PASSENGER AND IMMIGRATION LISTS INDEX

2002 Supplement

Part 1

Passenger and Immigration Lists Series

Passenger and Immigration Lists Index, First Edition

Passenger and Immigration Lists Index: 1982 Supplement

Passenger and Immigration Lists Index: 1983 Supplement

Passenger and Immigration Lists Index: 1984 Supplement

Passenger and Immigration Lists Index: 1985 Supplement

Passenger and Immigration Lists Index: 1982-85 Cumulated Supplements

Passenger and Immigration Lists Index: 1986 Supplement

Passenger and Immigration Lists Index: 1987 Supplement

Passenger and Immigration Lists Index: 1988 Supplement

Passenger and Immigration Lists Index: 1989 Supplement

Passenger and Immigration Lists Index: 1990 Supplement

Passenger and Immigration Lists Index: 1986-90 Cumulated Supplements

Passenger and Immigration Lists Index: 1991 Supplement

Passenger and Immigration Lists Index: 1992 Supplement

Passenger and Immigration Lists Index: 1993 Supplement

Passenger and Immigration Lists Index: 1994 Supplement

Passenger and Immigration Lists Index: 1995 Supplement

Passenger and Immigration Lists Index: 1991-95 Cumulated Supplements

Passenger and Immigration Lists Index: 1996 Supplement

Passenger and Immigration Lists Index: 1997 Supplement

Passenger and Immigration Lists Index: 1998 Supplement Part 1

Passenger and Immigration Lists Index: 1998 Supplement Part 2

Passenger and Immigration Lists Index: 1999 Supplement Part 1

Passenger and Immigration Lists Index: 1999 Supplement Part 2

Passenger and Immigration Lists Index: 2000 Supplement Part 1

Passenger and Immigration Lists Index: 2000 Supplement Part 2

Passenger and Immigration Lists Index: 1996-2000 Cumulated Supplements

Passenger and Immigration Lists Index: 2001 Supplement Part 1

Passenger and Immigration Lists Index: 2001 Supplement Part 2

Passenger and Immigration Lists Index: 2002 Supplement Part 1

Passenger and Immigration Lists Bibliography, 1538-1900, Second Edition

Philadelphia Naturalization Records

ISSN 0736-8267

PASSENGER AND IMMIGRATION LISTS INDEX

A Guide to Published Records of More Than 3,806,000 Immigrants Who Came to the New World between the Sixteenth and the Mid-Twentieth Centuries

2002 Supplement
Part 1

Edited by P. William Filby
and Katherine H. Nemeh

GALE GROUP

Detroit
New York
San Francisco
London
Boston
Woodbridge, CT

Staff

Editors: P. William Filby, Katherine H. Nemeh
Managing Editor: Bridget Travers
Assistant Editor: Noah Schusterbauer

Manufacturing Manager: Dorothy Maki
Buyer: Stacy L. Melson

Manager, Data Entry: Ronald D. Montgomery
Project Administrator: Gwendolyn S. Tucker

Manager, Technical Support Services: Theresa Rocklin
Oracle Applications Specialist: Carolin V. Jones

Product Design Manager: Kenn Zorn
Graphic Artist: Mike Logusz

Library of Congress Catalog Card Number 84-15404
ISBN 0-7876-3453-0
ISSN 0736-8267
Printed in the United States of America

Passenger and Immigration Lists Index
Advisory Board

Contents

Highlights

Passenger and Immigration Lists Index: 2002 Supplement Part 1 brings together in one alphabet more than 125,000 immigrants who arrived in the New World between the sixteenth and the mid-twentieth centuries. This book is the twenty-fifth supplement to the base set of *Passenger and Immigration Lists Index (PILI)* published in 1981. These names appear in a broad collection of more than 30 published passenger lists, naturalization records, church records, family and local histories, voter and land registrations, etc.

For the user's convenience, the following features appear in this supplement:

- The **User's Guide** section, which begins on page xiii, gives examples which show the user how index and bibliographic citations should be interpreted.

- Information as to where to find the sources indexed in *PILI* may be found in the **How to Locate Sources Indexed** section beginning on page xvii.

- Complete bibliographic citations to the sources indexed in *PILI 2002 Supplement Part 1*, and the codes used to refer to them, may be found in the **Bibliography of Sources Indexed** section, beginning on page xix.

Introduction

Passenger and Immigration Lists Index (PILI) was first published in 1981 in three volumes which indexed more than 300 published lists covering about 500,000 persons. *PILI* and its twenty-five supplements now cover more than 3,806,000 persons—still only a fraction of the over 35,000,000 immigrants who came to the New World. For the user's convenience, all material in the first four annual supplements to the *PILI* base set is also available in one alphabet in *PILI 1982-85 Cumulated Supplements.* The material indexed in the *PILI 1986* through *1990, 1991* through *1995,* and *1996* through *2000 Supplements* is also available in one alphabet in *PILI 1986-90 Cumulated Supplements*, *PILI 1991-95 Cumulated Supplements*, and *PILI 1996-2000 Cumulated Supplements,* respectively. Beginning with the 1998 supplements, two volumes are published annually. At this time, publication plans include a cumulation of supplements every five years.

Concept and Scope

Passenger lists, naturalization records, church records, etc. are primary sources for genealogists, since, in the case of passenger lists, almost all passengers arriving in the New World during the period covered were not casual travelers but immigrants intending to remain in America as permanent residents. Information which documents a specific time and location of an immigrant in the New World is an invaluable aid to research on the history of a family in America. In addition, any of the lists that furnish this information may also furnish clues to the country of origin and other crucial bits of genealogical information. This is true of all the lists indexed in *PILI,* and researchers will want to make certain to consult the sources themselves for additional information.

It should be noted that in some cases variant versions of lists have been indexed in *PILI,* since copying is notoriously inaccurate and it is not unusual to note variations from list to list. Likewise, different information is frequently given about the circumstances of the immigration. Since no library holds all of the lists, the researcher will have a better opportunity to locate one of the versions.

Most of the sources indexed in the three-volume base set of *PILI* were identified by Harold Lancour's *Bibliography of Ship Passenger Lists, 1538-1825: Being a Guide to Published Lists of Early Immigrants to North America* (third edition revised by Richard J. Wolfe, New York: New York Public Library, 1963). In 1981, P. William Filby edited a revised and updated edition of the Lancour bibliography, *Passenger and Immigration Lists Bibliography, 1538-1900: Being a Guide to Published Lists of Arrivals in the United States and Canada* (Detroit: Gale Research, 1981). Now in its second edition (published 1988), this bibliography identifies more than 2,550 published passenger and immigration lists, completely superseding Lancour's work. Many of the sources indexed in the earlier volumes of *PILI* are listed in *Passenger and Immigration Lists Bibliography,* Second Edition.

Editorial Practices

All names listed in *PILI* have been compiled directly from published sources; unpublished sources are never indexed. The information given in a source about each immigrant and those accompanying him or her was edited to a standard format. Cross-references were made for each of those individuals who accompanied the primary listee since, without those cross-references, much valuable information would be lost.

PILI does not index passenger lists only. Naturalization lists and other publications where immigration to the New World can be determined to have occurred are indexed as well. Early in the project, the editors decided that all names, including alternate forms of the surname, in a given source would be indexed unless there was a definite reason for omission. Examples of names that would not be indexed are those whose data reflects birth in America or those with no listed surname.

The date and place appearing in *PILI* do *not* necessarily equate to the date and port of *arrival.* Locations referred to in some sources are in fact sometimes destinations, the area where naturalization was filed, or the particular location of the immigrant on the date cited. Dates may reflect the date of death, the date the listee requested permission to emigrate, or the point in time when documents place that person in the New World at the location specified. Although they are not ports and dates of arrival, these references are retained because the editors feel that when someone is searching for an elusive ancestor, all information is helpful. It is felt that no researcher will object to the inclusion of her or his ancestor even if the person did not arrive precisely on the date listed in *PILI.* By consulting the complete bibliographic citation for the source cited in a *PILI* entry in the section "Bibliography of Sources Indexed" which begins on page xix, researchers can determine exactly what information the listed date and place represent.

While every attempt has been made to ensure accuracy, it has been impossible to search for corrections or errata in articles published after the ones indexed. Similarly, all names have been copied exactly as printed, even in cases where they might appear to be erroneous. Abbreviations, such as "Jno.," have been retained. Van, Van der, De, De La, von, van, etc. have been left as given in the source. Letters sometimes umlauted (¨) in German names (ü, ä, ö) have been spelled out (ue, ae, oe) in the bibliography but have *not* been spelled out in the index unless they are spelled out in the source document. The ess-tset symbol (ß) has been anglicized as "ss".

It should be remembered that names of emigrants were often recorded as they were heard, that many emigrants could not spell their own names, and that authorities were not as literate as one would wish. Thus, variations in spelling of names occur and members of the same family arriving at different times or places may be found under more than one spelling. In using *PILI,* the researcher should search for every conceivable spelling of the name sought as well as adaptations of the surname based on the customs of the ancestor's country of origin. (For example, if the ancestor is a female of German extraction, the surname may be listed with an "in" appended at the end. Thus, "Mayer" is listed as "Mayerin.")

When ages given in the source books contain fractions of years, these fractions have been dropped. (For example, 14 □ will appear in *PILI* as 14.) Ages of children of less than a year have been shown in months, weeks, or days.

Suggestions Are Welcome

PILI, which indexes only published material, has had an effect on genealogical publishing. Researchers have responded to *PILI* by increasing their efforts to have new lists published. Librarians and researchers are encouraged to inform the editors of further lists that could be indexed in the future. Questions, comments, and suggestions may be sent to Gale Group, Inc., *Passenger and Immigration Lists Index,* 27500 Drake Rd., Farmington Hills, MI 48331-3535 [phone: (248) 699-4253, toll-free: (800) 347-4253, fax: (248) 699-8062].

User's Guide

There are two main types of citations in *Passenger and Immigration Lists Index (PILI)*: Citations listing names of immigrants which appear in the main body or index portion of the book (beginning on page 1) and bibliographic citations which appear in the section "Bibliography of Sources Indexed" (beginning on page xix).

Index Citations

Citations in the main body of *PILI* can be of two types. The first type, the main entry, may read as follows:

(1) (2) (3) (4) (5) (6)
Bender, George 20; New York, NY, 1852 **8506** *p224*
Wife: Catharine 27
(7) *Son:* Jacob 4
Daughter: Catharine 2

The numbers in parentheses appearing in the above entry refer to the following explanations:

(1) Name of the immigrant, as spelled in the original published source
(2) Immigrant's age, when given
(3) Place of arrival, naturalization, or other record of immigration
(4) Year of arrival, naturalization, or other record of immigration
(5) Code that refers to the source in which the particular list can be found. **Complete bibliographic citations to the sources indexed which include an explanation as to what information is provided by the place and year cited, and the codes used to refer to them, may be found in the "Bibliography of Sources Indexed" section, beginning on page xix.**
(6) Page number on which that particular name is listed in the source cited
(7) Accompanying family members, if there are any, together with each person's relationship to the primary listee, and his or her age.

Occasionally a published list will not indicate a year of arrival or other reference year. In those instances the abbreviation *n.d.* (no date) is inserted:

Altomore, Mauro; Galveston, TX, n.d. **1004.5** *p17*

Some immigration lists note that the main listee was accompanied by other persons, with only the relationships indicated, and possibly the ages. Such information is included in the *PILI* listing:

Jacobs, Jan; New Netherland(s), 1659 **9143** *p174*
With wife & mother
With child 2
With child 4

The second type of citation found in *PILI* is the cross-reference. Cross-references have been generated by the computer for every accompanying relative whose name is provided in the source indexed in *PILI*. The only exception would be those lists where a relationship seemed obvious, but was not specified. Cross-references may read as follows:

(1) (2) (3)
Bauer, Katharina 6 *SEE* Bauer, Peter

The numbers in parentheses appearing in the preceding entry refer to the following explanations:

(1) Name of accompanying family member
(2) Family member's age, when given
(3) Name of the primary listee

Since cross-references are generated each time an accompanying individual is listed, duplicate cross-references will appear in *PILI* for names listed in more than one source or page:

Robertson, Jane *SEE* Robertson, James
Robertson, Jane *SEE* Robertson, James
Robertson, Jane *SEE* Robertson, James
Robertson, Jane *SEE* Robertson, James

This indicates to the researcher that there are four separate listings for James Robertson in *PILI* in which Jane is given as someone who accompanied him.

A wife whose maiden name is supplied in a source document may appear in three places in *PILI:* a) in the husband's main listing, b) under the maiden name, and c) as a cross-reference under the married name:

a) **Gardner,** Simeon; Nova Scotia, 1762 **8750.40** *p90*
Wife: Sarah Long

b) **Long,** Sarah; Nova Scotia, 1762 **8750.40** *p90*

c) **Gardner,** Sarah Long *SEE* Gardner, Simeon

For information concerning how names are selected and indexed in *PILI,* see the "Editorial Practices" section of the Introduction beginning on page xi.

Bibliographic Citations

Citations in the bibliography of *PILI* can also be of two types. The first type, indicating that the source indexed was a book, may read as follows:

(1)
***778.5**
(2) (3)
BRASSEAUX, CARL A. ***The "Foreign French:" Nineteenth-Century French Immigra-***
(4) (5) (6)
tion into Louisiana. Vol. 1: 1820-1839. Lafayette, LA: The Center for Louisiana Studies,
(7) (8)
University of Southwestern Louisiana, 1990. 569p.

The numbers in parentheses appearing in the above entry refer to the following explanations:

(1) Code cited in index citation referencing this source
(2) Author, editor, or compiler
(3) Title of book, pamphlet, or monograph
(4) Subtitle, volume, or edition information
(5) Place where source was published
(6) Name of publisher
(7) Year when published
(8) Number of pages in the source

The second type of bibliographic citation, indicating that the source indexed was a magazine or newspaper article or a chapter of a book may read as follows:

(1)
***7129**
(2) (3) (4) (5)
RACINE, JUANITA. "Caddo Parish Courthouse, Shreveport, LA. In *The Genie* (Ark-La-Tex
(6) (7) (8)
Genealogical Association, Shreveport), vol. 15:1 (Jan. 1981), pp. 44-46.

The numbers in parentheses appearing in the above entry refer to the following explanations:

(1) Code cited in index citation referencing this source
(2) Author or compiler of article
(3) Name of magazine article, book chapter, or newspaper article
(4) Name of the magazine, book, or newspaper in which the article or text appears
(5) Publisher of magazine or book and city (and, sometimes, state) where source was published
(6) Volume and issue number of magazine or newspaper
(7) Date when magazine, book, or newspaper was published
(8) Pages of article or chapter which were indexed

Both types of bibliographic citations will also have an annotation immediately following the citation:

(1) (2)
Date and place of first mention of residence in the New World. Extracted from records found
(3)
among the Bradford papers in the archives of the Pennsylvania Historical Society. Regiment,
company, place of birth, and other information provided.

The numbers in parentheses appearing in the above entry refer to the following explanations:

(1) Denotes what the date and place cited in the index citation represent
(2) Where the compiler or author of this source found his or her information
(3) What other information (not indexed in *PILI*) is provided by the compiler or author

Annotations may also contain other information:

English translation of the title if source is in a foreign language
The location of the original records
Address of author or compiler if source was self-published
Additional information that the staff of *PILI* feels will be of aid to the researcher

How to Locate Sources Indexed

Large public libraries, state libraries, libraries with genealogical or history collections, and libraries of family associations and genealogical or historical societies are excellent places to check for the sources listed in the "Bibliography of Sources Indexed" section of *PILI.* It should be noted that while many libraries do not have the staff to research sources, librarians can provide guidance to assist researchers in their own investigations. Some libraries may provide lists of researchers for hire. The publisher of the magazine or book indexed can also be contacted; magazine publishers often offer reprints of articles they publish. Also, the bibliographic citation in *PILI* (*see* "Bibliography of Sources Indexed," which begins on page xix) may provide information as to where the source may be found.

Many of the books and periodicals containing articles indexed in *PILI* are among the holdings of some of the institutions listed below. The *Bibliography of Genealogy and Local History Periodicals with Union List of Major U.S. Collections* edited by Michael Barren Clegg and published by the Allen County Public Library Foundation in Fort Wayne, Indiana, is helpful in determining which of the major genealogical libraries hold a specific periodical (those libraries surveyed by Clegg are indicated below by an asterisk).

A sampling of institutions and organizations with major holdings of genealogical publications follows:

*Allen County Public Library**
Genealogy Department
900 Webster Street
P.O. Box 2270
Fort Wayne, IN 46801-2270

*Atlanta-Fulton Public Library**
Special Collections Department
1 Margaret Mitchell Square NW
Atlanta, GA 30303-1022

Berkshire Athenaeum
Local History and Literature Services
1 Wendell Avenue
Pittsfield, MA 01201-6385

California State Library
Sutro Library Branch
480 Winston Drive
San Francisco, CA 94132-1777

The Church of Jesus Christ of Latter-day Saints
*Family History Library**
35 North West Temple Street
Salt Lake City, UT 84150-1003

The Connecticut Historical Society
1 Elizabeth Street
Hartford, CT 06105-2292

*Dallas Public Library**
Genealogy Collection
1515 Young Street
Dallas, TX 75201-5499

Denver Public Library
Western History/Genealogy Department
10 West 14th Avenue Parkway
Denver, CO 80204-2731

Detroit Public Library
Burton Historical Collection
5201 Woodward Avenue
Detroit, MI 48202-4093

The Filson Club Historical Society
1310 South Third Street
Louisville, KY 40208-5506

Houston Public Library
Clayton Library
Center for Genealogical Research
5300 Caroline Street
Houston, TX 77004-6896

*Library of Congress**
Local History and Genealogy Reading Room
Humanities and Social Sciences Division
Thomas Jefferson Building, Room LJ G42
Washington, DC 20540-4660

Library of Michigan
Michigan Library and Historical Center
717 W. Allegan Street
P.O. Box 30007
Lansing, MI 48909-7507

*Los Angeles Public Library**
History and Genealogy Department
630 West Fifth Street
Los Angeles, CA 90071-2097

National Society, Daughters of the American Revolution Library
1776 D Street, N.W.
Washington, DC 20006-5392

*New England Historic Genealogical Society**
101 Newbury Street
Boston, MA 02116-3007

*The New York Public Library**
Center for the Humanities
U.S. History, Local History and Genealogy Division
Fifth Avenue and 42nd Street, Room 315S
New York, NY 10018-2788

*Newberry Library**
Local & Family History Room
60 West Walton Street
Chicago, IL 60610-3380

Onondaga County Public Library
Local History and Special Collections
447 South Salina Street
Syracuse, NY 13202-2494

Orange County Library System
Genealogy Department
101 East Central Boulevard
Orlando, FL 32801-2471

*Public Library of Cincinnati and Hamilton County**
History Department
800 Vine Street
Library Square
Cincinnati, OH 45202-2071

*The State Historical Society of Wisconsin**
816 State Street
Madison, WI 53706-1482

Western Reserve Historical Society
Ohio Network of American History Research Centers
10825 East Boulevard
Cleveland, OH 44106-1788

Bibliography of Sources Indexed

★*Source Number*

★1220.25

COLDHAM, PETER WILSON. *Emigrants from England to the American Colonies, 1773-1776.* Baltimore, MD: Genealogical Publishing Co., Inc., 1988. 182p.

Date and port of arrival. Extracted from registers T 47/9-12, located at the Public Record Office in Kew, Surrey, England. Name of ship, country of origin, occupation and other historical information may also be provided.

★1224.1

COLDHAM, PETER WILSON. *English Estates of American Colonists, American Wills and Administrations in the Prerogative Court of Canterbury, 1610-1699.* Baltimore, MD: Genealogical Publishing Co., Inc., 1983. 72p.

Date and place of death, or date and place of will administration or place of mention in the New World. Extracted from several sources, including abstracts from the Prerogative Court of Canterbury Probate and Administration Act Books for the period 1610-1699. Name of executor, maritial status of testator, and other genealogical information may also be provided.

★1224.2

COLDHAM, PETER WILSON. *English Estates of American Colonists, American Wills and Administrations in the Prerogative Court of Canterbury, 1700-1799.* Baltimore, MD: Genealogical Publishing Co., Inc., 1980. 140p.

Date and place of death or date and place of mention in the New World. Extracted from Administration Act Books: PROB 6/76 (1700) to 175 (1799); Probate Act Books: PROB 8/93 (1700) to 192 (1799); and Limited Probate Act Book: PROB 9/1 (1781). Name and marital status of testator or intestate, name of executor, value of testator's personal estate, place of origin, and other genealogical information may also be provided.

★1224.3

COLDHAM, PETER WILSON. *English Estates of American Settlers, American Wills and Administrations in the Prerogative Court of Canterbury, 1800-1858.* Baltimore, MD: Genealogical Publishing Co., Inc., 1981. 103p.

Date and place of death or date and place of residence in the New World. Extracted from the following Prerogative Court of Canterbury Act Books: Administrations (Prob 6), Limited Administrations (PROB 7), Probates (PROB 8), and Limited Probates (PROB 9), all of which are located at the Public Record Office, Chancery Lane, London. Name and marital status of testator or intestate, name of executor, value of testator's personal estate, place of origin, and other genealogical information may also be provided.

★1640.10

DOBSON, DAVID. *Scots in Georgia and the Deep South, 1735-1845.* Baltimore, MD: Genealogical Publishing Co., Inc., 2000. 218p.

Most are date and port of arrival. Some are date and place of first mention of residence in the New World. Date and place of birth and/or death, place of settlement, occupation, name of ship, reference to original record, and other genealogical and historical information may also be provided.

★1640.13

DOBSON, DAVID. *Scottish-American Wills, 1650-1900.* Baltimore, MD: Genealogical Publishing Co., Inc., 1991. 137p.

Date and place of residence or place of death. Some are date of will registration. Extracted from records of the Commissariat Court of Edinburgh and the Sheriff Court of Edinburgh, located in the Scottish Record Office, Edinburgh. Supplementary data extracted from the publication entitled *Index to Personal Estates of Defuncts, 1846-1866.* (Edinburgh, 1866). Place of origin, occupation, and reference number of original record may also be provided.

★1823.15

ELLIOTT, BRUCE S. *Index to the 1871 Census of Ontario: Huron.* Toronto: Ontario Genealogical Society, 1986, 290p.

Date and place of census. Census films are available from the National Archives of Canada in Ottawa. Place of birth, sex of the immigrant, religion, ethnicity, occupation, district, subdistrict, division, and page number of original record are also provided.

★1823.22

ELLIOTT, BRUCE S. *Index to the 1871 Census of Ontario: Northumberland.* Toronto: Ontario Genealogical Society, 1990, 176p.

Date and place of census. Census films are available from the National Archives of Canada in Ottawa. Place of birth, sex of the immigrant, religion, ethnicity, occupation, district, subdistrict, division, and page number of original record are also provided.

★1823.28

ELLIOTT, BRUCE S. *Index to the 1871 Census of Ontario: Renfrew and the North.* Toronto: Ontario Genealogical Society, 1992, 107p.

Date and place of census. Census films are available from the National Archives of Canada in Ottawa. Place of birth, sex of the immigrant, religion, ethnicity, occupation, district, subdistrict, division, and page number of original record are also provided.

★1825.45

ELLIS, EILISH. *Emigrants from Ireland, 1847-1852, State-Aided Emigration Schemes from Crown Estates in Ireland.* Baltimore, MD: Genealogical Publishing Co., Inc., 1993. 68p.

Date and port of arrival. Extracted from the Quit Rent Office collection of books and papers located in the Public Record Office, Dublin. Date of departure, port of embarkation, and name of ship are also provided. Occupation and other personal and historical information may also be provided.

★2524.55

GIBB, CARSON. *A Supplement to The Early Settlers of Maryland.* Annapolis, MD: Maryland State Archives, 1997. 248p.

Date and port of arrival. Extracted from Maryland Land Office records of patents and warrants. Reference to original record or transcript and microfilm number are also provided. Other historical and genealogical information may also be provided. The first publication, *The Early Settlers of Maryland,* was indexed as source number 8510 in *PILI* 1982.

★2856.30

HACKER, WERNER. *Eighteenth Century Register of Emigrants from Southwest Germany to America and Other Countries.* Apollo, PA: Closson Press, 1994. 516p.

Date and place of intended destination. Place of origin and reference number to original source are also provided. Date of birth is sometimes listed. Section letters in the page number refer to Addendum pages.

★2896.25

HANCOCKS, ELIZABETH. *1861 Census of Ameliasburgh Township, Prince Edward County, Ontario, Canada.* Agincourt, ON: Generation Press, 1994. 82p.

Date and place of census. Extracted from microfilm numbers C-1069 and C-1070 in the National Archives of Canada at Ottawa, Ontario. Place of birth, marital status, occupation, religion, gender, and page and district number of original census record are also provided.

★2896.26

HANCOCKS, ELIZABETH. *1861 Census of Athol Township, Prince Edward County, Ontario, Canada.* Agincourt, ON: Generation Press, 1996. 45p.

Date and place of census. Extracted from microfilm numbers C-1069 and C-1070 in the National Archives of Canada at Ottawa, Ontario. Place of birth, marital status, occupation, religion, gender, and page and district number of original census record are also provided.

★2896.27

HANCOCKS, ELIZABETH. *1861 Census of Hallowell Township, Prince Edward County, Ontario, Canada.* Agincourt, ON: Generation Press, 1987. 79p.

Date and place of census. Extracted from microfilm number C-1069 in the National Archives of Canada at Ottawa, Ontario. Place of birth, marital status, occupation, religion, gender, and page and district number of original census record are also provided.

★2896.28

HANCOCKS, ELIZABETH. *1861 Census of Hillier Township, Prince Edward County, Ontario, Canada.* Agincourt, ON: Generation Press, 1995. 74p.

Date and place of census. Extracted from microfilm number C-1069 in the National Archives of Canada at Ottawa, Ontario. Place of birth, marital status, occupation, religion, gender, and page and district number of original census record are also provided.

★3259.35

HOLLOWAK, THOMAS L. *Polish Heads of Household in Maryland: An Index to the 1910 Census.* Westminister, MD: Family Line Publications, 1990. 74p.

Date and place of census. County, enumeration district, and page number of original census record are also provided.

★3437.14

INGMIRE, FRANCES T. *Hamilton County, Indiana Naturalization Certificates, 1855-1905.* Signal Mountain, TN: Mountain Press, 1980. 208p.

Date and port of arrival or date and place of naturalization.

★4537.32

LAWSON, BILL. *A Register of Emigrant Families from the Western Isles of Scotland to Ontario, Canada, Part 1 Bruce, Grey & Huron Counties.* Northton, Isle of Harris, Scotland: Bill Lawson Publications, 1996. 102p.

Date of emigration and place of settlement in Ontario. Port of embarkation, date of birth and/or death, marital information, and reference to original sources are also provided. Historical information is also provided.

★4537.35

LAWSON, BILL. *Register of Emigrants from the Western Isles of Scotland 1750-1900, Volume 1 Isle of Harris.* Northton, Isle of Harris, Scotland: Bill Lawson Publications, 1992. 87p.

Date of emigration and place of settlement in the New World. Port of embarkation, date of birth and/or death, marital information, and reference to original sources are also provided. Much historical and genealogical information are also provided.

★4537.37

LAWSON, BILL. *Register of Emigrants from the Western Isles of Scotland 1750-1900, Volume 2 Isles of South Uist and Benbecula, Part 2 1840-1900.* Northton, Isle of Harris, Scotland: Bill Lawson Publications, 1994. 137p.

Date of emigration and place of settlement in the New World. Port of embarkation, date of birth and/or death, marital information, and reference to original sources are also provided. Much historical and genealogical information are also provided.

★4628.40

LINEHAN, JOHN C. *The Irish Scots and the "Scotch—Irish", An Historical and Ethnological Monograph, with Some Reference to Scotia Major and Scotia Minor, To Which is Added a Chapter on "How the Irish Came as Builders of the Nation."* Bowie, MD: Heritage Books, Inc., 1997. 138p.

Date and port of arrival or date and place of first mention in the New World. The monograph on *The Irish Scots and the "Scotch—Irish"* originally appeared in the *The Granite Monthly,* (January-March, 1888), of Concord, New Hampshire. Extensive genealogical and historical data are also provided.

★4629.10

LINN, JOHN B., and WM. H. EGLE. *Names of Persons Who Took the Oath of Allegiance to the State of Pennsylvania.* Westminister, MD: Willow Bend Books, 2000. 118p.

Date and place of oath of allegiance. Country of origin, occupation and other historical and genealogical information may also be provided.

★5900.10

MURPHY, RONALD CHASE and JANICE CHURCH MURPHY. *Irish Famine Immigrants in the State of*

Vermont, Gravestone Inscriptions. Baltimore, MD: Clearfield Co., Inc., 2000. 723p.

Most are timespan between date of birth and date of death; some are just date of death with place of burial. Place of origin, gravestone inscriptions, and name and location of cemetary, may also be provided. Extensive historical data is also provided.

★6058.10

NEIDICH, JOYCE GRILL. *Venango County, Pennsylvania, Declarations of Intention and Petitions for Naturalization, 1806-1868.* Apollo, PA: Closson Press, 1998. 93p.

Date and place of declaration of intention or petition for naturalization. Extracted from Docket 1 records on file at the Venango County Courthouse. Country of nativity, page number of original record and other genealogical information may also be provided.

★6212.30

NOTTINGHAM, STRATTON. *Certificates and Rights, Accomack County, Virginia, 1663-1709.* Baltimore, MD: Clearfield Co., Inc., 1997. 91p.

Date when grant was received for land in area cited. Original certificates are on file at the Land Office, Richmond, Virginia. Other historical information is also provided.

★6688.10

PENSTONE, JACQUE. "Naturalization Records for A. Peterson/Petersen." In *Orange County, California Genealogical Society Quarterly,* Part 1, vol. 29:1 (March 1992), pp. 34-40; Part 2, vol. 29:2 (June 1992), pp. 61-66.

Date and place of naturalization or date and port of arrival. Extracted from Soundex P-362, located at the Chicago Branch of the National Archives. Date of birth, place of birth, and certificate number may also be provided.

★8197.10

SCOTT, KENNETH. *Early New York Naturalizations, Abstracts of Naturalization Records from Federal, State, and Local Courts, 1792-1840.* Baltimore, MD: Genealogical Publishing Co., Inc., 1999. 452p.

Most are date and place of naturalization or declaration of intention to become a citizen; a few are date and port of arrival. Extracted from records at the Federal Archives and Records Center Archives Branch in Bayonne, New Jersey. Name of court and other historical information are provided. Place of birth, port of departure, country of prior allegiance, and occupation may also be provided.

★9079.10

SUTTON, BETSY MILEY and SUSAN BECKMAN KOTTWITZ. *Germans from Russia in Russell County, Kansas, 1910 United States Census.* [Gretna, VA]: Jeruslan Nachrichten, 1995. 60p.

Date and place of census. Some dates include period between year of emigration and year of census. Place of birth, native language, citizenship status, marital status, occupation, and place of residence in Kansas are also provided.

★9196.1

TRACE, MARY KEARNS. *Canadian Border Entry Lists 1908-1918, Yukon Territory & British Columbia.* Part 1. Calgary, AB: Traces, 1997. 87p.

Date and port of arrival. Extracted from Immigration Records Group, RG 76 microfilm, available at the National Archives of Canada, Ottawa, Ontario. Place of birth, sex of the immigrant, country of origin, place of intended destination, and microfilm reel numbers are provided. Other historical data is also provided.

★9196.15

TRACE, MARY KEARNS. *Canadian Passengers Inward Bound 1856-1858.* Calgary, AB: Traces, 1997. 66p.

Date and port of arrival. Extracted from several issues of the *Canadian News (& North American Intelligencer.)* Name of ship, port of departure and other historical information are also provided.

A

Aamos, Thomas 40; Ontario, 1871 ***1823.15*** *p4*
Aarnold, L. 20; British Columbia, 1912 ***9196.1*** *p15*
Aaron, Henry; New York, 1794 ***8197.10*** *p1*
Aaron, John 46; Ontario, 1871 ***1823.22*** *p1*
Aaron, Peter; Port uncertain, 1765 ***2856.30*** *p1*
Abare, Joseph 32; Ontario, 1871 ***1823.28*** *p1*
Abare, Phoebe; Vermont, 1864-1944 ***5900.10*** *p440*
Abay, John; Maryland, 1665 ***2524.55*** *p9*
Abba, Elizabeth 20; Nova Scotia, 1774 ***1220.25*** *p14*
Abbereth, Adam 33; Ontario, 1871 ***1823.15*** *p1*
Abbereth, Sebastian 65; Ontario, 1871 ***1823.15*** *p1*
Abbert, Robert 15; Baltimore, 1775 ***1220.25*** *p119*
Abberton, Timothy 68; Ontario, 1871 ***1823.15*** *p1*
Abbes, Edward; Virginia, 1637 ***1224.1*** *p1*
Abbes, W. 24; Ontario, 1861 ***2896.28*** *p11*
Abbett, Edward; Maryland, 1669 ***2524.55*** *p45*
Abbey, Cornellus 36; Ontario, 1871 ***1823.15*** *p1*
Abbey, Janothin 74; Ontario, 1871 ***1823.15*** *p1*
Abbey, Shederic 57; Ontario, 1871 ***1823.15*** *p1*
Abbot, Eliza; Virginia, 1667-1668 ***6212.30*** *p39*
Abbot, John 20; Philadelphia, 1775 ***1220.25*** *p9*
Abbot, Michael; Maryland, 1671 ***2524.55*** *p9*
Abbot, Nathaniel; Maryland, 1682 ***2524.55*** *p9*
Abbot, Samuel; Maryland, 1671 ***2524.55*** *p9*
Abbott, Mr.; Quebec, 1858 ***9196.15*** *p33*
Abbott, Francise 41; Ontario, 1871 ***1823.28*** *p1*
Abbott, James; Charles Town, South Carolina, 1720 ***1224.2*** *p1*
Abbott, John 30; Ontario, 1871 ***1823.28*** *p1*
Abbott, Joseph; New York, New York, 1850 ***6058.10*** *p31*
Abbott, Josiah; New England, 1693 ***1224.1*** *p1*
Abbott, Richard; New York, 1836 ***8197.10*** *p205*
Abbott, Robert; Massachusetts, 1747 ***1224.2*** *p1*
Abbott, Susanna; Maryland, 1681 ***2524.55*** *p9*
Abbott, Thomas; Maryland, 1649 ***2524.55*** *p9*
Abbott, William; New York, 1840 ***8197.10*** *p206*
Abbott, William; New York, New York, 1844 ***1224.3*** *p1*
Abbott, William Van 10; Ontario, 1871 ***1823.28*** *p1*
Abbs, James; New York, New York, 1838 ***3437.14*** *p85*
Abchurch, Wm; Virginia, 1668-1669 ***6212.30*** *p40*
Abdengood, Amelia 11; Kansas, 1910 ***9079.10*** *p47*
Abdengood, David 7; Kansas, 1910 ***9079.10*** *p47*
Abdengood, Henry 3; Kansas, 1910 ***9079.10*** *p47*
Abdengood, Henry 33; Kansas, 1907-1910 ***9079.10*** *p47*
Abdengood, Lena 3 months; Kansas, 1910 ***9079.10*** *p47*
Abdengood, Sofhia 30; Kansas, 1910 ***9079.10*** *p47*
Abdy, Robert; Virginia, 1666-1667 ***6212.30*** *p33*
Abdy, Samll; Virginia, 1665-1666 ***6212.30*** *p23*
Abecacis, Salvador; New York, 1835 ***8197.10*** *p205*
Abeille, Francis; New York, 1827 ***8197.10*** *p347*
Abel, Anna Maria; Port uncertain, 1759 ***2856.30*** *p1*
Abel, Jacob; Pennsylvania, 1777 ***4629.10*** *p14*
Abel, John; Pennsylvania, 1786 ***4629.10*** *p54*
Abell, Gartrick *SEE* Abell, Hendrick
Abell, Georg; Port uncertain, 1751 ***2856.30*** *p1*
Abell, George; Charles Town, South Carolina, 1742 ***1224.2*** *p1*
Abell, Hendrick; Maryland, 1667 ***2524.55*** *p9*
Wife: Sophia
Child: Macklett
Child: Gartrick
Abell, John 31; Ontario, 1871 ***1823.15*** *p1*
Abell, Macklett *SEE* Abell, Hendrick
Abell, Martha; Vermont, 1845-1910 ***5900.10*** *p520*
Abell, Rose Brennan; Vermont, 1856-1933 ***5900.10*** *p485*
Abell, Sophia *SEE* Abell, Hendrick
Abendschon, Josef; Port uncertain, 1752 ***2856.30*** *p1*
With wife & children
Abercombie, James; Pennsylvania, 1777 ***4629.10*** *p27*
Abercorn, Isabella 61; Ontario, 1861 ***2896.27*** *p72*
Abercrombie, H. 35; Ontario, 1861 ***2896.26*** *p1*
Abercrombie, J. H. 5; Ontario, 1861 ***2896.26*** *p1*
Abercrombie, James; Boston, 1775 ***1224.2*** *p1*
Abercrombie, James; Philadelphia, 1761 ***1224.2*** *p1*
Abercrombie, Mary 27; Maryland, 1775 ***1220.25*** *p114*
Aberdeen, Charles 20; Tortola, 1773-1774 ***1220.25*** *p32*
Aberhard, William 22; Ontario, 1871 ***1823.15*** *p1*
Aberhart, Charles 27; Ontario, 1871 ***1823.15*** *p1*
Aberle, Konrad Israel; America, 1750 ***2856.30*** *p1*
Aberley, Katherin; Virginia, 1671-1672 ***6212.30*** *p47*
Abernethy, William 42; Ontario, 1871 ***1823.22*** *p1*
Abert, Jno; Virginia, 1664 ***6212.30*** *p10*
Abertson, Gullam, Jr.; Pennsylvania, 1780 ***4629.10*** *p43*
Abhardt, George 40; Ontario, 1871 ***1823.15*** *p1*
Abingdon, John; Maryland, 1651 ***2524.55*** *p9*
Abington, Mary; Virginia, 1667-1668 ***6212.30*** *p39*
Able, Adalaide 24; Ontario, 1861 ***2896.27*** *p73*
Able, Peter L. 2; Ontario, 1861 ***2896.27*** *p73*
Ableson, William 62; Ontario, 1871 ***1823.28*** *p1*
Ablett, Thomas; Maryland, 1755 ***1224.2*** *p1*
Abney, James; Virginia, 1666 ***6212.30*** *p30*
Abney, Thomas 48; Maryland, 1774 ***1220.25*** *p70*
Aborn, Anne; Providence, Rhode Island, 1828 ***1224.3*** *p1*
Aborn, William Wellington; Rhode Island, 1839 ***1224.3*** *p1*
Abraham, Cor.; Maryland, 1650 ***2524.55*** *p9*
Abraham, Isaac; Maryland, 1658 ***2524.55*** *p9*
Abraham, Isaac; Pennsylvania, 1777 ***4629.10*** *p25*
Abraham, John; Maryland, 1680 ***2524.55*** *p9*
Abraham, John; New York, 1807 ***8197.10*** *p33*
Abraham, Thomas 34; Ontario, 1871 ***1823.15*** *p1*
Abraham, William; New England, 1750 ***1224.2*** *p56*
Abraham, William 50; Ontario, 1871 ***1823.15*** *p1*
Abraham, William 60; Ontario, 1871 ***1823.15*** *p1*
Abrahams, Alexander 23; Philadelphia, 1774 ***1220.25*** *p81*
Abrahams, Benjamin; New Orleans, 1857 ***1224.3*** *p1*
Abrahams, Henry; Maryland, 1661 ***2524.55*** *p119*
Abrahamson, Cornelius; Maryland, 1651 ***2524.55*** *p9*
Abrahamson, Frances; Maryland, 1651-1659 ***2524.55*** *p9*
Abram, Leicester 11; Ontario, 1861 ***2896.28*** *p28*
Abram, Thomas; Virginia, 1671-1672 ***6212.30*** *p47*
Abram, William 45; Ontario, 1871 ***1823.15*** *p1*
Abreinski, Konstanty; Maryland, 1910 ***3259.35*** *p1*
Abry, Auguste, Jr.; New York, 1838 ***8197.10*** *p109*
Abstahs, Caroline; New York, 1896 ***1640.13*** *p1*
Abt, Hans Henrich; Port uncertain, 1724 ***2856.30*** *p1*
Abtill, Wm; Virginia, 1663 ***6212.30*** *p2*
Ace, Daniel; Philadelphia, 1794 ***4629.10*** *p78*
Acer, Charles 22; Ontario, 1871 ***1823.22*** *p1*
Acher, Barnabas 37; Ontario, 1871 ***1823.22*** *p1*
Acherly, Thomas; Maryland, 1672 ***2524.55*** *p9*
Acheson, George 39; Ontario, 1871 ***1823.15*** *p1*
Acheson, Hannah; Maryland, 1671 ***2524.55*** *p9*
Acheson, John 38; Ontario, 1871 ***1823.22*** *p1*
Acheson, Joseph 55; Ontario, 1871 ***1823.15*** *p1*
Acheson, May 42; Ontario, 1871 ***1823.15*** *p1*
Acheson, Robert 69; Ontario, 1871 ***1823.15*** *p1*
Acheson, Vincent; Maryland, 1671 ***2524.55*** *p9*
Achison, John 42; Ontario, 1871 ***1823.15*** *p1*
Achison, Robert 40; Ontario, 1871 ***1823.15*** *p1*
Achison, William 32; Ontario, 1871 ***1823.15*** *p1*
Achley, John; Virginia, 1666 ***1224.1*** *p1*
Achren, Otto; New York, 1839 ***8197.10*** *p134*
Achtern, Helena; Port uncertain, 1782 ***2856.30*** *p93*
Achtern, Helena; Port uncertain, 1794 ***2856.30*** *p93*
Acker, Miss; America, 1752 ***2856.30*** *p385*
Acker, Miss; America, 1762 ***2856.30*** *p385*
Acker, Maria Barbara; America, 1752 ***2856.30*** *p1*
With husband & child
Ackerman, Charles F.; New York, 1812-1834 ***8197.10*** *p304*
Ackermann, Anna Elisabeth; Port uncertain, 1749 ***2856.30*** *p1*
Ackermann, Anna Margarete; America, 1766 ***2856.30*** *p275*
Ackermann, Bernard; America, 1757 ***2856.30*** *p1*
With wife
Ackermann, Catharina; Port uncertain, 1765 ***2856.30*** *p1*
Ackermann, Elis. Catharina; America, 1771 ***2856.30*** *p1*
Ackermann, Elis. Catharina; America, 1771 ***2856.30*** *p1*
With son
Ackermann, Hans Georg; America, 1771 ***2856.30*** *p1*
Ackermann, Jakob; America, 1750 ***2856.30*** *p1*
With wife & 3 daughters
Ackermann, Johann Peter; Port uncertain, 1740 ***2856.30*** *p1*
Ackermann, Josef; Port uncertain, 1764 ***2856.30*** *p1*
Ackermann, Margarete; Port uncertain, 1734 ***2856.30*** *p1*
Ackermann, Mathias; Port uncertain, 1767 ***2856.30*** *p1*
Ackermann, Mathias; Port uncertain, 1781 ***2856.30*** *p1*
Ackeson, Archibald 46; Ontario, 1871 ***1823.28*** *p1*
Ackford, James 61; Ontario, 1871 ***1823.28*** *p1*
Ackher, Anna Maria; Port uncertain, 1728 ***2856.30*** *p1*
With husband & 2 children
Ackley, John Breintnall; Pennsylvania, 1787 ***4629.10*** *p50*
Ackley, Thomas; Pennsylvania, 1785 ***4629.10*** *p48*
Ackley, Thomas 24; Maryland, 1774 ***1220.25*** *p70*
Ackman, John; New York, 1807 ***8197.10*** *p33*
Ackrick, George; Maryland, 1647 ***2524.55*** *p9*
With wife
Ackroyd, John; Pennsylvania, 1777 ***4629.10*** *p23*
Ackva, E.; America, 1773 ***2856.30*** *p337*
Ackva, Elisabeth; America, 1773 ***2856.30*** *p1*
Acoste, Dominick; New York, 1826-1835 ***8197.10*** *p310*
Acreek, George; Maryland, 1647 ***2524.55*** *p9*
With wife
Acres, Margery; Virginia, 1665-1666 ***6212.30*** *p23*
Acrod, Benjamin; Pennsylvania, 1684 ***1224.1*** *p1*
Acton, Arthur 37; Ontario, 1871 ***1823.28*** *p1*
Acton, John 24; Philadelphia, 1774 ***1220.25*** *p67*
Acton, Philip 18; Ontario, 1871 ***1823.28*** *p1*
Acton, Richard 44; Ontario, 1871 ***1823.28*** *p1*
Acton, Walter; Virginia, 1664 ***6212.30*** *p11*
Acworth, John; Philadelphia, 1746 ***1224.2*** *p1*
Adair, . . .; South Carolina, 1750-1770 ***4628.40*** *p98*
Adair, Henry; New York, 1827 ***8197.10*** *p340*
Adair, James; Pennsylvania, 1777 ***4629.10*** *p20*
Adair, John 31; Ontario, 1871 ***1823.22*** *p1*
Adair, Robert; New York, 1807 ***8197.10*** *p326*
Adair, Susanah 71; Ontario, 1871 ***1823.22*** *p1*
Adair, William 31; Ontario, 1871 ***1823.22*** *p1*
Adam, Mr.; Portland, Maine, 1858 ***9196.15*** *p30*
Adam, Mrs.; Portland, Maine, 1858 ***9196.15*** *p30*
Adam, Alexander 34; Ontario, 1871 ***1823.15*** *p1*
Adam, Anna Maria; Port uncertain, 1766 ***2856.30*** *p1*
Adam, Anton; Port uncertain, 1760 ***2856.30*** *p1*
Adam, Ester; Vermont, 1800-1893 ***5900.10*** *p317*
Adam, Frank G.; Vermont, 1856-1915 ***5900.10*** *p118*
Adam, Georg; Port uncertain, 1736 ***2856.30*** *p1*
Adam, Georg; Port uncertain, 1783 ***2856.30*** *p1*

Adam, Hans, The Younger; Port uncertain, 1762 2856.30 p1
Adam, Hans Georg; Port uncertain, 1693 2856.30 p1
Adam, Hans Martins; Port uncertain, 1793 2856.30 p1
With 2 daughters
Adam, Henrich; Port uncertain, 1749 2856.30 p1
Adam, Jacob; Port uncertain, 1746 2856.30 p1
Adam, Johann; Port uncertain, 1734 2856.30 p1
Adam, John 42; Ontario, 1871 1823.15 p1
Adam, Mary E. Herbert 40; Vermont, 1904 5900.10 p118
Adam, Nikolaus; America, 1727 2856.30 p2
Adam, Patrick; Kingston, Jamaica, 1761 1640.13 p1
Adam, Peter; Vermont, 1797-1875 5900.10 p317
Adam, Samuel; Pennsylvania, 1785 4629.10 p48
Adam, William; Georgia, 1698 1640.13 p1
Adam, William 16; Philadelphia, 1775 1220.25 p8
Adames, Edward; Maryland, 1682 2524.55 p9
Adames, Robert; Maryland, 1677-1678 2524.55 p9
Adamikewich, Adam; Maryland, 1910 3259.35 p1
Adamoscky, John; Maryland, 1910 3259.35 p1
Adams, . . .; Virginia, 1660 1224.1 p1
Adams, Mr.; Quebec, 1857 9196.15 p18
Adams, Mr.; Quebec, 1857 9196.15 p23
Adams, Mr.; Quebec, 1858 9196.15 p46
Adams, Mrs.; Quebec, 1857 9196.15 p18
Adams, Mrs.; Quebec, 1857 9196.15 p20
Adams, Mrs.; Quebec, 1857 9196.15 p23
Adams, A. 8; Ontario, 1861 2896.25 p52
Adams, Abraham 23; Ontario, 1861 2896.25 p19
Adams, Allen 67; Ontario, 1871 1823.22 p1
Adams, Alpheus 25; Ontario, 1871 1823.28 p1
Adams, Ann; Maryland, 1673 2524.55 p9
Adams, Ann 43; Ontario, 1871 1823.28 p1
Adams, B. B.; Quebec, 1856 9196.15 p9
Adams, Benjamen 57; Ontario, 1871 1823.15 p1
Adams, Bill 1; Ontario, 1861 2896.28 p56
Adams, C. N. 5; Ontario, 1861 2896.25 p52
Adams, Catherine 17; Ontario, 1861 2896.25 p52
Adams, Catherine 77; Vermont, 1881 5900.10 p137
Adams, Charles 40; Ontario, 1871 1823.15 p1
Adams, Christie Ann 38; Ontario, 1871 1823.22 p1
Adams, Cinderilla 4; Ontario, 1861 2896.25 p19
Adams, David 14; Ontario, 1861 2896.25 p19
Adams, David 30; Ontario, 1871 1823.22 p1
Adams, David 41; Ontario, 1871 1823.15 p1
Adams, E. W. 15; Ontario, 1861 2896.25 p52
Adams, Edwin 48; Ontario, 1871 1823.28 p1
Adams, Eliza J. 26; Ontario, 1861 2896.28 p56
Adams, George *SEE* Adams, James
Adams, George; Maryland, 1681 2524.55 p9
Adams, George; New York, 1807 8197.10 p331
Adams, George 19; Ontario, 1861 2896.25 p19
Adams, George 25; Virginia, 1774 1220.25 p45
Adams, Grace; Portland, Maine, 1857 9196.15 p13
Adams, Henry; New York, 1802 8197.10 p18
Adams, Henry; New York, New York, 1848 1224.3 p1
Adams, Henry 28; Ontario, 1861 2896.27 p64
Adams, Isabell *SEE* Adams, James
Adams, Isabella 84; Ontario, 1871 1823.22 p1
Adams, J. L. 3; Ontario, 1861 2896.25 p52
Adams, Jacob 70; Ontario, 1861 2896.25 p12
Adams, James; Maryland, 1658 2524.55 p9
Wife: Margarett
Child: John
Child: Margarett
Child: Isabell
Child: George
Adams, James; North Carolina, 1711 1224.2 p1
Adams, James 19; Ontario, 1861 2896.25 p52
Adams, James 26; Ontario, 1861 2896.25 p19
Adams, James 39; Ontario, 1871 1823.22 p1
Adams, Jane 33; Ontario, 1871 1823.15 p1
Adams, Jane 35; Ontario, 1861 2896.25 p69
Adams, Jane 86; Ontario, 1871 1823.28 p1
Adams, Joane *SEE* Adams, John
Adams, John *SEE* Adams, James
Adams, John; Maryland, 1667 2524.55 p9
Daughter: Joane
Wife: Joane
Adams, John; Pennsylvania, 1777 4629.10 p21
Adams, John 20; Ontario, 1861 2896.25 p17
Adams, John 24; Ontario, 1861 2896.25 p52
Adams, John 30; Ontario, 1871 1823.28 p1
Adams, John 60; Ontario, 1871 1823.15 p1
Adams, John 65; Ontario, 1871 1823.22 p1
Adams, John, Jr.; New York, 1802 8197.10 p18
Adams, John A.; Mobile, Alabama, 1815-1845 1640.10 p1
Wife: Mary
Child: Robert
Child: Thomas
Child: Mary
Child: William
Adams, John T. 33; Ontario, 1871 1823.15 p1
Adams, Joseph; New York, 1830 8197.10 p313
Adams, Joseph; Vermont, 1841-1924 5900.10 p311
Adams, Joseph; Virginia, 1758 1224.2 p1
Adams, Joseph 8; Ontario, 1861 2896.25 p19
Adams, Joseph 28; Ontario, 1871 1823.15 p1
Adams, Joseph 60; Ontario, 1871 1823.15 p1
Adams, Kathrin; Maryland, 1667 2524.55 p9
Adams, Lydia 21; Maryland, 1774 1220.25 p61
Adams, M. A. 21; Ontario, 1861 2896.25 p52
Adams, Margaret 2; Ontario, 1861 2896.27 p64
Adams, Margaret 82; Vermont, 1882 5900.10 p615
Adams, Margarett *SEE* Adams, James
Adams, Margret; Maryland, 1673 2524.55 p9
Adams, Marilla 2; Ontario, 1861 2896.28 p56
Adams, Martha 54; Ontario, 1871 1823.28 p1
Adams, Mary *SEE* Adams, John A.
Adams, Mary; Maryland, 1667 2524.55 p9
Adams, Mary; Maryland, 1678 2524.55 p218
Adams, Mary; Vermont, 1843-1922 5900.10 p311
Adams, Mary; Virginia, 1672 6212.30 p49
Adams, Mary J. 12; Ontario, 1861 2896.25 p19
Adams, Mary L.; Vermont, 1859-1907 5900.10 p541
Adams, Mathew; Maryland, 1673 2524.55 p9
Adams, McBride 38; Ontario, 1871 1823.22 p1
Adams, Mich.; Port uncertain, 1788 2856.30 p362
Adams, Nathaniel 35; Virginia, 1774 1220.25 p92
Adams, Peter; New York, 1807 8197.10 p330
Adams, Philip 30; Philadelphia, 1774 1220.25 p50
With wife 26
Adams, Rebecca 10; Ontario, 1861 2896.25 p19
Adams, Robert *SEE* Adams, John A.
Adams, Robert; New York, 1802 8197.10 p17
Adams, Robert; Pennsylvania, 1700 1224.2 p1
Adams, Robert 24; Ontario, 1871 1823.22 p1
Adams, Robert 56; Ontario, 1861 2896.25 p19
Adams, Robert 57; Ontario, 1871 1823.28 p1
Adams, Robert S. 17; Ontario, 1861 2896.25 p19
Adams, Samuel; Pennsylvania, 1777 4629.10 p27
Adams, Samuel 17; Ontario, 1861 2896.25 p71
Adams, Samuel 20; Ontario, 1861 2896.25 p19
Adams, Samuel 32; Ontario, 1871 1823.28 p1
Adams, Samuel 57; Ontario, 1861 2896.25 p52
Adams, Samuel, Jr. 14; Ontario, 1861 2896.25 p52
Adams, Stephen 11; Ontario, 1861 2896.25 p52
Adams, Thomas *SEE* Adams, John A.
Adams, Thomas; New York, 1806 8197.10 p30
Adams, Thomas 5; Ontario, 1861 2896.28 p56
Adams, Thomas 26; Ontario, 1871 1823.28 p1
Adams, Thomas 32; Maryland, 1775 1220.25 p120
Adams, Thomas 35; Ontario, 1871 1823.15 p1
Adams, Thomas 35; Ontario, 1871 1823.22 p1
Adams, Thomas 38; Ontario, 1871 1823.22 p1
Adams, Thomas 45; Ontario, 1871 1823.22 p1
Adams, Thomas 55; Ontario, 1871 1823.15 p1
Adams, W. H. 35; Ontario, 1871 1823.28 p1
Adams, William *SEE* Adams, John A.
Adams, William; New York, 1803 8197.10 p10
Adams, William; Pennsylvania, 1781 4629.10 p42
Adams, William; Philadelphia, 1756 1224.2 p1
Adams, William 6; Ontario, 1861 2896.27 p64
Adams, William 22; Maryland, 1775 1220.25 p104
Adams, William 23; Maryland, 1775 1220.25 p104
Adams, William 45; Maryland, 1774 1220.25 p52
Adams, Wm; Virginia, 1688 6212.30 p57
Adams, Wm Henry 66; Ontario, 1871 1823.28 p1
Adamska, Katerzyna; Maryland, 1910 3259.35 p1
Adamski, Frank; Maryland, 1910 3259.35 p1
Adamski, John; Maryland, 1910 3259.35 p1
Adamski, Joseph; Maryland, 1910 3259.35 p1
Adamson, Henry; Georgia, 1815-1845 1640.10 p1
Adamson, John; New York, 1808 8197.10 p53
Adamson, Peter 45; Ontario, 1871 1823.15 p1
Adamson, Thomas; New York, 1835 8197.10 p316
Adamson, Thomas 21; Maryland, 1775 1220.25 p119
Adcock, James; New York, 1840 8197.10 p142
Adcock, William; Pennsylvania, 1779 4629.10 p35
Addams, John; Virginia, 1688 1224.1 p1
Addenbrooke, Edward; Maryland, 1662 2524.55 p9
Adding, Thomas 40; Maryland, 1774 1220.25 p7
Addis, Elizabeth 24; Philadelphia, 1774 1220.25 p42
Addison, Mr.; Quebec, 1856 9196.15 p11
Addison, Anthony; Maryland, 1838 1224.3 p1
Addison, Elizabeth 56; Ontario, 1871 1823.22 p1
Addison, George 31; Ontario, 1871 1823.15 p1
Addison, James 47; Ontario, 1871 1823.15 p1
Addison, John; New York, 1807 8197.10 p34
Addison, Margaret; Virginia, 1715 1224.2 p108
Addison, Robert 45; Ontario, 1871 1823.15 p1
Addley, John; New York, 1840 8197.10 p143
Addrian, J. 57; Vermont, 1870 5900.10 p528
Addrian, Mary Malaniff 57; Vermont, 1879 5900.10 p528
Adelberger, Ans Jorg; Port uncertain, 1752 2856.30 p2
Adelberger, Johann Georg; Port uncertain, 1752 2856.30 p2
Adelmann, Johann; Port uncertain, 1792 2856.30 p2
Adenbrooke, Edward; Maryland, 1662 2524.55 p9
Adenbrooke, Edward; Maryland, 1663 2524.55 p9
Ader, Leonard; Port uncertain, 1764 2856.30 p2
With wife
Aderne, John; Carolina, 1715 1224.2 p3
Aders, Leonard; Port uncertain, 1764 2856.30 p2
With wife
Aderson, Lawrence; Maryland, 1672 2524.55 p9
Aderton, John; Maryland, 1674 2524.55 p9
Adge, Henry 73; Montreal, 1775 1220.25 p106
Adge, Margaret 5 *SEE* Adge, Mary
Adge, Mary 14 *SEE* Adge, Mary
Adge, Mary 44; Montreal, 1775 1220.25 p106
Child: Samuel 16
Child: Mary 14
Child: Margaret 5
Child: William 9
Adge, Samuel 16 *SEE* Adge, Mary
Adge, William 9 *SEE* Adge, Mary
Adkinks, John 41; Philadelphia, 1774 1220.25 p69
Adkins, David 22; Carolina, 1774 1220.25 p75
Adkins, Lawrence; Virginia, 1674 6212.30 p52
Adkins, Robt; Virginia, 1671 6212.30 p42
Adkins, Robt; Virginia, 1671-1672 6212.30 p47
Adkinson, Francis; Maryland, 1682 2524.55 p10
Adlam, John 61; Ontario, 1871 1823.15 p1
Adleberger, Johann; America, 1753 2856.30 p2
Adler, Joseph; South Carolina, 1775 1224.2 p1
Adler, Rosina; Port uncertain, 1788 2856.30 p2
Adley, Godfrey; Pennsylvania, 1838 6058.10 p11
Adley, John; New York, 1840 8197.10 p143
Adley, Thomas; New York, 1840 8197.10 p206
Adrain, Peter; Pennsylvania, 1781 4629.10 p43
Adrenell, Thomas; Maryland, 1658 2524.55 p10
Adres, Leonard; Port uncertain, 1764 2856.30 p2
With wife
Adrian, John; New York, 1831 8197.10 p364
Adrianin, Anna Barbara; Port uncertain, 1746 2856.30 p2
Adriansen, Bartel; New York, 1839 8197.10 p206
Adrien, Ellen Reddy; Vermont, 1850-1924 5900.10 p531
Adrien, Thomas; Vermont, 1844-1927 5900.10 p531
Adshead, Mr.; Portland, Maine, 1858 9196.15 p27
Adsit, Elizabeth 23; Ontario, 1861 2896.28 p30
Adsit, Franklin 14; Ontario, 1861 2896.28 p22
Adsit, Jane 22; Ontario, 1861 2896.28 p22
Adsit, Nancy J. 2; Ontario, 1861 2896.28 p30
Adtalberger, Philipp; America, 1753 2856.30 p2
Adyson, John; Virginia, 1690-1691 6212.30 p59
Aeglowith, Joseph; Maryland, 1910 3259.35 p1
Affleck, Robert; Grenada, 1867 1640.13 p1
Afflick, Ann M. *SEE* Afflick, Hans
Afflick, Hans; Mississippi, 1843 1640.10 p1
Wife: Ann M.
Afflick, James 35; Jamaica, 1774 1220.25 p85
Aftaiken, F. 37; Alaska, 1918 9196.1 p55
Aftaiken, F. 37; Yukon, 1918 9196.1 p55
Agal, William Marius; New York, 1830 8197.10 p363
Agan, Amanda; Vermont, 1848-1911 5900.10 p300
Agan, Catherine; Vermont, 1817-1900 5900.10 p220
Agan, Cora Alice Safford; Vermont, 1854-1899 5900.10 p308
Agan, Dennis; New York, 1837 8197.10 p318
Agan, Ellen 36; Vermont, 1865 5900.10 p259
Agan, Ellen Enright; Vermont, 1835-1900 5900.10 p586
Agan, Frank W.; Vermont, 1869-1934 5900.10 p308
Agan, John; Vermont, 1845-1879 5900.10 p300
Agan, Mary 58; Vermont, 1885 5900.10 p259
Agan, Mary Ann 18; Vermont, 1880 5900.10 p83
Agan, Patrick 83; Vermont, 1876 5900.10 p259
Agan, Patrick 90; Vermont, 1895 5900.10 p218
Agan, Sarah Hanley 72; Vermont, 1891 5900.10 p218
Agan, William; Vermont, 1808-1883 5900.10 p586
Agar, Miss; Quebec, 1857 9196.15 p18
Agar, Benjamin 27; Virginia, 1774 1220.25 p91
Agar, Margaret Hayward; New Orleans, 1827 1224.3 p1
Agar, William; New York, 1807 8197.10 p34
Agard, Charles; Maryland, 1682 2524.55 p10
Agassiz, Mr.; Portland, Maine, 1858 9196.15 p27
Agassiz, Mrs.; Portland, Maine, 1858 9196.15 p27
Agawanakwat, Mrs. 31; Ontario, 1871 1823.28 p1
Agazis, Mr.; Quebec, 1857 9196.15 p19
Agen, Margaret 10; Vermont, 1857 5900.10 p449
Ager, Richard 17; Ontario, 1871 1823.28 p1
Agg, James; Maryland, 1682 2524.55 p10
Agin, Peter 62; Vermont, 1900 5900.10 p285
Aglionby, William; Savannah, Georgia, 1745 1224.2 p1

Agne, Johann Nickel; America, 1735 ***2856.30*** *p2*
Agne, Johann Nickel; America, 1736 ***2856.30*** *p2*
Agne, Magdalena; America, 1746 ***2856.30*** *p2*
Agne, Theobald; America, 1746 ***2856.30*** *p2*
Agnew, Andrew; Maryland, 1674 ***2524.55*** *p10*
Agnew, Catharine 36; Vermont, 1876 ***5900.10*** *p473*
Agnew, Elizabeth 49; Vermont, 1851 ***5900.10*** *p556*
Agnew, George; Georgia, 1699 ***1640.13*** *p1*
Agnew, Henry 60; Ontario, 1871 ***1823.15*** *p2*
Agnew, James; New York, 1807 ***8197.10*** *p329*
Agnew, James; North America, 1778 ***1224.2*** *p1*
Agnew, James 27; Ontario, 1871 ***1823.22*** *p1*
Agnew, James 29; Ontario, 1871 ***1823.28*** *p1*
Agnew, James 31; Ontario, 1871 ***1823.15*** *p2*
Agnew, James 49; Ontario, 1871 ***1823.15*** *p2*
Agnew, James 70; Ontario, 1871 ***1823.22*** *p1*
Agnew, John 35; Ontario, 1871 ***1823.15*** *p2*
Agnew, Mary 26; Ontario, 1871 ***1823.22*** *p1*
Agnew, Mary McGough 67; Vermont, 1874 ***5900.10*** *p470*
Agnew, Thomas; America, 1843 ***1640.13*** *p1*
Agnew, Thomas 24; Ontario, 1871 ***1823.15*** *p2*
Agnew, Thomas 29; Ontario, 1871 ***1823.15*** *p2*
Agnew, William 24; Ontario, 1871 ***1823.15*** *p2*
Agoff, A. 24; Alaska, 1916 ***9196.1*** *p43*
Agoff, A. 24; Whitehorse, Yukon, 1916 ***9196.1*** *p43*
Agoff, P. 25; Alaska, 1916 ***9196.1*** *p44*
Agoff, P. 25; Whitehorse, Yukon, 1916 ***9196.1*** *p44*
Agoff, P. 36; Alaska, 1917 ***9196.1*** *p45*
Agoff, P. 36; Whitehorse, Yukon, 1917 ***9196.1*** *p45*
Agowisse, Antoine 45; Ontario, 1871 ***1823.28*** *p1*
Agricola, Michael; Port uncertain, 1760 ***2856.30*** *p2*
Agricola, Michael; Port uncertain, 1781 ***2856.30*** *p2*
Agricola, Michael; Port uncertain, 1786 ***2856.30*** *p2*
Agustajmowics, Enacy; Maryland, 1910 ***3259.35*** *p1*
Aguzaroff, A. 35; Alaska, 1916 ***9196.1*** *p44*
Aguzaroff, A. 35; Whitehorse, Yukon, 1916 ***9196.1*** *p44*
Agwase, Dominic 37; Ontario, 1871 ***1823.28*** *p1*
Ahare, Patrick 45; Ontario, 1871 ***1823.28*** *p1*
Ahbetahkezhik, Francis Wahbegwowhnai 25; Ontario, 1871 ***1823.28*** *p1*
Ahbetahkezhik, John 35; Ontario, 1871 ***1823.28*** *p1*
Ahdahzhawa, John 70; Ontario, 1871 ***1823.28*** *p1*
Ahearn, Bridget Burke; Vermont, 1800-1899 ***5900.10*** *p186*
Ahearn, Catherine 78; Vermont, 1918 ***5900.10*** *p64*
Ahearn, Daniel; Vermont, 1838-1908 ***5900.10*** *p592*
Ahearn, Elizabeth; Vermont, 1877 ***5900.10*** *p191*
Ahearn, Hanora Murphy; Vermont, 1841-1892 ***5900.10*** *p592*
Ahearn, James 67; Vermont, 1908 ***5900.10*** *p589*
Ahearn, John 6; Vermont, 1863 ***5900.10*** *p176*
Ahearn, John 67; Vermont, 1909 ***5900.10*** *p508*
Ahearn, Joseph 60; Vermont, 1880 ***5900.10*** *p176*
Ahearn, Mary 67; Vermont, 1909 ***5900.10*** *p508*
Ahearn, Mary Murphy 60; Vermont, 1901 ***5900.10*** *p589*
Ahearn, Mary Murphy 75; Vermont, 1890 ***5900.10*** *p176*
Ahearn, Thomas; Vermont, 1837-1920 ***5900.10*** *p311*
Ahearn, Thomas F.; Vermont, 1852-1915 ***5900.10*** *p185*
Aher, John; Vermont, 1825-1897 ***5900.10*** *p119*
Aher, Margaret Stack; Vermont, 1843-1901 ***5900.10*** *p119*
Aher, Nellie E.; Vermont, 1884-1955 ***5900.10*** *p119*
Aher, Thomas J.; Vermont, 1874-1936 ***5900.10*** *p119*
Ahern, Catherine Griffin; Vermont, 1829-1905 ***5900.10*** *p507*
Ahern, Daniel 29; Vermont, 1887 ***5900.10*** *p114*
Ahern, Ellen O'Neill 56; Vermont, 1867 ***5900.10*** *p369*
Ahern, James 60; Vermont, 1866 ***5900.10*** *p368*
Ahern, Johanna 62; Vermont, 1888 ***5900.10*** *p106*
Ahern, Johanna 62; Vermont, 1888 ***5900.10*** *p114*
Ahern, Mary; Vermont, 1832-1913 ***5900.10*** *p59*
Ahern, Mary 37; Vermont, 1886 ***5900.10*** *p114*
Ahern, Mary Coffey; Vermont, 1838-1925 ***5900.10*** *p465*
Ahern, Michael; Vermont, 1826-1862 ***5900.10*** *p507*
Ahern, Patrick; Vermont, 1828-1909 ***5900.10*** *p465*
Ahern, William 51; Vermont, 1870 ***5900.10*** *p105*
Ahern, William 51; Vermont, 1870 ***5900.10*** *p114*
Aherne, Darby; Maryland, 1682 ***2524.55*** *p10*
Ahiabeus, Joseph 32; Ontario, 1871 ***1823.28*** *p1*
Ahl, Johann Adam; Port uncertain, 1752 ***2856.30*** *p2*
 With wife & 2 children
Ahl, Peter; Port uncertain, 1756 ***2856.30*** *p2*
Ahlmen, Henry; New York, 1807 ***8197.10*** *p33*
Ahlsbach, David; America, 1771 ***2856.30*** *p3*
Ahlstadter, Leonhard; Port uncertain, 1754 ***2856.30*** *p3*
Ahr, Johann Philipp; Port uncertain, 1775 ***2856.30*** *p3*
Ahrens, Albert; New York, 1840 ***8197.10*** *p142*
Ahrens, Fets 54; Ontario, 1871 ***1823.15*** *p2*
Ahrens, Frederick; New York, 1838 ***8197.10*** *p109*
Ahrens, George M.; New York, 1838 ***8197.10*** *p109*
Ahwonokemah, Peter 42; Ontario, 1871 ***1823.28*** *p1*
Ahwonoquet, Peter 33; Ontario, 1871 ***1823.28*** *p1*
Aichel, Franz; Port uncertain, 1752 ***2856.30*** *p3*
Aicheler, Johann; Port uncertain, 1738 ***2856.30*** *p3*
Aichenbrenner, Urban; America, 1740 ***2856.30*** *p3*
 With wife
Aicher, Willibald; Port uncertain, 1764 ***2856.30*** *p3*
Aichhorn, Anna Maria; Port uncertain, 1747 ***2856.30*** *p3*
Aichler, Johann; Port uncertain, 1738 ***2856.30*** *p3*
Aigst, Michael; Port uncertain, 1717 ***2856.30*** *p3*
Aiken, Alexander; Georgia, 1699 ***1640.13*** *p1*
Aiken, Peter 37; Ontario, 1871 ***1823.15*** *p2*
Aiken, Robert; Pennsylvania, 1779 ***4629.10*** *p39*
Aikenhead, James 55; Ontario, 1871 ***1823.15*** *p2*
Aikenhead, John 58; Ontario, 1871 ***1823.15*** *p2*
Aikens, Hannah; Ontario, 1861 ***2896.27*** *p53*
Aikens, William; New York, 1807 ***8197.10*** *p326*
Aikin, James 41; New York, 1774 ***1220.25*** *p141*
Aikins, Francis 40; Ontario, 1871 ***1823.22*** *p1*
Aikle, Henery 35; Ontario, 1871 ***1823.28*** *p1*
Aikman, George; Florida, 1781 ***1640.10*** *p1*
Aikman, Joseph; Mobile, Alabama, 1767 ***1640.10*** *p1*
Ailward, John; Maryland, 1675 ***2524.55*** *p10*
Ainkowicz, Alexander; Maryland, 1910 ***3259.35*** *p1*
Ainley, Ann 59; Ontario, 1871 ***1823.15*** *p2*
Ainley, Peter 39; Ontario, 1871 ***1823.15*** *p2*
Ainsley, Archibald 56; Ontario, 1871 ***1823.22*** *p1*
Ainslie, James; New York, 1834 ***8197.10*** *p71*
Ainslie, Robert; New York, 1805 ***8197.10*** *p28*
Ainson, Mary 1 *SEE* Ainson, Miles
Ainson, Mary 30 *SEE* Ainson, Miles
Ainson, Miles 6 *SEE* Ainson, Miles
Ainson, Miles 42; Fort Cumberland, Nova Scotia, 1774 ***1220.25*** *p18*
 Child: Mary 1
 Child: Miles 6
 Wife: Mary 30
 Child: Thomas 3
Ainson, Thomas 3 *SEE* Ainson, Miles
Ainsworth, Mr.; Quebec, 1856 ***9196.15*** *p10*
Ainsworth, Cornelius 63; Ontario, 1871 ***1823.22*** *p1*
Ainsworth, Eli 50; Ontario, 1871 ***1823.22*** *p1*
Aipen, Francis; Maryland, 1910 ***3259.35*** *p1*
Air, John; Georgia, 1752-1845 ***1640.10*** *p1*
Aird, Alexander 47; Ontario, 1871 ***1823.22*** *p1*
Aird, James; Pensacola, Florida, 1778 ***1640.10*** *p1*
Aird, James 50; Ontario, 1871 ***1823.22*** *p1*
Aird, William 52; Ontario, 1871 ***1823.22*** *p2*
Aire, Robert; New York, 1771 ***1224.2*** *p1*
Aires, John 27; Philadelphia, 1794 ***4629.10*** *p78*
Airey, Joseph; New York, 1764 ***1224.2*** *p1*
Airley, Robert 56; Ontario, 1871 ***1823.28*** *p1*
Airston, William Glen; Canada, 1890 ***1640.13*** *p1*
Airth, David 50; Ontario, 1871 ***1823.28*** *p1*
Airth, Henry 52; Ontario, 1871 ***1823.28*** *p1*
Airth, Henry 84; Ontario, 1871 ***1823.28*** *p1*
Airth, James 56; Ontario, 1871 ***1823.15*** *p2*
Airth, Mirion 80; Ontario, 1871 ***1823.28*** *p1*
Airth, Robert 49; Ontario, 1871 ***1823.28*** *p1*
Aishley, Edward; Virginia, 1656 ***1224.1*** *p3*
Aisquith, William; Maryland, 1681 ***2524.55*** *p10*
Aitcheson, Andrew 44; Ontario, 1871 ***1823.15*** *p2*
Aitcheson, James 17; Ontario, 1871 ***1823.15*** *p2*
Aitcheson, James 37; Ontario, 1871 ***1823.15*** *p2*
Aitchinson, Mr.; Quebec, 1857 ***9196.15*** *p16*
Aitchinson, Thomas 41; Ontario, 1871 ***1823.22*** *p2*
Aitchison, Christopher 40; Ontario, 1871 ***1823.22*** *p2*
Aitchison, Francis 57; Ontario, 1871 ***1823.22*** *p2*
Aitchison, James; New York, 1840 ***8197.10*** *p206*
Aitchison, Jannet 82; Ontario, 1871 ***1823.22*** *p2*
Aitchison, Peter; Jamaica, 1752 ***1640.13*** *p1*
Aitchison, William 66; Ontario, 1871 ***1823.22*** *p2*
Aitchson, Robert; New York, 1838 ***8197.10*** *p109*
Aitken, Mr.; Quebec, 1858 ***9196.15*** *p36*
Aitken, Mrs.; Quebec, 1858 ***9196.15*** *p36*
Aitken, Alexander; New York, 1831 ***8197.10*** *p367*
Aitken, George; Virgin Islands, 1815 ***1640.13*** *p1*
Aitken, James; America, 1783 ***1640.13*** *p1*
Aitken, James White; Vermont, 1860-1945 ***5900.10*** *p607*
Aitken, Mary Hill; Vermont, 1869-1945 ***5900.10*** *p607*
Aitken, Robert; Pennsylvania, 1777 ***4629.10*** *p19*
Aitkenhead, Mr.; Quebec, 1858 ***9196.15*** *p41*
Aitkenhead, Mr.; Quebec, 1858 ***9196.15*** *p42*
Aitkenhead, William; Jamaica, 1768 ***1640.13*** *p1*
Aitkin, John; New York, 1807 ***8197.10*** *p33*
Aitkin, John; New York, 1838 ***8197.10*** *p109*
Aitkin, William; New York, 1840 ***8197.10*** *p142*
Aitkin, William; Portland, Maine, 1858 ***9196.15*** *p27*
Ajawanakwah, J. Bte 35; Ontario, 1871 ***1823.28*** *p1*
Akaloff, . . . 23; Alaska, 1917 ***9196.1*** *p45*
Akaloff, . . . 23; Whitehorse, Yukon, 1917 ***9196.1*** *p45*
Akam, Henry 53; Ontario, 1871 ***1823.15*** *p2*
Akeeth, George; Maryland, 1670 ***2524.55*** *p10*
Akers, William; New York, 1794 ***8197.10*** *p1*
Akins, John 52; Ontario, 1871 ***1823.15*** *p2*
Akins, Patrik; Virginia, 1671 ***6212.30*** *p44*
Akins, Robert 43; Ontario, 1871 ***1823.22*** *p2*
Akins, William; Savannah, Georgia, 1810 ***1640.10*** *p1*
Alablaster, Ja; Virginia, 1665-1666 ***6212.30*** *p21*
Alander, H. 41; Alaska, 1917 ***9196.1*** *p53*
Alander, H. 41; Whitehorse, Yukon, 1917 ***9196.1*** *p53*
Alanson, Thomas; Maryland, 1659 ***2524.55*** *p10*
Alanston, Sarah; Maryland, 1659 ***2524.55*** *p10*
Albaret, Louis; New York, 1828 ***8197.10*** *p205*
Albee, Amos 50; Ontario, 1861 ***2896.28*** *p25*
Albee, Martha Ann 50; Ontario, 1861 ***2896.28*** *p25*
Alber, Matthaus; America, 1753 ***2856.30*** *p3*
 With wife & children
Albercrombie, Jemima 28; Ontario, 1871 ***1823.22*** *p2*
Alberding, August; Baltimore, 1852 ***3437.14*** *p64*
Alberg, Hilda 31; Vancouver, British Columbia, 1918 ***9196.1*** *p71*
Alberg, Hilda 31; Washington, 1918 ***9196.1*** *p71*
Alberg, Julius 34; Vancouver, British Columbia, 1918 ***9196.1*** *p71*
Alberg, Julius 34; Washington, 1918 ***9196.1*** *p71*
Albers, Peter; Port uncertain, 1754 ***2856.30*** *p3*
Alberson, Ruloff; Pennsylvania, 1777 ***4629.10*** *p10*
Alberstal, Franz Nickel; America, 1770 ***2856.30*** *p3*
Alberstal, Johann Nickel; America, 1770 ***2856.30*** *p3*
Alberstal, Nicol; America, 1763 ***2856.30*** *p3*
Alberstal, Nicol; America, 1764 ***2856.30*** *p3*
Albert, Adam; America, 1738 ***2856.30*** *p3*
Albert, Johann Adam; Port uncertain, 1781 ***2856.30*** *p3*
Albert, Johann Michael; America, 1737 ***2856.30*** *p3*
Albert, Johann Michael; America, 1748 ***2856.30*** *p3*
Albert, Margarete; Port uncertain, 1731 ***2856.30*** *p3*
Albert, Peter; Port uncertain, 1752 ***2856.30*** *p3*
Albert, Peter; Port uncertain, 1781 ***2856.30*** *p3*
Albert, Sebastian; America, 1739 ***2856.30*** *p3*
 With son
Albert, Wilhelm; America, 1752 ***2856.30*** *p3*
Albert, Wilhelm; Port uncertain, 1752 ***2856.30*** *p3*
Alberth, Wilhelm; Port uncertain, 1752 ***2856.30*** *p3*
Alberthal, Balthasar; Port uncertain, 1753 ***2856.30*** *p3*
Alberti, Clara Elisabeth; Port uncertain, 1736 ***2856.30*** *p3*
 With child
Alberts, William; New York, 1840 ***8197.10*** *p142*
Albertson, Carl 45; Seattle, 1917 ***9196.1*** *p52*
Albertson, Carl 45; Yukon, 1917 ***9196.1*** *p52*
Albes, Anna; Port uncertain, 1741 ***2856.30*** *p3*
Albes, Magdalena; Port uncertain, 1741 ***2856.30*** *p3*
Albig, Johann; Port uncertain, 1752 ***2856.30*** *p3*
Albin, Catherine; Charleston, South Carolina, 1854 ***1224.3*** *p44*
Albin, Thomas; Florida, 1800-1845 ***1640.10*** *p1*
Albinger, Mathias; Port uncertain, 1784 ***2856.30*** *p3*
 With wife
Albon, John; Virginia, 1672 ***6212.30*** *p50*
Albrecht, Barbara; Port uncertain, 1774 ***2856.30*** *p4*
 With husband
Albrecht, Friedrich; Port uncertain, 1796 ***2856.30*** *p3*
Albrecht, Jacob 68; Ontario, 1871 ***1823.15*** *p2*
Albrecht, Johann Michael; America, 1737 ***2856.30*** *p3*
Albrecht, Susanna Cathari; Port uncertain, 1769 ***2856.30*** *p3*
Albridge, Tho.; Maryland, 1681 ***2524.55*** *p10*
Albrigte, Christian 58; Ontario, 1871 ***1823.15*** *p2*
Albro, Maturian; Havana, 1765 ***1224.2*** *p1*
Albro, Maturian; Rhode Island, 1765 ***1224.2*** *p1*
Albu, Solomon; Philadelphia, 1857 ***6058.10*** *p49*
Alcock, Charles; New York, 1834 ***8197.10*** *p71*
Alcock, Richard 49; Ontario, 1871 ***1823.15*** *p2*
Alcock, Violet; Maryland, 1672 ***2524.55*** *p10*
Alcock, William 50; Ontario, 1871 ***1823.15*** *p2*
Alcorn, George; New York, 1838 ***8197.10*** *p109*
Alcorn, James; Pennsylvania, 1817 ***6058.10*** *p6*
Alcorn, William; New York, 1840 ***8197.10*** *p143*
Alcorn, William 40; Ontario, 1871 ***1823.22*** *p2*
Alcough, Abram; Virginia, 1664 ***6212.30*** *p7*
Alcraft, John; Maryland, 1660 ***2524.55*** *p10*
Alcroft, John; Maryland, 1660 ***2524.55*** *p10*
Alcut, Ellen 29; Ontario, 1871 ***1823.22*** *p2*
Alde, Henry; Maryland, 1653 ***2524.55*** *p10*
Alderchurch, . . .; Boston, 1737 ***4628.40*** *p114*
Alderdice, Eliza 8; Ontario, 1861 ***2896.28*** *p54*
Alderdice, Eliza 36; Ontario, 1861 ***2896.28*** *p54*
Alderdice, John 5; Ontario, 1861 ***2896.28*** *p54*
Alderdice, John 40; Ontario, 1861 ***2896.28*** *p54*
Alderdice, Margaret A. 3; Ontario, 1861 ***2896.28*** *p54*
Alderdice, Mary 9; Ontario, 1861 ***2896.28*** *p54*
Alderman, Thomas 33; Ontario, 1871 ***1823.28*** *p1*
Alderson, George; Maryland, 1663 ***2524.55*** *p10*
Alderson, John 55; Ontario, 1871 ***1823.15*** *p2*
Alderson, Robert; California, 1857 ***1224.3*** *p1*
Alderton, John 22; Maryland, 1774 ***1220.25*** *p71*
Aldfield, Elizabeth 25; Fort Cumberland, Nova Scotia, 1775 ***1220.25*** *p21*

Aldham, Daniel 27; Maryland, 1775 ***1220.25*** *p105*
Aldin, Thomas 21; Philadelphia, 1774 ***1220.25*** *p35*
Aldredge, Thomas; Maryland, 1668 ***2524.55*** *p10*
Aldrich, Peter; Maryland, 1673 ***2524.55*** *p10*
Aldrich, Sarah A. Kellett 57; Vermont, 1900-1909 ***5900.10*** *p310*
Aldrich, Truman 35; Ontario, 1871 ***1823.22*** *p2*
Aldridge, Ann; Maryland, 1667 ***2524.55*** *p10*
Aldridge, Christopher 24; Maryland, 1775 ***1220.25*** *p101*
Aldridge, George; Maryland, 1667 ***2524.55*** *p10*
With 4 children
Aldridge, Mary; Virginia, 1674 ***6212.30*** *p52*
Aldridge, Paul 68; Ontario, 1871 ***1823.15*** *p2*
Aldridge, Richard; Maryland, 1682 ***2524.55*** *p10*
Aldridge, Thomas; Maryland, 1674 ***2524.55*** *p10*
Aldridge, Thomas 21; Maryland, 1774 ***1220.25*** *p60*
Aldridge, Thomas 24; Maryland, 1774 ***1220.25*** *p47*
Aldrige, Richd; Virginia, 1671 ***6212.30*** *p45*
Aldsworth, Cicero 32; Ontario, 1871 ***1823.15*** *p2*
Aldwell, Mr.; Quebec, 1858 ***9196.15*** *p37*
Aleberry, Lewis; Virginia, 1665-1666 ***6212.30*** *p24*
Aleegof, Loverice; Maryland, 1680 ***2524.55*** *p10*
Alemby, Phillip; Maryland, 1657 ***2524.55*** *p10*
Alen, Genevieve P.; Vermont, 1825-1907 ***5900.10*** *p193*
Alexalzer, Ludwich; Maryland, 1910 ***3259.35*** *p1*
Alexander, Mr.; Quebec, 1856 ***9196.15*** *p8*
Alexander, Mr.; Quebec, 1857 ***9196.15*** *p14*
Alexander, Mr.; Quebec, 1858 ***9196.15*** *p45*
Alexander, Mrs.; Quebec, 1856 ***9196.15*** *p8*
Alexander, Mrs.; Quebec, 1858 ***9196.15*** *p36*
Alexander, Mrs.; Quebec, 1858 ***9196.15*** *p45*
Alexander, Adam; Georgia, 1735-1810 ***1640.10*** *p1*
Alexander, Adam; Port uncertain, 1789 ***2856.30*** *p4*
Alexander, Alexander; New York, 1840 ***8197.10*** *p143*
Alexander, Alexander 38; Ontario, 1871 ***1823.15*** *p2*
Alexander, Andrew; New York, 1802 ***8197.10*** *p18*
Alexander, Andrew; New York, 1803 ***8197.10*** *p10*
Alexander, Anthony; Maryland, 1682 ***2524.55*** *p10*
Alexander, Charles; London, England, 1861 ***1640.13*** *p1*
Alexander, David; Maryland, 1757 ***1224.2*** *p2*
Alexander, Ebenezer 35; Ontario, 1871 ***1823.15*** *p2*
Alexander, Francis; Alabama, 1806-1856 ***1640.10*** *p2*
Alexander, George; Halifax, Nova Scotia, 1872 ***1640.13*** *p1*
Alexander, George; Quebec, 1856 ***1640.13*** *p1*
Alexander, George; Savannah, Georgia, 1806 ***1640.10*** *p2*
Alexander, George 46; Ontario, 1871 ***1823.22*** *p2*
Alexander, Henry; Maryland, 1655 ***2524.55*** *p10*
Alexander, Isabella; Baltimore, 1839 ***1224.3*** *p1*
Alexander, Isabella; Grenada, 1869 ***1640.13*** *p2*
Alexander, James; Florida, 1826 ***1224.3*** *p1*
Alexander, James; Georgia, 1769 ***1640.10*** *p2*
Alexander, James 33; Ontario, 1861 ***2896.28*** *p28*
Alexander, James 49; Ontario, 1871 ***1823.22*** *p2*
Alexander, James 64; Ontario, 1871 ***1823.15*** *p2*
Alexander, Janet; Savannah, Georgia, 1774 ***1640.10*** *p2*
Alexander, Janet 60; Ontario, 1871 ***1823.28*** *p1*
Alexander, John; Carolina, 1699 ***1640.13*** *p2*
Alexander, John; Georgia, 1766 ***1640.10*** *p2*
Alexander, John; Pennsylvania, 1779 ***4629.10*** *p41*
Alexander, John 23; Philadelphia, 1774 ***1220.25*** *p81*
Alexander, John 40; Ontario, 1871 ***1823.15*** *p2*
Alexander, John 55; Ontario, 1871 ***1823.22*** *p2*
Alexander, John 62; Ontario, 1871 ***1823.15*** *p2*
Alexander, John 65; Ontario, 1871 ***1823.15*** *p2*
Alexander, L. S.; Alabama, 1843 ***1640.10*** *p2*
Wife: Margaret
Child: Sarah
Alexander, Margaret *SEE* Alexander, L. S.
Alexander, Mary; Windward Islands, 1818 ***1640.13*** *p2*
Alexander, Mary 64; Ontario, 1871 ***1823.15*** *p2*
Alexander, Matilda McDermott 60; Vermont, 1904 ***5900.10*** *p483*
Alexander, Matthew; New York, 1828 ***8197.10*** *p349*
Alexander, Perciville 44; Ontario, 1871 ***1823.28*** *p1*
Alexander, Robert; Kentucky, 1841 ***1224.3*** *p1*
Alexander, Robert; New York, 1821 ***8197.10*** *p205*
Alexander, Robert; New York, 1830 ***8197.10*** *p205*
Alexander, Robert; New York, 1866 ***1640.13*** *p2*
Alexander, Robert; Quebec, 1858 ***9196.15*** *p43*
Alexander, Robert 40; Ontario, 1871 ***1823.15*** *p2*
Alexander, Samuel; Pennsylvania, 1777 ***4629.10*** *p15*
Alexander, Samuel 33; Ontario, 1871 ***1823.28*** *p1*
Alexander, Samuel 45; Ontario, 1871 ***1823.15*** *p2*
Alexander, Sarah *SEE* Alexander, L. S.
Alexander, Sarah; New York, 1838 ***8197.10*** *p318*
Alexander, Sarah J. 2; Ontario, 1861 ***2896.28*** *p28*
Alexander, Thomas; Boston, n.d. ***1224.2*** *p2*
Alexander, Thomas; Nova Scotia, 1789 ***1224.2*** *p2*
Alexander, Thomas 65; Ontario, 1871 ***1823.22*** *p2*
Alexander, Walter 57; Ontario, 1871 ***1823.15*** *p3*
Alexander, William; Augusta, Georgia, 1757 ***1640.10*** *p2*
Alexander, William; Bahamas, 1783 ***1640.10*** *p2*
Alexander, William; Georgia, 1760 ***1640.10*** *p2*
Alexander, William; Georgia, 1774 ***1640.10*** *p3*
With wife & 3 children
Alexander, William; Philadelphia, 1727 ***1224.2*** *p2*
Alexander, William 32; Savannah, Georgia, 1774 ***1220.25*** *p139*
With wife & 3 children
Alexander, William 33; Ontario, 1871 ***1823.15*** *p3*
Alexander, William 51; Ontario, 1871 ***1823.22*** *p2*
Alexander, William 60; Ontario, 1871 ***1823.15*** *p3*
Alexander, William 65; Ontario, 1871 ***1823.15*** *p3*
Alexander, William S.; New York, 1830 ***8197.10*** *p360*
Alexander, Wm 33; Ontario, 1861 ***2896.28*** *p28*
Alexanderowicz, Stanislaw; Maryland, 1910 ***3259.35*** *p1*
Alexandre, Francis; New York, 1838 ***8197.10*** *p205*
Alexandre, Moine; New York, New York, 1898 ***3437.14*** *p169*
Alexanza, Konstantin; Maryland, 1910 ***3259.35*** *p1*
Alexon, Jasper; Virginia, 1706 ***1224.2*** *p2*
Aley, John; Philadelphia, 1783 ***1224.2*** *p2*
Alford, Anne *SEE* Alford, John
Alford, Elizabeth *SEE* Alford, John
Alford, Jno; Virginia, 1671-1672 ***6212.30*** *p46*
Alford, John; Maryland, 1665 ***2524.55*** *p10*
Wife: Elizabeth
Daughter: Anne
Daughter: Elizabeth
Alford, Mary 21; Maryland, 1774 ***1220.25*** *p84*
Alford, William 26; Maryland, 1774 ***1220.25*** *p84*
Alfred, Robert 22; Virginia, 1773 ***1220.25*** *p31*
Algate, Thomas; Virginia, 1665-1666 ***6212.30*** *p24*
Algeo, David; Quebec, 1792 ***1224.2*** *p2*
Algeo, Margaret; New York, New York, 1792 ***1224.2*** *p2*
Alger, Charles 78; Ontario, 1871 ***1823.22*** *p2*
Alger, Ellen Wall; Vermont, 1851-1915 ***5900.10*** *p538*
Alger, Mary; Maryland, 1676 ***2524.55*** *p10*
Alger, William H.; Vermont, 1853-1915 ***5900.10*** *p538*
Algernall, Jno; Virginia, 1665-1666 ***6212.30*** *p21*
Algie, Joseph 25; Ontario, 1871 ***1823.28*** *p1*
Alguire, Marion 64; Ontario, 1871 ***1823.22*** *p2*
Alicast, John; Maryland, 1660 ***2524.55*** *p10*
Alicee, Edward, Jr.; Maryland, 1668 ***2524.55*** *p10*
Alifford, Elizabeth; Maryland, 1666 ***2524.55*** *p10*
Alirich, G. 27; Alaska, 1917 ***9196.1*** *p46*
Alirich, G. 27; Whitehorse, Yukon, 1917 ***9196.1*** *p46*
Alison, Crow 25; Ontario, 1871 ***1823.15*** *p3*
Aliston, Elizabeth; Maryland, 1659-1661 ***2524.55*** *p10*
Alkemore, John; Maryland, 1661 ***2524.55*** *p119*
All, Isaac; Pennsylvania, 1777 ***4629.10*** *p25*
Allan, Master; Quebec, 1857 ***9196.15*** *p14*
Allan, Miss; Quebec, 1857 ***9196.15*** *p16*
Allan, Mr.; Quebec, 1858 ***9196.15*** *p32*
Allan, A.; Quebec, 1857 ***9196.15*** *p14*
Allan, Mrs. A.; Quebec, 1857 ***9196.15*** *p14*
Allan, Ann; Ontario, 1877 ***1640.13*** *p2*
Allan, Arthur Edward; Montreal, 1894 ***1640.13*** *p2*
Allan, B.; Quebec, 1857 ***9196.15*** *p14*
Allan, Christopher; Georgia, 1775 ***1640.10*** *p3*
Allan, Colin; Fredericton, New Brunswick, 1850 ***1640.13*** *p2*
Allan, David 54; Ontario, 1871 ***1823.22*** *p2*
Allan, Galdan 61; Ontario, 1871 ***1823.28*** *p1*
Allan, George 24; Ontario, 1871 ***1823.15*** *p3*
Allan, Henry 53; Ontario, 1871 ***1823.22*** *p2*
Allan, Hugh; Montreal, 1886 ***1640.13*** *p2*
Allan, James; Canada, 1853 ***1640.13*** *p2*
Allan, James; Quebec, 1857 ***9196.15*** *p15*
Allan, James 78; Ontario, 1871 ***1823.15*** *p3*
Allan, John 29; Ontario, 1871 ***1823.15*** *p3*
Allan, Jonathan 19; Philadelphia, 1774 ***1220.25*** *p82*
Allan, Robert; New Orleans, 1830 ***1640.10*** *p3*
Allan, Robert 44; Ontario, 1871 ***1823.15*** *p3*
Allan, Samuel 45; Ontario, 1871 ***1823.22*** *p2*
Allan, W.; Quebec, 1856 ***9196.15*** *p6*
Allan, Mrs. W.; Quebec, 1856 ***9196.15*** *p5*
Allan, William; New York, 1840 ***8197.10*** *p143*
Allan, William; Quebec, 1857 ***9196.15*** *p15*
Allan, William 49; Ontario, 1871 ***1823.15*** *p3*
Allan, William Spence; Canada, 1843 ***1640.13*** *p2*
Allanson, John; New York, 1837 ***8197.10*** *p318*
Allanson, X. P.; Virginia, 1664 ***6212.30*** *p14*
Allard, Elen A. 19; Ontario, 1861 ***2896.25*** *p26*
Allard, Elizabeth 63; Ontario, 1871 ***1823.22*** *p2*
Allard, William 22; Ontario, 1871 ***1823.28*** *p1*
Allardice, John; Savannah, Georgia, 1768 ***1640.10*** *p3*
Allat, Elizabeth; Maryland, 1679 ***2524.55*** *p11*
Allcock, Samuel; Maryland, 1649 ***2524.55*** *p11*
Allcock, Violetta; Maryland, 1657 ***2524.55*** *p11*
Allcoff, Boris; British Columbia, 1913 ***9196.1*** *p56*
Allcoff, Boris; Seattle, 1913 ***9196.1*** *p56*
Allebone, Thomas; Maryland, 1666 ***2524.55*** *p11*
Allecock, Christ'r Kelby; Pennsylvania, 1777 ***4629.10*** *p30*
Alleine, Josias; New England, 1678 ***1224.1*** *p1*
Alleman, William 15; Virginia, 1774 ***1220.25*** *p91*
Allemus, Jacob; Pennsylvania, 1786 ***4629.10*** *p54*
Allen, . . .; Boston, 1737 ***4628.40*** *p114*
Allen, Miss; Quebec, 1857 ***9196.15*** *p22*
Allen, Aaron; Pennsylvania, 1837 ***1224.3*** *p1*
Allen, Abijah; Pennsylvania, 1836 ***1224.3*** *p1*
Allen, Alexander 71; Ontario, 1871 ***1823.22*** *p2*
Allen, Alexr; Virginia, 1674 ***6212.30*** *p52*
Allen, Alfred 29; Ontario, 1871 ***1823.15*** *p3*
Allen, Alfred 40; Ontario, 1871 ***1823.15*** *p3*
Allen, Anthony 38; Ontario, 1871 ***1823.15*** *p3*
Allen, Arthur; Vermont, 1823-1896 ***5900.10*** *p338*
Allen, Benjamin 32; Ontario, 1871 ***1823.15*** *p3*
Allen, Bozonne; New England, 1647 ***1224.1*** *p1*
Allen, Catherine J. 8; Ontario, 1861 ***2896.25*** *p4*
Allen, Chamless; Pennsylvania, 1777 ***4629.10*** *p24*
Allen, Chamless; Pennsylvania, 1779 ***4629.10*** *p39*
Allen, Charles; Pennsylvania, 1777 ***4629.10*** *p11*
Allen, Cora Darcy; Vermont, 1859 ***5900.10*** *p308*
Allen, Daniel; Pennsylvania, 1836 ***1224.3*** *p1*
Allen, David; Georgia, 1699 ***1640.13*** *p2*
Allen, Edward Frederick; New York, 1839 ***8197.10*** *p134*
Allen, Eliza; Vermont, 1826-1875 ***5900.10*** *p338*
Allen, Elizabeth; Pennsylvania, 1836 ***1224.3*** *p1*
Allen, Elizabeth 38; Ontario, 1871 ***1823.15*** *p3*
Allen, Elizabeth 52; Ontario, 1871 ***1823.15*** *p3*
Allen, Ervin 41; Ontario, 1871 ***1823.22*** *p2*
Allen, Florence; Maryland, 1662 ***2524.55*** *p92*
Allen, Fra; Virginia, 1674 ***6212.30*** *p52*
Allen, George; Died enroute, 1673 ***1224.1*** *p1*
Allen, H.; Portland, Maine, 1858 ***9196.15*** *p30*
Allen, Hen; Virginia, 1692-1693 ***6212.30*** *p59*
Allen, Henry; Maryland, 1672 ***2524.55*** *p184*
Allen, Henry 50; Ontario, 1871 ***1823.22*** *p2*
Allen, Hobsen 34; Ontario, 1871 ***1823.15*** *p3*
Allen, Isaac C. 15; Ontario, 1861 ***2896.25*** *p4*
Allen, Isabella 40; Ontario, 1871 ***1823.22*** *p2*
Allen, James; Boston, 1763 ***1224.2*** *p2*
Allen, James; Maryland, 1652 ***2524.55*** *p11*
Allen, James; Maryland, 1666 ***2524.55*** *p11*
Allen, James; Pennsylvania, 1777 ***4629.10*** *p21*
Allen, James 5; Ontario, 1861 ***2896.27*** *p30*
Allen, James 24; Ontario, 1871 ***1823.15*** *p3*
Allen, James 44; Ontario, 1871 ***1823.15*** *p3*
Allen, James 45; Ontario, 1871 ***1823.15*** *p3*
Allen, James 48; Ontario, 1871 ***1823.22*** *p2*
Allen, James 58; Ontario, 1871 ***1823.15*** *p3*
Allen, James 65; Ontario, 1871 ***1823.15*** *p3*
Allen, John; America, 1722 ***1224.2*** *p2*
Allen, John; Maryland, 1664 ***2524.55*** *p11*
Allen, John; Maryland, 1675 ***1224.1*** *p1*
Allen, John; New York, 1807 ***8197.10*** *p33*
Allen, John; New York, 1840 ***8197.10*** *p142*
Allen, John; New York, 1840 ***8197.10*** *p143*
Allen, John; Philadelphia, 1779 ***1224.2*** *p2*
Allen, John 21; Philadelphia, 1774 ***1220.25*** *p82*
Allen, John 27; Ontario, 1871 ***1823.15*** *p3*
Allen, John 30; Ontario, 1871 ***1823.15*** *p3*
Allen, John 30; Ontario, 1871 ***1823.22*** *p2*
Allen, John 39; Ontario, 1861 ***2896.25*** *p4*
Allen, John 41; Ontario, 1871 ***1823.15*** *p3*
Allen, John 50; Ontario, 1871 ***1823.15*** *p3*
Allen, John 60; Ontario, 1871 ***1823.28*** *p1*
Allen, John 61; Ontario, 1871 ***1823.15*** *p3*
Allen, John W. 1; Ontario, 1861 ***2896.25*** *p4*
Allen, Joseph, Jr.; Pennsylvania, 1785 ***4629.10*** *p48*
Allen, Joseph M.; Vermont, 1848-1925 ***5900.10*** *p308*
Allen, Joseph S. 10; Ontario, 1861 ***2896.25*** *p4*
Allen, Mary *SEE* Allen, Richard
Allen, Mary 50; Ontario, 1871 ***1823.15*** *p3*
Allen, Mary A. 70; Vermont, 1921 ***5900.10*** *p445*
Allen, Michael; Pennsylvania, 1785 ***4629.10*** *p48*
Allen, Micheal 48; Ontario, 1871 ***1823.28*** *p1*
Allen, Nathaniel; Pennsylvania, 1777 ***4629.10*** *p7*
Allen, Patrick; Maryland, 1663 ***2524.55*** *p106*
Allen, Patrick 25; Maryland, 1773-1774 ***1220.25*** *p33*
Allen, Reuben Y. 6; Ontario, 1861 ***2896.25*** *p4*
Allen, Rich; Virginia, 1665 ***6212.30*** *p22*
Allen, Richard; Maryland, 1656 ***2524.55*** *p11*
Allen, Richard; Maryland, 1666 ***2524.55*** *p11*
Wife: Mary
Allen, Robert; Pennsylvania, 1777 ***4629.10*** *p14*
Allen, Robert; Pennsylvania, 1786 ***4629.10*** *p49*
Allen, Robert 16; Virginia, 1774 ***1220.25*** *p89*
Allen, Robert 55; Ontario, 1871 ***1823.15*** *p3*
Allen, Robert 80; Ontario, 1871 ***1823.22*** *p2*
Allen, Robert C. 92; Ontario, 1871 ***1823.28*** *p1*
Allen, Roger; New England, 1658 ***1224.1*** *p1*
Allen, Samuel; South Carolina, 1800 ***1224.3*** *p1*
Allen, Sarah; North Carolina, 1805 ***1224.3*** *p1*
Allen, Sarah; Pennsylvania, 1836 ***1224.3*** *p2*
Allen, Sarah Jane 11; Ontario, 1871 ***1823.28*** *p1*

Allen, Terrier; Vermont, 1861-1909 ***5900.10*** *p225*
Allen, Thomas; Maryland, 1662 ***2524.55*** *p11*
Allen, Thomas; Maryland, 1667 ***2524.55*** *p114*
Allen, Thomas; Maryland, 1669 ***2524.55*** *p11*
Allen, Thomas; South Carolina, 1729 ***1224.2*** *p2*
Allen, Thomas; Virginia, 1671-1672 ***6212.30*** *p46*
Allen, Thomas 22; Virginia, 1774 ***1220.25*** *p91*
Allen, Thomas 33; Ontario, 1871 ***1823.15*** *p3*
Allen, Thomas H. 17; Ontario, 1861 ***2896.25*** *p4*
Allen, W. W.; Quebec, 1858 ***9196.15*** *p42*
Allen, Mrs. W. W.; Quebec, 1858 ***9196.15*** *p42*
Allen, Walter D. 44; Ontario, 1871 ***1823.15*** *p3*
Allen, William; Maryland, 1665 ***2524.55*** *p11*
Allen, William; Maryland, 1673 ***2524.55*** *p11*
Allen, William; Pennsylvania, 1777 ***4629.10*** *p8*
Allen, William; Pennsylvania, 1777 ***4629.10*** *p10*
Allen, William 18; Ontario, 1871 ***1823.15*** *p3*
Allen, William 22; Philadelphia, 1775 ***1220.25*** *p122*
Allen, William 59; Ontario, 1871 ***1823.15*** *p3*
Allenbacher, Maria Elisabeth; Port uncertain, 1763 ***2856.30*** *p4*
Allenbacher, Peter; Port uncertain, 1748 ***2856.30*** *p4*
Allenbacher, Peter; Port uncertain, 1785 ***2856.30*** *p4*
Allenby, William Charles; Baltimore, 1801 ***1224.3*** *p2*
Allendar, William 39; Maryland, 1775 ***1220.25*** *p97*
Allenton, Elizabeth 21; Virginia, 1774 ***1220.25*** *p93*
Allerdyer, George 22; Jamaica, 1774 ***1220.25*** *p79*
Alles, Conrad 33; Ontario, 1871 ***1823.15*** *p4*
Alles, Conrad E. 63; Ontario, 1871 ***1823.15*** *p4*
Alles, Johann Jost; Port uncertain, 1733 ***2856.30*** *p4*
With 3 children
Alles, Philipp Michael; Port uncertain, 1787 ***2856.30*** *p4*
Allesch, Philipp Michael; Port uncertain, 1787 ***2856.30*** *p4*
Allet, James; Virginia, 1664 ***6212.30*** *p8*
Allet, Rebeckah; Maryland, 1670 ***2524.55*** *p11*
Allett, Edm; Virginia, 1679-1680 ***6212.30*** *p54*
Allett, Elizabeth; Maryland, 1665 ***2524.55*** *p11*
Allett, Rebecca; Maryland, 1675 ***2524.55*** *p11*
Alley, Albert 18; Ontario, 1861 ***2896.25*** *p47*
Alley, Caroline 11; Ontario, 1861 ***2896.25*** *p48*
Alley, David 24; Ontario, 1861 ***2896.25*** *p48*
Alley, E. 43; Ontario, 1861 ***2896.25*** *p47*
Alley, George 12; Ontario, 1861 ***2896.25*** *p48*
Alley, Jane 49; Ontario, 1861 ***2896.25*** *p48*
Alley, John 55; Ontario, 1861 ***2896.25*** *p48*
Alley, Joseph 3; Ontario, 1861 ***2896.25*** *p48*
Alley, Justice 14; Ontario, 1861 ***2896.25*** *p48*
Alley, Silles 8; Ontario, 1861 ***2896.25*** *p48*
Alley, William 40; Ontario, 1861 ***2896.25*** *p48*
Alleyn, Mr.; Quebec, 1856 ***9196.15*** *p9*
Alleyn, James; New York, 1838 ***8197.10*** *p109*
Allford, Dorothy; Pennsylvania, 1718 ***1224.2*** *p2*
Allgate, James E. 1; Ontario, 1861 ***2896.28*** *p34*
Allgate, Jane 34; Ontario, 1861 ***2896.28*** *p34*
Allgate, John H. 10; Ontario, 1861 ***2896.28*** *p34*
Allgate, Nancy J. 5; Ontario, 1861 ***2896.28*** *p34*
Allgate, William 8; Ontario, 1861 ***2896.28*** *p34*
Allgayer, Ignaz; Port uncertain, 1781 ***2856.30*** *p4*
Allgeo, David; Quebec, 1788 ***1224.2*** *p2*
Allgeo, John; North Carolina, 1788 ***1224.2*** *p2*
Allgeo, John; Quebec, n.d. ***1224.2*** *p2*
Allgeuer, Michael; Port uncertain, 1771 ***2856.30*** *p4*
Allgeyer, Jacob Heinr., The Younger; America, 1753 ***2856.30*** *p4*
Allgeyer, Johann; America, 1749 ***2856.30*** *p4*
Allgeyer, Johann; Port uncertain, 1744 ***2856.30*** *p4*
Allgood, Florance; Virginia, 1664 ***6212.30*** *p7*
Allibone, William; Pennsylvania, 1777 ***4629.10*** *p14*
Alliboone, Thomas; Maryland, 1666 ***2524.55*** *p11*
Allily, Edward, Jr.; Maryland, 1668 ***2524.55*** *p10*
Allin, Silvester; Died enroute, 1636 ***1224.1*** *p1*
Allin, Thomas 43; Ontario, 1871 ***1823.15*** *p4*
Allingham, Hugh 46; Ontario, 1871 ***1823.22*** *p3*
Allington, James; Virginia, 1666 ***6212.30*** *p25*
Allington, John 21; Maryland, 1775 ***1220.25*** *p108*
Allison, Mrs.; Quebec, 1857 ***9196.15*** *p14*
Allison, Able M. 37; Ontario, 1871 ***1823.15*** *p4*
Allison, Agnes; Pennsylvania, 1863 ***1640.13*** *p2*
Allison, C. R. 15; Ontario, 1861 ***2896.28*** *p58*
Allison, Charles R. 8; Ontario, 1861 ***2896.28*** *p58*
Allison, D.; Quebec, 1857 ***9196.15*** *p21*
Allison, Mrs. D.; Quebec, 1857 ***9196.15*** *p21*
Allison, David; Pennsylvania, 1777 ***4629.10*** *p10*
Allison, Eve 52; Ontario, 1861 ***2896.28*** *p58*
Allison, Hellen 5; Ontario, 1861 ***2896.28*** *p59*
Allison, J.; Quebec, 1857 ***9196.15*** *p14*
Allison, James; Savannah, Georgia, 1807 ***1640.10*** *p3*
Allison, John; Wisconsin, 1855 ***1224.3*** *p2*
Allison, John 44; Ontario, 1871 ***1823.15*** *p4*
Allison, Joseph 45; Ontario, 1871 ***1823.15*** *p4*
Allison, Phebe Jane 12; Ontario, 1861 ***2896.28*** *p58*
Allison, Sarah E. 18; Ontario, 1861 ***2896.28*** *p58*
Allison, Walter 34; Ontario, 1871 ***1823.15*** *p4*
Allison, William; Pennsylvania, 1777 ***4629.10*** *p16*
Allison, William 18; Virginia, 1773 ***1220.25*** *p29*
Allison, William H. 25; Ontario, 1861 ***2896.28*** *p58*
Allispach, John C.; New York, 1840 ***8197.10*** *p206*
Alliton, Lydia 29 *SEE* Alliton, Thomas
Alliton, Thomas 35; Maryland, 1775 ***1220.25*** *p99*
Wife: Lydia 29
Allman, Susanna Douglas; New York, New York, 1807 ***1224.3*** *p2*
Allmann, Georg Leonhard; Port uncertain, 1767 ***2856.30*** *p4*
Allmann, J. H.; America, 1764 ***2856.30*** *p432*
Allmann, Johann Henrich; America, 1764 ***2856.30*** *p4*
With wife & 6 children
Allmen, Henry; New York, New York, 1862 ***6058.10*** *p58*
Allom, S. 23; Philadelphia, 1775 ***1220.25*** *p9*
Allright, Margaret; New England, 1667 ***1224.1*** *p2*
Allsce, William; New York, 1793 ***8197.10*** *p1*
Allsopp, . . .; New England, 1647 ***1224.1*** *p2*
Allsopp, Miss; Quebec, 1858 ***9196.15*** *p42*
Allsworth, Cath 50; Ontario, 1871 ***1823.15*** *p4*
Allsworth, William 62; Ontario, 1871 ***1823.15*** *p4*
Allum, Carrol 32; Ontario, 1871 ***1823.28*** *p1*
Allwens, Bernard; Port uncertain, 1787 ***2856.30*** *p4*
Allwine, Lawrence; Pennsylvania, 1786 ***4629.10*** *p50*
Allwith, Sarah; Virginia, 1672 ***6212.30*** *p49*
Allwood, Robert; Jamaica, n.d. ***1224.3*** *p2*
Allwood, Robert; New York, 1839 ***1224.3*** *p2*
Alman, Charles; New York, 1840 ***8197.10*** *p143*
Almond, Edward 42; Ontario, 1871 ***1823.28*** *p1*
Alosfe, Geo; Virginia, 1664 ***6212.30*** *p15*
Alphonse, Alexis; New York, 1829 ***8197.10*** *p205*
Alricks, William; Pennsylvania, 1777 ***4629.10*** *p11*
Alridge, Thomas 70; Ontario, 1871 ***1823.22*** *p3*
Alsebrook, John 15; Antigua (Antego), 1775 ***1220.25*** *p97*
Alsebrook, Samuel 17; Antigua (Antego), 1775 ***1220.25*** *p97*
Alsnar, Otto 35; Ontario, 1871 ***1823.28*** *p1*
Alson, Hindrick; Maryland, 1672 ***2524.55*** *p11*
Alsop, . . .; New England, 1664 ***1224.1*** *p2*
Alsop, Christopher; Maryland, 1649 ***2524.55*** *p11*
Alsop, John 15; Philadelphia, 1774 ***1220.25*** *p81*
Alsope, John; Virginia, 1664 ***6212.30*** *p6*
Alston, David; New York, New York, 1806 ***1224.3*** *p2*
Alston, David; St. Vincent, 1831 ***1640.13*** *p2*
Alston, Humphry; Virginia, 1665 ***6212.30*** *p20*
Alston, John 50; Ontario, 1871 ***1823.28*** *p1*
Alsworth, Anges A. 2; Ontario, 1861 ***2896.27*** *p15*
Alsworth, Richard 64; Ontario, 1871 ***1823.15*** *p4*
Alt, Anna; Port uncertain, 1741 ***2856.30*** *p4*
Alt, Anna Apollonia; Port uncertain, 1752 ***2856.30*** *p4*
Alt, Elis. Catharina; Port uncertain, 1762 ***2856.30*** *p4*
Alt, Jacob; Pennsylvania, 1815 ***6058.10*** *p5*
Alt, Jacob; Port uncertain, 1764 ***2856.30*** *p4*
Alt, John; Pennsylvania, 1830 ***6058.10*** *p9*
Alt, Maria Margarete; Port uncertain, 1759 ***2856.30*** *p4*
Alt, Michael; Port uncertain, 1751 ***2856.30*** *p4*
Alt, Nicholas; Pennsylvania, 1815 ***6058.10*** *p5*
Altenbacher, Sofia; Port uncertain, 1767 ***2856.30*** *p5*
Altergott, Johann; Port uncertain, 1765 ***2856.30*** *p5*
Altham, Emmanuel; America, 1638 ***1224.1*** *p2*
Altham, John; Virginia, 1666-1667 ***6212.30*** *p33*
Althouse, Amelia 19; Ontario, 1861 ***2896.27*** *p69*
Althouse, Conrad; New York, 1827 ***8197.10*** *p341*
Althouse, Jacob; New York, 1830 ***8197.10*** *p363*
Althouse, Nicholas 38; Ontario, 1861 ***2896.27*** *p69*
Althouse, Phebe A. 2; Ontario, 1861 ***2896.27*** *p69*
Althus, Conrad; New York, 1821 ***8197.10*** *p205*
Altig, Johann; America, 1752 ***2856.30*** *p5*
Altman, Henry; New York, New York, 1862 ***6058.10*** *p58*
Altmont, William 30; Ontario, 1871 ***1823.15*** *p4*
Altomus, A. M.; America, 1739 ***2856.30*** *p450*
Altomus, Anna Margarete; America, 1739 ***2856.30*** *p5*
With husband
Altomus, Johann Peter; America, 1740 ***2856.30*** *p5*
With wife
Alton, Agnes 70; Ontario, 1871 ***1823.15*** *p4*
Alton, Daniel 37; Ontario, 1871 ***1823.15*** *p4*
Alton, Samuel 47; Ontario, 1871 ***1823.15*** *p4*
Alton, Valentine 50; Ontario, 1871 ***1823.15*** *p4*
Altrop, John; Maryland, 1674 ***2524.55*** *p11*
Altschuh, Johann; America, 1771 ***2856.30*** *p5*
Altstatt, Catharina; Port uncertain, 1783 ***2856.30*** *p5*
With husband
Alvany, James; New York, 1837 ***8197.10*** *p82*
Alverty, Raymond; New York, 1822 ***8197.10*** *p205*
Alvey, Elizabeth; Maryland, 1667 ***2524.55*** *p11*
Alvey, Samuel; New York, 1839 ***8197.10*** *p379*
Alwood, Elizabeth; Maryland, 1667 ***2524.55*** *p11*
Alxander, John 38; Ontario, 1871 ***1823.15*** *p4*
Alyea, Alan James 2; Ontario, 1861 ***2896.25*** *p21*
Alyea, Almer 15; Ontario, 1861 ***2896.25*** *p24*
Alyea, Almira 30; Ontario, 1861 ***2896.25*** *p21*
Alyea, Catherine 31; Ontario, 1861 ***2896.25*** *p19*
Alyea, David 32; Ontario, 1861 ***2896.25*** *p21*
Alyea, Elen 1; Ontario, 1861 ***2896.25*** *p19*
Alyea, Elizabeth 57; Ontario, 1861 ***2896.25*** *p23*
Alyea, Elizabeth A. 33; Ontario, 1861 ***2896.25*** *p24*
Alyea, Elizabeth L. 10; Ontario, 1861 ***2896.25*** *p19*
Alyea, H. J. S. 7; Ontario, 1861 ***2896.25*** *p19*
Alyea, Isaac 13; Ontario, 1861 ***2896.25*** *p23*
Alyea, James H. 5; Ontario, 1861 ***2896.25*** *p24*
Alyea, John 5; Ontario, 1861 ***2896.25*** *p19*
Alyea, Joseph 8; Ontario, 1861 ***2896.25*** *p21*
Alyea, M. Jane 18; Ontario, 1861 ***2896.25*** *p23*
Alyea, Margaret 26; Ontario, 1861 ***2896.25*** *p19*
Alyea, Maria 89; Ontario, 1861 ***2896.25*** *p31*
Alyea, Mary 1; Ontario, 1861 ***2896.25*** *p19*
Alyea, Mary E. 21; Ontario, 1861 ***2896.25*** *p24*
Alyea, Peter, Jr. 21; Ontario, 1861 ***2896.25*** *p23*
Alyea, Peter N. 12; Ontario, 1861 ***2896.25*** *p24*
Alyea, S. D. J. 3; Ontario, 1861 ***2896.25*** *p19*
Alyea, Sarah E. 15; Ontario, 1861 ***2896.25*** *p23*
Alyea, Simantha 11; Ontario, 1861 ***2896.25*** *p23*
Alyea, Smith 17; Ontario, 1861 ***2896.25*** *p23*
Alyea, Stephen 3; Ontario, 1861 ***2896.25*** *p19*
Alyea, William 1; Ontario, 1861 ***2896.25*** *p24*
Aman, C. 25; Alaska, 1917 ***9196.1*** *p49*
Aman, C. 25; Yukon, 1917 ***9196.1*** *p49*
Aman, H. 23; Alaska, 1917 ***9196.1*** *p49*
Aman, H. 23; Yukon, 1917 ***9196.1*** *p49*
Amann, Mary 70; Ontario, 1871 ***1823.15*** *p4*
Amans, Freeman C. 10; Ontario, 1861 ***2896.28*** *p19*
Amans, John S. 15; Ontario, 1861 ***2896.27*** *p59*
Amans, Rachel 17; Ontario, 1861 ***2896.28*** *p19*
Amans, Ruth 44; Ontario, 1861 ***2896.28*** *p19*
Amans, Thomas H. 13; Ontario, 1861 ***2896.28*** *p19*
Amar, John; Pensacola, Florida, n.d. ***1224.2*** *p2*
Ambery, Nelson 22; Ontario, 1871 ***1823.28*** *p1*
Ambioff, A. 24; Alaska, 1917 ***9196.1*** *p46*
Ambioff, A. 24; Whitehorse, Yukon, 1917 ***9196.1*** *p46*
Ambler, Ann 18 *SEE* Ambler, Benjamin
Ambler, Benjamin 45; New York, 1774 ***1220.25*** *p24*
Wife: Mary 40
Child: Ann 18
Child: John 14
Ambler, John 14 *SEE* Ambler, Benjamin
Ambler, John 35; Virginia, 1774 ***1220.25*** *p58*
Wife: Sarah 30
Ambler, Mary 40 *SEE* Ambler, Benjamin
Ambler, Sarah 30 *SEE* Ambler, John
Ambridge, Amy 22; Ontario, 1871 ***1823.28*** *p1*
Ambroise, Gard Pierre; New York, 1840 ***8197.10*** *p206*
Ambros, Boleslaw; Maryland, 1910 ***3259.35*** *p1*
Ambrose, Isabella; Newport, Rhode Island, 1802 ***1224.3*** *p2*
Ambrose, Michael 40; Ontario, 1871 ***1823.22*** *p3*
Ambrose, Robert 22; Maryland, 1774 ***1220.25*** *p84*
Ambsel, Johann Michael; Port uncertain, 1733 ***2856.30*** *p5*
Amckewa, Jacob 40; Ontario, 1871 ***1823.28*** *p1*
Amelung, Frederick Leopold Eberhard; New York, 1803 ***8197.10*** *p10*
Amenta, Emanuel; New York, 1806 ***8197.10*** *p323*
America, John; Virginia, 1671-1672 ***6212.30*** *p45*
America, Nicholas; Maryland, 1675 ***2524.55*** *p11*
Amerly, Elizabeth; Maryland, 1670 ***2524.55*** *p11*
Ames, Charles 29; Ontario, 1871 ***1823.28*** *p1*
Ames, Edw; Virginia, 1665-1666 ***6212.30*** *p21*
Ames, John 50; Ontario, 1871 ***1823.15*** *p4*
Ames, Joseph; Virginia, 1672 ***6212.30*** *p50*
Ames, Joseph 27; Ontario, 1871 ***1823.28*** *p1*
Ames, Thomas; Pennsylvania, 1786 ***4629.10*** *p50*
Amett, Thomas; Maryland, 1668 ***2524.55*** *p11*
Amezaga, Jose Manuel; Mexico, 1883 ***1640.13*** *p2*
Amhurst, Richard; Virginia, 1664 ***6212.30*** *p13*
Amias, . . .; Maryland, 1664 ***2524.55*** *p11*
Amias, Francis; Virginia, 1622 ***1224.1*** *p2*
Amiss, Thomas; Maryland, 1679 ***2524.55*** *p11*
Ammon, Anthony; Pennsylvania, 1777 ***4629.10*** *p16*
Amore, Hanor; Vermont, 1828-1901 ***5900.10*** *p123*
Amory, Catherine 44 *SEE* Amory, John
Amory, John 50; Boston, 1776 ***1220.25*** *p1*
Wife: Catherine 44
Amory, Simon; Pensacola, Florida, 1766 ***1224.2*** *p2*
Amos, Annie 19; Ontario, 1871 ***1823.15*** *p4*
Amos, Henry Thos 49; Ontario, 1871 ***1823.28*** *p2*
Amos, Johann Georg; Port uncertain, 1789 ***2856.30*** *p6*
Amos, John 27; Philadelphia, 1775 ***1220.25*** *p107*
Amos, Samuel 43; Ontario, 1871 ***1823.15*** *p4*
Amos, Valentin; Port uncertain, 1759 ***2856.30*** *p6*
Amos, William; Canada, 1866 ***1640.13*** *p2*

Amott, Richard 26; Maryland, 1774 **1220.25** *p38*
Amour, Eli; Vermont, 1845-1911 **5900.10** *p202*
Amour, Margaret Myers; Vermont, 1850-1934 **5900.10** *p202*
Amphlett, William; St. Louis, 1852 **1224.3** *p2*
Amsed, James; Virginia, 1696 **1224.1** *p2*
Amsley, Peter 36; Maryland, 1774 **1220.25** *p37*
Amsley, Sarah; Virginia, 1664 **6212.30** *p6*
Amy, Moses 39; Ontario, 1871 **1823.15** *p4*
Amy, Moses 67; Ontario, 1871 **1823.15** *p4*
Amyand, Isaac; Charles Town, South Carolina, 1739 **1224.2** *p2*
Anachutz, Aemelia 23; Kansas, 1907-1910 **9079.10** *p41*
Anachutz, Charley 30; Kansas, 1907-1910 **9079.10** *p41*
Anachutz, Christian 73; Kansas, 1879-1910 **9079.10** *p38*
Anachutz, George 53; Kansas, 1878-1910 **9079.10** *p41*
Anachutz, Mary 49; Kansas, 1881-1910 **9079.10** *p41*
Anastasi, Joseph, Jr.; New York, 1804 **8197.10** *p27*
Anastasia, Mary; Maryland, 1910 **3259.35** *p1*
Anau, Johann Georg; Port uncertain, 1808 **2856.30** *p7*
Anchinlock, Miss; Quebec, 1857 **9196.15** *p22*
Anchor, Alva 17; Ontario, 1861 **2896.27** *p66*
Anckner, Elisabeth; Port uncertain, 1765 **2856.30** *p6*
Ancram, Charles; Virginia, 1664 **6212.30** *p7*
Ancrum, George; Louisiana, 1764 **1640.10** *p3*
Andassano, Olive; Virginia, 1664 **6212.30** *p10*
Andelfinger, Anna Maria; Port uncertain, 1719 **2856.30** *p6*
Ander, Jacob; Port uncertain, 1764 **2856.30** *p6*
With 3 sons & 2 daughters
Anders, William 36; Ontario, 1871 **1823.28** *p2*
Andersen, Charles; New York, New York, 1888 **3437.14** *p150*
Anderson, . . .; Boston, 1765 **4628.40** *p114*
Anderson, Miss; Portland, Maine, 1858 **9196.15** *p29*
Anderson, Miss; Quebec, 1857 **9196.15** *p20*
Anderson, Miss; Quebec, 1857 **9196.15** *p22*
Anderson, Miss; Quebec, 1858 **9196.15** *p35*
Anderson, Miss; Quebec, 1858 **9196.15** *p45*
Anderson, Mr.; Portland, Maine, 1858 **9196.15** *p30*
Anderson, Mr.; Quebec, 1856 **9196.15** *p6*
Anderson, Mr.; Quebec, 1857 **9196.15** *p23*
Anderson, Mrs.; Quebec, 1858 **9196.15** *p35*
Anderson, Mrs.; Quebec, 1858 **9196.15** *p45*
Anderson, A. 7; Ontario, 1861 **2896.25** *p29*
Anderson, A. 30; Alaska, 1913 **9196.1** *p39*
Anderson, A. 30; Whitehorse, Yukon, 1913 **9196.1** *p39*
Anderson, A. 31; Alaska, 1917 **9196.1** *p47*
Anderson, A. 31; Whitehorse, Yukon, 1917 **9196.1** *p47*
Anderson, A. 48; Alaska, 1918 **9196.1** *p55*
Anderson, A. 48; Yukon, 1918 **9196.1** *p55*
Anderson, Adam; Pennsylvania, 1777 **4629.10** *p23*
Anderson, Agnes; Vermont, 1848-1930 **5900.10** *p375*
Anderson, Alex 58; Ontario, 1871 **1823.22** *p3*
Anderson, Alexander *SEE* Anderson, Hugh
Anderson, Alexander; Florida, 1767 **1640.10** *p3*
Anderson, Alexander; Georgia, 1699 **1640.13** *p2*
Anderson, Alexander; Pennsylvania, 1779 **4629.10** *p36*
Anderson, Alexander; Pennsylvania, 1781 **4629.10** *p42*
Anderson, Alexander; Quebec, 1882 **1640.13** *p3*
Anderson, Alexander 26; New York, 1774 **1220.25** *p92*
Anderson, Alexander 29; Ontario, 1871 **1823.22** *p3*
Anderson, Alexander 37; Ontario, 1871 **1823.22** *p3*
Anderson, Alexander 47; Ontario, 1871 **1823.15** *p4*
Anderson, Andrew; Long Island, 1785 **1224.2** *p2*
Anderson, Andrew; New York, 1829 **8197.10** *p351*
Anderson, Andrew; New York, New York, 1893 **3437.14** *p146*
Anderson, Andrew; West Indies, 1784 **1640.13** *p3*
Anderson, Andrew 36; Ontario, 1871 **1823.28** *p2*
Anderson, Ann 4; Ontario, 1861 **2896.25** *p58*
Anderson, Ann 5 *SEE* Anderson, Mary
Anderson, Ann 59; Vermont, 1874 **5900.10** *p283*
Anderson, Anne; Maryland, 1662 **2524.55** *p85*
Anderson, Archibald 50; Ontario, 1871 **1823.15** *p4*
Anderson, Archibald Thomas; Toronto, 1898 **1640.13** *p3*
Anderson, Asanath A. 22; Ontario, 1861 **2896.28** *p50*
Anderson, Barbra 18; Ontario, 1871 **1823.15** *p4*
Anderson, Bessie 65; Ontario, 1871 **1823.15** *p4*
Anderson, C. 29; Alaska, 1917 **9196.1** *p47*
Anderson, C. 29; Whitehorse, Yukon, 1917 **9196.1** *p47*
Anderson, C. F. 49; Alaska, 1917 **9196.1** *p51*
Anderson, C. F. 49; Yukon, 1917 **9196.1** *p51*
Anderson, C. J.; Portland, Maine, 1858 **9196.15** *p29*
Anderson, Catherine *SEE* Anderson, Hugh
Anderson, Charles; Jamaica, 1815 **1640.13** *p3*
Anderson, Charles; Jamaica, 1853 **1640.13** *p3*
Anderson, Charles; New York, New York, 1888 **3437.14** *p150*
Anderson, Charles 22; New York, 1774 **1220.25** *p49*
Anderson, Daniel 19; Ontario, 1861 **2896.28** *p50*
Anderson, David; Boston, 1678 **1224.1** *p2*
Anderson, David; New York, 1807 **8197.10** *p34*
Anderson, David; New York, 1830 **8197.10** *p66*
Anderson, David; New York, New York, 1821 **8197.10** *p205*
Anderson, David; Toronto, 1891 **1640.13** *p3*
Anderson, David 34; Ontario, 1871 **1823.15** *p4*
Anderson, David 50; Ontario, 1861 **2896.25** *p57*
Anderson, David 51; Ontario, 1871 **1823.15** *p4*
Anderson, Duncan 33; Ontario, 1871 **1823.15** *p4*
Anderson, Duncan 76; Ontario, 1871 **1823.28** *p2*
Anderson, Duncan, Sr. 73; Ontario, 1871 **1823.15** *p4*
Anderson, E. J. 19; Ontario, 1861 **2896.25** *p29*
Anderson, Ebenezer; Detroit, 1892 **1640.13** *p3*
Anderson, Edgar; Schuyler Co., Illinois, 1882 **1640.13** *p3*
Anderson, Edward 63; Ontario, 1871 **1823.28** *p2*
Anderson, Elinour; Maryland, 1663 **2524.55** *p11*
Anderson, Eliza 2; Ontario, 1861 **2896.25** *p40*
Anderson, Eliza J. 1; Ontario, 1861 **2896.28** *p50*
Anderson, Elizabeth *SEE* Anderson, Hugh
Anderson, Elizabeth; Maryland, 1668 **2524.55** *p11*
Anderson, Elizabeth; Maryland, 1672 **2524.55** *p11*
Anderson, Elizabeth; Savannah, Georgia, 1760 **1640.10** *p3*
Anderson, Elizabeth 14; Ontario, 1861 **2896.28** *p50*
Anderson, Elizabeth 16; Ontario, 1861 **2896.27** *p55*
Anderson, Elizabeth 36; Halifax, Nova Scotia, 1775 **1220.25** *p22*
Child: Mary 9
Child: William 4
Child: John 1
Child: Moses 5
Child: Jane 7
Anderson, Elizabeth 71; Ontario, 1871 **1823.22** *p3*
Anderson, Finley 30; Ontario, 1871 **1823.15** *p4*
Anderson, Flora; Georgia, 1774 **1640.10** *p3*
Anderson, Flora 25; Georgia, 1774 **1220.25** *p48*
Anderson, Frances; Vermont, 1911 **5900.10** *p81*
Anderson, Frances 22; British Columbia, 1909 **9196.1** *p28*
Anderson, Frances 22; Washington, 1909 **9196.1** *p28*
Anderson, Francis 85; Ontario, 1871 **1823.15** *p4*
Anderson, G. 18; Ontario, 1861 **2896.25** *p29*
Anderson, George; Georgia, 1698 **1640.13** *p2*
Anderson, George; Georgia, 1772 **1640.10** *p4*
Anderson, George; Georgia, 1777 **1224.2** *p2*
Anderson, George; New Orleans, 1827 **1640.10** *p4*
Anderson, George 12 *SEE* Anderson, Mary
Anderson, George 35; Ontario, 1871 **1823.22** *p3*
Anderson, George 50; Ontario, 1871 **1823.15** *p4*
Anderson, Gideon 17; Ontario, 1861 **2896.28** *p50*
Anderson, Gilbert 77; Ontario, 1871 **1823.15** *p4*
Anderson, Hamilon 44; Ontario, 1871 **1823.28** *p2*
Anderson, Hannah 30; Ontario, 1861 **2896.28** *p37*
Anderson, Harriet E. 9; Ontario, 1861 **2896.28** *p37*
Anderson, Henry; Maryland, 1662 **2524.55** *p85*
Anderson, Henry N. 50; Ontario, 1871 **1823.28** *p2*
Anderson, Hugh; Georgia, 1737 **1640.10** *p4*
Wife: Elizabeth
Daughter: Catherine
Son: Moore
Son: Alexander
Anderson, Hugh 45; Ontario, 1871 **1823.15** *p4*
Anderson, Hugh 46; Ontario, 1871 **1823.15** *p4*
Anderson, J. 3; Ontario, 1861 **2896.25** *p29*
Anderson, J. 9; Ontario, 1861 **2896.25** *p29*
Anderson, Miss J.; Quebec, 1857 **9196.15** *p19*
Anderson, James; Baltimore, 1846 **6058.10** *p41*
Anderson, James; Florida, 1766 **1640.10** *p4*
Anderson, James; Georgia, 1736 **1640.10** *p4*
Anderson, James; Georgia, 1762 **1640.10** *p4*
Anderson, James; Georgia, 1769 **1640.10** *p4*
Anderson, James; Jamaica, 1775 **1640.13** *p3*
Anderson, James; Jamaica, 1830 **1640.13** *p3*
Anderson, James; New York, 1807 **8197.10** *p331*
Anderson, James; New York, 1827 **8197.10** *p347*
Anderson, James; New York, 1832 **1224.3** *p2*
Anderson, James; New York, 1840 **8197.10** *p143*
Anderson, James; New York, New York, 1862 **6058.10** *p69*
Anderson, James; South Carolina, 1821 **1224.3** *p2*
Anderson, James; Virginia, 1788 **1640.13** *p3*
Anderson, James 19; Ontario, 1871 **1823.28** *p2*
Anderson, James 20; Ontario, 1871 **1823.22** *p3*
Anderson, James 33; Ontario, 1871 **1823.22** *p3*
Anderson, James 35; Ontario, 1871 **1823.15** *p4*
Anderson, James 39; Ontario, 1871 **1823.15** *p4*
Anderson, James 39; Ontario, 1871 **1823.28** *p2*
Anderson, James 40; Ontario, 1871 **1823.15** *p4*
Anderson, James 41; Ontario, 1871 **1823.22** *p3*
Anderson, James 42; British Columbia, 1909 **9196.1** *p28*
Anderson, James 42; Seattle, 1909 **9196.1** *p28*
Anderson, James 49; Ontario, 1871 **1823.15** *p4*
Anderson, James 54; Ontario, 1871 **1823.15** *p4*
Anderson, James 72; Ontario, 1871 **1823.15** *p4*
Anderson, James, Jr.; Augusta, Georgia, 1823 **1640.10** *p4*
Anderson, Jane; Maryland, 1681 **2524.55** *p166*
Anderson, Jane 7 *SEE* Anderson, Elizabeth
Anderson, Jane B. 10; Ontario, 1861 **2896.27** *p55*
Anderson, Jno; Virginia, 1664 **6212.30** *p10*
Anderson, Joe 35; Washington, 1914 **9196.1** *p64*
Anderson, John; Boston, 1676 **1224.1** *p2*
Anderson, John; Maryland, 1669 **2524.55** *p11*
Anderson, John; New England, 1678 **1224.1** *p2*
Anderson, John; New York, 1802 **8197.10** *p18*
Anderson, John; New York, 1822 **8197.10** *p205*
Anderson, John; New York, 1839 **8197.10** *p206*
Anderson, John; Vermont, 1808-1896 **5900.10** *p494*
Anderson, John; Virginia, 1665 **6212.30** *p20*
Anderson, John 1 *SEE* Anderson, Elizabeth
Anderson, John 26; Alaska, 1912 **9196.1** *p18*
Anderson, John 26; British Columbia, 1912 **9196.1** *p18*
Anderson, John 30; Ontario, 1871 **1823.15** *p5*
Anderson, John 31; Ontario, 1871 **1823.22** *p3*
Anderson, John 37; Ontario, 1871 **1823.28** *p2*
Anderson, John 39; Ontario, 1871 **1823.28** *p2*
Anderson, John 40; Ontario, 1871 **1823.15** *p5*
Anderson, John 40; Ontario, 1871 **1823.22** *p3*
Anderson, John 41; Ontario, 1871 **1823.15** *p4*
Anderson, John 44; Ontario, 1871 **1823.28** *p2*
Anderson, John 46; Ontario, 1871 **1823.15** *p4*
Anderson, John 56; Ontario, 1871 **1823.28** *p2*
Anderson, John 57; Ontario, 1871 **1823.22** *p3*
Anderson, John 68; Ontario, 1871 **1823.15** *p5*
Anderson, John David; Bermuda, 1857 **1640.13** *p3*
Anderson, John Henderson; Rhode Island, 1882 **1640.13** *p3*
Anderson, John L. 52; Ontario, 1871 **1823.15** *p5*
Anderson, John W. 5; Ontario, 1861 **2896.28** *p37*
Anderson, Jonas 36; Ontario, 1871 **1823.28** *p2*
Anderson, Jos 37; Alaska, 1917 **9196.1** *p53*
Anderson, Jos 37; Whitehorse, Yukon, 1917 **9196.1** *p53*
Anderson, Joseph; Pennsylvania, 1859 **6058.10** *p41*
Anderson, Joseph; Portland, Maine, 1858 **9196.15** *p31*
Anderson, Joseph 50; Ontario, 1871 **1823.15** *p5*
Anderson, Julia Ann; Detroit, 1845 **1224.3** *p2*
Anderson, Latitia 52; Ontario, 1871 **1823.22** *p3*
Anderson, Lauchlan; Detroit, 1785 **1224.2** *p2*
Anderson, Letitia 3 *SEE* Anderson, Mary
Anderson, Letty 8; Ontario, 1861 **2896.25** *p58*
Anderson, Lone 33; Washington, 1915 **9196.1** *p67*
Anderson, Louisa 7; Ontario, 1861 **2896.28** *p37*
Anderson, Louisa 11; Ontario, 1861 **2896.25** *p58*
Anderson, Lydia J. 21; Ontario, 1861 **2896.28** *p50*
Anderson, M. 5; Ontario, 1861 **2896.25** *p29*
Anderson, M. 12; Ontario, 1861 **2896.25** *p29*
Anderson, M. 14; Ontario, 1861 **2896.25** *p29*
Anderson, M. 37; Ontario, 1861 **2896.25** *p29*
Anderson, Malcolm; North Carolina, 1799 **1640.10** *p5*
Anderson, Margaret; New York, 1754-1845 **1640.10** *p5*
Anderson, Margaret; New York, 1882 **1640.13** *p3*
Anderson, Margaret 4; Ontario, 1861 **2896.25** *p40*
Anderson, Margaret 15; Ontario, 1871 **1823.22** *p3*
Anderson, Margaret 73; Ontario, 1871 **1823.15** *p5*
Anderson, Margret 33; Ontario, 1871 **1823.15** *p5*
Anderson, Maria 63; Vermont, 1878 **5900.10** *p494*
Anderson, Mary; Canada, 1871 **1640.13** *p3*
Anderson, Mary; Florida, 1777-1845 **1640.10** *p5*
Anderson, Mary; Vermont, 1847-1910 **5900.10** *p81*
Anderson, Mary 7; Ontario, 1861 **2896.25** *p58*
Anderson, Mary 9 *SEE* Anderson, Elizabeth
Anderson, Mary 31; Ontario, 1861 **2896.25** *p63*
Anderson, Mary 54; Virginia, 1775 **1220.25** *p106*
Child: George 12
Child: Letitia 3
Child: Ann 5
Child: Robert John 11
Anderson, Mary 69; Ontario, 1861 **2896.25** *p38*
Anderson, Mary F. 2; Ontario, 1861 **2896.28** *p40*
Anderson, Mary J. 15; Ontario, 1861 **2896.28** *p37*
Anderson, Mary J. 28; Ontario, 1861 **2896.28** *p40*
Anderson, Mat 25; British Columbia, 1909 **9196.1** *p28*
Anderson, Mat 25; Washington, 1909 **9196.1** *p28*
Anderson, Mathew; Mobile, Alabama, 1814-1845 **1640.10** *p5*
Anderson, Moore *SEE* Anderson, Hugh
Anderson, Moses 5 *SEE* Anderson, Elizabeth
Anderson, Nancy J. 7; Ontario, 1861 **2896.28** *p40*
Anderson, Nathan 15; Ontario, 1861 **2896.28** *p30*
Anderson, Mrs. Nolberg 24; British Columbia, 1917 **9196.1** *p69*
Anderson, Mrs. Nolberg 24; Washington, 1917 **9196.1** *p69*
Anderson, Nolow; Virginia, 1703-1704 **6212.30** *p62*
Anderson, Patrick 50; Ontario, 1871 **1823.22** *p3*
Anderson, Penelope 23; Maryland, 1774 **1220.25** *p83*

Anderson, Peter; New York, 1807 ***8197.10*** *p331*
Anderson, Peter 42; Ontario, 1871 ***1823.28*** *p2*
Anderson, Peter 71; Ontario, 1871 ***1823.22*** *p3*
Anderson, Porter; Schuyler Co., Illinois, 1882 ***1640.13*** *p3*
Anderson, Robert; Missouri, 1861 ***6058.10*** *p69*
Anderson, Robert; New York, 1807 ***8197.10*** *p33*
Anderson, Robert; New York, 1821 ***8197.10*** *p205*
Anderson, Robert; Nova Scotia, 1871 ***1640.13*** *p3*
Anderson, Robert; Virginia, 1664 ***6212.30*** *p9*
Anderson, Robert 16; Antigua (Antego), 1774 ***1220.25*** *p88*
Anderson, Robert 21; New York, 1822-1838 ***8197.10*** *p109*
Anderson, Robert 39; Ontario, 1871 ***1823.15*** *p5*
Anderson, Robert 49; Ontario, 1871 ***1823.15*** *p5*
Anderson, Robert John 11 *SEE* Anderson, Mary
Anderson, Robert N. 14; Ontario, 1861 ***2896.28*** *p37*
Anderson, Samuel 39; Ontario, 1871 ***1823.15*** *p5*
Anderson, Samuel J. 11; Ontario, 1861 ***2896.28*** *p37*
Anderson, Sarah 33; Ontario, 1861 ***2896.25*** *p40*
Anderson, Sibill; Maryland, 1681 ***2524.55*** *p11*
Anderson, T. 21; Ontario, 1861 ***2896.25*** *p38*
Anderson, Thomas; Maryland, 1673 ***2524.55*** *p11*
Anderson, Thomas; New Orleans, 1835 ***1640.10*** *p5*
Anderson, Thomas; New York, 1840 ***8197.10*** *p143*
Anderson, Thomas; Pennsylvania, 1786 ***4629.10*** *p50*
Anderson, Thomas; Pennsylvania, 1817 ***6058.10*** *p5*
Anderson, Thomas 10; Ontario, 1861 ***2896.25*** *p40*
Anderson, Thomas 22; Maryland, 1774 ***1220.25*** *p84*
Anderson, Thomas 23; Ontario, 1871 ***1823.15*** *p5*
Anderson, Thomas 24; Ontario, 1871 ***1823.22*** *p4*
Anderson, Thomas 31; Ontario, 1871 ***1823.28*** *p2*
Anderson, Thomas 39; Ontario, 1871 ***1823.15*** *p5*
Anderson, Thomas 42; Ontario, 1871 ***1823.15*** *p5*
Anderson, Thomas 44; Ontario, 1871 ***1823.15*** *p5*
Anderson, W. 17; Ontario, 1861 ***2896.25*** *p29*
Anderson, W. 42; Alaska, 1917 ***9196.1*** *p48*
Anderson, W. 42; Whitehorse, Yukon, 1917 ***9196.1*** *p48*
Anderson, W. G. 6; Ontario, 1861 ***2896.25*** *p40*
Anderson, W. M. 8; Ontario, 1861 ***2896.25*** *p40*
Anderson, Wilison 48; Ontario, 1871 ***1823.15*** *p5*
Anderson, William; Alabama, 1820-1845 ***1640.10*** *p5*
Anderson, William; Augusta, Georgia, 1806-1812 ***1640.10*** *p5*
Anderson, William; Georgia, 1698 ***1640.13*** *p4*
Anderson, William; Georgia, 1772 ***1640.10*** *p5*
Anderson, William; Maryland, 1668 ***2524.55*** *p11*
Anderson, William; Maryland, 1734 ***1224.2*** *p2*
Anderson, William; New York, 1829 ***8197.10*** *p352*
Anderson, William; Pennsylvania, 1777 ***4629.10*** *p13*
Anderson, William; Pennsylvania, 1785 ***4629.10*** *p48*
Anderson, William; Virginia, n.d. ***1224.2*** *p3*
Anderson, William; Virginia, 1680 ***1224.1*** *p2*
Anderson, William 4 *SEE* Anderson, Elizabeth
Anderson, William 4; Ontario, 1861 ***2896.28*** *p40*
Anderson, William 22; Ontario, 1871 ***1823.22*** *p4*
Anderson, William 31; Vermont, 1850 ***5900.10*** *p375*
Anderson, William 32; Ontario, 1871 ***1823.22*** *p4*
Anderson, William 34; Maryland, 1775 ***1220.25*** *p98*
Anderson, William 34; Maryland, 1775 ***1220.25*** *p101*
Anderson, William 40; Ontario, 1871 ***1823.28*** *p2*
Anderson, William 41; Ontario, 1871 ***1823.15*** *p5*
Anderson, William 46; Ontario, 1861 ***2896.27*** *p55*
Anderson, William 46; Ontario, 1871 ***1823.15*** *p5*
Anderson, William 48; Ontario, 1871 ***1823.15*** *p5*
Anderson, William 50; Ontario, 1871 ***1823.15*** *p5*
Anderson, William 54; Ontario, 1871 ***1823.22*** *p4*
Anderson, William 62; Ontario, 1871 ***1823.15*** *p5*
Anderson, William 66; Ontario, 1871 ***1823.15*** *p5*
Anderson, William 67; Ontario, 1871 ***1823.15*** *p5*
Anderson, William 75; Ontario, 1861 ***2896.25*** *p38*
Anderson, William A. 13; Ontario, 1861 ***2896.25*** *p38*
Anderson, William E. 2; Ontario, 1861 ***2896.25*** *p38*
Anderson, Wm 37; British Columbia, 1913 ***9196.1*** *p58*
Anderson, Wm 37; Seattle, 1913 ***9196.1*** *p58*
Anderson, Wm, Sr. 61; Ontario, 1861 ***2896.28*** *p50*
Anderton, Gertrude *SEE* Anderton, John
Anderton, Gertrude; Maryland, 1659 ***2524.55*** *p12*
Anderton, John; Maryland, 1659 ***2524.55*** *p12*
Wife: Gertrude
Anderton, Mary; Maryland, 1663 ***2524.55*** *p12*
Anderton, Mary; Maryland, 1666 ***2524.55*** *p12*
Anderton, Thomas; New York, New York, 1862 ***6058.10*** *p69*
Anderton, William; Maryland, 1665 ***2524.55*** *p96*
Anderton, William 18; Maryland, 1775 ***1220.25*** *p120*
Andes, Fred; Indiana, 1883-1884 ***3437.14*** *p198*
Andeyak, Agnizka; Maryland, 1910 ***3259.35*** *p1*
Andjeska, John; Maryland, 1910 ***3259.35*** *p1*
Andrada, Abraham; Ohio, 1826 ***1224.3*** *p2*
Andrade, Abraham; Ohio, 1826 ***1224.3*** *p2*
Andrade, Abraham 24; Philadelphia, 1774 ***1220.25*** *p43*
Andrae, Christoph; New York, 1838 ***8197.10*** *p109*
Andrchoski, Antonie; Maryland, 1910 ***3259.35*** *p1*
Andre, Abraham; New York, 1807 ***8197.10*** *p34*
Andre, Catharina; America, 1763 ***2856.30*** *p6*
Andre, John; North America, 1781 ***1224.2*** *p3*
Andreas, Hans; Port uncertain, 1766 ***2856.30*** *p6*
Andreas, Jacob; Port uncertain, 1782 ***2856.30*** *p6*
Andreas, Jacob; Port uncertain, 1785 ***2856.30*** *p6*
Andreas, Johann; Port uncertain, 1754 ***2856.30*** *p6*
Andreas, Margarethe; Port uncertain, 1753 ***2856.30*** *p6*
Andreas, Maria Catharina; Port uncertain, 1741 ***2856.30*** *p6*
Andren, Pedro A.; New York, 1839 ***8197.10*** *p206*
Andres, Adam; America, 1742 ***2856.30*** *p6*
Andres, Catharina Barba; Port uncertain, 1753 ***2856.30*** *p6*
Andres, Elisabet; Port uncertain, 1753 ***2856.30*** *p6*
Andres, Georg; Port uncertain, 1764 ***2856.30*** *p6*
Andres, Georg Emich; Port uncertain, 1764 ***2856.30*** *p6*
Andres, Georg Emich; Port uncertain, 1790 ***2856.30*** *p6*
Andres, Georg Michael; America, 1733 ***2856.30*** *p6*
Andres, Georg Nicolaus; Port uncertain, 1754 ***2856.30*** *p6*
Andres, Lorenz; Port uncertain, 1733 ***2856.30*** *p6*
Andres, Margarete; Port uncertain, 1753 ***2856.30*** *p6*
Andres, Martin; America, 1749 ***2856.30*** *p6*
With wife & 2 children
Andres, Melchior; Port uncertain, 1784 ***2856.30*** *p99*
Andres, Sybilla; Port uncertain, 1764 ***2856.30*** *p6*
Andresejeski, Sophia; Maryland, 1910 ***3259.35*** *p1*
Andress, Mary Doyle; Vermont, 1855-1919 ***5900.10*** *p495*
Andrevout, Elizabeth 31; Ontario, 1871 ***1823.28*** *p2*
Andrew, Alexander; Trinidad, 1840 ***1640.13*** *p4*
Andrew, Alexander 29; Virginia, 1774 ***1220.25*** *p88*
Andrew, Crozier 44; Ontario, 1871 ***1823.28*** *p2*
Andrew, Edmund 40; Ontario, 1871 ***1823.15*** *p5*
Andrew, Eliza 36; Ontario, 1871 ***1823.15*** *p5*
Andrew, Frank; Maryland, 1910 ***3259.35*** *p1*
Andrew, George 34; Ontario, 1871 ***1823.15*** *p1*
Andrew, James; Georgia, 1698 ***1640.13*** *p4*
Andrew, John 31; Ontario, 1871 ***1823.15*** *p5*
Andrew, John 38; Ontario, 1871 ***1823.28*** *p2*
Andrew, John 45; Ontario, 1871 ***1823.15*** *p5*
Andrew, John 79; Ontario, 1871 ***1823.15*** *p5*
Andrew, John F. 39; Ontario, 1871 ***1823.15*** *p5*
Andrew, Martin; Maryland, 1910 ***3259.35*** *p1*
Andrew, Moses 34; Nova Scotia, 1774 ***1220.25*** *p135*
Andrew, Osweld 35; Ontario, 1871 ***1823.15*** *p5*
Andrew, Philip 40; Ontario, 1871 ***1823.15*** *p5*
Andrew, William 33; Ontario, 1871 ***1823.15*** *p5*
Andrew, William 48; Ontario, 1871 ***1823.28*** *p2*
Andrew, William 64; Ontario, 1871 ***1823.15*** *p5*
Andrew, William 65; Ontario, 1871 ***1823.15*** *p5*
Andrewes, Breta; Maryland, 1659 ***2524.55*** *p197*
Andrewes, Edward; Maryland, 1672 ***2524.55*** *p12*
Andrewes, John; Barbados, 1649 ***1224.1*** *p2*
Andrewes, John; Virginia, 1616 ***1224.1*** *p2*
Andrews, A. 28; Alaska, 1917 ***9196.1*** *p46*
Andrews, A. 28; Whitehorse, Yukon, 1917 ***9196.1*** *p46*
Andrews, Abraham; Baltimore, 1801 ***1224.3*** *p2*
Andrews, Catherine F.; Vermont, 1850-1908 ***5900.10*** *p335*
Andrews, Charles; New York, 1839 ***8197.10*** *p134*
Andrews, Charles L.; Vermont, 1847-1947 ***5900.10*** *p335*
Andrews, David 19; Ontario, 1861 ***2896.25*** *p30*
Andrews, Elizabeth 66; Ontario, 1871 ***1823.15*** *p6*
Andrews, George; Maryland, 1668 ***2524.55*** *p12*
Andrews, Hannah 1 *SEE* Andrews, Thomas
Andrews, J. 20; Ontario, 1861 ***2896.25*** *p28*
Andrews, James 57; Ontario, 1871 ***1823.28*** *p2*
Andrews, James 69; Ontario, 1871 ***1823.15*** *p6*
Andrews, Jeremiah; Pennsylvania, 1777 ***4629.10*** *p13*
Andrews, Jno; Virginia, 1664 ***6212.30*** *p9*
Andrews, John; New York, 1832 ***8197.10*** *p357*
Andrews, John; New York, 1852 ***1224.3*** *p2*
Andrews, John; Vermont, 1816-1888 ***5900.10*** *p475*
Andrews, John 5 *SEE* Andrews, Thomas
Andrews, John 39; Ontario, 1871 ***1823.15*** *p6*
Andrews, Joseph; New York, 1802 ***8197.10*** *p17*
Andrews, Joshua 23; Maryland, 1774 ***1220.25*** *p40*
Andrews, Lilley 37 *SEE* Andrews, Thomas
Andrews, Margaret O'Brien; Vermont, 1846-1918 ***5900.10*** *p484*
Andrews, Mary 3 *SEE* Andrews, Thomas
Andrews, Mary 7 *SEE* Andrews, Thomas
Andrews, Mary A.; Vermont, 1853-1925 ***5900.10*** *p475*
Andrews, Mathew 33; Ontario, 1871 ***1823.28*** *p2*
Andrews, Matthew 52; Ontario, 1871 ***1823.22*** *p4*
Andrews, Mical 71; Ontario, 1871 ***1823.15*** *p6*
Andrews, Robert; Maryland, 1655-1656 ***2524.55*** *p12*
Andrews, Robert; Maryland, 1656 ***2524.55*** *p12*
Andrews, Robert 55; Ontario, 1871 ***1823.28*** *p2*
Andrews, Samuel; New York, 1812 ***8197.10*** *p371*
Andrews, Sarah A.; Vermont, 1850-1923 ***5900.10*** *p488*
Andrews, Sarah Tiffany; Vermont, 1817-1893 ***5900.10*** *p475*
Andrews, Sophia 56; Ontario, 1871 ***1823.28*** *p2*
Andrews, Stephen 27; Ontario, 1871 ***1823.15*** *p6*
Andrews, Theophilus 68; Ontario, 1871 ***1823.22*** *p4*
Andrews, Thomas 24; Ontario, 1871 ***1823.15*** *p6*
Andrews, Thomas 35; Carolina, 1774 ***1220.25*** *p74*
Andrews, Thomas 35; Ontario, 1871 ***1823.28*** *p2*
Andrews, Thomas 37; Nova Scotia, 1774 ***1220.25*** *p15*
Wife: Lilley 37
Child: John 5
Child: Hannah 1
Child: Mary 3
Child: Mary 7
Andrews, Thomas 39; Ontario, 1871 ***1823.28*** *p2*
Andrews, Thomas 53; Ontario, 1871 ***1823.15*** *p6*
Andrews, Treiva 20; Ontario, 1871 ***1823.15*** *p6*
Andrews, W.; Quebec, 1856 ***9196.15*** *p6*
Andrews, William; Virginia, 1726 ***1224.2*** *p3*
Andrews, William 25; Ontario, 1871 ***1823.15*** *p6*
Andrews, William 30; Ontario, 1871 ***1823.28*** *p2*
Andrews, William 31; North Carolina, 1774 ***1220.25*** *p65*
Andrews, William 54; Ontario, 1871 ***1823.15*** *p6*
Andreyewski, Stanislaus; Maryland, 1910 ***3259.35*** *p1*
Andrich, J. 34; British Columbia, 1909 ***9196.1*** *p27*
Andrich, J. 34; Seattle, 1909 ***9196.1*** *p27*
Andrie, Henrich; America, 1738 ***2856.30*** *p6*
Andrie, Philipp Heinric; America, 1738 ***2856.30*** *p7*
Andries, Anna Apollonia; America, 1769 ***2856.30*** *p6*
Andries, Cath. Margareta; America, 1769 ***2856.30*** *p6*
Andries, Maria Ursula; America, 1769 ***2856.30*** *p6*
Andries, Mathias; America, 1769 ***2856.30*** *p6*
Andrisski, Stoneslauce; Maryland, 1910 ***3259.35*** *p1*
Andrus, David; Connecticut, 1764 ***1224.2*** *p3*
Andrus, David; Havana, 1764 ***1224.2*** *p3*
Andrus, F. M. 3; Ontario, 1861 ***2896.26*** *p3*
Andrysiak, Walenty; Maryland, 1910 ***3259.35*** *p1*
Andryziak, Joseph; Maryland, 1910 ***3259.35*** *p1*
Andrzack, Joseph; Maryland, 1910 ***3259.35*** *p1*
Andrzeyewski, Felix; Maryland, 1910 ***3259.35*** *p1*
Andrzeyewski, Felix W.; Maryland, 1910 ***3259.35*** *p1*
Andrzeyewski, Frank; Maryland, 1910 ***3259.35*** *p1*
Andrzjieruski, John; Maryland, 1910 ***3259.35*** *p1*
Andrzyziak, John; Maryland, 1910 ***3259.35*** *p1*
Andy, Thomas 44; Ontario, 1871 ***1823.15*** *p1*
Andzyszek, Andrey F.; Maryland, 1910 ***3259.35*** *p1*
Aneckher, Ursula; Port uncertain, 1739 ***2856.30*** *p7*
Angel, Abraham 27; Maryland, 1774 ***1220.25*** *p38*
Angel, Charles; New York, 1831 ***8197.10*** *p313*
Angele, Georg; Port uncertain, 1743 ***2856.30*** *p7*
Angele, Georg; Port uncertain, 1775 ***2856.30*** *p7*
Angele, Maria; America, 1752 ***2856.30*** *p7*
Angele, Michael; Port uncertain, 1760 ***2856.30*** *p7*
Angell, Anthony; Maryland, 1661 ***2524.55*** *p12*
Angell, Audery; Virginia, 1664 ***6212.30*** *p10*
Angell, Audry; Virginia, 1664 ***6212.30*** *p5*
Angell, Jno; Virginia, 1663 ***6212.30*** *p4*
Angell, Thomas; New York, 1807 ***8197.10*** *p33*
Angelmeyer, Johann; Port uncertain, 1752 ***2856.30*** *p7*
Angene, Johann Nickel; America, 1735 ***2856.30*** *p2*
Angene, Johann Nickel; America, 1736 ***2856.30*** *p2*
Anger, Thomas 31; Ontario, 1871 ***1823.28*** *p2*
Angermeyer, Georg; Port uncertain, 1737 ***2856.30*** *p7*
Angers, Mr.; Quebec, 1857 ***9196.15*** *p23*
Angers, Mrs.; Quebec, 1857 ***9196.15*** *p23*
Angier, Edmund; New England, 1667 ***1224.1*** *p2*
Angier, Edmund; New England, 1678 ***1224.1*** *p2*
Angle, Jane; Virginia, 1664 ***6212.30*** *p6*
Angle, John; Maryland, 1681 ***2524.55*** *p12*
Anglen, Elenior; Maryland, 1668 ***2524.55*** *p12*
Anglerin, Maria; America, 1752 ***2856.30*** *p7*
Angley, Bridget 80; Vermont, 1880 ***5900.10*** *p617*
Anglim, Mary 65; Vermont, 1893 ***5900.10*** *p95*
Angliss, Alexander 48; Ontario, 1871 ***1823.22*** *p4*
Angne, Theobald; America, 1753 ***2856.30*** *p7*
With wife
Angove, Samuel 43; Ontario, 1871 ***1823.22*** *p4*
Angrove, George 35; Ontario, 1871 ***1823.22*** *p4*
Angst, Daniel; America, 1748 ***2856.30*** *p7*
Angst, Daniel; Port uncertain, 1748 ***2856.30*** *p7*
Angst, Solomon 27; Ontario, 1871 ***1823.15*** *p6*
Angst, Ulrick 31; Ontario, 1871 ***1823.15*** *p6*
Angst, Ulrick 69; Ontario, 1871 ***1823.15*** *p6*
Anguett, Margarett; Maryland, 1664 ***2524.55*** *p107*
Angur, Jacob; Virginia, 1664 ***6212.30*** *p7*
Angus, Mr.; Quebec, 1857 ***9196.15*** *p16*
Angus, Mrs.; Quebec, 1857 ***9196.15*** *p16*
Angus, George 51; Ontario, 1871 ***1823.22*** *p4*
Angus, Gilbert; Georgia, 1698 ***1640.13*** *p4*
Angus, James 28; Ontario, 1871 ***1823.15*** *p6*
Angus, James 43; Ontario, 1871 ***1823.22*** *p4*
Angus, John; Georgia, 1698 ***1640.13*** *p4*

Angus, John; New York, 1812 8197.10 p205
Angus, John 26; Ontario, 1871 1823.15 p6
Angus, John 65; Ontario, 1871 1823.15 p6
Angus, Robert; West Indies, 1859 1640.13 p4
Angus, Robert 44; Ontario, 1871 1823.15 p6
Angus, Thomas McQuiston; Jamaica, 1825 1640.13 p4
Angus, William; New York, 1826 8197.10 p335
Angus, William 39; Ontario, 1871 1823.15 p6
Anhausser, Johannetta; Port uncertain, 1726 2856.30 p7
Animikwaam, Paul 47; Ontario, 1871 1823.28 p2
Anis, Stephen; Virginia, 1666 6212.30 p26
Anker, Juliana; Port uncertain, 1766 2856.30 p7
Anketell, James; New York, 1840 8197.10 p143
Anktill, Elizabeth SEE Anktill, Francis
Anktill, Elizabeth; Maryland, 1659 2524.55 p12
Anktill, Francis; Maryland, 1659 2524.55 p12
Brother: John
Wife: Elizabeth
Anktill, John SEE Anktill, Francis
Anktill, John; Maryland, 1659 2524.55 p12
Anna, Johann Georg; Port uncertain, 1808 2856.30 p7
Annan, Bidina 69; Ontario, 1871 1823.15 p6
Annan, Robert; Pennsylvania, 1891 1640.13 p4
Annaud, Alexander 61; Ontario, 1871 1823.15 p6
Annell, Magnus; New York, 1790 1640.13 p4
Annely, Richard; New York, 1750 1224.2 p3
Annet, John; New York, 1806 8197.10 p324
Annett, William 30; Ontario, 1871 1823.15 p6
Annis, John Wm.; Pennsylvania, 1777 4629.10 p7
Annis, Thomas; Maryland, 1679 2524.55 p11
Annisly, Jno; Virginia, 1665-1666 6212.30 p22
Annisly, Jno; Virginia, 1666-1667 6212.30 p32
Annitt, Thomas 24; Ontario, 1861 2896.28 p49
Annsrewski, Joseph; Maryland, 1910 3259.35 p1
Ano., Mary; Maryland, 1682 2524.55 p12
Ansbro, Mary; Vermont, 1857-1919 5900.10 p206
Ansbro, William; Vermont, 1844-1921 5900.10 p206
Anschutz, David 44; Kansas, 1878-1910 9079.10 p39
Anschutz, Katie 42; Kansas, 1885-1910 9079.10 p39
Ansell, Asher 34; Ontario, 1871 1823.28 p2
Anselm, Christian; Port uncertain, 1796 2856.30 p7
Ansill, Robert; Maryland, 1664 2524.55 p12
Ansley, James 21; America, 1774 1220.25 p36
Ansley, Julius 74; Ontario, 1871 1823.28 p2
Anson, George 21; Maryland, 1775 1220.25 p105
Anson, Richard; Maryland, 1681 2524.55 p12
Anspach, Johann Peter; America, 1764 2856.30 p7
Anspach, Maria Elisabeth; America, 1754 2856.30 p7
Anspach, Nicolaus; America, 1764 2856.30 p7
Anstaet, Johann Georg; Port uncertain, 1790 2856.30 p7
Anstand, Johann Nickel; Port uncertain, 1761 2856.30 p7
Anstatt, C.; Port uncertain, 1783 2856.30 p317
Anstatt, Catharina; Port uncertain, 1783 2856.30 p5
With husband
Anstatt, Johann; America, 1749 2856.30 p7
Anstatt, Johann; Port uncertain, 1746 2856.30 p7
Anstatt, Margarete; Port uncertain, 1744 2856.30 p7
Anstatt, Maria Eva; Port uncertain, 1744 2856.30 p7
Anstatt, Maria Eva; Port uncertain, 1765 2856.30 p7
Anstattin, Elisabeth; Port uncertain, 1790 2856.30 p7
With husband
Anster, John 73; Ontario, 1871 1823.28 p2
Anstin, Moses; New York, 1835 8197.10 p71
Ant, Johann; Port uncertain, 1777 2856.30 p7
Ant, Michael; Maryland, 1910 3259.35 p1
Antes, Maria Sofia; Port uncertain, 1741 2856.30 p7
Anthes, Franz; America, 1757 2856.30 p7
Anthoney, Michael; Pennsylvania, 1777 4629.10 p9
Anthony, Mr.; Vermont, 1836-1911 5900.10 p431
Anthony, Mrs.; Vermont, 1845-1923 5900.10 p431
Anthony, David; Virginia, 1676 1224.1 p3
Anthony, Frederick; Pennsylvania, 1786 4629.10 p52
Anthony, Joane; Maryland, 1661 2524.55 p133
Anthony, John; Maryland, 1665 2524.55 p12
Anthony, John; New York, 1778 1224.2 p3
Anthony, John; New York, 1807 8197.10 p331
Anthony, John 21; Carolina, 1774 1220.25 p76
Anthony, Lucy; New York, 1838 8197.10 p109
Anthony, Mary; Maryland, 1661 2524.55 p133
Anthonye, Charles; Virginia, 1615 1224.1 p3
Antill, John; New York, 1819 1224.3 p2
Antill, Lewis; New York, 1786 1224.2 p3
Antkowiak, John; Maryland, 1910 3259.35 p1
Antkowiak, Martin J.; Maryland, 1910 3259.35 p1
Antkowski, John; Maryland, 1910 3259.35 p1
Antler, Charles 45; Ontario, 1871 1823.28 p2
Anton, Catharina; Port uncertain, 1792 2856.30 p7
Anton, Franz; Port uncertain, 1772 2856.30 p7
Antoni, Jacob; Port uncertain, 1785 2856.30 p8
Antoni, Michael; Port uncertain, 1753 2856.30 p8
Antonio, Joseph; New York, 1830 8197.10 p359
Antonziewski, Josef; Maryland, 1910 3259.35 p1
Antor, Henry; Maryland, 1668 2524.55 p12
Antowiak, Allan; Maryland, 1910 3259.35 p1
Antram, William; South Carolina, 1752 1224.2 p3
Antritt, Maria; Port uncertain, 1786 2856.30 p8
Antrum, Rich; Virginia, 1693-1694 6212.30 p60
Antryska, Edward; Maryland, 1910 3259.35 p1
Anuszewski, Andrew; Maryland, 1910 3259.35 p1
Anuzewski, Michel; Maryland, 1910 3259.35 p1
Anweiler, Ludwig; Port uncertain, 1791 2856.30 p8
With wife
Anwyle, Kenrick 27; Maryland, 1775 1220.25 p111
Anz, Frantz; New York, 1840 8197.10 p142
Anz, Philip; New York, 1840 8197.10 p206
Anzer, Wm; Virginia, 1674 6212.30 p52
Apel, Jonas; America, 1768 2856.30 p8
Apel, Jonas; America, 1782 2856.30 p8
With wife & 3 children
Apel, Mrs. Jonas; America, 1771 2856.30 p8
With 3 children
Apicarius, Maria Magdalena; Port uncertain, 1786 2856.30 p8
Appel, Anna Christina; Port uncertain, 1764 2856.30 p8
Appel, Michael; Port uncertain, 1733 2856.30 p8
Appel, Peter; Port uncertain, 1732 2856.30 p8
Appelhans, Henrich; Port uncertain, 1760 2856.30 p8
Appeman, George 62; Ontario, 1871 1823.15 p6
Appeman, Justus 36; Ontario, 1871 1823.15 p6
Applebe, Thomas 43; Ontario, 1871 1823.22 p4
Applebee, Benjamin; New York, 1744 1224.2 p3
Appleby, George 50; Ontario, 1871 1823.22 p4
Appleby, John 46; Ontario, 1871 1823.28 p2
Appleby, Robert 21; Nova Scotia, 1774 1220.25 p13
Appleby, Thomas; Pennsylvania, 1786 4629.10 p54
Appleby, Thomas 49; Ontario, 1871 1823.15 p6
Appleby, William; Maryland, 1657 2524.55 p12
Appleby, William; Maryland, 1660 2524.55 p12
Appleby, William 18; New York, 1774 1220.25 p24
Applegarth, George D.; Pennsylvania, 1862-1865 6058.10 p50
Appler, Godslip 45; Ontario, 1871 1823.28 p2
Appleton, Etherington; New York, 1821 8197.10 p205
Appleton, Frances; Vermont, 1838-1916 5900.10 p496
Appleton, Francis 22; Maryland, 1774 1220.25 p52
Appleton, Henry; Virginia, 1666-1667 6212.30 p34
Appleton, John; Boston, 1773 1224.2 p3
Appleton, Robert; New York, 1840 8197.10 p206
Appleton, Robert 24; Fort Cumberland, Nova Scotia, 1774 1220.25 p17
Appleton, Robert 48; Ontario, 1871 1823.15 p6
Appleton, Samuel; Boston, 1729 1224.2 p3
Appleton, Samuel; New England, 1638 1224.1 p48
Appleyard, Thomas; Maryland, 1673 2524.55 p12
Appleyard, William; New York, 1839 8197.10 p134
Appy, John; North America, 1763 1224.2 p3
Apreece, Robt; Virginia, 1665-1666 6212.30 p21
Aprice, Morgan; Virginia, 1667 6212.30 p36
Apted, Richard; New York, 1840 8197.10 p143
ApThomas, Richard; Maryland, 1663 2524.55 p12
Apthorp, Charles; Boston, 1784 1224.2 p3
Apthorp, John; Cambridge, Massachusetts, 1733 1224.2 p3
Apthorp, William Rice; Boston, n.d. 1224.3 p2
Apthorp, William Rice; West Indies, 1800 1224.3 p2
Aquart, Jean Marie; Windward Islands, 1838 1640.13 p4
Aram, Thomas; Maryland, 1673 2524.55 p12
Arbengast, Johann; America, 1751 2856.30 p8
Arbogast, Apollonia; Port uncertain, 1712 2856.30 p8
Arbogast, Frederick; New York, 1836 8197.10 p75
Arbogast, Georg; Port uncertain, 1770 2856.30 p8
Arbogast, Martin; Port uncertain, 1768 2856.30 p8
Arbogast, Martin; Port uncertain, 1771 2856.30 p8
Arbogast, Philipp; America, 1784 2856.30 p8
Arbon, Harry 18; Ontario, 1871 1823.22 p4
Arbona, Francis; New York, 1837 8197.10 p373
Arbot, Jno; Virginia, 1671-1672 6212.30 p47
Arbuckle, Hugh; Texas, 1808-1845 1640.10 p5
Arbuckle, Janet 85; Ontario, 1871 1823.15 p6
Arbuckle, Thomas; Vermont, 1837-1908 5900.10 p148
Arbuckle, William 62; Ontario, 1871 1823.15 p6
Arbuthnott, Thomas; Virginia, 1742 1640.13 p4
Arch, Thomas; Maryland, 1663 2524.55 p12
Archard, Thomas; New York, 1840 8197.10 p143
Archbell, John; Virginia, 1692 1224.1 p3
Archdale, Thomas 40; Maryland, 1774 1220.25 p78
Archdall, Lieutenant; Quebec, 1858 9196.15 p31
Archdeacon, James; Norfolk, Virginia, 1784 1224.2 p3
Archer, Mr.; Quebec, 1857 9196.15 p18
Archer, Mr.; St. John, New Brunswick, 1857 9196.15 p12
Archer, A.; Quebec, 1857 9196.15 p17
Archer, Amb; Virginia, 1672 6212.30 p49
Archer, Ambrose; Virginia, 1668-1669 6212.30 p40
Archer, Anto; Virginia, 1665-1666 6212.30 p22
Archer, Edmond; New York, 1794 8197.10 p1
Archer, Hugh 70; Ontario, 1871 1823.15 p6
Archer, Humphrey; Maryland, 1659 2524.55 p12
Archer, James 53; Ontario, 1871 1823.22 p4
Archer, Jane 28; Ontario, 1871 1823.22 p4
Archer, John; America, 1649 1224.1 p3
Archer, John 23; Maryland, 1775 1220.25 p97
Archer, John 46; Ontario, 1871 1823.15 p6
Archer, Joshua 44; Ontario, 1871 1823.22 p4
Archer, Moses; Pennsylvania, 1778 4629.10 p34
Archer, Richard; Virginia, 1665 6212.30 p17
Archer, Richard 50; Ontario, 1871 1823.28 p2
Archer, Robert; Carolina, 1691 1224.1 p3
Archer, Roger; Virginia, 1642 1224.1 p3
Archer, Samuel 40; Ontario, 1871 1823.15 p6
Archer, Sarah; Maryland, 1658 2524.55 p12
Archer, Thomas; New York, 1838 8197.10 p205
Archer, Thomas; New York, 1840 8197.10 p143
Archer, William; Savannah, Georgia, 1805 1640.10 p5
Archer, William 23; Maryland, 1774 1220.25 p77
Archer, William 28; Ontario, 1871 1823.22 p4
Archer, William 54; Ontario, 1871 1823.22 p4
Archibald, Mr. 93; Ontario, 1871 1823.22 p4
Archibald, Andrew 48; Ontario, 1871 1823.15 p6
Archibald, George; Virginia, 1676 6212.30 p53
Archibald, John; Georgia, 1698 1640.13 p4
Archibald, John; Georgia, 1883 1640.13 p5
Archibald, Robert; New York, 1812-1834 8197.10 p306
Archibold, Bartholomew; Pennsylvania, 1777 4629.10 p45
Archibold, William 30; Ontario, 1871 1823.15 p6
Arcles, Joseph 68; Ontario, 1871 1823.22 p4
Arcowski, Frank; Maryland, 1910 3259.35 p1
Arct, Frederick 54; Ontario, 1871 1823.15 p7
Ard, Peter; Maryland, 1657 2524.55 p12
Ard, Samuel 37; Ontario, 1871 1823.15 p7
Ardah, Mr.; Quebec, 1857 9196.15 p21
Ardein, Hans Adam; Port uncertain, 1752 2856.30 p8
With wife & children
Arderne, John; North Carolina, 1720 1224.2 p3
Ardla, Philip; Pennsylvania, 1777 4629.10 p12
Ardley, Mary; New York, 1832 8197.10 p303
Ardrion, Wm.; New York, 1819 8197.10 p205
Ards, Thomas; Maryland, 1662 2524.55 p12
Arenberg, Daniel; Port uncertain, 1749 2856.30 p8
Arend, Johann Jacob; Port uncertain, 1783 2856.30 p8
Arend, Leonhard; Port uncertain, 1720 2856.30 p8
Arendt, Michael; Maryland, 1910 3259.35 p1
Arens, Henry 30; Ontario, 1871 1823.28 p2
Arent, Antoine; New York, 1837 8197.10 p82
Arent, Johann Wilhelm; America, 1749 2856.30 p8
Arery, Wm.; Maryland, 1675 2524.55 p12
Arey, John; North Carolina, 1771 1224.2 p1
Arey, Thomas 26; Ontario, 1871 1823.15 p7
Argall, Samuel; Virginia, 1626 1224.1 p3
Argall, Thomas; Virginia, 1666-1667 6212.30 p33
Argall, William; New York, 1832 8197.10 p357
Argast, Johann; Port uncertain, 1751 2856.30 p8
Argast, Sophia Salome; Port uncertain, 1784 2856.30 p8
Argent, Adam 22; Maryland, 1774 1220.25 p41
Argent, Anne; Virginia, 1654 1224.1 p3
Argey, Jane 26; Ontario, 1871 1823.15 p7
Argey, Margaet 69; Ontario, 1871 1823.15 p7
Argors, Richard 16; Georgia, 1774 1220.25 p48
Argue, Andrew 51; Ontario, 1871 1823.22 p4
Argue, Henry 54; Ontario, 1871 1823.28 p2
Arington, Ann; Virginia, 1703-1704 6212.30 p62
Aris, Douglas; Jamaica, 1825 1640.13 p5
Arka, Francis; Maryland, 1910 3259.35 p1
Arkell, Mr.; Quebec, 1856 9196.15 p7
Arkett, Betsy 70; Ontario, 1861 2896.25 p14
Arkett, Lesly 5; Ontario, 1861 2896.27 p16
Arkett, Theodore 7; Ontario, 1861 2896.27 p16
Arking, Robert; New York, 1735 1224.2 p4
Arkinson, William 55; Ontario, 1871 1823.22 p4
Arkles, George; Savannah, Georgia, 1806 1640.10 p6
Arkley, William; Maryland, 1673 2524.55 p12
Arlington, Michael; Virginia, 1719 1224.2 p4
Arlington, Richd; Virginia, 1671-1672 6212.30 p47
Arlow, Jacob 45; Ontario, 1871 1823.28 p2
Arlsworth, Henry 28; Ontario, 1871 1823.15 p7
Armal, Daniel; Pennsylvania, 1778 4629.10 p32
Armatage, William 30; Maryland, 1773-1774 1220.25 p33
Armbrust, Johann; Port uncertain, 1736 2856.30 p9
Armbruster, Adam; Port uncertain, 1732 2856.30 p9
Armbruster, Anton; America, 1743 2856.30 p9
Armbruster, Anton; America, 1796 2856.30 p9
Armbruster, Georg; Port uncertain, 1736 2856.30 p9
Armbruster, Gottfried; America, 1818 2856.30 p9
With family
Armbruster, Gotthart; America, 1743 2856.30 p9
Armbruster, Hiob; America, 1753 2856.30 p9
Armbruster, Jakob; America, 1752 2856.30 p9

Arthur, Hugh 23; Ontario, 1861 ***2896.28*** *p40*
Arthur, Hugh 62; Ontario, 1861 ***2896.28*** *p40*
Arthur, James; Mississippi, 1805-1845 ***1640.10*** *p6*
Arthur, James; New York, 1806 ***8197.10*** *p30*
Arthur, James; Pennsylvania, 1779 ***4629.10*** *p38*
Arthur, James 27; Ontario, 1861 ***2896.28*** *p40*
Arthur, James 39; Ontario, 1861 ***2896.28*** *p32*
Arthur, John; San Francisco, 1856 ***1224.3*** *p3*
Arthur, John 8; Ontario, 1861 ***2896.28*** *p20*
Arthur, Joseph R. 14; Ontario, 1861 ***2896.28*** *p20*
Arthur, Margaret 1; Ontario, 1861 ***2896.28*** *p47*
Arthur, Mary; Boston, 1887 ***1640.13*** *p5*
Arthur, Mary; Jamaica, 1853 ***1640.13*** *p5*
Arthur, Mary 42; Ontario, 1861 ***2896.28*** *p47*
Arthur, Mary C. 6; Ontario, 1861 ***2896.28*** *p20*
Arthur, Mary J. 25; Ontario, 1861 ***2896.28*** *p40*
Arthur, Mary M. 16; Ontario, 1861 ***2896.28*** *p47*
Arthur, Mathew 4; Ontario, 1861 ***2896.28*** *p47*
Arthur, Mathew 36; Ontario, 1861 ***2896.27*** *p12*
Arthur, Mathew 55; Ontario, 1861 ***2896.28*** *p47*
Arthur, Nancy J. 10; Ontario, 1861 ***2896.28*** *p20*
Arthur, Phebe 20; Ontario, 1861 ***2896.28*** *p40*
Arthur, Robert 7; Ontario, 1861 ***2896.28*** *p47*
Arthur, Sarah A. 31; Ontario, 1861 ***2896.28*** *p40*
Arthur, Sarah C. 10; Ontario, 1861 ***2896.28*** *p47*
Arthur, Sarah E. 14; Ontario, 1861 ***2896.28*** *p40*
Arthur, Sarah E. 16; Ontario, 1861 ***2896.28*** *p20*
Arthur, Thomas 46; Ontario, 1871 ***1823.22*** *p5*
Arthur, William; New York, 1876 ***1640.13*** *p5*
Arthur, William; New York, New York, 1781 ***1224.2*** *p4*
Arthur, William; Ontario, 1861 ***2896.28*** *p49*
Arthur, William 44; Ontario, 1861 ***2896.28*** *p20*
Arthurs, Mary 36; Maryland, 1775 ***1220.25*** *p105*
Arthurs, Thomas 35; Maryland, 1775 ***1220.25*** *p105*
Artiguenave, Jean Francois; New York, 1826-1834 ***8197.10*** *p306*
Artiquenave, Jean Francois; Boston, 1826 ***8197.10*** *p315*
Arundell, Ezekiell; Virginia, 1666 ***6212.30*** *p28*
Arundell, Jno; Virginia, 1666 ***6212.30*** *p27*
Arundell, John; Maryland, 1673 ***2524.55*** *p13*
Arundell, Richard; Virginia, 1666 ***6212.30*** *p27*
Arundell, Robert; Nova Scotia, 1725 ***1224.2*** *p4*
Arundell, William; Maryland, 1673 ***2524.55*** *p13*
Arunthius, Johann; Port uncertain, 1732 ***2856.30*** *p10*
Arz, Peter; Canada, 1784 ***2856.30*** *p10*
Arz, Peter; Port uncertain, 1750 ***2856.30*** *p10*
Arzechowski, Lorenz; Maryland, 1910 ***3259.35*** *p1*
Asall, Jorg; Port uncertain, 1744 ***2856.30*** *p10*
Asand, Johann Nikolaus; Port uncertain, 1779 ***2856.30*** *p10*
Asand, Johann Nikolaus; Port uncertain, 1784 ***2856.30*** *p10*
Asche, Henry; New York, 1837 ***8197.10*** *p205*
Ascher, Mr.; Quebec, 1858 ***9196.15*** *p36*
Ascher, Mrs.; Quebec, 1858 ***9196.15*** *p36*
Asculoski, Walinti; Maryland, 1910 ***3259.35*** *p2*
Aseltyne, Mary 69; Vermont, 1874 ***5900.10*** *p500*
Asfalg, Franz; Port uncertain, 1729 ***2856.30*** *p10*
Asfalg, Josef; Port uncertain, 1789 ***2856.30*** *p10*
Ash, Anne; Charles Town, South Carolina, 1721 ***1224.2*** *p70*
Ash, Francis; Philadelphia, 1839 ***1224.3*** *p3*
Ash, Harry; New York, 1840 ***8197.10*** *p143*
Ash, Henry; Pennsylvania, 1777 ***4629.10*** *p22*
Ash, Hiram 80; Ontario, 1871 ***1823.22*** *p5*
Ash, James; Virginia, 1664 ***6212.30*** *p15*
Ash, John; Carolina, 1706 ***1224.2*** *p4*
Ash, John; New York, 1838 ***8197.10*** *p109*
Ash, John; New York, 1840 ***8197.10*** *p142*
Ash, John; South Carolina, 1721 ***1224.2*** *p4*
Ash, John 39; Ontario, 1871 ***1823.22*** *p5*
Ash, John Hill; Ontario, 1884 ***1640.13*** *p5*
Ash, Joseph; Vermont, 1862-1938 ***5900.10*** *p123*
Ash, Joseph; Virginia, 1679-1680 ***6212.30*** *p54*
Ash, Katherine M. Gill; Vermont, 1867-1952 ***5900.10*** *p123*
Ash, Mary 63; Vermont, 1886 ***5900.10*** *p59*
Ash, Michael; New York, 1826 ***8197.10*** *p335*
Ash, Michael; New York, 1840 ***8197.10*** *p143*
Ash, Roland; Virginia, 1665 ***6212.30*** *p20*
Ash, Samuell; Virginia, 1664 ***6212.30*** *p15*
Ash, Simon; New York, 1840 ***8197.10*** *p143*
Ashbee, John; Maryland, 1681 ***2524.55*** *p13*
Ashborne, Elizabeth; Maryland, 1650 ***2524.55*** *p13*
Ashborne, James; Maryland, 1650 ***2524.55*** *p13*
Ashborne, Peter; Maryland, 1656 ***2524.55*** *p13*
Ashbridge, Joseph; Pennsylvania, 1787 ***4629.10*** *p50*
Ashbrook, . . .; Maryland, 1648 ***2524.55*** *p13*
Ashbrooke, John; Maryland, 1677-1681 ***2524.55*** *p13*
Ashburn, John; Pennsylvania, 1777 ***4629.10*** *p13*
Ashburne, William 28; Virginia, 1773 ***1220.25*** *p30*
Ashburnham, Jno; Virginia, 1665-1666 ***6212.30*** *p23*
Ashby, James; Virginia, 1671-1672 ***6212.30*** *p47*
Ashby, John; Maryland, 1657 ***2524.55*** *p13*
Ashby, John; Maryland, 1681 ***2524.55*** *p13*
Ashby, John; New York, 1837 ***8197.10*** *p205*
Ashby, John; New York, 1838 ***8197.10*** *p205*
Ashby, William; Pennsylvania, 1786 ***4629.10*** *p50*
Ashby, Wm; Virginia, 1666 ***6212.30*** *p26*
Ashcomb, Charles *SEE* Ashcomb, John
Ashcomb, John *SEE* Ashcomb, John
Ashcomb, John; Maryland, 1650-1651 ***2524.55*** *p13*
Wife: Winifred
Son: Samuel
Son: John
Son: Nathaniel
Son: Charles
Ashcomb, John; Maryland, 1658 ***2524.55*** *p13*
With wife & family
Ashcomb, Lidia; Maryland, 1651 ***2524.55*** *p19*
Ashcomb, Nathaniel *SEE* Ashcomb, John
Ashcomb, Samuel *SEE* Ashcomb, John
Ashcomb, Winifred *SEE* Ashcomb, John
Ashdon, Eliza; Virginia, 1664 ***6212.30*** *p6*
Ashdown, James 46; Ontario, 1871 ***1823.28*** *p3*
Ashdown, William 31; Ontario, 1871 ***1823.28*** *p3*
Ashdown, William 51; Ontario, 1871 ***1823.15*** *p8*
Ashe, Agness Putnam; Vermont, 1850-1922 ***5900.10*** *p422*
Ashe, Eugene; Vermont, 1848-1935 ***5900.10*** *p422*
Ashe, Mary Batt; South Carolina, 1719 ***1224.2*** *p4*
Ashenburst, Jno; Virginia, 1665-1666 ***6212.30*** *p24*
Asher, John 28; Virginia, 1773 ***1220.25*** *p29*
Asheton, Thomas; Pennsylvania, 1777 ***4629.10*** *p21*
Ashey, John B. 43; Vermont, 1886 ***5900.10*** *p590*
Ashey, Joseph; Vermont, 1839-1912 ***5900.10*** *p593*
Ashey, Lucy 46; Vermont, 1885 ***5900.10*** *p590*
Ashey, Mary Tye; Vermont, 1846-1909 ***5900.10*** *p593*
Ashick, Fredrick 39; Ontario, 1871 ***1823.28*** *p3*
Ashley, Mr.; Quebec, 1858 ***9196.15*** *p34*
Ashley, Hattie M.; Vermont, 1848-1914 ***5900.10*** *p495*
Ashley, Henry; Maryland, 1649 ***2524.55*** *p13*
Ashley, John; Virginia, 1657 ***1224.1*** *p3*
Ashley, Nathaniel; Pennsylvania, 1777 ***4629.10*** *p25*
Ashley, Rich; Virginia, 1665-1666 ***6212.30*** *p21*
Ashley, Robert; New York, 1807 ***8197.10*** *p326*
Ashley, Robert; New York, 1822-1834 ***8197.10*** *p306*
Ashley, Wm; Virginia, 1663 ***6212.30*** *p4*
Ashlin, William; Philadelphia, 1828 ***1224.3*** *p3*
Ashling, George 35; Philadelphia, 1774 ***1220.25*** *p66*
Ashman, Richard; Maryland, 1665 ***2524.55*** *p13*
Ashmead, Alfred; New York, 1840 ***8197.10*** *p143*
Ashmead, John; Pennsylvania, 1777 ***4629.10*** *p9*
Ashmenall, John; Philadelphia, 1789 ***4629.10*** *p58*
Wife: Mary
Ashmenall, Mary *SEE* Ashmenall, John
Ashmenall, Michael 22; Philadelphia, 1789 ***4629.10*** *p58*
Ashton, Mrs.; Quebec, 1856 ***9196.15*** *p10*
Ashton, Benjamin; Quebec, 1856 ***9196.15*** *p11*
Ashton, Emanuel; New York, 1830 ***8197.10*** *p363*
Ashton, Francis 36; Ontario, 1871 ***1823.15*** *p8*
Ashton, Francis 54; Ontario, 1871 ***1823.15*** *p8*
Ashton, George; Pennsylvania, 1776 ***4629.10*** *p53*
Ashton, George 53; Ontario, 1871 ***1823.15*** *p8*
Ashton, Harry 31; Ontario, 1871 ***1823.22*** *p5*
Ashton, James; New York, 1831 ***8197.10*** *p367*
Ashton, James; Virginia, 1665-1666 ***6212.30*** *p25*
Ashton, James; Virginia, 1687 ***1224.1*** *p3*
Ashton, Jas.; Pennsylvania, 1781 ***4629.10*** *p42*
Ashton, John; New York, 1704 ***1224.2*** *p4*
Ashton, John 27; Maryland, 1775 ***1220.25*** *p106*
Ashton, John 35; Ontario, 1871 ***1823.22*** *p5*
Ashton, Joseph; Pennsylvania, 1777 ***4629.10*** *p27*
Ashton, Margaret 25; Ontario, 1871 ***1823.15*** *p8*
Ashton, Owen; Pennsylvania, 1777 ***4629.10*** *p17*
Ashton, Phillip; Quebec, 1856 ***9196.15*** *p11*
Ashton, Ralph; Virginia, 1665-1666 ***6212.30*** *p22*
Ashton, Saml; Quebec, 1856 ***9196.15*** *p11*
Ashton, Smith; New York, 1829 ***8197.10*** *p205*
Ashton, Stephen; New York, 1831 ***8197.10*** *p67*
Ashton, Tho; Virginia, 1665-1666 ***6212.30*** *p21*
Ashton, Thomas; Pennsylvania, 1777 ***4629.10*** *p27*
Ashton, Thomas 39; Ontario, 1871 ***1823.15*** *p9*
Ashton, William; Maryland, 1662 ***2524.55*** *p13*
Ashton, William 26; Ontario, 1871 ***1823.15*** *p9*
Ashton, William 26; Virginia, 1775 ***1220.25*** *p95*
Ashwell, Geo.; New York, 1840 ***8197.10*** *p142*
Ashwell, Samuel; New York, 1807 ***8197.10*** *p33*
Ashwith, George 30; Ontario, 1871 ***1823.15*** *p9*
Ashwith, Margaret 53; Ontario, 1871 ***1823.15*** *p9*
Ashwood, Mary Ann; Illinois, 1857 ***1224.3*** *p3*
Asinger, Peter; Port uncertain, 1788 ***2856.30*** *p10*
Asinus, Barbara; Port uncertain, 1792 ***2856.30*** *p10*
Askew, James; Virginia, 1698 ***6212.30*** *p61*
Askewe, Thomas; Maryland, 1658 ***2524.55*** *p13*
Askham, Mary; Maryland, 1649 ***2524.55*** *p13*
Askin, Henry 21; British Columbia, 1909 ***9196.1*** *p28*
Askin, Henry 21; Washington, 1909 ***9196.1*** *p28*
Askin, John; Maryland, 1674 ***2524.55*** *p13*
Askuith, Robert 53; Ontario, 1871 ***1823.15*** *p9*
Aslat, Edward; Galveston, Texas, 1840 ***1224.3*** *p3*
Asmalak, Mary; Maryland, 1910 ***3259.35*** *p2*
Aspeck, Anna Eva *SEE* Aspeck, Christian
Aspeck, Christian; America, 1736 ***2856.30*** *p10*
Wife: Anna Eva
Aspeck, Christian; America, 1737 ***2856.30*** *p10*
Asperkin, John 2 *SEE* Asperkin, William
Asperkin, Mary 26 *SEE* Asperkin, William
Asperkin, William 45; Philadelphia, 1774 ***1220.25*** *p25*
Wife: Mary 26
Child: John 2
Aspinall, Henry; Maryland, 1663 ***2524.55*** *p13*
Aspinall, Henry; Maryland, 1669 ***2524.55*** *p13*
Aspinall, John; Virginia, 1663 ***6212.30*** *p1*
Aspinwall, Anna Ross; Pittsburgh, 1895 ***1640.13*** *p5*
Aspitall, William; Florida, 1766 ***1224.2*** *p4*
Aspley, John 21; Virginia, 1774 ***1220.25*** *p75*
Asqua, Eledi *SEE* Asqua, Johelep
Asqua, Eledi; Maryland, 1671 ***2524.55*** *p13*
Asqua, Johelep; Maryland, 1671 ***2524.55*** *p13*
Wife: Eledi
Child: Mary
Asqua, Mary *SEE* Asqua, Johelep
Asqua, Mary; Maryland, 1671 ***2524.55*** *p13*
Assaf, Mike 33; British Columbia, 1909 ***9196.1*** *p27*
Assaf, Mike 33; Washington, 1909 ***9196.1*** *p27*
Asseter, William; Maryland, 1659 ***2524.55*** *p13*
With wife
Assfalg, Catharina; Port uncertain, 1782 ***2856.30*** *p10*
Assick, Richard 20; Maryland, 1774 ***1220.25*** *p77*
Assiginack, Benjamin 41; Ontario, 1871 ***1823.28*** *p3*
Assiginak, Amable 82; Ontario, 1871 ***1823.28*** *p3*
Assiginak, Daniel 40; Ontario, 1871 ***1823.28*** *p3*
Assiginak, Joseph 42; Ontario, 1871 ***1823.28*** *p3*
Assiginak, Louis 47; Ontario, 1871 ***1823.28*** *p3*
Assiniiwe, Jean Bte 64; Ontario, 1871 ***1823.28*** *p3*
Assiniwe, Vincent 59; Ontario, 1871 ***1823.28*** *p3*
Assister, Will.; Maryland, 1651 ***2524.55*** *p13*
With wife
Assister, William; Maryland, 1640 ***2524.55*** *p13*
Assiter, William; Maryland, 1659 ***2524.55*** *p13*
With wife
Assler, Johan; New York, 1838 ***8197.10*** *p109*
Assman, Henry; Baltimore, 1842 ***6058.10*** *p25*
Assmann, Catharina; Port uncertain, 1741 ***2856.30*** *p10*
Assmann, Catharina; Port uncertain, 1778 ***2856.30*** *p10*
Assmann, Johann Nikol; Port uncertain, 1785 ***2856.30*** *p10*
Assmann, Johann Thiel; Port uncertain, 1789 ***2856.30*** *p10*
Assmann, Ludwig; Port uncertain, 1784 ***2856.30*** *p10*
Assmann, Philipp; Port uncertain, 1750 ***2856.30*** *p10*
Asson, Mary; Maryland, 1671 ***2524.55*** *p13*
Asswald, Catharina; Port uncertain, 1782 ***2856.30*** *p10*
Ast, Elisabeth; Port uncertain, 1765 ***2856.30*** *p10*
Astbury, Thomas; New York, 1779 ***1224.2*** *p4*
Astinewski, Andrew; Maryland, 1910 ***3259.35*** *p2*
Astley, Robert 46; Ontario, 1871 ***1823.28*** *p3*
Aston, Richard 21; Maryland, 1774 ***1220.25*** *p40*
Aston, Richard 24; Maryland, 1774 ***1220.25*** *p8*
Aston, Robert 18; Maryland, 1774 ***1220.25*** *p7*
Astooria, George 30; British Columbia, 1910 ***9196.1*** *p31*
Astooria, George 30; Seattle, 1910 ***9196.1*** *p31*
Astor, Georg; Port uncertain, 1767 ***2856.30*** *p10*
Astor, Johann Jakob; America, 1783 ***2856.30*** *p10*
Astoyne, John; Maryland, 1665 ***2524.55*** *p87*
Astwood, John; New England, 1654 ***1224.1*** *p3*
Atawish, Cecil 60; Ontario, 1871 ***1823.28*** *p3*
Atcheson, Katherine; Maryland, 1665 ***2524.55*** *p14*
Atcheson, Lodwick; Maryland, 1664 ***2524.55*** *p14*
Atchinson, Frances; Maryland, 1670 ***2524.55*** *p14*
Atchinson, Lodowick; Maryland, 1661 ***2524.55*** *p14*
Atchion, John 58; Ontario, 1871 ***1823.15*** *p9*
Atchion, William 29; Ontario, 1871 ***1823.15*** *p9*
Atchison, Mrs.; Maryland, 1658 ***2524.55*** *p14*
Atchison, David 44; Ontario, 1871 ***1823.22*** *p5*
Atchison, George; Charles Town, South Carolina, 1728 ***1224.2*** *p4*
Atchison, George 53; Ontario, 1871 ***1823.28*** *p3*
Atchison, James 30; Ontario, 1871 ***1823.28*** *p3*
Atchison, Robert; New York, 1839 ***8197.10*** *p381*
Atchison, William 50; Ontario, 1871 ***1823.15*** *p9*
Atchitchakows, Joseph 29; Ontario, 1871 ***1823.28*** *p3*
Atckinson, Hanah; Maryland, 1673 ***2524.55*** *p14*
Atckinson, Vincent; Maryland, 1673 ***2524.55*** *p14*
Atfield, Moses 49; Ontario, 1871 ***1823.15*** *p9*
Atherden, George; New York, 1838 ***8197.10*** *p206*
Atheridge, John 37; Virginia, 1774 ***1220.25*** *p93*
Atherstone, William; America, 1836 ***1224.3*** *p3*

Athill, John; Antigua (Antego), 1842 ***1640.13*** *p5*
Athy, Marcus; Maryland, 1669 ***2524.55*** *p14*
Atkens, William 40; Ontario, 1871 ***1823.15*** *p9*
Atkin, James; New York, 1837 ***8197.10*** *p82*
Atkin, Scott 42; Ontario, 1871 ***1823.28*** *p3*
Atkin, Thomas 55; Ontario, 1871 ***1823.15*** *p9*
Atkin, William; New York, New York, 1852 ***6058.10*** *p40*
Atkins, . . .; Virginia, 1672 ***6212.30*** *p50*
Atkins, Abram; Virginia, 1665-1666 ***6212.30*** *p24*
Atkins, Ann 39 *SEE* Atkins, John
Atkins, Edw; Virginia, 1665-1666 ***6212.30*** *p21*
Atkins, Edward; America, 1652 ***1224.1*** *p3*
Atkins, Fanny 29 *SEE* Atkins, John
Atkins, George *SEE* Atkins, George
Atkins, George; Maryland, 1667 ***2524.55*** *p14*
Son: George
Atkins, George; Maryland, 1677 ***2524.55*** *p67*
Atkins, Herbert; New York, 1838 ***8197.10*** *p109*
Atkins, Humphry; Virginia, 1668-1669 ***6212.30*** *p40*
Atkins, John; Maryland, 1682 ***2524.55*** *p14*
Atkins, John; Virginia, 1624 ***1224.1*** *p3*
Atkins, John 23; Maryland, 1775 ***1220.25*** *p102*
Wife: Fanny 29
Atkins, John 60; Philadelphia, 1774 ***1220.25*** *p25*
Wife: Ann 39
Atkins, Martha; Virginia, 1663 ***6212.30*** *p2*
Atkins, Mary; Maryland, 1660 ***1224.1*** *p60*
Atkins, Mary; Virginia, 1666 ***6212.30*** *p30*
Atkins, Mary; Virginia, 1709 ***6212.30*** *p63*
Atkins, Oliver; Virginia, 1665-1666 ***6212.30*** *p24*
Atkins, Oliver; Virginia, 1666-1667 ***6212.30*** *p35*
Atkins, Richard; Maryland, 1669 ***1224.1*** *p4*
Atkins, Richard 22; Maryland, 1775 ***1220.25*** *p103*
Atkins, Samuel; New York, 1842 ***1224.3*** *p3*
Atkins, Sara; New England, 1707 ***1224.2*** *p4*
Atkins, Thomas 19; Virginia, 1775 ***1220.25*** *p110*
Atkins, Thomas 24; Virginia, 1774 ***1220.25*** *p74*
Atkins, William; Maryland, 1682 ***2524.55*** *p14*
Atkins, William; Ontario, 1861 ***2896.27*** *p31*
Atkinson, Mr.; Quebec, 1858 ***9196.15*** *p46*
Atkinson, Alice; Maryland, 1681 ***2524.55*** *p14*
Atkinson, Ann 19; Fort Cumberland, Nova Scotia, 1774 ***1220.25*** *p16*
Atkinson, Ann 21 *SEE* Atkinson, Robert
Atkinson, Charles; New York, 1840 ***8197.10*** *p143*
Atkinson, Charles 6 *SEE* Atkinson, John
Atkinson, Christopher; Maryland, 1681 ***2524.55*** *p14*
Atkinson, English 28; Boston, 1774 ***1220.25*** *p124*
Atkinson, Frances 30 *SEE* Atkinson, John
Atkinson, Francis; Virginia, 1695 ***1224.1*** *p4*
Atkinson, George; Charles Town, South Carolina, 1729 ***1224.2*** *p5*
Atkinson, George; Georgia, 1822 ***1640.10*** *p6*
Atkinson, George; Maryland, 1681 ***2524.55*** *p14*
Atkinson, George 55; Ontario, 1871 ***1823.15*** *p9*
Atkinson, J. P.; Quebec, 1857 ***9196.15*** *p18*
Atkinson, Jno; Virginia, 1667-1668 ***6212.30*** *p39*
Atkinson, Jno; Virginia, 1668-1669 ***6212.30*** *p40*
Atkinson, John; Maryland, 1682 ***2524.55*** *p14*
Atkinson, John; Portland, Maine, 1858 ***9196.15*** *p29*
Atkinson, John 1 *SEE* Atkinson, John
Atkinson, John 26; Maryland, 1775 ***1220.25*** *p116*
Wife: Mary 21
Atkinson, John 34; Ontario, 1871 ***1823.28*** *p3*
Atkinson, John 37; Ontario, 1871 ***1823.28*** *p3*
Atkinson, John 45; Fort Cumberland, Nova Scotia, 1774 ***1220.25*** *p16*
Child: Charles 6
Child: Martha 4
Wife: Frances 30
Child: John 1
Child: Michael 3
Atkinson, John 56; Ontario, 1871 ***1823.22*** *p5*
Atkinson, John 58; Ontario, 1871 ***1823.28*** *p3*
Atkinson, Martha 4 *SEE* Atkinson, John
Atkinson, Mary 21 *SEE* Atkinson, John
Atkinson, Mary Murphy; Vermont, n.d. ***5900.10*** *p481*
Atkinson, Michael; Vermont, n.d. ***5900.10*** *p481*
Atkinson, Michael 3 *SEE* Atkinson, John
Atkinson, Rich; Virginia, 1666 ***6212.30*** *p27*
Atkinson, Robert; New York, 1840 ***8197.10*** *p142*
Atkinson, Robert 28; Fort Cumberland, Nova Scotia, 1774 ***1220.25*** *p19*
Wife: Ann 21
Atkinson, Robert 38; Ontario, 1871 ***1823.28*** *p3*
Atkinson, Theodore; Portsmouth, New Hampshire, 1783 ***1224.2*** *p5*
Atkinson, Thomas; New York, 1821 ***8197.10*** *p205*
Atkinson, Thomas; Vermont, n.d. ***5900.10*** *p481*
Atkinson, Thomas 36; Ontario, 1871 ***1823.28*** *p3*
Atkinson, Timothy 73; Vermont, 1854 ***5900.10*** *p190*
Atkinson, William; Maryland, 1681 ***2524.55*** *p14*
Atkinson, William; Maryland, 1795 ***1224.2*** *p5*
Atkinson, William; Vermont, n.d. ***5900.10*** *p481*
Atkinson, William 16; Fort Cumberland, Nova Scotia, 1774 ***1220.25*** *p18*
Atkinson, William 18; Maryland, 1775 ***1220.25*** *p120*
Atkinson, William 48; Ontario, 1871 ***1823.22*** *p5*
Atkinson, William B. 50; Ontario, 1871 ***1823.15*** *p9*
Atkyns, Ringrose; California, 1855 ***1224.3*** *p3*
Atley, James; Virginia, 1702 ***6212.30*** *p62*
Atley, Marcus; Maryland, 1669 ***2524.55*** *p14*
Atmer, Edward 25; Maryland, 1774 ***1220.25*** *p53*
Atrington, W.; Quebec, 1857 ***9196.15*** *p16*
Atten, William; Philadelphia, 1790 ***4629.10*** *p83*
Atterberger, Jacob; New Orleans, 1853 ***3437.14*** *p3*
Atterbury, Richard; Virginia, 1638 ***1224.1*** *p4*
Atteridge, James; New York, 1840 ***8197.10*** *p142*
Attkins, Ann; Maryland, 1667 ***2524.55*** *p14*
Attkins, George; Maryland, 1662 ***2524.55*** *p14*
Attkins, George; Maryland, 1665 ***2524.55*** *p14*
Attkins, John; Maryland, 1662 ***2524.55*** *p14*
Attkins, Ralph; Maryland, 1665 ***2524.55*** *p210*
Attridge, James 52; Ontario, 1871 ***1823.28*** *p3*
Attwell, Ann; Maryland, 1661 ***2524.55*** *p14*
Attwell, James *SEE* Attwell, James
Attwell, James; New York, 1827 ***8197.10*** *p339*
Wife: Jane
Son: John
Son: William
Son: James
Attwell, Jane *SEE* Attwell, James
Attwell, John *SEE* Attwell, James
Attwell, William *SEE* Attwell, James
Attwood, Mr.; Quebec, 1858 ***9196.15*** *p38*
Attwood, Isaac; Perth Amboy, New Jersey, 1795 ***1224.2*** *p5*
Attwood, Richard; Maryland, 1668 ***2524.55*** *p14*
Atward, John; Virginia, 1666-1667 ***6212.30*** *p33*
Atwell, Eliza 14; Ontario, 1871 ***1823.22*** *p5*
Atwell, James 22; Ontario, 1871 ***1823.22*** *p5*
Atwell, Robert; Pennsylvania, 1808 ***6058.10*** *p2*
Atwell, Sabinia 13; Ontario, 1871 ***1823.22*** *p5*
Atwell, William; Pennsylvania, 1808 ***6058.10*** *p2*
Atwood, Anthony; Newport, Rhode Island, 1765 ***1224.2*** *p5*
Atwood, Elizabeth; Maryland, 1676 ***2524.55*** *p14*
Atwood, Frances E.; Vermont, 1835-1968 ***5900.10*** *p388*
Atwood, John 28; Ontario, 1871 ***1823.15*** *p9*
Atwood, Joseph; Havana, 1765 ***1224.2*** *p5*
Atwood, William; Maryland, 1669 ***2524.55*** *p30*
Auber, Peter 26; Virginia, 1773 ***1220.25*** *p30*
Aubery, Jean Louis; New York, 1805 ***8197.10*** *p28*
Aubony, Thomas 22; Virginia, 1774 ***1220.25*** *p93*
Aubray, Madame; Quebec, 1857 ***9196.15*** *p15*
Aubry, Charles; New York, 1835 ***8197.10*** *p317*
Aubry, John; Virginia, 1665 ***6212.30*** *p19*
Aucat, Richard; New York, 1803 ***8197.10*** *p10*
Auchenleck, John; Georgia, 1735 ***1640.10*** *p6*
Auchinvole, David; New York, 1803 ***8197.10*** *p10*
Auchterlonie, James Scott; Toronto, 1893 ***1640.13*** *p5*
Auclair, Annie E. Keeley; Vermont, 1857-1935 ***5900.10*** *p451*
Auclair, Arthur J.; Vermont, 1860-1940 ***5900.10*** *p451*
Audebert, Peter Benj'n; Pennsylvania, 1787 ***4629.10*** *p55*
Audes, Fred; Indiana, 1883-1884 ***3437.14*** *p198*
Audly, Thomas; Virginia, 1667-1668 ***6212.30*** *p38*
Auener, Nikolaus; Port uncertain, 1746 ***2856.30*** *p11*
Auer, Hans Martin; Port uncertain, 1758 ***2856.30*** *p10*
Auer, Hans Martin; Port uncertain, 1788 ***2856.30*** *p10*
Auer, Johann; America, 1753 ***2856.30*** *p10*
Auer, Johann; America, 1753 ***2856.30*** *p11*
With wife & children
Auge, Frederick; Baltimore, 1840 ***6058.10*** *p28*
Auge, John Frederick; New York, New York, 1854 ***6058.10*** *p38*
Augear, Mrs.; Quebec, 1857 ***9196.15*** *p15*
Augear, John M.; Quebec, 1857 ***9196.15*** *p15*
Augener, Charles E.; New York, 1838 ***8197.10*** *p318*
Augenstein, Abraham; America, 1751 ***2856.30*** *p11*
With 4 children
Augenstein, Anna Maria; America, 1751 ***2856.30*** *p11*
Augenstein, Caspar; America, 1751 ***2856.30*** *p11*
Augenstein, Christian; America, 1751 ***2856.30*** *p11*
Augenstein, Hans Georg; America, 1751 ***2856.30*** *p11*
Augenstein, Johann; America, 1751 ***2856.30*** *p11*
Augenstein, Johann Martin; America, 1738 ***2856.30*** *p11*
Augenstein, Marg. Barbara; America, 1770 ***2856.30*** *p11*
Auggelin, Barbara; Port uncertain, 1768 ***2856.30*** *p11*
Aught, Henry; New York, 1840 ***8197.10*** *p142*
Augst, Johann; Port uncertain, 1790 ***2856.30*** *p11*
With wife & children
Augur, Nicholas; New England, 1658 ***1224.1*** *p4*
Augustin, Anna Regina; Port uncertain, 1767 ***2856.30*** *p11*
Augustiniak, Valentin; Maryland, 1910 ***3259.35*** *p2*
Augustiniuk, Joseph; Maryland, 1910 ***3259.35*** *p2*
Augustinyak, John J.; Maryland, 1910 ***3259.35*** *p2*
Augustus, P. 68; Ontario, 1861 ***2896.28*** *p12*
Augustus, W. 17; Ontario, 1861 ***2896.28*** *p12*
Augustuski, Frank; Maryland, 1910 ***3259.35*** *p2*
Augustyniak, Michael; Maryland, 1910 ***3259.35*** *p2*
Augustyniski, Masim; Maryland, 1910 ***3259.35*** *p2*
Augustynowska, Eva; Maryland, 1910 ***3259.35*** *p2*
Auhoff, Johann Nickel; Port uncertain, 1737 ***2856.30*** *p11*
Auld, A.; Alabama, 1804-1845 ***1640.10*** *p6*
Auld, Alexander; Mobile, Alabama, 1805-1845 ***1640.10*** *p6*
Auld, Henry Alexander; New York, 1840 ***8197.10*** *p143*
Auld, James W. 48; Ontario, 1871 ***1823.15*** *p9*
Auld, John; Virginia, 1803 ***1640.13*** *p5*
Auld, Robert; Tobago, West Indies, 1862 ***1640.13*** *p5*
Auld, Samuel; New York, 1838 ***8197.10*** *p109*
Aulenbacher, Andreas; America, 1733 ***2856.30*** *p11*
Aulenbacher, Andreas; America, 1737 ***2856.30*** *p11*
With wife & children
Auler, Regina Margaret; Port uncertain, 1754 ***2856.30*** *p11*
Auman, Nicholas 27; Ontario, 1871 ***1823.15*** *p9*
Aumer, Nikolaus; Port uncertain, 1746 ***2856.30*** *p11*
Aumond, Janet 53; Ontario, 1871 ***1823.28*** *p3*
Aungier, John; Virginia, 1692 ***1224.1*** *p4*
Auschutz, Carl 50; Kansas, 1878-1910 ***9079.10*** *p49*
Auschutz, Emelie 43; Kansas, 1910 ***9079.10*** *p49*
Ausloch, Johann; Port uncertain, 1767 ***2856.30*** *p11*
Ausloch, Johann; Port uncertain, 1775 ***2856.30*** *p11*
Austell, Joseph; Boston, 1748 ***1224.2*** *p5*
Austen, James; Maryland, 1663 ***2524.55*** *p118*
Austin, . . .; Boston, 1765 ***4628.40*** *p114*
Austin, Ann 17 *SEE* Austin, Thomas
Austin, Bridget; Vermont, 1837-1894 ***5900.10*** *p101*
Austin, Bridget Curran 76; Vermont, 1905 ***5900.10*** *p113*
Austin, Catherine 36; Vermont, 1867 ***5900.10*** *p114*
Austin, Daniel, Jr.; Vermont, 1855-1895 ***5900.10*** *p387*
Austin, Delina; Vermont, 1856-1874 ***5900.10*** *p384*
Austin, Elizabeth Brosnahan; Vermont, 1839-1933 ***5900.10*** *p121*
Austin, Frances 64; Ontario, 1871 ***1823.22*** *p5*
Austin, Honora 73; Vermont, 1913 ***5900.10*** *p101*
Austin, Isaac; Pennsylvania, 1777 ***4629.10*** *p16*
Austin, Isaac 80; Ontario, 1871 ***1823.22*** *p5*
Austin, James; Pennsylvania, 1786 ***4629.10*** *p49*
Austin, James; Vermont, 1842-1929 ***5900.10*** *p101*
Austin, James; Virginia, 1664 ***6212.30*** *p7*
Austin, James; Virginia, 1664 ***6212.30*** *p9*
Austin, James; Virginia, 1665-1666 ***6212.30*** *p24*
Austin, James 55; Ontario, 1861 ***2896.25*** *p36*
Austin, James 76; Vermont, 1860 ***5900.10*** *p101*
Austin, Jane E.; Vermont, 1846-1884 ***5900.10*** *p282*
Austin, John; New York, New York, 1839 ***1224.3*** *p3*
Austin, John 76; Vermont, 1903 ***5900.10*** *p102*
Austin, Joseph; New England, 1679 ***1224.1*** *p4*
Austin, Joseph 18; Maryland, 1774 ***1220.25*** *p69*
Austin, Lacy 75; Ontario, 1871 ***1823.22*** *p5*
Austin, Margaret 72; Vermont, 1872 ***5900.10*** *p101*
Austin, Margaret Bowler 65; Vermont, 1894 ***5900.10*** *p102*
Austin, Martha 18 *SEE* Austin, Thomas
Austin, Martin; Vermont, 1838-1905 ***5900.10*** *p121*
Austin, Mary; Charles Town, South Carolina, 1762 ***1224.2*** *p5*
Austin, Mary 39; Vermont, 1871 ***5900.10*** *p114*
Austin, Mary Connell 75; Vermont, 1891 ***5900.10*** *p102*
Austin, Mary Kennedy; Vermont, 1856-1934 ***5900.10*** *p102*
Austin, Mary O'Donnell; Vermont, 1854-1925 ***5900.10*** *p387*
Austin, Maurice 76; Vermont, 1901 ***5900.10*** *p113*
Austin, Patrick, Sr. 45; Vermont, 1875 ***5900.10*** *p102*
Austin, Patrick, Jr. 58; Vermont, 1915 ***5900.10*** *p102*
Austin, Paulina 71; Vermont, 1899 ***5900.10*** *p520*
Austin, Philip 52; Ontario, 1871 ***1823.15*** *p9*
Austin, Richard; New York, 1840 ***8197.10*** *p142*
Austin, Robt; Virginia, 1665-1666 ***6212.30*** *p21*
Austin, Robt; Virginia, 1665-1666 ***6212.30*** *p23*
Austin, Sarah; Philadelphia, 1786 ***1224.2*** *p5*
Austin, Sarah 25; Baltimore, 1775 ***1220.25*** *p117*
Austin, Sophie; Vermont, 1853-1870 ***5900.10*** *p384*
Austin, Sophie Nolan; Vermont, 1821-1867 ***5900.10*** *p384*
Austin, Susan; Maryland, 1655-1656 ***2524.55*** *p14*
Austin, Thomas; New York, 1694 ***1224.1*** *p4*
Austin, Thomas; New York, 1839 ***8197.10*** *p206*
Austin, Thomas; New York, 1840 ***8197.10*** *p142*
Austin, Thomas 20; Jamaica, 1774 ***1220.25*** *p92*
Sister: Martha 18
Sister: Ann 17
Austin, William; Albany, New York, 1764 ***1224.2*** *p5*

B

B, Robt; Virginia, 1671 ***6212.30*** *p43*
Baack, Henry E.; New York, 1838 ***8197.10*** *p212*
Baad, Michel; Port uncertain, 1769 ***2856.30*** *p12*
Baader, Franz; Port uncertain, 1748 ***2856.30*** *p12*
Baader, Georg Christoph; America, 1730 ***2856.30*** *p12*
Baader, Johann; Port uncertain, 1721 ***2856.30*** *p12*
Baader, Kilian; Port uncertain, 1764 ***2856.30*** *p12*
Baader, Kilian; Port uncertain, 1767 ***2856.30*** *p12*
Baags, Henry; Pennsylvania, 1777 ***4629.10*** *p14*
Baague, John; Maryland, 1665 ***2524.55*** *p27*
Baale, Gabriel; Maryland, 1651 ***2524.55*** *p15*
Baalim, William 40; Ontario, 1871 ***1823.22*** *p6*
Baalino, Jane 29; Ontario, 1871 ***1823.22*** *p6*
Baanforth, Charles 33; Ontario, 1871 ***1823.15*** *p9*
Baargeldt, Johann; America, 1751 ***2856.30*** *p12*
Baargelt, Sebastian; Port uncertain, 1749 ***2856.30*** *p12*
Baas, Louis 33; Ontario, 1871 ***1823.15*** *p9*
Bab, Adam; Port uncertain, 1782 ***2856.30*** *p12*
Bab, Nathan; Maryland, 1660 ***2524.55*** *p15*
Babaud, Auguste; New York, 1830 ***8197.10*** *p353*
Babb, Catherine 12; British Columbia, 1917 ***9196.1*** *p71*
Babb, Catherine 12; Washington, 1917 ***9196.1*** *p71*
Babb, Catherine 39; British Columbia, 1917 ***9196.1*** *p71*
Babb, Catherine 39; Washington, 1917 ***9196.1*** *p71*
Babb, Fred W. 14; British Columbia, 1917 ***9196.1*** *p71*
Babb, Fred W. 14; Washington, 1917 ***9196.1*** *p71*
Babb, James; New York, 1803 ***8197.10*** *p11*
Babb, Thomas; New York, New York, 1800 ***1224.3*** *p3*
Babb, Thomas; Virginia, 1646 ***1224.1*** *p4*
Babb, William 28; Ontario, 1871 ***1823.15*** *p9*
Babbatt, N. 20; Ontario, 1861 ***2896.28*** *p14*
Babbett, Allis 32; Ontario, 1861 ***2896.28*** *p16*
Babbett, Joanna; Vermont, 1841-1893 ***5900.10*** *p306*
Babbit, Albert E. 15; Ontario, 1861 ***2896.28*** *p28*
Babbit, Catharine A. 28; Ontario, 1861 ***2896.28*** *p28*
Babbit, Elen 25; Ontario, 1861 ***2896.25*** *p38*
Babbit, Elizabeth 19; Ontario, 1861 ***2896.27*** *p45*
Babbit, Elizabeth 52; Ontario, 1861 ***2896.28*** *p28*
Babbit, Fred'k 6; Ontario, 1861 ***2896.28*** *p46*
Babbit, Jane A. 17; Ontario, 1861 ***2896.28*** *p26*
Babbit, Lida M. 10; Ontario, 1861 ***2896.28*** *p45*
Babbit, Phebe 52; Ontario, 1861 ***2896.27*** *p45*
Babbit, Sarah F. 11; Ontario, 1861 ***2896.28*** *p46*
Babbit, Sarah M. 21; Ontario, 1861 ***2896.28*** *p45*
Babbit, Wellington 11; Ontario, 1861 ***2896.28*** *p28*
Babbitt, C. M. 7; Ontario, 1861 ***2896.28*** *p3*
Babbitt, N. E. 4; Ontario, 1861 ***2896.28*** *p3*
Babbitt, Stephen N. 16; Ontario, 1861 ***2896.27*** *p29*
Babcock, A. 7; Ontario, 1861 ***2896.25*** *p48*
Babcock, A. 10; Ontario, 1861 ***2896.25*** *p48*
Babcock, A. J. 13; Ontario, 1861 ***2896.25*** *p46*
Babcock, Aaron 4; Ontario, 1861 ***2896.25*** *p46*
Babcock, Ann 3; Ontario, 1861 ***2896.25*** *p48*
Babcock, Anna Brewin; Vermont, 1857-1929 ***5900.10*** *p185*
Babcock, C. A. 20; Ontario, 1861 ***2896.25*** *p51*
Babcock, Charles M. 16; Ontario, 1861 ***2896.25*** *p45*
Babcock, Daniel 26; Ontario, 1861 ***2896.25*** *p46*
Babcock, E. 5; Ontario, 1861 ***2896.25*** *p48*
Babcock, E. 21; Ontario, 1861 ***2896.25*** *p46*
Babcock, E. 41; Ontario, 1861 ***2896.25*** *p51*
Babcock, E. J. 24; Ontario, 1861 ***2896.25*** *p9*
Babcock, Elizabeth 23; Ontario, 1861 ***2896.25*** *p46*
Babcock, George 9; Ontario, 1861 ***2896.25*** *p46*
Babcock, George H.; Vermont, 1851-1902 ***5900.10*** *p185*
Babcock, Henry A.; Vermont, 1854-1931 ***5900.10*** *p490*
Babcock, Horace 88; Vermont, 1908 ***5900.10*** *p183*
Babcock, Jacob 54; Ontario, 1871 ***1823.22*** *p6*
Babcock, John H. 25; Ontario, 1861 ***2896.25*** *p46*
Babcock, L. 17; Ontario, 1861 ***2896.25*** *p46*
Babcock, L. R. 7; Ontario, 1861 ***2896.25*** *p51*
Babcock, Laura A. O'Donnell; Vermont, 1852-1939 ***5900.10*** *p168*
Babcock, M. A. 14; Ontario, 1861 ***2896.25*** *p46*
Babcock, M. E. A. 10; Ontario, 1861 ***2896.25*** *p51*
Babcock, Margaret; Mississippi, 1810-1845 ***1640.10*** *p7*
Babcock, Mary 76; Vermont, 1897 ***5900.10*** *p183*
Babcock, Mary 78; Ontario, 1861 ***2896.25*** *p46*
Babcock, Mary J. Murphy; Vermont, 1856-1919 ***5900.10*** *p490*
Babcock, Matilda 12; Ontario, 1861 ***2896.25*** *p51*
Babcock, P. 35; Ontario, 1861 ***2896.25*** *p45*
Babcock, Phoebe 52; Ontario, 1861 ***2896.25*** *p46*
Babcock, R. 9; Ontario, 1861 ***2896.25*** *p48*
Babcock, S. A. 28; Ontario, 1861 ***2896.25*** *p48*
Babcock, Sarah 17; Ontario, 1861 ***2896.25*** *p46*
Babcock, Sophia 46; Ontario, 1861 ***2896.25*** *p46*
Babcock, William 21; Ontario, 1861 ***2896.25*** *p46*
Babcock, William H.; Vermont, 1855-1928 ***5900.10*** *p168*
Babcock, William J. 1; Ontario, 1861 ***2896.25*** *p9*
Babcock, William R. 11; Ontario, 1861 ***2896.25*** *p46*
Babcock, William R. 15; Ontario, 1861 ***2896.25*** *p51*
Babe, Richard; Pennsylvania, 1787 ***4629.10*** *p50*
Babear, John T.; New York, 1840 ***8197.10*** *p155*
Babell, Thomas; Virginia, 1665 ***6212.30*** *p17*
Baber, Charles; Illinois, 1855 ***1224.3*** *p3*
Babit, Esther 5; Ontario, 1861 ***2896.26*** *p21*
Babit, John H. 7; Ontario, 1861 ***2896.26*** *p21*
Babit, Sarah E. 27; Ontario, 1861 ***2896.26*** *p21*
Babst, Johann; Port uncertain, 1785 ***2856.30*** *p12*
Baby, Mr.; Quebec, 1857 ***9196.15*** *p26*
Bach, Amalie; Port uncertain, 1751 ***2856.30*** *p12*
Bach, Barbara; Port uncertain, 1752 ***2856.30*** *p12*
Bach, Bartel; America, 1738 ***2856.30*** *p12*
Bach, Bartel; America, 1738 ***2856.30*** *p12*
With wife & 2 children
Bach, Catharina; Port uncertain, 1788 ***2856.30*** *p12*
Bach, Christina; Port uncertain, 1752 ***2856.30*** *p12*
Bach, E. Schmelzler *SEE* Bach, Hans Georg
Bach, Elisabeth; Port uncertain, 1764 ***2856.30*** *p12*
Bach, Georg Daniel; America, 1739 ***2856.30*** *p12*
Bach, Hans Georg; America, 1744 ***2856.30*** *p12*
Wife: E. Schmelzler
Bach, Hans Georg; America, 1750 ***2856.30*** *p12*
Bach, Johann Nickel; America, 1770 ***2856.30*** *p12*
Bach, Johann Nickel; Port uncertain, 1778 ***2856.30*** *p12*
Bach, Johann Nikolaus; America, 1768 ***2856.30*** *p12*
Bach, Johann Nikolaus; America, 1770 ***2856.30*** *p12*
Bach, Jost; Port uncertain, 1735 ***2856.30*** *p12*
Bach, Ludwig; Port uncertain, 1735 ***2856.30*** *p12*
Bach, Mahlleben; Port uncertain, 1764 ***2856.30*** *p12*
Bach, Margarete; Port uncertain, 1790 ***2856.30*** *p12*
Bach, Maria; Port uncertain, 1752 ***2856.30*** *p12*
Bach, Philipp Jakob; America, 1739 ***2856.30*** *p12*
Bache, Richard; Pennsylvania, 1777 ***4629.10*** *p8*
Bachelle, David; New York, 1806 ***8197.10*** *p324*
Bachelor, Mrs.; Maryland, 1650 ***2524.55*** *p15*
Bachenski, Jacob; Maryland, 1910 ***3259.35*** *p2*
Bachenski, Martin; Maryland, 1910 ***3259.35*** *p2*
Bachler, Xaver; Port uncertain, 1791 ***2856.30*** *p61*
Bachman, Conrad; Pennsylvania, 1786 ***4629.10*** *p52*
Bachman, Isaack; New York, 1838 ***8197.10*** *p212*
Bachmann, Catharina; Port uncertain, 1751 ***2856.30*** *p12*
Bachmann, Christof Heinr.; Port uncertain, 1798 ***2856.30*** *p13*
With wife
Bachmann, Johann; America, 1752 ***2856.30*** *p12*
Bachmann, Johann; Canada, 1753 ***2856.30*** *p13*
Bachmann, Johanna; Port uncertain, 1784 ***2856.30*** *p13*
With husband
Bachmann, Michael; Port uncertain, 1788 ***2856.30*** *p13*
With wife & 4 children
Bachmeyer, Poppo; Port uncertain, 1771 ***2856.30*** *p13*
With wife & 4 children
Bachs, Martin Veisz; Virginia, 1775 ***1220.25*** *p123*
Bachs, Ottelia Veisz; Virginia, 1775 ***1220.25*** *p123*
Bachus, Henry 19; Philadelphia, 1774 ***1220.25*** *p67*
Back, John 47; Ontario, 1871 ***1823.15*** *p9*
Back, Kasimerz; Maryland, 1910 ***3259.35*** *p2*
Backe, Nicolaus; Port uncertain, 1749 ***2856.30*** *p13*
Backer, Adam 50; Ontario, 1871 ***1823.15*** *p9*
Backer, Anna Elisabeth; Port uncertain, 1792 ***2856.30*** *p61*
Backer, Christinia 31; Kansas, 1887-1910 ***9079.10*** *p23*
Backer, Hans Friedrich; Port uncertain, 1791 ***2856.30*** *p61*
Backer, J. G. 35; Kansas, 1887-1910 ***9079.10*** *p22*
Backer, Johann Friedric; Port uncertain, 1793 ***2856.30*** *p61*
Backer, John; Maryland, 1671 ***2524.55*** *p15*
Backer, Wm; Virginia, 1681-1682 ***6212.30*** *p55*
Backhouse, Edward; New York, 1802 ***8197.10*** *p18*
Backler, Catherine 25; Ontario, 1871 ***1823.15*** *p9*
Backlinski, John; Maryland, 1910 ***3259.35*** *p2*
Backman, Catherine; St. Louis, 1857 ***1224.3*** *p3*
Backman, James; Virginia, 1674 ***6212.30*** *p52*
Backman, O. 24; Alaska, 1917 ***9196.1*** *p46*
Backman, O. 24; Whitehorse, Yukon, 1917 ***9196.1*** *p46*
Backster, George 50; Ontario, 1861 ***2896.26*** *p34*
Backster, Margret 17; Ontario, 1861 ***2896.26*** *p34*
Backster, Mathew 24; Ontario, 1861 ***2896.26*** *p34*
Backster, Robert 21; Ontario, 1861 ***2896.26*** *p34*
Backster, Sarah 50; Ontario, 1861 ***2896.26*** *p34*
Backus, Oscar; New York, 1840 ***8197.10*** *p155*
Bacom, Henry 61; Ontario, 1871 ***1823.15*** *p9*
Bacom, James 51; Ontario, 1871 ***1823.15*** *p9*
Bacom, John 60; Ontario, 1871 ***1823.15*** *p9*
Bacom, Robert 28; Ontario, 1871 ***1823.15*** *p9*
Bacom, Robert 50; Ontario, 1871 ***1823.15*** *p9*
Bacon, . . .; New England, 1644 ***1224.1*** *p52*
Bacon, Mr.; Quebec, 1858 ***9196.15*** *p41*
Bacon, Butts; New England, 1726 ***1224.2*** *p5*
Bacon, Catherine A. Langan; Vermont, 1832-1900 ***5900.10*** *p186*
Bacon, Dan; Virginia, 1677 ***6212.30*** *p54*
Bacon, Edward; New York, 1806 ***8197.10*** *p30*
Bacon, Mary J. 25; Ontario, 1871 ***1823.15*** *p9*
Bacon, Nelson; Vermont, 1830-1899 ***5900.10*** *p186*
Bacon, Richard; Virginia, 1687 ***1224.1*** *p4*
Bacon, William; New York, 1840 ***8197.10*** *p145*
Baczak, Franciszek; Maryland, 1910 ***3259.35*** *p2*
Baddon, Sarah 44; Ontario, 1871 ***1823.15*** *p10*
Badelfyak, Simon; Maryland, 1910 ***3259.35*** *p2*
Badenach, Mr.; Quebec, 1857 ***9196.15*** *p26*
Badenach, Mrs.; Quebec, 1857 ***9196.15*** *p26*
Badenhop, Jesse; South Carolina, 1740 ***1224.2*** *p5*
Bader, Anna Barbara; America, 1765 ***2856.30*** *p13*
Bader, Anna Barbara; Port uncertain, 1759 ***2856.30*** *p13*
Bader, David; Port uncertain, 1783 ***2856.30*** *p13*
Bader, Dominikus; Port uncertain, 1785 ***2856.30*** *p13*
Bader, John; New York, 1838 ***8197.10*** *p110*
Bader, Mara Elisabeth; Port uncertain, 1766 ***2856.30*** *p13*
Bader, Mathias; America, 1754 ***2856.30*** *p13*
Bader, Nepomuk; Port uncertain, 1789 ***2856.30*** *p13*

Bader, Philipp Jacob; Port uncertain, 1784 ***2856.30*** *p61*
Baderman, Wm 25; Ontario, 1871 ***1823.28*** *p3*
Badgely, Dr.; Quebec, 1857 ***9196.15*** *p19*
Badger, Benjamin 22; Virginia, 1774 ***1220.25*** *p45*
Badger, Daniel; Pennsylvania, 1777 ***4629.10*** *p12*
Badger, James 53; Ontario, 1871 ***1823.28*** *p3*
Badger, John 22; Philadelphia, 1775 ***1220.25*** *p122*
Badger, Renald; Virginia, 1698 ***6212.30*** *p61*
Badger, Reynold; Virginia, 1690-1691 ***6212.30*** *p58*
Badger, Thomas; Maryland, 1681 ***2524.55*** *p15*
Badgley, Gilbert 1; Ontario, 1861 ***2896.28*** *p45*
Badgley, James 24; Ontario, 1861 ***2896.25*** *p37*
Badgley, Margaret 26; Ontario, 1861 ***2896.28*** *p45*
Badker, Frederick 47; Ontario, 1871 ***1823.15*** *p10*
Badnadge, Thomas; Died enroute, 1659 ***1224.1*** *p5*
Badter, Elisabeth Haas; Port uncertain, 1750 ***2856.30*** *p61*
With son
Badter, Hans Peter; Port uncertain, 1750 ***2856.30*** *p61*
Badter, Maria Margarete; Port uncertain, 1750 ***2856.30*** *p61*
Badter, Oswald; Port uncertain, 1750 ***2856.30*** *p61*
Badter, Philipp; Port uncertain, 1750 ***2856.30*** *p61*
Badter, Wendel; Port uncertain, 1753 ***2856.30*** *p61*
Baedier, Karl Ludwig; America, 1772 ***2856.30*** *p13*
Baehr, Georg; America, 1774 ***2856.30*** *p13*
Baer, Joseph; New York, 1837 ***8197.10*** *p84*
Bagby, Mrs.; Maryland, 1658 ***2524.55*** *p15*
Bagby, Amos *SEE* Bagby, John
Bagby, John *SEE* Bagby, John
Bagby, John; Maryland, 1652 ***2524.55*** *p15*
With wife
Son: John
Son: Amos
Bagby, John; Maryland, 1658 ***2524.55*** *p15*
With wife
Bagdanovich, M. 28; Alaska, 1917 ***9196.1*** *p50*
Bagdanovich, M. 28; Whitehorse, Yukon, 1917 ***9196.1*** *p50*
Bage, Robert; New York, 1836 ***8197.10*** *p76*
Bagensky, Alexander; Maryland, 1910 ***3259.35*** *p2*
Bagg, John; Maryland, 1661 ***2524.55*** *p120*
Bagg, John 19; Ontario, 1871 ***1823.15*** *p10*
Bagg, Mary Butler; Virginia, 1717 ***1224.2*** *p6*
Bagge, Andrew 23; Maryland, 1774 ***1220.25*** *p76*
Baggley, Phillip; Maryland, 1649 ***2524.55*** *p15*
Baggot, Louis; New York, 1834 ***8197.10*** *p358*
Baggott, Joseph; New York, 1827 ***8197.10*** *p338*
Baginski, John; Maryland, 1910 ***3259.35*** *p2*
Bagla, Henrich; America, 1749 ***2856.30*** *p13*
With 2 children
Bagler, Christy 56; Ontario, 1871 ***1823.15*** *p10*
Bagley, Catherine; Vermont, 1819-1890 ***5900.10*** *p485*
Bagley, Charles; Maryland, 1681 ***2524.55*** *p15*
Bagley, James T. 31; Ontario, 1871 ***1823.28*** *p3*
Bagley, Johanna; Vermont, 1836-1919 ***5900.10*** *p442*
Bagley, John; New York, 1839 ***8197.10*** *p380*
Bagley, William; Maryland, 1665 ***2524.55*** *p15*
Bagloe, Tho; Virginia, 1672 ***6212.30*** *p50*
Bagnall, James; Virginia, 1667 ***6212.30*** *p37*
Bagnall, Lawrence 28; Virginia, 1774 ***1220.25*** *p45*
Bagrowski, Joseph; Maryland, 1910 ***3259.35*** *p2*
Bagschaw, Alford 55; Ontario, 1871 ***1823.15*** *p10*
Bagshaw, Joseph; Philadelphia, 1797 ***1224.2*** *p6*
Bagwell, Robert 23; Virginia, 1773 ***1220.25*** *p28*
Bahdiwuayh, Pierre 28; Ontario, 1871 ***1823.28*** *p3*
Bahen, Denis 55; Ontario, 1871 ***1823.22*** *p6*
Bahl, Johann; Port uncertain, 1765 ***2856.30*** *p13*
Bahr, Hans Michael; Port uncertain, 1747 ***2856.30*** *p61*
Bahr, Jakob; Port uncertain, 1785 ***2856.30*** *p61*
Bahr, Johann; America, 1765 ***2856.30*** *p13*
Baibonerung, J. Baptiste 69; Ontario, 1871 ***1823.28*** *p3*
Baibonerung, Jean Baptiste 38; Ontario, 1871 ***1823.28*** *p3*
Baier, Josef; Port uncertain, 1771 ***2856.30*** *p13*
Bailey, Master; Quebec, 1858 ***9196.15*** *p45*
Bailey, Miss; Quebec, 1858 ***9196.15*** *p45*
Bailey, Mr.; Quebec, 1857 ***9196.15*** *p21*
Bailey, Mrs.; Quebec, 1858 ***9196.15*** *p45*
Bailey, Mrs. E. J. 48; Alaska, 1917 ***9196.1*** *p48*
Bailey, Mrs. E. J. 48; Whitehorse, Yukon, 1917 ***9196.1*** *p48*
Bailey, Edward 21; Maryland, 1774 ***1220.25*** *p57*
Bailey, Edward 28; Ontario, 1871 ***1823.28*** *p3*
Bailey, Emma J. 6; Ontario, 1861 ***2896.28*** *p39*
Bailey, Frederick 3; Ontario, 1861 ***2896.28*** *p39*
Bailey, George 43; Ontario, 1871 ***1823.22*** *p6*
Bailey, Mrs. H.; Quebec, 1857 ***9196.15*** *p21*
Bailey, Irvin 1; Ontario, 1861 ***2896.28*** *p39*
Bailey, Isaac 30; Maryland, 1775 ***1220.25*** *p101*
Bailey, Isaac 38; Ontario, 1871 ***1823.22*** *p6*
Bailey, James 8; Ontario, 1861 ***2896.28*** *p39*
Bailey, James 22; Philadelphia, 1774 ***1220.25*** *p43*
Bailey, James 27; Ontario, 1871 ***1823.28*** *p3*
Bailey, James 31; Maryland, 1774 ***1220.25*** *p37*
Bailey, James 46; Ontario, 1871 ***1823.15*** *p10*
Bailey, James 56; Ontario, 1871 ***1823.22*** *p6*
Bailey, James 58; Ontario, 1871 ***1823.15*** *p10*
Bailey, James 65; Ontario, 1871 ***1823.22*** *p6*
Bailey, John 15; Philadelphia, 1774 ***1220.25*** *p81*
Bailey, John 21; Virginia, 1774 ***1220.25*** *p87*
Bailey, John 23; Maryland, 1774 ***1220.25*** *p46*
Bailey, John 29; Ontario, 1871 ***1823.28*** *p3*
Bailey, John 31; Ontario, 1871 ***1823.15*** *p10*
Bailey, John 34; Ontario, 1871 ***1823.22*** *p6*
Bailey, John 45; Ontario, 1871 ***1823.28*** *p3*
Bailey, John 56; Ontario, 1871 ***1823.28*** *p3*
Bailey, John 59; Ontario, 1871 ***1823.15*** *p10*
Bailey, John 65; Ontario, 1871 ***1823.15*** *p10*
Bailey, John H. 44; Alaska, 1917 ***9196.1*** *p7*
Bailey, John H. 44; Yukon, 1917 ***9196.1*** *p7*
Bailey, Josiah 22; Virginia, 1775 ***1220.25*** *p95*
Bailey, Levi C. 31; Ontario, 1861 ***2896.28*** *p39*
Bailey, Richard 44; Ontario, 1871 ***1823.15*** *p10*
Bailey, Rishton Robbinson; New York, 1839 ***8197.10*** *p213*
Bailey, Robert 87; Ontario, 1871 ***1823.15*** *p10*
Bailey, Samuel; Pennsylvania, 1823 ***6058.10*** *p8*
Bailey, Sarah; Maryland, 1751 ***1224.2*** *p6*
Bailey, Seth 21; Maryland, 1774 ***1220.25*** *p72*
Bailey, Seth 21; Maryland, 1774 ***1220.25*** *p76*
Bailey, Thomas; New York, 1815 ***8197.10*** *p55*
Bailey, Thomas 17; Maryland, 1774 ***1220.25*** *p74*
Bailey, Thomas 21; Ontario, 1871 ***1823.28*** *p3*
Bailey, W. J.; Pennsylvania, 1868 ***6058.10*** *p76*
Bailey, William; Pennsylvania, 1864 ***6058.10*** *p48*
Bailey, William 27; Ontario, 1871 ***1823.22*** *p6*
Bailey, William 44; Ontario, 1871 ***1823.22*** *p6*
Bailey, William Hyde; New York, 1850 ***1224.3*** *p4*
Bailie, Evan 28; St. Vincent, 1775 ***1220.25*** *p129*
Bailie, J. 16; Ontario, 1861 ***2896.27*** *p6*
Bailie, John 53; Ontario, 1871 ***1823.15*** *p10*
Bailie, John 62; Ontario, 1871 ***1823.22*** *p6*
Baille, Jean; Philadelphia, 1793 ***4629.10*** *p70*
Bailley, John; Philadelphia, 1748 ***1224.2*** *p6*
Baillie, Alexander; Georgia, 1756 ***1640.10*** *p7*
Baillie, Elizabeth; Savannah, Georgia, 1767 ***1640.10*** *p7*
Baillie, George; Savannah, Georgia, 1763 ***1640.10*** *p7*
Baillie, Harriet; Georgia, 1812 ***1640.10*** *p7*
Baillie, Johanna; Georgia, 1812 ***1640.10*** *p7*
Baillie, John; Georgia, 1699 ***1640.13*** *p6*
Baillie, John; Georgia, 1733 ***1640.10*** *p7*
Baillie, John; Georgia, 1820 ***1640.10*** *p7*
Baillie, Kenneth; Georgia, 1737 ***1640.10*** *p7*
Baillie, Robert; Georgia, 1745 ***1640.10*** *p8*
Baillie, Thomas; Georgia, 1735 ***1640.10*** *p8*
Baillie, Thomas; Georgia, 1738 ***1640.10*** *p8*
Baillie, William; Georgia, 1699 ***1640.13*** *p6*
Baillie, William; Maryland, 1703 ***1224.2*** *p6*
Baillie, William; North America, 1759 ***1224.2*** *p6*
Baillie, William 44; Ontario, 1871 ***1823.28*** *p3*
Baillis, Mr.; Quebec, 1858 ***9196.15*** *p41*
Bailly, Simon Marie; New York, 1823 ***8197.10*** *p62*
Baily, Henry 28; Ontario, 1871 ***1823.15*** *p10*
Baily, John; Maryland, 1676 ***2524.55*** *p15*
Baily, Richard; Stoughton, Massachusetts, 1786 ***1224.2*** *p6*
Baily, Robert Nalder; New York, New York, 1847 ***1224.3*** *p3*
Baily, William 40; Ontario, 1871 ***1823.15*** *p10*
Bain, Alex 68; Ontario, 1871 ***1823.28*** *p3*
Bain, Alexander 26; Maryland, 1774 ***1220.25*** *p65*
Bain, Alexander 27; Maryland, 1774 ***1220.25*** *p39*
Bain, Alexander 46; Ontario, 1871 ***1823.28*** *p3*
Bain, Archibald; Antigua (Antego), 1812-1853 ***1640.13*** *p6*
Bain, Donald 60; Ontario, 1871 ***1823.15*** *p10*
Bain, Ella 37; British Columbia, 1912 ***9196.1*** *p17*
Bain, Ella 37; San Diego, 1912 ***9196.1*** *p17*
Bain, Henrietta; Savannah, Georgia, 1775 ***1640.10*** *p19*
Bain, Hugh 55; Ontario, 1871 ***1823.15*** *p10*
Bain, James; New York, 1840 ***8197.10*** *p153*
Bain, James; New York, 1848 ***1640.13*** *p6*
Bain, James 62; Ontario, 1871 ***1823.28*** *p3*
Bain, John 28; Ontario, 1871 ***1823.15*** *p10*
Bain, John 58; Ontario, 1871 ***1823.22*** *p6*
Bain, John MacIntosh; Georgia, 1739 ***1640.10*** *p8*
Bain, Thomas 47; Ontario, 1871 ***1823.28*** *p3*
Bain, William; Georgia, 1699 ***1640.13*** *p6*
Bain, William; Savannah, Georgia, 1749-1845 ***1640.10*** *p9*
Bain, William 43; Ontario, 1871 ***1823.28*** *p3*
Bain, William R. 35; Ontario, 1871 ***1823.15*** *p10*
Bainbridge, Mrs.; Quebec, 1858 ***9196.15*** *p44*
Bainbridge, Mary; America, 1898 ***1640.13*** *p6*
Baines, Caroline 70; Ontario, 1871 ***1823.15*** *p10*
Baines, Henry 55; Ontario, 1871 ***1823.15*** *p10*
Baines, William 47; Ontario, 1871 ***1823.15*** *p10*
Bain of Lochain, John; Georgia, 1736 ***1640.10*** *p8*
Bainton, Charles 40; Ontario, 1871 ***1823.15*** *p10*
Bainton, Hen; Virginia, 1665 ***6212.30*** *p17*
Bainton, Henry 38; Ontario, 1871 ***1823.15*** *p10*
Bair, Hendry; Pennsylvania, 1778 ***4629.10*** *p32*
Baird, Archibald; South Carolina, 1777 ***1224.2*** *p6*
Baird, Betsy 50; Ontario, 1861 ***2896.28*** *p20*
Baird, Charles; Vermont, 1820-1900 ***5900.10*** *p481*
Baird, David 1; Ontario, 1861 ***2896.28*** *p33*
Baird, David 21; Ontario, 1861 ***2896.28*** *p35*
Baird, David 22; Ontario, 1871 ***1823.15*** *p10*
Baird, David 35; Ontario, 1871 ***1823.28*** *p3*
Baird, Edgar 12; Ontario, 1861 ***2896.28*** *p35*
Baird, Eliza 18; Ontario, 1861 ***2896.28*** *p35*
Baird, Elizabeth 6; Ontario, 1861 ***2896.28*** *p36*
Baird, Elizabeth 24; Ontario, 1861 ***2896.28*** *p35*
Baird, Elizabeth 50; Ontario, 1861 ***2896.28*** *p36*
Baird, George 19; Ontario, 1861 ***2896.28*** *p20*
Baird, George 30; Ontario, 1871 ***1823.15*** *p10*
Baird, George 45; Ontario, 1861 ***2896.28*** *p49*
Baird, Hugh; New York, 1830 ***8197.10*** *p361*
Baird, Hugh 3; Ontario, 1861 ***2896.28*** *p33*
Baird, Hugh 48; Ontario, 1861 ***2896.28*** *p33*
Baird, Isabella 27; Ontario, 1861 ***2896.28*** *p33*
Baird, James; Georgia, 1763 ***1640.10*** *p9*
Baird, James; Vermont, 1856 ***5900.10*** *p187*
Baird, James 18; Ontario, 1861 ***2896.28*** *p42*
Baird, James 23; Ontario, 1861 ***2896.28*** *p20*
Baird, James 45; Ontario, 1871 ***1823.15*** *p10*
Baird, James 47; Ontario, 1871 ***1823.15*** *p10*
Baird, James 54; Ontario, 1861 ***2896.28*** *p42*
Baird, John; Oklahoma, 1889 ***1640.13*** *p6*
Baird, John 18; Ontario, 1861 ***2896.28*** *p20*
Baird, John 22; Ontario, 1861 ***2896.28*** *p41*
Baird, John 38; Ontario, 1871 ***1823.22*** *p6*
Baird, John 61; Ontario, 1861 ***2896.28*** *p20*
Baird, John H.; Vermont, 1852-1886 ***5900.10*** *p179*
Baird, John R. 10; Ontario, 1861 ***2896.28*** *p34*
Baird, Julia Duyea; Vermont, 1847-1913 ***5900.10*** *p481*
Baird, Margaret 15; Ontario, 1861 ***2896.28*** *p18*
Baird, Maria 84; Vermont, 1916 ***5900.10*** *p612*
Baird, Mary E. 7; Ontario, 1861 ***2896.28*** *p33*
Baird, Mary J. 12; Ontario, 1861 ***2896.28*** *p42*
Baird, Matthew; New York, 1806 ***8197.10*** *p322*
Baird, Nancy 18; Ontario, 1861 ***2896.28*** *p20*
Baird, Peter; Virginia, 1880 ***1640.13*** *p6*
Baird, Robert; New York, 1807 ***8197.10*** *p329*
Baird, Robert 45; Ontario, 1871 ***1823.15*** *p10*
Baird, Robert 47; Ontario, 1871 ***1823.15*** *p10*
Baird, Robert 51; Ontario, 1861 ***2896.28*** *p36*
Baird, Susan; Vermont, 1908 ***5900.10*** *p148*
Baird, Thomas; New York, 1837 ***8197.10*** *p85*
Baird, Thomas 57; Ontario, 1871 ***1823.15*** *p10*
Baird, Thomas W.; New York, 1840 ***8197.10*** *p145*
Baird, William; New York, 1838 ***8197.10*** *p311*
Baird, William; Pennsylvania, 1785 ***4629.10*** *p49*
Baird, William 5; Ontario, 1861 ***2896.28*** *p33*
Baird, William 14; Ontario, 1861 ***2896.28*** *p35*
Baird, William 20; Ontario, 1861 ***2896.28*** *p42*
Baird, William 28; Ontario, 1871 ***1823.15*** *p10*
Baird, William 45; Ontario, 1861 ***2896.28*** *p35*
Baird, William 51; Ontario, 1871 ***1823.15*** *p10*
Bairnsfather, William; Jamaica, 1791 ***1640.13*** *p6*
Baisch, Barbara; Port uncertain, 1737 ***2856.30*** *p13*
Baisch, Barbara; Port uncertain, 1738 ***2856.30*** *p13*
Baisch, Ernst Ludwig; America, 1773 ***2856.30*** *p13*
Baisch, Ernst Ludwig; America, 1786 ***2856.30*** *p14*
Baisch, Friedrich; America, 1752 ***2856.30*** *p14*
Baiser, Franz Anton; Port uncertain, 1803 ***2856.30*** *p14*
Baisley, Robert 39; Maryland, 1774 ***1220.25*** *p60*
Baisser, Johann; America, 1746 ***2856.30*** *p14*
With wife & children
Baistow, Richard, Jr.; New Jersey, 1832 ***8197.10*** *p153*
Baitauld, August 45; Ontario, 1871 ***1823.28*** *p3*
Baitsch, Johann Georg; Port uncertain, 1791 ***2856.30*** *p14*
Baj, Anna 30; Kansas, 1910 ***9079.10*** *p14*
Baj, Pauline 8; Kansas, 1910 ***9079.10*** *p14*
Baj, Reinhold 35; Kansas, 1904-1910 ***9079.10*** *p14*
Bakeland, Walter; Virginia, 1664 ***6212.30*** *p15*
Baker, Mr.; Quebec, 1857 ***9196.15*** *p24*
Baker, Abraham 17; Maryland, 1774 ***1220.25*** *p60*
Baker, Agnes E. 36; Vermont, 1888 ***5900.10*** *p287*
Baker, Alvey 27; Ontario, 1861 ***2896.27*** *p59*
Baker, Ann 16; Maryland, 1774 ***1220.25*** *p77*
Baker, Ann 52; Ontario, 1871 ***1823.15*** *p10*
Baker, Ann Casey; Vermont, 1844-1922 ***5900.10*** *p164*
Baker, Anne 42; Ontario, 1871 ***1823.22*** *p6*
Baker, Ashley Charles; New York, 1838 ***8197.10*** *p110*
Baker, Bartholomew; Pennsylvania, 1777 ***4629.10*** *p15*
Baker, Bartholomew; Pennsylvania, 1785 ***4629.10*** *p48*
Baker, Benjamin; New York, 1838 ***8197.10*** *p110*
Baker, Bridget; Vermont, 1916 ***5900.10*** *p134*

Baker, Caleb; Maryland, 1668 ***2524.55*** *p15*

Baker, Catherine; Vermont, 1897 ***5900.10*** *p103*

Baker, Catherine O'Connor; Vermont, 1829-1918 ***5900.10*** *p107*

Baker, Catherine O'Donnell 86; Vermont, 1909 ***5900.10*** *p103*

Baker, Catherine W. 20; Ontario, 1861 ***2896.27*** *p59*

Baker, Mrs. Christian; Florida, 1850 ***1640.10*** *p9*

Baker, Conrad; Pennsylvania, 1777 ***4629.10*** *p23*

Baker, Cory 12; Ontario, 1861 ***2896.28*** *p21*

Baker, Daniel 33; Ontario, 1871 ***1823.22*** *p6*

Baker, Daniel L.; Vermont, 1836-1914 ***5900.10*** *p597*

Baker, Daniell; Virginia, 1671 ***6212.30*** *p44*

Baker, Edwin D.; New York, 1839 ***8197.10*** *p212*

Baker, Eliza; Vermont, 1836-1920 ***5900.10*** *p390*

Baker, Eliza 87; Vermont, 1887 ***5900.10*** *p390*

Baker, Elizabeth H. McCauly; Vermont, 1852-1952 ***5900.10*** *p597*

Baker, Ellen Fitzgerald 44; Vermont, 1870 ***5900.10*** *p426*

Baker, Francis 86; Vermont, 1866 ***5900.10*** *p390*

Baker, Frank; Vermont, 1839-1916 ***5900.10*** *p390*

Baker, George; New York, 1840 ***8197.10*** *p155*

Baker, George 27; Ontario, 1871 ***1823.22*** *p6*

Baker, George 29; Maryland, 1774 ***1220.25*** *p39*

Baker, Godfrey 76; Ontario, 1871 ***1823.15*** *p10*

Baker, H. W. 25; Alaska, 1912 ***9196.1*** *p39*

Baker, H. W. 25; Whitehorse, Yukon, 1912 ***9196.1*** *p39*

Baker, Hannah 51; Ontario, 1861 ***2896.27*** *p59*

Baker, Hannah Connor 75; Vermont, 1909 ***5900.10*** *p103*

Baker, Harriet; Vermont, 1810-1882 ***5900.10*** *p221*

Baker, Henry; Maryland, 1649 ***2524.55*** *p15*

Baker, Henry; Maryland, 1650 ***2524.55*** *p15*

Baker, Henry; Maryland, 1663 ***2524.55*** *p18*

Baker, Henry; New York, 1821 ***8197.10*** *p208*

Baker, Henry 25; Ontario, 1871 ***1823.15*** *p10*

Baker, Honora 24; Vermont, 1860 ***5900.10*** *p105*

Baker, Isaac; Maryland, 1669 ***2524.55*** *p221*

Baker, Jacob; Pennsylvania, 1777 ***4629.10*** *p15*

Baker, Jacob; Pennsylvania, 1786 ***4629.10*** *p52*

Baker, James 13; Ontario, 1861 ***2896.28*** *p23*

Baker, James 22; Maryland, 1774 ***1220.25*** *p39*

Baker, Joanna Dulan; Vermont, 1799-1869 ***5900.10*** *p107*

Baker, Johanna Griffin 65; Vermont, 1890 ***5900.10*** *p108*

Baker, John; East New Jersey, 1709 ***1224.2*** *p6*

Baker, John; Maryland, 1671 ***2524.55*** *p15*

Baker, John; Maryland, 1673 ***2524.55*** *p15*

Baker, John; Maryland, 1680 ***2524.55*** *p15*

Baker, John; New England, 1678 ***1224.1*** *p5*

Baker, John; New York, 1839 ***8197.10*** *p213*

Baker, John; New York, 1845 ***1224.3*** *p4*

Baker, John; Vermont, 1831-1913 ***5900.10*** *p107*

Baker, John; Virginia, 1664 ***6212.30*** *p8*

Baker, John; Virginia, 1666-1667 ***6212.30*** *p34*

Baker, John 4; Vermont, 1888 ***5900.10*** *p106*

Baker, John 24; Ontario, 1871 ***1823.15*** *p11*

Baker, John 27; Ontario, 1871 ***1823.15*** *p11*

Baker, John 35; Ontario, 1871 ***1823.15*** *p10*

Baker, John 39; Ontario, 1871 ***1823.22*** *p6*

Baker, John 67; Ontario, 1871 ***1823.15*** *p10*

Baker, John 77; Vermont, 1908 ***5900.10*** *p426*

Baker, L. 11; Ontario, 1861 ***2896.26*** *p15*

Baker, Lorenz; Port uncertain, 1793 ***2856.30*** *p61*

Baker, Margaret 78; Vermont, 1879 ***5900.10*** *p105*

Baker, Margaret McDermott; Vermont, 1884-1978 ***5900.10*** *p606*

Baker, Martin; New York, 1821 ***8197.10*** *p208*

Baker, Martin; New York, 1839 ***8197.10*** *p129*

Baker, Mary 27; Ontario, 1871 ***1823.22*** *p6*

Baker, Mary 42; Vermont, 1878 ***5900.10*** *p105*

Baker, Mary 85; Vermont, 1927 ***5900.10*** *p139*

Baker, Mary Celia; Vermont, 1859-1897 ***5900.10*** *p115*

Baker, Mary Sweeney; Vermont, 1834-1926 ***5900.10*** *p76*

Baker, Merit 11; Ontario, 1861 ***2896.27*** *p59*

Baker, Michael 55; Vermont, 1900 ***5900.10*** *p103*

Baker, Michael 86; Vermont, 1912 ***5900.10*** *p108*

Baker, Nicholas; Maryland, 1766 ***1224.2*** *p6*

Baker, Nora; Vermont, 1855-1914 ***5900.10*** *p111*

Baker, Parker 29; Maryland, 1774 ***1220.25*** *p47*

Baker, Patrick; Vermont, 1830-1869 ***5900.10*** *p76*

Baker, Patrick 75; Vermont, 1900 ***5900.10*** *p103*

Baker, Paul; Maryland, 1910 ***3259.35*** *p2*

Baker, R. B.; Quebec, 1856 ***9196.15*** *p11*

Baker, Rebecca 25; Ontario, 1861 ***2896.27*** *p59*

Baker, Richard; New York, 1828 ***8197.10*** *p348*

Baker, Richard; Virginia, 1654 ***1224.1*** *p5*

Baker, Richard 11; Philadelphia, 1775 ***1220.25*** *p8*

Baker, Richard 50; Ontario, 1871 ***1823.28*** *p3*

Baker, Robert 31; Ontario, 1871 ***1823.15*** *p11*

Baker, Robert 58; Ontario, 1871 ***1823.15*** *p11*

Baker, Roger; Maryland, 1688 ***1224.1*** *p5*

Baker, Rosa 35; Ontario, 1871 ***1823.15*** *p11*

Baker, Samuel 55; Ontario, 1871 ***1823.28*** *p3*

Baker, Samuell; Maryland, 1669 ***2524.55*** *p15*

Baker, Sarah A. 23; Ontario, 1861 ***2896.27*** *p59*

Baker, Solomon 21; Maryland, 1774 ***1220.25*** *p46*

Baker, Stephen; Indiana, 1851 ***1224.3*** *p4*

Baker, Stephen; Maryland, 1910 ***3259.35*** *p2*

Baker, T. M.; Vermont, 1868-1943 ***5900.10*** *p606*

Baker, Thomas; New York, 1828 ***8197.10*** *p348*

Baker, Thomas; New York, 1839 ***8197.10*** *p128*

Baker, Thomas; Pennsylvania, 1786 ***4629.10*** *p49*

Baker, Thomas; Vermont, 1844-1922 ***5900.10*** *p164*

Baker, Thomas; Virginia, 1698 ***1224.1*** *p5*

Baker, Thomas 30; Ontario, 1871 ***1823.22*** *p6*

Baker, William; New York, 1820 ***8197.10*** *p207*

Baker, William; New York, 1821 ***8197.10*** *p208*

Baker, William; New York, 1838 ***8197.10*** *p110*

Baker, William 27; Ontario, 1871 ***1823.15*** *p11*

Baker, William 32; Ontario, 1871 ***1823.28*** *p3*

Baker, William 36; Ontario, 1871 ***1823.15*** *p11*

Baker, William 44; Ontario, 1871 ***1823.28*** *p3*

Baker, William 45; Ontario, 1871 ***1823.15*** *p11*

Baker, William 50; Ontario, 1871 ***1823.15*** *p11*

Baker, William 57; Ontario, 1871 ***1823.15*** *p11*

Bakich, P. 28; Alaska, 1916 ***9196.1*** *p44*

Bakich, P. 28; Whitehorse, Yukon, 1916 ***9196.1*** *p44*

Bakin, Christa 18; Ontario, 1871 ***1823.15*** *p11*

Bakman, John N.; New York, 1839 ***8197.10*** *p213*

Bakowski, George; Maryland, 1910 ***3259.35*** *p2*

Bakwill, John 38; Ontario, 1871 ***1823.15*** *p11*

Balantyne, Mr.; Quebec, 1857 ***9196.15*** *p13*

Balatine, Thomas 35; Ontario, 1871 ***1823.15*** *p11*

Balbey, Richard; Maryland, 1673 ***2524.55*** *p15*

Balbi, John Luc Jerome Armand; New York, 1809 ***8197.10*** *p55*

Balbierer, Philipp Michael; America, 1737 ***2856.30*** *p14*

Balbierer, Philipp Michael; America, 1786 ***2856.30*** *p14*

Balbzle, Mary 42; Ontario, 1871 ***1823.15*** *p11*

Balcera, Martin; Maryland, 1910 ***3259.35*** *p2*

Balcerowic, Walter; Maryland, 1910 ***3259.35*** *p2*

Balcerowicz, Czeslaw; Maryland, 1910 ***3259.35*** *p2*

Balcom, Robert 81; Ontario, 1871 ***1823.15*** *p11*

Balczerowski, Andrew; Maryland, 1910 ***3259.35*** *p2*

Balder, Francis; Maryland, 1673 ***2524.55*** *p15*

Baldock, Sarah 23; Maryland, 1773-1774 ***1220.25*** *p34*

Baldrey, John; Maryland, 1665 ***2524.55*** *p15*

Baldrick, William; Maryland, 1658 ***2524.55*** *p15*

Baldridge, F. 50; Alaska, 1917 ***9196.1*** *p47*

Baldridge, F. 50; Whitehorse, Yukon, 1917 ***9196.1*** *p47*

Baldry, John 22; Philadelphia, 1774 ***1220.25*** *p81*

Baldry, Wm; Virginia, 1672 ***6212.30*** *p48*

Balduff, Margarete; Port uncertain, 1795 ***2856.30*** *p14*

Baldwin, Bridget Pendergast 88; Vermont, 1899 ***5900.10*** *p387*

Baldwin, Charles; Virginia, 1664 ***6212.30*** *p11*

Baldwin, James 47; Ontario, 1871 ***1823.15*** *p11*

Baldwin, Jeffry; Virginia, 1666 ***6212.30*** *p26*

Baldwin, John 78; Vermont, 1893 ***5900.10*** *p387*

Baldwin, John E.; Vermont, 1847-1947 ***5900.10*** *p252*

Baldwin, Julia Quigley; Vermont, 1847-1902 ***5900.10*** *p252*

Baldwin, Margaret; Vermont, 1900 ***5900.10*** *p127*

Baldwin, Sabinia Shanahan; Vermont, 1878-1906 ***5900.10*** *p352*

Baldwin, William 22; Virginia, 1773 ***1220.25*** *p31*

Baldwin, William 24; Maryland, 1775 ***1220.25*** *p111*

Baldwin, William 43; Ontario, 1871 ***1823.15*** *p11*

Baldwin, William H. 17, Ontario, 1871 ***1823.28*** *p3*

Baldwin, Wm; Virginia, 1664 ***6212.30*** *p9*

Bale, Mr.; Quebec, 1858 ***9196.15*** *p34*

Bale, Mrs.; Quebec, 1858 ***9196.15*** *p34*

Bale, Adam 24; Maryland, 1775 ***1220.25*** *p106*

Bale, Charles; New York, 1840 ***8197.10*** *p145*

Bale, John 25; Maryland, 1774 ***1220.25*** *p46*

Bale, Thomas; New York, 1840 ***8197.10*** *p145*

Balen, Peter; New York, 1807 ***8197.10*** *p34*

Balestier, Joseph Neree; New York, 1817-1835 ***8197.10*** *p310*

Balestier, Joseph Nereus; New York, 1821 ***8197.10*** *p312*

Baley, Edmond 66; Vermont, 1871 ***5900.10*** *p501*

Balfour, Mr.; Quebec, 1858 ***9196.15*** *p38*

Balfour, John; Jamaica, 1750 ***1640.13*** *p6*

Balfour, John; South Carolina, 1781 ***1640.13*** *p6*

Balfour, Robert; Savannah, Georgia, 1756 ***1640.10*** *p9*

Balfour, Robert; Savannah, Georgia, 1837 ***1640.10*** *p9*

Balfour, William; Georgia, 1698 ***1640.13*** *p6*

Balfoure, William; Virginia, 1686 ***1224.1*** *p5*

Balger, John 40; Ontario, 1871 ***1823.28*** *p3*

Balger, Patrick 30; Ontario, 1871 ***1823.28*** *p3*

Balger, William 40; Ontario, 1871 ***1823.28*** *p3*

Balick, George; Maryland, 1650 ***2524.55*** *p15*

Baliga, Rosia; Maryland, 1910 ***3259.35*** *p2*

Balinski, Antoniatt; Maryland, 1910 ***3259.35*** *p2*

Balintine, Thomas 40; Ontario, 1871 ***1823.15*** *p11*

Balintyne, Elizabeth 5; Ontario, 1871 ***1823.15*** *p11*

Balintyne, Mary 43; Ontario, 1871 ***1823.15*** *p11*

Balintyne, Mary Jane 14; Ontario, 1871 ***1823.15*** *p11*

Balintyne, Robert 7; Ontario, 1871 ***1823.15*** *p11*

Balintyne, Robert 43; Ontario, 1871 ***1823.15*** *p11*

Balis, Michael; Maryland, 1910 ***3259.35*** *p2*

Balissa, John Solomon 31; Maryland, 1774 ***1220.25*** *p72*

Balkcoll, James 38; Ontario, 1871 ***1823.15*** *p11*

Balkwell, Jane 72; Ontario, 1871 ***1823.15*** *p11*

Balkwill, Hugh 76; Ontario, 1871 ***1823.15*** *p11*

Balkwill, John 40; Ontario, 1871 ***1823.15*** *p11*

Balkwill, John 45; Ontario, 1871 ***1823.15*** *p11*

Balkwill, Richard 78; Ontario, 1871 ***1823.15*** *p11*

Balkwill, Silas 37; Ontario, 1871 ***1823.15*** *p11*

Balkwill, William 31; Ontario, 1871 ***1823.15*** *p11*

Balkwill, William 40; Ontario, 1871 ***1823.15*** *p11*

Ball, . . .; Boston, 1765 ***4628.40*** *p114*

Ball, Mr.; Quebec, 1857 ***9196.15*** *p15*

Ball, A. 58; Ontario, 1861 ***2896.28*** *p10*

Ball, Archibald; New York, 1803 ***8197.10*** *p11*

Ball, Benjamin; Maryland, 1682 ***2524.55*** *p15*

Ball, Christopher; Maryland, 1667 ***2524.55*** *p15*

Ball, Edmd; Virginia, 1683 ***6212.30*** *p56*

Ball, Gabriel; Maryland, 1652 ***2524.55*** *p39*

Ball, George 63; Ontario, 1871 ***1823.28*** *p3*

Ball, Henery 33; Ontario, 1871 ***1823.15*** *p11*

Ball, Henry; New York, 1807 ***8197.10*** *p34*

Ball, Hermann; Port uncertain, 1751 ***2856.30*** *p14*

Ball, Ingram; Nova Scotia, 1807 ***1640.13*** *p6*

Ball, Ingram; Nova Scotia, 1888 ***1640.13*** *p6*

Ball, James; Watertown, Massachusetts, 1672 ***1224.1*** *p5*

Ball, James 47; Ontario, 1871 ***1823.15*** *p11*

Ball, James 60; Ontario, 1871 ***1823.15*** *p11*

Ball, John; Maryland, 1661 ***2524.55*** *p15*

Ball, John 41; Ontario, 1871 ***1823.15*** *p11*

Ball, Joseph; Pennsylvania, 1777 ***4629.10*** *p20*

Ball, L. 52; Ontario, 1861 ***2896.28*** *p10*

Ball, Lewis; Virginia, 1667 ***6212.30*** *p37*

Ball, Mary Ann 60; Ontario, 1871 ***1823.28*** *p3*

Ball, Mary Chichester; Virginia, 1790 ***1224.2*** *p6*

Ball, Peter; Ontario, 1871 ***1823.28*** *p3*

Ball, Peter; Virginia, 1666 ***6212.30*** *p29*

Ball, Philip; New York, 1837 ***8197.10*** *p95*

Ball, Silvanus 22; Virginia, 1774 ***1220.25*** *p90*

Ball, Stephen 57; Ontario, 1871 ***1823.15*** *p11*

Ball, Thomas 26; Ontario, 1871 ***1823.28*** *p4*

Ball, Thomas 33; Virginia, 1774 ***1220.25*** *p76*

Ball, Thomas 42; Ontario, 1871 ***1823.28*** *p3*

Ball, Thomas 52; Ontario, 1871 ***1823.22*** *p6*

Ball, William; Maryland, 1668 ***2524.55*** *p16*

Ball, William; Pennsylvania, 1777 ***4629.10*** *p27*

Ball, William; Pennsylvania, 1779 ***4629.10*** *p35*

Ball, William 48; Ontario, 1871 ***1823.15*** *p11*

Ball, William 51; Ontario, 1871 ***1823.22*** *p6*

Ball, William 71; Ontario, 1871 ***1823.15*** *p11*

Ballagh, John 48; Ontario, 1871 ***1823.22*** *p6*

Ballagh, Sarah 28; Ontario, 1871 ***1823.22*** *p6*

Ballagh, William; New York, 1819 ***8197.10*** *p207*

Ballantyne, Mr.; Quebec, 1857 ***9196.15*** *p24*

Ballantyne, Hannah 24; Ontario, 1871 ***1823.15*** *p11*

Ballantyne, Hugh; Virginia, 1736 ***1224.2*** *p6*

Ballantyne, John; Georgia, 1698 ***1640.13*** *p6*

Ballantyne, John; Savannah, Georgia, 1732 ***1640.10*** *p9*

Ballantyne, Robt 36; Ontario, 1871 ***1823.15*** *p11*

Ballantyne, William 32; Ontario, 1871 ***1823.15*** *p11*

Ballantyne, William 34; Ontario, 1871 ***1823.15*** *p11*

Ballantyne, William 37; Ontario, 1871 ***1823.15*** *p11*

Ballard, Elinor; Virginia, 1690 ***6212.30*** *p58*

Ballard, Geo.; Maryland, 1656 ***2524.55*** *p16*

Ballard, George 21; Virginia, 1774 ***1220.25*** *p75*

Ballard, Mary; Vermont, n.d. ***5900.10*** *p546*

Ballard, Mary; Virginia, 1672 ***6212.30*** *p50*

Ballard, William; Charleston, South Carolina, 1812 ***1224.3*** *p4*

Ballasteen, John; New York, 1831-1840 ***8197.10*** *p145*

Ballcott, Jeffry; Virginia, 1665-1666 ***6212.30*** *p25*

Ballemann, Josef; Port uncertain, 1787 ***2856.30*** *p14*

Ballentine, George; New York, 1840 ***8197.10*** *p153*

Ballentine, Richard; Texas, 1836 ***1640.10*** *p9*

Ballentine, Robert 30; Ontario, 1871 ***1823.28*** *p4*

Ballentyne, George; Georgia, 1699 ***1640.13*** *p6*

Ballerby, Edward 40; Ontario, 1871 ***1823.22*** *p6*

Ballet, Richard; Pennsylvania, 1842 ***6058.10*** *p23*

Ballett, Richard; Pennsylvania, 1842 ***6058.10*** *p23*

Ballew, Abraham; Virginia, 1709 ***1224.2*** *p6*

Balley, Ambrose; Maryland, 1669 ***2524.55*** *p16*

Balley, Andrew 45; Ontario, 1871 ***1823.15*** *p11*

Ballingal, Thomas; Ontario, 1888 ***1640.13*** *p7*

Ballinger, Cyprian; America, 1764 ***2856.30*** *p14*

Ballintine, James 59; Ontario, 1871 ***1823.15*** *p12*

Ballintine, William 25; Ontario, 1871 ***1823.15*** *p12*

Ballions, Barbara; Port uncertain, 1729 ***2856.30*** *p14*

Ballions, Clara; Port uncertain, 1729 ***2856.30*** *p14*

Ballions, Margarete; Port uncertain, 1729 ***2856.30*** *p14*

Balloch, Janet; Ontario, 1875 ***1640.13*** *p7*

Balloch, John; Jamaica, 1835 ***1640.13*** *p7*
Ballon, Angello; Georgia, 1698 ***1640.13*** *p7*
Bally, John; Maryland, 1662 ***2524.55*** *p16*
Balmain, William; Maryland, 1784 ***1224.2*** *p6*
Balman, Jacob 34; Ontario, 1871 ***1823.28*** *p4*
Balman, Thomas 53; Ontario, 1871 ***1823.15*** *p12*
Balmbach, Eva; Port uncertain, 1765 ***2856.30*** *p14*
Balmer, Mr.; Portland, Maine, 1858 ***9196.15*** *p29*
Balmer, Ann *SEE* Balmer, Thomas
Balmer, Georg Michel; Port uncertain, 1770 ***2856.30*** *p14*
Balmer, Philipp Adam; Port uncertain, 1770 ***2856.30*** *p14*
With family
Balmer, Robert; Montreal, 1860 ***1640.13*** *p7*
Balmer, Robert; Portland, Maine, 1857 ***9196.15*** *p11*
Balmer, Thomas; Maryland, 1651 ***2524.55*** *p16*
Wife: Ann
Balnaves, Robert; Georgia, 1698 ***1640.13*** *p7*
Balo, Peter 27; British Columbia, 1909 ***9196.1*** *p27*
Balo, Peter 27; Washington, 1909 ***9196.1*** *p27*
Balowitski, Thoman; Maryland, 1910 ***3259.35*** *p2*
Balsdon, George 35; Ontario, 1871 ***1823.15*** *p12*
Balsdon, James 51; Ontario, 1871 ***1823.15*** *p12*
Balsley, Priscilla Jope; Pittsburgh, 1837 ***1224.3*** *p4*
Balster, Helen; Maryland, 1910 ***3259.35*** *p2*
Baltauff, Georg; Port uncertain, 1738 ***2856.30*** *p14*
Balten, Frederick; New York, 1840 ***8197.10*** *p154*
Balthas, Miss; Port uncertain, 1784 ***2856.30*** *p266*
Balthas, Georg; Port uncertain, 1775 ***2856.30*** *p14*
Baltz, Adam; Port uncertain, 1736 ***2856.30*** *p14*
Baltz, Anton; Port uncertain, 1735 ***2856.30*** *p14*
Baltzer, Johann; Port uncertain, 1764 ***2856.30*** *p14*
Balyntine, Elizabeth 1; Ontario, 1861 ***2896.25*** *p39*
Balyntine, Simon 38; Ontario, 1861 ***2896.25*** *p39*
Balyntine, William 3; Ontario, 1861 ***2896.25*** *p39*
Balzer, Jacob; Port uncertain, 1790 ***2856.30*** *p14*
With family
Balzer, Susanna; America, 1747 ***2856.30*** *p14*
Balzinger, Christian; Port uncertain, 1738 ***2856.30*** *p15*
Bambach, Heinrich; Port uncertain, 1784 ***2856.30*** *p15*
Bamback, Charles 42; Ontario, 1871 ***1823.28*** *p4*
Bamber, Christina; Port uncertain, 1758 ***2856.30*** *p15*
Bamber, John 61; Ontario, 1871 ***1823.22*** *p7*
Bamber, Richard 58; Ontario, 1871 ***1823.22*** *p7*
Bamber, William; New York, 1731 ***1224.2*** *p6*
Bamberger, Anna Ursula; Port uncertain, 1759 ***2856.30*** *p15*
Bamberger, Cath. Sophia; Port uncertain, 1790 ***2856.30*** *p15*
Bamberger, Georg; Port uncertain, 1775 ***2856.30*** *p15*
Bamberger, Sybilla; Port uncertain, 1793 ***2856.30*** *p15*
Bame, Charles 47; Ontario, 1871 ***1823.28*** *p4*
Bamer, Frank; Maryland, 1910 ***3259.35*** *p2*
Bamer, Gotlip 56; Ontario, 1871 ***1823.28*** *p4*
Bamfeild, Jane; Virginia, 1666 ***6212.30*** *p29*
Bamfield, Edward; Portland, Maine, 1858 ***9196.15*** *p31*
Bamford, Catherine 47; Ontario, 1871 ***1823.22*** *p7*
Bampton, Charles 40; Ontario, 1871 ***1823.28*** *p4*
Banagan, Hugh J.; Vermont, 1847-1908 ***5900.10*** *p593*
Banagan, James 59; Vermont, 1900 ***5900.10*** *p589*
Banagan, Margaret; Vermont, 1843-1915 ***5900.10*** *p184*
Banagan, Mary Duffy 75; Vermont, 1883 ***5900.10*** *p585*
Banagan, Mary Godsill 39; Vermont, 1891 ***5900.10*** *p589*
Banagan, Minnie Morse; Vermont, 1858-1943 ***5900.10*** *p593*
Banahan, Ann; Vermont, 1840-1894 ***5900.10*** *p508*
Banahan, Catherine 63; Vermont, 1914 ***5900.10*** *p506*
Banahan, Maria D.; Vermont, 1848-1924 ***5900.10*** *p504*
Banahan, Maria Morris 54; Vermont, 1905 ***5900.10*** *p506*
Banahan, Mary Morris 83; Vermont, 1903 ***5900.10*** *p504*
Banahan, Michael; Vermont, 1851-1913 ***5900.10*** *p506*
Banahan, Patrick; Vermont, 1800-1870 ***5900.10*** *p508*
Banahan, Rose A. 42; Vermont, 1902 ***5900.10*** *p504*
Banashak, George; Maryland, 1910 ***3259.35*** *p2*
Banasjewski, Joe; Maryland, 1910 ***3259.35*** *p2*
Banatine, William 51; Ontario, 1871 ***1823.15*** *p12*
Banbury, Edw; Virginia, 1668-1669 ***6212.30*** *p40*
Banckes, George; Maryland, 1668 ***2524.55*** *p16*
Banckin, Maria Magdalene; Port uncertain, 1744 ***2856.30*** *p15*
Bancks, Eady; Maryland, 1673 ***2524.55*** *p16*
Bancks, Edith; Maryland, 1673 ***2524.55*** *p16*
Bancks, George; Maryland, 1673 ***2524.55*** *p16*
Bancks, Peter; Maryland, 1658 ***2524.55*** *p16*
Bancks, Richard; Carolina, 1682 ***1224.1*** *p5*
Bancroft, Ales; Maryland, 1651 ***2524.55*** *p45*
Bancroft, William; New York, 1811 ***8197.10*** *p57*
Band, George; Mississippi, 1792-1845 ***1640.10*** *p9*
Bandfield, Wm 12; Ontario, 1861 ***2896.28*** *p23*
Bandorska, Victoria; Maryland, 1910 ***3259.35*** *p2*
Bands, Mary 35; Maryland, 1774 ***1220.25*** *p65*
Bandy, Math; Virginia, 1672-1673 ***6212.30*** *p51*
Bandy, Richard 41; Ontario, 1871 ***1823.28*** *p4*
Bandy, Robert 39; Ontario, 1871 ***1823.28*** *p4*
Bandzwol, Joseph; Maryland, 1910 ***3259.35*** *p2*
Bane, Daniel 32; Ontario, 1871 ***1823.28*** *p4*
Bane, John 53; Ontario, 1871 ***1823.15*** *p12*
Banerle, William 29; Ontario, 1871 ***1823.28*** *p4*
Banes, Joseph 74; Ontario, 1871 ***1823.15*** *p12*
Banes, Philiph 67; Ontario, 1871 ***1823.15*** *p12*
Banes, William 50; Ontario, 1871 ***1823.15*** *p12*
Banestor, Petor; Maryland, 1654 ***2524.55*** *p16*
Banfield, Perlina 65; Ontario, 1861 ***2896.28*** *p21*
Banford, Charles; Boston, 1695 ***1224.1*** *p5*
Bang, David; Pennsylvania, 1777 ***4629.10*** *p12*
Banghen, Mr.; Quebec, 1856 ***9196.15*** *p11*
Banigan, Terrence; New York, 1821 ***8197.10*** *p208*
Baning, Allice 58; Ontario, 1871 ***1823.28*** *p4*
Banister, Mrs.; Maryland, 1648 ***2524.55*** *p16*
Banister, Henry; Maryland, 1655-1656 ***2524.55*** *p16*
Banister, Henry; Maryland, 1665 ***2524.55*** *p16*
Banister, Henry; Virginia, 1665-1666 ***6212.30*** *p24*
Banister, Jonas 31; Ontario, 1871 ***1823.22*** *p7*
Banister, Nathaniel 15; Philadelphia, 1774 ***1220.25*** *p34*
Banister, Nich; Virginia, 1664 ***6212.30*** *p14*
Banister, Richard; Maryland, 1648 ***2524.55*** *p16*
With wife
Banister, Thomas; Maryland, 1655-1656 ***2524.55*** *p16*
Banister, Thomas 19; Jamaica, 1774 ***1220.25*** *p85*
Banister, Wm; Virginia, 1663 ***6212.30*** *p4*
Bank, Gottfried; Port uncertain, 1770 ***2856.30*** *p15*
Bankerhie, James 21; Maryland, 1774 ***1220.25*** *p73*
Bankes, Elizabeth; Virginia, 1669-1670 ***6212.30*** *p41*
Bankes, Nicholas; Maryland, 1679 ***2524.55*** *p16*
Bankes, Wm; Virginia, 1665-1666 ***6212.30*** *p23*
Bankes, Wm; Virginia, 1666-1667 ***6212.30*** *p32*
Banks, Anne; Maryland, 1681 ***2524.55*** *p16*
Banks, David 15; Maryland, 1774 ***1220.25*** *p61*
Banks, Edward; Virginia, 1666-1667 ***6212.30*** *p34*
Banks, Eliza; Virginia, 1666 ***6212.30*** *p25*
Banks, James; New York, 1802 ***8197.10*** *p18*
Banks, John 28; Ontario, 1871 ***1823.28*** *p4*
Banks, Moses 21; Maryland, 1774 ***1220.25*** *p62*
Banks, Nicholas; Maryland, 1679 ***2524.55*** *p16*
Banks, William; New York, 1821 ***8197.10*** *p209*
Banks, William; New York, 1834 ***8197.10*** *p212*
Banks, William; New York, 1836 ***8197.10*** *p76*
Banks, William 24; Maryland, 1774 ***1220.25*** *p84*
Bann, Anna Margarete; Port uncertain, 1786 ***2856.30*** *p15*
Bannagan, Mary 80; Vermont, 1910 ***5900.10*** *p588*
Bannan, Robert; New York, 1807 ***8197.10*** *p325*
Bannatyne, William; Georgia, 1698 ***1640.13*** *p7*
Bannatyns, David 52; Ontario, 1871 ***1823.15*** *p12*
Banner, Thomas; New York, 1840 ***8197.10*** *p145*
Bannerman, Donald 66; Ontario, 1871 ***1823.15*** *p12*
Bannerman, Hugh 70; Ontario, 1871 ***1823.15*** *p12*
Bannerman, John 25; Ontario, 1871 ***1823.28*** *p4*
Bannerman, Mary 72; Ontario, 1871 ***1823.15*** *p12*
Bannerman, William 28; Ontario, 1871 ***1823.28*** *p4*
Bannerman, William 40; Ontario, 1871 ***1823.15*** *p12*
Bannester, Nicholas; Maryland, 1650 ***2524.55*** *p16*
With wife
Bannet, Ritcherd 30; Ontario, 1871 ***1823.15*** *p12*
Banning, James 21; Maryland, 1774 ***1220.25*** *p39*
Bannister, Edw; Quebec, 1857 ***9196.15*** *p25*
Bannister, Elizabeth; Maryland, 1681 ***2524.55*** *p16*
Bannister, Henry; Maryland, 1655-1656 ***2524.55*** *p16*
Bannister, Thomas; Maryland, 1655-1656 ***2524.55*** *p16*
Bannister, William; America, 1832 ***1224.3*** *p4*
Bannon, John; New York, 1839 ***8197.10*** *p379*
Bannon, Rose 81; Vermont, 1877 ***5900.10*** *p146*
Banon, John; Pennsylvania, 1777 ***4629.10*** *p14*
Banse, Mary 25; Maryland, 1775 ***1220.25*** *p114*
Bantel, Michel; Port uncertain, 1740 ***2856.30*** *p15*
Bantey, Andrew 40; Ontario, 1871 ***1823.22*** *p7*
Bantleon, Leonhard; Port uncertain, 1740 ***2856.30*** *p15*
Bantleon, Michel; Port uncertain, 1740 ***2856.30*** *p15*
Bantmann, Philipp; America, 1750 ***2856.30*** *p15*
Banton, Catherine 18; Ontario, 1861 ***2896.27*** *p2*
Banton, Hannah 15; Ontario, 1861 ***2896.27*** *p2*
Banton, Henry; Virginia, 1664 ***6212.30*** *p14*
Banton, Nancy 38; Ontario, 1861 ***2896.27*** *p2*
Banton, Robert 40; Ontario, 1861 ***2896.27*** *p2*
Banton, Samuell; Virginia, 1663-1664 ***6212.30*** *p5*
Banyar, William; Albany, New York, 1798 ***1224.2*** *p6*
Banz, Georg Michael; Port uncertain, 1765 ***2856.30*** *p15*
Banzdzicnck, Stanislas; Maryland, 1910 ***3259.35*** *p2*
Baoie, James; Quebec, 1858 ***9196.15*** *p32*
Baoie, Mrs. James; Quebec, 1858 ***9196.15*** *p32*
Baon, J. 24; British Columbia, 1909 ***9196.1*** *p27*
Baon, J. 24; Seattle, 1909 ***9196.1*** *p27*
Bapp, Mathias; New York, 1837 ***8197.10*** *p87*
Baptie, John; Georgia, 1698 ***1640.13*** *p7*
Baptist, Alexander 35; Ontario, 1871 ***1823.22*** *p7*
Baptist, George 30; Ontario, 1871 ***1823.22*** *p7*
Baptist, John 26; Virginia, 1774 ***1220.25*** *p89*
Baptist, John 34; Ontario, 1871 ***1823.22*** *p7*
Baptist, Mary 57; Ontario, 1871 ***1823.22*** *p7*
Baptista, Joannes; Georgia, 1698 ***1640.13*** *p7*
Baptista, John; Virginia, 1671 ***6212.30*** *p43*
Baptiste, Anthony; New York, 1840 ***8197.10*** *p155*
Bar, A. C. Marg. *SEE* Bar, Johann
Bar, Christian; America, 1743 ***2856.30*** *p61*
Bar, Eva Cath. Wedel *SEE* Bar, Johann Georg
Bar, Georg; America, 1752 ***2856.30*** *p61*
With wife & children
Bar, Hans; Port uncertain, 1739 ***2856.30*** *p61*
Bar, J.; America, 1749 ***2856.30*** *p291*
Bar, J. G.; America, 1752 ***2856.30*** *p482*
Bar, Jeremia; America, 1749 ***2856.30*** *p15*
With wife & children
Bar, Johann; America, 1743 ***2856.30*** *p61*
Bar, Johann; America, 1749 ***2856.30*** *p61*
Wife: A. C. Marg.
With child
Bar, Johann Georg; America, 1752 ***2856.30*** *p61*
Wife: Eva Cath. Wedel
Bar, Johann Georg; America, 1757 ***2856.30*** *p61*
With wife & 5 children
Bar, Melchior; America, 1743 ***2856.30*** *p61*
Barabine, Niccolas; New York, 1838 ***8197.10*** *p110*
Barabsz, Weczlaus; Maryland, 1910 ***3259.35*** *p2*
Baraby, John F.; Vermont, 1839-1903 ***5900.10*** *p186*
Baraby, Margaret Cummings; Vermont, 1849-1913 ***5900.10*** *p186*
Baraes, I. 27; Alaska, 1917 ***9196.1*** *p45*
Baraes, I. 27; Whitehorse, Yukon, 1917 ***9196.1*** *p45*
Baranger, Anjaline; Ontario, 1861 ***2896.25*** *p10*
Baranger, Rene; Philadelphia, 1793 ***4629.10*** *p71*
Baranoski, Jacob; Maryland, 1910 ***3259.35*** *p2*
Baranoski, John; Maryland, 1910 ***3259.35*** *p2*
Baranoski, Martin; Maryland, 1910 ***3259.35*** *p2*
Baranowski, Alexander; Maryland, 1910 ***3259.35*** *p2*
Baranowski, Francis; Maryland, 1910 ***3259.35*** *p2*
Baranowski, Max; Maryland, 1910 ***3259.35*** *p2*
Baraswerke, Frank; Maryland, 1910 ***3259.35*** *p2*
Barbarian, Ovnik 36; British Columbia, 1913 ***9196.1*** *p23*
Barbarian, Ovnik 36; Juneau, Alaska, 1913 ***9196.1*** *p23*
Barbaroues, Jean Andre, Sr.; Philadelphia, 1793 ***4629.10*** *p75*
Barben, Anna Maria; Port uncertain, 1765 ***2856.30*** *p15*
Barber, Mr.; Quebec, 1856 ***9196.15*** *p9*
Barber, Albert 50; Ontario, 1861 ***2896.28*** *p52*
Barber, Archibald 18; Ontario, 1871 ***1823.15*** *p12*
Barber, Charles 50; Ontario, 1871 ***1823.15*** *p12*
Barber, Chesheave 24; Georgia, 1774 ***1220.25*** *p48*
Barber, Francis; Maryland, 1660 ***2524.55*** *p16*
Barber, Geo.; Maryland, 1661 ***2524.55*** *p16*
Barber, Henry; Pennsylvania, 1777 ***4629.10*** *p13*
Barber, James 50; Ontario, 1871 ***1823.22*** *p7*
Barber, James 68; Ontario, 1871 ***1823.22*** *p7*
Barber, James R. 45; Ontario, 1871 ***1823.22*** *p7*
Barber, Jesse; New York, 1839 ***8197.10*** *p128*
Barber, John *SEE* Barber, John
Barber, John; Detroit, 1858 ***3437.14*** *p95*
Barber, John; Maryland, 1663 ***2524.55*** *p16*
Barber, John; Maryland, 1665 ***2524.55*** *p16*
Wife: Jone
Child: John
Child: Margarett
Child: Sarah
Child: Mary
Barber, John 41; Ontario, 1871 ***1823.15*** *p12*
Barber, John 62; Ontario, 1871 ***1823.28*** *p4*
Barber, Jone *SEE* Barber, John
Barber, Joseph; New York, 1838 ***8197.10*** *p110*
Barber, Margarett *SEE* Barber, John
Barber, Mary *SEE* Barber, John
Barber, Mary; New York, 1849 ***1224.3*** *p4*
Barber, Newman; Maryland, 1673 ***2524.55*** *p16*
Barber, Randall; Maryland, 1664 ***2524.55*** *p16*
Barber, Sarah *SEE* Barber, John
Barber, Tho; Virginia, 1672 ***6212.30*** *p50*
Barber, Thomas; Georgia, 1864 ***1640.10*** *p9*
Barber, William 44; Ontario, 1871 ***1823.15*** *p12*
Barber, William 45; Ontario, 1871 ***1823.15*** *p12*
Barbery, Thomas; Maryland, 1666 ***2524.55*** *p16*
Barbet, George; Maryland, 1743 ***1224.2*** *p6*
Barbet, John 21; Virginia, 1775 ***1220.25*** *p100*
Barbican, Oliver; Virginia, 1666-1667 ***6212.30*** *p35*
Barbich, L. 31; Alaska, 1917 ***9196.1*** *p47*
Barbich, L. 31; Whitehorse, Yukon, 1917 ***9196.1*** *p47*
Barbier, Georg; Port uncertain, 1770 ***2856.30*** *p15*
Barbinski, Heriman; Maryland, 1910 ***3259.35*** *p2*
Barbitch, Mike 28; British Columbia, 1909 ***9196.1*** *p27*
Barbitch, Mike 28; Seattle, 1909 ***9196.1*** *p27*
Barbot, Francis; South Carolina, 1739 ***1224.2*** *p6*
Barbot, James; Maryland, n.d. ***1224.2*** *p6*
Barbour, Letitia 23; Ontario, 1871 ***1823.15*** *p12*

Barbut, Theodore; Boston, 1700-1799 1224.2 p7
Barbut, Theodore; Quebec, 1700-1799 1224.2 p7
Barclay, Mr.; Quebec, 1857 9196.15 p19
Barclay, Mrs.; Quebec, 1857 9196.15 p16
Barclay, Andrew; Philadelphia, 1793 4629.10 p77
Barclay, George; New York, 1826 8197.10 p334
Barclay, Hugh; Georgia, 1699 1640.13 p7
Barclay, J.; Portland, Maine, 1858 9196.15 p29
Barclay, Jno; Portland, Maine, 1858 9196.15 p28
Barclay, John; New York, New York, 1779 1224.2 p7
Barclay, John 45; Ontario, 1871 1823.22 p7
Barclay, Peter; Wisconsin, 1876 1640.13 p7
Barclay, Thomas; America, 1831 1224.3 p4
Barclay, Thomas; Pennsylvania, 1777 4629.10 p7
Barclay, Thomas 16; Maryland, 1775 1220.25 p109
Barclay, William; Baltimore, 1814 1224.3 p4
Barclay, William; Georgia, 1699 1640.13 p7
Barclay, Wm.; Pennsylvania, 1781 4629.10 p43
Barcley, George 30; Ontario, 1871 1823.15 p12
Barcrak, Andres; Maryland, 1910 3259.35 p2
Bard, Charles 31; Ontario, 1871 1823.28 p4
Bard, Fredrick 27; Ontario, 1871 1823.28 p4
Bard, John; New York, 1807 8197.10 p34
Bard, Joseph; New York, 1821 8197.10 p208
Bardemess, Adam; Port uncertain, 1785 2856.30 p15
Bardon, Thomas; Maryland, 1663 2524.55 p16
Bare, Elizabeth; Maryland, 1674 2524.55 p16
Bare, James; Virginia, 1664 6212.30 p13
Bare, Polly 63; Ontario, 1861 2896.25 p55
Bare, Richard 26; Nova Scotia, 1774 1220.25 p14
Barefoot, Mary; Maryland, 1680 2524.55 p16
Barefoot, Thomas 25; Maryland, 1775 1220.25 p97
Barefoote, John; Maryland, 1681 2524.55 p17
Barefoote, Susanna; Maryland, 1681 2524.55 p17
Bareford, Thomas 26; Virginia, 1775 1220.25 p110
Barenger, John 18; Ontario, 1861 2896.25 p2
Baresek, Francis; Maryland, 1910 3259.35 p2
Baret, Christopher; New York, 1826 8197.10 p336
Barfe, Thomas; New York, 1808 8197.10 p34
Barford, Joane *SEE* Barford, John
Barford, John; Maryland, 1663 2524.55 p17
Wife: Joane
Barge, David 35; Ontario, 1871 1823.15 p12
Barget, Thomas 26; Virginia, 1773 1220.25 p31
Barham, Anthony; Virginia, 1640 1224.1 p5
Barham, Anthony; Virginia, 1641 1224.1 p5
Barick, Thomas; Virginia, 1671-1672 6212.30 p45
Barie, Elizabeth; Maryland, 1662 2524.55 p28
Baringer, Albert 11; Ontario, 1861 2896.25 p11
Baringer, Horace 1; Ontario, 1861 2896.25 p11
Baringer, Jacob 57; Ontario, 1871 1823.22 p7
Baringer, John 18; Ontario, 1861 2896.25 p10
Baringer, Loria A. 9; Ontario, 1861 2896.25 p11
Baringer, Lucinda 39; Ontario, 1861 2896.25 p10
Baringer, Smith 20; Ontario, 1861 2896.25 p10
Baringer, Wm 52; Ontario, 1861 2896.25 p10
Barington, Joane; Maryland, 1665 2524.55 p17
Barington, Jonathan; Pennsylvania, 1777 4629.10 p24
Barke, John; Maryland, 1661 2524.55 p17
Barke, John; Maryland, 1910 3259.35 p2
Barker, Mr.; Quebec, 1857 9196.15 p15
Barker, Mr.; Quebec, 1857 9196.15 p24
Barker, Abell; Virginia, 1664 6212.30 p11
Barker, Bartholomew 29; New York, 1774 1220.25 p20
Wife: Sarah 30
Barker, Brian; Pennsylvania, 1777 4629.10 p27
Barker, Charles 21; Maryland, 1775 1220.25 p121
Barker, Edward 24; Maryland, 1774 1220.25 p60
Barker, Elizabeth 19; Carolina, 1775 1220.25 p123
Barker, Emma 32; Ontario, 1861 2896.27 p24
Barker, Francis; Virginia, 1666 6212.30 p29
Barker, Frederick; New York, 1837 8197.10 p212
Barker, Frederick Henry; New York, 1823 8197.10 p209
Barker, George; Maryland, 1674 2524.55 p17
Barker, Hannah 70; Ontario, 1871 1823.15 p12
Barker, Harriette 6; Ontario, 1861 2896.27 p24
Barker, Jacob; Massachusetts, 1750 1224.2 p7
Barker, James; Pennsylvania, 1777 4629.10 p12
Barker, James 23; Maryland, 1774 1220.25 p76
Barker, James 63; Ontario, 1871 1823.15 p12
Barker, Jno; Virginia, 1676 6212.30 p53
Barker, John; Maryland, 1668 2524.55 p17
Barker, John; Maryland, 1671 2524.55 p17
Barker, John 42; Ontario, 1871 1823.15 p12
Barker, John 66; Ontario, 1871 1823.22 p7
Barker, Joseph 2; Ontario, 1861 2896.27 p54
Barker, Luke; New York, 1837 8197.10 p87
Barker, Mary 4; Ontario, 1861 2896.27 p24
Barker, Mary 31; Baltimore, 1775 1220.25 p116
Barker, Mary E. 19; Ontario, 1861 2896.27 p40
Barker, Mary J. 24; Ontario, 1861 2896.27 p21
Barker, Mathew 45; Ontario, 1871 1823.15 p12
Barker, Matilda 25; Ontario, 1861 2896.27 p54
Barker, Robert; West New Jersey, 1735 1224.2 p7
Barker, Robert 64; Ontario, 1871 1823.22 p7
Barker, Sarah 30 *SEE* Barker, Bartholomew
Barker, Thomas; Maryland, 1661 2524.55 p17
Barker, Thomas; Maryland, 1698 1224.1 p5
Barker, Thomas 5; Ontario, 1861 2896.27 p54
Barker, Thomas 24; Ontario, 1871 1823.22 p7
Barker, Thomas 50; Ontario, 1871 1823.22 p7
Barker, William 22; America, 1774 1220.25 p35
Barker, William 30; Jamaica, 1774 1220.25 p86
Barker, William 44; Ontario, 1871 1823.15 p12
Barker, William S. 1; Ontario, 1861 2896.27 p40
Barkley, Mr.; Quebec, 1858 9196.15 p42
Barkley, John 48; Ontario, 1871 1823.15 p12
Barkley, Nicholas; Maryland, 1664 2524.55 p17
Wife: Sarah
Barkley, Sarah *SEE* Barkley, Nicholas
Barkley, Thomas 40; Ontario, 1871 1823.15 p12
Barlee, Mr.; Portland, Maine, 1858 9196.15 p27
Barley, E. A. 28; Ontario, 1861 2896.28 p2
Barley, George, Sr. 58; Ontario, 1861 2896.28 p2
Barling, Aaron; Baltimore, 1810 1224.3 p4
Barlington, Wm; Virginia, 1666 6212.30 p25
Barloe, Samuel; Maryland, 1668 2524.55 p17
Barlow, Henry; Maryland, 1657 2524.55 p17
Barlow, Jane; Virginia, 1797 1224.2 p7
Barlow, John; Rochester, New York, 1841 1224.3 p4
Barlow, John 21; Maryland, 1775 1220.25 p108
Barlow, Jonathan 24; Nova Scotia, 1774 1220.25 p136
Barlow, Katherine; Maryland, 1675 2524.55 p17
Barlow, Nancy; Georgia, 1790-1845 1640.10 p9
Barlow, Samuel; Virginia, 1716 1224.2 p7
Barlow, Thomas; Virginia, 1797 1224.2 p7
Barmann, Ms.; Port uncertain, 1742 2856.30 p61
Barmby, Ellen; New York, 1846 1224.3 p4
Barn, Joseph 68; Philadelphia, 1774 1220.25 p25
Barnabe, John; Virginia, 1636 1224.1 p5
Barnaby, Elizabeth *SEE* Barnaby, James
Barnaby, James; Maryland, 1665 2524.55 p17
Relative: Mary
Relative: Elizabeth
Relative: Rebeccah
Barnaby, Jno; Virginia, 1665-1666 6212.30 p23
Barnaby, Mary *SEE* Barnaby, James
Barnaby, Mary; Maryland, 1668 2524.55 p17
Barnaby, Rebeccah *SEE* Barnaby, James
Barnard, John; Maryland, 1670 2524.55 p17
Wife: Thomasin
Barnard, John 24; Maryland, 1774 1220.25 p52
Barnard, John 24; Maryland, 1774 1220.25 p84
Barnard, Robt; Virginia, 1665-1666 6212.30 p21
Barnard, Thomasin *SEE* Barnard, John
Barnard, William 20; Virginia, 1774 1220.25 p94
Barnard, William 22; Baltimore, 1775 1220.25 p118
Barnare, Robt; Virginia, 1665-1666 6212.30 p21
Barnback, Otto 54; Ontario, 1871 1823.15 p13
Barnby, J.; Portland, Maine, 1857 9196.15 p13
Barnby, John 49; Ontario, 1871 1823.15 p13
Barnby, Thomas 45; Ontario, 1871 1823.15 p13
Barnby, William; Portland, Maine, 1857 9196.15 p13
Barne, Thomas 25; Maryland, 1775 1220.25 p113
Barne, Wm.; Maryland, 1669 2524.55 p17
Barnes, A. H. 24; Alaska, 1912 9196.1 p37
Barnes, A. H. 24; Whitehorse, Yukon, 1912 9196.1 p37
Barnes, Alice *SEE* Barnes, Francis
Barnes, Benjamin; Maryland, 1681 2524.55 p17
Barnes, Catherine; Vermont, 1883 5900.10 p603
Barnes, Charles; Kentucky, 1809 1224.3 p4
Barnes, Dorothy *SEE* Barnes, Francis, Jr.
Barnes, Edward; Maryland, 1679 2524.55 p17
Barnes, Edward 27; Philadelphia, 1775 1220.25 p8
Barnes, Edwin A. 38; Vermont, 1875 5900.10 p457
Barnes, Elizabeth; Maryland, 1666 2524.55 p17
Barnes, Elizabeth; Maryland, 1681 2524.55 p17
Barnes, Elizabeth 18; Maryland, 1775 1220.25 p109
Barnes, Esther; Vermont, 1836-1905 5900.10 p68
Barnes, Fran; Virginia, 1677 6212.30 p53
Barnes, Francis; Maryland, 1657 2524.55 p168
Barnes, Francis; Maryland, 1666 2524.55 p17
Wife: Isabell
Child: Thomas
Child: Alice
Barnes, Francis, Jr.; Maryland, 1666 2524.55 p17
Daughter: Mary
Daughter: Dorothy
Barnes, Frederick 33; Ontario, 1871 1823.15 p13
Barnes, Geo; Virginia, 1690-1691 6212.30 p59
Barnes, Henry; Maryland, 1651 2524.55 p17
Barnes, Henry; Virginia, 1678 6212.30 p54
Barnes, Isabell *SEE* Barnes, Francis
Barnes, James; New York, 1838 8197.10 p111
Barnes, James 75; Ontario, 1871 1823.15 p13
Barnes, Jno; Virginia, 1674 6212.30 p52
Barnes, John; Georgia, 1740 1224.2 p7
Barnes, John; Maryland, 1679 2524.55 p17
Barnes, John; New York, 1837 8197.10 p212
Barnes, John; New York, 1839 8197.10 p129
Barnes, John; Pennsylvania, 1777 4629.10 p23
Barnes, John; Pennsylvania, 1786 4629.10 p51
Barnes, John 59; Ontario, 1871 1823.15 p13
Barnes, Joshua; Maryland, 1672 2524.55 p17
Barnes, Margaret; Vermont, 1860-1940 5900.10 p351
Barnes, Mary *SEE* Barnes, Francis, Jr.
Barnes, Mary; Maryland, 1860 2524.55 p17
Barnes, Mary; New York, 1837 8197.10 p212
Barnes, Mary; North America, 1808 1224.3 p4
Barnes, Mary Carroll; Vermont, 1883 5900.10 p470
Barnes, Michael; Vermont, 1852-1920 5900.10 p488
Barnes, Nellie; Vermont, 1861-1951 5900.10 p488
Barnes, Patrick; Vermont, 1854-1935 5900.10 p351
Barnes, Patrick; Vermont, 1876 5900.10 p470
Barnes, R.; Mobile, Alabama, 1818-1845 1640.10 p9
Barnes, Richard; Maryland, 1680 2524.55 p168
Barnes, Richard; Virginia, 1664-1665 6212.30 p16
Barnes, Robert; New York, 1794 8197.10 p3
Barnes, Samuel C.; New York, 1836 8197.10 p212
Barnes, Samuel C.; New York, 1839 8197.10 p128
Barnes, Sarah; New England, 1646 1224.1 p9
Barnes, Sarah; New England, 1652 1224.1 p65
Barnes, Thomas *SEE* Barnes, Francis
Barnes, Thomas; New England, 1690 1224.1 p5
Barnes, William; New York, 1807 8197.10 p34
Barnes, Wm; Virginia, 1690-1691 6212.30 p59
Barnet, Fran; Virginia, 1684-1685 6212.30 p57
Barnet, George 40; Ontario, 1871 1823.15 p13
Barnet, Jacob; Virginia, 1683 6212.30 p56
Barnet, Jno; Virginia, 1693-1694 6212.30 p60
Barnet, Steph; Virginia, 1688 6212.30 p57
Barnet, Susan 49; Ontario, 1871 1823.28 p4
Barnet, Thomas 22; Maryland, 1775 1220.25 p106
Barnett, A. O. 5; Ontario, 1861 2896.27 p7
Barnett, Alfred 32; Ontario, 1861 2896.27 p7
Barnett, C. B. 7; Ontario, 1861 2896.27 p7
Barnett, Charles 45; Ontario, 1871 1823.22 p7
Barnett, Ed 10; Ontario, 1861 2896.27 p7
Barnett, F. J. 2; Ontario, 1861 2896.27 p7
Barnett, James 34; Ontario, 1871 1823.22 p7
Barnett, Jonathan; Maryland, 1654 2524.55 p17
Barnett, Mary; Maryland, 1682 2524.55 p17
Barnett, Nicholas; Maryland, 1665 2524.55 p24
Barnett, Thomas; Maryland, 1681 2524.55 p17
Barnett, William; New York, 1837 8197.10 p85
Barney, Adelaide; Vermont, 1827-1910 5900.10 p594
Barney, Byron B.; Vermont, 1828-1905 5900.10 p514
Barney, John 42; Ontario, 1871 1823.22 p7
Barney, Mary Quinn; Vermont, 1859-1924 5900.10 p514
Barney, Nancy 40; Vermont, 1855 5900.10 p190
Barney, Sarah J. Wallace; Vermont, 1840-1883 5900.10 p519
Barnfeild, John; Virginia, 1667 6212.30 p37
Barnham, Robert; Virginia, 1664 6212.30 p13
Barnhill, Robert; Pennsylvania, 1777 4629.10 p6
Barnhouse, Abigall; Virginia, 1666-1667 6212.30 p35
Barnicle, Catherine 71; Vermont, 1887 5900.10 p206
Barnier, Peter; Philadelphia, 1770 1224.2 p7
Barnim, Michael; Port uncertain, 1764 2856.30 p15
Barnowski, Joseph; Maryland, 1910 3259.35 p2
Barns, Aaron 33, Ontario, 1871 1823.22 p7
Barns, Frederick 45; Ontario, 1871 1823.15 p13
Barns, George; Pennsylvania, 1777 4629.10 p21
Barns, Jesse W. 5; Ontario, 1861 2896.28 p57
Barns, John 40; Ontario, 1871 1823.28 p4
Barnsby, Edward; New York, 1838 8197.10 p111
Barnsdall, John; New York, 1826 8197.10 p210
Barnsdall, John; New York, New York, 1836 8197.10 p311
Barnsley, Edward; New York, 1838 8197.10 p111
Barnsley, Thomas; Pennsylvania, 1774 1224.2 p7
Barnston, William; New York, 1807 8197.10 p34
Barnstow, John 42; Philadelphia, 1774 1220.25 p25
Barnwell, Luke; Maryland, 1667 2524.55 p17
Barnwell, T.; Quebec, 1858 9196.15 p35
Baro, Johann Adam; Port uncertain, 1788 2856.30 p15
Baro, Johann Adam; Port uncertain, 1789 2856.30 p15
Baroff, A. 23; Alaska, 1917 9196.1 p46
Baroff, A. 23; Whitehorse, Yukon, 1917 9196.1 p46
Barohn, Mary; Maryland, 1910 3259.35 p3
Baron, Gertrayt Van Heyst *SEE* Baron, Michael
Baron, Johann Adam; Port uncertain, 1788 2856.30 p15
Baron, Johann Adam; Port uncertain, 1789 2856.30 p15
Baron, Michael; Maryland, 1669 2524.55 p17
Wife: Gertrayt Van Heyst
With 2 stepchildren
Baronnet, Jean; New York, 1835 8197.10 p212
Barounies, M. 45; Juneau, Alaska, 1917 9196.1 p45
Barounies, M. 45; Whitehorse, Yukon, 1917 9196.1 p45

Barowski, Stanislaus; Maryland, 1910 **3259.35** *p3*
Barr, Mr.; Quebec, 1858 **9196.15** *p38*
Barr, Mr.; Quebec, 1858 **9196.15** *p41*
Barr, Mrs.; Quebec, 1858 **9196.15** *p38*
Barr, Alexander; Savannah, Georgia, 1801 **1640.10** *p10*
Barr, Alexander 45; Ontario, 1871 **1823.15** *p13*
Barr, Ann 49; Ontario, 1871 **1823.15** *p13*
Barr, Elizabeth; Canada, 1844 **1640.13** *p7*
Barr, Elizabeth 65; Ontario, 1871 **1823.28** *p4*
Barr, Hugh; New York, 1807 **8197.10** *p331*
Barr, James; New York, 1806 **8197.10** *p30*
Barr, James; Pennsylvania, 1777 **4629.10** *p17*
Barr, James 32; Maryland, 1775 **1220.25** *p101*
Barr, James 59; Ontario, 1871 **1823.15** *p13*
Barr, James 61; Ontario, 1871 **1823.28** *p4*
Barr, John; Pennsylvania, 1816 **6058.10** *p5*
Barr, John 51; Ontario, 1871 **1823.28** *p4*
Barr, Mathew 56; Ontario, 1871 **1823.15** *p13*
Barr, Matthew; New York, 1818 **8197.10** *p206*
Barr, Matthew 85; Ontario, 1871 **1823.28** *p4*
Barr, Philip; New York, 1806 **8197.10** *p324*
Barr, Robert; New York, 1805 **8197.10** *p28*
Barr, Robert; Pennsylvania, 1779 **4629.10** *p41*
Barr, Samuel 44; Ontario, 1871 **1823.15** *p13*
Barr, Thomas; Terre Haute, Indiana, 1884 **1640.13** *p7*
Barr, Thomas 22; Virginia, 1775 **1220.25** *p110*
Barr, William 54; Ontario, 1871 **1823.15** *p13*
Barra, John 61; Ontario, 1861 **2896.26** *p21*
Barrack, William; New York, New York, 1777 **1224.2** *p7*
Barrajyucki, Ramazki; Maryland, 1910 **3259.35** *p3*
Barranouski, Leona; Maryland, 1910 **3259.35** *p3*
Barras, Stephen; New York, 1803 **8197.10** *p10*
Barrat, Austin; Pennsylvania, 1866 **6058.10** *p52*
Barratt, James 25; Maryland, 1774 **1220.25** *p5*
Barrell, Francis; Virginia, 1664 **6212.30** *p14*
Barrell, John; Virginia, 1665-1666 **6212.30** *p24*
Barrell, Moses; Virginia, 1663 **6212.30** *p4*
Barrell, Theodore; New York, 1847 **1224.3** *p4*
Barrenger, William 25; Ontario, 1871 **1823.22** *p7*
Barres, Cars; New York, 1840 **8197.10** *p155*
Barret, William 28; Maryland, 1775 **1220.25** *p108*
Barrett, Mr.; Quebec, 1858 **9196.15** *p33*
Barrett, Alice *SEE* Barrett, Thomas
Barrett, Alice; Vermont, 1906 **5900.10** *p524*
Barrett, Alice 52; Vermont, 1880 **5900.10** *p525*
Barrett, Ann; Virginia, 1755 **1224.2** *p97*
Barrett, Anna Breen 72; Vermont, 1868 **5900.10** *p523*
Barrett, Bridget 34; Vermont, 1892 **5900.10** *p400*
Barrett, Bridget Cain; Vermont, 1849-1940 **5900.10** *p424*
Barrett, Catharine 35; Vermont, 1857 **5900.10** *p524*
Barrett, Catherine; Vermont, 1840-1921 **5900.10** *p181*
Barrett, Catherine Flannigan 28; Vermont, 1851 **5900.10** *p523*
Barrett, Celia; Vermont, 1830-1895 **5900.10** *p523*
Barrett, Charles; Vermont, n.d. **5900.10** *p523*
Barrett, Christopher; Maryland, 1666 **2524.55** *p205*
Barrett, Darby; Maryland, 1678 **2524.55** *p17*
Barrett, Dennis 50; Ontario, 1871 **1823.28** *p4*
Barrett, Diana *SEE* Barrett, Thomas
Barrett, Edward; Vermont, 1857-1925 **5900.10** *p59*
Barrett, Edward L. 23; Vermont, n.d. **5900.10** *p523*
Barrett, Elizabeth *SEE* Barrett, Thomas
Barrett, Elizabeth; Vermont, 1857-1938 **5900.10** *p535*
Barrett, Elizabeth A.; Vermont, 1857-1957 **5900.10** *p523*
Barrett, Elizabeth Breen; Vermont, 1827-1912 **5900.10** *p523*
Barrett, Elizabeth Brophy 75; Vermont, 1898 **5900.10** *p400*
Barrett, Elizabeth Conners 70; Vermont, 1868 **5900.10** *p523*
Barrett, Ellen E. 13; Vermont, 1875 **5900.10** *p523*
Barrett, Francis; Vermont, 1839-1905 **5900.10** *p532*
Barrett, Francis; Vermont, 1855-1856 **5900.10** *p523*
Barrett, Frank 1; Vermont, 1853 **5900.10** *p523*
Barrett, Frederick; Vermont, 1869-1888 **5900.10** *p523*
Barrett, Frederick H.; Vermont, 1862-1904 **5900.10** *p323*
Barrett, George; Maryland, 1657 **2524.55** *p18*
Barrett, George; Maryland, 1666 **2524.55** *p18*
Barrett, James; Kansas, 1861 **6058.10** *p68*
Barrett, James; Vermont, 1834-1934 **5900.10** *p167*
Barrett, James 18; Ontario, 1871 **1823.28** *p4*
Barrett, James 50; Ontario, 1871 **1823.15** *p13*
Barrett, Joanna; Vermont, 1835-1921 **5900.10** *p183*
Barrett, John; Maryland, 1666 **2524.55** *p205*
Barrett, John; Vermont, 1836-1925 **5900.10** *p307*
Barrett, John; Vermont, 1844-1909 **5900.10** *p424*
Barrett, John; Vermont, 1851-1928 **5900.10** *p400*
Barrett, John 19; Ontario, 1871 **1823.15** *p13*
Barrett, John 79; Vermont, 1871 **5900.10** *p523*
Barrett, John 83; Vermont, 1902 **5900.10** *p573*
Barrett, John H.; Vermont, 1866-1869 **5900.10** *p523*
Barrett, John W.; Vermont, 1854-1909 **5900.10** *p523*
Barrett, Julia; Vermont, 1830-1908 **5900.10** *p287*
Barrett, Luke 28; Vermont, 1855 **5900.10** *p523*
Barrett, Luke F.; Vermont, 1859-1959 **5900.10** *p523*
Barrett, Margaret; Vermont, 1836-1926 **5900.10** *p257*
Barrett, Margaret Durick 40; Vermont, 1874 **5900.10** *p573*
Barrett, Margaret K.; Vermont, 1860-1936 **5900.10** *p400*
Barrett, Margaret Tunney 40; Vermont, 1876 **5900.10** *p523*
Barrett, Margarett; Maryland, 1654 **2524.55** *p18*
Barrett, Mary; Vermont, 1844-1874 **5900.10** *p271*
Barrett, Mary; Vermont, 1861-1934 **5900.10** *p256*
Barrett, Mary 38; Vermont, 1863 **5900.10** *p524*
Barrett, Mary A.; Vermont, 1818-1903 **5900.10** *p529*
Barrett, Mary A. Jerry; Vermont, 1859-1935 **5900.10** *p400*
Barrett, Mary Cavanaugh; Vermont, 1832-1905 **5900.10** *p167*
Barrett, Mary E.; Vermont, n.d. **5900.10** *p523*
Barrett, Mary McTierney 38; Vermont, 1884 **5900.10** *p523*
Barrett, Mary T.; Vermont, 1864-1964 **5900.10** *p524*
Barrett, Mathias; Vermont, 1840-1918 **5900.10** *p307*
Barrett, Michael; Pennsylvania, 1867 **6058.10** *p57*
Barrett, Michael; Vermont, 1828-1888 **5900.10** *p523*
Barrett, Michael; Vermont, 1859-1878 **5900.10** *p523*
Barrett, Michael; Vermont, 1861-1961 **5900.10** *p523*
Barrett, Michael 75; Vermont, 1870 **5900.10** *p523*
Barrett, Nancy Doran; Vermont, 1843-1926 **5900.10** *p532*
Barrett, Patrick; Pennsylvania, 1867 **6058.10** *p57*
Barrett, Patrick; Vermont, 1829-1887 **5900.10** *p523*
Barrett, Patrick 27; Vermont, 1871 **5900.10** *p92*
Barrett, Patrick 28; Vermont, 1865 **5900.10** *p523*
Barrett, Patrick 80; Vermont, 1897 **5900.10** *p400*
Barrett, Patrick J.; Vermont, 1852-1903 **5900.10** *p400*
Barrett, Patrick Joseph; Vermont, 1857-1933 **5900.10** *p256*
Barrett, Patrick L.; Vermont, 1867-1967 **5900.10** *p524*
Barrett, Robert; Virginia, 1698 **1224.1** *p5*
Barrett, Sarah; Maryland, 1649 **2524.55** *p18*
Barrett, Sarah; Vermont, 1856-1936 **5900.10** *p528*
Barrett, Sarah 73; Ontario, 1871 **1823.15** *p13*
Barrett, Sarah Hogan; Vermont, 1859-1937 **5900.10** *p59*
Barrett, Thomas; Maryland, 1673 **2524.55** *p18*
Relative: Diana
Relative: Elizabeth
Relative: Alice
Barrett, Thomas; Vermont, 1853 **5900.10** *p523*
Barrett, Thomas F. 66; Vermont, 1913 **5900.10** *p164*
Barrett, Walter; Maryland, 1659 **2524.55** *p18*
Barrett, William 16; Philadelphia, 1774 **1220.25** *p44*
Barrett, William 67; Ontario, 1871 **1823.22** *p7*
Barrett, William H. 25; Ontario, 1871 **1823.22** *p7*
Barrey, Ann; Vermont, 1818-1894 **5900.10** *p529*
Barrey, Hannah; Vermont, 1831-1891 **5900.10** *p234*
Barrick, Jno; Virginia, 1677 **6212.30** *p53*
Barrick, John; Virginia, 1684-1685 **6212.30** *p57*
Barrido, L. 22; Washington, 1914 **9196.1** *p65*
Barrie, Andreas; America, 1744 **2856.30** *p15*
With family
Barrie, James; Savannah, Georgia, 1817 **1640,10** *p10*
Barrie, Robert; Florida, 1775 **1224.2** *p7*
Barrie, Robert; Florida, 1775 **1640.10** *p10*
Barrie, Robert; Pensacola, Florida, 1791 **1640.10** *p10*
Barrie, Robert 66; Ontario, 1871 **1823.28** *p4*
Barriff, Edwd; Virginia, 1671 **6212.30** *p44*
Barriger, William 95; Ontario, 1871 **1823.22** *p8*
Barrill, Edmd; Virginia, 1671 **6212.30** *p44*
Barringer, Angeline 18; Ontario, 1861 **2896.28** *p31*
Barringer, Mary 16; Ontario, 1861 **2896.28** *p31*
Barringer, Paul; New York, 1840 **8197.10** *p153*
Barrington, Edward A.; New York, 1839 **8197.10** *p127*
Barrington, John; Virginia, 1666-1667 **6212.30** *p33*
Barris, Simeon 35; Ontario, 1871 **1823.15** *p13*
Barritt, Joanna Scantlebury; New York, 1854 **1224.3** *p4*
Barrolett, William; Maryland, 1681 **2524.55** *p18*
Barron, Abraham *SEE* Barron, Michaell
Barron, Alexander; New York, 1810 **1640.10** *p10*
Barron, Alexander 48; Ontario, 1871 **1823.15** *p13*
Barron, Alexander 59; Ontario, 1871 **1823.28** *p4*
Barron, Anna Hickey 70; Vermont, 1917 **5900.10** *p378*
Barron, Charlotte Keith; Charles Town, South Carolina, 1807 **1224.3** *p4*
Barron, Frederick William 60; Ontario, 1871 **1823.22** *p8*
Barron, Gertrude *SEE* Barron, Michaell
Barron, James; Maryland, 1910 **3259.35** *p3*
Barron, John; New York, 1806 **8197.10** *p323*
Barron, John; New York, 1838 **8197.10** *p111*
Barron, John; Pennsylvania, 1777 **4629.10** *p24*
Barron, Julia Slattery 66; Vermont, 1892 **5900.10** *p167*
Barron, Margaret; Vermont, 1868-1946 **5900.10** *p256*
Barron, Michaell; Maryland, 1668 **2524.55** *p18*
Wife: Gertrude
Son: Abraham
Son: Rineres
Barron, Patrick; New York, 1837 **8197.10** *p84*
Barron, Patrick 58; Vermont, 1877 **5900.10** *p167*
Barron, Patrick 63; Vermont, 1901 **5900.10** *p378*
Barron, Rineres *SEE* Barron, Michaell
Barron, Sylvester 20; Vermont, 1878 **5900.10** *p155*
Barron, William 48; Ontario, 1871 **1823.22** *p8*
Barrot, Austin; Pennsylvania, 1866 **6058.10** *p52*
Barrow, Mr.; Quebec, 1858 **9196.15** *p41*
Barrow, Mrs.; Quebec, 1856 **9196.15** *p8*
Barrow, Alexander 47; Ontario, 1871 **1823.15** *p13*
Barrow, Charles; Portland, Maine, 1858 **9196.15** *p29*
Barrow, John; Quebec, 1856 **9196.15** *p5*
Barrow, John; Virginia, 1666-1667 **6212.30** *p33*
Barrow, John; Virginia, 1671 **6212.30** *p44*
Barrow, John 33; Georgia, 1774 **1220.25** *p47*
Barrows, George 26; Ontario, 1871 **1823.15** *p13*
Barrows, Jacob 30; Ontario, 1871 **1823.15** *p13*
Barrows, Peter 58; Vermont, 1874 **5900.10** *p543*
Barrows, Simeon 68; Ontario, 1871 **1823.15** *p13*
Barrsley, Hannah *SEE* Barrsley, John
Barrsley, Hannahmary *SEE* Barrsley, John
Barrsley, John; Maryland, 1666 **2524.55** *p18*
Wife: Hannahmary
Daughter: Rebecca
Daughter: Hannah
Barrsley, Rebecca *SEE* Barrsley, John
Barrt, Bridget; Vermont, 1813-1887 **5900.10** *p176*
Barrufskie, Andrew; Maryland, 1910 **3259.35** *p3*
Barry, . . . 3 days; Vermont, 1864 **5900.10** *p315*
Barry, Mr.; Quebec, 1857 **9196.15** *p21*
Barry, Mr.; Vermont, n.d. **5900.10** *p130*
Barry, Mrs.; Vermont, n.d. **5900.10** *p130*
Barry, Alexander A.; Vermont, 1852-1937 **5900.10** *p322*
Barry, Bridget; Vermont, 1852-1895 **5900.10** *p174*
Barry, Catherine Downs 69; Vermont, 1894 **5900.10** *p129*
Barry, Catherine Hanrahan; Vermont, 1833-1873 **5900.10** *p231*
Barry, David; New York, 1838 **8197.10** *p111*
Barry, David 75; Vermont, 1895 **5900.10** *p370*
Barry, Dennis 78; Vermont, 1892 **5900.10** *p71*
Barry, Edmund; New York, 1834 **8197.10** *p372*
Barry, Edward; New York, 1841 **1224.3** *p4*
Barry, Edward D.; New York, 1810 **8197.10** *p56*
Barry, Edward M.; Vermont, 1859-1941 **5900.10** *p67*
Barry, Eliza; Vermont, 1825-1900 **5900.10** *p95*
Barry, Ellen; Vermont, 1824-1897 **5900.10** *p187*
Barry, Ellen; Vermont, 1853-1932 **5900.10** *p445*
Barry, Ellen 59; Vermont, 1878 **5900.10** *p317*
Barry, Ellen Bowler; Vermont, 1857-1940 **5900.10** *p68*
Barry, Ellen Moore; Vermont, 1840-1882 **5900.10** *p81*
Barry, Florence 48; Ontario, 1871 **1823.15** *p13*
Barry, Francis; New York, 1839 **8197.10** *p128*
Barry, Garrett 84; Vermont, 1873 **5900.10** *p230*
Barry, Hannah Cronan; Vermont, 1854-1929 **5900.10** *p299*
Barry, Hanora; Vermont, 1816-1905 **5900.10** *p586*
Barry, Hanora Downs; Vermont, 1820-1893 **5900.10** *p159*
Barry, James; New York, 1812 **8197.10** *p206*
Barry, James; Vermont, 1818-1902 **5900.10** *p129*
Barry, James; Vermont, 1826-1881 **5900.10** *p315*
Barry, James 35; Vermont, 1887 **5900.10** *p299*
Barry, James 50; Ontario, 1871 **1823.28** *p4*
Barry, James 57; Vermont, 1908 **5900.10** *p509*
Barry, James G.; Vermont, 1852-1909 **5900.10** *p315*
Barry, Joe 25; Washington, 1912 **9196.1** *p36*
Barry, John; America, n.d. **4628.40** *p49*
Barry, John; Maryland, 1680 **2524.55** *p18*
Barry, John; Maryland, 1681 **2524.55** *p18*
Barry, John; Maryland, 1682 **2524.55** *p18*
Barry, John; New York, 1807 **8197.10** *p35*
Barry, John; New York, 1826 **8197.10** *p337*
Barry, John; New York, 1838 **8197.10** *p109*
Barry, John; Vermont, 1810-1894 **5900.10** *p159*
Barry, John; Vermont, 1818-1900 **5900.10** *p273*
Barry, John; Vermont, 1835-1916 **5900.10** *p231*
Barry, John 41; Ontario, 1871 **1823.28** *p4*
Barry, John 50; Ontario, 1871 **1823.15** *p13*
Barry, John 60; Ontario, 1871 **1823.15** *p13*
Barry, John 60; Ontario, 1871 **1823.22** *p8*
Barry, John 68; Vermont, 1877 **5900.10** *p405*
Barry, John J.; Vermont, 1855-1924 **5900.10** *p159*
Barry, Joseph; Pennsylvania, 1777 **4629.10** *p16*
Barry, Julia; Vermont, 1838-1916 **5900.10** *p316*
Barry, Julia; Vermont, 1852-1911 **5900.10** *p395*
Barry, Julia 76; Vermont, 1936 **5900.10** *p314*
Barry, Julia A.; Vermont, 1860-1949 **5900.10** *p316*
Barry, Julia A.; Vermont, 1868-1940 **5900.10** *p484*

Barry, Katherine; Vermont, 1783-1871 5900.10 p305
Barry, Katherine 88; Vermont, 1871 5900.10 p306
Barry, Lackey; New York, 1827 8197.10 p211
Barry, Lawrence; New York, 1829 8197.10 p351
Barry, Lawrence; Pennsylvania, 1777 4629.10 p16
Barry, Lois Eldred; Vermont, 1846-1912 5900.10 p71
Barry, M. Elizabeth; Vermont, 1858-1932 5900.10 p316
Barry, M. J.; Vermont, 1855-1926 5900.10 p129
Barry, Margaret; Maryland, 1680 2524.55 p18
Barry, Margaret; Vermont, n.d. 5900.10 p130
Barry, Margaret; Vermont, 1803-1878 5900.10 p81
Barry, Margaret 50; Vermont, 1890 5900.10 p176
Barry, Margaret 56; Vermont, 1898 5900.10 p612
Barry, Margaret Elizabeth 5 weeks; Vermont, 1847 5900.10 p315
Barry, Margaret O'Rourke; Vermont, 1830-1902 5900.10 p316
Barry, Maria; Vermont, 1851-1887 5900.10 p315
Barry, Marry 55; Vermont, 1901 5900.10 p510
Barry, Martin; Pennsylvania, 1778 4629.10 p45
Barry, Mary; Vermont, n.d. 5900.10 p130
Barry, Mary; Vermont, 1823-1887 5900.10 p231
Barry, Mary; Vermont, 1823-1912 5900.10 p424
Barry, Mary; Vermont, 1827-1889 5900.10 p446
Barry, Mary 37; Ontario, 1871 1823.22 p8
Barry, Mary 67; Ontario, 1871 1823.28 p4
Barry, Mary Ann 9; Vermont, 1864 5900.10 p315
Barry, Mary Daly 63; Vermont, 1883 5900.10 p315
Barry, Mary Dooley; Vermont, 1836-1908 5900.10 p273
Barry, Mary E. 75; Vermont, 1927 5900.10 p445
Barry, Mary Garvey; Vermont, 1859-1928 5900.10 p159
Barry, Mary Hanley; Vermont, 1831-1904 5900.10 p230
Barry, Mary J. Burke; Vermont, 1868-1937 5900.10 p129
Barry, Mary McGrath 70; Vermont, 1894 5900.10 p370
Barry, Mary Raleigh; Vermont, 1858-1905 5900.10 p115
Barry, Mary Rourke; Vermont, 1822-1901 5900.10 p315
Barry, Michael; Vermont, n.d. 5900.10 p130
Barry, Patrick; New York, 1807 8197.10 p325
Barry, Patrick; Vermont, 1829-1905 5900.10 p81
Barry, Patrick 45; Ontario, 1871 1823.22 p8
Barry, Patrick 50; Ontario, 1871 1823.15 p13
Barry, Patrick 71; Vermont, 1891 5900.10 p603
Barry, Patrick 72; Ontario, 1871 1823.15 p13
Barry, Patrick 72; Ontario, 1871 1823.22 p8
Barry, Patrick C.; Vermont, 1828-1912 5900.10 p230
Barry, Rose; Vermont, n.d. 5900.10 p130
Barry, Sophia Brunelle; Vermont, 1846-1937 5900.10 p322
Barry, Theodorous; Pennsylvania, 1777 4629.10 p16
Barry, Thomas; New York, 1837 8197.10 p84
Barry, Thomas; Pennsylvania, 1779 4629.10 p40
Barry, Thomas; Vermont, 1826-1863 5900.10 p316
Barry, Thomas; Vermont, 1828-1919 5900.10 p612
Barry, Thomas 40; Vermont, 1852 5900.10 p315
Barry, Thomas 71; Ontario, 1871 1823.15 p13
Barry, Vincent; Virginia, 1664 6212.30 p11
Barry, William; Vermont, n.d. 5900.10 p130
Barry, William 25; Maryland, 1774 1220.25 p7
Barry, William 41; Ontario, 1871 1823.22 p8
Barryk, Peter; Maryland, 1910 3259.35 p3
Barston, Thomas; Maryland, 1668 2524.55 p39
Barsy, Lydia; Maryland, 1658 2524.55 p237
Bart, Eva; Port uncertain, 1749 2856.30 p15
Bart, Juliana; Port uncertain, 1775 2856.30 p16
Bart, Maria Catharina; Port uncertain, 1783 2856.30 p16
Bart, Maria Christian; Port uncertain, 1787 2856.30 p16
Bart, Michael; Port uncertain, 1749 2856.30 p16
Bartecki, Thomas; Maryland, 1910 3259.35 p3
Bartell, Jane 20; Ontario, 1871 1823.15 p13
Bartemy, Caroline Miles; Vermont, 1840-1940 5900.10 p193
Bartemy, Edward; Vermont, 1836-1912 5900.10 p193
Bartenbach, Ferdinand; America, 1738 2856.30 p16
With wife
Bartenbach, Ferdinand; Port uncertain, 1735 2856.30 p16
Bartenbach, Ferdinand; Port uncertain, 1739 2856.30 p16
With wife
Barter, Mr.; Quebec, 1858 9196.15 p37
Barter, Mrs.; Quebec, 1858 9196.15 p37
Barter, John; Baltimore, 1817 8197.10 p62
Barter, William 41; Virginia, 1774 1220.25 p55
Barth, Anna Maria; Port uncertain, 1778 2856.30 p16
Barth, Anna Maria; Port uncertain, 1781 2856.30 p16
Barth, Barbara; Port uncertain, 1724 2856.30 p16
Barth, Barbara; Port uncertain, 1762 2856.30 p16
Barth, Bartol; Port uncertain, 1762 2856.30 p16
Barth, Caspar; Port uncertain, 1749 2856.30 p16
Barth, Catharina; Port uncertain, 1700-1799 2856.30 p16
Barth, Elisabeth; Port uncertain, 1763 2856.30 p16
Barth, Elisabeth; Port uncertain, 1775 2856.30 p16
Barth, Eva Catharina; Port uncertain, 1754 2856.30 p16
Barth, Jacob; America, 1736 2856.30 p16
Barth, Jacob; Port uncertain, 1731 2856.30 p16
Barth, Jacob; Port uncertain, 1784 2856.30 p16
Barth, Johann Jacob; Port uncertain, 1775 2856.30 p16
Barth, Johann Michael; Port uncertain, 1781 2856.30 p16
Barth, Johann Peter; Port uncertain, 1747 2856.30 p16
With wife & 4 children
Barth, Johann Wilhelm; America, 1773 2856.30 p16
Barth, Johann Wilhelm; America, 1784 2856.30 p16
Barth, John Michael; Pennsylvania, 1786 4629.10 p51
Barth, Konrad; Port uncertain, 1742 2856.30 p16
Barth, Peter; Port uncertain, 1727 2856.30 p16
Barth, Philipp; Port uncertain, 1752 2856.30 p16
Barth, Wilhelm; Port uncertain, 1751 2856.30 p16
Barth, Wilhelm; Port uncertain, 1783 2856.30 p16
Barth, Zacharias Karl; Port uncertain, 1791 2856.30 p16
Barthel, Anna Elisabeth; America, 1752 2856.30 p17
With child
Barthel, Conrad; New York, 1807 8197.10 p35
Barthemes, Peter; America, 1755 2856.30 p17
Barth Meyer, Christof; America, 1751 2856.30 p16
Barthol, Franz; Port uncertain, 1761 2856.30 p17
Bartholome, Andreas; Port uncertain, 1726 2856.30 p17
Bartholome, Johann; America, 1738 2856.30 p17
Bartholome, Peter; America, 1741 2856.30 p17
Bartholome, Peter; America, 1743 2856.30 p17
Bartholomew, Edward; Pennsylvania, 1779 4629.10 p41
Bartholomew, Mary; Maryland, 1672 2524.55 p18
Bartholomew, William 21; Virginia, 1774 1220.25 p55
Barthug, Christleb; Pennsylvania, 1777 4629.10 p8
Bartiff, James 49; Ontario, 1871 1823.15 p13
Bartin, Francis; Philadelphia, 1789 4629.10 p58
Wife: Mary
Bartin, H. 75; Ontario, 1861 2896.28 p13
Bartin, Joseph 28; Philadelphia, 1789 4629.10 p58
Bartin, Margarete; Port uncertain, 1758 2856.30 p17
Bartin, Mary *SEE* Bartin, Francis
Bartin, William; Pennsylvania, 1777 4629.10 p7
Bartkowak, Michael; Maryland, 1910 3259.35 p3
Bartkowiak, Frank; Maryland, 1910 3259.35 p3
Bartkowiak, Henry; Maryland, 1910 3259.35 p3
Bartkowiak, Stanley F.; Maryland, 1910 3259.35 p3
Bartkowska, Mary; Maryland, 1910 3259.35 p3
Bartkowski, Frank; Maryland, 1910 3259.35 p3
Bartkowski, Martin; Maryland, 1910 3259.35 p3
Bartle, John 42; Ontario, 1871 1823.28 p4
Bartle, Katherine; Maryland, 1673 2524.55 p18
Bartleson, Humming; Maryland, 1671 2524.55 p18
Bartlet, Mrs. 30; Grenada, 1776 1220.25 p129
Bartlet, Ellis; Virginia, 1666 6212.30 p30
Bartlet, James 30; Grenada, 1776 1220.25 p129
Bartlet, Thomas 52; Ontario, 1871 1823.15 p13
Bartlett, A.; Mississippi, 1800-1845 1640.10 p10
Bartlett, Daniel 22; Ontario, 1861 2896.26 p2
Bartlett, David 67; Ontario, 1871 1823.15 p13
Bartlett, Eliza 51; Ontario, 1861 2896.26 p2
Bartlett, G. W. 19; Ontario, 1871 1823.28 p4
Bartlett, George; Maryland, 1665 2524.55 p18
Bartlett, George 21; Ontario, 1871 1823.22 p8
Bartlett, John 12; Philadelphia, 1774 1220.25 p4
Bartlett, L. M. 8; Ontario, 1861 2896.26 p2
Bartlett, M. A. 13; Ontario, 1861 2896.26 p2
Bartlett, Margaret; Vermont, 1825-1903 5900.10 p437
Bartlett, R. A. 11; Ontario, 1861 2896.26 p2
Bartlett, Rachel Pheasant; Maryland, 1798 1224.2 p7
Bartlett, Richard 19; Ontario, 1871 1823.22 p8
Bartlett, Robert; Maryland, 1651 2524.55 p18
Bartlett, Sarah; New England, 1728 1224.2 p7
Bartlett, W. M. 51; Ontario, 1861 2896.26 p2
Bartlett, William 32; Ontario, 1871 1823.22 p8
Bartley, Bridget 60; Vermont, 1892 5900.10 p466
Bartley, Elizabeth Monty; Vermont, 1850-1938 5900.10 p539
Bartley, Ellen; Vermont, 1821-1897 5900.10 p530
Bartley, James; Vermont, 1811-1894 5900.10 p543
Bartley, James; Vermont, 1816-1898 5900.10 p530
Bartley, Jeremiah J.; Vermont, 1840-1916 5900.10 p539
Bartley, John; Vermont, 1838-1868 5900.10 p543
Bartley, Margaret Sullivan; Vermont, 1818-1846 5900.10 p543
Bartley, Michael; New York, 1834 8197.10 p74
Bartley, Michael; Vermont, 1848-1865 5900.10 p543
Bartley, Nicholas; Maryland, 1662 2524.55 p18
Wife: Sarah
Bartley, Patrick 82; Vermont, 1913 5900.10 p563
Bartley, Sarah *SEE* Bartley, Nicholas
Bartley, Winifred Murphy 60; Vermont, 1897 5900.10 p563
Bartmann, Johann Georg; Port uncertain, 1754 2856.30 p17
With wife & 2 children
Bartmess, Peter; Port uncertain, 1761 2856.30 p17
Bartmesser, Johann Adam; Port uncertain, 1759 2856.30 p17
Bartok, Stanislow; Maryland, 1910 3259.35 p3
Barton, . . .; Pennsylvania, 1697 1224.1 p5
Barton, Mrs.; Maryland, 1661 2524.55 p18
Barton, A.; Quebec, 1858 9196.15 p40
Barton, Agustus 31; Ontario, 1871 1823.15 p13
Barton, Christopher 80; Ontario, 1871 1823.15 p13
Barton, Geo; Virginia, 1667-1668 6212.30 p38
Barton, Henry Lane; New Jersey, 1801 1224.3 p4
Barton, Isaac 87; Ontario, 1861 2896.28 p26
Barton, J. 85; Ontario, 1861 2896.28 p13
Barton, J. W.; Quebec, 1858 9196.15 p40
Barton, James 18; New York, 1775 1220.25 p94
Barton, John; Maryland, 1666 2524.55 p18
Barton, John; Quebec, 1858 9196.15 p31
Barton, John 2; Ontario, 1861 2896.25 p65
Barton, Joshua Joseph; New Orleans, 1849 1224.3 p4
Barton, Margarett *SEE* Barton, William
Barton, Margarett; Maryland, 1663 2524.55 p18
Barton, Margart 62; Ontario, 1871 1823.15 p13
Barton, Marmaduke; Maryland, 1667 2524.55 p18
Barton, Mary; Virginia, 1668-1669 6212.30 p40
Barton, Mary 26; Ontario, 1861 2896.25 p65
Barton, Mary Hayes; Vermont, 1879-1919 5900.10 p355
Barton, Melissa 5; Ontario, 1861 2896.25 p65
Barton, Nath; Virginia, 1674 6212.30 p52
Barton, Richard; New York, 1810 8197.10 p56
Barton, Robert 36; Ontario, 1871 1823.15 p13
Barton, Tho; Virginia, 1670 6212.30 p42
Barton, Thomas; Maryland, 1654 2524.55 p18
Barton, Thomas; South Carolina, 1735 1224.2 p7
Barton, Valentine; Maryland, 1673 2524.55 p18
Barton, William *SEE* Barton, William
Barton, William; Maryland, 1663 2524.55 p18
With wife
Child: Margarett
Child: William
Barton, William; Maryland, 1663 2524.55 p18
Barton, William; New York, 1828 8197.10 p211
Barton, William 7; Ontario, 1861 2896.25 p65
Barton, William 35; Virginia, 1775 1220.25 p122
Bartonewicz, John; Maryland, 1910 3259.35 p3
Bartor, Ann *SEE* Bartor, Nathan
Bartor, Nathan; Maryland, 1665 2524.55 p18
Wife: Ann
Bartoss, Franciscek J.; Maryland, 1910 3259.35 p3
Bartow, William H.; Maryland, 1910 3259.35 p3
Bartowiak, Stanislaus; Maryland, 1910 3259.35 p3
Bartrage, William 50; Ontario, 1871 1823.28 p4
Bartram, Andrew; New York, 1832 8197.10 p357
Bartram, Christian; Georgia, 1698 1640.13 p7
Bartram, George; Pennsylvania, 1786 4629.10 p49
Bartsch, Jacob; America, 1749 2856.30 p17
With wife
Barturn, Henry 48; Ontario, 1871 1823.15 p14
Bartz, Johann Friedric; America, 1738 2856.30 p17
Barumler, John; New York, 1838 8197.10 p212
Barwell, John; Maryland, 1658 2524.55 p18
Barwick, Thomas 26; Dominica, 1773-1774 1220.25 p32
Barwis, John; Virginia, 1666 6212.30 p29
Barylski, Michael; Maryland, 1910 3259.35 p3
Basach'sche, . . .; America, 1750 2856.30 p17
Baser, Barbara; Port uncertain, 1755 2856.30 p17
Bashaw, Harriett; Vermont, 1861-1936 5900.10 p462
Bashaw Monteith, Mary Brown; Vermont, 1854-1920 5900.10 p406
Bashford, James; New York, 1817 8197.10 p206
Basil, John; Maryland, 1658 2524.55 p20
Baskerfeild, Jno; Virginia, 1665-1666 6212.30 p23
Baskerville, John; Virginia, 1676 1224.1 p5
Baslay, William 23; Philadelphia, 1775 1220.25 p107
Basler, Jacob; Port uncertain, 1769 2856.30 p17
Basler, Josef; Port uncertain, 1771 2856.30 p17
Basler, Josef; Port uncertain, 1802 2856.30 p17
Basler, Matthaus; Port uncertain, 1784 2856.30 p17
Basler, Michael; Port uncertain, 1771 2856.30 p17
Basler, Michael; Port uncertain, 1802 2856.30 p17
Basoff, Jim 26; Alaska, 1917 9196.1 p45
Basoff, Jim 26; Whitehorse, Yukon, 1917 9196.1 p45
Basoff, Paul 31; Alaska, 1917 9196.1 p47
Basoff, Paul 31; Whitehorse, Yukon, 1917 9196.1 p47
Bass, Abraham 25; Maryland, 1774 1220.25 p77
Bass, George; New York, 1828 8197.10 p350
Basse, John; New York, 1825 8197.10 p297
Basset, Arthur; Virginia, 1666 6212.30 p30
Bassett, Alice; Maryland, 1663 2524.55 p51
Bassett, Ann; Maryland, 1675 2524.55 p18
Bassett, Edward 36; Ontario, 1871 1823.28 p4
Bassett, H.; Mobile, Alabama, 1788-1845 1640.10 p10
Bassett, John; New York, 1838 8197.10 p110
Bassett, John; New York, 1840 8197.10 p213
Bassett, Margarett *SEE* Bassett, Thomas

Bassett, Margarett; Maryland, 1659 *2524.55 p18*
Bassett, Peter; Maryland, 1675 *2524.55 p18*
Bassett, Thomas; Maryland, 1659 *2524.55 p18*
Wife: Margarett
Bassett, Thomas; Virginia, 1665 *6212.30 p20*
Bassey, Edmond; Maryland, 1672 *2524.55 p18*
Bassindine, Charles Boyle; Virginia, 1740 *1224.2 p7*
Bassip, William 26; Ontario, 1861 *2896.28 p12*
Bassler, Franz Josef; Port uncertain, 1798 *2856.30 p17*
Bassler, Henrich; America, 1732 *2856.30 p17*
Bassler, Johann Georg; Port uncertain, 1757 *2856.30 p17*
Bassler, Maria Margarete; Port uncertain, 1757 *2856.30 p17*
Basso, Jean; New York, 1818 *8197.10 p207*
Bast, Christina; America, 1764 *2856.30 p17*
Bast, David; America, 1749 *2856.30 p17*
Bast, Michael; Port uncertain, 1749 *2856.30 p16*
Bastable, Edw; Virginia, 1666-1667 *6212.30 p35*
Bastard, Captain; Quebec, 1858 *9196.15 p38*
Bastard, Abraham 45; Ontario, 1871 *1823.15 p14*
Bastard, Joseph 36; Ontario, 1871 *1823.15 p14*
Bastian, Hans Michel; America, 1738 *2856.30 p17*
Bastian, Mathias; America, 1751 *2856.30 p18*
With wife
Bastian, Michael; America, 1749 *2856.30 p17*
Bastian, Michael; America, 1749 *2856.30 p18*
With wife & 2 children
Basticke, Thomas; Maryland, 1664 *2524.55 p19*
Batchelder, William; Massachusetts, 1819 *1224.3 p5*
Batchelor, Elizabeth; New York, New York, 1857 *1224.3 p5*
Batchelor, Francis; Maryland, 1662 *2524.55 p19*
Relative: Sarah
Batchelor, H. 33; Washington, 1915 *9196.1 p67*
Batchelor, Sarah *SEE* Batchelor, Francis
Batchelor, Thomas 22; Maryland, 1774 *1220.25 p84*
Batchelor, William; Maryland, 1681 *2524.55 p19*
Bate, Mr.; Quebec, 1856 *9196.15 p6*
Bate, Alice; New England, 1657 *1224.1 p5*
Bate, Thomas; Maryland, 1680 *2524.55 p19*
Bate, William 53; Ontario, 1871 *1823.22 p8*
Bate, William 55; Ontario, 1871 *1823.22 p8*
Batelle, Miss; Quebec, 1858 *9196.15 p42*
Bateman, Anto; Virginia, 1664 *6212.30 p14*
Bateman, Anto; Virginia, 1665-1666 *6212.30 p22*
Bateman, Anto; Virginia, 1666-1667 *6212.30 p32*
Bateman, Benjamin 35; Maryland, 1775 *1220.25 p109*
Bateman, Edward *SEE* Bateman, Elizabeth
Bateman, Elizabeth *SEE* Bateman, Elizabeth
Bateman, Elizabeth; Maryland, 1673 *2524.55 p19*
Husband: Edward
Relative: Elizabeth
Relative: John
Relative: William
Bateman, Elizabeth; Maryland, 1682 *2524.55 p19*
Bateman, John *SEE* Bateman, Elizabeth
Bateman, John 21; Ontario, 1871 *1823.15 p14*
Bateman, John 23; Virginia, 1774 *1220.25 p46*
Bateman, Mary; Maryland, 1659 *2524.55 p19*
Bateman, Robert; Charles Town, South Carolina, 1728 *1224.2 p7*
Bateman, Sarah 21; Maryland, 1775 *1220.25 p112*
Bateman, Stephen; New York, 1838 *8197.10 p111*
Bateman, William *SEE* Bateman, Elizabeth
Bateman, William 23; Philadelphia, 1774 *1220.25 p44*
Bateman, William 39; Ontario, 1871 *1823.28 p4*
Batemata, Thomas 41; Ontario, 1871 *1823.28 p4*
Baten, William 56; Ontario, 1871 *1823.28 p4*
Batenosen, Thomas; Maryland, 1651 *2524.55 p218*
Batenson, Thomas; Maryland, 1651 *2524.55 p218*
Bates, Belle; Vermont, 1861-1958 *5900.10 p495*
Bates, Charles E.; Vermont, 1836-1910 *5900.10 p308*
Bates, Christi 62; Ontario, 1871 *1823.22 p8*
Bates, Clark 88; Ontario, 1861 *2896.25 p68*
Bates, George 14; Ontario, 1861 *2896.25 p68*
Bates, George 50; Ontario, 1871 *1823.15 p14*
Bates, James; Cincinnati, 1851 *1224.3 p5*
Bates, John 21; Virginia, 1774 *1220.25 p86*
Bates, John 27; Philadelphia, 1775 *1220.25 p122*
Bates, Joseph; Boston, 1776 *1224.2 p7*
Bates, Joseph; New York, 1813 *8197.10 p206*
Bates, Joseph; New York, 1840 *8197.10 p155*
Bates, Margaret 60; Ontario, 1861 *2896.28 p28*
Bates, Mary Hart; Vermont, 1844-1908 *5900.10 p308*
Bates, Mathew 65; Ontario, 1871 *1823.28 p4*
Bates, Nancy 53; Ontario, 1861 *2896.25 p68*
Bates, Nicolas 18; Ontario, 1861 *2896.25 p68*
Bates, Robert; New York, 1836 *8197.10 p212*
Bates, Robert; New York, 1840 *8197.10 p155*
Bates, Sarah 11; Ontario, 1861 *2896.25 p68*
Bates, Thedah 16; Ontario, 1861 *2896.25 p68*
Bates, Thomas 48; Ontario, 1871 *1823.15 p14*
Bates, William 11; Ontario, 1861 *2896.28 p28*
Bates, William Davis; New York, 1818 *8197.10 p207*
Bateson, Christopher 53; Ontario, 1871 *1823.22 p8*
Bateson, Henry 23; Maryland, 1774 *1220.25 p40*
Bateson, Robert 11; Ontario, 1861 *2896.25 p3*
Bath, George F.; New York, 1834 *8197.10 p73*
Bath, James; Maryland, 1674 *2524.55 p19*
Bath, John 23; Annapolis, Nova Scotia, 1775 *1220.25 p22*
Bath, William 35; Ontario, 1871 *1823.15 p14*
Bathgate, Carles; New York, 1832 *8197.10 p357*
Bathgate, James; New York, 1803 *8197.10 p11*
Bathhouer, Alexander 3; Kansas, 1907-1910 *9079.10 p15*
Bathhouer, Alexander 31; Kansas, 1907-1910 *9079.10 p15*
Bathhouer, Anna 5; Kansas, 1907-1910 *9079.10 p15*
Bathhouer, Anna 33; Kansas, 1907-1910 *9079.10 p15*
Bathhouer, Julia 16; Kansas, 1907-1910 *9079.10 p15*
Bathin, Jacob; Port uncertain, 1785 *2856.30 p61*
Bathour, John 27; Kansas, 1908-1910 *9079.10 p40*
Bathour, Mary 3; Kansas, 1908-1910 *9079.10 p40*
Bathour, Mary 24; Kansas, 1908-1910 *9079.10 p40*
Bathwill, James 75; Ontario, 1871 *1823.15 p14*
Batie, William; New York, New York, 1852 *6058.10 p52*
Batley, John; Connecticut, 1851 *1224.3 p5*
Batley, Joseph 36; Ontario, 1871 *1823.22 p8*
Batmison, Thomas; Maryland, 1650 *2524.55 p19*
Batmrson, Thomas; Maryland, 1650 *2524.55 p19*
Batoff, Jim 22; Alaska, 1917 *9196.1 p45*
Batoff, Jim 22; Whitehorse, Yukon, 1917 *9196.1 p45*
Batornniere, Auguste; New York, 1832 *8197.10 p68*
Batotsky, Lawrance; Maryland, 1910 *3259.35 p3*
Batrsbee, Francis; New York, 1825-1834 *8197.10 p307*
Bats, William 48; Ontario, 1871 *1823.22 p8*
Batsch, Johann; Port uncertain, 1789 *2856.30 p18*
Batson, James; New York, 1839 *8197.10 p129*
Batson, Sarah; New England, 1728 *1224.2 p7*
Batster, John; Maryland, 1910 *3259.35 p3*
Batt, Mary; South Carolina, 1719 *1224.2 p4*
Batt, Samuel 22; Maryland, 1774 *1220.25 p39*
Batt, Thomas 25; Virginia, 1774 *1220.25 p90*
Batt, William; Pennsylvania, 1777 *4629.10 p29*
Battea, John; Maryland, 1674 *2524.55 p19*
Batteiger, Valentin; America, 1767 *2856.30 p18*
Batteiger, Valentin; America, 1777 *2856.30 p18*
Battell, William 74; Ontario, 1871 *1823.22 p8*
Battels, Bridget 68; Vermont, 1890 *5900.10 p535*
Batten, Francis; Maryland, 1661 *2524.55 p19*
Batten, Frederick; New York, 1840 *8197.10 p154*
Batten, Henry; Maryland, 1659 *2524.55 p19*
Batten, Margery *SEE* Batten, William
Batten, Mary; Maryland, 1681 *2524.55 p19*
Batten, William; Maryland, 1651 *2524.55 p19*
With stepchild
Wife: Margery
Batten, William; Maryland, 1658 *2524.55 p19*
With wife
Batten, Wm; Virginia, 1665-1666 *6212.30 p22*
Battenbergh, John; New York, 1794 *8197.10 p4*
Batter, Edmond; New England, 1645 *1224.1 p2*
Batter, William; Virginia, 1671-1672 *6212.30 p46*
Battersby, Mr.; Quebec, 1858 *9196.15 p38*
Battersbye, James; New York, 1717 *1224.2 p7*
Battin, Dina *SEE* Battin, Ferdinando
Battin, Ferdinando; Maryland, 1664 *2524.55 p19*
Wife: Millicent
Daughter: Mary
Daughter: Ruth
Son: Seaborne
Daughter: Dina
Battin, John; Pennsylvania, 1785 *4629.10 p48*
Battin, Mary *SEE* Battin, Ferdinando
Battin, Millicent *SEE* Battin, Ferdinando
Battin, Ruth *SEE* Battin, Ferdinando
Battin, Seaborne *SEE* Battin, Ferdinando
Batting, John; Virginia, 1664 *6212.30 p15*
Battis, Cathrin Moore 44; Vermont, 1880 *5900.10 p214*
Battisby, James 44; Ontario, 1871 *1823.22 p8*
Battles, Ann Brown 62; Vermont, 1899 *5900.10 p559*
Battles, Anna; Vermont, 1824-1909 *5900.10 p572*
Battles, Bridget; Vermont, 1849-1937 *5900.10 p572*
Battles, Catherine 45; Vermont, 1899 *5900.10 p562*
Battles, Catherine Walsh; Vermont, 1864-1937 *5900.10 p583*
Battles, Ellen 31; Vermont, 1887 *5900.10 p572*
Battles, James; Vermont, 1847-1915 *5900.10 p572*
Battles, John; Vermont, 1906 *5900.10 p575*
Battles, John J.; Vermont, 1851-1933 *5900.10 p583*
Battles, Julia Clancy 36; Vermont, 1886 *5900.10 p423*
Battles, Mary; Vermont, 1847-1904 *5900.10 p445*
Battles, Mary Pendergast; Vermont, 1830-1914 *5900.10 p575*
Battles, Thomas 40; Vermont, 1874 *5900.10 p570*
Battles, Thomas 75; Vermont, 1905 *5900.10 p559*
Batton, A. 5; Ontario, 1861 *2896.26 p14*
Batton, E. 3; Ontario, 1861 *2896.26 p14*
Batton, E. 6; Ontario, 1861 *2896.26 p14*
Batton, J. 38; Ontario, 1861 *2896.26 p14*
Batton, James; Pennsylvania, 1786 *4629.10 p55*
Batton, S. 35; Ontario, 1861 *2896.26 p14*
Batton, William 9; Ontario, 1861 *2896.26 p14*
Battram, John V. 33; Ontario, 1871 *1823.28 p4*
Batts, John; Maryland, 1681 *2524.55 p19*
Batts, Jonathan; Maryland, 1682 *2524.55 p19*
Batty, Barbary; Virginia, 1663 *6212.30 p2*
Batvel, Daniel 40; Maryland, 1774 *1220.25 p37*
Wife: Rachel 30
With 3 children
Batvel, Rachel 30 *SEE* Batvel, Daniel
Batz, Valtin 35; Ontario, 1871 *1823.28 p4*
Bauch, C.; Port uncertain, 1764 *2856.30 p43*
Bauch, Caspar; Port uncertain, 1764 *2856.30 p18*
Wife: M. Bohner
With 5 children
Bauch, M. Bohner *SEE* Bauch, Caspar
Baucke, Erdmann Ferdinand; New York, 1840 *8197.10 p144*
Bauckle, John; New York, 1839 *8197.10 p128*
Baudemont, Andreas; America, 1750 *2856.30 p18*
Baudemont, Andreas; America, 1762 *2856.30 p18*
Baudemont, Philipp; America, 1762 *2856.30 p18*
Bauden, James 46; Ontario, 1871 *1823.22 p8*
Baudrie, Mrs. 60; Ontario, 1871 *1823.28 p4*
Bauer, Miss; Port uncertain, 1763 *2856.30 p19*
Bauer, Andreas; America, 1742 *2856.30 p18*
Bauer, Anna; Port uncertain, 1740 *2856.30 p18*
Bauer, Anna Elisabeth; Port uncertain, 1787 *2856.30 p18*
Bauer, Anna Margarete; America, 1749 *2856.30 p20*
Bauer, Anna Margarete; Port uncertain, 1751 *2856.30 p18*
Bauer, Anna Maria; America, 1749 *2856.30 p20*
Bauer, Anna Maria; Port uncertain, 1746 *2856.30 p18*
Bauer, Apollonia; America, 1749 *2856.30 p20*
Bauer, Catharina; Port uncertain, 1752 *2856.30 p18*
Bauer, Catharina; Port uncertain, 1784 *2856.30 p18*
Bauer, Charles 37; Ontario, 1871 *1823.15 p14*
Bauer, Christian; Port uncertain, 1781 *2856.30 p18*
Bauer, Christina; Port uncertain, 1766 *2856.30 p18*
Bauer, Christina; Port uncertain, 1767 *2856.30 p18*
Bauer, Christof; Port uncertain, 1750 *2856.30 p18*
Bauer, Eva; Port uncertain, 1722 *2856.30 p18*
Bauer, Eva; Port uncertain, 1762 *2856.30 p18*
Bauer, Friedrich; Port uncertain, 1738 *2856.30 p18*
Bauer, Friedrich; Port uncertain, 1769 *2856.30 p18*
Bauer, Friedrich; Port uncertain, 1792 *2856.30 p20*
Bauer, George 67; Ontario, 1871 *1823.15 p14*
Bauer, Godfrey; New York, 1839 *8197.10 p127*
Bauer, Hans; Port uncertain, 1698 *2856.30 p20*
With wife & 3 daughters
Bauer, Hans Georg; America, 1750 *2856.30 p18*
Bauer, Hans Georg; America, 1750 *2856.30 p20*
With wife & children
Bauer, Henry 28; Ontario, 1871 *1823.15 p14*
Bauer, Jacob; Port uncertain, 1759 *2856.30 p19*
Bauer, Jacob; Port uncertain, 1778 *2856.30 p19*
Bauer, Jacob; Port uncertain, 1788 *2856.30 p19*
Bauer, Jacob; Port uncertain, 1789 *2856.30 p19*
Bauer, Johann; Port uncertain, 1735 *2856.30 p20*
With wife & 4 children
Bauer, Johann; Port uncertain, 1747 *2856.30 p19*
Bauer, Johann Adam; America, 1738 *2856.30 p19*
Bauer, Johann Georg; America, 1749 *2856.30 p20*
Bauer, Johann Philipp; Port uncertain, 1783 *2856.30 p20*
With wife & 3 daughters
Bauer, Josef; Port uncertain, 1763 *2856.30 p19*
Bauer, Josef; Port uncertain, 1769 *2856.30 p20*
Bauer, Jost; America, 1754 *2856.30 p19*
Bauer, Jost; Port uncertain, 1752 *2856.30 p19*
Bauer, Juliana; Port uncertain, 1722 *2856.30 p19*
Bauer, Karl; Port uncertain, 1785 *2856.30 p19*
Bauer, Konrad; Port uncertain, 1753 *2856.30 p19*
Bauer, Leonard; Port uncertain, 1752 *2856.30 p19*
Bauer, Maria Eva; Port uncertain, 1773 *2856.30 p19*
Bauer, Maria Margarete; Port uncertain, 1741 *2856.30 p19*
Bauer, Marx; Port uncertain, 1752 *2856.30 p19*
Bauer, Michael; America, 1737 *2856.30 p19*
Bauer, Michael; Port uncertain, 1736 *2856.30 p19*
Bauer, Michael; Port uncertain, 1752 *2856.30 p19*
Bauer, Michael; Port uncertain, 1788 *2856.30 p19*
Bauer, Nickel; America, 1738 *2856.30 p19*
Bauer, Peter; New York, 1838 *8197.10 p109*
Bauer, Peter; Port uncertain, 1783 *2856.30 p19*
Bauer, Philipp; America, 1769 *2856.30 p19*
Bauer, Philipp; America, 1784 *2856.30 p19*
Bauer, Philipp Adam; Port uncertain, 1776 *2856.30 p19*

Bauer, Sebastian; America, 1747 ***2856.30*** *p19*
Bauer, Sebastian; Port uncertain, 1747 ***2856.30*** *p20*
With wife & children
Bauer, Theobald; Port uncertain, 1770 ***2856.30*** *p19*
Bauer, Thomas; Port uncertain, 1737 ***2856.30*** *p19*
Bauer, Valentin; Port uncertain, 1783 ***2856.30*** *p19*
Bauerle, Anton; Port uncertain, 1796 ***2856.30*** *p61*
Bauerle, Ignaz; Port uncertain, 1764 ***2856.30*** *p61*
Bauerlin, Lucia; Port uncertain, 1799 ***2856.30*** *p20*
Bauerman, John 28; Ontario, 1871 ***1823.28*** *p4*
Bauermann, Anna Regina; America, 1777 ***2856.30*** *p20*
Bauersachs, Paul; America, 1771 ***2856.30*** *p20*
Bauersachs, Paul; Port uncertain, 1792 ***2856.30*** *p20*
Bauert, Johann Georg; Port uncertain, 1745 ***2856.30*** *p20*
Baugh, John; Virginia, 1664 ***6212.30*** *p11*
Baugh, Thomas; Rhode Island, 1781 ***1224.2*** *p8*
Baughan, Miss; Quebec, 1858 ***9196.15*** *p44*
Baum, Anna Catharina; Port uncertain, 1766 ***2856.30*** *p20*
Baum, Catharina; America, 1738 ***2856.30*** *p20*
Baum, Catharina; Port uncertain, 1747 ***2856.30*** *p20*
Baum, Jacob; America, 1752 ***2856.30*** *p20*
Baum, Konrad; Port uncertain, 1781 ***2856.30*** *p20*
Baum, Maria Catharina; Port uncertain, 1752 ***2856.30*** *p20*
Baum, Matthaus; Port uncertain, 1791 ***2856.30*** *p20*
Baum, Susanna Margare; Port uncertain, 1775 ***2856.30*** *p20*
Baum, Ulrich; Port uncertain, 1785 ***2856.30*** *p20*
Bauman, Mary 46; Ontario, 1871 ***1823.15*** *p14*
Baumann, Miss; America, 1763 ***2856.30*** *p21*
Baumann, Anna Catharina; America, 1752 ***2856.30*** *p21*
Baumann, Christof; Port uncertain, 1753 ***2856.30*** *p21*
With wife & 4 children
Baumann, Dorothea; Port uncertain, 1789 ***2856.30*** *p21*
Baumann, Ernst; Port uncertain, 1761 ***2856.30*** *p21*
Baumann, Ferdinand; Port uncertain, 1770 ***2856.30*** *p21*
Baumann, Ferdinand; Port uncertain, 1777 ***2856.30*** *p21*
Baumann, Friedrich; Port uncertain, 1774 ***2856.30*** *p21*
Baumann, Georg; Port uncertain, 1764 ***2856.30*** *p21*
Baumann, Gerhard Michel; Port uncertain, 1751 ***2856.30*** *p21*
With wife & 5 children
Baumann, Gertrud; Port uncertain, 1755 ***2856.30*** *p21*
With 3 children
Baumann, Hans Adam; Port uncertain, 1766 ***2856.30*** *p21*
Baumann, Johann; America, 1749 ***2856.30*** *p21*
With wife & 2 children
Baumann, Johann; Port uncertain, 1750 ***2856.30*** *p21*
Baumann, Johann; Port uncertain, 1765 ***2856.30*** *p21*
Baumann, Johann Adam; Port uncertain, 1785 ***2856.30*** *p21*
Baumann, Lorenz; Port uncertain, 1764 ***2856.30*** *p21*
Baumann, Magdalena; Port uncertain, 1694 ***2856.30*** *p21*
Baumann, Max; Port uncertain, 1792 ***2856.30*** *p21*
Baumann, Michael; America, 1744 ***2856.30*** *p21*
With wife & children
Baumann, Nabor; Port uncertain, 1765 ***2856.30*** *p21*
Baumann, Nicolaus; Port uncertain, 1785 ***2856.30*** *p21*
Baumann, Philipp; Port uncertain, 1783 ***2856.30*** *p21*
Baumann, Regina; Port uncertain, 1689 ***2856.30*** *p21*
Baumann, Regina; Port uncertain, 1729 ***2856.30*** *p21*
Baumberger, Paul; Port uncertain, 1763 ***2856.30*** *p21*
Baumer, Frantz; New York, 1839 ***8197.10*** *p127*
Baumgarth, Anna Magdalena; Port uncertain, 1731 ***2856.30*** *p21*
Baumgartner, Johann; Port uncertain, 1738 ***2856.30*** *p22*
Baumgartner, Johann; Port uncertain, 1768 ***2856.30*** *p21*
Baumgartner, Martin; Port uncertain, 1788 ***2856.30*** *p22*
Baumgartner, Michael; Port uncertain, 1783 ***2856.30*** *p22*
Baumgartner, Peter; America, 1737 ***2856.30*** *p22*
Baumgartner, Therese; Port uncertain, 1775 ***2856.30*** *p21*
Baumstarck, Franz Michael; Port uncertain, 1745 ***2856.30*** *p22*
Baumstarck, Mathes; Port uncertain, 1733 ***2856.30*** *p22*
Baumstarckh, Georg; Port uncertain, 1765 ***2856.30*** *p22*
Baumstark, Eva; Port uncertain, 1783 ***2856.30*** *p22*
Baumstark, Jacob; Port uncertain, 1765 ***2856.30*** *p22*
Baumstock, John 46; Ontario, 1871 ***1823.15*** *p14*
Baumstock, Louisa 79; Ontario, 1871 ***1823.15*** *p14*
Baunan, Edward 63; Ontario, 1871 ***1823.22*** *p8*
Baune, William 10; Ontario, 1871 ***1823.22*** *p8*
Bauner, Maria Catharina; Port uncertain, 1785 ***2856.30*** *p22*
Baungarder, John, Sr. 46; Kansas, 1890-1910 ***9079.10*** *p9*
Baungarder, Mary 53; Kansas, 1880-1910 ***9079.10*** *p9*
Bauniguany, K. 46; Ontario, 1871 ***1823.28*** *p4*
Baur, Adam; Port uncertain, 1752 ***2856.30*** *p22*
Baur, Anton; Port uncertain, 1803 ***2856.30*** *p22*
Baur, Georg; Port uncertain, 1715 ***2856.30*** *p22*
Baur, Jacob, Jr.; Port uncertain, 1744 ***2856.30*** *p22*
Baur, Johann; America, 1752 ***2856.30*** *p22*
Baur, Josef; Port uncertain, 1803 ***2856.30*** *p22*
Baurin, Anna Catharina; America, 1741 ***2856.30*** *p22*
Baurin, Elis. Catharina; Port uncertain, 1788 ***2856.30*** *p22*
Baurin, Eva Elisabeth; Port uncertain, 1771 ***2856.30*** *p22*
Baurin, Margarete; Port uncertain, 1775 ***2856.30*** *p22*
Baus, Adam; America, 1749 ***2856.30*** *p22*
Baus, Mathias; New York, 1833-1838 ***8197.10*** *p311*
Bausch, Miss; America, 1752 ***2856.30*** *p22*
With husband
Bausch, Bronislaus; Maryland, 1910 ***3259.35*** *p3*
Bauschlicher, Friedrich, Jr.; America, 1749 ***2856.30*** *p22*
Bauschlicher, Friedrich, Jr.; Port uncertain, 1744 ***2856.30*** *p22*
Bauss, Adam; America, 1754 ***2856.30*** *p22*
Bauss, Andreas; Port uncertain, 1791 ***2856.30*** *p22*
Bauss, Elisabeth; Port uncertain, 1749 ***2856.30*** *p22*
Baustain, Fred 56; Kansas, 1910 ***9079.10*** *p28*
Baustian, Alexander 5; Kansas, 1905-1910 ***9079.10*** *p28*
Baustian, Mary 7; Kansas, 1905-1910 ***9079.10*** *p28*
Baustian, Mary 35; Kansas, 1905-1910 ***9079.10*** *p28*
Baustian, Philip 56; Kansas, 1876-1910 ***9079.10*** *p28*
Bauston, Marke; Maryland, 1680 ***2524.55*** *p19*
Bauzak, Michael; Maryland, 1910 ***3259.35*** *p3*
Baven, John; Maryland, 1668 ***2524.55*** *p24*
Bavinder, George; Baltimore, 1846 ***6058.10*** *p20*
Baw, Edward; Maryland, 1672 ***2524.55*** *p19*
Bawasgak, Constantia; Maryland, 1910 ***3259.35*** *p3*
Bawbell, John 65; Ontario, 1871 ***1823.22*** *p8*
Bawcomb, Alice *SEE* Bawcomb, Peter
Bawcomb, Peter; Maryland, 1668 ***2524.55*** *p19*
Wife: Alice
Bawcombs, Peter; Maryland, 1667 ***2524.55*** *p19*
Bawden, Joseph, Sr. 69; Ontario, 1871 ***1823.22*** *p8*
Bawden, Joseph, Jr. 36; Ontario, 1871 ***1823.22*** *p8*
Bawden, William 29; Ontario, 1871 ***1823.22*** *p8*
Bawdler, Thomas 21; Maryland, 1774 ***1220.25*** *p70*
Bawer, Christof; Port uncertain, 1737 ***2856.30*** *p22*
Bawer, Friedrich; Port uncertain, 1729 ***2856.30*** *p22*
Bawer, Johann; Port uncertain, 1737 ***2856.30*** *p22*
With wife & children
Bawer, Michael; New York, 1839 ***8197.10*** *p129*
Bawer, Philip; New York, 1837 ***8197.10*** *p87*
Bawerin, Anna Eva; Port uncertain, 1734 ***2856.30*** *p22*
Bawldin, James; Maryland, 1649 ***2524.55*** *p20*
Bawldinge, James; Maryland, 1649 ***2524.55*** *p20*
Bawler, Henry 23; Ontario, 1871 ***1823.22*** *p8*
Bawman, Euphunie 72; Ontario, 1871 ***1823.15*** *p14*
Baxansky, Raymond; Maryland, 1910 ***3259.35*** *p3*
Baxster, Sarah; Maryland, 1658-1663 ***2524.55*** *p20*
Baxter, Mr.; Quebec, 1857 ***9196.15*** *p21*
Baxter, Mrs.; Maryland, 1658 ***2524.55*** *p20*
Baxter, Alice; Maryland, 1674 ***2524.55*** *p20*
Baxter, Barnaby 30; Maryland, 1774 ***1220.25*** *p40*
Baxter, Benjamin; Nantucket, Massachusetts, 1801 ***1224.3*** *p5*
Baxter, Catherine Sullivan 48; Vermont, 1876 ***5900.10*** *p614*
Baxter, David 24; Ontario, 1871 ***1823.28*** *p4*
Baxter, Henry 30; Ontario, 1861 ***2896.27*** *p73*
Baxter, Jane 48; Ontario, 1871 ***1823.15*** *p14*
Baxter, John; Grenada, 1822 ***1640.13*** *p8*
Baxter, John 36; Ontario, 1871 ***1823.22*** *p8*
Baxter, John 39; Ontario, 1871 ***1823.28*** *p4*
Baxter, John 61; Vermont, 1884 ***5900.10*** *p317*
Baxter, John, Jr.; New York, 1809 ***8197.10*** *p54*
Baxter, John Exall; Petersburg, Virginia, 1846 ***1224.3*** *p5*
Baxter, John Henry; New York, 1832 ***8197.10*** *p356*
Baxter, Margrett; Maryland, 1668 ***2524.55*** *p20*
Baxter, Mary; Maryland, 1645 ***2524.55*** *p20*
With husband & daughter
Baxter, Mary A.; Vermont, 1847-1931 ***5900.10*** *p340*
Baxter, Mary E. 80; Vermont, 1886 ***5900.10*** *p317*
Baxter, Patrick; New York, 1837 ***8197.10*** *p84*
Baxter, Peter 45; Ontario, 1871 ***1823.15*** *p14*
Baxter, Robert 23; Ontario, 1871 ***1823.22*** *p8*
Baxter, Robert 44; Ontario, 1871 ***1823.15*** *p14*
Baxter, Roger; Maryland, 1637 ***2524.55*** *p20*
With wife
Baxter, Sarah; Maryland, 1658-1663 ***2524.55*** *p20*
Baxter, Thomas 44; Ontario, 1871 ***1823.15*** *p14*
Baxter, William 45; Ontario, 1871 ***1823.15*** *p14*
Bay, Andrew 57; Ontario, 1871 ***1823.15*** *p14*
Bay, Charles 26; Maryland, 1774 ***1220.25*** *p38*
Bay, John 24; Maryland, 1774 ***1220.25*** *p38*
Bayand, John; New York, 1816 ***8197.10*** *p58*
Baybey, Amos *SEE* Baybey, John
Baybey, John *SEE* Baybey, John
Baybey, John; Maryland, 1652 ***2524.55*** *p15*
With wife
Son: Amos
Son: John
Bayer, Anna Margarete; Port uncertain, 1759 ***2856.30*** *p22*
Bayer, Ewald; America, 1749 ***2856.30*** *p22*
Bayer, Hans Adam; America, 1749 ***2856.30*** *p22*
Bayer, Hans Michael; Port uncertain, 1731 ***2856.30*** *p23*
With wife
Bayer, Isaac; America, 1749 ***2856.30*** *p22*
With son
Bayer, Joseph; New York, 1837 ***8197.10*** *p84*
Bayer, Louie; Indiana, 1900-1903 ***3437.14*** *p141*
Bayer, Magdalena; Port uncertain, 1725 ***2856.30*** *p23*
With husband
Bayer, Martin; Port uncertain, 1751 ***2856.30*** *p22*
Bayer, Peter; New York, New York, 1881 ***3437.14*** *p154*
Bayer, Valentine; Pennsylvania, 1777 ***4629.10*** *p14*
Bayere, Johann Michael; America, 1741 ***2856.30*** *p23*
Bayere, Johann Michael; America, 1746 ***2856.30*** *p23*
Bayerle, Hans; America, 1737 ***2856.30*** *p23*
Bayerle, Hans Michael; America, 1737 ***2856.30*** *p23*
Bayermeister, Johann Friedrch; America, 1764 ***2856.30*** *p23*
Bayermeister, Johann Friedrch; Port uncertain, 1764 ***2856.30*** *p23*
Baykoski, Mary; Maryland, 1910 ***3259.35*** *p3*
Bayle, Jno; Virginia, 1664 ***6212.30*** *p14*
Baylee, Alexander 38; Ontario, 1871 ***1823.28*** *p4*
Baylee, C. O'Dell 24; Ontario, 1871 ***1823.28*** *p4*
Bayley, Albert W. 11; Ontario, 1871 ***1823.15*** *p14*
Bayley, Barnard; New York, New York, 1833 ***1224.3*** *p3*
Bayley, Easter; Virginia, 1664 ***6212.30*** *p13*
Bayley, Elizabeth *SEE* Bayley, Richard
Bayley, Henry E. 14; Ontario, 1871 ***1823.15*** *p14*
Bayley, James Augustus; New York, 1855 ***1224.3*** *p3*
Bayley, Jno; Virginia, 1671 ***6212.30*** *p42*
Bayley, John *SEE* Bayley, Richard
Bayley, John; Maryland, 1676 ***2524.55*** *p20*
Bayley, John; Philadelphia, 1748 ***1224.2*** *p6*
Bayley, Mary; Virginia, 1666 ***6212.30*** *p27*
Bayley, Richard; Maryland, 1658-1663 ***2524.55*** *p20*
Son: John
Daughter: Elizabeth
Bayley, Richard; Maryland, 1659 ***2524.55*** *p20*
Bayley, Richard; Maryland, 1674 ***2524.55*** *p20*
Bayley, Thomas Elder; America, 1875 ***1640.13*** *p8*
Bayley, William 54; Ontario, 1871 ***1823.15*** *p14*
Bayley, Wm; Virginia, 1664 ***6212.30*** *p11*
Baylie, Joane; Maryland, 1673 ***2524.55*** *p20*
Baylife, John 38; Ontario, 1871 ***1823.15*** *p14*
Bayliff, Featherston; Georgia, 1750 ***1224.2*** *p8*
Baylis, John 21; Maryland, 1774 ***1220.25*** *p62*
Bayliss, Joseph; Boston, 1776 ***1224.2*** *p8*
Bayly, Amos *SEE* Bayly, John
Bayly, Elizabeth *SEE* Bayly, Richard
Bayly, Gerard; Maryland, 1658 ***2524.55*** *p20*
Bayly, Hen; Virginia, 1668-1669 ***6212.30*** *p41*
Bayly, John *SEE* Bayly, John
Bayly, John *SEE* Bayly, Richard
Bayly, John; Maryland, 1652 ***2524.55*** *p15*
With wife
Son: John
Son: Amos
Bayly, John; Maryland, 1662 ***2524.55*** *p16*
Bayly, John; Maryland, 1668 ***2524.55*** *p20*
Bayly, Melchizideck; Boston, 1720 ***1224.2*** *p6*
Bayly, Richard; Maryland, 1658-1663 ***2524.55*** *p20*
Son: John
Daughter: Elizabeth
Bayly, Robert; Maryland, 1681 ***2524.55*** *p20*
Bayly, William; Virginia, 1727 ***1224.2*** *p6*
Baylye, Rachell; Maryland, 1668 ***2524.55*** *p20*
Baynard, Tho; Virginia, 1666 ***6212.30*** *p31*
Bayne, Idith; Maryland, 1663 ***2524.55*** *p20*
Bayne, Penelope Sober; New York, 1884 ***1640.13*** *p8*
Bayne, Walter; Maryland, 1663 ***2524.55*** *p20*
Baynes, Henry; Virginia, 1705 ***1224.2*** *p8*
Baynham, Richard 22; Maryland, 1774 ***1220.25*** *p70*
Baynton, John; Died enroute, 1690 ***1224.1*** *p6*
Bayr, Barbara; America, 1744 ***2856.30*** *p23*
Bays, Mary 49; Ontario, 1871 ***1823.15*** *p14*
Bays, Solomon 56; Ontario, 1871 ***1823.22*** *p8*
Baysent, Thomas; Maryland, 1673 ***2524.55*** *p20*
Bayset, Richard W. 70; Ontario, 1871 ***1823.15*** *p14*
Baytop, Thomas; Virginia, 1692 ***1224.1*** *p6*
Bayzand, William Seddon; Baltimore, 1827 ***1224.3*** *p5*
Bazajou, Marie Antoine; New York, 1831 ***8197.10*** *p211*
Bazalee, John; Pennsylvania, 1777 ***4629.10*** *p17*
Bazill, Ralph; Maryland, 1665 ***2524.55*** *p20*
Bazin, Pierre Francois; New York, 1816 ***8197.10*** *p58*
Bazing, William Hamilton; New York, 1839 ***8197.10*** *p381*
Bazkowski, Joseph; Maryland, 1910 ***3259.35*** *p3*
Bazzick, John; Maryland, 1658 ***2524.55*** *p20*
Bea, Thomas; Maryland, 1670 ***2524.55*** *p20*
Beach, Alice T. 7; Ontario, 1861 ***2896.25*** *p5*
Beach, Alvaretta 2; Ontario, 1861 ***2896.27*** *p45*

Beach, Ann E. 9; Ontario, 1861 ***2896.25*** *p5*
Beach, Anna A. 11; Ontario, 1861 ***2896.25*** *p5*
Beach, Berintha 5; Ontario, 1861 ***2896.25*** *p5*
Beach, C. Jane 17; Ontario, 1861 ***2896.25*** *p5*
Beach, Catherine A. 16; Ontario, 1861 ***2896.25*** *p4*
Beach, Duellas 44; Ontario, 1861 ***2896.25*** *p5*
Beach, Elias; Maryland, 1649 ***2524.55*** *p20*
Beach, Elizabeth J. 23; Ontario, 1861 ***2896.25*** *p4*
Beach, Harlow 78; Ontario, 1861 ***2896.25*** *p4*
Beach, Julia A. 27; Ontario, 1861 ***2896.25*** *p4*
Beach, L. G. 18; Ontario, 1861 ***2896.25*** *p4*
Beach, Michael; Maryland, 1681 ***2524.55*** *p20*
Beach, Nancy 27; Ontario, 1861 ***2896.27*** *p45*
Beach, Peter V. 18; Ontario, 1861 ***2896.25*** *p5*
Beach, Phebe 51; Ontario, 1861 ***2896.25*** *p4*
Beach, Sarah 40; Ontario, 1861 ***2896.25*** *p5*
Beach, Sarah E. 13; Ontario, 1861 ***2896.25*** *p5*
Beach, Thomas; Maryland, 1667 ***2524.55*** *p20*
Beach, William; New York, 1839 ***8197.10*** *p128*
Beach, William J. 15; Ontario, 1861 ***2896.25*** *p5*
Beacham, William; Maryland, 1668 ***2524.55*** *p20*
Beachel, Catherine 46; Ontario, 1871 ***1823.15*** *p14*
Beachel, Conrad 18; Ontario, 1871 ***1823.15*** *p14*
Beachel, John 52; Ontario, 1871 ***1823.15*** *p14*
Beachel, William 22; Ontario, 1871 ***1823.15*** *p14*
Beacher, John; Pennsylvania, 1777 ***4629.10*** *p16*
Beachwell, Jane; Vermont, 1853-1939 ***5900.10*** *p410*
Beacom, David 43; Ontario, 1871 ***1823.15*** *p14*
Beacom, Henry 36; Ontario, 1871 ***1823.15*** *p14*
Beacom, Jemima 47; Ontario, 1871 ***1823.15*** *p14*
Beadellcombe, Tho.; Maryland, 1681 ***2524.55*** *p20*
Beadeneaff, Peter 29; Oregon, 1914 ***9196.1*** *p64*
Beaderman, Augustus 20; Ontario, 1871 ***1823.28*** *p4*
Beadle, George 36; Ontario, 1871 ***1823.15*** *p15*
Beadle, Henry 28; Ontario, 1871 ***1823.15*** *p15*
Beadle, Joseph; Maryland, 1681 ***2524.55*** *p20*
Beadle, Peter 33; Ontario, 1871 ***1823.15*** *p15*
Beadwort, Richard; Maryland, 1662 ***2524.55*** *p85*
Beahan, Sarah 73; Ontario, 1871 ***1823.28*** *p4*
Beake, George; Maryland, 1681 ***2524.55*** *p20*
Beaker, Jacob 50; Kansas, 1876-1910 ***9079.10*** *p2*
Beaker, Mallia 41; Kansas, 1876-1910 ***9079.10*** *p2*
Beal, Thomas; Pennsylvania, 1777 ***4629.10*** *p12*
Beale, Benjamin 21; Maryland, 1773-1774 ***1220.25*** *p33*
Beale, Elizabeth; Florida, 1772 ***1224.2*** *p8*
Beale, Henry; Virginia, 1671 ***6212.30*** *p44*
Beale, John; Pennsylvania, 1785 ***4629.10*** *p48*
Beale, John; Virginia, 1663 ***6212.30*** *p2*
Beale, Margaret; New England, 1651 ***1224.1*** *p6*
Beale, Ninian; Maryland, 1668 ***2524.55*** *p20*
Beale, Richard; Newport, Rhode Island, 1789 ***1224.2*** *p8*
Beale, Thomas; Maryland, 1666 ***2524.55*** *p46*
Beale, William; Maryland, 1665 ***2524.55*** *p20*
Beale, William 23; Ontario, 1871 ***1823.15*** *p15*
Beales, John Charles; New York, 1836 ***8197.10*** *p319*
Beall, William 63; Ontario, 1871 ***1823.28*** *p4*
Beam, August 29; Ontario, 1871 ***1823.28*** *p4*
Beam, Henry; Pennsylvania, 1786 ***4629.10*** *p49*
Beam, John G.; New York, 1840 ***8197.10*** *p143*
Beaman, Harman 28; Ontario, 1871 ***1823.28*** *p4*
Beamish, Allen 2; Ontario, 1861 ***2896.28*** *p44*
Beamish, Charles 50; Ontario, 1871 ***1823.22*** *p8*
Beamish, Henry 55; Ontario, 1871 ***1823.22*** *p9*
Beamish, Thomas 26; Ontario, 1861 ***2896.28*** *p44*
Beamont, George 21; New York, 1774 ***1220.25*** *p141*
Beamont, James; Maryland, 1775 ***1220.25*** *p113*
Bean, Mrs.; Maryland, 1648 ***2524.55*** *p20*
Bean, A. 60; Ontario, 1861 ***2896.28*** *p1*
Bean, Adelaide Barney; Vermont, 1827-1910 ***5900.10*** *p594*
Bean, Alexander; Georgia, 1775 ***1640.10*** *p10*
Wife: Christina
Bean, Alexander; Vermont, 1826-1911 ***5900.10*** *p390*
Bean, Alexander 23; Georgia, 1775 ***1220.25*** *p125*
Child: Christiana 18
Bean, Benjamin 84; Vermont, 1915 ***5900.10*** *p403*
Bean, Caleb; Boston, 1753 ***1224.2*** *p8*
Bean, Charles, Sr.; Vermont, 1847-1901 ***5900.10*** *p118*
Bean, Charles J.; Vermont, 1871-1901 ***5900.10*** *p118*
Bean, Christiana 18 *SEE* Bean, Alexander
Bean, Christina *SEE* Bean, Alexander
Bean, Ella L.; Vermont, 1885-1960 ***5900.10*** *p118*
Bean, F. A. 71; Ontario, 1861 ***2896.28*** *p1*
Bean, Florence; Vermont, 1887-1888 ***5900.10*** *p118*
Bean, Jane 33; Ontario, 1871 ***1823.22*** *p9*
Bean, John 16; Maryland, 1775 ***1220.25*** *p120*
Bean, John 35; Ontario, 1871 ***1823.15*** *p15*
Bean, Joseph; Vermont, 1817-1881 ***5900.10*** *p594*
Bean, Mary Jane; Vermont, 1852-1937 ***5900.10*** *p118*
Bean, Rebecca A. 36; Ontario, 1871 ***1823.15*** *p15*
Bean, Thomas 45; Maryland, 1775 ***1220.25*** *p99*
Beandry, J.; Quebec, 1856 ***9196.15*** *p6*
Beane, Mrs.; Maryland, 1648 ***2524.55*** *p20*
Beane, Anna; Vermont, 1855-1940 ***5900.10*** *p126*
Beane, Helena *SEE* Beane, Walter
Beane, Helena; Maryland, 1666 ***2524.55*** *p21*
Beane, John; Maryland, 1666 ***2524.55*** *p28*
Beane, Judith *SEE* Beane, Walter
Beane, Judith; Maryland, 1666 ***2524.55*** *p21*
Beane, Ralph; Maryland, 1639 ***2524.55*** *p21*
Beane, Walter; Maryland, 1666 ***2524.55*** *p21*
Wife: Helena
Daughter: Judith
Beanly, Anne; Virginia, 1667-1668 ***6212.30*** *p38*
Beans, William; Salem, Massachusetts, 1754 ***1224.2*** *p8*
Bear, Robert 23; Ontario, 1871 ***1823.22*** *p9*
Bear, Thomas; Virginia, 1666 ***6212.30*** *p31*
Bear, Thomas 21; Maryland, 1775 ***1220.25*** *p105*
Bear, William 52; Ontario, 1871 ***1823.22*** *p9*
Bearcroft, Jno; Virginia, 1664 ***6212.30*** *p9*
Beard, Alice *SEE* Beard, Robert
Beard, Alice 27 *SEE* Beard, Thomas
Beard, Ferdinand *SEE* Beard, Robert
Beard, John; New York, New York, 1854 ***3437.14*** *p28*
Beard, John 62; Ontario, 1871 ***1823.15*** *p15*
Beard, Margarett *SEE* Beard, Robert
Beard, Rachell *SEE* Beard, Richard
Beard, Rachell; Maryland, 1650 ***2524.55*** *p21*
Beard, Richard; Maryland, 1650 ***2524.55*** *p21*
Beard, Richard; Maryland, 1650 ***2524.55*** *p21*
Wife: Rachell
Beard, Robert; Maryland, 1680 ***2524.55*** *p21*
Beard, Robert; Maryland, 1681 ***2524.55*** *p21*
Wife: Alice
Child: Ferdinand
Child: Margarett
Beard, Robert 21; Maryland, 1774 ***1220.25*** *p70*
Beard, Robert 46; Ontario, 1871 ***1823.15*** *p15*
Beard, Stephen; Pennsylvania, 1777 ***4629.10*** *p29*
Beard, Thomas; Virginia, 1671 ***6212.30*** *p42*
Beard, Thomas 28; Philadelphia, 1774 ***1220.25*** *p42*
Wife: Alice 27
Beard, Thomas 39; Maryland, 1775 ***1220.25*** *p96*
Beard, Walter; Maryland, 1672 ***2524.55*** *p21*
Beard, William; Virginia, 1646 ***1224.1*** *p6*
Beard, William 24; Maryland, 1774 ***1220.25*** *p54*
Beardall, Robt 53; Seattle, 1917 ***9196.1*** *p51*
Beardall, Robt 53; Whitehorse, Yukon, 1917 ***9196.1*** *p51*
Beardmore, Miss; Quebec, 1856 ***9196.15*** *p10*
Beardmore, G. T.; Quebec, 1856 ***9196.15*** *p10*
Beardmore, John 23; Maryland, 1773-1774 ***1220.25*** *p33*
Beardsley, Gustavies Herbert; Portland, Maine, 1862 ***6058.10*** *p60*
Beare, Jno; Virginia, 1664 ***6212.30*** *p9*
Beare, Jno; Virginia, 1668-1669 ***6212.30*** *p40*
Beare, John; Virginia, 1674 ***6212.30*** *p52*
Beare, Richard; Virginia, 1667-1668 ***6212.30*** *p39*
Beare, Richard; Virginia, 1674 ***6212.30*** *p52*
Beare, Thomas; Maryland, 1681 ***2524.55*** *p21*
Bearliskie, Wadislouce; Maryland, 1910 ***3259.35*** *p3*
Bearns, Paul; Pennsylvania, 1777 ***4629.10*** *p13*
Bears, Helen F. Kennedy; Vermont, 1859-1898 ***5900.10*** *p186*
Beasant, Richard; New York, 1833 ***1224.3*** *p5*
Beascoecher, Francis; New York, 1830 ***8197.10*** *p362*
Beasland, Alexander; New York, 1714 ***1224.2*** *p10*
Beasley, Michael M.; Vermont, 1836-1888 ***5900.10*** *p62*
Beasley, Nora Keefe 55; Vermont, 1901 ***5900.10*** *p62*
Beasley, William 43; Ontario, 1871 ***1823.28*** *p5*
Beasly, Mr.; Quebec, 1858 ***9196.15*** *p33*
Beasly, Richard 53; Ontario, 1871 ***1823.15*** *p15*
Beasly, Stephen; Pennsylvania, 1779 ***4629.10*** *p36*
Beastly, Martin 31; Ontario, 1871 ***1823.28*** *p5*
Beastly, William 60; Ontario, 1871 ***1823.28*** *p5*
Beatie, John 45; Ontario, 1861 ***2896.28*** *p20*
Beaton, Angus *SEE* Beaton, Catherine MacIntyre
Beaton, Angus *SEE* Beaton, John
Beaton, Angus 60; Ontario, 1871 ***1823.15*** *p15*
Beaton, Ann *SEE* Beaton, Farquhar
Beaton, Ann; Ontario, 1840-1849 ***4537.37*** *p69*
Beaton, Catherine MacIntyre; Port uncertain, 1870-1879 ***4537.37*** *p105*
Child: Kenneth
Child: Janet
Child: Angus
Child: John
Child: Ranald
Beaton, Edward 20; Philadelphia, 1775 ***1220.25*** *p106*
Beaton, Farquhar; Saskatchewan, 1884 ***4537.37*** *p89*
Wife: Kirsty MacRury
Child: Mary
Child: Norman
Child: Ann
Beaton, George; Maryland, 1670 ***2524.55*** *p21*
Beaton, Gormelia; Port uncertain, 1840-1849 ***4537.37*** *p134*
Beaton, Janet *SEE* Beaton, Catherine MacIntyre
Beaton, John *SEE* Beaton, Catherine MacIntyre
Beaton, John; Nova Scotia, 1820 ***4537.35*** *p10*
Wife: Margaret MacAulay
Child: Kirsty
Child: Margaret
Child: Angus
Child: Roderick
Beaton, Kenneth *SEE* Beaton, Catherine MacIntyre
Beaton, Kirsty *SEE* Beaton, John
Beaton, Kirsty; Nova Scotia, 1828 ***4537.35*** *p25*
Beaton, Kirsty MacRury *SEE* Beaton, Farquhar
Beaton, Margaret *SEE* Beaton, John
Beaton, Margaret; Port uncertain, 1840-1849 ***4537.37*** *p119*
Beaton, Margaret MacAulay *SEE* Beaton, John
Beaton, Mary *SEE* Beaton, Farquhar
Beaton, Mary; Ontario, 1850-1859 ***4537.37*** *p49*
Beaton, Norman *SEE* Beaton, Farquhar
Beaton, Ranald *SEE* Beaton, Catherine MacIntyre
Beaton, Roderick *SEE* Beaton, John
Beatson, James; Canada, 1856 ***1640.13*** *p8*
Beattey, Mary Cronan 35; Vermont, 1886 ***5900.10*** *p52*
Beattie, Mr.; Quebec, 1857 ***9196.15*** *p26*
Beattie, Mr.; Quebec, 1858 ***9196.15*** *p32*
Beattie, David 45; Ontario, 1871 ***1823.22*** *p9*
Beattie, George 27; Ontario, 1871 ***1823.15*** *p15*
Beattie, George 53; Ontario, 1871 ***1823.15*** *p15*
Beattie, George 84; Ontario, 1871 ***1823.15*** *p15*
Beattie, James 32; Ontario, 1871 ***1823.15*** *p15*
Beattie, John; New York, 1834 ***8197.10*** *p74*
Beattie, John 38; Ontario, 1871 ***1823.15*** *p15*
Beattie, William; New York, 1807 ***8197.10*** *p34*
Beattman, John 25; Alaska, 1917 ***9196.1*** *p51*
Beattman, John 25; Whitehorse, Yukon, 1917 ***9196.1*** *p51*
Beatton, Norman 40; Ontario, 1871 ***1823.15*** *p15*
Beatty, Andrew 28; Ontario, 1871 ***1823.15*** *p15*
Beatty, Christina 23; Ontario, 1871 ***1823.15*** *p15*
Beatty, Christopher 45; Vermont, 1894 ***5900.10*** *p607*
Beatty, David; New York, 1821 ***8197.10*** *p207*
Beatty, David 34; Ontario, 1871 ***1823.15*** *p15*
Beatty, George 33; Ontario, 1871 ***1823.28*** *p5*
Beatty, James; New York, 1827 ***8197.10*** *p342*
Beatty, James; New York, 1834 ***8197.10*** *p371*
Beatty, James 68; Vermont, 1891 ***5900.10*** *p150*
Beatty, Jane 60; Ontario, 1871 ***1823.15*** *p15*
Beatty, John 14; Ontario, 1871 ***1823.15*** *p15*
Beatty, John 35; Ontario, 1871 ***1823.22*** *p9*
Beatty, John 61; Ontario, 1871 ***1823.22*** *p9*
Beatty, Joseph; New York, 1821 ***8197.10*** *p209*
Beatty, Margaret 65; Ontario, 1871 ***1823.22*** *p9*
Beatty, Mary 55; Ontario, 1871 ***1823.22*** *p9*
Beatty, Rebecca 88; Ontario, 1871 ***1823.22*** *p9*
Beatty, Samuel; New York, 1840 ***8197.10*** *p154*
Beatty, Samuel 35; Ontario, 1871 ***1823.15*** *p15*
Beatty, William; New York, 1802 ***8197.10*** *p18*
Beatty, William 30; Ontario, 1871 ***1823.22*** *p9*
Beatty, William 36; Ontario, 1871 ***1823.28*** *p5*
Beaty, Edward 52; Ontario, 1871 ***1823.15*** *p15*
Beaty, John; New York, 1803 ***8197.10*** *p11*
Beaty, Margaret 56; Ontario, 1871 ***1823.22*** *p9*
Beaty, William; New York, 1834 ***8197.10*** *p371*
Beaty, William 25; Ontario, 1871 ***1823.28*** *p5*
Beaucham, Joseph; Fredericksburg, Virginia, 1849 ***1224.3*** *p5*
Beauchamp, Abel; Virginia, 1678 ***1224.1*** *p6*
Beauchamp, Margret 64; Ontario, 1871 ***1823.28*** *p5*
Beaudette, N. 56; San Francisco, 1913 ***9196.1*** *p60*
Beaudry, Mr.; Quebec, 1857 ***9196.15*** *p13*
Beaudry, Mr.; Quebec, 1857 ***9196.15*** *p20*
Beaudry, Mr.; Quebec, 1858 ***9196.15*** *p44*
Beaukland, Elizabeth *SEE* Beaukland, Richard
Beaukland, Richard *SEE* Beaukland, Richard
Beaukland, Richard; Maryland, 1675 ***2524.55*** *p21*
Wife: Elizabeth
Son: Richard
Beaulac, Henry 64; Vermont, 1894 ***5900.10*** *p233*
Beaulac, Joseph H.; Vermont, 1852-1924 ***5900.10*** *p224*
Beaulac, Margaret M.; Vermont, 1845-1945 ***5900.10*** *p278*
Beaulac, Mary E. Roddy; Vermont, 1850-1932 ***5900.10*** *p224*
Beaulac, Mary O'Neil 74; Vermont, 1906 ***5900.10*** *p233*
Beaulieu, Mr.; Quebec, 1857 ***9196.15*** *p24*
Beaulieu, Mrs.; Quebec, 1857 ***9196.15*** *p24*
Beaumont, Miss; Quebec, 1858 ***9196.15*** *p39*
Beaumont, Mr.; Quebec, 1858 ***9196.15*** *p39*
Beaumont, Mrs.; Quebec, 1858 ***9196.15*** *p39*
Beaumont, Henry 46; Ontario, 1871 ***1823.22*** *p9*
Beaumont, John; Quebec, 1858 ***9196.15*** *p39*
Beauregard, Mr.; Quebec, 1858 ***9196.15*** *p38*
Beauregard, Josephine 67; Vermont, 1929 ***5900.10*** *p162*

Beauvais, Agnes M.; Vermont, 1866-1936 ***5900.10*** *p378*
Beauvais, Frank; Vermont, 1838-1907 ***5900.10*** *p380*
Beauvais, Mary J.; Vermont, 1833-1891 ***5900.10*** *p380*
Beavan, William; Pennsylvania, 1777 ***4629.10*** *p22*
Beavan, William; Pennsylvania, 1779 ***4629.10*** *p39*
Beavay, Thomas; Virginia, 1657 ***1224.1*** *p6*
Beaven, E. W. 37; Ontario, 1871 ***1823.28*** *p5*
Beavens, Thomas G. 39; Ontario, 1871 ***1823.22*** *p9*
Beaver, Benjamin 37; Ontario, 1871 ***1823.15*** *p15*
Beaver, Elizabeth 30; Fort Cumberland, Nova Scotia, 1775 ***1220.25*** *p21*
Beaver, John; New York, 1840 ***8197.10*** *p213*
Beavin, Charles; Maryland, 1671 ***2524.55*** *p21*
Beavour, John; Maryland, 1718 ***1224.2*** *p8*
Bebb, John 26; Maryland, 1775 ***1220.25*** *p100*
Bebe, Aaron 62; Ontario, 1871 ***1823.22*** *p9*
Bebe, Alice M. 16; Ontario, 1871 ***1823.22*** *p9*
Bebe, Caroline 32; Ontario, 1871 ***1823.22*** *p9*
Bebe, Frederick 13; Ontario, 1871 ***1823.22*** *p9*
Bebinski, Joseph; Maryland, 1910 ***3259.35*** *p3*
Beble, John 26; Maryland, 1775 ***1220.25*** *p97*
Bebley, Ann 58; Ontario, 1871 ***1823.15*** *p15*
Bebley, Richard 50; Ontario, 1871 ***1823.15*** *p15*
Bebley, William 84; Ontario, 1871 ***1823.15*** *p15*
Bebonise, Pierre 45; Ontario, 1871 ***1823.28*** *p5*
Becar, Noel J.; New York, 1824 ***8197.10*** *p209*
Becar, Noel J.; New York, 1829 ***8197.10*** *p299*
Becher, Jakob; Port uncertain, 1729 ***2856.30*** *p23*
Becher, Maria Catharina; America, 1741 ***2856.30*** *p23*
With 4 children
Bechler, Christian 42; Ontario, 1871 ***1823.15*** *p15*
Bechler, Otto Philipp; America, 1752 ***2856.30*** *p23*
With wife & 4 children
Bechler, Otto Philipp; Canada, 1752 ***2856.30*** *p23*
Bechler, Wilhelm; America, 1754 ***2856.30*** *p23*
With wife & 4 children
Bechman, John 45; Ontario, 1871 ***1823.15*** *p15*
Bechstein, Friedrich; New York, 1835 ***8197.10*** *p317*
Bechtel, John; America, 1726 ***2856.30*** *p23*
Bechtle, Laurence; America, 1732 ***2856.30*** *p23*
Bechtlin, Lorenz; Port uncertain, 1732 ***2856.30*** *p23*
With wife
Bechtold, Andreas; America, 1763 ***2856.30*** *p23*
Bechtold, Catharina; Port uncertain, 1769 ***2856.30*** *p23*
Bechtold, Heinrich; Port uncertain, 1787 ***2856.30*** *p23*
Bechtold, Jakob; Port uncertain, 1728 ***2856.30*** *p23*
Bechtold, Philipp Jacob; America, 1744 ***2856.30*** *p23*
With family
Bechtold, Veit; America, 1738 ***2856.30*** *p23*
Bechtold, Veit; America, 1738 ***2856.30*** *p23*
With wife
Bechtold, Wilhelmine; Port uncertain, 1781 ***2856.30*** *p23*
Beck, A. 39; Alaska, 1917 ***9196.1*** *p53*
Beck, A. 39; Whitehorse, Yukon, 1917 ***9196.1*** *p53*
Beck, A. Marg. *SEE* Beck, Heinrich
Beck, Amos 28; Virginia, 1774 ***1220.25*** *p87*
Beck, Andreas; Port uncertain, 1788 ***2856.30*** *p23*
Beck, Andrew; New York, 1839 ***8197.10*** *p128*
Beck, Andrew 34; Ontario, 1871 ***1823.15*** *p15*
Beck, Anna Maria; Port uncertain, 1750 ***2856.30*** *p24*
Beck, Barbara; Port uncertain, 1763 ***2856.30*** *p23*
Beck, Catharina; Port uncertain, 1795 ***2856.30*** *p23*
Beck, Catharina Louis; Port uncertain, 1755 ***2856.30*** *p23*
Beck, Christopher 21; Maryland, 1775 ***1220.25*** *p96*
Beck, Hans Adam; America, 1749 ***2856.30*** *p24*
With wife & 3 children
Beck, Hans Adam; America, 1749 ***2856.30*** *p24*
With wife & 4 children
Beck, Heinrich; America, 1751 ***2856.30*** *p24*
Wife: A. Marg.
With son
Beck, Jacob 34; Ontario, 1871 ***1823.28*** *p5*
Beck, James; New York, 1840 ***8197.10*** *p154*
Beck, James; Ontario, 1871 ***1823.28*** *p5*
Beck, Johann; Port uncertain, 1756 ***2856.30*** *p23*
Beck, John; New York, 1840 ***8197.10*** *p153*
Beck, John; Pennsylvania, 1777 ***4629.10*** *p7*
Beck, John; Pennsylvania, 1777 ***4629.10*** *p8*
Beck, John; Pennsylvania, 1778 ***4629.10*** *p32*
Beck, John 39; Ontario, 1871 ***1823.28*** *p5*
Beck, John George 46; Kansas, 1892-1910 ***9079.10*** *p50*
Beck, Karl; America, 1798-1799 ***2856.30*** *p24*
Beck, Kunigunda; Port uncertain, 1699 ***2856.30*** *p24*
Beck, Lewis; Maryland, 1666 ***2524.55*** *p21*
Beck, Lorenz; Port uncertain, 1754 ***2856.30*** *p24*
Beck, Maria Barbara; Port uncertain, 1751 ***2856.30*** *p24*
Beck, Maria Catharina; America, 1748 ***2856.30*** *p24*
Beck, Maria Elisabeth; Port uncertain, 1759 ***2856.30*** *p24*
Beck, Mary; Maryland, 1658 ***2524.55*** *p21*
Beck, Mary 49; Kansas, 1910 ***9079.10*** *p50*
Beck, Michael; New York, 1838 ***8197.10*** *p110*
Beck, Michael; New York, 1840 ***8197.10*** *p156*
Beck, Michael; Port uncertain, 1764 ***2856.30*** *p24*
Beck, Nora; Vermont, 1849-1928 ***5900.10*** *p310*
Beck, Paul; Pennsylvania, 1779 ***4629.10*** *p40*
Beck, Peter; Pennsylvania, 1786 ***4629.10*** *p51*
Beck, Ph.; Port uncertain, 1784 ***2856.30*** *p13*
Beck, Philippina; Port uncertain, 1731 ***2856.30*** *p24*
Beck, Richard; Maryland, 1666 ***2524.55*** *p21*
Beck, Richard; Maryland, 1680 ***2524.55*** *p21*
Beck, Richard; New York, 1839 ***8197.10*** *p127*
Beck, William 61; Ontario, 1871 ***1823.15*** *p15*
Beck, William J.; America, 1878 ***1640.13*** *p8*
Beckam, Adam 65; Ontario, 1871 ***1823.22*** *p9*
Beckel, Jakob; America, 1739 ***2856.30*** *p24*
With 3 children
Beckell, Peter; Maryland, 1653 ***2524.55*** *p21*
Beckenbach, Ms.; America, 1750 ***2856.30*** *p24*
Beckenbach, Ms.; America, 1751 ***2856.30*** *p24*
Beckenbach, Adam; America, 1751 ***2856.30*** *p24*
Beckenbach, Caspar; America, 1751 ***2856.30*** *p24*
Beckenbach, Catharina; Port uncertain, 1803 ***2856.30*** *p24*
Beckenbach, Georg Adam; America, 1751 ***2856.30*** *p24*
Beckenbach, Georg Leonhard; America, 1751 ***2856.30*** *p24*
Beckenbach, Johann Georg; America, 1751 ***2856.30*** *p24*
Beckenbach, Niklas; Port uncertain, 1788 ***2856.30*** *p24*
Beckenhaub, Albrecht; America, 1766 ***2856.30*** *p24*
Beckenhaupt, Johann Georg; Port uncertain, 1750 ***2856.30*** *p24*
Becker, Miss; America, 1782 ***2856.30*** *p26*
Becker, Miss; America, 1784 ***2856.30*** *p26*
Becker, Miss; Port uncertain, 1752 ***2856.30*** *p26*
Becker, Mr.; America, 1759 ***2856.30*** *p25*
Becker, Adam; Port uncertain, 1724 ***2856.30*** *p24*
Becker, Agnes; Port uncertain, 1784 ***2856.30*** *p27*
With husband
Becker, Amallia 41; Kansas, 1876-1910 ***9079.10*** *p23*
Becker, Anna Catharina; Port uncertain, 1754 ***2856.30*** *p24*
Becker, Anna Catharina; Port uncertain, 1773 ***2856.30*** *p24*
Becker, Anna Catharina; Port uncertain, 1791 ***2856.30*** *p24*
Becker, Anna Elisabeth; Port uncertain, 1754 ***2856.30*** *p24*
Becker, Anna Elisabeth; Port uncertain, 1784 ***2856.30*** *p24*
Becker, Anna Maria; America, 1758 ***2856.30*** *p24*
Becker, Anna Maria; Port uncertain, 1729 ***2856.30*** *p24*
Becker, Anna Maria; Port uncertain, 1764 ***2856.30*** *p24*
Becker, August 48; Ontario, 1871 ***1823.28*** *p5*
Becker, Barbara; Port uncertain, 1764 ***2856.30*** *p24*
Becker, Bernard; Port uncertain, 1726 ***2856.30*** *p24*
Becker, Carol 46; Ontario, 1871 ***1823.28*** *p5*
Becker, Caspar; Port uncertain, 1778 ***2856.30*** *p24*
Becker, Christian; Port uncertain, 1773 ***2856.30*** *p24*
Becker, Christina 65; Kansas, 1887-1910 ***9079.10*** *p34*
Becker, Christof; America, 1750 ***2856.30*** *p24*
Becker, Christof; America, 1793 ***2856.30*** *p24*
Becker, Christof; Port uncertain, 1791 ***2856.30*** *p25*
Becker, Eva E. 32; Kansas, 1902-1910 ***9079.10*** *p27*
Becker, Franz; Port uncertain, 1772 ***2856.30*** *p27*
With wife & children
Becker, Friedrich; Port uncertain, 1784 ***2856.30*** *p27*
Becker, Friedrich; Port uncertain, 1784 ***2856.30*** *p27*
With wife & 4 children
Becker, Georg; America, 1739 ***2856.30*** *p27*
With wife & 4 children
Becker, Georg; America, 1740 ***2856.30*** *p25*
Becker, Georg; Port uncertain, 1740 ***2856.30*** *p25*
Becker, Georg; Port uncertain, 1754 ***2856.30*** *p27*
With wife
Becker, Georg; Port uncertain, 1758 ***2856.30*** *p25*
Becker, George 36; Kansas, 1902-1910 ***9079.10*** *p27*
Becker, George M. 39; Kansas, 1887-1910 ***9079.10*** *p34*
Becker, Hans Adam; Port uncertain, 1790 ***2856.30*** *p25*
Becker, Heinrch; America, 1843 ***2856.30*** *p25*
Becker, Jacob; America, 1740 ***2856.30*** *p25*
Becker, Jacob; Port uncertain, 1764 ***2856.30*** *p25*
Becker, Jacob 50; Kansas, 1876-1910 ***9079.10*** *p23*
Becker, Johann; America, 1749 ***2856.30*** *p27*
With 5 children
Becker, Johann; America, 1750 ***2856.30*** *p25*
Becker, Johann; Port uncertain, 1750 ***2856.30*** *p27*
With wife
Becker, Johann; Port uncertain, 1764 ***2856.30*** *p25*
Becker, Johann; Port uncertain, 1777 ***2856.30*** *p25*
Becker, Johann; Port uncertain, 1783 ***2856.30*** *p25*
Becker, Johann; Port uncertain, 1785 ***2856.30*** *p25*
Becker, Johann; Port uncertain, 1790 ***2856.30*** *p25*
Becker, Johann Adam; Port uncertain, 1744 ***2856.30*** *p27*
With wife & 2 daughters
Becker, Johann Adam; Port uncertain, 1788 ***2856.30*** *p25*
Becker, Johann Engelhar; Port uncertain, 1745 ***2856.30*** *p28*
With wife & 6 children
Becker, Johann Georg; America, 1753 ***2856.30*** *p27*
With wife & children
Becker, Johann Jacob; America, 1749 ***2856.30*** *p27*
With wife & 3 children
Becker, Johann Jacob; Port uncertain, 1784 ***2856.30*** *p27*
With wife
Becker, Johann Melchior; England, 1774 ***2856.30*** *p25*
Becker, Johann Nicol; Port uncertain, 1752 ***2856.30*** *p26*
Becker, Johann Philipp; Port uncertain, 1752 ***2856.30*** *p25*
Becker, Johann Wendel; Port uncertain, 1739 ***2856.30*** *p25*
Becker, John 32; Ontario, 1871 ***1823.15*** *p15*
Becker, John 45; Ontario, 1871 ***1823.15*** *p15*
Becker, Josef; Port uncertain, 1790 ***2856.30*** *p25*
Becker, Juliane; Port uncertain, 1765 ***2856.30*** *p25*
Becker, Konrad; America, 1739 ***2856.30*** *p26*
With child
Becker, Lorenz; America, 1737 ***2856.30*** *p25*
Becker, Louis 61; Ontario, 1871 ***1823.15*** *p15*
Becker, Magnus; Port uncertain, 1770 ***2856.30*** *p25*
Becker, Margarete; America, 1752 ***2856.30*** *p25*
Becker, Margarete; Port uncertain, 1764 ***2856.30*** *p25*
Becker, Maria Catharina; Port uncertain, 1759 ***2856.30*** *p25*
Becker, Maria Magdalena; America, 1758 ***2856.30*** *p25*
Becker, Maria Magdalena; Port uncertain, 1775 ***2856.30*** *p25*
Becker, Maria Magdalena; Port uncertain, 1784 ***2856.30*** *p27*
With husband
Becker, Maria Margarete; Port uncertain, 1777 ***2856.30*** *p25*
Becker, Mary E. 37; Kansas, 1887-1910 ***9079.10*** *p34*
Becker, Michael; America, 1739 ***2856.30*** *p26*
Becker, Michael; America, 1749 ***2856.30*** *p26*
Becker, Michael; Port uncertain, 1774 ***2856.30*** *p26*
Becker, Michael; Port uncertain, 1776 ***2856.30*** *p25*
Becker, Nicol; Port uncertain, 1794 ***2856.30*** *p26*
Becker, Nikolaus; Port uncertain, 1748 ***2856.30*** *p27*
With wife & 4 daughters
Becker, Peter; America, 1739 ***2856.30*** *p26*
Becker, Peter; America, 1749 ***2856.30*** *p26*
Becker, Peter; America, 1786 ***2856.30*** *p26*
Becker, Peter; Port uncertain, 1729 ***2856.30*** *p26*
Becker, Peter; Port uncertain, 1785 ***2856.30*** *p26*
Becker, Philipp; America, 1754 ***2856.30*** *p26*
Becker, Philipp; Port uncertain, 1750 ***2856.30*** *p26*
Becker, Sabine; Port uncertain, 1779 ***2856.30*** *p26*
Becker, Sebastian; America, 1752 ***2856.30*** *p27*
With wife & 4 children
Becker, Theobald; America, 1752 ***2856.30*** *p27*
With wife & children
Becker, Theobald; Port uncertain, 1735 ***2856.30*** *p26*
Becker, Valentin; America, 1769 ***2856.30*** *p26*
Becker, Valentin; America, 1820 ***2856.30*** *p26*
Becker, Valentin; Port uncertain, 1787 ***2856.30*** *p26*
Becker, Valentin; Port uncertain, 1788 ***2856.30*** *p26*
Becker, Valten; America, 1739 ***2856.30*** *p26*
With child
Becker, Velten; Port uncertain, 1766 ***2856.30*** *p26*
Becker, Veronika; America, 1790 ***2856.30*** *p26*
Becker, Veronika; America, 1790 ***2856.30*** *p233*
Becker, Wendel; America, 1767 ***2856.30*** *p26*
Becker, Wendel; Port uncertain, 1749 ***2856.30*** *p26*
Becker, Wendel; Port uncertain, 1782 ***2856.30*** *p26*
Becker, Wendel; Port uncertain, 1783 ***2856.30*** *p26*
Becker, William 27; Ontario, 1871 ***1823.15*** *p15*
Becket, James 50; Ontario, 1871 ***1823.28*** *p5*
Becket, John 62; Ontario, 1871 ***1823.28*** *p5*
Becket, William 42; Ontario, 1871 ***1823.28*** *p5*
Becket, William 55; Ontario, 1871 ***1823.22*** *p9*
Beckett, Anna; Vermont, 1908 ***5900.10*** *p433*
Beckett, Hanorah; Vermont, 1895 ***5900.10*** *p433*
Beckett, Mary; Vermont, 1908 ***5900.10*** *p433*
Beckett, Simon; America, 1762 ***1224.2*** *p8*
Beckford, Mr.; Jamaica, 1774 ***1220.25*** *p132*
With family
Beckford, Jane 5; Ontario, 1871 ***1823.15*** *p15*
Beckh, Jakob; America, 1748 ***2856.30*** *p28*
Beckh, Jakob; Port uncertain, 1748 ***2856.30*** *p28*
Beckh, Johann Georg; Port uncertain, 1745 ***2856.30*** *p28*
Beckh, Johann Thiel; America, 1757 ***2856.30*** *p28*
Beckh, Magdalena; Port uncertain, 1768 ***2856.30*** *p28*
Beckh, Michael; Port uncertain, 1697 ***2856.30*** *p28*
Beckley, Jacob; Pennsylvania, 1777 ***4629.10*** *p26*
Beckwith, George; Maryland, 1631-1685 ***2524.55*** *p21*
Beckwith, George; Maryland, 1663 ***2524.55*** *p21*
Beckwith, John; Maryland, 1676 ***2524.55*** *p21*
Becniak, Maggie; Maryland, 1910 ***3259.35*** *p3*

Becon, John; Virginia, 1678 ***1224.1*** *p6*
Becroft, Alice 2; Ontario, 1861 ***2896.25*** *p2*
Becroft, Anna E. 6; Ontario, 1861 ***2896.25*** *p2*
Becroft, Eliza J. 25; Ontario, 1861 ***2896.25*** *p2*
Becroft, G. J. 28; Ontario, 1861 ***2896.25*** *p2*
Becroft, John 48; Ontario, 1871 ***1823.15*** *p15*
Becroft, William A. 3; Ontario, 1861 ***2896.25*** *p2*
Bedel, Edwin 10; Ontario, 1861 ***2896.27*** *p43*
Bedel, Elias 72; Ontario, 1861 ***2896.27*** *p43*
Bedel, Jane 29; Ontario, 1861 ***2896.27*** *p43*
Bedell, Charles 5; Ontario, 1861 ***2896.27*** *p41*
Bedell, Elizabeth 33; Ontario, 1861 ***2896.27*** *p41*
Bedell, Emmy L. 8; Ontario, 1861 ***2896.28*** *p27*
Bedell, Ida 9; Ontario, 1861 ***2896.27*** *p41*
Bedell, Margaret 45; Ontario, 1861 ***2896.28*** *p27*
Bedell, Mary E. 1; Ontario, 1861 ***2896.27*** *p55*
Bedell, Sarah; Maryland, 1665 ***2524.55*** *p21*
Bedell, Sarah 21; Ontario, 1861 ***2896.27*** *p54*
Bedell, Willet C. 20; Ontario, 1861 ***2896.28*** *p27*
Bedford, Myles; Maryland, 1652 ***2524.55*** *p21*
Bedford, Robert; Virginia, 1665 ***6212.30*** *p18*
Bedford, Thomas; Maryland, 1663 ***2524.55*** *p21*
Bedford, Thomas 35; Maryland, 1775 ***1220.25*** *p104*
Bedicker, Herman; New York, 1830 ***8197.10*** *p312*
Bedison, Robert; Pennsylvania, 1777 ***4629.10*** *p20*
Bedloe, Isaac; Maryland, 1662 ***2524.55*** *p116*
Bedon, Stephen; Charles Town, South Carolina, 1752 ***1224.2*** *p8*
Bedram, Doris 70; Ontario, 1871 ***1823.15*** *p16*
Bedrano, John 45; Ontario, 1871 ***1823.15*** *p16*
Bedson, Thomas; New York, 1807-1834 ***8197.10*** *p306*
Bedson, Thomas; New York, 1830 ***8197.10*** *p312*
Bedura, Shidurer; Maryland, 1910 ***3259.35*** *p3*
Bee, Henry; Virginia, 1708 ***1224.2*** *p8*
Beebe, Mr.; Quebec, 1858 ***9196.15*** *p36*
Beebe, Mrs.; Quebec, 1858 ***9196.15*** *p36*
Beebe, Nancy Manny; Vermont, n.d. ***5900.10*** *p320*
Beech, Ann; Maryland, 1651 ***2524.55*** *p21*
Beech, Elias; Maryland, 1651 ***2524.55*** *p22*
Beech, Elias; Maryland, 1670 ***2524.55*** *p21*
Beech, John 41; Ontario, 1871 ***1823.15*** *p16*
Beecham, Alfred 27; Alaska, 1912 ***9196.1*** *p18*
Beecham, Alfred 27; British Columbia, 1912 ***9196.1*** *p18*
Beecham, Hathfeild; Virginia, 1667 ***6212.30*** *p37*
Beechan, Miss; Quebec, 1856 ***9196.15*** *p7*
Beecher, James; Virginia, 1665 ***6212.30*** *p18*
Beeching, John; New York, 1840 ***8197.10*** *p145*
Beeching, Robert; New York, 1840 ***8197.10*** *p145*
Beechum, Roger; Virginia, 1671 ***6212.30*** *p45*
Beeck, Mathias; Port uncertain, 1792 ***2856.30*** *p28*
Beedell, Sarah *SEE* Beedell, Thomas
Beedell, Thomas; Maryland, 1665 ***2524.55*** *p22*
Wife: Sarah
Beederman, August 32; Ontario, 1871 ***1823.28*** *p5*
Beedle, Mercy 21; Maryland, 1775 ***1220.25*** *p101*
Beedler, Elizabeth 22; Maryland, 1775 ***1220.25*** *p102*
Beekman, Gerard; New York, 1823 ***1224.3*** *p5*
Beekman, Gerard G.; New York, 1823 ***1224.3*** *p5*
Beekman, Phillips 59; Ontario, 1871 ***1823.22*** *p9*
Beelow, Harman 23; Ontario, 1871 ***1823.28*** *p5*
Beeny, Edward; New York, 1840 ***8197.10*** *p153*
Beeny, Stephen; New York, 1840 ***8197.10*** *p153*
Beer, Cerf; New York, 1839 ***8197.10*** *p213*
Beer, Jakob; Port uncertain, 1785 ***2856.30*** *p61*
Beer, James 25; Ontario, 1871 ***1823.15*** *p16*
Beer, John; Pennsylvania, 1779 ***4629.10*** *p32*
Beer, Nich; Virginia, 1671-1672 ***6212.30*** *p46*
Beer, Thomas; Virginia, 1700 ***1224.2*** *p8*
Beere, Mr.; Quebec, 1858 ***9196.15*** *p31*
Beers, Jonathan; Pennsylvania, 1777 ***4629.10*** *p19*
Beesening, John; Maryland, 1663 ***2524.55*** *p22*
Beesley, George; New York, 1840 ***8197.10*** *p213*
Beesley, Samuel; Virginia, 1727 ***1224.2*** *p8*
Beetenson, Edmond; Maryland, 1669 ***2524.55*** *p22*
Beetham, William; South Carolina, 1783 ***1224.2*** *p8*
Beetle, Anne; Virginia, 1664 ***6212.30*** *p5*
Befiony, Frank; Maryland, 1910 ***3259.35*** *p3*
Befort, Barbara; Port uncertain, 1796 ***2856.30*** *p28*
With husband
Begg, John 80; Ontario, 1871 ***1823.22*** *p9*
Begg, Peter 37; Ontario, 1871 ***1823.22*** *p9*
Beggs, Geo 40; British Columbia, 1912 ***9196.1*** *p36*
Beggs, Geo 40; Seattle, 1912 ***9196.1*** *p36*
Beggs, Thomas; Savannah, Georgia, 1806 ***1640.10*** *p10*
Begier, Mary; Maryland, 1910 ***3259.35*** *p3*
Begins, John 28; New York, 1826-1840 ***8197.10*** *p155*
Begis, John 24; Alaska, 1917 ***9196.1*** *p7*
Begis, John 24; Yukon, 1917 ***9196.1*** *p7*
Begley, John 46; Ontario, 1871 ***1823.15*** *p16*
Behan, Alfred; Vermont, 1829-1906 ***5900.10*** *p378*
Behan, Angeline Carbans; Vermont, 1835-1897 ***5900.10*** *p378*
Behan, David 48; Ontario, 1871 ***1823.28*** *p5*
Behan, James 32; Ontario, 1871 ***1823.28*** *p5*
Beharell, Isaac 71; Ontario, 1871 ***1823.15*** *p16*
Beheathland, John; Died enroute, 1639 ***1224.1*** *p6*
Beherd, Margarett; Maryland, 1681 ***2524.55*** *p22*
Behm, August 32; Ontario, 1871 ***1823.28*** *p5*
Behm, Charles; Ontario, 1871 ***1823.28*** *p5*
Behmise, Frederick 21; Ontario, 1871 ***1823.28*** *p5*
Behmise, Julas 27; Ontario, 1871 ***1823.28*** *p5*
Behn, Johan; New York, 1839 ***8197.10*** *p213*
Behn, Peter; New Orleans, 1844 ***3437.14*** *p36*
Behnayne, William; Maryland, 1778 ***2524.55*** *p22*
Behnken, Henry; New York, 1839 ***8197.10*** *p213*
Behnken, Jacob; New York, 1839 ***8197.10*** *p213*
Behoment, Anne; Maryland, 1665 ***2524.55*** *p22*
Behr, Anna Elisabeth; America, 1788 ***2856.30*** *p28*
Behr, Jacob; America, 1765 ***2856.30*** *p28*
Behr, Jakob; America, 1749 ***2856.30*** *p28*
Behr, Jakob; Port uncertain, 1785 ***2856.30*** *p61*
Behr, Johann Wendel; Port uncertain, 1756 ***2856.30*** *p28*
Behr, Michael; Port uncertain, 1770 ***2856.30*** *p28*
Behren, Mrs. J. Georg; America, 1749 ***2856.30*** *p28*
With son
Behringer, Friedrich; Port uncertain, 1789 ***2856.30*** *p28*
Behringer, Joseph; Pennsylvania, 1786 ***4629.10*** *p50*
Behringer, Martin; America, 1754 ***2856.30*** *p28*
Beideman, Chas 28; Ontario, 1871 ***1823.28*** *p5*
Beiderman, Gotlip 55; Ontario, 1871 ***1823.28*** *p5*
Beifelder, Elisabeth; Port uncertain, 1794 ***2856.30*** *p28*
Beigbeder, Bertram Charles; New York, 1808 ***8197.10*** *p53*
Beigg, Ben 39; Ontario, 1871 ***1823.28*** *p5*
Beigin, Cath. Barbara; Port uncertain, 1747 ***2856.30*** *p28*
Beigin, Cath. Barbara; Port uncertain, 1747 ***2856.30*** *p53*
Beil, Elisabeth; Port uncertain, 1793 ***2856.30*** *p28*
Beil, Heinrich; Port uncertain, 1793 ***2856.30*** *p28*
Beil, Magdalena; Port uncertain, 1772 ***2856.30*** *p28*
Beiler, Vinzenz; America, 1738 ***2856.30*** *p28*
Beindar, Pantalron; New York, 1835 ***8197.10*** *p212*
Beinmuller, Christof; Port uncertain, 1768 ***2856.30*** *p29*
Beird, David 40; Ontario, 1871 ***1823.15*** *p16*
Beird, Humphry 65; Ontario, 1871 ***1823.15*** *p16*
Beirne, Margaret T. 76; Vermont, 1936 ***5900.10*** *p176*
Beirne, Martha; Vermont, 1861-1880 ***5900.10*** *p530*
Beirne, Michael 44; Vermont, 1851 ***5900.10*** *p522*
Beirnes, George 42; Ontario, 1871 ***1823.15*** *p16*
Beisch, Michael; Port uncertain, 1733 ***2856.30*** *p29*
Beisch, Ulrich; Port uncertain, 1624 ***2856.30*** *p29*
Beischer, Jacob; Port uncertain, 1820 ***2856.30*** *p36*
Beiser, Andrew; New York, 1839 ***8197.10*** *p128*
Beiser, Mrs. Martin; Port uncertain, 1746 ***2856.30*** *p29*
Beisher, Andrew; New York, 1839 ***8197.10*** *p128*
Beisin, Anna Maria; Port uncertain, 1769 ***2856.30*** *p29*
Beisin, Anna Maria; Port uncertain, 1770 ***2856.30*** *p29*
Beisinger, Augustin; New York, 1840 ***8197.10*** *p145*
Beissel, Johann Konrad; America, 1735 ***2856.30*** *p29*
Beisser, Konrad; Port uncertain, 1770 ***2856.30*** *p36*
Beith, Arch'd 63; Ontario, 1861 ***2896.28*** *p22*
Beith, Jane 23; Ontario, 1861 ***2896.28*** *p22*
Beith, Lanor 33; Ontario, 1861 ***2896.28*** *p22*
Beith, Malcolm 16; Ontario, 1861 ***2896.28*** *p22*
Beith, Mary 59; Ontario, 1861 ***2896.28*** *p22*
Beith, Susan 25; Ontario, 1861 ***2896.28*** *p22*
Bejlski, Michel; Maryland, 1910 ***3259.35*** *p3*
Bejoma, Stanislau; Maryland, 1910 ***3259.35*** *p3*
Bek, Friedrich; Port uncertain, 1784 ***2856.30*** *p29*
Bek, Friedrich; Port uncertain, 1785 ***2856.30*** *p29*
Bekczynki, Adam; Maryland, 1910 ***3259.35*** *p3*
Bekeff, L. 34; Alaska, 1916 ***9196.1*** *p42*
Bekeff, L. 34; Whitehorse, Yukon, 1916 ***9196.1*** *p42*
Beker, Catharina; Port uncertain, 1788 ***2856.30*** *p29*
Beker, Hans Nickel; America, 1788 ***2856.30*** *p29*
Beker, Hans Nickel; Port uncertain, 1780 ***2856.30*** *p29*
Beker, Maria Barbara; Port uncertain, 1774 ***2856.30*** *p29*
Bekowski, Jan J.; Maryland, 1910 ***3259.35*** *p3*
Belair, Michael; Maryland, 1910 ***3259.35*** *p3*
Belanger, Andrew 48; Ontario, 1871 ***1823.28*** *p5*
Belano, Joseph 38; British Columbia, 1910 ***9196.1*** *p31*
Belano, Joseph 38; Seattle, 1910 ***9196.1*** *p31*
Belbin, Edward; South Carolina, 1734 ***1224.2*** *p8*
Belcher, Charles; New York, 1824 ***8197.10*** *p209*
Belcher, Charles; New York, 1833 ***8197.10*** *p300*
Belcher, John; Virginia, 1740 ***1224.2*** *p8*
Belcher, Mary *SEE* Belcher, Thomas
Belcher, Thomas; Maryland, 1649 ***2524.55*** *p22*
Wife: Mary
Daughter: Mary
Belcher, Thomas; New York, 1824 ***8197.10*** *p209*
Belcher, William; Maryland, 1678 ***2524.55*** *p22*
Belcher, William; New York, 1824 ***8197.10*** *p209*
Belcher, William; New York, 1833 ***8197.10*** *p300*
Belcousen, Mary; Maryland, 1668 ***2524.55*** *p22*
Beldys, Andrew; Maryland, 1910 ***3259.35*** *p3*
Bele, Laurence; Virginia, 1664 ***6212.30*** *p15*
Belerly, William 64; Ontario, 1871 ***1823.22*** *p9*
Belesky, Albert 59; Ontario, 1871 ***1823.28*** *p5*
Beley, Benjamin Snowdri 30; Ontario, 1871 ***1823.28*** *p5*
Belford, Andrew 36; Ontario, 1871 ***1823.15*** *p16*
Belford, Catherine; Vermont, 1800-1852 ***5900.10*** *p238*
Belford, Henry 67; Ontario, 1871 ***1823.22*** *p9*
Belford, James 49; Ontario, 1871 ***1823.15*** *p16*
Belford, John 53; Ontario, 1871 ***1823.28*** *p5*
Belfou, Pierre Aman; Grenada, 1842 ***1640.13*** *p8*
Belin, Elizabeth; Charles Town, South Carolina, 1785 ***1224.2*** *p8*
Belin, Peter; Died enroute, 1843 ***1224.3*** *p5*
Beling, John; Maryland, 1910 ***3259.35*** *p3*
Belinski, Joseph; Maryland, 1910 ***3259.35*** *p3*
Belisario, Henry Mendes; Baltimore, 1855 ***1224.3*** *p5*
Beliski, Stephen; Maryland, 1910 ***3259.35*** *p3*
Belkowski, Henry; Maryland, 1910 ***3259.35*** *p3*
Bell, Mr.; Quebec, 1857 ***9196.15*** *p16*
Bell, Mr.; Quebec, 1857 ***9196.15*** *p26*
Bell, Mr.; Quebec, 1858 ***9196.15*** *p32*
Bell, Mrs.; Quebec, 1857 ***9196.15*** *p26*
Bell, Abraham; New York, 1803 ***8197.10*** *p11*
Bell, Ada 83; Vermont, 1930 ***5900.10*** *p374*
Bell, Adam 36; Ontario, 1871 ***1823.22*** *p9*
Bell, Agnes 42; Ontario, 1871 ***1823.22*** *p9*
Bell, Albert 62; Ontario, 1871 ***1823.28*** *p5*
Bell, Alexander 25; Ontario, 1871 ***1823.28*** *p5*
Bell, Alexander 72; Ontario, 1871 ***1823.15*** *p16*
Bell, Andrew; Georgia, 1735 ***1640.10*** *p10*
Bell, Ann 48; Ontario, 1871 ***1823.15*** *p16*
Bell, Ann 73; Ontario, 1871 ***1823.15*** *p16*
Bell, Antony 56; Ontario, 1871 ***1823.15*** *p16*
Bell, Catherine; New Orleans, 1858 ***1640.10*** *p10*
Bell, Daniel; Maryland, 1682 ***2524.55*** *p22*
Bell, Daniel 39; Ontario, 1871 ***1823.15*** *p16*
Bell, Daniel 45; Ontario, 1871 ***1823.15*** *p16*
Bell, David; Albany, New York, 1713 ***1224.2*** *p9*
Bell, David 3; Ontario, 1861 ***2896.28*** *p18*
Bell, David 11; Ontario, 1861 ***2896.28*** *p20*
Bell, David 49; Ontario, 1871 ***1823.28*** *p5*
Bell, David 50; Ontario, 1871 ***1823.22*** *p9*
Bell, Duncan 38; Ontario, 1871 ***1823.28*** *p5*
Bell, Edward 60; Ontario, 1871 ***1823.15*** *p16*
Bell, Eliza 17; Ontario, 1861 ***2896.25*** *p30*
Bell, Eliza Webb; Mobile, Alabama, 1827 ***1224.3*** *p5*
Bell, Elizabeth *SEE* Bell, Thomas
Bell, Ellen 20; Ontario, 1861 ***2896.25*** *p30*
Bell, George; Central America, 1841 ***1640.13*** *p8*
Bell, George; Florida, 1712 ***1640.10*** *p11*
Bell, George; New York, 1837 ***8197.10*** *p85*
Bell, George 2; Ontario, 1861 ***2896.28*** *p18*
Bell, George 60; Ontario, 1871 ***1823.28*** *p5*
Bell, George 76; Ontario, 1871 ***1823.22*** *p9*
Bell, Henry; Georgia, 1763 ***1640.10*** *p11*
Bell, Henry 27; Maryland, 1774 ***1220.25*** *p65*
Bell, Henry 40; Ontario, 1871 ***1823.15*** *p16*
Bell, Henry 60; Ontario, 1871 ***1823.15*** *p16*
Bell, Hugh 48; Ontario, 1871 ***1823.15*** *p16*
Bell, Isabella 35; Ontario, 1871 ***1823.15*** *p16*
Bell, Isabelle 54; Ontario, 1871 ***1823.22*** *p10*
Bell, James; New York, 1807 ***8197.10*** *p34*
Bell, James; Pennsylvania, 1777 ***4629.10*** *p25*
Bell, James 5; Ontario, 1861 ***2896.28*** *p18*
Bell, James 24; America, 1774 ***1220.25*** *p37*
Bell, James 24; Jamaica, 1773 ***1220.25*** *p31*
Bell, James 24; Ontario, 1871 ***1823.15*** *p16*
Bell, James 39; Ontario, 1871 ***1823.28*** *p5*
Bell, James 40; Maryland, 1774 ***1220.25*** *p71*
Bell, James 56; Ontario, 1871 ***1823.15*** *p16*
Bell, James 58; Ontario, 1871 ***1823.15*** *p16*
Bell, James 72; Ontario, 1871 ***1823.15*** *p16*
Bell, James, Sr. 60; Ontario, 1871 ***1823.22*** *p10*
Bell, James Christy; New York, 1836 ***8197.10*** *p76*
Bell, Jane 25; Maryland, 1775 ***1220.25*** *p12*
Bell, Jeanette; Georgia, 1770-1850 ***1640.10*** *p11*
Bell, John; Charleston, South Carolina, 1853 ***1224.3*** *p5*
Bell, John; Jamaica, 1773 ***1640.13*** *p8*
Bell, John; Jamaica, 1843 ***1640.13*** *p8*
Bell, John; Maryland, 1676 ***2524.55*** *p22*
Bell, John; Mexico, n.d. ***1224.3*** *p5*
Bell, John; New York, 1806 ***8197.10*** *p324*
Bell, John; New York, 1834 ***8197.10*** *p316*
Bell, John; Newport, Rhode Island, 1780 ***1224.2*** *p9*
Bell, John; Pennsylvania, 1785 ***4629.10*** *p48*
Bell, John; St. Louis, 1853 ***1224.3*** *p5*
Bell, John; St. Louis, 1860 ***1640.13*** *p8*
Bell, John; Virginia, 1698 ***6212.30*** *p61*
Bell, John 9; Ontario, 1861 ***2896.28*** *p18*
Bell, John 34; Ontario, 1871 ***1823.15*** *p16*
Bell, John 36; Philadelphia, 1774 ***1220.25*** *p86*
Bell, John 38; Ontario, 1871 ***1823.15*** *p16*
Bell, John 51; Ontario, 1871 ***1823.28*** *p5*
Bell, John 56; Ontario, 1871 ***1823.15*** *p16*

Bell, John M.; Savannah, Georgia, 1847 ***1640.10*** *p11*
Bell, Joseph; Maryland, 1681 ***2524.55*** *p22*
Bell, Joseph; New York, New York, 1849 ***6058.10*** *p30*
Bell, Joseph 35; Ontario, 1871 ***1823.15*** *p16*
Bell, Joseph 44; Ontario, 1871 ***1823.28*** *p5*
Bell, Margret 80; Ontario, 1871 ***1823.28*** *p5*
Bell, Mary; Maryland, 1671 ***2524.55*** *p22*
Bell, Mary 70; Ontario, 1871 ***1823.15*** *p16*
Bell, Mary A. 28; Ontario, 1861 ***2896.28*** *p18*
Bell, Maxwell 38; Ontario, 1871 ***1823.15*** *p16*
Bell, Michael; New York, 1837 ***8197.10*** *p84*
Bell, Pauld 41; Ontario, 1871 ***1823.15*** *p16*
Bell, Peter; Philadelphia, 1793 ***4629.10*** *p72*
Bell, R. M.; Quebec, 1857 ***9196.15*** *p19*
Bell, Rebecca H.; New York, 1835 ***8197.10*** *p70*
Bell, Richard; Maryland, 1663 ***2524.55*** *p22*
Bell, Richard; Maryland, 1665 ***2524.55*** *p22*
Bell, Richard; New York, 1857 ***1640.13*** *p8*
Bell, Richd James 39; Ontario, 1871 ***1823.28*** *p5*
Bell, Robert; New York, 1821 ***8197.10*** *p208*
Bell, Robert 39; Ontario, 1871 ***1823.15*** *p16*
Bell, Robert 40; Ontario, 1871 ***1823.22*** *p10*
Bell, Robert 44; Ontario, 1871 ***1823.15*** *p16*
Bell, Robert 48; Ontario, 1871 ***1823.28*** *p5*
Bell, Sarah; Quebec, 1858 ***9196.15*** *p40*
Bell, Silvester; Maryland, 1667 ***2524.55*** *p22*
Bell, Susan 32; Ontario, 1861 ***2896.28*** *p20*
Bell, Susanna; Maryland, 1672 ***2524.55*** *p22*
Bell, Thomas; Maryland, 1659 ***2524.55*** *p22*
Wife: Elizabeth
Bell, Thomas; New York, 1834 ***8197.10*** *p74*
Bell, Thomas; New York, 1838 ***8197.10*** *p212*
Bell, Thomas; Pennsylvania, 1777 ***4629.10*** *p7*
Bell, Thomas; Virginia, 1663 ***6212.30*** *p2*
Bell, Thomas; Virginia, 1668-1669 ***6212.30*** *p40*
Bell, Thomas 27; Ontario, 1871 ***1823.15*** *p16*
Bell, Thomas 38; Ontario, 1871 ***1823.15*** *p16*
Bell, Thomas 40; Ontario, 1871 ***1823.22*** *p10*
Bell, William; Maryland, 1677 ***2524.55*** *p22*
Bell, William; New Orleans, 1830 ***1640.10*** *p11*
Bell, William; New York, 1794 ***8197.10*** *p4*
Bell, William; New York, 1840 ***8197.10*** *p154*
Bell, William; New York, New York, 1831 ***8197.10*** *p153*
Bell, William; Norfolk, Virginia, 1795 ***1224.2*** *p9*
Bell, William; Pennsylvania, 1845 ***6058.10*** *p21*
Bell, William; Savannah, Georgia, 1758 ***1640.10*** *p11*
Bell, William; South Carolina, 1827 ***1224.3*** *p5*
Bell, William 7; Ontario, 1861 ***2896.28*** *p18*
Bell, William 29; New York, 1774 ***1220.25*** *p72*
Bell, William 39; Ontario, 1871 ***1823.15*** *p16*
Bell, William 40; Ontario, 1871 ***1823.15*** *p16*
Bell, William 46; Ontario, 1871 ***1823.28*** *p5*
Bell, William 50; Ontario, 1871 ***1823.22*** *p10*
Bell, William 50; Ontario, 1871 ***1823.28*** *p5*
Bell, William 56; Ontario, 1871 ***1823.15*** *p16*
Bell, William 79; Ontario, 1871 ***1823.28*** *p5*
Bell, William, Sr. 63; Ontario, 1871 ***1823.22*** *p10*
Bell, William J. 39; Ontario, 1871 ***1823.22*** *p10*
Bell, William W.; New York, 1808 ***8197.10*** *p34*
Bellacoosen, Mary *SEE* Bellacoosen, Michael
Bellacoosen, Michael; Maryland, 1667 ***2524.55*** *p22*
Wife: Mary
Bellacowson, Mary *SEE* Bellacowson, Michael
Bellacowson, Michael; Maryland, 1659 ***2524.55*** *p22*
Wife: Mary
Bellairs, Mr.; Quebec, 1858 ***9196.15*** *p33*
Bellamy, Samuel; New York, 1793 ***8197.10*** *p3*
Bellamy, Thomas; New York, 1806 ***8197.10*** *p323*
Bellamy, William 34; Ontario, 1871 ***1823.22*** *p10*
Bellanger, Isaac; Pennsylvania, 1777 ***4629.10*** *p19*
Bellarmin, Tho; Virginia, 1672 ***6212.30*** *p49*
Bellemere, Louis; New York, 1816-1834 ***8197.10*** *p307*
Beller, Martin; Port uncertain, 1708 ***2856.30*** *p29*
Bellerby, Henery 70; Ontario, 1871 ***1823.28*** *p5*
Bellet, Jean Noe; America, 1737 ***2856.30*** *p29*
With wife & child
Bellett, Michaell; Maryland, 1654 ***2524.55*** *p22*
Bellett, Richard; Pennsylvania, 1842 ***6058.10*** *p23*
Bellett, Thomas; Pennsylvania, 1842 ***6058.10*** *p21*
Bellew, Bridget; Vermont, 1921 ***5900.10*** *p271*
Bellew, Elizabeth 73; Vermont, 1907 ***5900.10*** *p271*
Bellinger, Maria Barbara; Port uncertain, 1734 ***2856.30*** *p29*
With husband
Bellinger, Mary 25; Kansas, 1908-1910 ***9079.10*** *p10*
Bellinger, Mike 23; Kansas, 1908-1910 ***9079.10*** *p10*
Bellings, Francis 47; Ontario, 1871 ***1823.28*** *p5*
Bellmaine, Jno; Virginia, 1676 ***6212.30*** *p53*
Bello, Anthony M.; New York, 1827 ***8197.10*** *p339*
Bellpot, Dr.; Portland, Maine, 1857 ***9196.15*** *p12*
Bellue, James; New York, 1840 ***8197.10*** *p156*
Bellwood, Robert; Maryland, 1681 ***2524.55*** *p22*
Belment, James 40; Ontario, 1871 ***1823.28*** *p6*
Belnap, David 14; Ontario, 1861 ***2896.25*** *p35*
Belnap, Fanny 17; Ontario, 1861 ***2896.25*** *p35*
Belnap, Louisa 22; Ontario, 1861 ***2896.28*** *p45*
Belnap, Sarah 9; Ontario, 1861 ***2896.25*** *p35*
Belondo, B. 42; British Columbia, 1910 ***9196.1*** *p29*
Belondo, B. 42; Washington, 1910 ***9196.1*** *p29*
Belrose, Joanna 39; Vermont, 1899 ***5900.10*** *p376*
Belson, Edward 70; Ontario, 1871 ***1823.22*** *p10*
Belt, Ann *SEE* Belt, Humphrey
Belt, Humphrey; Maryland, 1663 ***2524.55*** *p22*
Relative: John
Relative: Sarah
Relative: Ann
Belt, John *SEE* Belt, Humphrey
Belt, Sarah *SEE* Belt, Humphrey
Belton, James; Maryland, 1665 ***2524.55*** *p22*
Belyon, John 62; Ontario, 1861 ***2896.25*** *p25*
Belzer, Andreas; Port uncertain, 1786 ***2856.30*** *p29*
Beman, Thomas; Massachusetts, 1791 ***1224.2*** *p9*
Beman, William 39; Virginia, 1774 ***1220.25*** *p93*
Bemanakinang, Bernard 33; Ontario, 1871 ***1823.28*** *p6*
Bemanakinang, Fabien 40; Ontario, 1871 ***1823.28*** *p6*
Bemanakinang, Joseph 45; Ontario, 1871 ***1823.28*** *p6*
Bemanakinang, Louis 36; Ontario, 1871 ***1823.28*** *p6*
Bemanakinang, Margaret 42; Ontario, 1871 ***1823.28*** *p6*
Bemanakinang, Michel 72; Ontario, 1871 ***1823.28*** *p6*
Bemison, Thomas 32; Maryland, 1774 ***1220.25*** *p2*
Bemissenodawa, Pierre 43; Ontario, 1871 ***1823.28*** *p6*
Bemon, Francis; Maryland, 1670 ***2524.55*** *p22*
Bemond, Hannah Wood; Virginia, 1729 ***1224.2*** *p127*
Bemsel, David; America, 1752 ***2856.30*** *p29*
Bemsel, Friedrich; America, 1752 ***2856.30*** *p29*
Bemsel, Friedrich; Port uncertain, 1751 ***2856.30*** *p29*
Bemsel, Friedrich; Port uncertain, 1752 ***2856.30*** *p29*
Bemsel, Hans Georg; America, 1751 ***2856.30*** *p29*
With wife & children
Bemsel, Hans Georg; Port uncertain, 1752 ***2856.30*** *p29*
With wife & children
Bemsel, Johann; America, 1752 ***2856.30*** *p29*
Bemsel, Johann Georg; America, 1752 ***2856.30*** *p29*
Benack, William; New York, New York, 1777 ***1224.2*** *p7*
Benbow, John 21; Ontario, 1871 ***1823.28*** *p6*
Benbow, Wm 21; Ontario, 1871 ***1823.28*** *p6*
Bence, Jacob; America, 1749 ***2856.30*** *p29*
Bence, Johann Ludwig; America, 1749 ***2856.30*** *p29*
Benceno, Jacob; New York, 1838 ***8197.10*** *p212*
Benceno, Jacob; New York, 1840 ***8197.10*** *p153*
Benckert, Margarete; Port uncertain, 1752 ***2856.30*** *p29*
Bencroft, Alice; Maryland, 1658 ***2524.55*** *p45*
Bencroft, James 27; Maryland, 1774 ***1220.25*** *p84*
Bend, John 21; Maryland, 1775 ***1220.25*** *p121*
Bendal, Josiah 35; Maryland, 1775 ***1220.25*** *p99*
Bendel, Lorenz; Port uncertain, 1727 ***2856.30*** *p29*
Bendel, Maria; Port uncertain, 1774 ***2856.30*** *p30*
Bendelow, William; New York, 1857 ***1224.3*** *p5*
Bender, Amelia 19; Kansas, 1900-1910 ***9079.10*** *p10*
Bender, Anna L. 25; Kansas, 1889-1910 ***9079.10*** *p36*
Bender, Anna M. 39; Kansas, 1885-1910 ***9079.10*** *p27*
Bender, Anna Maria; Port uncertain, 1735 ***2856.30*** *p30*
Bender, Christopher; Pennsylvania, 1777 ***4629.10*** *p17*
Bender, Daniel; America, 1744 ***2856.30*** *p30*
Bender, Elisabeth; Port uncertain, 1781 ***2856.30*** *p30*
Bender, G. A. 36; Kansas, 1888-1910 ***9079.10*** *p49*
Bender, Georg Wilhelm; Port uncertain, 1785 ***2856.30*** *p30*
Bender, George 57; Kansas, 1886-1910 ***9079.10*** *p10*
Bender, George 79; Kansas, 1875-1910 ***9079.10*** *p26*
Bender, George, Jr. 27; Kansas, 1886-1910 ***9079.10*** *p10*
Bender, Henry 20; Ontario, 1871 ***1823.15*** *p17*
Bender, Henry 46; Kansas, 1875-1910 ***9079.10*** *p26*
Bender, Henry 50; Ontario, 1871 ***1823.15*** *p17*
Bender, Henry H. P. 26; Kansas, 1886-1910 ***9079.10*** *p36*
Bender, Henry L. 54; Kansas, 1876-1910 ***9079.10*** *p11*
Bender, Herman 24; Ontario, 1871 ***1823.15*** *p17*
Bender, Jacob; Port uncertain, 1771 ***2856.30*** *p30*
Bender, Jakob; America, 1749 ***2856.30*** *p30*
Bender, Jakob; Port uncertain, 1752 ***2856.30*** *p30*
Bender, Johann Karl; Port uncertain, 1789 ***2856.30*** *p30*
Bender, Johann Peter; Port uncertain, 1740 ***2856.30*** *p30*
Bender, John 46; Ontario, 1871 ***1823.15*** *p17*
Bender, Josef; Port uncertain, 1751 ***2856.30*** *p30*
Bender, Joseph; Maryland, 1910 ***3259.35*** *p3*
Bender, Julia Magdalena; Port uncertain, 1763 ***2856.30*** *p30*
Bender, Juliana Magdale; Port uncertain, 1763 ***2856.30*** *p30*
Bender, Katherine 51; Kansas, 1876-1910 ***9079.10*** *p11*
Bender, Katherine 52; Kansas, 1886-1910 ***9079.10*** *p10*
Bender, Lorenz; America, 1742 ***2856.30*** *p30*
Bender, Lorenz; America, 1751 ***2856.30*** *p30*
Bender, Margarete; Port uncertain, 1764 ***2856.30*** *p30*
Bender, Mary 26; Kansas, 1900-1910 ***9079.10*** *p11*
Bender, Mary 34; Kansas, 1910 ***9079.10*** *p49*
Bender, Mary C. 67; Kansas, 1875-1910 ***9079.10*** *p26*
Bender, Mathes; America, 1752 ***2856.30*** *p30*
Bender, Michael; Port uncertain, 1764 ***2856.30*** *p30*
Bender, Michael 31; Ontario, 1871 ***1823.15*** *p17*
Bender, Peter; Port uncertain, 1734 ***2856.30*** *p30*
Bender, Philipp; America, 1700-1799 ***2856.30*** *p30*
Bender, Theobald; Port uncertain, 1783 ***2856.30*** *p30*
With wife & son
Bender, Theobald; Port uncertain, 1784 ***2856.30*** *p30*
With wife & son
Bender, Urban; Port uncertain, 1734 ***2856.30*** *p30*
Bendish, Mr.; Quebec, 1857 ***9196.15*** *p26*
Bendish, John; Virginia, 1666-1667 ***6212.30*** *p33*
Bendle, Alfred 35; Ontario, 1871 ***1823.22*** *p10*
Bends, Stephen 70; Ontario, 1871 ***1823.22*** *p10*
Bene, Joan; Virginia, 1675 ***6212.30*** *p53*
Benedick, Jacob; America, 1741 ***2856.30*** *p30*
Benedick, Jacob; America, 1742 ***2856.30*** *p30*
Benedict, Daniel 55; Ontario, 1871 ***1823.22*** *p10*
Benedict, David 71; Ontario, 1871 ***1823.22*** *p10*
Benedict, Martin; New York, 1821 ***8197.10*** *p207*
Benedum, Henrich; America, 1753 ***2856.30*** *p30*
Benedum, Henrich; Port uncertain, 1770 ***2856.30*** *p31*
Benefeild, Mary; Maryland, 1665 ***2524.55*** *p22*
Benefeild, Rosa; Virginia, 1667 ***6212.30*** *p35*
Benefold, John 29; Maryland, 1774 ***1220.25*** *p77*
Benelski, Petin; Maryland, 1910 ***3259.35*** *p3*
Benet, Richard; Virginia, 1627 ***1224.1*** *p6*
Benett, Lawrence 49; Ontario, 1871 ***1823.15*** *p17*
Benewa, Ernest 28; Ontario, 1871 ***1823.15*** *p17*
Benezet, Daniel, Jr.; Pennsylvania, 1779 ***4629.10*** *p40*
Benezet, Philip; Pennsylvania, 1778 ***4629.10*** *p34*
Benezett, Daniel; Pennsylvania, 1777 ***4629.10*** *p24*
Benezett, Philip; Pennsylvania, 1777 ***4629.10*** *p23*
Benfield, John; Maryland, 1682 ***2524.55*** *p22*
Benford, John 59; Ontario, 1871 ***1823.22*** *p10*
Bengal, Conrad; New York, New York, 1847 ***3437.14*** *p31*
Bengeirigh, James 46; Ontario, 1871 ***1823.15*** *p17*
Bengel, Conrad; New York, New York, 1847 ***3437.14*** *p31*
Bengerth, Anna Catharina; Port uncertain, 1766 ***2856.30*** *p31*
Bengies, Andrew; Maryland, 1910 ***3259.35*** *p3*
Bengor, Ellenoer; Virginia, 1677 ***6212.30*** *p54*
Bengough, John Sowerby; Mexico, n.d. ***1224.3*** *p5*
Bengough, John Sowerby; New York, 1856 ***1224.3*** *p5*
Bengough, William 43; Ontario, 1871 ***1823.15*** *p17*
Benham, B. 4; Ontario, 1861 ***2896.27*** *p68*
Benham, James 3; Ontario, 1861 ***2896.27*** *p68*
Benham, John; New York, 1810 ***8197.10*** *p56*
Benham, John 27; Ontario, 1861 ***2896.28*** *p45*
Benham, Joseph 24; Ontario, 1861 ***2896.27*** *p70*
Benham, Margaret A. 28; Ontario, 1861 ***2896.27*** *p68*
Benham, Mary 16; Ontario, 1861 ***2896.27*** *p13*
Benham, Mary 70; Ontario, 1871 ***1823.15*** *p17*
Benham, W.; Quebec, 1857 ***9196.15*** *p23*
Benhoff, Steven; Maryland, 1910 ***3259.35*** *p3*
Benifin, Tho.; Maryland, 1682 ***2524.55*** *p22*
Benig, Sebastian; Port uncertain, 1766 ***2856.30*** *p31*
Benighoff, Jacob; Pennsylvania, 1777 ***4629.10*** *p29*
Benington, Edw.; Maryland, 1651 ***2524.55*** *p22*
Beniseska, Maryanna; Maryland, 1910 ***3259.35*** *p3*
Benison, William Lloyd; New York, 1818 ***8197.10*** *p207*
Benjamin, Mr.; Quebec, 1856 ***9196.15*** *p6*
Benjamin, Mr.; Quebec, 1857 ***9196.15*** *p24*
Benjamin, Mr.; Quebec, 1858 ***9196.15*** *p42*
Benjamin, Mrs.; Quebec, 1858 ***9196.15*** *p42*
Benjamin, G.; Quebec, 1858 ***9196.15*** *p42*
Benjamin, George 45; Ontario, 1871 ***1823.28*** *p6*
Benjamin, John; Vermont, 1817-1895 ***5900.10*** *p538*
Benjamin, John 40; Maryland, 1775 ***1220.25*** *p99*
Benjor, Robert; Maryland, 1665 ***2524.55*** *p22*
Benkard, James; New York, 1828 ***8197.10*** *p211*
Benkard, James; New York, 1830 ***8197.10*** *p66*
Benken, Christian; New York, 1837 ***8197.10*** *p212*
Benken, Christian; New York, 1839 ***8197.10*** *p129*
Bennefeild, Mary; Maryland, 1665 ***2524.55*** *p22*
Bennen, Hannah 37; Ontario, 1861 ***2896.27*** *p31*
Bennen, Mary E. 16; Ontario, 1861 ***2896.27*** *p31*
Bennen, Sarah C. 12; Ontario, 1861 ***2896.27*** *p31*
Bennen, William S. 8; Ontario, 1861 ***2896.27*** *p31*
Benner, Elisabeth; Port uncertain, 1769 ***2856.30*** *p52*
Benner, William 30; Ontario, 1871 ***1823.22*** *p10*
Bennet, Mr.; Quebec, 1858 ***9196.15*** *p44*
Bennet, Adam; New York, 1807 ***8197.10*** *p35*
Bennet, Arthur 20; Ontario, 1871 ***1823.15*** *p17*
Bennet, Elisha; Massachusetts, 1727 ***1224.2*** *p9*
Bennet, Fullarton; North Carolina, 1877 ***1640.13*** *p8*
Bennet, Giles; Virginia, 1665-1666 ***6212.30*** *p23*
Bennet, Henry 47; Ontario, 1871 ***1823.15*** *p17*
Bennet, James; New York, 1761 ***1224.2*** *p9*
Bennet, James; New York, 1824-1834 ***8197.10*** *p307*

Bennet, James 55; Ontario, 1871 *1823.22 p10*
Bennet, John; Maryland, 1669 *2524.55 p22*
Bennet, John; Maryland, 1681 *2524.55 p23*
Bennet, John 22; Ontario, 1871 *1823.15 p17*
Bennet, John 47; Ontario, 1871 *1823.15 p17*
Bennet, Lawrence; Maryland, 1670 *2524.55 p23*
Bennet, Moses 29; Ontario, 1871 *1823.28 p6*
Bennet, Peter; Ontario, 1871 *1823.28 p6*
Bennet, Richard 30; Ontario, 1871 *1823.28 p6*
Bennet, Richard 31; Ontario, 1871 *1823.15 p17*
Bennet, Richard 51; Ontario, 1871 *1823.15 p17*
Bennet, Robert; Maryland, 1680 *2524.55 p23*
Bennet, Tho; Virginia, 1664 *6212.30 p15*
Bennet, Thomas; New York, New York, 1853 *6058.10 p42*
Bennet, Wesley 42; Ontario, 1871 *1823.22 p10*
Bennet, William; Key West, Florida, 1862 *1640.13 p8*
Bennet, William; New York, 1840 *8197.10 p213*
Bennet, William; New York, New York, 1852 *6058.10 p42*
Bennet, William 48; Ontario, 1871 *1823.28 p6*
Bennett, . . .; Boston, 1737 *4628.40 p114*
Bennett, Mr.; Quebec, 1858 *9196.15 p36*
Bennett, Mr.; Quebec, 1858 *9196.15 p38*
Bennett, Mrs.; Maryland, 1646 *2524.55 p23*
Bennett, Mrs.; Quebec, 1858 *9196.15 p38*
Bennett, Adam 30; Georgia, 1774 *1220.25 p48*
Bennett, Ann; Maryland, 1672 *2524.55 p23*
Bennett, Arthur 58; Ontario, 1871 *1823.15 p17*
Bennett, Benjamin; Maryland, 1676 *2524.55 p23*
Bennett, Bridget 26; Ontario, 1871 *1823.28 p6*
Bennett, David 30; Fort Cumberland, Nova Scotia, 1774 *1220.25 p18*
Wife: Mary 30
Bennett, David 60; Vermont, 1855 *5900.10 p613*
Bennett, Dorothy *SEE* Bennett, Edward
Bennett, Dorothy; Maryland, 1680 *2524.55 p23*
Bennett, Edmond; Boston, 1743 *1224.2 p9*
Bennett, Edmund 32; Ontario, 1871 *1823.28 p6*
Bennett, Edward; Maryland, 1680 *2524.55 p23*
Wife: Dorothy
Daughter: Mary
Bennett, Edward; Maryland, 1681 *2524.55 p23*
Wife: Dorothy
Daughter: Mary
Bennett, Edward 27; Maryland, 1774 *1220.25 p7*
Bennett, Elizabeth *SEE* Bennett, Richard
Bennett, Elizabeth; Maryland, 1672 *2524.55 p23*
Bennett, Ellen Charlotte; Baltimore, 1828 *1224.3 p31*
Bennett, Francis; Pennsylvania, 1777 *4629.10 p15*
Bennett, George; Maryland, 1672 *2524.55 p23*
Bennett, George; New York, 1838 *8197.10 p212*
Bennett, Glover 75; Ontario, 1871 *1823.22 p10*
Bennett, Henry; North America, 1698 *1640.13 p8*
Bennett, Henry 23; Philadelphia, 1774 *1220.25 p44*
Bennett, James; Maryland, 1668 *2524.55 p23*
Bennett, James; New York, 1807 *8197.10 p34*
Bennett, James; Pennsylvania, 1777 *4629.10 p9*
Bennett, James 27; Ontario, 1871 *1823.28 p6*
Bennett, James 57; Ontario, 1871 *1823.28 p6*
Bennett, Jane; New England, 1663 *1224.1 p65*
Bennett, John; Boston, 1695 *1224.2 p9*
Bennett, John; Maryland, 1910 *3259.35 p4*
Bennett, John; New York, 1836 *8197.10 p76*
Bennett, John; New York, 1838 *8197.10 p111*
Bennett, John; Pennsylvania, 1785 *4629.10 p48*
Bennett, John 33; Ontario, 1871 *1823.15 p17*
Bennett, John 58; Ontario, 1871 *1823.28 p6*
Bennett, John Morris; Baltimore, 1831 *1224.3 p6*
Bennett, Joseph; New York, 1834 *1224.3 p6*
Bennett, Joseph 22; Virginia, 1774 *1220.25 p89*
Bennett, Lial 25; Ontario, 1871 *1823.22 p10*
Bennett, Margarett; Maryland, 1662 *2524.55 p23*
Bennett, Mary *SEE* Bennett, Edward
Bennett, Mary *SEE* Bennett, Richard
Bennett, Mary; Maryland, 1660 *2524.55 p23*
Bennett, Mary; Maryland, 1680 *2524.55 p23*
Bennett, Mary 30 *SEE* Bennett, David
Bennett, Matthias 54; Ontario, 1871 *1823.28 p6*
Bennett, Michael; Maryland, 1910 *3259.35 p4*
Bennett, Nicholas 35; Ontario, 1871 *1823.28 p6*
Bennett, Reuben; New York, 1832 *1224.3 p6*
Bennett, Richard *SEE* Bennett, Richard
Bennett, Richard; Maryland, 1649-1650 *2524.55 p23*
Bennett, Richard; Maryland, 1658 *2524.55 p23*
With wife
Bennett, Richard; Maryland, 1663 *2524.55 p23*
Wife: Elizabeth
Child: Richard
Child: Sarah
Child: Mary
Child: Thomas
Bennett, Richard; Maryland, 1666 *2524.55 p23*
Bennett, Richard; Maryland, 1750 *1224.2 p9*
Bennett, Richard; New England, 1665 *1224.1 p30*
Bennett, Richard; Virginia, 1676 *1224.1 p6*
Bennett, Richard 15; New York, 1775 *1220.25 p95*
Bennett, Richard 45; Ontario, 1871 *1823.22 p10*
Bennett, Robert; Charleston, South Carolina, 1817 *1224.3 p6*
Bennett, Robert; Maryland, 1682 *2524.55 p23*
Bennett, Robert 24; America, 1774 *1220.25 p36*
Bennett, Robert 33; Ontario, 1871 *1823.15 p17*
Bennett, Robert 36; Ontario, 1871 *1823.22 p10*
Bennett, Rossie D.; Vermont, 1863-1952 *5900.10 p49*
Bennett, Samuel; South Carolina, 1722 *1224.2 p9*
Bennett, Samuel 35; Ontario, 1871 *1823.22 p10*
Bennett, Sarah *SEE* Bennett, Richard
Bennett, Sarah 22; Maryland, 1775 *1220.25 p114*
Bennett, Thomas *SEE* Bennett, Richard
Bennett, Thomas; Maryland, 1668 *2524.55 p23*
Bennett, Thomas; Maryland, 1682 *2524.55 p23*
Bennett, Thomas; New York, New York, 1853 *6058.10 p42*
Bennett, Thomas; Pennsylvania, 1777 *4629.10 p8*
Bennett, Thomas 15; Philadelphia, 1774 *1220.25 p63*
Bennett, Thomas 19; Maryland, 1774 *1220.25 p58*
Bennett, Thomas 24; New York, 1774 *1220.25 p4*
Bennett, Thomas 50; Ontario, 1871 *1823.15 p17*
Bennett, William; New York, 1839 *8197.10 p129*
Bennett, William; New York, New York, 1852 *6058.10 p42*
Bennett, William 20; St. Vincent, 1774 *1220.25 p34*
Bennett, William 20; St. Vincent, 1774 *1220.25 p37*
Bennett, William 30; Ontario, 1861 *2896.28 p46*
Bennett, William 45; Ontario, 1871 *1823.22 p10*
Bennett, William 52; Ontario, 1871 *1823.15 p17*
Bennett, William 73; Ontario, 1871 *1823.28 p6*
Bennetthatt, Christian; Maryland, 1664 *2524.55 p23*
Bennetts, Hurbert 18; Ontario, 1871 *1823.28 p6*
Bennetts, Mary 19; Ontario, 1871 *1823.28 p6*
Benney, Thomas 59; Ontario, 1871 *1823.22 p10*
Bennie, Mathew; Virginia, 1663 *6212.30 p2*
Bennighoff, Jacob; Pennsylvania, 1777 *4629.10 p8*
Bennilson, Lesse; Maryland, 1671 *2524.55 p23*
Benning, Mr.; Quebec, 1856 *9196.15 p10*
Benning, James 25; Maryland, 1773-1774 *1220.25 p33*
Benninger, Peter; America, 1751 *2856.30 p31*
With wife & 4 children
Bennington, George 32; Savannah, Georgia, 1775 *1220.25 p139*
Bennington, Richard; Died enroute, 1612 *1224.1 p6*
Bennit, John; Maryland, 1670 *2524.55 p23*
Bennitt, Margarite; Maryland, 1664 *2524.55 p23*
Bennitt, Thomasin; Maryland, 1662 *2524.55 p23*
Bennoch, Alexander; Augusta, Georgia, 1809 *1640.10 p11*
Bennoch, Peter; Augusta, Georgia, 1805-1812 *1640.10 p11*
Bennose, Mr.; Quebec, 1857 *9196.15 p14*
Bennose, Mrs.; Quebec, 1857 *9196.15 p14*
Bennotski, Annie; Maryland, 1910 *3259.35 p4*
Benns, James; Maryland, 1681 *2524.55 p23*
Benns, Margaret 17; Ontario, 1871 *1823.22 p10*
Bennum, Rhoda A. 13; Ontario, 1861 *2896.25 p26*
Benny, George 60; Ontario, 1871 *1823.28 p6*
Benoit, Constant; New York, 1834 *8197.10 p74*
Benoit, Kattie Murphy; Vermont, 1879 *5900.10 p222*
Bensel, Friedrich Karl; Port uncertain, 1748 *2856.30 p31*
Bensel, Friedrich Karl; Port uncertain, 1772 *2856.30 p31*
Bensel, Friedrich Karl; Port uncertain, 1773 *2856.30 p31*
Bensel, Johann Georg; Port uncertain, 1793 *2856.30 p31*
Bensel, Johann Peter; America, 1773 *2856.30 p31*
Bensel, Johann Peter; Port uncertain, 1767 *2856.30 p31*
Bensel, Johann Peter; Port uncertain, 1788 *2856.30 p31*
Benselt, Johann Peter; America, 1773 *2856.30 p31*
Benselt, Johann Peter; Port uncertain, 1767 *2856.30 p31*
Bensen, John; New York, 1840 *8197.10 p155*
Bensist, James Mathwein; Philadelphia, 1793 *4629.10 p83*
Benskin, Henry; Virginia, 1692 *1224.1 p6*
Benskin, Thomas; Ohio, 1854 *1224.3 p6*
Bensly, Clement B.; New York, 1838 *8197.10 p110*
Benson, Mr.; Quebec, 1857 *9196.15 p18*
Benson, Mr.; Quebec, 1858 *9196.15 p38*
Benson, Mrs.; Quebec, 1857 *9196.15 p18*
Benson, Mrs.; Quebec, 1858 *9196.15 p38*
Benson, A. 20; Ontario, 1861 *2896.25 p29*
Benson, A. 28; Washington, 1914 *9196.1 p66*
Benson, Abagil 46; Ontario, 1861 *2896.25 p56*
Benson, Adam 2; Ontario, 1861 *2896.25 p62*
Benson, Angeline 23; Ontario, 1861 *2896.25 p13*
Benson, Asa T. 1; Ontario, 1861 *2896.25 p62*
Benson, Benjamin; New York, 1811 *8197.10 p57*
Benson, Catherine 12; Ontario, 1861 *2896.25 p62*
Benson, Catherine 30; Ontario, 1861 *2896.25 p62*
Benson, Catherine 41; Ontario, 1861 *2896.25 p52*
Benson, Cecilia 62; Ontario, 1871 *1823.22 p11*
Benson, Christ 48; British Columbia, 1909 *9196.1 p27*
Benson, Christ 48; Seattle, 1909 *9196.1 p27*
Benson, David 6; Ontario, 1861 *2896.25 p62*
Benson, David 16; Ontario, 1861 *2896.25 p56*
Benson, Elizabeth; Maryland, 1663 *2524.55 p23*
Benson, F. H. 9; Ontario, 1861 *2896.25 p29*
Benson, George 41; Ontario, 1871 *1823.22 p11*
Benson, Hanns; Virginia, 1703 *1224.2 p9*
Benson, Henry; New York, New York, 1747 *1224.2 p9*
Benson, Hugh; New York, 1750 *1224.2 p9*
Benson, J. 61; Ontario, 1861 *2896.25 p29*
Benson, J. A. 16; Ontario, 1861 *2896.25 p29*
Benson, J. A. 42; Ontario, 1861 *2896.25 p49*
Benson, James 43; Ontario, 1871 *1823.22 p11*
Benson, Jane 19; Ontario, 1861 *2896.25 p56*
Benson, John; New York, 1802 *8197.10 p18*
Benson, John; New York, 1840 *8197.10 p214*
Benson, John 10; Ontario, 1861 *2896.25 p62*
Benson, John 45; Ontario, 1871 *1823.22 p11*
Benson, Joseph 20; Ontario, 1861 *2896.25 p30*
Benson, M. A. 5; Ontario, 1861 *2896.25 p29*
Benson, Mary 10; Ontario, 1861 *2896.25 p56*
Benson, Mary 13; Ontario, 1861 *2896.25 p62*
Benson, Matilda J. 2; Ontario, 1861 *2896.25 p13*
Benson, Nancy 13; Ontario, 1861 *2896.25 p56*
Benson, O. E. 22; Ontario, 1861 *2896.25 p29*
Benson, Paul; New York, 1821 *8197.10 p208*
Benson, Phebe 23; Ontario, 1861 *2896.27 p17*
Benson, R. 46; Ontario, 1861 *2896.25 p29*
Benson, Richard; Maryland, 1663 *2524.55 p23*
Benson, Richard 59; Ontario, 1871 *1823.22 p11*
Benson, Samuel 9; Ontario, 1861 *2896.25 p52*
Benson, Sarah *SEE* Benson, Stephen
Benson, Sarah 74; Ontario, 1861 *2896.25 p48*
Benson, Stephen *SEE* Benson, Stephen
Benson, Stephen; Maryland, 1651 *2524.55 p23*
Wife: Sarah
Son: Stephen
Benson, Steven 8; Ontario, 1861 *2896.25 p62*
Benson, Thomas 29; Maryland, 1775 *1220.25 p9*
Benson, Thomas 60; Ontario, 1871 *1823.28 p6*
Benson, William 4; Ontario, 1861 *2896.25 p62*
Benson, William 21; Ontario, 1861 *2896.25 p56*
Benson, William 22; Ontario, 1861 *2896.25 p69*
Benson, William 23; Virginia, 1775 *1220.25 p95*
Benson, William 62; Ontario, 1861 *2896.25 p56*
Benson, William A. 13; Ontario, 1861 *2896.25 p29*
Benson, William George; Perth Amboy, New Jersey, 1811 *1224.3 p6*
Benson, William John Chapman; New York, 1851 *1224.3 p6*
Benson, William John Chapman; Quebec, 1851 *1224.3 p6*
Benson, Winifred; Vermont, 1820-1889 *5900.10 p400*
Bensson, Joseph; Pennsylvania, 1779 *4629.10 p39*
Bent, Maria; Port uncertain, 1776 *2856.30 p31*
Bent, Samll; Virginia, 1671-1672 *6212.30 p46*
Bent, William; New York, 1831 *8197.10 p313*
Bent, Wm; Virginia, 1664 *6212.30 p13*
Bentele, Josef; Port uncertain, 1743 *2856.30 p31*
Bentele, Josef; Port uncertain, 1770 *2856.30 p31*
Benteler, Jakob; Port uncertain, 1690 *2856.30 p31*
Benteler, Jakob; Port uncertain, 1740 *2856.30 p31*
Benten, Thomas, Jr. 37; Ontario, 1871 *1823.28 p6*
Benter, Jacob; New York, 1838 *8197.10 p110*
Bentinger, Andrias; Pennsylvania, 1777 *4629.10 p18*
Bentlett, John; Maryland, 1659 *2524.55 p23*
Bentley, Mr.; Portland, Maine, 1858 *9196.15 p27*
Bentley, Rev.; Quebec, 1857 *9196.15 p24*
Bentley, Henry 18; Ontario, 1861 *2896.26 p24*
Bentley, Henry 29; Ontario, 1871 *1823.22 p11*
Bentley, John 9; Ontario, 1861 *2896.26 p24*
Bentley, John 43; Ontario, 1871 *1823.15 p17*
Bentley, Lafeatt 8; Ontario, 1861 *2896.26 p24*
Bentley, Marian 16; Ontario, 1861 *2896.26 p24*
Bentley, Mary 65; Halifax, Nova Scotia, 1774 *1220.25 p138*
Bentley, Mathew; Maryland, 1665 *2524.55 p23*
Bentley, Susannah; New York, New York, 1845 *1224.3 p64*
Bentley, Thomas; New York, 1840 *8197.10 p144*
Bentley, W. 57; Ontario, 1861 *2896.26 p24*
Bentley, W. A. 6; Ontario, 1861 *2896.26 p24*
Bentley, William 15; Jamaica, 1774 *1220.25 p48*
Bently, A. 1; Ontario, 1861 *2896.26 p9*
Bently, George 41; Ontario, 1871 *1823.15 p17*
Bently, J. 21; Ontario, 1861 *2896.26 p9*
Bently, John; Maryland, 1659 *2524.55 p23*
Bently, John; Pennsylvania, 1779 *4629.10 p41*
Bently, M. 10; Ontario, 1861 *2896.26 p9*
Bently, M. 47; Ontario, 1861 *2896.26 p9*

Bently, Moses; Virginia, 1667 6212.30 p36
Bently, Richard; Maryland, 1658 2524.55 p23
Bently, Samuell; Maryland, 1654 2524.55 p24
Bently, Thomas; Maryland, 1681 2524.55 p24
Benton, Richard; Maryland, 1681 2524.55 p24
Benton, William 47; Ontario, 1871 1823.22 p11
Bentrum, William 70; Ontario, 1871 1823.28 p6
Bentsch, Jacob; America, 1749 2856.30 p31
Bentz, Barbara; America, 1732 2856.30 p31
Bentz, Jacob; New York, 1837 8197.10 p87
Bentz, Johann; America, 1748 2856.30 p31
Bentz, Johann; Port uncertain, 1775 2856.30 p31
Bentz, Jorg; America, 1749 2856.30 p31
Bentz, Peter; Port uncertain, 1770 2856.30 p31
Bentzel, Maria Ursula; Port uncertain, 1745 2856.30 p31
Bentzle, Adam; America, 1749 2856.30 p31
With wife
Bentzle, Adam; America, 1750 2856.30 p31
With wife
Bentzlin, Adam; America, 1749 2856.30 p31
With wife
Bentzlin, Adam; America, 1750 2856.30 p31
With wife
Benuto, Iam 25; British Columbia, 1910 9196.1 p29
Benuto, Iam 25; Washington, 1910 9196.1 p29
Benway, Julia A.; Vermont, 1858-1941 5900.10 p408
Benz, Anna Barbara; Port uncertain, 1751 2856.30 p31
Benz, Anton; Port uncertain, 1766 2856.30 p31
Benz, Catharina; Port uncertain, 1803 2856.30 p31
Benz, Friedrich; Port uncertain, 1795 2856.30 p31
Benz, Hans Georg; Port uncertain, 1749 2856.30 p31
Benz, Johann; America, 1787 2856.30 p31
Benz, Johann; Port uncertain, 1791 2856.30 p31
Benz, Josef; Port uncertain, 1795 2856.30 p31
Benz, Luise; Port uncertain, 1778 2856.30 p31
Benz, Magdalena; Port uncertain, 1752 2856.30 p31
Benz, Margarete; Port uncertain, 1739 2856.30 p31
Benz, Maria; Port uncertain, 1776 2856.30 p31
Benz, Mathias; New York, 1833-1838 8197.10 p311
Benz, Rudolf; Canada, 1751 2856.30 p31
Benz, Wilhelm; Port uncertain, 1783 2856.30 p31
Benz, Wilhelm; Port uncertain, 1787 2856.30 p31
Benzer, Johannes; New York, 1838 8197.10 p212
Benzinger, Fridne 34; Ontario, 1871 1823.28 p6
Beoen, John; Maryland, 1668 2524.55 p24
Beozkowski, Joseph; Maryland, 1910 3259.35 p4
Ber, Cath. Wengert *SEE* Ber, Christof
Ber, Christof; America, 1743 2856.30 p32
Wife: Cath. Wengert
Berbrick, Lydia L. 3; Ontario, 1861 2896.28 p22
Berbrick, Thomas 37; Ontario, 1861 2896.28 p22
Berch, John 70; Ontario, 1871 1823.15 p17
Bercher, Henry; Virginia, 1665-1666 6212.30 p21
Berckmann, Johann; America, 1793 2856.30 p32
Berduss, Johann Jacob; Port uncertain, 1759 2856.30 p32
Berdych, Mary; Maryland, 1910 3259.35 p4
Bere, Theodore; Virginia, 1757 1224.2 p8
Bere, Thomas 33; Ontario, 1871 1823.22 p11
Bereeth, Johann; Port uncertain, 1727 2856.30 p32
Berenstecher, Michael; America, 1747 2856.30 p32
Berer, Anna Maria; America, 1743 2856.30 p32
Beresford, Robert H.; New York, 1807 8197.10 p34
Bereuca, F. 31; Alaska, 1910 9196.1 p10
Bereuca, F. 31; Yukon, 1910 9196.1 p10
Berford, Francis M. 56; Ontario, 1871 1823.28 p6
Berg, A. 53; Alaska, 1918 9196.1 p56
Berg, A. 53; Yukon, 1918 9196.1 p56
Berg, Heinrich; Port uncertain, 1788 2856.30 p32
Berg, Henrich; Port uncertain, 1750 2856.30 p32
Berg, Jacob; America, 1788 2856.30 p32
Berg, Jacob; America, 1793 2856.30 p32
Berg, Jacob; Port uncertain, 1781 2856.30 p32
Berg, Jacob; Port uncertain, 1785 2856.30 p32
Berg, Joachim 50; Ontario, 1871 1823.15 p17
Berg, Johann Peter; Port uncertain, 1747 2856.30 p32
With wife & children
Berg, John 30; British Columbia, 1910 9196.1 p30
Berg, John 30; Seattle, 1910 9196.1 p30
Berg, Maria Elisabeth; Port uncertain, 1776 2856.30 p32
Berg, Mathes; Port uncertain, 1680 2856.30 p32
Berg, Michael; Port uncertain, 1728 2856.30 p32
Berg, Oliver 45; Alaska, 1917 9196.1 p52
Berg, Oliver 45; British Columbia, 1917 9196.1 p52
Bergdolti, . . .; America, 1793 2856.30 p32
Bergen, Daniel; New York, 1827 8197.10 p341
Bergen, William 18; Ontario, 1871 1823.15 p17
Berger, Andreas; Port uncertain, 1748 2856.30 p32
Berger, Caspar; America, 1752 2856.30 p32
Berger, Christian; Port uncertain, 1786 2856.30 p32
Berger, Jacob; Port uncertain, 1750 2856.30 p32
Berger, John; New York, 1834 8197.10 p74
Berger, Maria Magdalena; Port uncertain, 1749 2856.30 p32
Berger, Mathis; America, 1741 2856.30 p33
With wife & 4 children
Berger, Nikolaus; Port uncertain, 1733 2856.30 p32
Berger, Nikolaus; Port uncertain, 1763 2856.30 p32
Berger, William 27; Ontario, 1871 1823.28 p6
Bergh, Laurance 21; Maryland, 1773-1774 1220.25 p34
Bergin, Patrick; New York, 1827 8197.10 p344
Bergin, William; New York, 1827 8197.10 p347
Bergman, John; Pennsylvania, 1777 4629.10 p12
Bergmann, Jacob; Port uncertain, 1773 2856.30 p33
Bergmann, Johann Jacob; America, 1763 2856.30 p33
With wife & 5 children
Bergmann, Magdalene; Port uncertain, 1729 2856.30 p33
Bergmann, Maria Elisabeth; Port uncertain, 1778 2856.30 p33
Bergstrasser, Georg; Port uncertain, 1768 2856.30 p33
Bergwin, Edward; Pennsylvania, 1845 6058.10 p21
Berhand, Louis 23; Ontario, 1871 1823.15 p17
Berich, B. 26; Alaska, 1912 9196.1 p38
Berich, B. 26; Yukon, 1912 9196.1 p38
Beringer, Josef; Port uncertain, 1709 2856.30 p33
Beringer, Josef; Port uncertain, 1739 2856.30 p33
Berjeu, John; New York, 1783 1224.2 p9
Berkeley, William; Virginia, 1677 1224.1 p6
Berksby, Jno; Virginia, 1665-1666 6212.30 p21
Berkwell, Hugh 50; Ontario, 1871 1823.28 p6
Berleur, Eugene; New York, 1839 8197.10 p128
Berman, Joseph 40; Ontario, 1871 1823.28 p6
Bernadzikowski, Frank; Maryland, 1910 3259.35 p4
Bernard, Capt.; Quebec, 1857 9196.15 p16
Bernard, Mr.; Quebec, 1857 9196.15 p25
Bernard, Mrs.; Quebec, 1857 9196.15 p13
Bernard, Mrs.; Quebec, 1857 9196.15 p25
Bernard, Antoine; New York, 1823 8197.10 p62
Bernard, Benan 35; Ontario, 1871 1823.28 p6
Bernard, George 30; Ontario, 1871 1823.15 p17
Bernard, Jacob; Port uncertain, 1764 2856.30 p33
Bernard, Jno; Maryland, 1671 2524.55 p24
Wife: Thomasin
Bernard, Johann Adam; America, 1774 2856.30 p33
Bernard, Johann Christia; Port uncertain, 1744 2856.30 p33
Bernard, John 32; Ontario, 1871 1823.28 p6
Bernard, Nicholas; Pennsylvania, 1777 4629.10 p28
Bernard, Thomas 30; Ontario, 1871 1823.15 p17
Bernard, Thomasin *SEE* Bernard, Jno
Bernath, Conrad 34; Ontario, 1871 1823.15 p17
Bernauer, Johann; America, 1750 2856.30 p33
Bernauer, Johann; America, 1773 2856.30 p33
Berndt, Christian; America, 1749 2856.30 p33
Berndt, Christian; Port uncertain, 1749 2856.30 p33
Berndt, David 37; Ontario, 1871 1823.28 p6
Berndt, Johann Peter; Port uncertain, 1786 2856.30 p34
Berndt, Wilhelm; America, 1741 2856.30 p33
With wife & children
Berndtson, Eric; New York, 1825 8197.10 p210
Berndtus, Martin; Port uncertain, 1754 2856.30 p33
Berneholtz, Conrad; New York, 1838 8197.10 p110
Berner, Anna Maria; Port uncertain, 1747 2856.30 p33
Berner, Heinrich; Port uncertain, 1759 2856.30 p33
Berner, John 24; Philadelphia, 1774 1220.25 p35
Berner, Rosina; Port uncertain, 1749 2856.30 p33
Berners, Jane 29; Virginia, 1775 1220.25 p95
Berneskey, Anthony 60; Ontario, 1871 1823.28 p6
Bernetts, James 60; Ontario, 1871 1823.28 p6
Berney, Edward 36; Ontario, 1871 1823.15 p17
Bernhard, Anton; Port uncertain, 1766 2856.30 p33
Bernhard, Barbara; Port uncertain, 1788 2856.30 p33
Bernhard, Caspar; America, 1764 2856.30 p34
Bernhard, Caspar; America, 1767 2856.30 p34
Bernhard, Christof; America, 1738 2856.30 p33
Bernhard, Georg; Port uncertain, 1748 2856.30 p33
Bernhard, Henrich Valenti; America, 1748 2856.30 p34
Bernhard, Henry; New York, 1838 8197.10 p318
Bernhard, J. Peter Corneli; Port uncertain, 1771 2856.30 p34
Bernhard, Jakob; America, 1741 2856.30 p34
Bernhard, Johann; Port uncertain, 1753 2856.30 p34
Bernhard, Johann; Port uncertain, 1792 2856.30 p34
Bernhard, Johann Peter; Port uncertain, 1786 2856.30 p34
Bernhard, Karl; America, 1753 2856.30 p34
With wife & child
Bernhard, Karl; Port uncertain, 1753 2856.30 p34
With wife & child
Bernhard, Maria Margarete; Port uncertain, 1741 2856.30 p34
Bernhard, Wendel; Port uncertain, 1796 2856.30 p34
Bernhard, Wilhelm; America, 1764 2856.30 p34
Bernhard, Wilhelm; America, 1767 2856.30 p34
Bernhardt, Gustav; New York, 1840 8197.10 p153
Bernhardt, Jacob; Port uncertain, 1764 2856.30 p33
Bernhardt, Veronika; Port uncertain, 1766 2856.30 p34
Bernier, Captain; Quebec, 1857 9196.15 p19
Bernier, Ferdinand; Haiti, 1898 1640.13 p8
Berninger, Thomas; Port uncertain, 1728 2856.30 p34
Berny, Johann; Port uncertain, 1757 2856.30 p34
Berrent, Alexander; Maryland, 1910 3259.35 p4
Berrer, Elizabeth *SEE* Berrer, Phillip
Berrer, Griffes *SEE* Berrer, Phillip
Berrer, Olive *SEE* Berrer, Phillip
Berrer, Phillip; Maryland, 1665 2524.55 p24
Relative: Olive
Relative: Elizabeth
Relative: Griffes
Berridge, John; Maryland, 1664 2524.55 p24
Berrie, James; Ontario, 1864 1640.13 p8
Berriman, William; Pennsylvania, 1779 4629.10 p38
Berrist, John; Virginia, 1666-1667 6212.30 p34
Berrks, Sibell; Virginia, 1667 6212.30 p35
Berrks, Timothy; Virginia, 1667 6212.30 p35
Berron, Rice; Maryland, 1668 2524.55 p24
Berry, Dr.; Quebec, 1857 9196.15 p26
Berry, Miss; Quebec, 1856 9196.15 p6
Berry, Adam 53; Ontario, 1871 1823.15 p17
Berry, Bridget Walsh; Vermont, 1835-1909 5900.10 p406
Berry, Charles; New York, 1831 8197.10 p211
Berry, Edward; Virginia, 1664 6212.30 p9
Berry, Elizabeth *SEE* Berry, James
Berry, Ellen McGarghan; Vermont, 1849-1890 5900.10 p410
Berry, Francis; Georgia, 1698 1640.13 p9
Berry, George; Pennsylvania, 1777 4629.10 p11
Berry, George; Virginia, 1664 6212.30 p12
Berry, George Charles Bradbury; New York, 1850 1224.3 p6
Berry, Mrs. J.; Quebec, 1856 9196.15 p11
Berry, James; America, 1817 1640.13 p9
Berry, James; Maryland, 1652 2524.55 p24
Wife: Elizabeth
Relative: Roger
Relative: Martha
Relative: William
Berry, James 15; Salem, Massachusetts, 1774 1220.25 p83
Berry, James 31; Savannah, Georgia, 1774 1220.25 p139
With child
Berry, Jane Beachwell; Vermont, 1853-1939 5900.10 p410
Berry, John; New York, 1807 8197.10 p35
Berry, John; New York, 1840 8197.10 p213
Berry, John; New York, New York, 1802 1224.2 p9
Berry, John; New York, New York, 1802 1224.3 p6
Berry, John 26; Philadelphia, 1775 1220.25 p9
Berry, John 35; Ontario, 1871 1823.15 p17
Berry, John, Jr.; New York, 1794 8197.10 p4
Berry, John C.; Vermont, 1849-1934 5900.10 p410
Berry, Martha *SEE* Berry, James
Berry, Mary Phillips; Vermont, 1843-1903 5900.10 p413
Berry, Michael; Vermont, 1835-1919 5900.10 p406
Berry, Robert; Virginia, 1664 6212.30 p11
Berry, Robert C.; Vermont, 1847-1919 5900.10 p413
Berry, Roger *SEE* Berry, James
Berry, Thomas; New York, 1839 8197.10 p213
Berry, Thomas; Virginia, 1666 6212.30 p30
Berry, Thomas 16; Maryland, 1775 1220.25 p101
Berry, William *SEE* Berry, James
Berry, William; Maryland, 1681 2524.55 p24
Berryman, Michael; New York, 1837 8197.10 p212
Berstin, Anna Maria; Port uncertain, 1766 2856.30 p34
Bertack, Capt.; Quebec, 1856 9196.15 p10
Bertack, Mrs.; Quebec, 1856 9196.15 p10
Berthand, Abraham 21; Maryland, 1774 1220.25 p41
Bertie, Peregrine; Philadelphia, 1850 1224.3 p6
Bertold, Wilhelm; Port uncertain, 1776 2856.30 p35
Bertram, Alexander; Augusta, Georgia, 1827 1640.10 p11
Bertran, Christopher; New York, 1830 8197.10 p66
Bertrand, Charles Pierre; New York, 1807 8197.10 p35
Bertraud, Victor 21; Ontario, 1871 1823.15 p17
Bertre, Louis; New York, 1794 8197.10 p4
Bertsch, Anna; Port uncertain, 1761 2856.30 p35
Bertsch, Georg; America, 1752 2856.30 p35
With wife & child
Bertsch, Jacob; Port uncertain, 1772 2856.30 p35
Bertsch, Jakob; America, 1767 2856.30 p35
Bertsch, Nikolaus; Port uncertain, 1752 2856.30 p35
Bertsch, Susanna Maria; America, 1738 2856.30 p35
With husband 2 sons & 2 daughters
Bertsch, Susanna Maria; America, 1738 2856.30 p35
With husband & 4 children
Bertsche, Jacob; Port uncertain, 1790 2856.30 p35
Bertschmann, Johann; America, 1749 2856.30 p35
With wife & 3 children
Bertz, Martin; Port uncertain, 1716 2856.30 p35

Berwick, Mr.; Portland, Maine, 1858 9196.15 p47
Berwick, Mrs.; Portland, Maine, 1858 9196.15 p47
Besane, Francis; Maryland, 1666 2524.55 p24
Besanson, Henry 51; Ontario, 1871 1823.15 p17
Besau, Horace 33; Ontario, 1871 1823.28 p6
Besch, Jacob; New York, 1840 8197.10 p145
Besch, Johann Wilhelm; America, 1749 2856.30 p35
Besch, Konrad; America, 1764 2856.30 p35
Besch, Konrad; Canada, 1700-1799 2856.30 p35
Besch, Wilhelm; America, 1749 2856.30 p35
Besel, Jakob; Port uncertain, 1752 2856.30 p35
Besel, Johan; Port uncertain, 1752 2856.30 p35
Beser, Francis; Maryland, 1910 3259.35 p4
Besh, Sebastian; America, 1737 2856.30 p35
Besh, Sebastian; America, 1737 2856.30 p39
Besley, George Barlow 25; Ontario, 1871 1823.28 p6
Besley, William 28; Ontario, 1871 1823.28 p6
Besley, Wm Barlow 27; Ontario, 1871 1823.28 p6
Bessam, Sovefee 49; Ontario, 1871 1823.28 p6
Bessent, Richard 32; Ontario, 1871 1823.28 p6
Besser, Jacob; Port uncertain, 1744 2856.30 p35
Bessing, William; Maryland, 1665 2524.55 p24
Bessling, Henry; New York, 1839 8197.10 p128
Besson, Ann *SEE* Besson, Thomas
Besson, Thomas *SEE* Besson, Thomas
Besson, Thomas; Maryland, 1649 2524.55 p24
  Wife: Ann
  Child: Thomas
  Child: Ann
Bessy, Elizabeth Holland; Virginia, 1658 1224.1 p30
Best, Mr.; Quebec, 1857 9196.15 p18
Best, Abraham 67; Ontario, 1871 1823.15 p17
Best, Adam; Port uncertain, 1751 2856.30 p35
Best, Eliza; Pennsylvania, 1840 1224.3 p6
Best, Friedrich; America, 1783 2856.30 p35
Best, Geo 32; British Columbia, 1910 9196.1 p29
Best, Geo 32; Washington, 1910 9196.1 p29
Best, George; New Jersey, 1842 1224.3 p6
Best, Isabella; Pennsylvania, 1840 1224.3 p6
Best, Jacob 37; Ontario, 1871 1823.15 p17
Best, James 22; Maryland, 1774 1220.25 p39
Best, Jno; Virginia, 1665-1666 6212.30 p23
Best, Johann; Port uncertain, 1788 2856.30 p35
Best, Johann Adam; Port uncertain, 1788 2856.30 p35
Best, Johann Friedric; Port uncertain, 1763 2856.30 p35
Best, John; New York, 1826 8197.10 p333
Best, John; Virginia, 1664 6212.30 p13
Best, Joshriea 26; Ontario, 1871 1823.15 p17
Best, Nicholas; Maryland, 1686 1224.1 p6
Best, Sebastian; America, 1737 2856.30 p35
Best, Sebastian; America, 1737 2856.30 p35
  With wife & children
Best, Sebastian; America, 1737 2856.30 p39
Best, Wilhelm; Port uncertain, 1770 2856.30 p35
Best, Wilhelm; Port uncertain, 1771 2856.30 p35
Bestwick, W. W. 42; British Columbia, 1909 9196.1 p26
Bestwick, W. W. 42; Washington, 1909 9196.1 p26
Besuchet, Francois; New Orleans, 1849 1224.3 p6
Beswick, Mr.; Quebec, 1857 9196.15 p26
Beswick, Mrs.; Quebec, 1857 9196.15 p26
Beswicke, Charles; South Carolina, 1734 1224.2 p9
Beswicke, Mary Hill; Charles Town, South Carolina, 1749 1224.2 p9
Beswicke, Silence; Charles Town, South Carolina, 1740 1224.2 p9
Beswitheric, John 60; Ontario, 1871 1823.22 p11
Beswitheric, Joseph 33; Ontario, 1871 1823.22 p11
Beswitherick, James 50; Ontario, 1871 1823.15 p18
Betagh, Thomas; Pennsylvania, 1777 4629.10 p24
Betchen, Gottlieb 57; Ontario, 1871 1823.15 p18
Beteman, William 32; Ontario, 1871 1823.28 p6
Bethel, Daniel; Vermont, 1851-1924 5900.10 p393
Bethel, Ellen; Vermont, 1854-1928 5900.10 p397
Bethel, Ellen Collins 73; Vermont, 1893 5900.10 p397
Bethel, John T.; Vermont, 1850-1932 5900.10 p397
Bethel, Mary Holland; Vermont, 1856-1941 5900.10 p393
Bethel, Mary Mooney; Vermont, 1851-1930 5900.10 p397
Bethel, Mary Powers; Vermont, 1861-1942 5900.10 p397
Bethel, Sarah A.; Vermont, 1849-1910 5900.10 p397
Bethel, William; Vermont, 1852-1932 5900.10 p397
Bethel, William 75; Vermont, 1900 5900.10 p397
Bethell, Robert; Pennsylvania, 1777 4629.10 p18
Bethell, William; New York, 1807 8197.10 p35
Bethune, Angus *SEE* Bethune, John
Bethune, Benjamin Faneuil; Cambridge, Massachusetts, 1796 1224.2 p9
Bethune, George; Cambridge, Massachusetts, 1785 1224.2 p10
Bethune, John; Nova Scotia, 1820 4537.35 p10
  Wife: Margaret MacAulay
  Child: Kirsty
  Child: Margaret
  Child: Angus
  Child: Roderick
Bethune, Kirsty *SEE* Bethune, John
Bethune, Margaret *SEE* Bethune, John
Bethune, Margaret MacAulay *SEE* Bethune, John
Bethune, Mary; Cambridge, Massachusetts, 1796 1224.2 p9
Bethune, Robert; Ontario, 1864 1640.13 p9
Bethune, Robert Henry; Toronto, 1897 1640.13 p9
Bethune, Roderick *SEE* Bethune, John
Bethune, Unagh; Ontario, 1886 1640.13 p9
Betka, Frank; Maryland, 1910 3259.35 p4
Beton, John; Virginia, 1678 1224.1 p7
Betsch, Christian; America, 1789 2856.30 p35
Betsch, Christian; America, 1790 2856.30 p35
Betsch, Jakob; America, 1767 2856.30 p35
Betson, James; Pennsylvania, 1777 4629.10 p26
Bett, Philipp; Port uncertain, 1744 2856.30 p35
Bettejewski, John; Maryland, 1910 3259.35 p4
Bettejewski, Joseph; Maryland, 1910 3259.35 p4
Bettejewski, Marian; Maryland, 1910 3259.35 p4
Bettenfeld, Johann; America, 1750 2856.30 p35
  With wife 2 sons & 3 daughters
Better, Eva C. 20; Kansas, 1891-1910 9079.10 p22
Better, Henry 30; Kansas, 1907-1910 9079.10 p21
Betteridge, John 56; Philadelphia, 1774 1220.25 p67
Bettiason, James 25; Maryland, 1774 1220.25 p42
Bettle, Michael; America, 1727 2856.30 p35
Bettle, Samuel; Pennsylvania, 1786 4629.10 p54
Bettles, John 46; Ontario, 1871 1823.28 p6
Bettridge, Mr.; Quebec, 1856 9196.15 p7
Bettridge, Mrs.; Quebec, 1856 9196.15 p7
Betts, Mr.; Quebec, 1857 9196.15 p22
Betts, Mrs.; Quebec, 1857 9196.15 p22
Betts, Augusta; Quebec, 1857 9196.15 p23
Betts, Charles T.; New York, 1834 8197.10 p74
Betts, Clara; Quebec, 1857 9196.15 p23
Betts, Frederick; Quebec, 1857 9196.15 p23
Betts, George; Maryland, 1668 2524.55 p24
Betts, George; New York, 1840 8197.10 p144
Betts, George 47; Ontario, 1871 1823.15 p18
Betts, Henry; Quebec, 1857 9196.15 p23
Betts, Henry Augustus; Ontario, 1877 1640.13 p9
Betts, Hyla; Quebec, 1857 9196.15 p23
Betts, Isabella; Boston, 1725 1224.2 p98
Betts, Jabez; New York, 1820-1834 8197.10 p306
Betts, James 15; Maryland, 1774 1220.25 p46
Betts, John; Maryland, 1682 2524.55 p24
Betts, John; Quebec, 1857 9196.15 p23
Betts, John; Virginia, 1672 6212.30 p49
Betts, John 40; Ontario, 1871 1823.15 p18
Betts, Lucy; Quebec, 1857 9196.15 p22
Betts, Mary; Quebec, 1857 9196.15 p22
Betts, Newman 24; Maryland, 1775 1220.25 p101
Betts, William; New York, 1837 8197.10 p311
Bettur, William; Virginia, 1671-1672 6212.30 p47
Betty, John 29; Virginia, 1774 1220.25 p27
Betty, Robert Bell; Philadelphia, 1840 1224.3 p6
Betz, Adam; New York, 1839 8197.10 p128
Betzel, Heinrich; New York, 1807 8197.10 p35
Beucker, George; New York, 1840 8197.10 p145
Beukland, Elizabeth *SEE* Beukland, Richard
Beukland, Elizabeth; Maryland, 1672 2524.55 p24
Beukland, Richard *SEE* Beukland, Richard
Beukland, Richard; Maryland, 1631-1685 2524.55 p24
  Wife: Elizabeth
  Son: Richard
Beukland, Richard; Maryland, 1672 2524.55 p24
Beukland, Richard; Maryland, 1675 2524.55 p21
  Wife: Elizabeth
  Son: Richard
Beurbaum, Simon; New York, 1840 8197.10 p154
Beuschel, Georg; Port uncertain, 1772 2856.30 p35
Beuscher, Anna Gertraud; Port uncertain, 1760 2856.30 p36
Beuscher, Maria Barbara; Port uncertain, 1747 2856.30 p36
Beuscher, Nickel; Port uncertain, 1784 2856.30 p36
Beutel, Elisabeth; Port uncertain, 1764 2856.30 p36
Beutel, Henrich; Port uncertain, 1784 2856.30 p36
Beutel, Josef; Port uncertain, 1735 2856.30 p36
Beutel, Konrad; Port uncertain, 1783 2856.30 p36
Beutler, John C.; Pennsylvania, 1859 6058.10 p41
Bevad, William M. 48; Ontario, 1871 1823.15 p18
Beverage, John 20; Ontario, 1871 1823.15 p18
Beveridge, David; Pennsylvania, 1777 4629.10 p8
Beveridge, Mary 17; Maryland, 1774 1220.25 p59
Beverly, Jno; Virginia, 1664 6212.30 p9
Beverly, John; Maryland, 1659 2524.55 p24
Beverly, William; Virginia, 1665 6212.30 p17
Beverstock, Martha 30; Ontario, 1861 2896.26 p22
Beverstock, Robert 29; Ontario, 1861 2896.26 p22
Bevian, Mary; South Carolina, 1785 1224.2 p10
Bevis, Ann 33; Ontario, 1871 1823.22 p11
Bevis, Henry Basil 29; Ontario, 1871 1823.28 p6
Bevis, Nathan; Maryland, 1681 2524.55 p24
Bevis, William; Virginia, 1717 1224.2 p10
Bevis, William 35; Ontario, 1871 1823.22 p11
Bevridge, Robert 51; Ontario, 1871 1823.28 p6
Bew, Rigoult; Virginia, 1697 1224.1 p7
Bewfeild, Godfry; Virginia, 1667 6212.30 p37
Bewk, James 53; Ontario, 1871 1823.15 p18
Bewly, John Pearson; America, 1881 1640.13 p9
Bews, John; Savannah, Georgia, 1742-1845 1640.10 p11
Bews, William; Ontario, 1900 1640.13 p9
Bexfield, Joseph; Virginia, 1850 1224.3 p6
Bexley, Mary *SEE* Bexley, William
Bexley, Mary; Maryland, 1681 2524.55 p24
Bexley, William; Maryland, 1631-1685 2524.55 p24
  Wife: Mary
Bexley, William; Maryland, 1663 2524.55 p24
Beyer, Adam; America, 1741 2856.30 p36
Beyer, Hans Georg; Port uncertain, 1744 2856.30 p36
Beyer, Hans Georg; Port uncertain, 1774 2856.30 p36
Beyer, Johann Friedric; America, 1741 2856.30 p36
Beyerfalck, Michael; America, 1738 2856.30 p36
Beyerle, Daniel; America, 1738 2856.30 p36
Beyick, Paul; Maryland, 1910 3259.35 p4
Beykirch, Georg; Port uncertain, 1751 2856.30 p36
Beyl, Daniel; America, 1752 2856.30 p36
  With wife & child
Beyl, Johann; Port uncertain, 1745 2856.30 p36
  With wife & 2 children
Beynon, Evan; New York, 1810 8197.10 p56
Beynroth, William; Baltimore, 1793 4629.10 p78
Beys, John 24; Fort Cumberland, Nova Scotia, 1774 1220.25 p17
Beyscher, Jacob; Port uncertain, 1820 2856.30 p36
Beysel, Anna Maria; Port uncertain, 1754 2856.30 p36
  With 8 children
Beysiegel, Hans Peter; Port uncertain, 1724 2856.30 p36
Beysiegel, Johann Nicol; Port uncertain, 1751 2856.30 p36
Beysigel, Maria Elisabeth; Port uncertain, 1746 2856.30 p36
Beysiger, Peter Barthol; America, 1774 2856.30 p36
Beysiger, Peter Barthol; America, 1775 2856.30 p36
Beyss, Konrad; Port uncertain, 1770 2856.30 p36
Beytelt, Henrich; Port uncertain, 1784 2856.30 p36
Bez, Andreas; America, 1752 2856.30 p36
Bez, Anna Catharina; Port uncertain, 1792 2856.30 p36
Bez, Elisabeth; Port uncertain, 1774 2856.30 p36
Bez, Georg Peter; America, 1741 2856.30 p36
  With wife & 3 children
Bezinch, John 26; Washington, 1914 9196.1 p66
Bezkia, Frank; Maryland, 1910 3259.35 p4
Bezwah, J. Bte 56; Ontario, 1871 1823.28 p6
Biabot, Pierre; New York, 1840 8197.10 p213
Biago, Frank 22; British Columbia, 1910 9196.1 p29
Biago, Frank 22; Washington, 1910 9196.1 p29
Bialecki, Jan; Maryland, 1910 3259.35 p4
Bialek, Joseph; Maryland, 1910 3259.35 p4
Bialek, Joseph L.; Maryland, 1910 3259.35 p4
Bialek, Marga; Maryland, 1910 3259.35 p4
Bialek, Michael; Maryland, 1910 3259.35 p4
Bialek, Paul; Maryland, 1910 3259.35 p4
Bialobrzesky, Frank; Maryland, 1910 3259.35 p4
Bialosinski, Louis; Maryland, 1910 3259.35 p4
Bialosinski, Michael; Maryland, 1910 3259.35 p4
Bialozynska, Josephine; Maryland, 1910 3259.35 p4
Bialozynska, William; Maryland, 1910 3259.35 p4
Biart, John Peter; New York, 1807 8197.10 p35
Bibby, James; Maryland, 1681 2524.55 p24
Bibby, John 40; Ontario, 1871 1823.22 p11
Bibby, Margaret Johnson McEvers; New York, New York, 1823 1224.3 p6
Bibby, Nicholas 45; Ontario, 1871 1823.22 p11
Bibby, Robert 66; Ontario, 1871 1823.22 p11
Bibby, Thomas; New York, 1830 1224.3 p6
Bibby, Thomas 30; Ontario, 1871 1823.22 p11
Bibik, Adela; Maryland, 1910 3259.35 p4
Bibrim, Joseph; New York, 1837 8197.10 p375
Bicaterfeld, Christian 36; Kansas, 1878-1910 9079.10 p53
Bicaterfeld, Elizabeth 22; Kansas, 1893-1910 9079.10 p53
Bichno, Stanislaus; Maryland, 1910 3259.35 p4
Bick, Johann Henrich; America, 1733 2856.30 p37
Bicke, Conrad 61; Kansas, 1875-1910 9079.10 p9
Bicke, Mary 58; Kansas, 1875-1910 9079.10 p9
Bickel, Andreas; Port uncertain, 1749 2856.30 p37
Bickel, Anna Maria; Port uncertain, 1745 2856.30 p37
Bickel, Jacob; Port uncertain, 1780 2856.30 p37
Bickel, Jakob; Port uncertain, 1754 2856.30 p37
Bickel, Thomas 50; Ontario, 1871 1823.22 p11

Bickel, Xaver; Port uncertain, 1789 ***2856.30*** *p37*
Bickele, Peter; America, 1752 ***2856.30*** *p37*
Bicker, Flora 57; Kansas, 1875-1910 ***9079.10*** *p8*
Bicker, Michael 59; Ontario, 1871 ***1823.15*** *p18*
Bicker, Philip 58; Kansas, 1875-1910 ***9079.10*** *p8*
Bickerstaffe, Robt; Virginia, 1664 ***6212.30*** *p7*
Bickert, Jakob; Port uncertain, 1732 ***2856.30*** *p37*
Bickerton, Benjamin; Pennsylvania, 1777 ***4629.10*** *p17*
Bickerton, John; New York, New York, 1854 ***1224.3*** *p6*
Bickerton, Martha; New York, 1854 ***1224.3*** *p7*
Bicking, Caspar; America, 1749 ***2856.30*** *p37*
With wife & children
Bickle, Adam; America, 1751 ***2856.30*** *p37*
With wife & children
Bickle, Jane 33; Ontario, 1871 ***1823.15*** *p18*
Bickle, W. J.; Quebec, 1858 ***9196.15*** *p45*
Bickler, Anna; Port uncertain, 1750 ***2856.30*** *p37*
Bickler, Barbara; Port uncertain, 1748 ***2856.30*** *p37*
Bickler, Johann Adam; Port uncertain, 1790 ***2856.30*** *p37*
Bickler, Peter; New York, 1840 ***8197.10*** *p144*
Bickley, Abraham; Pennsylvania, 1776 ***4629.10*** *p53*
Bickley, Anne; Virginia, 1657 ***1224.1*** *p6*
Bickley, Henry; Pennsylvania, 1777 ***4629.10*** *p26*
Bickley, Lawrence; Pennsylvania, 1777 ***4629.10*** *p26*
Bickley, Thomas; Virginia, 1664 ***6212.30*** *p9*
Bickmore, Henry 27; Ontario, 1871 ***1823.28*** *p6*
Bicknall, Edward 40; Maryland, 1774 ***1220.25*** *p57*
Bicknell, Clare 29; Ontario, 1871 ***1823.15*** *p18*
Bicknell, Dorcas; New York, New York, 1856 ***1224.3*** *p7*
Bicknell, Mary; Philadelphia, 1812 ***1224.3*** *p7*
Bicknell, William; Annapolis, Maryland, 1764 ***1224.2*** *p10*
Biczuk, Peter; Maryland, 1910 ***3259.35*** *p4*
Biddle, Miss; Quebec, 1857 ***9196.15*** *p26*
Biddle, Edward; Pennsylvania, 1779 ***4629.10*** *p36*
Biddle, John; New York, 1821 ***8197.10*** *p208*
Biddle, John; Pennsylvania, 1777 ***4629.10*** *p13*
Biddle, John 25; Philadelphia, 1775 ***1220.25*** *p122*
Biddlecomb, Joseph 40; Ontario, 1871 ***1823.15*** *p18*
Biddulph, George 51; Ontario, 1871 ***1823.15*** *p18*
Biddulph, Tho; Virginia, 1664 ***6212.30*** *p15*
Bideau, Johann, The Older; Port uncertain, 1768 ***2856.30*** *p37*
Bidle, Thomas; Pennsylvania, 1779 ***4629.10*** *p38*
Bidmead, Samuel; Illinois, 1847 ***1224.3*** *p7*
Bido, Johann, The Older; Port uncertain, 1768 ***2856.30*** *p37*
Bidolph, Eliza; Virginia, 1663 ***6212.30*** *p4*
Bidwell, Mary 76; Ontario, 1871 ***1823.22*** *p11*
Bidwill, Harriet 48; Ontario, 1871 ***1823.22*** *p11*
Bidwill, William 45; Ontario, 1871 ***1823.22*** *p11*
Bieble, Edward 30; Ontario, 1871 ***1823.15*** *p18*
Bieck, Arend Hinrich; New York, 1837 ***8197.10*** *p212*
Biedronski, Frank; Maryland, 1910 ***3259.35*** *p4*
Biedrzyski, Vincent; Maryland, 1910 ***3259.35*** *p4*
Biegel, Henrich; Port uncertain, 1764 ***2856.30*** *p37*
Biegler, Leonard; Port uncertain, 1764 ***2856.30*** *p59*
Biehler, Georg; Port uncertain, 1762 ***2856.30*** *p37*
Biehler, Peter; New York, 1838 ***8197.10*** *p212*
Biehn, Peter; New Orleans, 1844 ***3437.14*** *p36*
Biehr, Johann Dietrich; America, 1770 ***2856.30*** *p37*
Biehy, John; New York, 1838 ***8197.10*** *p109*
Biel, Philipp; Port uncertain, 1767 ***2856.30*** *p37*
Bielat, Marcas; Maryland, 1910 ***3259.35*** *p4*
Bielle, John Baptiste Joseph; New York, 1820-1834 ***8197.10*** *p306*
Bielle, John Baptiste Joseph; New York, 1831 ***8197.10*** *p314*
Bien, Robert; Maryland, 1910 ***3259.35*** *p4*
Bienert, Theodore; Maryland, 1910 ***3259.35*** *p4*
Bienkowski, Anthony; Maryland, 1910 ***3259.35*** *p4*
Bienkowski, Joseph; Maryland, 1910 ***3259.35*** *p4*
Bier, Charles; New York, 1840 ***8197.10*** *p144*
Bier, Josef; America, 1739 ***2856.30*** *p37*
With wife
Bier, Joseph; New York, New York, 1892 ***3437.14*** *p143*
Biernacki, Antonia; Maryland, 1910 ***3259.35*** *p4*
Biesel, Mollie 58; Kansas, 1910 ***9079.10*** *p53*
Biesel, Rheinhardt 62; Kansas, 1900-1910 ***9079.10*** *p53*
Biesenthal, August 25; Ontario, 1871 ***1823.28*** *p6*
Biesenthal, Gottlaib 46; Ontario, 1871 ***1823.28*** *p6*
Biesenthal, John 17; Ontario, 1871 ***1823.28*** *p6*
Biesenthal, Michael 54; Ontario, 1871 ***1823.28*** *p6*
Biesenthal, William 26; Ontario, 1871 ***1823.28*** *p6*
Biesethal, Ferdinand 18; Ontario, 1871 ***1823.28*** *p6*
Biesterfeld, Carl J. 62; Kansas, 1878-1910 ***9079.10*** *p17*
Biesterfeld, Maria K. 56; Kansas, 1878-1910 ***9079.10*** *p17*
Bietanetay, Anna; Maryland, 1910 ***3259.35*** *p4*
Bietighofer, Philipp; America, 1752 ***2856.30*** *p37*
Biffart, Johann; America, 1751 ***2856.30*** *p37*
With wife & 3 children
Bifort, Jane; Virginia, 1666 ***6212.30*** *p26*
Bigby, Thomas 28; Tobago, West Indies, 1775 ***1220.25*** *p129*
Bigelow, Annie 8; Ontario, 1861 ***2896.28*** *p39*
Bigelow, Margaret 10; Ontario, 1861 ***2896.28*** *p39*
Bigelow, Rebecca 29; Ontario, 1861 ***2896.28*** *p39*
Biger, Franz Jakob; Port uncertain, 1786 ***2856.30*** *p59*
Bigg, George 23; Ontario, 1861 ***2896.27*** *p51*
Bigg, John; New England, 1643 ***1224.1*** *p7*
Bigg, Samuel; Maryland, 1703 ***1224.2*** *p10*
Bigg, William 20; Maryland, 1774 ***1220.25*** *p52*
Biggam, Hamilton; New York, 1826 ***8197.10*** *p333*
Biggam, Hugh 60; Ontario, 1871 ***1823.15*** *p18*
Biggar, George; New Jersey, 1899 ***1640.13*** *p9*
Biggard, Simon; Philadelphia, 1854 ***6058.10*** *p53*
Biggart, Margret 56; Ontario, 1871 ***1823.15*** *p18*
Bigges, John; Maryland, 1661 ***2524.55*** *p24*
Biggin, John 50; Ontario, 1871 ***1823.15*** *p18*
Biggings, Edward 40; Ontario, 1871 ***1823.28*** *p6*
Biggins, James 63; Ontario, 1871 ***1823.15*** *p18*
Biggs, Alexander 15; Philadelphia, 1775 ***1220.25*** *p8*
Biggs, Ambross; Maryland, 1658 ***2524.55*** *p24*
Biggs, Miss M.; Quebec, 1857 ***9196.15*** *p19*
Biggs, Richard; New York, 1794 ***1224.2*** *p10*
Biggs, Richard; Virginia, 1626 ***1224.1*** *p7*
Biggs, Richard 21; Maryland, 1775 ***1220.25*** *p111*
Bigham, Henderson 46; Ontario, 1871 ***1823.22*** *p11*
Bigher, James; New York, 1803 ***8197.10*** *p11*
Bigland, Mr.; Quebec, 1857 ***9196.15*** *p16*
Bigland, Henry; Virginia, 1664 ***6212.30*** *p15*
Bigler, George; Pennsylvania, 1785 ***4629.10*** *p48*
Biglow, J. L. 36; Ontario, 1871 ***1823.15*** *p18*
Bignel, James 62; Ontario, 1871 ***1823.15*** *p18*
Bignell, Jane 47; Carolina, 1774 ***1220.25*** *p79*
Bigney, Tho.; Maryland, 1676 ***2524.55*** *p24*
Bigoff, B. 32; Alaska, 1917 ***9196.1*** *p46*
Bigoff, B. 32; Whitehorse, Yukon, 1917 ***9196.1*** *p46*
Bigoff, M. 36; Alaska, 1916 ***9196.1*** *p42*
Bigoff, M. 36; Whitehorse, Yukon, 1916 ***9196.1*** *p42*
Bihlharz, John Baptist; New York, 1839 ***8197.10*** *p213*
Bihn, Andreas; Port uncertain, 1782 ***2856.30*** *p37*
Bihn, Andreas; Port uncertain, 1783 ***2856.30*** *p37*
Bihn, Jacob; America, 1738 ***2856.30*** *p37*
Bihn, Johann; America, 1749 ***2856.30*** *p37*
Bilby, John; New York, 1840 ***8197.10*** *p154*
Bildhausen, Anna Catharina; Port uncertain, 1744 ***2856.30*** *p38*
Bildhausen, Anna Margarete; Port uncertain, 1744 ***2856.30*** *p38*
Bildhausen, Jacob; Port uncertain, 1744 ***2856.30*** *p38*
Bildhous, Jacob; America, 1744 ***2856.30*** *p38*
Bildson, John 30; Ontario, 1871 ***1823.28*** *p7*
Biles, Thomas; New York, 1702 ***1224.2*** *p10*
Biles, William 18; Maryland, 1774 ***1220.25*** *p60*
Bilger, Barbara; Port uncertain, 1767 ***2856.30*** *p38*
Bilger, Christian; Port uncertain, 1770 ***2856.30*** *p38*
With wife
Bilger, Magdalena; Port uncertain, 1796 ***2856.30*** *p38*
Bilhard, Andreas; Port uncertain, 1751 ***2856.30*** *p38*
Biliny, S. E. 11; Ontario, 1861 ***2896.28*** *p6*
Bill, Hen; Virginia, 1664 ***6212.30*** *p9*
Bill, James; Maryland, 1675 ***2524.55*** *p24*
Bill, John; Virginia, 1664 ***6212.30*** *p5*
Billa, Andreas; Port uncertain, 1752 ***2856.30*** *p38*
Billado, H. C.; Vermont, 1860-1960 ***5900.10*** *p454*
Billado, J. E. McNaney; Vermont, 1850-1921 ***5900.10*** *p454*
Billany, William 40; Ontario, 1861 ***2896.28*** *p21*
Billcock, Richard 40; Ontario, 1871 ***1823.22*** *p11*
Biller, Andreas; Port uncertain, 1752 ***2856.30*** *p38*
Biller, Nicholas; Baltimore, 1833 ***8197.10*** *p128*
Billet, James; Virginia, 1666 ***6212.30*** *p27*
Billett, Grace; Maryland, 1663 ***2524.55*** *p24*
Billett, Michael; Maryland, 1665 ***2524.55*** *p24*
Billey, John; New York, 1840 ***8197.10*** *p154*
Billharz, Karl; Port uncertain, 1774 ***2856.30*** *p38*
Billing, Charles 50; Ontario, 1871 ***1823.22*** *p11*
Billing, Eliza; New York, 1854 ***1224.3*** *p7*
Billing, Jane 55; Vermont, 1874 ***5900.10*** *p62*
Billing, John; Virginia, 1666 ***6212.30*** *p27*
Billinger, Margarete; Port uncertain, 1754 ***2856.30*** *p38*
Billingly, Rebecca; Virginia, 1666 ***6212.30*** *p26*
Billings, Mr.; Quebec, 1858 ***9196.15*** *p34*
Billings, Ellen Butler; Vermont, 1838-1897 ***5900.10*** *p430*
Billings, Joseph 48; Ontario, 1871 ***1823.15*** *p18*
Billings, Joseph 71; Ontario, 1871 ***1823.22*** *p11*
Billings, Mary; Vermont, 1844-1907 ***5900.10*** *p439*
Billings, William; Pensacola, Florida, 1767 ***1224.2*** *p10*
Billingsley, Robert; Pennsylvania, 1844 ***6058.10*** *p19*
Billingsly, Francis; Maryland, 1652 ***2524.55*** *p25*
With wife
Son: John
Billingsly, John *SEE* Billingsly, Francis
Billingsly, Tho; Virginia, 1667-1668 ***6212.30*** *p39*
Billington, Thomas; Virginia, 1666-1667 ***6212.30*** *p35*
Billit, X. P.; Virginia, 1666 ***6212.30*** *p28*
Billite, Joseph; Virginia, 1674 ***6212.30*** *p52*
Billmann, Theobald; America, 1752 ***2856.30*** *p38*
Billney, Lydia 80; Ontario, 1861 ***2896.27*** *p38*
Billney, William 72; Ontario, 1861 ***2896.27*** *p38*
Billo, Andreas; Port uncertain, 1752 ***2856.30*** *p38*
Billopp, Joseph; New York, 1712 ***1224.2*** *p10*
Bills, William; Pennsylvania, 1781 ***4629.10*** *p42*
Billus, Samuel; Virginia, 1775 ***1220.25*** *p123*
Billy, John 26; Alaska, 1917 ***9196.1*** *p50*
Billy, John 26; Yukon, 1917 ***9196.1*** *p50*
Bilsberry, Ann; Maryland, 1652-1658 ***2524.55*** *p25*
Bilsberry, Hannah; Maryland, 1652-1658 ***2524.55*** *p138*
Bilsbery, Ann; Maryland, 1652-1658 ***2524.55*** *p25*
Biltis, William; New York, 1840 ***8197.10*** *p145*
Binch, Trustam; Maryland, 1666 ***2524.55*** *p25*
Bincker, Tho.; Maryland, 1652 ***2524.55*** *p25*
Bincom, George 24; Ontario, 1871 ***1823.15*** *p18*
Bincom, John 26; Ontario, 1871 ***1823.15*** *p18*
Binczkowski, Felix; Maryland, 1910 ***3259.35*** *p4*
Binder, Franz; Port uncertain, 1718 ***2856.30*** *p38*
Binder, Jacob; America, 1751 ***2856.30*** *p38*
Binder, Jacob; America, 1751 ***2856.30*** *p38*
With wife & children
Binder, Josef Bernhard; Port uncertain, 1748 ***2856.30*** *p38*
Bindinenski, Henry; Maryland, 1910 ***3259.35*** *p4*
Binding, Sarah; Boston, 1687 ***1224.1*** *p7*
Bindlos, Robt; Virginia, 1665 ***6212.30*** *p22*
Bindloss, Mrs.; Quebec, 1856 ***9196.15*** *p11*
Bindtnagel, Catharina; Port uncertain, 1740 ***2856.30*** *p38*
Bingener, Lewis; New York, 1838 ***8197.10*** *p212*
Bingenheimer, Regina; Port uncertain, 1776 ***2856.30*** *p38*
Bingham, Chas 42; Ontario, 1871 ***1823.15*** *p18*
Bingham, Edwin 36; Ontario, 1871 ***1823.15*** *p18*
Bingham, James; New York, 1803 ***8197.10*** *p11*
Bingham, Peter; Pennsylvania, 1777 ***4629.10*** *p11*
Bingham, William; Pennsylvania, 1781 ***4629.10*** *p42*
Bingham, William; Pennsylvania, 1781 ***4629.10*** *p43*
Bingham, William 48; Ontario, 1871 ***1823.15*** *p18*
Bingley, George; New York, 1820 ***8197.10*** *p207*
Bingley, William 18; New York, 1775 ***1220.25*** *p94*
Binion, Edward 24; Ontario, 1871 ***1823.28*** *p7*
Binke, Adam; Maryland, 1910 ***3259.35*** *p4*
Binkes, Henry; Virginia, 1666-1667 ***6212.30*** *p34*
Binkes, Thomas; Maryland, 1659 ***2524.55*** *p38*
Binkey, August 35; Ontario, 1871 ***1823.28*** *p7*
Binkey, Jacob 42; Ontario, 1871 ***1823.28*** *p7*
Binkowski, Emile; Maryland, 1910 ***3259.35*** *p4*
Binkowsky, Michael; Maryland, 1910 ***3259.35*** *p4*
Binks, George 22; Virginia, 1774 ***1220.25*** *p54*
Binnalls, John; Virginia, 1703-1704 ***6212.30*** *p63*
Binning, Mr.; Quebec, 1858 ***9196.15*** *p43*
Binning, Mrs.; Quebec, 1858 ***9196.15*** *p43*
Binsteed, Henry; America, 1778 ***1224.2*** *p10*
Bint, Michael; Maryland, 1910 ***3259.35*** *p4*
Binz, Margarete; Port uncertain, 1739 ***2856.30*** *p31*
Binzinger, Martin; Port uncertain, 1700-1799 ***2856.30*** *p38*
Binzkoski, Joseph; Maryland, 1910 ***3259.35*** *p4*
Biolozyaiski, John; Maryland, 1910 ***3259.35*** *p4*
Biper, M. 28; Alaska, 1914 ***9196.1*** *p41*
Bipett, John 47; Ontario, 1871 ***1823.15*** *p18*
Bir, J. Jos.; Port uncertain, 1784 ***2856.30*** *p73*
Biram, Jno; Virginia, 1666-1667 ***6212.30*** *p32*
Biram, Walter; Maryland, 1655 ***2524.55*** *p25*
Birbeck, William 16; Jamaica, 1774 ***1220.25*** *p141*
Birch, Chamberlain; Georgia, n.d. ***1224.2*** *p10*
Birch, Edward; New York, 1826 ***1224.3*** *p7*
Birch, Elizabeth; Pennsylvania, 1701 ***1224.2*** *p10*
Birch, Jno; Virginia, 1665-1666 ***6212.30*** *p23*
Birch, John Forbes; Mexico, 1884 ***1640.13*** *p9*
Birch, Matthew; Pennsylvania, 1701 ***1224.2*** *p10*
Birch, Samuel; Maryland, 1681 ***2524.55*** *p25*
Birch, William 27; Maryland, 1775 ***1220.25*** *p106*
Birchmeyer, Anna Maria; Port uncertain, 1746 ***2856.30*** *p38*
Birck, Mathias; New York, 1840 ***8197.10*** *p154*
Bircker, Franz Josef; Port uncertain, 1774 ***2856.30*** *p38*
Birckhead, Margaret; Maryland, 1666 ***2524.55*** *p25*
Birckherin, Therese; Port uncertain, 1737 ***2856.30*** *p38*
With husband & 2 children
Birckhin, Agathe; Port uncertain, 1747 ***2856.30*** *p39*
Bird, Mr.; Portland, Maine, 1858 ***9196.15*** *p47*
Bird, Mr.; Quebec, 1858 ***9196.15*** *p32*
Bird, Mrs.; Portland, Maine, 1858 ***9196.15*** *p47*
Bird, Mrs.; Quebec, 1858 ***9196.15*** *p32*
Bird, Charles; Maryland, 1663 ***2524.55*** *p212*
Bird, Daniel 67; Vermont, 1898 ***5900.10*** *p499*
Bird, Edward; Vermont, 1829-1908 ***5900.10*** *p97*
Bird, Edward; Virginia, 1664 ***6212.30*** *p6*
Bird, Edward 26; Philadelphia, 1775 ***1220.25*** *p122*

Bird, Elizabeth; Maryland, 1682 ***2524.55*** *p25*
Bird, Elizabeth; New England, 1698 ***1224.1*** *p64*
Bird, Ena 26; Ontario, 1871 ***1823.28*** *p7*
Bird, Frederick; Pennsylvania, 1777 ***4629.10*** *p11*
Bird, Gilbert 51; Ontario, 1871 ***1823.22*** *p11*
Bird, James; New York, 1839 ***8197.10*** *p213*
Bird, James 24; Maryland, 1774 ***1220.25*** *p52*
Bird, James 48; Ontario, 1871 ***1823.15*** *p18*
Bird, Jane 52; Ontario, 1871 ***1823.22*** *p11*
Bird, John; Maryland, 1679 ***2524.55*** *p25*
Bird, John; New York, 1840 ***8197.10*** *p155*
Bird, John; Pennsylvania, 1802 ***1224.3*** *p11*
Bird, John; Philadelphia, 1778 ***1224.2*** *p10*
Bird, John; Virginia, 1674 ***1224.1*** *p7*
Bird, John 16; Philadelphia, 1774 ***1220.25*** *p34*
Bird, Joseph; Pennsylvania, 1786 ***4629.10*** *p47*
Bird, Launcelot; New York, 1840 ***8197.10*** *p154*
Bird, Mary 26; Maryland, 1774 ***1220.25*** *p64*
Bird, Mary E.; Vermont, 1827-1908 ***5900.10*** *p97*
Bird, Michael; New York, 1805 ***8197.10*** *p28*
Bird, Philip; New York, 1840 ***8197.10*** *p145*
Bird, Samuel 20; Philadelphia, 1775 ***1220.25*** *p9*
Bird, Simon; Maryland, 1651 ***2524.55*** *p25*
Bird, Tho; Virginia, 1674-1675 ***6212.30*** *p53*
Bird, Thomas; New York, New York, 1808 ***1224.3*** *p11*
Bird, William 29; Virginia, 1774 ***1220.25*** *p92*
Birdsege, Ann; Maryland, 1670 ***2524.55*** *p25*
Biringer, Peter; Port uncertain, 1764 ***2856.30*** *p12*
Birk, Andrew 42; Ontario, 1871 ***1823.15*** *p18*
Birk, Henry 10; Ontario, 1871 ***1823.28*** *p7*
Birkby, Katherine; Maryland, 1654 ***2524.55*** *p25*
Birkby, Samuell; Maryland, 1657 ***2524.55*** *p25*
Birke, John; Maryland, 1667 ***2524.55*** *p25*
Birke, John; Maryland, 1681 ***2524.55*** *p25*
Birke, Joseph; Vermont, 1839-1913 ***5900.10*** *p140*
Birke, Matilda; Vermont, 1839 ***5900.10*** *p140*
Birke, Sisly; Virginia, 1668-1669 ***6212.30*** *p40*
Birken, Eliza; Virginia, 1664 ***6212.30*** *p9*
Birkenhead, Rupert; Maryland, 1673 ***2524.55*** *p25*
Birket, Grace 17; Ontario, 1861 ***2896.27*** *p67*
Birkett, Henry; Illinois, 1826 ***1224.3*** *p7*
Birketton, Francis; Maryland, 1666 ***2524.55*** *p25*
Birkinshaw, Joseph; New York, 1834 ***8197.10*** *p212*
Birkitt, Ruth; Maryland, 1668 ***2524.55*** *p25*
Birkitt, Thomas; Maryland, 1668 ***2524.55*** *p25*
Birkle, Ludwig; America, 1751 ***2856.30*** *p60*
Birkley, Alexander; Maryland, 1681 ***2524.55*** *p25*
Birkmyre, Mr.; Quebec, 1858 ***9196.15*** *p38*
Birkmyre, Mr., Jr.; Quebec, 1858 ***9196.15*** *p38*
Birkmyre, W.; Quebec, 1858 ***9196.15*** *p38*
Birleck, P. W. 18; St. Kitts, 1774 ***1220.25*** *p44*
Birmingham, Mrs.; Quebec, 1857 ***9196.15*** *p16*
Birmingham, Anna M. Smith; Vermont, 1857-1893 ***5900.10*** *p86*
Birmingham, E. 25; Ontario, 1861 ***2896.28*** *p10*
Birmingham, Henry; New York, 1829 ***8197.10*** *p312*
Birmingham, Henry; New York, 1832 ***8197.10*** *p68*
Birmingham, John; Vermont, 1838-1895 ***5900.10*** *p86*
Birmingham, Michael; New York, 1829 ***8197.10*** *p359*
Birmingham, Patrick; New York, 1832-1838 ***8197.10*** *p311*
Birmingham, W. 1; Ontario, 1861 ***2896.28*** *p10*
Birmingham, Wm 28; Ontario, 1861 ***2896.28*** *p10*
Birn, Laughlin 21; Philadelphia, 1774 ***1220.25*** *p82*
Birnbaum, Simon; New York, 1840 ***8197.10*** *p154*
Birne, Bridget 38 *SEE* Birne, Michael
Birne, Ellen 18 *SEE* Birne, Michael
Birne, John 8 *SEE* Birne, Michael
Birne, Michael 11 *SEE* Birne, Michael
Birne, Michael 41; Quebec, 1849 ***1825.45*** *p28*
  Wife: Bridget 38
  Son: John 8
  Son: Michael 11
  Daughter: Ellen 18
  Son: Timothy 4
Birne, Timothy 4 *SEE* Birne, Michael
Birney, Francis 26; Vermont, 1842 ***5900.10*** *p519*
Birney, Margaret 95; Vermont, 1897 ***5900.10*** *p323*
Birney, Mary 79; Vermont, 1890 ***5900.10*** *p514*
Birney, Mary Donaghue 65; Vermont, 1892 ***5900.10*** *p514*
Birney, Timothy; Vermont, 1830-1900 ***5900.10*** *p513*
Birnie, Alexr 27; Ontario, 1871 ***1823.28*** *p7*
Birnie, William; New York, 1839 ***8197.10*** *p128*
Birns, Christopher 25; Ontario, 1871 ***1823.22*** *p12*
Birom, Jno; Virginia, 1665-1666 ***6212.30*** *p23*
Biroth, Johann Bernhard; Port uncertain, 1748 ***2856.30*** *p39*
Birrell, James; Georgia, 1698 ***1640.13*** *p9*
Birrell, Margaret; Ontario, 1896 ***1640.13*** *p9*
Birrell, William; Savannah, Georgia, 1821 ***1640.10*** *p12*
Birrmann, Anna Elisabeth; America, 1743 ***2856.30*** *p39*
  With father
Birse, Alexander 34; Ontario, 1871 ***1823.15*** *p18*
Birt, Thomas; Boston, 1670 ***1224.1*** *p7*
Birtch, John; New York, 1807 ***8197.10*** *p35*
Birtt, Lenord 40; Washington, 1914 ***9196.1*** *p64*
Birum, Jno; Virginia, 1663 ***6212.30*** *p4*
Bisaker, Ambrose; Florida, 1766 ***1224.2*** *p10*
Bisby, John; Virginia, 1671-1672 ***6212.30*** *p48*
Biscar, Hugh; Virginia, 1666 ***6212.30*** *p27*
Biscawen, Cha; Virginia, 1666 ***6212.30*** *p29*
Bischof, Anton; Port uncertain, 1751 ***2856.30*** *p39*
Bischof, Johann, Jr.; America, 1749 ***2856.30*** *p39*
  With wife & 2 children
Bischof, Johann, Jr.; America, 1751 ***2856.30*** *p39*
Bischof, Johann Georg; Port uncertain, 1788 ***2856.30*** *p39*
Bischof, Maria Barbara; America, 1763 ***2856.30*** *p39*
  With husband
Bischof, Marx Franz; Port uncertain, 1751 ***2856.30*** *p39*
Bischof, Sebastian; America, 1743 ***2856.30*** *p39*
Bischofburger, Georg Michael; Port uncertain, 1771 ***2856.30*** *p39*
Bischoff, Adam; America, 1740 ***2856.30*** *p39*
Bischoff, Anna Catharina; America, 1747 ***2856.30*** *p39*
  With 3 children
Bischoff, Philipp Jakob; Port uncertain, 1749 ***2856.30*** *p39*
Bisdee, Edwin; New York, 1848 ***1224.3*** *p7*
Bisenbank, John 41; Ontario, 1871 ***1823.28*** *p7*
Bish, Robt; Virginia, 1664 ***6212.30*** *p7*
Bish, Sebastian; America, 1737 ***2856.30*** *p35*
Bish, Sebastian; America, 1737 ***2856.30*** *p39*
Bisher, John; New York, 1837 ***8197.10*** *p85*
Bishop, A.; Ontario, 1861 ***2896.28*** *p59*
Bishop, Aaron *SEE* Bishop, Henry, Sr.
Bishop, Abraham; Maryland, 1665 ***2524.55*** *p25*
Bishop, Ann *SEE* Bishop, Henry, Sr.
Bishop, Ann 21; Maryland, 1775 ***1220.25*** *p115*
Bishop, Ann Marie 75; Ontario, 1871 ***1823.22*** *p12*
Bishop, Archaba 40; Ontario, 1871 ***1823.15*** *p18*
Bishop, Cadwell 41; Ontario, 1861 ***2896.27*** *p14*
Bishop, Cintha A. 13; Ontario, 1861 ***2896.27*** *p15*
Bishop, David *SEE* Bishop, Henry, Sr.
Bishop, David C. 3; Ontario, 1861 ***2896.27*** *p15*
Bishop, Earnes 36; Boise, Idaho, 1918 ***9196.1*** *p14*
Bishop, Earnes 36; Vancouver, British Columbia, 1918 ***9196.1*** *p14*
Bishop, Edward W.; New York, New York, 1833 ***8197.10*** *p300*
Bishop, Elexandrina 10; Ontario, 1861 ***2896.27*** *p15*
Bishop, Elizabeth *SEE* Bishop, Henry, Sr.
Bishop, Elizabeth; Maryland, 1672 ***2524.55*** *p25*
Bishop, Elizabeth 48; Ontario, 1861 ***2896.27*** *p14*
Bishop, Emily A. 15; Ontario, 1861 ***2896.27*** *p15*
Bishop, Frank; Vermont, 1850-1934 ***5900.10*** *p440*
Bishop, George *SEE* Bishop, Henry, Sr.
Bishop, Geremiah 81; Ontario, 1861 ***2896.27*** *p14*
Bishop, Harison 45; Ontario, 1861 ***2896.27*** *p14*
Bishop, Harriet 39; Ontario, 1861 ***2896.27*** *p14*
Bishop, Henry; Maryland, 1640 ***2524.55*** *p25*
Bishop, Henry, Sr.; Maryland, 1672 ***2524.55*** *p25*
  Wife: Ann
  Son: Aaron
  Son: George
  Daughter: Sarah
  Stepchild: Mary
  Daughter: Ann
  Daughter: Elizabeth
  Son: David
  Son: John
  Son: Henry, Jr.
Bishop, Henry, Jr. *SEE* Bishop, Henry, Sr.
Bishop, James 37; Ontario, 1871 ***1823.15*** *p18*
Bishop, John *SEE* Bishop, Henry, Sr.
Bishop, John; New York, 1821 ***8197.10*** *p208*
Bishop, John 39; Ontario, 1871 ***1823.15*** *p18*
Bishop, John 53; Ontario, 1871 ***1823.28*** *p7*
Bishop, Joseph; New York, New York, 1784 ***1224.2*** *p10*
Bishop, Lucinda; Ontario, 1861 ***2896.28*** *p62*
Bishop, Lucinda 24; Ontario, 1861 ***2896.27*** *p25*
Bishop, Mahala; Ontario, 1861 ***2896.28*** *p62*
Bishop, Marsit E. 6; Ontario, 1861 ***2896.27*** *p15*
Bishop, Mary *SEE* Bishop, Henry, Sr.
Bishop, Mary E. 40; Ontario, 1861 ***2896.27*** *p15*
Bishop, Mathew; Virginia, 1667 ***6212.30*** *p37*
Bishop, Nathaniel; Canada, 1723 ***1224.2*** *p10*
Bishop, Phoebe Abare; Vermont, 1864-1944 ***5900.10*** *p440*
Bishop, R.; Ontario, 1861 ***2896.28*** *p59*
Bishop, Richard; North America, 1837 ***1224.3*** *p7*
Bishop, Sarah *SEE* Bishop, Henry, Sr.
Bishop, Thomas; New York, 1794 ***8197.10*** *p6*
Bishop, Thomas; New York, 1821 ***8197.10*** *p208*
Bishop, Thomas 19; Philadelphia, 1775 ***1220.25*** *p9*
Bishop, Thomas 21; Maryland, 1774 ***1220.25*** *p41*
Bishop, Welthian 71; Ontario, 1861 ***2896.27*** *p14*
Bishop, William; New York, 1838 ***8197.10*** *p212*
Bishop, William; New York, 1840 ***8197.10*** *p155*
Bishop, William; New York, 1840 ***8197.10*** *p214*
Bishop, Wm 35; Ontario, 1871 ***1823.28*** *p7*
Bishopp, Arthur; Virginia, 1666 ***6212.30*** *p26*
Bishopp, Charles; Virginia, 1664 ***6212.30*** *p13*
Bishopp, Edith; Virginia, 1674 ***6212.30*** *p52*
Bishopp, Humphry; Virginia, 1666-1667 ***6212.30*** *p32*
Bishopp, Mary; Virginia, 1657 ***1224.1*** *p37*
Biskupski, Frank; Maryland, 1910 ***3259.35*** *p4*
Biskupski, Theodore; Maryland, 1910 ***3259.35*** *p4*
Bisland, Alexander; New York, 1714 ***1224.2*** *p10*
Bisley, Alexander; New York, 1714 ***1224.2*** *p10*
Bispan, Robert; Maryland, 1661 ***2524.55*** *p25*
Bisse, Elizabeth; Maryland, 1663 ***2524.55*** *p25*
Bissell, John; Pennsylvania, 1786 ***4629.10*** *p47*
Bissell, Richard 59; Ontario, 1871 ***1823.15*** *p19*
Bissell, Robert; New York, 1807 ***8197.10*** *p35*
Bissell, Thomas 17; Philadelphia, 1774 ***1220.25*** *p81*
Bisset, George; St. Johns, Newfoundland, 1791 ***1224.2*** *p10*
Bisset, James 60; Ontario, 1871 ***1823.15*** *p19*
Bisset, Robert; Florida, 1767 ***1640.10*** *p12*
Bisset, Samuel; New York, 1821 ***8197.10*** *p208*
Bissett, Alexander; Georgia, 1791 ***1640.10*** *p12*
Bissett, James 52; Ontario, 1871 ***1823.15*** *p19*
Bissett, Margaret 59; Ontario, 1871 ***1823.15*** *p19*
Bissett, Richard 25; Ontario, 1871 ***1823.15*** *p19*
Bissett, Robert 38; Ontario, 1871 ***1823.15*** *p19*
Bissett, Robert 56; Ontario, 1871 ***1823.15*** *p19*
Bissett, Robert 57; Ontario, 1871 ***1823.15*** *p19*
Bissett, Thomas 42; Ontario, 1871 ***1823.15*** *p19*
Bissett, William 60; Ontario, 1871 ***1823.15*** *p19*
Bissill, William; Virginia, 1713 ***1224.2*** *p11*
Bissinger, Anna Maria; Port uncertain, 1773 ***2856.30*** *p39*
Bissinger, Johann; Port uncertain, 1783 ***2856.30*** *p39*
Bissinger, Johann Michael; America, 1747 ***2856.30*** *p39*
Bisterfeld, Carl 38; Kansas, 1906-1910 ***9079.10*** *p40*
Bisterfeld, Dora 11; Kansas, 1907-1910 ***9079.10*** *p40*
Bisterfeld, Dora 27; Kansas, 1906-1910 ***9079.10*** *p40*
Bisterfeld, Mary 41; Kansas, 1891-1910 ***9079.10*** *p40*
Bisterfeld, Peter 40; Kansas, 1891-1910 ***9079.10*** *p40*
Bistrick, Anna; Maryland, 1910 ***3259.35*** *p4*
Biterbey, Thomas; Maryland, 1664 ***2524.55*** *p25*
Bitigeman, John; New York, 1807 ***8197.10*** *p35*
Bitigheim, Balthasar; Port uncertain, 1755 ***2856.30*** *p39*
Bitlinger, Johann; Port uncertain, 1766 ***2856.30*** *p39*
Bittel, Sophia; Port uncertain, 1744 ***2856.30*** *p40*
Bitter, Andreas; Port uncertain, 1751 ***2856.30*** *p40*
Bittinger, Christof; Port uncertain, 1741 ***2856.30*** *p40*
Bittle, Richard; Nova Scotia, 1719 ***1224.2*** *p11*
Bittmann, Viktoria; Port uncertain, 1775 ***2856.30*** *p40*
Bitz, Velten; Port uncertain, 1753 ***2856.30*** *p40*
Bixby, Joanna Flaherty; Vermont, 1854-1915 ***5900.10*** *p307*
Bixby, John R.; Vermont, 1845-1916 ***5900.10*** *p307*
Bixby, Martha; Vermont, 1857-1909 ***5900.10*** *p225*
Bixlin, Michael; Port uncertain, 1714 ***2856.30*** *p40*
Bize, Hercules Daniel; New Jersey, 1800 ***1224.3*** *p7*
Blaau, Eleanor; New York, New York, 1803 ***1224.3*** *p7*
Blaau, Waldron; New York, New York, 1787 ***1224.2*** *p11*
Blacher, Christian; Port uncertain, 1751 ***2856.30*** *p42*
Blachomez, Rosie; Maryland, 1910 ***3259.35*** *p4*
Blachurst, Ja; Virginia, 1666-1667 ***6212.30*** *p32*
Black, . . .; Boston, 1765 ***4628.40*** *p114*
Black, A. J.; Quebec, 1858 ***9196.15*** *p45*
Black, Alexander *SEE* Black, Donald
Black, Alexander Leslie; New Orleans, 1837 ***1640.10*** *p12*
Black, Allan *SEE* Black, Joseph
Black, Allan; Pictou, Nova Scotia, 1848 ***4537.37*** *p29*
  Wife: Margaret MacDonald
  Child: Duncan
  Child: Roderick
  Child: John
  Child: Mary
Black, Andrew 29; Ontario, 1871 ***1823.15*** *p19*
Black, Andrew 39; Ontario, 1871 ***1823.22*** *p12*
Black, Andrew 58; Ontario, 1871 ***1823.22*** *p12*
Black, Angus; Ontario, 1840-1849 ***4537.37*** *p31*
  Wife: Ann Morrison
  Child: Donald
  Child: Catherine
  Child: John
  Child: Neil
  Child: Kirsty
  Child: Lachlan
Black, Angus; Ontario, 1849 ***4537.32*** *p4*
  Wife: Ann Morrison
  Child: Donald
  Child: Catherine
  Child: Neil
  Child: John

Blades, Robert; Maryland, 1678 ***2524.55*** *p26*
Wife: Sarah
Daughter: Mary
Blades, Sarah *SEE* Blades, Robert
Bladwell, Wm; Virginia, 1665-1666 ***6212.30*** *p21*
Blaes, Thomas; Virginia, 1666 ***6212.30*** *p27*
Blagborne, William; New York, New York, n.d. ***1224.3*** *p7*
Blagdon, Sweeting; North Carolina, 1761 ***1224.2*** *p11*
Blagge, Edward; Virginia, 1693 ***1224.1*** *p7*
Blagrave, Edward; Virginia, 1678 ***1224.1*** *p7*
Blagrave, Richd; Virginia, 1674-1675 ***6212.30*** *p53*
Blague, Newcombe; New England, 1718 ***1224.2*** *p11*
Blaikie, William; Ontario, 1859 ***1640.13*** *p10*
Blaiklock, Mr.; Quebec, 1857 ***9196.15*** *p20*
Blaiklock, Mr.; Quebec, 1858 ***9196.15*** *p43*
Blaiklock, Mrs.; Quebec, 1857 ***9196.15*** *p20*
Blain, James; Pennsylvania, 1778 ***4629.10*** *p34*
Blain, Matthew; Pennsylvania, 1814 ***6058.10*** *p4*
Blain, Robert; Pennsylvania, 1814 ***6058.10*** *p4*
Blair, Miss; Portland, Maine, 1858 ***9196.15*** *p27*
Blair, Mr.; Quebec, 1858 ***9196.15*** *p35*
Blair, Mrs. 50; Ontario, 1871 ***1823.28*** *p7*
Blair, Andrew; New York, 1821 ***8197.10*** *p208*
Blair, Andrew; New York, 1821 ***8197.10*** *p209*
Blair, Ann; South Carolina, 1797 ***1640.13*** *p10*
Blair, David; Georgia, 1736 ***1640.10*** *p12*
Blair, Edward; New York, 1834 ***8197.10*** *p315*
Blair, George; New York, 1830 ***8197.10*** *p211*
Blair, Grace Ann 35; Ontario, 1871 ***1823.15*** *p19*
Blair, Homer; Jamaica, 1832 ***1640.13*** *p10*
Blair, James 44; Ontario, 1871 ***1823.28*** *p7*
Blair, James 54; Ontario, 1871 ***1823.15*** *p19*
Blair, Joh; Jamaica, 1736 ***1640.13*** *p10*
Blair, John 50; Ontario, 1871 ***1823.28*** *p7*
Blair, John 61; Ontario, 1871 ***1823.15*** *p19*
Blair, John 74; Ontario, 1871 ***1823.28*** *p7*
Blair, Mary 13; Ontario, 1871 ***1823.15*** *p19*
Blair, Robert; New York, 1831 ***8197.10*** *p211*
Blair, Robert 55; Ontario, 1871 ***1823.28*** *p7*
Blair, Samuel; Pennsylvania, 1777 ***4629.10*** *p8*
Blair, William 40; Ontario, 1871 ***1823.15*** *p20*
Blair, William 43; Ontario, 1871 ***1823.15*** *p20*
Blair, William 60; Ontario, 1871 ***1823.28*** *p7*
Blair, William 67; Ontario, 1871 ***1823.15*** *p19*
Blair, William 78; Ontario, 1871 ***1823.28*** *p7*
Blake, Miss; Quebec, 1857 ***9196.15*** *p23*
Blake, Mr.; Quebec, 1857 ***9196.15*** *p21*
Blake, Mr.; Quebec, 1858 ***9196.15*** *p47*
Blake, Mrs.; Quebec, 1857 ***9196.15*** *p23*
Blake, Agnes A. White; Vermont, 1863-1923 ***5900.10*** *p122*
Blake, Andrew 37; Ontario, 1871 ***1823.22*** *p12*
Blake, Ann 25; New York, New York, 1852 ***1825.45*** *p58*
Blake, Ann Walsh; Vermont, 1837-1922 ***5900.10*** *p98*
Blake, Catherine O'Shea; Vermont, 1845-1915 ***5900.10*** *p255*
Blake, Charles; Maryland, 1734 ***1224.2*** *p11*
Blake, Charles; Quebec, 1857 ***9196.15*** *p23*
Blake, Edward 50; New York, New York, 1852 ***1825.45*** *p58*
Blake, Ellan 70; Vermont, 1891 ***5900.10*** *p550*
Blake, Emma; Quebec, 1857 ***9196.15*** *p23*
Blake, George 12; Ontario, 1861 ***2896.25*** *p36*
Blake, James 3; New York, New York, 1852 ***1825.45*** *p58*
Blake, James 11; Ontario, 1861 ***2896.25*** *p31*
Blake, James 30; Ontario, 1871 ***1823.15*** *p20*
Blake, Jas 39; Washington, 1913 ***9196.1*** *p59*
Blake, Jno; Virginia, 1664 ***6212.30*** *p7*
Blake, John; New York, 1825 ***8197.10*** *p210*
Blake, John; Pennsylvania, 1777 ***4629.10*** *p11*
Blake, John; Pennsylvania, 1777 ***4629.10*** *p29*
Blake, John; Vermont, 1834-1893 ***5900.10*** *p98*
Blake, John; Virginia, 1663 ***1224.1*** *p7*
Blake, John 45; Ontario, 1871 ***1823.15*** *p20*
Blake, John 64; Ontario, 1871 ***1823.22*** *p12*
Blake, John 68; Ontario, 1871 ***1823.15*** *p20*
Blake, John J.; Vermont, 1858-1928 ***5900.10*** *p122*
Blake, John Sayer; Maryland, 1760 ***1224.2*** *p11*
Blake, Joseph; South Carolina, 1751 ***1224.2*** *p11*
Blake, Leah 30; Ontario, 1861 ***2896.25*** *p32*
Blake, M. A. 18; Ontario, 1861 ***2896.25*** *p33*
Blake, Mary 6; Vermont, 1866 ***5900.10*** *p99*
Blake, Mary 10; Ontario, 1861 ***2896.25*** *p36*
Blake, Mary J. 2; Ontario, 1861 ***2896.25*** *p32*
Blake, Matthew 66; Ontario, 1871 ***1823.15*** *p20*
Blake, Michael; Vermont, 1867-1905 ***5900.10*** *p255*
Blake, Nehemiah; Virginia, 1667-1668 ***6212.30*** *p39*
Blake, Oner; Maryland, 1675 ***2524.55*** *p26*
Blake, Patrick; New York, 1837 ***8197.10*** *p87*
Blake, Patrick 30; Ontario, 1871 ***1823.15*** *p20*
Blake, Peter; Maryland, 1662 ***2524.55*** *p26*
Blake, Peter; New York, 1839 ***8197.10*** *p128*
Blake, Philemon Charles; Maryland, 1766 ***1224.2*** *p11*
Blake, Prissilla; Virginia, 1674 ***6212.30*** *p52*
Blake, Robert 40; Ontario, 1871 ***1823.15*** *p20*
Blake, Sarah 1; New York, New York, 1852 ***1825.45*** *p58*
Blake, Sarah 20; New York, New York, 1852 ***1825.45*** *p58*
Blake, Susan 42; Ontario, 1861 ***2896.25*** *p36*
Blake, Tho; Virginia, 1672 ***6212.30*** *p49*
Blake, Tho; Virginia, 1672 ***6212.30*** *p50*
Blake, Thomas; New York, 1828 ***8197.10*** *p211*
Blake, Thomas; Virginia, 1666 ***6212.30*** *p26*
Blake, Thomas; Virginia, 1668-1669 ***6212.30*** *p41*
Blake, Thomas 37; Ontario, 1871 ***1823.15*** *p20*
Blake, Thomas 73; Ontario, 1871 ***1823.15*** *p20*
Blake, Timothy 46; Ontario, 1871 ***1823.22*** *p12*
Blake, Timothy 70; Ontario, 1871 ***1823.15*** *p20*
Blake, William; Pennsylvania, 1777 ***4629.10*** *p11*
Blake, William 19; Maryland, 1775 ***1220.25*** *p103*
Blake, William 45; Ontario, 1871 ***1823.15*** *p20*
Blake, William A. 1; Ontario, 1861 ***2896.25*** *p32*
Blakelock, John; New York, 1838 ***8197.10*** *p110*
Blakelock, Richard A.; New York, 1838 ***8197.10*** *p111*
Blakely, A. 12; Ontario, 1861 ***2896.28*** *p11*
Blakely, C. 3; Ontario, 1861 ***2896.26*** *p11*
Blakely, C. 15; Ontario, 1861 ***2896.28*** *p11*
Blakely, Caroline 25; Ontario, 1861 ***2896.25*** *p6*
Blakely, E. 7; Ontario, 1861 ***2896.26*** *p11*
Blakely, Eliza A. 14; Ontario, 1861 ***2896.25*** *p6*
Blakely, F. 8; Ontario, 1861 ***2896.26*** *p11*
Blakely, H. 11; Ontario, 1861 ***2896.26*** *p11*
Blakely, John 65; Ontario, 1871 ***1823.22*** *p12*
Blakely, L. 39; Ontario, 1861 ***2896.26*** *p11*
Blakely, Lucy 19; Ontario, 1861 ***2896.25*** *p6*
Blakely, M. M. 14; Ontario, 1861 ***2896.26*** *p11*
Blakely, Mary A. 9; Ontario, 1861 ***2896.25*** *p6*
Blakely, Michael; New York, 1837 ***8197.10*** *p87*
Blakely, P. 55; Ontario, 1861 ***2896.28*** *p11*
Blakely, P. A. 20; Ontario, 1861 ***2896.28*** *p11*
Blakely, Philisina 38; Ontario, 1871 ***1823.22*** *p12*
Blakely, Richard 16; Ontario, 1861 ***2896.25*** *p6*
Blakely, Samuel, Sr. 76; Ontario, 1871 ***1823.22*** *p12*
Blakely, Sarah A. 12; Ontario, 1861 ***2896.25*** *p6*
Blakely, Vie 23; Ontario, 1861 ***2896.25*** *p6*
Blakely, W. S. 5; Ontario, 1861 ***2896.26*** *p11*
Blakeman, Samuel 33; Ontario, 1871 ***1823.15*** *p20*
Blaken, Judith; Maryland, 1659 ***2524.55*** *p26*
Blakie, James 82; Ontario, 1871 ***1823.22*** *p12*
Blakiman, Thomas 40; Ontario, 1871 ***1823.15*** *p20*
Blakley, Emmarilla 1; Ontario, 1861 ***2896.25*** *p19*
Blakley, J. P. 12; Ontario, 1861 ***2896.25*** *p28*
Blakley, James 35; Ontario, 1871 ***1823.15*** *p20*
Blakley, Joseph; Pennsylvania, 1831 ***6058.10*** *p10*
Blakley, Phila Ann 27; Ontario, 1861 ***2896.25*** *p19*
Blakley, William; New York, 1821 ***8197.10*** *p208*
Blakswik, James 21; North Carolina, 1774 ***1220.25*** *p49*
Blanch, John 51; Ontario, 1871 ***1823.22*** *p13*
Blanchard, Andrew; New York, 1807 ***8197.10*** *p34*
Blanchard, Elen 46; Ontario, 1871 ***1823.15*** *p20*
Blanchard, Emery 16; Ontario, 1861 ***2896.27*** *p15*
Blanchard, Frank; Vermont, 1857-1907 ***5900.10*** *p122*
Blanchard, George; New York, 1827 ***8197.10*** *p338*
Blanchard, Gustave; New York, 1840 ***8197.10*** *p143*
Blanchard, Hannah Murphey; Vermont, 1866-1950 ***5900.10*** *p122*
Blanchard, Henry L.; Vermont, 1853-1932 ***5900.10*** *p541*
Blanchard, James 50; Ontario, 1871 ***1823.22*** *p13*
Blanchard, Mary; Vermont, 1852-1902 ***5900.10*** *p297*
Blanchard, Mary A. O'Dowd; Vermont, 1853-1953 ***5900.10*** *p541*
Blanchard, Timothy; Vermont, 1838-1918 ***5900.10*** *p297*
Blanchard, William; Louisville, Kentucky, 1840 ***1224.3*** *p7*
Blanchet, A. M.; Quebec, 1856 ***9196.15*** *p5*
Blanck, Abraham; Virginia, 1666-1667 ***6212.30*** *p34*
Blanck, Philipp; Port uncertain, 1792 ***2856.30*** *p40*
Blancy, John 29; Maryland, 1774 ***1220.25*** *p41*
Bland, Mr.; Quebec, 1858 ***9196.15*** *p34*
Bland, Mrs.; Quebec, 1858 ***9196.15*** *p34*
Bland, Arthur 26; New York, 1774 ***1220.25*** *p141*
Bland, Edward; Virginia, 1652 ***1224.1*** *p7*
Bland, Elias; New York, 1781 ***1224.2*** *p11*
Bland, John 46; Ontario, 1871 ***1823.22*** *p13*
Bland, Ralph 18; Savannah, Georgia, 1775 ***1220.25*** *p139*
Bland, Sarah; Virginia, 1680 ***1224.1*** *p7*
Bland, Thomas; Virginia, 1666-1667 ***6212.30*** *p34*
Blandin, Anna Margarete; Port uncertain, 1751 ***2856.30*** *p40*
Blane, Charles Collins; Richmond, Virginia, 1855 ***1224.3*** *p7*
Blane, David 44; Ontario, 1871 ***1823.28*** *p7*
Blane, Marion 71; Ontario, 1871 ***1823.28*** *p7*
Blaney, Charles; New York, 1807 ***8197.10*** *p325*
Blank, Anthony 17; New York, 1775 ***1220.25*** *p94*
Blank, Elisabeth; Port uncertain, 1731 ***2856.30*** *p40*
Blanke, Sierich; New York, 1821 ***8197.10*** *p208*
Blanle, George; Maryland, 1910 ***3259.35*** *p4*
Blansheim, Mathys; America, 1663 ***2856.30*** *p40*
Blany, Tho; Virginia, 1665-1666 ***6212.30*** *p23*
Blar, Johann; America, 1753 ***2856.30*** *p40*
Blare, Mathew; Virginia, 1666 ***6212.30*** *p26*
Blare, William 40; Ontario, 1871 ***1823.15*** *p20*
Blarkowski, Marryanna; Maryland, 1910 ***3259.35*** *p5*
Blasack, Joseph; Maryland, 1910 ***3259.35*** *p5*
Blasdell, J. C. 67; Ontario, 1871 ***1823.28*** *p7*
Blaser, Christina; Port uncertain, 1694 ***2856.30*** *p40*
Blaser, Jacob; Port uncertain, 1694 ***2856.30*** *p40*
Blashell, Francis 29; Nova Scotia, 1774 ***1220.25*** *p135*
Blasin, Anna Maria; Port uncertain, 1784 ***2856.30*** *p401*
Blasius, Ms.; Port uncertain, 1775 ***2856.30*** *p40*
Blasius, Catharina; Port uncertain, 1759 ***2856.30*** *p40*
Blasius, Johann; America, 1765 ***2856.30*** *p40*
Blasius, Johann Adam; Port uncertain, 1765 ***2856.30*** *p40*
Blass, Johann; Port uncertain, 1758 ***2856.30*** *p42*
Blassle, Josef; Port uncertain, 1781 ***2856.30*** *p42*
Blaszezak, Nichlas; Maryland, 1910 ***3259.35*** *p5*
Blatchford, John 53; Ontario, 1871 ***1823.15*** *p20*
Blatchford, Richard 22; Ontario, 1871 ***1823.15*** *p20*
Blatchford, Richard 38; Ontario, 1871 ***1823.15*** *p20*
Blathurst, Ja; Virginia, 1665-1666 ***6212.30*** *p22*
Blatisque, Anna Maria; Port uncertain, 1764 ***2856.30*** *p40*
Blatling, Peter; Port uncertain, 1757 ***2856.30*** *p42*
Blatt, Johann Henrich; America, 1744 ***2856.30*** *p40*
Blattmann, Thaddaus; Port uncertain, 1788 ***2856.30*** *p40*
Blattner, Adam; Port uncertain, 1784 ***2856.30*** *p40*
Blattner, Jacob; America, 1738 ***2856.30*** *p40*
With wife
Blatz, Barbara; Port uncertain, 1749 ***2856.30*** *p40*
Blau, Han; Port uncertain, 1676 ***2856.30*** *p41*
With wife
Blau, Hans; Port uncertain, 1716 ***2856.30*** *p41*
With wife
Blauhorn, Jeremias; Port uncertain, 1791 ***2856.30*** *p40*
Blauhorn, Jeremias; Port uncertain, 1792 ***2856.30*** *p40*
Blaumer, Anna; Port uncertain, 1733 ***2856.30*** *p41*
Blaumerin, Anna; Port uncertain, 1733 ***2856.30*** *p41*
Blaw, Han; Port uncertain, 1676 ***2856.30*** *p41*
With wife
Blaw, Hans; Port uncertain, 1716 ***2856.30*** *p41*
With wife
Blawert, Maria Elisabeth; Port uncertain, 1754 ***2856.30*** *p41*
Blay, Mary; Maryland, 1658 ***2524.55*** *p26*
Blay, William; Maryland, 1669 ***2524.55*** *p26*
Blayard, Thomas; Maryland, 1664 ***2524.55*** *p26*
Blaydes, Samuel; Virginia, 1683 ***1224.1*** *p7*
Blayes, Robert; Virginia, 1664 ***6212.30*** *p14*
Blayin, Catharina; America, 1764 ***2856.30*** *p41*
Blayre, James; Maryland, 1681 ***2524.55*** *p26*
Blazard, Thomas; Maryland, 1664 ***2524.55*** *p26*
Blazer, Abraham 50; Ontario, 1871 ***1823.22*** *p13*
Blea, Mary 65; Ontario, 1871 ***1823.15*** *p20*
Bleakeman, George 30; Ontario, 1871 ***1823.28*** *p7*
Bleakley, Adam; New York, 1827 ***8197.10*** *p340*
Bleakney, Edward; Pennsylvania, 1777 ***4629.10*** *p22*
Blease, Frederick 33; Ontario, 1871 ***1823.28*** *p7*
Bleasner, Fernham 49; Ontario, 1871 ***1823.28*** *p7*
Blecha, Christian; Port uncertain, 1751 ***2856.30*** *p42*
Blechynden, Charles 20; Virginia, 1774 ***1220.25*** *p53*
Blehm, Adam 23; Kansas, 1900-1910 ***9079.10*** *p26*
Blehm, Catharine 36; Kansas, 1882-1910 ***9079.10*** *p18*
Blehm, Creata 2; Kansas, 1909-1910 ***9079.10*** *p20*
Blehm, David G. 37; Kansas, 1880-1910 ***9079.10*** *p18*
Blehm, Elizabeth 6; Kansas, 1909-1910 ***9079.10*** *p20*
Blehm, Elizabeth 36; Kansas, 1909-1910 ***9079.10*** *p20*
Blehm, Henry 9; Kansas, 1909-1910 ***9079.10*** *p20*
Blehm, Henry 38; Kansas, 1909-1910 ***9079.10*** *p20*
Blehm, Jacob 55; Kansas, 1876-1910 ***9079.10*** *p48*
Blehm, Kot 4; Kansas, 1909-1910 ***9079.10*** *p20*
Blehm, Lizzie 49; Kansas, 1910 ***9079.10*** *p48*
Blehm, Mary E. 13; Kansas, 1909-1910 ***9079.10*** *p20*
Bleidorn, Louis; New York, 1840 ***8197.10*** *p144*
Bleifuhs, Francis; New York, 1840 ***8197.10*** *p213*
Bleines, Ms.; Port uncertain, 1764 ***2856.30*** *p41*
Bleja, John; Maryland, 1910 ***3259.35*** *p5*
Blelam, George 28; Kansas, 1900-1910 ***9079.10*** *p24*
Blencoe, Mr.; Quebec, 1857 ***9196.15*** *p22*
Blencoe, Mrs.; Quebec, 1857 ***9196.15*** *p22*
Blencom, Mary; Virginia, 1666 ***6212.30*** *p29*
Blencowe, Richard 25; Boston, 1774 ***1220.25*** *p50*
Blenkarne, Captain; Quebec, 1858 ***9196.15*** *p36*
Blenkinson, Robt; Virginia, 1664 ***6212.30*** *p6*
Blennerhasset, James; Virginia, 1848 ***1224.3*** *p7*
Blersch, Aloys; Port uncertain, 1791 ***2856.30*** *p41*
Blertzner, Henry; Baltimore, 1854 ***6058.10*** *p42*
Blesch, Jonas; America, 1789 ***2856.30*** *p41*

Blesch, Jonas; America, 1793 2856.30 p41
Bleskey, Joseph 55; Ontario, 1871 1823.28 p7
Bleskey, Louis 30; Ontario, 1871 1823.28 p7
Bless, Johann Jacob; Port uncertain, 1770 2856.30 p41
Blessi, Herman; Port uncertain, 1777 2856.30 p41
Bletsch, Johann Peter; Port uncertain, 1752 2856.30 p41
Bletsoe, John Morgan; New York, 1820 8197.10 p207
Bletzner, Henry; Baltimore, 1854 6058.10 p42
Bleven, Bartholomew; Maryland, 1661 2524.55 p89
Blewer, Joseph; Pennsylvania, 1777 4629.10 p6
Blewer, William; Maryland, 1681 2524.55 p26
Blewett, Sarah; Ontario, 1861 2896.27 p9
Blewfeild, Rich; Virginia, 1667 6212.30 p37
Blewfeild, Robert; Virginia, 1667-1668 6212.30 p38
Bley, Adam; America, 1753 2856.30 p41
With wife & 2 children
Bley, Caspar; Port uncertain, 1737 2856.30 p41
With wife & children
Bley, Daniel; Pennsylvania, 1849 6058.10 p25
Bley, Georg; America, 1764 2856.30 p41
Bleyensteiner, Elisabeth; Port uncertain, 1730 2856.30 p41
Blezard, Anthony 78; Ontario, 1871 1823.22 p13
Blezard, Thomas 55; Ontario, 1871 1823.22 p13
Blick, William; New York, 1840 8197.10 p213
Blid, David; Pennsylvania, 1777 4629.10 p17
Blidder, Rowland; Maryland, 1667 2524.55 p26
Bliess, Jacob; America, 1749 2856.30 p41
Bligh, Jno; Virginia, 1666 6212.30 p28
Blight, John; New York, 1832 8197.10 p356
Blinco, George 26; Ontario, 1871 1823.28 p7
Blinco, James; Maryland, 1671 2524.55 p26
Blind, Joseph 25; Maryland, 1774 1220.25 p71
Blinille, Mrs. George; Port uncertain, 1772 2856.30 p41
Blinkey, Charles 33; Fort Cumberland, Nova Scotia, 1774 1220.25 p18
Wife: Sarah 33
Child: Mary 1
Child: Jane 6
Blinkey, Jane 6 *SEE* Blinkey, Charles
Blinkey, Mary 1 *SEE* Blinkey, Charles
Blinkey, Sarah 33 *SEE* Blinkey, Charles
Blinkhorn, Ann 3 *SEE* Blinkhorn, William
Blinkhorn, Ann 29 *SEE* Blinkhorn, William
Blinkhorn, Eleanor 1 *SEE* Blinkhorn, William
Blinkhorn, John 4 *SEE* Blinkhorn, William
Blinkhorn, William 7 *SEE* Blinkhorn, William
Blinkhorn, William 33; Nova Scotia, 1774 1220.25 p14
Wife: Ann 29
Child: William 7
Child: John 4
Child: Eleanor 1
Child: Ann 3
Blinkhorne, John *SEE* Blinkhorne, Robert
Blinkhorne, Mary *SEE* Blinkhorne, Robert
Blinkhorne, Robert *SEE* Blinkhorne, Robert
Blinkhorne, Robert; Maryland, 1652-1658 2524.55 p26
Wife: Mary
Son: John
Son: Robert
Blinkorne, John *SEE* Blinkorne, Robert
Blinkorne, Mary *SEE* Blinkorne, Robert
Blinkorne, Robert *SEE* Blinkorne, Robert
Blinkorne, Robert; Maryland, 1652-1658 2524.55 p26
Wife: Mary
Son: Robert
Son: John
Bliss, David; New York, 1807 8197.10 p35
Bliss, Jean; Philadelphia, 1820 1224.3 p7
Bliss, Theodore E.; New Haven, Connecticut, 1819 8197.10 p128
Bliss, Theodore E.; New York, 1836 8197.10 p212
Blisse, Mary; Virginia, 1655 1224.1 p7
Blitz, Georg; Port uncertain, 1788 2856.30 p41
Blitzhoffer, Feid; Port uncertain, 1752 2856.30 p41
With wife & children
Blizard, C. 8; Ontario, 1861 2896.28 p5
Blizard, J. C. 19; Ontario, 1861 2896.28 p5
Blizard, John 44; Ontario, 1871 1823.22 p13
Blizard, T. F. 2; Ontario, 1861 2896.28 p5
Blizard, William G. 16; Ontario, 1861 2896.28 p5
Bloch, Henry 40; Ontario, 1871 1823.15 p20
Bloch, Julius 69; Ontario, 1871 1823.15 p20
Bloch, Margaretha 68; Ontario, 1871 1823.15 p20
Bloch, Samuel; New York, 1838 8197.10 p111
Blochowiz, John; Maryland, 1910 3259.35 p5
Block, Albert; Maryland, 1673 2524.55 p26
Block, Elizabeth; Maryland, 1680 2524.55 p26
Block, John; Maryland, 1910 3259.35 p5
Block, Whilimene 35; Ontario, 1871 1823.28 p7
Blodget, Levi 72; Ontario, 1871 1823.22 p13
Blodt, Josef; Port uncertain, 1752 2856.30 p42
Blodt, Matern; Port uncertain, 1781 2856.30 p42
Bloedon, Ferdinand 28; Ontario, 1871 1823.28 p7
Blogg, Anna Maria; Savannah, Georgia, 1821 1224.3 p8
Bloies, Thomas; Virginia, 1665-1666 6212.30 p21
Bloise, Abraham 20; Maryland, 1774 1220.25 p39
Blomberger, Philipp; America, 1746 2856.30 p41
With wife & 3 children
Blomefeild, Wm; Virginia, 1676 6212.30 p53
Blomfeild, Dorothy; Maryland, 1671 2524.55 p27
Blomfield, Charles; Quebec, 1858 9196.15 p37
Blomstead, John; Maryland, 1670 2524.55 p27
Blondel, Peter; New York, 1821 8197.10 p209
Blondel, Peter; New York, 1826 8197.10 p333
Blonnik, Paul 33; Ontario, 1871 1823.28 p7
Blood, Harris; New York, 1827 8197.10 p298
Blood, Isabel; New England, 1646 1224.1 p64
Bloom, Bartholomew; Maryland, 1653 2524.55 p27
Bloom, Herman; Pennsylvania, 1845 6058.10 p21
Bloom, Sebastian; Pennsylvania, 1863 6058.10 p46
Bloome, William; Maryland, 1663 2524.55 p27
Bloomfield, Mr.; Quebec, 1858 9196.15 p43
Bloomfield, Mrs.; Quebec, 1858 9196.15 p43
Bloomfield, Isaac; New York, 1804 8197.10 p26
Bloomfield, Robert 44; Ontario, 1871 1823.15 p20
Bloomingdale, Solomon; Pennsylvania, 1857-1865 6058.10 p50
Bloore, Mr.; Quebec, 1857 9196.15 p16
Bloore, Mrs.; Quebec, 1857 9196.15 p16
Blos, Bartel; Port uncertain, 1785 2856.30 p42
Bloss, Joh. Frederick; New York, 1835 8197.10 p212
Bloth, Anna Margarete; Port uncertain, 1786 2856.30 p41
Bloth, Johann; Port uncertain, 1786 2856.30 p41
Blount, John 28; Maryland, 1775 1220.25 p108
Blount, Samuel; Jamaica, 1828 1640.13 p10
Blouse, Thomas; Maryland, 1663 2524.55 p29
Blow, Samuel 43; Ontario, 1871 1823.15 p20
Blowers, Archibald; Nova Scotia, 1895 1640.13 p10
Blowers, Mary; Maryland, 1680 2524.55 p27
Blowers, Samson 19; Boston, 1776 1220.25 p1
Blowey, Bessey Kate 15; Ontario, 1871 1823.15 p20
Bloxam, Jno; Virginia, 1672 6212.30 p49
Bloxerm, Elizabeth; Maryland, 1665-1666 2524.55 p27
Bloxom, Jno; Virginia, 1668-1669 6212.30 p41
Bloxon, Elizabeth; Maryland, 1665-1666 2524.55 p27
Bloxzerm, Elizabeth; Maryland, 1665-1666 2524.55 p27
Bloyce, Frances *SEE* Bloyce, Thomas
Bloyce, Judith *SEE* Bloyce, Thomas
Bloyce, Thomas; Maryland, 1662 2524.55 p27
Wife: Frances
Daughter: Frances
Daughter: Judith
Bloyce, Thomas; Maryland, 1666 2524.55 p27
Bloyd, Daniel; Maryland, 1658 2524.55 p27
Bloys, Daniel 18; Maryland, 1774 1220.25 p60
Bloysh, Thomas; Maryland, 1666 2524.55 p27
Blue, Daniel; Georgia, 1790-1812 1640.10 p13
Blue, William 33; Ontario, 1871 1823.22 p13
Blue, Wm; Virginia, 1666-1667 6212.30 p35
Bluett, Frederick B. 52; Ontario, 1871 1823.15 p20
Bluett, Ham 14; Ontario, 1861 2896.27 p9
Bluett, John 43; Ontario, 1861 2896.27 p9
Bluett, Nels 16; Ontario, 1861 2896.27 p9
Bluett, Mrs. Robt 28; Ontario, 1871 1823.15 p20
Bluett, S. J. 19; Ontario, 1861 2896.27 p9
Bluhm, Maria Elisabeth; Port uncertain, 1769 2856.30 p41
Bluhmling, Tobias; Port uncertain, 1742 2856.30 p42
Blum, Anna Catharina; Port uncertain, 1754 2856.30 p41
Blum, Apollonia; America, 1740 2856.30 p41
Blum, Apollonia; America, 1783 2856.30 p41
Blum, Caspar; Port uncertain, 1724 2856.30 p41
Blum, Christian; Port uncertain, 1795 2856.30 p42
With family
Blum, Christian; Port uncertain, 1796 2856.30 p42
With family
Blum, Christof; Port uncertain, 1764 2856.30 p41
Blum, Michel; Port uncertain, 1783 2856.30 p41
Blum, Nikolaus; America, 1737 2856.30 p42
With wife & children
Blum, Peter; America, 1786 2856.30 p41
Blum, Peter; Port uncertain, 1737 2856.30 p41
Blum, Sebastian; Pennsylvania, 1863 6058.10 p46
Blumberger, Philipp; America, 1746 2856.30 p42
With wife & 3 children
Blumly, George; Virginia, 1665-1666 6212.30 p21
Blundell, Anna; Maryland, 1662 2524.55 p27
Blundell, Charles 21; Maryland, 1774 1220.25 p61
Blundell, Charles 29; Maryland, 1775 1220.25 p110
Wife: Mary 29
Blundell, Hen; Virginia, 1665 6212.30 p17
Blundell, Mary 29 *SEE* Blundell, Charles
Blundell, Thomas; Maryland, 1671 2524.55 p27
Blunt, Mrs.; Maryland, 1649 2524.55 p27
Blunt, Abigail 30; Ontario, 1861 2896.28 p23
Blunt, Christopher; Maryland, 1660 2524.55 p27
Blunt, Eliday; Virginia, 1663 6212.30 p2
Blunt, Henry; Virginia, 1665-1666 6212.30 p21
Blunt, James; Maryland, 1656 2524.55 p27
Blunt, James; Maryland, 1665 2524.55 p27
Blunt, John; New England, 1712 1224.2 p11
Blunt, Magdalen; Virginia, 1666-1667 6212.30 p34
Blunt, Rebecca *SEE* Blunt, Richard
Blunt, Richard; Maryland, 1649 2524.55 p27
With wife
Daughter: Rebecca
Blunt, Stephen 9; Ontario, 1861 2896.28 p23
Blunt, Timothy; Virginia, 1667-1668 6212.30 p39
Blunt, William; Maryland, 1661 2524.55 p27
Blusewicz, Alexander; Maryland, 1910 3259.35 p5
Bluster, George 30; Ontario, 1871 1823.28 p7
Bluxome, Isaac; New York, 1823 8197.10 p209
Bluxome, Isaac; New York, 1828 8197.10 p62
Bluzczyk, Leokadza; Maryland, 1910 3259.35 p5
Bly, Daniel; Pennsylvania, 1849 6058.10 p25
Bly, Elizabeth 21; Virginia, 1774 1220.25 p91
Bly, John; Virginia, 1664 1224.1 p7
Blyth, David; Montreal, 1829 1640.13 p10
Blyth, John; Jamaica, 1835 1640.13 p10
Blyth, John; Pennsylvania, 1777 4629.10 p13
Blyth, William; Pennsylvania, 1777 4629.10 p6
Blythe, Joseph 30; Ontario, 1871 1823.15 p20
Boage, John; Maryland, 1658 2524.55 p27
Boague, John; Maryland, 1665 2524.55 p27
Boajanowski, Franz; Maryland, 1910 3259.35 p5
Boaker, John F.; Pennsylvania, 1861 6058.10 p51
Boal, John, Sr. 70; Ontario, 1871 1823.28 p7
Boalbla, Miss; Quebec, 1857 9196.15 p23
Boalbla, Mr.; Quebec, 1857 9196.15 p23
Boalbla, Mrs.; Quebec, 1857 9196.15 p23
Boane, John 38; Ontario, 1871 1823.15 p20
Board, John 36; Virginia, 1774 1220.25 p75
Board, John 42; Ontario, 1871 1823.28 p7
Boardman, Mr.; Quebec, 1857 9196.15 p24
Boardman, Wm.; Maryland, 1682 2524.55 p27
Boast, Francis 47; Nova Scotia, 1774 1220.25 p136
With wife & 5 children
Boast, John 56; Ontario, 1871 1823.28 p7
Boate, Alexander 34; Ontario, 1871 1823.22 p13
Bobel, Frank; Maryland, 1910 3259.35 p5
Bober, Edward; Maryland, 1910 3259.35 p5
Bober, Walter; Maryland, 1910 3259.35 p5
Boch, Andreas; America, 1744 2856.30 p42
With wife & 6 children
Boch, Johann; America, 1742 2856.30 p42
Boch, Leonhard; Port uncertain, 1783 2856.30 p42
Boch, Wendel; Port uncertain, 1737 2856.30 p42
Bochenski, Albert; Maryland, 1910 3259.35 p5
Bochenski, Joseph; Maryland, 1910 3259.35 p5
Bochiak, Kazmer; Maryland, 1910 3259.35 p5
Bochinski, Frank; Maryland, 1910 3259.35 p5
Bochius, Daniel; Pennsylvania, 1786 4629.10 p54
Bochter, Valentino 48; Ontario, 1871 1823.15 p20
Bochynck, Joseph; Maryland, 1910 3259.35 p5
Bock, Friedrich; Port uncertain, 1752 2856.30 p42
Bock, Jakob; Port uncertain, 1738 2856.30 p42
Bock, Johann; Port uncertain, 1753 2856.30 p42
Bock, Johann; Port uncertain, 1799 2856.30 p42
Bock, John; Maryland, 1659 2524.55 p27
Bock, Oliver 21; Maryland, 1774 1220.25 p74
Bock, Philipp; Port uncertain, 1752 2856.30 p42
Bocken, Margarete; Port uncertain, 1736 2856.30 p42
Bockenhaua, Henry 33; Ontario, 1871 1823.15 p20
Bockeus, Peter; Pennsylvania, 1776 4629.10 p53
Bockh, Jakob; Port uncertain, 1772 2856.30 p42
Bockh, Johann; Port uncertain, 1741 2856.30 p42
Bockh, Johann Peter; Port uncertain, 1738 2856.30 p42
Bocking, Reichard; America, 1741 2856.30 p62
Bocking, Reichard; Port uncertain, 1741 2856.30 p62
With wife & 5 children
Bocks, Andrew; Maryland, 1910 3259.35 p5
Bockstahler, Anna Maria; Port uncertain, 1747 2856.30 p42
Bockstahler, Catharina; Port uncertain, 1795 2856.30 p42
Bockstaler, Michael; Port uncertain, 1754 2856.30 p42
Bockus, Sarah E. 40; Ontario, 1861 2896.27 p18
Boddeker, John F.; Pennsylvania, 1861 6058.10 p51
Bodden, Jno.; Maryland, 1680 2524.55 p27
Boddie, Cornelius 9; Ontario, 1871 1823.22 p13
Boddie, James 21; Ontario, 1871 1823.22 p13
Boddie, James 61; Ontario, 1871 1823.22 p13
Boddily, Benjamin Peach; Newburyport, Massachusetts, 1827 1224.3 p8
Boddin, John 71; Ontario, 1871 1823.15 p20
Boddy, Mr.; Quebec, 1858 9196.15 p43
Boddy, Mrs.; Quebec, 1858 9196.15 p36
Boddy, Mrs.; Quebec, 1858 9196.15 p43
Boddy, John; Maryland, 1683 1224.1 p7

Boddy, Thomas K. 43; Ontario, 1871 ***1823.15*** *p20*
Boddy, William; Maryland, 1649 ***2524.55*** *p27*
Bodecker, John F.; Pennsylvania, 1861 ***6058.10*** *p51*
Bodell, Attwell; Maryland, 1662 ***2524.55*** *p27*
Bodell, Elizabeth; Maryland, 1662 ***2524.55*** *p27*
Bodella, Jacaminca; Virginia, 1663-1664 ***6212.30*** *p5*
Bodenmiller, Jakob; Port uncertain, 1689 ***2856.30*** *p43*
Bodenstein, Ehrhard; Port uncertain, 1764 ***2856.30*** *p43*
Bodey, William J. 32; Ontario, 1871 ***1823.15*** *p20*
Bodkin, Anthony 27; Philadelphia, 1789 ***4629.10*** *p58*
Bodkin, Bibian *SEE* Bodkin, James
Bodkin, James; Philadelphia, 1789 ***4629.10*** *p58*
Wife: Bibian
Bodkin, John 40; Ontario, 1871 ***1823.22*** *p13*
Bodle, George 38; Ontario, 1871 ***1823.15*** *p20*
Bodnick, Dora; Maryland, 1910 ***3259.35*** *p5*
Bodski, Francis; Maryland, 1910 ***3259.35*** *p5*
Bodt, Charles; New York, 1837 ***8197.10*** *p85*
Bodt, Henry; New York, 1840 ***8197.10*** *p144*
Bodwell, Attawell; Maryland, 1657 ***2524.55*** *p27*
Boeburger, G. Jacob 37; Kansas, 1878-1910 ***9079.10*** *p26*
Boeburger, Mary M. 37; Kansas, 1878-1910 ***9079.10*** *p26*
Boeffen, Matthaus; Port uncertain, 1783 ***2856.30*** *p43*
Boehnken, Henry; New York, 1840 ***8197.10*** *p144*
Boehnken, Johann Jacob; New York, 1840 ***8197.10*** *p144*
Boehr, Jakob; Port uncertain, 1785 ***2856.30*** *p61*
Boell, Frederick Charles; New York, 1827 ***8197.10*** *p210*
Boell, Frederick W.; New York, 1832 ***8197.10*** *p211*
Boell, Paul Joseph; New York, 1832 ***8197.10*** *p211*
Boeuf, Johann; Port uncertain, 1798 ***2856.30*** *p43*
Boffey, Barrick 18; Ontario, 1871 ***1823.28*** *p7*
Boffington, John Baptiste; New York, 1808 ***8197.10*** *p53*
Bogaciewicz, Maryanna; Maryland, 1910 ***3259.35*** *p5*
Bogan, Patrick 46; Ontario, 1871 ***1823.22*** *p13*
Bogan, Wm; Virginia, 1666 ***6212.30*** *p30*
Bogart, J. J.; Portland, Maine, 1858 ***9196.15*** *p28*
Bogartz, Anna Maria; Port uncertain, 1793 ***2856.30*** *p43*
Bogdan, Michael; Maryland, 1910 ***3259.35*** *p5*
Bogdansvich, M. 27; Alaska, 1917 ***9196.1*** *p47*
Bogdansvich, M. 27; British Columbia, 1917 ***9196.1*** *p47*
Bogdanweisch, Adam; Maryland, 1910 ***3259.35*** *p5*
Bogdinowicz, Julia; Maryland, 1910 ***3259.35*** *p5*
Bogdon, John; Maryland, 1910 ***3259.35*** *p5*
Bogenski, Alexander; Maryland, 1910 ***3259.35*** *p5*
Bogg, John; New York, 1802 ***8197.10*** *p18*
Boggas, John; Carolina, 1762 ***1224.2*** *p12*
Boggenstos, James 26; British Columbia, 1913 ***9196.1*** *p21*
Boggenstos, James 26; Juneau, Alaska, 1913 ***9196.1*** *p21*
Boggis, Benjamin *SEE* Boggis, Phillipp
Boggis, Mary *SEE* Boggis, Phillipp
Boggis, Phillipp; Maryland, 1664 ***2524.55*** *p27*
Wife: Mary
Daughter: Mary
Son: Benjamin
Boggs, Oliver 59; Ontario, 1871 ***1823.22*** *p13*
Boggs, Wm; Virginia, 1692-1693 ***6212.30*** *p59*
Boghick, Francis; New York, 1834 ***8197.10*** *p74*
Boghley, Donoh; Maryland, 1682 ***2524.55*** *p27*
Boghley, Margarett; Maryland, 1682 ***2524.55*** *p27*
Bogie, Andrew 36; Ontario, 1871 ***1823.15*** *p20*
Bogie, James 39; Ontario, 1871 ***1823.15*** *p21*
Bogle, Robert; New Orleans, 1826 ***1640.10*** *p13*
Bogle, William H.; New York, 1803 ***8197.10*** *p10*
Bogne, Henry 45; Ontario, 1871 ***1823.15*** *p21*
Bogue, William 27; Philadelphia, 1774 ***1220.25*** *p66*
Bogzomsky, Michael; Maryland, 1910 ***3259.35*** *p5*
Bohan, Michael 36; Ontario, 1871 ***1823.28*** *p7*
Bohanan, Flora 69; Ontario, 1871 ***1823.15*** *p21*
Bohannon, Wm.; Pennsylvania, 1777 ***4629.10*** *p25*
Bohement, Anne; Maryland, 1665 ***2524.55*** *p22*
Bohla, Maria Elisabeth; Port uncertain, 1764 ***2856.30*** *p43*
Bohler, Anna; Port uncertain, 1752 ***2856.30*** *p43*
With 4 children
Bohler, Henriette; Port uncertain, 1783 ***2856.30*** *p62*
Bohler, Jacob; America, 1766 ***2856.30*** *p62*
With wife & 5 children
Bohler, Maria Sybilla; America, 1759 ***2856.30*** *p62*
Bohler, Maria Sybilla; America, 1773 ***2856.30*** *p62*
Bohler, Maria Sybilla; America, 1774 ***2856.30*** *p253*
Bohler, Philipp Jacob; America, 1778 ***2856.30*** *p62*
With wife
Bohler, Philipp Jacob; America, 1782 ***2856.30*** *p62*
With wife
Bohlig, Hilligard; America, 1752 ***2856.30*** *p43*
With wife & daughter
Bohly, Hilligard; America, 1752 ***2856.30*** *p43*
With wife & daughter
Bohm, Anna Eva; Port uncertain, 1755 ***2856.30*** *p62*
Bohm, Josef; Port uncertain, 1782 ***2856.30*** *p62*
Bohm, Konrad; America, 1727 ***2856.30*** *p62*
Bohm, Lorenz; Port uncertain, 1749 ***2856.30*** *p43*
Bohmer, Philippine; Port uncertain, 1788 ***2856.30*** *p229*
Bohmer, Theodor; Port uncertain, 1783 ***2856.30*** *p62*
With wife & 2 daughters
Bohn, Jacob; Port uncertain, 1748 ***2856.30*** *p43*
Bohn, Maria Margarete; Port uncertain, 1782 ***2856.30*** *p43*
Bohn, Peter Tielmann; America, 1740 ***2856.30*** *p43*
Bohnenberger, Peter; Port uncertain, 1782 ***2856.30*** *p43*
Bohnenberger, Peter; Port uncertain, 1789 ***2856.30*** *p43*
Bohner, Anton; Port uncertain, 1769 ***2856.30*** *p43*
Bohner, Anton; Port uncertain, 1799 ***2856.30*** *p43*
Bohner, M.; Port uncertain, 1764 ***2856.30*** *p18*
Bohner, Margarete; Port uncertain, 1764 ***2856.30*** *p43*
With husband & 5 children
Bohnerd, Conrad; New York, 1839 ***8197.10*** *p382*
Bohnirt, George; New York, 1839 ***8197.10*** *p382*
Boholts, Charles 28; Ontario, 1871 ***1823.28*** *p7*
Boholts, Frances 53; Ontario, 1871 ***1823.28*** *p7*
Bohowich, Joseph; Maryland, 1910 ***3259.35*** *p5*
Bohr, Anna Gertrud; Port uncertain, 1752 ***2856.30*** *p43*
Bohr, Anna Maria; Port uncertain, 1747 ***2856.30*** *p43*
Bohr, Friedrich; Port uncertain, 1771 ***2856.30*** *p43*
Bohr, Johann Friedric; America, 1749 ***2856.30*** *p62*
Bohrer, Agnes; Port uncertain, 1769 ***2856.30*** *p43*
Bohrer, Anna Barbara; America, 1746 ***2856.30*** *p43*
Bohrer, Anna Barbara Risch; America, 1746 ***2856.30*** *p362*
With daughter
Bohrer, Anton; Port uncertain, 1752 ***2856.30*** *p43*
With wife & 3 children
Bohrer, Carl; New York, 1840 ***8197.10*** *p214*
Bohrer, Michael; Port uncertain, 1764 ***2856.30*** *p43*
Bohrin, Agnes; Port uncertain, 1769 ***2856.30*** *p43*
Bohringer, Johann; America, 1762 ***2856.30*** *p62*
Bohringer, Johann Georg; Port uncertain, 1774 ***2856.30*** *p62*
Bohringer, Sybilla; Port uncertain, 1765 ***2856.30*** *p62*
Boice, C. 23; Ontario, 1861 ***2896.28*** *p9*
Boice, C. H. 5; Ontario, 1861 ***2896.28*** *p9*
Boice, Charlotte 76; Ontario, 1871 ***1823.22*** *p13*
Boice, E. J. 3; Ontario, 1861 ***2896.28*** *p9*
Boice, G. 94; Ontario, 1861 ***2896.28*** *p9*
Boice, H. 66; Ontario, 1861 ***2896.28*** *p9*
Boice, J. C. 1; Ontario, 1861 ***2896.28*** *p9*
Boice, T. 28; Ontario, 1861 ***2896.28*** *p9*
Boice, Thomas; Maryland, 1675 ***2524.55*** *p27*
Boid, Samuel 58; Ontario, 1871 ***1823.15*** *p21*
Boidell, Mr.; Quebec, 1857 ***9196.15*** *p18*
Boigs, John; Georgia, 1699 ***1640.13*** *p10*
Boiko, John 30; Alaska, 1918 ***9196.1*** *p56*
Boiko, John 30; Yukon, 1918 ***9196.1*** *p56*
Boil, Ellen; Vermont, 1798-1875 ***5900.10*** *p586*
Boils, John; Philadelphia, 1819 ***6058.10*** *p13*
Bois, Anna Margarete; America, 1766 ***2856.30*** *p321*
Bois, William; Virginia, 1666-1667 ***6212.30*** *p32*
Bois, Wm; Virginia, 1665-1666 ***6212.30*** *p22*
Boisow, Charles 61; Ontario, 1871 ***1823.28*** *p8*
Boizard, Eustache Napoleon; New York, 1834 ***8197.10*** *p316*
Bojansky, Wojciech; Maryland, 1910 ***3259.35*** *p5*
Bojkowski, Adam; Maryland, 1910 ***3259.35*** *p5*
Boker, Edward; New York, 1838 ***8197.10*** *p111*
Boker, John G.; New York, 1830 ***8197.10*** *p353*
Bokowski, Stephen; Maryland, 1910 ***3259.35*** *p5*
Bolac, Catharine Cain 64; Vermont, 1884 ***5900.10*** *p280*
Bolan, Catherine; Vermont, 1839-1914 ***5900.10*** *p446*
Bolan, John 50; Ontario, 1871 ***1823.28*** *p8*
Bolan, Mary; Vermont, 1828-1928 ***5900.10*** *p567*
Boland, Catherine Ann 3; Ontario, 1861 ***2896.25*** *p69*
Boland, Catherine Ann 34; Ontario, 1861 ***2896.25*** *p69*
Boland, Elizabeth 80; Vermont, 1911 ***5900.10*** *p259*
Boland, James 33; Ontario, 1871 ***1823.22*** *p13*
Boland, James 71; Ontario, 1871 ***1823.22*** *p13*
Boland, John; Maryland, 1662 ***2524.55*** *p62*
Boland, John 56; Ontario, 1871 ***1823.28*** *p8*
Boland, Margaret; Vermont, 1834-1929 ***5900.10*** *p452*
Boland, Margaret M.; Vermont, 1852-1935 ***5900.10*** *p432*
Boland, Mary; Vermont, 1835-1930 ***5900.10*** *p452*
Boland, Mary 1; Ontario, 1861 ***2896.25*** *p69*
Boland, Mary 69; Vermont, 1888 ***5900.10*** *p257*
Boland, Michael 7; Ontario, 1861 ***2896.25*** *p69*
Boland, Patrick 50; Vermont, 1861 ***5900.10*** *p259*
Boland, Patrick 55; Ontario, 1861 ***2896.25*** *p69*
Boland, Patrick, Jr. 12; Ontario, 1861 ***2896.25*** *p69*
Boland, Thomas 19; Ontario, 1871 ***1823.28*** *p8*
Boland, Thomas 39; Ontario, 1871 ***1823.28*** *p8*
Boland, Timothy 10; Ontario, 1861 ***2896.25*** *p69*
Boland, William 21; Ontario, 1871 ***1823.28*** *p8*
Bolander, Fred; New Jersey, 1893 ***3437.14*** *p175*
Bolard, John; Maryland, 1664 ***2524.55*** *p27*
Boldry, Philip; Virginia, 1731 ***1224.2*** *p12*
Boldwinski, Joseph; Maryland, 1910 ***3259.35*** *p5*
Boldwinski, Ojoneck; Maryland, 1910 ***3259.35*** *p5*
Boleaw, Joseph 23; Ontario, 1871 ***1823.28*** *p8*
Bolen, Julia; Vermont, 1800-1872 ***5900.10*** *p560*
Bolender, Adam 42; Ontario, 1871 ***1823.15*** *p21*
Boleski, Ignatus; Maryland, 1910 ***3259.35*** *p5*
Bolesky, Antony; Maryland, 1910 ***3259.35*** *p5*
Bolewczynski, Alexander; Maryland, 1910 ***3259.35*** *p5*
Bolewick, John; Maryland, 1910 ***3259.35*** *p5*
Bolewicski, James; Maryland, 1910 ***3259.35*** *p5*
Bolewinsky, Michael; Maryland, 1910 ***3259.35*** *p5*
Bolfe, B. 33; Alaska, 1914 ***9196.1*** *p24*
Bolger, Catherine Leary; Vermont, 1861-1911 ***5900.10*** *p157*
Bolger, Edward 33; Vermont, 1875 ***5900.10*** *p267*
Bolger, Ellen; Vermont, 1854-1925 ***5900.10*** *p255*
Bolger, James; Vermont, 1825-1891 ***5900.10*** *p172*
Bolger, James F.; Vermont, 1863-1905 ***5900.10*** *p172*
Bolger, John; Vermont, 1848-1917 ***5900.10*** *p264*
Bolger, John; Vermont, 1851-1865 ***5900.10*** *p172*
Bolger, John 27; Kansas, 1909-1910 ***9079.10*** *p30*
Bolger, Katie 4; Kansas, 1908-1910 ***9079.10*** *p30*
Bolger, Luke B.; Vermont, 1855-1922 ***5900.10*** *p157*
Bolger, Margaret; Vermont, 1830-1877 ***5900.10*** *p172*
Bolger, Margaret; Vermont, 1855-1864 ***5900.10*** *p172*
Bolger, Maria C.; Vermont, 1860-1925 ***5900.10*** *p172*
Bolger, Martin 55; Ontario, 1871 ***1823.28*** *p8*
Bolger, Mary A.; Vermont, 1866-1880 ***5900.10*** *p172*
Bolger, Mary Hennessy; Vermont, 1816-1889 ***5900.10*** *p264*
Bolger, Salamon 29; Kansas, 1908-1910 ***9079.10*** *p30*
Bolger, Thomas; New York, 1828 ***8197.10*** *p211*
Bolger, Thomas; Vermont, 1868-1918 ***5900.10*** *p172*
Bolger, Thomas 66; Vermont, 1866 ***5900.10*** *p264*
Bolger, Tracy 24; Kansas, 1908-1910 ***9079.10*** *p30*
Bolin, John; Vermont, 1833-1914 ***5900.10*** *p403*
Bolin, Margaret Mary 75; Vermont, 1901 ***5900.10*** *p425*
Bolin, Martin 65; Vermont, 1885 ***5900.10*** *p425*
Bolin, Mary Driscoll; Vermont, 1831-1914 ***5900.10*** *p403*
Boll, Barbara; Port uncertain, 1772 ***2856.30*** *p44*
Boll, Franz; Port uncertain, 1772 ***2856.30*** *p44*
Bolland, Henry; New York, 1823 ***8197.10*** *p209*
Bollard, Mary 57; Vermont, 1897 ***5900.10*** *p83*
Bolle, Mr.; Portland, Maine, 1858 ***9196.15*** *p47*
Bolle, Mrs.; Portland, Maine, 1858 ***9196.15*** *p47*
Boller, Edw; Virginia, 1668-1669 ***6212.30*** *p40*
Boller, Henry 36; Ontario, 1871 ***1823.15*** *p21*
Bollerman, Charles; New York, 1840 ***8197.10*** *p156*
Bolles, Joseph; New England, 1666 ***1224.1*** *p7*
Bollier, Arnold; Indiana, 1900 ***3437.14*** *p185*
Bollinger, Christian; America, 1737 ***2856.30*** *p44*
Bollinger, George; New York, 1838 ***8197.10*** *p111*
Bollinger, Jakob; America, 1737 ***2856.30*** *p44*
Bollinger, Mathes; America, 1752 ***2856.30*** *p44*
With wife & 2 children
Bollmann, Johann Nickel; America, 1739 ***2856.30*** *p44*
Bollwein, Valentin; Port uncertain, 1764 ***2856.30*** *p44*
Bollwinkal, Karl Ludwig; New York, 1840 ***8197.10*** *p213*
Bolney, John 15; Maryland, 1775 ***1220.25*** *p120*
Bolon, Wilhelm; Port uncertain, 1736 ***2856.30*** *p44*
Bolser, Georges; Maryland, 1910 ***3259.35*** *p5*
Bolski, Julian; Maryland, 1910 ***3259.35*** *p5*
Bolster, John 51; Ontario, 1871 ***1823.22*** *p13*
Bolster, Thomas 57; Ontario, 1871 ***1823.22*** *p13*
Bolt, Emanuel 40; Ontario, 1871 ***1823.15*** *p21*
Bolt, John 53; Ontario, 1871 ***1823.28*** *p8*
Bolt, Thomas 31; Ontario, 1871 ***1823.15*** *p21*
Bolton, Mr.; Quebec, 1857 ***9196.15*** *p15*
Bolton, Barnet 54; Ontario, 1871 ***1823.15*** *p21*
Bolton, Francis; New York, 1826 ***8197.10*** *p333*
Bolton, George; Pennsylvania, 1860 ***6058.10*** *p45*
Bolton, George 65; Ontario, 1871 ***1823.15*** *p21*
Bolton, Harry 28; Ontario, 1871 ***1823.15*** *p21*
Bolton, Henry; Virginia, 1692 ***1224.1*** *p8*
Bolton, James; Maryland, 1665 ***2524.55*** *p27*
Bolton, James; New York, 1838 ***8197.10*** *p110*
Bolton, Jane 74; Vermont, 1874 ***5900.10*** *p246*
Bolton, John; Maryland, 1668 ***2524.55*** *p27*
Bolton, John 47; Ontario, 1871 ***1823.22*** *p13*
Bolton, Joseph 24; Vermont, 1864 ***5900.10*** *p246*
Bolton, Joseph 35; Ontario, 1871 ***1823.22*** *p13*
Bolton, Lorni 59; Ontario, 1871 ***1823.15*** *p21*
Bolton, Mary; Maryland, 1669 ***2524.55*** *p28*
Bolton, Philip; Virginia, 1673 ***1224.1*** *p7*
Bolton, Richard; New York, 1826 ***8197.10*** *p210*
Bolton, Richard 36; Maryland, 1773-1774 ***1220.25*** *p33*
Bolton, T. Carew; Quebec, 1857 ***9196.15*** *p25*
Bolton, William 34; Maryland, 1775 ***1220.25*** *p120*
Bolton, William 70; Vermont, 1866 ***5900.10*** *p246*
Bolts, Joseph 38; Maryland, 1774 ***1220.25*** *p51*
Boltz, Johann Jacob; America, 1752 ***2856.30*** *p44*
Boltz, Nicol; America, 1733 ***2856.30*** *p44*
With wife & children
Bolz, Christina; America, 1752 ***2856.30*** *p44*
Bolz, Christina; Port uncertain, 1752 ***2856.30*** *p44*
With daughter

Bolz, Michael, The Younger; America, 1737 2856.30 p44
Bolz, Michael, The Younger; Port uncertain, 1736 2856.30 p44
With wife & 3 children
Bolzer, Adam; Port uncertain, 1765 2856.30 p44
Bombach, Johann Nickel; America, 1743 2856.30 p44
Bomerscheim, Philipp; Port uncertain, 1785 2856.30 p44
Bomersheim, Philipp; Port uncertain, 1785 2856.30 p44
Bomgart, Henry 32; Kansas, 1892-1910 9079.10 p28
Bomgart, Molly 24; Kansas, 1906-1910 9079.10 p28
Bomkosski, Andrew; Maryland, 1910 3259.35 p5
Bommer, Eva; Port uncertain, 1756 2856.30 p44
Bommerman, Jennet 69; Ontario, 1871 1823.15 p21
Bonaffe, Edward; New York, 1815 8197.10 p55
Bonahue, Daniel; New York, 1837 8197.10 p87
Bonaparte, Napoleon 32; Alaska, 1918 9196.1 p8
Bonaparte, Napoleon 32; Yukon, 1918 9196.1 p8
Bonaszewski, Andrew; Maryland, 1910 3259.35 p5
Bonaszewski, John; Maryland, 1910 3259.35 p5
Bonbarger, Maggie 24; Kansas, 1899-1910 9079.10 p6
Bonchek, Anton; Maryland, 1910 3259.35 p5
Bonco, Anna; America, 1737 2856.30 p44
With husband & 2 children
Bond, Ann; Maryland, 1673 2524.55 p28
Bond, Barnet; Maryland, 1749 1224.2 p12
Bond, Bridget 60; Ontario, 1861 2896.26 p32
Bond, Elizabeth 20; Philadelphia, 1774 1220.25 p43
Bond, Henry; New York, 1826 8197.10 p333
Bond, James; Virginia, 1666 6212.30 p28
Bond, James 20; Ontario, 1861 2896.26 p32
Bond, John 50; Ontario, 1871 1823.28 p8
Bond, John 65; Ontario, 1871 1823.22 p13
Bond, Joseph; Maryland, 1663 2524.55 p28
Bond, Joseph; Pennsylvania, 1777 4629.10 p13
Bond, Margaret 18; Ontario, 1861 2896.26 p32
Bond, Moses 22; Ontario, 1861 2896.26 p32
Bond, Richard; Maryland, 1659 2524.55 p28
Bond, Richard; Virginia, 1652 1224.1 p8
Bond, Richard 17; Maryland, 1774 1220.25 p8
Bond, Robert; Pennsylvania, 1777 4629.10 p22
Bond, S. 27; Philadelphia, 1775 1220.25 p9
Bond, Thomas; Pennsylvania, 1777 4629.10 p21
Bond, Thomas; Pennsylvania, 1779 4629.10 p39
Bond, William 16; Maryland, 1775 1220.25 p103
Bond, William 21; New York, 1775 1220.25 p142
Bond, William 58; Ontario, 1871 1823.22 p13
Bondee, Hezekiah; Virginia, 1673 6212.30 p51
Bonden, William; Maryland, 1675 2524.55 p28
Bone, George 45; Ontario, 1871 1823.15 p21
Bone, Henry William 29; Ontario, 1871 1823.22 p13
Bone, John; Maryland, 1663 2524.55 p28
Bone, John; Maryland, 1666 2524.55 p28
Bone, John 52; Ontario, 1871 1823.28 p8
Bone, Thomas 36; Ontario, 1871 1823.15 p21
Bone, Thomas 38; Ontario, 1871 1823.22 p13
Bone, William; Chicago, 1870 1640.13 p11
Boneau, Kattie Ward 31; Vermont, 1887 5900.10 p601
Boneau, Thomas Frances 11 days; Vermont, 1887 5900.10 p601
Boneberger, Daniel; Port uncertain, 1777 2856.30 p44
Boneberger, Daniel; Port uncertain, 1784 2856.30 p44
Boner, Stephen; Virginia, 1674 6212.30 p52
Boney, Steve; Maryland, 1910 3259.35 p5
Boney, Thomas 59; Ontario, 1871 1823.22 p13
Bonfield, Ann; Vermont, 1839-1911 5900.10 p429
Bonfield, James 50; Ontario, 1871 1823.28 p8
Bongereau, Mrs.; Quebec, 1857 9196.15 p18
Bonham, Ephraim; Pennsylvania, 1777 4629.10 p7
Bonham, William; Pennsylvania, 1777 4629.10 p7
Boniface, Richard 16; Maryland, 1775 1220.25 p112
Bonis, Robert 46; Ontario, 1871 1823.15 p21
Bonky, William 39; Ontario, 1871 1823.28 p8
Bonn, Johann; Port uncertain, 1766 2856.30 p45
Bonn, Nicolaus; Port uncertain, 1767 2856.30 p45
Bonnany, Richard 41; Ontario, 1871 1823.15 p21
Bonne, Thomas; Maryland, 1652-1653 2524.55 p28
Bonnefond, John Baptist; New York, 1840 8197.10 p213
Bonnele, Amos; Virginia, 1674 6212.30 p51
Bonnell, Catherine; Vermont, n.d. 5900.10 p151
Bonnell, George; New York, 1830 8197.10 p211
Bonner, Lieut.; Quebec, 1857 9196.15 p17
Bonner, Abraham; Port uncertain, 1753 2856.30 p45
Bonner, Cornelius; New York, 1804 8197.10 p26
Bonner, George; New York, 1802 8197.10 p18
Bonner, John; New York, 1836 8197.10 p319
Bonner, John 50; Ontario, 1871 1823.22 p13
Bonner, Manus; New York, 1840 8197.10 p155
Bonner, Mathias 28; Maryland, 1774 1220.25 p84
Bonner, Patrick; New York, 1840 8197.10 p153
Bonner, Robert; Pennsylvania, 1777 4629.10 p27
Bonner, William 15; Philadelphia, 1774 1220.25 p35
Bonneskey, John 25; Ontario, 1871 1823.28 p8
Bonnet, Christian 49; Ontario, 1871 1823.15 p21
Bonnet, John; Pennsylvania, 1793 4629.10 p64
Bonnet, Leonard 27; Maryland, 1774 1220.25 p62
Bonnhart, Anton; Port uncertain, 1788 2856.30 p45
Bonnick, Ann; Maryland, 1664 2524.55 p28
Bonniwell, James; New York, 1836-1839 8197.10 p127
Bonny, John; Maryland, 1674 2524.55 p28
Bono, Cicely 60; Ontario, 1871 1823.28 p8
Bonoms, A. 30; Alaska, 1917 9196.1 p51
Bonoms, A. 30; British Columbia, 1917 9196.1 p51
Bonru, Anna 17; Ontario, 1861 2896.27 p29
Bonsall, Thomas; New York, 1835 8197.10 p316
Bonsfield, Rev.; Quebec, 1857 9196.15 p24
Bonsrewicz, Pawel; Maryland, 1910 3259.35 p5
Bontby, William 42; Ontario, 1871 1823.15 p21
Bontemps, Louis Claude; New York, 1840 8197.10 p213
Bonter, A. G. 18; Ontario, 1861 2896.25 p55
Bonter, Abraham J. 9; Ontario, 1861 2896.25 p26
Bonter, Arzelia 2; Ontario, 1861 2896.25 p23
Bonter, Asa 27; Ontario, 1861 2896.25 p26
Bonter, Charles 8; Ontario, 1861 2896.25 p50
Bonter, Charles 12; Ontario, 1861 2896.25 p23
Bonter, Clarissa 5; Ontario, 1861 2896.25 p23
Bonter, Colborn 16; Ontario, 1861 2896.25 p24
Bonter, Cornelius A. 12; Ontario, 1861 2896.25 p26
Bonter, Daniel G. 11; Ontario, 1861 2896.25 p23
Bonter, Edward 5; Ontario, 1861 2896.25 p24
Bonter, Fedora 12; Ontario, 1861 2896.25 p24
Bonter, Francis 8; Ontario, 1861 2896.25 p26
Bonter, George 13; Ontario, 1861 2896.25 p26
Bonter, George R. 2; Ontario, 1861 2896.25 p17
Bonter, Hannah 29; Ontario, 1861 2896.25 p17
Bonter, Henrietta 1; Ontario, 1861 2896.25 p26
Bonter, Israel 21; Ontario, 1861 2896.25 p24
Bonter, J. K. 2; Ontario, 1861 2896.25 p50
Bonter, Jacob R. 8; Ontario, 1861 2896.25 p23
Bonter, James 17; Ontario, 1861 2896.25 p26
Bonter, James G. 10; Ontario, 1861 2896.25 p23
Bonter, Jane 24; Ontario, 1861 2896.25 p14
Bonter, John A. 15; Ontario, 1861 2896.25 p26
Bonter, John G. 11; Ontario, 1861 2896.25 p23
Bonter, John W. 12; Ontario, 1861 2896.25 p23
Bonter, Joseph 16; Ontario, 1861 2896.25 p23
Bonter, L. 11; Ontario, 1861 2896.25 p50
Bonter, M. J. 45; Ontario, 1861 2896.25 p50
Bonter, Margaret 46; Ontario, 1861 2896.25 p24
Bonter, Margaret J. 9; Ontario, 1861 2896.25 p23
Bonter, Mary 18; Ontario, 1861 2896.25 p50
Bonter, Mary 20; Ontario, 1861 2896.25 p50
Bonter, Mary Ann 5; Ontario, 1861 2896.25 p23
Bonter, Mary Ann 37; Ontario, 1861 2896.25 p23
Bonter, Matilda C. 3; Ontario, 1861 2896.25 p26
Bonter, Moses 9; Ontario, 1861 2896.25 p23
Bonter, Nancy 15; Ontario, 1861 2896.25 p23
Bonter, Peggy 37; Ontario, 1861 2896.25 p23
Bonter, Polly 47; Ontario, 1861 2896.25 p26
Bonter, Saphronia 14; Ontario, 1861 2896.25 p24
Bonter, Sarah E. 15; Ontario, 1861 2896.25 p17
Bonter, Sarah J. 14; Ontario, 1861 2896.25 p23
Bonter, Smith 18; Ontario, 1861 2896.25 p23
Bonter, Sylvia 18; Ontario, 1861 2896.25 p26
Bonter, W. C. 13; Ontario, 1861 2896.25 p50
Bonter, Wesley 13; Ontario, 1861 2896.25 p50
Bonter, Wesley 19; Ontario, 1861 2896.25 p24
Bonter, Wesley G. 6; Ontario, 1861 2896.25 p26
Bonter, William F. 46; Ontario, 1861 2896.25 p50
Bonter, William R. 13; Ontario, 1861 2896.25 p23
Bonter, William R. 16; Ontario, 1861 2896.25 p26
Bonter, William W. 2; Ontario, 1861 2896.25 p14
Bonth, John; Maryland, 1663 2524.55 p28
Bonthron, Andrew; New Orleans, 1813 1640.10 p13
Bonthron, James; Georgia, 1698 1640.13 p11
Bonthron, James 29; Ontario, 1871 1823.15 p21
Bonthron, James 54; Ontario, 1871 1823.15 p21
Bonthron, John; Washington, District of Columbia, 1840 1224.3 p8
Bonthron, Thomas 40; Ontario, 1871 1823.15 p21
Bontkowski, Frank; Maryland, 1910 3259.35 p5
Bontz, William 40; Ontario, 1871 1823.28 p8
Bonus, William; New York, 1784 1224.2 p13
Bonzowiak, John; Maryland, 1910 3259.35 p5
Boodle, Robert; Virginia, 1686 1224.1 p61
Booke, Humphry; Maryland, 1666 2524.55 p28
Booker, Ann 19; Maryland, 1775 1220.25 p101
Booker, Edward; Maryland, 1651 2524.55 p28
Booker, George; New York, 1807 8197.10 p35
Booker, Mary; Maryland, 1672 2524.55 p28
Booker, Richard; Maryland, 1665 2524.55 p28
Booker, Thomas; Maryland, 1664 2524.55 p183
Booker, Thomas; Maryland, 1672 2524.55 p28
Bookstore, Martin; Pennsylvania, 1862 6058.10 p69
Boole, David; Maryland, 1681 2524.55 p28
Booles, Mary; Maryland, 1682 2524.55 p28
Boomhower, Nancy M.; Vermont, 1848-1943 5900.10 p517
Boomhower, Sarah; Vermont, n.d. 5900.10 p500
Boon, Elizabeth; Maryland, 1680 2524.55 p28
Boon, Franz; Port uncertain, 1746 2856.30 p45
With wife & 4 children
Boon, Joseph Henry; St. Kitts, 1880 1640.13 p11
Boon, William; Virginia, 1671 6212.30 p44
Boone, Elizabeth; Virginia, 1681-1682 6212.30 p56
Boones, Giles; Virginia, 1663 6212.30 p2
Boorer, George 24; Virginia, 1774 1220.25 p45
Boorgert, Henry; New York, 1827 8197.10 p210
Boorman, James; New York, 1805 8197.10 p28
Boorman, John; New York, 1796 1224.2 p12
Boorn, Christian 45; Ontario, 1871 1823.28 p8
Boorn, Earnest 36; Ontario, 1871 1823.28 p8
Boos, Adam; Port uncertain, 1785 2856.30 p45
Boos, Christian; Port uncertain, 1770 2856.30 p45
Boos, Jakob; Port uncertain, 1776 2856.30 p45
Boos, Jakob; Port uncertain, 1785 2856.30 p45
Boos, Ludwig; Port uncertain, 1776 2856.30 p45
Boos, Ludwig; Port uncertain, 1785 2856.30 p45
Boos, Philippine; Port uncertain, 1784 2856.30 p45
Boot, Thomas; New York, 1837 8197.10 p84
Boot, Thomas 21; Maryland, 1774 1220.25 p59
Boote, Mr.; Quebec, 1858 9196.15 p46
Booteflower, John; Virginia, 1663 1224.1 p8
Booten, Peter; Virginia, 1671 6212.30 p43
Booth, Mr.; Quebec, 1856 9196.15 p6
Booth, Benjamin; New York, 1821 8197.10 p208
Booth, Booth 35; Ontario, 1871 1823.15 p21
Booth, Francis 45; Ontario, 1871 1823.15 p21
Booth, George; Pennsylvania, 1843 6058.10 p20
Booth, George 26; Ontario, 1871 1823.15 p21
Booth, George 31; Maryland, 1775 1220.25 p98
Booth, H.; Portland, Maine, 1858 9196.15 p30
Booth, Henrietta; Ontario, 1861 2896.25 p16
Booth, Henry; Pennsylvania, 1823 6058.10 p13
Booth, Henry; Pennsylvania, 1844 6058.10 p14
Booth, James; Virginia, 1679 6212.30 p54
Booth, James 51; Ontario, 1871 1823.15 p21
Booth, John; Maryland, 1673 2524.55 p28
Booth, John; Maryland, 1681 2524.55 p28
Booth, John; Maryland, 1682 2524.55 p28
Booth, John; New York, 1840 8197.10 p145
Booth, John; Ontario, 1861 2896.25 p16
Booth, John; Virginia, 1694 1224.1 p8
Booth, Joseph; Maryland, 1673 2524.55 p28
Booth, Joseph; Maryland, 1681 2524.55 p28
Booth, Joseph; Maryland, 1682 2524.55 p28
Booth, Marty; Vermont, 1842-1876 5900.10 p55
Booth, Mary; Maryland, 1682 2524.55 p28
Booth, Paull; Virginia, 1671-1672 6212.30 p47
Booth, Robt; Virginia, 1664 6212.30 p10
Booth, Samuel; New York, 1839 8197.10 p382
Booth, Sarah; Richmond, Virginia, 1827 1224.3 p8
Booth, Thomas; Maryland, 1682 2524.55 p28
Booth, Walter; Virginia, 1665 6212.30 p19
Booth, William; New York, 1832 8197.10 p211
Booth, William; Philadelphia, 1817 1224.3 p8
Booth, William; Virginia, 1676 1224.1 p8
Booth, William 45; Ontario, 1871 1823.28 p8
Boothby, Geo; Virginia, 1664 6212.30 p8
Boothby, William; Virginia, 1666 6212.30 p29
Boothe, James N. 5; Ontario, 1861 2896.25 p7
Boothe, M. A. 15; Ontario, 1861 2896.25 p11
Boothe, Margaret 61; Ontario, 1861 2896.25 p11
Boothe, Robert 34; Ontario, 1861 2896.25 p7
Boothe, Robert 65; Ontario, 1861 2896.25 p11
Boothey, Joseph 19; New York, 1775 1220.25 p94
Boothman, John; New York, 1825 8197.10 p210
Boothman, John; New York, 1825 8197.10 p314
Bootwell, Elizabeth; Maryland, 1665 2524.55 p28
Boozan, Margaret Gedny 37; Vermont, 1866 5900.10 p229
Boozan, Richard 84; Vermont, 1903 5900.10 p229
Boozan, Richard G. 35; Vermont, 1887 5900.10 p229
Bopenmaier, Johann; Port uncertain, 1718 2856.30 p45
With wife
Bopp, Johann; America, 1738 2856.30 p45
Bopp, Nicolas; Port uncertain, 1738 2856.30 p45
Bopp, Valtin; Port uncertain, 1754 2856.30 p45
Boppert, John Peter; New York, 1837 8197.10 p85
Boracki, Martin; Maryland, 1910 3259.35 p5
Borasi, Ausilu; Maryland, 1910 3259.35 p6
Borazki, Frank; Maryland, 1910 3259.35 p6
Borbab, Bartholomew 38; Ontario, 1871 1823.15 p21
Borbinger, Jacob 55; Kansas, 1875-1910 9079.10 p13
Borbinger, Sarah 49; Kansas, 1870-1910 9079.10 p13
Borchardt, Anna Magdalena; America, 1752 2856.30 p45
With son & 2 daughters

Borchardt, Anna Magdalena; America, 1752 ***2856.30*** *p49*
Borchardt, Anna Margarete; America, 1752 ***2856.30*** *p45*
Borchardt, Anna Margarete; America, 1752 ***2856.30*** *p49*
Borchardt, Catharina; America, 1752 ***2856.30*** *p45*
Borchardt, Catharina; America, 1752 ***2856.30*** *p49*
Borchardt, Conrad; America, 1752 ***2856.30*** *p45*
Borchardt, Conrad; America, 1752 ***2856.30*** *p49*
Borchers, Jobst; New York, 1840 ***8197.10*** *p213*
Borchowicz, Jim; Maryland, 1910 ***3259.35*** *p6*
Borchowski, John; Maryland, 1910 ***3259.35*** *p6*
Borck, Nicolaus; Port uncertain, 1751 ***2856.30*** *p45*
Borczynsky, Pawel; Maryland, 1910 ***3259.35*** *p6*
Bord, Anna Maria; Port uncertain, 1771 ***2856.30*** *p45*
Bord, Barbara; Port uncertain, 1764 ***2856.30*** *p45*
Bordan, Henry; New York, 1824 ***8197.10*** *p209*
Bordas, Eli; New York, 1821 ***8197.10*** *p208*
Borden, Thomas 21; Virginia, 1773 ***1220.25*** *p29*
Border, Fredrick; Pennsylvania, 1829 ***6058.10*** *p9*
Border, Jacob Frederick; Pennsylvania, 1804-1823 ***6058.10*** *p7*
Bordiner, Maria Juliana; Port uncertain, 1771 ***2856.30*** *p45*
Bordley, Thomas; Annapolis, Maryland, 1747 ***1224.2*** *p12*
Bordman, Amos; Reading, Massachusetts, 1812 ***1224.3*** *p8*
Bordt, Matthaus; Port uncertain, 1748 ***2856.30*** *p45*
Borduzat, Anthony M.; New York, 1799 ***8197.10*** *p371*
Bordwine, Charles; Montreal, 1826 ***1224.3*** *p8*
Bordwine, Charles; New York, n.d. ***1224.3*** *p8*
Boreing, Ann *SEE* Boreing, John
Boreing, John; Maryland, 1670 ***2524.55*** *p28*
Daughter: Ann
Boreland, John; Jamaica, 1728 ***1640.13*** *p11*
Boreman, Mrs.; Maryland, 1631-1685 ***2524.55*** *p28*
Boreman, Thomas; Virginia, 1679 ***1224.1*** *p8*
Boreman, Wm; Virginia, 1665-1666 ***6212.30*** *p22*
Boresvski, Martin; Maryland, 1910 ***3259.35*** *p6*
Boreszki, Jacob; Maryland, 1910 ***3259.35*** *p6*
Borger, John, Jr.; New York, New York, 1842 ***6058.10*** *p33*
Borger, John, Jr.; Pennsylvania, 1856 ***6058.10*** *p38*
Borgner, Johann Peter; Port uncertain, 1740 ***2856.30*** *p45*
With wife
Borgors, Christian; New York, 1802 ***8197.10*** *p18*
Boriee, Olive *SEE* Boriee, Philip
Boriee, Philip; Maryland, 1662 ***2524.55*** *p28*
Wife: Olive
Boriniskie, Stonestonce; Maryland, 1910 ***3259.35*** *p6*
Borkne, Johann Jorg; Port uncertain, 1757 ***2856.30*** *p45*
Borkowski, Alex; Maryland, 1910 ***3259.35*** *p6*
Borkowski, Francis; Maryland, 1910 ***3259.35*** *p6*
Borkowski, John; Maryland, 1910 ***3259.35*** *p6*
Borkowski, Joseph; Maryland, 1910 ***3259.35*** *p6*
Borland, Francis; Boston, 1768 ***1224.2*** *p12*
Borland, John; Boston, 1779 ***1224.2*** *p12*
Borland, John; Canada, 1756-1760 ***4628.40*** *p45*
Borland, Mary Hamilton; Ontario, 1820 ***1640.13*** *p11*
Borland, William 54; Ontario, 1871 ***1823.15*** *p21*
Borman, Charles Frederick; Ontario, 1871 ***1823.28*** *p8*
Borman, Daniel; Pennsylvania, 1777 ***4629.10*** *p30*
Borman, Tho; Virginia, 1690 ***6212.30*** *p58*
Bormann, Michael; America, 1744 ***2856.30*** *p45*
Bormeth, John Valentine; New York, 1837 ***8197.10*** *p85*
Born, . . .; Port uncertain, 1786 ***2856.30*** *p46*
Born, Andreas; Port uncertain, 1768 ***2856.30*** *p45*
Born, Andreas Samuel; Port uncertain, 1752 ***2856.30*** *p46*
With wife
Born, Andreas Samuel; Port uncertain, 1773 ***2856.30*** *p46*
With wife
Born, Anna Catharina; America, 1709 ***2856.30*** *p45*
Born, Anna Catharina; America, 1724 ***2856.30*** *p45*
Born, Christof; Port uncertain, 1728 ***2856.30*** *p46*
Born, Ludwig; America, 1737 ***2856.30*** *p46*
With wife & children
Born, Maria Barbara; Port uncertain, 1760 ***2856.30*** *p46*
Born, Samuel; America, 1735 ***2856.30*** *p46*
Borne, Jefry; Virginia, 1671-1672 ***6212.30*** *p46*
Borne, Mary *SEE* Borne, William
Borne, Mary; Maryland, 1679 ***2524.55*** *p29*
Borne, Richard; Virginia, 1667 ***6212.30*** *p36*
Borne, William; Maryland, 1679 ***2524.55*** *p29*
Wife: Mary
Daughter: Mary
Bornefeld, William; New York, 1839 ***8197.10*** *p213*
Borner, Johannes Theodorus; New York, 1828 ***8197.10*** *p211*
Borner, Maria; America, 1775 ***2856.30*** *p62*
Borner, Maria; America, 1780 ***2856.30*** *p62*
Borner, Maria; Port uncertain, 1771 ***2856.30*** *p62*
Borner, Mathias; America, 1775 ***2856.30*** *p62*
Borner, Mathias; America, 1780 ***2856.30*** *p63*
Borner, Mathias; Port uncertain, 1771 ***2856.30*** *p62*
Bornhoaft, Ernest 40; Ontario, 1871 ***1823.15*** *p21*
Bornin, Elis. Margarete; Port uncertain, 1776 ***2856.30*** *p46*
Borodia, Anuffer; Maryland, 1910 ***3259.35*** *p6*
Boroff, A. 27; Alaska, 1916 ***9196.1*** *p42*
Boroff, A. 27; Whitehorse, Yukon, 1916 ***9196.1*** *p42*
Boromic, Andreas; Maryland, 1910 ***3259.35*** *p6*
Borosund, Olof 22; Alaska, 1913 ***9196.1*** *p22*
Borosund, Olof 22; British Columbia, 1913 ***9196.1*** *p22*
Boroughs, Thomas; Maryland, 1655 ***2524.55*** *p28*
Borowicz, Alexander; Maryland, 1910 ***3259.35*** *p6*
Borowski, John; Maryland, 1910 ***3259.35*** *p6*
Borowski, Peter; Maryland, 1910 ***3259.35*** *p6*
Borowski, Stanislai; Maryland, 1910 ***3259.35*** *p6*
Boroziak, Walter; Maryland, 1910 ***3259.35*** *p6*
Borre, John; Boston, 1701 ***1224.2*** *p12*
Borron, Edward B. 50; Ontario, 1871 ***1823.28*** *p8*
Borrosini, Anton; Port uncertain, 1783 ***2856.30*** *p46*
Borsdorffer, Lorenz; Port uncertain, 1772 ***2856.30*** *p63*
Borstler, Georg; America, 1765 ***2856.30*** *p46*
Borstler, Johann Georg; America, 1767 ***2856.30*** *p63*
Borstler, Johann Georg; Port uncertain, 1768 ***2856.30*** *p63*
Bortel, Maria Magdalena; Port uncertain, 1785 ***2856.30*** *p46*
Bortusskensur, Vincent; Maryland, 1910 ***3259.35*** *p6*
Bortzer, Jonas; New York, New York, 1853 ***6058.10*** *p47*
Borzt, Adam; Maryland, 1910 ***3259.35*** *p6*
Bos, Peter; Port uncertain, 1771 ***2856.30*** *p63*
Bosano, George; New York, 1838 ***8197.10*** *p110*
Bosca, William; Virginia, 1666 ***6212.30*** *p27*
Bosch, Jacob; New York, 1827 ***8197.10*** *p210*
Bosch, Klaus Martin; Port uncertain, 1762 ***2856.30*** *p46*
Boschen, Harman; New York, 1830 ***8197.10*** *p312*
Boschert, Xavier; New York, 1837 ***8197.10*** *p85*
Boscoy, Edw; Virginia, 1666 ***6212.30*** *p28*
Bosester, James 48; Ontario, 1871 ***1823.15*** *p21*
Bosewell, Anne 81; Ontario, 1871 ***1823.28*** *p8*
Boshard, Jacob 40; Ontario, 1871 ***1823.28*** *p8*
Bosinger, Hans; Port uncertain, 1770 ***2856.30*** *p63*
Boskopfsky, Joseph; Maryland, 1910 ***3259.35*** *p6*
Boskoski, John; Maryland, 1910 ***3259.35*** *p6*
Boskowski, Felix; Maryland, 1910 ***3259.35*** *p6*
Boskwell, Nicholas; Virginia, 1671 ***6212.30*** *p42*
Bosler, Antone; Pennsylvania, 1835 ***6058.10*** *p12*
Bosley, William 44; Ontario, 1871 ***1823.15*** *p21*
Bosman, Anne *SEE* Bosman, William
Bosman, Bridgett *SEE* Bosman, William
Bosman, Edward 37; Ontario, 1871 ***1823.15*** *p21*
Bosman, Elioner *SEE* Bosman, William
Bosman, George *SEE* Bosman, William
Bosman, John *SEE* Bosman, William
Bosman, Katherine *SEE* Bosman, William
Bosman, Katherine; Maryland, 1664 ***2524.55*** *p28*
Bosman, Mary *SEE* Bosman, William
Bosman, William *SEE* Bosman, William
Bosman, William; Maryland, 1663 ***2524.55*** *p29*
Wife: Elioner
Child: Mary
Child: John
Child: Bridgett
Child: Anne
Child: George
Child: William
Child: Katherine
Bosovich, A. 27; Alaska, 1912 ***9196.1*** *p38*
Bosovich, A. 27; Yukon, 1912 ***9196.1*** *p38*
Bosovich, G. 25; Alaska, 1912 ***9196.1*** *p38*
Bosovich, G. 25; Yukon, 1912 ***9196.1*** *p38*
Bosozowska, Julia; Maryland, 1910 ***3259.35*** *p6*
Bosque, Cayetano; New York, 1830 ***8197.10*** *p354*
Boss, Andrew; Wisconsin, 1868 ***1640.13*** *p11*
Boss, Ann; New York, 1779 ***1224.2*** *p12*
Boss, Johann; America, 1744 ***2856.30*** *p46*
With wife & children
Bossenberry, William 49; Ontario, 1871 ***1823.15*** *p21*
Bosser, Christina Magda; Port uncertain, 1795 ***2856.30*** *p46*
Bossert, Michael; America, 1751 ***2856.30*** *p46*
Bossile, Peter 21; Grenada, 1774 ***1220.25*** *p128*
Bossinger, Thomas; New England, 1698 ***1224.1*** *p8*
Bossington, Tho; Virginia, 1667-1668 ***6212.30*** *p39*
Bosson, August 28; Salt Lake City, 1911 ***9196.1*** *p33*
Bost, Anna Maria; Port uncertain, 1752 ***2856.30*** *p63*
Bostick, James; Pennsylvania, 1778 ***4629.10*** *p34*
Bostock, Wilcock; Virginia, 1709 ***1224.2*** *p12*
Boston, Miss; Quebec, 1857 ***9196.15*** *p22*
Boston, Mr.; Quebec, 1857 ***9196.15*** *p21*
Boston, Ann *SEE* Boston, Henry
Boston, Henry *SEE* Boston, Henry
Boston, Henry; Maryland, 1663 ***2524.55*** *p29*
Wife: Ann
Son: Henry
Boston, Isaack; Maryland, 1663 ***2524.55*** *p29*
Daughter: Rebeccah
Boston, John; New York, 1807 ***8197.10*** *p35*
Boston, Rebeccah *SEE* Boston, Isaack
Boston, Willm.; Maryland, 1658 ***2524.55*** *p29*
Bostwick, John 57; Ontario, 1871 ***1823.28*** *p8*
Boswell, Mrs.; Quebec, 1856 ***9196.15*** *p10*
Boswell, A. G.; Portland, Maine, 1858 ***9196.15*** *p28*
Boswell, Ann *SEE* Boswell, John
Boswell, Benjamin 15; Philadelphia, 1775 ***1220.25*** *p106*
Boswell, Charles; Portland, Maine, 1858 ***9196.15*** *p29*
Boswell, Eliza 52; Ontario, 1871 ***1823.22*** *p14*
Boswell, George M. 66; Ontario, 1871 ***1823.22*** *p14*
Boswell, J. Vance 69; Ontario, 1871 ***1823.22*** *p14*
Boswell, John *SEE* Boswell, John
Boswell, John; Maryland, 1680 ***2524.55*** *p29*
Wife: Ann
Son: John
Boswell, John C. 68; Ontario, 1871 ***1823.22*** *p14*
Boswell, Marmaduke; Maryland, 1663 ***2524.55*** *p29*
Boswell, Susannafi 63; Ontario, 1871 ***1823.22*** *p14*
Bote, Hans Henrik; America, 1748 ***2856.30*** *p46*
Bote, Johann Jonas; America, 1748 ***2856.30*** *p46*
Boteler, Francis; Virginia, 1665 ***6212.30*** *p18*
Botetourt, Norborne; Virginia, 1771 ***1224.2*** *p12*
Bothans, Mathew 44; Ontario, 1871 ***1823.15*** *p21*
Botheley, Joseph 22; Maryland, 1774 ***1220.25*** *p42*
Bothenschein, . . .; Port uncertain, 1736 ***2856.30*** *p46*
Bothlander, Johann, The Younger; Port uncertain, 1785 ***2856.30*** *p46*
With wife
Botliell, William 46; Ontario, 1871 ***1823.15*** *p21*
Botner, Elias; Pennsylvania, 1777 ***4629.10*** *p22*
Botner, Elias; Pennsylvania, 1779 ***4629.10*** *p40*
Botson, Elizabeth; North Carolina, 1818 ***1224.3*** *p20*
Botson, Mary; North Carolina, 1818 ***1224.3*** *p8*
Bott, Hans Georg; America, 1744 ***2856.30*** *p46*
Bottelberger, Georg Gottfried; Port uncertain, 1783 ***2856.30*** *p46*
With wife & 4 children
Bottelberger, Georg Gottfried; Port uncertain, 1785 ***2856.30*** *p46*
Bottlander, Johann Michael; Port uncertain, 1793 ***2856.30*** *p46*
Bottner, R. J.; Pennsylvania, 1868 ***6058.10*** *p64*
Bottomley, William; New York, 1838 ***8197.10*** *p212*
Bottrell, Mary 85; Ontario, 1871 ***1823.28*** *p8*
Bottrell, William 49; Ontario, 1871 ***1823.28*** *p8*
Bottrill, John 41; Ontario, 1871 ***1823.15*** *p21*
Botts, Thomas; Indiana, 1856 ***3437.14*** *p49*
Botz, Georg Peter; America, 1741 ***2856.30*** *p36*
With wife & 3 children
Botz, Valentin; Port uncertain, 1699 ***2856.30*** *p47*
Bouch, Anto; Virginia, 1666 ***6212.30*** *p29*
Bouche, H.; Quebec, 1858 ***9196.15*** *p34*
Boucher, Alfred; New York, 1839 ***8197.10*** *p213*
Boucher, Geo.; Maryland, 1651 ***2524.55*** *p29*
Boucher, Mary Heare; Vermont, 1853-1929 ***5900.10*** *p601*
Boucher, Pierre; Vermont, 1859-1918 ***5900.10*** *p601*
Boucher, Rose; Vermont, 1861-1918 ***5900.10*** *p514*
Boucher, Samuel; Pennsylvania, 1777 ***4629.10*** *p15*
Boucheron, Augustus; New York, 1803 ***8197.10*** *p11*
Bouchette, Mr.; Portland, Maine, 1858 ***9196.15*** *p27*
Bouchier, Col.; Quebec, 1856 ***9196.15*** *p8*
Bouchier, Mrs.; Quebec, 1856 ***9196.15*** *p8*
Bouchier, Edward Bass; New York, 1783 ***1224.2*** *p12*
Boucks, Miss; Quebec, 1857 ***9196.15*** *p15*
Bouden, Mary 60; Vermont, 1912 ***5900.10*** *p445*
Bouder, John 39; Ontario, 1871 ***1823.15*** *p21*
Boudette, Eugene; Vermont, 1855-1923 ***5900.10*** *p588*
Boudette, Isabelle Fitzgerald; Vermont, 1856-1938 ***5900.10*** *p588*
Boudren, John; New York, 1827 ***8197.10*** *p343*
Bouer, Jacob; New York, 1840 ***8197.10*** *p145*
Bouffler, Maria Ursula; Port uncertain, 1754 ***2856.30*** *p47*
Bough, Thomas; Rhode Island, 1781 ***1224.2*** *p8*
Boughall, Cornelius; Maryland, 1682 ***2524.55*** *p29*
Boughen, Margaret 80; Vermont, 1898 ***5900.10*** *p366*
Boughen, Richard; Maryland, 1677 ***2524.55*** *p29*
Bougher, Tobias; Pennsylvania, 1777 ***4629.10*** *p16*
Boughten, William; Maryland, 1673 ***2524.55*** *p29*
Boughton, Robert; New England, 1656 ***1224.1*** *p8*
Bouha, Phil. Jacob, Sr.; America, 1738 ***2856.30*** *p55*
Bouha, Phil. Jacob, Jr.; America, 1738 ***2856.30*** *p55*
Bouha, Philipp Jacob; America, 1738 ***2856.30*** *p55*
Bouha, Philipp Jacob; Port uncertain, 1755 ***2856.30*** *p55*
Bouholts, Francis 20; Ontario, 1871 ***1823.28*** *p8*
Bouldger, Thomas 58; Ontario, 1871 ***1823.15*** *p22*
Bouldin, Jacob; Pennsylvania, 1777 ***4629.10*** *p20*
Bouldridge, James; Georgia, 1774 ***1640.10*** *p13*
Boulger, Daniel; New York, 1840 ***8197.10*** *p213*
Boulger, John; New York, 1818 ***8197.10*** *p206*

Bowie, Catherine; Ontario, 1849 ***4537.37*** *p58*
Bowie, Catherine MacIntyre *SEE* Bowie, Neil
Bowie, Charles 60; Ontario, 1871 ***1823.28*** *p8*
Bowie, Donald *SEE* Bowie, John
Bowie, Donald *SEE* Bowie, Neil
Bowie, Donald *SEE* Bowie, Peter
Bowie, Effie MacLellan *SEE* Bowie, John
Bowie, Flora *SEE* Bowie, Neil
Bowie, Hector *SEE* Bowie, Neil
Bowie, John *SEE* Bowie, John
Bowie, John *SEE* Bowie, Neil
Bowie, John; Georgia, 1698 ***1640.13*** *p11*
Bowie, John; Georgia, 1801 ***1640.10*** *p13*
Bowie, John; Port uncertain, 1850-1859 ***4537.37*** *p105*
Wife: Effie MacLellan
Child: John
Child: Donald
Child: Angus
Bowie, Margaret *SEE* Bowie, Peter
Bowie, Margaret; Port uncertain, 1850-1859 ***4537.37*** *p119*
Bowie, Mary *SEE* Bowie, Neil
Bowie, Mary *SEE* Bowie, Peter
Bowie, Neil; Port uncertain, 1850-1859 ***4537.37*** *p105*
Wife: Catherine MacIntyre
Child: Flora
Child: Catherine
Child: Alexander
Child: John
Child: Angus
Child: Rachel
Child: Mary
Child: Hector
Child: Ann
Child: Donald
Bowie, Peter *SEE* Bowie, Peter
Bowie, Peter; Port uncertain, 1850-1859 ***4537.37*** *p105*
Child: Mary
Child: Margaret
Child: Catherine
Child: Donald
Child: Archie
Wife: Ann Wilson
Child: Peter
Bowie, Peter 52; Ontario, 1871 ***1823.28*** *p8*
Bowie, Rachel *SEE* Bowie, Neil
Bowie, William W. 50; Ontario, 1871 ***1823.15*** *p22*
Bowillson, Thomas; Maryland, 1665 ***2524.55*** *p30*
Bowin, Charles 57; Ontario, 1871 ***1823.22*** *p14*
Bowin, Githing; Maryland, 1664 ***2524.55*** *p30*
Bowin, Hugh; Virginia, 1668-1669 ***6212.30*** *p40*
Bowin, John; Virginia, 1664 ***6212.30*** *p6*
Bowing, Mary; Maryland, 1677 ***2524.55*** *p30*
Bowing, Richard; Maryland, 1631-1685 ***2524.55*** *p30*
Bowker, George H.; Vermont, 1828-1883 ***5900.10*** *p302*
Bowker, George H.; Vermont, 1856-1900 ***5900.10*** *p307*
Bowker, James; Vermont, 1858-1916 ***5900.10*** *p304*
Bowker, John 57; Ontario, 1871 ***1823.28*** *p8*
Bowker, Maggie A. Sullivan; Vermont, 1857-1946 ***5900.10*** *p304*
Bowker, Maria Tully; Vermont, 1836-1900 ***5900.10*** *p302*
Bowker, Mary Ann; Vermont, 1855-1934 ***5900.10*** *p303*
Bowkoski, Andrew; Maryland, 1910 ***3259.35*** *p6*
Bowland, James 45; Ontario, 1871 ***1823.15*** *p22*
Bowland, Thomas 60; Ontario, 1871 ***1823.28*** *p9*
Bowle, Rich; Virginia, 1664 ***6212.30*** *p15*
Bowler, Aaron 21; Philadelphia, 1774 ***1220.25*** *p80*
Bowler, Edward 18; Vermont, 1882 ***5900.10*** *p121*
Bowler, Ellen; Vermont, 1857-1940 ***5900.10*** *p68*
Bowler, Ellen J. Fitzgerald 68; Vermont, 1906 ***5900.10*** *p121*
Bowler, James Francis 85; Vermont, 1921 ***5900.10*** *p121*
Bowler, John 45; Ontario, 1871 ***1823.15*** *p22*
Bowler, John 48; Ontario, 1871 ***1823.15*** *p22*
Bowler, Margaret 65; Vermont, 1894 ***5900.10*** *p102*
Bowler, Mary 25; Vermont, 1873 ***5900.10*** *p108*
Bowler, Mary Austin 39; Vermont, 1871 ***5900.10*** *p114*
Bowler, Maurice 40; Ontario, 1871 ***1823.15*** *p22*
Bowler, Maurice 68; Vermont, 1897 ***5900.10*** *p114*
Bowler, Michael 40; Ontario, 1871 ***1823.15*** *p22*
Bowler, Patrick 50; Ontario, 1871 ***1823.15*** *p22*
Bowles, David; Maryland, 1682 ***2524.55*** *p30*
Bowles, Edward *SEE* Bowles, William
Bowles, Edward; Maryland, 1650 ***2524.55*** *p30*
With wife
Bowles, Elizabeth *SEE* Bowles, William
Bowles, Henry; Pennsylvania, 1786 ***4629.10*** *p54*
Bowles, James; Maryland, 1729 ***1224.2*** *p12*
Bowles, James; Pennsylvania, 1777 ***4629.10*** *p16*
Bowles, Jno; Virginia, 1664 ***6212.30*** *p15*
Bowles, John *SEE* Bowles, William
Bowles, John; Carolina, 1739 ***1224.2*** *p13*
Bowles, John 59; Ontario, 1871 ***1823.22*** *p14*
Bowles, Jonane *SEE* Bowles, William
Bowles, Norman *SEE* Bowles, William
Bowles, Peter 21; Maryland, 1775 ***1220.25*** *p99*
Bowles, Tobias; South Carolina, 1811 ***1224.3*** *p8*
Bowles, William; Maryland, 1650 ***2524.55*** *p30*
Relative: Edward
Relative: Jonane
Relative: Norman
Relative: Elizabeth
Relative: John
Bowles, William 70; Ontario, 1871 ***1823.22*** *p14*
Bowley, James; Virginia, 1671-1672 ***6212.30*** *p47*
Bowley, Jeremiah 23; Virginia, 1774 ***1220.25*** *p91*
Bowlin, Elisibeth 47; Ontario, 1871 ***1823.22*** *p14*
Bowling, James; Maryland, 1658 ***2524.55*** *p30*
Bowling, John 18; Maryland, 1775 ***1220.25*** *p102*
Bowman, Mr.; Quebec, 1856 ***9196.15*** *p6*
Bowman, Mr.; Vermont, n.d. ***5900.10*** *p286*
Bowman, A. 19; Ontario, 1861 ***2896.28*** *p6*
Bowman, C. 23; Ontario, 1861 ***2896.28*** *p6*
Bowman, C. 24; Ontario, 1861 ***2896.28*** *p6*
Bowman, C. E. 6; Ontario, 1861 ***2896.28*** *p6*
Bowman, Catherine Earley; Vermont, n.d. ***5900.10*** *p286*
Bowman, Elenor 77; Ontario, 1871 ***1823.22*** *p14*
Bowman, Elizabeth 31; Ontario, 1871 ***1823.22*** *p14*
Bowman, H. E. 2; Ontario, 1861 ***2896.28*** *p6*
Bowman, J. A. 9; Ontario, 1861 ***2896.28*** *p6*
Bowman, J. E. 2; Ontario, 1861 ***2896.28*** *p6*
Bowman, J. P. 24; Ontario, 1861 ***2896.28*** *p4*
Bowman, Jane McMath; America, 1895 ***1640.13*** *p11*
Bowman, John; Virginia, 1691 ***1224.1*** *p8*
Bowman, John 48; Ontario, 1871 ***1823.15*** *p22*
Bowman, John, Jr.; Florida, 1769 ***1640.10*** *p13*
Bowman, Joseph 13; Virginia, 1774 ***1220.25*** *p140*
Bowman, L. J. 3; Ontario, 1861 ***2896.28*** *p6*
Bowman, Mary A.; Vermont, 1846-1911 ***5900.10*** *p308*
Bowman, P. A. 28; Ontario, 1861 ***2896.28*** *p6*
Bowman, R. 33; Ontario, 1861 ***2896.28*** *p6*
Bowman, S. 27; Ontario, 1861 ***2896.28*** *p11*
Bowman, Samuel W. L.; New York, 1827 ***8197.10*** *p338*
Bowman, Sarah; New York, 1889 ***1640.13*** *p11*
Bowman, Thomas; Virginia, 1694 ***1224.1*** *p8*
Bown, Robert Tytherleigh; Mobile, Alabama, 1848 ***1224.3*** *p8*
Bown, Samuel Hasel; Chicago, 1856 ***1224.3*** *p8*
Bownass, William; New York, 1784 ***1224.2*** *p13*
Bowner, James; Maryland, 1659 ***2524.55*** *p30*
Bowness, George; Virginia, 1787 ***1224.2*** *p13*
Bowridge, Thomas; Maryland, 1662 ***2524.55*** *p30*
Bowridge, Thomas; Maryland, 1662 ***2524.55*** *p177*
Bowright, Eunase 71; Ontario, 1871 ***1823.22*** *p14*
Bowrin, Grace Eliza; Nevis, 1884 ***1640.13*** *p11*
Bowrin, Louisa; Ottawa, 1891 ***1640.13*** *p11*
Bowring, Mary Kelsey; North Carolina, 1824 ***1224.3*** *p8*
Bowry, James 21; Ontario, 1871 ***1823.15*** *p22*
Bowser, Ann 20; Nova Scotia, 1774 ***1220.25*** *p14*
Bowser, Ann 60; Nova Scotia, 1774 ***1220.25*** *p14*
Bowser, John; Philadelphia, 1831 ***6058.10*** *p13*
Bowser, Richard 29; Nova Scotia, 1774 ***1220.25*** *p14*
Bowser, William 20; Philadelphia, 1774 ***1220.25*** *p68*
Bowser, William 22; Boston, 1774 ***1220.25*** *p51*
Bowt, Charles; Maryland, 1671 ***2524.55*** *p30*
Bowtell, James 24; Virginia, 1775 ***1220.25*** *p110*
Bowyer, Robert; New York, 1817 ***8197.10*** *p206*
Bowyer, Thomas 38; Ontario, 1871 ***1823.15*** *p22*
Bowyer, William; Jamaica, 1707 ***1224.2*** *p13*
Bowyer, William; New York, 1707 ***1224.2*** *p13*
Box, Alexander 37; Ontario, 1871 ***1823.28*** *p9*
Box, James 51; Ontario, 1871 ***1823.15*** *p22*
Box, Jesophat; Maryland, 1910 ***3259.35*** *p6*
Box, John 26; Georgia, 1774 ***1220.25*** *p48*
Box, John 38; Ontario, 1871 ***1823.28*** *p9*
Box, Richard 25; Ontario, 1871 ***1823.15*** *p22*
Box, Thomas; Buffalo, New York, 1862 ***1640.13*** *p11*
Boxberger, George, Sr. 57; Kansas, 1878-1910 ***9079.10*** *p32*
Boxberger, George, Jr. 37; Kansas, 1878-1910 ***9079.10*** *p32*
Boxberger, Henry 41; Kansas, 1895-1910 ***9079.10*** *p32*
Boxberger, Kathie 33; Kansas, 1895-1910 ***9079.10*** *p32*
Boxberger, Katie 57; Kansas, 1878-1910 ***9079.10*** *p32*
Boxberger, Mary 35; Kansas, 1899-1910 ***9079.10*** *p32*
Boxborough, James 16; Virginia, 1774 ***1220.25*** *p140*
Boxburger, Eva 43; Kansas, 1885-1910 ***9079.10*** *p27*
Boxburger, Peeter 45; Kansas, 1879-1910 ***9079.10*** *p27*
Boxburger, Peeter 82; Kansas, 1879-1910 ***9079.10*** *p27*
Boxe, Tobias; Virginia, 1629 ***1224.1*** *p8*
Boxwel, Thomas 52; Ontario, 1871 ***1823.28*** *p9*
Boy, Theophilus; Maryland, 1663 ***2524.55*** *p30*
Boyant, Benjamin; Pennsylvania, 1777 ***4629.10*** *p16*
Boyce, Anna; Vermont, 1833-1912 ***5900.10*** *p287*
Boyce, Francis; New York, 1840 ***8197.10*** *p154*
Boyce, George 41; Ontario, 1871 ***1823.22*** *p14*
Boyce, James; Vermont, 1855-1935 ***5900.10*** *p276*
Boyce, Jennie C.; Vermont, 1855-1936 ***5900.10*** *p277*
Boyce, John; Maryland, 1658 ***2524.55*** *p30*
Boyce, John O.; Vermont, 1851-1926 ***5900.10*** *p276*
Boyce, Joseph 35; Ontario, 1871 ***1823.22*** *p14*
Boyce, Kathleen; Vermont, 1883-1914 ***5900.10*** *p172*
Boyce, Mary 33; Vermont, 1853 ***5900.10*** *p161*
Boyce, Matilda 69; Vermont, 1897 ***5900.10*** *p616*
Boyce, Robert 27; Ontario, 1871 ***1823.15*** *p22*
Boyce, Thomas 67; Ontario, 1871 ***1823.15*** *p22*
Boyce, William 47; Ontario, 1871 ***1823.22*** *p14*
Boyce, Wm; Virginia, 1664 ***6212.30*** *p13*
Boyd, . . .; Boston, 1737 ***4628.40*** *p114*
Boyd, Mrs. 39; Ontario, 1861 ***2896.26*** *p30*
Boyd, Agness 9; Ontario, 1861 ***2896.26*** *p30*
Boyd, Alexander *SEE* Boyd, Alexander
Boyd, Alexander; Ontario, 1851 ***4537.32*** *p5*
Wife: Ann MacDonald
Child: John
Child: Alexander
Child: Dougal
Child: Mary
Child: Angus
Child: Catherine
Child: Rachel
Child: Donald
Child: Marion
Boyd, Alexander; Savannah, Georgia, 1804 ***1224.3*** *p8*
Boyd, Alexander; Savannah, Georgia, 1804 ***1640.10*** *p13*
Boyd, Alexander 28; Ontario, 1871 ***1823.15*** *p22*
Boyd, Andrew; New York, 1831 ***8197.10*** *p354*
Boyd, Angus *SEE* Boyd, Alexander
Boyd, Ann 64; Ontario, 1871 ***1823.15*** *p22*
Boyd, Ann MacDonald *SEE* Boyd, Alexander
Boyd, Anthony 34; Ontario, 1871 ***1823.15*** *p22*
Boyd, Catherine *SEE* Boyd, Alexander
Boyd, Charles; Georgia, 1793 ***1640.10*** *p13*
Boyd, David; New York, 1821 ***8197.10*** *p207*
Boyd, Donald *SEE* Boyd, Alexander
Boyd, Donald 26; Ontario, 1871 ***1823.15*** *p22*
Boyd, Donald 40; Ontario, 1871 ***1823.15*** *p22*
Boyd, Dougal *SEE* Boyd, Alexander
Boyd, E. 19; Ontario, 1861 ***2896.26*** *p10*
Boyd, Elizabeth 80; Ontario, 1871 ***1823.22*** *p14*
Boyd, Gavin 57; Ontario, 1871 ***1823.22*** *p14*
Boyd, George; Portsmouth, New Hampshire, n.d. ***1224.3*** *p9*
Boyd, George 25; Maryland, 1775 ***1220.25*** *p103*
Boyd, George 29; Ontario, 1871 ***1823.22*** *p14*
Boyd, George 68; Ontario, 1871 ***1823.15*** *p22*
Boyd, Hugh 65; Ontario, 1871 ***1823.22*** *p14*
Boyd, James; New York, 1837 ***8197.10*** *p84*
Boyd, James; Pennsylvania, 1859 ***6058.10*** *p41*
Boyd, James; Virginia, 1672 ***6212.30*** *p50*
Boyd, John *SEE* Boyd, Alexander
Boyd, John; New Jersey, 1710 ***1640.13*** *p11*
Boyd, John; New York, 1803 ***8197.10*** *p10*
Boyd, John; New York, 1807 ***8197.10*** *p332*
Boyd, John 33; Ontario, 1871 ***1823.28*** *p9*
Boyd, John 35; Ontario, 1871 ***1823.15*** *p22*
Boyd, John 35; Ontario, 1871 ***1823.22*** *p14*
Boyd, John 49; Ontario, 1871 ***1823.22*** *p14*
Boyd, John 50; Ontario, 1871 ***1823.22*** *p14*
Boyd, Marion *SEE* Boyd, Alexander
Boyd, Mary *SEE* Boyd, Alexander
Boyd, Moore 52; Ontario, 1871 ***1823.15*** *p22*
Boyd, R. J. 5; Ontario, 1861 ***2896.26*** *p30*
Boyd, Rachel *SEE* Boyd, Alexander
Boyd, Robert; Ohio, 1890 ***1640.13*** *p12*
Boyd, Robert; Virginia, 1783 ***1640.13*** *p11*
Boyd, Robert 84; Ontario, 1871 ***1823.22*** *p15*
Boyd, Samuel; New York, 1821 ***8197.10*** *p207*
Boyd, Samuel; New York, New York, 1846 ***6058.10*** *p34*
Boyd, Thomas; Georgia, 1736 ***1640.10*** *p14*
Boyd, Thomas; New York, 1860 ***1640.13*** *p12*
Boyd, Thomas; Savannah, Georgia, 1808 ***1640.10*** *p14*
Boyd, Thomas 32; Ontario, 1871 ***1823.15*** *p22*
Boyd, W. J. 7; Ontario, 1861 ***2896.26*** *p30*
Boyd, William; Charleston, South Carolina, 1817 ***1224.3*** *p9*
Boyd, William; New York, 1821 ***8197.10*** *p207*
Boyd, William; New York, 1838 ***8197.10*** *p111*
Boyd, William; Pennsylvania, 1777 ***4629.10*** *p13*
Boyd, William 40; Ontario, 1871 ***1823.22*** *p15*
Boyde, Leonora 27 *SEE* Boyde, William
Boyde, Robert 28; New York, 1775 ***1220.25*** *p143*
With wife & child
Boyde, William 36; Maryland, 1775 ***1220.25*** *p100*
Wife: Leonora 27
Boyden, Elinor; Maryland, 1673 ***2524.55*** *p30*
Boyden, John 17; Maryland, 1774 ***1220.25*** *p70*
Boyen, Mary; Maryland, 1677 ***2524.55*** *p30*
Boyen, Richard; Maryland, 1631-1685 ***2524.55*** *p30*

Boyer, Miss; Quebec, 1857 ***9196.15*** *p15*
Boyer, Alice 1; Ontario, 1861 ***2896.28*** *p29*
Boyer, Amelia 12; Ontario, 1871 ***1823.28*** *p9*
Boyer, Blase; Pennsylvania, 1777 ***4629.10*** *p23*
Boyer, F. 22; Ontario, 1861 ***2896.27*** *p1*
Boyer, Grace 5; Ontario, 1861 ***2896.28*** *p29*
Boyer, Grace M. 29; Ontario, 1861 ***2896.28*** *p29*
Boyer, Harriet 16; Ontario, 1861 ***2896.25*** *p16*
Boyer, Henry 25; Ontario, 1871 ***1823.28*** *p9*
Boyer, James 36; Ontario, 1871 ***1823.28*** *p9*
Boyer, John; Maryland, 1910 ***3259.35*** *p6*
Boyer, Mary A. 55; Ontario, 1871 ***1823.22*** *p15*
Boyer, Peter; New York, New York, 1881 ***3437.14*** *p154*
Boyer, Roc 34; Ontario, 1861 ***2896.28*** *p29*
Boyer, Thomas 74; Ontario, 1871 ***1823.15*** *p22*
Boyes, Beiby 31; Ontario, 1871 ***1823.15*** *p22*
Boyes, Edward 26; Ontario, 1871 ***1823.15*** *p22*
Boyes, James 60; Ontario, 1871 ***1823.15*** *p22*
Boyes, John; Virginia, 1664 ***6212.30*** *p13*
Boyes, John; Virginia, 1665-1666 ***6212.30*** *p21*
Boyfield, Thomas 20; Maryland, 1774 ***1220.25*** *p74*
Boyington, Adda 1; Ontario, 1861 ***2896.27*** *p13*
Boyington, Alma 1; Ontario, 1861 ***2896.27*** *p13*
Boyington, Andrew 5; Ontario, 1861 ***2896.27*** *p13*
Boyington, Andrew 80; Ontario, 1861 ***2896.27*** *p13*
Boyington, Julian 66; Ontario, 1861 ***2896.27*** *p13*
Boyington, Louise 33; Ontario, 1861 ***2896.27*** *p13*
Boyington, Olive 23; Ontario, 1861 ***2896.27*** *p13*
Boylan, Bridget 28; Vermont, 1881 ***5900.10*** *p474*
Boylan, Catherine; Vermont, 1846-1921 ***5900.10*** *p407*
Boylan, Catherine 72; Vermont, 1875 ***5900.10*** *p234*
Boylan, George 40; Vermont, 1884 ***5900.10*** *p233*
Boylan, Hannah; Vermont, 1817-1897 ***5900.10*** *p312*
Boylan, James; Vermont, 1841-1913 ***5900.10*** *p52*
Boylan, John; New York, 1836 ***8197.10*** *p319*
Boylan, Lawrence 63; Vermont, 1881 ***5900.10*** *p238*
Boylan, Mary; Vermont, 1846-1924 ***5900.10*** *p174*
Boylan, Mary A.; Vermont, 1847-1942 ***5900.10*** *p312*
Boylan, Matthew; New York, 1839 ***8197.10*** *p383*
Boylan, Michael; New York, 1840 ***8197.10*** *p321*
Boylan, Michael; Vermont, 1817-1892 ***5900.10*** *p312*
Boylan, Michael, Jr.; Vermont, 1855-1890 ***5900.10*** *p312*
Boylan, Patrick; Charles Town, South Carolina, 1767 ***1224.2*** *p13*
Boylan, Patrick; New York, 1839 ***8197.10*** *p383*
Boylan, Patrick; New York, 1840 ***8197.10*** *p145*
Boylan, Patrick 24; Philadelphia, 1774 ***1220.25*** *p81*
Boylan, Peter; Vermont, n.d. ***5900.10*** *p233*
Boyland, James; New York, 1840 ***8197.10*** *p144*
Boyle, Mr.; Quebec, 1858 ***9196.15*** *p38*
Boyle, Anthony; Vermont, 1834-1958 ***5900.10*** *p181*
Boyle, Bridget 92; Vermont, 1893 ***5900.10*** *p250*
Boyle, Catherine; New York, New York, 1851 ***1224.3*** *p9*
Boyle, Dennis; New York, 1840 ***8197.10*** *p155*
Boyle, Elizabeth Fox 50; Vermont, 1885 ***5900.10*** *p251*
Boyle, Elizia 22; Ontario, 1871 ***1823.15*** *p23*
Boyle, Ellen 50; Ontario, 1871 ***1823.15*** *p23*
Boyle, Helen E.; Vermont, 1874-1935 ***5900.10*** *p181*
Boyle, Henry 26; Ontario, 1871 ***1823.15*** *p23*
Boyle, Henry 66; Ontario, 1871 ***1823.28*** *p9*
Boyle, James; New York, 1838 ***8197.10*** *p378*
Boyle, James; New York, 1840 ***8197.10*** *p144*
Boyle, James; New York, 1840 ***8197.10*** *p154*
Boyle, James; Virginia, 1667 ***6212.30*** *p35*
Boyle, Johanna; Vermont, n.d. ***5900.10*** *p66*
Boyle, John; New York, 1821 ***8197.10*** *p208*
Boyle, John; New York, 1827-1831 ***8197.10*** *p369*
Boyle, John; New York, 1838 ***8197.10*** *p111*
Boyle, John; Pennsylvania, 1777 ***4629.10*** *p20*
Boyle, John; Vermont, 1840-1919 ***5900.10*** *p269*
Boyle, John 50; Ontario, 1871 ***1823.15*** *p23*
Boyle, John 55; Ontario, 1871 ***1823.28*** *p9*
Boyle, John 74; Vermont, 1892 ***5900.10*** *p181*
Boyle, John 74; Vermont, 1919 ***5900.10*** *p70*
Boyle, John T.; Vermont, 1830-1901 ***5900.10*** *p309*
Boyle, Julia; Vermont, 1836-1912 ***5900.10*** *p197*
Boyle, Julia; Vermont, 1879 ***5900.10*** *p247*
Boyle, Katherine; Vermont, 1844-1914 ***5900.10*** *p309*
Boyle, Katherine J.; Vermont, 1868-1929 ***5900.10*** *p181*
Boyle, Kittie M.; Vermont, 1862-1891 ***5900.10*** *p181*
Boyle, Margaret Brown 76; Vermont, 1879 ***5900.10*** *p306*
Boyle, Margaret Brown 76; Vermont, 1879 ***5900.10*** *p309*
Boyle, Mary; Vermont, 1841-1916 ***5900.10*** *p304*
Boyle, Mary; Vermont, 1853-1933 ***5900.10*** *p444*
Boyle, Mary 57; Vermont, 1861 ***5900.10*** *p179*
Boyle, Mary Ann 51; Vermont, 1893 ***5900.10*** *p136*
Boyle, Mary Morrissey 80; Vermont, 1928 ***5900.10*** *p70*
Boyle, Michael; New York, 1832 ***8197.10*** *p356*
Boyle, Michael; New York, 1836 ***8197.10*** *p76*
Boyle, Patrick; New York, 1804 ***8197.10*** *p26*
Boyle, Patrick; New York, 1838 ***8197.10*** *p378*
Boyle, Patrick; New York, 1840 ***8197.10*** *p154*
Boyle, Richard 54; Ontario, 1871 ***1823.22*** *p15*
Boyle, Robert 21; Maryland, 1774 ***1220.25*** *p57*
Boyle, Robert 21; Maryland, 1775 ***1220.25*** *p115*
Boyle, Rose A.; Vermont, 1836-1913 ***5900.10*** *p592*
Boyle, Samuel 75; Ontario, 1871 ***1823.15*** *p23*
Boyle, Susan M.; Vermont, 1846-1905 ***5900.10*** *p127*
Boyle, Thomas; New York, 1804 ***8197.10*** *p26*
Boyle, Thomas 59; Ontario, 1871 ***1823.22*** *p15*
Boyle, Thomas 108; Vermont, 1886 ***5900.10*** *p306*
Boyle, Thomas 108; Vermont, 1886 ***5900.10*** *p309*
Boyle, William 26; Virginia, 1773 ***1220.25*** *p29*
Boyle, William 59; Ontario, 1871 ***1823.22*** *p15*
Boyle, William F.; New York, 1819 ***8197.10*** *p207*
Boylen, Thomas; New York, 1837 ***8197.10*** *p84*
Boyles, John; Philadelphia, 1819 ***6058.10*** *p13*
Boyles, Philip; New York, 1744 ***1224.2*** *p13*
Boyls, John; Philadelphia, 1819 ***6058.10*** *p13*
Boylston, John; Boston, n.d. ***1224.2*** *p13*
Boylston, Thomas; Boston, n.d. ***1224.2*** *p13*
Boylston, Ward Nicholas; Roxbury, Massachusetts, 1828 ***1224.3*** *p9*
Boyne, Alexander 28; Ontario, 1871 ***1823.28*** *p9*
Boyne, George 48; Vermont, 1914 ***5900.10*** *p90*
Boyne, Kathleen M. 62; Vermont, 1936 ***5900.10*** *p90*
Boyne, Thomas; Maryland, 1669 ***2524.55*** *p30*
Boynes, George; New York, 1838 ***8197.10*** *p110*
Boynton, Ann Eliza; Vermont, 1850-1872 ***5900.10*** *p303*
Boyovich, P. 28; Alaska, 1917 ***9196.1*** *p47*
Boyovich, P. 28; Yukon, 1917 ***9196.1*** *p47*
Boys, James 28; Ontario, 1871 ***1823.28*** *p9*
Boys, James 73; Ontario, 1871 ***1823.28*** *p9*
Boys, Jno; Virginia, 1665-1666 ***6212.30*** *p22*
Boys, John; Died enroute, 1650 ***1224.1*** *p8*
Boys, Nathan; Pennsylvania, 1777 ***4629.10*** *p6*
Boys, Nathan; Pennsylvania, 1779 ***4629.10*** *p36*
Boys, Thomas; Virginia, 1676 ***1224.1*** *p8*
Boyse, John; Virginia, 1710 ***1224.2*** *p13*
Boyse, Mary; Maryland, 1668 ***2524.55*** *p166*
Boyse, Thomas 15; Grenada, 1774 ***1220.25*** *p89*
Boyse, Wm; Virginia, 1671 ***6212.30*** *p42*
Boysen, Andrew F.; New York, 1838 ***8197.10*** *p111*
Boyst, Jane *SEE* Boyst, William
Boyst, Mary *SEE* Boyst, William
Boyst, William; Maryland, 1631-1685 ***2524.55*** *p30*
Relative: Mary
Relative: Jane
Boz, Philipp; Port uncertain, 1752 ***2856.30*** *p42*
Bozanovich, M. 26; Alaska, 1917 ***9196.1*** *p50*
Bozanovich, M. 26; Yukon, 1917 ***9196.1*** *p50*
Bozenhard, Bartolomaus; America, 1753 ***2856.30*** *p47*
With wife & children
Bozenhard, Bartolomaus; America, 1755 ***2856.30*** *p47*
With wife & children
Bozenhard, Bartolomaus; Port uncertain, 1754 ***2856.30*** *p47*
With wife & children
Bozenhart, Barbara; Port uncertain, 1609 ***2856.30*** *p47*
Bozenhart, Bartle; Port uncertain, 1585 ***2856.30*** *p47*
Bozenhart, Bartle; Port uncertain, 1608 ***2856.30*** *p47*
Bozenhart, Hans; Port uncertain, 1609 ***2856.30*** *p47*
Bozerin, Anna Maria; America, 1753 ***2856.30*** *p47*
Bozokowski, John; Maryland, 1910 ***3259.35*** *p6*
Bozonofski, Frank; Maryland, 1910 ***3259.35*** *p6*
Bozuchowski, Julian J.; Maryland, 1910 ***3259.35*** *p6*
Bozuzki, William; Maryland, 1910 ***3259.35*** *p6*
Bozwell, John 27; Maryland, 1774 ***1220.25*** *p61*
Bpiringer, Peter; Port uncertain, 1764 ***2856.30*** *p12*
Brabander, Jacob; America, 1743 ***2856.30*** *p47*
Braborne, William; Maryland, 1669 ***2524.55*** *p30*
Brabour, William 30; Ontario, 1871 ***1823.28*** *p9*
Brace, Hararvey 62; Ontario, 1871 ***1823.15*** *p23*
Brace, Phillip; Virginia, 1664 ***6212.30*** *p10*
Brace, T. M. 56; Ontario, 1871 ***1823.28*** *p9*
Brace, William 20; Jamaica, 1775 ***1220.25*** *p142*
Bracegirdle, John; Virginia, 1673 ***1224.1*** *p8*
Braceland, Alexander; New York, New York, 1833 ***6058.10*** *p22*
Brach, Caspar; Port uncertain, 1738 ***2856.30*** *p47*
Brachnicki, John; Maryland, 1910 ***3259.35*** *p6*
Brack, Conrad 38; Kansas, 1892-1910 ***9079.10*** *p18*
Brack, John 52; Ontario, 1871 ***1823.15*** *p23*
Brackel, Philipp; Port uncertain, 1785 ***2856.30*** *p50*
With wife
Bracken, Daniel R.; Vermont, 1838-1912 ***5900.10*** *p155*
Bracken, John; New York, 1837 ***8197.10*** *p87*
Bracken, Lochlin; New York, 1837 ***8197.10*** *p84*
Bracken, Sabina E. Downs; Vermont, 1836-1908 ***5900.10*** *p155*
Brackenbury, Robert 44; Ontario, 1871 ***1823.28*** *p9*
Brackett, William H.; New York, 1828 ***8197.10*** *p348*
Brackin, Andrew; New York, 1837 ***8197.10*** *p85*
Brackstone, Ann; Maryland, 1681 ***2524.55*** *p30*
Brackstone, Mary; Maryland, 1681 ***2524.55*** *p30*
Bracy, Elizabeth; Virginia, 1671-1672 ***6212.30*** *p46*
Bracy, Robert, Sr.; Virginia, 1671-1672 ***6212.30*** *p46*
Bracy, Robert, Jr.; Virginia, 1671-1672 ***6212.30*** *p46*
Bracy, Walter; Virginia, 1664 ***6212.30*** *p15*
Brad, Jno; Virginia, 1664 ***6212.30*** *p9*
Bradbrook, Robert; New York, 1840 ***8197.10*** *p154*
Bradburne, Richard; Boston, 1740 ***1224.2*** *p13*
Bradcock, Miss; Quebec, 1858 ***9196.15*** *p38*
Braddock, Edward; America, 1755 ***1224.2*** *p13*
Braddock, Nathaniel; Died enroute, 1636 ***1224.1*** *p8*
Braddon, Thomas 35; Ontario, 1871 ***1823.15*** *p23*
Brade, Isabell; Virginia, 1703-1704 ***6212.30*** *p62*
Braden, John; New York, 1830 ***8197.10*** *p361*
Braden, Robert 69; Ontario, 1871 ***1823.15*** *p23*
Braden, William J. 11; Ontario, 1861 ***2896.27*** *p56*
Bradey, Elizabeth Coffee 45; Vermont, 1863 ***5900.10*** *p246*
Bradey, James; New York, 1802 ***8197.10*** *p18*
Bradey, Terrence 40; Ontario, 1871 ***1823.28*** *p9*
Bradford, Ann *SEE* Bradford, John
Bradford, Bartholomew; Maryland, 1657 ***2524.55*** *p30*
Bradford, George *SEE* Bradford, John
Bradford, James; New York, 1825 ***8197.10*** *p210*
Bradford, John; Maryland, 1631-1685 ***2524.55*** *p30*
Wife: Ann
Brother: George
Bradford, John 18; Maryland, 1774 ***1220.25*** *p41*
Bradford, John 30; Maryland, 1775 ***1220.25*** *p103*
Bradford, Joseph; Pennsylvania, 1777 ***4629.10*** *p15*
Bradford, Richard; New York, 1840 ***8197.10*** *p145*
Bradford, Robert 43; Ontario, 1871 ***1823.15*** *p23*
Bradford, Susanna; Maryland, 1674 ***2524.55*** *p30*
Bradford, Thomas; Pennsylvania, 1777 ***4629.10*** *p13*
Bradford, Thomas; Virginia, 1671 ***1224.1*** *p8*
Bradford, William; Maryland, 1661 ***2524.55*** *p30*
Bradford, William; Maryland, 1669 ***2524.55*** *p30*
Bradford, William, Jr.; New York, 1838 ***8197.10*** *p110*
Bradgate, Katharine; Maryland, 1681 ***2524.55*** *p30*
Bradhurst, Jno; Virginia, 1702 ***6212.30*** *p62*
Bradigan, Frederick 56; Ontario, 1871 ***1823.15*** *p23*
Bradish, James; New York, 1794 ***8197.10*** *p4*
Bradle, Joseph; Pennsylvania, 1836 ***6058.10*** *p14*
Bradley, Alice 54; Vermont, 1872 ***5900.10*** *p249*
Bradley, Ann; Maryland, 1659 ***2524.55*** *p31*
Bradley, Ann; Wilmington, North Carolina, 1789 ***1224.2*** *p13*
Bradley, Anna; Wilmington, North Carolina, 1789 ***1224.3*** *p9*
Bradley, B. 24; Ontario, 1861 ***2896.25*** *p42*
Bradley, Catherine 37; Ontario, 1871 ***1823.22*** *p15*
Bradley, Catherine 70; Vermont, 1872 ***5900.10*** *p251*
Bradley, Christopher; Pennsylvania, 1777 ***4629.10*** *p14*
Bradley, Cornelius; Vermont, 1843-1906 ***5900.10*** *p385*
Bradley, Daniel; Virginia, 1669 ***1224.1*** *p8*
Bradley, Dennis 59; Vermont, 1897 ***5900.10*** *p422*
Bradley, Edward; Philadelphia, 1746 ***1224.2*** *p13*
Bradley, Ellen 75; Vermont, 1899 ***5900.10*** *p201*
Bradley, Francis 34; Ontario, 1871 ***1823.15*** *p23*
Bradley, George 24; Maryland, 1774 ***1220.25*** *p74*
Bradley, George 39; Ontario, 1871 ***1823.28*** *p9*
Bradley, George 48; Ontario, 1871 ***1823.22*** *p15*
Bradley, George 60; Ontario, 1871 ***1823.22*** *p15*
Bradley, Hannah; Vermont, 1857-1938 ***5900.10*** *p192*
Bradley, Hugh; New York, 1828 ***8197.10*** *p64*
Bradley, James; Maryland, 1681 ***2524.55*** *p30*
Bradley, Jane; Maryland, 1661 ***2524.55*** *p30*
Bradley, John; New York, 1821 ***8197.10*** *p208*
Bradley, John; New York, 1825 ***8197.10*** *p210*
Bradley, John; New York, 1830 ***8197.10*** *p66*
Bradley, John; New York, 1837 ***8197.10*** *p85*
Bradley, John; Vermont, 1862-1926 ***5900.10*** *p201*
Bradley, Joseph; Maryland, 1681 ***2524.55*** *p30*
Bradley, Lanag 2; Ontario, 1871 ***1823.22*** *p15*
Bradley, Lewis; South Carolina, 1735 ***1224.2*** *p13*
Bradley, Malinda Riley 58; Vermont, 1884 ***5900.10*** *p456*
Bradley, Mary Jane; Vermont, 1845-1915 ***5900.10*** *p385*
Bradley, Michael; Vermont, 1826-1908 ***5900.10*** *p201*
Bradley, Michael 65; Ontario, 1871 ***1823.22*** *p15*
Bradley, Miles; New York, 1837 ***8197.10*** *p84*
Bradley, Nicholas; Maryland, 1673 ***2524.55*** *p30*
Bradley, Patrick; Pennsylvania, 1786 ***4629.10*** *p49*
Bradley, Patrick 56; Ontario, 1871 ***1823.28*** *p9*
Bradley, Thomas; Maryland, 1663 ***2524.55*** *p242*
Bradley, William; Maryland, 1650 ***2524.55*** *p31*
Bradley, William 34; Virginia, 1774 ***1220.25*** *p46*
Bradlow, Arthur; Virginia, 1663 ***6212.30*** *p2*
Bradly, Henry; Maryland, 1674 ***2524.55*** *p31*
Bradly, Isaac; Virginia, 1668-1669 ***6212.30*** *p40*
Bradly, Joseph 71; Ontario, 1871 ***1823.15*** *p23*
Bradly, Mary; Maryland, 1674 ***2524.55*** *p31*
Bradly, Nic.; Maryland, 1675 ***2524.55*** *p31*
Bradly, Richard; Maryland, 1674 ***2524.55*** *p31*
Bradly, Samuell; Maryland, 1674 ***2524.55*** *p31*
Bradly, William; Maryland, 1674 ***2524.55*** *p31*

Bradmore, Elizabeth; Maryland, 1663 2524.55 p31
Bradmore, Katherine; Maryland, 1663 2524.55 p31
Bradnell, John; Maryland, 1658 2524.55 p31
Bradney, Owen 55; Ontario, 1871 1823.22 p15
Bradnock, David 36; Ontario, 1871 1823.15 p23
Bradnox, Mary *SEE* Bradnox, Thomas
Bradnox, Thomas; Maryland, 1644 2524.55 p31
Wife: Mary
Bradon, George; New York, 1837 8197.10 p84
Bradon, Mary Ann 50; Ontario, 1871 1823.22 p15
Bradowsky, Adam; Maryland, 1910 3259.35 p6
Bradshaw, Abel 37; Ontario, 1871 1823.15 p23
Bradshaw, Ann; Maryland, 1672 2524.55 p31
Bradshaw, Ann; Vermont, 1805-1896 5900.10 p396
Bradshaw, Caleb 1; Ontario, 1861 2896.27 p38
Bradshaw, Charles 8; Ontario, 1861 2896.27 p38
Bradshaw, Elizabeth; Maryland, 1672 2524.55 p31
Bradshaw, Ella; Vermont, 1925 5900.10 p188
Bradshaw, James 22; Maryland, 1775 1220.25 p111
Bradshaw, Jane 4; Ontario, 1861 2896.27 p38
Bradshaw, John; Maryland, 1672 2524.55 p31
Bradshaw, John 65; Ontario, 1871 1823.22 p15
Bradshaw, Kathrine; Maryland, 1672 2524.55 p31
Bradshaw, Margaret; Vermont, 1857-1930 5900.10 p424
Bradshaw, Margaret 25; Ontario, 1861 2896.27 p38
Bradshaw, Mary 83; Vermont, 1902 5900.10 p393
Bradshaw, Mary A.; Vermont, 1909 5900.10 p188
Bradshaw, Mary Murphy; Vermont, 1846-1904 5900.10 p609
Bradshaw, Nathaniel 34; Ontario, 1871 1823.22 p15
Bradshaw, Patrick; Vermont, 1840-1880 5900.10 p424
Bradshaw, Patrick 28; Ontario, 1871 1823.22 p15
Bradshaw, Peter 22; Maryland, 1775 1220.25 p108
Bradshaw, Richard; Maryland, 1672 2524.55 p31
Bradshaw, Robert; America, 1825 1224.3 p9
Bradshaw, Robert; New York, 1820 8197.10 p207
Bradshaw, Thomas; Maryland, 1681 2524.55 p31
Bradshaw, Thomas; Maryland, 1814 1224.3 p9
Bradshaw, Thomas 32; Virginia, 1774 1220.25 p89
Bradshaw, Thomas 67; Ontario, 1871 1823.22 p15
Bradstreet, Simon; Portsmouth, New Hampshire, 1783 1224.2 p13
Bradwart, Richard; Maryland, 1662 2524.55 p31
Bradwell, Mathew; Virginia, 1671 6212.30 p42
Bradwell, Thomas 37; Ontario, 1871 1823.15 p23
Brady, Agnes; Vermont, n.d. 5900.10 p52
Brady, Alice McGinn; Vermont, 1855-1907 5900.10 p50
Brady, Bernard; New York, 1837 8197.10 p87
Brady, Bridget; Vermont, 1853-1928 5900.10 p491
Brady, Bridget; Vermont, 1863-1951 5900.10 p398
Brady, Bridget 55; Ontario, 1871 1823.28 p9
Brady, Bridget 65; Ontario, 1871 1823.22 p15
Brady, Bridget 73; Vermont, 1922 5900.10 p391
Brady, Bridget Caffary 82; Vermont, 1892 5900.10 p51
Brady, Christina Sinnott; Vermont, 1845-1928 5900.10 p51
Brady, Edward; New York, 1830 8197.10 p360
Brady, Edward; New York, 1839 8197.10 p129
Brady, Edward; Vermont, 1848-1906 5900.10 p50
Brady, Edward 38; Ontario, 1861 2896.25 p1
Brady, Edward 47; Ontario, 1871 1823.22 p15
Brady, Eleanor; Vermont, n.d. 5900.10 p51
Brady, Elizabeth; Vermont, 1836-1910 5900.10 p192
Brady, Ellen; Vermont, 1841-1859 5900.10 p75
Brady, Ellen; Vermont, 1851-1918 5900.10 p55
Brady, Eva Thayer; Vermont, 1865-1941 5900.10 p499
Brady, Farrel 43; Ontario, 1871 1823.22 p15
Brady, Felix; New York, 1837 8197.10 p84
Brady, George F.; Vermont, 1856-1931 5900.10 p499
Brady, Hannah O'Conner; Vermont, 1835-1877 5900.10 p502
Brady, Hannah Real 75; Vermont, 1930 5900.10 p506
Brady, Hugh; New York, 1837 8197.10 p84
Brady, Hugh 55; Ontario, 1871 1823.28 p9
Brady, Isabella 73; Ontario, 1871 1823.28 p9
Brady, James; New York, 1827 8197.10 p210
Brady, James; New York, 1827-1834 8197.10 p306
Brady, James; New York, 1833 8197.10 p211
Brady, James; New York, 1834 8197.10 p372
Brady, James; Vermont, n.d. 5900.10 p52
Brady, James 87; Ontario, 1871 1823.22 p15
Brady, James 87; Vermont, 1885 5900.10 p51
Brady, John; New York, 1835 8197.10 p212
Brady, John; New York, 1836 8197.10 p76
Brady, John; New York, 1838 8197.10 p377
Brady, John; New York, 1838 8197.10 p378
Brady, John; Vermont, 1830-1910 5900.10 p464
Brady, John; Vermont, 1832-1888 5900.10 p52
Brady, John 61; Ontario, 1871 1823.22 p15
Brady, John 66; Ontario, 1871 1823.22 p15
Brady, Joseph; New York, 1840 8197.10 p153
Brady, Luke 23; Virginia, 1774 1220.25 p90
Brady, Margaret; Vermont, 1835-1911 5900.10 p218
Brady, Mary; Vermont, 1832-1917 5900.10 p132
Brady, Mary; Vermont, 1838-1918 5900.10 p52
Brady, Mary; Vermont, 1845-1928 5900.10 p309
Brady, Mary O'Rourke; Vermont, 1851-1916 5900.10 p464
Brady, Michael; New York, 1836 8197.10 p76
Brady, Michael; New York, 1838 8197.10 p213
Brady, Nancy 80; Vermont, 1887 5900.10 p226
Brady, Nellie A.; Vermont, 1855-1927 5900.10 p491
Brady, Owen; New York, 1827 8197.10 p345
Brady, Owen; New York, 1837 8197.10 p84
Brady, Owen; Vermont, 1831-1892 5900.10 p218
Brady, Patrick; New York, 1826 8197.10 p210
Brady, Patrick; New York, 1833-1838 8197.10 p311
Brady, Patrick; Vermont, 1825-1878 5900.10 p502
Brady, Patrick; Vermont, 1840-1928 5900.10 p51
Brady, Patrick; Vermont, 1912 5900.10 p458
Brady, Patrick; Virginia, 1703-1704 6212.30 p63
Brady, Peter 61; Ontario, 1871 1823.22 p15
Brady, Philip; New York, 1834 8197.10 p74
Brady, Philip; New York, 1837 8197.10 p85
Brady, Richard; New York, 1837 8197.10 p212
Brady, Richard; New York, 1840 8197.10 p153
Brady, Rolland; Vermont, n.d. 5900.10 p52
Brady, Rose 43; Vermont, 1877 5900.10 p51
Brady, Ruth E. 71; Vermont, 1871 5900.10 p196
Brady, Sampson; New York, 1840 8197.10 p145
Brady, Terrance 40; Ontario, 1871 1823.22 p15
Brady, Thomas; New York, 1840 8197.10 p153
Brady, Thomas; New York, 1840 8197.10 p154
Brady, Thomas; New York, 1840 8197.10 p155
Brady, Thomas R.; New York, 1840 8197.10 p145
Brady, William; Maryland, 1678 2524.55 p31
Brady, William 55; Vermont, 1861 5900.10 p196
Braem, Rudolph; New York, 1838 8197.10 p212
Braems, Arnold; Virginia, 1665-1666 6212.30 p22
Bragg, Ann 20; Virginia, 1774 1220.25 p140
Bragg, James; Virginia, 1666 6212.30 p30
Bragg, Mary 50; Virginia, 1774 1220.25 p140
Brago, William 60; Ontario, 1871 1823.15 p23
Bragos, Anthony; New York, 1828 8197.10 p348
Bragovich, G. 22; Alaska, 1912 9196.1 p38
Bragovich, G. 22; Yukon, 1912 9196.1 p38
Brahana, Bridget Kelty; Vermont, 1836-1909 5900.10 p298
Brahana, John; Vermont, 1826-1904 5900.10 p298
Brahm, Georg; America, 1738 2856.30 p47
Brahner, Jacob; Port uncertain, 1776 2856.30 p47
With 2 children
Braich, B. 35; Alaska, 1912 9196.1 p38
Braich, B. 35; Whitehorse, Yukon, 1912 9196.1 p38
Braich, B. 40; Alaska, 1917 9196.1 p54
Braich, B. 40; British Columbia, 1917 9196.1 p54
Braiden, James; New York, 1802 8197.10 p18
Braiemerdge, Joseph; Maryland, 1665 2524.55 p31
Brailsford, Edward; South Carolina, 1733 1224.2 p13
Brailsford, Samuel; New York, New York, 1819 1224.3 p9
Brain, A. W. 39; Vancouver, British Columbia, 1917 9196.1 p70
Brain, A. W. 39; Washington, 1917 9196.1 p70
Brain, Alexander 50; Ontario, 1871 1823.15 p24
Brain, Nellie 33; Vancouver, British Columbia, 1917 9196.1 p70
Brain, Nellie 33; Washington, 1917 9196.1 p70
Brainbridge, Samuel 24; Nova Scotia, 1774 1220.25 p135
Braine, James H.; New York, 1827 8197.10 p339
Brainey, Mary Ann Connolly; Vermont, 1837-1900 5900.10 p594
Brainey, Patrick; Vermont, 1837-1913 5900.10 p594
Brainger, Barbara; Port uncertain, 1696 2856.30 p47
Braithwait, John 24; Maryland, 1774 1220.25 p78
Braithwait, John 40; Ontario, 1871 1823.22 p15
Braithwait, Joseph 42; Ontario, 1871 1823.22 p15
Braithwaite, George 34; Ontario, 1871 1823.22 p15
Braithwaite, James 52; Ontario, 1871 1823.15 p23
Braithwaite, James 70; Ontario, 1871 1823.15 p23
Braithwaite, John 24; Ontario, 1871 1823.15 p23
Braithwaite, Joseph 70; Ontario, 1871 1823.22 p15
Braithwaite, William; New York, 1819 8197.10 p207
Braithwaite, William 22; Maryland, 1775 1220.25 p96
Braithwaite, William 45; Ontario, 1871 1823.22 p15
Braitmayer, Imanuel F.; New York, 1838 8197.10 p111
Brakeneczka, Joseph; Maryland, 1910 3259.35 p6
Brakin, Elisabeth; Port uncertain, 1736 2856.30 p47
Brakula, Petra 37; British Columbia, 1912 9196.1 p17
Brakula, Petra 37; California, 1912 9196.1 p17
Braley, Elizabeth Welsh; Vermont, 1839-1909 5900.10 p588
Braley, Elizabeth Welsh; Vermont, 1839-1909 5900.10 p592
Braley, John W.; Vermont, 1841-1922 5900.10 p588
Braley, John W.; Vermont, 1841-1922 5900.10 p592
Brallett, Ann; Maryland, 1657 2524.55 p31
Brallett, James; Maryland, 1657 2524.55 p31
Brallett, Walter; Maryland, 1657 2524.55 p31
Bram, John; Maryland, 1910 3259.35 p6
Bramberger, August 26; Ontario, 1871 1823.28 p9
Bramberger, Gotlip 53; Ontario, 1871 1823.28 p9
Bramble, John; Maryland, 1681 2524.55 p31
Brame, Christopher; Maryland, 1667 2524.55 p174
Bramfeild, Ralph; Virginia, 1664 6212.30 p8
Bramily, John 37; Ontario, 1871 1823.28 p9
Bramley, Elizabeth; Maryland, 1662 2524.55 p31
Brampton, Mr.; Quebec, 1857 9196.15 p25
Brampton, Briar 31; Virginia, 1774 1220.25 p56
Brams, Arnold; Virginia, 1664 6212.30 p14
Bramstone, Jno; Virginia, 1665-1666 6212.30 p23
Bramwall, Luke *SEE* Bramwall, Willm.
Bramwall, Mary *SEE* Bramwall, Willm.
Bramwall, Willm.; Maryland, 1651 2524.55 p31
Wife: Mary
Son: Luke
Branan, John; Pennsylvania, 1860 6058.10 p43
Branan, Mary Corblis 54; Vermont, 1850 5900.10 p242
Branan, Matthew 21; Maryland, 1774 1220.25 p77
Branan, William 50; Ontario, 1871 1823.22 p15
Branard, Wm; Virginia, 1663-1664 6212.30 p5
Branat, Charles 42; British Columbia, 1911 9196.1 p34
Branat, Charles 42; Seattle, 1911 9196.1 p34
Branch, Christopher; Maryland, 1652 2524.55 p31
Branch, Edward; Maryland, 1667 2524.55 p31
Wife: Marlett
Son: Morris
Branch, Marlett *SEE* Branch, Edward
Branch, Morris *SEE* Branch, Edward
Brand, Anna Apollonia; Port uncertain, 1740 2856.30 p47
Brand, Anna Catharina; Port uncertain, 1786 2856.30 p47
Brand, Christian Carl; Port uncertain, 1748 2856.30 p47
Brand, Christian Karl; America, 1748 2856.30 p47
With wife & 8 children
Brand, Christian Karl; America, 1748 2856.30 p47
Brand, Elisabeth; Port uncertain, 1752 2856.30 p47
Brand, Johann Philipp; Port uncertain, 1796 2856.30 p47
Brand, John; Virginia, 1676 1224.1 p8
Brand, John 40; Ontario, 1871 1823.15 p23
Brand, Jonathan; Philadelphia, 1749 1224.2 p13
Brand, Karl Christian; America, 1748 2856.30 p47
With wife & 8 children
Brand, Maria Margarete; Port uncertain, 1791 2856.30 p47
Brand, Michael; Port uncertain, 1738 2856.30 p47
Brand, Susanna; Port uncertain, 1768 2856.30 p47
Brande, John 23; Maryland, 1775 1220.25 p100
Brandell, Isack; Virginia, 1671 6212.30 p43
Brander, F. 43; Alaska, 1910 9196.1 p9
Brander, F. 43; Yukon, 1910 9196.1 p9
Brander, John; Grenada, 1806 1640.13 p12
Brander, John; Pennsylvania, 1863 1640.13 p12
Brander, O. 28; Alaska, 1910 9196.1 p9
Brander, O. 28; Yukon, 1910 9196.1 p9
Brandes, Henry 33; Virginia, 1773 1220.25 p30
Brandner, Johann Jacob; Port uncertain, 1770 2856.30 p48
Brandner, Kraft; Port uncertain, 1772 2856.30 p48
Brandner, Margarete; Port uncertain, 1766 2856.30 p48
Brandner, Maria Catharina; Port uncertain, 1771 2856.30 p48
Brandner, Paul; America, 1771 2856.30 p48
Brandner, Paul; America, 1772 2856.30 p48
Brandner, Paul; Port uncertain, 1752 2856.30 p48
Brandon, George 70; Ontario, 1871 1823.15 p23
Brandon, Isaac L.; New York, 1826 8197.10 p210
Brandon, Isaac L.; New York, 1829 8197.10 p65
Brandon, James 60; Ontario, 1871 1823.15 p23
Brandon, John; Pennsylvania, 1777 4629.10 p31
Brandon, John 65; Ontario, 1871 1823.15 p23
Brandon, John 70; Ontario, 1871 1823.15 p23
Brandon, Rachel; New York, 1836 8197.10 p212
Brandt, Anna Barbara; Port uncertain, 1757 2856.30 p48
Brandt, Anna Margarete; Port uncertain, 1763 2856.30 p48
Brandt, Jacob; Pennsylvania, 1777 4629.10 p7
Brandt, Johann; America, 1741 2856.30 p48
Brandt, Johann Adam; Port uncertain, 1758 2856.30 p48
Brandt, Margarete; Port uncertain, 1757 2856.30 p48
Branfield, Joseph 30; Ontario, 1871 1823.15 p23
Brang, Jacob; America, 1750 2856.30 p48
With child & mother
Brang, Jakob; America, 1750 2856.30 p48
With wife & child
Brang, Johann Jakob; America, 1750 2856.30 p48
Brangwell, Mary; Virginia, 1663-1664 6212.30 p5

Braniff, Patrick 52; Ontario, 1871 ***1823.22*** *p16*
Branigan, Mary Hagan; Vermont, 1837-1893 ***5900.10*** *p309*
Brankh, Anna Eva; Port uncertain, 1745 ***2856.30*** *p48*
Brann, John; Vermont, 1859-1886 ***5900.10*** *p86*
Brann, Mary Madden 66; Vermont, 1886 ***5900.10*** *p86*
Brann, Patrick 72; Vermont, 1888 ***5900.10*** *p86*
Brann, Thomas; Vermont, 1852-1885 ***5900.10*** *p86*
Brannaghan, John; New York, 1840 ***8197.10*** *p154*
Brannan, Bridget 68; Vermont, 1886 ***5900.10*** *p229*
Brannan, J. B.; Vermont, 1846-1902 ***5900.10*** *p242*
Brannan, James; New York, 1838 ***8197.10*** *p378*
Brannan, James 84; Vermont, 1861 ***5900.10*** *p227*
Brannan, John; Pennsylvania, 1860 ***6058.10*** *p43*
Brannan, Margaret 70; Vermont, 1872 ***5900.10*** *p240*
Brannan, Mary Ann 74; Vermont, 1911 ***5900.10*** *p598*
Brannan, Mary English; Vermont, 1825-1885 ***5900.10*** *p242*
Brannan, Mary J.; Vermont, 1856-1929 ***5900.10*** *p224*
Brannan, Michael; New York, 1834 ***8197.10*** *p316*
Brannan, P. J. 29; Ontario, 1871 ***1823.15*** *p23*
Brannan, Patrick; New York, 1840 ***8197.10*** *p155*
Brannan, Patrick; Vermont, 1817-1901 ***5900.10*** *p242*
Brannan, Patrick 65; Ontario, 1871 ***1823.28*** *p9*
Brannan, Peter 87; Vermont, 1873 ***5900.10*** *p240*
Branndes, August; New York, 1838 ***8197.10*** *p111*
Brannon, Andrew 20 *SEE* Brannon, William
Brannon, Christopher; New York, 1824 ***8197.10*** *p209*
Brannon, Daniel; New York, 1837 ***8197.10*** *p84*
Brannon, Daniel 24 *SEE* Brannon, William
Brannon, Gilbert 7 *SEE* Brannon, William
Brannon, Jane 18 *SEE* Brannon, William
Brannon, Roger 28 *SEE* Brannon, William
Brannon, William 26 *SEE* Brannon, William
Brannon, William 70; New York, New York, 1847 ***1825.45*** *p13*
Son: Andrew 20
Son: William 26
Daughter: Jane 18
Son: Roger 28
Son: Daniel 24
Son: Gilbert 7
Branon, Mary; Vermont, 1861 ***5900.10*** *p237*
Branscom, Polly 19; Ontario, 1861 ***2896.25*** *p18*
Branscombe, Alice M. 7; Ontario, 1861 ***2896.27*** *p41*
Branscombe, Anne M. 18; Ontario, 1861 ***2896.27*** *p41*
Branscombe, Arthur 7; Ontario, 1861 ***2896.27*** *p43*
Branscombe, Arthur 13; Ontario, 1861 ***2896.27*** *p40*
Branscombe, Catherine 54; Ontario, 1861 ***2896.27*** *p40*
Branscombe, Charlotte 43; Ontario, 1861 ***2896.27*** *p41*
Branscombe, Cynthia 19; Ontario, 1861 ***2896.27*** *p41*
Branscombe, David 2; Ontario, 1861 ***2896.27*** *p41*
Branscombe, Delilah 9; Ontario, 1861 ***2896.27*** *p41*
Branscombe, Elizabeth 20; Ontario, 1861 ***2896.27*** *p40*
Branscombe, Elizabeth 51; Ontario, 1861 ***2896.27*** *p40*
Branscombe, Elizabeth A. 10; Ontario, 1861 ***2896.27*** *p42*
Branscombe, Esther 39; Ontario, 1861 ***2896.27*** *p42*
Branscombe, Eve 41; Ontario, 1861 ***2896.27*** *p43*
Branscombe, Hannah 22; Ontario, 1861 ***2896.27*** *p40*
Branscombe, Henry 22; Ontario, 1861 ***2896.27*** *p55*
Branscombe, Huldah 15; Ontario, 1861 ***2896.27*** *p40*
Branscombe, James M. 1; Ontario, 1861 ***2896.27*** *p41*
Branscombe, John 55; Ontario, 1861 ***2896.27*** *p40*
Branscombe, John Y. 1; Ontario, 1861 ***2896.27*** *p43*
Branscombe, Joseph W. 8; Ontario, 1861 ***2896.27*** *p42*
Branscombe, Lydia 16; Ontario, 1861 ***2896.27*** *p43*
Branscombe, Martha 6; Ontario, 1861 ***2896.27*** *p41*
Branscombe, Martha A. 20; Ontario, 1861 ***2896.27*** *p43*
Branscombe, Mary C. 5; Ontario, 1861 ***2896.27*** *p41*
Branscombe, Matilda 33; Ontario, 1861 ***2896.27*** *p41*
Branscombe, Nathaniel 21; Ontario, 1861 ***2896.27*** *p40*
Branscombe, Nathaniel 85; Ontario, 1861 ***2896.27*** *p43*
Branscombe, Phebe 27; Ontario, 1861 ***2896.27*** *p40*
Branscombe, Polly 18; Ontario, 1861 ***2896.27*** *p43*
Branscombe, Robert 11; Ontario, 1861 ***2896.27*** *p43*
Branscombe, Robert 18; Ontario, 1861 ***2896.27*** *p40*
Branscombe, Samuel A. 17; Ontario, 1861 ***2896.27*** *p40*
Branscombe, Sarah E. 13; Ontario, 1861 ***2896.27*** *p41*
Branscombe, Sarah E. 14; Ontario, 1861 ***2896.27*** *p42*
Branscombe, Solomon 4; Ontario, 1861 ***2896.27*** *p41*
Branscombe, Sophiah 15; Ontario, 1861 ***2896.27*** *p40*
Branscombe, Stephen H. 12; Ontario, 1861 ***2896.27*** *p41*
Branscombe, Thomas H. 12; Ontario, 1861 ***2896.27*** *p41*
Branscombe, William H. 14; Ontario, 1861 ***2896.27*** *p43*
Branson, Francas; Virginia, 1663 ***6212.30*** *p3*
Branson, Thomas 21; Maryland, 1775 ***1220.25*** *p109*
Branson, William 26; Philadelphia, 1774 ***1220.25*** *p23*
Branston, William 48; Ontario, 1871 ***1823.22*** *p16*
Brant, Albert 20; Ontario, 1871 ***1823.28*** *p9*
Brant, Archibald 51; Ontario, 1871 ***1823.15*** *p23*
Brant, Caroline M. 34; Ontario, 1871 ***1823.22*** *p16*
Brant, Catherine 30; Ontario, 1861 ***2896.27*** *p63*
Brant, Christian 78; Ontario, 1871 ***1823.15*** *p23*
Brant, Fredrick 50; Ontario, 1871 ***1823.28*** *p9*
Brant, Henry; Maryland, 1662 ***2524.55*** *p31*
Brant, Jacob; New York, 1807 ***8197.10*** *p332*
Brant, James 48; Ontario, 1871 ***1823.15*** *p23*
Brant, John 71; Ontario, 1871 ***1823.15*** *p23*
Brant, Johnson 8; Ontario, 1861 ***2896.27*** *p63*
Brant, Joseph 10; Ontario, 1861 ***2896.27*** *p63*
Brant, Karl; Port uncertain, 1749 ***2856.30*** *p48*
Brant, Lucy 6; Ontario, 1861 ***2896.27*** *p63*
Brant, Peter; Port uncertain, 1733 ***2856.30*** *p48*
With 2 children
Brant, Sabbobag 58; Ontario, 1871 ***1823.15*** *p23*
Brant, Thomas; New York, 1826 ***8197.10*** *p210*
Brant, Thomas; New York, 1829 ***8197.10*** *p65*
Brant, Thomas 4; Ontario, 1861 ***2896.27*** *p63*
Brant, William 26; Maryland, 1775 ***1220.25*** *p121*
Brantingham, Thomas H.; New York, 1794 ***8197.10*** *p3*
Branum, Patrick; Pennsylvania, 1777 ***4629.10*** *p13*
Branwood, John; Carolina, 1706 ***1224.2*** *p13*
Brarenton, Thomas 21; Maryland, 1774 ***1220.25*** *p70*
Brasch, Louace; Ontario, 1871 ***1823.28*** *p9*
Brasine, Elinor; Maryland, 1669 ***2524.55*** *p31*
Daughter: Susanna
Brasine, Susanna *SEE* Brasine, Elinor
Brasington, Samuel 19; Maryland, 1775 ***1220.25*** *p101*
Brasinton, Robert; Maryland, 1678 ***2524.55*** *p31*
Brass, Mr.; St. John, New Brunswick, 1857 ***9196.15*** *p13*
Brass, Mrs.; St. John, New Brunswick, 1857 ***9196.15*** *p13*
Brass, Cristay 48; Ontario, 1871 ***1823.28*** *p9*
Brass, Thomas; Savannah, Georgia, 1774 ***1640.10*** *p14*
Brassal, John; New York, 1839 ***8197.10*** *p127*
Brasseur, Ann; South Carolina, 1742 ***1224.2*** *p13*
Braston, Tho; Virginia, 1674 ***6212.30*** *p52*
Brathwaite, John; South Carolina, 1740 ***1224.2*** *p14*
Bratock, John; Pennsylvania, 1868 ***6058.10*** *p73*
Bratt, Esther; Terre Haute, Indiana, 1842 ***1224.3*** *p9*
Bratz, Jerg; America, 1748 ***2856.30*** *p48*
Bratz, Jerg; Port uncertain, 1746 ***2856.30*** *p48*
Brauch, Mrs. Johann; Port uncertain, 1764 ***2856.30*** *p48*
Brauch, Michael; Port uncertain, 1780 ***2856.30*** *p48*
Braucheler, Theobald; America, 1741 ***2856.30*** *p48*
Braucher, Theobald; America, 1741 ***2856.30*** *p48*
Brauer, Martin; Port uncertain, 1781 ***2856.30*** *p48*
Brauffer, Anna Margarete; America, 1751 ***2856.30*** *p48*
Brauffer, Maria Salome; America, 1751 ***2856.30*** *p48*
Braumann, Anna; Port uncertain, 1741 ***2856.30*** *p48*
Braumbach, Eva; Port uncertain, 1739 ***2856.30*** *p48*
Braumlin, Maria Ursula; Port uncertain, 1776 ***2856.30*** *p55*
Braun, Adam; Port uncertain, 1747 ***2856.30*** *p48*
Braun, Adam; Port uncertain, 1764 ***2856.30*** *p48*
Braun, Anna Magdalena; America, 1752 ***2856.30*** *p49*
Braun, Anna Margarete; America, 1752 ***2856.30*** *p49*
Braun, Burkard; America, 1752 ***2856.30*** *p49*
With wife
Braun, Catharina; America, 1752 ***2856.30*** *p49*
Braun, Christian; Port uncertain, 1752 ***2856.30*** *p49*
Braun, Christof; America, 1750 ***2856.30*** *p49*
With father
Braun, Christof; Port uncertain, 1769 ***2856.30*** *p48*
Braun, Conrad; America, 1752 ***2856.30*** *p49*
Braun, Damian; Port uncertain, 1791 ***2856.30*** *p48*
Braun, Elis. Catharina; Port uncertain, 1788 ***2856.30*** *p48*
Braun, Friedrich; Port uncertain, 1781 ***2856.30*** *p48*
Braun, Friedrich Jacob; Port uncertain, 1752 ***2856.30*** *p50*
With wife & 3 children
Braun, Gottfried Andre; Port uncertain, 1752 ***2856.30*** *p49*
Braun, Jacob; America, 1752 ***2856.30*** *p49*
Braun, Jacob; Port uncertain, 1755 ***2856.30*** *p49*
Braun, Jacob Florian; Port uncertain, 1752 ***2856.30*** *p49*
Braun, Jakob; America, 1764 ***2856.30*** *p49*
Braun, Johann; Port uncertain, 1738 ***2856.30*** *p49*
Braun, Johann; Port uncertain, 1790 ***2856.30*** *p50*
With wife
Braun, Johann Adam; Port uncertain, 1770 ***2856.30*** *p49*
Braun, Johann Friedric; America, 1752 ***2856.30*** *p49*
Braun, Johann Georg; America, 1752 ***2856.30*** *p49*
Braun, Johann Georg; Port uncertain, 1752 ***2856.30*** *p50*
With wife & child
Braun, John 51; Ontario, 1871 ***1823.15*** *p24*
Braun, Lorenz; Port uncertain, 1757 ***2856.30*** *p49*
Braun, Lorenz; Port uncertain, 1762 ***2856.30*** *p49*
Braun, Magdalena; Port uncertain, 1764 ***2856.30*** *p49*
Braun, Maria; Port uncertain, 1782 ***2856.30*** *p49*
Braun, Marianna; Port uncertain, 1788 ***2856.30*** *p49*
Braun, Melchior; Cayenne, 1760 ***2856.30*** *p49*
Braun, Michael; Port uncertain, 1747 ***2856.30*** *p49*
Braun, Michael; Port uncertain, 1779 ***2856.30*** *p49*
Braun, Michael; Port uncertain, 1789 ***2856.30*** *p49*
Braun, Nicolas; Port uncertain, 1756 ***2856.30*** *p49*
Braun, Nicolaus; Port uncertain, 1793 ***2856.30*** *p49*
Braun, Peter; America, 1741 ***2856.30*** *p50*
With wife & children
Braun, Stefan; America, 1738 ***2856.30*** *p49*
Braun, Theobald; America, 1749 ***2856.30*** *p49*
With wife & 6 children
Braun, Theobald; America, 1749 ***2856.30*** *p50*
With wife & 5 children
Braunbach, Xaver; Port uncertain, 1791 ***2856.30*** *p50*
Braund, George 63; Ontario, 1871 ***1823.22*** *p16*
Braunewetter, Anna Elisabeth; Port uncertain, 1752 ***2856.30*** *p50*
Braunhold, Albert; New York, 1840 ***8197.10*** *p214*
Brauns, Andreas; America, 1749 ***2856.30*** *p50*
With wife
Brauns, Peter; America, 1749 ***2856.30*** *p50*
Brauss, Andreas; America, 1752 ***2856.30*** *p50*
With wife
Brauss, Peter; America, 1752 ***2856.30*** *p50*
With wife 3 sons & daughter
Bravin, Samuel; Maryland, 1682 ***2524.55*** *p31*
Brawley, Thomas; New York, 1828 ***8197.10*** *p350*
Brawn, Christian; New York, 1837 ***8197.10*** *p85*
Brawn, Digery 32; Ontario, 1871 ***1823.15*** *p24*
Brawn, John 17; Ontario, 1871 ***1823.15*** *p24*
Brawn, Mary 40; Ontario, 1871 ***1823.22*** *p16*
Brawne, Henry; Maryland, 1681 ***2524.55*** *p32*
Brawne, Margarett; Maryland, 1671 ***2524.55*** *p32*
Brawne, Mary; Maryland, 1681 ***2524.55*** *p32*
Brawski, Frank; Maryland, 1910 ***3259.35*** *p6*
Brax, Catharina; Port uncertain, 1778 ***2856.30*** *p50*
Bray, Mrs.; Quebec, 1858 ***9196.15*** *p36*
Bray, Benjamin 39; Ontario, 1871 ***1823.22*** *p16*
Bray, Catharine 75; Vermont, 1882 ***5900.10*** *p270*
Bray, Christopher; Maryland, 1660 ***2524.55*** *p32*
Bray, Daniel; Pennsylvania, 1787 ***4629.10*** *p55*
Bray, David 12; Vermont, 1863 ***5900.10*** *p509*
Bray, Edward; Virginia, 1664 ***6212.30*** *p12*
Bray, Edward 47; Ontario, 1871 ***1823.28*** *p9*
Bray, James; Pennsylvania, 1777 ***4629.10*** *p9*
Bray, John; New York, 1823 ***8197.10*** *p209*
Bray, John 40; Ontario, 1871 ***1823.22*** *p16*
Bray, John 43; Ontario, 1871 ***1823.28*** *p9*
Bray, John 46; Ontario, 1871 ***1823.15*** *p24*
Bray, Katie 8; Vermont, 1863 ***5900.10*** *p509*
Bray, Maggie 23; Ontario, 1871 ***1823.22*** *p16*
Bray, Margerett; Maryland, 1663 ***2524.55*** *p32*
Bray, Mary E. 23; Vermont, 1870 ***5900.10*** *p509*
Bray, Nicholas 38; Ontario, 1871 ***1823.22*** *p16*
Bray, Richard; Virginia, 1691 ***1224.1*** *p8*
Bray, Robert 16; Maryland, 1775 ***1220.25*** *p113*
Bray, Robert 71; Ontario, 1871 ***1823.15*** *p24*
Bray, Sarah 6; Vermont, 1863 ***5900.10*** *p509*
Bray, Thomas; New England, 1726 ***1224.2*** *p14*
Bray, Thomas 42; Ontario, 1871 ***1823.22*** *p16*
Bray, Walter; Maryland, 1657 ***2524.55*** *p32*
Bray, William 48; Ontario, 1871 ***1823.15*** *p24*
Bray, William 52; Ontario, 1871 ***1823.22*** *p16*
Brayfield, John; Pennsylvania, 1777 ***4629.10*** *p15*
Brayfield, John; Philadelphia, 1789 ***1224.2*** *p14*
Brayley, Mr.; Quebec, 1858 ***9196.15*** *p42*
Brays, James 46; Ontario, 1871 ***1823.22*** *p16*
Brayton, Hanorah Scannel; Vermont, 1860-1911 ***5900.10*** *p395*
Brayton, Patrick; Vermont, 1855-1934 ***5900.10*** *p395*
Brazier, John; New York, New York, 1810 ***1224.3*** *p9*
Brazier, William 19; Virginia, 1774 ***1220.25*** *p87*
Brazinsky, John; Maryland, 1910 ***3259.35*** *p6*
Bread, James 30; Virginia, 1774 ***1220.25*** *p27*
Breader, Tho; Virginia, 1665-1666 ***6212.30*** *p21*
Bready, Anne 48; Ontario, 1871 ***1823.28*** *p9*
Breakey, Andrew; New York, 1826 ***8197.10*** *p210*
Breakey, Andrew; New York, 1834 ***8197.10*** *p74*
Breakey, Catherine; Vermont, 1818-1879 ***5900.10*** *p495*
Breakey, Mary; Vermont, 1816-1904 ***5900.10*** *p495*
Breakinridge, C. 11; Ontario, 1861 ***2896.26*** *p10*
Breakinridge, E. 2; Ontario, 1861 ***2896.26*** *p10*
Breakinridge, J. 5; Ontario, 1861 ***2896.26*** *p10*
Breakinridge, L. 15; Ontario, 1861 ***2896.26*** *p10*
Breakinridge, M. 8; Ontario, 1861 ***2896.26*** *p10*
Breakinridge, M. C. 45; Ontario, 1861 ***2896.26*** *p10*
Breakinridge, R. 13; Ontario, 1861 ***2896.26*** *p10*
Breakinridge, W. 18; Ontario, 1861 ***2896.26*** *p10*
Bream, Edw; Virginia, 1667 ***6212.30*** *p36*
Brearly, Daniel 45; Philadelphia, 1774 ***1220.25*** *p80*
Brearton, Elizabeth; Vermont, 1867-1942 ***5900.10*** *p256*
Brechbuhl, Johann Wendel; America, 1744 ***2856.30*** *p50*
Brechbuhl, Wendel; America, 1732 ***2856.30*** *p50*
Brechbuhl, Wendel; America, 1744 ***2856.30*** *p50*
With wife
Brechel, Philipp; Port uncertain, 1785 ***2856.30*** *p50*
With wife
Brecheusin, Anna; Port uncertain, 1678 ***2856.30*** *p50*
With husband & 3 children

Brecht, Anna Catharina; America, 1726 ***2856.30*** *p50*
With 2 sons
Brecht, Charles; New York, New York, 1857 ***6058.10*** *p51*
Brecht, Christina; America, 1750 ***2856.30*** *p50*
Brecht, G.; Pennsylvania, 1834 ***6058.10*** *p11*
Brecht, Magdalena; America, 1750 ***2856.30*** *p50*
Brecht, Niklas; Port uncertain, 1738 ***2856.30*** *p50*
With wife & 3 children
Brecht, Stefan; America, 1737 ***2856.30*** *p50*
Breckels, Josephine; Maryland, 1910 ***3259.35*** *p6*
Breckenridge, David 35; Ontario, 1871 ***1823.15*** *p24*
Breckenridge, James 31; Ontario, 1871 ***1823.15*** *p24*
Breczke, Felix; Maryland, 1910 ***3259.35*** *p6*
Breda, Kenba; Maryland, 1910 ***3259.35*** *p6*
Bredall, Rasmus Christian; New York, 1828 ***8197.10*** *p211*
Bredan, Archibald 30; Ontario, 1861 ***2896.27*** *p36*
Bredan, Francis 2; Ontario, 1861 ***2896.27*** *p36*
Bredan, Margaret 9; Ontario, 1861 ***2896.27*** *p36*
Bredan, Reuben 6; Ontario, 1861 ***2896.27*** *p36*
Bredin, James; Maryland, 1681 ***2524.55*** *p32*
Bredin, John; New York, 1803 ***8197.10*** *p11*
Bree, Andrew; Vermont, 1859-1926 ***5900.10*** *p397*
Bree, Catherine; Vermont, 1844-1929 ***5900.10*** *p397*
Bree, Catherine 63; Vermont, 1886 ***5900.10*** *p265*
Bree, Daniel B.; Vermont, 1852-1915 ***5900.10*** *p397*
Bree, Ethel E.; Vermont, 1874-1906 ***5900.10*** *p397*
Bree, James; Vermont, 1861-1927 ***5900.10*** *p397*
Bree, John; Vermont, 1844-1895 ***5900.10*** *p397*
Bree, Martin H.; Vermont, 1848-1921 ***5900.10*** *p397*
Bree, Patrick 86; Vermont, 1894 ***5900.10*** *p265*
Bree, William; Maryland, 1667 ***2524.55*** *p32*
Breedborne, Ellinor; Maryland, 1671 ***2524.55*** *p32*
Breedborne, John; Maryland, 1666 ***2524.55*** *p32*
Breedon, Benjamin F.; New York, 1874 ***1640.13*** *p12*
Breedon, Thomas; New England, 1666 ***1224.1*** *p10*
Breedon, Zacheus; Died enroute, 1686 ***1224.1*** *p9*
Breen, Andrew 63; Ontario, 1871 ***1823.22*** *p16*
Breen, Ann 51; Vermont, 1850 ***5900.10*** *p524*
Breen, Ann Donahue; Vermont, 1839-1921 ***5900.10*** *p188*
Breen, Anna 72; Vermont, 1868 ***5900.10*** *p523*
Breen, Edward; Vermont, 1820-1829 ***5900.10*** *p523*
Breen, Edward 69; Ontario, 1871 ***1823.15*** *p24*
Breen, Elizabeth; Vermont, 1827-1912 ***5900.10*** *p523*
Breen, Elizabeth; Vermont, 1857-1861 ***5900.10*** *p536*
Breen, Elizabeth 4; Vermont, 1863 ***5900.10*** *p524*
Breen, Elizabeth B. 49; Vermont, 1875 ***5900.10*** *p190*
Breen, Ellen; Vermont, 1824-1893 ***5900.10*** *p527*
Breen, Ellen Moynihan 75; Vermont, 1897 ***5900.10*** *p117*
Breen, Evan; Pennsylvania, 1868 ***6058.10*** *p63*
Breen, George; Vermont, 1864-1869 ***5900.10*** *p536*
Breen, James; Vermont, 1822-1890 ***5900.10*** *p536*
Breen, Jennie; Vermont, 1852-1923 ***5900.10*** *p553*
Breen, John; Vermont, 1844-1901 ***5900.10*** *p188*
Breen, John 88; Vermont, 1896 ***5900.10*** *p117*
Breen, Katherine G.; Vermont, 1855-1893 ***5900.10*** *p117*
Breen, Katie 13; Vermont, 1886 ***5900.10*** *p523*
Breen, Mary; Vermont, 1823-1907 ***5900.10*** *p228*
Breen, Mary; Vermont, 1852-1893 ***5900.10*** *p536*
Breen, Mary; Vermont, 1855-1943 ***5900.10*** *p555*
Breen, Mary 32; Ontario, 1871 ***1823.28*** *p9*
Breen, Mary Barrett 38; Vermont, 1863 ***5900.10*** *p524*
Breen, Mary Cavanaugh 52; Vermont, 1889 ***5900.10*** *p523*
Breen, Moses; New York, 1840 ***8197.10*** *p144*
Breen, Moses; Vermont, 1868-1883 ***5900.10*** *p536*
Breen, Patrick 34; Ontario, 1871 ***1823.28*** *p9*
Breen, Peter; Vermont, 1848 ***5900.10*** *p536*
Breen, Robert 30; Ontario, 1871 ***1823.15*** *p24*
Breen, Rosanna 2; Vermont, 1853 ***5900.10*** *p524*
Breen, Rosannah 75; Vermont, 1863 ***5900.10*** *p523*
Breen, William 91; Vermont, 1903 ***5900.10*** *p524*
Breene, John 37; Ontario, 1871 ***1823.28*** *p9*
Breene, John 65; Ontario, 1871 ***1823.28*** *p9*
Breese, Evan; Pennsylvania, 1868 ***6058.10*** *p63*
Breese, Thomas; New York, 1834 ***8197.10*** *p306*
Breet, Charles; Virginia, 1664 ***6212.30*** *p9*
Breeze, William, Sr. 61; Ontario, 1871 ***1823.22*** *p16*
Breh, Michael; Port uncertain, 1776 ***2856.30*** *p50*
Brehm, Barbara; Port uncertain, 1760 ***2856.30*** *p50*
Brehm, Margarete; Port uncertain, 1774 ***2856.30*** *p50*
Breidgart, John J. 21; Kansas, 1892-1910 ***9079.10*** *p8*
Breisacher, Matthaus; Port uncertain, 1776 ***2856.30*** *p51*
Breit, Michael; Port uncertain, 1751 ***2856.30*** *p51*
Breitenbach, Peter; America, 1754 ***2856.30*** *p51*
Breithaupt, Thomas; Port uncertain, 1740 ***2856.30*** *p51*
Breithaupt, Thomas; Port uncertain, 1772 ***2856.30*** *p51*
Breither, Heinrich; Port uncertain, 1783 ***2856.30*** *p51*
With wife 3 sons & 3 daughters
Breitius, Jacob; America, 1749 ***2856.30*** *p53*
Breittmayer, Gaspard Andre Louis; New York, 1818 ***8197.10*** *p206*
Breitung, Maria Elisabeth; Port uncertain, 1786 ***2856.30*** *p51*
Brellbow, Mary J. 20; Ontario, 1871 ***1823.15*** *p24*
Bremer, Frederick; New York, 1837 ***8197.10*** *p85*
Bremer, Henry; New York, 1838 ***8197.10*** *p110*
Bremer, Peter; Port uncertain, 1762 ***2856.30*** *p51*
Bremford, Sisly; Virginia, 1666-1667 ***6212.30*** *p34*
Bremner, Mrs. 50; Ontario, 1871 ***1823.28*** *p9*
Bremner, Alexander; Colorado, 1887 ***1640.13*** *p12*
Bremner, Charles 70; Ontario, 1871 ***1823.15*** *p24*
Bremner, James; Pennsylvania, 1777 ***4629.10*** *p28*
Bremner, John 59; Ontario, 1871 ***1823.28*** *p9*
Bremner, Robert; Florida, 1767 ***1640.10*** *p14*
Bremson, Thomas; Maryland, 1672 ***2524.55*** *p32*
Brenan, Ann; Vermont, 1811-1893 ***5900.10*** *p569*
Brenan, Edward; New York, 1821 ***8197.10*** *p208*
Brenan, Michael 34; Ontario, 1871 ***1823.28*** *p9*
Brenan, Peter 29; Ontario, 1871 ***1823.15*** *p24*
Brenchley, Miss; Quebec, 1858 ***9196.15*** *p44*
Brenckir, John 74; Ontario, 1871 ***1823.15*** *p24*
Brendel, Hans; Port uncertain, 1790 ***2856.30*** *p51*
Brendel, Johann Marx; America, 1749 ***2856.30*** *p51*
Brendel, Johann Marx; Port uncertain, 1749 ***2856.30*** *p51*
Brendell, Robert; Maryland, 1664 ***2524.55*** *p32*
Brener, William 48; Ontario, 1871 ***1823.15*** *p24*
Brengel, Christian; America, 1754 ***2856.30*** *p51*
Brenmer, Edna; Vermont, 1871-1908 ***5900.10*** *p278*
Brenn, Catharina; Port uncertain, 1790 ***2856.30*** *p51*
Brennan, Alice S. Howrigan; Vermont, 1860-1928 ***5900.10*** *p227*
Brennan, Andrew 20 *SEE* Brennan, William
Brennan, Ann; Vermont, 1846-1913 ***5900.10*** *p258*
Brennan, Anna 72; Vermont, 1928 ***5900.10*** *p485*
Brennan, Anna T.; Vermont, 1858-1931 ***5900.10*** *p485*
Brennan, Anne Jane 27; Vermont, 1879 ***5900.10*** *p471*
Brennan, Annie; Vermont, 1855-1929 ***5900.10*** *p254*
Brennan, Bridget 34; Vermont, 1880 ***5900.10*** *p564*
Brennan, Bridget Cole; Vermont, 1813-1887 ***5900.10*** *p547*
Brennan, Bridget Geelan; Vermont, 1831-1902 ***5900.10*** *p254*
Brennan, Catharine; Vermont, 1883 ***5900.10*** *p67*
Brennan, Catherine; Vermont, 1848-1916 ***5900.10*** *p54*
Brennan, Catherine Bagley; Vermont, 1819-1890 ***5900.10*** *p485*
Brennan, Catherine Brough; Vermont, 1834-1896 ***5900.10*** *p195*
Brennan, Catherine Hanlon; Vermont, 1831-1903 ***5900.10*** *p506*
Brennan, Catherine Welch; Vermont, 1832-1912 ***5900.10*** *p547*
Brennan, Cathrine; Vermont, 1874-1966 ***5900.10*** *p254*
Brennan, Catie; Vermont, 1850-1870 ***5900.10*** *p227*
Brennan, Charles 70; Ontario, 1871 ***1823.22*** *p16*
Brennan, Daniel 24 *SEE* Brennan, William
Brennan, Daniel G.; Vermont, 1868-1950 ***5900.10*** *p254*
Brennan, Edward; Vermont, 1821-1895 ***5900.10*** *p485*
Brennan, Edward; Vermont, 1872-1895 ***5900.10*** *p254*
Brennan, Edward 50; Ontario, 1871 ***1823.28*** *p9*
Brennan, Eliza 45; Ontario, 1871 ***1823.28*** *p9*
Brennan, Elizabeth 55; Ontario, 1871 ***1823.28*** *p9*
Brennan, Elizabeth H.; Vermont, 1866-1904 ***5900.10*** *p254*
Brennan, Ellen; Vermont, 1855-1919 ***5900.10*** *p547*
Brennan, Ellen; Vermont, 1861-1939 ***5900.10*** *p235*
Brennan, Ellen 30; Ontario, 1861 ***2896.25*** *p69*
Brennan, Geoffrey; Castleton, Vermont, 1830 ***5900.10*** *p7*
Brennan, Geoffrey 52; Vermont, 1847 ***5900.10*** *p262*
Brennan, Gilbert 7 *SEE* Brennan, William
Brennan, James; New York, 1837 ***8197.10*** *p84*
Brennan, James; Vermont, 1820-1883 ***5900.10*** *p547*
Brennan, James; Vermont, 1831-1913 ***5900.10*** *p195*
Brennan, James 5; Vermont, 1856 ***5900.10*** *p67*
Brennan, James 64; Vermont, 1881 ***5900.10*** *p67*
Brennan, James 82; Vermont, 1896 ***5900.10*** *p235*
Brennan, James H.; Vermont, 1816-1884 ***5900.10*** *p227*
Brennan, James H.; Vermont, 1856-1929 ***5900.10*** *p227*
Brennan, Jane; Vermont, n.d. ***5900.10*** *p397*
Brennan, Jane 18 *SEE* Brennan, William
Brennan, Jeremiah 7; Vermont, 1860 ***5900.10*** *p67*
Brennan, John; New York, 1840 ***8197.10*** *p155*
Brennan, John; Vermont, 1827-1914 ***5900.10*** *p506*
Brennan, John; Vermont, 1847-1914 ***5900.10*** *p54*
Brennan, John; Vermont, 1847-1926 ***5900.10*** *p492*
Brennan, John; Vermont, 1856-1925 ***5900.10*** *p489*
Brennan, John 50; Ontario, 1871 ***1823.28*** *p9*
Brennan, John 73; Vermont, 1889 ***5900.10*** *p470*
Brennan, Kate 2; Vermont, 1857 ***5900.10*** *p67*
Brennan, Katharine; Vermont, 1853-1936 ***5900.10*** *p547*
Brennan, Lawrence 60; Ontario, 1871 ***1823.28*** *p9*
Brennan, Maggie; Vermont, 1861-1898 ***5900.10*** *p485*
Brennan, Margaret; Vermont, 1851-1909 ***5900.10*** *p547*
Brennan, Margaret; Vermont, 1853-1925 ***5900.10*** *p235*
Brennan, Margaret 27; Vermont, 1877 ***5900.10*** *p557*
Brennan, Margaret 27; Vermont, 1877 ***5900.10*** *p569*
Brennan, Margaret 43; Vermont, 1902 ***5900.10*** *p60*
Brennan, Margaret Dooley; Vermont, 1846-1917 ***5900.10*** *p579*
Brennan, Margaret Dowd; Vermont, 1857-1939 ***5900.10*** *p411*
Brennan, Margaret McCarty; Vermont, 1857-1929 ***5900.10*** *p395*
Brennan, Margaret McGookin; Vermont, 1854-1926 ***5900.10*** *p492*
Brennan, Margaret Murphy 45; Vermont, 1877 ***5900.10*** *p471*
Brennan, Maria L.; Vermont, 1853-1903 ***5900.10*** *p284*
Brennan, Martin; Vermont, 1820-1895 ***5900.10*** *p547*
Brennan, Mary; Vermont, 1803-1866 ***5900.10*** *p439*
Brennan, Mary; Vermont, 1831-1912 ***5900.10*** *p489*
Brennan, Mary; Vermont, 1858-1913 ***5900.10*** *p228*
Brennan, Mary 1; Vermont, 1857 ***5900.10*** *p67*
Brennan, Mary 17; Vermont, 1860 ***5900.10*** *p264*
Brennan, Mary 88; Vermont, 1881 ***5900.10*** *p89*
Brennan, Mary Mahar; Vermont, 1850-1909 ***5900.10*** *p267*
Brennan, Mary Thompson 75; Vermont, 1868 ***5900.10*** *p262*
Brennan, Mary Timbers; Vermont, 1824-1856 ***5900.10*** *p547*
Brennan, Michael; Vermont, 1846-1909 ***5900.10*** *p267*
Brennan, Nellie; Vermont, 1862-1945 ***5900.10*** *p485*
Brennan, Nora; Vermont, 1841-1921 ***5900.10*** *p510*
Brennan, Patrick; Vermont, 1847-1897 ***5900.10*** *p395*
Brennan, Patrick 22; Vermont, 1878 ***5900.10*** *p250*
Brennan, Patrick 32; Ontario, 1871 ***1823.28*** *p9*
Brennan, Patrick 40; Ontario, 1871 ***1823.22*** *p16*
Brennan, Patrick 60; Ontario, 1871 ***1823.28*** *p9*
Brennan, Peter; New York, 1840 ***8197.10*** *p145*
Brennan, Peter C. 42; Vermont, 1901 ***5900.10*** *p115*
Brennan, Philip; Vermont, 1845-1915 ***5900.10*** *p579*
Brennan, Roger 28 *SEE* Brennan, William
Brennan, Rose; Vermont, 1854-1939 ***5900.10*** *p241*
Brennan, Rose; Vermont, 1856-1933 ***5900.10*** *p485*
Brennan, Rose Carroll 46; Vermont, 1869 ***5900.10*** *p235*
Brennan, Samuel, Sr. 40; Ontario, 1871 ***1823.28*** *p9*
Brennan, Thomas; New York, 1823 ***8197.10*** *p209*
Brennan, Thos 18; Ontario, 1871 ***1823.28*** *p9*
Brennan, William; Vermont, 1820-1900 ***5900.10*** *p254*
Brennan, William 26 *SEE* Brennan, William
Brennan, William 70; New York, New York, 1847 ***1825.45*** *p13*
Son: Andrew 20
Daughter: Jane 18
Son: Daniel 24
Son: Gilbert 7
Son: William 26
Son: Roger 28
Brennan, William, Sr.; Vermont, 1780-1848 ***5900.10*** *p254*
Brennan, William, Jr.; Vermont, 1866-1928 ***5900.10*** *p254*
Brennan, Wm.; New York, 1840 ***8197.10*** *p155*
Brennand, David 22; Maryland, 1774 ***1220.25*** *p68*
Brennen, Kittie; Vermont, 1820-1862 ***5900.10*** *p227*
Brennen, Michael 48; Ontario, 1871 ***1823.28*** *p9*
Brenner, Christian; Port uncertain, 1773 ***2856.30*** *p51*
Brenner, Dorothea; Port uncertain, 1740 ***2856.30*** *p51*
Brenner, Elisabeth; Port uncertain, 1769 ***2856.30*** *p52*
Brenner, Eva Margarete; Port uncertain, 1754 ***2856.30*** *p51*
Brenner, Franz Peter; America, 1768 ***2856.30*** *p51*
Brenner, Georg; Port uncertain, 1612 ***2856.30*** *p51*
Brenner, George 76; Ontario, 1871 ***1823.28*** *p9*
Brenner, Hans Adam; America, 1753 ***2856.30*** *p51*
Brenner, Hans Adam; America, 1773 ***2856.30*** *p51*
Brenner, Hans Adam; Port uncertain, 1748 ***2856.30*** *p51*
Brenner, Hans Georg; Port uncertain, 1764 ***2856.30*** *p52*
With wife & 2 daughters
Brenner, Jacob 37; Ontario, 1871 ***1823.15*** *p24*
Brenner, Jacob, Sr. 34; Ontario, 1871 ***1823.15*** *p24*
Brenner, Johann Georg; Port uncertain, 1756 ***2856.30*** *p51*
Brenner, Johann Philipp; America, 1749 ***2856.30*** *p51*
Brenner, John; New York, 1838 ***8197.10*** *p111*
Brenner, Maria Juliana; Port uncertain, 1747 ***2856.30*** *p51*
Brenner, Peter; America, 1780 ***2856.30*** *p51*
Brenner, Peter; Port uncertain, 1768 ***2856.30*** *p52*
Brenner, Philipp; America, 1749 ***2856.30*** *p51*
Brenner, Philipp Adam; America, 1749 ***2856.30*** *p51*
Brenner, Sofie Elisabeth; Port uncertain, 1793 ***2856.30*** *p51*
Brenner, Sophia Elisabet; Port uncertain, 1741 ***2856.30*** *p52*
Brenner, Valentin; Port uncertain, 1788 ***2856.30*** *p52*

Brennesholtz, Christian; America, 1735 ***2856.30*** *p52*
Brennesholtz, Christian; America, 1750 ***2856.30*** *p52*
With wife & 4 children
Brennig, Elisabeth; America, 1752 ***2856.30*** *p52*
With husband
Brennig, Maria Eva; America, 1767 ***2856.30*** *p52*
Brennon, Catherine 45; Ontario, 1861 ***2896.27*** *p20*
Brenskie, Julius; Maryland, 1910 ***3259.35*** *p6*
Brent, Edward; Virginia, 1625 ***1224.1*** *p9*
Brent, Johann Nikolaus; Port uncertain, 1745 ***2856.30*** *p52*
Brent, Stephen; Virginia, 1665 ***6212.30*** *p22*
Brentnall, Catherine; New Jersey, 1856 ***1224.3*** *p9*
Brenton, William 27; Ontario, 1871 ***1823.22*** *p16*
Breo, Mary L.; Vermont, 1843-1910 ***5900.10*** *p285*
Breplur, Daniel 19; Maryland, 1774 ***1220.25*** *p51*
Brerely, Thomas; Maryland, 1679 ***2524.55*** *p32*
Brerenbucher, Adam; New York, 1837 ***8197.10*** *p84*
Bresinski, Michael; Maryland, 1910 ***3259.35*** *p6*
Breslin, Barney; Vermont, n.d. ***5900.10*** *p111*
Breslin, Ellen Hurd 30; Vermont, 1877 ***5900.10*** *p111*
Bresnaham, Francis 47; Ontario, 1871 ***1823.28*** *p9*
Bresnaham, Joseph 65; Ontario, 1871 ***1823.28*** *p9*
Bresnahan, Andrew; New York, 1805 ***8197.10*** *p28*
Bresnehan, Ann A. 27; Vermont, 1882 ***5900.10*** *p42*
Bresnehan, Ellen Kiernan; Vermont, 1853-1910 ***5900.10*** *p185*
Bresnehan, Ellen Oates; Vermont, 1860-1949 ***5900.10*** *p398*
Bresnehan, Joanna; Vermont, 1913 ***5900.10*** *p167*
Bresnehan, John; Vermont, 1849-1884 ***5900.10*** *p185*
Bresnehan, John 54; Vermont, 1871 ***5900.10*** *p208*
Bresnehan, K.; Vermont, 1853-1929 ***5900.10*** *p194*
Bresnehan, Mary; Vermont, 1845-1923 ***5900.10*** *p609*
Bresnehan, Patrick E.; Vermont, 1849-1934 ***5900.10*** *p398*
Bresnehen, Hannah; Vermont, 1845-1913 ***5900.10*** *p136*
Bresselan, Isaac; New York, 1829 ***8197.10*** *p212*
Bresselau, Isaac; New York, 1829 ***8197.10*** *p212*
Bressenham, Frances 58; Ontario, 1871 ***1823.28*** *p9*
Bressey, John; Maryland, 1723 ***1224.2*** *p14*
Bressler, Mr.; Quebec, 1856 ***9196.15*** *p9*
Brethauer, Amelia 59; Kansas, 1910 ***9079.10*** *p52*
Brethauer, Annie 23; Kansas, 1910 ***9079.10*** *p41*
Brethauer, George 29; Kansas, 1910 ***9079.10*** *p41*
Brethauer, George, Sr. 57; Kansas, 1910 ***9079.10*** *p52*
Brethauer, Henry 32; Kansas, 1900-1910 ***9079.10*** *p53*
Brethauer, Jacob 18; Kansas, 1910 ***9079.10*** *p52*
Brethauer, Mollie 30; Kansas, 1910 ***9079.10*** *p53*
Bretland, Elizabeth; Barbados, 1690 ***1224.1*** *p9*
Bretonnier, Auguste, Jr.; New York, 1835 ***8197.10*** *p70*
Brett, Elizabeth 25; Baltimore, 1775 ***1220.25*** *p119*
Brett, Elizabeth Jenkins; Savannah, Georgia, 1832 ***1224.3*** *p9*
Brett, James L.; New York, 1838 ***8197.10*** *p111*
Brett, Robert; Pennsylvania, 1701 ***1224.2*** *p14*
Brett, Robert 42; Ontario, 1871 ***1823.15*** *p24*
Brett, Stephen; Virginia, 1664 ***6212.30*** *p14*
Brett, Tho; Virginia, 1665-1666 ***6212.30*** *p21*
Brett, Thomas P.; New York, 1839 ***8197.10*** *p127*
Brettin, Jacob; Port uncertain, 1781 ***2856.30*** *p52*
Bretting, Jacob; Port uncertain, 1787 ***2856.30*** *p52*
Bretting, Jacob; Port uncertain, 1791 ***2856.30*** *p52*
Brettlell, Edmund; New York, 1839 ***8197.10*** *p128*
Bretton, George; Maryland, 1657 ***2524.55*** *p40*
Bretton, John; Maryland, 1672 ***2524.55*** *p32*
Bretton, Leayone; Maryland, 1654 ***2524.55*** *p32*
Bretton, Margarite; Maryland, 1664 ***2524.55*** *p32*
Bretton, Thomas; Maryland, 1681 ***2524.55*** *p32*
Bretton, William; Maryland, 1637 ***2524.55*** *p32*
With wife & child
Breuer, Peter; Port uncertain, 1792 ***2856.30*** *p52*
Breuer, Sebastian; Port uncertain, 1750 ***2856.30*** *p52*
Breuner, Caspar; Port uncertain, 1764 ***2856.30*** *p52*
Breuner, Johann Melcher; Port uncertain, 1747 ***2856.30*** *p52*
Breunig, Marx; Port uncertain, 1751 ***2856.30*** *p52*
Brevay, Victoria 14; Ontario, 1861 ***2896.25*** *p67*
Breverton, Thomas 29; Maryland, 1774 ***1220.25*** *p57*
Brevin, Martin 60; Ontario, 1871 ***1823.22*** *p16*
Brew, Arthur; Jamaica, 1788 ***1224.2*** *p14*
Brew, Arthur; Philadelphia, n.d. ***1224.2*** *p14*
Brewen, George; Maryland, 1656 ***2524.55*** *p32*
Brewen, Hubbard; Maryland, 1756 ***1224.2*** *p14*
Brewer, Alvah H. 16; Ontario, 1861 ***2896.28*** *p56*
Brewer, Ann; Maryland, 1658 ***2524.55*** *p32*
Brewer, Ann; Maryland, 1668 ***2524.55*** *p32*
Brewer, Benjamin 18; Ontario, 1861 ***2896.28*** *p56*
Brewer, Brock 17; Ontario, 1861 ***2896.27*** *p29*
Brewer, Charles 21; Maryland, 1775 ***1220.25*** *p99*
Brewer, Charles W. 3; Ontario, 1861 ***2896.28*** *p56*
Brewer, Daniel 42; Ontario, 1861 ***2896.28*** *p56*
Brewer, Daniel 52; Ontario, 1871 ***1823.22*** *p16*
Brewer, Eliza 51; Ontario, 1861 ***2896.27*** *p56*
Brewer, George; Maryland, 1658 ***2524.55*** *p32*
Brewer, George; Maryland, 1668 ***2524.55*** *p32*
Brewer, George 38; Ontario, 1871 ***1823.15*** *p24*
Brewer, Henry 77; Ontario, 1871 ***1823.22*** *p16*
Brewer, James J. 37; Ontario, 1871 ***1823.22*** *p16*
Brewer, John; Maryland, 1658 ***2524.55*** *p32*
Brewer, John; New York, 1840 ***8197.10*** *p213*
Brewer, John; Virginia, 1636 ***1224.1*** *p9*
Brewer, John 24; Jamaica, 1775 ***1220.25*** *p11*
Brewer, John 55; Ontario, 1871 ***1823.15*** *p24*
Brewer, Johnson, Jr. 24; Ontario, 1861 ***2896.27*** *p56*
Brewer, Margaret 8; Ontario, 1861 ***2896.28*** *p56*
Brewer, Nicholas R.; New York, 1823 ***8197.10*** *p209*
Brewer, Ruth 81; Ontario, 1861 ***2896.27*** *p41*
Brewer, Sarah 12; Ontario, 1861 ***2896.28*** *p56*
Brewer, Tho; Virginia, 1664 ***6212.30*** *p13*
Brewer, William; Maryland, 1676 ***2524.55*** *p32*
Brewer, William 70; Ontario, 1871 ***1823.15*** *p24*
Breweton, Sarah *SEE* Breweton, William
Breweton, William *SEE* Breweton, William
Breweton, William; Maryland, 1675 ***2524.55*** *p32*
Wife: Sarah
Son: William
Brewin, Anna; Vermont, 1857-1929 ***5900.10*** *p185*
Brewin, Ellen; Vermont, 1855-1914 ***5900.10*** *p184*
Brewster, James 50; Ontario, 1871 ***1823.22*** *p16*
Brewster, Thomas 56; Ontario, 1871 ***1823.22*** *p16*
Brewton, Miles; Charles Town, South Carolina, 1785 ***1224.2*** *p14*
Brewton, Robert; Pennsylvania, 1777 ***4629.10*** *p15*
Brey, Johann Caspar; America, 1740 ***2856.30*** *p52*
Breyer, Elisabeth; Port uncertain, 1755 ***2856.30*** *p52*
Breyer, Michael; Canada, 1751 ***2856.30*** *p52*
Breyl, Jacob; Port uncertain, 1771 ***2856.30*** *p52*
With wife
Breymeyer, George William; New York, 1840 ***8197.10*** *p213*
Brezel, Nikolaus; America, 1752 ***2856.30*** *p52*
With wife
Brezy, Henry; New York, 1803 ***8197.10*** *p10*
Briamcombe, Thomas 34; Ontario, 1871 ***1823.15*** *p24*
Brian, . . .; New Hampshire, 1641-1660 ***4628.40*** *p44*
Brian, Darby; Virginia, 1697 ***6212.30*** *p60*
Brian, Darby; Virginia, 1703-1704 ***6212.30*** *p63*
Brian, John; Maryland, 1665 ***2524.55*** *p32*
Brian, John; New York, 1839 ***8197.10*** *p320*
Briant, Darby; Maryland, 1680 ***2524.55*** *p32*
Briant, John C. 9; Ontario, 1861 ***2896.27*** *p66*
Briant, Mary A.; Ontario, 1861 ***2896.27*** *p66*
Briant, William; Maryland, 1664 ***2524.55*** *p32*
Briant, William; Ontario, 1861 ***2896.27*** *p66*
Bribner, William; Georgia, 1775 ***1640.10*** *p14*
Brice, Ellinor *SEE* Brice, William
Brice, Israel Bertram; New York, 1837 ***8197.10*** *p375*
Brice, John; New York, 1837 ***8197.10*** *p374*
Brice, Judith *SEE* Brice, William
Brice, William *SEE* Brice, William
Brice, William; Maryland, 1669 ***2524.55*** *p32*
Wife: Ellinor
Child: Judith
Child: William
Brich, Adam; New York, 1838 ***8197.10*** *p111*
Brickenden, Edward 40; Ontario, 1871 ***1823.15*** *p24*
Brickenden, John 35; Ontario, 1871 ***1823.15*** *p24*
Brickenden, Martha 9; Ontario, 1871 ***1823.15*** *p24*
Brickert, Matthaus; America, 1750 ***2856.30*** *p52*
Brickh, Lorenz; Port uncertain, 1746 ***2856.30*** *p52*
Brickhill, John; Virginia, 1667 ***6212.30*** *p36*
Brickin, Margarete; America, 1750 ***2856.30*** *p52*
Brickley, James 32; Ontario, 1871 ***1823.22*** *p16*
Brickley, John 40; Ontario, 1871 ***1823.22*** *p16*
Brickley, Julia 65; Ontario, 1871 ***1823.22*** *p16*
Brickman, A. E. 8; Ontario, 1861 ***2896.25*** *p29*
Brickman, A. M. 1; Ontario, 1861 ***2896.25*** *p42*
Brickman, A. M. 23; Ontario, 1861 ***2896.25*** *p42*
Brickman, Asa 19; Ontario, 1861 ***2896.25*** *p47*
Brickman, B. 18; Ontario, 1861 ***2896.25*** *p53*
Brickman, C. 8; Ontario, 1861 ***2896.25*** *p53*
Brickman, C. J. 31; Ontario, 1861 ***2896.25*** *p46*
Brickman, D. 32; Ontario, 1861 ***2896.25*** *p42*
Brickman, D. E. 5; Ontario, 1861 ***2896.25*** *p29*
Brickman, E. 31; Ontario, 1861 ***2896.25*** *p29*
Brickman, Edwin A. 7; Ontario, 1861 ***2896.25*** *p38*
Brickman, Eugenia 11; Ontario, 1861 ***2896.25*** *p38*
Brickman, F. 22; Ontario, 1861 ***2896.25*** *p47*
Brickman, F. E. 7; Ontario, 1861 ***2896.25*** *p29*
Brickman, Fanny 23; Ontario, 1861 ***2896.25*** *p50*
Brickman, H. B. 2; Ontario, 1861 ***2896.25*** *p47*
Brickman, H. V. 2; Ontario, 1861 ***2896.25*** *p50*
Brickman, Ida 3; Ontario, 1861 ***2896.25*** *p42*
Brickman, J. M. W. 15; Ontario, 1861 ***2896.25*** *p47*
Brickman, J. W. 3; Ontario, 1861 ***2896.25*** *p47*
Brickman, J. W. 5; Ontario, 1861 ***2896.25*** *p46*
Brickman, Jane A. 9; Ontario, 1861 ***2896.25*** *p38*
Brickman, Liza 16; Ontario, 1861 ***2896.25*** *p58*
Brickman, M. 44; Ontario, 1861 ***2896.25*** *p47*
Brickman, M. A. 10; Ontario, 1861 ***2896.25*** *p46*
Brickman, M. A. 13; Ontario, 1861 ***2896.25*** *p47*
Brickman, M. D. 8; Ontario, 1861 ***2896.25*** *p47*
Brickman, M. E. 9; Ontario, 1861 ***2896.25*** *p46*
Brickman, M. J. 23; Ontario, 1861 ***2896.25*** *p47*
Brickman, M. J. 36; Ontario, 1861 ***2896.25*** *p53*
Brickman, M. L. 11; Ontario, 1861 ***2896.25*** *p47*
Brickman, M. M. 12; Ontario, 1861 ***2896.25*** *p53*
Brickman, Mary A. 13; Ontario, 1861 ***2896.25*** *p38*
Brickman, N. J. 2; Ontario, 1861 ***2896.25*** *p46*
Brickman, R. 17; Ontario, 1861 ***2896.25*** *p53*
Brickman, R. W. 17; Ontario, 1861 ***2896.25*** *p47*
Brickman, Sarah 32; Ontario, 1861 ***2896.25*** *p38*
Brickman, Sophia 16; Ontario, 1861 ***2896.25*** *p53*
Brickman, W. A. S. 28; Ontario, 1861 ***2896.25*** *p42*
Brickman, W. B. 3; Ontario, 1861 ***2896.25*** *p29*
Brickman, W. F. 7; Ontario, 1861 ***2896.25*** *p46*
Brickman, William 17; Ontario, 1861 ***2896.25*** *p38*
Brickman, William 71; Ontario, 1861 ***2896.25*** *p42*
Brickman, William F. 4; Ontario, 1861 ***2896.25*** *p42*
Brickman, Wm A. 24; Ontario, 1861 ***2896.25*** *p48*
Bricks, Christifor 55; Ontario, 1871 ***1823.15*** *p24*
Brickstock, Roger 21; Maryland, 1775 ***1220.25*** *p102*
Brickstock, William 22; Maryland, 1775 ***1220.25*** *p103*
Brico, Leander 42; Ontario, 1871 ***1823.22*** *p16*
Bride, Mary 19; Ontario, 1871 ***1823.28*** *p10*
Briden, Barney; New York, 1840 ***8197.10*** *p154*
Bridge, Mr.; Quebec, 1857 ***9196.15*** *p25*
Bridge, Evelyn W.; Vermont, 1850-1905 ***5900.10*** *p598*
Bridge, John; Virginia, 1637 ***1224.1*** *p9*
Bridge, John 55; Ontario, 1871 ***1823.28*** *p10*
Bridge, Robt; Virginia, 1683 ***6212.30*** *p56*
Bridgeman, Bridget McGlynn; Vermont, 1822-1892 ***5900.10*** *p143*
Bridgeman, Edward J.; Vermont, 1845-1868 ***5900.10*** *p143*
Bridgeman, Helen M.; Vermont, 1844-1915 ***5900.10*** *p144*
Bridgeman, Johanna; Vermont, 1848-1866 ***5900.10*** *p143*
Bridgeman, John 70; Ontario, 1871 ***1823.28*** *p10*
Bridgeman, Mary; Vermont, 1854-1930 ***5900.10*** *p143*
Bridgeman, Maurice 40; Ontario, 1871 ***1823.28*** *p10*
Bridgeman, Michael; Vermont, 1814-1886 ***5900.10*** *p143*
Bridgeman, Michael; Vermont, 1856-1866 ***5900.10*** *p143*
Bridgeman, Thomas; Vermont, 1847-1867 ***5900.10*** *p143*
Bridgen, Charles 43; Ontario, 1871 ***1823.28*** *p10*
Bridgen, Thomas Bridgen; New Jersey, 1817 ***1224.3*** *p9*
Bridgens, William H.; New York, 1838 ***8197.10*** *p111*
Bridger, Benjamin; Quebec, 1858 ***9196.15*** *p31*
Bridger, James; Quebec, 1858 ***9196.15*** *p31*
Bridgers, J. A.; Quebec, 1856 ***9196.15*** *p9*
Bridges, Daniel 25; Jamaica, 1774 ***1220.25*** *p20*
Bridges, James; Maryland, 1666 ***2524.55*** *p32*
Bridges, John; New York, 1712 ***1224.2*** *p14*
Bridges, John; Virginia, 1637 ***1224.1*** *p9*
Bridges, John 53; Ontario, 1871 ***1823.28*** *p10*
Bridges, Robert; Pennsylvania, 1777 ***4629.10*** *p8*
Bridges, Robt; Virginia, 1663 ***6212.30*** *p4*
Bridges, Thomas 45; Ontario, 1871 ***1823.15*** *p24*
Bridges, William; New York, 1807 ***8197.10*** *p34*
Bridges, William; Virginia, 1665-1666 ***6212.30*** *p23*
Bridges, William 40; Ontario, 1871 ***1823.22*** *p16*
Bridgnorth, Mary; Virginia, 1663 ***6212.30*** *p1*
Bridigan, Christopher 79; Ontario, 1871 ***1823.15*** *p24*
Bridigan, Dorithy 82; Ontario, 1871 ***1823.15*** *p24*
Bridigan, Luthrink 56; Ontario, 1871 ***1823.15*** *p24*
Bridle, John; New York, 1827 ***8197.10*** *p338*
Bridloss, Mr.; Quebec, 1856 ***9196.15*** *p6*
Bridon, John 36; Ontario, 1871 ***1823.15*** *p24*
Bridwell, Mary; Maryland, 1680 ***2524.55*** *p33*
Briegel, Jacob; America, 1788 ***2856.30*** *p52*
Briegel, Jacob; Port uncertain, 1787 ***2856.30*** *p52*
Briegel, Michael; America, 1788 ***2856.30*** *p52*
Briegel, Michael; Port uncertain, 1787 ***2856.30*** *p52*
Brielmayer, Maria; Port uncertain, 1781 ***2856.30*** *p52*
Brien, Michael 22; Quebec, 1848 ***1825.45*** *p28*
Briens, Henery 58; Ontario, 1871 ***1823.28*** *p10*
Brier, Anne 9; Ontario, 1861 ***2896.28*** *p45*
Brier, Eliza 5; Ontario, 1861 ***2896.28*** *p45*
Brier, George 13; Ontario, 1861 ***2896.28*** *p45*
Brier, Hariet 15; Ontario, 1861 ***2896.28*** *p45*
Brier, John 35; Ontario, 1861 ***2896.28*** *p45*
Brier, Selina 33; Ontario, 1861 ***2896.28*** *p45*
Brierly, Thomas; New York, 1839 ***8197.10*** *p213*
Bries, Philipp; Port uncertain, 1777 ***2856.30*** *p53*
Briese, August 28; Ontario, 1871 ***1823.28*** *p10*
Briesemeister, William 46; Ontario, 1871 ***1823.28*** *p10*
Briesley, Edward; Maryland, 1649 ***2524.55*** *p33*
Briffith, Mrs.; Quebec, 1857 ***9196.15*** *p24*

Brigel, Maria Barbara; Port uncertain, 1752 ***2856.30*** *p53*
Briggs, David 37; New York, 1815-1820 ***8197.10*** *p207*
Briggs, E. H. 2; Ontario, 1861 ***2896.25*** *p1*
Briggs, Ephraim 43; Ontario, 1871 ***1823.15*** *p24*
Briggs, Frances 30; Ontario, 1861 ***2896.25*** *p1*
Briggs, Jane; Maryland, 1665 ***2524.55*** *p33*
Briggs, John; Maryland, 1673 ***2524.55*** *p33*
Briggs, John 21; Ontario, 1871 ***1823.22*** *p16*
Briggs, John 29; Maryland, 1775 ***1220.25*** *p106*
Briggs, John 59; Ontario, 1871 ***1823.22*** *p16*
Briggs, John R.; New York, 1838 ***8197.10*** *p212*
Briggs, John R.; New York, 1840 ***8197.10*** *p144*
Briggs, Martha E.; Vermont, 1855-1900 ***5900.10*** *p311*
Briggs, Richard; Virginia, 1701 ***1224.2*** *p14*
Briggs, Richard 25; Philadelphia, 1774 ***1220.25*** *p80*
Briggs, Robert; Antigua (Antego), 1841 ***1640.13*** *p12*
Briggs, Robert; Savannah, Georgia, 1768 ***1640.10*** *p14*
Briggs, Samuel; Georgia, 1775 ***1640.10*** *p14*
Briggs, Samuel 28; Georgia, 1775 ***1220.25*** *p124*
Briggs, Sarah; Vermont, 1863-1918 ***5900.10*** *p286*
Briggs, Thomas; Ontario, 1900 ***1640.13*** *p12*
Briggs, William; New York, 1838 ***8197.10*** *p213*
Brigham, George; Pennsylvania, 1827 ***6058.10*** *p9*
Brigham, John 24; Maryland, 1774 ***1220.25*** *p74*
Brigham, John 26; Ontario, 1871 ***1823.15*** *p24*
Brigham, John Harker 40; New York, 1835-1840 ***8197.10*** *p154*
Brighouse, James; Virginia, 1683 ***1224.1*** *p9*
Bright, Ann *SEE* Bright, Francis
Bright, Ann; Maryland, 1658 ***2524.55*** *p33*
Bright, Charles 31; Ontario, 1871 ***1823.22*** *p16*
Bright, Eliza; Virginia, 1666 ***6212.30*** *p25*
Bright, Francis; Maryland, 1651 ***2524.55*** *p33*
With wife
Son: Thomas
Bright, Francis; Maryland, 1658 ***2524.55*** *p33*
Wife: Ann
Bright, Jacob; Pennsylvania, 1777 ***4629.10*** *p8*
Bright, John; Maryland, 1682 ***2524.55*** *p33*
Bright, Thomas *SEE* Bright, Francis
Bright, William; Maryland, 1682 ***2524.55*** *p33*
Bright, William; Portland, Maine, 1857 ***9196.15*** *p13*
Brighton, Barney; New York, 1840 ***8197.10*** *p154*
Brightwell, Charles; Virginia, 1660 ***1224.1*** *p9*
Brighy, Thomas 45; Ontario, 1871 ***1823.22*** *p16*
Brigin, Cath. Barbara; Port uncertain, 1747 ***2856.30*** *p53*
Brigs, George; Pennsylvania, 1777 ***4629.10*** *p14*
Brigs, Rebecca 45; Ontario, 1871 ***1823.15*** *p24*
Brigs, Thomas 28; Nova Scotia, 1774 ***1220.25*** *p13*
Brikowski, Mary; Maryland, 1910 ***3259.35*** *p6*
Brill, Andreas; Port uncertain, 1755 ***2856.30*** *p53*
Brimacomb, William 68; Ontario, 1871 ***1823.22*** *p16*
Brimecombe, John 27; Ontario, 1871 ***1823.15*** *p25*
Brimicomb, Asarias 54; Ontario, 1871 ***1823.15*** *p25*
Brimicomb, John 56; Ontario, 1871 ***1823.15*** *p25*
Brimmerdge, Joseph; Maryland, 1665 ***2524.55*** *p31*
Brimscombe, George 35; Ontario, 1871 ***1823.22*** *p16*
Brimstead, William 23; Ontario, 1861 ***2896.27*** *p31*
Brimstin, James 36; Ontario, 1871 ***1823.28*** *p10*
Brind, Elizabeth 20; Maryland, 1775 ***1220.25*** *p116*
Brinder, Robert 32; Virginia, 1774 ***1220.25*** *p93*
Brindle, James, Sr. 59; Ontario, 1871 ***1823.28*** *p10*
Brindley, John; New York, 1825 ***8197.10*** *p209*
Brindly, John 61; Ontario, 1871 ***1823.15*** *p25*
Brine, Joseph 52; Ontario, 1871 ***1823.15*** *p25*
Bringes, John; New York, 1807 ***8197.10*** *p327*
Bringfortt, Bernard; Port uncertain, 1786 ***2856.30*** *p53*
Bringhurst, Samuel; Pennsylvania, 1786 ***4629.10*** *p54*
Brink, John H.; Maryland, 1910 ***3259.35*** *p6*
Brink, Rose; Maryland, 1910 ***3259.35*** *p6*
Brinkley, William; Rhode Island, 1781 ***1224.2*** *p14*
Brinkman, William 52; Ontario, 1871 ***1823.15*** *p25*
Brinkwell, William 22; Maryland, 1774 ***1220.25*** *p71*
Brinkworth, Samuel; New York, 1840 ***8197.10*** *p214*
Brinley, Elizabeth; Boston, n.d. ***1224.2*** *p14*
Brinley, Francis; Boston, 1721 ***1224.2*** *p14*
Brinley, Grissell; New England, 1661 ***1224.1*** *p9*
Brinn, Amelia; Vermont, 1855-1930 ***5900.10*** *p302*
Brinn, John 84; Vermont, 1904 ***5900.10*** *p301*
Brinn, Sarah E. 24; Vermont, 1884 ***5900.10*** *p302*
Brinn, Sarah R. 86; Vermont, 1914 ***5900.10*** *p301*
Brinn, Victor; Vermont, 1855-1941 ***5900.10*** *p302*
Brinnington, Jacob; Maryland, 1659 ***2524.55*** *p33*
Brinton, John 50; Ontario, 1871 ***1823.22*** *p16*
Brinton, Philip 52; Ontario, 1871 ***1823.22*** *p16*
Brinton, Thomas 26; Ontario, 1871 ***1823.22*** *p16*
Brinton, William 52; Ontario, 1871 ***1823.22*** *p17*
Brinz, Margarete; Port uncertain, 1739 ***2856.30*** *p31*
Briody, Nicholas; New York, 1838 ***8197.10*** *p110*
Brisbane, Robert; Georgia, 1764 ***1640.10*** *p14*
Brisbin, H. F.; Ontario, 1861 ***2896.27*** *p4*
Brisbin, Henery 55; Ontario, 1861 ***2896.27*** *p11*
Brisbin, Mary 42; Ontario, 1861 ***2896.27*** *p11*
Brisbin, Patric 82; Ontario, 1861 ***2896.27*** *p11*
Brisborne, John; Maryland, 1681 ***2524.55*** *p33*
Brisch, Engelhart; New York, 1837 ***8197.10*** *p85*
Brisco, Brian 37; Ontario, 1871 ***1823.28*** *p10*
Brisco, James 64; Ontario, 1871 ***1823.28*** *p10*
Brisco, William 62; Ontario, 1871 ***1823.28*** *p10*
Briscoe, Master; Quebec, 1857 ***9196.15*** *p20*
Briscoe, Miss; Quebec, 1857 ***9196.15*** *p20*
Briscoe, Mrs.; Quebec, 1857 ***9196.15*** *p20*
Briscoe, John; Virginia, 1716 ***1224.2*** *p14*
Briscoe, Miss S.; Quebec, 1857 ***9196.15*** *p20*
Brish, Adam; New York, 1838 ***8197.10*** *p111*
Brisky, August 34; Ontario, 1871 ***1823.28*** *p10*
Brislan, Patrick; New York, 1807 ***8197.10*** *p35*
Brisler, Christe 53; Ontario, 1871 ***1823.28*** *p10*
Brisley, John 28; Maryland, 1774 ***1220.25*** *p5*
Brislin, Bridget T.; Vermont, 1822-1868 ***5900.10*** *p447*
Brislin, Catherine Conerton; Vermont, 1845-1914 ***5900.10*** *p431*
Brislin, Henry E.; Vermont, 1853-1880 ***5900.10*** *p447*
Brislin, John W.; Vermont, 1845-1928 ***5900.10*** *p431*
Brislin, Margaret; Vermont, 1851-1872 ***5900.10*** *p447*
Brislin, Michael; Vermont, 1826-1907 ***5900.10*** *p436*
Brislin, Patrick; Vermont, 1820-1868 ***5900.10*** *p447*
Brissel, John; New York, 1840 ***8197.10*** *p155*
Brissel, Philip; New York, 1838 ***8197.10*** *p110*
Brisson, John 40; Ontario, 1871 ***1823.15*** *p25*
Bristoe, Edw; Virginia, 1665-1666 ***6212.30*** *p21*
Bristoe, Margret; Virginia, 1666 ***6212.30*** *p29*
Bristoe, Mary; Maryland, 1665 ***2524.55*** *p33*
Bristol, Caroline 30; Ontario, 1861 ***2896.27*** *p18*
Bristol, Jacob; Pennsylvania, 1779 ***4629.10*** *p40*
Bristol, Joseph; New York, 1764 ***1224.2*** *p14*
Bristol, Thomas; Pennsylvania, 1777 ***4629.10*** *p27*
Bristol, Thomas; Pennsylvania, 1779 ***4629.10*** *p41*
Bristoll, Jno; Virginia, 1665-1666 ***6212.30*** *p21*
Bristow, Mr.; Quebec, 1857 ***9196.15*** *p21*
Bristow, Robert; Virginia, 1755 ***1224.2*** *p14*
Britewell, Richard; Maryland, 1672 ***2524.55*** *p33*
Britsch, Tobias; Port uncertain, 1751 ***2856.30*** *p53*
Brittain, Alfred; New York, 1839 ***8197.10*** *p128*
Brittain, John; Maryland, 1661 ***2524.55*** *p177*
Brittain, William; Maryland, 1663 ***2524.55*** *p33*
Brittain, William; New York, 1840 ***8197.10*** *p214*
Brittan, Alfred 34; Ontario, 1871 ***1823.28*** *p10*
Brittan, Stephen; Maryland, 1661 ***2524.55*** *p33*
Brittan, Thomas; Maryland, 1669 ***2524.55*** *p33*
Britten, John; New York, 1807 ***8197.10*** *p34*
Britten, John; Virginia, 1637 ***1224.1*** *p9*
Brittingham, Wm; Virginia, 1663-1664 ***6212.30*** *p5*
Brittius, Mrs. Jacob; America, 1749 ***2856.30*** *p53*
With 4 children
Brittle, Joseph 28; Maryland, 1774 ***1220.25*** *p52*
Brittlebank, Elizabeth 21; Baltimore, 1775 ***1220.25*** *p119*
Britton, Christopher; New York, 1802 ***8197.10*** *p18*
Britton, James; New York, 1803 ***8197.10*** *p10*
Britton, John; Maryland, 1668 ***2524.55*** *p33*
Britton, John; New York, 1827 ***8197.10*** *p343*
Britton, Richard; Maryland, 1672 ***2524.55*** *p33*
Britton, Robert 60; Ontario, 1871 ***1823.15*** *p25*
Britton, Samuel; Pennsylvania, 1779 ***4629.10*** *p41*
Britz, Ulrich; America, 1749 ***2856.30*** *p53*
With wife & 5 children
Britzius, Jacob; America, 1749 ***2856.30*** *p53*
Britzius, Johann Adam; America, 1751 ***2856.30*** *p53*
Britzius, Johann Adam; America, 1758 ***2856.30*** *p53*
Broach, John 54; Ontario, 1871 ***1823.15*** *p25*
Broad, Amos; New York, 1810 ***8197.10*** *p56*
Broad, Isabel; Virginia, 1690-1691 ***6212.30*** *p59*
Broad, James 85; Ontario, 1871 ***1823.28*** *p10*
Broad, Jane; Virginia, 1671-1672 ***6212.30*** *p46*
Broad, Nich; Virginia, 1672 ***6212.30*** *p50*
Broad, Sarah; Maryland, 1664 ***2524.55*** *p33*
Broad, Thomas 36; Ontario, 1871 ***1823.15*** *p25*
Broad, Walter; Virginia, 1672 ***6212.30*** *p51*
Broadbent, Mr.; Quebec, 1856 ***9196.15*** *p10*
Broadbent, Ben.; New York, 1827 ***8197.10*** *p211*
Broadbent, Edward; New Orleans, 1851 ***1224.3*** *p9*
Broadbent, Henry 20; Ontario, 1871 ***1823.28*** *p10*
Broadbent, William 60; Ontario, 1871 ***1823.15*** *p25*
Broadbent, William, Jr. 29; Ontario, 1871 ***1823.15*** *p25*
Broader, John; Maryland, 1665 ***2524.55*** *p10*
Broades, William; Pennsylvania, 1779 ***4629.10*** *p37*
Broadfield, Richard 34; America, 1774 ***1220.25*** *p36*
Broadfoot, Alex 71; Ontario, 1871 ***1823.15*** *p25*
Broadfoot, James 68; Ontario, 1871 ***1823.15*** *p25*
Broadfoot, John; Pennsylvania, 1806 ***6058.10*** *p1*
Broadfoot, John 75; Ontario, 1871 ***1823.15*** *p25*
Broadfoot, William; Pennsylvania, 1806 ***6058.10*** *p1*
Broadhead, Dan'l, Jr.; Pennsylvania, 1777 ***4629.10*** *p30*
Broadhurst, Dorothy; Charleston, South Carolina, 1806 ***1224.3*** *p9*
Broadhurst, Hugh; Virginia, 1659 ***1224.1*** *p9*
Broadhurst, John; Virginia, 1701 ***1224.2*** *p14*
Broadlay, Francis; Maryland, 1681 ***2524.55*** *p33*
Broadley, Enos 27; Ontario, 1871 ***1823.28*** *p10*
Broadnax, Tho; Virginia, 1665-1666 ***6212.30*** *p23*
Broadnock, Edward; Maryland, 1666 ***2524.55*** *p33*
Wife: Jane
Broadnock, Jane *SEE* Broadnock, Edward
Broadnock, Jane; Maryland, 1666 ***2524.55*** *p33*
Broadnock, Tho; Virginia, 1664 ***6212.30*** *p14*
Broadribb, John; Maryland, 1687 ***1224.1*** *p9*
Broadson, Bridget; Mobile, Alabama, 1821-1845 ***1640.10*** *p14*
Broadway, Edwd; Virginia, 1671 ***6212.30*** *p43*
Broadway, Jean; Virginia, 1667 ***6212.30*** *p36*
Broadway, Jno; Virginia, 1666 ***6212.30*** *p30*
Broadway, Wm; Virginia, 1668-1669 ***6212.30*** *p41*
Broales, William 24; Ontario, 1871 ***1823.15*** *p25*
Broatch, James 52; Ontario, 1871 ***1823.22*** *p17*
Brobert, Kolumban; New York, 1840 ***8197.10*** *p154*
Brocas, Richard; North America, 1788 ***1224.2*** *p14*
Brocas, Simon; Charleston, South Carolina, 1792 ***4629.10*** *p73*
Brocas, Thomas; New England, 1751 ***1224.2*** *p14*
Brochauski, August; Maryland, 1910 ***3259.35*** *p6*
Brochaven, Jacob 65; Kansas, 1876-1910 ***9079.10*** *p11*
Brochaven, Mary M. 63; Kansas, 1876-1910 ***9079.10*** *p11*
Brochewisno, Michel; Maryland, 1910 ***3259.35*** *p6*
Brocinskey, Joseph; Maryland, 1910 ***3259.35*** *p6*
Brock, Mrs.; Quebec, 1857 ***9196.15*** *p21*
Brock, Andrew; Georgia, 1698 ***1640.13*** *p12*
Brock, Elizabeth; Dedham, Massachusetts, 1647 ***1224.1*** *p59*
Brock, Emanuel 40; Ontario, 1871 ***1823.15*** *p25*
Brock, James; Savannah, Georgia, 1775 ***1640.10*** *p14*
Brock, John 55; Ontario, 1871 ***1823.22*** *p17*
Brock, Rebecca; New York, 1840 ***8197.10*** *p144*
Brock, Robert 35; Ontario, 1871 ***1823.22*** *p17*
Brock, Samuel 30; Ontario, 1871 ***1823.15*** *p25*
Brock, Thomas 34; Ontario, 1871 ***1823.28*** *p10*
Brock, Thomas 43; Ontario, 1871 ***1823.22*** *p17*
Brock, William 23; Virginia, 1774 ***1220.25*** *p87*
Brock, William 48; Ontario, 1871 ***1823.15*** *p25*
Brockas, Clare *SEE* Brockas, George
Brockas, Elizabeth *SEE* Brockas, George
Brockas, George; Maryland, 1667 ***2524.55*** *p33*
Relative: William
Relative: Jane
Relative: Elizabeth
Relative: Clare
Relative: Mary
Relative: Susanna
Brockas, Jane *SEE* Brockas, George
Brockas, Mary *SEE* Brockas, George
Brockas, Susanna *SEE* Brockas, George
Brockas, William *SEE* Brockas, George
Brocke, James; Virginia, 1665-1666 ***6212.30*** *p21*
Brockett, Bryan; Maryland, 1669 ***2524.55*** *p33*
Brockett, William; Maryland, 1679 ***2524.55*** *p33*
Brockhall, James; Maryland, 1675 ***2524.55*** *p33*
Brockhall, John; South Carolina, 1742 ***1224.2*** *p14*
Brockhouse, Edw; Virginia, 1672 ***6212.30*** *p50*
Brocki, Michael; Maryland, 1910 ***3259.35*** *p7*
Brockley, Arthur; Virginia, 1665-1666 ***6212.30*** *p24*
Brockman, Henry; Maryland, 1674 ***2524.55*** *p33*
Brockney, Florence 73; Vermont, 1924 ***5900.10*** *p139*
Brockney, Joseph 76; Vermont, 1920 ***5900.10*** *p139*
Brockwell, Nathaniel; Pennsylvania, 1783 ***1224.2*** *p14*
Brocky, William; Maryland, 1910 ***3259.35*** *p7*
Brocosske, Julian; Maryland, 1910 ***3259.35*** *p7*
Broczkowski, Juljan; Maryland, 1910 ***3259.35*** *p7*
Broczkowsky, Antonie; Maryland, 1910 ***3259.35*** *p7*
Broda, Stephan; Maryland, 1910 ***3259.35*** *p7*
Brodbeck, Friedrich; Port uncertain, 1773 ***2856.30*** *p53*
Brodbeck, Maria Susanna; Port uncertain, 1755 ***2856.30*** *p53*
Broder, Mary; Maryland, 1658 ***2524.55*** *p34*
Broder, Philipp; Port uncertain, 1770 ***2856.30*** *p53*
With wife & 6 children
Broderick, Abigail; Vermont, 1830-1903 ***5900.10*** *p77*
Broderick, Bridget; Vermont, 1820-1903 ***5900.10*** *p206*
Broderick, Catherine; Vermont, 1816-1899 ***5900.10*** *p340*
Broderick, Edward 88; Vermont, 1878 ***5900.10*** *p543*
Broderick, Ellen 60; Vermont, 1898 ***5900.10*** *p74*
Broderick, Ellen Holden; Vermont, 1844-1894 ***5900.10*** *p61*
Broderick, Ellen Welch; Vermont, 1839-1913 ***5900.10*** *p596*
Broderick, George 43; Ontario, 1871 ***1823.15*** *p25*
Broderick, Honora 76; Vermont, 1866 ***5900.10*** *p543*
Broderick, J. W. 32; Ontario, 1871 ***1823.15*** *p25*
Broderick, James; Canada, 1756-1760 ***4628.40*** *p46*
Broderick, James; Vermont, 1833-1919 ***5900.10*** *p596*

Broderick, John; Vermont, 1789-1869 ***5900.10*** *p202*
Broderick, John W.; Vermont, 1847-1907 ***5900.10*** *p61*
Broderick, Michael 93; Vermont, 1869 ***5900.10*** *p202*
Broderick, Nich; Virginia, 1664 ***6212.30*** *p8*
Broderick, Robert 51; Ontario, 1871 ***1823.15*** *p25*
Broderick, Robert 87; Ontario, 1871 ***1823.15*** *p25*
Brodffeck, Maria Susanna; Port uncertain, 1755 ***2856.30*** *p53*
Brodhagen, August 32; Ontario, 1871 ***1823.15*** *p25*
Brodie, Charles 42; Ontario, 1871 ***1823.15*** *p25*
Brodie, David 75; Ontario, 1871 ***1823.22*** *p17*
Brodie, Francis; Georgia, 1698 ***1640.13*** *p12*
Brodie, James; New York, 1828 ***8197.10*** *p298*
Brodie, James; New York, 1830 ***8197.10*** *p360*
Brodie, James Arthur; Colorado, 1891 ***1640.13*** *p12*
Brodie, John; New York, 1819 ***8197.10*** *p207*
Brodie, John; Savannah, Georgia, 1737 ***1640.10*** *p15*
Brodie, John, Jr.; New York, 1831 ***8197.10*** *p366*
Brodie, Peter; New York, 1840 ***8197.10*** *p213*
Brodie, Rebecca 81; Ontario, 1871 ***1823.28*** *p10*
Brodie, William; Trinidad, 1883 ***1640.13*** *p12*
Brodowski, John; Maryland, 1910 ***3259.35*** *p7*
Brodrick, Dennis; New York, 1839 ***8197.10*** *p213*
Broell, Sebastian; Port uncertain, 1755 ***2856.30*** *p53*
Broffee, Edward 23; America, 1774 ***1220.25*** *p36*
Brogan, John 55; Vermont, 1863 ***5900.10*** *p238*
Brogan, Mathew; New York, 1834 ***8197.10*** *p372*
Brogden, George 22; Ontario, 1871 ***1823.15*** *p25*
Brogden, Richard, II; Maryland, 1669 ***2524.55*** *p33*
Brogden, Thomas 21; Maryland, 1775 ***1220.25*** *p111*
Brogen, Corne; Maryland, 1681 ***2524.55*** *p33*
Broguehen, Cornelius; Maryland, 1682 ***2524.55*** *p33*
Brohan, Bridget; Vermont, 1854-1903 ***5900.10*** *p418*
Brohan, Mary Caney; Vermont, 1826-1889 ***5900.10*** *p418*
Brohan, Patrick; Vermont, 1811-1901 ***5900.10*** *p418*
Broharts, Fredrick 44; Ontario, 1871 ***1823.28*** *p10*
Broheil, Kolumban; New York, 1840 ***8197.10*** *p154*
Brohert, Kolumban; New York, 1840 ***8197.10*** *p154*
Brohon, . . .; Vermont, 1847 ***5900.10*** *p26*
Brohy, Dennis; Maryland, 1678 ***2524.55*** *p34*
Brokenshire, Samuel 46; Ontario, 1871 ***1823.15*** *p25*
Brokenshire, Thomas 36; Ontario, 1871 ***1823.22*** *p17*
Brokey, Charles; Georgia, 1775 ***1640.10*** *p15*
Brokey, Charles 25; Georgia, 1775 ***1220.25*** *p125*
Brokle, John; Maryland, 1682 ***2524.55*** *p33*
Brokowsk, . . .; Maryland, 1910 ***3259.35*** *p7*
Brokowsky, Valentin; Maryland, 1910 ***3259.35*** *p7*
Brokshaw, James; Maryland, 1675 ***2524.55*** *p33*
Brokshaw, Mary; Maryland, 1675 ***2524.55*** *p33*
Bromall, Mrs.; Maryland, 1654 ***2524.55*** *p34*
Bromall, William; Maryland, 1654 ***2524.55*** *p34*
Brombacher, Anna Catharina; Port uncertain, 1741 ***2856.30*** *p53*
Brombacher, Anna Maria; Port uncertain, 1756 ***2856.30*** *p53*
Brombacher, Catharina; Port uncertain, 1792 ***2856.30*** *p53*
Brome, John; Maryland, 1668 ***2524.55*** *p34*
Bromell, Samuel; New York, 1815 ***8197.10*** *p55*
Bromer, Joseph; Maryland, 1910 ***3259.35*** *p7*
Bromer, Stanislaw; Maryland, 1910 ***3259.35*** *p7*
Bromfeild, Christian; Maryland, 1666 ***2524.55*** *p34*
Bromfeild, John; Maryland, 1651 ***2524.55*** *p34*
Bromfeild, John; Maryland, 1662 ***2524.55*** *p34*
Bromfeild, Margarett; Maryland, 1670 ***2524.55*** *p34*
Bromfield, J. W. 19; Ontario, 1871 ***1823.28*** *p10*
Bromfield, James; Boston, 1724 ***1224.2*** *p15*
Bromfield, Samuel 19; Ontario, 1871 ***1823.28*** *p10*
Bromfield, Thomas; Boston, 1787 ***1224.2*** *p15*
Bromfield, Thomas; Boston, 1787 ***1224.3*** *p9*
Bromfield, William; Virginia, 1702 ***1224.2*** *p15*
Bromily, James; New York, 1838 ***8197.10*** *p110*
Bromkin, Obediah; Virginia, 1679-1680 ***6212.30*** *p54*
Bromlee, Elizabeth 40; Ontario, 1871 ***1823.28*** *p10*
Bromley, Dury; New York, 1802 ***8197.10*** *p18*
Bromley, Edwin 20; Ontario, 1871 ***1823.28*** *p10*
Bromley, Henry; America, 1756 ***1224.2*** *p15*
Bromley, Henry 59; Ontario, 1871 ***1823.28*** *p10*
Bromley, James; Vermont, 1850-1920 ***5900.10*** *p464*
Bromley, James 47; Ontario, 1871 ***1823.28*** *p10*
Bromley, James 52; Ontario, 1871 ***1823.28*** *p10*
Bromley, James 63; Ontario, 1871 ***1823.28*** *p10*
Bromley, Joseph 22; Virginia, 1774 ***1220.25*** *p87*
Bromley, Matilda Dillon; Vermont, 1843-1918 ***5900.10*** *p464*
Brommer, Apollonia; America, 1752 ***2856.30*** *p53*
With 4 children
Bromrigg, Christopher; Maryland, 1651 ***2524.55*** *p34*
Bromsgrove, Jno; Virginia, 1674 ***6212.30*** *p52*
Bronatowski, Boleslaw; Maryland, 1910 ***3259.35*** *p7*
Bronecky, Pawel; Maryland, 1910 ***3259.35*** *p7*
Bronell, Sherman 17; Alaska, 1917 ***9196.1*** *p7*
Bronell, Sherman 17; Yukon, 1917 ***9196.1*** *p7*
Brongh, Mary 32; Ontario, 1871 ***1823.15*** *p25*
Bronikowsky, Tomasz; Maryland, 1910 ***3259.35*** *p7*
Bronn, Philipp; Port uncertain, 1785 ***2856.30*** *p53*
Bronner, Magdalena; Port uncertain, 1752 ***2856.30*** *p53*
Bronner, Maria Barbara; America, 1754 ***2856.30*** *p53*
Bronseniski, Michael; Maryland, 1910 ***3259.35*** *p7*
Brooder, Mary; Maryland, 1658 ***2524.55*** *p34*
Broofe, Thomas; Maryland, 1672 ***2524.55*** *p34*
Brook, Anne; Maryland, 1650 ***2524.55*** *p34*
Brook, James; Georgia, 1775 ***1640.10*** *p15*
Brook, James 60; Ontario, 1871 ***1823.15*** *p26*
Brook, Lawrance 21; Maryland, 1774 ***1220.25*** *p46*
Brook, Robert; Maryland, 1658 ***2524.55*** *p34*
With family
Brook, Robert 50; Ontario, 1871 ***1823.22*** *p17*
Brook, Robt.; Maryland, 1649 ***2524.55*** *p34*
With wife & 8 sons
Brook, Thomas; Maryland, 1656 ***2524.55*** *p34*
Brookan, Michael; New York, New York, 1863 ***3437.14*** *p166*
Brooke, Ann *SEE* Brooke, Sarah
Brooke, Ann; Maryland, 1676 ***2524.55*** *p34*
Brooke, Edward; Maryland, 1671 ***2524.55*** *p34*
Brooke, Elliner Jenkins *SEE* Brooke, Sarah
Brooke, Frances; Maryland, 1676 ***2524.55*** *p34*
Brooke, Francis; Maryland, 1676 ***2524.55*** *p34*
Brooke, Henry; Pennsylvania, 1737 ***1224.2*** *p15*
Brooke, James; Virginia, 1664 ***6212.30*** *p13*
Brooke, Mary *SEE* Brooke, Sarah
Brooke, Paulin; Virginia, 1748 ***1224.2*** *p15*
Brooke, Ricey; Virginia, 1740 ***1224.2*** *p15*
Brooke, Sarah; Maryland, 1667 ***2524.55*** *p34*
Daughter: Mary
Daughter: Ann
Daughter: Elliner Jenkins
Brooke, Sarah 21; Maryland, 1775 ***1220.25*** *p108*
Brooke, William; Maryland, 1674 ***2524.55*** *p34*
Brooker, Ann; Maryland, 1676 ***2524.55*** *p34*
Brooker, Joanna; Boston, 1763 ***1224.2*** *p15*
Brookes, Anne; Maryland, 1650 ***2524.55*** *p34*
Brookes, Edward; Virginia, 1666 ***6212.30*** *p26*
Brookes, Frances; Maryland, 1667 ***2524.55*** *p34*
Brookes, Henry; Maryland, 1640 ***2524.55*** *p34*
Brookes, Humphery; Virginia, 1664 ***6212.30*** *p14*
Brookes, James 27; Maryland, 1773-1774 ***1220.25*** *p33*
Brookes, James 51; Ontario, 1861 ***2896.25*** *p8*
Brookes, Jno; Virginia, 1674 ***6212.30*** *p52*
Brookes, John; Maryland, 1672 ***2524.55*** *p34*
Brookes, Joshua; New York, 1803 ***8197.10*** *p11*
Brookes, Mildred; Virginia, 1748 ***1224.2*** *p15*
Brookes, Samuel; Dorchester, Massachusetts, 1758 ***1224.2*** *p15*
Brookes, Sarah; Virginia, 1674-1675 ***6212.30*** *p53*
Brookes, Sisley; Virginia, 1664 ***6212.30*** *p6*
Brookes, Tho; Virginia, 1673 ***6212.30*** *p51*
Brookes, William; Maryland, 1668 ***2524.55*** *p110*
Brookes, William 15; Philadelphia, 1774 ***1220.25*** *p67*
Brookesbancke, Isaac; Died enroute, 1675 ***1224.1*** *p9*
Brookeshaw, James; Maryland, 1674 ***2524.55*** *p34*
Brookin, Michaell; Virginia, 1671-1672 ***6212.30*** *p47*
Brookman, Casper; New York, 1840 ***8197.10*** *p145*
Brooks, Mr.; Quebec, 1858 ***9196.15*** *p45*
Brooks, Mrs.; Maryland, 1654 ***2524.55*** *p34*
Brooks, Mrs.; Quebec, 1857 ***9196.15*** *p14*
Brooks, Mrs.; Quebec, 1858 ***9196.15*** *p45*
Brooks, A. C. 8; Ontario, 1861 ***2896.25*** *p52*
Brooks, A. L. 9; Ontario, 1861 ***2896.25*** *p44*
Brooks, A. S. 3; Ontario, 1861 ***2896.25*** *p44*
Brooks, Alice; Quebec, 1858 ***9196.15*** *p45*
Brooks, Amanda 11; Ontario, 1861 ***2896.25*** *p14*
Brooks, Ann 32; New York, 1774 ***1220.25*** *p26*
Brooks, Ann 59; Ontario, 1871 ***1823.15*** *p26*
Brooks, Benj'n 15; Ontario, 1861 ***2896.26*** *p22*
Brooks, Bowyer; Pennsylvania, 1777 ***4629.10*** *p25*
Brooks, C. 12; Ontario, 1861 ***2896.25*** *p44*
Brooks, C. E. 11; Ontario, 1861 ***2896.25*** *p52*
Brooks, Catharine 55; Ontario, 1871 ***1823.22*** *p17*
Brooks, Catherine 49; Ontario, 1861 ***2896.25*** *p14*
Brooks, Catherine 65; Ontario, 1861 ***2896.25*** *p52*
Brooks, Charles 9; Ontario, 1861 ***2896.25*** *p14*
Brooks, Charles 70; Ontario, 1871 ***1823.15*** *p26*
Brooks, Chauncey 36; Ontario, 1861 ***2896.25*** *p52*
Brooks, Content 30; Ontario, 1861 ***2896.25*** *p44*
Brooks, David 6; Ontario, 1861 ***2896.25*** *p14*
Brooks, David 75; Ontario, 1861 ***2896.25*** *p52*
Brooks, David G.; Vermont, 1808-1880 ***5900.10*** *p500*
Brooks, David H. 56; Ontario, 1871 ***1823.15*** *p26*
Brooks, E. C. 1; Ontario, 1861 ***2896.25*** *p52*
Brooks, Euseba Conner 79; Vermont, 1887 ***5900.10*** *p500*
Brooks, Fannie 2; Ontario, 1861 ***2896.28*** *p36*
Brooks, Francis 17; Philadelphia, 1774 ***1220.25*** *p67*
Brooks, George; Maryland, 1910 ***3259.35*** *p7*
Brooks, George 15; Baltimore, 1775 ***1220.25*** *p119*
Brooks, Henry; Maryland, 1640 ***2524.55*** *p34*
Brooks, Henry 23; Ontario, 1861 ***2896.25*** *p14*
Brooks, Hugh 60; Ontario, 1871 ***1823.15*** *p26*
Brooks, James 22; Baltimore, 1775 ***1220.25*** *p117*
Brooks, James 55; Ontario, 1871 ***1823.15*** *p26*
Brooks, Jane 32; Ontario, 1861 ***2896.25*** *p52*
Brooks, John; Maryland, 1667 ***2524.55*** *p207*
Brooks, John; Virginia, 1684 ***1224.1*** *p9*
Brooks, John 52; Ontario, 1871 ***1823.15*** *p26*
Brooks, John 65; Ontario, 1871 ***1823.22*** *p17*
Brooks, John A. 16; Ontario, 1861 ***2896.25*** *p14*
Brooks, Margaret 19; Ontario, 1861 ***2896.25*** *p14*
Brooks, Martha 18; Ontario, 1861 ***2896.25*** *p14*
Brooks, Mary 21; Georgia, 1774 ***1220.25*** *p48*
Brooks, Mary 24; Ontario, 1871 ***1823.15*** *p26*
Brooks, Mary J. 16; Ontario, 1861 ***2896.25*** *p37*
Brooks, Nancy 2; Ontario, 1861 ***2896.25*** *p14*
Brooks, Nicholas; Pennsylvania, 1777 ***4629.10*** *p10*
Brooks, Nicholas; Pennsylvania, 1777 ***4629.10*** *p22*
Brooks, Nicholas; Pennsylvania, 1779 ***4629.10*** *p40*
Brooks, P. 26; Ontario, 1861 ***2896.25*** *p52*
Brooks, Peter 7; Ontario, 1861 ***2896.25*** *p14*
Brooks, Philip; Florida, 1766 ***1224.2*** *p15*
Brooks, Philip 15; Philadelphia, 1774 ***1220.25*** *p66*
Brooks, Robert; Quebec, 1858 ***9196.15*** *p45*
Brooks, S. M. 3; Ontario, 1861 ***2896.25*** *p52*
Brooks, Sarah A. 13; Ontario, 1861 ***2896.25*** *p14*
Brooks, Sophia; Quebec, 1858 ***9196.15*** *p32*
Brooks, Thomas; New York, 1838 ***8197.10*** *p111*
Brooks, Thomas 30; Maryland, 1775 ***1220.25*** *p114*
Brooks, Thomas 48; Ontario, 1871 ***1823.15*** *p26*
Brooks, William; New York, 1838 ***8197.10*** *p212*
Brooks, William; New York, New York, 1882 ***3437.14*** *p127*
Brooks, William; Pennsylvania, 1777 ***4629.10*** *p20*
Brooks, William 30; Ontario, 1871 ***1823.15*** *p26*
Brooks, William 65; Ontario, 1871 ***1823.22*** *p17*
Brooks, William D. 6; Ontario, 1861 ***2896.25*** *p52*
Brookson, James 18; Jamaica, 1774 ***1220.25*** *p83*
Broom, Chas 52; Ontario, 1871 ***1823.28*** *p10*
Broom, Francis 50; Ontario, 1871 ***1823.28*** *p10*
Broom, Margarett; Maryland, 1652 ***2524.55*** *p216*
Broom, Thomas 53; Ontario, 1871 ***1823.28*** *p10*
Broom, William; New York, 1811 ***8197.10*** *p57*
Broomdonne, Joane *SEE* Broomdonne, Thomas
Broomdonne, Tho.; Maryland, 1677 ***2524.55*** *p34*
Broomdonne, Thomas; Maryland, 1667 ***2524.55*** *p35*
Wife: Joane
Broomdoone, Tho.; Maryland, 1677 ***2524.55*** *p34*
Broome, Edward; Maryland, 1658 ***2524.55*** *p34*
Broome, Francis 42; Maryland, 1775 ***1220.25*** *p112*
Broome, Sarah 27; Maryland, 1775 ***1220.25*** *p112*
Broome, Thomas; Died enroute, 1695 ***1224.1*** *p9*
Broomfield, John 36; Virginia, 1774 ***1220.25*** *p45*
Broomfield, Robert 66; Ontario, 1871 ***1823.22*** *p17*
Broomly, Alfred 22; Ontario, 1871 ***1823.28*** *p10*
Brophey, John 35; Ontario, 1871 ***1823.15*** *p26*
Brophy, Elizabeth 75; Vermont, 1898 ***5900.10*** *p400*
Brophy, Felicitas 7; Ontario, 1871 ***1823.22*** *p17*
Brophy, George 62; Ontario, 1871 ***1823.15*** *p26*
Brophy, John 38; Ontario, 1871 ***1823.15*** *p26*
Brophy, Margaret 55; Ontario, 1871 ***1823.22*** *p17*
Brosias, Henry; Pennsylvania, 1786 ***4629.10*** *p55*
Broske, Andrew; Maryland, 1910 ***3259.35*** *p7*
Brosky, Joseph; Maryland, 1910 ***3259.35*** *p7*
Brosnahan, Catherine 72; Vermont, 1888 ***5900.10*** *p121*
Brosnahan, Cornelius 73; Vermont, 1877 ***5900.10*** *p121*
Brosnahan, Daniel J.; Vermont, 1855-1927 ***5900.10*** *p70*
Brosnahan, Daniel M.; Vermont, 1846-1926 ***5900.10*** *p117*
Brosnahan, Dennis; Vermont, 1822-1879 ***5900.10*** *p65*
Brosnahan, Elizabeth; Vermont, 1839-1933 ***5900.10*** *p121*
Brosnahan, Ellen Lawlor 78; Vermont, 1908 ***5900.10*** *p55*
Brosnahan, Hannah Driscoll; Vermont, 1855-1914 ***5900.10*** *p70*
Brosnahan, Johanna; Vermont, 1823-1906 ***5900.10*** *p62*
Brosnahan, Johanna 23; Vermont, 1874 ***5900.10*** *p112*
Brosnahan, Johanna 78; Vermont, 1919 ***5900.10*** *p112*
Brosnahan, John 56; Vermont, 1878 ***5900.10*** *p55*
Brosnahan, Julia Dineen; Vermont, 1824-1903 ***5900.10*** *p105*
Brosnahan, Katie Sullivan 19; Vermont, 1864 ***5900.10*** *p109*
Brosnahan, Mary; Vermont, 1849-1917 ***5900.10*** *p121*
Brosnahan, Mary; Vermont, 1863 ***5900.10*** *p57*
Brosnahan, Mary A. Sullivan; Vermont, 1852-1932 ***5900.10*** *p102*
Brosnahan, Mary Howard; Vermont, 1832-1917 ***5900.10*** *p65*
Brosnahan, Mary Reddin; Vermont, 1861-1893 ***5900.10*** *p117*

Brosnahan, Mary Tibbert; Vermont, 1863-1924 ***5900.10*** *p117*
Brosnahan, Michael; Vermont, 1815-1893 ***5900.10*** *p105*
Brosnahan, Nellie M. 16; Vermont, 1881 ***5900.10*** *p55*
Brosnahan, Thomas P.; Vermont, 1857-1927 ***5900.10*** *p55*
Brosnan, Bridget Austin; Vermont, 1837-1894 ***5900.10*** *p101*
Brosnan, Mary 77; Vermont, 1904 ***5900.10*** *p103*
Brosnan, Nora 90; Vermont, 1920 ***5900.10*** *p104*
Bross, Catharina; Port uncertain, 1771 ***2856.30*** *p53*
Brossard, Claudius Francis Ferdinand; New York, 1830 ***8197.10*** *p353*
Brossel, Jacob; Port uncertain, 1791 ***2856.30*** *p53*
Brotchie, Robert 30; Ontario, 1871 ***1823.15*** *p26*
Brothers, Henry; Vermont, 1837-1926 ***5900.10*** *p225*
Brothers, John; Maryland, 1664 ***2524.55*** *p151*
Brothers, Mary Miller; Vermont, 1847-1926 ***5900.10*** *p225*
Brothers, T.; Vermont, 1837-1915 ***5900.10*** *p42*
Brothers, Winifred; Virginia, 1671 ***6212.30*** *p44*
Brotherton, Thomas 21; Maryland, 1775 ***1220.25*** *p114*
Brothy, Dennis; Maryland, 1678 ***2524.55*** *p34*
Brotschin, Anna Ursula; Port uncertain, 1751 ***2856.30*** *p53*
Brotsky, Ludwich; Maryland, 1910 ***3259.35*** *p7*
Brouase, Samuell; Maryland, 1661 ***2524.55*** *p34*
Brough, Mr.; Quebec, 1857 ***9196.15*** *p18*
Brough, Mr.; Quebec, 1858 ***9196.15*** *p39*
Brough, Ann; Maryland, 1674 ***2524.55*** *p34*
Brough, Anna F. Dunn; Vermont, n.d. ***5900.10*** *p392*
Brough, Barbara Leask *SEE* Brough, George
Brough, Catherine; Vermont, 1834-1896 ***5900.10*** *p195*
Brough, Christian *SEE* Brough, George
Brough, Elizabeth T. Dunn; Vermont, n.d. ***5900.10*** *p392*
Brough, George; Savannah, Georgia, 1774 ***1640.10*** *p15*
Wife: Barbara Leask
Child: Thomas
Child: James
Child: Helen
Child: Christian
Brough, Helen *SEE* Brough, George
Brough, James *SEE* Brough, George
Brough, James 40; Ontario, 1871 ***1823.22*** *p17*
Brough, Jane E. Watts; Vermont, 1816-1902 ***5900.10*** *p494*
Brough, John; Vermont, 1841-1912 ***5900.10*** *p195*
Brough, John T.; Vermont, n.d. ***5900.10*** *p392*
Brough, Joseph; Maryland, 1665 ***2524.55*** *p34*
Brough, Peter B.; Vermont, 1805-1895 ***5900.10*** *p494*
Brough, Sarah M. Doyle 24; Vermont, 1877 ***5900.10*** *p261*
Brough, Secker 56; Ontario, 1871 ***1823.15*** *p26*
Brough, Susanna Carmody; Vermont, 1849-1942 ***5900.10*** *p195*
Brough, Thomas *SEE* Brough, George
Broughall, Elizabeth 69; Ontario, 1871 ***1823.22*** *p17*
Brougham, George 23; Maryland, 1774 ***1220.25*** *p69*
Broughan, Jenett 28; Ontario, 1871 ***1823.28*** *p10*
Broughen, Patrick 38; Ontario, 1871 ***1823.28*** *p10*
Broughton, Banks 25; Virginia, 1774 ***1220.25*** *p54*
Broughton, Edmund; Charles Town, South Carolina, 1813 ***1224.3*** *p9*
Broughton, Edward; Quebec, 1854 ***1640.13*** *p12*
Broughton, Jno; Virginia, 1664 ***6212.30*** *p10*
Broughton, John; Virginia, 1667-1668 ***6212.30*** *p38*
Broughton, John; Virginia, 1671-1672 ***6212.30*** *p46*
Broughton, William 18; Maryland, 1775 ***1220.25*** *p98*
Broun, Georg; New York, 1840 ***8197.10*** *p214*
Brour, Jacob; New York, 1840 ***8197.10*** *p320*
Brour, John; New York, 1807 ***8197.10*** *p34*
Brousseau, J. T.; Quebec, 1858 ***9196.15*** *p31*
Broutich, Caroline 21; Ontario, 1871 ***1823.28*** *p10*
Brow, Eleanor 24; Philadelphia, 1774 ***1220.25*** *p23*
Browen, Robert 50; Ontario, 1871 ***1823.28*** *p10*
Browen, William 61; Ontario, 1871 ***1823.28*** *p10*
Brower, Jno; Virginia, 1674 ***6212.30*** *p52*
Browghan, William; Maryland, 1663 ***2524.55*** *p35*
Browkowski, Anthony; Maryland, 1910 ***3259.35*** *p7*
Browkowski, Stanislaw; Maryland, 1910 ***3259.35*** *p7*
Brown, Captain; Quebec, 1857 ***9196.15*** *p23*
Brown, Master; Quebec, 1856 ***9196.15*** *p8*
Brown, Master; Quebec, 1858 ***9196.15*** *p40*
Brown, Miss; Quebec, 1857 ***9196.15*** *p17*
Brown, Mr.; Quebec, 1856 ***9196.15*** *p5*
Brown, Mr.; Quebec, 1856 ***9196.15*** *p10*
Brown, Mr.; Quebec, 1857 ***9196.15*** *p26*
Brown, Mr.; Quebec, 1858 ***9196.15*** *p39*
Brown, Mr.; Quebec, 1858 ***9196.15*** *p44*
Brown, Mr. 36; Dominica, 1774 ***1220.25*** *p128*
Brown, Mrs.; Maryland, 1648 ***2524.55*** *p35*
Brown, Mrs.; Quebec, 1856 ***9196.15*** *p10*
Brown, Mrs.; Quebec, 1857 ***9196.15*** *p26*
Brown, Mrs.; Quebec, 1858 ***9196.15*** *p39*
Brown, Mrs.; Quebec, 1858 ***9196.15*** *p44*
Brown, Mrs.; Quebec, 1858 ***9196.15*** *p45*
Brown, Mrs.; Quebec, 1858 ***9196.15*** *p47*
Brown, Mrs. 30; Boston, 1774 ***1220.25*** *p56*
Brown, A. 1; Ontario, 1861 ***2896.28*** *p4*
Brown, Agness 60; Ontario, 1871 ***1823.15*** *p26*
Brown, Alex 42; Ontario, 1871 ***1823.28*** *p10*
Brown, Alex 45; Ontario, 1871 ***1823.28*** *p10*
Brown, Alexander; Georgia, 1760 ***1640.10*** *p15*
Brown, Alexander; Jamaica, 1770 ***1640.13*** *p12*
Brown, Alexander 32; Ontario, 1871 ***1823.15*** *p26*
Brown, Alexander 52; Ontario, 1871 ***1823.22*** *p17*
Brown, Alexander 57; Ontario, 1871 ***1823.15*** *p26*
Brown, Alexander 58; Ontario, 1871 ***1823.15*** *p26*
Brown, Alexander Ogilvy; New Brunswick, 1889 ***1640.13*** *p12*
Brown, Alfred 1; Ontario, 1861 ***2896.25*** *p26*
Brown, Alfred 24; Ontario, 1871 ***1823.28*** *p10*
Brown, Alfred F. 6; Ontario, 1861 ***2896.27*** *p46*
Brown, Alice; Ontario, 1871 ***1823.15*** *p26*
Brown, Alice; Vermont, 1845-1945 ***5900.10*** *p614*
Brown, Alison 60; Ontario, 1871 ***1823.15*** *p26*
Brown, Amelia 35; Ontario, 1861 ***2896.27*** *p7*
Brown, Ames 36; Ontario, 1861 ***2896.27*** *p17*
Brown, Anderson 10; Ontario, 1861 ***2896.27*** *p46*
Brown, Andrew; America, 1830 ***1640.10*** *p15*
Brown, Andrew; Georgia, 1707 ***1640.13*** *p13*
Brown, Andrew; New York, 1838 ***8197.10*** *p109*
Brown, Andrew 37; Ontario, 1871 ***1823.15*** *p26*
Brown, Ann 1; Ontario, 1861 ***2896.27*** *p54*
Brown, Ann 11; Ontario, 1861 ***2896.27*** *p7*
Brown, Ann 62; Vermont, 1899 ***5900.10*** *p559*
Brown, Annie Rooney; Vermont, 1850-1900 ***5900.10*** *p505*
Brown, Archibald; New York, 1840 ***8197.10*** *p144*
Brown, Audley; New York, 1829 ***8197.10*** *p312*
Brown, Bridget; Vermont, 1828-1898 ***5900.10*** *p60*
Brown, Bridget; Vermont, 1846-1915 ***5900.10*** *p180*
Brown, Bridget 72; Vermont, 1903 ***5900.10*** *p269*
Brown, Bridget 87; Vermont, 1883 ***5900.10*** *p61*
Brown, Bridget Kelly; Vermont, 1838-1870 ***5900.10*** *p113*
Brown, Bridget O'Shea; Vermont, 1839-1916 ***5900.10*** *p432*
Brown, Bridget Preston; Vermont, 1871 ***5900.10*** *p469*
Brown, C. M. 2; Ontario, 1861 ***2896.27*** *p7*
Brown, Car 8; Ontario, 1861 ***2896.27*** *p7*
Brown, Caroline 6; Ontario, 1861 ***2896.27*** *p19*
Brown, Catherine; Vermont, 1835-1908 ***5900.10*** *p535*
Brown, Catherine 15; Ontario, 1871 ***1823.15*** *p26*
Brown, Catherine 19; Ontario, 1861 ***2896.25*** *p18*
Brown, Catherine 26; Ontario, 1871 ***1823.15*** *p26*
Brown, Catherine D.; Vermont, 1854-1922 ***5900.10*** *p178*
Brown, Charles; Maryland, 1671 ***2524.55*** *p35*
Brown, Charles; New York, 1838 ***8197.10*** *p110*
Brown, Charles; Virginia, 1700-1799 ***1224.2*** *p15*
Brown, Charles 16; Ontario, 1871 ***1823.22*** *p17*
Brown, Charles 35; Ontario, 1871 ***1823.28*** *p10*
Brown, Charles 38; Ontario, 1871 ***1823.15*** *p26*
Brown, Charles 65; Ontario, 1871 ***1823.28*** *p10*
Brown, Charles 75; Ontario, 1871 ***1823.15*** *p26*
Brown, Charlotte; Quebec, 1858 ***9196.15*** *p45*
Brown, Chris 30; Alaska, 1917 ***9196.1*** *p51*
Brown, Chris 30; Whitehorse, Yukon, 1917 ***9196.1*** *p51*
Brown, Christian 54; Ontario, 1871 ***1823.22*** *p17*
Brown, Clare; Maryland, 1658 ***2524.55*** *p35*
Brown, D. W. 1; Ontario, 1861 ***2896.25*** *p36*
Brown, Daniel 2; Ontario, 1861 ***2896.27*** *p46*
Brown, Daniel 47; Ontario, 1871 ***1823.28*** *p10*
Brown, Daniel Obrien; New York, 1794 ***8197.10*** *p3*
Brown, Daniel S. 14; Ontario, 1861 ***2896.25*** *p18*
Brown, Daniell; Maryland, 1652-1658 ***2524.55*** *p35*
Brown, David; California, 1882 ***1640.13*** *p13*
Brown, David; Jamaica, 1822 ***1640.13*** *p13*
Brown, David; Maryland, 1697 ***1640.13*** *p13*
Brown, David; North America, 1814 ***1640.13*** *p13*
Brown, David; St. John, New Brunswick, 1812 ***1640.13*** *p13*
Brown, David; Vermont, 1846-1907 ***5900.10*** *p505*
Brown, David 11; Ontario, 1861 ***2896.27*** *p46*
Brown, David 23; Vermont, 1862 ***5900.10*** *p504*
Brown, David 30; Ontario, 1871 ***1823.15*** *p26*
Brown, David 35; Philadelphia, 1774 ***1220.25*** *p80*
Brown, David 63; Ontario, 1871 ***1823.28*** *p10*
Brown, Deborah 57; Ontario, 1861 ***2896.27*** *p65*
Brown, Denis, Sr. 75; Vermont, 1868 ***5900.10*** *p144*
Brown, Denis, Jr.; Vermont, 1840-1914 ***5900.10*** *p145*
Brown, E. 35; Ontario, 1861 ***2896.25*** *p49*
Brown, Mrs. E.; Quebec, 1858 ***9196.15*** *p33*
Brown, Edmund 73; Vermont, 1928 ***5900.10*** *p468*
Brown, Edward; Maryland, 1655 ***2524.55*** *p175*
Brown, Edward; Virginia, 1664 ***6212.30*** *p13*
Brown, Edward; Virginia, 1671 ***6212.30*** *p44*
Brown, Edward 53; Ontario, 1871 ***1823.22*** *p17*
Brown, Edward Cary; Pennsylvania, 1777 ***4629.10*** *p7*
Brown, Eliza; Vermont, 1844-1901 ***5900.10*** *p69*
Brown, Eliza 9; Ontario, 1861 ***2896.25*** *p36*
Brown, Eliza 17; Ontario, 1871 ***1823.22*** *p17*
Brown, Eliza 25; Ontario, 1861 ***2896.27*** *p54*
Brown, Elizabeth; Virginia, 1681 ***6212.30*** *p55*
Brown, Elizabeth 19; Maryland, 1775 ***1220.25*** *p114*
Brown, Elizabeth 22; Maryland, 1775 ***1220.25*** *p111*
Brown, Elizabeth 27; Ontario, 1861 ***2896.27*** *p69*
Brown, Elizabeth 30; Maryland, 1775 ***1220.25*** *p105*
Brown, Elizabeth 44; Ontario, 1871 ***1823.22*** *p17*
Brown, Elizabeth 57; Ontario, 1861 ***2896.25*** *p18*
Brown, Ellen; Vermont, 1826-1915 ***5900.10*** *p217*
Brown, Ellen 46; Ontario, 1871 ***1823.15*** *p26*
Brown, Ellen M. Hanley 28; Vermont, 1873 ***5900.10*** *p567*
Brown, Ethelonia Thurn; Vermont, 1848-1925 ***5900.10*** *p355*
Brown, Flaert 60; Ontario, 1861 ***2896.27*** *p65*
Brown, Frances 4; Ontario, 1861 ***2896.27*** *p46*
Brown, Francis; New York, 1840 ***8197.10*** *p213*
Brown, Francis; Philadelphia, 1738 ***1224.2*** *p15*
Brown, Francis; St. Vincent, 1829 ***1640.13*** *p13*
Brown, Francis; Vermont, 1834-1897 ***5900.10*** *p330*
Brown, Francis 20; St. Kitts, 1775 ***1220.25*** *p122*
Brown, Francis 22; Ontario, 1871 ***1823.28*** *p10*
Brown, Francis 42; Ontario, 1871 ***1823.15*** *p26*
Brown, Francis, Jr.; Vermont, 1858-1911 ***5900.10*** *p330*
Brown, Frank; Vermont, 1856-1932 ***5900.10*** *p142*
Brown, Fred 18; Ontario, 1871 ***1823.15*** *p26*
Brown, Fredrick 22; Ontario, 1871 ***1823.28*** *p10*
Brown, G.; Quebec, 1856 ***9196.15*** *p6*
Brown, G.; Quebec, 1857 ***9196.15*** *p16*
Brown, Garnet 48; Alaska, 1918 ***9196.1*** *p8*
Brown, Garnet 48; Yukon, 1918 ***9196.1*** *p8*
Brown, George; Buffalo, New York, 1863 ***1640.13*** *p13*
Brown, George; Maryland, 1673 ***2524.55*** *p36*
Brown, George 18; Maryland, 1774 ***1220.25*** *p60*
Brown, George 18; Ontario, 1871 ***1823.28*** *p10*
Brown, George 25; Washington, 1914 ***9196.1*** *p65*
Brown, George 41; Ontario, 1871 ***1823.15*** *p26*
Brown, George 44; Ontario, 1871 ***1823.22*** *p18*
Brown, George 46; Ontario, 1871 ***1823.15*** *p26*
Brown, George 50; Ontario, 1871 ***1823.15*** *p26*
Brown, George 53; Ontario, 1871 ***1823.15*** *p26*
Brown, George 64; Ontario, 1871 ***1823.22*** *p18*
Brown, George 71; Ontario, 1871 ***1823.28*** *p10*
Brown, George Allan; Antigua (Antego), 1861 ***1640.13*** *p13*
Brown, George B.; Vermont, 1854-1932 ***5900.10*** *p275*
Brown, Gerard; Maryland, 1672 ***2524.55*** *p35*
Brown, Gilbert 3; Ontario, 1861 ***2896.25*** *p22*
Brown, Gotlib 30; Ontario, 1871 ***1823.15*** *p26*
Brown, H. J. 4; Ontario, 1861 ***2896.28*** *p4*
Brown, Hamilton; New York, 1840 ***8197.10*** *p144*
Brown, Hannah 1; Ontario, 1861 ***2896.27*** *p46*
Brown, Hannah 42; Ontario, 1861 ***2896.27*** *p69*
Brown, Hanora 76; Vermont, 1899 ***5900.10*** *p113*
Brown, Hanora Sullivan; Vermont, 1821-1906 ***5900.10*** *p55*
Brown, Harriet; Quebec, 1858 ***9196.15*** *p45*
Brown, Hattie L.; Vermont, 1851-1885 ***5900.10*** *p348*
Brown, Hector 27; British Columbia, 1914 ***9196.1*** *p66*
Brown, Hector 27; San Francisco, 1914 ***9196.1*** *p66*
Brown, Henry; New York, 1834 ***8197.10*** *p74*
Brown, Henry 35; Maryland, 1774 ***1220.25*** *p47*
Brown, Hugh 65; Ontario, 1871 ***1823.28*** *p10*
Brown, Isabel; Cincinnati, 1851 ***1224.3*** *p9*
Brown, Isabella; Georgia, 1798 ***1640.10*** *p15*
Brown, J.; Quebec, 1856 ***9196.15*** *p8*
Brown, J.; Quebec, 1858 ***9196.15*** *p40*
Brown, Mrs. J.; Quebec, 1858 ***9196.15*** *p40*
Brown, J. A. 2; Ontario, 1861 ***2896.28*** *p4*
Brown, J. G.; Quebec, 1857 ***9196.15*** *p26*
Brown, Mrs. J. G.; Quebec, 1857 ***9196.15*** *p26*
Brown, James; Connecticut, 1764 ***1224.2*** *p15*
Brown, James; Georgia, 1804-1845 ***1640.10*** *p16*
Wife: Margaret Finlay
Brown, James; Georgia, 1851 ***1640.10*** *p16*
Brown, James; Georgia, 1851 ***1640.13*** *p13*
Brown, James; Havana, 1764 ***1224.2*** *p15*
Brown, James; Maryland, 1649 ***2524.55*** *p77*
Brown, James; Maryland, 1658 ***2524.55*** *p35*
Brown, James; Maryland, 1725 ***1224.2*** *p15*
Brown, James; New York, 1803 ***8197.10*** *p11*
Brown, James; New York, 1821 ***8197.10*** *p207*
Brown, James; New York, 1838 ***8197.10*** *p110*
Brown, James; New York, 1840 ***8197.10*** *p145*
Brown, James; Pennsylvania, 1777 ***4629.10*** *p11*
Brown, James; Pennsylvania, 1777 ***4629.10*** *p13*
Brown, James; Pennsylvania, 1777 ***4629.10*** *p27*

Brown, James; Pennsylvania, 1808 ***6058.10*** *p2*
Brown, James; Philadelphia, 1725 ***1224.2*** *p15*
Brown, James; Vermont, 1830-1910 ***5900.10*** *p65*
Brown, James 17; Nova Scotia, 1774 ***1220.25*** *p13*
Brown, James 22; New York, 1774 ***1220.25*** *p25*
Wife: Mary 25
Brown, James 23; Maryland, 1774 ***1220.25*** *p61*
Brown, James 27; Ontario, 1871 ***1823.28*** *p10*
Brown, James 30; Ontario, 1871 ***1823.15*** *p27*
Brown, James 31; Ontario, 1861 ***2896.27*** *p17*
Brown, James 35; Ontario, 1871 ***1823.22*** *p18*
Brown, James 36; Ontario, 1871 ***1823.28*** *p10*
Brown, James 42; Ontario, 1871 ***1823.22*** *p18*
Brown, James 47; Ontario, 1871 ***1823.15*** *p27*
Brown, James 55; Ontario, 1871 ***1823.22*** *p18*
Brown, James 56; Ontario, 1871 ***1823.22*** *p18*
Brown, James 57; Ontario, 1871 ***1823.15*** *p27*
Brown, James 59; Ontario, 1871 ***1823.15*** *p27*
Brown, James 60; Ontario, 1871 ***1823.28*** *p10*
Brown, James 62; Ontario, 1871 ***1823.22*** *p18*
Brown, James 71; Ontario, 1871 ***1823.22*** *p18*
Brown, James 95; Vermont, 1895 ***5900.10*** *p314*
Brown, James, Sr.; Augusta, Georgia, 1735-1810 ***1640.10*** *p16*
Brown, James Forrester; Chicago, 1888 ***1640.13*** *p13*
Brown, James J.; Vermont, 1854-1938 ***5900.10*** *p442*
Brown, James M. 36; Vermont, 1904 ***5900.10*** *p144*
Brown, James W. 37; Alaska, 1912 ***9196.1*** *p20*
Brown, James W. 37; British Columbia, 1912 ***9196.1*** *p20*
Brown, Jane 1 *SEE* Brown, William
Brown, Jane 21 *SEE* Brown, William
Brown, Jarvis 28; Ontario, 1871 ***1823.15*** *p27*
Brown, Jennett 31; Ontario, 1871 ***1823.22*** *p18*
Brown, Jerid 44; Ontario, 1871 ***1823.15*** *p27*
Brown, Joanna; Vermont, 1837-1872 ***5900.10*** *p432*
Brown, Job 19; Ontario, 1871 ***1823.15*** *p27*
Brown, Johannah Quinlan 78; Vermont, 1876 ***5900.10*** *p557*
Brown, John; Halifax, Nova Scotia, 1834 ***1640.13*** *p13*
Brown, John; Maryland, 1649 ***2524.55*** *p35*
Relative: Patient
Relative: Mary
Brown, John; Maryland, 1653 ***2524.55*** *p35*
Brown, John; Maryland, 1680 ***2524.55*** *p35*
Wife: Sarah
Child: Sarah
Child: William
Brown, John; New York, 1792-1840 ***8197.10*** *p324*
Brown, John; New York, 1802 ***8197.10*** *p18*
Brown, John; New York, 1803 ***8197.10*** *p10*
Brown, John; New York, 1806 ***8197.10*** *p322*
Brown, John; New York, 1807 ***8197.10*** *p34*
Brown, John; New York, 1807 ***8197.10*** *p35*
Brown, John; New York, 1807 ***8197.10*** *p325*
Brown, John; New York, 1821 ***8197.10*** *p207*
Brown, John; New York, 1821 ***8197.10*** *p208*
Brown, John; New York, 1828 ***8197.10*** *p211*
Brown, John; New York, 1834 ***8197.10*** *p73*
Brown, John; New York, 1837 ***8197.10*** *p84*
Brown, John; Pennsylvania, 1777 ***4629.10*** *p6*
Brown, John; Pennsylvania, 1777 ***4629.10*** *p9*
Brown, John; Pennsylvania, 1777 ***4629.10*** *p15*
Brown, John; Pennsylvania, 1777 ***4629.10*** *p19*
Brown, John; Pennsylvania, 1803-1816 ***6058.10*** *p6*
Brown, John; Philadelphia, 1794 ***4629.10*** *p81*
Brown, John; Vermont, 1822-1897 ***5900.10*** *p55*
Brown, John; Vermont, 1835-1887 ***5900.10*** *p469*
Brown, John; Virginia, 1727 ***1640.13*** *p13*
Brown, John 3; Ontario, 1861 ***2896.25*** *p26*
Brown, John 15; Ontario, 1871 ***1823.28*** *p11*
Brown, John 17; Philadelphia, 1774 ***1220.25*** *p81*
Brown, John 20; America, 1774 ***1220.25*** *p36*
Brown, John 20; Ontario, 1871 ***1823.28*** *p11*
Brown, John 21; Maryland, 1774 ***1220.25*** *p65*
Brown, John 21; Virginia, 1775 ***1220.25*** *p110*
Brown, John 22; Maryland, 1774 ***1220.25*** *p50*
Brown, John 22; Virginia, 1774 ***1220.25*** *p51*
Brown, John 23; Ontario, 1871 ***1823.15*** *p27*
Brown, John 23; Philadelphia, 1774 ***1220.25*** *p43*
Brown, John 23; Virginia, 1774 ***1220.25*** *p88*
Brown, John 24; Ontario, 1871 ***1823.28*** *p11*
Brown, John 25; Ontario, 1871 ***1823.15*** *p27*
Brown, John 26; Norfolk, Virginia, 1774 ***1220.25*** *p19*
Brown, John 29; Ontario, 1871 ***1823.15*** *p27*
Brown, John 30; New York, 1775 ***1220.25*** *p142*
Brown, John 30; Ontario, 1871 ***1823.28*** *p11*
Brown, John 33; Maryland, 1774 ***1220.25*** *p61*
Brown, John 33; Ontario, 1871 ***1823.15*** *p27*
Brown, John 34; Ontario, 1861 ***2896.27*** *p7*
Brown, John 39; Ontario, 1871 ***1823.22*** *p18*
Brown, John 40; Ontario, 1871 ***1823.22*** *p18*
Brown, John 42; Ontario, 1871 ***1823.15*** *p27*
Brown, John 45; Ontario, 1861 ***2896.27*** *p19*
Brown, John 50; Ontario, 1871 ***1823.28*** *p11*
Brown, John 51; Ontario, 1871 ***1823.15*** *p27*
Brown, John 52; Ontario, 1871 ***1823.15*** *p27*
Brown, John 58; Ontario, 1871 ***1823.15*** *p27*
Brown, John 78; Ontario, 1871 ***1823.15*** *p27*
Brown, John 80; Ontario, 1871 ***1823.22*** *p18*
Brown, John B.; New York, New York, 1856 ***3437.14*** *p42*
Brown, John H. 21; Ontario, 1861 ***2896.25*** *p18*
Brown, John S. 32; Ontario, 1871 ***1823.15*** *p27*
Brown, Jonathan; Pennsylvania, 1777 ***4629.10*** *p22*
Brown, Jonathan 55; Ontario, 1871 ***1823.22*** *p18*
Brown, Joseph; Pennsylvania, 1777 ***4629.10*** *p9*
Brown, Joseph; Quebec, 1858 ***9196.15*** *p40*
Brown, Joseph 13; Ontario, 1861 ***2896.27*** *p54*
Brown, Joseph 52; Ontario, 1871 ***1823.15*** *p27*
Brown, Julia 35; Vermont, 1888 ***5900.10*** *p113*
Brown, Julia 75; Vermont, 1894 ***5900.10*** *p65*
Brown, Julia Collins; Vermont, 1837-1911 ***5900.10*** *p433*
Brown, Julia E. Donovan 48; Vermont, 1901 ***5900.10*** *p468*
Brown, Julia E. Smith; Vermont, 1840-1889 ***5900.10*** *p545*
Brown, Kate; Vermont, 1847-1928 ***5900.10*** *p204*
Brown, Lillian M.; Vermont, 1867-1943 ***5900.10*** *p142*
Brown, Louisa; Quebec, 1858 ***9196.15*** *p45*
Brown, Lucy A. 23; Ontario, 1861 ***2896.25*** *p18*
Brown, Lydia 22; Ontario, 1861 ***2896.27*** *p69*
Brown, Lydia N. 28; Ontario, 1861 ***2896.27*** *p54*
Brown, M.; Alabama, 1821-1845 ***1640.10*** *p16*
Brown, M. 68; Ontario, 1861 ***2896.27*** *p7*
Brown, Miss M.; Quebec, 1858 ***9196.15*** *p45*
Brown, M. A. 17; Ontario, 1861 ***2896.25*** *p18*
Brown, Manuel; New York, 1831 ***8197.10*** *p354*
Brown, Margaret; Ontario, 1844 ***1640.13*** *p13*
Brown, Margaret; Vermont, 1829-1898 ***5900.10*** *p360*
Brown, Margaret 19; Georgia, 1775 ***1220.25*** *p126*
Brown, Margaret 28; Ontario, 1861 ***2896.27*** *p65*
Brown, Margaret 56; Vermont, 1893 ***5900.10*** *p145*
Brown, Margaret 76; Vermont, 1879 ***5900.10*** *p306*
Brown, Margaret 76; Vermont, 1879 ***5900.10*** *p309*
Brown, Margaret Carroll; Vermont, 1845-1905 ***5900.10*** *p113*
Brown, Margaret Craig; Manitoba, 1900 ***1640.13*** *p13*
Brown, Margaret E.; Vermont, 1844-1944 ***5900.10*** *p442*
Brown, Margaret Finlay *SEE* Brown, James
Brown, Margerett; Maryland, 1658 ***2524.55*** *p35*
Brown, Maria Oneida 41; Ontario, 1871 ***1823.15*** *p27*
Brown, Martha 40; Ontario, 1871 ***1823.22*** *p18*
Brown, Martha 63; Ontario, 1871 ***1823.28*** *p11*
Brown, Mary *SEE* Brown, John
Brown, Mary; Maryland, 1631-1685 ***2524.55*** *p35*
Brown, Mary; Vermont, 1827-1907 ***5900.10*** *p330*
Brown, Mary; Vermont, 1854-1920 ***5900.10*** *p406*
Brown, Mary 11; Ontario, 1861 ***2896.27*** *p65*
Brown, Mary 19; Ontario, 1871 ***1823.22*** *p18*
Brown, Mary 21; Maryland, 1775 ***1220.25*** *p114*
Brown, Mary 25 *SEE* Brown, James
Brown, Mary 26; Nova Scotia, 1774 ***1220.25*** *p13*
Brown, Mary 40; Ontario, 1861 ***2896.27*** *p17*
Brown, Mary 51; Ontario, 1871 ***1823.15*** *p27*
Brown, Mary 53; Vermont, 1871 ***5900.10*** *p56*
Brown, Mary 66; Ontario, 1861 ***2896.27*** *p17*
Brown, Mary 67; Ontario, 1871 ***1823.15*** *p27*
Brown, Mary 75; Vermont, 1877 ***5900.10*** *p314*
Brown, Mary A. McDonough; Vermont, 1851-1925 ***5900.10*** *p519*
Brown, Mary Ann; Vermont, 1854-1942 ***5900.10*** *p46*
Brown, Mary Ann Leonard; Vermont, 1858-1932 ***5900.10*** *p505*
Brown, Mary Devaney; Vermont, 1822-1900 ***5900.10*** *p507*
Brown, Mary E.; Vermont, 1862-1921 ***5900.10*** *p147*
Brown, Mary E. 1; Ontario, 1861 ***2896.25*** *p18*
Brown, Mary E. 25; Ontario, 1861 ***2896.25*** *p26*
Brown, Mary M. 2; Ontario, 1861 ***2896.25*** *p25*
Brown, Matilda 63; Ontario, 1861 ***2896.27*** *p69*
Brown, Matthew; New York, 1840 ***8197.10*** *p214*
Brown, Maurice 32; Vermont, 1855 ***5900.10*** *p113*
Brown, Michael; Vermont, 1855-1909 ***5900.10*** *p355*
Brown, Morris 1; Ontario, 1861 ***2896.27*** *p18*
Brown, Nancy 23; Ontario, 1861 ***2896.25*** *p22*
Brown, Nancy Eleanor; Vermont, 1830-1887 ***5900.10*** *p317*
Brown, Nathaniel; Connecticut, 1764 ***1224.2*** *p15*
Brown, Neil 45; Ontario, 1871 ***1823.15*** *p27*
Brown, Nicholas; Maryland, 1674 ***2524.55*** *p35*
Brown, Nora; Vermont, 1837-1919 ***5900.10*** *p69*
Brown, Nora; Vermont, 1854-1930 ***5900.10*** *p150*
Brown, Patient *SEE* Brown, John
Brown, Patrick; Pennsylvania, 1777 ***4629.10*** *p30*
Brown, Patrick; Vermont, 1821-1903 ***5900.10*** *p432*
Brown, Patrick; Vermont, 1851-1929 ***5900.10*** *p505*
Brown, Patrick 65; Ontario, 1871 ***1823.15*** *p27*
Brown, Patrick A.; Vermont, 1822-1897 ***5900.10*** *p507*
Brown, Patrick H. 49; Ontario, 1871 ***1823.22*** *p18*
Brown, Paul 24; Philadelphia, 1774 ***1220.25*** *p50*
Brown, Peter; Pennsylvania, n.d. ***1224.2*** *p16*
Brown, Peter 30; Ontario, 1871 ***1823.22*** *p18*
Brown, Peter 54; Ontario, 1871 ***1823.28*** *p11*
Brown, R.; Quebec, 1858 ***9196.15*** *p45*
Brown, Rachel; Pennsylvania, 1877 ***1640.13*** *p13*
Brown, Ralph; Pennsylvania, 1826 ***6058.10*** *p9*
Brown, Ralph 37; Ontario, 1871 ***1823.15*** *p27*
Brown, Richard; Maryland, 1650 ***2524.55*** *p35*
With wife
Brown, Richard; Maryland, 1673 ***2524.55*** *p35*
Brown, Richard; Maryland, 1679 ***2524.55*** *p35*
Brown, Richard; New York, 1794 ***8197.10*** *p3*
Brown, Richard; New York, 1840 ***8197.10*** *p154*
Brown, Richard; Pennsylvania, 1777 ***4629.10*** *p7*
Brown, Richard; Virginia, 1740 ***1224.2*** *p16*
Brown, Richard 22; Ontario, 1871 ***1823.15*** *p27*
Brown, Richard 27; Maryland, 1774 ***1220.25*** *p47*
Brown, Richard 40; Ontario, 1871 ***1823.15*** *p27*
Brown, Richard 62; Ontario, 1871 ***1823.15*** *p27*
Brown, Robert; Jamaica, 1837 ***1640.13*** *p14*
Brown, Robert; New York, 1834 ***8197.10*** *p212*
Brown, Robert; Pennsylvania, 1777 ***4629.10*** *p7*
Brown, Robert; Richmond, Virginia, 1785 ***1640.13*** *p14*
Brown, Robert; Savannah, Georgia, 1798 ***1224.2*** *p16*
Brown, Robert 28; Ontario, 1871 ***1823.22*** *p18*
Brown, Robert 32; Grenada, 1773-1774 ***1220.25*** *p124*
Brown, Robert 36; Ontario, 1871 ***1823.15*** *p27*
Brown, Robert 38; Ontario, 1871 ***1823.28*** *p11*
Brown, Robert 39; Ontario, 1871 ***1823.28*** *p11*
Brown, Robert 40; Ontario, 1871 ***1823.22*** *p18*
Brown, Robert 42; Ontario, 1871 ***1823.22*** *p18*
Brown, Robert 42; Ontario, 1871 ***1823.28*** *p11*
Brown, Robert 43; Ontario, 1871 ***1823.22*** *p18*
Brown, Robert 47; Ontario, 1871 ***1823.15*** *p27*
Brown, Robert 66; Ontario, 1871 ***1823.22*** *p18*
Brown, Robert J.; Vermont, 1841-1917 ***5900.10*** *p178*
Brown, Ronald K.; Indiana, 1897 ***3437.14*** *p172*
Brown, S. 29; Ontario, 1861 ***2896.28*** *p4*
Brown, S. E. 24; Ontario, 1861 ***2896.25*** *p36*
Brown, Samuel 6; Ontario, 1861 ***2896.27*** *p46*
Brown, Samuel 19; Virginia, 1774 ***1220.25*** *p87*
Brown, Samuel 63; Ontario, 1871 ***1823.22*** *p18*
Brown, Samuel 69; Ontario, 1871 ***1823.22*** *p18*
Brown, Sanger M. 10; Ontario, 1861 ***2896.27*** *p54*
Brown, Sara; Virginia, 1681-1682 ***6212.30*** *p56*
Brown, Sarah *SEE* Brown, John
Brown, Sarah; Maryland, 1672 ***2524.55*** *p35*
Brown, Sarah; Maryland, 1680 ***2524.55*** *p35*
Brown, Sarah 51; Ontario, 1871 ***1823.28*** *p11*
Brown, Sharlotte 34; Ontario, 1861 ***2896.27*** *p46*
Brown, Solomon 8; Ontario, 1861 ***2896.27*** *p46*
Brown, Sophia; Vermont, 1832-1901 ***5900.10*** *p334*
Brown, Stephen; Savannah, Georgia, 1768 ***1640.10*** *p16*
Brown, Stephen F.; Vermont, 1841-1903 ***5900.10*** *p519*
Brown, Susan; Maryland, 1659 ***2524.55*** *p35*
Brown, Susan; Vermont, 1845-1918 ***5900.10*** *p511*
Brown, Susan 54; Ontario, 1871 ***1823.28*** *p11*
Brown, Susanna 20; Philadelphia, 1774 ***1220.25*** *p50*
Brown, Susannah 38; Ontario, 1861 ***2896.27*** *p43*
Brown, Theodore; Vermont, 1827-1908 ***5900.10*** *p334*
Brown, Theodore 22; Ontario, 1861 ***2896.27*** *p65*
Brown, Thomas; New York, 1803 ***8197.10*** *p10*
Brown, Thomas; New York, 1807 ***8197.10*** *p34*
Brown, Thomas; New York, 1828-1830 ***8197.10*** *p307*
Brown, Thomas; New York, 1833 ***8197.10*** *p358*
Brown, Thomas; New York, 1834 ***8197.10*** *p73*
Brown, Thomas; New York, New York, 1769 ***1224.2*** *p16*
Brown, Thomas; Pennsylvania, 1777 ***4629.10*** *p26*
Brown, Thomas; Pennsylvania, 1862-1868 ***6058.10*** *p68*
Brown, Thomas; Savannah, Georgia, 1803 ***1640.10*** *p16*
Brown, Thomas; Vermont, 1826-1911 ***5900.10*** *p442*
Brown, Thomas 18; Ontario, 1861 ***2896.27*** *p65*
Brown, Thomas 21; Ontario, 1871 ***1823.15*** *p27*
Brown, Thomas 22; Maryland, 1774 ***1220.25*** *p78*
Brown, Thomas 22; Philadelphia, 1774 ***1220.25*** *p42*
Brown, Thomas 24; Ontario, 1861 ***2896.27*** *p69*
Brown, Thomas 29; Virginia, 1774 ***1220.25*** *p75*
Brown, Thomas 33; Ontario, 1871 ***1823.28*** *p11*
Brown, Thomas 37; Ontario, 1871 ***1823.15*** *p27*
Brown, Thomas 40; Ontario, 1871 ***1823.15*** *p27*
Brown, Thomas 45; Ontario, 1871 ***1823.15*** *p27*
Brown, Thomas 56; Ontario, 1871 ***1823.22*** *p18*
Brown, Thomas 60; Ontario, 1871 ***1823.15*** *p27*
Brown, Thomas 60; Ontario, 1871 ***1823.28*** *p11*
Brown, Thomas 86; Ontario, 1871 ***1823.22*** *p18*
Brown, Mrs. Thomas; Vermont, 1831-1891 ***5900.10*** *p442*
Brown, Thomas A. 34; Vermont, 1894 ***5900.10*** *p287*
Brown, Thomas M. 19; Ontario, 1861 ***2896.27*** *p29*

Brown, Thos; Portland, Maine, 1858 9196.15 p28
Brown, W. H. G. 24; Ontario, 1871 1823.15 p27
Brown, Walter; Georgia, 1780 1640.10 p16
Brown, Walter 51; Ontario, 1871 1823.28 p11
Brown, Watson 54; Ontario, 1871 1823.22 p19
Brown, William *SEE* Brown, John
Brown, William; Georgia, 1698 1640.13 p14
Brown, William; Maryland, 1633 2524.55 p35
Brown, William; Maryland, 1647 2524.55 p35
Brown, William; Maryland, 1672 2524.55 p35
Brown, William; Maryland, 1673 2524.55 p35
Brown, William; Maryland, 1680 2524.55 p35
Brown, William; Montreal, 1890 1640.13 p14
Brown, William; New York, 1826 8197.10 p337
Brown, William; New York, 1837 8197.10 p84
Brown, William; New York, 1840 8197.10 p156
Brown, William; Ontario, 1897 1640.13 p14
Brown, William; Pennsylvania, 1777 4629.10 p6
Brown, William; Pennsylvania, 1777 4629.10 p20
Brown, William; Quebec, 1858 9196.15 p46
Brown, William; Richmond, Virginia, 1815 1224.3 p10
Brown, William; Savannah, Georgia, 1768 1640.10 p16
Brown, William; Died enroute, 1849 1224.3 p10
Brown, William 5; Ontario, 1861 2896.27 p19
Brown, William 15; Philadelphia, 1775 1220.25 p107
Brown, William 21; Jamaica, 1774 1220.25 p79
Brown, William 21; Maryland, 1775 1220.25 p115
Brown, William 22; Nova Scotia, 1774 1220.25 p13
Wife: Jane 21
Child: Jane 1
Brown, William 22; Ontario, 1871 1823.15 p27
Brown, William 25; Ontario, 1871 1823.28 p11
Brown, William 26; Ontario, 1861 2896.25 p18
Brown, William 26; Ontario, 1871 1823.15 p27
Brown, William 26; Ontario, 1871 1823.28 p11
Brown, William 31; Ontario, 1871 1823.15 p28
Brown, William 33; Ontario, 1871 1823.22 p19
Brown, William 35; Ontario, 1871 1823.22 p19
Brown, William 38; Ontario, 1871 1823.15 p28
Brown, William 39; Ontario, 1871 1823.22 p19
Brown, William 40; Ontario, 1871 1823.15 p27
Brown, William 40; Ontario, 1871 1823.22 p19
Brown, William 47; Ontario, 1871 1823.28 p11
Brown, William 47; Vermont, 1883 5900.10 p314
Brown, William 50; Ontario, 1871 1823.15 p27
Brown, William 56; Ontario, 1871 1823.15 p27
Brown, William 57; Ontario, 1871 1823.15 p28
Brown, William 60; Ontario, 1871 1823.15 p27
Brown, William 67; Ontario, 1861 2896.27 p65
Brown, William 70; Ontario, 1871 1823.28 p11
Brown, William 73; Ontario, 1861 2896.27 p17
Brown, William 73; Ontario, 1871 1823.22 p19
Brown, William 84; Ontario, 1871 1823.22 p19
Brown, William A.; Vermont, 1859-1930 5900.10 p442
Brown, William E.; New York, 1840 8197.10 p213
Brown, William G. 5; Ontario, 1861 2896.27 p54
Brown, William H.; Vermont, 1877-1905 5900.10 p458
Brown, William Henry 36; Ontario, 1871 1823.28 p11
Brown, William Hugh; Jamaica, 1835 1224.3 p10
Brown, William Hugh; New York, 1835 1224.3 p10
Brown, William S. 5; Ontario, 1861 2896.25 p26
Brown, William T. 45; Ontario, 1871 1823.15 p28
Brown, Willie 34; Ontario, 1861 2896.27 p69
Brown, Willie E. 35; Vermont, 1893 5900.10 p287
Brown, Wm 58; Mexico, 1913 9196.1 p58
Brown, Wm 58; Vancouver, British Columbia, 1913 9196.1 p58
Brownall, Thomas; Rhode Island, 1659 1224.1 p65
Browndonne, Joane *SEE* Browndonne, Thomas
Browndonne, Thomas; Maryland, 1667 2524.55 p35
Wife: Joane
Browne, Miss; Quebec, 1856 9196.15 p10
Browne, Mrs.; Quebec, 1856 9196.15 p10
Browne, Ann; Maryland, 1679 2524.55 p35
Browne, Ann 52; Ontario, 1871 1823.28 p11
Browne, Anto; Virginia, 1665-1666 6212.30 p23
Browne, Anto; Virginia, 1666-1667 6212.30 p34
Browne, Benjamin; Salem, Massachusetts, 1712 1224.2 p15
Browne, Betty; Virginia, 1674 6212.30 p52
Browne, Charles; New York, 1802 8197.10 p18
Browne, Charles; Virginia, 1664 6212.30 p8
Browne, Edw; Virginia, 1668-1669 6212.30 p41
Browne, Edward; Maryland, 1655 2524.55 p35
Browne, Edward; Maryland, 1663 2524.55 p35
Browne, Eliza; New York, 1838 8197.10 p212
Browne, Elizabeth; Maryland, 1677 2524.55 p35
Browne, Ellis; Maryland, 1649 2524.55 p35
Browne, Francis; Maryland, 1664 2524.55 p35
Browne, Francis; Maryland, 1669 2524.55 p84
Browne, Francis; Vermont, 1833-1924 5900.10 p507
Browne, Gabriel; Maryland, 1679 2524.55 p35
Browne, Gabriell; Maryland, 1665 2524.55 p36
With wife
Son: William
Browne, Geo; Virginia, 1666-1667 6212.30 p34
Browne, George; Maryland, 1673 2524.55 p36
Browne, Gerrard; Maryland, 1670 2524.55 p36
Browne, Henry; Vermont, 1824-1889 5900.10 p432
Browne, Honora McCarthy; Vermont, 1833-1863 5900.10 p432
Browne, Isaac; Nova Scotia, 1789 1224.2 p15
Browne, James *SEE* Browne, John
Browne, James; Maryland, 1659-1662 2524.55 p36
Browne, James; Philadelphia, 1749 1224.2 p15
Browne, James; Virginia, 1671 6212.30 p44
Browne, Jani; Virginia, 1671 6212.30 p42
Browne, Johanna; Maryland, 1678 2524.55 p36
Browne, John; Maryland, 1659 2524.55 p36
Relative: James
Relative: Jonathan
Browne, John; Maryland, 1663 2524.55 p36
Browne, John; Maryland, 1668 2524.55 p36
Browne, John; Maryland, 1669 2524.55 p84
Browne, John; Maryland, 1671 2524.55 p36
Wife: Sarah
Child: William
Child: Sarah
Browne, John; Maryland, 1681 2524.55 p36
Browne, John; Maryland, 1682 2524.55 p36
Browne, John; Maryland, 1700 1224.2 p16
Browne, John; New York, 1818 8197.10 p206
Browne, John; New York, 1837 8197.10 p85
Browne, John; Pennsylvania, 1777 4629.10 p29
Browne, John; Virginia, 1665 6212.30 p19
Browne, John; Virginia, 1668 1224.1 p9
Browne, John; Virginia, 1671 6212.30 p42
Browne, Jonathan *SEE* Browne, John
Browne, Jonathan; Philadelphia, 1784 1224.2 p16
Browne, Josias Fairly; America, 1857 1640.13 p14
Browne, Lodwick; Virginia, 1665 6212.30 p17
Browne, Margaret; Vermont, 1830-1913 5900.10 p507
Browne, Margarett; Maryland, 1671 2524.55 p32
Browne, Margarett; Maryland, 1681 2524.55 p36
Browne, Mary; Maryland, 1659 2524.55 p36
Browne, Mary; Vermont, 1855-1900 5900.10 p432
Browne, Mary O'Sullivan; Vermont, 1800-1865 5900.10 p432
Browne, Nathaniel; Pennsylvania, 1779 4629.10 p36
Browne, Nicholas; Maryland, 1658 2524.55 p36
Browne, Peregrine; Maryland, 1712 1224.2 p16
Browne, Robert; Virginia, 1666 6212.30 p26
Browne, Sarah *SEE* Browne, John
Browne, Susan; Maryland, 1659 2524.55 p36
Browne, Thomas; Maryland, 1648 2524.55 p36
Browne, Thomas; New England, 1693 1224.1 p10
Browne, Thomas; Virginia, 1666-1667 6212.30 p34
Browne, William *SEE* Browne, Gabriell
Browne, William *SEE* Browne, John
Browne, William; Maryland, 1672 2524.55 p36
Browne, William; Maryland, 1681 2524.55 p36
Browne, William; Virginia, 1657 1224.1 p10
Browne, William; Virginia, 1668 1224.1 p10
Browne, William; Virginia, 1671-1672 6212.30 p45
Browne, Wm; Virginia, 1664 6212.30 p15
Browne, X. P.; Virginia, 1664 6212.30 p11
Brownejohn, Mary; New York, New York, 1786 1224.2 p16
Brownell, George 50; Ontario, 1871 1823.15 p28
Browning, Andrew H. 28; Ontario, 1871 1823.28 p11
Browning, Arthur 41; Ontario, 1871 1823.22 p19
Browning, Francis; Maryland, 1682 2524.55 p36
Browning, George F.; New York, 1839 8197.10 p128
Browning, George W.; Louisiana, 1805-1850 1640.10 p16
Browning, Hester; Maryland, 1679 2524.55 p36
Browning, J. W. 27; Ontario, 1871 1823.15 p28
Browning, John *SEE* Browning, Thomas
Browning, John; Maryland, 1679 2524.55 p36
Browning, John; Maryland, 1681 2524.55 p36
Browning, John; New England, 1702 1224.2 p16
Browning, John; New York, 1839 8197.10 p128
Browning, John; New York, 1839 8197.10 p213
Browning, Joseph 36; Maryland, 1774 1220.25 p51
Browning, Mathew; Maryland, 1652 2524.55 p36
Browning, Mathew; Maryland, 1662 2524.55 p36
Browning, Richard 21; Maryland, 1774 1220.25 p46
Browning, Thomas; Maryland, 1665 2524.55 p36
With wife
Son: John
Browning, Thomas; Maryland, 1679 2524.55 p36
Browning, Thomas Charles; New York, 1834 8197.10 p74
Browning, William 16; Maryland, 1775 1220.25 p120
Browning, William 21; Maryland, 1775 1220.25 p114
Browninge, Mary; New England, 1649 1224.1 p14
Browninge, William; Virginia, 1651 1224.1 p10
Brownjohn, William; New York, New York, 1785 1224.2 p16
Brownker, Wm; Virginia, 1664 6212.30 p15
Brownlee, David 46; Ontario, 1871 1823.22 p19
Brownlee, James 45; Ontario, 1871 1823.15 p28
Brownlee, James 48; Ontario, 1871 1823.15 p28
Brownlee, James 55; Ontario, 1871 1823.15 p28
Brownlee, Robert 70; Ontario, 1871 1823.15 p28
Brownlee, William; New York, 1838 8197.10 p111
Brownlee, Wm 46; Ontario, 1871 1823.15 p28
Brownlie, Elizabeth; Ontario, 1895 1640.13 p14
Brownlie, James 38; Ontario, 1871 1823.28 p11
Brownlow, Rich; Virginia, 1665-1666 6212.30 p22
Brownrigg, Henry; New Orleans, 1828 1224.3 p10
Brownsford, James; Virginia, 1684 1224.1 p10
Browonska, Valentine; Maryland, 1910 3259.35 p7
Broxam, Thomas; Maryland, 1673 2524.55 p36
Broyer, Claudius; New York, 1827 8197.10 p341
Brozkowski, Leonard; Maryland, 1910 3259.35 p7
Broźnowicz, Joseph; Maryland, 1910 3259.35 p7
Brtnikovosky, Antoni; Maryland, 1910 3259.35 p7
Brubacher, Abraham; Port uncertain, 1749 2856.30 p53
Brubaker, John; Pennsylvania, 1777 4629.10 p27
Bruce, Mrs. 30; Dominica, 1773-1774 1220.25 p127
Bruce, Alexander; New York, 1821 8197.10 p208
Bruce, Alexander; New York, 1827 8197.10 p347
Bruce, Alexander 40; Ontario, 1871 1823.15 p28
Bruce, Alexander 46; Ontario, 1871 1823.15 p28
Bruce, Charles Key; New York, 1827 1224.3 p10
Bruce, Collin 42; Ontario, 1871 1823.28 p11
Bruce, David; Florida, 1769 1640.10 p16
Bruce, Donald 60; Ontario, 1871 1823.15 p28
Bruce, Frances; New York, New York, 1821 1224.3 p10
Bruce, George 35; Dominica, 1773-1774 1220.25 p127
Bruce, James; Alabama, 1813-1845 1640.10 p16
Wife: Jane
Bruce, James; Florida, 1765 1640.10 p16
Bruce, James; Florida, 1820 1640.10 p17
Bruce, James 39; Ontario, 1871 1823.15 p28
Bruce, Jane *SEE* Bruce, James
Bruce, John; New York, 1839 8197.10 p128
Bruce, John 15; Philadelphia, 1774 1220.25 p67
Bruce, John 35; Ontario, 1871 1823.28 p11
Bruce, John 74; Ontario, 1871 1823.15 p28
Bruce, Mary *SEE* Bruce, Robert
Bruce, Robert; Mobile, Alabama, 1794-1845 1640.10 p17
Wife: Mary
Bruce, Robert 34; New England, 1774 1220.25 p56
Bruce, Robert 40; Ontario, 1871 1823.15 p28
Bruce, Robert 75; Ontario, 1871 1823.28 p11
Bruce, T.; Quebec, 1858 9196.15 p37
Bruce, Thomas; Georgia, 1757 1640.10 p17
Bruce, Thomas; Georgia, 1758 1640.10 p17
Bruce, Thomas; Mississippi, 1822-1845 1640.10 p17
Bruce, Thomas; Virgin Islands, 1863 1640.13 p14
Bruce, Thomas 40; Ontario, 1871 1823.28 p11
Bruce, Thomas Purves; Mississippi, 1896 1640.13 p14
Bruce, Walter Hamilton; Montreal, 1875 1640.13 p14
Bruce, William; Georgia, 1700 1640.13 p14
Bruce, William; New York, 1840 8197.10 p153
Bruce, William 15; Virginia, 1774 1220.25 p75
Brucek, Mary; Maryland, 1910 3259.35 p7
Bruch, Barbara; Port uncertain, 1764 2856.30 p54
Bruch, Jacob; Port uncertain, 1756 2856.30 p54
Bruch, Jacob; Port uncertain, 1781 2856.30 p54
Bruch, Trustam; Maryland, 1668 2524.55 p36
Bruchbacher, Abraham; America, 1754 2856.30 p54
Bruchels, Maria Margarete; America, 1764 2856.30 p55
Brucher, Johann Georg; Port uncertain, 1754 2856.30 p54
With 2 children
Bruchier, Miss; America, 1751 2856.30 p451
Bruchtt, James 28; Ontario, 1871 1823.15 p28
Bruck, Adam; Port uncertain, 1751 2856.30 p54
Bruck, Angelika; Port uncertain, 1751 2856.30 p55
Bruck, Catharina; Port uncertain, 1755 2856.30 p55
Bruck, Daniel; New York, 1839 8197.10 p127
Bruck, Jakob; America, 1737 2856.30 p54
With wife & 2 children
Bruck, Johann; Port uncertain, 1781 2856.30 p55
Bruck, Johann; Port uncertain, 1792 2856.30 p54
Bruck, Valden; Port uncertain, 1751 2856.30 p55
With wife & 3 children
Brucker, Henrich; Port uncertain, 1722 2856.30 p54
Brucker, Jacob; America, 1750 2856.30 p55
With wife & children
Brucker, Jacob; America, 1750 2856.30 p55
With wife & 7 daughters
Brucker, Johann; Port uncertain, 1785 2856.30 p54
Brucker, Konrad; Port uncertain, 1752 2856.30 p54
Bruckert, Matthaus; America, 1750 2856.30 p55

Bruckfield, Mary; Maryland, 1662 ***2524.55*** *p36*
Bruckhoffer, Johann; America, 1749 ***2856.30*** *p54*
Bruckle, Matthaus; America, 1744 ***2856.30*** *p55*
With family
Bruckler, Catharina; Port uncertain, 1724 ***2856.30*** *p54*
Bruckler, Johann Georg; Port uncertain, 1739 ***2856.30*** *p54*
Bruckner, Mr.; Port uncertain, 1784 ***2856.30*** *p27*
Bruckner, Margarete; Port uncertain, 1788 ***2856.30*** *p55*
Bruckner, Maria Elisabeth; Port uncertain, 1761 ***2856.30*** *p54*
Brucknier, Joseph; Pennsylvania, 1868 ***6058.10*** *p73*
Bruder, Frederick 18; Ontario, 1871 ***1823.15*** *p28*
Bruder, Heinrich; America, 1766 ***2856.30*** *p54*
Bruder, Martin; Port uncertain, 1741 ***2856.30*** *p54*
Bruder, Martin; Port uncertain, 1780 ***2856.30*** *p54*
Bruderlin, Johann; Port uncertain, 1793 ***2856.30*** *p55*
Bruechlin, Scholastika; Port uncertain, 1777 ***2856.30*** *p55*
Bruehl, Mathias; Port uncertain, 1751 ***2856.30*** *p55*
Bruehl, Scholastika; Port uncertain, 1777 ***2856.30*** *p55*
Bruen, Ann; Vermont, 1812-1863 ***5900.10*** *p430*
Bruen, Ann Barrey; Vermont, 1818-1894 ***5900.10*** *p529*
Bruen, Bernard; Vermont, 1850-1851 ***5900.10*** *p529*
Bruen, Elizabeth; Vermont, 1863-1874 ***5900.10*** *p529*
Bruen, Mathew; Vermont, 1814-1864 ***5900.10*** *p529*
Bruerton, George; New York, 1840 ***8197.10*** *p144*
Bruerton, John; New York, 1840 ***8197.10*** *p144*
Bruff, William 33; Maryland, 1775 ***1220.25*** *p104*
Bruffe, Susan; Maryland, 1665 ***2524.55*** *p36*
Bruffe, Susana; Maryland, 1679 ***2524.55*** *p36*
Bruffe, Thomas; Maryland, 1672 ***2524.55*** *p34*
Brug, Johann; Port uncertain, 1722 ***2856.30*** *p55*
Bruger, Vladislow; Maryland, 1910 ***3259.35*** *p7*
Bruges, William; New York, 1807 ***8197.10*** *p34*
Bruher, Jakob; Port uncertain, 1732 ***2856.30*** *p54*
Bruhl, Jacob; Port uncertain, 1763 ***2856.30*** *p55*
With wife & 6 children
Bruhl, Johann Jacob; Port uncertain, 1775 ***2856.30*** *p55*
Bruice, Wm Courtney 26; Ontario, 1871 ***1823.22*** *p19*
Bruin, Patrick 35; Ontario, 1871 ***1823.15*** *p28*
Bruing, Charles 23; Virginia, 1774 ***1220.25*** *p89*
Brujewska, Milka; Maryland, 1910 ***3259.35*** *p7*
Bruker, Peter; Port uncertain, 1757 ***2856.30*** *p55*
Brukonnings, John 38; Ontario, 1871 ***1823.15*** *p28*
Brulinski, Celestyn; Maryland, 1910 ***3259.35*** *p7*
Brumby, William 38; Ontario, 1871 ***1823.22*** *p19*
Brumell, Richd; Virginia, 1671-1672 ***6212.30*** *p47*
Brumfeild, John; Maryland, 1664 ***2524.55*** *p36*
Brumm, Adam; New York, 1836 ***8197.10*** *p212*
Brummer, Johann Adam; Port uncertain, 1754 ***2856.30*** *p55*
Brumridge, Joseph; Maryland, 1672 ***2524.55*** *p36*
Brun, John 50; Washington, 1910 ***9196.1*** *p30*
Brun, Louis Francis; Philadelphia, 1794 ***4629.10*** *p78*
Brun, Marianna; America, 1817 ***2856.30*** *p55*
Brun, Maurice 50; Ontario, 1871 ***1823.28*** *p11*
Brun, Victor L.; New York, 1816 ***8197.10*** *p58*
Brunck, Henrich; America, 1750 ***2856.30*** *p54*
With wife & 2 children
Brundage, Harry 69; Ontario, 1871 ***1823.22*** *p19*
Brunelle, Sophia; Vermont, 1846-1937 ***5900.10*** *p322*
Brunello, G. 29; Alaska, 1917 ***9196.1*** *p48*
Brunello, G. 29; Whitehorse, Yukon, 1917 ***9196.1*** *p48*
Brunen, Georg; Port uncertain, 1769 ***2856.30*** *p54*
Bruner, Cath. Elisabeth; Philadelphia, 1729 ***2856.30*** *p54*
With husband 2 sons & daughter
Bruner, Josef; Philadelphia, 1729 ***2856.30*** *p54*
With wife 2 sons & daughter
Brunily, Frederick 24; Ontario, 1871 ***1823.28*** *p11*
Brunlin, Maria Ursula; Port uncertain, 1776 ***2856.30*** *p55*
Brunn, Florian; America, 1750 ***2856.30*** *p54*
Brunnar, John; New York, 1837 ***8197.10*** *p85*
Brunnelle, P.; Quebec, 1857 ***9196.15*** *p19*
Brunner, Anna Catharina; America, 1785 ***2856.30*** *p219*
Brunner, Anna Margarete; Port uncertain, 1768 ***2856.30*** *p54*
Brunner, Cath. Elisabeth; Philadelphia, 1729 ***2856.30*** *p54*
With husband 2 sons & daughter
Brunner, Catharina; Port uncertain, 1761 ***2856.30*** *p54*
Brunner, Florian; America, 1750 ***2856.30*** *p54*
Brunner, Johann; Port uncertain, 1751 ***2856.30*** *p54*
Brunner, Johann Adam; Port uncertain, 1754 ***2856.30*** *p55*
Brunner, Josef; Philadelphia, 1729 ***2856.30*** *p54*
With wife 2 sons & daughter
Brunner, Michael; Port uncertain, 1765 ***2856.30*** *p54*
Brunner, Niklas; Port uncertain, 1754 ***2856.30*** *p54*
Brunner, William; New York, 1894 ***1640.13*** *p14*
Bruno, Agostino Maria; New York, 1807 ***8197.10*** *p332*
Brunow, Berndt John; New York, 1808 ***8197.10*** *p53*
Bruns, Behrent; New York, 1840 ***8197.10*** *p153*
Bruns, Christian L.; New York, 1837 ***8197.10*** *p85*
Bruns, Henry; New York, 1807 ***8197.10*** *p325*
Bruns, John; New York, 1828 ***8197.10*** *p211*
Bruns, Martin; New York, 1826 ***8197.10*** *p210*
Brunsdon, David 36; Ontario, 1871 ***1823.15*** *p28*
Brunsdon, John 35; Ontario, 1871 ***1823.15*** *p28*
Brunsdon, William 33; Ontario, 1871 ***1823.15*** *p28*
Brunsdon, William 60; Ontario, 1871 ***1823.15*** *p28*
Brunsen, Christopher William; New York, 1825 ***8197.10*** *p210*
Brunt, Robert; New York, 1825 ***8197.10*** *p209*
Brunton, Alexander 59; Ontario, 1871 ***1823.22*** *p19*
Brunton, Margaret; Quebec, 1841 ***1640.13*** *p14*
Brunton, Thomas 26; Ontario, 1871 ***1823.22*** *p19*
Brurain, Jacob; Port uncertain, 1744 ***2856.30*** *p54*
Brurain, Jacob; Port uncertain, 1754 ***2856.30*** *p55*
With wife & 3 children
Brus, Anthony; Philadelphia, 1793 ***4629.10*** *p73*
Bruse, Francis; Virginia, 1665 ***6212.30*** *p17*
Brush, Francis 20; Ontario, 1871 ***1823.28*** *p11*
Brush, Louace 35; Ontario, 1871 ***1823.28*** *p11*
Brusius, Ms.; Port uncertain, 1792 ***2856.30*** *p55*
Brusko, Paul; Maryland, 1910 ***3259.35*** *p7*
Brust, Catharina; Port uncertain, 1759 ***2856.30*** *p55*
Brust, Wm; Virginia, 1671 ***6212.30*** *p43*
Bruster, Johnston 57; Ontario, 1871 ***1823.22*** *p19*
Bruster, Peter; Pennsylvania, 1777 ***4629.10*** *p17*
Brustlin, Catharina; Port uncertain, 1795 ***2856.30*** *p55*
Brutache, John; Pennsylvania, 1868 ***6058.10*** *p73*
Bruten, John C.; Vermont, 1853-1934 ***5900.10*** *p429*
Bruten, Nellie E. Lynch; Vermont, 1863-1929 ***5900.10*** *p429*
Brutock, John; Pennsylvania, 1868 ***6058.10*** *p73*
Bruton, John; Maryland, 1656 ***2524.55*** *p36*
Bryam, Jno; Virginia, 1666-1667 ***6212.30*** *p32*
Bryan, Mr.; Quebec, 1857 ***9196.15*** *p15*
Bryan, Mr.; Quebec, 1858 ***9196.15*** *p32*
Bryan, Mrs.; Quebec, 1857 ***9196.15*** *p15*
Bryan, Mrs.; Quebec, 1858 ***9196.15*** *p32*
Bryan, Ann; Virginia, 1664 ***6212.30*** *p14*
Bryan, Catherine; Vermont, 1847-1892 ***5900.10*** *p454*
Bryan, Darby; Maryland, 1682 ***2524.55*** *p36*
Bryan, Derby; Maryland, 1668 ***2524.55*** *p37*
Bryan, Derby; Maryland, 1671 ***2524.55*** *p37*
Bryan, Edward 26; Ontario, 1871 ***1823.15*** *p28*
Bryan, Eliza Crowley; Vermont, 1841-1883 ***5900.10*** *p70*
Bryan, F. G. 2; Ontario, 1861 ***2896.28*** *p53*
Bryan, Frederick Henry Barker; New York, 1823-1836 ***8197.10*** *p310*
Bryan, G. F. 8; Ontario, 1861 ***2896.28*** *p53*
Bryan, George; Pennsylvania, 1775-1781 ***4628.40*** *p69*
Bryan, Grace; Maryland, 1682 ***2524.55*** *p37*
Bryan, J. W. 14; Ontario, 1861 ***2896.28*** *p53*
Bryan, James 38; Ontario, 1871 ***1823.15*** *p28*
Bryan, James 56; Vermont, 1882 ***5900.10*** *p238*
Bryan, James C.; Vermont, 1833-1911 ***5900.10*** *p70*
Bryan, John; Maryland, 1681 ***2524.55*** *p37*
Bryan, John; New York, 1807 ***8197.10*** *p34*
Bryan, John 30; Maryland, 1774 ***1220.25*** *p73*
Bryan, John 48; Ontario, 1871 ***1823.22*** *p19*
Bryan, Julyan; Maryland, 1669 ***2524.55*** *p37*
Bryan, M. A. 12; Ontario, 1861 ***2896.28*** *p53*
Bryan, M. A. 37; Ontario, 1861 ***2896.28*** *p53*
Bryan, Matilda 18; Ontario, 1861 ***2896.28*** *p53*
Bryan, Patrick; Quebec, 1814 ***5900.10*** *p33*
Bryan, Patrick; Vermont, 1814 ***5900.10*** *p33*
Bryan, Patrick 51; Vermont, 1847 ***5900.10*** *p148*
Bryan, Richard; New England, 1720 ***1224.2*** *p16*
Bryan, Sarah S.; Vermont, 1873 ***5900.10*** *p148*
Bryan, Silent; Maryland, 1682 ***2524.55*** *p37*
Bryan, Thomas; New York, 1825 ***8197.10*** *p210*
Bryan, Timothy; Maryland, 1682 ***2524.55*** *p37*
Bryan, W. J. 16; Ontario, 1861 ***2896.28*** *p53*
Bryan, William; Maryland, 1662 ***2524.55*** *p37*
Bryan, William; New York, 1794 ***8197.10*** *p4*
Bryan, William 27; Ontario, 1871 ***1823.22*** *p19*
Bryan, William, Sr.; New York, 1825 ***8197.10*** *p210*
Bryan, William, Jr.; New York, 1832 ***8197.10*** *p68*
Bryanes, Mick; New York, 1821 ***8197.10*** *p207*
Bryanoska, Eve; Maryland, 1910 ***3259.35*** *p7*
Bryans, William 30; Ontario, 1871 ***1823.15*** *p28*
Bryant, Aaron 8; Ontario, 1861 ***2896.25*** *p22*
Bryant, Abraham 22; Philadelphia, 1774 ***1220.25*** *p80*
Bryant, Alberta 1; Ontario, 1861 ***2896.25*** *p68*
Bryant, Alexander Drake; Cincinnati, 1836 ***1224.3*** *p10*
Bryant, Allice 1; Ontario, 1861 ***2896.25*** *p22*
Bryant, C. E. 8; Ontario, 1861 ***2896.25*** *p43*
Bryant, Caleb 7; Ontario, 1861 ***2896.28*** *p38*
Bryant, Charles 12; Ontario, 1861 ***2896.28*** *p38*
Bryant, Conger 20; Ontario, 1861 ***2896.25*** *p17*
Bryant, D. R. 12; Ontario, 1861 ***2896.25*** *p43*
Bryant, Daniel; Maryland, 1681 ***2524.55*** *p37*
Bryant, Derby; Maryland, 1681 ***2524.55*** *p37*
Bryant, Elin; Maryland, 1681 ***2524.55*** *p37*
Bryant, Elizabeth 6; Ontario, 1861 ***2896.25*** *p22*
Bryant, Hannah 2; Ontario, 1861 ***2896.25*** *p22*
Bryant, Hannah 7; Ontario, 1861 ***2896.25*** *p68*
Bryant, Henry 9; Ontario, 1861 ***2896.25*** *p22*
Bryant, Honour *SEE* Bryant, Robert
Bryant, James 16; Philadelphia, 1774 ***1220.25*** *p43*
Bryant, Jennet 19; Ontario, 1861 ***2896.25*** *p17*
Bryant, Jeremiah 32; America, 1774 ***1220.25*** *p36*
Bryant, John; Maryland, 1634 ***2524.55*** *p37*
Bryant, John; New York, 1840 ***8197.10*** *p144*
Bryant, John 21; Philadelphia, 1774 ***1220.25*** *p80*
Bryant, John 21; Virginia, 1774 ***1220.25*** *p56*
Bryant, John 76; Ontario, 1861 ***2896.25*** *p17*
Bryant, Joseph 5; Ontario, 1861 ***2896.25*** *p22*
Bryant, Lewis; Maryland, 1665 ***2524.55*** *p37*
With wife
Bryant, Lewis; Pennsylvania, 1777 ***4629.10*** *p13*
Bryant, Lewis 22; Virginia, 1773 ***1220.25*** *p28*
Bryant, M. E. 40; Ontario, 1861 ***2896.25*** *p43*
Bryant, Mary 18; Ontario, 1861 ***2896.28*** *p19*
Bryant, N. J. 15; Ontario, 1861 ***2896.25*** *p43*
Bryant, Rachel 40; Ontario, 1861 ***2896.28*** *p38*
Bryant, Robert; Maryland, 1672 ***2524.55*** *p37*
Wife: Honour
Bryant, Robert; Maryland, 1673 ***2524.55*** *p37*
Bryant, Robert 48; Ontario, 1871 ***1823.28*** *p11*
Bryant, S. E. 17; Ontario, 1861 ***2896.25*** *p43*
Bryant, Samuel Drake; Cincinnati, 1837 ***1224.3*** *p10*
Bryant, Sarah Jane 39; Ontario, 1861 ***2896.25*** *p68*
Bryant, Susan 43; Ontario, 1861 ***2896.25*** *p17*
Bryant, Thomas; Pennsylvania, 1777 ***4629.10*** *p13*
Bryant, Thomas 13; Ontario, 1861 ***2896.25*** *p68*
Bryant, Thomas 22; Maryland, 1774 ***1220.25*** *p3*
Bryant, Thomas H. 19; Ontario, 1861 ***2896.25*** *p43*
Bryant, William 17; Ontario, 1861 ***2896.28*** *p19*
Bryant, William 30; Ontario, 1871 ***1823.15*** *p28*
Bryant, William James 2; Ontario, 1861 ***2896.25*** *p43*
Bryaus, Robert 60; Ontario, 1871 ***1823.15*** *p28*
Bryce, Andrew Carter; Fargo, North Dakota, 1887 ***1640.13*** *p14*
Bryce, George 27; Ontario, 1871 ***1823.15*** *p28*
Bryce, Jessie; New Orleans, 1892 ***1640.13*** *p14*
Bryce, Thomas; Georgia, 1798-1850 ***1640.10*** *p17*
Bryce, Thomas; Illinois, 1886 ***1640.13*** *p14*
Bryden, Emma *SEE* Bryden, William
Bryden, Francis 29; Ontario, 1871 ***1823.15*** *p28*
Bryden, James; Boston, 1837 ***6058.10*** *p26*
Bryden, William; Alabama, 1804-1845 ***1640.10*** *p17*
Wife: Emma
Bryden, William; New York, 1807 ***8197.10*** *p35*
Brydia, William; Maryland, 1910 ***3259.35*** *p7*
Brydie, David; Georgia, 1770 ***1640.10*** *p17*
Brydon, Jane; Quebec, 1829 ***1640.13*** *p15*
Brydon, Marget 66; Ontario, 1871 ***1823.15*** *p28*
Bryed, J. 57; Ontario, 1861 ***2896.28*** *p8*
Bryed, M. A. 44; Ontario, 1861 ***2896.28*** *p8*
Bryer, Thomas; Maryland, 1662 ***2524.55*** *p180*
Bryers, Nelson 65; Ontario, 1871 ***1823.28*** *p11*
Bryers, Robert 21; Ontario, 1871 ***1823.28*** *p11*
Brykczenski, Vincenty; Maryland, 1910 ***3259.35*** *p7*
Brymer, Charles; St. Vincent, 1858 ***1640.13*** *p15*
Brymer, John; New York, 1840 ***8197.10*** *p154*
Brymer, Wm.; New York, 1840 ***8197.10*** *p156*
Brynall, Freke; Maryland, 1675 ***2524.55*** *p37*
Bryne, Michael 22; Quebec, 1848 ***1825.45*** *p28*
Bryne, William; Pennsylvania, 1867 ***6058.10*** *p60*
Brynell, Folke; Maryland, 1673 ***2524.55*** *p37*
Bryner, William 18; Philadelphia, 1774 ***1220.25*** *p80*
Bryns, Margret 54; Ontario, 1871 ***1823.15*** *p28*
Bryon, Master; Quebec, 1858 ***9196.15*** *p33*
Bryon, Miss; Quebec, 1858 ***9196.15*** *p33*
Bryon, Mr.; Quebec, 1858 ***9196.15*** *p33*
Bryon, Mrs.; Quebec, 1858 ***9196.15*** *p33*
Bryon, John; New York, 1840 ***8197.10*** *p153*
Bryon, Thomas 22; Philadelphia, 1775 ***1220.25*** *p9*
Bryson, Andrew; New York, 1802 ***8197.10*** *p206*
Bryson, Archibald; New York, 1807 ***8197.10*** *p34*
Bryson, James; New York, 1829 ***8197.10*** *p211*
Bryson, James; Pennsylvania, 1777 ***4629.10*** *p8*
Bryson, Robert; New York, 1794 ***8197.10*** *p4*
Brzczynski, Joseph; Maryland, 1910 ***3259.35*** *p7*
Brzecko, Stanislaw; Maryland, 1910 ***3259.35*** *p7*
Brzesiski, Jacob; Maryland, 1910 ***3259.35*** *p7*
Brzezenski, Walenty; Maryland, 1910 ***3259.35*** *p7*
Brzmavich, Nick 25; Alaska, 1914 ***9196.1*** *p11*
Brzozowska, Joseph; Maryland, 1910 ***3259.35*** *p7*
Brzozowski, Frank; Maryland, 1910 ***3259.35*** *p7*
Brzozowski, John; Maryland, 1910 ***3259.35*** *p7*
Brzozowsky, Wladislaw; Maryland, 1910 ***3259.35*** *p7*
Brzynski, Paul; Maryland, 1910 ***3259.35*** *p7*
Bterbey, Thomas; Maryland, 1664 ***2524.55*** *p25*
Buanojnoska, Eva; Maryland, 1910 ***3259.35*** *p7*
Buanojnoski, Peter; Maryland, 1910 ***3259.35*** *p7*

Bub, Apollonia; Port uncertain, 1751 2856.30 p55
Bub, Georg; America, 1766 2856.30 p55
Bub, Georg; America, 1773 2856.30 p55
Bub, Georg; America, 1774 2856.30 p55
With wife
Bub, Jacob; America, 1738 2856.30 p55
Bub, Jacob; Port uncertain, 1738 2856.30 p55
With wife
Bub, Mrs. Jacob; America, 1759 2856.30 p55
Bub, Johann Georg; America, 1774 2856.30 p55
Bub, Johann Georg; Port uncertain, 1773 2856.30 p55
Bub, Phil. Jacob, Sr.; America, 1738 2856.30 p55
Bub, Phil. Jacob, Jr.; America, 1738 2856.30 p55
Bub, Philipp Jacob; America, 1738 2856.30 p55
Bub, Philipp Jacob; Port uncertain, 1755 2856.30 p55
Bubazuk, Frank; Maryland, 1910 3259.35 p7
Bubb, Arthur; New York, 1854 1224.3 p10
Bubb, Mary Jane; New York, 1854 1224.3 p10
Bubear, Wm.; New York, 1827 8197.10 p210
Bubel, Bernhard; Port uncertain, 1785 2856.30 p56
Bubey, Fracis 40; Ontario, 1871 1823.28 p11
Bubi, Jac.; America, 1759 2856.30 p444
Bubi, Mrs. Jacob; America, 1759 2856.30 p55
Bubighoffer, Johann Henrich; Port uncertain, 1700-1799 2856.30 p56
Bubigkoffer, Josef; America, 1754 2856.30 p56
Bubilz, William 52; Ontario, 1871 1823.15 p28
Bubts, Josiah 78; Ontario, 1861 2896.27 p64
Buc, Joseph; Maryland, 1910 3259.35 p7
Buc, Teofila; Maryland, 1910 3259.35 p7
Bucaczinski, Theodore; Maryland, 1910 3259.35 p7
Bucannon, John; Virginia, 1775 1220.25 p122
Bucause, August 17; Ontario, 1871 1823.28 p11
Bucer, Elias; Virginia, 1671 6212.30 p44
Buch, Anna Margarete; Port uncertain, 1775 2856.30 p56
Buch, Elisabeth; Port uncertain, 1738 2856.30 p56
Buch, Georg Ludwig; Port uncertain, 1758 2856.30 p56
Buch, Heinrich; Port uncertain, 1741 2856.30 p56
Buch, Johann; Port uncertain, 1794 2856.30 p56
Buch, Margarete; Port uncertain, 1786 2856.30 p56
Buch, Maria Catharina; Port uncertain, 1758 2856.30 p56
Buch, Maria Margarete; Port uncertain, 1776 2856.30 p56
Buch, Mrs. Peter; Port uncertain, 1765 2856.30 p56
With 6 children
Buch, Rupert; Port uncertain, 1764 2856.30 p56
Buch, Sophia; Port uncertain, 1783 2856.30 p56
Buchaming, John 29; Ontario, 1871 1823.15 p28
Buchan, Mr.; Quebec, 1857 9196.15 p17
Buchan, Mrs.; Quebec, 1857 9196.15 p17
Buchan, Charles; Canada, 1853 1640.13 p15
Buchan, James; New York, 1840 8197.10 p144
Buchan, Jane 43; Ontario, 1871 1823.15 p28
Buchan, John 40; Ontario, 1871 1823.28 p11
Buchan, John Gentles; New York, 1884 1640.13 p15
Buchanan, Miss; Quebec, 1858 9196.15 p39
Buchanan, Mr.; Portland, Maine, 1857 9196.15 p13
Buchanan, Mrs.; Portland, Maine, 1857 9196.15 p13
Buchanan, Mrs.; Quebec, 1858 9196.15 p39
Buchanan, Agnes; Ontario, 1884 1640.13 p15
Buchanan, Agnes J. 10; Ontario, 1861 2896.28 p27
Buchanan, Alex; Pennsylvania, 1860 6058.10 p43
Buchanan, Alex 58; Ontario, 1871 1823.15 p28
Buchanan, Alexander *SEE* Buchanan, Angus
Buchanan, Alexander *SEE* Buchanan, James
Buchanan, Alexander; New York, 1835 8197.10 p212
Buchanan, Alex'r W. 1; Ontario, 1861 2896.28 p27
Buchanan, Alex'r W. 45; Ontario, 1861 2896.28 p27
Buchanan, Andrew 38; Ontario, 1871 1823.22 p19
Buchanan, Angus; Port uncertain, 1850-1859 4537.37 p105
Wife: Catherine MacLellan
Child: Alexander
Child: Kirsty
Child: Peggy
Child: John
Child: Donald
Child: Mary
Buchanan, Ann *SEE* Buchanan, James
Buchanan, Ann; Ontario, 1850-1859 4537.37 p31
Buchanan, Ann; Ontario, 1851 4537.32 p4
Buchanan, Ann 22; Ontario, 1871 1823.15 p28
Buchanan, Ann 42; Ontario, 1861 2896.25 p20
Buchanan, Ann MacDonald *SEE* Buchanan, James
Buchanan, Archibald; America, 1866 1640.13 p15
Buchanan, Archibald; Baltimore, 1786 1224.2 p16
Buchanan, Archibald; New York, 1775 1640.10 p17
Buchanan, Archibald; Pennsylvania, 1860 6058.10 p43
Buchanan, Catherine *SEE* Buchanan, James
Buchanan, Catherine; Ontario, 1850-1859 4537.37 p31
Buchanan, Catherine; Ontario, 1851 4537.32 p4
Buchanan, Catherine MacLellan *SEE* Buchanan, Angus
Buchanan, Charles; New York, 1807 8197.10 p35
Buchanan, David 3; Ontario, 1861 2896.25 p20
Buchanan, Donald *SEE* Buchanan, Angus
Buchanan, Donald *SEE* Buchanan, James
Buchanan, Donald 36; Ontario, 1871 1823.15 p29
Buchanan, Donald 69; Ontario, 1871 1823.15 p29
Buchanan, Duncan *SEE* Buchanan, James
Buchanan, Effie; Ontario, 1850-1859 4537.37 p64
Buchanan, Effie; Ontario, 1851 4537.32 p40
Buchanan, Eleanora 4; Ontario, 1861 2896.28 p27
Buchanan, Flora *SEE* Buchanan, James
Buchanan, Francis; Pennsylvania, 1807 6058.10 p1
Buchanan, Frederic 8; Ontario, 1861 2896.28 p27
Buchanan, George; New York, 1838 8197.10 p110
Buchanan, George; New York, New York, 1850 6058.10 p43
Buchanan, George 6; Ontario, 1861 2896.25 p20
Buchanan, George W. 6; Ontario, 1861 2896.28 p27
Buchanan, Isaac; Ontario, 1866 1640.13 p15
Buchanan, James *SEE* Buchanan, James
Buchanan, James; Ontario, 1850-1859 4537.37 p32
Wife: Ann MacDonald
Child: Ranald
Child: Duncan
Child: Donald
Child: Mary
Child: Ann
Child: Alexander
Child: Catherine
Child: Marion
Child: Penny
Buchanan, James; Ontario, 1850-1859 4537.37 p32
Wife: Flora
Child: Donald
Child: John
Child: Norman
Child: James
Child: Ann
Buchanan, James; Pennsylvania, 1856 6058.10 p37
Buchanan, James; Pennsylvania, 1856 6058.10 p43
Buchanan, James 10; Ontario, 1861 2896.25 p20
Buchanan, James 35; Ontario, 1871 1823.15 p29
Buchanan, James 42; Ontario, 1871 1823.15 p29
Buchanan, James 55; Ontario, 1871 1823.28 p11
Buchanan, James 62; Ontario, 1871 1823.15 p29
Buchanan, Jane 66; Ontario, 1871 1823.15 p29
Buchanan, John *SEE* Buchanan, Angus
Buchanan, John *SEE* Buchanan, James
Buchanan, John; Massachusetts, 1859 1640.13 p15
Buchanan, John; New York, 1794 8197.10 p4
Buchanan, John; New York, 1826 8197.10 p210
Buchanan, John; New York, 1837 8197.10 p85
Buchanan, John; New York, New York, 1850 6058.10 p43
Buchanan, John; Pennsylvania, 1845 6058.10 p21
Buchanan, John; Saskatchewan, 1883 4537.37 p89
Buchanan, John 40; Ontario, 1871 1823.15 p29
Buchanan, John 47; Ontario, 1871 1823.22 p19
Buchanan, John 49; Ontario, 1871 1823.15 p29
Buchanan, John 56; Ontario, 1871 1823.28 p11
Buchanan, Kirsty *SEE* Buchanan, Angus
Buchanan, Marion *SEE* Buchanan, James
Buchanan, Mary *SEE* Buchanan, Angus
Buchanan, Mary *SEE* Buchanan, James
Buchanan, Mary; Ontario, 1850-1859 4537.37 p32
Buchanan, Mary; Ontario, 1851 4537.32 p5
Buchanan, Mary A. 11; Ontario, 1861 2896.28 p27
Buchanan, Mary A. 35; Ontario, 1861 2896.28 p27
Buchanan, Mary Louisa; Ontario, 1882 1640.13 p15
Buchanan, Moses; Florida, 1822-1845 1640.10 p17
Buchanan, Norman *SEE* Buchanan, James
Buchanan, Peggy *SEE* Buchanan, Angus
Buchanan, Penny *SEE* Buchanan, James
Buchanan, Peter; Charleston, South Carolina, 1819 1640.13 p15
Buchanan, Ranald *SEE* Buchanan, James
Buchanan, Robert; New York, 1837 8197.10 p85
Buchanan, Robert; New York, 1840 8197.10 p386
Buchanan, Robert 42; Ontario, 1861 2896.25 p20
Buchanan, Robert, Jr. 8; Ontario, 1861 2896.25 p20
Buchanan, Robt 30; Ontario, 1871 1823.15 p29
Buchanan, S.; Quebec, 1856 9196.15 p5
Buchanan, Thomas; New York, 1829 8197.10 p352
Buchanan, Thomas 12; Ontario, 1861 2896.25 p20
Buchanan, William; Bermuda, 1839 1640.13 p15
Buchanan, William; Pennsylvania, 1839 6058.10 p15
Buchanan, William 25; Ontario, 1871 1823.28 p11
Buchanan, William 56; Ontario, 1871 1823.15 p29
Buchanan, William 66; Ontario, 1871 1823.15 p29
Buchanin, William 44; Ontario, 1871 1823.22 p19
Buchannan, David 63; Ontario, 1871 1823.28 p11
Buchannan, Robert 56; Ontario, 1871 1823.15 p29
Buchannan, Wm 32; Ontario, 1871 1823.15 p29
Buchannon, Mary A. 38; Ontario, 1871 1823.15 p29
Buchannon, Robert 46; Ontario, 1871 1823.22 p19
Buchcker, Valentin; America, 1747 2856.30 p56
Buchel, Jacob; Port uncertain, 1746 2856.30 p59
Buchele, Adam; Port uncertain, 1744 2856.30 p59
Buchele, Adam; Port uncertain, 1745 2856.30 p59
Buchele, Hans Martin; Port uncertain, 1733 2856.30 p59
Buchelin, Martin; America, 1744 2856.30 p59
Bucher, Mr.; Port uncertain, 1782 2856.30 p169
Bucher, Mr.; Port uncertain, 1786 2856.30 p169
Bucher, Franz Jakob; Port uncertain, 1786 2856.30 p59
Bucherer, Georg; Port uncertain, 1769 2856.30 p56
Bucherin, Barbara; Port uncertain, 1732 2856.30 p59
Buchert, Mrs. Bartel; America, 1741 2856.30 p56
With 4 children
Buchert, Jacob; Port uncertain, 1770 2856.30 p56
Buchert, Michael; Port uncertain, 1770 2856.30 p56
Buchert, Peter; America, 1741 2856.30 p56
With 2 children
Buchholz, Adam; America, 1752 2856.30 p56
With wife & 3 children
Buchler, Catharina; America, 1749 2856.30 p60
Buchler, Johann; America, 1749 2856.30 p60
Buchler, Leonard; Port uncertain, 1764 2856.30 p59
Buchler, Salomea; Port uncertain, 1765 2856.30 p59
Buchlin, Anastasia; Port uncertain, 1760 2856.30 p60
Buchmann, Maria Elisabeth; America, 1764 2856.30 p56
Buchtung, Maria Anna; Port uncertain, 1764 2856.30 p56
Buchucz, Peter; Maryland, 1910 3259.35 p7
Buchwalelski, Telfa; Maryland, 1910 3259.35 p8
Buck, Benjamin 40; Ontario, 1871 1823.22 p19
Buck, Bridget Casey; Vermont, 1844-1892 5900.10 p482
Buck, Daniel; New York, 1807 8197.10 p328
Buck, Francis; Pennsylvania, 1777 4629.10 p9
Buck, Frank; Maryland, 1910 3259.35 p8
Buck, Franz Josef; Port uncertain, 1755 2856.30 p56
Buck, Franz Josef; Port uncertain, 1791 2856.30 p56
Buck, John; Maryland, 1665 2524.55 p37
Buck, Josef; Port uncertain, 1797 2856.30 p56
Buck, Joseph; Pennsylvania, 1777 4629.10 p16
Buck, Konrad; Port uncertain, 1796 2856.30 p56
Buck, Lorenz; Port uncertain, 1764 2856.30 p56
Buck, Nathan A.; Vermont, 1840-1913 5900.10 p482
Buck, Peter; Virginia, 1674 1224.1 p4
Buck, Phebe; Maryland, 1658 2524.55 p37
Buck, Philip; Pennsylvania, 1777 4629.10 p15
Buck, Richard 29; Virginia, 1775 1220.25 p95
Buck, Therese; Port uncertain, 1794 2856.30 p56
Buck, Thomas 50; Ontario, 1871 1823.28 p11
Buck, William 41; Ontario, 1871 1823.22 p19
Buck, William 71; Ontario, 1871 1823.22 p19
Buck, Wm 45; Ontario, 1871 1823.28 p11
Buck, Wm, Jr. 20; Ontario, 1871 1823.28 p11
Buckel, Michael; Port uncertain, 1784 2856.30 p56
Buckerfield, William H. 34; Ontario, 1871 1823.28 p11
Buckey, Lewis 39; Ontario, 1871 1823.15 p29
Buckh, Johann; Port uncertain, 1770 2856.30 p56
Buckham, Andrew; New York, 1832 8197.10 p68
Buckham, Andrew, Jr.; New York, 1838 8197.10 p109
Buckhart, Frederick; New Orleans, 1856 3437.14 p32
Buckhurst, Jno; Virginia, 1665-1666 6212.30 p22
Buckingham, Samuel 41; Ontario, 1871 1823.15 p29
Buckinshaw, Edward 38; Ontario, 1871 1823.28 p11
Buckland, Amelia 21; Ontario, 1871 1823.28 p11
Buckland, Amelia 45; Ontario, 1871 1823.28 p11
Buckland, David; New York, 1837 1224.3 p10
Buckland, S. B. 36; Ontario, 1871 1823.15 p29
Buckland, William; New York, 1802 8197.10 p18
Buckle, Adam; America, 1751 2856.30 p37
With wife & children
Buckle, John 60; Ontario, 1871 1823.15 p29
Buckle, William; New York, 1804 8197.10 p26
Buckler, Benjamin; Maryland, 1682 2524.55 p37
Buckley, . . .; New Hampshire, 1641-1660 4628.40 p44
Buckley, Ann O'Connor; Vermont, 1827-1903 5900.10 p350
Buckley, Anna O'Connor; Vermont, n.d. 5900.10 p168
Buckley, Bridgett; Vermont, 1842-1922 5900.10 p510
Buckley, Catherine; Vermont, n.d. 5900.10 p319
Buckley, Cornelius 84; Vermont, 1907 5900.10 p310
Buckley, Darby 51; New York, New York, 1851 1825.45 p46
Wife: Mary 39
Son: Michael 16
Son: Tade 18
Daughter: Margaret 5
Daughter: Mary 12
Daughter: Johanna 9
Son: John 2
Buckley, Elizabeth Roach; Vermont, 1836-1921 5900.10 p314
Buckley, James; New York, 1803 8197.10 p11
Buckley, James; New York, 1819 8197.10 p61

Buckley, Johanna 9 *SEE* Buckley, Darby
Buckley, Johanna 60; Ontario, 1871 ***1823.15*** *p29*
Buckley, John 2 *SEE* Buckley, Darby
Buckley, John 24; Ontario, 1871 ***1823.28*** *p11*
Buckley, John 32; Ontario, 1871 ***1823.15*** *p29*
Buckley, John 60; Vermont, 1924 ***5900.10*** *p310*
Buckley, John 63; Vermont, 1886 ***5900.10*** *p319*
Buckley, Joseph; New York, New York, 1847 ***6058.10*** *p44*
Buckley, Joseph 45; Ontario, 1871 ***1823.22*** *p19*
Buckley, Lawrence; New York, 1836 ***8197.10*** *p317*
Buckley, Margaret 5 *SEE* Buckley, Darby
Buckley, Margaret 78; Vermont, 1891 ***5900.10*** *p169*
Buckley, Mary 12 *SEE* Buckley, Darby
Buckley, Mary 39 *SEE* Buckley, Darby
Buckley, Mary Crowley 74; Vermont, 1907 ***5900.10*** *p310*
Buckley, Mary Kiley; Vermont, 1826-1904 ***5900.10*** *p268*
Buckley, Mary Sullivan; Vermont, 1840-1916 ***5900.10*** *p507*
Buckley, Mathew; Vermont, 1822-1922 ***5900.10*** *p268*
Buckley, Michael; New York, 1820 ***8197.10*** *p61*
Buckley, Michael; New York, New York, 1840 ***1224.3*** *p10*
Buckley, Michael; Vermont, 1832-1896 ***5900.10*** *p507*
Buckley, Michael 16 *SEE* Buckley, Darby
Buckley, Michael 40; Ontario, 1871 ***1823.28*** *p11*
Buckley, Patrick; Vermont, 1831-1898 ***5900.10*** *p350*
Buckley, Patrick 32; Ontario, 1871 ***1823.15*** *p29*
Buckley, Patrick 40; Ontario, 1871 ***1823.28*** *p11*
Buckley, Patrick 60; Ontario, 1871 ***1823.15*** *p29*
Buckley, Robert 16; Ontario, 1871 ***1823.22*** *p19*
Buckley, Sarah Binding; Boston, 1687 ***1224.1*** *p7*
Buckley, Tade 18 *SEE* Buckley, Darby
Buckley, Thomas; New England, 1692 ***1224.1*** *p59*
Buckley, Thomas; Vermont, n.d. ***5900.10*** *p168*
Buckley, Thomas; Vermont, 1826-1919 ***5900.10*** *p314*
Buckley, William; Pennsylvania, 1785 ***4629.10*** *p47*
Buckmaker, Joseph; Maryland, 1681 ***2524.55*** *p37*
Buckmaster, Christopher; Ohio, 1853 ***1224.3*** *p10*
Bucknell, Sarah 77; Ontario, 1871 ***1823.22*** *p20*
Buckoll, William; New York, New York, 1829 ***1224.3*** *p10*
Buckout, Henry 71; Ontario, 1871 ***1823.22*** *p20*
Bucykowski, William; Maryland, 1910 ***3259.35*** *p8*
Buczek, Jan; Maryland, 1910 ***3259.35*** *p8*
Buczkowski, Frank; Maryland, 1910 ***3259.35*** *p8*
Buczkowski, Jacob; Maryland, 1910 ***3259.35*** *p8*
Buczkowski, John; Maryland, 1910 ***3259.35*** *p8*
Buczkowski, Victor; Maryland, 1910 ***3259.35*** *p8*
Buczkowski, Wojciek; Maryland, 1910 ***3259.35*** *p8*
Buczynski, George; Maryland, 1910 ***3259.35*** *p8*
Bud, Gyles; Maryland, 1659 ***2524.55*** *p38*
Budacz, Henry; Maryland, 1910 ***3259.35*** *p8*
Budacz, Melchior; Maryland, 1910 ***3259.35*** *p8*
Budacz, Thomas; Maryland, 1910 ***3259.35*** *p8*
Budam, Thomas; Maryland, 1674 ***2524.55*** *p37*
Budan, Frank 29; Juneau, Alaska, 1913 ***9196.1*** *p22*
Budd, Mr.; Quebec, 1858 ***9196.15*** *p46*
Budd, Mrs.; Maryland, 1650 ***2524.55*** *p37*
Budd, Joseph 38; Ontario, 1871 ***1823.22*** *p20*
Budd, Levy; Pennsylvania, 1777 ***4629.10*** *p10*
Budd, Peter; Maryland, 1661 ***2524.55*** *p37*
Budden, Mr.; Quebec, 1857 ***9196.15*** *p23*
Budden, Charles T. 21; Ontario, 1871 ***1823.28*** *p11*
Budden, James; Pennsylvania, 1777 ***4629.10*** *p6*
Budden, Samuel 22; Baltimore, 1775 ***1220.25*** *p118*
Budder, Fredrick 43; Ontario, 1871 ***1823.28*** *p11*
Budder, John 24; Ontario, 1871 ***1823.28*** *p11*
Buderick, Martin 58; Ontario, 1871 ***1823.28*** *p11*
Budge, James 75; Ontario, 1871 ***1823.15*** *p29*
Budge, Jane 72; Ontario, 1871 ***1823.15*** *p29*
Budge, John 50; Ontario, 1871 ***1823.15*** *p29*
Budge, William; Georgia, 1775 ***1640.10*** *p17*
Budge, William 22; Georgia, 1775 ***1220.25*** *p125*
Budgman, Jane 29; Virginia, 1774 ***1220.25*** *p89*
Budinich, Gus 26; Alaska, 1913 ***9196.1*** *p13*
Budrick, Martin 23; Ontario, 1871 ***1823.28*** *p12*
Budzanski, Frank; Maryland, 1910 ***3259.35*** *p8*
Budziski, Michael; Maryland, 1910 ***3259.35*** *p8*
Budzynski, Henry; Maryland, 1910 ***3259.35*** *p8*
Bueb, Jacob; America, 1738 ***2856.30*** *p55*
Bueb, Jacob; Port uncertain, 1738 ***2856.30*** *p55*
With wife
Buechel, Frederick; New York, 1810 ***8197.10*** *p56*
Buechmuller, Anton; Port uncertain, 1767 ***2856.30*** *p56*
Buel, William; Ontario, 1861 ***2896.25*** *p13*
Bueri, Frederick; Wilmington, Delaware, 1830 ***6058.10*** *p13*
Buerkle, Joseph; New York, 1837 ***8197.10*** *p87*
Bues, Johann; Port uncertain, 1755 ***2856.30*** *p57*
Bufenbach, Bernard; Port uncertain, 1750 ***2856.30*** *p57*
Buffan, M. S. 70; Ontario, 1871 ***1823.28*** *p12*
Buffel, Hans Adam; Port uncertain, 1746 ***2856.30*** *p60*
Buffel, Paul; America, 1738 ***2856.30*** *p60*
Buffin, John; Maryland, 1665 ***2524.55*** *p39*
Bug, Georg; America, 1781 ***2856.30*** *p57*
Bugge, Thomas; Virginia, 1656 ***1224.1*** *p10*
Buggins, Haniball; Virginia, 1666 ***6212.30*** *p27*
Buggions, Tho; Virginia, 1665-1666 ***6212.30*** *p22*
Buggnis, Wm; Virginia, 1664 ***6212.30*** *p14*
Buggy, James; New York, 1837 ***8197.10*** *p212*
Bugliss, Ralph 47; Ontario, 1871 ***1823.15*** *p29*
Buhhom, William 22; Ontario, 1871 ***1823.15*** *p29*
Buhl, Anna Barbara; Port uncertain, 1752 ***2856.30*** *p60*
Buhl, Eva Catharina; Port uncertain, 1783 ***2856.30*** *p57*
Buhl, Peter; America, 1739 ***2856.30*** *p60*
With wife & 3 children
Buhl, Peter; Port uncertain, 1754 ***2856.30*** *p57*
Buhler, Andreas; America, 1774 ***2856.30*** *p60*
Buhler, Andreas; America, 1775 ***2856.30*** *p60*
Buhler, Andreas; Port uncertain, 1762 ***2856.30*** *p60*
Buhler, Anna Catharina; Port uncertain, 1743 ***2856.30*** *p60*
Buhler, Catharina; Port uncertain, 1762 ***2856.30*** *p60*
Buhler, Christina; America, 1758 ***2856.30*** *p60*
Buhler, Christina; America, 1761 ***2856.30*** *p60*
Buhler, Friedrich; Port uncertain, 1744 ***2856.30*** *p60*
Buhler, Georg; Port uncertain, 1763 ***2856.30*** *p60*
Buhler, Jacob; Port uncertain, 1755 ***2856.30*** *p60*
Buhler, Johann Michael; Port uncertain, 1781 ***2856.30*** *p60*
Buhler, Karolina; America, 1774 ***2856.30*** *p60*
Buhler, Karolina; America, 1775 ***2856.30*** *p60*
Buhler, Kunigunda; Port uncertain, 1768 ***2856.30*** *p60*
Buhler, Martin; America, 1764 ***2856.30*** *p60*
With wife & children
Buhler, Martin; Port uncertain, 1752 ***2856.30*** *p60*
Buhler, Michael; Port uncertain, 1749 ***2856.30*** *p60*
Buhler, Vinzenz; America, 1738 ***2856.30*** *p60*
With wife & child
Buhlin, Elisabeth Von; Port uncertain, 1760 ***2856.30*** *p60*
Buhn, Andreas; Port uncertain, 1782 ***2856.30*** *p37*
Buhn, Andreas; Port uncertain, 1783 ***2856.30*** *p37*
Buhr, Martin; America, 1771 ***2856.30*** *p60*
Buhr, Michael; Port uncertain, 1764 ***2856.30*** *p57*
Buhrer, Jacob; Port uncertain, 1752 ***2856.30*** *p60*
Buice, John 51; Ontario, 1871 ***1823.15*** *p29*
Buist, Miss; Quebec, 1858 ***9196.15*** *p36*
Buist, Mr.; Quebec, 1858 ***9196.15*** *p37*
Buist, Andrew; New York, 1891 ***1640.13*** *p15*
Buist, John; New York, 1818-1834 ***8197.10*** *p304*
Bukwell, Mr.; Portland, Maine, 1857 ***9196.15*** *p13*
Bulatovich, M. 25; Alaska, 1916 ***9196.1*** *p44*
Bulatovich, M. 25; Whitehorse, Yukon, 1916 ***9196.1*** *p44*
Buler, Elis. Barbara; Port uncertain, 1796 ***2856.30*** *p60*
Bulfinch, Hannah; Boston, 1842 ***1224.3*** *p10*
Bulger, Alice Barrett; Vermont, 1906 ***5900.10*** *p524*
Bulger, Anna M.; Vermont, 1858-1911 ***5900.10*** *p533*
Bulger, Catherine 38; Vermont, 1885 ***5900.10*** *p268*
Bulger, Daniel 58; Ontario, 1871 ***1823.28*** *p12*
Bulger, Elizabeth; Vermont, 1844-1914 ***5900.10*** *p335*
Bulger, James 35; Ontario, 1871 ***1823.15*** *p29*
Bulger, John 66; Ontario, 1871 ***1823.15*** *p29*
Bulger, Julia 66; Ontario, 1871 ***1823.22*** *p20*
Bulger, Mary 6 months; Vermont, 1849 ***5900.10*** *p524*
Bulger, Mary 36; Ontario, 1871 ***1823.22*** *p20*
Bulger, Michael 45; Ontario, 1871 ***1823.22*** *p20*
Bulger, Moses 84; Vermont, 1890 ***5900.10*** *p524*
Bulger, Nion 30; Ontario, 1871 ***1823.15*** *p29*
Bulger, Patrick 7; Vermont, 1853 ***5900.10*** *p524*
Bulger, Thomas 40; Ontario, 1871 ***1823.22*** *p20*
Bulgin, Joseph 28; Maryland, 1774 ***1220.25*** *p53*
Bulkeley, Arthur; Died enroute, 1645 ***1224.1*** *p10*
Bulkeley, Thomas; New England, 1690 ***1224.1*** *p10*
Bulkley, Grace; New England, 1648 ***1224.1*** *p13*
Bulkley, Peter; Boston, 1761 ***1224.2*** *p16*
Bull, Miss; Quebec, 1857 ***9196.15*** *p22*
Bull, Mr. 40; Grenada, 1774-1775 ***1220.25*** *p129*
Bull, Absalom; Savannah, Georgia, 1797 ***1224.2*** *p16*
Bull, Albert 21; Ontario, 1861 ***2896.27*** *p53*
Bull, Alice 7; Ontario, 1861 ***2896.27*** *p53*
Bull, Amanda M. 12; Ontario, 1861 ***2896.27*** *p64*
Bull, Amos H. 19; Ontario, 1861 ***2896.27*** *p70*
Bull, Betsy; Ontario, 1861 ***2896.25*** *p9*
Bull, Caroline; Ontario, 1861 ***2896.25*** *p9*
Bull, Cory 20; Ontario, 1861 ***2896.27*** *p53*
Bull, Elizabeth 16; Ontario, 1861 ***2896.27*** *p70*
Bull, Elizabeth 53; Ontario, 1861 ***2896.27*** *p64*
Bull, Ezekiel; Pennsylvania, 1779 ***4629.10*** *p41*
Bull, Fanny 51; Ontario, 1861 ***2896.27*** *p53*
Bull, Frances 14; Ontario, 1861 ***2896.27*** *p53*
Bull, Harriet Ann 24; Ontario, 1861 ***2896.27*** *p53*
Bull, Herbert 15; Ontario, 1861 ***2896.27*** *p53*
Bull, Ida A. 10; Ontario, 1861 ***2896.27*** *p53*
Bull, James 15; Philadelphia, 1775 ***1220.25*** *p122*
Bull, James 20; Ontario, 1871 ***1823.15*** *p29*
Bull, John; Virginia, 1668-1669 ***6212.30*** *p40*
Bull, Jonathan; Boston, 1729 ***1224.2*** *p16*
Bull, Katharine; Maryland, 1680 ***2524.55*** *p37*
Bull, Martha 9; Ontario, 1861 ***2896.27*** *p70*
Bull, Martha 18; Ontario, 1861 ***2896.28*** *p30*
Bull, Mary; Maryland, 1661 ***2524.55*** *p37*
Bull, Mary A. 19; Ontario, 1861 ***2896.27*** *p64*
Bull, Mary E. 17; Ontario, 1861 ***2896.27*** *p53*
Bull, Mitchell B.; New York, 1802 ***8197.10*** *p18*
Bull, Permilia 40; Ontario, 1861 ***2896.27*** *p53*
Bull, Phebe 11; Ontario, 1861 ***2896.27*** *p53*
Bull, Sarah 18; Ontario, 1861 ***2896.27*** *p53*
Bull, Selick 23; Ontario, 1861 ***2896.27*** *p53*
Bull, Stephen; Ontario, 1861 ***2896.25*** *p9*
Bull, Stephen 10; Ontario, 1861 ***2896.27*** *p70*
Bull, Tho.; Maryland, 1674 ***2524.55*** *p37*
Bull, Thomas 37; Ontario, 1871 ***1823.15*** *p29*
Bull, Tobias; Virginia, 1664-1665 ***6212.30*** *p15*
Bull, William; New York, 1840 ***8197.10*** *p153*
Bullard, Abaham 59; Ontario, 1871 ***1823.15*** *p29*
Bullard, Anne Clark; Vermont, 1854-1924 ***5900.10*** *p184*
Bullard, Isaac; Virginia, 1667 ***6212.30*** *p37*
Bullard, John 30; Ontario, 1871 ***1823.15*** *p29*
Bullard, Tho; Virginia, 1666-1667 ***6212.30*** *p34*
Bullen, Charles 69; Ontario, 1871 ***1823.22*** *p20*
Bullen, Elinour *SEE* Bullen, Robert
Bullen, Elionor *SEE* Bullen, Robert
Bullen, James; Virginia, 1666 ***6212.30*** *p31*
Bullen, John 18; Maryland, 1775 ***1220.25*** *p98*
Bullen, Robert; Maryland, 1659 ***2524.55*** *p37*
Wife: Elinour
Bullen, Robert; Maryland, 1661 ***2524.55*** *p37*
Wife: Elionor
Bullen, Thomas; Virginia, 1690 ***1224.1*** *p10*
Bullens, James 32; Ontario, 1871 ***1823.15*** *p29*
Buller, Francis; Virginia, 1666 ***6212.30*** *p27*
Buller, John; Virginia, 1666 ***6212.30*** *p28*
Buller, Richard; Maryland, 1670 ***2524.55*** *p37*
Bullerant, Henry 30; Ontario, 1871 ***1823.28*** *p12*
Bullerant, Josephus 31; Ontario, 1871 ***1823.28*** *p12*
Bulley, Adeline; Vermont, n.d. ***5900.10*** *p543*
Bullin, Thomas; Boston, 1717 ***1224.2*** *p16*
Bulling, Diedrick; New York, 1837 ***8197.10*** *p85*
Bullinger, Christian; America, 1737 ***2856.30*** *p57*
Bullinger, Henry; New York, 1827 ***8197.10*** *p343*
Bullinger, Jakob; America, 1737 ***2856.30*** *p57*
Bullinger, Johann Georg; Port uncertain, 1780 ***2856.30*** *p57*
Bullinger, Johann Georg; Port uncertain, 1781 ***2856.30*** *p57*
Bullman, John 33; Ontario, 1871 ***1823.15*** *p29*
Bullmer, Jacob; New York, 1837 ***8197.10*** *p85*
Bullner, John 19; Ontario, 1871 ***1823.28*** *p12*
Bulloch, Ann Graham; Georgia, 1764 ***1640.10*** *p18*
Bullock, Bridget Walsh; Vermont, 1894 ***5900.10*** *p185*
Bullock, Francis; Maryland, 1660 ***2524.55*** *p37*
Bullock, Joseph 25; Ontario, 1871 ***1823.15*** *p29*
Bullock, Sarah; Vermont, 1845-1898 ***5900.10*** *p183*
Bullock, Sebella; Virginia, 1664-1665 ***6212.30*** *p15*
Bullock, Sibeel; Virginia, 1671-1672 ***6212.30*** *p47*
Bullock, Simon; Vermont, 1843-1931 ***5900.10*** *p183*
Bullock, Susan; Virginia, 1666 ***6212.30*** *p29*
Bullock, Thomas; New York, 1794 ***8197.10*** *p4*
Bullocke, William; Virginia, 1650 ***1224.1*** *p10*
Bullocke, William; Died enroute, 1650 ***1224.1*** *p10*
Bullpitt, John; Maryland, 1673 ***2524.55*** *p37*
Bulman, Diana *SEE* Bulman, George
Bulman, Diana 4 *SEE* Bulman, George
Bulman, Elizabeth *SEE* Bulman, George
Bulman, Elizabeth 36 *SEE* Bulman, George
Bulman, George *SEE* Bulman, George
Bulman, George; Georgia, 1775 ***1640.10*** *p18*
Wife: Elizabeth
Child: George
Child: Diana
Bulman, George 5 *SEE* Bulman, George
Bulman, George 46; Georgia, 1775 ***1220.25*** *p125*
Wife: Elizabeth 36
Child: George 5
Child: Diana 4
Bulmer, Annis *SEE* Bulmer, James
Bulmer, George 14 *SEE* Bulmer, John
Bulmer, Grace 46 *SEE* Bulmer, John
Bulmer, James; Maryland, 1658 ***2524.55*** *p38*
Wife: Annis
Bulmer, James 20 *SEE* Bulmer, John
Bulmer, John 45; Nova Scotia, 1774 ***1220.25*** *p14*
Wife: Grace 46
Child: James 20
Child: George 14
Child: Joseph 10
Bulmer, Joseph 10 *SEE* Bulmer, John

Bulmer, Mary; Maryland, 1658 ***2524.55*** *p38*
Bulmer, Robert 48; Ontario, 1871 ***1823.28*** *p12*
Bulmer, Thomas; Maryland, 1658 ***2524.55*** *p38*
Bulmer, Thomas 47; Ontario, 1871 ***1823.22*** *p20*
Bulpit, John; Maryland, 1669 ***2524.55*** *p38*
Bulwinkle, Henry; New York, 1807 ***8197.10*** *p326*
Bum, Andreas; America, 1738 ***2856.30*** *p57*
With wife 7 children & brother
Bumm, Jacob; Pennsylvania, 1777 ***4629.10*** *p24*
Bummel, Martin; Port uncertain, 1785 ***2856.30*** *p57*
Bummerer, Johann; Port uncertain, 1752 ***2856.30*** *p57*
Bumpus, Albreson *SEE* Bumpus, Thomas
Bumpus, Thomas; Maryland, 1662 ***2524.55*** *p38*
Wife: Albreson
Buna, Robert 40; Ontario, 1871 ***1823.15*** *p29*
Bunberry, Harry 35; Ontario, 1871 ***1823.22*** *p20*
Bunce, Charles; Pennsylvania, 1868 ***6058.10*** *p62*
Bunce, Edward 41; Ontario, 1871 ***1823.22*** *p20*
Bunce, Louisa 56; Ontario, 1871 ***1823.15*** *p29*
Bunch, Robert H.; New York, 1832 ***8197.10*** *p211*
Buncle, George; Georgia, 1738 ***1640.10*** *p18*
Bundell, Thomas; Maryland, 1665 ***2524.55*** *p38*
Bunel, Damas Napoleon; New York, 1831 ***8197.10*** *p367*
Bunfeild, James; Maryland, 1664 ***2524.55*** *p38*
Bungart, Eva 60; Kansas, 1910 ***9079.10*** *p49*
Bungart, Henry 61; Kansas, 1892-1910 ***9079.10*** *p49*
Bunger, George 42; Ontario, 1871 ***1823.15*** *p29*
Bunger, John; Maryland, 1910 ***3259.35*** *p8*
Bunion, John 70; Ontario, 1871 ***1823.28*** *p12*
Bunion, Michel 60; Ontario, 1871 ***1823.28*** *p12*
Bunk, Frank; Maryland, 1910 ***3259.35*** *p8*
Bunker, Francis 59; Ontario, 1871 ***1823.22*** *p20*
Bunn, George 37; Ontario, 1871 ***1823.28*** *p12*
Bunn, Wm; Virginia, 1672 ***6212.30*** *p50*
Bunne, John; Maryland, 1663 ***2524.55*** *p219*
Bunnell, Alvah 17; Vermont, 1851 ***5900.10*** *p151*
Bunney, Anna Coyne; Vermont, 1841-1914 ***5900.10*** *p266*
Bunney, Ellen; Vermont, n.d. ***5900.10*** *p266*
Bunney, James; Vermont, 1837-1913 ***5900.10*** *p266*
Bunney, John 27; Vermont, 1891 ***5900.10*** *p266*
Bunnie, Ellen Shea; Vermont, 1833-1915 ***5900.10*** *p251*
Bunnie, John; Vermont, 1832-1896 ***5900.10*** *p251*
Bunning, Nicholas R.; New York, 1829 ***8197.10*** *p351*
Buntin, Mr.; Quebec, 1858 ***9196.15*** *p41*
Buntin, Mrs.; Quebec, 1858 ***9196.15*** *p41*
Bunting, Benjamin; Pennsylvania, 1778 ***4629.10*** *p45*
Bunting, John; Pennsylvania, 1778 ***4629.10*** *p45*
Bunting, William; Pennsylvania, 1777 ***4629.10*** *p10*
Bunus, John 22; Ontario, 1871 ***1823.28*** *p12*
Buoby, William 33; Ontario, 1871 ***1823.15*** *p29*
Buons, Bridget 33; Ontario, 1871 ***1823.15*** *p29*
Buraham, Geo; Virginia, 1664 ***6212.30*** *p14*
Burbage, William 56; Ontario, 1871 ***1823.28*** *p12*
Burbidge, James 44; Ontario, 1871 ***1823.28*** *p12*
Burbowing, William; Maryland, 1910 ***3259.35*** *p8*
Burch, E. 24; Ontario, 1861 ***2896.28*** *p9*
Burch, Edward 36; Ontario, 1871 ***1823.22*** *p20*
Burch, Joan; Virginia, 1671-1672 ***6212.30*** *p46*
Burch, John 30; Maryland, 1775 ***1220.25*** *p108*
Burch, Thomas 16; Maryland, 1775 ***1220.25*** *p120*
Burchal, Edward 21; Maryland, 1774 ***1220.25*** *p83*
Burchall, John; Pennsylvania, 1786 ***4629.10*** *p54*
Burchert, Klaus; Port uncertain, 1770 ***2856.30*** *p57*
Burchett, Arthur Tertius Nicholas; Chicago, 1855 ***1224.3*** *p10*
Burchett, Frances Anne; Chicago, 1855 ***1224.3*** *p10*
Burchfeild, Samuell; Maryland, 1665 ***2524.55*** *p38*
Burchill, Arthur; New York, 1807 ***8197.10*** *p34*
Burchill, Samuel 18; Ontario, 1871 ***1823.15*** *p29*
Burchill, Thomas 53; Ontario, 1871 ***1823.15*** *p29*
Burchmayer, Anna Maria; Port uncertain, 1746 ***2856.30*** *p57*
Burckart, Philipp; Port uncertain, 1744 ***2856.30*** *p57*
Burckert, Philipp; Port uncertain, 1783 ***2856.30*** *p57*
Burckh, Anton; Port uncertain, 1753 ***2856.30*** *p57*
Burckhard, Anton; America, 1761 ***2856.30*** *p57*
Burckhard, Catharina; Port uncertain, 1773 ***2856.30*** *p57*
Burckhard, Klaus; Port uncertain, 1752 ***2856.30*** *p57*
Burckhardt, Josef; Port uncertain, 1740 ***2856.30*** *p57*
Burckhart, Bernhard; Port uncertain, 1752 ***2856.30*** *p57*
With family
Burckhmayer, Catharina; Port uncertain, 1755 ***2856.30*** *p57*
Burckhmeyer, Hans Georg; Port uncertain, 1754 ***2856.30*** *p57*
Burckholster, John; New York, 1838 ***8197.10*** *p212*
Burckholster, John; New York, 1840 ***8197.10*** *p144*
Burckin, Anna Maria; Port uncertain, 1744 ***2856.30*** *p60*
Burckin, Therese; Port uncertain, 1783 ***2856.30*** *p60*
Burckle, Ludwig; America, 1751 ***2856.30*** *p60*
Burcley, Thomas; Maryland, 1667 ***2524.55*** *p38*
Burd, Edward; Virginia, 1703-1704 ***6212.30*** *p63*
Burdel, Rosie; Maryland, 1910 ***3259.35*** *p8*
Burden, William 44; Ontario, 1871 ***1823.15*** *p29*
Burden, William F. 49; Ontario, 1871 ***1823.28*** *p12*
Burdett, Elizabeth 18; Philadelphia, 1774 ***1220.25*** *p42*
Burdett, Margrett *SEE* Burdett, Richard
Burdett, Richard; Maryland, 1674 ***2524.55*** *p38*
Wife: Margrett
Burdette, Jane U. 23; Ontario, 1861 ***2896.28*** *p49*
Burdette, Thomas; Maryland, 1659 ***2524.55*** *p38*
Burdette, Verlinda; Maryland, 1659 ***2524.55*** *p38*
Burdick, Aaron P.; Vermont, 1842-1916 ***5900.10*** *p281*
Burdick, Sarah Ann Keenan; Vermont, 1853-1934 ***5900.10*** *p281*
Burdin, Thomas 57; Ontario, 1871 ***1823.15*** *p29*
Burdock, Benjamin 23; Maryland, 1775 ***1220.25*** *p111*
Burdon, Hannah 27; Virginia, 1774 ***1220.25*** *p90*
Burdon, James; New York, 1837 ***8197.10*** *p87*
Burdon, John 28; Ontario, 1871 ***1823.22*** *p20*
Burdon, Wm.; New York, 1840 ***8197.10*** *p156*
Burdy, Joseph 13; Ontario, 1861 ***2896.27*** *p29*
Burford, Edward 21; Maryland, 1775 ***1220.25*** *p96*
Burford, Francis; Maryland, 1665 ***2524.55*** *p38*
Burg, Daniel; America, 1739 ***2856.30*** *p57*
Burg, Friedrich Karl; America, 1745 ***2856.30*** *p57*
Burg, Henry; New York, 1840 ***8197.10*** *p153*
Burg, Johann Henrich; America, 1745 ***2856.30*** *p57*
With wife
Burg, Martin; America, 1738 ***2856.30*** *p60*
Burgain, John; Virginia, 1665 ***6212.30*** *p18*
Burgardt, Antoni; Port uncertain, 1750 ***2856.30*** *p57*
Burgay, Peter; America, 1741 ***2856.30*** *p57*
Burge, Mr.; Portland, Maine, 1857 ***9196.15*** *p13*
Burge, Edward; New York, 1834 ***8197.10*** *p316*
Burge, J. 28; Alaska, 1908 ***9196.1*** *p36*
Burge, J. 28; Alaska, 1908 ***9196.1*** *p37*
Burgen, Ellen; Vermont, 1851-1921 ***5900.10*** *p201*
Burgen, Hannah Sexton; Vermont, 1838-1908 ***5900.10*** *p330*
Burgen, Stephen; Vermont, 1836-1886 ***5900.10*** *p330*
Burgep, Samuel 48; Ontario, 1871 ***1823.15*** *p30*
Burger, Elisabeth; Port uncertain, 1726 ***2856.30*** *p57*
Burger, Elizabeth; New York, 1750 ***1224.2*** *p16*
Burger, Johann; Port uncertain, 1783 ***2856.30*** *p58*
Burger, Michael; America, 1751 ***2856.30*** *p58*
With wife & sister
Burger, Michael; Port uncertain, 1745 ***2856.30*** *p58*
Burgert, Henry; New York, 1827 ***8197.10*** *p210*
Burges, Francis; New York, 1807 ***8197.10*** *p325*
Burges, Isaac; Virginia, 1664 ***6212.30*** *p15*
Burges, J. 21; Virginia, 1774 ***1220.25*** *p89*
Burges, John; New England, 1628 ***1224.1*** *p10*
Burges, Joseph; Maryland, n.d. ***1224.1*** *p10*
Burges, Mark 55; Ontario, 1871 ***1823.15*** *p30*
Burges, Mary A. 62; Ontario, 1871 ***1823.15*** *p30*
Burges, Phillip; Maryland, 1669 ***2524.55*** *p38*
Burges, Robert; Maryland, 1677 ***2524.55*** *p38*
Burges, Thomas; Maryland, 1681 ***2524.55*** *p38*
Burges, Thomas 47; Ontario, 1871 ***1823.28*** *p12*
Burges, William; Maryland, 1689 ***1224.1*** *p10*
Burges, Willm.; Maryland, 1650 ***2524.55*** *p38*
Burgess, Mr. 26; Dominica, 1774 ***1220.25*** *p128*
Burgess, Francis; Virginia, 1666 ***6212.30*** *p29*
Burgess, George 31; Ontario, 1871 ***1823.15*** *p30*
Burgess, James; New York, 1808 ***8197.10*** *p53*
Burgess, James 34; Ontario, 1871 ***1823.15*** *p30*
Burgess, James 35; Ontario, 1871 ***1823.15*** *p30*
Burgess, James 45; Ontario, 1871 ***1823.15*** *p30*
Burgess, John; New Jersey, 1878 ***1640.13*** *p15*
Burgess, John; New York, 1830 ***8197.10*** *p211*
Burgess, John; Virginia, 1666 ***6212.30*** *p27*
Burgess, John 35; Ontario, 1871 ***1823.15*** *p30*
Burgess, John 44; Ontario, 1871 ***1823.22*** *p20*
Burgess, Joseph; Georgia, 1736 ***1640.10*** *p18*
Burgess, Mack 56; Ontario, 1871 ***1823.15*** *p30*
Burgess, Richard; New York, 1802 ***8197.10*** *p18*
Burgess, William 34; Virginia, 1773 ***1220.25*** *p30*
Burgess, William 45; Ontario, 1871 ***1823.28*** *p12*
Burgess, William 70; Ontario, 1871 ***1823.22*** *p20*
Burgess, William L. 65; Ontario, 1871 ***1823.28*** *p12*
Burgett, Joseph 50; Ontario, 1871 ***1823.28*** *p12*
Burgey, Margaret; Vermont, 1835-1911 ***5900.10*** *p609*
Burggraf, Michael; Port uncertain, 1731 ***2856.30*** *p58*
Burgh, John 20; Philadelphia, 1774 ***1220.25*** *p4*
Burghard, Maria Agnes; Port uncertain, 1792 ***2856.30*** *p58*
Burgin, Grace Burke 84; Vermont, 1877 ***5900.10*** *p198*
Burgin, Johann; Port uncertain, 1770 ***2856.30*** *p60*
Burgin, Maria; Port uncertain, 1748 ***2856.30*** *p60*
Burgin, Maria; Port uncertain, 1784 ***2856.30*** *p60*
Burgin, Mary Carney 88; Vermont, 1901 ***5900.10*** *p198*
Burgin, Matth.; America, 1764 ***2856.30*** *p283*
Burgin, Michael 8; Vermont, 1857 ***5900.10*** *p198*
Burgin, Patrick J. 59; Vermont, 1873 ***5900.10*** *p198*
Burgis, Edward; Virginia, 1664 ***6212.30*** *p10*
Burgis, John; Virginia, 1712 ***1224.2*** *p17*
Burgis, Joseph; Virginia, 1749 ***1224.2*** *p17*
Burgly, George; Pennsylvania, 1865 ***6058.10*** *p50*
Burgstahler, Johann Adam; Port uncertain, 1739 ***2856.30*** *p58*
Burgstaler, Christof; Port uncertain, 1793 ***2856.30*** *p58*
Burgstaler, Margarete; Port uncertain, 1794 ***2856.30*** *p58*
Burgstaler, Rudolf; Port uncertain, 1793 ***2856.30*** *p58*
Burgwin, Edward; Pennsylvania, 1845 ***6058.10*** *p21*
Burgy, Henry; New York, 1836 ***8197.10*** *p76*
Burhem, Siebert; Baltimore, 1851 ***6058.10*** *p43*
Burhenn, Siebert; Baltimore, 1851 ***6058.10*** *p43*
Burin, Justina; Virginia, 1775 ***1220.25*** *p123*
Burjett, George; Ontario, 1871 ***1823.28*** *p12*
Burk, Carl 37; Ontario, 1871 ***1823.28*** *p12*
Burk, Elizabeth 1; Ontario, 1871 ***1823.28*** *p12*
Burk, Elizabeth 18; Maryland, 1774 ***1220.25*** *p59*
Burk, James 32; Ontario, 1871 ***1823.15*** *p30*
Burk, James 55; Ontario, 1871 ***1823.28*** *p12*
Burk, John; New York, 1807 ***8197.10*** *p35*
Burk, John; New York, 1840 ***8197.10*** *p144*
Burk, John; New York, 1840 ***8197.10*** *p153*
Burk, John; New York, 1840 ***8197.10*** *p154*
Burk, John 24; Maryland, 1774 ***1220.25*** *p52*
Burk, John 56; Ontario, 1871 ***1823.15*** *p30*
Burk, P. 47; Seattle, 1914 ***9196.1*** *p63*
Burk, Patrick; New York, 1840 ***8197.10*** *p154*
Burk, Samuel 35; Ontario, 1871 ***1823.15*** *p30*
Burk, Samuel 86; Ontario, 1871 ***1823.15*** *p30*
Burk, Thomas; New York, 1837 ***8197.10*** *p84*
Burk, Thomas 50; Ontario, 1871 ***1823.28*** *p12*
Burk, Walter; Maryland, 1681 ***2524.55*** *p38*
Burk, William; New York, 1837 ***8197.10*** *p84*
Burk, William; Pennsylvania, 1777 ***4629.10*** *p15*
Burkart, Jakob; Port uncertain, 1788 ***2856.30*** *p58*
Burkart, Wilhelm; Port uncertain, 1764 ***2856.30*** *p58*
Burkart, Wilhelm; Port uncertain, 1788 ***2856.30*** *p58*
Burke, Adaline; Vermont, 1836-1900 ***5900.10*** *p194*
Burke, Alexander *SEE* Burke, John
Burke, Ann *SEE* Burke, John
Burke, Ann *SEE* Burke, Murdo
Burke, Ann *SEE* Burke, Peter
Burke, Ann; Vermont, 1820-1902 ***5900.10*** *p161*
Burke, Ann; Vermont, 1851-1864 ***5900.10*** *p173*
Burke, Ann 68; Vermont, 1883 ***5900.10*** *p261*
Burke, Ann 70; Vermont, 1898 ***5900.10*** *p394*
Burke, Anna; Vermont, 1855-1916 ***5900.10*** *p472*
Burke, Anna; Vermont, 1860-1933 ***5900.10*** *p407*
Burke, Anna; Vermont, 1880 ***5900.10*** *p336*
Burke, Anna 60; Vermont, 1918 ***5900.10*** *p83*
Burke, Anna C. O'Neil; Vermont, 1849-1935 ***5900.10*** *p183*
Burke, Anna Cavanaugh; Vermont, 1827-1886 ***5900.10*** *p173*
Burke, Annie; Vermont, 1846-1903 ***5900.10*** *p267*
Burke, Annie C.; Vermont, 1885 ***5900.10*** *p133*
Burke, August 38; Ontario, 1871 ***1823.28*** *p12*
Burke, Aurelia Lafar; Vermont, 1852-1920 ***5900.10*** *p513*
Burke, Bessie Duffy; Vermont, 1889-1971 ***5900.10*** *p595*
Burke, Bridget; Vermont, 1800-1899 ***5900.10*** *p186*
Burke, Bridget; Vermont, 1828-1980 ***5900.10*** *p143*
Burke, Bridget; Vermont, 1856-1918 ***5900.10*** *p568*
Burke, Bridget 21; Vermont, 1855 ***5900.10*** *p264*
Burke, Bridget White; Vermont, 1825-1898 ***5900.10*** *p461*
Burke, Catharine; Vermont, 1801-1871 ***5900.10*** *p354*
Burke, Catherine *SEE* Burke, John
Burke, Catherine *SEE* Burke, Peter
Burke, Catherine; Vermont, 1825-1909 ***5900.10*** *p206*
Burke, Catherine; Vermont, 1844-1902 ***5900.10*** *p411*
Burke, Catherine 55; Vermont, 1883 ***5900.10*** *p250*
Burke, Catherine MacLeod *SEE* Burke, John
Burke, Catherine Maher 76; Vermont, 1892 ***5900.10*** *p330*
Burke, Catherine McGrath; Vermont, 1850-1922 ***5900.10*** *p143*
Burke, Charles E. 34; Vermont, 1897 ***5900.10*** *p271*
Burke, Daniel; Vermont, 1863-1904 ***5900.10*** *p173*
Burke, David; New York, 1837 ***8197.10*** *p87*
Burke, David; Vermont, 1809-1879 ***5900.10*** *p133*
Burke, Donald *SEE* Burke, John
Burke, Donald *SEE* Burke, Murdo
Burke, Duncan *SEE* Burke, Murdo
Burke, E. C. 76; Vermont, 1907 ***5900.10*** *p607*
Burke, Edmund; Vermont, 1830-1913 ***5900.10*** *p271*
Burke, Effie *SEE* Burke, John
Burke, Elenor A.; Vermont, 1835-1905 ***5900.10*** *p262*
Burke, Ellan Blake 70; Vermont, 1891 ***5900.10*** *p550*
Burke, Ellen; Vermont, 1834-1906 ***5900.10*** *p261*
Burke, Ellen; Vermont, 1856-1911 ***5900.10*** *p485*
Burke, Ellen; Vermont, 1858-1927 ***5900.10*** *p190*
Burke, Ellen; Vermont, 1860-1905 ***5900.10*** *p203*

Burke, Ellen; Vermont, 1860-1943 ***5900.10*** *p173*
Burke, Ellen Connell; Vermont, 1819-1904 ***5900.10*** *p357*
Burke, Ellen M. Foley 28; Vermont, 1874 ***5900.10*** *p570*
Burke, Frances 65; Vermont, 1874 ***5900.10*** *p264*
Burke, Grace 84; Vermont, 1877 ***5900.10*** *p198*
Burke, Hannah; Vermont, 1855-1933 ***5900.10*** *p423*
Burke, Honoria; Vermont, 1847-1920 ***5900.10*** *p403*
Burke, James; New York, 1837 ***8197.10*** *p87*
Burke, James; Vermont, 1816-1894 ***5900.10*** *p438*
Burke, James; Vermont, 1822-1909 ***5900.10*** *p161*
Burke, James; Vermont, 1839-1915 ***5900.10*** *p582*
Burke, James 3; Vermont, 1864 ***5900.10*** *p173*
Burke, James Edmund; Vermont, 1849-1943 ***5900.10*** *p176*
Burke, Jane; Vermont, 1854-1864 ***5900.10*** *p173*
Burke, Jane; Vermont, 1856-1937 ***5900.10*** *p161*
Burke, Jeremiah; Vermont, 1815-1891 ***5900.10*** *p380*
Burke, John *SEE* Burke, John
Burke, John; New York, 1827 ***8197.10*** *p343*
Burke, John; New York, New York, 1835 ***8197.10*** *p153*
Burke, John; Ontario, 1850-1859 ***4537.37*** *p32*
Wife: Catherine MacLeod
Child: William
Child: Alexander
Child: Effie
Child: John
Child: Ann
Child: Marion
Child: Donald
Child: Catherine
Child: Roderick
Child: Malcolm
Burke, John; Ontario, 1850-1859 ***4537.37*** *p32*
Wife: Mary Buchanan
Child: Catherine
Child: Ann
Burke, John; Ontario, 1851 ***4537.32*** *p5*
Wife: Mary Buchanan
Child: Catherine
Child: Ann
Burke, John; Vermont, 1820-1863 ***5900.10*** *p356*
Burke, John; Vermont, 1852-1892 ***5900.10*** *p143*
Burke, John; Vermont, 1894-1947 ***5900.10*** *p595*
Burke, John 10; Vermont, 1873 ***5900.10*** *p173*
Burke, John 16; Tortola, 1774 ***1220.25*** *p85*
Burke, John 19; Vermont, 1861 ***5900.10*** *p330*
Burke, John 24; Vermont, 1882 ***5900.10*** *p173*
Burke, John 27; Ontario, 1871 ***1823.15*** *p30*
Burke, John 53; Ontario, 1871 ***1823.28*** *p12*
Burke, John 57; Vermont, 1882 ***5900.10*** *p126*
Burke, John B.; Vermont, 1849-1874 ***5900.10*** *p133*
Burke, John E.; Vermont, 1854-1909 ***5900.10*** *p271*
Burke, John W.; Vermont, 1850-1888 ***5900.10*** *p93*
Burke, Joseph; Vermont, 1853-1901 ***5900.10*** *p193*
Burke, Josephine Lapierre; Vermont, 1854 ***5900.10*** *p193*
Burke, Julia; Vermont, 1893 ***5900.10*** *p53*
Burke, Julia A. 36; Vermont, 1895 ***5900.10*** *p206*
Burke, Kate; Vermont, 1855-1904 ***5900.10*** *p159*
Burke, Kate; Vermont, 1856 ***5900.10*** *p253*
Burke, Kate Murfy 57; Vermont, 1889 ***5900.10*** *p537*
Burke, Katherine 92; Vermont, 1923 ***5900.10*** *p126*
Burke, M. E. Sixby; Vermont, 1836-1919 ***5900.10*** *p607*
Burke, Malcolm *SEE* Burke, John
Burke, Margaret; Vermont, 1847-1924 ***5900.10*** *p253*
Burke, Margaret; Vermont, 1849-1924 ***5900.10*** *p394*
Burke, Margaret; Vermont, 1863-1904 ***5900.10*** *p173*
Burke, Margaret 80; Vermont, 1877 ***5900.10*** *p182*
Burke, Margaret E. McGreevy; Vermont, 1849-1883 ***5900.10*** *p182*
Burke, Margaret McCue; Vermont, 1832-1908 ***5900.10*** *p438*
Burke, Maria; Vermont, 1845-1933 ***5900.10*** *p271*
Burke, Maria; Vermont, 1856-1900 ***5900.10*** *p588*
Burke, Marion *SEE* Burke, John
Burke, Mary; Vermont, 1827-1881 ***5900.10*** *p52*
Burke, Mary; Vermont, 1856-1935 ***5900.10*** *p173*
Burke, Mary; Vermont, 1857-1921 ***5900.10*** *p380*
Burke, Mary; Vermont, 1905 ***5900.10*** *p171*
Burke, Mary; Port uncertain, 1850-1859 ***4537.37*** *p129*
Burke, Mary 46; Vermont, 1901 ***5900.10*** *p133*
Burke, Mary 64; Vermont, 1908 ***5900.10*** *p422*
Burke, Mary 78; Vermont, n.d. ***5900.10*** *p246*
Burke, Mary 85; Vermont, 1872 ***5900.10*** *p434*
Burke, Mary A.; Vermont, 1836-1914 ***5900.10*** *p356*
Burke, Mary Buchanan *SEE* Burke, John
Burke, Mary E.; Vermont, 1853-1893 ***5900.10*** *p461*
Burke, Mary E.; Vermont, 1862-1928 ***5900.10*** *p253*
Burke, Mary Flynn; Vermont, 1816-1898 ***5900.10*** *p133*
Burke, Mary Foley; Vermont, 1846-1874 ***5900.10*** *p563*
Burke, Mary Gleason; Vermont, 1834-1923 ***5900.10*** *p582*
Burke, Mary J.; Vermont, 1868-1937 ***5900.10*** *p129*
Burke, Mary MacDonald *SEE* Burke, Peter
Burke, Mary MacInnes *SEE* Burke, Murdo
Burke, Mary Medlar; Vermont, 1855-1942 ***5900.10*** *p340*
Burke, Mary Qualters; Vermont, 1854-1924 ***5900.10*** *p588*
Burke, Mary Ryan; Vermont, 1840-1885 ***5900.10*** *p557*
Burke, Mary Walsh 72; Vermont, 1896 ***5900.10*** *p271*
Burke, Michael; New York, 1837 ***8197.10*** *p87*
Burke, Michael; Pennsylvania, 1778 ***4629.10*** *p45*
Burke, Michael; Vermont, 1802-1866 ***5900.10*** *p354*
Burke, Michael; Vermont, 1825-1898 ***5900.10*** *p461*
Burke, Michael; Vermont, 1825-1899 ***5900.10*** *p173*
Burke, Michael; Vermont, 1848-1895 ***5900.10*** *p563*
Burke, Michael; Vermont, 1889 ***5900.10*** *p171*
Burke, Michael 40; Vermont, 1881 ***5900.10*** *p264*
Burke, Michael 41; Ontario, 1871 ***1823.22*** *p20*
Burke, Michael T.; Vermont, 1857-1929 ***5900.10*** *p253*
Burke, Murdo; Ontario, 1850-1859 ***4537.37*** *p33*
Child: Ann
Child: Ranald
Child: William
Child: Duncan
Child: Donald
Wife: Mary MacInnes
Burke, Murdo; Ontario, 1851 ***4537.32*** *p5*
Child: Duncan
Child: Donald
Wife: Mary MacInnes
Child: William
Child: Ranald
Child: Ann
Burke, Murdock 60; Ontario, 1871 ***1823.15*** *p30*
Burke, Nancy; Vermont, 1901 ***5900.10*** *p579*
Burke, Nancy Keating; Vermont, 1821-1905 ***5900.10*** *p380*
Burke, Nellie F. 24; Vermont, 1876 ***5900.10*** *p330*
Burke, Patrick; Vermont, 1817 ***5900.10*** *p550*
Burke, Patrick; Vermont, 1890 ***5900.10*** *p212*
Burke, Patrick 57; Vermont, 1882 ***5900.10*** *p246*
Burke, Patrick 63; Ontario, 1871 ***1823.15*** *p30*
Burke, Patrick C.; Vermont, 1836-1873 ***5900.10*** *p267*
Burke, Patrick K.; New York, 1837 ***8197.10*** *p87*
Burke, Patsy 3; Vermont, 1878 ***5900.10*** *p345*
Burke, Peter; Ontario, 1850-1859 ***4537.37*** *p33*
Wife: Mary MacDonald
Child: William
Child: Catherine
Child: Ann
Burke, Peter 40; Ontario, 1871 ***1823.28*** *p12*
Burke, Peter E.; Vermont, 1837-1897 ***5900.10*** *p411*
Burke, Philip; Pennsylvania, 1777 ***4629.10*** *p13*
Burke, Ranald *SEE* Burke, Murdo
Burke, Redmond; Philadelphia, 1814 ***1224.3*** *p10*
Burke, Richard; Vermont, 1832-1885 ***5900.10*** *p81*
Burke, Richard; Vermont, 1843-1927 ***5900.10*** *p183*
Burke, Robert; New York, 1819 ***8197.10*** *p207*
Burke, Robert; Vermont, 1853-1926 ***5900.10*** *p380*
Burke, Roderick *SEE* Burke, John
Burke, Rose Burns; Vermont, 1855-1930 ***5900.10*** *p379*
Burke, Sarah O'Rourke; Vermont, 1849-1926 ***5900.10*** *p176*
Burke, Stephen 29; Vermont, 1857 ***5900.10*** *p354*
Burke, Thomas; Maryland, 1660-1661 ***2524.55*** *p29*
Burke, Thomas; Maryland, 1660-1661 ***2524.55*** *p38*
Burke, Thomas; New York, 1807 ***8197.10*** *p329*
Burke, Thomas; North Carolina, 1775-1781 ***4628.40*** *p69*
Burke, Thomas; Vermont, 1841-1916 ***5900.10*** *p557*
Burke, Thomas; Vermont, 1855-1916 ***5900.10*** *p340*
Burke, Thomas 62; Vermont, 1877 ***5900.10*** *p264*
Burke, Thomas 65; Ontario, 1871 ***1823.15*** *p30*
Burke, Thomas 71; Ontario, 1871 ***1823.22*** *p20*
Burke, Thomas K.; Vermont, 1845-1927 ***5900.10*** *p379*
Burke, Thomas S.; Vermont, 1888-1935 ***5900.10*** *p595*
Burke, Tobias; Vermont, 1849-1925 ***5900.10*** *p588*
Burke, Walter 20; Vermont, 1863 ***5900.10*** *p330*
Burke, Walter 50; Ontario, 1871 ***1823.15*** *p30*
Burke, William *SEE* Burke, John
Burke, William *SEE* Burke, Murdo
Burke, William *SEE* Burke, Peter
Burke, William; Vermont, 1847-1920 ***5900.10*** *p568*
Burke, William; Vermont, 1852-1921 ***5900.10*** *p423*
Burke, William 22; Ontario, 1871 ***1823.15*** *p30*
Burke, William 61; Vermont, 1882 ***5900.10*** *p271*
Burke, Wm; Vermont, 1848-1915 ***5900.10*** *p513*
Burke Family ; Carolina, 1775-1781 ***4628.40*** *p81*
Burkel, Adam; Port uncertain, 1795 ***2856.30*** *p60*
Burkel, Adam; Port uncertain, 1796 ***2856.30*** *p60*
Burket, John; Pennsylvania, 1777 ***4629.10*** *p15*
Burkhard, Peter; New York, 1840 ***8197.10*** *p154*
Burkhardt, Anna Maria; Port uncertain, 1773 ***2856.30*** *p58*
Burkhart, Fredrik; New Orleans, 1856 ***3437.14*** *p32*
Burkhart, Martin; Pennsylvania, 1777 ***4629.10*** *p12*
Burkhart, Peter; New York, 1840 ***8197.10*** *p155*
Burkhart, William; Pennsylvania, 1777 ***4629.10*** *p11*
Burkhead, Tho.; Maryland, 1682 ***2524.55*** *p38*
Burkowing, Joseph; Maryland, 1910 ***3259.35*** *p8*
Burkum, Roger; Virginia, 1667 ***6212.30*** *p37*
Burlace, Nich; Virginia, 1666 ***6212.30*** *p27*
Burle, Cristop; Virginia, 1664 ***6212.30*** *p8*
Burle, Mary *SEE* Burle, Robert
Burle, Robert *SEE* Burle, Robert
Burle, Robert; Maryland, 1649 ***2524.55*** *p38*
Wife: Mary
Child: Stephen
Child: Robert
Burle, Robert; Maryland, 1649 ***2524.55*** *p38*
Wife: Sarah
Daughter: Sarah
Son: Thomas
Burle, Sarah *SEE* Burle, Robert
Burle, Stephen *SEE* Burle, Robert
Burle, Thomas *SEE* Burle, Robert
Burleigh, Alexander 16; Maryland, 1775 ***1220.25*** *p116*
Burleigh, Elizabeth A. 7; Ontario, 1861 ***2896.25*** *p27*
Burleigh, Freeman 4; Ontario, 1861 ***2896.28*** *p39*
Burleigh, George 35; Ontario, 1861 ***2896.25*** *p27*
Burleigh, Mary 4; Ontario, 1861 ***2896.25*** *p27*
Burleigh, William 8; Ontario, 1861 ***2896.25*** *p27*
Burlenguet, Elesebeth 56; Ontario, 1871 ***1823.28*** *p12*
Burley, Catharine 17; Ontario, 1861 ***2896.25*** *p44*
Burley, Catherine 34; Ontario, 1861 ***2896.25*** *p51*
Burley, Clarinda 23; Ontario, 1861 ***2896.25*** *p43*
Burley, E. J. 14; Ontario, 1861 ***2896.25*** *p44*
Burley, E. M. 37; Ontario, 1861 ***2896.25*** *p44*
Burley, George 47; Ontario, 1871 ***1823.22*** *p20*
Burley, Harriet 35; Ontario, 1861 ***2896.25*** *p44*
Burley, Henry; Maryland, 1673 ***2524.55*** *p38*
Burley, John 28; Baltimore, 1775 ***1220.25*** *p116*
Burley, John W. 4; Ontario, 1861 ***2896.25*** *p44*
Burley, M. A. 9; Ontario, 1861 ***2896.25*** *p44*
Burley, M. A. 12; Ontario, 1861 ***2896.25*** *p44*
Burley, M. E. 2; Ontario, 1861 ***2896.25*** *p44*
Burley, Maria 50; Ontario, 1861 ***2896.25*** *p44*
Burley, Marshall 15; Ontario, 1861 ***2896.25*** *p44*
Burley, Nancy 77; Ontario, 1871 ***1823.22*** *p20*
Burley, R. H. 13; Ontario, 1861 ***2896.25*** *p44*
Burley, S. E. 7; Ontario, 1861 ***2896.25*** *p44*
Burley, Samuel 17; Ontario, 1861 ***2896.28*** *p23*
Burley, Sophia 19; Ontario, 1861 ***2896.28*** *p56*
Burley, Susannah; Perth Amboy, New Jersey, 1746 ***1224.2*** *p64*
Burley, William; New York, 1727 ***1224.2*** *p17*
Burlin, Richard; New York, 1840 ***8197.10*** *p145*
Burling, Moses 44; Ontario, 1871 ***1823.15*** *p30*
Burling, Samuel; Nova Scotia, 1799 ***1224.3*** *p10*
Burlingham, Arthur 9; Ontario, 1861 ***2896.27*** *p48*
Burlingham, David 16; Ontario, 1861 ***2896.27*** *p64*
Burlingham, Elizabeth 23; Ontario, 1861 ***2896.26*** *p18*
Burlingham, Elizabeth 37; Ontario, 1861 ***2896.27*** *p65*
Burlingham, Freeman 4; Ontario, 1861 ***2896.27*** *p60*
Burlingham, Hannah 36; Ontario, 1861 ***2896.27*** *p65*
Burlingham, Helena A. 1; Ontario, 1861 ***2896.27*** *p65*
Burlingham, Hulda 27; Ontario, 1861 ***2896.27*** *p65*
Burlingham, James 8; Ontario, 1861 ***2896.27*** *p60*
Burlingham, Luke 15; Ontario, 1861 ***2896.27*** *p48*
Burlingham, Lydia 24; Ontario, 1861 ***2896.28*** *p41*
Burlingham, Marcus 7; Ontario, 1861 ***2896.27*** *p48*
Burlingham, Mary 11; Ontario, 1861 ***2896.27*** *p18*
Burlingham, Melissa 21; Ontario, 1861 ***2896.27*** *p60*
Burlingham, Obediah 13; Ontario, 1861 ***2896.27*** *p48*
Burlingham, Phebe 38; Ontario, 1861 ***2896.27*** *p64*
Burlingham, Phebe 40; Ontario, 1861 ***2896.27*** *p60*
Burlingham, Phebe 69; Ontario, 1861 ***2896.27*** *p65*
Burlingham, Phebe C. 13; Ontario, 1861 ***2896.27*** *p60*
Burlingham, Reuben B. 5 months; Ontario, 1861 ***2896.27*** *p48*
Burlingham, Sarah A. 11; Ontario, 1861 ***2896.27*** *p65*
Burlingham, Sarah E. 5; Ontario, 1861 ***2896.27*** *p48*
Burlingham, Varnum 63; Ontario, 1861 ***2896.26*** *p18*
Burlingham, William M. 5; Ontario, 1861 ***2896.26*** *p18*
Burly, D. A. 8; Ontario, 1861 ***2896.25*** *p52*
Burly, Deborah 19; Ontario, 1861 ***2896.27*** *p65*
Burly, Eliza; Virginia, 1666 ***6212.30*** *p30*
Burly, Emily 52; Ontario, 1861 ***2896.27*** *p65*
Burly, J. E. 4; Ontario, 1861 ***2896.25*** *p52*
Burly, John 11; Ontario, 1861 ***2896.27*** *p65*
Burly, Mary 13; Ontario, 1861 ***2896.25*** *p66*
Burly, Mary 45; Ontario, 1861 ***2896.25*** *p52*
Burly, Mary J. 14; Ontario, 1861 ***2896.25*** *p52*
Burly, Robert 16; Ontario, 1861 ***2896.27*** *p65*
Burly, Robt; Virginia, 1667 ***6212.30*** *p36*
Burly, Thomas 15; Ontario, 1861 ***2896.25*** *p66*
Burly, W. A. 1; Ontario, 1861 ***2896.25*** *p52*
Burly, William 20; Ontario, 1871 ***1823.22*** *p20*
Burmaster, Fredriek 37; Ontario, 1871 ***1823.28*** *p12*
Burn, Bryan 22; Philadelphia, 1775 ***1220.25*** *p121*

Burrows, Thomas 47; Ontario, 1871 ***1823.15*** *p30*
Bursey, Mary J. 84; Vermont, 1886 ***5900.10*** *p482*
Bursey, Peter; Vermont, 1827-1899 ***5900.10*** *p546*
Burskowski, Victor; Maryland, 1910 ***3259.35*** *p8*
Burstall, Mr.; Quebec, 1858 ***9196.15*** *p32*
Burstall, Mrs.; Quebec, 1857 ***9196.15*** *p25*
Bursted, Jeremy; Maryland, 1658 ***2524.55*** *p179*
Burston, Thomas; Maryland, 1668 ***2524.55*** *p39*
Burt, Benjamin; East New Jersey, 1733 ***1224.2*** *p17*
Burt, George; New Jersey, 1849 ***1224.3*** *p11*
Burt, Jane; Virginia, 1666 ***6212.30*** *p26*
Burt, Moses 15; Philadelphia, 1774 ***1220.25*** *p82*
Burt, Patrick; South Carolina, 1775 ***1640.13*** *p16*
Burt, William 15; Philadelphia, 1774 ***1220.25*** *p82*
Burtbey, Alice; Maryland, 1669 ***2524.55*** *p218*
Burtey, John; Maryland, 1675 ***2524.55*** *p39*
Burton, Dr.; Quebec, 1856 ***9196.15*** *p7*
Burton, Ann; Maryland, 1660 ***2524.55*** *p39*
Burton, Ann 55; Ontario, 1871 ***1823.15*** *p30*
Burton, Charles; New York, 1818 ***8197.10*** *p206*
Burton, Charles; New York, 1840 ***8197.10*** *p156*
Burton, Charlotte 13; St. John Island, 1775 ***1220.25*** *p121*
Burton, Edmond; Maryland, 1651 ***2524.55*** *p39*
Wife: Rebecca
Son: Edward
Burton, Edmond; Maryland, 1658 ***2524.55*** *p39*
Wife: Rebecca
Burton, Edward *SEE* Burton, Edmond
Burton, Francis; Virginia, 1665-1666 ***6212.30*** *p21*
Burton, Francis 21; Maryland, 1775 ***1220.25*** *p104*
Burton, George; Died enroute, 1637 ***1224.1*** *p11*
Burton, Isaac; Charles Town, South Carolina, 1788 ***1224.2*** *p17*
Burton, Jane 15; Ontario, 1871 ***1823.15*** *p30*
Burton, John; Maryland, 1674 ***2524.55*** *p39*
Burton, John; Texas, 1851 ***1224.3*** *p11*
Burton, John 21; Maryland, 1774 ***1220.25*** *p41*
Burton, John 22; Virginia, 1774 ***1220.25*** *p46*
Burton, Ralph 44; Ontario, 1871 ***1823.22*** *p21*
Burton, Rebecca *SEE* Burton, Edmond
Burton, Richard; Charles Town, South Carolina, 1763 ***1224.2*** *p17*
Burton, Richard; Virginia, 1656 ***1224.1*** *p11*
Burton, Robert; Richmond, Virginia, 1837 ***1640.13*** *p16*
Burton, Thomas; New England, 1689 ***1224.1*** *p11*
Burton, William; Maryland, 1681 ***2524.55*** *p39*
Burton, William 22; Maryland, 1775 ***1220.25*** *p98*
Burton, William 46; Ontario, 1871 ***1823.28*** *p12*
Burton, William 50; Philadelphia, 1774 ***1220.25*** *p66*
Burton, William, Sr. 74; Ontario, 1871 ***1823.28*** *p12*
Burtsch, Sebastian; Port uncertain, 1733 ***2856.30*** *p58*
Burwash, Janet A.; Ontario, 1871 ***1823.22*** *p21*
Burwell, Henry; Virginia, 1664 ***6212.30*** *p15*
Burwell, Thomas; Maryland, 1664 ***2524.55*** *p39*
Bury, Isaac 17; Maryland, 1774 ***1220.25*** *p77*
Bury, Jacob; Pennsylvania, 1777 ***4629.10*** *p25*
Bury, James 26; Ontario, 1861 ***2896.27*** *p72*
Bury, John; Virginia, 1666 ***6212.30*** *p31*
Bury, William 22; Maryland, 1775 ***1220.25*** *p115*
Busby, Henry 36; Ontario, 1871 ***1823.15*** *p31*
Busby, Isaac; Pennsylvania, 1777 ***4629.10*** *p27*
Busby, James; Maryland, 1709 ***1224.2*** *p17*
Busby, Mary 73; Ontario, 1871 ***1823.15*** *p31*
Busch, Christof; Port uncertain, 1766 ***2856.30*** *p58*
Busch, Elisabeth; Port uncertain, 1772 ***2856.30*** *p58*
Busch, Henrich; Port uncertain, 1754 ***2856.30*** *p58*
Busch, Jakob; Port uncertain, 1769 ***2856.30*** *p58*
Busch, Johann Karl; Port uncertain, 1756 ***2856.30*** *p58*
Busch, Johann Michael; America, 1733 ***2856.30*** *p59*
Busch, Johann Michael; Port uncertain, 1733 ***2856.30*** *p58*
Busch, Michael; America, 1740 ***2856.30*** *p59*
Busch, Michael; Port uncertain, 1777 ***2856.30*** *p58*
Busch, Nicolas; Port uncertain, 1770 ***2856.30*** *p59*
With wife & 3 children
Busch, Nicolas; Port uncertain, 1772 ***2856.30*** *p59*
With wife & 3 children
Busch, Urban; Port uncertain, 1741 ***2856.30*** *p59*
Buscher, Therese; Port uncertain, 1796 ***2856.30*** *p59*
Buschlen, Christian 44; Ontario, 1871 ***1823.15*** *p31*
Buse, Robert; Virginia, 1665 ***6212.30*** *p18*
Buser, Herman; Pennsylvania, 1868 ***6058.10*** *p77*
Buser, Jacob; Pennsylvania, 1868 ***6058.10*** *p77*
Busfield, John 30; Nova Scotia, 1774 ***1220.25*** *p13*
Bush, Barnabas 61; Ontario, 1871 ***1823.22*** *p21*
Bush, Bernard; Baltimore, 1840 ***6058.10*** *p46*
Bush, C. B. 34; Ontario, 1861 ***2896.25*** *p54*
Bush, Charles 18; Virginia, 1774 ***1220.25*** *p87*
Bush, Charles 31; Maryland, 1774 ***1220.25*** *p62*
Wife: Hepzibah 31
Bush, Daniel; Maryland, 1660 ***2524.55*** *p39*
Bush, Daniel; New York, 1807 ***8197.10*** *p35*
Bush, G. W. R. 18; Ontario, 1861 ***2896.25*** *p54*
Bush, George; Pennsylvania, 1781 ***4629.10*** *p42*
Bush, Gould; Maryland, 1665 ***2524.55*** *p39*
Bush, Harry; Maryland, 1910 ***3259.35*** *p8*
Bush, Henry; New York, 1806 ***8197.10*** *p323*
Bush, Hepzibah 31 *SEE* Bush, Charles
Bush, John 62; Ontario, 1871 ***1823.22*** *p21*
Bush, Ludwig; America, 1753 ***2856.30*** *p59*
Bush, Roger; New York, 1839 ***8197.10*** *p128*
Bush, Samuel; Pennsylvania, 1777 ***4629.10*** *p18*
Bush, William; New York, 1794 ***8197.10*** *p4*
Bush, William 31; Ontario, 1871 ***1823.28*** *p12*
Bush, William 43; Ontario, 1871 ***1823.15*** *p31*
Busha, Matilda; Vermont, 1836-1906 ***5900.10*** *p391*
Bushby, Captain; Quebec, 1857 ***9196.15*** *p17*
Bushby, Mrs.; Quebec, 1857 ***9196.15*** *p17*
Bushe, Elizabeth; New York, New York, n.d. ***1224.3*** *p57*
Bushel, Ann 40; Ontario, 1861 ***2896.26*** *p17*
Bushel, Elizabeth 9; Ontario, 1861 ***2896.26*** *p17*
Bushel, George 14; Ontario, 1861 ***2896.26*** *p17*
Bushel, John 12; Ontario, 1861 ***2896.26*** *p17*
Bushel, William 46; Ontario, 1861 ***2896.26*** *p17*
Bushel, William J. 2; Ontario, 1861 ***2896.26*** *p17*
Bushell, Mrs.; Maryland, 1649 ***2524.55*** *p39*
Bushell, Catherine 64; Vermont, 1890 ***5900.10*** *p578*
Bushell, Edwd.; Maryland, 1658 ***2524.55*** *p39*
Bushell, Edwd.; Maryland, 1658 ***2524.55*** *p207*
Bushell, Jno; Virginia, 1664 ***6212.30*** *p9*
Bushell, Patrick 91; Vermont, 1915 ***5900.10*** *p578*
Bushell, Thomas; Maryland, 1640 ***2524.55*** *p39*
Bushell, Thomas; Maryland, 1642 ***2524.55*** *p39*
Bushy, George *SEE* Bushy, George
Bushy, George; Maryland, 1653 ***2524.55*** *p39*
With wife
Son: Henry
Son: George
Bushy, Henry *SEE* Bushy, George
Businskie, Paul; Maryland, 1910 ***3259.35*** *p8*
Buskin, Ralph; Virginia, 1664 ***6212.30*** *p14*
Buskin, Ralph; Virginia, 1665-1666 ***6212.30*** *p23*
Busky, Jun 44; British Columbia, 1909 ***9196.1*** *p27*
Busky, Jun 44; Seattle, 1909 ***9196.1*** *p27*
Busonworth, John 39; Maryland, 1774 ***1220.25*** *p51*
Buss, Johann Michael; America, 1733 ***2856.30*** *p59*
Buss, Ludwig; Port uncertain, 1739 ***2856.30*** *p59*
With wife & 3 children
Bussa, Alexander Placide; Richmond, Virginia, 1837 ***1224.3*** *p11*
Busse, Willm; Maryland, 1672 ***2524.55*** *p39*
Bussenbaum, Peter; Port uncertain, 1720 ***2856.30*** *p59*
Bussert, Andreas; America, 1749 ***2856.30*** *p59*
With wife & children
Bussey, Ann *SEE* Bussey, George
Bussey, Ann; Maryland, 1654 ***2524.55*** *p39*
Bussey, George; Maryland, 1654 ***2524.55*** *p39*
Wife: Ann
With 2 sons
Bussey, Thomas 22; Philadelphia, 1774 ***1220.25*** *p43*
Bussin, John; Maryland, 1665 ***2524.55*** *p39*
Bussinger, Charles Ferdinand; New York, 1827 ***8197.10*** *p346*
Bussinick, Mary 31; British Columbia, 1912 ***9196.1*** *p17*
Bussinick, Mary 31; Seattle, 1912 ***9196.1*** *p17*
Bussy, George *SEE* Bussy, George
Bussy, George; Maryland, 1653 ***2524.55*** *p39*
With wife
Son: George
Son: Henry
Bussy, Henry *SEE* Bussy, George
Bussy, William; Virginia, 1665 ***6212.30*** *p19*
Bustamante, Jose; New York, 1830 ***8197.10*** *p363*
Busten, Christopher; Maryland, 1666 ***2524.55*** *p17*
With wife
Busten, Christopher; Maryland, 1666 ***2524.55*** *p39*
Busvine, Edward John; New York, 1833 ***8197.10*** *p315*
Buswell, George 54; Ontario, 1871 ***1823.15*** *p31*
Buszak, Wojciech; Maryland, 1910 ***3259.35*** *p8*
Buszinski, John; Maryland, 1910 ***3259.35*** *p8*
Butch, William; New York, New York, 1856 ***3437.14*** *p73*
Butchart, Elizabeth 30; Maryland, 1774 ***1220.25*** *p62*
Butchart, James C. 40; Ontario, 1871 ***1823.28*** *p13*
Butchart, John 50; Ontario, 1871 ***1823.15*** *p31*
Butcher, Ann; Maryland, 1659 ***2524.55*** *p39*
Butcher, Hannah 60; Ontario, 1871 ***1823.15*** *p31*
Butcher, James; Maryland, 1733 ***1224.2*** *p17*
Butcher, Job; Pennsylvania, 1777 ***4629.10*** *p24*
Butcher, Martha; Maryland, 1681 ***2524.55*** *p39*
Butcher, Robert; Maryland, 1681 ***2524.55*** *p39*
Butcher, Thomas 15; Maryland, 1775 ***1220.25*** *p102*
Butcher, William 29; Philadelphia, 1774 ***1220.25*** *p63*
Butchka, Joseph; Maryland, 1910 ***3259.35*** *p8*
Buther, Martin 50; Ontario, 1871 ***1823.28*** *p13*
Buthery, Henry 53; Ontario, 1871 ***1823.15*** *p31*
Butler, Mr.; Quebec, 1858 ***9196.15*** *p35*
Butler, Alice A. Mead 20; Vermont, 1876 ***5900.10*** *p283*
Butler, Alicia A. 2; Vermont, 1864 ***5900.10*** *p292*
Butler, Angeline 20; Vermont, 1831 ***5900.10*** *p463*
Butler, Ann; Vermont, 1829-1907 ***5900.10*** *p71*
Butler, Ann; Virginia, 1703-1704 ***6212.30*** *p63*
Butler, Ann 16; Maryland, 1775 ***1220.25*** *p21*
Butler, Ann 25 *SEE* Butler, John
Butler, Ann Anderson 59; Vermont, 1874 ***5900.10*** *p283*
Butler, Ann Jane 9; Vermont, 1847 ***5900.10*** *p281*
Butler, Anna E.; Vermont, 1854-1923 ***5900.10*** *p267*
Butler, Anna J. 19; Vermont, 1868 ***5900.10*** *p281*
Butler, Anne Haley; Vermont, 1850-1917 ***5900.10*** *p393*
Butler, Anthony; Pennsylvania, 1777 ***4629.10*** *p15*
Butler, Bridget 69; Vermont, 1898 ***5900.10*** *p124*
Butler, Bridget 89; Vermont, 1917 ***5900.10*** *p124*
Butler, Bridget Higgins; Vermont, 1837-1930 ***5900.10*** *p439*
Butler, Catherine; Vermont, 1850-1862 ***5900.10*** *p393*
Butler, Catherine Farrell; Vermont, 1834-1917 ***5900.10*** *p439*
Butler, Catherine Laughlin 76; Vermont, 1907 ***5900.10*** *p539*
Butler, Charles 93; Vermont, 1881 ***5900.10*** *p283*
Butler, Charles W.; Vermont, 1850-1923 ***5900.10*** *p282*
Butler, Daniel; Pennsylvania, 1777 ***4629.10*** *p12*
Butler, Edward; Maryland, 1651 ***2524.55*** *p90*
Butler, Edward; Vermont, 1802-1890 ***5900.10*** *p393*
Butler, Edward, Jr.; Vermont, 1852-1932 ***5900.10*** *p393*
Butler, Eleanor; Maryland, 1681 ***2524.55*** *p39*
Butler, Elizabeth; Cincinnati, 1847 ***1224.3*** *p11*
Butler, Elizabeth; Vermont, 1839-1913 ***5900.10*** *p605*
Butler, Elizabeth; Vermont, 1840-1906 ***5900.10*** *p281*
Butler, Elizabeth; Vermont, 1865-1934 ***5900.10*** *p441*
Butler, Elizabeth McMahon 55; Vermont, 1877 ***5900.10*** *p477*
Butler, Ellen; Vermont, 1838-1897 ***5900.10*** *p430*
Butler, Ellen 65; Vermont, 1876 ***5900.10*** *p547*
Butler, Ellen Dillon 74; Vermont, 1911 ***5900.10*** *p540*
Butler, Ellen Mitchell 73; Vermont, 1916 ***5900.10*** *p123*
Butler, Emma 40; Ontario, 1871 ***1823.15*** *p31*
Butler, Francis; New York, 1832 ***8197.10*** *p356*
Butler, Francis; Virginia, 1665-1666 ***6212.30*** *p21*
Butler, George; Maryland, 1657 ***2524.55*** *p39*
Butler, George; Maryland, 1698 ***1224.1*** *p11*
Butler, George 17; Philadelphia, 1774 ***1220.25*** *p4*
Butler, Hannah 27; Maryland, 1774 ***1220.25*** *p84*
Butler, Hannie; Vermont, 1863-1943 ***5900.10*** *p125*
Butler, Henry; Maryland, 1789 ***1224.2*** *p17*
Butler, Henry; Virginia, 1666 ***6212.30*** *p31*
Butler, James; Vermont, n.d. ***5900.10*** *p394*
Butler, James; Vermont, 1827-1917 ***5900.10*** *p439*
Butler, James 19; Vermont, 1919 ***5900.10*** *p463*
Butler, James 23; Vermont, 1871 ***5900.10*** *p587*
Butler, James 24; New York, 1775 ***1220.25*** *p94*
Butler, James 29; Maryland, 1774 ***1220.25*** *p7*
Butler, James 32; Ontario, 1871 ***1823.22*** *p21*
Butler, James 75; Ontario, 1861 ***2896.28*** *p40*
Butler, Jane; Vermont, n.d. ***5900.10*** *p190*
Butler, Jane; Vermont, 1845-1885 ***5900.10*** *p485*
Butler, John; Connecticut, 1698 ***1224.1*** *p11*
Butler, John; New York, 1837 ***8197.10*** *p84*
Butler, John; Pennsylvania, 1777 ***4629.10*** *p12*
Butler, John; Vermont, 1845-1925 ***5900.10*** *p488*
Butler, John; Vermont, 1855-1919 ***5900.10*** *p393*
Butler, John; Virginia, 1703-1704 ***6212.30*** *p63*
Butler, John 23; Maryland, 1774 ***1220.25*** *p78*
Butler, John 25; Carolina, 1774 ***1220.25*** *p74*
Wife: Ann 25
Butler, John 32; Ontario, 1871 ***1823.22*** *p21*
Butler, John 36; Ontario, 1871 ***1823.22*** *p21*
Butler, John 38; Ontario, 1871 ***1823.15*** *p31*
Butler, John 47; Ontario, 1871 ***1823.22*** *p21*
Butler, John 53; Ontario, 1871 ***1823.15*** *p31*
Butler, John 70; Vermont, 1874 ***5900.10*** *p281*
Butler, John 88; Vermont, 1898 ***5900.10*** *p477*
Butler, John, Jr. 46; Vermont, 1884 ***5900.10*** *p281*
Butler, Joseph; Vermont, 1740-1824 ***5900.10*** *p463*
Butler, Joseph 17; Maryland, 1775 ***1220.25*** *p104*
Butler, Julia; Vermont, 1889 ***5900.10*** *p273*
Butler, Julia Morrisey 59; Vermont, 1905 ***5900.10*** *p394*
Butler, Maggie 99; Vermont, 1908 ***5900.10*** *p394*
Butler, Margaret L.; Vermont, 1866-1899 ***5900.10*** *p439*
Butler, Margaret Salmon; Vermont, 1856-1915 ***5900.10*** *p439*
Butler, Mary; Vermont, 1827-1902 ***5900.10*** *p283*
Butler, Mary; Vermont, 1857-1900 ***5900.10*** *p544*
Butler, Mary; Vermont, 1860-1940 ***5900.10*** *p126*
Butler, Mary; Virginia, 1717 ***1224.2*** *p6*
Butler, Mary 43; Vermont, 1893 ***5900.10*** *p466*
Butler, Mary Ann McNamara; Vermont, 1848-1936 ***5900.10*** *p435*

Byworth, John; Maryland, 1658 ***2524.55*** *p40*

Bzesynski, Theodore; Maryland, 1910 ***3259.35*** *p8*

C

Caball, Rich; Virginia, 1666 ***6212.30*** *p31*
Cabarbe, Anne; Maryland, 1678 ***2524.55*** *p40*
Cabbin, Jno.; Maryland, 1679 ***2524.55*** *p127*
Cabell, Ann 27; Baltimore, 1775 ***1220.25*** *p119*
Cabineau, Joseph 60; Ontario, 1871 ***1823.28*** *p13*
Cable, John; Maryland, 1631-1685 ***2524.55*** *p40*
Cacace, Orestes; New York, 1820 ***8197.10*** *p215*
Cada, Mary 42; Ontario, 1871 ***1823.28*** *p13*
Cadagen, Daniel; Pennsylvania, 1866 ***6058.10*** *p56*
Cadd, Sarah; Maryland, 1662 ***2524.55*** *p40*
Cadden, Bridget 56; Ontario, 1871 ***1823.28*** *p13*
Caddy, Cyprian 46; Ontario, 1871 ***1823.22*** *p22*
Caddy, James 51; Ontario, 1871 ***1823.22*** *p22*
Cade, Mr.; Quebec, 1857 ***9196.15*** *p21*
Cade, Heinrich; Port uncertain, 1739 ***2856.30*** *p64*
Cade, Henry; Virginia, 1662 ***1224.1*** *p11*
Cade, Martin 38; Ontario, 1871 ***1823.15*** *p31*
Cade, Mary 70; Ontario, 1871 ***1823.15*** *p31*
Cade, Thomas; Maryland, 1674 ***2524.55*** *p40*
Caden, Bridget; Vermont, 1853-1924 ***5900.10*** *p416*
Caden, Hugh 29; New York, 1832-1840 ***8197.10*** *p161*
Caden, John 26; Vermont, 1874 ***5900.10*** *p416*
Caden, John 58; Vermont, 1899 ***5900.10*** *p416*
Caden, John 80; Vermont, 1878 ***5900.10*** *p416*
Caden, Kate; Vermont, 1840-1914 ***5900.10*** *p436*
Caden, Mary 73; Vermont, 1885 ***5900.10*** *p416*
Caden, Mary A.; Vermont, 1850-1924 ***5900.10*** *p416*
Caden, Thomas 29; Vermont, 1881 ***5900.10*** *p416*
Cadenhead, John; Georgia, 1735 ***1640.10*** *p19*
Cader, James; Maryland, 1668 ***2524.55*** *p40*
Caderman, Samuel; Maryland, 1649 ***2524.55*** *p40*
Cadger, Mary; Virginia, 1666 ***6212.30*** *p26*
Cadger, Thomas; Maryland, 1650 ***2524.55*** *p127*
Cadgow, Archibald 40; Ontario, 1871 ***1823.15*** *p32*
Cadieux, William 44; Ontario, 1871 ***1823.22*** *p22*
Cadigan, Denis T.; New York, 1838 ***8197.10*** *p112*
Cadigan, Ellen O'Connel; Vermont, n.d. ***5900.10*** *p55*
Cadiman, Johann; America, 1743 ***2856.30*** *p64*
Cadin, Hugh 29; New York, 1832-1840 ***8197.10*** *p161*
Cadman, Adalaide 20; Ontario, 1861 ***2896.28*** *p39*
Cadman, Arthur 9; Ontario, 1861 ***2896.28*** *p39*
Cadman, Clarissa 23; Ontario, 1861 ***2896.28*** *p39*
Cadman, Margaret 14; Ontario, 1861 ***2896.28*** *p39*
Cadman, Maria 45; Ontario, 1861 ***2896.28*** *p39*
Cadman, Pricilla 25; Ontario, 1861 ***2896.28*** *p39*
Cadman, William A. 18; Ontario, 1861 ***2896.28*** *p39*
Cadmore, Richard; Maryland, 1662 ***2524.55*** *p40*
Cadrain, Michael; Vermont, 1837-1916 ***5900.10*** *p97*
Cadwalladen, Captain; Portland, Maine, 1858 ***9196.15*** *p29*
Cadwallader, John; Pennsylvania, 1777 ***4629.10*** *p29*
Cadwallader, John; Pennsylvania, 1779 ***4629.10*** *p38*
Cadwallader, Thomas; Pennsylvania, 1842 ***1224.3*** *p12*
Cadwalleder, Lambert; Pennsylvania, 1777 ***4629.10*** *p10*
Caesar, Ellen 49; Ontario, 1871 ***1823.15*** *p32*
Caesar, Henry 40; Ontario, 1871 ***1823.15*** *p32*
Caesar, Joe; Pennsylvania, 1777 ***4629.10*** *p18*
Caffary, Bridget 82; Vermont, 1892 ***5900.10*** *p51*
Caffery, Alfred 34; Ontario, 1861 ***2896.27*** *p23*
Caffery, Rachel 30; Ontario, 1861 ***2896.27*** *p23*
Caffey, Jeremiah; New York, 1837 ***8197.10*** *p81*
Caffinch, John; New Haven, Connecticut, n.d. ***1224.1*** *p11*
Caffoe, John; Maryland, 1682 ***2524.55*** *p40*
Caffrey, Alice; Vermont, 1859-1906 ***5900.10*** *p123*
Caffrey, Anne Elizabeth 75; Vermont, 1924 ***5900.10*** *p318*
Caffrey, Bridget; Vermont, 1845-1905 ***5900.10*** *p370*
Caffrey, Bridget McCann 84; Vermont, 1907 ***5900.10*** *p318*
Caffrey, Charles; New York, 1825 ***8197.10*** *p217*
Caffrey, John 75; Vermont, 1889 ***5900.10*** *p318*
Caffrey, John T. 17; Vermont, 1861 ***5900.10*** *p318*
Caffrey, Morgan; New York, 1821 ***8197.10*** *p216*
Caffrey, Rose; Vermont, 1815-1896 ***5900.10*** *p49*
Caffrey, Wm. 62; Vermont, 1913 ***5900.10*** *p318*
Caffry, Barnard; New York, 1807 ***8197.10*** *p326*
Caffry, Catherine 32; Vermont, 1863 ***5900.10*** *p248*
Caffry, Patrick; New York, 1833 ***8197.10*** *p358*
Cagaux, Peter 26; Virginia, 1773 ***1220.25*** *p30*
Cage, Gilbert; Virginia, 1680 ***1224.1*** *p11*
Cage, John; Maryland, 1650 ***2524.55*** *p40*
Cage, John; Maryland, 1677 ***2524.55*** *p40*
Cage, Noragh; Maryland, 1658 ***2524.55*** *p99*
Cagney, Margaret Fean; Vermont, 1852-1902 ***5900.10*** *p428*
Cagney, William; Vermont, 1852-1915 ***5900.10*** *p428*
Cahalane, John 85; Vermont, 1916 ***5900.10*** *p469*
Cahalane, Mary 77; Vermont, 1917 ***5900.10*** *p469*
Cahill, Miss; Quebec, 1857 ***9196.15*** *p16*
Cahill, Barney; Vermont, 1807-1885 ***5900.10*** *p528*
Cahill, Bridget; Vermont, 1830-1913 ***5900.10*** *p362*
Cahill, Bryan; Died enroute, 1850 ***1224.3*** *p12*
Cahill, Catherine 87; Ontario, 1871 ***1823.28*** *p13*
Cahill, Cornelius; Maryland, 1671 ***2524.55*** *p40*
Cahill, Eliza; Vermont, 1828-1903 ***5900.10*** *p487*
Cahill, Eliza Lynch; Vermont, 1849-1902 ***5900.10*** *p395*
Cahill, Elizabeth; Vermont, 1850-1917 ***5900.10*** *p310*
Cahill, Francis; Vermont, n.d. ***5900.10*** *p528*
Cahill, Francis; Vermont, 1846-1914 ***5900.10*** *p536*
Cahill, James; New York, 1832 ***8197.10*** *p369*
Cahill, James 82; Vermont, 1859 ***5900.10*** *p481*
Cahill, James H.; Vermont, 1852-1952 ***5900.10*** *p487*
Cahill, John; Vermont, 1848-1903 ***5900.10*** *p395*
Cahill, John 33; Maryland, 1774 ***1220.25*** *p52*
Cahill, Lillian O. Webley; Vermont, 1883-1913 ***5900.10*** *p487*
Cahill, Lizzie Rice 30, Vermont, 1882 ***5900.10*** *p289*
Cahill, Margaret; Vermont, 1828-1911 ***5900.10*** *p309*
Cahill, Margaret Rice; Vermont, 1854-1930 ***5900.10*** *p48*
Cahill, Margaret Rice; Vermont, 1854-1930 ***5900.10*** *p292*
Cahill, Mary; Vermont, n.d. ***5900.10*** *p528*
Cahill, Mary; Vermont, 1841-1920 ***5900.10*** *p536*
Cahill, Mary 90; Vermont, 1892 ***5900.10*** *p481*
Cahill, Michael 55; Ontario, 1871 ***1823.28*** *p13*
Cahill, Robert; New York, 1840 ***8197.10*** *p159*
Cahill, Rose; Vermont, n.d. ***5900.10*** *p528*
Cahill, Susan Castle; Vermont, 1808-1892 ***5900.10*** *p528*
Cahill, Sylvester; New York, 1837 ***8197.10*** *p82*
Cahill, Thomas; Vermont, 1820-1897 ***5900.10*** *p487*
Cahill, Thomas 64; Vermont, 1909 ***5900.10*** *p48*
Cahill, Thomas 64; Vermont, 1909 ***5900.10*** *p292*
Cahill, William; Vermont, 1848-1916 ***5900.10*** *p289*
Cahill, William 8; Vermont, 1840 ***5900.10*** *p481*
Cahinael, Donald 30; Ontario, 1871 ***1823.15*** *p32*
Cahley, Charles 55; Ontario, 1871 ***1823.22*** *p22*
Caignet, Armand; Philadelphia, 1793 ***4629.10*** *p76*
Cailey, Dorcas 58; Ontario, 1861 ***2896.27*** *p18*
Cailey, R. J. 26; Ontario, 1861 ***2896.27*** *p18*
Cailloyell, Isaac; Boston, 1721 ***1224.2*** *p18*
Cain, Ann R. 23; Vermont, 1879 ***5900.10*** *p549*
Cain, Anna 24; Kansas, 1909-1910 ***9079.10*** *p35*
Cain, Bridget; Vermont, 1822-1918 ***5900.10*** *p245*
Cain, Bridget; Vermont, 1849-1940 ***5900.10*** *p424*
Cain, Bridget 32; Vermont, 1857 ***5900.10*** *p428*
Cain, Catharine 64; Vermont, 1884 ***5900.10*** *p280*
Cain, Catherine 45; Vermont, 1870 ***5900.10*** *p573*
Cain, Catherine 80; Vermont, 1894 ***5900.10*** *p614*
Cain, Cornelius 79; Vermont, 1925 ***5900.10*** *p464*
Cain, Daniel; Vermont, 1856-1930 ***5900.10*** *p274*
Cain, David 27; Kansas, 1909-1910 ***9079.10*** *p35*
Cain, David, Jr. 1; Kansas, 1909-1910 ***9079.10*** *p35*
Cain, Elizabeth C. 1; Vermont, 1851 ***5900.10*** *p283*
Cain, Ellen Murphy 74; Vermont, 1919 ***5900.10*** *p464*
Cain, Fanny Maroney; Vermont, 1830-1900 ***5900.10*** *p179*
Cain, Godfree; Maryland, 1661 ***2524.55*** *p40*
Cain, Hannah; Vermont, 1855-1908 ***5900.10*** *p248*
Cain, Honor; Vermont, 1824-1884 ***5900.10*** *p424*
Cain, Isac 60; Ontario, 1871 ***1823.28*** *p13*
Cain, James 22; Ontario, 1861 ***2896.27*** *p25*
Cain, James 45; Vermont, 1870 ***5900.10*** *p179*
Cain, Johannah 62; Vermont, 1880 ***5900.10*** *p270*
Cain, John; New Orleans, 1858 ***3437.14*** *p94*
Cain, John; New York, 1820-1834 ***8197.10*** *p307*
Cain, John 3; Vermont, n.d. ***5900.10*** *p245*
Cain, John 19; Ontario, 1861 ***2896.27*** *p30*
Cain, John 70; Vermont, 1875 ***5900.10*** *p325*
Cain, John 75; Vermont, 1904 ***5900.10*** *p247*
Cain, John 77; Vermont, 1900 ***5900.10*** *p399*
Cain, Lawrence 61; Vermont, 1913 ***5900.10*** *p549*
Cain, Mary; Vermont, 1790-1877 ***5900.10*** *p558*
Cain, Mary; Vermont, 1815-1883 ***5900.10*** *p379*
Cain, Mary 2; Vermont, n.d. ***5900.10*** *p245*
Cain, Mary 65; Vermont, 1885 ***5900.10*** *p564*
Cain, Mary Bolan; Vermont, 1828-1928 ***5900.10*** *p567*
Cain, Mary Butler; Vermont, 1827-1902 ***5900.10*** *p283*
Cain, Mary Cavanaugh; Vermont, 1832-1885 ***5900.10*** *p245*
Cain, Mary E. 75; Vermont, 1896 ***5900.10*** *p549*
Cain, Mary Grace 70; Vermont, 1862 ***5900.10*** *p179*
Cain, Mary Murphy; Vermont, 1861-1919 ***5900.10*** *p274*
Cain, Matthew 49; Vermont, 1887 ***5900.10*** *p567*
Cain, Michael; New York, New York, 1858 ***6058.10*** *p59*
Cain, Michael 45; Vermont, 1875 ***5900.10*** *p443*
Cain, Patrick; New York, 1839 ***8197.10*** *p382*
Cain, Patrick; Vermont, 1845-1927 ***5900.10*** *p424*
Cain, Patrick 63; Vermont, 1880 ***5900.10*** *p270*
Cain, Peter; New York, 1837 ***8197.10*** *p93*
Cain, Robert; New York, 1840 ***8197.10*** *p220*
Cain, Rose Coniff 38; Vermont, 1875 ***5900.10*** *p399*
Cain, Sarah Ryan 80; Vermont, 1909 ***5900.10*** *p248*
Cain, Thomas; Vermont, 1818-1890 ***5900.10*** *p283*
Cain, Thomas; Vermont, 1825-1884 ***5900.10*** *p245*
Cain, Timothy 70; Vermont, 1886 ***5900.10*** *p549*
Cain, William 38; Ontario, 1871 ***1823.15*** *p32*
Caine, Ann; Maryland, 1651-1662 ***2524.55*** *p85*
Caine, James; Maryland, 1665 ***2524.55*** *p40*
Caine, Lucy; Maryland, 1669 ***2524.55*** *p40*
Caines, George; America, 1797 ***8197.10*** *p19*
Cainey, John; New York, 1802 ***8197.10*** *p19*
Cairnduff, A. C. J. 9; Ontario, 1861 ***2896.26*** *p10*
Cairnduff, H. O. 7; Ontario, 1861 ***2896.26*** *p10*
Cairnduff, J. S. 34; Ontario, 1861 ***2896.26*** *p10*
Cairnduff, William H. 11; Ontario, 1861 ***2896.26*** *p10*
Cairnes, Alexander; Virginia, 1761 ***1224.2*** *p18*
Cairns, Agnes; Vermont, 1824-1903 ***5900.10*** *p322*
Cairns, Anstyss 23; Vermont, 1878 ***5900.10*** *p322*
Cairns, Bridget Mary; Vermont, 1840-1921 ***5900.10*** *p392*
Cairns, David 41; Ontario, 1871 ***1823.28*** *p13*
Cairns, George; New York, 1838 ***8197.10*** *p112*
Cairns, Janette; Vermont, 1852-1937 ***5900.10*** *p321*

Cairns, John; Vermont, 1817-1887 5900.10 p322
Cairns, Margaret 33; Vermont, 1887 5900.10 p405
Cairny, James 37; Ontario, 1871 1823.28 p13
Cairon, John; New York, 1827 8197.10 p344
Cairon, Peter; New York, 1803 8197.10 p11
Caja, Karol; Maryland, 1910 3259.35 p8
Cakos, Alex 28; Salt Lake City, 1911 9196.1 p33
Calaback, James 40; Ontario, 1871 1823.22 p22
Calaghan, Daniel 24; Maryland, 1774 1220.25 p53
Calaghan, John 23; Virginia, 1774 1220.25 p89
Calahan, Mrs.; Quebec, 1858 9196.15 p37
Calahan, B. A. 26; Ontario, 1861 2896.25 p49
Calahan, Bridget Collins; Vermont, 1829-1920 5900.10 p171
Calahan, Daniel; Pennsylvania, 1868 6058.10 p66
Calahan, E. C. 2; Ontario, 1861 2896.25 p49
Calahan, John 40; Ontario, 1871 1823.22 p22
Calahan, Sophia; Vermont, 1835-1897 5900.10 p280
Calahan, Thomas; Vermont, 1836-1907 5900.10 p280
Calahan, Thomas 45; Ontario, 1861 2896.25 p49
Calam, Michael 27; Maryland, 1775 1220.25 p96
Calawich, Michael; Maryland, 1910 3259.35 p8
Calbeck, Robert 37; Ontario, 1871 1823.28 p13
Calbirth, James 50; Ontario, 1871 1823.15 p32
Calcut, John 37; Ontario, 1871 1823.22 p22
Calcutt, Edward 43; Ontario, 1871 1823.22 p22
Calcutt, Kingsley 42; Ontario, 1871 1823.22 p22
Calcutt, William S. K. 48; Ontario, 1871 1823.22 p22
Calday, Timothy; New York, 1838 8197.10 p112
Caldbeck, Bridget Twohey; Vermont, 1804-1891 5900.10 p510
Caldbeck, Bridgett Buckley; Vermont, 1842-1922 5900.10 p510
Caldbeck, Jane McManus; Vermont, 1844-1880 5900.10 p510
Caldbeck, Mary J. Sinnott; Vermont, 1848-1926 5900.10 p503
Caldbeck, Matthew J.; Vermont, 1844-1912 5900.10 p503
Caldbeck, Michael M.; Vermont, 1842-1918 5900.10 p510
Caldbeck, William J.; Vermont, 1793-1874 5900.10 p510
Caldell, John 34; Ontario, 1871 1823.15 p32
Calder, Alexander; Savannah, Georgia, 1775 1640.10 p19
Wife: Henrietta Bain
Child: Katherine
Child: Robert
Child: John
Child: Christian
Child: Peggy
Child: James
Calder, Andrew 46; Ontario, 1871 1823.15 p32
Calder, Christian *SEE* Calder, Alexander
Calder, Henrietta Bain *SEE* Calder, Alexander
Calder, James *SEE* Calder, Alexander
Calder, James 70; Ontario, 1871 1823.15 p32
Calder, John *SEE* Calder, Alexander
Calder, Katherine *SEE* Calder, Alexander
Calder, Peggy *SEE* Calder, Alexander
Calder, Peter; New York, 1807 8197.10 p36
Calder, Richard 21; Maryland, 1775 1220.25 p103
Calder, Robert *SEE* Calder, Alexander
Calder, Robert 70; Ontario, 1871 1823.15 p32
Calder, Thomas 30; Ontario, 1871 1823.15 p32
Calder, William; Georgia, 1736 1640.10 p19
Calderhead, John; New York, 1838 8197.10 p111
Calderwood, . . .; Boston, 1765 4628.40 p114
Calderwood, George; Georgia, 1698 1640.13 p17
Caldway, Joshua 68; Ontario, 1871 1823.15 p32
Caldwell, . . .; Boston, 1765 4628.40 p114
Caldwell, Alexander 45; Ontario, 1871 1823.28 p13
Caldwell, Andrew; New York, 1827 8197.10 p218
Caldwell, Andrew; New York, 1829 8197.10 p359
Caldwell, Andrew; Pennsylvania, 1777 4629.10 p10
Caldwell, Andrew 67; Ontario, 1861 2896.28 p50
Caldwell, Andrew D. 5; Ontario, 1861 2896.28 p50
Caldwell, Bridget 62; Vermont, 1867 5900.10 p143
Caldwell, David; New York, 1840 8197.10 p160
Caldwell, George; New Jersey, 1832-1834 8197.10 p311
Caldwell, George F. 2; Ontario, 1861 2896.28 p50
Caldwell, J.; Quebec, 1857 9196.15 p19
Caldwell, James; Boston, 1774 1224.2 p18
Caldwell, James; Pennsylvania, 1777 4629.10 p10
Caldwell, Jane 70; Ontario, 1861 2896.28 p50
Caldwell, John; Georgia, 1698 1640.13 p17
Caldwell, Joseph J. 4; Ontario, 1861 2896.28 p50
Caldwell, Mary E. 27; Ontario, 1861 2896.28 p50
Caldwell, Robert; Georgia, 1699 1640.13 p17
Caldwell, Samuel; Pennsylvania, 1777 4629.10 p6
Caldwell, Thomas; Maryland, 1703 1224.2 p18
Cale, Albert 37; Ontario, 1871 1823.15 p32
Cale, Catherine Shanley 38; Vermont, 1854 5900.10 p524
Cale, James 36; Vermont, 1883 5900.10 p524
Cale, John 42; Maryland, 1774 1220.25 p78
Cale, Maria; Vermont, 1847-1925 5900.10 p531
Cale, Patrick 69; Vermont, 1883 5900.10 p524
Cale, Thomas; Maryland, 1681 2524.55 p40
Calegan, Martin; New York, 1837 8197.10 p81
Calery, Martha C. 15; Ontario, 1861 2896.27 p54
Caley, Jane Haynes; Vermont, 1842-1910 5900.10 p256
Caley, Katharine; Maryland, 1682 2524.55 p40
Caley, Timothy; Vermont, 1840-1888 5900.10 p256
Caley, William 64; Ontario, 1871 1823.22 p22
Calf, John 65; Ontario, 1871 1823.15 p32
Calhoon, James; New York, 1819 8197.10 p214
Calhoon, Mary 36; Ontario, 1871 1823.28 p13
Calhoun, . . .; South Carolina, 1750-1770 4628.40 p98
Calhoun, Elizabeth 72; Ontario, 1861 2896.26 p39
Calies, Charles 55; Ontario, 1871 1823.28 p13
Caligham, Bernard; New York, 1838 8197.10 p113
Call, Ebenezer; Pennsylvania, 1786 4629.10 p47
Call, Edward James; Portland, Maine, 1858 9196.15 p31
Call, Esther 61; Ontario, 1871 1823.15 p32
Call, James; Vermont, 1843-1894 5900.10 p275
Call, Jane Carrigan; Vermont, 1849-1941 5900.10 p275
Callaghan, Annie Murphy 74; Vermont, 1906 5900.10 p42
Callaghan, Barney; New York, 1821 8197.10 p216
Callaghan, David; Philadelphia, 1807 1224.3 p12
Callaghan, Elizabeth M.; Vermont, 1866-1937 5900.10 p273
Callaghan, Florence E. Holcombe; Vermont, 1852-1891 5900.10 p286
Callaghan, Henry; Pennsylvania, 1777 4629.10 p30
Callaghan, Hugh 77; Vermont, 1905 5900.10 p42
Callaghan, James; New York, 1835 8197.10 p220
Callaghan, James; Vermont, 1861-1935 5900.10 p42
Callaghan, Jeremiah; New York, 1837 8197.10 p81
Callaghan, John; Vermont, 1851-1913 5900.10 p273
Callaghan, John 22; Philadelphia, 1774 1220.25 p67
Callaghan, Launcelot; New York, 1819 8197.10 p215
Callaghan, Lawrence 20; Ontario, 1871 1823.22 p22
Callaghan, Margaret 62; Vermont, 1887 5900.10 p619
Callaghan, Patrick; New York, 1825 8197.10 p218
Callaghan, Patrick; New York, 1827-1831 8197.10 p370
Callaghan, Patrick 70; Ontario, 1871 1823.28 p13
Callaghan, Philip; New York, 1840 8197.10 p221
Callaghan, Roseannie 54; Vermont, 1906 5900.10 p42
Callagyn, Michael; New York, 1829 8197.10 p218
Callahan, Mr.; Vermont, 1841-1910 5900.10 p441
Callahan, Mrs.; Vermont, 1841-1910 5900.10 p441
Callahan, Anne; Vermont, n.d. 5900.10 p108
Callahan, Annie; Vermont, 1850-1930 5900.10 p120
Callahan, Bridget; Vermont, 1825-1912 5900.10 p467
Callahan, Bridget; Vermont, 1856-1924 5900.10 p551
Callahan, Bridget 43; Vermont, 1884 5900.10 p53
Callahan, Bridget A.; Vermont, 1861-1934 5900.10 p192
Callahan, Bridget Sullivan 72; Vermont, 1930 5900.10 p439
Callahan, Catherine Price; Vermont, 1842-1925 5900.10 p328
Callahan, Charles; Pennsylvania, 1786 4629.10 p50
Callahan, Charles; Vermont, n.d. 5900.10 p268
Callahan, Cornelius; New York, 1837 8197.10 p80
Callahan, Cornelius; Vermont, 1820-1908 5900.10 p467
Callahan, David 32; Vermont, 1879 5900.10 p328
Callahan, David H.; Vermont, n.d. 5900.10 p328
Callahan, Edward; Vermont, n.d. 5900.10 p268
Callahan, Edward; Vermont, 1854-1928 5900.10 p171
Callahan, Edward; Vermont, 1859-1891 5900.10 p550
Callahan, Elizabeth; Vermont, n.d. 5900.10 p268
Callahan, Elizabeth Mackey; Vermont, 1832-1911 5900.10 p444
Callahan, Ellen; Vermont, n.d. 5900.10 p268
Callahan, Ellen 68; Vermont, 1895 5900.10 p469
Callahan, Henry; Vermont, 1856-1891 5900.10 p432
Callahan, James; Pennsylvania, 1777 4629.10 p25
Callahan, James; Vermont, 1824-1894 5900.10 p171
Callahan, James; Vermont, 1862-1898 5900.10 p171
Callahan, James T. 50; Vermont, 1906 5900.10 p438
Callahan, John; Vermont, 1829-1905 5900.10 p444
Callahan, John J.; Vermont, 1864-1929 5900.10 p441
Callahan, Josephine J.; Vermont, n.d. 5900.10 p328
Callahan, Julia; Vermont, n.d. 5900.10 p196
Callahan, Katherine; Vermont, 1855-1880 5900.10 p108
Callahan, Katherine Lane; Vermont, 1855-1923 5900.10 p588
Callahan, Margaret; Vermont, 1859-1926 5900.10 p441
Callahan, Margaret; Vermont, 1867-1929 5900.10 p171
Callahan, Margaret 65; Vermont, 1890 5900.10 p438
Callahan, Martin 49; Vermont, 1889 5900.10 p585
Callahan, Mary; Vermont, n.d. 5900.10 p268
Callahan, Mary; Vermont, 1811 5900.10 p347
Callahan, Mary; Vermont, 1812 5900.10 p550
Callahan, Mary; Vermont, 1839-1884 5900.10 p280
Callahan, Mary; Vermont, 1856-1930 5900.10 p171
Callahan, Mary 43; Vermont, 1883 5900.10 p83
Callahan, Mary A.; Vermont, 1871-1895 5900.10 p340
Callahan, Mary E.; Vermont, 1856-1944 5900.10 p441
Callahan, Michael; Vermont, 1860-1916 5900.10 p171
Callahan, Michael; Vermont, 1898 5900.10 p579
Callahan, Michael 55; Ontario, 1871 1823.28 p13
Callahan, Michael 60; Ontario, 1871 1823.22 p22
Callahan, Nancy Burke; Vermont, 1901 5900.10 p579
Callahan, Nellie Simonds; Vermont, 1868-1945 5900.10 p550
Callahan, Patrick; Vermont, n.d. 5900.10 p108
Callahan, Patrick; Vermont, 1843-1929 5900.10 p328
Callahan, Patrick; Vermont, 1845-1912 5900.10 p588
Callahan, Patrick 57; Vermont, 1884 5900.10 p83
Callahan, Rose 54; Vermont, 1909 5900.10 p439
Callahan, Stephen; Vermont, 1864-1880 5900.10 p441
Callahan, Thomas; Vermont, 1852-1881 5900.10 p441
Callahan, Timothy 84; Vermont, 1894 5900.10 p550
Callahan, William; Vermont, n.d. 5900.10 p267
Callahan, William; Vermont, 1853-1891 5900.10 p551
Callahan, William; Vermont, 1870-1908 5900.10 p171
Callahone, Margaret; Maryland, 1671 2524.55 p40
Callahone, Teage; Maryland, 1671 2524.55 p40
Callan, Anastasia 39; Vermont, 1887 5900.10 p478
Callan, Catharine 23; Vermont, 1865 5900.10 p478
Callan, Edmond; Maryland, 1682 2524.55 p40
Callan, Elizabeth; Vermont, 1845-1906 5900.10 p478
Callan, Elizabeth; Vermont, 1846-1906 5900.10 p500
Callan, Francis; New York, 1824 8197.10 p217
Callan, James; New York, 1840 8197.10 p160
Callan, Libbie 39; Vermont, 1886 5900.10 p280
Callan, M. 25; Alaska, 1917 9196.1 p45
Callan, M. 25; Whitehorse, Yukon, 1917 9196.1 p45
Callan, Mary; Vermont, 1850-1921 5900.10 p487
Callan, Mary 80; Vermont, 1902 5900.10 p478
Callan, Michael 79; Vermont, 1886 5900.10 p478
Callan, Patrick 12; Vermont, 1863 5900.10 p478
Callan, Rosa; Vermont, 1838-1910 5900.10 p482
Callan, Sarah 24; Vermont, 1874 5900.10 p231
Callanan, Michael; Philadelphia, 1807 1224.3 p12
Callander, Mr.; Quebec, 1858 9196.15 p46
Callard, John C. 41; Ontario, 1871 1823.28 p13
Callary, James; New York, 1837 8197.10 p80
Callaway, Joseph 40; Ontario, 1871 1823.15 p32
Callaway, Joseph 67; Ontario, 1871 1823.15 p32
Callaway, Joshua 34; Ontario, 1871 1823.15 p32
Callaway, Thomas; New York, New York, 1846 1224.3 p12
Callen, Miss; Quebec, 1856 9196.15 p6
Callendar, Alexander; Florida, 1767 1640.10 p20
Callendar, John; Florida, 1767 1640.10 p20
Callendar, John; Toronto, 1853 1640.13 p17
Callender, George; New York, 1839 8197.10 p133
Callengwood, Daniel; Maryland, 1675 2524.55 p40
Caller, Jeremiah; Maryland, 1660 2524.55 p40
Callery, John; New York, 1831 8197.10 p219
Callery, John; New York, 1837 8197.10 p82
Callet, Eugene P.; New York, 1840 8197.10 p162
Callet, James; New York, 1815 8197.10 p55
Calley, Wm; Virginia, 1664 6212.30 p15
Calligan, Martin; New York, 1837 8197.10 p81
Calligan, Thomas 40; Ontario, 1871 1823.28 p13
Callighan, Bernard 60; Ontario, 1871 1823.22 p22
Callihan, James; New York, 1838 8197.10 p377
Callin, James 35; Ontario, 1871 1823.15 p32
Callinan, Ann Farrell; Vermont, 1874 5900.10 p616
Callinan, Margaret Rogers; Vermont, 1847-1921 5900.10 p217
Callinan, Patrick; Vermont, 1844-1906 5900.10 p217
Calling, Hugh; New York, 1807 8197.10 p37
Callis, Francis; Maryland, 1669 2524.55 p170
Callow, Rich; Virginia, 1664 6212.30 p9
Calloway, John; Maryland, 1673 2524.55 p40
Calloway, Peter; Maryland, 1673 2524.55 p40
Callum, D. A.; Portland, Maine, 1858 9196.15 p30
Callum, Edward 28; Ontario, 1871 1823.15 p32
Callum, Thomas; Quebec, 1846 1640.13 p17
Calmady, Josias; Virginia, 1666 6212.30 p30
Calmann, Bernhard; New York, 1833 8197.10 p219
Calnan, David 14; Ontario, 1861 2896.28 p62
Calnan, Dennis 51; Ontario, 1871 1823.22 p22
Calnan, Edward W. 12; Ontario, 1861 2896.28 p62
Calnan, Elizabeth 19; Ontario, 1861 2896.28 p62
Calnan, Fanny 1; Ontario, 1861 2896.28 p62
Calnan, James; Ontario, 1861 2896.28 p62
Calnan, James 23; Ontario, 1861 2896.28 p62
Calnan, M. E. 4; Ontario, 1861 2896.28 p62
Calnan, Margaret 50; Vermont, 1901 5900.10 p590
Calnan, Martin 64; Vermont, 1903 5900.10 p590
Calnan, Michael 54; Vermont, 1900 5900.10 p590

Calnan, Nora 83; Vermont, 1892 ***5900.10*** *p590*
Calnan, Oliver 9; Ontario, 1861 ***2896.28*** *p62*
Calnan, Richard S. 1; Ontario, 1861 ***2896.28*** *p62*
Calnan, Richard S. 57; Ontario, 1861 ***2896.28*** *p62*
Calnan, Sarah M. 6; Ontario, 1861 ***2896.28*** *p62*
Calnan, Sophia 49; Ontario, 1861 ***2896.28*** *p62*
Calnan, William; Ontario, 1861 ***2896.28*** *p62*
Calnon, Jeremiah; New York, 1837 ***8197.10*** *p80*
Calnon, Michael 42; Ontario, 1871 ***1823.22*** *p22*
Calton, Joseph 71; Ontario, 1871 ***1823.22*** *p22*
Calton, Thomas 58; Ontario, 1871 ***1823.22*** *p22*
Calvert, Mrs.; Quebec, 1857 ***9196.15*** *p15*
Calvert, Ann *SEE* Calvert, Philip
Calvert, Anthony 30; Carolina, 1774 ***1220.25*** *p12*
Calvert, Edward Henry; Annapolis, Maryland, 1730 ***1224.2*** *p18*
Calvert, George; America, 1635 ***1224.1*** *p11*
Calvert, Philip; Maryland, 1656 ***2524.55*** *p40*
Wife: Ann
Calvert, Reynard; South Carolina, 1767 ***1224.2*** *p18*
Calvet, Peter; Charles Town, South Carolina, 1765 ***1224.2*** *p18*
Calvey, Catharine Royston; Vermont, 1808-1880 ***5900.10*** *p605*
Calvey, Daniel J.; Vermont, 1840-1898 ***5900.10*** *p605*
Calvey, Elizabeth; Vermont, 1838-1879 ***5900.10*** *p605*
Calvey, Ellen McGrath; Vermont, 1847-1929 ***5900.10*** *p605*
Calvey, Patrick; Vermont, 1802-1874 ***5900.10*** *p605*
Calvey, William; Vermont, 1837-1865 ***5900.10*** *p605*
Calvin, Charles 34; Ontario, 1871 ***1823.28*** *p13*
Calvin, James 22; Ontario, 1871 ***1823.28*** *p13*
Calvin, William 16; Ontario, 1861 ***2896.28*** *p3*
Calwell, Elizabeth 80; Ontario, 1871 ***1823.15*** *p32*
Calwell, George 57; Ontario, 1871 ***1823.15*** *p32*
Calwell, James; Boston, 1774 ***1224.2*** *p18*
Cam, Godfery; Maryland, 1670 ***2524.55*** *p40*
Cam, Godfrey; Maryland, 1669 ***2524.55*** *p40*
Caman, John; Pennsylvania, 1777 ***4629.10*** *p11*
Camara, John 50; Ontario, 1871 ***1823.22*** *p22*
Camaran, John 52; Ontario, 1871 ***1823.28*** *p13*
Camaron, A. 48; Alaska, 1917 ***9196.1*** *p7*
Camaron, A. 48; Yukon, 1917 ***9196.1*** *p7*
Camaron, Sophie 60; Ontario, 1871 ***1823.28*** *p13*
Cambden, Thomas; Maryland, 1669 ***2524.55*** *p84*
Cambel, Edward 55; Ontario, 1871 ***1823.15*** *p32*
Cambell, Alexander 36; Ontario, 1871 ***1823.15*** *p32*
Cambell, Malcom 82; Ontario, 1871 ***1823.28*** *p13*
Cambile, Abram 45; Ontario, 1871 ***1823.15*** *p32*
Camblin, Robert; New York, 1807 ***8197.10*** *p327*
Cambridge, Miss; Quebec, 1858 ***9196.15*** *p34*
Camby, Jacob; Georgia, 1698 ***1640.13*** *p17*
Came, John 21; Maryland, 1774 ***1220.25*** *p3*
Camel, C. 23; Ontario, 1861 ***2896.26*** *p7*
Camel, George; Maryland, 1681 ***2524.55*** *p40*
Camel, James 24; Ontario, 1861 ***2896.28*** *p56*
Camel, James 35; Ontario, 1861 ***2896.27*** *p48*
Cameley, Terrance 35; Ontario, 1871 ***1823.28*** *p13*
Camell, Duncan 29; Ontario, 1871 ***1823.28*** *p13*
Camenek, David; Port uncertain, 1728 ***2856.30*** *p64*
Cameron, Miss; Portland, Maine, 1858 ***9196.15*** *p30*
Cameron, Mr.; Quebec, 1858 ***9196.15*** *p38*
Cameron, Aaron 35; Ontario, 1861 ***2896.28*** *p33*
Cameron, Abigail; New York, New York, 1808 ***1224.3*** *p12*
Cameron, Alex 19; Ontario, 1871 ***1823.15*** *p32*
Cameron, Alex 39; Ontario, 1871 ***1823.15*** *p32*
Cameron, Alex 42; Ontario, 1871 ***1823.15*** *p32*
Cameron, Alexander; Georgia, 1740 ***1640.10*** *p20*
Cameron, Alexander; Georgia, 1763 ***1640.10*** *p20*
Cameron, Alexander; New York, 1884 ***1640.13*** *p17*
Cameron, Alexander; New York, New York, 1802 ***1224.3*** *p12*
Cameron, Alexander; Savannah, Georgia, 1784 ***1224.2*** *p18*
Cameron, Alexander; South Carolina, 1763 ***1640.10*** *p20*
Cameron, Alexander 40; Ontario, 1871 ***1823.28*** *p13*
Cameron, Alexander 41; Ontario, 1871 ***1823.28*** *p13*
Cameron, Alexander 50; Ontario, 1871 ***1823.15*** *p32*
Cameron, Alexander 75; Ontario, 1871 ***1823.15*** *p32*
Cameron, Alexander 76; Ontario, 1871 ***1823.15*** *p32*
Cameron, Alexender 74; Ontario, 1871 ***1823.28*** *p13*
Cameron, Allan; New Jersey, 1765 ***1224.2*** *p18*
Cameron, Annabella *SEE* Cameron, Neil
Cameron, Angus *SEE* Cameron, Murdo
Cameron, Angus *SEE* Cameron, Neil
Cameron, Angus 36; Ontario, 1871 ***1823.28*** *p13*
Cameron, Angus 79; Ontario, 1871 ***1823.28*** *p13*
Cameron, Angus, Jr.; Georgia, 1743 ***1640.10*** *p20*
Cameron, Ann *SEE* Cameron, Ewen
Cameron, Ann *SEE* Cameron, Murdo
Cameron, Ann 35; Ontario, 1871 ***1823.28*** *p13*
Cameron, Catherina 59; Ontario, 1871 ***1823.15*** *p32*
Cameron, Catherine *SEE* Cameron, Donald
Cameron, Catherine *SEE* Cameron, Murdo
Cameron, Charles; Savannah, Georgia, 1782 ***1224.2*** *p18*
Cameron, Charles; Savannah, Georgia, 1782 ***1640.10*** *p20*
Cameron, Colin 52; Ontario, 1871 ***1823.28*** *p13*
Cameron, Don 52; Ontario, 1871 ***1823.15*** *p32*
Cameron, Donald *SEE* Cameron, Donald
Cameron, Donald *SEE* Cameron, Murdo
Cameron, Donald; Georgia, 1743 ***1640.10*** *p20*
Cameron, Donald; New York, 1807 ***8197.10*** *p37*
Cameron, Donald; Port uncertain, 1840-1849 ***4537.37*** *p105*
Wife: Effie Campbell
Child: Duncan
Child: Donald
Child: John
Child: Catherine
Child: Mary
Cameron, Donald 40; Ontario, 1871 ***1823.28*** *p13*
Cameron, Donald 61; Ontario, 1871 ***1823.15*** *p32*
Cameron, Donald 63; Ontario, 1871 ***1823.22*** *p22*
Cameron, Donald, Jr.; Georgia, 1743 ***1640.10*** *p20*
Cameron, Duncan *SEE* Cameron, Donald
Cameron, Duncan; Georgia, 1743 ***1640.10*** *p21*
Cameron, Duncan 18; Ontario, 1871 ***1823.22*** *p22*
Cameron, Duncan 23; Ontario, 1871 ***1823.15*** *p33*
Cameron, Duncan 39; Ontario, 1871 ***1823.15*** *p33*
Cameron, Duncan 52; Ontario, 1871 ***1823.15*** *p33*
Cameron, Effie Campbell *SEE* Cameron, Donald
Cameron, Ewan; Texas, 1843 ***1640.10*** *p21*
Cameron, Ewen; Port uncertain, 1840-1849 ***4537.37*** *p105*
Wife: Mary
Child: Kate
Child: John
Child: Mary
Child: Ann
Cameron, Ewen 72; Ontario, 1871 ***1823.15*** *p33*
Cameron, Flora; Port uncertain, 1840-1849 ***4537.37*** *p133*
Cameron, Frederick Gavin; New York, 1826 ***8197.10*** *p333*
Cameron, Geo 25; British Columbia, 1910 ***9196.1*** *p31*
Cameron, Geo 25; Washington, 1910 ***9196.1*** *p31*
Cameron, H.; Quebec, 1856 ***9196.15*** *p10*
Cameron, Hugh; New York, 1807 ***8197.10*** *p37*
Cameron, Hugh 36; Ontario, 1871 ***1823.28*** *p13*
Cameron, Hugh 56; Ontario, 1871 ***1823.15*** *p33*
Cameron, James 28; Pennsylvania, 1795 ***4629.10*** *p63*
Cameron, James K. 61; Ontario, 1871 ***1823.22*** *p22*
Cameron, Jane 24; Ontario, 1861 ***2896.27*** *p65*
Cameron, Jane E. 35; Ontario, 1861 ***2896.28*** *p33*
Cameron, Janet *SEE* Cameron, Murdo
Cameron, Janet; Georgia, 1738 ***1640.10*** *p21*
Cameron, Janet 30; Ontario, 1871 ***1823.28*** *p13*
Cameron, John *SEE* Cameron, Donald
Cameron, John *SEE* Cameron, Ewen
Cameron, John *SEE* Cameron, Neil
Cameron, John; Alabama, 1785-1845 ***1640.10*** *p21*
Cameron, John; Alabama, 1822-1845 ***1640.10*** *p22*
Cameron, John; Georgia, 1737 ***1640.10*** *p21*
Cameron, John; Georgia, 1738 ***1640.10*** *p21*
Cameron, John; New York, 1794 ***8197.10*** *p3*
Cameron, John 40; Ontario, 1871 ***1823.15*** *p33*
Cameron, John 45; Ontario, 1871 ***1823.28*** *p13*
Cameron, John 50; Ontario, 1871 ***1823.15*** *p33*
Cameron, John 53; Ontario, 1871 ***1823.15*** *p33*
Cameron, John 54; Ontario, 1871 ***1823.15*** *p33*
Cameron, John 55; Ontario, 1871 ***1823.15*** *p33*
Cameron, John 69; Ontario, 1871 ***1823.15*** *p33*
Cameron, John, Jr.; Georgia, 1743 ***1640.10*** *p21*
Cameron, John P. 5; Ontario, 1861 ***2896.28*** *p33*
Cameron, John S. 41; Ontario, 1871 ***1823.28*** *p13*
Cameron, Kate *SEE* Cameron, Ewen
Cameron, Kirsty *SEE* Cameron, Murdo
Cameron, Lewis 28; Maryland, 1774 ***1220.25*** *p47*
Cameron, Margaret; Ontario, 1884 ***1640.13*** *p17*
Cameron, Mary *SEE* Cameron, Donald
Cameron, Mary *SEE* Cameron, Ewen
Cameron, Mary Ann; Philadelphia, n.d. ***1224.3*** *p12*
Cameron, Murdo; Port uncertain, 1840-1849 ***4537.37*** *p105*
Child: Norman
Child: Ann
Child: Angus
Child: Kirsty
Wife: Janet
Child: Janet
Child: Catherine
Child: Donald
Cameron, Neil; Port uncertain, 1840-1849 ***4537.37*** *p105*
Wife: Annabella
Child: John
Child: Angus
Cameron, Norman *SEE* Cameron, Murdo
Cameron, Richard; Georgia, 1733 ***1640.10*** *p22*
Cameron, Robert 30; Ontario, 1871 ***1823.15*** *p33*
Cameron, Roderick 35; Ontario, 1871 ***1823.15*** *p33*
Cameron, Sarah 40; Ontario, 1871 ***1823.15*** *p33*
Cameron, Selina 48; Ontario, 1871 ***1823.22*** *p23*
Cameron, Thomas 18; Ontario, 1871 ***1823.15*** *p33*
Cameron, William 55; Ontario, 1871 ***1823.28*** *p13*
Cameron, William 61; Ontario, 1871 ***1823.28*** *p13*
Cames, James; Maryland, 1664 ***2524.55*** *p41*
Camis, Elizabeth; Vermont, 1850-1925 ***5900.10*** *p193*
Camm, John; Pennsylvania, 1778 ***4629.10*** *p34*
Camm, John 50; Ontario, 1871 ***1823.15*** *p33*
Camm, John B. 86; Ontario, 1871 ***1823.15*** *p33*
Cammel, Philipp; New York, 1703 ***1224.2*** *p18*
Cammeloe, Frederick; Pennsylvania, 1777 ***4629.10*** *p11*
Cammerer, Andreas; America, 1736 ***2856.30*** *p64*
With wife son & 2 daughters
Cammerer, Andreas; America, 1737 ***2856.30*** *p64*
Cammerer, Anna Maria; America, 1744 ***2856.30*** *p64*
With son & family
Cammerer, Anna Maria Neff; America, 1744 ***2856.30*** *p321*
Cammerer, Elisabeth; America, 1748 ***2856.30*** *p64*
Cammerer, Josef; America, 1752 ***2856.30*** *p64*
With wife & children
Cammerschmittin, Elisabeth; Port uncertain, 1730 ***2856.30*** *p64*
Cammeyer, Charles; New York, 1840 ***8197.10*** *p221*
Cammeyer, John C.; New York, 1840 ***8197.10*** *p221*
Cammusky, Christopher 52; Ontario, 1871 ***1823.22*** *p23*
Camp, George B. 54; Ontario, 1871 ***1823.28*** *p13*
Camp, Thomas 17; Philadelphia, 1774 ***1220.25*** *p42*
Campbel, Rachel 50; Ontario, 1861 ***2896.28*** *p58*
Campbell, . . .; Boston, 1765 ***4628.40*** *p114*
Campbell, . . .; Ontario, 1871 ***1823.15*** *p33*
Campbell, Miss; Quebec, 1858 ***9196.15*** *p44*
Campbell, Mr.; Quebec, 1856 ***9196.15*** *p6*
Campbell, Mr.; Quebec, 1858 ***9196.15*** *p31*
Campbell, Mr.; Quebec, 1858 ***9196.15*** *p32*
Campbell, Mr.; Quebec, 1858 ***9196.15*** *p40*
Campbell, Mr.; Quebec, 1858 ***9196.15*** *p43*
Campbell, Mrs.; Quebec, 1856 ***9196.15*** *p6*
Campbell, Mrs.; Quebec, 1857 ***9196.15*** *p13*
Campbell, Mrs.; Quebec, 1858 ***9196.15*** *p31*
Campbell, Mrs.; Quebec, 1858 ***9196.15*** *p32*
Campbell, Alexander *SEE* Campbell, Angus
Campbell, Alexander *SEE* Campbell, Donald
Campbell, Alexander *SEE* Campbell, Duncan
Campbell, Alexander *SEE* Campbell, Ewen
Campbell, Alexander *SEE* Campbell, Lachlan
Campbell, Alexander *SEE* Campbell, Norman
Campbell, Alexander; Jamaica, 1751 ***1640.13*** *p17*
Campbell, Alexander; Nova Scotia, 1830-1839 ***4537.35*** *p10*
Wife: Ann
Child: Roderick
Campbell, Alexander; Ontario, 1850-1859 ***4537.37*** *p33*
Wife: Mary Steele
Child: Flora
Child: Marion
Child: Roderick
Child: Mary
Child: Catherine
Campbell, Alexander; Ontario, 1864 ***4537.32*** *p6*
Wife: Margaret Morrison
Child: Angus
Child: Freddy
Child: Margaret
Child: Donald
Child: John
Child: Malcolm
Campbell, Alexander; Ontario, 1864 ***4537.35*** *p56*
Wife: Margaret Morrison
Child: John
Child: Angus
Child: Freddy
Child: Margaret
Child: Malcolm
Child: Donald
Campbell, Alexander; Pennsylvania, 1777 ***4629.10*** *p15*
Campbell, Alexander; Vermont, n.d. ***5900.10*** *p329*
Campbell, Alexander; Vermont, 1839-1905 ***5900.10*** *p329*
Campbell, Alexander; Port uncertain, 1850-1859 ***4537.37*** *p105*
Wife: Janet
Child: Margaret
Child: Kirsty
Child: Sally

Campbell, Margaret *SEE* Campbell, Alexander
Campbell, Margaret *SEE* Campbell, Angus
Campbell, Margaret *SEE* Campbell, Donald
Campbell, Margaret *SEE* Campbell, Ewen
Campbell, Margaret *SEE* Campbell, Finlay
Campbell, Margaret *SEE* Campbell, John
Campbell, Margaret; Ontario, 1840-1849 ***4537.37*** *p37*
Campbell, Margaret; Ontario, 1860-1869 ***4537.35*** *p60*
Campbell, Margaret; Ontario, 1862 ***4537.32*** *p70*
Campbell, Margaret; Vermont, 1840-1918 ***5900.10*** *p235*
Campbell, Margaret 8; Ontario, 1871 ***1823.15*** *p35*
Campbell, Margaret 50; Ontario, 1871 ***1823.15*** *p35*
Campbell, Margaret 100; Ontario, 1871 ***1823.15*** *p35*
Campbell, Margaret Kelley; Vermont, 1842-1909 ***5900.10*** *p510*
Campbell, Margaret MacLeod *SEE* Campbell, John
Campbell, Margaret MacPhee *SEE* Campbell, John
Campbell, Margaret Morrison *SEE* Campbell, Alexander
Campbell, Margret 79; Ontario, 1871 ***1823.15*** *p35*
Campbell, Marion *SEE* Campbell, Alexander
Campbell, Marion *SEE* Campbell, Angus
Campbell, Marion *SEE* Campbell, Donald
Campbell, Marion *SEE* Campbell, Duncan
Campbell, Marion *SEE* Campbell, Ewen
Campbell, Marion *SEE* Campbell, Finlay
Campbell, Marion *SEE* Campbell, John
Campbell, Marion *SEE* Campbell, Lachlan
Campbell, Marion; Ontario, 1840-1849 ***4537.37*** *p42*
Campbell, Marion MacAulay *SEE* Campbell, John
Campbell, Marion MacDonald *SEE* Campbell, Donald
Campbell, Marion MacLean *SEE* Campbell, Malcolm
Campbell, Martha F.; Vermont, 1851-1899 ***5900.10*** *p426*
Campbell, Martin; Augusta, Georgia, 1756 ***1640.10*** *p24*
Campbell, Mary *SEE* Campbell, Alexander
Campbell, Mary *SEE* Campbell, Angus
Campbell, Mary *SEE* Campbell, Catherine MacDonald
Campbell, Mary *SEE* Campbell, John
Campbell, Mary *SEE* Campbell, Lachlan
Campbell, Mary *SEE* Campbell, Neil
Campbell, Mary; Chile, 1880-1889 ***4537.35*** *p77*
Campbell, Mary; Nova Scotia, 1840-1849 ***4537.35*** *p13*
Campbell, Mary; Quebec, 1870-1879 ***4537.35*** *p64*
Campbell, Mary; Vermont, 1833-1933 ***5900.10*** *p555*
Campbell, Mary; Port uncertain, 1840-1849 ***4537.37*** *p115*
Campbell, Mary; Port uncertain, 1870-1879 ***4537.35*** *p78*
Campbell, Mary 69; Ontario, 1871 ***1823.15*** *p35*
Campbell, Mary 71; Vermont, 1908 ***5900.10*** *p269*
Campbell, Mary 73; Ontario, 1871 ***1823.15*** *p35*
Campbell, Mary Ann *SEE* Campbell, John
Campbell, Mary Ann; New York, 1885 ***1640.13*** *p18*
Campbell, Mary Campbell *SEE* Campbell, Donald
Campbell, Mary Emmons; Vermont, 1861-1883 ***5900.10*** *p337*
Campbell, Mary Gillies *SEE* Campbell, John
Campbell, Mary Lewis; Vermont, 1841-1925 ***5900.10*** *p128*
Campbell, Mary MacDonald *SEE* Campbell, John
Campbell, Mary MacIntyre *SEE* Campbell, Angus
Campbell, Mary MacIsaac *SEE* Campbell, Malcolm
Campbell, Mary MacLellan *SEE* Campbell, Donald
Campbell, Mary Melauen 54; Vermont, 1876 ***5900.10*** *p51*
Campbell, Mary Steele *SEE* Campbell, Alexander
Campbell, Mary Twigg 55; Vermont, 1895 ***5900.10*** *p235*
Campbell, Michael 74; Vermont, 1905 ***5900.10*** *p235*
Campbell, Mindoo 31; Ontario, 1871 ***1823.15*** *p35*
Campbell, Murdo *SEE* Campbell, John
Campbell, Neil *SEE* Campbell, Donald
Campbell, Neil *SEE* Campbell, Finlay
Campbell, Neil *SEE* Campbell, Lachlan
Campbell, Neil *SEE* Campbell, Malcolm
Campbell, Neil *SEE* Campbell, Neil
Campbell, Neil; Nova Scotia, 1833 ***4537.35*** *p10*
  With wife
  Child: Flora
  Son: Donald
  Child: Rachel
Campbell, Neil; Saskatchewan, 1884 ***4537.37*** *p90*
  Child: Neil
  Child: Ann
  Child: Mary
  Child: Penny
  Child: Effie
  Wife: Janet MacMillan
  Child: Colin
Campbell, Nora; Vermont, n.d. ***5900.10*** *p329*
Campbell, Norman *SEE* Campbell, Norman
Campbell, Norman; Canada, 1840-1849 ***4537.35*** *p71*
  Brother: Alexander
Campbell, Norman; Ontario, 1863 ***4537.32*** *p7*
  Wife: Kirsty MacLeod
  Child: Kirsty
  Child: Malcolm
  Child: Frances
  Child: Norman
  Child: Angus
  Child: Ann
  Child: John
  Child: Effie
Campbell, Owen 67; Vermont, 1883 ***5900.10*** *p51*
Campbell, Patrick; New York, New York, 1784 ***1224.2*** *p19*
Campbell, Patrick; Vermont, 1834-1918 ***5900.10*** *p530*
Campbell, Peggy *SEE* Campbell, John
Campbell, Peggy Ann *SEE* Campbell, Donald
Campbell, Penny *SEE* Campbell, John
Campbell, Penny *SEE* Campbell, Neil
Campbell, Peter; New York, 1840 ***8197.10*** *p221*
Campbell, Peter; St. Louis, 1878 ***1640.13*** *p18*
Campbell, Peter 50; Ontario, 1871 ***1823.15*** *p35*
Campbell, Peter 58; Ontario, 1871 ***1823.28*** *p14*
Campbell, Rachel *SEE* Campbell, John
Campbell, Rachel *SEE* Campbell, Neil
Campbell, Rachel; Nova Scotia, 1840-1849 ***4537.35*** *p22*
Campbell, Rachel MacAskill *SEE* Campbell, Lachlan
Campbell, Rachel MacAskill; Ontario, 1860-1869 ***4537.32*** *p7*
Campbell, Ranald *SEE* Campbell, Catherine MacDonald
Campbell, Randall; Georgia, 1778-1845 ***1640.10*** *p24*
Campbell, Rob 71; Ontario, 1871 ***1823.15*** *p35*
Campbell, Robert; Florida, 1767 ***1640.10*** *p24*
Campbell, Robert; Georgia, 1818 ***1640.10*** *p25*
Campbell, Robert; New York, 1829 ***8197.10*** *p352*
Campbell, Robert; New York, 1839 ***8197.10*** *p379*
Campbell, Robert 40; Ontario, 1871 ***1823.28*** *p14*
Campbell, Robert 45; Ontario, 1871 ***1823.15*** *p35*
Campbell, Robert 51; Ontario, 1871 ***1823.15*** *p35*
Campbell, Robert 60; Ontario, 1871 ***1823.15*** *p35*
Campbell, Robert 72; Ontario, 1861 ***2896.25*** *p26*
Campbell, Robert 103; Ontario, 1871 ***1823.15*** *p35*
Campbell, Roderick *SEE* Campbell, Alexander
Campbell, Roderick *SEE* Campbell, Angus
Campbell, Rollo; Portland, Maine, 1857 ***9196.15*** *p12*
Campbell, Mrs. Rollo; Portland, Maine, 1857 ***9196.15*** *p12*
Campbell, Sally *SEE* Campbell, Alexander
Campbell, Sally *SEE* Campbell, John
Campbell, Samuel; Florida, 1766 ***1640.10*** *p25*
Campbell, Samuel 39; Ontario, 1871 ***1823.28*** *p14*
Campbell, Sarah *SEE* Campbell, John
Campbell, Sarah; Vermont, 1848-1924 ***5900.10*** *p420*
Campbell, Sarah 42; Ontario, 1871 ***1823.15*** *p35*
Campbell, Sarah 65; Ontario, 1861 ***2896.25*** *p26*
Campbell, Stephen *SEE* Campbell, Malcolm
Campbell, Susan Conlin; Vermont, 1845-1910 ***5900.10*** *p45*
Campbell, Thomas 30; St. Vincent, 1775 ***1220.25*** *p129*
Campbell, Thomas 32; Ontario, 1871 ***1823.22*** *p23*
Campbell, Thomas 45; Ontario, 1871 ***1823.15*** *p35*
Campbell, Thomas 47; Ontario, 1871 ***1823.15*** *p35*
Campbell, Thomas 56; Ontario, 1871 ***1823.15*** *p35*
Campbell, Thomas 82; Vermont, 1878 ***5900.10*** *p235*
Campbell, Thomas 88; Vermont, 1884 ***5900.10*** *p268*
Campbell, Una *SEE* Campbell, Lachlan
Campbell, William *SEE* Campbell, John
Campbell, William; Florida, 1766 ***1640.10*** *p25*
Campbell, William; Georgia, 1699 ***1640.13*** *p18*
Campbell, William; Georgia, 1737 ***1640.10*** *p25*
Campbell, William; Jamaica, 1794 ***1640.13*** *p19*
Campbell, William; Maryland, 1718 ***1224.2*** *p19*
Campbell, William; New York, 1807 ***8197.10*** *p36*
Campbell, William; New York, 1845 ***1224.3*** *p12*
Campbell, William; Virginia, 1693 ***1224.1*** *p12*
Campbell, William 30; Ontario, 1871 ***1823.15*** *p35*
Campbell, William 36; Ontario, 1871 ***1823.15*** *p35*
Campbell, William 37; Ontario, 1871 ***1823.15*** *p35*
Campbell, William 45; Ontario, 1871 ***1823.28*** *p14*
Campbell, William 52; Ontario, 1871 ***1823.15*** *p35*
Campbell, William 52; Ontario, 1871 ***1823.22*** *p23*
Campbell, William 64; Ontario, 1871 ***1823.15*** *p35*
Campbell, William Mark; Bahamas, 1847 ***1640.13*** *p19*
Campbell, Wm.; New York, 1840 ***8197.10*** *p161*
Campbell, Wm 37; Ontario, 1871 ***1823.15*** *p35*
Campbell Family ; Vermont, 1850 ***5900.10*** *p320*
Campble, William; Pennsylvania, 1785 ***4629.10*** *p48*
Campeign, Nesbit 68; Ontario, 1871 ***1823.15*** *p35*
Campen, James 63; Ontario, 1861 ***2896.27*** *p45*
Camphier, Anne *SEE* Camphier, Thomas
Camphier, Thomas; Maryland, 1667 ***2524.55*** *p41*
  Wife: Anne
  With 2 children
Campiegan, Nesbit 34; Ontario, 1871 ***1823.15*** *p35*
Campier, Thomas; Maryland, 1663 ***2524.55*** *p41*
Campigne, Edward 39; Ontario, 1871 ***1823.15*** *p35*
Campion, Catharine; New York, 1836 ***8197.10*** *p317*
Campion, Catharine; New York, 1840 ***8197.10*** *p164*
Campion, David 52; Ontario, 1871 ***1823.15*** *p35*
Campion, Francis L.; Philadelphia, 1791 ***4629.10*** *p62*
Campion, German 29; Virginia, 1773 ***1220.25*** *p31*
Campion, J. S.; Quebec, 1858 ***9196.15*** *p35*
Campion, Michael 20; Ontario, 1871 ***1823.15*** *p35*
Campion, Timothy; Virginia, 1666-1667 ***6212.30*** *p35*
Campion, W. H.; Quebec, 1858 ***9196.15*** *p35*
Campire, Anne *SEE* Campire, Thomas
Campire, Mercy; Maryland, 1661 ***2524.55*** *p41*
Campire, Thomas; Maryland, 1661 ***2524.55*** *p41*
Campire, Thomas; Maryland, 1667 ***2524.55*** *p41*
  Wife: Anne
  With 2 children
Campney, Ann 38; Ontario, 1861 ***2896.27*** *p40*
Campney, Berta U. 3; Ontario, 1861 ***2896.27*** *p40*
Campney, Elizabeth 10; Ontario, 1861 ***2896.27*** *p40*
Campney, Happy O. 5; Ontario, 1861 ***2896.27*** *p40*
Campney, Jessy 13; Ontario, 1861 ***2896.27*** *p40*
Campney, Lucy Ann 8; Ontario, 1861 ***2896.27*** *p40*
Campney, Mary A. 5; Ontario, 1861 ***2896.27*** *p40*
Campny, William 16; Ontario, 1861 ***2896.27*** *p63*
Campo, Louisa 19; Ontario, 1861 ***2896.25*** *p7*
Campton, Bridget; Vermont, 1827-1881 ***5900.10*** *p502*
Campton, James; Vermont, 1816-1879 ***5900.10*** *p502*
Camq, Agustus 26; Ontario, 1871 ***1823.28*** *p14*
Can, Robert; Pennsylvania, 1777 ***4629.10*** *p19*
Can, Stephen 40; Ontario, 1871 ***1823.22*** *p23*
Can, Thomas 35; Ontario, 1871 ***1823.22*** *p23*
Cana, Michael; Vermont, 1850 ***5900.10*** *p158*
Canada, Cornelius; Maryland, 1652 ***2524.55*** *p41*
  Wife: Susan
  Son: James
Canada, Elizabeth 62; Ontario, 1861 ***2896.25*** *p63*
Canada, James *SEE* Canada, Cornelius
Canada, James; Ontario, 1861 ***2896.28*** *p59*
Canada, James 25; Ontario, 1861 ***2896.25*** *p63*
Canada, M.; Ontario, 1861 ***2896.28*** *p59*
Canada, Margaret; Ontario, 1861 ***2896.28*** *p59*
Canada, Margaret 19; Ontario, 1861 ***2896.25*** *p63*
Canada, Mary 29; Ontario, 1861 ***2896.25*** *p63*
Canada, Mitchell 21; Ontario, 1861 ***2896.25*** *p63*
Canada, Robert 27; Ontario, 1861 ***2896.28*** *p65*
Canada, Susan *SEE* Canada, Cornelius
Canadey, Cornelius; Maryland, 1648 ***2524.55*** *p41*
Canady, Cornelius; New York, 1828-1833 ***8197.10*** *p304*
Canan, Grace; Virginia, 1680 ***6212.30*** *p55*
Canan, James 20; Maryland, 1774 ***1220.25*** *p41*
Canary, Bridget; Vermont, 1831-1867 ***5900.10*** *p219*
Canary, James 35; Ontario, 1871 ***1823.22*** *p23*
Canary, Michael; Vermont, 1817-1895 ***5900.10*** *p219*
Canary, Michael 46; Ontario, 1871 ***1823.22*** *p23*
Canavan, Pat 25; British Columbia, 1917 ***9196.1*** *p52*
Canavan, Pat 25; Montana, 1917 ***9196.1*** *p52*
Canavan, Thomas; New York, 1838 ***8197.10*** *p112*
Canbarbe, Ann; Maryland, 1678 ***2524.55*** *p41*
Canby, Thomas; Pennsylvania, 1779 ***4629.10*** *p41*
Candee, Roger; Virginia, 1671-1672 ***6212.30*** *p46*
Candler, Anne; Virginia, 1733 ***1224.2*** *p19*
Candler, Robt; Virginia, 1664 ***6212.30*** *p9*
Candon, Ann; Vermont, 1843-1932 ***5900.10*** *p388*
Candon, John; Vermont, 1836-1899 ***5900.10*** *p388*
Candon, Patrick 51; Vermont, 1875 ***5900.10*** *p388*
Cane, Abigail; New England, 1714 ***1224.2*** *p99*
Cane, Charles; Maryland, 1656 ***2524.55*** *p41*
Cane, James 65; Ontario, 1871 ***1823.22*** *p23*
Cane, Jno; Virginia, 1664 ***6212.30*** *p13*
Cane, John; Maryland, 1659 ***2524.55*** *p41*
Cane, Mary 20; Ontario, 1871 ***1823.22*** *p23*
Cane, Walter; Virginia, 1664 ***6212.30*** *p12*
Cane, William; Maryland, 1680 ***2524.55*** *p41*
Caneer, Deborah 17; Ontario, 1861 ***2896.28*** *p55*
Caneer, Ellen 38; Ontario, 1861 ***2896.28*** *p55*
Caneer, Henry 50; Ontario, 1861 ***2896.28*** *p55*
Caneer, L. Jane 8; Ontario, 1861 ***2896.28*** *p56*
Caneer, Mary E. 4; Ontario, 1861 ***2896.28*** *p56*
Caneer, Rebecca 10; Ontario, 1861 ***2896.28*** *p56*
Caneer, S. B. 1; Ontario, 1861 ***2896.28*** *p56*
Caneer, William H. 13; Ontario, 1861 ***2896.28*** *p56*
Caner, Henry; Boston, 1793 ***1224.2*** *p19*
Canet, Joseph; New York, 1816 ***8197.10*** *p58*
Caney, Mary; Vermont, 1826-1889 ***5900.10*** *p418*
Canfall, Catharine 47; Vermont, 1849 ***5900.10*** *p473*
Canfield, Bridget Delaney 60; Vermont, 1904 ***5900.10*** *p44*
Canfield, James E.; Vermont, 1841-1916 ***5900.10*** *p45*
Canfield, Johanna Cullinan; Vermont, 1845-1913 ***5900.10*** *p45*
Canfield, John; Vermont, 1857-1923 ***5900.10*** *p514*
Canfield, Margaret Heyher 86; Vermont, 1910 ***5900.10*** *p558*
Canfield, Rose Boucher; Vermont, 1861-1918 ***5900.10*** *p514*

Canfield, Thomas 65; Vermont, 1884 5900.10 p557
Canham, Harry 71; Vermont, 1911 5900.10 p497
Canker, Mrs.; Maryland, 1663 2524.55 p41
Canker, Thomas; Maryland, 1664 2524.55 p41
Canling, Margret 20; Ontario, 1871 1823.15 p36
Cann, Elizabeth 56; Ontario, 1871 1823.15 p36
Cann, Johann; Port uncertain, 1762 2856.30 p64
Cann, Michael; Vermont, 1850 5900.10 p158
Cann, Robert 48; Ontario, 1871 1823.15 p36
Cann, Samuel 37; Ontario, 1871 1823.22 p23
Cann, Wm 52; Ontario, 1871 1823.28 p14
Cannaday, William; Maryland, 1669 2524.55 p41
Cannady, Ann; Maryland, 1673 2524.55 p41
Cannady, Cornelius; Maryland, 1659 2524.55 p128
Cannady, Dennis; Maryland, 1656 2524.55 p128
Cannady, Ellinour; Maryland, 1655 2524.55 p41
Cannamore, John; Maryland, 1650 2524.55 p41
Cannan, Bridget Keogh 71; Vermont, 1868 5900.10 p367
Cannan, Hanora; Vermont, 1836-1910 5900.10 p355
Cannan, Margaret 66; Vermont, 1897 5900.10 p369
Cannan, Mary Anna 17; Vermont, 1874 5900.10 p367
Cannan, Mary K. 81; Vermont, 1912 5900.10 p367
Cannan, Mathias 82; Vermont, 1878 5900.10 p367
Cannan, Patrick; Vermont, 1834-1913 5900.10 p357
Cannan, Thomas 45; Vermont, 1878 5900.10 p367
Cannan, Uria; Virginia, 1680 6212.30 p55
Cannan, Winifred Cronan; Vermont, 1841-1926 5900.10 p357
Cannawell, John; Maryland, 1650 2524.55 p41
Cannday, Edmund; Maryland, 1671 2524.55 p41
Canneen, Cornelius; Maryland, 1681 2524.55 p41
Cannell, Edward 55; Ontario, 1871 1823.28 p14
Cannell, Nell; Maryland, 1681 2524.55 p41
Canner, Jane 14; Ontario, 1871 1823.22 p23
Canner, John; Maryland, 1681 2524.55 p41
Canner, Suzan; Maryland, 1665 2524.55 p41
Canner, Thomas; Maryland, 1665 2524.55 p41
Canney, Catharine O'Mara 38; Vermont, 1875 5900.10 p263
Canney, John 70; Vermont, 1893 5900.10 p263
Canniers, James; Virginia, 1666-1667 6212.30 p34
Canniff, S. A. 7; Ontario, 1861 2896.27 p6
Cannine, Patrick 38; Ontario, 1871 1823.28 p14
Canning, Christopher; New York, 1836 8197.10 p317
Canning, Edward J. 19; Vermont, 1871 5900.10 p168
Canning, Edward Wm.; New York, 1836 8197.10 p220
Canning, Eliza 3; Vermont, 1849 5900.10 p346
Canning, Ellen 28; Vermont, n.d. 5900.10 p346
Canning, Francis 84; Vermont, 1891 5900.10 p168
Canning, John 46; Ontario, 1871 1823.28 p14
Canning, Judith Sullivan; Vermont, 1852-1896 5900.10 p168
Canning, Julia E. Roche; Vermont, 1853-1909 5900.10 p163
Canning, Maria; Vermont, 1843-1943 5900.10 p333
Canning, Teresa; Vermont, 1842-1888 5900.10 p332
Canning, Thomas 2; Vermont, 1853 5900.10 p346
Canning, William; Vermont, 1840-1901 5900.10 p332
Canning, William J.; Vermont, 1858-1914 5900.10 p163
Cannon, . . .; Vermont, n.d. 5900.10 p179
Cannon, Ann; Vermont, 1846-1907 5900.10 p191
Cannon, Bridget; Vermont, 1830-1906 5900.10 p564
Cannon, Bridget Glennon; Vermont, n.d. 5900.10 p357
Cannon, Bridget Loveday; Vermont, 1830-1919 5900.10 p415
Cannon, C.; Quebec, 1858 9196.15 p47
Cannon, Catharine Glennon; Vermont, 1850-1933 5900.10 p357
Cannon, Catherine; Vermont, 1798-1876 5900.10 p137
Cannon, Catherine 67; Vermont, 1884 5900.10 p156
Cannon, Clarinda 26; Ontario, 1861 2896.27 p50
Cannon, Daniel; New York, 1824 8197.10 p217
Cannon, Eliza M.; New York, 1881 1640.13 p19
Cannon, Ellen; Vermont, 1818-1878 5900.10 p294
Cannon, George; Maryland, 1682 2524.55 p41
Cannon, Henry; Maryland, 1680 2524.55 p41
Cannon, Henry; New York, 1825 8197.10 p218
Cannon, Honora 66; Vermont, 1893 5900.10 p530
Cannon, Hugh 63; Ontario, 1871 1823.15 p36
Cannon, James; New York, 1837 8197.10 p80
Cannon, James; Vermont, 1844-1920 5900.10 p357
Cannon, James J.; Vermont, 1855-1926 5900.10 p179
Cannon, Jennie Martin; Vermont, 1859-1914 5900.10 p407
Cannon, John 18; Philadelphia, 1774 1220.25 p42
Cannon, John 70; Ontario, 1871 1823.28 p14
Cannon, John 97; Vermont, 1891 5900.10 p294
Cannon, John J.; Vermont, 1853 5900.10 p407
Cannon, Lucy 59; Ontario, 1861 2896.27 p56
Cannon, Lucy A. 3; Ontario, 1861 2896.27 p50
Cannon, Margret 81; Ontario, 1871 1823.28 p14
Cannon, Mary; Vermont, 1852-1908 5900.10 p191
Cannon, Mary 2; Vermont, 1850 5900.10 p156
Cannon, Mary Cronin; Vermont, 1839-1910 5900.10 p357
Cannon, Mary Sheridan; Vermont, 1855-1930 5900.10 p179
Cannon, Mathias; Vermont, 1838-1925 5900.10 p357
Cannon, Michael 50; Vermont, 1890 5900.10 p357
Cannon, Patrick; New York, 1828 8197.10 p64
Cannon, Patrick 73; Vermont, 1890 5900.10 p156
Cannon, Sarah; Vermont, 1839-1912 5900.10 p137
Cannon, Stephen; Virginia, 1661 2524.55 p41
Cannon, Thomas; Vermont, 1826-1904 5900.10 p415
Cannon, William 28; Ontario, 1861 2896.27 p50
Cannon, William 54; Ontario, 1871 1823.28 p14
Cannordo, James 5; Ontario, 1871 1823.15 p36
Cannum, Thomas 17; Philadelphia, 1774 1220.25 p34
Canon, James; New York, 1837 8197.10 p80
Canovan, John; New York, 1834 8197.10 p219
Cantarali, Gregory; New York, 1827 8197.10 p339
Cantelian, Jane 50; Ontario, 1871 1823.15 p36
Cantell, Isaac; Texas, 1847 1224.3 p12
Cantelon, Arthur 42; Ontario, 1871 1823.15 p36
Cantelon, George 51; Ontario, 1871 1823.15 p36
Cantelon, John 49; Ontario, 1871 1823.15 p36
Cantelon, Peter 54; Ontario, 1871 1823.15 p36
Cantelon, Samuel 74; Ontario, 1871 1823.15 p36
Cantelon, William 40; Ontario, 1871 1823.15 p36
Canter, Rachel; New York, 1828 8197.10 p349
Canter, Thomas 18; Maryland, 1774 1220.25 p69
Canterbury, Samuel 16; Philadelphia, 1774 1220.25 p63
Cantillion, Mary Tehan; Vermont, 1847-1934 5900.10 p335
Cantillion, Patrick 34; Ontario, 1871 1823.15 p36
Cantillion, Thomas; Vermont, 1843-1910 5900.10 p335
Cantler, Baret; Pennsylvania, 1777 4629.10 p7
Cantlers, George; Pennsylvania, 1786 4629.10 p49
Cantlin, Arthur 38; Ontario, 1871 1823.15 p36
Cantlon, Adam 47; Ontario, 1871 1823.15 p36
Cantlon, Arthur 40; Ontario, 1871 1823.15 p36
Cantlon, Arthur 72; Ontario, 1871 1823.15 p36
Cantlon, David 60; Ontario, 1871 1823.15 p36
Cantlon, John 40; Ontario, 1871 1823.15 p36
Cantlon, John 93; Ontario, 1871 1823.15 p36
Cantlon, Mary A. 75; Ontario, 1871 1823.15 p36
Cantlon, Peter 42; Ontario, 1871 1823.15 p36
Cantlon, William 64; Ontario, 1871 1823.15 p36
Cantlow, Ellen 73; Vermont, 1909 5900.10 p117
Cantrell, John; New York, 1819-1834 8197.10 p307
Cantrell, Joseph; New York, 1819-1834 8197.10 p307
Cantrell, Peter; New York, 1839 8197.10 p133
Cantrell, Samuel; New York, 1839 8197.10 p132
Cantrell, Wm.; New York, 1840 8197.10 p161
Cantwell, Patrick 49; Ontario, 1871 1823.15 p36
Canty, Bridget Kelly; Vermont, 1836-1914 5900.10 p432
Canty, Catherine; Vermont, 1841-1916 5900.10 p429
Canty, Ellen Reagan; Vermont, 1825-1897 5900.10 p508
Canty, John L.; Vermont, 1820-1917 5900.10 p508
Canty, Julia Ellen; Vermont, 1851-1951 5900.10 p509
Canty, Mary; Vermont, 1863-1916 5900.10 p334
Canty, Thomas; Vermont, 1836-1929 5900.10 p432
Canty, William; New York, 1834 8197.10 p70
Cantzler, Marg. Elisabeth; Port uncertain, 1756 2856.30 p64
Canway, Patrick 55; Ontario, 1871 1823.28 p14
Canzler, Andreas; Port uncertain, 1769 2856.30 p64
Canzler, Andreas; Port uncertain, 1781 2856.30 p64
Caoll, James; Maryland, 1678 2524.55 p42
Capalia, Joseph; Maryland, 1910 3259.35 p8
Cape, John; New York, 1838 8197.10 p220
Capel, Mr.; Quebec, 1857 9196.15 p26
Capel, Anton; Port uncertain, 1743 2856.30 p64
Capel, George; Quebec, 1858 9196.15 p33
Capeless, Ellen; Vermont, 1842-1903 5900.10 p437
Capeless, John; Vermont, 1830-1911 5900.10 p420
Capeless, Julia Cronin; Vermont, 1843-1923 5900.10 p420
Capeless, Katie Gaffney 41; Vermont, 1888 5900.10 p420
Capeless, Michael 65; Vermont, 1913 5900.10 p420
Capeter, Josef; Port uncertain, 1773 2856.30 p64
Capmaker, Samuell; Virginia, 1663 6212.30 p2
Capp, Tho; Virginia, 1672 6212.30 p50
Capp, Thomas; New York, 1821 8197.10 p215
Cappel, Anna Maria; Port uncertain, 1791 2856.30 p64
Cappel, George Lewis; Virginia, 1768 1224.2 p19
Cappel, John; Pennsylvania, 1777 4629.10 p11
Capper, Henry; Philadelphia, 1794 1224.2 p19
Capper, Hy; Portland, Maine, 1858 9196.15 p28
Cappin, William 74; Ontario, 1871 1823.22 p23
Capreol, Mr.; Quebec, 1858 9196.15 p39
Caprtine Bapste, John 30; Ontario, 1871 1823.15 p36
Capsin, Barbara; America, 1754 2856.30 p64
Capurro, Luiz; Baltimore, 1834 8197.10 p159
Caradin, Peter; Maryland, 1565 2524.55 p41
Caradize, Henry; Maryland, 1675 2524.55 p41
Caraghen, Thomas 19; Philadelphia, 1774 1220.25 p44
Caragher, James; New York, 1840 8197.10 p220
Caraher, Mary; Vermont, n.d. 5900.10 p166
Carathers, John 40; Ontario, 1871 1823.15 p36
Carayon, Rev.; Quebec, 1856 9196.15 p8
Carayon, A.; Quebec, 1856 9196.15 p8
Carbach, Margarete; Port uncertain, 1736 2856.30 p64
Carbal, Conrad; Pennsylvania, 1838 6058.10 p15
Carbans, Angeline; Vermont, 1835-1897 5900.10 p378
Carbett, Thomas 42; Ontario, 1871 1823.15 p36
Carbine, Catherine Ward; Vermont, 1850-1935 5900.10 p420
Carbine, James C.; Vermont, 1847-1887 5900.10 p420
Carble, Samuel 41; Ontario, 1871 1823.15 p36
Carbo, Jean; America, 1737 2856.30 p64
Carbonell, Thomas; North America, 1759 1224.2 p19
Carbonnel, Joseph Hilary; Philadelphia, 1793 4629.10 p72
Carcaud, Mr.; Quebec, 1858 9196.15 p32
Carch, Corn 50; Ontario, 1871 1823.15 p36
Card, Truman 38; Ontario, 1871 1823.22 p23
Cardasis, Charlie 32; Washington, 1914 9196.1 p65
Cardiff, Mark 50; Ontario, 1871 1823.28 p14
Cardiff, Mark 63; Ontario, 1871 1823.15 p36
Cardiff, Richard 58; Ontario, 1871 1823.28 p14
Cardiff, Thos 58; Ontario, 1871 1823.28 p14
Cardiffe, George 62; Ontario, 1871 1823.28 p14
Cardinell, Lydia S. 1; Ontario, 1861 2896.28 p47
Cardinell, Philip K. 7; Ontario, 1861 2896.28 p47
Cardinell, Sarah O. 31; Ontario, 1861 2896.28 p47
Cardinell, Thomas 6; Ontario, 1861 2896.28 p47
Cardino, William 51; Ontario, 1871 1823.15 p36
Cardno, Alexander 44; Ontario, 1871 1823.15 p36
Cardwell, Samuel; New York, 1839 8197.10 p132
Cardwill, James; New York, 1803 8197.10 p11
Care, Jesse; Pennsylvania, 1786 4629.10 p53
Care, John 26; Maryland, 1774 1220.25 p71
Carew, Allen; Virginia, 1664 6212.30 p7
Carew, Evan; Maryland, 1672 2524.55 p41
Carew, James; Maryland, 1678 2524.55 p41
Carew, Joseph; New York, 1840 8197.10 p162
Carew, Katherine; Maryland, 1678 2524.55 p41
Carewood, Stephen; Maryland, 1664 2524.55 p44
Carey, Mrs.; Quebec, 1858 9196.15 p36
Carey, Abbie D.; Vermont, 1866-1956 5900.10 p225
Carey, Ann; Maryland, 1671 2524.55 p41
Carey, Catherine; Vermont, 1820-1900 5900.10 p441
Carey, Charles 45; Ontario, 1871 1823.15 p36
Carey, David; Vermont, 1850-1932 5900.10 p116
Carey, Edmund; Vermont, 1833-1904 5900.10 p114
Carey, Edward *SEE* Carey, Thomas
Carey, Elisabeth 79; Ontario, 1871 1823.15 p36
Carey, Hugh 72; Vermont, 1886 5900.10 p242
Carey, James; Maryland, 1678 2524.55 p42
Carey, James 60; Ontario, 1871 1823.22 p24
Carey, James 92; Ontario, 1871 1823.15 p36
Carey, Jane *SEE* Carey, Thomas
Carey, Jas; Portland, Maine, 1858 9196.15 p28
Carey, John *SEE* Carey, Thomas
Carey, John; New York, New York, 1851 6058.10 p54
Carey, John 52; Ontario, 1871 1823.15 p36
Carey, Katherine G. Breen; Vermont, 1855-1893 5900.10 p117
Carey, Lucius 50; Ontario, 1871 1823.15 p36
Carey, Margaret; Vermont, 1827-1901 5900.10 p528
Carey, Margaret; Vermont, 1861 5900.10 p318
Carey, Mary; Maryland, 1673 2524.55 p42
Carey, Mary; Vermont, 1847-1924 5900.10 p567
Carey, Mary; Vermont, 1855-1924 5900.10 p488
Carey, Mary A. Law; Vermont, 1854-1912 5900.10 p49
Carey, Mary Flavin; Vermont, 1836-1871 5900.10 p114
Carey, Mary Stewart 65; Vermont, 1883 5900.10 p242
Carey, Michael; New York, 1819 8197.10 p215
Carey, Michael; Vermont, 1853-1931 5900.10 p49
Carey, Nanno Butler; Vermont, 1850-1926 5900.10 p117
Carey, Patrick; New York, 1836 8197.10 p317
Carey, Patrick M.; New York, 1828-1834 8197.10 p305
Carey, Sarah 80; Ontario, 1871 1823.15 p36
Carey, Thomas *SEE* Carey, Thomas
Carey, Thomas; Maryland, 1673 2524.55 p42
Wife: Jane
Son: Thomas
Son: John
Son: Edward
Carey, Thomas 38; Ontario, 1871 1823.15 p37
Carey, Thomas 67; Ontario, 1871 1823.15 p37
Carey, Walter; Virginia, 1665 6212.30 p20
Carey, William; Vermont, 1837-1919 5900.10 p553
Carfeild, John; Virginia, 1666 6212.30 p27
Cargile, Adam; Georgia, 1774 1640.10 p25
Wife: Janet

Cargile, Janet *SEE* Cargile, Adam
Cargill, David; New Orleans, 1846 ***1640.10*** *p25*
Cargill, Louisa; Boston, 1893 ***1640.13*** *p19*
Carhard, Linard; America, 1740 ***2856.30*** *p64*
Carier, J. B. 45; Maryland, 1775 ***1220.25*** *p99*
Carile, Daniel; America, 1738 ***2856.30*** *p64*
Carius, Mr.; America, 1762 ***2856.30*** *p64*
With brother
Carius, Peter; America, 1764 ***2856.30*** *p64*
Carl, Luke; New York, 1825 ***8197.10*** *p217*
Carl, Michael 33; Ontario, 1871 ***1823.15*** *p37*
Carl, Nancy M. 48; Vermont, 1888 ***5900.10*** *p78*
Carl, Patrick 30; Ontario, 1871 ***1823.22*** *p24*
Carl, Thomas 37; Ontario, 1871 ***1823.28*** *p14*
Carlan, Patrick; Maryland, 1673 ***2524.55*** *p42*
Carlan, Patrick; Pennsylvania, 1839 ***6058.10*** *p16*
Carlau, William B.; New York, 1823 ***8197.10*** *p63*
Carlaw, Alexander; New York, 1821 ***8197.10*** *p216*
Carlbaum, Charles T.; New York, 1838 ***8197.10*** *p112*
Carle, Mathias; Port uncertain, 1748 ***2856.30*** *p64*
Carleton, Ann Jane 23; Ontario, 1861 ***2896.28*** *p22*
Carleton, Arthur; Maryland, 1681 ***1224.1*** *p12*
Carleton, Eliza; Maryland, 1668 ***2524.55*** *p42*
Carleton, Elizabeth *SEE* Carleton, Thomas
Carleton, James 26; Ontario, 1861 ***2896.28*** *p22*
Carleton, Richard; New York, 1819 ***8197.10*** *p215*
Carleton, Thomas; Maryland, 1668 ***2524.55*** *p42*
Wife: Elizabeth
Carleton, Wm; Virginia, 1664 ***6212.30*** *p7*
Carleton, Wm; Virginia, 1666 ***6212.30*** *p29*
Carley, Alexander 34; Ontario, 1871 ***1823.22*** *p24*
Carley, Andrew A. 20; Ontario, 1861 ***2896.27*** *p44*
Carley, Casper; New York, 1817 ***8197.10*** *p60*
Carley, Eliza 94; Ontario, 1861 ***2896.27*** *p44*
Carley, Eliza Crogan; Vermont, 1844-1898 ***5900.10*** *p499*
Carley, George 11; Ontario, 1861 ***2896.27*** *p44*
Carley, John; Vermont, 1836-1893 ***5900.10*** *p468*
Carley, John 45; Ontario, 1871 ***1823.15*** *p37*
Carley, Julia; Vermont, 1850-1923 ***5900.10*** *p468*
Carley, Mary 85; Ontario, 1861 ***2896.27*** *p44*
Carley, Moses; Vermont, 1844-1909 ***5900.10*** *p499*
Carley, Philip 2; Ontario, 1861 ***2896.27*** *p44*
Carley, Wesley 17; Ontario, 1861 ***2896.27*** *p44*
Carlieu, Henry; Maryland, 1651 ***2524.55*** *p42*
With wife
Carlile, Henry; Virginia, 1667-1668 ***6212.30*** *p38*
Carlile, John; Maryland, 1666 ***2524.55*** *p42*
Wife: Suzan
Daughter: Jone
Carlile, Jone *SEE* Carlile, John
Carlile, Robert 38; Ontario, 1871 ***1823.15*** *p37*
Carlile, Suzan *SEE* Carlile, John
Carlile, Thomas; New York, 1837 ***8197.10*** *p82*
Carlin, Annie Hinckey 62; Vermont, 1888 ***5900.10*** *p590*
Carlin, Bridget 18; New York, New York, 1847 ***1825.45*** *p13*
Carlin, Charles B.; Vermont, 1841-1941 ***5900.10*** *p448*
Carlin, Ellen 9; New York, New York, 1847 ***1825.45*** *p13*
Carlin, Honor 40 *SEE* Carlin, John
Carlin, James; New York, 1834 ***8197.10*** *p70*
Carlin, James; New York, 1839 ***8197.10*** *p132*
Carlin, John 30; New York, New York, 1847 ***1825.45*** *p13*
Wife: Honor 40
Carlin, Mary 7; New York, New York, 1847 ***1825.45*** *p13*
Carlin, Mary A. Kelley; Vermont, 1845-1917 ***5900.10*** *p448*
Carlin, Patrick; Pennsylvania, 1839 ***6058.10*** *p16*
Carlin, Thomas; New York, 1839 ***8197.10*** *p132*
Carlin, Thomas 76; Vermont, 1892 ***5900.10*** *p590*
Carlinger, George; Pennsylvania, 1777 ***4629.10*** *p13*
Carlington, Edw; Virginia, 1666-1667 ***6212.30*** *p34*
Carlington, James; Virginia, 1667-1668 ***6212.30*** *p38*
Carlington, Nehemiah; Virginia, 1664-1665 ***6212.30*** *p16*
Carlisle, Benjamin; New York, 1839 ***8197.10*** *p132*
Carlisle, George; Pennsylvania, 1786 ***4629.10*** *p54*
Carlisle, John H.; New York, 1830 ***8197.10*** *p218*
Carliw, Philip 60; Ontario, 1871 ***1823.15*** *p37*
Carlon, Bridget 18; New York, New York, 1847 ***1825.45*** *p13*
Carlon, Bridget 28; Vermont, 1862 ***5900.10*** *p210*
Carlon, Ellen 9; New York, New York, 1847 ***1825.45*** *p13*
Carlon, Honor 40 *SEE* Carlon, John
Carlon, James 52; Ontario, 1871 ***1823.15*** *p37*
Carlon, John 30; New York, New York, 1847 ***1825.45*** *p13*
Wife: Honor 40
Carlon, John 60; Ontario, 1871 ***1823.15*** *p37*
Carlon, Mary 7; New York, New York, 1847 ***1825.45*** *p13*
Carlon, Mary Flynn 77; Vermont, 1909 ***5900.10*** *p211*
Carlon, Owen; Vermont, 1835-1920 ***5900.10*** *p437*
Carlon, Thomas 32; Vermont, 1868 ***5900.10*** *p208*
Carlon, Thomas 60; Vermont, 1866 ***5900.10*** *p211*
Carlow, Bridget Murray; Vermont, 1850-1903 ***5900.10*** *p437*
Carlow, James, Sr. 58; Ontario, 1871 ***1823.22*** *p24*
Carlow, James, Jr. 36; Ontario, 1871 ***1823.22*** *p24*
Carlow, Thomas 32; Ontario, 1871 ***1823.22*** *p24*
Carlson, A. 34; Alaska, 1912 ***9196.1*** *p38*
Carlson, A. 34; Whitehorse, Yukon, 1912 ***9196.1*** *p38*
Carlson, C. F. 40; British Columbia, 1909 ***9196.1*** *p27*
Carlson, C. F. 40; Seattle, 1909 ***9196.1*** *p27*
Carlson, Chas 40; Alaska, 1913 ***9196.1*** *p20*
Carlson, Chas 40; British Columbia, 1913 ***9196.1*** *p20*
Carlson, Emil 28; Alaska, 1913 ***9196.1*** *p22*
Carlson, Emil 28; British Columbia, 1913 ***9196.1*** *p22*
Carlson, Franc; Boston, 1903 ***3437.14*** *p134*
Carlson, Gus 26; British Columbia, 1909 ***9196.1*** *p27*
Carlson, Gus 26; Washington, 1909 ***9196.1*** *p27*
Carlson, M. 49; Alaska, 1917 ***9196.1*** *p46*
Carlson, M. 49; Whitehorse, Yukon, 1917 ***9196.1*** *p46*
Carlson, O. C. 51; Alaska, 1916 ***9196.1*** *p6*
Carlson, O. C. 51; Alaska, 1917 ***9196.1*** *p46*
Carlson, O. C. 51; Whitehorse, Yukon, 1917 ***9196.1*** *p46*
Carlson, O. C. 51; Yukon, 1916 ***9196.1*** *p6*
Carlson, Ole 25; British Columbia, 1909 ***9196.1*** *p25*
Carlson, Ole 25; Washington, 1909 ***9196.1*** *p25*
Carlton, Mr.; Quebec, 1858 ***9196.15*** *p37*
Carlton, Arthur; Maryland, 1668 ***2524.55*** *p42*
Carlton, Mary 14; Ontario, 1861 ***2896.27*** *p62*
Carlton, Rebecca 62; Ontario, 1861 ***2896.27*** *p62*
Carlton, Richard; Pennsylvania, 1787 ***4629.10*** *p55*
Carlvon, Charles; Pennsylvania, 1786 ***4629.10*** *p49*
Carly, Owen; New York, 1839 ***8197.10*** *p383*
Carman, Andrew J.; Vermont, 1830-1907 ***5900.10*** *p518*
Carman, C. 34; Ontario, 1861 ***2896.26*** *p12*
Carman, Mary R. Donaldson; Vermont, 1840-1917 ***5900.10*** *p518*
Carman, Nicholas; New York, 1839 ***8197.10*** *p220*
Carman, Robert 57; Ontario, 1871 ***1823.15*** *p37*
Carman, S. 8; Ontario, 1861 ***2896.26*** *p12*
Carman, Sanford U.; Vermont, 1828-1907 ***5900.10*** *p282*
Carman, Susan D. Magowan; Vermont, 1835-1916 ***5900.10*** *p282*
Carmant, Peter; New York, 1824 ***8197.10*** *p64*
Carmelick, Marco; New York, 1838 ***8197.10*** *p220*
Carmich, Peter; Pennsylvania, 1777 ***4629.10*** *p29*
Carmichael, Alexander; Virgin Islands, 1782 ***1640.13*** *p19*
Carmichael, Andrew 26; Maryland, 1774 ***1220.25*** *p57*
Carmichael, Archibald; New York, 1829-1839 ***8197.10*** *p133*
Carmichael, Elizabeth 49; Ontario, 1871 ***1823.28*** *p14*
Carmichael, Euphemia Douglas; New York, 1899 ***1640.13*** *p19*
Carmichael, James; New York, 1840 ***8197.10*** *p162*
Carmichael, John 23; Ontario, 1871 ***1823.15*** *p37*
Carmichael, John 36; Ontario, 1871 ***1823.28*** *p14*
Carmichael, John 48; Ontario, 1871 ***1823.28*** *p14*
Carmichael, Mary 67; Ontario, 1871 ***1823.28*** *p14*
Carmichael, Robert 40; Ontario, 1871 ***1823.28*** *p14*
Carmichael, Robert 43; Ontario, 1871 ***1823.15*** *p37*
Carmichael, Thomas 49; Ontario, 1871 ***1823.28*** *p14*
Carmichael, William; Georgia, 1698 ***1640.13*** *p19*
Carmichul, Alexander 70; Ontario, 1871 ***1823.15*** *p37*
Carmody, Ann Davine; Vermont, 1840-1911 ***5900.10*** *p564*
Carmody, Bridget; Vermont, n.d. ***5900.10*** *p247*
Carmody, Bridget; Vermont, 1833-1890 ***5900.10*** *p247*
Carmody, Bridget 19; Vermont, 1869 ***5900.10*** *p564*
Carmody, Bridget A. Carvay; Vermont, 1865-1929 ***5900.10*** *p391*
Carmody, Bridget Carroll 30; Vermont, 1869 ***5900.10*** *p569*
Carmody, Bridget McNeal 31; Vermont, 1887 ***5900.10*** *p578*
Carmody, Catherine Spillane; Vermont, 1835-1916 ***5900.10*** *p464*
Carmody, Daniel 49; Vermont, 1864 ***5900.10*** *p573*
Carmody, Daniel F.; Vermont, 1857-1941 ***5900.10*** *p256*
Carmody, Dennis 60; Vermont, 1869 ***5900.10*** *p320*
Carmody, Edward; Vermont, 1857-1910 ***5900.10*** *p464*
Carmody, Ellen 44; Vermont, 1869 ***5900.10*** *p320*
Carmody, Frank, Sr.; Vermont, 1838-1904 ***5900.10*** *p437*
Carmody, James; Vermont, 1824-1892 ***5900.10*** *p247*
Carmody, James; Vermont, 1856-1910 ***5900.10*** *p464*
Carmody, James B.; Vermont, 1858-1918 ***5900.10*** *p391*
Carmody, James P.; Vermont, 1940 ***5900.10*** *p247*
Carmody, Jeremiah 60; Ontario, 1871 ***1823.28*** *p14*
Carmody, Johanna 32; Vermont, 1898 ***5900.10*** *p247*
Carmody, John; Vermont, 1833-1892 ***5900.10*** *p468*
Carmody, John; Vermont, 1865 ***5900.10*** *p468*
Carmody, John 16; Vermont, 1869 ***5900.10*** *p569*
Carmody, Julia Mahar; Vermont, 1853-1941 ***5900.10*** *p256*
Carmody, Kate; Vermont, 1817-1900 ***5900.10*** *p113*
Carmody, Margaret; Vermont, 1833-1890 ***5900.10*** *p247*
Carmody, Margaret; Vermont, 1851-1873 ***5900.10*** *p247*
Carmody, Margaret Keefe 35; Vermont, 1878 ***5900.10*** *p569*
Carmody, Margaret Lillis 72; Vermont, 1889 ***5900.10*** *p573*
Carmody, Maria Davine; Vermont, 1820-1893 ***5900.10*** *p574*
Carmody, Martha Fenton; Vermont, 1868-1914 ***5900.10*** *p405*
Carmody, Mary; Vermont, 1834-1915 ***5900.10*** *p437*
Carmody, Mary 28; Vermont, 1877 ***5900.10*** *p570*
Carmody, Mary Barrett; Vermont, 1861-1934 ***5900.10*** *p256*
Carmody, Mary Corbett; Vermont, 1830-1922 ***5900.10*** *p468*
Carmody, Mary E. 37; Vermont, 1896 ***5900.10*** *p562*
Carmody, Mary E. Griffith; Vermont, 1858-1932 ***5900.10*** *p394*
Carmody, Michael; New York, 1840 ***8197.10*** *p162*
Carmody, Michael J.; Vermont, 1849-1929 ***5900.10*** *p256*
Carmody, Michael Joseph; Vermont, 1853-1934 ***5900.10*** *p563*
Carmody, Patrick 70; Vermont, 1887 ***5900.10*** *p574*
Carmody, Patrick E.; Vermont, 1855-1935 ***5900.10*** *p394*
Carmody, Roger; Vermont, 1836-1875 ***5900.10*** *p564*
Carmody, Susanna; Vermont, 1849-1942 ***5900.10*** *p195*
Carmody, Thomas; New York, 1839 ***8197.10*** *p132*
Carmody, Thomas; Vermont, 1836-1906 ***5900.10*** *p464*
Carn, Thomas; Maryland, 1661 ***2524.55*** *p42*
Carnagie, Alexander 40; Ontario, 1871 ***1823.28*** *p14*
Carnagie, Alexander, Sr. 83; Ontario, 1871 ***1823.28*** *p14*
Carnagie, Daniel 37; Ontario, 1871 ***1823.28*** *p14*
Carnagie, William 37; Ontario, 1871 ***1823.28*** *p14*
Carnagie, William 42; Ontario, 1871 ***1823.15*** *p37*
Carnahan, Thomas H. 27; Ontario, 1861 ***2896.27*** *p20*
Carnall, George 66; Ontario, 1871 ***1823.22*** *p24*
Carnall, George W. 31; Ontario, 1871 ***1823.22*** *p24*
Carne, Thomas; Virginia, 1665 ***6212.30*** *p18*
Carnegie, J.; Quebec, 1856 ***9196.15*** *p6*
Carnegie, James; Augusta, Georgia, 1788 ***1640.10*** *p25*
Carnegie, John; Georgia, 1699 ***1640.13*** *p19*
Carnegy, John; Georgia, 1698 ***1640.13*** *p19*
Carnel, Mary J. 6; Ontario, 1861 ***2896.25*** *p3*
Carnel, Mathew 3; Ontario, 1861 ***2896.25*** *p3*
Carnel, Robert 38; Ontario, 1861 ***2896.25*** *p3*
Carnel, Sarah 30; Ontario, 1861 ***2896.25*** *p3*
Carnell, Daniel; Maryland, 1678 ***2524.55*** *p42*
Carnell, John; Maryland, 1658 ***2524.55*** *p42*
Carner, James; Virginia, 1667-1668 ***6212.30*** *p38*
Carnes, Burrell; Boston, n.d. ***1224.3*** *p12*
Carnes, Burrell; Guyana, 1805 ***1224.3*** *p12*
Carnes, Thomas; New York, 1837 ***8197.10*** *p82*
Carney, Agnes; Vermont, 1865-1886 ***5900.10*** *p551*
Carney, Ann Higgins 75; Vermont, 1900 ***5900.10*** *p544*
Carney, Anne 20; Quebec, 1848 ***1825.45*** *p28*
Carney, Annie E. 36; Vermont, 1891 ***5900.10*** *p228*
Carney, Bernard; Vermont, 1841-1917 ***5900.10*** *p398*
Carney, Bernard; Vermont, 1854-1919 ***5900.10*** *p327*
Carney, Bridget; Vermont, 1817-1887 ***5900.10*** *p99*
Carney, Bridget; Vermont, 1838-1916 ***5900.10*** *p404*
Carney, Catherine; Vermont, 1824-1899 ***5900.10*** *p220*
Carney, Catherine; Vermont, 1837-1907 ***5900.10*** *p261*
Carney, Catherine; Vermont, 1844 ***5900.10*** *p350*
Carney, Catherine Riley; Vermont, 1815-1904 ***5900.10*** *p231*
Carney, Daniel; Vermont, 1831-1891 ***5900.10*** *p231*
Carney, Daniel 55; Ontario, 1871 ***1823.28*** *p14*
Carney, Daniel, Jr.; Vermont, 1850-1874 ***5900.10*** *p232*
Carney, Erril 70; Vermont, 1877 ***5900.10*** *p211*
Carney, Erril P. 30; Vermont, 1873 ***5900.10*** *p213*
Carney, James; New York, 1821 ***8197.10*** *p215*
Carney, James; New York, 1824 ***8197.10*** *p215*
Carney, James; New York, 1840 ***8197.10*** *p160*
Carney, James; Vermont, 1814-1886 ***5900.10*** *p551*
Carney, James; Vermont, 1853-1881 ***5900.10*** *p213*
Carney, James; Vermont, 1854-1898 ***5900.10*** *p232*
Carney, James 44; Ontario, 1871 ***1823.28*** *p14*
Carney, James F.; Vermont, 1851-1926 ***5900.10*** *p398*
Carney, James J. 58; Vermont, 1887 ***5900.10*** *p485*
Carney, Jane; Vermont, 1828-1910 ***5900.10*** *p551*
Carney, Jane 88; Vermont, 1906 ***5900.10*** *p388*
Carney, John; Vermont, 1827-1899 ***5900.10*** *p350*
Carney, John; Vermont, 1849-1872 ***5900.10*** *p232*
Carney, John 2; Vermont, 1852 ***5900.10*** *p522*
Carney, John 39; Ontario, 1871 ***1823.28*** *p14*
Carney, John 65; Ontario, 1871 ***1823.28*** *p14*
Carney, Katharine; Maryland, 1682 ***2524.55*** *p42*
Carney, Katherine; Vermont, 1860-1933 ***5900.10*** *p240*

Carrigan, Mary Stack; Vermont, 1848-1905 ***5900.10*** *p358*
Carrigan, Mathew 65; Vermont, 1893 ***5900.10*** *p587*
Carrigan, Michael; Vermont, 1850-1926 ***5900.10*** *p389*
Carrigan, Mother; Vermont, 1847-1935 ***5900.10*** *p382*
Carrigan, Nellie McNamara; Vermont, 1864-1939 ***5900.10*** *p432*
Carrigan, Patrick; Vermont, 1827-1895 ***5900.10*** *p418*
Carrigan, Patrick; Vermont, 1836-1868 ***5900.10*** *p447*
Carrigan, Patrick 83; Vermont, 1853 ***5900.10*** *p383*
Carrigan, Richard; Vermont, 1830-1893 ***5900.10*** *p358*
Carrigan, Richard J. 20; Ontario, 1861 ***2896.25*** *p23*
Carrigan, Rose A. McEnany 26; Vermont, 1868 ***5900.10*** *p383*
Carrigan, Sarah M. 9; Ontario, 1861 ***2896.25*** *p23*
Carrigan, Thomas; Vermont, 1827-1902 ***5900.10*** *p84*
Carrigan, Walter; Vermont, 1830-1906 ***5900.10*** *p389*
Carrigan, William; Vermont, 1826-1896 ***5900.10*** *p467*
Carrigel, John; Georgia, 1775-1783 ***1640.10*** *p26*
Carrill, W. H.; Quebec, 1858 ***9196.15*** *p33*
Carrington, Henrietta 5; Ontario, 1861 ***2896.25*** *p23*
Carrington, John; Maryland, 1653 ***2524.55*** *p43*
Carrington, John 14; New York, New York, 1847 ***1825.45*** *p13*
Carrington, Wm 30; Ontario, 1861 ***2896.25*** *p23*
Carrman, Thomas; Maryland, 1658 ***2524.55*** *p43*
Carrol, Henry 21; Ontario, 1861 ***2896.27*** *p72*
Carrol, Henry 35; Ontario, 1871 ***1823.22*** *p24*
Carrol, James; Pennsylvania, 1836 ***6058.10*** *p14*
Carrol, James 25; Ontario, 1871 ***1823.15*** *p38*
Carrol, Lawrence; Pennsylvania, 1786 ***4629.10*** *p49*
Carrol, Thomas 18; Maryland, 1773-1774 ***1220.25*** *p34*
Carrol, Timothy; Maryland, 1682 ***2524.55*** *p43*
Carroll, Alice Casey 76; Vermont, 1896 ***5900.10*** *p271*
Carroll, Ann Cunningham 38; Vermont, 1874 ***5900.10*** *p210*
Carroll, Ann Quinn; Vermont, 1842-1903 ***5900.10*** *p273*
Carroll, Ann Rafferty 20; Quebec, 1849 ***1825.45*** *p28*
Carroll, Anna; Vermont, 1822-1888 ***5900.10*** *p312*
Carroll, Anna M. Bulger; Vermont, 1858-1911 ***5900.10*** *p533*
Carroll, B. 2; Ontario, 1861 ***2896.28*** *p9*
Carroll, Bartholomew 40; Ontario, 1871 ***1823.15*** *p38*
Carroll, Bernard 57; Vermont, 1889 ***5900.10*** *p436*
Carroll, Bernard 77; Vermont, 1889 ***5900.10*** *p613*
Carroll, Bridget; Vermont, 1834-1918 ***5900.10*** *p257*
Carroll, Bridget; Vermont, 1834-1937 ***5900.10*** *p581*
Carroll, Bridget 15 *SEE* Carroll, Thomas
Carroll, Bridget 23 *SEE* Carroll, Thomas
Carroll, Bridget 30; Ontario, 1871 ***1823.15*** *p38*
Carroll, Bridget 30; Vermont, 1869 ***5900.10*** *p569*
Carroll, Bridget Reynolds; Vermont, 1824-1898 ***5900.10*** *p468*
Carroll, Bridget Tierney 63; Vermont, 1875 ***5900.10*** *p328*
Carroll, Bridget Ward 87; Vermont, 1800-1899 ***5900.10*** *p231*
Carroll, C. 17; Ontario, 1861 ***2896.28*** *p9*
Carroll, Caroline J.; Vermont, 1851-1925 ***5900.10*** *p231*
Carroll, Catherine 62; Vermont, 1880 ***5900.10*** *p568*
Carroll, Catherine 88; Vermont, 1916 ***5900.10*** *p124*
Carroll, Catherine A. Ward; Vermont, 1920 ***5900.10*** *p558*
Carroll, Daniel 22; New York, 1834-1840 ***8197.10*** *p163*
Carroll, Daniel F.; Vermont, 1858-1888 ***5900.10*** *p486*
Carroll, Delia 56; Vermont, 1872 ***5900.10*** *p438*
Carroll, Dennis 58; Ontario, 1871 ***1823.15*** *p38*
Carroll, Dorothy; Maryland, 1760 ***1224.2*** *p19*
Carroll, Edward; New York, 1821 ***8197.10*** *p216*
Carroll, Edward; Pensacola, Florida, 1787 ***1224.2*** *p19*
Carroll, Edward; Vermont, 1859-1900 ***5900.10*** *p486*
Carroll, Edward 11; Vermont, 1870 ***5900.10*** *p448*
Carroll, Eliza Curley; Vermont, 1817-1885 ***5900.10*** *p338*
Carroll, Ellen 66; Vermont, 1910 ***5900.10*** *p443*
Carroll, Ellen O'Neil 67; Vermont, 1883 ***5900.10*** *p477*
Carroll, Ellen Regan; Vermont, 1863 ***5900.10*** *p351*
Carroll, George; New York, 1837 ***8197.10*** *p79*
Carroll, H. 21; Ontario, 1861 ***2896.28*** *p9*
Carroll, Hannah; Vermont, 1871-1878 ***5900.10*** *p486*
Carroll, Henry; Vermont, 1845-1923 ***5900.10*** *p589*
Carroll, Honor 56; Vermont, 1878 ***5900.10*** *p448*
Carroll, Hugh 70; Ontario, 1871 ***1823.15*** *p38*
Carroll, Isabel McIver; Vermont, 1838-1884 ***5900.10*** *p481*
Carroll, J. 6; Ontario, 1861 ***2896.28*** *p9*
Carroll, James; New York, 1839 ***8197.10*** *p132*
Carroll, James; Pennsylvania, 1777 ***4629.10*** *p11*
Carroll, James; Vermont, 1806-1871 ***5900.10*** *p557*
Carroll, James; Vermont, 1834-1912 ***5900.10*** *p479*
Carroll, James 45; Ontario, 1871 ***1823.15*** *p38*
Carroll, James 46; Ontario, 1861 ***2896.27*** *p24*
Carroll, James 60; Ontario, 1871 ***1823.22*** *p24*
Carroll, James 86; Vermont, 1883 ***5900.10*** *p231*
Carroll, James H.; Vermont, 1844-1914 ***5900.10*** *p531*
Carroll, James W. 42; Vermont, 1873 ***5900.10*** *p231*
Carroll, Jane; Vermont, 1857-1894 ***5900.10*** *p486*
Carroll, Jennie F. O'Donnell; Vermont, 1854-1917 ***5900.10*** *p148*
Carroll, Johannah Casey; Vermont, 1833-1921 ***5900.10*** *p486*
Carroll, John; New York, 1834 ***8197.10*** *p220*
Carroll, John; New York, 1840 ***8197.10*** *p221*
Carroll, John; Vermont, 1826-1896 ***5900.10*** *p486*
Carroll, John; Vermont, 1831-1898 ***5900.10*** *p216*
Carroll, John; Vermont, 1846-1928 ***5900.10*** *p557*
Carroll, John; Vermont, 1850-1933 ***5900.10*** *p533*
Carroll, John; Vermont, 1855-1914 ***5900.10*** *p351*
Carroll, John 12; Vermont, 1862 ***5900.10*** *p566*
Carroll, John 22 *SEE* Carroll, Thomas
Carroll, John 22; Maryland, 1774 ***1220.25*** *p78*
Carroll, John 60; Ontario, 1871 ***1823.15*** *p38*
Carroll, John 76; Vermont, 1866 ***5900.10*** *p328*
Carroll, John 82; Vermont, 1883 ***5900.10*** *p271*
Carroll, John F.; New York, 1840 ***8197.10*** *p159*
Carroll, John W.; Vermont, 1856-1898 ***5900.10*** *p486*
Carroll, Jom 19; Ontario, 1871 ***1823.15*** *p38*
Carroll, Joseph; Alaska, 1911 ***9196.1*** *p37*
Carroll, Joseph 35; Ontario, 1871 ***1823.15*** *p38*
Carroll, Julia 68; Vermont, 1914 ***5900.10*** *p581*
Carroll, Julia Barry; Vermont, 1838-1916 ***5900.10*** *p316*
Carroll, Julia Foster; Vermont, 1812-1887 ***5900.10*** *p557*
Carroll, M. 9; Ontario, 1861 ***2896.28*** *p9*
Carroll, M. 13; Ontario, 1861 ***2896.28*** *p9*
Carroll, M. 40; Ontario, 1861 ***2896.28*** *p9*
Carroll, Margaret; Vermont, 1826-1890 ***5900.10*** *p615*
Carroll, Margaret; Vermont, 1845-1905 ***5900.10*** *p113*
Carroll, Margaret 57; Vermont, 1880 ***5900.10*** *p616*
Carroll, Margaret 83; Vermont, 1905 ***5900.10*** *p359*
Carroll, Margaret A. Munday; Vermont, 1849-1928 ***5900.10*** *p557*
Carroll, Margaret M.; Vermont, 1834-1909 ***5900.10*** *p465*
Carroll, Margaret Reddy; Vermont, 1852-1935 ***5900.10*** *p531*
Carroll, Margaret W.; Vermont, 1838-1927 ***5900.10*** *p231*
Carroll, Martin 33; Vermont, 1893 ***5900.10*** *p129*
Carroll, Mary; Vermont, 1834-1916 ***5900.10*** *p548*
Carroll, Mary; Vermont, 1845-1910 ***5900.10*** *p446*
Carroll, Mary; Vermont, 1883 ***5900.10*** *p470*
Carroll, Mary 6 months; Quebec, 1849 ***1825.45*** *p28*
Carroll, Mary 36; Vermont, 1868 ***5900.10*** *p328*
Carroll, Mary 49; Vermont, 1883 ***5900.10*** *p233*
Carroll, Mary 70; Vermont, 1910 ***5900.10*** *p102*
Carroll, Mary 71; Vermont, 1897 ***5900.10*** *p558*
Carroll, Mary A. Ellis; Vermont, 1842-1921 ***5900.10*** *p288*
Carroll, Mary Ann 18 *SEE* Carroll, Thomas
Carroll, Mary Casey; Vermont, 1832-1887 ***5900.10*** *p216*
Carroll, Mary Cavanagh 80; Vermont, 1885 ***5900.10*** *p533*
Carroll, Mary E.; Vermont, 1851-1903 ***5900.10*** *p616*
Carroll, Mary E. 32; Vermont, 1867 ***5900.10*** *p231*
Carroll, Mary E. 75; Vermont, 1915 ***5900.10*** *p436*
Carroll, Mary Grace 53; Vermont, 1897 ***5900.10*** *p589*
Carroll, Mary Humphreys 26; Vermont, 1879 ***5900.10*** *p258*
Carroll, Mary Jane; Vermont, 1858-1923 ***5900.10*** *p461*
Carroll, Mary Moss 74; Vermont, 1891 ***5900.10*** *p486*
Carroll, Mary O'Neill; Vermont, 1846-1910 ***5900.10*** *p589*
Carroll, Mary Smith; Vermont, 1858-1942 ***5900.10*** *p490*
Carroll, Matilda; Vermont, 1823-1901 ***5900.10*** *p616*
Carroll, Maurice P.; Vermont, 1854-1886 ***5900.10*** *p486*
Carroll, Michael; Vermont, 1849-1921 ***5900.10*** *p148*
Carroll, Michael 24 *SEE* Carroll, Thomas
Carroll, Michael C.; Alaska, 1911 ***9196.1*** *p37*
Carroll, Mike; Vermont, 1928 ***5900.10*** *p322*
Carroll, Nora 50; Ontario, 1861 ***2896.27*** *p24*
Carroll, P. 4; Ontario, 1861 ***2896.28*** *p9*
Carroll, P. 11; Ontario, 1861 ***2896.28*** *p9*
Carroll, P. 42; Ontario, 1861 ***2896.28*** *p9*
Carroll, Patrick; New York, 1807 ***8197.10*** *p329*
Carroll, Patrick; New York, 1837 ***8197.10*** *p80*
Carroll, Patrick; New York, 1839 ***8197.10*** *p381*
Carroll, Patrick; Vermont, 1814-1890 ***5900.10*** *p338*
Carroll, Patrick; Vermont, 1833-1907 ***5900.10*** *p316*
Carroll, Patrick 25; Vermont, 1866 ***5900.10*** *p497*
Carroll, Patrick 32; Ontario, 1871 ***1823.22*** *p24*
Carroll, Patrick 47; Vermont, 1874 ***5900.10*** *p566*
Carroll, Patrick 53; Ontario, 1871 ***1823.15*** *p38*
Carroll, Paul; New York, 1833-1838 ***8197.10*** *p311*
Carroll, Peter 74; Ontario, 1871 ***1823.22*** *p24*
Carroll, Philin 38; Ontario, 1871 ***1823.22*** *p24*
Carroll, Philip 79; Vermont, 1877 ***5900.10*** *p533*
Carroll, Robert; New York, 1837 ***8197.10*** *p80*
Carroll, Robert 40; Ontario, 1871 ***1823.22*** *p24*
Carroll, Roger 45; Ontario, 1871 ***1823.15*** *p38*
Carroll, Rose 46; Vermont, 1869 ***5900.10*** *p235*
Carroll, Rose 49; Vermont, 1867 ***5900.10*** *p530*
Carroll, Sarah 70; Vermont, 1902 ***5900.10*** *p249*
Carroll, Stephen; Vermont, 1857-1929 ***5900.10*** *p490*
Carroll, Terrence; New York, 1837 ***8197.10*** *p81*
Carroll, Thomas; New York, 1836 ***8197.10*** *p79*
Carroll, Thomas; Vermont, 1815-1915 ***5900.10*** *p486*
Carroll, Thomas; Vermont, 1839-1916 ***5900.10*** *p273*
Carroll, Thomas 31; Quebec, 1849 ***1825.45*** *p28*
Wife: Bridget 23
Brother: John 22
Brother: Michael 24
Sister: Mary Ann 18
Sister: Bridget 15
Carroll, Thomas 84; Vermont, 1925 ***5900.10*** *p589*
Carroll, Thomas G. 77; Vermont, 1868 ***5900.10*** *p601*
Carroll, Timothy; Pennsylvania, 1777 ***4629.10*** *p24*
Carroll, Timothy; Pennsylvania, 1779 ***4629.10*** *p40*
Carroll, Timothy; Vermont, 1844-1893 ***5900.10*** *p288*
Carroll, Timothy 16; Vermont, 1870 ***5900.10*** *p448*
Carroll, Timothy E.; Vermont, 1863-1893 ***5900.10*** *p486*
Carroll, William; New York, 1840 ***8197.10*** *p159*
Carroll, William; Vermont, 1857-1904 ***5900.10*** *p271*
Carroll, William 29; Philadelphia, 1775 ***1220.25*** *p9*
Carroll Family ; Maryland, 1775-1781 ***4628.40*** *p81*
Carrothers, Matthew 65; Ontario, 1871 ***1823.15*** *p38*
Carrow, Joseph F.; Vermont, 1853-1918 ***5900.10*** *p333*
Carrow, Julia Smith; Vermont, 1863-1948 ***5900.10*** *p333*
Carrs, James S. 35; Ontario, 1871 ***1823.15*** *p38*
Carrull, John Frederick; New York, 1831 ***8197.10*** *p364*
Carruth, Andrew; Tobago, West Indies, 1845 ***1640.13*** *p19*
Carruthers, Mr.; Quebec, 1858 ***9196.15*** *p44*
Carruthers, Mrs.; Quebec, 1856 ***9196.15*** *p9*
Carruthers, Mrs.; Quebec, 1858 ***9196.15*** *p44*
Carruthers, Christopher 44; Ontario, 1871 ***1823.22*** *p25*
Carruthers, David 50; Ontario, 1871 ***1823.22*** *p25*
Carruthers, Francis 29; Ontario, 1871 ***1823.15*** *p38*
Carruthers, George 50; Ontario, 1871 ***1823.22*** *p25*
Carruthers, Herbert 30; Ontario, 1871 ***1823.22*** *p25*
Carruthers, James; Illinois, 1822 ***1640.13*** *p19*
Carruthers, James; Savannah, Georgia, 1815 ***1640.10*** *p26*
Carruthers, James 29; Ontario, 1871 ***1823.22*** *p25*
Carruthers, James 36; Ontario, 1871 ***1823.22*** *p25*
Carruthers, James 63; Ontario, 1871 ***1823.22*** *p25*
Carruthers, John; Quebec, 1858 ***9196.15*** *p44*
Carruthers, John; Savannah, Georgia, 1815 ***1640.10*** *p26*
Carruthers, Joseph; Savannah, Georgia, 1804 ***1640.10*** *p27*
Carruthers, Thos 32; Ontario, 1871 ***1823.15*** *p38*
Carruthers, William 50; Ontario, 1871 ***1823.22*** *p25*
Carry, John; New York, 1839 ***8197.10*** *p132*
Carry, John 24; Virginia, 1773 ***1220.25*** *p28*
Carry, William; Maryland, 1676 ***2524.55*** *p60*
Carryer, Mr.; Quebec, 1858 ***9196.15*** *p40*
Cars, Thomas; New York, 1807 ***8197.10*** *p36*
Carsan, James; Charles Town, South Carolina, n.d. ***1224.2*** *p19*
Carsewell, Thomas W.; Ontario, 1878 ***1640.13*** *p19*
Carsley, Joseph 19; Maryland, 1774 ***1220.25*** *p60*
Carsme, Edward 19; Ontario, 1871 ***1823.15*** *p38*
Carson, Alexander 35; Ontario, 1871 ***1823.15*** *p38*
Carson, Amelia 17; Ontario, 1861 ***2896.28*** *p29*
Carson, Andrew; Pennsylvania, 1777 ***4629.10*** *p20*
Carson, Ann 50; Ontario, 1871 ***1823.22*** *p25*
Carson, Daniel; Pennsylvania, 1868 ***6058.10*** *p71*
Carson, David 40; New York, 1775 ***1220.25*** *p142*
With wife & 4 children
Carson, George 40; Ontario, 1871 ***1823.28*** *p15*
Carson, Hugh 54; Ontario, 1871 ***1823.15*** *p38*
Carson, Jason 55; Ontario, 1871 ***1823.15*** *p38*
Carson, John; Mobile, Alabama, 1820-1845 ***1640.10*** *p27*
Carson, John; New York, 1827 ***8197.10*** *p347*
Carson, John; New York, 1831 ***8197.10*** *p365*
Carson, John; New York, 1831 ***8197.10*** *p370*
Carson, John; Virginia, 1666 ***6212.30*** *p29*
Carson, John 38; Ontario, 1871 ***1823.22*** *p25*
Carson, John 45; Ontario, 1871 ***1823.28*** *p15*
Carson, Johnson; New York, 1828 ***8197.10*** *p218*
Carson, Joseph; Pennsylvania, 1777 ***4629.10*** *p8*
Carson, Joseph; Pennsylvania, 1859 ***6058.10*** *p41*
Carson, Margarite 76; Ontario, 1871 ***1823.15*** *p38*
Carson, Marion Mary 67; Ontario, 1871 ***1823.15*** *p38*
Carson, Patrick; Baltimore, 1822 ***1224.3*** *p12*
Carson, Robert; Florida, 1766 ***1224.2*** *p19*
Carson, Robert; Florida, 1766 ***1640.10*** *p27*
Carson, Robert 20; Grenada, 1774 ***1220.25*** *p86*
Carson, William; Alabama, 1812-1845 ***1640.10*** *p27*
Carson, William 30; Ontario, 1871 ***1823.28*** *p15*
Carson, William 57; Ontario, 1871 ***1823.15*** *p38*
Carstairs, David 32; Ontario, 1871 ***1823.22*** *p25*

Carstairs, David 59; Ontario, 1871 ***1823.22*** *p25*
Carstairs, James; Canada, 1893 ***1640.13*** *p19*
Carstens, Gerhard Herman; New York, 1840 ***8197.10*** *p161*
Carswel, Agnes 17; Baltimore, 1775 ***1220.25*** *p116*
Carswell, Allan 40; Ontario, 1871 ***1823.28*** *p15*
Carswell, Allen 51; Ontario, 1871 ***1823.28*** *p15*
Carswell, John 44; Maryland, 1775 ***1220.25*** *p116*
Carswell, Margret 55; Ontario, 1871 ***1823.28*** *p15*
Carswell, Robert 45; Ontario, 1871 ***1823.28*** *p15*
Carswell, Robert Scott; New York, 1840 ***8197.10*** *p221*
Carswell, Samuel; Louisiana, 1797 ***1640.10*** *p27*
Carswell, Thomas 50; Ontario, 1871 ***1823.28*** *p15*
Carswell, William P. 48; Ontario, 1871 ***1823.22*** *p25*
Cartaright, Wm; Virginia, 1664 ***6212.30*** *p11*
Carter, Mr.; Quebec, 1858 ***9196.15*** *p41*
Carter, Anne; South Carolina, 1729 ***1224.2*** *p72*
Carter, Charles; New York, 1839 ***8197.10*** *p133*
Carter, Dennis 22; Maryland, 1775 ***1220.25*** *p99*
Carter, Edward 53; Ontario, 1871 ***1823.15*** *p38*
Carter, Eliza; Virginia, 1664 ***6212.30*** *p6*
Carter, Elizabeth; Virginia, 1694 ***1224.1*** *p36*
Carter, Ellen 65; Ontario, 1871 ***1823.22*** *p25*
Carter, Evans; Boston, 1691 ***1224.1*** *p12*
Carter, George 55; Ontario, 1871 ***1823.15*** *p38*
Carter, Henry; New York, 1840 ***8197.10*** *p161*
Carter, Jacob 27; Philadelphia, 1774 ***1220.25*** *p42*
Carter, James; Pennsylvania, 1777 ***4629.10*** *p12*
Carter, Jno; Virginia, 1671 ***6212.30*** *p42*
Carter, John; New York, 1834 ***8197.10*** *p73*
Carter, John; New York, 1837 ***8197.10*** *p219*
Carter, John 30; New York, 1774 ***1220.25*** *p4*
Carter, John 38; Ontario, 1871 ***1823.15*** *p38*
Carter, John 55; Ontario, 1871 ***1823.28*** *p15*
Carter, John 60; Ontario, 1871 ***1823.15*** *p38*
Carter, John James; Ohio, 1839 ***1224.3*** *p12*
Carter, Joseph; New York, 1832 ***8197.10*** *p357*
Carter, Joseph 26; Maryland, 1775 ***1220.25*** *p96*
Carter, Margret 42; Ontario, 1871 ***1823.15*** *p38*
Carter, Mary *SEE* Carter, Philip
Carter, Mary *SEE* Carter, Walter
Carter, Mary Carney 38; Vermont, 1874 ***5900.10*** *p575*
Carter, Mathew; Virginia, 1664-1665 ***6212.30*** *p16*
Carter, Nicolas 58; Ontario, 1861 ***2896.25*** *p60*
Carter, Philip; Maryland, 1682 ***2524.55*** *p43*
Wife: Mary
Daughter: Sarah Thomas
Carter, Rich; Virginia, 1666 ***6212.30*** *p30*
Carter, Richard; Maryland, 1665 ***2524.55*** *p43*
Carter, Richard; Maryland, 1672 ***2524.55*** *p43*
Carter, Richard; Maryland, 1708 ***1224.2*** *p19*
Carter, Richard 27; Fort Cumberland, Nova Scotia, 1774 ***1220.25*** *p19*
Carter, Robert; New York, 1837 ***8197.10*** *p79*
Carter, Robert 40; Ontario, 1871 ***1823.15*** *p38*
Carter, Robert 56; Ontario, 1871 ***1823.15*** *p38*
Carter, Sampson 24; Ontario, 1871 ***1823.15*** *p38*
Carter, Samuel, Jr.; New York, 1834 ***8197.10*** *p69*
Carter, Sara; Virginia, 1666-1667 ***6212.30*** *p35*
Carter, Sarah; Maryland, 1652 ***2524.55*** *p43*
Carter, Sarah Thomas *SEE* Carter, Philip
Carter, Thomas; New England, 1655 ***1224.1*** *p12*
Carter, Thomas; New York, 1819 ***8197.10*** *p61*
Carter, Thomas; Virginia, 1666 ***6212.30*** *p31*
Carter, Thomas 22; Maryland, 1775 ***1220.25*** *p115*
Carter, Thomas 26; Virginia, 1774 ***1220.25*** *p90*
Carter, Thomas 50; Ontario, 1871 ***1823.15*** *p38*
Carter, Thomas 63; Ontario, 1871 ***1823.15*** *p38*
Carter, Walter; Maryland, 1682 ***2524.55*** *p43*
Wife: Mary
Daughter: Mary
Carter, William; New York, 1838 ***8197.10*** *p112*
Carter, William; Pennsylvania, 1777 ***4629.10*** *p15*
Carter, William; Quebec, 1858 ***9196.15*** *p41*
Carter, William 25; Philadelphia, 1774 ***1220.25*** *p23*
Carter, William 44; Ontario, 1871 ***1823.22*** *p25*
Carter, William 55; Ontario, 1871 ***1823.28*** *p15*
Carter, William Morris; New York, 1808 ***8197.10*** *p53*
Carthew, Edmund 18; Maryland, 1774 ***1220.25*** *p41*
Carthney, John 45; Ontario, 1871 ***1823.15*** *p39*
Carthright, Sarah 57; Ontario, 1871 ***1823.15*** *p39*
Carthy, Ellin; Maryland, 1678 ***2524.55*** *p43*
Cartis, William 25; Virginia, 1773 ***1220.25*** *p31*
Cartland, Bridget 73; Vermont, 1892 ***5900.10*** *p392*
Cartlidge, Charles; New York, 1840 ***8197.10*** *p220*
Cartman, John 49; Ontario, 1871 ***1823.28*** *p15*
Cartman, Robert 51; Ontario, 1871 ***1823.28*** *p15*
Cartmel, Robert; New York, 1818 ***8197.10*** *p60*
Cartovicski, Thomas; Maryland, 1910 ***3259.35*** *p8*
Cartrite, Demetrius; Maryland, 1661 ***2524.55*** *p43*
Cartwright, Miss; Quebec, 1856 ***9196.15*** *p7*
Cartwright, Mrs.; Quebec, 1856 ***9196.15*** *p7*
Cartwright, Charles; Pennsylvania, 1777 ***4629.10*** *p15*
Cartwright, Thomas; Maryland, 1682 ***2524.55*** *p43*
Cartwright, Thomas 16; Philadelphia, 1774 ***1220.25*** *p4*
Cartwright, Timothy; Boston, 1787 ***1224.2*** *p19*
Cartwright, William 23; Jamaica, 1774 ***1220.25*** *p72*
Carty, Alice 8; Vermont, 1860 ***5900.10*** *p161*
Carty, Ann 2; New York, New York, 1848 ***1825.45*** *p29*
Carty, Bridget 55 *SEE* Carty, John
Carty, Catherine 20 *SEE* Carty, Owen
Carty, Charles; Maryland, 1680 ***2524.55*** *p43*
Carty, Daniel; Canada, 1756-1760 ***4628.40*** *p45*
Carty, Edward 12 *SEE* Carty, John
Carty, Elizabeth 77; Vermont, 1857 ***5900.10*** *p161*
Carty, Ellen; Maryland, 1682 ***2524.55*** *p43*
Carty, Francus 64; Ontario, 1871 ***1823.28*** *p15*
Carty, Gilbert 21; Maryland, 1775 ***1220.25*** *p112*
Carty, Hannah 73; Vermont, 1879 ***5900.10*** *p378*
Carty, James; New York, 1834 ***8197.10*** *p373*
Carty, James 28; Ontario, 1871 ***1823.28*** *p15*
Carty, James 77; Vermont, 1859 ***5900.10*** *p161*
Carty, Jeremiah; Canada, 1756-1760 ***4628.40*** *p45*
Carty, Jerry; Nova Scotia, 1745 ***4628.40*** *p45*
Carty, Joel S.; Vermont, 1854-1935 ***5900.10*** *p255*
Carty, John; Canada, 1756-1760 ***4628.40*** *p45*
Carty, John; New Hampshire, 1724 ***4628.40*** *p44*
Carty, John 14; Vermont, 1854 ***5900.10*** *p161*
Carty, John 26; Ontario, 1871 ***1823.28*** *p15*
Carty, John 40; Ontario, 1871 ***1823.28*** *p15*
Carty, John 60; New York, New York, 1848 ***1825.45*** *p29*
Wife: Bridget 55
Son: Peter 10
Daughter: Mary 25
Daughter: Peggy 21
Son: Thomas 14
Son: Martin 15
Son: Edward 12
Carty, Maria 14; Vermont, 1850 ***5900.10*** *p161*
Carty, Martin 15 *SEE* Carty, John
Carty, Mary 25 *SEE* Carty, John
Carty, Mary A. McCarragher; Vermont, 1854-1938 ***5900.10*** *p461*
Carty, Mary Culkins; Vermont, 1826-1905 ***5900.10*** *p255*
Carty, Owen 22; New York, New York, 1848 ***1825.45*** *p29*
Sister: Catherine 20
Carty, Patrick 75; Vermont, 1887 ***5900.10*** *p161*
Carty, Peggy 21 *SEE* Carty, John
Carty, Peter 10 *SEE* Carty, John
Carty, Simon; Vermont, 1813-1905 ***5900.10*** *p461*
Carty, Thomas; Maryland, 1681 ***2524.55*** *p43*
Carty, Thomas; Vermont, 1820-1902 ***5900.10*** *p255*
Carty, Thomas; Vermont, 1846-1916 ***5900.10*** *p461*
Carty, Thomas 14 *SEE* Carty, John
Carty, Thomas 40; Ontario, 1871 ***1823.28*** *p15*
Carty, Thomas Raymond; Vermont, 1927 ***5900.10*** *p255*
Carty, William; Maryland, 1682 ***2524.55*** *p43*
Caruise, Robert 22; Ontario, 1871 ***1823.28*** *p15*
Carus, Tho; Virginia, 1663 ***6212.30*** *p4*
Carvay, Bridget A.; Vermont, 1865-1929 ***5900.10*** *p391*
Carvay, Mary Mahar; Vermont, 1835-1899 ***5900.10*** *p395*
Carvay, Michael; Vermont, 1835-1898 ***5900.10*** *p395*
Carver, Alice; Vermont, 1835-1885 ***5900.10*** *p549*
Carver, Catherine Cawley 78; Vermont, 1902 ***5900.10*** *p591*
Carver, John 26; Georgia, 1774 ***1220.25*** *p48*
Carver, Mary E.; Vermont, 1847-1910 ***5900.10*** *p549*
Carver, Rowland; Virginia, 1667 ***6212.30*** *p36*
Carver, Sam; Virginia, 1674 ***6212.30*** *p52*
Carver, Samuel; Pennsylvania, 1786 ***4629.10*** *p50*
Carver, Tho; Virginia, 1665-1666 ***6212.30*** *p23*
Carver, Thomas; Vermont, 1837-1919 ***5900.10*** *p549*
Carver, William; New York, 1794 ***8197.10*** *p3*
Carvey, Mary; Vermont, 1831-1926 ***5900.10*** *p258*
Carvill, Charles; New York, 1828 ***8197.10*** *p64*
Carvill, George; New York, 1828 ***8197.10*** *p64*
Carvill, Thomas; Maryland, 1664 ***2524.55*** *p43*
Carwele, Henry 15; Philadelphia, 1774 ***1220.25*** *p80*
Carwithen, David; Boston, 1695 ***1224.1*** *p12*
Carwithen, Digery; New England, 1653 ***1224.1*** *p12*
Cary, Amie; Maryland, 1666 ***2524.55*** *p43*
Cary, Andrew; Virginia, 1666 ***6212.30*** *p29*
Cary, Bridgett 82; Vermont, 1900 ***5900.10*** *p371*
Cary, David 4; Ontario, 1861 ***2896.27*** *p11*
Cary, Edw; Virginia, 1664 ***6212.30*** *p10*
Cary, Edward *SEE* Cary, Thomas
Cary, Eliza 7; Ontario, 1861 ***2896.27*** *p11*
Cary, Ellen E. 23; Vermont, 1868 ***5900.10*** *p198*
Cary, Francis; Maryland, 1647 ***2524.55*** *p43*
Cary, Geo; Virginia, 1672 ***6212.30*** *p50*
Cary, Harriett Spafford; Vermont, 1845-1900 ***5900.10*** *p401*
Cary, Jane *SEE* Cary, Thomas
Cary, Jane 22; Ontario, 1861 ***2896.27*** *p11*
Cary, John *SEE* Cary, Thomas
Cary, John 13; Ontario, 1861 ***2896.27*** *p11*
Cary, John 89; Vermont, 1903 ***5900.10*** *p402*
Cary, Katharine; Maryland, 1682 ***2524.55*** *p43*
Cary, Katherin; Maryland, 1682 ***2524.55*** *p43*
Cary, Mariah 15; Ontario, 1861 ***2896.27*** *p11*
Cary, Mary; Maryland, 1673 ***2524.55*** *p42*
Cary, Mary; Maryland, 1673 ***2524.55*** *p43*
Cary, Mary 80; Vermont, 1892 ***5900.10*** *p371*
Cary, Mary Parkhurst 63; Vermont, 1882 ***5900.10*** *p402*
Cary, Meriah 47; Ontario, 1861 ***2896.27*** *p11*
Cary, Michael 23; Maryland, 1775 ***1220.25*** *p116*
Cary, Miles; Virginia, 1660 ***1224.1*** *p12*
Cary, Nancy 17; Ontario, 1861 ***2896.27*** *p11*
Cary, Patrick; New York, 1834 ***8197.10*** *p219*
Cary, Richard; Barbados, 1685 ***1224.1*** *p12*
Cary, Richard; Virginia, 1730 ***1224.2*** *p20*
Cary, Robert; New York, 1821 ***8197.10*** *p215*
Cary, Samuel; Maryland, 1770 ***1224.2*** *p20*
Cary, Sarah 11; Ontario, 1861 ***2896.27*** *p11*
Cary, Tarlo; Virginia, 1680 ***6212.30*** *p55*
Cary, Thomas; Maryland, 1657 ***2524.55*** *p43*
Cary, Thomas; Maryland, 1666 ***2524.55*** *p43*
Relative: Jane
Relative: Thomas, Jr.
Relative: John
Relative: Edward
Cary, Thomas 9; Ontario, 1861 ***2896.27*** *p11*
Cary, Thomas 47; Ontario, 1861 ***2896.27*** *p11*
Cary, Thomas, Jr. *SEE* Cary, Thomas
Cary, William W.; Vermont, 1844-1914 ***5900.10*** *p401*
Casadu, Catherin 18; Ontario, 1871 ***1823.28*** *p15*
Casan, Michael 23; Maryland, 1774 ***1220.25*** *p7*
Casares, Manuel; New York, 1827 ***8197.10*** *p338*
Casavant, Lizzie Moran 26; Vermont, 1868 ***5900.10*** *p595*
Casavaw, Anne Mullee; Vermont, 1849-1911 ***5900.10*** *p427*
Casavaw, Frank L.; Vermont, 1846-1904 ***5900.10*** *p427*
Casavaw, Louis; Vermont, 1838-1915 ***5900.10*** *p546*
Casavaw, Margaret O'Brien; Vermont, 1848-1912 ***5900.10*** *p546*
Casavitch, Annie; Maryland, 1910 ***3259.35*** *p8*
Cascaden, William; New York, 1834 ***8197.10*** *p358*
Case, Mr.; Portland, Maine, 1857 ***9196.15*** *p13*
Case, A. 36; Ontario, 1861 ***2896.26*** *p15*
Case, Abraham 31; Ontario, 1871 ***1823.15*** *p39*
Case, Benjamin 45; Ontario, 1871 ***1823.15*** *p39*
Case, C. 63; Ontario, 1861 ***2896.26*** *p8*
Case, E. 20; Ontario, 1861 ***2896.26*** *p8*
Case, Francis 37; Ontario, 1871 ***1823.15*** *p39*
Case, George 48; Ontario, 1871 ***1823.15*** *p39*
Case, H. 10; Ontario, 1861 ***2896.26*** *p15*
Case, H. 72; Ontario, 1861 ***2896.26*** *p8*
Case, H. C. 35; Ontario, 1861 ***2896.26*** *p15*
Case, H. W. 31; Ontario, 1861 ***2896.26*** *p15*
Case, J. 26; Ontario, 1861 ***2896.26*** *p8*
Case, John; Pennsylvania, 1786 ***4629.10*** *p51*
Case, Joseph 56; Ontario, 1871 ***1823.15*** *p39*
Case, K. 28; Ontario, 1861 ***2896.26*** *p8*
Case, L. 13; Ontario, 1861 ***2896.26*** *p15*
Case, M. 7; Ontario, 1861 ***2896.26*** *p15*
Case, M. 32; Ontario, 1861 ***2896.26*** *p15*
Case, R. A. 23; Ontario, 1861 ***2896.26*** *p8*
Case, Richard 42; Ontario, 1871 ***1823.15*** *p39*
Case, Thomas 52; Ontario, 1871 ***1823.15*** *p39*
Case, W. 15; Ontario, 1861 ***2896.28*** *p14*
Case, William 56; Ontario, 1871 ***1823.15*** *p39*
Casedy, Martin 58; Vermont, 1874 ***5900.10*** *p75*
Casent, William 39; Ontario, 1871 ***1823.22*** *p25*
Caset, Ellen Fitzgerald; Vermont, 1839-1937 ***5900.10*** *p539*
Casey, Alice; Vermont, 1888-1960 ***5900.10*** *p124*
Casey, Alice 76; Vermont, 1896 ***5900.10*** *p271*
Casey, Alice A. Tennien; Vermont, 1855-1928 ***5900.10*** *p444*
Casey, Alice E. 56; Vermont, 1914 ***5900.10*** *p124*
Casey, Alice Sadlier 89; Vermont, 1927 ***5900.10*** *p123*
Casey, Ambrose J.; Vermont, 1867 ***5900.10*** *p124*
Casey, Ann; Vermont, 1844-1922 ***5900.10*** *p164*
Casey, Ann 55; Ontario, 1871 ***1823.28*** *p15*
Casey, Ann 65; Vermont, 1912 ***5900.10*** *p72*
Casey, Ann Kinsella; Vermont, 1838-1900 ***5900.10*** *p158*
Casey, Ann Mangin; Vermont, 1831-1886 ***5900.10*** *p399*
Casey, Anna; Vermont, 1865-1934 ***5900.10*** *p128*
Casey, Anna Burke 60; Vermont, 1918 ***5900.10*** *p83*
Casey, Anna Conway; Vermont, 1864-1930 ***5900.10*** *p520*
Casey, Anna M.; Vermont, 1868-1948 ***5900.10*** *p554*
Casey, Anne; Maryland, 1663 ***2524.55*** *p44*
Casey, Annora 82; Vermont, 1940 ***5900.10*** *p124*
Casey, Annory Pierce 56; Vermont, 1860 ***5900.10*** *p521*
Casey, Bab 19 *SEE* Casey, John

Casey, Bartholomew; Vermont, 1852-1906 5900.10 p353
Casey, Bridget; Vermont, 1808-1890 5900.10 p82
Casey, Bridget; Vermont, 1816-1888 5900.10 p537
Casey, Bridget; Vermont, 1834-1915 5900.10 p151
Casey, Bridget; Vermont, 1836-1912 5900.10 p353
Casey, Bridget; Vermont, 1840-1842 5900.10 p82
Casey, Bridget; Vermont, 1844-1892 5900.10 p482
Casey, Bridget 27; Vermont, 1868 5900.10 p345
Casey, Bridget 52; Vermont, 1876 5900.10 p124
Casey, Bridget 56; Vermont, 1876 5900.10 p521
Casey, Catherine; Vermont, 1833-1901 5900.10 p136
Casey, Catherine; Vermont, 1849-1860 5900.10 p82
Casey, Catherine; Vermont, 1865-1950 5900.10 p124
Casey, Catherine; Vermont, 1866-1868 5900.10 p82
Casey, Catherine 2 months; Vermont, 1853 5900.10 p346
Casey, Catherine 54; Vermont, 1891 5900.10 p124
Casey, Catherine Carroll 88; Vermont, 1916 5900.10 p124
Casey, Catherine Gregory 68; Vermont, 1915 5900.10 p79
Casey, Cornelius 2 months; Vermont, 1849 5900.10 p346
Casey, Daniel; Pennsylvania, 1866 6058.10 p56
Casey, Daniel; Vermont, 1845-1917 5900.10 p82
Casey, Daniel 42; Ontario, 1861 2896.27 p20
Casey, David 60; Ontario, 1871 1823.22 p25
Casey, Dennie; Vermont, 1847-1890 5900.10 p82
Casey, Dennis; Vermont, 1868 5900.10 p124
Casey, Edward; Rhode Island, 1765 1224.2 p124
Casey, Eliza; Vermont, 1817-1872 5900.10 p71
Casey, Elizabeth M.; Vermont, 1868-1880 5900.10 p158
Casey, Ella Doon; Vermont, 1870-1913 5900.10 p531
Casey, Ellen; Vermont, 1834-1921 5900.10 p531
Casey, Ellen; Vermont, 1846-1917 5900.10 p410
Casey, Ellen; Vermont, 1882 5900.10 p92
Casey, Ellen 53; Vermont, 1870 5900.10 p528
Casey, Ellen Breen; Vermont, 1824-1893 5900.10 p527
Casey, Ellen D.; Vermont, 1865-1958 5900.10 p123
Casey, Ellen Evens 56; Vermont, 1877 5900.10 p346
Casey, Ellen Tobin 65; Vermont, 1861 5900.10 p73
Casey, Ellen Tyter 43; Vermont, 1857 5900.10 p59
Casey, Enos; Vermont, 1866-1868 5900.10 p158
Casey, Fanny; Vermont, 1837-1917 5900.10 p554
Casey, Francis; Vermont, 1846-1874 5900.10 p82
Casey, Hannora Connors 76; Vermont, 1896 5900.10 p173
Casey, Hanora; Vermont, 1867-1868 5900.10 p82
Casey, Hanora 4; Vermont, 1862 5900.10 p346
Casey, Hanora M.; Vermont, 1860-1929 5900.10 p568
Casey, Honora 76; Vermont, 1884 5900.10 p96
Casey, Hubert T.; Vermont, 1854-1927 5900.10 p123
Casey, Isaac 78; Ontario, 1871 1823.22 p25
Casey, James; New York, 1840 8197.10 p159
Casey, James; New York, 1840 8197.10 p162
Casey, James; Vermont, 1818-1907 5900.10 p151
Casey, James; Vermont, 1825-1899 5900.10 p158
Casey, James; Vermont, 1829-1904 5900.10 p452
Casey, James; Vermont, 1831-1924 5900.10 p531
Casey, James; Vermont, 1861-1892 5900.10 p527
Casey, James; Vermont, 1862-1864 5900.10 p158
Casey, James 45; Vermont, 1905 5900.10 p385
Casey, James 97; Vermont, 1890 5900.10 p526
Casey, James, Sr.; Vermont, 1847 5900.10 p385
Casey, James H. 51; Vermont, 1927 5900.10 p124
Casey, James M., Jr. 11; Vermont, 1886 5900.10 p526
Casey, James W.; Vermont, 1868-1932 5900.10 p123
Casey, Jane Wadick 78; Vermont, 1878 5900.10 p526
Casey, Jennie; Vermont, 1890 5900.10 p555
Casey, Joanna; Vermont, 1845-1905 5900.10 p407
Casey, Johanna 18 SEE Casey, John
Casey, Johannah; Vermont, 1833-1921 5900.10 p486
Casey, John; New York, 1840 8197.10 p161
Casey, John; Pennsylvania, 1868 6058.10 p72
Casey, John; Pennsylvania, 1868 6058.10 p77
Casey, John; Vermont, 1871-1878 5900.10 p158
Casey, John 16; New York, New York, 1848 1825.45 p29
Casey, John 21; Maryland, 1774 1220.25 p52
Casey, John 28; Ontario, 1871 1823.28 p15
Casey, John 33; Vermont, 1892 5900.10 p536
Casey, John 56; New York, New York, 1849 1825.45 p46
Son: Michael 13
Daughter: Johanna 18
Daughter: Rosean 16
Daughter: Bab 19
Casey, John 65; Vermont, 1907 5900.10 p164
Casey, John P. 61; Vermont, 1889 5900.10 p124
Casey, Julia; Vermont, 1852-1952 5900.10 p527
Casey, Julia 13; Vermont, 1869 5900.10 p346
Casey, Katherine C.; Vermont, 1860-1955 5900.10 p124
Casey, Maggie 10; Vermont, 1863 5900.10 p173
Casey, Margaret SEE Casey, Patrick
Casey, Margaret; Vermont, 1813-1878 5900.10 p537
Casey, Margaret; Vermont, 1858-1860 5900.10 p158
Casey, Margaret; Vermont, 1900 5900.10 p165
Casey, Margaret 6; Ontario, 1861 2896.27 p20
Casey, Margaret 42; Ontario, 1861 2896.27 p20
Casey, Margaret 56; Vermont, 1853 5900.10 p158
Casey, Margaret 63; Vermont, 1913 5900.10 p385
Casey, Margaret Boland; Vermont, 1834-1929 5900.10 p452
Casey, Margaret Jones; Vermont, 1858-1932 5900.10 p353
Casey, Margaret Mahoney; Vermont, 1855-1926 5900.10 p536
Casey, Martin; Vermont, 1860-1862 5900.10 p158
Casey, Mary; Vermont, n.d. 5900.10 p173
Casey, Mary; Vermont, 1819-1893 5900.10 p139
Casey, Mary; Vermont, 1832-1887 5900.10 p216
Casey, Mary; Vermont, 1834-1890 5900.10 p77
Casey, Mary; Vermont, 1841-1872 5900.10 p82
Casey, Mary; Vermont, 1854-1873 5900.10 p527
Casey, Mary; Vermont, 1868 5900.10 p82
Casey, Mary 46; Vermont, 1899 5900.10 p124
Casey, Mary 51; Vermont, 1915 5900.10 p124
Casey, Mary 70; Vermont, 1913 5900.10 p315
Casey, Mary 72; Vermont, 1882 5900.10 p385
Casey, Mary A.; Vermont, 1861-1943 5900.10 p174
Casey, Mary A. 8; Ontario, 1861 2896.27 p20
Casey, Mary Ann; Vermont, 1833-1903 5900.10 p486
Casey, Mary Ash 63; Vermont, 1886 5900.10 p59
Casey, Mary Bollard 57; Vermont, 1897 5900.10 p83
Casey, Mary P. O'Donnell; Vermont, 1843-1912 5900.10 p164
Casey, Mary Purcell; Vermont, 1844-1888 5900.10 p82
Casey, Mary Ryan 80; Vermont, 1896 5900.10 p83
Casey, Mathew; Vermont, 1815-1915 5900.10 p527
Casey, Maude C.; Vermont, 1890-1950 5900.10 p520
Casey, Michael; Florida, 1843 1224.3 p12
Casey, Michael; New York, 1840 8197.10 p162
Casey, Michael; Vermont, 1810-1875 5900.10 p82
Casey, Michael; Vermont, 1834-1888 5900.10 p410
Casey, Michael 13 SEE Casey, John
Casey, Michael 31; Ontario, 1861 2896.25 p15
Casey, Michael 44; Ontario, 1871 1823.22 p25
Casey, Michael 75; Vermont, 1879 5900.10 p173
Casey, Michael 81; Vermont, 1912 5900.10 p123
Casey, Michael R.; Vermont, 1863-1906 5900.10 p554
Casey, Nancy Kelty; Vermont, 1841-1922 5900.10 p553
Casey, Nellie Coughlin 42; Vermont, 1902 5900.10 p124
Casey, Pat 15; New York, New York, 1848 1825.45 p29
Casey, Patrick; New York, 1820 8197.10 p61
Wife: Margaret
Casey, Patrick; New York, 1838 8197.10 p378
Casey, Patrick; Vermont, 1892 5900.10 p58
Casey, Patrick 16; Ontario, 1861 2896.27 p20
Casey, Patrick 60; Ontario, 1871 1823.28 p15
Casey, Patrick 68; Vermont, 1893 5900.10 p124
Casey, Patrick 70; Vermont, 1877 5900.10 p83
Casey, Patrick 76; Ontario, 1871 1823.15 p39
Casey, Patrick J.; Vermont, 1839-1885 5900.10 p82
Casey, Patrick J.; Vermont, 1839-1928 5900.10 p539
Casey, Patrick W.; Vermont, 1855-1916 5900.10 p444
Casey, Philip 63; Vermont, 1894 5900.10 p79
Casey, Phillip; Vermont, 1897 5900.10 p555
Casey, Robert; Vermont, 1864-1866 5900.10 p158
Casey, Rosean 16 SEE Casey, John
Casey, T.; Vermont, n.d. 5900.10 p335
Casey, Thomas; Vermont, n.d. 5900.10 p6
Casey, Thomas; Vermont, 1827-1916 5900.10 p124
Casey, Thomas; Vermont, 1857-1859 5900.10 p158
Casey, Thomas; Vermont, 1867-1919 5900.10 p531
Casey, Thomas; Vermont, 1870-1872 5900.10 p82
Casey, Thomas 30; Ontario, 1871 1823.15 p39
Casey, Thomas 50; Ontario, 1871 1823.15 p39
Casey, Thomas 82; Vermont, 1874 5900.10 p521
Casey, Thomas C. 22; Vermont, 1881 5900.10 p124
Casey, Thomas M.; Vermont, 1862-1907 5900.10 p520
Casey, Timothy 2; Vermont, 1862 5900.10 p346
Casey, Timothy 75; Vermont, 1892 5900.10 p346
Casey, William; Vermont, 1824-1905 5900.10 p399
Casey, William; Vermont, 1832-1909 5900.10 p554
Casey, William; Vermont, 1842-1929 5900.10 p49
Casey, William 46; Vermont, 1908 5900.10 p83
Casey, William 59; Ontario, 1871 1823.22 p25
Casgrain, Rev.; Quebec, 1858 9196.15 p35
Cash, Daniel; New York, 1838 8197.10 p112
Cash, Edward 51; Ontario, 1871 1823.15 p39
Cash, John 40; Ontario, 1871 1823.15 p39
Cash, William 60; Ontario, 1871 1823.15 p39
Cashan, Dennis 31; Ontario, 1871 1823.15 p39
Cashen, Anthony; Vermont, 1780-1877 5900.10 p148
Cashen, Bridget Cahill; Vermont, 1830-1913 5900.10 p362
Cashen, Bridget Holland; Vermont, 1851-1889 5900.10 p359
Cashen, Catherine Cooney; Vermont, 1798-1862 5900.10 p148
Cashen, Dennis 45; Vermont, 1884 5900.10 p148
Cashen, John 80; Ontario, 1871 1823.22 p25
Cashen, Julia A.; Vermont, 1886-1887 5900.10 p359
Cashen, Margaret 50; Vermont, 1889 5900.10 p148
Cashen, Margaret E.; Vermont, 1884-1885 5900.10 p359
Cashen, Mary 65; Vermont, 1888 5900.10 p148
Cashen, Michael; Vermont, 1827-1895 5900.10 p362
Cashen, Timothy; Vermont, 1888 5900.10 p359
Casher, Jno; Virginia, 1663 6212.30 p4
Casher, Robt; Virginia, 1663 6212.30 p4
Cashine, William 33; Maryland, 1774 1220.25 p57
Cashion, James 60; Ontario, 1871 1823.22 p25
Cashman, Daniel; New York, 1819 8197.10 p61
Cashman, Hanora; Vermont, 1828-1908 5900.10 p590
Cashman, Joanna 83; Vermont, 1910 5900.10 p348
Cashman, Mary 68; Vermont, 1869 5900.10 p348
Cashman, Michael; New York, 1804 8197.10 p26
Cashman, Michael; Vermont, 1832-1932 5900.10 p277
Cashman, Timothy 60; Vermont, 1850 5900.10 p348
Cashmore, Thomas 39; Ontario, 1871 1823.28 p15
Cashon, John 75; Vermont, 1902 5900.10 p148
Cashon, Mary Griffin; Vermont, 1839-1913 5900.10 p148
Casil, Andrew; Pennsylvania, 1777 4629.10 p16
Casinger, Andreas; America, 1737 2856.30 p64
Caskey, Jane 70; Ontario, 1871 1823.28 p15
Caskey, Nathniel 28; Ontario, 1871 1823.15 p39
Caskey, Samuel; Pennsylvania, 1777 4629.10 p17
Caslin, Barbara Salmon 82; Vermont, 1915 5900.10 p419
Caslzle, James 79; Ontario, 1871 1823.15 p39
Caslzle, William 38; Ontario, 1871 1823.15 p39
Casman, Honora Casey 76; Vermont, 1884 5900.10 p96
Casman, Michael 83; Vermont, 1885 5900.10 p96
Casment, Joseph 42; Ontario, 1871 1823.22 p25
Casment, Samuel 70; Ontario, 1871 1823.22 p25
Casmiercz, Michael; Maryland, 1910 3259.35 p8
Casmore, George 84; Ontario, 1871 1823.15 p39
Casmunt, James; Ontario, 1871 1823.22 p25
Cason, Edward; Virginia, 1665-1666 6212.30 p21
Cason, Jno; Virginia, 1665-1666 6212.30 p21
Caspar, Antoni; Port uncertain, 1750 2856.30 p64
Caspar, Johann Michael; America, 1752 2856.30 p64
Caspar, Johann Nikolaus; Port uncertain, 1763 2856.30 p64
Caspar, Johann Nikolaus; Port uncertain, 1787 2856.30 p64
Caspar, Johann Nikolaus; Port uncertain, 1790 2856.30 p64
Caspar, Johanna; Port uncertain, 1751 2856.30 p65
Caspar, Magdalena; Port uncertain, 1726 2856.30 p65
Caspar, Maria Elisabeth; Port uncertain, 1759 2856.30 p65
Caspar, Nikolaus; America, 1753 2856.30 p65
Caspar, Susanna; Port uncertain, 1788 2856.30 p65
Cass, Anastasia; Vermont, 1841-1921 5900.10 p117
Cass, George 19; Nova Scotia, 1774 1220.25 p136
Cass, Jane; Philadelphia, 1832 1224.3 p79
Cass, John 18; Philadelphia, 1774 1220.25 p6
Cass, Thomas; New York, 1837 8197.10 p81
Cass, William; New York, 1837 8197.10 p81
Cassaday, Frances 62; Ontario, 1871 1823.15 p39
Cassady, Bernard; New York, New York, 1857 3437.14 p69
Cassady, Charles; New York, 1837 8197.10 p81
Cassady, Dennis; New York, 1802 8197.10 p19
Cassady, Hugh 60; Ontario, 1871 1823.22 p25
Cassady, John; New York, 1807 8197.10 p36
Cassady, John 65; Ontario, 1871 1823.22 p25
Cassady, Patrick 57; Ontario, 1871 1823.22 p25
Cassan, Edward 36; Ontario, 1871 1823.22 p25
Cassan, Joseph 44; Ontario, 1871 1823.22 p25
Cassan, Mathew 60; Ontario, 1871 1823.22 p25
Cassan, Matthew 40; Ontario, 1871 1823.22 p25
Cassar, D. 44; Alaska, 1917 9196.1 p48
Cassar, D. 44; Whitehorse, Yukon, 1917 9196.1 p48
Casse, Madame; Canada, 1858 9196.15 p46
Cassel, Peter; Port uncertain, 1764 2856.30 p65
Casselle, Freidrich Jakob; Port uncertain, 1764 2856.30 p65
Casselle, Mathias; Port uncertain, 1764 2856.30 p65
Cassels, Miss J.; Quebec, 1857 9196.15 p19
Cassels, Mark 41; Ontario, 1871 1823.15 p39
Cassels, Richard Scougall; Toronto, 1897 1640.13 p19
Casserty, Peter; New York, 1840 8197.10 p162
Cassey, Adam; Pennsylvania, 1777 4629.10 p15
Cassick, Jno; Virginia, 1663 6212.30 p4
Cassiday, Thomas 47; Ontario, 1871 1823.15 p39
Cassidy, Mr.; Vermont, n.d. 5900.10 p597
Cassidy, Mr.; Vermont, 1850-1935 5900.10 p501
Cassidy, Mrs.; Vermont, n.d. 5900.10 p597
Cassidy, Mrs.; Vermont, 1865-1935 5900.10 p501

Cassidy, Anna M. 6 months; Vermont, 1878 ***5900.10*** *p296*
Cassidy, Anne C.; Vermont, 1838-1897 ***5900.10*** *p509*
Cassidy, Annie; Vermont, 1868-1882 ***5900.10*** *p184*
Cassidy, Bernard; Vermont, n.d. ***5900.10*** *p597*
Cassidy, Bridget; Vermont, 1842-1915 ***5900.10*** *p352*
Cassidy, Bridget Rooney 72; Vermont, 1916 ***5900.10*** *p560*
Cassidy, Catharine; Vermont, 1837-1937 ***5900.10*** *p510*
Cassidy, Catharine Monahan 90; Vermont, 1880 ***5900.10*** *p201*
Cassidy, Catherine; Vermont, 1836-1921 ***5900.10*** *p155*
Cassidy, Cathrine; Vermont, 1850-1920 ***5900.10*** *p219*
Cassidy, Charles; New York, 1821 ***8197.10*** *p216*
Cassidy, Charles; Vermont, 1872-1914 ***5900.10*** *p117*
Cassidy, Ellen 35; Vermont, 1875 ***5900.10*** *p584*
Cassidy, Francis H.; Vermont, 1849-1911 ***5900.10*** *p391*
Cassidy, George; Vermont, 1852-1928 ***5900.10*** *p495*
Cassidy, Hugh; New York, 1826 ***8197.10*** *p219*
Cassidy, James; New York, 1821 ***8197.10*** *p215*
Cassidy, James; Vermont, 1828-1924 ***5900.10*** *p117*
Cassidy, James; Vermont, 1845-1911 ***5900.10*** *p48*
Cassidy, John; New York, 1802 ***8197.10*** *p19*
Cassidy, John; New York, 1826 ***8197.10*** *p219*
Cassidy, John; New York, 1838 ***8197.10*** *p113*
Cassidy, John 81; Vermont, 1896 ***5900.10*** *p509*
Cassidy, Lucy McDonough; Vermont, 1825-1860 ***5900.10*** *p184*
Cassidy, Luke; Vermont, 1858-1903 ***5900.10*** *p184*
Cassidy, Mary; Vermont, n.d. ***5900.10*** *p597*
Cassidy, Mary; Vermont, 1824-1898 ***5900.10*** *p205*
Cassidy, Mary; Vermont, 1829-1904 ***5900.10*** *p117*
Cassidy, Mary 60; Ontario, 1871 ***1823.22*** *p25*
Cassidy, Mary 60; Vermont, 1873 ***5900.10*** *p201*
Cassidy, Mary 72; Vermont, 1894 ***5900.10*** *p153*
Cassidy, Mary Ann Leamy; Vermont, 1850-1927 ***5900.10*** *p391*
Cassidy, Mary Cloutie 49; Vermont, 1870 ***5900.10*** *p509*
Cassidy, Mary Farrell; Vermont, 1848-1929 ***5900.10*** *p191*
Cassidy, Mary Keating; Vermont, 1853-1945 ***5900.10*** *p48*
Cassidy, Michael; New York, 1826 ***8197.10*** *p219*
Cassidy, Michael; Vermont, n.d. ***5900.10*** *p597*
Cassidy, Patrick; Vermont, 1821-1904 ***5900.10*** *p184*
Cassidy, Patrick 31; Vermont, 1879 ***5900.10*** *p265*
Cassidy, Patrick 50; Vermont, 1877 ***5900.10*** *p560*
Cassidy, Richard; New York, 1831 ***8197.10*** *p219*
Cassidy, Richard; New York, 1834 ***8197.10*** *p70*
Cassidy, Sabina; Vermont, 1905 ***5900.10*** *p87*
Cassidy, Sarah J.; Vermont, 1853-1886 ***5900.10*** *p495*
Cassidy, Theresa; Vermont, 1854-1922 ***5900.10*** *p504*
Cassidy, William; Vermont, 1837-1914 ***5900.10*** *p191*
Cassie, Clara 39; Ontario, 1871 ***1823.22*** *p25*
Cassie, George 38; Ontario, 1871 ***1823.15*** *p39*
Cassie, James; New York, 1802 ***8197.10*** *p19*
Cassills, John; Georgia, 1698 ***1640.13*** *p19*
Cassin, Catherine Tracy; Vermont, 1812-1870 ***5900.10*** *p539*
Cassin, Catherine Tracy; Vermont, 1857-1881 ***5900.10*** *p540*
Cassin, Mary; Vermont, 1851-1935 ***5900.10*** *p226*
Cassin, William; Vermont, 1802-1871 ***5900.10*** *p539*
Cassipede, Ann 62; Ontario, 1871 ***1823.15*** *p39*
Cassipede, Malcolm 68; Ontario, 1871 ***1823.15*** *p39*
Cassler, Daniel 58; Ontario, 1871 ***1823.22*** *p25*
Cassment, James 61; Ontario, 1871 ***1823.22*** *p25*
Cassocke, George; Maryland, 1651 ***2524.55*** *p44*
Casson, John A. 55; Ontario, 1871 ***1823.22*** *p25*
Cassons, Charles; Maryland, 1673 ***2524.55*** *p60*
Cassweller, Joseph 41; Ontario, 1871 ***1823.28*** *p15*
Castaffin, George; Halifax, Nova Scotia, 1774 ***1220.25*** *p12*
Castake, William 21; Virginia, 1774 ***1220.25*** *p75*
Castallo, Jordan 31; Maryland, 1775 ***1220.25*** *p120*
Castell, George 40; Maryland, 1775 ***1220.25*** *p101*
Castell, Ralphe; Maryland, 1668 ***2524.55*** *p44*
Caster, Eliza 30; Ontario, 1871 ***1823.15*** *p39*
Caster, George Oliver; New York, 1834 ***8197.10*** *p70*
Caster, Henry 30; Ontario, 1871 ***1823.15*** *p39*
Castets, Peter; Philadelphia, 1793 ***4629.10*** *p72*
Castide, Ralph; Maryland, 1653-1661 ***2524.55*** *p44*
Castine, John; New York, 1807 ***8197.10*** *p36*
Castle, Captain; Quebec, 1858 ***9196.15*** *p41*
Castle, Charles 46; Ontario, 1871 ***1823.22*** *p25*
Castle, George 41; Ontario, 1871 ***1823.15*** *p39*
Castle, George E. 45; Ontario, 1871 ***1823.22*** *p26*
Castle, James 46; Ontario, 1871 ***1823.15*** *p39*
Castle, Jeromy; Maryland, 1661 ***2524.55*** *p44*
Castle, John; Maryland, 1664 ***2524.55*** *p44*
Castle, Joy; Pennsylvania, 1779 ***4629.10*** *p41*
Castle, Mary 82; Ontario, 1871 ***1823.15*** *p39*
Castle, Ralph; Maryland, 1673 ***2524.55*** *p44*
Castle, Religoh 45; Ontario, 1871 ***1823.15*** *p39*
Castle, Robert; New York, 1807 ***8197.10*** *p36*
Castle, Susan; Vermont, 1808-1892 ***5900.10*** *p528*
Castle, Thomas; Virginia, 1666 ***6212.30*** *p28*
Castle, Thomas; Virginia, 1666 ***6212.30*** *p29*
Castle, William; Long Island, 1780 ***1224.2*** *p20*
Castle, William 23; Ontario, 1871 ***1823.15*** *p39*
Castlefield, Jane; Maryland, 1681 ***2524.55*** *p44*
Castles, Michael; New York, 1834 ***8197.10*** *p133*
Castles, Michael; New York, 1834 ***8197.10*** *p219*
Castles, William; Long Island, 1780 ***1224.2*** *p20*
Castleton, Ralph; Virginia, 1663 ***6212.30*** *p4*
Caston, Louis; Fairbanks, Alaska, 1909 ***9196.1*** *p8*
Caston, Louis; Yukon, 1909 ***9196.1*** *p8*
Castro, Henri; New York, 1827 ***8197.10*** *p298*
Caswall, Henry; Boston, 1748 ***1224.2*** *p20*
Caswell, Abigail; Vermont, 1817-1899 ***5900.10*** *p322*
Caswell, Lawrance 15; Maryland, 1774 ***1220.25*** *p5*
Caswell, Sarah E. 12; Ontario, 1861 ***2896.27*** *p18*
Caswell, Thomas 26; Ontario, 1871 ***1823.28*** *p15*
Cat, Robt; Virginia, 1665-1666 ***6212.30*** *p23*
Cataracy, Helen; Vermont, 1841-1909 ***5900.10*** *p322*
Catarius, Jakob; Port uncertain, 1768 ***2856.30*** *p65*
Catchme, Deborah; Virginia, 1663 ***6212.30*** *p30*
Caten, Daniel; Vermont, 1829-1902 ***5900.10*** *p437*
Caten, John J.; Vermont, 1857-1901 ***5900.10*** *p437*
Cateng, Margaret; Maryland, 1682 ***2524.55*** *p44*
Cater, John; Maryland, 1681 ***2524.55*** *p44*
Cater, John 47; Ontario, 1871 ***1823.15*** *p39*
Catesby, Edwin; Virginia, 1667-1668 ***6212.30*** *p38*
Catharin, Nicolaus; Port uncertain, 1769 ***2856.30*** *p65*
Cathcart, Mr.; Quebec, 1858 ***9196.15*** *p41*
Cathcart, Mrs.; Quebec, 1858 ***9196.15*** *p41*
Cathcart, Alexander 30; Ontario, 1871 ***1823.15*** *p39*
Cathcart, Alexander 35; Ontario, 1871 ***1823.15*** *p39*
Cathcart, Allan; Georgia, 1699 ***1640.13*** *p19*
Cathcart, Jane 50; Ontario, 1871 ***1823.15*** *p40*
Catheart, Henry 26; Ontario, 1871 ***1823.15*** *p40*
Cathell, E.; Portland, Maine, 1858 ***9196.15*** *p28*
Cather, Robert; Pennsylvania, 1777 ***4629.10*** *p9*
Catheral, John 38; Virginia, 1774 ***1220.25*** *p89*
Cathers, Robert 44; Ontario, 1871 ***1823.15*** *p40*
Catherwood, Joseph 56; Ontario, 1871 ***1823.15*** *p40*
Catherwood, Robert; Florida, 1771 ***1640.10*** *p27*
Catherwood, Robert; St. Augustine, Florida, 1787 ***1224.2*** *p20*
Cathwright, Susan N.; Vermont, 1859-1917 ***5900.10*** *p140*
Catina, Joseph 48; Washington, 1911 ***9196.1*** *p33*
Catkin, Anton; Maryland, 1910 ***3259.35*** *p8*
Catliffe, Mr.; Quebec, 1857 ***9196.15*** *p18*
Catlin, Henry; Maryland, 1649 ***2524.55*** *p44*
Wife: Jeane
Stepchild: Richd.
Catlin, Jeane *SEE* Catlin, Henry
Catlin, Richd. *SEE* Catlin, Henry
Catlyne, Anne *SEE* Catlyne, Robert
Catlyne, Joseph *SEE* Catlyne, Robert
Catlyne, Robert *SEE* Catlyne, Robert
Catlyne, Robert; Maryland, 1663 ***2524.55*** *p44*
Child: Robert
Wife: Anne
Child: Joseph
Child: Anne
Catmin, Mr.; Portland, Maine, 1858 ***9196.15*** *p27*
Cato, James 28; Maryland, 1775 ***1220.25*** *p106*
Caton, William 22; Maryland, 1775 ***1220.25*** *p98*
Caton, William 25; Ontario, 1871 ***1823.22*** *p26*
Catren, Margaret Sullivan; Vermont, 1831-1895 ***5900.10*** *p437*
Catrin, Anna Margarete; Port uncertain, 1754 ***2856.30*** *p65*
Catrup, Joane *SEE* Catrup, William
Catrup, William *SEE* Catrup, William
Catrup, William; Maryland, 1670 ***2524.55*** *p44*
Wife: Joane
Son: William
Catrup, William; Maryland, 1680 ***2524.55*** *p44*
Catt, John 28; Maryland, 1775 ***1220.25*** *p101*
Catt, Richard 37; Philadelphia, 1774 ***1220.25*** *p68*
Catt, Robt; Virginia, 1666-1667 ***6212.30*** *p32*
Catterson, Francis; Maryland, 1678 ***2524.55*** *p44*
Cattle, George 43; Ontario, 1871 ***1823.15*** *p40*
Cattle, Samuel 44; Ontario, 1871 ***1823.28*** *p15*
Cattline, Anne *SEE* Cattline, Robert
Cattline, Joseph *SEE* Cattline, Robert
Cattline, Robert *SEE* Cattline, Robert
Cattline, Robert; Maryland, 1663 ***2524.55*** *p44*
Wife: Anne
Child: Joseph
Child: Robert
Child: Anne
Cattling, Anne *SEE* Cattling, Robert
Cattling, Joseph *SEE* Cattling, Robert
Cattling, Robert *SEE* Cattling, Robert
Cattling, Robert; Maryland, 1663 ***2524.55*** *p44*
Wife: Anne
Child: Anne
Child: Joseph
Child: Robert
Catton, George; Pennsylvania, 1777 ***4629.10*** *p29*
Catts, Andrew 41; Ontario, 1871 ***1823.15*** *p40*
Cattswell, John; Virginia, 1665-1666 ***6212.30*** *p25*
Cauddle, David 45; Ontario, 1871 ***1823.15*** *p40*
Cauderry, James; Maryland, 1681 ***2524.55*** *p44*
Caufield, Catherine; Vermont, 1851-1916 ***5900.10*** *p118*
Caufield, Eliza T. Fenton; Vermont, 1842-1923 ***5900.10*** *p117*
Caufield, Hans 38; Ontario, 1871 ***1823.15*** *p40*
Caufield, James; Vermont, 1835-1918 ***5900.10*** *p587*
Caufield, James H. 50; Vermont, 1895 ***5900.10*** *p117*
Caufield, Mary O'Donnel; Vermont, 1837-1880 ***5900.10*** *p587*
Caughlin, Mathew 52; Ontario, 1871 ***1823.28*** *p15*
Caughlin, Patrick 22; Ontario, 1871 ***1823.15*** *p40*
Caul, Christopher; Pennsylvania, 1777 ***4629.10*** *p16*
Cauldwell, John; New York, 1803 ***8197.10*** *p11*
Cauley, Bridget McGettrick 59; Vermont, 1897 ***5900.10*** *p138*
Cauley, James; New York, 1840 ***8197.10*** *p221*
Cauley, John 40; Ontario, 1871 ***1823.22*** *p26*
Cauley, Joseph 45; Ontario, 1871 ***1823.15*** *p40*
Cauley, Margaret 27; Vermont, 1890 ***5900.10*** *p138*
Cauley, Martin 63; Vermont, 1893 ***5900.10*** *p138*
Cauley, Thomas 40; Ontario, 1871 ***1823.22*** *p26*
Caulson, Evelina 63; Ontario, 1871 ***1823.22*** *p26*
Cauly, Mary Ann 36; Ontario, 1871 ***1823.22*** *p26*
Cause, Catharine 36; Port uncertain, 1774 ***1220.25*** *p51*
Cause, John 36; Port uncertain, 1774 ***1220.25*** *p51*
Causin, Nicholas; Maryland, 1640 ***2524.55*** *p44*
Causin, Nicholas; Maryland, 1658 ***2524.55*** *p56*
Causin, Nick; Maryland, 1648 ***2524.55*** *p52*
Causlay, Soloman 78; Ontario, 1871 ***1823.28*** *p15*
Causton, Thomas; Savannah, Georgia, 1746 ***1224.2*** *p20*
Cauter, Johann; Port uncertain, 1764 ***2856.30*** *p65*
Cavallier, John; Long Island, 1783 ***1224.2*** *p20*
Cavan, John; Pennsylvania, 1786 ***4629.10*** *p47*
Cavan, Michael C. 38; Ontario, 1871 ***1823.28*** *p15*
Cavanagh, Alex 58; Vermont, 1895 ***5900.10*** *p499*
Cavanagh, Ann Eliza 38; Vermont, 1893 ***5900.10*** *p528*
Cavanagh, Ann McElroy; Vermont, 1834-1921 ***5900.10*** *p524*
Cavanagh, Arthur; Vermont, 1833-1914 ***5900.10*** *p524*
Cavanagh, Bridget 47; Ontario, 1871 ***1823.22*** *p26*
Cavanagh, John 28; Ontario, 1871 ***1823.15*** *p40*
Cavanagh, John 50; Ontario, 1871 ***1823.28*** *p15*
Cavanagh, Katherine; Vermont, 1843-1929 ***5900.10*** *p186*
Cavanagh, Mary; Vermont, 1857-1946 ***5900.10*** *p531*
Cavanagh, Mary 80; Vermont, 1885 ***5900.10*** *p533*
Cavanagh, Mathew; New York, 1840 ***8197.10*** *p163*
Cavanagh, Peter; New York, 1837 ***8197.10*** *p81*
Cavanagh, Sarah; Vermont, 1932 ***5900.10*** *p524*
Cavanah, Catherine 88; Vermont, 1872 ***5900.10*** *p413*
Cavanah, Edwd 41; Ontario, 1871 ***1823.28*** *p15*
Cavanaugh, Ann; Vermont, 1833-1917 ***5900.10*** *p166*
Cavanaugh, Ann; Vermont, 1842-1914 ***5900.10*** *p184*
Cavanaugh, Anna; Vermont, 1827-1886 ***5900.10*** *p173*
Cavanaugh, Bedelia; Vermont, 1844-1893 ***5900.10*** *p420*
Cavanaugh, Catherine; Vermont, 1834-1868 ***5900.10*** *p384*
Cavanaugh, Elizabeth 78; Vermont, 1887 ***5900.10*** *p413*
Cavanaugh, Ellen 70; Vermont, 1893 ***5900.10*** *p341*
Cavanaugh, Margaret Conway 58; Vermont, 1863 ***5900.10*** *p364*
Cavanaugh, Mary; Vermont, 1811-1873 ***5900.10*** *p166*
Cavanaugh, Mary; Vermont, 1832-1885 ***5900.10*** *p245*
Cavanaugh, Mary; Vermont, 1832-1905 ***5900.10*** *p167*
Cavanaugh, Mary 52; Vermont, 1889 ***5900.10*** *p523*
Cavanaugh, Patrick; Pennsylvania, 1846 ***6058.10*** *p22*
Cavanaugh, Stephen 23; Vermont, 1866 ***5900.10*** *p364*
Cavanaugh, Thomas; Vermont, 1847-1907 ***5900.10*** *p308*
Cave, Christopher; Pennsylvania, 1779 ***4629.10*** *p36*
Cave, James 46; Maryland, 1775 ***1220.25*** *p108*
Cave, John 60; Ontario, 1871 ***1823.15*** *p40*
Cave, Thomas; New York, 1807 ***8197.10*** *p36*
Cave, William; New York, 1807 ***8197.10*** *p37*
Cavenagh, Philip; New York, 1837 ***8197.10*** *p93*
Cavenaugh, Mary; Vermont, 1805-1906 ***5900.10*** *p476*
Cavender, Catherine 40; Vermont, 1861 ***5900.10*** *p73*
Caveney, Anne 7 *SEE* Caveney, Luke
Caveney, Catherine 1 *SEE* Caveney, Luke
Caveney, Edward 12 *SEE* Caveney, Luke
Caveney, Luke 10 *SEE* Caveney, Luke

Caveney, Luke 46; New York, New York, 1847 ***1825.45*** *p13*
Wife: Mary 40
Son: Thomas 15
Daughter: Catherine 1
Daughter: Mary 19
Daughter: Anne 7
Son: Patrick 17
Son: Edward 12
Son: Luke 10
Caveney, Mary 19 *SEE* Caveney, Luke
Caveney, Mary 40 *SEE* Caveney, Luke
Caveney, Patrick 17 *SEE* Caveney, Luke
Caveney, Thomas 15 *SEE* Caveney, Luke
Caverly, Amos; Ontario, 1861 ***2896.25*** *p72*
Caverly, Henry; Ontario, 1861 ***2896.25*** *p72*
Caves, Thomas 57; Ontario, 1871 ***1823.28*** *p15*
Cavie, Agnes; Ontario, 1879 ***1640.13*** *p20*
Cavillier, Miss; Quebec, 1857 ***9196.15*** *p17*
Cavillier, Mr.; Quebec, 1857 ***9196.15*** *p17*
Cavin, Elizabeth Mary 77; Vermont, 1891 ***5900.10*** *p413*
Cavinagh, Charles 35; Ontario, 1871 ***1823.15*** *p40*
Cavrup, Joane *SEE* Cavrup, William
Cavrup, William *SEE* Cavrup, William
Cavrup, William; Maryland, 1670 ***2524.55*** *p44*
Wife: Joane
Son: William
Cavrup, William; Maryland, 1680 ***2524.55*** *p44*
Cawfeild, Benjamin; Virginia, 1666-1667 ***6212.30*** *p33*
Cawgagib, John 38; Ontario, 1871 ***1823.28*** *p15*
Cawle, Joseph; Virginia, 1666 ***6212.30*** *p28*
Cawley, Catherine 78; Vermont, 1902 ***5900.10*** *p591*
Cawley, Catherine Foley 72; Vermont, 1914 ***5900.10*** *p570*
Cawley, Dennis 64; Vermont, 1879 ***5900.10*** *p416*
Cawley, Mary A. 91; Vermont, 1947 ***5900.10*** *p416*
Cawley, Mary Dyer 72; Vermont, 1889 ***5900.10*** *p416*
Cawley, Richard; Vermont, 1853-1923 ***5900.10*** *p496*
Cawley, Thomas 51; Ontario, 1871 ***1823.28*** *p15*
Cawly, Tho; Virginia, 1665-1666 ***6212.30*** *p21*
Cawood, Elizabeth; Boston, 1693 ***1224.1*** *p12*
Cawood, Stephen; Maryland, 1664 ***2524.55*** *p44*
Cawse, Elizabeth 80; Ontario, 1871 ***1823.22*** *p26*
Caxton, Bryan; Maryland, 1678 ***2524.55*** *p44*
Cay, David; Philadelphia, 1797 ***1224.2*** *p20*
Cay, Jonathan; Maryland, 1738 ***1224.2*** *p20*
Cayley, Master; Quebec, 1857 ***9196.15*** *p21*
Cayley, Miss; Quebec, 1857 ***9196.15*** *p21*
Cayley, Mr.; Quebec, 1857 ***9196.15*** *p14*
Cayley, Catherine 29; Ontario, 1871 ***1823.22*** *p26*
Cayley, Edward 48; Ontario, 1871 ***1823.22*** *p26*
Cayley, Henry 64; Ontario, 1871 ***1823.22*** *p26*
Cayley, William 68; Ontario, 1871 ***1823.22*** *p26*
Cayley, Wm; Quebec, 1858 ***9196.15*** *p46*
Caynes, William; Maryland, 1664 ***2524.55*** *p44*
Cazaley, Lewis 28; Grenada, 1774 ***1220.25*** *p51*
Cealard, Josiah 35; Ontario, 1871 ***1823.28*** *p15*
Ceanfas, Jonas Clean; Virginia, 1775 ***1220.25*** *p123*
Cearney, Catherine Gradey 42; Vermont, 1876 ***5900.10*** *p575*
Ceaser, James 64; Ontario, 1871 ***1823.15*** *p40*
Ceasy, Catherine Hayden 62; Vermont, 1890 ***5900.10*** *p564*
Ceballos, Ciracio; New Orleans, 1819 ***1224.3*** *p21*
Cebulski, Michael; Maryland, 1910 ***3259.35*** *p8*
Cecil, William; New York, 1840 ***8197.10*** *p320*
Cecill, Algernill; Virginia, 1665-1666 ***6212.30*** *p21*
Cecill, Wm; Virginia, 1665-1666 ***6212.30*** *p21*
Cee, John; Maryland, 1661 ***2524.55*** *p44*
Cegelsky, Frank; Maryland, 1910 ***3259.35*** *p8*
Cegielski, Michael; Maryland, 1910 ***3259.35*** *p8*
Ceisla, Katherine; Maryland, 1910 ***3259.35*** *p8*
Cekrer, Friederig; Virginia, 1775 ***1220.25*** *p123*
Celly, John; Virginia, 1663 ***6212.30*** *p3*
Centurier, Jean Jaques; Port uncertain, 1789 ***2856.30*** *p65*
Centurier, Jean Jaques; Port uncertain, 1801 ***2856.30*** *p65*
Cerdy, Bridget 3; Ontario, 1871 ***1823.15*** *p40*
Cerovich, M. 28; Alaska, 1917 ***9196.1*** *p46*
Cerovich, M. 28; Whitehorse, Yukon, 1917 ***9196.1*** *p46*
Cerwar, Rich; Virginia, 1664 ***6212.30*** *p9*
Ceslinski, Ignac; Maryland, 1910 ***3259.35*** *p9*
Cesselery, Patrick 33; Ontario, 1871 ***1823.22*** *p26*
Cetti, Abraham; America, 1752 ***2856.30*** *p65*
Cetti, Abraham; Port uncertain, 1752 ***2856.30*** *p65*
Ceur, Fredrick 25; Ontario, 1871 ***1823.28*** *p15*
Cexe, John; Maryland, 1661 ***2524.55*** *p44*
Cezinski, Kostak; Maryland, 1910 ***3259.35*** *p9*
Cgirzke, Wawrzeniec; Maryland, 1910 ***3259.35*** *p9*
Chabaud, James; Pennsylvania, 1777 ***4629.10*** *p12*
Chabert, Anthony; Baltimore, 1797 ***1224.2*** *p20*
Chacka, Vladislow; Maryland, 1910 ***3259.35*** *p9*
Chaderac, Chevalier; Pennsylvania, 1776 ***4629.10*** *p53*
Chadsey, Franklin 12; Ontario, 1861 ***2896.28*** *p24*
Chadsey, Ira 34; Ontario, 1861 ***2896.28*** *p24*
Chadsey, Jacob 27; Ontario, 1861 ***2896.28*** *p24*
Chadsey, Maria 61; Ontario, 1861 ***2896.28*** *p24*
Chadsey, Roxy 33; Ontario, 1861 ***2896.28*** *p24*
Chadsey, Wm J. 68; Ontario, 1861 ***2896.28*** *p24*
Chadwick, Mr.; Quebec, 1858 ***9196.15*** *p34*
Chadwick, Mrs.; Quebec, 1858 ***9196.15*** *p34*
Chadwick, Anne; Vermont, 1841-1921 ***5900.10*** *p508*
Chadwick, Catherine; Vermont, 1842-1930 ***5900.10*** *p289*
Chadwick, Catherine McGuire; Vermont, 1842-1907 ***5900.10*** *p288*
Chadwick, Gear; Pennsylvania, 1777 ***4629.10*** *p17*
Chadwick, Joseph; New York, 1807 ***8197.10*** *p36*
Chadwick, Prusella 37; Vermont, 1880 ***5900.10*** *p454*
Chadwick, Richard; Nantucket, Massachusetts, 1811 ***1224.3*** *p13*
Chadwick, William 24; Maryland, 1773-1774 ***1220.25*** *p34*
Chadwin, William; New York, 1818 ***8197.10*** *p214*
Chaerlski, Joseph; Maryland, 1910 ***3259.35*** *p9*
Chafe, James; Maryland, 1657 ***2524.55*** *p44*
Chaffin, Thomas; Virginia, 1664 ***6212.30*** *p9*
Chahalek, Mary; Maryland, 1910 ***3259.35*** *p9*
Chajenski, Andrew J.; Maryland, 1910 ***3259.35*** *p9*
Chalascombe, Miss; Quebec, 1857 ***9196.15*** *p18*
Chalaupka, Frank 52; Ontario, 1871 ***1823.22*** *p26*
Chalk, Ann *SEE* Chalk, Francis
Chalk, Francis; Maryland, 1658 ***2524.55*** *p44*
Wife: Ann
Chalk, James; New York, 1806 ***8197.10*** *p322*
Chalk, John Self; Buffalo, New York, 1851 ***1224.3*** *p13*
Chalk, Margret 71; Ontario, 1871 ***1823.15*** *p40*
Chalk, Stephen 32; Virginia, 1774 ***1220.25*** *p54*
Challcott, Tho; Virginia, 1665-1666 ***6212.30*** *p24*
Challe, Peter 23; Virginia, 1773 ***1220.25*** *p30*
Challener, Ralph; Maryland, 1664 ***2524.55*** *p44*
Challenge, John; Maryland, 1679-1681 ***2524.55*** *p44*
Challet, Francis 68; Ontario, 1871 ***1823.15*** *p40*
Challor, Robt; Virginia, 1664 ***6212.30*** *p9*
Chalmers, Mr.; Quebec, 1858 ***9196.15*** *p41*
Chalmers, Andrew; New York, 1807 ***8197.10*** *p36*
Chalmers, David; North America, 1787 ***1640.13*** *p20*
Chalmers, Gilbert; Savannah, Georgia, 1768 ***1640.10*** *p27*
Chalmers, Hector; Jamaica, 1831 ***1640.13*** *p20*
Chalmers, Jacob; Maryland, 1670 ***2524.55*** *p44*
Chalmers, James; California, 1882 ***1640.13*** *p20*
Chalmers, James; New York, 1807 ***8197.10*** *p36*
Chalmers, James; New York, 1887 ***1640.13*** *p20*
Chalmers, James; North America, 1787 ***1640.13*** *p20*
Chalmers, James; Portland, Maine, 1857 ***9196.15*** *p11*
Chalmers, Thomas H.; New York, 1821 ***8197.10*** *p215*
Chalmers, William; Dominica, 1811 ***1640.13*** *p20*
Chalmers, Wm 34; Ontario, 1871 ***1823.28*** *p15*
Chalwell, Thomas; Virginia, 1674 ***6212.30*** *p52*
Cham, Thomas; Maryland, 1677 ***2524.55*** *p44*
Chamberlain, Mr.; Quebec, 1858 ***9196.15*** *p46*
Chamberlain, Alice 56; Ontario, 1871 ***1823.15*** *p40*
Chamberlain, Jennie Murphy 27; Vermont, 1896 ***5900.10*** *p297*
Chamberlain, John 22; Maryland, 1775 ***1220.25*** *p96*
Chamberlain, John 48; Ontario, 1871 ***1823.22*** *p26*
Chamberlain, Jonas 22; Maryland, 1775 ***1220.25*** *p96*
Chamberlain, Kate Crawford; Vermont, 1852-1926 ***5900.10*** *p379*
Chamberlain, Philip 22; Maryland, 1775 ***1220.25*** *p96*
Chamberlain, William; Maryland, 1673 ***2524.55*** *p44*
Chamberlain, William A.; Vermont, 1851-1906 ***5900.10*** *p379*
Chamberlayne, Esther; Charleston, South Carolina, 1808 ***1224.3*** *p13*
Chamberlin, Benjamin 26; Maryland, 1774 ***1220.25*** *p61*
Chamberlin, Cha; Virginia, 1665-1666 ***6212.30*** *p21*
Chamberlin, James 23; Virginia, 1774 ***1220.25*** *p75*
Chamberlin, William; Boston, 1846 ***1224.3*** *p13*
Chamberlin, William 28; Baltimore, 1775 ***1220.25*** *p117*
Chamberlin, Wm; Virginia, 1664 ***6212.30*** *p11*
Chambers, Anne 28; Ontario, 1871 ***1823.28*** *p15*
Chambers, Charles; New York, 1808 ***8197.10*** *p214*
Chambers, Edmond 43; Ontario, 1871 ***1823.15*** *p40*
Chambers, Elizabeth; Maryland, 1666 ***2524.55*** *p203*
Chambers, Elizabeth Watson; Savannah, Georgia, 1770 ***1224.2*** *p87*
Chambers, Francis; Virginia, 1671 ***6212.30*** *p43*
Chambers, George 30; Maryland, 1775 ***1220.25*** *p104*
Chambers, George 35; Ontario, 1871 ***1823.28*** *p15*
Chambers, George Thomas 6; Ontario, 1871 ***1823.15*** *p40*
Chambers, Hannah 26; Ontario, 1871 ***1823.15*** *p40*
Chambers, James; Maryland, 1681 ***2524.55*** *p44*
Chambers, James; New York, 1806 ***8197.10*** *p323*
Chambers, John; Jamaica, 1831 ***1640.13*** *p20*
Chambers, John 60; Ontario, 1871 ***1823.28*** *p15*
Chambers, John 61; Ontario, 1871 ***1823.28*** *p15*
Chambers, John Ed. 5; Ontario, 1871 ***1823.15*** *p40*
Chambers, Joseph; Charles Town, South Carolina, 1737 ***1224.2*** *p20*
Chambers, Joseph; Ohio, 1843 ***1224.3*** *p13*
Chambers, Mary 38; Ontario, 1871 ***1823.15*** *p40*
Chambers, Mary Jane 2; Ontario, 1871 ***1823.15*** *p40*
Chambers, Mathew 30; Ontario, 1871 ***1823.15*** *p40*
Chambers, Rich; Virginia, 1674 ***6212.30*** *p52*
Chambers, Richard; Maryland, 1701 ***1224.2*** *p20*
Chambers, Richard; Virginia, 1667 ***6212.30*** *p37*
Chambers, Robert 59; Ontario, 1871 ***1823.15*** *p40*
Chambers, Samuel 30; Ontario, 1871 ***1823.15*** *p40*
Chambers, Sarah Elizabeth 9; Ontario, 1871 ***1823.15*** *p40*
Chambers, Tho; Virginia, 1681-1682 ***6212.30*** *p56*
Chambers, Thomas; New York, 1838 ***8197.10*** *p112*
Chambers, Thomas 40; Ontario, 1871 ***1823.15*** *p40*
Chambers, William; Carolina, 1683 ***1224.1*** *p12*
Chambers, William; Virginia, 1670 ***1224.1*** *p12*
Chambers, William 28; Maryland, 1775 ***1220.25*** *p114*
Chambliss, William P. 46; Ontario, 1871 ***1823.22*** *p26*
Chamier, Daniel; Baltimore, 1780 ***1224.2*** *p20*
Chamney, Richard 45; Ontario, 1871 ***1823.15*** *p40*
Chamon, John; Virginia, 1666 ***6212.30*** *p28*
Champ, Mathias; Pennsylvania, 1786 ***4629.10*** *p52*
Champ, William; Maryland, 1664 ***2524.55*** *p151*
Champaign, Stephen; Pennsylvania, 1777 ***4629.10*** *p28*
Champion, Chas; Quebec, 1857 ***9196.15*** *p13*
Champion, Francis; New York, 1839 ***8197.10*** *p220*
Champion, Richard; South Carolina, 1800 ***1224.3*** *p13*
Champion, Thomas 51; Ontario, 1871 ***1823.15*** *p40*
Champlain, Joe 63; Alaska, 1918 ***9196.1*** *p8*
Champlain, Joe 63; Yukon, 1918 ***9196.1*** *p8*
Champneys, Welden; Quebec, 1858 ***9196.15*** *p31*
Chanalia, Cath. 17; Ontario, 1861 ***2896.26*** *p38*
Chance, Elizabeth *SEE* Chance, Wm.
Chance, George; New York, 1826 ***8197.10*** *p336*
Chance, James 40; Ontario, 1871 ***1823.28*** *p15*
Chance, Thomas; St. Augustine, Florida, 1771 ***1224.2*** *p20*
Chance, Wm.; Maryland, 1668 ***2524.55*** *p44*
Wife: Elizabeth
Chancellor, William; Pennsylvania, 1777 ***4629.10*** *p22*
Chancellor, William; Pennsylvania, 1779 ***4629.10*** *p39*
Chancy, Henry; Virginia, 1668-1669 ***6212.30*** *p41*
Chandler, Ann *SEE* Chandler, Job
Chandler, Charlotte; New York, New York, 1853 ***1224.3*** *p13*
Chandler, Daniel; Virginia, 1651 ***1224.1*** *p12*
Chandler, Eliz.; Maryland, 1657 ***2524.55*** *p45*
Chandler, Hannah Lillis; Vermont, 1845-1904 ***5900.10*** *p105*
Chandler, Henry Whateley; New Orleans, 1854 ***1224.3*** *p13*
Chandler, Jane; Canada, 1864 ***1640.13*** *p20*
Chandler, Job; Maryland, 1651 ***2524.55*** *p45*
Wife: Ann
Daughter: Ann
Chandler, John 19; Maryland, 1774 ***1220.25*** *p84*
Chandler, John 22; Maryland, 1775 ***1220.25*** *p111*
Chandler, Mary; Maryland, 1667 ***2524.55*** *p45*
Chandler, Mary; Virginia, 1667 ***6212.30*** *p37*
Chandler, Nathaniel; Worcester, Massachusetts, 1801 ***1224.3*** *p13*
Chandler, R. 25; Boston, 1775 ***1220.25*** *p106*
Chandler, Richard; Maryland, 1657 ***2524.55*** *p45*
Chandler, Richard; Maryland, 1659 ***2524.55*** *p45*
Chandler, Richard; Virginia, 1667 ***6212.30*** *p36*
Chandler, Robert; New London, Connecticut, 1801 ***1224.3*** *p13*
Chandler, Samuel; Maryland, 1679 ***2524.55*** *p45*
Chandler, Samuel 22; Maryland, 1775 ***1220.25*** *p98*
Chandler, Sarah; Virginia, 1651 ***1224.1*** *p12*
Chandler, Thomas; Virginia, 1663 ***6212.30*** *p1*
Chandler, William; Maryland, 1651 ***2524.55*** *p45*
Chandler, William; North America, 1790 ***1224.2*** *p20*
Chandler, William; North Carolina, 1785 ***1224.2*** *p20*
Chandliss, Charles; Boston, 1775 ***1224.2*** *p21*
Chanellor, Thomas; Maryland, 1655 ***2524.55*** *p45*
Chaney, Thomas; Virginia, 1665 ***6212.30*** *p20*
Chank, Thomas 68; Ontario, 1871 ***1823.15*** *p42*
Channell, John; Maryland, 1650 ***2524.55*** *p45*
Chanowsky, Frances; Maryland, 1910 ***3259.35*** *p9*
Chant, Anna M. 22; Ontario, 1871 ***1823.28*** *p15*
Chantley, James 21; Maryland, 1775 ***1220.25*** *p97*
Chantrise, Eliz; Virginia, 1671 ***6212.30*** *p44*
Chapell, William; Virginia, 1682 ***1224.1*** *p13*
Chapin, Otis 42; Ontario, 1871 ***1823.22*** *p26*
Chapin, Roswell 73; Ontario, 1871 ***1823.22*** *p26*
Chaplain, Elizabeth *SEE* Chaplain, William
Chaplain, George; Pennsylvania, 1785 ***4629.10*** *p45*

Chaplain, William; Maryland, 1651 ***2524.55*** *p45*
Wife: Elizabeth
Daughter: Elizabeth
With stepchild
Chaplin, Elizabeth *SEE* Chaplin, Will.
Chaplin, George; Kingston, Jamaica, 1723 ***1640.13*** *p20*
Chaplin, Harriet; New York, 1846 ***1224.3*** *p56*
Chaplin, John; Pennsylvania, 1777 ***4629.10*** *p13*
Chaplin, Will.; Maryland, 1658 ***2524.55*** *p45*
Wife: Elizabeth
Daughter: Elizabeth
Chapline, Elizabeth Nourse; Missouri, 1847 ***1224.3*** *p13*
Chaplyn, Clement; New England, 1642 ***1224.1*** *p15*
Chapman, Captain; Quebec, 1857 ***9196.15*** *p25*
Chapman, Mr.; Quebec, 1858 ***9196.15*** *p45*
Chapman, Mrs.; Quebec, 1858 ***9196.15*** *p45*
Chapman, Mrs. 39; Ontario, 1861 ***2896.26*** *p25*
Chapman, Ann 1 *SEE* Chapman, William
Chapman, Ann 8 *SEE* Chapman, Lancelot
Chapman, Anne; Virginia, 1716 ***1224.2*** *p21*
Chapman, Benjamin; New York, 1802 ***8197.10*** *p19*
Chapman, Benjamin 21; Virginia, 1774 ***1220.25*** *p38*
Chapman, Cynthia 9; Ontario, 1861 ***2896.27*** *p31*
Chapman, Daniel; Maryland, 1665 ***2524.55*** *p45*
Chapman, Daniel; Maryland, 1669 ***2524.55*** *p45*
Chapman, David W. 35; Ontario, 1871 ***1823.22*** *p26*
Chapman, Edward; Virginia, 1664 ***6212.30*** *p10*
Chapman, Eliz Jane 26; Ontario, 1871 ***1823.28*** *p15*
Chapman, Emanuel 56; Ontario, 1871 ***1823.15*** *p40*
Chapman, Frances 12 *SEE* Chapman, Lancelot
Chapman, Frances 42 *SEE* Chapman, Lancelot
Chapman, George 42; Ontario, 1871 ***1823.22*** *p26*
Chapman, Hannah 4 *SEE* Chapman, Lancelot
Chapman, Harriett 56; Ontario, 1871 ***1823.22*** *p26*
Chapman, Henry 7 *SEE* Chapman, William
Chapman, Henry 33; Ontario, 1871 ***1823.15*** *p41*
Chapman, Henry 35; Ontario, 1871 ***1823.22*** *p26*
Chapman, James; Virginia, 1678 ***6212.30*** *p54*
Chapman, James 23; Baltimore, 1775 ***1220.25*** *p118*
Chapman, James 33; Ontario, 1871 ***1823.28*** *p15*
Chapman, James Holmes; New York, 1838 ***8197.10*** *p112*
Chapman, Jane 15 *SEE* Chapman, William
Chapman, John; Grenada, 1826 ***1640.13*** *p20*
Chapman, John; Maryland, 1676 ***2524.55*** *p45*
Chapman, John; Maryland, 1680 ***2524.55*** *p45*
Chapman, John; Ontario, 1871 ***1823.22*** *p26*
Chapman, John 13 *SEE* Chapman, William
Chapman, John 21; Maryland, 1775 ***1220.25*** *p106*
Chapman, John 22; Maryland, 1775 ***1220.25*** *p98*
Chapman, John 22; Maryland, 1775 ***1220.25*** *p101*
Chapman, John 29; Ontario, 1871 ***1823.22*** *p26*
Chapman, John 39; Ontario, 1871 ***1823.22*** *p26*
Chapman, John 40; Ontario, 1871 ***1823.15*** *p41*
Chapman, John Henry 5; Ontario, 1861 ***2896.27*** *p31*
Chapman, Jonathan 5 *SEE* Chapman, William
Chapman, Lancelot 6 *SEE* Chapman, Lancelot
Chapman, Lancelot 49; Fort Cumberland, Nova Scotia, 1774 ***1220.25*** *p16*
Wife: Frances 42
Child: Rachael 14
Child: Martin 10
Child: Lancelot 6
Child: Hannah 4
Child: Ann 8
Child: Frances 12
Child: Thomas 18
Chapman, Mariann 7; Ontario, 1861 ***2896.27*** *p31*
Chapman, Martin 10 *SEE* Chapman, Lancelot
Chapman, Mary; Philadelphia, 1839 ***1224.3*** *p13*
Chapman, Mary 9 *SEE* Chapman, William
Chapman, Mary 42 *SEE* Chapman, William
Chapman, Nicholas 54; Ontario, 1871 ***1823.22*** *p26*
Chapman, Peter 35; Maryland, 1774 ***1220.25*** *p41*
Chapman, Phoebe Ann 3; Ontario, 1861 ***2896.27*** *p31*
Chapman, Rachael 14 *SEE* Chapman, Lancelot
Chapman, Richard 28; Ontario, 1871 ***1823.28*** *p15*
Chapman, Richard 31; Ontario, 1861 ***2896.27*** *p31*
Chapman, Richard 45; Ontario, 1871 ***1823.15*** *p41*
Chapman, Richard 45; Ontario, 1871 ***1823.28*** *p15*
Chapman, Richard M. 1; Ontario, 1861 ***2896.27*** *p31*
Chapman, Robert; Maryland, 1673 ***2524.55*** *p45*
Chapman, Sarah 3 *SEE* Chapman, William
Chapman, Thomas; Maryland, 1659 ***2524.55*** *p45*
Chapman, Thomas 17 *SEE* Chapman, William
Chapman, Thomas 18 *SEE* Chapman, Lancelot
Chapman, William; New York, 1807 ***8197.10*** *p36*
Chapman, William; New York, 1810 ***8197.10*** *p214*
Chapman, William 18; Philadelphia, 1774 ***1220.25*** *p81*
Chapman, William 19 *SEE* Chapman, William
Chapman, William 27; Virginia, 1775 ***1220.25*** *p95*
Chapman, William 35; Ontario, 1871 ***1823.15*** *p41*
Chapman, William 38; Ontario, 1871 ***1823.28*** *p15*
Chapman, William 39; Ontario, 1871 ***1823.15*** *p41*
Chapman, William 44; Fort Cumberland, Nova Scotia, 1774 ***1220.25*** *p18*
Wife: Mary 42
Child: William 19
Child: Jane 15
Child: Mary 9
Child: John 13
Child: Ann 1
Child: Sarah 3
Child: Jonathan 5
Child: Henry 7
Child: Thomas 17
Chapman, William 60; Ontario, 1861 ***2896.26*** *p25*
Chapman, William 73; Ontario, 1871 ***1823.22*** *p26*
Chapman, William B.; New York, 1828 ***8197.10*** *p218*
Chapman, Wm; Virginia, 1665-1666 ***6212.30*** *p23*
Chappel, Gilbert H. 76; Vermont, 1919 ***5900.10*** *p517*
Chappel, Herman; Pennsylvania, 1777 ***4629.10*** *p11*
Chappel, Maggie Patton 54; Vermont, 1901 ***5900.10*** *p517*
Chappel, Thomas; Pennsylvania, 1779 ***4629.10*** *p41*
Chappel, Thomas 35; Ontario, 1871 ***1823.22*** *p26*
Chappell, Christopher; Virginia, 1855 ***1224.3*** *p13*
Chappell, Eleanor *SEE* Chappell, Thomas
Chappell, Thomas; Maryland, 1681 ***2524.55*** *p45*
Wife: Eleanor
Chappell, Thomas; New York, 1826 ***8197.10*** *p64*
Chappell, William; New York, 1840 ***8197.10*** *p160*
Chappell, William 32; Maryland, 1774 ***1220.25*** *p57*
Chapple, John 16; Philadelphia, 1774 ***1220.25*** *p35*
Chapple, John 64; Ontario, 1871 ***1823.15*** *p41*
Chapple, Robert 51; Ontario, 1871 ***1823.22*** *p26*
Chapple, Robert 75; Ontario, 1871 ***1823.22*** *p26*
Charbonnier, Powell 32; Philadelphia, 1774 ***1220.25*** *p43*
Chardon, Antoin Germain; Philadelphia, 1789 ***4629.10*** *p83*
Chardon, Henry; Charles Town, South Carolina, 1739 ***1224.2*** *p21*
Charitie, Philip 25; Grenada, 1774 ***1220.25*** *p128*
Charles, Mr.; Portland, Maine, 1857 ***9196.15*** *p12*
Charles, Anthony; New York, 1840 ***8197.10*** *p161*
Charles, Esther; Maryland, 1681 ***2524.55*** *p45*
Charles, Jacob; Pennsylvania, 1777 ***4629.10*** *p29*
Charles, James; Virginia, 1664 ***6212.30*** *p9*
Charles, James 41; Ontario, 1871 ***1823.28*** *p16*
Charles, Jno; Virginia, 1664 ***6212.30*** *p9*
Charles, Jno; Virginia, 1678 ***6212.30*** *p54*
Charles, John; Maryland, 1681 ***2524.55*** *p45*
Charles, John 47; Ontario, 1871 ***1823.28*** *p16*
Charles, William 24; Savannah, Georgia, 1775 ***1220.25*** *p139*
Charlesworth, Emma 61; Ontario, 1871 ***1823.15*** *p41*
Charlesworth, Henry 52; Ontario, 1871 ***1823.15*** *p41*
Charlesworth, John; Maryland, 1667 ***2524.55*** *p45*
Charlesworth, Martin 47; Ontario, 1871 ***1823.15*** *p41*
Charlesworth, Sarah 60; Ontario, 1871 ***1823.15*** *p41*
Charleton, Samuel; Maryland, 1681 ***2524.55*** *p45*
Charleton, William; Maryland, 1665 ***2524.55*** *p45*
Charlett, Richard; Maryland, 1694 ***1224.1*** *p13*
Charlsworth, Alexander 55; Ontario, 1871 ***1823.15*** *p41*
Charlton, Daniel; Maryland, 1757 ***1224.2*** *p21*
Charlton, Elling; Maryland, 1663 ***2524.55*** *p45*
Charlton, Emily Walters; Savannah, Georgia, 1821 ***1224.3*** *p13*
Charlton, Jno; Virginia, 1664 ***6212.30*** *p11*
Charlton, Job; Virginia, 1665-1666 ***6212.30*** *p23*
Charlton, Mary; Maryland, 1663 ***2524.55*** *p45*
Charlton, Oswell; Maryland, 1663 ***2524.55*** *p45*
Charlton, R.; Portland, Maine, 1858 ***9196.15*** *p31*
Charlton, Robert 17; Fort Cumberland, Nova Scotia, 1774 ***1220.25*** *p17*
Charlton, Walter; New York, 1834 ***8197.10*** *p70*
Charlton, William; Maryland, 1665 ***2524.55*** *p45*
Charlton, William; New York, 1831 ***8197.10*** *p355*
Charmichael, Samuel 10; Jamaica, 1773-1774 ***1220.25*** *p32*
Charmier, Johann; America, 1751 ***2856.30*** *p65*
Charne, Margaret; Virginia, 1671-1672 ***6212.30*** *p47*
Charnick, Henry 31; Fort Cumberland, Nova Scotia, 1774 ***1220.25*** *p18*
Charnock, Mrs.; Quebec, 1858 ***9196.15*** *p38*
Charnock, Henry; Virginia, 1665 ***6212.30*** *p20*
Charnock, John; Jamaica, 1850 ***1640.13*** *p20*
Charnock, Thomas 26; Maryland, 1774 ***1220.25*** *p78*
Charnocke, Elizabeth; Maryland, 1675 ***2524.55*** *p45*
Charras, James; New York, 1830 ***8197.10*** *p218*
Charslay, Charles 47; Ontario, 1871 ***1823.28*** *p16*
Charter, Andrew; Virginia, 1694 ***1224.1*** *p13*
Charters, George; Jamaica, 1841 ***1640.13*** *p20*
Charters, William 66; Ontario, 1871 ***1823.15*** *p41*
Chartre, Michael; New York, 1839 ***8197.10*** *p133*
Chartres, William; New York, 1816 ***8197.10*** *p214*
Chartting, F.; Portland, Maine, 1858 ***9196.15*** *p30*
Chase, Abram 3; Ontario, 1861 ***2896.25*** *p14*
Chase, Abram 13; Ontario, 1861 ***2896.25*** *p8*
Chase, Abram 77; Ontario, 1861 ***2896.25*** *p14*
Chase, Abram, Jr. 23; Ontario, 1861 ***2896.25*** *p14*
Chase, Abram J. 1; Ontario, 1861 ***2896.25*** *p14*
Chase, Andrew 19; Ontario, 1861 ***2896.25*** *p8*
Chase, Charles 54; Ontario, 1861 ***2896.25*** *p18*
Chase, Charles A. 5; Ontario, 1861 ***2896.25*** *p22*
Chase, Charles A. 19; Ontario, 1861 ***2896.25*** *p18*
Chase, Daniel 20; Ontario, 1861 ***2896.25*** *p18*
Chase, Daniel 36; Ontario, 1861 ***2896.25*** *p14*
Chase, Edgar 9; Ontario, 1861 ***2896.25*** *p14*
Chase, Eliza 54; Ontario, 1861 ***2896.25*** *p18*
Chase, Eliza A.; Ontario, 1861 ***2896.25*** *p10*
Chase, Elizabeth 4; Ontario, 1861 ***2896.25*** *p22*
Chase, Elizabeth 10; Ontario, 1861 ***2896.25*** *p8*
Chase, Francis A. 8; Ontario, 1861 ***2896.25*** *p14*
Chase, George 2; Ontario, 1861 ***2896.28*** *p41*
Chase, Gilford D. 6; Ontario, 1861 ***2896.25*** *p14*
Chase, H. M. 17; Ontario, 1861 ***2896.25*** *p8*
Chase, Hannah M. 17; Ontario, 1861 ***2896.25*** *p16*
Chase, Henry Case 2; Ontario, 1861 ***2896.25*** *p22*
Chase, Jacob 16; Ontario, 1861 ***2896.28*** *p41*
Chase, Jane 23; Ontario, 1861 ***2896.25*** *p14*
Chase, Jewit 17; Ontario, 1861 ***2896.25*** *p18*
Chase, Jo.; Maryland, 1681 ***2524.55*** *p45*
Chase, John 20; Ontario, 1861 ***2896.28*** *p41*
Chase, Joseph F. 1; Ontario, 1861 ***2896.25*** *p22*
Chase, Levi 13; Ontario, 1861 ***2896.25*** *p14*
Chase, Lewis; Ontario, 1861 ***2896.25*** *p10*
Chase, Lewis M. 23; Ontario, 1861 ***2896.25*** *p18*
Chase, M. A. 10; Ontario, 1861 ***2896.25*** *p8*
Chase, M. J. 32; Ontario, 1861 ***2896.25*** *p8*
Chase, Margaret J. 11; Ontario, 1861 ***2896.25*** *p14*
Chase, Marshall 5; Ontario, 1861 ***2896.25*** *p14*
Chase, Mary E. 3; Ontario, 1861 ***2896.25*** *p14*
Chase, Michael; Maryland, 1910 ***3259.35*** *p9*
Chase, Mortimer 5; Ontario, 1861 ***2896.25*** *p14*
Chase, Nelson 48; Ontario, 1861 ***2896.28*** *p41*
Chase, P. A. 22; Ontario, 1861 ***2896.25*** *p8*
Chase, Pheba 24; Ontario, 1861 ***2896.25*** *p22*
Chase, Rachel 10; Ontario, 1861 ***2896.28*** *p41*
Chase, Russel 14; Ontario, 1861 ***2896.25*** *p8*
Chase, S. 45; Ontario, 1861 ***2896.25*** *p8*
Chase, Sarah 47; Ontario, 1861 ***2896.25*** *p14*
Chase, Sarah J.; Vermont, 1852-1936 ***5900.10*** *p517*
Chase, Stewart 13; Ontario, 1861 ***2896.28*** *p41*
Chase, Susan 21; Ontario, 1861 ***2896.25*** *p18*
Chase, Susan 32; Ontario, 1861 ***2896.25*** *p14*
Chase, Thomas; Virginia, 1666 ***6212.30*** *p31*
Chase, Wilford 26; Ontario, 1861 ***2896.25*** *p18*
Chase, William; Massachusetts, 1896 ***1640.13*** *p20*
Chase, William 1; Ontario, 1861 ***2896.25*** *p14*
Chase, William 23; Philadelphia, 1775 ***1220.25*** *p107*
Chase, Zimerman 4; Ontario, 1861 ***2896.25*** *p14*
Chasemere, Edward; New York, 1840 ***8197.10*** *p163*
Chasmar, Thomas; New York, 1838 ***8197.10*** *p113*
Chasse, Thomas; Virginia, 1666-1667 ***6212.30*** *p34*
Chatard, Peter H.; New York, 1819 ***8197.10*** *p215*
Chatelle, Francis; New York, 1840 ***8197.10*** *p383*
Chatillon, George; New York, 1837 ***8197.10*** *p81*
Chatman, Caroline; Ontario, 1861 ***2896.25*** *p4*
Chatman, Duncan; Ontario, 1861 ***2896.25*** *p4*
Chatman, Jeremiah; Ontario, 1861 ***2896.25*** *p4*
Chatman, Louisa A.; Ontario, 1861 ***2896.25*** *p4*
Chatten, Charlotte 14; Ontario, 1871 ***1823.22*** *p27*
Chatten, James 28; Ontario, 1871 ***1823.22*** *p27*
Chatten, Thomas 49; Ontario, 1871 ***1823.22*** *p27*
Chatten, Thomas 80; Ontario, 1871 ***1823.22*** *p27*
Chatters, James; Pennsylvania, 1786 ***4629.10*** *p54*
Chatterson, Alonzo 6; Ontario, 1861 ***2896.25*** *p60*
Chatterson, Cornelius 8; Ontario, 1861 ***2896.25*** *p60*
Chatterson, Geo. 21; Ontario, 1861 ***2896.25*** *p60*
Chatterson, Matilda 19; Ontario, 1861 ***2896.25*** *p60*
Chatterson, Tressey 17; Ontario, 1861 ***2896.25*** *p60*
Chatterson, William 21; Ontario, 1861 ***2896.25*** *p60*
Chatterton, Richard D. 69; Ontario, 1871 ***1823.22*** *p27*
Chatterton, Wm Edward 41; Ontario, 1871 ***1823.28*** *p16*
Chatton, Albert 12; Ontario, 1871 ***1823.22*** *p27*
Chatwin, William; Pennsylvania, 1777 ***4629.10*** *p16*
Chauncy, Charles; New England, 1658 ***1224.1*** *p13*
Chavalier, John; Pennsylvania, 1777 ***4629.10*** *p23*
Chayer, John B.; Vermont, 1833-1892 ***5900.10*** *p534*
Chayer, Margaret Ryan; Vermont, 1829-1915 ***5900.10*** *p534*
Chayr, Mary; Virginia, 1666 ***6212.30*** *p27*
Chazarak, Charley; Maryland, 1910 ***3259.35*** *p9*
Chazournes, Felix; New York, 1821 ***8197.10*** *p215*
Cheap, Rowland; Virginia, 1666-1667 ***6212.30*** *p34*
Cheasman, Charles 75; Ontario, 1871 ***1823.15*** *p41*
Cheasman, Elizabeth 73; Ontario, 1871 ***1823.15*** *p41*
Cheauvant, Thomas 20; Virginia, 1773 ***1220.25*** *p30*

Checkley, Mr.; Quebec, 1857 ***9196.15*** *p15*
Checklinski, John; Maryland, 1910 ***3259.35*** *p9*
Cheeke, Thomas; Maryland, 1669 ***2524.55*** *p45*
Cheesebrough, John 21; Ontario, 1871 ***1823.28*** *p16*
Cheeseman, Clement 26; Maryland, 1774 ***1220.25*** *p64*
Cheeseman, Elizabeth; Maryland, 1672 ***2524.55*** *p45*
Cheesman, Johanna; Maryland, 1672 ***2524.55*** *p46*
Cheesman, John; Virginia, 1661 ***1224.1*** *p13*
Cheesman, Joseph; St. Augustine, Florida, 1778 ***1224.2*** *p21*
Cheesman, Maurice; New York, 1836 ***8197.10*** *p319*
Cheesman, Maurice; New York, 1840 ***8197.10*** *p160*
Cheesman, William; Maryland, 1672 ***2524.55*** *p46*
Cheetham, James; New York, 1797 ***8197.10*** *p9*
Cheetham, John; New York, 1802 ***8197.10*** *p19*
Cheevers, Samuel; New York, 1840 ***8197.10*** *p161*
Cheine, Elizabeth 24; Montreal, 1775 ***1220.25*** *p110*
Chelnar, Agness; Maryland, 1910 ***3259.35*** *p9*
Chelsea, Grace; Vermont, 1850-1916 ***5900.10*** *p145*
Cheltnam, Jacob; Maryland, 1675 ***2524.55*** *p46*
Cheltnam, John; Norfolk, Virginia, 1800 ***1224.3*** *p13*
Cheney, Charity; Maryland, 1658 ***2524.55*** *p46*
Cheney, Christopher; New York, 1821 ***8197.10*** *p216*
Cheney, Ellen I. Tynan; Vermont, 1854-1918 ***5900.10*** *p436*
Cheney, Frank; Vermont, 1817-1893 ***5900.10*** *p508*
Cheney, Henry C.; Vermont, 1846-1922 ***5900.10*** *p436*
Cheney, Richard; Maryland, 1658 ***2524.55*** *p46*
Cheney, Rose; Vermont, 1852-1928 ***5900.10*** *p508*
Cheney, Thomas 60; Ontario, 1871 ***1823.22*** *p27*
Chepell, Anne; Maryland, 1861 ***2524.55*** *p46*
Cheron, Mrs.; Maryland, 1657 ***2524.55*** *p46*
Cherriman, Mr.; Quebec, 1858 ***9196.15*** *p42*
Cherriman, Mrs.; Quebec, 1858 ***9196.15*** *p42*
Cherry, Edward; Maryland, 1681 ***2524.55*** *p46*
Cherry, John; Maryland, 1910 ***3259.35*** *p9*
Cherry, John; New York, 1817 ***8197.10*** *p60*
Cherry, Moses 70; Ontario, 1871 ***1823.28*** *p16*
Cherry, Sarah 22; Virginia, 1775 ***1220.25*** *p142*
Cherry, William 49; Ontario, 1871 ***1823.28*** *p16*
Cherubine, Mary; Maryland, 1910 ***3259.35*** *p9*
Chervinski, Agofia 33; Alaska, 1917 ***9196.1*** *p7*
Chervinski, Agofia 33; Yukon, 1917 ***9196.1*** *p7*
Chery, David; Ontario, 1861 ***2896.28*** *p55*
Chery, Margaret; Ontario, 1861 ***2896.28*** *p55*
Cherykee, Charles; Pennsylvania, 1777 ***4629.10*** *p11*
Chesaillez, Alexander 21; Virginia, 1773 ***1220.25*** *p30*
Cheshire, Mrs.; Maryland, 1665 ***2524.55*** *p46*
Cheshire, John; Maryland, 1655-1656 ***2524.55*** *p46*
Chesill, Francis; Maryland, 1672 ***2524.55*** *p46*
Chesley, Phillip; Virginia, 1675 ***1224.1*** *p13*
Chesney, Elizabeth 51; Ontario, 1871 ***1823.15*** *p41*
Chesney, Hugh 43; Ontario, 1871 ***1823.15*** *p41*
Chesney, James 50; Ontario, 1871 ***1823.15*** *p41*
Chesney, James 55; Ontario, 1871 ***1823.22*** *p27*
Chesshyre, H.; Quebec, 1857 ***9196.15*** *p17*
Chesson, John; Maryland, 1662 ***2524.55*** *p46*
Chester, Edward; Maryland, 1680 ***2524.55*** *p46*
Wife: Elinor
Chester, Elinor *SEE* Chester, Edward
Chester, Howard 13; Ontario, 1871 ***1823.28*** *p16*
Chester, Hugh *SEE* Chester, John
Chester, John *SEE* Chester, John
Chester, John; Maryland, 1666 ***2524.55*** *p46*
Wife: Mary
Brother: Hugh
Child: John
Child: Sarah
Chester, John; Pennsylvania, 1785 ***4629.10*** *p48*
Chester, John; Virginia, 1665 ***6212.30*** *p19*
Chester, Martin; Maryland, 1910 ***3259.35*** *p9*
Chester, Mary *SEE* Chester, John
Chester, Sarah *SEE* Chester, John
Chester, Tho; Virginia, 1666 ***6212.30*** *p25*
Chester, Thomas 23; Ontario, 1871 ***1823.28*** *p16*
Chester, William 24; Philadelphia, 1774 ***1220.25*** *p80*
Chesterfeild, Tho; Virginia, 1667 ***6212.30*** *p37*
Chesterfield, Henry 26; Ontario, 1871 ***1823.22*** *p27*
Chesterman, James; New York, 1807 ***8197.10*** *p36*
Chestmore, John 14; Philadelphia, 1775 ***1220.25*** *p8*
Cheston, Francina Augustina; Maryland, 1767 ***1224.2*** *p21*
Chettle, William 40; Ontario, 1871 ***1823.28*** *p16*
Chevaillier, Antony 21; Virginia, 1773 ***1220.25*** *p30*
Chevalier, Peter Renandet; Pennsylvania, 1779 ***4629.10*** *p40*
Cheverlin, John; Maryland, 1664 ***2524.55*** *p46*
Cheves, Eliza; Virginia, 1666-1667 ***6212.30*** *p33*
Cheves, William 35; Ontario, 1871 ***1823.15*** *p41*
Chew, Ann; Maryland, 1680 ***2524.55*** *p46*
Chew, Benjamin; Pennsylvania, 1777 ***4629.10*** *p23*
Chew, Benjamin, Jr.; Pennsylvania, 1777 ***4629.10*** *p23*
Chew, Richard; New York, 1807 ***8197.10*** *p35*
Chewing, James 35; Ontario, 1871 ***1823.15*** *p41*
Chewings, David 39; Ontario, 1871 ***1823.15*** *p41*
Cheyne, William; New York, 1842 ***1224.3*** *p13*
Cheyney, Charity; Maryland, 1658 ***2524.55*** *p46*
Cheyney, Richard; Maryland, 1658 ***2524.55*** *p46*
Chichely, Thomas; Maryland, 1672 ***2524.55*** *p46*
Chicherly, Thomas; Maryland, 1672 ***2524.55*** *p46*
Chichester, Edw; Virginia, 1667-1668 ***6212.30*** *p39*
Chichester, Ellen; Virginia, 1763 ***1224.2*** *p35*
Chichester, Ellen; Virginia, 1763 ***1224.2*** *p97*
Chichester, Hen; Virginia, 1667 ***6212.30*** *p37*
Chichester, John; Virginia, 1666 ***6212.30*** *p30*
Chichester, John; Virginia, 1763 ***1224.2*** *p21*
Chichester, John; Virginia, 1803 ***1224.3*** *p13*
Chichester, Mary; Virginia, 1790 ***1224.2*** *p6*
Chichester, Oliver; Virginia, 1665-1666 ***6212.30*** *p24*
Chichester, Richard; Virginia, 1746 ***1224.2*** *p21*
Chichester, Richard; Virginia, 1803 ***1224.3*** *p13*
Chichester, Robt; Virginia, 1667-1668 ***6212.30*** *p38*
Chichester, Tho; Virginia, 1666 ***6212.30*** *p28*
Chichowak, Josef; Maryland, 1910 ***3259.35*** *p9*
Chick, Elizabeth; Maryland, 1631-1685 ***2524.55*** *p46*
Chick, Thomas; Maryland, 1680 ***2524.55*** *p46*
Chicker, John; Maryland, 1652 ***2524.55*** *p46*
Chicking, Edward; Virginia, 1665-1666 ***6212.30*** *p20*
Chickley, Thomas; Maryland, 1672 ***2524.55*** *p46*
Chidley, George 34; Ontario, 1871 ***1823.15*** *p41*
Chidley, Joseph 39; Ontario, 1871 ***1823.15*** *p41*
Chidlow, John 29; Ontario, 1871 ***1823.15*** *p41*
Chie, Sarah; Maryland, 1663 ***2524.55*** *p46*
Chiene, Margaret; Philadelphia, 1834 ***1224.3*** *p13*
Chiffrill, Cleme; Maryland, 1665 ***2524.55*** *p46*
Chilcot, Thomas 25; Maryland, 1774 ***1220.25*** *p54*
Child, Abraham; Maryland, 1681 ***2524.55*** *p46*
Child, Francis; Maryland, 1664 ***2524.55*** *p46*
Child, Lewis; New York, 1807 ***8197.10*** *p37*
Child, Lewis; New York, 1839 ***8197.10*** *p132*
Child, Margaret; Boston, 1721 ***1224.2*** *p21*
Child, Mary; Ohio, 1829 ***1224.3*** *p54*
Child, Richard; America, 1822 ***1224.3*** *p14*
Child, Richard; New Haven, Connecticut, 1824 ***1224.3*** *p14*
Child, Robert 21; Maryland, 1775 ***1220.25*** *p119*
Child, Sarah; Cincinnati, 1857 ***1224.3*** *p14*
Child, William 21; Philadelphia, 1775 ***1220.25*** *p9*
Child, William 23; Maryland, 1774 ***1220.25*** *p47*
Child, Wm; Virginia, 1664 ***6212.30*** *p11*
Childerhose, Henry 52; Ontario, 1871 ***1823.28*** *p16*
Childerhose, John 31; Ontario, 1871 ***1823.28*** *p16*
Childerhose, John 63; Ontario, 1871 ***1823.28*** *p16*
Childerhose, Robert 75; Ontario, 1871 ***1823.28*** *p16*
Childerhose, Steven 38; Ontario, 1871 ***1823.28*** *p16*
Childerhose, Thomas 51; Ontario, 1871 ***1823.28*** *p16*
Childerhose, William 50; Ontario, 1871 ***1823.28*** *p16*
Chilinski, Ludwig; Maryland, 1910 ***3259.35*** *p9*
Chilinsky, Victor; Maryland, 1910 ***3259.35*** *p9*
Chillcock, Ann; Maryland, 1681 ***2524.55*** *p46*
Chillingworth, Ralph 35; Virginia, 1774 ***1220.25*** *p56*
Chillinworth, Dag 14; Ontario, 1871 ***1823.15*** *p41*
Chillinworth, Ellen 12; Ontario, 1871 ***1823.15*** *p41*
Chillinworth, Fanny 9; Ontario, 1871 ***1823.15*** *p41*
Chily, Nicholas 30; Maryland, 1775 ***1220.25*** *p98*
Chimelewski, Michael; Maryland, 1910 ***3259.35*** *p9*
Chiners, Michael; Maryland, 1679 ***2524.55*** *p46*
Chinery, James; New York, 1826-1836 ***8197.10*** *p310*
Chinery, James; New York, 1830 ***8197.10*** *p313*
Chinery, William; New York, 1830 ***8197.10*** *p313*
Chinery, William; New York, 1833 ***8197.10*** *p303*
Ching, Ann 73; Ontario, 1871 ***1823.15*** *p41*
Ching, Elizabeth 39; Ontario, 1871 ***1823.15*** *p41*
Ching, John 34; Ontario, 1871 ***1823.15*** *p41*
Ching, Thomas 44; Ontario, 1871 ***1823.15*** *p41*
Chiniski, Jacob; Maryland, 1910 ***3259.35*** *p9*
Chinner, Rebecca *SEE* Chinner, Thomas
Chinner, Thomas; Maryland, 1666 ***2524.55*** *p46*
Relative: Rebecca
Chinow, Anthony; Virginia, 1666 ***6212.30*** *p27*
Chipchase, Ann 35 *SEE* Chipchase, Thomas
Chipchase, Thomas 40; Maryland, 1774 ***1220.25*** *p58*
Wife: Ann 35
Chipman, Richard 39; Ontario, 1871 ***1823.28*** *p16*
Chipor, John 42; Ontario, 1871 ***1823.28*** *p16*
Chipp, Isaac; New York, 1821 ***8197.10*** *p216*
Chippeyur, Michael 50; Ontario, 1871 ***1823.28*** *p16*
Chips, James 64; Ontario, 1871 ***1823.22*** *p27*
Chipyere, Mathias 25; Ontario, 1871 ***1823.28*** *p16*
Chiquet, Lewis; New York, 1816 ***8197.10*** *p58*
Chirard, Margarete; Port uncertain, 1760 ***2856.30*** *p65*
Chirard, Peter; Port uncertain, 1751 ***2856.30*** *p65*
Chiseck, Annie; Maryland, 1910 ***3259.35*** *p9*
Chisham, Thomas 15; Jamaica, 1774 ***1220.25*** *p82*
Chisham, William 19; Philadelphia, 1774 ***1220.25*** *p81*
Chishollne, Elinor; Maryland, 1667 ***2524.55*** *p46*
Chisholm, Mr.; Quebec, 1857 ***9196.15*** *p21*
Chisholm, Ann 20; Ontario, 1871 ***1823.28*** *p16*
Chisholm, Elizabeth 47; Ontario, 1861 ***2896.27*** *p44*
Chisholm, Emely 22; Ontario, 1871 ***1823.28*** *p16*
Chisholm, Esther A. 15; Ontario, 1861 ***2896.27*** *p44*
Chisholm, James; Savannah, Georgia, 1771-1804 ***1640.10*** *p27*
Chisholm, James 22; Ontario, 1861 ***2896.27*** *p44*
Chisholm, Jessie 3; Ontario, 1871 ***1823.22*** *p27*
Chisholm, Joseph 58; Ontario, 1871 ***1823.22*** *p27*
Chisholm, Julie A. 11; Ontario, 1861 ***2896.27*** *p44*
Chisholm, Thomas; New York, 1807 ***8197.10*** *p37*
Chisney, George 41; Ontario, 1871 ***1823.15*** *p41*
Chisney, Henry 58; Ontario, 1871 ***1823.15*** *p41*
Chisney, William 47; Ontario, 1871 ***1823.15*** *p41*
Chison, Alexander; Florida, 1824 ***1640.10*** *p27*
Chitry, Peter; New York, 1826 ***8197.10*** *p334*
Chittek, John 38; Ontario, 1871 ***1823.15*** *p41*
Chitterell, Elizabeth; Maryland, 1674 ***2524.55*** *p46*
Chitty, Ann; Maryland, 1650 ***2524.55*** *p46*
Chiverell, Clement; Maryland, 1673 ***2524.55*** *p46*
Chivers, John 23; Virginia, 1774 ***1220.25*** *p54*
Chivers, Robert; New York, 1838 ***8197.10*** *p112*
Chiverton, Thomas; New York, 1840 ***8197.10*** *p387*
Chiwatkiewicz, W.; Maryland, 1910 ***3259.35*** *p9*
Chmelewsky, Steve; Maryland, 1910 ***3259.35*** *p9*
Chmiel, Valentine; Maryland, 1910 ***3259.35*** *p9*
Chmielewsky, Antony; Maryland, 1910 ***3259.35*** *p9*
Chmieliski, Joseph; Maryland, 1910 ***3259.35*** *p9*
Chmiluski, Frank; Maryland, 1910 ***3259.35*** *p9*
Choate, Mr.; Quebec, 1856 ***9196.15*** *p6*
Choate, Elizabeth A.; Ontario, 1861 ***2896.25*** *p6*
Choinsky, Febs; Maryland, 1910 ***3259.35*** *p9*
Chojnacka, Fodajyia; Maryland, 1910 ***3259.35*** *p9*
Chojnacki, Franzerez; Maryland, 1910 ***3259.35*** *p9*
Chojnowski, James; Maryland, 1910 ***3259.35*** *p9*
Chojnowski, John; Maryland, 1910 ***3259.35*** *p9*
Cholewerzuski, Antone; Maryland, 1910 ***3259.35*** *p9*
Cholewinski, Joseph; Maryland, 1910 ***3259.35*** *p9*
Chollet, Abraham Louis; Charleston, South Carolina, 1821 ***1224.3*** *p14*
Cholmondeley, Mr.; Quebec, 1858 ***9196.15*** *p43*
Chondron, Jacob; America, 1749 ***2856.30*** *p65*
Choni, John Peter 63; Ontario, 1871 ***1823.28*** *p16*
Chorazy, John; Maryland, 1910 ***3259.35*** *p9*
Choresel, Johann Daniel; Port uncertain, 1781 ***2856.30*** *p65*
Choreselin, Catharina; Port uncertain, 1779 ***2856.30*** *p66*
Chorhummel, Mathes; Port uncertain, 1745 ***2856.30*** *p66*
Chorly, Alford 40; Ontario, 1871 ***1823.15*** *p41*
Chossen, James; Philadelphia, 1793 ***4629.10*** *p72*
Chot, Hans Peter; America, 1754 ***2856.30*** *p410*
Chot, Ludwig; America, 1754 ***2856.30*** *p410*
Chotes, Ann 57; Ontario, 1861 ***2896.25*** *p68*
Chotes, Benjamin 15; Ontario, 1861 ***2896.25*** *p68*
Chotes, Catherine 4; Ontario, 1861 ***2896.25*** *p68*
Chotes, Durinda 1; Ontario, 1861 ***2896.25*** *p68*
Chotes, Elizabeth 22; Ontario, 1861 ***2896.25*** *p68*
Chotes, Irene 7; Ontario, 1861 ***2896.25*** *p68*
Chotes, Jane 8; Ontario, 1861 ***2896.25*** *p68*
Chotes, Jason 14; Ontario, 1861 ***2896.25*** *p68*
Chotes, John 10; Ontario, 1861 ***2896.25*** *p68*
Chotes, Joseph 9; Ontario, 1861 ***2896.25*** *p68*
Chotes, Unis 36; Ontario, 1861 ***2896.25*** *p68*
Chovet, Abraham; Pennsylvania, 1777 ***4629.10*** *p24*
Chowe, Malcolm 15; Ontario, 1861 ***2896.27*** *p29*
Chowing, William 36; Ontario, 1871 ***1823.15*** *p41*
Chown, Henry; Virginia, 1664 ***6212.30*** *p9*
Choyce, Elizabeth; Maryland, 1661 ***2524.55*** *p46*
Chraby, Stephen; Maryland, 1910 ***3259.35*** *p9*
Chranch, Mrs.; Quebec, 1856 ***9196.15*** *p11*
Chrawa, Stanslaw; Maryland, 1910 ***3259.35*** *p9*
Chrbim, John; Maryland, 1910 ***3259.35*** *p9*
Chrisholm, Robert 42; Ontario, 1871 ***1823.15*** *p41*
Chrisnowski, John; Maryland, 1910 ***3259.35*** *p9*
Chrisolme, John; Carolina, 1801 ***1224.3*** *p14*
Christ, Anna Barbara; America, 1742 ***2856.30*** *p66*
With 3 children
Christ, Anna Catharina; Port uncertain, 1792 ***2856.30*** *p66*
Christ, Anna Maria; Port uncertain, 1786 ***2856.30*** *p66*
Christ, Apollonia; Port uncertain, 1749 ***2856.30*** *p66*
Christ, Christian; Port uncertain, 1749 ***2856.30*** *p66*
Christ, Clara; Port uncertain, 1734 ***2856.30*** *p66*
Christ, George; New York, 1838 ***8197.10*** *p220*
Christ, Hans Michael; Port uncertain, 1781 ***2856.30*** *p66*
Christ, Henrich; America, 1749 ***2856.30*** *p66*
Christ, Henrich; Port uncertain, 1747 ***2856.30*** *p66*
Christ, James 36; New York, 1774 ***1220.25*** *p24*
Christ, Maria Catharina; Port uncertain, 1754 ***2856.30*** *p66*
Christ, Maria Dorothea; Port uncertain, 1753 ***2856.30*** *p66*

Christ, Maria Eva; Port uncertain, 1745 ***2856.30*** *p66*
Christ, Peter; Port uncertain, 1793 ***2856.30*** *p66*
Christ, Valentin; Port uncertain, 1770 ***2856.30*** *p66*
Christ, Wendel; Port uncertain, 1791 ***2856.30*** *p66*
Christadler, Konrad; Port uncertain, 1703 ***2856.30*** *p66*
Christadler, Konrad; Port uncertain, 1733 ***2856.30*** *p66*
Christafsen, Herman; Alaska, 1915 ***9196.1*** *p11*
Christafsen, Herman; British Columbia, 1915 ***9196.1*** *p11*
Christe, Ann 50; Ontario, 1871 ***1823.15*** *p41*
Christe, Elizabeth 16; Ontario, 1871 ***1823.15*** *p41*
Christe, John 23; Ontario, 1871 ***1823.15*** *p41*
Christe, Kate 20; Ontario, 1871 ***1823.15*** *p41*
Christe, William 18; Ontario, 1871 ***1823.15*** *p41*
Christen, Jacob; America, 1752 ***2856.30*** *p66*
Christensen, . . .; Chicago, 1862 ***3437.14*** *p115*
Christian, Adam; Maryland, 1650 ***2524.55*** *p47*
Christian, Adam; Maryland, 1658 ***2524.55*** *p47*
Christian, Charles; New York, 1802 ***8197.10*** *p19*
Christian, Felika; Maryland, 1910 ***3259.35*** *p9*
Christian, Stephen 45; Ontario, 1871 ***1823.15*** *p41*
Christian, William; New York, 1803 ***8197.10*** *p214*
Christians, Alice; Maryland, 1666 ***2524.55*** *p52*
Christiansen, C. 28; Alaska, 1912 ***9196.1*** *p37*
Christiansen, C. 28; Yukon, 1912 ***9196.1*** *p37*
Christianson, Carl 38; Alaska, 1916 ***9196.1*** *p6*
Christianson, Carl 38; Yukon, 1916 ***9196.1*** *p6*
Christie, Adam; Florida, 1774 ***1640.10*** *p27*
Christie, Alexander; New York, 1815-1831 ***8197.10*** *p307*
Christie, Alexander; New York, 1831 ***8197.10*** *p355*
Christie, Duncan; South Carolina, 1882 ***1640.13*** *p20*
Christie, Francis Carnegie; Belize, 1854 ***1640.13*** *p21*
Christie, James; New York, 1794 ***8197.10*** *p3*
Christie, James; New York, 1806 ***8197.10*** *p30*
Christie, John; Pennsylvania, 1777 ***4629.10*** *p17*
Christie, Peter; Canada, 1827 ***1640.13*** *p21*
Christie, Robert; Florida, 1667 ***1640.10*** *p28*
Christie, Robert Stuart; Canada, 1892 ***1640.13*** *p21*
Christie, Thomas; Georgia, 1733 ***1640.10*** *p28*
Christie, Thomas; Georgia, 1760 ***1640.10*** *p28*
Christie, William; Charleston, South Carolina, 1838 ***1224.3*** *p14*
Christie, William; Georgia, 1776-1829 ***1640.10*** *p28*
Christis, Edward 24; Ontario, 1871 ***1823.15*** *p42*
Christison, Ann Hay; Colorado, 1892 ***1640.13*** *p21*
Christler, Georg; Port uncertain, 1738 ***2856.30*** *p66*
Christler, Jacob; Pennsylvania, 1777 ***4629.10*** *p25*
Christman, Charles G.; New York, 1823 ***8197.10*** *p217*
Christman, Daniel William; New York, 1834 ***8197.10*** *p358*
Christmann, Miss; Port uncertain, 1737 ***2856.30*** *p66*
Christmann, Adam; New York, 1837 ***8197.10*** *p80*
Christmann, Anna Catharina; Port uncertain, 1751 ***2856.30*** *p66*
Christmann, Anna Margarete; Port uncertain, 1767 ***2856.30*** *p66*
Christmann, Christof; Port uncertain, 1736 ***2856.30*** *p66*
With wife & 5 children
Christmann, Mrs. Daniel; America, 1730 ***2856.30*** *p66*
Christmann, Mrs. Daniel; America, 1743 ***2856.30*** *p66*
Christmann, Mrs. Franz Wilhelm; Port uncertain, 1790 ***2856.30*** *p66*
Christmann, Henrich; America, 1741 ***2856.30*** *p66*
Christmann, Maria Christina; Port uncertain, 1750 ***2856.30*** *p66*
Christmann, Peter; Port uncertain, 1760 ***2856.30*** *p66*
Christmann, Philippina; Port uncertain, 1751 ***2856.30*** *p66*
Christmas, George, Sr.; Vermont, 1847-1922 ***5900.10*** *p390*
Christmas, Kate Lander; Vermont, 1850-1917 ***5900.10*** *p390*
Christo, Mary Ann 67; Ontario, 1871 ***1823.22*** *p27*
Christy, Charles 14; Ontario, 1861 ***2896.27*** *p59*
Christy, Elizabeth 67; Ontario, 1861 ***2896.27*** *p69*
Christy, Elmira 18; Ontario, 1861 ***2896.27*** *p44*
Christy, Gideon 21; Ontario, 1861 ***2896.27*** *p69*
Christy, Henry W. 15; Ontario, 1861 ***2896.27*** *p44*
Christy, James A. 8; Ontario, 1861 ***2896.27*** *p44*
Christy, Jane 24; Ontario, 1861 ***2896.27*** *p69*
Christy, John; Pennsylvania, 1787 ***4629.10*** *p50*
Christy, John 26; Ontario, 1861 ***2896.27*** *p69*
Christy, Joseph; New York, 1830 ***8197.10*** *p353*
Christy, Mary 18; Ontario, 1861 ***2896.27*** *p59*
Christy, Mary 29; Ontario, 1861 ***2896.27*** *p68*
Christy, Mary 31; Ontario, 1861 ***2896.27*** *p59*
Christy, Sharlotte 42; Ontario, 1861 ***2896.27*** *p44*
Christy, Sophiah 5; Ontario, 1861 ***2896.27*** *p44*
Christy, Stuart 65; Ontario, 1861 ***2896.27*** *p69*
Christy, Thomas 16; Ontario, 1861 ***2896.27*** *p59*
Chrobak, Peter; Maryland, 1910 ***3259.35*** *p9*
Chrobak, Wadislaw; Maryland, 1910 ***3259.35*** *p9*
Chropshear, Mrs.; Maryland, 1658 ***2524.55*** *p47*
Husband: Thomas
Chropshear, Thomas *SEE* Chropshear, Mrs.
Chrowowska, Joseph; Maryland, 1910 ***3259.35*** *p9*
Chruschmak, Harry; Maryland, 1910 ***3259.35*** *p9*
Chrystie, Andrew; New York, 1807 ***8197.10*** *p36*
Chrystie, John; Virginia, 1718 ***1224.2*** *p21*
Chrzanouski, John; Maryland, 1910 ***3259.35*** *p9*
Chrzanowsky, Bronislawa; Maryland, 1910 ***3259.35*** *p9*
Chrzawski, John; Maryland, 1910 ***3259.35*** *p9*
Chswinka, Andrew; Maryland, 1910 ***3259.35*** *p9*
Chtteinken, Janthena; Pennsylvania, 1784 ***4629.10*** *p43*
Chubb, Jeremiah; New York, 1820 ***8197.10*** *p215*
Chubb, Lydia; New York, 1851 ***1224.3*** *p14*
Chuck, Joseph 26; Ontario, 1871 ***1823.28*** *p16*
Chuffey, Miss; Quebec, 1856 ***9196.15*** *p7*
Churasach, Joe 32; Washington, 1912 ***9196.1*** *p36*
Church, Daniel 21; Ontario, 1861 ***2896.25*** *p16*
Church, Deliah 69; Ontario, 1871 ***1823.15*** *p42*
Church, Edward 23; Maryland, 1775 ***1220.25*** *p116*
Church, George; New York, 1807 ***8197.10*** *p36*
Church, Hester 2; Ontario, 1861 ***2896.26*** *p35*
Church, John B. 9; Ontario, 1861 ***2896.25*** *p24*
Church, Marthy 23; Ontario, 1861 ***2896.26*** *p35*
Church, Mary; New Hampshire, 1746 ***1224.2*** *p21*
Church, Mary 17; Ontario, 1861 ***2896.26*** *p35*
Church, Mary J. 27; Ontario, 1861 ***2896.25*** *p24*
Church, Peter S. 4; Ontario, 1861 ***2896.25*** *p24*
Church, Richard L. 2; Ontario, 1861 ***2896.25*** *p24*
Church, Sarah 54; Ontario, 1861 ***2896.26*** *p35*
Church, Sarah 77; Ontario, 1871 ***1823.15*** *p42*
Church, Sarah M. 21; Ontario, 1861 ***2896.25*** *p24*
Church, Silvester 19; Ontario, 1861 ***2896.26*** *p35*
Church, Smith 13; Ontario, 1861 ***2896.26*** *p35*
Church, William; New York, 1838 ***8197.10*** *p113*
Church, William J. 6; Ontario, 1861 ***2896.25*** *p24*
Churchill, Arthur 48; Ontario, 1871 ***1823.15*** *p42*
Churchill, Asa 70; Ontario, 1871 ***1823.28*** *p16*
Churchill, Dorothy; Virginia, 1664 ***6212.30*** *p6*
Churchill, James 34; Ontario, 1871 ***1823.15*** *p42*
Churchill, John 59; Ontario, 1871 ***1823.15*** *p42*
Churchill, William 32; Ontario, 1871 ***1823.15*** *p42*
Churchill, William 64; Ontario, 1871 ***1823.15*** *p42*
Churll, Jno; Virginia, 1664 ***6212.30*** *p9*
Churnesko, Jozef; Maryland, 1910 ***3259.35*** *p9*
Churnley, Robert; New York, 1805 ***8197.10*** *p29*
Churton, Sarah; New York, 1843 ***1224.3*** *p14*
Chute, Henry; Virginia, 1664 ***6212.30*** *p8*
Chutkowski, Ignatius; New York, 1840 ***8197.10*** *p221*
Chwinsky, Vladislow; Maryland, 1910 ***3259.35*** *p10*
Chwinsky, Wladislow; Maryland, 1910 ***3259.35*** *p10*
Chymny, Michael; Maryland, 1910 ***3259.35*** *p10*
Ciant, Marke; Maryland, 1680 ***2524.55*** *p47*
Cibisky, Alexander A.; Maryland, 1910 ***3259.35*** *p10*
Cichocki, John; Maryland, 1910 ***3259.35*** *p10*
Cichocki, Martin; Maryland, 1910 ***3259.35*** *p10*
Cichon, Antonina; Maryland, 1910 ***3259.35*** *p10*
Cichon, Frank; Maryland, 1910 ***3259.35*** *p10*
Cichy, Frank; Maryland, 1910 ***3259.35*** *p10*
Cid, Arthur 43; Ontario, 1871 ***1823.22*** *p27*
Ciechanowski, Martin; Maryland, 1910 ***3259.35*** *p10*
Cieminsky, Tomas; Maryland, 1910 ***3259.35*** *p10*
Ciernikowsky, Joseph; Maryland, 1910 ***3259.35*** *p10*
Cieslak, Joseph; Maryland, 1910 ***3259.35*** *p10*
Cieslik, John; Maryland, 1910 ***3259.35*** *p10*
Ciewiskie, John; Maryland, 1910 ***3259.35*** *p10*
Ciolba, Mary A.; Maryland, 1910 ***3259.35*** *p10*
Cipes, Thomas; Maryland, 1681 ***2524.55*** *p47*
Cipinski, Frances; Maryland, 1910 ***3259.35*** *p10*
Ciszechowicz, John; Maryland, 1910 ***3259.35*** *p10*
Ciszek, George; Maryland, 1910 ***3259.35*** *p10*
City, Samuel G.; New York, 1832 ***8197.10*** *p356*
Ciutpimmeki, Peter; Maryland, 1910 ***3259.35*** *p10*
Ciyapinska, Antoni; Maryland, 1910 ***3259.35*** *p10*
Ckwill, William 21; Ontario, 1871 ***1823.15*** *p42*
Claas, Jacob; Port uncertain, 1775 ***2856.30*** *p66*
Claassen, Gerhard; New York, 1828 ***8197.10*** *p218*
Clachay, Arthur; Maryland, 1649 ***2524.55*** *p47*
Wife: Mary
Son: Charles
Clachay, Charles *SEE* Clachay, Arthur
Clachay, Mary *SEE* Clachay, Arthur
Clack, Abraham 23; Maryland, 1774 ***1220.25*** *p57*
Clack, Ellen Murphy; Vermont, 1859-1935 ***5900.10*** *p95*
Clack, Thomas; Vermont, 1852-1916 ***5900.10*** *p95*
Clackford, Jacob; Virginia, 1664 ***6212.30*** *p7*
Cladworthy, William John 50; Ontario, 1871 ***1823.28*** *p16*
Claffery, Margaret; Vermont, n.d. ***5900.10*** *p110*
Claffey, Edward; Pennsylvania, 1862 ***6058.10*** *p72*
Claffey, James; New York, 1840 ***8197.10*** *p163*
Claffey, John; New York, 1839 ***8197.10*** *p381*
Claiborne, William; Virginia, 1746 ***1224.2*** *p22*
Clair, Catherine Barnes; Vermont, 1883 ***5900.10*** *p603*
Clak, William 42; Ontario, 1871 ***1823.15*** *p42*
Clamer, Johann Peter; Port uncertain, 1748 ***2856.30*** *p67*
Clamm, Georg Michael; Port uncertain, 1764 ***2856.30*** *p67*
Clampton, Philip 26; Philadelphia, 1774 ***1220.25*** *p68*
Clampton, Thomas 21; Philadelphia, 1774 ***1220.25*** *p68*
Clancey, Margaret 73; Ontario, 1871 ***1823.15*** *p42*
Clancey, Mary 80; Ontario, 1871 ***1823.22*** *p27*
Clancey, Patrick; New York, 1836 ***8197.10*** *p79*
Clancy, . . .; Vermont, 1843 ***5900.10*** *p5*
Clancy, Catherine; Vermont, 1836-1914 ***5900.10*** *p447*
Clancy, Daniel 62; Vermont, 1891 ***5900.10*** *p587*
Clancy, Elizabeth E.; Vermont, 1861-1939 ***5900.10*** *p369*
Clancy, Ellen; Vermont, 1824-1859 ***5900.10*** *p585*
Clancy, Hanorah Maloney; Vermont, 1811-1898 ***5900.10*** *p369*
Clancy, Henry; Vermont, 1853-1918 ***5900.10*** *p369*
Clancy, James; Pennsylvania, 1868 ***6058.10*** *p74*
Clancy, Jeremiah; Philadelphia, 1819 ***6058.10*** *p8*
Clancy, John; New York, 1837 ***8197.10*** *p81*
Clancy, Julia 36; Vermont, 1886 ***5900.10*** *p423*
Clancy, Mary 50; Vermont, 1859 ***5900.10*** *p360*
Clancy, Mary 68; Vermont, 1899 ***5900.10*** *p587*
Clancy, Mary Dunn; Vermont, 1839-1924 ***5900.10*** *p491*
Clancy, Michael; Vermont, 1836-1908 ***5900.10*** *p491*
Clancy, Patrick 50; Ontario, 1871 ***1823.22*** *p27*
Clancy, Thomas; New York, 1840 ***8197.10*** *p163*
Clancy, Thomas; Vermont, 1818-1900 ***5900.10*** *p369*
Clancy, William; New York, 1828 ***1224.3*** *p14*
Clandellan, George; Maryland, 1682 ***2524.55*** *p47*
Clanell, William; Virginia, 1671 ***6212.30*** *p44*
Claney, James; New York, 1839 ***8197.10*** *p220*
Clangs, Daniel; Pennsylvania, 1776 ***4629.10*** *p53*
Clanny, James; New York, 1839 ***8197.10*** *p220*
Clanon, Simon; New York, 1820 ***8197.10*** *p215*
Clanon, Simon; New York, 1829 ***8197.10*** *p65*
Clansie, William; New York, 1828 ***1224.3*** *p14*
Clanson, Daniel; Maryland, 1670 ***2524.55*** *p47*
Clapham, Glover; New York, 1838 ***8197.10*** *p220*
Clapham, Samuel; New York, 1836 ***8197.10*** *p220*
Clapp, Miss 1; Ontario, 1861 ***2896.26*** *p26*
Clapp, Mrs. 27; Ontario, 1861 ***2896.26*** *p26*
Clapp, Allan 5; Ontario, 1861 ***2896.26*** *p26*
Clapp, Anson 2; Ontario, 1861 ***2896.26*** *p26*
Clapp, Catharine 20; Ontario, 1861 ***2896.26*** *p24*
Clapp, Cornelius 5; Ontario, 1861 ***2896.28*** *p50*
Clapp, E. 17; Ontario, 1861 ***2896.28*** *p10*
Clapp, Hannah M. 15; Ontario, 1861 ***2896.28*** *p44*
Clapp, Herbert S. 3; Ontario, 1861 ***2896.28*** *p46*
Clapp, Howard 5; Ontario, 1861 ***2896.26*** *p24*
Clapp, J. 4; Ontario, 1861 ***2896.28*** *p10*
Clapp, J. P. 23; Ontario, 1861 ***2896.28*** *p10*
Clapp, James 18; Ontario, 1861 ***2896.26*** *p24*
Clapp, Jane 8; Ontario, 1861 ***2896.26*** *p24*
Clapp, John 7; Ontario, 1861 ***2896.26*** *p26*
Clapp, Jonathon 10; Ontario, 1861 ***2896.26*** *p24*
Clapp, Joseph 14; Ontario, 1861 ***2896.26*** *p24*
Clapp, K. A. 40; Ontario, 1861 ***2896.28*** *p10*
Clapp, Lucetta 1; Ontario, 1861 ***2896.28*** *p50*
Clapp, Lucretia 35; Ontario, 1861 ***2896.28*** *p44*
Clapp, Lydia 36; Ontario, 1861 ***2896.28*** *p50*
Clapp, Margaret 7; Ontario, 1861 ***2896.28*** *p50*
Clapp, Margaret 15; Ontario, 1861 ***2896.28*** *p50*
Clapp, Margaret 23; Ontario, 1861 ***2896.28*** *p46*
Clapp, Margaret 69; Ontario, 1861 ***2896.28*** *p45*
Clapp, Nancy 62; Ontario, 1861 ***2896.28*** *p45*
Clapp, Nansey 22; Ontario, 1861 ***2896.26*** *p24*
Clapp, Phebe H. 10; Ontario, 1861 ***2896.28*** *p50*
Clapp, S. 10; Ontario, 1861 ***2896.28*** *p14*
Clapp, S. 11; Ontario, 1861 ***2896.28*** *p10*
Clapp, Samuel; New York, 1794 ***8197.10*** *p2*
Clapp, Samuel 56; Ontario, 1861 ***2896.26*** *p24*
Clapp, Sarah 19; Ontario, 1861 ***2896.28*** *p42*
Clapp, Sarah 30; Ontario, 1861 ***2896.28*** *p50*
Clapp, Sarah Ann 12; Ontario, 1861 ***2896.26*** *p24*
Clapp, Susan 11; Ontario, 1861 ***2896.28*** *p44*
Clapp, Susan 16; Ontario, 1861 ***2896.26*** *p24*
Clapp, William; New York, 1807 ***8197.10*** *p37*
Clapperton, James 55; Ontario, 1871 ***1823.22*** *p28*
Clapperton, Robert 53; Ontario, 1871 ***1823.22*** *p28*
Clappison, David C. 52; Ontario, 1871 ***1823.15*** *p42*
Clar, Jacob; America, 1740 ***2856.30*** *p67*
Clar, Stephan; America, 1738 ***2856.30*** *p68*
Clarck, Robert; Virginia, 1690-1691 ***6212.30*** *p59*
Clare, Alfred; Philadelphia, 1835 ***1224.3*** *p14*
Clare, Bridgett; Virginia, 1672 ***6212.30*** *p48*
Clare, Charlotte Susannah; Galveston, Texas, 1855 ***1224.3*** *p82*
Clare, Frances; Maryland, 1681 ***2524.55*** *p47*
Clare, John; Maryland, 1666 ***2524.55*** *p47*
Clare, John 22; Philadelphia, 1774 ***1220.25*** *p80*
Clare, John-George; Maryland, 1680 ***2524.55*** *p47*

Clare, Joseph; South Carolina, 1731 1224.2 p21
Clareston, Ann; Maryland, 1666 2524.55 p47
Claret, Rev.; Quebec, 1857 9196.15 p24
Clarey, Adward 4; Ontario, 1861 2896.27 p71
Clarey, Bridget 51; Vermont, 1878 5900.10 p228
Clarey, Clarinda 8; Ontario, 1861 2896.27 p71
Clarey, Elizabeth 11; Ontario, 1861 2896.27 p71
Clarey, Ella Driscoll; Vermont, 1850-1933 5900.10 p243
Clarey, Ellen J. 13; Ontario, 1861 2896.27 p71
Clarey, Luis 17; Ontario, 1861 2896.27 p71
Clarey, Margaret; Vermont, 1847-1932 5900.10 p176
Clarey, Michael 39; Ontario, 1861 2896.27 p71
Clarey, Patrick; Maryland, 1676 2524.55 p47
Claridge, James; New York, 1821 8197.10 p216
Claridge, Thomas; Pennsylvania, 1777 4629.10 p25
Claringburn, Charles; New York, 1821 8197.10 p215
Clark, . . .; Boston, 1737 4628.40 p114
Clark, . . .; Georgia, 1737 1640.10 p30
Clark, Miss; Quebec, 1858 9196.15 p34
Clark, Mrs. 28; Ontario, 1861 2896.26 p25
Clark, Mrs. 48; Ontario, 1861 2896.26 p24
Clark, Mrs. 55; Ontario, 1871 1823.15 p43
Clark, A. Jane 16; Ontario, 1861 2896.25 p4
Clark, A. L. 5; Ontario, 1861 2896.25 p3
Clark, A. M. 23; Ontario, 1861 2896.28 p15
Clark, Adlaid 19; Ontario, 1861 2896.28 p18
Clark, Agnes 32; Ontario, 1861 2896.27 p30
Clark, Alex 26; Vancouver, British Columbia, 1913 9196.1 p58
Clark, Alex 26; Washington, 1913 9196.1 p58
Clark, Alexander; Georgia, 1739 1640.10 p28
Clark, Alexander; Maryland, 1681 2524.55 p47
Clark, Alexander; New Jersey, 1877 1640.13 p21
Clark, Alexander; New York, 1802 8197.10 p19
Clark, Alexander; Virginia, 1665 6212.30 p20
Clark, Alexander 3; Ontario, 1861 2896.26 p22
Clark, Alexander 30; Ontario, 1871 1823.15 p42
Clark, Alexander 73; Ontario, 1871 1823.22 p28
Clark, Alice Gormley 70; Vermont, 1903 5900.10 p177
Clark, Alinda 34; Ontario, 1861 2896.28 p7
Clark, Allan; New York, 1805 8197.10 p29
Clark, Allice 5; Ontario, 1861 2896.25 p2
Clark, Almira 4; Ontario, 1861 2896.25 p8
Clark, Almon J.; Vermont, 1853-1932 5900.10 p164
Clark, Alvaretta 3; Ontario, 1861 2896.28 p32
Clark, Alzina 1; Ontario, 1861 2896.25 p21
Clark, Amarilla 7; Ontario, 1861 2896.25 p21
Clark, Amelia 22; Ontario, 1861 2896.27 p54
Clark, Andrew; Virginia, 1664 6212.30 p11
Clark, Ann SEE Clark, John
Clark, Ann; Vermont, 1830-1875 5900.10 p131
Clark, Ann; Vermont, 1839-1887 5900.10 p542
Clark, Ann 36; Ontario, 1861 2896.28 p42
Clark, Ann 69; Ontario, 1871 1823.15 p42
Clark, Anne; Vermont, 1854-1924 5900.10 p184
Clark, Anne T. Kennedy 58; Vermont, 1903 5900.10 p164
Clark, Annie 14 days; Vermont, 1867 5900.10 p177
Clark, Archibald 85; Ontario, 1871 1823.22 p28
Clark, Beatman 15; Ontario, 1861 2896.27 p46
Clark, Benjamin 18; Ontario, 1861 2896.27 p42
Clark, Betsey Almira 64; Vermont, 1878 5900.10 p493
Clark, Bridget A. 38; Vermont, 1896 5900.10 p581
Clark, Bridget Corley; Vermont, 1920 5900.10 p175
Clark, Bridget McDonough; Vermont, 1832-1878 5900.10 p184
Clark, Bridget McEneany; Vermont, 1813-1883 5900.10 p233
Clark, C. 17; Ontario, 1861 2896.28 p12
Clark, C. 19; Ontario, 1861 2896.28 p17
Clark, C. V. 24; Ontario, 1861 2896.27 p9
Clark, Catharine Bray 75; Vermont, 1882 5900.10 p270
Clark, Catherine; Vermont, 1859-1902 5900.10 p409
Clark, Catherine S. 12; Ontario, 1861 2896.27 p42
Clark, Charles 12; Ontario, 1861 2896.28 p32
Clark, Charles 54; Ontario, 1871 1823.22 p28
Clark, Charles G. 3; Ontario, 1861 2896.27 p47
Clark, Charles Henry; Vermont, 1853-1925 5900.10 p176
Clark, Chester 9; Ontario, 1861 2896.27 p53
Clark, Christina 1; Ontario, 1861 2896.25 p21
Clark, Collin 40; Ontario, 1871 1823.15 p42
Clark, Cory S. 17; Ontario, 1861 2896.27 p53
Clark, D. Clinton 49; Ontario, 1871 1823.22 p28
Clark, Dama 17; Ontario, 1861 2896.28 p32
Clark, Danail 38; Ontario, 1871 1823.15 p42
Clark, Daniel; Augusta, Georgia, 1757 1224.2 p21
Clark, Daniel; Georgia, 1739 1640.10 p28
Clark, Daniel; Vermont, 1838-1884 5900.10 p187
Clark, Daniel 6 months; Vermont, 1862 5900.10 p177
Clark, Daniel 45; Ontario, 1871 1823.22 p28
Clark, Daniel W.; New York, 1840 8197.10 p159
Clark, Daniel W. 6; Ontario, 1861 2896.27 p46
Clark, David; New York, 1839 8197.10 p133
Clark, David; Pennsylvania, 1778 4629.10 p35
Clark, David; Pennsylvania, 1779 4629.10 p37
Clark, David 6; Ontario, 1861 2896.26 p25
Clark, David 50; Ontario, 1871 1823.15 p42
Clark, Davis 2; Ontario, 1861 2896.28 p44
Clark, Deborah Ann 27; Ontario, 1861 2896.27 p54
Clark, Dennis; Pennsylvania, 1779 4629.10 p37
Clark, Donald; Georgia, 1739 1640.10 p29
Clark, Duncan 33; Ontario, 1871 1823.22 p28
Clark, Duncan 47; Ontario, 1871 1823.22 p28
Clark, Duncan 59; Ontario, 1871 1823.22 p28
Clark, E.; Mobile, Alabama, 1824-1845 1640.10 p29
Clark, E. 6; Ontario, 1861 2896.28 p15
Clark, Edward; Vermont, 1833-1926 5900.10 p459
Clark, Edwd 36; Ontario, 1871 1823.28 p16
Clark, Eleanor 72; Ontario, 1871 1823.22 p28
Clark, Elgin 6; Ontario, 1861 2896.26 p24
Clark, Elias; Ontario, 1861 2896.25 p2
Clark, Elias 1; Ontario, 1861 2896.28 p44
Clark, Elias 11; Ontario, 1861 2896.25 p4
Clark, Eliza; Vermont, 1916 5900.10 p390
Clark, Eliza 21; Ontario, 1871 1823.15 p42
Clark, Elizabeth SEE Clark, John
Clark, Elizabeth 65; Ontario, 1861 2896.28 p32
Clark, Elizabeth A. 11; Ontario, 1861 2896.25 p21
Clark, Elizabeth D.; Vermont, 1867-1957 5900.10 p187
Clark, Elizabeth McKenna; Vermont, 1841-1910 5900.10 p441
Clark, Ellen; Ontario, 1861 2896.25 p4
Clark, Ellen 29; Ontario, 1861 2896.25 p2
Clark, Ellen 30; Vermont, 1850-1859 5900.10 p189
Clark, Ellen 80; Ontario, 1871 1823.22 p28
Clark, Elly 53; Ontario, 1861 2896.27 p54
Clark, Emily 22; Ontario, 1861 2896.27 p54
Clark, Emily A. 3; Ontario, 1861 2896.27 p43
Clark, Emma 3; Ontario, 1861 2896.28 p18
Clark, Emma 21; Ontario, 1861 2896.28 p18
Clark, Emma L. 11; Ontario, 1861 2896.25 p3
Clark, Emphumia 53; Ontario, 1871 1823.15 p42
Clark, Enock 66; Ontario, 1861 2896.26 p29
Clark, Ephraim; Pennsylvania, 1777 4629.10 p24
Clark, Ester A. 20; Ontario, 1861 2896.27 p42
Clark, Ester J. 12; Ontario, 1861 2896.27 p47
Clark, Esther; Vermont, 1861-1917 5900.10 p206
Clark, Ezekiel 13; Ontario, 1861 2896.27 p33
Clark, Fanny V. 5; Ontario, 1861 2896.27 p42
Clark, Flora 9; Ontario, 1861 2896.27 p42
Clark, Francis; Virginia, 1664 6212.30 p13
Clark, Frederick; New York, 1833 8197.10 p219
Clark, G. 40; Ontario, 1861 2896.26 p25
Clark, George; Jamaica, 1781 1640.13 p21
Clark, George; New Castle Co., Delaware, 1812 1224.3 p14
Clark, George 13; Ontario, 1861 2896.28 p32
Clark, George 18; Virginia, 1773 1220.25 p29
Clark, George 32; Ontario, 1871 1823.28 p16
Clark, George 35; Ontario, 1871 1823.15 p42
Clark, Godfry; Virginia, 1666 6212.30 p29
Clark, Hannah 26; Ontario, 1861 2896.28 p44
Clark, Harriet A. 19; Ontario, 1861 2896.27 p53
Clark, Helen; Vermont, 1824-1918 5900.10 p321
Clark, Henry; Ontario, 1861 2896.28 p32
Clark, Henry; Pennsylvania, 1727 1224.2 p21
Clark, Henry 20; Ontario, 1861 2896.25 p21
Clark, Henry 33; Vermont, 1869 5900.10 p382
Clark, Herman 1; Ontario, 1861 2896.25 p8
Clark, Hester 18; Ontario, 1861 2896.26 p24
Clark, Honora 27; Vermont, 1862 5900.10 p177
Clark, Hugh; Georgia, 1757 1640.10 p29
Clark, Hugh; New York, 1802 8197.10 p19
Clark, Hugh 64; Ontario, 1871 1823.15 p42
Clark, Isaac 58; Ontario, 1871 1823.28 p16
Clark, Isabella 11; Ontario, 1861 2896.28 p19
Clark, Isabella 14; Ontario, 1861 2896.27 p29
Clark, J.; Portland, Maine, 1857 9196.15 p12
Clark, J. 17; Ontario, 1861 2896.28 p15
Clark, J. P.; Quebec, 1857 9196.15 p18
Clark, J. W. 16; Ontario, 1861 2896.28 p6
Clark, Jacob 13; Ontario, 1861 2896.25 p21
Clark, Jacob 23; Maryland, 1774 1220.25 p65
Clark, Jacob 50; Ontario, 1871 1823.22 p28
Clark, Jacob 64; Ontario, 1861 2896.28 p32
Clark, James; Florida, 1786 1640.10 p29
Clark, James; Illinois, 1842 1224.3 p14
Clark, James; Maryland, 1680 2524.55 p47
Clark, James; New York, 1830 8197.10 p362
Clark, James; New York, 1837 8197.10 p81
Clark, James; Pennsylvania, 1777 4629.10 p31
Clark, James; Pennsylvania, 1862 6058.10 p45
Clark, James; Vermont, 1820-1900 5900.10 p616
Clark, James 6; Ontario, 1861 2896.27 p63
Clark, James 9; Ontario, 1861 2896.28 p32
Clark, James 17; Ontario, 1861 2896.26 p22
Clark, James 24; Ontario, 1871 1823.15 p42
Clark, James 31; Ontario, 1871 1823.28 p16
Clark, James 32; Ontario, 1871 1823.22 p28
Clark, James 38; Ontario, 1871 1823.15 p42
Clark, James 42; Ontario, 1871 1823.28 p16
Clark, James 43; British Columbia, 1909 9196.1 p25
Clark, James 43; Ontario, 1871 1823.22 p28
Clark, James 43; Washington, 1909 9196.1 p25
Clark, James 66; Ontario, 1871 1823.15 p42
Clark, James Alderson; Savannah, Georgia, 1829 1224.3 p14
Clark, James H. 11; Ontario, 1861 2896.27 p47
Clark, James Richard; Vermont, 1856-1886 5900.10 p176
Clark, James W. 42; Ontario, 1861 2896.25 p3
Clark, Jane; Ontario, 1861 2896.25 p2
Clark, Jane 11; Ontario, 1861 2896.26 p22
Clark, Jane 27; Ontario, 1861 2896.27 p47
Clark, Janet; Ontario, 1874 1640.13 p21
Clark, Jared 13; Ontario, 1861 2896.28 p18
Clark, Jno; Vermont, n.d. 5900.10 p106
Clark, Jno; Virginia, 1671 6212.30 p42
Clark, Johanna Fitzgibbons 65; Vermont, 1889 5900.10 p106
Clark, John SEE Clark, John
Clark, John; Georgia, 1699 1640.13 p21
Clark, John; Georgia, 1738 1640.10 p29
Clark, John; Louisiana, 1779-1845 1640.10 p29
Clark, John; Maryland, 1650 2524.55 p47
Wife: Elizabeth
Child: John
Child: Ann
Clark, John; New Orleans, 1800-1845 1640.10 p29
Clark, John; New York, 1807 8197.10 p325
Clark, John; New York, 1834 8197.10 p70
Clark, John; New York, 1840 8197.10 p159
Clark, John; Pennsylvania, 1786 4629.10 p54
Clark, John; Pennsylvania, 1846 1224.3 p14
Clark, John; South Carolina, 1758-1789 1640.10 p29
Clark, John; Vermont, 1821-1899 5900.10 p184
Clark, John; Vermont, 1843-1909 5900.10 p187
Clark, John; Virginia, 1664 6212.30 p11
Clark, John; Virginia, 1666 6212.30 p25
Clark, John 1; Ontario, 1861 2896.25 p2
Clark, John 18; Philadelphia, 1774 1220.25 p80
Clark, John 23; Maryland, 1775 1220.25 p111
Clark, John 24; Ontario, 1861 2896.26 p22
Clark, John 28; Virginia, 1774 1220.25 p87
Clark, John 33; Vermont, 1875 5900.10 p411
Clark, John 40; Ontario, 1871 1823.15 p42
Clark, John 41; Ontario, 1871 1823.15 p42
Clark, John 44; Ontario, 1871 1823.22 p28
Clark, John 47; Ontario, 1871 1823.15 p42
Clark, John 50; Ontario, 1871 1823.22 p28
Clark, John 52; Ontario, 1871 1823.28 p16
Clark, John 54; Ontario, 1871 1823.22 p28
Clark, John 55; Nova Scotia, 1774 1220.25 p135
Clark, John 55; Ontario, 1871 1823.22 p28
Clark, John 60; Ontario, 1871 1823.15 p42
Clark, John 72; Ontario, 1871 1823.15 p42
Clark, John 82; Ontario, 1871 1823.22 p28
Clark, John A.; Vermont, 1857-1953 5900.10 p233
Clark, John A. 10; Ontario, 1861 2896.27 p47
Clark, John C.; Vermont, 1826-1888 5900.10 p441
Clark, John F. 2; Ontario, 1861 2896.27 p53
Clark, John P. 25; Ontario, 1871 1823.22 p28
Clark, Jonathan A. 9; Ontario, 1861 2896.27 p63
Clark, Joseph; New York, 1766 1224.2 p22
Clark, Joseph; New York, 1834 8197.10 p359
Clark, Joseph 18; Philadelphia, 1774 1220.25 p34
Clark, Joseph 21; Virginia, 1774 1220.25 p45
Clark, Joseph 43; Ontario, 1871 1823.15 p42
Clark, Joseph 58; Ontario, 1871 1823.15 p42
Clark, Joseph B. 14; Ontario, 1861 2896.25 p3
Clark, Joseph George; New York, 1845 1224.3 p15
Clark, Julia A. 5; Ontario, 1861 2896.28 p32
Clark, Katherine J.; Vermont, 1847-1914 5900.10 p489
Clark, Katherine Sheehan; Vermont, 1848-1935 5900.10 p187
Clark, Leonorah 9; Ontario, 1861 2896.27 p42
Clark, Levi 44; Ontario, 1871 1823.22 p28
Clark, Lewis 4; Ontario, 1861 2896.26 p24
Clark, Lewis W. 5; Ontario, 1861 2896.27 p47
Clark, Lucinda 45; Ontario, 1861 2896.28 p18
Clark, Luke 12; Ontario, 1861 2896.26 p24
Clark, Lyda 4; Ontario, 1861 2896.27 p63
Clark, Lydia; Ontario, 1861 2896.28 p43
Clark, Lydia 11; Ontario, 1861 2896.27 p30
Clark, Lydia 14; Ontario, 1861 2896.27 p29
Clark, Lydia 33; Ontario, 1861 2896.28 p32
Clark, Lydia 94; Ontario, 1871 1823.22 p28
Clark, Lydia C. 1; Ontario, 1861 2896.27 p42

Clark, Lydia J. 1; Ontario, 1861 ***2896.27*** *p43*
Clark, M. 27; Ontario, 1861 ***2896.27*** *p9*
Clark, Malcolm; New York, 1837 ***8197.10*** *p82*
Clark, Marcus 2; Ontario, 1861 ***2896.27*** *p63*
Clark, Margaret; Vermont, 1826-1903 ***5900.10*** *p445*
Clark, Margaret 7; Ontario, 1861 ***2896.26*** *p22*
Clark, Margaret 8; Ontario, 1861 ***2896.25*** *p8*
Clark, Margaret 16; Ontario, 1861 ***2896.28*** *p18*
Clark, Margaret 26; Baltimore, 1775 ***1220.25*** *p119*
Clark, Margaret 36; Ontario, 1861 ***2896.27*** *p46*
Clark, Margaret 36; Ontario, 1871 ***1823.15*** *p42*
Clark, Margaret 40; Ontario, 1871 ***1823.15*** *p42*
Clark, Margaret 41; Vermont, 1882 ***5900.10*** *p294*
Clark, Margaret 88; Vermont, 1906 ***5900.10*** *p567*
Clark, Margaret J. 16; Ontario, 1861 ***2896.27*** *p42*
Clark, Margarett; Maryland, 1680 ***2524.55*** *p47*
Clark, Margerat 78; Ontario, 1871 ***1823.15*** *p42*
Clark, Mariah 2; Ontario, 1861 ***2896.26*** *p22*
Clark, Mark 39; Ontario, 1871 ***1823.15*** *p42*
Clark, Martha A. 4; Ontario, 1861 ***2896.27*** *p47*
Clark, Martin; Vermont, 1899 ***5900.10*** *p175*
Clark, Martin 33; Ontario, 1871 ***1823.22*** *p28*
Clark, Mary; Vermont, 1815-1892 ***5900.10*** *p205*
Clark, Mary; Vermont, 1863-1935 ***5900.10*** *p177*
Clark, Mary 9; Ontario, 1861 ***2896.26*** *p24*
Clark, Mary 13 *SEE* Clark, William
Clark, Mary 22; Ontario, 1861 ***2896.27*** *p43*
Clark, Mary 30; Ontario, 1861 ***2896.25*** *p8*
Clark, Mary 96; Vermont, 1903 ***5900.10*** *p412*
Clark, Mary A. 6; Ontario, 1861 ***2896.28*** *p18*
Clark, Mary A. 24; Vermont, 1872 ***5900.10*** *p159*
Clark, Mary A. 45; Ontario, 1871 ***1823.15*** *p42*
Clark, Mary Ann 9; Vermont, 1861 ***5900.10*** *p176*
Clark, Mary Ann 57; Ontario, 1871 ***1823.22*** *p28*
Clark, Mary E. 16; Ontario, 1861 ***2896.27*** *p47*
Clark, Mary E. 21; Ontario, 1861 ***2896.27*** *p42*
Clark, Mary Jane; Vermont, 1856-1900 ***5900.10*** *p184*
Clark, Mary M. 17; Ontario, 1861 ***2896.25*** *p2*
Clark, Mathew; New York, 1821 ***8197.10*** *p216*
Clark, Matilda 31; Ontario, 1861 ***2896.28*** *p32*
Clark, Matilda Carroll; Vermont, 1823-1901 ***5900.10*** *p616*
Clark, Michael; Vermont, 1798-1886 ***5900.10*** *p233*
Clark, Michael 59; Vermont, 1873 ***5900.10*** *p570*
Clark, Michael 60; Vermont, 1892 ***5900.10*** *p177*
Clark, Nathan; New York, 1820 ***8197.10*** *p61*
Clark, Nellie 4; Vermont, 1876 ***5900.10*** *p177*
Clark, Newton 18; Ontario, 1871 ***1823.15*** *p43*
Clark, Nicholas; Vermont, 1837-1902 ***5900.10*** *p233*
Clark, Nicholas J. 27; Ontario, 1871 ***1823.15*** *p43*
Clark, Norman 18; Ontario, 1871 ***1823.28*** *p16*
Clark, Orig 24; Ontario, 1871 ***1823.15*** *p43*
Clark, P. H.; Quebec, 1856 ***9196.15*** *p10*
Clark, Parsons; Pennsylvania, 1777 ***4629.10*** *p16*
Clark, Patrick; Canada, 1756-1760 ***4628.40*** *p45*
Clark, Patrick; Vermont, 1827-1918 ***5900.10*** *p176*
Clark, Patrick; Vermont, 1834-1915 ***5900.10*** *p47*
Clark, Patrick 62; Ontario, 1871 ***1823.15*** *p43*
Clark, Patrick William 1; Vermont, 1863 ***5900.10*** *p176*
Clark, Permilla 37; Ontario, 1861 ***2896.26*** *p20*
Clark, Peter; Maryland, 1680 ***2524.55*** *p47*
Clark, Peter 27; Ontario, 1861 ***2896.25*** *p2*
Clark, Phebe 42; Ontario, 1861 ***2896.27*** *p42*
Clark, Phebe A. 10; Ontario, 1861 ***2896.25*** *p21*
Clark, Phebe A. 16; Ontario, 1861 ***2896.27*** *p63*
Clark, Phebe Ann 16; Ontario, 1861 ***2896.28*** *p29*
Clark, Phebe E. 6; Ontario, 1861 ***2896.27*** *p42*
Clark, Phebe J. 15; Ontario, 1861 ***2896.27*** *p53*
Clark, Philip 8; Ontario, 1861 ***2896.28*** *p19*
Clark, Phinley M. 17; Ontario, 1861 ***2896.27*** *p63*
Clark, Pryd; Maryland, 1681 ***2524.55*** *p47*
Clark, Pulaster 27; Ontario, 1871 ***1823.28*** *p16*
Clark, R. P. 54; Ontario, 1861 ***2896.28*** *p15*
Clark, Rachael 3 *SEE* Clark, William
Clark, Ranston 5; Ontario, 1861 ***2896.25*** *p21*
Clark, Rebecca Sullivan; Vermont, 1840-1878 ***5900.10*** *p187*
Clark, Richard 9 *SEE* Clark, William
Clark, Richard 15; Ontario, 1871 ***1823.15*** *p43*
Clark, Richard 25; Ontario, 1871 ***1823.28*** *p16*
Clark, Richard 30; Jamaica, 1774 ***1220.25*** *p86*
Clark, Richard 41; Ontario, 1871 ***1823.22*** *p28*
Clark, Richard 50; Nova Scotia, 1774 ***1220.25*** *p135*
Clark, Richard W.; New York, 1840 ***8197.10*** *p162*
Clark, Robert; Maryland, 1636 ***2524.55*** *p47*
Clark, Robert 1; Ontario, 1861 ***2896.27*** *p47*
Clark, Robert 25; Maryland, 1774 ***1220.25*** *p70*
Clark, Robert 34; Ontario, 1871 ***1823.15*** *p43*
Clark, Robert 36; Ontario, 1871 ***1823.15*** *p43*
Clark, Robert 45; Ontario, 1871 ***1823.15*** *p43*
Clark, Robert 54; Ontario, 1871 ***1823.15*** *p43*
Clark, Robert C.; New York, 1839 ***8197.10*** *p133*
Clark, Rose; Vermont, 1854-1928 ***5900.10*** *p564*
Clark, Rose Ann 59; Vermont, 1887 ***5900.10*** *p570*
Clark, S. 9; Ontario, 1861 ***2896.28*** *p15*
Clark, S. J. 1; Ontario, 1861 ***2896.28*** *p15*
Clark, Samuel 50; Ontario, 1871 ***1823.15*** *p43*
Clark, Sarah; Vermont, 1838-1907 ***5900.10*** *p47*
Clark, Sarah; Virginia, 1835 ***1224.3*** *p15*
Clark, Sarah 14; Ontario, 1861 ***2896.26*** *p24*
Clark, Sarah 17; Ontario, 1861 ***2896.25*** *p3*
Clark, Sarah 20; Ontario, 1861 ***2896.27*** *p29*
Clark, Sarah 32; Ontario, 1861 ***2896.27*** *p63*
Clark, Sarah A. 42; Ontario, 1861 ***2896.25*** *p21*
Clark, Sarah E. 12; Ontario, 1861 ***2896.27*** *p53*
Clark, Sarah E. 14; Ontario, 1861 ***2896.27*** *p63*
Clark, Sarah E. 18; Ontario, 1861 ***2896.27*** *p47*
Clark, Sarah J. 2; Ontario, 1861 ***2896.27*** *p47*
Clark, Selick 53; Ontario, 1861 ***2896.27*** *p53*
Clark, Sidney 17; Ontario, 1861 ***2896.26*** *p25*
Clark, Smith; New York, 1820 ***8197.10*** *p214*
Clark, Solomon 16; Ontario, 1861 ***2896.28*** *p33*
Clark, Stephen 8; Ontario, 1861 ***2896.27*** *p63*
Clark, Stephen 13; Ontario, 1861 ***2896.25*** *p8*
Clark, Stephen H. 2; Ontario, 1861 ***2896.28*** *p42*
Clark, Susan 25; Ontario, 1861 ***2896.28*** *p50*
Clark, Susan 38; Ontario, 1861 ***2896.25*** *p3*
Clark, Susan H. 11; Ontario, 1861 ***2896.28*** *p18*
Clark, Susanna 17; Maryland, 1773-1774 ***1220.25*** *p33*
Clark, Thomas; New York, 1840 ***8197.10*** *p163*
Clark, Thomas; Pennsylvania, 1777 ***4629.10*** *p22*
Clark, Thomas 18; Virginia, 1774 ***1220.25*** *p74*
Clark, Thomas 21; Baltimore, 1775 ***1220.25*** *p117*
Clark, Thomas 28; Ontario, 1871 ***1823.15*** *p43*
Clark, Thomas 33; America, 1774 ***1220.25*** *p35*
Clark, Thomas 39; Maryland, 1774 ***1220.25*** *p74*
Clark, Thomas 40; Maryland, 1774 ***1220.25*** *p37*
Clark, Thomas 59; Ontario, 1871 ***1823.15*** *p43*
Clark, Thomas 59; Vermont, 1868 ***5900.10*** *p205*
Clark, Thomas 67; Ontario, 1871 ***1823.22*** *p29*
Clark, Thomas 70; Ontario, 1871 ***1823.15*** *p43*
Clark, Thomas, Sr. 80; Ontario, 1871 ***1823.28*** *p16*
Clark, Thomas B.; New York, 1806 ***8197.10*** *p322*
Clark, Thomas H.; New York, 1840 ***8197.10*** *p159*
Clark, Thomas W.; New York, 1840 ***8197.10*** *p163*
Clark, Timothy; Vermont, 1818-1902 ***5900.10*** *p445*
Clark, Walter Riley 53; Ontario, 1871 ***1823.22*** *p29*
Clark, Westor; Pennsylvania, 1786 ***4629.10*** *p49*
Clark, William; Georgia, 1757 ***1640.10*** *p30*
Clark, William; Illinois, 1842 ***1224.3*** *p15*
Clark, William; New York, 1821 ***8197.10*** *p216*
Clark, William; New York, 1838 ***8197.10*** *p112*
Clark, William; New York, 1839 ***8197.10*** *p382*
Clark, William; Ohio, 1877 ***1640.13*** *p21*
Clark, William; Pennsylvania, 1777 ***4629.10*** *p7*
Clark, William; Pennsylvania, 1783 ***1224.2*** *p22*
Clark, William 10 *SEE* Clark, William
Clark, William 19; Maryland, 1774 ***1220.25*** *p64*
Clark, William 22; Jamaica, 1773 ***1220.25*** *p28*
Clark, William 25; Ontario, 1871 ***1823.15*** *p43*
Clark, William 27; Ontario, 1871 ***1823.15*** *p43*
Clark, William 29; Maryland, 1775 ***1220.25*** *p102*
Clark, William 30; America, 1774 ***1220.25*** *p35*
Clark, William 30; Ontario, 1871 ***1823.15*** *p43*
Clark, William 38; Ontario, 1871 ***1823.15*** *p43*
Clark, William 42; Annapolis, Nova Scotia, 1775 ***1220.25*** *p21*
Child: Mary 13
Child: William 10
Child: Richard 9
Child: Rachael 3
Clark, William 43; Ontario, 1871 ***1823.15*** *p43*
Clark, William 44; Ontario, 1871 ***1823.15*** *p43*
Clark, William 49; Ontario, 1871 ***1823.15*** *p43*
Clark, William 55; Ontario, 1861 ***2896.26*** *p22*
Clark, William 60; Ontario, 1871 ***1823.22*** *p29*
Clark, William 62; Ontario, 1871 ***1823.15*** *p43*
Clark, William 63; Ontario, 1871 ***1823.22*** *p29*
Clark, William 66; Ontario, 1871 ***1823.15*** *p43*
Clark, William 80; Ontario, 1861 ***2896.27*** *p42*
Clark, William A. 11; Ontario, 1861 ***2896.27*** *p63*
Clark, William B. 4; Ontario, 1861 ***2896.27*** *p42*
Clark, William Bennet; Texas, 1886 ***1640.13*** *p21*
Clark, William H. 4; Ontario, 1861 ***2896.27*** *p53*
Clark, William H. 73; Vermont, 1887 ***5900.10*** *p294*
Clark, William J. 23; Ontario, 1861 ***2896.25*** *p3*
Clark, William W. 3; Ontario, 1861 ***2896.25*** *p2*
Clark, Wm 40; Ontario, 1871 ***1823.28*** *p16*
Clarke, Captain; Quebec, 1858 ***9196.15*** *p46*
Clarke, Mr.; Portland, Maine, 1858 ***9196.15*** *p47*
Clarke, Mr.; Quebec, 1856 ***9196.15*** *p7*
Clarke, Mr. 38; Dominica, 1774 ***1220.25*** *p128*
Clarke, Mrs.; Portland, Maine, 1858 ***9196.15*** *p29*
Clarke, Mrs.; Quebec, 1858 ***9196.15*** *p46*
Clarke, Abraham; Maryland, 1655 ***2524.55*** *p47*
Clarke, Abraham; Maryland, 1680 ***2524.55*** *p47*
Clarke, Alexander 53; Ontario, 1871 ***1823.28*** *p16*
Clarke, Andrew; Maryland, 1691 ***1224.1*** *p13*
Clarke, Andrew; New York, 1839 ***8197.10*** *p220*
Clarke, Ann *SEE* Clarke, John
Clarke, Ann; Maryland, 1668 ***2524.55*** *p47*
Clarke, Ann 56; Ontario, 1871 ***1823.28*** *p16*
Clarke, Annie; Vermont, 1822-1894 ***5900.10*** *p302*
Clarke, Barnabas 21; Virginia, 1775 ***1220.25*** *p109*
Clarke, Catherine Maloney; Vermont, 1853-1918 ***5900.10*** *p477*
Clarke, Charles 33; Ontario, 1871 ***1823.15*** *p43*
Clarke, Daniel; New York, 1836 ***8197.10*** *p319*
Clarke, David; Portland, Maine, 1858 ***9196.15*** *p29*
Clarke, Donald, Sr. 40; Ontario, 1871 ***1823.28*** *p16*
Clarke, Donald, Jr. 30; Ontario, 1871 ***1823.28*** *p16*
Clarke, E. 60; Ontario, 1861 ***2896.26*** *p14*
Clarke, Edward; Maryland, 1675 ***2524.55*** *p47*
Clarke, Edward; New York, 1840 ***8197.10*** *p163*
Clarke, Edwin; Portland, Maine, 1858 ***9196.15*** *p30*
Clarke, Elizabeth; Long Island, 1845 ***1224.3*** *p14*
Clarke, Ellen; Vermont, 1837-1853 ***5900.10*** *p477*
Clarke, Fanny A. 3; Ontario, 1861 ***2896.27*** *p40*
Clarke, Francis; Maryland, 1669 ***2524.55*** *p221*
Clarke, Frank 48; Ontario, 1871 ***1823.28*** *p16*
Clarke, Frank X.; Vermont, 1839-1886 ***5900.10*** *p477*
Clarke, Frederick; Carolina, 1700 ***1224.2*** *p21*
Clarke, Frederick; Quebec, 1858 ***9196.15*** *p45*
Clarke, George; Maryland, 1680 ***2524.55*** *p47*
Clarke, George; New England, 1700 ***1224.2*** *p21*
Clarke, George; New York, 1810 ***8197.10*** *p214*
Clarke, George; New York, 1838 ***1224.3*** *p14*
Clarke, George 36; Ontario, 1871 ***1823.15*** *p43*
Clarke, George 37; Ontario, 1871 ***1823.28*** *p16*
Clarke, George 60; Ontario, 1871 ***1823.28*** *p16*
Clarke, Grace; Maryland, 1660 ***2524.55*** *p47*
Clarke, Harry M.; Vermont, 1822-1881 ***5900.10*** *p302*
Clarke, Henry; Portland, Maine, 1858 ***9196.15*** *p29*
Clarke, Hutchinson; Havana, 1765 ***1224.2*** *p21*
Clarke, Hutchinson; Rhode Island, 1765 ***1224.2*** *p21*
Clarke, J. 60; Ontario, 1861 ***2896.26*** *p12*
Clarke, James *SEE* Clarke, John
Clarke, James; New England, 1641 ***1224.1*** *p13*
Clarke, James; New York, 1836 ***8197.10*** *p79*
Clarke, James; Virginia, 1658 ***1224.1*** *p13*
Clarke, James 21; Philadelphia, 1775 ***1220.25*** *p10*
Clarke, James 44; Ontario, 1871 ***1823.15*** *p43*
Clarke, James Henry; New Orleans, 1831 ***1224.3*** *p14*
Clarke, Jeremiah; Maryland, 1661 ***2524.55*** *p177*
Clarke, Jeremy; Maryland, 1663 ***2524.55*** *p47*
Clarke, Jno; Virginia, 1671 ***6212.30*** *p44*
Clarke, John; Illinois, 1842 ***1224.3*** *p14*
Clarke, John; Maryland, 1664 ***2524.55*** *p47*
Wife: Susanna
Relative: Ann
Relative: James
Clarke, John; Maryland, 1682 ***2524.55*** *p47*
Clarke, John; Pennsylvania, 1777 ***4629.10*** *p24*
Clarke, John; Virginia, 1710 ***1224.2*** *p22*
Clarke, John; Virginia, 1757 ***1224.2*** *p22*
Clarke, John 60; Ontario, 1871 ***1823.22*** *p29*
Clarke, Joseph; New York, New York, 1844 ***1224.3*** *p14*
Clarke, Joseph; Virginia, 1738 ***1224.2*** *p22*
Clarke, Joseph 75; Ontario, 1871 ***1823.22*** *p29*
Clarke, Joshua; New York, 1833 ***8197.10*** *p301*
Clarke, Lardner; Pennsylvania, 1777 ***4629.10*** *p27*
Clarke, Lewis O. 6; Ontario, 1861 ***2896.27*** *p40*
Clarke, Margaret; Maryland, 1673 ***2524.55*** *p47*
Clarke, Margaret; Vermont, 1855-1891 ***5900.10*** *p472*
Clarke, Margarett; Maryland, 1665 ***2524.55*** *p47*
Clarke, Maria; Portland, Maine, 1858 ***9196.15*** *p29*
Clarke, Martha F. 5; Ontario, 1861 ***2896.27*** *p40*
Clarke, Mary; Maryland, 1665 ***2524.55*** *p129*
Clarke, Mary; Maryland, 1669 ***2524.55*** *p47*
Clarke, Mary; Portland, Maine, 1858 ***9196.15*** *p30*
Clarke, Mathew; Maryland, 1650 ***2524.55*** *p48*
Clarke, Mathew; Maryland, 1651 ***2524.55*** *p47*
Clarke, Miles 45; Ontario, 1871 ***1823.28*** *p16*
Clarke, Neale; Maryland, 1649 ***2524.55*** *p38*
Clarke, Neall; Maryland, 1659 ***2524.55*** *p48*
Clarke, Patrick; New York, 1837 ***8197.10*** *p80*
Clarke, Patrick; Vermont, 1808-1865 ***5900.10*** *p469*
Clarke, Patrick; Virginia, 1703-1704 ***6212.30*** *p63*
Clarke, Patrick 21; Philadelphia, 1774 ***1220.25*** *p86*
Clarke, Philip 21; Philadelphia, 1774 ***1220.25*** *p86*
Clarke, R. C.; Alabama, 1814-1845 ***1640.10*** *p30*
Clarke, Rebecca J. 24; Ontario, 1861 ***2896.27*** *p40*
Clarke, Richard; Boston, n.d. ***1224.2*** *p22*
Clarke, Richard; Maryland, 1680 ***2524.55*** *p48*
Clarke, Richard; New York, 1834 ***8197.10*** *p219*
Clarke, Richard; Virginia, 1686 ***1224.1*** *p13*
Clarke, Robert *SEE* Clarke, Thomas
Clarke, Robert; Maryland, n.d. ***1224.1*** *p13*
Clarke, Robert; New England, 1663 ***1224.1*** *p13*

Clarke, Robt 24; Ontario, 1871 ***1823.15*** *p43*
Clarke, S. E. 10; Ontario, 1861 ***2896.26*** *p8*
Clarke, Samuel 45; Ontario, 1871 ***1823.15*** *p43*
Clarke, Sarah *SEE* Clarke, Tho.
Clarke, Sarah *SEE* Clarke, Thomas
Clarke, Sarah Duffey; Vermont, 1806-1877 ***5900.10*** *p469*
Clarke, Susanna *SEE* Clarke, John
Clarke, Susanna; Maryland, 1681 ***2524.55*** *p48*
Clarke, Tho.; Maryland, 1675 ***2524.55*** *p48*
Wife: Sarah
Daughter: Sarah
Clarke, Tho.; Maryland, 1681 ***2524.55*** *p48*
Clarke, Thomas; Maryland, 1665 ***2524.55*** *p48*
Wife: Sarah
Son: Robert
Daughter: Sarah
Clarke, Thomas; Maryland, 1709 ***1224.2*** *p22*
Clarke, Thomas; Virginia, 1667-1668 ***6212.30*** *p39*
Clarke, Thomas; York, Virginia, 1670 ***1224.1*** *p13*
Clarke, Thomas 18; Maryland, 1773-1774 ***1220.25*** *p33*
Clarke, Thos 35; Ontario, 1871 ***1823.28*** *p17*
Clarke, William; Boston, 1687 ***1224.1*** *p13*
Clarke, William; Maryland, 1682 ***2524.55*** *p48*
Clarke, William; New York, 1827 ***8197.10*** *p339*
Clarke, William; Virginia, 1701 ***1224.2*** *p22*
Clarke, William 18; Maryland, 1775 ***1220.25*** *p103*
Clarke, William 21; Virginia, 1775 ***1220.25*** *p110*
Clarke, Wm 57; Ontario, 1871 ***1823.28*** *p17*
Clarkson, Charles 19; Fort Cumberland, Nova Scotia, 1774 ***1220.25*** *p19*
Clarkson, James 66; Ontario, 1871 ***1823.22*** *p29*
Clarkson, Mathew M.; Pennsylvania, 1785 ***4629.10*** *p48*
Clarkson, Matthew, Jr.; Pennsylvania, 1779 ***4629.10*** *p41*
Clarkson, Robert; Maryland, 1649 ***2524.55*** *p48*
Clarkson, Thomas; Pennsylvania, 1777 ***4629.10*** *p17*
Clarkson, William 18; Ontario, 1871 ***1823.28*** *p17*
Clarry, John; New York, 1825 ***8197.10*** *p218*
Clarson, Frederick; New York, 1838 ***8197.10*** *p112*
Clarvis, Robert; Long Island, 1780 ***1224.2*** *p22*
Clarvise, Robert; Long Island, 1780 ***1224.2*** *p22*
Clary, Daniel 51; Ontario, 1871 ***1823.22*** *p29*
Clary, John 50; Ontario, 1871 ***1823.22*** *p29*
Clary, John H. 51; Vermont, 1905 ***5900.10*** *p68*
Clary, Patrick 42; Ontario, 1871 ***1823.22*** *p29*
Clary, Patrick 52; Vermont, 1883 ***5900.10*** *p482*
Clary, Patrick, Jr. 17; Vermont, 1876 ***5900.10*** *p295*
Clary, Sarah 71; Ontario, 1871 ***1823.22*** *p29*
Clary, William; Canada, 1756-1760 ***4628.40*** *p46*
Clask, William 101; Ontario, 1871 ***1823.15*** *p43*
Class, Anna Margarete; Port uncertain, 1745 ***2856.30*** *p67*
With husband
Clatham, John; Maryland, 1658 ***2524.55*** *p48*
Clauncey, Margaret 20; Ontario, 1871 ***1823.22*** *p29*
Claus, Catherine 25; Ontario, 1861 ***2896.27*** *p64*
Claus, Daw 26; Ontario, 1871 ***1823.22*** *p29*
Claus, Delanci 23; Ontario, 1871 ***1823.22*** *p29*
Claus, Henry; Maryland, 1661 ***2524.55*** *p48*
Claus, Nathan 62; Ontario, 1871 ***1823.22*** *p29*
Claus, Sarah 3; Ontario, 1861 ***2896.27*** *p64*
Claus, Wellington 8; Ontario, 1861 ***2896.27*** *p64*
Clause, Peter; Virginia, 1663-1664 ***6212.30*** *p5*
Clauson, John; Maryland, 1661 ***2524.55*** *p48*
Clauss, Jacob; Port uncertain, 1741 ***2856.30*** *p67*
Clauss, Jacob; Port uncertain, 1742 ***2856.30*** *p67*
Clauss, Philipp Jakob; Port uncertain, 1739 ***2856.30*** *p67*
Clauss, Philipp Jakob; Port uncertain, 1741 ***2856.30*** *p67*
Clauth, Georg; Port uncertain, 1763 ***2856.30*** *p67*
Clavater, Wm.; Maryland, 1675 ***2524.55*** *p48*
Clavein, Gertraude; Port uncertain, 1796 ***2856.30*** *p67*
Clawson, Abbott; Maryland, 1659 ***2524.55*** *p48*
Clawson, Elizabeth; Maryland, 1673 ***2524.55*** *p48*
Clawson, Mary; Maryland, 1673 ***2524.55*** *p48*
Clawson, Tobias; Maryland, 1663 ***2524.55*** *p48*
Claxton, Mr.; Quebec, 1858 ***9196.15*** *p41*
Claxton, J. J.; Quebec, 1857 ***9196.15*** *p20*
Claxton, T. J.; Portland, Maine, 1857 ***9196.15*** *p12*
Clay, Curtis; Pennsylvania, 1777 ***4629.10*** *p21*
Clay, Curtis; Pennsylvania, 1779 ***4629.10*** *p41*
Clay, Henry; Maryland, 1650 ***2524.55*** *p48*
Clay, John; New York, 1838 ***8197.10*** *p111*
Clay, Richard; New York, 1838 ***8197.10*** *p111*
Clay, Robert; New York, 1838 ***8197.10*** *p111*
Clay, Stephen; Virginia, 1734 ***1224.2*** *p22*
Clayce, Jno; Virginia, 1672 ***6212.30*** *p50*
Claydon, Charles 29; Ontario, 1871 ***1823.15*** *p43*
Clayford, John; Maryland, 1681 ***2524.55*** *p48*
Clayman, Simon; Maryland, 1673 ***2524.55*** *p48*
Clayne, Nickol; America, 1741 ***2856.30*** *p67*
Claypoole, John; Pennsylvania, 1777 ***4629.10*** *p9*
Claypoole, Joseph; Pennsylvania, 1777 ***4629.10*** *p27*
Clayton, Charles; Maryland, 1666 ***2524.55*** *p46*
Clayton, Charles 29; Ontario, 1871 ***1823.15*** *p43*
Clayton, Eliza; Virginia, 1692-1693 ***6212.30*** *p59*
Clayton, Elizabeth 63; Ontario, 1871 ***1823.15*** *p43*
Clayton, Ellinor; Maryland, 1673 ***2524.55*** *p48*
Clayton, Francis; Wilmington, North Carolina, 1791 ***1640.13*** *p21*
Clayton, Henry 36; Maryland, 1773-1774 ***1220.25*** *p34*
Clayton, John; New York, 1838 ***8197.10*** *p376*
Clayton, John; Virginia, 1791 ***1224.2*** *p22*
Clayton, Richard 21; Maryland, 1774 ***1220.25*** *p73*
Clayton, Sarah 17; Maryland, 1774 ***1220.25*** *p59*
Clayton, Thomas; New York, 1794 ***8197.10*** *p3*
Clayton, William; Maryland, 1681 ***2524.55*** *p48*
Clayton, William 37; Ontario, 1871 ***1823.22*** *p29*
Clayton, William Robert 28; Ontario, 1871 ***1823.15*** *p43*
Clayton, Wm; Virginia, 1664 ***6212.30*** *p11*
Cleafford, Ann; Virginia, 1669-1670 ***6212.30*** *p41*
Clean, Richard 34; Virginia, 1774 ***1220.25*** *p93*
Clear, Thomas; Pennsylvania, 1777 ***4629.10*** *p16*
Cleare, Ambrose; Virginia, 1697 ***1224.1*** *p13*
Cleare, Joseph; Maryland, 1682 ***2524.55*** *p48*
Cleare, Locklyn; Maryland, 1669 ***2524.55*** *p48*
Cleare, Marish; Maryland, 1681 ***2524.55*** *p48*
Cleare, Nathaniel; Maryland, 1642 ***2524.55*** *p48*
Cleare, Thomas; Maryland, 1681 ***2524.55*** *p48*
Cleary, Bridget 81; Vermont, 1879 ***5900.10*** *p618*
Cleary, Charlie W. 20; Vermont, 1874 ***5900.10*** *p538*
Cleary, Dora; Vermont, 1822-1899 ***5900.10*** *p508*
Cleary, James; New York, 1826-1834 ***8197.10*** *p307*
Cleary, James 19; Vermont, 1873 ***5900.10*** *p538*
Cleary, Jennie A. 25; Vermont, 1871 ***5900.10*** *p538*
Cleary, John; Vermont, 1849-1914 ***5900.10*** *p310*
Cleary, John P.; Vermont, 1854-1916 ***5900.10*** *p284*
Cleary, Louise McArthur; Vermont, 1863-1955 ***5900.10*** *p310*
Cleary, Margaret 42; Ontario, 1871 ***1823.15*** *p43*
Cleary, Mary L.; Vermont, 1830-1910 ***5900.10*** *p476*
Cleary, Michael; New York, 1840 ***8197.10*** *p221*
Cleather, Col.; Quebec, 1858 ***9196.15*** *p38*
Cleaton, Robert John 20; Jamaica, 1773-1774 ***1220.25*** *p32*
Cleave, Francis; Maryland, 1660 ***2524.55*** *p48*
Cleave, Joyce; Maryland, 1666 ***2524.55*** *p48*
Cleave, Nathaniell; Maryland, 1631-1685 ***2524.55*** *p48*
Cleave, Paul 52; Ontario, 1871 ***1823.15*** *p43*
Cleaveland, Ann 14; St. John Island, 1775 ***1220.25*** *p121*
Cleaver, Matthew; New York, 1837 ***8197.10*** *p81*
Cleaver, Thomas 22; Maryland, 1775 ***1220.25*** *p111*
Cleaworth, Peter 72; Ontario, 1871 ***1823.15*** *p43*
Cleaworth, Thomas 43; Ontario, 1871 ***1823.15*** *p43*
Cleckner, Adam; Pennsylvania, 1777 ***4629.10*** *p8*
Clee, Miss; Port uncertain, 1726 ***2856.30*** *p67*
Cleeman, Gustavus; New York, 1815 ***8197.10*** *p55*
Cleens, Johann; Port uncertain, 1753 ***2856.30*** *p67*
Cleer, Tobius; Virginia, 1665-1666 ***6212.30*** *p21*
Cleere, Fabius; Virginia, 1664 ***6212.30*** *p13*
Clegg, Henery 30; Ontario, 1871 ***1823.22*** *p29*
Clegg, Isaac; New York, 1821 ***8197.10*** *p216*
Clegg, James 70; Ontario, 1871 ***1823.15*** *p43*
Clegg, James Wilson; Georgia, 1796 ***1224.2*** *p22*
Clegg, Mary 65; Ontario, 1871 ***1823.15*** *p43*
Clegg, William 61; Ontario, 1871 ***1823.15*** *p43*
Cleghorn, Adam 28; Ontario, 1871 ***1823.15*** *p43*
Cleghorn, John; Frederick Co., Maryland, 1824 ***1224.3*** *p15*
Cleghorn, William; Georgia, 1897 ***1640.13*** *p21*
Clein, Augustus; Indiana, 1879-1884 ***3437.14*** *p206*
Clein, Gabriel; Virginia, 1775 ***1220.25*** *p123*
Clein, George Adam; Virginia, 1775 ***1220.25*** *p123*
Cleitin, James; Maryland, 1678 ***2524.55*** *p48*
Cleland, James; Georgia, 1699 ***1640.13*** *p21*
Cleland, James; New York, 1822 ***8197.10*** *p217*
Cleland, James; New York, 1828 ***8197.10*** *p64*
Clelone, Robert; Georgia, 1699 ***1640.13*** *p21*
Cleman, George; New York, 1802 ***8197.10*** *p19*
Clemance, Wm; Virginia, 1666 ***6212.30*** *p26*
Clemann, Johann Adam; Port uncertain, 1750 ***2856.30*** *p67*
With wife
Clemens, Elizabeth; Maryland, 1652 ***2524.55*** *p48*
Clemens, Elizabeth; Maryland, 1662 ***2524.55*** *p48*
Clemens, Juliana; America, 1754 ***2856.30*** *p67*
Clemens, Michael; America, 1738 ***2856.30*** *p67*
Clemenshaw, Walter 24; Maryland, 1775 ***1220.25*** *p98*
Clemenson, Andreas *SEE* Clemenson, Andrew
Clemenson, Andrew; Maryland, 1661 ***2524.55*** *p49*
With wife
Son: Andreas
Son: Clement
Clemenson, Clement *SEE* Clemenson, Andrew
Clemenson, Wm 24; Ontario, 1861 ***2896.28*** *p14*
Clement, Anton 45; Alaska, 1914 ***9196.1*** *p11*
Clement, Elizabeth Fawne; New England, 1666 ***1224.1*** *p21*
Clement, Joseph; New York, 1840 ***8197.10*** *p161*
Clement, Thomas 54; Ontario, 1871 ***1823.15*** *p44*
Clement, William; New York, 1839 ***8197.10*** *p132*
Clements, Miss; Quebec, 1858 ***9196.15*** *p45*
Clements, Mrs.; Quebec, 1858 ***9196.15*** *p45*
Clements, Bernard 39; Ontario, 1871 ***1823.15*** *p44*
Clements, George; Maryland, 1667 ***2524.55*** *p48*
Clements, Hannah; Maryland, 1655 ***2524.55*** *p175*
Clements, James; New York, 1817 ***8197.10*** *p214*
Clements, James; New York, New York, 1831 ***1224.3*** *p15*
Clements, John; New York, 1838 ***8197.10*** *p112*
Clements, Margaret Dummer; New England, 1650 ***1224.1*** *p19*
Clements, Nicholas; New York, 1821 ***8197.10*** *p216*
Clements, Tessa 36; Ontario, 1871 ***1823.15*** *p44*
Clements, Thomas; New York, New York, 1847 ***6058.10*** *p60*
Clements, William; Savannah, Georgia, 1809 ***1640.10*** *p30*
Clements, William 20; Maryland, 1775 ***1220.25*** *p111*
Clementson, Andreas *SEE* Clementson, Andrew
Clementson, Andrew; Maryland, 1661 ***2524.55*** *p49*
With wife
Son: Clement
Son: Andreas
Clementson, Andrew; Maryland, 1664 ***2524.55*** *p48*
With wife
Son: Andreas
Son: Clement
Clementson, Clement *SEE* Clementson, Andrew
Clementz, Ms.; America, 1754 ***2856.30*** *p67*
With husband & 2 children
Clementz, Georg; America, 1753 ***2856.30*** *p67*
Clementz, Jacob; America, 1753 ***2856.30*** *p67*
With wife
Clementz, Mrs. Johann; Port uncertain, 1755 ***2856.30*** *p67*
Clementz, Johann Nickel; America, 1748 ***2856.30*** *p67*
With wife & 4 children
Clementz, Valentin; America, 1754 ***2856.30*** *p67*
Clemenz, Catharina; Port uncertain, 1790 ***2856.30*** *p67*
Clemenz, Catharina; Port uncertain, 1791 ***2856.30*** *p67*
Clemenz, Maria Catharina; Port uncertain, 1781 ***2856.30*** *p67*
Clench, Freeman S. 75; Ontario, 1871 ***1823.22*** *p29*
Clenddenning, Ann 72; Ontario, 1871 ***1823.15*** *p44*
Clendenen, Alexander; New York, 1807 ***8197.10*** *p330*
Clendenning, William 60; Ontario, 1871 ***1823.15*** *p44*
Clendinen, Elizabeth Ann Stewart; Baltimore, 1836 ***1224.3*** *p15*
Clenhenning, Robert 42; Ontario, 1871 ***1823.15*** *p44*
Clennan, James 26; Ontario, 1871 ***1823.15*** *p44*
Clennan, John 40; Ontario, 1871 ***1823.15*** *p44*
Clennan, Pearce 72; Ontario, 1871 ***1823.15*** *p44*
Clennan, Perce 3; Ontario, 1871 ***1823.15*** *p44*
Clennan, William 30; Ontario, 1871 ***1823.15*** *p44*
Cleor, Patrick 50; Ontario, 1871 ***1823.15*** *p44*
Clephan, George; New York, 1777 ***1224.2*** *p22*
Clephan, James; New York, 1777 ***1224.2*** *p22*
Clephan, James; New York, 1783 ***1224.2*** *p22*
Clere, Johannah 70; Ontario, 1871 ***1823.15*** *p44*
Clere, Michael 40; Ontario, 1871 ***1823.15*** *p44*
Clere, Patrick 41; Ontario, 1871 ***1823.15*** *p44*
Clere, Thomas 44; Ontario, 1871 ***1823.15*** *p44*
Clerk, Fredric 19; Ontario, 1871 ***1823.22*** *p29*
Clerk, George 45; Ontario, 1871 ***1823.15*** *p44*
Clerk, Mary Ann 44; Ontario, 1871 ***1823.15*** *p44*
Clerk, Stephen 26; Grenada, 1774 ***1220.25*** *p128*
Clerk, William 60; Ontario, 1871 ***1823.15*** *p44*
Clerke, Christian; Maryland, 1669 ***2524.55*** *p49*
Clerke, Francis; Virginia, 1665-1666 ***6212.30*** *p22*
Clerke, Robert; Maryland, 1672 ***2524.55*** *p49*
Clerke, Thomas; Maryland, 1673 ***2524.55*** *p49*
Clerl, Christ 44; Kansas, 1910 ***9079.10*** *p44*
Clerl, Katie 44; Kansas, 1910 ***9079.10*** *p44*
Clernon, Emilia 20; Ontario, 1871 ***1823.15*** *p44*
Clerry, Lettice *SEE* Clerry, Peter
Clerry, Peter; Maryland, 1663 ***2524.55*** *p49*
Relative: Lettice
Clery, Curnilus 36; Ontario, 1871 ***1823.28*** *p17*
Cleugh, Lancaster 41; Ontario, 1871 ***1823.22*** *p29*
Cleugh, Robert 79; Ontario, 1871 ***1823.22*** *p29*
Cleuhayle, Christopher; Maryland, 1682 ***2524.55*** *p49*
Cleury, John 77; Vermont, 1889 ***5900.10*** *p358*
Cleury, Johnie 33; Vermont, 1887 ***5900.10*** *p359*
Cleury, Margaret Carroll 83; Vermont, 1905 ***5900.10*** *p359*
Cleve, Daniell; Maryland, 1665 ***2524.55*** *p49*
Daughter: Jane
Brother: John
Cleve, Jane *SEE* Cleve, Daniell
Cleve, John *SEE* Cleve, Daniell

Clever, Thomas; Virginia, 1700 ***1224.2*** *p22*
Cleverill, Clement; Maryland, 1672 ***2524.55*** *p49*
Cleverill, Mary; Maryland, 1672 ***2524.55*** *p49*
Cleverly, Constant; Virginia, 1671 ***6212.30*** *p43*
Clevertt, John; Maryland, 1679 ***2524.55*** *p49*
Clewelin, David; Maryland, 1680 ***2524.55*** *p49*
Clewellin, Dunkin; Maryland, 1651 ***2524.55*** *p49*
Clewes, Elizabeth; Maryland, 1665 ***2524.55*** *p49*
Clewet, George 23; Ontario, 1871 ***1823.15*** *p44*
Clewit, John 55; Ontario, 1871 ***1823.15*** *p44*
Clewitt, James 40; Ontario, 1871 ***1823.15*** *p44*
Clifford, . . .; Vermont, 1847 ***5900.10*** *p26*
Clifford, Abigail; Vermont, 1826-1894 ***5900.10*** *p266*
Clifford, Ann 65; Vermont, 1890 ***5900.10*** *p418*
Clifford, Anne; Virginia, 1672 ***6212.30*** *p49*
Clifford, Bridget; Vermont, n.d. ***5900.10*** *p449*
Clifford, Bridget Holleran; Vermont, 1840-1906 ***5900.10*** *p427*
Clifford, Bridget M.; Vermont, 1847-1936 ***5900.10*** *p441*
Clifford, Caroline A. McCoy; Vermont, 1839-1909 ***5900.10*** *p196*
Clifford, Catherine 60; Vermont, 1917 ***5900.10*** *p585*
Clifford, Catherine Foley; Vermont, 1845-1928 ***5900.10*** *p425*
Clifford, Edward; Vermont, 1824-1906 ***5900.10*** *p559*
Clifford, Edward 41; Ontario, 1871 ***1823.28*** *p17*
Clifford, Edwin 45; Ontario, 1871 ***1823.15*** *p44*
Clifford, Gilbert 46; Ontario, 1871 ***1823.22*** *p29*
Clifford, Hannah; Vermont, 1833-1894 ***5900.10*** *p418*
Clifford, Hannora Hickey 65; Vermont, 1866 ***5900.10*** *p418*
Clifford, Henry 60; Ontario, 1871 ***1823.28*** *p17*
Clifford, Henry F. 65; Vermont, 1903 ***5900.10*** *p48*
Clifford, Hugh; Pennsylvania, 1811 ***6058.10*** *p4*
Clifford, James; New York, 1802 ***8197.10*** *p19*
Clifford, James; Virginia, 1666 ***6212.30*** *p31*
Clifford, John; New York, 1823 ***8197.10*** *p217*
Clifford, John 85; Vermont, 1895 ***5900.10*** *p441*
Clifford, Joseph A.; Vermont, 1839-1887 ***5900.10*** *p196*
Clifford, Julia Lee; Vermont, 1830-1927 ***5900.10*** *p583*
Clifford, Martha S. 79; Vermont, 1919 ***5900.10*** *p48*
Clifford, Martin 55; Ontario, 1871 ***1823.15*** *p44*
Clifford, Mary 47; Vermont, 1876 ***5900.10*** *p261*
Clifford, Mary Ann; Vermont, 1857-1933 ***5900.10*** *p393*
Clifford, Mary E. Carmody 37; Vermont, 1896 ***5900.10*** *p562*
Clifford, Mary McGrath; Vermont, 1828-1903 ***5900.10*** *p559*
Clifford, Mary Sheridan 68; Vermont, 1899 ***5900.10*** *p441*
Clifford, Michael; Vermont, 1833-1905 ***5900.10*** *p583*
Clifford, Nicholas; Vermont, 1842-1899 ***5900.10*** *p425*
Clifford, Patrick 70; Vermont, 1853 ***5900.10*** *p418*
Clifford, Peter; North America, 1715 ***1224.2*** *p22*
Clifford, Tho; Virginia, 1666 ***6212.30*** *p30*
Clifford, Thomas; New York, 1833 ***8197.10*** *p219*
Clifford, Timothy 55; Vermont, 1853 ***5900.10*** *p58*
Clifford, Timothy 55; Vermont, 1871 ***5900.10*** *p266*
Clifford, William; Vermont, 1832-1904 ***5900.10*** *p427*
Clifford, William 22; Maryland, 1774 ***1220.25*** *p77*
Cliford, James; Pennsylvania, 1778 ***4629.10*** *p32*
Clifton, Anne *SEE* Clifton, James
Clifton, James; Maryland, 1660-1663 ***2524.55*** *p49*
Wife: Anne
Clifton, James 50; St. Kitts, 1774-1775 ***1220.25*** *p129*
Clifton, Thomas; Maryland, 1681 ***2524.55*** *p49*
Clifton, Thomas; Virginia, 1671 ***6212.30*** *p42*
Clifton, William; Florida, 1783 ***1224.2*** *p22*
Climmonse, Nicholas; Maryland, 1664 ***2524.55*** *p49*
Climo, Thomas 50; Ontario, 1871 ***1823.22*** *p29*
Climon, Symon; Maryland, 1664 ***2524.55*** *p49*
Climur, John; Maryland, 1667 ***2524.55*** *p49*
Clinch, Vincent; Maryland, 1666 ***2524.55*** *p49*
Cline, Ann; Vermont, 1810-1892 ***5900.10*** *p219*
Cline, Annie; Vermont, 1888 ***5900.10*** *p433*
Cline, B. M.; Vermont, 1855-1923 ***5900.10*** *p433*
Cline, Daniel; Vermont, 1849-1934 ***5900.10*** *p446*
Cline, Elizabeth; Vermont, 1810-1878 ***5900.10*** *p214*
Cline, Ellen; Vermont, 1842-1908 ***5900.10*** *p444*
Cline, Hugh; Vermont, 1861 ***5900.10*** *p433*
Cline, Jennie; Vermont, 1851-1925 ***5900.10*** *p433*
Cline, Jennie Hackett; Vermont, 1857-1913 ***5900.10*** *p446*
Cline, John 89; Ontario, 1871 ***1823.15*** *p44*
Cline, Mary Duclos; Vermont, 1851-1922 ***5900.10*** *p256*
Cline, Mathias; Pennsylvania, 1777 ***4629.10*** *p12*
Cline, Mitchell; Vermont, 1834-1916 ***5900.10*** *p256*
Cline, Philip; Pennsylvania, 1777 ***4629.10*** *p12*
Cline, Thomas; Vermont, 1859-1936 ***5900.10*** *p433*
Cline, Thomas; Vermont, 1936 ***5900.10*** *p433*
Cline, William 58; New York, New York, 1848 ***1825.45*** *p13*
Clines, Bridget Carney; Vermont, 1817-1887 ***5900.10*** *p99*
Clines, James; Vermont, 1844-1865 ***5900.10*** *p99*
Clines, Margaret 79; Vermont, 1901 ***5900.10*** *p98*
Clines, Patrick; Vermont, 1807-1893 ***5900.10*** *p99*
Cling, Richard 51; Ontario, 1871 ***1823.15*** *p44*
Clinre, Hanorah Beckett; Vermont, 1895 ***5900.10*** *p433*
Clinton, Ann J. 55; Ontario, 1861 ***2896.28*** *p25*
Clinton, Anne; New York, 1746 ***1224.2*** *p22*
Clinton, Bartholomew; New York, 1828 ***8197.10*** *p350*
Clinton, Bridget O'Kane; Vermont, 1856-1926 ***5900.10*** *p326*
Clinton, David 20; Ontario, 1861 ***2896.27*** *p67*
Clinton, Eliza O'Kane; Vermont, 1853-1909 ***5900.10*** *p326*
Clinton, George; New England, 1775-1781 ***4628.40*** *p68*
Clinton, George 9; Ontario, 1861 ***2896.28*** *p25*
Clinton, Henry; Vermont, 1839-1906 ***5900.10*** *p326*
Clinton, Hugh; New York, 1837 ***8197.10*** *p80*
Clinton, Jane; Vermont, 1803-1905 ***5900.10*** *p323*
Clinton, Jemima 14; Ontario, 1861 ***2896.28*** *p25*
Clinton, Jno 19; Ontario, 1861 ***2896.28*** *p11*
Clinton, John; Vermont, 1784-1887 ***5900.10*** *p326*
Clinton, John; Vermont, 1835-1908 ***5900.10*** *p326*
Clinton, John 16; Ontario, 1861 ***2896.28*** *p25*
Clinton, John 55; Ontario, 1861 ***2896.28*** *p25*
Clinton, Margaret; Vermont, 1845-1910 ***5900.10*** *p463*
Clinton, Margaret Kern; Vermont, 1810-1867 ***5900.10*** *p326*
Clinton, Phebe Jane 2; Ontario, 1861 ***2896.27*** *p67*
Clinton, Susan 34; Ontario, 1861 ***2896.27*** *p67*
Clinton, William; New York, 1834 ***8197.10*** *p70*
Clintrie, Archibald; Georgia, 1698 ***1640.13*** *p21*
Clipsham, Michael 31; Ontario, 1871 ***1823.28*** *p17*
Clitheroe, James 47; Ontario, 1871 ***1823.22*** *p29*
Clivedon, Jane; Virginia, 1672 ***6212.30*** *p50*
Cliverdon, Walter 38; Ontario, 1871 ***1823.22*** *p29*
Clliford, Thomas 26; Ontario, 1871 ***1823.28*** *p17*
Cloake, Francis; Maryland, 1656 ***2524.55*** *p49*
Cloakey, George 32; Ontario, 1871 ***1823.15*** *p44*
Cloakey, James 36; Ontario, 1871 ***1823.15*** *p44*
Cloates, Jacob; America, 1738 ***2856.30*** *p67*
Clocker, Daniel; Maryland, 1636 ***2524.55*** *p49*
Cloheim, John; Maryland, 1678 ***2524.55*** *p49*
Clokey, Andrew 38; Ontario, 1871 ***1823.15*** *p44*
Clokey, John 48; Ontario, 1871 ***1823.15*** *p44*
Clonney, James G.; New York, 1840 ***8197.10*** *p159*
Clony, Jno; Virginia, 1672 ***6212.30*** *p50*
Clood, John; Maryland, 1660-1661 ***2524.55*** *p81*
Cloode, John; Maryland, 1660-1661 ***2524.55*** *p49*
Cloon, John; New York, 1839 ***8197.10*** *p380*
Cloonan, Patrick; New York, 1839 ***8197.10*** *p379*
Clor, Christof; America, 1749 ***2856.30*** *p67*
With wife & 4 children
Clor, Jakob; America, 1749 ***2856.30*** *p67*
With wife & child
Clore, James 28; Ontario, 1871 ***1823.15*** *p44*
Cloredge, Thomas; Pennsylvania, 1779 ***4629.10*** *p41*
Cloren, Bridget 62; Vermont, 1903 ***5900.10*** *p136*
Clorin, Ann Hynes; Vermont, 1817-1898 ***5900.10*** *p136*
Clorin, Martin C.; Vermont, 1807-1892 ***5900.10*** *p136*
Clorin, Mary; Vermont, 1843-1928 ***5900.10*** *p136*
Clos, Anna Catharina; Port uncertain, 1766 ***2856.30*** *p67*
Close, Captain; Quebec, 1858 ***9196.15*** *p38*
Close, David 56; Ontario, 1871 ***1823.28*** *p17*
Close, Geo; Virginia, 1681-1682 ***6212.30*** *p56*
Close, Hugh 50; Ontario, 1871 ***1823.22*** *p29*
Close, James 56; Ontario, 1871 ***1823.22*** *p29*
Close, John; New York, 1839 ***8197.10*** *p383*
Closey, William; New York, 1840 ***8197.10*** *p161*
Closs, . . .; Port uncertain, 1722 ***2856.30*** *p67*
Closs, . . .; Port uncertain, 1728 ***2856.30*** *p67*
Closs, . . .; Port uncertain, 1773 ***2856.30*** *p67*
Closs, Miss; America, 1771 ***2856.30*** *p306*
Closs, Miss; America, 1772 ***2856.30*** *p306*
Closs, Miss 11; Ontario, 1861 ***2896.26*** *p9*
Closs, Anna Christina; Port uncertain, 1746 ***2856.30*** *p67*
Closs, Anna Gertrud; Port uncertain, 1773 ***2856.30*** *p67*
Closs, Anna Maria; America, 1749 ***2856.30*** *p67*
Closs, J. 9; Ontario, 1861 ***2896.26*** *p9*
Closs, Johann Henrich; Port uncertain, 1746 ***2856.30*** *p67*
Closs, Marg. Catharina; America, 1771 ***2856.30*** *p67*
With husband
Closs, Marg. Catharina; America, 1772 ***2856.30*** *p67*
With husband
Closs, Peter; Port uncertain, 1730 ***2856.30*** *p67*
Clossey, Christina; Vermont, 1845-1933 ***5900.10*** *p548*
Clossey, Elizabeth Kirk; Vermont, 1854-1940 ***5900.10*** *p605*
Clossey, George; Vermont, 1895-1986 ***5900.10*** *p605*
Clossey, William H.; Vermont, 1847-1932 ***5900.10*** *p548*
Closson, William 48; Ontario, 1871 ***1823.22*** *p29*
Clough, Catherine 60; Ontario, 1871 ***1823.15*** *p44*
Clough, Jesse; New York, 1838 ***8197.10*** *p220*
Clough, Jesse; New York, 1840 ***8197.10*** *p163*
Clough, John 40; Virginia, 1775 ***1220.25*** *p110*
Clough, Thomas; Maryland, 1674 ***2524.55*** *p49*
Cloughton, James; Maryland, 1640 ***2524.55*** *p49*
Father: James, Sr.
Mother: Jane
Cloughton, James, Sr.; Maryland, 1640 ***2524.55*** *p49*
Wife: Jane
Son: James, Jr.
Cloughton, James, Sr. *SEE* Cloughton, James
Cloughton, James, Jr. *SEE* Cloughton, James, Sr.
Cloughton, Jane *SEE* Cloughton, James
Cloughton, Jane *SEE* Cloughton, James, Sr.
Clous, Jacob; Pennsylvania, 1777 ***4629.10*** *p9*
Clous, Joseph; New York, 1839 ***8197.10*** *p133*
Clouston, John D. 40; Ontario, 1871 ***1823.22*** *p29*
Clouston, Joseph 30; Ontario, 1871 ***1823.22*** *p30*
Cloutie, Mary 49; Vermont, 1870 ***5900.10*** *p509*
Clover, Edward; New York, 1840 ***8197.10*** *p162*
Clow, James 29; Ontario, 1871 ***1823.15*** *p44*
Clow, James 60; Ontario, 1871 ***1823.15*** *p44*
Clow, Robert; Illinois, 1874 ***1640.13*** *p21*
Clowes, Gerhardus; St. John, New Brunswick, 1795 ***1224.2*** *p23*
Clowes, John; Long Island, 1795 ***1224.2*** *p23*
Clowes, Martha; Virginia, 1666-1667 ***6212.30*** *p34*
Cloyden, Samuel; Maryland, 1674 ***2524.55*** *p49*
Cloyson, James; Maryland, 1669 ***2524.55*** *p49*
Clozier, . . . 21; Grenada, 1774 ***1220.25*** *p128*
Clucas, Henry 23; Ontario, 1871 ***1823.15*** *p44*
Cludius, Charles; New York, 1838 ***8197.10*** *p220*
Cluff, Hannah 54; Ontario, 1871 ***1823.15*** *p44*
Cluff, James 60; Ontario, 1871 ***1823.15*** *p45*
Cluff, John; New York, 1837 ***8197.10*** *p219*
Cluff, Joseph; New York, 1833 ***8197.10*** *p219*
Cluff, Richard 45; Ontario, 1871 ***1823.15*** *p45*
Cluff, Robert 60; Ontario, 1871 ***1823.15*** *p45*
Cluff, Thomas 57; Ontario, 1871 ***1823.15*** *p45*
Cluff, William; New York, 1839 ***8197.10*** *p220*
Cluff, William 24; Ontario, 1871 ***1823.28*** *p17*
Cluff, William 61; Ontario, 1871 ***1823.15*** *p45*
Cluft, Maria 60; Ontario, 1861 ***2896.26*** *p39*
Cullingworth, Emma 18; Ontario, 1871 ***1823.15*** *p45*
Clumer, John; Maryland, 1668 ***2524.55*** *p49*
Clump, Adam 50; Ontario, 1871 ***1823.15*** *p45*
Clump, Michael 39; Ontario, 1871 ***1823.15*** *p45*
Clunas, Alexander; Georgia, 1737 ***1640.10*** *p30*
Clune, Balthomy 47; Ontario, 1871 ***1823.22*** *p30*
Clune, Patrick; Pennsylvania, 1867 ***6058.10*** *p58*
Clunesse, Elizabeth; Maryland, 1664 ***2524.55*** *p49*
Clure, Bridget A. Maroney; Vermont, 1855-1940 ***5900.10*** *p117*
Clure, Catherine A.; Vermont, 1878-1962 ***5900.10*** *p120*
Clure, Catherine Murphy; Vermont, 1851-1913 ***5900.10*** *p120*
Clure, James; Vermont, 1850-1897 ***5900.10*** *p117*
Clure, Patrick; Pennsylvania, 1867 ***6058.10*** *p58*
Clure, Patrick; Vermont, 1848-1931 ***5900.10*** *p120*
Cluskey, Cathrine Meighan 62; Vermont, 1869 ***5900.10*** *p233*
Cluskey, Elizabeth O'Brien 80; Vermont, 1843 ***5900.10*** *p601*
Clusky, James 39; Ontario, 1871 ***1823.15*** *p45*
Clute, C. Eliza 17; Ontario, 1861 ***2896.25*** *p2*
Clute, Ellen M. 6; Ontario, 1861 ***2896.25*** *p2*
Clute, Fred 4; Ontario, 1861 ***2896.25*** *p2*
Clute, John R. 15; Ontario, 1861 ***2896.25*** *p2*
Clute, Margaret J. 20; Ontario, 1861 ***2896.25*** *p2*
Clute, Mary A. 38; Ontario, 1861 ***2896.25*** *p2*
Clute, Mary Ann 48; Ontario, 1871 ***1823.22*** *p30*
Clute, Rachel M. 10; Ontario, 1861 ***2896.25*** *p2*
Clute, Richard G. 82; Ontario, 1871 ***1823.22*** *p30*
Clute, Richard J. 12; Ontario, 1861 ***2896.25*** *p2*
Clute, Richard J. 42; Ontario, 1861 ***2896.25*** *p2*
Clutterbooke, Elizabeth; Maryland, 1679 ***2524.55*** *p49*
Clutterbrooke, Elizabeth; Maryland, 1679 ***2524.55*** *p49*
Clutterbuck, William; New England, 1680 ***1224.1*** *p26*
Clutton, William 33; Ontario, 1871 ***1823.15*** *p45*
Clutton, William 54; Ontario, 1871 ***1823.15*** *p45*
Cluxton, Bryan; Maryland, 1678 ***2524.55*** *p49*
Cluzet, Charles; New York, 1816 ***8197.10*** *p58*
Clyde, George; New York, 1839 ***8197.10*** *p220*
Clyde, James; New York, 1802 ***8197.10*** *p19*
Clydesdale, Thomas 26; Ontario, 1871 ***1823.28*** *p17*
Clymer, Anne; Maryland, 1691 ***1224.1*** *p14*
Clymer, Daniel; Pennsylvania, 1777 ***4629.10*** *p7*
Clymer, George; Pennsylvania, 1777 ***4629.10*** *p8*
Clyne, Frank 49; Ontario, 1871 ***1823.15*** *p45*
Clyver, Jacob; Pennsylvania, 1777 ***4629.10*** *p8*
Cnefelius, Henrich; Port uncertain, 1783 ***2856.30*** *p68*
Coachafer, Henry J. 27; Ontario, 1871 ***1823.22*** *p30*
Coachy, William; Maryland, 1660 ***2524.55*** *p49*
Coad, Richard 58; Ontario, 1871 ***1823.15*** *p45*
Coady, Bridget 35; Ontario, 1871 ***1823.22*** *p30*

Coady, Peter 32; Ontario, 1871 ***1823.22*** *p30*
Coafer, John; Maryland, 1658 ***2524.55*** *p49*
Coaig, James 45; Ontario, 1871 ***1823.15*** *p45*
Coakley, Catherine Harrington 78; Vermont, n.d. ***5900.10*** *p437*
Coakley, Ella; Vermont, 1876-1953 ***5900.10*** *p437*
Coakley, James; Vermont, 1835-1911 ***5900.10*** *p507*
Coakley, Mary A.; Vermont, 1860-1923 ***5900.10*** *p505*
Coakley, Mary A. Glynn; Vermont, 1844-1877 ***5900.10*** *p507*
Coakley, Timothy 70; Vermont, n.d. ***5900.10*** *p437*
Coapland, Lettice; Maryland, 1678 ***2524.55*** *p50*
Coarr, Rose Ann; Vermont, 1855-1938 ***5900.10*** *p512*
Coast, John; New York, 1840 ***8197.10*** *p221*
Coate, D.; Quebec, 1857 ***9196.15*** *p17*
Coate, Eliza 40; Ontario, 1871 ***1823.22*** *p30*
Coates, Alfred; Virginia, 1841 ***1224.3*** *p15*
Coates, Benjamin; Pennsylvania, 1777 ***4629.10*** *p26*
Coates, Christopher 44; Ontario, 1871 ***1823.15*** *p45*
Coates, Edward; New York, 1813 ***8197.10*** *p214*
Coates, Fanny Dean; Boston, 1830 ***1224.3*** *p15*
Coates, Isaac; Pennsylvania, 1777 ***4629.10*** *p27*
Coates, James; New York, 1840 ***8197.10*** *p160*
Coates, John; Virginia, 1664 ***6212.30*** *p12*
Coates, John 33; Ontario, 1871 ***1823.15*** *p45*
Coates, Samuel; Maryland, 1682 ***2524.55*** *p50*
Coates, Sarah; Baltimore, 1772 ***1224.2*** *p23*
Coates, Thomas 39; Ontario, 1871 ***1823.15*** *p45*
Coates, William 32; Ontario, 1871 ***1823.15*** *p45*
Coates, William 61; Ontario, 1871 ***1823.22*** *p30*
Coatraine, George; Maryland, 1671 ***2524.55*** *p50*
Coats, Benjamin; Pennsylvania, 1779 ***4629.10*** *p41*
Coats, Henry 37; Virginia, 1773 ***1220.25*** *p31*
Coats, James 38; Ontario, 1871 ***1823.15*** *p45*
Coats, James 41; Ontario, 1871 ***1823.22*** *p30*
Coats, John; New York, 1809 ***8197.10*** *p55*
Coats, John 18; Ontario, 1871 ***1823.15*** *p45*
Coats, Richard 52; Ontario, 1871 ***1823.22*** *p30*
Coats, Robert 41; Ontario, 1871 ***1823.15*** *p45*
Coats, Septimus; Pennsylvania, 1777 ***4629.10*** *p28*
Coats, Thomas; Pennsylvania, 1779 ***4629.10*** *p40*
Coats, William 47; Ontario, 1871 ***1823.15*** *p45*
Cobb, Arthur; Died enroute, 1666 ***1224.1*** *p14*
Cobb, John; Georgia, 1775 ***1640.10*** *p30*
Cobb, John 31; Georgia, 1775 ***1220.25*** *p125*
Cobb, Thomas; Virginia, 1664 ***6212.30*** *p12*
Cobb, Thomas; Virginia, 1665-1666 ***6212.30*** *p20*
Cobb, Woolley; Virginia, 1732 ***1224.2*** *p23*
Cobbs, Elizabeth; Maryland, 1669 ***2524.55*** *p50*
Cober, George; New York, 1838-1840 ***8197.10*** *p300*
Coberthwaites, Ann; Maryland, 1658 ***2524.55*** *p50*
Cobham, Mr.; Quebec, 1858 ***9196.15*** *p41*
Cobham, George Ashworth; New York, 1835 ***8197.10*** *p220*
Cobham, Robert 39; Philadelphia, 1774 ***1220.25*** *p82*
Cobhane, Miss; Quebec, 1857 ***9196.15*** *p16*
Cobin, Derman; Virginia, 1672 ***6212.30*** *p50*
Cobler, Mary; Maryland, 1681 ***2524.55*** *p50*
Cobourn, Alexander 60; Ontario, 1871 ***1823.28*** *p17*
Cobourn, Benjamin 30; Ontario, 1871 ***1823.28*** *p17*
Cobourn, George 32; Ontario, 1871 ***1823.28*** *p17*
Cobourn, James; Pennsylvania, 1777 ***4629.10*** *p20*
Cobourn, John; Pennsylvania, 1777 ***4629.10*** *p21*
Cobourn, John 40; Ontario, 1871 ***1823.28*** *p17*
Cobourn, John 45; Ontario, 1871 ***1823.28*** *p17*
Cobourn, John 76; Ontario, 1871 ***1823.28*** *p17*
Cobourn, William 50; Ontario, 1871 ***1823.28*** *p17*
Cobudge, Joseph 22; Virginia, 1774 ***1220.25*** *p89*
Coburn, Frank; Vermont, 1869-1946 ***5900.10*** *p460*
Coburn, James 56; Ontario, 1871 ***1823.28*** *p17*
Coburn, James M.; Vermont, 1841-1909 ***5900.10*** *p379*
Coburn, Katherine McAuley; Vermont, 1845-1916 ***5900.10*** *p379*
Coburn, Robt 58; Ontario, 1871 ***1823.28*** *p17*
Coburn, Sally; Vermont, 1799-1892 ***5900.10*** *p207*
Coburn, Samuel; New York, 1816 ***8197.10*** *p58*
Coch, William; New York, New York, 1831 ***6058.10*** *p38*
Coch, William; New York, New York, 1831 ***6058.10*** *p46*
Coch, William; Pennsylvania, 1839 ***6058.10*** *p16*
Cochaska, William; Maryland, 1910 ***3259.35*** *p10*
Cochel, Edmond; Pennsylvania, 1779 ***4629.10*** *p33*
Cochems, John 65; Ontario, 1871 ***1823.15*** *p45*
Cocherline, Anthony Johnson 44; Ontario, 1871 ***1823.15*** *p45*
Cocherline, Hannah 70; Ontario, 1871 ***1823.15*** *p45*
Cochlin, Catherine Malone; Vermont, 1863-1919 ***5900.10*** *p443*
Cochlin, Cornelius J.; Vermont, 1852-1928 ***5900.10*** *p443*
Cochran, Alexander; New York, 1829 ***8197.10*** *p312*
Cochran, George; Pennsylvania, 1777 ***4629.10*** *p12*
Cochran, Henry; Alabama, 1889 ***1640.13*** *p22*
Cochran, Hugh; Pennsylvania, 1827 ***6058.10*** *p9*
Cochran, James; Georgia, 1737 ***1640.10*** *p30*
Cochran, James; Pennsylvania, 1779 ***4629.10*** *p40*
Cochran, James; Savannah, Georgia, 1752-1845 ***1640.10*** *p30*
Cochran, James; Savannah, Georgia, 1781 ***1224.2*** *p23*
Cochran, John; Pennsylvania, 1777 ***4629.10*** *p12*
Cochran, John; Pennsylvania, 1786 ***4629.10*** *p51*
Cochran, John 35; Ontario, 1871 ***1823.15*** *p45*
Cochran, John 50; Ontario, 1871 ***1823.22*** *p30*
Cochran, Mary 52; Ontario, 1871 ***1823.28*** *p17*
Cochran, Michael 22; Maryland, 1775 ***1220.25*** *p10*
Cochran, Nathan; New York, 1832 ***8197.10*** *p357*
Cochran, Richard; New York, 1862 ***6058.10*** *p67*
Cochran, Robert; New York, 1788-1845 ***1640.10*** *p30*
Cochran, Robert; New York, 1832 ***8197.10*** *p219*
Cochran, Robert; New York, 1834 ***8197.10*** *p70*
Cochran, Samuel 32; Ontario, 1871 ***1823.28*** *p17*
Cochran, Thomas 70; Ontario, 1871 ***1823.28*** *p17*
Cochran, W.; Quebec, 1856 ***9196.15*** *p8*
Cochran, William; New York, 1821 ***8197.10*** *p215*
Cochran, William 46; Ontario, 1871 ***1823.28*** *p17*
Cochran, William Johnson 32; New York, 1820-1834 ***8197.10*** *p305*
Cochrane, Archibald; Ohio, 1891 ***1640.13*** *p22*
Cochrane, George 50; Ontario, 1871 ***1823.22*** *p30*
Cochrane, James; New York, 1832 ***8197.10*** *p356*
Cochrane, James 32; Ontario, 1871 ***1823.15*** *p45*
Cochrane, John 38; Ontario, 1871 ***1823.15*** *p45*
Cochrane, John 41; Ontario, 1871 ***1823.22*** *p30*
Cochrane, John 59; Ontario, 1871 ***1823.28*** *p17*
Cochrane, John 66; Ontario, 1871 ***1823.15*** *p45*
Cochrane, William Johnson; New York, 1829 ***8197.10*** *p312*
Cochrane, William W.; Mississippi, 1823-1845 ***1640.10*** *p31*
Cochrin, Samuel 75; Ontario, 1871 ***1823.22*** *p30*
Cock, An; Virginia, 1680 ***6212.30*** *p55*
Cock, David; Jamaica, 1799 ***1640.13*** *p22*
Cock, Edwd; Virginia, 1671 ***6212.30*** *p43*
Cock, Frederick 56; Ontario, 1871 ***1823.28*** *p17*
Cock, Jacob 20; Philadelphia, 1774 ***1220.25*** *p3*
Cock, John; Maryland, 1681 ***2524.55*** *p50*
Cock, Ralph; Savannah, Georgia, 1774 ***1640.10*** *p31*
With wife
Cock, Ralph; Virginia, 1671-1672 ***6212.30*** *p46*
Cock, Ralph 37; Savannah, Georgia, 1774 ***1220.25*** *p139*
With wife
Cock, Robert 25; Georgia, 1774 ***1220.25*** *p48*
Cock, Thomas; Maryland, 1669 ***2524.55*** *p50*
Cock, William; New York, New York, 1831 ***6058.10*** *p46*
Cock, William; Pennsylvania, 1839 ***6058.10*** *p16*
Cock, William 15; Maryland, 1774 ***1220.25*** *p61*
Cockayne, Mr.; Quebec, 1857 ***9196.15*** *p24*
Cockayne, Francis Henry; California, 1898 ***1640.13*** *p22*
Cockburn, Mrs. 26; Grenada, 1774 ***1220.25*** *p127*
Cockburn, Alexander 30; Grenada, 1774 ***1220.25*** *p127*
Cockburn, David 38; Ontario, 1871 ***1823.28*** *p17*
Cockburn, George 29; Ontario, 1871 ***1823.22*** *p30*
Cockburn, George 46; Ontario, 1871 ***1823.22*** *p30*
Cockburn, Henry; Grenada, 1854 ***1640.13*** *p22*
Cockburn, James; Georgia, 1698 ***1640.13*** *p22*
Cockburn, James H. 51; Ontario, 1871 ***1823.22*** *p30*
Cockburn, John; New England, 1700 ***1224.2*** *p23*
Cockburn, John 38; Ontario, 1871 ***1823.28*** *p17*
Cockburn, John 56; Ontario, 1871 ***1823.15*** *p45*
Cockburn, William 55; Ontario, 1871 ***1823.22*** *p30*
Cockburne, George 22; Ontario, 1871 ***1823.28*** *p17*
Cockburne, Thomas; Pennsylvania, 1725 ***1224.2*** *p23*
Cocke, Catesby; Virginia, 1773 ***1224.2*** *p23*
Cocke, Christopher; New York, 1714 ***1224.2*** *p23*
Cocke, George; Maryland, 1665 ***2524.55*** *p50*
Cocke, John; Maryland, 1668 ***2524.55*** *p50*
Cocke, Thomas; Virginia, 1712 ***1224.2*** *p23*
Cockee, Edward; Maryland, 1672 ***2524.55*** *p50*
Cockeline, John 49; Ontario, 1871 ***1823.15*** *p45*
Cockely, Timothy; Pennsylvania, 1839 ***6058.10*** *p20*
Cocker, George; Portland, Maine, 1857 ***9196.15*** *p12*
Cocker, John 63; Ontario, 1871 ***1823.15*** *p45*
Cocker, Richard; Maryland, 1682 ***2524.55*** *p50*
Cockerell, Eleanor; Maryland, 1681 ***2524.55*** *p50*
Cockerell, John; Maryland, 1681 ***2524.55*** *p50*
Cockerell, Susanna; Maryland, 1681 ***2524.55*** *p50*
Cockerline, George 42; Ontario, 1871 ***1823.15*** *p45*
Cockerton, Robert 22; Maryland, 1774 ***1220.25*** *p58*
Cockes, John; Maryland, 1668 ***2524.55*** *p50*
Cockes, Rich; Virginia, 1669-1670 ***6212.30*** *p41*
Cockey, Tho; Virginia, 1672-1673 ***6212.30*** *p51*
Cockfield, Thomas Nelson; St. Kitts, 1869 ***1640.13*** *p22*
Cockhead, Richd; Virginia, 1671-1672 ***6212.30*** *p47*
Cockin, Stephen; Boston, 1701 ***1224.2*** *p23*
Cocklewood, Robert 48; Ontario, 1871 ***1823.22*** *p30*
Cocklin, Daniel J.; Vermont, 1833-1893 ***5900.10*** *p431*
Cocklin, Elizabeth D.; Vermont, 1832-1918 ***5900.10*** *p431*
Cocklina, Robert 37; Ontario, 1871 ***1823.15*** *p45*
Cockram, Charles 22; Ontario, 1871 ***1823.28*** *p17*
Cockran, Francis; New York, 1802 ***8197.10*** *p19*
Cockran, James; Pennsylvania, 1777 ***4629.10*** *p21*
Cockran, Michael; New York, 1821 ***8197.10*** *p216*
Cocks, Henry; New York, 1840 ***8197.10*** *p159*
Cocks, Jno; Virginia, 1665-1666 ***6212.30*** *p23*
Cocks, Richd; Virginia, 1671 ***6212.30*** *p42*
Cocks, Robert; Pennsylvania, 1777 ***4629.10*** *p23*
Cocks, Robert; Pennsylvania, 1779 ***4629.10*** *p40*
Cocks, Robt; Virginia, 1674-1675 ***6212.30*** *p53*
Cockshot, Jane *SEE* Cockshot, John
Cockshot, John; Maryland, 1641 ***2524.55*** *p50*
Wife: Jane
Daughter: Jane
Daughter: Mary
Cockshot, Mary *SEE* Cockshot, John
Cockshutt, Geoffrey; Virginia, 1710 ***1224.2*** *p23*
Cockwill, William 50; Ontario, 1871 ***1823.15*** *p45*
Codant, James; Maryland, 1910 ***3259.35*** *p10*
Codd, Thomas; New York, 1808 ***8197.10*** *p53*
Coddon, Jno; Virginia, 1673 ***6212.30*** *p51*
Code, James 60; Ontario, 1871 ***1823.28*** *p17*
Code, Patrick; New York, 1828 ***8197.10*** *p350*
Codenham, Robert; New York, 1700 ***1224.2*** *p23*
Codey, John 29; Ontario, 1861 ***2896.27*** *p27*
Codmore, John; Maryland, 1681 ***2524.55*** *p50*
Codrington, Mr.; Quebec, 1858 ***9196.15*** *p39*
Cody, Bridget; Vermont, 1840-1898 ***5900.10*** *p467*
Coe, Charlotte 23; Ontario, 1871 ***1823.22*** *p30*
Coe, Margaret 40; Ontario, 1871 ***1823.15*** *p45*
Coe, Robert; Pennsylvania, 1777 ***4629.10*** *p25*
Coe, William 45; Ontario, 1871 ***1823.15*** *p45*
Coen, Philipp; America, 1738 ***2856.30*** *p68*
Coffee, Ann 75; Ontario, 1871 ***1823.28*** *p17*
Coffee, Charles Michael; Vermont, 1851-1915 ***5900.10*** *p257*
Coffee, Elizabeth 45; Vermont, 1863 ***5900.10*** *p246*
Coffee, Elizabeth J.; Vermont, 1862-1930 ***5900.10*** *p162*
Coffee, Mary 59; Vermont, 1882 ***5900.10*** *p410*
Coffee, Mary J. O'Brien; Vermont, 1859-1936 ***5900.10*** *p257*
Coffee, Patrick 30; Maryland, 1774 ***1220.25*** *p41*
Coffee, Patrick H.; Vermont, 1856-1925 ***5900.10*** *p162*
Coffee, Richard 50; Ontario, 1871 ***1823.22*** *p30*
Coffee, Samuel 50; Ontario, 1871 ***1823.22*** *p30*
Coffee, Sarah Hays; Vermont, 1825-1880 ***5900.10*** *p270*
Coffee, Thomas 43; Ontario, 1871 ***1823.22*** *p30*
Coffer, John; Maryland, 1669 ***2524.55*** *p50*
With wife
Coffey, Ann 5; Vermont, 1853 ***5900.10*** *p567*
Coffey, Ann 75; Vermont, 1886 ***5900.10*** *p567*
Coffey, Anna B.; Vermont, n.d. ***5900.10*** *p127*
Coffey, Bridget 2; Vermont, 1855 ***5900.10*** *p567*
Coffey, Bridget Sheehan; Vermont, 1838-1912 ***5900.10*** *p127*
Coffey, Catharine O'Brien; Vermont, 1891 ***5900.10*** *p215*
Coffey, Daniel; Vermont, 1906 ***5900.10*** *p214*
Coffey, Elizabeth; Vermont, 1842-1915 ***5900.10*** *p465*
Coffey, Ellen; Vermont, 1835-1920 ***5900.10*** *p216*
Coffey, Ellenor; Vermont, 1826-1890 ***5900.10*** *p88*
Coffey, Hanorah Hayes; Vermont, 1810-1895 ***5900.10*** *p166*
Coffey, Henry J.; Vermont, n.d. ***5900.10*** *p127*
Coffey, James; Virginia, 1698 ***6212.30*** *p61*
Coffey, Jennie M.; Vermont, n.d. ***5900.10*** *p127*
Coffey, John; Pennsylvania, 1833 ***6058.10*** *p11*
Coffey, John 39; Vermont, 1886 ***5900.10*** *p290*
Coffey, John W.; Vermont, 1853-1930 ***5900.10*** *p255*
Coffey, Kate; Vermont, 1854-1916 ***5900.10*** *p147*
Coffey, Margaret Keough 55; Vermont, 1865 ***5900.10*** *p252*
Coffey, Mary; Vermont, 1838-1925 ***5900.10*** *p465*
Coffey, Mary 56; Vermont, 1879 ***5900.10*** *p82*
Coffey, Mary 75; Vermont, 1875 ***5900.10*** *p390*
Coffey, Mary E.; Vermont, 1864-1940 ***5900.10*** *p421*
Coffey, Mary Galvin 78; Vermont, 1891 ***5900.10*** *p290*
Coffey, Michael; Vermont, n.d. ***5900.10*** *p252*
Coffey, Michael 20; New York, New York, 1848 ***1825.45*** *p29*
Coffey, Patrick 81; Vermont, 1894 ***5900.10*** *p290*
Coffey, Patrick 95; Vermont, 1896 ***5900.10*** *p567*
Coffey, Phillip 41; Ontario, 1871 ***1823.22*** *p30*
Coffey, Selina Durivage; Vermont, 1858-1936 ***5900.10*** *p255*
Coffey, Thomas B.; Vermont, 1840-1919 ***5900.10*** *p127*
Coffey, Timothy 70; Vermont, 1889 ***5900.10*** *p82*
Coffey, William; Vermont, 1815-1872 ***5900.10*** *p166*
Coffie, Ann 65; Ontario, 1871 ***1823.22*** *p30*
Coffie, Eleanor; New York, 1830 ***8197.10*** *p353*
Coffin, Abraham; Maryland, 1659 ***2524.55*** *p50*
Coffin, Anne; Maryland, 1681 ***2524.55*** *p50*
Coffin, Clinton 5; Ontario, 1861 ***2896.27*** *p32*

Coffin, David; Maryland, 1681 ***2524.55*** *p50*
Coffin, Gregory; Died enroute, 1662 ***1224.1*** *p14*
Coffin, Jacob 30; Ontario, 1861 ***2896.27*** *p32*
Coffin, Mary 27; Ontario, 1861 ***2896.27*** *p32*
Coffin, Peter; New York, 1807 ***8197.10*** *p36*
Coffin, Robert; Maryland, 1681 ***2524.55*** *p50*
Coffin, Tyler 1; Ontario, 1861 ***2896.27*** *p32*
Coffman, Jacob; Pennsylvania, 1777 ***4629.10*** *p15*
Coffy, John; New York, 1822 ***8197.10*** *p217*
Cofie, George 39; Ontario, 1871 ***1823.15*** *p45*
Cofue, Philip; Maryland, 1672 ***2524.55*** *p50*
Cogach, Angus *SEE* Cogach, John
Cogach, Anne Mackay *SEE* Cogach, John
Cogach, Christiana *SEE* Cogach, John
Cogach, Isabel *SEE* Cogach, John
Cogach, John; Georgia, 1741 ***1640.10*** *p31*
Wife: Anne Mackay
Daughter: Christiana
Son: Angus
Daughter: Isabel
Son: William
Cogach, William *SEE* Cogach, John
Cogan, John 26; Ontario, 1861 ***2896.25*** *p30*
Cogan, John 30; Ontario, 1871 ***1823.22*** *p30*
Cogan, Katie 2 days; Vermont, 1865 ***5900.10*** *p199*
Cogan, Margaret Larkin; Vermont, n.d. ***5900.10*** *p199*
Cogan, Mary A. 4; Vermont, 1863 ***5900.10*** *p199*
Cogan, Minnie 6; Vermont, 1874 ***5900.10*** *p199*
Cogan, Owen; Vermont, n.d. ***5900.10*** *p199*
Cogan, Patrick F. 11; Vermont, 1874 ***5900.10*** *p199*
Cogan, Peter; New York, 1838 ***8197.10*** *p112*
Cogan, Thomas 6; Vermont, 1863 ***5900.10*** *p199*
Cogans, Julia; Vermont, 1845-1928 ***5900.10*** *p452*
Cogans, Mary; Vermont, 1872-1940 ***5900.10*** *p452*
Cogans, Michael; Vermont, 1874-1940 ***5900.10*** *p452*
Cogans, Patrick; Vermont, 1848-1918 ***5900.10*** *p452*
Cogans, Thomas 76; Vermont, 1906 ***5900.10*** *p452*
Cogell, William; New York, 1792 ***1224.2*** *p23*
Cogell, Wm; Virginia, 1673 ***6212.30*** *p51*
Coger, John; New York, 1807 ***8197.10*** *p37*
Coggan, Bartley; New York, 1837 ***8197.10*** *p80*
Coggan, Geo 27; Alaska, 1916 ***9196.1*** *p43*
Coggan, Geo 27; Whitehorse, Yukon, 1916 ***9196.1*** *p43*
Coggay, William J.; New York, 1828-1832 ***8197.10*** *p307*
Coggeshall, Giles; Havana, 1765 ***1224.2*** *p23*
Coggeshall, Giles; Portsmouth, 1765 ***1224.2*** *p23*
Coggeshall, James; Newport, Rhode Island, n.d. ***1224.2*** *p23*
Coggeshall, James; Nova Scotia, 1790 ***1224.2*** *p23*
Coggeshall, John; New England, 1648 ***1224.1*** *p14*
Coggill, George; New York, 1818 ***8197.10*** *p60*
Coggin, Thomas P.; New York, 1837 ***8197.10*** *p374*
Coggins, Bridget; Vermont, 1810-1898 ***5900.10*** *p190*
Coggins, Daniel 66; Vermont, 1897 ***5900.10*** *p127*
Coggins, Ike 39; Seattle, 1913 ***9196.1*** *p60*
Coggins, James 65; Ontario, 1871 ***1823.15*** *p45*
Coggins, Michael 43; Vermont, 1856 ***5900.10*** *p612*
Coggins, Thomas 39; Ontario, 1871 ***1823.15*** *p45*
Coghlan, Daniel; New York, 1822 ***8197.10*** *p217*
Coghlan, Harriet Jarvis; Vermont, 1855-1908 ***5900.10*** *p339*
Coghlan, James; New York, 1815 ***8197.10*** *p214*
Coghlan, James; New York, 1819 ***8197.10*** *p61*
Coghlan, James; New York, 1838 ***8197.10*** *p112*
Coghlan, James 37; Ontario, 1871 ***1823.28*** *p17*
Coghlan, John; New York, 1831 ***8197.10*** *p367*
Coghlan, John; Vermont, 1849-1921 ***5900.10*** *p339*
Coghlan, John D.; New York, 1838 ***8197.10*** *p112*
Coghlan, Patrick 32; Ontario, 1871 ***1823.28*** *p17*
Coghlan, Thomas 64; Ontario, 1871 ***1823.28*** *p17*
Coghlin, Honner; Maryland, 1679 ***2524.55*** *p50*
Coghlin, Thomas; New York, 1840 ***8197.10*** *p221*
Coghlin, Timothy 60; Ontario, 1871 ***1823.15*** *p45*
Cogle, David; Georgia, 1698 ***1640.13*** *p22*
Cogswell, Nathaniel; New York, New York, 1834 ***1224.3*** *p15*
Cohalan, Ellen; Vermont, 1822-1892 ***5900.10*** *p421*
Cohan, Abraham; Pennsylvania, 1777 ***4629.10*** *p29*
Cohen, Mr.; Quebec, 1858 ***9196.15*** *p42*
Cohen, Cleomenes Charles Colman; New York, 1831 ***8197.10*** *p219*
Cohen, Jacob; Pennsylvania, 1777 ***4629.10*** *p24*
Cohen, Jacob Aron; South Carolina, 1813 ***1224.3*** *p15*
Cohen, Mayer; New York, 1831 ***8197.10*** *p313*
Cohen, Mordecai; New York, 1840 ***8197.10*** *p160*
Cohen, Moses; New York, 1840 ***8197.10*** *p159*
Cohen, Samuel; New York, New York, 1857 ***6058.10*** *p70*
Cohen, Solomon Meyers; Pennsylvania, 1777 ***4629.10*** *p14*
Coheran, William; Maryland, 1678 ***2524.55*** *p50*
Cohhone, Joane; Maryland, 1681 ***2524.55*** *p50*
Cohn, Hirsch Casper; New York, 1833 ***8197.10*** *p219*
Cohu, William; New York, 1831 ***8197.10*** *p355*
Coine, John; Ontario, 1871 ***1823.28*** *p17*
Cok, Jane; Virginia, 1703 ***6212.30*** *p62*
Coke, Jno; Virginia, 1674 ***6212.30*** *p51*
Coker, Henry; Virginia, 1665 ***6212.30*** *p19*
Coker, Robert; Virginia, 1666 ***6212.30*** *p31*
Coker, William Lawrence; Boston, 1777 ***1224.2*** *p23*
Cola, Mike 32; Alaska, 1917 ***9196.1*** *p51*
Cola, Mike 32; British Columbia, 1917 ***9196.1*** *p51*
Colahan, James J.; New York, 1840 ***8197.10*** *p221*
Colan, Michael 49; Ontario, 1871 ***1823.22*** *p30*
Colbay, Rielie 22; Ontario, 1871 ***1823.28*** *p17*
Colbert, John; New York, 1828 ***8197.10*** *p349*
Colbick, John 65; Ontario, 1871 ***1823.15*** *p46*
Colbourne, Thomas 36; Ontario, 1871 ***1823.15*** *p46*
Colbrook, Robert 28; Philadelphia, 1774 ***1220.25*** *p80*
Colburn, Elizabeth; Vermont, 1920 ***5900.10*** *p593*
Colburn, John 75; Ontario, 1861 ***2896.27*** *p9*
Colburn, Mary 70; Ontario, 1861 ***2896.27*** *p9*
Colburn, Sarah 25; Ontario, 1861 ***2896.27*** *p9*
Colby, Fred N.; Vermont, 1851 ***5900.10*** *p308*
Colby, Jane E. Henry; Vermont, 1842-1919 ***5900.10*** *p308*
Colby, Jess M.; Vermont, 1840-1905 ***5900.10*** *p308*
Colby, John 73; Ontario, 1871 ***1823.22*** *p31*
Colby, L. E.; Vermont, 1825-1904 ***5900.10*** *p300*
Colby, Mary C. Curran; Vermont, 1862 ***5900.10*** *p308*
Colby, Timothy 78; Ontario, 1871 ***1823.22*** *p31*
Colchester, Thomas; Virginia, 1703 ***1224.2*** *p23*
Colcott, Thomas; Maryland, 1668 ***2524.55*** *p50*
Colcutt, William; Virginia, 1659 ***1224.1*** *p14*
Colden, Alexander; New York, New York, 1784 ***1224.2*** *p23*
Colden, Catharine; Vermont, 1864-1865 ***5900.10*** *p111*
Colden, G. 8; Ontario, 1861 ***2896.26*** *p16*
Colden, Henery 68; Ontario, 1861 ***2896.27*** *p8*
Colden, J. 3; Ontario, 1861 ***2896.26*** *p16*
Colden, J. 38; Ontario, 1861 ***2896.26*** *p16*
Colden, James H. 2; Ontario, 1861 ***2896.27*** *p8*
Colden, Louisa 32; Ontario, 1861 ***2896.27*** *p8*
Colden, Marget 65; Ontario, 1861 ***2896.27*** *p8*
Colden, S. M. 5; Ontario, 1861 ***2896.26*** *p16*
Coldeway, F. 32; British Columbia, 1912 ***9196.1*** *p15*
Coldeway, F. 32; San Francisco, 1912 ***9196.1*** *p15*
Coldisell, William 39; Ontario, 1871 ***1823.15*** *p46*
Coldstream, William; Savannah, Georgia, 1781 ***1224.2*** *p24*
Coldwell, George; New York, 1807 ***8197.10*** *p37*
Coldwell, Samuel 42; Ontario, 1871 ***1823.15*** *p46*
Coldwill, John 40; Ontario, 1871 ***1823.15*** *p46*
Cole, Mrs.; Maryland, 1652-1653 ***2524.55*** *p50*
Cole, Mrs. 28; Ontario, 1861 ***2896.26*** *p29*
Cole, A. Lowry; Quebec, 1856 ***9196.15*** *p5*
Cole, Abram 90; Ontario, 1861 ***2896.27*** *p33*
Cole, Adelaide 14; Ontario, 1861 ***2896.27*** *p29*
Cole, Alexander; Virginia, 1664 ***6212.30*** *p14*
Cole, Andrew; New York, 1802 ***8197.10*** *p19*
Cole, Ann; Maryland, 1682 ***2524.55*** *p50*
Cole, Ann 43; Ontario, 1861 ***2896.25*** *p31*
Cole, Ann 69; Ontario, 1861 ***2896.27*** *p36*
Cole, Austin 20; Maryland, 1774 ***1220.25*** *p53*
Cole, B. 52; Ontario, 1861 ***2896.28*** *p9*
Cole, Benjamin; New York, 1807 ***8197.10*** *p36*
Cole, Bridget; Vermont, 1813-1887 ***5900.10*** *p547*
Cole, Cecelia 7; Ontario, 1861 ***2896.27*** *p36*
Cole, Charles; Annapolis, Maryland, 1759 ***1224.2*** *p24*
Cole, Charles; New York, 1821 ***8197.10*** *p216*
Cole, Charles 45; Ontario, 1861 ***2896.27*** *p39*
Cole, Charles Hugal 1; Ontario, 1871 ***1823.22*** *p31*
Cole, Cynthia J. 20; Ontario, 1861 ***2896.25*** *p31*
Cole, Daniel 22; Ontario, 1861 ***2896.26*** *p39*
Cole, Edmond 2; Ontario, 1871 ***1823.22*** *p31*
Cole, Edmund H. 49; Ontario, 1871 ***1823.22*** *p31*
Cole, Edward 17; Philadelphia, 1775 ***1220.25*** *p9*
Cole, Elijah 3; Ontario, 1861 ***2896.27*** *p39*
Cole, Elisha 65; Ontario, 1861 ***2896.26*** *p29*
Cole, Elizabeth; New England, 1653 ***1224.1*** *p14*
Cole, Elizabeth 37; Ontario, 1861 ***2896.26*** *p34*
Cole, Emily 17; Ontario, 1861 ***2896.27*** *p39*
Cole, Farnting 37; Ontario, 1861 ***2896.26*** *p39*
Cole, Felix; New York, 1837 ***8197.10*** *p82*
Cole, Flora; Maryland, 1660 ***2524.55*** *p50*
Cole, Francis; Maryland, 1659 ***2524.55*** *p50*
Cole, Frank 24; Ontario, 1861 ***2896.26*** *p39*
Cole, Fredrick 33; Ontario, 1871 ***1823.28*** *p17*
Cole, George 8; Ontario, 1861 ***2896.25*** *p31*
Cole, George 19; Ontario, 1871 ***1823.15*** *p46*
Cole, George W. 4; Ontario, 1861 ***2896.27*** *p36*
Cole, Gibes; Maryland, 1680 ***2524.55*** *p50*
Cole, Guy 27; Maryland, 1774 ***1220.25*** *p5*
Cole, Henry 24; Maryland, 1774 ***1220.25*** *p56*
Cole, Henry 25; Ontario, 1871 ***1823.15*** *p46*
Cole, Henry 55; Ontario, 1871 ***1823.15*** *p46*
Cole, Henry 56; Ontario, 1871 ***1823.15*** *p46*
Cole, Irena 15; Ontario, 1861 ***2896.26*** *p34*
Cole, J. 15; Ontario, 1861 ***2896.26*** *p9*
Cole, Jacob M. 1; Ontario, 1861 ***2896.27*** *p36*
Cole, James; Maryland, 1672 ***2524.55*** *p50*
Cole, James; Virginia, 1666-1667 ***6212.30*** *p34*
Cole, James 20; Ontario, 1861 ***2896.26*** *p39*
Cole, John; Maryland, 1678 ***2524.55*** *p218*
Cole, John; Nova Scotia, 1774 ***1220.25*** *p137*
Cole, John; Pennsylvania, 1693 ***1224.1*** *p14*
Cole, John 21; Virginia, 1773 ***1220.25*** *p31*
Cole, John 25; Ontario, 1871 ***1823.28*** *p17*
Cole, John 35; Ontario, 1861 ***2896.27*** *p36*
Cole, John 68; Ontario, 1871 ***1823.15*** *p46*
Cole, John 86; Ontario, 1861 ***2896.25*** *p37*
Cole, John, Sr. 75; Ontario, 1861 ***2896.26*** *p39*
Cole, Joseph 58; Ontario, 1871 ***1823.28*** *p17*
Cole, Joseph 77; Vermont, 1888 ***5900.10*** *p98*
Cole, July Ann 12; Ontario, 1861 ***2896.27*** *p39*
Cole, Kate C. Quinn; Vermont, 1857-1903 ***5900.10*** *p354*
Cole, Ludwig; America, 1741 ***2856.30*** *p68*
Cole, M. J. 17; Ontario, 1861 ***2896.26*** *p29*
Cole, Martin 38; Ontario, 1871 ***1823.28*** *p17*
Cole, Mary 41; Ontario, 1871 ***1823.15*** *p46*
Cole, Mary 49; Vermont, 1890 ***5900.10*** *p361*
Cole, Mary Ann 38; Ontario, 1861 ***2896.27*** *p39*
Cole, Nathaniel B. 9; Ontario, 1861 ***2896.27*** *p36*
Cole, Olaver 18; Ontario, 1861 ***2896.26*** *p34*
Cole, Patrick 33; Ontario, 1871 ***1823.22*** *p31*
Cole, Peter; Maryland, 1669 ***2524.55*** *p50*
Cole, Peter 50; Ontario, 1871 ***1823.15*** *p46*
Cole, Philip; Maryland, 1682 ***2524.55*** *p50*
Cole, Priscilla *SEE* Cole, Thomas
Cole, Rebecca; Maryland, 1658 ***2524.55*** *p51*
Cole, Richard 24; Ontario, 1871 ***1823.15*** *p46*
Cole, Richard 52; Ontario, 1871 ***1823.15*** *p46*
Cole, Robert; Maryland, 1654 ***2524.55*** *p51*
Cole, Roscoe R.; Vermont, 1865-1941 ***5900.10*** *p354*
Cole, Samuel 31; Ontario, 1871 ***1823.15*** *p46*
Cole, Sarah *SEE* Cole, William
Cole, Simon; Boston, 1674 ***1224.1*** *p14*
Cole, Sophia 70; Vermont, 1889 ***5900.10*** *p98*
Cole, Sophia 73; Ontario, 1861 ***2896.25*** *p37*
Cole, Susan *SEE* Cole, William
Cole, Thomas; Maryland, 1649 ***2524.55*** *p51*
Wife: Priscilla
Cole, Thomas; Maryland, 1658 ***2524.55*** *p51*
Cole, Thomas; Maryland, 1672 ***2524.55*** *p51*
Cole, Thomas; Virginia, 1664 ***6212.30*** *p14*
Cole, Thomas 14; Ontario, 1861 ***2896.27*** *p39*
Cole, Thomas 50; Ontario, 1871 ***1823.15*** *p46*
Cole, Thomas 52; Ontario, 1871 ***1823.22*** *p31*
Cole, William; Maryland, 1650 ***2524.55*** *p51*
Wife: Sarah
Daughter: Susan
Cole, William; Maryland, 1673 ***2524.55*** *p51*
Cole, William; Maryland, 1680 ***2524.55*** *p51*
Cole, William; Maryland, 1681 ***2524.55*** *p51*
Cole, William; New York, 1834 ***8197.10*** *p315*
Cole, William; New York, 1839 ***8197.10*** *p132*
Cole, William 13; Ontario, 1861 ***2896.26*** *p34*
Cole, William 16; Philadelphia, 1774 ***1220.25*** *p34*
Cole, William 19; Ontario, 1861 ***2896.27*** *p39*
Cole, William 21; Maryland, 1775 ***1220.25*** *p102*
Cole, William 22; Baltimore, 1775 ***1220.25*** *p117*
Cole, William 22; Ontario, 1861 ***2896.28*** *p9*
Cole, William 52; Ontario, 1861 ***2896.28*** *p9*
Cole, Wright 25; Ontario, 1871 ***1823.28*** *p17*
Colealough, James 24; Philadelphia, 1775 ***1220.25*** *p121*
Colebourne, Ann *SEE* Colebourne, William
Colebourne, William; Maryland, 1661 ***2524.55*** *p51*
Wife: Ann
Child: William, Jr.
Colebourne, William; Maryland, 1681 ***2524.55*** *p51*
Colebourne, William, Jr. *SEE* Colebourne, William
Colebrook, Johanna Murphy; Vermont, 1856-1919 ***5900.10*** *p120*
Colebrook, Martha J.; Vermont, 1863-1933 ***5900.10*** *p119*
Colebrooke, Harriet 21; Maryland, 1775 ***1220.25*** *p114*
Coleburn, Ann *SEE* Coleburn, William
Coleburn, Mary *SEE* Coleburn, William
Coleburn, William; Maryland, 1663 ***2524.55*** *p51*
Wife: Ann
Son: Wm.
Daughter: Mary
Coleburn, Wm. *SEE* Coleburn, William
Coleby, John 21; Maryland, 1775 ***1220.25*** *p114*
Coleford, Richard; Maryland, 1638 ***2524.55*** *p51*
Colegeora, Jos 20; Washington, 1911 ***9196.1*** *p33*
Colehan, John Hughes; New York, 1840 ***8197.10*** *p221*
Colelough, John 50; Ontario, 1871 ***1823.15*** *p46*
Colelough, Samuel 50; Ontario, 1871 ***1823.15*** *p46*

Colelough, William 60; Ontario, 1871 ***1823.15*** *p46*
Coleman, Anna; Vermont, 1831-1891 ***5900.10*** *p220*
Coleman, Annie; Vermont, 1877-1900 ***5900.10*** *p118*
Coleman, Annie; Vermont, 1894-1990 ***5900.10*** *p483*
Coleman, Bailey; Ohio, 1854 ***1224.3*** *p15*
Coleman, Bernard; New York, 1834 ***8197.10*** *p70*
Coleman, Catherine; Vermont, 1834-1864 ***5900.10*** *p560*
Coleman, Catherine Caufield; Vermont, 1851-1916 ***5900.10*** *p118*
Coleman, Charles 45; Ontario, 1861 ***2896.25*** *p71*
Coleman, Christopher; America, 1823 ***1224.3*** *p15*
Coleman, Conrad; Pennsylvania, 1777 ***4629.10*** *p25*
Coleman, Cornelius; Vermont, 1825-1910 ***5900.10*** *p509*
Coleman, David 7; Ontario, 1861 ***2896.25*** *p72*
Coleman, David 47; Ontario, 1861 ***2896.25*** *p71*
Coleman, David 50; Ontario, 1871 ***1823.15*** *p46*
Coleman, Denis; New York, 1840 ***8197.10*** *p160*
Coleman, Frances 13; Ontario, 1861 ***2896.25*** *p71*
Coleman, Francis 41; Ontario, 1871 ***1823.15*** *p46*
Coleman, Frederick; Vermont, 1883-1911 ***5900.10*** *p118*
Coleman, Geo; Virginia, 1666-1667 ***6212.30*** *p34*
Coleman, George; New York, 1839 ***8197.10*** *p220*
Coleman, George; Vermont, 1870-1930 ***5900.10*** *p459*
Coleman, Hannah; Vermont, 1850-1925 ***5900.10*** *p489*
Coleman, Hellen 38; Ontario, 1861 ***2896.25*** *p71*
Coleman, Henry; Vermont, 1850-1913 ***5900.10*** *p489*
Coleman, Isaiah 15; Ontario, 1861 ***2896.25*** *p71*
Coleman, James 36; Ontario, 1871 ***1823.28*** *p17*
Coleman, James 60; Ontario, 1871 ***1823.22*** *p31*
Coleman, Jane 11; Ontario, 1861 ***2896.25*** *p71*
Coleman, Jane 40; Ontario, 1861 ***2896.25*** *p69*
Coleman, Joan; Maryland, 1681 ***2524.55*** *p51*
Coleman, Johannah; Vermont, 1808-1891 ***5900.10*** *p348*
Coleman, John 9; Ontario, 1861 ***2896.25*** *p69*
Coleman, John 22; Virginia, 1774 ***1220.25*** *p54*
Coleman, Lucy Ann 42; Vermont, 1866 ***5900.10*** *p463*
Coleman, Margaret 5; Ontario, 1861 ***2896.25*** *p71*
Coleman, Margaret 70; Vermont, 1859 ***5900.10*** *p342*
Coleman, Margaret 94; Vermont, 1888 ***5900.10*** *p545*
Coleman, Margaret M.; Vermont, 1890-1982 ***5900.10*** *p483*
Coleman, Margaret McCarl; Vermont, 1862-1957 ***5900.10*** *p123*
Coleman, Margarett; Maryland, 1681 ***2524.55*** *p51*
Coleman, Martha 13; Ontario, 1861 ***2896.25*** *p69*
Coleman, Mary; Maryland, 1655-1656 ***2524.55*** *p54*
Coleman, Mary Doon; Vermont, 1857-1951 ***5900.10*** *p483*
Coleman, Mary E.; Vermont, 1892-1898 ***5900.10*** *p483*
Coleman, Michael; New York, 1837 ***8197.10*** *p82*
Coleman, Obed Mitchell; New York, 1846 ***1224.3*** *p15*
Coleman, Patrick; New York, 1826 ***8197.10*** *p218*
Coleman, Patrick 55; Ontario, 1871 ***1823.15*** *p46*
Coleman, Peter; Marblehead, Massachusetts, 1800 ***1224.3*** *p15*
Coleman, Robert 15; Ontario, 1861 ***2896.25*** *p69*
Coleman, Robert 35; Ontario, 1861 ***2896.25*** *p71*
Coleman, Robert 37; Ontario, 1871 ***1823.15*** *p46*
Coleman, Robert 40; Ontario, 1871 ***1823.15*** *p46*
Coleman, Robt 35; Ontario, 1871 ***1823.15*** *p46*
Coleman, Sarah 13; Ontario, 1861 ***2896.25*** *p71*
Coleman, Sarah Harrington; Vermont, 1826-1904 ***5900.10*** *p509*
Coleman, Sarah Stickney; Newbury, Massachusetts, 1801 ***1224.3*** *p15*
Coleman, Thomas; New York, 1840 ***8197.10*** *p163*
Coleman, Thomas; Vermont, 1841-1911 ***5900.10*** *p497*
Coleman, Thomas; Vermont, 1853-1887 ***5900.10*** *p118*
Coleman, Thomas; Vermont, 1861-1938 ***5900.10*** *p483*
Coleman, Thomas; Vermont, 1888-1889 ***5900.10*** *p483*
Coleman, Thomas 35; Vermont, 1861 ***5900.10*** *p516*
Coleman, Thomas 35; Vermont, 1875 ***5900.10*** *p440*
Coleman, Timothy Theobold 42; Ontario, 1871 ***1823.15*** *p46*
Coleman, William; Vermont, 1841-1927 ***5900.10*** *p545*
Colemore, Richard; Maryland, 1663 ***2524.55*** *p51*
Colenutt, Edwin 56; Ontario, 1871 ***1823.15*** *p46*
Colenutt, Elizabeth 24; Ontario, 1871 ***1823.15*** *p46*
Colenutt, James 44; Ontario, 1871 ***1823.15*** *p46*
Coles, Charles; New York, 1839 ***8197.10*** *p132*
Coles, Edward; Maryland, 1673 ***2524.55*** *p51*
Coles, George 15; Virginia, 1774 ***1220.25*** *p89*
Coles, John; New London, Connecticut, 1827 ***1224.3*** *p15*
Coles, John; Pennsylvania, 1693 ***1224.1*** *p14*
Coles, John 26; Ontario, 1871 ***1823.22*** *p31*
Coles, Phillip; Virginia, 1663 ***6212.30*** *p4*
Coles, Tho; Virginia, 1663 ***6212.30*** *p4*
Coles, Thomas 64; Ontario, 1871 ***1823.22*** *p31*
Colesford, Richard; Maryland, 1638 ***2524.55*** *p51*
Colestain, Mary *SEE* Colestain, Robert
Colestain, Robert *SEE* Colestain, Robert
Colestain, Robert; Maryland, 1670 ***2524.55*** *p51*
  Wife: Mary
  Son: Robert
Colestone, Mary *SEE* Colestone, Robert
Colestone, Robert *SEE* Colestone, Robert
Colestone, Robert; Maryland, 1670 ***2524.55*** *p51*
  Son: Robert
  Wife: Mary
Coletsch, Johann Nicolas; Port uncertain, 1770 ***2856.30*** *p72*
  With wife
Colett, Margarete; Port uncertain, 1754 ***2856.30*** *p68*
Coleus, Peter 25; Washington, 1911 ***9196.1*** *p33*
Colgan, Anne 7 *SEE* Colgan, Patrick
Colgan, Anne 12 *SEE* Colgan, Patrick
Colgan, Anne 40 *SEE* Colgan, Patrick
Colgan, Bernard 8 *SEE* Colgan, Patrick
Colgan, Betty 6 *SEE* Colgan, Patrick
Colgan, Bridget 12 *SEE* Colgan, Patrick
Colgan, Dominick; New York, 1824 ***8197.10*** *p217*
Colgan, Dominick; New York, 1828 ***8197.10*** *p64*
Colgan, Edward; New York, 1823 ***8197.10*** *p217*
Colgan, Edward; New York, 1834 ***8197.10*** *p373*
Colgan, Honor 30 *SEE* Colgan, Margaret
Colgan, Margaret 16 *SEE* Colgan, Patrick
Colgan, Margaret 66; New York, New York, 1848 ***1825.45*** *p13*
  Daughter: Honor 30
  Daughter: Mary 28
Colgan, Mary 15 *SEE* Colgan, Patrick
Colgan, Mary 28 *SEE* Colgan, Margaret
Colgan, Mary 40 *SEE* Colgan, Patrick
Colgan, Michael 4 *SEE* Colgan, Patrick
Colgan, Michael 19 *SEE* Colgan, Patrick
Colgan, Neil; New York, 1834 ***8197.10*** *p373*
Colgan, Owen; New York, 1830 ***8197.10*** *p360*
Colgan, Patrick 8 *SEE* Colgan, Patrick
Colgan, Patrick 36; New York, New York, 1847 ***1825.45*** *p13*
  Wife: Mary 40
  Daughter: Bridget 12
  Daughter: Margaret 16
  Daughter: Anne 7
  Son: Michael 19
  Son: Patrick 8
Colgan, Patrick 44; New York, New York, 1847 ***1825.45*** *p13*
  Son: William 1
  Daughter: Anne 12
  Son: Bernard 8
  Wife: Anne 40
  Daughter: Mary 15
  Son: Michael 4
  Daughter: Betty 6
Colgan, William 1 *SEE* Colgan, Patrick
Colgrove, John 23; Virginia, 1774 ***1220.25*** *p88*
Colins, Margaret 25; Ontario, 1861 ***2896.26*** *p30*
Coll, Edward 21; Maryland, 1774 ***1220.25*** *p65*
Coll, William; Maryland, 1680 ***2524.55*** *p51*
Collamer, George B.; Vermont, 1864-1906 ***5900.10*** *p122*
Collan, Peter; New York, 1831 ***8197.10*** *p314*
Collar, A. 11; Ontario, 1861 ***2896.25*** *p45*
Collar, Caroline 38; Ontario, 1861 ***2896.25*** *p45*
Collar, G. W. 1; Ontario, 1861 ***2896.25*** *p45*
Collar, J. L. 15; Ontario, 1861 ***2896.25*** *p45*
Collart, William; Norfolk, Virginia, 1776 ***1224.2*** *p24*
Collas, Mr.; Quebec, 1858 ***9196.15*** *p32*
Colldron, Robert; Virginia, 1665-1666 ***6212.30*** *p23*
Colle, Francis 25; Barbados, 1774 ***1220.25*** *p90*
Collect, Joane; Maryland, 1671 ***2524.55*** *p51*
Collect, John; Philadelphia, 1790 ***4629.10*** *p60*
Colledge, Ruth; Virginia, 1663 ***6212.30*** *p2*
Collemore, Richard; Maryland, 1665 ***2524.55*** *p51*
Collen, Ann 61; Vermont, 1895 ***5900.10*** *p229*
Collen, Lizzie 40; Vermont, 1862 ***5900.10*** *p229*
Collen, Mary C. 38; Vermont, 1906 ***5900.10*** *p229*
Collen, Nancy McCana; Vermont, 1824-1901 ***5900.10*** *p227*
Collen, Owen 75; Vermont, 1889 ***5900.10*** *p227*
Collen, Peter 70; Vermont, 1892 ***5900.10*** *p229*
Collender, Richard 36; Ontario, 1871 ***1823.28*** *p17*
Collens, James 39; Ontario, 1871 ***1823.15*** *p46*
Collens, Richard; Maryland, 1667 ***2524.55*** *p51*
Collerton, Edward; Maryland, 1668 ***2524.55*** *p52*
Colles, Thomas; Virginia, 1706 ***1224.2*** *p24*
Collet, Anna Maria; Port uncertain, 1786 ***2856.30*** *p68*
Collet, Gabriel; New York, 1826 ***8197.10*** *p219*
Collet, George 37; Ontario, 1871 ***1823.28*** *p17*
Collet, John; Washington, District of Columbia, 1822 ***1224.3*** *p15*
Collet, Margarete; Port uncertain, 1770 ***2856.30*** *p68*
Collet, Nicolaus; Port uncertain, 1773 ***2856.30*** *p68*
Collet, Peter; Port uncertain, 1771 ***2856.30*** *p68*
Colleton, John; South Carolina, 1751 ***1224.2*** *p24*
Colleton, John; South Carolina, 1779 ***1224.2*** *p24*
Colleton, Peter; South Carolina, 1754 ***1224.2*** *p24*
Colleton, Peter; South Carolina, 1756 ***1224.2*** *p24*
Collett, Ann *SEE* Collett, John
Collett, Arthur 29; Ontario, 1871 ***1823.28*** *p17*
Collett, George *SEE* Collett, John
Collett, John *SEE* Collett, John
Collett, John; Maryland, 1659 ***2524.55*** *p51*
  Wife: Ann
  Son: George
  Son: Samuel
  Son: John
Collett, Samuel *SEE* Collett, John
Collett, William; Maryland, 1666 ***2524.55*** *p51*
Collidge, William 65; Ontario, 1871 ***1823.28*** *p17*
Collie, Thomas; Jamaica, 1836 ***1640.13*** *p22*
Collie, William; Norfolk, Virginia, 1900 ***1640.13*** *p22*
Collier, Alexander; Virginia, 1739 ***1224.2*** *p24*
Collier, Ann 30; Ontario, 1861 ***2896.26*** *p9*
Collier, Daniel; Maryland, 1681 ***2524.55*** *p51*
Collier, Daniel; New York, 1763 ***1224.2*** *p24*
Collier, E. 1; Ontario, 1861 ***2896.26*** *p11*
Collier, E. 23; Ontario, 1861 ***2896.26*** *p11*
Collier, Frances 56; Ontario, 1861 ***2896.26*** *p11*
Collier, H. 20; Ontario, 1861 ***2896.26*** *p11*
Collier, J. 1; Ontario, 1861 ***2896.26*** *p11*
Collier, J. 19; Ontario, 1861 ***2896.26*** *p9*
Collier, J. R. 7; Ontario, 1861 ***2896.26*** *p9*
Collier, James; Maryland, 1672 ***2524.55*** *p51*
Collier, John; Maryland, 1653 ***2524.55*** *p51*
Collier, Joseph; Ontario, 1871 ***1823.22*** *p31*
Collier, Joseph; South Carolina, 1730 ***1224.2*** *p24*
Collier, Julia Burns 69; Vermont, 1895 ***5900.10*** *p169*
Collier, M. 17; Ontario, 1861 ***2896.26*** *p11*
Collier, M. 25; Ontario, 1861 ***2896.26*** *p9*
Collier, Mathew; New York, 1803 ***8197.10*** *p11*
Collier, Richard; Pennsylvania, 1779 ***4629.10*** *p37*
Collier, Robert 20; Maryland, 1672 ***2524.55*** *p51*
Collier, S. 4; Ontario, 1861 ***2896.26*** *p9*
Collier, Tho; Virginia, 1665-1666 ***6212.30*** *p22*
Collier, Thomas; New York, 1766 ***1224.2*** *p24*
Collier, Thomas 21; Maryland, 1774 ***1220.25*** *p65*
Colligan, Catherine Carroll 62; Vermont, 1880 ***5900.10*** *p568*
Colligan, James; New York, 1827 ***8197.10*** *p218*
Colligan, John F.; Vermont, 1845-1912 ***5900.10*** *p558*
Colligan, Mary E.; Vermont, 1854-1940 ***5900.10*** *p558*
Collin, George 30; Maryland, 1775 ***1220.25*** *p116*
Collin, Joseph; New York, 1798-1817 ***8197.10*** *p214*
Collin, Mary 22; Philadelphia, 1774 ***1220.25*** *p82*
Collin, Michel 74; Ontario, 1871 ***1823.28*** *p17*
Collin, Morris; New York, 1840 ***8197.10*** *p221*
Colling, Aaron 25; Philadelphia, 1775 ***1220.25*** *p122*
Collinge, J.; Quebec, 1856 ***9196.15*** *p9*
Collingham, Barnard; Providence, Rhode Island, 1881 ***1640.13*** *p22*
Collings, Elizabeth; Maryland, 1666 ***2524.55*** *p61*
Collings, Hamel H. M. 10; Ontario, 1861 ***2896.27*** *p24*
Collings, Matilda 12; Ontario, 1861 ***2896.27*** *p24*
Collings, Richard; Maryland, 1666 ***2524.55*** *p61*
Collings, Robert; Pennsylvania, 1777 ***4629.10*** *p26*
Collings, Samuel 49; Ontario, 1871 ***1823.22*** *p31*
Collings, Samuel R.; New York, 1831 ***8197.10*** *p365*
Collings, Samuel R.; New York, 1831 ***8197.10*** *p370*
Collings, William; Maryland, 1666 ***2524.55*** *p61*
Collington, Geo.; Maryland, 1663 ***2524.55*** *p51*
Collington, Isabell; New England, 1660 ***1224.1*** *p14*
Collingwood, Charles; Pennsylvania, 1835 ***6058.10*** *p12*
Collingwood, Gerard; Virginia, 1732 ***1224.2*** *p24*
Collingwood, Hannah 50; Ontario, 1871 ***1823.15*** *p46*
Collingwood, John 29; Ontario, 1871 ***1823.15*** *p46*
Collingwood, Thomas 35; Ontario, 1871 ***1823.15*** *p46*
Collingwood, Thomas 59; Ontario, 1871 ***1823.15*** *p46*
Collins, Alfred 44; Ontario, 1871 ***1823.15*** *p46*
Collins, Ann; Vermont, 1851-1926 ***5900.10*** *p584*
Collins, Ann Gilrain 54; Vermont, 1870 ***5900.10*** *p451*
Collins, Ann Slattery 59; Vermont, 1891 ***5900.10*** *p565*
Collins, Ann Tobin; Vermont, 1844-1880 ***5900.10*** *p133*
Collins, Anne; Virginia, 1657 ***1224.1*** *p14*
Collins, Anneky *SEE* Collins, Johnathan
Collins, Annie 48; Vermont, 1899 ***5900.10*** *p477*
Collins, Bartholomew; New York, 1802 ***8197.10*** *p19*
Collins, Bartholomew 68; Vermont, 1887 ***5900.10*** *p451*
Collins, Bartholomew 74; Vermont, 1903 ***5900.10*** *p61*
Collins, Bridget; Vermont, n.d. ***5900.10*** *p165*
Collins, Bridget; Vermont, 1829-1920 ***5900.10*** *p171*
Collins, Bridget; Vermont, 1832-1907 ***5900.10*** *p161*
Collins, Bridget; Vermont, 1852 ***5900.10*** *p444*
Collins, Bridget; Vermont, 1857-1891 ***5900.10*** *p215*
Collins, Bridget 56; Vermont, 1864 ***5900.10*** *p343*
Collins, Bridget 87; Vermont, 1917 ***5900.10*** *p564*
Collins, C. 26; Ontario, 1871 ***1823.15*** *p46*

Collins, Catherine; Vermont, 1838-1924 ***5900.10*** *p167*
Collins, Catherine; Vermont, 1840-1900 ***5900.10*** *p133*
Collins, Catherine; Vermont, 1851-1885 ***5900.10*** *p584*
Collins, Catherine 65; Ontario, 1871 ***1823.28*** *p17*
Collins, Catherine Kennedy; Vermont, 1843-1918 ***5900.10*** *p142*
Collins, Catherine S.; Vermont, 1845-1922 ***5900.10*** *p310*
Collins, Charles A.; Vermont, 1842-1915 ***5900.10*** *p312*
Collins, Cornelius; Vermont, 1854-1910 ***5900.10*** *p92*
Collins, Daniel; Vermont, 1827-1917 ***5900.10*** *p351*
Collins, Daniel; Vermont, 1842-1899 ***5900.10*** *p345*
Collins, Daniel 34; Ontario, 1871 ***1823.22*** *p31*
Collins, Daniel 47; Ontario, 1871 ***1823.15*** *p46*
Collins, Daniel 60; Ontario, 1871 ***1823.22*** *p31*
Collins, Dennie 18; Vermont, 1880 ***5900.10*** *p110*
Collins, Dennis 36; Vermont, 1853 ***5900.10*** *p315*
Collins, Dennis 38; Ontario, 1871 ***1823.15*** *p46*
Collins, Dennis 69; Vermont, 1885 ***5900.10*** *p110*
Collins, Edward 32; Vermont, 1878 ***5900.10*** *p215*
Collins, Edward 65; Ontario, 1871 ***1823.28*** *p17*
Collins, Eliza 21; Ontario, 1861 ***2896.27*** *p40*
Collins, Elizabeth Ann 15; Ontario, 1871 ***1823.22*** *p31*
Collins, Elizabeth Hart 76; Vermont, 1885 ***5900.10*** *p315*
Collins, Ellen; Portland, Maine, 1858 ***9196.15*** *p29*
Collins, Ellen; Quebec, 1858 ***9196.15*** *p45*
Collins, Ellen; Vermont, 1827-1902 ***5900.10*** *p87*
Collins, Ellen; Vermont, 1839-1931 ***5900.10*** *p62*
Collins, Ellen; Vermont, 1856-1942 ***5900.10*** *p553*
Collins, Ellen 65; Vermont, 1895 ***5900.10*** *p102*
Collins, Ellen 73; Vermont, 1893 ***5900.10*** *p397*
Collins, Ellen 85; Vermont, 1867 ***5900.10*** *p73*
Collins, Ellen Cohalan; Vermont, 1822-1892 ***5900.10*** *p421*
Collins, Ellen Donnelly; Vermont, 1839-1927 ***5900.10*** *p312*
Collins, Ferdinand; Vermont, 1839-1919 ***5900.10*** *p553*
Collins, Frances 48; Ontario, 1861 ***2896.27*** *p24*
Collins, Francis; New York, 1836 ***8197.10*** *p79*
Collins, Fredrich *SEE* Collins, Johnathan
Collins, George; Maryland, 1665 ***2524.55*** *p51*
Son: William
Collins, George 11; Ontario, 1861 ***2896.28*** *p52*
Collins, George 28; Ontario, 1871 ***1823.28*** *p17*
Collins, Hannah 29; Vermont, 1881 ***5900.10*** *p110*
Collins, Hanora; Vermont, 1853-1873 ***5900.10*** *p141*
Collins, Harriet 38; Ontario, 1871 ***1823.22*** *p31*
Collins, Henrietta E.; Vermont, 1857-1935 ***5900.10*** *p598*
Collins, Henrietta E.; Vermont, 1857-1935 ***5900.10*** *p599*
Collins, Henry; New York, 1824 ***8197.10*** *p217*
Collins, Henry 49; Ontario, 1861 ***2896.27*** *p33*
Collins, Herbert; Maryland, 1656 ***2524.55*** *p51*
Collins, James; Vermont, n.d. ***5900.10*** *p367*
Collins, James; Vermont, 1906 ***5900.10*** *p159*
Collins, James; Virginia, 1665 ***6212.30*** *p19*
Collins, James 19; Maryland, 1774 ***1220.25*** *p41*
Collins, James 38; Ontario, 1871 ***1823.28*** *p17*
Collins, James 60; Ontario, 1871 ***1823.28*** *p17*
Collins, James 77; Ontario, 1871 ***1823.15*** *p46*
Collins, James 77; Vermont, 1907 ***5900.10*** *p367*
Collins, James E. 19; Vermont, 1870 ***5900.10*** *p315*
Collins, Jane; Virginia, 1666-1667 ***6212.30*** *p34*
Collins, Jane 47; Vermont, 1876 ***5900.10*** *p613*
Collins, Jane 69; Ontario, 1871 ***1823.22*** *p31*
Collins, Jeremiah; New York, 1840 ***8197.10*** *p161*
Collins, Jeremiah; New York, 1840 ***8197.10*** *p163*
Collins, Jeremiah; Vermont, 1814-1870 ***5900.10*** *p421*
Collins, Jeremiah 36; Ontario, 1871 ***1823.22*** *p31*
Collins, Jess; Canada, 1895 ***1640.13*** *p22*
Collins, Jno; Virginia, 1664 ***6212.30*** *p15*
Collins, Jno; Virginia, 1672 ***6212.30*** *p49*
Collins, Johanna 86; Vermont, 1887 ***5900.10*** *p574*
Collins, Johannah 80; Vermont, 1880 ***5900.10*** *p177*
Collins, John; Cape Fear, North Carolina, 1753 ***1224.2*** *p24*
Collins, John; Delaware, 1775-1781 ***4628.40*** *p69*
Collins, John; New York, 1729 ***1224.2*** *p24*
Collins, John; New York, 1837 ***8197.10*** *p374*
Collins, John; New York, 1840 ***8197.10*** *p221*
Collins, John; New York, 1840 ***8197.10*** *p385*
Collins, John; Vermont, 1835-1910 ***5900.10*** *p407*
Collins, John; Vermont, 1837-1906 ***5900.10*** *p132*
Collins, John; Vermont, 1840-1929 ***5900.10*** *p224*
Collins, John; Vermont, 1845 ***5900.10*** *p223*
Collins, John; Vermont, 1846-1904 ***5900.10*** *p215*
Collins, John; Vermont, 1855-1923 ***5900.10*** *p574*
Collins, John; Virginia, 1663 ***6212.30*** *p3*
Collins, John 25; Virginia, 1775 ***1220.25*** *p95*
Collins, John 39; Maryland, 1773-1774 ***1220.25*** *p34*
Collins, John 42; Philadelphia, 1775 ***1220.25*** *p122*
Collins, John 46; Vermont, 1872 ***5900.10*** *p267*
Collins, John 61; Ontario, 1871 ***1823.22*** *p31*
Collins, John 63; Ontario, 1871 ***1823.15*** *p47*
Collins, John 72; Vermont, 1886 ***5900.10*** *p92*
Collins, John E. 46; Ontario, 1871 ***1823.28*** *p17*
Collins, John J. 30; Vermont, 1874 ***5900.10*** *p262*
Collins, John P.; Vermont, 1851-1919 ***5900.10*** *p421*
Collins, Johnathan; Maryland, 1667 ***2524.55*** *p52*
Wife: Veny
Child: Anneky
Child: Fredrich
Collins, Joseph; Vermont, 1851-1932 ***5900.10*** *p194*
Collins, Joseph 20; Maryland, 1774 ***1220.25*** *p69*
Collins, Joshua; Pennsylvania, 1777 ***4629.10*** *p28*
Collins, Julia; Vermont, 1837-1911 ***5900.10*** *p433*
Collins, Julia; Vermont, 1875-1930 ***5900.10*** *p192*
Collins, Katherine Riley; Vermont, 1850-1932 ***5900.10*** *p92*
Collins, Kathrine Fitzgerald; Vermont, 1903 ***5900.10*** *p159*
Collins, Katie 23; Vermont, 1876 ***5900.10*** *p110*
Collins, Levi 42; Ontario, 1861 ***2896.27*** *p23*
Collins, Louise M. Russell; Vermont, 1852-1928 ***5900.10*** *p194*
Collins, M.; Vermont, 1852-1923 ***5900.10*** *p127*
Collins, Margaret; Vermont, 1810-1883 ***5900.10*** *p592*
Collins, Margaret; Vermont, 1837-1915 ***5900.10*** *p63*
Collins, Margaret 56; Vermont, 1884 ***5900.10*** *p465*
Collins, Margaret Holleran; Vermont, 1854-1893 ***5900.10*** *p574*
Collins, Margarite 21; Ontario, 1871 ***1823.28*** *p17*
Collins, Margret 50; Ontario, 1871 ***1823.15*** *p47*
Collins, Margrett; Maryland, 1678 ***2524.55*** *p52*
Collins, Mariah; Vermont, 1837-1897 ***5900.10*** *p460*
Collins, Mark; Pennsylvania, 1786 ***4629.10*** *p46*
Collins, Mary; Vermont, 1847-1944 ***5900.10*** *p240*
Collins, Mary; Vermont, 1864-1940 ***5900.10*** *p65*
Collins, Mary 27; New York, New York, 1850 ***1825.45*** *p46*
Collins, Mary 34; Vermont, 1859 ***5900.10*** *p367*
Collins, Mary 50; Vermont, 1875 ***5900.10*** *p267*
Collins, Mary 60; Vermont, 1875 ***5900.10*** *p173*
Collins, Mary 62; Vermont, 1895 ***5900.10*** *p57*
Collins, Mary Anne 50; Ontario, 1871 ***1823.15*** *p47*
Collins, Mary Brady; Vermont, 1832-1917 ***5900.10*** *p132*
Collins, Mary Culligan; Vermont, 1841-1918 ***5900.10*** *p407*
Collins, Mary Cushing 62; Vermont, 1900 ***5900.10*** *p367*
Collins, Mary E.; Vermont, 1859-1955 ***5900.10*** *p485*
Collins, Mary E. 77; Vermont, 1922 ***5900.10*** *p315*
Collins, Mary J. Brannan; Vermont, 1856-1929 ***5900.10*** *p224*
Collins, Mary McMahon; Vermont, 1838-1912 ***5900.10*** *p351*
Collins, Mary Murphy 96; Vermont, 1915 ***5900.10*** *p92*
Collins, Mary Potter; Vermont, 1848-1948 ***5900.10*** *p215*
Collins, Mary Sullivan 33; Vermont, 1855 ***5900.10*** *p347*
Collins, Mary Toomey; Vermont, 1801-1887 ***5900.10*** *p132*
Collins, Mathew; Maryland, 1662 ***2524.55*** *p52*
Collins, Mathew; Maryland, 1682 ***2524.55*** *p52*
Collins, Matthew; Vermont, 1845-1913 ***5900.10*** *p133*
Collins, Maurice; Vermont, 1834-1908 ***5900.10*** *p215*
Collins, Michael; Maryland, 1655-1656 ***2524.55*** *p52*
Collins, Michael; Pennsylvania, 1867 ***6058.10*** *p57*
Collins, Michael; Vermont, 1844-1915 ***5900.10*** *p177*
Collins, Michael; Vermont, 1853-1908 ***5900.10*** *p444*
Collins, Michael 24; Vermont, 1869 ***5900.10*** *p215*
Collins, Michael 63; Vermont, 1896 ***5900.10*** *p367*
Collins, Michael 86; Vermont, 1886 ***5900.10*** *p177*
Collins, Nancy; Vermont, 1844-1900 ***5900.10*** *p224*
Collins, Nancy; Vermont, 1845-1936 ***5900.10*** *p357*
Collins, Nancy Killy 101; Vermont, 1867 ***5900.10*** *p226*
Collins, Nancy Kingston 64; Vermont, 1876 ***5900.10*** *p362*
Collins, Nicholas 29; Ontario, 1871 ***1823.22*** *p31*
Collins, Nora; Vermont, 1857-1909 ***5900.10*** *p353*
Collins, P. H.; Vermont, 1853-1920 ***5900.10*** *p224*
Collins, Palfrey; Boston, 1787 ***1224.2*** *p24*
Collins, Patrick; New York, 1836 ***8197.10*** *p317*
Collins, Patrick; Vermont, 1804-1903 ***5900.10*** *p142*
Collins, Patrick 25; Maryland, 1775 ***1220.25*** *p97*
Collins, Patrick 28; Vermont, 1870 ***5900.10*** *p362*
Collins, Patrick 45; Ontario, 1871 ***1823.28*** *p18*
Collins, Patrick 65; Ontario, 1871 ***1823.22*** *p31*
Collins, Patrick 104; Vermont, 1852 ***5900.10*** *p226*
Collins, Peter; New York, 1818 ***8197.10*** *p214*
Collins, Peter 40; Virginia, 1774 ***1220.25*** *p45*
Collins, Richard; Virginia, 1667 ***1224.1*** *p14*
Collins, Richard 5; Ontario, 1871 ***1823.22*** *p31*
Collins, Richard 37; Virginia, 1775 ***1220.25*** *p100*
Collins, Richard 60; Ontario, 1871 ***1823.28*** *p18*
Collins, Roger 80; Vermont, 1895 ***5900.10*** *p223*
Collins, Rosa Woods; Vermont, 1860-1901 ***5900.10*** *p224*
Collins, Rosemond 60; Ontario, 1871 ***1823.15*** *p47*
Collins, Samuell; Maryland, 1679 ***2524.55*** *p52*
Collins, Sarah; Vermont, 1822-1895 ***5900.10*** *p592*
Collins, Sarah J. Miles; Vermont, 1853-1889 ***5900.10*** *p223*
Collins, Sarah Morris 84; Vermont, 1931 ***5900.10*** *p61*
Collins, Stephen; Pennsylvania, 1777 ***4629.10*** *p21*
Collins, Stephen; Vermont, 1837-1926 ***5900.10*** *p167*
Collins, Stephen S.; Vermont, 1812-1885 ***5900.10*** *p500*
Collins, Steven; Maryland, 1910 ***3259.35*** *p10*
Collins, Susan 25; Ontario, 1871 ***1823.28*** *p18*
Collins, Thankful W. Connor; Vermont, 1817-1860 ***5900.10*** *p500*
Collins, Thomas; Delaware, 1775-1781 ***4628.40*** *p69*
Collins, Thomas; Maryland, 1725-1726 ***1224.2*** *p25*
Collins, Thomas; Pennsylvania, 1867 ***6058.10*** *p60*
Collins, Thomas 28; Maryland, 1774 ***1220.25*** *p52*
Collins, Thomas 32; Maryland, 1774 ***1220.25*** *p52*
Collins, Thomas 36; Ontario, 1871 ***1823.28*** *p18*
Collins, Thomas 52; Ontario, 1871 ***1823.28*** *p18*
Collins, Thomas 90; Vermont, 1883 ***5900.10*** *p574*
Collins, Timothy; Vermont, 1829-1907 ***5900.10*** *p87*
Collins, Timothy 55; Ontario, 1871 ***1823.22*** *p31*
Collins, Timothy 65; Vermont, 1897 ***5900.10*** *p565*
Collins, Timothy 77; Vermont, 1877 ***5900.10*** *p226*
Collins, Tommy 13; Vermont, 1888 ***5900.10*** *p110*
Collins, Veny *SEE* Collins, Johnathan
Collins, W. H. 12; Ontario, 1861 ***2896.26*** *p3*
Collins, William *SEE* Collins, George
Collins, William; Maryland, 1655 ***2524.55*** *p175*
Collins, William; Maryland, 1658 ***2524.55*** *p52*
Collins, William; Maryland, 1679 ***2524.55*** *p52*
Collins, William; New York, 1830 ***8197.10*** *p360*
Collins, William; New York, 1837 ***8197.10*** *p80*
Collins, William 14; Philadelphia, 1775 ***1220.25*** *p8*
Collins, William 24; Maryland, 1774 ***1220.25*** *p76*
Collins, William 24; Maryland, 1775 ***1220.25*** *p104*
Collins, William 40; Ontario, 1871 ***1823.28*** *p18*
Collins, William 60; Ontario, 1871 ***1823.15*** *p47*
Collinson, George 28; Ontario, 1871 ***1823.15*** *p47*
Collinson, William; Maryland, 1672 ***2524.55*** *p52*
Collinson, William 42; Ontario, 1871 ***1823.15*** *p47*
Collis, William 45; Ontario, 1871 ***1823.22*** *p31*
Collison, Ellen 82; Vermont, 1905 ***5900.10*** *p445*
Collison, George F.; Vermont, 1843-1932 ***5900.10*** *p146*
Collison, Mary A. Mullins; Vermont, 1848-1916 ***5900.10*** *p147*
Colliver, Almeda 4; Ontario, 1861 ***2896.27*** *p31*
Colliver, Charlotte E. 2; Ontario, 1861 ***2896.27*** *p31*
Colliver, John 41; Ontario, 1861 ***2896.27*** *p31*
Colliver, John H. 11; Ontario, 1861 ***2896.27*** *p31*
Colliver, Jonathan R. 7; Ontario, 1861 ***2896.27*** *p31*
Colliver, Mary J. 10; Ontario, 1861 ***2896.27*** *p31*
Collmar, Maria Catharina; America, 1738 ***2856.30*** *p68*
Collmer, Jakob; Port uncertain, 1768 ***2856.30*** *p68*
Collons, William 72; Ontario, 1871 ***1823.15*** *p47*
Collopy, Margaret; Vermont, 1821-1907 ***5900.10*** *p300*
Collosky, John 53; Ontario, 1871 ***1823.15*** *p47*
Colloway, Anthony; Maryland, 1644-1650 ***2524.55*** *p52*
Colltsch, Johann Nicolas; Port uncertain, 1770 ***2856.30*** *p72*
With wife
Collup, William 15; Philadelphia, 1774 ***1220.25*** *p34*
Colly, Sylvanus; Virginia, 1698 ***6212.30*** *p61*
Collyer, Francis; Pennsylvania, 1866 ***6058.10*** *p53*
Collyer, James; Pennsylvania, 1844 ***1224.3*** *p15*
Collyer, Jane Curtyce; New England, 1660 ***1224.1*** *p16*
Collyer, Richard; New York, 1840 ***8197.10*** *p160*
Collyer, Samuel Charles; New York, New York, 1837 ***1224.3*** *p15*
Collyer, Walter; Virginia, 1671-1672 ***6212.30*** *p47*
Colman, Sebastian; America, 1738 ***2856.30*** *p68*
Colmar, Barbara; Port uncertain, 1792 ***2856.30*** *p68*
Colmer, George 44; Maryland, 1774 ***1220.25*** *p64*
Cologan, Patrick; New York, 1839 ***8197.10*** *p381*
Colon, John; Virginia, 1666 ***6212.30*** *p28*
Colona, Owen; Virginia, 1663 ***6212.30*** *p2*
Colonon, Ogin; Virginia, 1671 ***6212.30*** *p43*
Colopy, Bridget 63; Vermont, 1882 ***5900.10*** *p540*
Colose, Fredrick 44; Ontario, 1871 ***1823.28*** *p18*
Coloton, James 50; Ontario, 1871 ***1823.15*** *p47*
Colpits, Robert 28; Fort Cumberland, Nova Scotia, 1775 ***1220.25*** *p21*
Colquhoun, Angus; Georgia, 1782-1812 ***1640.10*** *p31*
Colquhoun, Jas; Quebec, 1858 ***9196.15*** *p47*
Colquhoun, John; New York, 1839 ***8197.10*** *p132*
Colsey, Henry James Chitty; New York, 1836 ***8197.10*** *p79*
Colsin, Nicholas; Maryland, 1658 ***2524.55*** *p56*
Colsin, Nick; Maryland, 1648 ***2524.55*** *p52*
Colson, Charles 63; Ontario, 1871 ***1823.28*** *p18*
Colson, Elizabeth; Charles Town, South Carolina, 1751 ***1224.2*** *p25*
Colson, Jane 5; Ontario, 1871 ***1823.15*** *p47*
Colson, Maria 18; Ontario, 1871 ***1823.15*** *p47*
Colson, Robert 13; Ontario, 1871 ***1823.15*** *p47*

Colson, Thomas 32; Ontario, 1871 ***1823.28*** *p18*
Colson, William 27; Ontario, 1871 ***1823.15*** *p47*
Colsova, Ann 20; Ontario, 1871 ***1823.28*** *p18*
Colston, Rawleigh; Virginia, 1827 ***1224.3*** *p16*
Colston, Tho; Virginia, 1665-1666 ***6212.30*** *p21*
Colston, Thomas 29; Philadelphia, 1774 ***1220.25*** *p2*
Colsworthy, George; Maryland, 1704 ***1224.2*** *p25*
Colt, Andrew; Georgia, 1698 ***1640.13*** *p22*
Colt, Eliza; Virginia, 1667 ***6212.30*** *p36*
Colter, Benjamin; New York, 1840 ***8197.10*** *p302*
Colter, George 59; Ontario, 1871 ***1823.28*** *p18*
Colter, John 51; Ontario, 1871 ***1823.15*** *p47*
Colter, Mary 30; Ontario, 1871 ***1823.15*** *p47*
Colter, Samuel 45; Ontario, 1871 ***1823.15*** *p47*
Colter, Thomas 64; Ontario, 1871 ***1823.15*** *p47*
Colterton, Edward; Maryland, 1668 ***2524.55*** *p52*
Colthred, John; Georgia, 1737 ***1640.10*** *p31*
Colthred, William; Georgia, 1738 ***1640.10*** *p31*
Coltis, Robert 40; Ontario, 1871 ***1823.15*** *p47*
Coltman, . . .; Virginia, 1623 ***1224.1*** *p14*
Coltman, Robert; Pennsylvania, 1781 ***4629.10*** *p42*
Coltman, William; Virginia, 1666 ***1224.1*** *p14*
Colton, Amy 86; Vermont, 1846 ***5900.10*** *p376*
Colton, Edward; New York, 1825 ***8197.10*** *p217*
Colton, James 50; Ontario, 1871 ***1823.28*** *p18*
Colton, Mary; Vermont, 1854-1930 ***5900.10*** *p44*
Colton, Rose; Vermont, 1807-1882 ***5900.10*** *p561*
Colton, Thomas 40; Ontario, 1871 ***1823.28*** *p18*
Colton, W. H. 61; Ontario, 1871 ***1823.22*** *p31*
Colton, William 22; Virginia, 1774 ***1220.25*** *p94*
Coltropp, Jno; Virginia, 1665-1666 ***6212.30*** *p21*
Coluskey, Margaret 49; Ontario, 1871 ***1823.15*** *p47*
Colvan, James 40; Ontario, 1871 ***1823.28*** *p18*
Colven, George 62; Ontario, 1871 ***1823.15*** *p47*
Colvill, John; Georgia, 1699 ***1640.13*** *p22*
Colvill, John; New England, 1695 ***1224.1*** *p14*
Colvill, Matthew; Cape Fear, North Carolina, 1790 ***1224.2*** *p25*
Colville, James 42; Ontario, 1871 ***1823.15*** *p47*
Colville, Thomas Low; America, 1875 ***1640.13*** *p22*
Colvin, Miss; Quebec, 1856 ***9196.15*** *p9*
Colvin, Harriet 30; Ontario, 1861 ***2896.28*** *p21*
Colvin, James Kennedy; Providence, Rhode Island, 1896 ***1640.13*** *p23*
Colvin, Robert 63; Ontario, 1871 ***1823.22*** *p31*
Colwell, William 37; Ontario, 1871 ***1823.22*** *p31*
Colwill, Joseph 34; Ontario, 1871 ***1823.15*** *p47*
Colyer, Francis; Pennsylvania, 1866 ***6058.10*** *p53*
Colyer, George; New York, 1838 ***8197.10*** *p112*
Coman, John 50; Ontario, 1871 ***1823.15*** *p47*
Coman, John, II; Maryland, 1671 ***2524.55*** *p52*
Comando, Joseph 70; Ontario, 1871 ***1823.28*** *p18*
Comasky, James; New York, 1826 ***8197.10*** *p218*
Comb, Fredrick 40; Ontario, 1871 ***1823.28*** *p18*
Comb, John; New York, 1840 ***8197.10*** *p159*
Combault, Peter Estaniselas; New York, 1818 ***8197.10*** *p214*
Combault, Pierre Estaniselas; New York, 1823 ***8197.10*** *p62*
Combe, James 36; Ontario, 1871 ***1823.15*** *p47*
Comber, Abraham; Maryland, 1680 ***2524.55*** *p52*
Daughter: Sarah
Comber, Rodrick 49; Ontario, 1871 ***1823.28*** *p18*
Comber, Samsom 62; Ontario, 1871 ***1823.28*** *p18*
Comber, Sarah *SEE* Comber, Abraham
Combes, Edmond 50; Ontario, 1871 ***1823.15*** *p47*
Combes, Elizabeth; Maryland, 1658 ***2524.55*** *p52*
Combes, Maryann 55; Ontario, 1871 ***1823.22*** *p31*
Combes, Philip; Maryland, 1664 ***2524.55*** *p52*
Combes, Phillip; Maryland, 1659 ***2524.55*** *p52*
Combes, William 15; Baltimore, 1775 ***1220.25*** *p116*
Combest, John; Maryland, 1682 ***2524.55*** *p52*
Combs, John 30; Ontario, 1871 ***1823.22*** *p31*
Combs, Mary; Maryland, 1659 ***2524.55*** *p33*
Combs, Richard; Virginia, 1665-1666 ***6212.30*** *p21*
Combs, Richard 24; Ontario, 1871 ***1823.15*** *p47*
Combs, Thomas; New York, 1840 ***8197.10*** *p163*
Combs, Thomas 30; Ontario, 1871 ***1823.15*** *p47*
Comegys, Cornelius *SEE* Comegys, Cornelius
Comegys, Cornelius; Maryland, 1666 ***2524.55*** *p52*
Wife: Willemyntye
Son: Cornelius
Comegys, John; Pennsylvania, 1777 ***4629.10*** *p10*
Comegys, Willemyntye *SEE* Comegys, Cornelius
Comer, Charles; New York, 1687 ***1224.1*** *p14*
Comer, Henry 31; Ontario, 1871 ***1823.15*** *p47*
Comer, John; New York, 1736 ***1224.2*** *p25*
Comer, M. A. 62; Ontario, 1861 ***2896.28*** *p13*
Comer, Maria 85; Vermont, 1899 ***5900.10*** *p258*
Comer, Mary; Vermont, 1820-1920 ***5900.10*** *p206*
Comerford, Ann 47; Vermont, 1891 ***5900.10*** *p547*
Comerford, Ellen Butler 65; Vermont, 1876 ***5900.10*** *p547*
Comerford, John 83; Vermont, 1888 ***5900.10*** *p547*
Comerford, John Francis; America, 1794 ***1224.3*** *p16*
Comerford, Mary A.; Vermont, 1837-1907 ***5900.10*** *p547*
Comerford, Nellie B. 92; Vermont, 1932 ***5900.10*** *p547*
Comerford, Patrick L. 83; Vermont, 1930 ***5900.10*** *p547*
Comerford, Thomas 56; Vermont, 1886 ***5900.10*** *p547*
Comery, Peter 57; Ontario, 1871 ***1823.28*** *p18*
Comes, Abraham; Maryland, 1670 ***2524.55*** *p52*
Daughter: Sarah
Comes, Barbary *SEE* Comes, Enoch
Comes, Enoch *SEE* Comes, Enoch
Comes, Enoch; Maryland, 1664 ***2524.55*** *p52*
Wife: Barbary
Son: Enoch
Comes, Fennekey *SEE* Comes, Walter
Comes, Sarah *SEE* Comes, Abraham
Comes, Walter; Maryland, 1666 ***2524.55*** *p52*
Wife: Fennekey
Comey, Edward; Vermont, 1851-1923 ***5900.10*** *p394*
Comey, Ellen; Vermont, 1859-1947 ***5900.10*** *p394*
Comforter, James 34; Ontario, 1871 ***1823.28*** *p18*
Comin, Grace; Virginia, 1672 ***6212.30*** *p48*
Comin, Uriah; Virginia, 1672 ***6212.30*** *p48*
Comins, Robert; Maryland, 1661 ***2524.55*** *p52*
Comins, Robert; Maryland, 1664 ***2524.55*** *p52*
Commander, Charles 54; Ontario, 1871 ***1823.15*** *p47*
Commins, Edward; Maryland, 1639 ***2524.55*** *p52*
Wife: Elizabeth
Commins, Elizabeth *SEE* Commins, Edward
Commins, Elizabeth; Maryland, 1639 ***2524.55*** *p52*
Comor, Patrick 30; Ontario, 1871 ***1823.28*** *p18*
Comp, William; Maryland, 1663 ***2524.55*** *p52*
Compa, Maria Elisabeth; Port uncertain, 1768 ***2856.30*** *p68*
Comper, Mathes; Port uncertain, 1751 ***2856.30*** *p68*
Comport, Katherine; Maryland, 1669 ***2524.55*** *p52*
Compthall, Elizabeth; Maryland, 1676 ***2524.55*** *p52*
Compton, Christopher; Maryland, 1681 ***2524.55*** *p52*
Compton, Francis; Virginia, 1665-1666 ***6212.30*** *p21*
Compton, John; New York, 1837 ***8197.10*** *p219*
Compton, Jonathan; Maryland, 1680 ***2524.55*** *p52*
Compton, Robert; Virginia, 1664 ***6212.30*** *p11*
Compton, William 25; Maryland, 1775 ***1220.25*** *p100*
Comrie, James 60; Ontario, 1871 ***1823.22*** *p32*
Comrin, John; Boston, 1765 ***1224.2*** *p25*
Comron, Abraham; Pennsylvania, 1779 ***4629.10*** *p41*
Comstock, James W.; Vermont, 1846-1928 ***5900.10*** *p196*
Comstock, Mary Jane McMullen; Vermont, 1836-1906 ***5900.10*** *p196*
Comyn, Frederick Duke; Florida, 1778 ***1224.2*** *p25*
Comyn, Thomas; Florida, 1769 ***1640.10*** *p31*
Comyn, Valence Stephen; Florida, 1778 ***1224.2*** *p25*
Con, Thomas; New York, 1779 ***1224.2*** *p25*
Conacheche, Joseph; New York, 1794 ***8197.10*** *p2*
Conaly, Andrew 23; Maryland, 1775 ***1220.25*** *p96*
Conaten, James; New York, 1840 ***8197.10*** *p161*
Concannon, James; Virginia, 1764 ***1224.2*** *p25*
Conchy, James; Pennsylvania, 1777 ***4629.10*** *p22*
Conchy, James; Pennsylvania, 1779 ***4629.10*** *p40*
Condell, Charles 35; Ontario, 1871 ***1823.28*** *p18*
Condell, John 30; Ontario, 1871 ***1823.28*** *p18*
Condell, Patrick 30; Ontario, 1871 ***1823.28*** *p18*
Condey, James 51; Ontario, 1871 ***1823.15*** *p47*
Condie, James 70; Ontario, 1871 ***1823.28*** *p18*
Condle, Patrick 41; Ontario, 1871 ***1823.28*** *p18*
Condon, Bridget; Vermont, 1833-1893 ***5900.10*** *p221*
Condon, Catherine 68; Vermont, 1914 ***5900.10*** *p466*
Condon, Catherine Halleran 44; Vermont, 1868 ***5900.10*** *p201*
Condon, Catherine McDonough; Vermont, 1853-1917 ***5900.10*** *p95*
Condon, Eliza; Vermont, 1821-1902 ***5900.10*** *p215*
Condon, Eliza C.; Vermont, 1852-1923 ***5900.10*** *p54*
Condon, Elizabeth; Vermont, 1838-1893 ***5900.10*** *p461*
Condon, Elizabeth 14; Vermont, 1887 ***5900.10*** *p315*
Condon, Elizabeth F.; Vermont, 1793-1858 ***5900.10*** *p461*
Condon, Elizabeth Hodges 74; Vermont, 1916 ***5900.10*** *p317*
Condon, Ellen 32; Vermont, 1874 ***5900.10*** *p317*
Condon, Ellen 74; Vermont, 1891 ***5900.10*** *p68*
Condon, Ellen 87; Vermont, 1890 ***5900.10*** *p461*
Condon, Ellen Barry 59; Vermont, 1878 ***5900.10*** *p317*
Condon, Ellen Hanning; Vermont, 1849-1897 ***5900.10*** *p466*
Condon, George; Vermont, 1831-1893 ***5900.10*** *p221*
Condon, James J.; Vermont, 1853-1924 ***5900.10*** *p95*
Condon, John; Vermont, 1834-1899 ***5900.10*** *p45*
Condon, John 10 months; Vermont, 1870 ***5900.10*** *p315*
Condon, John 40; Ontario, 1871 ***1823.22*** *p32*
Condon, John 56; Ontario, 1871 ***1823.28*** *p18*
Condon, John 58; Vermont, 1866 ***5900.10*** *p317*
Condon, John 61; Vermont, 1907 ***5900.10*** *p466*
Condon, John C.; Vermont, 1856-1932 ***5900.10*** *p221*
Condon, Julia 14; Vermont, 1865 ***5900.10*** *p317*
Condon, Kate Haley; Vermont, 1869-1937 ***5900.10*** *p221*
Condon, Kattie 8; Vermont, 1865 ***5900.10*** *p317*
Condon, Marie; Vermont, 1847-1947 ***5900.10*** *p213*
Condon, Mary; Vermont, 1833-1909 ***5900.10*** *p461*
Condon, Mary; Vermont, 1920 ***5900.10*** *p65*
Condon, Mary; Vermont, 1935 ***5900.10*** *p45*
Condon, Mary 21; Vermont, 1865 ***5900.10*** *p317*
Condon, Mary E. Collins 77; Vermont, 1922 ***5900.10*** *p315*
Condon, Michael James; New York, 1840 ***8197.10*** *p221*
Condon, O. 28; British Columbia, 1916 ***9196.1*** *p68*
Condon, O. 28; Washington, 1916 ***9196.1*** *p68*
Condon, Patrick; Vermont, 1843-1896 ***5900.10*** *p466*
Condon, Patrick 20; Vermont, 1881 ***5900.10*** *p201*
Condon, Patrick 66; Vermont, 1910 ***5900.10*** *p315*
Condon, Patrick 80; Vermont, 1917 ***5900.10*** *p317*
Condon, Sarah Cunningham 40; Vermont, 1867 ***5900.10*** *p210*
Condon, Terry; Vermont, 1791-1888 ***5900.10*** *p461*
Condon, Thomas 51; Ontario, 1871 ***1823.15*** *p47*
Condon, William; New York, 1840 ***8197.10*** *p162*
Condon, William 42; Vermont, 1882 ***5900.10*** *p54*
Condrip, Anne; Virginia, 1672 ***6212.30*** *p51*
Condrip, Elizabeth; Virginia, 1672 ***6212.30*** *p51*
Condy, Benj.; Pennsylvania, 1777 ***4629.10*** *p14*
Condy, William; Pennsylvania, 1779 ***4629.10*** *p39*
Cone, Abigail Broderick; Vermont, 1830-1903 ***5900.10*** *p77*
Cone, Bridget Gibney 62; Vermont, 1896 ***5900.10*** *p72*
Cone, David H. 37; Ontario, 1871 ***1823.28*** *p18*
Cone, Delia 68; Vermont, 1901 ***5900.10*** *p77*
Cone, Ellen O'Mara; Vermont, 1846-1914 ***5900.10*** *p79*
Cone, Ellen Ryan 82; Vermont, 1889 ***5900.10*** *p85*
Cone, Francis; Maryland, 1670 ***2524.55*** *p53*
Cone, Henry 39; Ontario, 1871 ***1823.28*** *p18*
Cone, James; Vermont, 1851-1923 ***5900.10*** *p79*
Cone, John; Maryland, 1665 ***2524.55*** *p53*
Cone, John 75; Vermont, 1860 ***5900.10*** *p75*
Cone, John 76; Vermont, 1908 ***5900.10*** *p72*
Cone, Julia; Vermont, 1851-1889 ***5900.10*** *p87*
Cone, Martin 58; Vermont, 1895 ***5900.10*** *p77*
Cone, Mary 60; Vermont, 1908 ***5900.10*** *p85*
Cone, Patrick; Vermont, 1829-1915 ***5900.10*** *p76*
Cone, Thomas 86; Vermont, 1892 ***5900.10*** *p85*
Coneire, Mrs.; Maryland, 1655 ***2524.55*** *p53*
Conelly, Nicholes; New York, New York, 1856 ***6058.10*** *p53*
Conerton, Catherine; Vermont, 1845-1914 ***5900.10*** *p431*
Conery, Edmond; Maryland, 1655 ***2524.55*** *p53*
Conesy, William 40; Ontario, 1871 ***1823.15*** *p47*
Coney, Francis; Maryland, 1667 ***2524.55*** *p53*
Congdon, John I.; Vermont, 1852-1919 ***5900.10*** *p547*
Congdon, Mary Mulqueen; Vermont, 1862-1936 ***5900.10*** *p547*
Congdrin, Walter 38; Ontario, 1871 ***1823.15*** *p47*
Conger, Alice C. McIntosh; Vermont, 1844-1910 ***5900.10*** *p500*
Conger, Angeline 6; Ontario, 1861 ***2896.27*** *p13*
Conger, Anna M. 42; Ontario, 1861 ***2896.27*** *p13*
Conger, Betsy 59; Ontario, 1861 ***2896.27*** *p19*
Conger, Gertrude 25; Ontario, 1861 ***2896.27*** *p18*
Conger, Hannah 51; Ontario, 1861 ***2896.27*** *p19*
Conger, James A. 18; Ontario, 1861 ***2896.27*** *p19*
Conger, John W. 23; Ontario, 1861 ***2896.27*** *p18*
Conger, Lavina 4; Ontario, 1861 ***2896.27*** *p13*
Conger, Margaret R. 16; Ontario, 1861 ***2896.27*** *p18*
Conger, Mariah 62; Ontario, 1861 ***2896.27*** *p18*
Conger, Nelson B. 25; Ontario, 1861 ***2896.27*** *p19*
Conger, Rebecca 2; Ontario, 1861 ***2896.27*** *p13*
Conger, Ruth 47; Ontario, 1861 ***2896.27*** *p70*
Conger, Ruth M. 6; Ontario, 1861 ***2896.27*** *p70*
Conger, Stephen M. 26; Ontario, 1861 ***2896.27*** *p18*
Conger, Warren W.; Vermont, 1842-1930 ***5900.10*** *p500*
Conger, William O. 42; Ontario, 1861 ***2896.27*** *p13*
Congrave, John 23; Virginia, 1774 ***1220.25*** *p55*
Conier, Quinton; Maryland, 1659 ***2524.55*** *p53*
Coniff, Ann Owens 65; Vermont, 1896 ***5900.10*** *p558*
Coniff, John 58; Vermont, 1880 ***5900.10*** *p558*
Coniff, Rose 38; Vermont, 1875 ***5900.10*** *p399*
Conillan, James; New York, 1837 ***8197.10*** *p80*
Coningham, Grove; New York, 1807 ***8197.10*** *p36*
Coningham, Thomas; Virginia, 1671-1672 ***6212.30*** *p46*
Coningsby, Hen; Virginia, 1665-1666 ***6212.30*** *p21*
Coningsby, Tho; Virginia, 1665-1666 ***6212.30*** *p23*
Conington, Bridget 49; Vermont, 1891 ***5900.10*** *p415*
Conise, Mr.; Quebec, 1857 ***9196.15*** *p16*
Conkler, Charles; Pennsylvania, 1777 ***4629.10*** *p27*
Conklin, Debra 17; Ontario, 1861 ***2896.25*** *p71*
Conklin, Mary; Vermont, 1851-1927 ***5900.10*** *p560*
Conklin, William 10; Ontario, 1861 ***2896.25*** *p60*
Conlan, Francis; New York, 1840 ***8197.10*** *p162*
Conlan, James; New York, 1840 ***8197.10*** *p162*

Conlan, John; New York, 1837 8197.10 p80
Conlan, John; New York, 1837 8197.10 p81
Conlan, Mathew; New York, 1837 8197.10 p81
Conley, Catherine 27; Vermont, 1870 5900.10 p239
Conley, James 40; Ontario, 1871 1823.28 p18
Conley, John 19; Ontario, 1861 2896.27 p4
Conley, Mary Ann O'Brien; Vermont, 1904 5900.10 p50
Conley, Mary McKenna 84; Vermont, 1897 5900.10 p230
Conley, Michael 80; Vermont, 1885 5900.10 p230
Conley, Nancy 19; Vermont, 1879 5900.10 p239
Conley, Nancy Brady 80; Vermont, 1887 5900.10 p226
Conley, Patrick; New York, 1837 8197.10 p81
Conley, Patrick 24; Vermont, 1865 5900.10 p239
Conley, Peter 22; Vermont, 1877 5900.10 p239
Conley, Peter 75; Vermont, 1883 5900.10 p226
Conley, William 61; Ontario, 1871 1823.15 p47
Conlin, Mrs. 65; Ontario, 1861 2896.26 p28
Conlin, Alice; Vermont, 1792-1878 5900.10 p442
Conlin, Ann Radigan; Vermont, 1823-1907 5900.10 p560
Conlin, Bernard; Vermont, 1825-1907 5900.10 p560
Conlin, Bernard; Vermont, 1857-1911 5900.10 p560
Conlin, Bridget A. Gibbons; Vermont, 1867-1897 5900.10 p332
Conlin, Catherine; Vermont, 1831-1890 5900.10 p324
Conlin, Catherine H.; Vermont, 1864-1962 5900.10 p596
Conlin, Delia Jellett 28; Vermont, 1883 5900.10 p596
Conlin, Ellen; Vermont, 1861-1932 5900.10 p560
Conlin, Ellen E.; Vermont, 1862-1931 5900.10 p594
Conlin, James; Vermont, n.d. 5900.10 p463
Conlin, James; Vermont, 1804-1860 5900.10 p442
Conlin, James; Vermont, 1836-1912 5900.10 p419
Conlin, James 39; Vermont, 1873 5900.10 p463
Conlin, James 63; Vermont, 1915 5900.10 p596
Conlin, James 79; Ontario, 1871 1823.22 p32
Conlin, Jane 58; Vermont, 1904 5900.10 p463
Conlin, Jane Clinton; Vermont, 1803-1905 5900.10 p323
Conlin, Jennie; Vermont, 1847-1915 5900.10 p442
Conlin, John; New York, 1838 8197.10 p377
Conlin, John; Vermont, 1833-1907 5900.10 p442
Conlin, John; Vermont, 1853-1901 5900.10 p560
Conlin, John 32; Ontario, 1871 1823.22 p32
Conlin, John 73; Vermont, 1892 5900.10 p596
Conlin, John M.; Vermont, 1854-1927 5900.10 p595
Conlin, Margaret; Vermont, 1852-1923 5900.10 p464
Conlin, Margaret Fell; Vermont, 1842-1919 5900.10 p419
Conlin, Martin; Vermont, 1866-1934 5900.10 p594
Conlin, Mary; Vermont, 1829-1906 5900.10 p557
Conlin, Mary; Vermont, 1841-1859 5900.10 p442
Conlin, Mary 79; Vermont, 1903 5900.10 p386
Conlin, Mary A.; Vermont, 1856-1943 5900.10 p594
Conlin, Mary Mann 31; Vermont, 1892 5900.10 p596
Conlin, Mary Moran; Vermont, 1837-1922 5900.10 p332
Conlin, Mary Sears 63; Vermont, 1891 5900.10 p596
Conlin, Nicholas 45; Ontario, 1871 1823.22 p32
Conlin, Owen; Vermont, 1832-1905 5900.10 p323
Conlin, Patrick; Vermont, 1817-1893 5900.10 p332
Conlin, Patrick; Vermont, 1859-1865 5900.10 p560
Conlin, Robert 40; Ontario, 1861 2896.26 p28
Conlin, Rose McManus; Vermont, 1849-1927 5900.10 p596
Conlin, Samuel 26; Ontario, 1861 2896.26 p28
Conlin, Susan; Vermont, 1845-1910 5900.10 p45
Conlin, William; Vermont, 1858-1906 5900.10 p594
Conlin, William 70; Ontario, 1861 2896.26 p28
Conline, Anna M.; Vermont, 1852-1913 5900.10 p447
Conline, James; Vermont, 1848-1915 5900.10 p430
Conline, Margaret Kellt; Vermont, 1862-1912 5900.10 p430
Conline, Mary Cunningham 54; Vermont, 1870 5900.10 p451
Conline, Thomas 68; Vermont, 1862 5900.10 p451
Conlley, Ellen; Vermont, 1845-1920 5900.10 p341
Conlon, Ann E. 52; Vermont, 1904 5900.10 p414
Conlon, Bridget; Vermont, 1827-1894 5900.10 p158
Conlon, Bridget; Vermont, 1839-1883 5900.10 p569
Conlon, Catharine Moran; Vermont, 1858-1913 5900.10 p332
Conlon, Charles; New York, 1837 8197.10 p80
Conlon, James 69; Vermont, 1898 5900.10 p569
Conlon, Margaret Gavin; Vermont, 1836-1900 5900.10 p570
Conlon, Margaret T.; Vermont, 1840-1928 5900.10 p443
Conlon, Mary 70; Vermont, 1901 5900.10 p570
Conlon, Mary O'Meara; Vermont, 1825-1909 5900.10 p158
Conlon, Michael 24; Maryland, 1774 1220.25 p68
Conlon, Michael 72; Vermont, 1871 5900.10 p569
Conlon, Patrick; New York, 1838 8197.10 p378
Conlon, Patrick; Vermont, 1818-1893 5900.10 p158
Conlon, Patrick; Vermont, 1824-1886 5900.10 p570
Conlon, Patrick 54; Ontario, 1871 1823.22 p32
Conlon, Thomas J.; Vermont, 1858-1914 5900.10 p332
Conn, Lewis 67; Vermont, 1889 5900.10 p91
Conn, Margaret; Canada, 1853 1640.13 p23
Conn, Mary 75; Vermont, 1903 5900.10 p91
Conn, Michael 36; Vermont, 1893 5900.10 p91
Connacher, Donald 57; Ontario, 1871 1823.22 p32
Connagay, Edw; Virginia, 1668-1669 6212.30 p41
Connal, Michael 10; Vermont, 1851 5900.10 p613
Connal, Robert Meiklejohn; New York, 1892 1640.13 p23
Connaley, Michael 55; Ontario, 1871 1823.28 p18
Connally, James; New York, 1856 6058.10 p53
Connally, Mary 65; Vermont, 1886 5900.10 p197
Connally, Nicholes; New York, New York, 1856 6058.10 p53
Connally, William 63; Vermont, 1883 5900.10 p197
Connarn, Bridget Greaney; Vermont, 1854-1923 5900.10 p118
Connarn, Patrick; Vermont, 1850-1916 5900.10 p118
Connaty, Charles; New York, New York, 1834 8197.10 p163
Connaughton, Patrick; New York, 1840 8197.10 p221
Connaughty, William 62; Ontario, 1871 1823.22 p32
Connaway, John; Maryland, 1682 2524.55 p53
Connel, Catharine 68; Ontario, 1871 1823.15 p47
Connel, John 38; Ontario, 1871 1823.15 p48
Connel, William 45; Ontario, 1871 1823.15 p48
Connell, Alexander Hutchison; Montreal, 1898 1640.13 p23
Connell, Ann 78; Ontario, 1871 1823.15 p48
Connell, Anne 66; Vermont, 1921 5900.10 p423
Connell, Bernard; Vermont, 1831-1900 5900.10 p363
Connell, Bridget Keough; Vermont, 1833-1919 5900.10 p363
Connell, Bridget O'Brien; Vermont, 1847-1896 5900.10 p388
Connell, Cornelius 35; Vermont, 1882 5900.10 p104
Connell, Dan 15 SEE Connell, David
Connell, Dan 16 SEE Connell, Patrick
Connell, Daniel; Maryland, 1682 2524.55 p53
Connell, David 45; New York, New York, 1849 1825.45 p46
  Wife: Margaret 35
  Son: Pat 3
  Daughter: Johanna 8
  Daughter: Mary 5
  Daughter: Margaret 9
  Daughter: Eileen 6 months
  Son: John 13
  Son: Dan 15
  Son: Jerry 10
Connell, Dennis; Vermont, 1840-1902 5900.10 p613
Connell, Edward 59; Vermont, 1901 5900.10 p422
Connell, Eileen 6 months SEE Connell, David
Connell, Elizabeth; Vermont, 1824-1910 5900.10 p605
Connell, Elizabeth 14; Ontario, 1861 2896.28 p59
Connell, Elizabeth 46; Ontario, 1861 2896.28 p59
Connell, Ellen; Vermont, 1819-1904 5900.10 p357
Connell, Ellen 44 SEE Connell, Patrick
Connell, Ellen B.; Vermont, 1857-1888 5900.10 p359
Connell, Hanorah; Vermont, n.d. 5900.10 p134
Connell, Hugh; Maryland, 1672 2524.55 p53
Connell, James; Maryland, 1680 2524.55 p53
Connell, James 5; Ontario, 1861 2896.28 p59
Connell, Janet; New York, 1883 1640.13 p23
Connell, Jerry 10 SEE Connell, David
Connell, Johanna 4 SEE Connell, Patrick
Connell, Johanna 8 SEE Connell, David
Connell, John; New York, 1804 8197.10 p26
Connell, John; New York, 1839 8197.10 p379
Connell, John; New York, 1839 8197.10 p382
Connell, John; Virginia, 1675 1224.1 p15
Connell, John 13 SEE Connell, David
Connell, John 13 SEE Connell, Patrick
Connell, John 39; Maryland, 1774 1220.25 p72
Connell, John 64; Ontario, 1871 1823.15 p48
Connell, John 80; Ontario, 1871 1823.28 p18
Connell, Joseph 45; Ontario, 1871 1823.15 p48
Connell, Judy 15 SEE Connell, Patrick
Connell, Lawrence 51; Ontario, 1861 2896.28 p59
Connell, Malisa A. 16; Ontario, 1861 2896.27 p67
Connell, Margaret 7 SEE Connell, Patrick
Connell, Margaret 9 SEE Connell, David
Connell, Margaret 35 SEE Connell, David
Connell, Martin 62; Ontario, 1871 1823.22 p32
Connell, Mary; Vermont, 1842-1905 5900.10 p183
Connell, Mary; Vermont, 1853-1924 5900.10 p338
Connell, Mary 5 SEE Connell, David
Connell, Mary 22 SEE Connell, Patrick
Connell, Mary 69; Vermont, 1902 5900.10 p233
Connell, Mary 75; Vermont, 1891 5900.10 p102
Connell, Mary Burke 64; Vermont, 1908 5900.10 p422
Connell, Maurice 70; Vermont, 1856 5900.10 p359
Connell, Michael; New York, 1825 8197.10 p217
Connell, Michael 60; Ontario, 1871 1823.15 p48
Connell, Pat 3 SEE Connell, David
Connell, Patrick; Pennsylvania, 1868 6058.10 p73
Connell, Patrick 50; New York, New York, 1849 1825.45 p47
  Daughter: Margaret 7
  Daughter: Mary 22
  Daughter: Johanna 4
  Son: Philip 19
  Son: John 13
  Son: Dan 16
  Wife: Ellen 44
  Daughter: Judy 15
Connell, Patrick 67; Vermont, 1880 5900.10 p134
Connell, Philip 19 SEE Connell, Patrick
Connell, Richd 55; Ontario, 1871 1823.22 p32
Connell, Robert 56; Ontario, 1871 1823.22 p32
Connell, Robert Hutchison; Montreal, 1898 1640.13 p23
Connell, Thomas; Pennsylvania, 1785 4629.10 p44
Connell, William; Pennsylvania, 1777 4629.10 p20
Connell, William 19; Ontario, 1871 1823.15 p48
Connell, William 26; Ontario, 1871 1823.28 p18
Connellan, James; New York, 1840 8197.10 p221
Connellan, Patrick; Maryland, 1682 2524.55 p53
Connelley, James 40; Ontario, 1871 1823.15 p48
Connelly, David 60; Ontario, 1871 1823.22 p32
Connelly, Edward; New York, New York, 1856 6058.10 p53
Connelly, James; New York, 1840 8197.10 p384
Connelly, James; New York, 1856 6058.10 p53
Connelly, James 44; Ontario, 1871 1823.22 p32
Connelly, Jeremiah 59; Ontario, 1871 1823.22 p32
Connelly, Jno; Vermont, n.d. 5900.10 p421
Connelly, Johanna 60; Vermont, 1896 5900.10 p56
Connelly, John; New York, 1838 8197.10 p318
Connelly, Kate; Vermont, 1840-1885 5900.10 p587
Connelly, Thos 34; Ontario, 1871 1823.28 p18
Connelly, Timothy 22; Philadelphia, 1774 1220.25 p6
Connelly, William J.; Pennsylvania, 1864 6058.10 p75
Conner, Arvesta J.; Vermont, 1829-1899 5900.10 p500
Conner, Daniel 22; Vermont, 1849 5900.10 p192
Conner, Elizabeth 87; Vermont, 1872 5900.10 p283
Conner, Euseba 79; Vermont, 1887 5900.10 p500
Conner, Hannah; Maryland, 1679 2524.55 p53
Conner, Hannah; Vermont, 1839-1913 5900.10 p552
Conner, Honner; Maryland, 1678 2524.55 p53
Conner, John; Canada, 1756-1760 4628.40 p46
Conner, John 39; Ontario, 1871 1823.22 p32
Conner, John P.; Vermont, 1828-1880 5900.10 p500
Conner, Jonathan; Canada, 1756-1760 4628.40 p45
Conner, M. O. 65; Ontario, 1861 2896.28 p5
Conner, Peter; New York, 1838 8197.10 p113
Conner, Philip; Maryland, 1636 2524.55 p53
Conner, Sarah Boomhower; Vermont, n.d. 5900.10 p500
Conner, Thankful Weeks; Vermont, 1793-1876 5900.10 p500
Conner, Thomas; Pennsylvania, 1867 6058.10 p60
Conner, Thomas 60; Ontario, 1871 1823.22 p32
Conner, Thomas 67; Vermont, 1873 5900.10 p283
Conner, W. W. 55; Ontario, 1871 1823.15 p48
Conner, William 60; Vermont, 1837 5900.10 p283
Conners, Bridget 65; Vermont, 1885 5900.10 p82
Conners, Catherine; Vermont, 1808-1883 5900.10 p462
Conners, Catherine 23; Vermont, 1862 5900.10 p473
Conners, Catherine O'Brien 25; Vermont, 1848 5900.10 p348
Conners, Dennis 30; Vermont, 1846 5900.10 p348
Conners, Elizabeth; Vermont, 1856-1918 5900.10 p191
Conners, Elizabeth 70; Vermont, 1868 5900.10 p523
Conners, Hugh 27; Ontario, 1871 1823.28 p18
Conners, James 21; Vermont, 1886 5900.10 p82
Conners, James 65; Vermont, 1872 5900.10 p473
Conners, Joanna 39; Vermont, 1893 5900.10 p473
Conners, Johanna; Vermont, 1855 5900.10 p159
Conners, Johanna 29; Vermont, 1881 5900.10 p82
Conners, John; Vermont, 1847-1912 5900.10 p473
Conners, John; Died enroute, 1654 1224.1 p15
Conners, John 63; Ontario, 1871 1823.15 p48
Conners, Mary; Vermont, 1826-1913 5900.10 p483
Conners, Mary; Vermont, 1875 5900.10 p170
Conners, Mary 78; Vermont, 1889 5900.10 p473
Conners, Michael 20; Vermont, 1880 5900.10 p82
Conners, Michael 49; Ontario, 1871 1823.28 p18
Conners, Patrick 48; Vermont, 1866 5900.10 p82
Conners, Rose F.; Vermont, 1849-1918 5900.10 p473
Conners, Stephen 82; Vermont, 1887 5900.10 p170
Conners, Thomas 17; Vermont, 1880 5900.10 p82
Conners, William 36; Ontario, 1871 1823.22 p32
Connery, John; Maryland, 1682 2524.55 p53
Connery, John 40; Virginia, 1774 1220.25 p45
Conney, John; Maryland, 1669 2524.55 p53
Conney, Mark 32; Washington, 1911 9196.1 p33

Conniff, Ann 63; Vermont, 1892 ***5900.10*** *p400*
Conniff, Bridget; Vermont, 1838-1926 ***5900.10*** *p569*
Conniff, Frank; Vermont, 1842-1922 ***5900.10*** *p430*
Conniff, Norah; Vermont, 1843-1921 ***5900.10*** *p431*
Connill, Alexander 24; New York, 1775 ***1220.25*** *p142*
With wife
Connill, Dennis; Maryland, 1674 ***2524.55*** *p53*
Connillen, Peter Patrick; New York, 1838 ***8197.10*** *p112*
Connington, William; Maryland, 1676 ***1224.1*** *p15*
Connoghan, John 28; Ontario, 1871 ***1823.28*** *p18*
Connoghan, John 55; Ontario, 1871 ***1823.28*** *p18*
Connoley, Owen; New York, 1837 ***8197.10*** *p81*
Connoley, Patrick; New York, 1807 ***8197.10*** *p330*
Connolly, Mr.; Vermont, 1842-1928 ***5900.10*** *p302*
Connolly, Mrs.; Vermont, 1853-1922 ***5900.10*** *p302*
Connolly, Aileen; Vermont, 1832-1920 ***5900.10*** *p389*
Connolly, Anna Mullin; Vermont, 1844-1938 ***5900.10*** *p388*
Connolly, Bartholomew; New York, 1840 ***8197.10*** *p161*
Connolly, Bridget; Vermont, 1838-1908 ***5900.10*** *p115*
Connolly, Bridget Ann; Vermont, 1855-1929 ***5900.10*** *p91*
Connolly, Catherine; Vermont, 1851-1935 ***5900.10*** *p546*
Connolly, Catherine 69; Vermont, 1874 ***5900.10*** *p209*
Connolly, Christopher; New York, 1836 ***8197.10*** *p220*
Connolly, Daniel; Vermont, 1848-1926 ***5900.10*** *p169*
Connolly, Edward; New York, 1806 ***8197.10*** *p30*
Connolly, Edward; New York, 1825 ***8197.10*** *p218*
Connolly, Edward; New York, 1838 ***8197.10*** *p220*
Connolly, Edward; New York, 1840 ***8197.10*** *p160*
Connolly, Elizabeth; Vermont, 1845-1926 ***5900.10*** *p547*
Connolly, Hanora Houlihan; Vermont, 1842-1911 ***5900.10*** *p169*
Connolly, Honoria Burke; Vermont, 1847-1920 ***5900.10*** *p403*
Connolly, James; New York, 1826 ***8197.10*** *p334*
Connolly, James; New York, 1838 ***8197.10*** *p113*
Connolly, James; Vermont, 1810-1886 ***5900.10*** *p546*
Connolly, James; Vermont, 1847-1929 ***5900.10*** *p546*
Connolly, James; Vermont, 1854-1947 ***5900.10*** *p443*
Connolly, James 21; Ontario, 1871 ***1823.28*** *p18*
Connolly, James 48; Ontario, 1871 ***1823.28*** *p18*
Connolly, Jane; Vermont, 1845-1899 ***5900.10*** *p193*
Connolly, John; Canada, 1756-1760 ***4628.40*** *p45*
Connolly, John; New York, 1840 ***8197.10*** *p161*
Connolly, John; Vermont, 1812-1854 ***5900.10*** *p439*
Connolly, John; Vermont, 1838-1849 ***5900.10*** *p546*
Connolly, John; Vermont, 1853-1947 ***5900.10*** *p91*
Connolly, John 65; Vermont, 1898 ***5900.10*** *p594*
Connolly, Katie; Vermont, 1840-1885 ***5900.10*** *p592*
Connolly, Margaret; Vermont, 1821-1880 ***5900.10*** *p546*
Connolly, Mrs. Martin; Vermont, 1825-1911 ***5900.10*** *p388*
Connolly, Mary; Vermont, 1816-1892 ***5900.10*** *p439*
Connolly, Mary; Vermont, 1843-1903 ***5900.10*** *p546*
Connolly, Mary; Vermont, 1855-1936 ***5900.10*** *p353*
Connolly, Mary; Vermont, 1860-1899 ***5900.10*** *p388*
Connolly, Mary 18; New York, New York, 1849 ***1825.45*** *p36*
Connolly, Mary Ann; Vermont, 1837-1900 ***5900.10*** *p594*
Connolly, Mary Curtin; Vermont, 1855-1917 ***5900.10*** *p443*
Connolly, Michael; Vermont, 1850-1932 ***5900.10*** *p388*
Connolly, Michael 38; Ontario, 1871 ***1823.22*** *p32*
Connolly, Michael 60; Ontario, 1871 ***1823.22*** *p32*
Connolly, Patrick; New York, 1838 ***8197.10*** *p113*
Connolly, Patrick 42; Vermont, 1868 ***5900.10*** *p265*
Connolly, Patrick 47; Ontario, 1871 ***1823.28*** *p18*
Connolly, Patrick 48; Ontario, 1871 ***1823.22*** *p32*
Connolly, Richard 52; Vermont, 1869 ***5900.10*** *p265*
Connolly, Thomas; New York, 1840 ***8197.10*** *p160*
Connolly, Thomas; Vermont, 1841-1891 ***5900.10*** *p546*
Connolly, Thomas; Vermont, 1844-1920 ***5900.10*** *p403*
Connolly, William; New York, 1802 ***8197.10*** *p19*
Connoly, Dennis 43; Ontario, 1871 ***1823.22*** *p32*
Connoly, Michael; New York, 1840 ***8197.10*** *p162*
Connop, John; Virginia, 1706 ***1224.2*** *p25*
Connor, . . .; New Hampshire, 1641-1660 ***4628.40*** *p44*
Connor, A. 23; Ontario, 1861 ***2896.28*** *p10*
Connor, Ann Conniff 63; Vermont, 1892 ***5900.10*** *p400*
Connor, Anne; Vermont, 1841-1904 ***5900.10*** *p225*
Connor, Annie; Vermont, 1862-1893 ***5900.10*** *p50*
Connor, Barney; Vermont, 1823-1898 ***5900.10*** *p408*
Connor, Bartholomew 62; Vermont, 1885 ***5900.10*** *p431*
Connor, Benjamin; Pennsylvania, 1777 ***4629.10*** *p8*
Connor, Bridget 49; Vermont, 1875 ***5900.10*** *p468*
Connor, Bridget Collins; Vermont, 1832-1907 ***5900.10*** *p161*
Connor, Bridget Crowe 85; Vermont, 1924 ***5900.10*** *p428*
Connor, Carnolian 28; Ontario, 1871 ***1823.15*** *p48*
Connor, Catherine; Vermont, 1852-1904 ***5900.10*** *p598*
Connor, Catherine 27; New York, New York, 1847 ***1825.45*** *p14*
Connor, Catherine 70; Vermont, 1879 ***5900.10*** *p312*
Connor, Catherine Daly 28; Vermont, 1866 ***5900.10*** *p337*
Connor, Cornelius; New York, 1840 ***8197.10*** *p159*
Connor, Daniel J. 70; Vermont, 1901 ***5900.10*** *p428*
Connor, Edward; New York, 1826 ***8197.10*** *p337*
Connor, Ellen 50; Ontario, 1871 ***1823.15*** *p48*
Connor, Gillian; Virginia, 1688 ***6212.30*** *p57*
Connor, Hannah 75; Vermont, 1909 ***5900.10*** *p103*
Connor, Honor 44 *SEE* Connor, James
Connor, Hugh; New Hampshire, 1724 ***4628.40*** *p44*
Connor, James; Canada, 1756-1760 ***4628.40*** *p46*
Connor, James; New York, 1837 ***8197.10*** *p81*
Connor, James; New York, 1837 ***8197.10*** *p82*
Connor, James; Vermont, 1818-1916 ***5900.10*** *p212*
Connor, James; Vermont, 1856-1936 ***5900.10*** *p190*
Connor, James 24; Maryland, 1775 ***1220.25*** *p98*
Connor, James 45; New York, New York, 1848 ***1825.45*** *p14*
Wife: Honor 44
Son: Martin 22
Connor, James 82; Vermont, 1910 ***5900.10*** *p400*
Connor, Janet 68; Ontario, 1871 ***1823.15*** *p48*
Connor, Jeremiah; Canada, 1756-1760 ***4628.40*** *p45*
Connor, Jeremiah 32; Ontario, 1871 ***1823.15*** *p48*
Connor, Jerry; New Hampshire, 1710 ***4628.40*** *p44*
Connor, John; Charles Town, South Carolina, 1768 ***1224.2*** *p25*
Connor, John; New York, 1839 ***8197.10*** *p379*
Connor, John 19; Virginia, 1775 ***1220.25*** *p95*
Connor, John 21; Maryland, 1775 ***1220.25*** *p109*
Connor, John 37; Died enroute, 1847 ***1825.45*** *p14*
Connor, John 68; Vermont, 1893 ***5900.10*** *p542*
Connor, Josie Coursey; Vermont, 1859-1936 ***5900.10*** *p190*
Connor, Kate 47; Vermont, 1882 ***5900.10*** *p207*
Connor, Katy 45; Vermont, 1879 ***5900.10*** *p110*
Connor, Levi; Canada, 1756-1760 ***4628.40*** *p46*
Connor, Margaret 86; Vermont, 1894 ***5900.10*** *p312*
Connor, Margaret Gill; Vermont, 1848-1882 ***5900.10*** *p239*
Connor, Margaret Grady; Vermont, 1831-1907 ***5900.10*** *p212*
Connor, Martin 22 *SEE* Connor, James
Connor, Mary; Maryland, 1648 ***2524.55*** *p53*
Connor, Mary; Vermont, n.d. ***5900.10*** *p350*
Connor, Mary 11 *SEE* Connor, Terence
Connor, Mary 35 *SEE* Connor, Terence
Connor, Mary 48; Ontario, 1871 ***1823.15*** *p48*
Connor, Matthew; New York, 1840 ***8197.10*** *p220*
Connor, Matthew 60; Ontario, 1871 ***1823.15*** *p48*
Connor, Michael; New York, 1840 ***8197.10*** *p221*
Connor, Michael 45; Ontario, 1871 ***1823.28*** *p18*
Connor, Moses; New Hampshire, 1724 ***4628.40*** *p44*
Connor, Patrick; New York, 1807 ***8197.10*** *p326*
Connor, Patrick; New York, New York, 1849 ***6058.10*** *p52*
Connor, Patrick 34; Ontario, 1871 ***1823.15*** *p48*
Connor, Patrick 35; St. Vincent, 1775 ***1220.25*** *p129*
Connor, Philip; Maryland, 1648 ***2524.55*** *p53*
Connor, Richard; Vermont, 1840-1923 ***5900.10*** *p239*
Connor, Samuel; Canada, 1756-1760 ***4628.40*** *p45*
Connor, Samuel; Nova Scotia, 1745 ***4628.40*** *p45*
Connor, Terence 50; New York, New York, 1847 ***1825.45*** *p14*
Wife: Mary 35
Son: Thomas 20
Daughter: Mary 11
Connor, Thankful W.; Vermont, 1817-1860 ***5900.10*** *p500*
Connor, Thomas; Pennsylvania, 1868 ***6058.10*** *p65*
Connor, Thomas 20 *SEE* Connor, Terence
Connor, Thomas 60; Ontario, 1871 ***1823.28*** *p18*
Connor, Timothy; New Hampshire, 1710 ***4628.40*** *p44*
Connor, William; New York, 1840 ***8197.10*** *p160*
Connors, Ann 83; Vermont, 1900 ***5900.10*** *p183*
Connors, Bridget Cosgriff 59; Vermont, 1882 ***5900.10*** *p614*
Connors, Ellen Magner 83; Vermont, 1913 ***5900.10*** *p433*
Connors, Hannora 76; Vermont, 1896 ***5900.10*** *p173*
Connors, Jesy 24; Ontario, 1871 ***1823.28*** *p18*
Connors, Joanna; Vermont, 1842-1866 ***5900.10*** *p542*
Connors, John; Pennsylvania, 1868 ***6058.10*** *p65*
Connors, John 32; Ontario, 1871 ***1823.28*** *p18*
Connors, John 37; Ontario, 1871 ***1823.28*** *p18*
Connors, John 40; Ontario, 1871 ***1823.28*** *p18*
Connors, John 43; Vermont, 1852 ***5900.10*** *p614*
Connors, John 56; Vermont, 1899 ***5900.10*** *p433*
Connors, John 62; Ontario, 1871 ***1823.28*** *p18*
Connors, Joseph; Vermont, 1857-1923 ***5900.10*** *p303*
Connors, Martin 36; Ontario, 1871 ***1823.28*** *p18*
Connors, Mary; Vermont, 1851-1912 ***5900.10*** *p429*
Connors, Mary Ann Bowker; Vermont, 1855-1934 ***5900.10*** *p303*
Connors, Mary Sullivan; Vermont, 1853-1920 ***5900.10*** *p301*
Connors, Michael; Maryland, 1910 ***3259.35*** *p10*
Connors, Patrick 26; Vermont, 1853 ***5900.10*** *p183*
Connors, Patrick 34; Ontario, 1871 ***1823.28*** *p18*
Connors, Patrick 39; Vermont, 1884 ***5900.10*** *p614*
Connors, Thomas; Pennsylvania, 1868 ***6058.10*** *p65*
Connors, Thomas 30; Ontario, 1871 ***1823.15*** *p48*
Connors, Thomas W.; Vermont, 1855-1885 ***5900.10*** *p301*
Connors, William 2; Vermont, 1851 ***5900.10*** *p188*
Connory, Daniel; Maryland, 1682 ***2524.55*** *p53*
Connoys, W. W.; Quebec, 1858 ***9196.15*** *p33*
Cono, Pete 21; British Columbia, 1910 ***9196.1*** *p29*
Cono, Pete 21; Washington, 1910 ***9196.1*** *p29*
Conock, Jno; Virginia, 1666 ***6212.30*** *p29*
Conolin, Michael 45; Ontario, 1871 ***1823.22*** *p32*
Conolly, David 21; Maryland, 1775 ***1220.25*** *p97*
Conolly, James; New York, 1821 ***8197.10*** *p216*
Conolly, James 22; Maryland, 1774 ***1220.25*** *p54*
Conolly, Patrick; New York, 1821 ***8197.10*** *p215*
Conolly, William; New York, 1802 ***8197.10*** *p19*
Conoly, Anne 22; Ontario, 1871 ***1823.28*** *p18*
Conoly, John 50; Ontario, 1871 ***1823.22*** *p32*
Conon, Quinton; Maryland, 1658 ***2524.55*** *p53*
Conors, Catherine 75; Vermont, 1883 ***5900.10*** *p461*
Conors, Mary 70; Ontario, 1871 ***1823.15*** *p48*
Conoway, William 33; Ontario, 1861 ***2896.25*** *p65*
Conquest, Edm; Virginia, 1673 ***6212.30*** *p51*
Conquest, George; New York, New York, 1835 ***1224.3*** *p16*
Conrad, Anna Catharina; America, 1740 ***2856.30*** *p68*
Conrad, Anna Margarete; Port uncertain, 1754 ***2856.30*** *p68*
Conrad, Anna Maria; Port uncertain, 1745 ***2856.30*** *p68*
Conrad, Blandina Cath.; Port uncertain, 1759 ***2856.30*** *p68*
Conrad, Cath. Magdalena; Port uncertain, 1757 ***2856.30*** *p68*
Conrad, Charles; Pennsylvania, 1786 ***4629.10*** *p52*
Conrad, Georg Magnus; Port uncertain, 1754 ***2856.30*** *p68*
Conrad, Georg Yerrick; America, 1740 ***2856.30*** *p68*
Conrad, Gorg; America, 1740 ***2856.30*** *p68*
Conrad, Henrich; Port uncertain, 1736 ***2856.30*** *p68*
Conrad, Henrich; Port uncertain, 1754 ***2856.30*** *p69*
With wife
Conrad, Mrs. J. Adam; Port uncertain, 1784 ***2856.30*** *p68*
Conrad, Jacob; New York, New York, 1852 ***6058.10*** *p47*
Conrad, Jacob, Jr.; America, 1740 ***2856.30*** *p68*
Conrad, Johann; Port uncertain, 1792 ***2856.30*** *p68*
Conrad, Johann Georg; Port uncertain, 1754 ***2856.30*** *p69*
Conrad, Johann Jakob; Port uncertain, 1752 ***2856.30*** *p69*
Conrad, Johann Martin; Port uncertain, 1759 ***2856.30*** *p69*
Conrad, Johann Nickel; Port uncertain, 1754 ***2856.30*** *p69*
Conrad, Johann Valentin; Port uncertain, 1750 ***2856.30*** *p69*
Conrad, John; Pennsylvania, 1786 ***4629.10*** *p54*
Conrad, Joseph 23; Ontario, 1861 ***2896.25*** *p48*
Conrad, Lorenz; Port uncertain, 1756 ***2856.30*** *p69*
Conrad, Maria Magdalena; Port uncertain, 1764 ***2856.30*** *p69*
Conrad, Mathew; Pennsylvania, 1786 ***4629.10*** *p53*
Conrad, Matthaus; Port uncertain, 1768 ***2856.30*** *p69*
Conrad, Peter; America, 1747 ***2856.30*** *p69*
With wife & children
Conrad, Peter; Port uncertain, 1761 ***2856.30*** *p69*
Conrad, Peter; Port uncertain, 1793 ***2856.30*** *p69*
Conrad, Valentin; Port uncertain, 1773 ***2856.30*** *p69*
Conrad, Wilhamina 42; Ontario, 1871 ***1823.28*** *p18*
Conradi, Hans Ulrich; Port uncertain, 1753 ***2856.30*** *p69*
With wife
Conradin, Elis. Margarete; Port uncertain, 1785 ***2856.30*** *p69*
Conradus, Conrad; America, 1746 ***2856.30*** *p69*
Conradus, Conrad; America, 1788 ***2856.30*** *p69*
Conright, George W. 13; Ontario, 1861 ***2896.27*** *p1*
Conrodsmeyer, Daniel; Georgia, 1698 ***1640.13*** *p23*
Conroy, Annie 50; Vermont, 1894 ***5900.10*** *p423*
Conroy, Ellen; Vermont, 1853-1925 ***5900.10*** *p513*
Conroy, James 57; Ontario, 1871 ***1823.22*** *p32*
Conroy, John; New York, 1836 ***8197.10*** *p319*
Conroy, Mary 90; Vermont, 1903 ***5900.10*** *p440*
Conroy, Mary A.; Vermont, 1850-1893 ***5900.10*** *p430*
Conroy, Matthias R. 32; Vermont, 1831 ***5900.10*** *p519*
Conroy, Michael; New York, 1837 ***8197.10*** *p80*
Conroy, Michael; New York, 1837 ***8197.10*** *p82*
Conroy, Michael 50; Ontario, 1871 ***1823.22*** *p32*

Conroy, Michael 63; Ontario, 1871 ***1823.22*** *p32*
Conroy, Patrick; New York, 1838 ***8197.10*** *p220*
Conroy, Patrick; New York, 1838-1840 ***8197.10*** *p301*
Conroy, Patrick; Pennsylvania, 1868 ***6058.10*** *p75*
Conroy, Thomas 60; Ontario, 1871 ***1823.22*** *p32*
Conroy, William; New York, 1807 ***8197.10*** *p328*
Conroy, William; New York, 1837 ***8197.10*** *p81*
Conroy, William 39; Vermont, 1895 ***5900.10*** *p440*
Conry, Catherine Griffin 62; Vermont, 1917 ***5900.10*** *p93*
Conry, Patrick 63; Vermont, 1893 ***5900.10*** *p93*
Consalvi, Camillo; New York, 1827 ***8197.10*** *p339*
Consaul, Eliza 4; Ontario, 1861 ***2896.25*** *p59*
Consaul, George 2; Ontario, 1861 ***2896.25*** *p59*
Consaul, Jane 22; Ontario, 1861 ***2896.25*** *p59*
Consaul, Mary 13; Ontario, 1861 ***2896.25*** *p59*
Consaul, Samuel 10; Ontario, 1861 ***2896.25*** *p59*
Consaul, Stewart 7; Ontario, 1861 ***2896.25*** *p59*
Consedine, Timothy; Maryland, 1665-1666 ***2524.55*** *p53*
Conser, George; Pennsylvania, 1779 ***4629.10*** *p38*
Considine, Carroll; New York, 1836 ***8197.10*** *p220*
Consit, John 42; Ontario, 1871 ***1823.15*** *p48*
Consody, Mary 45; Ontario, 1871 ***1823.22*** *p32*
Constable, Alexander; Charles Town, South Carolina, 1781 ***1224.2*** *p25*
Constable, Charles 13; Philadelphia, 1774 ***1220.25*** *p55*
Constable, Charles 19; America, 1774 ***1220.25*** *p85*
Constable, James; New York, 1807 ***8197.10*** *p329*
Constable, John; Philadelphia, 1791 ***1224.2*** *p25*
Constable, John 24; Baltimore, 1775 ***1220.25*** *p116*
Constable, Mary; Virginia, 1672 ***6212.30*** *p51*
Constable, Mary J. 50; Ontario, 1871 ***1823.15*** *p48*
Constable, William; Pennsylvania, 1777 ***4629.10*** *p21*
Constant, Thomas; New York, 1779 ***1224.2*** *p25*
Constantine, Mrs.; Quebec, 1857 ***9196.15*** *p16*
Constantine, Rev.; Quebec, 1857 ***9196.15*** *p16*
Constantinide, Laisio 34; Washington, 1913 ***9196.1*** *p59*
Conver, Peter; Pennsylvania, 1777 ***4629.10*** *p8*
Conver, Peter; Pennsylvania, 1777 ***4629.10*** *p29*
Convey, Bridget 27; Ontario, 1871 ***1823.22*** *p32*
Convey, Morris 50; Ontario, 1871 ***1823.22*** *p32*
Convey, Patrick 48; Ontario, 1871 ***1823.22*** *p32*
Convy, John 58; Ontario, 1871 ***1823.22*** *p32*
Conway, Mrs. 60; Ontario, 1871 ***1823.28*** *p18*
Conway, Agnes M. Beauvais; Vermont, 1866-1936 ***5900.10*** *p378*
Conway, Ann 23; Vermont, 1861 ***5900.10*** *p520*
Conway, Ann 40; Vermont, 1865 ***5900.10*** *p172*
Conway, Ann 53; Vermont, 1887 ***5900.10*** *p272*
Conway, Anna; Vermont, 1864-1930 ***5900.10*** *p520*
Conway, Biddy 20 *SEE* Conway, John
Conway, Bridget 18; Vermont, 1855 ***5900.10*** *p520*
Conway, Bridget 42; New York, New York, 1848 ***1825.45*** *p29*
Daughter: Mary 12
Son: Pat 16
Conway, Bridget McKeough 73; Vermont, 1910 ***5900.10*** *p150*
Conway, Catherine 33; Vermont, 1898 ***5900.10*** *p291*
Conway, Catherine 36 *SEE* Conway, John
Conway, Catherine 55; Vermont, 1888 ***5900.10*** *p506*
Conway, Catherine Bulger 38; Vermont, 1885 ***5900.10*** *p268*
Conway, Catherine Griffin; Vermont, 1805-1879 ***5900.10*** *p520*
Conway, Cormack; New York, 1840 ***8197.10*** *p221*
Conway, Ellen Bolger; Vermont, 1854-1925 ***5900.10*** *p255*
Conway, Ellen M.; Vermont, 1850-1919 ***5900.10*** *p553*
Conway, Francis; New York, 1821 ***8197.10*** *p216*
Conway, George 60; Ontario, 1871 ***1823.28*** *p18*
Conway, Hanora; Vermont, 1820-1898 ***5900.10*** *p370*
Conway, Honora; Vermont, 1841-1913 ***5900.10*** *p378*
Conway, James; New York, 1838 ***8197.10*** *p113*
Conway, James; Vermont, 1800-1905 ***5900.10*** *p520*
Conway, James; Vermont, 1860-1929 ***5900.10*** *p520*
Conway, James 27; New York, New York, 1848 ***1825.45*** *p29*
Wife: Margaret 24
Son: Pat 2
Son: Thomas 7
Daughter: Margaret 3
Conway, John; New York, 1802 ***8197.10*** *p19*
Conway, John 31; New York, New York, 1849 ***1825.45*** *p29*
Sister: Biddy 20
Sister: Catherine 36
Sister: Mary 25
Sister: Mary Ann 41
Conway, John E.; Vermont, 1855-1936 ***5900.10*** *p378*
Conway, Lawrence 52; Vermont, 1865 ***5900.10*** *p364*
Conway, Lawyer; Mississippi, 1829-1845 ***1640.10*** *p31*
Conway, Margaret; Vermont, 1853-1927 ***5900.10*** *p378*
Conway, Margaret 3 *SEE* Conway, James
Conway, Margaret 24 *SEE* Conway, James
Conway, Margaret 58; Vermont, 1863 ***5900.10*** *p364*
Conway, Mary 12 *SEE* Conway, Bridget
Conway, Mary 25 *SEE* Conway, John
Conway, Mary 45; Vermont, 1873 ***5900.10*** *p247*
Conway, Mary Ann 41 *SEE* Conway, John
Conway, Mary Ann Donahue; Vermont, 1845-1930 ***5900.10*** *p370*
Conway, Mary Tobin; Vermont, 1835-1921 ***5900.10*** *p520*
Conway, Mathew 25; Vermont, 1876 ***5900.10*** *p381*
Conway, Michael; Vermont, 1837-1914 ***5900.10*** *p553*
Conway, Michael 19; Ontario, 1861 ***2896.25*** *p15*
Conway, Michael 43; Ontario, 1871 ***1823.28*** *p18*
Conway, Michael 44; Ontario, 1871 ***1823.28*** *p18*
Conway, Michael 49; Ontario, 1871 ***1823.28*** *p18*
Conway, Michael J.; Vermont, 1840-1914 ***5900.10*** *p370*
Conway, Pat 2 *SEE* Conway, James
Conway, Pat 16 *SEE* Conway, Bridget
Conway, Patrick; New York, 1838 ***8197.10*** *p112*
Conway, Patrick; New York, 1840 ***8197.10*** *p163*
Conway, Patrick; Vermont, 1805-1865 ***5900.10*** *p520*
Conway, Patrick 34; Vermont, 1873 ***5900.10*** *p150*
Conway, Patrick 50; Ontario, 1871 ***1823.28*** *p18*
Conway, Patrick 56; Ontario, 1871 ***1823.22*** *p32*
Conway, Patrick 75; Ontario, 1871 ***1823.22*** *p32*
Conway, Richard 68; Vermont, 1908 ***5900.10*** *p268*
Conway, Thomas; New England, 1775-1781 ***4628.40*** *p68*
Conway, Thomas 7 *SEE* Conway, James
Conway, Thomas 30; Vermont, 1864 ***5900.10*** *p520*
Conway, Thomas 55; Ontario, 1871 ***1823.15*** *p48*
Conway, Thos 56; Ontario, 1871 ***1823.28*** *p18*
Conwell, Margaret; Vermont, 1830-1908 ***5900.10*** *p354*
Conwell, William; Vermont, 1839-1911 ***5900.10*** *p354*
Conworth, Master; Quebec, 1857 ***9196.15*** *p21*
Conworth, Miss; Quebec, 1857 ***9196.15*** *p21*
Conworth, Mr.; Quebec, 1857 ***9196.15*** *p21*
Cony, Mary; Maryland, 1659 ***2524.55*** *p53*
Conyers, Richard; Boston, 1709 ***1224.2*** *p25*
Coo, George 55; Ontario, 1871 ***1823.15*** *p48*
Cooch, Richard; Maryland, 1665 ***2524.55*** *p53*
Coock, Annie 16; Ontario, 1871 ***1823.15*** *p48*
Coock, Edw; Virginia, 1663 ***6212.30*** *p2*
Coock, John 51; Ontario, 1871 ***1823.15*** *p48*
Coofer, John; Maryland, 1668 ***2524.55*** *p53*
With wife
Coogan, John 41; Ontario, 1871 ***1823.22*** *p32*
Coogan, Richard B.; Pennsylvania, 1867 ***6058.10*** *p60*
Coogen, John 66; Ontario, 1871 ***1823.22*** *p32*
Cook, Lieut.; Quebec, 1857 ***9196.15*** *p23*
Cook, Mr.; Portland, Maine, 1858 ***9196.15*** *p28*
Cook, Mr.; Vermont, 1810-1855 ***5900.10*** *p153*
Cook, Mrs.; Portland, Maine, 1858 ***9196.15*** *p28*
Cook, Mrs.; Quebec, 1856 ***9196.15*** *p5*
Cook, Mrs.; Vermont, 1822-1897 ***5900.10*** *p153*
Cook, Aaron 61; Ontario, 1871 ***1823.28*** *p18*
Cook, Adam 55; Ontario, 1871 ***1823.15*** *p48*
Cook, Alexander; Georgia, 1698 ***1640.13*** *p23*
Cook, Alexander 60; Ontario, 1871 ***1823.22*** *p32*
Cook, Alveretta 2; Ontario, 1861 ***2896.27*** *p36*
Cook, Amy 26; Ontario, 1861 ***2896.27*** *p36*
Cook, Andrew; New York, 1838 ***8197.10*** *p112*
Cook, Andrew 7; Ontario, 1861 ***2896.27*** *p24*
Cook, Andrew 52; Ontario, 1871 ***1823.15*** *p48*
Cook, Ann 70; Ontario, 1871 ***1823.15*** *p48*
Cook, Ann C. 64; Vermont, 1880 ***5900.10*** *p49*
Cook, Ann E. 4; Ontario, 1861 ***2896.27*** *p24*
Cook, Anne 77; Vermont, 1877 ***5900.10*** *p618*
Cook, Catharine Keenan 62; Vermont, 1899 ***5900.10*** *p512*
Cook, Catherine Flynn; Vermont, 1852-1916 ***5900.10*** *p153*
Cook, Charles; Pennsylvania, 1779 ***4629.10*** *p40*
Cook, Charles 23; Maryland, 1774 ***1220.25*** *p79*
Cook, Charles 23; Ontario, 1871 ***1823.28*** *p18*
Cook, Cornelius 85; Vermont, 1877 ***5900.10*** *p618*
Cook, David 45; Ontario, 1871 ***1823.15*** *p48*
Cook, Edmund; Maryland, 1747 ***1224.2*** *p25*
Cook, Edward; Maryland, 1680 ***2524.55*** *p53*
Cook, Edward; Portland, Maine, 1858 ***9196.15*** *p28*
Cook, Eliza; Quebec, 1858 ***9196.15*** *p35*
Cook, Elizabeth 72; Ontario, 1871 ***1823.15*** *p48*
Cook, Ellen; Vermont, 1850-1919 ***5900.10*** *p462*
Cook, Ellen; Vermont, 1857-1952 ***5900.10*** *p462*
Cook, Ellis; New Jersey, 1855 ***1224.3*** *p16*
Cook, Elvira; Vermont, 1846-1919 ***5900.10*** *p48*
Cook, Emily M. 47; Vermont, 1884 ***5900.10*** *p279*
Cook, George; Virginia, 1671 ***6212.30*** *p42*
Cook, George 18; Ontario, 1861 ***2896.27*** *p49*
Cook, Gilbert 22; Ontario, 1861 ***2896.27*** *p49*
Cook, Harman 40; Ontario, 1871 ***1823.15*** *p48*
Cook, Henery 40; Ontario, 1871 ***1823.15*** *p48*
Cook, Henry; Pennsylvania, 1785 ***4629.10*** *p47*
Cook, Henry 25; Ontario, 1871 ***1823.28*** *p18*
Cook, Henry 32; Virginia, 1775 ***1220.25*** *p110*
Cook, Henry 42; Ontario, 1871 ***1823.15*** *p48*
Cook, Henry 50; Ontario, 1871 ***1823.15*** *p48*
Cook, Isabel; New Jersey, 1855 ***1224.3*** *p16*
Cook, Jacob 79; Ontario, 1871 ***1823.15*** *p48*
Cook, James 58; Ontario, 1871 ***1823.15*** *p49*
Cook, James 60; Ontario, 1871 ***1823.22*** *p33*
Cook, James 60; Ontario, 1871 ***1823.28*** *p18*
Cook, Jane 89; Vermont, 1892 ***5900.10*** *p279*
Cook, Jasper 40; Ontario, 1871 ***1823.22*** *p33*
Cook, Jenette 9; Ontario, 1861 ***2896.27*** *p24*
Cook, Jenette 32; Ontario, 1861 ***2896.27*** *p24*
Cook, John; New York, 1807 ***8197.10*** *p37*
Cook, John; New York, 1830 ***8197.10*** *p362*
Cook, John; New York, 1840 ***8197.10*** *p161*
Cook, John; Quebec, 1790 ***1224.2*** *p26*
Cook, John; West Indies, 1699 ***1640.13*** *p23*
Cook, John 15; Philadelphia, 1774 ***1220.25*** *p34*
Cook, John 21; Maryland, 1774 ***1220.25*** *p72*
Cook, John 21; Virginia, 1774 ***1220.25*** *p92*
Cook, John 23; Ontario, 1871 ***1823.15*** *p49*
Cook, John 29; Maryland, 1775 ***1220.25*** *p101*
Cook, John 40; Ontario, 1871 ***1823.15*** *p49*
Cook, John 57; Ontario, 1871 ***1823.15*** *p49*
Cook, John 58; Ontario, 1871 ***1823.28*** *p18*
Cook, John 61; Ontario, 1871 ***1823.15*** *p49*
Cook, John H.; New York, 1837 ***8197.10*** *p81*
Cook, Joseph 19; Ontario, 1861 ***2896.27*** *p49*
Cook, Joseph 19; Ontario, 1871 ***1823.28*** *p18*
Cook, Joseph 24; Virginia, 1774 ***1220.25*** *p74*
Cook, Josiah 31; Ontario, 1871 ***1823.28*** *p18*
Cook, Julia A. 26; Vermont, 1874 ***5900.10*** *p49*
Cook, Marey 24; Ontario, 1871 ***1823.28*** *p18*
Cook, Margaret Doyle 51; Vermont, 1892 ***5900.10*** *p130*
Cook, Mary; Portland, Maine, 1858 ***9196.15*** *p28*
Cook, Mary; Vermont, 1852-1936 ***5900.10*** *p516*
Cook, Mary E. McGinn; Vermont, n.d. ***5900.10*** *p49*
Cook, Michael; Vermont, 1845 ***5900.10*** *p153*
Cook, Michael 43; Ontario, 1871 ***1823.22*** *p33*
Cook, Michael P. 20; Vermont, 1877 ***5900.10*** *p49*
Cook, Miles; Maryland, 1659 ***2524.55*** *p53*
Cook, Myles; Maryland, 1658 ***2524.55*** *p53*
Cook, Nathan; Pennsylvania, 1777 ***4629.10*** *p22*
Cook, Nathan; Pennsylvania, 1779 ***4629.10*** *p39*
Cook, Nichalas 35; Ontario, 1871 ***1823.15*** *p49*
Cook, Peter; New York, 1840 ***8197.10*** *p161*
Cook, Peter 63; Vermont, 1833 ***5900.10*** *p49*
Cook, Richard; New York, 1823 ***8197.10*** *p217*
Cook, Richard; Vermont, 1835-1916 ***5900.10*** *p90*
Cook, Robert 44; Ontario, 1871 ***1823.15*** *p49*
Cook, Robert 44; Ontario, 1871 ***1823.22*** *p33*
Cook, Robert 73; Ontario, 1871 ***1823.15*** *p49*
Cook, Rubin 62; Ontario, 1871 ***1823.22*** *p33*
Cook, Samuel; New York, 1834 ***8197.10*** *p70*
Cook, Samuel 47; Ontario, 1871 ***1823.15*** *p49*
Cook, Samuel 52; Vermont, 1853 ***5900.10*** *p279*
Cook, Samuel C.; New York, 1840 ***8197.10*** *p161*
Cook, Sandy; Vermont, 1840-1894 ***5900.10*** *p47*
Cook, Sarah A.; Vermont, 1846-1933 ***5900.10*** *p90*
Cook, Sebastian; Pennsylvania, 1839 ***6058.10*** *p15*
Cook, Solomon; Maryland, 1663 ***2524.55*** *p53*
Cook, Thomas; New York, 1807 ***8197.10*** *p36*
Cook, Thomas 23; Philadelphia, 1774 ***1220.25*** *p42*
Cook, Thomas 30; Ontario, 1871 ***1823.15*** *p49*
Cook, Thomas 32; Ontario, 1871 ***1823.28*** *p18*
Cook, Thomas 43; Ontario, 1871 ***1823.15*** *p49*
Cook, Thomas 47; Ontario, 1871 ***1823.15*** *p49*
Cook, Thomas 50; Vermont, 1892 ***5900.10*** *p130*
Cook, Thomas 64; Ontario, 1871 ***1823.28*** *p19*
Cook, Virginia Raymond; Vermont, 1846-1934 ***5900.10*** *p279*
Cook, Walter 44; Ontario, 1871 ***1823.15*** *p49*
Cook, William; America, 1890 ***1640.13*** *p23*
Cook, William; New York, 1838 ***1224.3*** *p16*
Cook, William; New York, 1840 ***8197.10*** *p160*
Cook, William; New York, 1840 ***8197.10*** *p162*
Cook, William; Vermont, 1830-1903 ***5900.10*** *p279*
Cook, William; Vermont, 1851-1905 ***5900.10*** *p153*
Cook, William; Wilmington, North Carolina, 1824 ***1224.3*** *p16*
Cook, William 21; Maryland, 1774 ***1220.25*** *p85*
Cook, William 21; Maryland, 1775 ***1220.25*** *p105*
Cook, William 24; Maryland, 1774 ***1220.25*** *p84*
Cook, William 24; Ontario, 1861 ***2896.25*** *p65*
Cook, William 30; Ontario, 1871 ***1823.15*** *p49*
Cook, William 36; Ontario, 1871 ***1823.15*** *p49*
Cook, William 42; Ontario, 1871 ***1823.15*** *p49*
Cook, William 48; Ontario, 1871 ***1823.22*** *p33*
Cook, William 50; Ontario, 1871 ***1823.15*** *p49*
Cook, William 51; Ontario, 1871 ***1823.15*** *p49*
Cook, William 54; Ontario, 1871 ***1823.22*** *p33*
Cook, William 69; Ontario, 1861 ***2896.27*** *p49*

Cook, William H.; Vermont, 1854-1925 ***5900.10*** *p49*
Cook, William John; New York, 1840 ***8197.10*** *p162*
Cook, Willian 25; Ontario, 1871 ***1823.28*** *p19*
Cooke, Mrs.; Quebec, 1857 ***9196.15*** *p23*
Cooke, Amos; Virginia, 1668-1669 ***6212.30*** *p40*
Cooke, Amos; Virginia, 1672 ***6212.30*** *p49*
Cooke, Benjamin; Maryland, 1658 ***2524.55*** *p200*
Cooke, Edmond; Maryland, 1665 ***2524.55*** *p53*
Cooke, Edward; Maryland, 1669 ***2524.55*** *p218*
Cooke, Edward; Maryland, 1673 ***2524.55*** *p53*
Cooke, Elinor; Maryland, 1671 ***2524.55*** *p53*
Cooke, Eliza; Virginia, 1663 ***6212.30*** *p4*
Cooke, Elizabeth; Maryland, 1668 ***2524.55*** *p53*
Cooke, George; New York, 1807 ***8197.10*** *p325*
Cooke, George; South Carolina, 1755 ***1224.2*** *p26*
Cooke, George 30; Ontario, 1871 ***1823.28*** *p19*
Cooke, Henry; Maryland, 1655 ***2524.55*** *p53*
Cooke, Henry 41; Ontario, 1871 ***1823.15*** *p49*
Cooke, Henry J.; New York, 1840 ***8197.10*** *p160*
Cooke, James; Virginia, 1656 ***1224.1*** *p15*
Cooke, Janet; Quebec, 1858 ***9196.15*** *p41*
Cooke, Jno; Virginia, 1674 ***6212.30*** *p52*
Cooke, John *SEE* Cooke, John
Cooke, John; Maryland, 1660 ***2524.55*** *p53*
With wife
Child: John
Child: Margarett
Child: Thomas
Cooke, John; New York, 1834 ***8197.10*** *p373*
Cooke, John; North America, 1778 ***1224.2*** *p26*
Cooke, John; South Carolina, 1755 ***1224.2*** *p26*
Cooke, Margarett *SEE* Cooke, John
Cooke, Mark 18; Kingston, Jamaica, 1774 ***1220.25*** *p13*
Cooke, Mary 53; Ontario, 1871 ***1823.28*** *p19*
Cooke, Michael 50; Ontario, 1871 ***1823.28*** *p19*
Cooke, Nicholas; Virginia, 1700 ***1224.2*** *p26*
Cooke, Rebecca; South Carolina, 1755 ***1224.2*** *p26*
Cooke, Richard; Maryland, 1682 ***2524.55*** *p54*
Cooke, Richard; Virginia, 1666 ***6212.30*** *p30*
Cooke, Robert; Maryland, 1663 ***2524.55*** *p54*
Cooke, Samuel; Virginia, 1686 ***1224.1*** *p15*
Cooke, Samuell; Maryland, 1658 ***2524.55*** *p54*
Cooke, Sarah; Maryland, 1681 ***2524.55*** *p54*
Cooke, Sarah; New York, New York, 1797 ***1224.2*** *p26*
Cooke, Suzanna; Maryland, 1654 ***2524.55*** *p54*
Cooke, Thomas *SEE* Cooke, John
Cooke, Thomas; Maryland, 1662 ***2524.55*** *p54*
Cooke, Thomas; Maryland, 1666 ***2524.55*** *p54*
Cooke, Thomas; Maryland, 1666 ***2524.55*** *p189*
Cooke, Thomas; Maryland, 1681 ***2524.55*** *p54*
Cooke, Thomas; New York, 1838 ***8197.10*** *p376*
Cooke, William; Maryland, 1681 ***2524.55*** *p54*
Cooke, William 30; Virginia, 1774 ***1220.25*** *p89*
Cooke, X. P.; Virginia, 1666 ***6212.30*** *p28*
Cookeman, Joane; Maryland, 1666 ***2524.55*** *p54*
Cookeman, Rice; Maryland, 1667 ***2524.55*** *p54*
Cookes, Thomas; Maryland, 1664 ***2524.55*** *p189*
Cookhart, Jacob; America, 1739 ***2856.30*** *p69*
Cookhart, Jakob; America, 1739 ***2856.30*** *p69*
Cookman, Thomas 56; Ontario, 1871 ***1823.28*** *p19*
Cookson, George; St. Augustine, Florida, 1777 ***1224.2*** *p26*
Cookson, John 26; Virginia, 1774 ***1220.25*** *p91*
Coolas, Albert 52; Ontario, 1871 ***1823.28*** *p19*
Coolas, Jacob 65; Ontario, 1871 ***1823.28*** *p19*
Cooley, Alice; Vermont, 1858-1893 ***5900.10*** *p554*
Cooley, Bridget; Vermont, 1854-1900 ***5900.10*** *p430*
Cooley, Elizabeth Halpin; Vermont, 1843-1881 ***5900.10*** *p384*
Cooley, George; Pennsylvania, 1777 ***4629.10*** *p7*
Cooley, H. 20; Ontario, 1861 ***2896.28*** *p7*
Cooley, Hugh 59; Ontario, 1861 ***2896.28*** *p7*
Cooley, John 16; Virginia, 1774 ***1220.25*** *p45*
Cooley, Joseph 12; Virginia, 1774 ***1220.25*** *p45*
Cooley, Mary E.; Vermont, 1852-1902 ***5900.10*** *p349*
Cooley, Patrick; New York, 1838 ***8197.10*** *p113*
Cooley, Peter 38; Virginia, 1774 ***1220.25*** *p45*
Cooley, Peter, Jr. 18; Virginia, 1774 ***1220.25*** *p45*
Cooley, William 21; Maryland, 1774 ***1220.25*** *p77*
Coolihan, Alice; Vermont, 1857-1934 ***5900.10*** *p317*
Coolihan, Margaret 64; Vermont, 1882 ***5900.10*** *p317*
Coolihan, Phelps; Vermont, 1857-1921 ***5900.10*** *p317*
Coolihan, William 63; Vermont, 1882 ***5900.10*** *p317*
Coolihan, Willie 21; Vermont, 1875 ***5900.10*** *p317*
Cooling, George; Georgia, 1736 ***1640.10*** *p31*
Coolman, Mary; Maryland, 1655-1656 ***2524.55*** *p54*
Coombe, Rich; Virginia, 1672-1673 ***6212.30*** *p51*
Coombes, Miss; Quebec, 1857 ***9196.15*** *p21*
Coombes, Nathaniel; New Jersey, 1822 ***1224.3*** *p16*
Coombs, Abraham; Maryland, 1670 ***2524.55*** *p52*
Daughter: Sarah
Coombs, Edward 21; Virginia, 1774 ***1220.25*** *p87*
Coombs, Joseph 36; Ontario, 1871 ***1823.15*** *p49*
Coombs, Richard; New York, 1840 ***8197.10*** *p384*
Coombs, Sarah *SEE* Coombs, Abraham
Coombs, Thomas; New York, 1840 ***8197.10*** *p163*
Coome, Mathew; Virginia, 1666 ***6212.30*** *p26*
Coomes, . . .; Maryland, 1655-1656 ***2524.55*** *p54*
Coon, George 37; Ontario, 1871 ***1823.22*** *p33*
Coonan, Edward 50; Ontario, 1871 ***1823.28*** *p19*
Coonan, Jerry 23; Vermont, 1866 ***5900.10*** *p364*
Coonerty, Catherine Corley; Vermont, 1836-1900 ***5900.10*** *p131*
Coonerty, Ellen 84; Vermont, 1907 ***5900.10*** *p521*
Coonerty, John J.; Vermont, 1833-1907 ***5900.10*** *p131*
Coonerty, Mary A. Moran; Vermont, 1853-1916 ***5900.10*** *p595*
Coonerty, Nancy 38; Vermont, 1860 ***5900.10*** *p124*
Coonerty, Thomas B.; Vermont, 1859-1906 ***5900.10*** *p595*
Cooney, Alice; Vermont, 1835-1864 ***5900.10*** *p566*
Cooney, Alice; Vermont, 1835-1864 ***5900.10*** *p576*
Cooney, Bernard; Vermont, 1807-1872 ***5900.10*** *p157*
Cooney, Catherine; Vermont, 1798-1862 ***5900.10*** *p148*
Cooney, Catherine; Vermont, 1829-1885 ***5900.10*** *p449*
Cooney, Cecelia; Vermont, 1812-1857 ***5900.10*** *p157*
Cooney, Dennis 38; Ontario, 1871 ***1823.22*** *p33*
Cooney, Edward 48; Ontario, 1871 ***1823.22*** *p33*
Cooney, Elizabeth 77; Vermont, 1884 ***5900.10*** *p449*
Cooney, George 52; Ontario, 1871 ***1823.22*** *p33*
Cooney, John 50; Ontario, 1871 ***1823.22*** *p33*
Cooney, Martha 33; Ontario, 1871 ***1823.28*** *p19*
Cooney, Mary; Vermont, 1847-1906 ***5900.10*** *p84*
Cooney, Mary Hayes; Vermont, 1837-1894 ***5900.10*** *p582*
Cooney, Matthew 87; Vermont, 1890 ***5900.10*** *p84*
Cooney, Patrick; Vermont, n.d. ***5900.10*** *p386*
Cooney, Sarah 90; Vermont, 1899 ***5900.10*** *p84*
Cooney, Thomas; Vermont, 1833-1913 ***5900.10*** *p566*
Cooney, Thomas; Vermont, 1833-1914 ***5900.10*** *p576*
Cooney, Thomas; Vermont, 1840-1922 ***5900.10*** *p157*
Cooney, Thomas; Vermont, 1855 ***5900.10*** *p518*
Cooney, William 29; Ontario, 1871 ***1823.22*** *p33*
Coons, Johann; America, 1738 ***2856.30*** *p69*
Coons, Peter Jost; America, 1738 ***2856.30*** *p69*
Cooper, Miss; Quebec, 1856 ***9196.15*** *p9*
Cooper, Mr.; Quebec, 1857 ***9196.15*** *p19*
Cooper, Alexander 42; Ontario, 1871 ***1823.28*** *p19*
Cooper, Alice; Vermont, 1827-1901 ***5900.10*** *p550*
Cooper, Alice M.; Vermont, 1861-1931 ***5900.10*** *p291*
Cooper, Allexr; Virginia, 1671 ***6212.30*** *p45*
Cooper, Amos 12; Ontario, 1861 ***2896.27*** *p35*
Cooper, Ann *SEE* Cooper, Walter
Cooper, Anne 76; Ontario, 1871 ***1823.15*** *p49*
Cooper, Anne M. 49; Ontario, 1871 ***1823.15*** *p49*
Cooper, Catherine *SEE* Cooper, Walter
Cooper, Charles; Virginia, 1679 ***6212.30*** *p54*
Cooper, Delilah J. 17; Ontario, 1861 ***2896.27*** *p54*
Cooper, Dorithy *SEE* Cooper, Walter
Cooper, Dorothy *SEE* Cooper, Walter
Cooper, Edmon 30; Ontario, 1871 ***1823.28*** *p19*
Cooper, Edward; Boston, 1809 ***1224.3*** *p16*
Cooper, Edward; Maryland, 1682 ***2524.55*** *p54*
Cooper, Edward; New York, 1819 ***8197.10*** *p214*
Cooper, Elizabeth *SEE* Cooper, Walter
Cooper, Elizabeth 49; Ontario, 1861 ***2896.27*** *p54*
Cooper, Elizabeth Susannah; New Jersey, n.d. ***1224.3*** *p46*
Cooper, Emanuel 40; Ontario, 1871 ***1823.28*** *p19*
Cooper, Esther Ritchie; Jamaica, 1844 ***1640.13*** *p23*
Cooper, Francis; Maryland, 1662 ***2524.55*** *p54*
Cooper, Francis 49; Ontario, 1871 ***1823.15*** *p49*
Cooper, Freeman 18; Ontario, 1861 ***2896.27*** *p31*
Cooper, George; New York, 1840 ***8197.10*** *p162*
Cooper, George 31; Ontario, 1871 ***1823.22*** *p33*
Cooper, George 45; Ontario, 1871 ***1823.15*** *p49*
Cooper, Gilbert; Maryland, 1668 ***2524.55*** *p54*
Wife: Katherine
Cooper, Hannah 32; Ontario, 1871 ***1823.15*** *p49*
Cooper, Henry; Virginia, 1667 ***6212.30*** *p37*
Cooper, Henry 22; Baltimore, 1775 ***1220.25*** *p117*
Cooper, Hugh 62; Ontario, 1871 ***1823.22*** *p33*
Cooper, Irish; Virginia, 1673 ***6212.30*** *p51*
Cooper, James; New York, 1827 ***8197.10*** *p342*
Cooper, James; Pennsylvania, 1777 ***4629.10*** *p25*
Cooper, James 52; Ontario, 1871 ***1823.28*** *p19*
Cooper, James M.; Vermont, 1853-1943 ***5900.10*** *p291*
Cooper, Jane; Maryland, 1665 ***2524.55*** *p54*
Cooper, Jane 35; Ontario, 1861 ***2896.27*** *p35*
Cooper, Joane; Maryland, 1667 ***2524.55*** *p54*
Cooper, Joane; Maryland, 1670 ***2524.55*** *p54*
Cooper, John; New York, 1807 ***8197.10*** *p36*
Cooper, John; New York, 1840 ***8197.10*** *p160*
Cooper, John 15; Ontario, 1861 ***2896.27*** *p35*
Cooper, John 16; Tortola, 1773-1774 ***1220.25*** *p32*
Cooper, John 28; Ontario, 1861 ***2896.27*** *p54*
Cooper, John 29; Maryland, 1774 ***1220.25*** *p84*
Cooper, John 45; Ontario, 1871 ***1823.15*** *p49*
Cooper, John 53; Ontario, 1871 ***1823.15*** *p49*
Cooper, John Knor; Pennsylvania, 1777 ***4629.10*** *p21*
Cooper, Jonathan 54; Ontario, 1871 ***1823.15*** *p49*
Cooper, Joseph 26; Virginia, 1774 ***1220.25*** *p89*
Cooper, Justinian; Virginia, 1655 ***1224.1*** *p15*
Cooper, Katherine *SEE* Cooper, Gilbert
Cooper, Luke B. 26; Ontario, 1861 ***2896.27*** *p54*
Cooper, Margrett; Virginia, 1677 ***6212.30*** *p53*
Cooper, Marrion 45; Ontario, 1871 ***1823.15*** *p49*
Cooper, Mary; Charles Town, South Carolina, n.d. ***1224.2*** *p26*
Cooper, Mary 29; Maryland, 1774 ***1220.25*** *p47*
Cooper, Mary 30; Maryland, 1775 ***1220.25*** *p105*
Cooper, Mary Ann 26; Ontario, 1861 ***2896.27*** *p54*
Cooper, Mary Ann 27; Ontario, 1861 ***2896.27*** *p31*
Cooper, Mary Jane 1; Ontario, 1861 ***2896.27*** *p35*
Cooper, Mechetabel; Boston, 1705 ***1224.2*** *p80*
Cooper, Minnie A. 3; Ontario, 1861 ***2896.28*** *p53*
Cooper, P.; Alabama, 1829-1845 ***1640.10*** *p31*
Cooper, Peter; Pennsylvania, 1777 ***4629.10*** *p21*
Cooper, Phillip 22; Ontario, 1871 ***1823.22*** *p33*
Cooper, Ransalaer B. 14; Ontario, 1861 ***2896.27*** *p54*
Cooper, Rebecca 52; Ontario, 1861 ***2896.27*** *p54*
Cooper, Rich; Virginia, 1677 ***6212.30*** *p54*
Cooper, Richard; Maryland, 1682 ***2524.55*** *p54*
Cooper, Robert; Mississippi, 1810-1845 ***1640.10*** *p32*
Cooper, Robert 45; Ontario, 1871 ***1823.15*** *p50*
Cooper, Robert 60; Ontario, 1871 ***1823.28*** *p19*
Cooper, Robt.; Maryland, 1658 ***2524.55*** *p54*
Cooper, Samuel 22; Maryland, 1774 ***1220.25*** *p47*
Cooper, Samuell; Maryland, 1680 ***2524.55*** *p54*
Cooper, Stephen; Maryland, 1656 ***2524.55*** *p54*
Cooper, Stephen 31; Maryland, 1774 ***1220.25*** *p39*
Cooper, Susan *SEE* Cooper, Walter
Cooper, Susan; New England, 1705 ***1224.2*** *p26*
Cooper, Susan 31; Ontario, 1861 ***2896.28*** *p53*
Cooper, Susanna *SEE* Cooper, Walter
Cooper, Tho; Virginia, 1673 ***6212.30*** *p51*
Cooper, Thomas; Maryland, 1671 ***2524.55*** *p54*
Cooper, Thomas; Philadelphia, 1793 ***4629.10*** *p73*
Cooper, Thomas; Philadelphia, 1806 ***1224.3*** *p16*
Cooper, Thomas 21; Maryland, 1774 ***1220.25*** *p5*
Cooper, Thomas 22; Virginia, 1775 ***1220.25*** *p95*
Cooper, Thomas 30; Ontario, 1871 ***1823.15*** *p50*
Cooper, Thomas 63; Ontario, 1871 ***1823.15*** *p50*
Cooper, Timothy; New England, 1655 ***1224.1*** *p15*
Cooper, W. H. 54; Ontario, 1871 ***1823.15*** *p50*
Cooper, Walter; Maryland, 1651 ***2524.55*** *p54*
Wife: Ann
Daughter: Susanna
Daughter: Catherine
Daughter: Elizabeth
Daughter: Dorithy
Cooper, Walter; Maryland, 1659 ***2524.55*** *p54*
Wife: Ann
Daughter: Dorothy
Daughter: Catherine
Daughter: Susan
Daughter: Elizabeth
Cooper, William; Maryland, 1679 ***2524.55*** *p54*
Cooper, William; Virginia, 1667-1668 ***6212.30*** *p39*
Cooper, William 27; Philadelphia, 1774 ***1220.25*** *p67*
Cooper, William 40; Maryland, 1775 ***1220.25*** *p104*
Cooper, William 47; Ontario, 1871 ***1823.15*** *p50*
Cooper, William B. 20; Ontario, 1861 ***2896.27*** *p31*
Cooper, Wills; Virginia, 1671-1672 ***6212.30*** *p47*
Coote, Richard; New York, 1839 ***8197.10*** *p132*
Coote, Teremy; Maryland, 1639 ***2524.55*** *p54*
Coots, John; New York, 1837 ***8197.10*** *p81*
Cope, Barth; Virginia, 1672 ***6212.30*** *p50*
Cope, Henry; New York, 1744 ***1224.2*** *p26*
Cope, John; Maryland, 1724 ***1224.2*** *p26*
Cope, Nathaniel; Pennsylvania, 1777 ***4629.10*** *p16*
Cope, Peter 13; Ontario, 1861 ***2896.27*** *p72*
Cope, Thomas; Virginia, 1664 ***6212.30*** *p11*
Cope, William; New York, 1840 ***8197.10*** *p161*
Cope, William; Virginia, 1666-1667 ***6212.30*** *p34*
Copeland, Miss; Quebec, 1857 ***9196.15*** *p18*
Copeland, Catherine 84; Ontario, 1871 ***1823.15*** *p50*
Copeland, Frederick; Pennsylvania, 1856 ***6058.10*** *p38*
Copeland, James 24; Ontario, 1871 ***1823.15*** *p50*
Copeland, Jas 59; Ontario, 1871 ***1823.28*** *p19*
Copeland, John 30; Ontario, 1871 ***1823.15*** *p50*
Copeland, John 33; Ontario, 1871 ***1823.15*** *p50*
Copeland, Samuel; Maryland, 1660 ***2524.55*** *p54*
Copeman, Jno; Virginia, 1664 ***6212.30*** *p5*
Copes, Frances *SEE* Copes, John
Copes, Francis; Maryland, 1681 ***2524.55*** *p54*
Copes, John *SEE* Copes, John
Copes, John; Maryland, 1681 ***2524.55*** *p54*
Wife: Frances
Son: John

Copestak, John C.; Portland, Maine, 1858 ***9196.15*** *p47*
Copinsher, Mrs. 30; Boston, 1774 ***1220.25*** *p56*
Copland, George; New York, 1794 ***8197.10*** *p3*
Copland, James 38; Ontario, 1871 ***1823.15*** *p50*
Copland, John 40; Maryland, 1774 ***1220.25*** *p61*
Copland, John C. 55; Ontario, 1871 ***1823.15*** *p50*
Copland, Robert 70; Ontario, 1871 ***1823.15*** *p50*
Copland, William H. 35; Ontario, 1871 ***1823.15*** *p50*
Coplestone, Mr.; Quebec, 1856 ***9196.15*** *p9*
Coplestone, Mr.; Quebec, 1857 ***9196.15*** *p24*
Coplestone, Mrs.; Quebec, 1856 ***9196.15*** *p9*
Copley, Abraham 22; New York, 1774 ***1220.25*** *p24*
Copley, Janet; New York, 1850 ***1640.13*** *p23*
Copley, Savell; Maryland, 1653 ***2524.55*** *p54*
Copman, James 70; Ontario, 1871 ***1823.15*** *p50*
Copp, Miss; Quebec, 1857 ***9196.15*** *p20*
Copp, Mrs.; Quebec, 1857 ***9196.15*** *p20*
Copp, D.; Quebec, 1857 ***9196.15*** *p20*
Copp, Jonas 52; Ontario, 1871 ***1823.15*** *p50*
Copp, Micheal 40; Ontario, 1871 ***1823.28*** *p19*
Copp, Samuel 40; Ontario, 1871 ***1823.15*** *p50*
Copp, W. G.; Quebec, 1857 ***9196.15*** *p20*
Copp, William; New England, 1654 ***1224.1*** *p15*
Copp, William 65; Ontario, 1871 ***1823.15*** *p50*
Coppel, Jane 45; New York, 1774 ***1220.25*** *p25*
Copper, Norris; Pennsylvania, 1777 ***4629.10*** *p16*
Copper, Robt.; Maryland, 1658 ***2524.55*** *p54*
Copper, Thomas 16; Virginia, 1774 ***1220.25*** *p89*
Copperthwaite, Harold 57; Ontario, 1871 ***1823.22*** *p33*
Coppin, John; New York, 1803 ***8197.10*** *p11*
Copping, Edward; Maryland, 1650 ***2524.55*** *p54*
Copping, James; Virginia, 1664 ***6212.30*** *p9*
Coppinger, . . .; Boston, 1765 ***4628.40*** *p114*
Coppinger, Bridget; Vermont, 1868-1962 ***5900.10*** *p443*
Coppoway, Richard 20; Ontario, 1871 ***1823.22*** *p33*
Copps, Ann Ryan 82; Vermont, 1907 ***5900.10*** *p561*
Copps, B. J. Moloney 46; Vermont, 1902 ***5900.10*** *p583*
Copps, Daniel 39; Ontario, 1871 ***1823.28*** *p19*
Copps, Dennis 71; Vermont, 1898 ***5900.10*** *p561*
Copps, Edward R. 32; Vermont, 1886 ***5900.10*** *p583*
Copps, Ellen Gaffney; Vermont, 1852-1881 ***5900.10*** *p567*
Copps, Hannah Darmody 74; Vermont, 1907 ***5900.10*** *p561*
Copps, Helen; Vermont, 1833-1901 ***5900.10*** *p274*
Copps, John 36; Ontario, 1871 ***1823.28*** *p19*
Copps, John 71; Vermont, 1892 ***5900.10*** *p561*
Cops, Frederick; New York, 1830 ***8197.10*** *p313*
Copson, John; Maryland, 1740 ***1224.2*** *p26*
Coquebert, Hanibal Henri Felix; New York, 1808 ***8197.10*** *p53*
Coquelet, John B.; Pennsylvania, 1821 ***6058.10*** *p8*
Coragon, William 28; Ontario, 1871 ***1823.28*** *p19*
Coram, William; Maryland, 1673 ***2524.55*** *p54*
Corazzi, A. 39; Ontario, 1871 ***1823.28*** *p19*
Corbe, Peter; Port uncertain, 1761 ***2856.30*** *p69*
Corbeau, Jean; America, 1736 ***2856.30*** *p69*
Corbert, Margret 60; Ontario, 1871 ***1823.15*** *p50*
Corbet, Mr.; Quebec, 1857 ***9196.15*** *p15*
Corbet, Alexander; Pennsylvania, 1777 ***4629.10*** *p22*
Corbet, John; New Orleans, 1882 ***1640.13*** *p23*
Corbett, . . .; New Hampshire, 1641-1660 ***4628.40*** *p44*
Corbett, Mrs. 50; Ontario, 1871 ***1823.28*** *p19*
Corbett, Abigail; Vermont, 1801-1894 ***5900.10*** *p442*
Corbett, Agnes B. Cox; Vermont, 1849-1934 ***5900.10*** *p285*
Corbett, Ann Eliza Cavanagh 38; Vermont, 1893 ***5900.10*** *p528*
Corbett, Anne; Virginia, 1664 ***6212.30*** *p6*
Corbett, Catharine Canfall 47; Vermont, 1849 ***5900.10*** *p473*
Corbett, Catherine 37; Vermont, 1866 ***5900.10*** *p372*
Corbett, Catherine Burke 55; Vermont, 1883 ***5900.10*** *p250*
Corbett, Edmond; Vermont, 1851-1929 ***5900.10*** *p528*
Corbett, Ellen; Vermont, 1862-1950 ***5900.10*** *p189*
Corbett, Ellen 64; Vermont, 1886 ***5900.10*** *p551*
Corbett, Flora; Ontario, 1851 ***4537.32*** *p31*
Corbett, Henry; Maryland, 1656 ***2524.55*** *p55*
Corbett, Henry 52; Ontario, 1871 ***1823.22*** *p33*
Corbett, James; Pennsylvania, 1868 ***6058.10*** *p76*
Corbett, James 52; Ontario, 1871 ***1823.22*** *p33*
Corbett, Jane Sexton 46; Vermont, 1876 ***5900.10*** *p469*
Corbett, Julia 19; Vermont, 1872 ***5900.10*** *p250*
Corbett, Maggie 20; Vermont, 1885 ***5900.10*** *p250*
Corbett, Margaret Carey; Vermont, 1827-1901 ***5900.10*** *p528*
Corbett, Margaret O'Brien 38; Vermont, 1887 ***5900.10*** *p250*
Corbett, Mary; Vermont, 1830-1922 ***5900.10*** *p468*
Corbett, Mary; Vermont, 1852-1920 ***5900.10*** *p585*
Corbett, Mary; Vermont, 1858-1951 ***5900.10*** *p189*
Corbett, Mary 21; Ontario, 1861 ***2896.25*** *p15*
Corbett, Mary Welch 33; Vermont, 1878 ***5900.10*** *p469*
Corbett, Michael 21; Vermont, 1872 ***5900.10*** *p250*
Corbett, Michael 58; Vermont, 1887 ***5900.10*** *p469*
Corbett, Nora; Vermont, 1855-1922 ***5900.10*** *p252*
Corbett, Patrick; New York, 1840 ***8197.10*** *p162*
Corbett, Patrick; Vermont, 1810-1872 ***5900.10*** *p528*
Corbett, Patrick 55; Vermont, 1872 ***5900.10*** *p527*
Corbett, Rodger 42; Vermont, 1883 ***5900.10*** *p250*
Corbett, Sarah Barrett; Vermont, 1856-1936 ***5900.10*** *p528*
Corbett, Thomas 17; Vermont, 1885 ***5900.10*** *p250*
Corbett, Thomas 55; Ontario, 1871 ***1823.15*** *p50*
Corbett, Valentine 45; Ontario, 1871 ***1823.22*** *p33*
Corbett, William; Georgia, 1812 ***1640.10*** *p32*
Corbett, William; Vermont, 1855-1918 ***5900.10*** *p528*
Corbett, William 73; Vermont, 1868 ***5900.10*** *p473*
Corbey, Jacob; Port uncertain, 1727 ***2856.30*** *p69*
Corbiere, William; New York, 1821 ***8197.10*** *p216*
Corbin, Francis; Maryland, 1671 ***2524.55*** *p55*
Corbisley, Samuel; Maryland or Virginia, 1720 ***1224.2*** *p26*
Corbith, Christopher 60; Ontario, 1871 ***1823.15*** *p50*
Corbitt, John 47; Ontario, 1871 ***1823.15*** *p50*
Corbitt, Joseph; New York, 1805 ***8197.10*** *p28*
Corbitt, Margaret Torpey; Vermont, 1830-1903 ***5900.10*** *p465*
Corbitt, Mathew 49; Vermont, 1879 ***5900.10*** *p81*
Corbitt, Michael; Vermont, 1828-1876 ***5900.10*** *p465*
Corbless, James 69; Vermont, 1861 ***5900.10*** *p230*
Corbless, Margaret 73; Vermont, 1876 ***5900.10*** *p230*
Corbless, Nicholas 90; Vermont, 1882 ***5900.10*** *p230*
Corbley, Thomas; New York, 1830 ***8197.10*** *p354*
Corblis, Mary 54; Vermont, 1850 ***5900.10*** *p242*
Corbman, Emily 21; Ontario, 1861 ***2896.25*** *p20*
Corbman, Sarah A. 50; Ontario, 1861 ***2896.25*** *p20*
Corbman, William 30; Ontario, 1861 ***2896.25*** *p20*
Corbo, Jean; America, 1737 ***2856.30*** *p64*
Corby, Miss; Quebec, 1857 ***9196.15*** *p16*
Corby, Mr.; Quebec, 1857 ***9196.15*** *p16*
Corby, Benjamin 15; Maryland, 1775 ***1220.25*** *p111*
Corcoran, Anna; Vermont, 1854-1929 ***5900.10*** *p327*
Corcoran, Bridget 40; Ontario, 1871 ***1823.15*** *p50*
Corcoran, Cornelius 30; Vermont, 1890 ***5900.10*** *p361*
Corcoran, Daniel; Vermont, 1852-1922 ***5900.10*** *p491*
Corcoran, Daniel 19; Vermont, 1887 ***5900.10*** *p361*
Corcoran, Dominick; Vermont, 1846-1918 ***5900.10*** *p432*
Corcoran, Ella; Vermont, 1854-1913 ***5900.10*** *p140*
Corcoran, Ellen Doyle; Vermont, 1839-1916 ***5900.10*** *p433*
Corcoran, Ellen McGuire; Vermont, 1860-1894 ***5900.10*** *p351*
Corcoran, Francis; Pennsylvania, 1777 ***4629.10*** *p13*
Corcoran, Hannah; Vermont, 1860-1942 ***5900.10*** *p231*
Corcoran, James 40; Vermont, 1879 ***5900.10*** *p433*
Corcoran, John; Vermont, 1846-1916 ***5900.10*** *p351*
Corcoran, Katherine A.; Vermont, 1856-1925 ***5900.10*** *p443*
Corcoran, Lucy Gallagher; Vermont, 1852-1929 ***5900.10*** *p128*
Corcoran, Margaret; Vermont, 1853-1903 ***5900.10*** *p175*
Corcoran, Mary; Vermont, 1837-1910 ***5900.10*** *p80*
Corcoran, Mary; Vermont, 1844-1915 ***5900.10*** *p334*
Corcoran, Mary Barry; Vermont, 1823-1887 ***5900.10*** *p231*
Corcoran, Michael; New York, 1839 ***8197.10*** *p382*
Corcoran, Michael; Vermont, 1844-1914 ***5900.10*** *p128*
Corcoran, Michael; Vermont, 1848-1918 ***5900.10*** *p351*
Corcoran, Michael 78; Vermont, 1902 ***5900.10*** *p361*
Corcoran, Norah Kinnaley 70; Vermont, 1891 ***5900.10*** *p80*
Corcoran, Peter; Vermont, 1833-1924 ***5900.10*** *p433*
Corcoran, Sarah 60; Vermont, 1891 ***5900.10*** *p361*
Corcoran, Thomas; New York, 1831 ***8197.10*** *p366*
Corcoran, Timothy; Vermont, 1829-1916 ***5900.10*** *p231*
Corcoran, Timothy; Vermont, 1855-1934 ***5900.10*** *p327*
Corcoran, William 21; Vermont, 1886 ***5900.10*** *p91*
Corcoran, William 90; Vermont, 1888 ***5900.10*** *p80*
Corcoran, Winifred A.; Vermont, 1849-1929 ***5900.10*** *p432*
Corcran, Richard; New York, 1862 ***6058.10*** *p67*
Corcrane, John; Maryland, 1678 ***2524.55*** *p55*
Corderoy, William; Virginia, 1667 ***1224.1*** *p15*
Cordery, Anne; Maryland, 1668 ***2524.55*** *p55*
Daughter: Elizabeth
Cordery, Elizabeth *SEE* Cordery, Anne
Cordier, David; Port uncertain, 1783 ***2856.30*** *p69*
Cordies, Heinrich; Port uncertain, 1764 ***2856.30*** *p69*
Cordill, James; Pennsylvania, 1777 ***4629.10*** *p29*
Cordin, Roger; Maryland, 1667 ***2524.55*** *p174*
Cordiner, James; Rappahannock, Virginia, 1724 ***1640.13*** *p23*
Cordis, Hannah; Boston, n.d. ***1224.2*** *p26*
Cordland, Hans; Pennsylvania, 1786 ***4629.10*** *p49*
Cordon, Margaret; Vermont, 1824-1900 ***5900.10*** *p117*
Core, Lucey 48; Ontario, 1871 ***1823.15*** *p50*
Core, Patrick 65; Ontario, 1871 ***1823.22*** *p33*
Core, Ralph 22; Maryland, 1775 ***1220.25*** *p121*
Core, William 58; Ontario, 1871 ***1823.15*** *p50*
Corell, Adam; Port uncertain, 1748 ***2856.30*** *p69*
Corell, George; Maryland, 1673 ***2524.55*** *p55*
Corell, Johann; Port uncertain, 1748 ***2856.30*** *p69*
Corell, Philipp; America, 1741 ***2856.30*** *p70*
With wife & children
Corett, Johann; Port uncertain, 1748 ***2856.30*** *p69*
Corey, Ann; Vermont, 1836-1886 ***5900.10*** *p579*
Corey, Edward; Vermont, 1804-1879 ***5900.10*** *p561*
Corey, Hugh; Vermont, 1836-1916 ***5900.10*** *p561*
Corey, James 49; Vermont, 1885 ***5900.10*** *p581*
Corey, John; Vermont, 1849-1879 ***5900.10*** *p561*
Corey, John 54; Ontario, 1871 ***1823.22*** *p34*
Corey, Julia Carroll 68; Vermont, 1914 ***5900.10*** *p581*
Corey, Mary; Vermont, 1818-1906 ***5900.10*** *p570*
Corey, Mary; Vermont, 1840-1905 ***5900.10*** *p579*
Corey, Mary 70; Vermont, 1904 ***5900.10*** *p580*
Corey, Mary A. Young; Vermont, 1852-1933 ***5900.10*** *p217*
Corey, Robina 23; Ontario, 1861 ***2896.27*** *p55*
Corey, Rose Colton; Vermont, 1807-1882 ***5900.10*** *p561*
Corey, Sarah; Vermont, 1827-1907 ***5900.10*** *p579*
Corey, Sarah; Vermont, 1834-1890 ***5900.10*** *p561*
Corey, William; Vermont, 1844-1944 ***5900.10*** *p217*
Corfield, Richard; Charleston, South Carolina, 1807 ***1224.3*** *p16*
Corgan, Mary; New York, 1831 ***8197.10*** *p370*
Corgen, John; New York, 1806 ***8197.10*** *p30*
Corgill, John; Georgia, 1775 ***1640.10*** *p32*
Corigan, El 23; Ontario, 1861 ***2896.25*** *p1*
Corigan, Ellen 24; Ontario, 1871 ***1823.22*** *p34*
Corigan, Margaret 55; Vermont, 1873 ***5900.10*** *p282*
Coriveau, Hannah; Vermont, 1838-1916 ***5900.10*** *p288*
Cork, E. N. 5; Ontario, 1861 ***2896.26*** *p27*
Cork, Eliza 16; Ontario, 1861 ***2896.26*** *p27*
Cork, Elizabeth 7; Ontario, 1861 ***2896.26*** *p27*
Cork, Emanuel 9; Ontario, 1861 ***2896.26*** *p27*
Cork, Henry 14; Ontario, 1861 ***2896.26*** *p27*
Cork, Mary J. 12; Ontario, 1861 ***2896.26*** *p27*
Cork, Samuel 44; Ontario, 1861 ***2896.26*** *p27*
Cork, William 24; Ontario, 1861 ***2896.26*** *p27*
Corke, Robert; Maryland, 1665 ***2524.55*** *p55*
Corke, Robert; Maryland, 1668 ***2524.55*** *p55*
Corken, James; New York, 1840 ***8197.10*** *p301*
Corker, Ann; Virginia, 1665-1666 ***6212.30*** *p21*
Corker, Susan Blackmore; Virginia, 1664 ***1224.1*** *p7*
Corker, Thomas; Charles Town, South Carolina, 1772 ***1224.2*** *p26*
Corkerell, John; Maryland, 1677 ***2524.55*** *p55*
Corkerell, Mary; Maryland, 1677 ***2524.55*** *p55*
Corkery, Bridget 75; Vermont, 1883 ***5900.10*** *p344*
Corkery, Catherine; Vermont, 1846-1912 ***5900.10*** *p345*
Corkery, Dennis 44; Ontario, 1871 ***1823.22*** *p34*
Corkery, Dennis 80; Vermont, 1885 ***5900.10*** *p344*
Corkery, Ellen 27; Vermont, 1883 ***5900.10*** *p106*
Corkery, Jane 1; Vermont, 1861 ***5900.10*** *p106*
Corkery, John 37; Ontario, 1871 ***1823.22*** *p34*
Corkery, John 77; Vermont, 1892 ***5900.10*** *p106*
Corkery, Martha 2; Vermont, 1855 ***5900.10*** *p106*
Corkery, Mary; Vermont, 1853-1929 ***5900.10*** *p106*
Corkery, Michael; Vermont, 1847-1907 ***5900.10*** *p106*
Corkery, Nora 60; Vermont, 1884 ***5900.10*** *p106*
Corkery, Richard 79; Ontario, 1871 ***1823.22*** *p34*
Corkery, Timothy 52; Ontario, 1871 ***1823.22*** *p34*
Corkhill, Mr.; Quebec, 1857 ***9196.15*** *p26*
Corkhill, Mrs.; Quebec, 1857 ***9196.15*** *p26*
Corkin, Julia; Vermont, 1826-1891 ***5900.10*** *p538*
Corlett, Michael 50; Ontario, 1871 ***1823.22*** *p34*
Corley, Ann; Vermont, 1832-1923 ***5900.10*** *p142*
Corley, Ann Clark; Vermont, 1830-1875 ***5900.10*** *p131*
Corley, Ann Glynn; Vermont, 1838-1920 ***5900.10*** *p206*
Corley, Bartholomew; Vermont, 1784-1866 ***5900.10*** *p144*
Corley, Bridget; Vermont, 1802-1875 ***5900.10*** *p144*
Corley, Bridget; Vermont, 1920 ***5900.10*** *p175*
Corley, Catherine; Vermont, 1836-1900 ***5900.10*** *p131*
Corley, Catherine; Vermont, 1846-1926 ***5900.10*** *p143*
Corley, Ellen B.; Vermont, 1860-1916 ***5900.10*** *p193*
Corley, Helen M. Bridgeman; Vermont, 1844-1915 ***5900.10*** *p144*
Corley, Maria Hogan; Vermont, 1826-1904 ***5900.10*** *p152*
Corley, Maria Hogan; Vermont, 1826-1904 ***5900.10*** *p182*
Corley, Martin H.; Vermont, 1855-1934 ***5900.10*** *p140*
Corley, Mary; Vermont, 1824-1906 ***5900.10*** *p182*
Corley, Mary 57; Vermont, 1889 ***5900.10*** *p141*
Corley, Michael; New York, 1839 ***8197.10*** *p220*
Corley, Michael B.; Vermont, 1822-1910 ***5900.10*** *p131*
Corley, Michael J.; Vermont, 1833-1909 ***5900.10*** *p206*
Corley, Patrick H.; Vermont, 1841-1923 ***5900.10*** *p144*

Corley, Susan N. Cathwright; Vermont, 1859-1917 ***5900.10*** *p140*
Corley, Thomas 60; Ontario, 1871 ***1823.22*** *p34*
Corley, Thomas R. 29; Ontario, 1871 ***1823.22*** *p34*
Corly, John; New York, 1818 ***8197.10*** *p60*
Corly, John; Virginia, 1666 ***6212.30*** *p30*
Corly, Margaret; Vermont, 1825-1861 ***5900.10*** *p205*
Cormack, Miss; Quebec, 1857 ***9196.15*** *p14*
Cormack, Mrs.; Quebec, 1857 ***9196.15*** *p14*
Cormack, L.; Quebec, 1857 ***9196.15*** *p14*
Cormack, M.; Quebec, 1857 ***9196.15*** *p14*
Cormagh, Neil 36; Ontario, 1871 ***1823.28*** *p19*
Corman, Mary A.; Vermont, 1855-1916 ***5900.10*** *p452*
Cormelly, Dennis 23; Maryland, 1774 ***1220.25*** *p57*
Cormichael, James 89; Ontario, 1871 ***1823.28*** *p19*
Cormick, Francis 68; Ontario, 1871 ***1823.22*** *p34*
Cormick, Mary 24; Maryland, 1774 ***1220.25*** *p76*
Cormier, Lewis; New York, 1830 ***8197.10*** *p362*
Cormity, Adam; Virginia, 1741 ***1224.2*** *p28*
Cornand, Marques 12; Ontario, 1861 ***2896.27*** *p17*
Corneforth, Leonard; Virginia, 1681 ***1224.1*** *p15*
Cornein, Cornelius; Vermont, 1843-1918 ***5900.10*** *p426*
Cornein, Mary; Vermont, 1839-1922 ***5900.10*** *p426*
Cornel, Alexander 10; Ontario, 1861 ***2896.25*** *p56*
Cornel, Annetta 2; Ontario, 1861 ***2896.27*** *p39*
Cornel, Daniel 42; Ontario, 1861 ***2896.25*** *p56*
Cornel, John A. 2; Ontario, 1861 ***2896.25*** *p57*
Cornel, Mary J. 31; Ontario, 1861 ***2896.27*** *p39*
Cornel, Richard 7; Ontario, 1861 ***2896.25*** *p56*
Cornel, Sophia 9; Ontario, 1861 ***2896.27*** *p39*
Cornelis, Gartrid; Maryland, 1659-1661 ***2524.55*** *p55*
Cornelis, Tenus; Maryland, 1659-1661 ***2524.55*** *p55*
Cornelison, Hanse; Virginia, 1682 ***1224.1*** *p15*
Cornelius, Alicia *SEE* Cornelius, Mathias
Cornelius, Andrew; Maryland, 1666 ***2524.55*** *p52*
Cornelius, Anniken Engels *SEE* Cornelius, John
Cornelius, Cloud; Port uncertain, 1758 ***2856.30*** *p70*
Cornelius, Cornelius *SEE* Cornelius, John
Cornelius, Elioner *SEE* Cornelius, John
Cornelius, Elliston; Maryland, 1664 ***2524.55*** *p55*
Cornelius, Gartrid; Maryland, 1659-1661 ***2524.55*** *p55*
Cornelius, Gertruyd *SEE* Cornelius, John
Cornelius, Gertruyd; Maryland, 1668 ***2524.55*** *p55*
Father: John
Cornelius, Hendrick *SEE* Cornelius, John
Cornelius, Hough; Maryland, 1631-1685 ***2524.55*** *p55*
Wife: Mary
Child: Mary Coke
Cornelius, James 21; Ontario, 1871 ***1823.15*** *p50*
Cornelius, John *SEE* Cornelius, Gertruyd
Cornelius, John; Maryland, 1652 ***2524.55*** *p55*
Wife: Elioner
Cornelius, John; Maryland, 1669 ***2524.55*** *p55*
Wife: Anniken Engels
Child: Hendrick
Child: Gertruyd
Child: Cornelius
Cornelius, Joseph 22; Ontario, 1871 ***1823.15*** *p50*
Cornelius, Margaret *SEE* Cornelius, Mathias
Cornelius, Margaret 42; Ontario, 1871 ***1823.15*** *p50*
Cornelius, Mary *SEE* Cornelius, Hough
Cornelius, Mary Coke *SEE* Cornelius, Hough
Cornelius, Mathias; Maryland, 1658 ***2524.55*** *p55*
Wife: Margaret
Daughter: Alicia
Cornelius, Tenus; Maryland, 1659-1661 ***2524.55*** *p55*
Cornell, Elizabeth 46; Ontario, 1861 ***2896.28*** *p22*
Cornell, Hiram 8; Ontario, 1861 ***2896.28*** *p22*
Cornell, John; Vermont, 1848-1899 ***5900.10*** *p218*
Cornell, Malissa A. 16; Ontario, 1861 ***2896.28*** *p22*
Cornell, Nancy A. 12; Ontario, 1861 ***2896.28*** *p22*
Cornell, Samuel; New Bern, North Carolina, n.d. ***1224.2*** *p26*
Cornell, Sarah 17; Ontario, 1861 ***2896.27*** *p18*
Cornell, Sarah Garvey; Vermont, 1854-1930 ***5900.10*** *p218*
Cornell, Sarah Jane 14; Ontario, 1861 ***2896.28*** *p22*
Cornell, Susan E. 6; Ontario, 1861 ***2896.28*** *p22*
Corner, John; Maryland, 1680 ***2524.55*** *p55*
Corners, Ann 67; Vermont, 1885 ***5900.10*** *p283*
Cornett, Ellinor; Maryland, 1674 ***2524.55*** *p55*
Corney, Francis 6; Ontario, 1871 ***1823.28*** *p19*
Corney, John 14; Ontario, 1871 ***1823.28*** *p19*
Cornforth, Elizabeth 4 *SEE* Cornforth, William
Cornforth, Henry 45; Ontario, 1871 ***1823.28*** *p19*
Cornforth, Mary 1 *SEE* Cornforth, William
Cornforth, Mary 26 *SEE* Cornforth, William
Cornforth, Paul 70; Fort Cumberland, Nova Scotia, 1774 ***1220.25*** *p16*
Wife: Phillis 68
Cornforth, Phillis 68 *SEE* Cornforth, Paul
Cornforth, William 34; Fort Cumberland, Nova Scotia, 1774 ***1220.25*** *p16*
Wife: Mary 26
Child: Mary 1
Child: Elizabeth 4
Cornhill, Tho.; Maryland, 1670 ***2524.55*** *p55*
Corniek, Joseph; Maryland, 1910 ***3259.35*** *p10*
Cornilus, Thomas 56; Ontario, 1871 ***1823.15*** *p50*
Cornish, Mr.; Quebec, 1857 ***9196.15*** *p18*
Cornish, Francis 41; Ontario, 1871 ***1823.15*** *p50*
Cornish, George 27; Ontario, 1871 ***1823.15*** *p50*
Cornish, Henry; New York, 1847 ***1224.3*** *p16*
Cornish, James; Pennsylvania, 1786 ***4629.10*** *p52*
Cornish, John; Maryland, 1681 ***2524.55*** *p55*
Cornish, John; New England, 1695 ***1224.1*** *p15*
Cornish, John; New York, 1836 ***8197.10*** *p220*
Cornish, John; New York, 1838 ***8197.10*** *p113*
Cornish, John 38; Maryland, 1775 ***1220.25*** *p99*
Cornish, John 53; Ontario, 1871 ***1823.15*** *p50*
Cornish, Samuel 44; Ontario, 1871 ***1823.15*** *p50*
Cornish, Thomas 40; Ontario, 1871 ***1823.15*** *p50*
Cornish, William 50; Ontario, 1871 ***1823.15*** *p50*
Cornlane, Patrick; Maryland, 1673 ***2524.55*** *p42*
Cornock, Samuel; South Carolina, 1733 ***1224.2*** *p26*
Cornwaleys, Penelope; Maryland, 1656 ***2524.55*** *p55*
Cornwall, Alexander; Maryland, 1704 ***1224.2*** *p27*
Cornwall, C. 50; Ontario, 1861 ***2896.27*** *p19*
Cornwall, John 58; Ontario, 1871 ***1823.22*** *p34*
Cornwall, Regnoll; Virginia, 1665-1666 ***6212.30*** *p23*
Cornwallis, Lieut.; Quebec, 1857 ***9196.15*** *p14*
Cornwell, James 33; Ontario, 1871 ***1823.28*** *p19*
Cornwell, Thomas; Maryland, 1695 ***1224.1*** *p15*
Cornwell, William 27; Maryland, 1774 ***1220.25*** *p65*
Cornwright, Fanny 18; Ontario, 1861 ***2896.27*** *p34*
Cornyn, Mary 63; Ontario, 1871 ***1823.15*** *p50*
Coronell, Cornelius; Maryland, 1668 ***2524.55*** *p55*
Coronell, Francis; Maryland, 1668 ***2524.55*** *p55*
Corper, Johann Matthaus; Port uncertain, 1752 ***2856.30*** *p70*
Corr, David; New York, 1830 ***8197.10*** *p363*
Corr, Hugh; New York, 1837 ***8197.10*** *p79*
Corr, Peter; New York, 1821 ***8197.10*** *p216*
Corr, Susanna O'Neill 83; Vermont, 1900 ***5900.10*** *p295*
Corrall, Catharin; Virginia, 1667 ***6212.30*** *p36*
Corran, Alexander 30; Ontario, 1871 ***1823.15*** *p51*
Corran, James; New York, 1821 ***1224.3*** *p16*
Corran, James 33; Ontario, 1871 ***1823.15*** *p51*
Corran, Margret 68; Ontario, 1871 ***1823.15*** *p51*
Corre, Helene Florentine; Charleston, South Carolina, 1805 ***1224.3*** *p16*
Correa, Emanuel Alvares; New York, 1837 ***8197.10*** *p219*
Correa, Sarah; New York, 1826 ***8197.10*** *p218*
Correa, Sarah; New York, 1838 ***8197.10*** *p113*
Correll, Friederich; New York, 1837 ***8197.10*** *p81*
Correy, Robert; Pennsylvania, 1777 ***4629.10*** *p29*
Corrick, Roger; Virginia, 1671-1672 ***6212.30*** *p47*
Corrie, Mr.; Quebec, 1857 ***9196.15*** *p23*
Corrie, Jasper; Pennsylvania, 1777 ***4629.10*** *p16*
Corrigan, Mr. 40; Ontario, 1871 ***1823.22*** *p34*
Corrigan, Andrew; New York, 1822 ***8197.10*** *p217*
Corrigan, Annie English; Vermont, 1853-1934 ***5900.10*** *p173*
Corrigan, Catherine 50; Ontario, 1871 ***1823.28*** *p19*
Corrigan, E. L. Jamieson 42; Vermont, 1892 ***5900.10*** *p243*
Corrigan, Eliza J. Farrell; Vermont, 1860-1912 ***5900.10*** *p135*
Corrigan, Ellen Potter; Vermont, 1855-1926 ***5900.10*** *p333*
Corrigan, George; Vermont, 1850-1917 ***5900.10*** *p243*
Corrigan, James; New York, 1829 ***8197.10*** *p352*
Corrigan, James E.; Vermont, 1839-1901 ***5900.10*** *p243*
Corrigan, John; Vermont, 1851-1930 ***5900.10*** *p173*
Corrigan, Luke; New York, 1829 ***8197.10*** *p351*
Corrigan, Martin 32; Ontario, 1871 ***1823.28*** *p19*
Corrigan, Mary 19; Ontario, 1871 ***1823.15*** *p51*
Corrigan, Mary 23; Ontario, 1871 ***1823.28*** *p19*
Corrigan, Michael 28; Ontario, 1871 ***1823.28*** *p19*
Corrigan, Sarah J.; Vermont, 1838-1909 ***5900.10*** *p243*
Corrigan, Sarah J. Minor; Vermont, 1863-1921 ***5900.10*** *p243*
Corrigan, Thomas; Vermont, 1859-1909 ***5900.10*** *p135*
Corrigan, William; Vermont, 1852-1935 ***5900.10*** *p333*
Corrigil, Adam; Savannah, Georgia, 1775 ***1640.10*** *p32*
Wife: Janet
Child: Robert
Child: William
Child: Katherine
Corrigil, Elizabeth; Savannah, Georgia, 1775 ***1640.10*** *p32*
Corrigil, Janet *SEE* Corrigil, Adam
Corrigil, Katherine *SEE* Corrigil, Adam
Corrigil, Robert *SEE* Corrigil, Adam
Corrigil, William *SEE* Corrigil, Adam
Corrill, George; Maryland, 1674 ***2524.55*** *p55*
Corris, John; New York, 1819 ***8197.10*** *p215*
Corry, Bridget 26; Vermont, 1865 ***5900.10*** *p329*
Corry, Frank M.; Vermont, 1855-1941 ***5900.10*** *p331*
Corry, Katharine Donahue; Vermont, 1855-1912 ***5900.10*** *p356*
Corry, Margaret Cotter; Vermont, 1857-1938 ***5900.10*** *p331*
Corry, Mary 84; Vermont, 1891 ***5900.10*** *p329*
Corry, Michael M.; Vermont, 1843-1914 ***5900.10*** *p335*
Corry, Patrick; New York, 1828-1831 ***8197.10*** *p369*
Corry, Patrick 84; Vermont, 1886 ***5900.10*** *p329*
Corry, Samuel; Pennsylvania, 1777 ***4629.10*** *p28*
Corry, Thomas 44; New York, 1774 ***1220.25*** *p20*
Corry, Thomas H.; Vermont, 1840-1925 ***5900.10*** *p337*
Corry, Walter; Pennsylvania, 1777 ***4629.10*** *p8*
Corsar, Mrs. 30; Grenada, 1774 ***1220.25*** *p127*
Corsar, Frederick 35; Grenada, 1774 ***1220.25*** *p127*
Corson, Isaac; Pennsylvania, 1777 ***4629.10*** *p17*
Cortilli, Augustus; New York, 1817 ***8197.10*** *p60*
Cortney, John; Pennsylvania, 1777 ***4629.10*** *p31*
Corton, Henry; Virginia, 1664 ***6212.30*** *p15*
Cortswick, Martin 48; Ontario, 1871 ***1823.28*** *p19*
Corvan, Philip James; New York, 1837 ***8197.10*** *p80*
Corven, Katherine; Vermont, 1857-1952 ***5900.10*** *p340*
Corven, Thomas; Vermont, 1848-1907 ***5900.10*** *p340*
Corvin, Bridget Harrington; Vermont, 1843-1932 ***5900.10*** *p161*
Corvin, Catherine C.; Vermont, 1842-1916 ***5900.10*** *p407*
Corvin, John; Vermont, 1843-1923 ***5900.10*** *p161*
Corvisier, Bartholomew; Philadelphia, 1793 ***4629.10*** *p83*
Corwinn, Thomas; Maryland, 1681 ***2524.55*** *p55*
Cory, Abner 58; Ontario, 1861 ***2896.28*** *p34*
Cory, Amanda A. 14; Ontario, 1861 ***2896.28*** *p34*
Cory, Benjamin 19; Ontario, 1861 ***2896.28*** *p34*
Cory, David 17; Ontario, 1861 ***2896.28*** *p34*
Cory, Fannie E. 21; Ontario, 1861 ***2896.28*** *p34*
Cory, Lewin 21; Philadelphia, 1774 ***1220.25*** *p82*
Cory, Nancy Y. 23; Ontario, 1861 ***2896.25*** *p16*
Cory, Randolph 23; Ontario, 1861 ***2896.28*** *p34*
Cory, Robert 16; Philadelphia, 1774 ***1220.25*** *p76*
Cory, Sarah J. 24; Ontario, 1861 ***2896.28*** *p34*
Coryhlin, Patrick; Cleveland, Ohio, 1858 ***3437.14*** *p58*
Coryhlin, Patrick; Cleveland, Ohio, 1858 ***3437.14*** *p65*
Corzyski, Michael; Maryland, 1910 ***3259.35*** *p10*
Cosack, Geo 32; British Columbia, 1910 ***9196.1*** *p31*
Cosack, Geo 32; Seattle, 1910 ***9196.1*** *p31*
Cosby, Henry; New York, 1754 ***1224.2*** *p27*
Cosby, Jonathan; Maryland, 1677 ***2524.55*** *p55*
Cosby, Thomas; Maryland, 1660 ***2524.55*** *p55*
Coscaden, David 31; Ontario, 1871 ***1823.15*** *p51*
Cosden, Elizabeth *SEE* Cosden, Thomas
Cosden, Sarah *SEE* Cosden, Thomas
Cosden, Stephen; Maryland, 1680 ***2524.55*** *p55*
Cosden, Thomas; Maryland, 1668 ***2524.55*** *p55*
Wife: Sarah
Daughter: Elizabeth
Daughter: Sarah
Cosey, Anne; Maryland, 1663 ***2524.55*** *p44*
Cosgrave, Ann 34 *SEE* Cosgrave, John
Cosgrave, Anne 12 *SEE* Cosgrave, James
Cosgrave, Anne 18 *SEE* Cosgrave, Bridget
Cosgrave, Bridget 3 *SEE* Cosgrave, Pat
Cosgrave, Bridget 12 *SEE* Cosgrave, John
Cosgrave, Bridget 22 *SEE* Cosgrave, James
Cosgrave, Bridget 50; New York, New York, 1848 ***1825.45*** *p29*
Son: James 13
Son: Michael 16
Son: Pat 7
Son: Thomas 20
Daughter: Margaret 17
Daughter: Mary 10
Daughter: Anne 18
Son: Peter 29
Son: John 26
Cosgrave, Catherine 2 *SEE* Cosgrave, James
Cosgrave, Ellen 19 *SEE* Cosgrave, William
Cosgrave, Ellen 24; New York, New York, 1849 ***1825.45*** *p30*
Cosgrave, Francis 20 *SEE* Cosgrave, John
Cosgrave, Hannah 1 *SEE* Cosgrave, Thomas
Cosgrave, Hannah 23 *SEE* Cosgrave, Thomas
Cosgrave, James 1 *SEE* Cosgrave, John
Cosgrave, James 13 *SEE* Cosgrave, Bridget
Cosgrave, James 41; New York, New York, 1848 ***1825.45*** *p30*
Wife: Mary 37
Son: Thomas 3
Daughter: Catherine 2
Sister: Anne 12

Coughlin, Daniel 72; Vermont, 1900 ***5900.10*** *p598*
Coughlin, Delia M. Gregg; Vermont, 1858-1935 ***5900.10*** *p45*
Coughlin, Ellen Collins; Vermont, 1839-1931 ***5900.10*** *p62*
Coughlin, James 55; Vermont, 1890 ***5900.10*** *p543*
Coughlin, Joanna Cullen 69; Vermont, 1908 ***5900.10*** *p146*
Coughlin, John J.; Vermont, 1848-1916 ***5900.10*** *p45*
Coughlin, Mary Ann Brannan 74; Vermont, 1911 ***5900.10*** *p598*
Coughlin, Nancy Coonerty 38; Vermont, 1860 ***5900.10*** *p124*
Coughlin, Nellie 42; Vermont, 1902 ***5900.10*** *p124*
Coughlin, Patrick; Cleveland, Ohio, 1858 ***3437.14*** *p58*
Coughlin, Patrick; Cleveland, Ohio, 1858 ***3437.14*** *p65*
Coughlin, Patrick; Pennsylvania, 1868 ***6058.10*** *p61*
Coughlin, Patrick 69; Vermont, 1891 ***5900.10*** *p146*
Coughlin, Thomas 60; Ontario, 1871 ***1823.28*** *p19*
Coughlin, William; Vermont, 1840-1918 ***5900.10*** *p62*
Coughoon, Anne; Maryland, 1681 ***2524.55*** *p56*
Coughran, John; New York, 1815 ***8197.10*** *p55*
Coulaska, Joseph; Maryland, 1910 ***3259.35*** *p10*
Couley, Henry 21; Baltimore, 1775 ***1220.25*** *p117*
Couling, George 31; Maryland, 1775 ***1220.25*** *p121*
Couling, James 21; Maryland, 1775 ***1220.25*** *p121*
Coull, John; Georgia, 1740 ***1640.10*** *p32*
Coulon, Frederick; New York, 1838 ***8197.10*** *p112*
Coulson, Mr.; Quebec, 1857 ***9196.15*** *p26*
Coulson, Adam; New England, 1690 ***1224.1*** *p9*
Coulson, Daniell; Virginia, 1672 ***6212.30*** *p49*
Coulson, John 20; Fort Cumberland, Nova Scotia, 1774 ***1220.25*** *p15*
Wife: Mary 20
Coulson, John 37; Ontario, 1871 ***1823.28*** *p19*
Coulson, Mary 20 *SEE* Coulson, John
Coulston, Mr.; Quebec, 1857 ***9196.15*** *p17*
Coulston, Mrs.; Quebec, 1857 ***9196.15*** *p17*
Coulter, Mrs.; Ontario, 1861 ***2896.28*** *p50*
Coulter, Francis 26; Ontario, 1871 ***1823.15*** *p51*
Coulter, Hugh; Maryland, 1763 ***1640.13*** *p23*
Coulter, James B.; Pennsylvania, 1842-1846 ***6058.10*** *p22*
Coulter, John; Philadelphia, 1838 ***6058.10*** *p39*
Coulter, John 55; Ontario, 1871 ***1823.15*** *p51*
Coulter, John 56; Ontario, 1871 ***1823.22*** *p34*
Coulter, John 72; Ontario, 1871 ***1823.15*** *p51*
Coulter, John 84; Ontario, 1871 ***1823.15*** *p51*
Coulter, Joseph 40; Ontario, 1871 ***1823.28*** *p19*
Coulter, Margret 42; Ontario, 1871 ***1823.15*** *p51*
Coulter, Matilda; Ontario, 1861 ***2896.28*** *p50*
Coulter, Robert; Pennsylvania, 1861 ***6058.10*** *p45*
Coulter, Robert 44; Ontario, 1871 ***1823.28*** *p19*
Coulter, Samuel; New York, 1807 ***8197.10*** *p328*
Coulter, Samuel; Pennsylvania, 1846 ***6058.10*** *p24*
Coulter, William; New York, 1840 ***8197.10*** *p160*
Coulter, William 40; Ontario, 1871 ***1823.15*** *p51*
Coulthard, Mrs.; Quebec, 1858 ***9196.15*** *p47*
Coulthart, Mr.; Quebec, 1857 ***9196.15*** *p15*
Coulthart, Mrs.; Quebec, 1857 ***9196.15*** *p15*
Coulton, Ann; Maryland, 1673 ***2524.55*** *p56*
Coulton, Mary; Maryland, 1673 ***2524.55*** *p56*
Coulton, Thomas; Maryland, 1673 ***2524.55*** *p56*
Couman, John; New York, 1803 ***8197.10*** *p11*
Councell, Thomas; Maryland, 1663 ***2524.55*** *p56*
Councellour, Thomas; Maryland, 1657 ***2524.55*** *p84*
Counerty, Hannah 63; Vermont, 1899 ***5900.10*** *p122*
Counerty, Mary Nichols; Vermont, 1851-1935 ***5900.10*** *p125*
Counerty, Patrick 63; Vermont, 1906 ***5900.10*** *p125*
Counter, Mr.; Quebec, 1858 ***9196.15*** *p36*
Counter, Kate Shanty 48; Vermont, 1901 ***5900.10*** *p310*
Counter, Moses 26; Ontario, 1871 ***1823.15*** *p51*
Counter, Oliver; Vermont, 1844-1910 ***5900.10*** *p310*
Coupar, James; Georgia, 1698 ***1640.13*** *p24*
Coupar, John; Georgia, 1804 ***1640.10*** *p32*
Coupland, Richard; New York, 1840 ***8197.10*** *p159*
Couray, Richard; New York, 1838 ***8197.10*** *p113*
Couretry, Hen; Virginia, 1683 ***6212.30*** *p56*
Courney, John 30; Ontario, 1871 ***1823.15*** *p51*
Coursey, Catherine *SEE* Coursey, Henry
Coursey, Catherine Malana; Vermont, 1832-1915 ***5900.10*** *p126*
Coursey, David; Maryland, 1682 ***2524.55*** *p56*
Coursey, Edward 28; Maryland, 1773-1774 ***1220.25*** *p33*
Coursey, Henry; Maryland, 1653 ***2524.55*** *p56*
Brother: John
Sister: Katheren
Brother: William
Coursey, Henry; Maryland, 1658 ***2524.55*** *p56*
Sister: Catherine
Coursey, Henry; Maryland, 1658 ***2524.55*** *p56*
Coursey, Henry; Maryland, 1658 ***2524.55*** *p56*
Wife: Mary
Coursey, Jane; Maryland, 1666 ***2524.55*** *p205*
Coursey, John *SEE* Coursey, Henry
Coursey, John; Maryland, 1658 ***2524.55*** *p56*
Coursey, Josie; Vermont, 1859-1936 ***5900.10*** *p190*
Coursey, Katheren *SEE* Coursey, Henry
Coursey, Mary *SEE* Coursey, Henry
Coursey, Mary; Vermont, 1814-1893 ***5900.10*** *p543*
Coursey, Richard; Vermont, 1826-1908 ***5900.10*** *p125*
Coursey, William *SEE* Coursey, Henry
Coursey, Willm.; Maryland, 1658 ***2524.55*** *p56*
Courson, Adolphus 27; Ontario, 1871 ***1823.22*** *p34*
Court, Miss; Quebec, 1858 ***9196.15*** *p42*
Court, Mr.; Quebec, 1858 ***9196.15*** *p42*
Court, Charles 18; Dominica, 1774 ***1220.25*** *p127*
Court, Edward; Virginia, 1664 ***6212.30*** *p7*
Court, Fredrick 29; Ontario, 1871 ***1823.28*** *p19*
Court, Fredrick 51; Ontario, 1871 ***1823.28*** *p19*
Court, Margarett; Maryland, 1649 ***2524.55*** *p56*
Court, William; Maryland, 1671 ***2524.55*** *p56*
Court, William 18; Maryland, 1775 ***1220.25*** *p103*
Court, Wm; Virginia, 1668-1669 ***6212.30*** *p41*
Courtenay, Charles; New York, 1840 ***8197.10*** *p221*
Courtenay, Charles Edward Foster; Georgia, 1854 ***1224.3*** *p16*
Courtis, Raphaell; Maryland, 1667 ***2524.55*** *p56*
Courtis, Robert; Maryland, 1651 ***2524.55*** *p56*
Courtman, Thomas 28; Baltimore, 1775 ***1220.25*** *p117*
Courtney, . . .; Maryland, 1651 ***2524.55*** *p56*
Courtney, Alexander; Vermont, 1836-1869 ***5900.10*** *p140*
Courtney, Elizabeth McKaige; Vermont, 1852-1875 ***5900.10*** *p509*
Courtney, George; Maryland, 1665 ***2524.55*** *p114*
Courtney, George; New York, 1794 ***8197.10*** *p3*
Courtney, Hugh; Virginia, 1666 ***6212.30*** *p27*
Courtney, James; Virginia, 1666 ***6212.30*** *p29*
Courtney, Jno; Virginia, 1663 ***6212.30*** *p4*
Courtney, Jno; Virginia, 1668-1669 ***6212.30*** *p41*
Courtney, Margaret; Vermont, 1840-1894 ***5900.10*** *p139*
Courtney, Margaret E.; Vermont, n.d. ***5900.10*** *p188*
Courtney, Michael; Vermont, 1835-1917 ***5900.10*** *p139*
Courtney, Michael 40; Ontario, 1871 ***1823.15*** *p51*
Courtney, Miles; Virginia, 1666 ***6212.30*** *p26*
Courtney, Paul 23; Philadelphia, 1775 ***1220.25*** *p107*
Courtney, Peter; Virginia, 1666 ***6212.30*** *p27*
Courtney, Thomas 15; Vermont, 1867 ***5900.10*** *p143*
Courtney, Wm; Virginia, 1666 ***6212.30*** *p27*
Courtou, George; New York, 1806 ***8197.10*** *p30*
Courts, John; Maryland, 1639 ***2524.55*** *p56*
Courts, John; Maryland, 1645 ***2524.55*** *p56*
Courts, Mary; Maryland, 1663 ***2524.55*** *p18*
Cousen, William; Maryland, 1673 ***2524.55*** *p56*
Cousin, William; Maryland, 1668 ***2524.55*** *p56*
Cousine, Joan; Maryland, 1658 ***2524.55*** *p56*
Cousine, Nicholas; Maryland, 1658 ***2524.55*** *p56*
Cousins, Catherine 46; Ontario, 1871 ***1823.15*** *p51*
Cousins, Edward 19; Maryland, 1774 ***1220.25*** *p57*
Cousins, James 73; Ontario, 1871 ***1823.15*** *p51*
Cousins, John 54; Ontario, 1871 ***1823.28*** *p19*
Cousins, Nathan 53; Ontario, 1871 ***1823.15*** *p51*
Cousins, Robert; New York, 1835 ***8197.10*** *p317*
Cousseman, Geo 26; Seattle, 1917 ***9196.1*** *p51*
Cousseman, Geo 26; Whitehorse, Yukon, 1917 ***9196.1*** *p51*
Coustoun, Robert; Georgia, 1698 ***1640.13*** *p24*
Couthard, Isaac; New York, 1807 ***8197.10*** *p37*
Couthland, Margarett; Maryland, 1668 ***2524.55*** *p56*
Couts, John 18; Ontario, 1871 ***1823.15*** *p51*
Couts, Nelly 23; Ontario, 1871 ***1823.15*** *p51*
Couttes, Henry; Pennsylvania, 1709 ***1224.2*** *p27*
Coutts, James; Florida, 1766 ***1640.10*** *p32*
Coutts, John 48; Ontario, 1871 ***1823.15*** *p51*
Coutts, Thomas; Florida, 1766 ***1640.10*** *p33*
Couture, Mary; Vermont, 1857-1935 ***5900.10*** *p224*
Couzens, John; Oswego, New York, 1757 ***1224.2*** *p27*
Covell, Daniel; Maryland, 1679 ***2524.55*** *p56*
Covell, Samuel; Pennsylvania, 1777 ***4629.10*** *p22*
Covell, Thomas; Maryland, 1651 ***2524.55*** *p57*
Coveney, Margaret Nelson; Vermont, 1855-1924 ***5900.10*** *p505*
Coveney, Michael J.; Vermont, 1844-1903 ***5900.10*** *p505*
Coventon, Ann *SEE* Coventon, Thomas
Coventon, Jane *SEE* Coventon, Nehemiah
Coventon, John *SEE* Coventon, Nehemiah
Coventon, Katherine *SEE* Coventon, Nehemiah
Coventon, Margarett *SEE* Coventon, Nehemiah
Coventon, Mary *SEE* Coventon, Nehemiah
Coventon, Nehemiah *SEE* Coventon, Nehemiah
Coventon, Nehemiah; Maryland, 1665 ***2524.55*** *p57*
Child: Nehemiah
Child: John
Wife: Mary
Child: Sarah
Child: Katherine
Child: Margarett
Child: Jane
Coventon, Sarah *SEE* Coventon, Nehemiah
Coventon, Thomas; Maryland, 1665 ***2524.55*** *p57*
Relative: Ann
Coventry, David 22; Ontario, 1871 ***1823.15*** *p52*
Coventry, David Sandeman; America, 1899 ***1640.13*** *p24*
Coventry, George; New York, 1777 ***1224.2*** *p27*
Coventry, William; Maryland, 1661 ***2524.55*** *p57*
Coventry, William 27; Virginia, 1774 ***1220.25*** *p45*
Coveny, Bernard; Vermont, 1814-1883 ***5900.10*** *p508*
Coveny, Mary; Vermont, 1821-1881 ***5900.10*** *p508*
Coveny, Peter; Maryland, 1631-1685 ***2524.55*** *p56*
Coverane, John; Maryland, 1678 ***2524.55*** *p55*
Coverdale, Grace; Maryland, 1672 ***2524.55*** *p57*
Coverdale, Richard 38; Ontario, 1871 ***1823.28*** *p19*
Coverdale, Thomas; Maryland, 1680 ***2524.55*** *p57*
Coversly, Jno; Virginia, 1667-1668 ***6212.30*** *p38*
Covert, Mr.; Quebec, 1857 ***9196.15*** *p26*
Covert, Albina 11; Ontario, 1861 ***2896.25*** *p64*
Covert, Almira 33; Ontario, 1861 ***2896.25*** *p64*
Covert, John 5; Ontario, 1861 ***2896.25*** *p64*
Covert, Margaret 8; Ontario, 1861 ***2896.25*** *p64*
Covert, Mary; Ontario, 1861 ***2896.25*** *p64*
Covert, Sarah; Ontario, 1861 ***2896.25*** *p64*
Covert, Wm; Virginia, 1664 ***6212.30*** *p8*
Covett, Ann Sanders *SEE* Covett, John
Covett, John; Maryland, 1649 ***2524.55*** *p57*
Covett, John; Maryland, 1652 ***2524.55*** *p57*
Wife: Sarah
Stepchild: Ann Sanders
Covett, Sarah *SEE* Covett, John
Covill, William; Maryland, 1681 ***2524.55*** *p57*
Covington, Ann *SEE* Covington, Thomas
Covington, Jane *SEE* Covington, Nehemiah
Covington, John *SEE* Covington, Nehemiah
Covington, Katherine *SEE* Covington, Nehemiah
Covington, Margarett *SEE* Covington, Nehemiah
Covington, Mary *SEE* Covington, Nehemiah
Covington, Nehemiah *SEE* Covington, Nehemiah
Covington, Nehemiah; Maryland, 1665 ***2524.55*** *p57*
Wife: Mary
Child: Margarett
Child: Katherine
Child: Sarah
Child: Jane
Child: John
Child: Nehemiah
Covington, Sarah *SEE* Covington, Nehemiah
Covington, Thomas; Maryland, 1665 ***2524.55*** *p57*
Relative: Ann
Covintry, Joseph 30; Ontario, 1871 ***1823.15*** *p52*
Covner, Francis 39; Ontario, 1871 ***1823.28*** *p19*
Cowalick, Charles; Maryland, 1910 ***3259.35*** *p10*
Cowan, Miss; Quebec, 1857 ***9196.15*** *p18*
Cowan, Mr.; Quebec, 1858 ***9196.15*** *p47*
Cowan, Mrs.; Quebec, 1858 ***9196.15*** *p47*
Cowan, Alexander; Portland, Maine, 1857 ***9196.15*** *p12*
Cowan, Alexander 34; Ontario, 1871 ***1823.15*** *p52*
Cowan, Alexander 40; Ontario, 1871 ***1823.28*** *p19*
Cowan, Alexander 50; Ontario, 1871 ***1823.15*** *p52*
Cowan, Alexander 65; Ontario, 1871 ***1823.28*** *p19*
Cowan, Alice 8; Ontario, 1861 ***2896.28*** *p36*
Cowan, Andrew 43; Ontario, 1871 ***1823.15*** *p52*
Cowan, Bridget; Vermont, 1846-1920 ***5900.10*** *p600*
Cowan, David 43; Ontario, 1871 ***1823.15*** *p52*
Cowan, Edward 4; Ontario, 1861 ***2896.28*** *p36*
Cowan, Elizabeth 15; Ontario, 1861 ***2896.28*** *p36*
Cowan, Elizabeth 26; Ontario, 1861 ***2896.25*** *p1*
Cowan, Francis; San Francisco, 1852 ***1640.13*** *p24*
Cowan, Frank; Vermont, 1869-1893 ***5900.10*** *p600*
Cowan, George; New York, 1832 ***8197.10*** *p357*
Cowan, Isabella 28; Ontario, 1861 ***2896.28*** *p36*
Cowan, Jane 25; Ontario, 1861 ***2896.28*** *p36*
Cowan, Jane 59; Vermont, 1904 ***5900.10*** *p600*
Cowan, John; New York, 1802 ***8197.10*** *p19*
Cowan, John; New York, 1822-1834 ***8197.10*** *p307*
Cowan, John; Pennsylvania, 1786 ***4629.10*** *p49*
Cowan, John; St. Johns, Newfoundland, 1820 ***1640.13*** *p24*
Cowan, John; Savannah, Georgia, 1803-1812 ***1640.10*** *p33*
Cowan, John 36; Ontario, 1871 ***1823.15*** *p52*
Cowan, John 42; Ontario, 1871 ***1823.15*** *p52*
Cowan, John 55; Ontario, 1871 ***1823.15*** *p52*
Cowan, John 57; Ontario, 1871 ***1823.15*** *p52*
Cowan, John 59; Ontario, 1871 ***1823.15*** *p52*
Cowan, Joseph; New York, n.d. ***1224.3*** *p16*
Cowan, Joseph; New York, New York, n.d. ***1224.2*** *p27*
Cowan, Martha 68; Ontario, 1861 ***2896.25*** *p1*
Cowan, Mary J. 53; Ontario, 1871 ***1823.15*** *p52*
Cowan, Mary R. 6; Ontario, 1861 ***2896.28*** *p36*
Cowan, Miles 50; Ontario, 1871 ***1823.22*** *p34*

Cowan, Owen 72; Vermont, 1881 *5900.10 p600*
Cowan, Patrick 69; Ontario, 1871 *1823.22 p34*
Cowan, Peter 30; Ontario, 1871 *1823.15 p52*
Cowan, R.; Quebec, 1857 *9196.15 p18*
Cowan, Mrs. R.; Quebec, 1857 *9196.15 p18*
Cowan, Richard 4; Ontario, 1861 *2896.28 p36*
Cowan, Richard 8; Ontario, 1861 *2896.28 p36*
Cowan, Robert; New York, 1839 *8197.10 p132*
Cowan, Robert 29; Ontario, 1871 *1823.22 p34*
Cowan, Robert J. 17; Ontario, 1861 *2896.28 p36*
Cowan, Sarah Kirk; Vermont, 1842-1930 *5900.10 p600*
Cowan, Thomas; Vermont, 1832-1912 *5900.10 p600*
Cowan, Thomas 12; Ontario, 1861 *2896.28 p36*
Cowan, Thomas 35; Ontario, 1861 *2896.28 p36*
Cowan, Thomas 38; Ontario, 1861 *2896.28 p36*
Cowan, Thomas 48; Ontario, 1871 *1823.22 p34*
Cowan, Walter 37; Ontario, 1871 *1823.15 p52*
Cowan, William 32; Ontario, 1871 *1823.15 p52*
Cowan, William 40; Ontario, 1871 *1823.15 p52*
Cowan, Young 35; Ontario, 1871 *1823.15 p52*
Coward, John; North Carolina, 1772 *1224.2 p27*
Coward, James 21; America, 1774 *1220.25 p36*
Coward, Jane; Virginia, 1671-1672 *6212.30 p45*
Coward, Nick; Virginia, 1663 *6212.30 p2*
Coward, Robert 60; Ontario, 1871 *1823.15 p52*
Coward, William; Boston, 1691 *1224.1 p15*
Coward, William 39; Ontario, 1871 *1823.28 p20*
Cowbie, Marton 30; Ontario, 1871 *1823.28 p20*
Cowdell, Robert 17; Virginia, 1774 *1220.25 p45*
Cowden, John; Virginia, 1777 *1224.2 p27*
Cowder, Edward; Maryland, 1658 *2524.55 p57*
Cowder, James 40; Ontario, 1871 *1823.15 p52*
Cowder, John; Maryland, 1678 *2524.55 p57*
Cowdery, Mrs.; Maryland, 1666 *2524.55 p57*
Cowdonski, John; Maryland, 1910 *3259.35 p10*
Cowe, Geo; Virginia, 1703 *6212.30 p62*
Cowell, Elizabeth; Charles Town, South Carolina, 1797 *1224.2 p27*
Cowen, A. 21; Ontario, 1861 *2896.28 p14*
Cowen, Thomas 21; Maryland, 1774 *1220.25 p74*
Cowen, William 40; Ontario, 1871 *1823.15 p52*
Cowey, John 71; Ontario, 1871 *1823.22 p34*
Cowey, John C. 38; Ontario, 1871 *1823.22 p34*
Cowey, Robert 47; Ontario, 1871 *1823.22 p34*
Cowgill, Joseph; Maryland, 1675 *2524.55 p57*
Cowham, Mr.; Portland, Maine, 1858 *9196.15 p30*
Cowham, Mrs.; Portland, Maine, 1858 *9196.15 p30*
Cowherd, Thomas 44; Ontario, 1871 *1823.15 p52*
Cowhey, Michael; New York, 1827 *8197.10 p340*
Cowie, James; Colorado, 1896 *1640.13 p24*
Cowie, James 52; Ontario, 1871 *1823.15 p52*
Cowie, John 40; Ontario, 1871 *1823.28 p20*
Cowie, Margaret D. 87; Ontario, 1871 *1823.15 p52*
Cowie, Robert 42; Ontario, 1871 *1823.22 p34*
Cowin, Ellen 20; Ontario, 1861 *2896.25 p18*
Cowin, James 31; Ontario, 1861 *2896.25 p18*
Cowles, Joseph B.; New York, 1839 *8197.10 p133*
Cowles, Thomas; Virginia, 1665-1666 *6212.30 p23*
Cowley, Harriet 44; Vermont, 1884 *5900.10 p472*
Cowley, J.; Portland, Maine, 1858 *9196.15 p30*
Cowley, John; New York, 1840 *8197.10 p162*
Cowley, John; Vermont, 1830-1894 *5900.10 p460*
Cowley, Margaret 58; Vermont, 1874 *5900.10 p283*
Cowley, Mary 38; Vermont, 1872 *5900.10 p478*
Cowley, Richard B.; New York, 1819 *8197.10 p214*
Cowley, Richard B.; New York, 1828 *8197.10 p218*
Cowley, Robert 27; Maryland, 1774 *1220.25 p70*
Cowley, Sarah; Virginia, 1647 *1224.1 p18*
Cowley, Thomas; New York, 1833 *8197.10 p315*
Cowley, Thomas; Virginia, 1666 *6212.30 p26*
Cowley, Thomas 78; Vermont, 1867 *5900.10 p283*
Cowley, Thomas, Jr.; Vermont, 1853 *5900.10 p283*
Cowley, William; New York, 1839 *8197.10 p133*
Cowling, Agnes 60; Ontario, 1871 *1823.22 p34*
Cowling, William 38; Ontario, 1871 *1823.22 p34*
Cowman, John; New York, New York, 1833 *1224.3 p17*
Cowper, Basil; Savannah, Georgia, 1774-1775 *1640.10 p33*
Cowper, Mary; Savannah, Georgia, 1822 *1224.3 p17*
Cowper, Mary; Savannah, Georgia, 1822 *1640.10 p33*
Cowper, Sarah Mew; New England, 1671 *1224.1 p39*
Cowten, Charles; New York, 1839 *8197.10 p132*
Cox, Mr.; Quebec, 1856 *9196.15 p9*
Cox, Mr.; Quebec, 1858 *9196.15 p42*
Cox, Mrs.; Maryland, 1674 *2524.55 p57*
Cox, Agnes B.; Vermont, 1849-1934 *5900.10 p285*
Cox, Albane; Virginia, 1665-1666 *6212.30 p21*
Cox, Ambrose; Maryland, 1681 *2524.55 p57*
Cox, Andrew; Virginia, 1764 *1224.2 p27*
Cox, Ann 62; Vermont, 1900 *5900.10 p558*
Cox, Ann 70; Vermont, 1893 *5900.10 p292*
Cox, Bridgett; Maryland, 1665 *2524.55 p57*
Cox, Catherlin 58; Ontario, 1871 *1823.22 p35*
Cox, Charles; New York, 1803 *8197.10 p11*
Cox, Charles; New York, 1832 *8197.10 p219*
Cox, Charles; New York, 1834 *8197.10 p70*
Cox, Charles; New York, 1840 *8197.10 p161*
Cox, Charles; Pennsylvania, 1785 *4629.10 p47*
Cox, Charles; Virginia, 1666-1667 *6212.30 p33*
Cox, Charles 26; America, 1774 *1220.25 p35*
Cox, Darby 98; Vermont, 1885 *5900.10 p233*
Cox, David 40; Ontario, 1871 *1823.15 p52*
Cox, David 50; Ontario, 1871 *1823.15 p52*
Cox, Edward; Maryland, 1649 *2524.55 p57*
Cox, Edward; Maryland, 1658 *2524.55 p57*
Wife: Joan
Cox, Edward 74; Vermont, 1920 *5900.10 p242*
Cox, Ellen; Vermont, 1826-1896 *5900.10 p524*
Cox, Fred H. 49; Vancouver, British Columbia, 1917 *9196.1 p70*
Cox, Fred H. 49; Washington, 1917 *9196.1 p70*
Cox, George; Maryland, 1663 *2524.55 p57*
Cox, George 54; Ontario, 1871 *1823.15 p52*
Cox, Henry; Maryland, 1653 *2524.55 p57*
Cox, Henry; Maryland, 1668 *2524.55 p57*
Cox, Henry; New York, 1818 *1224.3 p17*
Cox, Hugh 48; Ontario, 1871 *1823.28 p20*
Cox, Isaac; Pennsylvania, 1777 *4629.10 p9*
Cox, Isaac; Philadelphia, 1784 *1224.2 p27*
Cox, James; Maryland, 1667 *2524.55 p57*
Cox, James; Maryland, 1680 *1224.1 p15*
Cox, James; New York, 1822 *8197.10 p217*
Cox, James; Pennsylvania, 1785 *4629.10 p47*
Cox, James 29; Ontario, 1871 *1823.28 p20*
Cox, James 32; Ontario, 1871 *1823.28 p20*
Cox, James 46; Ontario, 1871 *1823.15 p52*
Cox, James 61; Ontario, 1871 *1823.15 p52*
Cox, James 88; Ontario, 1871 *1823.15 p52*
Cox, James C. 27; Ontario, 1871 *1823.15 p52*
Cox, Jane 70; Ontario, 1871 *1823.15 p52*
Cox, Jennie; Vermont, 1838-1931 *5900.10 p285*
Cox, Joan *SEE* Cox, Edward
Cox, Joan; Maryland, 1658 *2524.55 p57*
Cox, John; Maryland, 1660 *2524.55 p57*
Cox, John; Maryland, 1665 *2524.55 p232*
Cox, John; Maryland, 1667 *2524.55 p57*
Cox, John; Maryland, 1671 *2524.55 p57*
Cox, John; Maryland, 1674 *2524.55 p57*
Cox, John; Maryland, 1702 *1224.2 p27*
Cox, John; New York, 1834 *8197.10 p306*
Cox, John; North America, 1778 *1224.2 p27*
Cox, John; Pennsylvania, 1777 *4629.10 p12*
Cox, John; Pennsylvania, 1777 *4629.10 p14*
Cox, John; Pennsylvania, 1785 *4629.10 p48*
Cox, John 29; Ontario, 1871 *1823.15 p52*
Cox, John 40; Ontario, 1871 *1823.15 p52*
Cox, John 54; Ontario, 1871 *1823.22 p35*
Cox, John 57; Ontario, 1871 *1823.15 p52*
Cox, John 58; Ontario, 1871 *1823.15 p52*
Cox, John, Jr.; Pennsylvania, 1777 *4629.10 p25*
Cox, Joseph; New York, 1834 *8197.10 p306*
Cox, Joseph; Virginia, 1667 *6212.30 p37*
Cox, Margaret H.; Vermont, 1843-1926 *5900.10 p285*
Cox, Margarett; Maryland, 1681 *2524.55 p57*
Cox, Mary; Maryland, 1671 *2524.55 p57*
Cox, Mary 60; Ontario, 1871 *1823.22 p35*
Cox, Mary Ann; Vermont, 1843-1912 *5900.10 p284*
Cox, Mary Flanagan 65; Vermont, 1880 *5900.10 p242*
Cox, Mary McLaughlin 78; Vermont, 1881 *5900.10 p242*
Cox, Michael; New York, 1834 *8197.10 p70*
Cox, Michael 31; Ontario, 1871 *1823.28 p20*
Cox, Moses; Pennsylvania, 1777 *4629.10 p22*
Cox, Paul; Pennsylvania, 1777 *4629.10 p6*
Cox, Peter 44; Vermont, 1850 *5900.10 p242*
Cox, Philip 46; Ontario, 1871 *1823.22 p35*
Cox, R. 33; Alaska, 1915 *9196.1 p42*
Cox, Rich; Virginia, 1672 *6212.30 p49*
Cox, Richard; Maryland, 1643 *2524.55 p57*
Cox, Samuel; Barbados, 1726 *1224.2 p27*
Cox, Samuel; Maryland, 1726 *1224.2 p27*
Cox, Samuel 44; Ontario, 1871 *1823.15 p52*
Cox, Sem; Richmond, Virginia, 1711 *1224.2 p27*
Cox, T.; Quebec, 1857 *9196.15 p16*
Cox, Tench; Pennsylvania, 1777 *4629.10 p21*
Cox, Terrence; New York, 1837 *8197.10 p80*
Cox, Thomas; Maryland, 1672 *2524.55 p57*
Cox, Thomas; Virginia, 1663-1664 *6212.30 p5*
Cox, Thomas; Virginia, 1671 *6212.30 p42*
Cox, Thomas; Virginia, 1697 *1224.1 p15*
Cox, Thomas 35; Vermont, 1890 *5900.10 p136*
Cox, Thomas 99; Vermont, 1906 *5900.10 p242*
Cox, W. J. 40; San Francisco, 1917 *9196.1 p51*
Cox, W. J. 40; Whitehorse, Yukon, 1917 *9196.1 p51*
Cox, W. M.; Portland, Maine, 1858 *9196.15 p31*
Cox, William; Georgia, 1735 *1224.2 p28*
Cox, William; New York, 1839 *8197.10 p220*
Cox, William; Philadelphia, 1789 *4629.10 p83*
Cox, William 47; Ontario, 1871 *1823.28 p20*
Cox, William 55; Ontario, 1871 *1823.15 p52*
Cox, William A.; New York, 1840 *8197.10 p163*
Cox, William J. 38; Ontario, 1871 *1823.15 p52*
Cox, William J. 38; Vermont, 1896 *5900.10 p83*
Cox, Willm.; Maryland, 1651 *2524.55 p57*
Coxford, John 40; Ontario, 1871 *1823.28 p20*
Coxhall, William; Maryland, 1682 *2524.55 p57*
Coxon, Charles H.; Vermont, 1853-1943 *5900.10 p402*
Coxson, Charles S.; Pennsylvania, 1868 *6058.10 p72*
Coxton, Bryan; Maryland, 1678 *2524.55 p44*
Coxwell, Sarah; Virginia, 1684-1685 *6212.30 p57*
Coy, Catherine Cavender 40; Vermont, 1861 *5900.10 p73*
Coy, Mary 16; Ontario, 1861 *2896.27 p19*
Coyle, Anna; Vermont, 1842-1923 *5900.10 p444*
Coyle, Aurelia; Vermont, 1861-1942 *5900.10 p594*
Coyle, Charles; New York, 1823 *8197.10 p217*
Coyle, Daniel; New York, 1802 *8197.10 p19*
Coyle, Edward; New York, 1840 *8197.10 p221*
Coyle, Mary; Vermont, 1828-1903 *5900.10 p140*
Coyle, Mary Newman; Vermont, 1815-1869 *5900.10 p140*
Coyle, Matthew; New York, 1834 *8197.10 p315*
Coyle, Micheal F.; Vermont, 1855-1934 *5900.10 p594*
Coyle, Owen; New York, 1837 *8197.10 p80*
Coyle, Patrick; New York, 1831 *8197.10 p364*
Coyle, Patrick; Vermont, 1810-1870 *5900.10 p140*
Coyle, Peter; New York, 1838 *8197.10 p112*
Coyle, Philip; New York, 1837 *8197.10 p80*
Coyle, Robert 64; Ontario, 1871 *1823.22 p35*
Coyle, Sarah 36; Vermont, 1884 *5900.10 p83*
Coyle, Thomas; Vermont, 1853-1891 *5900.10 p140*
Coyle, William 27; Ontario, 1871 *1823.22 p35*
Coyle, William 60; Ontario, 1871 *1823.22 p35*
Coyne, Ann 89; Vermont, 1922 *5900.10 p591*
Coyne, Anna; Vermont, 1841-1914 *5900.10 p266*
Coyne, Catherine 55; Vermont, 1876 *5900.10 p611*
Coyne, Ellen; Vermont, 1846-1920 *5900.10 p290*
Coyne, James; New York, 1840 *8197.10 p221*
Coyne, John 66; Ontario, 1871 *1823.28 p20*
Coyne, Lawrence; New York, 1840 *8197.10 p159*
Coyne, Margaret M.; Vermont, 1870-1929 *5900.10 p178*
Coyne, Patrick 46; Ontario, 1871 *1823.28 p20*
Coyne, Phineus 40; Ontario, 1871 *1823.28 p20*
Coyne, Thomas; Vermont, 1813-1897 *5900.10 p266*
Cozettd, Christian 49; Ontario, 1871 *1823.28 p20*
Crab, John 22; Philadelphia, 1775 *1220.25 p107*
Crabb, Christopher 60; Ontario, 1871 *1823.15 p52*
Crabb, Mathew; Maryland, 1649 *2524.55 p58*
Crabb, Robert; South Carolina, 1811 *1640.13 p24*
Crabb, Samuel; New England, 1694 *1224.1 p16*
Crabb, Tho; Virginia, 1672 *6212.30 p51*
Crabb, Thomas; Virginia, 1667-1668 *6212.30 p38*
Crabbe, John; Virginia, 1695 *1224.1 p15*
Crabtrece, Grace 41; Alaska, 1917 *9196.1 p7*
Crabtrece, Grace 41; British Columbia, 1917 *9196.1 p7*
Crabtree, Jno; Virginia, 1677 *6212.30 p53*
Crabtree, Mary; Virginia, 1690-1691 *6212.30 p59*
Crabtree, Mary; Virginia, 1703-1704 *6212.30 p62*
Crachter, John; Georgia, 1698 *1640.13 p24*
Cracklow, January; Pennsylvania, 1727 *1224.2 p28*
Cracks, Witherald 57; Ontario, 1871 *1823.15 p52*
Cradick, Thomas 16; Virginia, 1774 *1220.25 p94*
Cradock, Sarah; Boston, 1799 *1224.2 p28*
Craf, Edm.; Maryland, 1678 *2524.55 p58*
Craffon, Mary; Maryland, 1665 *2524.55 p58*
Crafford, George; Maryland, 1658 *2524.55 p58*
Craffort, William; Maryland, 1659 *2524.55 p58*
Craford, Alexander 47; Ontario, 1871 *1823.15 p52*
Craford, Joseph; Pennsylvania, 1778 *4629.10 p32*
Craft, Albert 12; Ontario, 1861 *2896.27 p44*
Craft, Anderson 68; Ontario, 1861 *2896.27 p62*
Craft, Charity 66; Ontario, 1861 *2896.27 p62*
Craft, Clisty A. 10; Ontario, 1861 *2896.27 p44*
Craft, John; Pennsylvania, 1777 *4629.10 p11*
Craft, John; Virginia, 1683 *6212.30 p56*
Craft, Jul.; Maryland, 1679 *2524.55 p58*
Craft, Levinia 35; Ontario, 1861 *2896.27 p43*
Craft, Sarah 18; Ontario, 1861 *2896.27 p61*
Crag, John; Pennsylvania, 1780 *4629.10 p43*
Craggs, George 25; Maryland, 1773-1774 *1220.25 p33*
Cragin, Catherine 80; Vermont, 1938 *5900.10 p271*
Crago, Francis 30; Maryland, 1775 *1220.25 p120*
Crahan, Anne Webb; Vermont, n.d. *5900.10 p386*
Crahan, Bridget 33; Vermont, 1868 *5900.10 p76*
Crahan, Bryan 45; Vermont, 1867 *5900.10 p76*
Crahan, Catherine Robinson 68; Vermont, 1904 *5900.10 p78*
Crahan, Eliza Clark; Vermont, 1916 *5900.10 p390*
Crahan, John; Vermont, n.d. *5900.10 p386*
Crahan, John 59; Vermont, 1886 *5900.10 p78*
Crahan, Laurence; Vermont, 1844-1915 *5900.10 p387*

Crahan, Lawrence A.; Vermont, n.d. ***5900.10*** *p386*
Crahan, Mary; Vermont, 1842-1884 ***5900.10*** *p562*
Crahan, Mary A.; Vermont, 1879-1979 ***5900.10*** *p386*
Crahan, Mary Cunningham; Vermont, 1848-1926 ***5900.10*** *p387*
Crahan, Richard; Vermont, 1852-1923 ***5900.10*** *p390*
Crahan, William; Vermont, 1861-1923 ***5900.10*** *p386*
Craich, John; Georgia, 1698 ***1640.13*** *p24*
Craig, Mr.; Quebec, 1858 ***9196.15*** *p36*
Craig, Albert 41; Ontario, 1871 ***1823.15*** *p52*
Craig, Alexander; New York, 1806 ***8197.10*** *p324*
Craig, Andrew; Trinidad, 1784 ***1640.13*** *p24*
Craig, Archibald Cummings; Philadelphia, 1802 ***1224.3*** *p17*
Craig, Beatrice; Mississippi, 1805-1845 ***1640.10*** *p33*
Craig, Edward 39; Ontario, 1871 ***1823.15*** *p52*
Craig, Eleanor; Died enroute, 1855 ***1224.3*** *p17*
Craig, Elen 5; Ontario, 1861 ***2896.27*** *p4*
Craig, Frank 1; Ontario, 1861 ***2896.27*** *p4*
Craig, Frederick 6; Ontario, 1871 ***1823.15*** *p52*
Craig, Gavin 56; Ontario, 1871 ***1823.22*** *p35*
Craig, George; Barbados, 1776 ***1220.25*** *p134*
Craig, George 27; Virginia, 1773 ***1220.25*** *p31*
Craig, George 45; Ontario, 1871 ***1823.28*** *p20*
Craig, Hector; New York, 1803 ***8197.10*** *p11*
Craig, Henry 44; Ontario, 1871 ***1823.22*** *p35*
Craig, Henry 54; Ontario, 1871 ***1823.15*** *p52*
Craig, Hugh; New York, 1839 ***8197.10*** *p133*
Craig, James; Pennsylvania, 1777 ***4629.10*** *p24*
Craig, James; Pennsylvania, 1779 ***4629.10*** *p40*
Craig, James; Vermont, 1886-1901 ***5900.10*** *p281*
Craig, James 3; Ontario, 1861 ***2896.27*** *p4*
Craig, James 27; Ontario, 1861 ***2896.27*** *p4*
Craig, James 30; Ontario, 1871 ***1823.15*** *p53*
Craig, James, Sr. 70; Ontario, 1871 ***1823.22*** *p35*
Craig, James, Jr. 45; Ontario, 1871 ***1823.22*** *p35*
Craig, John; Albany, New York, 1833 ***1224.3*** *p17*
Craig, John; New York, 1803 ***8197.10*** *p11*
Craig, John; New York, 1840 ***8197.10*** *p159*
Craig, John; Ontario, 1897 ***1640.13*** *p24*
Craig, John; Pennsylvania, 1781 ***4629.10*** *p42*
Craig, John; Philadelphia, 1810 ***1224.3*** *p17*
Craig, John; Portland, Maine, 1857 ***9196.15*** *p12*
Craig, John 4; Ontario, 1861 ***2896.27*** *p4*
Craig, John 50; Ontario, 1871 ***1823.15*** *p53*
Craig, John 72; Ontario, 1871 ***1823.15*** *p53*
Craig, Joseph; Pennsylvania, 1777 ***4629.10*** *p25*
Craig, Joseph 36; Ontario, 1871 ***1823.15*** *p53*
Craig, Margaret; Georgia, 1774 ***1640.10*** *p33*
Craig, Margaret; Minnesota, 1895 ***1640.13*** *p24*
Craig, Margaret 40; Ontario, 1871 ***1823.15*** *p53*
Craig, Margret 89; Ontario, 1871 ***1823.15*** *p53*
Craig, Mary 30; Ontario, 1861 ***2896.27*** *p4*
Craig, Mary 65; Ontario, 1871 ***1823.22*** *p35*
Craig, Patrick; Georgia, 1698 ***1640.13*** *p24*
Craig, Peter; Connecticut, 1854 ***1640.13*** *p24*
Craig, R. S.; Mississippi, 1814-1845 ***1640.10*** *p33*
Craig, Robert; Pennsylvania, 1777 ***4629.10*** *p8*
Craig, Robert 48; Ontario, 1871 ***1823.22*** *p35*
Craig, Samuel 79; Ontario, 1871 ***1823.22*** *p35*
Craig, Thomas 22; Jamaica, 1774 ***1220.25*** *p79*
Craig, William; Georgia, 1740 ***1640.10*** *p33*
Craig, William; New York, 1794 ***8197.10*** *p3*
Craig, William; Pennsylvania, 1777 ***4629.10*** *p22*
Craig, William; Pennsylvania, 1781 ***4629.10*** *p42*
Craig, William 30; Ontario, 1871 ***1823.22*** *p35*
Craig, William 57; Ontario, 1871 ***1823.22*** *p35*
Craigen, Dennis 37; Virginia, 1774 ***1220.25*** *p93*
Craigg, William 38; Ontario, 1871 ***1823.22*** *p35*
Craighead, Alexander 44; Ontario, 1871 ***1823.22*** *p35*
Craighead, George 50; Ontario, 1871 ***1823.22*** *p35*
Craighead, William 39; Ontario, 1871 ***1823.22*** *p35*
Craighead, William 51; Ontario, 1871 ***1823.22*** *p35*
Craigie, William; Helena, Montana, 1893 ***1640.13*** *p25*
Craike, George 28; Virginia, 1775 ***1220.25*** *p141*
Crain, Robert; East New Jersey, 1747 ***1224.2*** *p28*
Crake, Mr.; Quebec, 1856 ***9196.15*** *p6*
Crake, Mrs.; Quebec, 1856 ***9196.15*** *p6*
Cram, Charles; Vermont, 1817-1863 ***5900.10*** *p96*
Cram, Dorothy; Philadelphia, 1837 ***1224.3*** *p17*
Cram, Elizabeth E.; Vermont, 1842-1902 ***5900.10*** *p97*
Cram, Ellen A.; Vermont, 1849-1866 ***5900.10*** *p96*
Cram, George 28; Ontario, 1871 ***1823.28*** *p20*
Cram, Henry D.; Vermont, 1853-1897 ***5900.10*** *p97*
Cram, James 53; Ontario, 1871 ***1823.28*** *p20*
Cram, John C.; Vermont, 1851-1907 ***5900.10*** *p97*
Cram, Katherine S.; Vermont, 1852-1931 ***5900.10*** *p97*
Cram, Mary C.; Vermont, 1814-1892 ***5900.10*** *p96*
Cram, Mary H.; Vermont, 1845-1868 ***5900.10*** *p97*
Cram, William 60; Ontario, 1871 ***1823.28*** *p20*
Cramer, Albrecht Daniel; Canada, 1791 ***2856.30*** *p70*
Cramer, Andreas; Port uncertain, 1771 ***2856.30*** *p70*
Cramer, Anna; Port uncertain, 1752 ***2856.30*** *p70*
Cramer, Charles; New York, 1834 ***8197.10*** *p219*
Cramer, Francis; New York, 1807 ***8197.10*** *p37*
Cramer, Johann Andreas; Port uncertain, 1729 ***2856.30*** *p70*
Cramer, Johann Dietrich; Port uncertain, 1750 ***2856.30*** *p71*
Cramer, John; New York, 1826 ***8197.10*** *p219*
Cramer, John; Pennsylvania, 1825 ***6058.10*** *p8*
Cramer, Peter; Port uncertain, 1738 ***2856.30*** *p70*
Cramond, James; Philadelphia, n.d. ***1224.2*** *p28*
Cramp, Elizabeth *SEE* Cramp, William
Cramp, Francis *SEE* Cramp, William
Cramp, Francis; Maryland, 1663 ***2524.55*** *p58*
Cramp, John *SEE* Cramp, William
Cramp, William *SEE* Cramp, William
Cramp, William; Maryland, 1663 ***2524.55*** *p58*
Relative: Francis
Son: William
Relative: John
Relative: Elizabeth
Cramp, William; Maryland, 1663 ***2524.55*** *p58*
Crampton, Thomas; New York, 1835 ***8197.10*** *p371*
Crampton, Thomas 15; Maryland, 1775 ***1220.25*** *p112*
Cran, William; Toronto, 1878 ***1640.13*** *p25*
Cranan, Patrick; Virginia, 1702 ***6212.30*** *p62*
Cranbrough, Nell; Maryland, 1678 ***2524.55*** *p58*
Cranch, Nathaniel; Pennsylvania, 1779 ***4629.10*** *p38*
Crandall, H. 34; Ontario, 1861 ***2896.28*** *p16*
Crandall, P. H. 9; Ontario, 1861 ***2896.28*** *p16*
Crandall, S. 15; Ontario, 1861 ***2896.28*** *p16*
Crandell, Fanny 50; Ontario, 1861 ***2896.28*** *p43*
Crandell, Jane 51; Ontario, 1871 ***1823.22*** *p35*
Crandell, Stephen 22; Ontario, 1861 ***2896.28*** *p43*
Crandle, Emma 6; Ontario, 1861 ***2896.26*** *p20*
Crandle, Phebe 28; Ontario, 1861 ***2896.26*** *p20*
Crane, Edward 40; Ontario, 1871 ***1823.28*** *p20*
Crane, Henry 18; Maryland, 1774 ***1220.25*** *p60*
Crane, John; Virginia, 1671-1672 ***6212.30*** *p45*
Crane, Lawrance 23; Maryland, 1775 ***1220.25*** *p109*
Crane, Margaret; New England, 1655 ***1224.1*** *p16*
Crane, William 26; Baltimore, 1775 ***1220.25*** *p117*
Crane, Wm; Virginia, 1671 ***6212.30*** *p44*
Cranford, Nathaniel; Maryland, 1682 ***2524.55*** *p58*
Cranmer, James; Virginia, 1666-1667 ***6212.30*** *p33*
Cransbrough, Nell; Maryland, 1678 ***2524.55*** *p58*
Cransdorf, Barthel; America, 1738 ***2856.30*** *p70*
With wife & children
Cranston, J. G. 37; Ontario, 1871 ***1823.28*** *p20*
Cranston, James 25; Maryland, 1775 ***1220.25*** *p109*
Cranston, Robert 50; Ontario, 1871 ***1823.15*** *p53*
Cranstoun, Thomas; New York, 1807 ***8197.10*** *p37*
Crantz, John; New York, 1837 ***8197.10*** *p81*
Crantzgen, Johann; Port uncertain, 1767 ***2856.30*** *p145*
Cranzbihler, Georg; Port uncertain, 1773 ***2856.30*** *p70*
Cranzbihler, Georg; Port uncertain, 1780 ***2856.30*** *p70*
Cranzbihler, Matheis; Port uncertain, 1773 ***2856.30*** *p70*
Cranzbihler, Matheis; Port uncertain, 1780 ***2856.30*** *p70*
Crapp, Conrad; Baltimore, 1832 ***6058.10*** *p13*
Crapp, Cornelius 61; Ontario, 1871 ***1823.22*** *p35*
Craske, John; Virginia, 1705 ***1224.2*** *p28*
Crasler, Philipp; America, 1732 ***2856.30*** *p70*
Crassen, Joaquin M.; New York, 1830 ***8197.10*** *p362*
Crassman, James; Boston, 1854 ***3437.14*** *p113*
Crasson, Mary; Maryland, 1663 ***2524.55*** *p58*
Craswell, Charles; Pennsylvania, 1777 ***4629.10*** *p12*
Cratcherly, Jno.; Virginia, 1667-1668 ***6212.30*** *p39*
Crate, Joseph Henshaw; Mississippi, 1856 ***1224.3*** *p17*
Crater, Roger; Virginia, 1680 ***6212.30*** *p55*
Crath, John 28; Ontario, 1871 ***1823.15*** *p53*
Craton, David; New York, 1826 ***8197.10*** *p219*
Cratton, William 83; Ontario, 1871 ***1823.28*** *p20*
Craufurd, James; New York, New York, 1812 ***1224.3*** *p17*
Craughwell, Ann 22 *SEE* Craughwell, Michael
Craughwell, Bridget 14 *SEE* Craughwell, Peter
Craughwell, Catherine 18 *SEE* Craughwell, Peter
Craughwell, Ellen 11 *SEE* Craughwell, Peter
Craughwell, Ellen 16 *SEE* Craughwell, Michael
Craughwell, Honoria 18 *SEE* Craughwell, Thomas
Craughwell, John 4 *SEE* Craughwell, Peter
Craughwell, John 15 *SEE* Craughwell, Nancy
Craughwell, Kitty 20 *SEE* Craughwell, Peter
Craughwell, Margaret 17 *SEE* Craughwell, Nancy
Craughwell, Mary 16 *SEE* Craughwell, Peter
Craughwell, Mary 16 *SEE* Craughwell, Thomas
Craughwell, Michael 20; New York, New York, 1849 ***1825.45*** *p31*
Sister: Ann 22
Sister: Ellen 16
Craughwell, Nancy 41; New York, New York, 1849 ***1825.45*** *p31*
Son: Pat 20
Sister: Peggy 40
Nephew: Thomas 7
Nephew: John 15
Daughter: Margaret 17
Craughwell, Pat 15 *SEE* Craughwell, Thomas
Craughwell, Pat 20 *SEE* Craughwell, Nancy
Craughwell, Patrick 6 *SEE* Craughwell, Peter
Craughwell, Peggy 40 *SEE* Craughwell, Nancy
Craughwell, Peter 40; New York, New York, 1848 ***1825.45*** *p31*
Wife: Winifred 36
Son: Patrick 6
Daughter: Bridget 14
Daughter: Ellen 11
Daughter: Mary 16
Daughter: Rose 13
Daughter: Kitty 20
Daughter: Catherine 18
Son: John 4
Craughwell, Rose 13 *SEE* Craughwell, Peter
Craughwell, Thomas 7 *SEE* Craughwell, Nancy
Craughwell, Thomas 20; New York, New York, 1848 ***1825.45*** *p31*
Brother: Pat 15
Sister: Mary 16
Sister: Honoria 18
Craughwell, Winifred 36 *SEE* Craughwell, Peter
Craven, Catherine S.; Vermont, 1849-1873 ***5900.10*** *p78*
Craven, John; Pennsylvania, 1787 ***4629.10*** *p56*
Craven, John; Philadelphia, 1705 ***1224.2*** *p28*
Craven, John; Vermont, 1848-1937 ***5900.10*** *p78*
Craven, Julia Cone; Vermont, 1851-1889 ***5900.10*** *p87*
Craven, Lawrence; Baltimore, 1772 ***1224.2*** *p28*
Craven, Mary; Vermont, 1846-1937 ***5900.10*** *p90*
Craven, Mary 35; Vermont, 1872 ***5900.10*** *p72*
Craven, Mary Connolly; Vermont, 1855-1936 ***5900.10*** *p353*
Craven, Michael; Vermont, n.d. ***5900.10*** *p72*
Craven, Michael; Vermont, 1855-1917 ***5900.10*** *p353*
Craven, Patrick; New York, 1840 ***8197.10*** *p385*
Craven, Patrick 65; Vermont, 1872 ***5900.10*** *p72*
Craven, Richard Charles 27; Ontario, 1871 ***1823.15*** *p53*
Craven, Sarah; New York, New York, 1851 ***1224.3*** *p17*
Craven, William 69; Ontario, 1871 ***1823.15*** *p53*
Cravy, Alvin 46; Ontario, 1871 ***1823.22*** *p35*
Crawfoot, Thomas; Maryland, 1652-1659 ***2524.55*** *p58*
Crawfoott, Thomas; Maryland, 1652-1659 ***2524.55*** *p58*
Crawford, Miss; Quebec, 1857 ***9196.15*** *p14*
Crawford, Mr.; Quebec, 1857 ***9196.15*** *p24*
Crawford, Mr.; Quebec, 1858 ***9196.15*** *p35*
Crawford, Mrs.; Quebec, 1857 ***9196.15*** *p14*
Crawford, Mrs.; Quebec, 1857 ***9196.15*** *p24*
Crawford, A.; Portland, Maine, 1857 ***9196.15*** *p12*
Crawford, A.; Quebec, 1856 ***9196.15*** *p6*
Crawford, Adam; Illinois, 1891 ***1640.13*** *p25*
Crawford, Alexander; Florida, 1767 ***1640.10*** *p33*
Crawford, Alexander; Georgia, 1763 ***1640.10*** *p33*
Crawford, Alexander; Pennsylvania, 1777 ***4629.10*** *p9*
Crawford, Alexander 28; Ontario, 1871 ***1823.15*** *p53*
Crawford, Andrew 23; Nova Scotia, 1774 ***1220.25*** *p15*
Crawford, Angus 55; Ontario, 1871 ***1823.22*** *p35*
Crawford, Annie; Portland, Maine, 1858 ***9196.15*** *p47*
Crawford, Archibald 44; Ontario, 1871 ***1823.28*** *p20*
Crawford, Benj'n; Pennsylvania, 1785 ***4629.10*** *p48*
Crawford, Bridget 58; Ontario, 1871 ***1823.22*** *p35*
Crawford, David; New York, 1807 ***8197.10*** *p37*
Crawford, David 30; Ontario, 1871 ***1823.15*** *p53*
Crawford, David 45; Ontario, 1871 ***1823.28*** *p20*
Crawford, E.; Pennsylvania, 1781 ***4629.10*** *p42*
Crawford, Flora; Port uncertain, 1870-1879 ***4537.37*** *p123*
Crawford, George; Jamaica, 1802 ***1640.13*** *p25*
Crawford, Hugh 44; Ontario, 1871 ***1823.15*** *p53*
Crawford, James; Georgia, 1699 ***1640.13*** *p25*
Crawford, James; Pennsylvania, 1777 ***4629.10*** *p28*
Crawford, James; Quebec, 1857 ***9196.15*** *p24*
Crawford, James 30; Ontario, 1871 ***1823.15*** *p53*
Crawford, James 50; Ontario, 1871 ***1823.15*** *p53*
Crawford, Mrs. James; Quebec, 1857 ***9196.15*** *p24*
Crawford, Jane 20; Ontario, 1871 ***1823.15*** *p53*
Crawford, Janet; Massachusetts, 1886 ***1640.13*** *p25*
Crawford, Janus 33; Ontario, 1871 ***1823.22*** *p35*
Crawford, John; Georgia, 1751 ***1640.10*** *p33*
Crawford, John; Jamaica, 1771 ***1640.13*** *p25*
Crawford, John; New York, 1840 ***8197.10*** *p160*
Crawford, John; Pennsylvania, 1777 ***4629.10*** *p15*
Crawford, John; Pennsylvania, 1785 ***4629.10*** *p45*
Crawford, John; Pennsylvania, 1841 ***6058.10*** *p17*
Crawford, John 26; Ontario, 1871 ***1823.15*** *p53*
Crawford, John 32; Ontario, 1871 ***1823.15*** *p53*
Crawford, John 61; Ontario, 1871 ***1823.15*** *p53*
Crawford, John W. 52; Ontario, 1871 ***1823.28*** *p20*
Crawford, Joseph; Pennsylvania, 1777 ***4629.10*** *p9*
Crawford, Kate; Vermont, 1852-1926 ***5900.10*** *p379*

Crawford, Margaret 60; Ontario, 1871 *1823.15 p53*
Crawford, Mary; Ontario, 1851 *4537.32 p75*
Crawford, Mary 8; Ontario, 1871 *1823.15 p53*
Crawford, Robert; Georgia, 1775 *1640.10 p34*
Crawford, Robert; Pennsylvania, 1838 *6058.10 p15*
Crawford, Robert 16; Georgia, 1775 *1220.25 p125*
Crawford, Robert 22; Maryland, 1774 *1220.25 p3*
Crawford, Robert 36; Ontario, 1871 *1823.28 p20*
Crawford, Robert 47; Ontario, 1871 *1823.15 p53*
Crawford, Robert 63; Ontario, 1871 *1823.15 p53*
Crawford, Samuel; Pennsylvania, 1777 *4629.10 p22*
Crawford, Samuel; Pennsylvania, 1785 *4629.10 p48*
Crawford, Sarah 45; Ontario, 1871 *1823.15 p53*
Crawford, Thomas 47; Ontario, 1871 *1823.15 p53*
Crawford, Thomas 63; Ontario, 1871 *1823.28 p20*
Crawford, William; America, 1751 *1640.10 p34*
Crawford, William; Dominica, 1850 *1640.13 p25*
Crawford, William; Georgia, 1809 *1640.10 p34*
Crawford, William; New York, 1840 *8197.10 p221*
Crawford, William; Pennsylvania, 1838 *6058.10 p15*
Crawford, William 53; Ontario, 1871 *1823.15 p53*
Crawford, William 60; Ontario, 1871 *1823.28 p20*
Crawford and Lindsay, George; Florida, 1767 *1640.10 p34*
Crawley, Dewsberry; New York, 1807 *8197.10 p36*
Crawley, Jacob; New York, New York, 1837 *1224.3 p17*
Crawley, John; New Jersey, 1800 *1224.3 p17*
Crawley, John 60; Ontario, 1871 *1823.15 p53*
Crawley, Mary; New Jersey, 1823 *1224.3 p54*
Crawley, Mary; Vermont, 1853-1928 *5900.10 p273*
Crawley, Mary Preston 31; Vermont, 1863 *5900.10 p245*
Crawley, Patrick; New York, 1803 *8197.10 p11*
Crawly, Fran; Virginia, 1663 *6212.30 p4*
Crawly, Richard; Virginia, 1665 *6212.30 p20*
Crawshawe, John 55; Ontario, 1871 *1823.22 p35*
Cray, Annie M. Eagan; Vermont, 1856-1903 *5900.10 p62*
Cray, Bridget F. Pierce; Vermont, 1856-1915 *5900.10 p66*
Cray, Dennis E.; Vermont, 1857-1943 *5900.10 p62*
Cray, Ellen; Vermont, n.d. *5900.10 p55*
Cray, Eugene; Vermont, 1820-1905 *5900.10 p62*
Cray, Eugene E.; Vermont, 1855-1932 *5900.10 p54*
Cray, Eugene E.; Vermont, 1855-1932 *5900.10 p62*
Cray, Hannah; Vermont, n.d. *5900.10 p67*
Cray, Johanna Brosnahan; Vermont, 1823-1906 *5900.10 p62*
Cray, John; New York, 1840 *8197.10 p160*
Cray, John E.; Vermont, 1857-1917 *5900.10 p55*
Cray, John H.; Vermont, 1847-1934 *5900.10 p71*
Cray, John S. 40; Vermont, 1888 *5900.10 p60*
Cray, Julia Finn 40; Vermont, 1888 *5900.10 p60*
Cray, Margaret D.; Vermont, 1852-1924 *5900.10 p71*
Cray, Margaret W. Crehan; Vermont, 1855-1929 *5900.10 p54*
Cray, Margaret W. Grehan; Vermont, 1855-1929 *5900.10 p62*
Cray, Mary; Vermont, 1845-1929 *5900.10 p71*
Cray, Mary; Vermont, 1854-1919 *5900.10 p67*
Cray, Mary C. 70; Vermont, 1900 *5900.10 p68*
Cray, Mary V. Slattery; Vermont, 1855-1926 *5900.10 p55*
Cray, Micheal 47; Ontario, 1871 *1823.15 p53*
Cray, P. J.; Vermont, 1815-1882 *5900.10 p55*
Cray, Patrick; Vermont, 1849-1925 *5900.10 p66*
Craye, Miss; Quebec, 1858 *9196.15 p44*
Crea, Agnes Marcus *SEE* Crea, John
Crea, John; Philadelphia, 1789 *4629.10 p58*
Wife: Agnes Marcus
Crea, John 24; Philadelphia, 1789 *4629.10 p58*
Crea, Samuel; New York, 1838 *8197.10 p112*
Creacroft, Anne *SEE* Creacroft, John
Creacroft, John; Maryland, 1665 *2524.55 p58*
Wife: Anne
Cready, James 66; Vermont, 1858 *5900.10 p248*
Creagan, Dennis; Pennsylvania, 1866 *6058.10 p55*
Creagan, Henry 70; Vermont, 1865 *5900.10 p335*
Creagan, Margaret 49; Vermont, 1864 *5900.10 p335*
Creagh, Mr.; Quebec, 1856 *9196.15 p8*
Creake, Samuel; Maryland, 1716 *1224.2 p28*
Creamer, William 35; New York, 1775 *1220.25 p94*
Crean, Ira; Vermont, 1850-1853 *5900.10 p343*
Crean, Jeremiah; Vermont, 1818 *5900.10 p343*
Crean, Mary Moriarty; Vermont, 1817-1884 *5900.10 p343*
Crean, Richard; Pennsylvania, 1787 *4629.10 p56*
Crearar, Peter 49; Ontario, 1871 *1823.15 p53*
Crease, Alfred; Philadelphia, 1836 *1224.3 p17*
Creathby, John; Maryland, 1681 *2524.55 p58*
Crebe, Alfred 37; Ontario, 1871 *1823.28 p20*
Crebel, Peter; Port uncertain, 1752 *2856.30 p70*
Crebo, Philip 29; Ontario, 1871 *1823.28 p20*
Crebo, William 44; Ontario, 1871 *1823.28 p20*
Credy, Mary; Vermont, 1825-1902 *5900.10 p378*
Credy, Peter 25; Maryland, 1774 *1220.25 p78*
Cree, Cleland; Jamaica, 1838 *1640.13 p25*
Cree, James; New Mexico, 1891 *1640.13 p25*
Creech, James 33; Ontario, 1871 *1823.15 p53*
Creech, William 28; Ontario, 1871 *1823.15 p53*
Creed, Annie Tiernan; Vermont, 1860-1925 *5900.10 p447*
Creed, James E.; Vermont, 1854-1936 *5900.10 p447*
Creed, John; Virginia, 1635 *1224.1 p16*
Creed, Nancy Starr; Vermont, 1852-1924 *5900.10 p432*
Creedwell, George; Maryland, 1665 *2524.55 p58*
Creef, Sebastian; America, 1727 *2856.30 p70*
Creeley, John 38; Ontario, 1871 *1823.28 p20*
Crego, Stephen; New York, 1692 *1224.1 p16*
Crehan, Annie; Vermont, 1853-1886 *5900.10 p54*
Crehan, Carl 58; Ontario, 1871 *1823.28 p20*
Crehan, Margaret W.; Vermont, 1855-1929 *5900.10 p54*
Creighton, Adam 40; Ontario, 1871 *1823.28 p20*
Creighton, Alexander; Georgia, 1770 *1640.10 p34*
Creighton, Anthony; Pennsylvania, 1868 *6058.10 p64*
Creighton, El 55; Ontario, 1861 *2896.27 p1*
Creighton, James; New York, 1822 *8197.10 p61*
Creighton, James; Pennsylvania, 1777 *4629.10 p17*
Creighton, James 33; Maryland, 1774 *1220.25 p53*
Creighton, James 63; Ontario, 1861 *2896.27 p1*
Creighton, John; Oswego, New York, 1846 *1224.3 p17*
Creighton, John 50; Ontario, 1871 *1823.22 p35*
Creighton, John 74; Ontario, 1871 *1823.22 p35*
Creiman, Charles 45; Ontario, 1871 *1823.15 p53*
Creiton, John; Virginia, 1666 *6212.30 p28*
Crelock, Richard 47; Ontario, 1871 *1823.22 p36*
Cremarse, Johnakin; Maryland, 1669 *2524.55 p238*
Cremin, John 28; New York, New York, 1849 *1825.45 p47*
Wife: Kitty 25
Son: Timothy 3 months
Cremin, Kitty 25 *SEE* Cremin, John
Cremin, Timothy 3 months *SEE* Cremin, John
Creor, Ann 11; Ontario, 1871 *1823.28 p20*
Creor, Christiana 38; Ontario, 1871 *1823.28 p20*
Crerich, Margaret; St. Augustine, Florida, 1786 *1640.10 p34*
Cresbach, Philipp; Port uncertain, 1735 *2856.30 p70*
Cresol, Jone; Maryland, 1672 *2524.55 p58*
Cresoll, Johnny 35; Ontario, 1871 *1823.28 p20*
Cresor, George 40; Ontario, 1871 *1823.28 p20*
Cresor, Henry 40; Ontario, 1871 *1823.28 p20*
Cresor, John 34; Ontario, 1871 *1823.28 p20*
Cresor, Maria 32; Ontario, 1871 *1823.28 p20*
Cressey, John; North America, 1812 *1224.3 p17*
Cresson, Jeremiah; Pennsylvania, 1786 *4629.10 p54*
Cresswell, Miss; Quebec, 1856 *9196.15 p10*
Cresswell, Edwin 38; Ontario, 1871 *1823.15 p53*
Cresswell, Estcourt; New Jersey, 1843 *1224.3 p18*
Cresswell, Joseph; Pennsylvania, 1856 *1224.3 p18*
Cressy, Samuel; Maryland, 1673 *2524.55 p58*
Crestye, Samuell; Maryland, 1658 *2524.55 p58*
Creswell, Mr.; Quebec, 1857 *9196.15 p24*
Creswell, Frederick; Baltimore, 1857 *1224.3 p18*
Creswell, George; New York, 1854 *1224.3 p18*
Creucas, Jaque; America, 1737 *2856.30 p70*
Creuil, Nicolas Antoine Gabriel 36; Pennsylvania, 1793 *4629.10 p64*
Creur, Daniel 65; Ontario, 1871 *1823.28 p20*
Creutz, Anna Christina; Port uncertain, 1752 *2856.30 p70*
Creutz, Elisabeth; Port uncertain, 1771 *2856.30 p70*
Creutz, Johann Henrich; America, 1753 *2856.30 p145*
Creutz, Johann Jacob; America, 1753 *2856.30 p70*
Creutzer, Anna Catharina; Port uncertain, 1775 *2856.30 p70*
Creutzer, Mathes; Port uncertain, 1752 *2856.30 p70*
Creutzer, Phil. Dorothea; Port uncertain, 1754 *2856.30 p70*
Creuzbauer, Jacob; America, 1768 *2856.30 p70*
Crevensac, Mr.; Port uncertain, 1700 *2856.30 p70*
With wife
Crevesac, Mr.; America, 1737 *2856.30 p44*
Crevesac, Jaque; America, 1737 *2856.30 p70*
With wife & 2 children
Crevier, Julien; New York, 1838 *8197.10 p113*
Crew, Miss; Quebec, 1856 *9196.15 p6*
Crew, Dorothy; Maryland, 1660 *2524.55 p58*
Crew, Martin 29; Maryland, 1774 *1220.25 p77*
Wife: Mary 28
Crew, Mary 28 *SEE* Crew, Martin
Crew, Mary 30; Ontario, 1871 *1823.15 p53*
Crew, Tho.; Maryland, 1681 *2524.55 p58*
Crewes, James; Virginia, 1677 *1224.1 p16*
Crews, William 58; Ontario, 1871 *1823.15 p54*
Crewsell, Miss; Quebec, 1858 *9196.15 p41*
Crey, Thomas; New York, 1827 *8197.10 p218*
Creychgauer, Dorothea; Port uncertain, 1791 *2856.30 p70*
Crias, Franns 29; Ontario, 1871 *1823.28 p20*
Crich, James 40; Ontario, 1871 *1823.15 p54*
Crich, John 48; Ontario, 1871 *1823.15 p54*
Crich, Joseph 54; Ontario, 1871 *1823.15 p54*
Crich, Samuel 44; Ontario, 1871 *1823.15 p54*
Crich, Thomas 59; Ontario, 1871 *1823.15 p54*
Crichton, Miss; Quebec, 1857 *9196.15 p27*
Crichton, James; Prince Edward Island, 1820 *1640.13 p25*
Crichton, James Maitland; Jamaica, 1877 *1640.13 p25*
Crickland, Wm 42; Ontario, 1871 *1823.28 p20*
Crickmare, Mrs.; Quebec, 1858 *9196.15 p41*
Cridland, John; Pennsylvania, 1777 *4629.10 p8*
Crief, John; Jamaica, 1776 *1220.25 p134*
Crighton, Alexander; St. Augustine, Florida, 1817 *1640.10 p34*
Crighton, Anthony; Pennsylvania, 1868 *6058.10 p64*
Crighton, Emma 21; Ontario, 1871 *1823.15 p54*
Crighton, James 82; Ontario, 1871 *1823.15 p54*
Crimere, Alexander 27; Ontario, 1871 *1823.15 p54*
Crimm, Peter; America, 1752 *2856.30 p70*
Crimmins, Catherine H.; Vermont, 1835-1908 *5900.10 p361*
Crimmins, John; Vermont, 1836-1895 *5900.10 p361*
Crimmins, Julia; Vermont, 1856-1884 *5900.10 p134*
Crimmins, Katherine; Vermont, 1832-1913 *5900.10 p356*
Cripin, Ashahel 75; Ontario, 1861 *2896.26 p39*
Cripp, George; New York, New York, 1856 *6058.10 p46*
Crippin, Tho; Virginia, 1681-1682 *6212.30 p56*
Cripps, Christian; Pennsylvania, 1819 *6058.10 p6*
Cripps, Sarah 25; America, 1774 *1220.25 p35*
Cripps, Wm; Virginia, 1674-1675 *6212.30 p53*
Cripts, Philip; Pennsylvania, 1777 *4629.10 p15*
Crisfield, John; New York, 1825-1831 *8197.10 p370*
Crisley, Mary; Maryland, 1681 *2524.55 p58*
Crisp, Francis 25; Maryland, 1774 *1220.25 p59*
Crisp, Tho; Virginia, 1665-1666 *6212.30 p22*
Crisp, Thomas; Virginia, 1663 *6212.30 p4*
Crisp, Thomas; Virginia, 1666-1667 *6212.30 p32*
Crisp, Thomas 41; Ontario, 1871 *1823.15 p54*
Crispe, Jemima Humphreys; Buffalo, New York, 1840 *1224.3 p18*
Crispe, John; Buffalo, New York, 1840 *1224.3 p18*
Crispe, Thomas; Virginia, 1664 *6212.30 p14*
Crispe, Thomas; Virginia, 1704 *1224.2 p28*
Crispin, Silas; Pennsylvania, 1777 *4629.10 p27*
Crispin, Thomas; Pennsylvania, 1777 *4629.10 p14*
Crispin, Thomas; Pennsylvania, 1777 *4629.10 p28*
Crispin, William; Pennsylvania, 1777 *4629.10 p6*
Crispin, William; Pennsylvania, 1777 *4629.10 p18*
Crispin, William; Pennsylvania, 1779 *4629.10 p35*
Crissell, Clem; Maryland, 1666 *2524.55 p58*
Crissrell, Clem; Maryland, 1666 *2524.55 p58*
Cristadoro, Joseph; New York, 1838 *8197.10 p113*
Cristfield, Charles 26; Ontario, 1871 *1823.28 p20*
Cristoll, Frank 20; Ontario, 1861 *2896.27 p12*
Cristy, John 78; Vermont, 1867 *5900.10 p293*
Cristy, Roxanna B. 70; Vermont, 1866 *5900.10 p293*
Criswell, Alan; New York, 1827-1834 *8197.10 p305*
Critchell, Michael; Ohio, 1851 *1224.3 p18*
Critchlow, Thomas; Portland, Maine, 1857 *9196.15 p12*
Crittendon, Hannah 70; Ontario, 1871 *1823.15 p54*
Croake, M. Ellen; Vermont, 1861-1916 *5900.10 p540*
Croake, Robert; Georgia, 1698 *1640.13 p25*
Crobubski, Charles; Maryland, 1910 *3259.35 p10*
Crock, John 33; Ontario, 1871 *1823.28 p20*
Crockatt, John; Georgia, 1751 *1640.10 p34*
Crocker, Mrs.; Quebec, 1856 *9196.15 p8*
Crocker, James; Virginia, 1666 *6212.30 p29*
Crocker, James 29; Ontario, 1871 *1823.15 p54*
Crocker, James 39; Ontario, 1871 *1823.15 p54*
Crocker, John 18; Philadelphia, 1774 *1220.25 p4*
Crocker, John V. 36; Ontario, 1871 *1823.15 p54*
Crocker, S.; Quebec, 1856 *9196.15 p8*
Crocket, Henry 21; Maryland, 1775 *1220.25 p114*
Crocket, William; New York, 1825 *8197.10 p217*
Crockett, . . .; South Carolina, 1750-1770 *4628.40 p98*
Crockett, Richard; Maryland, 1672 *2524.55 p58*
Crockett, Richard; Maryland, 1673 *2524.55 p58*
Crockett, Richard; Maryland, 1676 *2524.55 p58*
Crockett, William; New York, 1837 *8197.10 p219*
Crockett, William; South Carolina, 1730 *1224.2 p28*
Croferd, John 40; Ontario, 1861 *2896.27 p67*
Crofert, John 52; Ontario, 1871 *1823.22 p36*
Croffts, Edm; Virginia, 1665 *6212.30 p17*
Croford, Georgina 29; Ontario, 1871 *1823.15 p54*
Croft, Miss; Quebec, 1858 *9196.15 p46*
Croft, Mr.; Quebec, 1858 *9196.15 p44*
Croft, Mrs.; Quebec, 1858 *9196.15 p44*
Croft, Harbert; Maryland, 1667 *2524.55 p58*
Croft, Harbert; Maryland, 1670 *2524.55 p58*

Cross, Wilson 42; Ontario, 1871 ***1823.22*** *p36*
Crossan, Thomas 32; Ontario, 1871 ***1823.15*** *p54*
Crosse, Charles; Virginia, 1671 ***6212.30*** *p45*
Crosse, Nathaniel; Maryland, 1675 ***2524.55*** *p59*
Crosse, Nathaniell; Virginia, 1661 ***2524.55*** *p58*
Crosse, S.; Quebec, 1856 ***9196.15*** *p6*
Crosse, William; Maryland, 1683 ***1224.1*** *p16*
Crossen, Jackson 69; Ontario, 1871 ***1823.22*** *p36*
Crossen, James 43; Ontario, 1871 ***1823.22*** *p36*
Crossen, John 37; Ontario, 1871 ***1823.22*** *p36*
Crossen, Robert 41; Ontario, 1871 ***1823.22*** *p36*
Crossett, J. E.; Vermont, 1854-1916 ***5900.10*** *p554*
Crossett, Mary Breen; Vermont, 1855-1943 ***5900.10*** *p555*
Crossett, Mary J. McMullen; Vermont, 1856-1926 ***5900.10*** *p554*
Crossett, Willis H. 44; Vermont, 1892 ***5900.10*** *p555*
Crossey, Allan 55; Ontario, 1871 ***1823.15*** *p54*
Crossfeild, Joseph; Virginia, 1666-1667 ***6212.30*** *p34*
Crossingham, George; New York, 1839 ***8197.10*** *p132*
Crossley, Leonard; America, 1773 ***1224.2*** *p28*
Crossley, William; New York, 1788 ***1224.2*** *p28*
Crossley, William; New York, 1839 ***8197.10*** *p132*
Crossly, Thomas Baldwin; New Jersey, 1897 ***1640.13*** *p26*
Crossman, George 56; Ontario, 1871 ***1823.15*** *p54*
Crosson, James 49; Ontario, 1871 ***1823.22*** *p36*
Crosson, Thomas 67; Ontario, 1871 ***1823.22*** *p36*
Crosss, P. 32; Alaska, 1912 ***9196.1*** *p38*
Crosss, P. 32; Yukon, 1912 ***9196.1*** *p38*
Crosswill, William 49; Ontario, 1871 ***1823.15*** *p54*
Croston, Alice; New York, 1831 ***8197.10*** *p219*
Croston, Frances; Virginia, 1681 ***6212.30*** *p55*
Crothers, George F. 11; Ontario, 1861 ***2896.28*** *p48*
Crothers, Margaret 32; Ontario, 1861 ***2896.28*** *p48*
Crothers, Mary J. 14; Ontario, 1861 ***2896.28*** *p48*
Crothers, Sarah 2; Ontario, 1861 ***2896.28*** *p48*
Crothers, William 45; Ontario, 1861 ***2896.28*** *p48*
Crotty, David; Pennsylvania, 1777 ***4629.10*** *p9*
Crotty, Ellen 60; Vermont, 1879 ***5900.10*** *p154*
Crotty, John 19; Vermont, 1873 ***5900.10*** *p166*
Crouch, Mrs.; Maryland, 1650 ***2524.55*** *p59*
Crouch, Elizabeth *SEE* Crouch, William
Crouch, George; Maryland, 1640 ***2524.55*** *p59*
Crouch, James; Maryland, 1679 ***2524.55*** *p59*
Crouch, James; Virginia, 1664 ***6212.30*** *p9*
Crouch, John *SEE* Crouch, William
Crouch, Josias *SEE* Crouch, William
Crouch, Margaret 27; Baltimore, 1775 ***1220.25*** *p119*
Crouch, Mary *SEE* Crouch, William
Crouch, Mary; Maryland, 1640-1650 ***2524.55*** *p59*
Crouch, Rachell *SEE* Crouch, William
Crouch, Richard; Maryland, 1648 ***2524.55*** *p59*
Crouch, Thomas; Philadelphia, 1779 ***1224.2*** *p29*
Crouch, Thomas 25; Maryland, 1774 ***1220.25*** *p47*
Crouch, William; Maryland, 1650 ***2524.55*** *p59*
Wife: Mary
Child: Elizabeth
Child: John
Child: Rachell
Child: Josias
Crouch, William; New England, 1660 ***1224.1*** *p16*
Croucher, Henry; New York, New York, 1768 ***1224.2*** *p29*
Crouchland, Margaret; Maryland, 1671 ***2524.55*** *p59*
Crough, James; Maryland, 1678 ***2524.55*** *p59*
Crouly, Timothy 40; Ontario, 1871 ***1823.15*** *p54*
Crouse, B. 21; Ontario, 1861 ***2896.26*** *p12*
Crouse, C. 5; Ontario, 1861 ***2896.26*** *p12*
Crouse, C. 40; Ontario, 1861 ***2896.26*** *p12*
Crouse, C. A. 12; Ontario, 1861 ***2896.26*** *p12*
Crouse, E. 10; Ontario, 1861 ***2896.26*** *p12*
Crouse, R. 14; Ontario, 1861 ***2896.26*** *p12*
Crouse, S. 7; Ontario, 1861 ***2896.26*** *p12*
Crout, Frederick; Pennsylvania, 1777 ***4629.10*** *p8*
Croutch, Edward; Virginia, 1667-1668 ***6212.30*** *p38*
Crouthers, Henry; Virginia, 1674-1675 ***6212.30*** *p53*
Crow, Alison 25; Ontario, 1871 ***1823.15*** *p54*
Crow, Ann; Maryland, 1666 ***2524.55*** *p59*
Crow, Cornelius 48; Virginia, 1774 ***1220.25*** *p93*
Crow, Dorothy; Maryland, 1660 ***2524.55*** *p58*
Crow, Ellen 29; Vermont, 1845 ***5900.10*** *p612*
Crow, John; New York, 1808 ***8197.10*** *p53*
Crow, John; New York, 1840 ***8197.10*** *p160*
Crow, John; Virginia, 1710 ***1224.2*** *p29*
Crow, Mary Hagerty 73; Vermont, 1893 ***5900.10*** *p414*
Crow, Michael 83; Vermont, 1894 ***5900.10*** *p414*
Crow, Oliver; Virginia, 1665-1666 ***6212.30*** *p24*
Crow, William 45; Ontario, 1871 ***1823.28*** *p20*
Crowden, Samuel 22; Jamaica, 1774 ***1220.25*** *p49*
Crowder, Alicia; Maryland, 1649-1658 ***2524.55*** *p59*
Crowder, Elizabeth; Maryland, 1655 ***2524.55*** *p59*
Crowder, Elizabeth; Maryland, 1673 ***2524.55*** *p59*
Crowder, Joseph; Maryland, 1681 ***2524.55*** *p60*
Crowder, Thomas; Maryland, 1672 ***2524.55*** *p60*
Crowdson, Robt; Virginia, 1690-1691 ***6212.30*** *p59*
Crowe, Bridget 85; Vermont, 1924 ***5900.10*** *p428*
Crowe, Bridget 90; Vermont, 1906 ***5900.10*** *p181*
Crowe, James 42; Ontario, 1871 ***1823.22*** *p36*
Crowe, John; New York, 1838 ***8197.10*** *p113*
Crowe, Jos; British Columbia, 1917 ***9196.1*** *p69*
Crowe, Jos; California, 1917 ***9196.1*** *p69*
Crowe, Margaret 44; Vermont, 1881 ***5900.10*** *p417*
Crowe, Margaret 44; Vermont, 1881 ***5900.10*** *p428*
Crowe, Mary 24; Vermont, 1859 ***5900.10*** *p181*
Crowe, Mary Wynn 59; Vermont, 1898 ***5900.10*** *p405*
Crowe, Michael; Vermont, 1836-1906 ***5900.10*** *p417*
Crowe, Michael; Vermont, 1836-1909 ***5900.10*** *p428*
Crowell, Elisha; Pennsylvania, 1785 ***4629.10*** *p48*
Crowle, Mr.; Quebec, 1857 ***9196.15*** *p27*
Crowle, Mrs.; Quebec, 1857 ***9196.15*** *p27*
Crowler, Anthony 28; Ontario, 1861 ***2896.25*** *p51*
Crowler, Mary 52; Ontario, 1861 ***2896.25*** *p51*
Crowley, Mr.; Vermont, 1832-1877 ***5900.10*** *p251*
Crowley, Mrs.; Vermont, 1839-1895 ***5900.10*** *p251*
Crowley, Agnes 43; Ontario, 1871 ***1823.22*** *p36*
Crowley, Ann Corley; Vermont, 1832-1923 ***5900.10*** *p142*
Crowley, Bedelia Cavanaugh; Vermont, 1844-1893 ***5900.10*** *p420*
Crowley, Bridget; Vermont, 1853-1935 ***5900.10*** *p170*
Crowley, Bridget 87; Vermont, 1946 ***5900.10*** *p124*
Crowley, Bridget Coppinger; Vermont, 1868-1962 ***5900.10*** *p443*
Crowley, Bridget McCue 53; Vermont, 1873 ***5900.10*** *p202*
Crowley, Bridget Ryan; Vermont, 1860-1938 ***5900.10*** *p252*
Crowley, Catherine; Vermont, 1820-1884 ***5900.10*** *p474*
Crowley, Catherine 40; Vermont, 1898 ***5900.10*** *p108*
Crowley, Catherine 83; Vermont, 1900 ***5900.10*** *p108*
Crowley, Catherine Hennessey 70; Vermont, 1899 ***5900.10*** *p475*
Crowley, Clara L. Cronkrite; Vermont, 1852-1934 ***5900.10*** *p494*
Crowley, Cornelius; Vermont, 1848-1870 ***5900.10*** *p160*
Crowley, Cornelius 65; Vermont, 1887 ***5900.10*** *p108*
Crowley, Cornelius E.; Vermont, 1841-1918 ***5900.10*** *p452*
Crowley, Daniel; Vermont, 1836-1906 ***5900.10*** *p339*
Crowley, Daniel 67; Vermont, 1880 ***5900.10*** *p250*
Crowley, Daniel E.; Vermont, 1848-1923 ***5900.10*** *p120*
Crowley, Dennis; Vermont, 1864-1939 ***5900.10*** *p192*
Crowley, Edwin Hubert; New York, 1838 ***8197.10*** *p114*
Crowley, Eleanor N.; Vermont, n.d. ***5900.10*** *p399*
Crowley, Eliza; Vermont, 1841-1883 ***5900.10*** *p70*
Crowley, Elizabeth 16; Ontario, 1871 ***1823.22*** *p36*
Crowley, Elizabeth Conners; Vermont, 1856-1918 ***5900.10*** *p191*
Crowley, Ellen; Vermont, 1853-1941 ***5900.10*** *p588*
Crowley, Ellen 61; Vermont, 1868 ***5900.10*** *p498*
Crowley, Ellen Driscoll 65; Vermont, 1886 ***5900.10*** *p250*
Crowley, Flora E.; Vermont, 1868-1932 ***5900.10*** *p125*
Crowley, Florence; Vermont, 1840-1914 ***5900.10*** *p421*
Crowley, Gerritt D.; Vermont, 1852-1920 ***5900.10*** *p125*
Crowley, Hannah; Vermont, 1892 ***5900.10*** *p481*
Crowley, Hannie 5; Vermont, 1869 ***5900.10*** *p126*
Crowley, Honora; Vermont, 1850-1937 ***5900.10*** *p435*
Crowley, Isaac J.; Vermont, 1830-1903 ***5900.10*** *p494*
Crowley, James E.; Vermont, 1848-1908 ***5900.10*** *p170*
Crowley, James P.; Vermont, 1849-1903 ***5900.10*** *p418*
Crowley, Jeremiah; Vermont, 1816-1887 ***5900.10*** *p542*
Crowley, Jeremiah; Vermont, 1822-1889 ***5900.10*** *p142*
Crowley, Jeremiah; Vermont, 1848-1859 ***5900.10*** *p160*
Crowley, Jeremiah; Vermont, 1859-1906 ***5900.10*** *p252*
Crowley, Jeremiah J.; Vermont, 1855-1873 ***5900.10*** *p543*
Crowley, Joanna Hannon; Vermont, 1852-1920 ***5900.10*** *p125*
Crowley, John; Vermont, 1815-1892 ***5900.10*** *p160*
Crowley, John; Vermont, 1850-1927 ***5900.10*** *p125*
Crowley, John D. 10 months; Vermont, 1855 ***5900.10*** *p108*
Crowley, John J.; Vermont, 1853-1933 ***5900.10*** *p191*
Crowley, John P.; Vermont, 1843-1918 ***5900.10*** *p420*
Crowley, Julia C.; Vermont, 1854-1939 ***5900.10*** *p185*
Crowley, Julia Collins; Vermont, 1875-1930 ***5900.10*** *p192*
Crowley, Margaret; Vermont, 1850-1925 ***5900.10*** *p137*
Crowley, Margaret; Vermont, 1860-1951 ***5900.10*** *p120*
Crowley, Margaret A. Dower; Vermont, 1848-1923 ***5900.10*** *p452*
Crowley, Margaret DeCoursey 51; Vermont, 1915 ***5900.10*** *p126*
Crowley, Margaret Fitzgerald 72; Vermont, 1904 ***5900.10*** *p126*
Crowley, Margaret McCormick 22; Vermont, 1861 ***5900.10*** *p254*
Crowley, Mary; Vermont, 1834-1896 ***5900.10*** *p588*
Crowley, Mary; Vermont, 1837-1911 ***5900.10*** *p339*
Crowley, Mary; Vermont, 1840-1906 ***5900.10*** *p565*
Crowley, Mary 74; Vermont, 1907 ***5900.10*** *p310*
Crowley, Mary 95; Vermont, 1879 ***5900.10*** *p585*
Crowley, Mary A.; Vermont, 1860-1877 ***5900.10*** *p543*
Crowley, Mary A. Marlow 26; Vermont, 1878 ***5900.10*** *p202*
Crowley, Mary Coursey; Vermont, 1814-1893 ***5900.10*** *p543*
Crowley, Mary Mulcahy; Vermont, 1818-1907 ***5900.10*** *p160*
Crowley, Mary Sullivan 42; Vermont, 1871 ***5900.10*** *p575*
Crowley, Mary White; Vermont, 1834-1906 ***5900.10*** *p274*
Crowley, Matthew; Vermont, 1851-1919 ***5900.10*** *p253*
Crowley, Micah 8; Vermont, 1871 ***5900.10*** *p108*
Crowley, Michael; Vermont, 1829-1889 ***5900.10*** *p566*
Crowley, Michael; Vermont, 1858-1920 ***5900.10*** *p160*
Crowley, Michael 69; Vermont, 1884 ***5900.10*** *p126*
Crowley, Michael E. 64; Vermont, 1931 ***5900.10*** *p126*
Crowley, Mikie 1; Vermont, 1863 ***5900.10*** *p126*
Crowley, Patrick; Vermont, 1830-1911 ***5900.10*** *p274*
Crowley, Patrick; Vermont, 1847-1944 ***5900.10*** *p443*
Crowley, Peter 68; Vermont, 1894 ***5900.10*** *p475*
Crowley, Robert; New York, 1838 ***8197.10*** *p220*
Crowley, Rosalie; Vermont, 1857-1939 ***5900.10*** *p253*
Crowley, Thomas; Vermont, 1863-1882 ***5900.10*** *p160*
Crowley, Timothy; Vermont, 1846-1868 ***5900.10*** *p421*
Crowley, Timothy; Vermont, 1846-1902 ***5900.10*** *p160*
Crowley, Timothy 39; Ontario, 1871 ***1823.15*** *p54*
Crowley, Timothy 75; Vermont, 1873 ***5900.10*** *p202*
Crowley, W. W. 51; Alaska, 1918 ***9196.1*** *p54*
Crowley, W. W. 51; Whitehorse, Yukon, 1918 ***9196.1*** *p54*
Crowley, William P. 26; Vermont, 1890 ***5900.10*** *p251*
Crowly, John 27; Ontario, 1871 ***1823.15*** *p54*
Crown, Anthony; New York, 1838 ***8197.10*** *p113*
Crown, Henry 43; Maryland, 1774 ***1220.25*** *p52*
Crown, John; New York, 1803 ***8197.10*** *p11*
Crowne, David; Maryland, 1649 ***2524.55*** *p60*
Crowningshield, Johanna 60; Vermont, 1891 ***5900.10*** *p112*
Crowston, William 26; Ontario, 1871 ***1823.15*** *p54*
Crowter, J. E. 14; Ontario, 1861 ***2896.25*** *p54*
Crowter, James H. 4; Ontario, 1861 ***2896.25*** *p54*
Crowter, Jane 7; Ontario, 1861 ***2896.25*** *p54*
Crowter, Peter E. 12; Ontario, 1861 ***2896.25*** *p54*
Crowter, S. A. 32; Ontario, 1861 ***2896.25*** *p54*
Crowther, Richard; New York, 1838 ***8197.10*** *p220*
Crowther, William; New York, 1838 ***8197.10*** *p220*
Crowther, William; New York, 1840 ***8197.10*** *p159*
Croxford, Henry 29; Ontario, 1871 ***1823.22*** *p36*
Croxford, Joseph 23; Virginia, 1774 ***1220.25*** *p90*
Croydon, Glanville Henry; New York, 1840 ***8197.10*** *p221*
Crozer, Robert; Pennsylvania, 1784 ***4629.10*** *p44*
Crozier, Agnes Ann 67; Ontario, 1871 ***1823.22*** *p36*
Crozier, Andrew 44; Ontario, 1871 ***1823.28*** *p20*
Crozier, Christopher 37; Ontario, 1871 ***1823.28*** *p20*
Crozier, Christopher 75; Ontario, 1871 ***1823.28*** *p20*
Crozier, Hugh 40; Ontario, 1871 ***1823.22*** *p37*
Crozier, John 41; Ontario, 1871 ***1823.15*** *p54*
Crozier, M. Jane; Ontario, 1871 ***1823.22*** *p37*
Crozier, Margt 40; Ontario, 1871 ***1823.28*** *p20*
Crozier, Octave 50; Ontario, 1871 ***1823.28*** *p20*
Crozier, Roland 30; Ontario, 1871 ***1823.28*** *p20*
Crozier, Samuel; New York, New York, 1801 ***1224.3*** *p18*
Crozier, William 29; Ontario, 1871 ***1823.15*** *p54*
Crozier, William 50; Ontario, 1871 ***1823.15*** *p54*
Cruce, Richard; Maryland, 1680 ***2524.55*** *p60*
Cruckshank, Thomas 44; Ontario, 1871 ***1823.15*** *p54*
Cruden, Miss; Quebec, 1856 ***9196.15*** *p7*
Cruden, Alexander; Virginia, n.d. ***1224.2*** *p29*
Cruer, Francis 17; Ontario, 1871 ***1823.28*** *p20*
Cruer, John 41; Ontario, 1871 ***1823.28*** *p20*
Cruer, Mary 13; Ontario, 1871 ***1823.28*** *p20*
Cruer, William 56; Ontario, 1871 ***1823.28*** *p20*
Cruger, Catharine; New York, New York, 1840 ***1224.3*** *p18*
Cruger, Henry; New York, New York, n.d. ***1224.2*** *p29*
Cruger, John; New York, 1825 ***1224.3*** *p18*
Cruger, John 50; Ontario, 1871 ***1823.28*** *p20*
Cruger, Nicholas; New York, New York, 1805 ***1224.3*** *p18*
Cruickshank, James; St. Vincent, 1817 ***1640.13*** *p26*
Cruikshank, Charles 36; Ontario, 1871 ***1823.15*** *p54*
Cruikshank, William 57; Ontario, 1871 ***1823.22*** *p37*
Cruikshanks, Wm 21; Ontario, 1861 ***2896.25*** *p9*

Cruise, Patrick; New York, 1836 ***8197.10*** *p79*
Cruise, Patrick Russel; New York, 1830 ***8197.10*** *p218*
Crumbauer, Anna Christina; Port uncertain, 1752 ***2856.30*** *p71*
Crumbie, Robert; Pennsylvania, 1777 ***4629.10*** *p14*
Crumby, David 65; Ontario, 1871 ***1823.22*** *p37*
Crumlisk, John; New York, 1833-1838 ***8197.10*** *p311*
Crummel, William 40; Ontario, 1871 ***1823.15*** *p54*
Crummenauer, Nickel; Port uncertain, 1766 ***2856.30*** *p71*
Crummey, Michael; New York, 1838 ***8197.10*** *p376*
Crummey, Thomas; New York, 1840 ***8197.10*** *p385*
Crump, Elizabeth *SEE* Crump, William
Crump, Elizabeth; Maryland, 1672 ***2524.55*** *p60*
Crump, Francis *SEE* Crump, William
Crump, Francis Robert; New York, 1840 ***8197.10*** *p162*
Crump, John *SEE* Crump, William
Crump, John; Maryland, 1672 ***2524.55*** *p60*
Crump, William *SEE* Crump, William
Crump, William; Maryland, 1664 ***2524.55*** *p60*
Child: William
Child: Francis
Child: Elizabeth
Child: John
Crumpe, Anto; Virginia, 1664 ***6212.30*** *p9*
Crumpe, Mary; Virginia, 1656 ***1224.1*** *p27*
Crumpler, Daniel 26; Maryland, 1775 ***1220.25*** *p106*
Crumpton, Robert; Virginia, 1665 ***6212.30*** *p17*
Crunedge, Henry 18; Maryland, 1774 ***1220.25*** *p60*
Cruse, Edward 67; Vermont, 1913 ***5900.10*** *p596*
Cruse, Margaret Riley B. 82; Vermont, 1932 ***5900.10*** *p596*
Cruse, Robert 35; Maryland, 1774 ***1220.25*** *p70*
Crusius, Anna Maria; Port uncertain, 1751 ***2856.30*** *p71*
Crusius, Maria Sophia; Port uncertain, 1793 ***2856.30*** *p71*
Cruso, Henry B. 36; Ontario, 1871 ***1823.22*** *p37*
Cruso, Michael D. 69; Ontario, 1871 ***1823.22*** *p37*
Cruss, William 35; Ontario, 1871 ***1823.15*** *p55*
Crut, John 36; Maryland, 1775 ***1220.25*** *p99*
Crutchfield, John; Pensacola, Florida, 1766 ***1224.2*** *p29*
Crutchill, Samuel; Maryland, 1669 ***2524.55*** *p60*
Cruter, Agnes 23; Ontario, 1861 ***2896.25*** *p33*
Cruter, E. J. 3; Ontario, 1861 ***2896.25*** *p33*
Cruter, G. E. 1; Ontario, 1861 ***2896.25*** *p33*
Crux, Thomas; New York, 1829 ***8197.10*** *p218*
Cryer, George 30; Ontario, 1871 ***1823.22*** *p37*
Cryson, Albert 1; Ontario, 1861 ***2896.26*** *p35*
Cryson, Catherine 29; Ontario, 1861 ***2896.26*** *p35*
Cryson, Rocksy 6; Ontario, 1861 ***2896.26*** *p35*
Crystal, Andrew; Ontario, 1885 ***1640.13*** *p26*
Crystal, Christina 58; Ontario, 1871 ***1823.15*** *p55*
Cryz, Anthony; Maryland, 1910 ***3259.35*** *p10*
Csary, Robert 50; Ontario, 1871 ***1823.15*** *p55*
Ctisp, Nicholas; Maryland, 1675 ***2524.55*** *p60*
Cubb, The; Virginia, 1668-1669 ***6212.30*** *p40*
Cubitt, Robert; Virginia, 1675 ***1224.1*** *p16*
Cubler, Jacob; Virginia, 1775 ***1220.25*** *p123*
Cudbord, Leonard; Maryland, 1655 ***2524.55*** *p60*
Cuddie, Jean; Philadelphia, 1831 ***1640.13*** *p26*
Cuddy, Margret 50; Ontario, 1871 ***1823.28*** *p20*
Cuddy, Michael 24; Ontario, 1871 ***1823.28*** *p20*
Cudlipp, David; New York, 1824 ***8197.10*** *p217*
Cudlipp, David; New York, 1827 ***8197.10*** *p340*
Cudlipp, Eliza 21; Ontario, 1861 ***2896.28*** *p32*
Cudlipp, Jonathan; New York, 1849 ***1224.3*** *p18*
Cudlipp, Joseph; New York, 1820 ***8197.10*** *p221*
Cudlipp, Mary 56; Ontario, 1861 ***2896.28*** *p38*
Cudlipp, Priccilla 23; Ontario, 1861 ***2896.28*** *p38*
Cudmore, Annie; Vermont, 1843-1908 ***5900.10*** *p466*
Cudmore, Emma Jane 1; Ontario, 1871 ***1823.15*** *p55*
Cudmore, George 32; Ontario, 1871 ***1823.15*** *p55*
Cudmore, Grace 60; Ontario, 1871 ***1823.15*** *p55*
Cudmore, Henry 14; Ontario, 1871 ***1823.15*** *p55*
Cudmore, John 26; Ontario, 1871 ***1823.15*** *p55*
Cudmore, John 61; Ontario, 1871 ***1823.15*** *p55*
Cudmore, Mary Ellen 3; Ontario, 1871 ***1823.15*** *p55*
Cudmore, Mary Jane 27; Ontario, 1871 ***1823.15*** *p55*
Cudmore, Sarah 20; Ontario, 1871 ***1823.15*** *p55*
Cudmore, Susan 18; Ontario, 1871 ***1823.15*** *p55*
Cudmore, Thomas 35; Ontario, 1871 ***1823.15*** *p55*
Cudmore, William 36; Ontario, 1871 ***1823.15*** *p55*
Cuendet, Eugene; New York, 1835 ***8197.10*** *p317*
Cuendet, Eugene; New York, 1838 ***8197.10*** *p113*
Cuesla, Stephen 36; Ontario, 1871 ***1823.28*** *p20*
Cufe, Hans Georg; Port uncertain, 1774 ***2856.30*** *p71*
Cuff, Ann 48; Ontario, 1871 ***1823.22*** *p37*
Cuff, Anthony M. 27; Ontario, 1871 ***1823.22*** *p37*
Cuff, John; New York, 1840 ***8197.10*** *p162*
Cuff, William 57; Ontario, 1871 ***1823.22*** *p37*
Cuffe, Thomas; Virginia, 1679-1680 ***6212.30*** *p54*
Cuhlmann, Maria Elisabeth; America, 1764 ***2856.30*** *p71*
Cuiltis, Richard 41; Ontario, 1871 ***1823.15*** *p55*
Culas, Anthony 60; Ontario, 1871 ***1823.28*** *p20*
Culbert, Ellinor 21; Ontario, 1871 ***1823.15*** *p55*
Culbert, John; New York, 1828 ***8197.10*** *p349*
Culbert, Thomas 47; Ontario, 1871 ***1823.15*** *p55*
Culbertson, James; Pennsylvania, 1779 ***4629.10*** *p40*
Culbertson, John; Pennsylvania, 1838 ***6058.10*** *p14*
Culbertson, Thomas 38; Ontario, 1871 ***1823.28*** *p20*
Culhane, Daniel 28; Ontario, 1871 ***1823.28*** *p20*
Culhane, Daniel 50; Ontario, 1871 ***1823.28*** *p20*
Culhane, Daniel, Sr. 60; Ontario, 1871 ***1823.28*** *p20*
Culhane, Dan'l 60; Ontario, 1871 ***1823.28*** *p20*
Culhane, John 60; Ontario, 1871 ***1823.28*** *p20*
Culin, Louis A.; New York, 1840 ***8197.10*** *p160*
Culiver, Annie 1; Ontario, 1861 ***2896.27*** *p10*
Culiver, Franky 1; Ontario, 1861 ***2896.27*** *p8*
Culiver, George 26; Ontario, 1861 ***2896.27*** *p8*
Culiver, Jo; Ontario, 1861 ***2896.27*** *p9*
Culiver, Joseph 3; Ontario, 1861 ***2896.27*** *p8*
Culiver, Josepha 27; Ontario, 1861 ***2896.27*** *p8*
Culiver, Josepha 71; Ontario, 1861 ***2896.27*** *p8*
Culiver, M. 4; Ontario, 1861 ***2896.27*** *p10*
Culiver, M. J. 7; Ontario, 1861 ***2896.27*** *p10*
Culiver, Thomas 40; Ontario, 1861 ***2896.27*** *p8*
Culiver, Thomas 69; Ontario, 1861 ***2896.27*** *p8*
Culiver, William 6; Ontario, 1861 ***2896.27*** *p10*
Culiver, William 30; Ontario, 1861 ***2896.27*** *p10*
Culkeen, James 55; Ontario, 1871 ***1823.22*** *p37*
Culkins, Bridget; Vermont, 1875 ***5900.10*** *p269*
Culkins, Hannah; Vermont, 1900 ***5900.10*** *p269*
Culkins, Lovina; Vermont, 1907 ***5900.10*** *p269*
Culkins, Mary; Vermont, 1826-1905 ***5900.10*** *p255*
Culkins, Sophia; Vermont, 1885 ***5900.10*** *p269*
Cull, Caleb 42; Ontario, 1871 ***1823.15*** *p55*
Cull, John 35; Ontario, 1871 ***1823.28*** *p20*
Cull, John 68; Ontario, 1871 ***1823.28*** *p20*
Cull, Michael 33; Ontario, 1871 ***1823.28*** *p20*
Cull, Thomas 27; Ontario, 1871 ***1823.28*** *p20*
Cull, William 32; Ontario, 1871 ***1823.28*** *p20*
Cullen, Alexander 27; Ontario, 1871 ***1823.22*** *p37*
Cullen, Anna Ravey; Vermont, 1857-1933 ***5900.10*** *p407*
Cullen, Daniel; New York, 1840 ***8197.10*** *p161*
Cullen, David 31; Ontario, 1871 ***1823.15*** *p55*
Cullen, Edward; Vermont, 1854-1917 ***5900.10*** *p407*
Cullen, Elizabeth; Vermont, 1831-1907 ***5900.10*** *p333*
Cullen, Ellen; Vermont, 1830-1890 ***5900.10*** *p92*
Cullen, Geo; Virginia, 1664 ***6212.30*** *p7*
Cullen, Isabella; Jamaica, 1834 ***1640.13*** *p26*
Cullen, James; Maryland, 1660 ***2524.55*** *p60*
Cullen, James; Maryland, 1681 ***2524.55*** *p60*
Cullen, James 8; Vermont, 1861 ***5900.10*** *p529*
Cullen, Joanna 69; Vermont, 1908 ***5900.10*** *p146*
Cullen, John; New York, 1838 ***8197.10*** *p113*
Cullen, John; New York, New York, 1854 ***6058.10*** *p75*
Cullen, John; Vermont, 1880 ***5900.10*** *p331*
Cullen, John 42; Ontario, 1871 ***1823.22*** *p37*
Cullen, Katherine; Vermont, n.d. ***5900.10*** *p529*
Cullen, Mary 77; Vermont, 1907 ***5900.10*** *p331*
Cullen, Patrick; New York, New York, 1847 ***6058.10*** *p75*
Cullen, Patrick 83; Vermont, 1904 ***5900.10*** *p529*
Cullen, Patrick J. 27; Vermont, 1883 ***5900.10*** *p469*
Cullen, Tho; Virginia, 1672 ***6212.30*** *p51*
Cullenar, William; Maryland, 1669 ***2524.55*** *p60*
Cullender, Mr.; Quebec, 1856 ***9196.15*** *p7*
Cullens, Peter; New York, 1803 ***8197.10*** *p11*
Culler, Isaac; Virginia, 1668-1669 ***6212.30*** *p40*
Cullerton, John 60; Ontario, 1871 ***1823.22*** *p37*
Culliford, Robert; Virginia, 1666-1667 ***6212.30*** *p32*
Culligan, Betsey; Vermont, 1828-1917 ***5900.10*** *p412*
Culligan, John; Vermont, 1854-1944 ***5900.10*** *p408*
Culligan, Maria; Vermont, 1858-1940 ***5900.10*** *p552*
Culligan, Mary; Vermont, 1841-1918 ***5900.10*** *p407*
Culligan, Michael 17; Ontario, 1871 ***1823.28*** *p21*
Culligan, Patrick 40; Ontario, 1871 ***1823.28*** *p21*
Culligan, Peter; Vermont, 1829-1894 ***5900.10*** *p412*
Culligan, Winifred; Vermont, 1859-1954 ***5900.10*** *p408*
Cullin, Geo; Virginia, 1668-1669 ***6212.30*** *p41*
Cullin, Jeremiah; Pennsylvania, 1777 ***4629.10*** *p11*
Cullinan, Bridget; Vermont, 1850-1910 ***5900.10*** *p93*
Cullinan, Bridget Mann; Vermont, 1851-1934 ***5900.10*** *p44*
Cullinan, Bridget Nash; Vermont, 1846-1926 ***5900.10*** *p44*
Cullinan, Catherine Hand; Vermont, 1869-1909 ***5900.10*** *p44*
Cullinan, Edmond; Vermont, 1826-1887 ***5900.10*** *p42*
Cullinan, Ellen Morrissey; Vermont, 1832-1887 ***5900.10*** *p42*
Cullinan, Johanna; Vermont, 1845-1913 ***5900.10*** *p45*
Cullinan, Julia; Vermont, 1851-1934 ***5900.10*** *p44*
Cullinan, Margaret; Vermont, 1851-1906 ***5900.10*** *p43*
Cullinan, Margaret 92; Vermont, 1911 ***5900.10*** *p99*
Cullinan, Margaret Hanley; Vermont, 1868-1926 ***5900.10*** *p46*
Cullinan, Margaret Whalen; Vermont, 1820-1902 ***5900.10*** *p44*
Cullinan, Mary; Vermont, 1822-1900 ***5900.10*** *p44*
Cullinan, Mary; Vermont, 1831-1889 ***5900.10*** *p43*
Cullinan, Mary 80; Vermont, 1899 ***5900.10*** *p204*
Cullinan, Mary Hays; Vermont, 1852-1918 ***5900.10*** *p42*
Cullinan, Patrick; Vermont, 1850-1915 ***5900.10*** *p46*
Cullinan, Patrick; Vermont, 1850-1921 ***5900.10*** *p44*
Cullinan, Patrick 83; Vermont, 1893 ***5900.10*** *p99*
Cullinan, Philip; Vermont, 1816-1882 ***5900.10*** *p44*
Cullinan, Philip C.; Vermont, 1850-1921 ***5900.10*** *p44*
Cullinan, Philip E.; Vermont, 1853-1904 ***5900.10*** *p42*
Cullinan, Thomas; Vermont, 1820-1898 ***5900.10*** *p44*
Cullinan, Thomas; Vermont, 1842-1913 ***5900.10*** *p44*
Cullinan, Thomas; Vermont, 1872-1946 ***5900.10*** *p44*
Cullingford, John 70; Ontario, 1871 ***1823.22*** *p37*
Cullion, Daniel; Vermont, 1820-1899 ***5900.10*** *p78*
Cullion, Mary Woods; Vermont, 1906 ***5900.10*** *p78*
Cullion, Roseay 77; Vermont, 1875 ***5900.10*** *p77*
Cullis, Elizabeth 58; Ontario, 1871 ***1823.22*** *p37*
Cullis, John 45; Ontario, 1871 ***1823.22*** *p37*
Cullis, John 49; Ontario, 1871 ***1823.15*** *p55*
Cullis, Richard 34; Ontario, 1871 ***1823.22*** *p37*
Cullis, Richard 48; Ontario, 1871 ***1823.28*** *p21*
Culliton, Anastasia O'Connell; Vermont, 1857-1929 ***5900.10*** *p84*
Culliton, M. 14; Ontario, 1861 ***2896.28*** *p1*
Culliton, Margaret O'Donnell; Vermont, 1847-1894 ***5900.10*** *p84*
Culliton, Mortimer; Vermont, 1848-1907 ***5900.10*** *p84*
Cullmann, Miss; America, 1764 ***2856.30*** *p338*
Cullmann, A. E.; America, 1738 ***2856.30*** *p128*
Cullmann, A. E.; America, 1739 ***2856.30*** *p128*
Cullmann, Anna Elisabeth; America, 1738 ***2856.30*** *p71*
With husband
Cullmann, Anna Elisabeth; America, 1739 ***2856.30*** *p71*
With husband
Cullmann, Burkhardt; America, 1764 ***2856.30*** *p71*
Cullmann, Catharina; Port uncertain, 1784 ***2856.30*** *p254*
Cullmann, Elis. Catharina; Port uncertain, 1774 ***2856.30*** *p71*
Cullmann, Johann; Port uncertain, 1784 ***2856.30*** *p254*
Cullmann, Johann Burkhard; America, 1764 ***2856.30*** *p71*
Cullmann, Johann Georg; Port uncertain, 1774 ***2856.30*** *p71*
Cullmann, Johann Nikol; America, 1756 ***2856.30*** *p71*
With wife & 4 children
Cullmann, Konrad; America, 1787 ***2856.30*** *p71*
Cullmann, Maria Christina; Port uncertain, 1775 ***2856.30*** *p71*
Cullmann, Maria Elisabeth; Port uncertain, 1738 ***2856.30*** *p71*
Cullmann, Maria Elisabeth; Port uncertain, 1739 ***2856.30*** *p71*
Cullmann, Maria Juliana; Port uncertain, 1741 ***2856.30*** *p71*
Cullmann, Maria Margarete; America, 1764 ***2856.30*** *p71*
With husband & 4 children
Cullmann, Peter; Port uncertain, 1784 ***2856.30*** *p255*
Cullmann, Sybille; Port uncertain, 1764 ***2856.30*** *p71*
Cully, Abraham; Virginia, 1694 ***1224.1*** *p16*
Cully, Thomas; New York, 1838 ***8197.10*** *p112*
Culmann, Eva Elisabeth; Port uncertain, 1745 ***2856.30*** *p72*
Culmann, Johann Friedric; Port uncertain, 1746 ***2856.30*** *p72*
Culmann, Maria Elisabeth; Port uncertain, 1746 ***2856.30*** *p72*
Culme, Benjamin; Virginia, 1666-1667 ***6212.30*** *p32*
Culpepper, Ja; Virginia, 1665-1666 ***6212.30*** *p22*
Culpepper, Ja; Virginia, 1666-1667 ***6212.30*** *p32*
Culpepper, Jno; Virginia, 1664 ***6212.30*** *p13*
Culpepper, Jno; Virginia, 1665-1666 ***6212.30*** *p22*
Culpepper, Tho; Virginia, 1664 ***6212.30*** *p12*
Culuris, J. 25; Alaska, 1917 ***9196.1*** *p47*
Culuris, J. 25; Whitehorse, Yukon, 1917 ***9196.1*** *p47*
Culver, Abraham 78; Ontario, 1871 ***1823.22*** *p37*
Culy, John 72; Ontario, 1871 ***1823.15*** *p55*
Cumar, Sebastian; Port uncertain, 1767 ***2856.30*** *p72*
Cumasky, Cornelius; New York, 1838 ***8197.10*** *p112*
Cumber, John 39; Ontario, 1871 ***1823.28*** *p21*
Cumberland, Elizabeth; New York, 1830 ***8197.10*** *p303*
Cumberland, William; New York, 1839 ***8197.10*** *p133*
Cuming, Elias 38; Ontario, 1871 ***1823.15*** *p55*
Cuming, Elias Williams 72; Ontario, 1871 ***1823.15*** *p55*
Cuming, George; New York, 1808 ***8197.10*** *p53*
Cuming, John 43; Ontario, 1871 ***1823.15*** *p55*
Cuming, Nicholas 33; Ontario, 1871 ***1823.15*** *p55*
Cuming, Robert; South Carolina, 1754 ***1224.2*** *p29*
Cumings, James; Pennsylvania, 1777 ***4629.10*** *p7*
Cumiskey, John; New York, 1836 ***8197.10*** *p319*
Cummeskey, John; New York, 1837 ***8197.10*** *p81*
Cummin, William 20; Ontario, 1861 ***2896.28*** *p42*

Cumming, Miss; Quebec, 1857 ***9196.15*** *p21*
Cumming, Miss; Quebec, 1858 ***9196.15*** *p36*
Cumming, Mr.; Quebec, 1858 ***9196.15*** *p34*
Cumming, Abel 77; Ontario, 1871 ***1823.22*** *p37*
Cumming, Alexander *SEE* Cumming, David
Cumming, Alexr 48; Ontario, 1871 ***1823.28*** *p21*
Cumming, Ann *SEE* Cumming, George S.
Cumming, Ann; Port uncertain, 1850-1859 ***4537.37*** *p110*
Cumming, Catherine *SEE* Cumming, David
Cumming, Charles 26; Maryland, 1775 ***1220.25*** *p111*
Cumming, Christine *SEE* Cumming, David
Cumming, Cuthburt 83; Ontario, 1871 ***1823.22*** *p37*
Cumming, Daniel; Georgia, 1698 ***1640.13*** *p26*
Cumming, Daniel 81; Ontario, 1871 ***1823.22*** *p37*
Cumming, David; Alabama, 1842-1845 ***1640.10*** *p35*
Wife: Janet
Daughter: Mary
Daughter: Christine
Son: James
Son: Ogan
Son: Alexander
Daughter: Catherine
Daughter: Janet
Cumming, Elizabeth 25; Ontario, 1871 ***1823.22*** *p37*
Cumming, Flora 99; Ontario, 1871 ***1823.22*** *p37*
Cumming, George S.; Alabama, 1816-1845 ***1640.10*** *p35*
Wife: Ann
Cumming, Isabella 21; Ontario, 1871 ***1823.22*** *p37*
Cumming, James *SEE* Cumming, David
Cumming, James; Savannah, Georgia, 1820 ***1640.10*** *p35*
Cumming, James 29; Ontario, 1871 ***1823.15*** *p55*
Cumming, Janet *SEE* Cumming, David
Cumming, Jessie; Ontario, 1849 ***4537.37*** *p85*
Cumming, John; New York, 1840 ***8197.10*** *p159*
Cumming, John 57; Ontario, 1871 ***1823.15*** *p55*
Cumming, John 62; Ontario, 1871 ***1823.22*** *p37*
Cumming, Joseph; Grenada, 1786 ***1640.13*** *p26*
Cumming, Mary *SEE* Cumming, David
Cumming, Ogan *SEE* Cumming, David
Cumming, Robert 17; Ontario, 1871 ***1823.22*** *p37*
Cumming, Thomas; Georgia, 1699 ***1640.13*** *p26*
Cumming, William; Kingston, Jamaica, 1803 ***1640.13*** *p26*
Cumming, William; New York, 1834 ***8197.10*** *p219*
Cummings, . . .; Vermont, 1844-1925 ***5900.10*** *p379*
Cummings, Adelia; Vermont, 1844-1920 ***5900.10*** *p419*
Cummings, Alice Newan; Vermont, 1847-1888 ***5900.10*** *p379*
Cummings, Ann 67; Vermont, 1878 ***5900.10*** *p110*
Cummings, Anna; Vermont, 1858-1860 ***5900.10*** *p179*
Cummings, Annie; Vermont, 1837-1910 ***5900.10*** *p591*
Cummings, Archibald; Philadelphia, 1741 ***1224.2*** *p29*
Cummings, Bridget M. Price; Vermont, 1860-1921 ***5900.10*** *p353*
Cummings, Bridget Welsh; Vermont, 1855-1926 ***5900.10*** *p119*
Cummings, Catherine Powers; Vermont, 1816-1904 ***5900.10*** *p179*
Cummings, D. J. M. 7; Ontario, 1861 ***2896.28*** *p8*
Cummings, Donald 38; Ontario, 1871 ***1823.15*** *p55*
Cummings, Eliza A.; Vermont, 1861-1906 ***5900.10*** *p86*
Cummings, Elizabeth; Vermont, 1840-1907 ***5900.10*** *p430*
Cummings, Elizabeth Peach; Newburyport, Massachusetts, 1827 ***1224.3*** *p18*
Cummings, Elizabeth Powers; Vermont, 1848-1930 ***5900.10*** *p352*
Cummings, G. 10; Ontario, 1861 ***2896.28*** *p8*
Cummings, George; Pennsylvania, 1831 ***6058.10*** *p10*
Cummings, George 43; Ontario, 1871 ***1823.15*** *p55*
Cummings, Honora; Vermont, 1830-1911 ***5900.10*** *p90*
Cummings, Honora Moynihan 75; Vermont, 1898 ***5900.10*** *p104*
Cummings, Hugh; Vermont, 1877-1954 ***5900.10*** *p352*
Cummings, James; Vermont, 1840-1924 ***5900.10*** *p265*
Cummings, Johanna E.; Vermont, 1850-1896 ***5900.10*** *p179*
Cummings, John; New York, 1804 ***8197.10*** *p26*
Cummings, John; New York, 1827-1831 ***8197.10*** *p370*
Cummings, John; Pennsylvania, 1779 ***4629.10*** *p41*
Cummings, John 78; Vermont, 1886 ***5900.10*** *p265*
Cummings, M. 52; Ontario, 1861 ***2896.28*** *p8*
Cummings, Margaret; Vermont, 1849-1913 ***5900.10*** *p186*
Cummings, Margaret; Vermont, 1855-1932 ***5900.10*** *p256*
Cummings, Martin F.; Vermont, 1852-1909 ***5900.10*** *p352*
Cummings, Mary; Vermont, 1854-1927 ***5900.10*** *p90*
Cummings, Mary; Vermont, 1930-1999 ***5900.10*** *p254*
Cummings, Mary Cain; Vermont, 1815-1883 ***5900.10*** *p379*
Cummings, Mary Hughes; Vermont, 1810-1906 ***5900.10*** *p265*
Cummings, Mary Salome; Vermont, 1843-1914 ***5900.10*** *p135*
Cummings, Mary Walsh; Vermont, 1860-1931 ***5900.10*** *p421*
Cummings, Michael; Vermont, 1810-1882 ***5900.10*** *p379*
Cummings, Patrick; New York, 1840 ***8197.10*** *p159*
Cummings, Patrick; Vermont, 1850-1902 ***5900.10*** *p119*
Cummings, Peter; Vermont, 1837-1886 ***5900.10*** *p430*
Cummings, R. 16; Ontario, 1861 ***2896.28*** *p8*
Cummings, R. M. 18; Ontario, 1861 ***2896.25*** *p44*
Cummings, Samuel 40; Ontario, 1861 ***2896.28*** *p55*
Cummings, Susan T. G. 28; Vermont, 1884 ***5900.10*** *p597*
Cummings, Thomas; Vermont, 1814-1886 ***5900.10*** *p179*
Cummings, Thomas; Vermont, 1853-1947 ***5900.10*** *p421*
Cummings, Thomas; Vermont, 1872-1931 ***5900.10*** *p352*
Cummings, Thomas 41; Vermont, 1871 ***5900.10*** *p110*
Cummings, Thomas 50; Ontario, 1871 ***1823.22*** *p37*
Cummings, William; Vermont, 1905 ***5900.10*** *p110*
Cummings, William 14; Vermont, 1867 ***5900.10*** *p265*
Cummings, Wm 64; Ontario, 1871 ***1823.15*** *p55*
Cummins, Adeline; Vermont, 1809-1888 ***5900.10*** *p145*
Cummins, Catherine 6; Ontario, 1861 ***2896.28*** *p45*
Cummins, Celia 12; Ontario, 1861 ***2896.28*** *p45*
Cummins, Hugh; New York, 1832 ***8197.10*** *p219*
Cummins, James 34; Ontario, 1861 ***2896.28*** *p45*
Cummins, James 63; Ontario, 1871 ***1823.15*** *p55*
Cummins, James 67; Ontario, 1871 ***1823.22*** *p37*
Cummins, John 31; New York, 1819-1827 ***8197.10*** *p307*
Cummins, John 42; Ontario, 1871 ***1823.22*** *p37*
Cummins, Margaret; Vermont, 1860-1938 ***5900.10*** *p166*
Cummins, Mary 10; Ontario, 1861 ***2896.28*** *p45*
Cummins, Patrick; New York, 1828 ***8197.10*** *p350*
Cummins, Patrick; New York, 1840 ***8197.10*** *p159*
Cummins, Sarah 8; Ontario, 1861 ***2896.28*** *p45*
Cummins, Sarah 39; Ontario, 1861 ***2896.28*** *p45*
Cummisky, Patrick; New York, 1840 ***8197.10*** *p384*
Cummuskey, Margaret; Vermont, 1857-1888 ***5900.10*** *p509*
Cumusky, Cornelius; New York, 1838 ***8197.10*** *p112*
Cunaughan, James; New York, 1826 ***8197.10*** *p219*
Cundy, William; Texas, 1852 ***1224.3*** *p18*
Cunell, Edward 42; Ontario, 1871 ***1823.15*** *p55*
Cunell, George 45; Ontario, 1871 ***1823.15*** *p55*
Cuner, Mrs. Johann; Port uncertain, 1784 ***2856.30*** *p72*
Cuningham, Gustavus; Pennsylvania, 1787 ***4629.10*** *p50*
Cuningham, Hugh 49; Ontario, 1871 ***1823.15*** *p55*
Cuninghame, William; New York, New York, 1789 ***1224.2*** *p29*
Cuningsby, Sara; Virginia, 1666-1667 ***6212.30*** *p34*
Cunior, William 50; Ontario, 1871 ***1823.15*** *p55*
Cunius, Anna Martha; Port uncertain, 1734 ***2856.30*** *p72*
Cunliffe, Esther 28; Maryland, 1775 ***1220.25*** *p112*
Cunliffe, J. W. 22; Virginia, 1775 ***1220.25*** *p95*
Cunliffe, John 27; New York, 1774 ***1220.25*** *p25*
Cunneen, John; New York, 1827 ***8197.10*** *p218*
Cunnell, Honor; Maryland, 1681 ***2524.55*** *p60*
Cunnick, Robert 21; America, 1774 ***1220.25*** *p35*
Cunning, David; Pennsylvania, 1777 ***4629.10*** *p24*
Cunningham, Miss; Quebec, 1857 ***9196.15*** *p16*
Cunningham, Mr.; Quebec, 1857 ***9196.15*** *p20*
Cunningham, Mr.; Quebec, 1858 ***9196.15*** *p36*
Cunningham, Mr.; Quebec, 1858 ***9196.15*** *p42*
Cunningham, Abagail 12; Ontario, 1861 ***2896.27*** *p50*
Cunningham, Alexander; Georgia, 1698 ***1640.13*** *p26*
Cunningham, Alexander; New York, 1892 ***1640.13*** *p26*
Cunningham, Andrew; Maryland, 1663 ***2524.55*** *p60*
Cunningham, Ann 12; Ontario, 1861 ***2896.27*** *p21*
Cunningham, Ann 38; Vermont, 1874 ***5900.10*** *p210*
Cunningham, Ann 60; Ontario, 1871 ***1823.28*** *p21*
Cunningham, Annie; Vermont, 1835-1906 ***5900.10*** *p590*
Cunningham, Bridget; Vermont, n.d. ***5900.10*** *p415*
Cunningham, Bridget 59; Vermont, 1882 ***5900.10*** *p102*
Cunningham, Bridget Igoe; Vermont, 1837-1912 ***5900.10*** *p217*
Cunningham, Bridget McKenney 89; Vermont, 1886 ***5900.10*** *p474*
Cunningham, Catherine 1; Vermont, 1858 ***5900.10*** *p101*
Cunningham, Catherine 20; Ontario, 1861 ***2896.25*** *p38*
Cunningham, Charles; Alabama, 1826 ***1224.3*** *p18*
Cunningham, Charles 7; Ontario, 1861 ***2896.27*** *p21*
Cunningham, Charles A. 8; Ontario, 1861 ***2896.27*** *p50*
Cunningham, Chas 38; Ontario, 1861 ***2896.25*** *p58*
Cunningham, Conrad 1; Ontario, 1861 ***2896.25*** *p58*
Cunningham, Cynthis 23; Ontario, 1861 ***2896.25*** *p58*
Cunningham, Daniel; New York, 1837 ***8197.10*** *p79*
Cunningham, Daniel 18; Ontario, 1861 ***2896.27*** *p21*
Cunningham, Darby; Maryland, 1664 ***2524.55*** *p197*
Cunningham, David; Savannah, Georgia, 1757 ***1640.10*** *p35*
Cunningham, Deby 2; Ontario, 1861 ***2896.25*** *p59*
Cunningham, Delila J. 7; Ontario, 1861 ***2896.27*** *p50*
Cunningham, Elias 14; Ontario, 1861 ***2896.27*** *p50*
Cunningham, Eliza 8; Ontario, 1861 ***2896.25*** *p38*
Cunningham, Elizabeth 56; Ontario, 1871 ***1823.22*** *p37*
Cunningham, Elizabeth 65; Vermont, 1875 ***5900.10*** *p385*
Cunningham, Elizy 22; Ontario, 1861 ***2896.27*** *p49*
Cunningham, Elizy F. 4; Ontario, 1861 ***2896.27*** *p50*
Cunningham, Ella 42; Vermont, 1880 ***5900.10*** *p474*
Cunningham, Ellen; Vermont, 1812-1884 ***5900.10*** *p506*
Cunningham, Ellen; Vermont, 1829-1893 ***5900.10*** *p352*
Cunningham, Ellen 96; Vermont, 1926 ***5900.10*** *p197*
Cunningham, Ellen Lavell; Vermont, 1868-1936 ***5900.10*** *p132*
Cunningham, Elvira 13; Ontario, 1861 ***2896.25*** *p58*
Cunningham, Fanny 33; Ontario, 1861 ***2896.25*** *p58*
Cunningham, Frank M.; Vermont, 1855-1885 ***5900.10*** *p506*
Cunningham, George; Florida, 1772 ***1640.10*** *p35*
Cunningham, George; Ontario, 1866 ***1640.13*** *p26*
Cunningham, George 56; Ontario, 1871 ***1823.15*** *p55*
Cunningham, Hannah 49; Ontario, 1871 ***1823.15*** *p55*
Cunningham, Hannah M. 11; Ontario, 1861 ***2896.27*** *p50*
Cunningham, Helen D. 5; Ontario, 1861 ***2896.27*** *p50*
Cunningham, Hellen 9; Ontario, 1861 ***2896.25*** *p58*
Cunningham, Henry; Jamaica, 1730-1739 ***1640.13*** *p26*
Cunningham, Henry; St. Augustine, Florida, 1771 ***1640.10*** *p35*
Cunningham, Henry; St. Augustine, Florida, 1792 ***1640.13*** *p26*
Cunningham, Henry 1; Ontario, 1861 ***2896.25*** *p58*
Cunningham, Henry 1; Ontario, 1861 ***2896.27*** *p70*
Cunningham, Henry 3; Ontario, 1861 ***2896.27*** *p21*
Cunningham, Henry 4; Ontario, 1861 ***2896.25*** *p59*
Cunningham, Henry 25; Ontario, 1861 ***2896.25*** *p38*
Cunningham, Hester 8; Ontario, 1861 ***2896.25*** *p58*
Cunningham, Hester 43; Ontario, 1861 ***2896.25*** *p61*
Cunningham, Hugh 33; Vermont, 1858 ***5900.10*** *p101*
Cunningham, James; Florida, 1769 ***1224.2*** *p29*
Cunningham, James; New York, 1807 ***8197.10*** *p36*
Cunningham, James; New York, 1807 ***8197.10*** *p326*
Cunningham, James; New York, 1838 ***8197.10*** *p220*
Cunningham, James; New York, 1840 ***8197.10*** *p163*
Cunningham, James 62; Vermont, 1872 ***5900.10*** *p385*
Cunningham, Jane *SEE* Cunningham, Keith
Cunningham, Jane 18; Ontario, 1861 ***2896.25*** *p38*
Cunningham, Jessie; Port uncertain, 1860-1869 ***4537.35*** *p84*
Cunningham, John; Canada, 1756-1760 ***4628.40*** *p45*
Cunningham, John; New York, 1803 ***8197.10*** *p11*
Cunningham, John; New York, 1819 ***8197.10*** *p215*
Cunningham, John; New York, 1839 ***8197.10*** *p379*
Cunningham, John; Pennsylvania, 1777 ***4629.10*** *p19*
Cunningham, John; Vermont, 1826 ***5900.10*** *p13*
Cunningham, John; Vermont, 1853-1917 ***5900.10*** *p385*
Cunningham, John; Vermont, 1859-1917 ***5900.10*** *p334*
Cunningham, John 18; Vermont, 1837 ***5900.10*** *p610*
Cunningham, John 21; Ontario, 1861 ***2896.25*** *p38*
Cunningham, John 28; Ontario, 1871 ***1823.28*** *p21*
Cunningham, John 36; Ontario, 1871 ***1823.22*** *p38*
Cunningham, John 39; Ontario, 1871 ***1823.28*** *p21*
Cunningham, John 50; Ontario, 1871 ***1823.22*** *p38*
Cunningham, Joseph 9; Ontario, 1861 ***2896.27*** *p21*
Cunningham, Joshua 17; Ontario, 1861 ***2896.27*** *p21*
Cunningham, Kate; Vermont, 1849-1869 ***5900.10*** *p288*
Cunningham, Katherine; Vermont, 1843-1903 ***5900.10*** *p74*
Cunningham, Keith; Alabama, 1814-1845 ***1640.10*** *p35*
Wife: Jane
Cunningham, Louisa 12; Ontario, 1861 ***2896.25*** *p38*
Cunningham, Lydia 30; Ontario, 1861 ***2896.27*** *p21*
Cunningham, Margaret; Florida, 1772 ***1640.10*** *p35*
Cunningham, Margaret; Vermont, 1842-1900 ***5900.10*** *p216*
Cunningham, Margaret 11; Ontario, 1861 ***2896.25*** *p58*
Cunningham, Margaret B.; Vermont, 1864-1915 ***5900.10*** *p374*
Cunningham, Margaret McMahon; Vermont, 1870-1970 ***5900.10*** *p334*
Cunningham, Marion; Canada, 1860-1869 ***4537.35*** *p72*
Cunningham, Mary; Vermont, 1848-1926 ***5900.10*** *p387*
Cunningham, Mary 10; Ontario, 1861 ***2896.25*** *p58*
Cunningham, Mary 14; Ontario, 1861 ***2896.27*** *p21*
Cunningham, Mary 15; Ontario, 1861 ***2896.25*** *p38*
Cunningham, Mary 35; Ontario, 1861 ***2896.27*** *p55*
Cunningham, Mary 54; Vermont, 1870 ***5900.10*** *p451*
Cunningham, Mary J. Farrell; Vermont, 1854-1919 ***5900.10*** *p506*
Cunningham, Mary Mooney; Vermont, 1856-1931 ***5900.10*** *p352*
Cunningham, Mary Mylott; Vermont, 1844-1926 ***5900.10*** *p218*
Cunningham, Mathew 45; Ontario, 1871 ***1823.15*** *p55*

Cunningham, Michael; New York, 1831 8197.10 p355
Cunningham, Michael; New York, 1837 8197.10 p80
Cunningham, Michael; Vermont, 1833-1891 5900.10 p217
Cunningham, Michael; Vermont, 1835-1915 5900.10 p217
Cunningham, Michael; Vermont, 1858-1917 5900.10 p216
Cunningham, Michael 21; Vermont, 1855 5900.10 p603
Cunningham, Michael 30; Ontario, 1871 1823.28 p21
Cunningham, Michael 40; Ontario, 1871 1823.28 p21
Cunningham, Michael 58; Ontario, 1871 1823.22 p38
Cunningham, Miles; Vermont, 1855-1938 5900.10 p132
Cunningham, Nellie 18; Vermont, 1865 5900.10 p165
Cunningham, O. E.; Vermont, 1855-1934 5900.10 p384
Cunningham, Owen; New York, 1840 8197.10 p162
Cunningham, Owen; Vermont, 1800-1863 5900.10 p506
Cunningham, P.; Vermont, 1839-1904 5900.10 p118
Cunningham, Patrick; New York, 1840 8197.10 p161
Cunningham, Patrick; New York, 1840 8197.10 p221
Cunningham, Patrick; Vermont, 1842-1899 5900.10 p506
Cunningham, Patrick 54; Vermont, 1871 5900.10 p618
Cunningham, Patrick 55; Ontario, 1871 1823.28 p21
Cunningham, Patrick 60; Vermont, n.d. 5900.10 p102
Cunningham, Paul; Vermont, 1834-1904 5900.10 p352
Cunningham, Perlina 32; Ontario, 1861 2896.25 p58
Cunningham, Peter; New York, 1819 8197.10 p215
Cunningham, Phebe 49; Ontario, 1861 2896.25 p38
Cunningham, Phelix; New York, 1806 8197.10 p324
Cunningham, Phelix; New York, 1827 8197.10 p347
Cunningham, Philip; New York, 1834 8197.10 p70
Cunningham, R. 24; Ontario, 1861 2896.26 p4
Cunningham, Rachel 16; Ontario, 1861 2896.27 p50
Cunningham, Rebecca 24; Ontario, 1861 2896.27 p72
Cunningham, Rebecca 25; Ontario, 1861 2896.27 p50
Cunningham, Richard; New York, 1838 8197.10 p376
Cunningham, Robert; New York, 1836 8197.10 p79
Cunningham, Robert; Savannah, Georgia, 1804 1640.10 p36
Cunningham, Robert 14; Ontario, 1861 2896.27 p55
Cunningham, Robert 19; Ontario, 1861 2896.25 p61
Cunningham, Sarah 1; Ontario, 1861 2896.27 p50
Cunningham, Sarah 40; Vermont, 1867 5900.10 p210
Cunningham, Sarah 47; Ontario, 1861 2896.27 p49
Cunningham, Sarah 56; Ontario, 1861 2896.25 p54
Cunningham, Sarah 71; Ontario, 1861 2896.27 p50
Cunningham, Sarah E. 20; Ontario, 1861 2896.27 p49
Cunningham, Sarah E. 22; Ontario, 1861 2896.27 p21
Cunningham, Simon 31; Vermont, 1883 5900.10 p165
Cunningham, Stephen 60; Vermont, 1893 5900.10 p415
Cunningham, Tho; Virginia, 1672 6212.30 p50
Cunningham, Thomas; New York, 1821 8197.10 p216
Cunningham, Thomas; New York, 1834 8197.10 p373
Cunningham, Thomas; Pennsylvania, 1777 4629.10 p19
Cunningham, Thomas; Vermont, 1856-1878 5900.10 p470
Cunningham, Thomas 1; Ontario, 1861 2896.27 p21
Cunningham, Thomas 40; Vermont, 1880 5900.10 p469
Cunningham, Thos 34; Ontario, 1871 1823.28 p21
Cunningham, Timothy 34; Ontario, 1871 1823.28 p21
Cunningham, Vic 23; Ontario, 1861 2896.25 p38
Cunningham, Will; Pennsylvania, 1779 4629.10 p39
Cunningham, William; Bahamas, 1791 1224.2 p29
Cunningham, William; St. Augustine, Florida, n.d. 1224.2 p29
Cunningham, William; St. Augustine, Florida, 1735-1791 1640.10 p36
Cunningham, William 9 months; Vermont, 1855 5900.10 p603
Cunningham, William 2; Ontario, 1861 2896.25 p61
Cunningham, William 12; Ontario, 1861 2896.25 p58
Cunningham, William 42; Ontario, 1871 1823.15 p55
Cunningham, William 54; Ontario, 1871 1823.15 p55
Cunningham, William 60; Ontario, 1871 1823.28 p21
Cunningham, William W. 20; Ontario, 1861 2896.27 p21
Cunningham, Younges 50; Ontario, 1861 2896.27 p49
Cunnisby, William; Maryland, 1671 2524.55 p60
Cuntz, Anna Elizabeth; Port uncertain, 1791 2856.30 p72
Cuntz, Daniel; America, 1744 2856.30 p72
With wife & 3 children
Cuntz, Jacob 41; Ontario, 1871 1823.15 p55
Cuntz, Jakob; America, 1727 2856.30 p72
Cuntz, Jakob; America, 1729 2856.30 p72
Cuntz, Johann Theobald; Port uncertain, 1738 2856.30 p252
Cuntz, Ludwig; America, 1737 2856.30 p72
Cuntz, Maria Agnes; Port uncertain, 1756 2856.30 p72
Cuntz, Michael; Port uncertain, 1764 2856.30 p72
Cuntz, Philipp; America, 1740 2856.30 p72
Cuntz, Philipp; America, 1741 2856.30 p72
Cuntz, Philipp; Port uncertain, 1751 2856.30 p72
With wife & 8 children
Cuntz, Veltin; America, 1784 2856.30 p72
Cuntze, Johann Michael; America, 1739 2856.30 p72
Cuntzer, Jacob; America, 1739 2856.30 p72
Cuntzer, Michael; America, 1739 2856.30 p72
Cuny, Mrs. Blasii; Port uncertain, 1789 2856.30 p72
Cunz, Henrich; Port uncertain, 1750 2856.30 p72
Cunz, Johann Nickel; Port uncertain, 1750 2856.30 p72
Cunzin, Maria Elisabeth; Port uncertain, 1778 2856.30 p72
Cuor, Martin 44; Ontario, 1871 1823.28 p21
Cuorie, John 21; Ontario, 1871 1823.15 p56
Cup, William 40; Ontario, 1871 1823.15 p56
Cupman, John; Maryland, 1678 2524.55 p60
Wife: Sarah
Cupman, Sarah SEE Cupman, John
Cupor, John; Maryland, 1663 2524.55 p60
Curavoo, Joseph 77; Vermont, 1905 5900.10 p200
Curavoo, Margaret Mahoney 74; Vermont, 1904 5900.10 p200
Curby, Katharine; Maryland, 1681 2524.55 p60
Curchin, Abraham J.; New York, 1840 8197.10 p162
Curchin, Jacob; New York, 1840 8197.10 p161
Cure, Charles; Rappahannock, Virginia, 1734 1224.2 p29
Cure, Joseph; Maryland, 1668 2524.55 p60
Cure, Mary 19; Baltimore, 1775 1220.25 p119
Curl, John; New York, 1838 8197.10 p113
Curlane, Annie; Vermont, 1843-1894 5900.10 p220
Curle, Jno; Virginia, 1664 6212.30 p15
Curle, Robert 56; Ontario, 1871 1823.22 p38
Curlett, A. 38; Ontario, 1861 2896.28 p5
Curlett, E. 4; Ontario, 1861 2896.28 p5
Curlett, H. 16; Ontario, 1861 2896.28 p5
Curlett, J. 1; Ontario, 1861 2896.28 p5
Curlett, James 17; Ontario, 1861 2896.28 p2
Curlett, P. 14; Ontario, 1861 2896.28 p5
Curlett, T. 6; Ontario, 1861 2896.28 p5
Curley, Armina A. King; Vermont, 1844-1929 5900.10 p244
Curley, Biddy 5 SEE Curley, Margaret
Curley, Cathrine; Vermont, 1819-1883 5900.10 p604
Curley, Eliza; Vermont, 1817-1885 5900.10 p338
Curley, Hue 50; Ontario, 1871 1823.28 p21
Curley, Lawrence 63; Ontario, 1871 1823.28 p21
Curley, Margaret 30; New York, New York, 1849 1825.45 p31
Daughter: Biddy 5
Curley, Peter R.; Vermont, 1844-1900 5900.10 p244
Curlin, Frances; Virginia, 1671 6212.30 p43
Curling, Mr.; Quebec, 1857 9196.15 p22
Curling, R.; Quebec, 1857 9196.15 p22
Curling, Saunders; New York, 1838 8197.10 p113
Curnane, John 60; Ontario, 1871 1823.28 p21
Curney, John 66; Ontario, 1871 1823.22 p38
Curow, Thomas; New York, 1838 8197.10 p377
Curpisz, Michael; Maryland, 1910 3259.35 p10
Curr, William; New York, 1830 8197.10 p354
Curran, Mr.; Quebec, 1857 9196.15 p22
Curran, Ann M.; Vermont, 1829-1915 5900.10 p45
Curran, Bridget 76; Vermont, 1905 5900.10 p113
Curran, Catherine Coyne 55; Vermont, 1876 5900.10 p611
Curran, Charles; New York, 1821 8197.10 p216
Curran, Elizabeth 82; Vermont, 1916 5900.10 p541
Curran, Joseph; New York, 1838 8197.10 p311
Curran, Julia Barrett; Vermont, 1830-1908 5900.10 p287
Curran, Lucy; Buffalo, New York, 1851 1224.3 p19
Curran, Margaret; Vermont, 1836-1906 5900.10 p110
Curran, Martin; New York, 1838 8197.10 p220
Curran, Mary C.; Vermont, 1862 5900.10 p308
Curran, Mary Stephenson; Vermont, 1833-1941 5900.10 p447
Curran, Michael; Vermont, 1915 5900.10 p446
Curran, Patrick; New York, 1840 8197.10 p163
Curran, Patrick; Vermont, 1818-1905 5900.10 p287
Curran, Patrick; Vermont, 1824-1902 5900.10 p45
Curran, Robert 58; Ontario, 1871 1823.15 p56
Curran, Sarah; Vermont, 1834-1861 5900.10 p293
Currant, Nicholas; New York, 1807 8197.10 p36
Curre, Angus; New York, 1794 8197.10 p3
Curree, Mary; Maryland, 1682 2524.55 p60
Currey, James 42; Ontario, 1871 1823.15 p56
Currey, John; New York, 1807 8197.10 p327
Currey, Samuel; Pennsylvania, 1777 4629.10 p20
Currey, William 63; Ontario, 1871 1823.22 p38
Currey, William 66; Ontario, 1871 1823.15 p56
Currie, Major; Quebec, 1858 9196.15 p33
Currie, Agnes; Jamaica, 1850 1640.13 p27
Currie, Agnes; Jamaica, 1853 1640.13 p27
Currie, Alexander SEE Currie, Archie
Currie, Alexander; Curacao, 1728 1640.13 p27
Currie, Alexander; Jamaica, 1828 1640.13 p27
Currie, Alexander; Saskatchewan, 1883 4537.37 p90
Currie, Alexander; Savannah, Georgia, 1813 1640.10 p36
Currie, Alexander; Tobago, West Indies, 1828 1640.13 p27
Currie, Alexander; Port uncertain, 1850-1859 4537.37 p107
Wife: Mary
Child: Ann
Child: John
Child: Catherine
Child: Marion
Child: Angus
Child: Donald
Currie, Allan SEE Currie, Archie
Currie, Andrew 45; Ontario, 1871 1823.15 p56
Currie, Angus SEE Currie, Alexander
Currie, Angus SEE Currie, John Roy
Currie, Ann SEE Currie, Alexander
Currie, Ann SEE Currie, John Roy
Currie, Ann; Ontario, 1850-1859 4537.37 p40
Currie, Ann; Ontario, 1851 4537.32 p18
Currie, Ann 42; Ontario, 1871 1823.15 p56
Currie, Archibald; New York, 1807 8197.10 p36
Currie, Archie; Ontario, 1850-1859 4537.37 p34
Wife: Eliza MacEachan
Child: Allan
Child: Mary
Child: Simon
Child: Alexander
Child: Flora
Child: Marion
Child: Catherine
Child: John
Child: Donald
Currie, Archie; Ontario, 1851 4537.32 p8
Wife: Eliza MacEachan
Child: Mary
Child: Simon
Child: Alexander
Child: Marion
Child: Flora
Child: Marion
Child: Donald
Child: Catherine
Child: Allan
Child: John
Currie, Catherine SEE Currie, Alexander
Currie, Catherine SEE Currie, Archie
Currie, Catherine; Port uncertain, 1840-1849 4537.37 p112
Currie, Catherine; Port uncertain, 1850-1859 4537.37 p117
Currie, Catherine MacDonald SEE Currie, Ranald
Currie, Christopher 53; Ontario, 1871 1823.15 p56
Currie, Donald SEE Currie, Alexander
Currie, Donald SEE Currie, Archie
Currie, Donald SEE Currie, John Roy
Currie, Ebenezer; Pennsylvania, 1747 1224.2 p29
Currie, Eliza MacEachan SEE Currie, Archie
Currie, Flora SEE Currie, Archie
Currie, Flora SEE Currie, John Roy
Currie, Flora Gillies SEE Currie, John Roy
Currie, Flora Gillies; Ontario, 1851 4537.32 p8
Currie, Flora MacDonald SEE Currie, John Roy
Currie, Francis William; Ontario, 1896 1640.13 p27
Currie, George; New Orleans, 1829 1640.10 p36
Currie, Janet Smith; Ontario, 1851 4537.37 p35
Child: John
Child: Neil
Child: Mary
Currie, Jessie; Ontario, 1851 4537.32 p74
Currie, Jessie; Ontario, 1851 4537.37 p74
Currie, John SEE Currie, Alexander
Currie, John SEE Currie, Archie
Currie, John SEE Currie, Janet Smith
Currie, John SEE Currie, John Roy
Currie, John; Jamaica, 1747 1640.13 p27
Currie, John; New York, 1806 8197.10 p322
Currie, John; Savannah, Georgia, 1799 1640.10 p36
Currie, John 52; Ontario, 1871 1823.15 p56
Currie, John G.; New York, 1794 8197.10 p3
Currie, John Roy; Ontario, 1850-1859 4537.37 p35
Wife: Flora Gillies
Child: John
Child: Ann
Child: Donald
Currie, John Roy; Ontario, 1851 4537.32 p8
Wife: Flora MacDonald
Child: Ann
Child: Flora
Child: Mary
Child: Donald

Child: John
Child: Angus
Child: Kenneth
Currie, Kenneth *SEE* Currie, John Roy
Currie, Marg 60; Ontario, 1871 ***1823.15*** *p56*
Currie, Margaret 46; Ontario, 1871 ***1823.15*** *p56*
Currie, Marion *SEE* Currie, Alexander
Currie, Marion *SEE* Currie, Archie
Currie, Mary *SEE* Currie, Alexander
Currie, Mary *SEE* Currie, Archie
Currie, Mary *SEE* Currie, Janet Smith
Currie, Mary *SEE* Currie, John Roy
Currie, Mary; Ontario, 1840-1849 ***4537.37*** *p60*
Currie, Mary; Ontario, 1851 ***4537.32*** *p60*
Currie, Mary; Ontario, 1851 ***4537.37*** *p68*
Currie, Mary; Port uncertain, 1840-1849 ***4537.37*** *p125*
Currie, Mary; Port uncertain, 1850-1859 ***4537.37*** *p115*
Currie, Michael; New York, 1832 ***8197.10*** *p356*
Currie, Michael; New York, 1838 ***8197.10*** *p220*
Currie, Neil *SEE* Currie, Janet Smith
Currie, Patrick 30; Ontario, 1871 ***1823.15*** *p56*
Currie, Peggy; Port uncertain, 1840-1849 ***4537.37*** *p119*
Currie, Pete 50; Ontario, 1871 ***1823.15*** *p56*
Currie, Ranald; Port uncertain, 1840-1849 ***4537.37*** *p107*
Wife: Catherine MacDonald
Currie, Robert 41; Ontario, 1871 ***1823.15*** *p56*
Currie, Simon *SEE* Currie, Archie
Currie, William; New York, 1827 ***8197.10*** *p344*
Currier, Francis 28; Ontario, 1871 ***1823.28*** *p21*
Currin, John; Virginia, 1671 ***6212.30*** *p42*
Currin, Mary; Vermont, 1859-1894 ***5900.10*** *p132*
Currin, Mathew; Maryland, 1682 ***2524.55*** *p60*
Curror, Jno.; Maryland, 1680 ***2524.55*** *p60*
Curry, A.; Mississippi, 1781-1833 ***1640.10*** *p36*
Curry, Almira O'Dell; Vermont, 1843-1906 ***5900.10*** *p495*
Curry, Bridget Tivanan; Vermont, 1796-1880 ***5900.10*** *p45*
Curry, Catherine; Vermont, 1877-1879 ***5900.10*** *p560*
Curry, Catherine Coleman; Vermont, 1834-1864 ***5900.10*** *p560*
Curry, Christy 28; Ontario, 1861 ***2896.27*** *p3*
Curry, Dennis 60; Ontario, 1871 ***1823.15*** *p56*
Curry, Donald 46; Ontario, 1871 ***1823.15*** *p56*
Curry, Eleanor 79; Ontario, 1871 ***1823.15*** *p56*
Curry, Frances 40; Ontario, 1871 ***1823.28*** *p21*
Curry, George; Georgia, 1736 ***1640.10*** *p36*
Curry, George 32; Ontario, 1871 ***1823.15*** *p56*
Curry, Hector 71; Ontario, 1871 ***1823.22*** *p38*
Curry, Honora; Vermont, 1874-1949 ***5900.10*** *p117*
Curry, Isaac 38; Ontario, 1871 ***1823.15*** *p56*
Curry, James; Vermont, 1843-1920 ***5900.10*** *p495*
Curry, James 15; Maryland, 1774 ***1220.25*** *p61*
Curry, James 67; Ontario, 1871 ***1823.28*** *p21*
Curry, John; Pennsylvania, 1703 ***1224.2*** *p29*
Curry, John 45; Ontario, 1871 ***1823.28*** *p21*
Curry, John D.; Vermont, 1830-1913 ***5900.10*** *p560*
Curry, Lucret 5; Ontario, 1861 ***2896.27*** *p3*
Curry, M. A. 4; Ontario, 1861 ***2896.27*** *p3*
Curry, Margaret 64; Ontario, 1871 ***1823.15*** *p56*
Curry, Mary; Mississippi, 1788-1845 ***1640.10*** *p36*
Curry, Mary; Vermont, 1844-1913 ***5900.10*** *p400*
Curry, Mary 80; Ontario, 1871 ***1823.22*** *p38*
Curry, P. E. 2; Ontario, 1861 ***2896.27*** *p3*
Curry, Philip 43; Ontario, 1871 ***1823.15*** *p56*
Curry, Robert 57; Ontario, 1871 ***1823.15*** *p56*
Curry, Samuel; Boston, 1737 ***1224.2*** *p29*
Curry, Thomas; Maryland, 1674 ***2524.55*** *p60*
Curry, Thomas 62; Ontario, 1871 ***1823.22*** *p38*
Curry, Thomas 70; Ontario, 1871 ***1823.28*** *p21*
Curry, William; Maryland, 1676 ***2524.55*** *p60*
Curry, William 42; Ontario, 1871 ***1823.15*** *p56*
Curry, William 54; Ontario, 1871 ***1823.15*** *p56*
Curson, Richard; Baltimore, 1809 ***1224.3*** *p19*
Curtain, Morris 40; Ontario, 1871 ***1823.28*** *p21*
Curtain, Thomas 60; Ontario, 1871 ***1823.22*** *p38*
Curten, Catharine E. Murphy; Vermont, 1841-1865 ***5900.10*** *p480*
Curtes, Mary *SEE* Curtes, Robt.
Curtes, Robt.; Maryland, 1664 ***2524.55*** *p60*
Wife: Mary
Daughter: Mary
Curtin, Dennis; New York, 1838 ***8197.10*** *p320*
Curtin, James; Pennsylvania, 1777 ***4629.10*** *p22*
Curtin, John; New York, 1837 ***8197.10*** *p80*
Curtin, Mary; Vermont, 1855-1917 ***5900.10*** *p443*
Curtin, Patrick 60; Ontario, 1871 ***1823.28*** *p21*
Curtin, Thomas 44; Ontario, 1871 ***1823.15*** *p56*
Curtis, Mr.; Quebec, 1856 ***9196.15*** *p11*
Curtis, Mrs.; Quebec, 1856 ***9196.15*** *p11*
Curtis, Anna W.; Vermont, 1859-1936 ***5900.10*** *p183*
Curtis, Betsey; Halifax, Nova Scotia, 1851 ***1224.3*** *p19*
Curtis, Chester 23; Ontario, 1861 ***2896.25*** *p51*
Curtis, Daniel; Maryland, 1666 ***2524.55*** *p60*
Wife: Mary
Daughter: Elizabeth
Curtis, Elizabeth *SEE* Curtis, Daniel
Curtis, Febey 70; Ontario, 1871 ***1823.22*** *p38*
Curtis, Geo; Virginia, 1665-1666 ***6212.30*** *p21*
Curtis, George; Virginia, 1664 ***6212.30*** *p13*
Curtis, Henry; New York, 1839 ***8197.10*** *p132*
Curtis, Ida Margaret; Vermont, 1858-1895 ***5900.10*** *p133*
Curtis, James; New York, 1837 ***8197.10*** *p82*
Curtis, James 46; Ontario, 1871 ***1823.28*** *p21*
Curtis, Jno; Virginia, 1665-1666 ***6212.30*** *p22*
Curtis, John; Boston, 1680 ***1224.1*** *p16*
Curtis, John; Maryland, 1682 ***2524.55*** *p60*
Curtis, John; Virginia, 1684 ***1224.1*** *p16*
Curtis, John 27; Virginia, 1774 ***1220.25*** *p88*
Curtis, Mary *SEE* Curtis, Daniel
Curtis, Michael; Vermont, 1852-1928 ***5900.10*** *p183*
Curtis, Norton; Virginia, 1664 ***6212.30*** *p14*
Curtis, Richard; New York, 1830 ***8197.10*** *p363*
Curtis, Richard 41; Ontario, 1871 ***1823.15*** *p56*
Curtis, Robert; Maryland, 1670 ***2524.55*** *p60*
Curtis, Robert; New York, 1803 ***8197.10*** *p11*
Curtis, Robert; New York, 1840 ***8197.10*** *p160*
Curtis, Thomas 24; Philadelphia, 1774 ***1220.25*** *p44*
Curtis, Uriah; New York, 1790 ***1224.2*** *p29*
Curtis, Walter; Maryland, 1661 ***2524.55*** *p60*
Curtius, John; New York, 1824 ***8197.10*** *p217*
Curty, Thomas; Maryland, 1675 ***2524.55*** *p60*
Curtyce, Jane; New England, 1660 ***1224.1*** *p16*
Curwen, Edward; Iowa, 1857 ***1224.3*** *p19*
Curwen, Henry 35; Ontario, 1871 ***1823.15*** *p56*
Curwithy, Jno; Virginia, 1667-1668 ***6212.30*** *p38*
Curwithy, Morris; Virginia, 1667 ***6212.30*** *p37*
Curye, Patrick 70; Ontario, 1871 ***1823.15*** *p56*
Curzon, H.; Quebec, 1857 ***9196.15*** *p25*
Cusac, John 31; Ontario, 1871 ***1823.22*** *p38*
Cusack, Bridget; Vermont, 1841-1909 ***5900.10*** *p399*
Cusack, Helen; Vermont, n.d. ***5900.10*** *p416*
Cusack, Mrs. J. C.; Quebec, 1856 ***9196.15*** *p6*
Cusack, James 73; Vermont, 1890 ***5900.10*** *p416*
Cusack, Katherine; Vermont, 1854-1924 ***5900.10*** *p541*
Cush, Charles 31; Ontario, 1871 ***1823.28*** *p21*
Cushen, William 62; Ontario, 1871 ***1823.22*** *p38*
Cushing, Edward; Vermont, 1839-1921 ***5900.10*** *p357*
Cushing, Edward; Vermont, 1848-1889 ***5900.10*** *p509*
Cushing, Emely; Vermont, 1844-1909 ***5900.10*** *p349*
Cushing, Johanna Shea; Vermont, 1841-1923 ***5900.10*** *p175*
Cushing, Margaret Corcoran; Vermont, 1853-1903 ***5900.10*** *p175*
Cushing, Margaret Cummuskey; Vermont, 1857-1888 ***5900.10*** *p509*
Cushing, Mary; Vermont, 1849-1927 ***5900.10*** *p357*
Cushing, Mary; Vermont, 1852 ***5900.10*** *p593*
Cushing, Mary 62; Vermont, 1900 ***5900.10*** *p367*
Cushing, Mary S.; Vermont, 1855-1922 ***5900.10*** *p287*
Cushing, Richard; Vermont, 1834-1896 ***5900.10*** *p175*
Cushing, Thomas; Vermont, 1832-1912 ***5900.10*** *p175*
Cushman, Charles; Vermont, 1816-1883 ***5900.10*** *p145*
Cushman, Elijah J. 49; Vermont, 1884 ***5900.10*** *p134*
Cushman, Katie M.; Vermont, n.d. ***5900.10*** *p134*
Cushny, Thomas; Georgia, 1837 ***1640.10*** *p36*
Cusic, Mary 72; Vermont, 1896 ***5900.10*** *p140*
Cusic, Michael; Vermont, 1869 ***5900.10*** *p140*
Cusick, Bridget; Vermont, 1842-1917 ***5900.10*** *p156*
Cusick, Mary 15; Vermont, 1870 ***5900.10*** *p171*
Cuskye, Peter; Virginia, 1671-1672 ***6212.30*** *p47*
Cusler, Henrich; Port uncertain, 1739 ***2856.30*** *p72*
Cusostki, Adam; Maryland, 1910 ***3259.35*** *p10*
Cussey, Bridget 90; Ontario, 1871 ***1823.15*** *p56*
Cussins, John; Georgia, 1698 ***1640.13*** *p27*
Cusson, Ann Corners 67; Vermont, 1885 ***5900.10*** *p283*
Cusson, George C. 74; Vermont, 1882 ***5900.10*** *p283*
Cussons, Charles; Maryland, 1673 ***2524.55*** *p60*
Custand, Francis; Maryland, 1667 ***2524.55*** *p60*
Custard, Adam; Pennsylvania, 1777 ***4629.10*** *p7*
Custer, Peter; Port uncertain, 1756 ***2856.30*** *p72*
Custis, Daniel Parke; Virginia, 1758 ***1224.2*** *p29*
Custis, John; Maryland, 1682 ***2524.55*** *p60*
Custis, John; Virginia, 1671 ***6212.30*** *p44*
Custis, John; Virginia, 1671-1672 ***6212.30*** *p46*
Custis, John; Virginia, 1753 ***1224.2*** *p30*
Custis, Joseph; Virginia, 1656 ***1224.1*** *p16*
Custis, William; Virginia, 1669-1670 ***6212.30*** *p41*
Custwicz, Kasmier; Maryland, 1910 ***3259.35*** *p10*
Cutbert, Tho; Virginia, 1665-1666 ***6212.30*** *p23*
Cutbush, Edward; Pennsylvania, 1777 ***4629.10*** *p26*
Cutbush, Edward; Pennsylvania, 1779 ***4629.10*** *p41*
Cutchuck, Peter 41; Ontario, 1871 ***1823.28*** *p21*
Cutclift, William 28; Maryland, 1774 ***1220.25*** *p70*
Cute, Elizabeth; Maryland, 1665 ***2524.55*** *p60*
Cuthbartson, Benjamin 75; Ontario, 1871 ***1823.15*** *p56*
Cuthbartson, John 46; Ontario, 1871 ***1823.15*** *p56*
Cuthbert, Mrs.; Quebec, 1857 ***9196.15*** *p22*
Cuthbert, Alexander; Ontario, 1871 ***1823.22*** *p38*
Cuthbert, Alexander 28; Ontario, 1871 ***1823.22*** *p38*
Cuthbert, Anne; Savannah, Georgia, 1757 ***1640.10*** *p69*
Cuthbert, Anthony; Pennsylvania, 1777 ***4629.10*** *p7*
Cuthbert, David 19; Maryland, 1774 ***1220.25*** *p41*
Cuthbert, George; Georgia, 1736 ***1640.10*** *p37*
Cuthbert, George; Georgia, 1756 ***1640.10*** *p37*
Cuthbert, H.; Quebec, 1858 ***9196.15*** *p31*
Cuthbert, James; Georgia, 1770 ***1640.10*** *p37*
Cuthbert, James 58; Ontario, 1871 ***1823.28*** *p21*
Cuthbert, James Evans 46; Ontario, 1871 ***1823.28*** *p21*
Cuthbert, Janet; Michigan, 1874 ***1640.13*** *p27*
Cuthbert, Jarvis; Maryland, 1667 ***2524.55*** *p60*
Cuthbert, John; Georgia, 1736 ***1640.10*** *p37*
Cuthbert, John; Georgia, 1739 ***1640.10*** *p37*
Cuthbert, John; Georgia, 1742 ***1640.10*** *p38*
Cuthbert, Joseph; Savannah, Georgia, 1783 ***1640.10*** *p38*
Cuthbert, Thomas; New York, 1840 ***8197.10*** *p161*
Cuthbert, Thomas; Pennsylvania, 1777 ***4629.10*** *p19*
Cuthbert, Thomas, Jr.; Pennsylvania, 1777 ***4629.10*** *p6*
Cuthbertson, John; Havana, 1854 ***1640.13*** *p27*
Cuthbertson, John; Louisiana, 1850 ***1640.10*** *p38*
Cuthbertson, John; Virginia, 1727 ***1224.2*** *p30*
Cuthbertson, William; Virginia, 1678 ***1224.1*** *p17*
Cuthill, Alexander; New York, 1802 ***8197.10*** *p19*
Cuthill, James 33; Ontario, 1871 ***1823.15*** *p56*
Cuthill, John 51; Ontario, 1871 ***1823.15*** *p56*
Cutler, James L.; Vermont, 1851-1867 ***5900.10*** *p338*
Cutler, John; Virginia, 1671-1672 ***6212.30*** *p46*
Cutler, Marshall; Alabama, 1800-1845 ***1640.10*** *p38*
Cutler, Mary L.; Vermont, 1858-1947 ***5900.10*** *p339*
Cutler, Rich; Virginia, 1672 ***6212.30*** *p49*
Cutlip, John 22; Ontario, 1861 ***2896.25*** *p3*
Cutlip, Rebecca 21; Ontario, 1861 ***2896.25*** *p10*
Cutmore, Ann Cole Reddicliffe; Illinois, 1853 ***1224.3*** *p19*
Cutreil, George 22; Ontario, 1871 ***1823.15*** *p56*
Cutt, Richard; Portsmouth, New Hampshire, 1682 ***1224.1*** *p17*
Cutter, Robert B.; Indiana, 1843-1856 ***3437.14*** *p13*
Cuttings, John; Maryland, 1675 ***2524.55*** *p60*
Cuttler, Benjamin; Maryland, 1677-1681 ***2524.55*** *p61*
Cuttler, Eliza; Virginia, 1668-1669 ***6212.30*** *p40*
Cuttler, Mary; Maryland, 1680 ***2524.55*** *p61*
Cuttler, Rich; Virginia, 1668-1669 ***6212.30*** *p41*
Cutts, Sarah; Virginia, 1674 ***6212.30*** *p52*
Cutts, Tho; Virginia, 1672-1673 ***6212.30*** *p51*
Cuture, Joseph 33; British Columbia, 1911 ***9196.1*** *p33*
Cuture, Joseph 33; Washington, 1911 ***9196.1*** *p33*
Cuvillier, Mr.; Quebec, 1858 ***9196.15*** *p33*
Cuvillier, Mrs.; Quebec, 1858 ***9196.15*** *p33*
Cuyler, Abraham; Albany, New York, 1816 ***1224.3*** *p19*
Cuyler, Abraham; Montreal, 1816 ***1224.3*** *p19*
Cuyler, Edward; New York, 1840 ***8197.10*** *p321*
Cuyler, Henry; New York, 1806 ***1224.3*** *p19*
Cwiek, Machiey; Maryland, 1910 ***3259.35*** *p10*
Cwisi, John 50; Ontario, 1871 ***1823.28*** *p21*
Cywinski, William; Maryland, 1910 ***3259.35*** *p10*
Cywinsky, Stanislaw; Maryland, 1910 ***3259.35*** *p10*
Czajkowska, Francis; Maryland, 1910 ***3259.35*** *p10*
Czajkowski, Joseph; Maryland, 1910 ***3259.35*** *p10*
Czapski, Joseph; Maryland, 1910 ***3259.35*** *p10*
Czapsky, Vicenty; Maryland, 1910 ***3259.35*** *p10*
Czarnowsk, Ferdinand E.; Maryland, 1910 ***3259.35*** *p10*
Czarski, John; Maryland, 1910 ***3259.35*** *p10*
Czarski, Walenty; Maryland, 1910 ***3259.35*** *p10*
Czekai, Jan; Maryland, 1910 ***3259.35*** *p10*
Czerwinski, Malenty; Maryland, 1910 ***3259.35*** *p10*
Czerwinski, Peter; Maryland, 1910 ***3259.35*** *p11*
Czeshl, John; Maryland, 1910 ***3259.35*** *p11*
Czeswinski, Isidore; Maryland, 1910 ***3259.35*** *p11*
Czsinski, Joseph; Maryland, 1910 ***3259.35*** *p11*
Czwek, Martin; Maryland, 1910 ***3259.35*** *p11*
Czyrniesvski, Franziek; Maryland, 1910 ***3259.35*** *p11*
Czyzinski, Joseph; Maryland, 1910 ***3259.35*** *p11*

D

Dabell, William J.; New York, 1861 ***6058.10*** *p68*
Dabidge, Robert; Maryland, 1670 ***2524.55*** *p61*
Dabney, Henry; Maryland, 1666 ***2524.55*** *p61*
Daborne, Thomas; Maryland, 1659 ***2524.55*** *p61*
Dabrall, Willson 25; Carolina, 1774 ***1220.25*** *p83*
Dabrowski, John; Maryland, 1910 ***3259.35*** *p11*
Dabrowski, Martin; Maryland, 1910 ***3259.35*** *p11*
Dabuck, Incah 46; Ontario, 1871 ***1823.28*** *p21*
Dabulski, Walter; Maryland, 1910 ***3259.35*** *p11*
Dacas, Ann; Maryland, 1664 ***2524.55*** *p61*
Dacas, Nicholas; Maryland, 1664 ***2524.55*** *p61*
Dacer, Thomas; Virginia, 1666 ***6212.30*** *p29*
Dacewicz, Antone; Maryland, 1910 ***3259.35*** *p11*
Dacey, Margaret 74; Vermont, 1894 ***5900.10*** *p484*
Dachsteiner, Georg; Port uncertain, 1753 ***2856.30*** *p73*
With mother
Dachsteiner, Mrs. Jacob; Port uncertain, 1752 ***2856.30*** *p73*
Dacie, Thomas; Virginia, 1681-1682 ***6212.30*** *p56*
Dack, Mr.; Quebec, 1858 ***9196.15*** *p41*
Dack, Jane 60; Ontario, 1871 ***1823.15*** *p56*
Dackert, Johann Michael; America, 1749 ***2856.30*** *p73*
Dacks, Georg; Port uncertain, 1774 ***2856.30*** *p73*
Dacres, Robert; Charles Town, South Carolina, 1707 ***1224.2*** *p30*
Dacy, John 9; Vermont, 1865 ***5900.10*** *p210*
Dade, Mary; Alabama, 1806-1829 ***1640.10*** *p38*
Dady, Catherine 18; Vermont, 1862 ***5900.10*** *p144*
Dady, Johannah 71; Vermont, 1889 ***5900.10*** *p144*
Dady, John 43; Vermont, 1899 ***5900.10*** *p144*
Dady, John 69; Vermont, 1890 ***5900.10*** *p144*
Dady, Mary Frances 15; Vermont, 1875 ***5900.10*** *p144*
Dady, Michael 29; Vermont, 1880 ***5900.10*** *p144*
Daeck, Nicholas; Pennsylvania, 1840 ***6058.10*** *p24*
Daenzler, Frederick; New York, 1837 ***8197.10*** *p107*
Daer, John 59; Ontario, 1871 ***1823.15*** *p57*
Daffee, Niel; New York, 1838 ***8197.10*** *p107*
Da Fies, A. 26; Alaska, 1917 ***9196.1*** *p53*
Da Fies, A. 26; Whitehorse, Yukon, 1917 ***9196.1*** *p53*
Daft, Charles; Maryland, 1681 ***2524.55*** *p61*
Daft, Thomas; New York, New York, 1792 ***1224.2*** *p30*
Dagen, Elias; Port uncertain, 1752 ***2856.30*** *p90*
With family
Dagenais, Mr.; Vermont, 1816-1904 ***5900.10*** *p253*
Dagenais, Mrs.; Vermont, 1828-1887 ***5900.10*** *p253*
Dagenais, Joseph; Vermont, 1850-1929 ***5900.10*** *p252*
Dagenais, Rosalie Crowley; Vermont, 1857-1939 ***5900.10*** *p253*
Daggan, Dr.; Portland, Maine, 1857 ***9196.15*** *p12*
Dagger, Elizabeth; Maryland, 1663 ***2524.55*** *p61*
Dagger, Michael; Maryland, 1663 ***2524.55*** *p61*
Daggett, George; New York, 1828-1831 ***8197.10*** *p370*
Daggitt, Richard; Maryland, 1681 ***2524.55*** *p61*
Daggor, Isack; Virginia, 1671-1672 ***6212.30*** *p46*
Dagley, Elizabeth; Charleston, South Carolina, 1856 ***1224.3*** *p19*
Dagnan, Elizabeth; Vermont, 1838-1913 ***5900.10*** *p487*
Dagworthy, Ely; Trenton, New Jersey, 1780 ***1224.2*** *p30*
Dahl, Andreas; Port uncertain, 1782 ***2856.30*** *p73*
Dahler, Catharina; Port uncertain, 1752 ***2856.30*** *p90*
Dahlinger, Caspar; America, 1752 ***2856.30*** *p73*
With wife & 2 children
Dahlinger, Christina; Port uncertain, 1787 ***2856.30*** *p73*
Dahlinger, Friedrich; Port uncertain, 1770 ***2856.30*** *p73*
Dahlinger, Sibylla Cath.; Port uncertain, 1794 ***2856.30*** *p73*
Dahll, Mr.; Quebec, 1858 ***9196.15*** *p32*
Dahlroot, Albin 25; British Columbia, 1909 ***9196.1*** *p28*
Dahlroot, Albin 25; Washington, 1909 ***9196.1*** *p28*
Dahn, Jacob; Port uncertain, 1769 ***2856.30*** *p73*
Dahn, Maria Eva; Port uncertain, 1769 ***2856.30*** *p73*
Dahnin, Margarete; Port uncertain, 1768 ***2856.30*** *p73*
Dahoney, Pat 35; Ontario, 1871 ***1823.15*** *p57*
Daile, Robert 21; Maryland, 1775 ***1220.25*** *p115*
Dailey, Bridget; Vermont, 1844-1933 ***5900.10*** *p306*
Dailey, Bridget; Vermont, 1844-1933 ***5900.10*** *p308*
Dailey, Bridget; Vermont, 1857-1930 ***5900.10*** *p305*
Dailey, Daniel 67; Ontario, 1871 ***1823.22*** *p38*
Dailey, Daniel S.; Vermont, 1897 ***5900.10*** *p306*
Dailey, Edward L.; Vermont, 1870-1913 ***5900.10*** *p351*
Dailey, Elizabeth N. Gilligan; Vermont, 1857-1936 ***5900.10*** *p308*
Dailey, Ellen; Vermont, 1869-1937 ***5900.10*** *p352*
Dailey, Ellen 40; Ontario, 1871 ***1823.28*** *p21*
Dailey, Ellen 47; Vermont, 1870 ***5900.10*** *p414*
Dailey, Hanora 85; Vermont, 1826 ***5900.10*** *p304*
Dailey, Hugh; New York, 1802 ***8197.10*** *p20*
Dailey, Joanna Babbett; Vermont, 1841-1893 ***5900.10*** *p306*
Dailey, John; Vermont, 1838-1911 ***5900.10*** *p303*
Dailey, John 19; Ontario, 1861 ***2896.27*** *p19*
Dailey, Margaret 18; Vermont, 1871 ***5900.10*** *p364*
Dailey, Mary Boyle; Vermont, 1841-1916 ***5900.10*** *p304*
Dailey, Mary Sullivan; Vermont, 1854-1908 ***5900.10*** *p306*
Dailey, Michael; Vermont, 1839-1920 ***5900.10*** *p306*
Dailey, Michael; Vermont, 1839-1920 ***5900.10*** *p308*
Dailey, Patrick; New York, 1839 ***8197.10*** *p380*
Dailey, Patrick 66; Vermont, 1876 ***5900.10*** *p591*
Dailey, Peter 25; Ontario, 1871 ***1823.28*** *p21*
Dailey, Robert 26; Ontario, 1871 ***1823.28*** *p21*
Dailey, T. S.; Vermont, 1848-1904 ***5900.10*** *p308*
Dailey, Thomas 24; Philadelphia, 1774 ***1220.25*** *p81*
Dailey, Timothy; Vermont, 1807-1892 ***5900.10*** *p306*
Dailey, William 28; Vermont, 1873 ***5900.10*** *p411*
Dailey, William H.; Vermont, 1844-1929 ***5900.10*** *p306*
Daily, Catherine 76; Vermont, 1873 ***5900.10*** *p541*
Daily, Charles; New York, 1802 ***8197.10*** *p20*
Daily, John; New York, New York, 1832 ***6058.10*** *p30*
Daily, John 50; Ontario, 1871 ***1823.22*** *p38*
Daily, Margaret 55; Vermont, 1871 ***5900.10*** *p208*
Daily, Michael; New York, 1836 ***8197.10*** *p317*
Daily, Michael 30; Ontario, 1871 ***1823.22*** *p38*
Daily, Peter; New York, 1840 ***8197.10*** *p159*
Daily, Peter 20; Ontario, 1871 ***1823.15*** *p57*
Dain, John 47; Ontario, 1871 ***1823.28*** *p21*
Dainard, Ally 4; Ontario, 1861 ***2896.26*** *p32*
Dainard, Luther 19; Ontario, 1861 ***2896.26*** *p1*
Dainard, Mahaly 1; Ontario, 1861 ***2896.26*** *p39*
Dainard, Marilla 9; Ontario, 1861 ***2896.26*** *p39*
Dainard, Mary 24; Ontario, 1861 ***2896.26*** *p39*
Dainard, Mary Ann 27; Ontario, 1861 ***2896.26*** *p32*
Dainard, Phebe C. 3; Ontario, 1861 ***2896.26*** *p32*
Dainard, William 26; Ontario, 1861 ***2896.26*** *p1*
Dainlog, Miss; Quebec, 1856 ***9196.15*** *p10*
Daintry, John 38; Ontario, 1871 ***1823.22*** *p38*
Dairdron, Thomas 56; Ontario, 1871 ***1823.15*** *p57*
Daisey, Daniel 30; Ontario, 1871 ***1823.28*** *p21*
Dakers, Mr.; Quebec, 1856 ***9196.15*** *p7*
Dakers, Mrs.; Quebec, 1856 ***9196.15*** *p7*
Dakse, Ludwig; New York, 1840 ***8197.10*** *p156*
D'Albertanson, Adolphus; Halifax, Nova Scotia, 1861 ***1640.13*** *p28*
Dale, Christopher 32; Ontario, 1871 ***1823.15*** *p57*
Dale, Christopher 54; Ontario, 1871 ***1823.15*** *p57*
Dale, David; Maryland, 1665 ***2524.55*** *p61*
Relative: Elizabeth
Relative: Rachaell
Dale, Edward; Virginia, 1671-1672 ***6212.30*** *p45*
Dale, Elizabeth *SEE* Dale, David
Dale, Ester 25; Ontario, 1871 ***1823.28*** *p21*
Dale, James 22; Maryland, 1775 ***1220.25*** *p105*
Dale, John; Virginia, 1667 ***6212.30*** *p37*
Dale, John 26; Ontario, 1871 ***1823.15*** *p57*
Dale, John 33; Ontario, 1871 ***1823.22*** *p39*
Dale, Mary *SEE* Dale, Thomas
Dale, Mary A.; Vermont, 1855-1909 ***5900.10*** *p62*
Dale, Rachaell *SEE* Dale, David
Dale, Richard; Pennsylvania, 1785 ***4629.10*** *p48*
Dale, Samuel 26; Ontario, 1871 ***1823.28*** *p21*
Dale, Thomas *SEE* Dale, Thomas
Dale, Thomas; Maryland, 1667 ***2524.55*** *p61*
Wife: Mary
Son: Thomas
Dale, Thomas; Maryland, 1681 ***2524.55*** *p61*
Dalem, Christina; Port uncertain, 1784 ***2856.30*** *p73*
With husband
Daley, Mr.; Portland, Maine, 1858 ***9196.15*** *p28*
Daley, Mr.; Quebec, 1857 ***9196.15*** *p18*
Daley, Mr.; Quebec, 1857 ***9196.15*** *p21*
Daley, Bridget E.; Vermont, 1842-1909 ***5900.10*** *p65*
Daley, Bridget L. Kelly; Vermont, 1857-1917 ***5900.10*** *p350*
Daley, Catharine H.; Vermont, 1831-1914 ***5900.10*** *p488*
Daley, Catherine B. Donoghue 75; Vermont, 1897 ***5900.10*** *p294*
Daley, Catheslin 38; Ontario, 1871 ***1823.22*** *p39*
Daley, Daniel 71; Vermont, 1903 ***5900.10*** *p220*
Daley, Daniel V. 25; Ontario, 1861 ***2896.27*** *p23*
Daley, Eliza 32; Ontario, 1861 ***2896.27*** *p23*
Daley, Elizabeth; Vermont, 1862-1929 ***5900.10*** *p583*
Daley, Emmett B.; Vermont, 1855-1917 ***5900.10*** *p79*
Daley, George W.; New York, 1816 ***8197.10*** *p221*
Daley, Harriet Horsford; Vermont, 1852-1922 ***5900.10*** *p79*
Daley, Hugh; Vermont, 1856-1934 ***5900.10*** *p192*
Daley, J. W.; Vermont, 1852-1932 ***5900.10*** *p132*
Daley, James; New York, 1838 ***8197.10*** *p226*
Daley, James; Vermont, 1856-1916 ***5900.10*** *p435*
Daley, John; Vermont, 1859-1889 ***5900.10*** *p435*
Daley, John 35; Ontario, 1871 ***1823.28*** *p21*
Daley, John C.; Vermont, 1830-1907 ***5900.10*** *p488*
Daley, Joseph 28; Ontario, 1871 ***1823.15*** *p57*
Daley, Margaret; Vermont, 1861-1924 ***5900.10*** *p435*
Daley, Margaret Cauley 27; Vermont, 1890 ***5900.10*** *p138*
Daley, Margaret G.; Vermont, 1856-1956 ***5900.10*** *p192*
Daley, Martin; Vermont, 1820-1893 ***5900.10*** *p147*
Daley, Mary; Vermont, 1853-1854 ***5900.10*** *p147*
Daley, Mary 58; Ontario, 1861 ***2896.27*** *p23*
Daley, Mary A.; Vermont, 1855-1889 ***5900.10*** *p435*
Daley, Mary A. 36; Ontario, 1861 ***2896.27*** *p23*
Daley, Mary Reddington; Vermont, 1852-1913 ***5900.10*** *p132*
Daley, Michael; Pennsylvania, 1867 ***6058.10*** *p59*
Daley, Michael; Vermont, 1830-1900 ***5900.10*** *p435*
Daley, Michael 36; Ontario, 1871 ***1823.28*** *p21*
Daley, Patrick 42; Vermont, 1870 ***5900.10*** *p541*
Daley, Patrick 60; Vermont, 1888 ***5900.10*** *p570*
Daley, Peter 72; Vermont, 1897 ***5900.10*** *p294*
Daley, R.; Quebec, 1856 ***9196.15*** *p6*
Daley, Richard; New York, 1838 ***8197.10*** *p108*
Daley, Sarah; Vermont, 1849-1854 ***5900.10*** *p147*

Daley, Sarah Gallagher; Vermont, 1826-1914 ***5900.10*** *p147*
Daley, Sarah McPhilmy 62; Vermont, 1901 ***5900.10*** *p570*
Daley, Susan McDevitt; Vermont, 1840-1920 ***5900.10*** *p220*
Daley, Thomas P.; Vermont, 1854-1922 ***5900.10*** *p350*
Daley, Thomas P.; Vermont, 1855-1920 ***5900.10*** *p138*
Dalgaly, Robert 49; Ontario, 1871 ***1823.15*** *p57*
Dalgarno, George 43; Ontario, 1871 ***1823.15*** *p57*
Dalgety, Jane Bowhill; Powhatan Co., Virginia, 1900 ***1640.13*** *p28*
Dalgleish, Thomas; Canada, 1876 ***1640.13*** *p28*
Dalglish, Peter 50; Ontario, 1871 ***1823.28*** *p21*
Dalheimer, Anna Dorothea; Port uncertain, 1786 ***2856.30*** *p73*
Dalhoffer, Salome; Port uncertain, 1768 ***2856.30*** *p73*
Dalinger, Christian, The Old; America, 1762 ***2856.30*** *p73*
With wife
Dalker, Elisabeth; Port uncertain, 1740 ***2856.30*** *p73*
Dalkin, Mr.; Quebec, 1857 ***9196.15*** *p21*
Dalkin, Mr.; Quebec, 1858 ***9196.15*** *p44*
Dalkin, Mrs.; Quebec, 1858 ***9196.15*** *p44*
Dall, Robert; Jamaica, 1852 ***1640.13*** *p28*
Dallas, Demster 23; Washington, 1914 ***9196.1*** *p64*
Dallas, Duncan; Georgia, 1737 ***1640.10*** *p38*
Dallas, James; Ontario, 1872 ***1640.13*** *p28*
Dallas, James 49; Ontario, 1871 ***1823.15*** *p57*
Dalle, Henry; Maryland, 1665 ***2524.55*** *p61*
Dalle, William; Maryland, 1665 ***2524.55*** *p61*
Dallett, Judith; Philadelphia, 1854 ***1224.3*** *p19*
Dalley, David; Maryland, 1665 ***2524.55*** *p61*
Relative: Elizabeth
Relative: Rachaell
Dalley, Elizabeth *SEE* Dalley, David
Dalley, Rachaell *SEE* Dalley, David
Dallimore, Obediah *SEE* Dallimore, Robert
Dallimore, Peter *SEE* Dallimore, Robert
Dallimore, Robert *SEE* Dallimore, Robert
Dallimore, Robert; Maryland, 1666 ***2524.55*** *p61*
Wife: Sarah
Son: Robert
Relative: Obediah
Relative: Peter
Dallimore, Sarah *SEE* Dallimore, Robert
Dalliston, Jno; Virginia, 1665-1666 ***6212.30*** *p22*
Dalma, Tho; Virginia, 1664 ***6212.30*** *p9*
Dalond, Ann 15; Ontario, 1861 ***2896.25*** *p32*
Dalond, Franc 19; Ontario, 1861 ***2896.25*** *p32*
Dalrumble, Alexander; New England, 1747 ***1224.2*** *p30*
Dalrumple, Alexander; New England, 1747 ***1224.2*** *p30*
Dalrymple, Alexander; New England, 1747 ***1224.2*** *p30*
Dalrymple, Alexander; New York, 1839 ***8197.10*** *p129*
Dalrymple, John; North Carolina, 1767 ***1224.2*** *p30*
Dalrymple, Martha; North Carolina, 1787 ***1224.2*** *p30*
Dalrymple, Thomas; Savannah, Georgia, 1811-1812 ***1640.10*** *p38*
Dalrymple, William; Jamaica, 1860 ***1640.13*** *p28*
Dalston, Mr.; Quebec, 1858 ***9196.15*** *p42*
Dalston, James; Virginia, 1665 ***6212.30*** *p18*
Dalton, Bridget 20; Ontario, 1871 ***1823.15*** *p57*
Dalton, Bridget Conington 49; Vermont, 1891 ***5900.10*** *p415*
Dalton, Catherine; Vermont, 1842-1932 ***5900.10*** *p542*
Dalton, Catherine 65; Vermont, 1869 ***5900.10*** *p542*
Dalton, Charles 34; Ontario, 1871 ***1823.15*** *p57*
Dalton, Daniel 72; Vermont, 1877 ***5900.10*** *p540*
Dalton, Edward 28; New England, 1774 ***1220.25*** *p56*
Dalton, Edward 31; Virginia, 1774 ***1220.25*** *p56*
Dalton, Ellan; Maryland, 1678 ***2524.55*** *p61*
Dalton, Ellen 90; Vermont, 1885 ***5900.10*** *p612*
Dalton, Ellen Fannin; Vermont, 1829-1909 ***5900.10*** *p220*
Dalton, Esther 77; Vermont, 1960 ***5900.10*** *p318*
Dalton, Finora J.; Vermont, 1858-1945 ***5900.10*** *p123*
Dalton, Henry; New York, 1837 ***8197.10*** *p86*
Dalton, Henry; New York, New York, 1825 ***1224.3*** *p19*
Dalton, Henry 40; Ontario, 1871 ***1823.15*** *p57*
Dalton, James; New York, 1805 ***8197.10*** *p29*
Dalton, James; Pennsylvania, 1868 ***6058.10*** *p74*
Dalton, James; Vermont, 1859-1884 ***5900.10*** *p220*
Dalton, James 7; Ontario, 1871 ***1823.15*** *p57*
Dalton, James 40; Ontario, 1871 ***1823.15*** *p57*
Dalton, Jane; New York, 1829 ***8197.10*** *p351*
Dalton, Jane Gorman 68; Vermont, 1875 ***5900.10*** *p540*
Dalton, John; New York, 1839 ***8197.10*** *p129*
Dalton, John; Virginia, 1666 ***6212.30*** *p30*
Dalton, John 35; Ontario, 1871 ***1823.15*** *p57*
Dalton, John 50; Ontario, 1871 ***1823.22*** *p39*
Dalton, John 67; Ontario, 1871 ***1823.15*** *p57*
Dalton, Joseph; Virginia, 1720 ***1224.2*** *p30*
Dalton, Julia 74; Ontario, 1871 ***1823.15*** *p57*
Dalton, Margaret; Vermont, 1856-1932 ***5900.10*** *p354*
Dalton, Maurice 43; Ontario, 1871 ***1823.15*** *p57*
Dalton, Maurice, Sr. 55; Ontario, 1871 ***1823.15*** *p57*
Dalton, Michael; New York, 1838 ***8197.10*** *p377*
Dalton, Michael 30; Ontario, 1871 ***1823.15*** *p57*
Dalton, Patrick; New York, 1840 ***8197.10*** *p158*
Dalton, Patrick; Vermont, 1836-1912 ***5900.10*** *p415*
Dalton, Richard; New York, 1829-1831 ***8197.10*** *p370*
Dalton, Rosella; Vermont, 1835-1890 ***5900.10*** *p396*
Dalton, Thomas; Vermont, 1827-1896 ***5900.10*** *p220*
Dalton, Thomas 66; Ontario, 1871 ***1823.22*** *p39*
Dalton, William; Vermont, 1856-1936 ***5900.10*** *p354*
Dalton, William; Virginia, 1666 ***6212.30*** *p29*
Daly, Ann Leonard; Vermont, 1829-1904 ***5900.10*** *p588*
Daly, Bessy 25 *SEE* Daly, Margaret
Daly, Bridget; Vermont, 1816-1906 ***5900.10*** *p391*
Daly, Bryan; New York, 1819 ***8197.10*** *p222*
Daly, Bryan; New York, 1825 ***8197.10*** *p297*
Daly, Catherine 28; Vermont, 1866 ***5900.10*** *p337*
Daly, Catherine 58; Vermont, 1866 ***5900.10*** *p504*
Daly, Charles H. 34; Vermont, 1889 ***5900.10*** *p485*
Daly, Cornelius; New York, 1827 ***8197.10*** *p224*
Daly, Daniel; Vermont, 1855-1915 ***5900.10*** *p488*
Daly, Daniel 50; Died enroute, 1849 ***1825.45*** *p47*
Daly, Ellen 31; Vermont, 1868 ***5900.10*** *p235*
Daly, Esther Ellen Sherlock; Vermont, 1852-1907 ***5900.10*** *p488*
Daly, Florence 30; Ontario, 1871 ***1823.15*** *p57*
Daly, Hannah 77; Ontario, 1861 ***2896.25*** *p25*
Daly, James; New York, 1838 ***8197.10*** *p108*
Daly, James; Vermont, 1788-1879 ***5900.10*** *p419*
Daly, James 40; Ontario, 1871 ***1823.28*** *p21*
Daly, Johannah 16; Ontario, 1871 ***1823.15*** *p57*
Daly, John; Charles Town, South Carolina, 1768 ***1224.2*** *p32*
Daly, John; New York, 1807 ***8197.10*** *p329*
Daly, John; New York, 1837 ***8197.10*** *p83*
Daly, John; New York, 1839 ***8197.10*** *p226*
Daly, John; Vermont, 1849-1903 ***5900.10*** *p339*
Daly, John 16; Ontario, 1871 ***1823.15*** *p57*
Daly, John 26 *SEE* Daly, Margaret
Daly, John 46; British Columbia, 1915 ***9196.1*** *p68*
Daly, John 46; Washington, 1915 ***9196.1*** *p68*
Daly, John 55; Ontario, 1871 ***1823.15*** *p57*
Daly, John 65; Ontario, 1871 ***1823.15*** *p57*
Daly, Joseph 45; Ontario, 1871 ***1823.28*** *p21*
Daly, Judy 20 *SEE* Daly, Margaret
Daly, Julia C. 28; Vermont, 1861 ***5900.10*** *p502*
Daly, Kate Henesy 47; Vermont, 1882 ***5900.10*** *p482*
Daly, Margaret 19 *SEE* Daly, Margaret
Daly, Margaret 19; Ontario, 1871 ***1823.15*** *p57*
Daly, Margaret 50; New York, New York, 1849 ***1825.45*** *p47*
Son: John 26
Daughter: Margaret 19
Daughter: Bessy 25
Daughter: Judy 20
Daly, Margaret 78; Vermont, 1876 ***5900.10*** *p262*
Daly, Margaret O'Neil; Vermont, 1855-1908 ***5900.10*** *p339*
Daly, Mary; New York, New York, 1851 ***1825.45*** *p56*
With daughter & mother
Daly, Mary 30; Vermont, 1859 ***5900.10*** *p363*
Daly, Mary 48; Ontario, 1871 ***1823.15*** *p57*
Daly, Mary 56; Ontario, 1871 ***1823.15*** *p57*
Daly, Mary 63; Vermont, 1883 ***5900.10*** *p315*
Daly, Mary Ann; Vermont, 1827-1881 ***5900.10*** *p419*
Daly, Mathew A.; New York, 1821 ***8197.10*** *p223*
Daly, Michael; Pennsylvania, 1867 ***6058.10*** *p59*
Daly, Michael 25; Ontario, 1871 ***1823.15*** *p57*
Daly, Michael 46; Ontario, 1871 ***1823.28*** *p21*
Daly, Nicholas; New York, 1803 ***8197.10*** *p12*
Daly, Owen; New York, 1840 ***8197.10*** *p157*
Daly, Patrick; New York, 1827 ***8197.10*** *p298*
Daly, Patrick; Vermont, 1828-1908 ***5900.10*** *p588*
Daly, Richard; New York, 1836 ***8197.10*** *p225*
Daly, Robert 77; Ontario, 1871 ***1823.22*** *p39*
Daly, Steven 60; Ontario, 1871 ***1823.28*** *p21*
Daly, Thomas; New York, 1803 ***8197.10*** *p12*
Daly, Thomas; New York, 1838 ***8197.10*** *p107*
Daly, Thomas 15; Vermont, 1845 ***5900.10*** *p348*
Daly, Thomas 25; Ontario, 1871 ***1823.28*** *p21*
Daly, Thomas 60; Ontario, 1871 ***1823.28*** *p21*
Dalye, William 65; Ontario, 1871 ***1823.22*** *p39*
Dalyell, James; New York, 1807 ***8197.10*** *p329*
Dalziel, James; New York, 1838 ***8197.10*** *p108*
Dalziel, Robert; Memphis, Tennessee, 1864 ***1640.10*** *p38*
Dalziell, Charles; Georgia, 1699 ***1640.13*** *p28*
Dam, Apoll. Schwarz *SEE* Dam, Michael
Dam, Michael; Port uncertain, 1770 ***2856.30*** *p73*
Wife: Apoll. Schwarz
Damainville, Denis Auguste; New York, 1837 ***8197.10*** *p225*
Damarell, . . .; Maryland, 1631-1685 ***2524.55*** *p157*
Damarell, Mrs.; Maryland, 1658 ***2524.55*** *p61*
Damarell, John; Maryland, 1658 ***2524.55*** *p61*
Dambacher, Caspar; Port uncertain, 1783 ***2856.30*** *p73*
Dame, George 33; Virginia, 1773 ***1220.25*** *p30*
Damead, William 21; Philadelphia, 1774 ***1220.25*** *p5*
Damer, Bessie 32; Alaska, 1918 ***9196.1*** *p55*
Damer, Bessie 32; British Columbia, 1918 ***9196.1*** *p55*
Damerel, George; New York, 1826 ***8197.10*** *p224*
Dameres, Thomas; Maryland, 1668-1669 ***2524.55*** *p61*
Dames, Richard; Maryland, 1679 ***2524.55*** *p61*
Dames, William 48; Ontario, 1871 ***1823.15*** *p57*
Damesyc, Francis; Maryland, 1910 ***3259.35*** *p11*
Damideryk, Anton; Maryland, 1910 ***3259.35*** *p11*
Damien, Bernard; Vermont, 1843-1910 ***5900.10*** *p593*
Damien, Mary Roy; Vermont, 1853-1929 ***5900.10*** *p593*
Damisyn, Michael; Maryland, 1910 ***3259.35*** *p11*
Damm, Georg; Port uncertain, 1764 ***2856.30*** *p88*
With wife & 7 children
Damm, Philippina; Port uncertain, 1764 ***2856.30*** *p73*
Damm, Therese; Port uncertain, 1795 ***2856.30*** *p73*
Dampan, Elinor; Virginia, 1701-1702 ***6212.30*** *p61*
Danah, Sidney 88; Ontario, 1871 ***1823.15*** *p57*
Danaher, Timothy L.; New York, 1839 ***8197.10*** *p129*
Danard, A. E. 18; Ontario, 1861 ***2896.27*** *p38*
Danard, Alferd 21; Ontario, 1861 ***2896.26*** *p21*
Danard, Amelia 19; Ontario, 1861 ***2896.26*** *p21*
Danard, Brittan 13; Ontario, 1861 ***2896.26*** *p21*
Danard, Byron 30; Ontario, 1861 ***2896.26*** *p21*
Danard, David 16; Ontario, 1861 ***2896.26*** *p21*
Danard, Eleanor 59; Ontario, 1861 ***2896.27*** *p10*
Danard, Emma 1; Ontario, 1861 ***2896.26*** *p19*
Danard, Irena 14; Ontario, 1861 ***2896.26*** *p21*
Danard, Lesle B. 8; Ontario, 1861 ***2896.26*** *p21*
Danard, Louisa 34; Ontario, 1861 ***2896.26*** *p21*
Danard, M. E. 3; Ontario, 1861 ***2896.27*** *p10*
Danard, Manerva 24; Ontario, 1861 ***2896.26*** *p21*
Danard, Moris 3; Ontario, 1861 ***2896.26*** *p19*
Danard, Synthia 25; Ontario, 1861 ***2896.26*** *p19*
Danard, Wellington 22; Ontario, 1861 ***2896.26*** *p21*
Danard, Werden 10; Ontario, 1861 ***2896.26*** *p21*
Danby, John 50; Ontario, 1871 ***1823.15*** *p57*
Dance, John; America, 1754 ***2856.30*** *p73*
Dance, Thomas; Maryland, 1682 ***2524.55*** *p61*
Dancer, Brill 18; Maryland, 1775 ***1220.25*** *p115*
Dancer, William 21; Maryland, 1774 ***1220.25*** *p47*
Dancomb, James; Virginia, 1665 ***6212.30*** *p20*
Dancy, Elizabeth 50; Ontario, 1871 ***1823.22*** *p39*
Dancyger, Lewis; New York, New York, 1859 ***3437.14*** *p84*
Dandecoate, Wm.; Maryland, 1681 ***2524.55*** *p61*
Dando, Stephen; New York, 1802 ***8197.10*** *p20*
Dandres, Catharina; America, 1796 ***2856.30*** *p73*
Dandson, James 26; Ontario, 1871 ***1823.15*** *p57*
Dane, Anthony; New York, New York, 1854 ***6058.10*** *p52*
Dane, Archibald; New York, 1803 ***8197.10*** *p12*
Dane, George 68; Ontario, 1871 ***1823.15*** *p57*
Dane, James 34; Ontario, 1871 ***1823.15*** *p57*
Dane, Jane 70; Ontario, 1871 ***1823.15*** *p57*
Dane, John 38; Ontario, 1871 ***1823.15*** *p57*
Dane, Paul 60; Ontario, 1871 ***1823.28*** *p21*
Danear, Grace; Virginia, 1665 ***6212.30*** *p17*
Danellson, John; Maryland, 1673 ***2524.55*** *p61*
Daner, Lukas; Port uncertain, 1754 ***2856.30*** *p73*
Daney, William 35; Ontario, 1871 ***1823.15*** *p57*
Danger, Lewis; New York, 1839 ***8197.10*** *p129*
Danial, Peter 36; Ontario, 1871 ***1823.28*** *p21*
Daniecki, Jacob; Maryland, 1910 ***3259.35*** *p11*
Daniel, Alexander 15; America, 1774 ***1220.25*** *p36*
Daniel, Alice; Virginia, 1693-1694 ***6212.30*** *p60*
Daniel, Charles; New York, 1840 ***8197.10*** *p157*
Daniel, Edmond; Maryland, 1678 ***2524.55*** *p61*
Daniel, Edward; Maryland, 1673 ***2524.55*** *p61*
Daniel, Francis 27; Maryland, 1774 ***1220.25*** *p65*
Daniel, Galip 31; Ontario, 1871 ***1823.15*** *p57*
Daniel, Henry; New York, 1800 ***1224.3*** *p19*
Daniel, Jacob; America, 1742 ***2856.30*** *p73*
Daniel, James; New York, 1782 ***1224.2*** *p30*
Daniel, Jane; Maryland, 1672 ***2524.55*** *p61*
Daniel, John; Maryland, 1682 ***2524.55*** *p61*
Daniel, John 21; Maryland, 1774 ***1220.25*** *p74*
Daniel, Joseph 29; Virginia, 1774 ***1220.25*** *p93*
Daniel, Leonard; Maryland, 1672 ***2524.55*** *p61*
Daniel, Thomas; Maryland, 1681 ***2524.55*** *p61*
Daniel, Thomas 21; Maryland, 1774 ***1220.25*** *p61*
Daniel, Wilhelm; America, 1742 ***2856.30*** *p73*
Daniel, William; Maryland, 1681 ***2524.55*** *p61*
Danielak, Joseph; Maryland, 1910 ***3259.35*** *p11*
Daniell, Constant; Maryland, 1667 ***2524.55*** *p62*
Daniell, Edmond; Maryland, 1678 ***2524.55*** *p62*
Daniell, Elizabeth; Ontario, 1891 ***1640.13*** *p28*
Daniell, Isaac; Maryland, 1669 ***2524.55*** *p62*
Daniell, James; Ontario, 1891 ***1640.13*** *p28*
Daniell, Jane; Maryland, 1673 ***2524.55*** *p62*

Dauler, Hans Michael; Port uncertain, 1742 ***2856.30*** *p74*
With wife & children
Daum, Elisabeth; Port uncertain, 1773 ***2856.30*** *p74*
Daum, Johann Philipp; America, 1740 ***2856.30*** *p74*
Daume, Michael; Port uncertain, 1776 ***2856.30*** *p74*
Daun, Johann Philipp; America, 1741 ***2856.30*** *p74*
Dauncey, Anne Wallin; New England, 1699 ***1224.1*** *p17*
Dauner, Adam; Port uncertain, 1741 ***2856.30*** *p74*
Dauner, Michael; America, 1752 ***2856.30*** *p74*
With wife & children
Daunn, Johann; America, 1742 ***2856.30*** *p74*
Dauns, Johann; America, 1742 ***2856.30*** *p74*
Daurschauer, Jacob; America, 1744 ***2856.30*** *p74*
Dausacker, Sebastian; Port uncertain, 1764 ***2856.30*** *p74*
With wife & 3 children
Dausicke, Charles; Maryland, 1659 ***2524.55*** *p62*
Davany, James; New York, 1840 ***8197.10*** *p156*
Dave, Henry; Maryland, 1659 ***2524.55*** *p62*
Davell, Robt; Virginia, 1665-1666 ***6212.30*** *p24*
Davenant, James; Virginia, 1664 ***6212.30*** *p15*
Davenport, Addington; Boston, 1747 ***1224.2*** *p30*
Davenport, Ann; Boston, 1745 ***1224.2*** *p30*
Davenport, J. 14; Ontario, 1861 ***2896.26*** *p2*
Davenport, L. 20; Ontario, 1861 ***2896.25*** *p38*
Davenport, L. M. 22; Ontario, 1861 ***2896.25*** *p38*
Davenport, Martha 68; Vermont, 1892 ***5900.10*** *p303*
Davenport, Michael; Pennsylvania, 1777 ***4629.10*** *p14*
Davenport, Thomas; New York, 1716 ***1224.2*** *p31*
Davenport, Thomas Donald; Cincinnati, 1852 ***1224.3*** *p19*
Davenport, William; Virginia, 1796 ***1224.2*** *p31*
Davenport, William 15; Philadelphia, 1774 ***1220.25*** *p80*
Davenport, William A. F.; New York, 1835 ***8197.10*** *p225*
Davern, Harriet 8; Ontario, 1861 ***2896.28*** *p43*
Davern, James 3; Ontario, 1861 ***2896.28*** *p43*
Davern, Mary 88; Vermont, 1894 ***5900.10*** *p123*
Davern, Rebekah 34; Ontario, 1861 ***2896.28*** *p43*
Davern, Sarah 13; Ontario, 1861 ***2896.28*** *p43*
Davernier, Peter; Port uncertain, 1736 ***2856.30*** *p75*
Davers, Henry; America, 1759 ***1224.2*** *p31*
Davers, Jermyn; Virginia, 1751 ***1224.2*** *p31*
Davey, Mr.; Portland, Maine, 1858 ***9196.15*** *p29*
Davey, Mr.; St. John, New Brunswick, 1857 ***9196.15*** *p12*
Davey, Henry 37; Ontario, 1871 ***1823.22*** *p39*
Davey, John 38; Ontario, 1871 ***1823.22*** *p39*
Davey, Joseph 40; Ontario, 1871 ***1823.22*** *p39*
Davey, Peter; New York, 1828 ***8197.10*** *p349*
Davey, Peter 63; Ontario, 1871 ***1823.22*** *p39*
Davey, Robert P.; New York, 1834 ***8197.10*** *p72*
Davey, Thomas Henry; Memphis, Tennessee, 1855 ***1224.3*** *p19*
Davey, Tighe; New York, 1827 ***8197.10*** *p338*
Davey, William; Pennsylvania, 1777 ***4629.10*** *p15*
David, Alexander; Maryland, 1910 ***3259.35*** *p11*
David, August 53; Ontario, 1871 ***1823.28*** *p21*
David, Charles 26; Maryland, 1774 ***1220.25*** *p78*
David, David; New York, 1807 ***8197.10*** *p38*
David, Ezekiel; Charles Town, South Carolina, 1769 ***1224.2*** *p31*
David, Fred 28; Kansas, 1910 ***9079.10*** *p45*
David, Joane; Maryland, 1672 ***2524.55*** *p62*
David, Mathis; Port uncertain, 1792 ***2856.30*** *p75*
David, Zebadiah; Pennsylvania, 1777 ***4629.10*** *p21*
Davids, Heinrich; America, 1753 ***2856.30*** *p75*
With wife & 4 children
Davidshofer, Johann Nepomuk; Port uncertain, 1794 ***2856.30*** *p75*
Davidson, . . .; Georgia, 1737 ***1640.10*** *p40*
Davidson, Miss; Quebec, 1858 ***9196.15*** *p33*
Davidson, Mr.; Quebec, 1857 ***9196.15*** *p20*
Davidson, Adam; Savannah, Georgia, 1811-1812 ***1640.10*** *p39*
Davidson, Adam 68; Ontario, 1871 ***1823.22*** *p39*
Davidson, Agness 51; Ontario, 1871 ***1823.22*** *p39*
Davidson, Alexander; Savannah, Georgia, 1825 ***1640.10*** *p39*
Davidson, Mrs. C. 69; Ontario, 1871 ***1823.15*** *p58*
Davidson, Charles; New York, 1840 ***8197.10*** *p158*
Davidson, Charles Felix; Augusta, Maine, 1887 ***1640.13*** *p28*
Davidson, David; Virginia, 1690-1691 ***6212.30*** *p59*
Davidson, David 64; Ontario, 1871 ***1823.22*** *p39*
Davidson, David William; Omaha, Nebraska, 1887 ***1640.13*** *p28*
Davidson, Duncan; Florida, 1767 ***1640.10*** *p39*
Davidson, Edward; Georgia, 1738 ***1640.10*** *p39*
Davidson, Elizabeth *SEE* Davidson, Robert
Davidson, Elizabeth 21; Maryland, 1775 ***1220.25*** *p104*
Davidson, Euphemia; Albany, New York, 1874 ***1640.13*** *p28*
Davidson, Francis; Ontario, 1861 ***2896.28*** *p56*
Davidson, George 27; Ontario, 1871 ***1823.15*** *p58*
Davidson, George 38; Virginia, 1774 ***1220.25*** *p88*
Davidson, George 45; Ontario, 1871 ***1823.28*** *p21*
Davidson, George 76; Ontario, 1871 ***1823.22*** *p39*
Davidson, H. C.; Quebec, 1857 ***9196.15*** *p13*
Davidson, Harry; Jamaica, 1874 ***1640.13*** *p29*
Davidson, Henry; Florida, 1767 ***1640.10*** *p39*
Davidson, Hugh 45; Ontario, 1871 ***1823.15*** *p58*
Davidson, Hugh 78; Ontario, 1871 ***1823.15*** *p58*
Davidson, James; Jamaica, 1869 ***1640.13*** *p29*
Davidson, James; Louisiana, 1850 ***1640.10*** *p39*
Davidson, James 41; Ontario, 1871 ***1823.22*** *p39*
Davidson, James 44; Ontario, 1871 ***1823.15*** *p58*
Davidson, James 46; Ontario, 1871 ***1823.15*** *p58*
Davidson, James 49; Ontario, 1871 ***1823.15*** *p58*
Davidson, James 52; Ontario, 1871 ***1823.15*** *p58*
Davidson, James 60; Ontario, 1871 ***1823.28*** *p22*
Davidson, James 71; Ontario, 1871 ***1823.15*** *p58*
Davidson, John; Louisiana, 1850 ***1640.10*** *p39*
Davidson, John; New York, 1807 ***8197.10*** *p38*
Davidson, John; Tennessee, 1808-1845 ***1640.10*** *p39*
Wife: Margaret
Davidson, John 22; Maryland, 1774 ***1220.25*** *p84*
Davidson, John 24; Ontario, 1871 ***1823.22*** *p39*
Davidson, John 41; Ontario, 1871 ***1823.22*** *p39*
Davidson, John 47; Ontario, 1871 ***1823.15*** *p58*
Davidson, John 55; Ontario, 1871 ***1823.28*** *p22*
Davidson, John 63; Ontario, 1871 ***1823.22*** *p39*
Davidson, John 88; Ontario, 1871 ***1823.22*** *p39*
Davidson, Joseph; Georgia, 1698 ***1640.13*** *p29*
Davidson, Margaret *SEE* Davidson, John
Davidson, Margaret; Ontario, 1861 ***2896.28*** *p56*
Davidson, Margret 30; Ontario, 1871 ***1823.15*** *p58*
Davidson, Mary; Port uncertain, 1850-1859 ***4537.37*** *p120*
Davidson, Mary 54; Ontario, 1871 ***1823.15*** *p58*
Davidson, Mary 70; Ontario, 1871 ***1823.22*** *p39*
Davidson, Mary 71; Ontario, 1871 ***1823.15*** *p58*
Davidson, Nathaniel 61; Ontario, 1871 ***1823.22*** *p40*
Davidson, Nelson 42; Ontario, 1871 ***1823.15*** *p58*
Davidson, Robert; Georgia, 1698 ***1640.13*** *p29*
Davidson, Robert; Maryland, 1667 ***2524.55*** *p62*
Wife: Elizabeth
Davidson, Robert 21; Philadelphia, 1774 ***1220.25*** *p43*
Davidson, Robert 36; Ontario, 1871 ***1823.22*** *p40*
Davidson, Robert 46; Ontario, 1871 ***1823.15*** *p58*
Davidson, Robert 50; Ontario, 1871 ***1823.15*** *p58*
Davidson, Robert 54; Ontario, 1871 ***1823.15*** *p58*
Davidson, Robert 72; Ontario, 1871 ***1823.22*** *p40*
Davidson, Robert T.; Texas, 1838 ***1640.10*** *p39*
Davidson, Rosa Larkin; Vermont, 1862-1937 ***5900.10*** *p91*
Davidson, Samuel 15; Maryland, 1774 ***1220.25*** *p84*
Davidson, Thomas; Pennsylvania, 1808 ***6058.10*** *p2*
Davidson, Thomas 35; Ontario, 1871 ***1823.15*** *p58*
Davidson, Thomas 37; Ontario, 1871 ***1823.22*** *p40*
Davidson, Thomas 42; Ontario, 1871 ***1823.22*** *p40*
Davidson, William; Georgia, 1698 ***1640.13*** *p29*
Davidson, William; Georgia, 1801 ***1640.10*** *p39*
Davidson, William 41; Ontario, 1871 ***1823.28*** *p22*
Davidson, William A. 40; Ontario, 1871 ***1823.22*** *p40*
Davidtshofer, Christina; Port uncertain, 1756 ***2856.30*** *p75*
Davie, Mr.; Quebec, 1858 ***9196.15*** *p36*
Davie, Mr.; Quebec, 1858 ***9196.15*** *p41*
Davie, Mrs.; Quebec, 1858 ***9196.15*** *p36*
Davie, Humphrey; Boston, 1674 ***1224.1*** *p63*
Davie, James; New York, 1807 ***8197.10*** *p37*
Davies, . . .; Pennsylvania, 1777 ***4629.10*** *p21*
Davies, Mr.; Quebec, 1857 ***9196.15*** *p19*
Davies, Charles 37; Ontario, 1871 ***1823.15*** *p58*
Davies, David; Maryland, 1659 ***2524.55*** *p62*
Davies, David; Maryland, 1675 ***2524.55*** *p62*
Davies, David; New York, 1839 ***8197.10*** *p382*
Davies, E.; Quebec, 1857 ***9196.15*** *p18*
Davies, Elizabeth *SEE* Davies, Hopkin
Davies, Elizabeth; Maryland, 1665 ***2524.55*** *p62*
Davies, Elizabeth Lee *SEE* Davies, Hopkin
Davies, Emanuel; New York, 1830 ***8197.10*** *p225*
Davies, Francis; Maryland, 1666 ***2524.55*** *p130*
Davies, Hopkin; Maryland, 1662 ***2524.55*** *p62*
Wife: Elizabeth
Daughter: Elizabeth Lee
Davies, Isaack; Virginia, 1658 ***1224.1*** *p17*
Davies, J. R.; Portland, Maine, 1857 ***9196.15*** *p12*
Davies, James; Maryland, 1665 ***2524.55*** *p62*
Relative: Margarett
Relative: Sarah
Davies, James; New York, 1773 ***1224.2*** *p31*
Davies, John; Maryland, 1658 ***2524.55*** *p62*
Wife: Mary
Davies, John; Maryland, 1665 ***2524.55*** *p63*
Davies, John; Maryland, 1665 ***2524.55*** *p63*
Son: John, Jr.
Wife: Mary
Davies, John; New York, 1783 ***1224.2*** *p31*
Davies, John, Jr. *SEE* Davies, John
Davies, John D.; New York, 1838 ***8197.10*** *p375*
Davies, John Mayer; New York, 1826 ***8197.10*** *p334*
Davies, Leona E. 4; Ontario, 1861 ***2896.28*** *p40*
Davies, Margaret 27; Ontario, 1861 ***2896.28*** *p40*
Davies, Margarett *SEE* Davies, James
Davies, Margarett; Maryland, 1665 ***2524.55*** *p63*
Davies, Mary *SEE* Davies, John
Davies, Mary; Maryland, 1658 ***2524.55*** *p63*
Davies, Mary; Maryland, 1671 ***2524.55*** *p63*
Davies, Richard; Maryland, 1681 ***2524.55*** *p63*
Davies, Richard; New Orleans, 1818 ***1224.3*** *p20*
Davies, Richard; St. Louis, 1853 ***1224.3*** *p20*
Davies, Richard; Virginia, 1661 ***1224.1*** *p17*
Davies, Sarah *SEE* Davies, James
Davies, Sarah; Maryland, 1665 ***2524.55*** *p63*
Davies, Stephen; Virginia, 1704 ***1224.2*** *p31*
Davies, Sutherton R.; New York, 1831 ***8197.10*** *p364*
Davies, Thomas; New York, 1807 ***8197.10*** *p37*
Davies, Thomas; New York, 1807 ***8197.10*** *p331*
Davies, Thomas; North Carolina, 1707 ***1224.2*** *p31*
Davies, Thomas; Philadelphia, 1793 ***4629.10*** *p67*
Davies, Thomas; Virginia, 1735 ***1224.2*** *p31*
Davies, William; America, 1802 ***1224.3*** *p20*
Davies, William; Maryland, 1649 ***2524.55*** *p77*
Davies, William; Maryland, 1679 ***2524.55*** *p63*
Davies, William; Virginia, 1775 ***1224.2*** *p31*
Davies, William 2; Ontario, 1861 ***2896.28*** *p40*
Davies, William, II; Maryland, 1665 ***2524.55*** *p63*
Davin, Katherine; Vermont, 1860-1890 ***5900.10*** *p584*
Davin, Thomas 32; Vermont, 1866 ***5900.10*** *p575*
Davine, Ann; Vermont, 1840-1911 ***5900.10*** *p564*
Davine, Bridget 62; Vermont, 1896 ***5900.10*** *p564*
Davine, James 60; Vermont, 1888 ***5900.10*** *p563*
Davine, John; Vermont, 1839-1902 ***5900.10*** *p563*
Davine, Margaret; Vermont, 1830-1893 ***5900.10*** *p563*
Davine, Margaret Smith; Vermont, 1849-1921 ***5900.10*** *p563*
Davine, Maria; Vermont, 1820-1893 ***5900.10*** *p574*
Davine, Mary Moylan; Vermont, 1837-1871 ***5900.10*** *p564*
Davine, Patrick; Vermont, 1820-1886 ***5900.10*** *p564*
Daviner, William 16; New York, 1774 ***1220.25*** *p24*
Daving, Joseph; Maryland, 1910 ***3259.35*** *p11*
Daviorinjinski, William; Maryland, 1910 ***3259.35*** *p11*
Davis, Mrs.; Portland, Maine, 1858 ***9196.15*** *p27*
Davis, Mrs. 78; Ontario, 1861 ***2896.26*** *p30*
Davis, Aaron; New York, 1833 ***8197.10*** *p358*
Davis, Alexander; Maryland, 1661 ***2524.55*** *p63*
Davis, Alice; Maryland, 1681 ***2524.55*** *p63*
Davis, Alice; Maryland, 1682 ***2524.55*** *p63*
Davis, Andrew; Maryland, 1666 ***2524.55*** *p63*
Davis, Ann *SEE* Davis, Francis
Davis, Ann; Maryland, 1672 ***2524.55*** *p63*
Davis, Ann; Maryland, 1682 ***2524.55*** *p63*
Davis, Ann; New York, 1839 ***8197.10*** *p226*
Davis, Anne *SEE* Davis, William
Davis, Annie 1; Ontario, 1861 ***2896.28*** *p39*
Davis, Annie Cudmore; Vermont, 1843-1908 ***5900.10*** *p466*
Davis, Benjamin; Pennsylvania, 1777 ***4629.10*** *p12*
Davis, Benjamin, Jr.; Pennsylvania, 1777 ***4629.10*** *p12*
Davis, Catharon; Maryland, 1658 ***2524.55*** *p63*
Davis, Charles 25; Maryland, 1774 ***1220.25*** *p64*
Davis, D. H. 3; Ontario, 1861 ***2896.26*** *p30*
Davis, Daniell; Virginia, 1703-1704 ***6212.30*** *p62*
Davis, David *SEE* Davis, William
Davis, David; Maryland, 1663 ***2524.55*** *p63*
Davis, David; New York, 1834 ***8197.10*** *p372*
Davis, David; New York, 1839 ***8197.10*** *p380*
Davis, David 20; Maryland, 1774 ***1220.25*** *p69*
Davis, David 76; Ontario, 1871 ***1823.28*** *p22*
Davis, E. 3; Ontario, 1861 ***2896.26*** *p7*
Davis, Edmund; New York, 1838 ***8197.10*** *p377*
Davis, Edward; Maryland, 1673 ***2524.55*** *p61*
Davis, Edward 17; Jamaica, 1774 ***1220.25*** *p60*
Davis, Edward 25; Maryland, 1774 ***1220.25*** *p79*
Davis, Edward 25; Maryland, 1775 ***1220.25*** *p120*
Davis, Edward 77; Ontario, 1871 ***1823.28*** *p22*
Davis, Eliz; Virginia, 1693-1694 ***6212.30*** *p60*
Davis, Eliza 46; Ontario, 1871 ***1823.22*** *p40*
Davis, Elizabeth *SEE* Davis, Hopkin
Davis, Elizabeth *SEE* Davis, Thomas
Davis, Elizabeth *SEE* Davis, William
Davis, Elizabeth; Maryland, 1664 ***2524.55*** *p63*
Davis, Elizabeth; Maryland, 1682 ***2524.55*** *p63*
Davis, Elizabeth 21; Virginia, 1774 ***1220.25*** *p76*
Davis, Elizabeth Botson; North Carolina, 1818 ***1224.3*** *p20*
Davis, Elizabeth Lee *SEE* Davis, Hopkin
Davis, Elonzo 1; Ontario, 1861 ***2896.26*** *p30*
Davis, Evan; Maryland, 1679 ***2524.55*** *p63*
Davis, Evan; Maryland, 1681 ***2524.55*** *p63*

Davis, Evan; New York, 1834 ***8197.10*** *p372*
Davis, Evan 24; Maryland, 1774 ***1220.25*** *p61*
Davis, Evan Jones; New York, 1837 ***8197.10*** *p225*
Davis, Evan Jones; New York, 1838 ***8197.10*** *p108*
Davis, Ezekiel; Philadelphia, 1802 ***6058.10*** *p39*
Davis, Fannie 20; Ontario, 1861 ***2896.28*** *p39*
Davis, Francis; Maryland, 1657 ***2524.55*** *p63*
Wife: Ann
Daughter: Jennett
Davis, Francis; Virginia, 1671-1672 ***6212.30*** *p47*
Davis, Frank L. 2; Ontario, 1861 ***2896.27*** *p23*
Davis, Freeman 24; Ontario, 1861 ***2896.27*** *p23*
Davis, G. M. 39; Ontario, 1871 ***1823.15*** *p59*
Davis, George; Pennsylvania, 1776 ***4629.10*** *p53*
Davis, George; Philadelphia, 1822 ***1224.3*** *p20*
Davis, George; Virginia, 1681 ***6212.30*** *p55*
Davis, George 27; Ontario, 1871 ***1823.15*** *p59*
Davis, George S. 4; Ontario, 1861 ***2896.27*** *p23*
Davis, Griffith 54; Ontario, 1871 ***1823.15*** *p59*
Davis, Hannah; Maryland, 1659 ***2524.55*** *p63*
Davis, Hannah; Vermont, 1846-1922 ***5900.10*** *p494*
Davis, Henery 41; Ontario, 1871 ***1823.28*** *p22*
Davis, Henry; Maryland, 1673 ***2524.55*** *p64*
Davis, Henry; New York, 1826 ***8197.10*** *p224*
Davis, Henry 27; Ontario, 1871 ***1823.15*** *p59*
Davis, Hester; Maryland, 1682 ***2524.55*** *p63*
Davis, Hopkin; Maryland, 1664 ***2524.55*** *p63*
Wife: Elizabeth
Daughter: Elizabeth Lee
Davis, Humphry; Virginia, 1668-1669 ***6212.30*** *p40*
Davis, Israel; Pennsylvania, 1779 ***4629.10*** *p36*
Davis, James; Maryland, 1665 ***2524.55*** *p63*
Davis, James; Maryland, 1681 ***2524.55*** *p63*
Davis, James; New York, 1830 ***8197.10*** *p225*
Davis, James; Pennsylvania, 1777 ***4629.10*** *p29*
Davis, James; Virginia, 1674-1675 ***6212.30*** *p53*
Davis, James 21; Maryland, 1774 ***1220.25*** *p47*
Davis, James 34; Ontario, 1871 ***1823.28*** *p22*
Davis, James 39; Ontario, 1871 ***1823.15*** *p59*
Davis, James 52; Ontario, 1871 ***1823.15*** *p59*
Davis, James 76; Ontario, 1861 ***2896.28*** *p39*
Davis, Jane *SEE* Davis, Thomas
Davis, Jane *SEE* Davis, William
Davis, Jane 29; Maryland, 1774 ***1220.25*** *p59*
Davis, Jennett *SEE* Davis, Francis
Davis, Jno.; Maryland, 1680 ***2524.55*** *p64*
Davis, Jno.; Maryland, 1682 ***2524.55*** *p64*
Davis, Jno; Virginia, 1668-1669 ***6212.30*** *p40*
Davis, Jno; Virginia, 1674 ***6212.30*** *p52*
Davis, John *SEE* Davis, Thomas
Davis, John; Boston, 1725 ***1224.2*** *p31*
Davis, John; Maryland, 1653 ***2524.55*** *p64*
Davis, John; Maryland, 1658 ***2524.55*** *p64*
Wife: Mary
Davis, John; Maryland, 1673 ***2524.55*** *p64*
Davis, John; Nantucket, Massachusetts, 1843 ***1224.3*** *p20*
Davis, John; New York, 1827 ***8197.10*** *p224*
Davis, John; New York, 1829 ***8197.10*** *p65*
Davis, John; New York, 1840 ***8197.10*** *p158*
Davis, John; Pennsylvania, 1778 ***4629.10*** *p32*
Davis, John; Philadelphia, 1779 ***1224.2*** *p31*
Davis, John 21; Maryland, 1774 ***1220.25*** *p53*
Davis, John 21; Maryland, 1774 ***1220.25*** *p64*
Davis, John 26; Virginia, 1775 ***1220.25*** *p95*
Davis, John 35; Ontario, 1871 ***1823.15*** *p59*
Davis, John 54; Ontario, 1871 ***1823.22*** *p40*
Davis, John Joseph; New York, 1839 ***8197.10*** *p226*
Davis, Jonathan; Virginia, 1684 ***1224.1*** *p17*
Davis, Joseph; Pennsylvania, 1777 ***4629.10*** *p27*
Davis, Judith; Maryland, 1672 ***2524.55*** *p64*
Davis, Katharine; Maryland, 1681 ***2524.55*** *p64*
Davis, Katharine; Virginia, 1703-1704 ***6212.30*** *p62*
Davis, L. 22; Ontario, 1861 ***2896.26*** *p7*
Davis, Lewellyn; Pennsylvania, 1781 ***4629.10*** *p42*
Davis, Lewis; New England, 1702 ***1224.2*** *p31*
Davis, Lydia 32; Maryland, 1775 ***1220.25*** *p96*
Davis, M. 32; Ontario, 1861 ***2896.28*** *p2*
Davis, M. C. 4; Ontario, 1861 ***2896.26*** *p7*
Davis, Margaret; Boston, 1662 ***1224.1*** *p47*
Davis, Margaret 74; Ontario, 1871 ***1823.15*** *p59*
Davis, Margarett; Maryland, 1681 ***2524.55*** *p64*
Davis, Margarett; Maryland, 1682 ***2524.55*** *p64*
Davis, Mary *SEE* Davis, John
Davis, Mary; Maryland, 1682 ***2524.55*** *p64*
Davis, Mary; Virginia, 1664 ***6212.30*** *p10*
Davis, Mary; Virginia, 1673 ***6212.30*** *p51*
Davis, Mary 69; Ontario, 1871 ***1823.22*** *p40*
Davis, Mathew; Virginia, 1666-1667 ***6212.30*** *p32*
Davis, Michael; Canada, 1756-1760 ***4628.40*** *p45*
Davis, Morrice; Maryland, 1669 ***2524.55*** *p64*
Davis, Nathaniel; Maryland, 1681 ***2524.55*** *p64*
Davis, Patrick 40; Ontario, 1871 ***1823.15*** *p59*
Davis, Patrick J.; New York, New York, 1868 ***3437.14*** *p111*
Davis, Richard; New York, 1840 ***8197.10*** *p156*
Davis, Richard; St. Louis, 1853 ***1224.3*** *p20*
Davis, Richard 12; Philadelphia, 1774 ***1220.25*** *p4*
Davis, Richard 40; Ontario, 1871 ***1823.28*** *p22*
Davis, Richard 44; Ontario, 1871 ***1823.15*** *p59*
Davis, Richd 57; Ontario, 1871 ***1823.28*** *p22*
Davis, Robert; Maryland, 1658 ***2524.55*** *p64*
Davis, Robert; Pennsylvania, 1785 ***4629.10*** *p44*
Davis, Robert; Virginia, 1671 ***6212.30*** *p43*
Davis, Robert 56; Ontario, 1871 ***1823.15*** *p59*
Davis, Roger; Maryland, 1674 ***2524.55*** *p64*
Davis, Ruth 46; Ontario, 1871 ***1823.28*** *p22*
Davis, Samll; Virginia, 1671-1672 ***6212.30*** *p47*
Davis, Samuel; Pennsylvania, 1777 ***4629.10*** *p14*
Davis, Samuel; Pennsylvania, 1786 ***4629.10*** *p55*
Davis, Samuel 28; Maryland, 1774 ***1220.25*** *p59*
Davis, Samuel 44; Ontario, 1871 ***1823.15*** *p59*
Davis, Sarah; Maryland, 1665 ***2524.55*** *p64*
Davis, Sarah; Vermont, 1836-1871 ***5900.10*** *p74*
Davis, Sarah 10; Ontario, 1861 ***2896.26*** *p30*
Davis, Serintha 54; Ontario, 1861 ***2896.28*** *p39*
Davis, Silas 32; Ontario, 1871 ***1823.15*** *p59*
Davis, Solomon; New York, 1832 ***8197.10*** *p356*
Davis, Stoakes; Virginia, 1703-1704 ***6212.30*** *p62*
Davis, Tho; Virginia, 1677 ***6212.30*** *p54*
Davis, Thomas; Maryland, 1670 ***2524.55*** *p64*
Wife: Jane
Child: Elizabeth
Child: John
Davis, Thomas; Maryland, 1671 ***2524.55*** *p64*
Davis, Thomas; Maryland, 1673 ***2524.55*** *p64*
Davis, Thomas; Maryland, 1682 ***2524.55*** *p64*
Davis, Thomas; New York, 1839 ***8197.10*** *p380*
Davis, Thomas; Pennsylvania, 1777 ***4629.10*** *p23*
Davis, Thomas; Pennsylvania, 1777 ***4629.10*** *p25*
Davis, Thomas; Pennsylvania, 1779 ***4629.10*** *p38*
Davis, Thomas; Virginia, 1668-1669 ***6212.30*** *p40*
Davis, Thomas; Virginia, 1671 ***6212.30*** *p45*
Davis, Thomas 19; Maryland, 1774 ***1220.25*** *p70*
Davis, Thomas 22; Maryland, 1775 ***1220.25*** *p111*
Davis, Thomas 26; Philadelphia, 1774 ***1220.25*** *p63*
Davis, Thomas 40; Virginia, 1774 ***1220.25*** *p46*
Davis, Thomas 45; Ontario, 1871 ***1823.28*** *p22*
Davis, Thomas 55; Ontario, 1871 ***1823.15*** *p59*
Davis, W. 35; British Columbia, 1913 ***9196.1*** *p62*
Davis, W. 35; Washington, 1913 ***9196.1*** *p62*
Davis, Watkin; Pennsylvania, 1867 ***6058.10*** *p57*
Davis, Wells; Virginia, 1732 ***1224.2*** *p31*
Davis, Wesley 8; Ontario, 1861 ***2896.26*** *p30*
Davis, William; Maryland, 1665 ***2524.55*** *p64*
Davis, William; Maryland, 1672 ***2524.55*** *p64*
Wife: Elizabeth
Child: David
Child: Anne
Child: Jane
Davis, William; Maryland, 1673 ***2524.55*** *p64*
Davis, William; Maryland, 1679 ***2524.55*** *p63*
Davis, William; New Orleans, 1828 ***1224.3*** *p20*
Davis, William; New York, 1694 ***1224.1*** *p17*
Davis, William; Pennsylvania, 1777 ***4629.10*** *p6*
Davis, William; Pennsylvania, 1846 ***6058.10*** *p27*
Davis, William; Vermont, 1842-1916 ***5900.10*** *p466*
Davis, William; Virginia, 1668-1669 ***6212.30*** *p40*
Davis, William 6; Ontario, 1861 ***2896.26*** *p30*
Davis, William 40; Ontario, 1871 ***1823.15*** *p59*
Davis, William 42; Ontario, 1871 ***1823.15*** *p59*
Davis, William 58; Ontario, 1871 ***1823.28*** *p22*
Davis, Wm; Virginia, 1672 ***6212.30*** *p49*
Davis, Zadock Abraham; New York, 1825 ***8197.10*** *p222*
Davise, Henry; Maryland, 1673 ***2524.55*** *p64*
Davison, Alexander 23; Ontario, 1871 ***1823.15*** *p59*
Davison, Alexander 84; Ontario, 1871 ***1823.15*** *p59*
Davison, Amarilla 20; Ontario, 1861 ***2896.25*** *p67*
Davison, Ann *SEE* Davison, John
Davison, Daniel *SEE* Davison, John
Davison, David 5; Ontario, 1861 ***2896.25*** *p63*
Davison, Eliza 23; Ontario, 1861 ***2896.25*** *p66*
Davison, Elizabeth *SEE* Davison, John
Davison, Emeline 3; Ontario, 1861 ***2896.25*** *p63*
Davison, George; Maryland, 1670 ***2524.55*** *p64*
Davison, George 28; Maryland, 1774 ***1220.25*** *p53*
Davison, Henry 4 *SEE* Davison, Sarah
Davison, Henry 8; Ontario, 1861 ***2896.25*** *p63*
Davison, James 20; Ontario, 1861 ***2896.25*** *p63*
Davison, James 22; Maryland, 1775 ***1220.25*** *p105*
Davison, James 45; Ontario, 1871 ***1823.28*** *p22*
Davison, James 48; Ontario, 1871 ***1823.15*** *p59*
Davison, Jane *SEE* Davison, John
Davison, Jane 19; Ontario, 1861 ***2896.25*** *p63*
Davison, John; Maryland, 1670 ***2524.55*** *p64*
Wife: Elizabeth
Child: Jane
Child: Daniel
Child: Ann
Davison, John 10; Ontario, 1861 ***2896.25*** *p63*
Davison, Margaret 21; Ontario, 1861 ***2896.25*** *p66*
Davison, Martha 47; Ontario, 1861 ***2896.25*** *p66*
Davison, Mary 13; Ontario, 1861 ***2896.25*** *p63*
Davison, Mary Anne 57; Ontario, 1871 ***1823.28*** *p22*
Davison, R. 19; Ontario, 1861 ***2896.25*** *p29*
Davison, Richard 8 *SEE* Davison, Sarah
Davison, Robert 25; Ontario, 1861 ***2896.25*** *p66*
Davison, Robert 50; Ontario, 1871 ***1823.28*** *p22*
Davison, Sarah 34; Georgia, 1774 ***1220.25*** *p65*
Child: Thomas 9
Child: Richard 8
Child: Henry 4
Davison, Thomas 9 *SEE* Davison, Sarah
Davison, Thomas 45; Ontario, 1861 ***2896.25*** *p63*
Davison, Thomas, Jr. 16; Ontario, 1861 ***2896.25*** *p63*
Davison, William; Boston, 1776 ***1224.2*** *p31*
Davison, William; Maryland, 1649 ***2524.55*** *p65*
Davison, William 18; Ontario, 1861 ***2896.25*** *p63*
Davison, William 29; Maryland, 1775 ***1220.25*** *p113*
Davison, William 36; Ontario, 1871 ***1823.28*** *p22*
Davock, Mary Sherlock; Vermont, 1831-1906 ***5900.10*** *p84*
Davock, Michael E.; New York, 1836 ***8197.10*** *p319*
Davock, Patrick; Vermont, 1830-1903 ***5900.10*** *p84*
Davran, Anna Coughlin; Vermont, 1809-1906 ***5900.10*** *p614*
Davran, Jeremiah 75; Vermont, 1875 ***5900.10*** *p614*
Davy, Eliz.; Maryland, 1649 ***2524.55*** *p77*
Davy, John; Virginia, 1649 ***1224.1*** *p17*
Davy, John; Virginia, 1666 ***6212.30*** *p30*
Davy, Richard; New York, 1834 ***8197.10*** *p72*
Davyes, Roger; Maryland, 1667 ***2524.55*** *p65*
Daw, Anne 20 *SEE* Daw, Thomas
Daw, Biddy 4 *SEE* Daw, Thomas
Daw, Bridget 28 *SEE* Daw, Thomas
Daw, James 20 *SEE* Daw, Thomas
Daw, John; Maryland, 1666 ***2524.55*** *p244*
Daw, John 18 *SEE* Daw, Thomas
Daw, John 44; Ontario, 1871 ***1823.15*** *p59*
Daw, Mary 16 *SEE* Daw, Thomas
Daw, Mary Ann 6 months *SEE* Daw, Thomas
Daw, Pat 2 *SEE* Daw, Thomas
Daw, Thomas 32; New York, New York, 1848 ***1825.45*** *p31*
Sister: Anne 20
Sister: Mary 16
Brother: James 20
Daughter: Mary Ann 6 months
Daughter: Biddy 4
Son: Pat 2
Wife: Bridget 28
Brother: John 18
Dawcy, John; Maryland, 1660 ***2524.55*** *p65*
Dawe, Anne 20 *SEE* Dawe, Thomas
Dawe, Biddy 4 *SEE* Dawe, Thomas
Dawe, Bridget 28 *SEE* Dawe, Thomas
Dawe, George 67; Ontario, 1871 ***1823.22*** *p40*
Dawe, James 20 *SEE* Dawe, Thomas
Dawe, John 18 *SEE* Dawe, Thomas
Dawe, John 41; Ontario, 1871 ***1823.22*** *p40*
Dawe, John 73; Ontario, 1871 ***1823.22*** *p40*
Dawe, Mary 16 *SEE* Dawe, Thomas
Dawe, Mary Ann 6 months *SEE* Dawe, Thomas
Dawe, Pat 2 *SEE* Dawe, Thomas
Dawe, Thomas 32; New York, New York, 1848 ***1825.45*** *p31*
Wife: Bridget 28
Son: Pat 2
Brother: James 20
Sister: Anne 20
Sister: Mary 16
Brother: John 18
Daughter: Mary Ann 6 months
Daughter: Biddy 4
Dawes, Francis; New York, 1837 ***8197.10*** *p83*
Dawes, John; Virginia, 1664 ***6212.30*** *p8*
Dawes, Samuel 26; Philadelphia, 1774 ***1220.25*** *p55*
Dawin, Hirominns 56; Ontario, 1871 ***1823.15*** *p59*
Dawison, Robert 51; Ontario, 1871 ***1823.15*** *p59*
Dawkin, Elizabeth; Maryland, 1665 ***2524.55*** *p65*
Dawkins, Edward 29; Philadelphia, 1774 ***1220.25*** *p35*
Dawkins, Joseph; Maryland, 1656 ***2524.55*** *p65*
Dawkins, Mary 61; Ontario, 1871 ***1823.22*** *p40*
Dawkins, Simon; Long Island, 1675 ***1224.1*** *p17*
Dawney, Bryan; Virginia, 1722 ***1224.2*** *p31*
Dawpool, Richard; Virginia, 1667-1668 ***6212.30*** *p39*
Dawsett, George; New York, 1840 ***8197.10*** *p158*

Dawsey, Ralph; Maryland, 1660 ***2524.55*** *p65*
Dawson, Mr.; Quebec, 1858 ***9196.15*** *p32*
Dawson, Mr.; Quebec, 1858 ***9196.15*** *p34*
Dawson, Abraham; Maryland, 1664 ***2524.55*** *p65*
Dawson, Abraham; New York, 1794 ***8197.10*** *p5*
Dawson, Abram 53; Ontario, 1871 ***1823.28*** *p22*
Dawson, Alexander 27; Ontario, 1871 ***1823.15*** *p59*
Dawson, Anthony *SEE* Dawson, William, Sr.
Dawson, Benedict; New Orleans, 1856 ***3437.14*** *p16*
Dawson, Doratha; Virginia, 1703-1704 ***6212.30*** *p63*
Dawson, Dougald; Trinidad, 1841 ***1640.13*** *p29*
Dawson, Eleanor; Baltimore, 1834 ***1224.3*** *p20*
Dawson, Eliza 21; Philadelphia, 1774 ***1220.25*** *p63*
Dawson, Elizabeth; New York, 1839 ***8197.10*** *p226*
Dawson, Elizabeth 8; Ontario, 1871 ***1823.22*** *p40*
Dawson, Frederick 39; Maryland, 1774 ***1220.25*** *p73*
Dawson, Frederick 39; Maryland, 1774 ***1220.25*** *p77*
Dawson, George 30; Ontario, 1871 ***1823.15*** *p59*
Dawson, Hanrey 50; Ontario, 1871 ***1823.15*** *p59*
Dawson, J.; Quebec, 1856 ***9196.15*** *p11*
Dawson, James; Pennsylvania, 1808 ***6058.10*** *p2*
Dawson, James 25; Maryland, 1775 ***1220.25*** *p108*
Dawson, James 61; Ontario, 1871 ***1823.28*** *p22*
Dawson, Jane; Maryland, 1672 ***2524.55*** *p65*
Dawson, John; Maryland, 1672 ***2524.55*** *p65*
Dawson, John; Maryland, 1681 ***2524.55*** *p65*
Dawson, John 22; Virginia, 1773 ***1220.25*** *p30*
Dawson, John 55; Ontario, 1871 ***1823.22*** *p40*
Dawson, John 64; Ontario, 1871 ***1823.15*** *p59*
Dawson, Jone *SEE* Dawson, William, Sr.
Dawson, Mabell *SEE* Dawson, Ralph
Dawson, Margret 52; Ontario, 1871 ***1823.15*** *p59*
Dawson, Mary; Maryland, 1660 ***2524.55*** *p65*
Dawson, Mary 62; Ontario, 1871 ***1823.15*** *p59*
Dawson, Michael; Pennsylvania, 1777 ***4629.10*** *p7*
Dawson, Patrick; Philadelphia, 1785 ***1224.2*** *p31*
Dawson, Peter 40; Ontario, 1871 ***1823.22*** *p40*
Dawson, Ralph; Maryland, 1662 ***2524.55*** *p65*
Wife: Mabell
Dawson, Richd; Virginia, 1690-1691 ***6212.30*** *p59*
Dawson, Robert 28; Virginia, 1775 ***1220.25*** *p95*
Dawson, Robt; Virginia, 1671-1672 ***6212.30*** *p47*
Dawson, Susanna 16; Jamaica, 1774 ***1220.25*** *p91*
Dawson, Tho.; Maryland, 1682 ***2524.55*** *p65*
Dawson, Thomas; Georgia, 1734 ***1640.10*** *p40*
Dawson, Thomas; New York, 1807 ***8197.10*** *p37*
Dawson, Thomas; New York, 1807 ***8197.10*** *p38*
Dawson, Thomas; Pennsylvania, 1821 ***6058.10*** *p6*
Dawson, Thomas C.; New York, 1830 ***8197.10*** *p360*
Dawson, Thomas J. 22; Ontario, 1871 ***1823.28*** *p22*
Dawson, Timothy; New York, 1840 ***8197.10*** *p226*
Dawson, William; Baltimore, 1828 ***1224.3*** *p20*
Dawson, William; Georgia, 1775 ***1640.10*** *p40*
Dawson, William; Maryland, 1822 ***1224.3*** *p20*
Dawson, William; Pensacola, Florida, 1770 ***1640.13*** *p29*
Dawson, William; Pensacola, Florida, 1770-1845 ***1640.10*** *p40*
Dawson, William 17; Philadelphia, 1774 ***1220.25*** *p81*
Dawson, William 40; Ontario, 1871 ***1823.28*** *p22*
Dawson, William 65; Ontario, 1871 ***1823.22*** *p40*
Dawson, William, Sr.; Maryland, 1665 ***2524.55*** *p65*
Son: William, Jr.
Relative: Jone
Relative: Anthony
Dawson, William, Jr. *SEE* Dawson, William, Sr.
Dawson, William Alfred; Mobile, Alabama, 1842-1845 ***1640.10*** *p40*
Dawsonson, Cornelius; Maryland, 1659 ***2524.55*** *p65*
Wife: Ellynor
Daughter: Cristine
Dawsonson, Cristine *SEE* Dawsonson, Cornelius
Dawsonson, Ellynor *SEE* Dawsonson, Cornelius
Dawsye, James; Virginia, 1671-1672 ***6212.30*** *p47*
Dax, Cornelius 26; Philadelphia, 1774 ***1220.25*** *p63*
Dax, John; New York, 1840 ***8197.10*** *p157*
Dax, Thomas; Maryland, 1678 ***2524.55*** *p65*
Daxheimer, Daniel; Port uncertain, 1754 ***2856.30*** *p75*
Day, Mrs.; Maryland, 1652 ***2524.55*** *p65*
Day, Mrs.; Maryland, 1659 ***2524.55*** *p65*
Day, Mrs.; Quebec, 1858 ***9196.15*** *p35*
Day, Alexander 31; Ontario, 1871 ***1823.15*** *p59*
Day, Ann; Vermont, 1841-1916 ***5900.10*** *p349*
Day, Benjamin; Pennsylvania, 1805 ***1224.3*** *p20*
Day, C. J.; Portland, Maine, 1858 ***9196.15*** *p29*
Day, Mrs. C. J.; Portland, Maine, 1858 ***9196.15*** *p29*
Day, Charlotte 19; Ontario, 1861 ***2896.27*** *p56*
Day, Eliza 44; Ontario, 1871 ***1823.22*** *p40*
Day, Elizabeth 50; Ontario, 1871 ***1823.15*** *p59*
Day, Francis 30; Maryland, 1775 ***1220.25*** *p104*
Day, George 72; Ontario, 1871 ***1823.22*** *p40*
Day, Hannah A.; Vermont, 1843-1885 ***5900.10*** *p549*
Day, Humphrey; Maryland, 1681 ***2524.55*** *p65*
Day, J.; Quebec, 1856 ***9196.15*** *p7*
Day, Mrs. J.; Quebec, 1856 ***9196.15*** *p7*
Day, James; Maryland, 1660 ***2524.55*** *p65*
Day, James 24; Maryland, 1774 ***1220.25*** *p57*
Day, John; Maryland, 1652 ***2524.55*** *p65*
With wife & daughter
Day, John; New York, 1829 ***8197.10*** *p299*
Day, John; New York, 1852 ***1224.3*** *p20*
Day, John; Virginia, 1672 ***1224.1*** *p17*
Day, John 44; Ontario, 1871 ***1823.28*** *p22*
Day, John 50; Ontario, 1871 ***1823.15*** *p59*
Day, John P.; New York, 1839 ***8197.10*** *p129*
Day, Joseph; New York, 1839 ***8197.10*** *p380*
Day, Margaret Langley; Maryland, 1699 ***1224.1*** *p35*
Day, Mary; Virginia, 1721 ***1224.2*** *p45*
Day, Richard; Maryland, 1681 ***2524.55*** *p65*
Day, Roger; Maryland, 1668 ***2524.55*** *p62*
Day, Thomas; Charles Town, South Carolina, 1765 ***1224.2*** *p32*
Day, Thomas; Maryland, 1728 ***1224.2*** *p31*
Day, Thomas 42; Ontario, 1871 ***1823.28*** *p22*
Day, Thomas 45; Ontario, 1871 ***1823.22*** *p40*
Day, William; New Jersey, 1706 ***1224.2*** *p32*
Day, Wiloughby 14; Barbados, 1774 ***1220.25*** *p82*
Daye, George; Virginia, 1671-1672 ***6212.30*** *p46*
Dayley, Jno; Virginia, 1664 ***6212.30*** *p11*
Dayly, John; Charles Town, South Carolina, 1768 ***1224.2*** *p32*
Dayman, Joseph 21; Philadelphia, 1774 ***1220.25*** *p81*
Daymon, Francis; Pennsylvania, 1777 ***4629.10*** *p7*
Daymond, John 43; Ontario, 1871 ***1823.15*** *p59*
Daymond, Tho; Virginia, 1672 ***6212.30*** *p50*
Daymont, Charles 54; Ontario, 1871 ***1823.15*** *p59*
Dayne, Thomas; Maryland, 1665 ***2524.55*** *p65*
Dayrell, Paul; New York, New York, 1805 ***1224.3*** *p20*
Days, Hannah 38; Ontario, 1871 ***1823.15*** *p59*
Dczensky, Stanislaw; Maryland, 1910 ***3259.35*** *p11*
Deacon, Charles; Maryland, 1655 ***2524.55*** *p65*
Deacon, Henry 43; Ontario, 1871 ***1823.22*** *p41*
Deacon, Henry 68; Ontario, 1871 ***1823.15*** *p59*
Deacon, James 15; Maryland, 1775 ***1220.25*** *p104*
Deacon, John 15; Georgia, 1774 ***1220.25*** *p47*
Deacon, Peter 25; Maryland, 1774 ***1220.25*** *p85*
Deacon, Thomas; Virginia, 1652 ***1224.1*** *p17*
Deacon, William 22; Maryland, 1774 ***1220.25*** *p42*
Deacon, William 67; Ontario, 1871 ***1823.15*** *p60*
Deacy, Anthony; Vermont, 1849-1918 ***5900.10*** *p557*
Deacy, Maria Holleran; Vermont, 1844-1932 ***5900.10*** *p557*
Deadlo, Daniel; America, 1754 ***2856.30*** *p84*
Deadman, Charity; Maryland, 1681 ***2524.55*** *p65*
Deady, Bridget M. 76; Vermont, 1898 ***5900.10*** *p165*
Deady, Ellen O'Brine; Vermont, 1847-1916 ***5900.10*** *p144*
Deady, Jeremiah; Vermont, 1847-1913 ***5900.10*** *p144*
Deady, Katherine C.; Vermont, n.d. ***5900.10*** *p144*
Deady, Mary 75; Vermont, 1911 ***5900.10*** *p144*
Deagh, Joseph; Maryland, 1672 ***2524.55*** *p65*
Deags, Joseph; Maryland, 1672 ***2524.55*** *p65*
Deal, Conrad; New York, 1807 ***8197.10*** *p38*
Deal, John; New York, 1828 ***8197.10*** *p225*
Deal, John; Pennsylvania, 1777 ***4629.10*** *p9*
Deal, Maria L. Brennan; Vermont, 1853-1903 ***5900.10*** *p284*
Deal, Ralph M.; Vermont, 1847-1932 ***5900.10*** *p284*
Dealy, Charles; New York, 1807 ***8197.10*** *p327*
Dealy, John 31; Maryland, 1775 ***1220.25*** *p109*
Dealy, Joseph 40; Ontario, 1871 ***1823.28*** *p22*
Dealy, Martin 40; Ontario, 1871 ***1823.28*** *p22*
Dealy, Mary 22; Maryland, 1775 ***1220.25*** *p109*
Dean, Anthony; New York, New York, 1854 ***6058.10*** *p52*
Dean, Benjamin; Pennsylvania, 1777 ***4629.10*** *p29*
Dean, Charles; Maryland, 1775 ***1220.25*** *p113*
Dean, Corbin 69; Ontario, 1871 ***1823.22*** *p41*
Dean, Eliza 18; Ontario, 1871 ***1823.28*** *p22*
Dean, Fanny; Boston, 1830 ***1224.3*** *p15*
Dean, Jane; New York, 1890 ***1640.13*** *p29*
Dean, John; Pennsylvania, 1777 ***4629.10*** *p8*
Dean, John 18; Philadelphia, 1774 ***1220.25*** *p4*
Dean, John 19; Georgia, 1775 ***1220.25*** *p124*
Dean, John 77; Ontario, 1871 ***1823.15*** *p60*
Dean, Joseph; New York, 1805 ***8197.10*** *p29*
Dean, Joseph; Pennsylvania, 1777 ***4629.10*** *p6*
Dean, Lawrence; New York, New York, 1854 ***6058.10*** *p52*
Dean, Michael; New York, New York, 1850 ***6058.10*** *p59*
Dean, Robert 28; Nova Scotia, 1774 ***1220.25*** *p136*
Dean, Thos 46; Ontario, 1871 ***1823.28*** *p22*
Dean, William 19; Maryland, 1775 ***1220.25*** *p102*
Dean, William 35; Maryland, 1775 ***1220.25*** *p111*
Deane, George; New England, 1693 ***1224.1*** *p17*
Deane, John; Maryland, 1681 ***2524.55*** *p65*
Deane, John; Virginia, 1684-1685 ***6212.30*** *p57*
Deane, Thomas; Boston, n.d. ***1224.1*** *p17*
Deane, Thomas 27; Maryland, 1774 ***1220.25*** *p70*
Deane, William; Maryland, 1680 ***2524.55*** *p65*
Deane, William 36; Maryland, 1775 ***1220.25*** *p100*
Deans, Peter 48; Ontario, 1871 ***1823.15*** *p60*
Deans, Robert 31; Ontario, 1871 ***1823.22*** *p41*
Deape, Alice; Maryland, 1672 ***2524.55*** *p65*
Dear, Edward 40; Ontario, 1871 ***1823.22*** *p41*
Dear, Samuel 55; Ontario, 1871 ***1823.22*** *p41*
Dear, William 48; Ontario, 1871 ***1823.28*** *p22*
Dearden, Mary 81; Vermont, 1877 ***5900.10*** *p494*
Dearin, Andrew; New York, 1837 ***8197.10*** *p86*
Dearing, Abraham 35; Ontario, 1871 ***1823.15*** *p60*
Dearing, Jane 74; Ontario, 1871 ***1823.15*** *p60*
Dearing, Thomas 44; Ontario, 1871 ***1823.15*** *p60*
Dearing, William 39; Ontario, 1871 ***1823.15*** *p60*
Deary, Barney; New York, 1840 ***8197.10*** *p158*
Deary, Bernard; New York, 1840 ***8197.10*** *p158*
Deary, James; New York, 1803 ***8197.10*** *p12*
Deas, David; New York, 1794 ***8197.10*** *p5*
Deasaimue, Jeane; Maryland, 1631-1685 ***2524.55*** *p30*
Dease, Patrick; New York, 1837 ***8197.10*** *p83*
Deaver, Mary 45; Vermont, 1849 ***5900.10*** *p279*
Deaver, Richard; Maryland, 1664 ***2524.55*** *p65*
Deaves, Henry; New York, 1799 ***8197.10*** *p9*
Deavitt, Julia Ann 25; Vermont, 1835 ***5900.10*** *p373*
Deavour, Richard; Maryland, 1666 ***2524.55*** *p65*
Deayes, Joseph; Maryland, 1673 ***2524.55*** *p65*
Debald, Peter; Maryland, 1910 ***3259.35*** *p11*
Debarats, Mr.; Quebec, 1858 ***9196.15*** *p42*
De Barcaiztequi, Joseph Michael; New York, 1831 ***8197.10*** *p356*
DeBarthot, David; Pennsylvania, 1777 ***4629.10*** *p11*
De Beaufain, Hector Beringer; Charles Town, South Carolina, 1767 ***1224.2*** *p32*
de Begnis, Giuseppe; New York, 1849 ***1224.3*** *p20*
De Belenhard, John 37; Ontario, 1871 ***1823.28*** *p22*
De Belleville, Colonel; Quebec, 1858 ***9196.15*** *p46*
Debescon, Lewis; Philadelphia, 1793 ***4629.10*** *p73*
Debeski, George A.; Maryland, 1910 ***3259.35*** *p11*
Debinski, Nicholas; Maryland, 1910 ***3259.35*** *p11*
De Blaguiere, Lord; Quebec, 1857 ***9196.15*** *p16*
Deboben, Elisabeth; Port uncertain, 1732 ***2856.30*** *p75*
De Boever, J. 39; Alaska, 1917 ***9196.1*** *p50*
De Boever, J. 39; Yukon, 1917 ***9196.1*** *p50*
Debor, J.; Portland, Maine, 1857 ***9196.15*** *p13*
Deborox, Joseph 22; Maryland, 1774 ***1220.25*** *p59*
DeBray, Daniel; Pennsylvania, 1787 ***4629.10*** *p55*
De Brey, Fusiens; Philadelphia, 1793 ***4629.10*** *p70*
De Brot, Henry; New York, 1818 ***8197.10*** *p222*
DeBrynn, Dirick Tomson; Maryland, 1664 ***2524.55*** *p65*
Debuke, Thomas; Boston, 1748 ***1224.2*** *p32*
Debus, Conrad 31; Ontario, 1871 ***1823.15*** *p60*
Debus, Dorothea; Port uncertain, 1781 ***2856.30*** *p75*
De Bussey, Thomas; New York, 1838 ***8197.10*** *p109*
De Butts, Mary; Virginia, 1831 ***1224.3*** *p20*
De Butts, Samuel; Maryland, 1816 ***1224.3*** *p20*
Decaadia, Mr.; Quebec, 1858 ***9196.15*** *p37*
Decaadia, Mrs.; Quebec, 1858 ***9196.15*** *p37*
Decasse, Cecile M.; New York, 1833 ***8197.10*** *p68*
De Castro, Emanuel; New York, 1838 ***8197.10*** *p225*
De Cazes, C. H., Sr.; Portland, Maine, 1857 ***9196.15*** *p12*
De Cazes, C. H., Jr.; Portland, Maine, 1857 ***9196.15*** *p12*
De Cazes, L.; Portland, Maine, 1857 ***9196.15*** *p12*
Decerf, Sebastian; New York, 1805 ***8197.10*** *p29*
De Cevallos, Ciracio; New Orleans, 1819 ***1224.3*** *p21*
Decevee, Pierre T.; New York, 1821 ***8197.10*** *p223*
Dech, Jakob; America, 1741 ***2856.30*** *p75*
With wife & children
Dechant, Catherine 53; Kansas, 1874-1910 ***9079.10*** *p9*
Dechant, John, Jr. 67; Kansas, 1875-1910 ***9079.10*** *p9*
De Charbonnel, Bishop; Quebec, 1858 ***9196.15*** *p33*
Decher, John 39; Ontario, 1871 ***1823.15*** *p60*
Dechert, Lorenz 35; Ontario, 1871 ***1823.15*** *p60*
Dechruski, Richard; Maryland, 1910 ***3259.35*** *p11*
Deck, Barbara; Port uncertain, 1768 ***2856.30*** *p75*
Deck, Friedrich; Port uncertain, 1749 ***2856.30*** *p75*
Deckener, Augustus William; New York, 1821 ***8197.10*** *p223*
Decker, Anna Maria Muller; Port uncertain, 1742 ***2856.30*** *p316*
Decker, Anton; Port uncertain, 1791 ***2856.30*** *p75*
Decker, Augustus; New York, 1832 ***8197.10*** *p368*
Decker, Catharina; Port uncertain, 1786 ***2856.30*** *p75*
Decker, Jacob; America, 1751 ***2856.30*** *p75*
Decker, Jacob; America, 1752 ***2856.30*** *p75*
Decker, John; New York, 1838 ***8197.10*** *p108*
Decker, Maria Barbara; America, 1748 ***2856.30*** *p75*
Decker, Thomas 34; Ontario, 1871 ***1823.15*** *p60*
Deckeson, William; Maryland, 1666 ***2524.55*** *p65*
Deck'sche, . . .; America, 1785 ***2856.30*** *p75*
Decon, Charles; Maryland, 1659 ***2524.55*** *p66*
De Conty, Esther; New York, 1819 ***1224.3*** *p21*

DeCost, Elizabeth *SEE* DeCost, Mathias
DeCost, Mathias; Maryland, 1665 ***2524.55*** *p66*
Wife: Elizabeth
DeCoursey, Edward; Vermont, 1819-1899 ***5900.10*** *p541*
DeCoursey, Garrett 96; Vermont, 1868 ***5900.10*** *p542*
DeCoursey, Margaret; Vermont, 1884 ***5900.10*** *p542*
DeCoursey, Margaret 51; Vermont, 1915 ***5900.10*** *p126*
DeCoursey, Margaret 72; Vermont, 1904 ***5900.10*** *p541*
DeCoursey, Mary A. Mullings 41; Vermont, 1915 ***5900.10*** *p126*
DeCoursey, Mary Sullivan 90; Vermont, 1928 ***5900.10*** *p541*
DeCoursey, Richard; Vermont, n.d. ***5900.10*** *p126*
De Courtney, Mr.; Quebec, 1858 ***9196.15*** *p33*
De Courtney, Mrs.; Quebec, 1858 ***9196.15*** *p33*
Decouses, Peter; New York, 1821 ***8197.10*** *p223*
De Cousse, Philip; New York, 1822 ***8197.10*** *p223*
De Covarrubias, Gabriel; New York, 1834 ***8197.10*** *p316*
DeCurinen, John; Maryland, 1664 ***2524.55*** *p66*
Dedebant, Mr.; Quebec, 1858 ***9196.15*** *p45*
Dedicott, John; South Carolina, 1718 ***1224.2*** *p32*
Dedrierski, Joseph; Maryland, 1910 ***3259.35*** *p11*
Dee, Robert 33; Georgia, 1775 ***1220.25*** *p122*
Dee, Saml.; Maryland, 1659 ***2524.55*** *p66*
Dee, Samll.; Maryland, 1656 ***2524.55*** *p66*
Dee, Thomas M.; Indiana, 1880 ***3437.14*** *p118*
Deeg, Andreas; America, 1740 ***2856.30*** *p86*
With wife & children
Deeg, Andreas; America, 1741 ***2856.30*** *p76*
Deeg, Andreas; America, 1741 ***2856.30*** *p78*
Deeg, Andreas; America, 1742 ***2856.30*** *p78*
Deeg, Elias; Port uncertain, 1752 ***2856.30*** *p76*
With family
Deeg, Johann Michael; America, 1742 ***2856.30*** *p76*
Deemondedier, Anthony; Maryland, 1656 ***2524.55*** *p66*
Deepe, Gregory; Maryland, 1661 ***2524.55*** *p66*
Deer, Mrs.; Maryland, 1647 ***2524.55*** *p66*
Deer, Edward 47; Ontario, 1871 ***1823.15*** *p60*
Deer, Henry 64; Ontario, 1871 ***1823.15*** *p60*
Deer, John; Maryland, 1647 ***2524.55*** *p66*
With wife
Deere, Elizabeth; Maryland, 1659 ***2524.55*** *p66*
Deering, Edmond; Maryland, 1639 ***2524.55*** *p66*
Deering, Marion; Vermont, 1841-1915 ***5900.10*** *p597*
Deering, Osmond; Virginia, 1668-1669 ***6212.30*** *p40*
Deering, William 50; Ontario, 1871 ***1823.22*** *p41*
Dees, Andreas; Port uncertain, 1764 ***2856.30*** *p76*
Deese, Benonie; Maryland, 1664 ***2524.55*** *p66*
Deesing, Peter 46; Ontario, 1871 ***1823.15*** *p60*
Deetz, John; Pennsylvania, 1825 ***6058.10*** *p7*
Deeves, John 40; Ontario, 1871 ***1823.15*** *p60*
Deeves, John 64; Ontario, 1871 ***1823.15*** *p60*
de Fermoy, Roche; New England, 1775-1781 ***4628.40*** *p68*
Deffely, Bridget 14 *SEE* Deffely, Patrick
Deffely, George 26; New York, New York, 1847 ***1825.45*** *p14*
Deffely, James 20; New York, New York, 1847 ***1825.45*** *p14*
Deffely, Mary 55 *SEE* Deffely, Patrick
Deffely, Mary 60; New York, New York, 1847 ***1825.45*** *p14*
Deffely, Patrick 60; New York, New York, 1847 ***1825.45*** *p14*
Wife: Mary 55
Daughter: Bridget 14
Deffley, Bridget 14 *SEE* Deffley, Patrick
Deffley, George 26; New York, New York, 1847 ***1825.45*** *p14*
Deffley, James 20; New York, New York, 1847 ***1825.45*** *p14*
Deffley, Mary 55 *SEE* Deffley, Patrick
Deffley, Mary 60; New York, New York, 1847 ***1825.45*** *p14*
Deffley, Patrick 60; New York, New York, 1847 ***1825.45*** *p14*
Wife: Mary 55
Daughter: Bridget 14
De Figaniere, Lewis F.; New York, 1835 ***8197.10*** *p70*
Defino, Mike 51; Alaska, 1914 ***9196.1*** *p40*
de Fontaines, James Alexander; Philadelphia, 1793 ***4629.10*** *p71*
Defresnaye, Nicolas Louis Fontaine 30; Pennsylvania, 1794 ***4629.10*** *p63*
Defscoate, Dermot; Maryland, 1671 ***2524.55*** *p66*
Degan, Patrick; New York, 1840 ***8197.10*** *p226*
Degarne, Madam 27; Grenada, 1774-1775 ***1220.25*** *p128*
Degarne, Jean 30; Grenada, 1774-1775 ***1220.25*** *p128*
de Gazon, Jean Francis Boisbuille; Philadelphia, 1792 ***4629.10*** *p70*
Degelmann, Maria Elisabeth; Port uncertain, 1783 ***2856.30*** *p76*
Degelmann, Maria Elisabeth Kullman; Port uncertain, 1786 ***2856.30*** *p76*
Degelmann, Maria Elisabeth Kullman; Port uncertain, 1788 ***2856.30*** *p76*
Degen, . . .; America, 1737 ***2856.30*** *p76*
With wife & children
Degen, Elias; Port uncertain, 1752 ***2856.30*** *p76*
With family
Degen, Elizabeth; New Orleans, 1825 ***1224.3*** *p21*
Degen, Johann Henrich; America, 1738 ***2856.30*** *p76*
Degenhard, Peter; Port uncertain, 1774 ***2856.30*** *p76*
De Gerate, Eugenio Roque; New York, 1827 ***8197.10*** *p347*
De Gerstner, Francis Anthony Chevalier; Philadelphia, 1840 ***1224.3*** *p21*
Degez, John; New York, 1810 ***8197.10*** *p57*
Degge, Simon; Virginia, 1666 ***6212.30*** *p29*
Degger, Elizabeth; Maryland, 1663 ***2524.55*** *p66*
Degger, Michael; Maryland, 1663 ***2524.55*** *p66*
Degin, Anna Barbara; Port uncertain, 1746 ***2856.30*** *p76*
Deglapion, . . . 23; Grenada, 1774 ***1220.25*** *p128*
Degnan, Bridget; Vermont, 1823-1898 ***5900.10*** *p155*
Degnan, Johanna Gleason; Vermont, 1834-1907 ***5900.10*** *p587*
Degnan, Margaret 52; Vermont, 1862 ***5900.10*** *p149*
Degnan, Patrick; Vermont, 1828-1904 ***5900.10*** *p587*
Degrechts, Philipp Hermann; Port uncertain, 1744 ***2856.30*** *p76*
With wife & 8 children
Degroff, W. H. 18; Ontario, 1861 ***2896.27*** *p36*
Deguerre, Joseph F.; New York, 1827 ***8197.10*** *p224*
Degutes, Michael; Maryland, 1910 ***3259.35*** *p11*
De Haas, John P.; Pennsylvania, 1776 ***4629.10*** *p53*
Dehanne, Jean Vilodorez; New York, 1818 ***8197.10*** *p222*
Dehart, Martin; Pennsylvania, 1779 ***4629.10*** *p36*
Deharty, Barnard; New York, New York, 1843 ***3437.14*** *p70*
DeHattway, Jacob; Maryland, 1649-1652 ***2524.55*** *p67*
Dehaven, Abraham; Pennsylvania, 1777 ***4629.10*** *p24*
Dehn, . . .; America, 1792 ***2856.30*** *p76*
Dehoff, Henrich; America, 1742 ***2856.30*** *p76*
With wife & children
Dehogues, Magloire; Philadelphia, 1793 ***4629.10*** *p81*
Dehost, Philipp Hermann; Port uncertain, 1744 ***2856.30*** *p76*
With wife & 8 children
Dehrer, Hans Georg; Port uncertain, 1753 ***2856.30*** *p76*
Deibel, Ernst; Port uncertain, 1759 ***2856.30*** *p76*
Deicher, Christina; Port uncertain, 1792 ***2856.30*** *p76*
Deichert, Elizabeth 70; Ontario, 1871 ***1823.15*** *p60*
Deichert, John 30; Ontario, 1871 ***1823.15*** *p60*
Deichert, Nickolous 27; Ontario, 1871 ***1823.15*** *p60*
Deickert, Johann Michael; Port uncertain, 1747 ***2856.30*** *p76*
Deickert, Johann Michael; Port uncertain, 1749 ***2856.30*** *p76*
Deidge, Wm; Virginia, 1672 ***6212.30*** *p49*
Deigan, Patrick; New York, 1840 ***8197.10*** *p226*
Deighton, John; Pennsylvania, 1777 ***4629.10*** *p24*
Deighton, John; Pennsylvania, 1779 ***4629.10*** *p38*
Deighton, Thomas 20; New York, 1774 ***1220.25*** *p24*
Deines, Anna Elizabeth 39; Kansas, 1910 ***9079.10*** *p43*
Deines, Cadrina W. 62; Kansas, 1901-1910 ***9079.10*** *p21*
Deines, Catherine 14; Kansas, 1898-1910 ***9079.10*** *p19*
Deines, Christian 40; Kansas, 1898-1910 ***9079.10*** *p19*
Deines, Elizabeth 41; Kansas, 1898-1910 ***9079.10*** *p19*
Deines, Frederick 62; Kansas, 1876-1910 ***9079.10*** *p27*
Deines, George 13; Kansas, 1898-1910 ***9079.10*** *p19*
Deines, George 18; Kansas, 1883-1910 ***9079.10*** *p33*
Deines, George 34; Kansas, 1901-1910 ***9079.10*** *p20*
Deines, George H. 43; Kansas, 1883-1910 ***9079.10*** *p33*
Deines, Henry 43; Kansas, 1875-1910 ***9079.10*** *p34*
Deines, J. J. 40; Kansas, 1910 ***9079.10*** *p43*
Deines, Jacob 38; Kansas, 1890-1910 ***9079.10*** *p49*
Deines, Jacob 67; Kansas, 1901-1910 ***9079.10*** *p21*
Deines, Lena 36; Kansas, 1910 ***9079.10*** *p49*
Deines, Lydia 30; Kansas, 1900-1910 ***9079.10*** *p33*
Deines, Mary 37; Kansas, 1887-1910 ***9079.10*** *p34*
Deines, Mary M. 29; Kansas, 1900-1910 ***9079.10*** *p27*
Deines, Mollie 28; Kansas, 1901-1910 ***9079.10*** *p20*
Deininger, Christoph; New York, 1807 ***8197.10*** *p327*
Deis, John; Pennsylvania, 1860 ***6058.10*** *p42*
Deiss, Jakob; Port uncertain, 1739 ***2856.30*** *p76*
Deissler, Johann Helferic; Port uncertain, 1746 ***2856.30*** *p76*
Deist, Catharina; Port uncertain, 1762 ***2856.30*** *p76*
Deist, Catharina; Port uncertain, 1762 ***2856.30*** *p268*
Deitz, Conrad 38; Ontario, 1871 ***1823.15*** *p60*
De Jong, Roedolph, Jr.; New York, 1840 ***8197.10*** *p157*
De Jong, Roedolph Jacob, Sr.; New York, 1840 ***8197.10*** *p226*
Dek, Jakob; Port uncertain, 1752 ***2856.30*** *p76*
Dekanatter, Christopher 53; Ontario, 1871 ***1823.28*** *p22*
Dekins, James; New York, 1840 ***8197.10*** *p157*
Dekins, William; New York, 1840 ***8197.10*** *p158*
Dekowski, John; Maryland, 1910 ***3259.35*** *p11*
Delabarre, Lewis Hyppolite; Philadelphia, 1793 ***4629.10*** *p69*
De La Cadena, Mariano Velazquez; New York, 1818 ***8197.10*** *p222*
DeLacey, Matthew P.; New York, 1831 ***8197.10*** *p364*
De La Chauvetiere, Charles Louis; Philadelphia, 1793 ***4629.10*** *p70*
de la Combe, John Anselmo Douin; Pennsylvania, 1785 ***4629.10*** *p48*
Delacroix, Louis; New York, 1807 ***8197.10*** *p38*
Delader, David; America, 1741 ***2856.30*** *p76*
Delader, Jacob; America, 1749 ***2856.30*** *p76*
With wife & son
Delafield, Charles; Milwaukee, 1844 ***1224.3*** *p21*
Delagal, John; South Carolina, 1769 ***1224.2*** *p32*
Delago, Andre; Philadelphia, 1794 ***4629.10*** *p62*
Delahay, Arthur; Maryland, 1637 ***2524.55*** *p66*
Wife: Mary
Son: Charles
Delahay, Charles *SEE* Delahay, Arthur
Delahay, James *SEE* Delahay, John
Delahay, Jane *SEE* Delahay, John
Delahay, John; Maryland, 1661 ***2524.55*** *p66*
Wife: Jane
Stepchild: James
Delahay, John; Maryland, 1663 ***2524.55*** *p66*
Wife: Jane
Stepchild: James
Delahay, Mary *SEE* Delahay, Arthur
Delahay, Robt 43; Ontario, 1871 ***1823.28*** *p22*
Delahunty, Mary A. Kennedy 67; Vermont, 1922 ***5900.10*** *p165*
Delahunty, Michael 67; Vermont, 1914 ***5900.10*** *p165*
Delaistre, Marianne; New York, 1814 ***8197.10*** *p58*
De La March, John; Virginia, 1723 ***1224.2*** *p32*
Delamue, Joane; Maryland, 1665 ***2524.55*** *p66*
De Lancey, Oliver; New York, n.d. ***1224.3*** *p21*
De Lancy, James; London, England, 1857 ***1640.13*** *p29*
De Lancy, Oliver; New York, New York, 1786 ***1224.2*** *p32*
Delancy, Patrick; New York, 1839 ***8197.10*** *p226*
Delane, John; Maryland, 1681 ***2524.55*** *p66*
de la Newville, Nicholas; Philadelphia, 1790 ***4629.10*** *p77*
Delaney, Ann 45; Ontario, 1871 ***1823.22*** *p41*
Delaney, Bridget 60; Vermont, 1904 ***5900.10*** *p44*
Delaney, Catherine 61; Vermont, 1868 ***5900.10*** *p64*
Delaney, Catherine Bowen; Vermont, n.d. ***5900.10*** *p64*
Delaney, Daniel 46; Ontario, 1871 ***1823.28*** *p22*
Delaney, Dennis; Vermont, n.d. ***5900.10*** *p64*
Delaney, Ellen; Vermont, 1842-1909 ***5900.10*** *p165*
Delaney, Fanny 70; Ontario, 1871 ***1823.22*** *p41*
Delaney, James; New York, 1838 ***8197.10*** *p108*
Delaney, John; New York, 1831 ***8197.10*** *p225*
Delaney, John; New York, 1834 ***8197.10*** *p316*
Delaney, John; New York, 1839 ***8197.10*** *p226*
Delaney, John 23; Ontario, 1871 ***1823.22*** *p41*
Delaney, John 35; Ontario, 1871 ***1823.22*** *p41*
Delaney, John P.; Vermont, 1840-1914 ***5900.10*** *p165*
Delaney, Joseph; Vermont, 1850-1919 ***5900.10*** *p458*
Delaney, Joseph 25; Ontario, 1871 ***1823.22*** *p41*
Delaney, Julia A. Sexton; Vermont, 1854-1900 ***5900.10*** *p186*
Delaney, Julia Jackson; Vermont, 1839-1910 ***5900.10*** *p46*
Delaney, Kate; Vermont, 1843-1896 ***5900.10*** *p64*
Delaney, Mary Clark; Vermont, 1863-1935 ***5900.10*** *p177*
Delaney, Michael 18; Maryland, 1774 ***1220.25*** *p69*
Delaney, Michael 21; Carolina, 1774 ***1220.25*** *p76*
Delaney, Patrick; New York, 1839 ***8197.10*** *p226*
Delaney, Richard; Vermont, 1837-1927 ***5900.10*** *p46*
Delaney, Sarah 47; Ontario, 1871 ***1823.22*** *p41*
Delaney, Thomas 34; Ontario, 1871 ***1823.28*** *p22*
Delaney, Thomas Alban; Vermont, 1862-1928 ***5900.10*** *p177*
Delaney-Clark, . . .; Vermont, n.d. ***5900.10*** *p177*
De Lanne, John; South Carolina, 1728 ***1224.2*** *p32*
Delany, Andrew 16; Ontario, 1861 ***2896.27*** *p67*
Delany, Ann 11; Ontario, 1861 ***2896.27*** *p67*
Delany, Ann 44; Ontario, 1861 ***2896.27*** *p67*
Delany, Ann 60; Ontario, 1871 ***1823.22*** *p41*
Delany, Charles E. 21; Vermont, 1871 ***5900.10*** *p330*
Delany, Cornelius 53; Ontario, 1871 ***1823.22*** *p41*
Delany, Daniel; New York, 1837 ***8197.10*** *p83*
Delany, Edward 59; Vermont, 1862 ***5900.10*** *p330*
Delany, G. 65; Ontario, 1861 ***2896.26*** *p11*
Delany, Henry; New York, 1836 ***8197.10*** *p78*
Delany, James; New York, 1834 ***8197.10*** *p73*
Delany, Julia 54; Ontario, 1871 ***1823.28*** *p22*
Delany, July A. 19; Ontario, 1861 ***2896.27*** *p67*
Delany, Lawrence 50; Vermont, 1881 ***5900.10*** *p364*
Delany, Martin 70; Ontario, 1871 ***1823.22*** *p41*

Delany, Mary 75; Vermont, 1905 5900.10 p360
Delany, Nicholas; New York, 1821 8197.10 p223
Delany, Rose Ann 9; Vermont, 1857 5900.10 p330
Delany, Thomas; New York, 1831 8197.10 p365
Delany, Thomas; New York, 1840 8197.10 p156
Delany, Thomas 14; Ontario, 1861 2896.27 p67
De Laperelle, Mr.; Portland, Maine, 1858 9196.15 p31
De la Porta, Pedro Ramon; Philadelphia, 1794 4629.10 p82
De la Quintana, Manuel; New York, 1830 8197.10 p361
De la Quintana, Pedro; New York, 1830 8197.10 p361
Delargey, Mrs.; Ontario, 1861 2896.26 p26
Delargey, P.; Ontario, 1861 2896.26 p26
Delaroche, Peter; Maryland, 1675 2524.55 p66
Delaroy, William; Maryland, 1676 2524.55 p66
Delarue, Louis; New York, 1806 8197.10 p30
Delary, John 84; Ontario, 1871 1823.22 p41
Delastions, Sevat; Virginia, 1668-1669 6212.30 p41
Delater, Peter; America, 1740 2856.30 p76
Delater, Peter; America, 1750 2856.30 p77
Delater, Peter; Port uncertain, 1740 2856.30 p77
Delatour, Louis Antoine Jousseaum; New York, 1826 8197.10 p335
De Launce, John; South Carolina, 1728 1224.2 p32
Delauney, Pierre A.; New York, 1838 8197.10 p108
De Lavall, Thomas; New York, New York, 1683 1224.1 p17
Delawood, Joseph; Maryland, 1672 2524.55 p66
Delbridge, Richard 30; Ontario, 1871 1823.15 p60
Delbridge, Richard 67; Ontario, 1871 1823.15 p60
Delbridge, Robert 21; Baltimore, 1775 1220.25 p118
Del Castillo, Manuel Samaniego; New Orleans, 1833 1224.3 p21
Del Corral, Atanasio Gutienez; New Orleans, n.d. 1224.3 p21
Deldine, John; Pennsylvania, 1777 4629.10 p14
Deledicq, Lawrence; Died enroute, 1691 1224.1 p18
Delegal, Eleanor; Georgia, 1764 1224.2 p32
Delegal, Philip; Georgia, 1764 1224.2 p32
Delehanty, Allice Kelley 36; Vermont, 1873 5900.10 p476
Delehanty, Ann; Vermont, n.d. 5900.10 p392
Delehanty, Bridget; Vermont, 1852-1901 5900.10 p273
Delehanty, Bridget; Vermont, 1858-1934 5900.10 p274
Delehanty, Edward; Vermont, 1849-1906 5900.10 p274
Delehanty, Hannah M.; Vermont, 1868-1958 5900.10 p256
Delehanty, James; Vermont, 1844-1917 5900.10 p257
Delehanty, John; Vermont, 1851-1916 5900.10 p256
Delehanty, Mary; Vermont, 1814-1864 5900.10 p264
Delehanty, Mary; Vermont, 1847-1888 5900.10 p257
Delehanty, Mary M. 55; Vermont, 1862 5900.10 p245
Delehanty, Mathias; Vermont, 1842-1899 5900.10 p273
Delehanty, Patrick; Vermont, 1809-1888 5900.10 p264
Delehanty, Patrick; Vermont, 1852-1888 5900.10 p264
Delehanty, Richard 66; Vermont, 1872 5900.10 p245
Delehay, John 21; Ontario, 1871 1823.28 p22
Deleny, Cornilious 42; Ontario, 1871 1823.15 p60
Delfe, Anne; Virginia, 1664 6212.30 p7
Delgatty, Alescander 24; Ontario, 1871 1823.15 p60
Del Hoyo, Francis; New York, 1827 8197.10 p345
Del Hoyo, Francis; New York, 1837 8197.10 p82
Delich, M. 27; Alaska, 1917 9196.1 p47
Delich, M. 27; Whitehorse, Yukon, 1917 9196.1 p47
Delisle, Enemmond; New York, 1823 8197.10 p224
Delius, Henry; New York, 1831 8197.10 p365
Delius, Henry; New York, 1831 8197.10 p369
Delke, Elizabeth Kenythorpe; Virginia, 1629 1224.1 p18
Dell, Mary; Maryland, 1656 2524.55 p66
Dell, William; Maryland, 1655 2524.55 p66
Della Torre, Joseph; New York, 1821 8197.10 p223
Dellemore, Robert 22; Virginia, 1773 1220.25 p28
Delle Piane, Bernardino; New York, 1834 8197.10 p316
Deller, Mathes; Port uncertain, 1749 2856.30 p77
Delligan, Bernard; Vermont, 1849-1937 5900.10 p474
Delligan, Bridget; Vermont, 1859-1935 5900.10 p490
Delligan, Fannie Gallagher; Vermont, 1813-1893 5900.10 p474
Delligan, Katherine A. 40; Vermont, 1902 5900.10 p513
Delligan, Mary Ann McDonald; Vermont, 1859-1940 5900.10 p474
Delligan, Mary Dion; Vermont, 1855-1892 5900.10 p513
Delligan, Philip; Vermont, 1812-1901 5900.10 p474
Delligan, Philip; Vermont, 1851-1922 5900.10 p513
Delligan, Rose Mossey; Vermont, 1866-1931 5900.10 p513
Delluc, Francis; New York, 1838 8197.10 p107
Delmont, Luce; New York, 1814 8197.10 p58
Del Noce, Gennaro; New York, 1829 8197.10 p351
Delohery, Daniel 36; Vermont, 1864 5900.10 p254
Delolme, John Charles; New York, 1827 8197.10 p225
Delone, Barnet 20; Ontario, 1861 2896.27 p13
Delone, Catharine 12; Ontario, 1861 2896.26 p23
Delone, Charles 8; Ontario, 1861 2896.26 p23
Delone, E. 24; Ontario, 1861 2896.26 p4
Delone, Emeline 24; Ontario, 1861 2896.26 p23
Delone, John 26; Ontario, 1861 2896.26 p23
Delone, Lucinda 10; Ontario, 1861 2896.26 p23
Delone, Mary 5; Ontario, 1861 2896.26 p23
Delone, Sylvester 15; Ontario, 1861 2896.26 p23
Delong, A. 7; Ontario, 1861 2896.25 p9
Delong, Ann 15; Ontario, 1861 2896.25 p70
Delong, Ann 33; Ontario, 1861 2896.28 p27
Delong, Antoinette 18; Ontario, 1861 2896.25 p70
Delong, Ara 24; Ontario, 1861 2896.28 p27
Delong, Ara 60; Ontario, 1861 2896.28 p27
Delong, Betsy J. 18; Ontario, 1861 2896.28 p27
Delong, C. 6; Ontario, 1861 2896.25 p45
Delong, Catherine 19; Ontario, 1861 2896.25 p71
Delong, Catherine Dempsey 51; Ontario, 1861 2896.25 p71
Delong, Christopher 10; Ontario, 1861 2896.25 p65
Delong, Clarissa 18; Ontario, 1861 2896.25 p65
Delong, Comfort 58; Ontario, 1861 2896.28 p27
Delong, David 9; Ontario, 1861 2896.25 p66
Delong, David 20; Ontario, 1861 2896.25 p65
Delong, David 72; Ontario, 1861 2896.25 p52
Delong, David H. 4; Ontario, 1861 2896.28 p27
Delong, E. 8; Ontario, 1861 2896.25 p45
Delong, Egbert 6; Ontario, 1861 2896.28 p27
Delong, Egbert 22; Ontario, 1861 2896.28 p27
Delong, Elizabeth 24; Ontario, 1861 2896.28 p23
Delong, Ella 9; Ontario, 1861 2896.25 p70
Delong, Emma 11; Ontario, 1861 2896.25 p70
Delong, Esther D. 8; Ontario, 1861 2896.28 p27
Delong, Ezra O. 3; Ontario, 1861 2896.25 p9
Delong, Franklin 1; Ontario, 1861 2896.28 p27
Delong, George 20; Ontario, 1861 2896.25 p46
Delong, George E. 4; Ontario, 1861 2896.28 p27
Delong, Henry 1; Ontario, 1861 2896.25 p66
Delong, Isaac 27; Ontario, 1861 2896.28 p27
Delong, Isaiah 13; Ontario, 1861 2896.25 p66
Delong, J. 1; Ontario, 1861 2896.25 p46
Delong, J. G. 4; Ontario, 1861 2896.25 p45
Delong, Jacob 4; Ontario, 1861 2896.25 p66
Delong, James 27; Ontario, 1861 2896.25 p46
Delong, Jane 7; Ontario, 1861 2896.25 p70
Delong, John 2; Ontario, 1861 2896.28 p27
Delong, Joseph 22; Ontario, 1861 2896.25 p59
Delong, Letitia 42; Ontario, 1861 2896.25 p70
Delong, Lizabeth 38; Ontario, 1861 2896.25 p66
Delong, Martha 16; Ontario, 1861 2896.28 p27
Delong, Mary 30; Ontario, 1861 2896.25 p69
Delong, Mary 33; Ontario, 1861 2896.25 p9
Delong, Mary 46; Ontario, 1861 2896.25 p65
Delong, Mary E. 9; Ontario, 1861 2896.28 p27
Delong, Mary E. 23; Ontario, 1861 2896.28 p27
Delong, P. J. 1; Ontario, 1861 2896.25 p45
Delong, Pheba J. 7; Ontario, 1861 2896.28 p27
Delong, R. 8; Ontario, 1861 2896.25 p45
Delong, R. 31; Ontario, 1861 2896.25 p45
Delong, Richard 52; Ontario, 1861 2896.25 p45
Delong, Robert J. 10; Ontario, 1861 2896.25 p9
Delong, S. E. 25; Ontario, 1861 2896.25 p46
Delong, S. L. 10; Ontario, 1861 2896.25 p45
Delong, S. N. H. 2; Ontario, 1861 2896.25 p70
Delong, Sarah 12; Ontario, 1861 2896.25 p65
Delong, Sarah 23; Ontario, 1861 2896.25 p71
Delong, Sarah E. 5; Ontario, 1861 2896.25 p9
Delong, Sarah J. 2; Ontario, 1861 2896.28 p27
Delong, Sidney 2; Ontario, 1861 2896.25 p45
Delong, Sinthey 5; Ontario, 1861 2896.25 p66
Delong, Theadora 20; Ontario, 1861 2896.25 p66
Delong, William 25; Ontario, 1861 2896.25 p66
Delong, William C. 11; Ontario, 1861 2896.25 p69
Delong, Willie 5; Ontario, 1861 2896.25 p70
De Longueil, Madame; Quebec, 1858 9196.15 p39
Delonguemare, James Stanislaus; New York, 1814 8197.10 p58
Delort, Theophilus; New York, 1815 8197.10 p55
Deloughery, Michael 62; Ontario, 1871 1823.28 p22
Deloughry, Joseph 27; Ontario, 1871 1823.28 p22
Deloughry, Thos 60; Ontario, 1871 1823.28 p22
De Loynes, George; New York, 1835 8197.10 p225
De Loynes, George; New York, 1838 8197.10 p108
Delphick, George 26; Ontario, 1871 1823.22 p41
Delsch, Franziska; Port uncertain, 1731 2856.30 p77
Del Vecchio, Charles; New York, 1816 8197.10 p58
Del Vecchio, John; New York, 1807 8197.10 p37
Delworth, Jeremiah; New York, 1837 8197.10 p86
Delworth, Jno.; Pennsylvania, 1778 4629.10 p34
Delyeer, A. 1; Ontario, 1861 2896.28 p6
Delyeer, C. A. 3; Ontario, 1861 2896.28 p6
Delyeer, R. 23; Ontario, 1861 2896.28 p6
DeMaherne, . . .; Quebec, 1857 9196.15 p15
Demall, John; Maryland, 1651 2524.55 p66
Demall, John; Maryland, 1658 2524.55 p61
Demalt, Anna A. 54; Kansas, 1878-1910 9079.10 p23
Demalt, George J. 56; Kansas, 1878-1910 9079.10 p23
Demant, Peter; Port uncertain, 1739 2856.30 p77
DeMartin, John; Maryland, 1910 3259.35 p11
Demaszewicz, Michael; Maryland, 1910 3259.35 p11
de Mazas, Francisco; Mexico, n.d. 1224.3 p21
de Mazas, Francisco; Philadelphia, 1831 1224.3 p21
Dembeck, Anton; Maryland, 1910 3259.35 p11
Dembeck, August; Maryland, 1910 3259.35 p11
Dembeck, Frank; Maryland, 1910 3259.35 p11
Dembeck, John; Maryland, 1910 3259.35 p11
Dembeck, Valenty; Maryland, 1910 3259.35 p11
Dembezysky, Nellie M.; Maryland, 1910 3259.35 p11
Dembick, Michael; Maryland, 1910 3259.35 p11
Dembkowski, Pioter; Maryland, 1910 3259.35 p11
Dembowsky, John; Maryland, 1910 3259.35 p11
Dembroski, Joseph; Maryland, 1910 3259.35 p11
Demeiere, Philippe; New York, 1821 8197.10 p223
De Mello, Theophilas; New York, 1815 8197.10 p55
Demend, Jacob; Pennsylvania, 1777 4629.10 p11
Demensky, Michael 40; Ontario, 1871 1823.28 p22
Demer, John; New York, 1840 8197.10 p159
Demere, Paul; South Carolina, 1765 1224.2 p32
Demerostes, N. 36; Alaska, 1917 9196.1 p46
Demerostes, N. 36; Whitehorse, Yukon, 1917 9196.1 p46
Demick, Martin; Pennsylvania, 1868 6058.10 p77
Demill, Daniel; Ontario, 1861 2896.25 p10
Demill, William A.; Ontario, 1861 2896.25 p10
Deming, Anne; Vermont, 1819-1875 5900.10 p175
Deming, Fanny Follett; Vermont, 1788-1878 5900.10 p174
Deming, Maria; Vermont, 1817-1904 5900.10 p174
Demlenski, Katie; Maryland, 1910 3259.35 p11
Demler, Gottlieb; Port uncertain, 1795 2856.30 p77
Demler, Gottlieb; Port uncertain, 1796 2856.30 p77
Demluck, Walter; Maryland, 1910 3259.35 p11
Demmel, Philipp; Port uncertain, 1785 2856.30 p77
Demmer, Anna Maria; Port uncertain, 1791 2856.30 p77
Demmler, Georg; Port uncertain, 1786 2856.30 p77
Demont, Joseph; New York, 1840 8197.10 p226
Demonte, J. 34; Alaska, 1918 9196.1 p55
Demonte, J. 34; Yukon, 1918 9196.1 p55
De Montmollein, Frederick; Pennsylvania, 1787 4629.10 p54
Demorest, Mary; Vermont, 1852-1923 5900.10 p340
Demorest, T. H.; Vermont, 1841-1910 5900.10 p340
Demoski, Boleslaus; Maryland, 1910 3259.35 p11
Demountede, Anthony; Maryland, 1656 2524.55 p66
Demper, Emma L. Lovern; Vermont, 1855-1925 5900.10 p539
Demper, John B.; Vermont, 1852-1920 5900.10 p539
Dempey, John 26; Ontario, 1871 1823.15 p60
Dempsey, A. M. 3; Ontario, 1861 2896.25 p48
Dempsey, Aaron 6; Ontario, 1861 2896.25 p48
Dempsey, Adrew 28; Ontario, 1871 1823.15 p60
Dempsey, Ann 5 *SEE* Dempsey, John
Dempsey, Anne 13 *SEE* Dempsey, Henry
Dempsey, Annie; Vermont, 1861-1943 5900.10 p195
Dempsey, B. M. G. 11; Ontario, 1861 2896.25 p49
Dempsey, Barney; New York, 1836 8197.10 p78
Dempsey, Biddy 30 *SEE* Dempsey, John
Dempsey, Bridget 8 *SEE* Dempsey, Michael
Dempsey, Bridget 55 *SEE* Dempsey, John
Dempsey, C. 16; Ontario, 1861 2896.25 p54
Dempsey, Catherine 1 *SEE* Dempsey, Henry
Dempsey, Catherine 1 *SEE* Dempsey, John
Dempsey, Catherine 31 *SEE* Dempsey, Michael
Dempsey, Catherine 47 *SEE* Dempsey, Henry
Dempsey, Charles 18; Ontario, 1861 2896.25 p48
Dempsey, Charlotte 20; Ontario, 1861 2896.25 p48
Dempsey, Charlotte 40; Ontario, 1861 2896.25 p49
Dempsey, D. L. 18; Ontario, 1861 2896.25 p49
Dempsey, Daniel; New York, 1838 8197.10 p318
Dempsey, David R. 10; Ontario, 1861 2896.25 p54
Dempsey, E. 25; Ontario, 1861 2896.25 p48
Dempsey, E. C. 5; Ontario, 1861 2896.25 p48
Dempsey, E. S. 14; Ontario, 1861 2896.25 p49
Dempsey, Elizabeth 28; Ontario, 1861 2896.25 p48
Dempsey, Elizabeth 45; Ontario, 1861 2896.25 p54
Dempsey, G. E. R. 4; Ontario, 1861 2896.25 p48
Dempsey, George 2; Ontario, 1861 2896.25 p48
Dempsey, Henry 4 *SEE* Dempsey, Henry
Dempsey, Henry 50; New York, New York, 1848 1825.45 p32
Wife: Catherine 47
Son: John 13
Son: Patrick 21
Daughter: Catherine 1
Daughter: Mary 15
Daughter: Margaret 18
Daughter: Anne 13

Son: Michael 10
Son: Henry 4
Dempsey, James; Vermont, 1835-1883 ***5900.10*** *p112*
Dempsey, James 15; Ontario, 1861 ***2896.25*** *p48*
Dempsey, Jane 10; Ontario, 1861 ***2896.25*** *p48*
Dempsey, Johanna; Vermont, 1818-1906 ***5900.10*** *p438*
Dempsey, John; New York, 1821 ***8197.10*** *p223*
Dempsey, John 13 *SEE* Dempsey, Henry
Dempsey, John 22; Ontario, 1861 ***2896.25*** *p54*
Dempsey, John 30 *SEE* Dempsey, John
Dempsey, John 56; Ontario, 1871 ***1823.15*** *p60*
Dempsey, John 57; New York, New York, 1848 ***1825.45*** *p32*
Wife: Bridget 55
Granddaughter: Ann 5
Granddaughter: Margaret 6
Granddaughter: Catherine 1
Daughter-In-Law: Biddy 30
Son: John 30
Dempsey, M. A. 30; Ontario, 1861 ***2896.25*** *p48*
Dempsey, M. J. 15; Ontario, 1861 ***2896.25*** *p48*
Dempsey, Margaret; Vermont, 1839-1887 ***5900.10*** *p112*
Dempsey, Margaret 6 *SEE* Dempsey, John
Dempsey, Margaret 18 *SEE* Dempsey, Henry
Dempsey, Margaret McLoughlin; Vermont, 1840-1924 ***5900.10*** *p572*
Dempsey, Mary 15 *SEE* Dempsey, Henry
Dempsey, Mary Ann 38; Vermont, 1876 ***5900.10*** *p268*
Dempsey, Michael 10 *SEE* Dempsey, Henry
Dempsey, Michael 32; New York, New York, 1848 ***1825.45*** *p32*
Wife: Catherine 31
Daughter: Bridget 8
Son: Pat 5
Dempsey, Micheal; Vermont, 1816-1896 ***5900.10*** *p438*
Dempsey, Pat 5 *SEE* Dempsey, Michael
Dempsey, Patrick; Vermont, 1841-1889 ***5900.10*** *p572*
Dempsey, Patrick 21 *SEE* Dempsey, Henry
Dempsey, Peter 76; Ontario, 1861 ***2896.25*** *p49*
Dempsey, S. E. 10; Ontario, 1861 ***2896.25*** *p48*
Dempsey, S. W. 19; Ontario, 1861 ***2896.25*** *p54*
Dempsey, Sarah 62; Ontario, 1861 ***2896.25*** *p48*
Dempsey, Sarah A. 13; Ontario, 1861 ***2896.25*** *p54*
Dempsey, Sarah A. 24; Ontario, 1861 ***2896.25*** *p48*
Dempsey, Sophia 63; Ontario, 1861 ***2896.25*** *p49*
Dempsey, Stephen; Vermont, 1858-1896 ***5900.10*** *p438*
Dempsey, Thomas 43; Ontario, 1861 ***2896.25*** *p48*
Dempsey, Thos 50; Ontario, 1871 ***1823.28*** *p22*
Dempsey, William; Vermont, 1856-1941 ***5900.10*** *p195*
Dempsey, William 35; Ontario, 1871 ***1823.28*** *p22*
Dempster, George; Florida, 1766 ***1640.10*** *p40*
Dempster, George; Georgia, 1734 ***1640.10*** *p40*
Dempster, George; South Carolina, 1734 ***1640.10*** *p40*
Dempster, James; New York, 1840 ***8197.10*** *p156*
Dempster, James; Savannah, Georgia, 1802 ***1640.10*** *p40*
Dempster, John 48; Ontario, 1871 ***1823.22*** *p41*
Demsay, James 21; Virginia, 1773 ***1220.25*** *p28*
Demstoll, Edw; Virginia, 1667-1668 ***6212.30*** *p39*
Demuth, Anna Maria; Port uncertain, 1758 ***2856.30*** *p77*
Demuth, Mathias; America, 1748 ***2856.30*** *p77*
Denahoe, Daniel; Maryland, 1678 ***2524.55*** *p66*
Denar, Elizabeth *SEE* Denar, John
Denar, John; Maryland, 1671 ***2524.55*** *p66*
Wife: Elizabeth
Stepchild: William
Stepchild: Mary Empson
Denar, Mary Empson *SEE* Denar, John
Denar, William *SEE* Denar, John
Denard, Lewin *SEE* Denard, Lewin
Denard, Lewin; Maryland, 1680 ***2524.55*** *p66*
Son: Lewin
Denbige, Jno; Virginia, 1667 ***6212.30*** *p37*
Denbow, John 60; Ontario, 1871 ***1823.15*** *p60*
Denby, Mary; Maryland, 1654 ***2524.55*** *p66*
Dench, John 69; Ontario, 1871 ***1823.22*** *p41*
Dench, Jona; Maryland, 1678 ***2524.55*** *p67*
Dench, R.; Quebec, 1857 ***9196.15*** *p13*
Dencin, Christy 56; Ontario, 1871 ***1823.28*** *p22*
Dendy, Samuel; North America, 1808 ***1224.3*** *p21*
Deneau, Edmund 45; Virginia, 1773 ***1220.25*** *p28*
Denecke, George Joseph; New York, 1840 ***8197.10*** *p156*
Deneen, Lillian; Vermont, n.d. ***5900.10*** *p158*
De Negre, John; New York, 1803 ***8197.10*** *p12*
Denehan, William 28; Ontario, 1871 ***1823.28*** *p22*
De Neufville, John; Cambridge, Massachusetts, 1801 ***1224.3*** *p21*
Dengel, Anton; Port uncertain, 1756 ***2856.30*** *p77*
Dengel, Michael; America, 1731 ***2856.30*** *p77*
Dengeler, Johann; Port uncertain, 1715 ***2856.30*** *p77*
Denger, Mr.; America, 1749 ***2856.30*** *p450*
Denger, Anna Maria; Port uncertain, 1789 ***2856.30*** *p77*
Denger, Christof; America, 1749 ***2856.30*** *p77*
Denham, Robert; Savannah, Georgia, 1786 ***1640.13*** *p29*
Denham, Thomas; Pennsylvania, 1777 ***4629.10*** *p11*
Denholm, John; Grenada, 1793 ***1640.13*** *p29*
Denholm, Robert; Savannah, Georgia, 1786-1845 ***1640.10*** *p40*
Deniard, Richard S.; New York, 1839 ***8197.10*** *p226*
Denies, Anth; Virginia, 1672 ***6212.30*** *p50*
Denihan, James 55; Ontario, 1871 ***1823.28*** *p22*
Denike, L. A. 69; Ontario, 1861 ***2896.25*** *p35*
Deninth, Frederick 25; Ontario, 1871 ***1823.15*** *p60*
Denio, John 45; Ontario, 1871 ***1823.28*** *p22*
Deniord, Richard S.; New York, 1839 ***8197.10*** *p226*
Denis, Mr.; Quebec, 1857 ***9196.15*** *p21*
Denis, Mrs.; Quebec, 1857 ***9196.15*** *p21*
Denis, Rich; Virginia, 1668-1669 ***6212.30*** *p41*
Denison, Francis 21; Ontario, 1871 ***1823.28*** *p22*
Denison, Henry 37; Ontario, 1871 ***1823.22*** *p41*
Denison, James 23; Maryland, 1774 ***1220.25*** *p65*
Denison, John 70; Ontario, 1871 ***1823.28*** *p22*
Denison, Joseph; New York, 1838 ***8197.10*** *p108*
Denison, Margaret 35; Maryland, 1775 ***1220.25*** *p108*
Denison, Patrick 17; Maryland, 1774 ***1220.25*** *p65*
Denison, Samuel 40; Ontario, 1871 ***1823.15*** *p60*
Deniver, John H. 46; Vermont, 1867 ***5900.10*** *p232*
Deniver, Mary A. 41; Vermont, 1870 ***5900.10*** *p232*
Denley, William 58; Ontario, 1871 ***1823.28*** *p22*
Denmark, Alexander 64; Ontario, 1871 ***1823.22*** *p41*
Denn, Basil 18; Maryland, 1774 ***1220.25*** *p64*
Denn, Christopher *SEE* Denn, Christopher
Denn, Christopher; Maryland, 1665 ***2524.55*** *p67*
Son: Robert
Son: Christopher
Denn, Robert *SEE* Denn, Christopher
Dennan, Michael; New York, 1838 ***8197.10*** *p301*
Dennan, Thomas; New York, 1840 ***8197.10*** *p158*
Dennehy, William Henry; Vermont, 1875-1904 ***5900.10*** *p415*
Denner, Andreas; America, 1781 ***2856.30*** *p77*
Denner, Mathias; Port uncertain, 1792 ***2856.30*** *p77*
With wife
Dennestone, James; Georgia, 1751 ***1640.10*** *p41*
Dennet, Alfred 24; Ontario, 1861 ***2896.27*** *p69*
Dennett, Edward; Maryland, 1681 ***2524.55*** *p67*
Denney, Christopher *SEE* Denney, Christopher
Denney, Christopher; Maryland, 1665 ***2524.55*** *p67*
Son: Robert
Son: Christopher
Denney, Robert *SEE* Denney, Christopher
Denney, Wm; Virginia, 1671-1672 ***6212.30*** *p46*
Dennhard, Eva Margarete; Port uncertain, 1777 ***2856.30*** *p77*
Dennie, John 62; Ontario, 1871 ***1823.15*** *p60*
Dennig, Anna Barbara; America, 1749 ***2856.30*** *p77*
Dennig, Christof; America, 1737 ***2856.30*** *p77*
Denniger, Andreas; Port uncertain, 1764 ***2856.30*** *p77*
Dennin, John; New York, 1837 ***8197.10*** *p86*
Dennin, Margaret Hays; Vermont, 1860-1926 ***5900.10*** *p272*
Dennin, William; Vermont, 1859-1899 ***5900.10*** *p272*
Denning, Bernard; Vermont, 1832-1912 ***5900.10*** *p386*
Denning, Bridget 38; Vermont, 1876 ***5900.10*** *p162*
Denning, Caroline Elliott; Vermont, 1837-1906 ***5900.10*** *p182*
Denning, Jane B.; Vermont, 1839-1912 ***5900.10*** *p386*
Denning, Jerry; Vermont, 1825-1899 ***5900.10*** *p508*
Denning, Mary Lynch; Vermont, 1831-1870 ***5900.10*** *p508*
Denning, William; Vermont, 1837-1901 ***5900.10*** *p182*
Denninger, Anna Maria; Port uncertain, 1751 ***2856.30*** *p77*
Dennins, John; Maryland, 1677 ***2524.55*** *p67*
Dennis, Barbra *SEE* Dennis, Justinean
Dennis, Dornick; Maryland, 1668 ***2524.55*** *p67*
Wife: Ellis
Child: Elizabeth
Child: William
Dennis, Edward 21; Maryland, 1775 ***1220.25*** *p114*
Dennis, Elizabeth *SEE* Dennis, Dornick
Dennis, Ellis *SEE* Dennis, Dornick
Dennis, James; Ontario, 1871 ***1823.28*** *p22*
Dennis, Janet 35; Ontario, 1871 ***1823.15*** *p60*
Dennis, Jeane *SEE* Dennis, Justinean
Dennis, John; Maryland, 1649 ***2524.55*** *p67*
Dennis, John; Maryland, 1649 ***2524.55*** *p206*
Dennis, John; Pennsylvania, 1777 ***4629.10*** *p20*
Dennis, John 73; Ontario, 1871 ***1823.15*** *p60*
Dennis, Joseph 21; Maryland, 1775 ***1220.25*** *p108*
Dennis, Justinean *SEE* Dennis, Justinean
Dennis, Justinean; Maryland, 1668 ***2524.55*** *p67*
Wife: Katherin
Child: Barbra
Child: Mary
Child: Justinean
Child: Jeane
Dennis, Katherin *SEE* Dennis, Justinean
Dennis, Mary *SEE* Dennis, Justinean
Dennis, Mary *SEE* Dennis, Peter
Dennis, Mary Ann 45; Vermont, 1887 ***5900.10*** *p240*
Dennis, Moore; Virginia, 1663 ***6212.30*** *p4*
Dennis, Morris; Virginia, 1663 ***6212.30*** *p4*
Dennis, Nicholas; Virginia, 1666 ***6212.30*** *p30*
Dennis, Peter; Maryland, 1668 ***2524.55*** *p67*
Wife: Mary
Dennis, Richard; New York, 1840 ***8197.10*** *p157*
Dennis, Richard 24; Virginia, 1773 ***1220.25*** *p31*
Dennis, Samuel 21; Baltimore, 1775 ***1220.25*** *p117*
Dennis, Thomas 41; Ontario, 1871 ***1823.15*** *p60*
Dennis, William *SEE* Dennis, Dornick
Dennis, William; America, 1722 ***1224.2*** *p32*
Dennis, William C. 24; Ontario, 1871 ***1823.28*** *p22*
Dennison, Bridget Mullaney; Vermont, 1852-1930 ***5900.10*** *p204*
Dennison, Catherine 73; Ontario, 1871 ***1823.15*** *p60*
Dennison, Dominic F.; Vermont, 1847-1935 ***5900.10*** *p204*
Dennison, James; New York, 1839 ***8197.10*** *p381*
Dennison, Michael; Pennsylvania, 1776 ***4629.10*** *p53*
Dennison, Thomas 30; Maryland, 1775 ***1220.25*** *p105*
Dennison, William 16; Maryland, 1775 ***1220.25*** *p112*
Denniston, James; New York, 1834 ***8197.10*** *p305*
Denniston, John Alexander; New York, 1839 ***8197.10*** *p226*
Denniston, Robert; Philadelphia, 1794 ***4629.10*** *p79*
Denniston, Thomas; Pennsylvania, 1777 ***4629.10*** *p12*
Dennon, Owen; New York, 1837 ***8197.10*** *p87*
Dennon, Thomas; New York, 1840 ***8197.10*** *p158*
Denny, Alexander; South Carolina, 1730 ***1224.2*** *p32*
Denny, Catharina; Port uncertain, 1761 ***2856.30*** *p77*
Denny, James; New York, 1839 ***8197.10*** *p381*
Denny, John; Virginia, 1684-1685 ***6212.30*** *p57*
Denny, John; Virginia, 1688 ***6212.30*** *p57*
Denny, Walter; Georgia, 1741 ***1640.10*** *p41*
De Noielle, Peter; New York, 1837 ***8197.10*** *p83*
Denoon, David; Charleston, South Carolina, 1823 ***1224.3*** *p21*
Denoon, John; Georgia, 1736 ***1640.10*** *p41*
Denow, Stanislaus; Maryland, 1910 ***3259.35*** *p11*
Denoyelle, Paul; New York, 1806 ***8197.10*** *p324*
Denritta, Emarila 4; Ontario, 1861 ***2896.27*** *p71*
Denritta, Louisa 2; Ontario, 1861 ***2896.27*** *p71*
Densley, Edith; Alexandria, Virginia, 1800 ***1224.3*** *p21*
Densley, Jerome; Maryland, 1668 ***2524.55*** *p67*
Dent, Andrew; Virginia, 1671 ***6212.30*** *p42*
Dent, Esther; Vermont, 1819-1905 ***5900.10*** *p496*
Dent, George; North America, 1791 ***1224.2*** *p32*
Dent, George 32; Maryland, 1774 ***1220.25*** *p64*
Dent, George 35; Ontario, 1871 ***1823.15*** *p61*
Dent, John; Maryland, 1672 ***2524.55*** *p67*
Dent, John; North America, 1791 ***1224.2*** *p32*
Dent, Thomas; Maryland, 1680 ***2524.55*** *p67*
Dent, Thomas; Virginia, 1709 ***6212.30*** *p64*
Dent, William; Virginia, 1886 ***1640.13*** *p29*
Denton, Mrs.; Maryland, 1665 ***2524.55*** *p67*
Denton, George; Virginia, 1666 ***6212.30*** *p29*
Denton, James 21; Ontario, 1871 ***1823.15*** *p61*
Denton, John; Virginia, 1665 ***6212.30*** *p20*
Denton, Thomas; Virginia, 1666 ***6212.30*** *p30*
Denton, William 23; Maryland, 1775 ***1220.25*** *p100*
Dentzler, Lorenz; Port uncertain, 1722 ***2856.30*** *p77*
Denwood, Laban; Maryland, 1665 ***2524.55*** *p245*
Denwood, Mary; Maryland, 1753 ***1224.2*** *p32*
Denwood, Sarah; Maryland, 1665 ***2524.55*** *p245*
Deny, Friedrich; Port uncertain, 1758 ***2856.30*** *p77*
Denz, Johann; Port uncertain, 1725 ***2856.30*** *p77*
Denzer, Hans Georg; Port uncertain, 1795 ***2856.30*** *p78*
Denzi, Louis Anthony; New York, 1836-1840 ***8197.10*** *p300*
De Olazabal, Jose Javier; New Orleans, 1833 ***1224.3*** *p21*
Depatie, Melchor 23; Vermont, 1855 ***5900.10*** *p498*
De Pedro, Joseph; New York, 1833 ***8197.10*** *p358*
De Perdreanville, Rene Elizabeth David; New York, 1816 ***8197.10*** *p58*
De Peyster, Frederick; New York, New York, 1836 ***1224.3*** *p21*
Depont, James; New York, 1706 ***1224.2*** *p33*
Dequas, Nicholas; Maryland, 1674 ***2524.55*** *p67*
deQurinen, John; Maryland, 1661 ***2524.55*** *p67*
Dera, Stanislaus; Maryland, 1910 ***3259.35*** *p11*
Deraismes, Hippolite; New York, 1838 ***8197.10*** *p109*
Deraismes, John Francis Joseph; New York, 1838 ***8197.10*** *p108*
Deran, Mr.; Quebec, 1857 ***9196.15*** *p16*
Deran, Mrs.; Quebec, 1857 ***9196.15*** *p16*
Derbishire, Miss; Quebec, 1857 ***9196.15*** *p19*
Derbishire, Mr.; Quebec, 1857 ***9196.15*** *p19*
Derby, . . .; Boston, 1765 ***4628.40*** *p114*
Derbyshire, Annetta J. 3; Ontario, 1861 ***2896.27*** *p32*

Derbyshire, Elizabeth 21; Maryland, 1774 1220.25 p77
Derbyshire, Erwin 12; Ontario, 1861 2896.27 p32
Derbyshire, Eugene 3; Ontario, 1861 2896.27 p51
Derbyshire, Eva 7; Ontario, 1861 2896.27 p51
Derbyshire, George 5; Ontario, 1861 2896.27 p32
Derbyshire, Hiram 18; Ontario, 1861 2896.27 p51
Derbyshire, Margaret 28; Ontario, 1861 2896.27 p51
Derbyshire, Martha E. 1; Ontario, 1861 2896.27 p32
Derbyshire, Mary E. 9; Ontario, 1861 2896.27 p32
Derbyshire, Sarah A. 1; Ontario, 1861 2896.27 p51
Derbyshire, Sarah Ann 28; Ontario, 1861 2896.27 p32
Derbyshire, William 10; Ontario, 1861 2896.27 p51
Derczyk, Stanislaus; Maryland, 1910 3259.35 p11
Derda, Thomas; Maryland, 1910 3259.35 p12
Derder, F.; Portland, Maine, 1857 9196.15 p13
Derdtler, Peter; America, 1754 2856.30 p78
Derecke, Joseph; Maryland, 1910 3259.35 p12
Deremo, Albert 23; Ontario, 1861 2896.25 p11
Deremo, Clark 22; Ontario, 1861 2896.27 p21
Deremo, Eliza; Ontario, 1861 2896.25 p12
Deremo, George 51; Ontario, 1861 2896.25 p12
Deremo, Martha 10; Ontario, 1861 2896.25 p12
Deremo, Mary 17; Ontario, 1861 2896.25 p12
Derendinger, Lorenz; Port uncertain, 1783 2856.30 p78
Derendinger, Maria Theresia; Port uncertain, 1795 2856.30 p78
Derendinger, Salome; Port uncertain, 1773 2856.30 p78
Deress, Valentin; America, 1747 2856.30 p87
Dereux, Jacob Heinrich; Port uncertain, 1755 2856.30 p78
Derg, Andreas; America, 1741 2856.30 p78
Derg, Andreas; America, 1742 2856.30 p78
Derham, James; New York, 1840 8197.10 p156
Derick, Lawrence; Philadelphia, 1794 4629.10 p82
Derickson, George; Virginia, 1685 1224.1 p18
Derickson, Harman; Virginia, 1676 1224.1 p18
Derin, Lewis; Maryland, 1674 2524.55 p67
Derine, Elizabeth; Maryland, 1674 2524.55 p67
Derkheim, Moses Myer; Norfolk, Virginia, 1817 1224.3 p21
Dermin, Patrick 60; Ontario, 1871 1823.15 p61
Derming, Edw; Virginia, 1665-1666 6212.30 p22
Dermit, John; New York, 1827 8197.10 p345
Dermody, Catherine; Vermont, 1847-1912 5900.10 p354
Dermon, Danll; Virginia, 1664 6212.30 p6
Dermot, Patrick; New York, 1807 8197.10 p327
Dermot, Patrick 22; Ontario, 1871 1823.22 p42
Dermot, Thomas 25; Maryland, 1774 1220.25 p52
Dermott, . . .; New Hampshire, 1641-1660 4628.40 p44
Dermott, Elizabeth 68; Ontario, 1871 1823.22 p42
Derniewicz, Bartreni; Maryland, 1910 3259.35 p12
Dernimple, James; Maryland, 1672 2524.55 p67
Deroche, Cleophes 22; Ontario, 1871 1823.28 p22
de Ronchamp, Bartholomew; Philadelphia, 1794 4629.10 p82
Derose, John J.; New York, 1802 8197.10 p20
De Rossett, Lewis Henry; North Carolina, n.d. 1224.2 p33
Derrick, Henry; Virginia, 1677 1224.1 p18
Derricke, Hen; Virginia, 1672-1673 6212.30 p51
Derring, Chas 26; Ontario, 1871 1823.28 p23
Derring, William 40; Ontario, 1871 1823.28 p23
Derry, George 25; Philadelphia, 1774 1220.25 p66
Derry, John 45; Georgia, 1775 1220.25 p126
Derry, Joseph 86; Vermont, 1888 5900.10 p365
Derusha, Charles; Vermont, 1833-1880 5900.10 p351
Derusha, Mary Griffin; Vermont, 1836-1924 5900.10 p351
De Ruyter, John C.; New York, 1831 8197.10 p354
Derven, Bridget Conniff; Vermont, 1838-1926 5900.10 p569
Derven, John C.; Vermont, 1829-1901 5900.10 p569
Dervin, Daniel; Vermont, 1832-1909 5900.10 p445
Dervin, Mary McLaughlin; Vermont, 1840-1912 5900.10 p445
Derwin, . . .; Castleton, Vermont, 1837 5900.10 p7
With mother & daughter
Dery, Barney; New York, 1840 8197.10 p158
Dery, Bernard; New York, 1840 8197.10 p158
Desaa, Arnaud; Philadelphia, 1792 4629.10 p80
De Saumarez, Mr.; Quebec, 1858 9196.15 p31
Des Bouttels, Claude Francois Jean Bellanger; New Orleans, 1837 1224.3 p22
Desbrisay, Albert; Georgia, 1751 1224.2 p33
Desbrosses, James; New York, New York, 1808 1224.3 p22
Desbrosses, Magdalen; New York, New York, 1796 1224.2 p33
Desch, Abraham; Port uncertain, 1764 2856.30 p78
Deschamps, Mr. 40; Grenada, 1774-1775 1220.25 p128
Des Champs, Auguste Francois; Philadelphia, 1793 4629.10 p70
Deschler, David; Port uncertain, 1700 2856.30 p78
Deschler, Jacob; Port uncertain, 1744 2856.30 p78
Deschner, Michael; America, 1737 2856.30 p78
With wife & 3 children
Descury, Simon; Ohio, 1763 1224.2 p33
Desdemonds, Mike 32; Seattle, 1911 9196.1 p34
Desdoity, John Baptist; New York, 1794 8197.10 p5
Desertembo, John 25; Maryland, 1775 1220.25 p111
Desgranges, Hans Peter; America, 1790 2856.30 p78
Deshner, John George; Baltimore, 1840 6058.10 p21
De Silvie, Manuel; New York, New York, 1771 1224.2 p33
Desjardin, Abare; Ontario, 1871 1823.28 p23
Deslandes, Charles Francis; Philadelphia, 1794 4629.10 p80
Desmon, Alonzo 6; Ontario, 1861 2896.28 p54
Desmon, Elizabeth 33; Ontario, 1861 2896.28 p54
Desmon, Emma 1; Ontario, 1861 2896.28 p54
Desmon, Hetty 4; Ontario, 1861 2896.28 p54
Desmon, Jane S. 10; Ontario, 1861 2896.28 p54
Desmond, Catherine Mahaney 60; Vermont, 1889 5900.10 p466
Desmond, John 75; Ontario, 1871 1823.15 p61
Desmond, John 79; Vermont, 1905 5900.10 p466
Desmond, Michael; Pennsylvania, 1868 6058.10 p66
Desnones, Joseph; New York, 1821 8197.10 p63
Desombrages, Marie Joseph Adine Vezien; New Orleans, 1833 1224.3 p22
De Soye, Martin; America, 1748 2856.30 p75
With wife & 6 children
De Soyin, Anna Catharina; Port uncertain, 1745 2856.30 p75
Despard, Green; New York, 1819 8197.10 p222
Despe, Niklas; Port uncertain, 1726 2856.30 p78
D'Espinose, Jerome Francois; Savannah, Georgia, 1830 1224.3 p22
Dessardius, Hester *SEE* Dessardius, John
Dessardius, John *SEE* Dessardius, John
Dessardius, John; Maryland, 1677 2524.55 p67
Wife: Hester
Son: John
Dessardius, John; Maryland, 1677 2524.55 p67
Dessloch, Gorg; America, 1754 2856.30 p78
With wife & 5 children
Destein, Peter; Port uncertain, 1829 2856.30 p78
Desterberg, Henry 16; Maryland, 1774 1220.25 p76
D'Estrange, Lieut.; Quebec, 1857 9196.15 p14
De Strzelecki, Paul Edmond; New York, 1834 8197.10 p226
Detchevary, Joseph; Philadelphia, 1791-1792 4629.10 p65
Detiman, Fredrich 33; Ontario, 1871 1823.15 p61
Detken, . . .; America, 1785 2856.30 p85
Detlaf, John 30; Carolina, 1774 1220.25 p71
Wife: Sarah 25
Detlaf, Sarah 25 *SEE* Detlaf, John
Detrick, Lewis; New Orleans, 1850 3437.14 p23
Dettwanger, Jacob; Port uncertain, 1749 2856.30 p78
Detzler, Kilian; Port uncertain, 1755 2856.30 p78
Detzler, Margarete; Port uncertain, 1757 2856.30 p78
Deuch, Jona; Maryland, 1678 2524.55 p67
Deuchar, Alexander; Barbados, 1732 1640.13 p29
Deuchler, Maximiliam; America, 1820 2856.30 p78
With wife & children
Deumair, James 46; Ontario, 1871 1823.15 p61
Deuniston, John Alexander; New York, 1839 8197.10 p226
Deunor, Frederick 47; Ontario, 1871 1823.28 p23
Deupey, Sarah; Carolina, 1715 1224.2 p33
Deurer, Ferdinand; West Indies, 1775 2856.30 p78
Deuring, Johann Georg; Port uncertain, 1742 2856.30 p79
Deutch, Levi 15; Philadelphia, 1774 1220.25 p3
Deutz, Hans Michael; Port uncertain, 1748 2856.30 p89
Deutz, Josef; Port uncertain, 1764 2856.30 p78
Devalley, Charles; Maryland, 1649 2524.55 p67
Devaney, Mary; Vermont, 1822-1900 5900.10 p507
Devaney, Mary; Vermont, 1830-1915 5900.10 p406
Deveaux, Andrew; New York, 1813 1224.3 p22
Develin, Francis; New York, 1824 8197.10 p64
Devenish, Jno; Virginia, 1668-1669 6212.30 p41
Devenish, John; Maryland, 1681 2524.55 p67
Devenish, John; Virginia, 1672 6212.30 p49
De Vent, Daniel; America, 1727 2856.30 p75
Dever, Ann McMahan 87; Vermont, 1896 5900.10 p572
Dever, Elizabeth; Vermont, 1854-1937 5900.10 p93
Dever, Thomas; Vermont, 1857-1925 5900.10 p93
Dever, William; Vermont, 1826-1889 5900.10 p572
Deverall, Benjamin; Virginia, 1720 1224.2 p33
Deverax, Elizabeth *SEE* Deverax, John
Deverax, Elizabeth; Maryland, 1678 2524.55 p67
Deverax, John; Maryland, 1678 2524.55 p67
Wife: Elizabeth
Child: Mary Empson
Child: William
Deverax, Mary Empson *SEE* Deverax, John
Deverax, William *SEE* Deverax, John
Devereaux, Peter; Vermont, 1852-1903 5900.10 p187
Deverell, Benjamin; Virginia, 1720 1224.2 p33
Devereux, James; New York, 1827 8197.10 p346
Devereux, Joan; Maryland, 1659 2524.55 p51
Devereux, Olivia Camilla; America, 1804 1224.3 p22
Devers, Robert 24; Ontario, 1871 1823.28 p23
Devery, Kearn; New York, 1840 8197.10 p158
Devill, James; Maryland, 1671 2524.55 p67
Devin, James 45; Ontario, 1871 1823.22 p42
Devin, Magdalen; Philadelphia, n.d. 1224.2 p33
Devin, Patrick; New York, 1837 8197.10 p83
Devine, Andrew 54; Ontario, 1871 1823.28 p23
Devine, Anna Martin; Vermont, 1879-1912 5900.10 p553
Devine, Bernard 62; Vermont, 1901 5900.10 p433
Devine, Bridget Meehan 74; Vermont, 1905 5900.10 p465
Devine, Bridget Monahan; Vermont, 1829-1905 5900.10 p336
Devine, Bridget Morrow; Vermont, 1839-1923 5900.10 p553
Devine, Catharine 9; Vermont, 1862 5900.10 p344
Devine, Catherine; Vermont, 1865 5900.10 p121
Devine, Catherine Dooling; Vermont, 1917 5900.10 p115
Devine, Christopher 29; Vermont, 1867 5900.10 p358
Devine, Daniel 2; Vermont, 1862 5900.10 p344
Devine, Elizabeth 26; Vermont, 1871 5900.10 p358
Devine, Elizabeth 26; Vermont, 1877 5900.10 p345
Devine, Elizabeth Moran; Vermont, 1834-1916 5900.10 p121
Devine, Ellen M.; Vermont, 1854-1892 5900.10 p336
Devine, Felix 49; Ontario, 1871 1823.28 p23
Devine, H. 6; Ontario, 1861 2896.28 p11
Devine, James 29; Vermont, 1886 5900.10 p358
Devine, Jno 8; Ontario, 1861 2896.28 p11
Devine, John; Vermont, 1826-1911 5900.10 p336
Devine, John; Vermont, 1834-1910 5900.10 p115
Devine, John; Vermont, 1834-1914 5900.10 p338
Devine, John 40; Ontario, 1871 1823.28 p23
Devine, L. 11; Ontario, 1861 2896.28 p11
Devine, M. 3; Ontario, 1861 2896.28 p11
Devine, M. 14; Ontario, 1861 2896.28 p11
Devine, M. 51; Vermont, 1900 5900.10 p358
Devine, Magdalen; Philadelphia, n.d. 1224.2 p33
Devine, Mary; Vermont, 1837-1920 5900.10 p113
Devine, Mary; Vermont, 1877-1937 5900.10 p115
Devine, Mary C.; Vermont, 1865-1943 5900.10 p553
Devine, Mary Eliott 49; Vermont, 1866 5900.10 p358
Devine, Mary M. 29; Vermont, 1862 5900.10 p344
Devine, Matthew 56; Ontario, 1871 1823.28 p23
Devine, Michael; Vermont, 1824-1915 5900.10 p553
Devine, Michael; Vermont, 1833-1914 5900.10 p121
Devine, Robert; Vermont, 1832-1914 5900.10 p338
Devine, Robert 45; Ontario, 1871 1823.28 p23
Devine, S. 38; Ontario, 1861 2896.28 p11
Devine, Thomas; New York, 1826 8197.10 p224
Devine, Thomas 43; Vermont, 1890 5900.10 p358
Devine, Thomas 50; Vermont, 1857 5900.10 p344
Devine, Thomas 50; Vermont, 1857 5900.10 p358
Devine, Thomas 78; Vermont, 1925 5900.10 p465
Devine, Thomas M.; Vermont, 1866-1936 5900.10 p553
Devine, W. R.; Vermont, 1887-1937 5900.10 p121
Devine, William; Vermont, 1864-1945 5900.10 p553
Devine, William 39; Ontario, 1861 2896.28 p11
Devine, William 58; Ontario, 1871 1823.28 p23
Deviney, Hugh 57; Ontario, 1871 1823.22 p42
Deviney, James 62; Ontario, 1871 1823.22 p42
Deviney, Jane 77; Ontario, 1871 1823.22 p42
Deviney, John 47; Ontario, 1871 1823.22 p42
Deviney, Mary 17; Ontario, 1871 1823.22 p42
Devins, Ellen Lynch 48; Vermont, 1889 5900.10 p589
Devins, James E.; Vermont, 1848-1916 5900.10 p589
Devisme, Peter; New York, New York, 1781 1224.2 p33
Devlin, Arthur; New York, 1840 8197.10 p157
Devlin, Barnard; New York, 1821 8197.10 p223
Devlin, Charles; New York, 1839 8197.10 p129
Devlin, Francis; New York, 1838 8197.10 p108
Devlin, John; New York, 1837 8197.10 p83
Devlin, Margaret 68; Vermont, 1898 5900.10 p581
Devlin, Michael; New York, 1837 8197.10 p84
Devlin, Peter; New York, 1837 8197.10 p86
Devlin, Thomas 30; New York, 1826-1837 8197.10 p310
Devon, John; Maryland, 1679 2524.55 p67
Devonald, Thomas; Philadelphia, 1794 1224.2 p33
Devonish, Margaret; Maryland, 1657 2524.55 p67
Devos, Salvator 33; British Columbia, 1910 9196.1 p31
Devos, Salvator 33; Seattle, 1910 9196.1 p31

Dickson, William; New York, 1821 ***8197.10*** *p222*
Dickson, William; New York, 1869 ***1640.13*** *p30*
Dickson, William; Norfolk, Virginia, 1823 ***1224.3*** *p22*
Dickson, William; Ontario, 1861 ***2896.28*** *p55*
Dickson, William; Virginia, 1686 ***1224.1*** *p18*
Dickson, William 45; Ontario, 1871 ***1823.15*** *p62*
Dickson, William 57; Ontario, 1871 ***1823.15*** *p62*
Dickvendorf, George; Pennsylvania, 1777 ***4629.10*** *p24*
Dicky, John 30; Ontario, 1871 ***1823.22*** *p42*
Diddall, William; Maryland, 1674 ***2524.55*** *p68*
Didier, Magdalena; Port uncertain, 1758 ***2856.30*** *p79*
Didier, Regina; Port uncertain, 1795 ***2856.30*** *p79*
Didier, Regina; Port uncertain, 1797 ***2856.30*** *p79*
Didion, Peter; Port uncertain, 1786 ***2856.30*** *p79*
Didlo, Henry 28; Ontario, 1871 ***1823.28*** *p23*
Didnot, Edwd; Virginia, 1671 ***6212.30*** *p42*
Didziedzic, Kazimer; Maryland, 1910 ***3259.35*** *p12*
Diebendorffer, Johann; America, 1727 ***2856.30*** *p79*
With wife
Diebold, Hans Georg; Port uncertain, 1747 ***2856.30*** *p79*
Dieboldt, Barbara; Port uncertain, 1738 ***2856.30*** *p79*
Diedela, Daniel; America, 1754 ***2856.30*** *p84*
Diedenhofen, Anton; Port uncertain, 1772 ***2856.30*** *p79*
Diederich, Michael; America, 1754 ***2856.30*** *p80*
Diederich, Peter; Port uncertain, 1750 ***2856.30*** *p80*
Diedrichsen, Peter; New York, New York, 1882 ***3437.14*** *p167*
Diefenbacher, Caspar; America, 1749 ***2856.30*** *p80*
With wife & 4 children
Diefenbacher, Caspar; America, 1750 ***2856.30*** *p80*
With wife & 3 children
Diefenbacher, Elisabeth; America, 1793 ***2856.30*** *p80*
Diefenbacher, Elisabeth; Port uncertain, 1792 ***2856.30*** *p80*
Diefenbacher, Jacob; Port uncertain, 1769 ***2856.30*** *p80*
Dieffenbach, John Henry; New York, 1838 ***8197.10*** *p226*
Dieffenbacher, . . .; America, 1793 ***2856.30*** *p80*
Diehl, Anna Maria; Port uncertain, 1747 ***2856.30*** *p80*
Diehl, Anna Maria; Port uncertain, 1793 ***2856.30*** *p80*
Diehl, Apollonia; Port uncertain, 1742 ***2856.30*** *p80*
Diehl, Christof; Port uncertain, 1749 ***2856.30*** *p80*
With wife & 6 children
Diehl, George 42; Ontario, 1871 ***1823.15*** *p62*
Diehl, Jacob 50; Ontario, 1871 ***1823.15*** *p62*
Diehl, Johann Nikolaus; Port uncertain, 1763 ***2856.30*** *p80*
Diehl, Klemens; Port uncertain, 1765 ***2856.30*** *p80*
Diehl, Maria; Port uncertain, 1736 ***2856.30*** *p80*
Diehl, Michael; America, 1738 ***2856.30*** *p80*
Diehl, Theobald; America, 1738 ***2856.30*** *p80*
Diehl, Valentin; America, 1745 ***2856.30*** *p80*
Diehl, Valintine 48; Ontario, 1871 ***1823.15*** *p62*
Diehl, Wilhelm; Port uncertain, 1764 ***2856.30*** *p80*
Diehl, William; New York, New York, 1882 ***3437.14*** *p162*
Diehm, Johann; Port uncertain, 1751 ***2856.30*** *p80*
Diehr, Elias; Port uncertain, 1755 ***2856.30*** *p80*
Diel, Anna 17; Kansas, 1898-1910 ***9079.10*** *p33*
Diel, Catharena 46; Kansas, 1898-1910 ***9079.10*** *p33*
Diel, Fredrick 15; Kansas, 1898-1910 ***9079.10*** *p33*
Diel, Friedrich; Port uncertain, 1764 ***2856.30*** *p80*
Diel, Jacob 13; Kansas, 1898-1910 ***9079.10*** *p33*
Diel, Jacob 45; Kansas, 1898-1910 ***9079.10*** *p33*
Diel, Johann; Port uncertain, 1783 ***2856.30*** *p80*
Diel, Johann Adam; America, 1782 ***2856.30*** *p80*
Diel, Michael; America, 1727 ***2856.30*** *p80*
Diel, Peter; America, 1739 ***2856.30*** *p80*
Diel, Peter; Port uncertain, 1782 ***2856.30*** *p80*
Diel, Simon Jakob; America, 1742 ***2856.30*** *p80*
Dieler, Caspar Elias; America, 1733 ***2856.30*** *p80*
With wife & children
Dielport, Johann; Port uncertain, 1788 ***2856.30*** *p81*
Diem, Christian; New York, New York, 1845 ***6058.10*** *p40*
Diem, John; Philadelphia, 1842 ***6058.10*** *p27*
Diemer, Henrich; Port uncertain, 1734 ***2856.30*** *p81*
Dien, Gottlieb; New York, 1835 ***8197.10*** *p225*
Diener, Johann Henrich; Port uncertain, 1734 ***2856.30*** *p81*
Diener, Marianna; Port uncertain, 1790 ***2856.30*** *p81*
Dienstler, Anna; Port uncertain, 1729 ***2856.30*** *p81*
Dier, E. F. 6; Ontario, 1861 ***2896.28*** *p65*
Dier, Mahala 47; Ontario, 1861 ***2896.28*** *p65*
Dier, Samuell; Virginia, 1665 ***6212.30*** *p20*
Dierker, Henry; New York, 1838 ***8197.10*** *p226*
Dierks, Charles 35; Ontario, 1871 ***1823.28*** *p23*
Dierks, Henry 36; Ontario, 1871 ***1823.28*** *p23*
Dierr, Augustus; New York, 1839 ***8197.10*** *p129*
Dierr, Johannes; New York, 1839 ***8197.10*** *p129*
Dies, John; Pennsylvania, 1860 ***6058.10*** *p42*
Dies, Peter 35; Kansas, 1910 ***9079.10*** *p45*
Diess, Konrad; America, 1749 ***2856.30*** *p81*
Dieter, Jeremia; Port uncertain, 1739 ***2856.30*** *p81*
Dieterich, Franz; Port uncertain, 1791 ***2856.30*** *p81*
Dieterich, Friedrich Karl; Port uncertain, 1790 ***2856.30*** *p81*
Dieterich, Georg Henrich; Port uncertain, 1769 ***2856.30*** *p81*
Dieterich, Johann Jacob; Port uncertain, 1785 ***2856.30*** *p81*
Dieterich, Johann Wilhelm; Port uncertain, 1785 ***2856.30*** *p81*
Dieterich, Maria Sophia; America, 1742 ***2856.30*** *p81*
Dieterich, Peter; Port uncertain, 1792 ***2856.30*** *p81*
Dieterle, Johann Jacob; America, 1774 ***2856.30*** *p81*
Diether, Henrich; Port uncertain, 1749 ***2856.30*** *p81*
Dietherich, Jacob; New York, 1792-1840 ***8197.10*** *p86*
Dietrich, Edward 36; Ontario, 1871 ***1823.15*** *p62*
Dietrich, Gregor; America, 1721 ***2856.30*** *p81*
Dietrich, Gregor; Port uncertain, 1720 ***2856.30*** *p81*
Dietrich, Isaac; America, 1740 ***2856.30*** *p81*
Dietrich, Johann Heinrich; Port uncertain, 1790 ***2856.30*** *p81*
Dietrich, Johann Nickel; Port uncertain, 1784 ***2856.30*** *p81*
Dietrich, Maria Barbara; Port uncertain, 1763 ***2856.30*** *p81*
Diets, George N. 54; Kansas, 1875-1910 ***9079.10*** *p24*
Diets, Maria E. 54; Kansas, 1875-1910 ***9079.10*** *p24*
Diett, Robert 45; Ontario, 1871 ***1823.15*** *p62*
Dietterich, Michael; New York, 1840 ***8197.10*** *p156*
Dietz, Adam 73; Kansas, 1873-1910 ***9079.10*** *p24*
Dietz, Anna 73; Kansas, 1873-1910 ***9079.10*** *p24*
Dietz, Catherine 25; Kansas, 1901-1910 ***9079.10*** *p24*
Dietz, Cristina 38; Kansas, 1905-1910 ***9079.10*** *p20*
Dietz, Elisabeth; Port uncertain, 1743 ***2856.30*** *p81*
Dietz, Hans Jacob; Port uncertain, 1753 ***2856.30*** *p81*
Dietz, Henry 4; Kansas, 1907-1910 ***9079.10*** *p7*
Dietz, Henry 24; Kansas, 1907-1910 ***9079.10*** *p6*
Dietz, Henry 47; Ontario, 1871 ***1823.15*** *p62*
Dietz, Jacob 13; Kansas, 1905-1910 ***9079.10*** *p20*
Dietz, Johann Georg; Port uncertain, 1743 ***2856.30*** *p82*
Dietz, Johann Jakob; Port uncertain, 1750 ***2856.30*** *p82*
Dietz, Johann Michael; England, 1700-1799 ***2856.30*** *p82*
Dietz, John 8; Kansas, 1905-1910 ***9079.10*** *p20*
Dietz, Lizzie 24; Kansas, 1907-1910 ***9079.10*** *p7*
Dietz, Lydia 5; Kansas, 1905-1910 ***9079.10*** *p20*
Dietz, Margarete; Port uncertain, 1788 ***2856.30*** *p82*
Dietz, Martin; America, 1751 ***2856.30*** *p82*
Dietz, Martin; Port uncertain, 1751 ***2856.30*** *p82*
Dietz, Mrs. Martin; America, 1753 ***2856.30*** *p82*
Dietz, Peter; Port uncertain, 1838 ***2856.30*** *p82*
With wife
Dietz, Susana C. 28; Kansas, 1900-1910 ***9079.10*** *p22*
Dietz, Wilhilm 60; Kansas, 1905-1910 ***9079.10*** *p20*
Dietz, William 37; Kansas, 1905-1910 ***9079.10*** *p20*
Dietzel, Bernard; Port uncertain, 1774 ***2856.30*** *p82*
Dieulafoy, Joseph Michael; Philadelphia, 1793 ***4629.10*** *p74*
Dieulourd, Charles Joseph; Philadelphia, 1793 ***4629.10*** *p69*
Diez, Apollonia; America, 1752 ***2856.30*** *p82*
With child
Diez, Caspar; Port uncertain, 1751 ***2856.30*** *p82*
Diez, Phil. Leonhard; Port uncertain, 1776 ***2856.30*** *p82*
Diffley, Bridget; Vermont, 1865-1932 ***5900.10*** *p216*
Diffley, Catherine 79; Vermont, 1892 ***5900.10*** *p92*
Diffley, Edward 45; Vermont, 1893 ***5900.10*** *p212*
Difley, Bridget; Vermont, 1844-1875 ***5900.10*** *p583*
Difley, Mary; Vermont, 1819-1867 ***5900.10*** *p558*
Difley, Mary E.; Vermont, 1849-1904 ***5900.10*** *p579*
Difley, Patrick; Vermont, 1815-1858 ***5900.10*** *p558*
Difnesh, Jno; Virginia, 1663 ***6212.30*** *p4*
Digary, Jno; Virginia, 1666 ***6212.30*** *p28*
Digbey, Salter 32; Ontario, 1871 ***1823.22*** *p42*
Digby, James; Maryland, 1666 ***2524.55*** *p68*
Digel, Peter; Port uncertain, 1797 ***2856.30*** *p82*
Digg, Maurice; Virginia, 1665-1666 ***6212.30*** *p21*
Diggins, Hannah Fagan 31; Vermont, 1872 ***5900.10*** *p402*
Diggins, Honora 76; Vermont, 1904 ***5900.10*** *p57*
Diggins, James 73; Vermont, 1896 ***5900.10*** *p57*
Diggins, James J.; Vermont, 1858-1882 ***5900.10*** *p57*
Diggins, Maria Hackett 77; Vermont, 1925 ***5900.10*** *p68*
Diggins, Michael 63; Vermont, 1902 ***5900.10*** *p68*
Diggins, Nora E.; Vermont, 1854-1895 ***5900.10*** *p57*
Diggle, Jane 45; Ontario, 1871 ***1823.15*** *p62*
Diggs, Edward; Virginia, 1686 ***1224.1*** *p18*
Diggs, Morris; Virginia, 1664 ***6212.30*** *p14*
Dignan, Patrick; New York, 1839 ***8197.10*** *p320*
Dihl, Adam; America, 1737 ***2856.30*** *p82*
Dihl, Anna Margarete; Port uncertain, 1754 ***2856.30*** *p82*
Dihl, Margarete; Port uncertain, 1763 ***2856.30*** *p82*
Dihl, Maria Martha; Port uncertain, 1748 ***2856.30*** *p82*
Dikczykski, John; Maryland, 1910 ***3259.35*** *p12*
Dike, Thomas 56; Ontario, 1871 ***1823.15*** *p62*
Dikes, Ann; Maryland, 1678 ***2524.55*** *p68*
Dikes, Ann; Maryland, 1679 ***2524.55*** *p68*
Dikes, Edw; Virginia, 1672 ***6212.30*** *p49*
Dikes, Jeremy; Virginia, 1672 ***6212.30*** *p49*
Dikes, Phillip; Maryland, 1678 ***2524.55*** *p68*
Dikins, Mary; Virginia, 1668-1669 ***6212.30*** *p40*
Dikins, Michael; New York, 1804 ***8197.10*** *p28*
Dilck, Johann Nickel; Port uncertain, 1754 ***2856.30*** *p82*
Dilger, Gottfried Paul; Port uncertain, 1748 ***2856.30*** *p82*
With child
Dilger, Gottfried Paul; Port uncertain, 1749 ***2856.30*** *p82*
With child
Dilgerin, Gottfried Paul; Port uncertain, 1748 ***2856.30*** *p82*
With child
Dilgerin, Gottfried Paul; Port uncertain, 1749 ***2856.30*** *p82*
With child
Dilgin, Ursula; Port uncertain, 1749 ***2856.30*** *p82*
Diliam, Henry 25; Ontario, 1871 ***1823.28*** *p23*
Dilke, Thomas; New York, New York, 1831 ***8197.10*** *p158*
Dill, Charles Henry 45; Ontario, 1871 ***1823.28*** *p23*
Dill, John; Maryland, 1659 ***2524.55*** *p68*
Dill, John 46; Ontario, 1871 ***1823.15*** *p62*
Dill, Robert; Pennsylvania, 1777 ***4629.10*** *p7*
Dill, Simon; Port uncertain, 1779 ***2856.30*** *p82*
Dillan, Darby; Maryland, 1678 ***2524.55*** *p68*
Dillan, James 30; Ontario, 1871 ***1823.28*** *p23*
Dillcunz, Magdalena; Port uncertain, 1740 ***2856.30*** *p82*
Dillen, Richard 19; Ontario, 1871 ***1823.15*** *p62*
Dillenberger, Philipp; Port uncertain, 1753 ***2856.30*** *p82*
Dillenburg, Gerhard; Port uncertain, 1740 ***2856.30*** *p82*
With wife & children
Dillier, Franz; America, 1752 ***2856.30*** *p82*
Dilling, John 44; Ontario, 1871 ***1823.15*** *p62*
Dilling, Pearce; Virginia, 1671 ***6212.30*** *p43*
Dillinger, Johann; Port uncertain, 1760 ***2856.30*** *p82*
Dillion, D. R.; Quebec, 1858 ***9196.15*** *p44*
Dillmann, Catharina; Port uncertain, 1784 ***2856.30*** *p83*
Dillmann, Franz Josef; Port uncertain, 1790 ***2856.30*** *p83*
Dillmann, Georg Martin; Port uncertain, 1759 ***2856.30*** *p83*
Dillmann, Hans Georg; America, 1751 ***2856.30*** *p83*
With wife & 2 children
Dillmann, Hans Georg; Port uncertain, 1746 ***2856.30*** *p83*
Dillmann, Hans Georg; Port uncertain, 1750 ***2856.30*** *p83*
Dillmann, Johann; Port uncertain, 1765 ***2856.30*** *p83*
Dillon, Mr.; Quebec, 1857 ***9196.15*** *p22*
Dillon, Mrs.; Quebec, 1857 ***9196.15*** *p22*
Dillon, Agnes M.; Vermont, 1867-1937 ***5900.10*** *p596*
Dillon, Alexander; New York, 1821 ***8197.10*** *p222*
Dillon, Alice 54; Vermont, 1892 ***5900.10*** *p278*
Dillon, Andrew J. 80; Vermont, 1918 ***5900.10*** *p124*
Dillon, Ann G. Shanahan 64; Vermont, 1911 ***5900.10*** *p125*
Dillon, Austni 55; Ontario, 1871 ***1823.15*** *p62*
Dillon, Bridget Hannan; Vermont, 1832-1906 ***5900.10*** *p540*
Dillon, Catherine 73; Vermont, 1892 ***5900.10*** *p540*
Dillon, Catherine Donnelly 63; Vermont, 1898 ***5900.10*** *p540*
Dillon, Dennis 43; Ontario, 1871 ***1823.28*** *p23*
Dillon, Edward 22; Maryland, 1775 ***1220.25*** *p99*
Dillon, Edward 35; Ontario, 1871 ***1823.28*** *p23*
Dillon, Edward 59; Vermont, 1877 ***5900.10*** *p540*
Dillon, Ellen; Vermont, 1826-1861 ***5900.10*** *p182*
Dillon, Ellen; Vermont, 1833-1923 ***5900.10*** *p468*
Dillon, Ellen 74; Vermont, 1911 ***5900.10*** *p540*
Dillon, Hugh 54; Ontario, 1871 ***1823.22*** *p42*
Dillon, James; New York, 1839 ***8197.10*** *p226*
Dillon, James 55; Ontario, 1871 ***1823.22*** *p42*
Dillon, James H. 5; Vermont, 1864 ***5900.10*** *p346*
Dillon, James H. 6; Vermont, 1865 ***5900.10*** *p346*
Dillon, John; New York, 1807 ***8197.10*** *p326*
Dillon, John; New York, 1822 ***8197.10*** *p224*
Dillon, John; New York, 1837 ***8197.10*** *p83*
Dillon, John; New York, 1838 ***8197.10*** *p109*
Dillon, John 60; Ontario, 1871 ***1823.28*** *p23*
Dillon, John E.; Vermont, 1850-1922 ***5900.10*** *p596*
Dillon, Judy 51 *SEE* Dillon, Pat
Dillon, Margaret; Vermont, 1844-1905 ***5900.10*** *p428*
Dillon, Margaret 23 *SEE* Dillon, Pat
Dillon, Margaret 73; Vermont, 1877 ***5900.10*** *p278*
Dillon, Margaret Halpin 48; Vermont, 1875 ***5900.10*** *p540*
Dillon, Mary Boylan; Vermont, 1846-1924 ***5900.10*** *p174*
Dillon, Matilda; Vermont, 1843-1918 ***5900.10*** *p464*
Dillon, Matthew; New York, 1840 ***8197.10*** *p158*
Dillon, Pat 47; New York, New York, 1850 ***1825.45*** *p48*
Wife: Judy 51
Daughter: Margaret 23
Dillon, Patrick; Vermont, 1824-1884 ***5900.10*** *p174*
Dillon, Patrick 60; Vermont, 1884 ***5900.10*** *p540*
Dillon, T. H. 50; Ontario, 1871 ***1823.28*** *p23*

Dillon, Thomas; Vermont, 1828-1908 ***5900.10*** *p540*
Dillon, William; Vermont, 1834-1892 ***5900.10*** *p468*
Dilworth, Ellen; Vermont, 1818-1886 ***5900.10*** *p303*
Dilworth, John; Pennsylvania, 1777 ***4629.10*** *p26*
Dilworth, Robt 24; Ontario, 1871 ***1823.28*** *p23*
DiMartin, Andrew; Maryland, 1910 ***3259.35*** *p12*
Dimbolski, Peter; Maryland, 1910 ***3259.35*** *p12*
Dimmon, William 66; Ontario, 1871 ***1823.15*** *p62*
Dimock, Jno; Virginia, 1665-1666 ***6212.30*** *p23*
Dimock, John; Virginia, 1664 ***6212.30*** *p14*
Dimond, Alice 24; Fort Cumberland, Nova Scotia, 1774 ***1220.25*** *p18*
Dimond, Denis; New York, 1831-1837 ***8197.10*** *p311*
Dimond, Jacob; Pennsylvania, 1779 ***4629.10*** *p38*
Dimond, Nancy; Vermont, 1830-1914 ***5900.10*** *p103*
Dimpsey, James 23; Baltimore, 1775 ***1220.25*** *p117*
Dimsdale, Mrs.; Quebec, 1856 ***9196.15*** *p7*
Dimski, Leonard; Maryland, 1910 ***3259.35*** *p12*
Dinan, Patrick R.; New York, 1834 ***8197.10*** *p72*
Dinan, Peter; New York, 1807 ***8197.10*** *p328*
Dinckel, Conrad; New York, 1835 ***8197.10*** *p225*
Dinckley, Hannah; Maryland, 1669 ***2524.55*** *p221*
Dindiska, Mary; Maryland, 1910 ***3259.35*** *p12*
Dineen, Denis; Vermont, 1878-1915 ***5900.10*** *p483*
Dineen, Julia; Vermont, 1824-1903 ***5900.10*** *p105*
Dines, Ann 67; Ontario, 1871 ***1823.15*** *p62*
Dines, Christina 57; Kansas, 1876-1910 ***9079.10*** *p23*
Dines, David 33; Ontario, 1871 ***1823.22*** *p42*
Dines, Edward 28; Ontario, 1871 ***1823.15*** *p62*
Dines, John 23; Ontario, 1871 ***1823.15*** *p62*
Dines, Leticia 25; Ontario, 1871 ***1823.15*** *p62*
Dines, Potter, Sr. 59; Kansas, 1876-1910 ***9079.10*** *p23*
Dines, Richard 26; Ontario, 1871 ***1823.15*** *p62*
Dines, William; Virginia, 1665 ***6212.30*** *p19*
Dinger, Wilhelm; Port uncertain, 1767 ***2856.30*** *p83*
Dinges, Gerhard; Port uncertain, 1730 ***2856.30*** *p83*
Dinges, J.; America, 1750 ***2856.30*** *p231*
Dinges, J.; America, 1778 ***2856.30*** *p231*
Dinges, J.; Port uncertain, 1765 ***2856.30*** *p231*
Dinges, Johann; America, 1775 ***2856.30*** *p83*
With wife
Dinges, Johann; America, 1778 ***2856.30*** *p83*
With wife
Dingle, John 40; Ontario, 1871 ***1823.22*** *p42*
Dingman, Allan 13; Ontario, 1861 ***2896.27*** *p38*
Dingman, Archibald 11; Ontario, 1861 ***2896.27*** *p38*
Dingman, Chester 3; Ontario, 1861 ***2896.27*** *p3*
Dingman, Clarissa 16; Ontario, 1861 ***2896.27*** *p38*
Dingman, David 18; Ontario, 1861 ***2896.27*** *p38*
Dingman, Dugakd 22; Ontario, 1861 ***2896.27*** *p38*
Dingman, Garrett, Sr. 77; Ontario, 1871 ***1823.22*** *p43*
Dingman, Henry; Ontario, 1861 ***2896.25*** *p12*
Dingman, John 9; Ontario, 1861 ***2896.27*** *p3*
Dingman, Margaret 36; Ontario, 1861 ***2896.27*** *p3*
Dingman, Milicent 49; Ontario, 1861 ***2896.27*** *p38*
Dingman, N. J. 16; Ontario, 1861 ***2896.27*** *p3*
Dingman, Nelson 24; Ontario, 1861 ***2896.27*** *p38*
Dingman, O. H. 5; Ontario, 1861 ***2896.27*** *p3*
Dingman, Oliver 38; Ontario, 1861 ***2896.27*** *p3*
Dingman, Oliver 75; Ontario, 1861 ***2896.27*** *p3*
Dingman, P. S. 14; Ontario, 1861 ***2896.27*** *p3*
Dingnan, William 64; Ontario, 1871 ***1823.15*** *p62*
Dingwall, Donald; Nova Scotia, 1820-1829 ***4537.35*** *p10*
Child: Mary
Child: Kirsty
Child: Rachel
Dingwall, Kirsty *SEE* Dingwall, Donald
Dingwall, Mary *SEE* Dingwall, Donald
Dingwall, Rachel *SEE* Dingwall, Donald
Dingwell, Alexander 46; Ontario, 1871 ***1823.15*** *p62*
Dingwell, Edward 23; Ontario, 1871 ***1823.22*** *p43*
Dinko, Ignatius; Maryland, 1910 ***3259.35*** *p12*
Dinkovitz, Wishtor; Maryland, 1910 ***3259.35*** *p12*
Dinmby, Peter 38; Ontario, 1871 ***1823.15*** *p62*
Dinn, Ellen M.; Vermont, 1847-1899 ***5900.10*** *p422*
Dinnen, George; New York, 1807 ***8197.10*** *p38*
Dinnen, James; New York, 1838 ***8197.10*** *p108*
Dinner, William 47; Ontario, 1871 ***1823.28*** *p23*
Dinney, Charles 40; Ontario, 1871 ***1823.15*** *p62*
Dinnin, Joseph 45; Ontario, 1871 ***1823.15*** *p62*
Dinnin, Joseph 89; Ontario, 1871 ***1823.15*** *p63*
Dinnin, William 58; Ontario, 1871 ***1823.15*** *p63*
Dinning, Miss; Quebec, 1857 ***9196.15*** *p22*
Dinning, Mrs.; Quebec, 1857 ***9196.15*** *p22*
Dinning, James; Portland, Maine, 1858 ***9196.15*** *p29*
Dinny, Hampdin 26; Ontario, 1871 ***1823.15*** *p63*
Dinsdale, Thomas 40; Ontario, 1871 ***1823.15*** *p63*
Dinsley, Edward 56; Ontario, 1871 ***1823.15*** *p63*
Dinsley, John 27; Ontario, 1871 ***1823.15*** *p63*
Dinsmore, John 68; Ontario, 1871 ***1823.15*** *p63*
Dinsmore, Robert 38; Ontario, 1871 ***1823.15*** *p63*
Dintelmann, Johann Adam; Port uncertain, 1754 ***2856.30*** *p83*
Dinwiddie, Robert; Virginia, n.d. ***1224.2*** *p33*
Dinwoodie, James 43; Ontario, 1871 ***1823.22*** *p43*
Dinwoodie, James 73; Ontario, 1871 ***1823.22*** *p43*
Dion, Mary; Vermont, 1855-1892 ***5900.10*** *p513*
Diorush, Antoni; Maryland, 1910 ***3259.35*** *p12*
Dippel, Anton; Port uncertain, 1782 ***2856.30*** *p83*
Dirrick, Henry; Virginia, 1671-1672 ***6212.30*** *p46*
Dirry, Caspar; America, 1738 ***2856.30*** *p83*
Dirry, Jakob; America, 1752 ***2856.30*** *p83*
With wife & 5 children
Dirry, Philipp; America, 1752 ***2856.30*** *p83*
With wife & 3 children
Dirsewiecki, Wojciech; Maryland, 1910 ***3259.35*** *p12*
Dirstein, Henry 40; Ontario, 1871 ***1823.15*** *p63*
Disbonne, Charles 30; Virginia, 1773 ***1220.25*** *p30*
Dischbein, Magdalena; Port uncertain, 1729 ***2856.30*** *p83*
Dischbeinin, Magdalena; Port uncertain, 1729 ***2856.30*** *p83*
Discher, . . .; Port uncertain, 1799 ***2856.30*** *p83*
Disher, Thomas 42; Ontario, 1871 ***1823.15*** *p63*
Disley, Maria; Vermont, 1840-1912 ***5900.10*** *p479*
Dismore, Henry 21; Maryland, 1775 ***1220.25*** *p98*
Disney, Cahel 37; Ontario, 1871 ***1823.15*** *p63*
Disney, Elias 30; Ontario, 1871 ***1823.15*** *p63*
Disney, Robert 73; Ontario, 1871 ***1823.15*** *p63*
Disque, Georg Nicolas; Port uncertain, 1776 ***2856.30*** *p83*
Distin, Mr.; Quebec, 1858 ***9196.15*** *p34*
Distler, Elisabeth; Port uncertain, 1777 ***2856.30*** *p83*
Distler, Philipp; Port uncertain, 1793 ***2856.30*** *p83*
Ditchburn, John 32; Ontario, 1871 ***1823.28*** *p23*
Ditchburn, Thomas Lee 35; Ontario, 1871 ***1823.22*** *p43*
Ditchett, Richard; New York, 1837 ***8197.10*** *p82*
Ditchfield, Jno.; Maryland, 1673 ***2524.55*** *p68*
Diterich, Maria Catharina; Port uncertain, 1764 ***2856.30*** *p83*
Ditrich, Anna Elisabeth; Port uncertain, 1777 ***2856.30*** *p83*
Ditsbarer, Henry; Pennsylvania, 1856 ***6058.10*** *p36*
Ditter, Joseph; New York, 1838 ***8197.10*** *p108*
Dittler, Georg Jacob; Port uncertain, 1770 ***2856.30*** *p84*
Dittler, Johann Peter; Port uncertain, 1754 ***2856.30*** *p84*
Dittlo, Daniel; America, 1754 ***2856.30*** *p84*
Dittmann, Christina; Port uncertain, 1748 ***2856.30*** *p84*
Ditton, Robert; New York, 1840 ***8197.10*** *p158*
Dittrich, Rudolph Moritz; Mexico, 1851 ***1224.3*** *p22*
Dittrich, Rudolph Moritz; New Orleans, 1851 ***1224.3*** *p22*
Ditz, Adam; America, 1739 ***2856.30*** *p84*
Ditz, Hans Georg; America, 1738 ***2856.30*** *p84*
Ditz, Jakob; America, 1738 ***2856.30*** *p84*
Ditz, Konrad; America, 1738 ***2856.30*** *p84*
With wife & children
Divar, William 26; Ontario, 1871 ***1823.28*** *p23*
Divau, Nikolaus; Port uncertain, 1784 ***2856.30*** *p456*
With family
Divenger, Gerard Henry; New York, 1839 ***8197.10*** *p129*
Divger, John 37; Ontario, 1871 ***1823.15*** *p63*
Divin, John; New York, 1831 ***8197.10*** *p355*
Divine, Francis; New York, 1834 ***8197.10*** *p72*
Divine, James; New York, 1839 ***8197.10*** *p380*
Divine, John; New York, 1802 ***8197.10*** *p20*
Divine, Thmas 62; Ontario, 1871 ***1823.15*** *p63*
Divine, Thomas; New York, 1838 ***8197.10*** *p108*
Divine, William 28; Ontario, 1871 ***1823.15*** *p63*
Dix, Augustine; Maryland, 1672 ***2524.55*** *p68*
Dix, Frank; Maryland, 1910 ***3259.35*** *p12*
Dix, Isack; Virginia, 1671 ***6212.30*** *p44*
Dix, Peter; Port uncertain, 1737 ***2856.30*** *p84*
Dix, Thomas; Maryland, 1910 ***3259.35*** *p12*
Dix, Wilhelm; Port uncertain, 1770 ***2856.30*** *p84*
Dixcon, Wm; Virginia, 1681 ***6212.30*** *p55*
Dixey, Thomas; Pennsylvania, 1777 ***4629.10*** *p45*
Dixey, Thomas; Pennsylvania, 1785 ***4629.10*** *p48*
Dixon, Alice 1; Vermont, 1863 ***5900.10*** *p96*
Dixon, Ambrose *SEE* Dixon, Ambrose
Dixon, Ambrose; Maryland, 1661 ***2524.55*** *p68*
Wife: Mary
Child: Sarah
Child: Grace
Child: Elizabeth
Child: Mary
Child: Ambrose
Child: Thomas
Dixon, Ann 43; Ontario, 1871 ***1823.22*** *p43*
Dixon, Ann 68; Vermont, 1937 ***5900.10*** *p191*
Dixon, Catherine 74; Vermont, 1892 ***5900.10*** *p96*
Dixon, David 42; Ontario, 1871 ***1823.28*** *p23*
Dixon, Dorothy 68; Vermont, 1885 ***5900.10*** *p191*
Dixon, Edward; New York, 1839 ***8197.10*** *p129*
Dixon, Eliza McGowan; Vermont, 1813-1875 ***5900.10*** *p377*
Dixon, Elizabeth *SEE* Dixon, Ambrose
Dixon, Elizabeth 44; Vermont, 1902 ***5900.10*** *p96*
Dixon, Ellen; Vermont, 1842-1915 ***5900.10*** *p99*
Dixon, Ellen 76; Vermont, 1876 ***5900.10*** *p411*
Dixon, Frans; Virginia, 1690 ***6212.30*** *p58*
Dixon, George; New York, 1794 ***8197.10*** *p5*
Dixon, Grace *SEE* Dixon, Ambrose
Dixon, Henderson 37; Ontario, 1871 ***1823.22*** *p43*
Dixon, Horatio; New York, 1840 ***8197.10*** *p385*
Dixon, James 25; America, 1774 ***1220.25*** *p35*
Dixon, James 33; Ontario, 1871 ***1823.28*** *p23*
Dixon, John; New York, 1823 ***8197.10*** *p224*
Dixon, John 38; Vermont, 1898 ***5900.10*** *p191*
Dixon, John 44; Ontario, 1871 ***1823.22*** *p43*
Dixon, John A. 79; Vermont, 1898 ***5900.10*** *p191*
Dixon, Jonas; Virginia, 1699 ***1224.1*** *p18*
Dixon, Joshua; New York, 1831 ***8197.10*** *p225*
Dixon, Julia A. McLaine; Vermont, 1853-1918 ***5900.10*** *p532*
Dixon, L. 18; Ontario, 1861 ***2896.26*** *p14*
Dixon, Margaret 80; Vermont, n.d. ***5900.10*** *p191*
Dixon, Margaret 85; Vermont, n.d. ***5900.10*** *p191*
Dixon, Margaret Clines 79; Vermont, 1901 ***5900.10*** *p98*
Dixon, Mary *SEE* Dixon, Ambrose
Dixon, Mary 77; Ontario, 1871 ***1823.15*** *p63*
Dixon, Michael; Vermont, 1855-1926 ***5900.10*** *p532*
Dixon, Michael 30; Vermont, 1872 ***5900.10*** *p96*
Dixon, Michael 72; Vermont, 1886 ***5900.10*** *p96*
Dixon, Miles; Virginia, 1660 ***1224.1*** *p18*
Dixon, Phillip 15; Vermont, 1863 ***5900.10*** *p96*
Dixon, Richard; North America, 1711 ***1224.2*** *p33*
Dixon, Richard 24; Maryland, 1774 ***1220.25*** *p41*
Dixon, Richard 38; Vermont, n.d. ***5900.10*** *p191*
Dixon, Roger; Virginia, 1671-1672 ***6212.30*** *p45*
Dixon, Sarah *SEE* Dixon, Ambrose
Dixon, Thomas *SEE* Dixon, Ambrose
Dixon, Thomas; Georgia, n.d. ***1224.2*** *p34*
Dixon, Thomas 32; Vermont, 1877 ***5900.10*** *p96*
Dixon, Thomas 45; Ontario, 1871 ***1823.15*** *p63*
Dixon, Thomas 48; Ontario, 1871 ***1823.22*** *p43*
Dixon, Thomas 56; Ontario, 1871 ***1823.15*** *p63*
Dixon, William 34; Ontario, 1871 ***1823.15*** *p63*
Dixon, William 43; Vermont, 1879 ***5900.10*** *p98*
Dixon, William 49; Vermont, 1904 ***5900.10*** *p96*
Dixon, William 52; Ontario, 1871 ***1823.22*** *p43*
Dixson, Augustus 28; Ontario, 1871 ***1823.28*** *p23*
Dixson, James 54; Ontario, 1871 ***1823.28*** *p23*
Dixson, Jane *SEE* Dixson, John
Dixson, John; Maryland, 1665 ***2524.55*** *p68*
Wife: Jane
Dizaloff, J. 21; Alaska, 1916 ***9196.1*** *p42*
Dizaloff, J. 21; Whitehorse, Yukon, 1916 ***9196.1*** *p42*
Dlugobarski, Frank; Maryland, 1910 ***3259.35*** *p12*
Doak, Joseph 50; Ontario, 1871 ***1823.22*** *p43*
Doaks, Anne E. 37; Ontario, 1871 ***1823.15*** *p63*
Doaks, David 40; Ontario, 1871 ***1823.15*** *p63*
Doane, William; Maryland, 1680 ***2524.55*** *p68*
Dobberhow, William 23; Maryland, 1775 ***1220.25*** *p114*
Dobbie, George 68; Ontario, 1871 ***1823.15*** *p63*
Dobbin, John 33; Ontario, 1871 ***1823.28*** *p23*
Dobbins, Ellen; Maryland, 1666 ***2524.55*** *p68*
Dobbins, Ellen; Maryland, 1666 ***2524.55*** *p169*
Dobbins, Ellinor; Maryland, 1651 ***2524.55*** *p169*
Dobbins, James; New York, 1837 ***8197.10*** *p374*
Dobbins, Mary; Virginia, 1677 ***6212.30*** *p54*
Dobbins, Nicholas; New York, 1840 ***8197.10*** *p386*
Dobbis, Edward 21; Maryland, 1775 ***1220.25*** *p112*
Dobbis, Mary 29; Maryland, 1775 ***1220.25*** *p112*
Dobbs, Mrs.; Quebec, 1858 ***9196.15*** *p43*
Dobbs, Ambrose; New York, 1834 ***8197.10*** *p359*
Dobbs, Arthur; North Carolina, 1766 ***1224.2*** *p34*
Dobbs, Gerard; Maryland, 1659 ***2524.55*** *p68*
Dobbs, Samuel 21; Maryland, 1774 ***1220.25*** *p69*
Dobbyn, Richard; Savannah, Georgia, 1770 ***1224.2*** *p34*
Dobele, Mr.; Quebec, 1857 ***9196.15*** *p18*
Dobelski, William; Maryland, 1910 ***3259.35*** *p12*
Dobie, George C. 37; Ontario, 1871 ***1823.15*** *p63*
Dobie, John 53; Ontario, 1871 ***1823.15*** *p63*
Dobie, Joseph 54; Ontario, 1871 ***1823.15*** *p63*
Dobie, William; New York, 1824 ***8197.10*** *p224*
Dobie, William 32; Ontario, 1871 ***1823.28*** *p23*
Dobie, William 43; Ontario, 1871 ***1823.15*** *p63*
Dobiecz, Joseph; Maryland, 1910 ***3259.35*** *p12*
Dobmajcki, Nicolaus; Maryland, 1910 ***3259.35*** *p12*
Dobridge, Robert; New Jersey, 1846 ***1224.3*** *p22*
Dobring, Martin; Ontario, 1871 ***1823.28*** *p23*
Dobring, Martin 16; Ontario, 1871 ***1823.28*** *p23*
Dobrochowsky, Tomas; Maryland, 1910 ***3259.35*** *p12*
Dobrowski, Yan; Maryland, 1910 ***3259.35*** *p12*
Dobrsykowski, John; Maryland, 1910 ***3259.35*** *p12*
Dobrzykaiski, Martin A.; Maryland, 1910 ***3259.35*** *p12*
Dobrzykauski, Walenty; Maryland, 1910 ***3259.35*** *p12*
Dobson, Charles 34; Ontario, 1871 ***1823.15*** *p63*
Dobson, David 40; Ontario, 1871 ***1823.15*** *p63*
Dobson, George; Ohio, 1889 ***1640.13*** *p30*
Dobson, George 37; Ontario, 1871 ***1823.15*** *p63*

Dobson, Henry; New York, 1837 ***8197.10*** *p375*
Dobson, James 46; Ontario, 1871 ***1823.28*** *p23*
Dobson, James 62; Ontario, 1871 ***1823.22*** *p43*
Dobson, Lawrence 47; Ontario, 1871 ***1823.15*** *p63*
Dobson, Lucy *SEE* Dobson, Samuel
Dobson, Lucy; Maryland, 1668 ***2524.55*** *p68*
Dobson, Richard 72; Fort Cumberland, Nova Scotia, 1774 ***1220.25*** *p17*
Dobson, Samuel; Maryland, 1661 ***2524.55*** *p68*
Relative: Lucy
Dobson, Samuel; New England, 1690 ***1224.1*** *p18*
Dobson, Sarah 17; Baltimore, 1775 ***1220.25*** *p119*
Dobson, Tho.; Maryland, 1681 ***2524.55*** *p68*
Dobson, W.; Quebec, 1856 ***9196.15*** *p10*
Dobson, William 72; Ontario, 1871 ***1823.22*** *p43*
Dobson, William 72; Ontario, 1871 ***1823.28*** *p23*
Dobson, William A. 40; Ontario, 1871 ***1823.15*** *p63*
Dobson, William B.; New York, 1807 ***8197.10*** *p37*
Dobzyn, Frances; Maryland, 1910 ***3259.35*** *p12*
Docherty, Sarah Jane 34; Ontario, 1871 ***1823.28*** *p23*
Dockenbach, Anna Eva; Port uncertain, 1764 ***2856.30*** *p84*
Docker, Elizabeth Smith Shakespear; Missouri, 1855 ***1224.3*** *p22*
Docker, Timothy Strickland; New Orleans, 1839 ***1224.3*** *p22*
Docker, William; Missouri, 1857 ***1224.3*** *p22*
Dockerly, Nathaniel; Virginia, 1679 ***6212.30*** *p54*
Dockery, Thomas; Maryland, 1675 ***2524.55*** *p68*
Dockly, Ralph; Virginia, 1665-1666 ***6212.30*** *p21*
Dockly, Thomas; Virginia, 1668-1669 ***6212.30*** *p41*
Dockry, Bridget 69; Vermont, 1877 ***5900.10*** *p478*
Docksteader, Christina 67; Ontario, 1871 ***1823.15*** *p63*
Dockweiler, Peter; New York, 1838 ***8197.10*** *p108*
Dockwray, Tho; Virginia, 1665-1666 ***6212.30*** *p21*
Docto, Suca 26; Kansas, 1900-1910 ***9079.10*** *p28*
Dod, Anne; Maryland, 1681 ***2524.55*** *p69*
Dod, Elizabeth; Maryland, 1682 ***2524.55*** *p69*
Dod, Thomas 50; Ontario, 1871 ***1823.22*** *p43*
Doda, Julian; Maryland, 1910 ***3259.35*** *p12*
Dodd, Agnes Donald; Vermont, 1790-1862 ***5900.10*** *p375*
Dodd, Bridget 40; Ontario, 1871 ***1823.22*** *p43*
Dodd, Catherine 36; Ontario, 1861 ***2896.25*** *p60*
Dodd, Daniel 18; Georgia, 1774 ***1220.25*** *p47*
Dodd, Henry 40; Ontario, 1871 ***1823.15*** *p64*
Dodd, James; Boston, 1774 ***1224.2*** *p34*
Dodd, James; Vermont, 1788-1856 ***5900.10*** *p375*
Dodd, Jane 8; Ontario, 1861 ***2896.25*** *p60*
Dodd, John 27; Ontario, 1871 ***1823.15*** *p64*
Dodd, John B. 31; New York, 1818-1834 ***8197.10*** *p307*
Dodd, Joshua 11; Ontario, 1861 ***2896.25*** *p60*
Dodd, Thomas 31; Ontario, 1871 ***1823.28*** *p23*
Dodd, Thomas 52; Ontario, 1871 ***1823.15*** *p64*
Dodd, Thomas Anderson; Puerto Rico, 1897 ***1640.13*** *p30*
Dodd, William 17; Philadelphia, 1774 ***1220.25*** *p81*
Dodd, William 44; Ontario, 1871 ***1823.15*** *p64*
Dodd, William, Jr.; New York, 1838 ***8197.10*** *p377*
Dodds, Agnes B.; Vermont, 1843-1900 ***5900.10*** *p374*
Dodds, Alexander 42; Ontario, 1871 ***1823.15*** *p64*
Dodds, Andrew 43; Ontario, 1871 ***1823.15*** *p64*
Dodds, Andrew 50; Ontario, 1871 ***1823.15*** *p64*
Dodds, Charles 38; Ontario, 1871 ***1823.15*** *p64*
Dodds, David 62; Vermont, 1890 ***5900.10*** *p375*
Dodds, Elein 37; Ontario, 1871 ***1823.15*** *p64*
Dodds, Hulda A. Hazen; Vermont, 1823-1879 ***5900.10*** *p375*
Dodds, James 38; Ontario, 1871 ***1823.15*** *p64*
Dodds, James 40; Ontario, 1871 ***1823.15*** *p64*
Dodds, James 52; Ontario, 1871 ***1823.15*** *p64*
Dodds, James 56; Vermont, 1876 ***5900.10*** *p375*
Dodds, James Addison; Vermont, 1846-1912 ***5900.10*** *p375*
Dodds, James Bird 22; Vermont, 1870 ***5900.10*** *p374*
Dodds, Jennie Kingsley; Vermont, 1859-1941 ***5900.10*** *p375*
Dodds, John; Vermont, 1818-1893 ***5900.10*** *p375*
Dodds, John 25; Ontario, 1871 ***1823.15*** *p64*
Dodds, John 68; Vermont, 1832 ***5900.10*** *p375*
Dodds, Mary Harrington 56; Vermont, 1883 ***5900.10*** *p374*
Dodds, Matthew W.; Vermont, 1854-1940 ***5900.10*** *p375*
Dodds, Samuel; New York, 1836 ***8197.10*** *p78*
Dodds, Sarah Hutchins; Vermont, 1857-1937 ***5900.10*** *p375*
Dodds, Sarah Jane 39; Vermont, 1881 ***5900.10*** *p375*
Dodds, Thomas 45; Ontario, 1871 ***1823.15*** *p64*
Dodds, William 40; Ontario, 1871 ***1823.15*** *p64*
Dodey, Augustine; New York, 1821 ***8197.10*** *p223*
Dodge, Nicholas 41; Ontario, 1871 ***1823.22*** *p43*
Dodk, Rosanah 65; Ontario, 1871 ***1823.15*** *p64*
Dods, John; Trinidad, 1865 ***1640.13*** *p30*
Dods, Robert Young; Puerto Rico, 1869 ***1640.13*** *p30*
Dods, William Anderson; Puerto Rico, 1869 ***1640.13*** *p30*
Dodson, Henry 23; America, 1774 ***1220.25*** *p36*
Dodsworth, Anthy 61; Ontario, 1871 ***1823.15*** *p64*
Dodsworth, James 25; Maryland, 1775 ***1220.25*** *p120*
Dodsworth, Sarah Mary; Ohio, 1854 ***1224.3*** *p22*
Dodsworth, Timothy; New York, 1838 ***8197.10*** *p108*
Dodsworth, Walter 35; Ontario, 1871 ***1823.15*** *p64*
Doe, Elizabeth; Maryland, 1681 ***2524.55*** *p69*
Doe, Roger; Virginia, 1688 ***6212.30*** *p58*
Doeff, M. 27; Alaska, 1916 ***9196.1*** *p44*
Doeff, M. 27; Whitehorse, Yukon, 1916 ***9196.1*** *p44*
Doeherty, Tamalson 41; Ontario, 1871 ***1823.15*** *p64*
Doering, Henrygtia; Ontario, 1871 ***1823.28*** *p24*
Does, Sylvester; Pennsylvania, 1825 ***6058.10*** *p8*
Doess, Bernard; America, 1780 ***2856.30*** *p84*
Doess, Bernard; Port uncertain, 1763 ***2856.30*** *p84*
Dogger, Elizabeth; Maryland, 1663 ***2524.55*** *p66*
Dogger, Michael; Maryland, 1663 ***2524.55*** *p66*
Dogharty, John 21; Maryland, 1774 ***1220.25*** *p40*
Dogherty, John 48; Ontario, 1871 ***1823.22*** *p44*
Dogue, John; Maryland, 1682 ***2524.55*** *p69*
Dohana, Darby; Pennsylvania, 1786 ***4629.10*** *p52*
Doharty, David; New York, 1839 ***8197.10*** *p129*
Doharty, Ellen 42; Vermont, 1863 ***5900.10*** *p611*
Doheny, Edward; Vermont, 1873-1916 ***5900.10*** *p359*
Doheny, Edward 35; Vermont, 1866 ***5900.10*** *p146*
Doheny, James; Vermont, 1828-1917 ***5900.10*** *p359*
Doheny, Katherine C.; Vermont, 1876-1953 ***5900.10*** *p359*
Doheny, Margaret A.; Vermont, 1878-1941 ***5900.10*** *p359*
Doheny, Mary O'Connor; Vermont, 1849-1912 ***5900.10*** *p359*
Doheny, Michael; Vermont, 1879-1885 ***5900.10*** *p359*
Doherty, Mr.; Quebec, 1857 ***9196.15*** *p17*
Doherty, Bridget; Vermont, 1811-1903 ***5900.10*** *p371*
Doherty, Bridget; Vermont, 1841-1912 ***5900.10*** *p330*
Doherty, Catherine; Vermont, 1828-1902 ***5900.10*** *p129*
Doherty, Catherine 69; Ontario, 1871 ***1823.15*** *p64*
Doherty, Clara Belle; Vermont, 1890 ***5900.10*** *p413*
Doherty, Constantine; New York, 1766 ***1224.2*** *p34*
Doherty, D. J.; Vermont, 1849-1884 ***5900.10*** *p413*
Doherty, Elizabeth; Vermont, 1840-1893 ***5900.10*** *p130*
Doherty, Elizabeth Mary Cavin 77; Vermont, 1891 ***5900.10*** *p413*
Doherty, Ellen; Vermont, 1832-1913 ***5900.10*** *p340*
Doherty, Francis; New York, 1837 ***8197.10*** *p86*
Doherty, Hannah J.; Vermont, 1859-1943 ***5900.10*** *p602*
Doherty, Hugh; New York, 1837 ***8197.10*** *p87*
Doherty, J. 53; Alaska, 1918 ***9196.1*** *p55*
Doherty, J. 53; Yukon, 1918 ***9196.1*** *p55*
Doherty, James; New York, 1834 ***8197.10*** *p373*
Doherty, James 46; Ontario, 1871 ***1823.22*** *p44*
Doherty, John; New York, 1829-1840 ***8197.10*** *p158*
Doherty, John; New York, 1837 ***8197.10*** *p82*
Doherty, John 27; Ontario, 1871 ***1823.28*** *p24*
Doherty, John 28; Ontario, 1871 ***1823.28*** *p24*
Doherty, John 40; Ontario, 1871 ***1823.15*** *p64*
Doherty, Johnny 8 months; Vermont, n.d. ***5900.10*** *p413*
Doherty, Julia B. O'Clair; Vermont, 1856-1920 ***5900.10*** *p552*
Doherty, Mary 59; Vermont, 1886 ***5900.10*** *p370*
Doherty, Mary Agnes; Vermont, 1878 ***5900.10*** *p413*
Doherty, Michael; Vermont, 1837-1906 ***5900.10*** *p130*
Doherty, Michael 90; Vermont, 1880 ***5900.10*** *p413*
Doherty, Patrick; New York, 1840 ***8197.10*** *p156*
Doherty, William 49; Ontario, 1871 ***1823.28*** *p24*
Doheyzoski, Wladyslaw; Maryland, 1910 ***3259.35*** *p12*
Dohm, Lubbe; New York, 1837 ***8197.10*** *p86*
Dohr, Hans Georg; Port uncertain, 1747 ***2856.30*** *p84*
With wife & 2 children
Dohrmann, Neclaus; New York, 1840 ***8197.10*** *p226*
Dohrmann, Otto; New York, 1839 ***8197.10*** *p226*
Doidge, George 36; Ontario, 1871 ***1823.22*** *p44*
Doidge, Thomas 39; Ontario, 1871 ***1823.22*** *p44*
Doidge, Thomas 75; Ontario, 1871 ***1823.22*** *p44*
Doig, Alexander; Alabama, 1820-1845 ***1640.10*** *p41*
Doig, Alexander; New York, 1807 ***8197.10*** *p37*
Doig, Paul; Jamaica, 1847 ***1640.13*** *p30*
Doig, Paul 33; Ontario, 1871 ***1823.15*** *p64*
Doig, Robert 63; Ontario, 1871 ***1823.15*** *p64*
Doig, William; Savannah, Georgia, 1807 ***1640.10*** *p41*
Doil, John 55; Ontario, 1871 ***1823.28*** *p24*
Doinnen, John 40; Ontario, 1871 ***1823.22*** *p44*
Dokendorf, Johann Jakob; Port uncertain, 1754 ***2856.30*** *p84*
Dokes, Henry 46; Ontario, 1871 ***1823.15*** *p64*
Dokes, Mary 70; Ontario, 1871 ***1823.15*** *p64*
Dokes, William 48; Ontario, 1871 ***1823.15*** *p64*
Dol, Michael; Port uncertain, 1786 ***2856.30*** *p84*
Dolan, Amasa H.; Vermont, 1849-1920 ***5900.10*** *p287*
Dolan, Ann; Vermont, 1833-1907 ***5900.10*** *p132*
Dolan, Ann 35; Vermont, 1851 ***5900.10*** *p191*
Dolan, Anna; Vermont, 1862-1944 ***5900.10*** *p394*
Dolan, Bedsey K. 65; Vermont, 1867 ***5900.10*** *p371*
Dolan, Bernard; Vermont, 1827-1893 ***5900.10*** *p80*
Dolan, Bridget; Vermont, 1852 ***5900.10*** *p373*
Dolan, Bridget 66; Vermont, 1899 ***5900.10*** *p600*
Dolan, Bryan 17; New York, New York, 1848 ***1825.45*** *p32*
Dolan, Catherine; Vermont, 1862-1936 ***5900.10*** *p80*
Dolan, Catherine 35; Vermont, 1861 ***5900.10*** *p373*
Dolan, Catherine Cragin 80; Vermont, 1938 ***5900.10*** *p271*
Dolan, Charles L.; Vermont, 1847-1947 ***5900.10*** *p160*
Dolan, Elizabeth; Vermont, 1864-1865 ***5900.10*** *p160*
Dolan, Elizabeth Bellew 73; Vermont, 1907 ***5900.10*** *p271*
Dolan, Elizabeth Toole; Vermont, 1827-1905 ***5900.10*** *p80*
Dolan, George T.; Vermont, n.d. ***5900.10*** *p271*
Dolan, Honora 6; Ontario, 1871 ***1823.28*** *p24*
Dolan, James; New York, 1837 ***8197.10*** *p83*
Dolan, James; New York, 1837 ***8197.10*** *p86*
Dolan, James; New York, 1840 ***8197.10*** *p157*
Dolan, James; Vermont, 1826-1896 ***5900.10*** *p160*
Dolan, James; Vermont, 1827-1888 ***5900.10*** *p354*
Dolan, Jane; Vermont, 1849-1926 ***5900.10*** *p258*
Dolan, Jennie; Vermont, 1866-1873 ***5900.10*** *p160*
Dolan, Jennie A. Tabor; Vermont, 1858-1906 ***5900.10*** *p243*
Dolan, John; New York, 1840 ***8197.10*** *p156*
Dolan, John; Vermont, 1846-1916 ***5900.10*** *p243*
Dolan, John 15; New York, New York, 1848 ***1825.45*** *p32*
Dolan, John 56; Vermont, 1917 ***5900.10*** *p271*
Dolan, John 59; Vermont, 1866 ***5900.10*** *p209*
Dolan, John 94; Vermont, 1893 ***5900.10*** *p468*
Dolan, Joseph; Vermont, 1854-1872 ***5900.10*** *p80*
Dolan, Kate; Vermont, 1839-1918 ***5900.10*** *p98*
Dolan, Katherine L.; Vermont, 1856-1956 ***5900.10*** *p160*
Dolan, Katherine O'Brien; Vermont, 1855-1919 ***5900.10*** *p250*
Dolan, Margaret Conwell; Vermont, 1830-1908 ***5900.10*** *p354*
Dolan, Mary; Vermont, 1822-1915 ***5900.10*** *p511*
Dolan, Mary; Vermont, 1837-1906 ***5900.10*** *p93*
Dolan, Mary; Vermont, 1856-1872 ***5900.10*** *p80*
Dolan, Mary; Vermont, 1862-1944 ***5900.10*** *p357*
Dolan, Mary; Vermont, 1863-1963 ***5900.10*** *p160*
Dolan, Mary 31; Vermont, 1863 ***5900.10*** *p371*
Dolan, Mary 70; Vermont, 1901 ***5900.10*** *p124*
Dolan, Mary F. 26; Vermont, 1889 ***5900.10*** *p271*
Dolan, Mary Murray; Vermont, 1829-1907 ***5900.10*** *p160*
Dolan, Mary Smullin; Vermont, 1825-1916 ***5900.10*** *p156*
Dolan, Maurice; New York, 1840 ***8197.10*** *p158*
Dolan, Michael; New York, 1838 ***8197.10*** *p318*
Dolan, Michael 60; Ontario, 1871 ***1823.28*** *p24*
Dolan, Owen; Vermont, 1831-1910 ***5900.10*** *p156*
Dolan, Patrick; New York, 1834 ***8197.10*** *p72*
Dolan, Patrick 35; Ontario, 1871 ***1823.28*** *p24*
Dolan, Patrick 81; Vermont, 1886 ***5900.10*** *p138*
Dolan, Peter; Vermont, 1814-1890 ***5900.10*** *p98*
Dolan, Peter; Vermont, 1823-1891 ***5900.10*** *p93*
Dolan, Philip F.; Vermont, 1862-1890 ***5900.10*** *p160*
Dolan, Rose E.; Vermont, 1872-1939 ***5900.10*** *p355*
Dolan, Thomas 15; New York, New York, 1848 ***1825.45*** *p32*
Dolan, Thomas 56; Vermont, 1883 ***5900.10*** *p271*
Dolan, William; Pennsylvania, 1866 ***6058.10*** *p56*
Dolan, William; Vermont, 1831-1903 ***5900.10*** *p80*
Dolbeare, Grizzle; Boston, 1828 ***1224.3*** *p22*
Dolbery, Andrew; New England, 1694 ***1224.1*** *p18*
Dolby, Samuel; Pennsylvania, 1777 ***4629.10*** *p17*
Dolch, Ursula; Port uncertain, 1790 ***2856.30*** *p84*
Dolding, Richard; Boston, 1712 ***1224.2*** *p34*
Dolehay, John 60; Ontario, 1871 ***1823.15*** *p64*
Dolen, John 62; Ontario, 1871 ***1823.22*** *p44*
Dolfin, Nathaniel; Maryland, 1662 ***2524.55*** *p69*
Dolfiski, Michael; Maryland, 1910 ***3259.35*** *p12*
Dolin, Manly 21; Ontario, 1861 ***2896.25*** *p71*
Dolinas, Louis 27; Washington, 1914 ***9196.1*** *p64*
Doll, Miss; America, 1739 ***2856.30*** *p37*
Doll, Anton; Port uncertain, 1724 ***2856.30*** *p84*
With wife & 5 children
Doll, Bastian; America, 1739 ***2856.30*** *p84*
Doll, Christian; America, 1737 ***2856.30*** *p84*
Doll, Christof; America, 1739 ***2856.30*** *p84*
With son
Doll, Hans Michael; America, 1742 ***2856.30*** *p84*
Doll, Johann Nickel; America, 1739 ***2856.30*** *p84*
Doll, Konrad; America, 1753 ***2856.30*** *p84*
Doll, Maria Catharina; America, 1741 ***2856.30*** *p84*
Doll, Michael; America, 1769 ***2856.30*** *p84*
Doll, Michael; Port uncertain, 1783 ***2856.30*** *p84*
With wife son & 2 daughters
Doll, Philipp; Port uncertain, 1725 ***2856.30*** *p84*
Doll, Philipp; Port uncertain, 1796 ***2856.30*** *p84*

Doll, Stoffel; America, 1739 ***2856.30*** *p84*
Doll, Stoffel; America, 1739 ***2856.30*** *p85*
With wife
Dollar, Robert 45; Ontario, 1871 ***1823.28*** *p24*
Doller, Wm; Virginia, 1698 ***6212.30*** *p60*
Dollet, Nicholas; New York, 1797 ***8197.10*** *p8*
Dolling, . . .; America, 1785 ***2856.30*** *p85*
Dolling, John; Virginia, 1666-1667 ***6212.30*** *p33*
Dollmeyer, Henry; New York, New York, 1853 ***6058.10*** *p39*
Dollmyer, Henry; New York, New York, 1853 ***6058.10*** *p39*
Dolly, Peter 65; Ontario, 1871 ***1823.22*** *p44*
Dolmage, James 50; Ontario, 1871 ***1823.15*** *p64*
Dolman, Samuel; Detroit, 1898 ***3437.14*** *p178*
Dolon, Catherine 20; Ontario, 1871 ***1823.15*** *p64*
Dolovich, R. 35; Alaska, 1917 ***9196.1*** *p7*
Dolovich, R. 35; Yukon, 1917 ***9196.1*** *p7*
Dolphin, John; Georgia, 1745 ***1224.2*** *p34*
Dolphine, Nathaniel; Maryland, 1662 ***2524.55*** *p69*
Dolpir, Peter 54; Ontario, 1871 ***1823.15*** *p64*
Dolrowalski, Anton; Maryland, 1910 ***3259.35*** *p12*
Dolrzykowski, James; Maryland, 1910 ***3259.35*** *p12*
Dolson, Martha; Maryland, 1651 ***2524.55*** *p90*
Dolten, James 60; Ontario, 1861 ***2896.27*** *p5*
Dolton, John 60; Vermont, 1850 ***5900.10*** *p279*
Dolton, Patrick; New York, 1838 ***8197.10*** *p226*
Doltzer, Michael; Port uncertain, 1752 ***2856.30*** *p90*
Doly, John; New York, 1834 ***8197.10*** *p72*
Dombkowsky, Antony; Maryland, 1910 ***3259.35*** *p12*
Dombrowski, Joseph; Maryland, 1910 ***3259.35*** *p12*
Dombrowsky, Antony; Maryland, 1910 ***3259.35*** *p12*
Dombrusky, Addam 49; Ontario, 1871 ***1823.28*** *p24*
Dombrusky, Christie 47; Ontario, 1871 ***1823.28*** *p24*
Domec, John; New York, 1815 ***8197.10*** *p55*
Domelaw, Richard; Virginia, 1624 ***1224.1*** *p18*
Domenes, A. 26; Alaska, 1908 ***9196.1*** *p36*
Domenes, A. 26; Alaska, 1908 ***9196.1*** *p37*
Domey, John; Vermont, 1823-1873 ***5900.10*** *p482*
Dominato, F. 25; Seattle, 1912 ***9196.1*** *p20*
Dominguez, Manuel; New York, 1824 ***8197.10*** *p224*
Dominiak, Frank; Maryland, 1910 ***3259.35*** *p12*
Dominica, Peter 17; Philadelphia, 1774 ***1220.25*** *p35*
Dominick, Frederick; Pennsylvania, 1779 ***4629.10*** *p36*
Dominik, Sabolo; Maryland, 1910 ***3259.35*** *p12*
Dominikus, Anna Maria; Port uncertain, 1752 ***2856.30*** *p85*
Dommeneck, Andreas; America, 1752 ***2856.30*** *p85*
Dommeneckh, Johann; America, 1752 ***2856.30*** *p85*
With wife & 2 children
Dommi, Hans; America, 1752 ***2856.30*** *p85*
Domporowski, Ignatius; Maryland, 1910 ***3259.35*** *p12*
Don, John; Augusta, Georgia, 1810 ***1640.10*** *p41*
Donage, John; Virginia, 1666 ***6212.30*** *p29*
Donaghue, Mary 65; Vermont, 1892 ***5900.10*** *p514*
Donaghy, Patrick; Pennsylvania, 1867 ***6058.10*** *p59*
Donahan, John 38; Ontario, 1871 ***1823.22*** *p44*
Donahoe, Cornelius 26; Vermont, 1883 ***5900.10*** *p477*
Donahoe, Dennis 57; Vermont, 1865 ***5900.10*** *p324*
Donahoe, Joseph 28; Vermont, 1867 ***5900.10*** *p324*
Donahoe, Margaret; Vermont, n.d. ***5900.10*** *p129*
Donahoe, Mary 30; Vermont, 1800-1899 ***5900.10*** *p151*
Donahoe, Michael; New York, 1821 ***8197.10*** *p223*
Donahoe, Michael; New York, 1828 ***8197.10*** *p225*
Donahoe, Patrick; New York, 1821 ***8197.10*** *p223*
Donahoe, Patrick; New York, 1837 ***8197.10*** *p83*
Donahoe, Rodger 53; Vermont, 1857 ***5900.10*** *p362*
Donahoe, Rodger 53; Vermont, 1857 ***5900.10*** *p366*
Donahoe, Thomas 60; Ontario, 1871 ***1823.28*** *p24*
Donahowe, Teag...; Maryland, 1661 ***2524.55*** *p69*
Donahue, Abbie D. Carey; Vermont, 1866-1956 ***5900.10*** *p225*
Donahue, Ann; Vermont, 1835-1926 ***5900.10*** *p355*
Donahue, Ann; Vermont, 1839-1921 ***5900.10*** *p188*
Donahue, Ann Mattamore; Vermont, 1827-1880 ***5900.10*** *p326*
Donahue, Ann Mee; Vermont, 1851-1930 ***5900.10*** *p334*
Donahue, Anthony; Vermont, 1834-1916 ***5900.10*** *p277*
Donahue, Bridget 68; Vermont, 1912 ***5900.10*** *p432*
Donahue, Bridget Caffrey; Vermont, 1845-1905 ***5900.10*** *p370*
Donahue, Bridget Mooney 36; Vermont, 1883 ***5900.10*** *p396*
Donahue, Catherine 72; Vermont, 1890 ***5900.10*** *p343*
Donahue, Dennis; Vermont, 1811-1875 ***5900.10*** *p356*
Donahue, Dennis; Vermont, 1847-1920 ***5900.10*** *p356*
Donahue, Elizabeth 51; Vermont, 1897 ***5900.10*** *p117*
Donahue, Ellen; Vermont, 1810-1898 ***5900.10*** *p103*
Donahue, Ellen; Vermont, 1815-1875 ***5900.10*** *p304*
Donahue, Ellen; Vermont, 1853-1916 ***5900.10*** *p130*
Donahue, Ellen Lee Sheridan; Vermont, 1839-1918 ***5900.10*** *p277*
Donahue, Ellen M.; Vermont, 1845-1926 ***5900.10*** *p356*
Donahue, Ellen McCarty; Vermont, 1845-1914 ***5900.10*** *p225*
Donahue, Francis 79; Vermont, 1884 ***5900.10*** *p343*
Donahue, Hugh 57; Vermont, 1892 ***5900.10*** *p290*
Donahue, James; Vermont, 1848-1918 ***5900.10*** *p277*
Donahue, James; Vermont, 1856-1913 ***5900.10*** *p326*
Donahue, James 28; Vermont, 1885 ***5900.10*** *p343*
Donahue, James A.; Vermont, 1853-1929 ***5900.10*** *p326*
Donahue, Jerry; Vermont, 1849-1864 ***5900.10*** *p370*
Donahue, Johanna; Vermont, 1806-1870 ***5900.10*** *p139*
Donahue, Johanna; Vermont, 1859-1877 ***5900.10*** *p370*
Donahue, Johanna Lynch; Vermont, 1808-1903 ***5900.10*** *p356*
Donahue, Johannah 65; Vermont, 1914 ***5900.10*** *p426*
Donahue, John; Vermont, 1809-1893 ***5900.10*** *p370*
Donahue, John; Vermont, 1839-1915 ***5900.10*** *p225*
Donahue, John; Vermont, 1842-1864 ***5900.10*** *p356*
Donahue, John; Vermont, 1853-1903 ***5900.10*** *p334*
Donahue, John 62; Vermont, 1869 ***5900.10*** *p365*
Donahue, Josephine E.; Vermont, 1865-1949 ***5900.10*** *p326*
Donahue, Julia L.; Vermont, 1857-1947 ***5900.10*** *p355*
Donahue, Katharine; Vermont, 1855-1912 ***5900.10*** *p356*
Donahue, Margaret; Vermont, 1833-1913 ***5900.10*** *p311*
Donahue, Margaret; Vermont, 1845-1923 ***5900.10*** *p396*
Donahue, Margaret; Vermont, 1851-1914 ***5900.10*** *p583*
Donahue, Margaret 35; Vermont, 1876 ***5900.10*** *p106*
Donahue, Margaret 63; Vermont, 1879 ***5900.10*** *p337*
Donahue, Margaret Loveday; Vermont, 1840-1922 ***5900.10*** *p304*
Donahue, Margaret Shea; Vermont, n.d. ***5900.10*** *p370*
Donahue, Mary; Vermont, 1857-1938 ***5900.10*** *p356*
Donahue, Mary 24; Vermont, 1885 ***5900.10*** *p271*
Donahue, Mary 77; Vermont, 1884 ***5900.10*** *p345*
Donahue, Mary A. Neenan; Vermont, 1856-1925 ***5900.10*** *p326*
Donahue, Mary Ann; Vermont, 1845-1930 ***5900.10*** *p370*
Donahue, Mary Boyle 57; Vermont, 1861 ***5900.10*** *p179*
Donahue, Mary Doherty 59; Vermont, 1886 ***5900.10*** *p370*
Donahue, Mary E.; Vermont, 1857-1908 ***5900.10*** *p186*
Donahue, Mary Fitzpatrick; Vermont, 1857-1937 ***5900.10*** *p590*
Donahue, Mary J. 25; Vermont, 1879 ***5900.10*** *p337*
Donahue, Michael; New York, 1837 ***8197.10*** *p82*
Donahue, Michael; Vermont, 1833-1917 ***5900.10*** *p326*
Donahue, Michael 61; Vermont, 1865 ***5900.10*** *p179*
Donahue, Michael 71; Vermont, 1917 ***5900.10*** *p337*
Donahue, Owen; Vermont, 1838-1912 ***5900.10*** *p304*
Donahue, Patrick; Vermont, 1817-1907 ***5900.10*** *p311*
Donahue, Patrick 50; Ontario, 1871 ***1823.22*** *p44*
Donahue, Peter; Vermont, 1919 ***5900.10*** *p432*
Donahue, Robert 28; Ontario, 1871 ***1823.28*** *p24*
Donahue, Roger; Vermont, 1847-1906 ***5900.10*** *p370*
Donahue, Roger J.; Vermont, 1848-1909 ***5900.10*** *p590*
Donahue, Sophia; Vermont, 1856-1936 ***5900.10*** *p333*
Donahue, Susan Mulheron; Vermont, 1852-1915 ***5900.10*** *p186*
Donahue, Thomas 70; Vermont, 1875 ***5900.10*** *p337*
Donahue, Timothy 75; Vermont, 1896 ***5900.10*** *p370*
Donahue, William; Vermont, 1840-1924 ***5900.10*** *p396*
Donahuy, William 40; Ontario, 1871 ***1823.28*** *p24*
Donahy, Nora 40; Ontario, 1871 ***1823.22*** *p44*
Donaiski, Marton; Maryland, 1910 ***3259.35*** *p12*
Donal, George; Pennsylvania, 1777 ***4629.10*** *p16*
Donald, Agnes; Vermont, 1790-1862 ***5900.10*** *p375*
Donald, Alexander; Virginia, 1806 ***1640.13*** *p30*
Donald, Alexander 55; Ontario, 1871 ***1823.22*** *p44*
Donald, Alex'r 32; Ontario, 1861 ***2896.28*** *p33*
Donald, Anne; New Orleans, 1858 ***1640.10*** *p42*
Donald, David; Georgia, 1699 ***1640.13*** *p30*
Donald, David; Georgia, 1699 ***1640.13*** *p31*
Donald, James; Florida, 1776 ***1640.10*** *p42*
Donald, James 60; Ontario, 1871 ***1823.22*** *p44*
Donald, John; Jamaica, 1819 ***1640.13*** *p31*
Donald, Martha 28; Ontario, 1861 ***2896.28*** *p33*
Donald, Robert; Florida, 1776 ***1640.10*** *p42*
Donald, Robert; Petersburg, Virginia, 1806 ***1640.13*** *p31*
Donald, W.; Mississippi, 1813-1845 ***1640.10*** *p42*
Donald, William; New York, 1807 ***8197.10*** *p37*
Donalds, Curtis 60; Ontario, 1871 ***1823.22*** *p44*
Donaldson, Albert M.; Vermont, 1842-1939 ***5900.10*** *p517*
Donaldson, Alexander; Tobago, West Indies, 1852 ***1640.13*** *p31*
Donaldson, Alexander 43; Ontario, 1871 ***1823.15*** *p64*
Donaldson, Amanda; Vermont, 1852-1937 ***5900.10*** *p517*
Donaldson, Angeline; Vermont, 1845-1914 ***5900.10*** *p513*
Donaldson, Arthur; Pennsylvania, 1785 ***4629.10*** *p48*
Donaldson, Cornelia M. Hazen; Vermont, 1845-1932 ***5900.10*** *p517*
Donaldson, Emily; Vermont, 1845-1929 ***5900.10*** *p517*
Donaldson, George; Mobile, Alabama, 1767 ***1640.10*** *p42*
Donaldson, James; Jamaica, 1828 ***1640.13*** *p31*
Donaldson, James; New York, 1802 ***8197.10*** *p20*
Donaldson, James; New York, 1840 ***8197.10*** *p159*
Donaldson, Jane; Vermont, 1843-1921 ***5900.10*** *p518*
Donaldson, Jane 43; Ontario, 1871 ***1823.15*** *p64*
Donaldson, John; Pennsylvania, 1777 ***4629.10*** *p15*
Donaldson, Joseph; New York, 1834 ***8197.10*** *p73*
Donaldson, Joseph; Pennsylvania, 1777 ***4629.10*** *p22*
Donaldson, Joseph; Pennsylvania, 1779 ***4629.10*** *p41*
Donaldson, Lillie; Vermont, 1863-1930 ***5900.10*** *p517*
Donaldson, Mary; Vermont, 1850-1943 ***5900.10*** *p517*
Donaldson, Mary E. Town; Vermont, 1844-1906 ***5900.10*** *p374*
Donaldson, Mary P.; Vermont, 1844-1937 ***5900.10*** *p517*
Donaldson, Mary R.; Vermont, 1840-1917 ***5900.10*** *p518*
Donaldson, Nancy M. Boomhower; Vermont, 1848-1943 ***5900.10*** *p517*
Donaldson, Peter 33; Dominica, 1773 ***1220.25*** *p31*
Donaldson, Phebe Anna; Vermont, 1837-1906 ***5900.10*** *p517*
Donaldson, Robert; Georgia, 1769 ***1640.10*** *p42*
Donaldson, Robert; New York, 1807 ***8197.10*** *p221*
Donaldson, Robert; New York, 1807 ***8197.10*** *p326*
Donaldson, Robert; Ottawa, 1865 ***1640.13*** *p31*
Donaldson, Robert 28; Ontario, 1871 ***1823.22*** *p44*
Donaldson, Robert 60; Ontario, 1871 ***1823.15*** *p64*
Donaldson, Robert 63; Ontario, 1871 ***1823.15*** *p64*
Donaldson, Sabins W.; Vermont, 1845-1932 ***5900.10*** *p517*
Donaldson, Sylvester; Vermont, 1837-1911 ***5900.10*** *p517*
Donaldson, Thomas; New York, 1819 ***8197.10*** *p222*
Donaldson, William; New York, 1807 ***8197.10*** *p38*
Donaldson, William 56; Ontario, 1871 ***1823.22*** *p44*
Donaldson, William R.; Vermont, 1842-1917 ***5900.10*** *p374*
Donaldson, Wm 33; Ontario, 1871 ***1823.15*** *p64*
Donaldson, Wm 59; Ontario, 1871 ***1823.15*** *p64*
Donally, Francis; New York, 1837 ***8197.10*** *p86*
Donally, Robert 52; Ontario, 1871 ***1823.28*** *p24*
Donan, A.; Mississippi, 1849 ***1640.10*** *p42*
Donan, Martin 37; Ontario, 1871 ***1823.28*** *p24*
Donan, Martin 38; Ontario, 1871 ***1823.28*** *p24*
Donaugho, Elizabeth 22; Dominica, 1774 ***1220.25*** *p128*
Donaugho, John 34; Dominica, 1774 ***1220.25*** *p128*
Donavan, David 62; Ontario, 1871 ***1823.22*** *p44*
Donavan, Ellen; Maryland, 1682 ***2524.55*** *p69*
Donavan, John; Maryland, 1674 ***2524.55*** *p69*
Donavan, Mathew 74; Ontario, 1871 ***1823.22*** *p44*
Donavan, Thomas 28; Ontario, 1871 ***1823.22*** *p44*
Donazski, Sophie; Maryland, 1910 ***3259.35*** *p12*
Doncaster, Ann; Maryland, 1672 ***2524.55*** *p69*
Doncett, John; Nova Scotia, 1727 ***1224.2*** *p34*
Dondwill, John; Maryland, 1681 ***2524.55*** *p69*
Done, John; Maryland, 1681 ***2524.55*** *p69*
Donegan, Edward; Vermont, 1807-1882 ***5900.10*** *p350*
Donegan, Elizabeth; Vermont, n.d. ***5900.10*** *p62*
Donegan, Joseph 60; Ontario, 1871 ***1823.28*** *p24*
Donegan, Josie S.; Vermont, 1855-1924 ***5900.10*** *p350*
Donegan, Lizzie; Vermont, 1846-1931 ***5900.10*** *p350*
Donegan, Margaret Parker; Vermont, 1818-1890 ***5900.10*** *p350*
Donegan, Mary A.; Vermont, 1848-1920 ***5900.10*** *p563*
Donegan, Owen; Vermont, 1817-1882 ***5900.10*** *p350*
Donegan, Sarah Bowe; Vermont, 1812-1879 ***5900.10*** *p350*
Donegan, Thomas; New York, 1837 ***8197.10*** *p86*
Donehue, John; Indiana, 1873-1884 ***3437.14*** *p200*
Donehue, Peter 77; Ontario, 1871 ***1823.15*** *p65*
Donehue, Timothy 50; Ontario, 1871 ***1823.15*** *p65*
Donel, William 27; Ontario, 1871 ***1823.15*** *p65*
Donellan, Mr.; Quebec, 1857 ***9196.15*** *p17*
Donelly, Bridget Kannon; Vermont, 1895 ***5900.10*** *p536*
Donelly, Ellen 43; Vermont, 1899 ***5900.10*** *p536*
Donelly, Ellen Welch; Vermont, n.d. ***5900.10*** *p482*
Donelly, Fanny 53; Ontario, 1871 ***1823.28*** *p24*
Donelly, Julia Corkin; Vermont, 1826-1891 ***5900.10*** *p538*
Donelly, Katherine Meehan; Vermont, 1836-1914 ***5900.10*** *p357*
Donelly, Michael; Vermont, 1836-1917 ***5900.10*** *p357*
Donelly, Patrick; Vermont, 1817-1892 ***5900.10*** *p536*
Donelly, Philip 11; Ontario, 1861 ***2896.27*** *p69*
Donelly, Thomas; Vermont, 1836-1886 ***5900.10*** *p538*
Donelly, William 44; Ontario, 1871 ***1823.28*** *p24*
Donelly, William 62; Ontario, 1871 ***1823.28*** *p24*
Donelson, George; New York, 1838 ***8197.10*** *p109*
Doney, Joseph 44; Ontario, 1871 ***1823.28*** *p24*
Dongan, Thomas; New York, 1775-1781 ***4628.40*** *p69*
Donigan, Patrick 46; Ontario, 1871 ***1823.22*** *p44*
Donion, John 45; Ontario, 1871 ***1823.15*** *p65*
Donk, William 4; Ontario, 1871 ***1823.22*** *p44*
Donkester, William; Boston, 1730 ***1224.2*** *p34*
Donlan, Catherine Dermody; Vermont, 1847-1912 ***5900.10*** *p354*

Donlan, Edward 25 *SEE* Donlan, Patrick
Donlan, John; Vermont, 1839-1925 ***5900.10*** *p354*
Donlan, John 36 *SEE* Donlan, Patrick
Donlan, Margaret 14 *SEE* Donlan, Patrick
Donlan, Martin 32; New York, New York, 1847 ***1825.45*** *p14*
Donlan, Mary 67; Vermont, 1876 ***5900.10*** *p287*
Donlan, Mary 88; Vermont, 1907 ***5900.10*** *p343*
Donlan, Mary Ann Kane; Vermont, 1833-1906 ***5900.10*** *p180*
Donlan, Patrick; Vermont, 1829-1881 ***5900.10*** *p180*
Donlan, Patrick 27 *SEE* Donlan, Patrick
Donlan, Patrick 60; New York, New York, 1847 ***1825.45*** *p14*
Son: Edward 25
Son: John 36
Son: William 16
Daughter: Margaret 14
Son: Patrick 27
Donlan, William 16 *SEE* Donlan, Patrick
Donley, Elizabeth 50; Ontario, 1871 ***1823.15*** *p65*
Donley, Hannah 32; Vermont, 1880 ***5900.10*** *p237*
Donley, John 43; Ontario, 1871 ***1823.15*** *p65*
Donley, John 44; Ontario, 1871 ***1823.15*** *p65*
Donley, Mathew 67; Ontario, 1871 ***1823.15*** *p65*
Donley, Nancy 60; Vermont, 1845 ***5900.10*** *p235*
Donlin, Jane A.; Vermont, 1859 ***5900.10*** *p158*
Donlin, John; Vermont, 1818-1904 ***5900.10*** *p130*
Donlin, Katherine M. Minahan; Vermont, 1863-1907 ***5900.10*** *p130*
Donlin, Mary McSherry; Vermont, 1825-1907 ***5900.10*** *p130*
Donlin, Patrick J.; Vermont, 1857-1930 ***5900.10*** *p130*
Donlon, Anne 27 *SEE* Donlon, Patrick
Donlon, Bridget 17 *SEE* Donlon, Catherine
Donlon, Catherine 33 *SEE* Donlon, Catherine
Donlon, Catherine 55; New York, New York, 1848 ***1825.45*** *p32*
Son: John 26
Son: Pat 20
Son: Thomas 30
Daughter: Catherine 33
Daughter: Bridget 17
Donlon, John; New York, 1838 ***8197.10*** *p377*
Donlon, John 26 *SEE* Donlon, Catherine
Donlon, Martin F.; Vermont, 1848-1911 ***5900.10*** *p406*
Donlon, Mary J. Roystan; Vermont, 1852-1915 ***5900.10*** *p406*
Donlon, Mary O'Brien 67; Vermont, 1887 ***5900.10*** *p601*
Donlon, Pat 20 *SEE* Donlon, Catherine
Donlon, Patrick 28; New York, New York, 1847 ***1825.45*** *p14*
Wife: Anne 27
Donlon, Susan 1; Vermont, 1857 ***5900.10*** *p601*
Donlon, Thomas 30 *SEE* Donlon, Catherine
Donnaghan, William; Maryland, 1682 ***2524.55*** *p69*
Donnahey, Timothy; New York, 1834 ***8197.10*** *p372*
Donnal, James; Pennsylvania, 1777 ***4629.10*** *p8*
Donnally, Catharine 58; Vermont, 1885 ***5900.10*** *p537*
Donnally, John; Pennsylvania, 1777 ***4629.10*** *p11*
Donnally, Matthew; New York, 1837 ***8197.10*** *p86*
Donnally, Peter; Vermont, n.d. ***5900.10*** *p537*
Donnavan, Cornelius; Maryland, 1682 ***2524.55*** *p69*
Donnavan, Darby; Maryland, 1682 ***2524.55*** *p69*
Donnecker, Philipp; Port uncertain, 1783 ***2856.30*** *p85*
With 4 sons & 2 daughters
Donnell, Patrick; Canada, 1756-1760 ***4628.40*** *p45*
Donnellan, Bridget 17 *SEE* Donnellan, Catherine
Donnellan, Catherine 33 *SEE* Donnellan, Catherine
Donnellan, Catherine 55; New York, New York, 1848 ***1825.45*** *p32*
Son: John 26
Daughter: Catherine 33
Daughter: Bridget 17
Son: Pat 20
Son: Thomas 30
Donnellan, John 26 *SEE* Donnellan, Catherine
Donnellan, Martin 32; New York, New York, 1847 ***1825.45*** *p14*
Donnellan, Pat 20 *SEE* Donnellan, Catherine
Donnellan, Thomas 30 *SEE* Donnellan, Catherine
Donnellan, Thomas T.; New York, 1822 ***8197.10*** *p223*
Donnellon, Edward; New York, 1825-1831 ***8197.10*** *p307*
Donnellon, James; New York, 1839 ***8197.10*** *p129*
Donnelly, Ann 81; Vermont, 1922 ***5900.10*** *p445*
Donnelly, Anna Hogan; Vermont, 1850-1908 ***5900.10*** *p147*
Donnelly, Annie; Vermont, 1847-1899 ***5900.10*** *p346*
Donnelly, Anthony; Vermont, 1838-1911 ***5900.10*** *p452*
Donnelly, Anthony; Vermont, 1844-1944 ***5900.10*** *p162*
Donnelly, Bernard 62; Vermont, 1873 ***5900.10*** *p234*
Donnelly, Bridget A. Clark 38; Vermont, 1896 ***5900.10*** *p581*
Donnelly, Bridget Lynch; Vermont, 1855-1934 ***5900.10*** *p398*
Donnelly, Catherine 46; Vermont, 1858 ***5900.10*** *p74*
Donnelly, Catherine 63; Vermont, 1898 ***5900.10*** *p540*
Donnelly, Charles; New York, 1830 ***8197.10*** *p362*
Donnelly, Daniel F.; Vermont, 1854-1937 ***5900.10*** *p464*
Donnelly, Edward J.; Vermont, 1849-1927 ***5900.10*** *p353*
Donnelly, Eliza; Vermont, 1854-1947 ***5900.10*** *p114*
Donnelly, Elizabeth Kirbee 55; Vermont, 1904 ***5900.10*** *p163*
Donnelly, Ellen; Vermont, 1839-1927 ***5900.10*** *p312*
Donnelly, Ellen; Vermont, 1856-1899 ***5900.10*** *p536*
Donnelly, Ellen; Vermont, 1867-1935 ***5900.10*** *p452*
Donnelly, Ellen Kane; Vermont, 1848-1948 ***5900.10*** *p162*
Donnelly, Hugh; New York, 1837 ***8197.10*** *p86*
Donnelly, James; New York, 1837 ***8197.10*** *p86*
Donnelly, James; New York, 1840 ***8197.10*** *p157*
Donnelly, James P.; Vermont, 1858-1880 ***5900.10*** *p542*
Donnelly, John; New York, 1837 ***8197.10*** *p225*
Donnelly, John; New York, 1838 ***8197.10*** *p225*
Donnelly, John; Vermont, 1830-1901 ***5900.10*** *p355*
Donnelly, John; Vermont, 1843-1911 ***5900.10*** *p147*
Donnelly, John; Vermont, 1856-1925 ***5900.10*** *p96*
Donnelly, John 44; Vermont, 1851 ***5900.10*** *p258*
Donnelly, John 65; Ontario, 1871 ***1823.28*** *p24*
Donnelly, John H.; Vermont, 1855-1931 ***5900.10*** *p542*
Donnelly, K. M.; Vermont, 1866-1933 ***5900.10*** *p542*
Donnelly, Margaret; Vermont, 1872-1948 ***5900.10*** *p452*
Donnelly, Margaret McGrath; Vermont, 1835-1897 ***5900.10*** *p452*
Donnelly, Mary A. Mahar; Vermont, 1857-1933 ***5900.10*** *p464*
Donnelly, Mary A. McDonnell; Vermont, 1832-1905 ***5900.10*** *p542*
Donnelly, Mary A. Nash; Vermont, 1863-1927 ***5900.10*** *p353*
Donnelly, Mary Ann; Vermont, 1854-1894 ***5900.10*** *p300*
Donnelly, Mary Lynch; Vermont, 1860-1919 ***5900.10*** *p96*
Donnelly, Michael; New York, 1837 ***8197.10*** *p107*
Donnelly, Michael; Vermont, 1853-1916 ***5900.10*** *p398*
Donnelly, Patrick; New York, 1807 ***8197.10*** *p331*
Donnelly, Patrick; New York, 1820 ***8197.10*** *p222*
Donnelly, Patrick; New York, 1821 ***8197.10*** *p223*
Donnelly, Patrick; Vermont, 1845-1924 ***5900.10*** *p97*
Donnelly, Peter 22; Vermont, 1864 ***5900.10*** *p258*
Donnelly, Philip B.; Vermont, 1855-1891 ***5900.10*** *p88*
Donnelly, Rose Tennien; Vermont, 1848-1880 ***5900.10*** *p97*
Donnelly, Sophia 69; Vermont, 1879 ***5900.10*** *p346*
Donnelly, Thomas; New York, 1827 ***8197.10*** *p339*
Donnelly, Thomas; New York, 1837 ***8197.10*** *p82*
Donnelly, Thomas; New York, 1840 ***8197.10*** *p384*
Donnelly, Thomas 12; Ontario, 1871 ***1823.22*** *p44*
Donnelly, Thomas T.; Vermont, 1830-1909 ***5900.10*** *p542*
Donnelly, William; Newfoundland, 1864 ***1640.13*** *p31*
Donnelly, William D.; Vermont, 1872-1889 ***5900.10*** *p542*
Donnely, Michael 50; Ontario, 1871 ***1823.15*** *p65*
Donnen, John; New York, 1802 ***8197.10*** *p20*
Donner, William; Pennsylvania, 1785 ***4629.10*** *p48*
Donnily, Hannora 20; Ontario, 1871 ***1823.28*** *p24*
Donninger, Lorenz; Port uncertain, 1721 ***2856.30*** *p90*
Donnolly, Mr.; Quebec, 1857 ***9196.15*** *p14*
Donnovan, Catherine; Vermont, 1834-1903 ***5900.10*** *p75*
Donogh, J. 21; Ontario, 1861 ***2896.28*** *p8*
Donogh, John 48; Ontario, 1871 ***1823.15*** *p65*
Donoghue, Catherine B. 75; Vermont, 1897 ***5900.10*** *p294*
Donoghue, Ellen Tierney 49; Vermont, 1889 ***5900.10*** *p226*
Donoghue, M. O. 73; Vermont, 1898 ***5900.10*** *p226*
Donoghy, William 29; Ontario, 1871 ***1823.15*** *p65*
Donoho, Barney; New York, 1839 ***8197.10*** *p226*
Donoho, William; New York, 1839 ***8197.10*** *p379*
Donohoe, Humphrey; Pennsylvania, 1779 ***4629.10*** *p38*
Donohoe, Jane 54; Ontario, 1871 ***1823.28*** *p24*
Donohoe, Julie; Maryland, 1682 ***2524.55*** *p69*
Donohoe, Julie, II; Maryland, 1682 ***2524.55*** *p69*
Donohoe, Peter; New York, 1826 ***8197.10*** *p224*
Donohoe, Thomas 33; Ontario, 1871 ***1823.28*** *p24*
Donohogh, Margarett; Maryland, 1682 ***2524.55*** *p69*
Donohue, Bridget 36; Ontario, 1871 ***1823.22*** *p44*
Donohue, John 45; Ontario, 1871 ***1823.15*** *p65*
Donohue, John A.; New York, 1840 ***8197.10*** *p163*
Donohue, Margaret 25; Ontario, 1871 ***1823.15*** *p65*
Donohue, Timothy 45; Ontario, 1871 ***1823.28*** *p24*
Donolan, Bridget 17 *SEE* Donolan, Catherine
Donolan, Catherine 33 *SEE* Donolan, Catherine
Donolan, Catherine 55; New York, New York, 1848 ***1825.45*** *p32*
Son: John 26
Son: Thomas 30
Daughter: Bridget 17
Daughter: Catherine 33
Son: Pat 20
Donolan, John 26 *SEE* Donolan, Catherine
Donolan, Pat 20 *SEE* Donolan, Catherine
Donolan, Thomas 30 *SEE* Donolan, Catherine
Donoly, Peter; New York, 1838 ***8197.10*** *p377*
Donongh, Anne 73; Ontario, 1871 ***1823.15*** *p65*
Donough, Alexander 70; Ontario, 1871 ***1823.15*** *p65*
Donough, Ester 37; Ontario, 1871 ***1823.15*** *p65*
Donoughan, Elioner; Maryland, 1658 ***2524.55*** *p90*
Donovan, Ann 58; Vermont, 1902 ***5900.10*** *p419*
Donovan, Ann Dolan 35; Vermont, 1851 ***5900.10*** *p191*
Donovan, Bartholomew; New York, 1837 ***8197.10*** *p86*
Donovan, Bridget; Vermont, 1836-1889 ***5900.10*** *p78*
Donovan, Bridget; Vermont, 1877 ***5900.10*** *p543*
Donovan, Bridget 95; Vermont, 1898 ***5900.10*** *p213*
Donovan, Catherine 10; Vermont, 1853 ***5900.10*** *p191*
Donovan, Cathrine; Vermont, 1844-1906 ***5900.10*** *p489*
Donovan, Cornelius; Vermont, 1805-1879 ***5900.10*** *p58*
Donovan, Daniel 16; Philadelphia, 1774 ***1220.25*** *p34*
Donovan, Daniel 30; Ontario, 1871 ***1823.28*** *p24*
Donovan, Daniel 53; Vermont, 1880 ***5900.10*** *p577*
Donovan, Dennis 27; Vermont, 1842 ***5900.10*** *p58*
Donovan, Dennis 38; Vermont, 1883 ***5900.10*** *p347*
Donovan, Dennis 39; New York, 1832-1840 ***8197.10*** *p157*
Donovan, Donald 60; Ontario, 1871 ***1823.15*** *p65*
Donovan, Edward; New York, 1837 ***8197.10*** *p107*
Donovan, Ellen; Vermont, 1804-1873 ***5900.10*** *p73*
Donovan, Ellen; Vermont, 1834-1873 ***5900.10*** *p79*
Donovan, Ellen 74; Vermont, 1897 ***5900.10*** *p555*
Donovan, Ellen K.; Vermont, 1859-1922 ***5900.10*** *p423*
Donovan, Ellen Murphy 50; Vermont, 1882 ***5900.10*** *p345*
Donovan, James 27; Philadelphia, 1774 ***1220.25*** *p35*
Donovan, James 49; Vermont, 1899 ***5900.10*** *p377*
Donovan, Jane; Vermont, 1849-1905 ***5900.10*** *p458*
Donovan, Jennie A. Hale; Vermont, 1853-1922 ***5900.10*** *p497*
Donovan, Johanna King; Vermont, n.d. ***5900.10*** *p58*
Donovan, Johanna Reardon; Vermont, 1809-1860 ***5900.10*** *p58*
Donovan, John; Vermont, 1849-1917 ***5900.10*** *p496*
Donovan, John 8; Ontario, 1861 ***2896.25*** *p49*
Donovan, John 33; Vermont, 1867 ***5900.10*** *p58*
Donovan, John 40; Ontario, 1871 ***1823.28*** *p24*
Donovan, John 45; Vermont, 1875 ***5900.10*** *p466*
Donovan, John 74; Vermont, 1881 ***5900.10*** *p191*
Donovan, Julia; Vermont, 1798-1870 ***5900.10*** *p75*
Donovan, Julia; Vermont, 1822-1858 ***5900.10*** *p75*
Donovan, Julia E. 48; Vermont, 1901 ***5900.10*** *p468*
Donovan, Kate Cotter 56; Vermont, 1889 ***5900.10*** *p371*
Donovan, Margaret; Vermont, 1849-1919 ***5900.10*** *p590*
Donovan, Margaret; Vermont, 1850-1922 ***5900.10*** *p474*
Donovan, Mary; Vermont, 1825-1895 ***5900.10*** *p168*
Donovan, Mary; Vermont, 1830-1881 ***5900.10*** *p441*
Donovan, Mary; Vermont, 1845-1898 ***5900.10*** *p365*
Donovan, Mary 32; Vermont, 1873 ***5900.10*** *p213*
Donovan, Mary 65; Vermont, 1885 ***5900.10*** *p260*
Donovan, Mary A.; Vermont, 1838-1906 ***5900.10*** *p486*
Donovan, Mary A.; Vermont, 1842-1928 ***5900.10*** *p58*
Donovan, Mary A. 19; Vermont, 1868 ***5900.10*** *p347*
Donovan, Mary Feeley; Vermont, 1838-1911 ***5900.10*** *p466*
Donovan, Michael; New York, 1840 ***8197.10*** *p158*
Donovan, Michael 56; Vermont, 1903 ***5900.10*** *p419*
Donovan, Michael 60; Ontario, 1871 ***1823.22*** *p44*
Donovan, Michael 67; Vermont, 1910 ***5900.10*** *p543*
Donovan, P. W.; Pennsylvania, 1868 ***6058.10*** *p66*
Donovan, Patrick 3; Vermont, 1864 ***5900.10*** *p260*
Donovan, Patrick 45; Ontario, 1871 ***1823.28*** *p24*
Donovan, Patrick 59; Ontario, 1871 ***1823.22*** *p44*
Donovan, Patrick 67; Vermont, 1866 ***5900.10*** *p213*
Donovan, Richard; New York, 1802 ***8197.10*** *p20*
Donovan, Richard; New York, 1837 ***8197.10*** *p83*
Donovan, Richard; Vermont, 1834-1863 ***5900.10*** *p75*
Donovan, Sarah A. Macomber 69; Vermont, 1922 ***5900.10*** *p377*
Donovan, Thomas; Maryland, 1682 ***2524.55*** *p69*
Donovan, Thomas; Vermont, 1815-1893 ***5900.10*** *p75*
Donovan, Thomas 30; Ontario, 1871 ***1823.28*** *p24*
Donovan, Thomas J.; Vermont, 1855-1889 ***5900.10*** *p423*
Donovan, Timothy; New York, 1837 ***8197.10*** *p83*
Donovan, Timothy; New York, 1839 ***8197.10*** *p226*
Donovan, Timothy 23; Maryland, 1775 ***1220.25*** *p96*
Donovan, Timothy 66; Ontario, 1871 ***1823.28*** *p24*
Donovan, Timothy 74; Vermont, 1887 ***5900.10*** *p543*
Donovan, William; New York, 1802 ***8197.10*** *p20*

Donovan, William; New York, 1837 ***8197.10*** *p83*
Donovan, William 49; Ontario, 1871 ***1823.28*** *p24*
Donovane, Daniell; Maryland, 1678 ***2524.55*** *p69*
Donoven, Mary 20; Vermont, 1866 ***5900.10*** *p110*
Donoway, Ellen; Vermont, 1843-1927 ***5900.10*** *p540*
Donoway, James; Vermont, 1841-1919 ***5900.10*** *p540*
Donoyki, Joseph; Maryland, 1910 ***3259.35*** *p12*
Donsbach, Maria Agnes; Port uncertain, 1776 ***2856.30*** *p85*
Donski, Lucas; Maryland, 1910 ***3259.35*** *p12*
Doody, Jeremiah; Vermont, 1817-1904 ***5900.10*** *p312*
Doody, John H.; Vermont, 1853-1940 ***5900.10*** *p312*
Doody, Lillian V. Foote; Vermont, 1861-1933 ***5900.10*** *p312*
Doody, Mary; Vermont, 1812-1906 ***5900.10*** *p312*
Doogan, Michael; Pennsylvania, 1777 ***4629.10*** *p21*
Dool, John 57; Ontario, 1871 ***1823.28*** *p24*
Doolan, James 65; Vermont, 1894 ***5900.10*** *p251*
Doolan, Mary Ryan 40; Vermont, 1877 ***5900.10*** *p251*
Doolan, Timothy 38; Ontario, 1871 ***1823.28*** *p24*
Dooley, Alice; Vermont, 1834-1926 ***5900.10*** *p423*
Dooley, Anna M. Pickett; Vermont, n.d. ***5900.10*** *p178*
Dooley, Bridget 26; Vermont, 1860 ***5900.10*** *p567*
Dooley, Elizabeth Sloan; Vermont, 1855-1928 ***5900.10*** *p257*
Dooley, Ellen 74; Vermont, 1885 ***5900.10*** *p237*
Dooley, Ellen Moore; Vermont, 1852-1873 ***5900.10*** *p173*
Dooley, James; Vermont, 1847-1916 ***5900.10*** *p579*
Dooley, James 59; Vermont, 1900 ***5900.10*** *p273*
Dooley, Katharine; Vermont, 1848-1914 ***5900.10*** *p358*
Dooley, Margaret; Vermont, 1846-1917 ***5900.10*** *p579*
Dooley, Margaret 78; Vermont, 1876 ***5900.10*** *p250*
Dooley, Martin 25; Vermont, 1871 ***5900.10*** *p368*
Dooley, Martin H.; Vermont, 1852-1913 ***5900.10*** *p257*
Dooley, Mary; Vermont, 1818-1901 ***5900.10*** *p262*
Dooley, Mary; Vermont, 1836-1908 ***5900.10*** *p273*
Dooley, Mathew; Vermont, 1814-1868 ***5900.10*** *p262*
Dooley, Mathew, Jr.; Vermont, 1859-1879 ***5900.10*** *p262*
Dooley, Roseanna McMahon; Vermont, 1897 ***5900.10*** *p422*
Dooley, Sarah 44; Vermont, 1893 ***5900.10*** *p273*
Dooley, Thomas 1; New York, New York, 1848 ***1825.45*** *p32*
Dooley, Thomas E.; Vermont, 1847-1928 ***5900.10*** *p178*
Dooley, Thomas J.; Vermont, 1930 ***5900.10*** *p422*
Doolin, Agnes E. Baker 36; Vermont, 1888 ***5900.10*** *p287*
Doolin, Ann; Vermont, 1841-1913 ***5900.10*** *p383*
Doolin, Dell Johnson; Vermont, 1863-1919 ***5900.10*** *p457*
Doolin, Edward 45; Vermont, 1875 ***5900.10*** *p381*
Doolin, James; Vermont, 1839-1924 ***5900.10*** *p388*
Doolin, James; Vermont, 1858-1914 ***5900.10*** *p457*
Doolin, James 80; Vermont, 1901 ***5900.10*** *p286*
Doolin, Johannah 32; Vermont, 1862 ***5900.10*** *p286*
Doolin, John; New York, 1807 ***8197.10*** *p37*
Doolin, Kate 84; Vermont, 1905 ***5900.10*** *p381*
Doolin, Kate Shelvey 73; Vermont, 1910 ***5900.10*** *p381*
Doolin, Katie A. 31; Vermont, 1887 ***5900.10*** *p121*
Doolin, Margaret; Vermont, 1840-1911 ***5900.10*** *p388*
Doolin, Martha A.; Vermont, 1855-1906 ***5900.10*** *p286*
Doolin, Mary L. Kelley; Vermont, 1836-1905 ***5900.10*** *p286*
Doolin, Mary White; Vermont, 1823-1901 ***5900.10*** *p381*
Doolin, Patrick; Vermont, 1812-1907 ***5900.10*** *p381*
Doolin, Rosa Armstrong; Vermont, 1819-1858 ***5900.10*** *p381*
Dooling, Abbie 67; Vermont, 1896 ***5900.10*** *p113*
Dooling, Ann Swanton 92; Vermont, 1889 ***5900.10*** *p475*
Dooling, Catherine; Vermont, 1917 ***5900.10*** *p115*
Dooling, Catherine 21; Ontario, 1871 ***1823.15*** *p65*
Dooling, Mary Ann; Vermont, 1837-1897 ***5900.10*** *p515*
Dooling, Michael 65; Ontario, 1871 ***1823.15*** *p65*
Dooling, Nellie; Vermont, 1859-1943 ***5900.10*** *p118*
Dooling, Patrick 54; Vermont, 1880 ***5900.10*** *p113*
Dooling, Patrick 82; Vermont, 1877 ***5900.10*** *p475*
Doolittle, Mr. 1; Ontario, 1861 ***2896.28*** *p63*
Doolittle, Mr. 7; Ontario, 1861 ***2896.28*** *p63*
Doolittle, Ms. 3; Ontario, 1861 ***2896.28*** *p63*
Doolittle, Aurelius 21; Ontario, 1861 ***2896.28*** *p62*
Doolittle, Barbara; Vermont, 1840-1902 ***5900.10*** *p70*
Doolittle, Catharine 7; Ontario, 1861 ***2896.28*** *p61*
Doolittle, Densmor 3; Ontario, 1861 ***2896.28*** *p63*
Doolittle, Eliza 5; Ontario, 1861 ***2896.28*** *p61*
Doolittle, Elizabeth 36; Ontario, 1861 ***2896.28*** *p62*
Doolittle, Ephraim 83; Ontario, 1871 ***1823.22*** *p44*
Doolittle, George 5; Ontario, 1861 ***2896.28*** *p63*
Doolittle, Hannah 73; Ontario, 1861 ***2896.28*** *p63*
Doolittle, Jane 23; Ontario, 1861 ***2896.28*** *p62*
Doolittle, Jasper 2; Ontario, 1861 ***2896.28*** *p63*
Doolittle, John N. 2; Ontario, 1861 ***2896.28*** *p61*
Doolittle, Limon 78; Ontario, 1861 ***2896.28*** *p63*
Doolittle, Lucinda 16; Ontario, 1861 ***2896.28*** *p62*
Doolittle, Malissa 17; Ontario, 1861 ***2896.28*** *p63*
Doolittle, Manly 10; Ontario, 1861 ***2896.28*** *p62*
Doolittle, Margaret 32; Ontario, 1861 ***2896.28*** *p63*
Doolittle, Mary 20; Ontario, 1861 ***2896.28*** *p63*
Doolittle, Mary 45; Ontario, 1861 ***2896.28*** *p63*
Doolittle, Mary 70; Ontario, 1861 ***2896.28*** *p11*
Doolittle, Morenus 20; Ontario, 1861 ***2896.28*** *p62*
Doolittle, Orrilla 31; Ontario, 1861 ***2896.28*** *p63*
Doolittle, Patrick O. 32; Vermont, 1900 ***5900.10*** *p54*
Doolittle, Percilla 31; Ontario, 1861 ***2896.28*** *p61*
Doolittle, Sarah 19; Ontario, 1861 ***2896.28*** *p63*
Doolittle, Stephen 13; Ontario, 1861 ***2896.28*** *p62*
Doolittle, Victoria 10; Ontario, 1861 ***2896.28*** *p63*
Dooly, Dora 50; Ontario, 1871 ***1823.22*** *p44*
Dooly, Jeremiah 45; Ontario, 1871 ***1823.28*** *p24*
Dooly, Patrick 26; Ontario, 1871 ***1823.28*** *p24*
Dooly, William 70; Ontario, 1871 ***1823.28*** *p24*
Doon, Anna; Vermont, 1873-1973 ***5900.10*** *p538*
Doon, Catharine Barrett 35; Vermont, 1857 ***5900.10*** *p524*
Doon, Elizabeth; Vermont, 1858-1912 ***5900.10*** *p512*
Doon, Ella; Vermont, 1870-1913 ***5900.10*** *p531*
Doon, Ellen 25; Vermont, 1871 ***5900.10*** *p525*
Doon, Ellen Cox; Vermont, 1826-1896 ***5900.10*** *p524*
Doon, Felix; Vermont, 1853-1937 ***5900.10*** *p531*
Doon, Felix 84; Vermont, 1890 ***5900.10*** *p525*
Doon, Frances M.; Vermont, 1889-1902 ***5900.10*** *p525*
Doon, Francis; Vermont, 1862-1932 ***5900.10*** *p538*
Doon, Henery 13; Vermont, 1853 ***5900.10*** *p524*
Doon, James; Vermont, 1850-1919 ***5900.10*** *p525*
Doon, John; Vermont, n.d. ***5900.10*** *p525*
Doon, John; Vermont, 1806-1898 ***5900.10*** *p524*
Doon, John; Vermont, 1841-1908 ***5900.10*** *p516*
Doon, Laura Duffey; Vermont, 1863-1950 ***5900.10*** *p531*
Doon, Margaret McIver; Vermont, 1817-1900 ***5900.10*** *p516*
Doon, Margrett Malone 76; Vermont, 1883 ***5900.10*** *p525*
Doon, Mary; Vermont, 1797-1888 ***5900.10*** *p513*
Doon, Mary; Vermont, 1838-1909 ***5900.10*** *p225*
Doon, Mary; Vermont, 1857-1951 ***5900.10*** *p483*
Doon, Mary Fay 81; Vermont, 1868 ***5900.10*** *p525*
Doon, Mary J. Hanley; Vermont, 1852-1952 ***5900.10*** *p525*
Doon, Michael J.; Vermont, 1881-1940 ***5900.10*** *p525*
Doon, Neal; Vermont, 1816-1886 ***5900.10*** *p515*
Doon, Patrick 28; Vermont, 1867 ***5900.10*** *p513*
Doon, Rose; Vermont, 1795-1877 ***5900.10*** *p513*
Doon, Rose 40; Vermont, 1831 ***5900.10*** *p515*
Doon, William E. 8 months; Vermont, 1867 ***5900.10*** *p345*
Dooner, Bernard 52; Ontario, 1871 ***1823.28*** *p24*
Dooner, Francis 65; Ontario, 1871 ***1823.28*** *p24*
Dooner, James 64; Ontario, 1871 ***1823.28*** *p24*
Dooner, John 56; Ontario, 1871 ***1823.28*** *p24*
Doorley, John; New York, 1838 ***8197.10*** *p376*
Doppert, Johann; America, 1752 ***2856.30*** *p85*
With wife & child
Dopre, Jakob; America, 1738 ***2856.30*** *p85*
Doran, Ann; Vermont, 1827-1869 ***5900.10*** *p236*
Doran, Ann 66; Vermont, 1896 ***5900.10*** *p484*
Doran, Bridget 16; Ontario, 1861 ***2896.25*** *p42*
Doran, Catherine; Vermont, 1844-1933 ***5900.10*** *p255*
Doran, Catherine; Vermont, 1848-1918 ***5900.10*** *p170*
Doran, David 38; Ontario, 1871 ***1823.15*** *p68*
Doran, Edward; New York, 1828 ***8197.10*** *p348*
Doran, Edward L. 9; Vermont, 1866 ***5900.10*** *p522*
Doran, Eliza J. 3; Vermont, 1866 ***5900.10*** *p522*
Doran, Ellen 45; Ontario, 1861 ***2896.25*** *p42*
Doran, Emily A. 2; Vermont, 1862 ***5900.10*** *p522*
Doran, Emily A. Ellsworth 40; Vermont, 1873 ***5900.10*** *p522*
Doran, Henry; Pennsylvania, 1777 ***4629.10*** *p20*
Doran, James; New York, 1806 ***8197.10*** *p324*
Doran, James A. 2 months; Vermont, 1858 ***5900.10*** *p522*
Doran, John; Vermont, 1797-1870 ***5900.10*** *p529*
Doran, John 19; Ontario, 1861 ***2896.25*** *p42*
Doran, Joseph; Portland, Maine, 1858 ***9196.15*** *p29*
Doran, M. 45; Ontario, 1861 ***2896.25*** *p42*
Doran, Margaret; Vermont, 1839-1921 ***5900.10*** *p354*
Doran, Mary; Vermont, 1857-1922 ***5900.10*** *p170*
Doran, Mary A. Barrett; Vermont, 1818-1903 ***5900.10*** *p529*
Doran, Mary Nugant 95; Vermont, 1872 ***5900.10*** *p522*
Doran, Michael; New York, 1837 ***8197.10*** *p83*
Doran, Michael 4; Ontario, 1861 ***2896.25*** *p42*
Doran, Nancy; Vermont, 1843-1926 ***5900.10*** *p532*
Doran, Nancy 21; Ontario, 1861 ***2896.25*** *p42*
Doran, Owen; Vermont, 1846-1924 ***5900.10*** *p255*
Doran, Patrick 78; Vermont, 1862 ***5900.10*** *p522*
Doran, Peter 68; Vermont, 1871 ***5900.10*** *p503*
Doran, Susan 5; Vermont, 1866 ***5900.10*** *p522*
Doran, Thomas 5 months; Vermont, 1847 ***5900.10*** *p522*
Doran, Thomas 45; Vermont, 1871 ***5900.10*** *p522*
Doran, William 31; Ontario, 1871 ***1823.28*** *p24*
Dorcey, Matthew 23; Ontario, 1871 ***1823.15*** *p65*
Dorcy, Michael 62; Ontario, 1871 ***1823.15*** *p65*
Dorcy, William 29; Ontario, 1871 ***1823.15*** *p65*
Dordino, Peter; Maryland, 1674 ***2524.55*** *p69*
Dore, Garrat; Maryland, 1676 ***2524.55*** *p69*
Dore, Machael 59; Ontario, 1871 ***1823.28*** *p24*
Dore, Thomas 23; Virginia, 1774 ***1220.25*** *p87*
Dorent, John; Virginia, 1673 ***6212.30*** *p51*
Dorer, Jacob; America, 1744 ***2856.30*** *p90*
Dorer, Johann; America, 1752 ***2856.30*** *p90*
With wife
Dorey, Ellen Phalen; Vermont, 1851-1905 ***5900.10*** *p532*
Dorey, Louis; Vermont, 1845-1945 ***5900.10*** *p532*
Dorey, Mathew 63; Ontario, 1871 ***1823.15*** *p65*
Dorfflinger, Johann; America, 1742 ***2856.30*** *p90*
Dorfling, Johann Adam; America, 1742 ***2856.30*** *p90*
Dorflinger, . . .; America, 1764 ***2856.30*** *p90*
Dorflinger, Mr.; America, 1761 ***2856.30*** *p90*
Dorflinger, Anna Margarete; Port uncertain, 1788 ***2856.30*** *p90*
Dorflinger, Friedrich, The Younger; America, 1749 ***2856.30*** *p90*
Dorflinger, Friedrich, The Younger; America, 1750 ***2856.30*** *p90*
Dorflinger, Friedrich, The Younger; America, 1759 ***2856.30*** *p90*
Dorflinger, Martin; America, 1748 ***2856.30*** *p90*
Dorgan, Morty; New York, 1840 ***8197.10*** *p156*
Doringer, Anton; Port uncertain, 1782 ***2856.30*** *p90*
Doringer, Jacob; Port uncertain, 1742 ***2856.30*** *p90*
Doringer, Jacob; Port uncertain, 1767 ***2856.30*** *p90*
Dorington, Robt; Virginia, 1667-1668 ***6212.30*** *p39*
Doritty, Mary Jane 19; Ontario, 1871 ***1823.22*** *p44*
Dorkray, Jno; Virginia, 1665-1666 ***6212.30*** *p21*
Dorland, A. 6; Ontario, 1861 ***2896.28*** *p8*
Dorland, A. J. 6; Ontario, 1861 ***2896.26*** *p1*
Dorland, Alonzo 23; Ontario, 1861 ***2896.28*** *p46*
Dorland, Andrew 4; Ontario, 1861 ***2896.27*** *p67*
Dorland, Annah M. 18; Ontario, 1861 ***2896.28*** *p46*
Dorland, Arnoldi 10; Ontario, 1861 ***2896.28*** *p26*
Dorland, Augusta 1; Ontario, 1861 ***2896.28*** *p48*
Dorland, B. 15; Ontario, 1861 ***2896.28*** *p8*
Dorland, B. 58; Ontario, 1861 ***2896.28*** *p14*
Dorland, C. E. 20; Ontario, 1861 ***2896.28*** *p14*
Dorland, E. 79; Ontario, 1861 ***2896.28*** *p1*
Dorland, E. A. 2; Ontario, 1861 ***2896.28*** *p14*
Dorland, Elizabeth 16; Ontario, 1861 ***2896.27*** *p30*
Dorland, Elizabeth 17; Ontario, 1861 ***2896.27*** *p70*
Dorland, Elizabeth 83; Ontario, 1861 ***2896.28*** *p46*
Dorland, G. M. 19; Ontario, 1861 ***2896.28*** *p8*
Dorland, Gilbert 16; Ontario, 1861 ***2896.27*** *p70*
Dorland, Hannah 44; Ontario, 1861 ***2896.27*** *p67*
Dorland, J. 1; Ontario, 1861 ***2896.28*** *p8*
Dorland, Jane 6; Ontario, 1861 ***2896.28*** *p48*
Dorland, Jane Ann 51; Ontario, 1861 ***2896.28*** *p46*
Dorland, John 17; Ontario, 1861 ***2896.28*** *p50*
Dorland, M. 9; Ontario, 1861 ***2896.28*** *p8*
Dorland, M. A. 46; Ontario, 1861 ***2896.28*** *p8*
Dorland, M. J. 22; Ontario, 1861 ***2896.28*** *p14*
Dorland, Martha 77; Ontario, 1861 ***2896.27*** *p73*
Dorland, Martha Jane 19; Ontario, 1861 ***2896.28*** *p29*
Dorland, Mary E. 29; Ontario, 1861 ***2896.28*** *p48*
Dorland, Mary M. 5; Ontario, 1861 ***2896.28*** *p48*
Dorland, Nancy 10; Ontario, 1861 ***2896.28*** *p46*
Dorland, Patty G. 34; Ontario, 1861 ***2896.28*** *p26*
Dorland, Phebe E. 7; Ontario, 1861 ***2896.28*** *p26*
Dorland, Philip A. 6; Ontario, 1861 ***2896.28*** *p46*
Dorland, Philip N. 2; Ontario, 1861 ***2896.28*** *p26*
Dorland, Robert 29; Ontario, 1861 ***2896.28*** *p47*
Dorland, Ruth A. 11; Ontario, 1861 ***2896.27*** *p70*
Dorland, Samuel 66; Ontario, 1861 ***2896.27*** *p73*
Dorland, Susan 39; Ontario, 1861 ***2896.28*** *p46*
Dorland, Susan 52; Ontario, 1861 ***2896.27*** *p70*
Dorland, Tabitha 20; Ontario, 1861 ***2896.28*** *p50*
Dorland, Thomas 19; Ontario, 1861 ***2896.27*** *p29*
Dorland, Thomas 19; Ontario, 1861 ***2896.28*** *p46*
Dorland, Thomas C. 23; Ontario, 1861 ***2896.28*** *p8*
Dorland, Wm Davis 15; Ontario, 1861 ***2896.28*** *p46*
Dorlin, Antho; Virginia, 1674-1675 ***6212.30*** *p53*
Dorling, John 50; Ontario, 1871 ***1823.15*** *p65*
Dorly, Jeremy; Virginia, 1667-1668 ***6212.30*** *p38*
Dormain, William 59; Ontario, 1871 ***1823.15*** *p65*
Dorman, Hugh 57; Vermont, 1855 ***5900.10*** *p154*
Dorman, Jacob; Maryland, 1674 ***2524.55*** *p69*
Dorman, James; New York, 1839 ***8197.10*** *p226*
Dorman, Jane 72; Vermont, 1879 ***5900.10*** *p133*
Dorman, John; Maryland, 1670 ***2524.55*** *p69*
Dorman, Loveland; Maryland, 1682 ***2524.55*** *p69*
Dorman, Mathew; Maryland, 1670 ***2524.55*** *p69*
Dorman, Robert; Maryland, 1663 ***2524.55*** *p29*
Dorman, Sarah; Maryland, 1674 ***2524.55*** *p69*
Dormant, William 25; Philadelphia, 1775 ***1220.25*** *p8*
Dormer, Robert; Virginia, 1664 ***6212.30*** *p11*
Dormoore, Gabriell; Maryland, 1654 ***2524.55*** *p69*

Dorn, Christian; America, 1765 **2856.30** *p85*
With wife & 3 children
Dorn, Frederick 35; Ontario, 1871 **1823.15** *p65*
Dornberger, Andreas; Port uncertain, 1730 **2856.30** *p85*
Dornberger, Andreas; Port uncertain, 1770 **2856.30** *p85*
Dornbush, Albert 31; Ontario, 1871 **1823.28** *p24*
Dorner, Caspar Friedric; America, 1744 **2856.30** *p90*
With wife
Dorner, Jakob; America, 1771 **2856.30** *p90*
Dorner, Jakob; Port uncertain, 1746 **2856.30** *p90*
Dorner, Maria Catharina; America, 1767 **2856.30** *p90*
Dorner, Maria Catharina; Port uncertain, 1746 **2856.30** *p90*
Dorner, Sebastian; Port uncertain, 1746 **2856.30** *p90*
Dorney, James 53; Vermont, 1891 **5900.10** *p66*
Dorney, James, Jr. 38; Vermont, 1895 **5900.10** *p66*
Dorney, Mary Farrell 64; Vermont, 1892 **5900.10** *p66*
Dorney, Morris 27; Vermont, 1881 **5900.10** *p66*
Dornin, Andrew 34; Ontario, 1871 **1823.15** *p65*
Dornu, Lewis Joseph; Pennsylvania, 1779 **4629.10** *p36*
Dornyan, Edward 45; Ontario, 1871 **1823.15** *p65*
Doroan, John 40; Ontario, 1871 **1823.22** *p45*
Doroba, Ludwick; Maryland, 1910 **3259.35** *p12*
Dorolranie, Mr.; Canada, 1858 **9196.15** *p45*
Doron, Samuel 39; Ontario, 1871 **1823.15** *p65*
Dorow, Richard 56; Ontario, 1871 **1823.22** *p45*
Dorpert, Andreas; Port uncertain, 1781 **2856.30** *p85*
Dorpfing, Jakob; Port uncertain, 1736 **2856.30** *p85*
Dorr, . . .; Port uncertain, 1786 **2856.30** *p90*
Dorr, Adam; America, 1749 **2856.30** *p90*
Dorr, Anna Barbara; Port uncertain, 1770 **2856.30** *p90*
Dorr, Anna Barbara; Port uncertain, 1785 **2856.30** *p152*
Dorr, Balthasar; Port uncertain, 1781 **2856.30** *p90*
Dorr, Balthasar; Port uncertain, 1783 **2856.30** *p90*
Dorr, Georg Peter; Port uncertain, 1764 **2856.30** *p90*
Dorr, Jacob; Port uncertain, 1738 **2856.30** *p90*
Dorr, Johann Georg; Port uncertain, 1752 **2856.30** *p90*
Dorr, Josef; Port uncertain, 1782 **2856.30** *p91*
With wife & children
Dorr, Katherine; Vermont, 1841-1913 **5900.10** *p452*
Dorr, Paul; America, 1782 **2856.30** *p91*
With wife
Dorr, Paul; America, 1787 **2856.30** *p91*
With wife
Dorr, Peter; America, 1752 **2856.30** *p91*
With wife & 3 children
Dorr, Peter; America, 1764 **2856.30** *p90*
Dorr, Peter; America, 1782 **2856.30** *p125*
Dorr, Peter; America, 1787 **2856.30** *p125*
Dorrance, David 51; Ontario, 1871 **1823.15** *p65*
Dorrance, George 47; Ontario, 1871 **1823.15** *p65*
Dorrance, James 38; Ontario, 1871 **1823.15** *p65*
Dorrance, Samuel 44; Ontario, 1871 **1823.15** *p65*
Dorrance, William 40; Ontario, 1871 **1823.15** *p65*
Dorrbach, Anton; America, 1764 **2856.30** *p91*
Dorrbach, Barbara; America, 1764 **2856.30** *p91*
Dorrbach, Michael; America, 1764 **2856.30** *p91*
Dorrell, Elizabeth; Maryland, 1653 **2524.55** *p69*
Dorrell, Myles; Maryland, 1649 **2524.55** *p69*
Dorrer, Jacob; America, 1737 **2856.30** *p91*
Dorrer, Josef; Port uncertain, 1752 **2856.30** *p91*
With wife & children
Dorrer, Ursula; Port uncertain, 1765 **2856.30** *p91*
Dorrer, Ursula; Port uncertain, 1766 **2856.30** *p91*
Dorril, Josophat; Maryland, 1667 **2524.55** *p69*
Dorrington, Nicholas; Maryland, 1661 **2524.55** *p133*
Dorrmann, Johann Georg; America, 1752 **2856.30** *p91*
Dorrstein, Samuel; America, 1737 **2856.30** *p91*
Dorrwachter, Charles; Pennsylvania, 1868 **6058.10** *p61*
Dorrwackter, Charles; Pennsylvania, 1868 **6058.10** *p61*
Dorschheimer, Jakob; Port uncertain, 1764 **2856.30** *p85*
Dorsching, Simon; Port uncertain, 1726 **2856.30** *p85*
Dorsett, Marke; Maryland, 1657 **2524.55** *p69*
Dorsey, Bessie O'Donnell; Vermont, 1837-1929 **5900.10** *p585*
Dorsey, Bridget 72; Ontario, 1871 **1823.15** *p65*
Dorsey, Edward; Maryland, 1661 **2524.55** *p37*
Dorsey, Hannah 72; Vermont, 1925 **5900.10** *p467*
Dorsey, Jacob 75; Ontario, 1871 **1823.15** *p65*
Dorsey, James 35; Ontario, 1871 **1823.15** *p65*
Dorsey, John; Vermont, 1847-1918 **5900.10** *p585*
Dorsey, John 24; Ontario, 1871 **1823.15** *p65*
Dorsey, John 35; Vermont, 1843 **5900.10** *p319*
Dorsey, John 75; Vermont, 1885 **5900.10** *p253*
Dorsey, Joseph T. 78; Vermont, 1923 **5900.10** *p467*
Dorsey, Julia 45; Vermont, 1850 **5900.10** *p319*
Dorsey, Margaret; Vermont, 1833-1910 **5900.10** *p306*
Dorsey, Martin 17; Vermont, 1848 **5900.10** *p319*
Dorsey, Mary; Vermont, 1816-1881 **5900.10** *p251*
Dorsey, Mary Lyons; Vermont, 1848-1876 **5900.10** *p585*
Dorsey, Michael; Vermont, 1835-1898 **5900.10** *p306*
Dorsey, Patrick 68; Ontario, 1871 **1823.15** *p65*
Dorsey, Phebe J. 53; Ontario, 1871 **1823.15** *p65*
Dorsey, Ralph; Maryland, 1665 **2524.55** *p69*
Dorsey, Thomas; New York, 1836 **8197.10** *p78*
Dorsey, Thomas; Pennsylvania, 1777 **4629.10** *p20*
Dorsheimer, Christof; Port uncertain, 1751 **2856.30** *p85*
Dorsheimer, Jakob; Port uncertain, 1764 **2856.30** *p85*
Dorst, Peter; America, 1762 **2856.30** *p85*
Dorst, Peter; America, 1764 **2856.30** *p85*
Dorst, Peter; America, 1768 **2856.30** *p85*
Dorsy, Ralph; Maryland, 1665 **2524.55** *p69*
Dorter, Cath. Elisabeth; Port uncertain, 1775 **2856.30** *p91*
Dorter, Karolina; Port uncertain, 1793 **2856.30** *p91*
Dorter, Peter; America, 1754 **2856.30** *p78*
Dorthion, Roger; Virginia, 1677 **6212.30** *p54*
Dortic, Sebastien C.; New York, 1837 **8197.10** *p225*
Dortner, Anton; Port uncertain, 1749 **2856.30** *p91*
Dortzbacher, Hans Georg; Port uncertain, 1745 **2856.30** *p91*
Dortzbacher, Hans Georg; Port uncertain, 1748 **2856.30** *p91*
Dorvill, Joseph; Pennsylvania, 1777 **4629.10** *p15*
Dorwart, Miss; America, 1775 **2856.30** *p85*
With sister
Dory, William 36; Ontario, 1871 **1823.15** *p65*
Dorzazki, Stanislaw; Maryland, 1910 **3259.35** *p12*
Doschen, Claus; New York, 1840 **8197.10** *p321*
Doset, Cristian; Virginia, 1663-1664 **6212.30** *p5*
Doss, Bernard; America, 1780 **2856.30** *p84*
Doss, Bernard; Port uncertain, 1763 **2856.30** *p84*
Dossen, Katherine; Maryland, 1667 **2524.55** *p69*
Dota, Albert 25; Ontario, 1871 **1823.28** *p24*
Dotson, Abram; Virginia, 1663 **6212.30** *p3*
Dotterer, Johann; Port uncertain, 1768 **2856.30** *p86*
Dotterer, Johannes; New York, 1840 **8197.10** *p156*
Dottons, Michael 29; Ontario, 1871 **1823.22** *p45*
Doty, Hattie; Ontario, 1871 **1823.28** *p24*
Doty, Jasper; Ontario, 1871 **1823.28** *p24*
Doty, Lewey 11; Ontario, 1871 **1823.28** *p24*
Double, Lucy; Falkland Islands, 1880-1889 **4537.35** *p74*
Doubleday, Mr.; Quebec, 1856 **9196.15** *p7*
Doubledee, Edward 80; Ontario, 1871 **1823.15** *p65*
Doubledee, Eliza 58; Ontario, 1871 **1823.28** *p24*
Doubledee, Frederick 37; Ontario, 1871 **1823.15** *p66*
Doubledee, James 35; Ontario, 1871 **1823.15** *p66*
Douch, Hugh; Maryland, 1682 **2524.55** *p69*
Doud, Emelie; Vermont, 1837-1915 **5900.10** *p608*
Doude, Catharine 59; Vermont, 1900 **5900.10** *p113*
Doude, Catharine 65; Vermont, 1864 **5900.10** *p113*
Douden, Richd; Virginia, 1683 **6212.30** *p56*
Doudy, James; Maryland, 1667 **2524.55** *p69*
Dougal, Andrew 64; Ontario, 1871 **1823.15** *p66*
Dougal, Peter 35; Ontario, 1871 **1823.28** *p24*
Dougall, David 43; Ontario, 1871 **1823.15** *p66*
Dougall, James 59; Ontario, 1871 **1823.15** *p66*
Dougall, John; Georgia, 1699 **1640.13** *p31*
Dougall, William 53; Ontario, 1871 **1823.15** *p66*
Dougan, Christopher; New York, New York, 1850 **3437.14** *p2*
Dougan, Christopher; New York, New York, 1850 **3437.14** *p5*
Dougen, John 40; Ontario, 1871 **1823.15** *p66*
Dougharty, Edward 20; Virginia, 1774 **1220.25** *p45*
Dougharty, Mary 52; Vermont, 1827 **5900.10** *p511*
Dougherty, Andrew 21; Vermont, 1864 **5900.10** *p324*
Dougherty, Andrew 63; Vermont, 1881 **5900.10** *p476*
Dougherty, Ann; Vermont, 1854-1931 **5900.10** *p304*
Dougherty, Ann 46; Vermont, 1872 **5900.10** *p463*
Dougherty, Ann Cox 70; Vermont, 1893 **5900.10** *p292*
Dougherty, Barney; New York, 1839 **8197.10** *p380*
Dougherty, Bernard 27; Ontario, 1871 **1823.22** *p45*
Dougherty, Catharine 25; Vermont, 1842 **5900.10** *p324*
Dougherty, Catharine 43; Vermont, 1866 **5900.10** *p324*
Dougherty, Catherine; Vermont, 1838-1916 **5900.10** *p436*
Dougherty, Celia Hall; Vermont, 1800-1836 **5900.10** *p293*
Dougherty, Charles; New York, 1794 **8197.10** *p5*
Dougherty, Charles; New York, 1802 **8197.10** *p20*
Dougherty, Constantine; New York, 1838-1840 **8197.10** *p300*
Dougherty, Cornelius; New York, 1837 **8197.10** *p107*
Dougherty, Daniel; New York, 1837 **8197.10** *p375*
Dougherty, Dennis; New York, 1806 **8197.10** *p324*
Dougherty, Dennis; Pennsylvania, 1777 **4629.10** *p22*
Dougherty, Dennis; Pennsylvania, 1779 **4629.10** *p40*
Dougherty, Didly; New York, 1821 **8197.10** *p223*
Dougherty, Dominie 48; Ontario, 1871 **1823.28** *p24*
Dougherty, Edward; New York, 1840 **8197.10** *p301*
Dougherty, Ellen Rowland; Vermont, 1900 **5900.10** *p426*
Dougherty, Ervin 32; Ontario, 1871 **1823.15** *p66*
Dougherty, George; New York, 1827 **8197.10** *p224*
Dougherty, George; New York, 1834 **8197.10** *p373*
Dougherty, Henry; Pennsylvania, 1777 **4629.10** *p6*
Dougherty, James; New York, 1807 **8197.10** *p38*
Dougherty, James; New York, 1837 **8197.10** *p82*
Dougherty, James; Pennsylvania, 1777 **4629.10** *p12*
Dougherty, James; Vermont, 1796-1878 **5900.10** *p292*
Dougherty, James; Vermont, 1845-1913 **5900.10** *p463*
Dougherty, James 36; Ontario, 1871 **1823.15** *p66*
Dougherty, James 72; Vermont, 1877 **5900.10** *p292*
Dougherty, James S.; Pennsylvania, 1786 **4629.10** *p54*
Dougherty, John; New York, 1807 **8197.10** *p332*
Dougherty, John; New York, 1830 **8197.10** *p361*
Dougherty, John; New York, 1840 **8197.10** *p158*
Dougherty, John 32; Ontario, 1871 **1823.22** *p45*
Dougherty, Joseph; Vermont, 1888 **5900.10** *p426*
Dougherty, Katherine J. Clark; Vermont, 1847-1914 **5900.10** *p489*
Dougherty, Margaret; Vermont, n.d. **5900.10** *p507*
Dougherty, Margaret 52; Ontario, 1861 **2896.27** *p12*
Dougherty, Margaret Clinton; Vermont, 1845-1910 **5900.10** *p463*
Dougherty, Margaret E. 94; Vermont, 1914 **5900.10** *p444*
Dougherty, Martin 73; Vermont, 1883 **5900.10** *p324*
Dougherty, Mary O'Brine; Vermont, 1900 **5900.10** *p476*
Dougherty, Michael; New York, 1839 **8197.10** *p381*
Dougherty, P. J.; Vermont, 1849-1884 **5900.10** *p489*
Dougherty, Patrick; New York, 1792-1840 **8197.10** *p380*
Dougherty, Patrick; New York, 1836 **8197.10** *p317*
Dougherty, Philip; New York, 1803 **8197.10** *p12*
Dougherty, Sarah 38; Ontario, 1871 **1823.28** *p24*
Dougherty, Sarah Curran; Vermont, 1834-1861 **5900.10** *p293*
Dougherty, Theresa; Vermont, 1855 **5900.10** *p359*
Dougherty, Thomas; New York, 1807 **8197.10** *p325*
Dougherty, Thomas; New York, 1826 **8197.10** *p337*
Dougherty, William; New York, 1828 **8197.10** *p350*
Dougherty, William; New York, 1837 **8197.10** *p375*
Dougherty, William 55; Ontario, 1871 **1823.15** *p66*
Doughorty, David; Maryland, 1658 **2524.55** *p69*
Doughtery, Francis 60; Ontario, 1871 **1823.28** *p24*
Doughty, Enoch; Maryland, 1680 **2524.55** *p70*
Doughty, Robert; Maryland, 1668 **2524.55** *p70*
Douglas, Dr.; Portland, Maine, 1858 **9196.15** *p30*
Douglas, Mr.; Florida, 1776 **1640.10** *p44*
Douglas, Mr.; Quebec, 1857 **9196.15** *p15*
Douglas, Mr.; Quebec, 1858 **9196.15** *p33*
Douglas, Mrs.; Portland, Maine, 1858 **9196.15** *p30*
Douglas, Mrs.; Quebec, 1858 **9196.15** *p34*
Douglas, Rev.; Quebec, 1858 **9196.15** *p34*
Douglas, Agnes 46; Ontario, 1871 **1823.15** *p66*
Douglas, Alexander; New York, 1840 **8197.10** *p157*
Douglas, Alexander 22; Carolina, 1774 **1220.25** *p91*
Douglas, Alexander 42; Ontario, 1871 **1823.15** *p66*
Douglas, Aleyr 36; Ontario, 1871 **1823.28** *p24*
Douglas, Allen 35; Ontario, 1871 **1823.15** *p66*
Douglas, Charles; Vermont, 1854-1954 **5900.10** *p541*
Douglas, Colin; Georgia, 1820 **1640.10** *p42*
Douglas, Colin; Mississippi, 1815-1845 **1640.10** *p42*
Douglas, David; Augusta, Georgia, 1758 **1640.10** *p43*
Douglas, David; Savannah, Georgia, 1736 **1640.10** *p42*
Douglas, Elison 70; Ontario, 1871 **1823.15** *p66*
Douglas, Elizabeth Garrow; Vermont, 1842-1917 **5900.10** *p203*
Douglas, George; Georgia, 1699 **1640.13** *p31*
Douglas, George; Georgia, 1741 **1640.10** *p43*
Wife: Margaret Monro
Daughter: Isabel
Douglas, George; Maryland, 1677 **2524.55** *p70*
Douglas, George 25; Ontario, 1871 **1823.28** *p24*
Douglas, George 35; Ontario, 1871 **1823.15** *p66*
Douglas, George 61; Ontario, 1871 **1823.22** *p45*
Douglas, Isabel *SEE* Douglas, George
Douglas, Isabella 80; Ontario, 1871 **1823.15** *p66*
Douglas, Jacob O.; Vermont, 1828-1909 **5900.10** *p203*
Douglas, James; Georgia, 1698 **1640.13** *p31*
Douglas, James; St. Johns, Newfoundland, 1854 **1640.13** *p31*
Douglas, James; Vermont, 1836-1936 **5900.10** *p541*
Douglas, James 48; Ontario, 1871 **1823.28** *p24*
Douglas, James 49; Ontario, 1871 **1823.15** *p66*
Douglas, James 60; Ontario, 1871 **1823.28** *p24*
Douglas, Janet; Savannah, Georgia, 1736 **1640.10** *p43*
Douglas, John; Alabama, 1822-1845 **1640.10** *p43*
Douglas, John; America, 1836 **1640.13** *p31*
Douglas, John; California, 1891 **1640.13** *p31*
Douglas, John; Georgia, 1775 **1640.10** *p43*
Douglas, John; Grenada, 1838 **1640.13** *p31*
Douglas, John; Mobile, Alabama, 1823-1845 **1640.10** *p43*
Douglas, John; Ontario, 1871 **1823.28** *p24*
Douglas, John 20; Georgia, 1775 **1220.25** *p124*
Douglas, John 48; Ontario, 1871 **1823.22** *p45*
Douglas, John 53; Ontario, 1871 **1823.28** *p24*
Douglas, John 62; Ontario, 1871 **1823.15** *p66*
Douglas, John 68; Ontario, 1871 **1823.28** *p24*

Douglas, John 89; Vermont, 1891 ***5900.10*** *p541*
Douglas, John C.; New York, 1827 ***8197.10*** *p224*
Douglas, John C.; New York, 1830 ***8197.10*** *p303*
Douglas, John P. 56; Ontario, 1871 ***1823.22*** *p45*
Douglas, Joseph; Baltimore, 1774 ***1224.2*** *p34*
Douglas, Julia; Vermont, 1851-1919 ***5900.10*** *p541*
Douglas, Margaret Monro *SEE* Douglas, George
Douglas, Mary 35; Ontario, 1871 ***1823.15*** *p66*
Douglas, Mary Ann; Vermont, 1805-1882 ***5900.10*** *p539*
Douglas, Mary L. Adams; Vermont, 1859-1907 ***5900.10*** *p541*
Douglas, Nicholas J.; Vermont, 1850-1943 ***5900.10*** *p539*
Douglas, Robert; Tobago, West Indies, 1859 ***1640.13*** *p31*
Douglas, Robert 35; Ontario, 1871 ***1823.15*** *p66*
Douglas, Robert 38; Ontario, 1871 ***1823.15*** *p66*
Douglas, Robert 47; Ontario, 1871 ***1823.15*** *p66*
Douglas, Samuel; Savannah, Georgia, 1735-1823 ***1640.10*** *p43*
Douglas, Sarah; Vermont, 1837-1917 ***5900.10*** *p464*
Douglas, Sholto; North America, 1759 ***1224.2*** *p34*
Douglas, Susanna; New York, New York, 1807 ***1224.3*** *p2*
Douglas, Thomas; Maryland, 1677 ***2524.55*** *p70*
Douglas, William; Baltimore, 1895 ***1640.13*** *p32*
Douglas, William; Boston, 1753 ***1224.2*** *p34*
Douglas, William; Georgia, 1734 ***1640.10*** *p43*
Douglas, William 40; Ontario, 1871 ***1823.15*** *p66*
Douglas, William 47; Ontario, 1871 ***1823.15*** *p66*
Douglas, Wm.; New York, 1840 ***8197.10*** *p157*
Douglass, Christine 40; Ontario, 1871 ***1823.15*** *p66*
Douglass, George; Pennsylvania, 1777 ***4629.10*** *p12*
Douglass, George; Pennsylvania, 1777 ***4629.10*** *p22*
Douglass, James; New York, 1807 ***8197.10*** *p37*
Douglass, John; Bahamas, 1820 ***1224.3*** *p22*
Douglass, John; New York, 1821 ***8197.10*** *p223*
Douglass, John; St. Augustine, Florida, n.d. ***1224.3*** *p22*
Douglass, John; St. Augustine, Florida, 1735-1820 ***1640.10*** *p43*
Douglass, John 72; Ontario, 1871 ***1823.28*** *p24*
Douglass, John C.; New York, 1821 ***8197.10*** *p222*
Douglass, Mary *SEE* Douglass, William
Douglass, Mary; Vermont, 1854-1902 ***5900.10*** *p68*
Douglass, Peter 37; Ontario, 1871 ***1823.15*** *p66*
Douglass, Robert; New York, 1821 ***8197.10*** *p222*
Douglass, Samuel; Jamaica, 1800 ***1224.3*** *p22*
Douglass, Samuel; Savannah, Georgia, n.d. ***1224.3*** *p22*
Douglass, William *SEE* Douglass, William
Douglass, William; Louisiana, 1844 ***1640.10*** *p44*
Relative: William
Relative: Mary
Douglass, William; New York, 1828 ***8197.10*** *p225*
Douglass, William 29; Ontario, 1871 ***1823.22*** *p45*
Dougles, Robert 33; Ontario, 1871 ***1823.15*** *p66*
Dougless, James 46; Ontario, 1871 ***1823.28*** *p24*
Dougreity, John 28; Ontario, 1871 ***1823.15*** *p66*
Douguty, Robert; Maryland, 1668 ***2524.55*** *p70*
Doulan, William 24; Virginia, 1774 ***1220.25*** *p94*
Doull, David 38; Ontario, 1871 ***1823.15*** *p66*
Doull, William 32; Ontario, 1871 ***1823.22*** *p45*
Doumas, Geo 23; Juneau, Alaska, 1917 ***9196.1*** *p45*
Doumas, Geo 23; Whitehorse, Yukon, 1917 ***9196.1*** *p45*
Doupe, Henry 58; Ontario, 1871 ***1823.15*** *p66*
Dourille, Mrs.; Quebec, 1857 ***9196.15*** *p15*
Dourille, Taylor; Quebec, 1857 ***9196.15*** *p15*
Douslin, Richard 50; Ontario, 1871 ***1823.15*** *p66*
Douslin, Robert 51; Ontario, 1871 ***1823.15*** *p66*
Douty, Enoch; Maryland, 1667 ***2524.55*** *p70*
Wife: Mary
Relative: Joy
Douty, Joy *SEE* Douty, Enoch
Douty, Mary *SEE* Douty, Enoch
Douzabre, Jean Baptiste; New York, 1794 ***8197.10*** *p5*
Dovby, Thomas; Maryland, 1910 ***3259.35*** *p12*
Dove, Andrew 15; Maryland, 1775 ***1220.25*** *p114*
Dove, Elizabeth 73; Ontario, 1871 ***1823.22*** *p45*
Dove, Robert; Maryland, 1669 ***2524.55*** *p70*
Dove, William 24; Philadelphia, 1774 ***1220.25*** *p67*
Dover, John; Maryland, 1673 ***2524.55*** *p70*
Dover, John; New England, 1718 ***1224.2*** *p34*
Dover, Philip; Pennsylvania, 1777 ***4629.10*** *p10*
Dover, William; Virginia, 1706 ***1224.2*** *p34*
Doves, James 28; Virginia, 1774 ***1220.25*** *p94*
Dovrier, John 67; Ontario, 1871 ***1823.28*** *p24*
Dow, Alexander; Plymouth, Massachusetts, 1750 ***1224.2*** *p34*
Dow, Alexander Drysdale; Honolulu, 1876 ***1640.13*** *p32*
Dow, Edward; New York, 1840 ***8197.10*** *p159*
Dow, Elijah; Pennsylvania, 1777 ***4629.10*** *p7*
Dow, Henry; New York, 1802 ***8197.10*** *p20*
Dow, James; Pennsylvania, 1777 ***4629.10*** *p20*
Dow, James; West Indies, 1698 ***1640.13*** *p32*
Dow, John; New York, 1808 ***8197.10*** *p53*
Dow, Mary Ann 28; Ontario, 1871 ***1823.15*** *p66*
Dow, Robert; New Orleans, 1843 ***1640.10*** *p44*
Dowad, Ellenor 45; Ontario, 1871 ***1823.22*** *p45*
Dowager, Mrs. 72; Ontario, 1871 ***1823.15*** *p66*
Dowan, J.; Mississippi, 1800-1845 ***1640.10*** *p44*
Dowane, Margarett; Maryland, 1678 ***2524.55*** *p70*
Dowbjetzke, Martin; Maryland, 1910 ***3259.35*** *p12*
Dowd, Andrew 30; Vermont, 1884 ***5900.10*** *p603*
Dowd, Bridget; Vermont, 1829-1907 ***5900.10*** *p411*
Dowd, Bridget Murray; Vermont, 1838-1916 ***5900.10*** *p76*
Dowd, Dennis 54; Vermont, 1879 ***5900.10*** *p411*
Dowd, Elizabeth 22; Ontario, 1871 ***1823.22*** *p45*
Dowd, Ellen Clark 30; Vermont, 1850-1859 ***5900.10*** *p189*
Dowd, Emma 24; Vermont, 1874 ***5900.10*** *p189*
Dowd, Farrell 75; Vermont, 1873 ***5900.10*** *p608*
Dowd, Francis 20; Vermont, 1868 ***5900.10*** *p603*
Dowd, James; Vermont, 1825-1879 ***5900.10*** *p411*
Dowd, James H. 70; Vermont, 1934 ***5900.10*** *p107*
Dowd, John; New York, 1838 ***8197.10*** *p107*
Dowd, John C. 61; Vermont, 1916 ***5900.10*** *p107*
Dowd, John H. 30; Vermont, 1892 ***5900.10*** *p189*
Dowd, John J.; Vermont, 1835-1899 ***5900.10*** *p76*
Dowd, Katherine A. 67; Vermont, 1921 ***5900.10*** *p107*
Dowd, Margaret; Vermont, 1857-1939 ***5900.10*** *p411*
Dowd, Mary 20; New York, New York, 1848 ***1825.45*** *p33*
Dowd, Mary A. 76; Vermont, 1942 ***5900.10*** *p107*
Dowd, Mary Flanagan; Vermont, n.d. ***5900.10*** *p107*
Dowd, Mary Flannagan 70; Vermont, 1897 ***5900.10*** *p104*
Dowd, Mary McGinnis; Vermont, n.d. ***5900.10*** *p603*
Dowd, Patrick; New York, 1840 ***8197.10*** *p226*
Dowd, Patrick 57; Vermont, 1882 ***5900.10*** *p189*
Dowd, Patrick 61; Vermont, 1888 ***5900.10*** *p103*
Dowd, Patrick F. 24; Vermont, 1893 ***5900.10*** *p189*
Dowd, Peter; Vermont, 1861-1925 ***5900.10*** *p411*
Dowd, Thomas 13; Vermont, 1870 ***5900.10*** *p107*
Dowdale, James; Maryland, 1673 ***2524.55*** *p70*
Dowdel, Richard; Pennsylvania, 1777 ***4629.10*** *p19*
Dowden, Thomas 72; Ontario, 1871 ***1823.15*** *p66*
Dowding, George; New York, 1837 ***8197.10*** *p86*
Dowdney, John; New York, 1827 ***8197.10*** *p225*
Dowdney, John; Pennsylvania, 1779 ***4629.10*** *p37*
Dowe, Christopher; Maryland, 1673 ***2524.55*** *p70*
Dowe, Rich; Virginia, 1664 ***6212.30*** *p9*
Dowell, Francis 38; Ontario, 1871 ***1823.28*** *p24*
Dowell, M.; Quebec, 1857 ***9196.15*** *p15*
Dowenhime, John; Pennsylvania, 1777 ***4629.10*** *p28*
Dower, Conrad; Baltimore, 1840 ***6058.10*** *p34*
Dower, Ellen; Vermont, 1850-1920 ***5900.10*** *p174*
Dower, Hanora 76; Vermont, 1902 ***5900.10*** *p171*
Dower, Henry; Baltimore, 1840 ***6058.10*** *p25*
Dower, James N. 87; Vermont, 1904 ***5900.10*** *p411*
Dower, Kathleen Boyce; Vermont, 1883-1914 ***5900.10*** *p172*
Dower, Margaret 1; Vermont, 1859 ***5900.10*** *p171*
Dower, Margaret A.; Vermont, 1848-1923 ***5900.10*** *p452*
Dower, Mary 2; Vermont, 1864 ***5900.10*** *p171*
Dower, Mary Welch 63; Vermont, 1878 ***5900.10*** *p411*
Dower, Philip 73; Vermont, 1900 ***5900.10*** *p171*
Dowers, John; Pennsylvania, 1777 ***4629.10*** *p24*
Dowers, John; Pennsylvania, 1779 ***4629.10*** *p39*
Dowie, Henry; New York, 1829 ***8197.10*** *p351*
Dowis, William 30; Ontario, 1871 ***1823.28*** *p24*
Dowland, Mr.; Quebec, 1858 ***9196.15*** *p35*
Dowland, Anthony; Pennsylvania, 1785 ***4629.10*** *p48*
Dowland, William; Maryland, 1667 ***2524.55*** *p70*
Dowlar, Ezabella 44; Ontario, 1871 ***1823.28*** *p24*
D'Owleans, Albert M.; New York, 1839 ***8197.10*** *p226*
Dowler, John 41; Ontario, 1871 ***1823.28*** *p24*
Dowles, Richard 58; Ontario, 1871 ***1823.22*** *p45*
Dowlies, Sarah; Virginia, 1672 ***6212.30*** *p49*
Dowlin, Barbarah; Maryland, 1656 ***2524.55*** *p70*
Dowlin, Dennis 27; Virginia, 1774 ***1220.25*** *p90*
Dowlin, John; Maryland, 1663 ***2524.55*** *p70*
Dowlin, Patrick; Maryland, 1680 ***2524.55*** *p70*
Dowling, Charles 30; Maryland, 1775 ***1220.25*** *p99*
Dowling, Edward; Pennsylvania, 1777 ***4629.10*** *p11*
Dowling, John; Maryland, 1669 ***2524.55*** *p70*
Dowling, John 76; Ontario, 1871 ***1823.15*** *p66*
Dowling, Margaret 75; Ontario, 1871 ***1823.22*** *p45*
Dowling, Mary; Vermont, 1830-1893 ***5900.10*** *p85*
Dowling, Mary; Vermont, 1834-1911 ***5900.10*** *p423*
Dowling, Mary 66; Ontario, 1871 ***1823.15*** *p66*
Dowling, Mary 67; Vermont, 1876 ***5900.10*** *p287*
Dowling, Michael; New York, New York, 1850 ***6058.10*** *p54*
Dowling, Nancy; Vermont, 1840-1920 ***5900.10*** *p389*
Dowling, Patrick; Vermont, 1829-1904 ***5900.10*** *p423*
Dowling, Peter; New York, 1837 ***8197.10*** *p87*
Dowling, Richard 30; Ontario, 1871 ***1823.15*** *p66*
Dowly, James; Maryland, 1668 ***2524.55*** *p70*
Dowly, Jane; Maryland, 1664 ***2524.55*** *p70*
Dowman, Jno; Virginia, 1677 ***6212.30*** *p54*
Down, James 34; Ontario, 1871 ***1823.15*** *p66*
Down, Robert 40; Ontario, 1871 ***1823.28*** *p24*
Down, William 35; Ontario, 1871 ***1823.22*** *p45*
Down, William 43; Ontario, 1871 ***1823.15*** *p66*
Downe, Jas; Ontario, 1871 ***1823.22*** *p45*
Downe, Joane; Virginia, 1653 ***1224.1*** *p18*
Downe, William; Boston, 1753 ***1224.2*** *p34*
Downes, Mrs.; Maryland, 1665 ***2524.55*** *p70*
Downes, Bridget; Vermont, 1851-1912 ***5900.10*** *p274*
Downes, Catherine; Vermont, 1829-1901 ***5900.10*** *p258*
Downes, Daniell; Virginia, 1667 ***6212.30*** *p35*
Downes, James; Maryland, 1681 ***2524.55*** *p70*
Son: James, Jr.
Relative: Sarah
Downes, James 29; Virginia, 1774 ***1220.25*** *p46*
Downes, James, Jr. *SEE* Downes, James
Downes, John; New York, 1807 ***8197.10*** *p38*
Downes, John E.; Vermont, 1856-1886 ***5900.10*** *p258*
Downes, Katharine; Maryland, 1681 ***2524.55*** *p70*
Downes, Katie; Vermont, 1864-1892 ***5900.10*** *p258*
Downes, Mary L. 20; Vermont, 1871 ***5900.10*** *p258*
Downes, Patrick H.; Vermont, 1847-1902 ***5900.10*** *p274*
Downes, Sarah *SEE* Downes, James
Downes, Thomas B.; Vermont, 1857-1885 ***5900.10*** *p258*
Downes, Thomas J.; Vermont, 1817-1885 ***5900.10*** *p258*
Downes, William; Maryland, 1677 ***2524.55*** *p70*
Downes, William 22; New York, 1774 ***1220.25*** *p26*
Downey, Ann; Vermont, 1817-1872 ***5900.10*** *p267*
Downey, Bridget 33; Vermont, 1868 ***5900.10*** *p185*
Downey, Bryan 34; Ontario, 1871 ***1823.15*** *p66*
Downey, David 19; Ontario, 1861 ***2896.25*** *p38*
Downey, Edward J. 11; Ontario, 1861 ***2896.27*** *p45*
Downey, Eliza Casey; Vermont, 1817-1872 ***5900.10*** *p71*
Downey, Francis P. 5; Ontario, 1861 ***2896.27*** *p45*
Downey, Hattie M. Ashley; Vermont, 1848-1914 ***5900.10*** *p495*
Downey, Helen 78; Vermont, 1897 ***5900.10*** *p583*
Downey, Henry 58; Ontario, 1871 ***1823.22*** *p45*
Downey, Hiram 67; Ontario, 1871 ***1823.22*** *p45*
Downey, James 49; Ontario, 1871 ***1823.28*** *p24*
Downey, James 57; Ontario, 1871 ***1823.15*** *p67*
Downey, Joannah 10; Ontario, 1861 ***2896.27*** *p45*
Downey, John; New York, 1802 ***8197.10*** *p20*
Downey, John; New York, 1840 ***8197.10*** *p158*
Downey, John; Pennsylvania, 1781 ***4629.10*** *p42*
Downey, John 22; Ontario, 1871 ***1823.28*** *p24*
Downey, John 30; Ontario, 1871 ***1823.15*** *p67*
Downey, Louisa 7; Ontario, 1861 ***2896.27*** *p45*
Downey, Margaret; Vermont, 1837-1910 ***5900.10*** *p185*
Downey, Margaret; Died enroute, 1849 ***1224.3*** *p23*
Downey, Marshall H.; Vermont, 1843-1916 ***5900.10*** *p495*
Downey, Mary; Died enroute, 1849 ***1224.3*** *p23*
Downey, Mary 16; Ontario, 1861 ***2896.27*** *p45*
Downey, Mary 73; Ontario, 1871 ***1823.15*** *p67*
Downey, Mary E. 54; Vermont, 1904 ***5900.10*** *p496*
Downey, Mercilla 13; Ontario, 1861 ***2896.27*** *p45*
Downey, Micle 9; Ontario, 1861 ***2896.27*** *p45*
Downey, Mortimer; Vermont, n.d. ***5900.10*** *p337*
Downey, Patrick; Vermont, 1806-1881 ***5900.10*** *p267*
Downey, Patrick 43; Ontario, 1861 ***2896.27*** *p45*
Downey, Russel B.; Vermont, 1814-1859 ***5900.10*** *p71*
Downey, Samuel 30; Ontario, 1871 ***1823.28*** *p24*
Downey, Stephen 39; Ontario, 1871 ***1823.15*** *p67*
Downey, Thomas 42; Ontario, 1871 ***1823.15*** *p67*
Downey, Thomas 62; Ontario, 1871 ***1823.28*** *p24*
Downey, Timothy 2; Ontario, 1861 ***2896.27*** *p45*
Downey, William 64; Vermont, 1852 ***5900.10*** *p228*
Downie, David; Augusta, Georgia, 1796 ***1640.10*** *p44*
Downie, Elizabeth 61; Ontario, 1871 ***1823.15*** *p67*
Downie, George 65; Ontario, 1871 ***1823.15*** *p67*
Downie, James; Georgia, 1698 ***1640.13*** *p32*
Downing, Jacob; Pennsylvania, 1776 ***4629.10*** *p52*
Downing, James 20; Tortola, 1774 ***1220.25*** *p85*
Downing, Mary; Maryland, 1670 ***2524.55*** *p70*
Downing, William 33; Ontario, 1871 ***1823.15*** *p67*
Downing, William 37; Ontario, 1871 ***1823.22*** *p45*
Downman, Ellen Chichester; Virginia, 1763 ***1224.2*** *p35*
Downman, Frances; Virginia, 1782 ***1224.2*** *p35*
Downman, Rawleigh; Virginia, 1782 ***1224.2*** *p35*
Downs, Anna; Vermont, 1855-1928 ***5900.10*** *p272*
Downs, Bridget Brown; Vermont, 1846-1915 ***5900.10*** *p180*
Downs, Catherine 69; Vermont, 1894 ***5900.10*** *p129*
Downs, Hanora; Vermont, 1820-1893 ***5900.10*** *p159*
Downs, James 32; Ontario, 1871 ***1823.22*** *p45*
Downs, James 53; Ontario, 1871 ***1823.22*** *p45*
Downs, John; Philadelphia, 1793 ***4629.10*** *p77*
Downs, John 43; Ontario, 1871 ***1823.22*** *p45*
Downs, John 58; Ontario, 1871 ***1823.22*** *p45*
Downs, Joseph 22; Ontario, 1871 ***1823.22*** *p45*
Downs, Mary Ann 79; Vermont, 1898 ***5900.10*** *p224*
Downs, Michael 68; Vermont, 1907 ***5900.10*** *p352*
Downs, Patrick; Vermont, 1837-1916 ***5900.10*** *p180*

Downs, Patrick 53; Ontario, 1871 ***1823.22*** *p45*
Downs, Patrick 81; Ontario, 1861 ***2896.25*** *p15*
Downs, Robert 38; Ontario, 1871 ***1823.15*** *p67*
Downs, Sabina E.; Vermont, 1836-1908 ***5900.10*** *p155*
Downs, Sophie; Maryland, 1910 ***3259.35*** *p12*
Downs, Thomas 20; Vermont, 1865 ***5900.10*** *p262*
Downs, William 26; Ontario, 1871 ***1823.15*** *p67*
Dowring, John; Maryland, 1664 ***2524.55*** *p70*
Dowry, Mr.; Quebec, 1857 ***9196.15*** *p15*
Dows, Mr.; Quebec, 1857 ***9196.15*** *p27*
Dows, Mrs.; Quebec, 1857 ***9196.15*** *p27*
Dowsett, George; New York, 1840 ***8197.10*** *p158*
Dowsing, Ann; New York, 1825 ***1224.3*** *p23*
Dowsing, Jeremiah 30; Philadelphia, 1775 ***1220.25*** *p122*
Dowsley, Martin 58; Ontario, 1871 ***1823.28*** *p24*
Dowsley, Samuel 30; Ontario, 1871 ***1823.28*** *p25*
Dowson, Ellen C. 58; Ontario, 1871 ***1823.28*** *p25*
Dowson, George 16; Philadelphia, 1774 ***1220.25*** *p80*
Dowswell, A. H. 61; Ontario, 1871 ***1823.28*** *p25*
Dowsy, Jane; Maryland, 1664 ***2524.55*** *p70*
Dowty, Enoch; Maryland, 1667 ***2524.55*** *p70*
Wife: Mary
Relative: Joy
Dowty, Jove; Maryland, 1663 ***2524.55*** *p70*
Dowty, Joy *SEE* Dowty, Enoch
Dowty, Mary *SEE* Dowty, Enoch
Doxee, Hiram 41; Ontario, 1871 ***1823.22*** *p45*
Doxey, Ann; Maryland, 1669 ***2524.55*** *p70*
Doxey, Thomas; Maryland, 1669 ***2524.55*** *p70*
Doxsee, John 52; Ontario, 1871 ***1823.22*** *p45*
Doxtater, John 76; Ontario, 1871 ***1823.22*** *p45*
Doyas, John L.; Maryland, 1910 ***3259.35*** *p12*
Doyemoke, John; Maryland, 1910 ***3259.35*** *p13*
Doyl, Patrick 40; Ontario, 1871 ***1823.22*** *p45*
Doyle, Mrs. 55; Ontario, 1871 ***1823.28*** *p25*
Doyle, A. 29; Ontario, 1861 ***2896.28*** *p2*
Doyle, A. E.; Vermont, n.d. ***5900.10*** *p333*
Doyle, Ann Mullen; Vermont, 1833-1904 ***5900.10*** *p476*
Doyle, Anna; New York, 1830 ***8197.10*** *p363*
Doyle, Anne 50; Ontario, 1871 ***1823.15*** *p67*
Doyle, Barney M.; New York, 1837 ***8197.10*** *p375*
Doyle, Bartholomew; New York, 1837 ***8197.10*** *p86*
Doyle, Bridget; Vermont, 1830-1914 ***5900.10*** *p103*
Doyle, Bridget; Vermont, 1843-1905 ***5900.10*** *p201*
Doyle, Bridget 31; Vermont, 1849 ***5900.10*** *p612*
Doyle, Bridget Kendy 83; Vermont, 1872 ***5900.10*** *p109*
Doyle, Bridget Reynolds 35; Vermont, 1874 ***5900.10*** *p538*
Doyle, Catherine; Vermont, 1855-1930 ***5900.10*** *p221*
Doyle, Catherine; Vermont, 1857-1931 ***5900.10*** *p60*
Doyle, Catherine 22; Ontario, 1871 ***1823.22*** *p45*
Doyle, Catherine 52; Vermont, 1880 ***5900.10*** *p270*
Doyle, Catherine 65; Vermont, 1918 ***5900.10*** *p102*
Doyle, Catherine O'Brine; Vermont, 1840-1934 ***5900.10*** *p269*
Doyle, Cathrine; Vermont, 1875 ***5900.10*** *p482*
Doyle, Celia; Vermont, 1833-1904 ***5900.10*** *p476*
Doyle, Cornelius; Vermont, 1857-1917 ***5900.10*** *p60*
Doyle, Cornellis 64; Ontario, 1871 ***1823.15*** *p67*
Doyle, Daniel 23; Philadelphia, 1789 ***4629.10*** *p58*
Doyle, Daniel 33; Ontario, 1871 ***1823.22*** *p45*
Doyle, Delia 28; Ontario, 1871 ***1823.22*** *p45*
Doyle, Denis 40; Ontario, 1871 ***1823.28*** *p25*
Doyle, Denis 70; Ontario, 1871 ***1823.28*** *p25*
Doyle, Dennis; New York, 1804 ***8197.10*** *p26*
Doyle, Dennis; New York, 1807 ***8197.10*** *p38*
Doyle, Dennis; Philadelphia, 1789 ***4629.10*** *p58*
Wife: Sarah
Doyle, Dennis, Jr.; New York, 1818 ***8197.10*** *p221*
Doyle, Edward; New York, 1816 ***8197.10*** *p221*
Doyle, Edward; Vermont, 1841-1890 ***5900.10*** *p476*
Doyle, Elizabeth G. Fleming; Vermont, 1863-1939 ***5900.10*** *p403*
Doyle, Ellen; Vermont, 1839-1916 ***5900.10*** *p433*
Doyle, Ellen 57; Vermont, 1884 ***5900.10*** *p105*
Doyle, Ellon 66; Ontario, 1871 ***1823.15*** *p67*
Doyle, Elmore B.; Vermont, 1857-1947 ***5900.10*** *p403*
Doyle, Ethel P.; Vermont, 1876 ***5900.10*** *p308*
Doyle, F. L.; Vermont, 1856-1904 ***5900.10*** *p47*
Doyle, Henry 34; Ontario, 1871 ***1823.15*** *p67*
Doyle, Henry 40; Ontario, 1871 ***1823.22*** *p46*
Doyle, Honora 35; Vermont, 1878 ***5900.10*** *p138*
Doyle, James; New York, 1834 ***8197.10*** *p315*
Doyle, James; New York, 1836 ***8197.10*** *p78*
Doyle, James 28; Virginia, 1774 ***1220.25*** *p93*
Doyle, James 46; Ontario, 1871 ***1823.22*** *p46*
Doyle, James 65; Ontario, 1871 ***1823.28*** *p25*
Doyle, James 66; Vermont, 1892 ***5900.10*** *p77*
Doyle, James E.; Vermont, 1857-1946 ***5900.10*** *p308*
Doyle, Jno 31; Ontario, 1861 ***2896.28*** *p2*
Doyle, John; New York, 1821 ***8197.10*** *p223*
Doyle, John; Vermont, 1845-1930 ***5900.10*** *p221*
Doyle, John 18; Vermont, 1868 ***5900.10*** *p113*
Doyle, John 41; Vermont, 1869 ***5900.10*** *p261*
Doyle, John 46; Vermont, 1886 ***5900.10*** *p141*
Doyle, John 59; Ontario, 1871 ***1823.28*** *p25*
Doyle, John 80; Ontario, 1871 ***1823.22*** *p46*
Doyle, Joseph 24; Philadelphia, 1774 ***1220.25*** *p81*
Doyle, Joseph 30; Ontario, 1871 ***1823.28*** *p25*
Doyle, Joseph 42; Vermont, 1885 ***5900.10*** *p497*
Doyle, Kate Carmody; Vermont, 1817-1900 ***5900.10*** *p113*
Doyle, M. J.; Vermont, n.d. ***5900.10*** *p333*
Doyle, Margaret 51; Vermont, 1892 ***5900.10*** *p130*
Doyle, Margaret 69; Vermont, 1888 ***5900.10*** *p261*
Doyle, Margaret Mahan 78; Vermont, 1905 ***5900.10*** *p78*
Doyle, Martin; Vermont, 1823-1901 ***5900.10*** *p486*
Doyle, Martin 22; Virginia, 1774 ***1220.25*** *p93*
Doyle, Martin 27; Ontario, 1861 ***2896.27*** *p40*
Doyle, Mary; Vermont, 1817-1896 ***5900.10*** *p504*
Doyle, Mary; Vermont, 1825-1905 ***5900.10*** *p479*
Doyle, Mary; Vermont, 1825-1913 ***5900.10*** *p302*
Doyle, Mary; Vermont, 1831-1909 ***5900.10*** *p368*
Doyle, Mary; Vermont, 1833-1890 ***5900.10*** *p86*
Doyle, Mary; Vermont, 1855-1919 ***5900.10*** *p495*
Doyle, Mary 25; Ontario, 1871 ***1823.15*** *p67*
Doyle, Mary 40; Ontario, 1871 ***1823.22*** *p46*
Doyle, Mary 43; Vermont, 1847 ***5900.10*** *p610*
Doyle, Mary 55; Vermont, 1887 ***5900.10*** *p86*
Doyle, Mary C.; Vermont, 1848-1913 ***5900.10*** *p410*
Doyle, Mary E.; Vermont, 1867-1948 ***5900.10*** *p472*
Doyle, Mary E. 19; Vermont, 1890 ***5900.10*** *p221*
Doyle, Mary McGrath; Vermont, 1850-1895 ***5900.10*** *p604*
Doyle, Michael; Vermont, 1816-1864 ***5900.10*** *p368*
Doyle, Michael; Vermont, 1833-1909 ***5900.10*** *p88*
Doyle, Morace 50; Ontario, 1871 ***1823.28*** *p25*
Doyle, Nora C.; Vermont, 1864-1916 ***5900.10*** *p119*
Doyle, Owen 42; Ontario, 1871 ***1823.15*** *p67*
Doyle, Patrick; New York, 1840 ***8197.10*** *p157*
Doyle, Patrick; Vermont, 1843-1911 ***5900.10*** *p604*
Doyle, Patrick 45; Vermont, 1875 ***5900.10*** *p105*
Doyle, Patrick 50; Ontario, 1871 ***1823.15*** *p67*
Doyle, Patrick 58; Ontario, 1871 ***1823.15*** *p67*
Doyle, Patrick 65; Ontario, 1871 ***1823.22*** *p46*
Doyle, Philip; New York, 1823 ***8197.10*** *p224*
Doyle, Robert; New York, 1816 ***8197.10*** *p221*
Doyle, Rose McBride; Vermont, 1825-1892 ***5900.10*** *p486*
Doyle, Sarah *SEE* Doyle, Dennis
Doyle, Sarah M. 24; Vermont, 1877 ***5900.10*** *p261*
Doyle, Simon; Quebec, 1818 ***6058.10*** *p39*
Doyle, Thomas; New York, 1821 ***8197.10*** *p222*
Doyle, Thomas; New York, 1837 ***8197.10*** *p86*
Doyle, Thomas 19; Vermont, 1874 ***5900.10*** *p538*
Doyle, Thomas 22; Virginia, 1774 ***1220.25*** *p88*
Doyle, Thomas 32; Ontario, 1871 ***1823.22*** *p46*
Doyle, Timothy; New York, 1840 ***8197.10*** *p156*
Doyle, William 52; Ontario, 1871 ***1823.15*** *p67*
Doyle, William 70; Ontario, 1871 ***1823.22*** *p46*
Doyley, Cope, Sr.; Virginia, 1706 ***1224.2*** *p35*
Doyley, Cope, Jr.; Virginia, 1713 ***1224.2*** *p35*
Doyley, James 26; Maryland, 1775 ***1220.25*** *p97*
Doyley, Robt.; Maryland, 1657 ***2524.55*** *p70*
D'Ozeville, Lewis; New York, 1830 ***8197.10*** *p360*
Drabwell, Charles 29; Maryland, 1775 ***1220.25*** *p110*
Drach, Miss; America, 1788 ***2856.30*** *p86*
Drach, Miss; Port uncertain, 1748 ***2856.30*** *p86*
Drach, Elisabeth; Port uncertain, 1732 ***2856.30*** *p86*
With husband
Drach, Rudolf; America, 1749 ***2856.30*** *p86*
Drachin, Anna Catharina; Port uncertain, 1764 ***2856.30*** *p86*
Dradge, John 24; Philadelphia, 1774 ***1220.25*** *p35*
Dragor, August 28; Ontario, 1871 ***1823.28*** *p25*
Dragor, Fredrica 67; Ontario, 1871 ***1823.28*** *p25*
Drahmer, Paul; England, 1768 ***2856.30*** *p86*
Drain, James 43; Ontario, 1871 ***1823.22*** *p46*
Drainey, George 33; Ontario, 1871 ***1823.15*** *p67*
Drais, Daniel; Pennsylvania, 1777 ***4629.10*** *p14*
Drake, Ann; Maryland, 1682 ***2524.55*** *p70*
Drake, Charles; New York, 1838 ***8197.10*** *p108*
Drake, David; New York, 1825 ***8197.10*** *p222*
Drake, Enoch 64; Ontario, 1871 ***1823.22*** *p46*
Drake, George 26; Ontario, 1871 ***1823.15*** *p67*
Drake, James; Maryland, 1682 ***2524.55*** *p71*
Drake, Joseph 54; Ontario, 1871 ***1823.15*** *p67*
Drake, Mary E. Fitzpatrick; Vermont, 1865-1939 ***5900.10*** *p387*
Drake, Robert Henry; Vermont, 1847-1929 ***5900.10*** *p387*
Drake, William; Maryland, 1677 ***2524.55*** *p71*
Drake, William; Pennsylvania, 1786 ***4629.10*** *p55*
Drake, Winifred; Maryland, 1677 ***2524.55*** *p71*
Drakula, Petra 37; British Columbia, 1912 ***9196.1*** *p17*
Drakula, Petra 37; California, 1912 ***9196.1*** *p17*
Drandower, Nogweek; Maryland, 1910 ***3259.35*** *p13*
Draney, Alexander 31; Ontario, 1871 ***1823.15*** *p67*
Draney, Andrew 40; Ontario, 1871 ***1823.15*** *p67*
Draney, Henery 74; Ontario, 1871 ***1823.15*** *p67*
Drankliwez, Kate; Maryland, 1910 ***3259.35*** *p13*
Draper, . . .; Boston, 1765 ***4628.40*** *p114*
Draper, Mr.; Quebec, 1858 ***9196.15*** *p34*
Draper, Alexander; Maryland, 1663 ***2524.55*** *p71*
Wife: Catherine
Draper, Anne; Virginia, 1671 ***6212.30*** *p44*
Draper, Catherine *SEE* Draper, Alexander
Draper, Elizabeth 26; Baltimore, 1775 ***1220.25*** *p119*
Draper, George 33; Ontario, 1871 ***1823.15*** *p67*
Draper, James; Virginia, 1664 ***6212.30*** *p11*
Draper, Jno; Virginia, 1664 ***6212.30*** *p9*
Draper, Jno; Virginia, 1664 ***6212.30*** *p12*
Draper, Jno; Virginia, 1667-1668 ***6212.30*** *p38*
Draper, Lewis; Maryland, 1666 ***2524.55*** *p71*
Draper, Ralph; Maryland, 1681 ***2524.55*** *p71*
Draper, Roger; Virginia, 1665-1666 ***6212.30*** *p25*
Draper, Thomas 22; Virginia, 1773 ***1220.25*** *p28*
Draper, William; Maryland, 1666 ***2524.55*** *p71*
Draper, William; New York, 1838 ***8197.10*** *p377*
Draper, William 26; Ontario, 1871 ***1823.15*** *p67*
Drapezynski, Alexander; Maryland, 1910 ***3259.35*** *p13*
Draton, Walter; Maryland, 1661 ***2524.55*** *p71*
Drawyer, John; New York, 1840 ***8197.10*** *p158*
Draxel, Johann; America, 1737 ***2856.30*** *p86*
With wife & children
Draxel, Johann; America, 1737 ***2856.30*** *p86*
Drayer, Johann; America, 1738 ***2856.30*** *p86*
Draysey, Thomas 15; Philadelphia, 1775 ***1220.25*** *p8*
Drayton, Mr.; Quebec, 1858 ***9196.15*** *p44*
Drayton, Mrs.; Quebec, 1858 ***9196.15*** *p44*
Dreast, Samuel 50; Ontario, 1871 ***1823.15*** *p67*
Dredzinsky, Eva; Maryland, 1910 ***3259.35*** *p13*
Drega, Frank; Maryland, 1910 ***3259.35*** *p13*
Drega, Sigmund; Maryland, 1910 ***3259.35*** *p13*
Dregas, Devorax; Maryland, 1680 ***2524.55*** *p71*
Dreghorn, Robert; Savannah, Georgia, 1823 ***1640.10*** *p44*
Drehen, Anna 59; Kansas, 1876-1910 ***9079.10*** *p8*
Drehen, John 62; Kansas, 1876-1910 ***9079.10*** *p8*
Dreher, A. Marg. *SEE* Dreher, Johann
Dreher, Anna Elisabeth; Port uncertain, 1792 ***2856.30*** *p86*
Dreher, Apollonia; America, 1764 ***2856.30*** *p86*
With 4 daughters
Dreher, Elisabeth; Port uncertain, 1750 ***2856.30*** *p86*
Dreher, Johan; America, 1738 ***2856.30*** *p86*
Dreher, Johann; America, 1738 ***2856.30*** *p86*
Dreher, Johann; America, 1764 ***2856.30*** *p86*
Wife: A. Marg.
With 5 children
Dreher, Johann Georg; Port uncertain, 1774 ***2856.30*** *p86*
Dreher, Margarete; America, 1754 ***2856.30*** *p86*
Dreher, Maria Elisabeth; Port uncertain, 1788 ***2856.30*** *p86*
Dreher, Petronella Loscher; America, 1764 ***2856.30*** *p86*
Dreier, A. Marg. Juliana; Port uncertain, 1784 ***2856.30*** *p86*
Drenan, James; New York, 1838 ***8197.10*** *p226*
Drennan, George 41; Ontario, 1871 ***1823.15*** *p67*
Drennan, James; New York, 1840 ***8197.10*** *p158*
Drennan, James 43; Ontario, 1871 ***1823.15*** *p67*
Drennan, Jenett 78; Ontario, 1871 ***1823.15*** *p67*
Drennan, John; New York, 1802 ***8197.10*** *p20*
Drennan, John 39; Ontario, 1871 ***1823.15*** *p67*
Drennon, Andrew; New York, 1807 ***8197.10*** *p327*
Drenry, William; Pennsylvania, 1777 ***4629.10*** *p11*
Drerubuski, Walter; Maryland, 1910 ***3259.35*** *p13*
Dres, Christina; Port uncertain, 1751 ***2856.30*** *p86*
Drescher, Mrs. Friedrich; Port uncertain, 1754 ***2856.30*** *p86*
Drescher, Philipp; America, 1743 ***2856.30*** *p86*
Dresel, Friederich; New York, 1821 ***8197.10*** *p223*
Dresky, William; Pennsylvania, 1788 ***4629.10*** *p56*
Drespack, Henry; New York, 1840 ***8197.10*** *p158*
Dress, Valentin; America, 1747 ***2856.30*** *p87*
Dressler, Georg; Port uncertain, 1761 ***2856.30*** *p86*
Dressler, Johann Gotthard; Port uncertain, 1741 ***2856.30*** *p86*
Dressler, Therese; Port uncertain, 1780 ***2856.30*** *p86*
Drether, . . .; Port uncertain, 1773 ***2856.30*** *p86*
Dreusch, Jakob; Port uncertain, 1757 ***2856.30*** *p86*
Drew, Alfred 25; Ontario, 1871 ***1823.15*** *p67*
Drew, Catherine; Vermont, 1847-1915 ***5900.10*** *p90*
Drew, Edred 34; Ontario, 1871 ***1823.15*** *p67*
Drew, Edward; New York, 1821 ***8197.10*** *p222*
Drew, Francis; Virginia, 1666 ***6212.30*** *p30*
Drew, James; New York, New York, 1803 ***1224.3*** *p23*
Drew, John 29; Ontario, 1871 ***1823.15*** *p67*
Drew, William 43; Ontario, 1871 ***1823.15*** *p67*
Drew, William Carfrae; Denver, Colorado, 1894 ***1640.13*** *p32*
Drewe, Emanuel; Maryland, 1659 ***2524.55*** *p71*

Drewe, Hugh; Maryland, 1659 ***2524.55*** *p71*
Drewery, Charles 28; Ontario, 1861 ***2896.25*** *p71*
Drewery, H. 16; Ontario, 1861 ***2896.28*** *p5*
Drewery, W. M. 44; Ontario, 1861 ***2896.28*** *p5*
Drewing, George 72; Ontario, 1871 ***1823.22*** *p46*
Drexhagen, Jane Medland; New York, New York, 1856 ***1224.3*** *p23*
Drey, Andreas; America, 1740 ***2856.30*** *p86*
With wife & children
Drey, Andreas; America, 1741 ***2856.30*** *p76*
Drey, Andreas; America, 1741 ***2856.30*** *p78*
Drey, Andreas; America, 1742 ***2856.30*** *p78*
Dreycott, Thomas 45; Ontario, 1871 ***1823.28*** *p25*
Dreyer, Lorenz; Port uncertain, 1725 ***2856.30*** *p86*
Dreyer, Lorenz; Port uncertain, 1765 ***2856.30*** *p86*
Dreyfelcher, Carl; New York, 1840 ***8197.10*** *p156*
Dricker, Hans Michael; Port uncertain, 1749 ***2856.30*** *p86*
Driffill, John; South Carolina, 1797 ***1224.2*** *p35*
Drigas, Devorax; Maryland, 1677 ***2524.55*** *p71*
Driminuell, William; Maryland, 1674 ***2524.55*** *p71*
Dring, Mathias; Maryland, 1671 ***2524.55*** *p71*
Dring, Stephen; Virginia, 1675 ***1224.1*** *p19*
Dringe, Mathias; Maryland, 1671 ***2524.55*** *p71*
Drinker, John; Pennsylvania, 1777 ***4629.10*** *p14*
Drinkle, John; Maryland, 1671 ***2524.55*** *p71*
Drinkwater, Abagail 29; Ontario, 1861 ***2896.27*** *p50*
Drinkwater, Elizy G. 4; Ontario, 1861 ***2896.27*** *p50*
Drinkwater, George E. 2; Ontario, 1861 ***2896.27*** *p50*
Drinkwater, Matthew; New York, 1840 ***8197.10*** *p226*
Drinkwater, William A. 7; Ontario, 1861 ***2896.27*** *p50*
Drinnan, James 34; Ontario, 1871 ***1823.28*** *p25*
Drinnen, Catherine 75; Ontario, 1871 ***1823.22*** *p46*
Driscol, M. 66; Vermont, 1868 ***5900.10*** *p64*
Driscoll, Addie M. Foster; Vermont, n.d. ***5900.10*** *p244*
Driscoll, Bridget Agnes; Vermont, 1862-1898 ***5900.10*** *p68*
Driscoll, Bridget Drum 82; Vermont, 1899 ***5900.10*** *p483*
Driscoll, Bridget S.; Vermont, 1846-1926 ***5900.10*** *p490*
Driscoll, Catharine 61; Vermont, 1872 ***5900.10*** *p473*
Driscoll, Catherine Dalton; Vermont, 1842-1932 ***5900.10*** *p542*
Driscoll, Catherine Griffin 35; Vermont, 1856 ***5900.10*** *p58*
Driscoll, Cornelius; New Hampshire, 1710 ***4628.40*** *p44*
Driscoll, Cornelius; New York, 1837 ***8197.10*** *p83*
Driscoll, Daniel; Canada, 1756-1760 ***4628.40*** *p45*
Driscoll, Daniel; Canada, 1756-1760 ***4628.40*** *p46*
Driscoll, Dennis A.; Vermont, 1857-1935 ***5900.10*** *p589*
Driscoll, Edward; Vermont, 1849-1949 ***5900.10*** *p394*
Driscoll, Edward; Vermont, 1918 ***5900.10*** *p394*
Driscoll, Edward 27; Ontario, 1871 ***1823.15*** *p67*
Driscoll, Ella; Vermont, 1850-1933 ***5900.10*** *p243*
Driscoll, Ellen 42; Vermont, 1864 ***5900.10*** *p233*
Driscoll, Ellen 65; Vermont, 1886 ***5900.10*** *p250*
Driscoll, Ellen Ryan; Vermont, 1831-1914 ***5900.10*** *p473*
Driscoll, Florence; Maryland, 1674 ***2524.55*** *p71*
Driscoll, Hannah; Vermont, 1832-1924 ***5900.10*** *p607*
Driscoll, Hannah; Vermont, 1855-1914 ***5900.10*** *p70*
Driscoll, James Francis; Vermont, n.d. ***5900.10*** *p397*
Driscoll, Jane Brennan; Vermont, n.d. ***5900.10*** *p397*
Driscoll, Jeremiah; New York, 1821 ***8197.10*** *p223*
Driscoll, Joan; Vermont, n.d. ***5900.10*** *p398*
Driscoll, Johanna McCarty 62; Vermont, 1890 ***5900.10*** *p476*
Driscoll, John; Canada, 1756-1760 ***4628.40*** *p45*
Driscoll, John; New Hampshire, 1710 ***4628.40*** *p44*
Driscoll, John; New York, 1837 ***8197.10*** *p86*
Driscoll, John; Vermont, n.d. ***5900.10*** *p397*
Driscoll, John; Vermont, 1827-1920 ***5900.10*** *p542*
Driscoll, John; Vermont, 1856-1910 ***5900.10*** *p243*
Driscoll, John; Vermont, 1907 ***5900.10*** *p482*
Driscoll, John 30; Ontario, 1871 ***1823.15*** *p67*
Driscoll, John G. 56; Vermont, 1880 ***5900.10*** *p473*
Driscoll, Kate; Vermont, 1842-1922 ***5900.10*** *p585*
Driscoll, Margaret McNamara; Vermont, 1845-1909 ***5900.10*** *p589*
Driscoll, Martin 52; Vermont, 1887 ***5900.10*** *p396*
Driscoll, Martin Richard; Vermont, n.d. ***5900.10*** *p398*
Driscoll, Mary; Vermont, n.d. ***5900.10*** *p398*
Driscoll, Mary; Vermont, 1812-1890 ***5900.10*** *p393*
Driscoll, Mary; Vermont, 1831-1914 ***5900.10*** *p403*
Driscoll, Mary; Vermont, 1855-1928 ***5900.10*** *p71*
Driscoll, Mary; Vermont, 1886 ***5900.10*** *p53*
Driscoll, Mary Ann Cross; Vermont, 1846-1946 ***5900.10*** *p394*
Driscoll, Mary J.; Vermont, 1851-1927 ***5900.10*** *p243*
Driscoll, Mary Kiely; Vermont, 1852-1933 ***5900.10*** *p397*
Driscoll, Mary Ryan; Vermont, 1838-1907 ***5900.10*** *p243*
Driscoll, Matilda J. Spaulding; Vermont, n.d. ***5900.10*** *p244*
Driscoll, Michael 57; Vermont, 1884 ***5900.10*** *p476*
Driscoll, Nellie; Vermont, 1861-1882 ***5900.10*** *p243*
Driscoll, Patrick; Pennsylvania, 1868 ***6058.10*** *p72*
Driscoll, Patrick; Vermont, 1820-1912 ***5900.10*** *p243*
Driscoll, Peter; Canada, 1756-1760 ***4628.40*** *p46*
Driscoll, Sarah; Vermont, 1856-1925 ***5900.10*** *p243*
Driscoll, Susan 60; Ontario, 1871 ***1823.15*** *p67*
Driscoll, Thomas 44; Vermont, 1886 ***5900.10*** *p53*
Driscoll, Timothy 97; Vermont, 1901 ***5900.10*** *p483*
Driscoll, William; Vermont, n.d. ***5900.10*** *p398*
Driscoll, William 31; Vermont, 1864 ***5900.10*** *p473*
Driscoll, William Alexander 5 months; Vermont, 1855 ***5900.10*** *p498*
Driscoll, William H.; Vermont, n.d. ***5900.10*** *p244*
Drisdale, Alexander 19; Philadelphia, 1774 ***1220.25*** *p44*
Drislane, Bridget Agnes Driscoll; Vermont, 1862-1898 ***5900.10*** *p68*
Drislane, Dennis; Vermont, 1832-1892 ***5900.10*** *p422*
Drislane, Dennis D.; Vermont, 1830-1918 ***5900.10*** *p68*
Drislane, Ellen 76; Vermont, 1912 ***5900.10*** *p426*
Drislane, Hanora; Vermont, 1832-1922 ***5900.10*** *p422*
Drislane, Johanna Roche; Vermont, 1835-1897 ***5900.10*** *p68*
Drislane, John J.; Vermont, 1856-1937 ***5900.10*** *p68*
Drislane, Margaret O'Connor; Vermont, 1836-1909 ***5900.10*** *p58*
Drislane, Mary 89; Vermont, 1908 ***5900.10*** *p55*
Drislane, Patrick; Vermont, 1832-1906 ***5900.10*** *p58*
Drislawn, James 76; Vermont, 1902 ***5900.10*** *p57*
Drislawn, Mary Collins 62; Vermont, 1895 ***5900.10*** *p57*
Drisler, Henry; New York, 1823 ***8197.10*** *p222*
Driss, Ms.; Quebec, 1856 ***9196.15*** *p8*
Dristle, William 34; Ontario, 1861 ***2896.27*** *p22*
Driver, Edward 19; Maryland, 1774 ***1220.25*** *p72*
Driver, George 31; Ontario, 1871 ***1823.15*** *p67*
Driver, Joseph; Maryland, 1677-1681 ***2524.55*** *p71*
Driver, Joseph 23; Ontario, 1871 ***1823.15*** *p67*
Driver, Joseph 35; Ontario, 1871 ***1823.15*** *p67*
Driver, Joseph 67; Ontario, 1871 ***1823.15*** *p67*
Driver, Thomas; Salem, Massachusetts, 1800 ***1224.3*** *p23*
Driver, Thomas 26; Georgia, 1774 ***1220.25*** *p48*
Driver, Thomas 65; Ontario, 1871 ***1823.15*** *p68*
Driver, William; Virginia, 1681 ***1224.1*** *p19*
Driver, William 39; Ontario, 1871 ***1823.15*** *p68*
Drohan, Robert 24; Ontario, 1871 ***1823.28*** *p25*
Droll, A. M. Elis. *SEE* Droll, Sigmund Friedri
Droll., Margarete; America, 1743 ***2856.30*** *p278*
Droll, Michael; Port uncertain, 1790 ***2856.30*** *p87*
Droll, Sigmund Friedri; America, 1737 ***2856.30*** *p87*
Wife: A. M. Elis.
Drolling, Margarete; America, 1743 ***2856.30*** *p278*
Drollinger, Miss; America, 1744 ***2856.30*** *p87*
Drollinger, Adam; America, 1738 ***2856.30*** *p87*
Drollinger, Adam; Port uncertain, 1737 ***2856.30*** *p87*
Drollinger, Eberhard; America, 1738 ***2856.30*** *p87*
Drollinger, Eberhard; Port uncertain, 1737 ***2856.30*** *p87*
Drollinger, Gabriel; America, 1743 ***2856.30*** *p87*
Drollinger, Hans Michael; America, 1740 ***2856.30*** *p87*
With wife & children
Drollinger, Hans Michael; America, 1743 ***2856.30*** *p87*
Drollinger, Hans Michael; America, 1743 ***2856.30*** *p87*
With wife & son
Dromay, Simon; New York, 1837 ***8197.10*** *p82*
Drommond, William E.; New York, 1832 ***8197.10*** *p225*
Drommond, William E.; New York, 1835 ***8197.10*** *p70*
Dron, Christian; America, 1737 ***2856.30*** *p87*
Dron, Christian; Canada, 1789 ***2856.30*** *p87*
Dron, Christian; Port uncertain, 1780 ***2856.30*** *p87*
Dron, William; Augusta, Georgia, 1839-1879 ***1640.10*** *p44*
Dronecker, Philipp; Port uncertain, 1783 ***2856.30*** *p87*
With 4 sons & 2 daughters
Dronscher, Anna Elisabeth; Port uncertain, 1775 ***2856.30*** *p87*
Dronzkiewicz, Tomas; Maryland, 1910 ***3259.35*** *p13*
Drope, Robert 71; Ontario, 1871 ***1823.22*** *p46*
Drope, William 50; Ontario, 1871 ***1823.22*** *p46*
Droper, Alexander; Maryland, 1663 ***2524.55*** *p71*
Wife: Catherine
Droper, Catherine *SEE* Droper, Alexander
Droper, T.; Quebec, 1857 ***9196.15*** *p19*
Dross, Valentin; America, 1747 ***2856.30*** *p87*
Drossmann, Mrs. Jacob; America, 1761 ***2856.30*** *p87*
Drossmann, Philipp; Port uncertain, 1761 ***2856.30*** *p87*
Drought, George 66; Ontario, 1871 ***1823.15*** *p68*
Droutwine, William; New York, 1806 ***8197.10*** *p30*
Drozd, Thomas; Maryland, 1910 ***3259.35*** *p13*
Druckert, Anna Margarete; America, 1759 ***2856.30*** *p87*
With father
Drucklo, John; Maryland, 1671 ***2524.55*** *p71*
Drueman, John; Maryland, 1652 ***2524.55*** *p71*
Druer, Chn.; Port uncertain, 1739 ***2856.30*** *p472*
Druer, Christian; Port uncertain, 1734 ***2856.30*** *p87*
With wife & 3 children
Druer, Joseph 33; Ontario, 1871 ***1823.15*** *p68*
Druga, Leopold; Maryland, 1910 ***3259.35*** *p13*
Druitt, Robert; Maryland, 1659 ***2524.55*** *p71*
Drum, Bridget 82; Vermont, 1899 ***5900.10*** *p483*
Drum, Mary 32; Vermont, 1853 ***5900.10*** *p484*
Drum, Patrick 40; Ontario, 1871 ***1823.22*** *p46*
Drum, Simon; America, 1739 ***2856.30*** *p87*
Drumm, Adam; America, 1737 ***2856.30*** *p87*
Drumm, Adam; America, 1737 ***2856.30*** *p87*
With wife
Drumm, Agusta 42; Ontario, 1871 ***1823.15*** *p68*
Drumm, Simon; America, 1739 ***2856.30*** *p87*
With wife & 2 children
Drumm, Simon; America, 1742 ***2856.30*** *p87*
Drumm, Simon; America, 1754 ***2856.30*** *p87*
Drumm, Simon; Port uncertain, 1741 ***2856.30*** *p87*
Drummer, Patrick; Maryland, 1681 ***2524.55*** *p71*
Drummer, Steven; Maryland, 1659 ***2524.55*** *p71*
Drummond, . . .; Boston, 1737 ***4628.40*** *p114*
Drummond, Mr.; Quebec, 1857 ***9196.15*** *p15*
Drummond, Agnes; Grenada, 1876 ***1640.13*** *p32*
Drummond, Andrew; Jamaica, 1851 ***1640.13*** *p32*
Drummond, Andrew; Mississippi, 1818-1845 ***1640.10*** *p44*
Drummond, Charles; Bermuda, 1858 ***1640.13*** *p32*
Drummond, Co P. 35; Ontario, 1871 ***1823.22*** *p46*
Drummond, David; Savannah, Georgia, 1771 ***1640.10*** *p44*
Drummond, Elizabeth 56; Ontario, 1871 ***1823.22*** *p46*
Drummond, James; New York, 1794 ***8197.10*** *p5*
Drummond, James; New York, 1801 ***1640.13*** *p32*
Drummond, John 46; Ontario, 1871 ***1823.15*** *p68*
Drummond, John 55; Ontario, 1871 ***1823.15*** *p68*
Drummond, Peter; Pennsylvania, 1777 ***4629.10*** *p17*
Drummond, Robert; New York, 1718 ***1224.2*** *p35*
Drummond, Robert; New York, 1869 ***1640.13*** *p32*
Drummond, Robert 70; Ontario, 1871 ***1823.15*** *p68*
Drummond, Thomas; Georgia, 1699 ***1640.13*** *p32*
Drummond, Thomas; Louisiana, 1890 ***1640.13*** *p32*
Drummond, Thomas; Pennsylvania, 1777 ***4629.10*** *p6*
Drummond, W. H.; Montreal, 1896 ***4628.40*** *p99*
Drummond, Walter; Savannah, Georgia, 1801-1812 ***1640.10*** *p44*
Drummond, William; New York, 1807 ***8197.10*** *p38*
Drummond, Wm 44; Ontario, 1871 ***1823.15*** *p68*
Drumond, William; Virginia, 1677 ***1224.1*** *p19*
Drumont, James; Virginia, 1667 ***1224.1*** *p19*
Drury, Ann 24; Vermont, 1865 ***5900.10*** *p596*
Drury, Edward; Philadelphia, 1779 ***1224.2*** *p35*
Drury, James; New York, 1779 ***1224.2*** *p35*
Drury, Richard; Maryland, 1673 ***2524.55*** *p71*
Drury, Robert; Maryland, 1673 ***2524.55*** *p71*
Drury, Robt; Virginia, 1663 ***6212.30*** *p4*
Drury, Thomas; Maryland, 1674 ***2524.55*** *p71*
Drush, Sima; Maryland, 1910 ***3259.35*** *p13*
Drusth, Andrew; Maryland, 1910 ***3259.35*** *p13*
Drustka, William; Maryland, 1910 ***3259.35*** *p13*
Druve, William 38; Ontario, 1871 ***1823.28*** *p25*
Dry, John; Virginia, 1663 ***6212.30*** *p4*
Dryburgh, Andrew; Canada, 1878 ***1640.13*** *p32*
Dryden, Adam; Savannah, Georgia, 1774 ***1640.10*** *p45*
Dryden, Adam 28; Savannah, Georgia, 1774 ***1220.25*** *p139*
Drygasz, Pawel; Maryland, 1910 ***3259.35*** *p13*
Drysdale, Andrew; New York, 1839 ***8197.10*** *p129*
Drysdale, Ann 59; Ontario, 1871 ***1823.15*** *p68*
Drysdale, Christina 29; Ontario, 1871 ***1823.22*** *p46*
Drysdale, David; Georgia, 1699 ***1640.13*** *p32*
Drysdale, Henry 40; Ontario, 1871 ***1823.22*** *p46*
Drysdale, Hugh; Virginia, 1726 ***1224.2*** *p35*
Drysdale, James; Georgia, 1740 ***1640.10*** *p45*
Drysdale, John; St. Louis, 1869 ***1640.13*** *p32*
Drysdale, Robert 24; Ontario, 1871 ***1823.15*** *p68*
Drysdall, William; Boston, 1750 ***1224.2*** *p35*
Drysdel, James 32; Ontario, 1871 ***1823.28*** *p25*
Drzewiezki, Wladyslaw; Maryland, 1910 ***3259.35*** *p13*
Duane, Dennis; Maryland, 1739 ***1224.2*** *p35*
Duane, Maurice; New York, 1837 ***8197.10*** *p83*
Duanohall, Daniell; Maryland, 1631-1685 ***2524.55*** *p30*
Dubarry, Jean; Philadelphia, 1793 ***4629.10*** *p75*
Dube, Jane Queen 74; Vermont, 1898 ***5900.10*** *p600*
Dube, John M. 77; Vermont, 1897 ***5900.10*** *p600*
Dubeal, John; Maryland, 1910 ***3259.35*** *p13*
Dubendorfer, Alexander; America, 1727 ***2856.30*** *p89*
Duberidge, Elizabeth; Maryland, 1673 ***2524.55*** *p71*
Dubernel, Hans Theobald; America, 1783 ***2856.30*** *p88*
Duberville, Thomas 22; Ontario, 1871 ***1823.28*** *p25*
Dubicen, Fred 25; Alaska, 1912 ***9196.1*** *p13*
Dubich, J. 32; Alaska, 1912 ***9196.1*** *p37*
Dubich, J. 32; Whitehorse, Yukon, 1912 ***9196.1*** *p37*
Dubinski, Lasky; Maryland, 1910 ***3259.35*** *p13*
Dubisky, Frank; Maryland, 1910 ***3259.35*** *p13*
Duble, Walter; Virginia, 1664 ***6212.30*** *p9*
Dubois, Francis Blake; New York, 1834 ***8197.10*** *p316*
Du Bois, Walter; New York, 1793 ***1224.2*** *p35*

Dubord, Mr.; Quebec, 1857 ***9196.15*** *p14*
Dubring, Martin 50; Ontario, 1871 ***1823.28*** *p25*
Dubue, Mr.; Quebec, 1858 ***9196.15*** *p34*
Ducasse, James; New York, 1827 ***8197.10*** *p344*
Ducey, Ann; Vermont, 1843-1915 ***5900.10*** *p246*
Ducey, Ellen Donahue; Vermont, 1810-1898 ***5900.10*** *p103*
Ducey, Henry; Vermont, 1836-1912 ***5900.10*** *p246*
Ducey, James; Vermont, 1822-1897 ***5900.10*** *p103*
Ducey, Thomas; New York, 1837 ***8197.10*** *p83*
Duchake, Nath; Virginia, 1672 ***6212.30*** *p50*
Ducharme, Aurilla 68; Vermont, 1892 ***5900.10*** *p298*
Ducharme, Mrs. L. 33; Alaska, 1914 ***9196.1*** *p41*
Duche, Jacob; Philadelphia, n.d. ***1224.2*** *p35*
Duche, John; Pennsylvania, 1777 ***4629.10*** *p13*
Ducheman, Francis Christopher Ambrose; Montreal, 1826 ***1224.3*** *p23*
Duchesne, Peter; New York, 1794 ***8197.10*** *p5*
Duchmann, Stephan; New York, 1837 ***8197.10*** *p83*
Duck, Daniel; New York, 1830 ***8197.10*** *p225*
Duck, Joseph 40; Ontario, 1871 ***1823.28*** *p25*
Duck, Martin 22; Ontario, 1871 ***1823.28*** *p25*
Duck, Nicholas; Virginia, 1666 ***6212.30*** *p30*
Duck, Richard; Virginia, 1664 ***6212.30*** *p13*
Duck, Thomas; New York, 1778 ***1224.2*** *p35*
Duckelin, Elisabeth; Port uncertain, 1755 ***2856.30*** *p89*
Ducken, Jno; Virginia, 1665-1666 ***6212.30*** *p23*
Duckers, Henry; New York, 1838 ***8197.10*** *p108*
Ducket, Loyd 40; Ontario, 1871 ***1823.15*** *p68*
Duckett, Jno; Virginia, 1665 ***6212.30*** *p17*
Duckett, Wm; Virginia, 1671-1672 ***6212.30*** *p47*
Duckham, John 28; Ontario, 1871 ***1823.15*** *p68*
Ducklow, John 50; Ontario, 1871 ***1823.15*** *p68*
Ducle, Tho; Virginia, 1664 ***6212.30*** *p9*
Duclos, Anne Rose de Kater; New York, 1805 ***8197.10*** *p29*
Duclos, Mary; Vermont, 1851-1922 ***5900.10*** *p256*
Du Cornan, John; Philadelphia, 1793 ***4629.10*** *p73*
Du Crit, Jean Louis; Philadelphia, 1793 ***4629.10*** *p71*
Ducro, Frederick 50; Ontario, 1871 ***1823.15*** *p68*
Duda, Michael; Maryland, 1910 ***3259.35*** *p13*
Dudek, Joseph; Maryland, 1910 ***3259.35*** *p13*
Dudgeon, Ann 70; Ontario, 1871 ***1823.28*** *p25*
Dudgeon, Patrick; Boston, 1702 ***1224.2*** *p116*
Dudgeon, Patrick; West Indies, 1702 ***1224.2*** *p116*
Dudley, Charles Edward; New York, 1803 ***8197.10*** *p12*
Dudley, Honor; Maryland, 1673 ***2524.55*** *p71*
Dudley, Honr; Virginia, 1671 ***6212.30*** *p42*
Dudley, James; Virginia, 1664 ***6212.30*** *p11*
Dudley, John 73; Ontario, 1871 ***1823.22*** *p46*
Dudley, Joseph; Maryland, 1682 ***2524.55*** *p71*
Dudley, Joshua; New York, 1840 ***8197.10*** *p157*
Dudley, Josua 50; Ontario, 1871 ***1823.28*** *p25*
Dudley, Levi 62; Ontario, 1871 ***1823.22*** *p46*
Dudley, Margaret Riley 36; Vermont, 1865 ***5900.10*** *p395*
Dudley, Mary Ann Sarah; New York, New York, 1854 ***1224.3*** *p23*
Dudley, Thomas; New England, 1696 ***1224.1*** *p19*
Dudley, Thomas 28; Ontario, 1871 ***1823.28*** *p25*
Dudley, Thomas 36; Vermont, 1893 ***5900.10*** *p461*
Dudley, William; Pennsylvania, 1777 ***4629.10*** *p8*
Dudley, William 75; Vermont, 1901 ***5900.10*** *p395*
Dudman, Mr.; Quebec, 1857 ***9196.15*** *p15*
Dudrick, Martin; Maryland, 1910 ***3259.35*** *p13*
Dudridge, Elizabeth; Maryland, 1673 ***2524.55*** *p71*
Dues, Edwd; Virginia, 1698 ***6212.30*** *p61*
Duetta, E. A. 19; Ontario, 1861 ***2896.28*** *p10*
Duetta, J. B. 2; Ontario, 1861 ***2896.28*** *p10*
Duetta, W. 22; Ontario, 1861 ***2896.28*** *p10*
Dufey, Sara 51; Vermont, 1848 ***5900.10*** *p471*
Duff, Alexander; St. Vincent, 1819 ***1640.13*** *p32*
Duff, Andrew 31; Ontario, 1871 ***1823.15*** *p68*
Duff, Ann 10; Jamaica, 1773-1774 ***1220.25*** *p32*
Duff, Archibald; Florida, 1774 ***1640.10*** *p45*
Duff, Charles 35; Ontario, 1871 ***1823.22*** *p46*
Duff, Edward 40; Ontario, 1871 ***1823.22*** *p46*
Duff, Ellen 60; Ontario, 1871 ***1823.22*** *p46*
Duff, Fintan; New York, 1821 ***8197.10*** *p222*
Duff, Izett 67; Ontario, 1871 ***1823.28*** *p25*
Duff, John; New York, 1828 ***8197.10*** *p64*
Duff, John 43; Ontario, 1871 ***1823.28*** *p25*
Duff, Mary E. 64; Vermont, 1896 ***5900.10*** *p594*
Duff, Michael; Pennsylvania, 1777 ***4629.10*** *p13*
Duff, Peter 30; Ontario, 1871 ***1823.28*** *p25*
Duff, Robert 62; Ontario, 1871 ***1823.15*** *p68*
Duff, Thomas; New York, 1821 ***8197.10*** *p222*
Duff, Thomas; New York, 1840 ***8197.10*** *p158*
Duffacy, Kate 61; Vermont, 1884 ***5900.10*** *p448*
Duffain, Cath. *SEE* Duffain, Johann Georg
Duffain, Johann Georg; Cayenne, 1764 ***2856.30*** *p88*
Wife: Cath.
With 4 children
Duffany, Father 71; Vermont, 1864 ***5900.10*** *p363*
Duffany, John L.; Vermont, 1854-1895 ***5900.10*** *p255*
Duffany, Mary L.; Vermont, 1822-1919 ***5900.10*** *p255*
Dufferin, Cath. *SEE* Dufferin, Johann Georg
Dufferin, Johann Georg; Cayenne, 1764 ***2856.30*** *p88*
Wife: Cath.
With 4 children
Duffett, Frederick 31; Ontario, 1871 ***1823.22*** *p46*
Duffey, Bridget 55; Vermont, 1875 ***5900.10*** *p259*
Duffey, Bridget 62; Ontario, 1871 ***1823.22*** *p46*
Duffey, Edward 60; Ontario, 1871 ***1823.22*** *p46*
Duffey, Elizabeth; Vermont, 1837 ***5900.10*** *p528*
Duffey, Ellen D. Hanley; Vermont, 1836-1936 ***5900.10*** *p532*
Duffey, Ellen F. 25; Vermont, 1864 ***5900.10*** *p230*
Duffey, Francis 46; Vermont, 1880 ***5900.10*** *p525*
Duffey, James; New York, 1839 ***8197.10*** *p383*
Duffey, James 20; Ontario, 1871 ***1823.28*** *p25*
Duffey, James 65; Ontario, 1871 ***1823.22*** *p46*
Duffey, John; Vermont, 1835-1900 ***5900.10*** *p532*
Duffey, Kate; Vermont, 1842-1931 ***5900.10*** *p225*
Duffey, Laura; Vermont, 1863-1950 ***5900.10*** *p531*
Duffey, Mary; Vermont, 1800-1918 ***5900.10*** *p525*
Duffey, Mary; Vermont, 1857-1928 ***5900.10*** *p174*
Duffey, Mary 32; Vermont, 1873 ***5900.10*** *p525*
Duffey, Mary Moan 72; Vermont, 1877 ***5900.10*** *p530*
Duffey, Patrick 68; Vermont, 1864 ***5900.10*** *p530*
Duffey, Sarah; Vermont, 1806-1877 ***5900.10*** *p469*
Duffey, Thomas; Pennsylvania, 1867 ***6058.10*** *p60*
Dufficy, . . .; Vermont, n.d. ***5900.10*** *p417*
Dufficy, Bridget; Vermont, 1848-1878 ***5900.10*** *p417*
Dufficy, Bridget; Vermont, 1851-1939 ***5900.10*** *p303*
Dufficy, Darby; Vermont, 1899 ***5900.10*** *p417*
Dufficy, Jeremiah; Vermont, 1820-1905 ***5900.10*** *p422*
Dufficy, Mary Higgins; Vermont, 1813-1896 ***5900.10*** *p422*
Duffield, John; Pennsylvania, 1777 ***4629.10*** *p17*
Duffield, Joseph; Pennsylvania, 1777 ***4629.10*** *p27*
Duffield, Thomas 29; Ontario, 1871 ***1823.15*** *p68*
Duffins, John 45; Ontario, 1871 ***1823.15*** *p68*
Duffner, Anton; America, 1780 ***2856.30*** *p88*
Duffner, Georg; Port uncertain, 1785 ***2856.30*** *p88*
Duffner, Josef; Port uncertain, 1715 ***2856.30*** *p88*
Duffour, Amedee; New York, 1829 ***8197.10*** *p225*
Duffus, Jane; New Jersey, 1858 ***1640.13*** *p33*
Duffy, Ann E. Carrigan; Vermont, 1836-1922 ***5900.10*** *p383*
Duffy, Ann Fay; Vermont, 1830-1883 ***5900.10*** *p322*
Duffy, Ann Glynn; Vermont, 1830-1909 ***5900.10*** *p507*
Duffy, Ann Padgin 62; Vermont, 1892 ***5900.10*** *p580*
Duffy, Anna; Vermont, 1849-1904 ***5900.10*** *p157*
Duffy, Anna Keenan; Vermont, 1869-1928 ***5900.10*** *p420*
Duffy, Barney; Pennsylvania, 1831 ***6058.10*** *p10*
Duffy, Bessie; Vermont, 1889-1971 ***5900.10*** *p595*
Duffy, Bridget 38; Vermont, 1858 ***5900.10*** *p238*
Duffy, Bridget C.; Vermont, 1840-1927 ***5900.10*** *p139*
Duffy, Bridget Carroll; Vermont, 1834-1937 ***5900.10*** *p581*
Duffy, Catharine 43; Vermont, 1875 ***5900.10*** *p323*
Duffy, Catherine; Vermont, 1829-1903 ***5900.10*** *p238*
Duffy, Catherine; Vermont, 1833-1887 ***5900.10*** *p157*
Duffy, Catherine; Vermont, 1840-1908 ***5900.10*** *p111*
Duffy, Daniel; New York, 1840 ***8197.10*** *p321*
Duffy, Daniel; Vermont, 1836-1883 ***5900.10*** *p581*
Duffy, Daniel; Vermont, 1851-1920 ***5900.10*** *p453*
Duffy, Daniel H. 40; Ontario, 1871 ***1823.28*** *p25*
Duffy, David; Vermont, 1847-1873 ***5900.10*** *p388*
Duffy, Edward; New York, 1836 ***8197.10*** *p319*
Duffy, Elizabeth 57; Ontario, 1871 ***1823.15*** *p68*
Duffy, Elizabeth Kelly 65; Vermont, 1882 ***5900.10*** *p580*
Duffy, Ellenor Sinnott 25; Vermont, 1864 ***5900.10*** *p51*
Duffy, Francis Thomas; New York, New York, 1841 ***1224.3*** *p23*
Duffy, Frank; Vermont, 1868-1873 ***5900.10*** *p111*
Duffy, George; Vermont, 1825-1891 ***5900.10*** *p429*
Duffy, Hugh; Vermont, 1855-1920 ***5900.10*** *p420*
Duffy, James; New York, 1827 ***8197.10*** *p343*
Duffy, James; New York, 1837 ***8197.10*** *p83*
Duffy, James; Toronto, 1886 ***1640.13*** *p33*
Duffy, James; Vermont, 1829-1915 ***5900.10*** *p322*
Duffy, James 38; Ontario, 1871 ***1823.22*** *p47*
Duffy, James C.; Vermont, 1860-1908 ***5900.10*** *p323*
Duffy, John; New York, 1839 ***8197.10*** *p383*
Duffy, John; Vermont, 1826 ***5900.10*** *p22*
Duffy, John; Vermont, 1831-1901 ***5900.10*** *p383*
Duffy, John 64; Ontario, 1871 ***1823.28*** *p25*
Duffy, John 72; Vermont, 1869 ***5900.10*** *p388*
Duffy, John 75; Vermont, 1895 ***5900.10*** *p237*
Duffy, Julia; Vermont, 1856-1875 ***5900.10*** *p507*
Duffy, Julia O'Donnell; Vermont, 1830-1909 ***5900.10*** *p419*
Duffy, Katherine Hale; Vermont, 1885-1919 ***5900.10*** *p323*
Duffy, Katie; Vermont, 1851-1874 ***5900.10*** *p507*
Duffy, Margaret; Vermont, 1835-1922 ***5900.10*** *p387*
Duffy, Margaret A.; Vermont, 1864-1922 ***5900.10*** *p323*
Duffy, Margaret Kennedy 65; Vermont, 1866 ***5900.10*** *p231*
Duffy, Mary; Vermont, 1831-1899 ***5900.10*** *p429*
Duffy, Mary; Vermont, 1848-1913 ***5900.10*** *p388*
Duffy, Mary; Vermont, 1864-1865 ***5900.10*** *p111*
Duffy, Mary 32; Ontario, 1871 ***1823.22*** *p47*
Duffy, Mary 73; Vermont, 1878 ***5900.10*** *p388*
Duffy, Mary 75; Vermont, 1883 ***5900.10*** *p585*
Duffy, Mary Ann; Vermont, 1862-1865 ***5900.10*** *p323*
Duffy, Mary Ann Mahonbey; Vermont, 1829-1906 ***5900.10*** *p324*
Duffy, Mary E.; Vermont, 1857-1921 ***5900.10*** *p487*
Duffy, Mary McCoy; Vermont, 1802-1881 ***5900.10*** *p388*
Duffy, Mary Riley; Vermont, 1811-1863 ***5900.10*** *p157*
Duffy, Matthew; Vermont, 1804-1860 ***5900.10*** *p157*
Duffy, Michael; Vermont, 1801-1886 ***5900.10*** *p388*
Duffy, Michael 16; Vermont, 1877 ***5900.10*** *p580*
Duffy, Michael 84; Vermont, 1899 ***5900.10*** *p580*
Duffy, Michael A.; Vermont, 1872-1898 ***5900.10*** *p322*
Duffy, Michael C. 18; Vermont, 1869 ***5900.10*** *p580*
Duffy, Nancy; Vermont, 1846-1921 ***5900.10*** *p531*
Duffy, Owen 64; Ontario, 1871 ***1823.22*** *p47*
Duffy, Patrick; New York, 1825 ***8197.10*** *p222*
Duffy, Patrick; New York, 1832 ***8197.10*** *p356*
Duffy, Patrick; New York, 1836 ***8197.10*** *p78*
Duffy, Patrick; New York, 1840 ***8197.10*** *p157*
Duffy, Patrick; New York, 1840 ***8197.10*** *p321*
Duffy, Patrick; Vermont, 1806-1878 ***5900.10*** *p111*
Duffy, Patrick; Vermont, 1820-1901 ***5900.10*** *p324*
Duffy, Patrick 29; Ontario, 1871 ***1823.22*** *p47*
Duffy, Patrick 50; Ontario, 1871 ***1823.15*** *p68*
Duffy, Patrick 50; Vermont, 1869 ***5900.10*** *p230*
Duffy, Patrick 74; Vermont, 1865 ***5900.10*** *p238*
Duffy, Patrick S.; Vermont, 1870-1943 ***5900.10*** *p323*
Duffy, Peter; New York, 1819 ***8197.10*** *p61*
Duffy, Peter; New York, New York, 1841 ***1224.3*** *p23*
Duffy, Peter; Vermont, 1827-1903 ***5900.10*** *p507*
Duffy, Peter 65; Vermont, 1851 ***5900.10*** *p522*
Duffy, Philip; New York, 1818 ***8197.10*** *p60*
Duffy, Philip; New York, 1837 ***8197.10*** *p83*
Duffy, Rose; Vermont, 1851-1917 ***5900.10*** *p111*
Duffy, Rose 84; Vermont, 1868 ***5900.10*** *p238*
Duffy, Rose A.; Vermont, 1858-1891 ***5900.10*** *p486*
Duffy, Rose Ellen; Vermont, 1859-1876 ***5900.10*** *p323*
Duffy, Sarah; Vermont, 1857-1890 ***5900.10*** *p111*
Duffy, Sarah Gero; Vermont, 1851-1951 ***5900.10*** *p453*
Duffy, Susan; Vermont, 1817-1873 ***5900.10*** *p111*
Duffy, Thomas; New York, 1837 ***8197.10*** *p83*
Duffy, Thomas; Vermont, 1828-1917 ***5900.10*** *p419*
Duffy, Thomas; Vermont, 1838-1872 ***5900.10*** *p111*
Duffy, William J.; Vermont, 1868-1886 ***5900.10*** *p323*
Duflon, John P.; New York, 1803 ***8197.10*** *p12*
Dufner, Josef; America, 1822 ***2856.30*** *p88*
With 2 sons & daughter
Dufour, Lawrence; New York, 1840 ***8197.10*** *p157*
Dufour, Paul; New York, 1840 ***8197.10*** *p157*
Dufour, Thomas; New York, 1840 ***8197.10*** *p157*
Dufourg, John R.; New York, 1815 ***8197.10*** *p55*
Dufresne, Mary A. Manahan; Vermont, 1846-1928 ***5900.10*** *p472*
Dufresne, Wilfred M.; Vermont, 1848-1921 ***5900.10*** *p472*
Dufton, John 27; Baltimore, 1775 ***1220.25*** *p118*
Dugald, Smith 51; Ontario, 1871 ***1823.15*** *p68*
Dugan, A. 21; Ontario, 1861 ***2896.25*** *p29*
Dugan, A. J. 9; Ontario, 1861 ***2896.25*** *p41*
Dugan, Agnes 14; Ontario, 1861 ***2896.25*** *p41*
Dugan, Alex 11; Ontario, 1861 ***2896.25*** *p41*
Dugan, Alexander 51; Ontario, 1861 ***2896.25*** *p35*
Dugan, Ann 13; Ontario, 1861 ***2896.25*** *p41*
Dugan, Ann 63; Vermont, 1894 ***5900.10*** *p424*
Dugan, Bridget 70; Vermont, 1890 ***5900.10*** *p448*
Dugan, Bridget Morris; Vermont, 1829-1884 ***5900.10*** *p467*
Dugan, C. M. 3; Ontario, 1861 ***2896.25*** *p41*
Dugan, D. 29; Alaska, 1917 ***9196.1*** *p46*
Dugan, D. 29; Whitehorse, Yukon, 1917 ***9196.1*** *p46*
Dugan, Frank M.; Vermont, 1858-1935 ***5900.10*** *p401*
Dugan, George 27; Ontario, 1871 ***1823.28*** *p25*
Dugan, H. 4; Ontario, 1861 ***2896.25*** *p41*
Dugan, Hannora 72; Vermont, 1891 ***5900.10*** *p327*
Dugan, Henry; Vermont, 1829-1901 ***5900.10*** *p467*
Dugan, Henry; Vermont, 1878 ***5900.10*** *p516*
Dugan, Jane; Vermont, 1832-1918 ***5900.10*** *p467*
Dugan, John; New York, 1840 ***8197.10*** *p226*
Dugan, John; Pennsylvania, 1777 ***4629.10*** *p25*
Dugan, John 17; Ontario, 1861 ***2896.25*** *p35*
Dugan, Maria; Vermont, 1833-1901 ***5900.10*** *p440*
Dugan, Mary 74; Vermont, 1894 ***5900.10*** *p467*
Dugan, Mary A. Haley; Vermont, 1856-1941 ***5900.10*** *p401*

Dugan, Mary Mullaney; Vermont, 1905 ***5900.10*** *p436*
Dugan, Michael; Vermont, 1818-1899 ***5900.10*** *p424*
Dugan, Michael; Vermont, 1929 ***5900.10*** *p436*
Dugan, Neil; New York, 1840 ***8197.10*** *p226*
Dugan, O. 7; Ontario, 1861 ***2896.25*** *p41*
Dugan, Patrick; Pennsylvania, 1777 ***4629.10*** *p18*
Dugan, Patrick; Vermont, 1823-1895 ***5900.10*** *p440*
Dugan, Rachel; Vermont, 1844-1915 ***5900.10*** *p512*
Dugan, Thomas; New York, 1840 ***8197.10*** *p157*
Dugan, Thomas 1; Ontario, 1861 ***2896.25*** *p41*
Dugan, William 19; Ontario, 1861 ***2896.25*** *p35*
Dugdale, John; Boston, 1702 ***1224.2*** *p35*
Dugen, Roseann 45; Ontario, 1871 ***1823.28*** *p25*
Duggan, . . .; New Hampshire, 1641-1660 ***4628.40*** *p44*
Duggan, Ann Conway 53; Vermont, 1887 ***5900.10*** *p272*
Duggan, Bridget 30; Ontario, 1871 ***1823.15*** *p68*
Duggan, Bridget Kane; Vermont, 1833-1869 ***5900.10*** *p263*
Duggan, Daniel 57; Ontario, 1871 ***1823.28*** *p25*
Duggan, Daniel L.; Vermont, 1856-1936 ***5900.10*** *p110*
Duggan, Denis 27; New York, New York, 1850 ***1825.45*** *p48*
Duggan, Denis 40; Ontario, 1871 ***1823.22*** *p47*
Duggan, Edward 52; Ontario, 1871 ***1823.15*** *p68*
Duggan, Eileen 25 *SEE* Duggan, Margaret
Duggan, Hannah; Vermont, 1840-1921 ***5900.10*** *p355*
Duggan, Henry J. 17; Ontario, 1871 ***1823.15*** *p68*
Duggan, Jane 57; Ontario, 1861 ***2896.25*** *p40*
Duggan, Jeremiah 104; Vermont, 1865 ***5900.10*** *p371*
Duggan, John; Vermont, 1833-1914 ***5900.10*** *p263*
Duggan, Julia; Vermont, 1831-1904 ***5900.10*** *p301*
Duggan, Margaret 29; New York, New York, 1850 ***1825.45*** *p49*
Sister: Eileen 25
Duggan, Martin 42; Vermont, 1858 ***5900.10*** *p371*
Duggan, Mary; Vermont, 1850-1928 ***5900.10*** *p333*
Duggan, Michael; New York, 1830 ***8197.10*** *p360*
Duggan, Michael 25; Vermont, 1878 ***5900.10*** *p81*
Duggan, Nancy Grandfield; Vermont, 1835-1902 ***5900.10*** *p365*
Duggan, Patrick; Vermont, 1825-1893 ***5900.10*** *p365*
Duggan, Patrick 34; Ontario, 1871 ***1823.28*** *p25*
Duggan, Phill 35; Ontario, 1871 ***1823.28*** *p25*
Duggan, Rose 79; Ontario, 1871 ***1823.15*** *p68*
Duggan, Sarah; Vermont, 1847-1931 ***5900.10*** *p110*
Duggan, William 61; Ontario, 1861 ***2896.25*** *p40*
Duggen, Isabelle; Vermont, 1822-1857 ***5900.10*** *p372*
Duglas, James 40; Ontario, 1871 ***1823.15*** *p68*
Duglas, John; Maryland, 1682 ***2524.55*** *p71*
Duglas, John 39; Ontario, 1871 ***1823.28*** *p25*
Duglas, John 40; Ontario, 1871 ***1823.15*** *p68*
Duglas, Nichol 40; Ontario, 1871 ***1823.22*** *p47*
Duglass, James 66; Ontario, 1871 ***1823.15*** *p68*
Duglass, John 53; Ontario, 1871 ***1823.15*** *p68*
Duglasse, Robert; Maryland, 1658 ***2524.55*** *p71*
Dugles, Donald 55; Ontario, 1871 ***1823.22*** *p47*
Dugless, John 55; Ontario, 1871 ***1823.22*** *p47*
Dugless, John 72; Ontario, 1871 ***1823.22*** *p47*
Duguid, Deidaina; America, 1853 ***1640.13*** *p33*
Duguid, Eleanor; America, 1853 ***1640.13*** *p33*
Duguid, William; New York, 1854 ***1640.13*** *p33*
Duikoisky, James; Maryland, 1910 ***3259.35*** *p13*
Duke, Mrs.; Maryland, 1653 ***2524.55*** *p71*
Duke, Adam 30; Ontario, 1871 ***1823.15*** *p68*
Duke, Andrew 22; Ontario, 1871 ***1823.15*** *p68*
Duke, David; New York, 1838 ***8197.10*** *p108*
Duke, David 67; Ontario, 1871 ***1823.15*** *p68*
Duke, John 25; Nova Scotia, 1774 ***1220.25*** *p135*
Duke, John 35; Ontario, 1871 ***1823.28*** *p25*
Duke, Lory Ann 17; Ontario, 1861 ***2896.25*** *p70*
Duke, Rich; Virginia, 1665-1666 ***6212.30*** *p22*
Duke, Rich; Virginia, 1666-1667 ***6212.30*** *p32*
Duke, William 34; Ontario, 1871 ***1823.15*** *p68*
Dukes, Robert; Maryland, 1672 ***2524.55*** *p71*
Dukleow, Charles 45; Ontario, 1871 ***1823.22*** *p47*
Dulan, Joanna; Vermont, 1799-1869 ***5900.10*** *p107*
Dulany, Rebecca; Newport, Rhode Island, 1826 ***1224.3*** *p23*
Dulenkopf, Sebastian; Port uncertain, 1750 ***2856.30*** *p88*
With wife & child
Dulin, Charles 9; Ontario, 1861 ***2896.25*** *p57*
Dulin, Francis 7; Ontario, 1861 ***2896.25*** *p57*
Dulin, James 13; Ontario, 1861 ***2896.25*** *p57*
Dulin, Jane 45; Ontario, 1861 ***2896.25*** *p57*
Dulin, John 12; Ontario, 1861 ***2896.25*** *p57*
Dulin, John 50; Ontario, 1861 ***2896.25*** *p57*
Dulin, Richard 5; Ontario, 1861 ***2896.25*** *p57*
Dulin, Thomas 2; Ontario, 1861 ***2896.25*** *p57*
Duling, Anne N.; Vermont, 1838-1901 ***5900.10*** *p470*
Duling, James Knox Polk; Vermont, 1844-1904 ***5900.10*** *p487*
Duling, John 30; Vermont, 1865 ***5900.10*** *p477*
Duling, Mary Eustace 83; Vermont, 1922 ***5900.10*** *p477*
Duling, Thomas; Vermont, 1835-1909 ***5900.10*** *p470*
Dull, Abraham; Pennsylvania, 1786 ***4629.10*** *p51*
Dull, Johann Nickel; America, 1739 ***2856.30*** *p84*
Dullahan, Edward 42; Vermont, 1886 ***5900.10*** *p477*
Dullahan, Ellen Dwyer; Vermont, 1850-1901 ***5900.10*** *p139*
Dullahan, John; Vermont, 1868-1936 ***5900.10*** *p458*
Dullahan, Michael; Vermont, 1849-1922 ***5900.10*** *p139*
Dulmadge, Mrs. 47; Ontario, 1861 ***2896.26*** *p25*
Dulmadge, Patience 16; Ontario, 1861 ***2896.26*** *p25*
Dulmadge, Philip 15; Ontario, 1861 ***2896.26*** *p25*
Dulmage, Anson 18; Ontario, 1861 ***2896.26*** *p37*
Dulmage, Calvin 4; Ontario, 1861 ***2896.26*** *p18*
Dulmage, Charles H. 8; Ontario, 1861 ***2896.26*** *p32*
Dulmage, Christian 46; Ontario, 1861 ***2896.26*** *p37*
Dulmage, Christopher 50; Ontario, 1871 ***1823.15*** *p68*
Dulmage, Daniel 12; Ontario, 1861 ***2896.26*** *p37*
Dulmage, Daniel 70; Ontario, 1861 ***2896.25*** *p4*
Dulmage, David A. 6; Ontario, 1861 ***2896.26*** *p17*
Dulmage, Edward C. 9; Ontario, 1861 ***2896.26*** *p17*
Dulmage, Emily 4; Ontario, 1861 ***2896.26*** *p32*
Dulmage, George 18; Ontario, 1861 ***2896.26*** *p17*
Dulmage, Hariet 5; Ontario, 1861 ***2896.26*** *p37*
Dulmage, Henry C. 12; Ontario, 1861 ***2896.26*** *p17*
Dulmage, Jane Ann 14; Ontario, 1861 ***2896.26*** *p37*
Dulmage, John W. 5; Ontario, 1861 ***2896.26*** *p18*
Dulmage, Lucy 17; Ontario, 1861 ***2896.26*** *p37*
Dulmage, Lydia 6; Ontario, 1861 ***2896.26*** *p32*
Dulmage, Lydia A. 16; Ontario, 1861 ***2896.26*** *p17*
Dulmage, Malcolm 1; Ontario, 1861 ***2896.26*** *p38*
Dulmage, Manerva 30; Ontario, 1861 ***2896.26*** *p32*
Dulmage, Margret 27; Ontario, 1861 ***2896.26*** *p38*
Dulmage, Mary 22; Ontario, 1861 ***2896.26*** *p37*
Dulmage, Mary J. 10; Ontario, 1861 ***2896.26*** *p32*
Dulmage, Philip M. 11; Ontario, 1861 ***2896.26*** *p38*
Dulmage, Robert 20; Ontario, 1861 ***2896.26*** *p37*
Dulmage, Sarah 2; Ontario, 1861 ***2896.26*** *p32*
Dulmage, Sarah 8; Ontario, 1861 ***2896.26*** *p37*
Dulmage, Sylida 36; Ontario, 1861 ***2896.26*** *p18*
Dulmage, Ureta 10; Ontario, 1861 ***2896.26*** *p37*
Dulmage, William 8; Ontario, 1861 ***2896.26*** *p37*
Duluce, Andrew; New York, 1803 ***8197.10*** *p12*
Duly, John; Maryland, 1656 ***2524.55*** *p73*
Duman, Josephine; Vermont, 1856 ***5900.10*** *p378*
Dumastier, Anne; New York, 1831 ***8197.10*** *p225*
Dumbal, Frederick; Pennsylvania, 1778 ***4629.10*** *p32*
Dumban, James 32; Ontario, 1871 ***1823.15*** *p68*
Dumble, Albert 30; Ontario, 1871 ***1823.22*** *p47*
Dumble, John 41; Ontario, 1871 ***1823.22*** *p47*
Dumble, Thomas 69; Ontario, 1871 ***1823.22*** *p47*
Dumbler, Frederick 25; Kansas, 1910 ***9079.10*** *p52*
Dumbler, Jacob 54; Kansas, 1890-1910 ***9079.10*** *p52*
Dumbler, Mary 50; Kansas, 1910 ***9079.10*** *p52*
Dumbler, Molly 22; Kansas, 1910 ***9079.10*** *p52*
Dumbresky, Thomas 26; Ontario, 1871 ***1823.28*** *p25*
Dumenit, Guilliaume Francois; Philadelphia, 1793 ***4629.10*** *p75*
Dumler, Amalia 31; Kansas, 1892-1910 ***9079.10*** *p31*
Dumler, Anna 66; Kansas, 1910 ***9079.10*** *p51*
Dumler, Catherine 20; Kansas, 1891-1910 ***9079.10*** *p14*
Dumler, Catherine E. 53; Kansas, 1891-1910 ***9079.10*** *p14*
Dumler, Claude 19; Kansas, 1891-1910 ***9079.10*** *p29*
Dumler, Dave 17; Kansas, 1910 ***9079.10*** *p50*
Dumler, Dave 69; Kansas, 1900 1910 ***9079.10*** *p51*
Dumler, Dave R. 35; Kansas, 1899-1910 ***9079.10*** *p12*
Dumler, David 19; Kansas, 1892-1910 ***9079.10*** *p31*
Dumler, David 23; Kansas, 1891-1910 ***9079.10*** *p14*
Dumler, David 30; Kansas, 1892-1910 ***9079.10*** *p6*
Dumler, Elizabeth 35; Kansas, 1898-1910 ***9079.10*** *p29*
Dumler, Emma 25; Kansas, 1890-1910 ***9079.10*** *p13*
Dumler, Eva 75; Kansas, 1889-1910 ***9079.10*** *p12*
Dumler, Eva H. 39; Kansas, 1900-1910 ***9079.10*** *p36*
Dumler, Fred, Sr. 53; Kansas, 1891-1910 ***9079.10*** *p29*
Dumler, Fred, Jr. 39; Kansas, 1891-1910 ***9079.10*** *p29*
Dumler, Fred B. 25; Kansas, 1892-1910 ***9079.10*** *p35*
Dumler, Frederick 12; Kansas, 1900-1910 ***9079.10*** *p36*
Dumler, George 37; Kansas, 1889-1910 ***9079.10*** *p13*
Dumler, George, Sr. 61; Kansas, 1892-1910 ***9079.10*** *p31*
Dumler, George J. 42; Kansas, 1900-1910 ***9079.10*** *p36*
Dumler, George J., Jr. 15; Kansas, 1900-1910 ***9079.10*** *p36*
Dumler, Gotfried 14; Kansas, 1910 ***9079.10*** *p50*
Dumler, Gotfried 35; Kansas, 1900-1910 ***9079.10*** *p50*
Dumler, Jacob 12; Kansas, 1910 ***9079.10*** *p50*
Dumler, Jacob 53; Kansas, 1891-1910 ***9079.10*** *p14*
Dumler, Jacob, Jr. 27; Kansas, 1891-1910 ***9079.10*** *p29*
Dumler, Jacob R. 32; Kansas, 1889-1910 ***9079.10*** *p12*
Dumler, John 14; Kansas, 1910 ***9079.10*** *p50*
Dumler, John 47; Kansas, 1900-1910 ***9079.10*** *p50*
Dumler, Julia 35; Kansas, 1910 ***9079.10*** *p50*
Dumler, Katherine 39; Kansas, 1887-1910 ***9079.10*** *p7*
Dumler, Katie 47; Kansas, 1910 ***9079.10*** *p50*
Dumler, Marie D. 61; Kansas, 1892-1910 ***9079.10*** *p31*
Dumler, Mary 11; Kansas, 1900-1910 ***9079.10*** *p36*
Dumler, Mary 23; Kansas, 1892-1910 ***9079.10*** *p29*
Dumler, Mary 52; Kansas, 1891-1910 ***9079.10*** *p29*
Dumler, Mike 77; Kansas, 1889-1910 ***9079.10*** *p12*
Dumler, Susie 12; Kansas, 1910 ***9079.10*** *p50*
Dumlick, Peter; Maryland, 1910 ***3259.35*** *p13*
Dumm, Georg; Port uncertain, 1764 ***2856.30*** *p88*
With wife & 7 children
Dumm, Valentin; America, 1764 ***2856.30*** *p88*
With wife & 3 children
Dumma, Adam 42; Ontario, 1871 ***1823.22*** *p47*
Dummer, Elizabeth; New England, 1741 ***1224.2*** *p35*
Dummer, Margaret; New England, 1650 ***1224.1*** *p19*
Dummick, Henry; New York, 1840 ***8197.10*** *p158*
Dumois, Lewis James; Philadelphia, 1793 ***4629.10*** *p69*
Dumont, Franz; Port uncertain, 1761 ***2856.30*** *p88*
Dumont, Franz; Port uncertain, 1762 ***2856.30*** *p88*
Du Moulin, James; Baltimore, 1821 ***1224.3*** *p23*
Dumphosky, John; Maryland, 1910 ***3259.35*** *p13*
Dumphrey, Catherine; Vermont, 1855-1906 ***5900.10*** *p425*
Dumpkowsky, Valentine; Maryland, 1910 ***3259.35*** *p13*
Dumser, Georg; Port uncertain, 1760 ***2856.30*** *p88*
Dumser, Georg; Port uncertain, 1780 ***2856.30*** *p88*
Dumser, Georg; Port uncertain, 1785 ***2856.30*** *p88*
Dumser, Mathias; Port uncertain, 1760 ***2856.30*** *p88*
Dumser, Mathias; Port uncertain, 1780 ***2856.30*** *p88*
Dumser, Mathias; Port uncertain, 1785 ***2856.30*** *p88*
Dumski, John; Maryland, 1910 ***3259.35*** *p13*
Dumun, David; Maryland, 1662 ***2524.55*** *p71*
Dun, Robert; Maryland, 1649 ***2524.55*** *p72*
Dunaname, George; Maryland, 1674 ***2524.55*** *p72*
Dunant, George John; New York, 1821 ***1224.3*** *p23*
Dundone, George; Maryland, 1674 ***2524.55*** *p72*
Dunavanne, Teage; Maryland, 1673 ***2524.55*** *p72*
Dunbar, Charles 51; Ontario, 1871 ***1823.15*** *p68*
Dunbar, David; New Hampshire, 1775-1781 ***4628.40*** *p69*
Dunbar, David 45; Ontario, 1871 ***1823.15*** *p68*
Dunbar, David M.; New York, 1838 ***8197.10*** *p108*
Dunbar, Elizabeth 20; Ontario, 1861 ***2896.27*** *p28*
Dunbar, Elizabeth 60; Ontario, 1861 ***2896.27*** *p28*
Dunbar, Emeline 21; Ontario, 1861 ***2896.27*** *p28*
Dunbar, George; Georgia, 1733 ***1640.10*** *p45*
Dunbar, George; New York, 1807 ***1224.3*** *p23*
Dunbar, Isabella 18; Ontario, 1861 ***2896.27*** *p28*
Dunbar, James; New York, 1783 ***1224.2*** *p35*
Dunbar, James 33; Ontario, 1871 ***1823.15*** *p68*
Dunbar, James 55; Ontario, 1871 ***1823.28*** *p25*
Dunbar, James 63; Ontario, 1861 ***2896.27*** *p28*
Dunbar, Jane Ann 25; Ontario, 1861 ***2896.27*** *p28*
Dunbar, Jane E. 6; Ontario, 1861 ***2896.27*** *p28*
Dunbar, John; Georgia, 1736 ***1640.10*** *p45*
Dunbar, John; Georgia, 1768-1769 ***1640.10*** *p45*
Dunbar, John; Louisiana, 1764 ***1640.10*** *p45*
Dunbar, John; Savannah, Georgia, 1737 ***1640.10*** *p45*
Dunbar, Joseph 43; Ontario, 1871 ***1823.15*** *p68*
Dunbar, Margaret; Georgia, 1740 ***1640.10*** *p46*
Dunbar, Margret 70; Ontario, 1871 ***1823.15*** *p69*
Dunbar, Priscilla; Georgia, 1736 ***1640.10*** *p46*
Dunbar, Sally B. 41; Vermont, 1839 ***5900.10*** *p518*
Dunbar, Sellinda 75; Vermont, 1939 ***5900.10*** *p401*
Dunbar, Theodore 7; Ontario, 1861 ***2896.27*** *p28*
Dunbar, Tryphena; Savannah, Georgia, 1810 ***1224.3*** *p53*
Dunbar, William; Maryland, 1649 ***2524.55*** *p72*
Dunbar, William; Philadelphia, 1771 ***1640.10*** *p46*
Dunbar, William; Quebec, 1857 ***9196.15*** *p18*
Dunbee, Joseph; Maryland, 1677-1681 ***2524.55*** *p72*
Dunbowsky, Konstantin; Maryland, 1910 ***3259.35*** *p13*
Duncan, . . .; Boston, 1737 ***4628.40*** *p114*
Duncan, Miss; Quebec, 1858 ***9196.15*** *p42*
Duncan, Alexander; Florida, 1766 ***1640.10*** *p46*
Duncan, Alexander; New York, 1828 ***8197.10*** *p348*
Duncan, Alexander; Providence, Rhode Island, 1890 ***1640.13*** *p33*
Duncan, Alexander; Savannah, Georgia, 1842 ***1640.10*** *p46*
Duncan, Alexander 41; Ontario, 1871 ***1823.15*** *p69*
Duncan, Alexander 62; Ontario, 1871 ***1823.15*** *p69*
Duncan, Alexander 65; Ontario, 1871 ***1823.15*** *p69*
Duncan, Alexander 70; Ontario, 1871 ***1823.15*** *p69*
Duncan, Alexander, Jr.; New York, New York, 1822 ***8197.10*** *p339*
Duncan, Andrew; Prince Edward Island, 1830 ***1640.13*** *p33*
Duncan, Andrew 67; Ontario, 1871 ***1823.15*** *p69*
Duncan, Ann 49; Ontario, 1871 ***1823.15*** *p69*
Duncan, Charles 27; Ontario, 1861 ***2896.26*** *p1*
Duncan, Daniel; Pennsylvania, 1777 ***4629.10*** *p7*
Duncan, David 48; Ontario, 1871 ***1823.15*** *p69*
Duncan, Donald Shaw; Mississippi, 1804-1845 ***1640.10*** *p46*
Duncan, Flora *SEE* Duncan, Neil

Duncan, George; Charles Town, South Carolina, 1784 1224.2 p35
Duncan, George; Georgia, 1738 1640.10 p47
Duncan, George; Savannah, Georgia, 1737 1640.10 p47
Duncan, George 36; Ontario, 1871 1823.15 p69
Duncan, H.; Quebec, 1858 9196.15 p35
Duncan, James *SEE* Duncan, Neil
Duncan, James; Pennsylvania, 1777 4629.10 p20
Duncan, James; Pennsylvania, 1777 4629.10 p29
Duncan, James; Savannah, Georgia, 1798 1640.10 p47
Duncan, James 19; Ontario, 1871 1823.28 p25
Duncan, James 32; Ontario, 1871 1823.15 p69
Duncan, James 60; Ontario, 1871 1823.15 p69
Duncan, James 67; Ontario, 1871 1823.15 p69
Duncan, Jane 100; Ontario, 1871 1823.15 p69
Duncan, John; Georgia, 1734 1640.10 p47
Duncan, John; Georgia, 1759 1640.10 p47
Duncan, John; New York, 1823 8197.10 p224
Duncan, John; New York, 1840 8197.10 p158
Duncan, John; Port uncertain, 1850-1859 4537.37 p107
Wife: Rachel MacLellan
Child: Kirsty
Duncan, John 36; Ontario, 1871 1823.15 p69
Duncan, John 50; Ontario, 1871 1823.22 p47
Duncan, John 58; Ontario, 1871 1823.22 p47
Duncan, Johnson 35; Ontario, 1871 1823.15 p69
Duncan, Julius 37; Ontario, 1871 1823.15 p69
Duncan, Kirsty *SEE* Duncan, John
Duncan, Marion *SEE* Duncan, Neil
Duncan, Matthew; Pennsylvania, 1779 4629.10 p37
Duncan, Neil; Port uncertain, 1860-1869 4537.37 p107
Wife: Marion
Child: Flora
Child: James
Duncan, Paul 24; Alaska, 1914 9196.1 p24
Duncan, Peter 59; Ontario, 1871 1823.22 p47
Duncan, Phebee 44; Ontario, 1871 1823.22 p47
Duncan, Rachel MacLellan *SEE* Duncan, John
Duncan, Richard 30; Ontario, 1871 1823.15 p69
Duncan, Robert; Georgia, 1804 1640.10 p47
Duncan, Robert; Pennsylvania, 1777 4629.10 p28
Duncan, Robert; Pennsylvania, 1779 4629.10 p35
Duncan, Robert 21; Ontario, 1871 1823.15 p69
Duncan, Robert 40; Ontario, 1871 1823.15 p69
Duncan, Robert 45; Ontario, 1871 1823.22 p47
Duncan, Samuel 71; Ontario, 1871 1823.15 p69
Duncan, Thomas; Mississippi, 1820-1845 1640.10 p47
Duncan, Thomas; Ontario, 1854 1640.13 p33
Duncan, Thomas 45; Ontario, 1871 1823.28 p25
Duncan, Walter; Georgia, 1699 1640.13 p33
Duncan, William; America, 1735-1776 1640.10 p47
Duncan, William; Guadeloupe, 1762 1640.13 p33
Duncan, William; New York, 1837 8197.10 p83
Duncan, William; New York, 1838 8197.10 p226
Duncan, William 18; Ontario, 1871 1823.28 p25
Duncan, William 21; Virginia, 1774 1220.25 p92
Duncan, William 25; Ontario, 1871 1823.28 p25
Duncan, William 29; Ontario, 1871 1823.15 p69
Duncan, William 32; Ontario, 1871 1823.22 p47
Duncan, William 36; Ontario, 1871 1823.15 p69
Duncan, William 52; Ontario, 1871 1823.22 p47
Duncanson, Archibald 33; Ontario, 1871 1823.15 p69
Duncanson, Archibald 70; Ontario, 1871 1823.15 p69
Duncanson, John; Manitoba, 1891 1640.13 p33
Duncanson, Neil 35; Ontario, 1871 1823.15 p69
Duncanson, William; Georgia, 1761 1640.10 p47
Duncason, Hugh 18; St. Vincent, 1774 1220.25 p44
Duncaster, Anne; Maryland, 1673 2524.55 p72
Dunce, Margarett; Maryland, 1657 2524.55 p72
Dunch, Peter; Maryland, 1656 2524.55 p72
Dunch, Samuel; Maryland, 1656 2524.55 p72
Duncking, John; Maryland, 1663 2524.55 p72
Duncomb, Roger; Virginia, 1664 6212.30 p7
Duncombe, Susanna; Virginia, 1694 1224.1 p33
Duncoms, Miles; Maryland, 1666 2524.55 p72
Dunda, George; Maryland, 1665 2524.55 p72
Dundar, Joseph 53; Ontario, 1871 1823.15 p69
Dundas, George Younger; St. Vincent, 1881 1640.13 p33
Dundas, John 39; Ontario, 1871 1823.15 p69
Dundass, James; Pennsylvania, 1777 4629.10 p8
Dundass, John; Pennsylvania, 1777 4629.10 p8
Dundass, Margaret; Vermont, 1824-1890 5900.10 p619
Dundass, Robert 75; Ontario, 1871 1823.15 p69
Dundass, William 26; Ontario, 1871 1823.22 p47
Dunderdale, John; New York, 1830 8197.10 p313
Dundodell, William; Maryland, 1668 2524.55 p72
Dundodells, William; Maryland, 1668 2524.55 p72
Dundon, Hannah Fleming 87; Vermont, 1934 5900.10 p113
Dundon, Hanora Hogan; Vermont, 1830-1910 5900.10 p393
Dundon, Mary; Vermont, n.d. 5900.10 p393
Dundon, Michael 55; Vermont, 1903 5900.10 p113
Dunela, Darby; Maryland, 1671 2524.55 p72
Dunella, Darby; Maryland, 1680 2524.55 p72
Dunew, William 51; Ontario, 1871 1823.15 p69
Dunfield, George 40; Ontario, 1871 1823.28 p25
Dunfield, James 50; Ontario, 1871 1823.28 p25
Dunfield, James 73; Ontario, 1871 1823.15 p69
Dunfield, William 60; Ontario, 1871 1823.28 p25
Dunford, John 46; Ontario, 1871 1823.15 p69
Dunges, Johann Adam; Port uncertain, 1765 2856.30 p89
Dunham, David 39; Ontario, 1861 2896.26 p22
Dunham, Hiram 34; Ontario, 1861 2896.26 p22
Dunham, Sarah 42; Ontario, 1871 1823.15 p69
Dunigan, Daniel 49; Vermont, 1862 5900.10 p572
Dunigan, Eliza 51; Ontario, 1871 1823.22 p47
Dunigan, James 40; Ontario, 1871 1823.28 p25
Dunigan, Katherine Hart 75; Vermont, 1894 5900.10 p572
Dunigan, Michael 70; Ontario, 1871 1823.22 p47
Dunigan, Patrick 36; Ontario, 1871 1823.28 p25
Dunigan, Patrick 50; Ontario, 1871 1823.28 p25
Dunihue, Patrick 24; Vermont, 1862 5900.10 p320
Dunill, John 67; Ontario, 1871 1823.22 p47
Dunilton, John 21; Philadelphia, 1774 1220.25 p80
Dunivan, Alice 5; Ontario, 1861 2896.27 p74
Dunivan, Bridget 2; Ontario, 1861 2896.27 p74
Dunivan, David 42; Ontario, 1861 2896.27 p74
Dunivan, Dennis 40; Ontario, 1861 2896.27 p74
Dunivan, Elizabeth 13; Ontario, 1861 2896.27 p71
Dunivan, Ellen 4; Ontario, 1861 2896.27 p74
Dunivan, Ellen 36; Ontario, 1861 2896.27 p74
Dunivan, Ellen 40; Ontario, 1861 2896.27 p74
Dunivan, Mary 19; Ontario, 1861 2896.27 p74
Dunivan, Michael 48; Ontario, 1861 2896.27 p74
Dunivan, William B. 7; Ontario, 1861 2896.27 p74
Dunk, Alonzo 55; Ontario, 1871 1823.22 p47
Dunk, George 42; Ontario, 1871 1823.22 p47
Dunk, John 31; Ontario, 1871 1823.28 p25
Dunk, Lewis 54; Ontario, 1871 1823.22 p47
Dunk, Mary Jane 29; Ontario, 1871 1823.28 p25
Dunk, Sophia 66; Ontario, 1871 1823.28 p25
Dunk, William 46; Ontario, 1871 1823.22 p47
Dunkan, John; Virginia, 1714 1224.2 p36
Dunkarn, Thomas 20; Philadelphia, 1774 1220.25 p3
Dunkel, Alexander 7; Kansas, 1908-1910 9079.10 p10
Dunkel, Andrew 15; Kansas, 1908-1910 9079.10 p10
Dunkel, Andrew 35; Kansas, 1908-1910 9079.10 p10
Dunkel, Anna 38; Kansas, 1908-1910 9079.10 p10
Dunkel, Eva; Port uncertain, 1757 2856.30 p88
Dunkel, Johann Melchior; Port uncertain, 1762 2856.30 p88
Dunkel, Johann Melchior; Port uncertain, 1792 2856.30 p88
Dunkel, Johann Melchior; Port uncertain, 1793 2856.30 p88
Dunkel, Joseph 3; Kansas, 1908-1910 9079.10 p10
Dunkel, Margaret 9; Kansas, 1908-1910 9079.10 p10
Dunkeld, William 40; Ontario, 1871 1823.15 p69
Dunkin, Anthony Parker; Philadelphia, 1826 1224.3 p23
Dunkin, Henry; Philadelphia, 1826 1224.3 p23
Dunkin, John; Maryland, 1659 2524.55 p72
Dunkin, John; Maryland, 1664 2524.55 p72
Dunkin, John; New York, 1840 1224.3 p23
Dunkin, Robert; Philadelphia, 1784 1224.2 p36
Dunkley, Carleton; Charleston, South Carolina, 1817 1224.3 p23
Dunkley, George 39; Ontario, 1871 1823.15 p69
Dunkley, George 82; Ontario, 1871 1823.15 p69
Dunkley, William 18; Maryland, 1775 1220.25 p96
Dunlap, James; New York, 1840 8197.10 p157
Dunlap, James; Pennsylvania, 1786 4629.10 p50
Dunlap, John; New York, 1839 8197.10 p226
Dunlap, William; New York, 1834 8197.10 p315
Dunlavay, Mary J.; Vermont, 1880-1950 5900.10 p603
Dunlea, Jeremiah; Vermont, 1851-1873 5900.10 p246
Dunleavy, Mary; Vermont, 1830-1930 5900.10 p473
Dunlevy, John B.; Vermont, 1847-1910 5900.10 p115
Dunlevy, Margaret 60; Vermont, 1884 5900.10 p111
Dunlevy, Sarah J. Hurley; Vermont, 1854-1942 5900.10 p115
Dunley, Bridget Starr; Vermont, 1835-1912 5900.10 p586
Dunley, Patrick; Vermont, 1834-1914 5900.10 p586
Dunley, William; New York, 1834 8197.10 p72
Dunley, William 50; Ontario, 1871 1823.22 p47
Dunlop, Mr.; Quebec, 1857 9196.15 p17
Dunlop, Agness 50; Ontario, 1871 1823.15 p69
Dunlop, C.; Quebec, 1857 9196.15 p14
Dunlop, Colin McKenzie; Virginia, 1876 1640.13 p33
Dunlop, James; New York, 1840 8197.10 p157
Dunlop, James 30; Ontario, 1871 1823.28 p26
Dunlop, James 53; Ontario, 1871 1823.28 p26
Dunlop, John; New York, 1839 8197.10 p226
Dunlop, John 53; Ontario, 1871 1823.15 p69
Dunlop, John 57; Ontario, 1871 1823.28 p26
Dunlop, John Alexander; Jamaica, 1844 1640.13 p33
Dunlop, Nathaniel; New York, 1822 8197.10 p223
Dunlop, William; Cincinnati, 1869 1640.13 p33
Dunlop, William; New York, 1820 8197.10 p222
Dunlop, William; New York, 1825 8197.10 p297
Dunlop, William 50; Ontario, 1871 1823.15 p69
Dunmore, William; New York, 1807 8197.10 p38
Dunn, Miss 20; Barbados, 1774 1220.25 p62
Dunn, Mr.; Quebec, 1857 9196.15 p26
Dunn, Mrs.; Quebec, 1857 9196.15 p21
Dunn, Mrs.; Quebec, 1857 9196.15 p26
Dunn, Albert T.; Vermont, 1850-1903 5900.10 p244
Dunn, Amelia; New York, 1899 1640.13 p34
Dunn, Anastasia Cass; Vermont, 1841-1921 5900.10 p117
Dunn, Ann 43 *SEE* Dunn, William
Dunn, Ann Delehanty; Vermont, n.d. 5900.10 p392
Dunn, Anna F.; Vermont, n.d. 5900.10 p392
Dunn, Arthur F. 20; British Columbia, 1914 9196.1 p66
Dunn, Arthur F. 20; Portland, Oregon, 1914 9196.1 p66
Dunn, Arvilla H.; Vermont, 1824-1904 5900.10 p244
Dunn, B. 50; Ontario, 1861 2896.28 p5
Dunn, Bernard; New York, 1826-1831 8197.10 p369
Dunn, Biddy 19 *SEE* Dunn, William
Dunn, Bridget; Vermont, 1861-1862 5900.10 p248
Dunn, Bridget; Vermont, 1899 5900.10 p392
Dunn, Bridget 53; Vermont, 1882 5900.10 p248
Dunn, Bridget 73; Ontario, 1871 1823.15 p69
Dunn, Bridget Daly; Vermont, 1816-1906 5900.10 p391
Dunn, Bridget Hickey; Vermont, 1834-1889 5900.10 p427
Dunn, Bridget Moren 36; Vermont, 1878 5900.10 p148
Dunn, Catharine 29; Vermont, 1862 5900.10 p325
Dunn, Catherine A.; Vermont, n.d. 5900.10 p130
Dunn, Charles; Nova Scotia, 1722 1224.2 p36
Dunn, Cora L.; Vermont, n.d. 5900.10 p130
Dunn, Cornelia A.; Vermont, 1844-1910 5900.10 p244
Dunn, Daniel; Vermont, 1845-1911 5900.10 p441
Dunn, David; New York, 1840 8197.10 p159
Dunn, Dennis; New York, 1840 8197.10 p226
Dunn, Edward; New York, 1807 8197.10 p328
Dunn, Edward 21; Maryland, 1774 1220.25 p77
Dunn, Eliza 26; Ontario, 1861 2896.28 p44
Dunn, Elizabeth *SEE* Dunn, Obediah
Dunn, Elizabeth; Maryland, 1682 2524.55 p72
Dunn, Elizabeth; Vermont, 1827-1897 5900.10 p254
Dunn, Elizabeth Butler; Vermont, 1865-1934 5900.10 p441
Dunn, Elizabeth T.; Vermont, n.d. 5900.10 p392
Dunn, Ellen; Vermont, 1816-1897 5900.10 p324
Dunn, Esther Shippe; Vermont, 1835-1899 5900.10 p350
Dunn, Fintan; New York, 1823 8197.10 p224
Dunn, George 42; Ontario, 1871 1823.22 p47
Dunn, George A.; Vermont, n.d. 5900.10 p244
Dunn, Helen; New York, 1839 8197.10 p381
Dunn, Henry; New York, 1837 8197.10 p83
Dunn, Honora Purtell; Vermont, 1818-1891 5900.10 p216
Dunn, Hugh 43; Ontario, 1871 1823.15 p69
Dunn, Idalette; Vermont, 1856-1907 5900.10 p244
Dunn, James; Pennsylvania, 1777 4629.10 p16
Dunn, James; Pennsylvania, 1790 4629.10 p59
Dunn, James; Pennsylvania, 1839 6058.10 p16
Dunn, James 2; Ontario, 1861 2896.28 p44
Dunn, James 8 *SEE* Dunn, William
Dunn, James 28; Ontario, 1871 1823.22 p47
Dunn, James 65; Ontario, 1871 1823.28 p26
Dunn, James 82; Vermont, 1903 5900.10 p56
Dunn, Jane; Quebec, 1858 9196.15 p38
Dunn, Jane 20; Georgia, 1775 1220.25 p126
Dunn, Jemia. 57; Vermont, 1876 5900.10 p295
Dunn, Jno; Vermont, n.d. 5900.10 p100
Dunn, Jno 16; Ontario, 1861 2896.28 p5
Dunn, John; Maryland, 1664 2524.55 p72
Dunn, John; Maryland, 1676 2524.55 p72
Dunn, John; Pennsylvania, 1839 6058.10 p15
Dunn, John; Vermont, n.d. 5900.10 p393
Dunn, John; Vermont, 1817-1907 5900.10 p216
Dunn, John; Vermont, 1853-1922 5900.10 p441
Dunn, John 35; Pennsylvania, 1790 4629.10 p59
Dunn, John N.; Vermont, 1855-1928 5900.10 p244
Dunn, John Ritchie; San Francisco, 1881 1640.13 p34
Dunn, Jonathan 39; Ontario, 1871 1823.22 p47
Dunn, Joseph; Maryland, 1718 1224.2 p36
Dunn, Joseph; Vermont, 1813-1898 5900.10 p301
Dunn, Joseph; Virginia, 1666-1667 6212.30 p35
Dunn, Joseph 50; Ontario, 1871 1823.22 p47
Dunn, Kate Smith; Vermont, 1853-1877 5900.10 p544
Dunn, Katherine; Vermont, n.d. 5900.10 p392
Dunn, L. A.; Vermont, 1814-1888 5900.10 p244
Dunn, Lizzie 19; Vermont, 1874 5900.10 p56
Dunn, Lucinda M.; Vermont, 1808-1881 5900.10 p301
Dunn, Lucy A.; Vermont, 1852-1922 5900.10 p244

Dunn, Lucy A. T.; Vermont, 1811-1853 ***5900.10*** *p244*
Dunn, M. 14; Ontario, 1861 ***2896.28*** *p5*
Dunn, M. 60; Ontario, 1861 ***2896.28*** *p5*
Dunn, Margaret; Pennsylvania, 1790 ***4629.10*** *p59*
Dunn, Margaret 80; Vermont, 1907 ***5900.10*** *p46*
Dunn, Margaret Cunningham; Vermont, 1842-1900 ***5900.10*** *p216*
Dunn, Maria; New York, 1834 ***8197.10*** *p225*
Dunn, Maria; Vermont, n.d. ***5900.10*** *p392*
Dunn, Martha E.; Vermont, 1844-1926 ***5900.10*** *p301*
Dunn, Martha M.; Vermont, 1879-1944 ***5900.10*** *p392*
Dunn, Martin; Vermont, 1837-1913 ***5900.10*** *p117*
Dunn, Martin; Vermont, 1847-1896 ***5900.10*** *p544*
Dunn, Martin F.; Vermont, 1863-1925 ***5900.10*** *p115*
Dunn, Mary; Vermont, 1839-1924 ***5900.10*** *p491*
Dunn, Mary; Vermont, 1850-1928 ***5900.10*** *p483*
Dunn, Mary; Vermont, 1854-1912 ***5900.10*** *p43*
Dunn, Mary; Vermont, 1855-1932 ***5900.10*** *p288*
Dunn, Mary 11; Vermont, 1861 ***5900.10*** *p248*
Dunn, Mary 55; Vermont, 1868 ***5900.10*** *p102*
Dunn, Mary A.; Vermont, n.d. ***5900.10*** *p130*
Dunn, Mary A.; Vermont, 1857-1900 ***5900.10*** *p439*
Dunn, Mary A.; Vermont, 1863-1880 ***5900.10*** *p244*
Dunn, Mary Ann Macksey; Vermont, 1847-1885 ***5900.10*** *p81*
Dunn, Mary Butler; Vermont, 1857-1900 ***5900.10*** *p544*
Dunn, Mary Celia Baker; Vermont, 1859-1897 ***5900.10*** *p115*
Dunn, Mary Feighelle 40; Vermont, 1844 ***5900.10*** *p148*
Dunn, Mary O'Neill 85; Vermont, 1899 ***5900.10*** *p294*
Dunn, Matthew 60; Ontario, 1871 ***1823.22*** *p47*
Dunn, Michael; New York, 1824 ***8197.10*** *p224*
Dunn, Michael; New York, 1838 ***8197.10*** *p378*
Dunn, Michael; New York, 1840 ***8197.10*** *p159*
Dunn, Michael 76; Ontario, 1871 ***1823.22*** *p48*
Dunn, Nathan; Philadelphia, 1845 ***1224.3*** *p23*
Dunn, Nich; Virginia, 1678 ***6212.30*** *p54*
Dunn, Nicholas; Vermont, 1880-1933 ***5900.10*** *p117*
Dunn, Obediah; Maryland, 1676 ***2524.55*** *p72*
Wife: Elizabeth
Dunn, Owen 32; Maryland, 1774 ***1220.25*** *p65*
Dunn, Patrick; New York, 1821 ***8197.10*** *p223*
Dunn, Patrick; Vermont, n.d. ***5900.10*** *p248*
Dunn, Patrick; Vermont, n.d. ***5900.10*** *p393*
Dunn, Patrick; Vermont, 1836-1912 ***5900.10*** *p216*
Dunn, Patrick 19; Ontario, 1861 ***2896.28*** *p7*
Dunn, Patrick 30; Ontario, 1871 ***1823.15*** *p69*
Dunn, Patrick 84; Vermont, 1878 ***5900.10*** *p148*
Dunn, Richard 10 weeks; Vermont, 1879 ***5900.10*** *p294*
Dunn, Richard 37; Ontario, 1871 ***1823.28*** *p26*
Dunn, Robert 1; Vermont, 1860 ***5900.10*** *p210*
Dunn, Rosanna Smith 87; Vermont, 1905 ***5900.10*** *p56*
Dunn, Rose Anna; Vermont, 1830-1906 ***5900.10*** *p46*
Dunn, Sophia 45; Ontario, 1871 ***1823.22*** *p48*
Dunn, Thomas; Vermont, 1828-1928 ***5900.10*** *p350*
Dunn, Thomas; Vermont, 1835-1890 ***5900.10*** *p427*
Dunn, Thomas; Virginia, 1664 ***6212.30*** *p11*
Dunn, Thomas 28; Ontario, 1861 ***2896.28*** *p44*
Dunn, Thomas 35; Ontario, 1871 ***1823.22*** *p48*
Dunn, Thomas 55; Ontario, 1871 ***1823.15*** *p69*
Dunn, Thomas 57; Vermont, 1874 ***5900.10*** *p46*
Dunn, Thomas 60; Ontario, 1871 ***1823.22*** *p48*
Dunn, Thomas L.; Vermont, n.d. ***5900.10*** *p130*
Dunn, Walter; Virginia, 1820 ***1224.3*** *p23*
Dunn, William; Maryland, 1678 ***2524.55*** *p72*
Dunn, William; New York, 1836 ***8197.10*** *p78*
Dunn, William; New York, 1840 ***8197.10*** *p157*
Dunn, William; New York, 1842 ***1224.3*** *p24*
Dunn, William; Vermont, 1841-1902 ***5900.10*** *p148*
Dunn, William; Vermont, 1875-1896 ***5900.10*** *p117*
Dunn, William 6 *SEE* Dunn, William
Dunn, William 21; Ontario, 1871 ***1823.28*** *p26*
Dunn, William 36; Virginia, 1774 ***1220.25*** *p45*
Dunn, William 40; Ontario, 1871 ***1823.28*** *p26*
Dunn, William 45; New York, New York, 1852 ***1825.45*** *p58*
Wife: Ann 43
Son: James 8
Son: William 6
Daughter: Biddy 19
Dunn, William 67; Ontario, 1871 ***1823.28*** *p26*
Dunn, William, Sr.; Vermont, n.d. ***5900.10*** *p392*
Dunn, William H., Jr.; Vermont, n.d. ***5900.10*** *p392*
Dunne, Mr.; Quebec, 1858 ***9196.15*** *p46*
Dunne, Alice; Vermont, 1853-1925 ***5900.10*** *p300*
Dunne, James; Vermont, 1845-1924 ***5900.10*** *p291*
Dunne, James 58; Ontario, 1871 ***1823.28*** *p26*
Dunne, Mary; Vermont, 1849-1925 ***5900.10*** *p291*
Dunnelly, Joseph 32; Ontario, 1871 ***1823.28*** *p26*
Dunnett, Miss; Quebec, 1857 ***9196.15*** *p25*
Dunnett, Mr.; Quebec, 1857 ***9196.15*** *p25*
Dunnett, James 54; Ontario, 1871 ***1823.22*** *p48*
Dunnett, Robert 49; Ontario, 1871 ***1823.22*** *p48*
Dunnigs, J. 18; Ontario, 1861 ***2896.25*** *p47*
Dunniken, William 28; Ontario, 1871 ***1823.15*** *p69*
Dunning, . . .; Boston, 1765 ***4628.40*** *p114*
Dunning, Jeremiah 67; Ontario, 1871 ***1823.22*** *p48*
Dunning, John 24; Fort Cumberland, Nova Scotia, 1774 ***1220.25*** *p17*
Dunning, L. J. 25; Ontario, 1861 ***2896.28*** *p11*
Dunning, Mary; Vermont, 1837-1912 ***5900.10*** *p512*
Dunning, Theophilus 15; Philadelphia, 1775 ***1220.25*** *p107*
Dunning, Thomas; New York, 1806 ***8197.10*** *p324*
Dunning, William 16; Ontario, 1861 ***2896.27*** *p12*
Dunnitt, William 42; Ontario, 1871 ***1823.22*** *p48*
Dunnock, Mr.; Maryland, 1657 ***2524.55*** *p72*
Dunnock, Margaret; Maryland, 1657 ***2524.55*** *p72*
Dunogh, Derby; Maryland, 1678 ***2524.55*** *p72*
Dunoon, Mary A. Shannon; Vermont, 1845-1926 ***5900.10*** *p386*
Dunoon, Thomas E.; Vermont, 1845-1922 ***5900.10*** *p386*
Dunovan, P. W.; Pennsylvania, 1868 ***6058.10*** *p66*
Dunphy, Joseph 44; Vermont, 1872 ***5900.10*** *p159*
Dunscorad, George Hoyles 53; Ontario, 1871 ***1823.22*** *p48*
Dunsell, Phillis; Maryland, 1675 ***2524.55*** *p72*
Dunsford, Catherine 66; Ontario, 1871 ***1823.15*** *p70*
Dunshee, Robert; New York, 1839 ***8197.10*** *p129*
Dunsmore, Henry 40; Ontario, 1871 ***1823.15*** *p70*
Dunson, Joseph; Maryland, 1910 ***3259.35*** *p13*
Dunster, Charles; New Jersey, 1732 ***1224.2*** *p36*
Dunster, Elizabeth 21 *SEE* Dunster, William
Dunster, Tobias; Virginia, 1663 ***6212.30*** *p1*
Dunster, William 22; Baltimore, 1775 ***1220.25*** *p117*
Dunster, William 40; Maryland, 1774 ***1220.25*** *p84*
Wife: Elizabeth 21
Dunton, Cleora P.; Vermont, 1829-1901 ***5900.10*** *p276*
Dunton, Ida A. McFeeters; Vermont, 1857-1934 ***5900.10*** *p457*
Dunton, William Henry; Vermont, 1854-1933 ***5900.10*** *p457*
Duntz, Hans Michael; Port uncertain, 1748 ***2856.30*** *p89*
Duntz, Josef; Port uncertain, 1764 ***2856.30*** *p78*
Dunwoodie, Robert 46; Ontario, 1871 ***1823.22*** *p48*
Dunworth, . . .; Boston, 1765 ***4628.40*** *p114*
Dunz, Josef; Port uncertain, 1789 ***2856.30*** *p89*
Dunzweiler, Jakob; Port uncertain, 1751 ***2856.30*** *p89*
Duoney, Margaret 48; Vermont, 1854 ***5900.10*** *p74*
Dupant, Sicame; New York, 1812-1834 ***8197.10*** *p305*
Duparke, Eliza *SEE* Duparke, Thomas
Duparke, Thomas; Maryland, 1662 ***2524.55*** *p72*
Wife: Eliza
Dupaw, Catharine McDonal; Vermont, 1847-1882 ***5900.10*** *p142*
Duphiney, Father 71; Vermont, 1864 ***5900.10*** *p363*
Dupich, John 25; Alaska, 1917 ***9196.1*** *p50*
Dupich, John 25; Yukon, 1917 ***9196.1*** *p50*
Duplex, George; New York, 1794 ***8197.10*** *p5*
Dupont, Catharine; Vermont, 1834-1896 ***5900.10*** *p265*
Dupont, Catherine *SEE* Dupont, Francis
Dupont, Catherine Caffry 32; Vermont, 1863 ***5900.10*** *p248*
Dupont, Francis; Philadelphia, 1789 ***4629.10*** *p59*
Wife: Catherine
Dupont, Francis Clery 28; Philadelphia, 1789 ***4629.10*** *p59*
Dupont, Gideon; Charles Town, South Carolina, 1788 ***1224.2*** *p36*
Dupont, L. 45; Fairbanks, Alaska, 1910 ***9196.1*** *p9*
Dupont, L. 45; Yukon, 1910 ***9196.1*** *p9*
Dupont, Louis 24; Alaska, 1917 ***9196.1*** *p48*
Dupont, Louis 24; Whitehorse, Yukon, 1917 ***9196.1*** *p48*
Dupont, Louis 47; Alaska, 1916 ***9196.1*** *p6*
Dupont, Louis 47; Yukon, 1916 ***9196.1*** *p6*
Duport, Peter L.; New York, 1809 ***8197.10*** *p55*
Dupper, Ann; Virginia, 1678 ***6212.30*** *p54*
Dupras, Christine; Alabama, 1810-1834 ***1640.10*** *p47*
Dupre, Jacob; America, 1738 ***2856.30*** *p89*
Dupre, Julius A.; New York, 1830 ***8197.10*** *p362*
Dupuis, Abraham; America, 1752 ***2856.30*** *p89*
With wife & children
Dupuis, Frank; Vermont, 1852-1925 ***5900.10*** *p429*
Dupuis, Henry 22; Ontario, 1871 ***1823.28*** *p26*
Dupuis, Lucy Lynch; Vermont, 1851-1934 ***5900.10*** *p429*
Dupuy, Alexander; Philadelphia, 1792 ***4629.10*** *p65*
Dupuy, Daniel; Pennsylvania, 1777 ***4629.10*** *p25*
Dupuy, Stephen; Philadelphia, 1792 ***4629.10*** *p75*
Durack, John; Vermont, 1876-1926 ***5900.10*** *p459*
Durack, John 57; Vermont, 1866 ***5900.10*** *p602*
Durack, Sarah 45; Vermont, 1854 ***5900.10*** *p602*
Duran, William; Pennsylvania, 1866 ***6058.10*** *p56*
Durand, Miss; Quebec, 1857 ***9196.15*** *p17*
Durand, Mr.; Quebec, 1857 ***9196.15*** *p17*
Durand, Benjamin; New York, 1827 ***8197.10*** *p224*
Durand, Elizabeth *SEE* Durand, William
Durand, William; Maryland, 1648 ***2524.55*** *p72*
With wife
Daughter: Elizabeth
Durando, Paul M. Piccard; New York, 1828 ***8197.10*** *p351*
Duranquit, Domnick 58; Ontario, 1871 ***1823.28*** *p26*
Durant, Elizabeth *SEE* Durant, William
Durant, John; New York, 1829 ***8197.10*** *p225*
Durant, Thomas; New York, 1827 ***8197.10*** *p225*
Durant, Thomas; South Carolina, 1744 ***1224.2*** *p36*
Durant, Thomas 20; Maryland, 1774 ***1220.25*** *p77*
Durant, William; Maryland, 1648 ***2524.55*** *p72*
With wife
Daughter: Elizabeth
Durant, William; New York, 1840 ***8197.10*** *p157*
Durban, Anna Magdalena; America, 1749 ***2856.30*** *p89*
Durban, Edward S.; New York, New York, 1830 ***6058.10*** *p30*
Durbrow, Thomas 60; Ontario, 1871 ***1823.28*** *p26*
Durck, Anna Margarete; Port uncertain, 1731 ***2856.30*** *p89*
Dure, Duncan 55; Ontario, 1871 ***1823.28*** *p26*
Durey, Thomas; Maryland, 1675 ***2524.55*** *p72*
Durford, William; Virginia, 1646 ***1224.1*** *p19*
Durham, Miss; Quebec, 1857 ***9196.15*** *p22*
Durham, Miss E.; Quebec, 1857 ***9196.15*** *p22*
Durham, Miss J.; Quebec, 1857 ***9196.15*** *p22*
Durham, John W.; Vermont, 1855-1929 ***5900.10*** *p373*
Durham, Mary 21; Baltimore, 1775 ***1220.25*** *p116*
Durham, Mary McBride; Vermont, 1857-1928 ***5900.10*** *p373*
Durham, Peter E.; Vermont, 1852-1924 ***5900.10*** *p147*
Durham, Richard; Maryland, 1659 ***2524.55*** *p72*
Durham, Robert; Maryland, 1681 ***2524.55*** *p72*
Durich, M. J. 22; British Columbia, 1909 ***9196.1*** *p27*
Durich, M. J. 22; Seattle, 1909 ***9196.1*** *p27*
Durick, Anna Barbara; Port uncertain, 1738 ***2856.30*** *p89*
Durick, Bridget Lewis; Vermont, 1845-1917 ***5900.10*** *p252*
Durick, Daniel 46; Ontario, 1871 ***1823.28*** *p26*
Durick, Helen Copps; Vermont, 1833-1901 ***5900.10*** *p274*
Durick, Jeremiah 48; Vermont, 1884 ***5900.10*** *p252*
Durick, John; Vermont, 1835-1906 ***5900.10*** *p274*
Durick, Margaret 40; Vermont, 1874 ***5900.10*** *p573*
Durick, Margaret Kain 60; Vermont, 1907 ***5900.10*** *p580*
Durick, Patrick 63; Vermont, 1889 ***5900.10*** *p580*
Duricker, Anna Barbar; America, 1738 ***2856.30*** *p89*
Durie, Lieutenant-Colonel; Quebec, 1858 ***9196.15*** *p36*
Durie, Robert; Kansas City, 1893 ***1640.13*** *p34*
Durivage, Selina; Vermont, 1858-1936 ***5900.10*** *p255*
Durk, Johann Reinhard; Port uncertain, 1725 ***2856.30*** *p79*
With wife & 4 children
Durkee, Jay W.; Vermont, 1852-1921 ***5900.10*** *p283*
Durkee, Mary E. Hanna; Vermont, 1857-1939 ***5900.10*** *p283*
Durkin, Bridget; Vermont, 1908 ***5900.10*** *p145*
Durkin, Jennie; Vermont, 1849-1913 ***5900.10*** *p401*
Durkin, Julia Richardson; Vermont, 1857-1911 ***5900.10*** *p207*
Durkin, Martin; Vermont, 1847-1926 ***5900.10*** *p207*
Durkin, Thomas 33; Vermont, 1886 ***5900.10*** *p207*
Durler, . . .; Port uncertain, 1716 ***2856.30*** *p89*
With mother
Durlin, Honor; Maryland, 1682 ***2524.55*** *p72*
Durly, William; Virginia, 1741 ***1224.2*** *p36*
Durmowiz, Anthony; Maryland, 1910 ***3259.35*** *p13*
Durney, Michael; Pennsylvania, 1779 ***4629.10*** *p38*
Durnher, Caspar; Port uncertain, 1752 ***2856.30*** *p89*
With mother
Durnian, Charles 42; Ontario, 1871 ***1823.15*** *p70*
Durnian, Ellen 82; Ontario, 1871 ***1823.15*** *p70*
Durnian, James 35; Ontario, 1871 ***1823.15*** *p70*
Durnian, William 51; Ontario, 1871 ***1823.15*** *p70*
Durnien, Robert 43; Ontario, 1871 ***1823.15*** *p70*
Durning, James; New York, 1840 ***8197.10*** *p226*
Durr, Anna Maria; Port uncertain, 1752 ***2856.30*** *p89*
Durr, Augustus; New York, 1839 ***8197.10*** *p129*
Durr, Georg; Port uncertain, 1770 ***2856.30*** *p89*
Durr, Hans Georg; America, 1747 ***2856.30*** *p89*
With wife
Durr, Hans Georg; America, 1751 ***2856.30*** *p89*
Durr, Jakob Simon; New York, 1838 ***8197.10*** *p225*
Durr, Johannes; New York, 1839 ***8197.10*** *p129*
Durr, Peter; Port uncertain, 1734 ***2856.30*** *p89*
Durrance, John; Virginia, 1705 ***1224.2*** *p36*
Durrant, Robert 23; Ontario, 1871 ***1823.15*** *p70*
Durred, William 15; Virginia, 1773 ***1220.25*** *p31*
Durrfussin, Cath. Margarete; America, 1750 ***2856.30*** *p89*
With husband & son
Durrick, Patrick 33; Ontario, 1871 ***1823.28*** *p26*
Durrmajer, Johann Georg; Port uncertain, 1751 ***2856.30*** *p89*

Durrmeyer, Germann; Port uncertain, 1738 2856.30 p89
Durrmeyer, Hans Georg; Port uncertain, 1727 2856.30 p89
Durrmeyer, Hans Georg; Port uncertain, 1769 2856.30 p89
Durrmeyer, Johann; Port uncertain, 1727 2856.30 p89
Durrmeyer, Johann; Port uncertain, 1769 2856.30 p90
Durrstein, Samuel; Port uncertain, 1738 2856.30 p90
Durrstein, Samuel; Port uncertain, 1751 2856.30 p90
Durrum, Henry; Maryland, 1663 2524.55 p72
Dursdall, D. M.; Quebec, 1857 9196.15 p25
Durst, Adam 66; Ontario, 1871 1823.15 p70
Durst, Hans; America, 1765 2856.30 p89
Durst, Peter; America, 1764 2856.30 p85
Durstler, Adam; America, 1765 2856.30 p90
Durston, Elizabeth; Wisconsin, 1856 1224.3 p24
Dury, Thomas; Maryland, 1675 2524.55 p72
Dury, William; New York, 1839 8197.10 p129
Dusbury, Thomas; Maryland, 1672 2524.55 p73
Dusenbury, William 5; Ontario, 1871 1823.22 p48
Duslan, John P.; New York, 1803 8197.10 p12
Duss, Christof; Port uncertain, 1742 2856.30 p89
Dussen, Christof; Port uncertain, 1742 2856.30 p89
Dussler, Jakob; America, 1752 2856.30 p89
Dussler, Maria; America, 1752 2856.30 p89
Dusterkotter, Henrich; New York, 1830 8197.10 p312
Dustow, James 47; Ontario, 1871 1823.15 p70
Duszewski, John; Maryland, 1910 3259.35 p13
Duszynski, Roman; Maryland, 1910 3259.35 p13
Dutch, Cornelius 27; Maryland, 1775 1220.25 p98
Dutch, James 16; Maryland, 1775 1220.25 p98
Dutch, John 23; Maryland, 1775 1220.25 p99
Wife: Mary 23
Dutch, Mary 23 *SEE* Dutch, John
Dutch, Susana; Virginia, 1674-1675 6212.30 p53
Dutch, Thomas 21; Maryland, 1775 1220.25 p99
Dutchman, Isacc; Virginia, 1672 6212.30 p49
Duthie, James Cowe; Denver, Colorado, 1887 1640.13 p34
Duttenhofer, Augustus; New York, 1826 8197.10 p224
Dutton, Bridget 63; Vermont, 1894 5900.10 p297
Dutton, Cecelia Kennedy; Vermont, 1940 5900.10 p323
Dutton, Harry N.; Vermont, 1941 5900.10 p323
Dutton, John 15; Grenada, 1773-1774 1220.25 p124
Dutton, Mary A. Goeg 43; Vermont, 1899 5900.10 p188
Dutton, Thomas 23; Maryland, 1775 1220.25 p96
Duty, John; Maryland, 1656 2524.55 p73
Duval, . . . 16; Grenada, 1774 1220.25 p128
Duval, Jean; Port uncertain, 1752 2856.30 p89
Duvan, Charles; New York, 1805 8197.10 p29
Duvban, Edward S.; New York, New York, 1830 6058.10 p30
Duvine, Michael 39; Ontario, 1871 1823.15 p70
Duvivier, Peter; Philadelphia, 1792 4629.10 p75
Duxen, George; Philadelphia, 1793 4629.10 p69
Duyea, Julia; Vermont, 1847-1913 5900.10 p481
Duzack, Stan; Maryland, 1910 3259.35 p13
Dwan, Ellen Crow 29; Vermont, 1845 5900.10 p612
Dwane, James; New York, 1840 8197.10 p226
Dwiderski, John; Maryland, 1910 3259.35 p13
Dwire, Margaret 97; Vermont, 1910 5900.10 p123
Dwire, Olive; Vermont, 1852-1932 5900.10 p414
Dwire, Thomas 49; Ontario, 1871 1823.28 p26
Dwyer, Mr.; Quebec, 1858 9196.15 p37
Dwyer, Mrs.; Quebec, 1858 9196.15 p37
Dwyer, Bridget; Vermont, 1826-1873 5900.10 p561
Dwyer, Bridget; Vermont, 1835-1909 5900.10 p331
Dwyer, Bridget; Vermont, 1844-1924 5900.10 p257
Dwyer, Bridget 58; Vermont, 1881 5900.10 p614
Dwyer, Bridget 87; Vermont, 1894 5900.10 p582
Dwyer, Catherine; Vermont, 1896 5900.10 p116
Dwyer, Catherine 40; Vermont, 1872 5900.10 p200
Dwyer, Charles; Vermont, 1921 5900.10 p425
Dwyer, Connor 56; Ontario, 1871 1823.28 p26
Dwyer, Daniel; Vermont, 1830-1910 5900.10 p590
Dwyer, Edmund; Maryland, 1682 2524.55 p73
Dwyer, Edward; Vermont, 1834-1919 5900.10 p136
Dwyer, Ellen; Vermont, 1850-1901 5900.10 p139
Dwyer, Ellen 50; Vermont, 1870 5900.10 p189
Dwyer, Hanora; Vermont, 1826-1906 5900.10 p422
Dwyer, Herbert; Vermont, 1841-1936 5900.10 p520
Dwyer, James; New York, 1838 8197.10 p108
Dwyer, James 63; Vermont, 1913 5900.10 p425
Dwyer, Johanna Fean 74; Vermont, 1918 5900.10 p425
Dwyer, Johannah 55; Vermont, 1911 5900.10 p582
Dwyer, John; New York, 1837 8197.10 p86
Dwyer, John; New York, 1838 8197.10 p108
Dwyer, John; New York, 1838 8197.10 p375
Dwyer, John 68; Ontario, 1871 1823.28 p26
Dwyer, Julia 60; Vermont, 1873 5900.10 p590
Dwyer, Margaret 39; Vermont, 1887 5900.10 p582
Dwyer, Margaret 48; Vermont, 1877 5900.10 p571
Dwyer, Margaret Donovan; Vermont, 1849-1919 5900.10 p590
Dwyer, Margaret J.; Vermont, 1861-1939 5900.10 p490
Dwyer, Margaret McSweeney 99; Vermont, 1937 5900.10 p186
Dwyer, Martha Abell; Vermont, 1845-1910 5900.10 p520
Dwyer, Martin; New York, 1840 8197.10 p157
Dwyer, Martin 60; Ontario, 1871 1823.15 p70
Dwyer, Mary; Vermont, 1847-1904 5900.10 p399
Dwyer, Mary; Vermont, 1866-1945 5900.10 p490
Dwyer, Mary 38; Vermont, 1883 5900.10 p280
Dwyer, Mary 80; Vermont, 1897 5900.10 p177
Dwyer, Mary A. 68; Vermont, 1898 5900.10 p590
Dwyer, Mary Ann Boyle 51; Vermont, 1893 5900.10 p136
Dwyer, Mary Casey; Vermont, 1819-1893 5900.10 p139
Dwyer, Mary Riley 72; Vermont, 1913 5900.10 p465
Dwyer, Maty 36; Vermont, 1846 5900.10 p64
Dwyer, Michael; Vermont, 1856-1888 5900.10 p139
Dwyer, Nancy; Vermont, 1869-1900 5900.10 p332
Dwyer, Nancy 74; Vermont, 1901 5900.10 p466
Dwyer, Nora Fean 49; Vermont, 1896 5900.10 p425
Dwyer, Patrick; Vermont, 1838-1896 5900.10 p186
Dwyer, Patrick; Vermont, 1838-1896 5900.10 p581
Dwyer, Mrs. Patrick; Vermont, 1840-1913 5900.10 p581
Dwyer, Sarah; Vermont, 1834-1906 5900.10 p560
Dwyer, Thomas; Vermont, 1818-1878 5900.10 p139
Dwyer, Thomas 52; Ontario, 1871 1823.22 p48
Dwyer, Thomas 73; Vermont, 1911 5900.10 p464
Dwyer, Thomas E.; New York, 1840 8197.10 p156
Dwyer, William; Vermont, 1827-1881 5900.10 p331
Dwyer, William 67; Vermont, 1853 5900.10 p189
Dwyre, John 52; Ontario, 1871 1823.28 p26
Dwyret, Patrick 28; Ontario, 1871 1823.15 p70
Dya, Warren; Maryland, 1672 2524.55 p184
Dyal, Mary 23; Jamaica, 1775 1220.25 p113
Dyar, Edmond; Maryland, 1676 2524.55 p73
Dybies, Wladyslaw; Maryland, 1910 3259.35 p13
Dyck, Daniel; New York, 1806 8197.10 p324
Dyde, Robert; New York, 1810 8197.10 p56
Dye, J. S.; Quebec, 1856 9196.15 p6
Dye, Mrs. J. S.; Quebec, 1856 9196.15 p6
Dyell, Captain; Quebec, 1858 9196.15 p33
Dyer, Alexander 36; Ontario, 1871 1823.15 p70
Dyer, Ann Kelty; Vermont, 1838-1925 5900.10 p296
Dyer, Catherine; Vermont, 1866-1942 5900.10 p434
Dyer, Frank; Vermont, 1852-1908 5900.10 p74
Dyer, George; Vermont, 1852-1917 5900.10 p292
Dyer, John; Maryland, 1676 2524.55 p73
Dyer, John B.; Vermont, 1853-1935 5900.10 p434
Dyer, Joseph 17; New York, 1775 1220.25 p94
Dyer, Joseph 21; Maryland, 1774 1220.25 p73
Dyer, Joseph 21; South Carolina, 1774 1220.25 p83
Dyer, Manda; Vermont, 1860-1940 5900.10 p292
Dyer, Margaret; Vermont, 1845-1918 5900.10 p443
Dyer, Margaret; Vermont, 1850-1908 5900.10 p74
Dyer, Martin 36; Ontario, 1871 1823.15 p70
Dyer, Mary 72; Vermont, 1889 5900.10 p416
Dyer, Michael; Vermont, 1839-1913 5900.10 p296
Dyer, Patrick; Vermont, 1827-1899 5900.10 p443
Dyer, Peter; Maryland, 1667 2524.55 p73
Dyer, Philip; Maryland, 1681 2524.55 p73
Dyer, Robert; Virginia, 1718 1224.2 p36
Dyer, Thomas; Virginia, 1665 6212.30 p18
Dyett, John; Maryland, 1661 2524.55 p73
Dyinkinska, Regina; Maryland, 1910 3259.35 p13
Dyke, James; New York, 1807 8197.10 p37
Dyke, John 27; Ontario, 1871 1823.28 p26
Dyke, Samuel 33; Ontario, 1871 1823.15 p70
Dykes, Francis; New York, 1840 8197.10 p157
Dymant, Humphry 30; Ontario, 1871 1823.15 p70
Dymant, William 76; Ontario, 1871 1823.15 p70
Dynan, Mary Lynch 86; Vermont, 1917 5900.10 p396
Dynan, Michael 35; Vermont, 1871 5900.10 p396
Dyne, William; Maryland, 1672 2524.55 p73
Dynes, Edward 29; Ontario, 1871 1823.15 p70
Dynes, William 33; Ontario, 1871 1823.15 p70
Dyre, A. 5; Ontario, 1861 2896.26 p8
Dyre, E. 28; Ontario, 1861 2896.26 p8
Dyre, J. J. 7; Ontario, 1861 2896.26 p8
Dyre, M. C. 64; Ontario, 1861 2896.26 p8
Dyre, William; Pennsylvania, 1690 1224.1 p19
Dyre, William 53; Ontario, 1861 2896.26 p21
Dyrgosh, Stephen; Maryland, 1910 3259.35 p13
Dyrolf, Johann; Port uncertain, 1775 2856.30 p462
Dysart, James 61; Ontario, 1871 1823.15 p70
Dyson, Dunbar Smith; New York, 1831 1640.10 p47
Dyson, Edward; Savannah, Georgia, 1740 1224.2 p36
Dyson, John; New York, 1838 8197.10 p108
Dytche, William 20; Virginia, 1774 1220.25 p91
Dyton, Jane; Virginia, 1676 6212.30 p53
Dyunnik, Frank S.; Maryland, 1910 3259.35 p13
Dzautek, Alex; Maryland, 1910 3259.35 p13
Dzcanocack, Hedwig; Maryland, 1910 3259.35 p13
Dzestoe, P. 35; Alaska, 1917 9196.1 p45
Dzestoe, P. 35; Whitehorse, Yukon, 1917 9196.1 p45
Dzienlewska, Mary; Maryland, 1910 3259.35 p13
Dziewandowski, Alexander; Maryland, 1910 3259.35 p13
Dzinck, Anna; Maryland, 1910 3259.35 p13
Dzunik, Augusta; Maryland, 1910 3259.35 p13

E

Eachus, Robert; Pennsylvania, 1777 ***4629.10*** *p18*
Eackman, Elizabeth; Virginia, 1704 ***1224.2*** *p36*
Eacreth, Charles 29; Ontario, 1871 ***1823.15*** *p70*
Eacreth, George 39; Ontario, 1871 ***1823.15*** *p70*
Eacrett, Michal 33; Ontario, 1871 ***1823.15*** *p70*
Eacritt, Christiphor 36; Ontario, 1871 ***1823.15*** *p70*
Eade, James 33; Ontario, 1871 ***1823.28*** *p26*
Eades, John; New England, 1698 ***1224.1*** *p19*
Eadie, George Frederick; New York, 1866 ***1640.13*** *p35*
Eadie, Thomas 58; Ontario, 1871 ***1823.15*** *p70*
Eady, George, Sr. 57; Ontario, 1871 ***1823.28*** *p26*
Eaed, John 60; Ontario, 1871 ***1823.15*** *p70*
Eagan, Annie M.; Vermont, 1856-1903 ***5900.10*** *p62*
Eagan, Catharine; Vermont, 1815-1879 ***5900.10*** *p346*
Eagan, Ellen 23; Vermont, 1869 ***5900.10*** *p368*
Eagan, John; Vermont, 1796-1877 ***5900.10*** *p346*
Eagan, John 78; Vermont, 1864 ***5900.10*** *p105*
Eagan, Mary Lillis 65; Vermont, 1874 ***5900.10*** *p105*
Eagan, Patrick; Vermont, 1811-1853 ***5900.10*** *p346*
Eagan, Robert; Vermont, 1845-1865 ***5900.10*** *p346*
Eagar, George 38; Ontario, 1871 ***1823.15*** *p70*
Eagar, Robert 35; Ontario, 1871 ***1823.15*** *p70*
Eagen, Honora; Vermont, 1846-1911 ***5900.10*** *p193*
Eager, Henry; New York, 1803 ***8197.10*** *p12*
Eager, Joseph; Pennsylvania, 1777 ***4629.10*** *p31*
Eagle, Alexander 37; Ontario, 1871 ***1823.15*** *p70*
Eagle, Henry; New York, 1802 ***8197.10*** *p20*
Eaglefeild, Ann; Maryland, 1637 ***2524.55*** *p73*
Eagles, Richard; New York, 1839 ***8197.10*** *p130*
Eaglesen, Margaret 20; Ontario, 1871 ***1823.22*** *p48*
Eagleson, Charles 46; Ontario, 1871 ***1823.22*** *p48*
Eagleson, David 50; Ontario, 1871 ***1823.22*** *p48*
Eagleson, James 52; Ontario, 1871 ***1823.22*** *p48*
Eagleson, James 53; Ontario, 1871 ***1823.22*** *p48*
Eagleson, Jane 70; Ontario, 1871 ***1823.15*** *p70*
Eagleson, John 38; Ontario, 1871 ***1823.15*** *p70*
Eagleson, John 56; Ontario, 1871 ***1823.22*** *p48*
Eagleson, Mathew 20; Ontario, 1871 ***1823.22*** *p48*
Eagleson, Matthew 47; Ontario, 1871 ***1823.22*** *p48*
Eagleson, Noble 40; Ontario, 1871 ***1823.15*** *p70*
Eagleson, Robert 40; Ontario, 1871 ***1823.22*** *p48*
Eagleson, William 59; Ontario, 1871 ***1823.22*** *p48*
Eagleson, Willson 26; Ontario, 1871 ***1823.15*** *p70*
Eagleton, Archibald; Georgia, 1698 ***1640.13*** *p35*
Eagleton, Bridgett; Vermont, 1844-1940 ***5900.10*** *p602*
Eagrs, George; Virginia, 1671 ***6212.30*** *p44*
Eahart, William 11; Ontario, 1871 ***1823.22*** *p48*
Eaket, Simon 40; Ontario, 1871 ***1823.15*** *p70*
Eakin, Benjamin; Pennsylvania, 1778 ***4629.10*** *p32*
Eakin, David; Pennsylvania, 1841 ***6058.10*** *p17*
Eakin, James; Philadelphia, 1837 ***6058.10*** *p29*
Eakin, John; Pennsylvania, 1810 ***6058.10*** *p3*
Eakin, John; Pennsylvania, 1849 ***6058.10*** *p25*
Eakin, Joseph; Pennsylvania, 1844 ***6058.10*** *p19*
Eakin, Samuel; Pennsylvania, 1811 ***6058.10*** *p4*
Eakin, Thomas A.; Pennsylvania, 1848 ***6058.10*** *p24*
Eales, Francis 21; Maryland, 1775 ***1220.25*** *p115*
Ealon, Elizabeth; Maryland, 1679 ***2524.55*** *p73*
Ealy, Andrew; Pennsylvania, 1786 ***4629.10*** *p54*
Eames, Thomas; New York, 1824 ***8197.10*** *p227*
Eamond, James 33; Ontario, 1871 ***1823.15*** *p70*
Eams, William 38; Ontario, 1871 ***1823.28*** *p26*
Eana, Margaret 20; Ontario, 1861 ***2896.27*** *p60*
Eargen, West 30; Ontario, 1871 ***1823.15*** *p70*
Earl, Barton 30; Ontario, 1871 ***1823.22*** *p48*
Earl, James 61; Ontario, 1871 ***1823.22*** *p48*
Earl, John; New York, 1794 ***8197.10*** *p5*
Earl, John; New York, New York, 1819 ***8197.10*** *p227*
Earl, Mary 20; Ontario, 1871 ***1823.15*** *p71*
Earl, Thomas 40; Ontario, 1871 ***1823.22*** *p48*
Earl, Thos 55; Ontario, 1871 ***1823.28*** *p26*
Earl, William 40; Ontario, 1871 ***1823.22*** *p48*
Earle, James 26; Ontario, 1871 ***1823.15*** *p71*
Earle, John; Pennsylvania, 1777 ***4629.10*** *p7*
Earle, John 25; Philadelphia, 1774 ***1220.25*** *p26*
Earle, Joseph; New York, 1785 ***1224.2*** *p36*
Earle, Rich; Virginia, 1665-1666 ***6212.30*** *p23*
Earle, Richard; Virginia, 1666-1667 ***6212.30*** *p32*
Earle, William; New York, 1840 ***8197.10*** *p167*
Earle, William 28; Ontario, 1871 ***1823.15*** *p71*
Earley, Mr.; Vermont, n.d. ***5900.10*** *p286*
Earley, Ann McTague 80; Vermont, 1897 ***5900.10*** *p286*
Earley, Catherine; Vermont, n.d. ***5900.10*** *p286*
Earley, Catherine J. O'Hara; Vermont, 1855-1914 ***5900.10*** *p184*
Earley, Esther Mina; Vermont, n.d. ***5900.10*** *p286*
Earley, Francis 67; Vermont, 1888 ***5900.10*** *p286*
Earley, John; Vermont, 1831-1907 ***5900.10*** *p225*
Earley, Margaret; Vermont, 1838-1910 ***5900.10*** *p505*
Earley, Melvin J.; Vermont, 1849-1927 ***5900.10*** *p184*
Earley, Michael; Vermont, 1824-1895 ***5900.10*** *p128*
Earley, Sarah McLane; Vermont, 1833-1913 ***5900.10*** *p225*
Earley, William; Vermont, 1820-1899 ***5900.10*** *p128*
Earls, James 27; Ontario, 1871 ***1823.15*** *p71*
Earlsman, Edward 30; Jamaica, 1774 ***1220.25*** *p72*
Early, Bridget 73; Vermont, 1891 ***5900.10*** *p145*
Early, Catherine; Vermont, 1860-1942 ***5900.10*** *p121*
Early, Charles; New York, 1833-1838 ***8197.10*** *p115*
Early, George 20; Ontario, 1871 ***1823.22*** *p48*
Early, John; Maryland, 1669 ***2524.55*** *p73*
Early, John; New York, New York, 1856 ***6058.10*** *p64*
Early, Mary 92; Vermont, 1878 ***5900.10*** *p145*
Early, Patrick; New York, 1837 ***8197.10*** *p86*
Early, Patrick; New York, 1840 ***8197.10*** *p167*
Early, Peter; Georgia, 1775-1781 ***4628.40*** *p69*
Early, Thomas; New York, 1840 ***8197.10*** *p167*
Earnert, John 19; Kansas, 1908-1910 ***9079.10*** *p32*
Earngey, William 51; Ontario, 1871 ***1823.15*** *p71*
Earp, William; New York, 1840 ***8197.10*** *p387*
Easing, William; Maryland, 1665 ***2524.55*** *p24*
Easler, John; New York, New York, 1856 ***3437.14*** *p12*
Eason, John; New York, New York, 1853 ***6058.10*** *p42*
Eason, Thomas; Maryland, 1681 ***2524.55*** *p73*
East, Francis; Maryland, 1670 ***2524.55*** *p73*
East, John; Pennsylvania, 1699 ***1224.1*** *p62*
East, Martha; Virginia, 1666 ***6212.30*** *p26*
East, Miles; Virginia, 1666-1667 ***6212.30*** *p35*
East, Thomas 41; Ontario, 1871 ***1823.15*** *p71*
East, William 49; Ontario, 1871 ***1823.22*** *p48*
Eastall, William; Virginia, 1668 ***1224.1*** *p19*
Eastburn, Robert; Pennsylvania, 1777 ***4629.10*** *p6*
Eastcott, Anne Maria 53; Ontario, 1871 ***1823.15*** *p71*
Eastcott, John 64; Ontario, 1871 ***1823.15*** *p71*
Eastend, Thomas; Virginia, 1667-1668 ***6212.30*** *p38*
Easterbrook, John 39; Ontario, 1871 ***1823.15*** *p71*
Eastfeild, Tho; Virginia, 1666 ***6212.30*** *p25*
Eastgate, Caleb; Maryland, 1667 ***2524.55*** *p73*
Eastgate, Francis; Maryland, 1680 ***2524.55*** *p73*
Easthum, James; New York, 1807 ***8197.10*** *p38*
Eastman, Charles 28; Ontario, 1871 ***1823.15*** *p71*
Eastman, Joseph; Maryland, 1775 ***1220.25*** *p113*
Eastman, Mary; Maryland, 1671 ***2524.55*** *p73*
Eastmond, John; New York, 1830 ***8197.10*** *p66*
Eastneck, Susanna; Maryland, 1663 ***2524.55*** *p73*
Easton, Agnes 53; Ontario, 1871 ***1823.15*** *p71*
Easton, George; St. John, New Brunswick, 1888 ***1640.13*** *p35*
Easton, Lydia C. 13; Ontario, 1871 ***1823.22*** *p48*
Easton, Peter; Nantucket, Massachusetts, 1819 ***1224.3*** *p24*
Easton, Thomas; New York, 1828 ***8197.10*** *p227*
Easton, Thomas; St. Vincent, 1873 ***1640.13*** *p35*
Easton, William 62; Ontario, 1871 ***1823.22*** *p48*
Eastrey, John; Maryland, 1665 ***2524.55*** *p73*
Eastrop, Harry 23; Ontario, 1871 ***1823.28*** *p26*
Eastwick, Suzannah; Maryland, 1663 ***2524.55*** *p73*
Eastwood, Sarah 16; South Carolina, 1774 ***1220.25*** *p83*
Eastwood, Sophiah 26; Ontario, 1861 ***2896.27*** *p54*
Easun, William 37; Maryland, 1774 ***1220.25*** *p50*
Easy, George; Virginia, 1664 ***6212.30*** *p8*
Eatles, John 31; Ontario, 1871 ***1823.15*** *p71*
Eaton, Miss; Quebec, 1858 ***9196.15*** *p40*
Eaton, Alce; Virginia, 1703-1704 ***6212.30*** *p63*
Eaton, Anne; Virginia, 1667-1668 ***6212.30*** *p39*
Eaton, Catharine C.; Vermont, 1846-1905 ***5900.10*** *p275*
Eaton, Charles G.; New York, 1818 ***8197.10*** *p227*
Eaton, Eliza.; Maryland, 1678 ***2524.55*** *p73*
Eaton, Elizabeth 34; Ontario, 1861 ***2896.25*** *p59*
Eaton, Jacob; Virginia, 1665-1666 ***6212.30*** *p21*
Eaton, James 27; Ontario, 1861 ***2896.26*** *p3*
Eaton, James 32; Maryland, 1775 ***1220.25*** *p96*
Eaton, James S.; Vermont, 1856-1931 ***5900.10*** *p490*
Eaton, John 16; New York, 1774 ***1220.25*** *p24*
Eaton, John C.; Vermont, 1847-1947 ***5900.10*** *p275*
Eaton, Martha; New England, 1667 ***1224.1*** *p35*
Eaton, Mary Dwyer; Vermont, 1866-1945 ***5900.10*** *p490*
Eaton, Patrick; Virginia, 1668-1669 ***6212.30*** *p40*
Eaton, William 46; Ontario, 1871 ***1823.15*** *p71*
Eatton, Margaret; Georgia, 1774 ***1640.10*** *p48*
Eatton, Thomas; Savannah, Georgia, 1761 ***1640.10*** *p48*
Eaves, Thomas; Philadelphia, 1809 ***1224.3*** *p24*
Ebbler, Johann; America, 1737 ***2856.30*** *p102*
Ebbs, Edward; Maryland, 1643 ***2524.55*** *p73*
Ebbs, Mathew; Maryland, 1682 ***2524.55*** *p73*
Ebel, Adam 36; Kansas, 1887-1910 ***9079.10*** *p31*
Ebel, Anna Catherina 72; Kansas, 1910 ***9079.10*** *p45*
Ebel, Elizabeth 31; Kansas, 1890-1910 ***9079.10*** *p34*
Ebel, Frederick 46; Ontario, 1871 ***1823.28*** *p26*
Ebel, Henry 42; Kansas, 1910 ***9079.10*** *p45*
Ebel, Henry F. 23; Kansas, 1910 ***9079.10*** *p46*
Ebel, Jacob J. 38; Kansas, 1887-1910 ***9079.10*** *p34*
Ebel, Katarina 30; Kansas, 1899-1910 ***9079.10*** *p31*
Ebel, Mary W. 39; Kansas, 1910 ***9079.10*** *p45*
Ebeling, Martin; Port uncertain, 1736 ***2856.30*** *p92*
Eberanz, Johann; Port uncertain, 1788 ***2856.30*** *p92*
Eberdt, Leonhard; Port uncertain, 1767 ***2856.30*** *p92*
Eberhand, Edward 51; Kansas, 1870-1910 ***9079.10*** *p35*
Eberhard, Anna; America, 1752 ***2856.30*** *p92*
Eberhard, Christof; Port uncertain, 1763 ***2856.30*** *p92*
Eberhard, Mrs. Georg; Port uncertain, 1789 ***2856.30*** *p92*
With 8 children
Eberhard, Georg Adam; Port uncertain, 1778 ***2856.30*** *p92*
Eberhard, Georg Martin; America, 1779 ***2856.30*** *p92*
Eberhard, Georg Martin; America, 1781 ***2856.30*** *p92*
Eberhard, Johann; Port uncertain, 1759 ***2856.30*** *p92*
Eberhard, Johann; Port uncertain, 1795 ***2856.30*** *p92*
Eberhard, Johann; Port uncertain, 1796 ***2856.30*** *p92*
Eberhard, Johann Peter; Port uncertain, 1739 ***2856.30*** *p92*
With wife & 5 children
Eberhard, Johann Peter; Port uncertain, 1748 ***2856.30*** *p92*

Eberhard, Joseph; New York, 1837 ***8197.10*** *p86*
Eberhard, Michael; Port uncertain, 1765 ***2856.30*** *p92*
Eberhard, Nicolaus; Port uncertain, 1749 ***2856.30*** *p92*
Eberhard, Philipp; America, 1750 ***2856.30*** *p92*
Eberhard, Philipp; America, 1769 ***2856.30*** *p92*
Eberhard, Philipp; Port uncertain, 1749 ***2856.30*** *p92*
Eberhardt, Andreas; America, 1740 ***2856.30*** *p92*
Eberhardt, Andreas; America, 1786 ***2856.30*** *p92*
Eberhardt, Andreas; Port uncertain, 1752 ***2856.30*** *p92*
Eberhardt, Cath. Barbara; Port uncertain, 1767 ***2856.30*** *p92*
Eberhardt, Hans Georg; America, 1752 ***2856.30*** *p92*
Eberhardt, Johann Jakob; Port uncertain, 1744 ***2856.30*** *p92*
Eberhardt, Johann Nicol; Port uncertain, 1767 ***2856.30*** *p92*
Eberhart, Anna Ursula; Port uncertain, 1766 ***2856.30*** *p92*
Eberhart, Elisabeth; Port uncertain, 1746 ***2856.30*** *p92*
Eberhart, Henrich; Port uncertain, 1746 ***2856.30*** *p92*
Eberhart, Oswald; Port uncertain, 1764 ***2856.30*** *p92*
Eberhart, Paul; America, 1744 ***2856.30*** *p92*
With wife & 3 children
Eberhart, Paul; Port uncertain, 1744 ***2856.30*** *p92*
With wife & 3 children
Eberhart, Wendel; Port uncertain, 1746 ***2856.30*** *p92*
Eberherth, Christ 46; Ontario, 1871 ***1823.15*** *p71*
Eberle, Bartolome; America, 1728 ***2856.30*** *p92*
Eberle, Johann; America, 1749 ***2856.30*** *p93*
With wife & 4 children
Eberle, Johann Adam; America, 1750 ***2856.30*** *p92*
Eberle, Johann Adam; Port uncertain, 1750 ***2856.30*** *p92*
Eberle, John; New York, 1839 ***8197.10*** *p130*
Eberle, Leonhard; America, 1749 ***2856.30*** *p93*
With wife & 3 children
Eberle, Simon; Port uncertain, 1783 ***2856.30*** *p92*
Eberlens, Mrs. Joh. Gottl; America, 1769 ***2856.30*** *p93*
With 6 children
Eberlin, Anna Margarete; America, 1764 ***2856.30*** *p93*
Eberlin, Magdalena; Port uncertain, 1770 ***2856.30*** *p93*
Eberlin, Michael; Port uncertain, 1781 ***2856.30*** *p93*
Eberlin, Rosina Barbara; Port uncertain, 1773 ***2856.30*** *p93*
Eberling, Martin 44; Ontario, 1871 ***1823.15*** *p71*
Ebersold, Peter; America, 1739 ***2856.30*** *p93*
Eberstein, Johann; Port uncertain, 1753 ***2856.30*** *p93*
Ebert, Michael; America, 1763 ***2856.30*** *p93*
Ebert, Philipp; America, 1740 ***2856.30*** *p93*
Ebert, Philipp; America, 1741 ***2856.30*** *p93*
Ebington, Obediah; Virginia, 1666-1667 ***6212.30*** *p34*
Ebitany, Paul 47; Ontario, 1871 ***1823.28*** *p26*
Ebling, Konrad; America, 1744 ***2856.30*** *p93*
Ebrington, Mr.; Quebec, 1858 ***9196.15*** *p34*
Ebrington, Mrs.; Quebec, 1858 ***9196.15*** *p34*
Ebster, F. 27; Alaska, 1912 ***9196.1*** *p38*
Ebster, F. 27; Yukon, 1912 ***9196.1*** *p38*
Ecckoffi, Franz Ludwig; Port uncertain, 1765 ***2856.30*** *p93*
Eccles, Capt.; Quebec, 1857 ***9196.15*** *p20*
Eccles, George; Jamaica, 1799 ***1640.13*** *p35*
Eccleston, Edward; New York, 1824 ***8197.10*** *p227*
Eccleston, Edward; New York, 1826 ***8197.10*** *p227*
Eccoff, Franz Ludwig; Port uncertain, 1765 ***2856.30*** *p93*
Echternach, Helena; Port uncertain, 1782 ***2856.30*** *p93*
Echternach, Helena; Port uncertain, 1794 ***2856.30*** *p93*
Echternacht, Catharina; Port uncertain, 1766 ***2856.30*** *p93*
Eck, Jakob; Port uncertain, 1754 ***2856.30*** *p93*
Eck, Johan Daniel; New York, 1829 ***8197.10*** *p227*
Eck, Johann; Port uncertain, 1771 ***2856.30*** *p93*
Eck, John Daniel; New York, 1829 ***8197.10*** *p315*
Eck, Matthaus, The Younger; America, 1752 ***2856.30*** *p93*
With family
Eck, Matthaus, The Younger; Port uncertain, 1752 ***2856.30*** *p93*
With family
Eck, Michael; Port uncertain, 1753 ***2856.30*** *p93*
Eckard, Friedrich Anton; Port uncertain, 1765 ***2856.30*** *p93*
Eckart, Seibert; America, 1771 ***2856.30*** *p93*
Eckart, William; Pennsylvania, 1777 ***4629.10*** *p16*
Eckel, Johann; Port uncertain, 1749 ***2856.30*** *p93*
Eckel, Jorg Peter; America, 1752 ***2856.30*** *p93*
Eckel, Jorg Peter; America, 1764 ***2856.30*** *p93*
Eckels, John J., Sr.; Vermont, 1855-1926 ***5900.10*** *p119*
Eckels, Katherine Magee; Vermont, 1854-1943 ***5900.10*** *p119*
Eckelson, Wilson 29; Ontario, 1871 ***1823.15*** *p71*
Ecker, Jacob; America, 1737 ***2856.30*** *p93*
With wife & children
Ecker, Jakob; Port uncertain, 1730 ***2856.30*** *p93*
Ecker, Leonard; America, 1777 ***2856.30*** *p93*
Ecker, Philip; Pennsylvania, 1777 ***4629.10*** *p14*
Eckert, Alice 2; Ontario, 1861 ***2896.28*** *p27*
Eckert, Alvin 22; Ontario, 1861 ***2896.26*** *p2*
Eckert, David 10; Ontario, 1861 ***2896.26*** *p2*
Eckert, David 10; Ontario, 1861 ***2896.27*** *p62*
Eckert, Deborah 15; Ontario, 1861 ***2896.26*** *p2*
Eckert, Deborah E. 16; Ontario, 1861 ***2896.27*** *p62*
Eckert, Eliza 17; Ontario, 1861 ***2896.26*** *p2*
Eckert, Elzira 29; Ontario, 1861 ***2896.26*** *p3*
Eckert, Emily M. 22; Ontario, 1861 ***2896.28*** *p27*
Eckert, Esther 3; Ontario, 1861 ***2896.26*** *p3*
Eckert, George A. 6; Ontario, 1861 ***2896.27*** *p62*
Eckert, Hannah 33; Ontario, 1861 ***2896.26*** *p2*
Eckert, Henry; New York, New York, 1856 ***6058.10*** *p54*
Eckert, John; New York, 1839 ***8197.10*** *p129*
Eckert, John 18; Ontario, 1861 ***2896.28*** *p27*
Eckert, John 35; Ontario, 1861 ***2896.26*** *p3*
Eckert, Martha 32; Ontario, 1861 ***2896.26*** *p19*
Eckert, Mary 12; Ontario, 1861 ***2896.27*** *p62*
Eckert, Nancy 38; Ontario, 1861 ***2896.27*** *p62*
Eckert, Peter 62; Ontario, 1861 ***2896.26*** *p2*
Eckert, Rebecca 71; Ontario, 1861 ***2896.27*** *p62*
Eckert, Sarah 4; Ontario, 1861 ***2896.28*** *p27*
Eckert, Tunis 25; Ontario, 1861 ***2896.27*** *p62*
Eckert, Valrin; New York, 1838 ***8197.10*** *p115*
Eckert, William 6; Ontario, 1861 ***2896.26*** *p19*
Eckfield, Jacob; Pennsylvania, 1777 ***4629.10*** *p8*
Eckford, George 29; Ontario, 1871 ***1823.28*** *p26*
Eckford, Henry; New York, 1803 ***8197.10*** *p12*
Eckford, John; Ontario, 1882 ***1640.13*** *p35*
Eckford, William 64; Ontario, 1871 ***1823.28*** *p26*
Eckh, Jakob; America, 1754 ***2856.30*** *p94*
With wife & children
Eckhardt, Philipp; Port uncertain, 1743 ***2856.30*** *p94*
Eckhart, Jos 37; Alaska, 1917 ***9196.1*** *p50*
Eckhart, Jos 37; Yukon, 1917 ***9196.1*** *p50*
Eckherle, Matthaus; Port uncertain, 1749 ***2856.30*** *p94*
Eckhstein, Martin; Port uncertain, 1746 ***2856.30*** *p94*
Eckley, Mr.; Quebec, 1856 ***9196.15*** *p9*
Eckley, John; Philadelphia, 1699 ***1224.1*** *p19*
Eckley, Sarah; Philadelphia, 1698 ***1224.1*** *p19*
Eckmann, Konrad; Port uncertain, 1744 ***2856.30*** *p94*
Eckmire, Daniel 47; Ontario, 1871 ***1823.15*** *p71*
Eckstein, John; Pennsylvania, 1777 ***4629.10*** *p17*
Eckstein, John 63; Ontario, 1871 ***1823.15*** *p71*
Eddingbrough, William; Maryland, 1660 ***2524.55*** *p73*
Edds, William; America, 1722 ***1224.2*** *p36*
Eddy, Dr.; Quebec, 1857 ***9196.15*** *p26*
Eddy, Asinith 35; Ontario, 1871 ***1823.22*** *p49*
Eddy, Bags 28; Ontario, 1871 ***1823.22*** *p48*
Eddy, Caspar Wistar; New York, 1838 ***1224.3*** *p24*
Eddy, Elizabeth 55; Ontario, 1871 ***1823.22*** *p49*
Eddy, Harnden 74; Ontario, 1871 ***1823.22*** *p49*
Eddy, John 24; Ontario, 1871 ***1823.28*** *p26*
Eddy, Joseph 68; Ontario, 1871 ***1823.28*** *p26*
Ede, John; North Carolina, 1760 ***1224.2*** *p36*
Edel, Peter; Port uncertain, 1800 ***2856.30*** *p94*
Edelen, Elizabeth *SEE* Edelen, Richard
Edelen, Richard; Maryland, 1663 ***2524.55*** *p73*
Wife: Elizabeth
Edelmann, David; America, 1733 ***2856.30*** *p94*
With wife & children
Edelmann, Franz; Port uncertain, 1771 ***2856.30*** *p94*
Edelmann, Hans Adam; Port uncertain, 1731 ***2856.30*** *p94*
Edelmann, Hans Georg; America, 1749 ***2856.30*** *p94*
Edelmann, Margarete; Port uncertain, 1775 ***2856.30*** *p94*
Edelmann, Philipp; America, 1733 ***2856.30*** *p94*
With wife & children
Eden, Thomas; Florida, 1788 ***1224.2*** *p37*
Edenburn, Philip; Pennsylvania, 1786 ***4629.10*** *p53*
Ederich, Jacob; Port uncertain, 1755 ***2856.30*** *p94*
Ederich, Johann Adam; Port uncertain, 1786 ***2856.30*** *p94*
Ederich, Josef; Port uncertain, 1788 ***2856.30*** *p94*
Edey, Henry; New York, 1840 ***8197.10*** *p167*
Edey, Matthew; New York, 1839 ***8197.10*** *p130*
Edgar, . . .; Boston, 1765 ***4628.40*** *p114*
Edgar, Alexander; Jamaica, 1821 ***1640.13*** *p35*
Edgar, Alexander; New York, 1825 ***8197.10*** *p227*
Edgar, Alexander 38; Ontario, 1871 ***1823.15*** *p71*
Edgar, Bridget Harlan; Vermont, 1846-1925 ***5900.10*** *p351*
Edgar, Handasyde; Jamaica, 1814 ***1640.13*** *p35*
Edgar, James 37; Ontario, 1871 ***1823.15*** *p71*
Edgar, John; Maryland, 1711 ***1224.2*** *p37*
Edgar, Mary 60; Ontario, 1871 ***1823.22*** *p49*
Edgar, Richard; Maryland, 1681 ***2524.55*** *p73*
Edgar, Robert; New York, 1825 ***8197.10*** *p227*
Edgar, Samuel; New York, 1807 ***8197.10*** *p325*
Edgar, William; Vermont, 1846-1923 ***5900.10*** *p351*
Edge, Daniell; Maryland, 1663 ***2524.55*** *p77*
Edge, John; Boston, 1724 ***1224.2*** *p37*
Edgecomb, John; Virginia, 1666 ***6212.30*** *p27*
Edgecombe, George 27; Ontario, 1871 ***1823.22*** *p49*
Edger, Charles; New York, 1834 ***8197.10*** *p73*
Edger, David 40; New York, 1775 ***1220.25*** *p143*
With wife & 2 children
Edgerler, John 24; Maryland, 1774 ***1220.25*** *p51*
Edgerton, Frank; Vermont, 1851-1912 ***5900.10*** *p43*
Edgerton, Mary; Virginia, 1666-1667 ***6212.30*** *p35*
Edgerton, Mary E. Morrissey; Vermont, 1853-1883 ***5900.10*** *p43*
Edgson, William; New York, 1830 ***8197.10*** *p66*
Edgworth, John; Pennsylvania, 1786 ***4629.10*** *p47*
Edholm, Edwin 38; British Columbia, 1909 ***9196.1*** *p28*
Edholm, Edwin 38; Washington, 1909 ***9196.1*** *p28*
Edie, George; Virginia, 1781 ***1224.2*** *p37*
Edie, George 28; Virginia, 1775 ***1220.25*** *p110*
Edighofer, Adam 24; Ontario, 1871 ***1823.15*** *p71*
Edin, John 26; Alaska, 1915 ***9196.1*** *p42*
Edinger, Heinrich; Port uncertain, 1784 ***2856.30*** *p94*
With wife
Edinger, Philipp; America, 1739 ***2856.30*** *p94*
Edinger, Philipp; America, 1756 ***2856.30*** *p94*
Edinger, R.; America, 1764 ***2856.30*** *p146*
Edinger, Reinhard; America, 1764 ***2856.30*** *p94*
With wife & 4 children
Edington, Gerret; Virginia, 1658 ***1224.1*** *p56*
Edington, Robert 45; Ontario, 1871 ***1823.22*** *p49*
Edington, Robert 64; Ontario, 1871 ***1823.22*** *p49*
Edloe, Joseph; Maryland, 1682 ***2524.55*** *p73*
Edlow, Elioner; Maryland, 1641 ***2524.55*** *p73*
Edmans, John 40; Ontario, 1861 ***2896.26*** *p36*
Edmans, Sarah J. 20; Ontario, 1861 ***2896.26*** *p36*
Edmans, Thomas 66; Ontario, 1861 ***2896.26*** *p36*
Edmeston, John 50; Ontario, 1871 ***1823.15*** *p71*
Edminson, Robert; Portland, Maine, 1857 ***9196.15*** *p11*
Edmison, Alex 50; Ontario, 1871 ***1823.22*** *p49*
Edmond, Father; Vermont, 1844-1911 ***5900.10*** *p339*
Edmonds, Benjamin; Boston, 1741 ***1224.2*** *p37*
Edmonds, Bridgett; Maryland, 1664 ***2524.55*** *p73*
Edmonds, Ellinor; Maryland, 1671 ***2524.55*** *p73*
Edmonds, Evan 46; Maryland, 1775 ***1220.25*** *p105*
Edmonds, Harriet 25; Ontario, 1861 ***2896.26*** *p17*
Edmonds, James; Boston, 1677 ***1224.1*** *p19*
Edmonds, James; Georgia, 1821 ***1640.10*** *p48*
Edmonds, Joan; Maryland, 1662 ***2524.55*** *p116*
Edmonds, John; Maryland, 1668 ***2524.55*** *p73*
Edmonds, John; Philadelphia, 1776 ***1224.2*** *p37*
Edmonds, John; Virginia, 1672 ***1224.1*** *p19*
Edmonds, John 12; Dominica, 1774 ***1220.25*** *p128*
Edmonds, John, Sr.; Maryland, 1676 ***2524.55*** *p126*
Edmonds, John, Jr.; Maryland, 1676 ***2524.55*** *p126*
Edmonds, Mary; Maryland, 1668 ***2524.55*** *p73*
Edmonds, Olliver; Virginia, 1666-1667 ***6212.30*** *p34*
Edmonds, Rebecca; Maryland, 1676 ***2524.55*** *p126*
Edmonds, Richard; Maryland, 1659 ***2524.55*** *p73*
Edmonds, Richard; Maryland, 1665 ***2524.55*** *p73*
Edmonds, Richard; Maryland, 1671 ***2524.55*** *p73*
Edmonds, Thomas; Maryland, 1664 ***2524.55*** *p73*
Edmonds, Thomas; Virginia, 1667 ***6212.30*** *p36*
Edmonds, Thomas 19; St. John Island, 1775 ***1220.25*** *p121*
Edmondski, Jacob; Maryland, 1910 ***3259.35*** *p13*
Edmondson, John; Maryland, 1662 ***2524.55*** *p74*
Edmondson, John 88; Ontario, 1871 ***1823.15*** *p71*
Edmonston, Sarah 18; Ontario, 1871 ***1823.15*** *p71*
Edmonstone, James; New York, 1819 ***8197.10*** *p61*
Edmunds, Bridget *SEE* Edmunds, Thomas
Edmunds, George; Maryland, 1668 ***2524.55*** *p55*
Edmunds, James; Maryland, 1666 ***2524.55*** *p74*
Edmunds, Thomas; Maryland, 1661 ***2524.55*** *p74*
Relative: Bridget
Ednons, William; Maryland, 1673 ***2524.55*** *p74*
Edowwishkosh, John 36; Ontario, 1871 ***1823.28*** *p26*
Edowwishkosh, Mrs. Joseph 32; Ontario, 1871 ***1823.28*** *p26*
Edowwishkosh, Samson 60; Ontario, 1871 ***1823.28*** *p26*
Edrington, Tho; Virginia, 1668-1669 ***6212.30*** *p40*
Edrington, Thomosin; Virginia, 1681-1682 ***6212.30*** *p56*
Edward, Benjamin 59; Ontario, 1871 ***1823.15*** *p71*
Edward, Eliza 51; Vermont, 1878 ***5900.10*** *p247*
Edward, George 42; Ontario, 1871 ***1823.15*** *p71*
Edward, James; New York, 1839 ***1640.10*** *p48*
Edward, James 36; Ontario, 1871 ***1823.15*** *p71*
Edward, Jane 27 *SEE* Edward, John
Edward, John 26; South Carolina, 1774 ***1220.25*** *p25*
Wife: Jane 27
Edward, John 36; Ontario, 1871 ***1823.15*** *p71*
Edward, John 70; Ontario, 1871 ***1823.15*** *p71*
Edward, Michael 77; Vermont, 1889 ***5900.10*** *p247*
Edward, Peter 44; Ontario, 1871 ***1823.15*** *p71*
Edward, Pinta 23; British Columbia, 1910 ***9196.1*** *p29*
Edward, Pinta 23; Washington, 1910 ***9196.1*** *p29*
Edward, William 38; Ontario, 1871 ***1823.15*** *p71*
Edward, William 70; Ontario, 1871 ***1823.15*** *p71*

Edwards, Mr.; Quebec, 1857 ***9196.15*** *p23*
Edwards, Mr.; Quebec, 1858 ***9196.15*** *p46*
Edwards, Ann; Charles Town, South Carolina, 1789 ***1224.2*** *p37*
Edwards, Ann 18; Philadelphia, 1774 ***1220.25*** *p44*
Edwards, Arthur; Virginia, 1663 ***6212.30*** *p2*
Edwards, Bartholomew; Virginia, 1671-1672 ***6212.30*** *p46*
Edwards, Benjamin 22; Virginia, 1773 ***1220.25*** *p29*
Edwards, Catherine 64; Ontario, 1871 ***1823.15*** *p71*
Edwards, Charles; New York, 1831 ***8197.10*** *p67*
Edwards, Charles; Pennsylvania, 1777 ***4629.10*** *p23*
Edwards, Charles 15; Philadelphia, 1774 ***1220.25*** *p66*
Edwards, Charles Henry; New York, 1819-1834 ***8197.10*** *p306*
Edwards, David; Boston, 1698 ***1224.1*** *p19*
Edwards, David; Virginia, 1663-1664 ***6212.30*** *p5*
Edwards, Edward 22; Maryland, 1775 ***1220.25*** *p101*
Edwards, Edwin W. 56; Ontario, 1871 ***1823.22*** *p49*
Edwards, Evan; Pennsylvania, 1777 ***4629.10*** *p30*
Edwards, George; New York, 1807 ***8197.10*** *p38*
Edwards, George; Pennsylvania, 1777 ***4629.10*** *p12*
Edwards, Henry; Virginia, 1656 ***1224.1*** *p19*
Edwards, Henry 17; Virginia, 1774 ***1220.25*** *p76*
Edwards, Jane 50; Ontario, 1871 ***1823.15*** *p71*
Edwards, Jno; Virginia, 1666 ***6212.30*** *p29*
Edwards, Joanna 21; Vermont, 1869 ***5900.10*** *p236*
Edwards, Joanna Lawler 67; Vermont, 1876 ***5900.10*** *p226*
Edwards, John; Jamaica, 1848 ***1640.13*** *p35*
Edwards, John; Maryland, 1661 ***2524.55*** *p74*
Edwards, John; Maryland, 1663 ***2524.55*** *p74*
Edwards, John; Maryland, 1669 ***2524.55*** *p221*
Edwards, John; Maryland, 1679 ***2524.55*** *p74*
Edwards, John; Maryland, 1680 ***2524.55*** *p74*
Edwards, John; New York, 1806 ***8197.10*** *p30*
Edwards, John; New York, 1840 ***8197.10*** *p167*
Edwards, John; Virginia, 1668 ***1224.1*** *p19*
Edwards, John 16; Maryland, 1774 ***1220.25*** *p40*
Edwards, John 20; Philadelphia, 1774 ***1220.25*** *p3*
Edwards, John 21; Ontario, 1871 ***1823.28*** *p26*
Edwards, John 37; Ontario, 1871 ***1823.15*** *p71*
Edwards, John, Jr.; New York, 1806 ***8197.10*** *p324*
Edwards, John, Jr.; New York, 1807 ***8197.10*** *p38*
Edwards, Joseph; Maryland, 1648 ***2524.55*** *p224*
Edwards, Joseph 22; Ontario, 1871 ***1823.28*** *p26*
Edwards, Joseph 54; Ontario, 1871 ***1823.22*** *p49*
Edwards, Lovan 22; Ontario, 1871 ***1823.28*** *p26*
Edwards, Margaret 29; Vermont, 1870 ***5900.10*** *p236*
Edwards, Margaret 58; Ontario, 1871 ***1823.28*** *p26*
Edwards, Mary; Maryland, 1681 ***2524.55*** *p74*
Edwards, Mordecay; Virginia, 1674 ***6212.30*** *p52*
Edwards, Mordica; Virginia, 1664 ***6212.30*** *p6*
Edwards, Nancy 6; Vermont, 1854 ***5900.10*** *p236*
Edwards, Nich; Virginia, 1684-1685 ***6212.30*** *p57*
Edwards, Patrick 23; Vermont, 1864 ***5900.10*** *p236*
Edwards, Penelope; Maryland, 1681 ***2524.55*** *p74*
Edwards, Rebecca 67; Ontario, 1871 ***1823.28*** *p26*
Edwards, Richard; North Carolina, 1757 ***1224.2*** *p37*
Edwards, Richard 23; Philadelphia, 1775 ***1220.25*** *p9*
Edwards, Robert 22; Virginia, 1774 ***1220.25*** *p92*
Edwards, Samuel 15; Maryland, 1775 ***1220.25*** *p9*
Edwards, Sweet; New England, 1705 ***1224.2*** *p37*
Edwards, Thomas; Maryland, 1660 ***2524.55*** *p74*
Edwards, Thomas; Maryland, 1665 ***2524.55*** *p74*
Edwards, Thomas; Maryland, 1667 ***2524.55*** *p74*
Edwards, Thomas; Maryland, 1668 ***2524.55*** *p74*
Edwards, Thomas 19; Maryland, 1774 ***1220.25*** *p79*
Edwards, Thomas 21; Baltimore, 1775 ***1220.25*** *p117*
Edwards, Thomas 50; Ontario, 1871 ***1823.15*** *p71*
Edwards, Thomas 56; Vermont, 1857 ***5900.10*** *p226*
Edwards, Thos 40; Ontario, 1871 ***1823.28*** *p27*
Edwards, Wakeman Jc 30; Ontario, 1871 ***1823.28*** *p27*
Edwards, William; Pennsylvania, 1777 ***4629.10*** *p27*
Edwards, William 32; Ontario, 1871 ***1823.15*** *p72*
Edwards, William 36; Philadelphia, 1775 ***1220.25*** *p107*
Edwards, William 40; Philadelphia, 1774 ***1220.25*** *p68*
Edwards, William 56; Ontario, 1871 ***1823.22*** *p49*
Edwards, William 62; Ontario, 1871 ***1823.28*** *p27*
Edwarthy, George 50; Ontario, 1871 ***1823.15*** *p72*
Edwerds, James 29; Ontario, 1871 ***1823.15*** *p72*
Edwerds, Jane 69; Ontario, 1871 ***1823.15*** *p72*
Edwin, Margarett *SEE* Edwin, William
Edwin, William; Maryland, 1647 ***2524.55*** *p74*
Edwin, William; Maryland, 1656 ***2524.55*** *p74*
Wife: Margarett
Edwins, Edward; Maryland, 1664 ***2524.55*** *p74*
Edworthy, Manal 28; Ontario, 1871 ***1823.15*** *p72*
Edy, John; Maryland, 1664 ***2524.55*** *p217*
Eeche, Chistian 37; Ontario, 1871 ***1823.28*** *p27*
Eedin, Benjamin 53; Ontario, 1871 ***1823.15*** *p72*
Eeles, John; Virginia, 1678 ***1224.1*** *p19*
Eells, Hannah; Massachusetts, 1792 ***1224.2*** *p37*
Efame, Elizabeth; Maryland, 1665 ***2524.55*** *p230*
Effle, Johann Wendel; Port uncertain, 1785 ***2856.30*** *p94*
Efftinger, Clara; Port uncertain, 1784 ***2856.30*** *p94*
Efthim, Peter 28; Alaska, 1916 ***9196.1*** *p43*
Efthim, Peter 28; Whitehorse, Yukon, 1916 ***9196.1*** *p43*
Egab, Catherine; Vermont, 1843-1909 ***5900.10*** *p382*
Egan, Bridget; Vermont, 1825-1894 ***5900.10*** *p435*
Egan, Bridget 51; New York, New York, 1849 ***1825.45*** *p33*
Son: John 18
Son: Michael 10
Egan, Daniel; New York, 1834-1838 ***8197.10*** *p115*
Egan, Denis 40; Ontario, 1871 ***1823.15*** *p72*
Egan, Dennis; Vermont, 1810-1883 ***5900.10*** *p537*
Egan, Dominica; Dominica, 1789 ***1224.2*** *p37*
Egan, Edward 50; Ontario, 1871 ***1823.28*** *p27*
Egan, Ellen; Vermont, 1856-1933 ***5900.10*** *p407*
Egan, Ellen Sheehan; Vermont, 1841-1922 ***5900.10*** *p535*
Egan, Francis 60; Ontario, 1871 ***1823.15*** *p72*
Egan, Hannah; Vermont, 1848-1868 ***5900.10*** *p537*
Egan, Hanora 99; Vermont, 1881 ***5900.10*** *p591*
Egan, James; New York, 1837 ***8197.10*** *p85*
Egan, Jennie; Vermont, 1859-1887 ***5900.10*** *p537*
Egan, Joanna E. Neville; Vermont, 1855-1917 ***5900.10*** *p163*
Egan, John; Vermont, 1855-1880 ***5900.10*** *p537*
Egan, John 18 *SEE* Egan, Bridget
Egan, John 28; Ontario, 1871 ***1823.28*** *p27*
Egan, John 48; Ontario, 1871 ***1823.28*** *p27*
Egan, John 77; Ontario, 1871 ***1823.28*** *p27*
Egan, Luke 60; Ontario, 1871 ***1823.22*** *p49*
Egan, Mary; Vermont, 1819-1902 ***5900.10*** *p537*
Egan, Mary; Vermont, 1839-1868 ***5900.10*** *p403*
Egan, Mary 20; New York, New York, 1849 ***1825.45*** *p33*
Egan, Mary Hines; Vermont, 1846-1919 ***5900.10*** *p253*
Egan, Michael; New York, 1840 ***8197.10*** *p167*
Egan, Michael 10 *SEE* Egan, Bridget
Egan, Michael 70; Ontario, 1871 ***1823.28*** *p27*
Egan, Nicholas; Pennsylvania, 1777 ***4629.10*** *p14*
Egan, Pat 14; Died enroute, 1849 ***1825.45*** *p33*
Egan, Patrick; Vermont, n.d. ***5900.10*** *p163*
Egan, Patrick; Vermont, 1831-1888 ***5900.10*** *p535*
Egan, Patrick; Vermont, 1840-1894 ***5900.10*** *p253*
Egan, Patrick 70; Ontario, 1871 ***1823.22*** *p49*
Egan, Sarah; Vermont, 1828-1910 ***5900.10*** *p442*
Egan, Stephen; Florida, n.d. ***1224.2*** *p37*
Egan, Thomas; New York, 1839 ***8197.10*** *p228*
Egan, Timothy 62; Ontario, 1871 ***1823.28*** *p27*
Egan, William 30; Ontario, 1871 ***1823.28*** *p27*
Egart, . . .; Boston, 1737 ***4628.40*** *p114*
Egart, John 41; Ontario, 1871 ***1823.15*** *p72*
Egart, John 54; Ontario, 1871 ***1823.15*** *p72*
Egel, Daniel; America, 1751 ***2856.30*** *p94*
Egel, Dietrich; Port uncertain, 1786 ***2856.30*** *p94*
Egele, Friedrich; Port uncertain, 1786 ***2856.30*** *p94*
Egenton, Thomas; New York, 1802 ***8197.10*** *p20*
Eger, John 41; Ontario, 1871 ***1823.15*** *p72*
Egerly, William; Virginia, 1667-1668 ***6212.30*** *p38*
Egger, J. 31; Alaska, 1912 ***9196.1*** *p37*
Egger, J. 31; Yukon, 1912 ***9196.1*** *p37*
Eggleston, Hezekiah; Boston, 1744 ***1224.2*** *p37*
Eggleston, Newton 46; Ontario, 1871 ***1823.28*** *p27*
Egin, Nicolaus; Port uncertain, 1738 ***2856.30*** *p94*
Egin, Regina; Port uncertain, 1760 ***2856.30*** *p94*
Egin, Regina; Port uncertain, 1761 ***2856.30*** *p94*
Egker, Michael 47; Ontario, 1871 ***1823.15*** *p72*
Eglehon, David; Maryland, 1681 ***2524.55*** *p74*
Egler, Josef; Port uncertain, 1738 ***2856.30*** *p94*
Egler, Josef; Port uncertain, 1762 ***2856.30*** *p94*
Egleson, James; Pennsylvania, 1777 ***4629.10*** *p24*
Egleson, William 33; Ontario, 1871 ***1823.15*** *p72*
Eglin, Stephen 25; Carolina, 1774 ***1220.25*** *p82*
Eglington, Peter 24; Maryland, 1773-1774 ***1220.25*** *p33*
Egneu, James; Pennsylvania, 1779 ***4629.10*** *p33*
Egnew, Thomas 60; Ontario, 1871 ***1823.15*** *p72*
Egvel, George 20; Ontario, 1871 ***1823.15*** *p72*
Ehe, Johann Georg; Port uncertain, 1740 ***2856.30*** *p95*
Ehemann, Hans Georg; America, 1769 ***2856.30*** *p95*
With wife & 3 children
Ehewald, Eva Margarete; Port uncertain, 1768 ***2856.30*** *p95*
Ehewald, Karl; America, 1751 ***2856.30*** *p95*
Ehewald, Karl; America, 1755 ***2856.30*** *p95*
Ehinger, Ambros; Venezuela, 1532 ***2856.30*** *p95*
Ehl, Jakob; America, 1756 ***2856.30*** *p95*
Ehler, William 38; Ontario, 1871 ***1823.15*** *p72*
Ehlhard, Johann Adam; Port uncertain, 1761 ***2856.30*** *p95*
Ehlhard, Johann Adam; Port uncertain, 1787 ***2856.30*** *p95*
Ehmke, Charles 29; Ontario, 1871 ***1823.15*** *p72*
Ehrat, Anton; Canada, 1752 ***2856.30*** *p95*
Ehrat, Christof; America, 1752 ***2856.30*** *p95*
With wife & children
Ehrat, Martin; America, 1752 ***2856.30*** *p95*
With wife
Ehrbach, Balthasar; Port uncertain, 1748 ***2856.30*** *p102*
With wife & 4 children
Ehrbart, Sebastian; Port uncertain, 1752 ***2856.30*** *p95*
With wife & children
Ehrenhard, Anna Maria Mutol; England, 1786 ***2856.30*** *p95*
Ehret, Anna Maria; Port uncertain, 1785 ***2856.30*** *p95*
Ehret, John S.; New York, New York, 1847 ***6058.10*** *p32*
Ehret, Peter; America, 1749 ***2856.30*** *p95*
Ehrhard, Georg; Port uncertain, 1770 ***2856.30*** *p95*
Ehrhard, Gertrud; Port uncertain, 1786 ***2856.30*** *p95*
Ehrhard, Michael Christi; Port uncertain, 1764 ***2856.30*** *p95*
Ehrhardt, Georg; Port uncertain, 1791 ***2856.30*** *p95*
With wife
Ehring, Anna Margarete; Port uncertain, 1797 ***2856.30*** *p95*
With husband
Ehrinskowski, John; Maryland, 1910 ***3259.35*** *p13*
Ehrit, John S.; New York, New York, 1847 ***6058.10*** *p32*
Ehrle, Friedrich; America, 1738 ***2856.30*** *p95*
Ehrle, Friedrich; Port uncertain, 1738 ***2856.30*** *p95*
Ehrle, Martin; America, 1738 ***2856.30*** *p95*
Ehrle, Martin; America, 1742 ***2856.30*** *p95*
Ehrle, Martin; Port uncertain, 1738 ***2856.30*** *p95*
Ehrler, Friedrich; Port uncertain, 1796 ***2856.30*** *p95*
Ehrler, Matthaus; Port uncertain, 1748 ***2856.30*** *p95*
Ehrler, Matthaus; Port uncertain, 1783 ***2856.30*** *p95*
Ehrlich, Eva C. 47; Kansas, 1891-1910 ***9079.10*** *p33*
Ehrlich, Fred 49; Kansas, 1891-1910 ***9079.10*** *p33*
Ehrlich, Marie 34; Kansas, 1879-1910 ***9079.10*** *p41*
Ehrlich, Waldemar 34; Kansas, 1892-1910 ***9079.10*** *p41*
Ehrly, Michael; Port uncertain, 1777 ***2856.30*** *p95*
Ehrmann, Friedrich; Port uncertain, 1720 ***2856.30*** *p95*
Ehrmannstraut, Michael; Port uncertain, 1736 ***2856.30*** *p96*
With wife & 6 children
Eib, Jacob; America, 1733 ***2856.30*** *p96*
Eibach, Henrich; America, 1712 ***2856.30*** *p96*
Eich, Christof; America, 1749 ***2856.30*** *p96*
Eich, Jakobina; Port uncertain, 1754 ***2856.30*** *p96*
Eich, Maria Elisabeth; Port uncertain, 1784 ***2856.30*** *p96*
Eich, Maria Margarete; Port uncertain, 1746 ***2856.30*** *p96*
Eich, Nickel; America, 1749 ***2856.30*** *p96*
Eich, Susanna Magdale; Port uncertain, 1749 ***2856.30*** *p96*
Eichaker, Daniel; New York, 1838 ***8197.10*** *p228*
Eichel, Leonhard; America, 1738 ***2856.30*** *p96*
With wife & daughter
Eichenauer, Eva Maria; Port uncertain, 1751 ***2856.30*** *p96*
Eicher, Anna; America, 1725 ***2856.30*** *p96*
Eicher, Barbara; America, 1725 ***2856.30*** *p96*
Eichert, Christian; Canada, 1752 ***2856.30*** *p96*
With wife & children
Eichholz, Bernhard; America, 1763 ***2856.30*** *p96*
With wife son & daughter
Eichhorn, Matthaus, Jr.; America, 1742 ***2856.30*** *p96*
Eichiman, Catherine 18; Kansas, 1904-1910 ***9079.10*** *p24*
Eichiman, Catherine 43; Kansas, 1904-1910 ***9079.10*** *p24*
Eichiman, Frederick 21, Kansas, 1904-1910 ***9079.10*** *p24*
Eichiman, Frederick 50; Kansas, 1904-1910 ***9079.10*** *p24*
Eichiman, Godfried 15; Kansas, 1904-1910 ***9079.10*** *p24*
Eichiman, John G. 12; Kansas, 1904-1910 ***9079.10*** *p24*
Eichiman, Susanna 9; Kansas, 1904-1910 ***9079.10*** *p24*
Eichinger, Jacob; America, 1738 ***2856.30*** *p96*
With wife & 5 children
Eichler, Christian 43; Ontario, 1871 ***1823.15*** *p72*
Eichler, Franz; Port uncertain, 1748 ***2856.30*** *p96*
With wife & children
Eichman, Catherine 25; Kansas, 1892-1910 ***9079.10*** *p21*
Eichman, Christina 26; Kansas, 1900-1910 ***9079.10*** *p21*
Eichman, Elizabeth 13; Kansas, 1899-1910 ***9079.10*** *p32*
Eichman, Elizabeth 35; Kansas, 1899-1910 ***9079.10*** *p32*
Eichman, Elizabeth 45; Kansas, 1907-1910 ***9079.10*** *p29*
Eichman, Eva 35; Kansas, 1910 ***9079.10*** *p48*
Eichman, Fred D. 46; Kansas, 1907-1910 ***9079.10*** *p29*
Eichman, George 27; Kansas, 1900-1910 ***9079.10*** *p30*
Eichman, George B. 30; Kansas, 1909-1910 ***9079.10*** *p31*
Eichman, George G. 21; Kansas, 1907-1910 ***9079.10*** *p29*
Eichman, Gothfred 6; Kansas, 1907-1910 ***9079.10*** *p29*
Eichman, Jacob 45; Kansas, 1899-1910 ***9079.10*** *p32*
Eichman, Katie 23; Kansas, 1899-1910 ***9079.10*** *p32*
Eichman, Mary 18; Kansas, 1899-1910 ***9079.10*** *p32*
Eichman, Mary 23; Kansas, 1900-1910 ***9079.10*** *p30*
Eichman, Mary 62; Kansas, 1900-1910 ***9079.10*** *p21*
Eichman, Peter 22; Kansas, 1900-1910 ***9079.10*** *p21*
Eichner, Christopher; New York, New York, 1854 ***6058.10*** *p54*

Eichsteller, Anna Margarete; Port uncertain, 1761 2856.30 p96
Eichsteller, Josef Wilhelm; Port uncertain, 1737 2856.30 p96
Eichtern, Catharina; Port uncertain, 1766 2856.30 p93
Eiden, Johann; Port uncertain, 1756 2856.30 p96
Eidmann, Johann Daniel; Port uncertain, 1750 2856.30 p96
Eidmann, Konrad; England, 1784 2856.30 p96
Eidmeyer, Martin; Port uncertain, 1783 2856.30 p96
Eier, Christiana; Port uncertain, 1754 2856.30 p96
Eier, Frederick; New York, 1837 8197.10 p86
Eierk, Edward 44; Ontario, 1871 1823.28 p27
Eifert, John; New York, 1840 8197.10 p175
Eifler, Mrs. Nikol; America, 1757 2856.30 p96
With daughter
Eigenmann, Hans Georg; Port uncertain, 1752 2856.30 p96
With wife & children
Eigler, Franziska; Port uncertain, 1765 2856.30 p96
Eihenbaugh, Henry; Baltimore, 1845 6058.10 p36
Eikert, Wilhelm; Port uncertain, 1764 2856.30 p96
Eilbeck, John; America, 1821 1224.3 p24
Eilbeck, Jonathan; Norfolk, Virginia, 1821 1224.3 p24
Eilber, Charles 44; Ontario, 1871 1823.15 p72
Eilber, Christopher 42; Ontario, 1871 1823.15 p72
Eilber, Frederick 79; Ontario, 1871 1823.15 p72
Eilber, Friderick 46; Ontario, 1871 1823.15 p72
Eilber, Jacob 41; Ontario, 1871 1823.15 p72
Eiler, Yerrick; America, 1754 2856.30 p96
Eillen, Francis; Maryland, 1667 2524.55 p74
Wife: Mary
Eillen, Mary *SEE* Eillen, Francis
Eimvachter, Henry 30; Ontario, 1871 1823.15 p72
Einsmann, Michael; Port uncertain, 1764 2856.30 p96
With wife & 7 children
Einstein, Daniel; Pennsylvania, 1866 6058.10 p56
Einstein, F. H.; New York, New York, 1860 6058.10 p57
Einwachter, George; Pennsylvania, 1786 4629.10 p52
Eipin, Maria; Port uncertain, 1769 2856.30 p97
Eisdell, Thomas; Illinois, 1842 1224.3 p24
Eisel, Hans Adam; Port uncertain, 1758 2856.30 p97
Eiselin, Margarete; Port uncertain, 1751 2856.30 p97
Eisen, John; Maryland, 1910 3259.35 p13
Eisenbach, George 47; Ontario, 1871 1823.15 p72
Eisenbeiss, Hans Adam; America, 1741 2856.30 p97
Eisenhard, Sybille; Port uncertain, 1790 2856.30 p97
Eisenhauer, Anna Margarethe; Port uncertain, 1747 2856.30 p97
Eisenhauer, Bernhard; Port uncertain, 1805 2856.30 p97
With 6 children
Eisenhauer, Friedrich; Port uncertain, 1787 2856.30 p97
Eisenhauer, Jacob; Port uncertain, 1774 2856.30 p97
Eisenhauer, Johann Adam; America, 1751 2856.30 p97
Eisenhauer, Johann Heinrich; Canada, 1700-1799 2856.30 p97
With wife & children
Eisenhauer, Johann Heinrich; Canada, 1751 2856.30 p97
With wife & children
Eisenhauer, Johann Niklas; Port uncertain, 1774 2856.30 p97
Eisenhauer'sche, Miss; Port uncertain, 1781 2856.30 p97
With 2 sisters
Eisenhuth, Albert; America, 1742 2856.30 p97
Eisenloffel, Johann Nikolaus; Port uncertain, 1769 2856.30 p97
Eisenloffel, Konrad; Port uncertain, 1730 2856.30 p97
Eisenmanger, Balthasar; America, 1751 2856.30 p97
Eisenmanger, Christof; America, 1751 2856.30 p97
Eisenmenger, Friedrich; Port uncertain, 1751 2856.30 p97
Eisenmenger, Friedrich; Port uncertain, 1791 2856.30 p97
Eisenschmid, Josef; Port uncertain, 1773 2856.30 p97
Eisert, Catharina; Port uncertain, 1791 2856.30 p97
Eiskirch, Thomas; America, 1764 2856.30 p97
Eison, Thomas 25; Nova Scotia, 1774 1220.25 p136
Eisselin, Catharina; Port uncertain, 1752 2856.30 p97
Eissinger, Jakob; America, 1731 2856.30 p97
Eiszler, Andrew; New York, 1834 8197.10 p73
Eives, Elizabeth 24 *SEE* Eives, John
Eives, John 31; Georgia, 1775 1220.25 p126
Wife: Elizabeth 24
Child: William 7
Eives, William 7 *SEE* Eives, John
Ekardt, Martin; America, 1752 2856.30 p97
Ekel, John; New York, 1835 8197.10 p310
Ekerlin, Carls; New York, 1837 8197.10 p82
Ekielsca, Felix A.; Maryland, 1910 3259.35 p13
Eklevim, Victor 23; Washington, 1914 9196.1 p66
Ekon, Adam *SEE* Ekon, Hugh
Ekon, Hugh; Maryland, 1665 2524.55 p74
Wife: Mary
Son: Adam
With 2 daughters
Ekon, Mary *SEE* Ekon, Hugh
Ekson, Sarah; Mobile, Alabama, 1826-1845 1640.10 p48
Ekubek, Antwan 48; Ontario, 1871 1823.28 p27
Elam, Joseph; Philadelphia, 1794 1224.2 p37
Elam, Joseph 50; Norfolk, Virginia, 1774 1220.25 p20
Elam, Samuel; Rhode Island, 1815 1224.3 p24
Elbert, Eva; Port uncertain, 1786 2856.30 p97
Elbing, Martin; Port uncertain, 1736 2856.30 p92
Elbling, Wenzel; Port uncertain, 1749 2856.30 p97
Elbrow, John; Maryland, 1709 1224.2 p37
Elcker, Franz; Port uncertain, 1791 2856.30 p97
Elcoat, Appleton 50; Ontario, 1871 1823.15 p72
Elcock, Robert 22; Baltimore, 1775 1220.25 p117
Elder, Alexander 30; Ontario, 1871 1823.22 p49
Elder, Jane 75; Ontario, 1871 1823.28 p27
Elder, John; Canada, 1880 1640.13 p35
Elder, John; Pennsylvania, 1810 6058.10 p3
Elder, Stewart; New York, 1816 8197.10 p59
Elder, Thomas 30; Ontario, 1871 1823.22 p49
Elder, William 27; Ontario, 1871 1823.28 p27
Elder, William 42; Ontario, 1871 1823.15 p72
Eldred, Lois; Vermont, 1846-1912 5900.10 p71
Eldred, William; Virginia, 1660 1224.1 p20
Eldridge, John; New York, 1827 8197.10 p344
Eldridge, John; Pennsylvania, 1786 4629.10 p54
Eldridge, Thomas 26; Baltimore, 1775 1220.25 p119
Elefvern, B. 27; Alaska, 1916 9196.1 p43
Elefvern, B. 27; Whitehorse, Yukon, 1916 9196.1 p43
Elena, Andrew; Maryland, 1644 2524.55 p74
Elenberger, Christian; America, 1741 2856.30 p97
Elert, Ignacy; Maryland, 1910 3259.35 p13
Elestree, Roger; Virginia, 1666 6212.30 p29
Elett, Jocm; Virginia, 1680 6212.30 p55
Elett, Lewis; Maryland, 1682 2524.55 p74
Eley, William 50; Ontario, 1871 1823.22 p49
Elford, Michael 37; Ontario, 1871 1823.15 p72
Elgar, Charles 29; Ontario, 1871 1823.28 p27
Elgar, John 75; Ontario, 1871 1823.22 p49
Elgas, Catharina; Port uncertain, 1760 2856.30 p97
Elgian, James 23; Virginia, 1774 1220.25 p89
Elgie, Charles; New York, 1865 6058.10 p71
Elgie, Robert 48; Ontario, 1871 1823.15 p72
Elgo, Patrick; New York, 1834 8197.10 p73
Elgren, Alexander; New York, 1834 8197.10 p359
Elibank, Patrick; Florida, 1766 1640.10 p48
Elice, Jane; Maryland, 1661 2524.55 p74
Elich, John 32; Alaska, 1917 9196.1 p46
Elich, John 32; Whitehorse, Yukon, 1917 9196.1 p46
Elie, A. F.; Vermont, 1859-1928 5900.10 p291
Elie, Catherine Conway 33; Vermont, 1898 5900.10 p291
Eligmear, Frederick 24; Dominica, 1774 1220.25 p128
Elina, Andrew; Maryland, 1644 2524.55 p74
Elines, Joyce *SEE* Elines, Thomas
Elines, Thomas; Maryland, 1665 2524.55 p74
Wife: Joyce
Elinor, John 74; Ontario, 1871 1823.22 p49
Eliot, Miss; Quebec, 1858 9196.15 p42
Eliot, John; Florida, 1769 1224.2 p38
Eliot, Robert 50; Ontario, 1871 1823.15 p72
Eliot, Thomas 60; Ontario, 1871 1823.15 p72
Eliott, Charles 42; Ontario, 1871 1823.22 p49
Eliott, James 81; Ontario, 1871 1823.22 p49
Eliott, Mary 49; Vermont, 1866 5900.10 p358
Elis, Emmy 1; Ontario, 1861 2896.25 p70
Elis, Hester 16; Ontario, 1861 2896.25 p70
Elis, John 20; Ontario, 1861 2896.25 p68
Elison, Franz Josef; Port uncertain, 1769 2856.30 p98
Elison, Jacob; Port uncertain, 1769 2856.30 p98
Elison, Maria Elisabeth; Port uncertain, 1762 2856.30 p98
Elison, Marianna; Port uncertain, 1762 2856.30 p98
Elison, Michael; Port uncertain, 1734 2856.30 p98
Elison, Robert 16; Ontario, 1861 2896.25 p50
Elkin, Elizabeth; Barbados, 1752 1224.2 p37
Elkin, Elizabeth; Virginia, 1752 1224.2 p37
Elkin, Eneas 57; Ontario, 1871 1823.15 p72
Elkins, William 25; Maryland, 1774 1220.25 p79
Elkinston, James; Maryland, 1681 2524.55 p74
Elks, Rich; Virginia, 1668-1669 6212.30 p40
Ellard, G.; Quebec, 1858 9196.15 p35
Ellard, J.; Quebec, 1858 9196.15 p35
Ellard, J., Jr.; Quebec, 1858 9196.15 p35
Ellas, George 42; Ontario, 1871 1823.15 p72
Ellaway, Edward; New York, 1816 1224.3 p24
Ellaway, Edward; Surinam, n.d. 1224.3 p24
Elldin, William 38; Ontario, 1871 1823.28 p27
Elleiot, George 41; Ontario, 1871 1823.15 p72
Ellems, Robert 25; Maryland, 1774 1220.25 p3
Ellen, Miss L.; Quebec, 1858 9196.15 p38
Ellenberger, Nikolaus; America, 1739 2856.30 p98
Ellenor, Andrew; Maryland, 1644 2524.55 p74
Ellens, Sarah Elizabeth; Louisiana, 1845 1224.3 p24
Eller, Jakob; Port uncertain, 1780 2856.30 p98
Eller, Wilhelm; Port uncertain, 1764 2856.30 p98
Ellerd, Luke 43; Ontario, 1871 1823.15 p72
Ellerston, Niels; Philadelphia, 1700-1799 1224.2 p38
Ellery, Henry; Maryland, 1663 2524.55 p74
Ellesdon, Wm; Virginia, 1666-1667 6212.30 p34
Elleser, Jakob; Port uncertain, 1754 2856.30 p98
Elletson, Goodin; North Carolina, 1790 1224.2 p37
Ellett, Rebeckah; Maryland, 1670 2524.55 p11
Ellford, Marth; Virginia, 1664 6212.30 p7
Ellford, William 44; Ontario, 1871 1823.22 p49
Ellgate, William; Maryland, 1661 2524.55 p74
Elliason, Gospar; Maryland, 1668 2524.55 p74
Elliason, Jesper; Maryland, 1671 2524.55 p74
Ellice, E.; Quebec, 1858 9196.15 p38
Ellice, George; Philadelphia, 1753 1224.2 p38
Ellingsworth, Richard; Maryland, 1654 2524.55 p74
Ellinor, Thomas; Maryland, 1673 2524.55 p74
Ellins, George; Maryland, 1671 2524.55 p74
Ellins, Henry; Virginia, 1663 6212.30 p3
Ellinsworth, Christian; Maryland, 1663 2524.55 p75
Elliot, . . .; Boston, 1765 4628.40 p114
Elliot, Mrs.; Quebec, 1856 9196.15 p9
Elliot, Alice; Vermont, 1830-1901 5900.10 p358
Elliot, Andrew; Rhode Island, 1778 1224.2 p37
Elliot, Andrew; Savannah, Georgia, 1775 1640.10 p48
Elliot, Christopher; Vermont, 1863-1898 5900.10 p360
Elliot, Edward; Virginia, 1666 6212.30 p29
Elliot, Edward 42; Ontario, 1871 1823.15 p72
Elliot, George; Died enroute, 1665 1224.1 p20
Elliot, Hattie W.; Vermont, 1869-1953 5900.10 p360
Elliot, James; Pennsylvania, 1777 4629.10 p14
Elliot, James; Savannah, Georgia, 1774 1640.10 p48
With wife
Elliot, James 35; Savannah, Georgia, 1774 1220.25 p139
With wife
Elliot, James 50; Ontario, 1871 1823.15 p72
Elliot, James 61; Ontario, 1871 1823.15 p73
Elliot, Jane 19; Ontario, 1871 1823.15 p73
Elliot, Jane 43; Ontario, 1871 1823.15 p73
Elliot, John; Alabama, 1839 1640.10 p48
Elliot, John; Florida, 1769 1640.10 p48
Elliot, John; Virginia, 1664 6212.30 p9
Elliot, John; Virginia, 1666 6212.30 p27
Elliot, John 45; Ontario, 1871 1823.28 p27
Elliot, Julia; Vermont, 1854-1879 5900.10 p360
Elliot, Mary Delany 75; Vermont, 1905 5900.10 p360
Elliot, Patrick H.; Vermont, 1860-1902 5900.10 p360
Elliot, Phoebe; Vermont, 1832-1898 5900.10 p563
Elliot, Robert; New York, 1807 8197.10 p38
Elliot, Robert 21; Ontario, 1871 1823.28 p27
Elliot, Robert 45; Ontario, 1871 1823.15 p73
Elliot, Robert 47; Ontario, 1871 1823.15 p73
Elliot, Robert 80; Ontario, 1871 1823.15 p73
Elliot, Thomas; New York, 1829 8197.10 p227
Elliot, Thomas 43; Ontario, 1871 1823.15 p73
Elliot, Thomas 46; Ontario, 1871 1823.15 p73
Elliot, Thomas 68; Vermont, 1896 5900.10 p360
Elliot, Thomas, Jr.; Vermont, 1868-1912 5900.10 p360
Elliot, William 38; Ontario, 1871 1823.15 p73
Elliot, William 40; Ontario, 1871 1823.15 p73
Elliot, William 50; Ontario, 1871 1823.15 p73
Elliot, William 59; Ontario, 1871 1823.22 p49
Elliot, Wm; Virginia, 1664 6212.30 p8
Elliott, Mr.; Quebec, 1856 9196.15 p5
Elliott, Mr.; Quebec, 1858 9196.15 p32
Elliott, Alexander 30; Ontario, 1871 1823.15 p73
Elliott, Alexander 50; Ontario, 1871 1823.15 p73
Elliott, Alexander 81; Ontario, 1871 1823.15 p73
Elliott, Andrew; Savannah, Georgia, 1775 1224.2 p37
Elliott, Anna M. 79; Ontario, 1871 1823.15 p73
Elliott, Anthony 60; Ontario, 1871 1823.15 p73
Elliott, Archibald 47; Ontario, 1871 1823.15 p73
Elliott, Arthur 42; Ontario, 1871 1823.22 p49
Elliott, Barnabus 55; Ontario, 1871 1823.22 p49
Elliott, Benjam V. 56; Ontario, 1871 1823.15 p73
Elliott, Caroline; Vermont, 1837-1906 5900.10 p182
Elliott, Catherine 70; Vermont, 1894 5900.10 p587
Elliott, Charles; Pennsylvania, 1821 6058.10 p6
Elliott, Daniel; Pennsylvania, 1777 4629.10 p18
Elliott, David 49; Ontario, 1871 1823.22 p49
Elliott, David 50; Ontario, 1871 1823.15 p73
Elliott, Dawson 41; Ontario, 1871 1823.28 p27
Elliott, Elizabeth; Vermont, 1869-1920 5900.10 p386
Elliott, Farncis 42; Ontario, 1871 1823.15 p73
Elliott, Gabriel 35; Ontario, 1871 1823.15 p73
Elliott, Gary A.; Vermont, 1852-1908 5900.10 p540
Elliott, George 36; Ontario, 1871 1823.15 p73
Elliott, George 43; Ontario, 1871 1823.28 p27
Elliott, George 49; Ontario, 1871 1823.15 p73

Elliott, Gray; Georgia, n.d. ***1224.2*** *p37*
Elliott, Henry 42; Ontario, 1871 ***1823.28*** *p27*
Elliott, Isabella 74; Ontario, 1871 ***1823.15*** *p73*
Elliott, James; Vermont, 1853-1887 ***5900.10*** *p386*
Elliott, James 32; Philadelphia, 1774 ***1220.25*** *p81*
Elliott, James 51; Ontario, 1871 ***1823.22*** *p49*
Elliott, James 62; Ontario, 1871 ***1823.15*** *p73*
Elliott, Jane 32 *SEE* Elliott, William
Elliott, John; New York, 1816 ***8197.10*** *p59*
Elliott, John; North Carolina, 1738 ***1224.2*** *p38*
Elliott, John; Portland, Maine, 1857 ***9196.15*** *p12*
Elliott, John 38; Ontario, 1871 ***1823.15*** *p73*
Elliott, John 44; Ontario, 1871 ***1823.15*** *p73*
Elliott, John 45; Ontario, 1871 ***1823.15*** *p73*
Elliott, John 47; Ontario, 1871 ***1823.15*** *p73*
Elliott, John 60; Ontario, 1871 ***1823.15*** *p73*
Elliott, Kate; Vermont, 1855-1917 ***5900.10*** *p387*
Elliott, M. Ellen Croake; Vermont, 1861-1916 ***5900.10*** *p540*
Elliott, Margaret 96; Ontario, 1871 ***1823.15*** *p73*
Elliott, Margaret E.; Vermont, 1865-1931 ***5900.10*** *p386*
Elliott, Mary; Vermont, 1835-1911 ***5900.10*** *p386*
Elliott, Mary 70; Ontario, 1871 ***1823.15*** *p73*
Elliott, Mary 87; Ontario, 1871 ***1823.15*** *p73*
Elliott, Moses 62; Ontario, 1871 ***1823.15*** *p73*
Elliott, Richard 28; Ontario, 1871 ***1823.15*** *p73*
Elliott, Robert; New York, 1821 ***8197.10*** *p227*
Elliott, Robert; Vermont, 1827-1895 ***5900.10*** *p386*
Elliott, Robert; Vermont, 1859-1915 ***5900.10*** *p386*
Elliott, Robert 47; Ontario, 1871 ***1823.15*** *p73*
Elliott, Samuel M.; New York, 1837 ***8197.10*** *p318*
Elliott, Samuel M.; New York, 1839 ***8197.10*** *p130*
Elliott, Sarah 40; Ontario, 1871 ***1823.15*** *p73*
Elliott, Thomas; Vermont, 1857-1881 ***5900.10*** *p386*
Elliott, Thomas 43; Ontario, 1871 ***1823.28*** *p27*
Elliott, Thomas 48; Ontario, 1871 ***1823.15*** *p73*
Elliott, Thomas 63; Ontario, 1871 ***1823.15*** *p73*
Elliott, Vincent; Maryland, 1678 ***2524.55*** *p75*
Elliott, William; Maryland, 1681 ***2524.55*** *p75*
Elliott, William; Nova Scotia, 1712 ***1224.2*** *p38*
Elliott, William 30; Ontario, 1871 ***1823.28*** *p27*
Elliott, William 33; New York, 1774 ***1220.25*** *p124*
Wife: Jane 32
Elliott, William 38; Philadelphia, 1774 ***1220.25*** *p66*
Elliott, William 41; Ontario, 1871 ***1823.15*** *p74*
Elliott, William 57; Ontario, 1871 ***1823.15*** *p74*
Elliott, William 60; Ontario, 1871 ***1823.15*** *p73*
Ellis, A. M. 17; Ontario, 1861 ***2896.28*** *p13*
Ellis, Adam Gibb; Jamaica, 1895 ***1640.13*** *p35*
Ellis, Alexander; New York, 1818 ***8197.10*** *p227*
Ellis, Anthony Hardy; Toronto, 1856 ***1640.13*** *p35*
Ellis, Benjamin F. 3; Ontario, 1861 ***2896.27*** *p57*
Ellis, Charles; New York, 1831 ***8197.10*** *p67*
Ellis, Charles Edward; New York, 1826 ***8197.10*** *p227*
Ellis, David H.; New York, 1837 ***8197.10*** *p86*
Ellis, E. 44; Ontario, 1861 ***2896.28*** *p13*
Ellis, Edward 27; Virginia, 1774 ***1220.25*** *p91*
Ellis, Emeline 36; Ontario, 1861 ***2896.27*** *p57*
Ellis, Evan; Virginia, 1666 ***6212.30*** *p26*
Ellis, Fanny M. 10; Ontario, 1861 ***2896.27*** *p57*
Ellis, Francis; Pennsylvania, 1777 ***4629.10*** *p30*
Ellis, Frederick 27; Ontario, 1871 ***1823.15*** *p74*
Ellis, G. 16; Ontario, 1861 ***2896.28*** *p13*
Ellis, G. 19; Ontario, 1861 ***2896.28*** *p13*
Ellis, G. J. 11; Ontario, 1861 ***2896.28*** *p13*
Ellis, Griffith; America, 1732 ***1224.2*** *p38*
Ellis, H. T. 11; Ontario, 1861 ***2896.28*** *p13*
Ellis, Henry; New York, 1840 ***8197.10*** *p167*
Ellis, Isabella 60; Ontario, 1871 ***1823.15*** *p74*
Ellis, J. B. 13; Ontario, 1861 ***2896.28*** *p13*
Ellis, James; Maryland, 1681 ***2524.55*** *p75*
Ellis, James; New York, 1717 ***1224.2*** *p38*
Ellis, James; New York, 1839 ***8197.10*** *p129*
Ellis, James 47; Ontario, 1871 ***1823.28*** *p27*
Ellis, Jason 52; Ontario, 1871 ***1823.15*** *p74*
Ellis, John; Maryland, 1663 ***2524.55*** *p75*
Ellis, John; Maryland, 1680 ***2524.55*** *p75*
Ellis, John; Maryland, 1682 ***2524.55*** *p75*
Ellis, John; New York, 1819 ***8197.10*** *p61*
Ellis, John; North America, 1785 ***1224.2*** *p38*
Ellis, John; Virginia, 1659 ***1224.1*** *p20*
Ellis, John 43; Alaska, 1918 ***9196.1*** *p12*
Ellis, John 43; British Columbia, 1918 ***9196.1*** *p12*
Ellis, John 50; Ontario, 1871 ***1823.28*** *p27*
Ellis, John 58; Ontario, 1871 ***1823.15*** *p74*
Ellis, Joseph H.; Pennsylvania, 1779 ***4629.10*** *p35*
Ellis, M. 9; Ontario, 1861 ***2896.28*** *p13*
Ellis, M. J. 11; Ontario, 1861 ***2896.28*** *p13*
Ellis, Mary A.; Vermont, 1842-1921 ***5900.10*** *p288*
Ellis, Nicholas; Maryland, 1667 ***2524.55*** *p75*
Ellis, Peter; Maryland, 1664 ***2524.55*** *p75*
Ellis, Phebe J. 13; Ontario, 1861 ***2896.27*** *p57*
Ellis, Robert 29; Georgia, 1774 ***1220.25*** *p48*
Ellis, S. M. 9; Ontario, 1861 ***2896.28*** *p13*
Ellis, Samuel 55; Ontario, 1871 ***1823.28*** *p27*
Ellis, Samuell; Virginia, 1668-1669 ***6212.30*** *p40*
Ellis, Stephen 21; Maryland, 1774 ***1220.25*** *p71*
Ellis, Thomas 28; Ontario, 1871 ***1823.15*** *p74*
Ellis, William; New York, 1840 ***8197.10*** *p167*
Ellis, William 24; Nova Scotia, 1774 ***1220.25*** *p135*
With wife & child
Ellis, William M. 44; Ontario, 1871 ***1823.15*** *p74*
Ellis, Wm; Virginia, 1664 ***6212.30*** *p5*
Ellison, . . .; Boston, 1765 ***4628.40*** *p114*
Ellison, Ellen; New York, 1852 ***1224.3*** *p24*
Ellison, Jane; Maryland, 1681 ***2524.55*** *p75*
Ellison, John 19; Maryland, 1774 ***1220.25*** *p41*
Ellison, John 20; British Columbia, 1910 ***9196.1*** *p29*
Ellison, John 20; Washington, 1910 ***9196.1*** *p29*
Ellison, Joseph 36; Ontario, 1871 ***1823.15*** *p74*
Ellison, Robert; Albany, New York, 1756 ***1224.2*** *p38*
Ellist, Lewis 39; Ontario, 1871 ***1823.15*** *p74*
Elliston, Mrs. 50; Jamaica, 1776 ***1220.25*** *p134*
Elliston, Elizabeth; Maryland, 1659-1661 ***2524.55*** *p10*
Elliston, Robert; New York, 1759 ***1224.2*** *p38*
Ellixon, Jasper; Virginia, 1706 ***1224.2*** *p2*
Ellmann, Hans Georg; America, 1744 ***2856.30*** *p98*
Ellmer, Jno; Portland, Maine, 1858 ***9196.15*** *p28*
Ellmes, Thomas; Maryland, 1665 ***2524.55*** *p75*
Ellmore, William; Maryland, 1682 ***2524.55*** *p75*
Ellsasser, Conrad 39; Kansas, 1876-1910 ***9079.10*** *p22*
Ellson, Ann; Maryland, 1659 ***2524.55*** *p76*
Ellson, John; Maryland, 1659 ***2524.55*** *p76*
Ellstone, Ellinour *SEE* Ellstone, Ralph
Ellstone, Ralph; Maryland, 1661-1662 ***2524.55*** *p75*
Wife: Ellinour
Son: Ralph, Jr.
Ellstone, Ralph, Jr. *SEE* Ellstone, Ralph
Ellsworth, Albert 14; Ontario, 1861 ***2896.28*** *p43*
Ellsworth, Almira 35; Ontario, 1861 ***2896.27*** *p36*
Ellsworth, Chancy 11; Ontario, 1861 ***2896.28*** *p43*
Ellsworth, Charlotte 3; Ontario, 1861 ***2896.28*** *p43*
Ellsworth, Emily A. 40; Vermont, 1873 ***5900.10*** *p522*
Ellsworth, Lorena 18; Ontario, 1861 ***2896.28*** *p43*
Ellsworth, Nial 9; Ontario, 1861 ***2896.28*** *p43*
Ellsworth, Olive 41; Ontario, 1861 ***2896.28*** *p43*
Ellsworth, Ruth 10; Ontario, 1861 ***2896.28*** *p43*
Ellsworth, Stephen 20; Ontario, 1861 ***2896.28*** *p43*
Ellton, James; Maryland, 1662 ***2524.55*** *p76*
Ellys, Mary; Maryland, 1676 ***2524.55*** *p75*
Ellys, Robert; Maryland, 1676 ***2524.55*** *p75*
Elmar, Charles; Maryland, 1673 ***2524.55*** *p75*
Elmer, Sarah 23; Ontario, 1871 ***1823.22*** *p49*
Elmes, Elizabeth *SEE* Elmes, William
Elmes, James 18; Georgia, 1774 ***1220.25*** *p48*
Elmes, Martha; Virginia, 1664 ***6212.30*** *p9*
Elmes, Rich; Virginia, 1665-1666 ***6212.30*** *p21*
Elmes, William; Maryland, 1673 ***2524.55*** *p75*
Wife: Elizabeth
Elmes, William 30; Baltimore, 1775 ***1220.25*** *p118*
Elmore, John; Maryland, 1681 ***2524.55*** *p75*
Elmsley, Miss; Quebec, 1857 ***9196.15*** *p24*
Elmsley, Mrs.; Quebec, 1857 ***9196.15*** *p24*
Elmsman, Edw; Virginia, 1664-1665 ***6212.30*** *p16*
Eloden, Benjamin; New York, 1804 ***8197.10*** *p26*
Elphinstone, Anne *SEE* Elphinstone, William
Elphinstone, William; Georgia, 1734 ***1640.10*** *p49*
Wife: Anne
Elrich, Caspar; America, 1733 ***2856.30*** *p98*
With wife & children
Elringinton, Mark 38; Ontario, 1871 ***1823.15*** *p74*
Elsam, Dorothy; New England, 1684 ***1224.1*** *p20*
Elsasser, Johann Michael; Port uncertain, 1764 ***2856.30*** *p98*
Elsden, Benjamin; New York, 1807 ***8197.10*** *p330*
Elser, Anna Barbara; America, 1744 ***2856.30*** *p98*
Elser, Johann Georg; Port uncertain, 1741 ***2856.30*** *p98*
Elser, Johann Michael; America, 1799 ***2856.30*** *p98*
Elser, Johann Michael; Port uncertain, 1764 ***2856.30*** *p98*
Elser, Michael; America, 1775 ***2856.30*** *p98*
Elser, Peter; America, 1749 ***2856.30*** *p98*
Elsey, Nicholas; New England, 1649 ***1224.1*** *p20*
Elsey, Peter; Virginia, 1671 ***6212.30*** *p45*
Elsigood, Edmund 24; St. Kitts, 1773 ***1220.25*** *p30*
Elson, John 49; Ontario, 1871 ***1823.15*** *p74*
Elson, Samuel; New England, 1707 ***1224.2*** *p38*
Elsse, Edward; New York, 1838 ***8197.10*** *p228*
Elsser, Margarete; America, 1749 ***2856.30*** *p98*
With son
Elsser, Margarete; America, 1749 ***2856.30*** *p160*
Elstad, Sam 27; Alaska, 1917 ***9196.1*** *p7*
Elstad, Sam 27; Yukon, 1917 ***9196.1*** *p7*
Elster, Christof; Port uncertain, 1764 ***2856.30*** *p98*
Elston, David; New Jersey, 1857 ***1224.3*** *p24*
Elston, Elinor; Maryland, 1664 ***2524.55*** *p75*
Elston, John 41; Ontario, 1871 ***1823.15*** *p74*
Elston, Ralph; Maryland, 1664 ***2524.55*** *p75*
Elston, Richard 35; Ontario, 1871 ***1823.15*** *p74*
Elston, Robert 61; Ontario, 1871 ***1823.15*** *p74*
Elston, Thomas 29; Ontario, 1871 ***1823.15*** *p74*
Elsvetak, Mary; Maryland, 1910 ***3259.35*** *p13*
Elsworth, A. 85; Ontario, 1861 ***2896.26*** *p5*
Elsworth, A. A. 14; Ontario, 1861 ***2896.26*** *p5*
Elsworth, A. M. 20; Ontario, 1861 ***2896.26*** *p5*
Elsworth, D. 17; Ontario, 1861 ***2896.26*** *p5*
Elsworth, D. L. 12; Ontario, 1861 ***2896.26*** *p5*
Elsworth, D. R. 16; Ontario, 1861 ***2896.26*** *p5*
Elsworth, Dinah 47; Ontario, 1861 ***2896.26*** *p5*
Elsworth, E. 14; Ontario, 1861 ***2896.26*** *p5*
Elsworth, E. J. 12; Ontario, 1861 ***2896.26*** *p5*
Elsworth, G. H. 22; Ontario, 1861 ***2896.26*** *p5*
Elsworth, H. E. 18; Ontario, 1861 ***2896.26*** *p5*
Elsworth, J. T. 3; Ontario, 1861 ***2896.26*** *p5*
Elsworth, L. B. 27; Ontario, 1861 ***2896.26*** *p5*
Elsworth, M. 52; Ontario, 1861 ***2896.26*** *p5*
Elsworth, Olive 18; Ontario, 1861 ***2896.28*** *p26*
Elsworth, S.; Ontario, 1861 ***2896.26*** *p8*
Elsworth, S. N. 11; Ontario, 1861 ***2896.26*** *p5*
Elsworth, S. W. 19; Ontario, 1861 ***2896.26*** *p5*
Elsworth, Waty 41; Ontario, 1861 ***2896.26*** *p5*
Elthringham, George; Maryland, 1665 ***2524.55*** *p75*
Elton, Marcus; Maryland, 1673 ***2524.55*** *p75*
Eltonhead, Edward; Maryland, 1655 ***2524.55*** *p75*
Eltz, Ludwig; Port uncertain, 1729 ***2856.30*** *p98*
Elvidge, Ellen; Vermont, 1860-1954 ***5900.10*** *p504*
Elvin, Delilah 52; Ontario, 1861 ***2896.27*** *p37*
Elvin, Edward 15; Ontario, 1861 ***2896.27*** *p37*
Elvin, Edward 61; Ontario, 1871 ***1823.22*** *p50*
Elvin, John 56; Ontario, 1861 ***2896.27*** *p37*
Elvin, Wm; Virginia, 1674 ***6212.30*** *p52*
Elwell, William; New York, 1835 ***8197.10*** *p227*
Elwood, Bridget; Vermont, 1816-1902 ***5900.10*** *p376*
Elwood, E. L. 60; Ontario, 1871 ***1823.15*** *p74*
Elwood, Ellen 50; Ontario, 1871 ***1823.15*** *p74*
Elwood, John Y. 32; Ontario, 1871 ***1823.15*** *p74*
Elwood, Macy 25; Ontario, 1861 ***2896.27*** *p29*
Elworthy, Thomas 21; Maryland, 1775 ***1220.25*** *p103*
Elwyn, Thomas Langdon; Portsmouth, New Hampshire, 1818 ***1224.3*** *p24*
Ely, Isaac; Pennsylvania, 1777 ***4629.10*** *p19*
Ely, Johann Georg; Port uncertain, 1785 ***2856.30*** *p98*
Emalinska, Wladislaw; Maryland, 1910 ***3259.35*** *p14*
Embar, L. 21; Alaska, 1913 ***9196.1*** *p40*
Emblen, Caleb; Pennsylvania, 1777 ***4629.10*** *p19*
Embs, Georg; America, 1741 ***2856.30*** *p98*
Embser, Anton; Port uncertain, 1765 ***2856.30*** *p98*
Embser, Peter; Port uncertain, 1762 ***2856.30*** *p98*
With wife & 7 children
Embury, Cecilia 20; Ontario, 1861 ***2896.28*** *p18*
Embury, Philip; America, 1790 ***4628.40*** *p29*
Emel, Gabriel; Port uncertain, 1754 ***2856.30*** *p98*
Emelicki, Gasta; Maryland, 1910 ***3259.35*** *p14*
Emeridge, Ralph; Virginia, 1667-1668 ***6212.30*** *p38*
Emerson, Miss; Quebec, 1857 ***9196.15*** *p24*
Emerson, Mr.; Quebec, 1857 ***9196.15*** *p14*
Emerson, Mrs.; Quebec, 1857 ***9196.15*** *p14*
Emerson, Andrew 65; Ontario, 1871 ***1823.15*** *p74*
Emerson, James; New York, 1810-1834 ***8197.10*** *p307*
Emerson, John 71; Ontario, 1871 ***1823.28*** *p27*
Emerson, Mary; Bristol, Rhode Island, 1748 ***1224.2*** *p38*
Emerson, Matthew 29; Ontario, 1871 ***1823.28*** *p27*
Emerson, Melchizedel 27; Ontario, 1871 ***1823.28*** *p27*
Emerson, Paull; Virginia, 1664 ***6212.30*** *p7*
Emerson, Robert 38; Ontario, 1871 ***1823.15*** *p74*
Emerson, Thomas; Maryland, 1658 ***2524.55*** *p75*
Emerson, Thomas; Pennsylvania, 1785 ***4629.10*** *p48*
Emerton, Henry 21; Maryland, 1775 ***1220.25*** *p112*
Emerton, John 37; Ontario, 1871 ***1823.15*** *p74*
Emerton, Joseph 21; Maryland, 1775 ***1220.25*** *p112*
Emerton, William 28; Maryland, 1774 ***1220.25*** *p41*
Emery, Miss; Quebec, 1857 ***9196.15*** *p17*
Emery, Ann; Iowa, 1856 ***1224.3*** *p24*
Emery, C. E. 7; Ontario, 1861 ***2896.28*** *p11*
Emery, E. N. A. 1; Ontario, 1861 ***2896.28*** *p11*
Emery, G. W. 4; Ontario, 1861 ***2896.28*** *p11*
Emery, Mary; Maryland, 1666 ***2524.55*** *p75*
With 2 children
Emery, W. W. 9; Ontario, 1861 ***2896.28*** *p11*
Emery, W. W. 43; Ontario, 1861 ***2896.28*** *p11*
Emery, William; Maryland, 1668 ***2524.55*** *p75*
Emery, William; Pennsylvania, 1868 ***6058.10*** *p74*
Emes, Worsley; Pennsylvania, 1781 ***4629.10*** *p42*
Emett, Thomas; Maryland, 1668 ***2524.55*** *p11*
Emich, Adam; Port uncertain, 1732 ***2856.30*** *p98*
Emicke, Justas Peter; Baltimore, 1854 ***6058.10*** *p42*
Emig, Catharina; America, 1793 ***2856.30*** *p98*
Emig, Johann; America, 1752 ***2856.30*** *p98*
Emig, Konrad; America, 1752 ***2856.30*** *p98*
With wife & 3 children

Emigh, Eunic Aida 12; Ontario, 1871 ***1823.22*** *p50*
Emigh, Mary M. 31; Ontario, 1871 ***1823.22*** *p50*
Emigin, Agnes; America, 1742 ***2856.30*** *p98*
With 2 children
Eminger, Georg; America, 1768 ***2856.30*** *p98*
Emlach, James; New York, 1807 ***8197.10*** *p328*
Emlah, Louis 25; Ontario, 1871 ***1823.22*** *p50*
Emmel, Johann Nickel; Port uncertain, 1758 ***2856.30*** *p98*
Emmel, Juliana; Port uncertain, 1747 ***2856.30*** *p98*
Emmerich, Andreas; America, 1764 ***2856.30*** *p99*
With wife & 2 children
Emmerich, Anna Christina; Port uncertain, 1754 ***2856.30*** *p98*
Emmerich, Anna Margarete; Port uncertain, 1754 ***2856.30*** *p98*
Emmerich, Catharina; Port uncertain, 1794 ***2856.30*** *p99*
Emmerich, Catharina; Port uncertain, 1796 ***2856.30*** *p99*
Emmerich, Christian; Port uncertain, 1782 ***2856.30*** *p98*
Emmerich, Franz; Cayenne, 1764 ***2856.30*** *p99*
With child
Emmerich, Jakob; Port uncertain, 1783 ***2856.30*** *p98*
Emmerich, Mrs. Johann; America, 1741 ***2856.30*** *p99*
With daughter
Emmerich, Johann Georg; America, 1752 ***2856.30*** *p99*
Emmerich, Niklas; Port uncertain, 1783 ***2856.30*** *p99*
Emmerich, Valentin; Port uncertain, 1789 ***2856.30*** *p99*
Emmerling, John; Pennsylvania, 1833 ***6058.10*** *p11*
Emmerson, Nicholas; Maryland, 1650 ***2524.55*** *p75*
Emmerson, Phebe; Maryland, 1650 ***2524.55*** *p75*
Emmerson, Thomas; Maryland, 1659 ***2524.55*** *p75*
Emmert, Francis; New York, 1836-1838 ***8197.10*** *p115*
Emmert, Peter; America, 1752 ***2856.30*** *p99*
Emmert, Peter; America, 1770 ***2856.30*** *p99*
Emmes, John; Pennsylvania, 1777 ***4629.10*** *p9*
Emmett, Henry 32; Philadelphia, 1775 ***1220.25*** *p9*
Emmig, Georg; America, 1766 ***2856.30*** *p99*
Emmins, William 27; Virginia, 1773 ***1220.25*** *p28*
Emmons, John; Vermont, 1855-1915 ***5900.10*** *p340*
Emmons, Margaret Mee; Vermont, 1854-1935 ***5900.10*** *p340*
Emmons, Mary; Vermont, 1861-1883 ***5900.10*** *p337*
Emney, Christine; Canada, 1828 ***1640.13*** *p35*
Emons, Andrew 39; Ontario, 1861 ***2896.25*** *p19*
Emons, Harvey 3; Ontario, 1861 ***2896.25*** *p21*
Emons, William H. 7; Ontario, 1861 ***2896.25*** *p21*
Empfinger, Georg; America, 1752 ***2856.30*** *p99*
Empfinger, Georg, Sr.; America, 1752 ***2856.30*** *p99*
Empson, Mrs.; Maryland, 1651 ***2524.55*** *p76*
Empson, Mary; Maryland, 1671 ***2524.55*** *p66*
Empson, Mary; Maryland, 1671 ***2524.55*** *p76*
Empson, Mary; Maryland, 1678 ***2524.55*** *p67*
Empson, Mary; Maryland, 1678 ***2524.55*** *p76*
Empson, William; Maryland, 1671 ***2524.55*** *p76*
Empson, William; Maryland, 1678 ***2524.55*** *p76*
Emrich, Friedrich; Port uncertain, 1789 ***2856.30*** *p99*
Enck, Christian; Port uncertain, 1751 ***2856.30*** *p99*
Enck, Jakob; Port uncertain, 1723 ***2856.30*** *p99*
Enck, Maria Anna; Port uncertain, 1784 ***2856.30*** *p99*
Enckteller, Michael; New York, 1840 ***8197.10*** *p167*
Ende, Nikolaus; Port uncertain, 1764 ***2856.30*** *p99*
Enderle, Mathias; America, 1832 ***2856.30*** *p99*
Enderlin, Eva; America, 1754 ***2856.30*** *p99*
Enderlin, Franziska; Port uncertain, 1743 ***2856.30*** *p99*
Enderlin, Johann; Port uncertain, 1755 ***2856.30*** *p99*
With wife
Enderlin, Salome; Port uncertain, 1757 ***2856.30*** *p99*
With husband
Enders, Anna Margarete; Port uncertain, 1784 ***2856.30*** *p99*
Enders, Benedikt; Port uncertain, 1776 ***2856.30*** *p99*
Enders, Johann Eberhard; Port uncertain, 1764 ***2856.30*** *p99*
Enders, Melchior; Port uncertain, 1784 ***2856.30*** *p99*
Endgles, Anny 46; Ontario, 1871 ***1823.28*** *p27*
Endicott, John; New England, 1695 ***1224.1*** *p20*
Endicott, William; Boston, 1887 ***3437.14*** *p148*
Endinger, Johann; Port uncertain, 1753 ***2856.30*** *p99*
Endlich, Johann Jakob; Port uncertain, 1803 ***2856.30*** *p99*
Endlich, Johann Jakob; Port uncertain, 1804 ***2856.30*** *p99*
Endres, Anna Catharina; Port uncertain, 1747 ***2856.30*** *p99*
Endres, Christof; Port uncertain, 1760 ***2856.30*** *p99*
Endres, Elisabeth; Port uncertain, 1755 ***2856.30*** *p99*
Endres, Georg; Port uncertain, 1746 ***2856.30*** *p99*
Endres, Melchior; Port uncertain, 1784 ***2856.30*** *p99*
Endress, Jacob; Pennsylvania, 1786 ***4629.10*** *p52*
Ends, George; Maryland, 1670 ***2524.55*** *p76*
Enefer, James; Philadelphia, 1793 ***4629.10*** *p68*
Enell, Lucke; Maryland, 1670 ***2524.55*** *p76*
Enery, Henry; Virginia, 1666 ***6212.30*** *p30*
Enes, George; Maryland, 1670 ***2524.55*** *p76*
Enes, Philipp; America, 1751 ***2856.30*** *p100*
With wife & child
Enes, Veit; Port uncertain, 1765 ***2856.30*** *p100*
Enever, John; New York, 1807 ***8197.10*** *p328*
Enew, James; Pennsylvania, 1787 ***4629.10*** *p50*
Enfeild, James; Virginia, 1666 ***6212.30*** *p25*
Enfield, Nellie Manley 44; Vermont, 1899 ***5900.10*** *p579*
Engbarr, Anna Maria; Port uncertain, 1792 ***2856.30*** *p100*
Engbart, Johann; Port uncertain, 1736 ***2856.30*** *p100*
Engbaum, Jno 76; British Columbia, 1917 ***9196.1*** *p69*
Engbaum, Jno 76; Washington, 1917 ***9196.1*** *p69*
Engehard, Franz; Port uncertain, 1741 ***2856.30*** *p100*
Engel, Casper 40; Ontario, 1871 ***1823.15*** *p74*
Engel, Catharina; Port uncertain, 1784 ***2856.30*** *p100*
Engel, Catharina; Port uncertain, 1784 ***2856.30*** *p405*
Engel, Dietrich; Port uncertain, 1786 ***2856.30*** *p94*
Engel, Dor.; America, 1771 ***2856.30*** *p455*
Engel, Dor.; America, 1772 ***2856.30*** *p455*
Engel, Dor.; America, 1773 ***2856.30*** *p455*
Engel, Dor.; America, 1774 ***2856.30*** *p455*
Engel, Georg; Port uncertain, 1764 ***2856.30*** *p100*
Engel, Georg; Port uncertain, 1765 ***2856.30*** *p100*
Engel, Heinrich; Port uncertain, 1763 ***2856.30*** *p100*
Engel, Henrich; Port uncertain, 1764 ***2856.30*** *p100*
Engel, Jakob; America, 1744 ***2856.30*** *p100*
With wife & 6 children
Engel, Johann; Port uncertain, 1742 ***2856.30*** *p100*
Engel, Peter; America, 1748 ***2856.30*** *p100*
Engel, Sofie Dorothea; America, 1773 ***2856.30*** *p100*
Engel, Sofie Dorothea; Port uncertain, 1771 ***2856.30*** *p100*
Engel, Wilhelm; America, 1753 ***2856.30*** *p296*
Engelfrid, Wilhelm; America, 1786 ***2856.30*** *p100*
Engelhard, Johann; Port uncertain, 1735 ***2856.30*** *p100*
Engelhard, Valentin; Port uncertain, 1734 ***2856.30*** *p100*
Engelhardt, Anna Maria; Port uncertain, 1785 ***2856.30*** *p100*
Engelhardt, Anna Maria; Port uncertain, 1786 ***2856.30*** *p100*
Engelhardt, Johann Adam; Port uncertain, 1775 ***2856.30*** *p100*
Engelhardt, Johann Adam; Port uncertain, 1779 ***2856.30*** *p100*
Engelhorn, Stefan; Port uncertain, 1751 ***2856.30*** *p100*
Engelin, Catharina; Port uncertain, 1769 ***2856.30*** *p100*
Engelke, John; New York, 1839 ***8197.10*** *p129*
Engelkirch, Maria Catharina; Port uncertain, 1775 ***2856.30*** *p100*
Engelman, Frederick; New York, 1838 ***8197.10*** *p115*
Engelmann, Anna Elisabeth; Port uncertain, 1739 ***2856.30*** *p100*
Engelmann, Elis. Catharina; Port uncertain, 1762 ***2856.30*** *p100*
Engelmann, Jacob; America, 1741 ***2856.30*** *p100*
Engelmann, Jacob; America, 1766 ***2856.30*** *p100*
Engelmann, Jacob; Port uncertain, 1773 ***2856.30*** *p100*
Engelmann, Jacob, Jr.; America, 1741 ***2856.30*** *p101*
Engelmann, Johann Jakob; Port uncertain, 1751 ***2856.30*** *p101*
With wife & children
Engelmann, Margarete; America, 1766 ***2856.30*** *p101*
Engelmann, Maria Elisabeth; Port uncertain, 1763 ***2856.30*** *p101*
Engelmann, Michael; Port uncertain, 1751 ***2856.30*** *p101*
Engels, Anniken; Maryland, 1669 ***2524.55*** *p55*
Enger, Adam; Port uncertain, 1777 ***2856.30*** *p101*
Enger, Melchior; Port uncertain, 1784 ***2856.30*** *p101*
Engert, Christina Gais; Port uncertain, 1785 ***2856.30*** *p128*
Engisch, John; New York, 1838 ***8197.10*** *p228*
Engl, Johann Niklas; Port uncertain, 1786 ***2856.30*** *p101*
England, Adam 49; Ontario, 1871 ***1823.15*** *p74*
England, Albert 21; Ontario, 1871 ***1823.15*** *p74*
England, Ben 58; Ontario, 1871 ***1823.28*** *p27*
England, E. 24; Washington, 1914 ***9196.1*** *p66*
England, Edward; New York, 1840 ***8197.10*** *p167*
England, Edwin; New York, 1840 ***8197.10*** *p167*
England, Elizabeth 35; Ontario, 1871 ***1823.15*** *p74*
England, James 30; Ontario, 1871 ***1823.15*** *p74*
England, John; Maryland, 1739 ***1224.2*** *p38*
England, John 18; Ontario, 1871 ***1823.22*** *p50*
England, John 49; Ontario, 1871 ***1823.15*** *p74*
England, John 52; Ontario, 1871 ***1823.22*** *p50*
England, Joseph 44; Ontario, 1871 ***1823.15*** *p74*
England, Rodolphus 26; Ontario, 1871 ***1823.15*** *p74*
England, William 45; Ontario, 1871 ***1823.22*** *p50*
Engle, Benjamin; Pennsylvania, 1777 ***4629.10*** *p28*
Engle, Joseph; Pennsylvania, 1779 ***4629.10*** *p41*
Engle, Michael; Pennsylvania, 1777 ***4629.10*** *p27*
Engle, Silas; Pennsylvania, 1779 ***4629.10*** *p41*
Engler, Charles; New York, 1836 ***8197.10*** *p227*
Engler, Georg; Port uncertain, 1790 ***2856.30*** *p101*
Engler, Johann; Port uncertain, 1742 ***2856.30*** *p101*
Engler, Johann; Port uncertain, 1755 ***2856.30*** *p101*
Engler, Johann; Port uncertain, 1788 ***2856.30*** *p101*
Engler, Theresia; Port uncertain, 1734 ***2856.30*** *p101*
Englert, Valentin; Port uncertain, 1786 ***2856.30*** *p101*
Engles, Antwine 73; Ontario, 1871 ***1823.28*** *p27*
Engles, Silas; Pennsylvania, 1777 ***4629.10*** *p10*
Englesdon, Isack; Virginia, 1679-1680 ***6212.30*** *p54*
Englin, Anna Maria; Port uncertain, 1764 ***2856.30*** *p101*
English, Agnes 23; Ontario, 1861 ***2896.27*** *p30*
English, Alexander 20; Jamaica, 1773-1774 ***1220.25*** *p32*
English, Annie; Vermont, 1853-1934 ***5900.10*** *p173*
English, Bridget; Vermont, 1826-1879 ***5900.10*** *p173*
English, Catherine 13; Ontario, 1861 ***2896.27*** *p35*
English, David 1; Ontario, 1861 ***2896.27*** *p35*
English, Ellen; Maryland, 1682 ***2524.55*** *p76*
English, George; Maryland, 1664 ***2524.55*** *p76*
Relative: Mary
Son: George, Jr.
English, George, Jr. *SEE* English, George
English, Jane 53; Ontario, 1861 ***2896.27*** *p1*
English, John; Maryland, 1674 ***2524.55*** *p76*
English, John; New York, 1804 ***8197.10*** *p26*
English, John; New York, 1807 ***8197.10*** *p38*
English, John 6; Ontario, 1861 ***2896.27*** *p1*
English, John 45; Ontario, 1871 ***1823.15*** *p74*
English, John 53; Ontario, 1871 ***1823.28*** *p27*
English, John 65; Ontario, 1861 ***2896.27*** *p1*
English, Kate; Vermont, 1832-1897 ***5900.10*** *p242*
English, King 35; Maryland, 1775 ***1220.25*** *p115*
English, Lyman; Ontario, 1889 ***1640.13*** *p35*
English, Martha J. 15; Ontario, 1861 ***2896.27*** *p35*
English, Mary *SEE* English, George
English, Mary; Vermont, 1825-1885 ***5900.10*** *p242*
English, Mary E.; Vermont, 1846-1928 ***5900.10*** *p173*
English, Mat 26; Ontario, 1861 ***2896.27*** *p1*
English, Middleton; New York, 1802 ***8197.10*** *p20*
English, Robert 56; Ontario, 1871 ***1823.15*** *p74*
English, Robert 81; Ontario, 1871 ***1823.22*** *p50*
English, Samuel 23; Maryland, 1775 ***1220.25*** *p112*
English, Sarah 76; Ontario, 1861 ***2896.27*** *p1*
English, Thomas; New York, 1818 ***8197.10*** *p227*
English, William; Pennsylvania, 1786 ***4629.10*** *p49*
English, William 40; Ontario, 1861 ***2896.27*** *p30*
English, William Molesworth; Boston, n.d. ***1224.3*** *p24*
Engstler, Michael; Port uncertain, 1712 ***2856.30*** *p101*
Engstler, Michael; Port uncertain, 1752 ***2856.30*** *p101*
Enlicknay, James 61; Ontario, 1871 ***1823.15*** *p74*
Ennis, Anne; Maryland, 1691 ***1224.1*** *p14*
Ennis, Bridget Friel; Vermont, 1833-1901 ***5900.10*** *p548*
Ennis, John; Canada, 1756-1760 ***4628.40*** *p46*
Ennis, John 70; Ontario, 1871 ***1823.28*** *p27*
Ennis, Nathan; Vermont, 1865-1900 ***5900.10*** *p548*
Ennis, Nathaniel F.; Vermont, 1832-1932 ***5900.10*** *p548*
Ennis, Robert 37; Ontario, 1871 ***1823.28*** *p27*
Ennis, Samuell; Virginia, 1666 ***6212.30*** *p28*
Ennis, Thomas 36; Ontario, 1871 ***1823.15*** *p74*
Ennis, William 46; Ontario, 1871 ***1823.28*** *p27*
Eno, George 40; Ontario, 1871 ***1823.15*** *p74*
Enoffi, Franz Ludwig; Port uncertain, 1765 ***2856.30*** *p93*
Enos, Bridget Casey; Vermont, 1816-1888 ***5900.10*** *p537*
Enos, Matthew; Vermont, 1811-1876 ***5900.10*** *p537*
Enous, Edward W.; Vermont, 1858-1911 ***5900.10*** *p524*
Enous, Margaret A. Hanley; Vermont, 1856-1938 ***5900.10*** *p524*
Enright, Anna Hyland; Vermont, 1858-1937 ***5900.10*** *p184*
Enright, Bridget A. Mattimore; Vermont, 1855-1914 ***5900.10*** *p406*
Enright, Dennis 30; Ontario, 1871 ***1823.28*** *p27*
Enright, Donald 47; Ontario, 1871 ***1823.28*** *p27*
Enright, Edward 50; Vermont, 1875 ***5900.10*** *p586*
Enright, Eliza A. Cummings; Vermont, 1861-1906 ***5900.10*** *p86*
Enright, Eliza Hanna; Vermont, 1859-1921 ***5900.10*** *p406*
Enright, Ellen; Vermont, 1835-1900 ***5900.10*** *p586*
Enright, Ellen Boil; Vermont, 1798-1875 ***5900.10*** *p586*
Enright, Hannibal; Vermont, 1856-1956 ***5900.10*** *p406*
Enright, James 55; Ontario, 1871 ***1823.28*** *p27*
Enright, Jeremiah; Vermont, 1815-1881 ***5900.10*** *p406*
Enright, Jeremiah 68; Vermont, 1881 ***5900.10*** *p222*
Enright, Johanna 20; Vermont, 1849 ***5900.10*** *p158*
Enright, Johanna Ormond; Vermont, 1832-1904 ***5900.10*** *p187*
Enright, John; Vermont, 1820-1896 ***5900.10*** *p187*
Enright, John 24; Ontario, 1871 ***1823.28*** *p27*
Enright, John 26; Ontario, 1871 ***1823.28*** *p27*
Enright, John 30; Ontario, 1871 ***1823.28*** *p27*
Enright, John 65; Ontario, 1871 ***1823.28*** *p27*
Enright, John J.; Vermont, 1843-1919 ***5900.10*** *p406*
Enright, Kate 55; Vermont, 1893 ***5900.10*** *p240*
Enright, Mary Ann Simm; Vermont, 1817-1904 ***5900.10*** *p406*
Enright, Mary E.; Vermont, 1859-1929 ***5900.10*** *p187*
Enright, Mary Kessane 53; Vermont, 1874 ***5900.10*** *p586*

Enright, Mary Mattimore; Vermont, 1837-1917 ***5900.10*** *p406*
Enright, Matthew P.; Vermont, 1857-1906 ***5900.10*** *p86*
Enright, Michael; Vermont, 1858-1930 ***5900.10*** *p184*
Enright, Michael 48; Ontario, 1871 ***1823.15*** *p74*
Enright, Owen 32; Ontario, 1871 ***1823.28*** *p27*
Enright, Patrick; Vermont, 1855-1919 ***5900.10*** *p187*
Enright, Patrick 34; Ontario, 1871 ***1823.28*** *p27*
Enright, Patrick 47; Ontario, 1871 ***1823.28*** *p27*
Enright, Stephen 29; Ontario, 1871 ***1823.28*** *p27*
Enright, Thomas 22; Vermont, 1863 ***5900.10*** *p240*
Enright, Thos 53; Ontario, 1871 ***1823.28*** *p27*
Enright, Thos 60; Ontario, 1871 ***1823.28*** *p27*
Enright, Timothy 60; Ontario, 1871 ***1823.28*** *p27*
Enright, William; Vermont, 1845-1930 ***5900.10*** *p406*
Enroight, James 35; Ontario, 1871 ***1823.22*** *p50*
Ensam, Robert; Maryland, 1668 ***2524.55*** *p76*
Ensell, Robert; Maryland, 1669 ***2524.55*** *p76*
Ensigne, Thomas; New England, 1658 ***1224.1*** *p20*
With children
Ensill, Robert; Maryland, 1665 ***2524.55*** *p76*
Ensinger, Maria Eva; Port uncertain, 1734 ***2856.30*** *p101*
Ensinger, Thomas; Port uncertain, 1753 ***2856.30*** *p101*
Enska, Micheal 56; Ontario, 1871 ***1823.28*** *p27*
Ensley, Effa 5; Ontario, 1861 ***2896.27*** *p73*
Ensley, George 8; Ontario, 1861 ***2896.27*** *p73*
Ensley, Hannah 27; Ontario, 1861 ***2896.27*** *p73*
Ensley, Hannah E. 2; Ontario, 1861 ***2896.27*** *p73*
Ensom, Robert; Maryland, 1673 ***2524.55*** *p76*
Ensom, Robert; Maryland, 1679 ***2524.55*** *p76*
Enson, George; Pennsylvania, 1777 ***4629.10*** *p14*
Ent, Jacob; Virginia, 1666-1667 ***6212.30*** *p34*
Enteman, Christoph; New York, 1807 ***8197.10*** *p38*
Entivis, Jno; Virginia, 1666-1667 ***6212.30*** *p32*
Enton, John; Virginia, 1691 ***1224.1*** *p20*
Entoska, Frank; Maryland, 1910 ***3259.35*** *p14*
Entrem, Richard; Virginia, 1671-1672 ***6212.30*** *p47*
Entrican, Wright 41; Ontario, 1871 ***1823.15*** *p74*
Ents, Ann; Maryland, 1663 ***2524.55*** *p76*
Entwis, Jno; Virginia, 1665-1666 ***6212.30*** *p22*
Entwisle, Henry; New York, 1840 ***8197.10*** *p167*
Enty, Edward 46; Ontario, 1871 ***1823.28*** *p27*
Enwaosl, Daniel 62; Ontario, 1871 ***1823.28*** *p27*
Enzinger, Anna Maria; Port uncertain, 1760 ***2856.30*** *p101*
Epes, Francis; Virginia, 1688 ***1224.1*** *p20*
Eppert, Hans; America, 1752 ***2856.30*** *p102*
With wife & 4 children
Eppinger, Niklas; Port uncertain, 1750 ***2856.30*** *p102*
Eppler, Johann; America, 1737 ***2856.30*** *p102*
Eppler, Johann; America, 1742 ***2856.30*** *p102*
Epplett, John 54; Ontario, 1871 ***1823.15*** *p74*
Equidoney, Peter 15; Maryland, 1775 ***1220.25*** *p102*
Erath, Aloys; New York, 1840 ***8197.10*** *p228*
Erath, Heinrich; New York, 1840 ***8197.10*** *p228*
Erb, A. M. Sauter *SEE* Erb, Johann Jacob
Erb, Johann Jacob; America, 1754 ***2856.30*** *p102*
Wife: A. M. Sauter
With father
Erbach, Balthasar; Port uncertain, 1748 ***2856.30*** *p102*
With wife & 4 children
Erbach, Lorenz; Port uncertain, 1743 ***2856.30*** *p102*
Erber, Christian; New York, New York, 1857 ***3437.14*** *p61*
Erbery, Edward; Maryland, 1663 ***2524.55*** *p76*
Erbin, James; New York, 1836 ***8197.10*** *p76*
Erdmann, Jacob; America, 1732 ***2856.30*** *p102*
Erdmann, Regina; Port uncertain, 1732 ***2856.30*** *p102*
Erels, Andrew 57; Ontario, 1871 ***1823.15*** *p74*
Erels, George 53; Ontario, 1871 ***1823.15*** *p74*
Erels, John 55; Ontario, 1871 ***1823.15*** *p75*
Eremeath, Johanna 15; Maryland, 1775 ***1220.25*** *p102*
Ergatt, George F.; New York, 1838 ***8197.10*** *p115*
Ergelin, Anna Maria; America, 1751 ***2856.30*** *p102*
Ergesaged, R. 19; Jamaica, 1774 ***1220.25*** *p60*
Erhard, Johann; America, 1752 ***2856.30*** *p102*
Erhard, Johann Daniel; England, 1779 ***2856.30*** *p102*
Erhard, Johann Daniel; Port uncertain, 1784 ***2856.30*** *p102*
Erhard, Martin; America, 1752 ***2856.30*** *p102*
Erhard, Michael Christi; Port uncertain, 1764 ***2856.30*** *p95*
Erhard, Peter; America, 1731 ***2856.30*** *p102*
Erhardt, Andreas; America, 1745 ***2856.30*** *p102*
Erhardt, Maria Elisabeth; Port uncertain, 1774 ***2856.30*** *p102*
Erhart, Maria; Port uncertain, 1628 ***2856.30*** *p102*
With husband
Erhart, Peter; America, 1750 ***2856.30*** *p102*
Erhwald, Karl; America, 1754 ***2856.30*** *p102*
Erian, Stephen 47; Ontario, 1871 ***1823.15*** *p75*
Erichson, Swerin; Pennsylvania, 1778 ***4629.10*** *p34*
Ericksen, Selma 30; Alaska, 1916 ***9196.1*** *p44*
Ericksen, Selma 30; Yukon, 1916 ***9196.1*** *p44*
Erickson, Con 43; Alaska, 1913 ***9196.1*** *p21*
Erickson, Con 43; British Columbia, 1913 ***9196.1*** *p21*
Erickson, Elizabeth *SEE* Erickson, John
Erickson, Hjalmir 25; Alaska, 1915 ***9196.1*** *p42*
Erickson, J. O. 40; Alaska, 1918 ***9196.1*** *p54*
Erickson, J. O. 40; Whitehorse, Yukon, 1918 ***9196.1*** *p54*
Erickson, John; Maryland, 1652 ***2524.55*** *p76*
Wife: Elizabeth
Erickson, Mrs. Svenborg 30; British Columbia, 1917 ***9196.1*** *p16*
Erickson, Mrs. Svenborg 30; Washington, 1917 ***9196.1*** *p16*
Erickson, Wm 42; Alaska, 1915 ***9196.1*** *p42*
Ericson, Carl 32; British Columbia, 1909 ***9196.1*** *p26*
Ericson, Carl 32; Washington, 1909 ***9196.1*** *p26*
Erington, William 28; Ontario, 1871 ***1823.22*** *p50*
Erisly, Rich; Virginia, 1666 ***6212.30*** *p30*
Eritchik, Albert 10; Ontario, 1871 ***1823.28*** *p27*
Eritchik, Catharine 17; Ontario, 1871 ***1823.28*** *p27*
Erler, Mrs. Andreas; America, 1751 ***2856.30*** *p102*
With 4 children
Erlich, Anna 20; Kansas, 1891-1910 ***9079.10*** *p30*
Erlich, Anna 49; Kansas, 1891-1910 ***9079.10*** *p29*
Erlich, George 22; Kansas, 1907-1910 ***9079.10*** *p30*
Erlich, Gotfried 51; Kansas, 1891-1910 ***9079.10*** *p29*
Erlick, Alex 58; Kansas, 1890-1910 ***9079.10*** *p53*
Erlick, Eva 34; Kansas, 1910 ***9079.10*** *p50*
Erlick, G. R. 36; Kansas, 1897-1910 ***9079.10*** *p50*
Erlick, Katherina 61; Kansas, 1910 ***9079.10*** *p53*
Ermel, Abraham; Port uncertain, 1751 ***2856.30*** *p102*
Ermel, Johann Peter; America, 1752 ***2856.30*** *p102*
Ermel, Peter; Port uncertain, 1781 ***2856.30*** *p102*
Ermson, John; Virginia, 1671 ***6212.30*** *p44*
Ernenputsch, John C.; New York, 1836 ***8197.10*** *p227*
Ernest, Henry; Pennsylvania, 1777 ***4629.10*** *p9*
Ernest, Sarah 77; Ontario, 1871 ***1823.15*** *p75*
Ernest, William 57; Ontario, 1871 ***1823.15*** *p75*
Ernich, Philipp; Port uncertain, 1752 ***2856.30*** *p102*
Ernst, . . .; America, 1735 ***2856.30*** *p103*
Ernst, Anna 21; Kansas, 1910 ***9079.10*** *p45*
Ernst, Friedrich; America, 1741 ***2856.30*** *p102*
Ernst, Georg; America, 1751 ***2856.30*** *p103*
With 2 children
Ernst, Henrich; America, 1739 ***2856.30*** *p103*
Ernst, Johann; Port uncertain, 1768 ***2856.30*** *p103*
Ernst, Johann Georg; America, 1751 ***2856.30*** *p103*
With wife & children
Ernst, Johann Jacob; America, 1752 ***2856.30*** *p103*
Ernst, Johann Konrad; America, 1737 ***2856.30*** *p103*
Ernst, Johann Michael; America, 1741-1799 ***2856.30*** *p103*
Ernst, Johann Wendel; America, 1737 ***2856.30*** *p103*
Ernst, Konrad; America, 1737 ***2856.30*** *p103*
Ernst, Konrad; Port uncertain, 1737 ***2856.30*** *p103*
Ernst, Ludwig; Port uncertain, 1788 ***2856.30*** *p103*
Ernst, Margarete; Port uncertain, 1786 ***2856.30*** *p103*
With husband & 3 children
Ernst, Maria Anna; Port uncertain, 1817 ***2856.30*** *p103*
Ernst, Maria Magdalena; Port uncertain, 1783 ***2856.30*** *p103*
Ernst, Maria Margareta; Port uncertain, 1749 ***2856.30*** *p103*
Ernst, Paulin; Port uncertain, 1749 ***2856.30*** *p103*
Ernst, Philipp; Port uncertain, 1738 ***2856.30*** *p103*
With wife
Ernst, Sebastian; Port uncertain, 1761 ***2856.30*** *p103*
Erquart, George 42; Ontario, 1871 ***1823.15*** *p75*
Errah, Isaac 71; Ontario, 1871 ***1823.15*** *p75*
Errin, George 44; Ontario, 1871 ***1823.15*** *p75*
Errington, Lanclott; Virginia, 1674-1675 ***6212.30*** *p53*
Erschwey, Johann; Port uncertain, 1733 ***2856.30*** *p103*
Ersfeld, Johann Peter; Port uncertain, 1744 ***2856.30*** *p103*
Erskin, William 37; Ontario, 1871 ***1823.22*** *p50*
Erskine, Alexander; Toronto, 1867 ***1640.13*** *p35*
Erskine, David; Jamaica, 1798 ***1640.13*** *p35*
Ertel, Velten; America, 1739 ***2856.30*** *p103*
Erule, Jno; Virginia, 1664 ***6212.30*** *p15*
Ervin, Eliza 52; Ontario, 1871 ***1823.15*** *p75*
Ervin, James; New York, 1807 ***8197.10*** *p330*
Ervin, Margart 26; Ontario, 1871 ***1823.15*** *p75*
Ervin, William 66; Ontario, 1871 ***1823.15*** *p75*
Erving, Mary E.; Vermont, 1853-1889 ***5900.10*** *p361*
Erwach, Edward 50; Ontario, 1871 ***1823.15*** *p75*
Erwin, Allen 26; Ontario, 1871 ***1823.15*** *p75*
Erwin, Annie; Vermont, 1857-1957 ***5900.10*** *p456*
Erwin, David; Vermont, 1853-1934 ***5900.10*** *p456*
Erwin, Eliza Ann; Vermont, 1854-1912 ***5900.10*** *p457*
Erwin, Eliza Gilbart 65; Vermont, 1893 ***5900.10*** *p456*
Erwin, George; Vermont, 1850-1926 ***5900.10*** *p224*
Erwin, George 71; Ontario, 1871 ***1823.15*** *p75*
Erwin, J. B.; Vermont, 1848-1926 ***5900.10*** *p457*
Erwin, J. W.; Vermont, 1839-1920 ***5900.10*** *p457*
Erwin, James; Pennsylvania, 1777 ***4629.10*** *p13*
Erwin, James; Vermont, 1833-1905 ***5900.10*** *p456*
Erwin, James 38; Ontario, 1871 ***1823.28*** *p27*
Erwin, James 45; Ontario, 1871 ***1823.15*** *p75*
Erwin, James 60; Ontario, 1871 ***1823.15*** *p75*
Erwin, Jane 83; Vermont, 1870 ***5900.10*** *p456*
Erwin, Jane Riley 82; Vermont, 1893 ***5900.10*** *p457*
Erwin, John; New York, 1802 ***8197.10*** *p20*
Erwin, John 86; Vermont, 1871 ***5900.10*** *p456*
Erwin, Lucy J.; Vermont, 1855-1943 ***5900.10*** *p456*
Erwin, Margaret I. Sanborn; Vermont, 1849-1914 ***5900.10*** *p456*
Erwin, Maria 67; Vermont, 1894 ***5900.10*** *p456*
Erwin, Mary 79; Vermont, 1915 ***5900.10*** *p89*
Erwin, Mary Ann; Vermont, 1824-1881 ***5900.10*** *p457*
Erwin, Mary Couture; Vermont, 1857-1935 ***5900.10*** *p224*
Erwin, Mary M. 28; Vermont, 1875 ***5900.10*** *p456*
Erwin, Matty E. McMeekin; Vermont, 1817-1894 ***5900.10*** *p456*
Erwin, Ralph 85; Vermont, 1884 ***5900.10*** *p457*
Erwin, Robert; Pennsylvania, 1777 ***4629.10*** *p28*
Erwin, Sarah; Vermont, 1818-1899 ***5900.10*** *p457*
Erwin, Susan; Vermont, 1814-1892 ***5900.10*** *p222*
Erwin, Thomas 80; Vermont, 1886 ***5900.10*** *p456*
Erwin, William; Vermont, 1809-1881 ***5900.10*** *p455*
Erwin, William 31; Ontario, 1871 ***1823.15*** *p75*
Erwin, William 50; Ontario, 1871 ***1823.15*** *p75*
Erwin, William J.; Vermont, 1861-1874 ***5900.10*** *p456*
Erwin, William J. 13; Vermont, 1874 ***5900.10*** *p456*
Erwin, William J. 24; Vermont, 1858 ***5900.10*** *p457*
Erwine, George 39; Ontario, 1871 ***1823.15*** *p75*
Esaly, Ludwick R. E.; New York, New York, 1850 ***3437.14*** *p24*
Esbach, Johann Heinrich; America, 1738 ***2856.30*** *p103*
Esch, Abraham; Port uncertain, 1736 ***2856.30*** *p103*
Esch, Henry; New York, New York, 1880 ***3437.14*** *p187*
Esch, Nikolaus; America, 1754 ***2856.30*** *p103*
Eschbach, Jakob; America, 1753 ***2856.30*** *p103*
Eschbach, Johann; America, 1750 ***2856.30*** *p103*
With wife & 6 children
Eschbach, Johann Heinrich; America, 1738 ***2856.30*** *p103*
Eschbach, Peter; Port uncertain, 1771 ***2856.30*** *p103*
Eschelmann, Johann; America, 1731 ***2856.30*** *p103*
Eschenbrenner, Jacob; Port uncertain, 1776 ***2856.30*** *p103*
Escher, George; New York, 1831 ***8197.10*** *p365*
Escher, Henry; New York, 1838 ***8197.10*** *p228*
Escher, Josef; Port uncertain, 1781 ***2856.30*** *p103*
Eschwege, Herz; New York, 1838 ***8197.10*** *p228*
Escot, John Peter; New York, 1807 ***8197.10*** *p38*
Escott, Gabriel; South Carolina, 1741 ***1224.2*** *p38*
Esdale, Wm 44; Ontario, 1871 ***1823.15*** *p75*
Esenpreis, Magdalene; Cayenne, 1764 ***2856.30*** *p103*
Eshott, Will.; Maryland, 1641 ***2524.55*** *p76*
Eskillion, Francis; Pennsylvania, 1777 ***4629.10*** *p22*
Eskillion, Francis; Pennsylvania, 1778 ***4629.10*** *p35*
Eslor, James 28; Ontario, 1871 ***1823.15*** *p75*
Eslor, John 38; Ontario, 1871 ***1823.15*** *p75*
Eslor, John 61; Ontario, 1871 ***1823.15*** *p75*
Esoney, . . .; Maryland, 1631-1685 ***2524.55*** *p76*
Esoney, Rose; Maryland, 1680 ***2524.55*** *p128*
Espach, Peter; Port uncertain, 1771 ***2856.30*** *p103*
Espada, Joseph M.; New York, 1818 ***8197.10*** *p227*
Espie, James; New York, 1834 ***8197.10*** *p315*
Espie, James; New York, 1839 ***8197.10*** *p130*
Esplin, Michael; New York, 1806 ***8197.10*** *p324*
Esser, Maria Margarete; Port uncertain, 1754 ***2856.30*** *p103*
Essery, John 45; Ontario, 1871 ***1823.15*** *p75*
Essery, John 70; Ontario, 1871 ***1823.15*** *p75*
Essery, Samuel 28; Ontario, 1871 ***1823.15*** *p75*
Essery, William 60; Ontario, 1871 ***1823.15*** *p75*
Essewein, Johann; America, 1750 ***2856.30*** *p103*
Essex, John 25; Ontario, 1871 ***1823.28*** *p27*
Essig, Christof; America, 1754 ***2856.30*** *p104*
Essling, Johann Peter; Port uncertain, 1748 ***2856.30*** *p104*
With wife & 3 children
Esson, Mrs.; Quebec, 1857 ***9196.15*** *p14*
Esson, Ann; Maryland, 1659 ***2524.55*** *p76*
Esson, John; Maryland, 1659 ***2524.55*** *p76*
Estcourt, Jno; Virginia, 1664 ***6212.30*** *p15*
Estcourt, Martha; Virginia, 1665 ***6212.30*** *p18*
Estcourt, Richard; Virginia, 1664 ***6212.30*** *p15*
Esterfeild, Mary; Virginia, 1667 ***6212.30*** *p37*
Estes, Rebecca; Virginia, 1671 ***6212.30*** *p43*
Esthop, Mary; Virginia, 1663 ***6212.30*** *p1*
Estleford, Joseph 34; Ontario, 1871 ***1823.15*** *p75*
Eston, James; Maryland, 1662 ***2524.55*** *p76*
Esuki, Geo 40; British Columbia, 1910 ***9196.1*** *p31*
Esuki, Geo 40; Seattle, 1910 ***9196.1*** *p31*
Etcher, John 42; Ontario, 1871 ***1823.22*** *p50*
Eten, Jnoathan; Virginia, 1663 ***6212.30*** *p2*

Etheredge, Thomas; New York, 1840 *8197.10 p167*
Etheridge, Mr.; Portland, Maine, 1858 *9196.15 p30*
Etheridge, Mrs.; Portland, Maine, 1858 *9196.15 p30*
Ethringham, George; Maryland, 1665 *2524.55 p75*
Etienne, Denis Germain; New York, 1831 *8197.10 p355*
Etienne, Denis Germaine; New York, 1831 *8197.10 p370*
Etridge, Thomas 26; Virginia, 1774 *1220.25 p90*
Etsberger, Johann Jakob; Port uncertain, 1746 *2856.30 p104*
Etson, Alfred 22; Ontario, 1871 *1823.28 p27*
Ettlinger, George; New York, 1839 *8197.10 p228*
Ettricke, John; Charles Town, South Carolina, 1766 *1224.2 p38*
Etty, Arthur *SEE* Etty, Arthur
Etty, Arthur; Maryland, 1682 *2524.55 p76*
Wife: Joane
Son: Arthur
Son: Nathaniel
Etty, Joane *SEE* Etty, Arthur
Etty, Nathaniel *SEE* Etty, Arthur
Euen, Griffit; Virginia, 1681 *6212.30 p55*
Euen, Vayned; Virginia, 1681 *6212.30 p55*
Eugen, Paul; New York, 1838 *8197.10 p120*
Euler, Adam; Port uncertain, 1746 *2856.30 p104*
Euler, Anna Catharina; Port uncertain, 1783 *2856.30 p104*
Euler, Cath. Elisabeth; Port uncertain, 1760 *2856.30 p104*
Euler, Cath. Elisabeth; Port uncertain, 1778 *2856.30 p104*
Euler, Johann; America, 1749 *2856.30 p104*
Euler, Johann; America, 1750 *2856.30 p104*
Euler, Johann Nickel; Port uncertain, 1775 *2856.30 p104*
Euler, Maria Ursula; Port uncertain, 1756 *2856.30 p104*
Eunson, George; Savannah, Georgia, 1774 *1640.10 p49*
Euphrosine, Mary; Maryland, 1910 *3259.35 p14*
Eurcheke, Robert 14; Ontario, 1871 *1823.28 p27*
Eure, Peter *SEE* Eure, Thomas
Eure, Peter; Maryland, 1669 *2524.55 p76*
Eure, Thomas; Maryland, 1658 *2524.55 p76*
Relative: Peter
Eurich, Hans; America, 1752 *2856.30 p104*
Eurich, Matthaus; America, 1750 *2856.30 p104*
Euryss, Matthaus; America, 1750 *2856.30 p104*
Euska, Frank; Maryland, 1910 *3259.35 p14*
Euson, John; New York, 1802 *8197.10 p20*
Eussel, Dieterich; Port uncertain, 1764 *2856.30 p104*
Eust, Harle 34; Ontario, 1871 *1823.15 p75*
Eustace, Alexander; Vermont, 1855-1930 *5900.10 p428*
Eustace, Charles; Pennsylvania, 1777 *4629.10 p27*
Eustace, Edward; Vermont, 1830-1911 *5900.10 p424*
Eustace, Esther; Vermont, 1843-1907 *5900.10 p324*
Eustace, John; Vermont, 1819-1901 *5900.10 p437*
Eustace, Julia Foley; Vermont, 1865-1945 *5900.10 p428*
Eustace, Margaret Bartlett; Vermont, 1825-1903 *5900.10 p437*
Eustace, Mary 27; Vermont, n.d. *5900.10 p151*
Eustace, Mary 83; Vermont, 1922 *5900.10 p477*
Eustace, Mary M.; Vermont, 1840-1905 *5900.10 p424*
Eustace, Nellie M. McLaughlin; Vermont, 1855-1881 *5900.10 p437*
Eustace, Thomas 87; Vermont, 1886 *5900.10 p477*
Eustice, Ellen L.; Vermont, 1835-1910 *5900.10 p491*
Eustis, Herman; New York, New York, 1880 *3437.14 p181*
Eutken, Janet 77; Ontario, 1871 *1823.15 p75*
Eva, Hannah; Charles Town, South Carolina, 1771 *1224.2 p38*
Evan, Morgan; Virginia, 1666-1667 *6212.30 p35*
Evander, Edward 23; Philadelphia, 1775 *1220.25 p122*
Evans, Mr.; Portland, Maine, 1858 *9196.15 p28*
Evans, Mrs.; Quebec, 1857 *9196.15 p15*
Evans, Amy; Maryland, 1665 *2524.55 p76*
Evans, Andrew 55; Ontario, 1871 *1823.15 p75*
Evans, Anne; Virginia, 1681 *1224.1 p20*
Evans, Anthony; Maryland, 1681 *2524.55 p76*
Evans, Benjamin; New Hampshire, n.d. *4628.40 p76*
Evans, Benjamin; Pennsylvania, 1786 *4629.10 p49*
Evans, Benjamin 22; Carolina, 1774 *1220.25 p75*
Evans, Benjamin 28; Maryland, 1774 *1220.25 p52*
Evans, Benjamin 42; Ontario, 1871 *1823.15 p75*
Evans, C.; Portland, Maine, 1857 *9196.15 p12*
Evans, Charles 32; Maryland, 1775 *1220.25 p113*
Evans, Cicily; Maryland, 1673 *2524.55 p76*
Evans, Daniel; New York, New York, 1845 *6058.10 p28*
Evans, Daniel; Pennsylvania, 1777 *4629.10 p23*
Evans, Daniel M.; New York, 1837 *8197.10 p318*
Evans, David; New York, 1807 *8197.10 p331*
Evans, David; New York, 1827 *8197.10 p338*
Evans, David; New York, 1838 *8197.10 p228*
Evans, Dewbery; Maryland, 1665 *2524.55 p76*
Evans, Edward; Maryland, 1671 *2524.55 p34*
Evans, Edward; Pennsylvania, 1777 *4629.10 p7*
Evans, Emma 10; Ontario, 1871 *1823.15 p75*
Evans, Ephraim; Pennsylvania, 1778 *4629.10 p34*
Evans, Evan; Maryland, 1729 *1224.2 p38*
Evans, Evan; Pennsylvania, 1777 *4629.10 p22*
Evans, Evan; Pennsylvania, 1779 *4629.10 p38*
Evans, Florence; Virginia, 1665 *6212.30 p19*
Evans, Floyd 45; Maryland, 1774 *1220.25 p52*
Evans, George 38; Ontario, 1871 *1823.15 p75*
Evans, Griffin; Maryland, 1681 *2524.55 p77*
Evans, Mrs. H. 35; Alaska, 1918 *9196.1 p55*
Evans, Mrs. H. 35; British Columbia, 1918 *9196.1 p55*
Evans, Henry 48; Ontario, 1871 *1823.15 p75*
Evans, Henry 60; Ontario, 1871 *1823.22 p50*
Evans, Henry B. 40; Ontario, 1871 *1823.15 p75*
Evans, Hugh; Maryland, 1672 *2524.55 p77*
Evans, Humphry; Virginia, 1671 *6212.30 p44*
Evans, Isaac 18; Ontario, 1871 *1823.15 p75*
Evans, James; New York, 1830 *8197.10 p353*
Evans, James 55; Ontario, 1871 *1823.15 p76*
Evans, Jno; Virginia, 1663 *6212.30 p4*
Evans, John; Maryland, 1671 *2524.55 p34*
Evans, John; Maryland, 1673 *2524.55 p77*
Evans, John; Maryland, 1676 *2524.55 p77*
Evans, John; Maryland, 1679 *2524.55 p77*
Evans, John; New York, 1818 *8197.10 p227*
Evans, John; Pennsylvania, 1777 *4629.10 p21*
Evans, John; Virginia, 1663 *6212.30 p2*
Evans, John; Virginia, 1672 *6212.30 p48*
Evans, John 24; Maryland, 1774 *1220.25 p41*
Evans, John 24; Maryland, 1775 *1220.25 p10*
Evans, John 34; Ontario, 1871 *1823.28 p27*
Evans, Joseph; New York, 1816 *8197.10 p58*
Evans, Joseph; New York, 1839 *1224.3 p25*
Evans, Joseph 48; Ontario, 1871 *1823.15 p76*
Evans, L. 51; Washington, 1914 *9196.1 p64*
Evans, Laurence; Virginia, 1642 *1224.1 p20*
Evans, Lewis; Maryland, 1663 *2524.55 p77*
Evans, Lewis 52; Seattle, 1914 *9196.1 p66*
Evans, Lewis 52; Vancouver, British Columbia, 1914 *9196.1 p66*
Evans, Margaret 23; Maryland, 1775 *1220.25 p115*
Evans, Martin; Pennsylvania, 1777 *4629.10 p10*
Evans, Mary; Maryland, 1671 *2524.55 p34*
Evans, Mary; Maryland, 1673 *2524.55 p77*
Evans, Mary; North Carolina, 1794 *1224.2 p38*
Evans, Mary; Virginia, 1671-1672 *6212.30 p47*
Evans, Mary; Virginia, 1759 *1224.2 p90*
Evans, Mary 54; Ontario, 1871 *1823.15 p76*
Evans, Meridath; Virginia, 1667-1668 *6212.30 p39*
Evans, Morgan; Maryland, 1670 *2524.55 p77*
Evans, Morgan; Maryland, 1678 *2524.55 p218*
Evans, Morgan; Virginia, 1665 *6212.30 p20*
Evans, Oliver; Virginia, 1665 *6212.30 p18*
Evans, Peter; Pennsylvania, 1777 *4629.10 p16*
Evans, R.; Quebec, 1858 *9196.15 p38*
Evans, Richard; Maryland, 1671 *2524.55 p34*
Evans, Richard; Virginia, 1673 *1224.1 p20*
Evans, Richard 17; Maryland, 1774 *1220.25 p64*
Evans, Robert; New York, 1807 *8197.10 p38*
Evans, Robert; New York, 1840 *8197.10 p167*
Evans, Robert 15; Maryland, 1774 *1220.25 p7*
Evans, Samuel 52; Ontario, 1871 *1823.28 p27*
Evans, Sarah; Maryland, 1668 *2524.55 p77*
Evans, Sisley; Virginia, 1664 *6212.30 p15*
Evans, Thomas; Maryland, 1661 *2524.55 p77*
Evans, Thomas; Maryland, 1664 *2524.55 p122*
Evans, Thomas; New York, 1836 *8197.10 p227*
Evans, Thomas; Vermont, 1859-1894 *5900.10 p400*
Evans, Thomas; Virginia, 1663 *6212.30 p1*
Evans, Thomas 1 month; Vermont, 1868 *5900.10 p83*
Evans, Thomas 26; Barbados, 1774 *1220.25 p82*
Evans, Thomas 29; Maryland, 1774 *1220.25 p57*
Evans, Thomas 36; Virginia, 1774 *1220.25 p55*
Evans, Thomas 79; Ontario, 1871 *1823.28 p27*
Evans, Timothy 9; Vermont, 1881 *5900.10 p83*
Evans, W. C.; Quebec, 1857 *9196.15 p15*
Evans, William; Maryland, 1671 *2524.55 p34*
Evans, William; Maryland, 1678 *2524.55 p218*
Evans, William; Maryland, 1681 *2524.55 p77*
Evans, William; New York, 1828 *8197.10 p227*
Evans, William; Ohio, 1853 *1224.3 p25*
Evans, William; Ontario, n.d. *1224.3 p25*
Evans, William; Pennsylvania, 1815 *6058.10 p5*
Evans, William 1; Vermont, 1874 *5900.10 p83*
Evans, William 19; Virginia, 1775 *1220.25 p95*
Evans, William 33; Ontario, 1871 *1823.15 p76*
Evans, William 34; Ontario, 1871 *1823.15 p76*
Evans, William 35; Maryland, 1774 *1220.25 p39*
Evans, William 40; Philadelphia, 1774 *1220.25 p43*
Evans, William Henry; Charleston, South Carolina, 1833 *1224.3 p25*
Evard, Francois J.; New York, 1837 *8197.10 p86*
Evatt, Humphrey; New York, 1840 *8197.10 p167*
Eveleigh, Samuel; Charles Town, South Carolina, n.d. *1224.2 p38*
Eveling, James; Virginia, 1665 *6212.30 p17*
Eveling, Jno; Virginia, 1664 *6212.30 p12*
Eveling, Jno; Virginia, 1664 *6212.30 p15*
Eveling, Jno; Virginia, 1665-1666 *6212.30 p22*
Eveling, Rich; Virginia, 1664 *6212.30 p7*
Evelling, Geo; Virginia, 1665 *6212.30 p17*
Evelling, Jane; Virginia, 1665 *6212.30 p17*
Evelling, Mountjoy; Virginia, 1665 *6212.30 p17*
Evelling, Rebecca; Virginia, 1665 *6212.30 p17*
Evelyn, Martha Boscawen; Charleston, South Carolina, 1815 *1224.3 p81*
Evenett, Elizabeth 21; Virginia, 1774 *1220.25 p89*
Evens, Ann 30; Ontario, 1871 *1823.22 p50*
Evens, Ellen 56; Vermont, 1877 *5900.10 p346*
Evens, Joseph 22; Vermont, 1850 *5900.10 p605*
Evens, Thomas 26; Ontario, 1871 *1823.22 p50*
Evens, William 37; Ontario, 1871 *1823.22 p50*
Evenson, Catherine 30; Ontario, 1871 *1823.15 p76*
Evenson, Gustav 32; Alaska, 1913 *9196.1 p22*
Evenson, Gustav 32; British Columbia, 1913 *9196.1 p22*
Everard, Thomas; Maryland, 1681 *2524.55 p77*
Everest, Richard; Georgia, 1789 *1224.2 p39*
Everet, Ambrose; Virginia, 1671-1672 *6212.30 p47*
Everett, Elizabeth; Virginia, 1671-1672 *6212.30 p46*
Everett, Jno; Virginia, 1671 *6212.30 p42*
Everett, Mary 58; Vermont, 1865 *5900.10 p362*
Everett, Mary 58; Vermont, 1865 *5900.10 p365*
Everett, Patrick 80; Vermont, 1915 *5900.10 p589*
Everett, Robert 21; Virginia, 1774 *1220.25 p53*
Everett, Thomas 63; Vermont, 1864 *5900.10 p362*
Everett, Thomas 63; Vermont, 1864 *5900.10 p365*
Everhard, Fred 24; Kansas, 1909-1910 *9079.10 p31*
Everigin, Catherine; Virginia, 1698 *1224.1 p20*
Everin, Bridget Kennedy 67; Vermont, 1909 *5900.10 p571*
Everin, Catherine Flood 38; Vermont, 1865 *5900.10 p574*
Everin, Cathrine Trainor; Vermont, 1832-1858 *5900.10 p565*
Everin, Margaret Farrell 68; Vermont, 1893 *5900.10 p574*
Everin, Patrick 83; Vermont, 1914 *5900.10 p574*
Everin, Peter; Vermont, 1835-1862 *5900.10 p565*
Everin, William 78; Vermont, 1918 *5900.10 p571*
Everist, Richard; Georgia, 1789 *1224.2 p39*
Everitt, Richard 34; Ontario, 1871 *1823.15 p76*
Everry, Susanna; Maryland, 1658 *2524.55 p77*
Eversalt, Philip Jacob; New York, 1837 *8197.10 p85*
Eves, George; Maryland, 1672 *2524.55 p77*
Eves, John; Virginia, 1672 *6212.30 p48*
Evett, Mary; Boston, 1744 *1224.2 p39*
Evett, William 37; Ontario, 1871 *1823.15 p76*
Evetts, James; New York, 1707 *1224.2 p39*
Evill, Luke; Wilmington, North Carolina, 1849 *1224.3 p25*
Evins, Madalen; Maryland, 1661 *2524.55 p77*
Evit, Margaret 52; Ontario, 1871 *1823.28 p28*
Evit, Mary; Boston, 1744 *1224.2 p39*
Evitt, Mr.; Quebec, 1858 *9196.15 p35*
Evitt, Mrs.; Quebec, 1858 *9196.15 p35*
Evitts, Ellen *SEE* Evitts, Nathaniell
Evitts, Mary *SEE* Evitts, Nathaniell
Evitts, Nathaniell; Maryland, 1665 *2524.55 p77*
Wife: Ellen
Child: Mary
Evyom, William 60; Ontario, 1871 *1823.15 p76*
Ewald, Johann Adam; Port uncertain, 1762 *2856.30 p104*
Ewald, Johann Adam; Port uncertain, 1766 *2856.30 p104*
Ewald, Johann Adam; Port uncertain, 1792 *2856.30 p104*
Ewald, Johann Michael; Port uncertain, 1762 *2856.30 p104*
Ewald, Johann Michael; Port uncertain, 1766 *2856.30 p104*
Ewald, Johann Michael; Port uncertain, 1792 *2856.30 p104*
Ewan, William; Georgia, 1735 *1640.10 p49*
Ewang, George 19; Dominica, 1773 *1220.25 p31*
Ewart, Miss; Quebec, 1857 *9196.15 p21*
Ewart, Mr.; Quebec, 1857 *9196.15 p17*
Ewart, Mrs.; Quebec, 1857 *9196.15 p21*
Ewart, George; Pennsylvania, 1787 *4629.10 p52*
Ewart, Helen; Kingston, Jamaica, 1891 *1640.13 p36*
Ewart, John; Albany, New York, 1825 *1224.3 p25*
Ewart, John 45; Ontario, 1871 *1823.22 p50*
Ewart, Mathilde; Kingston, Jamaica, 1891 *1640.13 p36*
Ewel, John 24; Ontario, 1871 *1823.15 p76*
Ewen, Alexander 47; Ontario, 1871 *1823.15 p76*
Ewen, Ann *SEE* Ewen, Richard
Ewen, Ann *SEE* Ewen, William
Ewen, David *SEE* Ewen, Richard
Ewen, Elizabeth *SEE* Ewen, Richard

F

Faath, Georg; Port uncertain, 1755 ***2856.30*** *p106*
Faber, Adamine; New York, 1840 ***8197.10*** *p231*
Faber, Conrad William; New York, 1855 ***1224.3*** *p25*
Faber, Elisabeth; Port uncertain, 1738 ***2856.30*** *p106*
Faber, Frederick 23; Grenada, 1773 ***1220.25*** *p30*
Faber, Henrich; Port uncertain, 1775 ***2856.30*** *p106*
Faber, John H.; New York, 1840 ***8197.10*** *p231*
Faber, Maria Elisabeth; Port uncertain, 1775 ***2856.30*** *p106*
Fabian, Josef; Port uncertain, 1741 ***2856.30*** *p106*
Fabian, Simon; Virginia, 1668 ***1224.1*** *p21*
Fabian, William; New York, 1817 ***8197.10*** *p228*
Fabishak, Joseph; Maryland, 1910 ***3259.35*** *p14*
Fabishak, William; Maryland, 1910 ***3259.35*** *p14*
Fabissak, John; Maryland, 1910 ***3259.35*** *p14*
Fabiszak, Thomas; Maryland, 1910 ***3259.35*** *p14*
Fable, Julean; Maryland, 1649 ***2524.55*** *p77*
Fabre, Mr.; Quebec, 1857 ***9196.15*** *p21*
Fabre, Mr.; Quebec, 1857 ***9196.15*** *p22*
Fabri, Dolovico; New York, 1830 ***8197.10*** *p230*
Fabway, Christian 39; Ontario, 1871 ***1823.28*** *p28*
Fabyssa, Joseph; Maryland, 1910 ***3259.35*** *p14*
Fach, George 34; Ontario, 1871 ***1823.15*** *p76*
Fachrie, James; Savannah, Georgia, 1809 ***1640.10*** *p50*
Facile, Mr.; Quebec, 1857 ***9196.15*** *p17*
Facile, Mr.; Quebec, 1858 ***9196.15*** *p39*
Facile, T.; Quebec, 1858 ***9196.15*** *p40*
Fadagan, John; New York, 1840 ***8197.10*** *p231*
Fader, Alexander; Mississippi, 1832-1845 ***1640.10*** *p50*
Faesh, John; America, 1767 ***1224.2*** *p39*
Fagan, Alice 66; Vermont, 1872 ***5900.10*** *p402*
Fagan, Barnard; New York, 1821 ***8197.10*** *p229*
Fagan, Edward; New York, 1821 ***8197.10*** *p229*
Fagan, Edward; New York, 1840 ***8197.10*** *p164*
Fagan, Elizabeth A. 18; Ontario, 1861 ***2896.27*** *p52*
Fagan, Francis; New York, 1826 ***8197.10*** *p336*
Fagan, Hannah 31; Vermont, 1872 ***5900.10*** *p402*
Fagan, Hugh 23; Ontario, 1861 ***2896.27*** *p52*
Fagan, James; New York, 1821 ***8197.10*** *p228*
Fagan, James; New York, 1840 ***8197.10*** *p164*
Fagan, James; New York, 1840 ***8197.10*** *p165*
Fagan, James 64; Ontario, 1871 ***1823.15*** *p76*
Fagan, Jane; Vermont, 1828-1912 ***5900.10*** *p145*
Fagan, John; New York, 1840 ***8197.10*** *p167*
Fagan, John 62; Vermont, 1849 ***5900.10*** *p146*
Fagan, L. 49; Vermont, 1876 ***5900.10*** *p451*
Fagan, Margaret 55; Vermont, 1879 ***5900.10*** *p451*
Fagan, Margaret McDermott 73; Vermont, 1922 ***5900.10*** *p422*
Fagan, Margaret T. Conlon; Vermont, 1840-1928 ***5900.10*** *p443*
Fagan, Mary Malony 78; Vermont, 1921 ***5900.10*** *p402*
Fagan, Michael 17; Vermont, 1847 ***5900.10*** *p146*
Fagan, Michael 64; Vermont, 1880 ***5900.10*** *p422*
Fagan, Patrick 35; Vermont, 1878 ***5900.10*** *p402*
Fagan, Patrick 58; Vermont, 1904 ***5900.10*** *p443*
Fagan, Patrick 61; Vermont, 1886 ***5900.10*** *p450*
Fagan, Peter; New York, 1840 ***8197.10*** *p164*
Fagan, Peter; Vermont, n.d. ***5900.10*** *p451*
Fagan, Rose Bannon 81; Vermont, 1877 ***5900.10*** *p146*
Fagan, Sarah W.; Vermont, 1868 ***5900.10*** *p451*
Fagan, Simon; New York, 1840 ***8197.10*** *p164*
Fagan, Thomas 88; Vermont, 1889 ***5900.10*** *p402*
Fagan, William 56; Vermont, 1899 ***5900.10*** *p580*
Fage, Susan; Maryland, 1650 ***2524.55*** *p77*
Fagg, Francis; Philadelphia, 1829 ***1224.3*** *p25*
Faggett, Robert; New York, 1792-1840 ***8197.10*** *p375*
Faghojowska, Joseph; Maryland, 1910 ***3259.35*** *p14*
Fagregoe, Moses; Maryland, 1674 ***2524.55*** *p77*
Faherty, Patrick; New York, 1831 ***8197.10*** *p367*
Fahey, Margaret 87; Vermont, 1901 ***5900.10*** *p590*
Fahey, Nicholas 64; Ontario, 1871 ***1823.28*** *p28*
Fahlstrom, N. 24; Alaska, 1917 ***9196.1*** *p48*
Fahlstrom, N. 24; Whitehorse, Yukon, 1917 ***9196.1*** *p48*
Fahner, Georg Adolf; Port uncertain, 1759 ***2856.30*** *p106*
Fahns, Christian; Pennsylvania, 1777 ***4629.10*** *p23*
Fahr, Maria Elisabeth; Port uncertain, 1765 ***2856.30*** *p106*
Fahrin, Maria Elisabeth; Port uncertain, 1765 ***2856.30*** *p106*
Fahsenmoyer, Blatzer; New York, New York, 1828 ***6058.10*** *p12*
Fahuer, Jacob 66; Ontario, 1871 ***1823.15*** *p76*
Fahuer, Tobias 50; Ontario, 1871 ***1823.15*** *p76*
Fahy, Allice; Vermont, 1885 ***5900.10*** *p469*
Fahy, Bridget 69; Vermont, 1891 ***5900.10*** *p436*
Fahy, Hanora 18; Vermont, 1887 ***5900.10*** *p436*
Fahy, James G.; Vermont, 1845-1925 ***5900.10*** *p212*
Fahy, Mary Houlihan; Vermont, 1855-1923 ***5900.10*** *p212*
Fahy, Peter 62; Vermont, 1885 ***5900.10*** *p436*
Fahy, Winnie 22; Vermont, 1877 ***5900.10*** *p436*
Faichney, Ann; South Carolina, 1797 ***1640.13*** *p37*
Faigle, Jon.; Maryland, 1675 ***2524.55*** *p214*
Faikbuin, George 27; Ontario, 1871 ***1823.15*** *p76*
Failey, Annie; Vermont, 1873-1954 ***5900.10*** *p475*
Failey, Catharine; Vermont, 1841-1903 ***5900.10*** *p234*
Failey, Catharine 77; Vermont, 1881 ***5900.10*** *p234*
Failey, Catherine McNalley 93; Vermont, 1866 ***5900.10*** *p604*
Failey, Elizabeth Owen 54; Vermont, 1898 ***5900.10*** *p229*
Failey, Francis 25; Vermont, 1864 ***5900.10*** *p234*
Failey, Lawrence, Sr. 81; Vermont, 1881 ***5900.10*** *p234*
Failey, Margaret 29; Vermont, 1863 ***5900.10*** *p229*
Failey, Mary A. 35; Vermont, 1881 ***5900.10*** *p234*
Failey, Patrick; Vermont, 1838-1915 ***5900.10*** *p229*
Failin, Margaret 50; Ontario, 1871 ***1823.15*** *p76*
Failin, William 50; Ontario, 1871 ***1823.15*** *p76*
Faillon, Rev.; Quebec, 1857 ***9196.15*** *p26*
Faily, John 95; Vermont, 1867 ***5900.10*** *p240*
Fainan, Patrick 48; Ontario, 1871 ***1823.15*** *p76*
Fair, Adam; New York, 1840 ***8197.10*** *p165*
Fair, E. Neil 30; Ontario, 1871 ***1823.15*** *p76*
Fair, James; Canada, 1854 ***1640.13*** *p37*
Fair, James 34; Ontario, 1871 ***1823.15*** *p76*
Fair, Janet 60; Ontario, 1871 ***1823.15*** *p76*
Fair, Thomas 37; Ontario, 1871 ***1823.15*** *p76*
Fair, William 22; Philadelphia, 1775 ***1220.25*** *p8*
Fairar, John 16; Nevis, 1773 ***1220.25*** *p30*
Fairback, Christian; New York, 1839 ***8197.10*** *p231*
Fairbairn, Allan; Chicago, 1896 ***1640.13*** *p37*
Fairbairn, Francis; New York, 1805 ***8197.10*** *p29*
Fairbairn, Henry Brougham; Chicago, 1896 ***1640.13*** *p37*
Fairbairn, James Newell; Chicago, 1896 ***1640.13*** *p37*
Fairbairn, Maud; Chicago, 1896 ***1640.13*** *p37*
Fairbairn, Robert; Canada, 1881 ***1640.13*** *p37*
Fairbairn, Robert; Chicago, 1896 ***1640.13*** *p37*
Fairbairn, William; New York, 1840 ***8197.10*** *p166*
Fairbank, Daniel; Maryland, 1667 ***2524.55*** *p77*
Fairbarn, John 19; Ontario, 1871 ***1823.15*** *p76*
Fairbarn, Thomas 43; Ontario, 1871 ***1823.15*** *p76*
Fairbrother, Eliza Elvara *SEE* Fairbrother, William
Fairbrother, William; New York, 1837 ***8197.10*** *p89*
Wife: Eliza Elvara
Fairclough, Henry; New York, 1840 ***8197.10*** *p166*
Fairer, Joseph 33; Ontario, 1871 ***1823.28*** *p28*
Fairface, James 20; Georgia, 1775 ***1220.25*** *p124*
Fairfax, George William; Virginia, n.d. ***1224.2*** *p39*
Fairfeild, Eliza.; Virginia, 1668-1669 ***6212.30*** *p41*
Fairfield, Henrietta 29; Ontario, 1871 ***1823.15*** *p76*
Fairfield, Julie E. St. Johns; Vermont, 1846-1913 ***5900.10*** *p474*
Fairfield, Lewis C.; Vermont, 1846-1875 ***5900.10*** *p474*
Fairholm, Thomas; Tobago, West Indies, 1791 ***1640.13*** *p37*
Fairley, Alexander; New York, 1807 ***8197.10*** *p42*
Fairley, Hugh; New York, 1807 ***8197.10*** *p42*
Fairley, James; Virginia, 1735-1781 ***1640.10*** *p50*
Fairman, Susannah 44; Ontario, 1861 ***2896.28*** *p31*
Fairservice, James 34; Ontario, 1871 ***1823.15*** *p76*
Fairservice, Thomas 55; Ontario, 1871 ***1823.15*** *p76*
Fairwether, William 60; Ontario, 1871 ***1823.15*** *p76*
Faist, Bernard 43; Ontario, 1871 ***1823.15*** *p76*
Fakulek, Steven; Maryland, 1910 ***3259.35*** *p14*
Falck, Johann; Port uncertain, 1738 ***2856.30*** *p106*
Falckel, Nicolaus; America, 1763 ***2856.30*** *p109*
Falckel, Nicolaus; America, 1783 ***2856.30*** *p109*
Falckenberger, Caspar; Port uncertain, 1737 ***2856.30*** *p106*
Falckenberger, Caspar; Port uncertain, 1767 ***2856.30*** *p106*
Falcon, Thomas; Roxbury, Massachusetts, 1856 ***1224.3*** *p25*
Falconer, Alexir 60; Ontario, 1871 ***1823.15*** *p76*
Falconer, Archibald Cowan; Boston, 1900 ***1640.13*** *p37*
Falconer, James 51; Ontario, 1871 ***1823.15*** *p76*
Falconer, John; Mobile, Alabama, 1766 ***1640.10*** *p50*
Falconer, Margaret 60; Ontario, 1871 ***1823.15*** *p76*
Falconer, Thomas; Philadelphia, 1767 ***1224.2*** *p39*
Falconer, William; Mississippi, 1794 ***1640.10*** *p50*
Falcott, Emily 1; Ontario, 1861 ***2896.27*** *p51*
Falcott, Eunice 16; Ontario, 1861 ***2896.27*** *p50*
Falcott, Freeman 11; Ontario, 1861 ***2896.27*** *p50*
Falcott, James W. 14; Ontario, 1861 ***2896.27*** *p50*
Falcott, Lydia M. 8; Ontario, 1861 ***2896.27*** *p50*
Falcott, Philip 3; Ontario, 1861 ***2896.27*** *p51*
Falcott, Sarah 36; Ontario, 1861 ***2896.27*** *p50*
Faldo, Charles; Carolina, 1729 ***1224.2*** *p39*
Fal...er, Mr.; Portland, Maine, 1858 ***9196.15*** *p47*
Faler, Andreas; Port uncertain, 1698 ***2856.30*** *p106*
With 7 children
Falewich, Alfons; Maryland, 1910 ***3259.35*** *p14*
Falion, Mary 18 *SEE* Falion, Thomas
Falion, Thomas 43; New York, New York, 1847 ***1825.45*** *p15*
Wife: Mary 18
Falishinick, Andrew; Maryland, 1910 ***3259.35*** *p14*
Falk, Heinrich; New York, 1837 ***8197.10*** *p89*
Falkner, Dorothy 45 *SEE* Falkner, Ralph
Falkner, Mary 30 *SEE* Falkner, Ralph
Falkner, Ralph 30; Philadelphia, 1774 ***1220.25*** *p26*
Wife: Mary 30
Falkner, Ralph 50; Philadelphia, 1774 ***1220.25*** *p26*
Wife: Dorothy 45
Falkner, Thomas; New York, 1837 ***8197.10*** *p89*
Falkner, William 21; Maryland, 1774 ***1220.25*** *p40*
Falkner, William B. 54; Ontario, 1871 ***1823.22*** *p50*
Fall, John; New York, 1825 ***8197.10*** *p229*
Fallaize, James Louis; Pennsylvania, 1779 ***4629.10*** *p39*
Fallan, Winefred; Vermont, 1817-1896 ***5900.10*** *p340*
Fallane, Richard 50; Ontario, 1871 ***1823.28*** *p28*
Fallenberger, Nicolaus; America, 1749 ***2856.30*** *p106*
With wife & children

Faller, Cath. Elisabeth; Port uncertain, 1744 ***2856.30*** *p106*
Faller, Christian; Port uncertain, 1756 ***2856.30*** *p106*
Faller, Elisabeth; Port uncertain, 1762 ***2856.30*** *p106*
Faller, Konrad; Port uncertain, 1743 ***2856.30*** *p106*
Faller, Maria Anna; Port uncertain, 1758 ***2856.30*** *p106*
Faller, Matthaus; Port uncertain, 1765 ***2856.30*** *p106*
Falles, Ann 21; Maryland, 1775 ***1220.25*** *p104*
Fallevolte, Benedetto 40; Maryland, 1775 ***1220.25*** *p114*
Fallon, Mr.; Quebec, 1857 ***9196.15*** *p22*
Fallon, Anne 32 *SEE* Fallon, Thomas
Fallon, Bridget 20 *SEE* Fallon, Garret
Fallon, Bridget 25 *SEE* Fallon, Thomas
Fallon, Catharine 50; Vermont, 1870 ***5900.10*** *p198*
Fallon, Catherine E. Solomon; Vermont, 1868-1944 ***5900.10*** *p607*
Fallon, Edward; New York, 1837 ***8197.10*** *p90*
Fallon, Eliza 26 *SEE* Fallon, Garret
Fallon, Elizabeth; Vermont, 1845-1910 ***5900.10*** *p157*
Fallon, Ellen 8 *SEE* Fallon, Thomas
Fallon, Garret 32; New York, New York, 1847 ***1825.45*** *p14*
Wife: Eliza 26
Sister: Bridget 20
Fallon, James; New York, 1833 ***8197.10*** *p230*
Fallon, James; Pennsylvania, 1779 ***4629.10*** *p37*
Fallon, James 36; Ontario, 1871 ***1823.28*** *p28*
Fallon, James 98; Vermont, 1897 ***5900.10*** *p181*
Fallon, John 48; Ontario, 1871 ***1823.28*** *p28*
Fallon, John 50; Vermont, 1867 ***5900.10*** *p498*
Fallon, John Jay; Vermont, 1840-1913 ***5900.10*** *p607*
Fallon, Kate; Vermont, 1859-1942 ***5900.10*** *p477*
Fallon, Katie Fitzgerald 86; Vermont, 1883 ***5900.10*** *p181*
Fallon, Martin 5 *SEE* Fallon, Thomas
Fallon, Mary 1 *SEE* Fallon, Thomas
Fallon, Patrick 16 *SEE* Fallon, Thomas
Fallon, Sarah Nugent 34; Vermont, 1838 ***5900.10*** *p181*
Fallon, Thomas 33; New York, New York, 1847 ***1825.45*** *p15*
Wife: Anne 32
Sister: Bridget 25
Son: Martin 5
Daughter: Ellen 8
Brother: Patrick 16
Daughter: Mary 1
Fallon, Thomas 62; Vermont, 1886 ***5900.10*** *p198*
Fallon, Thomas, Jr. 19; Vermont, 1873 ***5900.10*** *p199*
Falloon, Catherine A.; Vermont, 1858-1914 ***5900.10*** *p390*
Falloon, James F. 10; Vermont, 1872 ***5900.10*** *p383*
Falloon, Mary; Vermont, 1839-1914 ***5900.10*** *p389*
Falloon, Mary A.; Vermont, 1839-1914 ***5900.10*** *p390*
Falls, Henry 24; Ontario, 1871 ***1823.15*** *p76*
Falls, Margaret 65; Ontario, 1871 ***1823.15*** *p76*
Falls, Robert 30; Ontario, 1871 ***1823.15*** *p76*
Fallydown, Patience 22; Halifax, Nova Scotia, 1775 ***1220.25*** *p22*
Falon, Bernard; New York, 1835-1838 ***8197.10*** *p118*
Faloney, Catherine 20; Ontario, 1861 ***2896.28*** *p61*
Faloney, Hugh 23; Ontario, 1861 ***2896.28*** *p61*
Faloney, Hugh 60; Ontario, 1861 ***2896.28*** *p61*
Faloney, Jane 25; Ontario, 1861 ***2896.28*** *p61*
Faloney, Jane 55; Ontario, 1861 ***2896.28*** *p61*
Falque, Charles; New York, 1829 ***8197.10*** *p230*
Faltor, Lewes 27; Ontario, 1871 ***1823.15*** *p77*
Falvey, Jeremiah; New York, 1837 ***8197.10*** *p89*
Falvey, Thomas; Pennsylvania, 1868 ***6058.10*** *p73*
Falwell, Samuel; Pennsylvania, 1787 ***4629.10*** *p55*
Famanel, William 62; Ontario, 1871 ***1823.15*** *p77*
Fame, Francis; Virginia, 1665-1666 ***6212.30*** *p23*
Fame, Francis; Virginia, 1666-1667 ***6212.30*** *p32*
Famine, John; Maryland, 1655 ***2524.55*** *p77*
Fananhone, Carl 47; Ontario, 1871 ***1823.28*** *p28*
Fandrich, Miss; Port uncertain, 1763 ***2856.30*** *p126*
Fandrich, Georg; Port uncertain, 1782 ***2856.30*** *p126*
Fandschilling, Michael; Port uncertain, 1775 ***2856.30*** *p106*
With wife
Fane, Francis; Virginia, 1664 ***6212.30*** *p15*
Fane, George; New York, 1709 ***1224.2*** *p39*
Fanell, Francis; New York, 1834 ***8197.10*** *p315*
Fanen, Thomas; Pennsylvania, 1777 ***4629.10*** *p17*
Fanerbach, Peter; Port uncertain, 1771 ***2856.30*** *p106*
Fanestial, Catherina 39; Kansas, 1888-1910 ***9079.10*** *p42*
Fanestial, Ferdinand 44; Kansas, 1888-1910 ***9079.10*** *p42*
Faneuil, Andrew; Boston, 1738 ***1224.2*** *p39*
Faneuil, Benjamin; Boston, 1787 ***1224.2*** *p39*
Faneuil, Peter; Boston, 1743 ***1224.2*** *p39*
Faning, Joseph; Pennsylvania, 1777 ***4629.10*** *p6*
Fanley, Daniel; Pennsylvania, 1864 ***6058.10*** *p75*
Fann, Charles; Maryland, 1663 ***2524.55*** *p77*
Fannin, Ellen; Vermont, 1829-1909 ***5900.10*** *p220*
Fanning, Edward J.; Vermont, 1834-1928 ***5900.10*** *p309*
Fanning, John; Virginia, 1672 ***1224.1*** *p21*
Fanning, Mary; Vermont, 1818-1907 ***5900.10*** *p391*
Fanning, Thomas 73; Ontario, 1871 ***1823.22*** *p51*
Fannon, Thomas; New York, 1828 ***8197.10*** *p230*
Fanshaw, Thomas; Virginia, 1666-1667 ***6212.30*** *p33*
Fanshawe, John; New York, 1817 ***8197.10*** *p228*
Fanson, John 32; Ontario, 1871 ***1823.15*** *p77*
Fanson, Richard 26; Ontario, 1871 ***1823.15*** *p77*
Fanson, Richard 71; Ontario, 1871 ***1823.15*** *p77*
Fanson, Robert 43; Ontario, 1871 ***1823.15*** *p77*
Fanson, William 29; Ontario, 1871 ***1823.15*** *p77*
Fanson, William 34; Ontario, 1871 ***1823.15*** *p77*
Fant, Ann 59; Vermont, 1880 ***5900.10*** *p618*
Fant, James 68; Vermont, 1878 ***5900.10*** *p618*
Fantly, Wm; Virginia, 1666-1667 ***6212.30*** *p34*
Fanton, Lucy R.; Vermont, 1857-1949 ***5900.10*** *p241*
Fanton, Peter; New York, 1794 ***8197.10*** *p1*
Fantz, Eva; Port uncertain, 1764 ***2856.30*** *p106*
Faote, John, Sr. 56; Ontario, 1871 ***1823.15*** *p77*
Faram, Cottain; Maryland, 1657 ***2524.55*** *p78*
Farant, Pete 47; Washington, 1912 ***9196.1*** *p36*
Farar, James; Virginia, 1666 ***6212.30*** *p26*
Farcee, Margret; Virginia, 1664 ***6212.30*** *p6*
Fardell, William; Maryland, 1664-1665 ***2524.55*** *p78*
Farding, Mathew; Maryland, 1682 ***2524.55*** *p78*
Farell, Bridget; Vermont, 1821-1889 ***5900.10*** *p511*
Farenton, Robert; Maryland, 1661 ***2524.55*** *p78*
Farflar, George; Pennsylvania, 1777 ***4629.10*** *p17*
Fargason, Christian *SEE* Fargason, Nyles
Fargason, Ellin *SEE* Fargason, Nyles
Fargason, Nyles; Maryland, 1661 ***2524.55*** *p78*
Wife: Ellin
Daughter: Christian
Fargie, John F.; New York, 1837 ***8197.10*** *p88*
Farguarson, Alexander 33; Ontario, 1871 ***1823.15*** *p77*
Farguharson, William 29; Ontario, 1871 ***1823.15*** *p77*
Fargusion, Robert; New England, 1698 ***1224.1*** *p21*
Farguson, Edward 32; Ontario, 1871 ***1823.15*** *p77*
Farguson, William 30; Ontario, 1871 ***1823.28*** *p28*
Farguson, William 49; Ontario, 1871 ***1823.15*** *p77*
Farhan, Daniel; New York, 1834 ***8197.10*** *p373*
Farington, Anne *SEE* Farington, Robert
Farington, Anne; Maryland, 1673 ***2524.55*** *p78*
Farington, Francis 24; Ontario, 1861 ***2896.27*** *p47*
Farington, Jane *SEE* Farington, Robert
Farington, Jane; Maryland, 1673 ***2524.55*** *p78*
Farington, Robert; Maryland, 1673 ***2524.55*** *p78*
Wife: Anne
Daughter: Jane
Faris, Rie 52; Washington, 1912 ***9196.1*** *p36*
Faris, Tee 17; Washington, 1912 ***9196.1*** *p36*
Farish, David 30; Ontario, 1871 ***1823.15*** *p77*
Farley, Andrew; New York, 1838 ***8197.10*** *p230*
Farley, Annie Farrell 53; Vermont, 1909 ***5900.10*** *p516*
Farley, Cornelius 71; Vermont, 1868 ***5900.10*** *p320*
Farley, Edward 53; Ontario, 1871 ***1823.15*** *p77*
Farley, George 52; Ontario, 1861 ***2896.28*** *p14*
Farley, H. 13; Ontario, 1861 ***2896.28*** *p14*
Farley, James; New York, 1821 ***8197.10*** *p228*
Farley, James; New York, 1838 ***8197.10*** *p119*
Farley, M. 52; Ontario, 1861 ***2896.28*** *p14*
Farley, Mary; Vermont, 1830-1893 ***5900.10*** *p311*
Farley, Michael; Pennsylvania, 1827 ***6058.10*** *p10*
Farley, P. A. 10; Ontario, 1861 ***2896.28*** *p14*
Farley, Philip; New York, 1839 ***8197.10*** *p130*
Farley, Sarah; Savannah, Georgia, 1814 ***1224.3*** *p25*
Farley, Sarah; Savannah, Georgia, 1814 ***1640.10*** *p50*
Farley, Sarah 20; Virginia, 1775 ***1220.25*** *p95*
Farley, Susanna; Virginia, 1656 ***1224.1*** *p21*
Farley, Timothy; Nova Scotia, 1745 ***4628.40*** *p45*
Farley, William; Vermont, 1891 ***5900.10*** *p459*
Farley, William 19; Ontario, 1861 ***2896.28*** *p14*
Farlow, Robert; Virginia, 1667 ***6212.30*** *p36*
Farmar, Robert; Florida, 1784 ***1224.2*** *p39*
Farmar, Samuel; Norfolk, Virginia, 1791 ***1224.2*** *p39*
Farmar, Susan Ravand; New York, New York, 1841 ***1224.3*** *p25*
Farmer, Archibald 68; Ontario, 1871 ***1823.22*** *p51*
Farmer, Catherine; Vermont, n.d. ***5900.10*** *p180*
Farmer, Edward; New York, 1838 ***8197.10*** *p118*
Farmer, Felix 61; Ontario, 1871 ***1823.22*** *p51*
Farmer, James 55; Ontario, 1871 ***1823.22*** *p51*
Farmer, Jamima 66; Ontario, 1871 ***1823.22*** *p51*
Farmer, Jasper; Barbados, n.d. ***1224.3*** *p25*
Farmer, Jasper; New York, 1801 ***1224.3*** *p25*
Farmer, John 22; Maryland, 1775 ***1220.25*** *p100*
Farmer, Richard; Pennsylvania, 1777 ***4629.10*** *p27*
Farmer, Richard; Pennsylvania, 1777 ***4629.10*** *p29*
Farmer, Richard; Pennsylvania, 1779 ***4629.10*** *p40*
Farmer, Richard; Virginia, 1689 ***1224.1*** *p21*
Farmer, Shepard; Maryland, 1640 ***2524.55*** *p78*
Farmer, William; South Carolina, 1739 ***1224.2*** *p39*
Farmer, William 23; Ontario, 1871 ***1823.28*** *p28*
Farmor, John; Virginia, 1664-1665 ***6212.30*** *p15*
Farms, Margaret; New Jersey, 1895 ***1640.13*** *p37*
Farn, John 37; Ontario, 1871 ***1823.15*** *p77*
Farnando, Peter; Maryland, 1672 ***2524.55*** *p78*
Farnell, Elizabeth *SEE* Farnell, Thomas
Farnell, John *SEE* Farnell, Thomas
Farnell, Mary *SEE* Farnell, Thomas
Farnell, Thomas *SEE* Farnell, Thomas
Farnell, Thomas; Maryland, 1682 ***2524.55*** *p78*
Wife: Elizabeth
Child: John
Child: Thomas
Child: Mary
Farner, Michael; Pennsylvania, 1777 ***4629.10*** *p11*
Farnham, John 65; Vermont, 1892 ***5900.10*** *p343*
Farnham, Paulina 22; Vermont, 1880 ***5900.10*** *p343*
Farnham, Pauline 92; Vermont, 1916 ***5900.10*** *p343*
Farnham, William; Vermont, 1824-1894 ***5900.10*** *p460*
Farnsworth, John 32; Ontario, 1871 ***1823.15*** *p77*
Farnsworth, Willm 37; Ontario, 1871 ***1823.28*** *p28*
Faroll, William; New York, 1838 ***8197.10*** *p378*
Faron, John; New York, 1837 ***8197.10*** *p89*
Farquaharson, David 49; Ontario, 1871 ***1823.28*** *p28*
Farquareson, William 48; Ontario, 1871 ***1823.15*** *p77*
Farquhar, David; Kingston, Jamaica, 1758 ***1640.13*** *p37*
Farquhar, George; Savannah, Georgia, 1768 ***1640.10*** *p50*
Farquhar, George Peat; Windward Islands, 1860 ***1640.13*** *p37*
Farquhar, James 27; Ontario, 1871 ***1823.15*** *p77*
Farquhar, Jean; Boston, 1893 ***1640.13*** *p37*
Farquhar, John; Jamaica, 1767 ***1640.13*** *p37*
Farquhar, John 45; Ontario, 1871 ***1823.15*** *p77*
Farquhar, Thomas 50; Ontario, 1871 ***1823.15*** *p77*
Farquhar, Thomas 56; Ontario, 1871 ***1823.15*** *p77*
Farquhar, William 45; Ontario, 1871 ***1823.15*** *p77*
Farquhar, William P.; Worcester, Massachusetts, 1882 ***1640.13*** *p37*
Farquharson, John; Charles Town, South Carolina, n.d. ***1224.2*** *p39*
Farquharson, Margret 32; Ontario, 1871 ***1823.28*** *p28*
Farquharson, Robert; Nashville, Tennessee, 1856 ***1640.10*** *p51*
Farr, Arthur 18; Ontario, 1871 ***1823.28*** *p28*
Farr, Christopher 55; Ontario, 1871 ***1823.28*** *p28*
Farr, Edward 18; Virginia, 1774 ***1220.25*** *p92*
Farr, George 40; Ontario, 1871 ***1823.22*** *p51*
Farr, John; Pennsylvania, 1777 ***4629.10*** *p11*
Farr, John C. 27; Ontario, 1871 ***1823.28*** *p28*
Farr, Mary R.; Vermont, 1816-1897 ***5900.10*** *p198*
Farr, Robert; New Orleans, 1857 ***1224.3*** *p25*
Farr, Robert; New York, 1831 ***8197.10*** *p313*
Farr, Russell H.; Vermont, 1852-1913 ***5900.10*** *p401*
Farr, Sarah; New York, 1820 ***1224.3*** *p69*
Farr, Susie McNulty; Vermont, 1857-1918 ***5900.10*** *p401*
Farr, William; New York, 1840 ***8197.10*** *p165*
Farrall, Margaret 23; Vermont, 1867 ***5900.10*** *p328*
Farrall, Patrick; New York, 1838 ***8197.10*** *p375*
Farrandall, Richard; Maryland, 1665 ***2524.55*** *p78*
Farrant, Charlotte Caroline; New Jersey, n.d. ***1224.3*** *p25*
Farrant, Henry; New York, 1768 ***1224.2*** *p39*
Farrant, Thomas; New York, 1855 ***1224.3*** *p25*
Farrar, George 49; Ontario, 1871 ***1823.22*** *p51*
Farrar, John; Virginia, 1665-1666 ***6212.30*** *p21*
Farrel, Edward; New York, 1816 ***8197.10*** *p228*
Farrel, Edward 48; Ontario, 1871 ***1823.15*** *p77*
Farrel, Lewis; Portland, Maine, 1858 ***9196.15*** *p28*
Farrel, Mary; Vermont, 1826-1906 ***5900.10*** *p200*
Farrel, Patrick 38; Maryland, 1774 ***1220.25*** *p52*
Farrel, Poartlz 36; Ontario, 1871 ***1823.28*** *p28*
Farrel, Samuel 37; Ontario, 1871 ***1823.15*** *p77*
Farrell, Alexander; Maryland, 1673 ***2524.55*** *p78*
Farrell, Andrew 60; Vermont, 1898 ***5900.10*** *p559*
Farrell, Ann; Vermont, 1874 ***5900.10*** *p616*
Farrell, Annie 53; Vermont, 1909 ***5900.10*** *p516*
Farrell, Annie Naven 29; Vermont, 1882 ***5900.10*** *p448*
Farrell, Bernard; New York, 1840 ***8197.10*** *p164*
Farrell, Bridget; Vermont, 1819-1919 ***5900.10*** *p205*
Farrell, Bridget; Vermont, 1855-1893 ***5900.10*** *p311*
Farrell, Bridget 14 *SEE* Farrell, Pat
Farrell, Bridget 36; New York, New York, 1848 ***1825.45*** *p15*
Farrell, Bridget 59; Vermont, 1904 ***5900.10*** *p560*
Farrell, Bridget 69; Vermont, 1903 ***5900.10*** *p135*
Farrell, Bridget 71; Vermont, 1905 ***5900.10*** *p439*
Farrell, Bridget Battels 68; Vermont, 1890 ***5900.10*** *p535*
Farrell, Bridget Campbell; Vermont, 1860-1936 ***5900.10*** *p535*
Farrell, Bridget Kennedy 70; Vermont, 1873 ***5900.10*** *p591*
Farrell, Bryan; New York, 1838 ***8197.10*** *p119*
Farrell, Catherine; Vermont, n.d. ***5900.10*** *p153*
Farrell, Catherine; Vermont, 1834-1917 ***5900.10*** *p439*

Farrell, Catherine Gilfeather 65; Vermont, 1919 ***5900.10*** *p559*
Farrell, Catherine Golden; Vermont, 1813-1888 ***5900.10*** *p527*
Farrell, Christopher; New York, 1840 ***8197.10*** *p165*
Farrell, Christopher; Vermont, n.d. ***5900.10*** *p153*
Farrell, Edward; New York, 1839 ***8197.10*** *p231*
Farrell, Edward 63; Ontario, 1871 ***1823.28*** *p28*
Farrell, Edward 73; Vermont, 1887 ***5900.10*** *p530*
Farrell, Eleanor; Maryland, 1681 ***2524.55*** *p78*
Farrell, Eliza; Vermont, 1819-1901 ***5900.10*** *p453*
Farrell, Eliza J.; Vermont, 1860-1912 ***5900.10*** *p135*
Farrell, Elizabeth; Vermont, 1836-1910 ***5900.10*** *p504*
Farrell, Elizabeth 58; Vermont, 1891 ***5900.10*** *p559*
Farrell, Ellen; Vermont, 1846-1924 ***5900.10*** *p491*
Farrell, Ellen Cline; Vermont, 1842-1908 ***5900.10*** *p444*
Farrell, Ellen Hurley; Vermont, 1843-1889 ***5900.10*** *p339*
Farrell, Ellen Neary; Vermont, 1833-1897 ***5900.10*** *p424*
Farrell, James; New York, 1802 ***8197.10*** *p20*
Farrell, James; New York, 1836-1838 ***8197.10*** *p119*
Farrell, James; New York, 1840 ***8197.10*** *p231*
Farrell, James; Vermont, 1831-1903 ***5900.10*** *p316*
Farrell, James 21; Maryland, 1774 ***1220.25*** *p41*
Farrell, James 32; Vermont, 1876 ***5900.10*** *p361*
Farrell, James 52; Vermont, 1883 ***5900.10*** *p509*
Farrell, James E.; Vermont, 1850-1898 ***5900.10*** *p516*
Farrell, James H.; Vermont, 1838-1913 ***5900.10*** *p174*
Farrell, Jerry 81; Vermont, 1912 ***5900.10*** *p376*
Farrell, Joanna Belrose 39; Vermont, 1899 ***5900.10*** *p376*
Farrell, John; New York, 1839 ***8197.10*** *p382*
Farrell, John; Vermont, n.d. ***5900.10*** *p140*
Farrell, John; Vermont, 1808-1888 ***5900.10*** *p559*
Farrell, John 25; Maryland, 1773-1774 ***1220.25*** *p34*
Farrell, John 48; Vermont, 1880 ***5900.10*** *p448*
Farrell, John 49; Vermont, 1884 ***5900.10*** *p560*
Farrell, John 82; Vermont, 1898 ***5900.10*** *p531*
Farrell, John, Jr. 37; Vermont, 1876 ***5900.10*** *p591*
Farrell, John B.; New York, 1803 ***8197.10*** *p12*
Farrell, John C.; Vermont, 1842-1906 ***5900.10*** *p140*
Farrell, Kennedy; Detroit, 1771 ***1224.2*** *p39*
Farrell, Lewis; New York, 1837 ***8197.10*** *p89*
Farrell, Lizzie Gale 30; Vermont, 1873 ***5900.10*** *p530*
Farrell, Marcella; Vermont, 1848-1918 ***5900.10*** *p160*
Farrell, Margaret; Vermont, 1834-1913 ***5900.10*** *p150*
Farrell, Margaret; Vermont, 1873-1936 ***5900.10*** *p352*
Farrell, Margaret 68; Vermont, 1893 ***5900.10*** *p574*
Farrell, Margaret M.; Vermont, 1849-1902 ***5900.10*** *p140*
Farrell, Maria 35; Vermont, 1888 ***5900.10*** *p192*
Farrell, Maria Manying; Vermont, 1810-1860 ***5900.10*** *p160*
Farrell, Martin 61; Vermont, 1893 ***5900.10*** *p439*
Farrell, Mary; Vermont, 1848-1929 ***5900.10*** *p191*
Farrell, Mary 16 *SEE* Farrell, Pat
Farrell, Mary 50 *SEE* Farrell, Pat
Farrell, Mary 64; Vermont, 1892 ***5900.10*** *p66*
Farrell, Mary 75; Vermont, 1888 ***5900.10*** *p503*
Farrell, Mary 88; Vermont, 1932 ***5900.10*** *p361*
Farrell, Mary A.; Vermont, 1883-1952 ***5900.10*** *p149*
Farrell, Mary Ann; Vermont, n.d. ***5900.10*** *p191*
Farrell, Mary Ann; Vermont, 1844-1912 ***5900.10*** *p160*
Farrell, Mary Connell; Vermont, 1842-1905 ***5900.10*** *p183*
Farrell, Mary Cook; Vermont, 1852-1936 ***5900.10*** *p516*
Farrell, Mary Duffey; Vermont, 1857-1928 ***5900.10*** *p174*
Farrell, Mary Filbon; Vermont, 1853-1882 ***5900.10*** *p176*
Farrell, Mary Fitzmorris; Vermont, n.d. ***5900.10*** *p591*
Farrell, Mary Foster 33; Vermont, 1878 ***5900.10*** *p564*
Farrell, Mary J.; Vermont, 1854-1919 ***5900.10*** *p506*
Farrell, Mary Kennedy; Vermont, 1841-1910 ***5900.10*** *p164*
Farrell, Mary Lynch; Vermont, 1851-1927 ***5900.10*** *p334*
Farrell, Mathew; New York, 1833-1838 ***8197.10*** *p119*
Farrell, Mathew; New York, 1837 ***8197.10*** *p89*
Farrell, Matilda; Alabama, 1828-1845 ***1640.10*** *p50*
Farrell, Michael; New York, 1840 ***8197.10*** *p165*
Farrell, Michael; Vermont, 1809-1849 ***5900.10*** *p160*
Farrell, Michael; Vermont, 1832-1876 ***5900.10*** *p424*
Farrell, Michael; Vermont, 1852-1924 ***5900.10*** *p465*
Farrell, Murt; Vermont, n.d. ***5900.10*** *p153*
Farrell, Nellie K.; Vermont, 1861-1952 ***5900.10*** *p465*
Farrell, Pat 55; New York, New York, 1848 ***1825.45*** *p15*
  Wife: Mary 50
  Son: William 18
  Daughter: Bridget 14
  Daughter: Mary 16
Farrell, Patrick; Long Island, 1783 ***1224.2*** *p40*
Farrell, Patrick; New York, 1840 ***8197.10*** *p166*
Farrell, Patrick; Vermont, 1834-1905 ***5900.10*** *p444*
Farrell, Patrick; Vermont, 1834-1915 ***5900.10*** *p339*
Farrell, Patrick; Vermont, 1842-1920 ***5900.10*** *p183*
Farrell, Patrick 84; Vermont, 1874 ***5900.10*** *p367*
Farrell, Patrick 84; Vermont, 1902 ***5900.10*** *p535*
Farrell, Patrick 92; Vermont, 1865 ***5900.10*** *p163*
Farrell, Peter; New York, 1827 ***8197.10*** *p338*
Farrell, Phillip; Vermont, 1852-1934 ***5900.10*** *p535*
Farrell, Richard; New York, 1802 ***8197.10*** *p20*
Farrell, Richard; New York, 1840 ***8197.10*** *p166*
Farrell, Robert; New York, 1829 ***8197.10*** *p230*
Farrell, Robert; Vermont, 1800-1888 ***5900.10*** *p527*
Farrell, Rose; Vermont, 1855-1939 ***5900.10*** *p130*
Farrell, Rose Ann T. Hart 32; Vermont, 1872 ***5900.10*** *p509*
Farrell, Rose Carroll 49; Vermont, 1867 ***5900.10*** *p530*
Farrell, Theresa; Vermont, 1855-1936 ***5900.10*** *p149*
Farrell, Thomas; New Orleans, 1848 ***6058.10*** *p26*
Farrell, Thomas; New York, 1840 ***8197.10*** *p165*
Farrell, Thomas; Pennsylvania, 1868 ***6058.10*** *p71*
Farrell, Thomas; Vermont, 1848-1921 ***5900.10*** *p334*
Farrell, Thomas; Vermont, 1854-1942 ***5900.10*** *p352*
Farrell, Thomas; Virginia, 1671 ***6212.30*** *p43*
Farrell, William 18 *SEE* Farrell, Pat
Farrelly, Bernard; New York, 1821 ***8197.10*** *p229*
Farrelly, Bernard; New York, 1827 ***8197.10*** *p343*
Farren, Hugh; New York, 1806 ***8197.10*** *p323*
Farrendell, Richard; Maryland, 1667 ***2524.55*** *p78*
Farrest, John 66; Ontario, 1871 ***1823.28*** *p28*
Farrill, Thomas; New Orleans, 1848 ***6058.10*** *p26*
Farrill, William 46; Ontario, 1871 ***1823.15*** *p77*
Farrin, Anna Maria; America, 1750 ***2856.30*** *p106*
Farrington, Anne *SEE* Farrington, Robert
Farrington, Anne; Maryland, 1673 ***2524.55*** *p78*
Farrington, Charles; America, 1817 ***1224.3*** *p26*
Farrington, Hen; Virginia, 1663 ***6212.30*** *p4*
Farrington, Jane *SEE* Farrington, Robert
Farrington, Jane; Maryland, 1673 ***2524.55*** *p78*
Farrington, John; Maryland, 1662 ***2524.55*** *p78*
Farrington, John; Maryland, 1672 ***2524.55*** *p78*
Farrington, John; Virginia, 1664 ***6212.30*** *p8*
Farrington, Robert; Maryland, 1673 ***2524.55*** *p78*
  Wife: Anne
  Daughter: Jane
Farris, John 56; Ontario, 1871 ***1823.15*** *p77*
Farrish, Ann 84; Ontario, 1871 ***1823.15*** *p77*
Farrish, Isibela 52; Ontario, 1871 ***1823.15*** *p77*
Farrish, John 39; Ontario, 1871 ***1823.15*** *p77*
Farrish, Robert 47; Ontario, 1871 ***1823.15*** *p77*
Farrish, Robert 50; Ontario, 1871 ***1823.15*** *p77*
Farro, James; Maryland, 1673 ***2524.55*** *p78*
Farro, Jonas; Maryland, 1681 ***2524.55*** *p78*
Farrow, Asher 28; Ontario, 1871 ***1823.15*** *p77*
Farrow, George 32; Ontario, 1871 ***1823.22*** *p51*
Farrow, Henry 42; Ontario, 1871 ***1823.15*** *p77*
Farrow, James; Georgia, 1748 ***1224.2*** *p40*
Farrow, James; Maryland, 1673 ***2524.55*** *p78*
Farrow, John 39; Ontario, 1871 ***1823.15*** *p77*
Farrow, Martin 65; Ontario, 1871 ***1823.15*** *p77*
Farrow, Thomas 39; Ontario, 1871 ***1823.15*** *p77*
Farrow, William; Maryland, 1653 ***2524.55*** *p78*
Farry, Patrick 6; Vermont, 1849 ***5900.10*** *p477*
Farthing, Tho.; Maryland, 1681 ***2524.55*** *p78*
Farwell, Alice E.; Vermont, 1848-1926 ***5900.10*** *p322*
Farwell, David; Vermont, 1815-1892 ***5900.10*** *p300*
Farwell, Julia B. Locke; Vermont, 1822-1849 ***5900.10*** *p300*
Farwell, Julia M.; Vermont, 1844-1908 ***5900.10*** *p300*
Fary, Joseph; Maryland, 1695 ***1224.1*** *p21*
Fasecki, Martin; Maryland, 1910 ***3259.35*** *p14*
Fasheira, Joseph; New York, 1807 ***8197.10*** *p51*
Fassaker, Richard; Virginia, 1676 ***1224.1*** *p21*
Fassall, Christopher; New York, 1838 ***8197.10*** *p230*
Fassbender, Maria Magdalena; Port uncertain, 1775 ***2856.30*** *p106*
Fassert, Alex. Friedrich; America, 1751 ***2856.30*** *p106*
Fassler, Maria; Port uncertain, 1728 ***2856.30*** *p126*
  With daughter
Fassler, Therese; Port uncertain, 1781 ***2856.30*** *p126*
Fastex, Macey; Maryland, 1910 ***3259.35*** *p14*
Fasurer, Daniel 30; Ontario, 1871 ***1823.15*** *p77*
Fath, Adam; Port uncertain, 1777 ***2856.30*** *p107*
Fath, Catharina; Port uncertain, 1756 ***2856.30*** *p107*
Fath, Catharina; Port uncertain, 1779 ***2856.30*** *p107*
Fatscher, Peter; New York, 1838 ***8197.10*** *p119*
Fattgers, Mrs. Michael; Port uncertain, 1750 ***2856.30*** *p107*
Faubel, Catharina; Port uncertain, 1765 ***2856.30*** *p107*
Faucett, John; Maryland, 1664 ***2524.55*** *p78*
Faucks, Jerrick; America, 1754 ***2856.30*** *p107*
Faughdelbaug, John; Pennsylvania, 1817 ***6058.10*** *p7*
Faughnau, James 30; Ontario, 1871 ***1823.28*** *p28*
Faught, Lawerence 50; Ontario, 1871 ***1823.28*** *p28*
Fauh, Christopher 28; Ontario, 1871 ***1823.15*** *p77*
Faul, Miss; America, 1764 ***2856.30*** *p107*
Faul, Friedrich; New York, 1840 ***8197.10*** *p165*
Faul, John 63; Ontario, 1871 ***1823.22*** *p51*
Faul, William 18; Ontario, 1861 ***2896.27*** *p18*
Faulhaber, Anna Maria; Port uncertain, 1742 ***2856.30*** *p107*
Faulhaber, Anna Maria; Port uncertain, 1748 ***2856.30*** *p107*
Faulhaber, Michael; New York, 1840 ***8197.10*** *p164*
Faulkener, Mr.; Quebec, 1856 ***9196.15*** *p10*
Faulkener, Mrs.; Quebec, 1856 ***9196.15*** *p10*
Faulkner, Mr.; Quebec, 1857 ***9196.15*** *p16*
Faulkner, Mr.; Quebec, 1858 ***9196.15*** *p36*
Faulkner, Mrs.; Quebec, 1857 ***9196.15*** *p16*
Faulkner, Edw; Virginia, 1664 ***6212.30*** *p12*
Faulkner, Elizabeth *SEE* Faulkner, John
Faulkner, Ephraim; Pennsylvania, 1777 ***4629.10*** *p7*
Faulkner, Francis *SEE* Faulkner, John
Faulkner, George; New York, 1837 ***8197.10*** *p374*
Faulkner, James 20; Philadelphia, 1774 ***1220.25*** *p6*
Faulkner, John *SEE* Faulkner, John
Faulkner, John; Maryland, 1665 ***2524.55*** *p78*
  Wife: Elizabeth
  Child: Francis
  Child: John
  Child: Thomas
Faulkner, Joseph; Pennsylvania, 1777 ***4629.10*** *p18*
Faulkner, Nathaniel; Pennsylvania, 1777 ***4629.10*** *p7*
Faulkner, Sarah E.; Vermont, 1852-1893 ***5900.10*** *p441*
Faulkner, Thomas *SEE* Faulkner, John
Faulkner, Thomas; New York, 1834 ***8197.10*** *p315*
Faulkner, Thomas W.; New York, 1840 ***8197.10*** *p165*
Faulkrode, Philip; Pennsylvania, 1777 ***4629.10*** *p23*
Fauquier, Francis; Virginia, 1771 ***1224.2*** *p40*
Faurbach, Adam; Port uncertain, 1771 ***2856.30*** *p107*
Faure, John P.; New York, 1816 ***8197.10*** *p59*
Faussat, John William; Philadelphia, 1792 ***4629.10*** *p79*
Faust, Henry 49; Ontario, 1871 ***1823.15*** *p77*
Faust, Henry C. 53; Ontario, 1871 ***1823.15*** *p77*
Faust, Johann Nikolaus; Port uncertain, 1776 ***2856.30*** *p107*
Faust, Johann Peter; America, 1750 ***2856.30*** *p107*
Faust, Mathias; Port uncertain, 1764 ***2856.30*** *p107*
Faust, Mrs. Melchior; America, 1739 ***2856.30*** *p107*
  With son
Faust, Philipp; Port uncertain, 1775 ***2856.30*** *p107*
  With wife & children
Fauth, Andreas; Port uncertain, 1754 ***2856.30*** *p107*
Fauth, Johann Jacob; America, 1765 ***2856.30*** *p107*
Fautz, Elisabeth; America, 1738 ***2856.30*** *p107*
Fautzin, Elisabeth; America, 1738 ***2856.30*** *p107*
Favanaugh, Arthur 55; Ontario, 1871 ***1823.22*** *p51*
Favell, James 26; Maryland, 1775 ***1220.25*** *p115*
Favors, Thomas; Virginia, 1671 ***6212.30*** *p44*
Favre, Jean Jacques; Philadelphia, 1791 ***4629.10*** *p61*
Fawceit, Jane 28 *SEE* Fawceit, John
Fawceit, John 29; Nova Scotia, 1774 ***1220.25*** *p15*
  Wife: Jane 28
  Child: Mary 4
Fawceit, Mary 4 *SEE* Fawceit, John
Fawcett, Charles; Savannah, Georgia, 1805 ***1640.10*** *p51*
Fawcett, Joseph; Pennsylvania, 1777 ***4629.10*** *p24*
Fawcett, Thomas 22; Ontario, 1871 ***1823.28*** *p28*
Fawconer, Edward; New England, 1663 ***1224.1*** *p21*
Fawlon, Joseph; Pennsylvania, 1777 ***4629.10*** *p12*
Fawne, Charles; Maryland, 1664 ***2524.55*** *p78*
Fawne, Elizabeth; New England, 1666 ***1224.1*** *p21*
Fawne, Thomas; Virginia, 1652 ***1224.1*** *p21*
Fawsett, Charles *SEE* Fawsett, Rhodah
Fawsett, Elizabeth *SEE* Fawsett, Rhodah
Fawsett, John; Maryland, 1682 ***2524.55*** *p78*
Fawsett, Rhodah; Maryland, 1680 ***2524.55*** *p78*
  Child: Charles
  Child: William
  Child: Thomas
  Child: Elizabeth
Fawsett, Thomas *SEE* Fawsett, Rhodah
Fawsett, William *SEE* Fawsett, Rhodah
Fay, Ann; Vermont, 1830-1883 ***5900.10*** *p322*
Fay, David; New York, 1839 ***8197.10*** *p383*
Fay, Honor McGarry 27; Vermont, 1852 ***5900.10*** *p606*
Fay, John 74; Vermont, 1926 ***5900.10*** *p606*
Fay, John Francis; New York, 1829 ***8197.10*** *p230*
Fay, John Francis; New York, 1832 ***8197.10*** *p68*
Fay, Julia Margaret; New York, New York, 1843 ***1224.3*** *p26*
Fay, Luke; New York, 1821 ***8197.10*** *p229*
Fay, Mary 47; Vermont, 1861 ***5900.10*** *p524*
Fay, Mary 81; Vermont, 1868 ***5900.10*** *p525*
Fay, Rose; Vermont, 1836-1889 ***5900.10*** *p323*
Fay, William; New York, 1819 ***8197.10*** *p228*
Fay, William H. 22; Vermont, 1855 ***5900.10*** *p530*
Fayerweather, Alexander; Pennsylvania, 1785 ***4629.10*** *p48*
Fayne, John 21; Maryland, 1774 ***1220.25*** *p71*
Feagan, William 54; Ontario, 1871 ***1823.15*** *p77*
Feager, D. 24; Ontario, 1861 ***2896.28*** *p15*

Feake, Mary; Maryland, 1665 ***2524.55*** *p98*
Feakes, Sarah; Maryland, 1663 ***2524.55*** *p78*
Fean, Ann 45; Vermont, 1884 ***5900.10*** *p399*
Fean, Edward 66; Vermont, 1905 ***5900.10*** *p399*
Fean, Johanna 74; Vermont, 1918 ***5900.10*** *p425*
Fean, Margaret; Vermont, 1852-1902 ***5900.10*** *p428*
Fean, Mary A. 19; Vermont, 1886 ***5900.10*** *p399*
Fean, Nora 49; Vermont, 1896 ***5900.10*** *p425*
Feany, Cormick; New York, 1827 ***8197.10*** *p229*
Fear, Thomas; Rhode Island, 1781 ***1224.2*** *p40*
Fear, Thomas 49; Ontario, 1871 ***1823.15*** *p77*
Feare, Reynold; Maryland, 1668 ***2524.55*** *p78*
Fearis, Bernard; Pennsylvania, 1777 ***4629.10*** *p24*
Fearnhead, William; New York, 1831 ***8197.10*** *p365*
Fearnley, Anthony; Canada, 1848 ***1224.3*** *p26*
Fearnley, John; New York, 1827 ***8197.10*** *p337*
Featherston, John 26; Ontario, 1871 ***1823.22*** *p51*
Featherstone, John; New York, 1834 ***8197.10*** *p71*
Featherstonehaff, Thomas; New York, 1840 ***8197.10*** *p167*
Featler, Nich; Virginia, 1665-1666 ***6212.30*** *p23*
Featler, Nich; Virginia, 1666-1667 ***6212.30*** *p32*
Featson, Henry 22; Virginia, 1774 ***1220.25*** *p46*
Fecher, Adam; New York, 1838 ***8197.10*** *p231*
Fechtman, Henry; New York, 1821 ***8197.10*** *p229*
Fecy, A. Mertin 77; Ontario, 1871 ***1823.15*** *p78*
Feda, Theodore; Maryland, 1910 ***3259.35*** *p14*
Feder, George Simon; New York, 1840 ***8197.10*** *p165*
Feder, Hans Friedrich; Port uncertain, 1769 ***2856.30*** *p107*
Federenko, Mike; Maryland, 1910 ***3259.35*** *p14*
Federmann, Balthasar; Port uncertain, 1750 ***2856.30*** *p108*
With wife & 4 children
Federmann, Nikolaus; Venezuela, 1542 ***2856.30*** *p107*
Federolff, Nikolas; America, 1754 ***2856.30*** *p108*
With wife & 3 children
Federwolf, Anna Catharina; America, 1752 ***2856.30*** *p108*
With husband & 3 daughters
Federwolf, Johann; America, 1752 ***2856.30*** *p108*
With wife & 3 daughters
Fee, Catherine; Vermont, 1856-1926 ***5900.10*** *p443*
Fee, Edward 45; Ontario, 1871 ***1823.15*** *p78*
Fee, James 48; Ontario, 1871 ***1823.22*** *p51*
Fee, James 83; Vermont, 1897 ***5900.10*** *p228*
Fee, Katherine McGinn; Vermont, 1822-1919 ***5900.10*** *p228*
Fee, Mary 71; Vermont, 1904 ***5900.10*** *p487*
Fee, Michael 78; Ontario, 1871 ***1823.22*** *p51*
Fee, Robert; New York, 1807 ***8197.10*** *p43*
Fee, Thomas 38; Ontario, 1871 ***1823.22*** *p51*
Fee, Walter 42; Ontario, 1871 ***1823.15*** *p78*
Fee, William 60; Ontario, 1871 ***1823.15*** *p78*
Feebey, Edward; Maryland, 1666 ***2524.55*** *p171*
Feedes, Henry; Maryland, 1666 ***2524.55*** *p78*
Feehan, Patrick 50; Ontario, 1871 ***1823.22*** *p51*
Feek, Charles; New York, 1806 ***8197.10*** *p323*
Feeld, Hannah; Maryland, 1666 ***2524.55*** *p78*
Feeley, Mary; Vermont, 1838-1911 ***5900.10*** *p466*
Feely, Cornelius 60; Ontario, 1871 ***1823.22*** *p51*
Feely, Thomas 40; Ontario, 1871 ***1823.28*** *p28*
Feeney, Edward 36; New York, 1833-1840 ***8197.10*** *p165*
Feeney, Esther; Vermont, 1862-1950 ***5900.10*** *p163*
Feeney, John; New York, 1840 ***8197.10*** *p165*
Feeney, Thomas; New York, 1837 ***8197.10*** *p89*
Feeny, John 50; Ontario, 1871 ***1823.22*** *p51*
Feeston, John; Pennsylvania, 1777 ***4629.10*** *p16*
Fegan, Patrick; New York, 1827 ***8197.10*** *p346*
Fehland, Mr.; Portland, Maine, 1857 ***9196.15*** *p12*
Fehlinger, Hans Philipp; America, 1744 ***2856.30*** *p108*
Fehlinger, Johann; Port uncertain, 1781 ***2856.30*** *p108*
Fehner, Johann Georg; Port uncertain, 1738 ***2856.30*** *p108*
Fehr, Andreas; America, 1738 ***2856.30*** *p108*
Fehr, Johann; Port uncertain, 1769 ***2856.30*** *p108*
Feighelle, Mary 40; Vermont, 1844 ***5900.10*** *p148*
Feighoney, Ann; Vermont, n.d. ***5900.10*** *p155*
Feighoney, Thomas; Vermont, n.d. ***5900.10*** *p155*
Feigler, Catharina; Port uncertain, 1769 ***2856.30*** *p108*
Feil, Andrew 6; Kansas, 1905-1910 ***9079.10*** *p17*
Feil, Andrew 21; Kansas, 1896-1910 ***9079.10*** *p14*
Feil, Andrew 59; Kansas, 1896-1910 ***9079.10*** *p14*
Feil, Andrew L. 35; Kansas, 1905-1910 ***9079.10*** *p17*
Feil, David 10; Kansas, 1905-1910 ***9079.10*** *p17*
Feil, David 25; Kansas, 1896-1910 ***9079.10*** *p14*
Feil, Julia 22; Kansas, 1891-1910 ***9079.10*** *p14*
Feil, Mary 31; Kansas, 1905-1910 ***9079.10*** *p17*
Feil, Mary 56; Kansas, 1905-1910 ***9079.10*** *p17*
Feil, Peter Hinrich; New York, 1828 ***8197.10*** *p230*
Feil, Wilhelm; America, 1749 ***2856.30*** *p108*
With wife & 3 children
Feild, Edw; Virginia, 1665-1666 ***6212.30*** *p21*
Feild, John; Maryland, 1655 ***2524.55*** *p78*
Feild, Mary; Virginia, 1664 ***6212.30*** *p11*
Feilding, Edgar; Virginia, 1667-1668 ***6212.30*** *p38*
Feilding, Miles; Virginia, 1667-1668 ***6212.30*** *p39*
Feilding, Tho; Virginia, 1665-1666 ***6212.30*** *p24*
Feiler, Catharina; Port uncertain, 1768 ***2856.30*** *p108*
Feindel, Andreas; Port uncertain, 1736 ***2856.30*** *p108*
Feiner, Michael; Port uncertain, 1763 ***2856.30*** *p108*
Feinnan, Joseph; New York, 1838 ***8197.10*** *p377*
Feinthel, Georg Jakob; Canada, 1754 ***2856.30*** *p108*
Feir, Eliza 48; Ontario, 1871 ***1823.22*** *p51*
Feist, Michael Charles; New York, 1839 ***8197.10*** *p231*
Feistel, Anthony; New York, 1836 ***8197.10*** *p75*
Feit, Jacob; Pennsylvania, 1777 ***4629.10*** *p10*
Feiter, Christian; New Orleans, 1852 ***6058.10*** *p47*
Feix, Michael; Port uncertain, 1766 ***2856.30*** *p108*
With wife & 5 children
Fela, John; Maryland, 1910 ***3259.35*** *p14*
Feld, Konrad; Port uncertain, 1750 ***2856.30*** *p108*
Feld, Richard; Virginia, 1663 ***6212.30*** *p2*
Feldberger, Melchior; Port uncertain, 1764 ***2856.30*** *p108*
Felder, Franz Xaver; Port uncertain, 1773 ***2856.30*** *p108*
Feldmann, Johann Kilian; Port uncertain, 1751 ***2856.30*** *p108*
Feldtmann, Anna Eva Margar; Port uncertain, 1758 ***2856.30*** *p108*
Felk, Konrad; Port uncertain, 1750 ***2856.30*** *p108*
Felkner, George; Pennsylvania, 1777 ***4629.10*** *p8*
Fell, Edward; Maryland, 1657 ***2524.55*** *p79*
Fell, Franz Martin; Port uncertain, 1780 ***2856.30*** *p108*
Fell, Frederick 49; Ontario, 1871 ***1823.15*** *p78*
Fell, George 48; Ontario, 1871 ***1823.15*** *p78*
Fell, James; New York, 1818 ***8197.10*** *p228*
Fell, James; Virginia, 1704 ***1224.2*** *p40*
Fell, Margaret; Vermont, 1842-1919 ***5900.10*** *p419*
Fell, Margarete; America, 1754 ***2856.30*** *p108*
Fell, Pete 27; British Columbia, 1909 ***9196.1*** *p28*
Fell, Pete 27; Washington, 1909 ***9196.1*** *p28*
Fell, Thomas; Pennsylvania, 1777 ***4629.10*** *p6*
Felland, William 37; Ontario, 1871 ***1823.15*** *p78*
Fellentzer, Nicolas; Port uncertain, 1768 ***2856.30*** *p108*
Fellenzer, Elis. Catharina; Port uncertain, 1784 ***2856.30*** *p108*
Fellers, Sarah 22; Ontario, 1861 ***2896.26*** *p37*
Felles, Matthew; Pennsylvania, 1777 ***4629.10*** *p24*
Felleter, William 67; Ontario, 1871 ***1823.28*** *p28*
Fellett, Abell; Maryland, 1660 ***2524.55*** *p79*
Fellett, Abell; Maryland, 1660 ***2524.55*** *p81*
Fellett, Thomas 22; Philadelphia, 1774 ***1220.25*** *p4*
Felley, John 17; Maryland, 1774 ***1220.25*** *p7*
Fellgate, James 24; Philadelphia, 1774 ***1220.25*** *p43*
Fellgate, Tobias; Virginia, 1635 ***1224.1*** *p21*
Fellmoore, Edw; Virginia, 1664 ***6212.30*** *p14*
Felloon, Arthur; New York, 1840 ***8197.10*** *p166*
Fellow, Daniell; Maryland, 1670 ***2524.55*** *p79*
Fellowes, William; Virginia, 1682 ***1224.1*** *p21*
Fellows, Joseph 39; Maryland, 1775 ***1220.25*** *p113*
Fellows, S. M. 23; Ontario, 1861 ***2896.26*** *p25*
Fells, Samuel 39; Ontario, 1871 ***1823.15*** *p78*
Fels, Henrich; Port uncertain, 1784 ***2856.30*** *p109*
With wife
Felstead, Elizabeth; Maryland, 1680 ***2524.55*** *p79*
Felter, Hans Jurg; America, 1738 ***2856.30*** *p109*
Felton, Eli, Jr.; New York, 1840 ***8197.10*** *p164*
Felton, George; New York, 1840 ***8197.10*** *p164*
Felton, Katherine; Maryland, 1653-1657 ***2524.55*** *p79*
Felton, Philip; Maryland, 1653-1657 ***2524.55*** *p79*
Felton, Thomas 21; Virginia, 1774 ***1220.25*** *p89*
Feltonaen, H. 31; Alaska, 1917 ***9196.1*** *p48*
Feltonaen, H. 31; Whitehorse, Yukon, 1917 ***9196.1*** *p48*
Feltus, Henry James; New York, 1810 ***8197.10*** *p57*
Feltz, Harman 21; Ontario, 1871 ***1823.28*** *p28*
Fen, David; Pennsylvania, 1777 ***4629.10*** *p23*
Fenan, Felix; New York, 1818 ***8197.10*** *p228*
Fenby, Robert 26; Nova Scotia, 1774 ***1220.25*** *p14*
Fenchel, Lorenz; Port uncertain, 1762 ***2856.30*** *p109*
Fend, John; Maryland, 1659 ***2524.55*** *p79*
Fendall, Josias; Maryland, 1658 ***2524.55*** *p79*
Wife: Mary
Fendall, Mary *SEE* Fendall, Josias
Fendi, Joseph Gustave; New York, 1839 ***8197.10*** *p130*
Feneick, Peter; Pennsylvania, 1777 ***4629.10*** *p27*
Fenelly, Nicholas; New York, 1839 ***8197.10*** *p231*
Fenen, Thomas 46; Ontario, 1871 ***1823.15*** *p78*
Fenerty, Peter 56; Ontario, 1871 ***1823.28*** *p28*
Fenex, George; Maryland, 1653 ***2524.55*** *p79*
Fenigan, Daniel 55; New York, New York, 1849 ***1825.45*** *p49*
Wife: Johanna 48
Daughter: Johanna 20
Daughter: Judy 7
Daughter: Mary 22
Daughter: Kitty 10
Fenigan, Johanna 20 *SEE* Fenigan, Daniel
Fenigan, Johanna 48 *SEE* Fenigan, Daniel
Fenigan, Judy 7 *SEE* Fenigan, Daniel
Fenigan, Kitty 10 *SEE* Fenigan, Daniel
Fenigan, Mary 22 *SEE* Fenigan, Daniel
Fenkel, Nicolaus; America, 1763 ***2856.30*** *p109*
Fenkel, Nicolaus; America, 1783 ***2856.30*** *p109*
Fenn, Benjamin; Connecticut, 1675 ***1224.1*** *p21*
Fenn, Deborah; Boston, 1649 ***1224.1*** *p2*
Fenn, James; Norfolk, Virginia, 1794 ***1224.2*** *p40*
Fenn, Jno; Virginia, 1703-1704 ***6212.30*** *p62*
Fenn, John; New York, 1840 ***8197.10*** *p166*
Fenn, John; Virginia, 1663 ***6212.30*** *p3*
Fenn, Stephen 22; Georgia, 1774 ***1220.25*** *p48*
Fenn, Thomas; Maryland, 1679 ***2524.55*** *p79*
Fennegan, Mary Tierney 57; Vermont, 1872 ***5900.10*** *p475*
Fennell, Abel 81; Ontario, 1871 ***1823.22*** *p51*
Fennell, Arthur; New York, 1830 ***8197.10*** *p361*
Fennell, James; Philadelphia, 1817 ***1224.3*** *p26*
Fennell, Wm; Virginia, 1666 ***6212.30*** *p26*
Fennemore, Joseph; Maryland, 1668 ***2524.55*** *p79*
Fennemore, Peter; Pennsylvania, 1779 ***4629.10*** *p37*
Fenner, Ann Reeve; Baltimore, 1848 ***1224.3*** *p26*
Fenner, Joseph; New York, 1838 ***8197.10*** *p231*
Fenner, Jost H.; New York, New York, 1867 ***3437.14*** *p106*
Fenner, Margaret; Rochester, New York, 1854 ***1224.3*** *p26*
Fenner, William; New York, 1838 ***8197.10*** *p119*
Fennicks, Margaret 40; Ontario, 1871 ***1823.22*** *p51*
Fennie, Richard; Maryland, 1638-1643 ***2524.55*** *p79*
Fenning, James 21; America, 1774 ***1220.25*** *p36*
Fenning, John 28; Maryland, 1774 ***1220.25*** *p54*
Fenninge, William; Died enroute, 1623 ***1224.1*** *p21*
Fennis, Richard; Maryland, 1638-1643 ***2524.55*** *p79*
Fenson, Isaac; Maryland, 1668 ***2524.55*** *p79*
Fenstermacher, Jakob; America, 1738 ***2856.30*** *p109*
Fenstermacher, Mathes; America, 1738 ***2856.30*** *p109*
With wife
Fenton, Bartholomew; Vermont, 1843-1923 ***5900.10*** *p405*
Fenton, Daniel 33; Alaska, 1913 ***9196.1*** *p20*
Fenton, Daniel 33; British Columbia, 1913 ***9196.1*** *p20*
Fenton, Elaine Fitzgerald 71; Vermont, 1893 ***5900.10*** *p110*
Fenton, Eliza Ann; Vermont, 1843-1927 ***5900.10*** *p109*
Fenton, Eliza T.; Vermont, 1842-1923 ***5900.10*** *p117*
Fenton, James; Florida, 1767 ***1640.10*** *p51*
Fenton, Jeremiah; Vermont, 1818-1894 ***5900.10*** *p431*
Fenton, John 36; Ontario, 1871 ***1823.22*** *p51*
Fenton, John 76; Ontario, 1871 ***1823.22*** *p51*
Fenton, John A.; Vermont, 1856-1940 ***5900.10*** *p118*
Fenton, Joseph 90; Vermont, 1901 ***5900.10*** *p110*
Fenton, Katie A. Doolin 31; Vermont, 1887 ***5900.10*** *p121*
Fenton, Martha; Vermont, 1868-1914 ***5900.10*** *p405*
Fenton, Martha Griffin; Vermont, 1851-1880 ***5900.10*** *p405*
Fenton, Mary 9; Halifax, Nova Scotia, 1775 ***1220.25*** *p22*
Fenton, Mary 70; Vermont, 1880 ***5900.10*** *p347*
Fenton, Mary E.; Vermont, 1847-1940 ***5900.10*** *p119*
Fenton, Mary Ferriter 78; Vermont, 1891 ***5900.10*** *p121*
Fenton, Michael 39; Vermont, 1857 ***5900.10*** *p347*
Fenton, Nellie Dooling; Vermont, 1859-1943 ***5900.10*** *p118*
Fenton, Patrick J.; Vermont, 1846-1931 ***5900.10*** *p119*
Fenton, Patrick Joseph; Vermont, 1841-1916 ***5900.10*** *p116*
Fenton, Richard; Savannah, Georgia, 1774 ***1640.10*** *p51*
Fenton, Richard 26; Savannah, Georgia, 1774 ***1220.25*** *p139*
With wife & children
Fenton, Samuel; New York, 1807 ***8197.10*** *p330*
Fenton, Sarah 15; Halifax, Nova Scotia, 1775 ***1220.25*** *p22*
Fenton, Sarah Frances Hart; Vermont, 1848-1898 ***5900.10*** *p116*
Fenton, Thomas 15; Philadelphia, 1774 ***1220.25*** *p81*
Fenton, Thomas 52; Vermont, 1904 ***5900.10*** *p121*
Fenton, William 23; Maryland, 1775 ***1220.25*** *p99*
Fenton, William 45; Ontario, 1871 ***1823.15*** *p78*
Fenwick, Cornelius C.; New York, 1840 ***8197.10*** *p164*
Fenwick, Edward 28; Fort Cumberland, Nova Scotia, 1774 ***1220.25*** *p17*
Fenwick, Harriet 26; Ontario, 1871 ***1823.15*** *p78*
Fenwick, John; New York, 1830 ***8197.10*** *p360*
Fenwick, John 28; Ontario, 1871 ***1823.28*** *p28*
Fenwick, John 29; Ontario, 1871 ***1823.15*** *p78*
Fenwick, Mathew 16; Fort Cumberland, Nova Scotia, 1774 ***1220.25*** *p19*
Fenwick, Robert; New York, 1780 ***1224.2*** *p40*
Fenwick, Thomas; New York, 1804 ***8197.10*** *p27*
Fenwick, Thomas 26; Ontario, 1871 ***1823.15*** *p78*

Fenwick, William; Boston, 1763 ***1224.2*** *p40*
Fenwick, William 32; Ontario, 1871 ***1823.15*** *p78*
Fenwicke, John; South Carolina, n.d. ***1224.2*** *p40*
Fenworth, John; Maryland, 1659 ***2524.55*** *p79*
Ferand, Charles 43; Ontario, 1871 ***1823.15*** *p78*
Ferand, Sarah 74; Ontario, 1871 ***1823.15*** *p78*
Ferand, Zatus 80; Ontario, 1871 ***1823.15*** *p78*
Ferara, Vicenzo Francisco; New York, 1838 ***8197.10*** *p119*
Ferard, Martin 54; Ontario, 1871 ***1823.28*** *p28*
Fercy, Peter 25; Maryland, 1774 ***1220.25*** *p59*
Ferdinandez, Pedro; Maryland, 1670 ***2524.55*** *p79*
Ference, Mary; Maryland, 1910 ***3259.35*** *p14*
Ferencz, Peter; Maryland, 1910 ***3259.35*** *p14*
Ferer, David 35; Ontario, 1871 ***1823.28*** *p28*
Fergason, Charity 54; Ontario, 1861 ***2896.26*** *p20*
Fergason, Cornelia A. 25; Ontario, 1861 ***2896.26*** *p20*
Fergason, Elizabeth 27; Ontario, 1861 ***2896.26*** *p20*
Fergason, Hester 23; Ontario, 1861 ***2896.26*** *p22*
Fergason, James M. 3; Ontario, 1861 ***2896.26*** *p22*
Fergason, Jane 1; Ontario, 1861 ***2896.26*** *p22*
Fergason, John F. 10; Ontario, 1861 ***2896.26*** *p20*
Fergason, Phebe Jane 30; Ontario, 1861 ***2896.26*** *p20*
Fergason, William H. 17; Ontario, 1861 ***2896.26*** *p20*
Fergerson, Angus 51; Ontario, 1871 ***1823.28*** *p28*
Fergie, Alexander 53; Ontario, 1871 ***1823.15*** *p78*
Fergupon, James 39; Ontario, 1871 ***1823.15*** *p78*
Fergupon, Peter 63; Ontario, 1871 ***1823.15*** *p78*
Fergurson, Minerva 63; Vermont, 1870 ***5900.10*** *p293*
Fergurson, Willard 43; Vermont, 1861 ***5900.10*** *p293*
Fergus, John 61; Ontario, 1871 ***1823.28*** *p28*
Fergus, Patrick 22; Ontario, 1871 ***1823.28*** *p28*
Ferguson, . . .; Boston, 1765 ***4628.40*** *p114*
Ferguson, Mr.; Quebec, 1856 ***9196.15*** *p6*
Ferguson, Mr.; Quebec, 1858 ***9196.15*** *p43*
Ferguson, A. 20; Ontario, 1861 ***2896.28*** *p1*
Ferguson, Adam; Newport, Rhode Island, 1802 ***1224.3*** *p26*
Ferguson, Adam 57; Ontario, 1871 ***1823.15*** *p78*
Ferguson, Agnes 8; Ontario, 1861 ***2896.27*** *p27*
Ferguson, Agnes 66; Ontario, 1871 ***1823.15*** *p78*
Ferguson, Alex 34; Ontario, 1871 ***1823.22*** *p51*
Ferguson, Alexander *SEE* Ferguson, Archie
Ferguson, Alexander *SEE* Ferguson, John
Ferguson, Alexander; Georgia, 1699 ***1640.13*** *p37*
Ferguson, Alexander; Georgia, 1775 ***1640.10*** *p51*
Ferguson, Alexander; Jamaica, 1836 ***1640.13*** *p38*
Ferguson, Alexander 24; Ontario, 1871 ***1823.22*** *p51*
Ferguson, Angus *SEE* Ferguson, Donald
Ferguson, Angus *SEE* Ferguson, Kenneth
Ferguson, Angus *SEE* Ferguson, Ranald
Ferguson, Angus; Nova Scotia, 1820-1829 ***4537.35*** *p12*
Brother: Donald
Brother: Norman
Ferguson, Angus; Nova Scotia, 1828 ***4537.35*** *p11*
Wife: Margaret Morrison
Ferguson, Ann; Alabama, 1820-1845 ***1640.10*** *p51*
Ferguson, Ann; Nova Scotia, 1840-1849 ***4537.35*** *p29*
Ferguson, Ann 63; Vermont, 1875 ***5900.10*** *p374*
Ferguson, Anna 7; Ontario, 1861 ***2896.26*** *p18*
Ferguson, Annetta A. 3; Ontario, 1861 ***2896.27*** *p23*
Ferguson, Annie; Vermont, 1817-1904 ***5900.10*** *p249*
Ferguson, Archibald 51; Ontario, 1871 ***1823.15*** *p78*
Ferguson, Archie; Saskatchewan, 1889 ***4537.35*** *p65*
Wife: Mary MacLeod
Child: Jane
Child: Alexander
Child: Joan
Child: Marion
Ferguson, Barbara 60; Ontario, 1871 ***1823.15*** *p78*
Ferguson, Benjamin; Pennsylvania, 1854 ***6058.10*** *p33*
Ferguson, Benjamin 26; Ontario, 1861 ***2896.28*** *p20*
Ferguson, C. 4; Ontario, 1861 ***2896.25*** *p43*
Ferguson, C. A. 10; Ontario, 1861 ***2896.28*** *p1*
Ferguson, Catherine *SEE* Ferguson, Kenneth
Ferguson, Catherine *SEE* Ferguson, Kirsty Laing
Ferguson, Catherine *SEE* Ferguson, Malcolm
Ferguson, Catherine *SEE* Ferguson, Neil
Ferguson, Catherine; Nova Scotia, 1840-1849 ***4537.37*** *p9*
Child: Donald
Child: Flora
Child: Neil
Child: Isabella
Child: Marion
Child: Fergus
Ferguson, Catherine; Port uncertain, 1850-1859 ***4537.37*** *p118*
Ferguson, Catherine 27; Ontario, 1861 ***2896.27*** *p27*
Ferguson, Catherine Robertson *SEE* Ferguson, Roderick
Ferguson, Charles; New York, 1807 ***8197.10*** *p42*
Ferguson, Charles 70; Ontario, 1871 ***1823.22*** *p51*
Ferguson, D. A. 46; Ontario, 1861 ***2896.28*** *p1*
Ferguson, Daniel; Savannah, Georgia, 1805 ***1640.10*** *p51*
Ferguson, Daniel 27; Ontario, 1871 ***1823.15*** *p78*
Ferguson, Daniel 56; Ontario, 1861 ***2896.26*** *p19*
Ferguson, David 22; Ontario, 1861 ***2896.28*** *p58*
Ferguson, David 32; Ontario, 1871 ***1823.22*** *p51*
Ferguson, David 48; Ontario, 1871 ***1823.15*** *p78*
Ferguson, Donald *SEE* Ferguson, Angus
Ferguson, Donald *SEE* Ferguson, Catherine
Ferguson, Donald *SEE* Ferguson, Donald
Ferguson, Donald *SEE* Ferguson, John
Ferguson, Donald *SEE* Ferguson, Kirsty Laing
Ferguson, Donald *SEE* Ferguson, Malcolm
Ferguson, Donald *SEE* Ferguson, Roderick
Ferguson, Donald; Nova Scotia, 1840-1849 ***4537.35*** *p11*
Wife: Una
Child: Kenneth
Son: Donald
Child: Marion
Child: Hugh
Son: Angus
Child: Margaret
Ferguson, Donald; Port uncertain, 1860-1869 ***4537.35*** *p78*
Wife: Mary MacLeod
Child: Malcolm
Ferguson, Donald 34; Ontario, 1871 ***1823.22*** *p52*
Ferguson, Donald 52; Ontario, 1871 ***1823.22*** *p52*
Ferguson, Duncan; Idaho, 1894 ***1640.13*** *p38*
Ferguson, Duncan 51; Ontario, 1871 ***1823.28*** *p28*
Ferguson, Duncan 52; Ontario, 1871 ***1823.28*** *p28*
Ferguson, Duncan 60; Ontario, 1871 ***1823.15*** *p78*
Ferguson, E. J. 12; Ontario, 1861 ***2896.28*** *p1*
Ferguson, Edward H. 1; Ontario, 1861 ***2896.28*** *p20*
Ferguson, Effie *SEE* Ferguson, Neil
Ferguson, Effie *SEE* Ferguson, Ranald
Ferguson, Eliza *SEE* Ferguson, Ranald
Ferguson, Eliza 9; Ontario, 1871 ***1823.22*** *p52*
Ferguson, Elizabeth 24; Ontario, 1861 ***2896.27*** *p12*
Ferguson, Elizabeth 31; Ontario, 1861 ***2896.28*** *p21*
Ferguson, Elizabeth 46; Ontario, 1861 ***2896.27*** *p12*
Ferguson, Elizabeth 93; Ontario, 1861 ***2896.26*** *p19*
Ferguson, Emelia S. 3; Ontario, 1861 ***2896.27*** *p12*
Ferguson, Emily; Ontario, 1849 ***4537.37*** *p52*
Ferguson, Fergus *SEE* Ferguson, Catherine
Ferguson, Fidelia 5; Ontario, 1861 ***2896.25*** *p13*
Ferguson, Flora *SEE* Ferguson, Catherine
Ferguson, Flora *SEE* Ferguson, Malcolm
Ferguson, Frank 40; Ontario, 1871 ***1823.15*** *p78*
Ferguson, George; Georgia, 1737 ***1640.10*** *p51*
Ferguson, George 5; Ontario, 1861 ***2896.27*** *p27*
Ferguson, George 6; Ontario, 1861 ***2896.25*** *p43*
Ferguson, George 18; Ontario, 1861 ***2896.28*** *p20*
Ferguson, Gilbert 32; Ontario, 1861 ***2896.27*** *p23*
Ferguson, H. 20; Jamaica, 1773 ***1220.25*** *p28*
Ferguson, Henry; Georgia, 1783 ***1640.10*** *p51*
Ferguson, Henry; New Orleans, 1859 ***1640.10*** *p51*
Ferguson, Henry; New Orleans, 1859 ***1640.13*** *p38*
Ferguson, Hermon 10; Ontario, 1861 ***2896.27*** *p12*
Ferguson, Hugh *SEE* Ferguson, Donald
Ferguson, Hugh; New York, 1820 ***8197.10*** *p228*
Ferguson, Ida A. 3; Ontario, 1861 ***2896.28*** *p20*
Ferguson, Isaac 59; Ontario, 1861 ***2896.27*** *p23*
Ferguson, Isabel; Tennessee, 1815 ***1640.10*** *p51*
Ferguson, Isabella *SEE* Ferguson, Catherine
Ferguson, James; Georgia, 1698 ***1640.13*** *p38*
Ferguson, James; Louisiana, 1807-1812 ***1640.10*** *p52*
Ferguson, James; New York, 1837 ***8197.10*** *p89*
Ferguson, James; Pennsylvania, 1777 ***4629.10*** *p31*
Ferguson, James; Texas, 1735-1845 ***1640.10*** *p52*
Ferguson, James 33; Ontario, 1871 ***1823.15*** *p78*
Ferguson, James 33; Ontario, 1871 ***1823.28*** *p28*
Ferguson, James 38; Ontario, 1871 ***1823.15*** *p78*
Ferguson, James 64; Ontario, 1861 ***2896.28*** *p58*
Ferguson, James 72; Ontario, 1871 ***1823.22*** *p52*
Ferguson, James A. 7; Ontario, 1861 ***2896.25*** *p43*
Ferguson, Jane *SEE* Ferguson, Archie
Ferguson, Jane 51; Ontario, 1861 ***2896.25*** *p57*
Ferguson, Jane 65; Ontario, 1871 ***1823.15*** *p78*
Ferguson, Janet; Prince Edward Island, 1848 ***4537.37*** *p26*
Ferguson, Joan *SEE* Ferguson, Archie
Ferguson, John *SEE* Ferguson, Kirsty Laing
Ferguson, John *SEE* Ferguson, Neil
Ferguson, John *SEE* Ferguson, Roderick
Ferguson, John; Kingston, Jamaica, 1856 ***1640.13*** *p38*
Ferguson, John; New York, 1802 ***8197.10*** *p20*
Ferguson, John; New York, 1807 ***8197.10*** *p42*
Ferguson, John; New York, 1818 ***8197.10*** *p228*
Ferguson, John; New York, 1840 ***8197.10*** *p165*
Ferguson, John; Nova Scotia, 1820-1829 ***4537.35*** *p11*
With wife
Child: Alexander
Child: Peter
Ferguson, John; Nova Scotia, 1820-1829 ***4537.35*** *p11*
Wife: Margaret Shaw
Child: Donald
Ferguson, John; Pennsylvania, 1777 ***4629.10*** *p14*
Ferguson, John; Saskatchewan, 1883 ***4537.37*** *p90*
Ferguson, John 30; Ontario, 1871 ***1823.15*** *p78*
Ferguson, John 31; Ontario, 1871 ***1823.28*** *p28*
Ferguson, John 47; Ontario, 1861 ***2896.25*** *p57*
Ferguson, John B. 9; Ontario, 1861 ***2896.28*** *p21*
Ferguson, John Proctor; Chicago, 1900 ***1640.13*** *p38*
Ferguson, Joseph; Pennsylvania, 1777 ***4629.10*** *p10*
Ferguson, Joseph; Vermont, 1836-1913 ***5900.10*** *p464*
Ferguson, Josephine 2; Ontario, 1861 ***2896.25*** *p13*
Ferguson, Kellen 35; Ontario, 1871 ***1823.15*** *p78*
Ferguson, Kenneth *SEE* Ferguson, Donald
Ferguson, Kenneth *SEE* Ferguson, Kenneth
Ferguson, Kenneth *SEE* Ferguson, Ranald
Ferguson, Kenneth *SEE* Ferguson, Roderick
Ferguson, Kenneth; Nova Scotia, 1820-1829 ***4537.35*** *p11*
Wife: Catherine
Child: Angus
Child: Rachel
Child: Kenneth
Ferguson, Kirsty; Nova Scotia, 1840-1849 ***4537.35*** *p32*
Ferguson, Kirsty Laing; Nova Scotia, 1840-1849 ***4537.37*** *p9*
Child: John
Child: Donald
Child: Catherine
Child: Malcolm
Child: Mary
Child: Peter
Ferguson, Kirsty MacDermid *SEE* Ferguson, Ranald
Ferguson, Kirsty MacDermid *SEE* Ferguson, Roderick
Ferguson, Lucy A. 20; Ontario, 1861 ***2896.27*** *p23*
Ferguson, M. A. 36; Ontario, 1861 ***2896.25*** *p43*
Ferguson, M. E. 18; Ontario, 1861 ***2896.28*** *p1*
Ferguson, Malcolm *SEE* Ferguson, Donald
Ferguson, Malcolm *SEE* Ferguson, Kirsty Laing
Ferguson, Malcolm; Nova Scotia, 1840-1849 ***4537.35*** *p11*
Wife: Mary Morrison
Child: Flora
Child: Rachel
Child: Catherine
Child: Mary
Child: Margaret
Child: Donald
Ferguson, Manley 1; Ontario, 1861 ***2896.27*** *p27*
Ferguson, Margaret *SEE* Ferguson, Donald
Ferguson, Margaret *SEE* Ferguson, Malcolm
Ferguson, Margaret *SEE* Ferguson, Neil
Ferguson, Margaret *SEE* Ferguson, Roderick
Ferguson, Margaret; Nova Scotia, 1840-1849 ***4537.35*** *p28*
Ferguson, Margaret 67; Ontario, 1871 ***1823.15*** *p78*
Ferguson, Margaret A. 32; Ontario, 1861 ***2896.25*** *p13*
Ferguson, Margaret Morrison *SEE* Ferguson, Angus
Ferguson, Margaret Shaw *SEE* Ferguson, John
Ferguson, Maria 52; Ontario, 1861 ***2896.27*** *p37*
Ferguson, Marion *SEE* Ferguson, Archie
Ferguson, Marion *SEE* Ferguson, Catherine
Ferguson, Marion *SEE* Ferguson, Donald
Ferguson, Marion *SEE* Ferguson, Neil
Ferguson, Marion *SEE* Ferguson, Roderick
Ferguson, Marion; Port uncertain, 1860-1869 ***4537.35*** *p80*
Ferguson, Marjory; Port uncertain, 1850-1859 ***4537.37*** *p123*
Ferguson, Mary *SEE* Ferguson, Kirsty Laing
Ferguson, Mary *SEE* Ferguson, Malcolm
Ferguson, Mary *SEE* Ferguson, Neil
Ferguson, Mary *SEE* Ferguson, Ranald
Ferguson, Mary; Georgia, 1821-1845 ***1640.10*** *p52*
Ferguson, Mary; Nova Scotia, 1826-1829 ***4537.35*** *p20*
Ferguson, Mary; Vermont, 1861-1939 ***5900.10*** *p464*
Ferguson, Mary 11; Ontario, 1861 ***2896.28*** *p58*
Ferguson, Mary 53; Ontario, 1861 ***2896.27*** *p12*
Ferguson, Mary 62; Ontario, 1861 ***2896.28*** *p58*
Ferguson, Mary 72; Ontario, 1871 ***1823.22*** *p52*
Ferguson, Mary Hanning 71; Vermont, 1890 ***5900.10*** *p466*
Ferguson, Mary L. 9; Ontario, 1861 ***2896.25*** *p13*
Ferguson, Mary MacLeod *SEE* Ferguson, Archie
Ferguson, Mary MacLeod *SEE* Ferguson, Donald
Ferguson, Mary Morrison *SEE* Ferguson, Malcolm
Ferguson, Michael; New York, 1820 ***8197.10*** *p228*
Ferguson, Miriam 22; Ontario, 1861 ***2896.28*** *p20*
Ferguson, Neil *SEE* Ferguson, Catherine
Ferguson, Neil; Port uncertain, 1840-1849 ***4537.37*** *p107*
Wife: Effie
Child: Marion
Child: Margaret

Field, Thomas 32; Ontario, 1871 ***1823.22*** *p52*
Field, William 25; Ontario, 1871 ***1823.28*** *p28*
Field, William 28; Ontario, 1861 ***2896.26*** *p1*
Field, William 43; Ontario, 1871 ***1823.22*** *p52*
Fieldhouse, Henry 60; Ontario, 1871 ***1823.22*** *p52*
Fielding, Ambrose; Virginia, 1675 ***1224.1*** *p21*
Fielding, Arnistead 42; Nova Scotia, 1774 ***1220.25*** *p14*
Wife: Elizabeth 40
Child: John 15
Child: Nicholas 12
Child: Esther 5
Child: Joseph 2
Child: Hannah 8
Child: William 14
Fielding, Cornelius; Maryland, 1783 ***1224.2*** *p40*
Fielding, Elizabeth 40 *SEE* Fielding, Arnistead
Fielding, Esther 5 *SEE* Fielding, Arnistead
Fielding, Hannah 8 *SEE* Fielding, Arnistead
Fielding, Henry; Maryland, 1681 ***2524.55*** *p79*
Fielding, Henry; Virginia, 1712 ***1224.2*** *p40*
Fielding, Jeremiah; New York, 1837 ***8197.10*** *p88*
Fielding, John; Illinois, 1845 ***1224.3*** *p26*
Fielding, John 15 *SEE* Fielding, Arnistead
Fielding, Joseph 2 *SEE* Fielding, Arnistead
Fielding, Magdlena 45; Ontario, 1871 ***1823.15*** *p79*
Fielding, Nicholas 12 *SEE* Fielding, Arnistead
Fielding, Robert; New York, 1837 ***8197.10*** *p89*
Fielding, William 14 *SEE* Fielding, Arnistead
Fier, William 70; Ontario, 1871 ***1823.22*** *p52*
Fieron, John Lewis; Pennsylvania, 1792 ***4629.10*** *p63*
Fierrier, John Peter; New York, 1838 ***8197.10*** *p231*
Fiers, James; Virginia, 1664 ***6212.30*** *p11*
Fieser, Christina; Port uncertain, 1774 ***2856.30*** *p111*
With husband
Fieser, Georg; Port uncertain, 1770 ***2856.30*** *p111*
Fieser, Georg; Port uncertain, 1774 ***2856.30*** *p111*
Fiess, Johann Michael; Port uncertain, 1733 ***2856.30*** *p111*
Fiethinger, Johann Philipp; Port uncertain, 1753 ***2856.30*** *p111*
Fife, Alexander 24; Jamaica, 1774 ***1220.25*** *p49*
Fife, Amos E. 49; Ontario, 1871 ***1823.22*** *p52*
Fife, Charles 32; Ontario, 1871 ***1823.28*** *p28*
Fife, Lawrence 34; Ontario, 1871 ***1823.15*** *p79*
Figel, John; Pennsylvania, 1777 ***4629.10*** *p13*
Figg, William 19; Virginia, 1775 ***1220.25*** *p109*
Figner, Paul; Pennsylvania, 1777 ***4629.10*** *p12*
Filbon, Mary; Vermont, 1853-1882 ***5900.10*** *p176*
Filbon, Mary Gill 83; Vermont, 1910 ***5900.10*** *p176*
Filbon, Patrick 85; Vermont, 1896 ***5900.10*** *p176*
Filbrick, Robert; New England, 1649 ***1224.1*** *p21*
Filbrigg, John; Virginia, 1638 ***1224.1*** *p21*
Filby, Frank 7; Ontario, 1871 ***1823.22*** *p52*
Filce, Thomas 23; Maryland, 1774 ***1220.25*** *p53*
Filds, Ann L. 14; Ontario, 1871 ***1823.15*** *p79*
Files, John; St. Augustine, Florida, 1780 ***1224.2*** *p40*
Filgsowitz, Konstanta; Maryland, 1910 ***3259.35*** *p14*
Filhaber, Francis 42; Ontario, 1871 ***1823.28*** *p28*
Filipak, George; Maryland, 1910 ***3259.35*** *p14*
Filipkowsky, Joseph; Maryland, 1910 ***3259.35*** *p14*
Fillet, Antoine Joseph; Pennsylvania, 1784 ***4629.10*** *p43*
Filleter, Anne; Virginia, 1659 ***1224.1*** *p21*
Filley, Sophia 62; Ontario, 1871 ***1823.22*** *p52*
Fillingham, Richard; Maryland, 1672 ***2524.55*** *p79*
Fillmarsh, John; Maryland, 1659 ***2524.55*** *p79*
Fills, Priscilla; Virginia, 1664 ***6212.30*** *p6*
Filly, James 60; Ontario, 1871 ***1823.28*** *p28*
Filmann, Wendel; Port uncertain, 1752 ***2856.30*** *p111*
Filmer, Samuel; Virginia, n.d. ***1224.1*** *p22*
Filnor, William; New York, 1837 ***8197.10*** *p374*
Filpott, Jerome; Maryland, 1659 ***2524.55*** *p79*
Fimpel, Michael; Port uncertain, 1736 ***2856.30*** *p111*
Fimpel, Michael; Port uncertain, 1770 ***2856.30*** *p111*
Fimstlerin, Barbara; America, 1744 ***2856.30*** *p111*
With husband & 2 children
Finan, John 60; Ontario, 1871 ***1823.28*** *p28*
Finana, Daniel 36; Virginia, 1775 ***1220.25*** *p95*
Finch, Adam; Virginia, 1667-1668 ***6212.30*** *p39*
Finch, Edw; Virginia, 1664 ***6212.30*** *p14*
Finch, Immanuel 57; Ontario, 1871 ***1823.15*** *p79*
Finch, J. 20; Alaska, 1912 ***9196.1*** *p37*
Finch, J. 20; Whitehorse, Yukon, 1912 ***9196.1*** *p37*
Finch, Jno; Virginia, 1664 ***6212.30*** *p10*
Finch, John; New York, 1810 ***1224.3*** *p26*
Finch, John; Virginia, 1667-1668 ***6212.30*** *p39*
Finch, John 15; Philadelphia, 1774 ***1220.25*** *p35*
Finch, William 11; Jamaica, 1774 ***1220.25*** *p79*
Fincher, Charles 30; Maryland, 1774 ***1220.25*** *p59*
Finck, Anna Maria; Port uncertain, 1755 ***2856.30*** *p111*
Finck, Friedrich; America, 1752 ***2856.30*** *p111*
Finck, Henrich; America, 1750 ***2856.30*** *p111*
With wife & 4 children
Finck, Henrich; Port uncertain, 1755 ***2856.30*** *p111*
Finck, Johann; Port uncertain, 1786 ***2856.30*** *p111*
Finck, Johann; Port uncertain, 1791 ***2856.30*** *p111*
Finck, Johann Adam; Port uncertain, 1781 ***2856.30*** *p111*
Finck, Margarete; Port uncertain, 1750 ***2856.30*** *p111*
Finckenauer, Philipp; Port uncertain, 1735 ***2856.30*** *p111*
Finckin, Margarete; Port uncertain, 1750 ***2856.30*** *p111*
Findlan, Edward 60; Ontario, 1871 ***1823.22*** *p52*
Findlay, Alexander; Georgia, 1699 ***1640.13*** *p39*
Findlay, Alexander; Savannah, Georgia, 1767 ***1640.10*** *p53*
Findlay, Alexander 52; Ontario, 1871 ***1823.28*** *p28*
Findlay, Arthur Stephen; Windward Islands, 1897 ***1640.13*** *p39*
Findlay, James 26; Ontario, 1871 ***1823.22*** *p52*
Findlay, James 53; Ontario, 1871 ***1823.15*** *p79*
Findlay, Kenneth; Alabama, 1828 ***1640.10*** *p53*
Findlay, Robert; New York, 1828 ***1640.10*** *p53*
Findlay, Robert; Pensacola, Florida, 1777 ***1640.10*** *p53*
Findlay, Thomas; New Orleans, 1840 ***1640.10*** *p53*
Findlay, Walter 48; Ontario, 1871 ***1823.28*** *p28*
Findley, Alexander 60; Ontario, 1871 ***1823.15*** *p79*
Findley, George; Pennsylvania, 1778 ***4629.10*** *p32*
Findley, John 28; Ontario, 1871 ***1823.15*** *p79*
Findley, L. 25; Ontario, 1861 ***2896.28*** *p17*
Findley, W. Y.; Quebec, 1856 ***9196.15*** *p9*
Findley, William 35; Ontario, 1871 ***1823.15*** *p79*
Findling, Ignaz; Port uncertain, 1795 ***2856.30*** *p111*
Findling, Ignaz; Port uncertain, 1796 ***2856.30*** *p111*
Findly, James 45; Ontario, 1871 ***1823.28*** *p29*
Finegan, Edward; New York, 1837 ***8197.10*** *p89*
Finegan, John; New York, 1840 ***8197.10*** *p231*
Finemore, William H. 27; Ontario, 1871 ***1823.22*** *p52*
Finerty, John 26; Ontario, 1871 ***1823.28*** *p29*
Fines, Sarah 22; Georgia, 1774 ***1220.25*** *p48*
Fineur, Joseph; Pennsylvania, 1777 ***4629.10*** *p12*
Finigan, Eleanor 8; Ontario, 1861 ***2896.27*** *p23*
Finigan, Elizabeth 12; Ontario, 1861 ***2896.27*** *p23*
Finigan, James 14; Ontario, 1861 ***2896.27*** *p23*
Finigan, Joanna 41; Ontario, 1861 ***2896.27*** *p23*
Finigan, John 8; Ontario, 1861 ***2896.27*** *p23*
Finigan, John 46; Ontario, 1861 ***2896.27*** *p23*
Finigan, Mary A. 10; Ontario, 1861 ***2896.27*** *p23*
Finigan, Patrick; New York, 1827 ***8197.10*** *p340*
Finigan, William E. 4; Ontario, 1861 ***2896.27*** *p23*
Finigin, John; New York, 1827 ***8197.10*** *p230*
Finigine, John; New York, 1827 ***8197.10*** *p230*
Finin, Roger; New York, 1828 ***8197.10*** *p230*
Finingan, Thomas; New York, 1830 ***8197.10*** *p361*
Fink, James 14; Ontario, 1871 ***1823.22*** *p52*
Fink, Nicol; Port uncertain, 1786 ***2856.30*** *p111*
Fink, Nicol; Port uncertain, 1791 ***2856.30*** *p111*
Finkbiner, Jacob 30; Ontario, 1871 ***1823.15*** *p79*
Finkbiner, Jacob 50; Ontario, 1871 ***1823.15*** *p79*
Finkbiner, Mathew 23; Ontario, 1871 ***1823.15*** *p79*
Finkbiner, Mathew 55; Ontario, 1871 ***1823.15*** *p79*
Finkbiner, Michael 46; Ontario, 1871 ***1823.15*** *p79*
Finke, Ellenor; Virginia, 1672 ***6212.30*** *p49*
Finke, John Frederick; New York, 1838 ***8197.10*** *p318*
Finlan, Martin 51; Ontario, 1871 ***1823.15*** *p79*
Finlan, Thomas 56; Ontario, 1871 ***1823.15*** *p79*
Finland, Thomas 56; Ontario, 1871 ***1823.15*** *p79*
Finlason, William 31; Ontario, 1871 ***1823.15*** *p79*
Finlay, James; New York, 1817 ***8197.10*** *p228*
Finlay, James; New York, 1831 ***8197.10*** *p314*
Finlay, James; New York, 1831 ***8197.10*** *p315*
Finlay, James 33; Ontario, 1871 ***1823.15*** *p79*
Finlay, James A. 38; Ontario, 1871 ***1823.22*** *p52*
Finlay, James Watson; New Brunswick, 1878 ***1640.13*** *p39*
Finlay, John; Georgia, 1736 ***1640.10*** *p53*
Finlay, Margaret; Georgia, 1804-1845 ***1640.10*** *p16*
Finlay, Robert 29; Ontario, 1871 ***1823.22*** *p52*
Finlay, Robert 35; Ontario, 1871 ***1823.22*** *p52*
Finlay, William; Vermont, 1881-1909 ***5900.10*** *p494*
Finlay, William 44; Ontario, 1871 ***1823.22*** *p52*
Finlay, William Achison; Georgia, 1733 ***1640.10*** *p53*
Finlay, William M.; New York, 1803 ***8197.10*** *p12*
Finlayson, Alexander 53; Ontario, 1871 ***1823.15*** *p79*
Finlayson, Angus; Georgia, 1821 ***1640.10*** *p53*
Finlayson, Ann *SEE* Finlayson, John
Finlayson, Donald *SEE* Finlayson, John
Finlayson, George 21; Maryland, 1774 ***1220.25*** *p83*
Finlayson, J. McNair 52; Ontario, 1871 ***1823.28*** *p29*
Finlayson, Janet *SEE* Finlayson, John
Finlayson, John; Georgia, 1821 ***1640.10*** *p54*
Finlayson, John; Ontario, 1863 ***4537.32*** *p8*
Child: Janet
Child: Kenneth
Child: Mary
Wife: Mary Smith
Child: Ann
Child: Donald
Finlayson, John 50; Ontario, 1871 ***1823.15*** *p79*
Finlayson, John 70; Ontario, 1871 ***1823.15*** *p79*
Finlayson, Kenneth *SEE* Finlayson, John
Finlayson, Mary *SEE* Finlayson, John
Finlayson, Mary Smith *SEE* Finlayson, John
Finlayson, Roderick 56; Ontario, 1871 ***1823.15*** *p79*
Finlayson, William; America, 1707 ***1640.13*** *p39*
Finlayson, William Thomas; Detroit, 1879 ***1640.13*** *p39*
Finlen, Miss; Quebec, 1856 ***9196.15*** *p10*
Finley, Mrs.; Grenada, 1775 ***1220.25*** *p133*
Finley, David; Maryland, 1667 ***2524.55*** *p79*
Finley, George 51; Vermont, 1897 ***5900.10*** *p281*
Finley, James; Maryland, 1667 ***2524.55*** *p79*
Finley, James; New York, 1827-1833 ***8197.10*** *p303*
Finley, James Edward; Pennsylvania, 1777 ***4629.10*** *p15*
Finley, John; New York, 1837 ***8197.10*** *p89*
Finley, John 70; Ontario, 1871 ***1823.22*** *p53*
Finley, Nancy McKillop; Vermont, 1836-1901 ***5900.10*** *p510*
Finley, Richard; New York, 1834-1838 ***8197.10*** *p118*
Finley, Thomas; Pennsylvania, 1785 ***4629.10*** *p48*
Finley, Thomas 41; Ontario, 1871 ***1823.15*** *p80*
Finley, Timothy 62; Ontario, 1871 ***1823.22*** *p53*
Finmore, Francis 50; Georgia, 1775 ***1220.25*** *p122*
Finn, Bridget 20 *SEE* Finn, Patrick
Finn, Catherine 50; Vermont, 1876 ***5900.10*** *p372*
Finn, Catherine 55; Ontario, 1871 ***1823.15*** *p80*
Finn, Cornelius 59; Vermont, 1865 ***5900.10*** *p342*
Finn, Elizabeth Mee; Vermont, 1852-1948 ***5900.10*** *p332*
Finn, Ellen; Vermont, 1843-1901 ***5900.10*** *p327*
Finn, Ellen 63; Vermont, 1912 ***5900.10*** *p482*
Finn, Francis 43; Ontario, 1871 ***1823.22*** *p53*
Finn, Francis M. 39; Ontario, 1871 ***1823.22*** *p53*
Finn, Henry; New York, 1840 ***8197.10*** *p167*
Finn, Hugh; New York, 1835-1838 ***8197.10*** *p118*
Finn, James 55; Ontario, 1871 ***1823.15*** *p80*
Finn, James 69; Ontario, 1871 ***1823.22*** *p53*
Finn, James C.; Vermont, 1851-1941 ***5900.10*** *p332*
Finn, James S.; Vermont, 1849-1918 ***5900.10*** *p491*
Finn, Jane 3; Vermont, 1849 ***5900.10*** *p343*
Finn, John; Maryland, 1665 ***2524.55*** *p79*
Finn, John; New York, 1840 ***8197.10*** *p231*
Finn, John; Vermont, 1857-1931 ***5900.10*** *p56*
Finn, John 50; Ontario, 1871 ***1823.15*** *p80*
Finn, Julia; Vermont, 1861 ***5900.10*** *p372*
Finn, Julia 40; Vermont, 1888 ***5900.10*** *p60*
Finn, Julia 88; Vermont, 1911 ***5900.10*** *p369*
Finn, Katherine Leary 46; Vermont, n.d. ***5900.10*** *p56*
Finn, Margaret; Vermont, 1849-1937 ***5900.10*** *p342*
Finn, Margaret; Vermont, 1854-1923 ***5900.10*** *p491*
Finn, Margaret; Vermont, 1928 ***5900.10*** *p151*
Finn, Margaret 9 *SEE* Finn, Patrick
Finn, Margaret 24 *SEE* Finn, Patrick
Finn, Margaret E.; Vermont, 1864-1902 ***5900.10*** *p486*
Finn, Mary; Vermont, 1856-1940 ***5900.10*** *p70*
Finn, Mary 19; Vermont, 1859 ***5900.10*** *p342*
Finn, Mary Reynolds 77; Vermont, 1897 ***5900.10*** *p342*
Finn, Michael 22 *SEE* Finn, Patrick
Finn, Michael 56; Vermont, n.d. ***5900.10*** *p56*
Finn, Michael C.; Vermont, 1855-1937 ***5900.10*** *p486*
Finn, Nathaniel 52; Ontario, 1871 ***1823.22*** *p53*
Finn, Patrick 35; New York, New York, 1847 ***1825.45*** *p15*
Wife: Margaret 24
Brother: Michael 22
Sister: Bridget 20
Sister: Margaret 9
Finn, Thomas 24; Ontario, 1871 ***1823.15*** *p80*
Finn, William; New York, 1840 ***8197.10*** *p165*
Finn, William; Vermont, 1851-1921 ***5900.10*** *p56*
Finncane, Patrick 50; Ontario, 1871 ***1823.28*** *p29*
Finne, Bridget 20 *SEE* Finne, Patrick
Finne, Margaret 9 *SEE* Finne, Patrick
Finne, Margaret 24 *SEE* Finne, Patrick
Finne, Michael 22 *SEE* Finne, Patrick
Finne, Patrick 35; New York, New York, 1847 ***1825.45*** *p15*
Wife: Margaret 24
Sister: Bridget 20
Sister: Margaret 9
Brother: Michael 22
Finne, Teak; Maryland, 1658 ***2524.55*** *p79*
Finnegan, Alice E.; Vermont, 1856-1919 ***5900.10*** *p187*
Finnegan, Anastasia; Vermont, 1851-1887 ***5900.10*** *p255*
Finnegan, Ann Reilly 52; Vermont, 1885 ***5900.10*** *p298*
Finnegan, Annie Failey; Vermont, 1873-1954 ***5900.10*** *p475*
Finnegan, Bernard 44; Vermont, 1862 ***5900.10*** *p475*
Finnegan, Bridget; Vermont, 1831-1916 ***5900.10*** *p288*
Finnegan, Catharine; Vermont, 1823-1858 ***5900.10*** *p299*
Finnegan, Catherine; Vermont, 1850-1893 ***5900.10*** *p475*
Finnegan, Catherine Chadwick; Vermont, 1842-1930 ***5900.10*** *p289*

Finnegan, Catherine McAnaney 86; Vermont, 1907 ***5900.10*** *p615*
Finnegan, Charles A.; Vermont, 1850-1889 ***5900.10*** *p285*
Finnegan, Edward 63; Vermont, 1895 ***5900.10*** *p289*
Finnegan, Eleanor; Vermont, 1842-1920 ***5900.10*** *p475*
Finnegan, Eliza L.; Vermont, 1852-1893 ***5900.10*** *p475*
Finnegan, James B.; Vermont, 1846-1922 ***5900.10*** *p475*
Finnegan, John; America, 1790 ***4628.40*** *p29*
Finnegan, John 49; Ontario, 1871 ***1823.15*** *p80*
Finnegan, John 90; Vermont, 1915 ***5900.10*** *p298*
Finnegan, Katherine L.; Vermont, 1858-1888 ***5900.10*** *p290*
Finnegan, M. Anne; Vermont, 1855-1888 ***5900.10*** *p475*
Finnegan, Margaret 57; Vermont, 1888 ***5900.10*** *p285*
Finnegan, Mary Ann; Vermont, 1839-1920 ***5900.10*** *p285*
Finnegan, Patrick; Vermont, n.d. ***5900.10*** *p298*
Finnegan, Patrick 71; Vermont, 1889 ***5900.10*** *p615*
Finnegan, Patrick, Jr. 29; Vermont, 1879 ***5900.10*** *p615*
Finnegan, Peter; Vermont, 1848-1918 ***5900.10*** *p475*
Finnegan, Terrance; Vermont, 1829-1915 ***5900.10*** *p285*
Finnegan, Thomas; New York, 1834-1838 ***8197.10*** *p118*
Finnel, John 34; Ontario, 1871 ***1823.28*** *p29*
Finnell, Samuel 69; Ontario, 1871 ***1823.28*** *p29*
Finnelly, Catherine Mulhern; Vermont, 1840-1913 ***5900.10*** *p584*
Finnelly, Michael 30; Vermont, 1873 ***5900.10*** *p584*
Finnemor, Joseph; New York, 1828 ***8197.10*** *p230*
Finnen, James; New York, 1840 ***8197.10*** *p200*
Finner, Henry; Pennsylvania, 1777 ***4629.10*** *p19*
Finnerty, Bridget 56; Vermont, 1852 ***5900.10*** *p228*
Finnessey, John 65; Vermont, 1911 ***5900.10*** *p177*
Finnessey, Michael 53; Vermont, 1895 ***5900.10*** *p177*
Finnessy, Elizabeth 87; Vermont, 1920 ***5900.10*** *p141*
Finnessy, Kate 72; Vermont, 1930 ***5900.10*** *p452*
Finnessy, Margaret; Vermont, 1850-1934 ***5900.10*** *p129*
Finney, Charles; Pennsylvania, 1777 ***4629.10*** *p25*
Finney, Ellen; Vermont, 1837-1921 ***5900.10*** *p170*
Finney, Israel John 23; Ontario, 1871 ***1823.28*** *p29*
Finney, John 32; Maryland, 1774 ***1220.25*** *p70*
Finney, Patrick; New York, 1834 ***8197.10*** *p373*
Finnie, William; Boston, 1775 ***1224.2*** *p40*
Finnigan, Charles C.; Vermont, 1841-1907 ***5900.10*** *p159*
Finnigan, Daniel 90; Vermont, 1888 ***5900.10*** *p468*
Finnigan, Elizabeth McNaboe 79; Vermont, 1893 ***5900.10*** *p468*
Finnigan, James 84; Vermont, 1906 ***5900.10*** *p612*
Finnigan, John 37; Vermont, 1870 ***5900.10*** *p55*
Finnigan, John 46; Vermont, 1869 ***5900.10*** *p265*
Finnigan, Maria Baird 84; Vermont, 1916 ***5900.10*** *p612*
Finnigan, Maria J.; Vermont, 1849-1907 ***5900.10*** *p159*
Finnigan, Timothy 61; Vermont, 1877 ***5900.10*** *p265*
Finnil, Michael; New York, 1823 ***8197.10*** *p229*
Finnisey, Mary 47; Vermont, 1889 ***5900.10*** *p142*
Finnissy, Daniel; Vermont, 1856-1901 ***5900.10*** *p170*
Finnissy, Mary Doran; Vermont, 1857-1922 ***5900.10*** *p170*
Finny, Hugh 31; Ontario, 1871 ***1823.15*** *p80*
Finoka, Charles; Pennsylvania, 1840 ***6058.10*** *p17*
Finter, Christof; America, 1748 ***2856.30*** *p112*
Finter, Jacob; America, 1771 ***2856.30*** *p112*
With wife & 4 children
Finther, Michael, Jr.; America, 1737 ***2856.30*** *p112*
Finucane, John 60; Ontario, 1871 ***1823.28*** *p29*
Fiol, Jan; Maryland, 1910 ***3259.35*** *p14*
Firby, Cornelius; Maryland, 1658 ***2524.55*** *p79*
Firby, Henry; Maryland, 1657 ***2524.55*** *p79*
Firby, James; Maryland, 1654 ***2524.55*** *p80*
Firestone, Conrad; Pennsylvania, 1777 ***4629.10*** *p11*
Firman, Charles 42; Ontario, 1871 ***1823.22*** *p53*
Firmins, William 23; Maryland, 1774 ***1220.25*** *p72*
Firmundt, Franz Konrad; Port uncertain, 1745 ***2856.30*** *p112*
Firriby, George 54; Ontario, 1871 ***1823.15*** *p80*
Firriby, Mary 78; Ontario, 1871 ***1823.15*** *p80*
Firth, George; New York, 1840 ***8197.10*** *p166*
Firth, George 30; Nova Scotia, 1774 ***1220.25*** *p13*
Firth, John; Georgia, 1783 ***1640.10*** *p54*
Firth, John 29; Ontario, 1871 ***1823.28*** *p29*
Firth, Samuel; New York, 1834 ***8197.10*** *p71*
Firtzel, Mrs. Paul; Port uncertain, 1732 ***2856.30*** *p112*
Firum, Mathias; Port uncertain, 1745 ***2856.30*** *p112*
Fischbach, Johann; Port uncertain, 1736 ***2856.30*** *p112*
Fischborn, Philipp; America, 1789 ***2856.30*** *p112*
Fischel, Frederick S.; New York, 1837 ***8197.10*** *p90*
Fischel, Johann; Port uncertain, 1741 ***2856.30*** *p112*
Fischel, Johann Peter; Port uncertain, 1764 ***2856.30*** *p112*
Fischer, Ambrosius; America, 1752 ***2856.30*** *p113*
With wife & children
Fischer, Anna Maria; America, 1752 ***2856.30*** *p113*
With husband
Fischer, Anton; Port uncertain, 1719 ***2856.30*** *p112*
Fischer, Anton; Port uncertain, 1749 ***2856.30*** *p112*
Fischer, Antoni; Port uncertain, 1736 ***2856.30*** *p112*
Fischer, Bernhard; Port uncertain, 1796 ***2856.30*** *p112*
Fischer, Catharina; America, 1752 ***2856.30*** *p112*
Fischer, Elisabeth; America, 1752 ***2856.30*** *p112*
Fischer, Eva; America, 1758 ***2856.30*** *p113*
With husband & 3 children
Fischer, Ferdinand, Jr.; Port uncertain, 1762 ***2856.30*** *p112*
Fischer, Gabriel; America, 1731 ***2856.30*** *p112*
Fischer, Georg; America, 1752 ***2856.30*** *p112*
Fischer, Georg; America, 1765 ***2856.30*** *p112*
Fischer, Georg; America, 1786 ***2856.30*** *p112*
Fischer, Georg; Port uncertain, 1764 ***2856.30*** *p112*
Fischer, Georg Adam; America, 1818 ***2856.30*** *p113*
With wife & 2 sons
Fischer, Hans Michael; America, 1744 ***2856.30*** *p112*
Fischer, Hans Nichel; America, 1739 ***2856.30*** *p113*
Fischer, Jacob; America, 1765 ***2856.30*** *p113*
With father
Fischer, Jacob; Port uncertain, 1794 ***2856.30*** *p112*
Fischer, Johann; New York, 1835-1836 ***8197.10*** *p118*
Fischer, Johann; Port uncertain, 1777 ***2856.30*** *p112*
Fischer, Johann Bernhard; New York, 1794 ***8197.10*** *p1*
Fischer, Johann Georg; America, 1749 ***2856.30*** *p113*
With 5 children
Fischer, Johann Georg; America, 1752 ***2856.30*** *p113*
With wife & child
Fischer, Johann Georg; Port uncertain, 1777 ***2856.30*** *p112*
Fischer, Johann Ludwig; Port uncertain, 1771 ***2856.30*** *p112*
Fischer, Johann Ludwig; Port uncertain, 1772 ***2856.30*** *p112*
Fischer, Johann Peter; Port uncertain, 1778 ***2856.30*** *p112*
Fischer, Johann Philipp; America, 1752 ***2856.30*** *p112*
Fischer, Johann Philipp; America, 1755 ***2856.30*** *p112*
Fischer, Josef; Port uncertain, 1729 ***2856.30*** *p112*
Fischer, Josef; Port uncertain, 1754 ***2856.30*** *p113*
With wife & 4 children
Fischer, Karl; Port uncertain, 1796 ***2856.30*** *p112*
Fischer, Maria Catharina; Port uncertain, 1788 ***2856.30*** *p112*
Fischer, Maria Dorothea; Port uncertain, 1790 ***2856.30*** *p112*
Fischer, Nickel; America, 1738 ***2856.30*** *p113*
Fischer, Philipp; America, 1774 ***2856.30*** *p113*
Fischer, Philipp Jakob; America, 1791 ***2856.30*** *p113*
Fischer, Philipp Jakob; Port uncertain, 1790 ***2856.30*** *p113*
Fischer, Sarah; Vermont, 1863-1936 ***5900.10*** *p357*
Fischer, Ulrich; America, 1752 ***2856.30*** *p113*
Fischer, Ulrich; Port uncertain, 1752 ***2856.30*** *p113*
With wife & child
Fischer, Valentin; Port uncertain, 1789 ***2856.30*** *p113*
Fischer, Walpurga; Port uncertain, 1796 ***2856.30*** *p113*
Fiscus, Veronika; Port uncertain, 1729 ***2856.30*** *p113*
Fisel, Niklas; Port uncertain, 1748 ***2856.30*** *p113*
Fisel, Niklas; Port uncertain, 1778 ***2856.30*** *p113*
Fish, Mr.; Quebec, 1857 ***9196.15*** *p20*
Fish, Mr.; Quebec, 1858 ***9196.15*** *p43*
Fish, Mrs.; Quebec, 1858 ***9196.15*** *p43*
Fish, Alexander; New York, 1838 ***8197.10*** *p118*
Fish, Ann; Virginia, 1688 ***6212.30*** *p57*
Fish, Charles 37; Ontario, 1871 ***1823.22*** *p53*
Fish, James; New York, 1838 ***8197.10*** *p119*
Fish, James 34; Ontario, 1871 ***1823.22*** *p53*
Fish, Joshua 19; Virginia, 1773 ***1220.25*** *p31*
Fish, Leander 64; Ontario, 1871 ***1823.22*** *p53*
Fish, Philip; Pennsylvania, 1785 ***4629.10*** *p48*
Fish, William; New England, 1647 ***1224.1*** *p22*
Fishbourne, William; Pennsylvania, 1777 ***4629.10*** *p14*
Fishburn, John 44; Ontario, 1871 ***1823.15*** *p80*
Fishe, Wm; Virginia, 1664 ***6212.30*** *p14*
Fisher, Capt.; Portland, Maine, 1858 ***9196.15*** *p30*
Fisher, Dr.; Quebec, 1858 ***9196.15*** *p33*
Fisher, Mr.; Portland, Maine, 1858 ***9196.15*** *p30*
Fisher, Mr.; Quebec, 1857 ***9196.15*** *p16*
Fisher, Mr.; Quebec, 1858 ***9196.15*** *p41*
Fisher, Mrs.; Maryland, 1666 ***2524.55*** *p80*
Fisher, Mrs.; Quebec, 1858 ***9196.15*** *p33*
Fisher, Albert 24; Ontario, 1871 ***1823.28*** *p29*
Fisher, Alexander; New York, 1802 ***8197.10*** *p20*
Fisher, Alexander 27; Ontario, 1871 ***1823.28*** *p29*
Fisher, Alfred R. 40; Ontario, 1871 ***1823.22*** *p53*
Fisher, Andrew; New York, 1829 ***8197.10*** *p352*
Fisher, Ann; Maryland, 1665 ***2524.55*** *p238*
Fisher, Ann; Maryland, 1679 ***2524.55*** *p80*
Fisher, Annie; Maryland, 1658 ***2524.55*** *p80*
Fisher, August; Maryland, 1910 ***3259.35*** *p14*
Fisher, Barbery; Virginia, 1665 ***6212.30*** *p20*
Fisher, Benjamin 25; Dominica, 1774 ***1220.25*** *p128*
Fisher, Catharine 82; Ontario, 1871 ***1823.28*** *p29*
Fisher, Catherine 50; Ontario, 1871 ***1823.28*** *p29*
Fisher, Christopher 50; Ontario, 1871 ***1823.15*** *p80*
Fisher, Daniel; New York, 1803 ***8197.10*** *p12*
Fisher, Donald; Mississippi, 1816-1821 ***1640.10*** *p54*
Fisher, Duncan 36; Ontario, 1871 ***1823.15*** *p80*
Fisher, Edward; Maryland, 1678 ***2524.55*** *p80*
Fisher, Edward; Maryland, 1679 ***2524.55*** *p80*
Fisher, Edward; Maryland, 1681 ***2524.55*** *p80*
Fisher, Edward; South Carolina, 1783 ***1224.2*** *p40*
Fisher, Edward 28; New York, 1775 ***1220.25*** *p142*
With wife & 2 children
Fisher, Edward D.; Pennsylvania, 1865 ***6058.10*** *p62*
Fisher, Elisha; Pennsylvania, 1786 ***4629.10*** *p53*
Fisher, George; Pennsylvania, 1868 ***6058.10*** *p74*
Fisher, George 35; Ontario, 1871 ***1823.28*** *p29*
Fisher, George 36; Philadelphia, 1774 ***1220.25*** *p43*
Fisher, George 38; Ontario, 1871 ***1823.15*** *p80*
Fisher, George Barton; Vancouver, British Columbia, 1895 ***1640.13*** *p39*
Fisher, Giles; Savannah, Georgia, 1845 ***1224.3*** *p26*
Fisher, Henry 26; Virginia, 1774 ***1220.25*** *p27*
Fisher, Henry 30; Maryland, 1775 ***1220.25*** *p105*
Fisher, Henry N.; New York, 1838 ***8197.10*** *p119*
Fisher, Herman 33; Ontario, 1871 ***1823.15*** *p80*
Fisher, James; America, 1847 ***1224.3*** *p26*
Fisher, James; Jamaica, 1789 ***1640.13*** *p39*
Fisher, James; New York, 1803 ***8197.10*** *p12*
Fisher, James C.; Pennsylvania, 1786 ***4629.10*** *p51*
Fisher, James Campbell; St. Kitts, 1853 ***1640.13*** *p39*
Fisher, Jeremiah; Pennsylvania, 1777 ***4629.10*** *p9*
Fisher, Johann; America, 1731 ***2856.30*** *p113*
Fisher, John; Maryland, 1658 ***2524.55*** *p80*
Fisher, John; Maryland, 1681 ***2524.55*** *p80*
Fisher, John; New York, 1794 ***8197.10*** *p1*
Fisher, John; New York, 1794 ***8197.10*** *p2*
Fisher, John; New York, 1826 ***8197.10*** *p229*
Fisher, John; Pennsylvania, 1777 ***4629.10*** *p27*
Fisher, John; Pennsylvania, 1786 ***4629.10*** *p50*
Fisher, John; Pennsylvania, 1786 ***4629.10*** *p54*
Fisher, John; Quebec, 1899 ***1640.13*** *p39*
Fisher, John; Virginia, 1654 ***1224.1*** *p22*
Fisher, John; Virginia, 1680 ***6212.30*** *p55*
Fisher, John; Virginia, 1723 ***1224.2*** *p41*
Fisher, John 33; Ontario, 1871 ***1823.28*** *p29*
Fisher, John 39; Ontario, 1871 ***1823.22*** *p53*
Fisher, John 52; Ontario, 1871 ***1823.22*** *p53*
Fisher, John 68; Ontario, 1871 ***1823.15*** *p80*
Fisher, John, Jr.; New York, 1837 ***8197.10*** *p375*
Fisher, John George; New York, 1840 ***8197.10*** *p165*
Fisher, John T.; New York, 1840 ***8197.10*** *p164*
Fisher, Joseph; North America, 1839 ***1224.3*** *p26*
Fisher, Katharine; Maryland, 1681 ***2524.55*** *p80*
Fisher, Kathrin; Virginia, 1663 ***6212.30*** *p2*
Fisher, Miers; Philadelphia, 1815 ***1224.3*** *p26*
Fisher, P. 48; Alaska, 1909 ***9196.1*** *p8*
Fisher, P. 48; Yukon, 1909 ***9196.1*** *p8*
Fisher, Paul Carl; Indiana, 1879-1884 ***3437.14*** *p201*
Fisher, Peter 39; Ontario, 1871 ***1823.15*** *p80*
Fisher, Pratt 40; Ontario, 1871 ***1823.15*** *p80*
Fisher, Rebeka 77; Ontario, 1871 ***1823.28*** *p29*
Fisher, Richard; Maryland, 1682 ***2524.55*** *p80*
Fisher, Richard 69; Ontario, 1871 ***1823.28*** *p29*
Fisher, Richard 74; Ontario, 1871 ***1823.15*** *p80*
Fisher, Robert 56; Ontario, 1871 ***1823.15*** *p80*
Fisher, Samuel; Maryland, 1680 ***2524.55*** *p80*
Fisher, Stephen 30; New York, 1774 ***1220.25*** *p20*
Fisher, Thomas; Maryland, 1672 ***2524.55*** *p80*
Fisher, Thomas 19; Maryland, 1774 ***1220.25*** *p70*
Fisher, Thomas 27; Virginia, 1774 ***1220.25*** *p27*
Fisher, Thomas 40; Ontario, 1871 ***1823.28*** *p29*
Fisher, Tobias; Pennsylvania, 1777 ***4629.10*** *p26*
Fisher, William; Maryland, 1665 ***2524.55*** *p80*
Fisher, William; New York, 1840 ***8197.10*** *p231*
Fisher, William; Pennsylvania, 1777 ***4629.10*** *p16*
Fisher, William; Philadelphia, 1791 ***1224.2*** *p41*
Fisher, William 40; Ontario, 1871 ***1823.28*** *p29*
Fisher, William, Jr.; Pennsylvania, 1779 ***4629.10*** *p41*
Fisher, Wm; Virginia, 1664 ***6212.30*** *p14*
Fishermann, John; New York, 1840 ***8197.10*** *p231*
Fishermann, John William; New York, 1837 ***8197.10*** *p89*
Fisk, Mr.; Quebec, 1856 ***9196.15*** *p7*
Fisk, Jennette McDonnell; Vermont, 1836-1890 ***5900.10*** *p616*
Fisk, Jerome B.; Vermont, 1832-1901 ***5900.10*** *p616*
Fisk, Ole 32; British Columbia, 1909 ***9196.1*** *p28*
Fisk, Ole 32; Washington, 1909 ***9196.1*** *p28*
Fiskey, Garet; Pennsylvania, 1778 ***4629.10*** *p32*
Fiskey, John; Pennsylvania, 1778 ***4629.10*** *p32*
Fiskorowiz, Wladislaw; Maryland, 1910 ***3259.35*** *p14*
Fisse, Wm; Virginia, 1665-1666 ***6212.30*** *p23*
Fisse, Wm; Virginia, 1666-1667 ***6212.30*** *p32*
Fissel, Kilian; America, 1742 ***2856.30*** *p113*
Fiste, John; Maryland, 1665 ***2524.55*** *p80*
Fistik, Wincenty; Maryland, 1910 ***3259.35*** *p14*

Fitch, Adam A. 60; Ontario, 1871 ***1823.22*** *p53*
Fitch, John; New York, 1838 ***8197.10*** *p118*
Fitch, John; Pennsylvania, 1777 ***4629.10*** *p20*
Fitch, Michael; New York, 1840 ***8197.10*** *p166*
Fitch, Patrick; New York, 1751 ***1224.2*** *p41*
Fitch, Thomas; Boston, 1737 ***1224.2*** *p41*
FitchAllen, Richard; Maryland, 1663 ***2524.55*** *p80*
Fitcher, Sam.; Maryland, 1659 ***2524.55*** *p80*
Fitching, Eliza; Virginia, 1667-1668 ***6212.30*** *p38*
Fite, Christian; Pennsylvania, 1777 ***4629.10*** *p10*
Fitlon, Thomas 34; Ontario, 1871 ***1823.15*** *p80*
Fitmarsh, John; Maryland, 1659 ***2524.55*** *p80*
Fitsimmons, Mary McGinnis; Vermont, 1865-1941 ***5900.10*** *p82*
Fitspatrick, George M. 42; Ontario, 1871 ***1823.15*** *p81*
Fitting, Caspar; America, 1764 ***2856.30*** *p113*
Fitting, Caspar; America, 1764 ***2856.30*** *p114*
Fitting, Henrich; Port uncertain, 1764 ***2856.30*** *p114*
Fitting, Johann Caspar; America, 1752 ***2856.30*** *p114*
Fitting, Johann Peter; America, 1764 ***2856.30*** *p113*
Fitting, Vinzenz-Kuhn; America, 1764 ***2856.30*** *p113*
Fittler, Mathias Kern; America, 1747 ***2856.30*** *p114*
Fittler, Philipp; America, 1747 ***2856.30*** *p114*
Fitton, Mr.; Quebec, 1857 ***9196.15*** *p14*
Fitton, Mrs.; Quebec, 1857 ***9196.15*** *p14*
Fitts, John M. 28; Alaska, 1914 ***9196.1*** *p24*
Fitts, Mary; Vermont, 1858-1923 ***5900.10*** *p314*
Fitty, Mary; Maryland, 1680 ***2524.55*** *p80*
Fitz, Jno; Virginia, 1664 ***6212.30*** *p14*
Fitz, Randolph; New York, 1838 ***8197.10*** *p118*
Fitzakerly, Timothy 67; Ontario, 1871 ***1823.15*** *p81*
Fitzer, John; Maryland, 1683 ***1224.1*** *p22*
Fitzgerald, . . .; Vermont, 1847 ***5900.10*** *p26*
Fitzgerald, Col.; Quebec, 1856 ***9196.15*** *p7*
Fitzgerald, Mrs.; Quebec, 1856 ***9196.15*** *p7*
Fitzgerald, Amy Colton 86; Vermont, 1846 ***5900.10*** *p376*
Fitzgerald, Andrew; New York, 1840 ***8197.10*** *p166*
Fitzgerald, Andrew; Vermont, 1818-1890 ***5900.10*** *p508*
Fitzgerald, Ann; Vermont, 1825-1874 ***5900.10*** *p336*
Fitzgerald, Anna Lynaugh; Vermont, 1843-1905 ***5900.10*** *p429*
Fitzgerald, Anne; Vermont, 1822-1903 ***5900.10*** *p227*
Fitzgerald, Anne Wing; Vermont, 1856-1943 ***5900.10*** *p165*
Fitzgerald, Annie E. Carney 36; Vermont, 1891 ***5900.10*** *p228*
Fitzgerald, Arthur 32; British Columbia, 1909 ***9196.1*** *p28*
Fitzgerald, Arthur 32; Washington, 1909 ***9196.1*** *p28*
Fitzgerald, Bartholemew 59; Ontario, 1871 ***1823.22*** *p53*
Fitzgerald, Bridget; Vermont, 1846-1928 ***5900.10*** *p167*
Fitzgerald, Bridget D.; Vermont, 1853-1944 ***5900.10*** *p333*
Fitzgerald, Bridget M.; Vermont, 1858-1937 ***5900.10*** *p333*
Fitzgerald, C. D. 30; Maryland, 1775 ***1220.25*** *p109*
Fitzgerald, Catherine; Vermont, 1824-1895 ***5900.10*** *p121*
Fitzgerald, Catherine; Vermont, 1844-1910 ***5900.10*** *p339*
Fitzgerald, Catherine 70; Vermont, 1892 ***5900.10*** *p114*
Fitzgerald, Catherine Broderick; Vermont, 1816-1899 ***5900.10*** *p340*
Fitzgerald, Catherine Brown; Vermont, 1835-1908 ***5900.10*** *p535*
Fitzgerald, Catherine Doyle 52; Vermont, 1880 ***5900.10*** *p270*
Fitzgerald, Catherine J.; Vermont, 1832-1895 ***5900.10*** *p589*
Fitzgerald, Catherine Mangin 67; Vermont, 1887 ***5900.10*** *p165*
Fitzgerald, Catherine Mead; Vermont, 1819-1899 ***5900.10*** *p165*
Fitzgerald, Cornelius; Vermont, 1852-1927 ***5900.10*** *p115*
Fitzgerald, Daniel; Vermont, 1816-1866 ***5900.10*** *p113*
Fitzgerald, David; Vermont, 1847-1930 ***5900.10*** *p228*
Fitzgerald, David 12; Ontario, 1871 ***1823.28*** *p29*
Fitzgerald, Denis 12 *SEE* Fitzgerald, John
Fitz Gerald, Edmond; New York, 1803 ***8197.10*** *p228*
Fitzgerald, Edmund 82; Vermont, 1896 ***5900.10*** *p165*
Fitzgerald, Edward; Vermont, 1822-1850 ***5900.10*** *p473*
Fitzgerald, Edward 21; Vermont, 1872 ***5900.10*** *p165*
Fitzgerald, Edward A.; Vermont, 1858-1939 ***5900.10*** *p340*
Fitzgerald, Edward J.; Vermont, 1860-1918 ***5900.10*** *p333*
Fitzgerald, Elaine 71; Vermont, 1893 ***5900.10*** *p110*
Fitzgerald, Eliza; Ontario, 1861 ***2896.27*** *p53*
Fitzgerald, Elizabeth; Vermont, 1863-1931 ***5900.10*** *p189*
Fitzgerald, Elizabeth 16; Maryland, 1775 ***1220.25*** *p21*
Fitzgerald, Elizabeth Cullen; Vermont, 1831-1907 ***5900.10*** *p333*
Fitzgerald, Ella M. Hennessey; Vermont, 1857-1950 ***5900.10*** *p115*
Fitzgerald, Ellen; Vermont, 1829-1919 ***5900.10*** *p107*
Fitzgerald, Ellen; Vermont, 1839-1937 ***5900.10*** *p539*
Fitzgerald, Ellen; Vermont, 1844-1911 ***5900.10*** *p291*
Fitzgerald, Ellen; Vermont, 1851-1898 ***5900.10*** *p535*
Fitzgerald, Ellen; Vermont, 1856-1940 ***5900.10*** *p469*
Fitzgerald, Ellen; Vermont, 1897 ***5900.10*** *p191*
Fitzgerald, Ellen 24; Ontario, 1871 ***1823.22*** *p53*
Fitzgerald, Ellen 30 *SEE* Fitzgerald, John
Fitzgerald, Ellen 44; Vermont, 1870 ***5900.10*** *p426*
Fitzgerald, Ellen J. 68; Vermont, 1906 ***5900.10*** *p121*
Fitzgerald, Emma; Vermont, 1869-1918 ***5900.10*** *p234*
Fitzgerald, Frederick J.; Ontario, 1861 ***2896.27*** *p53*
Fitzgerald, Garret; New York, 1821 ***8197.10*** *p229*
Fitzgerald, Garret; New York, 1823 ***8197.10*** *p229*
Fitzgerald, Garrett; New York, 1840 ***8197.10*** *p166*
Fitzgerald, George; Vermont, 1855-1933 ***5900.10*** *p333*
Fitzgerald, Hannah; Vermont, 1832-1914 ***5900.10*** *p126*
Fitzgerald, Hannah; Vermont, 1856-1859 ***5900.10*** *p234*
Fitzgerald, Hannah Barrey; Vermont, 1831-1891 ***5900.10*** *p234*
Fitzgerald, Hanoria 18 *SEE* Fitzgerald, James
Fitzgerald, Honora; Vermont, 1905 ***5900.10*** *p352*
Fitzgerald, Honora Magner; Vermont, 1827-1866 ***5900.10*** *p113*
Fitzgerald, Isabelle; Vermont, 1856-1938 ***5900.10*** *p588*
Fitzgerald, James; New York, 1821 ***8197.10*** *p229*
Fitzgerald, James; New York, 1840 ***8197.10*** *p166*
Fitzgerald, James; Vermont, 1821-1871 ***5900.10*** *p165*
Fitzgerald, James; Vermont, 1854-1889 ***5900.10*** *p113*
Fitzgerald, James; Vermont, 1855-1859 ***5900.10*** *p234*
Fitzgerald, James; Vermont, 1855-1922 ***5900.10*** *p165*
Fitzgerald, James 16 *SEE* Fitzgerald, James
Fitzgerald, James 22; Vermont, 1857 ***5900.10*** *p236*
Fitzgerald, James 35; Vermont, 1882 ***5900.10*** *p62*
Fitzgerald, James 55; New York, New York, 1852 ***1825.45*** *p58*
Wife: Margaret 58
Daughter: Hanoria 18
Daughter: Margaret 19
Son: James 16
Fitzgerald, James 63; Ontario, 1871 ***1823.15*** *p81*
Fitzgerald, James 75; Vermont, 1896 ***5900.10*** *p417*
Fitzgerald, James B.; Vermont, 1822-1898 ***5900.10*** *p589*
Fitzgerald, James R. 27; Vermont, 1899 ***5900.10*** *p233*
Fitzgerald, Jane 5; Vermont, 1862 ***5900.10*** *p527*
Fitzgerald, Jennie McRavy; Vermont, 1847-1907 ***5900.10*** *p131*
Fitzgerald, Jeremiah; Vermont, 1802-1896 ***5900.10*** *p475*
Fitzgerald, Joanna; Vermont, 1817-1905 ***5900.10*** *p234*
Fitzgerald, Johanna; Vermont, 1861-1873 ***5900.10*** *p113*
Fitzgerald, Johanna 55; Vermont, 1875 ***5900.10*** *p112*
Fitzgerald, Johannah; Vermont, 1858-1908 ***5900.10*** *p353*
Fitzgerald, John; New York, 1826 ***8197.10*** *p337*
Fitzgerald, John; New York, 1837 ***8197.10*** *p89*
Fitzgerald, John; New York, 1837 ***8197.10*** *p230*
Fitzgerald, John; New York, 1838 ***8197.10*** *p118*
Fitzgerald, John; Vermont, 1848-1883 ***5900.10*** *p131*
Fitzgerald, John; Vermont, 1848-1913 ***5900.10*** *p238*
Fitzgerald, John; Vermont, 1849-1933 ***5900.10*** *p147*
Fitzgerald, John; Vermont, 1852-1859 ***5900.10*** *p234*
Fitzgerald, John; Vermont, 1853-1932 ***5900.10*** *p469*
Fitzgerald, John; Vermont, 1858-1923 ***5900.10*** *p234*
Fitzgerald, John; Vermont, 1887 ***5900.10*** *p352*
Fitzgerald, John 37; Ontario, 1871 ***1823.15*** *p81*
Fitzgerald, John 37; Ontario, 1871 ***1823.22*** *p53*
Fitzgerald, John 42; New York, New York, 1852 ***1825.45*** *p58*
Wife: Ellen 30
Son: Denis 12
Son: Thomas 8
Daughter: Margaret 10
Fitzgerald, John 56; Ontario, 1871 ***1823.28*** *p29*
Fitzgerald, John 70; Vermont, 1870 ***5900.10*** *p520*
Fitzgerald, John 76; Vermont, 1883 ***5900.10*** *p240*
Fitzgerald, John P.; Vermont, 1853-1925 ***5900.10*** *p378*
Fitzgerald, Joseph; Vermont, 1824-1899 ***5900.10*** *p333*
Fitzgerald, Joseph M.; Vermont, 1851-1911 ***5900.10*** *p340*
Fitzgerald, Joseph M.; Vermont, 1857-1940 ***5900.10*** *p333*
Fitzgerald, Josephine Duman; Vermont, 1856 ***5900.10*** *p378*
Fitzgerald, Kate 35; Ontario, 1871 ***1823.22*** *p53*
Fitzgerald, Kate Coffey; Vermont, 1854-1916 ***5900.10*** *p147*
Fitzgerald, Katherine 69; Vermont, 1872 ***5900.10*** *p121*
Fitzgerald, Katherine Carney; Vermont, 1860-1933 ***5900.10*** *p240*
Fitzgerald, Kathrine; Vermont, 1903 ***5900.10*** *p159*
Fitzgerald, Katie 86; Vermont, 1883 ***5900.10*** *p181*
Fitzgerald, Katie A.; Vermont, 1850-1902 ***5900.10*** *p438*
Fitzgerald, Lawrence; Vermont, 1825-1897 ***5900.10*** *p336*
Fitzgerald, Lyia 74; Ontario, 1871 ***1823.22*** *p53*
Fitzgerald, Maggie 19; Vermont, 1871 ***5900.10*** *p165*
Fitzgerald, Margaret; Vermont, 1845-1895 ***5900.10*** *p437*
Fitzgerald, Margaret; Vermont, 1848-1906 ***5900.10*** *p194*
Fitzgerald, Margaret 10 *SEE* Fitzgerald, John
Fitzgerald, Margaret 19 *SEE* Fitzgerald, James
Fitzgerald, Margaret 58 *SEE* Fitzgerald, James
Fitzgerald, Margaret 72; Vermont, 1904 ***5900.10*** *p126*
Fitzgerald, Margaret A.; Vermont, 1836-1918 ***5900.10*** *p508*
Fitzgerald, Martin; Vermont, 1811-1866 ***5900.10*** *p340*
Fitzgerald, Martin 55; Vermont, 1865 ***5900.10*** *p327*
Fitzgerald, Martin M.; Vermont, 1869-1911 ***5900.10*** *p333*
Fitzgerald, Mary; Vermont, 1810-1903 ***5900.10*** *p508*
Fitzgerald, Mary; Vermont, 1824-1884 ***5900.10*** *p431*
Fitzgerald, Mary; Vermont, 1826-1898 ***5900.10*** *p336*
Fitzgerald, Mary; Vermont, 1841-1913 ***5900.10*** *p511*
Fitzgerald, Mary; Vermont, 1843-1916 ***5900.10*** *p165*
Fitzgerald, Mary; Vermont, 1844-1918 ***5900.10*** *p107*
Fitzgerald, Mary; Vermont, 1851-1925 ***5900.10*** *p234*
Fitzgerald, Mary; Vermont, 1852-1892 ***5900.10*** *p471*
Fitzgerald, Mary; Vermont, 1853-1920 ***5900.10*** *p334*
Fitzgerald, Mary; Vermont, 1860-1923 ***5900.10*** *p270*
Fitzgerald, Mary; Vermont, 1861-1904 ***5900.10*** *p355*
Fitzgerald, Mary 31; Vermont, 1895 ***5900.10*** *p233*
Fitzgerald, Mary 52; Vermont, 1894 ***5900.10*** *p111*
Fitzgerald, Mary 65; Ontario, 1871 ***1823.15*** *p81*
Fitzgerald, Mary 68; Vermont, 1859 ***5900.10*** *p521*
Fitzgerald, Mary 81; Vermont, 1910 ***5900.10*** *p503*
Fitzgerald, Mary A.; Vermont, 1852-1937 ***5900.10*** *p340*
Fitzgerald, Mary A.; Vermont, 1855-1884 ***5900.10*** *p508*
Fitzgerald, Mary A.; Vermont, 1867-1941 ***5900.10*** *p333*
Fitzgerald, Mary Connell 69; Vermont, 1902 ***5900.10*** *p233*
Fitzgerald, Mary E.; Vermont, 1845-1918 ***5900.10*** *p138*
Fitzgerald, Mary E. Gorman; Vermont, 1852-1913 ***5900.10*** *p340*
Fitzgerald, Mary Foley 76; Vermont, 1886 ***5900.10*** *p515*
Fitzgerald, Mary Gilwee; Vermont, 1855-1930 ***5900.10*** *p238*
Fitzgerald, Mary J.; Ontario, 1861 ***2896.27*** *p53*
Fitzgerald, Mary Kelly 32; Vermont, 1874 ***5900.10*** *p62*
Fitzgerald, Michael; Pennsylvania, 1861 ***6058.10*** *p63*
Fitzgerald, Michael; Vermont, 1808-1892 ***5900.10*** *p234*
Fitzgerald, Michael; Vermont, 1824-1903 ***5900.10*** *p534*
Fitzgerald, Michael; Vermont, 1857-1859 ***5900.10*** *p234*
Fitzgerald, Michael 4; Vermont, 1862 ***5900.10*** *p527*
Fitzgerald, Michael 58; Vermont, 1882 ***5900.10*** *p270*
Fitzgerald, Michael F.; Vermont, n.d. ***5900.10*** *p241*
Fitzgerald, Nancy 76; Vermont, 1907 ***5900.10*** *p417*
Fitzgerald, Nancy Sloan 67; Vermont, 1914 ***5900.10*** *p241*
Fitzgerald, Patrick; New York, 1839 ***8197.10*** *p320*
Fitzgerald, Patrick; Vermont, 1826-1903 ***5900.10*** *p508*
Fitzgerald, Patrick 40; Ontario, 1871 ***1823.22*** *p53*
Fitzgerald, Patrick 54; Ontario, 1871 ***1823.28*** *p29*
Fitzgerald, Richard; Nova Scotia, 1745 ***4628.40*** *p44*
Fitz Gerald, Robert 33; Ontario, 1871 ***1823.15*** *p81*
Fitzgerald, Sarah 1; Vermont, 1862 ***5900.10*** *p527*
Fitzgerald, Susan Sullivan 55; Vermont, 1874 ***5900.10*** *p475*
Fitzgerald, Thomas; Pennsylvania, 1779 ***4629.10*** *p41*
Fitzgerald, Thomas; Vermont, 1840-1898 ***5900.10*** *p165*
Fitzgerald, Thomas; Vermont, 1842-1917 ***5900.10*** *p189*
Fitzgerald, Thomas; Vermont, 1855-1910 ***5900.10*** *p240*
Fitzgerald, Thomas 8 *SEE* Fitzgerald, John
Fitzgerald, Thomas 29; Vermont, 1878 ***5900.10*** *p471*
Fitzgerald, Thomas J.; Vermont, 1842-1899 ***5900.10*** *p429*
Fitzgerald, William; Vermont, 1843-1898 ***5900.10*** *p138*
Fitzgerald, William H.; Vermont, 1861-1930 ***5900.10*** *p333*
Fitzgerrard, Gerrard; Maryland, 1672 ***2524.55*** *p80*
Fitzgibbon, Michael; New York, 1840 ***8197.10*** *p384*
Fitzgibbons, Johanna 65; Vermont, 1889 ***5900.10*** *p106*
Fitzgibbons, Michael; Vermont, 1871-1900 ***5900.10*** *p117*
Fitzherbert, Francis; Maryland, 1671 ***2524.55*** *p80*
Fitzhugh, Robert; Boston, 1696 ***1224.1*** *p58*
Fitzmarice, John 70; Ontario, 1871 ***1823.28*** *p29*
Fitzmarice, Michael 37; Ontario, 1871 ***1823.28*** *p29*
Fitzmaurice, Catherine 40; Ontario, 1871 ***1823.22*** *p53*
Fitzmorris, Edward 33; Ontario, 1871 ***1823.28*** *p29*
Fitzmorris, Jane Young 55; Vermont, 1895 ***5900.10*** *p589*
Fitzmorris, Katherine; Vermont, 1835-1907 ***5900.10*** *p369*
Fitzmorris, Mary; Vermont, n.d. ***5900.10*** *p591*
Fitzmorris, Michael 46; Vermont, 1866 ***5900.10*** *p369*
Fitzmorris, Thomas 31; Ontario, 1871 ***1823.28*** *p29*
Fitzmorris, Thomas 67; Ontario, 1871 ***1823.28*** *p29*
Fitzmurice, James 28; Ontario, 1871 ***1823.28*** *p29*
Fitzner, Adam 25; Ontario, 1871 ***1823.28*** *p29*
Fitzner, Bernard 17; Ontario, 1871 ***1823.28*** *p29*

Fitzner, Fredrick 21; Ontario, 1871 ***1823.28*** *p29*
Fitzner, Harmen 24; Ontario, 1871 ***1823.28*** *p29*
Fitzner, Julius 19; Ontario, 1871 ***1823.28*** *p29*
Fitzner, William 30; Ontario, 1871 ***1823.28*** *p29*
Fitzpatrick, Ann; Vermont, 1824-1910 ***5900.10*** *p388*
Fitzpatrick, Anna; Vermont, 1833-1901 ***5900.10*** *p508*
Fitzpatrick, Barnard 53; Ontario, 1871 ***1823.15*** *p81*
Fitzpatrick, Bridget Regan 70; Vermont, 1914 ***5900.10*** *p272*
Fitzpatrick, Bridget Reilly 75; Vermont, 1878 ***5900.10*** *p613*
Fitzpatrick, Edward; New York, 1803 ***8197.10*** *p12*
Fitzpatrick, Edward; New York, 1838 ***8197.10*** *p118*
Fitzpatrick, Edward 31; Virginia, 1774 ***1220.25*** *p45*
Fitzpatrick, Edward 64; Vermont, 1894 ***5900.10*** *p508*
Fitzpatrick, Emily Donaldson; Vermont, 1845-1929 ***5900.10*** *p517*
Fitzpatrick, Henry 60; Ontario, 1871 ***1823.28*** *p29*
Fitzpatrick, Hugh 26; Ontario, 1871 ***1823.22*** *p53*
Fitzpatrick, James; New York, 1802 ***8197.10*** *p20*
Fitzpatrick, James; Vermont, 1837-1906 ***5900.10*** *p590*
Fitzpatrick, James 52; Ontario, 1871 ***1823.28*** *p29*
Fitzpatrick, James 56; Vermont, 1886 ***5900.10*** *p272*
Fitzpatrick, Jas 37; British Columbia, 1917 ***9196.1*** *p51*
Fitzpatrick, Jas 37; Seattle, 1917 ***9196.1*** *p51*
Fitzpatrick, John; New York, 1822 ***8197.10*** *p61*
Fitzpatrick, John; New York, 1835-1838 ***8197.10*** *p119*
Fitzpatrick, John 24; Philadelphia, 1774 ***1220.25*** *p43*
Fitzpatrick, John 25; Ontario, 1871 ***1823.15*** *p81*
Fitzpatrick, John, Jr.; New York, 1840 ***8197.10*** *p166*
Fitzpatrick, John Henry 17; Vermont, 1880 ***5900.10*** . *p501*
Fitzpatrick, Joseph; Philadelphia, 1792 ***4629.10*** *p75*
Fitzpatrick, Katherine A.; Vermont, 1858-1937 ***5900.10*** *p387*
Fitzpatrick, Margaret 50; Ontario, 1871 ***1823.28*** *p29*
Fitzpatrick, Margaret 65; Vermont, 1898 ***5900.10*** *p560*
Fitzpatrick, Margaret Duffy; Vermont, 1835-1922 ***5900.10*** *p387*
Fitzpatrick, Margaret Hanrahan; Vermont, 1841-1896 ***5900.10*** *p590*
Fitzpatrick, Martin; Vermont, 1818-1909 ***5900.10*** *p387*
Fitzpatrick, Martin; Vermont, 1853-1931 ***5900.10*** *p387*
Fitzpatrick, Mary; Vermont, 1857-1937 ***5900.10*** *p590*
Fitzpatrick, Mary; Vermont, 1859-1937 ***5900.10*** *p387*
Fitzpatrick, Mary 32; Vermont, 1860 ***5900.10*** *p618*
Fitzpatrick, Mary 68; Vermont, 1900 ***5900.10*** *p508*
Fitzpatrick, Mary 69; Vermont, 1864 ***5900.10*** *p502*
Fitzpatrick, Mary E.; Vermont, 1865-1939 ***5900.10*** *p387*
Fitzpatrick, Michael 52; Vermont, 1877 ***5900.10*** *p578*
Fitzpatrick, Owen; New York, 1827 ***8197.10*** *p345*
Fitzpatrick, Patrick; New York, 1837 ***8197.10*** *p88*
Fitzpatrick, Peter; New York, 1839 ***8197.10*** *p130*
FitzPatrick, Philip; Maryland, 1682 ***2524.55*** *p80*
Fitzpatrick, Phillip 23; Vermont, 1871 ***5900.10*** *p428*
Fitzpatrick, Thomas; New York, 1837 ***8197.10*** *p89*
Fitzpatrick, Thomas 69; Vermont, 1875 ***5900.10*** *p610*
Fitzpatrick, William; New York, 1807 ***8197.10*** *p42*
Fitzpatrick, William; New York, 1840 ***8197.10*** *p166*
Fitzpen, David; New England, 1652 ***1224.1*** *p22*
Fitzrandolph, Edward; Pennsylvania, 1779 ***4629.10*** *p37*
Fitzsimmons, Brian 54; Ontario, 1871 ***1823.22*** *p53*
Fitzsimmons, Bridget Barry; Vermont, 1852-1895 ***5900.10*** *p174*
Fitzsimmons, Edward; Vermont, 1834-1908 ***5900.10*** *p68*
Fitzsimmons, Esther Barnes; Vermont, 1836-1905 ***5900.10*** *p68*
Fitzsimmons, James; New York, 1836 ***8197.10*** *p230*
Fitzsimmons, John; New York, 1837 ***8197.10*** *p89*
Fitzsimmons, John; Vermont, 1852-1929 ***5900.10*** *p82*
Fitzsimmons, John; Vermont, 1857-1928 ***5900.10*** *p407*
Fitzsimmons, John M.; Vermont, 1879-1947 ***5900.10*** *p174*
Fitzsimmons, Maria Hogan; Vermont, 1851-1894 ***5900.10*** *p128*
Fitzsimmons, Mary Cavanagh; Vermont, 1857-1946 ***5900.10*** *p531*
Fitzsimmons, Mary Sullivan; Vermont, 1871-1932 ***5900.10*** *p174*
Fitzsimmons, Owen 79; Ontario, 1871 ***1823.22*** *p53*
Fitzsimmons, Patrick; Vermont, 1845-1918 ***5900.10*** *p174*
Fitzsimmons, Samuel 49; Ontario, 1871 ***1823.15*** *p81*
Fitzsimmons, Sarah T. Smith; Vermont, 1857-1934 ***5900.10*** *p407*
Fitzsimmons, Thomas; Vermont, 1846-1932 ***5900.10*** *p128*
Fitzsimmons, Thomas 52; Vermont, 1878 ***5900.10*** *p82*
Fitzsimonds, John 48; Vermont, 1882 ***5900.10*** *p532*
Fitzsimonds, Margaret McNulty 73; Vermont, 1908 ***5900.10*** *p532*
Fitzsimons, Bridget 74; Vermont, 1900 ***5900.10*** *p532*
Fitzsimons, George W.; Vermont, 1854-1937 ***5900.10*** *p531*
Fitzsimons, James 82; Vermont, 1912 ***5900.10*** *p532*
Fitzsimons, Lawrence; New York, 1827 ***8197.10*** *p229*
Fitzsimons, Nicholas; Pennsylvania, 1777 ***4629.10*** *p17*
Fitzsimons, Nicholas; Pennsylvania, 1779 ***4629.10*** *p36*
Fitzsimons, Rose; Vermont, 1855-1918 ***5900.10*** *p532*
Fitzwater, Thomas; Maryland, 1682 ***2524.55*** *p80*
Fitzwilliam, Bridget 35; Ontario, 1871 ***1823.28*** *p29*
Fitzwilliams, Sarah 40; Ontario, 1871 ***1823.15*** *p81*
Fixin, Catharina; Port uncertain, 1754 ***2856.30*** *p114*
Fixin, Elisabeth; America, 1769 ***2856.30*** *p114*
Fiz, Catharina; Port uncertain, 1735 ***2856.30*** *p114*
Fiz, Peter; America, 1750 ***2856.30*** *p114*
With 5 children
Flach, Johann; Port uncertain, 1732 ***2856.30*** *p114*
Flach, Martin; Port uncertain, 1779 ***2856.30*** *p114*
Flacher, Martin; Port uncertain, 1753 ***2856.30*** *p115*
Flachsbord, August 40; Ontario, 1871 ***1823.15*** *p81*
Flachsbord, Christoph 72; Ontario, 1871 ***1823.15*** *p81*
Flack, Elizabeth; Maryland, 1680 ***2524.55*** *p80*
Flack, Jno; Virginia, 1668-1669 ***6212.30*** *p40*
Flack, John; New York, 1802 ***8197.10*** *p20*
Flack, Joseph 21; Maryland, 1774 ***1220.25*** *p59*
Flack, Joseph 39; Ontario, 1871 ***1823.15*** *p81*
Flack, Philip; Pennsylvania, 1777 ***4629.10*** *p10*
Flagg, Charles; Maryland, 1682 ***2524.55*** *p80*
Flagherty, John 35; Ontario, 1871 ***1823.22*** *p53*
Flagherty, Michael 40; Ontario, 1871 ***1823.22*** *p53*
Flagler, Annie A. 4; Ontario, 1861 ***2896.28*** *p33*
Flahavan, John; Pennsylvania, 1779 ***4629.10*** *p38*
Flahavan, Roger; Pennsylvania, 1777 ***4629.10*** *p22*
Flaherty, Ellen Coyne; Vermont, 1846-1920 ***5900.10*** *p290*
Flaherty, Ellen Fitzgerald; Vermont, 1897 ***5900.10*** *p191*
Flaherty, Hannah 60; Vermont, 1891 ***5900.10*** *p291*
Flaherty, James; Vermont, 1855 ***5900.10*** *p433*
Flaherty, James 39; Ontario, 1871 ***1823.28*** *p29*
Flaherty, Joanna; Vermont, 1854-1915 ***5900.10*** *p307*
Flaherty, John; New York, 1833 ***8197.10*** *p230*
Flaherty, John J.; Vermont, 1893 ***5900.10*** *p191*
Flaherty, Mary; Vermont, 1830 ***5900.10*** *p433*
Flaherty, Mary; Vermont, 1852-1902 ***5900.10*** *p433*
Flaherty, Patrick; Vermont, 1853-1901 ***5900.10*** *p290*
Flahive, Mary Long 46; Vermont, 1865 ***5900.10*** *p113*
Flaker, Sarah 16; Maryland, 1774 ***1220.25*** *p77*
Flamang, Jacob; Port uncertain, 1785 ***2856.30*** *p114*
Flamang, Jacob; Port uncertain, 1787 ***2856.30*** *p114*
Flambeth, Abell; Maryland, 1654 ***2524.55*** *p80*
Flamies, A. 43; Alaska, 1912 ***9196.1*** *p39*
Flamies, A. 43; Whitehorse, Yukon, 1912 ***9196.1*** *p39*
Flammann, Peter; Port uncertain, 1764 ***2856.30*** *p114*
With wife & children
Flammer, Jacob; New York, 1834-1838 ***8197.10*** *p118*
Flanagan, Abby 37; Vermont, 1871 ***5900.10*** *p164*
Flanagan, Bridget Farell; Vermont, 1821-1889 ***5900.10*** *p511*
Flanagan, Catherine 61; Vermont, 1920 ***5900.10*** *p578*
Flanagan, Christopher; New York, 1802 ***8197.10*** *p21*
Flanagan, D. 8; Ontario, 1861 ***2896.28*** *p11*
Flanagan, Dennis; Vermont, 1829-1890 ***5900.10*** *p479*
Flanagan, Dennis 35; Vermont, 1887 ***5900.10*** *p561*
Flanagan, E. 3; Ontario, 1861 ***2896.28*** *p11*
Flanagan, Edward; New York, 1821 ***8197.10*** *p229*
Flanagan, Eliza 42; Vermont, 1887 ***5900.10*** *p561*
Flanagan, Ellen; Vermont, 1855-1861 ***5900.10*** *p511*
Flanagan, Ellen S. 20; Vermont, 1893 ***5900.10*** *p342*
Flanagan, Francis 4; Ontario, 1861 ***2896.28*** *p11*
Flanagan, James; Pennsylvania, 1868 ***6058.10*** *p65*
Flanagan, James 15; Vermont, 1873 ***5900.10*** *p561*
Flanagan, James 21; Jamaica, 1774 ***1220.25*** *p79*
Flanagan, Jane 40; Vermont, 1863 ***5900.10*** *p561*
Flanagan, Joanna Cashman 83; Vermont, 1910 ***5900.10*** *p348*
Flanagan, John 80; Vermont, 1880 ***5900.10*** *p348*
Flanagan, John A.; Vermont, 1848-1892 ***5900.10*** *p511*
Flanagan, John B.; Vermont, 1842-1914 ***5900.10*** *p399*
Flanagan, John G.; Vermont, 1860-1929 ***5900.10*** *p342*
Flanagan, Josephine E.; Vermont, 1861-1934 ***5900.10*** *p405*
Flanagan, Julia A. 16; Vermont, 1885 ***5900.10*** *p342*
Flanagan, Julia Martin 74; Vermont, 1896 ***5900.10*** *p206*
Flanagan, Julia Whalen 67; Vermont, 1899 ***5900.10*** *p342*
Flanagan, M. 6; Ontario, 1861 ***2896.28*** *p11*
Flanagan, Mary; Vermont, n.d. ***5900.10*** *p107*
Flanagan, Mary; Vermont, 1828-1870 ***5900.10*** *p479*
Flanagan, Mary; Vermont, 1842-1870 ***5900.10*** *p511*
Flanagan, Mary; Vermont, 1858-1939 ***5900.10*** *p268*
Flanagan, Mary 57; Vermont, 1876 ***5900.10*** *p601*
Flanagan, Mary 65; Vermont, 1880 ***5900.10*** *p242*
Flanagan, Mary 75; Vermont, 1875 ***5900.10*** *p341*
Flanagan, Mary Ann 15; Vermont, 1869 ***5900.10*** *p206*
Flanagan, Mary Dwyer; Vermont, 1847-1904 ***5900.10*** *p399*
Flanagan, Mary Noone; Vermont, 1845-1924 ***5900.10*** *p393*
Flanagan, Michael; Vermont, 1810-1892 ***5900.10*** *p511*
Flanagan, Michael; Vermont, 1844-1859 ***5900.10*** *p511*
Flanagan, Michael 80; Vermont, 1896 ***5900.10*** *p561*
Flanagan, Nancie J. Hutchins; Vermont, 1858-1932 ***5900.10*** *p555*
Flanagan, P. 34; Ontario, 1861 ***2896.28*** *p11*
Flanagan, Patrick; Vermont, 1824-1898 ***5900.10*** *p393*
Flanagan, Patrick 46; Ontario, 1871 ***1823.22*** *p53*
Flanagan, Patrick 50; Vermont, 1873 ***5900.10*** *p206*
Flanagan, Patrick 51; Ontario, 1871 ***1823.22*** *p53*
Flanagan, Peter M.; Vermont, 1853-1909 ***5900.10*** *p405*
Flanagan, Robert; New York, 1815-1834 ***8197.10*** *p304*
Flanagan, Rose Johnson; Vermont, 1831-1911 ***5900.10*** *p479*
Flanagan, S. 17; Ontario, 1861 ***2896.28*** *p8*
Flanagan, Sarah A.; Vermont, 1858-1890 ***5900.10*** *p479*
Flanagan, Thomas; New York, 1837 ***8197.10*** *p89*
Flanagan, Timothy W.; Vermont, 1854-1932 ***5900.10*** *p555*
Flanagan, William 73; Vermont, 1883 ***5900.10*** *p342*
Flanagan, William P.; Vermont, 1859-1878 ***5900.10*** *p511*
Flanary, Catherine 8 *SEE* Flanary, Nicholas
Flanary, Ellen 5 *SEE* Flanary, Nicholas
Flanary, John 6 months *SEE* Flanary, Nicholas
Flanary, Margaret 7 *SEE* Flanary, Nicholas
Flanary, Mary 10 *SEE* Flanary, Nicholas
Flanary, Michael 12 *SEE* Flanary, Nicholas
Flanary, Nancy 38 *SEE* Flanary, Nicholas
Flanary, Nicholas 40; New York, New York, 1848 ***1825.45*** *p33*
Wife: Nancy 38
Daughter: Margaret 7
Daughter: Winifred 4
Daughter: Mary 10
Daughter: Ellen 5
Son: John 6 months
Son: Michael 12
Daughter: Catherine 8
Son: Pat 13
Flanary, Pat 13 *SEE* Flanary, Nicholas
Flanary, Winifred 4 *SEE* Flanary, Nicholas
Flanders, Annie Cunningham; Vermont, 1835-1906 ***5900.10*** *p590*
Flanery, William 61; Ontario, 1871 ***1823.15*** *p81*
Flangan, John 23; Ontario, 1871 ***1823.15*** *p81*
Flangen, Thomas 60; Ontario, 1871 ***1823.28*** *p29*
Flanigan, James 31; Ontario, 1871 ***1823.22*** *p53*
Flanigan, John S. 42; Vermont, 1906 ***5900.10*** *p348*
Flanley, Hugh; New York, 1826 ***8197.10*** *p229*
Flanly, Martin 87; Vermont, 1868 ***5900.10*** *p201*
Flannagan, Bridget 63; Vermont, 1896 ***5900.10*** *p104*
Flannagan, Mary 70; Vermont, 1897 ***5900.10*** *p104*
Flannahan, Patrick; Ontario, 1871 ***1823.28*** *p29*
Flannelly, Ann 39; Vermont, 1860 ***5900.10*** *p180*
Flannery, Anna; Vermont, 1837-1854 ***5900.10*** *p434*
Flannery, Anne McCormack; Vermont, 1841-1923 ***5900.10*** *p434*
Flannery, Bridget Hayes 75; Vermont, 1883 ***5900.10*** *p59*
Flannery, Catherine 8 *SEE* Flannery, Nicholas
Flannery, Catherine 35; Ontario, 1871 ***1823.28*** *p29*
Flannery, Catherine 42; Vermont, 1879 ***5900.10*** *p413*
Flannery, Catherine 87; Vermont, 1883 ***5900.10*** *p368*
Flannery, Cornelius; Vermont, 1832-1855 ***5900.10*** *p434*
Flannery, Ellen 5 *SEE* Flannery, Nicholas
Flannery, Ellen 43; Ontario, 1871 ***1823.15*** *p81*
Flannery, James 18; Vermont, 1865 ***5900.10*** *p368*
Flannery, John 6 months *SEE* Flannery, Nicholas
Flannery, John 62; Vermont, 1905 ***5900.10*** *p368*
Flannery, Katherine M.; Vermont, 1847-1903 ***5900.10*** *p434*
Flannery, Margaret; Vermont, 1800-1884 ***5900.10*** *p434*
Flannery, Margaret 7 *SEE* Flannery, Nicholas
Flannery, Margaret 87; Ontario, 1871 ***1823.15*** *p81*
Flannery, Martin J.; Vermont, 1830-1909 ***5900.10*** *p534*
Flannery, Mary 10 *SEE* Flannery, Nicholas
Flannery, Mary A. Tunney; Vermont, 1834-1876 ***5900.10*** *p534*
Flannery, Mary Jane; Vermont, 1856-1914 ***5900.10*** *p120*
Flannery, Michael 12 *SEE* Flannery, Nicholas
Flannery, Michael 30; Ontario, 1871 ***1823.15*** *p81*
Flannery, Michael 88; Vermont, 1890 ***5900.10*** *p368*
Flannery, Nancy 38 *SEE* Flannery, Nicholas
Flannery, Nicholas 40; New York, New York, 1848 ***1825.45*** *p33*
Wife: Nancy 38
Daughter: Ellen 5
Daughter: Mary 10
Daughter: Winifred 4
Daughter: Margaret 7
Daughter: Catherine 8

Son: John 6 months
Son: Michael 12
Son: Pat 13
Flannery, P. H.; Vermont, 1838-1867 ***5900.10*** *p433*
Flannery, Pat 13 *SEE* Flannery, Nicholas
Flannery, Patrick; Vermont, 1788-1854 ***5900.10*** *p434*
Flannery, Peter 62; Vermont, 1896 ***5900.10*** *p413*
Flannery, Timothy; Vermont, 1843-1883 ***5900.10*** *p434*
Flannery, Timothy 32; Vermont, 1876 ***5900.10*** *p368*
Flannery, Winifred 4 *SEE* Flannery, Nicholas
Flannigan, Bridget 34; Vermont, 1872 ***5900.10*** *p568*
Flannigan, Catherine 28; Vermont, 1851 ***5900.10*** *p523*
Flannigan, Elizabeth; Vermont, 1869 ***5900.10*** *p566*
Flannigan, James 67; Vermont, 1868 ***5900.10*** *p106*
Flannigan, Larry 42; British Columbia, 1910 ***9196.1*** *p30*
Flannigan, Larry 42; Seattle, 1910 ***9196.1*** *p30*
Flannigan, Peter; Vermont, 1904 ***5900.10*** *p566*
Flarnechin, Elizabeth 60; Ontario, 1871 ***1823.15*** *p81*
Flarty, John; Maryland, 1682 ***2524.55*** *p80*
Flatman, John 35; Maryland, 1774 ***1220.25*** *p54*
Flatt, James 25; Carolina, 1774 ***1220.25*** *p85*
Flatt, Leonard, The Older; Port uncertain, 1741 ***2856.30*** *p114*
Flatt, Leonard, The Younger; Port uncertain, 1741 ***2856.30*** *p114*
Flavell, Mr.; Quebec, 1858 ***9196.15*** *p33*
Flavin, Catherine Neilan; Vermont, 1839-1928 ***5900.10*** *p55*
Flavin, Dennis; Vermont, 1840-1903 ***5900.10*** *p55*
Flavin, Eugene E.; Vermont, 1855-1930 ***5900.10*** *p57*
Flavin, James; Vermont, n.d. ***5900.10*** *p66*
Flavin, James 90; Vermont, 1887 ***5900.10*** *p60*
Flavin, James W.; Vermont, 1857-1925 ***5900.10*** *p60*
Flavin, Johanna Rady 52; Vermont, 1903 ***5900.10*** *p67*
Flavin, Julia M. Sullivan; Vermont, 1854-1947 ***5900.10*** *p57*
Flavin, Katherine; Vermont, 1855-1929 ***5900.10*** *p66*
Flavin, Margaret E.; Vermont, 1856-1947 ***5900.10*** *p60*
Flavin, Mary; Vermont, 1836-1871 ***5900.10*** *p114*
Flavin, Mary Stack 95; Vermont, 1921 ***5900.10*** *p66*
Flavin, Patrick 31; Ontario, 1871 ***1823.28*** *p29*
Flavin, Thomas; Vermont, 1853-1927 ***5900.10*** *p57*
Flavin, William; Vermont, 1821-1906 ***5900.10*** *p60*
Flavin, William 25; Vermont, 1885 ***5900.10*** *p66*
Flavin, Winifred Sullivan; Vermont, 1826-1903 ***5900.10*** *p60*
Flawski, Mike; Maryland, 1910 ***3259.35*** *p14*
Flaxman, Thomas 44; Maryland, 1775 ***1220.25*** *p119*
Flaxmayer, Anton; Port uncertain, 1746 ***2856.30*** *p114*
Flaxon, Thomas; Maryland, 1664 ***2524.55*** *p80*
Flecher, Thomas 25; Ontario, 1871 ***1823.15*** *p81*
Fleck, Johann; Port uncertain, 1780 ***2856.30*** *p114*
Fleck, Lukas; America, 1747 ***2856.30*** *p114*
Fleck, Peter; Port uncertain, 1776 ***2856.30*** *p114*
Fleckenstein, Johann Georg; Port uncertain, 1768 ***2856.30*** *p114*
Fleckenstein, Philipp Jakob; Port uncertain, 1752 ***2856.30*** *p114*
Fleece, Albert 80; Ontario, 1871 ***1823.28*** *p29*
Fleece, John 38; Ontario, 1871 ***1823.28*** *p29*
Fleeman, Robert; Pennsylvania, 1778 ***4629.10*** *p32*
Fleeson, Plunket; Pennsylvania, 1777 ***4629.10*** *p14*
Fleet, Benjamin 21; Virginia, 1774 ***1220.25*** *p55*
Fleet, Rich; Virginia, 1665-1666 ***6212.30*** *p23*
Fleet, Richard; Virginia, 1666-1667 ***6212.30*** *p32*
Fleet, William; Maryland, 1733 ***1224.2*** *p41*
Fleete, Henry; Virginia, 1652 ***1224.1*** *p22*
Fleetwood, Edward; Virginia, 1663 ***6212.30*** *p4*
Fleetwood, Edward; Virginia, 1665 ***6212.30*** *p22*
Fleetwood, Robt; Virginia, 1663 ***6212.30*** *p4*
Fleetwood, Tho; Virginia, 1664 ***6212.30*** *p12*
Flegen, George; Maryland, 1670 ***2524.55*** *p127*
Flegler, Alice 4; Ontario, 1861 ***2896.28*** *p48*
Flegler, Caroline 6; Ontario, 1861 ***2896.28*** *p48*
Flegler, Catharine 33; Ontario, 1861 ***2896.28*** *p48*
Flegler, Emma 4; Ontario, 1861 ***2896.28*** *p48*
Flegler, Jacob 40; Kansas, 1891-1910 ***9079.10*** *p25*
Flegler, John 8; Ontario, 1861 ***2896.28*** *p48*
Flegler, Mary E. 17; Ontario, 1861 ***2896.28*** *p48*
Flegler, Mary E. 34; Kansas, 1891-1910 ***9079.10*** *p25*
Flegler, Milla 12; Ontario, 1861 ***2896.28*** *p48*
Flegler, Philip 2; Ontario, 1861 ***2896.28*** *p48*
Flegler, Samuel W. 21; Ontario, 1861 ***2896.28*** *p49*
Flegler, Stephen 10; Ontario, 1861 ***2896.28*** *p48*
Flegler, Thomas 23; Ontario, 1861 ***2896.28*** *p49*
Flehr, Anna Margarete; Port uncertain, 1749 ***2856.30*** *p114*
Flehrmann, Gottfried; America, 1773 ***2856.30*** *p114*
Flein, Thomas 18; Ontario, 1861 ***2896.28*** *p55*
Fleming, Aileen Connolly; Vermont, 1832-1920 ***5900.10*** *p389*
Fleming, Alexander; Georgia, 1698 ***1640.13*** *p39*
Fleming, Beatrice; Georgia, 1806 ***1640.10*** *p54*
Fleming, Catherine; Vermont, 1840-1895 ***5900.10*** *p116*
Fleming, Catherine Early; Vermont, 1860-1942 ***5900.10*** *p121*
Fleming, Dan 20; Ontario, 1871 ***1823.28*** *p29*
Fleming, David 67; Vermont, 1904 ***5900.10*** *p300*
Fleming, E. 22; Alaska, 1912 ***9196.1*** *p37*
Fleming, E. 22; Whitehorse, Yukon, 1912 ***9196.1*** *p37*
Fleming, Elizabeth 59; Ontario, 1871 ***1823.15*** *p81*
Fleming, Elizabeth G.; Vermont, 1863-1939 ***5900.10*** *p403*
Fleming, Ellen; Vermont, 1839-1901 ***5900.10*** *p76*
Fleming, Ellen; Vermont, 1857-1919 ***5900.10*** *p389*
Fleming, George; Georgia, 1699 ***1640.13*** *p39*
Fleming, Hannah 87; Vermont, 1934 ***5900.10*** *p113*
Fleming, James; New York, 1834 ***8197.10*** *p315*
Fleming, James; New York, 1840 ***8197.10*** *p164*
Fleming, James; Pennsylvania, 1788 ***4629.10*** *p56*
Fleming, James 27; Ontario, 1871 ***1823.28*** *p29*
Fleming, James 64; Ontario, 1871 ***1823.22*** *p53*
Fleming, Jennie; Vermont, 1861-1913 ***5900.10*** *p389*
Fleming, Jessie; Ontario, 1866 ***4537.35*** *p60*
Fleming, John; Maryland, 1659 ***2524.55*** *p80*
Fleming, John; Maryland, 1665 ***2524.55*** *p80*
Wife: Susanna
Daughter: Mary
Fleming, John; Maryland, 1665 ***2524.55*** *p107*
Wife: Susanna
Daughter: Mary
Fleming, John; New England, 1659 ***1224.1*** *p22*
Fleming, John; New York, 1829 ***1224.3*** *p26*
Fleming, John; Vermont, 1826-1902 ***5900.10*** *p389*
Fleming, John; Vermont, 1833-1916 ***5900.10*** *p403*
Fleming, John; Vermont, 1845-1930 ***5900.10*** *p200*
Fleming, John 21; Philadelphia, 1774 ***1220.25*** *p6*
Fleming, John 23; Ontario, 1871 ***1823.28*** *p29*
Fleming, John 39; Ontario, 1871 ***1823.15*** *p81*
Fleming, John 65; Ontario, 1871 ***1823.28*** *p29*
Fleming, John B.; New York, 1812 ***8197.10*** *p57*
Fleming, John B.; New York, 1820 ***8197.10*** *p61*
Fleming, Kate; Vermont, 1856-1921 ***5900.10*** *p200*
Fleming, Kathrin; Virginia, 1666 ***6212.30*** *p29*
Fleming, Kenneth J.; Vermont, 1901-1983 ***5900.10*** *p351*
Fleming, M. T.; Vermont, 1814-1900 ***5900.10*** *p200*
Fleming, Maria; Vermont, 1853-1912 ***5900.10*** *p389*
Fleming, Martin; Vermont, 1863 ***5900.10*** *p389*
Fleming, Mary *SEE* Fleming, John
Fleming, Mary; Vermont, 1854-1911 ***5900.10*** *p200*
Fleming, Mary 46; Ontario, 1871 ***1823.22*** *p53*
Fleming, Mary E. 22; Vermont, 1877 ***5900.10*** *p297*
Fleming, Mary Farrel; Vermont, 1826-1906 ***5900.10*** *p200*
Fleming, Mary Hickey; Vermont, 1833-1908 ***5900.10*** *p403*
Fleming, Mary Murphy; Vermont, 1900-1977 ***5900.10*** *p351*
Fleming, Mary Welch 95; Vermont, 1881 ***5900.10*** *p121*
Fleming, Michael; Vermont, 1814-1900 ***5900.10*** *p200*
Fleming, Michael 28; Vermont, 1865 ***5900.10*** *p539*
Fleming, Millar; Georgia, 1810 ***1640.10*** *p54*
Fleming, Millar; Ontario, 1897 ***1640.13*** *p39*
Fleming, Patrick; Vermont, 1848-1923 ***5900.10*** *p121*
Fleming, Patrick 65; Ontario, 1871 ***1823.15*** *p81*
Fleming, Robert; Pennsylvania, 1777 ***4629.10*** *p14*
Fleming, Susanna *SEE* Fleming, John
Fleming, T. S.; Nashville, Tennessee, 1849 ***1640.10*** *p54*
Fleming, Theresa A.; Vermont, 1855-1907 ***5900.10*** *p389*
Fleming, Thomas; New York, 1840 ***8197.10*** *p165*
Fleming, Thomas; Vermont, 1848-1899 ***5900.10*** *p350*
Fleming, William 31; Ontario, 1871 ***1823.22*** *p53*
Flemings, Thomas 63; Vermont, 1868 ***5900.10*** *p207*
Flemming, Agnes 25; Ontario, 1871 ***1823.22*** *p53*
Flemming, Eliza 35; Ontario, 1861 ***2896.28*** *p34*
Flemming, Esther J. 10; Ontario, 1861 ***2896.28*** *p34*
Flemming, James 26; Virginia, 1773 ***1220.25*** *p30*
Flemming, James A. 13; Ontario, 1861 ***2896.28*** *p34*
Flemming, James E.; Vermont, 1858-1900 ***5900.10*** *p387*
Flemming, John 2; Ontario, 1861 ***2896.28*** *p34*
Flemming, John 27; Virginia, 1775 ***1220.25*** *p110*
Flemming, Julia D.; Vermont, 1850-1929 ***5900.10*** *p387*
Flemming, Mary J. 5; Ontario, 1861 ***2896.28*** *p34*
Flemming, Sarah 7; Ontario, 1861 ***2896.28*** *p34*
Flemming, Sarah 60; Ontario, 1871 ***1823.22*** *p54*
Flemming, Thomas; New York, 1837 ***8197.10*** *p89*
Flemming, William 17; Ontario, 1861 ***2896.28*** *p34*
Flemming, Wilson 45; Ontario, 1861 ***2896.28*** *p34*
Flennock, John; Pennsylvania, 1860 ***6058.10*** *p44*
Flesh, Henry 50; Ontario, 1871 ***1823.22*** *p54*
Flesh, Patrick 30; Ontario, 1871 ***1823.22*** *p54*
Fleshman, William 38; Ontario, 1871 ***1823.28*** *p29*
Fletcher, Lieut.; Quebec, 1858 ***9196.15*** *p46*
Fletcher, Mr.; Portland, Maine, 1858 ***9196.15*** *p27*
Fletcher, Mr.; Quebec, 1858 ***9196.15*** *p32*
Fletcher, Mrs.; Quebec, 1858 ***9196.15*** *p46*
Fletcher, Alexander 45; Ontario, 1871 ***1823.22*** *p54*
Fletcher, Andrew; New York, 1840 ***8197.10*** *p166*
Fletcher, Ann; Maryland, 1681 ***2524.55*** *p80*
Fletcher, Charles 50; Ontario, 1871 ***1823.28*** *p29*
Fletcher, Charles 60; Ontario, 1871 ***1823.15*** *p81*
Fletcher, Frances; Maryland, 1674 ***2524.55*** *p80*
Fletcher, Frederick 20; Ontario, 1871 ***1823.15*** *p81*
Fletcher, Geo; Virginia, 1666 ***6212.30*** *p30*
Fletcher, H.; Quebec, 1857 ***9196.15*** *p17*
Fletcher, James; Pennsylvania, 1777 ***4629.10*** *p27*
Fletcher, James; Pennsylvania, 1779 ***4629.10*** *p37*
Fletcher, James H.; New York, 1840 ***8197.10*** *p231*
Fletcher, Jno; Virginia, 1668-1669 ***6212.30*** *p40*
Fletcher, John; Maryland, 1663 ***2524.55*** *p80*
Fletcher, John 48; Ontario, 1871 ***1823.28*** *p29*
Fletcher, John 60; Ontario, 1871 ***1823.22*** *p54*
Fletcher, Joseph; New York, 1804-1834 ***8197.10*** *p307*
Fletcher, Mary 60; Ontario, 1871 ***1823.15*** *p81*
Fletcher, Michel 50; Ontario, 1871 ***1823.15*** *p81*
Fletcher, Michial 49; Ontario, 1871 ***1823.28*** *p29*
Fletcher, Neill 60; Ontario, 1871 ***1823.22*** *p54*
Fletcher, Patrick; New York, 1836 ***8197.10*** *p77*
Fletcher, Reuben; Indiana, 1856 ***1224.3*** *p26*
Fletcher, Robert 40; Ontario, 1871 ***1823.28*** *p29*
Fletcher, Robert 65; Ontario, 1871 ***1823.15*** *p81*
Fletcher, Samuel 16; Virginia, 1774 ***1220.25*** *p91*
Fletcher, Susan; Virginia, 1668-1669 ***6212.30*** *p40*
Fletcher, Thomas 26; Philadelphia, 1774 ***1220.25*** *p6*
Fletcher, Thomas 29; Maryland, 1774 ***1220.25*** *p47*
Fletcher, William; Augusta, Georgia, 1836 ***1640.10*** *p54*
Fletcher, William; Augusta, Georgia, 1836 ***1640.13*** *p39*
Fletcher, William; Boston, 1746 ***1224.2*** *p41*
Fletcher, William; Died enroute, 1659 ***1224.1*** *p22*
Fletcher, Wm T. 24; Ontario, 1871 ***1823.28*** *p29*
Fleth, John Christoph; New York, 1840 ***8197.10*** *p164*
Fletnitz, William T. 42; Kansas, 1896-1910 ***9079.10*** *p37*
Flets, Johannes; New York, 1838 ***8197.10*** *p118*
Flett, C. L.; Alabama, 1813-1845 ***1640.10*** *p54*
Flett, Isobel; Savannah, Georgia, 1775 ***1640.10*** *p89*
Flett, William; Canada, 1823 ***1640.13*** *p39*
Fleurey, Andrew 25; Ontario, 1871 ***1823.28*** *p29*
Fleury, Rev.; Quebec, 1858 ***9196.15*** *p37*
Fleury, Berteyer; New York, 1816 ***8197.10*** *p59*
Flewelling, Samuel; New York, 1840 ***8197.10*** *p165*
Flick, Jacob 47; Ontario, 1871 ***1823.15*** *p81*
Flick, John; Pennsylvania, 1777 ***4629.10*** *p29*
Flick, Philip; Pennsylvania, 1777 ***4629.10*** *p7*
Flick, Wilhelm; Port uncertain, 1727 ***2856.30*** *p114*
Flick, William; Pennsylvania, 1786 ***4629.10*** *p49*
Flicker, John Adam; New York, 1840 ***8197.10*** *p165*
Flickmann, Peter; America, 1744 ***2856.30*** *p114*
With wife & children
Fliegauf, Josef; Port uncertain, 1726 ***2856.30*** *p114*
Fliem, Andreas; Port uncertain, 1710 ***2856.30*** *p114*
With wife & 14 children
Flight, Elizabeth; Virginia, 1671-1672 ***6212.30*** *p45*
Flilliall, Will.; Maryland, 1670 ***2524.55*** *p80*
Flimaning, John 31; Maryland, 1775 ***1220.25*** *p99*
Flinbidy, Timothy 40; Ontario, 1871 ***1823.28*** *p29*
Flinch, Edw; Virginia, 1665-1666 ***6212.30*** *p22*
Flinch, Edw; Virginia, 1666-1667 ***6212.30*** *p32*
Flindall, Caroline 61; Ontario, 1871 ***1823.22*** *p54*
Flindall, George 55; Ontario, 1871 ***1823.22*** *p54*
Flindall, Stephen 62; Ontario, 1871 ***1823.22*** *p54*
Fling, Roger; Virginia, 1703-1704 ***6212.30*** *p63*
Flinloff, Andrew 72; Ontario, 1871 ***1823.15*** *p81*
Flinn, Anna; Vermont, 1848-1881 ***5900.10*** *p343*
Flinn, Anna B.; Vermont, 1849-1862 ***5900.10*** *p343*
Flinn, David; New York, 1840 ***8197.10*** *p165*
Flinn, Edward; New York, 1836-1838 ***8197.10*** *p118*
Flinn, Edward 35; Ontario, 1871 ***1823.15*** *p81*
Flinn, Ellen; Vermont, 1837-1917 ***5900.10*** *p477*
Flinn, Hannah 35; Ontario, 1871 ***1823.15*** *p81*
Flinn, James; New York, 1803 ***8197.10*** *p12*
Flinn, Mary; Vermont, 1847-1862 ***5900.10*** *p343*
Flinn, Mary; Vermont, 1870-1931 ***5900.10*** *p356*
Flinn, Mary Donlan 88; Vermont, 1907 ***5900.10*** *p343*
Flinn, Michael; Vermont, 1854-1931 ***5900.10*** *p356*
Flinn, Pamer 61; Ontario, 1871 ***1823.15*** *p81*
Flinn, Thomas; Vermont, 1820-1862 ***5900.10*** *p343*
Flinn, Thomas; Vermont, 1841-1922 ***5900.10*** *p150*
Flinn, Thomas; Vermont, 1851-1862 ***5900.10*** *p343*
Flinn, Thomas 42; Vermont, 1862 ***5900.10*** *p343*
Flint, Henry A. 70; Vermont, 1905 ***5900.10*** *p292*
Flint, James 15; Maryland, 1774 ***1220.25*** *p61*
Flint, Jon; Virginia, 1674-1675 ***6212.30*** *p53*
Flint, Sarah R. 60; Vermont, 1904 ***5900.10*** *p292*
Flint, Thomas; New England, 1706 ***1224.2*** *p41*
Flint, Tobias; Maryland, 1659 ***2524.55*** *p81*
Flint, William 26; Maryland, 1775 ***1220.25*** *p112*
Flintoft, Francis; New York, 1838 ***8197.10*** *p378*
Flite, Richard; Virginia, 1703-1704 ***6212.30*** *p63*
Floard, George; Virginia, 1676 ***6212.30*** *p53*

Flock, Elisabeth; Port uncertain, 1775 2856.30 p114
Flock, Elizabeth 42; Ontario, 1871 1823.15 p81
Flock, John 15; Ontario, 1871 1823.15 p81
Flock, William 17; Ontario, 1871 1823.15 p81
Flogden, Andrew 16; Philadelphia, 1774 1220.25 p81
Flohausen, Konrad; Port uncertain, 1739 2856.30 p114
With wife & 4 children
Flohr, Jerg Anton; Port uncertain, 1785 2856.30 p114
Flojenski, Frank; Maryland, 1910 3259.35 p14
Flood, Mr.; Portland, Maine, 1858 9196.15 p30
Flood, Ann 75; Vermont, 1908 5900.10 p231
Flood, Ann 88; Vermont, 1888 5900.10 p226
Flood, Ann Burke 68; Vermont, 1883 5900.10 p261
Flood, Arthur 37; New York, 1838-1840 8197.10 p165
Flood, Bridget; Vermont, 1832-1916 5900.10 p240
Flood, Bridget; Vermont, 1835-1915 5900.10 p355
Flood, Bridget; Vermont, 1835-1916 5900.10 p357
Flood, Bridget; Vermont, 1847-1889 5900.10 p89
Flood, Bridget Melady 78; Vermont, 1864 5900.10 p72
Flood, Catherine 38; Vermont, 1865 5900.10 p574
Flood, Catherine Morgan 53; Vermont, 1879 5900.10 p591
Flood, Christopher 73; Vermont, 1877 5900.10 p72
Flood, Elizabeth; Vermont, 1838-1918 5900.10 p47
Flood, Elizabeth T.; Vermont, 1865-1926 5900.10 p120
Flood, Gregory 37; Vermont, 1880 5900.10 p506
Flood, Isaac 61; Ontario, 1871 1823.22 p54
Flood, James 67; Ontario, 1871 1823.15 p81
Flood, James 71; Ontario, 1871 1823.22 p54
Flood, John; Canada, 1756-1760 4628.40 p45
Flood, John; New York, 1834 8197.10 p315
Flood, John; Vermont, 1849-1915 5900.10 p395
Flood, John 63; Vermont, 1875 5900.10 p109
Flood, John 72; Ontario, 1871 1823.22 p54
Flood, John 76; Vermont, 1885 5900.10 p261
Flood, John 76; Vermont, 1899 5900.10 p591
Flood, John S.; Vermont, 1853-1936 5900.10 p120
Flood, Mary; Vermont, 1812-1887 5900.10 p89
Flood, Mary; Vermont, 1831-1888 5900.10 p83
Flood, Mary 26; Vermont, 1882 5900.10 p181
Flood, Mary 30; Vermont, 1877 5900.10 p580
Flood, Mary A.; Vermont, 1860-1954 5900.10 p395
Flood, Mary A. 70; Vermont, 1897 5900.10 p109
Flood, Mathew; New York, 1840 8197.10 p164
Flood, Nicholas; Vermont, 1839-1915 5900.10 p357
Flood, Nicholas; Vermont, 1839-1919 5900.10 p355
Flood, Patrick; New York, 1836 8197.10 p77
Flood, Patrick; New York, 1840 8197.10 p167
Flood, Patrick 67; Vermont, 1871 5900.10 p226
Flood, Peter; Canada, 1756-1760 4628.40 p46
Flood, Philip; New York, 1837 8197.10 p89
Flood, Robert; New York, 1840 8197.10 p164
Flood, Sarah; Vermont, 1853-1932 5900.10 p505
Flood, Sophia; Mobile, Alabama, 1790-1845 1640.10 p54
Flood, Stephen; Nova Scotia, 1745 4628.40 p45
Flood, Thomas; Vermont, 1845-1902 5900.10 p505
Flood, Thomas; Vermont, 1850-1911 5900.10 p120
Flood, Thomas 36; Vermont, 1883 5900.10 p476
Flood, William; Maryland, 1666 2524.55 p81
Flood, William 79; Ontario, 1871 1823.28 p29
Floody, Charles 48; Ontario, 1871 1823.15 p81
Flor, Georg; Port uncertain, 1783 2856.30 p115
Flor, Jerg Anton; Port uncertain, 1785 2856.30 p114
Flor, Nikolas; Port uncertain, 1783 2856.30 p115
Flore, Emile 32; Seattle, 1910 9196.1 p30
Flore, M. A. 30; Seattle, 1910 9196.1 p30
Florence, James 29; Ontario, 1871 1823.28 p29
Florer, Jose 30; Washington, 1913 9196.1 p59
Floud, Emily 40; Ontario, 1861 2896.28 p30
Floud, Fannie 13; Ontario, 1861 2896.28 p30
Floud, Hiram 4; Ontario, 1861 2896.28 p30
Floud, Isaac 50; Ontario, 1861 2896.28 p30
Floud, James E. 6; Ontario, 1861 2896.28 p30
Floud, Ross 11; Ontario, 1861 2896.28 p30
Floud, Susan E. 9; Ontario, 1861 2896.28 p30
Floud, Thomas 17; Ontario, 1861 2896.28 p30
Floud, William M. 1; Ontario, 1861 2896.28 p30
Flower, Elizabeth; Illinois, 1847 1224.3 p27
Flower, Hen; Virginia, 1672 6212.30 p50
Flower, Jane; Maryland, 1681 2524.55 p81
Flower, John 21; Virginia, 1774 1220.25 p87
Flower, Richard; Illinois, 1830 1224.3 p27
Flower, Thomas 28; Virginia, 1775 1220.25 p95
Flower, Walter; Virginia, 1726 1224.2 p41
Flower, William 21; Virginia, 1774 1220.25 p56
Flower, Wm; Virginia, 1678 6212.30 p54
Flowerdew, James Gray; America, 1873 1640.13 p39
Flowers, Mr.; Grenada, 1775 1220.25 p133
Flowers, Christopher; Pennsylvania, 1777 4629.10 p15
Flowers, Henry; Virginia, 1671 6212.30 p42
Flowers, Jonah; Virginia, 1666-1667 6212.30 p35
Floy, Michael; New York, 1807 8197.10 p42
Floyd, Ebenezer; New York, 1817 8197.10 p228
Floyd, J. 19; Ontario, 1861 2896.26 p11
Floyd, Jeane; Maryland, 1671 2524.55 p81
Floyd, John; Maryland, 1660-1661 2524.55 p49
Floyd, John; Maryland, 1660-1661 2524.55 p81
Floyd, John; Maryland, 1663 2524.55 p81
Floyd, John; Maryland, 1666 2524.55 p81
Floyd, John; Maryland, 1681 2524.55 p81
Floyd, John; Pennsylvania, 1832 6058.10 p11
Floyd, Joseph 16; Maryland, 1775 1220.25 p115
Floyd, Margaret; Georgia, 1774 1640.10 p54
Floyd, Margaret; Maryland, 1674 2524.55 p81
Floyd, Marmaduke; Maryland, 1679 2524.55 p81
Floyd, William H. 43; Ontario, 1871 1823.22 p54
Floyde, Edwd; Virginia, 1674-1675 6212.30 p53
Floyde, Marmaduke; Maryland, 1679 2524.55 p81
Floyde, Tho.; Maryland, 1672 2524.55 p81
Floyer, James; Virginia, 1666-1667 6212.30 p32
Flucher, John 22; Ontario, 1871 1823.28 p29
Flucker, Mary; Alabama, 1818-1845 1640.10 p54
Flud, Tho; Virginia, 1665-1666 6212.30 p22
Flud, Wm; Virginia, 1665-1666 6212.30 p21
Flude, Tho; Virginia, 1664 6212.30 p13
Fluegel, Charles; New York, 1807 8197.10 p42
Fluhr, Maria Catharina; Port uncertain, 1753 2856.30 p115
Fluits, Hannah; Maryland, 1665 2524.55 p81
Fluke, James; Maryland, 1679 2524.55 p81
Fluker, George 40; Ontario, 1871 1823.28 p29
Flukes, James; Maryland, 1679 2524.55 p81
Flukiger, John; New York, 1834 8197.10 p230
Flunker, Catherine 55; Ontario, 1871 1823.15 p81
Flunker, Mary 25; Ontario, 1871 1823.15 p81
Flunker, Sarah 18; Ontario, 1871 1823.15 p82
Flunker, William 55; Ontario, 1871 1823.15 p82
Flurgenner, Druscila 47; Ontario, 1861 2896.27 p74
Flurgenner, Egerton R. 18; Ontario, 1861 2896.27 p74
Flurgenner, James 20; Ontario, 1861 2896.27 p74
Flurgenner, Mary A. 11; Ontario, 1861 2896.27 p74
Flurgenner, Rachel M. 16; Ontario, 1861 2896.27 p74
Flurgenner, Sarah Elma 12; Ontario, 1861 2896.27 p74
Flurschutz, John 60; Ontario, 1871 1823.15 p82
Flury, Wilhelm; Port uncertain, 1773 2856.30 p115
Flute, Alice; Maryland, 1656 2524.55 p81
Flute, Jarvis; Maryland, 1657 2524.55 p81
Flute, Tho; Virginia, 1665-1666 6212.30 p23
Flute, Thomas; Virginia, 1666-1667 6212.30 p32
Fly, John; New England, 1698 1224.1 p22
Fly, Susan; Virginia, 1666 6212.30 p31
Flyharty, John; Maryland, 1680 2524.55 p81
Flyharty, Margaret; Maryland, 1680 2524.55 p81
Flyn, Catherine 44; Ontario, 1871 1823.22 p54
Flyn, James 50; Ontario, 1871 1823.15 p82
Flyn, Michael; New York, 1794 8197.10 p1
Flynn, Ann; Vermont, 1836-1928 5900.10 p563
Flynn, Ann; Vermont, 1838-1901 5900.10 p528
Flynn, Ann Maguire; Vermont, 1833-1889 5900.10 p618
Flynn, Augustus; New York, 1838 8197.10 p231
Flynn, Bridget; Vermont, 1822-1885 5900.10 p567
Flynn, Bridget 91; Vermont, 1897 5900.10 p342
Flynn, Bridget Collins; Vermont, n.d. 5900.10 p165
Flynn, Catherine; Vermont, n.d. 5900.10 p230
Flynn, Catherine; Vermont, 1850-1926 5900.10 p213
Flynn, Catherine; Vermont, 1852-1916 5900.10 p153
Flynn, Catherine; Vermont, 1855-1883 5900.10 p535
Flynn, Catherine 68; Vermont, 1894 5900.10 p577
Flynn, Catherine 73; Vermont, 1859 5900.10 p181
Flynn, Catherine H.; Vermont, 1854-1917 5900.10 p563
Flynn, Catherine Shea; Vermont, 1826-1911 5900.10 p220
Flynn, Charles 24; Maryland, 1775 1220.25 p114
Flynn, Charlotte Kennedy; Vermont, 1846-1934 5900.10 p489
Flynn, Daniel; New York, 1840 8197.10 p164
Flynn, David E.; Vermont, 1849-1927 5900.10 p184
Flynn, Edward 65; Ontario, 1871 1823.22 p54
Flynn, Eliza 80; Ontario, 1871 1823.15 p82
Flynn, Elizabeth; Vermont, 1832-1904 5900.10 p433
Flynn, Elizabeth; Vermont, 1853-1931 5900.10 p160
Flynn, Elizabeth C. 49; Vermont, 1883 5900.10 p107
Flynn, Ella; Vermont, 1852-1925 5900.10 p244
Flynn, Ellen; Vermont, 1831-1914 5900.10 p483
Flynn, Ellen; Vermont, 1842-1910 5900.10 p241
Flynn, Ellen 20; Ontario, 1861 2896.27 p19
Flynn, Ellen 83; Vermont, 1904 5900.10 p181
Flynn, Ellen Bartley; Vermont, 1821-1897 5900.10 p530
Flynn, Ellen Brewin; Vermont, 1855-1914 5900.10 p184
Flynn, Ellen Mullen; Vermont, 1854-1911 5900.10 p507
Flynn, Ellen Scanlen; Vermont, 1820-1898 5900.10 p219
Flynn, James; Vermont, 1824-1897 5900.10 p220
Flynn, James; Vermont, 1845-1913 5900.10 p160
Flynn, James; Vermont, 1850-1921 5900.10 p507
Flynn, James; Vermont, 1857-1925 5900.10 p554
Flynn, James 31; Vermont, 1875 5900.10 p529
Flynn, James 59; Ontario, 1871 1823.22 p54
Flynn, James 60; Ontario, 1871 1823.15 p82
Flynn, Jane; Vermont, n.d. 5900.10 p230
Flynn, Jane 36; Vermont, 1872 5900.10 p417
Flynn, Jeremiah 47; Ontario, 1871 1823.22 p54
Flynn, Jermiah 68; Ontario, 1871 1823.15 p82
Flynn, Joan Shanley; Vermont, 1853-1931 5900.10 p531
Flynn, John; New York, 1837 8197.10 p230
Flynn, John; Vermont, 1813-1890 5900.10 p342
Flynn, John; Vermont, 1821-1887 5900.10 p528
Flynn, John; Vermont, 1827-1896 5900.10 p219
Flynn, John 60; Vermont, 1872 5900.10 p77
Flynn, John 66; Ontario, 1871 1823.15 p82
Flynn, John Patrick; New York, 1835-1838 8197.10 p118
Flynn, Joseph; New York, 1823 8197.10 p229
Flynn, Joseph 15; Vermont, 1897 5900.10 p529
Flynn, Joseph 46; Ontario, 1871 1823.22 p54
Flynn, Katherine A.; Vermont, 1865-1943 5900.10 p554
Flynn, Katie McFarland 27; Vermont, 1877 5900.10 p181
Flynn, Lawrence 80; Vermont, 1880 5900.10 p229
Flynn, Louisa; Vermont, 1845-1890 5900.10 p477
Flynn, Martha F.; Vermont, 1863-1911 5900.10 p529
Flynn, Martha J.; Vermont, 1853-1856 5900.10 p530
Flynn, Martin; Vermont, 1816-1898 5900.10 p530
Flynn, Mary; Vermont, 1816-1898 5900.10 p133
Flynn, Mary; Vermont, 1848-1909 5900.10 p230
Flynn, Mary; Vermont, 1851-1946 5900.10 p323
Flynn, Mary; Vermont, 1852-1930 5900.10 p88
Flynn, Mary 31; Vermont, 1887 5900.10 p561
Flynn, Mary 34; Vermont, 1883 5900.10 p577
Flynn, Mary 77; Vermont, 1909 5900.10 p211
Flynn, Mary A.; Vermont, 1855-1919 5900.10 p68
Flynn, Mary Maher; Vermont, 1852-1928 5900.10 p429
Flynn, Mary O'Brien 70; Vermont, 1890 5900.10 p77
Flynn, Mathew; Vermont, 1863-1945 5900.10 p429
Flynn, Mattie E.; Vermont, 1858-1879 5900.10 p530
Flynn, Maurice; Vermont, n.d. 5900.10 p165
Flynn, Michael; New York, 1837 8197.10 p90
Flynn, Michael; Vermont, 1826-1888 5900.10 p433
Flynn, Michael 74; Vermont, 1892 5900.10 p181
Flynn, Patrick; New York, 1836 8197.10 p77
Flynn, Patrick; New York, 1838 8197.10 p231
Flynn, Patrick; Vermont, 1841-1927 5900.10 p489
Flynn, Patrick 51; Vermont, 1863 5900.10 p150
Flynn, Peter 55; Ontario, 1871 1823.15 p82
Flynn, Sarah Meighan; Vermont, 1819-1886 5900.10 p342
Flynn, Thomas; Vermont, n.d. 5900.10 p469
Flynn, Thomas; Vermont, 1845-1911 5900.10 p477
Flynn, Thomas 52; Vermont, 1861 5900.10 p230
Flynn, Thomas 60; Ontario, 1871 1823.15 p82
Flynn, William; New York, 1840 8197.10 p164
Flynn, William; Vermont, 1849-1922 5900.10 p531
Flynn, William 23; Ontario, 1871 1823.15 p82
Flyod, George 46; Ontario, 1871 1823.15 p82
Foard, John; Virginia, 1666 6212.30 p26
Foard, Wm; Virginia, 1663 6212.30 p2
Foceman, Thomas 37; Ontario, 1871 1823.15 p82
Focke, Charles A.; New York, 1840 8197.10 p167
Focley, James 60; Ontario, 1871 1823.15 p82
Foebek, J. 23; Alaska, 1912 9196.1 p38
Foebek, J. 23; Yukon, 1912 9196.1 p38
Foersch, John Augustus; New York, 1838 8197.10 p318
Foesyth, Frederick 31; Ontario, 1871 1823.15 p82
Fogarty, Bridget 65; Vermont, 1899 5900.10 p381
Fogarty, Cornelius 30; Virginia, 1774 1220.25 p91
Fogarty, Dennis 49; Vermont, 1879 5900.10 p245
Fogarty, Edward; New York, 1839 8197.10 p320
Fogarty, Ellen; Vermont, 1847-1880 5900.10 p269
Fogarty, Michael; New York, 1807 8197.10 p327
Fogel, Adam 30; Kansas, 1910 9079.10 p47
Fogel, Katie 7; Kansas, 1910 9079.10 p47
Fogel, Lea 4; Kansas, 1910 9079.10 p47
Fogel, Mollie 26; Kansas, 1910 9079.10 p47
Fogerty, James 27; Virginia, 1774 1220.25 p91
Fogerty, John; New York, 1837 8197.10 p89
Fogerty, Mary 54; Vermont, 1887 5900.10 p245
Fogg, Benjamin 19; Maryland, 1774 1220.25 p52
Fogg, John; Mississippi, 1823-1845 1640.10 p55
Fogg, William 23; Virginia, 1773 1220.25 p30
Foggett, Charles 17; Philadelphia, 1774 1220.25 p80
Fogle, Henry; Pennsylvania, 1840 6058.10 p16
Fogle, Jno; Virginia, 1664 6212.30 p15
Foglebaugher, John; Pennsylvania, 1829 6058.10 p9
Fogler, Henry; Pennsylvania, 1836 6058.10 p14
Fogler, Joseph; Pennsylvania, 1836 6058.10 p14
Fohet, Augustus; New York, 1838 8197.10 p119
Fohrin, Eva; Port uncertain, 1729 2856.30 p115
Fohrs, Georg; Port uncertain, 1780 2856.30 p115
Fohrs, Georg; Port uncertain, 1781 2856.30 p115
Foight, David; New York, New York, 1852 3437.14 p37
Foight, Jacob; New York, New York, 1856 3437.14 p33

Foiling, Col.; Quebec, 1856 ***9196.15*** *p10*
Foissin, John; Virginia, 1694 ***1224.1*** *p22*
Fojkowski, Handrey; Maryland, 1910 ***3259.35*** *p14*
Fokkes, Itje; New York, 1829 ***8197.10*** *p312*
Fokkes, Teunis; New York, 1836 ***8197.10*** *p77*
Folan, Mary 64; Vermont, 1894 ***5900.10*** *p290*
Folan, Thomas Edward; New York, 1840 ***8197.10*** *p231*
Folch, Urenund 36; Alaska, 1917 ***9196.1*** *p11*
Folch, Urenund 36; British Columbia, 1917 ***9196.1*** *p11*
Foldersby, Thomas; Maryland, 1666 ***2524.55*** *p81*
Foldwell, Joseph; Pennsylvania, 1777 ***4629.10*** *p8*
Foley, Ann; Vermont, 1828-1909 ***5900.10*** *p542*
Foley, Ann 62; Vermont, 1892 ***5900.10*** *p564*
Foley, Ann Flannelly 39; Vermont, 1860 ***5900.10*** *p180*
Foley, Ann O'Bryan 71; Vermont, 1903 ***5900.10*** *p188*
Foley, Annie; Vermont, 1839-1939 ***5900.10*** *p423*
Foley, Annie 10; Vermont, 1883 ***5900.10*** *p106*
Foley, Bartholmew; Buffalo, New York, 1854 ***6058.10*** *p51*
Foley, Bridget; Vermont, 1853-1897 ***5900.10*** *p252*
Foley, Bridget 29; Vermont, 1871 ***5900.10*** *p582*
Foley, Bridget Hanly; Vermont, 1829-1899 ***5900.10*** *p584*
Foley, Bryan; New York, 1837 ***8197.10*** *p89*
Foley, Bryan 76; Vermont, 1900 ***5900.10*** *p180*
Foley, Catharine Ryan 71; Vermont, 1905 ***5900.10*** *p342*
Foley, Catherine; Vermont, 1845-1928 ***5900.10*** *p425*
Foley, Catherine 72; Vermont, 1914 ***5900.10*** *p570*
Foley, Catherine Heffron; Vermont, 1829-1897 ***5900.10*** *p116*
Foley, Catherine Keniry; Vermont, 1815-1892 ***5900.10*** *p220*
Foley, Charlotte 73; Vermont, 1913 ***5900.10*** *p564*
Foley, Dan 18 *SEE* Foley, John
Foley, David; New York, 1821 ***8197.10*** *p229*
Foley, Delia B.; Vermont, 1867-1898 ***5900.10*** *p291*
Foley, Dennis; Vermont, 1846-1872 ***5900.10*** *p563*
Foley, Edward; Vermont, 1841-1908 ***5900.10*** *p357*
Foley, Eileen 28 *SEE* Foley, John
Foley, Eileen 50 *SEE* Foley, John
Foley, Eliza 66; Vermont, 1870 ***5900.10*** *p582*
Foley, Elizabeth B. 26; Vermont, 1886 ***5900.10*** *p188*
Foley, Ellen M. 28; Vermont, 1874 ***5900.10*** *p570*
Foley, Hannah McCarty; Vermont, n.d. ***5900.10*** *p396*
Foley, Hugh; Vermont, 1831-1894 ***5900.10*** *p116*
Foley, Isabella M. 3; Vermont, 1884 ***5900.10*** *p222*
Foley, James; Pennsylvania, 1868 ***6058.10*** *p73*
Foley, James; Vermont, 1824-1873 ***5900.10*** *p584*
Foley, James; Vermont, 1850-1917 ***5900.10*** *p94*
Foley, James; Vermont, 1858-1907 ***5900.10*** *p255*
Foley, James 59; Ontario, 1871 ***1823.22*** *p54*
Foley, James 68; Vermont, 1885 ***5900.10*** *p99*
Foley, James 87; Vermont, 1896 ***5900.10*** *p582*
Foley, James D. 37; Vermont, 1878 ***5900.10*** *p188*
Foley, Jennie E. Manor; Vermont, 1861-1919 ***5900.10*** *p318*
Foley, Johanna 11 *SEE* Foley, John
Foley, John; New York, 1829 ***8197.10*** *p359*
Foley, John; Vermont, 1831-1897 ***5900.10*** *p267*
Foley, John; Vermont, 1849-1905 ***5900.10*** *p318*
Foley, John 21 *SEE* Foley, John
Foley, John 37; Ontario, 1871 ***1823.28*** *p29*
Foley, John 40; Ontario, 1871 ***1823.28*** *p29*
Foley, John 52; New York, New York, 1849 ***1825.45*** *p49*
 Wife: Eileen 50
 Son: Pat 16
 Daughter: Johanna 11
 Daughter: Julea 8
 Daughter: Eileen 28
 Son: John 21
 Son: Dan 18
Foley, John 60; Vermont, 1910 ***5900.10*** *p149*
Foley, John 64; Vermont, 1919 ***5900.10*** *p290*
Foley, John J.; Vermont, 1838-1938 ***5900.10*** *p423*
Foley, Julea 8 *SEE* Foley, John
Foley, Julia; Vermont, 1865-1945 ***5900.10*** *p428*
Foley, Kate Tierney 71; Vermont, 1898 ***5900.10*** *p290*
Foley, Katherine; Vermont, 1857-1937 ***5900.10*** *p132*
Foley, Katherine; Vermont, 1863-1943 ***5900.10*** *p255*
Foley, Lucy E.; Vermont, 1860-1941 ***5900.10*** *p94*
Foley, Margaret; Vermont, 1827-1915 ***5900.10*** *p489*
Foley, Margaret; Vermont, 1833-1871 ***5900.10*** *p447*
Foley, Margaret; Vermont, 1834-1910 ***5900.10*** *p527*
Foley, Margaret 49; Vermont, 1885 ***5900.10*** *p106*
Foley, Margaret McQuire 77; Vermont, 1886 ***5900.10*** *p570*
Foley, Margaret Ryle; Vermont, 1841-1926 ***5900.10*** *p357*
Foley, Margaret Sheehan; Vermont, 1839-1891 ***5900.10*** *p267*
Foley, Martin; Vermont, 1816-1898 ***5900.10*** *p220*
Foley, Martin 45; Ontario, 1871 ***1823.28*** *p29*
Foley, Mary; Vermont, 1828-1878 ***5900.10*** *p196*
Foley, Mary; Vermont, 1834-1934 ***5900.10*** *p488*
Foley, Mary; Vermont, 1846-1874 ***5900.10*** *p563*
Foley, Mary; Vermont, 1856-1936 ***5900.10*** *p213*
Foley, Mary 42; Vermont, 1870 ***5900.10*** *p501*
Foley, Mary 42; Vermont, 1870 ***5900.10*** *p510*
Foley, Mary 76; Vermont, 1886 ***5900.10*** *p515*
Foley, Mary Carmody 28; Vermont, 1877 ***5900.10*** *p570*
Foley, Mary D. 24; Vermont, 1884 ***5900.10*** *p106*
Foley, Mary Kennedy 80; Vermont, 1906 ***5900.10*** *p247*
Foley, Mary Murray 70; Vermont, 1915 ***5900.10*** *p118*
Foley, Mary Rice; Vermont, 1861-1920 ***5900.10*** *p579*
Foley, Matthew 30; Ontario, 1871 ***1823.15*** *p82*
Foley, Michael 28; Ontario, 1871 ***1823.28*** *p29*
Foley, Michael 40; Vermont, 1863 ***5900.10*** *p247*
Foley, Michael 57; Ontario, 1871 ***1823.28*** *p29*
Foley, Michael 88; Vermont, 1886 ***5900.10*** *p570*
Foley, Miles; Vermont, 1855-1920 ***5900.10*** *p396*
Foley, Nellie 15; Vermont, 1883 ***5900.10*** *p106*
Foley, Nellie 56; Vermont, 1876 ***5900.10*** *p99*
Foley, Nora Brown; Vermont, 1854-1930 ***5900.10*** *p150*
Foley, Nora Corbett; Vermont, 1855-1922 ***5900.10*** *p252*
Foley, Owen 60; Vermont, 1901 ***5900.10*** *p118*
Foley, Pat 16 *SEE* Foley, John
Foley, Patrick; New York, 1835-1838 ***8197.10*** *p119*
Foley, Patrick; Vermont, 1827-1898 ***5900.10*** *p291*
Foley, Patrick; Vermont, 1853-1903 ***5900.10*** *p252*
Foley, Patsey 31; Vermont, 1885 ***5900.10*** *p290*
Foley, Richard; Vermont, 1850-1917 ***5900.10*** *p579*
Foley, Sarah 52; Vermont, 1913 ***5900.10*** *p290*
Foley, Tho; Virginia, 1664 ***6212.30*** *p10*
Foley, Thomas; Vermont, 1824-1899 ***5900.10*** *p418*
Foley, Thomas 21; Vermont, 1873 ***5900.10*** *p288*
Foley, Thomas 63; Vermont, 1926 ***5900.10*** *p290*
Foley, Thomas 75; Vermont, 1902 ***5900.10*** *p290*
Foley, Thomas 80; Vermont, 1886 ***5900.10*** *p342*
Foley, William; New York, 1826 ***8197.10*** *p337*
Foley, William; Vermont, 1863 ***5900.10*** *p247*
Foley, William 37; Ontario, 1871 ***1823.22*** *p54*
Folgaringle, Godtlip 40; Ontario, 1871 ***1823.28*** *p29*
Folie, Robert 27; Ontario, 1871 ***1823.15*** *p82*
Folkard, P. 28; St. Kitts, 1774 ***1220.25*** *p44*
Folkard, Philip 29; Virginia, 1775 ***1220.25*** *p95*
Folks, John 59; Ontario, 1871 ***1823.28*** *p29*
Follan, Thomas; Vermont, n.d. ***5900.10*** *p477*
Folland, Henry 53; Ontario, 1871 ***1823.15*** *p82*
Folland, Thomas 36; Ontario, 1871 ***1823.15*** *p82*
Follard, John 20; Virginia, 1774 ***1220.25*** *p94*
Follen, William 27; Ontario, 1871 ***1823.15*** *p82*
Follet, David 70; Ontario, 1871 ***1823.22*** *p54*
Follett, Abell; Maryland, 1660 ***2524.55*** *p79*
Follett, Abell; Maryland, 1660 ***2524.55*** *p81*
Follett, Asneath 24; Ontario, 1861 ***2896.25*** *p13*
Follett, Charlotte 26; Ontario, 1861 ***2896.25*** *p13*
Follett, Fanny; Vermont, 1788-1878 ***5900.10*** *p174*
Follett, John; Virginia, 1692 ***1224.1*** *p22*
Follette, William 43; Ontario, 1871 ***1823.15*** *p82*
Folliard, Bridget 72; Vermont, 1909 ***5900.10*** *p605*
Follingsayne, Anne; Maryland, 1666 ***2524.55*** *p81*
Follington, Ann; Maryland, 1667 ***2524.55*** *p81*
Follis, James 41; Ontario, 1871 ***1823.15*** *p82*
Follis, William 55; Ontario, 1871 ***1823.15*** *p82*
Follon, John 76; Vermont, 1856 ***5900.10*** *p477*
Folly, William 35; Ontario, 1871 ***1823.15*** *p82*
Folmar, Andrew; New York, 1810-1816 ***8197.10*** *p59*
 Wife: Louisa L.
 Child: Jane
 Child: John
 Child: Francis
 Child: Mary
Folmar, Francis *SEE* Folmar, Andrew
Folmar, Jane *SEE* Folmar, Andrew
Folmar, John *SEE* Folmar, Andrew
Folmar, John; New York, 1810-1816 ***8197.10*** *p59*
Folmar, Louisa L. *SEE* Folmar, Andrew
Folmar, Mary *SEE* Folmar, Andrew
Fols, Eva; Port uncertain, 1764 ***2856.30*** *p115*
Fols, Johann Baptist; America, 1764 ***2856.30*** *p126*
Foltz, Anna Maria; Port uncertain, 1786 ***2856.30*** *p115*
Foltz, Gertrud; Port uncertain, 1786 ***2856.30*** *p115*
Foltz, Maria Anna; Port uncertain, 1786 ***2856.30*** *p115*
Foman, John; Pennsylvania, 1837 ***6058.10*** *p14*
Fones, D. B. 47; Ontario, 1861 ***2896.28*** *p15*
Fones, Ida 5; Ontario, 1861 ***2896.28*** *p15*
Fones, M. 1; Ontario, 1861 ***2896.28*** *p15*
Font, Geog; Virginia, 1671 ***6212.30*** *p42*
Fontaine, Frances Antoinette; New York, 1831 ***8197.10*** *p355*
Fontaine, Francis Antoinette; New York, 1831 ***8197.10*** *p370*
Fontius, Johann; America, 1752 ***2856.30*** *p115*
 With wife & 8 children
Fontius, Mrs. Valentin; America, 1752 ***2856.30*** *p115*
Fooke, Samuel; Maryland, 1661 ***2524.55*** *p81*
Fooke, William; Virginia, 1664 ***6212.30*** *p13*
Fookes, Amy; Maryland, 1672 ***2524.55*** *p81*
Fookes, Arthur; Virginia, 1666-1667 ***6212.30*** *p34*
Fooks, Paul; Pennsylvania, 1778 ***4629.10*** *p35*
Foones, Gilbert; Maryland, 1665 ***2524.55*** *p81*
Foord, Gabriel; South Carolina, 1719 ***1224.2*** *p41*
Foord, Jane 23; Ontario, 1871 ***1823.15*** *p82*
Foord, Lettis; Maryland, 1674 ***2524.55*** *p81*
Foord, Robert 60; Ontario, 1871 ***1823.15*** *p82*
Foord, Stephen; New York, 1840 ***8197.10*** *p165*
Foord, William; Georgia, 1698 ***1640.13*** *p39*
Foorte, Richard; Maryland, 1659 ***2524.55*** *p81*
Foos, Johann; Port uncertain, 1751 ***2856.30*** *p115*
Foose, George; New York, 1794 ***8197.10*** *p1*
Foost, Caspar; New York, 1838 ***8197.10*** *p231*
Foot, Mrs.; Maryland, 1665 ***2524.55*** *p81*
Foot, Alexander 42; Ontario, 1871 ***1823.22*** *p54*
Foot, Alexander 45; Ontario, 1871 ***1823.15*** *p82*
Foot, Mary; Maryland, 1658 ***2524.55*** *p223*
Foot, Mary; Maryland, 1666 ***2524.55*** *p223*
Foot, Richd.; Maryland, 1657 ***2524.55*** *p81*
Foot, Thomas; New York, 1802 ***8197.10*** *p20*
Foote, Geneva C.; Vermont, 1854-1918 ***5900.10*** *p50*
Foote, Henry; Maryland, 1681 ***2524.55*** *p81*
Foote, James; Maryland, 1659 ***2524.55*** *p81*
Foote, James; Maryland, 1665 ***2524.55*** *p81*
Foote, Lillian V.; Vermont, 1861-1933 ***5900.10*** *p312*
Footman, Richard; Pennsylvania, 1777 ***4629.10*** *p21*
Footman, Richard; Pennsylvania, 1779 ***4629.10*** *p40*
Foott, Helen 2; Ontario, 1871 ***1823.28*** *p29*
Foott, Wade George 43; Ontario, 1871 ***1823.28*** *p29*
Foran, Mr.; Quebec, 1856 ***9196.15*** *p11*
Foran, Mrs.; Quebec, 1856 ***9196.15*** *p11*
Foran, Catherine; Vermont, 1851-1930 ***5900.10*** *p137*
Foran, Dennis; Vermont, 1843-1912 ***5900.10*** *p136*
Foran, John 55; Ontario, 1871 ***1823.28*** *p30*
Foran, Julia 75; Vermont, n.d. ***5900.10*** *p136*
Foran, Julia Sullivan; Vermont, 1847-1908 ***5900.10*** *p75*
Foran, Mary; Vermont, 1832-1914 ***5900.10*** *p340*
Foran, Mary Clorin; Vermont, 1843-1928 ***5900.10*** *p136*
Foran, Michael, Sr. 64; Ontario, 1871 ***1823.28*** *p30*
Foran, Michael, Jr. 33; Ontario, 1871 ***1823.28*** *p30*
Foran, Patrick 32; Ontario, 1871 ***1823.28*** *p30*
Foran, Patrick 62; Ontario, 1871 ***1823.28*** *p30*
Forbes, Miss; Portland, Maine, 1858 ***9196.15*** *p47*
Forbes, Mrs.; Quebec, 1857 ***9196.15*** *p13*
Forbes, Alexander; Kingston, Jamaica, 1803 ***1640.13*** *p40*
Forbes, Alexander; San Francisco, 1884 ***1640.13*** *p40*
Forbes, Alexander 28; Ontario, 1871 ***1823.22*** *p54*
Forbes, Alexander 50; Ontario, 1871 ***1823.15*** *p82*
Forbes, Alexander 65; Ontario, 1871 ***1823.22*** *p54*
Forbes, Ann 51; Ontario, 1871 ***1823.15*** *p82*
Forbes, Ann Katherine; Charleston, South Carolina, 1824 ***1224.3*** *p40*
Forbes, C. G.; Mobile, Alabama, 1844 ***1640.10*** *p55*
Forbes, Daniel; New York, 1807 ***8197.10*** *p42*
Forbes, Daniel; Pennsylvania, 1777 ***4629.10*** *p25*
Forbes, Donald; Georgia, 1743 ***1640.10*** *p55*
Forbes, Esther 30; Ontario, 1871 ***1823.22*** *p54*
Forbes, George; Maryland, 1742 ***1224.2*** *p41*
Forbes, George 45; Ontario, 1871 ***1823.15*** *p82*
Forbes, Hugh; Georgia, 1736 ***1640.10*** *p55*
Forbes, Hugh; South Carolina, 1734 ***1640.10*** *p55*
Forbes, Jack 69; Ontario, 1871 ***1823.22*** *p54*
Forbes, James; Long Island, 1782 ***1224.2*** *p41*
Forbes, James; New York, 1805 ***8197.10*** *p29*
Forbes, James; Pennsylvania, 1777 ***4629.10*** *p15*
Forbes, James; Savannah, Georgia, 1818 ***1640.10*** *p55*
Forbes, John; Georgia, 1715-1845 ***1640.10*** *p55*
Forbes, John; St. Augustine, Florida, 1764-1783 ***1640.10*** *p55*
Forbes, John; St. Augustine, Florida, 1784 ***1640.10*** *p56*
Forbes, John; Savannah, Georgia, 1775 ***1640.10*** *p55*
Forbes, John 25; Jamaica, 1774 ***1220.25*** *p79*
Forbes, John 30; Philadelphia, 1774 ***1220.25*** *p68*
Forbes, John 49; Ontario, 1871 ***1823.22*** *p54*
Forbes, John 60; Ontario, 1871 ***1823.15*** *p82*
Forbes, John 62; Ontario, 1871 ***1823.15*** *p82*
Forbes, John Stuart; America, 1877 ***1640.13*** *p40*
Forbes, Mary Ann 27; Ontario, 1871 ***1823.22*** *p54*
Forbes, Robert 63; Ontario, 1871 ***1823.15*** *p82*
Forbes, Thomas; Pennsylvania, 1739 ***1224.2*** *p41*
Forbes, Thomas; St. Augustine, Florida, 1775 ***1640.10*** *p56*
Forbes, Thomas W. 35; Ontario, 1871 ***1823.22*** *p54*
Forbes, William; Florida, 1770-1845 ***1640.10*** *p56*
Forbes, William; North America, 1890 ***1640.13*** *p40*
Forbes, William; Pennsylvania, 1777 ***4629.10*** *p24*
Forbes, William 30; Tobago, West Indies, 1775 ***1220.25*** *p129*
Forbey, William 15; Baltimore, 1775 ***1220.25*** *p116*
Forbie, Margarett *SEE* Forbie, William
Forbie, William *SEE* Forbie, William

Forbie, William; Maryland, 1682 2524.55 p81
Wife: Margarett
Son: William
Forbis, John 41; Ontario, 1871 1823.28 p30
Forby, . . .; Virginia, 1661 1224.1 p22
Forby, Thomas; Maryland, 1649 2524.55 p81
Force, Helen O'Neil; Vermont, 1860-1947 5900.10 p560
Force, Robert; Vermont, 1844-1917 5900.10 p560
Forch, Catherina; America, 1768 2856.30 p115
Forch, Elisabeth; America, 1768 2856.30 p115
Forcier, Loude; Vermont, 1847-1921 5900.10 p379
Ford, Mr.; Quebec, 1856 9196.15 p9
Ford, Mr.; Quebec, 1857 9196.15 p14
Ford, Alex 64; Ontario, 1871 1823.15 p83
Ford, Alexander 26; Virginia, 1774 1220.25 p89
Ford, Ann 53; Ontario, 1871 1823.15 p83
Ford, Arthur Perroneau; Charleston, South Carolina, 1849 1224.3 p27
Ford, Benjamin; Virginia, 1664 6212.30 p15
Ford, Betsey Westover; Vermont, 1841-1930 5900.10 p520
Ford, Catharine; Vermont, 1830-1923 5900.10 p489
Ford, Charles 53; Ontario, 1871 1823.22 p54
Ford, Constance; Maryland, 1660 2524.55 p81
Ford, Daniel; Vermont, 1850-1905 5900.10 p70
Ford, Dennis 50; Ontario, 1871 1823.15 p83
Ford, Edmund 73; Vermont, 1881 5900.10 p297
Ford, Edward; Vermont, 1861-1894 5900.10 p286
Ford, Elijah; New York, 1839 8197.10 p231
Ford, George 57; Ontario, 1871 1823.15 p83
Ford, George 58; Ontario, 1871 1823.15 p83
Ford, Gilbert 83; Ontario, 1871 1823.22 p54
Ford, H.; Quebec, 1856 9196.15 p10
Ford, Henry; Virginia, 1664 6212.30 p15
Ford, Henry 39; Ontario, 1871 1823.22 p54
Ford, James 26; Ontario, 1871 1823.15 p83
Ford, James 39; Ontario, 1871 1823.22 p54
Ford, Jane 53; Ontario, 1871 1823.15 p83
Ford, Jennie; Vermont, 1868-1890 5900.10 p286
Ford, John; New York, 1806 8197.10 p322
Ford, John; New York, 1832 8197.10 p299
Ford, John; Pennsylvania, 1837 6058.10 p12
Ford, John; Vermont, 1837 5900.10 p190
Ford, John; Vermont, 1845-1899 5900.10 p412
Ford, John; Vermont, 1847-1902 5900.10 p520
Ford, John; Vermont, 1857-1889 5900.10 p286
Ford, John; Virginia, 1665-1666 6212.30 p24
Ford, John 17; Philadelphia, 1774 1220.25 p81
Ford, John 21; Ontario, 1871 1823.15 p83
Ford, John 37; Ontario, 1871 1823.15 p83
Ford, John 60; Ontario, 1871 1823.15 p83
Ford, John Ross; New York, 1897 1640.13 p40
Ford, Joni; Maryland, 1663 2524.55 p242
Ford, Lidia *SEE* Ford, Robert
Ford, Margaret; Vermont, 1855-1922 5900.10 p286
Ford, Margaret 58; Vermont, 1870 5900.10 p412
Ford, Margaret Stack; Vermont, 1852-1931 5900.10 p412
Ford, Mary; Vermont, 1857 5900.10 p566
Ford, Mary A. Murray; Vermont, 1822-1883 5900.10 p286
Ford, Mary E. Higgins 20; Vermont, 1876 5900.10 p53
Ford, Menery 46; Ontario, 1871 1823.15 p83
Ford, N. C.; Quebec, 1858 9196.15 p45
Ford, Ralph 22; Maryland, 1775 1220.25 p105
Ford, Rebeccah; Maryland, 1659 2524.55 p82
Ford, Robert; Maryland, 1667 2524.55 p82
Wife: Lidia
Ford, Robert 9; Maryland, 1647 2524.55 p82
Ford, Robert 40; Carolina, 1775 1220.25 p123
Ford, Samuel; Pennsylvania, 1777 4629.10 p17
Ford, Samuel 72; Ontario, 1871 1823.15 p83
Ford, Thomas; Vermont, 1822-1892 5900.10 p286
Ford, Thomas 31; Ontario, 1871 1823.15 p83
Ford, Thomas 32; Virginia, 1774 1220.25 p45
Ford, Thomas 39; Ontario, 1871 1823.28 p30
Ford, William; New York, 1838 8197.10 p376
Ford, Wm; Virginia, 1663 6212.30 p2
Forder, Charles; Pennsylvania, 1777 4629.10 p14
Forderer, Elisabeth; Port uncertain, 1735 2856.30 p115
Forderer, Michael; Port uncertain, 1768 2856.30 p115
Fordyce, Charles; Virginia, 1777 1224.2 p41
Fordyce, Peter; Tobago, West Indies, 1830 1640.13 p40
Fore, Henry 14; Kansas, 1906-1910 9079.10 p9
Fore, Thomas 55; Ontario, 1871 1823.15 p83
Fore, William 40; Ontario, 1871 1823.15 p83
Forecythe, Frances 35; Ontario, 1871 1823.28 p30
Forehand, Gillian; Maryland, 1671 2524.55 p82
Forehen, John 29; Ontario, 1871 1823.15 p83
Foreland, Mathew; Virginia, 1667 6212.30 p37
Foreman, Eleanor 20; Georgia, 1775 1220.25 p126
Foreman, Mary 40; Ontario, 1871 1823.22 p54
Foreman, Richard; Maryland, 1652-1658 2524.55 p138
Foreman, Richd.; Maryland, 1652-1658 2524.55 p82
Foreman, Stephen; Pennsylvania, 1777 4629.10 p14
Foreman, William 47; Ontario, 1871 1823.28 p30
Foren, Catherine 55; Vermont, 1854 5900.10 p348
Forenz, Frank; Maryland, 1910 3259.35 p14
Forepaugh, George; Pennsylvania, 1777 4629.10 p10
Fores, Sebastian; Port uncertain, 1752 2856.30 p115
Forest, Charles 19; Ontario, 1871 1823.28 p30
Forest, John 84; Ontario, 1871 1823.28 p30
Forest, Peter A.; New York, 1831 8197.10 p367
Forest, Thomas 24; Virginia, 1774 1220.25 p55
Forest, William 43; Ontario, 1871 1823.15 p83
Forestreet, Thomas 24; Jamaica, 1774 1220.25 p90
Foresyth, Archie 60; Ontario, 1871 1823.22 p55
Forfar, Alexander 20; Tortola, 1773-1774 1220.25 p32
Forge, Frank 33; Ontario, 1871 1823.28 p30
Forge, Tho; Virginia, 1665-1666 6212.30 p24
Forkey, Edward; Vermont, 1840-1911 5900.10 p552
Forkey, Lizzie Myott; Vermont, 1843-1938 5900.10 p552
Forle, Johann; Port uncertain, 1776 2856.30 p126
Forler, Andreas; Port uncertain, 1698 2856.30 p106
With 7 children
Forler, Jacob; America, 1750 2856.30 p115
With wife & children
Forler, Jacob; Port uncertain, 1750 2856.30 p115
With wife & children
Forler, Jacob, Jr.; America, 1750 2856.30 p115
With wife & children
Forlong, Benjamin 71; Ontario, 1871 1823.22 p55
Forman, William; New York, 1775 1224.2 p41
Forner, Elizabeth 46; Ontario, 1871 1823.22 p55
Forrer, Abraham; America, 1765 2856.30 p115
Forrest, Mrs.; Quebec, 1858 9196.15 p36
Forrest, Andrew; Pennsylvania, 1777 4629.10 p30
Forrest, Andrew 55; Ontario, 1871 1823.28 p30
Forrest, Charles 70; Ontario, 1871 1823.15 p83
Forrest, Cooper 43; Ontario, 1871 1823.15 p83
Forrest, David; New York, 1837 8197.10 p89
Forrest, Elizabeth 26; Baltimore, 1775 1220.25 p119
Forrest, George 48; Ontario, 1871 1823.15 p83
Forrest, George 83; Ontario, 1871 1823.15 p83
Forrest, James; Minnesota, 1888 1640.13 p40
Forrest, James; New York, 1806 8197.10 p322
Forrest, James; New York, 1858 1640.13 p40
Forrest, James; Savannah, Georgia, 1820 1640.10 p56
Forrest, James; Virginia, 1667 6212.30 p36
Forrest, James 39; Ontario, 1871 1823.15 p83
Forrest, James 57; Ontario, 1871 1823.15 p83
Forrest, John 39; Ontario, 1871 1823.15 p83
Forrest, Mary; New Orleans, 1853 1640.10 p56
Forrest, Patrick; Maryland, 1654 2524.55 p82
Forrest, Robert; Virginia, 1664 6212.30 p12
Forrest, Thomas; Pennsylvania, 1781 4629.10 p42
Forrest, Timo; Virginia, 1666 6212.30 p25
Forrest, William; New York, 1807 8197.10 p42
Forrest, William 21; Ontario, 1871 1823.15 p83
Forrest, William 45; Ontario, 1871 1823.22 p55
Forrester, Andrew; New York, 1808 8197.10 p53
Forrester, Arabella; Mississippi, 1845 1640.10 p56
Forrester, James 20; Philadelphia, 1774 1220.25 p76
Forrester, John; Honduras, 1872 1640.13 p40
Forrester, John; St. Augustine, Florida, 1787 1640.10 p56
Forrester, John Young; America, 1869 1640.13 p40
Forrester, Margaret; Mississippi, 1822 1640.10 p56
Forrester, Robert; Mississippi, 1815 1640.10 p56
Forrester, Somerville; Jamaica, 1804 1640.13 p40
Forrester, Thomas 31; Ontario, 1871 1823.28 p30
Forrister, Garrald; Pennsylvania, 1777 4629.10 p22
Forrister, Gerald; Pennsylvania, 1779 4629.10 p41
Forsch, J. P.; America, 1697 2856.30 p362
Forsch, Johann Peter; America, 1697 2856.30 p115
Forschges, Wilhelm; Port uncertain, 1775 2856.30 p126
Forschges, Wilhelm; Port uncertain, 1793 2856.30 p127
Forschner, Johann; Canada, 1751 2856.30 p115
Forse, John; Alaska, 1915 9196.1 p11
Forse, John; British Columbia, 1915 9196.1 p11
Forsen, John; Maryland, 1662 2524.55 p82
Forset, Thomas; Maryland, 1667 2524.55 p82
Forsey, Jeremiah; Maryland, 1658 2524.55 p82
Forsham, John 54; Ontario, 1871 1823.15 p83
Forshea, Benjamin 14; Ontario, 1861 2896.28 p63
Forshea, Hiram 26; Ontario, 1861 2896.28 p65
Forshea, Mary; Ontario, 1861 2896.28 p64
Forshea, Peter 23; Ontario, 1861 2896.28 p64
Forson, Thomas; Virginia, 1671 6212.30 p44
Forss, Elisabeth; America, 1796 2856.30 p115
Forster, Mr.; Quebec, 1858 9196.15 p43
Forster, Ann *SEE* Forster, Richard
Forster, Anna Maria Kraft; America, 1764 2856.30 p126
Forster, Henry; New York, 1807 8197.10 p42
Forster, Jane *SEE* Forster, Richard
Forster, Johann; Port uncertain, 1736 2856.30 p116
Forster, Johann Georg; America, 1763 2856.30 p116
With wife
Forster, Johann Georg; America, 1764 2856.30 p116
With wife
Forster, John; Maryland, 1662 2524.55 p82
Forster, John 17; Philadelphia, 1774 1220.25 p81
Forster, John 24; North Carolina, 1774 1220.25 p65
Forster, John 30; Philadelphia, 1775 1220.25 p107
Forster, Jonathan 20; Virginia, 1774 1220.25 p90
Forster, Mrs. Michael; Port uncertain, 1762 2856.30 p126
Forster, Nickolous 48; Ontario, 1871 1823.15 p83
Forster, Nikolaus; Port uncertain, 1736 2856.30 p116
Forster, Richard *SEE* Forster, Richard
Forster, Richard; Maryland, 1653 2524.55 p82
Wife: Ann
Child: Jane
Child: Ann
Child: Richard
Forster, Thomas 18; Maryland, 1774 1220.25 p8
Forster, William T. 42; Ontario, 1871 1823.28 p30
Forstges, Wilhelm; Port uncertain, 1770 2856.30 p126
With wife & children
Forstges, Wilhelm; Port uncertain, 1775 2856.30 p126
Forstges, Wilhelm; Port uncertain, 1793 2856.30 p127
Forsyght, Simon 28; Ontario, 1871 1823.15 p83
Forsyth, Mr.; Quebec, 1857 9196.15 p22
Forsyth, Alesean 70; Ontario, 1871 1823.15 p83
Forsyth, Alexander 38; Ontario, 1871 1823.15 p83
Forsyth, Alexander 46; Ontario, 1871 1823.15 p83
Forsyth, Berobeer 22; Carolina, 1774 1220.25 p83
Forsyth, Catherine; Georgia, 1738 1640.10 p56
Forsyth, David 42; Ontario, 1871 1823.15 p83
Forsyth, Donald 50; Ontario, 1871 1823.28 p30
Forsyth, Ebenezar 45; Ontario, 1871 1823.15 p83
Forsyth, George 38; Ontario, 1871 1823.15 p83
Forsyth, George 50; Ontario, 1871 1823.15 p83
Forsyth, Henry 42; Ontario, 1871 1823.15 p83
Forsyth, Hugh 35; Ontario, 1871 1823.15 p83
Forsyth, James 44; Ontario, 1871 1823.15 p83
Forsyth, John; Jamaica, 1854 1640.13 p40
Forsyth, John 34; Ontario, 1871 1823.15 p83
Forsyth, John 34; Ontario, 1871 1823.28 p30
Forsyth, John 42; Ontario, 1871 1823.22 p55
Forsyth, John 64; Ontario, 1871 1823.28 p30
Forsyth, Margaret; Georgia, 1738 1640.10 p56
Forsyth, Robert 50; Ontario, 1871 1823.15 p84
Forsyth, Roderick 27; Ontario, 1871 1823.15 p84
Forsyth, Sarah 60; Ontario, 1871 1823.15 p84
Forsyth, Thomas; Maryland, 1910 3259.35 p14
Forsyth, Thomas 47; Maryland, 1775 1220.25 p110
Forsyth, William; Georgia, 1743 1640.10 p57
Forsyth, William; New York, 1840 8197.10 p231
Forsyth, William; North America, 1797 1640.13 p40
Forsyth, William 17; Jamaica, 1774 1220.25 p49
Forsyth, William 36; Ontario, 1871 1823.15 p84
Forsythe, Francis 31; Ontario, 1871 1823.28 p30
Forsythe, John; Chicago, 1886 1640.13 p40
Forsythe, William 17; Ontario, 1861 2896.28 p15
Fort, Jno.; Maryland, 1680 2524.55 p82
Fortchunch, Miss; Quebec, 1857 9196.15 p26
Forte, Marmaduke; Maryland, 1653 2524.55 p82
Fortee, Henry; Virginia, 1691 1224.1 p22
Forteen, David; New York, 1803 8197.10 p12
Forten, Thomas; Rhode Island, 1765 1224.2 p41
Fortenback, Wenselaus; New York, 1840 8197.10 p167
Fortescue, Miles; Virginia, 1666-1667 6212.30 p35
Fortescue, Robt; Virginia, 1666 6212.30 p31
Fortescue, William; Virginia, 1667 6212.30 p36
Forth, John; Georgia, 1775 1640.10 p57
Fortibaur, Maria Elisabeth; America, 1743 2856.30 p116
Fortibaurin, Maria Elisabeth; America, 1743 2856.30 p116
Fortier, Louis Henry; New York, 1807 8197.10 p331
Fortin, Robert; Maryland, 1676 2524.55 p82
Fortree, Thomas; Virginia, 1665-1666 6212.30 p21
Fortun, David; New York, 1803 8197.10 p12
Fortune, David; America, 1739 2856.30 p116
Fortune, George 44; Ontario, 1871 1823.15 p84
Fortune, John 48; Ontario, 1871 1823.15 p84
Fortune, John 63; Ontario, 1871 1823.15 p84
Fortune, Robert 38; Ontario, 1871 1823.15 p84
Fortune, Thomas; Rhode Island, 1765 1224.2 p41
Fortune, Thomas 46; Ontario, 1871 1823.15 p84
Forty, Richard; Maryland, 1681 2524.55 p83
Forvell, John; Vermont, 1855 5900.10 p225
Forvell, Terrier Allen; Vermont, 1861-1909 5900.10 p225
Forward, William 16; Ontario, 1861 2896.25 p35
Fosbrook, William; New York, 1807 8197.10 p42
Fosburg, C. 61; Ontario, 1861 2896.27 p1
Fosburg, Elizabeth 45; Ontario, 1861 2896.27 p1
Fosburg, Martin 75; Ontario, 1861 2896.27 p1

Fose, Adam 23; Kansas, 1910 ***9079.10*** *p47*
Fose, Adam 26; Kansas, 1910 ***9079.10*** *p48*
Fose, Anne 60; Ontario, 1871 ***1823.15*** *p84*
Fose, Catherine 28; Kansas, 1901-1910 ***9079.10*** *p25*
Fose, Charles 29; Kansas, 1886-1910 ***9079.10*** *p25*
Fose, Charlotte 7; Kansas, 1907-1910 ***9079.10*** *p25*
Fose, Christina 17; Kansas, 1910 ***9079.10*** *p47*
Fose, Eva E. 16; Kansas, 1907-1910 ***9079.10*** *p25*
Fose, Eva E. 40; Kansas, 1907-1910 ***9079.10*** *p25*
Fose, Henry 14; Kansas, 1907-1910 ***9079.10*** *p25*
Fose, Henry 31; Kansas, 1910 ***9079.10*** *p44*
Fose, Henry M. 32; Kansas, 1900-1910 ***9079.10*** *p20*
Fose, Jacob 12; Kansas, 1907-1910 ***9079.10*** *p25*
Fose, Jacob 40; Kansas, 1907-1910 ***9079.10*** *p25*
Fose, Katherine 65; Kansas, 1910 ***9079.10*** *p48*
Fose, Katie 27; Kansas, 1910 ***9079.10*** *p48*
Fose, Mary C. 10; Kansas, 1907-1910 ***9079.10*** *p25*
Fose, Michael 28; Ontario, 1871 ***1823.15*** *p84*
Fose, Mollie 25; Kansas, 1910 ***9079.10*** *p47*
Fose, Peter 49; Ontario, 1871 ***1823.15*** *p84*
Fose, Phillip 30; Kansas, 1910 ***9079.10*** *p47*
Fose, Teralis 4; Kansas, 1907-1910 ***9079.10*** *p25*
Fose, Thomas 26; Ontario, 1871 ***1823.15*** *p84*
Fosh, Abraham; Pennsylvania, 1840 ***6058.10*** *p17*
Foshay, David S. 6; Ontario, 1861 ***2896.27*** *p45*
Foshay, George B. 5; Ontario, 1861 ***2896.27*** *p45*
Foshay, Philip S. 3; Ontario, 1861 ***2896.27*** *p45*
Foshay, Rhody 31; Ontario, 1861 ***2896.27*** *p45*
Foshay, William H. 8; Ontario, 1861 ***2896.27*** *p45*
Foshea, John 18; Ontario, 1861 ***2896.28*** *p43*
Foss, Follrath 46; Ontario, 1871 ***1823.15*** *p84*
Foss, Fred 71; Ontario, 1871 ***1823.28*** *p30*
Foss, Henry 59; Ontario, 1871 ***1823.15*** *p84*
Foss, Orway 60; Ontario, 1871 ***1823.15*** *p84*
Fosse, John; Maryland, 1663 ***2524.55*** *p82*
Fosse, John; Maryland, 1666 ***2524.55*** *p82*
Fosse, John; Maryland, 1682 ***2524.55*** *p82*
Fossett, Anthony; Maryland, 1664 ***2524.55*** *p82*
Fossett, Anthony; Maryland, 1665 ***2524.55*** *p82*
Fossett, John; Maryland, 1657 ***2524.55*** *p82*
Fossett, Pattericke; Maryland, 1657 ***2524.55*** *p82*
Fossit, Thomas 39; Ontario, 1871 ***1823.22*** *p55*
Fossitt, Anthony; Maryland, 1664 ***2524.55*** *p82*
Fossold, George 38; Ontario, 1871 ***1823.15*** *p84*
Fosster, Thomas 36; Ontario, 1871 ***1823.22*** *p55*
Fost, Charles 41; Ontario, 1871 ***1823.15*** *p84*
Foster, Dr. 25; Ontario, 1861 ***2896.28*** *p12*
Foster, Mr.; Quebec, 1856 ***9196.15*** *p5*
Foster, Mr.; Quebec, 1857 ***9196.15*** *p23*
Foster, Mr.; Quebec, 1858 ***9196.15*** *p36*
Foster, Mrs.; Quebec, 1856 ***9196.15*** *p5*
Foster, Mrs.; Quebec, 1857 ***9196.15*** *p23*
Foster, Addie M.; Vermont, n.d. ***5900.10*** *p244*
Foster, Albert E. 12; Ontario, 1861 ***2896.27*** *p12*
Foster, Alexander; Pennsylvania, 1777 ***4629.10*** *p28*
Foster, Alexander 22; Ontario, 1871 ***1823.15*** *p84*
Foster, Alexander P. 2; Ontario, 1861 ***2896.27*** *p12*
Foster, Alex'r; Pennsylvania, 1784 ***4629.10*** *p44*
Foster, Alice 18; Ontario, 1871 ***1823.15*** *p84*
Foster, Amanda Donaldson; Vermont, 1852-1937 ***5900.10*** *p517*
Foster, Ann *SEE* Foster, Richard
Foster, Ann 70; Ontario, 1871 ***1823.15*** *p84*
Foster, Ann J. 72; Ontario, 1871 ***1823.15*** *p84*
Foster, Annetta 5; Ontario, 1861 ***2896.27*** *p12*
Foster, Archibald; Pennsylvania, 1836 ***6058.10*** *p14*
Foster, Bridget 30; Vermont, 1863 ***5900.10*** *p239*
Foster, Charles; Pennsylvania, 1777 ***4629.10*** *p15*
Foster, Charles 65; Ontario, 1871 ***1823.15*** *p84*
Foster, Edward 52; Ontario, 1871 ***1823.15*** *p84*
Foster, Elizabeth; Maryland, 1681 ***2524.55*** *p82*
Foster, Elizabeth; Maryland, 1682 ***2524.55*** *p82*
Foster, Elizabeth 32; Ontario, 1871 ***1823.15*** *p84*
Foster, Ervin 40; Ontario, 1871 ***1823.15*** *p84*
Foster, F. F. 5; Ontario, 1861 ***2896.27*** *p48*
Foster, Florence; Vermont, 1878-1927 ***5900.10*** *p255*
Foster, Frank H.; Vermont, 1852-1907 ***5900.10*** *p517*
Foster, George; Georgia, 1737 ***1640.10*** *p57*
Foster, George; New York, 1827 ***8197.10*** *p340*
Foster, George 53; Ontario, 1871 ***1823.28*** *p30*
Foster, George A. 2; Ontario, 1861 ***2896.27*** *p39*
Foster, Gershum 7; Ontario, 1861 ***2896.27*** *p39*
Foster, Henry; New York, 1838 ***8197.10*** *p119*
Foster, Henry; Portland, Maine, 1857 ***9196.15*** *p12*
Foster, Henry; Virginia, 1674 ***1224.1*** *p22*
Foster, Isaac; Philadelphia, 1781 ***1224.2*** *p41*
Foster, J. 37; Ontario, 1861 ***2896.28*** *p16*
Foster, James; Virginia, 1677 ***6212.30*** *p54*
Foster, James 38; Ontario, 1871 ***1823.15*** *p84*
Foster, James Montague; Richmond, Virginia, 1826 ***1224.3*** *p27*
Foster, Jane *SEE* Foster, Richard
Foster, John; Boston, 1711 ***1224.2*** *p42*
Foster, John; Maryland, 1661 ***2524.55*** *p82*
Foster, John; Maryland, 1665 ***2524.55*** *p185*
Foster, John; Maryland, 1669 ***2524.55*** *p82*
Foster, John; New York, 1807 ***8197.10*** *p42*
Foster, John; New York, New York, 1844 ***1224.3*** *p27*
Foster, John; Pennsylvania, 1808 ***6058.10*** *p2*
Foster, John; Richmond, Virginia, 1826 ***1224.3*** *p27*
Foster, John; Sacramento, California, 1850 ***1224.3*** *p27*
Foster, John 20; New York, New York, 1848 ***1825.45*** *p33*
Foster, John 25; Ontario, 1871 ***1823.28*** *p30*
Foster, John 26; Maryland, 1774 ***1220.25*** *p7*
Foster, John 32; Ontario, 1871 ***1823.15*** *p84*
Foster, John 33; Ontario, 1871 ***1823.15*** *p84*
Foster, John 40; Boston, 1774 ***1220.25*** *p51*
Foster, John 49; Ontario, 1871 ***1823.28*** *p30*
Foster, John 62; Ontario, 1871 ***1823.22*** *p55*
Foster, John 63; Ontario, 1871 ***1823.28*** *p30*
Foster, John 65; Ontario, 1871 ***1823.15*** *p84*
Foster, John 78; Ontario, 1871 ***1823.15*** *p84*
Foster, John B. 15; Ontario, 1861 ***2896.27*** *p12*
Foster, John William 30; Ontario, 1871 ***1823.28*** *p30*
Foster, Joseph; Pennsylvania, 1777 ***4629.10*** *p27*
Foster, Joseph 62; Ontario, 1871 ***1823.15*** *p84*
Foster, Judith; Maryland, 1664 ***2524.55*** *p82*
Foster, Julia; Vermont, 1812-1887 ***5900.10*** *p557*
Foster, Kittie M. Boyle; Vermont, 1862-1891 ***5900.10*** *p181*
Foster, M. 10; Ontario, 1861 ***2896.28*** *p16*
Foster, Mahala 26; Ontario, 1861 ***2896.27*** *p48*
Foster, Margaret 64; Ontario, 1871 ***1823.15*** *p84*
Foster, Martha; New York, New York, 1844 ***1224.3*** *p27*
Foster, Mary; Maryland, 1672 ***2524.55*** *p82*
Foster, Mary 18; Georgia, 1775 ***1220.25*** *p126*
Foster, Mary 33; Vermont, 1878 ***5900.10*** *p564*
Foster, Mary M. 24; Ontario, 1861 ***2896.27*** *p12*
Foster, Maturah 20; Ontario, 1861 ***2896.27*** *p16*
Foster, Mich.; Maryland, 1670 ***2524.55*** *p82*
Foster, Michael; Maryland, 1669 ***2524.55*** *p82*
Foster, Nickolous 49; Ontario, 1871 ***1823.15*** *p84*
Foster, Perina E. 22; Ontario, 1861 ***2896.27*** *p12*
Foster, Reuben F. 4; Ontario, 1861 ***2896.27*** *p39*
Foster, Richard *SEE* Foster, Richard
Foster, Richard; Maryland, 1659 ***2524.55*** *p82*
Son: Richard
Wife: Ann
Daughter: Ann
Daughter: Jane
Foster, Richard; Maryland, 1665 ***2524.55*** *p82*
Foster, Richard; Maryland, 1667 ***2524.55*** *p82*
Foster, Richard 22; Ontario, 1871 ***1823.15*** *p84*
Foster, Richard 56; Ontario, 1871 ***1823.15*** *p84*
Foster, Robert; Maryland, 1672 ***2524.55*** *p83*
Foster, Robert 52; Ontario, 1871 ***1823.22*** *p55*
Foster, Roel; Maryland, 1674 ***2524.55*** *p83*
Foster, Samuel 32; Ontario, 1871 ***1823.15*** *p84*
Foster, Sarah 27; Ontario, 1861 ***2896.27*** *p39*
Foster, Sintha E. 9; Ontario, 1861 ***2896.27*** *p12*
Foster, Susanna 46; Ontario, 1861 ***2896.27*** *p12*
Foster, Thomas; Maryland, 1681 ***2524.55*** *p83*
Foster, Thomas; Pennsylvania, 1777 ***4629.10*** *p15*
Foster, Thomas; Virginia, 1671 ***6212.30*** *p44*
Foster, Thomas 29; America, 1774 ***1220.25*** *p35*
Foster, Thomas 42; Ontario, 1871 ***1823.28*** *p30*
Foster, Thomas 44; Ontario, 1871 ***1823.15*** *p84*
Foster, William; Maryland, 1665-1666 ***2524.55*** *p83*
Foster, William; New England, 1664 ***1224.1*** *p26*
Foster, William; New York, New York, 1852 ***6058.10*** *p58*
Foster, William; Vermont, 1847-1922 ***5900.10*** *p414*
Foster, William 17; Philadelphia, 1774 ***1220.25*** *p35*
Foster, William 43; Ontario, 1871 ***1823.28*** *p30*
Foster, William 65; Ontario, 1871 ***1823.22*** *p55*
Foster, William H. 17; Ontario, 1861 ***2896.27*** *p12*
Foster, William J. 9; Ontario, 1861 ***2896.27*** *p39*
Fostion, John; Maryland, 1910 ***3259.35*** *p14*
Fothergill, Mr.; Quebec, 1857 ***9196.15*** *p21*
Fothergill, Anthony; Philadelphia, n.d. ***1224.3*** *p27*
Fothergill, John; Portland, Maine, 1858 ***9196.15*** *p29*
Fotheringham, Rev.; Quebec, 1857 ***9196.15*** *p26*
Fotheringham, Adam; Georgia, 1698 ***1640.13*** *p40*
Fotheringham, James; New Hampshire, 1877 ***1640.13*** *p41*
Fottrell, Edward; Baltimore, 1748 ***1224.2*** *p42*
Fotts, Hannah 22; Maryland, 1775 ***1220.25*** *p102*
Fouace, Sarah; Philadelphia, 1785 ***1224.2*** *p85*
Fougaroly, Andrew F.; New York, 1815 ***8197.10*** *p55*
Foukes, Robert; Maryland, 1673 ***2524.55*** *p83*
Foukett, Mr. 30; Grenada, 1774 ***1220.25*** *p127*
Foulchier, Henry; Maryland, 1672 ***2524.55*** *p83*
Foulds, Mr.; Quebec, 1856 ***9196.15*** *p8*
Foulds, John; Portland, Maine, 1857 ***9196.15*** *p11*
Foule, Anto; Virginia, 1665-1666 ***6212.30*** *p21*
Foulger, Benjamin 14 *SEE* Foulger, Thomas
Foulger, Mary 40 *SEE* Foulger, Thomas
Foulger, Rebecca 18 *SEE* Foulger, Thomas
Foulger, Thomas 16 *SEE* Foulger, Thomas
Foulger, Thomas 42; Philadelphia, 1774 ***1220.25*** *p88*
Wife: Mary 40
Child: Rebecca 18
Child: Thomas 16
Child: Benjamin 14
Foulke, Jno.; Pennsylvania, 1779 ***4629.10*** *p41*
Foulke, John; Pennsylvania, 1777 ***4629.10*** *p28*
Foulke, John; Pennsylvania, 1785 ***4629.10*** *p47*
Foulkes, Mr.; Quebec, 1858 ***9196.15*** *p36*
Foulkner, Edward; Maryland, 1675 ***2524.55*** *p83*
Foulks, John Lawrence; Virginia, 1737 ***1224.2*** *p42*
Foulks, Thomas; Virginia, 1692 ***1224.1*** *p22*
Foull, Anto; Virginia, 1664 ***6212.30*** *p14*
Foull, Rich; Virginia, 1664 ***6212.30*** *p14*
Fouller, Thomas; Georgia, 1698 ***1640.13*** *p41*
Found, Anne; Virginia, 1663 ***6212.30*** *p4*
Found, James 35; Ontario, 1871 ***1823.15*** *p84*
Founier, Isaac 24; Baltimore, 1775 ***1220.25*** *p118*
Fountain, Lewis 28; Maryland, 1775 ***1220.25*** *p97*
Fountain, Thomas; Wisconsin, 1857 ***1224.3*** *p27*
Fountaine, Richard; Maryland, 1671 ***2524.55*** *p83*
Fourby, Richard 60; Ontario, 1871 ***1823.15*** *p84*
Fourdrimer, Mr.; Portland, Maine, 1857 ***9196.15*** *p12*
Fourdrinier, Mr.; Quebec, 1858 ***9196.15*** *p36*
Fourdrinier, Mrs.; Quebec, 1858 ***9196.15*** *p36*
Fournier, Antonie 19; Ontario, 1871 ***1823.28*** *p30*
Fournier, John 40; Ontario, 1871 ***1823.28*** *p30*
Fournier, Levis 26; Ontario, 1871 ***1823.28*** *p30*
Fournier, Lewis 23; Ontario, 1871 ***1823.28*** *p30*
Fourt, Samuel 23; Ontario, 1871 ***1823.22*** *p55*
Fourthy, Richard; Maryland, 1681 ***2524.55*** *p83*
Fouse, Luke 33; Ontario, 1871 ***1823.15*** *p85*
Foust, Adam 30; Ontario, 1871 ***1823.15*** *p85*
Fout, Aughter; Maryland, 1681 ***2524.55*** *p83*
Foutis, A. 25; Alaska, 1917 ***9196.1*** *p45*
Foutis, A. 25; Whitehorse, Yukon, 1917 ***9196.1*** *p45*
Fowell, Edmond; Virginia, 1666 ***6212.30*** *p30*
Fowell, John; Virginia, 1666 ***6212.30*** *p30*
Fowen, Francis 15; Philadelphia, 1774 ***1220.25*** *p63*
Fower, Johann Leonhard; America, 1742 ***2856.30*** *p116*
Fowke, Amy; Maryland, 1672 ***2524.55*** *p83*
Fowke, Amy; Maryland, 1680 ***2524.55*** *p83*
Fowkes, Anne; Virginia, 1671 ***6212.30*** *p44*
Fowkes, Hester; Maryland, 1678 ***2524.55*** *p83*
Fowkes, Jacob; Virginia, 1674 ***6212.30*** *p52*
Fowkes, James; Virginia, 1671 ***6212.30*** *p45*
Fowkes, Thomas; Virginia, 1671 ***6212.30*** *p44*
Fowl, Peter; Virginia, 1700 ***1224.2*** *p42*
Fowl, Sarah 52; Ontario, 1871 ***1823.15*** *p85*
Fowlds, Henry M. 45; Ontario, 1871 ***1823.22*** *p55*
Fowlds, James S. 51; Ontario, 1871 ***1823.22*** *p55*
Fowler, Mr.; Quebec, 1857 ***9196.15*** *p24*
Fowler, Mr.; Quebec, 1858 ***9196.15*** *p40*
Fowler, Mrs. 23; Jamaica, 1774 ***1220.25*** *p50*
Fowler, Charels 36; Ontario, 1871 ***1823.15*** *p85*
Fowler, Charity; Maryland, 1681 ***2524.55*** *p83*
Fowler, Charles; New York, 1803 ***8197.10*** *p12*
Fowler, Dina 63; Ontario, 1871 ***1823.15*** *p85*
Fowler, Edward; Maryland, 1681 ***2524.55*** *p83*
Fowler, Francis 40; Ontario, 1871 ***1823.15*** *p85*
Fowler, Francis 57; Ontario, 1871 ***1823.15*** *p85*
Fowler, George 59; Ontario, 1871 ***1823.15*** *p85*
Fowler, Hanah; Maryland, 1649-1650 ***2524.55*** *p83*
Fowler, James; Virginia, 1709 ***1224.2*** *p42*
Fowler, James 46; Ontario, 1871 ***1823.15*** *p85*
Fowler, James 48; Ontario, 1871 ***1823.15*** *p85*
Fowler, John; New York, 1807 ***8197.10*** *p42*
Fowler, John; Pennsylvania, 1779 ***4629.10*** *p36*
Fowler, John; Virginia, 1667 ***6212.30*** *p37*
Fowler, John 25; Ontario, 1871 ***1823.15*** *p85*
Fowler, John 34; Ontario, 1871 ***1823.28*** *p30*
Fowler, John 36; Maryland, 1775 ***1220.25*** *p102*
Fowler, John 49; Ontario, 1871 ***1823.15*** *p85*
Fowler, John 50; Ontario, 1871 ***1823.22*** *p55*
Fowler, John 70; Ontario, 1871 ***1823.15*** *p85*
Fowler, John 92; Ontario, 1871 ***1823.15*** *p85*
Fowler, Joshua; Maryland, 1682 ***2524.55*** *p83*
Fowler, Mary; Maryland, 1660 ***2524.55*** *p83*
Fowler, Mary; Maryland, 1665 ***2524.55*** *p83*
Fowler, Mary 22; Maryland, 1775 ***1220.25*** *p105*
Fowler, Mary 22; Philadelphia, 1774 ***1220.25*** *p63*
Fowler, Mary 87; Ontario, 1871 ***1823.22*** *p55*
Fowler, Peter 42; Ontario, 1871 ***1823.15*** *p85*
Fowler, Richard; Virginia, 1664 ***6212.30*** *p11*
Fowler, Robert 44; Ontario, 1871 ***1823.15*** *p85*
Fowler, Robert 48; Ontario, 1871 ***1823.22*** *p55*
Fowler, Robt; Virginia, 1665 ***6212.30*** *p22*
Fowler, Samuel; New York, 1828 ***1224.3*** *p27*
Fowler, Sarah; Maryland, 1677-1681 ***2524.55*** *p83*

Fowler, Stephen; Maryland, 1652 2524.55 p83
Fowler, Thomas 29; Ontario, 1871 1823.15 p85
Fowler, Thomas 46; Ontario, 1871 1823.15 p85
Fowler, Walter 84; Ontario, 1871 1823.22 p55
Fowler, William; Maryland, 1670 2524.55 p83
Fowler, William; Maryland, 1677-1681 2524.55 p83
Fowler, William 43; Ontario, 1871 1823.15 p85
Fowler, William 45; Ontario, 1871 1823.15 p85
Fowler, William H.; Pennsylvania, 1868 6058.10 p73
Fowles, Allan; Dominican Republic, 1824 1640.13 p41
Fowles, Archibald Primrose; Dominican Republic, 1824 1640.13 p41
Fowles, George; Dominican Republic, 1820 1640.13 p41
Fowles, John 58; Ontario, 1871 1823.22 p55
Fowley, Dan 18 *SEE* Fowley, John
Fowley, Eileen 28 *SEE* Fowley, John
Fowley, Eileen 50 *SEE* Fowley, John
Fowley, James 51; Ontario, 1871 1823.15 p85
Fowley, Johanna 11 *SEE* Fowley, John
Fowley, John 21 *SEE* Fowley, John
Fowley, John 52; New York, New York, 1849 1825.45 p49
Wife: Eileen 50
Son: John 21
Daughter: Eileen 28
Daughter: Julea 8
Daughter: Johanna 11
Son: Pat 16
Son: Dan 18
Fowley, Julea 8 *SEE* Fowley, John
Fowley, Margret 62; Ontario, 1871 1823.15 p85
Fowley, Pat 16 *SEE* Fowley, John
Fowley, Thomas 28; Ontario, 1871 1823.15 p85
Fowlis, John; Jamaica, 1804 1640.13 p41
Fownes, John; Virginia, 1625 1224.1 p22
Fowns, John; Virginia, 1666 6212.30 p31
Fox, Mrs.; Maryland, 1653 2524.55 p83
Fox, Mrs.; Maryland, 1659 2524.55 p173
Fox, Abraham; Pennsylvania, 1777 4629.10 p11
Fox, Ann; Maryland, 1667 2524.55 p83
Fox, Anna 25; Ontario, 1861 2896.25 p53
Fox, Anora Sheridan; Vermont, 1843-1930 5900.10 p388
Fox, Bridget; Vermont, 1840-1920 5900.10 p251
Fox, Bridget Dwyer 58; Vermont, 1881 5900.10 p614
Fox, Catherine 16 *SEE* Fox, Francis
Fox, Charity 65; Ontario, 1861 2896.25 p53
Fox, Christopher 6; Ontario, 1861 2896.25 p60
Fox, D. B. 3; Ontario, 1861 2896.25 p53
Fox, Dennis; Vermont, 1814-1863 5900.10 p613
Fox, E. J. 2; Ontario, 1861 2896.25 p39
Fox, Edgerton R. 3; Ontario, 1861 2896.25 p60
Fox, Edmd.; Maryland, 1681 2524.55 p83
Fox, Edward; Pennsylvania, 1868 6058.10 p77
Fox, Edward 21; Maryland, 1774 1220.25 p61
Fox, Edwin 38; Ontario, 1871 1823.22 p55
Fox, Elinor; Maryland, 1680 2524.55 p83
Fox, Elizabeth 4; Ontario, 1861 2896.25 p39
Fox, Elizabeth 50; Vermont, 1885 5900.10 p251
Fox, Elizabeth 87; Ontario, 1871 1823.22 p55
Fox, Elizabeth Farrell 58; Vermont, 1891 5900.10 p559
Fox, Ellen; Vermont, n.d. 5900.10 p213
Fox, Ellen Kieley; Vermont, 1852-1903 5900.10 p424
Fox, Frances E. Atwood; Vermont, 1835-1968 5900.10 p388
Fox, Francis 4 *SEE* Fox, Francis
Fox, Francis 35; New York, New York, 1848 1825.45 p15
Wife: Mary 33
Son: Pat 7
Brother: Thomas 26
Sister: Catherine 16
Son: Francis 4
Fox, Gilbert; Charleston, South Carolina, 1829 1224.3 p27
Fox, Grace 23; Maryland, 1773-1774 1220.25 p34
Fox, H. E. 11; Ontario, 1861 2896.25 p53
Fox, Harrison; Vermont, 1831-1901 5900.10 p459
Fox, Henry Stephen; Washington, District of Columbia, 1846 1224.3 p27
Fox, Isabella 35; Ontario, 1861 2896.25 p64
Fox, J. William 26; Ontario, 1871 1823.28 p30
Fox, James; America, 1843 1224.3 p27
Fox, James; Maryland, 1650 2524.55 p83
Fox, James; New York, 1818 8197.10 p228
Fox, James; New York, 1820 8197.10 p228
Fox, James; New York, 1837 8197.10 p89
Fox, James; New York, 1840 8197.10 p164
Fox, James; Vermont, 1821-1899 5900.10 p254
Fox, James 35; Ontario, 1871 1823.22 p55
Fox, James 60; Ontario, 1871 1823.15 p85
Fox, Jane *SEE* Fox, John
Fox, Jane 40; Ontario, 1871 1823.22 p55
Fox, Johanna 60; Ontario, 1871 1823.28 p30
Fox, Johanna Cronin; Vermont, 1846-1919 5900.10 p448
Fox, John; Boston, 1713 1224.2 p42
Fox, John; Maryland, 1677 2524.55 p83
Fox, John; Philadelphia, 1789 4629.10 p57
Wife: Jane
Fox, John; Vermont, 1847-1920 5900.10 p448
Fox, John; Virginia, 1668 1224.1 p22
Fox, John 16; Maryland, 1774 1220.25 p70
Fox, John 21; America, 1774 1220.25 p35
Fox, John 26; Maryland, 1773-1774 1220.25 p34
Fox, John 27; Ontario, 1871 1823.28 p30
Fox, John 33; Ontario, 1871 1823.22 p55
Fox, John 40; Ontario, 1871 1823.22 p55
Fox, John G.; New York, 1840 8197.10 p166
Fox, John O.; Vermont, 1841-1899 5900.10 p251
Fox, John W. 26; Ontario, 1871 1823.28 p30
Fox, Joseph; Pennsylvania, 1777 4629.10 p25
Fox, Joseph; Pennsylvania, 1779 4629.10 p39
Fox, Joseph, Jr.; Pennsylvania, 1779 4629.10 p39
Fox, Juliana Cronan 56; Vermont, 1873 5900.10 p251
Fox, Justus; America, 1750 2856.30 p125
Fox, Levi 42; Ontario, 1871 1823.22 p55
Fox, Margaret; Vermont, 1829-1910 5900.10 p183
Fox, Margaret 8; Ontario, 1861 2896.25 p64
Fox, Margaret Moloney; Vermont, 1825-1896 5900.10 p254
Fox, Martha 30; Ontario, 1861 2896.25 p60
Fox, Mary 21; Ontario, 1861 2896.25 p9
Fox, Mary 33 *SEE* Fox, Francis
Fox, Mary A. Moore 27; Vermont, 1888 5900.10 p228
Fox, Mary E.; Ontario, 1861 2896.28 p37
Fox, Mathew 63; Vermont, 1899 5900.10 p559
Fox, Matthew 21; Maryland, 1774 1220.25 p58
Fox, Matthew M.; Vermont, 1829-1904 5900.10 p388
Fox, Michael; New York, 1838 8197.10 p118
Fox, Michael; Vermont, 1853-1937 5900.10 p424
Fox, Michael 40; Ontario, 1871 1823.22 p55
Fox, Michael 68; Ontario, 1871 1823.22 p55
Fox, Nancy 31; Ontario, 1861 2896.25 p53
Fox, Nephua; Maryland, 1910 3259.35 p14
Fox, Pat 7 *SEE* Fox, Francis
Fox, Patrick; New York, 1839 8197.10 p382
Fox, Patrick 77; Vermont, 1875 5900.10 p384
Fox, Phillips; North America, 1829 1224.3 p27
Fox, Richard 26; Ontario, 1871 1823.28 p30
Fox, Robert; Maryland, 1649 2524.55 p83
Fox, Robert 28; Philadelphia, 1789 4629.10 p57
Fox, Robert 36; Ontario, 1871 1823.15 p85
Fox, Samuel 22; Virginia, 1774 1220.25 p89
Fox, Sarah J. 29; Ontario, 1861 2896.25 p39
Fox, Stephen; New England, 1663 1224.1 p22
Fox, Stephen; Virginia, 1664 6212.30 p9
Fox, Theodore 39; Ontario, 1871 1823.22 p55
Fox, Thomas; Maryland, 1662 2524.55 p126
Fox, Thomas; New York, 1807 8197.10 p42
Fox, Thomas; New York, 1839 8197.10 p383
Fox, Thomas 26 *SEE* Fox, Francis
Fox, Thomas 41; Ontario, 1871 1823.28 p30
Fox, Thomas 64; Ontario, 1871 1823.22 p55
Fox, Thomas 83; Vermont, 1894 5900.10 p251
Fox, W. S. 1; Ontario, 1861 2896.25 p53
Fox, Warren; New York, 1802 8197.10 p21
Fox, William; New York, 1854 1224.3 p27
Fox, William 26; Virginia, 1775 1220.25 p110
Foxall, Catherine; Washington, District of Columbia, 1848 1224.3 p27
Foxall, Thomas; Virginia, 1671-1672 6212.30 p47
Foxcroft, Daniell; Virginia, 1671 6212.30 p44
Foxcroft, John; Cambridge, Massachusetts, 1804 1224.3 p27
Foxcroft, John; New York, New York, 1791 1224.2 p42
Foxcroft, Sarah; Cambridge, Massachusetts, 1802 1224.3 p27
Foxe, John; Virginia, 1681-1682 6212.30 p56
Foxhall, John; Maryland, 1665 2524.55 p83
Wife: Martha
Child: Mary
Foxhall, John; Virginia, 1704 1224.2 p42
Foxhall, Martha *SEE* Foxhall, John
Foxhall, Mary *SEE* Foxhall, John
Foxwell, George; Virginia, 1673 1224.1 p22
Foy, Benjamin; New York, 1834-1838 8197.10 p119
Foy, Catherine; Vermont, 1861 5900.10 p101
Foy, Ellen 19; Vermont, 1865 5900.10 p101
Foy, Henry; Maryland, 1651 2524.55 p83
Foy, John; Nova Scotia, 1745 4628.40 p45
Foy, John 45; Ontario, 1871 1823.28 p30
Foy, John 66; Ontario, 1871 1823.15 p85
Foy, John H.; Vermont, 1851-1902 5900.10 p274
Foy, Margaret D. McDonough; Vermont, 1852-1913 5900.10 p274
Foy, Margaret Lang; Vermont, 1769-1878 5900.10 p612
Foy, Michael 55; Ontario, 1871 1823.28 p30
Foy, Nicholas 28; Ontario, 1871 1823.28 p30
Foy, Patrick 60; Ontario, 1871 1823.28 p30
Foya, John; New York, New York, 1850-1859 6058.10 p47
Foyght, Jacob; New York, New York, 1856 3437.14 p33
Foyle, Harrison; New York, 1837 8197.10 p89
Foyle, John; Virginia, 1665 6212.30 p18
Fraherty, William; New York, 1828 8197.10 p349
Frahill, Ellen McCarty; Vermont, 1886 5900.10 p549
Frahill, James; Vermont, 1868 5900.10 p549
Frahill, Michael J.; Vermont, 1931 5900.10 p549
Fraind, Lauro; New York, 1838 8197.10 p119
Frainer, Bridget 45; Ontario, 1871 1823.15 p85
Fraiser, John 28; Baltimore, 1775 1220.25 p118
Fraizer, Catherine; Maryland, 1765 1224.2 p55
Fraizor, James; Pennsylvania, 1785 4629.10 p44
Frake, Robert; Virginia, 1666-1667 6212.30 p33
Fraleigh, Mrs. 66; Ontario, 1861 2896.26 p24
Fraleigh, A. Jordan 17; Ontario, 1861 2896.27 p35
Fraleigh, C. 14; Ontario, 1861 2896.26 p14
Fraleigh, C. E. 13; Ontario, 1861 2896.26 p24
Fraleigh, Charlotte E. 7; Ontario, 1861 2896.27 p35
Fraleigh, George 14; Ontario, 1861 2896.27 p35
Fraleigh, H. L. 11; Ontario, 1861 2896.26 p14
Fraleigh, John 22; Ontario, 1861 2896.27 p29
Fraleigh, Jonathan 77; Ontario, 1861 2896.26 p24
Fraleigh, Mary A. 9; Ontario, 1861 2896.27 p35
Fraleigh, Sarah 20; Ontario, 1861 2896.27 p35
Fraleigh, Sarah E. 20; Ontario, 1861 2896.27 p35
Fraleigh, Thomas 12; Ontario, 1861 2896.27 p35
Fraleigh, Victoria 16; Ontario, 1861 2896.27 p30
Fraleigh, Willard 10; Ontario, 1861 2896.27 p35
Fraleigh, William 8; Ontario, 1861 2896.26 p14
Fralhowski, Jacob; Maryland, 1910 3259.35 p14
Fralick, Charles G. 2; Ontario, 1861 2896.27 p20
Fralick, Clarissy 20; Ontario, 1861 2896.27 p20
Frame, Arthur James; Grenada, 1871 1640.13 p41
Frame, John; Maryland, 1674 2524.55 p83
Frame, Robert; New York, 1831 8197.10 p365
Frampton, Joseph 29; Ontario, 1871 1823.28 p30
Franar, Ann; Maryland, 1659 2524.55 p38
Franar, Christian; Maryland, 1659 2524.55 p38
Franar, Domingo; Maryland, 1659 2524.55 p38
Franar, Edward; Maryland, 1659 2524.55 p38
France, Robert; New York, 1840 8197.10 p166
France, Thomas 53; Ontario, 1871 1823.22 p55
Frances, Samual 56; Ontario, 1871 1823.28 p30
Francey, George 36; Ontario, 1871 1823.22 p56
Francey, John 45; Ontario, 1871 1823.22 p56
Francey, Joseph H. 52; Ontario, 1871 1823.22 p56
Francey, William 30; Virginia, 1774 1220.25 p86
Franchowiak, Marks; Maryland, 1910 3259.35 p14
Franchowitz, Anton; Maryland, 1910 3259.35 p14
Francis, Andrew; Maryland, 1910 3259.35 p14
Francis, Ann; Virginia, 1668-1669 6212.30 p41
Francis, Anne; Philadelphia, 1818 1224.3 p28
Francis, Edward; Vermont, 1844-1894 5900.10 p409
Francis, Elizabeth; Maryland, 1664 2524.55 p83
Francis, Ellen Kavanaugh; Vermont, 1843-1873 5900.10 p409
Francis, Francis 27; America, 1774 1220.25 p36
Francis, Henry 41; Ontario, 1871 1823.15 p85
Francis, Henry 50; Ontario, 1871 1823.15 p85
Francis, Hu 62; Ontario, 1871 1823.28 p30
Francis, James 56; Ontario, 1871 1823.15 p85
Francis, Jane; New York, 1833-1838 8197.10 p119
Francis, Kate 22; Vermont, 1880 5900.10 p63
Francis, Leonard; Maryland, 1664 2524.55 p83
Francis, Philip; Pennsylvania, 1778 4629.10 p43
Francis, Richard 26; Philadelphia, 1774 1220.25 p81
Francis, Tarbutt; Philadelphia, 1782 1224.2 p42
Francis, Thomas; Connecticut, 1827 1224.3 p28
Francis, W. B. 23; Ontario, 1871 1823.28 p30
Francis, Walter; Maryland, 1664 2524.55 p122
Francis, William 15; Virginia, 1775 1220.25 p110
Francis, William 33; Maryland, 1774 1220.25 p65
Francis, William 68; Vermont, 1911 5900.10 p141
Francizkowska, Frank; Maryland, 1910 3259.35 p14
Franck, Mr.; Quebec, 1856 9196.15 p8
Franck, A. Urs. *SEE* Franck, Adam
Franck, Adam; America, 1764 2856.30 p116
Franck, Adam; America, 1764 2856.30 p117
Wife: A. Urs.
With 2 children
Franck, Andreas; America, 1741 2856.30 p116
Franck, Andreas; Port uncertain, 1752 2856.30 p116
Franck, Anna Barbara; America, 1752 2856.30 p116
Franck, Anna Barbara; America, 1752 2856.30 p117
Franck, Anna Catharina; Port uncertain, 1739 2856.30 p117
Franck, Anna Maria; Port uncertain, 1750 2856.30 p117
With 3 children
Franck, Chr. M. *SEE* Franck, Johann Nikolaus

Franck, Daniel; America, 1764 2856.30 p116
Franck, Elisabeth; Port uncertain, 1778 2856.30 p116
Franck, Johann; Port uncertain, 1771 2856.30 p116
Franck, Johann; Port uncertain, 1793 2856.30 p116
Franck, Johann Adam; America, 1764 2856.30 p116
Franck, Johann Georg; America, 1732 2856.30 p116
Franck, Johann Georg; America, 1776 2856.30 p116
Franck, Johann Nikolaus; America, 1764 2856.30 p117
Wife: Chr. M.
With 3 children
Franck, Josef Christian; America, 1752 2856.30 p116
Franck, Mrs. Ludwig; Port uncertain, 1764 2856.30 p116
Franck, Maria Catharina; America, 1752 2856.30 p116
Franck, Maria Catharina; America, 1752 2856.30 p117
Franck, Maria Elisabeth; America, 1752 2856.30 p116
Franck, Maria Elisabeth; America, 1752 2856.30 p117
Franck, Nickel; Port uncertain, 1729 2856.30 p116
Franck, Nicolaus; Cayenne, 1764 2856.30 p117
Franck, Peter; America, 1750 2856.30 p117
With wife & children
Franck, Peter; America, 1761 2856.30 p116
Franck, Peter; America, 1765 2856.30 p117
With son
Franck, Peter; Port uncertain, 1749 2856.30 p116
Franck, Peter; Port uncertain, 1765 2856.30 p117
With son
Franck, Peter; Port uncertain, 1788 2856.30 p116
Franck, Philipp; Port uncertain, 1755 2856.30 p116
Franck, Sara Catharina; Port uncertain, 1774 2856.30 p117
With husband
Franck, Stephan; America, 1748 2856.30 p117
With wife & 4 children
Franck, Wilhelm; America, 1753 2856.30 p116
Franck, Wilhelm Heinric; Port uncertain, 1776 2856.30 p116
Francke, Anna Maria; Port uncertain, 1736 2856.30 p117
Franckh, Franz Josef; Port uncertain, 1771 2856.30 p117
Franckh, Johann Michael; Port uncertain, 1745 2856.30 p117
Franckh, Michael; Mississippi, 1724 2856.30 p117
Franckh, Nicolaus; Port uncertain, 1758 2856.30 p117
Franckh, Philipp; Port uncertain, 1757 2856.30 p117
Franckh, Valentin; Port uncertain, 1754 2856.30 p117
Franckham, Joane *SEE* Franckham, Richard
Franckham, Richard; Maryland, 1668 2524.55 p84
Relative: Joane
Relative: Thomas
Franckham, Thomas *SEE* Franckham, Richard
Franckin, Anna Catharina; Port uncertain, 1739 2856.30 p117
Francklin, Henry; Maryland, 1649 2524.55 p84
Francklin, Idia; Virginia, 1671 6212.30 p44
Francklin, Jane *SEE* Francklin, Jane
Francklin, Jane; Virginia, 1673 6212.30 p51
Child: Jane
Francklin, Joane *SEE* Francklin, Richard
Francklin, John; Virginia, 1693-1694 6212.30 p60
Francklin, Jone; Virginia, 1666 6212.30 p26
Francklin, Rich; Virginia, 1663-1664 6212.30 p5
Francklin, Richard; Maryland, 1667 2524.55 p84
Relative: Joane
Relative: Thomas
Francklin, Robert; Maryland, 1667 2524.55 p84
Francklin, Thomas *SEE* Francklin, Richard
Francklin, Walter; Virginia, 1664 6212.30 p15
Francklyn, Henry; Boston, 1725 1224.2 p42
Franclham, Elizabeth; Maryland, 1680 2524.55 p84
Francock, Walter; Maryland, 1910 3259.35 p14
Francois, Jean 28; Maryland, 1774 1220.25 p62
Francolin, Louis Robert; New York, 1806 8197.10 p31
Francomb, George; America, 1722 1224.2 p42
Francy, John 50; Ontario, 1871 1823.22 p56
Frand, Josef; Port uncertain, 1774 2856.30 p117
Frank, Adam; Baltimore, 1847 6058.10 p23
Frank, Andrew 51; Ontario, 1871 1823.15 p85
Frank, Barbara Mechtel; Cayenne, 1764 2856.30 p294
Frank, Daniel; America, 1758 2856.30 p117
Frank, Mrs. Friedrich; Port uncertain, 1783 2856.30 p117
Frank, Geo 27; British Columbia, 1913 9196.1 p62
Frank, Geo 27; Washington, 1913 9196.1 p62
Frank, Gerog; Port uncertain, 1788 2856.30 p117
Frank, Johann; Port uncertain, 1784 2856.30 p117
With 3 children
Frank, Johanna; America, 1774 2856.30 p117
Frank, Joseph; New York, New York, 1856 3437.14 p26
Frank, Julius; Pennsylvania, 1859-1865 6058.10 p50
Frank, Peter; New York, 1839 8197.10 p231
Frank, Thomas 55; Ontario, 1871 1823.22 p56
Frank, Ursula; Port uncertain, 1787 2856.30 p117
Franke, Eliz; Virginia, 1672 6212.30 p48
Franke, Fredrick 30; Ontario, 1871 1823.28 p30
Franke, Martin; Port uncertain, 1757 2856.30 p117
Frankes, David; Pennsylvania, 1779 4629.10 p40
Frankes, Henry; Virginia, 1664 6212.30 p9
Frankland, Mr. 58; Philadelphia, 1775 1220.25 p132
Franklin, Benjamin 58; Ontario, 1871 1823.22 p56
Franklin, James 52; Ontario, 1871 1823.15 p85
Franklin, John; Virginia, 1664 6212.30 p10
Franklin, John; Virginia, 1671 6212.30 p42
Franklin, Margarett; Maryland, 1661 2524.55 p68
Franklin, Thomas; Pennsylvania, 1777 4629.10 p27
Franklin, Thomas; Pennsylvania, 1779 4629.10 p35
Franklin, Walter; Virginia, 1665-1666 6212.30 p22
Frankling, John 48; Ontario, 1871 1823.15 p85
Franklyn, Henry; Maryland, 1649 2524.55 p84
Franklyn, Jonathan; Boston, 1759 1224.2 p42
Franklyn, Peter 24; Philadelphia, 1775 1220.25 p9
Frankon, John; Maryland, 1670 2524.55 p84
Frankowski, Joseph; Maryland, 1910 3259.35 p14
Frankpitt, James; New York, 1825 8197.10 p229
Franks, Charles; New York, 1818 8197.10 p228
Franks, Charles 45; Ontario, 1871 1823.22 p56
Franks, David; Pennsylvania, 1777 4629.10 p25
Franks, David; Philadelphia, 1794 1224.2 p42
Franks, John; New York, 1829 8197.10 p230
Franler, John 38; Maryland, 1774 1220.25 p65
Frans, Martin; Port uncertain, 1752 2856.30 p117
Fransin, William 40; Ontario, 1871 1823.22 p56
Frantz, Anna Maria; Port uncertain, 1733 2856.30 p117
Frantz, Anna Susanna; Port uncertain, 1746 2856.30 p117
Frantz, Astmus; America, 1739 2856.30 p118
With wife & 7 children
Frantz, Johann Peter; Port uncertain, 1750 2856.30 p117
Frantz, Maria Catharina; Port uncertain, 1758 2856.30 p117
Frantz, Maria Elisabeth; Port uncertain, 1775 2856.30 p117
Frantz, Susanna Margare; Port uncertain, 1746 2856.30 p118
Frantz, Wilhelm; Port uncertain, 1754 2856.30 p118
Frantzke, Wilhelm Friderick; New York, 1834 8197.10 p71
Franz, Ms.; America, 1752 2856.30 p118
With husband
Franz, Catharina; Port uncertain, 1759 2856.30 p118
Franz, Christian; Port uncertain, 1753 2856.30 p118
Franz, Dorothea; Port uncertain, 1744 2856.30 p118
Franz, Elisabeth; Port uncertain, 1790 2856.30 p118
Franz, Jacob; America, 1751 2856.30 p118
Franz, Jacob; Port uncertain, 1751 2856.30 p118
Franz, Johann; Port uncertain, 1763 2856.30 p118
Franz, Konrad; Port uncertain, 1784 2856.30 p118
Franz, Maria Elisabeth; Port uncertain, 1773 2856.30 p118
Franz, Mathes; Port uncertain, 1746 2856.30 p118
Franz, Mathes; Port uncertain, 1784 2856.30 p118
Frarley, John 32; Ontario, 1871 1823.15 p85
Fraser, . . .; Mobile, Alabama, 1768 1640.10 p60
Fraser, Miss; Quebec, 1857 9196.15 p22
Fraser, Mrs.; Quebec, 1857 9196.15 p22
Fraser, Mrs., Sr.; Quebec, 1857 9196.15 p22
Fraser, A.; Quebec, 1856 9196.15 p9
Fraser, Abraham 45; Ontario, 1871 1823.28 p30
Fraser, Alexander; Annapolis, Maryland, 1732 1640.13 p41
Fraser, Alexander; Georgia, 1698 1640.13 p41
Fraser, Alexander; Georgia, 1699 1640.13 p41
Fraser, Alexander; Georgia, 1743 1640.10 p57
Fraser, Alexander; New York, 1889 1640.13 p41
Fraser, Alexander; Savannah, Georgia, 1783 1224.2 p42
Fraser, Alexander; Savannah, Georgia, 1783 1640.10 p57
Fraser, Alexander; Toronto, 1880 1640.13 p41
Fraser, Alexander 23; Ontario, 1871 1823.28 p30
Fraser, Alexander 26; Ontario, 1871 1823.22 p56
Fraser, Alexander 31; Ontario, 1871 1823.15 p86
Fraser, Alexander 34; Ontario, 1871 1823.28 p30
Fraser, Alexander 41; Ontario, 1871 1823.15 p86
Fraser, Alexander 46; Ontario, 1871 1823.22 p56
Fraser, Alexander 50; Ontario, 1871 1823.28 p30
Fraser, Alexander 54; Ontario, 1871 1823.15 p86
Fraser, Alexander 64; Ontario, 1871 1823.15 p85
Fraser, Alexander 76; Ontario, 1871 1823.28 p30
Fraser, Andrew 57; Ontario, 1871 1823.22 p56
Fraser, Anna Laughton; New Jersey, 1841 1224.3 p28
Fraser, Anne; Georgia, 1738 1640.10 p57
Fraser, Archibald 60; Ontario, 1871 1823.22 p56
Fraser, Catherine; Georgia, 1738 1640.10 p57
Fraser, Catherine 32; Ontario, 1871 1823.15 p86
Fraser, Charles 33; Ontario, 1871 1823.28 p30
Fraser, Charles 33; Ontario, 1871 1823.28 p31
Fraser, Charles 67; Ontario, 1871 1823.28 p30
Fraser, D.; Quebec, 1857 9196.15 p22
Fraser, Donald *SEE* Fraser, John
Fraser, Donald; Georgia, 1734 1640.10 p57
Fraser, Donald; Georgia, 1736 1640.10 p57
Fraser, Donald; Georgia, 1736 1640.10 p58
Fraser, Donald; Georgia, 1768 1640.10 p58
Fraser, Donald; Georgia, 1827 1640.10 p58
Fraser, Donald 48; Ontario, 1871 1823.15 p86
Fraser, Donald 60; Ontario, 1871 1823.15 p86
Fraser, Douglas; Buffalo, New York, 1868 1640.13 p41
Fraser, Effie; Saskatchewan, 1880-1889 4537.35 p70
Fraser, Finlay *SEE* Fraser, John
Fraser, Finlay 56; Ontario, 1871 1823.15 p86
Fraser, George; Georgia, 1755 1640.10 p58
Fraser, George; Savannah, Georgia, 1775 1640.10 p58
Fraser, George 25; Ontario, 1871 1823.15 p86
Fraser, George 41; Ontario, 1871 1823.28 p31
Fraser, George 64; Ontario, 1871 1823.15 p86
Fraser, Henrietta; Georgia, 1738 1640.10 p58
Fraser, Hugh; Antigua (Antego), 1750 1640.13 p41
Fraser, Hugh; Georgia, 1698 1640.13 p41
Fraser, Hugh; Georgia, 1733 1640.10 p58
Fraser, Hugh; Georgia, 1738 1640.10 p58
Fraser, Hugh; Georgia, 1741 1640.10 p59
Fraser, Hugh; Pennsylvania, 1777 4629.10 p8
Fraser, Hugh 63; Ontario, 1871 1823.28 p31
Fraser, Hugh Grant; New York, 1893 1640.13 p41
Fraser, Isaac 67; Ontario, 1871 1823.22 p56
Fraser, James; Augusta, Georgia, 1749 1640.10 p59
Fraser, James; Augusta, Georgia, 1807-1812 1640.10 p59
Fraser, James; Charleston, South Carolina, 1807 1224.3 p28
Fraser, James; Georgia, 1743 1640.10 p59
Fraser, James; Georgia, 1828 1640.10 p59
Fraser, James 36; Ontario, 1871 1823.28 p31
Fraser, James A. 36; Ontario, 1871 1823.28 p31
Fraser, Janet; Georgia, 1738 1640.10 p59
Fraser, John *SEE* Fraser, John
Fraser, John; Florida, 1769 1640.10 p59
Fraser, John; Georgia, 1737 1640.10 p59
Fraser, John; Georgia, 1737 1640.10 p117
Fraser, John; Georgia, 1841 1224.3 p28
Fraser, John; Georgia, 1841 1640.10 p59
Fraser, John; Manitoba, 1888 4537.35 p65
Child: Mary
Child: Donald
Child: Rachel
Child: John
Child: Finlay
Fraser, John; New York, 1838 8197.10 p231
Fraser, John; Ohio, 1893 1640.13 p42
Fraser, John; Ontario, 1885 1640.13 p42
Fraser, John 60; Ontario, 1871 1823.15 p86
Fraser, Josanna; Wisconsin, 1882 1640.13 p42
Fraser, Joseph; Maryland, 1910 3259.35 p14
Fraser, Margaret; Georgia, 1741 1640.10 p60
Fraser, Margory; Georgia, 1736 1640.10 p119
Fraser, Margret 55; Ontario, 1871 1823.15 p86
Fraser, Mary *SEE* Fraser, John
Fraser, Mary 30; Philadelphia, 1774 1220.25 p75
Fraser, Matthew Moncrieff; Kansas City, 1885 1640.13 p42
Fraser, Patrick; Long Island, 1795 1224.2 p42
Fraser, Rachel *SEE* Fraser, John
Fraser, Rebecca E.; New York, 1887 1640.13 p42
Fraser, Robert F.; New York, 1837 8197.10 p90
Fraser, Simon; Georgia, 1762 1640.10 p60
Fraser, Simon; Georgia, 1812 1640.10 p60
Fraser, Simon; Mississippi, 1819 1640.10 p60
Fraser, Thomas; Georgia, 1734 1640.10 p60
Fraser, Thomas; Georgia, 1759 1640.10 p60
Fraser, Thomas; Norfolk, Virginia, 1790 1224.2 p42
Fraser, Thomas; Philadelphia, 1823 1224.3 p28
Fraser, Thomas; Virginia, 1782 1224.2 p42
Fraser, Thomas 41; Ontario, 1871 1823.28 p31
Fraser, William; Georgia, 1734 1640.10 p60
Fraser, William; Georgia, 1743 1640.10 p60
Fraser, William; Georgia, 1828 1640.10 p60
Fraser, William; Kingston, Jamaica, 1839 1640.13 p42
Fraser, William; New York, 1835-1838 8197.10 p119
Fraser, William 28; Ontario, 1871 1823.15 p86
Fraser, William 34; Ontario, 1871 1823.28 p31
Fraser, William 36; Ontario, 1871 1823.22 p56
Fraser, William 40; Philadelphia, 1774 1220.25 p75
With 3 children
Fraser, William 44; Ontario, 1871 1823.22 p56
Fraser, William 50; Ontario, 1871 1823.28 p31
Fraser, William 58; Ontario, 1871 1823.15 p86
Fraser, Wm 51; British Columbia, 1910 9196.1 p32
Fraser, Wm 51; Washington, 1910 9196.1 p32
Frasier, John 55; Ontario, 1871 1823.28 p31
Frass, Henrich; America, 1739 2856.30 p118
Fratebas, Jerome; Philadelphia, 1815 8197.10 p297
Frati, Severc 44; British Columbia, 1910 9196.1 p31
Frati, Severc 44; Seattle, 1910 9196.1 p31
Frauenberger, Jacob; Port uncertain, 1790 2856.30 p118

Frauenfeld, Jacob; America, 1768 2856.30 p118
Frauenfeld, Jacob; America, 1773 2856.30 p118
Frauenfeld, Jacob; America, 1785 2856.30 p118
Frauenfelder, Jakob; America, 1793 2856.30 p118
Frawinski, Mike M.; Maryland, 1910 3259.35 p14
Frawiski, John; Maryland, 1910 3259.35 p14
Frawk, Mr.; Quebec, 1857 9196.15 p14
Frawley, Catherine 70; Vermont, 1903 5900.10 p115
Frawley, Edward 60; Vermont, n.d. 5900.10 p58
Frawley, James M. 55; Vermont, 1903 5900.10 p487
Frawley, Margaret 65; Vermont, 1875 5900.10 p372
Frawley, Mary; Vermont, 1852-1939 5900.10 p44
Frawley, Michael; Pennsylvania, 1827 6058.10 p10
Frawley, Michael 70; Vermont, 1864 5900.10 p372
Frawley, Patrick 37; Vermont, 1857 5900.10 p59
Frawley, Thomas 60; Ontario, 1871 1823.15 p86
Frayer, Benjamin 25; Ontario, 1861 2896.28 p58
Frayer, Catherine 15; Ontario, 1861 2896.28 p58
Frayer, John 32; Ontario, 1861 2896.28 p58
Frayer, John J. 66; Ontario, 1861 2896.28 p58
Frayer, Levi 21; Ontario, 1861 2896.28 p58
Frayer, Sarah 17; Ontario, 1861 2896.28 p58
Frayer, Sarah A. 25; Ontario, 1861 2896.28 p58
Frayne, Robert 50; Ontario, 1871 1823.15 p86
Frazer, Alexander; New York, 1807 8197.10 p329
Frazer, Arthur; New York, 1807 8197.10 p42
Frazer, Donald 53; Ontario, 1871 1823.15 p86
Frazer, Francis 15; Maryland, 1775 1220.25 p100
Frazer, John; New York, 1807 8197.10 p42
Frazer, John; New York, 1840 8197.10 p166
Frazer, John; New York, 1840 8197.10 p167
Frazer, Mary Ann 48; Ontario, 1871 1823.15 p86
Frazer, Robert; New York, 1807 8197.10 p42
Frazer, Roderick 44; Ontario, 1871 1823.15 p86
Frazer, Susan; Ontario, 1861 2896.28 p62
Frazer, Thomas; Virginia, 1782 1224.2 p42
Frazer, William; New York, 1807 8197.10 p42
Frazier, Danial 68; Ontario, 1871 1823.28 p31
Frazier, Daniel; Virginia, 1702 6212.30 p62
Frazier, Lewis 23; Ontario, 1861 2896.28 p24
Frazior, Simond 40; Ontario, 1871 1823.28 p31
Frazon, Samuel; Barbados, 1705 1224.2 p43
Frazon, Samuel; Boston, 1705 1224.2 p43
Freake, Henry; Maryland, 1682 2524.55 p84
Freake, Thomas; Virginia, 1666 6212.30 p31
Freame, Thomas; Philadelphia, 1744 1224.2 p43
Freaton, Ann; Maryland, 1675 2524.55 p222
Freck, Ralph; Virginia, 1664 6212.30 p15
Frede, Christian; New York, 1807 8197.10 p42
Frederick, Anthony; Germantown, Pennsylvania, 1778 1224.2 p43
Frederick, Hannah 51; Ontario, 1861 2896.25 p34
Frederick, Irvine 13; Ontario, 1861 2896.25 p34
Frederick, Isaac 27; Ontario, 1861 2896.25 p34
Frederick, J. A. 10; Ontario, 1861 2896.25 p34
Frederick, Peter 18; Ontario, 1861 2896.25 p34
Frederick, Sarah 21; Ontario, 1861 2896.25 p34
Frederofsky, Stanislow; Maryland, 1910 3259.35 p15
Fredrick, Amelia 40; Ontario, 1871 1823.28 p31
Fredrick, Chas 35; Ontario, 1871 1823.28 p31
Fredrick, John 30; Ontario, 1871 1823.28 p31
Fredrick, Stanley; Maryland, 1910 3259.35 p15
Free, Abraham 59; Ontario, 1871 1823.22 p56
Free, John 60; Ontario, 1871 1823.22 p56
Free, William; New York, 1840 8197.10 p164
Free, William 61; Ontario, 1871 1823.22 p56
Freeborn, Andrew; New York, 1840 8197.10 p165
Freeborn, Thomas; New York, 1802 8197.10 p20
Freeburn, Robert; New York, 1807 8197.10 p42
Freed, Elizabeth Woodgate; New York, 1844 1224.3 p28
Freed, Simon 15; Pennsylvania, 1857 6058.10 p50
Freel, Hugh; New York, 1835 8197.10 p371
Freel, James; New York, 1835 8197.10 p371
Freel, James; New York, 1840 8197.10 p231
Freeland, . . .; Boston, 1737 4628.40 p114
Freeland, George 65; Ontario, 1871 1823.28 p31
Freeland, John; New York, 1807 8197.10 p42
Freeland, P.; Quebec, 1857 9196.15 p17
Freeland, Robt; Quebec, 1858 9196.15 p47
Freeland, William; Ottawa, 1873 1640.13 p42
Freeman, Alexander; Pennsylvania, 1787 4629.10 p55
Freeman, Charles; Pennsylvania, 1777 4629.10 p15
Freeman, Edw; Virginia, 1665-1666 6212.30 p23
Freeman, Edward 43; Alaska, 1912 9196.1 p19
Freeman, Edward 43; British Columbia, 1912 9196.1 p19
Freeman, Edward 48; Ontario, 1871 1823.22 p56
Freeman, Eliza; Virginia, 1664 6212.30 p10
Freeman, Henry 40; Ontario, 1871 1823.15 p86
Freeman, James; Vermont, n.d. 5900.10 p188
Freeman, James 20; Virginia, 1774 1220.25 p45
Freeman, Jno; Virginia, 1669-1670 6212.30 p41
Freeman, Jno; Virginia, 1672 6212.30 p49
Freeman, John; Maryland, 1668 2524.55 p84
Freeman, John; New Jersey, 1717 1224.2 p43
Freeman, John; Virginia, 1664 6212.30 p8
Freeman, John; Virginia, 1739 1224.2 p43
Freeman, John 23; Maryland, 1774 1220.25 p83
Freeman, Joseph; Maryland, 1672 2524.55 p84
Freeman, Margaret; Vermont, n.d. 5900.10 p188
Freeman, Maria Murray; Vermont, n.d. 5900.10 p188
Freeman, Mark; Pennsylvania, 1777 4629.10 p21
Freeman, Mary; Vermont, 1849-1942 5900.10 p125
Freeman, Patrick 27; Ontario, 1871 1823.15 p86
Freeman, Ralph; Virginia, 1665-1666 6212.30 p21
Freeman, Richard; Pennsylvania, 1777 4629.10 p22
Freeman, Robert; Maryland, 1668 2524.55 p84
Freeman, Robert; Maryland, 1678 2524.55 p84
Freeman, Samuel 27; Maryland, 1774 1220.25 p84
Freeman, Sylvenis 65; Ontario, 1871 1823.22 p56
Freeman, William; Virginia, 1663 6212.30 p3
Freeman, William 20; Maryland, 1774 1220.25 p52
Freeman, William 26; Ontario, 1871 1823.15 p86
Freeman, William 30; Ontario, 1871 1823.28 p31
Freeman, William Y.; New York, 1830 8197.10 p360
Freemore, Joseph; Maryland, 1668 2524.55 p79
Freemount, Robert 23; Maryland, 1774 1220.25 p65
Freer, John; Maryland, 1680 2524.55 p84
Freeston, William; Maryland, 1681 2524.55 p84
Frei, Ludwig; Port uncertain, 1791 2856.30 p118
Freidenberger, Henrich; Port uncertain, 1781 2856.30 p118
Frelech, William; New York, 1840 8197.10 p165
Freleigh, Jacob H. 20; Ontario, 1861 2896.27 p65
Freleigh, John 22; Ontario, 1861 2896.27 p65
Freleigh, Juliann 42; Ontario, 1861 2896.27 p65
Freleigh, Mariah V. 17; Ontario, 1861 2896.27 p65
Freleigh, William P. 16; Ontario, 1861 2896.27 p65
Fremis, Cath. Hugel *SEE* Fremis, Jean Demi
Fremis, Jean Demi; Port uncertain, 1769 2856.30 p118
Fremis, Jean Demi; Port uncertain, 1769 2856.30 p118
Wife: Cath. Hugel
Fremore, John 84; Vermont, 1872 5900.10 p514
Fremore, Mary 59; Vermont, 1876 5900.10 p514
Fremstad, Hoakon 21; Alaska, 1913 9196.1 p22
Fremstad, Hoakon 21; British Columbia, 1913 9196.1 p22
French, Mr.; Quebec, 1857 9196.15 p18
French, Mr.; Quebec, 1858 9196.15 p42
French, Ann 71; Ontario, 1871 1823.22 p56
French, Elizabeth A. 43; Ontario, 1861 2896.27 p21
French, Emily E. 15; Ontario, 1861 2896.27 p21
French, Frances 63; Ontario, 1871 1823.28 p31
French, Francis 31; Ontario, 1871 1823.28 p31
French, Georgina 49; Ontario, 1871 1823.15 p86
French, Henry; New York, 1840 8197.10 p166
French, James; New York, 1840 8197.10 p166
French, James 25; Maryland, 1775 1220.25 p111
French, James 55; Ontario, 1871 1823.28 p31
French, John; Alabama, 1846 1224.3 p28
French, John 29; Ontario, 1871 1823.22 p56
French, Luke 3; Ontario, 1861 2896.25 p30
French, Margaret 48; Ontario, 1871 1823.22 p56
French, Margarett *SEE* French, Nathaniell
French, Maria 24; Ontario, 1861 2896.25 p30
French, Mary Dolan; Vermont, 1863-1963 5900.10 p160
French, Micheal 30; Ontario, 1871 1823.28 p31
French, Nathan; New York, 1837 8197.10 p319
French, Nathaniell; Maryland, 1665 2524.55 p84
Wife: Margarett
French, Peter 30; Ontario, 1861 2896.27 p21
French, Peter 48; Ontario, 1871 1823.22 p56
French, Robert 42; Ontario, 1871 1823.15 p86
French, Sarah A. McCollum 68; Vermont, 1887 5900.10 p301
French, Sheldon 7; Ontario, 1861 2896.27 p21
French, Thomas; America, 1795 1224.2 p43
French, Thomas 73; Vermont, 1888 5900.10 p301
French, Willet 5; Ontario, 1861 2896.25 p30
French, Willet 5; Ontario, 1861 2896.25 p65
French, William; New York, 1840 8197.10 p166
French, William 22; Ontario, 1861 2896.27 p21
French, William 25; Virginia, 1774 1220.25 p53
French, William 46; America, 1774 1220.25 p36
French, William 47; Ontario, 1871 1823.22 p56
Frenchen, Frances; Maryland, 1910 3259.35 p15
Frenchman, Henry; Virginia, 1668-1669 6212.30 p41
Frenchman, Phillip; Virginia, 1669-1670 6212.30 p41
Frentzel, Franz; Port uncertain, 1783 2856.30 p118
Frere, S. Ermand; New York, 1807 8197.10 p42
Fresen, Will.; Maryland, 1658 2524.55 p84
Fresh, John; Maryland, 1664 2524.55 p84
Freshwater, William; Virginia, 1706 1224.2 p43
Frett, Ann 22; Tortola, 1773-1774 1220.25 p32
Frett, Florence 21; Tortola, 1773-1774 1220.25 p32
Freudenreich, Johann; Port uncertain, 1746 2856.30 p119
Frevet, Gustave 31; Ontario, 1871 1823.28 p31
Frew, Miss; Quebec, 1858 9196.15 p42
Frew, Mrs.; Quebec, 1858 9196.15 p42
Frew, Hugh; Pennsylvania, 1808 6058.10 p2
Frew, Stewart 48; Ontario, 1871 1823.22 p56
Frewen, Thomas; Pennsylvania, 1868 6058.10 p72
Frewin, Anne; Virginia, 1664-1665 6212.30 p16
Frewin, Thomas 21; Philadelphia, 1774 1220.25 p63
Frey, Mr.; Port uncertain, 1788 2856.30 p170
Frey, Abraham; America, 1752 2856.30 p120
With wife & children
Frey, Albertina; Port uncertain, 1764 2856.30 p119
Frey, Andreas; America, 1750 2856.30 p120
With 5 children
Frey, Andreas; Port uncertain, 1750 2856.30 p120
With 5 children
Frey, Anna Maria; Port uncertain, 1788 2856.30 p119
Frey, Anton; Port uncertain, 1791 2856.30 p119
Frey, Christina; Port uncertain, 1761 2856.30 p119
Frey, Elisabeth; America, 1754 2856.30 p119
Frey, Eva Barbara; Port uncertain, 1754 2856.30 p119
Frey, Georg Peter; Port uncertain, 1757 2856.30 p119
Frey, Hans Heinrich; Port uncertain, 1739 2856.30 p119
Frey, Heinrich; Port uncertain, 1784 2856.30 p119
Frey, Henrich; America, 1787 2856.30 p119
Frey, Henrich; America, 1788 2856.30 p119
Frey, Henrich; America, 1795 2856.30 p119
Frey, Henrich; Port uncertain, 1778 2856.30 p119
Frey, J. P.; Port uncertain, 1755 2856.30 p475
Frey, Jacob; America, 1744 2856.30 p119
Frey, Jacob; Port uncertain, 1752 2856.30 p119
Frey, Jacob; Port uncertain, 1761 2856.30 p119
Frey, Jakob; Port uncertain, 1750 2856.30 p119
Frey, Jakob; Port uncertain, 1751 2856.30 p119
Frey, Jakob; Port uncertain, 1775 2856.30 p119
Frey, Joahnn; Port uncertain, 1734 2856.30 p119
Frey, Johann; America, 1780 2856.30 p120
Frey, Johann; Port uncertain, 1754 2856.30 p120
With wife & 2 sons
Frey, Johann; Port uncertain, 1762 2856.30 p120
Frey, Johann Christof; Port uncertain, 1753 2856.30 p119
Frey, Johann Georg; Port uncertain, 1773 2856.30 p119
Frey, Johann Ludwig; Port uncertain, 1751 2856.30 p119
Frey, Magdalena; Port uncertain, 1754 2856.30 p119
Frey, Martin; America, 1780 2856.30 p120
Frey, Martin; Port uncertain, 1762 2856.30 p120
Frey, Melchior; Port uncertain, 1771 2856.30 p119
Frey, Nikolaus; Port uncertain, 1737 2856.30 p119
Frey, Paul; Port uncertain, 1760 2856.30 p120
Frey, Peter; Port uncertain, 1754 2856.30 p120
Frey, Philipp Adam; Port uncertain, 1785 2856.30 p120
Frey, Tob.; America, 1727 2856.30 p336
Frey, Tobias; America, 1727 2856.30 p120
Frey, Tobias; America, 1727 2856.30 p120
With wife & children
Frey, Xaver; Port uncertain, 1796 2856.30 p120
Freyburg, Ludwig; America, 1764 2856.30 p120
With wife & children
Freyd, Adam; Port uncertain, 1783 2856.30 p120
With wife son & 2 daughters
Freyfogel, Jacob F.; New York, 1840 8197.10 p231
Freymann, Barbara; America, 1752 2856.30 p116
With parents
Freymann, Johann; America, 1752 2856.30 p116
With wife & daughter
Freymann, Johann; America, 1752 2856.30 p120
Freymuth, Johann; Port uncertain, 1749 2856.30 p120
With wife & children
Freyss, Franz; America, 1750 2856.30 p120
Freytag, Erhard Friedric; Port uncertain, 1771 2856.30 p120
Freytag, Erhard Friedric; Port uncertain, 1772 2856.30 p120
Freytag, Johann Friedric; Port uncertain, 1771 2856.30 p120
Freytag, Johann Friedric; Port uncertain, 1772 2856.30 p120
Freyvogel, Hans Michael; America, 1754 2856.30 p120
With wife & 7 children
Friand, Louis; New York, 1838 8197.10 p119
Friar, Francis 1; Ontario, 1861 2896.27 p58
Friar, Isaac N. 5; Ontario, 1861 2896.27 p58
Friar, Levi 21; Ontario, 1861 2896.27 p61
Friar, M. E. 19; Ontario, 1861 2896.27 p1
Friar, Margaret E. 10; Ontario, 1861 2896.27 p58
Friar, Rebecca 3; Ontario, 1861 2896.27 p58
Friar, Sarah 17; Ontario, 1861 2896.27 p62
Friar, Sophiah 42; Ontario, 1861 2896.27 p58
Fribber, Anna Margarete; Port uncertain, 1773 2856.30 p120
Fribiss, Johann; New York, 1840 8197.10 p321

Frice, Benjamin 24; Ontario, 1861 ***2896.28*** *p36*
Frick, Anna Rosina; Port uncertain, 1742 ***2856.30*** *p120*
Frick, Georg; Port uncertain, 1756 ***2856.30*** *p120*
Frick, Hans Georg; Port uncertain, 1753 ***2856.30*** *p120*
Frick, Hans Georg; Port uncertain, 1779 ***2856.30*** *p121*
Fricker, Antoni; Port uncertain, 1729 ***2856.30*** *p121*
Frickert, Anna Elisabeth; Port uncertain, 1794 ***2856.30*** *p121*
Frickert, Johann Georg; Port uncertain, 1791 ***2856.30*** *p121*
Fricketton, Evans; New York, 1807 ***8197.10*** *p42*
Frickher, Josef; Port uncertain, 1741 ***2856.30*** *p121*
Frickher, Josef; Port uncertain, 1753 ***2856.30*** *p121*
Frickher, Josef; Port uncertain, 1771 ***2856.30*** *p121*
Friday, Henry; Pennsylvania, 1777 ***4629.10*** *p20*
Friday, Henry 42; Ontario, 1871 ***1823.28*** *p31*
Friday, Mary 66; Ontario, 1871 ***1823.28*** *p31*
Friday, Philip Lawrence; New York, 1838 ***8197.10*** *p231*
Fridd, John; Maryland, 1637-1641 ***2524.55*** *p84*
Fridemann, Josef; Port uncertain, 1741 ***2856.30*** *p121*
Friderich, Konrad; Port uncertain, 1761 ***2856.30*** *p121*
Friderich, Konrad; Port uncertain, 1781 ***2856.30*** *p121*
Friderich, Konrad; Port uncertain, 1789 ***2856.30*** *p121*
Friderich, Philipp; Port uncertain, 1788 ***2856.30*** *p121*
Fridinger, Benedikt; Port uncertain, 1724 ***2856.30*** *p121*
Fridinger, Benedikt; Port uncertain, 1774 ***2856.30*** *p121*
Fridinger, Maxi; Port uncertain, 1724 ***2856.30*** *p121*
Fridinger, Maxi; Port uncertain, 1774 ***2856.30*** *p121*
Fridli, Michael; Port uncertain, 1781 ***2856.30*** *p121*
With wife
Fridmann, Hans Georg; Port uncertain, 1721 ***2856.30*** *p121*
Fridmann, Theresia; Port uncertain, 1723 ***2856.30*** *p121*
Fridrichin, Margarete; Port uncertain, 1732 ***2856.30*** *p121*
Friebel, Anna Maria; Port uncertain, 1743 ***2856.30*** *p121*
Frieberg, G. 27; Alaska, 1913 ***9196.1*** *p39*
Frieberg, G. 27; Whitehorse, Yukon, 1913 ***9196.1*** *p39*
Friebolin, Felicitas; America, 1750 ***2856.30*** *p121*
Friebus, Anna 44; Kansas, 1884-1910 ***9079.10*** *p40*
Friebus, Fredrick 30; Kansas, 1883-1910 ***9079.10*** *p38*
Friebus, Fredrick 59; Kansas, 1883-1910 ***9079.10*** *p38*
Friebus, John 35; Kansas, 1883-1910 ***9079.10*** *p38*
Friebus, John C. 44; Kansas, 1884-1910 ***9079.10*** *p40*
Friebus, Katherine 54; Kansas, 1883-1910 ***9079.10*** *p38*
Friebus, Mary 57; Kansas, 1910 ***9079.10*** *p40*
Fried, Konrad; Port uncertain, 1784 ***2856.30*** *p121*
Fried, Simon 15; Pennsylvania, 1857 ***6058.10*** *p50*
Friederich, Johann; Port uncertain, 1785 ***2856.30*** *p121*
Friederich, Johann Georg; America, 1736 ***2856.30*** *p121*
Friederich, Johann Georg; America, 1737 ***2856.30*** *p121*
Friederich, Maria Elisabeth; Port uncertain, 1775 ***2856.30*** *p121*
Friedering, George Neinrich; Virginia, 1775 ***1220.25*** *p123*
Friedle, Christian; New York, 1840 ***8197.10*** *p164*
Friedle, John; New York, 1840 ***8197.10*** *p164*
Friedler, Anna Maria; Port uncertain, 1751 ***2856.30*** *p121*
Friedmann, Michael; Port uncertain, 1764 ***2856.30*** *p121*
With wife
Friedmann, Solomon; New York, 1840 ***8197.10*** *p231*
Friedrich, Miss; Port uncertain, 1763 ***2856.30*** *p122*
With sister
Friedrich, Mr.; Port uncertain, 1774 ***2856.30*** *p111*
Friedrich, Anna Maria; Port uncertain, 1752 ***2856.30*** *p121*
Friedrich, Anna Maria; Port uncertain, 1755 ***2856.30*** *p121*
Friedrich, Elisabeth; Port uncertain, 1758 ***2856.30*** *p121*
Friedrich, Friedrich; America, 1764 ***2856.30*** *p122*
Friedrich, Jacob; America, 1750 ***2856.30*** *p122*
Friedrich, Johann; Port uncertain, 1758 ***2856.30*** *p122*
Friedrich, Matheis; Port uncertain, 1754 ***2856.30*** *p122*
Friedrich, Sebastian; Canada, 1763 ***2856.30*** *p122*
With wife & child
Friedrichs, Claus Rickmer; New York, 1835-1838 ***8197.10*** *p118*
Friedrichssohn, Jacob; America, 1750 ***2856.30*** *p122*
Friel, Bridget; Vermont, 1833-1901 ***5900.10*** *p548*
Friel, Hugh; New York, 1821 ***8197.10*** *p229*
Friel, John; New York, 1827 ***8197.10*** *p230*
Friel, Mary 57; Ontario, 1871 ***1823.28*** *p31*
Friel, Patrick; Vermont, 1838-1911 ***5900.10*** *p596*
Friel, William; New York, 1826 ***8197.10*** *p334*
Friell, James; New York, 1802 ***8197.10*** *p228*
Friend, Henry; New Orleans, 1857 ***1224.3*** *p28*
Friend, John; New York, 1840 ***8197.10*** *p386*
Friend, John; Virginia, 1671-1672 ***6212.30*** *p47*
Frier, Sarah 34; Ontario, 1871 ***1823.28*** *p31*
Fries, Caspar; Port uncertain, 1764 ***2856.30*** *p122*
Fries, G. 6; Alaska, 1912 ***9196.1*** *p37*
Fries, G. 6; Yukon, 1912 ***9196.1*** *p37*
Fries, Georg; Port uncertain, 1754 ***2856.30*** *p122*
With wife & child
Fries, Johann Georg; Port uncertain, 1761 ***2856.30*** *p122*
Fries, John; Pennsylvania, 1779 ***4629.10*** *p40*
Friess, Jacob; America, 1774 ***2856.30*** *p122*
Friess, Maria Anna; Port uncertain, 1776 ***2856.30*** *p122*
Frietsch, Hans Adam; Port uncertain, 1769 ***2856.30*** *p122*
Frietsch, Hans Adam; Port uncertain, 1781 ***2856.30*** *p122*
Frieuscoski, John; Maryland, 1910 ***3259.35*** *p15*
Friganza, Romeo; New York, 1837 ***8197.10*** *p374*
Frigg, Andrew; Jamaica, 1769 ***1640.13*** *p42*
Fright, Mathew 33; Virginia, 1774 ***1220.25*** *p45*
Frigot, Dick; Virginia, 1666 ***6212.30*** *p26*
Frik, Adrian; Port uncertain, 1763 ***2856.30*** *p122*
Frik, Adrian; Port uncertain, 1793 ***2856.30*** *p122*
Frilan, Mary 56; Ontario, 1871 ***1823.15*** *p86*
Frinch, James 61; Ontario, 1871 ***1823.22*** *p56*
Frinck, Sarah Noyes; New England, 1699 ***1224.1*** *p42*
Frink, Anna 33; Kansas, 1902-1910 ***9079.10*** *p11*
Frink, Jacob 34; Kansas, 1902-1910 ***9079.10*** *p11*
Frink, Jake 10; Kansas, 1902-1910 ***9079.10*** *p11*
Frink, Lizzie 8; Kansas, 1902-1910 ***9079.10*** *p11*
Friory, Barnard; New York, 1840 ***8197.10*** *p167*
Friot, Francis; Vermont, 1837-1922 ***5900.10*** *p282*
Friot, Mary McCummings; Vermont, 1851-1911 ***5900.10*** *p282*
Frippey, Margaret; Maryland, 1669 ***2524.55*** *p222*
Frippey, Nicholas; Maryland, 1669 ***2524.55*** *p222*
Frisard, Victor L.; New York, 1840 ***8197.10*** *p165*
Frisby, James *SEE* Frisby, James
Frisby, James; Maryland, 1665 ***2524.55*** *p84*
Wife: Mary
Child: William
Child: Mary
Child: Jonas
Child: Thomas
Child: James
Frisby, James; Maryland, 1703 ***1224.2*** *p43*
Frisby, Jonas *SEE* Frisby, James
Frisby, Mary *SEE* Frisby, James
Frisby, Thomas *SEE* Frisby, James
Frisby, William *SEE* Frisby, James
Frisell, John; Maryland, 1652 ***2524.55*** *p41*
Frisk, Moresk; Maryland, 1681 ***2524.55*** *p84*
Friss, Jacob; Pennsylvania, 1786 ***4629.10*** *p54*
Frissell, Patrick; Maryland, 1658 ***2524.55*** *p84*
Frist, John 46; Ontario, 1871 ***1823.22*** *p57*
Frith, Edward; New York, 1835 ***8197.10*** *p316*
Frith, Mathew; Virginia, 1666 ***6212.30*** *p25*
Frith, Thomas 20; Grenada, 1774 ***1220.25*** *p127*
Fritot, Charles E.; New York, 1803 ***8197.10*** *p12*
Fritsch, Annie; Maryland, 1910 ***3259.35*** *p15*
Fritsch, Benedikt; Port uncertain, 1787 ***2856.30*** *p122*
Fritsch, Dorothea; Port uncertain, 1789 ***2856.30*** *p122*
Fritsch, Franz Josef; Port uncertain, 1793 ***2856.30*** *p122*
Fritsch, Friedrich; Port uncertain, 1776 ***2856.30*** *p122*
Fritsch, Jacob; Port uncertain, 1783 ***2856.30*** *p122*
Fritsch, Jacob; Port uncertain, 1796 ***2856.30*** *p122*
Fritsch, Johann; Port uncertain, 1759 ***2856.30*** *p122*
Fritsch, Johann Adam; Port uncertain, 1763 ***2856.30*** *p122*
Fritsch, Josef; Port uncertain, 1788 ***2856.30*** *p122*
Fritsch, Magdalena; Port uncertain, 1788 ***2856.30*** *p122*
Fritsche, Benedikt; Port uncertain, 1795 ***2856.30*** *p122*
Fritsche, Benedikt; Port uncertain, 1796 ***2856.30*** *p122*
Fritsley, Joseph 55; Ontario, 1871 ***1823.15*** *p86*
Fritsley, Robert 38; Ontario, 1871 ***1823.15*** *p87*
Frittan, James 40; Ontario, 1871 ***1823.15*** *p87*
Fritz, Anton; Port uncertain, 1764 ***2856.30*** *p122*
Fritz, Barbara; Port uncertain, 1754 ***2856.30*** *p122*
Fritz, Cath. Elisabeth; America, 1754 ***2856.30*** *p123*
With husband
Fritz, Conrad Aaron; New York, 1807 ***8197.10*** *p43*
Fritz, Elis. C.; America, 1754 ***2856.30*** *p488*
Fritz, Elisabeth; Port uncertain, 1764 ***2856.30*** *p122*
Fritz, Georg; Port uncertain, 1799 ***2856.30*** *p122*
Fritz, George; New York, 1839 ***8197.10*** *p130*
Fritz, Henrich; America, 1737 ***2856.30*** *p123*
With wife & children
Fritz, Jacob; New York, 1839 ***8197.10*** *p130*
Fritz, Margarete; Port uncertain, 1778 ***2856.30*** *p123*
Fritz, Martin J.; Maryland, 1910 ***3259.35*** *p15*
Fritz, Nicolas; Port uncertain, 1737 ***2856.30*** *p123*
Fritz, Valtin; Port uncertain, 1754 ***2856.30*** *p123*
Fritzler, Henry 37; Kansas, 1902-1910 ***9079.10*** *p47*
Fritzler, Katie 8; Kansas, 1910 ***9079.10*** *p47*
Fritzler, Mollie 30; Kansas, 1910 ***9079.10*** *p47*
Fritzsch, Johann; Port uncertain, 1739 ***2856.30*** *p123*
Frivolt, August 45; Ontario, 1871 ***1823.28*** *p31*
Friz, Maria Christina; Port uncertain, 1795 ***2856.30*** *p123*
Frizby, Elizabeth; Maryland, 1649 ***2524.55*** *p84*
Frizell, Alexander; Maryland, 1657 ***2524.55*** *p84*
Wife: Sarah
Daughter: Rebeccha
Frizell, Patrick; Maryland, 1666 ***2524.55*** *p84*
Frizell, Rebeccha *SEE* Frizell, Alexander
Frizell, Sarah *SEE* Frizell, Alexander
Frizell, William; Maryland, 1663 ***2524.55*** *p84*
Frizin, Sabine; America, 1791 ***2856.30*** *p123*
Frizzell, Patrick; Maryland, 1666 ***2524.55*** *p204*
Frohlich, Ap. Rapp *SEE* Frohlich, Valentin
Frohlich, Bernard; Port uncertain, 1740 ***2856.30*** *p123*
Frohlich, Catharina; Port uncertain, 1779 ***2856.30*** *p123*
Frohlich, Jakob; Port uncertain, 1760 ***2856.30*** *p123*
Frohlich, Valentin; America, 1723 ***2856.30*** *p123*
Wife: Ap. Rapp
Frohmann, Michael; Port uncertain, 1750 ***2856.30*** *p123*
Frohnder, Ursula; Port uncertain, 1728 ***2856.30*** *p123*
With children
Frohner, Georg Jacob; Port uncertain, 1791 ***2856.30*** *p124*
Frohnmuller, Rosina; Port uncertain, 1795 ***2856.30*** *p123*
Frokey, Mary 51; Vermont, 1878 ***5900.10*** *p611*
Frolicker, John; British Columbia, 1913 ***9196.1*** *p56*
Frolicker, John; Seattle, 1913 ***9196.1*** *p56*
Frolin, Agathe; Port uncertain, 1796 ***2856.30*** *p123*
Froly, John 24; Ontario, 1871 ***1823.28*** *p31*
Fromacki, John; Maryland, 1910 ***3259.35*** *p15*
Froman, Andrew; Virginia, 1666-1667 ***6212.30*** *p34*
Fromberger, John; Pennsylvania, 1777 ***4629.10*** *p14*
Fromlet, Dominik; Port uncertain, 1745 ***2856.30*** *p123*
Fromlet, Johann; Port uncertain, 1745 ***2856.30*** *p123*
Fromstone, William 46; Ontario, 1871 ***1823.28*** *p31*
Fronmy, James 32; Virginia, 1774 ***1220.25*** *p87*
Frood, Hugh 51; Ontario, 1871 ***1823.28*** *p31*
Frood, John Andrew 42; Ontario, 1871 ***1823.22*** *p57*
Frood, Thomas 55; Ontario, 1871 ***1823.28*** *p31*
Froome, Mr.; Quebec, 1857 ***9196.15*** *p19*
Frosch, Johann; Port uncertain, 1752 ***2856.30*** *p123*
Frose, John 53; Vermont, 1871 ***5900.10*** *p178*
Frosh, Anthony Lawrence; New York, 1837 ***8197.10*** *p230*
Frosh, John Colleral; Pennsylvania, 1786 ***4629.10*** *p55*
Frost, Alexander; Maryland, 1657 ***2524.55*** *p84*
Frost, Arthur; Virginia, 1666-1667 ***6212.30*** *p35*
Frost, Augustine; North America, 1759 ***1224.2*** *p43*
Frost, Jacob; Port uncertain, 1796 ***2856.30*** *p123*
Frost, John; New York, 1840 ***8197.10*** *p164*
Frost, John; New York, New York, 1843 ***1224.3*** *p28*
Frost, John; Vermont, 1877-1927 ***5900.10*** *p459*
Frost, John 25; Philadelphia, 1774 ***1220.25*** *p81*
Frost, John 53; Vermont, 1871 ***5900.10*** *p192*
Frost, John 75; Ontario, 1871 ***1823.22*** *p57*
Frost, Michaell; Virginia, 1667 ***6212.30*** *p37*
Frost, Miles; Virginia, 1665-1666 ***6212.30*** *p25*
Frost, Rachael; Maryland, 1655 ***2524.55*** *p84*
Frost, Thomas 57; Ontario, 1871 ***1823.22*** *p57*
Frost, Valentine; Maryland, 1657 ***2524.55*** *p84*
Froste, Miss; America, 1752 ***2856.30*** *p282*
Froste, Elisabeth; America, 1752 ***2856.30*** *p123*
Froste, Margarete; America, 1752 ***2856.30*** *p123*
With husband
Frowne, John; Virginia, 1666 ***6212.30*** *p31*
Fruchtner, Johann; Port uncertain, 1754 ***2856.30*** *p123*
Frue, William B. 42; Ontario, 1871 ***1823.28*** *p31*
Fruel, Barnard O.; New York, New York, 1860 ***3437.14*** *p71*
Fruerin, Maria; Port uncertain, 1614 ***2856.30*** *p123*
With mother
Frugoni, Matthew; New York, 1829 ***8197.10*** *p359*
Fruh, Eva; Port uncertain, 1754 ***2856.30*** *p123*
With family
Fruhauf, Adam; Port uncertain, 1766 ***2856.30*** *p123*
Fruhauf, Adam; Port uncertain, 1769 ***2856.30*** *p123*
Fruhauf, Dorothea Elisab; Port uncertain, 1790 ***2856.30*** *p123*
Fruhaus, Elis. Catharina; Port uncertain, 1783 ***2856.30*** *p123*
Fruin, Marrian; Virginia, 1668-1669 ***6212.30*** *p40*
Frusilla, Philpot 26; Jamaica, 1773 ***1220.25*** *p31*
Fruten, William 44; Ontario, 1871 ***1823.28*** *p31*
Frwid, James; Maryland, 1725 ***1224.2*** *p43*
Fry, Captain; Quebec, 1857 ***9196.15*** *p24*
Fry, Miss; Quebec, 1856 ***9196.15*** *p5*
Fry, Mr.; Quebec, 1858 ***9196.15*** *p33*
Fry, Abraham 74; Ontario, 1861 ***2896.27*** *p15*
Fry, C.; Quebec, 1857 ***9196.15*** *p16*
Fry, David; Maryland, 1662 ***2524.55*** *p85*
Fry, David; Maryland, 1669 ***2524.55*** *p84*
Relative: Edmund
Fry, Edmund *SEE* Fry, David
Fry, Edward 50; Ontario, 1871 ***1823.15*** *p87*
Fry, Elenor 27; Ontario, 1861 ***2896.27*** *p15*
Fry, George; Indiana, 1846 ***1224.3*** *p28*

G

Gaa, Katharina; Port uncertain, 1796 ***2856.30*** *p128*
Gaarthuis, Hendrick; New York, 1839 ***8197.10*** *p130*
Gabbett, Thomas 49; Vermont, 1890 ***5900.10*** *p88*
Gabbraith, William 48; Ontario, 1871 ***1823.15*** *p87*
Gabel, A. E. Cullmann *SEE* Gabel, Johann Philipp
Gabel, George 67; Ontario, 1871 ***1823.15*** *p87*
Gabel, Jakob; Port uncertain, 1768 ***2856.30*** *p128*
With wife
Gabel, Johann Friedric; America, 1739 ***2856.30*** *p128*
Gabel, Johann Friedric; America, 1739 ***2856.30*** *p128*
Wife: M. M. Spies
With daughter
Gabel, Johann Philipp; America, 1738 ***2856.30*** *p128*
Wife: A. E. Cullmann
Gabel, Johann Philipp; America, 1739 ***2856.30*** *p128*
Wife: A. E. Cullmann
Gabel, Konrad; America, 1773 ***2856.30*** *p128*
With wife & children
Gabel, Konrad; Port uncertain, 1759 ***2856.30*** *p128*
With wife & children
Gabel, M. M. Spies *SEE* Gabel, Johann Friedric
Gabel, Maria Magdalena Spies; America, 1738 ***2856.30*** *p435*
Gabel, Michael; Maryland, 1910 ***3259.35*** *p15*
Gaberdam, Anna Maria; Port uncertain, 1769 ***2856.30*** *p128*
Gaberdan, Anna Maria; Port uncertain, 1760 ***2856.30*** *p128*
Gaberdan, Barbara; Port uncertain, 1778 ***2856.30*** *p128*
Gaberdo, Maria Barbara; Port uncertain, 1746 ***2856.30*** *p128*
Gaberie, Eliza 66; Vermont, 1889 ***5900.10*** *p222*
Gaberthan, Johann; Port uncertain, 1766 ***2856.30*** *p128*
Gaberthan, Magdalena; Port uncertain, 1766 ***2856.30*** *p128*
Gabhart, Nicholas; America, 1747 ***2856.30*** *p128*
Gable, Gottlob 59; Ontario, 1871 ***1823.28*** *p31*
Gable, John; New York, 1807 ***8197.10*** *p39*
Gabler, John 74; Ontario, 1871 ***1823.15*** *p87*
Gabotis, John 75; Ontario, 1871 ***1823.22*** *p57*
Gabourel, Joshua; Cape Fear, North Carolina, 1737 ***1224.2*** *p44*
Gabovsky, Joseph; Maryland, 1910 ***3259.35*** *p15*
Gabriell, John; Maryland, 1659 ***2524.55*** *p85*
Gackowski, John; Maryland, 1910 ***3259.35*** *p15*
Gackowski, Tomisz; Maryland, 1910 ***3259.35*** *p15*
Gactins, Thomas; New York, 1840 ***8197.10*** *p168*
Gacturads, Julious; Maryland, 1910 ***3259.35*** *p15*
Gaczar, Felicks; Maryland, 1910 ***3259.35*** *p15*
Gaczkowski, Mike; Maryland, 1910 ***3259.35*** *p15*
Gadd, Lewis; New York, 1836 ***8197.10*** *p79*
Gaddis, John 36; Maryland, 1774 ***1220.25*** *p52*
Gadek, John; Maryland, 1910 ***3259.35*** *p15*
Gades, Harman 25; Jamaica, 1774 ***1220.25*** *p49*
Gadke, Christie 35; Ontario, 1871 ***1823.15*** *p87*
Gadley, John; Vermont, 1828-1917 ***5900.10*** *p510*
Gadsby, Edward; Died enroute, 1696 ***1224.1*** *p23*
Gadsby, John 19; Maryland, 1774 ***1220.25*** *p51*
Gadsby, Ralph 21; Maryland, 1775 ***1220.25*** *p99*
Gadwiga, Annie; Maryland, 1910 ***3259.35*** *p15*
Gaebel, Albin; New York, New York, 1903 ***3437.14*** *p133*
Gaeling, John 33; Maryland, 1774 ***1220.25*** *p39*
Gaertner, John Samuel; New York, 1807 ***8197.10*** *p39*
Gaertner, William; New York, 1807 ***8197.10*** *p39*
Gafeny, Charles; Vermont, 1831-1896 ***5900.10*** *p459*
Gaff, John; New York, 1840 ***8197.10*** *p168*
Gaffany, Ellen; Vermont, 1830-1904 ***5900.10*** *p201*
Gaffany, Margaret; Vermont, 1828-1908 ***5900.10*** *p200*
Gaffany, Michael 56; Vermont, 1881 ***5900.10*** *p200*
Gaffenay, James 47; Ontario, 1871 ***1823.28*** *p31*
Gaffield, Jonathan 81; Ontario, 1871 ***1823.22*** *p57*
Gaffney, Bridget; Vermont, 1849-1875 ***5900.10*** *p567*
Gaffney, Bridget 25; Vermont, 1875 ***5900.10*** *p567*
Gaffney, Bridget Flynn; Vermont, 1822-1885 ***5900.10*** *p567*
Gaffney, Catherine 69; Vermont, 1899 ***5900.10*** *p507*
Gaffney, Catherine Lyons; Vermont, 1833-1901 ***5900.10*** *p564*
Gaffney, Charles; New York, 1831 ***8197.10*** *p234*
Gaffney, Charles; Vermont, 1859-1861 ***5900.10*** *p567*
Gaffney, Dennis; New York, 1837 ***8197.10*** *p87*
Gaffney, Dennis B.; New York, 1827 ***8197.10*** *p234*
Gaffney, Edward; Vermont, 1863-1903 ***5900.10*** *p567*
Gaffney, Ellen; Vermont, 1852-1881 ***5900.10*** *p567*
Gaffney, Ellen; Vermont, 1857-1899 ***5900.10*** *p562*
Gaffney, Ellen 86; Vermont, 1872 ***5900.10*** *p199*
Gaffney, Ellen Leahy 44; Vermont, 1877 ***5900.10*** *p63*
Gaffney, James; New York, 1837 ***8197.10*** *p88*
Gaffney, James; Vermont, 1845-1899 ***5900.10*** *p567*
Gaffney, James 50; Ontario, 1871 ***1823.28*** *p31*
Gaffney, James 80; Vermont, 1890 ***5900.10*** *p507*
Gaffney, Jane; Vermont, 1851-1896 ***5900.10*** *p567*
Gaffney, Katherine Prior 53; Vermont, 1890 ***5900.10*** *p505*
Gaffney, Katie 41; Vermont, 1888 ***5900.10*** *p420*
Gaffney, Margaret; Vermont, 1860-1897 ***5900.10*** *p567*
Gaffney, Margaret Dougherty; Vermont, n.d. ***5900.10*** *p507*
Gaffney, Mary; Vermont, 1843-1922 ***5900.10*** *p567*
Gaffney, Mary 41; Vermont, 1881 ***5900.10*** *p536*
Gaffney, Mary J. 34; Vermont, 1884 ***5900.10*** *p559*
Gaffney, Michael; New York, 1836-1838 ***8197.10*** *p114*
Gaffney, Michael, Jr. 45; Vermont, 1880 ***5900.10*** *p536*
Gaffney, Owen 65; Vermont, 1879 ***5900.10*** *p559*
Gaffney, Patrick; New York, 1837 ***8197.10*** *p87*
Gaffney, Patrick; New York, 1838 ***8197.10*** *p235*
Gaffney, Peter; Vermont, 1820-1885 ***5900.10*** *p567*
Gaffney, Peter; Vermont, 1855-1916 ***5900.10*** *p567*
Gaffney, Philip; New York, 1821 ***8197.10*** *p232*
Gaffney, T. J.; Vermont, 1843-1906 ***5900.10*** *p446*
Gaffney, Thomas; New York, 1840 ***8197.10*** *p236*
Gaffney, Thomas 80; Vermont, 1903 ***5900.10*** *p63*
Gaffney, William; Vermont, 1834-1899 ***5900.10*** *p564*
Gafney, Michael; New York, 1832 ***8197.10*** *p368*
Gagaghan, Margaret 46; Ontario, 1871 ***1823.22*** *p57*
Gagaghan, Thomas 78; Ontario, 1871 ***1823.22*** *p57*
Gagan, James 35; Ontario, 1871 ***1823.28*** *p31*
Gagberg, Henrich Martin; Port uncertain, 1765 ***2856.30*** *p128*
Gagen, Richard S. 50; Ontario, 1871 ***1823.15*** *p87*
Gagew, George 52; Ontario, 1871 ***1823.15*** *p87*
Gagnon, Asa; Ontario, 1871 ***1823.22*** *p57*
Gaherty, Patrick; Vermont, 1831-1910 ***5900.10*** *p212*
Gahring, George; New York, New York, 1842 ***6058.10*** *p41*
Gahring, Godfrey; New York, New York, 1846 ***6058.10*** *p56*
Gahring, Jacob; New York, New York, 1844 ***6058.10*** *p36*
Gahring, Jacob; New York, New York, 1853 ***6058.10*** *p36*
Gahring, Jacob; New York, New York, 1853 ***6058.10*** *p55*
Gahring, John; New York, New York, 1843 ***6058.10*** *p28*
Gahringer, Johann Georg; America, 1753 ***2856.30*** *p153*
Gaiger, Henrich; America, 1767 ***2856.30*** *p128*
Gaiger, Henrich; America, 1770 ***2856.30*** *p128*
Gaiger, Jakob; America, 1770 ***2856.30*** *p128*
Gailfuss, Hans Adam; Port uncertain, 1791 ***2856.30*** *p128*
Gaine, Ann; Maryland, 1651-1662 ***2524.55*** *p85*
Gaine, John; Maryland, 1667 ***2524.55*** *p85*
Gainer, Edward 70; Ontario, 1871 ***1823.15*** *p87*
Gainer, Thomas 35; Ontario, 1871 ***1823.15*** *p87*
Gainey, John; Vermont, 1803-1887 ***5900.10*** *p610*
Gainforth, James 59; Ontario, 1871 ***1823.22*** *p57*
Gainforth, Thomas 55; Ontario, 1871 ***1823.15*** *p87*
Gainforth, Thomas 90; Ontario, 1871 ***1823.15*** *p87*
Gains, Thomas 59; Ontario, 1871 ***1823.22*** *p57*
Gainsford, Erasmus; Virginia, 1664 ***6212.30*** *p8*
Gainsford, Mathias 28; Maryland, 1774 ***1220.25*** *p65*
Gaird, Miss; Quebec, 1857 ***9196.15*** *p25*
Gairdner, James; Charleston, South Carolina, 1780 ***1640.10*** *p61*
Gairdner, James 50; Ontario, 1871 ***1823.15*** *p87*
Gairdner, Robert Hutch 45; Ontario, 1871 ***1823.15*** *p87*
Gairdner, William; Georgia, 1698 ***1640.13*** *p44*
Gais, Christina; Port uncertain, 1785 ***2856.30*** *p128*
Gaiser, George; New York, New York, 1856 ***3437.14*** *p20*
Gaisford, John; Charles Town, South Carolina, 1796 ***1224.2*** *p44*
Gait, John 81; Ontario, 1871 ***1823.15*** *p87*
Gait, Sydenham; New York, 1840 ***8197.10*** *p169*
Gait, Sydenham; New York, 1840 ***8197.10*** *p235*
Gaitley, Patrick; Pennsylvania, 1846 ***6058.10*** *p22*
Gajdzicki, Wladislaus; Maryland, 1910 ***3259.35*** *p15*
Gajeski, Martin; Maryland, 1910 ***3259.35*** *p15*
Gajewski, August; Maryland, 1910 ***3259.35*** *p15*
Gajewski, Michael; Maryland, 1910 ***3259.35*** *p15*
Gajkowska, Bronislawa; Maryland, 1910 ***3259.35*** *p15*
Gakel, Karl; Port uncertain, 1764 ***2856.30*** *p128*
Gakelsin, Anna Barbara; Port uncertain, 1746 ***2856.30*** *p128*
Gakerlin, Mary; Maryland, 1658 ***2524.55*** *p85*
Gakes, John 30; Washington, 1914 ***9196.1*** *p64*
Galaczynski, Joseph; Maryland, 1910 ***3259.35*** *p15*
Galagan, William 40; Ontario, 1871 ***1823.15*** *p87*
Galager, Robert 39; Ontario, 1871 ***1823.15*** *p87*
Galagher, John; New York, 1837 ***8197.10*** *p88*
Galahar, James 33; Ontario, 1871 ***1823.15*** *p87*
Galaher, Catherine 7; Ontario, 1861 ***2896.27*** *p61*
Galaher, Elizabeth 4; Ontario, 1861 ***2896.27*** *p61*
Galaher, Francis 2; Ontario, 1861 ***2896.27*** *p61*
Galaher, Margaret 11; Ontario, 1861 ***2896.27*** *p61*
Galaher, Margaret 32; Ontario, 1861 ***2896.27*** *p61*
Galaher, Mary 13; Ontario, 1861 ***2896.27*** *p61*
Galaher, Mary 70; Ontario, 1861 ***2896.27*** *p61*
Galaher, Thomas 9; Ontario, 1861 ***2896.27*** *p61*
Galaher, Thomas 49; Ontario, 1861 ***2896.27*** *p61*
Galaspie, John 60; Ontario, 1871 ***1823.15*** *p87*
Galaway, Michael; Maryland, 1682 ***2524.55*** *p85*
Galbraith, Archibald 32; Ontario, 1871 ***1823.15*** *p87*
Galbraith, Benjamin; New York, 1836 ***8197.10*** *p79*
Galbraith, David 50; Ontario, 1871 ***1823.15*** *p87*
Galbraith, David, Sr. 79; Ontario, 1871 ***1823.15*** *p87*
Galbraith, Elizabeth; Savannah, Georgia, 1821-1845 ***1640.10*** *p61*
Galbraith, Isabella 28; Ontario, 1871 ***1823.15*** *p87*
Galbraith, James; New York, 1836 ***8197.10*** *p234*
Galbraith, John 36; Ontario, 1871 ***1823.15*** *p87*
Galbraith, John 39; Ontario, 1871 ***1823.15*** *p87*
Galbraith, Mary 80; Ontario, 1871 ***1823.15*** *p88*
Galbraith, Sarah 56; Ontario, 1871 ***1823.22*** *p57*

Galbraith, William; Jamaica, 1768 ***1640.13*** *p44*
Galbraith, William 26; Ontario, 1871 ***1823.15*** *p88*
Galbrath, Allen 44; Ontario, 1871 ***1823.15*** *p88*
Galbreath, James 50; Ontario, 1871 ***1823.15*** *p88*
Gale, Catherine Shanley 38; Vermont, 1854 ***5900.10*** *p524*
Gale, Emma 14; Ontario, 1871 ***1823.15*** *p88*
Gale, Francis 40; Ontario, 1871 ***1823.22*** *p57*
Gale, James 36; Vermont, 1883 ***5900.10*** *p524*
Gale, John 25; Maryland, 1774 ***1220.25*** *p57*
Gale, Lizzie 30; Vermont, 1873 ***5900.10*** *p530*
Gale, Mary McMannis 57; Vermont, 1878 ***5900.10*** *p527*
Gale, Patrick 69; Vermont, 1883 ***5900.10*** *p524*
Gale, Thomas; New York, New York, 1823 ***1224.3*** *p29*
Gale, Thomas 48; Ontario, 1871 ***1823.22*** *p57*
Gales, Richard; Virginia, 1666-1667 ***6212.30*** *p34*
Galette, Henrich; America, 1738 ***2856.30*** *p128*
Galewicz, Kazmierz; Maryland, 1910 ***3259.35*** *p15*
Galey, Thomas; Florida, 1766 ***1224.2*** *p44*
Galgey, Barbara *SEE* Galgey, Richard
Galgey, Richard; Philadelphia, 1789 ***4629.10*** *p57*
Wife: Barbara
Galgey, Thomas 34; Philadelphia, 1789 ***4629.10*** *p57*
Gall, Johann Michael; Port uncertain, 1766 ***2856.30*** *p128*
Gallacher, John 60; Ontario, 1871 ***1823.15*** *p88*
Gallagar, Elizabeth Cavanaugh 78; Vermont, 1887 ***5900.10*** *p413*
Gallagar, John G. 81; Vermont, 1880 ***5900.10*** *p413*
Gallaghan, Bernard; New York, 1839 ***8197.10*** *p130*
Gallaghar, Sarah 84; Vermont, 1892 ***5900.10*** *p91*
Gallagher, Mr.; Vermont, 1857-1921 ***5900.10*** *p206*
Gallagher, Adelia McClure 17; Vermont, 1863 ***5900.10*** *p500*
Gallagher, Alice L. Slade; Vermont, 1862-1927 ***5900.10*** *p594*
Gallagher, Ann 52; Vermont, 1904 ***5900.10*** *p441*
Gallagher, Ann Killgallen; Vermont, 1821-1877 ***5900.10*** *p205*
Gallagher, Anna McDonough; Vermont, 1816-1899 ***5900.10*** *p176*
Gallagher, Anna Sloway 35; Vermont, 1879 ***5900.10*** *p573*
Gallagher, Bernard; Vermont, 1812-1897 ***5900.10*** *p176*
Gallagher, Bernard 47; Ontario, 1871 ***1823.28*** *p31*
Gallagher, Brian 45; Ontario, 1871 ***1823.15*** *p88*
Gallagher, Bridget; Vermont, 1856-1946 ***5900.10*** *p394*
Gallagher, Cathrine; Vermont, 1818-1894 ***5900.10*** *p205*
Gallagher, Clara Renfrew; Vermont, 1861-1909 ***5900.10*** *p206*
Gallagher, Daniel; New York, 1826 ***8197.10*** *p233*
Gallagher, Edmond; Vermont, 1818-1904 ***5900.10*** *p205*
Gallagher, Edward M.; Vermont, 1855-1928 ***5900.10*** *p206*
Gallagher, Elizabeth; Vermont, n.d. ***5900.10*** *p583*
Gallagher, Elizabeth; Vermont, 1857-1861 ***5900.10*** *p176*
Gallagher, Emma W. Laselle; Vermont, 1854-1926 ***5900.10*** *p500*
Gallagher, Fannie; Vermont, 1813-1893 ***5900.10*** *p474*
Gallagher, Farigal 50; Ontario, 1871 ***1823.28*** *p31*
Gallagher, Frances; Vermont, 1852-1920 ***5900.10*** *p127*
Gallagher, Hanora; Vermont, 1831-1918 ***5900.10*** *p379*
Gallagher, Hugh; New York, 1837 ***8197.10*** *p88*
Gallagher, Hugh; Vermont, 1791-1854 ***5900.10*** *p147*
Gallagher, Hugh 30; Ontario, 1871 ***1823.22*** *p58*
Gallagher, Hugh 33; Ontario, 1871 ***1823.28*** *p31*
Gallagher, Hugh 34; Ontario, 1871 ***1823.28*** *p31*
Gallagher, Hugh 44; Ontario, 1871 ***1823.22*** *p58*
Gallagher, James; Pennsylvania, 1779 ***4629.10*** *p39*
Gallagher, James; Vermont, 1832-1920 ***5900.10*** *p583*
Gallagher, James; Vermont, 1836-1902 ***5900.10*** *p582*
Gallagher, James 31; Vermont, 1889 ***5900.10*** *p168*
Gallagher, James 39; Ontario, 1861 ***2896.25*** *p32*
Gallagher, James 53; Ontario, 1871 ***1823.15*** *p88*
Gallagher, Jane McClinton; Vermont, 1818-1905 ***5900.10*** *p595*
Gallagher, Jennie; Vermont, 1854-1912 ***5900.10*** *p595*
Gallagher, John; New York, 1828 ***8197.10*** *p349*
Gallagher, John; New York, 1839 ***8197.10*** *p130*
Gallagher, John; New York, 1840 ***8197.10*** *p168*
Gallagher, John; New York, 1840 ***8197.10*** *p236*
Gallagher, John; Vermont, 1810-1865 ***5900.10*** *p595*
Gallagher, John 25; Ontario, 1871 ***1823.22*** *p58*
Gallagher, John 46; Ontario, 1871 ***1823.28*** *p32*
Gallagher, John 50; Ontario, 1871 ***1823.22*** *p58*
Gallagher, John W.; Vermont, 1852-1908 ***5900.10*** *p594*
Gallagher, Joseph 76; Vermont, 1800-1899 ***5900.10*** *p500*
Gallagher, Julia McNamara; Vermont, 1861-1911 ***5900.10*** *p216*
Gallagher, Kate 49; Vermont, 1894 ***5900.10*** *p205*
Gallagher, Kate Waters; Vermont, 1857-1939 ***5900.10*** *p206*
Gallagher, Katherine; Vermont, 1858-1909 ***5900.10*** *p595*
Gallagher, Lucy; Vermont, 1852-1929 ***5900.10*** *p128*
Gallagher, Margaret 20 *SEE* Gallagher, Michael
Gallagher, Margaret O'Donnell; Vermont, 1835-1899 ***5900.10*** *p582*
Gallagher, Mary; Vermont, 1847-1897 ***5900.10*** *p176*
Gallagher, Mary 5; Ontario, 1861 ***2896.25*** *p32*
Gallagher, Mary 28; Ontario, 1861 ***2896.25*** *p32*
Gallagher, Mary 28; Ontario, 1871 ***1823.22*** *p58*
Gallagher, Mary 34; Vermont, 1872 ***5900.10*** *p557*
Gallagher, Mary A.; Vermont, 1858-1922 ***5900.10*** *p583*
Gallagher, Mary Corey 70; Vermont, 1904 ***5900.10*** *p580*
Gallagher, Mary J.; Vermont, 1851-1923 ***5900.10*** *p277*
Gallagher, Matilda; Vermont, 1849-1919 ***5900.10*** *p576*
Gallagher, Michael 24; New York, New York, 1847 ***1825.45*** *p15*
Sister: Margaret 20
Gallagher, Michael 35; Ontario, 1871 ***1823.28*** *p32*
Gallagher, Mor 3; Ontario, 1861 ***2896.25*** *p32*
Gallagher, Nancy 1; Ontario, 1861 ***2896.25*** *p32*
Gallagher, Niel; New York, 1838 ***8197.10*** *p378*
Gallagher, Nora M.; Vermont, 1850-1930 ***5900.10*** *p277*
Gallagher, Nora McKern; Vermont, 1834-1896 ***5900.10*** *p595*
Gallagher, Patrick; New York, 1838-1840 ***8197.10*** *p301*
Gallagher, Patrick; Philadelphia, 1827 ***6058.10*** *p23*
Gallagher, Patrick; Vermont, 1837-1896 ***5900.10*** *p595*
Gallagher, Patrick 36; Ontario, 1871 ***1823.22*** *p58*
Gallagher, Patrick 39; Ontario, 1871 ***1823.15*** *p88*
Gallagher, Patrick 55; Ontario, 1871 ***1823.22*** *p58*
Gallagher, Peter; New York, 1837 ***8197.10*** *p88*
Gallagher, Peter; Pennsylvania, 1777 ***4629.10*** *p9*
Gallagher, Philip; Vermont, 1848-1927 ***5900.10*** *p216*
Gallagher, Robert; New York, 1864 ***6058.10*** *p66*
Gallagher, Rosamond; Vermont, 1830-1907 ***5900.10*** *p172*
Gallagher, Sarah; Vermont, 1826-1914 ***5900.10*** *p147*
Gallagher, Sarah O'Neill; Vermont, 1803-1847 ***5900.10*** *p147*
Gallagher, Susan 72; Vermont, 1905 ***5900.10*** *p562*
Gallagher, Thomas 55; Ontario, 1871 ***1823.28*** *p32*
Gallagher, Thomas A.; Vermont, 1853-1926 ***5900.10*** *p500*
Gallagher, William 50; Ontario, 1871 ***1823.28*** *p32*
Gallagher, William 56; Vermont, 1890 ***5900.10*** *p580*
Gallaher, Charles; New York, 1807 ***8197.10*** *p331*
Gallaher, Charles 38; Ontario, 1871 ***1823.22*** *p58*
Gallaher, John; New York, 1838 ***8197.10*** *p115*
Gallaher, John 46; Ontario, 1871 ***1823.28*** *p32*
Galland, Samuel 39; Maryland, 1775 ***1220.25*** *p97*
Gallant, Allexander; Maryland, 1676 ***2524.55*** *p85*
Gallaran, Johannah; Vermont, 1867 ***5900.10*** *p63*
Gallaspy, Valentine; Pennsylvania, 1777 ***4629.10*** *p12*
Gallauer, Dorothea; Port uncertain, 1736 ***2856.30*** *p128*
Gallaugher, Hannorah 64; Ontario, 1871 ***1823.22*** *p58*
Gallaugher, Patrick; New York, 1807 ***8197.10*** *p327*
Gallaway, Isaac; Baltimore, 1847 ***6058.10*** *p29*
Gallaway, John 30; Ontario, 1871 ***1823.15*** *p88*
Gallaway, Robert 42; Ontario, 1871 ***1823.15*** *p88*
Galle, Johann Georg; America, 1788 ***2856.30*** *p128*
Galle, Johann Georg; America, 1789 ***2856.30*** *p128*
Galle, Johann Georg; Port uncertain, 1768 ***2856.30*** *p128*
Galle, Johann Nickel; Port uncertain, 1764 ***2856.30*** *p128*
Galle, Johann Nickel; Port uncertain, 1788 ***2856.30*** *p128*
Gallen, Alice *SEE* Gallen, Joseph
Gallen, Joseph; Maryland, 1665 ***2524.55*** *p85*
Wife: Alice
Gallen, Patrick; New York, 1837 ***8197.10*** *p88*
Gallenz, Michael; Port uncertain, 1749 ***2856.30*** *p128*
Galles, Jacob Frederick; New York, 1825 ***8197.10*** *p233*
Galles, Joseph; New York, 1838 ***8197.10*** *p113*
Galletly, Janet; New York, 1883 ***1640.13*** *p44*
Gallett, Mrs.; Maryland, 1631-1685 ***2524.55*** *p85*
Galley, Mathew; Maryland, 1667 ***2524.55*** *p85*
Galley, William 19; Ontario, 1871 ***1823.15*** *p88*
Galliart, Adam 40; Kansas, 1887-1910 ***9079.10*** *p15*
Galliart, Anna 36; Kansas, 1910 ***9079.10*** *p15*
Galliart, Katie 34; Kansas, 1910 ***9079.10*** *p39*
Gallie, Alexander; Jamaica, 1831 ***1640.13*** *p44*
Galliegan, William 50; Ontario, 1871 ***1823.15*** *p88*
Gallies, Joseph; New York, 1827 ***8197.10*** *p342*
Galligan, Dennis; New York, 1838 ***8197.10*** *p114*
Galligan, John; Vermont, 1845-1907 ***5900.10*** *p549*
Galligan, Patrick; New York, 1825 ***8197.10*** *p233*
Galliger, Richard 24; Ontario, 1871 ***1823.28*** *p32*
Gallimore, Christopher; Georgia, 1734 ***1640.10*** *p65*
Gallin, Francis D. 2; Vermont, 1859 ***5900.10*** *p498*
Gallion, Catharina; Port uncertain, 1755 ***2856.30*** *p128*
Gallivan, Catherine 77; Vermont, 1883 ***5900.10*** *p298*
Gallivan, James; New York, 1823 ***8197.10*** *p233*
Gallivan, Mary 52; Ontario, 1871 ***1823.22*** *p58*
Gallivan, Michel 30; Ontario, 1871 ***1823.22*** *p58*
Gallman, John 65; Ontario, 1871 ***1823.15*** *p88*
Gallop, George 50; Ontario, 1871 ***1823.15*** *p88*
Gallot, John; New York, 1838 ***8197.10*** *p114*
Galloway, Miss; Quebec, 1857 ***9196.15*** *p17*
Galloway, A.; Savannah, Georgia, 1854 ***1640.10*** *p61*
Galloway, Alexander; Jackson, Mississippi, 1858 ***1640.10*** *p61*
Galloway, David; Savannah, Georgia, 1854 ***1640.10*** *p62*
Galloway, David 38; Ontario, 1871 ***1823.28*** *p32*
Galloway, Gallia 21 *SEE* Galloway, John
Galloway, James; Georgia, 1738 ***1640.10*** *p62*
Galloway, James 29; Ontario, 1871 ***1823.15*** *p88*
Galloway, John; Georgia, 1699 ***1640.13*** *p44*
Galloway, John 22; Philadelphia, 1774 ***1220.25*** *p42*
Wife: Gallia 21
Galloway, Lucey; Maryland, 1658 ***2524.55*** *p86*
Gallup, Joseph A.; Vermont, 1848-1921 ***5900.10*** *p598*
Gallup, Sarah A. Shaw; Vermont, 1856-1933 ***5900.10*** *p598*
Gallwey, James; New York, 1837 ***8197.10*** *p234*
Gallwith, John; Maryland, 1681 ***2524.55*** *p86*
Gally, Christian; Pennsylvania, 1777 ***4629.10*** *p8*
Galovich, M. 40; Alaska, 1917 ***9196.1*** *p46*
Galovich, M. 40; Whitehorse, Yukon, 1917 ***9196.1*** *p46*
Galoway, James; New York, 1840 ***8197.10*** *p170*
Galpin, Joseph; North America, 1790 ***1224.2*** *p44*
Galroth, Henry 6; Kansas, 1910 ***9079.10*** *p48*
Galroth, Jacob 28; Kansas, 1908-1910 ***9079.10*** *p47*
Galroth, Leda 2; Kansas, 1910 ***9079.10*** *p48*
Galroth, Mollie 25; Kansas, 1910 ***9079.10*** *p48*
Galster, Christian 23; Ontario, 1871 ***1823.15*** *p88*
Galster, Servatuss 54; Ontario, 1871 ***1823.15*** *p88*
Galt, Mr.; Quebec, 1857 ***9196.15*** *p24*
Galtt, James; Virginia, 1697 ***1224.1*** *p23*
Galuska, George; Maryland, 1910 ***3259.35*** *p15*
Galvin, Mr.; Vermont, 1828-1901 ***5900.10*** *p312*
Galvin, Mrs.; Vermont, 1833-1900 ***5900.10*** *p312*
Galvin, Biddy 6 *SEE* Galvin, John
Galvin, Bridget Madigan; Vermont, 1910 ***5900.10*** *p466*
Galvin, Bridget Splain; Vermont, 1839-1918 ***5900.10*** *p174*
Galvin, Catharine Duffy 43; Vermont, 1875 ***5900.10*** *p323*
Galvin, Dennis; New York, 1839 ***8197.10*** *p235*
Galvin, Dennis J.; Vermont, 1868-1892 ***5900.10*** *p312*
Galvin, Edward 46; Vermont, 1901 ***5900.10*** *p568*
Galvin, Edward 47; Vermont, n.d. ***5900.10*** *p568*
Galvin, Ellen; Vermont, 1867-1894 ***5900.10*** *p312*
Galvin, Henry; Vermont, 1855-1932 ***5900.10*** *p317*
Galvin, James; Vermont, 1833-1917 ***5900.10*** *p174*
Galvin, John; New York, 1840 ***8197.10*** *p168*
Galvin, John; Vermont, 1854-1911 ***5900.10*** *p120*
Galvin, John 19; Vermont, 1863 ***5900.10*** *p317*
Galvin, John 32; New York, New York, 1849 ***1825.45*** *p49*
Wife: Margaret 30
Son: Tade 4
Daughter: Biddy 6
Son: Patrick 2
Galvin, John 40; Vermont, 1854 ***5900.10*** *p317*
Galvin, Katherine; Vermont, 1874-1897 ***5900.10*** *p312*
Galvin, Margaret 30 *SEE* Galvin, John
Galvin, Margaret 94; Vermont, 1906 ***5900.10*** *p317*
Galvin, Martha Henry; Vermont, n.d. ***5900.10*** *p568*
Galvin, Mary 78; Vermont, 1891 ***5900.10*** *p290*
Galvin, Mary A.; Vermont, 1857-1896 ***5900.10*** *p312*
Galvin, Mary A. 74; Vermont, 1926 ***5900.10*** *p122*
Galvin, Mary Jane Flannery; Vermont, 1856-1914 ***5900.10*** *p120*
Galvin, Michael; Vermont, 1894 ***5900.10*** *p466*
Galvin, Patrick 2 *SEE* Galvin, John
Galvin, Patrick 68; Vermont, 1916 ***5900.10*** *p317*
Galvin, Tade 4 *SEE* Galvin, John
Galvin, Tade 30; New York, New York, 1849 ***1825.45*** *p49*
Galvin, Thomas; Vermont, 1855-1936 ***5900.10*** *p317*
Galway, Bridget Cody; Vermont, 1840-1898 ***5900.10*** *p467*
Galway, John; Vermont, 1848-1920 ***5900.10*** *p467*
Galway, Michael; New York, 1821 ***8197.10*** *p232*
Galyardt, Anna 27; Kansas, 1878-1910 ***9079.10*** *p8*
Galyardt, David 27; Kansas, 1878-1910 ***9079.10*** *p8*
Galyardt, Mary 57; Kansas, 1878-1910 ***9079.10*** *p8*
Galyardt, Molly 22; Kansas, 1904-1910 ***9079.10*** *p8*
Galyardt, Rinhart 32; Kansas, 1878-1910 ***9079.10*** *p8*
Galyardt, Rinhart 52; Kansas, 1878-1910 ***9079.10*** *p8*
Gamball, William; Maryland, 1668 ***2524.55*** *p86*
Gambell, Elisabeth 33; Ontario, 1871 ***1823.15*** *p88*
Gambert, Johann; America, 1749 ***2856.30*** *p129*
With 3 children
Gambert, Wilhelm; America, 1749 ***2856.30*** *p129*
With 3 children
Gamble, Capt.; Quebec, 1857 ***9196.15*** *p15*
Gamble, Mr.; Quebec, 1856 ***9196.15*** *p10*
Gamble, Mr.; Quebec, 1858 ***9196.15*** *p33*
Gamble, Mrs.; Quebec, 1857 ***9196.15*** *p15*

Gamble, Eliza 21; Philadelphia, 1774 1220.25 p63
Gamble, James; Pennsylvania, 1786 4629.10 p46
Gamble, James 28; Ontario, 1871 1823.15 p88
Gamble, Jane 31; Ontario, 1871 1823.15 p88
Gamble, John; Pennsylvania, 1786 4629.10 p47
Gamble, Joseph; Pennsylvania, 1777 4629.10 p7
Gamble, Rebeca 41; Ontario, 1871 1823.15 p88
Gamble, Robert; New York, 1822 8197.10 p232
Gamble, Robert 30; Ontario, 1871 1823.15 p88
Gamble, William; Pennsylvania, 1786 4629.10 p47
Gamenski, Stanislaus; Maryland, 1910 3259.35 p15
Gamer, Cath. Margarete; Port uncertain, 1790 2856.30 p129
Gamer, Walter; Maryland, 1651 2524.55 p86
Games, Edward; Virginia, 1665 6212.30 p18
Games, Elizabeth; Maryland, 1665 2524.55 p86
Games, Joane; Maryland, 1675 2524.55 p86
Games, Thomas; Maryland, 1675 2524.55 p86
Gamet, Konrad; Port uncertain, 1749 2856.30 p129
Gammack, John; New York, 1811 8197.10 p57
Gams, Margarete; Port uncertain, 1791 2856.30 p129
Gams, Maria Anna; Port uncertain, 1769 2856.30 p129
Gams, Maria Catharina; Port uncertain, 1790 2856.30 p129
Gamsby, Ann 8 *SEE* Gamsby, John
Gamsby, Dorothy 10 *SEE* Gamsby, John
Gamsby, George 6 *SEE* Gamsby, John
Gamsby, John 7 *SEE* Gamsby, John
Gamsby, John 33; Boston, 1774 1220.25 p124
Wife: Margaret 30
Child: Peter 1
Child: Dorothy 10
Child: Ann 8
Child: George 6
Child: John 7
Gamsby, Margaret 30 *SEE* Gamsby, John
Gamsby, Peter 1 *SEE* Gamsby, John
Ganbaim, John 40; Ontario, 1871 1823.15 p88
Gancoe, Edward 39; Ontario, 1871 1823.15 p88
Gander, Adam; Port uncertain, 1754 2856.30 p129
Gander, Karl; America, 1746 2856.30 p129
With wife & children
Gander, Philipp Jakob; Port uncertain, 1777 2856.30 p129
Gandolfo, Jerolamo; New York, 1831 8197.10 p367
Gandolfo, Joseph; New York, 1830 8197.10 p362
Gandy, Absolon; Virginia, 1663 6212.30 p2
Ganey, Bridget C. Duffy; Vermont, 1840-1927 5900.10 p139
Ganey, Francis 22; Vermont, 1871 5900.10 p614
Ganey, John; Vermont, 1839-1884 5900.10 p139
Ganey, Margaret Ring 82; Vermont, 1883 5900.10 p139
Ganey, Mary; Vermont, 1835-1897 5900.10 p135
Ganey, Matthew 90; Vermont, 1879 5900.10 p139
Ganey, Matthew, II; Vermont, 1843-1917 5900.10 p139
Gang, Jacob; Port uncertain, 1749 2856.30 p129
Gang, Jakob; Port uncertain, 1733 2856.30 p153
Gang, Jakob; Port uncertain, 1766 2856.30 p154
Ganglof, Joseph; New York, 1838 8197.10 p115
Gangloff, Johann Nikolas; Port uncertain, 1785 2856.30 p129
Gangolff, Cath. Barbara; America, 1749 2856.30 p129
Gangolff, Cath. Barbara; Port uncertain, 1748 2856.30 p129
Gangolff, Cath. Barbara; Port uncertain, 1749 2856.30 p129
Gangrich, Jakobea; Port uncertain, 1773 2856.30 p154
Ganly, William; New York, 1838 8197.10 p114
Gannet, Charles 45; Ontario, 1871 1823.15 p88
Gannock, Wm; Virginia, 1664 6212.30 p11
Gannon, Cornelius 94; Ontario, 1871 1823.22 p58
Gannon, Edward 40; Ontario, 1871 1823.28 p32
Gannon, John; New York, 1840 8197.10 p236
Gannon, John F.; New York, 1823 8197.10 p233
Gannon, Margaret 62; Vermont, 1875 5900.10 p330
Gannon, Margaret 76; Vermont, 1916 5900.10 p330
Gannon, Mary 56; Vermont, 1895 5900.10 p331
Gannon, Mary 58; Vermont, 1883 5900.10 p546
Gannon, Michael; New York, 1838 8197.10 p377
Gannon, Michael 52; Ontario, 1871 1823.28 p32
Gannon, Michael 80; Ontario, 1871 1823.28 p32
Gannon, Patrick 46; Ontario, 1871 1823.28 p32
Gannon, Thomas; New York, 1840 8197.10 p168
Gannon, Thomas; New York, 1840 8197.10 p170
Gannon, Thomas 87; Vermont, 1879 5900.10 p330
Ganns, Benedikt; Port uncertain, 1763 2856.30 p129
Ganns, Gabriel; Port uncertain, 1784 2856.30 p129
Ganns, Jacob; Port uncertain, 1791 2856.30 p129
Gannsin, Maria Elisabeth; Port uncertain, 1762 2856.30 p154
Gannt, Robert; Savannah, Georgia, 1821 1640.10 p62
Gannt, Thomas; Maryland, 1654 2524.55 p86
Gans, Anna Elisabeth; Port uncertain, 1747 2856.30 p129
Gans, Franz; Port uncertain, 1747 2856.30 p129
Gans, Franz Henrich; America, 1747 2856.30 p129
Gans, Franz Henrich; Port uncertain, 1747 2856.30 p129
Gans, Johann Georg; Port uncertain, 1754 2856.30 p129
Gans, Meyer; New York, 1839 8197.10 p320
Gansert, Cornelia; Port uncertain, 1750 2856.30 p129
Gansert, Matthes; Port uncertain, 1750 2856.30 p129
Ganshorn, Johann Georg; Port uncertain, 1812 2856.30 p129
Ganshorn, Johann Georg; Port uncertain, 1813 2856.30 p129
Gansin, Anna Catharina; Port uncertain, 1756 2856.30 p129
Gansin, Anna Margarete; Port uncertain, 1769 2856.30 p129
Ganson, James; Virginia, 1672 6212.30 p50
Ganson, John 54; Vermont, 1838 5900.10 p454
Ganson, Mary 74; Vermont, 1860 5900.10 p454
Ganss, Otto; Port uncertain, 1785 2856.30 p129
Ganssel, Jakob; America, 1748 2856.30 p154
Gansshorn, Johann Georg; America, 1750 2856.30 p129
Gansshorn, Johann Georg; Port uncertain, 1750 2856.30 p129
Gant, Harmen 30; Ontario, 1871 1823.28 p32
Ganter, Johann; Port uncertain, 1763 2856.30 p129
Ganter, John, Jr.; New York, 1838 8197.10 p114
Ganter, Peter; New York, 1837 8197.10 p88
Ganther, Anna Maria; Port uncertain, 1765 2856.30 p130
Ganther, Jacob; America, 1754 2856.30 p130
With wife
Ganther, Jacob; Port uncertain, 1747 2856.30 p130
Gantzmann, Friedrich; Port uncertain, 1769 2856.30 p130
Gantzmann, Jacob; Port uncertain, 1769 2856.30 p130
Ganz, Peter; Port uncertain, 1751 2856.30 p130
With wife & children
Ganzmann, Elisabeth; Port uncertain, 1764 2856.30 p130
Gaphney, Francis 20; Ontario, 1861 2896.27 p12
Gaphney, Mary McLaughlin 48; Vermont, 1863 5900.10 p572
Gapper, Susan Maria; Philadelphia, 1838 1224.3 p29
Garapee, John; New York, 1839 8197.10 p131
Garason, Charles 9; Ontario, 1861 2896.26 p38
Garason, David 11; Ontario, 1861 2896.26 p38
Garason, Lyda 46; Ontario, 1861 2896.26 p38
Garason, Matilda 24; Ontario, 1861 2896.26 p38
Garason, Rheuben 18; Ontario, 1861 2896.26 p38
Garason, Samual 15; Ontario, 1861 2896.26 p38
Garason, William 20; Ontario, 1861 2896.26 p38
Garbal, Conrad; Pennsylvania, 1838 6058.10 p15
Garbet, George 40; Ontario, 1871 1823.15 p88
Garbet, Henry 47; Ontario, 1871 1823.22 p58
Garbet, John 46; Ontario, 1871 1823.28 p32
Garbet, Sarah 78; Ontario, 1871 1823.15 p88
Garbi, John 73; Ontario, 1871 1823.15 p88
Garbit, Robert 44; Ontario, 1871 1823.15 p88
Garbutt, John 31; Ontario, 1871 1823.15 p88
Garbutt, Richard 34; Nova Scotia, 1774 1220.25 p135
With wife & 6 children
Garbutt, Thomas 48; Ontario, 1871 1823.22 p58
Garceau, Celina; Vermont, 1850-1911 5900.10 p336
Gard, Eliz; Virginia, 1672 6212.30 p50
Garden, Anthony A.; New York, 1826 8197.10 p233
Garden, John; Philadelphia, 1801 1224.3 p29
Garden, Robert; New York, 1840 8197.10 p170
Gardenance, James; Maryland, 1672 2524.55 p86
Gardener, Miss; Quebec, 1857 9196.15 p23
Gardener, Edward 18; Maryland, 1775 1220.25 p120
Gardener, James; Augusta, Georgia, 1811 1640.10 p62
Gardener, John M.; New York, 1840 8197.10 p169
Gardener, Peter; Pennsylvania, 1777 4629.10 p10
Gardener, Peter 68; Ontario, 1871 1823.22 p58
Gardiner, Aleander 26; Ontario, 1871 1823.15 p88
Gardiner, Benjamin 12; Ontario, 1861 2896.28 p24
Gardiner, Charles 39; Ontario, 1871 1823.28 p32
Gardiner, Elizabeth *SEE* Gardiner, Luke
Gardiner, Hugh 36; Ontario, 1871 1823.15 p88
Gardiner, John *SEE* Gardiner, Luke
Gardiner, John; Maryland, 1681 2524.55 p86
Gardiner, John; Virginia, 1816 1224.3 p29
Gardiner, Julian *SEE* Gardiner, Luke
Gardiner, Julian; Maryland, 1637 2524.55 p86
Gardiner, Luke; Maryland, 1637 2524.55 p86
Father: Richard
With mother
Son: John
Daughter: Elizabeth
Daughter: Julian
Son: Richard
Gardiner, Mary Ann 60; Ontario, 1871 1823.15 p88
Gardiner, P. 11; Ontario, 1861 2896.28 p3
Gardiner, Richard *SEE* Gardiner, Luke
Gardiner, Richard; Maryland, 1637 2524.55 p86
Gardiner, Silvester; Boston, n.d. 1224.2 p44
Gardiner, Thomas; Boston, 1776 1224.2 p44
Gardiner, Thomas; Maryland, 1680 2524.55 p86
Gardiner, Thomas 16; Ontario, 1861 2896.28 p3
Gardiner, William 16; Ontario, 1861 2896.28 p18
Gardiner, William 27; Ontario, 1871 1823.15 p88
Gardiner, William 60; Ontario, 1871 1823.15 p88
Gardnaw, James 49; Ontario, 1871 1823.15 p88
Gardner, Alexander; Pennsylvania, 1777 4629.10 p8
Gardner, Alexander 74; Ontario, 1871 1823.15 p88
Gardner, Allen 6; Ontario, 1861 2896.25 p31
Gardner, Anna; Augusta, Georgia, 1813 1640.10 p62
Gardner, Anna; Port uncertain, 1739 2856.30 p130
Gardner, Archibald; Pennsylvania, 1777 4629.10 p30
Gardner, Cannif 10; Ontario, 1861 2896.25 p31
Gardner, Caroline 41; Ontario, 1871 1823.28 p32
Gardner, Edward 18; Maryland, 1774 1220.25 p60
Gardner, Emma C.; Vermont, 1855-1923 5900.10 p189
Gardner, George 19; Maryland, 1774 1220.25 p72
Gardner, Henry 21; Maryland, 1775 1220.25 p104
Gardner, Isaac; Pennsylvania, 1777 4629.10 p11
Gardner, Issabella 78; Ontario, 1861 2896.25 p19
Gardner, James; Jamaica, 1802 1640.13 p44
Gardner, James Corbet; Mobile, Alabama, 1844 1640.10 p62
Gardner, James Ogilvie; Nashville, Tennessee, 1847 1640.10 p62
Gardner, John; Maryland, 1664 2524.55 p86
Gardner, John; New York, 1839 8197.10 p130
Gardner, John; Vermont, n.d. 5900.10 p91
Gardner, John 18; Ontario, 1861 2896.27 p66
Gardner, John 30; Virginia, 1774 1220.25 p54
Gardner, John 35; Ontario, 1871 1823.15 p89
Gardner, John J. 31; Ontario, 1871 1823.15 p89
Gardner, Joseph; Maryland, 1667 2524.55 p86
Gardner, Lewis 11; Ontario, 1861 2896.25 p43
Gardner, Margaret 43 *SEE* Gardner, Thomas
Gardner, Mary 66; Ontario, 1871 1823.15 p89
Gardner, Mary 87; Vermont, 1928 5900.10 p298
Gardner, Peter 52; Ontario, 1871 1823.15 p89
Gardner, Peter M. 66; Vermont, 1899 5900.10 p298
Gardner, Rebecca 7 *SEE* Gardner, Thomas
Gardner, Richard; Boston, 1820 1224.3 p29
Gardner, Richard; Maryland, 1660 2524.55 p86
Gardner, Richard; Maryland, 1665 2524.55 p86
Gardner, Richard 21; Maryland, 1774 1220.25 p73
Gardner, Robert; Augusta, Georgia, 1791 1640.10 p62
Gardner, Robert; Virginia, 1710 1224.2 p44
Gardner, Sandford 14; Ontario, 1861 2896.25 p19
Gardner, Sarah 22; Ontario, 1861 2896.25 p31
Gardner, Simon 16 *SEE* Gardner, Thomas
Gardner, Theophilus; Pennsylvania, 1777 4629.10 p28
Gardner, Thomas; Augusta, Georgia, 1822 1640.10 p62
Gardner, Thomas; New York, 1838 8197.10 p115
Gardner, Thomas 20 *SEE* Gardner, Thomas
Gardner, Thomas 38; Ontario, 1871 1823.15 p89
Gardner, Thomas 44; Boston, 1774 1220.25 p58
Wife: Margaret 43
Child: Rebecca 7
Child: Thomas 20
Child: Simon 16
Gardner, William; New York, 1807 8197.10 p39
Gardner, William; Pennsylvania, 1777 4629.10 p18
Gardner, William 76; Ontario, 1861 2896.25 p19
Gardner, William II. 24; Ontario, 1861 2896.25 p12
Gardner, Wm; Virginia, 1668-1669 6212.30 p40
Gardner, Wm; Virginia, 1672 6212.30 p49
Gardner, X. P.; Virginia, 1664 6212.30 p9
Gardwell, Isabella; Maryland, 1670 2524.55 p86
Gardyne, Mr.; Quebec, 1858 9196.15 p34
Gardyne, Mr.; Quebec, 1858 9196.15 p45
Gardyne, Mr., Jr.; Quebec, 1858 9196.15 p34
Gardyne, Mrs.; Quebec, 1858 9196.15 p34
Garee, Richard; Maryland, 1665 2524.55 p86
Garesche, Alphonse P.; New York, 1828-1834 8197.10 p306
Garesche, Paul; New York, 1834 8197.10 p304
Garety, Thomas; New York, 1839 8197.10 p131
Garey, Joanna H.; Vermont, 1857-1951 5900.10 p48
Garey, Miama 50; Vermont, 1867 5900.10 p302
Garford, Richard; Maryland, 1651 2524.55 p86
Gargill, Anne; Maryland, 1670 2524.55 p86
Gargill, Benjamin; Maryland, 1667 2524.55 p86
Gargill, Nicholas; Maryland, 1681 2524.55 p86
Gariahan, Peter; New York, 1827 8197.10 p233
Garigan, Philip; New York, 1834 8197.10 p316
Garilski, John; Maryland, 1910 3259.35 p15
Garin, Rev.; Quebec, 1858 9196.15 p32
Garioch, Alexander; San Francisco, 1889 1640.13 p44
Garity, Patrick 36; Ontario, 1871 1823.22 p58
Garjsick, Donald 25; Ontario, 1871 1823.15 p89
Garjsick, Helen 22; Ontario, 1871 1823.15 p89
Garjsick, John 20; Ontario, 1871 1823.15 p89

Garland, Alfred; Vermont, n.d. ***5900.10*** *p280*
Garland, Ann 68; Vermont, 1901 ***5900.10*** *p404*
Garland, Bernard 67; Vermont, 1906 ***5900.10*** *p404*
Garland, Bridget Burns 41; Vermont, 1881 ***5900.10*** *p534*
Garland, George; Pennsylvania, 1777 ***4629.10*** *p8*
Garland, George; Pennsylvania, 1779 ***4629.10*** *p36*
Garland, George 54; Ontario, 1871 ***1823.22*** *p58*
Garland, Humphry; Virginia, 1664-1665 ***6212.30*** *p16*
Garland, Isabell 78; Vermont, 1890 ***5900.10*** *p377*
Garland, James; Pennsylvania, 1867 ***6058.10*** *p59*
Garland, James; Virginia, 1666 ***6212.30*** *p25*
Garland, James 40; Ontario, 1871 ***1823.15*** *p89*
Garland, John 55; Ontario, 1871 ***1823.15*** *p89*
Garland, John 73; Vermont, 1820 ***5900.10*** *p124*
Garland, Margaret 87; Vermont, 1822 ***5900.10*** *p124*
Garland, Mary 44; Ontario, 1871 ***1823.28*** *p32*
Garland, Richard 33; Ontario, 1871 ***1823.22*** *p58*
Garland, Richard 45; Ontario, 1871 ***1823.22*** *p58*
Garland, William; Maryland, 1679 ***2524.55*** *p86*
Garland, William 26; Ontario, 1871 ***1823.22*** *p58*
Garland, William 85; Vermont, 1886 ***5900.10*** *p280*
Garlick, J. W. 40; Vermont, 1881 ***5900.10*** *p616*
Garman, Daniel 35; Ontario, 1871 ***1823.28*** *p32*
Garn, Magdalena; America, 1756 ***2856.30*** *p272*
Garn, Magdalena; Port uncertain, 1751 ***2856.30*** *p272*
Garn, Magdalena; Port uncertain, 1752 ***2856.30*** *p272*
Garn, Magdalena; Port uncertain, 1754 ***2856.30*** *p272*
Garneau, Mr.; Quebec, 1856 ***9196.15*** *p6*
Garneau, Mr.; Quebec, 1857 ***9196.15*** *p20*
Garneau, Mr.; Quebec, 1858 ***9196.15*** *p31*
Garneau, Mrs.; Quebec, 1858 ***9196.15*** *p31*
Garnel, Michael; New York, 1838 ***8197.10*** *p235*
Garnep, Francis 44; Ontario, 1871 ***1823.15*** *p89*
Garnep, Robert 30; Ontario, 1871 ***1823.15*** *p89*
Garnep, William 27; Ontario, 1871 ***1823.15*** *p89*
Garner, Andrew 54; Ontario, 1871 ***1823.15*** *p89*
Garner, C. 40; Ontario, 1861 ***2896.25*** *p46*
Garner, Henry; New York, 1830 ***8197.10*** *p362*
Garner, J. 45; Ontario, 1861 ***2896.25*** *p46*
Garner, J. G. T.; Quebec, 1856 ***9196.15*** *p8*
Garner, James; New York, 1840 ***8197.10*** *p171*
Garner, John; New York, 1826 ***8197.10*** *p333*
Garner, John 26; Ontario, 1871 ***1823.15*** *p89*
Garner, Margarete; Port uncertain, 1752 ***2856.30*** *p196*
Garner, Thomas; New York, 1830 ***8197.10*** *p353*
Garner, Thomas, Jr.; New York, 1830 ***8197.10*** *p362*
Garner, William 26; Ontario, 1871 ***1823.15*** *p89*
Garness, Henry 46; Ontario, 1871 ***1823.15*** *p89*
Garness, John 30; Ontario, 1871 ***1823.15*** *p89*
Garness, Thomas 70; Ontario, 1871 ***1823.15*** *p89*
Garnett, Elizabeth *SEE* Garnett, Richard
Garnett, Elizabeth 19 *SEE* Garnett, Richard
Garnett, Henry; New Jersey, 1835 ***1224.3*** *p29*
Garnett, John; New Jersey, 1822 ***1224.3*** *p29*
Garnett, John 4 *SEE* Garnett, Richard
Garnett, Julian 6 *SEE* Garnett, Richard
Garnett, Richard; Maryland, 1637 ***2524.55*** *p86*
  Wife: Elizabeth
  Daughter: Julian 6
  Son: Richard 21
  Son: John 4
  Daughter: Elizabeth 19
Garnett, Richard 21 *SEE* Garnett, Richard
Garnham, Mr.; Quebec, 1858 ***9196.15*** *p42*
Garnier, Lieut.; Quebec, 1856 ***9196.15*** *p7*
Garnier, Charles; New York, 1817 ***8197.10*** *p60*
Garnier, Xaver; Port uncertain, 1730 ***2856.30*** *p130*
Garnier, Xaver; Port uncertain, 1757 ***2856.30*** *p130*
Garnin, John; New York, 1840 ***8197.10*** *p383*
Garniss, Philip; New York, 1807 ***8197.10*** *p39*
Garniss, Thomas; New York, 1792 ***8197.10*** *p1*
Garniss, Thomas 39; Ontario, 1871 ***1823.15*** *p89*
Garnner, Ellen 86; Vermont, 1915 ***5900.10*** *p125*
Garnoch, Archibd 50; Ontario, 1871 ***1823.28*** *p32*
Garnsney, Edward; Maryland, 1658 ***2524.55*** *p86*
Garon, John 60; Ontario, 1871 ***1823.22*** *p58*
Garr, Andrew S.; New York, 1806 ***8197.10*** *p31*
Garraghty, John; New York, 1840 ***8197.10*** *p170*
Garrard, William H.; New York, 1839 ***8197.10*** *p235*
Garratsee, Sarah P. 19; Ontario, 1861 ***2896.27*** *p37*
Garratt, Anna 40; Ontario, 1861 ***2896.28*** *p19*
Garratt, Ashley 1; Ontario, 1861 ***2896.28*** *p22*
Garratt, Beatrice 3; Ontario, 1861 ***2896.28*** *p19*
Garratt, Caleb 75; Ontario, 1861 ***2896.28*** *p19*
Garratt, Catharine 18; Ontario, 1861 ***2896.28*** *p22*
Garratt, Dorcas; Ontario, 1861 ***2896.27*** *p66*
Garratt, Dorcas 71; Ontario, 1861 ***2896.28*** *p19*
Garratt, E. 37; Ontario, 1861 ***2896.28*** *p10*
Garratt, E. L. 11; Ontario, 1861 ***2896.28*** *p10*
Garratt, Eleanor 25; Ontario, 1861 ***2896.28*** *p22*
Garratt, Eliza 25; Ontario, 1861 ***2896.28*** *p22*
Garratt, Eliza A. 38; Ontario, 1861 ***2896.28*** *p22*
Garratt, Elizabeth 1; Ontario, 1861 ***2896.28*** *p24*
Garratt, Elwood 2; Ontario, 1861 ***2896.28*** *p19*
Garratt, Estella 5; Ontario, 1861 ***2896.28*** *p22*
Garratt, Finley 8; Ontario, 1861 ***2896.28*** *p22*
Garratt, H. S. 13; Ontario, 1861 ***2896.28*** *p10*
Garratt, Isaac B. 62; Ontario, 1861 ***2896.28*** *p22*
Garratt, J. B. 25; Ontario, 1861 ***2896.25*** *p42*
Garratt, John; Ontario, 1861 ***2896.27*** *p66*
Garratt, Joseph 68; Ontario, 1861 ***2896.28*** *p22*
Garratt, Lydia 10; Ontario, 1861 ***2896.28*** *p22*
Garratt, Lydia 17; Ontario, 1861 ***2896.28*** *p22*
Garratt, Manerva; Ontario, 1861 ***2896.27*** *p66*
Garratt, Mary 63; Ontario, 1861 ***2896.28*** *p22*
Garratt, Mary Jane 26; Ontario, 1861 ***2896.28*** *p19*
Garratt, Mary L. 11; Ontario, 1861 ***2896.28*** *p22*
Garratt, P. E. 14; Ontario, 1861 ***2896.28*** *p10*
Garratt, Phebe J. 19; Ontario, 1861 ***2896.28*** *p22*
Garratt, Philo; Ontario, 1861 ***2896.27*** *p66*
Garratt, Ralph 5; Ontario, 1861 ***2896.28*** *p10*
Garratt, Robert; New York, 1832 ***1224.3*** *p29*
Garratt, Robert A. 6; Ontario, 1861 ***2896.28*** *p19*
Garratt, Roda R. 39; Ontario, 1861 ***2896.27*** *p66*
Garratt, Rufus 3; Ontario, 1861 ***2896.28*** *p10*
Garratt, Ruth A. 12; Ontario, 1861 ***2896.28*** *p24*
Garratt, S. 28; Ontario, 1861 ***2896.28*** *p10*
Garratt, S. E. 16; Ontario, 1861 ***2896.28*** *p10*
Garratt, Sarah 66; Ontario, 1861 ***2896.28*** *p24*
Garratt, Sarah M. 31; Ontario, 1861 ***2896.28*** *p24*
Garratt, Susan C. 4; Ontario, 1861 ***2896.28*** *p24*
Garratt, Thomas 69; Ontario, 1861 ***2896.25*** *p42*
Garratt, Townsend 19; Ontario, 1861 ***2896.28*** *p22*
Garratt, Wallace E. 8; Ontario, 1861 ***2896.28*** *p19*
Garrattsee, T. H. 15; Ontario, 1861 ***2896.25*** *p42*
Garraty, James; New York, 1840 ***8197.10*** *p302*
Garraway, Richard; New England, 1668 ***1224.1*** *p23*
Garrawich, John; Maryland, 1660 ***2524.55*** *p86*
Garret, Elizabeth; Virginia, 1681-1682 ***6212.30*** *p56*
Garret, George; Maryland, 1676 ***2524.55*** *p86*
Garret, Harriet 28; Ontario, 1861 ***2896.25*** *p16*
Garret, Ida Augusta 5; Ontario, 1861 ***2896.25*** *p16*
Garret, Jane 26; Ontario, 1861 ***2896.25*** *p16*
Garret, Jessie 1; Ontario, 1861 ***2896.25*** *p16*
Garret, Katherine; Maryland, 1676 ***2524.55*** *p86*
Garret, Leroy 3; Ontario, 1861 ***2896.25*** *p16*
Garret, Philip; Maryland, 1668 ***2524.55*** *p86*
Garret, Wallace 3; Ontario, 1861 ***2896.25*** *p16*
Garretsey, Mary 24; Ontario, 1861 ***2896.28*** *p44*
Garretsie, Anna 20; Ontario, 1861 ***2896.28*** *p49*
Garrett, Adam 22; Maryland, 1775 ***1220.25*** *p98*
Garrett, Amos; Maryland, 1728 ***1224.2*** *p44*
Garrett, Charles 27; Ontario, 1861 ***2896.27*** *p73*
Garrett, George; Charles Town, South Carolina, 1769 ***1224.2*** *p44*
Garrett, John 15; Philadelphia, 1774 ***1220.25*** *p34*
Garrett, John 33; Ontario, 1861 ***2896.27*** *p73*
Garrett, John Philip 26; Ontario, 1871 ***1823.22*** *p58*
Garrett, Patience 62; Ontario, 1861 ***2896.27*** *p73*
Garrett, Rachaiell; Maryland, 1666 ***2524.55*** *p87*
Garrett, Samuel; Pennsylvania, 1777 ***4629.10*** *p27*
Garrett, Sarah 35; Ontario, 1861 ***2896.27*** *p73*
Garrett, William 50; Ontario, 1871 ***1823.15*** *p89*
Garrick, John 69; Ontario, 1871 ***1823.15*** *p89*
Garrick, Saturnin Bernard; Philadelphia, 1792 ***4629.10*** *p69*
Garrick, William; Pennsylvania, 1787 ***4629.10*** *p56*
Garrigan, Patrick; New York, 1840 ***8197.10*** *p235*
Garrigues, Samuel; Pennsylvania, 1777 ***4629.10*** *p20*
Garrington, Mr.; Portland, Maine, 1858 ***9196.15*** *p47*
Garriott, James 24; Maryland, 1774 ***1220.25*** *p65*
Garrison, H. A. 6; Ontario, 1861 ***2896.28*** *p4*
Garrison, J. H. 15; Ontario, 1861 ***2896.28*** *p4*
Garrison, R. E. 17; Ontario, 1861 ***2896.28*** *p4*
Garrison, S. L. 12; Ontario, 1861 ***2896.28*** *p4*
Garriss, Amos; Virginia, 1675 ***6212.30*** *p53*
Garritt, Abraham; Maryland, 1680 ***2524.55*** *p87*
Garritt, Richard, Sr.; Maryland, 1680 ***2524.55*** *p87*
Garritt, Richd., Jr.; Maryland, 1680 ***2524.55*** *p87*
Garrity, Lydia Ann Spry; Vermont, 1855-1921 ***5900.10*** *p591*
Garrity, William; Vermont, 1857-1932 ***5900.10*** *p591*
Garrott, Phillip; Maryland, 1660 ***2524.55*** *p87*
Garrow, Edward 65; Ontario, 1871 ***1823.15*** *p89*
Garrow, Elizabeth; Vermont, 1842-1917 ***5900.10*** *p203*
Garry, Ann 65; Ontario, 1871 ***1823.22*** *p58*
Garry, Benjamian 36; Ontario, 1871 ***1823.15*** *p89*
Garry, Ellen J.; Vermont, 1881 ***5900.10*** *p603*
Garry, John 40; Ontario, 1871 ***1823.15*** *p89*
Garry, John L. 59; Vermont, 1902 ***5900.10*** *p84*
Garry, Patrick; Vermont, 1849-1902 ***5900.10*** *p459*
Garry, Phelemy; Maryland, 1681 ***2524.55*** *p87*
Garry, Thomas 79; Ontario, 1871 ***1823.15*** *p89*
Garsed, Edward; New York, 1822 ***8197.10*** *p232*
Garsed, Joshua; New York, 1822 ***8197.10*** *p232*
Garsford, John 22; Maryland, 1774 ***1220.25*** *p3*
Garside, Joseph; New York, 1888 ***1640.13*** *p44*
Garsinski, Henry; Maryland, 1910 ***3259.35*** *p15*
Garson, John 39; Ontario, 1871 ***1823.28*** *p32*
Garson, Mary 16; Ontario, 1871 ***1823.15*** *p89*
Garson, Robert; Savannah, Georgia, 1775 ***1640.10*** *p62*
Garszynsky, Pawel; Maryland, 1910 ***3259.35*** *p15*
Garth, George; Virginia, 1664 ***6212.30*** *p8*
Garth, George 24; Philadelphia, 1774 ***1220.25*** *p66*
Garth, John 39; Virginia, 1773 ***1220.25*** *p29*
Garthan, Thomas 19; Maryland, 1774 ***1220.25*** *p52*
Garthner, Johann Nickel; Port uncertain, 1745 ***2856.30*** *p154*
Garthwaitt, Jane 22; Georgia, 1775 ***1220.25*** *p126*
Gartlan, Thomas; New York, 1821 ***8197.10*** *p232*
Gartland, Hanora 63; Vermont, 1869 ***5900.10*** *p75*
Gartland, Margaret; Vermont, 1833-1895 ***5900.10*** *p311*
Gartland, Mary; Vermont, 1847-1912 ***5900.10*** *p231*
Gartland, Mary 83; Vermont, 1889 ***5900.10*** *p75*
Gartland, Mary Brennan; Vermont, 1831-1912 ***5900.10*** *p489*
Gartland, Mary Ward 25; Vermont, 1852 ***5900.10*** *p239*
Gartland, Nicholas 50; Vermont, 1856 ***5900.10*** *p75*
Gartland, Patrick; Vermont, 1823-1900 ***5900.10*** *p489*
Gartlin, Hugh 22; Vermont, 1869 ***5900.10*** *p242*
Gartlin, Mary Kerley 61; Vermont, 1876 ***5900.10*** *p242*
Gartmann, Josef; Port uncertain, 1741 ***2856.30*** *p130*
Gartner, Johann; Port uncertain, 1782 ***2856.30*** *p154*
Gartner, Johann Georg; America, 1737 ***2856.30*** *p154*
Garton, James 16; Maryland, 1774 ***1220.25*** *p53*
Garton, Samuel 28; Ontario, 1871 ***1823.15*** *p89*
Gartshore, John S. 54; Ontario, 1871 ***1823.22*** *p58*
Garttach, Johann Adam; Port uncertain, 1746 ***2856.30*** *p130*
Garvan, John 62; Ontario, 1871 ***1823.28*** *p32*
Garvay, Mary E.; Vermont, 1896 ***5900.10*** *p393*
Garven, Miss; Portland, Maine, 1858 ***9196.15*** *p27*
Garvey, Ann 37; Vermont, 1867 ***5900.10*** *p217*
Garvey, Annie; Vermont, 1850-1931 ***5900.10*** *p47*
Garvey, Barney; Vermont, 1824-1889 ***5900.10*** *p217*
Garvey, E. 27; Ontario, 1861 ***2896.27*** *p9*
Garvey, George 30; Ontario, 1871 ***1823.28*** *p32*
Garvey, Henry 27; Ontario, 1871 ***1823.15*** *p89*
Garvey, Hugh; Vermont, 1844-1904 ***5900.10*** *p47*
Garvey, John; New York, 1840 ***8197.10*** *p170*
Garvey, John 32; Ontario, 1871 ***1823.28*** *p32*
Garvey, Julia Ann 46; Ontario, 1871 ***1823.15*** *p89*
Garvey, Margaret; Vermont, 1828-1895 ***5900.10*** *p176*
Garvey, Margaret 64; Vermont, 1877 ***5900.10*** *p378*
Garvey, Mary; Vermont, 1847-1919 ***5900.10*** *p46*
Garvey, Mary; Vermont, 1859-1928 ***5900.10*** *p159*
Garvey, Mary McGinn 54; Vermont, 1890 ***5900.10*** *p233*
Garvey, Michael; Vermont, 1828-1872 ***5900.10*** *p141*
Garvey, Michael; Vermont, 1847-1906 ***5900.10*** *p46*
Garvey, Michael 65; Vermont, 1884 ***5900.10*** *p233*
Garvey, Michael 66; Vermont, 1877 ***5900.10*** *p378*
Garvey, Patrick; New York, 1839 ***8197.10*** *p131*
Garvey, Rose; Vermont, 1856-1899 ***5900.10*** *p472*
Garvey, Roseanna; Vermont, 1840-1920 ***5900.10*** *p379*
Garvey, Sarah; Vermont, 1854-1930 ***5900.10*** *p218*
Garvey, William 35; Ontario, 1871 ***1823.28*** *p32*
Garvie, David 45; Ontario, 1871 ***1823.15*** *p89*
Garvie, Hugh 35; Ontario, 1871 ***1823.28*** *p32*
Garvie, John; Mississippi, 1870 ***1640.13*** *p44*
Garvill, James 35; Vermont, 1885 ***5900.10*** *p525*
Garvill, Mary Duffey; Vermont, 1800-1918 ***5900.10*** *p525*
Garvin, Patrick; New York, 1838 ***8197.10*** *p115*
Garvin, Patrick 32; Ontario, 1871 ***1823.28*** *p32*
Garvin, Patrick 38; Vermont, 1872 ***5900.10*** *p260*
Garvin, Thomas; New York, 1838 ***8197.10*** *p114*
Garvis, Thomas; Maryland, 1659 ***2524.55*** *p121*
Garvy, James 62; Ontario, 1871 ***1823.22*** *p58*
Garvy, John 70; Ontario, 1871 ***1823.22*** *p58*
Garvy, Mary 50; Ontario, 1871 ***1823.15*** *p89*
Garvy, Owen; Maryland, 1682 ***2524.55*** *p87*
Gary, Elizabeth *SEE* Gary, John
Gary, Elizabeth *SEE* Gary, John, Sr.
Gary, Elizabeth; Vermont, 1804-1875 ***5900.10*** *p156*
Gary, Jane *SEE* Gary, John, Sr.
Gary, Jean *SEE* Gary, John
Gary, John; Maryland, 1651 ***2524.55*** *p87*
  Relative: Judith, Jr.
  Relative: Judith, Sr.
  Relative: John, Jr.
  Relative: Jean
  Relative: Elizabeth
Gary, John, Sr.; Maryland, 1651 ***2524.55*** *p87*
  Relative: Judith, Jr.
  Relative: Judith, Sr.
  Relative: John, Jr.
  Relative: Jane
  Relative: Elizabeth
Gary, John, Jr. *SEE* Gary, John

Gary, John, Jr. *SEE* Gary, John, Sr.
Gary, Judith, Sr. *SEE* Gary, John
Gary, Judith, Sr. *SEE* Gary, John, Sr.
Gary, Judith, Jr. *SEE* Gary, John
Gary, Judith, Jr. *SEE* Gary, John, Sr.
Gary, Michael 60; Ontario, 1871 ***1823.22*** *p58*
Gary, Richard; Maryland, 1663 ***2524.55*** *p87*
Gary, Sarah; Maryland, 1656 ***2524.55*** *p87*
Gary, Sarah; Maryland, 1672 ***2524.55*** *p87*
Gary, Stephen; Maryland, 1650 ***2524.55*** *p87*
Gascho, Georg; Port uncertain, 1760 ***2856.30*** *p130*
Gascho, John 32; Ontario, 1871 ***1823.15*** *p89*
Gascho, Joseph 77; Ontario, 1871 ***1823.15*** *p89*
Gascoign, Francis; Georgia, 1698 ***1640.13*** *p44*
Gascoyne, Thomas 22; Maryland, 1774 ***1220.25*** *p58*
Gash, Mathew 21; New York, 1774 ***1220.25*** *p141*
Gasho, Andreas 29; Ontario, 1871 ***1823.15*** *p89*
Gasionawski, William; Maryland, 1910 ***3259.35*** *p15*
Gaskell, James 32; Ontario, 1871 ***1823.28*** *p32*
Gaskell, Lawrence 24; Maryland, 1774 ***1220.25*** *p40*
Gaskill, Ellis; Maryland, 1682 ***2524.55*** *p87*
Gaskin, Margarett *SEE* Gaskin, William, Sr.
Gaskin, William, Sr.; Maryland, 1666 ***2524.55*** *p87*
Wife: Margarett
Gaskins, William; Maryland, 1666 ***2524.55*** *p87*
Gaskolski, Mary; Maryland, 1910 ***3259.35*** *p15*
Gasmann, Johann Adam; Port uncertain, 1780 ***2856.30*** *p130*
Gasoloff, A. 34; Alaska, 1916 ***9196.1*** *p42*
Gasoloff, A. 34; Whitehorse, Yukon, 1916 ***9196.1*** *p42*
Gaspart, Jean; New York, 1836 ***8197.10*** *p319*
Gasper, Mathew 46; Alaska, 1912 ***9196.1*** *p13*
Gasper, Mathew 46; British Columbia, 1912 ***9196.1*** *p13*
Gasquet, Joseph; New York, 1827 ***8197.10*** *p308*
Gass, Catharina; Port uncertain, 1765 ***2856.30*** *p130*
Gass, Franz; Port uncertain, 1776 ***2856.30*** *p130*
Gass, Johann Georg; America, 1751 ***2856.30*** *p130*
Gass, John; Pennsylvania, 1785 ***4629.10*** *p48*
Gass, Susanna; Port uncertain, 1778 ***2856.30*** *p130*
Gassaway, Nicholas; Maryland, 1650 ***2524.55*** *p87*
Gassel, Michael; America, 1736 ***2856.30*** *p130*
With wife & 5 children
Gasser, Maria Barbara; Port uncertain, 1795 ***2856.30*** *p130*
Gassert, Apollonia; Port uncertain, 1787 ***2856.30*** *p130*
Gassett, Hannah McNeill; Vermont, 1796-1887 ***5900.10*** *p401*
Gassett, Levi; Vermont, 1797-1869 ***5900.10*** *p401*
Gassler, Jakob; Port uncertain, 1761 ***2856.30*** *p130*
Gassler, Jakob; Port uncertain, 1762 ***2856.30*** *p130*
Gassler, Martin; Port uncertain, 1758 ***2856.30*** *p130*
Gassler, Martin; Port uncertain, 1759 ***2856.30*** *p130*
Gassmann, . . .; Port uncertain, 1783 ***2856.30*** *p130*
Gassmann, Friedrich; Port uncertain, 1780 ***2856.30*** *p130*
Gassmann, Johann; Port uncertain, 1735 ***2856.30*** *p130*
Gassmann, Johann; Port uncertain, 1746 ***2856.30*** *p130*
Gassmann, Johann; Port uncertain, 1747 ***2856.30*** *p130*
Gassmann, Johann; Port uncertain, 1777 ***2856.30*** *p130*
Gassmann, Phil. Reinhard; America, 1750 ***2856.30*** *p131*
With wife & 3 children
Gassmann, Phil. Reinhard; America, 1750 ***2856.30*** *p131*
Gassner, Martin; America, 1731 ***2856.30*** *p131*
Gassner, Martin; America, 1732 ***2856.30*** *p131*
Gassoway, Nicholas; Maryland, 1649 ***2524.55*** *p166*
Gastburger, Johann; America, 1736 ***2856.30*** *p131*
With wife
Gastburger, Johann; Port uncertain, 1750 ***2856.30*** *p131*
With wife
Gastellin, John; Virginia, 1671-1672 ***6212.30*** *p45*
Gastinger, Konrad; America, 1769 ***2856.30*** *p131*
With wife & 5 children
Gastle, William 30; Ontario, 1871 ***1823.28*** *p32*
Gastman, Eilt Jansen; New York, 1840 ***8197.10*** *p235*
Gastoyne, John; Maryland, 1665 ***2524.55*** *p87*
Gate, John; Virginia, 1665 ***1224.1*** *p26*
Gate, Robert 52; Ontario, 1871 ***1823.22*** *p58*
Gatehouse, Edward; New York, 1746 ***1224.2*** *p44*
Gatehouse, Richard; New York, 1761 ***1224.2*** *p44*
Gately, Patrick; Pennsylvania, 1846 ***6058.10*** *p22*
Gatenby, Robert 42; Ontario, 1871 ***1823.15*** *p89*
Gatenby, Thomas 46; Ontario, 1871 ***1823.15*** *p89*
Gater, Charles; Maryland, 1659 ***2524.55*** *p87*
Gaterau, Cesar; New York, 1830 ***8197.10*** *p353*
Gates, Conrod 50; Ontario, 1871 ***1823.15*** *p89*
Gates, George; New York, 1807 ***8197.10*** *p39*
Gates, James; Maryland, 1655 ***2524.55*** *p87*
Gates, John 17; Maryland, 1774 ***1220.25*** *p76*
Gates, John W.; Vermont, 1807-1888 ***5900.10*** *p194*
Gates, Matilda; Vermont, 1845-1923 ***5900.10*** *p194*
Gates, Nicholas; New York, New York, 1856 ***3437.14*** *p19*
Gates, Thomas; Charleston, South Carolina, 1853 ***1224.3*** *p29*
Gates, Thomas; Maryland, 1649 ***2524.55*** *p87*
Gatkey, Mathew 48; Ontario, 1871 ***1823.28*** *p32*
Gatley, Thomas 17; Baltimore, 1775 ***1220.25*** *p116*
Gator, Mathew; Maryland, 1661 ***2524.55*** *p87*
Gattens, William 26; Maryland, 1774 ***1220.25*** *p51*
Gattge, Michael; Port uncertain, 1776 ***2856.30*** *p131*
Gattge, Michael; Port uncertain, 1784 ***2856.30*** *p131*
Gattinger, Elisabeth; Port uncertain, 1764 ***2856.30*** *p131*
Gattung, Johann; Port uncertain, 1754 ***2856.30*** *p131*
Gatty, Lieutenant; Quebec, 1858 ***9196.15*** *p41*
Gauch, Josef; Port uncertain, 1739 ***2856.30*** *p131*
Gauch, Maria Barbara; Port uncertain, 1773 ***2856.30*** *p131*
Gauchman, Joseph; Maryland, 1910 ***3259.35*** *p15*
Gauckhler, Franz; Port uncertain, 1754 ***2856.30*** *p131*
Gaudard, John Francis Rodolphus; New York, 1831 ***8197.10*** *p363*
Gaudin, Francis; New York, 1809 ***8197.10*** *p55*
Gaudin, Francois; New York, 1803 ***8197.10*** *p12*
Gaudin, Louis; New York, 1807 ***8197.10*** *p39*
Gaudin, Louis Frederick; New York, 1827 ***8197.10*** *p346*
Gaudy, George; Maryland, 1680 ***2524.55*** *p87*
Gaul, Joanna 82; Vermont, 1922 ***5900.10*** *p541*
Gaul, John Valentine; Pennsylvania, 1777 ***4629.10*** *p29*
Gaul, Mina 43; Ontario, 1871 ***1823.22*** *p58*
Gauld, Caroline; Prince Edward Island, 1892 ***4537.35*** *p39*
Gauley, Thomas; New York, 1840 ***8197.10*** *p170*
Gauling, James; Maryland, 1673 ***2524.55*** *p87*
Gault, Mr.; Portland, Maine, 1858 ***9196.15*** *p29*
Gault, Mr.; Quebec, 1858 ***9196.15*** *p41*
Gault, James; Virginia, 1697 ***1224.1*** *p23*
Gault, Patrick; Nova Scotia, 1745 ***4628.40*** *p44*
Gauly, Abraham 29; Ontario, 1871 ***1823.15*** *p89*
Gauly, Ann 20; Ontario, 1871 ***1823.15*** *p89*
Gauly, Hugh 46; Ontario, 1871 ***1823.15*** *p89*
Gauly, Thomas 26; Ontario, 1871 ***1823.15*** *p89*
Gaum, Johann Bernard; Port uncertain, 1765 ***2856.30*** *p131*
Gaun, Clement; Maryland, 1660 ***2524.55*** *p87*
Gaun, George 33; Ontario, 1871 ***1823.15*** *p89*
Gaunt, Edward 40; Ontario, 1871 ***1823.15*** *p89*
Gaunt, James; New York, 1838 ***8197.10*** *p234*
Gaunt, John 42; Ontario, 1871 ***1823.15*** *p90*
Gaunt, Samuel; New York, 1840 ***8197.10*** *p168*
Gaus, Emma Mary 26; Ontario, 1871 ***1823.15*** *p90*
Gaus, Meyer; New York, 1839 ***8197.10*** *p320*
Gauss, Anton; Port uncertain, 1736 ***2856.30*** *p131*
Gauthier, Lemial; Ontario, 1871 ***1823.28*** *p32*
Gauthier, Margaret McCormick; Vermont, 1849-1920 ***5900.10*** *p601*
Gavagon, Ellen 19; Ontario, 1861 ***2896.25*** *p39*
Gavara, Sina 22; Seattle, 1910 ***9196.1*** *p30*
Gavaran, John; Pennsylvania, 1777 ***4629.10*** *p15*
Gaven, Joseph; Pennsylvania, 1777 ***4629.10*** *p11*
Gavin, Ann 38; Vermont, 1875 ***5900.10*** *p75*
Gavin, Ann A.; Vermont, 1848-1927 ***5900.10*** *p437*
Gavin, Ann Flynn; Vermont, 1836-1928 ***5900.10*** *p563*
Gavin, John; New York, 1891 ***1640.13*** *p44*
Gavin, John; Vermont, 1829-1879 ***5900.10*** *p563*
Gavin, Margaret; Vermont, 1836-1900 ***5900.10*** *p570*
Gavin, Thomas; New York, 1839 ***8197.10*** *p235*
Gavin, Thomas 24; Maryland, 1774 ***1220.25*** *p52*
Gavrish, Annie; Maryland, 1910 ***3259.35*** *p15*
Gaw, Robert 35; Ontario, 1871 ***1823.15*** *p90*
Gawd, Anna; Maryland, 1910 ***3259.35*** *p15*
Gawdey, Alexander 47; Ontario, 1871 ***1823.15*** *p90*
Gawlik, Cazmer; Maryland, 1910 ***3259.35*** *p15*
Gawlik, Michael; Maryland, 1910 ***3259.35*** *p15*
Gawran, Jan; Maryland, 1910 ***3259.35*** *p15*
Gawronski, Leon; New York, 1840 ***8197.10*** *p235*
Gawrys, George; Maryland, 1910 ***3259.35*** *p15*
Gay, Mrs.; Quebec, 1857 ***9196.15*** *p26*
Gay, Elizabeth 30; Ontario, 1871 ***1823.28*** *p32*
Gay, John; Maryland, 1641 ***2524.55*** *p87*
Gay, Michael; Maryland, 1910 ***3259.35*** *p15*
Gay, Michael 65; Ontario, 1871 ***1823.22*** *p58*
Gay, Thomas; New York, 1840 ***8197.10*** *p170*
Gaych, James; Virginia, 1709 ***1224.2*** *p44*
Gaye, Jo.; Maryland, 1681 ***2524.55*** *p87*
Gayer, Casper; Pennsylvania, 1777 ***4629.10*** *p7*
Gayers, Sarah 84; Vermont, 1878 ***5900.10*** *p580*
Gaykowski, Michal; Maryland, 1910 ***3259.35*** *p15*
Gaylard, Robert; Virginia, 1657 ***1224.1*** *p23*
Gayner, Henry; South Carolina, 1733 ***1224.2*** *p44*
Gaynor, Dennis; New York, 1826 ***8197.10*** *p233*
Gaynor, William; New York, 1807 ***8197.10*** *p327*
Gaynox, C.; Quebec, 1858 ***9196.15*** *p44*
Gayny, Anne; Virginia, 1643 ***1224.1*** *p23*
Gayr, Frances; Maryland, 1659 ***2524.55*** *p87*
Gayr, George; Georgia, 1734 ***1640.10*** *p63*
Gayton, Roger 26; Maryland, 1774 ***1220.25*** *p3*
Gaze, John C.; New York, 1839 ***8197.10*** *p235*
Gazell, Michael; America, 1737 ***2856.30*** *p131*
Gazell, Michael; Port uncertain, 1736 ***2856.30*** *p130*
With wife & 5 children
Gazo, Miss; Port uncertain, 1795 ***2856.30*** *p450*
Gdaski, Joseph; Maryland, 1910 ***3259.35*** *p15*
Gear, John 17; Virginia, 1774 ***1220.25*** *p76*
Gearey, William; New York, 1807 ***8197.10*** *p38*
Gearin, Patrick 42; Ontario, 1871 ***1823.22*** *p58*
Gearing, Colin 27; Ontario, 1861 ***2896.28*** *p37*
Gearing, Thomas 1; Ontario, 1861 ***2896.28*** *p37*
Gearity, Daniel; Vermont, 1841-1921 ***5900.10*** *p445*
Gearity, Mary Battles; Vermont, 1847-1904 ***5900.10*** *p445*
Gearity, Mary Gillfeather 67; Vermont, 1888 ***5900.10*** *p422*
Gearity, Michael 70; Vermont, 1899 ***5900.10*** *p422*
Gearle, Gairde; Maryland, 1671 ***2524.55*** *p87*
Gearns, John 40; Ontario, 1871 ***1823.22*** *p58*
Geary, Catherine 71; Vermont, 1863 ***5900.10*** *p542*
Geary, Daniel; Vermont, 1878 ***5900.10*** *p194*
Geary, Daniel 39; Vermont, 1874 ***5900.10*** *p542*
Geary, Edmond 75; Vermont, 1865 ***5900.10*** *p542*
Geary, Hannah; Vermont, 1840-1916 ***5900.10*** *p127*
Geary, James; New York, 1840 ***8197.10*** *p236*
Geary, Joseph 45; Ontario, 1871 ***1823.22*** *p58*
Geary, Mary; Vermont, 1875-1931 ***5900.10*** *p124*
Geary, Mary 83; Vermont, 1916 ***5900.10*** *p542*
Geary, Mary Ryan 63; Vermont, 1891 ***5900.10*** *p614*
Geary, Michael; New York, New York, 1855 ***6058.10*** *p54*
Gease, David; Maryland, 1910 ***3259.35*** *p15*
Gease, Thomas; Maryland, 1650 ***2524.55*** *p87*
Geass, John; Maryland, 1910 ***3259.35*** *p15*
Geay, Peter; New York, 1829 ***8197.10*** *p312*
Gebaner, Frederick 45; Ontario, 1871 ***1823.15*** *p90*
Gebauer, Georg; Port uncertain, 1771 ***2856.30*** *p131*
Geber, Konrad; America, 1792 ***2856.30*** *p132*
Gebert, Johann Diel; Port uncertain, 1791 ***2856.30*** *p132*
Gebert, Johann Nickel; Port uncertain, 1759 ***2856.30*** *p132*
Geberth, Anna Eva; Port uncertain, 1741 ***2856.30*** *p132*
Geberz, Mgdl.; Port uncertain, 1785 ***2856.30*** *p218*
Geberzt, Bronslawa; Maryland, 1910 ***3259.35*** *p15*
Gebhard, . . .; America, 1790 ***2856.30*** *p132*
Gebhard, Albrecht; America, 1765 ***2856.30*** *p132*
Gebhard, Gorg Philipp; America, 1738 ***2856.30*** *p132*
Gebhard, Michael; America, 1741 ***2856.30*** *p132*
Gebhard, Nickel; America, 1741 ***2856.30*** *p132*
Gebhard, Peter; America, 1741 ***2856.30*** *p132*
Gebhardt, Barbara; Port uncertain, 1731 ***2856.30*** *p132*
Gebhardt, Christian; Port uncertain, 1764 ***2856.30*** *p132*
Gebhardt, Philipp Jacob; Port uncertain, 1737 ***2856.30*** *p132*
Gebhart, Christian; Port uncertain, 1771 ***2856.30*** *p132*
Gebhart, Niclas; America, 1747 ***2856.30*** *p132*
Gebisky, Joseph M.; Maryland, 1910 ***3259.35*** *p15*
Gebler, Fredrick 33; Ontario, 1871 ***1823.28*** *p32*
Gebowski, Walter; Maryland, 1910 ***3259.35*** *p15*
Gece, James J.; Maryland, 1910 ***3259.35*** *p15*
Geddes, David 43; Ontario, 1871 ***1823.15*** *p90*
Geddes, James; Georgia, 1737 ***1640.10*** *p63*
Geddes, James; Georgia, 1738 ***1640.10*** *p63*
Geddes, John; America, 1894 ***1640.13*** *p44*
Geddes, John; Georgia, 1738 ***1640.10*** *p63*
Geddes, William 50; Ontario, 1871 ***1823.15*** *p90*
Geddis, David 9; Ontario, 1861 ***2896.28*** *p35*
Geddis, Elizabeth 44; Ontario, 1861 ***2896.28*** *p35*
Geddis, James 16; Ontario, 1861 ***2896.28*** *p35*
Geddis, Joseph 18; Ontario, 1861 ***2896.28*** *p35*
Geddis, Mary A. 15; Ontario, 1861 ***2896.28*** *p35*
Geddis, Matthew 46; Ontario, 1861 ***2896.28*** *p35*
Geddis, Robert 13; Ontario, 1861 ***2896.28*** *p35*
Geddis, Sarah 10; Ontario, 1861 ***2896.28*** *p35*
Geddis, William 23; Ontario, 1861 ***2896.28*** *p35*
Gedel, Judith; Port uncertain, 1775 ***2856.30*** *p132*
Gedny, Margaret 37; Vermont, 1866 ***5900.10*** *p229*
Gee, Miss; Quebec, 1857 ***9196.15*** *p16*
Gee, Charles E.; Vermont, 1854-1895 ***5900.10*** *p318*
Gee, John; New York, 1836-1838 ***8197.10*** *p114*
Gee, Joseph; Pennsylvania, 1777 ***4629.10*** *p25*
Gee, Richard 21; Maryland, 1774 ***1220.25*** *p74*
Gee, William; New York, 1853 ***1224.3*** *p29*
Geehan, Dennis 56; Vermont, 1892 ***5900.10*** *p305*
Geehan, Katharine 67; Vermont, 1902 ***5900.10*** *p305*
Geehan, Margaret 52; Vermont, 1903 ***5900.10*** *p306*
Geekie, Daniel; South Carolina, 1740 ***1224.2*** *p44*
Geelan, Bridget; Vermont, 1831-1902 ***5900.10*** *p254*
Geelan, Mary Ann; Vermont, 1826-1912 ***5900.10*** *p397*
Geelen, Catherine 58; Vermont, 1880 ***5900.10*** *p270*
Geely, Thomas; Virginia, 1665 ***6212.30*** *p20*
Geenty, Bernard 14 *SEE* Geenty, Margaret
Geenty, Bridget 16 *SEE* Geenty, Margaret

German, Phebe Ann 61; Ontario, 1861 ***2896.28*** *p23*
German, Phebe E. 11; Ontario, 1861 ***2896.28*** *p21*
German, Phila A. 19; Ontario, 1861 ***2896.28*** *p21*
German, Samuel J. 33; Ontario, 1861 ***2896.28*** *p26*
German, Sharlotte S. 7; Ontario, 1861 ***2896.28*** *p21*
German, Susan 38; Ontario, 1861 ***2896.28*** *p21*
German, Thomas 26; Virginia, 1773 ***1220.25*** *p28*
German, William M. 9; Ontario, 1861 ***2896.28*** *p21*
Germandong, Friedrich; America, 1742 ***2856.30*** *p136*
Germandong, Friedrich; Port uncertain, 1770 ***2856.30*** *p136*
Germann, Catharina; Port uncertain, 1740 ***2856.30*** *p136*
Germann, Johann; Port uncertain, 1771 ***2856.30*** *p136*
Germann, Johann Philipp; America, 1785 ***2856.30*** *p136*
Germann, Magdalena; Port uncertain, 1740 ***2856.30*** *p136*
Germann, Magdalena; Port uncertain, 1748 ***2856.30*** *p136*
Germann, Wilhelm; America, 1738 ***2856.30*** *p136*
Germanton, Friedrich; America, 1742 ***2856.30*** *p136*
With wife & children
Germer, Ludolph; New York, 1840 ***8197.10*** *p235*
Germich, Johann Adam; Port uncertain, 1754 ***2856.30*** *p136*
Gerner, Johann Mathes; America, 1750 ***2856.30*** *p137*
Gerninhead, John 45; Ontario, 1871 ***1823.15*** *p90*
Gernish, Samuel; Pennsylvania, 1786 ***4629.10*** *p49*
Gero, Henry J.; Vermont, 1847-1925 ***5900.10*** *p510*
Gero, Julia A. Murphy; Vermont, 1849-1921 ***5900.10*** *p510*
Gero, Sarah; Vermont, 1851-1951 ***5900.10*** *p453*
Geromo, Liberato; New York, 1817 ***8197.10*** *p60*
Gerow, A. 7; Ontario, 1861 ***2896.25*** *p34*
Gerow, A. 9; Ontario, 1861 ***2896.25*** *p34*
Gerow, A. 27; Ontario, 1861 ***2896.25*** *p34*
Gerow, Adelaide 20; Ontario, 1861 ***2896.27*** *p56*
Gerow, Allice 2; Ontario, 1861 ***2896.26*** *p21*
Gerow, Almira 21; Ontario, 1861 ***2896.27*** *p60*
Gerow, Amy J. 1; Ontario, 1861 ***2896.27*** *p60*
Gerow, Arnold 11; Ontario, 1861 ***2896.27*** *p52*
Gerow, Bernard 22; Ontario, 1861 ***2896.26*** *p20*
Gerow, Daniel 81; Ontario, 1861 ***2896.25*** *p35*
Gerow, Deborah 41; Ontario, 1861 ***2896.27*** *p56*
Gerow, Delilah 18; Ontario, 1861 ***2896.27*** *p46*
Gerow, Edward 8; Ontario, 1861 ***2896.27*** *p56*
Gerow, Eliza J. 26; Ontario, 1861 ***2896.25*** *p35*
Gerow, Elizabeth 3; Ontario, 1861 ***2896.25*** *p35*
Gerow, Elizabeth 11; Ontario, 1861 ***2896.26*** *p21*
Gerow, Emma 8; Ontario, 1861 ***2896.26*** *p21*
Gerow, Esther 62; Ontario, 1861 ***2896.27*** *p45*
Gerow, Esther Jane 9; Ontario, 1861 ***2896.27*** *p45*
Gerow, Gilbert 17; Ontario, 1861 ***2896.27*** *p45*
Gerow, Henry 5; Ontario, 1861 ***2896.26*** *p21*
Gerow, Henry 100; Ontario, 1861 ***2896.27*** *p46*
Gerow, Hezikiah 16; Ontario, 1861 ***2896.27*** *p46*
Gerow, Ichabod 6; Ontario, 1861 ***2896.27*** *p56*
Gerow, J. A. 20; Ontario, 1861 ***2896.25*** *p35*
Gerow, J. P. 25; Ontario, 1861 ***2896.25*** *p29*
Gerow, John 4; Ontario, 1861 ***2896.26*** *p21*
Gerow, Louisa C. 2; Ontario, 1861 ***2896.27*** *p47*
Gerow, M. 4; Ontario, 1861 ***2896.25*** *p34*
Gerow, M. 24; Ontario, 1861 ***2896.28*** *p6*
Gerow, M. 32; Ontario, 1861 ***2896.25*** *p34*
Gerow, M. 43; Ontario, 1861 ***2896.25*** *p34*
Gerow, M. R. 2; Ontario, 1861 ***2896.25*** *p34*
Gerow, Margaret 1; Ontario, 1861 ***2896.25*** *p35*
Gerow, Martha A. 18; Ontario, 1861 ***2896.27*** *p56*
Gerow, Mary 9; Ontario, 1861 ***2896.25*** *p35*
Gerow, Mary 76; Ontario, 1861 ***2896.25*** *p35*
Gerow, Mary J. 8; Ontario, 1861 ***2896.25*** *p35*
Gerow, Peter 22; Ontario, 1861 ***2896.27*** *p64*
Gerow, Phebe 6; Ontario, 1861 ***2896.25*** *p35*
Gerow, Ryal 12; Ontario, 1861 ***2896.27*** *p46*
Gerow, S. A. 3; Ontario, 1861 ***2896.25*** *p34*
Gerow, S. A. 9; Ontario, 1861 ***2896.25*** *p35*
Gerow, Sarah 14; Ontario, 1861 ***2896.27*** *p65*
Gerow, Sarah A. 12; Ontario, 1861 ***2896.26*** *p19*
Gerow, Sarah E. 4; Ontario, 1861 ***2896.27*** *p56*
Gerow, W. 11; Ontario, 1861 ***2896.25*** *p34*
Gerow, William A. 13; Ontario, 1861 ***2896.27*** *p56*
Gerrard, Mrs.; Portland, Maine, 1858 ***9196.15*** *p30*
Gerrard, Ann 33 *SEE* Gerrard, Thomas
Gerrard, C.; Portland, Maine, 1858 ***9196.15*** *p30*
Gerrard, Elizabeth *SEE* Gerrard, Thomas
Gerrard, Elizabeth; Maryland, 1659 ***2524.55*** *p88*
Gerrard, Ferdinand; Virginia, 1693 ***1224.1*** *p23*
Gerrard, Frances *SEE* Gerrard, Thomas
Gerrard, Henry; Virginia, 1693 ***1224.1*** *p23*
Gerrard, Justinian *SEE* Gerrard, Thomas
Gerrard, Nicholas; Virginia, 1693 ***1224.1*** *p23*
Gerrard, Susan *SEE* Gerrard, Thomas
Gerrard, Temperance *SEE* Gerrard, Thomas
Gerrard, Thomas; Maryland, 1633 ***2524.55*** *p88*
Gerrard, Thomas; Maryland, 1650 ***2524.55*** *p88*
With wife
Child: Temperance
Child: Elizabeth
Child: Frances
Child: Justinian
Child: Susan
Gerrard, Thomas 28; Philadelphia, 1774 ***1220.25*** *p67*
Wife: Ann 33
Gerraty, Thomas; New York, 1838 ***8197.10*** *p114*
Gerrell, Alexander 52; Ontario, 1871 ***1823.15*** *p90*
Gerrell, William 60; Ontario, 1871 ***1823.15*** *p90*
Gerres, Peter; America, 1742 ***2856.30*** *p137*
Gerris, John 34; Ontario, 1871 ***1823.22*** *p59*
Gerrond, William 43; Ontario, 1871 ***1823.15*** *p90*
Gerrow, Aaron 12; Ontario, 1861 ***2896.28*** *p39*
Gerrow, Annie 16; Ontario, 1861 ***2896.28*** *p39*
Gerrow, Cory L.; Ontario, 1861 ***2896.28*** *p39*
Gerrow, Diana 32; Ontario, 1861 ***2896.28*** *p39*
Gerrow, Wilber 10; Ontario, 1861 ***2896.28*** *p39*
Gerrow, William H. 14; Ontario, 1861 ***2896.28*** *p39*
Gerst, Adam; New York, 1837 ***8197.10*** *p88*
Gerst, Henry P.; New York, 1840 ***8197.10*** *p235*
Gerstel, Johann; Port uncertain, 1784 ***2856.30*** *p137*
Gerstenlauer, Barbara; Port uncertain, 1752 ***2856.30*** *p137*
With 2 daughters
Gerster, Antoni; Port uncertain, 1712 ***2856.30*** *p137*
Gerstner, Catharina; Port uncertain, 1759 ***2856.30*** *p137*
Gerstner, Johann; Port uncertain, 1696 ***2856.30*** *p137*
Gerstner, Josef; Port uncertain, 1765 ***2856.30*** *p137*
Gerthner, Peter; Port uncertain, 1737 ***2856.30*** *p137*
With wife & children
Gertling, Georg Adam; America, 1773 ***2856.30*** *p137*
With wife
Gervais, James 5; Ontario, 1861 ***2896.25*** *p39*
Gervaize, John Marie; New York, 1803 ***8197.10*** *p13*
Gervan, Richard 18; Maryland, 1773-1774 ***1220.25*** *p33*
Gervis, Edward 25; Ontario, 1871 ***1823.15*** *p90*
Gervise, Robert; Maryland, 1658-1663 ***2524.55*** *p88*
Gerweig, Frederick; New York, New York, 1848 ***3437.14*** *p96*
Gerwig, Bechtold; Port uncertain, 1748 ***2856.30*** *p137*
Gerwig, Jacob; Port uncertain, 1750 ***2856.30*** *p137*
With wife & 3 children
Gery, Edwd; Virginia, 1671 ***6212.30*** *p42*
Gery, Elinr; Virginia, 1671 ***6212.30*** *p42*
Gery, Ellinor; Maryland, 1681 ***2524.55*** *p88*
Gery, Lawrence; Virginia, 1671 ***6212.30*** *p42*
Gery, Margery; Virginia, 1671 ***6212.30*** *p42*
Gescheidt, Lewis Anthony; New York, 1840 ***8197.10*** *p170*
Geschwinder, Andreas; Port uncertain, 1779 ***2856.30*** *p137*
With son
Gesinn, Henrich; Port uncertain, 1762 ***2856.30*** *p137*
Gesinn, Henrich; Port uncertain, 1774 ***2856.30*** *p137*
Gessner, George; Pennsylvania, 1856 ***6058.10*** *p36*
Gessner, Jacob; Port uncertain, 1784 ***2856.30*** *p137*
Gessner, Jacob; Port uncertain, 1788 ***2856.30*** *p137*
Gest, Thomas 25; Philadelphia, 1774 ***1220.25*** *p66*
Gesting, Margarete; Port uncertain, 1760 ***2856.30*** *p137*
Gesun, Heinrich; Port uncertain, 1782 ***2856.30*** *p137*
Gesun, Johann Martin; Port uncertain, 1783 ***2856.30*** *p137*
Gethen, Thomas; New York, 1835-1838 ***8197.10*** *p115*
Gethen, Thomas, Jr.; New York, 1839 ***8197.10*** *p130*
Gething, Jane; Virginia, 1668-1669 ***6212.30*** *p40*
Gething, Thomas; Virginia, 1664 ***6212.30*** *p10*
Getting, John 23; Philadelphia, 1774 ***1220.25*** *p80*
Gettings, John; Vermont, 1858-1893 ***5900.10*** *p253*
Gettings, Sarah; Maryland, 1681 ***2524.55*** *p88*
Gettings, Sarah; Vermont, 1856-1919 ***5900.10*** *p253*
Getty, Samuel 39; Ontario, 1871 ***1823.15*** *p90*
Getty, William 56; Ontario, 1871 ***1823.28*** *p33*
Gettys, James; America, n.d. ***4628.40*** *p56*
Getz, Henry; Georgia, 1858 ***6058.10*** *p52*
Geuse, James; Maryland, 1910 ***3259.35*** *p16*
Geven, Mr.; Portland, Maine, 1858 ***9196.15*** *p31*
Gewalt, Anna Margarete; Port uncertain, 1765 ***2856.30*** *p137*
Geyer, Adam; Port uncertain, 1781 ***2856.30*** *p137*
Wife: M. Schroder
Geyer, Anna; Port uncertain, 1737 ***2856.30*** *p137*
Geyer, Elisabeth; Port uncertain, 1732 ***2856.30*** *p137*
Geyer, Georg Philipp; Port uncertain, 1750 ***2856.30*** *p137*
Geyer, Johann Heinrich; Port uncertain, 1753 ***2856.30*** *p137*
Geyer, M. Schroder *SEE* Geyer, Adam
Geyer, Maria Schroder; Port uncertain, 1781 ***2856.30*** *p137*
Geyger, Valentin; America, 1768 ***2856.30*** *p137*
Geyser, Adam 48; Ontario, 1871 ***1823.15*** *p91*
Geyss, Johann Adam; Port uncertain, 1749 ***2856.30*** *p137*
Geysselhard, Franziska; Port uncertain, 1746 ***2856.30*** *p138*
Geywitz, Hans; America, 1752 ***2856.30*** *p138*
With wife & children
Gezerak, Victorie; Maryland, 1910 ***3259.35*** *p16*
Gezeshkowiak, Harry; Maryland, 1910 ***3259.35*** *p16*
Gfaller, Johann; America, 1737 ***2856.30*** *p138*
Gharing, Christain; Pennsylvania, 1851 ***6058.10*** *p28*
Gharing, John; New York, New York, 1843 ***6058.10*** *p28*
Gharing, Leonard; New York, New York, 1844 ***6058.10*** *p31*
Gher, James; Pennsylvania, 1778 ***4629.10*** *p32*
Ghirardini, Vincent; New York, 1784 ***4629.10*** *p78*
Ghoghotty, John B.; New York, 1806 ***8197.10*** *p323*
Ghurst, Simon; Virginia, 1664 ***6212.30*** *p15*
Giambony, Lionzio; New York, 1838 ***8197.10*** *p114*
Gibald, James 35; Ontario, 1871 ***1823.15*** *p91*
Gibb, . . .; Quebec, 1856 ***9196.15*** *p11*
Gibb, Mr.; Quebec, 1858 ***9196.15*** *p35*
Gibb, Alexander; New York, 1840 ***8197.10*** *p168*
Gibb, Alexander; Ontario, 1884 ***1640.13*** *p44*
Gibb, Benjamin; Pennsylvania, 1786 ***4629.10*** *p51*
Gibb, Christina; Virginia, 1861 ***1640.13*** *p44*
Gibb, Hugh 47; Ontario, 1871 ***1823.22*** *p59*
Gibb, James; Georgia, 1699 ***1640.13*** *p45*
Gibb, John; Georgia, 1698 ***1640.13*** *p45*
Gibb, John; Maryland, 1681 ***2524.55*** *p88*
Gibb, Thomas; Virginia, 1671-1672 ***6212.30*** *p47*
Gibb, Thomas 36; British Columbia, 1911 ***9196.1*** *p15*
Gibb, William; San Francisco, 1872 ***1640.13*** *p45*
Gibbard, Henry 35; Virginia, 1774 ***1220.25*** *p93*
Gibbin, Thomas 31; Nova Scotia, 1774 ***1220.25*** *p136*
Gibbings, Jonas 67; Ontario, 1871 ***1823.15*** *p91*
Gibbins, Bridget 44; Ontario, 1871 ***1823.15*** *p91*
Gibbins, Bridget 62; Ontario, 1871 ***1823.15*** *p91*
Gibbins, John; Havana, 1765 ***1224.2*** *p44*
Gibbins, John; Newport, Rhode Island, 1765 ***1224.2*** *p44*
Gibbins, Mary Ann 11; Ontario, 1871 ***1823.15*** *p91*
Gibbins, Oner 9; Ontario, 1871 ***1823.15*** *p91*
Gibbins, Patrick 47; Ontario, 1871 ***1823.15*** *p91*
Gibbins, Thomas 21; Maryland, 1774 ***1220.25*** *p57*
Gibbins, Thomas 42; Ontario, 1871 ***1823.15*** *p91*
Gibbins, William 16; Ontario, 1871 ***1823.28*** *p33*
Gibbins, William 47; Ontario, 1871 ***1823.15*** *p91*
Gibbon, . . .; New Hampshire, 1641-1660 ***4628.40*** *p44*
Gibbon, Miss; Quebec, 1857 ***9196.15*** *p20*
Gibbon, Anto; Virginia, 1664 ***6212.30*** *p15*
Gibbon, C.; Quebec, 1857 ***9196.15*** *p20*
Gibbon, H.; Quebec, 1857 ***9196.15*** *p20*
Gibbon, James; Pennsylvania, 1777 ***4629.10*** *p30*
Gibbon, James S.; Alabama, 1822-1845 ***1640.10*** *p63*
Gibbon, John; New York, 1794 ***8197.10*** *p1*
Gibbons, B. Ellen; Vermont, 1850-1937 ***5900.10*** *p488*
Gibbons, Bridget A.; Vermont, 1867-1897 ***5900.10*** *p332*
Gibbons, Catherine; Vermont, 1812-1876 ***5900.10*** *p331*
Gibbons, Catherine; Vermont, 1833-1906 ***5900.10*** *p328*
Gibbons, David; Vermont, n.d. ***5900.10*** *p328*
Gibbons, David 70; Vermont, 1863 ***5900.10*** *p331*
Gibbons, Francis; New York, 1818 ***8197.10*** *p232*
Gibbons, George 55; Ontario, 1871 ***1823.28*** *p33*
Gibbons, Henry; Virginia, 1676 ***6212.30*** *p53*
Gibbons, James; New York, 1807 ***8197.10*** *p39*
Gibbons, James 50; Vermont, 1861 ***5900.10*** *p263*
Gibbons, John; Maryland, 1681 ***2524.55*** *p88*
Gibbons, John B. 44; Ontario, 1871 ***1823.28*** *p33*
Gibbons, Katie; Vermont, n.d. ***5900.10*** *p328*
Gibbons, M. J.; Vermont, 1853-1905 ***5900.10*** *p334*
Gibbons, Margaret; New England, 1657 ***1224.1*** *p23*
Gibbons, Margaret Ryan 76; Vermont, 1878 ***5900.10*** *p331*
Gibbons, Martin 22; Vermont, 1877 ***5900.10*** *p263*
Gibbons, Mary; Virginia, 1665-1666 ***6212.30*** *p24*
Gibbons, Mary 45; Vermont, 1870 ***5900.10*** *p263*
Gibbons, Mary Gannon 56; Vermont, 1895 ***5900.10*** *p331*
Gibbons, Michael; Vermont, n.d. ***5900.10*** *p328*
Gibbons, Nora; Vermont, 1852-1908 ***5900.10*** *p331*
Gibbons, Patrick; Pennsylvania, 1868 ***6058.10*** *p65*
Gibbons, Patrick; Vermont, 1836-1867 ***5900.10*** *p328*
Gibbons, Robert 59; Ontario, 1871 ***1823.15*** *p91*
Gibbons, Thomas; Savannah, Georgia, 1798-1800 ***1640.10*** *p63*
Gibbons, Thomas; Virginia, 1666-1667 ***6212.30*** *p32*
Gibbons, William 63; Ontario, 1871 ***1823.28*** *p33*
Gibbons, William 82; Vermont, 1912 ***5900.10*** *p331*
Gibbons, Wm Joseph 38; Ontario, 1871 ***1823.28*** *p33*
Gibborn, Hen; Virginia, 1665-1666 ***6212.30*** *p22*
Gibbs, . . .; Boston, 1737 ***4628.40*** *p114*
Gibbs, Catherine Kirley; Vermont, 1837-1914 ***5900.10*** *p456*
Gibbs, Edward; Maryland, 1663 ***2524.55*** *p88*
Gibbs, Elizabeth; Maryland, 1675 ***2524.55*** *p88*
Gibbs, George 21; Virginia, 1774 ***1220.25*** *p87*

Gibbs, Gregory; Virginia, 1666-1667 ***6212.30*** *p32*
Gibbs, Henry; New York, 1834-1838 ***8197.10*** *p114*
Gibbs, Horace S.; Vermont, 1849-1948 ***5900.10*** *p400*
Gibbs, Isaac; Vermont, 1842-1911 ***5900.10*** *p456*
Gibbs, James; New York, 1807 ***8197.10*** *p39*
Gibbs, Jennie Durkin; Vermont, 1849-1913 ***5900.10*** *p401*
Gibbs, John *SEE* Gibbs, John
Gibbs, John; Maryland, 1667 ***2524.55*** *p88*
With wife
Son: John
Gibbs, John; New York, 1838 ***8197.10*** *p235*
Gibbs, John 27; Virginia, 1775 ***1220.25*** *p110*
Gibbs, John Jones; New York, 1840 ***8197.10*** *p236*
Gibbs, Joseph; New York, 1840 ***8197.10*** *p236*
Gibbs, Joseph 25; Baltimore, 1775 ***1220.25*** *p117*
Gibbs, Joseph 26; Maryland, 1774 ***1220.25*** *p83*
Gibbs, Mary; Maryland, 1663 ***2524.55*** *p88*
Gibbs, Nathaniel; Maryland, 1663 ***2524.55*** *p88*
Gibbs, Philip; Died enroute, 1674 ***1224.1*** *p23*
Gibbs, Richard; Maryland, 1660 ***2524.55*** *p88*
Gibbs, Richard; Maryland, 1665 ***2524.55*** *p88*
Gibbs, Richard; New York, 1683 ***1224.1*** *p23*
Gibbs, Richard; Philadelphia, 1804 ***1224.3*** *p29*
Gibbs, Richard; Virginia, 1665-1666 ***6212.30*** *p23*
Gibbs, Robert 19; Tortola, 1773-1774 ***1220.25*** *p32*
Gibbs, Robert 23; Ontario, 1871 ***1823.28*** *p33*
Gibbs, Thomas; Long Island, 1784 ***1224.2*** *p45*
Gibbs, Thomas; Virginia, 1665 ***6212.30*** *p17*
Gibbs, William; Maryland, 1663 ***2524.55*** *p88*
Gibbs, William; Pennsylvania, 1787 ***4629.10*** *p55*
Giberson, Gilbert; Pennsylvania, 1791 ***1224.2*** *p45*
Gibhert, Gorg Philipp; America, 1738 ***2856.30*** *p138*
Gibhert, Philipp; America, 1738 ***2856.30*** *p138*
Gibidwegijy, Michel 58; Ontario, 1871 ***1823.28*** *p33*
Giblett, Jacob; Philadelphia, 1790 ***4629.10*** *p61*
Giblin, Peter; New York, 1837 ***8197.10*** *p88*
Gibney, Ann; Vermont, 1834-1888 ***5900.10*** *p93*
Gibney, Bridget 62; Vermont, 1896 ***5900.10*** *p72*
Gibney, Ellen; Vermont, 1847-1923 ***5900.10*** *p107*
Gibney, Jennie; Vermont, 1859-1925 ***5900.10*** *p109*
Gibney, Margaret; Vermont, 1846-1924 ***5900.10*** *p87*
Gibney, Mary; Vermont, 1829-1890 ***5900.10*** *p581*
Gibney, Mary Cone 60; Vermont, 1908 ***5900.10*** *p85*
Gibney, Patrick; New York, 1828-1840 ***8197.10*** *p300*
Gibney, Patrick; New York, 1839 ***8197.10*** *p235*
Gibney, Patrick 47; Vermont, 1884 ***5900.10*** *p85*
Gibney, Patrick S.; New York, 1836 ***8197.10*** *p302*
Gibons, Henry; Maryland, 1681 ***2524.55*** *p88*
Gibracz, Alexander; Maryland, 1910 ***3259.35*** *p16*
Gibsin, Huson 45; Ontario, 1871 ***1823.15*** *p91*
Gibson, . . .; Newport, Rhode Island, 1782 ***1224.2*** *p45*
Gibson, Mr.; Quebec, 1858 ***9196.15*** *p38*
Gibson, Mrs. 50; Ontario, 1861 ***2896.26*** *p28*
Gibson, Abraham Priest; Boston, 1852 ***1224.3*** *p29*
Gibson, Agnes 1; Ontario, 1861 ***2896.26*** *p17*
Gibson, Alex 38; Ontario, 1871 ***1823.28*** *p33*
Gibson, Alexander; America, 1861 ***1640.13*** *p45*
Gibson, Alexander 43; Ontario, 1871 ***1823.15*** *p91*
Gibson, Alison 41; Ontario, 1871 ***1823.15*** *p91*
Gibson, Ann 9; Ontario, 1861 ***2896.25*** *p57*
Gibson, Bridget 67; Ontario, 1871 ***1823.15*** *p91*
Gibson, Catharine 20; Ontario, 1861 ***2896.26*** *p28*
Gibson, Catherine 28; Ontario, 1861 ***2896.25*** *p57*
Gibson, Catherine 66; Ontario, 1861 ***2896.25*** *p72*
Gibson, Cathrine 42; Ontario, 1871 ***1823.22*** *p59*
Gibson, Charles 5; Ontario, 1861 ***2896.25*** *p57*
Gibson, D. 61; Ontario, 1861 ***2896.25*** *p28*
Gibson, David 36; Ontario, 1871 ***1823.22*** *p59*
Gibson, Deby Ann 3; Ontario, 1861 ***2896.25*** *p57*
Gibson, Edward 40; Ontario, 1871 ***1823.15*** *p91*
Gibson, Edward 61; Ontario, 1861 ***2896.26*** *p28*
Gibson, Edwards 26; Ontario, 1871 ***1823.15*** *p91*
Gibson, Elisa 10; Ontario, 1861 ***2896.26*** *p38*
Gibson, Eliza Finch; Antigua (Antego), 1867 ***1640.13*** *p45*
Gibson, Elizabeth 19; Maryland, 1775 ***1220.25*** *p98*
Gibson, Ellinor; Maryland, 1669 ***2524.55*** *p88*
Gibson, Freeman 15; Ontario, 1861 ***2896.27*** *p65*
Gibson, George; Georgia, 1699 ***1640.13*** *p45*
Gibson, George; Ontario, 1861 ***2896.28*** *p34*
Gibson, George 5; Ontario, 1861 ***2896.26*** *p38*
Gibson, George 5; Ontario, 1861 ***2896.28*** *p51*
Gibson, George 30; Ontario, 1871 ***1823.15*** *p91*
Gibson, George 36; Fort Cumberland, Nova Scotia, 1774 ***1220.25*** *p19*
Gibson, George 46; Ontario, 1871 ***1823.15*** *p91*
Gibson, Hamilton 55; Ontario, 1871 ***1823.15*** *p91*
Gibson, Hellen 1; Ontario, 1861 ***2896.25*** *p57*
Gibson, Ida M.; Vermont, 1865-1958 ***5900.10*** *p402*
Gibson, Isaack; Maryland, 1679 ***2524.55*** *p88*
Wife: Katherine
Gibson, James; Georgia, 1698 ***1640.13*** *p45*
Gibson, James; Montreal, 1849 ***1640.13*** *p45*
Gibson, James; New York, 1839 ***8197.10*** *p130*
Gibson, James; New York, 1860 ***1640.13*** *p45*
Gibson, James; Pennsylvania, 1777 ***4629.10*** *p14*
Gibson, James; Philadelphia, 1842 ***6058.10*** *p29*
Gibson, James 28; Ontario, 1861 ***2896.26*** *p38*
Gibson, James 42; Ontario, 1871 ***1823.22*** *p59*
Gibson, James 51; Ontario, 1871 ***1823.22*** *p59*
Gibson, James 53; Ontario, 1861 ***2896.27*** *p65*
Gibson, James 56; Ontario, 1871 ***1823.15*** *p91*
Gibson, James 64; Ontario, 1871 ***1823.15*** *p91*
Gibson, James Allen 21; Ontario, 1861 ***2896.27*** *p30*
Gibson, James Taylor; New Orleans, 1849 ***1640.10*** *p64*
Gibson, Jane 33; Ontario, 1861 ***2896.26*** *p38*
Gibson, Jane 74; Ontario, 1871 ***1823.15*** *p91*
Gibson, John; Maryland, 1650 ***2524.55*** *p207*
Gibson, John; Maryland, 1658 ***2524.55*** *p88*
Gibson, John; Mobile, Alabama, 1845 ***1640.10*** *p64*
Gibson, John; New York, 1806 ***8197.10*** *p322*
Gibson, John; New York, 1839 ***8197.10*** *p235*
Gibson, John; New York, 1839 ***8197.10*** *p380*
Gibson, John; Virginia, 1692 ***1224.1*** *p23*
Gibson, John 7; Ontario, 1861 ***2896.25*** *p57*
Gibson, John 22; Maryland, 1775 ***1220.25*** *p97*
Gibson, John 23; Ontario, 1861 ***2896.26*** *p28*
Gibson, John 33; Ontario, 1871 ***1823.15*** *p91*
Gibson, John 52; Ontario, 1871 ***1823.15*** *p91*
Gibson, John 56; Ontario, 1871 ***1823.22*** *p59*
Gibson, John 58; Ontario, 1871 ***1823.15*** *p91*
Gibson, John 70; Ontario, 1871 ***1823.15*** *p91*
Gibson, John W.; Mississippi, 1828 ***1640.10*** *p64*
Gibson, Joseph 5; Ontario, 1861 ***2896.26*** *p38*
Gibson, Katherine *SEE* Gibson, Isaack
Gibson, Larence; Virginia, 1690-1691 ***6212.30*** *p59*
Gibson, Malcolm; Georgia, 1699 ***1640.13*** *p45*
Gibson, Margaret 30; Ontario, 1871 ***1823.15*** *p91*
Gibson, Margret 8; Ontario, 1861 ***2896.26*** *p38*
Gibson, Maria 23; Ontario, 1861 ***2896.27*** *p30*
Gibson, Mark; Virginia, 1690-1691 ***6212.30*** *p59*
Gibson, Marshall F. 6; Ontario, 1861 ***2896.27*** *p60*
Gibson, Mary 17; Ontario, 1871 ***1823.15*** *p91*
Gibson, Mary 20; Ontario, 1861 ***2896.28*** *p34*
Gibson, Mary 27; Ontario, 1861 ***2896.26*** *p38*
Gibson, Mary 68; Ontario, 1861 ***2896.26*** *p38*
Gibson, Mary A. 24; Ontario, 1861 ***2896.26*** *p17*
Gibson, Mathew 44; Ontario, 1871 ***1823.15*** *p91*
Gibson, Matilda 23; Ontario, 1861 ***2896.27*** *p65*
Gibson, Michael 40; Ontario, 1871 ***1823.15*** *p91*
Gibson, Miles; Maryland, 1668 ***2524.55*** *p88*
Gibson, Patrick 78; Ontario, 1861 ***2896.25*** *p72*
Gibson, Rachel 14; Ontario, 1871 ***1823.15*** *p91*
Gibson, Robert; New York, 1840 ***8197.10*** *p168*
Gibson, Robert; Ontario, 1861 ***2896.28*** *p56*
Gibson, Robert 24; Ontario, 1861 ***2896.25*** *p57*
Gibson, Robert 25; Ontario, 1861 ***2896.27*** *p65*
Gibson, Robert 41; Ontario, 1871 ***1823.15*** *p91*
Gibson, Robert 50; Ontario, 1871 ***1823.15*** *p91*
Gibson, Robert 54; Ontario, 1871 ***1823.15*** *p91*
Gibson, Robert 57; Ontario, 1871 ***1823.15*** *p91*
Gibson, Robert 73; Ontario, 1871 ***1823.15*** *p91*
Gibson, Samuel 55; Ontario, 1871 ***1823.15*** *p91*
Gibson, T. H.; Quebec, 1857 ***9196.15*** *p17*
Gibson, Thomas; New York, 1802 ***8197.10*** *p21*
Gibson, Thomas 35; Ontario, 1871 ***1823.15*** *p92*
Gibson, Thomas 46; Ontario, 1871 ***1823.15*** *p92*
Gibson, Thomas 70; Ontario, 1871 ***1823.28*** *p33*
Gibson, Thomas S. 57; Ontario, 1871 ***1823.15*** *p92*
Gibson, Use; Virginia, 1709 ***1224.2*** *p45*
Gibson, William; Maryland, 1681 ***2524.55*** *p88*
Gibson, William; Montreal, 1893 ***1640.13*** *p45*
Gibson, William; Virgin Islands, 1841 ***1640.13*** *p45*
Gibson, William 2; Ontario, 1861 ***2896.26*** *p38*
Gibson, William 27; Ontario, 1871 ***1823.15*** *p92*
Gibson, William 38; Ontario, 1871 ***1823.15*** *p92*
Gibson, William 65; Ontario, 1871 ***1823.15*** *p92*
Gibson, William 68; Ontario, 1861 ***2896.26*** *p38*
Gibson, William 68; Ontario, 1871 ***1823.28*** *p33*
Gibson, Wm 58; British Columbia, 1913 ***9196.1*** *p58*
Gibson, Wm 58; Washington, 1913 ***9196.1*** *p58*
Gibson, Wood; New York, 1821 ***8197.10*** *p232*
Gibson, Wood, Jr.; New York, 1827 ***8197.10*** *p339*
Giddings, Arthur 29; Ontario, 1871 ***1823.22*** *p59*
Giddings, Charles 32; Virginia, 1774 ***1220.25*** *p56*
Giddings, George 41; Ontario, 1871 ***1823.22*** *p59*
Giddings, Henry 34; Ontario, 1871 ***1823.22*** *p60*
Giddings, James 35; Ontario, 1871 ***1823.22*** *p60*
Giddings, John 44; Ontario, 1871 ***1823.22*** *p60*
Giddons, James 25; Jamaica, 1774 ***1220.25*** *p86*
Gideon, Archdeacon; Quebec, 1858 ***9196.15*** *p47*
Gideon, George H. 37; Kansas, 1900-1910 ***9079.10*** *p26*
Gidley, Charles 32; Ontario, 1871 ***1823.15*** *p92*
Gidley, Richard 34; Ontario, 1871 ***1823.15*** *p92*
Gidley, Samuel 30; Ontario, 1871 ***1823.15*** *p92*
Gidley, Samuel 55; Ontario, 1871 ***1823.28*** *p33*
Gielerski, Julian; Maryland, 1910 ***3259.35*** *p16*
Giemski, Jan; Maryland, 1910 ***3259.35*** *p16*
Gierich, Florian; Port uncertain, 1701 ***2856.30*** *p138*
Gierich, Florian; Port uncertain, 1714 ***2856.30*** *p138*
Gierich, Florian; Port uncertain, 1728 ***2856.30*** *p138*
Gierke, Martin 60; Ontario, 1871 ***1823.28*** *p33*
Gies, Anthony 60; Ontario, 1871 ***1823.15*** *p92*
Gies, Ernest 31; Ontario, 1871 ***1823.15*** *p92*
Gies, Henry 33; Ontario, 1871 ***1823.15*** *p92*
Gies, Johann Adam; Port uncertain, 1754 ***2856.30*** *p138*
Giesser, Barbara; America, 1742 ***2856.30*** *p138*
With son
Giesser, Georg; America, 1738 ***2856.30*** *p138*
Giesser, Hans; Port uncertain, 1794 ***2856.30*** *p138*
Giessert, Hans Adam; Port uncertain, 1732 ***2856.30*** *p138*
Giessler, Jakob; Port uncertain, 1751 ***2856.30*** *p138*
Giessler, Johann; Port uncertain, 1749 ***2856.30*** *p138*
Giessler, Johann; Port uncertain, 1792 ***2856.30*** *p138*
Giesz, Anthony; New York, 1821 ***8197.10*** *p232*
Giesz, Anthony; New York, 1827 ***8197.10*** *p345*
Giffen, John 40; Ontario, 1871 ***1823.15*** *p92*
Giffen, Thomas; Maryland, 1664 ***2524.55*** *p88*
Giffin, Gerry 50; Ontario, 1871 ***1823.15*** *p100*
Giffin, John; Pennsylvania, 1777 ***4629.10*** *p31*
Gifford, Mr.; Quebec, 1858 ***9196.15*** *p41*
Gifford, Mrs.; Quebec, 1858 ***9196.15*** *p41*
Gifford, Alice; Virginia, 1665 ***6212.30*** *p17*
Gifford, Charles 49; Ontario, 1871 ***1823.22*** *p60*
Gifford, Henry; Maryland, 1668 ***2524.55*** *p88*
Gifford, Jno.; Maryland, 1681 ***2524.55*** *p88*
Gifford, Jno; Virginia, 1666 ***6212.30*** *p30*
Gifford, John; Philadelphia, 1790 ***4629.10*** *p61*
Gifford, Wearman; Houston, 1855 ***1224.3*** *p29*
Giggles, William; Maryland, 1665 ***2524.55*** *p88*
Gignoux, Claudius; New York, 1834 ***8197.10*** *p234*
Gilbard, John 38; Ontario, 1871 ***1823.22*** *p60*
Gilbart, Eliza 65; Vermont, 1893 ***5900.10*** *p456*
Gilbert, Mr.; Quebec, 1856 ***9196.15*** *p6*
Gilbert, Ann 76; Ontario, 1871 ***1823.22*** *p60*
Gilbert, Annie Starr; Vermont, 1863-1954 ***5900.10*** *p588*
Gilbert, Barbary; Maryland, 1670 ***2524.55*** *p88*
Gilbert, Catharine A.; New York, 1837 ***8197.10*** *p88*
Gilbert, Charles; New York, 1794 ***8197.10*** *p4*
Gilbert, Charles; New York, 1839 ***8197.10*** *p235*
Gilbert, Edward; New York, 1806 ***8197.10*** *p322*
Gilbert, Eli; Vermont, 1844-1913 ***5900.10*** *p287*
Gilbert, Elizabeth *SEE* Gilbert, Richard
Gilbert, Ellen; Vermont, 1835-1915 ***5900.10*** *p362*
Gilbert, Francis; Maryland, 1665 ***2524.55*** *p89*
Gilbert, George 29; Ontario, 1871 ***1823.28*** *p33*
Gilbert, George 33; Maryland, 1775 ***1220.25*** *p99*
Gilbert, Grace *SEE* Gilbert, Richard
Gilbert, Henry 67; Ontario, 1871 ***1823.28*** *p33*
Gilbert, Henry, Jr. 33; Ontario, 1871 ***1823.28*** *p33*
Gilbert, James 65; Ontario, 1871 ***1823.15*** *p92*
Gilbert, James A.; Vermont, 1858-1926 ***5900.10*** *p588*
Gilbert, Jane; New England, 1664 ***1224.1*** *p5*
Gilbert, Jesse; New York, 1839 ***8197.10*** *p131*
Gilbert, Johann; America, 1752 ***2856.30*** *p134*
Gilbert, John; Maryland, 1668 ***2524.55*** *p89*
Gilbert, John; New York, 1840 ***8197.10*** *p171*
Gilbert, John 16; Virginia, 1774 ***1220.25*** *p92*
Gilbert, John 20; Maryland, 1774 ***1220.25*** *p64*
Gilbert, John 70; Vermont, 1894 ***5900.10*** *p297*
Gilbert, Mary Killen 69; Vermont, 1901 ***5900.10*** *p297*
Gilbert, Mary S. Cushing; Vermont, 1855-1922 ***5900.10*** *p287*
Gilbert, Mary Woods 73; Vermont, 1902 ***5900.10*** *p297*
Gilbert, Nicolaus; America, 1741 ***2856.30*** *p138*
With wife & 2 children
Gilbert, P.; Vermont, 1833-1916 ***5900.10*** *p361*
Gilbert, Peter; Port uncertain, 1785 ***2856.30*** *p138*
Gilbert, Richard; Maryland, 1638 ***2524.55*** *p89*
Wife: Rose
Child: Elizabeth
Child: Grace
Gilbert, Richard; Maryland, 1666 ***2524.55*** *p204*
Gilbert, Robert 30; Ontario, 1871 ***1823.28*** *p33*
Gilbert, Robert 54; Ontario, 1871 ***1823.22*** *p60*
Gilbert, Rosa 11; Ontario, 1871 ***1823.28*** *p33*
Gilbert, Rose *SEE* Gilbert, Richard
Gilbert, Thomas 26; Maryland, 1775 ***1220.25*** *p104*
Gilbert, Thomas 65; Vermont, 1897 ***5900.10*** *p297*
Gilbert, William 17; Maryland, 1774 ***1220.25*** *p57*
Gilbert, William 25; Jamaica, 1775 ***1220.25*** *p144*
Gilbons, John 32; Ontario, 1871 ***1823.28*** *p33*
Gilbons, Patrick 55; Ontario, 1871 ***1823.28*** *p33*
Gilbrandson, Kasper; New York, New York, 1903 ***3437.14*** *p130*
Gilbrath, John 84; Ontario, 1871 ***1823.15*** *p92*
Gilbreath, Thomas 33; Ontario, 1871 ***1823.28*** *p33*
Gilbride, John; New York, 1834 ***8197.10*** *p316*
Gilbride, Thomas 50; Ontario, 1871 ***1823.22*** *p60*

Gilcher, Hans Jakob; America, 1744 ***2856.30*** *p138*
Gilcher, Thomas; America, 1744 ***2856.30*** *p138*
With wife & 6 children
Gilchrest, John 36; Ontario, 1871 ***1823.15*** *p92*
Gilchrist, Adam; Charleston, South Carolina, 1818 ***1224.3*** *p29*
Gilchrist, Adam; New York, 1819 ***1224.3*** *p29*
Gilchrist, Andrew; Virginia, 1700-1799 ***1640.13*** *p45*
Gilchrist, Charles E.; Vermont, 1855-1917 ***5900.10*** *p197*
Gilchrist, Chonie A.; Alabama, 1735-1845 ***1640.10*** *p64*
Gilchrist, Edmund 36; Ontario, 1871 ***1823.28*** *p33*
Gilchrist, Elizabeth C.; Vermont, 1855-1931 ***5900.10*** *p197*
Gilchrist, Gilles 50; Ontario, 1871 ***1823.15*** *p92*
Gilchrist, Henry; Georgia, 1698 ***1640.13*** *p45*
Gilchrist, James; South Carolina, 1819 ***1224.3*** *p29*
Gilchrist, James 74; Ontario, 1871 ***1823.28*** *p33*
Gilchrist, James A. 61; Ontario, 1871 ***1823.22*** *p60*
Gilchrist, John 67; Ontario, 1871 ***1823.15*** *p92*
Gilchrist, Margaret; Montreal, 1891 ***1640.13*** *p45*
Gilchrist, Petter 40; Ontario, 1871 ***1823.28*** *p33*
Gilchrist, Robert; Barbados, 1649 ***1640.13*** *p45*
Gilchrist, Robert; New York, 1802 ***8197.10*** *p21*
Gilchrist, Robert; New York, New York, 1819 ***1224.3*** *p29*
Gilchrist, Thomas 27; Maryland, 1774 ***1220.25*** *p84*
Gilchrist, William; Mobile, Alabama, 1800-1845 ***1640.10*** *p64*
Gildart, Francis; Mississippi, 1816 ***1224.3*** *p29*
Gildart, John 19; Fort Cumberland, Nova Scotia, 1774 ***1220.25*** *p18*
Gildart, Joshua 48; Fort Cumberland, Nova Scotia, 1774 ***1220.25*** *p18*
Gildart, Richard 30; New York, 1774 ***1220.25*** *p141*
Gildea, Frank 22; Alaska, 1916 ***9196.1*** *p43*
Gildea, Frank 22; Whitehorse, Yukon, 1916 ***9196.1*** *p43*
Gildemaster, Christopher; East New Jersey, 1736 ***1224.2*** *p45*
Gildemeester, Hugo C.; New York, 1831 ***8197.10*** *p234*
Gildemeister, Charles A.; New York, 1813 ***8197.10*** *p232*
Gilder, William 78; Ontario, 1871 ***1823.15*** *p92*
Gildermerscher, Charles A.; New York, 1813 ***8197.10*** *p232*
Gildersleeve, Miss; Quebec, 1857 ***9196.15*** *p26*
Gilderslieve, Mr.; Portland, Maine, 1858 ***9196.15*** *p29*
Gile, Thomas 55; Ontario, 1871 ***1823.28*** *p33*
Giler, Maria Sophia; Port uncertain, 1740 ***2856.30*** *p138*
Giles, Alexander; New Orleans, 1830 ***1640.10*** *p64*
Giles, Cyrus 20; Ontario, 1861 ***2896.25*** *p42*
Giles, E. J. 2; Ontario, 1861 ***2896.25*** *p34*
Giles, Edward; New York, 1838 ***8197.10*** *p235*
Giles, Eleazar; Beverly, Massachusetts, 1809 ***1224.3*** *p30*
Giles, Grace Fraser; New Orleans, 1838 ***1640.10*** *p64*
Giles, Henery 68; Ontario, 1871 ***1823.28*** *p33*
Giles, Isaac; Virginia, 1730 ***1224.2*** *p45*
Giles, Jean; Charles Town, South Carolina, 1797 ***1224.2*** *p45*
Giles, John; Charles Town, South Carolina, 1798 ***1224.2*** *p45*
Giles, John 32; Tortola, 1773-1774 ***1220.25*** *p32*
Giles, Jonell; Maryland, 1648 ***2524.55*** *p89*
Giles, Maria 59; Ontario, 1861 ***2896.25*** *p42*
Giles, Martha 55; Ontario, 1871 ***1823.28*** *p33*
Giles, Mary 32; Ontario, 1861 ***2896.25*** *p34*
Giles, Nelson 26; Ontario, 1861 ***2896.25*** *p42*
Giles, Robert; New York, 1830 ***8197.10*** *p361*
Giles, Robert; Philadelphia, 1846 ***1224.3*** *p30*
Giles, S. M. 12; Ontario, 1861 ***2896.25*** *p34*
Giles, William; New York, 1703 ***1224.2*** *p45*
Giles, William N. 6; Ontario, 1861 ***2896.25*** *p34*
Giles, William T. 65; Ontario, 1861 ***2896.25*** *p42*
Gilespie, James 38; Ontario, 1871 ***1823.15*** *p92*
Gilfeather, Catherine 65; Vermont, 1919 ***5900.10*** *p559*
Gilfert, Charles; Pennsylvania, 1837 ***6058.10*** *p13*
Gilfether, Catherine; Vermont, 1835-1914 ***5900.10*** *p45*
Gilfether, John; Vermont, 1833-1917 ***5900.10*** *p45*
Gilfillan, James; New York, 1827 ***8197.10*** *p341*
Gilfillan, William 52; Ontario, 1871 ***1823.15*** *p92*
Gilford, Mrs.; Quebec, 1856 ***9196.15*** *p11*
Gilford, Charles; Pennsylvania, 1837 ***6058.10*** *p13*
Gilford, Mary; Maryland, 1651-1652 ***2524.55*** *p89*
Gilgan, John; New York, 1829 ***8197.10*** *p234*
Gilgan, John; New York, 1840 ***8197.10*** *p168*
Gilgunn, Denis 55; Ontario, 1871 ***1823.22*** *p60*
Gilhooly, John; New York, 1840 ***8197.10*** *p169*
Gilhooly, Michael J.; New York, 1840 ***8197.10*** *p168*
Giligan, Elenor 20; Ontario, 1861 ***2896.27*** *p17*
Gilkinson, William 42; Ontario, 1871 ***1823.15*** *p92*
Gilkisson, Elizabeth 36; Ontario, 1871 ***1823.15*** *p92*
Gilks, Edward 22; North Carolina, 1774 ***1220.25*** *p65*
Gill, Mrs.; Philadelphia, 1774 ***1220.25*** *p73*
With children
Gill, Andrew 3 *SEE* Gill, Bernard
Gill, Ann 8 months; Vermont, 1853 ***5900.10*** *p525*
Gill, Ann 10 *SEE* Gill, Richard
Gill, Ann 41; Ontario, 1861 ***2896.25*** *p47*
Gill, Ann 46 *SEE* Gill, Richard
Gill, Austin 70; Vermont, 1908 ***5900.10*** *p171*
Gill, Bernard 30; New York, New York, 1848 ***1825.45*** *p15*
Wife: Catherine 25
Son: Andrew 3
Son: Pat 2
Gill, Bridget 44; Vermont, 1899 ***5900.10*** *p171*
Gill, Bridget 45; Vermont, 1854 ***5900.10*** *p521*
Gill, Catherine 25 *SEE* Gill, Bernard
Gill, Charles P.; Vermont, 1832-1939 ***5900.10*** *p339*
Gill, Edward 32; Ontario, 1871 ***1823.15*** *p92*
Gill, Elizabeth *SEE* Gill, Thomas
Gill, Elizabeth 20; Philadelphia, 1774 ***1220.25*** *p23*
Gill, Ellen 36; Vermont, 1899 ***5900.10*** *p313*
Gill, Emma 36; Ontario, 1871 ***1823.22*** *p60*
Gill, Faithfull; Maryland, 1681 ***2524.55*** *p89*
Gill, Francis 24; Ontario, 1871 ***1823.15*** *p92*
Gill, Georgeana 24; Ontario, 1871 ***1823.15*** *p92*
Gill, Hannah; Vermont, 1840-1890 ***5900.10*** *p302*
Gill, Hanor Amore; Vermont, 1828-1901 ***5900.10*** *p123*
Gill, Henry; Maryland, 1674 ***2524.55*** *p89*
Gill, Henry; Ontario, 1871 ***1823.28*** *p33*
Gill, Henry 20; Ontario, 1871 ***1823.28*** *p33*
Gill, Hugh 37; San Francisco, 1910 ***9196.1*** *p16*
Gill, Irene 55; Ontario, 1871 ***1823.15*** *p92*
Gill, Isacc 30; Ontario, 1871 ***1823.15*** *p92*
Gill, James 55; Ontario, 1871 ***1823.22*** *p60*
Gill, James H. 73; Vermont, 1928 ***5900.10*** *p125*
Gill, John; Maryland, 1652-1658 ***2524.55*** *p89*
Gill, John; Pennsylvania, 1786 ***4629.10*** *p53*
Gill, John; Virginia, 1665-1666 ***6212.30*** *p24*
Gill, John 15; Vermont, 1853 ***5900.10*** *p525*
Gill, John 34; Ontario, 1871 ***1823.15*** *p92*
Gill, John 35; Ontario, 1871 ***1823.28*** *p33*
Gill, John 40; Ontario, 1871 ***1823.15*** *p92*
Gill, John 71; Ontario, 1871 ***1823.15*** *p92*
Gill, Jona; Vermont, 1837-1884 ***5900.10*** *p302*
Gill, Joseph 30; Ontario, 1871 ***1823.15*** *p92*
Gill, Joseph 65; Ontario, 1871 ***1823.15*** *p92*
Gill, Katherine M.; Vermont, 1867-1952 ***5900.10*** *p123*
Gill, Margaret; Vermont, 1848-1882 ***5900.10*** *p239*
Gill, Margaret Leddy 25; Vermont, 1881 ***5900.10*** *p526*
Gill, Mary; Vermont, 1861-1914 ***5900.10*** *p123*
Gill, Mary 46; Ontario, 1871 ***1823.22*** *p60*
Gill, Mary 83; Vermont, 1910 ***5900.10*** *p176*
Gill, Mary A. 32; Vermont, 1884 ***5900.10*** *p526*
Gill, Mary A. Callahan; Vermont, 1871-1895 ***5900.10*** *p340*
Gill, Mary A. White; Vermont, 1872-1961 ***5900.10*** *p340*
Gill, Mary E. Hannon 52; Vermont, 1913 ***5900.10*** *p125*
Gill, Mary Joice 63; Vermont, 1863 ***5900.10*** *p525*
Gill, Mary Lavelle; Vermont, 1848-1924 ***5900.10*** *p129*
Gill, Michael; Vermont, 1843-1916 ***5900.10*** *p129*
Gill, Pat 2 *SEE* Gill, Bernard
Gill, Patrick; Vermont, 1826-1908 ***5900.10*** *p123*
Gill, Richard; Maryland, 1668 ***2524.55*** *p89*
Gill, Richard 6 *SEE* Gill, Richard
Gill, Richard 40; New York, 1774 ***1220.25*** *p24*
Wife: Sarah 41
Child: Ann 10
Sister: Ann 46
Child: Richard 6
Gill, Robert; Philadelphia, 1797 ***4629.10*** *p62*
Gill, Robert 40; Ontario, 1871 ***1823.15*** *p92*
Gill, Sarah; Virginia, 1663 ***6212.30*** *p3*
Gill, Sarah 41 *SEE* Gill, Richard
Gill, Stephen; Maryland, 1665 ***2524.55*** *p187*
Gill, Steven; Maryland, 1659-1664 ***2524.55*** *p187*
Gill, Thomas; Maryland, 1658 ***2524.55*** *p89*
Wife: Elizabeth
Gill, Thomas; Vermont, 1856-1880 ***5900.10*** *p123*
Gill, Timothy 76; Ontario, 1871 ***1823.22*** *p60*
Gill, William; Virginia, 1668 ***1224.1*** *p24*
Gill, William 30; Virginia, 1774 ***1220.25*** *p93*
Gill, William H. 28; Ontario, 1871 ***1823.15*** *p92*
Gillaland, James 67; Ontario, 1871 ***1823.22*** *p60*
Gillan, John 54; Ontario, 1871 ***1823.28*** *p33*
Gillan, Thomas; Vermont, 1830 ***5900.10*** *p13*
Gillan, William; New York, 1837 ***8197.10*** *p234*
Gillard, James 64; Ontario, 1871 ***1823.22*** *p60*
Gillard, Jarvis 77; Ontario, 1871 ***1823.22*** *p60*
Gillard, Josias 48; Ontario, 1871 ***1823.22*** *p60*
Gillard, Thomas 21; Maryland, 1774 ***1220.25*** *p2*
Gillas, Charles; New York, 1834 ***8197.10*** *p373*
Gillatt, Isabella 8; British Columbia, 1910 ***9196.1*** *p13*
Gillatt, J. B. 36; British Columbia, 1910 ***9196.1*** *p13*
Gillatt, Mrs. J. B. 30; British Columbia, 1910 ***9196.1*** *p13*
Gillatt, Margaret 5; British Columbia, 1910 ***9196.1*** *p13*
Gillbard, Thomas 45; Ontario, 1871 ***1823.22*** *p60*
Gillbert, Wallter; Maryland, 1680 ***2524.55*** *p89*
Gille, John; Maryland, 1665 ***2524.55*** *p143*
Gille, Mary; Maryland, 1665 ***2524.55*** *p143*
Gille, Thomas; Maryland, 1665 ***2524.55*** *p143*
Gillen, Ambrose; New York, 1840 ***8197.10*** *p236*
Gillen, Anthony; New York, 1839 ***8197.10*** *p380*
Gillen, Dennis; New York, 1839 ***8197.10*** *p235*
Gillen, Margaret A.; Vermont, 1827-1894 ***5900.10*** *p285*
Gillen, Patrick; Vermont, 1821-1906 ***5900.10*** *p285*
Gillen, Thomas 17; Maryland, 1774 ***1220.25*** *p70*
Gillender, Ann; New York, 1833 ***8197.10*** *p358*
Gillender, James; New York, 1794 ***8197.10*** *p4*
Giller, Anna Maria; Port uncertain, 1794 ***2856.30*** *p138*
Giller, John E.; New York, 1803 ***8197.10*** *p13*
Gilles, John 29; Ontario, 1871 ***1823.15*** *p92*
Gilles, Narie Pierre; New York, 1827 ***8197.10*** *p233*
Gillespey, Martin; New York, 1838 ***8197.10*** *p376*
Gillespie, Miss; Quebec, 1858 ***9196.15*** *p39*
Gillespie, Annie 40; Ontario, 1871 ***1823.28*** *p33*
Gillespie, Dominick; New York, 1835-1838 ***8197.10*** *p115*
Gillespie, Elizabeth Daley; Vermont, 1862-1929 ***5900.10*** *p583*
Gillespie, George; Jamaica, 1782 ***1224.2*** *p45*
Gillespie, George; Maryland, 1724 ***1224.2*** *p45*
Gillespie, George; Pennsylvania, 1782 ***1224.2*** *p45*
Gillespie, George Hamilton; Ontario, 1900 ***1640.13*** *p46*
Gillespie, James; Boston, 1898 ***1640.13*** *p46*
Gillespie, James; New York, 1828 ***8197.10*** *p64*
Gillespie, James; St. Vincent, 1821 ***1640.13*** *p46*
Gillespie, James; Vermont, 1854-1939 ***5900.10*** *p583*
Gillespie, Jas; Quebec, 1857 ***9196.15*** *p14*
Gillespie, Mrs. Jas; Quebec, 1857 ***9196.15*** *p14*
Gillespie, John; Georgia, 1775 ***1640.10*** *p64*
Gillespie, John; New York, 1836 ***8197.10*** *p79*
Gillespie, Thomas; Georgia, 1775 ***1640.10*** *p64*
Gillespie, William; Jamaica, 1812 ***1640.13*** *p46*
Gillespie, William J.; New York, 1831 ***8197.10*** *p366*
Gillet, Thomas W.; New York, 1807 ***8197.10*** *p29*
Gillett, George 55; Ontario, 1871 ***1823.22*** *p60*
Gillett, German; Maryland, 1663 ***2524.55*** *p89*
Wife: Sarah
Gillett, Sarah *SEE* Gillett, German
Gillett, William; Maryland, 1663 ***2524.55*** *p89*
Gillfeather, Mary 67; Vermont, 1888 ***5900.10*** *p422*
Gillford, Mr.; Maryland, 1651-1652 ***2524.55*** *p89*
Wife: Mary
Gillford, Mary *SEE* Gillford, Mr.
Gillford, Mary; Maryland, 1651-1652 ***2524.55*** *p89*
Gillian, John Arthur 36; Ontario, 1871 ***1823.28*** *p33*
Gilliard, Andrew; Virginia, 1656 ***1224.1*** *p24*
Gilliat, Elizabeth 4 *SEE* Gilliat, William
Gilliat, Mary 1 *SEE* Gilliat, William
Gilliat, Rebecca 30 *SEE* Gilliat, William
Gilliat, Thomas; Richmond, Virginia, 1810 ***1224.3*** *p30*
Gilliat, William 3 *SEE* Gilliat, William
Gilliat, William 34; Nova Scotia, 1774 ***1220.25*** *p136*
Child: Mary 1
Child: William 3
Child: Elizabeth 4
Wife: Rebecca 30
Gillick, James; New York, 1836 ***8197.10*** *p234*
Gillick, James; New York, 1840 ***8197.10*** *p170*
Gillick, Joseph; New York, 1840 ***8197.10*** *p235*
Gillie, James 21; Philadelphia, 1774 ***1220.25*** *p43*
Gillies, Mrs.; Quebec, 1858 ***9196.15*** *p41*
Gillies, Alexander *SEE* Gillies, Kenneth
Gillies, Alexander; Pictou, Nova Scotia, 1848 ***4537.37*** *p29*
Wife: Flora
Child: Bella
Gillies, Angus *SEE* Gillies, Duncan
Gillies, Angus *SEE* Gillies, Kenneth
Gillies, Angus *SEE* Gillies, Neil
Gillies, Angus; Ontario, 1855 ***4537.32*** *p9*
Wife: Sarah Matheson
Child: Donald
Child: Margaret
Child: Kirsty
Child: Jessie
Child: George
Child: John
Gillies, Ann *SEE* Gillies, Ann
Gillies, Ann *SEE* Gillies, Donald
Gillies, Ann; Nova Scotia, 1840-1849 ***4537.35*** *p25*
Gillies, Ann; Port uncertain, 1840-1849 ***4537.35*** *p78*
Child: Ann
Child: Marion
Child: Mary
Child: Donald
Gillies, Ann MacEachan *SEE* Gillies, John
Gillies, Annabella; Ontario, 1855 ***4537.32*** *p52*
Gillies, Bella *SEE* Gillies, Alexander

Glenn, Susan 36; Ontario, 1861 ***2896.25*** *p9*
Glenn, Thomas E. 7; Ontario, 1861 ***2896.25*** *p22*
Glenn, William 31; Ontario, 1861 ***2896.25*** *p45*
Glenn, William 50; Ontario, 1871 ***1823.15*** *p94*
Glenn, William H. 11; Ontario, 1861 ***2896.25*** *p45*
Glennan, Peter; New York, 1807 ***8197.10*** *p327*
Glennon, Bridget; Vermont, n.d. ***5900.10*** *p357*
Glennon, Catharine; Vermont, 1850-1933 ***5900.10*** *p357*
Glennon, Catherine Ryan 74; Vermont, 1886 ***5900.10*** *p370*
Glennon, Daniel; New York, 1837 ***8197.10*** *p88*
Glennon, Thomas; Vermont, 1849-1931 ***5900.10*** *p370*
Glennon, Timothy 82; Vermont, 1894 ***5900.10*** *p370*
Glennon, Timothy, Jr.; Vermont, 1852-1914 ***5900.10*** *p370*
Glenny, Isaac 28; Ontario, 1871 ***1823.22*** *p61*
Glenny, James 52; Ontario, 1871 ***1823.22*** *p61*
Glers, Simon; America, 1739 ***2856.30*** *p140*
Gleser, Peter; New York, New York, 1848 ***3437.14*** *p9*
Glessing, Henry; Indiana, 1836 ***1224.3*** *p30*
Gleven, Bartholomew; Maryland, 1661 ***2524.55*** *p89*
Glevin, Mary; Maryland, 1667 ***2524.55*** *p89*
Glew, John 58; Ontario, 1871 ***1823.15*** *p94*
Glew, Thomas; Virginia, 1663-1664 ***6212.30*** *p5*
Glewbocky, Mateusz; Maryland, 1910 ***3259.35*** *p16*
Gliddon, James 42; Ontario, 1871 ***1823.22*** *p61*
Gliddon, William 45; Ontario, 1871 ***1823.22*** *p61*
Glinck, Christian; New York, 1807 ***8197.10*** *p330*
Glinday, Elizabeth 35; Ontario, 1871 ***1823.28*** *p34*
Glindinning, John; Maryland, 1665 ***2524.55*** *p89*
Glinka, Ignacy S.; Maryland, 1910 ***3259.35*** *p16*
Glinney, Bridget Doherty; Vermont, 1841-1912 ***5900.10*** *p330*
Glinney, Elizabeth Sexton; Vermont, 1840-1906 ***5900.10*** *p330*
Glinney, John; Vermont, 1839-1916 ***5900.10*** *p330*
Glinney, Julia Paine; Vermont, 1827-1877 ***5900.10*** *p330*
Glinney, Patrick; Vermont, 1831-1911 ***5900.10*** *p330*
Glipp, Andreas; America, 1749 ***2856.30*** *p140*
With wife & 4 children
Glisson, Francis; Maryland, 1652-1659 ***2524.55*** *p89*
Glitton, William 45; Ontario, 1871 ***1823.15*** *p94*
Glixby, Eliza 60; Ontario, 1871 ***1823.22*** *p61*
Glocester, Robert; Virginia, 1670 ***1224.1*** *p24*
Glocker, Maria; Port uncertain, 1792 ***2856.30*** *p140*
Glocker, Maria Catharina; Port uncertain, 1794 ***2856.30*** *p140*
Glocker, Martin; Port uncertain, 1735 ***2856.30*** *p140*
Glocker, Martin; Port uncertain, 1768 ***2856.30*** *p140*
Glockler, Jacob; America, 1752 ***2856.30*** *p140*
Glockler, Mrs. Jacob; America, 1752 ***2856.30*** *p141*
With 3 children
Glockler, Leonhard; America, 1765 ***2856.30*** *p141*
Glockner, Agnes; Port uncertain, 1765 ***2856.30*** *p141*
Glockner, Mathis; Port uncertain, 1780 ***2856.30*** *p140*
Glodek, Joseph; Maryland, 1910 ***3259.35*** *p16*
Glodek, Stanaslonce; Maryland, 1910 ***3259.35*** *p16*
Glodek, Walenty; Maryland, 1910 ***3259.35*** *p16*
Glodek, Wojciech; Maryland, 1910 ***3259.35*** *p16*
Glombiensky, Waclaw; Maryland, 1910 ***3259.35*** *p16*
Glorve, Ernest 48; Ontario, 1871 ***1823.15*** *p94*
Glory, James; New York, 1837 ***8197.10*** *p88*
Glory, John; New York, 1837 ***8197.10*** *p88*
Gloss, Andrew; New York, 1838 ***8197.10*** *p115*
Glov, Evan 25; British Columbia, 1910 ***9196.1*** *p29*
Glov, Evan 25; Washington, 1910 ***9196.1*** *p29*
Glover, Mr.; Quebec, 1857 ***9196.15*** *p24*
Glover, Mrs.; Quebec, 1856 ***9196.15*** *p9*
Glover, Alexander Johnston; Washington, 1896 ***1640.13*** *p46*
Glover, Alice; Maryland, 1675 ***2524.55*** *p89*
Glover, Benjamin; Maryland, 1652-1659 ***2524.55*** *p166*
Glover, Bennett; Virginia, 1661 ***1224.1*** *p24*
Glover, Clement; Maryland, 1673 ***2524.55*** *p89*
Glover, Giles; Maryland, 1663 ***2524.55*** *p137*
Glover, John; Maryland, 1660 ***2524.55*** *p90*
Glover, John; Maryland, 1681 ***2524.55*** *p90*
Glover, John 28; New York, 1774 ***1220.25*** *p49*
Glover, Jose; New England, 1638 ***1224.1*** *p24*
Glover, Nicholas; Virginia, 1612 ***1224.1*** *p24*
Glover, Richard; Virginia, 1684 ***1224.1*** *p24*
Glover, Thomas; Charles Town, South Carolina, 1730 ***1224.2*** *p46*
Glover, Thomas; Maryland, 1655-1656 ***2524.55*** *p90*
Glover, Thomas 24; Maryland, 1775 ***1220.25*** *p120*
Glover, William 16; Maryland, 1775 ***1220.25*** *p120*
Glover, William 88; Ontario, 1871 ***1823.22*** *p61*
Glover, William H. 41; Ontario, 1871 ***1823.15*** *p94*
Glowacki, Thomas; Maryland, 1910 ***3259.35*** *p16*
Gluck, Johann Konrad; Port uncertain, 1749 ***2856.30*** *p140*
Glue, Charles 61; Ontario, 1871 ***1823.15*** *p94*
Glue, Jean; Virginia, 1681-1682 ***6212.30*** *p56*
Glue, Marshall 25; Ontario, 1871 ***1823.15*** *p94*
Glue, Mesiah 21; Ontario, 1871 ***1823.15*** *p94*
Glue, Nelson 45; Ontario, 1871 ***1823.15*** *p94*
Gluitz, Jakob; Port uncertain, 1706 ***2856.30*** *p140*
Gluitz, Jakob; Port uncertain, 1722 ***2856.30*** *p140*
Glusex, Peter; Maryland, 1910 ***3259.35*** *p16*
Glynn, Ann; Vermont, 1830-1909 ***5900.10*** *p507*
Glynn, Ann; Vermont, 1838-1920 ***5900.10*** *p206*
Glynn, Bridget; Vermont, 1855-1928 ***5900.10*** *p504*
Glynn, Bridget 26 *SEE* Glynn, Michael
Glynn, Catherine; Vermont, 1844-1878 ***5900.10*** *p204*
Glynn, Catherine 75; Vermont, 1896 ***5900.10*** *p225*
Glynn, Catherine 82; Vermont, 1886 ***5900.10*** *p204*
Glynn, James 80; Vermont, 1897 ***5900.10*** *p225*
Glynn, John; New York, 1840 ***8197.10*** *p170*
Glynn, John; Oregon, 1852 ***1224.3*** *p30*
Glynn, Julia 53 *SEE* Glynn, Michael
Glynn, Margaret 19 *SEE* Glynn, Michael
Glynn, Maria A.; Vermont, 1836-1857 ***5900.10*** *p204*
Glynn, Mary 24 *SEE* Glynn, Michael
Glynn, Mary 82; Vermont, 1907 ***5900.10*** *p94*
Glynn, Mary A.; Vermont, 1844-1877 ***5900.10*** *p507*
Glynn, Michael 21 *SEE* Glynn, Michael
Glynn, Michael 55; New York, New York, 1849 ***1825.45*** *p33*
Daughter: Bridget 26
Daughter: Margaret 19
Son: Pat 16
Son: Michael 21
Wife: Julia 53
Daughter: Mary 24
Son: Timothy 8
Glynn, Pat 16 *SEE* Glynn, Michael
Glynn, Patrick; New York, 1840 ***8197.10*** *p235*
Glynn, Patrick 75; Vermont, 1874 ***5900.10*** *p204*
Glynn, Patrick T. 5; Vermont, 1857 ***5900.10*** *p507*
Glynn, Peter 58; Vermont, 1893 ***5900.10*** *p207*
Glynn, Timothy 8 *SEE* Glynn, Michael
Gmahler, Jacob; Port uncertain, 1766 ***2856.30*** *p141*
Gmehlin, Dietrich; Port uncertain, 1762 ***2856.30*** *p141*
Gmehlin, Johann David; America, 1748 ***2856.30*** *p141*
Gnan, Christian; America, 1752 ***2856.30*** *p141*
With wife & children
Gnanth, Hans; Port uncertain, 1712 ***2856.30*** *p141*
Gnanth, Hans; Port uncertain, 1723 ***2856.30*** *p141*
Gnatowski, Antonie; Maryland, 1910 ***3259.35*** *p16*
Gniewkoski, Anthony; New York, 1838 ***8197.10*** *p235*
Goacher, Mark 40; Ontario, 1871 ***1823.22*** *p61*
Goad, Alice; Maryland, 1681 ***2524.55*** *p90*
Goal, Thomas; Virginia, 1666-1667 ***6212.30*** *p34*
Goald, Arthur; Virginia, 1693-1694 ***6212.30*** *p60*
Goalen, Alexander James; West Indies, 1890 ***1640.13*** *p47*
Gobel, Hans Georg; Philadelphia, 1733 ***2856.30*** *p141*
With wife & children
Gobel, Hans Jerg; Philadelphia, 1733 ***2856.30*** *p141*
With wife 3 sons & 2 daughters
Gobel, Susanna Elisabe; Port uncertain, 1775 ***2856.30*** *p154*
Gobert, Louis; Baltimore, 1792 ***4629.10*** *p78*
Goch, Johann Peter; America, 1744 ***2856.30*** *p141*
With wife & 4 children
Gockelmann, Hans Thomas; Port uncertain, 1758 ***2856.30*** *p154*
With wife & 4 children
Godbery, James; New York, 1803 ***8197.10*** *p12*
Godbolt, George 51; Ontario, 1871 ***1823.15*** *p94*
Godby, Miss; Quebec, 1858 ***9196.15*** *p32*
Goddard, Mr.; Quebec, 1858 ***9196.15*** *p42*
Goddard, Mrs.; Quebec, 1858 ***9196.15*** *p42*
Goddard, A. H. 32; Alaska, 1917 ***9196.1*** *p49*
Goddard, A. H. 32; Whitehorse, Yukon, 1917 ***9196.1*** *p49*
Goddard, Edmond 46; Ontario, 1871 ***1823.28*** *p34*
Goddard, Edmund; Virginia, 1681 ***1224.1*** *p24*
Goddard, Edw; Virginia, 1664 ***6212.30*** *p15*
Goddard, Elmira; Vermont, 1841-1924 ***5900.10*** *p299*
Goddard, George; Maryland, 1673 ***2524.55*** *p90*
Goddard, John; Maryland, 1663 ***2524.55*** *p90*
Goddard, Joseph; Vermont, 1846-1927 ***5900.10*** *p299*
Goddard, Judith; Maryland, 1682 ***2524.55*** *p90*
Goddard, Mary 63; Ontario, 1871 ***1823.22*** *p61*
Goddard, Mary Hamilton; Vermont, 1857-1941 ***5900.10*** *p299*
Goddard, Thomas; Maryland, 1665 ***2524.55*** *p90*
Goddard, Thomas; Maryland, 1687 ***1224.1*** *p24*
Goddard, William; South Carolina, 1740 ***1224.2*** *p46*
Godden, William; Massachusetts, 1823 ***1224.3*** *p46*
Godel, Cath. Elisabeth; Port uncertain, 1791 ***2856.30*** *p154*
Godey, James; Vermont, 1844-1904 ***5900.10*** *p218*
Godey, Margaret 72; Vermont, 1892 ***5900.10*** *p218*
Godey, Nancy Kelley; Vermont, 1851-1889 ***5900.10*** *p218*
Godey, William 76; Vermont, 1892 ***5900.10*** *p218*
Godffry, Thomas; Virginia, 1664 ***6212.30*** *p13*
Godfree, Judith; Virginia, 1667 ***6212.30*** *p37*
Godfrey, Miss; Quebec, 1856 ***9196.15*** *p7*
Godfrey, Mr.; Quebec, 1857 ***9196.15*** *p17*
Godfrey, Mr.; Quebec, 1858 ***9196.15*** *p46*
Godfrey, Elizabeth; Maryland, 1678 ***2524.55*** *p90*
Godfrey, James; New York, 1840 ***8197.10*** *p169*
Godfrey, John; Philadelphia, 1784 ***4629.10*** *p64*
Godfrey, John 22; Virginia, 1774 ***1220.25*** *p92*
Godfrey, Joseph 21; Maryland, 1774 ***1220.25*** *p73*
Godfrey, Mary; Maryland, 1668 ***2524.55*** *p22*
Godfrey, Tho; Virginia, 1665-1666 ***6212.30*** *p22*
Godfrey, William 56; Ontario, 1871 ***1823.22*** *p61*
Godfrie, Andrew; Maryland, 1682 ***2524.55*** *p90*
Godfroid, William; New York, 1803 ***8197.10*** *p13*
Godie, William 42; Ontario, 1871 ***1823.15*** *p94*
Godin, Abner; Ontario, 1871 ***1823.28*** *p34*
Godin, Gregoire; Ontario, 1871 ***1823.28*** *p34*
Godin, Joseph; Ontario, 1871 ***1823.28*** *p34*
Godin, Theophile; Ontario, 1871 ***1823.28*** *p34*
Godjenski, James; Maryland, 1910 ***3259.35*** *p16*
Godkins, Saml 39; Ontario, 1871 ***1823.28*** *p34*
Godler, Peter; Port uncertain, 1766 ***2856.30*** *p154*
Godlington, Thomas; Maryland, 1657 ***2524.55*** *p90*
Godlington, Thomas; Maryland, 1659 ***2524.55*** *p90*
Godnoralski, Joseph; Maryland, 1910 ***3259.35*** *p16*
Godona, Peter 17; Maryland, 1775 ***1220.25*** *p97*
Godoy, Louis; New York, 1803 ***8197.10*** *p12*
Godriski, Frank; Maryland, 1910 ***3259.35*** *p16*
Godry, Frederick; New York, 1833-1837 ***8197.10*** *p310*
Godsgrace, Hannah *SEE* Godsgrace, James
Godsgrace, James; Maryland, 1652 ***2524.55*** *p90*
Godsgrace, James; Maryland, 1658 ***2524.55*** *p90*
Wife: Hannah
Godsill, Arthur 73; Vermont, 1881 ***5900.10*** *p587*
Godsill, Margaret 74; Vermont, 1897 ***5900.10*** *p587*
Godsill, Mary 39; Vermont, 1891 ***5900.10*** *p589*
Godsill, Mary Morse; Vermont, 1857-1911 ***5900.10*** *p593*
Godsill, Mathew J.; Vermont, 1855-1918 ***5900.10*** *p593*
Godson, Richard; New York, 1702 ***1224.2*** *p46*
Godtschalk, Sebastian; New York, 1807 ***8197.10*** *p39*
Godwalvouch, Geo 20; Alaska, 1908 ***9196.1*** *p37*
Godwin, Thomas; New York, 1837 ***8197.10*** *p88*
Godziewski, Joseph; Maryland, 1910 ***3259.35*** *p16*
Godzik, Andrey; Maryland, 1910 ***3259.35*** *p16*
Goe, William; Philadelphia, 1821 ***1224.3*** *p30*
Goebel, Anna Maria; Port uncertain, 1761 ***2856.30*** *p141*
Goebel, Conrad; New York, 1840 ***8197.10*** *p168*
Goebel, Johann; Port uncertain, 1803 ***2856.30*** *p141*
With wife & child
Goeg, Hanora Reagan; Vermont, 1827-1864 ***5900.10*** *p150*
Goeg, James; Vermont, 1815-1891 ***5900.10*** *p150*
Goeg, James 97; Vermont, 1859 ***5900.10*** *p188*
Goeg, Jeremiah 78; Vermont, 1901 ***5900.10*** *p188*
Goeg, Mary A. 43; Vermont, 1899 ***5900.10*** *p188*
Goeg, Mary Mellendy 77; Vermont, 1902 ***5900.10*** *p188*
Goehl, Eva Elisabeth; Port uncertain, 1769 ***2856.30*** *p141*
Goehl, Henry; New York, 1840 ***8197.10*** *p235*
Goeller, John M.; New York, 1840 ***8197.10*** *p168*
Goep, Philip Henry; New York, 1834 ***8197.10*** *p234*
Goeth, Daniel; Port uncertain, 1764 ***2856.30*** *p141*
Goett, Christof; Port uncertain, 1774 ***2856.30*** *p141*
Goett, Daniel; Port uncertain, 1764 ***2856.30*** *p141*
Goett, Johann Adam; Port uncertain, 1774 ***2856.30*** *p141*
Goettler, Georg; Port uncertain, 1774 ***2856.30*** *p141*
With wife
Goetz, Christina 66; Kansas, 1892-1910 ***9079.10*** *p9*
Goetz, Mike E. 31; Kansas, 1892-1910 ***9079.10*** *p9*
Goetz, Peter 67; Kansas, 1892-1910 ***9079.10*** *p9*
Goff, Cathrine 34; Vermont, 1872 ***5900.10*** *p591*
Goff, Samuel; Pennsylvania, 1777 ***4629.10*** *p27*
Goff, Thomas; Pennsylvania, 1777 ***4629.10*** *p27*
Goffe, Daniel; America, 1744 ***1224.2*** *p47*
Goffe, Deborah; New England, 1654 ***1224.1*** *p45*
Goffe, Mary; Maryland, 1861 ***2524.55*** *p90*
Goffe, William; Maryland, 1673 ***2524.55*** *p90*
Gofton, John 55; Ontario, 1871 ***1823.15*** *p94*
Goggin, Ellen; Vermont, 1831-1907 ***5900.10*** *p365*
Goggin, John; New York, 1834 ***8197.10*** *p73*
Goggin, William 50; Ontario, 1871 ***1823.28*** *p34*
Goggings, William 12; Ontario, 1871 ***1823.28*** *p34*
Gogin, James 22; Virginia, 1774 ***1220.25*** *p89*
Gogin, John; New York, 1837 ***8197.10*** *p87*
Gohalia, Thomas 60; Ontario, 1871 ***1823.28*** *p34*
Goheen, Samuel 76; Ontario, 1871 ***1823.22*** *p61*
Gohl, Anna Elisabeth; Port uncertain, 1732 ***2856.30*** *p154*
Gohl, Elisabeth; Port uncertain, 1744 ***2856.30*** *p141*
Gohler, Friedrich; Port uncertain, 1751 ***2856.30*** *p154*
Gohler, Jacob; Port uncertain, 1764 ***2856.30*** *p154*

Gohler, Johann Philipp; Port uncertain, 1752 ***2856.30*** *p154*
With wife & 4 children
Gohler, Ludwig; Port uncertain, 1790 ***2856.30*** *p154*
Gohler, Ludwig; Port uncertain, 1791 ***2856.30*** *p154*
Gohler, Matthaus; America, 1738 ***2856.30*** *p154*
With family
Gohn, Fielip; America, 1738 ***2856.30*** *p68*
Gohn, Philipp; Port uncertain, 1733 ***2856.30*** *p141*
Gohn, Philipp; Port uncertain, 1734 ***2856.30*** *p141*
Gohring, Christian; New York, New York, 1843 ***6058.10*** *p30*
Gohring, Friedrich; Port uncertain, 1770 ***2856.30*** *p154*
Gohringer, Johann Georg; America, 1753 ***2856.30*** *p154*
With wife & children
Gohun, Mary Ann 39; Ontario, 1871 ***1823.22*** *p61*
Goin, Charles; New York, 1840 ***8197.10*** *p386*
Gokow, John 23; Alaska, 1917 ***9196.1*** *p45*
Gokow, John 23; Whitehorse, Yukon, 1917 ***9196.1*** *p45*
Golabiecki, Joseph; Maryland, 1910 ***3259.35*** *p16*
Golabosbka, George M.; Maryland, 1910 ***3259.35*** *p16*
Golaner, Anna; Maryland, 1910 ***3259.35*** *p16*
Golanska, Stefania; Maryland, 1910 ***3259.35*** *p16*
Golansky, Maximilian; Maryland, 1910 ***3259.35*** *p16*
Golasynska, Rosie; Maryland, 1910 ***3259.35*** *p16*
Golbuski, James; Maryland, 1910 ***3259.35*** *p16*
Golczynski, Maryanna; Maryland, 1910 ***3259.35*** *p16*
Gold, Anna Elisabeth; Port uncertain, 1794 ***2856.30*** *p141*
Gold, Anna Maria; Port uncertain, 1751 ***2856.30*** *p141*
Gold, J. 26; Ontario, 1861 ***2896.26*** *p11*
Gold, John; Maryland, 1671 ***2524.55*** *p90*
Gold, M. 28; Ontario, 1861 ***2896.28*** *p1*
Gold, Nehemiah; Virginia, 1666-1667 ***6212.30*** *p35*
Gold, Philip; Maryland, 1682 ***2524.55*** *p90*
Gold, Richard; Boston, 1777 ***1224.2*** *p47*
Gold, Richard; Maryland, 1668 ***2524.55*** *p92*
Relative: Ursula
Gold, Ursula *SEE* Gold, Richard
Goldberg, Heres Lyon; New York, 1840 ***8197.10*** *p170*
Golden, Catherine; Vermont, 1813-1888 ***5900.10*** *p527*
Golden, Felix; New York, 1822 ***8197.10*** *p61*
Golden, Hannah Grady 24 *SEE* Golden, Michael
Golden, Hugh; New York, 1837 ***8197.10*** *p88*
Golden, Lillian Deneen; Vermont, n.d. ***5900.10*** *p158*
Golden, Marcus 31; Seattle, 1914 ***9196.1*** *p63*
Golden, Mary 3 *SEE* Golden, Michael
Golden, Mary 76; Vermont, 1908 ***5900.10*** *p59*
Golden, Michael; New York, 1838 ***8197.10*** *p318*
Golden, Michael 24; New York, New York, 1848 ***1825.45*** *p33*
Wife: Hannah Grady 24
Daughter: Mary 3
Son: Thomas 1
Golden, Owen 77; Vermont, 1873 ***5900.10*** *p158*
Golden, Patrick; New York, 1838 ***8197.10*** *p114*
Golden, Thomas 1 *SEE* Golden, Michael
Golden, Thomas 72; Vermont, 1903 ***5900.10*** *p59*
Golder, Miss; Quebec, 1857 ***9196.15*** *p16*
Golder, George 70; Ontario, 1871 ***1823.22*** *p61*
Golder, Joseph; New York, 1840 ***8197.10*** *p170*
Golder, Robert 22; Ontario, 1871 ***1823.15*** *p94*
Goldey, Jane; Savannah, Georgia, 1823 ***1640.10*** *p66*
Goldie, Catherine; Virginia, 1788 ***1640.13*** *p47*
Goldie, William; Charles Town, South Carolina, 1736 ***1224.2*** *p46*
Goldie, William 38; Virginia, 1774 ***1220.25*** *p92*
Goldin, John 25; Virginia, 1774 ***1220.25*** *p46*
Golding, . . . 34; Washington, 1914 ***9196.1*** *p64*
Golding, David 42; Ontario, 1871 ***1823.15*** *p94*
Golding, James; Virginia, 1667 ***6212.30*** *p37*
Golding, John; Virginia, 1665-1666 ***6212.30*** *p25*
Goldmann, Peter; Port uncertain, 1764 ***2856.30*** *p141*
Goldrick, Thomas; Pennsylvania, 1867 ***6058.10*** *p58*
Goldsberry, Judith; Maryland, 1672 ***2524.55*** *p90*
Goldsborough, John 24; Maryland, 1774 ***1220.25*** *p56*
Goldsborough, William; Maryland, 1766 ***1224.2*** *p46*
Goldsbury, Judith; Maryland, 1674 ***2524.55*** *p92*
Goldscheuer, Ignaz; Port uncertain, 1772 ***2856.30*** *p141*
Goldschmid, Wendel; Port uncertain, 1791 ***2856.30*** *p141*
Goldschmidt, John Meyer; New York, 1838 ***8197.10*** *p114*
Goldschmidt, Ludwig; New York, 1838 ***8197.10*** *p318*
Goldsmith, Lieutenant; Quebec, 1858 ***9196.15*** *p41*
Goldsmith, Andrew 16; Ontario, 1861 ***2896.26*** *p39*
Goldsmith, Audrey 39; Ontario, 1861 ***2896.26*** *p39*
Goldsmith, Blanche *SEE* Goldsmith, Samuel
Goldsmith, Elisa 7; Ontario, 1861 ***2896.26*** *p39*
Goldsmith, George *SEE* Goldsmith, George
Goldsmith, George; Maryland, 1656 ***2524.55*** *p90*
Wife: Mary
Son: George
Goldsmith, George; Maryland, 1663 ***2524.55*** *p90*
Goldsmith, George 2; Ontario, 1861 ***2896.26*** *p39*
Goldsmith, Hannah 26; Ontario, 1861 ***2896.27*** *p19*
Goldsmith, Joanah 12; Ontario, 1861 ***2896.26*** *p39*
Goldsmith, Johanna *SEE* Goldsmith, Samuel
Goldsmith, John *SEE* Goldsmith, John
Goldsmith, John; Maryland, 1650 ***2524.55*** *p90*
Goldsmith, John; Maryland, 1658 ***2524.55*** *p90*
Goldsmith, John; Maryland, 1665 ***2524.55*** *p90*
Relative: Mary
Relative: John
Goldsmith, John Thomas; New York, 1840 ***8197.10*** *p171*
Goldsmith, Joseph; New York, 1838 ***8197.10*** *p301*
Goldsmith, Margaret; Alabama, 1847 ***1640.10*** *p66*
Goldsmith, Martha 29; Ontario, 1861 ***2896.27*** *p19*
Goldsmith, Mary *SEE* Goldsmith, George
Goldsmith, Mary *SEE* Goldsmith, John
Goldsmith, Mary 17; Ontario, 1861 ***2896.26*** *p39*
Goldsmith, Matthew; Maryland, 1658 ***2524.55*** *p90*
Goldsmith, Roger 10; Ontario, 1861 ***2896.26*** *p39*
Goldsmith, Samuel; Maryland, 1658 ***2524.55*** *p90*
Wife: Johanna
Daughter: Susanna
Daughter: Blanche
Goldsmith, Susanna *SEE* Goldsmith, Samuel
Goldsmith, Thomas; Maryland, 1658 ***2524.55*** *p90*
Goldsmith, William; Baltimore, 1834 ***8197.10*** *p169*
Goldsmith, William 27; Ontario, 1871 ***1823.15*** *p94*
Goldsmyth, William; Maryland, 1668 ***2524.55*** *p90*
Goldson, Danl.; Maryland, 1659 ***2524.55*** *p90*
Wife: Sarah
Relative: Martha
Goldson, Martha *SEE* Goldson, Danl.
Goldson, Sarah *SEE* Goldson, Danl.
Goldthorp, Joseph 43; Ontario, 1871 ***1823.15*** *p94*
Goldthwaite, Joseph; New York, New York, 1780 ***1224.2*** *p46*
Goldworth, James Chapman; Augusta, Georgia, 1851 ***1224.3*** *p30*
Goldys, John; Maryland, 1910 ***3259.35*** *p16*
Golebienska, Jozefa; Maryland, 1910 ***3259.35*** *p16*
Golfin, Ann Walsh; Vermont, 1871-1899 ***5900.10*** *p559*
Golfin, Michael; Vermont, 1847-1921 ***5900.10*** *p559*
Goliart, Anna 10; Kansas, 1906-1910 ***9079.10*** *p18*
Goliart, Catherine 36; Kansas, 1906-1910 ***9079.10*** *p18*
Goliart, David 12; Kansas, 1906-1910 ***9079.10*** *p18*
Goliart, Frederic 7; Kansas, 1906-1910 ***9079.10*** *p18*
Goliart, George 40; Kansas, 1906-1910 ***9079.10*** *p18*
Goliezewski, Felix; Maryland, 1910 ***3259.35*** *p16*
Golightly, Culchett; South Carolina, 1756 ***1224.2*** *p46*
Golinski, Henry; Maryland, 1910 ***3259.35*** *p16*
Goll, Amelia 16; Ontario, 1871 ***1823.28*** *p34*
Goll, Frederica 60; Ontario, 1871 ***1823.28*** *p34*
Goll, Frederick P., Jr.; New York, 1840 ***8197.10*** *p169*
Goll, George Frederic; New York, 1830 ***8197.10*** *p363*
Goll, John 58; Ontario, 1871 ***1823.28*** *p34*
Gollacher, Thomas 53; Ontario, 1871 ***1823.22*** *p61*
Goller, Charlotta; Port uncertain, 1766 ***2856.30*** *p141*
Golley, Joseph 49; Ontario, 1871 ***1823.15*** *p94*
Golliart, Andrew 28; Kansas, 1900-1910 ***9079.10*** *p19*
Golliart, Dora 27; Kansas, 1894-1910 ***9079.10*** *p19*
Golligley, Francis 72; Vermont, 1872 ***5900.10*** *p617*
Golling, Peter; Port uncertain, 1765 ***2856.30*** *p142*
Gollinger, Jakob; Port uncertain, 1729 ***2856.30*** *p142*
Gollinger, Josef; Port uncertain, 1751 ***2856.30*** *p142*
Gollington, Ja; Virginia, 1667 ***6212.30*** *p37*
Gollmann, Franz; Port uncertain, 1768 ***2856.30*** *p142*
Gollmann, Franz; Port uncertain, 1782 ***2856.30*** *p142*
Gollward, Thomas; New York, 1839 ***8197.10*** *p130*
Golobauski, Walter; Maryland, 1910 ***3259.35*** *p16*
Golombowsky, Joseph; Maryland, 1910 ***3259.35*** *p16*
Golovich, M. 35; Alaska, 1916 ***9196.1*** *p43*
Golovich, M. 35; Whitehorse, Yukon, 1916 ***9196.1*** *p43*
Golovich, R. 32; Alaska, 1917 ***9196.1*** *p47*
Golovich, R. 32; Whitehorse, Yukon, 1917 ***9196.1*** *p47*
Golsborrog, Ralph; Virginia, 1665-1666 ***6212.30*** *p24*
Golson, Daniel; Maryland, 1650 ***2524.55*** *p90*
Wife: Sarah
Child: Mathew
Child: Grisell
Golson, Daniel; Maryland, 1651 ***2524.55*** *p90*
Wife: Sarah
Golson, Danl.; Maryland, 1659 ***2524.55*** *p90*
Wife: Sarah
Relative: Martha
Golson, Grisell *SEE* Golson, Daniel
Golson, Martha *SEE* Golson, Danl.
Golson, Mathew *SEE* Golson, Daniel
Golson, Sarah *SEE* Golson, Daniel
Golson, Sarah *SEE* Golson, Danl.
Golt, Marx; Port uncertain, 1800 ***2856.30*** *p142*
Golter, A.; America, 1763 ***2856.30*** *p39*
Golton, Brooke 18; Ontario, 1871 ***1823.28*** *p34*
Goltz, Jacob; Port uncertain, 1748 ***2856.30*** *p154*
With wife 3 children & mother
Goltzer, Miss; America, 1740 ***2856.30*** *p154*
Goltzer, Jacob; Port uncertain, 1764 ***2856.30*** *p154*
Golubevich, B. 35; Alaska, 1917 ***9196.1*** *p53*
Golubevich, B. 35; Whitehorse, Yukon, 1917 ***9196.1*** *p53*
Golubski, Jacob; Maryland, 1910 ***3259.35*** *p17*
Golubski, Paul P.; Maryland, 1910 ***3259.35*** *p17*
Golzlin, Annamaria; Port uncertain, 1753 ***2856.30*** *p154*
Gom, Therese; Port uncertain, 1799 ***2856.30*** *p142*
Goman, John 20; Maryland, 1775 ***1220.25*** *p10*
Gomboski, Peter; Maryland, 1910 ***3259.35*** *p17*
Gometz, Matthias; Pennsylvania, 1777 ***4629.10*** *p30*
Gometz, Moses; Pennsylvania, 1778 ***4629.10*** *p34*
Gomez, Francis; New York, 1840 ***8197.10*** *p171*
Gomez, Raphael M.; New York, 1839 ***8197.10*** *p130*
Gomis, Abrm 63; Ontario, 1871 ***1823.28*** *p34*
Gomme, James; St. Vincent, 1787 ***1224.2*** *p46*
Gomond, Arthur; Virginia, 1665-1666 ***6212.30*** *p23*
Gomstomski, Frances; Maryland, 1910 ***3259.35*** *p17*
Gomulka, George; Maryland, 1910 ***3259.35*** *p17*
Gonaroot, Valantine 31; Ontario, 1871 ***1823.28*** *p34*
Gondry, William; Died enroute, 1638 ***1224.1*** *p24*
Gonheimer, A. M. Kunigunda; Port uncertain, 1765 ***2856.30*** *p155*
Gonner, Magdalena; Port uncertain, 1795 ***2856.30*** *p155*
Gonsals, Emannuel 18; Maryland, 1774 ***1220.25*** *p59*
Gonts, Mrs.; Quebec, 1858 ***9196.15*** *p32*
Gonzell, Moses; Maryland, 1679 ***2524.55*** *p91*
Gooch, John; New York, 1831 ***8197.10*** *p234*
Gooch, William; Virginia, 1744 ***1224.2*** *p46*
Good, Ann; Maryland, 1663 ***2524.55*** *p91*
Good, Benjamin; Virginia, 1672 ***1224.1*** *p24*
Good, Brent; New York, 1835 ***1224.3*** *p30*
Good, Charles; Vermont, 1843-1927 ***5900.10*** *p616*
Good, Grace; Maryland, 1669 ***2524.55*** *p91*
Good, John 17; Philadelphia, 1774 ***1220.25*** *p66*
Good, John 64; Ontario, 1871 ***1823.15*** *p94*
Good, Joseph; Pennsylvania, 1786 ***4629.10*** *p50*
Good, Mary E. Carroll; Vermont, 1851-1903 ***5900.10*** *p616*
Good, Thomas 54; Ontario, 1871 ***1823.28*** *p34*
Good, William 21; Philadelphia, 1774 ***1220.25*** *p80*
Good, William 50; Ontario, 1871 ***1823.15*** *p94*
Goodaile, Wm; Virginia, 1671-1672 ***6212.30*** *p45*
Goodale, Ann *SEE* Goodale, Peter
Goodale, Gilbert; Maryland, 1680 ***2524.55*** *p91*
Goodale, Humphry *SEE* Goodale, Peter
Goodale, Isabell; Maryland, 1680 ***2524.55*** *p91*
Goodale, John *SEE* Goodale, Peter
Goodale, Peter; Maryland, 1666 ***2524.55*** *p91*
Brother: John
Sister: Ann
Brother: Humphry
Goodall, Andrew 27; Ontario, 1871 ***1823.15*** *p94*
Goodall, Elizabeth; New England, 1651 ***1224.1*** *p24*
Goodall, James; New York, 1826 ***8197.10*** *p233*
Goodall, John; New York, 1831 ***8197.10*** *p234*
Goodall, John 30; Ontario, 1871 ***1823.15*** *p94*
Goodbern, Francis 25; Maryland, 1775 ***1220.25*** *p113*
GoodChild, Wm; Virginia, 1663 ***6212.30*** *p2*
Goode, John; Virginia, 1678 ***1224.1*** *p24*
Goodell, John 60; Ontario, 1871 ***1823.22*** *p61*
Gooden, Ms. 22; Ontario, 1861 ***2896.26*** *p14*
Gooder, William 24; Ontario, 1871 ***1823.28*** *p34*
Goodery, James; Maryland, 1681 ***2524.55*** *p91*
Goodeve, G. M. 61; Ontario, 1871 ***1823.22*** *p61*
Goodeve, John; New York, New York, 1843 ***1224.3*** *p30*
Goodfellow, George 30; Ontario, 1871 ***1823.22*** *p61*
Goodfellow, John 47; Ontario, 1871 ***1823.28*** *p34*
Goodfellow, Robert; Jamaica, 1827 ***1640.13*** *p47*
Goodfellow, William 42; Ontario, 1871 ***1823.22*** *p61*
Goodfellowe, Alin; Virginia, 1638 ***1224.1*** *p24*
Goodgame, Mary; Maryland, 1658 ***2524.55*** *p91*
Goodheart, Jerry 60; Vermont, 1850 ***5900.10*** *p279*
Goodin, William; New York, 1832 ***8197.10*** *p234*
Gooding, Mary 55; Ontario, 1871 ***1823.15*** *p95*
Gooding, Stephen; New York, 1838 ***8197.10*** *p318*
Goodjean, Robert; Maryland, 1649 ***2524.55*** *p38*
Goodleski, Blanche C.; Maryland, 1910 ***3259.35*** *p17*
Goodlet, Jane; New York, 1836 ***1640.13*** *p47*
Goodley, John 23; Virginia, 1773 ***1220.25*** *p31*
Goodman, Amos 32; Ontario, 1871 ***1823.15*** *p95*
Goodman, Daniel; Pennsylvania, 1777 ***4629.10*** *p9*
Goodman, Edward; Maryland, 1658 ***2524.55*** *p91*
Goodman, Gabriell; Maryland, 1657 ***2524.55*** *p91*
Goodman, George; Maryland, 1679 ***2524.55*** *p91*
Goodman, George; Pennsylvania, 1779 ***4629.10*** *p36*
Goodman, Jennie 34; British Columbia, 1918 ***9196.1*** *p72*
Goodman, Jennie 34; Washington, 1918 ***9196.1*** *p72*
Goodman, John; Pennsylvania, 1779 ***4629.10*** *p38*
Goodman, Michael; Pennsylvania, 1777 ***4629.10*** *p9*
Goodman, Richard; Maryland, 1653 ***2524.55*** *p91*
Goodman, S. H. 37; British Columbia, 1918 ***9196.1*** *p72*
Goodman, S. H. 37; Washington, 1918 ***9196.1*** *p72*

Gorman, Constant 21; Ontario, 1871 1823.28 p34
Gorman, Daniel 53; Ontario, 1871 1823.28 p34
Gorman, Daniel 54; Ontario, 1871 1823.28 p34
Gorman, David; Vermont, 1848-1905 5900.10 p562
Gorman, Denis 13; Ontario, 1871 1823.28 p34
Gorman, Edward; Vermont, 1833-1905 5900.10 p168
Gorman, Edward; Vermont, 1837-1914 5900.10 p47
Gorman, Edward; Vermont, 1850-1920 5900.10 p65
Gorman, Eliza Jane 15; Vermont, 1853 5900.10 p319
Gorman, Elizabeth Flood; Vermont, 1838-1918 5900.10 p47
Gorman, Ellen; Vermont, 1840-1920 5900.10 p335
Gorman, Ellen; Vermont, 1858-1939 5900.10 p562
Gorman, Fred A. 18; Ontario, 1871 1823.28 p34
Gorman, Hanna 24; Ontario, 1871 1823.28 p34
Gorman, Hanora Kelly; Vermont, 1839-1879 5900.10 p266
Gorman, Henry 3; Vermont, 1868 5900.10 p344
Gorman, James 28; Ontario, 1871 1823.22 p62
Gorman, James 65; Vermont, 1871 5900.10 p319
Gorman, James H. 43; Ontario, 1871 1823.22 p62
Gorman, Jane 68; Vermont, 1875 5900.10 p540
Gorman, Johanna Lynch 52; Vermont, 1895 5900.10 p396
Gorman, John; New York, 1808 8197.10 p54
Gorman, John; New York, 1840 8197.10 p168
Gorman, John; Vermont, 1830-1898 5900.10 p138
Gorman, John; Vermont, 1836-1916 5900.10 p266
Gorman, John 32; Ontario, 1871 1823.22 p62
Gorman, John 47; Ontario, 1871 1823.28 p34
Gorman, John 50; Ontario, 1871 1823.22 p62
Gorman, John 50; Ontario, 1871 1823.28 p34
Gorman, John 55; Ontario, 1871 1823.15 p95
Gorman, John 60; Ontario, 1871 1823.22 p62
Gorman, John 62; Vermont, 1907 5900.10 p396
Gorman, John G.; Vermont, 1852-1935 5900.10 p295
Gorman, Katherine Lambert; Vermont, 1840-1912 5900.10 p168
Gorman, Lawrance 23; Philadelphia, 1774 1220.25 p44
Gorman, Martin 37; Ontario, 1871 1823.28 p34
Gorman, Mary Corcoran; Vermont, 1844-1915 5900.10 p334
Gorman, Mary E.; Vermont, 1852-1913 5900.10 p340
Gorman, Mary Hannon; Vermont, 1865-1932 5900.10 p65
Gorman, Mich L. 47; Ontario, 1871 1823.28 p34
Gorman, Michael 50; Ontario, 1871 1823.28 p34
Gorman, Patrick; Vermont, 1842-1900 5900.10 p334
Gorman, Patrick 58; Ontario, 1871 1823.28 p34
Gorman, Patrick 65; Ontario, 1871 1823.28 p34
Gorman, Peter 40; Ontario, 1871 1823.28 p34
Gorman, Sarah 55; Ontario, 1871 1823.15 p95
Gorman, Simon 45; Ontario, 1871 1823.28 p34
Gorman, Susan D.; Vermont, 1852-1927 5900.10 p295
Gorman, Thomas; Maryland, 1682 2524.55 p91
Gorman, Thomas 34; Ontario, 1871 1823.22 p62
Gorman, Thomas 53; Ontario, 1871 1823.28 p34
Gorman, Thos 40; Ontario, 1871 1823.28 p34
Gorman, Timothy 37; Ontario, 1871 1823.28 p34
Gorman, William; New York, 1838 8197.10 p234
Gorman, William 45; Ontario, 1871 1823.22 p62
Gorman, William 70; Ontario, 1871 1823.28 p34
Gorman, Winifred Lang; Vermont, 1834-1907 5900.10 p138
Gormlay, James; New York, 1831 8197.10 p234
Gormley, Alice 70; Vermont, 1903 5900.10 p177
Gormley, Bridget 11 *SEE* Gormley, Mary
Gormley, Catherine 9 *SEE* Gormley, Mary
Gormley, Henry 13; Philadelphia, 1839 6058.10 p31
Gormley, James; New York, 1840 8197.10 p167
Gormley, John; New York, 1826 8197.10 p233
Gormley, John; New York, 1838 8197.10 p114
Gormley, John 13 *SEE* Gormley, Mary
Gormley, Margaret; Vermont, 1840-1898 5900.10 p163
Gormley, Margaret McDevitt 41; Vermont, 1895 5900.10 p221
Gormley, Martin 50; Ontario, 1871 1823.22 p62
Gormley, Mary 36; New York, New York, 1848 1825.45 p34
Son: John 13
Daughter: Bridget 11
Daughter: Catherine 9
Son: Thady 4
Gormley, Michael 70; Ontario, 1871 1823.15 p95
Gormley, Philip; New York, 1840 8197.10 p236
Gormley, Robert; Vermont, 1840-1920 5900.10 p221
Gormley, Thady 4 *SEE* Gormley, Mary
Gormley, William; New York, 1826 8197.10 p233
Gormly, Henry 13; Philadelphia, 1839 6058.10 p31
Gormon, John 41; Ontario, 1861 2896.27 p17
Gormon, Michael; New Orleans, 1855 3437.14 p72
Gornal, Mrs.; Quebec, 1857 9196.15 p18
Gorne, Mary; Savannah, Georgia, 1774 1640.10 p190
Gornig, Josef; Port uncertain, 1779 2856.30 p155
Gornly, Bernard; New York, 1828-1834 8197.10 p308
Gornowitz, Frank; Maryland, 1910 3259.35 p17
Gornowitz, Michael; Maryland, 1910 3259.35 p17
Gorny, Vincenty; Maryland, 1910 3259.35 p17
Goroode, John; Maryland, 1658 2524.55 p91
Gorr, Frdrick 52; Ontario, 1871 1823.28 p34
Gorr, Louise 18; Ontario, 1871 1823.28 p35
Gorr, William 28; Ontario, 1871 1823.28 p35
Gorriby, Maria Mona 39; Ontario, 1871 1823.15 p95
Gorrie, Daniel 29; Maryland, 1775 1220.25 p102
Gorsch, Jacob; America, 1767 2856.30 p142
Gorski, Andlcek; Maryland, 1910 3259.35 p17
Gorski, Andy; Maryland, 1910 3259.35 p17
Gorski, Ludwiga; Maryland, 1910 3259.35 p17
Gorski, Stanislaw; Maryland, 1910 3259.35 p17
Gorski, Walenty; Maryland, 1910 3259.35 p17
Gorsoski, Henrietta 17; Ontario, 1871 1823.28 p35
Gorssline, Adaline 25; Ontario, 1861 2896.28 p50
Gorstich, Thomas; New York, 1714 1224.2 p47
Gorsuch, Elizabeth; Maryland, 1661 2524.55 p177
Gorsuch, Richard; Maryland, 1661 2524.55 p177
Gorton, Mary; New England, 1671 1224.1 p38
Gorton, Mary Maplet; New England, 1647 1224.1 p38
Gortz, Mathes Gerhard; Port uncertain, 1784 2856.30 p155
Gortz, Mathes Gerhard; Port uncertain, 1785 2856.30 p155
Gorvjleki, Stephen; Maryland, 1910 3259.35 p17
Gorza, Katherine; Maryland, 1910 3259.35 p17
Gorzenski, John; Maryland, 1910 3259.35 p17
Gos, Frank; Maryland, 1910 3259.35 p17
Gos, Henry; New York, 1840 8197.10 p236
Goscinsky, Joseph; Maryland, 1910 3259.35 p17
Gose, Ann; Maryland, 1680 2524.55 p91
Gose, Thomas; Maryland, 1680 2524.55 p91
Gosfright, Charles; Maryland, 1678 2524.55 p91
Goship, John; Maryland, 1682 2524.55 p91
Gosinskie, Vincens; Maryland, 1910 3259.35 p17
Goslett, Henry; Maryland, 1660 2524.55 p91
Goslin, Edw; Virginia, 1666 6212.30 p26
Goslin, Hollet; Ontario, 1861 2896.27 p45
Goslin, Thomas 40; Ontario, 1871 1823.28 p35
Gosline, Joseph 14; New York, New York, 1861 6058.10 p57
Gosline, Thomas; Pennsylvania, 1868 6058.10 p61
Gosling, James 34; Maryland, 1774 1220.25 p84
Gosling, Louisa 40; Ontario, 1871 1823.22 p62
Gosling, Mathew; Maryland, 1655 2524.55 p91
Gosling, Mathew; Virginia, 1665-1666 6212.30 p24
Gosling, Wm; Virginia, 1666 6212.30 p27
Gosnell, Robt.; Maryland, 1656 2524.55 p91
Gosner, George; Pennsylvania, 1779 4629.10 p39
Gosnold, Anthony; Virginia, 1615 1224.1 p24
Gosnold, Mary 67; Ontario, 1871 1823.22 p62
Goss, Miss; Quebec, 1857 9196.15 p25
Goss, Aaron 56; Ontario, 1871 1823.22 p62
Goss, John; Maryland, 1654 2524.55 p91
With wife
Gosse, David; Virginia, 1665-1666 6212.30 p20
Gosse, Frances *SEE* Gosse, John
Gosse, Hans Ellery *SEE* Gosse, John
Gosse, John; Maryland, 1654 2524.55 p91
Wife: Frances
Daughter: Hans Ellery
Gosse, Margrtt.; Maryland, 1659 2524.55 p92
Gosse, Samuell; Maryland, 1665 2524.55 p92
Gosse, William; Maryland, 1675 2524.55 p92
Gossiss, Rose; Virginia, 1672 6212.30 p50
Gosso, George 28; Seattle, 1911 9196.1 p34
Gossocke, Jerome; Maryland, 1657 2524.55 p92
Gosson, Anthony; Maryland, 1659 2524.55 p92
Gossun, Elizabeth *SEE* Gossun, Patrick
Gossun, Elizabeth; Maryland, 1658 2524.55 p92
Husband: Patrick
Gossun, Patrick *SEE* Gossun, Elizabeth
Gossun, Patrick; Maryland, 1658 2524.55 p92
Wife: Elizabeth
Gostelowe, Jonathan; Pennsylvania, 1777 4629.10 p10
Gostenia, Wladislow; Maryland, 1910 3259.35 p17
Gostomski, John; Maryland, 1910 3259.35 p17
Gostomski, Karel; Maryland, 1910 3259.35 p17
Gostowski, John; Maryland, 1910 3259.35 p17
Goswell, John; Virginia, 1734 1224.2 p47
Goswell, Richard; Maryland, 1663 2524.55 p92
Goszczynski, Stanislaus; Maryland, 1910 3259.35 p17
Goszka, Mary; Maryland, 1910 3259.35 p17
Got, Juliallia *SEE* Got, Richard
Got, Richard; Maryland, 1650 2524.55 p92
Wife: Susan
Child: Juliallia
Child: Sarah
Got, Sarah *SEE* Got, Richard
Got, Susan *SEE* Got, Richard
Goth, John 84; Ontario, 1871 1823.28 p35
Gotier, Joseph; New York, 1802 8197.10 p21
Gotschel, Andreas; America, 1742 2856.30 p142
Gott, Edward 30; Ontario, 1861 2896.27 p47
Gott, Franz; Port uncertain, 1784 2856.30 p155
Gott, Franz; Port uncertain, 1785 2856.30 p155
Gott, James 34; Ontario, 1871 1823.28 p35
Gott, Jane 26; Ontario, 1861 2896.27 p47
Gott, Thomas 21; Ontario, 1861 2896.27 p47
Gottel, Henrich; Port uncertain, 1785 2856.30 p155
Gottel, Jakob; Port uncertain, 1785 2856.30 p155
Gottgen, Johann; America, 1751 2856.30 p155
Gottgen, Johann; America, 1751 2856.30 p155
With wife & 6 children
Gotthard, Henrich; America, 1737 2856.30 p142
Gotthilff, August Philip Jurdes; New York, 1832 8197.10 p368
Gottileb, Ketterer 46; Ontario, 1871 1823.15 p95
Gottinger, Catharina; Port uncertain, 1749 2856.30 p155
Gottinger, Josef; Port uncertain, 1751 2856.30 p142
Gottlieb, Frederick William; New York, 1840 8197.10 p236
Gottlitt, Johann Bernhard; Port uncertain, 1801 2856.30 p142
Gottlitt, Johann Bernhard; Port uncertain, 1802 2856.30 p142
Gottlitt, Johann Bernhard; Port uncertain, 1804 2856.30 p142
Gottschalk, Louis 48; Ontario, 1871 1823.15 p95
Gotz, . . .; America, 1751 2856.30 p156
Gotz, Andreas; Port uncertain, 1766 2856.30 p155
Gotz, Christian; Philadelphia, 1729 2856.30 p156
With wife son & daughter
Gotz, Christian; Philadelphia, 1729 2856.30 p156
Gotz, Christof; Port uncertain, 1730 2856.30 p155
Gotz, Elisabeth; America, 1783 2856.30 p155
Gotz, Franz; Port uncertain, 1785 2856.30 p155
Gotz, Hans; Port uncertain, 1764 2856.30 p155
Gotz, Hans Georg; Port uncertain, 1733 2856.30 p156
Gotz, Jacob; America, 1752 2856.30 p156
With wife & daughter
Gotz, Johann; Port uncertain, 1760 2856.30 p156
Gotz, Johann; Port uncertain, 1770 2856.30 p156
With wife & children
Gotz, Johann Peter; America, 1744 2856.30 p141
With wife & 4 children
Gotz, Maria Catharina; Port uncertain, 1754 2856.30 p156
Gotz, Marianna; Port uncertain, 1748 2856.30 p156
Gotz, Sebastian; Port uncertain, 1735 2856.30 p156
Gotzendanner, Christian; Philadelphia, 1729 2856.30 p156
Gotzmann, Catharina; Port uncertain, 1759 2856.30 p156
Gouce, John 50; Ontario, 1871 1823.28 p35
Goud, John 34; Ontario, 1871 1823.15 p95
Goude, John; Maryland, 1672 2524.55 p92
Goudy, William 44; Ontario, 1871 1823.22 p62
Gouge, Phillip; Maryland, 1658 2524.55 p92
Gouges, Joseph H.; New York, 1815 8197.10 p56
Gough, Charles; Maryland, 1699 1224.1 p25
Gough, Charles; Maryland, 1700 1224.2 p47
Gough, George 41; Ontario, 1871 1823.15 p95
Gough, Harry; Harford Co., Maryland, 1829 1224.3 p31
Gough, Harry Dorsey; Baltimore, 1822 1224.3 p31
Gough, Henry 46; Ontario, 1871 1823.15 p95
Gough, James 27; Ontario, 1861 2896.27 p54
Gough, John 33; Maryland, 1775 1220.25 p114
Gough, Margaret E. 1; Ontario, 1861 2896.27 p54
Gough, Perry Hall; Baltimore, 1822 1224.3 p31
Gough, Phillip; Maryland, 1658 2524.55 p92
Gough, Richard 15; Philadelphia, 1775 1220.25 p8
Gouin, Joseph; New York, 1806 8197.10 p31
Goulby, John 24; Maryland, 1774 1220.25 p60
Gould, Abram 24; Ontario, 1871 1823.22 p62
Gould, Ann; Maryland, 1651 2524.55 p92
Gould, Annie; Vermont, 1842-1925 5900.10 p578
Gould, C. H.; Quebec, 1857 9196.15 p15
Gould, George 82; Ontario, 1871 1823.22 p62
Gould, Hannah; Maryland, 1659 2524.55 p92
Gould, Irvine 50; Ontario, 1871 1823.22 p62
Gould, James; Trenton, New Jersey, 1742 1224.2 p47
Gould, James; Vermont, 1842-1906 5900.10 p578
Gould, James; Virginia, 1666-1667 6212.30 p32
Gould, John; Maryland, 1651 2524.55 p92
Gould, John 25; Ontario, 1871 1823.15 p96
Gould, John 37; Ontario, 1871 1823.15 p96
Gould, John 60; Ontario, 1871 1823.28 p35
Gould, Joseph; Quebec, 1857 9196.15 p15
Gould, Joseph 55; Ontario, 1871 1823.15 p96
Gould, Joseph 81; Ontario, 1871 1823.22 p62
Gould, Katherine; Maryland, 1665 2524.55 p92
Gould, Mary A. 16; Ontario, 1861 2896.28 p39

Gould, Nathan; New England, 1650 ***1224.1*** *p25*
Gould, Richard; Maryland, 1668 ***2524.55*** *p92*
Relative: Ursula
Gould, Richard 30; Ontario, 1871 ***1823.15*** *p96*
Gould, Robert 38; Ontario, 1871 ***1823.28*** *p35*
Gould, Thomas 21; Maryland, 1775 ***1220.25*** *p121*
Gould, Ursula *SEE* Gould, Richard
Gould, William 39; Ontario, 1871 ***1823.15*** *p96*
Gould, William 40; Ontario, 1871 ***1823.28*** *p35*
Gouldsbury, Judith; Maryland, 1674 ***2524.55*** *p92*
Gouldsmith, Elizabeth; Maryland, 1662 ***2524.55*** *p92*
Gouldsmith, George; Maryland, 1663 ***2524.55*** *p92*
Gouldson, Daniell; Maryland, 1659 ***2524.55*** *p92*
Wife: Sarah
Gouldson, Sarah *SEE* Gouldson, Daniell
Goulson, Daniell; Maryland, 1659 ***2524.55*** *p92*
Wife: Sarah
Goulson, Sarah *SEE* Goulson, Daniell
Gourlay, John; Ohio, 1857 ***1224.3*** *p31*
Gourlay, Robert; New York, 1794 ***8197.10*** *p4*
Gourley, George 50; Ontario, 1871 ***1823.28*** *p35*
Gourley, John 45; Ontario, 1871 ***1823.28*** *p35*
Gourley, William 51; Ontario, 1871 ***1823.15*** *p96*
Gourlie, Robert; New York, 1807 ***8197.10*** *p327*
Gourly, John 37; Ontario, 1871 ***1823.15*** *p96*
Gourney, Joseph; Maryland, 1910 ***3259.35*** *p17*
Gouro, Francis John Mary Vincent; Philadelphia, 1793 ***4629.10*** *p66*
Gouskowski, Stanislau; Maryland, 1910 ***3259.35*** *p17*
Gouther, William; Maryland, 1681 ***2524.55*** *p92*
Gouttie, Caspar; Port uncertain, 1780 ***2856.30*** *p153*
Gouttie, Caspar; Port uncertain, 1788 ***2856.30*** *p153*
Govalsky, Marton; Maryland, 1910 ***3259.35*** *p17*
Govan, James; Mobile, Alabama, 1849 ***1640.10*** *p68*
Govan, James; Mobile, Alabama, 1849 ***1640.13*** *p48*
Govatzski, Joseph; Maryland, 1910 ***3259.35*** *p17*
Goven, John; New York, 1747 ***1224.2*** *p47*
Govenlock, John 50; Ontario, 1871 ***1823.15*** *p96*
Govenlock, Robert 44; Ontario, 1871 ***1823.15*** *p96*
Govenlock, Thomas 50; Ontario, 1871 ***1823.15*** *p96*
Gover, Aaron 16; Philadelphia, 1775 ***1220.25*** *p8*
Gover, Clement; Maryland, 1665 ***2524.55*** *p92*
Gover, Elizabeth *SEE* Gover, Robert
Gover, Elizabeth; Maryland, 1674 ***2524.55*** *p92*
Gover, John 15; Maryland, 1775 ***1220.25*** *p120*
Gover, Robert *SEE* Gover, Robert
Gover, Robert; Maryland, 1674 ***2524.55*** *p92*
Relative: Robert
Wife: Elizabeth
Gover, Robert; Maryland, 1679 ***2524.55*** *p92*
Wife: Elizabeth
Son: Robert
Gover, William 22; Maryland, 1774 ***1220.25*** *p57*
Govier, Ann 71; Ontario, 1871 ***1823.15*** *p96*
Govier, John 42; Ontario, 1871 ***1823.15*** *p96*
Govier, Richard 51; Ontario, 1871 ***1823.15*** *p96*
Govier, William 36; Ontario, 1871 ***1823.15*** *p96*
Govinlock, Andrew 40; Ontario, 1871 ***1823.15*** *p96*
Gow, David; New York, 1838 ***8197.10*** *p234*
Gow, David; New York, 1840 ***8197.10*** *p169*
Gow, George F. 35; Ontario, 1871 ***1823.28*** *p35*
Gowan, Alexander; New York, 1800 ***1224.3*** *p31*
Gowan, John; Ontario, 1862 ***1640.13*** *p48*
Gowance, John 45; Ontario, 1871 ***1823.15*** *p96*
Gowans, James 53; Ontario, 1871 ***1823.22*** *p62*
Gowans, John; Tennessee, 1829 ***1640.10*** *p68*
Gowdey, Adam; New York, 1840 ***8197.10*** *p170*
Gowdey, John, Jr.; New York, 1840 ***8197.10*** *p170*
Gowdey, William; New York, 1806 ***8197.10*** *p323*
Gowen, Charles 62; Ontario, 1871 ***1823.22*** *p62*
Gower, Henry 23; Philadelphia, 1775 ***1220.25*** *p9*
Gowey, James 43; Ontario, 1871 ***1823.22*** *p62*
Gowie, Alexander 23; Jamaica, 1774 ***1220.25*** *p60*
Gowing, Samuel 49; Ontario, 1871 ***1823.15*** *p96*
Gowlan, Robert; Maryland, 1662 ***2524.55*** *p92*
Goy, Peter; Port uncertain, 1794 ***2856.30*** *p142*
Goy, Thomas; Port uncertain, 1794 ***2856.30*** *p142*
Goyet, Mary A.; Vermont, 1850-1901 ***5900.10*** *p507*
Goyou, John B.; New York, 1816 ***8197.10*** *p59*
Goz, Elisabeth; Port uncertain, 1795 ***2856.30*** *p156*
Goz, Johann; Port uncertain, 1769 ***2856.30*** *p156*
With 2 children
Goz, Magdalena; Port uncertain, 1796 ***2856.30*** *p156*
Gozeczki, Michael; Maryland, 1910 ***3259.35*** *p17*
Gozeczki, Stephen; Maryland, 1910 ***3259.35*** *p18*
Gozeleski, Joseph; Maryland, 1910 ***3259.35*** *p18*
Gozenberger, Ferdinand; Port uncertain, 1776 ***2856.30*** *p156*
Gozeski, Ludwika; Maryland, 1910 ***3259.35*** *p18*
Graaf, Maria Dorothea; Port uncertain, 1777 ***2856.30*** *p142*
Graafin, C.; America, 1763 ***2856.30*** *p215*
Grab, Henry 30; Ontario, 1871 ***1823.28*** *p35*
Grab, Michael 31; Ontario, 1871 ***1823.28*** *p35*
Grabb, Tho; Virginia, 1664 ***6212.30*** *p14*
Grabecki, Stanislaus; Maryland, 1910 ***3259.35*** *p18*
Grabenne, William 29; Ontario, 1871 ***1823.15*** *p96*
Grabenstetter, Hans Georg, The Younger; Port uncertain, 1693 ***2856.30*** *p142*
Grabenstetter, Jacob; Port uncertain, 1812 ***2856.30*** *p142*
Graber, Emanuel; America, 1752 ***2856.30*** *p151*
With family
Graber, Margarete; Port uncertain, 1739 ***2856.30*** *p142*
Graber, William 34; Ontario, 1871 ***1823.28*** *p35*
Grabherr, Johann; Port uncertain, 1742 ***2856.30*** *p142*
Grabherr, Johann; Port uncertain, 1758 ***2856.30*** *p142*
Grabius, Nickel; America, 1784 ***2856.30*** *p142*
With 3 children
Grabon, Blaze; Maryland, 1910 ***3259.35*** *p18*
Grabowska, Mary; Maryland, 1910 ***3259.35*** *p18*
Grabowski, Boleslaw; Maryland, 1910 ***3259.35*** *p18*
Grabowski, John; Maryland, 1910 ***3259.35*** *p18*
Grabowski, Valentine; Maryland, 1910 ***3259.35*** *p18*
Grabski, John; Maryland, 1910 ***3259.35*** *p18*
Grace, Mr.; Vermont, 1806-1850 ***5900.10*** *p312*
Grace, Mrs.; Vermont, 1818-1890 ***5900.10*** *p312*
Grace, Ann; Maryland, 1672 ***2524.55*** *p92*
Grace, Barbara Thurn; Vermont, 1855-1914 ***5900.10*** *p356*
Grace, Benjerman 35; Ontario, 1871 ***1823.28*** *p35*
Grace, Bridget 56; Vermont, 1902 ***5900.10*** *p272*
Grace, Catharine 65; Vermont, 1869 ***5900.10*** *p72*
Grace, Catherine Noonan 68; Vermont, 1878 ***5900.10*** *p269*
Grace, Catherine Trainer; Vermont, 1843-1897 ***5900.10*** *p548*
Grace, Edward; Vermont, 1864 ***5900.10*** *p72*
Grace, Edward 63; Vermont, 1865 ***5900.10*** *p72*
Grace, Ellen Dalton 90; Vermont, 1885 ***5900.10*** *p612*
Grace, Henry Jonathan; New York, 1824 ***8197.10*** *p233*
Grace, Jacob; Pennsylvania, 1786 ***4629.10*** *p55*
Grace, James; Vermont, 1840-1898 ***5900.10*** *p74*
Grace, James 19; Maryland, 1774 ***1220.25*** *p7*
Grace, James 35; Vermont, 1844 ***5900.10*** *p610*
Grace, James 50; Ontario, 1871 ***1823.28*** *p35*
Grace, John; Maryland, 1673 ***2524.55*** *p92*
Grace, John; Vermont, 1829-1875 ***5900.10*** *p492*
Grace, John; Vermont, 1848-1926 ***5900.10*** *p275*
Grace, John 18; Ontario, 1871 ***1823.28*** *p35*
Grace, Julia; Vermont, 1853-1910 ***5900.10*** *p275*
Grace, Margaret; Vermont, 1846-1879 ***5900.10*** *p74*
Grace, Margaret DeCoursey 72; Vermont, 1904 ***5900.10*** *p541*
Grace, Mary; Vermont, 1840-1893 ***5900.10*** *p405*
Grace, Mary; Vermont, 1845-1930 ***5900.10*** *p255*
Grace, Mary 53; Vermont, 1897 ***5900.10*** *p589*
Grace, Mary 70; Vermont, 1862 ***5900.10*** *p179*
Grace, Mary Kelly; Vermont, 1833-1912 ***5900.10*** *p492*
Grace, Michael; Maryland, 1672 ***2524.55*** *p92*
Grace, Michael 54; Ontario, 1871 ***1823.28*** *p35*
Grace, Michael 69; Vermont, 1889 ***5900.10*** *p541*
Grace, Miles; Virginia, 1668-1669 ***6212.30*** *p41*
Grace, Nicholas; Nova Scotia, 1745 ***4628.40*** *p45*
Grace, Patrick 44; Vermont, 1886 ***5900.10*** *p272*
Grace, Piere B.; New York, 1840 ***8197.10*** *p321*
Grace, William; Boston, 1748 ***1224.2*** *p47*
Grace, William; Maryland, 1660 ***2524.55*** *p175*
Grace, William; Maryland, 1672 ***2524.55*** *p92*
Gracie, James; Baltimore, 1817 ***1224.3*** *p31*
Graczavski, Phillip; Maryland, 1910 ***3259.35*** *p18*
Graczkowski, Jacob; Maryland, 1910 ***3259.35*** *p18*
Gradee, Bryan; Virginia, 1702 ***6212.30*** *p62*
Gradey, Catherine 42; Vermont, 1876 ***5900.10*** *p575*
Gradon, W. 25; Ontario, 1861 ***2896.25*** *p50*
Gradt, Wendel; Port uncertain, 1751 ***2856.30*** *p142*
With wife & children
Gradwell, Jacob; South Carolina, 1699 ***1224.1*** *p25*
Grady, Abbie; Vermont, 1868-1921 ***5900.10*** *p116*
Grady, Abbie McSweeney; Vermont, 1838-1926 ***5900.10*** *p116*
Grady, Adeline; Vermont, 1858-1889 ***5900.10*** *p543*
Grady, Adeline Bulley; Vermont, n.d. ***5900.10*** *p543*
Grady, Andrew; Vermont, 1826-1890 ***5900.10*** *p543*
Grady, Andrew; Vermont, 1853-1887 ***5900.10*** *p543*
Grady, Ann 11 *SEE* Grady, Thomas
Grady, Bridget 4 *SEE* Grady, Thomas
Grady, Bridget 83; Vermont, 1902 ***5900.10*** *p479*
Grady, Bridget Mahar 52; Vermont, 1896 ***5900.10*** *p254*
Grady, Catherine 2; Died enroute, 1849 ***1825.45*** *p34*
Grady, Catherine 36 *SEE* Grady, Thomas
Grady, Catherine Austin 36; Vermont, 1867 ***5900.10*** *p114*
Grady, Catherine Fitzgerald 70; Vermont, 1892 ***5900.10*** *p114*
Grady, Clement; Canada, 1756-1760 ***4628.40*** *p46*
Grady, Denis 30; New York, New York, 1848 ***1825.45*** *p34*
Brother: John 21
Sister: Honoria 20
Grady, Dennis 55; Vermont, 1879 ***5900.10*** *p114*
Grady, Edmund; Maryland, 1673 ***2524.55*** *p92*
Grady, Eliza Donnelly; Vermont, 1854-1947 ***5900.10*** *p114*
Grady, Elizabeth; Vermont, 1866-1948 ***5900.10*** *p116*
Grady, Frederick; Vermont, 1872-1940 ***5900.10*** *p544*
Grady, Mrs. Frederick; Vermont, 1873-1955 ***5900.10*** *p544*
Grady, Hannah; Vermont, 1864-1943 ***5900.10*** *p116*
Grady, Hannah 24; New York, New York, 1848 ***1825.45*** *p33*
Grady, Hannorah 74; Vermont, 1896 ***5900.10*** *p275*
Grady, Helena; Vermont, 1883-1902 ***5900.10*** *p116*
Grady, Honoria 20 *SEE* Grady, Denis
Grady, James; Vermont, 1855-1935 ***5900.10*** *p114*
Grady, James; Vermont, 1869-1900 ***5900.10*** *p116*
Grady, James H.; New York, 1840 ***8197.10*** *p169*
Grady, Jeremiah; Vermont, 1830-1895 ***5900.10*** *p195*
Grady, Jeremiah 75; Vermont, 1897 ***5900.10*** *p214*
Grady, Johannah; Vermont, 1860-1911 ***5900.10*** *p422*
Grady, John; Vermont, 1823-1906 ***5900.10*** *p247*
Grady, John 14 *SEE* Grady, Thomas
Grady, John 21 *SEE* Grady, Denis
Grady, John 75; Vermont, 1895 ***5900.10*** *p254*
Grady, John T.; Vermont, 1870-1950 ***5900.10*** *p116*
Grady, Katherine; Vermont, 1879-1897 ***5900.10*** *p116*
Grady, Margaret; Vermont, 1831-1907 ***5900.10*** *p212*
Grady, Mary 27 *SEE* Grady, Peter
Grady, Mary Hanon; Vermont, 1821-1909 ***5900.10*** *p247*
Grady, Mary Moran; Vermont, 1869-1949 ***5900.10*** *p116*
Grady, Mary O'Brien 72; Vermont, 1903 ***5900.10*** *p214*
Grady, Michael 3 months *SEE* Grady, Thomas
Grady, Nazarus; Vermont, 1856-1870 ***5900.10*** *p543*
Grady, Norah; Vermont, 1875-1938 ***5900.10*** *p116*
Grady, Pat 6 *SEE* Grady, Thomas
Grady, Patrick; Vermont, 1821-1892 ***5900.10*** *p116*
Grady, Peter; Vermont, 1860-1885 ***5900.10*** *p543*
Grady, Peter 31; New York, New York, 1849 ***1825.45*** *p34*
Wife: Mary 27
Grady, Stephen; Vermont, 1862-1865 ***5900.10*** *p543*
Grady, Susan; Vermont, 1837-1897 ***5900.10*** *p195*
Grady, Thomas 6 months; Died enroute, 1849 ***1825.45*** *p34*
Grady, Thomas 2 *SEE* Grady, Thomas
Grady, Thomas 41; New York, New York, 1849 ***1825.45*** *p34*
Wife: Catherine 36
Son: Thomas 2
Daughter: Bridget 4
Daughter: Ann 11
Son: Pat 6
Son: John 14
Son: Michael 3 months
Graebe, Charles; New York, 1827 ***8197.10*** *p339*
Graeme, David; Charles Town, South Carolina, 1778 ***1224.2*** *p47*
Graeme, William; Savannah, Georgia, 1770 ***1640.10*** *p68*
Graeslin, Maria; Port uncertain, 1785 ***2856.30*** *p143*
Graf, Anna Dorothea; Port uncertain, 1758 ***2856.30*** *p143*
Graf, Anna Maria; Port uncertain, 1787 ***2856.30*** *p143*
With husband
Graf, Anton; Port uncertain, 1742 ***2856.30*** *p143*
Graf, Christian; America, 1749 ***2856.30*** *p143*
Graf, Franz Simon; Port uncertain, 1784 ***2856.30*** *p143*
Graf, George; New York, 1838 ***8197.10*** *p114*
Graf, Johann; Port uncertain, 1762 ***2856.30*** *p143*
Graf, Johann; Port uncertain, 1787 ***2856.30*** *p143*
Graf, Johann; Port uncertain, 1788 ***2856.30*** *p143*
Graf, Johann; Port uncertain, 1791 ***2856.30*** *p143*
Graf, Lenhard; Port uncertain, 1785 ***2856.30*** *p143*
Graf, Martin; Port uncertain, 1771 ***2856.30*** *p143*
Graf, Peter; Port uncertain, 1781 ***2856.30*** *p143*
With 2 sons & 2 daughters
Graf, Sebastian, q; Port uncertain, 1727 ***2856.30*** *p151*
Graff, Bernhard; Port uncertain, 1765 ***2856.30*** *p143*
Graff, Johann Philipp; Port uncertain, 1730 ***2856.30*** *p143*
Graff, John 67; Ontario, 1871 ***1823.28*** *p35*
Graff, John Jacob; Pennsylvania, 1805-1814 ***6058.10*** *p4*
Graff, Mrs. Michael; Port uncertain, 1746 ***2856.30*** *p143*
Graff, Philipp; America, 1741 ***2856.30*** *p143*
Graff, Sebastian; America, 1727 ***2856.30*** *p70*
Graffert, Anna Margarete; Port uncertain, 1735 ***2856.30*** *p143*
Graft, Anth; Virginia, 1683 ***6212.30*** *p56*
Grafton, Woodbridge; Philadelphia, 1826 ***1224.3*** *p31*
Graham, Miss; Quebec, 1857 ***9196.15*** *p14*
Graham, Mr.; Georgia, 1735-1845 ***1640.10*** *p70*
Graham, Mr.; Quebec, 1856 ***9196.15*** *p7*

Graham, Mrs.; Quebec, 1856 ***9196.15*** *p7*
Graham, A.; Quebec, 1858 ***9196.15*** *p35*
Graham, Albert J.; Vermont, 1839-1899 ***5900.10*** *p186*
Graham, Alex 26; Alaska, 1912 ***9196.1*** *p20*
Graham, Alex 26; British Columbia, 1912 ***9196.1*** *p20*
Graham, Alexander *SEE* Graham, William
Graham, Alexander; Florida, 1769 ***1640.10*** *p69*
Graham, Alexander; New York, 1826-1834 ***8197.10*** *p308*
Graham, Alexander 26; Ontario, 1871 ***1823.15*** *p96*
Graham, Alexander 52; Ontario, 1871 ***1823.28*** *p35*
Graham, Allen; New York, 1807 ***8197.10*** *p38*
Graham, Andrew 21; Ontario, 1861 ***2896.28*** *p39*
Graham, Andrew 45; Ontario, 1871 ***1823.22*** *p62*
Graham, Andrew 70; Ontario, 1871 ***1823.15*** *p96*
Graham, Andrew 72; Ontario, 1871 ***1823.22*** *p63*
Graham, Angus; Ontario, 1851 ***4537.32*** *p9*
Wife: Catherine MacLeod
Child: Margaret
Child: Janet
Child: Ann
Child: Mary
Graham, Ann *SEE* Graham, Angus
Graham, Ann *SEE* Graham, Donald
Graham, Ann; Ontario, 1863 ***4537.32*** *p88*
Graham, Ann 55; Ontario, 1871 ***1823.15*** *p96*
Graham, Ann 84; Ontario, 1871 ***1823.22*** *p63*
Graham, Ann Campbell *SEE* Graham, William
Graham, Anne; Savannah, Georgia, 1757 ***1640.10*** *p69*
Graham, B.; Quebec, 1857 ***9196.15*** *p25*
Graham, Barney 99; Vermont, 1901 ***5900.10*** *p162*
Graham, Ben; New York, 1835-1838 ***8197.10*** *p114*
Graham, Benjamin 22; Ontario, 1871 ***1823.15*** *p96*
Graham, Bryce; Alabama, 1839 ***1640.10*** *p69*
Graham, Catherine; Georgia, 1738 ***1640.10*** *p69*
Graham, Catherine MacDonald *SEE* Graham, Donald
Graham, Catherine MacDonald *SEE* Graham, John
Graham, Catherine MacLeod *SEE* Graham, Angus
Graham, Charles; Maryland, 1682 ***2524.55*** *p92*
Graham, Charles 42; Ontario, 1871 ***1823.28*** *p35*
Graham, Charles 60; Ontario, 1871 ***1823.15*** *p96*
Graham, Charlotte 16; Ontario, 1861 ***2896.28*** *p39*
Graham, Charlotte 17; Ontario, 1861 ***2896.28*** *p34*
Graham, Christopher 37; Ontario, 1871 ***1823.22*** *p63*
Graham, D.; Quebec, 1857 ***9196.15*** *p25*
Graham, Dan 28; Ontario, 1871 ***1823.15*** *p96*
Graham, Daniel 25; Virginia, 1774 ***1220.25*** *p76*
Graham, Daniel 50; Ontario, 1871 ***1823.15*** *p96*
Graham, Daniel 60; Ontario, 1871 ***1823.15*** *p96*
Graham, David; Georgia, 1752 ***1640.10*** *p69*
Graham, David; New York, 1812 ***8197.10*** *p231*
Graham, David; New York, 1840 ***8197.10*** *p167*
Graham, David 43; Ontario, 1871 ***1823.28*** *p35*
Graham, Dilman 27; Ontario, 1871 ***1823.15*** *p96*
Graham, Donald *SEE* Graham, William
Graham, Donald; Ontario, 1863 ***4537.32*** *p9*
Wife: Catherine MacDonald
Child: Ann
Child: Jane
Child: Norman
Child: Margaret
Child: John
Graham, Donald; Ontario, 1863 ***4537.32*** *p9*
Wife: Mary MacDonald
Child: Norman
Child: John
Graham, Duncan; New York, 1810 ***8197.10*** *p57*
Graham, E. D. 27; Ontario, 1861 ***2896.26*** *p3*
Graham, Edward 36; Ontario, 1871 ***1823.15*** *p96*
Graham, Effie *SEE* Graham, William
Graham, Effie; Ontario, 1855 ***4537.32*** *p28*
Graham, Elizabeth 25; Ontario, 1861 ***2896.27*** *p28*
Graham, Elizabeth 60; Ontario, 1871 ***1823.15*** *p96*
Graham, Elizabeth 66; Ontario, 1871 ***1823.15*** *p96*
Graham, Elizabeth 80; Ontario, 1871 ***1823.15*** *p96*
Graham, Ellen Ready; Vermont, 1839-1909 ***5900.10*** *p186*
Graham, Francis; New York, 1802 ***8197.10*** *p21*
Graham, Francis 66; Ontario, 1871 ***1823.15*** *p96*
Graham, George; New York, 1807 ***8197.10*** *p39*
Graham, George; New York, 1832-1838 ***8197.10*** *p114*
Graham, George; Pennsylvania, 1777 ***4629.10*** *p11*
Graham, George 17; Maryland, 1774 ***1220.25*** *p84*
Graham, George 37; Ontario, 1871 ***1823.15*** *p96*
Graham, George 40; Ontario, 1871 ***1823.15*** *p96*
Graham, George 53; Ontario, 1871 ***1823.15*** *p96*
Graham, Henry; Georgia, 1775 ***1640.10*** *p69*
Graham, Henry 26; Georgia, 1775 ***1220.25*** *p126*
Graham, Hugh; New York, 1837 ***8197.10*** *p88*
Graham, Hugh; Philadelphia, 1727 ***1224.2*** *p47*
Graham, Isaac 38; Ontario, 1871 ***1823.15*** *p96*
Graham, Israel 38; Ontario, 1861 ***2896.28*** *p31*
Graham, J. 32; Alaska, 1912 ***9196.1*** *p37*
Graham, J. 32; Yukon, 1912 ***9196.1*** *p37*
Graham, Jacob 25; Ontario, 1871 ***1823.28*** *p35*
Graham, James; Georgia, 1698 ***1640.13*** *p48*
Graham, James; Georgia, 1758 ***1640.10*** *p69*
Graham, James; New York, 1835 ***8197.10*** *p70*
Graham, James; New York, 1838 ***8197.10*** *p235*
Graham, James; New York, 1839 ***8197.10*** *p235*
Graham, James; Pennsylvania, 1843 ***6058.10*** *p16*
Graham, James; Savannah, Georgia, 1760 ***1640.10*** *p69*
Graham, James; Trinidad, 1806 ***1640.13*** *p48*
Graham, James 28; Ontario, 1871 ***1823.15*** *p96*
Graham, James 38; Ontario, 1871 ***1823.15*** *p96*
Graham, James 40; Ontario, 1871 ***1823.15*** *p96*
Graham, James 57; Ontario, 1861 ***2896.28*** *p39*
Graham, James 61; Ontario, 1871 ***1823.28*** *p35*
Graham, James 62; Ontario, 1871 ***1823.15*** *p96*
Graham, James 80; Ontario, 1871 ***1823.15*** *p96*
Graham, James H. 2; Ontario, 1861 ***2896.27*** *p25*
Graham, James L.; New York, 1840 ***8197.10*** *p168*
Graham, James W.; Pennsylvania, 1868 ***6058.10*** *p72*
Graham, Jane *SEE* Graham, Donald
Graham, Jane *SEE* Graham, William
Graham, Jane 48; Ontario, 1871 ***1823.28*** *p35*
Graham, Janet *SEE* Graham, Angus
Graham, Janet; Ontario, 1863 ***4537.32*** *p64*
Graham, Jhonson 55; Ontario, 1871 ***1823.15*** *p96*
Graham, Jno; Virginia, 1665-1666 ***6212.30*** *p23*
Graham, Johan; New York, 1834 ***8197.10*** *p73*
Graham, John *SEE* Graham, Donald
Graham, John *SEE* Graham, William
Graham, John; Charles Town, South Carolina, 1755 ***1224.2*** *p47*
Graham, John; Florida, 1769 ***1640.10*** *p70*
Graham, John; Georgia, 1738 ***1640.10*** *p69*
Graham, John; Georgia, 1753 ***1640.10*** *p69*
Graham, John; New York, 1821 ***8197.10*** *p232*
Graham, John; New York, 1838 ***8197.10*** *p235*
Graham, John; New York, New York, 1853 ***6058.10*** *p44*
Graham, John; Pennsylvania, 1840 ***6058.10*** *p16*
Graham, John; Quebec, 1850-1859 ***4537.32*** *p10*
Wife: Catherine MacDonald
Graham, John 25; Ontario, 1871 ***1823.28*** *p35*
Graham, John 26; Ontario, 1871 ***1823.15*** *p96*
Graham, John 30; Ontario, 1871 ***1823.15*** *p97*
Graham, John 30; Ontario, 1871 ***1823.28*** *p35*
Graham, John 32; Ontario, 1871 ***1823.15*** *p97*
Graham, John 35; Ontario, 1871 ***1823.15*** *p96*
Graham, John 35; Ontario, 1871 ***1823.22*** *p63*
Graham, John 38; Ontario, 1871 ***1823.15*** *p97*
Graham, John 40; Ontario, 1871 ***1823.28*** *p35*
Graham, John 65; Ontario, 1871 ***1823.15*** *p97*
Graham, John B.; New York, 1834 ***8197.10*** *p372*
Graham, Joseph; New Orleans, 1856 ***1224.3*** *p31*
Graham, Julia Ann; Vermont, 1856-1889 ***5900.10*** *p419*
Graham, Kenneth *SEE* Graham, William
Graham, Kirsty; Ontario, 1863 ***4537.32*** *p49*
Graham, Kirsty; Ontario, 1863 ***4537.32*** *p85*
Graham, Miss L.; Quebec, 1858 ***9196.15*** *p40*
Graham, Langford 28; Ontario, 1871 ***1823.15*** *p97*
Graham, Lecie 37; Ontario, 1871 ***1823.15*** *p97*
Graham, Lewis; New York, 1800 ***1224.3*** *p31*
Graham, Lydia 21; Ontario, 1861 ***2896.27*** *p25*
Graham, Margaret *SEE* Graham, Angus
Graham, Margaret *SEE* Graham, Donald
Graham, Margaret; Ontario, 1851 ***4537.32*** *p46*
Graham, Martha Ann 48; Ontario, 1871 ***1823.15*** *p97*
Graham, Mary *SEE* Graham, Angus
Graham, Mary; Ontario, 1861 ***2896.25*** *p1*
Graham, Mary 24; Ontario, 1861 ***2896.28*** *p31*
Graham, Mary 25; Ontario, 1871 ***1823.28*** *p35*
Graham, Mary 33; Ontario, 1861 ***2896.28*** *p31*
Graham, Mary 34; Virginia, 1775 ***1220.25*** *p142*
Graham, Mary A. 16; Ontario, 1861 ***2896.28*** *p31*
Graham, Mary MacDonald *SEE* Graham, Donald
Graham, Michael; Vermont, 1844-1917 ***5900.10*** *p276*
Graham, Mungo; Georgia, 1755 ***1640.10*** *p70*
Graham, Nancy 40; Ontario, 1871 ***1823.22*** *p63*
Graham, Norman *SEE* Graham, Donald
Graham, Norman *SEE* Graham, William
Graham, Norman; Quebec, 1841 ***4537.32*** *p10*
With parents
Graham, Ophelia 16; Ontario, 1861 ***2896.27*** *p25*
Graham, Patrick; Georgia, 1736 ***1640.10*** *p70*
Graham, Patrick; New York, New York, 1848 ***6058.10*** *p33*
Graham, Peter; New York, 1807 ***8197.10*** *p39*
Graham, Peter 18; Maryland, 1774 ***1220.25*** *p5*
Graham, Richard 37; Ontario, 1871 ***1823.28*** *p35*
Graham, Robert; Dominica, 1780 ***1640.13*** *p48*
Graham, Robert 25; Ontario, 1871 ***1823.28*** *p35*
Graham, Robert 40; Ontario, 1871 ***1823.15*** *p97*
Graham, Robert 42; Ontario, 1871 ***1823.15*** *p97*
Graham, Robert 46; Ontario, 1871 ***1823.22*** *p63*
Graham, Robert 61; Ontario, 1871 ***1823.28*** *p35*
Graham, Robert 63; Ontario, 1871 ***1823.15*** *p97*
Graham, Robert 71; Ontario, 1871 ***1823.28*** *p35*
Graham, Ronald 45; Ontario, 1871 ***1823.15*** *p97*
Graham, Rosanna Black; Vermont, 1832-1896 ***5900.10*** *p162*
Graham, Samuel; Pennsylvania, 1840 ***6058.10*** *p18*
Graham, Stephen E. 11; Ontario, 1861 ***2896.28*** *p31*
Graham, Susan 19; Ontario, 1861 ***2896.28*** *p39*
Graham, Susan 67; Ontario, 1871 ***1823.28*** *p35*
Graham, Thomas 30; Ontario, 1871 ***1823.15*** *p97*
Graham, Thomas 46; Ontario, 1871 ***1823.28*** *p35*
Graham, Thomas 55; Ontario, 1871 ***1823.15*** *p97*
Graham, Thomas R. 4; Ontario, 1861 ***2896.28*** *p31*
Graham, Thos 32; Ontario, 1871 ***1823.28*** *p35*
Graham, U. 18; Ontario, 1861 ***2896.26*** *p15*
Graham, William; New York, 1821 ***8197.10*** *p232*
Graham, William; New York, 1827 ***8197.10*** *p344*
Graham, William; New York, 1834 ***8197.10*** *p234*
Graham, William; New York, 1840 ***8197.10*** *p169*
Graham, William; Ontario, 1863 ***4537.32*** *p10*
Wife: Ann Campbell
Child: Norman
Child: Effie
Child: John
Child: Alexander
Child: Kenneth
Child: Donald
Child: Jane
Graham, William; Pennsylvania, 1840 ***6058.10*** *p16*
Graham, William 4; Ontario, 1861 ***2896.27*** *p28*
Graham, William 14; St. John Island, 1775 ***1220.25*** *p121*
Graham, William 32; Ontario, 1871 ***1823.22*** *p63*
Graham, William 39; Ontario, 1871 ***1823.28*** *p35*
Graham, William 40; Ontario, 1871 ***1823.15*** *p97*
Graham, William 48; Ontario, 1871 ***1823.15*** *p97*
Graham, William 49; Ontario, 1871 ***1823.28*** *p35*
Graham, William 50; Ontario, 1871 ***1823.15*** *p97*
Graham, William 53; Ontario, 1871 ***1823.15*** *p97*
Graham, William 58; Ontario, 1871 ***1823.15*** *p97*
Graham, William 60; Ontario, 1871 ***1823.15*** *p97*
Graham, William 60; Ontario, 1871 ***1823.22*** *p63*
Graham, William F. 14; Ontario, 1861 ***2896.28*** *p31*
Graham, William Leckie; Virgin Islands, 1843 ***1640.13*** *p48*
Grahame, Peter; Jamaica, 1755 ***1640.13*** *p48*
Grahand, Charles; Maryland, 1680 ***2524.55*** *p92*
Grahme, Richard; New York, 1803 ***8197.10*** *p13*
Graidy, James; New York, New York, 1870 ***3437.14*** *p116*
Grainger, Charels 32; Ontario, 1871 ***1823.15*** *p97*
Grainger, Edward; Maryland, 1661 ***2524.55*** *p177*
Grainger, James; St. Kitts, 1790 ***1640.13*** *p48*
Grainger, Willm.; Maryland, 1658 ***2524.55*** *p93*
Grallet, John; Maryland, 1658 ***2524.55*** *p93*
Gram, Hans; America, 1738 ***2856.30*** *p143*
Graman, Thomas; Maryland, 1672 ***2524.55*** *p93*
Grames, James 40; Ontario, 1871 ***1823.22*** *p63*
Gramling, Georg; Port uncertain, 1764 ***2856.30*** *p143*
Grammeyer, Matthaus; America, 1761 ***2856.30*** *p143*
Grams, Anna Maria; Port uncertain, 1751 ***2856.30*** *p143*
Granahan, Edward; New York, 1840 ***8197.10*** *p169*
Grandfield, Nancy; Vermont, 1835-1902 ***5900.10*** *p365*
Grandgerard, Joseph; New York, 1840 ***8197.10*** *p235*
Grandison, Isabella; Mississippi, 1780-1845 ***1640.10*** *p70*
Grandom, John; Pennsylvania, 1786 ***4629.10*** *p53*
Grandy, Catherine 60; Ontario, 1871 ***1823.15*** *p97*
Grandy, Mary 88; Ontario, 1871 ***1823.22*** *p63*
Graneis, Anna; America, 1735 ***2856.30*** *p143*
Graneling, James; Virginia, 1666-1667 ***6212.30*** *p35*
Grange, Mrs.; Quebec, 1856 ***9196.15*** *p5*
Grange, Peter 86; Vermont, 1891 ***5900.10*** *p52*
Grange, Robert 35; Ontario, 1871 ***1823.22*** *p63*
Grange, Stephen 38; Virginia, 1775 ***1220.25*** *p95*
Granger, Early; New York, 1840 ***8197.10*** *p170*
Granger, Geog; Virginia, 1671 ***6212.30*** *p44*
Granger, James; Maryland, 1680 ***2524.55*** *p93*
Granger, James 50; Ontario, 1871 ***1823.15*** *p97*
Granger, James 64; Ontario, 1871 ***1823.15*** *p97*
Granger, John; New York, 1838 ***8197.10*** *p114*
Granger, John; New York, 1838 ***8197.10*** *p379*
Granger, John 45; Ontario, 1871 ***1823.15*** *p97*
Granger, Robert; Maryland, 1690 ***1224.1*** *p25*
Granger, Thomas 26; Ontario, 1871 ***1823.15*** *p97*
Granger, William; New York, 1840 ***8197.10*** *p170*
Granges, Benjamin; Maryland, 1664 ***2524.55*** *p93*
Granier, Caspar; Port uncertain, 1769 ***2856.30*** *p143*
Granilln, Matette 18; Ontario, 1871 ***1823.15*** *p97*
Granka, Andrew; Maryland, 1910 ***3259.35*** *p18*
Grannis, F. 18; Ontario, 1861 ***2896.26*** *p15*
Grannis, H. 14; Ontario, 1861 ***2896.26*** *p15*
Grannis, L. 11; Ontario, 1861 ***2896.26*** *p15*

Gray, Joseph 19; Maryland, 1775 ***1220.25*** *p120*
Gray, Judith, Sr. *SEE* Gray, John
Gray, Judith, Jr. *SEE* Gray, John
Gray, Katharine *SEE* Gray, John
Gray, Katharine *SEE* Gray, Katharine
Gray, Katharine; Maryland, 1682 ***2524.55*** *p93*
Husband: John
Daughter: Katharine
Gray, Katharine; Maryland, 1682 ***2524.55*** *p93*
Father: John
Mother: Katharine
Gray, Leonard 55; Ontario, 1871 ***1823.15*** *p98*
Gray, Margaret; Georgia, 1741 ***1640.10*** *p74*
Gray, Mary; Maryland, 1666 ***2524.55*** *p244*
Gray, Mary 83; Ontario, 1871 ***1823.15*** *p98*
Gray, Michael 5; Vermont, 1861 ***5900.10*** *p527*
Gray, Michael 25; Maryland, 1775 ***1220.25*** *p100*
Gray, Miles; Maryland, 1672 ***2524.55*** *p93*
Gray, Nicholas; New York, 1809-1810 ***8197.10*** *p231*
Gray, Richard; Virginia, 1664-1665 ***6212.30*** *p16*
Gray, Richard K.; New York, 1840 ***8197.10*** *p236*
Gray, Robert; Maryland, 1660 ***2524.55*** *p93*
Gray, Robert; Pennsylvania, 1777 ***4629.10*** *p8*
Gray, Robert 15; Maryland, 1775 ***1220.25*** *p98*
Gray, Robert 56; Ontario, 1871 ***1823.28*** *p35*
Gray, Roderick; Florida, 1820 ***1640.10*** *p74*
Gray, Samuel 16; Baltimore, 1775 ***1220.25*** *p119*
Gray, Sarah J.; Vermont, 1854-1930 ***5900.10*** *p70*
Gray, T.; Quebec, 1858 ***9196.15*** *p35*
Gray, Thomas *SEE* Gray, Andrew
Gray, Thomas; Boston, 1782 ***1224.2*** *p48*
Gray, Thomas; New York, 1831 ***8197.10*** *p365*
Gray, Thomas; New York, 1831 ***8197.10*** *p370*
Gray, Thomas; Pennsylvania, 1777 ***4629.10*** *p21*
Gray, Thomas; Virginia, 1664 ***6212.30*** *p9*
Gray, Thomas 23; Philadelphia, 1774 ***1220.25*** *p43*
Gray, Thomas 31; Nova Scotia, 1774 ***1220.25*** *p135*
Gray, Thomas 60; Ontario, 1871 ***1823.15*** *p98*
Gray, Valentine; Vermont, 1849-1944 ***5900.10*** *p70*
Gray, William *SEE* Gray, Andrew
Gray, William; Augusta, Georgia, 1739 ***1640.10*** *p74*
Gray, William; Maryland, 1660 ***2524.55*** *p93*
Gray, William; New York, 1839 ***8197.10*** *p235*
Gray, William 17; Virginia, 1774 ***1220.25*** *p87*
Gray, William 21; Philadelphia, 1775 ***1220.25*** *p107*
Gray, William, Jr.; New York, 1840 ***8197.10*** *p385*
Gray, Willm.; Maryland, 1662 ***2524.55*** *p93*
Graybel, Michael; America, 1793 ***2856.30*** *p244*
Graybum, John; Buffalo, New York, 1846 ***6058.10*** *p44*
Graydon, John 57; Ontario, 1861 ***2896.28*** *p47*
Graydon, Samuel; New York, 1840 ***8197.10*** *p168*
Graydon, Samuel 43; Ontario, 1871 ***1823.28*** *p35*
Graysbury, Joseph; Pennsylvania, 1777 ***4629.10*** *p6*
Graysbury, Joseph; Pennsylvania, 1777 ***4629.10*** *p30*
Graysbury, Joseph; Pennsylvania, 1779 ***4629.10*** *p39*
Grayson, Anthony; New York, 1806 ***8197.10*** *p324*
Grayson, James; Pennsylvania, 1777 ***4629.10*** *p23*
Grayson, John; Virginia, 1733 ***1224.2*** *p48*
Graystock, Lucy 21; Maryland, 1775 ***1220.25*** *p102*
Graz, Minne 15; Ontario, 1871 ***1823.28*** *p35*
Grazdowski, Wetales; Maryland, 1910 ***3259.35*** *p18*
Grbich, Steve 25; Alaska, 1914 ***9196.1*** *p11*
Grcszeyniski, Piotr; Maryland, 1910 ***3259.35*** *p18*
Grczuzk, Josephh; Maryland, 1910 ***3259.35*** *p18*
Gready, Ann 11 *SEE* Gready, Thomas
Gready, Bridget 4 *SEE* Gready, Thomas
Gready, Catherine 2; Died enroute, 1849 ***1825.45*** *p34*
Gready, Catherine 36 *SEE* Gready, Thomas
Gready, Charles 35; Ontario, 1871 ***1823.15*** *p98*
Gready, Denis 30; New York, New York, 1848 ***1825.45*** *p34*
Brother: John 21
Sister: Honoria 20
Gready, Honoria 20 *SEE* Gready, Denis
Gready, John 14 *SEE* Gready, Thomas
Gready, John 21 *SEE* Gready, Denis
Gready, Lawrence; New York, New York, 1858 ***3437.14*** *p60*
Gready, Mary 18; New York, New York, 1848 ***1825.45*** *p34*
Gready, Mary 27 *SEE* Gready, Peter
Gready, Michael 3 months *SEE* Gready, Thomas
Gready, Pat 6 *SEE* Gready, Thomas
Gready, Peter 31; New York, New York, 1849 ***1825.45*** *p34*
Wife: Mary 27
Gready, Thomas 6 months; Died enroute, 1849 ***1825.45*** *p34*
Gready, Thomas 2 *SEE* Gready, Thomas
Gready, Thomas 41; New York, New York, 1849 ***1825.45*** *p34*
Wife: Catherine 36
Son: Pat 6
Daughter: Ann 11
Daughter: Bridget 4
Son: Thomas 2
Son: Michael 3 months
Son: John 14
Greanall, Richd; Virginia, 1671-1672 ***6212.30*** *p47*
Greaney, Bridget; Vermont, 1854-1923 ***5900.10*** *p118*
Greaney, Cornelius; Vermont, 1803-1888 ***5900.10*** *p140*
Greaney, Dennis 62; Vermont, 1880 ***5900.10*** *p144*
Greaney, Elizabeth; Vermont, 1836-1919 ***5900.10*** *p141*
Greaney, Johanna 22; Vermont, 1873 ***5900.10*** *p111*
Greaney, Katy Connor 45; Vermont, 1879 ***5900.10*** *p110*
Greaney, Mary Deady 75; Vermont, 1911 ***5900.10*** *p144*
Greaney, Maurice; Vermont, 1857-1868 ***5900.10*** *p141*
Greasen, Thomas 45; Ontario, 1871 ***1823.22*** *p63*
Greasley, Thomas Taft; New York, 1840 ***8197.10*** *p170*
Greason, George; New York, 1828-1834 ***8197.10*** *p307*
Greatrex, Brown 27; Ontario, 1871 ***1823.28*** *p35*
Greaves, Adam; Charles Town, South Carolina, 1738 ***1224.2*** *p48*
Greaves, James W.; Vermont, 1844-1931 ***5900.10*** *p443*
Greb, Henry 41; Ontario, 1871 ***1823.15*** *p98*
Greber, Dorothea; America, 1750 ***2856.30*** *p144*
Grebonoski, Leokadia; Maryland, 1910 ***3259.35*** *p18*
Grebs, Adam; America, 1738 ***2856.30*** *p245*
Grecz, Madeline; Maryland, 1910 ***3259.35*** *p18*
Greda, Kundigunda; Maryland, 1910 ***3259.35*** *p18*
Greedy, William 28; Maryland, 1775 ***1220.25*** *p105*
Greel, Arnold; Port uncertain, 1788 ***2856.30*** *p144*
Greem, Feltin; America, 1740 ***2856.30*** *p144*
Green, Dr.; Quebec, 1856 ***9196.15*** *p9*
Green, Miss; Quebec, 1856 ***9196.15*** *p11*
Green, Miss; Quebec, 1857 ***9196.15*** *p23*
Green, Miss; Quebec, 1857 ***9196.15*** *p26*
Green, Mr.; Quebec, 1857 ***9196.15*** *p24*
Green, Mr.; Quebec, 1858 ***9196.15*** *p38*
Green, Mrs.; Maryland, 1669 ***2524.55*** *p93*
Green, Mrs.; Quebec, 1857 ***9196.15*** *p24*
Green, Abram; Virginia, 1671-1672 ***6212.30*** *p47*
Green, Adam 54; Ontario, 1871 ***1823.15*** *p98*
Green, Alexander; Mississippi, 1828-1845 ***1640.10*** *p74*
Green, Alice; Maryland, 1678 ***2524.55*** *p93*
Green, Andrew 72; Ontario, 1871 ***1823.15*** *p98*
Green, Andrew H. 41; Ontario, 1871 ***1823.15*** *p98*
Green, Andy; Maryland, 1910 ***3259.35*** *p18*
Green, Ann Murphy 48; Vermont, 1892 ***5900.10*** *p239*
Green, Annie 1; Ontario, 1861 ***2896.27*** *p2*
Green, B.; Quebec, 1858 ***9196.15*** *p40*
Green, Betsy 22; Ontario, 1871 ***1823.15*** *p98*
Green, Bridget; Vermont, 1846-1929 ***5900.10*** *p538*
Green, Bridget Murphy; Vermont, 1835-1911 ***5900.10*** *p248*
Green, C. 40; Ontario, 1861 ***2896.26*** *p13*
Green, Caroline 7; Ontario, 1861 ***2896.27*** *p2*
Green, Catherine; Vermont, 1847-1926 ***5900.10*** *p380*
Green, Catherine 28; Ontario, 1861 ***2896.27*** *p2*
Green, Charles S.; Vermont, 1852-1888 ***5900.10*** *p181*
Green, Cornclins 35; Ontario, 1871 ***1823.15*** *p98*
Green, David 33; Ontario, 1871 ***1823.15*** *p98*
Green, Delia; Vermont, 1867-1958 ***5900.10*** *p298*
Green, Edward; Vermont, 1836-1916 ***5900.10*** *p77*
Green, Edward 32; Ontario, 1871 ***1823.15*** *p98*
Green, Edward 42; Baltimore, 1775 ***1220.25*** *p117*
Green, Edward 84; Ontario, 1871 ***1823.15*** *p98*
Green, Eliza McChesney 75; Vermont, 1883 ***5900.10*** *p493*
Green, Ellen 13; Ontario, 1861 ***2896.28*** *p22*
Green, Ellen 65; Vermont, 1907 ***5900.10*** *p380*
Green, Ellen Charlotte Bennett; Baltimore, 1828 ***1224.3*** *p31*
Green, Francis 32; Ontario, 1871 ***1823.28*** *p36*
Green, Frederick 30; Ontario, 1871 ***1823.15*** *p98*
Green, G. 2; Ontario, 1861 ***2896.26*** *p13*
Green, George; Maryland, 1667 ***2524.55*** *p93*
Green, George 15; Maryland, 1775 ***1220.25*** *p102*
Green, George 39; Ontario, 1871 ***1823.15*** *p98*
Green, Helen; Vermont, 1858-1920 ***5900.10*** *p96*
Green, Henry; Maryland, 1661 ***2524.55*** *p177*
Green, Henry 48; Ontario, 1871 ***1823.15*** *p98*
Green, Isaac; New York, 1838 ***8197.10*** *p234*
Green, Isaac, Jr.; Pennsylvania, 1777 ***4629.10*** *p26*
Green, J. 15; Ontario, 1861 ***2896.26*** *p13*
Green, Jacob 56; Ontario, 1871 ***1823.22*** *p63*
Green, James; New York, 1840 ***8197.10*** *p236*
Green, James 55; Ontario, 1871 ***1823.15*** *p98*
Green, Jane 63; Vermont, 1891 ***5900.10*** *p212*
Green, Joan 39; Ontario, 1871 ***1823.15*** *p98*
Green, Johannah Reagan; Vermont, 1847-1921 ***5900.10*** *p137*
Green, John; Maryland, 1668 ***2524.55*** *p42*
Green, John; New York, 1807 ***8197.10*** *p39*
Green, John; New York, 1826 ***8197.10*** *p233*
Green, John; New York, 1840 ***8197.10*** *p236*
Green, John; Pennsylvania, 1777 ***4629.10*** *p28*
Green, John; Vermont, 1820-1902 ***5900.10*** *p216*
Green, John; Vermont, 1849-1928 ***5900.10*** *p96*
Green, John; Virginia, 1694 ***1224.1*** *p25*
Green, John 25; Virginia, 1774 ***1220.25*** *p93*
Green, John 35; Ontario, 1871 ***1823.15*** *p98*
Green, Joseph; Kingston, Jamaica, 1847 ***1640.13*** *p49*
Green, Joseph; Virginia, 1679 ***6212.30*** *p54*
Green, L. 7; Ontario, 1861 ***2896.26*** *p13*
Green, L. 18; Vancouver, British Columbia, 1910 ***9196.1*** *p15*
Green, Mary; Vermont, 1826-1901 ***5900.10*** *p216*
Green, Mary; Vermont, 1885 ***5900.10*** *p298*
Green, Mary Burns; Vermont, 1843-1910 ***5900.10*** *p77*
Green, Mary Roddy 27; Vermont, 1886 ***5900.10*** *p569*
Green, Matthew; New York, New York, 1852 ***1224.3*** *p31*
Green, Michael 48; Vermont, 1888 ***5900.10*** *p239*
Green, Michael J.; New York, 1840 ***8197.10*** *p169*
Green, Michal 47; Ontario, 1871 ***1823.22*** *p63*
Green, Moses 60; Ontario, 1871 ***1823.15*** *p99*
Green, Patrick; New York, 1830 ***8197.10*** *p353*
Green, Patrick H.; Vermont, 1837-1911 ***5900.10*** *p248*
Green, Peter 25; Baltimore, 1775 ***1220.25*** *p117*
Green, Peter 37; Ontario, 1871 ***1823.15*** *p99*
Green, Peter 38; Ontario, 1871 ***1823.15*** *p99*
Green, Peter 69; Ontario, 1871 ***1823.15*** *p99*
Green, Philip, Sr. 68; Ontario, 1871 ***1823.28*** *p36*
Green, Richard; Jamaica, 1794 ***1224.2*** *p48*
Green, Richard; New York, New York, 1794 ***1224.2*** *p48*
Green, Richard 18; Virginia, 1774 ***1220.25*** *p87*
Green, Richard 22; Ontario, 1871 ***1823.15*** *p99*
Green, Richard 35; Maryland, 1774 ***1220.25*** *p42*
Green, Richard 35; Virginia, 1774 ***1220.25*** *p46*
Green, Robert; Vermont, 1838-1923 ***5900.10*** *p137*
Green, Robert 5; Ontario, 1861 ***2896.27*** *p2*
Green, Robert 40; Ontario, 1871 ***1823.15*** *p99*
Green, Rosa 55; Vermont, 1891 ***5900.10*** *p536*
Green, Samuel 26; Maryland, 1774 ***1220.25*** *p51*
Green, Sarah A.; Vermont, 1851-1912 ***5900.10*** *p496*
Green, Sarah E. 29; Vermont, 1868 ***5900.10*** *p516*
Green, Simon 63; Ontario, 1871 ***1823.22*** *p63*
Green, Susan; Maryland, 1678 ***2524.55*** *p93*
Green, Thomas; Maryland, 1633 ***2524.55*** *p88*
Green, Thomas; Maryland, 1644 ***2524.55*** *p93*
Green, Thomas; Virginia, 1729 ***1224.2*** *p48*
Green, Thomas 15; Baltimore, 1775 ***1220.25*** *p119*
Green, Thomas 50; Ontario, 1871 ***1823.15*** *p99*
Green, Thomas 69; Ontario, 1871 ***1823.15*** *p99*
Green, Walter 65; Ontario, 1871 ***1823.22*** *p63*
Green, Will.; Maryland, 1652 ***2524.55*** *p93*
Green, William; Maryland, 1681 ***2524.55*** *p93*
Green, William; New York, 1802 ***8197.10*** *p21*
Green, William 4; Ontario, 1861 ***2896.26*** *p13*
Green, William 15; America, 1774 ***1220.25*** *p36*
Green, William 37; Ontario, 1871 ***1823.15*** *p99*
Green, William 49; Ontario, 1871 ***1823.15*** *p99*
Green, William 60; Ontario, 1871 ***1823.28*** *p36*
Green, William 63; Ontario, 1871 ***1823.15*** *p99*
Green, William 67; Ontario, 1871 ***1823.15*** *p99*
Green, William Alexander; New York, 1840 ***8197.10*** *p168*
Greenacre, James; New York, 1834 ***8197.10*** *p234*
Greenall, Rich; Virginia, 1672 ***6212.30*** *p50*
Greenan, Thomas 60; Ontario, 1871 ***1823.15*** *p99*
Greenaway, Edward; Maryland, 1665 ***2524.55*** *p93*
Greenaway, G.; Quebec, 1856 ***9196.15*** *p8*
Greenaway, Robert 34; Ontario, 1871 ***1823.15*** *p99*
Greenaway, William 32; Ontario, 1871 ***1823.22*** *p63*
Greene, Mr.; Quebec, 1856 ***9196.15*** *p10*
Greene, Ann; Maryland, 1663 ***2524.55*** *p93*
Greene, Edward; New York, 1840 ***8197.10*** *p236*
Greene, Edward; Virginia, 1698 ***1224.1*** *p25*
Greene, Erasmus; Maryland, 1682 ***2524.55*** *p93*
Greene, Geo.; Maryland, 1653 ***2524.55*** *p93*
Greene, George; Virginia, 1666 ***6212.30*** *p25*
Greene, H.; New York, 1845 ***1640.10*** *p74*
Wife: Margaret
Greene, Jane; Maryland, 1664 ***2524.55*** *p94*
Greene, Jane; Virginia, 1664 ***6212.30*** *p9*
Greene, Jean; Virginia, 1664 ***6212.30*** *p9*
Greene, John; Maryland, 1654 ***2524.55*** *p94*
Greene, John; Maryland, 1662 ***2524.55*** *p94*
Greene, John; Maryland, 1667 ***2524.55*** *p94*
Greene, Leonard; Maryland, 1644 ***2524.55*** *p94*
Greene, Margaret *SEE* Greene, H.
Greene, Margarett; Maryland, 1682 ***2524.55*** *p94*
Greene, Mary Fitzgerald; Vermont, 1852-1892 ***5900.10*** *p471*
Greene, Maudley; Maryland, 1665 ***2524.55*** *p210*
Greene, Michael; New York, 1839 ***8197.10*** *p131*
Greene, Peter; Virginia, 1678 ***1224.1*** *p25*
Greene, Rich; Virginia, 1664 ***6212.30*** *p9*

Greene, Samuel 46; Ontario, 1871 ***1823.28*** *p36*
Greene, Samuel Davis; Pennsylvania, 1785 ***4629.10*** *p44*
Greene, Suzanna; Maryland, 1661 ***2524.55*** *p94*
Greene, Thomas; Maryland, 1644 ***2524.55*** *p94*
Greene, Thomas; Maryland, 1667 ***2524.55*** *p94*
Greene, Thomas; Maryland, 1672 ***2524.55*** *p94*
Greene, Thomas; Virginia, 1663 ***6212.30*** *p2*
Greene, W. P.; Quebec, 1856 ***9196.15*** *p5*
Greene, Mrs. W. P.; Quebec, 1856 ***9196.15*** *p5*
Greene, William; Virginia, 1667 ***6212.30*** *p36*
Greene, Wm; Virginia, 1666 ***6212.30*** *p25*
Greener, James 48; Ontario, 1861 ***2896.25*** *p33*
Greener, Jane 45; Ontario, 1861 ***2896.25*** *p33*
Greenfield, George; New York, 1838 ***8197.10*** *p114*
Greenfield, James; New York, 1900 ***1640.13*** *p49*
Greenfield, Thomas; Maryland, 1666 ***2524.55*** *p94*
Greenham, Mrs.; Quebec, 1857 ***9196.15*** *p20*
Greening, Thomas 33; Ontario, 1871 ***1823.15*** *p99*
Greenish, Henry; Maryland, 1670 ***2524.55*** *p94*
Greenleaf, John; New York, 1828 ***8197.10*** *p234*
Greenley, James 62; Ontario, 1871 ***1823.22*** *p63*
Greenman, Lot 30; Ontario, 1871 ***1823.28*** *p36*
Greenough, William; Boston, 1684 ***1224.1*** *p25*
Greenshields, Mr.; Portland, Maine, 1858 ***9196.15*** *p30*
Greenshields, Mr.; Quebec, 1857 ***9196.15*** *p22*
Greenside, Matthew 40; Ontario, 1871 ***1823.15*** *p99*
Greenslade, Francis; Illinois, 1838 ***1224.3*** *p31*
Greensled, George 50; Ontario, 1871 ***1823.15*** *p99*
Greenvill, Bernard; Virginia, 1666 ***6212.30*** *p28*
Greenway, Mrs.; Maryland, 1650 ***2524.55*** *p94*
Greenway, John 30; Ontario, 1871 ***1823.15*** *p99*
Greenway, William; Pennsylvania, 1777 ***4629.10*** *p7*
Greenwell, Bridgett; Maryland, 1658 ***2524.55*** *p94*
Greenwell, James *SEE* Greenwell, John
Greenwell, John; Maryland, 1658 ***2524.55*** *p94*
Wife: Mary
Son: James
Greenwell, Mary *SEE* Greenwell, John
Greenwood, Armiger; Maryland, 1659 ***2524.55*** *p94*
Wife: Christian
Greenwood, Christian *SEE* Greenwood, Armiger
Greenwood, Elizabeth 36 *SEE* Greenwood, John
Greenwood, George 47; Ontario, 1871 ***1823.22*** *p63*
Greenwood, Henry 61; Ontario, 1871 ***1823.22*** *p63*
Greenwood, Isaac; Barbados, 1700 ***1224.2*** *p48*
Greenwood, Isaac; Boston, 1700 ***1224.2*** *p48*
Greenwood, James 29; Ontario, 1871 ***1823.15*** *p99*
Greenwood, John 40; Halifax, Nova Scotia, 1774 ***1220.25*** *p138*
Wife: Elizabeth 36
With child 8
With child 6
With child 4
With child 10
Greenwood, John 40; Ontario, 1871 ***1823.22*** *p63*
Greenwood, John 55; Ontario, 1871 ***1823.22*** *p63*
Greenwood, Philip 58; Ontario, 1871 ***1823.15*** *p99*
Greenwood, Thomas 40; Ontario, 1871 ***1823.22*** *p63*
Greenwood, William; New York, 1840 ***8197.10*** *p235*
Greeor, James 60; Ontario, 1871 ***1823.28*** *p36*
Greeovich, N. J. 25; Alaska, 1912 ***9196.1*** *p38*
Greeovich, N. J. 25; Yukon, 1912 ***9196.1*** *p38*
Greepwick, Mr.; Quebec, 1856 ***9196.15*** *p11*
Greer, Edward 50; Ontario, 1871 ***1823.28*** *p36*
Greer, George; New York, 1829 ***8197.10*** *p351*
Greer, George 40; Ontario, 1871 ***1823.15*** *p99*
Greer, John; Pennsylvania, 1787 ***4629.10*** *p55*
Greer, John 45; Ontario, 1871 ***1823.15*** *p99*
Greer, Joseph; New York, 1831 ***8197.10*** *p355*
Greer, Samuel 36; Ontario, 1871 ***1823.15*** *p99*
Greer, Thomas 58; Ontario, 1871 ***1823.22*** *p63*
Greer, William 50; Ontario, 1871 ***1823.15*** *p99*
Greere, John; Maryland, 1661 ***2524.55*** *p94*
Wife: Margarett
Greere, Margarett *SEE* Greere, John
Greete, Conrad; New York, 1821 ***8197.10*** *p232*
Greeve, Archibald; New York, 1840 ***8197.10*** *p169*
Greeves, David 44; Ontario, 1871 ***1823.22*** *p64*
Greeves, James 36; Ontario, 1871 ***1823.22*** *p64*
Greeves, Jane 35; Ontario, 1871 ***1823.28*** *p36*
Greeves, Nathaniel 40; Ontario, 1871 ***1823.28*** *p36*
Greey, Mr.; Quebec, 1856 ***9196.15*** *p9*
Greey, Mrs.; Quebec, 1856 ***9196.15*** *p9*
Greff, Jakob; Port uncertain, 1757 ***2856.30*** *p144*
Greffen, Stephen; New Orleans, 1791 ***4629.10*** *p76*
Greffs, Margarete; Canada, 1764 ***2856.30*** *p144*
Greg, John 56; Ontario, 1871 ***1823.15*** *p99*
Greg, Thomas; West Indies, 1699 ***1640.13*** *p49*
Gregar, August 32; Ontario, 1871 ***1823.28*** *p36*
Gregg, Captain; Georgia, 1765 ***1640.10*** *p74*
Gregg, Alexander 40; Ontario, 1871 ***1823.22*** *p64*
Gregg, Catharine Lillis 59; Vermont, 1900 ***5900.10*** *p108*
Gregg, Daniel; Philadelphia, 1837 ***6058.10*** *p29*
Gregg, Delia M.; Vermont, 1858-1935 ***5900.10*** *p45*
Gregg, George 31; Ontario, 1871 ***1823.28*** *p36*
Gregg, Morris 67; Vermont, 1899 ***5900.10*** *p320*
Gregg, Patrick 58; Vermont, 1900 ***5900.10*** *p108*
Gregg, Thomas; New York, 1825-1834 ***8197.10*** *p308*
Gregg, William 34; Ontario, 1871 ***1823.28*** *p36*
Gregg, William 42; Ontario, 1871 ***1823.15*** *p99*
Gregg, William 46; Ontario, 1871 ***1823.15*** *p99*
Gregg, William T.; New York, 1838 ***8197.10*** *p114*
Greggor, Henrietta 69; Ontario, 1871 ***1823.22*** *p64*
Gregon, James 39; Ontario, 1871 ***1823.22*** *p64*
Gregor, John 29; Ontario, 1871 ***1823.28*** *p36*
Gregor, Theodore 38; Ontario, 1871 ***1823.15*** *p99*
Gregorek, John; Maryland, 1910 ***3259.35*** *p18*
Gregory, Mrs.; Maryland, 1651 ***2524.55*** *p94*
Gregory, Caroline; Vermont, 1834-1896 ***5900.10*** *p195*
Gregory, Catherine 68; Vermont, 1915 ***5900.10*** *p79*
Gregory, Edward 38; Maryland, 1774 ***1220.25*** *p72*
Gregory, Elizabeth; Vermont, 1845-1880 ***5900.10*** *p76*
Gregory, Ellen; Vermont, 1843-1922 ***5900.10*** *p76*
Gregory, George; Rhode Island, 1855 ***1224.3*** *p31*
Gregory, Henry; New England, 1652 ***1224.1*** *p25*
Gregory, Humphry; Virginia, 1665-1666 ***6212.30*** *p23*
Gregory, James; Georgia, 1766 ***1640.10*** *p75*
Gregory, James; Pennsylvania, 1777 ***4629.10*** *p15*
Gregory, John; Maryland, 1671 ***2524.55*** *p94*
Gregory, John; New York, 1837 ***8197.10*** *p374*
Gregory, John; Pennsylvania, 1785 ***4629.10*** *p48*
Gregory, John; Virginia, 1702 ***1224.2*** *p48*
Gregory, John 46; Ontario, 1871 ***1823.15*** *p99*
Gregory, Josephine; Vermont, 1854-1911 ***5900.10*** *p274*
Gregory, Sarah; Vermont, 1832-1919 ***5900.10*** *p88*
Gregory, Susanna Farley; Virginia, 1656 ***1224.1*** *p21*
Gregory, T. A.; St. John, New Brunswick, 1857 ***9196.15*** *p12*
Gregory, Thomas; Pennsylvania, 1777 ***4629.10*** *p9*
Gregory, Thomas 39; Ontario, 1871 ***1823.15*** *p99*
Gregory, William 22; Ontario, 1871 ***1823.22*** *p64*
Gregson, Mrs.; Portland, Maine, 1858 ***9196.15*** *p31*
Gregson, Anthony 69; British Columbia, 1917 ***9196.1*** *p70*
Gregson, Anthony 69; Oregon, 1917 ***9196.1*** *p70*
Gregson, James 63; Ontario, 1871 ***1823.28*** *p36*
Gregson, Thomas; New England, 1640 ***1224.1*** *p25*
Greham, David 42; Ontario, 1871 ***1823.28*** *p36*
Greham, John; New York, New York, 1853 ***6058.10*** *p44*
Greham, Patrick; New York, New York, 1848 ***6058.10*** *p33*
Grehan, Margaret W.; Vermont, 1855-1929 ***5900.10*** *p62*
Grehl, Maria Barbara; America, 1770 ***2856.30*** *p144*
Greiason, William 42; Ontario, 1871 ***1823.15*** *p99*
Greiff, David; Port uncertain, 1774 ***2856.30*** *p144*
Greiffenstein, Valentin; Port uncertain, 1732 ***2856.30*** *p144*
Greig, Alexander; Jamaica, 1776 ***1640.13*** *p50*
Greig, Alexander Mount; New York, 1835 ***8197.10*** *p316*
Greig, David; New York, 1788 ***1224.2*** *p48*
Greig, James; New York, 1807 ***8197.10*** *p39*
Greig, John M. 34; Ontario, 1871 ***1823.28*** *p36*
Greig, John Whittet; New Orleans, 1848 ***1640.10*** *p75*
Greig, Robert; Mobile, Alabama, 1840 ***1640.10*** *p75*
Greig, William; Mobile, Alabama, 1828-1845 ***1640.10*** *p75*
Greig, William; New York, 1834-1838 ***8197.10*** *p114*
Greimm, Veltin; America, 1740 ***2856.30*** *p144*
Grein, Anna Magdalena; Port uncertain, 1786 ***2856.30*** *p144*
Grein, Juliana; Port uncertain, 1749 ***2856.30*** *p144*
Grein, Peter; Port uncertain, 1749 ***2856.30*** *p144*
Greiner, Andreas; America, 1766 ***2856.30*** *p144*
Greiner, Georg; Port uncertain, 1767 ***2856.30*** *p144*
Greiner, Hans Adam; America, 1766 ***2856.30*** *p144*
Greiner, Heinrich; Port uncertain, 1768 ***2856.30*** *p144*
With wife & children
Greing, Patrick; New Hampshire, 1724 ***4628.40*** *p44*
Greinood, Joseph 59; Ontario, 1871 ***1823.15*** *p99*
Greinthowski, John; Maryland, 1910 ***3259.35*** *p18*
Greischer, Margarete; Port uncertain, 1754 ***2856.30*** *p144*
Greitz, Johann Henrich; America, 1753 ***2856.30*** *p145*
Greive, George; America, n.d. ***1224.3*** *p32*
Greive, Oswell 35; Ontario, 1871 ***1823.22*** *p64*
Greives, John 40; Ontario, 1871 ***1823.15*** *p99*
Grell, Christian 57; Ontario, 1871 ***1823.15*** *p99*
Grelle, Peter; Port uncertain, 1783 ***2856.30*** *p145*
Grelle, Peter; Port uncertain, 1785 ***2856.30*** *p151*
Grellet, Stephen; New York, 1803 ***8197.10*** *p12*
Grelling, John; Savannah, Georgia, 1768 ***1640.10*** *p75*
Grenda, Joseph; Maryland, 1910 ***3259.35*** *p18*
Grendon, Thomas; Virginia, 1685 ***1224.1*** *p25*
Greneway, Jacob 39; Ontario, 1871 ***1823.22*** *p64*
Grenfell, Edwin 30; Ontario, 1871 ***1823.28*** *p36*
Grenfell, John 46; Ontario, 1871 ***1823.28*** *p36*
Grenier, Felix James; New York, 1806 ***8197.10*** *p31*
Greniker, Thomas; New York, 1827 ***8197.10*** *p344*
Grennan, Jane; Vermont, 1836-1891 ***5900.10*** *p76*
Grennan, Michael; Vermont, 1831-1907 ***5900.10*** *p76*
Grenoway, James; Maryland, 1665 ***2524.55*** *p94*
Grensbrack, Machol; Maryland, 1910 ***3259.35*** *p18*
Grenville, Edward 29; Georgia, 1774 ***1220.25*** *p48*
Grenzel, Johann; Port uncertain, 1767 ***2856.30*** *p145*
Grescher, Johann Georg; Port uncertain, 1776 ***2856.30*** *p145*
Greser, Johann Adam; Port uncertain, 1753 ***2856.30*** *p145*
Gresham, James; Virginia, 1664 ***6212.30*** *p8*
Gresham, Mark; Virginia, 1665-1666 ***6212.30*** *p22*
Gresham, Mary; Maryland, 1659 ***2524.55*** *p215*
Gresham, Otway; Boston, 1717 ***1224.2*** *p48*
Gresham, Wm; Virginia, 1664 ***6212.30*** *p7*
Gresie, Frederick 47; Ontario, 1871 ***1823.28*** *p36*
Gresinski, Aleck; Maryland, 1910 ***3259.35*** *p18*
Gresley, Jeffery; Virginia, 1791 ***1224.2*** *p48*
Gresor, Frederick 32; Ontario, 1871 ***1823.28*** *p36*
Gress, Philipp; America, 1788 ***2856.30*** *p151*
Gressam, John; Maryland, 1682 ***2524.55*** *p94*
Gretereck, Daniel; Maryland, 1681 ***2524.55*** *p94*
Grether, . . .; Port uncertain, 1689 ***2856.30*** *p145*
With 3 siblings
Grether, . . .; Port uncertain, 1719 ***2856.30*** *p145*
With 3 siblings
Grether, Anna Maria; Port uncertain, 1775 ***2856.30*** *p145*
Gretton, George 19; Virginia, 1774 ***1220.25*** *p89*
Gretz, Anna Margarete; Port uncertain, 1786 ***2856.30*** *p144*
Gretz, Jacob; Port uncertain, 1739 ***2856.30*** *p145*
Greudly, Margt; Maryland, 1674 ***2524.55*** *p94*
Greulich, Johann; Port uncertain, 1728 ***2856.30*** *p145*
Greulich, Johann Adam; Port uncertain, 1767 ***2856.30*** *p145*
Greulich, Philipp; Port uncertain, 1727 ***2856.30*** *p145*
Greville, James; New York, 1839 ***8197.10*** *p130*
Greville, Nellie; Vermont, 1947 ***5900.10*** *p551*
Grevin, Maria Elisabeth; Port uncertain, 1778 ***2856.30*** *p145*
Grew, Ludwell Dampier; New York, 1840 ***8197.10*** *p169*
Grey, Clara 38; Ontario, 1871 ***1823.15*** *p99*
Grey, Edward 36; Ontario, 1871 ***1823.22*** *p64*
Grey, Geo; Virginia, 1674 ***6212.30*** *p52*
Grey, Henry; Virginia, 1675 ***1224.1*** *p25*
Grey, James; Maryland, 1665 ***2524.55*** *p94*
Grey, John; New England, 1663 ***1224.1*** *p25*
Grey, John 48; Ontario, 1871 ***1823.28*** *p36*
Grey, Joseph 27; Alaska, 1914 ***9196.1*** *p24*
Grey, Martin; Milwaukee, 1899 ***1640.13*** *p50*
Grey, Robert 34; Ontario, 1871 ***1823.22*** *p64*
Grey, Stephen 45; Ontario, 1871 ***1823.15*** *p99*
Grey, William 30; Ontario, 1871 ***1823.15*** *p99*
Greyling, Susanna; Port uncertain, 1751 ***2856.30*** *p145*
Greyson, William; New York, 1807 ***8197.10*** *p39*
Grezer, Josef; Port uncertain, 1790 ***2856.30*** *p145*
Grgegonak, Teofil; Maryland, 1910 ***3259.35*** *p18*
Grian, Andrew 38; Ontario, 1871 ***1823.15*** *p99*
Gribb, John; Virginia, 1698 ***1224.1*** *p25*
Gribbin, James; Vermont, 1833-1903 ***5900.10*** *p145*
Gribbin, Nancy McLane; Vermont, 1831-1908 ***5900.10*** *p145*
Gribbin, Sarah A. 33; Vermont, 1872 ***5900.10*** *p323*
Gribbon, Jane; Vermont, 1842-1906 ***5900.10*** *p592*
Gribling, Jean; Port uncertain, 1770 ***2856.30*** *p145*
Grice, Caesar; Maryland, 1754 ***1224.2*** *p48*
Grice, Charles; New York, 1838 ***8197.10*** *p115*
Grice, John; New York, 1804 ***8197.10*** *p27*
Grice, John; New York, 1807 ***8197.10*** *p330*
Grice, John; Virginia, 1686 ***1224.1*** *p58*
Grice, Peter; New York, 1853 ***1224.3*** *p32*
Grice, Robt; Virginia, 1671 ***6212.30*** *p44*
Gricz, Mary; Maryland, 1910 ***3259.35*** *p18*
Griebel, Jakob; Port uncertain, 1783 ***2856.30*** *p145*
Griebel, Konrad; Port uncertain, 1772 ***2856.30*** *p145*
Grief, Charles; Ontario, 1871 ***1823.28*** *p36*
Grief, Jacob; Port uncertain, 1753 ***2856.30*** *p145*
Grier, Alex 57; Ontario, 1861 ***2896.28*** *p6*
Grier, E. A. 5; Ontario, 1861 ***2896.28*** *p6*
Grier, E. W. 9; Ontario, 1861 ***2896.28*** *p6*
Grier, G. 14; Ontario, 1861 ***2896.28*** *p6*
Grier, H. M. 32; Ontario, 1861 ***2896.28*** *p6*
Grier, J.; Pennsylvania, 1781 ***4629.10*** *p42*
Grier, John; Pennsylvania, 1868 ***6058.10*** *p77*
Grier, Patrick 46; Ontario, 1871 ***1823.28*** *p36*
Grier, S. 27; Ontario, 1861 ***2896.28*** *p6*
Grier, Samuel 27; Ontario, 1871 ***1823.28*** *p36*
Grierson, Mr.; Quebec, 1858 ***9196.15*** *p38*
Grierson, Mrs.; Quebec, 1858 ***9196.15*** *p38*
Grierson, Arabella 52; Ontario, 1871 ***1823.22*** *p64*
Grierson, James; Augusta, Georgia, 1776 ***1640.10*** *p75*
Grierson, James; Augusta, Georgia, 1789 ***1224.2*** *p48*

Grierson, John 66; Ontario, 1871 ***1823.22*** *p64*
Grierson, Joseph; Jamaica, 1849 ***1640.13*** *p50*
Grierson, William 35; Ontario, 1871 ***1823.28*** *p36*
Gries, Anna Maria; Port uncertain, 1764 ***2856.30*** *p145*
Gries, Johanna; Maryland, 1910 ***3259.35*** *p18*
Griesang, Konrad; Port uncertain, 1783 ***2856.30*** *p145*
Griesbach, Elisabeth; Port uncertain, 1776 ***2856.30*** *p145*
Griesemer, Theobald; Port uncertain, 1777 ***2856.30*** *p146*
Grieser, Miss; Port uncertain, 1764 ***2856.30*** *p146*
Grieser, Konrad; Canada, 1752 ***2856.30*** *p146*
Griesinger, Georg; Port uncertain, 1785 ***2856.30*** *p146*
Griesinger, Michael; America, 1744 ***2856.30*** *p146*
Griesmeyer, Jakob; Port uncertain, 1754 ***2856.30*** *p146* With wife
Griess, Jakob; America, 1749 ***2856.30*** *p146*
Griess, Johann; Port uncertain, 1694 ***2856.30*** *p146*
Griessbach, Sophia; Port uncertain, 1731 ***2856.30*** *p146*
Griesser, Anna Maria; Port uncertain, 1760 ***2856.30*** *p146*
Griestlinger, Jakob; Port uncertain, 1751 ***2856.30*** *p146*
Grieve, George 54; Ontario, 1871 ***1823.22*** *p64*
Grieve, Hugh 58; Ontario, 1871 ***1823.15*** *p99*
Grieve, James; Canada, 1889 ***1640.13*** *p50*
Grieve, James 40; Ontario, 1871 ***1823.22*** *p64*
Grieve, James 66; Ontario, 1871 ***1823.22*** *p64*
Grieve, James 70; Ontario, 1871 ***1823.15*** *p100*
Grieve, Janet; Port uncertain, 1850-1859 ***4537.37*** *p109*
Grieve, Janet 45; Ontario, 1871 ***1823.15*** *p100*
Grieve, John 60; Ontario, 1871 ***1823.15*** *p100*
Grieve, John B. 54; Ontario, 1871 ***1823.15*** *p100*
Grieve, Thomas 56; Ontario, 1871 ***1823.15*** *p100*
Grieve, Walter; Ontario, 1889 ***1640.13*** *p50*
Grieve, William; Georgia, 1699 ***1640.13*** *p50*
Grieves, Henry 56; Ontario, 1871 ***1823.22*** *p64*
Grieves, Thomas 45; Ontario, 1871 ***1823.22*** *p64*
Grieves, William 36; Ontario, 1871 ***1823.15*** *p100*
Grife, Charles 44; Ontario, 1871 ***1823.28*** *p36*
Griffa, Louis; Quebec, 1858 ***9196.15*** *p33*
Griffen, Lewis; Maryland, 1670 ***2524.55*** *p94*
Griffen, Michel 30; Ontario, 1871 ***1823.15*** *p100*
Griffen, Timothy 56; Ontario, 1871 ***1823.15*** *p100*
Griffies, Mary; Maryland, 1668 ***2524.55*** *p94*
Griffin, Master; Quebec, 1858 ***9196.15*** *p46*
Griffin, Mrs.; Maryland, 1652 ***2524.55*** *p94*
Griffin, Mrs.; Portland, Maine, 1858 ***9196.15*** *p47*
Griffin, Abbie; Vermont, 1856-1925 ***5900.10*** *p108*
Griffin, Abbie; Vermont, 1865-1928 ***5900.10*** *p114*
Griffin, Alice *SEE* Griffin, Samll.
Griffin, Alice; Maryland, 1658 ***2524.55*** *p94*
Griffin, Alice 73; Vermont, 1892 ***5900.10*** *p415*
Griffin, Ann; Vermont, n.d. ***5900.10*** *p166*
Griffin, Ann McGrath; Vermont, 1833-1908 ***5900.10*** *p80*
Griffin, Annie; Vermont, 1873-1888 ***5900.10*** *p114*
Griffin, Annie Collins 48; Vermont, 1899 ***5900.10*** *p477*
Griffin, Anthony; Maryland, 1657 ***2524.55*** *p94*
Griffin, Bartholomew; Pennsylvania, 1844 ***6058.10*** *p19*
Griffin, Bridget 79; Vermont, 1907 ***5900.10*** *p73*
Griffin, Bridget Casey; Vermont, 1836-1912 ***5900.10*** *p353*
Griffin, Bridget Harty; Vermont, 1846-1918 ***5900.10*** *p61*
Griffin, Catherine; Vermont, 1805-1879 ***5900.10*** *p520*
Griffin, Catherine; Vermont, 1829-1905 ***5900.10*** *p507*
Griffin, Catherine; Vermont, 1847-1906 ***5900.10*** *p289*
Griffin, Catherine; Vermont, 1858-1934 ***5900.10*** *p352*
Griffin, Catherine 35; Vermont, 1856 ***5900.10*** *p58*
Griffin, Catherine 41; Vermont, 1872 ***5900.10*** *p613*
Griffin, Catherine 62; Vermont, 1917 ***5900.10*** *p93*
Griffin, Daniel; New York, New York, 1848 ***1825.45*** *p56* With wife & 3 sons
Griffin, Edwin 50; Ontario, 1871 ***1823.28*** *p36*
Griffin, Eliza 72; Vermont, 1885 ***5900.10*** *p125*
Griffin, Elizabeth; Maryland, 1652 ***2524.55*** *p94*
Griffin, Elizabeth; Virginia, 1689 ***1224.1*** *p25*
Griffin, Ellen; Vermont, 1845-1919 ***5900.10*** *p483*
Griffin, Ellen 29; Vermont, 1913 ***5900.10*** *p103*
Griffin, Ellen 78; Vermont, 1892 ***5900.10*** *p467*
Griffin, Ellen 79; Vermont, 1905 ***5900.10*** *p405*
Griffin, Ellen 87; Ontario, 1871 ***1823.15*** *p100*
Griffin, Ellen Capeless; Vermont, 1842-1903 ***5900.10*** *p437*
Griffin, Eugene; Vermont, 1846-1926 ***5900.10*** *p553*
Griffin, George; Pennsylvania, 1775 ***4629.10*** *p48*
Griffin, George 7; Ontario, 1861 ***2896.27*** *p23*
Griffin, Hannah E. 11; Ontario, 1861 ***2896.27*** *p14*
Griffin, Hanora; Vermont, 1856-1934 ***5900.10*** *p428*
Griffin, Hanora Rooney; Vermont, 1813-1871 ***5900.10*** *p166*
Griffin, Henry 62; Ontario, 1871 ***1823.22*** *p64*
Griffin, James; Massachusetts, 1773 ***1224.2*** *p48*
Griffin, James; New York, 1837 ***8197.10*** *p87*
Griffin, James; Vermont, 1809-1893 ***5900.10*** *p166*
Griffin, James; Virginia, 1666 ***6212.30*** *p26*
Griffin, James 20; Ontario, 1871 ***1823.15*** *p100*
Griffin, James 45; Vermont, 1901 ***5900.10*** *p108*
Griffin, James 63; Vermont, 1888 ***5900.10*** *p576*
Griffin, James 76; Vermont, 1882 ***5900.10*** *p405*
Griffin, James A.; Vermont, 1867-1937 ***5900.10*** *p103*
Griffin, Jno.; Nova Scotia, 1745 ***4628.40*** *p45*
Griffin, Job; New York, 1840 ***8197.10*** *p387*
Griffin, Johanna 65; Vermont, 1890 ***5900.10*** *p108*
Griffin, John; New York, 1840 ***8197.10*** *p170*
Griffin, John; Vermont, 1836-1897 ***5900.10*** *p88*
Griffin, John; Vermont, 1843-1900 ***5900.10*** *p437*
Griffin, John; Vermont, 1868-1943 ***5900.10*** *p115*
Griffin, John 20; Maryland, 1775 ***1220.25*** *p101*
Griffin, John 50; Vermont, 1899 ***5900.10*** *p166*
Griffin, John 55; Vermont, 1863 ***5900.10*** *p105*
Griffin, John 60; Vermont, 1889 ***5900.10*** *p587*
Griffin, Mrs. John 89; Vermont, 1815 ***5900.10*** *p377*
Griffin, Margaret; Vermont, 1831-1887 ***5900.10*** *p86*
Griffin, Margaret J. 31; Vermont, 1892 ***5900.10*** *p108*
Griffin, Martha; Vermont, 1851-1880 ***5900.10*** *p405*
Griffin, Martin; New York, 1837 ***8197.10*** *p88*
Griffin, Mary; Maryland, 1682 ***2524.55*** *p94*
Griffin, Mary; Vermont, 1830-1902 ***5900.10*** *p73*
Griffin, Mary; Vermont, 1836-1924 ***5900.10*** *p351*
Griffin, Mary; Vermont, 1839-1913 ***5900.10*** *p148*
Griffin, Mary; Vermont, 1848-1914 ***5900.10*** *p101*
Griffin, Mary; Vermont, 1860-1935 ***5900.10*** *p115*
Griffin, Mary 74; Vermont, 1906 ***5900.10*** *p112*
Griffin, Mary 75; Vermont, 1912 ***5900.10*** *p55*
Griffin, Mary 89; Vermont, 1884 ***5900.10*** *p54*
Griffin, Mary A.; Vermont, 1870-1935 ***5900.10*** *p103*
Griffin, Mary Hartley 70; Vermont, 1894 ***5900.10*** *p117*
Griffin, Mary Leonard; Vermont, 1825-1893 ***5900.10*** *p88*
Griffin, Mary Lynch 78; Vermont, 1937 ***5900.10*** *p438*
Griffin, Mary McNamara; Vermont, 1834-1914 ***5900.10*** *p576*
Griffin, Mary Moynihan 69; Vermont, 1888 ***5900.10*** *p105*
Griffin, Mary O'Neil; Vermont, 1838-1911 ***5900.10*** *p114*
Griffin, Mary W. 40; Vermont, 1880 ***5900.10*** *p148*
Griffin, Michael; New York, 1840 ***8197.10*** *p170*
Griffin, Michael; Vermont, n.d. ***5900.10*** *p477*
Griffin, Michael; Vermont, 1834-1899 ***5900.10*** *p114*
Griffin, Michael; Vermont, 1858-1870 ***5900.10*** *p114*
Griffin, Michael 21; Maryland, 1775 ***1220.25*** *p109*
Griffin, Michael 69; Vermont, 1885 ***5900.10*** *p437*
Griffin, Michael H. 44; Vermont, 1900 ***5900.10*** *p438*
Griffin, Patrick; New York, 1839 ***8197.10*** *p379*
Griffin, Patrick; Vermont, 1820-1897 ***5900.10*** *p353*
Griffin, Patrick; Vermont, 1841-1911 ***5900.10*** *p80*
Griffin, Patrick 23; Vermont, 1873 ***5900.10*** *p415*
Griffin, Patrick 75; Vermont, 1900 ***5900.10*** *p117*
Griffin, Richard 15; Philadelphia, 1774 ***1220.25*** *p35*
Griffin, Roger; Virginia, 1664 ***6212.30*** *p12*
Griffin, Samll.; Maryland, 1658 ***2524.55*** *p95* *Wife:* Alice
Griffin, Samuel; Virginia, 1679 ***1224.1*** *p25*
Griffin, Sarah 66; Vermont, 1873 ***5900.10*** *p405*
Griffin, Thomas; Maryland, 1665 ***2524.55*** *p95*
Griffin, Thomas; New York, 1834 ***8197.10*** *p234*
Griffin, Thomas; New York, 1840 ***8197.10*** *p168*
Griffin, Thomas; Vermont, 1841-1927 ***5900.10*** *p60*
Griffin, Thomas; Vermont, 1877-1914 ***5900.10*** *p103*
Griffin, Thomas; Virginia, 1697 ***1224.1*** *p26*
Griffin, Thomas 56; Vermont, 1873 ***5900.10*** *p287*
Griffin, Thos 28; Arizona, 1917 ***9196.1*** *p52*
Griffin, Thos 28; Whitehorse, Yukon, 1917 ***9196.1*** *p52*
Griffin, William 24; Baltimore, 1775 ***1220.25*** *p116*
Griffing, Jane; Virginia, 1663 ***6212.30*** *p4*
Griffing, Seth; Pennsylvania, 1777 ***4629.10*** *p14*
Griffis, Edward 25; Philadelphia, 1774 ***1220.25*** *p42*
Griffit, Thomas 50; Ontario, 1871 ***1823.15*** *p100*
Griffith, Asa 24; Ontario, 1871 ***1823.28*** *p36*
Griffith, Bridget; Maryland, 1679 ***2524.55*** *p95*
Griffith, Edmund W.; Vermont, 1845-1916 ***5900.10*** *p195*
Griffith, Edward; Charles Town, South Carolina, n.d. ***1224.2*** *p49*
Griffith, Edward; Pennsylvania, 1811 ***6058.10*** *p3*
Griffith, Edward; Vermont, 1849-1870 ***5900.10*** *p395*
Griffith, Edward Moule; New York, 1837 ***8197.10*** *p87*
Griffith, George 30; Ontario, 1871 ***1823.28*** *p36*
Griffith, Hamilton 54; Ontario, 1871 ***1823.15*** *p100*
Griffith, John; Maryland, 1668 ***2524.55*** *p95*
Griffith, John; Maryland, 1672 ***2524.55*** *p95*
Griffith, John; New York, 1832 ***8197.10*** *p234*
Griffith, John 36; Ontario, 1871 ***1823.28*** *p36*
Griffith, Jone; Maryland, 1668 ***2524.55*** *p95*
Griffith, Levi; Pennsylvania, 1781 ***4629.10*** *p42*
Griffith, Mary C.; Vermont, 1865-1939 ***5900.10*** *p195*
Griffith, Mary E.; Vermont, 1858-1932 ***5900.10*** *p394*
Griffith, Mary Melvin; Vermont, 1825-1906 ***5900.10*** *p395*
Griffith, Robert; Maryland, 1681 ***2524.55*** *p95*
Griffith, Samuel 28; Ontario, 1871 ***1823.28*** *p36*
Griffith, Thomas; New York, 1805 ***8197.10*** *p30*
Griffith, Thomas; Vermont, 1828-1902 ***5900.10*** *p395*
Griffith, Thomas 57; Ontario, 1871 ***1823.28*** *p36*
Griffith, Thomas J.; Vermont, 1860-1886 ***5900.10*** *p395*
Griffith, William 51; Ontario, 1871 ***1823.22*** *p64*
Griffiths, Andrew; New York, 1782 ***1224.2*** *p49*
Griffiths, David; New York, 1807 ***8197.10*** *p29*
Griffiths, David; New York, 1834 ***8197.10*** *p73*
Griffiths, Griffith; Pennsylvania, 1777 ***4629.10*** *p13*
Griffiths, James; Carolina, 1709 ***1224.2*** *p49*
Griffiths, James 16; Maryland, 1775 ***1220.25*** *p9*
Griffiths, Jane 23; Maryland, 1774 ***1220.25*** *p38*
Griffiths, John; New York, 1807 ***8197.10*** *p326*
Griffiths, John; New York, 1825 ***8197.10*** *p233*
Griffiths, John; New York, 1839 ***8197.10*** *p130*
Griffiths, John; New York, New York, 1799 ***1224.2*** *p49*
Griffiths, John 19; Maryland, 1775 ***1220.25*** *p10*
Griffiths, John 22; Maryland, 1774 ***1220.25*** *p3*
Griffiths, John 26; Maryland, 1774 ***1220.25*** *p85*
Griffiths, Joseph 30; Philadelphia, 1774 ***1220.25*** *p44*
Griffiths, Richard; New York, 1803 ***8197.10*** *p12*
Griffiths, Samuel 19; Maryland, 1774 ***1220.25*** *p78*
Griffiths, Samuel 22; Maryland, 1775 ***1220.25*** *p111*
Griffiths, William; New York, 1839 ***8197.10*** *p130*
Griffiths, William 52; Ontario, 1871 ***1823.28*** *p36*
Griffitt, Henery 24; Ontario, 1871 ***1823.15*** *p100*
Griffony, Augustine; Philadelphia, 1793 ***4629.10*** *p68*
Griffyn, Joanna; Virginia, 1661 ***1224.1*** *p26*
Grifith, John 26; Ontario, 1871 ***1823.15*** *p100*
Grig, Lily 75; Ontario, 1871 ***1823.15*** *p100*
Griger, Mary 16; Ontario, 1871 ***1823.28*** *p36*
Grigg, James 44; Ontario, 1871 ***1823.15*** *p100*
Grigg, John 64; Ontario, 1871 ***1823.15*** *p100*
Grigg, Joseph 37; Ontario, 1871 ***1823.15*** *p100*
Grigg, Robert; Mobile, Alabama, 1848 ***1224.3*** *p32*
Grigg, Thomas 52; Ontario, 1871 ***1823.22*** *p64*
Grigg, William 50; Ontario, 1871 ***1823.15*** *p100*
Griggs, Michael; Virginia, 1688 ***1224.1*** *p26*
Grill, Maria Dorothea; America, 1764 ***2856.30*** *p146* With husband
Grills, Charles; Virginia, 1666 ***6212.30*** *p27*
Grills, Charles; Virginia, 1666 ***6212.30*** *p29*
Grills, Nathan 42; Ontario, 1871 ***1823.22*** *p64*
Grills, Thomas 56; Ontario, 1871 ***1823.22*** *p64*
Grim, Catharine; New York, 1837 ***8197.10*** *p88*
Grimaldy, Christopher 25; Ontario, 1871 ***1823.15*** *p100*
Grimaldy, John 73; Ontario, 1871 ***1823.15*** *p100*
Grimbaldby, Ruben 30; Ontario, 1871 ***1823.15*** *p100*
Grimditch, Thomas; New York, 1684 ***1224.1*** *p26*
Grime, John; Maryland, 1665 ***2524.55*** *p95*
Grimes, Arthur; Virginia, 1664-1665 ***6212.30*** *p16*
Grimes, Austin 54; Ontario, 1871 ***1823.28*** *p36*
Grimes, Catharine 60; Ontario, 1871 ***1823.28*** *p36*
Grimes, Eliz; Virginia, 1671 ***6212.30*** *p44*
Grimes, Francis; Maryland, 1667 ***2524.55*** *p170*
Grimes, George; Maryland, 1665 ***2524.55*** *p95*
Grimes, George; Pennsylvania, 1777 ***4629.10*** *p22*
Grimes, Gilbert; Panama, 1722 ***1224.2*** *p49*
Grimes, James; Virginia, 1667 ***6212.30*** *p36*
Grimes, James 33; Vermont, 1866 ***5900.10*** *p380*
Grimes, John; Vermont, 1826-1894 ***5900.10*** *p545*
Grimes, John 25; Virginia, 1773 ***1220.25*** *p31*
Grimes, John 49; Ontario, 1871 ***1823.28*** *p36*
Grimes, M. A.; Vermont, n.d. ***5900.10*** *p380*
Grimes, Mary Scanlon; Vermont, 1834-1898 ***5900.10*** *p461*
Grimes, Patrick; Vermont, 1836-1933 ***5900.10*** *p461*
Grimes, Roger; Virginia, 1666-1667 ***6212.30*** *p35*
Grimes, Rosanna; Vermont, 1828-1896 ***5900.10*** *p545*
Grimes, Thomas; Maryland, 1654 ***2524.55*** *p95*
Grimes, Thomas 65; Ontario, 1871 ***1823.28*** *p36*
Grimm, Abrm; Pennsylvania, 1867 ***6058.10*** *p60*
Grimm, Catharina; Port uncertain, 1787 ***2856.30*** *p146*
Grimm, Charles A.; New York, 1832-1838 ***8197.10*** *p114*
Grimm, Daniel; Pennsylvania, 1863 ***6058.10*** *p47*
Grimm, Feltin; America, 1740 ***2856.30*** *p146*
Grimm, Heinrich; America, 1741 ***2856.30*** *p146* With wife & 6 children
Grimm, Henrich; America, 1737 ***2856.30*** *p146*
Grimm, Henrich; America, 1741 ***2856.30*** *p146*
Grimm, Johann; America, 1738 ***2856.30*** *p246*
Grimm, Johann; America, 1747 ***2856.30*** *p146*
Grimm, Johann; America, 1750 ***2856.30*** *p146* With wife & children
Grimm, Johann; Port uncertain, 1750 ***2856.30*** *p146* With wife & children
Grimm, Mrs. Johann; Port uncertain, 1764 ***2856.30*** *p146* With children
Grimm, Johann Nikolaus; America, 1764 ***2856.30*** *p146* With wife & 3 children
Grimm, Maria Elisabeth; America, 1764 ***2856.30*** *p146* With husband
Grimm, Martin; America, 1738 ***2856.30*** *p146*

Grimm, Martin; America, 1738 ***2856.30*** *p246*
Grimm, Michael; Port uncertain, 1737 ***2856.30*** *p146*
Grimm, Michael; Port uncertain, 1742 ***2856.30*** *p146*
Grimm, Peter; America, 1752 ***2856.30*** *p146*
With wife & 6 children
Grimm, Wendel; America, 1754 ***2856.30*** *p146*
With wife & 6 children
Grimme, Charles A.; New York, 1832 ***8197.10*** *p234*
Grimme, Henry Augustus; New York, 1839 ***8197.10*** *p235*
Grimme, Johann; America, 1747 ***2856.30*** *p146*
Grimmer, Peter; Port uncertain, 1770 ***2856.30*** *p146*
Grimmon, A. 3; Ontario, 1861 ***2896.27*** *p6*
Grimmon, Jane 33; Ontario, 1861 ***2896.27*** *p6*
Grimmon, John 6; Ontario, 1861 ***2896.27*** *p6*
Grimmon, R. 8; Ontario, 1861 ***2896.27*** *p6*
Grimmon, Rebecca 80; Ontario, 1861 ***2896.27*** *p6*
Grimon, E. 6; Ontario, 1861 ***2896.27*** *p7*
Grimon, L. 8; Ontario, 1861 ***2896.27*** *p7*
Grimon, Sarah 32; Ontario, 1861 ***2896.27*** *p7*
Grims, John W. 47; Ontario, 1871 ***1823.22*** *p64*
Grimsditch, William; Maryland, 1659 ***2524.55*** *p95*
Grimshaw, Mr.; Quebec, 1858 ***9196.15*** *p42*
Grimshaw, Elizabeth; Virginia, 1693-1694 ***6212.30*** *p60*
Grimshaw, John; New York, 1821 ***8197.10*** *p232*
Grimshaw, John; New York, 1827 ***8197.10*** *p338*
Grimshaw, John; New York, 1840 ***8197.10*** *p170*
Grimshaw, Thomas 56; Ontario, 1871 ***1823.22*** *p64*
Grimshaw, William 21; Ontario, 1871 ***1823.15*** *p100*
Grimston, James; Virginia, 1665-1666 ***6212.30*** *p21*
Grimvill, James; Virginia, 1666 ***6212.30*** *p27*
Grindal, Elizabeth 32; Baltimore, 1775 ***1220.25*** *p117*
Grindige, Charles; Maryland, 1681 ***2524.55*** *p95*
Grindlay, Capt.; Quebec, 1857 ***9196.15*** *p20*
Grindlay, John; America, 1806 ***1640.13*** *p50*
Grindley, Mr.; Quebec, 1858 ***9196.15*** *p41*
Grindley, Mrs.; Quebec, 1858 ***9196.15*** *p41*
Grindy, Mrs.; Quebec, 1856 ***9196.15*** *p10*
Grinfield, Thomas; Maryland, 1682 ***2524.55*** *p95*
Grinion, Peter; Pennsylvania, 1777 ***4629.10*** *p11*
Grinsden, Dorcas; Virginia, 1672 ***6212.30*** *p50*
Grintoun, Alexander; Georgia, 1700 ***1640.13*** *p50*
Grippin, Catharine 73; Ontario, 1861 ***2896.26*** *p19*
Grisch, Anthony; New York, 1840 ***8197.10*** *p169*
Grischele, Hypolite; New York, 1837 ***8197.10*** *p88*
Grischele, John; New York, 1836 ***8197.10*** *p319*
Grischele, John; New York, 1837 ***8197.10*** *p88*
Grischelen, Martin; Port uncertain, 1790 ***2856.30*** *p147*
Griskin, Dederick 30; Philadelphia, 1774 ***1220.25*** *p82*
Grismond, Charles; Nova Scotia, 1723 ***1224.2*** *p49*
Grist, David; New York, 1836-1838 ***8197.10*** *p115*
Grist, Henry; Maryland, 1667 ***2524.55*** *p95*
Gristoe, Mrs.; Maryland, 1667 ***2524.55*** *p95*
Griswold, Maryett Kelley 23; Vermont, 1849 ***5900.10*** *p194*
Grives, James 37; Ontario, 1871 ***1823.28*** *p36*
Grjgich, Mike 44; Alaska, 1914 ***9196.1*** *p11*
Grob, Catharina; Port uncertain, 1759 ***2856.30*** *p147*
Grob, Josef Heinrich; Port uncertain, 1767 ***2856.30*** *p147*
With children
Grob, Salome; America, 1750 ***2856.30*** *p147*
Grob, Simon; Port uncertain, 1764 ***2856.30*** *p147*
Grober, Josef; Port uncertain, 1744 ***2856.30*** *p147*
Grober, Josef; Port uncertain, 1784 ***2856.30*** *p147*
Groberger, Daniel; America, 1749 ***2856.30*** *p147*
Groce, Franc; Maryland, 1653 ***2524.55*** *p95*
Groce, Francis; Maryland, 1653 ***2524.55*** *p95*
Grocer, Thomas W.; New York, 1840 ***8197.10*** *p169*
Grochowski, John; Maryland, 1910 ***3259.35*** *p18*
Grocka, Theresa; Maryland, 1910 ***3259.35*** *p18*
Grocki, Frank; Maryland, 1910 ***3259.35*** *p18*
Groff, Stepen; New York, 1838 ***8197.10*** *p115*
Groffe, Roger; Maryland, 1658 ***2524.55*** *p95*
With wife
Grogan, Anthony 55; Ontario, 1871 ***1823.28*** *p36*
Grogan, Ellen; Vermont, 1868-1929 ***5900.10*** *p137*
Grogan, James 60; Vermont, 1889 ***5900.10*** *p136*
Grogan, Lawrence Edward 26; Vermont, 1884 ***5900.10*** *p136*
Grogan, Margaret; Vermont, 1894 ***5900.10*** *p136*
Grogan, Mary; Vermont, 1805-1896 ***5900.10*** *p485*
Grogan, Patrick 51; Ontario, 1871 ***1823.28*** *p36*
Grogan, William 31; Vermont, 1886 ***5900.10*** *p136*
Grogen, Bernard; New York, 1821 ***8197.10*** *p232*
Grogen, Hanora 82; Vermont, 1914 ***5900.10*** *p68*
Grogen, William; Charleston, South Carolina, 1818 ***1224.3*** *p32*
Groh, Johann Christof; Port uncertain, 1785 ***2856.30*** *p147*
Grohe, Johann; Port uncertain, 1756 ***2856.30*** *p147*
Grohn, Konrad; Port uncertain, 1784 ***2856.30*** *p147*
Grohn, Philipp; America, 1738 ***2856.30*** *p147*
With wife & children
Grohs, Joseph; New York, New York, 1891 ***3437.14*** *p157*
Grohuert, W. 33; British Columbia, 1917 ***9196.1*** *p51*
Grohuert, W. 33; Seattle, 1917 ***9196.1*** *p51*
Grojean, Alexander Jonas; New York, 1828 ***8197.10*** *p233*
Groll, Maria Anna; Port uncertain, 1755 ***2856.30*** *p147*
Grolle, Peter; Port uncertain, 1783 ***2856.30*** *p145*
Grolmann, Walter; Port uncertain, 1729 ***2856.30*** *p147*
Groly, Peter; Port uncertain, 1783 ***2856.30*** *p145*
Groly, Peter; Port uncertain, 1785 ***2856.30*** *p151*
Gromacka, Boleslawa; Maryland, 1910 ***3259.35*** *p18*
Gromer, Peter; Maryland, 1658 ***2524.55*** *p95*
Gromid, John; New York, New York, 1851 ***3437.14*** *p74*
Grominger, Leonhard; Philadelphia, 1749 ***2856.30*** *p147*
Gron, John; New York, 1840 ***8197.10*** *p321*
Grona, Dora; Maryland, 1910 ***3259.35*** *p18*
Grondeki, Stanislaw; Maryland, 1910 ***3259.35*** *p18*
Grone, William 71; Vermont, 1883 ***5900.10*** *p378*
Groner, Barbara; America, 1752 ***2856.30*** *p151*
Groner, Jacob, Jr.; America, 1751 ***2856.30*** *p151*
Groner, Maria; America, 1750 ***2856.30*** *p147*
With husband & 2 children
Groner, Matthaus; America, 1749 ***2856.30*** *p151*
Groninger, Georg; America, 1749 ***2856.30*** *p147*
With wife & children
Gronner, Maria; America, 1767 ***2856.30*** *p151*
With child
Gronns, James; Maryland, 1676 ***2524.55*** *p95*
Gronsky, Joseph; Maryland, 1910 ***3259.35*** *p18*
Groom, George; Boston, 1808 ***1224.3*** *p32*
Groombridge, Walter; Philadelphia, 1710 ***1224.2*** *p49*
Groome, Hannah; Maryland, 1657 ***2524.55*** *p95*
Groome, Mary *SEE* Groome, William
Groome, Nicholas; Virginia, 1652 ***1224.1*** *p26*
Groome, Thomas; New England, 1698 ***1224.1*** *p26*
Groome, William; Maryland, 1666 ***2524.55*** *p95*
Wife: Mary
Groppin, Jane; Maryland, 1680 ***2524.55*** *p95*
Groree, James 15; Maryland, 1774 ***1220.25*** *p8*
Gros, Jakob; Port uncertain, 1739 ***2856.30*** *p147*
Gros, Johann; America, 1749 ***2856.30*** *p147*
Gros, Johann; Port uncertain, 1782 ***2856.30*** *p147*
Gros, Maria Christina; Port uncertain, 1765 ***2856.30*** *p147*
Gros, Nicolas; Port uncertain, 1754 ***2856.30*** *p147*
With wife & daughter
Grosclaude, Frederick; New York, 1840 ***8197.10*** *p168*
Grose, John 27; Ontario, 1871 ***1823.28*** *p36*
Grose, Matthew 31; Ontario, 1871 ***1823.28*** *p36*
Grosew, Henry 62; Ontario, 1871 ***1823.28*** *p36*
Groshaw, Joseph 32; Ontario, 1871 ***1823.22*** *p64*
Grosholz, Adolf; Port uncertain, 1799 ***2856.30*** *p147*
Grosinski, Thomas; Maryland, 1910 ***3259.35*** *p18*
Grosjean, F. W. 29; Ontario, 1871 ***1823.22*** *p64*
Grosjean, Francis 63; Ontario, 1871 ***1823.22*** *p64*
Grosjean, Nicholas 65; Ontario, 1871 ***1823.22*** *p64*
Grosjean, Peter 25; Ontario, 1871 ***1823.22*** *p64*
Grosmann, Hans Georg; Port uncertain, 1765 ***2856.30*** *p147*
Gross, Felix; America, 1732 ***2856.30*** *p148*
Gross, George H. 30; Kansas, 1887-1910 ***9079.10*** *p53*
Gross, Helene; Port uncertain, 1763 ***2856.30*** *p148*
Gross, Johann Jakob; Port uncertain, 1751 ***2856.30*** *p148*
Gross, Johann Nikolaus; Port uncertain, 1741 ***2856.30*** *p148*
Gross, Konrad; Port uncertain, 1783 ***2856.30*** *p149*
With wife 2 sons & 2 daughters
Gross, Lewis; New York, 1839 ***8197.10*** *p235*
Gross, Maria Catharina; Port uncertain, 1759 ***2856.30*** *p148*
Gross, Mathew; Virginia, 1665-1666 ***6212.30*** *p24*
Gross, Michael; America, 1752 ***2856.30*** *p148*
Gross, Nicola; Port uncertain, 1742 ***2856.30*** *p148*
Gross, Peter; Pennsylvania, 1778 ***4629.10*** *p32*
Gross, Peter; Port uncertain, 1768 ***2856.30*** *p148*
Gross, Peter; Port uncertain, 1783 ***2856.30*** *p148*
Gross, Petkin 78; Ontario, 1871 ***1823.22*** *p64*
Grossart, Anna Maria; Port uncertain, 1784 ***2856.30*** *p149*
Grossart, Anton; America, 1741 ***2856.30*** *p149*
Grossart, Anton; Port uncertain, 1740 ***2856.30*** *p149*
Grossart, Peter; America, 1741 ***2856.30*** *p149*
Grossart, Peter; Port uncertain, 1740 ***2856.30*** *p149*
Grosse, Jane 15; Ontario, 1861 ***2896.28*** *p29*
Grosse, Roger; Maryland, 1658 ***2524.55*** *p95*
With wife
Grosse, Roger; Maryland, 1663 ***2524.55*** *p95*
Grosselas, Carles 44; Ontario, 1871 ***1823.28*** *p36*
Grossen, Peter 21; Seattle, 1913 ***9196.1*** *p62*
Grosser, Franziska; Port uncertain, 1722 ***2856.30*** *p151*
Grossie, George 30; Ontario, 1871 ***1823.15*** *p100*
Grossmann, Dietrich; America, 1740 ***2856.30*** *p149*
With wife & children
Grossmann, Michael; America, 1741 ***2856.30*** *p149*
Grosso, Peter 41; Seattle, 1911 ***9196.1*** *p33*
Grossschmied, Johann; Port uncertain, 1678 ***2856.30*** *p149*
With wife & 3 children
Groszkowski, Felix; Maryland, 1910 ***3259.35*** *p18*
Grotan, Evis; Maryland, 1666 ***2524.55*** *p95*
Grotoskey, Albert 35; Ontario, 1871 ***1823.28*** *p36*
Grotzek, Pawel; Maryland, 1910 ***3259.35*** *p18*
Grotzinger, Johann Konrad; America, 1759 ***2856.30*** *p151*
With family
Grotzinger, Johann Konrad; America, 1760 ***2856.30*** *p151*
With family
Groudnoski, Michael 40; Ontario, 1871 ***1823.28*** *p36*
Ground, John; New York, New York, 1851 ***3437.14*** *p74*
Groundwell, John; New York, 1807 ***8197.10*** *p39*
Group, Conrad; Pennsylvania, 1840 ***6058.10*** *p16*
Group, Jacob; Pennsylvania, 1838 ***6058.10*** *p16*
Group, John; Pennsylvania, 1840 ***6058.10*** *p15*
Grous, Johann Georg; America, 1754 ***2856.30*** *p149*
Grousset, Alexandre Eugene; New York, 1830 ***8197.10*** *p360*
Grout, John; Maryland, 1673 ***2524.55*** *p95*
Grove, Alexander; Maryland, 1655 ***2524.55*** *p95*
Grove, Allice; Maryland, 1656 ***2524.55*** *p95*
Grove, Dorothy; Maryland, 1658 ***2524.55*** *p95*
Grove, Elizabeth; Maryland, 1660 ***2524.55*** *p95*
Grove, Francis; Maryland, 1653 ***2524.55*** *p95*
Grove, George; Maryland, 1667 ***2524.55*** *p95*
Grove, Grey; New York, 1777 ***1224.2*** *p49*
Grove, John 23; Baltimore, 1775 ***1220.25*** *p118*
Grove, Samuel; South Carolina, 1777 ***1224.2*** *p49*
Grover, John; Georgia, 1774 ***1224.2*** *p49*
Grover, John; Pennsylvania, 1779 ***4629.10*** *p40*
Grover, Jonathan 17; Philadelphia, 1774 ***1220.25*** *p82*
Grover, William; Florida, 1768 ***1224.2*** *p49*
Groves, Duncan 36; Ontario, 1871 ***1823.15*** *p100*
Groves, Elizabeth; Charleston, South Carolina, 1810 ***1224.3*** *p32*
Groves, George; Maryland, 1673 ***2524.55*** *p95*
Groves, James 48; Ontario, 1871 ***1823.15*** *p100*
Groves, Jno; Virginia, 1668-1669 ***6212.30*** *p40*
Groves, John; Maryland, 1675 ***2524.55*** *p96*
Groves, John; Pennsylvania, 1777 ***4629.10*** *p23*
Groves, John; Pennsylvania, 1778 ***4629.10*** *p35*
Groves, John 44; Maryland, 1775 ***1220.25*** *p104*
Groves, Joseph; Maryland, 1678 ***2524.55*** *p96*
Groves, Katherine; Maryland, 1680 ***2524.55*** *p96*
Groves, Peter; New York, 1847 ***1224.3*** *p32*
Groves, William 49; Ontario, 1871 ***1823.28*** *p36*
Grovski, Lilly; Maryland, 1910 ***3259.35*** *p18*
Growak, John; Maryland, 1910 ***3259.35*** *p18*
Growski, James; Maryland, 1910 ***3259.35*** *p18*
Grub, Andreas; Port uncertain, 1754 ***2856.30*** *p149*
Grub, Henrich; Port uncertain, 1770 ***2856.30*** *p247*
Grub, Henrich; Port uncertain, 1783 ***2856.30*** *p149*
Grub, Henrich; Port uncertain, 1783 ***2856.30*** *p149*
With wife 4 sons & 2 daughters
Grub, Peter; America, 1739 ***2856.30*** *p150*
Grubank, William 32; Ontario, 1871 ***1823.22*** *p65*
Grubb, Adam; Pennsylvania, 1777 ***4629.10*** *p16*
Grubb, Janet; New York, 1828 ***8197.10*** *p225*
Grubb, John; Maryland, 1666 ***2524.55*** *p96*
Grubb, Wm; Virginia, 1665 ***6212.30*** *p17*
Grubbe, John; Maryland, 1666 ***2524.55*** *p96*
Grubel, Catharina; Port uncertain, 1755 ***2856.30*** *p149*
Gruber, Georg; America, 1751 ***2856.30*** *p149*
Gruber, Margarete; Port uncertain, 1750 ***2856.30*** *p149*
Grubham, Jno; Virginia, 1666-1667 ***6212.30*** *p34*
Grubich, John 26; British Columbia, 1909 ***9196.1*** *p27*
Grubich, John 26; Seattle, 1909 ***9196.1*** *p27*
Grubig, Bechtold; Port uncertain, 1748 ***2856.30*** *p149*
Gruczczynski, Vincenty; Maryland, 1910 ***3259.35*** *p18*
Grudgzieki, John; Maryland, 1910 ***3259.35*** *p18*
Gruebel, Josef; Port uncertain, 1755 ***2856.30*** *p149*
With wife & children
Grueber, Anton; Port uncertain, 1761 ***2856.30*** *p149*
Gruenenwald, Anna Catharina; America, 1752 ***2856.30*** *p150*
With 8 children
Gruenenwaldt, Anna Catharina; Port uncertain, 1744 ***2856.30*** *p150*
Gruer, John; Montana, 1898 ***1640.13*** *p50*
Gruet, Peggy; New Jersey, 1838 ***1224.3*** *p32*
Grumbach, Konrad; America, 1749 ***2856.30*** *p150*
With 2 children
Grumball, Thomas; Maryland, 1681 ***2524.55*** *p96*
Grumble, David 21; Maryland, 1775 ***1220.25*** *p10*
Grumell, Wm.; Maryland, 1664 ***2524.55*** *p97*
Grummet, Godard 42; Ontario, 1871 ***1823.15*** *p100*
Grummett, John 61; Ontario, 1871 ***1823.15*** *p100*

Grummett, Thomas 37; Ontario, 1871 ***1823.15*** *p101*
Grun, Anton; America, 1750 ***2856.30*** *p150*
Grun, Barbara; Port uncertain, 1752 ***2856.30*** *p150*
Grun, Christian; America, 1744 ***2856.30*** *p150*
Grun, Hans David; America, 1744 ***2856.30*** *p150*
Grun, Hans Georg; Port uncertain, 1761 ***2856.30*** *p150*
Grun, Jacob, Sr.; Port uncertain, 1755 ***2856.30*** *p150*
Grun, Johann; Port uncertain, 1764 ***2856.30*** *p150*
Grun, Johann; Port uncertain, 1791 ***2856.30*** *p150*
Grun, Maria Martha; Port uncertain, 1791 ***2856.30*** *p178*
Grun, Martin; America, 1738 ***2856.30*** *p146*
Grun, Martin; America, 1752 ***2856.30*** *p150*
With 3 daughters
Grun, Michael; Port uncertain, 1767 ***2856.30*** *p150*
Grunand, Mary 56; Ontario, 1871 ***1823.15*** *p101*
Grunard, John 25; Ontario, 1871 ***1823.15*** *p101*
Grunbacher, Josef; Port uncertain, 1742 ***2856.30*** *p150*
Grund, Johann Bernhard; Port uncertain, 1764 ***2856.30*** *p150*
Grund, Maria; Port uncertain, 1765 ***2856.30*** *p150*
Grund, Nikl.; Port uncertain, 1774 ***2856.30*** *p117*
Grundler, Maria; Port uncertain, 1741 ***2856.30*** *p150*
Grundler, Mathis; Port uncertain, 1741 ***2856.30*** *p150*
Grundoy, Mr.; Quebec, 1857 ***9196.15*** *p26*
Grundtin, Sara Catharina; Port uncertain, 1783 ***2856.30*** *p150*
Grundy, Jacob 55; Ontario, 1871 ***1823.22*** *p65*
Grundy, Oswell 61; Ontario, 1871 ***1823.22*** *p65*
Grunenthal, William Theodore; New York, 1835 ***8197.10*** *p234*
Grunenwald, Anna Gertrud; Port uncertain, 1772 ***2856.30*** *p150*
Grunenwald, Anna Rosina; America, 1752 ***2856.30*** *p150*
With husband & 4 children
Grunewald, Barbara; Port uncertain, 1774 ***2856.30*** *p150*
Grunewald, Maria Catharina; America, 1752 ***2856.30*** *p150*
Grunnett, Emily; Ontario, 1871 ***1823.15*** *p101*
Gruno, John; Maryland, 1910 ***3259.35*** *p18*
Grunrernauer, Jacob; Port uncertain, 1760 ***2856.30*** *p151*
Grunt, John 58; Ontario, 1871 ***1823.28*** *p36*
Grunwald, Anna Catharina; Port uncertain, 1785 ***2856.30*** *p151*
Grunwald, Anna Christina; Port uncertain, 1746 ***2856.30*** *p150*
Grunwald, Barbara; Port uncertain, 1753 ***2856.30*** *p151*
Grunwald, Nicolaus; Port uncertain, 1725 ***2856.30*** *p151*
Grunwald, William 40; Ontario, 1871 ***1823.22*** *p65*
Grusemeyer, George; New York, 1838 ***8197.10*** *p235*
Grusnonski, John; Maryland, 1910 ***3259.35*** *p18*
Grute, Charles; Pennsylvania, 1844 ***6058.10*** *p20*
Gruve, William E. 46; Ontario, 1871 ***1823.15*** *p100*
Gryar, John; Maryland, 1661 ***2524.55*** *p94*
Wife: Margarett
Gryar, Margarett *SEE* Gryar, John
Grybe, Joseph; Maryland, 1910 ***3259.35*** *p18*
Gryglik, Alexander, Sr.; Maryland, 1910 ***3259.35*** *p18*
Gryglik, Frank; Maryland, 1910 ***3259.35*** *p19*
Grymes, Thomas; Maryland, 1654 ***2524.55*** *p95*
Gryning, Edward 23; Vermont, 1872 ***5900.10*** *p163*
Gryning, Michael 85; Vermont, 1880 ***5900.10*** *p163*
Gryning, Nancy 67; Vermont, 1876 ***5900.10*** *p163*
Gryseicka, Mary; Maryland, 1910 ***3259.35*** *p19*
Gryzankowski, Alexandria; Maryland, 1910 ***3259.35*** *p19*
Gryzsbski, Stephen; Maryland, 1910 ***3259.35*** *p19*
Grzchowiax, Joseph; Maryland, 1910 ***3259.35*** *p19*
Grzybowski, Julius; Maryland, 1910 ***3259.35*** *p19*
Grzyma, Felix; Maryland, 1910 ***3259.35*** *p19*
Gsbulski, Joseph; Maryland, 1910 ***3259.35*** *p19*
Gschwind, Josef Jacob; Port uncertain, 1758 ***2856.30*** *p151*
Guanaski, Sophia; Maryland, 1910 ***3259.35*** *p19*
Guard, Peter; Virginia, 1664 ***6212.30*** *p8*
Guare, John; Vermont, 1832-1900 ***5900.10*** *p328*
Guare, Sarah McMahon; Vermont, 1844-1926 ***5900.10*** *p328*
Gubbins, James 70; Vermont, 1858 ***5900.10*** *p365*
Gubbins, Mary; Maryland, 1679 ***2524.55*** *p96*
Gubbor, Henry; Maryland, 1655 ***2524.55*** *p96*
Gubbott, George; Maryland, 1659 ***2524.55*** *p96*
Guck, James 65; Ontario, 1871 ***1823.15*** *p101*
Guckelsperger, Catharina; Port uncertain, 1761 ***2856.30*** *p151*
Guckert, Arnold; America, 1742 ***2856.30*** *p151*
Gudanovski, John 59; Washington, 1911 ***9196.1*** *p34*
Gudge, Mr.; Quebec, 1858 ***9196.15*** *p33*
Gudge, Mrs.; Quebec, 1858 ***9196.15*** *p33*
Gudgeon, Henry; Oswego, New York, 1765 ***1224.2*** *p49*
Gudgeon, Robert; Maryland, 1675 ***2524.55*** *p96*
Gueguin, John 31; Ontario, 1871 ***1823.28*** *p36*
Guental, Charles; New York, 1840 ***8197.10*** *p171*
Guenther, George; New York, New York, 1854 ***6058.10*** *p39*
Gueran, Margaret 52; Ontario, 1871 ***1823.15*** *p101*
Guerin, Elizabeth; Maryland, 1661 ***2524.55*** *p96*
Guerin, Gasper; Maryland, 1664 ***2524.55*** *p96*
Guerin, John; New York, 1834 ***8197.10*** *p73*
Guerin, Peter; New York, 1834 ***8197.10*** *p73*
Guerine, Elizabeth *SEE* Guerine, Jesper
Guerine, Jesper; Maryland, 1661 ***2524.55*** *p96*
Relative: Elizabeth
Guerout, L.; Quebec, 1858 ***9196.15*** *p44*
Guest, Edwin; New York, 1840 ***8197.10*** *p171*
Guest, Eliza 60; Ontario, 1871 ***1823.28*** *p36*
Guest, Elizabeth; Maryland, 1649 ***2524.55*** *p97*
Guest, Francis; Maryland, 1653 ***2524.55*** *p96*
Guest, Francis 34; Ontario, 1871 ***1823.28*** *p36*
Guest, George 32; Ontario, 1871 ***1823.28*** *p36*
Guest, James 44; Ontario, 1871 ***1823.28*** *p36*
Guest, John; Philadelphia, 1708 ***1224.2*** *p49*
Guest, Robert; Maryland, 1653 ***2524.55*** *p96*
Guest, Thomas 36; Ontario, 1871 ***1823.28*** *p36*
Guest, Walter; Maryland, 1646 ***2524.55*** *p96*
Guest, Walter; Maryland, 1646 ***2524.55*** *p97*
Gueth, Anna Maria; Port uncertain, 1725 ***2856.30*** *p152*
Gugele, Johann; America, 1752 ***2856.30*** *p152*
With wife & son
Gugelmayer, Christian; Port uncertain, 1707 ***2856.30*** *p152*
Gugelmayer, Christian; Port uncertain, 1727 ***2856.30*** *p152*
Gugelmayer, Christian; Port uncertain, 1735 ***2856.30*** *p152*
Gugelmayer, Norbert; Port uncertain, 1707 ***2856.30*** *p152*
Gugelmayer, Norbert; Port uncertain, 1727 ***2856.30*** *p152*
Gugelmayer, Norbert; Port uncertain, 1735 ***2856.30*** *p152*
Guggenberger, Hans Adam; Port uncertain, 1745 ***2856.30*** *p152*
With wife & 2 children
Guggenheimer, Jakob; Port uncertain, 1773 ***2856.30*** *p152*
Gugule, Johann; America, 1752 ***2856.30*** *p152*
With wife & son
Guide, Thomas 23; New York, 1774 ***1220.25*** *p25*
Guided, Matthew 60; Ontario, 1871 ***1823.15*** *p101*
Guiderupt, James; Maryland, 1658 ***2524.55*** *p96*
Guidi, Joseph 28; Ontario, 1871 ***1823.28*** *p36*
Guier, John; New York, 1840 ***8197.10*** *p169*
Guier, William; Pennsylvania, 1787 ***4629.10*** *p56*
Guiheen, John; Vermont, 1842-1932 ***5900.10*** *p107*
Guiheen, Mary Fitzgerald; Vermont, 1844-1918 ***5900.10*** *p107*
Guild, Alexander; New York, 1894 ***1640.13*** *p50*
Guilderfeild, Tho; Virginia, 1666-1667 ***6212.30*** *p34*
Guilders, Thomas 51; Ontario, 1871 ***1823.15*** *p101*
Guilford, Mary *SEE* Guilford, Willm.
Guilford, Mary; Maryland, 1651-1652 ***2524.55*** *p89*
Guilford, Paul *SEE* Guilford, Willm.
Guilford, Susan *SEE* Guilford, Willm.
Guilford, Willm.; Maryland, 1658 ***2524.55*** *p96*
Wife: Mary
Child: Paul
Child: Susan
Guilgot, Jacob Philip; Philadelphia, 1790 ***4629.10*** *p60*
Guillaume, Anna Barbara Dorr; Port uncertain, 1785 ***2856.30*** *p152*
Guillett, John 68; Ontario, 1871 ***1823.22*** *p65*
Guillot, Joseph; New York, 1815 ***8197.10*** *p55*
Guillume, Peter; Virginia, 1702 ***1224.2*** *p49*
Guilmette, Theodore 60; Ontario, 1871 ***1823.28*** *p36*
Guilsbury, John 17; Virginia, 1774 ***1220.25*** *p75*
Guiltinan, Bridget; Vermont, 1839-1914 ***5900.10*** *p86*
Guiltinan, Francis; Vermont, 1839-1909 ***5900.10*** *p86*
Guiltinane, Margaret Hogan 60; Vermont, 1888 ***5900.10*** *p73*
Guiltinane, Mary 50; Vermont, 1888 ***5900.10*** *p86*
Guinan, Lack; New York, 1832 ***8197.10*** *p234*
Guinane, Ann 75; Vermont, 1878 ***5900.10*** *p371*
Guinen, William 35; Ontario, 1871 ***1823.15*** *p101*
Guiner, Clause; Maryland, 1670 ***2524.55*** *p96*
Guiney, Ben 5 *SEE* Guiney, Darby
Guiney, Ben 8 *SEE* Guiney, Mary
Guiney, Biddy 9 *SEE* Guiney, Darby
Guiney, Cornelius 31; Ontario, 1871 ***1823.28*** *p36*
Guiney, Dan 17 *SEE* Guiney, Darby
Guiney, Dan 23 *SEE* Guiney, Mary
Guiney, Daniel 35; Ontario, 1871 ***1823.28*** *p36*
Guiney, Darby 3 *SEE* Guiney, Darby
Guiney, Darby 45; New York, New York, 1850 ***1825.45*** *p49*
Daughter: Joney 13
Daughter: Eileen 11
Daughter: Biddy 9
Son: Tade 5
Son: Darby 3
Son: Dan 17
Son: Ben 5
Wife: Kitty 37
Guiney, Eileen 11 *SEE* Guiney, Darby
Guiney, Ellen 68; Ontario, 1871 ***1823.28*** *p36*
Guiney, Gubby 11 *SEE* Guiney, Mary
Guiney, Joney 13 *SEE* Guiney, Darby
Guiney, Kitty 37 *SEE* Guiney, Darby
Guiney, Mary 50; New York, New York, 1850 ***1825.45*** *p50*
Son: Ben 8
Son: Tade 14
Son: Dan 23
Daughter: Gubby 11
Guiney, Tade 5 *SEE* Guiney, Darby
Guiney, Tade 14 *SEE* Guiney, Mary
Guinlon, Patrick; New Hampshire, n.d. ***4628.40*** *p76*
Guinnessy, Ann 14 *SEE* Guinnessy, Pat
Guinnessy, Bridget 20 *SEE* Guinnessy, Thomas
Guinnessy, Catherine 3 *SEE* Guinnessy, Pat
Guinnessy, Hanora 25 *SEE* Guinnessy, John
Guinnessy, James 20 *SEE* Guinnessy, Pat
Guinnessy, John 2 *SEE* Guinnessy, John
Guinnessy, John 27; New York, New York, 1849 ***1825.45*** *p34*
Wife: Hanora 25
Son: Thomas 3 months
Son: John 2
Guinnessy, Malachy 16 *SEE* Guinnessy, Pat
Guinnessy, Mary 51 *SEE* Guinnessy, Pat
Guinnessy, Pat 13 *SEE* Guinnessy, Pat
Guinnessy, Pat 55; New York, New York, 1849 ***1825.45*** *p35*
Wife: Mary 51
Daughter: Catherine 3
Daughter: Ann 14
Son: James 20
Son: Malachy 16
Son: Pat 13
Guinnessy, Thomas 3 months *SEE* Guinnessy, John
Guinnessy, Thomas 22; New York, New York, 1848 ***1825.45*** *p35*
Sister: Bridget 20
Guire, Adam; Pennsylvania, 1777 ***4629.10*** *p9*
Guischard, Henry; New York, 1834 ***8197.10*** *p359*
Guispys, Beagan 26; Alaska, 1908 ***9196.1*** *p36*
Guispys, Bragon 26; Alaska, 1908 ***9196.1*** *p37*
Guizer, Adam 47; Ontario, 1871 ***1823.15*** *p101*
Gulcher, Theobald; Port uncertain, 1764 ***2856.30*** *p153*
Gulcsynski, Wawsyn; Maryland, 1910 ***3259.35*** *p19*
Gulczewski, John; Maryland, 1910 ***3259.35*** *p19*
Guld, Robert 21; St. Kitts, 1774 ***1220.25*** *p88*
Gulden, Jacob; New York, 1840 ***8197.10*** *p168*
Guler, Jakob; Port uncertain, 1612 ***2856.30*** *p152*
Gullet, James 57; Ontario, 1871 ***1823.15*** *p101*
Gullett, Mrs.; Maryland, 1631-1685 ***2524.55*** *p85*
Gullett, Dorothy; Maryland, 1661 ***2524.55*** *p96*
Gullich, Heinrich; America, 1752 ***2856.30*** *p153*
With wife & 2 children
Gulliford, Mary 24; Maryland, 1775 ***1220.25*** *p12*
Gullikson, Jackima 41; Ontario, 1871 ***1823.28*** *p37*
Gulline, William; Havana, 1763 ***1224.2*** *p49*
Gulline, William; New York, 1763 ***1224.2*** *p49*
Gulliver, Elijah; New England, 1754 ***1224.2*** *p49*
Gulliver, Samuel; New England, 1754 ***1224.2*** *p49*
Gully, Samuell; Virginia, 1666 ***6212.30*** *p28*
Gulmann, Daniel; America, 1741 ***2856.30*** *p152*
Gumbe, Francis; Maryland, 1668 ***2524.55*** *p96*
Gumbert, Catharina; Port uncertain, 1743 ***2856.30*** *p152*
Gumenznia, Peter; Maryland, 1910 ***3259.35*** *p19*
Gummel, Georg; Port uncertain, 1745 ***2856.30*** *p152*
Gummer, John 39; Ontario, 1871 ***1823.22*** *p65*
Gummer, John 47; Ontario, 1871 ***1823.22*** *p65*
Gummow, James 36; Ontario, 1871 ***1823.22*** *p65*
Gummow, Robert 57; Ontario, 1871 ***1823.22*** *p65*
Gummow, Thomas 44; Ontario, 1871 ***1823.22*** *p65*
Gummow, William 53; Ontario, 1871 ***1823.22*** *p65*
Gumpe, John; Virginia, 1683 ***6212.30*** *p56*
Gun, Margret 30; Ontario, 1871 ***1823.22*** *p65*
Gunas, Elizabeth 40; Ontario, 1871 ***1823.15*** *p101*
Gunas, Elizabeth Anne 3; Ontario, 1871 ***1823.15*** *p101*
Gunas, Mary Jane 11; Ontario, 1871 ***1823.15*** *p101*
Gunbee, Francis; Maryland, 1668 ***2524.55*** *p96*
Gunbert, Joshua; Maryland, 1664 ***2524.55*** *p96*
Gundray, Mr.; Portland, Maine, 1857 ***9196.15*** *p12*
Gundray, Mrs.; Portland, Maine, 1857 ***9196.15*** *p12*
Gundry, Gidion *SEE* Gundry, Joseph
Gundry, Joseph; Maryland, 1665 ***2524.55*** *p96*
Relative: Gidion
Gunis, Elizabeth *SEE* Gunis, Leonard
Gunis, Leonard; Maryland, 1651 ***2524.55*** *p96*
Wife: Elizabeth
Gunk, Thomas 60; Ontario, 1871 ***1823.28*** *p37*
Gunley, John 22; Virginia, 1774 ***1220.25*** *p56*

Gunn, Miss; Quebec, 1856 ***9196.15*** *p7*
Gunn, Mr.; Quebec, 1858 ***9196.15*** *p42*
Gunn, Mrs.; Quebec, 1858 ***9196.15*** *p42*
Gunn, Arthur; Maryland, 1665 ***2524.55*** *p96*
Gunn, Bernard; Vermont, 1819-1891 ***5900.10*** *p289*
Gunn, Donald; Florida, 1824 ***1640.10*** *p75*
Wife: Mary
Gunn, Elizabeth; Virginia, 1663-1664 ***6212.30*** *p5*
Gunn, Elizabeth Kane; Vermont, 1820-1920 ***5900.10*** *p289*
Gunn, George; Georgia, 1738 ***1640.10*** *p75*
Gunn, James; New York, 1840 ***8197.10*** *p168*
Gunn, James 58; Ontario, 1871 ***1823.15*** *p101*
Gunn, John; Maryland, 1660 ***2524.55*** *p96*
Gunn, John; Maryland, 1664 ***2524.55*** *p97*
Gunn, John; New York, 1837 ***8197.10*** *p87*
Gunn, Mary *SEE* Gunn, Donald
Gunn, Patrick 44; Ontario, 1871 ***1823.15*** *p101*
Gunn, William; Georgia, 1736 ***1640.10*** *p75*
Gunn, William 32; Virginia, 1773 ***1220.25*** *p29*
Gunne, Mr.; Portland, Maine, 1858 ***9196.15*** *p29*
Gunnell, George; Virginia, 1674 ***1224.1*** *p26*
Gunnell, Wm.; Maryland, 1664 ***2524.55*** *p97*
Gunner, James 23; Maryland, 1774 ***1220.25*** *p73*
Gunnill, Edward; Maryland, 1672 ***2524.55*** *p97*
Gunnill, George; Maryland, 1672 ***2524.55*** *p97*
Gunnin, Ann 51; Ontario, 1871 ***1823.22*** *p65*
Gunning, Bernard 81; Vermont, 1906 ***5900.10*** *p192*
Gunning, Maria Farrell 35; Vermont, 1888 ***5900.10*** *p192*
Gunning, Peter; Pennsylvania, 1850 ***1224.3*** *p32*
Gunningham, W. 87; Ontario, 1871 ***1823.22*** *p65*
Gunnis, Janie; Maryland, 1663 ***2524.55*** *p97*
Gunnis, Leonard; Maryland, 1663 ***2524.55*** *p97*
Gunnison, John 43; Alaska, 1918 ***9196.1*** *p8*
Gunnison, John 43; Yukon, 1918 ***9196.1*** *p8*
Gunrey, Robert; Maryland, 1651 ***2524.55*** *p97*
Gunshannon, Ann Gavin 38; Vermont, 1875 ***5900.10*** *p75*
Gunshannon, Bridget E.; Vermont, 1868-1935 ***5900.10*** *p85*
Gunshannon, Edward 53; Vermont, 1883 ***5900.10*** *p75*
Gunshannon, Edward J.; Vermont, 1864-1916 ***5900.10*** *p85*
Gunshannon, Elizabeth A.; Vermont, 1856-1909 ***5900.10*** *p85*
Gunshannon, James 60; Vermont, 1895 ***5900.10*** *p84*
Gunshannon, James H.; Vermont, 1858-1903 ***5900.10*** *p85*
Gunshannon, Mary; Vermont, 1849-1877 ***5900.10*** *p546*
Gunshannon, Michael; Vermont, 1825-1882 ***5900.10*** *p85*
Gunshannon, Thomas F.; Vermont, 1860-1931 ***5900.10*** *p85*
Gunsheimer, Anna Catharina; Port uncertain, 1789 ***2856.30*** *p152*
Gunter, Anton; America, 1730 ***2856.30*** *p153*
Gunter, Bartholomew; Pennsylvania, 1836 ***6058.10*** *p14*
Gunter, Friedrich; Port uncertain, 1768 ***2856.30*** *p153*
Gunter, Gustav 48; Ontario, 1871 ***1823.28*** *p37*
Gunter, James; Virginia, 1666 ***6212.30*** *p25*
Gunter, John; Maryland, 1649 ***2524.55*** *p97*
Gunter, John 53; Ontario, 1871 ***1823.28*** *p37*
Guntert, Anna; Port uncertain, 1784 ***2856.30*** *p153*
Guntert, Jacob; Port uncertain, 1787 ***2856.30*** *p153*
Gunther, Andreas; Port uncertain, 1770 ***2856.30*** *p153*
Gunther, Georg; America, 1738 ***2856.30*** *p153*
Gunther, Johann; Port uncertain, 1752 ***2856.30*** *p152*
Gunther, Johann; Port uncertain, 1755 ***2856.30*** *p153*
Gunther, Josef; Port uncertain, 1802 ***2856.30*** *p153*
Gunther, Peter; America, 1738 ***2856.30*** *p153*
Guntly, Herbert; Maryland, 1659 ***2524.55*** *p97*
Guntner, Franz Josef; Port uncertain, 1785 ***2856.30*** *p153*
Gunton, Mark; New York, 1802 ***8197.10*** *p21*
Gunto'r, Mathew; Maryland, 1658 ***2524.55*** *p97*
Guntzer, Georg; America, 1765 ***2856.30*** *p153*
Guntzer, Georg; Port uncertain, 1765 ***2856.30*** *p152*
Gunwald, William 40; Ontario, 1871 ***1823.22*** *p65*
Gunz, Georg; Port uncertain, 1766 ***2856.30*** *p153*
Gunzler, Christof; America, 1738 ***2856.30*** *p153*
With wife
Guppy, Henery 44; Ontario, 1871 ***1823.28*** *p37*
Gurbelski, Paul; Maryland, 1910 ***3259.35*** *p19*
Gurdwell, Thomas 60; Ontario, 1871 ***1823.15*** *p101*
Gurecki, John; Maryland, 1910 ***3259.35*** *p19*
Gurling, Richard; Maryland, 1675 ***2524.55*** *p97*
Gurly, John 53; Ontario, 1871 ***1823.22*** *p65*
Gurman, Alexander; Maryland, 1910 ***3259.35*** *p19*
Gurney, Daniel; North America, 1788 ***1224.2*** *p50*
Gurney, Frances; Virginia, 1666-1667 ***6212.30*** *p34*
Gurney, Francis; Pennsylvania, 1777 ***4629.10*** *p16*
Gurney, Henry; Pennsylvania, 1777 ***4629.10*** *p21*
Gurney, John 25; Maryland, 1774 ***1220.25*** *p51*
Gurney, Robert 56; Ontario, 1871 ***1823.15*** *p101*
Gurney, Rowland; Virginia, 1667-1668 ***6212.30*** *p39*
Gurney, William 26; Ontario, 1871 ***1823.15*** *p101*
Guromski, Albert; Maryland, 1910 ***3259.35*** *p19*
Gurr, Johann; America, 1752 ***2856.30*** *p153*
With children
Gurry, John 40; Ontario, 1871 ***1823.22*** *p65*
Gurt, Frederick 40; Ontario, 1871 ***1823.28*** *p37*
Gurt, Godfortz 48; Ontario, 1871 ***1823.28*** *p37*
Gurtz, Louis 42; Ontario, 1871 ***1823.28*** *p37*
Guschwa, Johann; America, 1750 ***2856.30*** *p152*
With wife & 2 children
Guse, Conrad 39; Kansas, 1907-1910 ***9079.10*** *p46*
Guse, Mollie 12; Kansas, 1910 ***9079.10*** *p46*
Guse, Mollie 37; Kansas, 1910 ***9079.10*** *p46*
Gushbush, Joseph 60; Ontario, 1871 ***1823.15*** *p101*
Gusina, K. 38; Alaska, 1916 ***9196.1*** *p43*
Gusina, K. 38; Whitehorse, Yukon, 1916 ***9196.1*** *p43*
Guskie, Michael; Maryland, 1910 ***3259.35*** *p19*
Guskrick, William 17; Philadelphia, 1774 ***1220.25*** *p6*
Guss, Miss; Port uncertain, 1745 ***2856.30*** *p267*
Gussy, Thomas 40; Ontario, 1871 ***1823.15*** *p101*
Gusta, Rose; Ontario, 1871 ***1823.28*** *p37*
Gustavson, W. 51; Alaska, 1918 ***9196.1*** *p55*
Gustavson, W. 51; Yukon, 1918 ***9196.1*** *p55*
Gustier, Maria; Port uncertain, 1726 ***2856.30*** *p152*
Guston, George; Maryland, 1910 ***3259.35*** *p19*
Gutenberg, Johann Jakob; Port uncertain, 1748 ***2856.30*** *p152*
Guter, Martin; Port uncertain, 1772 ***2856.30*** *p153*
Gutewski, Jacob; Maryland, 1910 ***3259.35*** *p19*
Guth, Niklas; Port uncertain, 1766 ***2856.30*** *p152*
Guth, Peter; America, 1754 ***2856.30*** *p152*
With family
Guthknecht, Georg; Port uncertain, 1754 ***2856.30*** *p152*
Guthmann, Jacob; Port uncertain, 1765 ***2856.30*** *p152*
Guthre, Jamie 23; Ontario, 1871 ***1823.15*** *p101*
Guthrie, Adam *SEE* Guthrie, Thomas
Guthrie, Helen *SEE* Guthrie, Thomas
Guthrie, James; Georgia, 1699 ***1640.13*** *p50*
Guthrie, Janet *SEE* Guthrie, Thomas
Guthrie, Jean *SEE* Guthrie, Thomas
Guthrie, John *SEE* Guthrie, Thomas
Guthrie, Margaret *SEE* Guthrie, Thomas
Guthrie, Thomas *SEE* Guthrie, Thomas
Guthrie, Thomas; Savannah, Georgia, 1774 ***1640.10*** *p76*
Wife: Jean
Child: Janet
Child: Jean
Child: Margaret
Child: Adam
Child: Thomas
Child: John
Child: Helen
Guthrie, William; New York, 1794 ***8197.10*** *p4*
Gutling, Benjamin 32; Maryland, 1774 ***1220.25*** *p3*
Gutlinger, Konrad; America, 1749 ***2856.30*** *p153*
Gutmann, Joseph; New York, 1832 ***8197.10*** *p234*
Gutowki, Alexander; Maryland, 1910 ***3259.35*** *p19*
Gutowska, Kazmiera; Maryland, 1910 ***3259.35*** *p19*
Gutowski, Alexander; Maryland, 1910 ***3259.35*** *p19*
Gutowski, John; Maryland, 1910 ***3259.35*** *p19*
Gutowski, Peter; Maryland, 1910 ***3259.35*** *p19*
Gutscher, Michael; Port uncertain, 1795 ***2856.30*** *p253*
Gutsman, Frederick 38; Ontario, 1871 ***1823.28*** *p37*
Gutt, William 21; Maryland, 1775 ***1220.25*** *p112*
Gutteridge, Richard; Maryland, 1680 ***2524.55*** *p97*
Guttermann, Christian; Port uncertain, 1752 ***2856.30*** *p153*
Guttiger, Caspar; Port uncertain, 1780 ***2856.30*** *p153*
Guttiger, Caspar; Port uncertain, 1788 ***2856.30*** *p153*
Guttinger, Caspar; Port uncertain, 1780 ***2856.30*** *p153*
Guttinger, Caspar; Port uncertain, 1788 ***2856.30*** *p153*
Guttmann, Catharina; Port uncertain, 1785 ***2856.30*** *p153*
Guttree, Thomas; Maryland, 1656 ***2524.55*** *p97*
Guttree, Thomas; Maryland, 1666 ***2524.55*** *p97*
Gutzeit, Bertha 10; Ontario, 1871 ***1823.28*** *p37*
Gutzeit, Ernest 45; Ontario, 1871 ***1823.28*** *p37*
Gutzeit, Frederica 46; Ontario, 1871 ***1823.28*** *p37*
Gutzeit, Ida 7; Ontario, 1871 ***1823.28*** *p37*
Gutzeit, Johanna 13; Ontario, 1871 ***1823.28*** *p37*
Gutzeit, Paul 1; Ontario, 1871 ***1823.28*** *p37*
Guvashki, Thomas; Maryland, 1910 ***3259.35*** *p19*
Guy, Edward; Philadelphia, 1698 ***1224.1*** *p26*
Guy, Elizabeth 54; Ontario, 1871 ***1823.15*** *p101*
Guy, James; Virginia, 1679 ***6212.30*** *p54*
Guy, John; Maryland, 1641 ***2524.55*** *p87*
Guy, John 80; Ontario, 1871 ***1823.15*** *p101*
Guy, Thomas; New York, 1836-1838 ***8197.10*** *p115*
Guy, Thomas 40; Ontario, 1871 ***1823.15*** *p101*
Guy, William 50; Ontario, 1871 ***1823.15*** *p101*
Guyacyk, John; Maryland, 1910 ***3259.35*** *p19*
Guyer, John; New York, New York, 1856 ***3437.14*** *p50*
Guyer, Susan Riley 37; Vermont, 1881 ***5900.10*** *p505*
Guyette, Victoria Riley 44; Vermont, 1894 ***5900.10*** *p194*
Guyger, Gasper; Pennsylvania, 1777 ***4629.10*** *p27*
Guyger, Gasper; Pennsylvania, 1779 ***4629.10*** *p40*
Guyger, Jesse; Pennsylvania, 1777 ***4629.10*** *p30*
Guyjelska, John; Maryland, 1910 ***3259.35*** *p19*
Guylielma, L..alli; British Columbia, 1913 ***9196.1*** *p56*
Guylielma, L..alli; Seattle, 1913 ***9196.1*** *p56*
Guynne, Evan 22; Maryland, 1773-1774 ***1220.25*** *p34*
Guyon, Stephen; North America, 1784 ***1224.2*** *p50*
Guyser, Jacob; New Orleans, 1856 ***3437.14*** *p52*
Guzinski, Peter; Maryland, 1910 ***3259.35*** *p19*
Gwalina, Boleslaw; Maryland, 1910 ***3259.35*** *p19*
Gwawoski, Adolph; Maryland, 1910 ***3259.35*** *p19*
Gweast, Elizabeth; Maryland, 1649 ***2524.55*** *p97*
Gweast, Walter; Maryland, 1646 ***2524.55*** *p97*
Gwenly, Edwd; Virginia, 1671 ***6212.30*** *p44*
Gwin, John; Virginia, 1684 ***1224.1*** *p26*
Gwin, Michael; Maryland, 1658 ***2524.55*** *p97*
Gwinn, James; Nantucket, Massachusetts, 1818 ***1224.3*** *p32*
Gwinner, John A.; New York, 1840 ***8197.10*** *p235*
Gwinnett, Ann; Georgia, 1785 ***1224.2*** *p50*
Gwither, Mary; Maryland, 1658 ***2524.55*** *p97*
Gwither, Nicholas; Maryland, 1658 ***2524.55*** *p97*
Gwy, John; Maryland, 1640 ***2524.55*** *p97*
Gwyn, John; Charles Town, South Carolina, 1757 ***1224.2*** *p50*
Gwynn, James 26; Maryland, 1774 ***1220.25*** *p57*
Gwyther, Nicholas; Maryland, 1649 ***2524.55*** *p97*
Gyerzynski, Konstancy; Maryland, 1910 ***3259.35*** *p19*
Gyet, John; Maryland, 1673 ***2524.55*** *p97*
Gygur, Franaszek; Maryland, 1910 ***3259.35*** *p19*
Gyles, William; Fredericksburg, Virginia, 1769 ***1224.2*** *p45*
Gyles, William 22; Philadelphia, 1774 ***1220.25*** *p35*
Gymer, Robert; Maryland, 1658 ***2524.55*** *p97*
Gyssi, Andreas; Port uncertain, 1775 ***2856.30*** *p153*
Gyssi, Andreas; Port uncertain, 1781 ***2856.30*** *p153*
Gyvh, Eva; Maryland, 1910 ***3259.35*** *p19*
Gzelecky, Joseph; Maryland, 1910 ***3259.35*** *p19*

H

Haaber, Philipp; Port uncertain, 1768 2856.30 p157
Haab-Lutzelin, Eva; Port uncertain, 1761 2856.30 p157
Haacke, Maria 47; Ontario, 1871 1823.15 p101
Haader, Max; Port uncertain, 1714 2856.30 p157
Haader, Michael; Port uncertain, 1725 2856.30 p161
Haaf, Jakob; Port uncertain, 1785 2856.30 p157
Haag, Johann Adam; New York, 1838 8197.10 p117
Haag, Johann Georg; America, 1748 2856.30 p157
Haag, Johann Georg; Port uncertain, 1745 2856.30 p157
With wife & children
Haag, Johann Peter; Port uncertain, 1789 2856.30 p157
Haag, Ludwig; Port uncertain, 1765 2856.30 p157
With wife & 2 children
Haage, Friedrich; America, 1739 2856.30 p157
Haager, Erasmus; Port uncertain, 1782 2856.30 p157
Haal, Konrad; America, 1731 2856.30 p157
Haar, Ludwig, The Younger; America, 1754 2856.30 p157
Haarstrich, Carl; New York, 1839 8197.10 p131
Haas, Mr.; Port uncertain, 1787 2856.30 p476
Haas, Anna Eva; Port uncertain, 1755 2856.30 p157
Haas, Anna Maria; Port uncertain, 1785 2856.30 p157
Haas, Anton; Port uncertain, 1771 2856.30 p157
Haas, Casimir; Port uncertain, 1764 2856.30 p158
With wife & 3 children
Haas, Catharina; Port uncertain, 1774 2856.30 p158
Haas, David; New York, 1840 8197.10 p173
Haas, Elisabeth; America, 1826 2856.30 p158
With husband
Haas, Elisabeth; Port uncertain, 1750 2856.30 p61
Haas, Franziska; America, 1826 2856.30 p157
Haas, Gailack; Pennsylvania, 1777 4629.10 p9
Haas, Gottlob; New York, 1839 8197.10 p131
Haas, Hans Adam; Port uncertain, 1736 2856.30 p158
With wife & 2 children
Haas, Heinrich; Port uncertain, 1747 2856.30 p157
Haas, Jakob; Port uncertain, 1764 2856.30 p158
Haas, Johann; America, 1740 2856.30 p157
Haas, Johann; America, 1741 2856.30 p157
Haas, Johann; Port uncertain, 1740 2856.30 p158
With wife
Haas, Johann; Port uncertain, 1755 2856.30 p157
Haas, Johann; Port uncertain, 1758 2856.30 p157
Haas, Johann; Port uncertain, 1765 2856.30 p157
Haas, Johann Lorenz; Port uncertain, 1738 2856.30 p157
Haas, Josef; Port uncertain, 1747 2856.30 p157
Haas, Ludwig, The Younger; America, 1754 2856.30 p157
Haas, Martin; New York, 1838 8197.10 p118
Haas, Michael; America, 1749 2856.30 p158
Haas, Michael; America, 1790 2856.30 p158
Haas, Michael; New York, 1840 8197.10 p174
Haas, Michael; Port uncertain, 1764 2856.30 p158
Haas, Michael 60; Ontario, 1871 1823.15 p101
Haas, Nikolaus; Port uncertain, 1764 2856.30 p158
Haas, Philipp Karl; America, 1748 2856.30 p158
Haase, Elisabeth; Port uncertain, 1750 2856.30 p233
Haase, Herman; New York, New York, 1876 3437.14 p117
Haase, John; New York, 1839 8197.10 p242
Haase, Louis; New York, New York, 1869 3437.14 p114
Haasel, Burkhard; Port uncertain, 1764 2856.30 p158
Haasmann, Margarete; Port uncertain, 1740 2856.30 p158
Haass, Christof; Port uncertain, 1732 2856.30 p158
Haass, Georg; America, 1754 2856.30 p158
Haass, Hans Jacob; Port uncertain, 1694 2856.30 p158
Haass, Johann Abraham; America, 1740 2856.30 p158
Haass, Johann Henrich; Port uncertain, 1750 2856.30 p158
Haass, Johann Michael; America, 1752 2856.30 p158
Haass, Johann Michael; Port uncertain, 1748 2856.30 p158
With wife & 4 children
Haass, Ludwig, The Younger; America, 1754 2856.30 p158
With wife & children
Haass, Marg. Walk *SEE* Haass, Peter
Haass, Peter; Port uncertain, 1756 2856.30 p467
Haass, Peter; Port uncertain, 1779 2856.30 p158
Wife: Marg. Walk
Haass, Sebastian; Port uncertain, 1738 2856.30 p158
Haasserin, Ludgardis; Port uncertain, 1754 2856.30 p158
Habbkirk, A. A. 22; Ontario, 1871 1823.15 p101
Habe, Andreas; Port uncertain, 1753 2856.30 p158
Habe, Johann; Port uncertain, 1756 2856.30 p158
Habe, Mathias; Port uncertain, 1758 2856.30 p158
Habele, Hans Adam; Port uncertain, 1749 2856.30 p158
With wife & children
Haber, Franz; Port uncertain, 1790 2856.30 p158
Haber, Philipp; America, 1749 2856.30 p158
With wife & 3 children
Haber, Wilhelm; Port uncertain, 1781 2856.30 p158
Haberer, Georg Ernst; Port uncertain, 1764 2856.30 p158
Haberer, Johann Georg; Port uncertain, 1756 2856.30 p158
Haberland, Mary 93; Vermont, 1892 5900.10 p165
Haberle, Karl; New York, New York, 1893 3437.14 p145
Haberlin, James; New York, New York, 1851 6058.10 p70
Habermann, Catharina; Port uncertain, 1737 2856.30 p158
Habermann, Sophia; Port uncertain, 1752 2856.30 p158
Habermiller, Magdalena; Port uncertain, 1791 2856.30 p158
Habersack, Michael; America, 1741 2856.30 p158
Haberstich, Susanna Maria; America, 1750 2856.30 p158
Haberstroh, Anton; Port uncertain, 1768 2856.30 p159
Haberstroh, Christof; Port uncertain, 1790 2856.30 p159
Haberstroh, Georg Adam; America, 1788 2856.30 p159
Haberstroh, Michael; America, 1744 2856.30 p159
Haberstroh, Wendel; America, 1744 2856.30 p159
Haberstroh, Xaver; America, 1840 2856.30 p159
Habich, Marianna; Port uncertain, 1793 2856.30 p159
Habishaw, William 18; Nova Scotia, 1774 1220.25 p135
Habkirk, William 37; Ontario, 1871 1823.15 p101
Habkirk, William 75; Ontario, 1871 1823.15 p101
Habluzlerin, Eva; Port uncertain, 1761 2856.30 p159
Hacett, Nicholas; Maryland, 1665 2524.55 p97
Hack, Anna Elisabeth; Port uncertain, 1773 2856.30 p159
Hack, Johann Ludwig; Port uncertain, 1787 2856.30 p159
Hack, Johann Ludwig; Port uncertain, 1788 2856.30 p159
Hack, Maria Elisabeth; Port uncertain, 1764 2856.30 p159
Hack, Valentin; America, 1749 2856.30 p159
Hackatt, John; Pennsylvania, 1777 4629.10 p12
Hacke, Christian; New York, 1840 8197.10 p171
Hacker, Christof; America, 1752 2856.30 p159
Hacker, Christof; Port uncertain, 1752 2856.30 p159
Hacker, Elizabeth *SEE* Hacker, Richard
Hacker, John *SEE* Hacker, Richard
Hacker, John; Virginia, 1690 1224.1 p26
Hacker, Mary *SEE* Hacker, Richard
Hacker, Nathaniel; Maryland, 1666 2524.55 p97
Hacker, Rachell *SEE* Hacker, Richard
Hacker, Richard; Maryland, 1672 2524.55 p97
Wife: Mary
Son: John
Daughter: Elizabeth
Daughter: Rachell
Daughter: Mary
Hacket, Elisa 45; Ontario, 1871 1823.15 p101
Hacket, Ellen 29; Ontario, 1871 1823.15 p101
Hacket, James 35; Ontario, 1871 1823.15 p101
Hacket, Joseph 50; Ontario, 1871 1823.15 p102
Hacket, Joseph 77; Ontario, 1871 1823.15 p102
Hacket, Mathew; New York, 1828 8197.10 p240
Hacket, Thomas 60; Ontario, 1871 1823.15 p102
Hackett, Bridget 49; Vermont, 1895 5900.10 p60
Hackett, Cathrine O'Bryan; Vermont, 1834-1911 5900.10 p90
Hackett, Charles 22; Maryland, 1774 1220.25 p70
Hackett, Elizabeth 49; Ontario, 1871 1823.22 p65
Hackett, Ellen Condon 74; Vermont, 1891 5900.10 p68
Hackett, Ellen M. Ward; Vermont, 1854-1928 5900.10 p89
Hackett, Ellen Murphey; Vermont, n.d. 5900.10 p68
Hackett, James; New York, 1818 8197.10 p236
Hackett, James; Pennsylvania, 1868 6058.10 p72
Hackett, James; Vermont, n.d. 5900.10 p68
Hackett, James 33; Vermont, 1893 5900.10 p196
Hackett, James H. 25; Vermont, 1890 5900.10 p116
Hackett, Jennie; Vermont, 1857-1913 5900.10 p446
Hackett, John; Maryland, 1729 1224.2 p50
Hackett, John; New York, 1838 8197.10 p241
Hackett, John; Pennsylvania, 1731 1224.2 p50
Hackett, John; Vermont, 1832-1923 5900.10 p90
Hackett, John; Vermont, 1854-1921 5900.10 p583
Hackett, John 41; Maryland, 1774 1220.25 p47
Hackett, John E.; Vermont, 1854-1928 5900.10 p89
Hackett, Lawrance 32; Maryland, 1774 1220.25 p77
Hackett, Margaret 7; Vermont, 1865 5900.10 p196
Hackett, Margaret A. Hanley; Vermont, 1833-1901 5900.10 p557
Hackett, Maria 77; Vermont, 1925 5900.10 p68
Hackett, Mary; Vermont, 1864-1942 5900.10 p196
Hackett, Mary A. Gallagher; Vermont, 1858-1922 5900.10 p583
Hackett, Mary Foley; Vermont, 1828-1878 5900.10 p196
Hackett, Mathias 43; Vermont, 1890 5900.10 p196
Hackett, Matilda; Vermont, 1856-1932 5900.10 p196
Hackett, Michael; Vermont, 1832-1908 5900.10 p557
Hackett, Nicholas; Maryland, 1665 2524.55 p97
Hackett, Onnoria 19; Ontario, 1871 1823.15 p102
Hackett, Patrick 47; Vermont, 1891 5900.10 p60
Hackett, Richard; New York, 1837 8197.10 p90
Hackett, Richard; Pennsylvania, 1777 4629.10 p20
Hackett, Susan; Vermont, 1854-1934 5900.10 p196
Hackett, Thomas; Maryland, 1682 2524.55 p97
Hackett, Thomas; Vermont, 1817-1910 5900.10 p196
Hackett, Thomas 79; Vermont, 1887 5900.10 p68
Hackett, Watty 47; Ontario, 1871 1823.15 p102
Hackett, William; New York, 1837 8197.10 p90
Hackett, William 25; Vermont, 1892 5900.10 p196
Hackhel, Jerg; America, 1751 2856.30 p197G
Hackister, John; Maryland, 1674 2524.55 p97
Hackley, Thomas 29; Virginia, 1774 1220.25 p55
Hackman, Sam 29; Alaska, 1917 9196.1 p50
Hackman, Sam 29; Whitehorse, Yukon, 1917 9196.1 p50
Hackmann, Abraham; Port uncertain, 1754 2856.30 p159

Hackney, James 42; Ontario, 1871 *1823.15 p102*
Hackney, John; Maryland, 1675 *2524.55 p97*
Hackney, Joseph; Maryland, 1665 *2524.55 p97*
Hackny, Frans; Virginia, 1674-1675 *6212.30 p53*
Hacoth, Edward; Virginia, 1671-1672 *6212.30 p46*
Hadden, James 37; Ontario, 1861 *2896.28 p11*
Hadden, Jane 19; Ontario, 1861 *2896.28 p28*
Hadden, M. 30; Ontario, 1861 *2896.28 p11*
Hadden, M. 59; Ontario, 1861 *2896.28 p11*
Hadden, R. 23; Ontario, 1861 *2896.28 p11*
Hadden, William 22; Ontario, 1861 *2896.28 p48*
Hadden, William 71; Ontario, 1871 *1823.15 p102*
Haddin, M. 15; Ontario, 1861 *2896.28 p4*
Haddin, Robert; Pennsylvania, 1868 *6058.10 p62*
Haddock, Thomas; Maryland, 1681 *2524.55 p97*
Haddock, W. 31; Alaska, 1917 *9196.1 p53*
Haddock, W. 31; Whitehorse, Yukon, 1917 *9196.1 p53*
Haddocke, William; Virginia, 1649 *1224.1 p26*
Haddow, Margaret 18; Ontario, 1871 *1823.28 p37*
Hadfield, George; Washington, District of Columbia, 1827 *1224.3 p32*
Hadikoff, George 31; Alaska, 1917 *9196.1 p47*
Hadikoff, George 31; Whitehorse, Yukon, 1917 *9196.1 p47*
Hadley, Caroline; Vermont, 1849-1920 *5900.10 p500*
Hadley, John 25; Virginia, 1774 *1220.25 p89*
Hadley, Maria S.; Vermont, 1856-1936 *5900.10 p197*
Hadley, Thomas H.; Vermont, 1858-1910 *5900.10 p197*
Hadline, John; New York, New York, 1859 *3437.14 p76*
Hadlington, William; Virginia, 1663 *6212.30 p1*
Hadoway, Mrs.; Maryland, 1665 *2524.55 p97*
Haduck, Alice; Virginia, 1703-1704 *6212.30 p63*
Hadzicki, John; Maryland, 1910 *3259.35 p19*
Haeffile, Moritz; New York, 1839 *8197.10 p131*
Haeg, Christian; Port uncertain, 1791 *2856.30 p159*
Haentshal, Charles 36; Ontario, 1871 *1823.28 p37*
Haering, Maria Sara Stuhlfaud; Port uncertain, 1770 *2856.30 p159*
Haescher, Samuel; New York, 1837 *8197.10 p91*
Haeselbarth, Adam C.; New York, 1836 *8197.10 p75*
Haeussler, Heinrich; Port uncertain, 1777 *2856.30 p159*
With wife
Hafard, Anthony; New York, 1840 *8197.10 p171*
Haff, Miss; Port uncertain, 1785 *2856.30 p475*
Haffee, John; New York, 1806 *8197.10 p323*
Haffele, Karl; Port uncertain, 1736 *2856.30 p197G*
With wife & children
Haffeli, Montz; New York, New York, 1854 *6058.10 p42*
Hafflin, Maria; Port uncertain, 1769 *2856.30 p197G*
Haffner, Albert; Port uncertain, 1764 *2856.30 p159*
Haffner, Johann; America, 1749 *2856.30 p159*
Haffner, Johann; America, 1750 *2856.30 p159*
Haffner, John Christian 28; Maryland, 1774 *1220.25 p78*
Haffner, Margarete; America, 1750 *2856.30 p159*
Hafford, John; Vermont, 1821-1870 *5900.10 p511*
Hafford, Mary Dolan; Vermont, 1822-1915 *5900.10 p511*
Haffy, Edward; New York, 1840 *8197.10 p386*
Hafner, Catharina; Port uncertain, 1766 *2856.30 p197G*
Hafner, Maria Elisabeth; Port uncertain, 1792 *2856.30 p197G*
Hafzinger, Peter 64; Ontario, 1871 *1823.15 p102*
Hag, Anna Margarete; Port uncertain, 1751 *2856.30 p160*
Hag, Jakob; Port uncertain, 1734 *2856.30 p159*
Hag, Margarete; Port uncertain, 1743 *2856.30 p159*
Hag, Michael; Port uncertain, 1791 *2856.30 p159*
With wife & 5 children
Hagair, Martin 28; Ontario, 1871 *1823.15 p102*
Hagan, Ann 73; Vermont, 1891 *5900.10 p345*
Hagan, Darby 22; Maryland, 1774 *1220.25 p70*
Hagan, Edmond; Maryland, 1682 *2524.55 p98*
Hagan, Francis; New York, 1827-1834 *8197.10 p308*
Hagan, Hugh 64; Ontario, 1871 *1823.22 p65*
Hagan, James 36; Ontario, 1871 *1823.15 p102*
Hagan, James 50; Ontario, 1871 *1823.15 p102*
Hagan, Jas 48; Alaska, 1917 *9196.1 p44*
Hagan, Jas 48; Whitehorse, Yukon, 1917 *9196.1 p44*
Hagan, John 40; Ontario, 1871 *1823.15 p102*
Hagan, Margaret 72; Ontario, 1871 *1823.15 p102*
Hagan, Mary; Vermont, 1837-1893 *5900.10 p309*
Hagan, Mary 64; Vermont, 1900 *5900.10 p608*
Hagan, Mary E. Horton; Vermont, 1843-1904 *5900.10 p385*
Hagan, Michael; New York, 1840 *8197.10 p172*
Hagan, Robert; Pennsylvania, 1777 *4629.10 p28*
Hagan, Robert 36; Ontario, 1871 *1823.15 p102*
Hagan, Samuel 31; Ontario, 1871 *1823.15 p102*
Hagan, Thomas J.; Vermont, 1841-1912 *5900.10 p385*
Hagard, Rev.; Portland, Maine, 1858 *9196.15 p47*
Hagarty, Anthony; Vermont, 1823-1884 *5900.10 p585*
Hagarty, Catherine; Vermont, 1837-1897 *5900.10 p585*
Hagarty, Cornelius 19; Baltimore, 1775 *1220.25 p116*
Hagarty, Joseph; New York, 1840 *8197.10 p174*
Hagbig, A. 27; Alaska, 1912 *9196.1 p37*
Hagbig, A. 27; British Columbia, 1912 *9196.1 p37*
Hage, John; Maryland, 1650 *2524.55 p98*
Hagel, Heinrich; America, 1739 *2856.30 p160*
Hagel, Johann; Port uncertain, 1771 *2856.30 p160*
With wife & children
Hagelberger, Benjamin; America, 1752 *2856.30 p160*
With wife & 5 children
Hagelberger, Catharina; America, 1752 *2856.30 p160*
Hagelberger, H. Zacharias; America, 1752 *2856.30 p160*
Hagelstein, Alexander 44; Ontario, 1871 *1823.28 p37*
Hageman, Nelson; New York, 1807 *8197.10 p40*
Hagen, Archibald; New York, 1835-1838 *8197.10 p117*
Hagen, George; Vermont, 1854 *1224.3 p32*
Hagen, John O. 80; Vermont, 1881 *5900.10 p608*
Hagen, Margaret 38; Vermont, 1850 *5900.10 p281*
Hagen, Mary Melissa; Vermont, 1821-1902 *5900.10 p281*
Hagen, O. C. 31; Alaska, 1909 *9196.1 p8*
Hagen, O. C. 31; Yukon, 1909 *9196.1 p8*
Hagen, Thomas; Vermont, 1856 *5900.10 p281*
Hagen, Thomas 64; Vermont, 1870 *5900.10 p281*
Hagenauer, Johann; Port uncertain, 1795 *2856.30 p160*
Hagenauer, Johann; Port uncertain, 1796 *2856.30 p160*
Hagener, Johann Peter; America, 1740 *2856.30 p160*
Hagenmuller, Melchior; Port uncertain, 1727 *2856.30 p160*
Hagenmuller, Melchior; Port uncertain, 1752 *2856.30 p160*
Hager, Catharina; America, 1749 *2856.30 p513*
Hager, Catharina Zimmermann; America, 1749 *2856.30 p160*
Hager, Georg; Port uncertain, 1756 *2856.30 p160*
Hager, Margarete Elsser; America, 1749 *2856.30 p160*
With children
Hagerthy, Timothy; New York, 1833 *8197.10 p240*
Hagerty, Andrew N. 19; Vermont, 1853 *5900.10 p615*
Hagerty, Edward K. 21; Vermont, 1862 *5900.10 p615*
Hagerty, Ellen 48; Vermont, 1875 *5900.10 p55*
Hagerty, Margaret Adams 82; Vermont, 1882 *5900.10 p615*
Hagerty, Mary 33; Vermont, 1864 *5900.10 p100*
Hagerty, Mary 73; Vermont, 1893 *5900.10 p414*
Hagerty, Michael 84; Vermont, 1876 *5900.10 p615*
Hagerty, Timothy 40; Ontario, 1871 *1823.28 p37*
Hagerty, William; New York, 1837 *8197.10 p91*
Hagerty, William 48; Ontario, 1871 *1823.28 p37*
Hagerty, William H. 16; Vermont, 1854 *5900.10 p615*
Haggans, Uriah; Vermont, 1842-1901 *5900.10 p459*
Haggans, William; Vermont, 1836-1901 *5900.10 p459*
Haggard, David 28; Ontario, 1871 *1823.15 p102*
Haggard, Richard; Maryland, 1672 *2524.55 p98*
Haggard, Thomas 29; Ontario, 1871 *1823.15 p102*
Haggard, Thomas 59; Ontario, 1871 *1823.15 p102*
Haggart, Ann 37; Ontario, 1871 *1823.15 p116*
Haggart, Archibald 67; Ontario, 1871 *1823.22 p65*
Haggart, James; New York, 1832 *8197.10 p240*
Haggart, Martha 59; Ontario, 1871 *1823.22 p65*
Haggarty, Abigail 25; Ontario, 1861 *2896.27 p30*
Haggarty, Bridget 48; Ontario, 1871 *1823.28 p37*
Haggerty, Mr.; Vermont, n.d. *5900.10 p37*
Haggerty, Ann; Vermont, 1803-1887 *5900.10 p534*
Haggerty, Barney; New York, 1838 *8197.10 p117*
Haggerty, John; New York, 1840 *8197.10 p173*
Haggerty, Manric 70; Vermont, 1875 *5900.10 p530*
Haggerty, Margaret 70; Ontario, 1861 *2896.27 p40*
Haggerty, Mary 68; Vermont, 1920 *5900.10 p114*
Haggerty, Mary A. 31; Vermont, 1881 *5900.10 p529*
Haggett, Anne; Maryland, 1663 *2524.55 p98*
Haggin, Therese; Port uncertain, 1725 *2856.30 p160*
With husband
Haggins, Catherine 40; Ontario, 1861 *2896.27 p67*
Haggins, John 70; Ontario, 1861 *2896.27 p67*
Haggister, John; Maryland, 1674 *2524.55 p97*
Haggit, Edward 50; Ontario, 1871 *1823.15 p102*
Haggon, Cornelius; Maryland, 1658 *2524.55 p98*
Haghue, Patrick; New York, 1837 *8197.10 p90*
Hagin, Anna Margarete; Port uncertain, 1751 *2856.30 p160*
Hagin, Jerg; Port uncertain, 1771 *2856.30 p160*
Hagin, Jerg; Port uncertain, 1781 *2856.30 p160*
Hagle, Jane 35; Ontario, 1871 *1823.28 p37*
Hagner, Frederick; Pennsylvania, 1777 *4629.10 p7*
Hagner, Philip; Pennsylvania, 1777 *4629.10 p9*
Hagoe, Mary; Maryland, 1672 *2524.55 p98*
Hagoff, Nick 26; Alaska, 1917 *9196.1 p47*
Hagoff, Nick 26; Whitehorse, Yukon, 1917 *9196.1 p47*
Hagon, Mary; Maryland, 1672 *2524.55 p98*
Hague, Ralph 24; Maryland, 1774 *1220.25 p83*
Hahanan, Tomas; Pennsylvania, 1779 *4629.10 p40*
Hahar, Ellen; Vermont, 1815-1898 *5900.10 p578*
Haher, Mary; Vermont, 1841-1924 *5900.10 p579*
Hahn, Adam; America, 1762 *2856.30 p160*
Hahn, Adam; America, 1769 *2856.30 p160*
Hahn, Anna Barbara; Port uncertain, 1775 *2856.30 p160*
Hahn, Anna Catharina; Port uncertain, 1745 *2856.30 p160*
Hahn, Anna Margarete; Port uncertain, 1790 *2856.30 p160*
Hahn, Anna Margarete; Port uncertain, 1791 *2856.30 p160*
Hahn, Anton; Port uncertain, 1777 *2856.30 p160*
Hahn, Heymann; New York, 1839 *8197.10 p320*
Hahn, Josef; Port uncertain, 1773 *2856.30 p160*
Hahn, Maria Catharina; Port uncertain, 1774 *2856.30 p160*
Hahn, Mathes Nickhel; Port uncertain, 1745 *2856.30 p160*
Hahn, Michael; America, 1751 *2856.30 p160*
Hahn, Nickel; Port uncertain, 1759 *2856.30 p160*
Hahn, Paul; Port uncertain, 1786 *2856.30 p160*
Hahn, Peter; America, 1744 *2856.30 p160*
Hahn, Philipp; Port uncertain, 1789 *2856.30 p160*
Hahnengrath, Margarete; Port uncertain, 1793 *2856.30 p160*
Hai, Elisabeth; Port uncertain, 1734 *2856.30 p160*
Haider, Max; Port uncertain, 1714 *2856.30 p157*
Haider, Michael; Port uncertain, 1725 *2856.30 p161*
Haiderich, Abraham; America, 1739 *2856.30 p161*
With wife & 4 children
Haidon, Gideon; Virginia, 1666-1667 *6212.30 p32*
Haies, Patrick; Virginia, 1663 *6212.30 p2*
Haig, Mr.; Quebec, 1857 *9196.15 p27*
Haig, Andrew 47; Ontario, 1871 *1823.22 p65*
Haig, Archibald 32; Ontario, 1871 *1823.22 p65*
Haig, David 46; Ontario, 1871 *1823.22 p65*
Haig, David 50; Ontario, 1871 *1823.22 p65*
Haig, James 28; Ontario, 1871 *1823.22 p66*
Haig, James 49; Ontario, 1871 *1823.22 p65*
Haig, John 54; Ontario, 1871 *1823.22 p66*
Haig, Mary 30; Ontario, 1871 *1823.28 p37*
Haig, Susan; Ontario, 1885 *1640.13 p51*
Haig, Susan McEwan; Charleston, South Carolina, 1883 *1640.13 p51*
Haig, Thomas 43; Ontario, 1871 *1823.22 p66*
Haig, Thomas 61; Ontario, 1871 *1823.22 p66*
Haigh, Samuel; New Orleans, 1834 *1224.3 p32*
Haighes, John; Virginia, 1628 *1224.1 p28*
Haight, Miss 1; Ontario, 1861 *2896.28 p13*
Haight, A. 32; Ontario, 1861 *2896.28 p13*
Haight, Angeline 36; Ontario, 1861 *2896.27 p30*
Haight, B. L. 4; Ontario, 1861 *2896.28 p13*
Haight, Daniel D. 14; Ontario, 1861 *2896.28 p14*
Haight, Deborah 14; Ontario, 1861 *2896.27 p29*
Haight, Ed; Virginia, 1683 *6212.30 p56*
Haight, Eliza 41; Ontario, 1861 *2896.28 p27*
Haight, Elizabeth 56; Ontario, 1871 *1823.22 p66*
Haight, H. A. 47; Ontario, 1861 *2896.28 p14*
Haight, H. M. 28; Ontario, 1861 *2896.28 p14*
Haight, J. D. 18; Ontario, 1861 *2896.28 p13*
Haight, J. E. 2; Ontario, 1861 *2896.28 p14*
Haight, J. E. 6; Ontario, 1861 *2896.28 p13*
Haight, J. W. 12; Ontario, 1861 *2896.28 p14*
Haight, Joel 17; Ontario, 1861 *2896.28 p14*
Haight, John 22; Ontario, 1861 *2896.25 p16*
Haight, John William 9; Ontario, 1861 *2896.27 p49*
Haight, L. 19; Ontario, 1861 *2896.28 p14*
Haight, L. 57; Ontario, 1861 *2896.28 p14*
Haight, M. 44; Ontario, 1861 *2896.28 p14*
Haight, M. A. 38; Ontario, 1861 *2896.28 p13*
Haight, M. E. 12; Ontario, 1861 *2896.28 p13*
Haight, Minerva A. 16; Ontario, 1861 *2896.27 p49*
Haight, P. 10; Ontario, 1861 *2896.28 p14*
Haight, P. A. 6; Ontario, 1861 *2896.28 p13*
Haight, P. C. 15; Ontario, 1861 *2896.28 p13*
Haight, Peter 19; Ontario, 1861 *2896.28 p14*
Haight, Phebe J. 18; Ontario, 1861 *2896.27 p49*
Haight, R. 6; Ontario, 1861 *2896.28 p14*
Haight, S. 27; Ontario, 1861 *2896.28 p14*
Haight, Sarah 38; Ontario, 1861 *2896.27 p49*
Haight, Thomas H. 11; Ontario, 1861 *2896.27 p49*
Haight, W. A. 8; Ontario, 1861 *2896.28 p13*
Haight, W. W. 2; Ontario, 1861 *2896.28 p14*
Haight, William 4; Ontario, 1861 *2896.28 p13*
Haile, William 22; Philadelphia, 1774 *1220.25 p4*
Hailey, John 49; Ontario, 1871 *1823.22 p66*
Hailey, Peter 50; Ontario, 1871 *1823.22 p66*
Hailey, William 63; Ontario, 1871 *1823.28 p37*
Hailshorn, John; New York, 1807 *8197.10 p329*
Haily, James 64; Ontario, 1871 *1823.28 p37*
Hain, Andrew 29; Ontario, 1871 *1823.15 p102*
Hain, Job 32; Maryland, 1775 *1220.25 p111*
Hain, Lorenz; America, 1738 *2856.30 p161*
Hain, Robert 34; Ontario, 1871 *1823.28 p37*
Haines, Mr.; Portland, Maine, 1858 *9196.15 p29*
Haines, Mr.; Quebec, 1856 *9196.15 p8*

Haines, Mrs.; Portland, Maine, 1858 ***9196.15*** *p29*
Haines, Mrs.; Quebec, 1856 ***9196.15*** *p9*
Haines, Andrew 16; Virginia, 1774 ***1220.25*** *p89*
Haines, Anna Maria; Virginia, 1700-1799 ***1224.2*** *p54*
Haines, Catherine; Vermont, 1858-1938 ***5900.10*** *p434*
Haines, Daniel; Pennsylvania, 1777 ***4629.10*** *p20*
Haines, Edw; Virginia, 1665-1666 ***6212.30*** *p21*
Haines, Homer 26; Ontario, 1871 ***1823.28*** *p37*
Haines, John; Pennsylvania, 1777 ***4629.10*** *p20*
Haines, John; Pennsylvania, 1777 ***4629.10*** *p22*
Hainlewski, Stanislaus; Maryland, 1910 ***3259.35*** *p19*
Hainpeaux, Joseph 66; Ontario, 1871 ***1823.28*** *p37*
Hains, Cassen; New York, 1807 ***8197.10*** *p40*
Hains, Ranseler 64; Ontario, 1871 ***1823.22*** *p66*
Hainzmann, Michael; Port uncertain, 1623 ***2856.30*** *p161*
Hainzmann, Michael; Port uncertain, 1623 ***2856.30*** *p161*
With wife & father
Hair, Maria 30; Ontario, 1871 ***1823.22*** *p66*
Hair, William 41; Ontario, 1871 ***1823.15*** *p102*
Haire, Henry; Maryland, 1665 ***2524.55*** *p98*
Haisler, Christian; Port uncertain, 1733 ***2856.30*** *p161*
Haisley, Mary Ann 45; Ontario, 1871 ***1823.22*** *p66*
Haisong, Friedrich; Canada, 1751 ***2856.30*** *p161*
Haist, Catherina 55; Ontario, 1871 ***1823.15*** *p102*
Haist, Christian 64; Ontario, 1871 ***1823.15*** *p102*
Haiste, James 34; Virginia, 1774 ***1220.25*** *p91*
Haiston, Francis; New York, 1838 ***8197.10*** *p378*
Haize, John; Maryland, 1682 ***2524.55*** *p98*
Haize, Thomas; Maryland, 1655 ***2524.55*** *p98*
Hajek, Mr.; Port uncertain, 1776 ***2856.30*** *p497*
Hake, Lucy; Wisconsin, 1857 ***1224.3*** *p32*
Hala, Thomas; New York, 1838 ***8197.10*** *p318*
Haland, Lawrence; Maryland, 1678 ***2524.55*** *p105*
Halbert, Adam; America, 1738 ***2856.30*** *p161*
Halbert, Miles; Virginia, 1669-1670 ***6212.30*** *p41*
Halbert, Rene; New York, 1840 ***8197.10*** *p171*
Halbert, Richard; Maryland, 1657 ***2524.55*** *p98*
Halbham, Mr.; Quebec, 1856 ***9196.15*** *p11*
Halcorne, Andrew; Maryland, 1674 ***2524.55*** *p98*
Halcro, Elizabeth *SEE* Halcro, Magnus
Halcro, Hugh *SEE* Halcro, Magnus
Halcro, Magnus; Savannah, Georgia, 1774 ***1640.10*** *p76*
Wife: Elizabeth
Son: Hugh
Haldane, Miss; Quebec, 1858 ***9196.15*** *p41*
Haldane, John; New York, 1840 ***8197.10*** *p172*
Halde, Christian; America, 1749 ***2856.30*** *p161*
Halder, Hans; Port uncertain, 1687 ***2856.30*** *p161*
Halder, Hans; Port uncertain, 1726 ***2856.30*** *p161*
Halder, Jacob; Port uncertain, 1678 ***2856.30*** *p161*
With wife & 3 children
Halder, Johann; Port uncertain, 1714 ***2856.30*** *p161*
Halder, Johann; Port uncertain, 1717 ***2856.30*** *p161*
Halder, Michael; Port uncertain, 1792 ***2856.30*** *p161*
Hale, Miss; Quebec, 1858 ***9196.15*** *p39*
Hale, Mr.; Portland, Maine, 1858 ***9196.15*** *p28*
Hale, Mrs.; Portland, Maine, 1858 ***9196.15*** *p28*
Hale, Ann Burns 80; Vermont, 1891 ***5900.10*** *p228*
Hale, Anna L. Maloney; Vermont, 1868-1915 ***5900.10*** *p278*
Hale, Anthony 17; Maryland, 1775 ***1220.25*** *p121*
Hale, Bartholomew; Vermont, 1839-1918 ***5900.10*** *p233*
Hale, Bridget; Vermont, 1861-1928 ***5900.10*** *p503*
Hale, Carrie Barton; California, 1894 ***1640.13*** *p51*
Hale, Daniel Horatio; Los Angeles, 1888 ***1640.13*** *p51*
Hale, Edward; Virginia, 1663-1664 ***6212.30*** *p5*
Hale, Edward; Watertown, Massachusetts, 1811 ***1224.3*** *p32*
Hale, Henry H.; Vermont, 1847-1916 ***5900.10*** *p278*
Hale, Horatio 50; Ontario, 1871 ***1823.15*** *p102*
Hale, Jennie A.; Vermont, 1853-1922 ***5900.10*** *p497*
Hale, John; Maryland, 1681 ***2524.55*** *p98*
Hale, John 38; Ontario, 1871 ***1823.28*** *p37*
Hale, Katherine; Vermont, 1885-1919 ***5900.10*** *p323*
Hale, Laura McGowan; Vermont, 1829-1876 ***5900.10*** *p377*
Hale, Mary 48; Vermont, 1859 ***5900.10*** *p228*
Hale, Mary 63; Vermont, 1883 ***5900.10*** *p494*
Hale, Robert; Maryland, 1668 ***2524.55*** *p98*
Hale, Robert; Maryland, 1672 ***2524.55*** *p98*
Hale, Samuel; Maryland, 1658 ***2524.55*** *p237*
Hale, Sarah; Vermont, 1847-1925 ***5900.10*** *p233*
Hale, Thomas; New York, 1834 ***8197.10*** *p240*
Hale, Thomas 65; Vermont, 1864 ***5900.10*** *p228*
Hale, Warwick; Pennsylvania, 1777 ***4629.10*** *p13*
Hale, William; Philadelphia, 1832 ***1224.3*** *p32*
Halegan, Mary; Vermont, 1821-1881 ***5900.10*** *p231*
Halen, Emily A.; Vermont, 1848-1929 ***5900.10*** *p197*
Haler, Daniel; Pennsylvania, 1786 ***4629.10*** *p49*
Hales, Mrs.; Maryland, 1631-1636 ***2524.55*** *p98*
Hales, Edw; Virginia, 1665-1666 ***6212.30*** *p22*
Hales, Jno; Virginia, 1665-1666 ***6212.30*** *p21*
Hales, Mary 80; Ontario, 1871 ***1823.22*** *p66*
Hales, Sarah; New England, 1696 ***1224.1*** *p26*
Hales, Wm; Virginia, 1665-1666 ***6212.30*** *p21*
Haleson, William; Maryland, 1682 ***2524.55*** *p98*
Haletade, John 75; Ontario, 1871 ***1823.22*** *p66*
Halewell, John; Maryland, 1663 ***2524.55*** *p98*
Haley, Anne; Vermont, 1850-1917 ***5900.10*** *p393*
Haley, Catherine; Vermont, 1845-1919 ***5900.10*** *p135*
Haley, Catherine E.; Vermont, 1853-1925 ***5900.10*** *p399*
Haley, Cornelius 30; Ontario, 1871 ***1823.28*** *p37*
Haley, Hannah Sheehan; Vermont, 1822-1897 ***5900.10*** *p401*
Haley, Hanora 56; Vermont, 1868 ***5900.10*** *p502*
Haley, Hanora Lawton 50; Vermont, 1866 ***5900.10*** *p577*
Haley, Hugh 28; Ontario, 1871 ***1823.22*** *p66*
Haley, James; Vermont, 1814-1897 ***5900.10*** *p401*
Haley, James; Vermont, 1839-1915 ***5900.10*** *p316*
Haley, James E.; Vermont, 1852-1926 ***5900.10*** *p399*
Haley, Jane; Vermont, 1842-1925 ***5900.10*** *p349*
Haley, Jeremiah 44; Vermont, 1845 ***5900.10*** *p316*
Haley, Jeremiah F. 29; Vermont, 1873 ***5900.10*** *p316*
Haley, John; Canada, 1756-1760 ***4628.40*** *p45*
Haley, John 49; Vermont, 1876 ***5900.10*** *p593*
Haley, John 76; Vermont, 1886 ***5900.10*** *p365*
Haley, Kate; Vermont, 1869-1937 ***5900.10*** *p221*
Haley, Margaret; Vermont, 1820-1863 ***5900.10*** *p562*
Haley, Margaret E. Courtney; Vermont, n.d. ***5900.10*** *p188*
Haley, Mary A.; Vermont, 1856-1941 ***5900.10*** *p401*
Haley, Mary A. McMahon 91; Vermont, 1934 ***5900.10*** *p316*
Haley, Mary Harrington; Vermont, 1827-1916 ***5900.10*** *p593*
Haley, Mary L.; Vermont, 1840-1914 ***5900.10*** *p313*
Haley, Patrick; Vermont, 1800-1888 ***5900.10*** *p562*
Haley, Robert; Maryland, 1668 ***2524.55*** *p98*
Haley, Samuel; Maryland, 1670 ***2524.55*** *p107*
Haley, Samuell; Maryland, 1673 ***2524.55*** *p98*
Haley, Thomas; New York, 1837 ***8197.10*** *p90*
Haley, Thomas; Nova Scotia, 1745 ***4628.40*** *p45*
Haley, Thomas; Pennsylvania, 1777 ***4629.10*** *p20*
Halfeway, John; Maryland, 1665 ***2524.55*** *p168*
Halfhead, Ann; Maryland, 1649 ***2524.55*** *p98*
Halfhead, Anne; Maryland, 1649 ***2524.55*** *p98*
Halfhead, Julian; Maryland, 1649 ***2524.55*** *p98*
Halfoard, John; Maryland, 1674 ***2524.55*** *p98*
Halford, J.; Quebec, 1856 ***9196.15*** *p9*
Halford, John; Virginia, 1690 ***1224.1*** *p26*
Halford, Richard 21; Maryland, 1775 ***1220.25*** *p115*
Halfpenny, Martin 67; Ontario, 1871 ***1823.15*** *p102*
Haliburton, Thomas; West Indies, 1790-1795 ***1640.13*** *p51*
Halick, Caspar; America, 1743 ***2856.30*** *p168*
Haliday, Allice 41; Ontario, 1871 ***1823.15*** *p102*
Haliday, Jane 70; Ontario, 1871 ***1823.15*** *p102*
Haliday, John 70; Ontario, 1871 ***1823.22*** *p66*
Haliday, Samuel 54; Ontario, 1871 ***1823.15*** *p102*
Haliday, William 51; Ontario, 1871 ***1823.15*** *p102*
Halinan, James 74; Vermont, 1910 ***5900.10*** *p161*
Halkett, John; Georgia, 1699 ***1640.13*** *p51*
Hall, . . .; Boston, 1765 ***4628.40*** *p114*
Hall, Mr.; Quebec, 1856 ***9196.15*** *p10*
Hall, Mr.; Quebec, 1857 ***9196.15*** *p14*
Hall, Mr.; Quebec, 1858 ***9196.15*** *p46*
Hall, Mrs.; Quebec, 1857 ***9196.15*** *p16*
Hall, Mrs.; Quebec, 1857 ***9196.15*** *p21*
Hall, Mrs.; Quebec, 1858 ***9196.15*** *p46*
Hall, Adam; New York, 1837 ***8197.10*** *p302*
Hall, Alexander; Savannah, Georgia, 1804 ***1640.10*** *p76*
Hall, Alexander 50; Ontario, 1871 ***1823.22*** *p66*
Hall, Alexander 56; Ontario, 1871 ***1823.22*** *p66*
Hall, Ann; Maryland, 1673 ***2524.55*** *p98*
Hall, Ann 60; Ontario, 1871 ***1823.15*** *p102*
Hall, Anto; Virginia, 1664 ***6212.30*** *p15*
Hall, Archibald; New York, 1807 ***8197.10*** *p40*
Hall, Archibald Glen; Montreal, 1867 ***1640.13*** *p51*
Hall, Celia; Vermont, 1800-1836 ***5900.10*** *p293*
Hall, Charles; Maryland, 1665 ***2524.55*** *p98*
Relative: Ellis
Hall, Charles; Virginia, 1699 ***1224.1*** *p26*
Hall, Charles 16; Virginia, 1775 ***1220.25*** *p110*
Hall, Christopher; Maryland, 1667 ***2524.55*** *p15*
Hall, Daniel; New York, 1840 ***8197.10*** *p386*
Hall, David; New York, 1834-1838 ***8197.10*** *p116*
Hall, David; Pennsylvania, 1777 ***4629.10*** *p16*
Hall, E.; Quebec, 1858 ***9196.15*** *p32*
Hall, Mrs. E.; Quebec, 1858 ***9196.15*** *p32*
Hall, E. H.; Quebec, 1856 ***9196.15*** *p5*
Hall, Easah; Maryland, 1677 ***2524.55*** *p98*
Hall, Edward; Maryland, 1682 ***2524.55*** *p98*
Hall, Edward; New York, 1840 ***8197.10*** *p242*
Hall, Edward; Pennsylvania, 1823 ***6058.10*** *p8*
Hall, Elizabeth *SEE* Hall, Richard
Hall, Elizabeth *SEE* Hall, Thomas
Hall, Elizabeth; Maryland, 1672 ***2524.55*** *p98*
Hall, Ellis *SEE* Hall, Charles
Hall, Francis; Maryland, 1652 ***2524.55*** *p98*
Hall, Francis 33; Ontario, 1871 ***1823.22*** *p66*
Hall, Frederick; New York, 1816 ***8197.10*** *p237*
Hall, Frederick 47; Ontario, 1871 ***1823.22*** *p66*
Hall, George *SEE* Hall, Thomas
Hall, George; Maryland, 1681 ***2524.55*** *p98*
Hall, George; New York, 1826 ***8197.10*** *p335*
Hall, George; Norfolk, Virginia, 1828 ***1224.3*** *p32*
Hall, George 10; Ontario, 1871 ***1823.28*** *p37*
Hall, Grace; Maryland, 1673 ***2524.55*** *p98*
Hall, H. H.; Mississippi, 1821-1845 ***1640.10*** *p76*
Hall, Henry; Charleston, South Carolina, 1804 ***1224.3*** *p33*
Hall, Henry; Maryland, 1670 ***2524.55*** *p117*
Hall, Henry 26; Maryland, 1774 ***1220.25*** *p74*
Hall, Henry Long; New York, 1816 ***8197.10*** *p237*
Hall, Hugh 68; Ontario, 1871 ***1823.15*** *p102*
Hall, Humphery; Maryland, 1665 ***2524.55*** *p98*
Hall, Humphrey; Maryland, 1680 ***2524.55*** *p98*
Hall, Isaac; New York, 1840 ***8197.10*** *p172*
Hall, Isaac; New York, 1840 ***8197.10*** *p386*
Hall, Isaiah 48; Ontario, 1871 ***1823.15*** *p103*
Hall, James; Maryland, 1682 ***2524.55*** *p98*
Hall, James; New York, 1838 ***8197.10*** *p116*
Hall, James; Virginia, 1664 ***6212.30*** *p9*
Hall, James 41; Ontario, 1871 ***1823.15*** *p103*
Hall, James 62; Ontario, 1871 ***1823.15*** *p103*
Hall, James 66; Ontario, 1871 ***1823.22*** *p66*
Hall, Jeffry; Virginia, 1665 ***6212.30*** *p20*
Hall, Johannes; America, 1740 ***2856.30*** *p161*
Hall, John; Maryland, 1673 ***2524.55*** *p98*
Hall, John; New England, 1663 ***1224.1*** *p27*
Hall, John; New York, 1807 ***8197.10*** *p41*
Hall, John; New York, 1813 ***1224.3*** *p33*
Hall, John; Pennsylvania, 1777 ***4629.10*** *p8*
Hall, John; Pennsylvania, 1777 ***4629.10*** *p10*
Hall, John; Pennsylvania, 1777 ***4629.10*** *p23*
Hall, John; Pennsylvania, 1777 ***4629.10*** *p25*
Hall, John; Virginia, 1787 ***1224.2*** *p50*
Hall, John 15; Philadelphia, 1774 ***1220.25*** *p42*
Hall, John 21; Maryland, 1774 ***1220.25*** *p73*
Hall, John 22; Maryland, 1775 ***1220.25*** *p102*
Hall, John 22; Philadelphia, 1774 ***1220.25*** *p42*
Hall, John 25; Maryland, 1774 ***1220.25*** *p71*
Hall, John 27; Ontario, 1871 ***1823.15*** *p103*
Hall, John 40; Ontario, 1861 ***2896.27*** *p23*
Hall, John 41; Ontario, 1871 ***1823.22*** *p66*
Hall, John 50; Ontario, 1871 ***1823.22*** *p66*
Hall, John 60; Ontario, 1871 ***1823.15*** *p103*
Hall, Jonathan; New York, 1768 ***1224.2*** *p50*
Hall, Joseph; New York, 1807 ***8197.10*** *p40*
Hall, Joseph; Virginia, 1666-1667 ***6212.30*** *p33*
Hall, Joseph; Virginia, 1671-1672 ***6212.30*** *p46*
Hall, Joseph 23; Maryland, 1774 ***1220.25*** *p52*
Hall, Margaret; Maryland, 1672 ***2524.55*** *p99*
Hall, Margaret; Virginia, 1665-1666 ***6212.30*** *p25*
Hall, Margrett; Virginia, 1663 ***6212.30*** *p3*
Hall, Marshall 22; Philadelphia, 1775 ***1220.25*** *p121*
Hall, Martha; Maryland, 1676 ***2524.55*** *p99*
Hall, Mary; Maryland, 1673 ***2524.55*** *p99*
Hall, Mary 26; Maryland, 1775 ***1220.25*** *p100*
Hall, Oliver; Maryland, 1665 ***2524.55*** *p99*
Hall, Parthenia; Maryland, 1680 ***2524.55*** *p99*
Hall, Peter; New York, 1808 ***8197.10*** *p54*
Hall, Philipp; America, 1763 ***2856.30*** *p161*
With wife & son
Hall, R.; Quebec, 1857 ***9196.15*** *p27*
Hall, Richard; Maryland, 1658 ***2524.55*** *p99*
Wife: Elizabeth
Hall, Richard; Maryland, 1666 ***2524.55*** *p99*
Wife: Elizabeth
Hall, Richard; New York, 1816 ***8197.10*** *p237*
Hall, Richard; Virginia, 1668 ***1224.1*** *p27*
Hall, Richard 16; Virginia, 1774 ***1220.25*** *p91*
Hall, Richard 19; Maryland, 1774 ***1220.25*** *p71*
Hall, Richard 31; Ontario, 1871 ***1823.28*** *p37*
Hall, Richard Y.; New York, 1838 ***8197.10*** *p116*
Hall, Robert; Maryland, 1720 ***1224.2*** *p50*
Hall, Robert 40; Ontario, 1871 ***1823.15*** *p103*
Hall, Roger; Maryland, 1657 ***2524.55*** *p99*
Hall, Samll; Virginia, 1673 ***6212.30*** *p51*
Hall, Samuel; New York, 1816 ***6058.10*** *p6*
Hall, Samuel; Pennsylvania, 1786 ***4629.10*** *p55*
Hall, Samuel; Pennsylvania, 1826 ***6058.10*** *p9*
Hall, Samuell; Maryland, 1673 ***2524.55*** *p117*
Hall, Steven; Maryland, 1657 ***2524.55*** *p99*
Hall, Thomas; Maryland, 1657 ***2524.55*** *p99*
Hall, Thomas; Maryland, 1680 ***2524.55*** *p99*
Wife: Elizabeth
Son: George
Hall, Thomas; New York, 1807 ***8197.10*** *p329*

Hall, Thomas; New York, 1816 ***8197.10*** *p237*
Hall, Thomas; New York, 1828 ***8197.10*** *p240*
Hall, Thomas; Virginia, 1664 ***6212.30*** *p15*
Hall, Thomas 28; Maryland, 1775 ***1220.25*** *p103*
Hall, Thomas 30; Ontario, 1871 ***1823.15*** *p103*
Hall, Thomas 51; Ontario, 1871 ***1823.22*** *p66*
Hall, Thomas 59; Ontario, 1871 ***1823.15*** *p103*
Hall, Thomas 65; Ontario, 1871 ***1823.22*** *p66*
Hall, Thomas 69; Ontario, 1871 ***1823.15*** *p103*
Hall, Thomas 71; Ontario, 1871 ***1823.22*** *p66*
Hall, William; Maryland, 1668 ***2524.55*** *p99*
Hall, William; New York, 1832 ***8197.10*** *p357*
Hall, William; New York, 1837 ***8197.10*** *p374*
Hall, William; Pennsylvania, 1777 ***4629.10*** *p7*
Hall, William; Pennsylvania, 1777 ***4629.10*** *p8*
Hall, William; Portland, Maine, 1857 ***9196.15*** *p12*
Hall, William; South Carolina, 1786 ***1224.2*** *p50*
Hall, William; Virginia, 1713 ***1224.2*** *p50*
Hall, William 16; Jamaica, 1774 ***1220.25*** *p82*
Hall, William 17; Philadelphia, 1775 ***1220.25*** *p8*
Hall, William 21; Maryland, 1774 ***1220.25*** *p3*
Hall, William 28; Ontario, 1871 ***1823.15*** *p103*
Hall, William 28; Ontario, 1871 ***1823.22*** *p66*
Hall, William 40; Halifax, Nova Scotia, 1774 ***1220.25*** *p138*
Hall, William 40; Ontario, 1871 ***1823.15*** *p103*
Hall, William 54; Ontario, 1871 ***1823.15*** *p103*
Hall, William 56; Ontario, 1871 ***1823.22*** *p66*
Hall, William John 48; Ontario, 1871 ***1823.15*** *p103*
Hall, Wm; Virginia, 1665-1666 ***6212.30*** *p23*
Hall, Wm; Virginia, 1677 ***6212.30*** *p54*
Hallahan, Johanna Connelly 60; Vermont, 1896 ***5900.10*** *p56*
Hallahan, Michael; Vermont, 1788-1873 ***5900.10*** *p56*
Hallahan, Thomas; Vermont, 1824-1887 ***5900.10*** *p56*
Hallam, John; Portland, Maine, 1857 ***9196.15*** *p12*
Hallaren, Margaret 57; Vermont, 1865 ***5900.10*** *p110*
Hallaron, James 47; Vermont, 1899 ***5900.10*** *p132*
Hallaron, Mary 43; Vermont, 1892 ***5900.10*** *p132*
Hallas, Anna Dorothea; Port uncertain, 1773 ***2856.30*** *p161*
Hallau, Anna Dorothea; Port uncertain, 1773 ***2856.30*** *p161*
Hallcock, John; Virginia, 1699 ***6212.30*** *p61*
Hallebread, Daniel; New York, 1840 ***8197.10*** *p171*
Hallenan, Mary 55; Vermont, 1871 ***5900.10*** *p100*
Haller, Hans Georg; Port uncertain, 1736 ***2856.30*** *p161*
Haller, Hans Georg; Port uncertain, 1758 ***2856.30*** *p161*
Haller, Henry; Pennsylvania, 1777 ***4629.10*** *p8*
Haller, J. F. 19; Philadelphia, 1774 ***1220.25*** *p66*
Haller, Jakob; Port uncertain, 1747 ***2856.30*** *p161*
Haller, Johann; Port uncertain, 1755 ***2856.30*** *p161*
Haller, Johann; Port uncertain, 1785 ***2856.30*** *p161*
Halleran, Catherine 44; Vermont, 1868 ***5900.10*** *p201*
Hallet, Jno; Virginia, 1693-1694 ***6212.30*** *p60*
Hallett, Charles 21; Philadelphia, 1774 ***1220.25*** *p80*
Hallett, Elizabeth; New York, 1723 ***1224.2*** *p50*
Hallett, Lancelott; Maryland, 1671 ***1224.1*** *p27*
Halley, Ellen 42; Vermont, 1902 ***5900.10*** *p200*
Halley, Francis; Virginia, 1702 ***1224.2*** *p50*
Halley, Robert; New York, 1839 ***8197.10*** *p131*
Halley, W.; Quebec, 1858 ***9196.15*** *p35*
Halliburton, Lawden 25; Philadelphia, 1774 ***1220.25*** *p86*
Hallican, Edmond; Maryland, 1678 ***2524.55*** *p99*
Halliday, Amelia 25; Ontario, 1871 ***1823.22*** *p66*
Halliday, Andrew 60; Ontario, 1871 ***1823.22*** *p66*
Halliday, George; New York, 1839 ***8197.10*** *p242*
Halliday, James 40; Ontario, 1871 ***1823.15*** *p103*
Halliday, John 26; Maryland, 1775 ***1220.25*** *p108*
Halliday, John 67; Ontario, 1871 ***1823.28*** *p37*
Hallidy, James 35; Ontario, 1871 ***1823.28*** *p37*
Hallidy, James 57; Ontario, 1871 ***1823.22*** *p66*
Halligan, Anna; Vermont, 1859-1946 ***5900.10*** *p277*
Halligan, Hugh 58; Ontario, 1871 ***1823.22*** *p66*
Halligan, James 33; Ontario, 1871 ***1823.22*** *p66*
Halligan, Patrick; Vermont, 1860-1931 ***5900.10*** *p277*
Hallihan, Eliza; Vermont, 1845-1922 ***5900.10*** *p132*
Hallihan, Mary A.; Vermont, 1853-1933 ***5900.10*** *p131*
Hallinan, Ann Mellen 40; Vermont, 1867 ***5900.10*** *p232*
Hallinan, Ellen A. Moran 56; Vermont, 1905 ***5900.10*** *p51*
Hallinan, Hannah; Vermont, 1876 ***5900.10*** *p98*
Hallinan, James 37; Vermont, 1891 ***5900.10*** *p51*
Hallinan, Patrick; Vermont, 1888 ***5900.10*** *p98*
Hallinan, Stephen 53; Vermont, 1873 ***5900.10*** *p232*
Halling, Michael; Pennsylvania, 1777 ***4629.10*** *p8*
Halliran, Mary Ann 26; Ontario, 1871 ***1823.22*** *p67*
Halliran, Thomas 41; Ontario, 1871 ***1823.22*** *p67*
Halliwell, Richard 25; New York, 1774 ***1220.25*** *p24*
Hallman, John; Pennsylvania, 1786 ***4629.10*** *p51*
Hallmayer, Josef; Port uncertain, 1728 ***2856.30*** *p161*
Hallmayer, Josef; Port uncertain, 1758 ***2856.30*** *p161*
Hallon, Charles 55; Ontario, 1871 ***1823.28*** *p37*
Halloran, Delia Tracy; Vermont, 1840-1897 ***5900.10*** *p289*
Halloran, Ellen 79; Vermont, 1916 ***5900.10*** *p609*
Halloran, John; Vermont, 1829-1910 ***5900.10*** *p289*
Halloran, Lawrence 36; Vermont, 1863 ***5900.10*** *p246*
Halloran, Margaret 58; Vermont, 1900 ***5900.10*** *p128*
Halloran, Margaret Hogan 38; Vermont, 1857 ***5900.10*** *p577*
Halloran, Mary Madden 80; Vermont, 1905 ***5900.10*** *p79*
Halloran, Michael 42; Vermont, 1870 ***5900.10*** *p79*
Halloran, Nellie M.; Vermont, 1862-1917 ***5900.10*** *p609*
Halloran, Patrick; New York, 1840 ***8197.10*** *p171*
Halloran, Patrick 48; Vermont, 1893 ***5900.10*** *p128*
Halloran, Simon 60; Vermont, 1887 ***5900.10*** *p609*
Hallow, John; Maryland, 1661 ***2524.55*** *p99*
Hallowell, Robert; Massachusetts, 1818 ***1224.3*** *p33*
Hallowran, Michael; Pennsylvania, 1868 ***6058.10*** *p73*
Halls, Ellen 45; Ontario, 1871 ***1823.15*** *p103*
Halls, George 4; Ontario, 1871 ***1823.15*** *p103*
Halls, James 41; Ontario, 1871 ***1823.15*** *p103*
Halls, John 44; Ontario, 1871 ***1823.15*** *p103*
Halls, Mathew; Virginia, 1666 ***6212.30*** *p31*
Halls, Samuel 32; Ontario, 1871 ***1823.15*** *p103*
Halls, Samuel 51; Ontario, 1871 ***1823.15*** *p103*
Halls, William 45; Ontario, 1871 ***1823.15*** *p103*
Hallsey, Edgar; Virginia, 1665-1666 ***6212.30*** *p25*
Hallsey, Hannorah; Vermont, 1843-1925 ***5900.10*** *p272*
Hallsteed, Jno; Virginia, 1665-1666 ***6212.30*** *p22*
Hallsteed, Jno; Virginia, 1666-1667 ***6212.30*** *p32*
Hally, Andrew 23; Ontario, 1871 ***1823.15*** *p103*
Hally, James; Quebec, 1894 ***1640.13*** *p51*
Hally, Johane 40; Ontario, 1871 ***1823.28*** *p37*
Hally, John 24; Ontario, 1871 ***1823.28*** *p37*
Hallyard, Ann; Maryland, 1662 ***2524.55*** *p200*
Hallyburton, William; Georgia, 1699 ***1640.13*** *p51*
Hallyday, Henry; New York, 1794 ***8197.10*** *p5*
Halm, Johann Peter; Port uncertain, 1748 ***2856.30*** *p161*
With wife & children
Halm, Maria Elisabeth; Port uncertain, 1752 ***2856.30*** *p161*
Halm, Maria Margarete; Port uncertain, 1788 ***2856.30*** *p161*
Halmon, Catherine Dalton 65; Vermont, 1869 ***5900.10*** *p542*
Halnon, Elizabeth; Vermont, 1850-1933 ***5900.10*** *p318*
Halnon, Isabelle Tully 85; Vermont, 1936 ***5900.10*** *p318*
Halnon, James 87; Vermont, 1885 ***5900.10*** *p318*
Halnon, John 75; Vermont, 1907 ***5900.10*** *p318*
Halnon, William; Vermont, 1841-1926 ***5900.10*** *p318*
Halpin, Andrew 42; Vermont, 1867 ***5900.10*** *p521*
Halpin, Bridget Meehan 68; Vermont, 1879 ***5900.10*** *p314*
Halpin, Elizabeth; Vermont, 1816-1878 ***5900.10*** *p384*
Halpin, Elizabeth; Vermont, 1843-1881 ***5900.10*** *p384*
Halpin, Ellen Barry; Vermont, 1853-1932 ***5900.10*** *p445*
Halpin, Hannah Roch; Vermont, 1842-1923 ***5900.10*** *p314*
Halpin, James; Vermont, 1845-1927 ***5900.10*** *p387*
Halpin, James 28; Vermont, 1887 ***5900.10*** *p169*
Halpin, Johannah 28; Vermont, 1855 ***5900.10*** *p521*
Halpin, John; Vermont, 1843-1902 ***5900.10*** *p428*
Halpin, Julia Barry 76; Vermont, 1936 ***5900.10*** *p314*
Halpin, Margaret 48; Vermont, 1875 ***5900.10*** *p540*
Halpin, Margaret Dillon; Vermont, 1844-1905 ***5900.10*** *p428*
Halpin, Margaret Marshall 35; Vermont, 1879 ***5900.10*** *p540*
Halpin, Mary; Vermont, 1841-1909 ***5900.10*** *p314*
Halpin, Mary J.; Vermont, 1840-1875 ***5900.10*** *p384*
Halpin, Mary O'Brien; Vermont, 1842-1915 ***5900.10*** *p387*
Halpin, Michael; Vermont, 1809-1865 ***5900.10*** *p384*
Halpin, Michael; Vermont, 1842-1916 ***5900.10*** *p314*
Halpin, Michael; Vermont, 1852-1877 ***5900.10*** *p384*
Halpin, Patrick 45; Ontario, 1871 ***1823.15*** *p103*
Halpin, Patrick 73; Vermont, 1918 ***5900.10*** *p314*
Halpin, Philip; Vermont, 1838-1869 ***5900.10*** *p384*
Halpin, Thomas 67; Vermont, 1872 ***5900.10*** *p314*
Halpin, Timothy C.; Vermont, 1853-1927 ***5900.10*** *p445*
Halse, Mr.; Quebec, 1857 ***9196.15*** *p15*
Halse, Abraham; Maryland, 1673 ***2524.55*** *p99*
Halser, James; Virginia, 1666-1667 ***6212.30*** *p35*
Halsey, Esau; New England, 1677 ***1224.1*** *p27*
Halsey, Mary; Maryland, 1667 ***2524.55*** *p99*
Halsey, Thomas; Virginia, 1665 ***6212.30*** *p20*
Halstead, Albert 22; Ontario, 1871 ***1823.22*** *p67*
Halstead, Hargrave 28; Ontario, 1871 ***1823.22*** *p67*
Halstead, James; New York, 1837 ***8197.10*** *p91*
Halsted, . . .; New England, 1651 ***1224.1*** *p27*
Halsted, Ann B.; New York, 1832 ***8197.10*** *p358*
Halt, George; Pennsylvania, 1825 ***6058.10*** *p8*
Halter, Johann; Port uncertain, 1775 ***2856.30*** *p162*
Haltin, Mr.; Port uncertain, 1752 ***2856.30*** *p299*
Halton, James 16; Maryland, 1775 ***1220.25*** *p116*
Halton, Joseph; New York, 1837 ***8197.10*** *p91*
Haltz, Caroline 22; Ontario, 1871 ***1823.28*** *p37*
Haltzhimer, Jacob; Pennsylvania, 1777 ***4629.10*** *p18*
Halworth, Henry 23; Maryland, 1774 ***1220.25*** *p79*
Haly, Richard; Maryland, 1682 ***2524.55*** *p99*
Halyer, Thomas 36; Maryland, 1774 ***1220.25*** *p39*
Ham, Barbarah; Maryland, 1650 ***2524.55*** *p99*
Ham, Catharina; Port uncertain, 1767 ***2856.30*** *p162*
Ham, George; Maryland, 1660 ***2524.55*** *p99*
Ham, James; Pennsylvania, 1777 ***4629.10*** *p13*
Ham, James; Pennsylvania, 1779 ***4629.10*** *p37*
Ham, James 21; Maryland, 1775 ***1220.25*** *p115*
Ham, James, Jr.; Pennsylvania, 1779 ***4629.10*** *p39*
Ham, Johann Jacob; America, 1753 ***2856.30*** *p162*
Ham, Richard 16; Philadelphia, 1774 ***1220.25*** *p34*
Ham, Samuel; Portsmouth, New Hampshire, 1815 ***1224.3*** *p33*
Ham, Stefan; Port uncertain, 1741 ***2856.30*** *p163*
With family
Hamaker, Livy 34; Ontario, 1871 ***1823.15*** *p103*
Haman, Ann; Virginia, 1703 ***6212.30*** *p62*
Haman, Isack; Virginia, 1671 ***6212.30*** *p44*
Haman, Richard; New York, 1717 ***1224.2*** *p50*
Hamann, Martin; Port uncertain, 1795 ***2856.30*** *p162*
Hambacher, Bernard; America, 1752 ***2856.30*** *p162*
With wife & 3 children
Hambalin, Maria Margarete; Port uncertain, 1774 ***2856.30*** *p162*
Hambel, Jakob; Port uncertain, 1792 ***2856.30*** *p162*
Hamberger, Anna Barbara; Port uncertain, 1752 ***2856.30*** *p162*
Hamberry, Catherine 36; New York, New York, 1849 ***1825.45*** *p35*
Hamble, George; Pennsylvania, 1786 ***4629.10*** *p53*
Hambleton, John; Maryland, 1661 ***2524.55*** *p99*
Hambleton, John; Maryland, 1662 ***2524.55*** *p99*
Hambleton, Peter; Maryland, 1656 ***2524.55*** *p99*
Hamblton, Temperance; Maryland, 1652 ***2524.55*** *p99*
Hambly, Edwin 37; Ontario, 1871 ***1823.22*** *p67*
Hambly, William 43; Ontario, 1871 ***1823.22*** *p67*
Hamburger, Philipp; Port uncertain, 1771 ***2856.30*** *p162*
Hambury, Benjamin 15; Virginia, 1774 ***1220.25*** *p94*
Hambury, Catherine 36; New York, New York, 1849 ***1825.45*** *p35*
Hambury, Judy 23; New York, New York, 1848 ***1825.45*** *p35*
Hamby, Mary *SEE* Hamby, Richard
Hamby, Richard; Maryland, 1658 ***2524.55*** *p99*
Wife: Mary
Son: William
Hamby, William *SEE* Hamby, Richard
Hamel, Johann Adam; Port uncertain, 1741 ***2856.30*** *p162*
Hamel, Mary Tierney; Vermont, 1842-1907 ***5900.10*** *p47*
Hamel, Nelson; Vermont, 1839-1923 ***5900.10*** *p47*
Hamen, Lorenz; America, 1748 ***2856.30*** *p162*
Hamer, Edw; Virginia, 1667 ***6212.30*** *p37*
Hamerhly, Thomas; Maryland, 1665 ***2524.55*** *p99*
Hamerston, Thomas 22; Virginia, 1774 ***1220.25*** *p86*
Hamerton, Pinchback; Virginia, 1729 ***1224.2*** *p50*
Hametton, Amoss; Maryland, 1650 ***2524.55*** *p99*
Hamigar, James; Savannah, Georgia, 1774 ***1640.10*** *p76*
Wife: Jean
Hamigar, Jean *SEE* Hamigar, James
Hamill, Daniel; Philadelphia, 1789 ***4629.10*** *p57*
Wife: Issamiah
Hamill, Henry; New York, 1840 ***8197.10*** *p242*
Hamill, Issamiah *SEE* Hamill, Daniel
Hamill, Mary 26; Vermont, 1860 ***5900.10*** *p513*
Hamill, Patrick; New York, 1826 ***8197.10*** *p334*
Hamill, Peter; New York, 1837 ***8197.10*** *p90*
Hamill, Roger 28; Philadelphia, 1789 ***4629.10*** *p57*
Hamilton, . . .; Boston, 1765 ***4628.40*** *p114*
Hamilton, Miss; Quebec, 1858 ***9196.15*** *p36*
Hamilton, Mrs.; Quebec, 1858 ***9196.15*** *p33*
Hamilton, Alexander; Georgia, 1698 ***1640.13*** *p51*
Hamilton, Alexander; Georgia, 1699 ***1640.13*** *p51*
Hamilton, Alexander 55; Ontario, 1871 ***1823.15*** *p103*
Hamilton, Andrew; Philadelphia, 1742 ***1224.2*** *p50*
Hamilton, Andrew 50; Ontario, 1871 ***1823.28*** *p37*
Hamilton, Andrew, Sr. 68; Ontario, 1871 ***1823.28*** *p37*
Hamilton, Ann 65; Ontario, 1871 ***1823.15*** *p103*
Hamilton, Archibald; Georgia, 1699 ***1640.13*** *p51*
Hamilton, Archibald; Georgia, 1739 ***1640.10*** *p76*
Hamilton, Archibald; Kingston, Jamaica, 1799 ***1640.13*** *p51*
Hamilton, Bustard 38; Ontario, 1871 ***1823.22*** *p67*
Hamilton, Caroline *SEE* Hamilton, William
Hamilton, Caroline; New York, 1899 ***1640.13*** *p51*
Hamilton, Catherin; Vermont, 1810-1880 ***5900.10*** *p42*
Hamilton, Charles; Georgia, 1698 ***1640.13*** *p51*
Hamilton, Charles 16; Antigua (Antego), 1773-1774 ***1220.25*** *p32*

Hamilton, D.; Quebec, 1856 ***9196.15*** *p8*
Hamilton, David; Chicago, 1889 ***1640.13*** *p52*
Hamilton, David 39; Ontario, 1871 ***1823.28*** *p37*
Hamilton, Douglas; Virginia, 1783 ***1224.2*** *p51*
Hamilton, Edward 26; Ontario, 1871 ***1823.28*** *p37*
Hamilton, Elizebe 67; Ontario, 1871 ***1823.28*** *p37*
Hamilton, Francis; New York, 1839 ***8197.10*** *p242*
Hamilton, Francis; Philadelphia, 1790 ***4629.10*** *p60*
Hamilton, Gavin 42; Ontario, 1871 ***1823.15*** *p103*
Hamilton, Gavin 70; Ontario, 1871 ***1823.15*** *p103*
Hamilton, George 19; Maryland, 1774 ***1220.25*** *p79*
Hamilton, George 23; Virginia, 1774 ***1220.25*** *p140*
Hamilton, Hamlin 56; Ontario, 1871 ***1823.15*** *p103*
Hamilton, Hans 58; Ontario, 1871 ***1823.15*** *p103*
Hamilton, Henry; Georgia, 1756 ***1640.10*** *p76*
Hamilton, Henry; New York, 1821 ***8197.10*** *p238*
Hamilton, Hugh; Pensacola, Florida, 1793 ***1224.2*** *p51*
Hamilton, Hugh; Pensacola, Florida, 1793 ***1640.10*** *p76*
Hamilton, Hugh 53; Ontario, 1871 ***1823.28*** *p37*
Hamilton, Hugh 57; Ontario, 1871 ***1823.15*** *p103*
Hamilton, James; Georgia, 1699 ***1640.13*** *p52*
Hamilton, James; Maryland, 1772 ***1224.2*** *p51*
Hamilton, James; New Orleans, 1832-1845 ***1640.10*** *p77*
Hamilton, James; New York, 1781 ***1640.13*** *p52*
Hamilton, James; New York, 1818-1834 ***8197.10*** *p308*
Hamilton, James; New York, 1834 ***8197.10*** *p240*
Hamilton, James; New York, 1837 ***8197.10*** *p374*
Hamilton, James; New York, 1840 ***8197.10*** *p172*
Hamilton, James; Pennsylvania, 1781 ***4629.10*** *p43*
Hamilton, James; Philadelphia, 1829 ***1640.10*** *p76*
Hamilton, James 41; Ontario, 1871 ***1823.22*** *p67*
Hamilton, James 42; Ontario, 1871 ***1823.15*** *p104*
Hamilton, James 46; Ontario, 1871 ***1823.15*** *p104*
Hamilton, James 58; Ontario, 1871 ***1823.15*** *p104*
Hamilton, James 65; Ontario, 1871 ***1823.28*** *p37*
Hamilton, John; Florida, 1765 ***1640.10*** *p77*
Hamilton, John; Harrisburg, Pennsylvania, 1823 ***1224.3*** *p33*
Hamilton, John; Jamaica, 1786 ***1640.13*** *p52*
Hamilton, John; Maryland, 1680 ***2524.55*** *p99*
Wife: Temperance
Hamilton, John; Maryland, 1681 ***2524.55*** *p99*
Hamilton, John; Montreal, 1888 ***1640.13*** *p52*
Hamilton, John; New York, 1830 ***8197.10*** *p313*
Hamilton, John; New York, 1839 ***8197.10*** *p242*
Hamilton, John; Pennsylvania, 1777 ***4629.10*** *p14*
Hamilton, John; Savannah, Georgia, 1809 ***1640.10*** *p77*
Hamilton, John 21; Maryland, 1774 ***1220.25*** *p52*
Hamilton, John 22; Maryland, 1775 ***1220.25*** *p96*
Hamilton, John 32; Virginia, 1774 ***1220.25*** *p94*
Hamilton, John 40; Ontario, 1871 ***1823.15*** *p104*
Hamilton, John 92; Vermont, 1911 ***5900.10*** *p567*
Hamilton, John, Sr. 63; Ontario, 1871 ***1823.28*** *p37*
Hamilton, John L.; New York, 1830 ***8197.10*** *p66*
Hamilton, John Robert; New York, 1876 ***1640.13*** *p52*
Hamilton, John Stuart; Mexico, 1900 ***1640.13*** *p52*
Hamilton, Jos 42; Oregon, 1914 ***9196.1*** *p64*
Hamilton, Joseph; Baltimore, 1774 ***1224.2*** *p34*
Hamilton, Luke 50; Ontario, 1871 ***1823.22*** *p67*
Hamilton, Margaret 84; Ontario, 1871 ***1823.28*** *p37*
Hamilton, Margaret Clark 88; Vermont, 1906 ***5900.10*** *p567*
Hamilton, Mary; Philadelphia, 1794 ***1224.2*** *p51*
Hamilton, Mary; Vermont, 1857-1941 ***5900.10*** *p299*
Hamilton, Mary 45; Ontario, 1871 ***1823.22*** *p67*
Hamilton, Mary A. 24; Ontario, 1871 ***1823.28*** *p37*
Hamilton, Owen; New York, 1838 ***8197.10*** *p116*
Hamilton, Past; Pennsylvania, 1777 ***4629.10*** *p14*
Hamilton, Paul; Charleston, South Carolina, n.d. ***1224.2*** *p51*
Hamilton, Paul; Georgia, 1735 ***1640.10*** *p77*
Hamilton, Peter; New York, New York, 1887 ***3437.14*** *p177*
Hamilton, Peter Alexander; Philadelphia, 1895 ***3437.14*** *p180*
Hamilton, Robert; Canada, 1857 ***1640.13*** *p52*
Hamilton, Robert; London, England, 1840 ***1640.13*** *p52*
Hamilton, Robert; New York, 1826 ***8197.10*** *p335*
Hamilton, Robert 24; Maryland, 1775 ***1220.25*** *p120*
Hamilton, Robert 30; Ontario, 1871 ***1823.15*** *p104*
Hamilton, Robert 33; Ontario, 1871 ***1823.15*** *p104*
Hamilton, Robert 42; New York, 1775 ***1220.25*** *p142*
With wife & 3 children
Hamilton, Robert 44; Ontario, 1871 ***1823.15*** *p104*
Hamilton, Robert 57; Ontario, 1871 ***1823.15*** *p104*
Hamilton, Robert D.; Canada, 1857 ***1640.13*** *p52*
Hamilton, Robert Day 65; Ontario, 1871 ***1823.28*** *p37*
Hamilton, Robert Douglas; Canada, 1860 ***1640.13*** *p52*
Hamilton, Samuel 24; Ontario, 1871 ***1823.28*** *p37*
Hamilton, Sara; Vermont, 1848-1918 ***5900.10*** *p579*
Hamilton, Temperance *SEE* Hamilton, John
Hamilton, Thomas; Georgia, 1698 ***1640.13*** *p52*
Hamilton, Thomas; Georgia, 1699 ***1640.13*** *p52*
Hamilton, Thomas; Savannah, Georgia, 1761 ***1640.10*** *p77*
Hamilton, Thomas 30; Ontario, 1871 ***1823.28*** *p37*
Hamilton, Thomas 40; Ontario, 1871 ***1823.15*** *p104*
Hamilton, W. P. J.; Quebec, 1857 ***9196.15*** *p16*
Hamilton, William; Georgia, 1698 ***1640.13*** *p52*
Hamilton, William; Mobile, Alabama, 1862 ***1640.13*** *p53*
Hamilton, William; New Brunswick, 1888 ***1640.13*** *p53*
Hamilton, William; New York, 1806 ***8197.10*** *p31*
Hamilton, William; New York, 1807 ***8197.10*** *p40*
Hamilton, William; New York, 1825 ***1640.13*** *p52*
Hamilton, William; New York, 1829-1845 ***1640.10*** *p77*
Wife: Caroline
Hamilton, William; New York, 1836-1838 ***8197.10*** *p117*
Hamilton, William; New York, 1840 ***8197.10*** *p242*
Hamilton, William; New York, New York, 1887 ***3437.14*** *p176*
Hamilton, William; Pennsylvania, 1777 ***4629.10*** *p15*
Hamilton, William; Pennsylvania, 1779 ***4629.10*** *p41*
Hamilton, William 14; Ontario, 1861 ***2896.27*** *p12*
Hamilton, William 42; Ontario, 1871 ***1823.28*** *p37*
Hamilton, William 45; Ontario, 1871 ***1823.28*** *p37*
Hamilton, William 70; Ontario, 1871 ***1823.15*** *p104*
Hamilton, William B.; Pennsylvania, 1836 ***6058.10*** *p14*
Hamilton, Willm.; Maryland, 1657 ***2524.55*** *p99*
Hamkin, Konrad; Port uncertain, 1752 ***2856.30*** *p162*
Hamlet, Christopher 42; New York, 1774 ***1220.25*** *p26*
Hamleton, David; Virginia, 1664 ***6212.30*** *p6*
Hamley, John; Maryland, 1681 ***2524.55*** *p99*
Hamlin, George; Maryland, 1675 ***2524.55*** *p99*
Hamlin, James 64; Ontario, 1871 ***1823.15*** *p104*
Hamlin, John 49; Ontario, 1871 ***1823.15*** *p104*
Hamlin, William 61; Ontario, 1871 ***1823.15*** *p104*
Hamm, Anna Margarete; Port uncertain, 1741 ***2856.30*** *p162*
Hamm, Daniel; America, 1754 ***2856.30*** *p162*
With wife
Hamm, Elisabeth; Port uncertain, 1791 ***2856.30*** *p162*
Hamm, Jacob; America, 1753 ***2856.30*** *p162*
With wife
Hamm, Jacob; Port uncertain, 1745 ***2856.30*** *p162*
Hamm, Margarete; Port uncertain, 1734 ***2856.30*** *p162*
Hamm, Maria Catharina; Port uncertain, 1772 ***2856.30*** *p162*
Hamm, Maria Gertrud; Port uncertain, 1772 ***2856.30*** *p162*
Hamman, Maria Catharina; America, 1738 ***2856.30*** *p162*
Hammand, Thomas; North America, 1786 ***1224.2*** *p51*
Hammann, Maria Catharina; America, 1750 ***2856.30*** *p162*
Hammel, Cath. Elisabeth; Port uncertain, 1783 ***2856.30*** *p162*
Hammel, Ellen 53; Vermont, 1892 ***5900.10*** *p380*
Hammel, Henrich; Port uncertain, 1746 ***2856.30*** *p162*
With wife & 3 children
Hammel, Johann; Port uncertain, 1765 ***2856.30*** *p162*
Hammel, Johann Leonhard; Port uncertain, 1760 ***2856.30*** *p162*
Hammel, John 35; Vermont, 1897 ***5900.10*** *p297*
Hammel, John B. 49; Vermont, 1883 ***5900.10*** *p297*
Hammel, Mary 30; Ontario, 1861 ***2896.25*** *p49*
Hammel, Mary E.; Vermont, 1860-1938 ***5900.10*** *p441*
Hammel, Peter; Port uncertain, 1752 ***2856.30*** *p162*
Hammell, John; New York, 1797 ***1224.2*** *p51*
Hammell, John 37; Ontario, 1871 ***1823.28*** *p37*
Hammen, Philip; Vermont, n.d. ***5900.10*** *p148*
Hammer, Adam; Port uncertain, 1751 ***2856.30*** *p162*
Hammer, Anna Magdalena; Port uncertain, 1746 ***2856.30*** *p162*
Hammer, Anna Margarete; Port uncertain, 1765 ***2856.30*** *p162*
Hammer, Catharina; Port uncertain, 1749 ***2856.30*** *p162*
Hammer, Franz; America, 1747 ***2856.30*** *p162*
Hammer, Franz; Port uncertain, 1747 ***2856.30*** *p162*
Hammer, Hans Georg; Port uncertain, 1751 ***2856.30*** *p162*
Hammer, Johann; New York, 1838 ***8197.10*** *p117*
Hammer, Johann Friedric; America, 1748 ***2856.30*** *p162*
Hammer, John Michael; New York, 1839 ***8197.10*** *p242*
Hammer, Joseph; New York, 1838 ***8197.10*** *p117*
Hammer, Martin; Virginia, 1704 ***1224.2*** *p51*
Hammer, Michael; America, 1733 ***2856.30*** *p163*
With wife
Hammer, Michael; America, 1733 ***2856.30*** *p163*
With wife & children
Hammer, Philipp; Port uncertain, 1784 ***2856.30*** *p162*
Hammer, Samuel; Port uncertain, 1744 ***2856.30*** *p163*
Hammerer, Josef; Port uncertain, 1763 ***2856.30*** *p163*
Hammerling, Johann; Port uncertain, 1786 ***2856.30*** *p197G*
Hammerschmidt, David; Port uncertain, 1739 ***2856.30*** *p163*
Hammerton, Elizabeth; Charles Town, South Carolina, 1750 ***1224.2*** *p51*
Hammess, Peter; Port uncertain, 1752 ***2856.30*** *p162*
Hammet, Frances Hutchins; Philadelphia, 1819 ***1224.3*** *p33*
Hammle, Fredrick 37; Ontario, 1871 ***1823.28*** *p37*
Hammon, Mary 28; Ontario, 1861 ***2896.27*** *p17*
Hammon, William; Pennsylvania, 1777 ***4629.10*** *p9*
Hammond, Miss; Quebec, 1858 ***9196.15*** *p37*
Hammond, Mr.; Quebec, 1857 ***9196.15*** *p22*
Hammond, Mr.; Quebec, 1858 ***9196.15*** *p37*
Hammond, Abbie M.; Vermont, 1823-1908 ***5900.10*** *p308*
Hammond, Abijah; New York, 1838 ***1224.3*** *p33*
Hammond, B. 21; Ontario, 1871 ***1823.28*** *p37*
Hammond, Catherine Hartigan; Vermont, 1827-1906 ***5900.10*** *p462*
Hammond, Charles; Pennsylvania, 1777 ***4629.10*** *p7*
Hammond, Daniell; Maryland, 1673 ***2524.55*** *p99*
Hammond, Henery 30; Ontario, 1871 ***1823.22*** *p67*
Hammond, Henry 5 *SEE* Hammond, Henry
Hammond, Henry 31; Fort Cumberland, Nova Scotia, 1774 ***1220.25*** *p18*
Wife: Margaret 27
Child: Jane 3
Child: Margaret 1
Child: Henry 5
Hammond, James; Ohio, 1834 ***1224.3*** *p33*
Hammond, Jane 3 *SEE* Hammond, Henry
Hammond, John; Rhode Island, 1844 ***1224.3*** *p33*
Hammond, John 37; Virginia, 1774 ***1220.25*** *p93*
Hammond, Joseph 21; Maryland, 1774 ***1220.25*** *p63*
Hammond, Judah; New York, 1806 ***8197.10*** *p323*
Hammond, Lewis; Vermont, 1828-1887 ***5900.10*** *p462*
Hammond, M. P.; Alabama, 1814-1843 ***1640.10*** *p77*
Hammond, Margaret 1 *SEE* Hammond, Henry
Hammond, Margaret 27 *SEE* Hammond, Henry
Hammond, Philip; Maryland, 1681 ***2524.55*** *p99*
Hammond, Samuel; New York, New York, 1852 ***1224.3*** *p33*
Hamon, Phillip; Virginia, 1679 ***6212.30*** *p54*
Hamond, Ann *SEE* Hamond, John
Hamond, Bernard *SEE* Hamond, John
Hamond, Daniel *SEE* Hamond, John
Hamond, Daniel; Maryland, 1673 ***2524.55*** *p100*
Hamond, Elizabeth; Maryland, 1673 ***2524.55*** *p100*
Hamond, Jno; Virginia, 1663 ***6212.30*** *p2*
Hamond, John; Maryland, 1653 ***2524.55*** *p100*
Wife: Ann
Child: Bernard
Child: Ann
Child: Daniel
Child: Mordecai
Hamond, Mordecai *SEE* Hamond, John
Hamond, Mordica; Virginia, 1663 ***6212.30*** *p3*
Hamond, Thomas; Maryland, 1649 ***2524.55*** *p100*
With wife
Hamor, John; Virginia, 1703-1704 ***6212.30*** *p62*
Hampar, Christopher; Maryland, 1666 ***2524.55*** *p113*
Hampel, Oswall 38; Ontario, 1871 ***1823.28*** *p38*
Hamper, Mrs.; Maryland, 1652 ***2524.55*** *p100*
Hamper, Mrs.; Maryland, 1658 ***2524.55*** *p100*
Hamper, William; Maryland, 1666 ***2524.55*** *p113*
Hampshire, William 27; Ontario, 1871 ***1823.22*** *p67*
Hampson, Joseph; Quebec, 1858 ***9196.15*** *p33*
Hampstead, Mrs.; Maryland, 1650 ***2524.55*** *p100*
Hampstead, Mrs.; Maryland, 1659 ***2524.55*** *p100*
Hampstead, James; West Indies, 1869 ***1640.13*** *p53*
Hampstead, William; Maryland, 1659 ***2524.55*** *p100*
Hampton, Hannah *SEE* Hampton, William
Hampton, Hannah; Maryland, 1668 ***2524.55*** *p100*
Hampton, John; Maryland, 1656 ***2524.55*** *p100*
Hampton, John; Maryland, 1722 ***1224.2*** *p51*
Hampton, Joseph; New York, 1838 ***8197.10*** *p241*
Hampton, Phillis *SEE* Hampton, William
Hampton, William; Maryland, 1668 ***2524.55*** *p100*
Wife: Phillis
Daughter: Phillis
Daughter: Hannah
Hampton, William 33; Maryland, 1774 ***1220.25*** *p72*
Hamsler, Christof; America, 1754 ***2856.30*** *p163*
Hamson, Mark; Maryland, 1663 ***2524.55*** *p100*
Hamstead, Mrs.; Maryland, 1659 ***2524.55*** *p100*
Hamstead, Richard; Virginia, 1665 ***6212.30*** *p19*
Hamstead, William; Maryland, 1659 ***2524.55*** *p100*
Han, Anna Catharina; Port uncertain, 1792 ***2856.30*** *p163*
Han, Anna Magdalena; Port uncertain, 1790 ***2856.30*** *p163*
Han, Johann Mathes; Port uncertain, 1788 ***2856.30*** *p197G*
Han, Johann Nickel; Port uncertain, 1738 ***2856.30*** *p163*
Han, Michael; America, 1752 ***2856.30*** *p163*
With wife & child

Han, Michael; America, 1752 ***2856.30*** *p164*
With wife
Hanan, Cornelious 3; Vermont, 1856 ***5900.10*** *p363*
Hanan, Henry; New York, 1821 ***8197.10*** *p238*
Hanan, Joseph; New York, 1837 ***8197.10*** *p90*
Hanan, Patrick; Pennsylvania, 1868 ***6058.10*** *p75*
Hanan, Patrick; Pennsylvania, 1868 ***6058.10*** *p77*
Hanan, William 2; Vermont, 1857 ***5900.10*** *p363*
Hanauer, Johann Henrich; Port uncertain, 1751 ***2856.30*** *p163*
Hanauer, Maria Margarete; Port uncertain, 1754 ***2856.30*** *p163*
Hanay, John; New York, 1837 ***8197.10*** *p91*
Hanborough, Martha; Maryland, 1654 ***2524.55*** *p100*
Hanbury, Mr.; Quebec, 1857 ***9196.15*** *p23*
Hanbury, Mr.; Quebec, 1858 ***9196.15*** *p33*
Hanbury, Catherine 36; New York, New York, 1849 ***1825.45*** *p35*
Hanbury, Peter; New England, 1647 ***1224.1*** *p27*
Hanby, John; Savannah, Georgia, 1806 ***1640.10*** *p77*
Hance, John; Maryland, 1666 ***2524.55*** *p100*
Hance, Moses; Maryland, 1665 ***2524.55*** *p100*
Hance, Peter; Virginia, 1708 ***1224.2*** *p51*
Hance, Rawleigh; Virginia, 1673 ***1224.1*** *p27*
Hancock, Edward; New York, 1840 ***8197.10*** *p172*
Hancock, George; New York, 1840 ***8197.10*** *p172*
Hancock, James 42; Ontario, 1871 ***1823.22*** *p67*
Hancock, Jno; Virginia, 1663 ***6212.30*** *p4*
Hancock, Jno; Virginia, 1668-1669 ***6212.30*** *p41*
Hancock, John; New Orleans, 1836 ***1224.3*** *p33*
Hancock, John; New York, 1829 ***8197.10*** *p351*
Hancock, John 46; Ontario, 1871 ***1823.28*** *p38*
Hancock, John 68; Ontario, 1871 ***1823.15*** *p104*
Hancock, Richard 21; America, 1774 ***1220.25*** *p36*
Hancock, Robert 15; Philadelphia, 1774 ***1220.25*** *p63*
Hancock, Samuel 49; Ontario, 1871 ***1823.15*** *p104*
Hancock, Samuel 52; Ontario, 1871 ***1823.28*** *p38*
Hancock, Stephen 16; Maryland, 1775 ***1220.25*** *p121*
Hancock, Thomas 29; Maryland, 1775 ***1220.25*** *p114*
Hancock, Thomas 57; Ontario, 1871 ***1823.15*** *p104*
Hancock, Thomas John; New York, 1819 ***8197.10*** *p237*
Hancocke, Martha; Maryland, 1668 ***2524.55*** *p100*
Hancom, Miss; Quebec, 1857 ***9196.15*** *p23*
Hancox, O.; Quebec, 1857 ***9196.15*** *p15*
Hand, Catherine; Vermont, 1869-1909 ***5900.10*** *p44*
Hand, Daniel 45; Ontario, 1871 ***1823.22*** *p67*
Hand, Edward; New England, 1775-1781 ***4628.40*** *p68*
Hand, Gartrid; Virginia, 1663 ***6212.30*** *p3*
Hand, Gartrude; Virginia, 1672 ***6212.30*** *p49*
Hand, James 49; Vermont, 1877 ***5900.10*** *p474*
Hand, Joane; Maryland, 1666 ***2524.55*** *p100*
Hand, John; Maryland, 1666 ***2524.55*** *p100*
Hand, Rose; Vermont, 1837-1916 ***5900.10*** *p490*
Handcock, Robert 59; Ontario, 1871 ***1823.15*** *p104*
Handcock, Stephen; Maryland, 1667 ***2524.55*** *p100*
Handford, James 31; Ontario, 1871 ***1823.15*** *p104*
Handford, John 70; Ontario, 1871 ***1823.15*** *p104*
Handford, Richard 29; Ontario, 1871 ***1823.15*** *p104*
Handford, Richard 62; Ontario, 1871 ***1823.15*** *p104*
Handford, Tobias; Virginia, n.d. ***1224.1*** *p27*
Handford, Tobias; Virginia, 1670 ***1224.1*** *p27*
Handie, Robert; Pennsylvania, 1777 ***4629.10*** *p6*
Handiesyde, James; Georgia, 1698 ***1640.13*** *p53*
Handle, Adam; Pennsylvania, 1777 ***4629.10*** *p16*
Handlen, Ernest; Alaska, 1915 ***9196.1*** *p11*
Handlen, Ernest; British Columbia, 1915 ***9196.1*** *p11*
Handley, Deborah; Maryland, 1663 ***2524.55*** *p100*
Handley, Edward 8; Ontario, 1861 ***2896.27*** *p18*
Handley, George 37; Ontario, 1871 ***1823.28*** *p38*
Handley, Hannah 6; Ontario, 1861 ***2896.27*** *p18*
Handley, Hannah 72; Ontario, 1861 ***2896.27*** *p18*
Handley, Harper 4; Ontario, 1861 ***2896.27*** *p18*
Handley, Henry 34; Ontario, 1861 ***2896.27*** *p18*
Handley, James 21; Maryland, 1775 ***1220.25*** *p108*
Handley, John; Pennsylvania, 1777 ***4629.10*** *p9*
Handley, Rebeca 26; Ontario, 1861 ***2896.27*** *p18*
Handley, William J. 9; Ontario, 1861 ***2896.27*** *p18*
Handlin, John; Maryland, 1681 ***2524.55*** *p100*
Handlin, Katharine; Maryland, 1681 ***2524.55*** *p100*
Handlon, James; New York, 1837 ***8197.10*** *p91*
Handly, John 46; Ontario, 1871 ***1823.22*** *p67*
Handman, James N.; Pennsylvania, 1850 ***6058.10*** *p28*
Handor, Edward; Virginia, 1666 ***6212.30*** *p29*
Handrup, Axel 35; Vancouver, British Columbia, 1913 ***9196.1*** *p57*
Handrup, Axel 35; Washington, 1913 ***9196.1*** *p57*
Hands, Emily 48; Ontario, 1871 ***1823.15*** *p104*
Hands, Herbert 19; Ontario, 1871 ***1823.28*** *p38*
Hands, John; New York, 1837 ***8197.10*** *p90*
Handson, Harry; Virginia, 1681 ***6212.30*** *p55*
Handtschue, Friedrich; Port uncertain, 1773 ***2856.30*** *p163*
Handushiski, Joseph; Maryland, 1910 ***3259.35*** *p19*
Handwerk, Susanna; Port uncertain, 1783 ***2856.30*** *p163*
Handwick, Elizabeth 24 *SEE* Handwick, James
Handwick, James 34; Fort Cumberland, Nova Scotia, 1774 ***1220.25*** *p17*
Wife: Elizabeth 24
Handy, Charles; Newport, Rhode Island, 1796 ***1224.2*** *p51*
Handy, George 54; Ontario, 1871 ***1823.15*** *p104*
Handy, P. L.; Quebec, 1858 ***9196.15*** *p31*
Handyside, Mr.; Quebec, 1856 ***9196.15*** *p9*
Haneck, Catharina; Port uncertain, 1780 ***2856.30*** *p163*
Hanegan, James; New York, 1836 ***8197.10*** *p75*
Hanegan, Patrick; Pennsylvania, 1850 ***6058.10*** *p28*
Hanemann, Johann; Port uncertain, 1773 ***2856.30*** *p163*
With wife
Hanemann, Mrs. Peter; America, 1700-1799 ***2856.30*** *p163*
Hanemann, Mrs. Peter; Port uncertain, 1732 ***2856.30*** *p163*
Haner, John 24; America, 1774 ***1220.25*** *p36*
Hanerberger, Henrich; America, 1751 ***2856.30*** *p197H*
Hanerley, John; Virginia, 1671-1672 ***6212.30*** *p47*
Haney, Andrew; Pennsylvania, 1786 ***4629.10*** *p52*
Haney, Bridget Toohey; Vermont, 1846-1913 ***5900.10*** *p420*
Haney, Charles 65; Vermont, 1894 ***5900.10*** *p405*
Haney, James; Vermont, 1852-1940 ***5900.10*** *p399*
Haney, James E.; Vermont, 1910 ***5900.10*** *p399*
Haney, Mary A.; Vermont, 1846-1946 ***5900.10*** *p443*
Haney, Mary A. Tree; Vermont, 1861-1932 ***5900.10*** *p399*
Haney, Mary Grace; Vermont, 1840-1893 ***5900.10*** *p405*
Haney, Michael B.; Vermont, 1851-1927 ***5900.10*** *p420*
Haney, William 28; Ontario, 1871 ***1823.15*** *p104*
Hanfield, Lewis; Vermont, 1847-1925 ***5900.10*** *p461*
Hanfield, Mary E. Burke; Vermont, 1853-1893 ***5900.10*** *p461*
Hanford, Elnathan; Connecticut, 1769 ***1224.2*** *p51*
Hang, Maria Apollonia; Port uncertain, 1788 ***2856.30*** *p163*
Hangen, Nikol; Port uncertain, 1784 ***2856.30*** *p163*
Hangen, Peter; Port uncertain, 1781 ***2856.30*** *p163*
Hanger, Ann; Virginia, 1671 ***6212.30*** *p43*
Hangin, Maria Apollonia; Port uncertain, 1788 ***2856.30*** *p163*
Hangner, Johann; Port uncertain, 1792 ***2856.30*** *p163*
Hanham, Thomas 21; Virginia, 1773 ***1220.25*** *p28*
Hanich, Jakob; Port uncertain, 1764 ***2856.30*** *p163*
Hanie, Moses; Maryland, 1664 ***2524.55*** *p100*
Hanifan, Bridget 27; Vermont, 1869 ***5900.10*** *p109*
Hanifen, Dan 2 *SEE* Hanifen, Ulick
Hanifen, Mary 6 *SEE* Hanifen, Ulick
Hanifen, Mary 31 *SEE* Hanifen, Ulick
Hanifen, Ulick 30; New York, New York, 1851 ***1825.45*** *p56*
Wife: Mary 31
Daughter: Mary 6
Son: Dan 2
Hanigan, Henry; New York, 1840 ***8197.10*** *p173*
Hanigan, Hugh; New York, 1826 ***8197.10*** *p337*
Hanigan, Patrick; Pennsylvania, 1866 ***6058.10*** *p51*
Hanisworth, George; Maryland, 1662 ***2524.55*** *p100*
Hanker, John Henry; New York, 1838 ***8197.10*** *p241*
Hankilh, John 31; Washington, 1913 ***9196.1*** *p60*
Hanks, Edward 16; Maryland, 1775 ***1220.25*** *p116*
Hanks, Isaac 25; Philadelphia, 1775 ***1220.25*** *p122*
Hanlan, James 29; Maryland, 1775 ***1220.25*** *p110*
Hanlan, Michael; New York, 1840 ***8197.10*** *p242*
Hanlan, Richard; Vermont, n.d. ***5900.10*** *p211*
Hanley, Andrew; Vermont, 1854-1925 ***5900.10*** *p568*
Hanley, Ann Eliza; Vermont, 1840-1916 ***5900.10*** *p303*
Hanley, Bernard; Vermont, 1816-1891 ***5900.10*** *p217*
Hanley, Betty 54 *SEE* Hanley, James
Hanley, Bridget; Vermont, 1846-1917 ***5900.10*** *p266*
Hanley, Bridget; Vermont, 1914 ***5900.10*** *p400*
Hanley, Bridget 74; Vermont, 1872 ***5900.10*** *p172*
Hanley, Bridget O'Donnell 84; Vermont, 1897 ***5900.10*** *p267*
Hanley, Catherine; Vermont, 1829-1893 ***5900.10*** *p535*
Hanley, Catherine Kenian 67; Vermont, 1878 ***5900.10*** *p163*
Hanley, Darby 16 *SEE* Hanley, Thomas
Hanley, Dennis 24; New York, 1834-1840 ***8197.10*** *p171*
Hanley, Edward 18 *SEE* Hanley, Thomas
Hanley, Edward 67; Vermont, 1871 ***5900.10*** *p163*
Hanley, Edward M. 64; Vermont, 1875 ***5900.10*** *p524*
Hanley, Ellen; Vermont, 1831-1903 ***5900.10*** *p487*
Hanley, Ellen 67; Vermont, 1896 ***5900.10*** *p567*
Hanley, Ellen D.; Vermont, 1836-1936 ***5900.10*** *p532*
Hanley, Ellen M. 28; Vermont, 1873 ***5900.10*** *p567*
Hanley, Ema 9; Ontario, 1861 ***2896.26*** *p39*
Hanley, Gilbert 47; Vermont, 1884 ***5900.10*** *p567*
Hanley, Hanah 12; Ontario, 1861 ***2896.26*** *p39*
Hanley, Hannora 67; Vermont, 1882 ***5900.10*** *p221*
Hanley, Hanora M. Casey; Vermont, 1860-1929 ***5900.10*** *p568*
Hanley, Henry; New York, 1821 ***8197.10*** *p238*
Hanley, Henry; New York, 1827 ***8197.10*** *p346*
Hanley, Hester Ann 10; Ontario, 1861 ***2896.26*** *p39*
Hanley, Honor 22 *SEE* Hanley, Thomas
Hanley, James; Vermont, n.d. ***5900.10*** *p46*
Hanley, James 14 *SEE* Hanley, James
Hanley, James 30; New York, New York, 1847 ***1825.45*** *p16*
Wife: Susan 30
Son: John 7
Son: Peter 5
Hanley, James 38; Ontario, 1861 ***2896.26*** *p39*
Hanley, James 64; New York, New York, 1847 ***1825.45*** *p15*
Wife: Betty 54
Son: John 18
Son: Patrick 20
Son: Mary 17
Son: Roger 12
Son: Martin 22
Son: James 14
Hanley, James 69; Vermont, 1893 ***5900.10*** *p567*
Hanley, Joanna Reynolds; Vermont, 1847-1923 ***5900.10*** *p532*
Hanley, John; Vermont, 1830-1902 ***5900.10*** *p225*
Hanley, John; Vermont, 1830-1920 ***5900.10*** *p577*
Hanley, John 7 *SEE* Hanley, James
Hanley, John 18 *SEE* Hanley, James
Hanley, John 75; Vermont, 1894 ***5900.10*** *p558*
Hanley, John 82; Vermont, 1877 ***5900.10*** *p190*
Hanley, Julia; Vermont, 1857-1920 ***5900.10*** *p275*
Hanley, Kate Duffey; Vermont, 1842-1931 ***5900.10*** *p225*
Hanley, Laurence; Vermont, 1821-1897 ***5900.10*** *p487*
Hanley, Mrs. Lawrence; Vermont, 1843-1911 ***5900.10*** *p247*
Hanley, Margaret; Vermont, 1862-1919 ***5900.10*** *p568*
Hanley, Margaret; Vermont, 1868-1926 ***5900.10*** *p46*
Hanley, Margaret 41; Vermont, 1880 ***5900.10*** *p567*
Hanley, Margaret 54; Vermont, 1872 ***5900.10*** *p558*
Hanley, Margaret 81; Vermont, 1878 ***5900.10*** *p190*
Hanley, Margaret A.; Vermont, 1833-1901 ***5900.10*** *p557*
Hanley, Margaret A.; Vermont, 1856-1938 ***5900.10*** *p524*
Hanley, Margaret Gormley; Vermont, 1840-1898 ***5900.10*** *p163*
Hanley, Maria; Vermont, 1825-1902 ***5900.10*** *p526*
Hanley, Martha 32; Ontario, 1861 ***2896.26*** *p39*
Hanley, Martin 22 *SEE* Hanley, James
Hanley, Martin D.; Vermont, 1839-1899 ***5900.10*** *p163*
Hanley, Mary; Vermont, 1830-1910 ***5900.10*** *p577*
Hanley, Mary; Vermont, 1831-1904 ***5900.10*** *p230*
Hanley, Mary 17 *SEE* Hanley, James
Hanley, Mary 20 *SEE* Hanley, Thomas
Hanley, Mary 50 *SEE* Hanley, Thomas
Hanley, Mary 65; Vermont, 1888 ***5900.10*** *p46*
Hanley, Mary 72; Vermont, 1899 ***5900.10*** *p218*
Hanley, Mary Doon; Vermont, 1838-1909 ***5900.10*** *p225*
Hanley, Mary J.; Vermont, 1852-1952 ***5900.10*** *p525*
Hanley, Michael; Vermont, 1831-1903 ***5900.10*** *p459*
Hanley, Michael; Vermont, 1845-1913 ***5900.10*** *p274*
Hanley, Michael 13 *SEE* Hanley, Thomas
Hanley, Nancy; Vermont, 1834-1901 ***5900.10*** *p534*
Hanley, Nathan 26; Vermont, 1865 ***5900.10*** *p164*
Hanley, Patrick 20 *SEE* Hanley, James
Hanley, Patrick 24 *SEE* Hanley, Thomas
Hanley, Patrick 25; Vermont, 1876 ***5900.10*** *p582*
Hanley, Peter 5 *SEE* Hanley, James
Hanley, Rebecca 4; Ontario, 1861 ***2896.26*** *p39*
Hanley, Robert; Vermont, 1850-1903 ***5900.10*** *p275*
Hanley, Robert 2; Ontario, 1861 ***2896.26*** *p39*
Hanley, Robert 64; Vermont, 1873 ***5900.10*** *p267*
Hanley, Roger 12 *SEE* Hanley, James
Hanley, Ruth Walsh; Vermont, 1854-1914 ***5900.10*** *p274*
Hanley, Sarah 72; Vermont, 1891 ***5900.10*** *p218*
Hanley, Susan 30 *SEE* Hanley, James
Hanley, Thomas 60; New York, New York, 1847 ***1825.45*** *p16*
Wife: Mary 50
Daughter: Mary 20
Daughter: Honor 22
Son: Darby 16
Son: Edward 18
Son: Patrick 24
Son: Michael 13
Hanley, Thomas B.; Vermont, 1838-1905 ***5900.10*** *p225*
Hanley, William; Vermont, 1839-1891 ***5900.10*** *p396*
Hanley, William 76; Vermont, 1893 ***5900.10*** *p221*
Hanley, William 95; Vermont, 1897 ***5900.10*** *p164*
Hanley, Wm J.; Vermont, 1844-1921 ***5900.10*** *p532*
Hanlin, Catharine; New York, 1833 ***8197.10*** *p358*
Hanlin, James 29; Ontario, 1871 ***1823.28*** *p38*

Hanlin, John H. 72; Vermont, 1919 ***5900.10*** *p122*
Hanlin, Mary A. Slattery 73; Vermont, 1922 ***5900.10*** *p122*
Hanlon, Bernard; New York, 1836 ***8197.10*** *p75*
Hanlon, Catherine; Vermont, 1831-1903 ***5900.10*** *p506*
Hanlon, Catherine Linehan 35; Vermont, 1876 ***5900.10*** *p101*
Hanlon, Ellen McBride; Vermont, 1844-1944 ***5900.10*** *p220*
Hanlon, Felix 45; Ontario, 1871 ***1823.15*** *p104*
Hanlon, John; Vermont, 1855-1917 ***5900.10*** *p162*
Hanlon, Margaret A. Lynch 26; Vermont, 1893 ***5900.10*** *p467*
Hanlon, Mary; Vermont, 1834-1916 ***5900.10*** *p357*
Hanlon, Mary Currin; Vermont, 1859-1894 ***5900.10*** *p132*
Hanlon, Mary O'Day 91; Vermont, 1924 ***5900.10*** *p595*
Hanlon, Michael; New York, 1840 ***8197.10*** *p174*
Hanlon, Michael 55; Vermont, 1889 ***5900.10*** *p595*
Hanlon, Owen; Vermont, 1846-1915 ***5900.10*** *p220*
Hanlon, Patrick 26; Ontario, 1871 ***1823.22*** *p67*
Hanlon, Sarah; Vermont, n.d. ***5900.10*** *p359*
Hanlon, Sarah E.; Vermont, 1858-1926 ***5900.10*** *p162*
Hanlon, Thomas 77; Vermont, 1904 ***5900.10*** *p101*
Hanlon, William T.; Vermont, 1859-1929 ***5900.10*** *p132*
Hanly, Ann Kearigan 34; Vermont, 1866 ***5900.10*** *p209*
Hanly, Betty 54 *SEE* Hanly, James
Hanly, Bridget; Vermont, 1829-1899 ***5900.10*** *p584*
Hanly, Daniel 26; Vermont, 1870 ***5900.10*** *p573*
Hanly, Darby 16 *SEE* Hanly, Thomas
Hanly, Edward 18 *SEE* Hanly, Thomas
Hanly, Honor 22 *SEE* Hanly, Thomas
Hanly, James 14 *SEE* Hanly, James
Hanly, James 30; New York, New York, 1847 ***1825.45*** *p16*
Wife: Susan 30
Son: Peter 5
Son: John 7
Hanly, James 64; New York, New York, 1847 ***1825.45*** *p15*
Wife: Betty 54
Son: Martin 22
Son: Roger 12
Son: Mary 17
Son: Patrick 20
Son: John 18
Son: James 14
Hanly, John; New York, 1834 ***8197.10*** *p373*
Hanly, John 7 *SEE* Hanly, James
Hanly, John 18 *SEE* Hanly, James
Hanly, John 52; Ontario, 1871 ***1823.15*** *p104*
Hanly, Martin 22 *SEE* Hanly, James
Hanly, Mary 17 *SEE* Hanly, James
Hanly, Mary 20 *SEE* Hanly, Thomas
Hanly, Mary 50 *SEE* Hanly, Thomas
Hanly, Michael 13 *SEE* Hanly, Thomas
Hanly, Patrick 20 *SEE* Hanly, James
Hanly, Patrick 24 *SEE* Hanly, Thomas
Hanly, Peter 5 *SEE* Hanly, James
Hanly, Roger 12 *SEE* Hanly, James
Hanly, Susan 30 *SEE* Hanly, James
Hanly, Thomas 60; New York, New York, 1847 ***1825.45*** *p16*
Wife: Mary 50
Daughter: Mary 20
Son: Darby 16
Son: Michael 13
Son: Patrick 24
Daughter: Honor 22
Son: Edward 18
Hann, John; Maryland, 1681 ***2524.55*** *p100*
Hann, Peter; America, 1744 ***2856.30*** *p163*
Hann, Stefan; Port uncertain, 1741 ***2856.30*** *p163*
With family
Hanna, Andrew; Vermont, 1832-1899 ***5900.10*** *p279*
Hanna, Andrew 50; Ontario, 1871 ***1823.28*** *p38*
Hanna, Bridget; Vermont, 1823-1884 ***5900.10*** *p278*
Hanna, Bridget 62; Vermont, 1884 ***5900.10*** *p280*
Hanna, Campbell 40; Ontario, 1871 ***1823.15*** *p104*
Hanna, Eliza; Vermont, 1859-1921 ***5900.10*** *p406*
Hanna, George 52; Ontario, 1871 ***1823.15*** *p104*
Hanna, George 55; Ontario, 1871 ***1823.22*** *p67*
Hanna, Henry Nelson; New York, 1840 ***8197.10*** *p174*
Hanna, Hugh 43; Ontario, 1871 ***1823.15*** *p104*
Hanna, James; New York, 1835-1840 ***8197.10*** *p173*
Hanna, James; New York, 1840 ***8197.10*** *p173*
Hanna, James; Vermont, 1830-1900 ***5900.10*** *p280*
Hanna, James 68; Vermont, 1892 ***5900.10*** *p279*
Hanna, John; New York, 1839 ***8197.10*** *p320*
Hanna, John; Pennsylvania, 1807 ***6058.10*** *p2*
Hanna, John; Vermont, 1830 ***5900.10*** *p13*
Hanna, John; Vermont, 1832-1901 ***5900.10*** *p280*
Hanna, John 32; Ontario, 1871 ***1823.15*** *p104*
Hanna, John 35; Ontario, 1871 ***1823.15*** *p104*
Hanna, John 47; Ontario, 1871 ***1823.22*** *p67*
Hanna, John 61; Ontario, 1871 ***1823.15*** *p104*
Hanna, John 81; Ontario, 1871 ***1823.15*** *p104*
Hanna, Margaret McMahon 58; Vermont, 1894 ***5900.10*** *p279*
Hanna, Mary 72; Ontario, 1871 ***1823.15*** *p104*
Hanna, Mary Dwyer 38; Vermont, 1883 ***5900.10*** *p280*
Hanna, Mary E.; Vermont, 1857-1939 ***5900.10*** *p283*
Hanna, Mary E.; Vermont, 1859 ***5900.10*** *p278*
Hanna, Mary Murphy; Vermont, 1821-1902 ***5900.10*** *p279*
Hanna, Matthew; New York, 1832 ***8197.10*** *p357*
Hanna, Moses 45; Ontario, 1871 ***1823.15*** *p104*
Hanna, Nancy 74; Vermont, 1862 ***5900.10*** *p279*
Hanna, Nicholas; Vermont, 1789-1883 ***5900.10*** *p280*
Hanna, Richard 53; Ontario, 1871 ***1823.22*** *p67*
Hanna, Robert 43; Ontario, 1871 ***1823.15*** *p104*
Hanna, Samuel S. 65; Ontario, 1871 ***1823.15*** *p105*
Hanna, William; New York, 1802 ***8197.10*** *p21*
Hanna, William; New York, 1836 ***8197.10*** *p75*
Hannaford, George 41; Ontario, 1871 ***1823.15*** *p105*
Hannagan, Bridget 63; Vermont, 1871 ***5900.10*** *p616*
Hannah, Charles M. 15; Ontario, 1861 ***2896.27*** *p16*
Hannah, Daniel; New York, 1838 ***8197.10*** *p241*
Hannah, Edward; Pennsylvania, 1777 ***4629.10*** *p26*
Hannah, Francis 49; Ontario, 1871 ***1823.28*** *p38*
Hannah, Hamlet 65; Ontario, 1871 ***1823.15*** *p105*
Hannah, Harison B. 12; Ontario, 1861 ***2896.27*** *p16*
Hannah, James L.; New York, 1834 ***8197.10*** *p69*
Hannah, John; Pennsylvania, 1777 ***4629.10*** *p8*
Hannah, John; Pennsylvania, 1777 ***4629.10*** *p14*
Hannah, John 40; Ontario, 1871 ***1823.28*** *p38*
Hannah, John 69; Ontario, 1871 ***1823.15*** *p105*
Hannah, Margret 59; Ontario, 1871 ***1823.15*** *p105*
Hannah, Mariah 48; Ontario, 1861 ***2896.27*** *p16*
Hannah, Marilla 16; Ontario, 1861 ***2896.27*** *p16*
Hannah, Mary; Chicago, 1896 ***1640.13*** *p53*
Hannah, William 60; Ontario, 1871 ***1823.15*** *p105*
Hannah, William, Sr. 62; Ontario, 1871 ***1823.15*** *p105*
Hannahan, Christian 49; Ontario, 1871 ***1823.28*** *p38*
Hannahan, Patrick 34; Ontario, 1871 ***1823.28*** *p38*
Hannahan, Timothy 30; Ontario, 1871 ***1823.28*** *p38*
Hannam, James 45; New York, 1774 ***1220.25*** *p24*
Hannam, John 30; New York, 1774 ***1220.25*** *p24*
Hannam, Minty; Maryland, 1791 ***1224.2*** *p51*
Hannam, William; New York, 1806 ***1224.3*** *p33*
Hannan, Annora Casey 82; Vermont, 1940 ***5900.10*** *p124*
Hannan, Bridget; Vermont, 1832-1906 ***5900.10*** *p540*
Hannan, Catherine Ryan; Vermont, 1861-1917 ***5900.10*** *p394*
Hannan, Edmond; Vermont, 1857-1944 ***5900.10*** *p124*
Hannan, Ellen Coonerty 84; Vermont, 1907 ***5900.10*** *p521*
Hannan, Ellen Stapleton 41; Vermont, 1895 ***5900.10*** *p521*
Hannan, Francis 12; Vermont, 1878 ***5900.10*** *p521*
Hannan, Francis 67; Vermont, 1890 ***5900.10*** *p521*
Hannan, George 18; Vermont, 1894 ***5900.10*** *p521*
Hannan, Hannie 8; Vermont, 1878 ***5900.10*** *p521*
Hannan, Hanorah Ryan; Vermont, 1849-1903 ***5900.10*** *p394*
Hannan, James; New York, 1840 ***8197.10*** *p173*
Hannan, James; Pennsylvania, 1867 ***6058.10*** *p58*
Hannan, James; Vermont, 1850-1898 ***5900.10*** *p394*
Hannan, James 61; Ontario, 1871 ***1823.15*** *p105*
Hannan, John; Vermont, 1844-1898 ***5900.10*** *p393*
Hannan, John W. 62; Vermont, 1916 ***5900.10*** *p124*
Hannan, Margaret; Vermont, 1851-1923 ***5900.10*** *p559*
Hannan, Margaret; Vermont, 1861-1923 ***5900.10*** *p125*
Hannan, Mary 23; Vermont, 1878 ***5900.10*** *p521*
Hannan, Mary Fitzgerald 68; Vermont, 1859 ***5900.10*** *p521*
Hannan, Mary Geary; Vermont, 1875-1931 ***5900.10*** *p124*
Hannan, Thomas 87; Vermont, 1902 ***5900.10*** *p521*
Hannan, Thomas C. 44; Vermont, 1897 ***5900.10*** *p520*
Hannay, Mr.; Portland, Maine, 1858 ***9196.15*** *p28*
Hannay, Mrs.; Portland, Maine, 1858 ***9196.15*** *p28*
Hannay, George; St. Augustine, Florida, 1783 ***1640.10*** *p77*
Hannay, Patrick; Virginia, 1823 ***1640.13*** *p53*
Hanne, Johannes Thiel; Port uncertain, 1775 ***2856.30*** *p163*
Hanneford, Mr.; Quebec, 1857 ***9196.15*** *p14*
Hannemann, Margarete; Port uncertain, 1731 ***2856.30*** *p163*
Hannen, Johannes Thiel; Port uncertain, 1775 ***2856.30*** *p163*
Hannen, Julia; Vermont, n.d. ***5900.10*** *p149*
Hannen, Mathew; Vermont, n.d. ***5900.10*** *p149*
Hannen, Michael; New York, 1840 ***8197.10*** *p171*
Hanner, Johann Jost; America, 1763 ***2856.30*** *p197H*
Hannewell, Wm; Virginia, 1669-1670 ***6212.30*** *p41*
Hannhofer, Johann; Port uncertain, 1795 ***2856.30*** *p163*
Hannhofer, Johann; Port uncertain, 1796 ***2856.30*** *p163*
Hanni, M. 28; Alaska, 1917 ***9196.1*** *p46*
Hanni, M. 28; Whitehorse, Yukon, 1917 ***9196.1*** *p46*
Hannifin, Mary; Vermont, n.d. ***5900.10*** *p122*
Hannigan, Anthony; New York, 1837 ***8197.10*** *p91*
Hannigan, Edward; New York, 1837 ***8197.10*** *p91*
Hannigan, Terry; New York, 1840 ***8197.10*** *p242*
Hannigan, Thomas; New York, 1834 ***8197.10*** *p315*
Hanning, Ellen; Vermont, 1849-1897 ***5900.10*** *p466*
Hanning, Ellen Callahan 68; Vermont, 1895 ***5900.10*** *p469*
Hanning, John; Virginia, 1671-1672 ***6212.30*** *p45*
Hanning, John 80; Vermont, 1903 ***5900.10*** *p469*
Hanning, Mary 71; Vermont, 1890 ***5900.10*** *p466*
Hanning, William; New York, 1836-1838 ***8197.10*** *p117*
Hannock, Michael 58; Ontario, 1871 ***1823.22*** *p67*
Hannon, Bridget; Vermont, 1840-1873 ***5900.10*** *p112*
Hannon, Daniel 55; Vermont, 1869 ***5900.10*** *p300*
Hannon, Dominick; New York, 1834 ***8197.10*** *p69*
Hannon, Edmond; Vermont, 1818-1898 ***5900.10*** *p125*
Hannon, Edmond; Vermont, 1864-1930 ***5900.10*** *p125*
Hannon, Edward; Vermont, 1855 ***5900.10*** *p120*
Hannon, Elizabeth J.; Vermont, 1858-1932 ***5900.10*** *p125*
Hannon, Ellen Garnner 86; Vermont, 1915 ***5900.10*** *p125*
Hannon, Francis; Vermont, n.d. ***5900.10*** *p6*
Hannon, George 60; Ontario, 1871 ***1823.22*** *p67*
Hannon, Hannie Butler; Vermont, 1863-1943 ***5900.10*** *p125*
Hannon, Henry; Vermont, 1869-1922 ***5900.10*** *p112*
Hannon, Henry; Vermont, 1881 ***5900.10*** *p120*
Hannon, Isabell; Vermont, 1858 ***5900.10*** *p120*
Hannon, James; Vermont, 1840-1917 ***5900.10*** *p112*
Hannon, Joanna; Vermont, 1852-1920 ***5900.10*** *p125*
Hannon, Julia 85; Vermont, 1895 ***5900.10*** *p289*
Hannon, Margaret Hogan; Vermont, 1828-1901 ***5900.10*** *p125*
Hannon, Margaret Leathede 69; Vermont, 1883 ***5900.10*** *p301*
Hannon, Mary; Vermont, 1865-1932 ***5900.10*** *p65*
Hannon, Mary E. 52; Vermont, 1913 ***5900.10*** *p125*
Hannon, Michael; Vermont, 1858-1924 ***5900.10*** *p125*
Hannon, Michael 57; Vermont, 1885 ***5900.10*** *p125*
Hannon, Thomas; Vermont, 1848 ***5900.10*** *p6*
Hannon, Thomas; Vermont, 1849-1913 ***5900.10*** *p430*
Hannon, Thomas; Vermont, 1850-1926 ***5900.10*** *p120*
Hannon, Thomas; Vermont, 1852-1912 ***5900.10*** *p106*
Hannon, Walter; Vermont, 1863-1864 ***5900.10*** *p112*
Hannough, Susanna; Maryland, 1670 ***2524.55*** *p100*
Hannyford, Edward; Virginia, 1656 ***1224.1*** *p27*
Hanon, Mary; Vermont, 1821-1909 ***5900.10*** *p247*
Hanrahan, Bridget 70; Ontario, 1871 ***1823.28*** *p38*
Hanrahan, Bridget Harrow 80; Vermont, 1901 ***5900.10*** *p77*
Hanrahan, Bridget Slattery; Vermont, 1847-1923 ***5900.10*** *p588*
Hanrahan, Catharine Ronan; Vermont, 1833-1908 ***5900.10*** *p275*
Hanrahan, Catherine; Vermont, 1833-1873 ***5900.10*** *p231*
Hanrahan, Ellen; Vermont, 1818 ***5900.10*** *p416*
Hanrahan, Frances M.; Vermont, 1860-1900 ***5900.10*** *p416*
Hanrahan, James; New York, 1802 ***8197.10*** *p21*
Hanrahan, James; Pennsylvania, 1868 ***6058.10*** *p61*
Hanrahan, James; Vermont, 1820-1888 ***5900.10*** *p416*
Hanrahan, John; Vermont, 1843-1920 ***5900.10*** *p416*
Hanrahan, John 50; Ontario, 1871 ***1823.28*** *p38*
Hanrahan, John, Sr.; Vermont, 1804-1901 ***5900.10*** *p588*
Hanrahan, John Francis; Vermont, 1848-1931 ***5900.10*** *p588*
Hanrahan, Margaret; Vermont, 1841-1896 ***5900.10*** *p590*
Hanrahan, Margaret 30; Vermont, 1881 ***5900.10*** *p336*
Hanrahan, Patrick 49; Ontario, 1871 ***1823.28*** *p38*
Hanrahan, Richard; Vermont, 1828-1907 ***5900.10*** *p275*
Hanrahan, Timothy 70; Vermont, 1891 ***5900.10*** *p77*
Hans, Jacob; Pennsylvania, 1777 ***4629.10*** *p8*
Hans, Lasten; Maryland, 1666 ***2524.55*** *p100*
Hans, Peter; Virginia, 1708 ***1224.2*** *p51*
Hans, Rowland; Maryland, 1666 ***2524.55*** *p100*
Hansbury, Judy 23; New York, New York, 1848 ***1825.45*** *p35*
Hansch, Jakob; America, 1748 ***2856.30*** *p164*
Hansell, John A.; New York, 1838 ***8197.10*** *p118*
Hanselmann, Anna; America, 1771 ***2856.30*** *p164*
With child
Hansen, Anna Dorothea; Port uncertain, 1788 ***2856.30*** *p164*
Hansen, Hy 21; British Columbia, 1911 ***9196.1*** *p15*
Hansen, Pete 32; British Columbia, 1911 ***9196.1*** *p33*
Hansen, Pete 32; Seattle, 1911 ***9196.1*** *p33*
Hanser, Johann; Port uncertain, 1744 ***2856.30*** *p164*
Hanser, Willm; Maryland, 1673 ***2524.55*** *p100*
Hanslap, Elizabeth, Sr.; Maryland, 1682 ***2524.55*** *p100*

Hanslap, Elizabeth, Jr.; Maryland, 1682 2524.55 p100
Hanslap, Frances; Maryland, 1682 2524.55 p100
Hanslap, Joseph; Maryland, 1682 2524.55 p101
Hansler, John; New York, 1836-1838 8197.10 p116
Hansley, Edmond; Maryland, 1673 2524.55 p101
Hansman, Jacob 33; Ontario, 1871 1823.15 p105
Hansminger, John; Pennsylvania, 1779 4629.10 p38
Hanson, Andrew; Maryland, 1659 2524.55 p101
Wife: Ann
With 4 children
Hanson, Ann *SEE* Hanson, Andrew
Hanson, Ann; Maryland, 1659 2524.55 p101
Hanson, Anthony; Maryland, 1673 2524.55 p101
Hanson, Cornelius; Maryland, 1671 2524.55 p101
Hanson, Edward 89; Ontario, 1871 1823.15 p105
Hanson, H. 35; Alaska, 1910 9196.1 p10
Hanson, H. 35; Yukon, 1910 9196.1 p10
Hanson, Hance; Maryland, 1673 2524.55 p101
Hanson, Henry C.; New York, 1840 8197.10 p171
Hanson, James; New York, 1899 1640.13 p53
Hanson, Jno; Virginia, 1674 6212.30 p52
Hanson, John 27; Ontario, 1871 1823.28 p38
Hanson, John 32; British Columbia, 1909 9196.1 p28
Hanson, John 32; Washington, 1909 9196.1 p28
Hanson, Louis 27; British Columbia, 1909 9196.1 p28
Hanson, Louis 27; Washington, 1909 9196.1 p28
Hanson, Ole 30; British Columbia, 1913 9196.1 p23
Hanson, Ole 30; Seattle, 1913 9196.1 p23
Hanson, Patrick 45; Vermont, 1863 5900.10 p565
Hanson, Peter; Maryland, 1673 2524.55 p101
Hanson, Samuel 15; Maryland, 1775 1220.25 p116
Hanson, Walter 45; Ontario, 1871 1823.15 p105
Hanson, William; Pennsylvania, 1777 4629.10 p17
Hanson, William 55; Ontario, 1871 1823.28 p38
Hanstock, Henry 8; Ontario, 1871 1823.15 p105
Hanstock, Joseph 57; Ontario, 1871 1823.15 p105
Hantchar, Thomas; Maryland, 1659 2524.55 p101
Hanton, John 17; Ontario, 1871 1823.22 p67
Hants, Captain; Canada, 1858 9196.15 p45
Hanwell, Henry T. 49; Ontario, 1871 1823.28 p38
Hany, Catharine 33; Maryland, 1775 1220.25 p113
Hanzel, Georg; Port uncertain, 1772 2856.30 p197H
Hanzel, Peter; Port uncertain, 1783 2856.30 p164
Hapeny, John; Maryland, 1665 2524.55 p101
Hapin, Thomas 14; Ontario, 1871 1823.15 p105
Happel, Hartman 24; Ontario, 1871 1823.15 p105
Happel, Jacob 51; Ontario, 1871 1823.15 p105
Happes, George; America, 1751 2856.30 p164
Happes, Jorg; Port uncertain, 1751 2856.30 p164
Happeth, Martin 30; Ontario, 1871 1823.28 p38
Hapyard, Thos Robt 26; Ontario, 1871 1823.15 p105
Har, Daniel 30; Maryland, 1775 1220.25 p96
Harald, Henry 25; Ontario, 1871 1823.22 p67
Harbach, Anna Ottilia; Port uncertain, 1757 2856.30 p197A
Harbard, Shilby; Maryland, 1668 2524.55 p101
Harberger, Christopher; Pennsylvania, 1779 4629.10 p40
Harbert, Clement; Maryland, 1667 2524.55 p101
Wife: Elizabeth
Harbert, Elizabeth *SEE* Harbert, Clement
Harbert, Rich; Virginia, 1669-1670 6212.30 p41
Harbinger, William; Maryland, 1679 2524.55 p101
Harbinson, John; New York, 1826 8197.10 p335
Harbor, William 75; Ontario, 1871 1823.22 p67
Harbot, William 29; Ontario, 1871 1823.15 p105
Harbottle, John 40; Ontario, 1871 1823.15 p105
Harby, Erasmus; Virginia, 1665-1666 6212.30 p21
Harcort, John 29; Ontario, 1871 1823.15 p105
Harcourt, Mr.; Quebec, 1856 9196.15 p7
Harcourt, Mr.; Quebec, 1857 9196.15 p20
Harcourt, Mrs.; Quebec, 1856 9196.15 p7
Harcourt, Mrs.; Quebec, 1857 9196.15 p20
Harcourt, J.; Portland, Maine, 1857 9196.15 p12
Harcourt, John; Maryland, 1658 2524.55 p101
Harcourt, Phillip; Virginia, 1664 6212.30 p12
Hard, Johann; Port uncertain, 1769 2856.30 p164
Hard, William 54; Ontario, 1871 1823.28 p38
Hardacre, Catherine O'Sullivan; Vermont, 1841-1915 5900.10 p140
Hardacre, William 62; Vermont, 1901 5900.10 p140
Hardcastle, Elizabeth 27 *SEE* Hardcastle, Samuel
Hardcastle, George 54; Ontario, 1871 1823.22 p67
Hardcastle, Samuel 28; Maryland, 1775 1220.25 p119
Wife: Elizabeth 27
Hardcastle, William 42; Ontario, 1871 1823.22 p67
Hardcastle, William 69; Ontario, 1871 1823.22 p67
Hardeck, Henry; Maryland, 1681 2524.55 p101
Harden, Mr.; Quebec, 1856 9196.15 p10
Hardesty, George; Maryland, 1662 2524.55 p101
Hardey, George Newman; New York, 1818 8197.10 p236
Hardgrave, William 36; Maryland, 1774 1220.25 p62
Hardi, Peter; Port uncertain, 1764 2856.30 p164
With wife & children
Hardich, William; Virginia, 1669 1224.1 p27
Hardick, Francis; Maryland, 1664 2524.55 p101
Hardidge, Willm.; Maryland, 1650 2524.55 p101
Hardie, Miss; Quebec, 1858 9196.15 p39
Hardie, Mr.; Quebec, 1858 9196.15 p44
Hardie, Alexander 28; Ontario, 1871 1823.28 p38
Hardie, Elizabeth 78; Ontario, 1871 1823.22 p67
Hardie, George; Georgia, 1818 1640.10 p77
Hardie, James; Mississippi, 1845 1640.10 p77
Wife: Jane
Hardie, Jane *SEE* Hardie, James
Hardie, Robert; Maryland, 1662 2524.55 p101
Hardie, Thomas 21; Philadelphia, 1774 1220.25 p43
Hardigan, Maggie A. 29; Vermont, 1876 5900.10 p338
Hardin, Elizabeth; New York, 1882 1640.13 p53
Hardin, Mary; Maryland, 1681 2524.55 p101
Harding, Miss; Quebec, 1858 9196.15 p34
Harding, Ann, Sr.; Maryland, 1669 2524.55 p84
Harding, Ann, Jr.; Maryland, 1669 2524.55 p84
Harding, Charles 21; Maryland, 1775 1220.25 p109
Harding, David; Pennsylvania, 1786 4629.10 p50
Harding, Easter 63; Ontario, 1871 1823.15 p105
Harding, Geo; Portland, Maine, 1857 9196.15 p13
Harding, George 21; Maryland, 1775 1220.25 p115
Harding, Jno; Virginia, 1664 6212.30 p11
Harding, John; Pennsylvania, 1777 4629.10 p20
Harding, John; Virginia, 1666-1667 6212.30 p33
Harding, John; Virginia, 1671 6212.30 p45
Harding, John 22; Maryland, 1775 1220.25 p97
Harding, John 22; Maryland, 1775 1220.25 p101
Harding, John 23; Maryland, 1774 1220.25 p39
Harding, Joseph; Maryland, 1674 2524.55 p101
Harding, M. E. L. 2; Ontario, 1861 2896.25 p44
Harding, Martha 50; Ontario, 1871 1823.28 p38
Harding, Philip 73; Ontario, 1871 1823.15 p105
Harding, Richard; Kentucky, 1832 1224.3 p33
Harding, S. M. 22; Ontario, 1861 2896.25 p44
Harding, Thomas; Maryland, 1657 2524.55 p40
Harding, William; Virginia, 1742 1224.2 p52
Harding, Wm 13; Ontario, 1871 1823.28 p38
Hardinge, Mr.; Quebec, 1858 9196.15 p46
Hardinge, Frederick 36; Ontario, 1871 1823.22 p67
Hardman, F.; Portland, Maine, 1858 9196.15 p28
Hardman, Hendrikin; Maryland, 1665 2524.55 p101
Hardman, James; Montreal, 1876 1640.13 p53
Hardman, James Nicholas; Pennsylvania, 1850 6058.10 p28
Hardman, Jeoffrey; Maryland, 1681 2524.55 p101
Hardman, Michael; New York, New York, 1835 6058.10 p37
Hardman, Moritz; Grenada, 1818 1640.13 p53
Hardman, Nicholas; New York, New York, 1836 6058.10 p35
Hardman, Peter; New York, New York, 1832 6058.10 p15
Hardmann, Elisabeth; America, 1767 2856.30 p164
Hardmann, Elisabeth; America, 1792 2856.30 p164
Hardmann, Elisabeth; Port uncertain, 1754 2856.30 p164
Hardness, Rich; Virginia, 1665-1666 6212.30 p22
Hardness, Tho; Virginia, 1665-1666 6212.30 p21
Hardres, Tho; Virginia, 1664 6212.30 p14
Hardrick, John; Maryland, 1680 2524.55 p101
Hardt, Philipp; America, 1743 2856.30 p164
With wife & 3 children
Hardwick, George; Maryland, 1659 2524.55 p101
Hardwick, Joseph; New York, 1840 8197.10 p173
Hardwick, Mary Ann; New York, 1850 1224.3 p75
Hardwick, Willm.; Maryland, 1650 2524.55 p101
Hardwik, William 62; Ontario, 1871 1823.15 p105
Hardy, Mr.; Quebec, 1856 9196.15 p7
Hardy, Mr.; Quebec, 1858 9196.15 p34
Hardy, Ann *SEE* Hardy, Robert
Hardy, Antho; Virginia, 1674 6212.30 p52
Hardy, David 31; Ontario, 1871 1823.15 p105
Hardy, Elizabeth A. 5; Ontario, 1861 2896.28 p28
Hardy, Henry; Maryland, 1673 2524.55 p101
Hardy, J. L.; Portland, Maine, 1858 9196.15 p27
Hardy, James; Georgia, 1699 1640.13 p53
Hardy, Jane 43; Ontario, 1861 2896.28 p28
Hardy, John; Florida, 1775 1224.2 p52
Hardy, John; Virginia, 1666-1667 6212.30 p33
Hardy, Lance 32; Ontario, 1871 1823.15 p105
Hardy, Mary J. 19; Ontario, 1861 2896.28 p47
Hardy, Mary Jane 19; Ontario, 1861 2896.28 p29
Hardy, Remy; New York, 1815 8197.10 p56
Hardy, Robert; Maryland, 1666 2524.55 p101
Wife: Ann
Hardy, Robt.; Maryland, 1665 2524.55 p101
Hardy, Robt; Virginia, 1684-1685 6212.30 p57
Hardy, Samuel; New England, 1678 1224.1 p40
Hardy, Thomas; New York, 1827 8197.10 p237
Hardy, Thomas; New York, 1840 8197.10 p386
Hardy, Thomas 47; Ontario, 1861 2896.28 p28
Hardy, Thomas 51; Ontario, 1871 1823.15 p105
Hardy, Thomas M. 7; Ontario, 1861 2896.28 p28
Hardy, William; New York, 1821 8197.10 p238
Hardy, William 25; Nova Scotia, 1774 1220.25 p136
Hardy, William H.; New York, 1823 8197.10 p238
Hare, A. 7; Ontario, 1861 2896.26 p2
Hare, Alice 3; Ontario, 1861 2896.26 p2
Hare, Charles 22; Maryland, 1775 1220.25 p98
Hare, Chester 19; Ontario, 1861 2896.26 p20
Hare, Dexter 20; Ontario, 1861 2896.27 p56
Hare, Dorcas 47; Ontario, 1861 2896.26 p2
Hare, Edmund 18; Ontario, 1861 2896.26 p2
Hare, Emarilla 21; Ontario, 1861 2896.26 p2
Hare, George 16; Ontario, 1861 2896.26 p2
Hare, Huldah 73; Ontario, 1861 2896.26 p2
Hare, Jacob; Pennsylvania, 1777 4629.10 p9
Hare, John; New York, 1840 8197.10 p172
Hare, Margaret; Pennsylvania, 1819 1224.3 p33
Hare, Margaret 50; Ontario, 1861 2896.25 p7
Hare, Mary 46; Ontario, 1861 2896.27 p56
Hare, Rose; Maryland, 1861 2524.55 p101
Hare, Thomas 21; Maryland, 1774 1220.25 p39
Hare, W. 5; Ontario, 1861 2896.26 p2
Hare, W. B. 10; Ontario, 1861 2896.26 p2
Hared, Rachel 8; Ontario, 1861 2896.27 p69
Haren, Andrew; New York, 1821 8197.10 p237
Harenin, Bridget 43; Ontario, 1871 1823.28 p38
Harer, Andrew; New York, 1821 8197.10 p237
Hares, Henrey 29; Ontario, 1871 1823.28 p38
Harewski, John; Maryland, 1910 3259.35 p19
Harff, Johann Nickel; America, 1773 2856.30 p164
Harff, Johann Nickel; America, 1774 2856.30 p164
Harff, Johann Nickel; Port uncertain, 1771 2856.30 p164
Harford, Robert; Virginia, 1703-1704 6212.30 p62
Harford, Samuel; New York, 1839 1224.3 p33
Hargart, Philipp; Port uncertain, 1766 2856.30 p164
Hargesheimer, Michael; America, 1741 2856.30 p164
With wife & 8 children
Hargesheimer, Michael; America, 1749 2856.30 p164
Hargesse, Ann; Maryland, 1668 2524.55 p101
Hargesse, William; Maryland, 1668 2524.55 p101
Hargiens, Jacob; America, 1790 2856.30 p164
Hargiens, Jacob; America, 1791 2856.30 p164
Hargish, Thomas; Maryland, 1663 2524.55 p133
Hargraft, Dorathea 79; Ontario, 1871 1823.22 p68
Hargraft, William 41; Ontario, 1871 1823.22 p68
Hargrave, George; New York, 1837 8197.10 p91
Hargrave, Michael; New York, 1840 8197.10 p171
Hargrave, William; Maryland, 1667 2524.55 p101
Harigan, Catharine 17; Ontario, 1861 2896.28 p46
Harigan, James 39; Ontario, 1871 1823.22 p68
Harigan, Timothy 12; Ontario, 1861 2896.28 p46
Haris, Elizabeth; Maryland, 1682 2524.55 p101
Harisine, Mathew 43; Ontario, 1871 1823.15 p105
Harison, James 35; Ontario, 1871 1823.15 p105
Harison, James 69; Ontario, 1871 1823.15 p105
Harison, Sarah 70; Ontario, 1871 1823.15 p105
Harken, Archibald; Pennsylvania, 1811 6058.10 p16
Harker, Mary; Maryland, 1681 2524.55 p101
Harkett, John 32; Georgia, 1774 1220.25 p47
Harkey, Ann; Virginia, 1679-1680 6212.30 p54
Harkin, Mr.; Portland, Maine, 1858 9196.15 p31
Harkin, Michael; New York, 1837 8197.10 p241
Harkins, Patrick; New York, 1840 8197.10 p385
Harkling, John; Maryland, 1672 2524.55 p101
Harkmonder, Joseph; Pennsylvania, 1777 4629.10 p12
Harkness, Mr.; Quebec, 1857 9196.15 p24
Harkness, Mrs.; Quebec, 1857 9196.15 p24
Harkness, James; Canada, 1841 1640.13 p53
Harkout, Michael; Maryland, 1910 3259.35 p19
Harkurle, William 30; Ontario, 1871 1823.15 p105
Harlan, Bridget; Vermont, 1846-1925 5900.10 p351
Harlan, Phineas; Pennsylvania, 1777 4629.10 p22
Harland, John; Pennsylvania, 1777 4629.10 p23
Harland, John 30; Halifax, Nova Scotia, 1774 1220.25 p138
Harland, William 23; Fort Cumberland, Nova Scotia, 1774 1220.25 p15
Harland, William 60; Ontario, 1871 1823.15 p106
Harle, Thomas; Maryland, 1668 2524.55 p118
Harley, Cesper 30; Ontario, 1871 1823.15 p106
Harley, David; Montreal, 1870 1640.13 p53
Harley, Henry; Virginia, 1665-1666 6212.30 p23
Harley, Jane 22; Maryland, 1775 1220.25 p111
Harley, John; Long Island, 1781 1224.2 p52
Harley, John; Maryland, 1910 3259.35 p19
Harley, John; New Jersey, 1848 1640.13 p53
Harley, Patrick 40; Ontario, 1871 1823.15 p106
Harley, Thomas; New York, 1818 8197.10 p236
Harley, Thomas; New York, 1824 8197.10 p297
Harlfinger, Franz; Port uncertain, 1747 2856.30 p164

Harlin, Anna Maria; Port uncertain, 1725 ***2856.30*** *p197H*
Harling, James 17; Philadelphia, 1774 ***1220.25*** *p66*
Harlington, Edward; Virginia, 1664 ***6212.30*** *p5*
Harloe, Ja; Virginia, 1674 ***6212.30*** *p52*
Harlow, James; Virginia, 1666 ***6212.30*** *p25*
Harlow, John 30; Dominica, 1773 ***1220.25*** *p28*
Harman, Andrew; New York, 1838 ***8197.10*** *p116*
Harman, Arian; Maryland, 1666 ***2524.55*** *p52*
Harman, Francis; Vermont, n.d. ***5900.10*** *p6*
Harman, Hendrikin; Maryland, 1665 ***2524.55*** *p101*
Harman, Jacob; Pennsylvania, 1777 ***4629.10*** *p21*
Harman, James 20; Maryland, 1774 ***1220.25*** *p39*
Harman, John; Maryland, 1660-1663 ***2524.55*** *p101*
Harman, John; Virginia, 1728 ***1224.2*** *p52*
Harman, John 32; Ontario, 1871 ***1823.15*** *p106*
Harman, Joseph S.; New York, 1826 ***8197.10*** *p239*
Harman, Patrick 30; Ontario, 1871 ***1823.15*** *p106*
Harman, Thomas; Virginia, 1701 ***1224.2*** *p52*
Harman, Thomas 65; Ontario, 1871 ***1823.15*** *p106*
Harmeld, Mary 13; Ontario, 1871 ***1823.28*** *p38*
Harmer, Charles; Virginia, 1639 ***1224.1*** *p27*
Harmer, George; Virginia, 1799 ***1224.2*** *p52*
Harmer, Jno; Virginia, 1677 ***6212.30*** *p54*
Harmive, Ivon 24; Washington, 1915 ***9196.1*** *p67*
Harmmoni, C. T. 62; Ontario, 1871 ***1823.28*** *p38*
Harmon, Absolon; Maryland, 1653 ***2524.55*** *p101*
Harmon, John; Vermont, 1831-1905 ***5900.10*** *p532*
Harmon, William; Pennsylvania, 1777 ***4629.10*** *p9*
Harmony, Peter; New York, 1805 ***8197.10*** *p29*
Harms, Claus; New York, 1828-1834 ***8197.10*** *p308*
Harmum, William 25; Philadelphia, 1775 ***1220.25*** *p8*
Harne, Wm; Virginia, 1671 ***6212.30*** *p43*
Harned, Jonathan; Pennsylvania, 1777 ***4629.10*** *p13*
Harned, Josiah; Pennsylvania, 1777 ***4629.10*** *p18*
Harned, Patrick; New York, 1838 ***8197.10*** *p240*
Harned, Patrick; New York, 1840 ***8197.10*** *p173*
Harnek, John H.; Maryland, 1910 ***3259.35*** *p19*
Harnes, Edward; Virginia, 1666-1667 ***6212.30*** *p34*
Harnes, John; Virginia, 1681 ***6212.30*** *p56*
Harness, Isaac *SEE* Harness, William
Harness, Susan *SEE* Harness, William
Harness, William *SEE* Harness, William
Harness, William; Maryland, 1658 ***2524.55*** *p102*
Wife: Susan
Child: William
Child: Isaac
Harnett, Kate 19; Vermont, 1873 ***5900.10*** *p197*
Harney, Bridget 98; Vermont, 1910 ***5900.10*** *p253*
Harney, Bridget Brady 73; Vermont, 1922 ***5900.10*** *p391*
Harney, Catharine 20; Vermont, 1859 ***5900.10*** *p190*
Harney, Ellen; Vermont, 1825-1901 ***5900.10*** *p202*
Harney, James; Vermont, 1859-1910 ***5900.10*** *p391*
Harney, John 66; Vermont, 1851 ***5900.10*** *p189*
Harney, Joseph; New York, 1840 ***8197.10*** *p174*
Harney, Mary 20; Vermont, 1852 ***5900.10*** *p189*
Harney, Mary Helen Moloney; Vermont, 1852-1914 ***5900.10*** *p391*
Harney, Thomas; Vermont, 1845-1899 ***5900.10*** *p391*
Harns, Jason 16; Ontario, 1861 ***2896.25*** *p69*
Harny, John; Maryland, 1676 ***2524.55*** *p102*
Harold, James; New York, 1838 ***8197.10*** *p116*
Haron, Robert; Pennsylvania, 1777 ***4629.10*** *p15*
Harpen, William 57; Ontario, 1871 ***1823.22*** *p68*
Harper, Mr.; Quebec, 1857 ***9196.15*** *p15*
Harper, Catharine 7 *SEE* Harper, Christopher
Harper, Charlotte 6 *SEE* Harper, Christopher
Harper, Christopher 40; Nova Scotia, 1774 ***1220.25*** *p15*
Harper, Christopher 45; Fort Cumberland, Nova Scotia, 1775 ***1220.25*** *p21*
Wife: Elizabeth 40
Child: John 13
Child: Catharine 7
Child: William 4
Child: Charlotte 6
Child: Thomas 12
Child: Elizabeth 14
Child: Hannah 15
Harper, David; Georgia, 1698 ***1640.13*** *p53*
Harper, Elizabeth 14 *SEE* Harper, Christopher
Harper, Elizabeth 40 *SEE* Harper, Christopher
Harper, Ephraim 33; Ontario, 1871 ***1823.22*** *p68*
Harper, Hannah 15 *SEE* Harper, Christopher
Harper, Helen; Maryland, 1656 ***2524.55*** *p40*
Harper, Hellen 46; Ontario, 1871 ***1823.15*** *p106*
Harper, Henry 48; Ontario, 1871 ***1823.28*** *p38*
Harper, James; New York, New York, 1854 ***6058.10*** *p43*
Harper, James; New York, New York, 1854 ***6058.10*** *p47*
Harper, James 15; Philadelphia, 1774 ***1220.25*** *p43*
Harper, John; Maryland, 1657 ***2524.55*** *p102*
Harper, John; Virginia, 1666 ***6212.30*** *p29*
Harper, John 13 *SEE* Harper, Christopher
Harper, John 40; Ontario, 1871 ***1823.22*** *p68*
Harper, Margarett; Maryland, 1668 ***2524.55*** *p92*
Harper, Mary 32; Ontario, 1871 ***1823.15*** *p106*
Harper, Richard 40; Ontario, 1871 ***1823.22*** *p68*
Harper, Richard 77; Ontario, 1871 ***1823.22*** *p68*
Harper, Robert; Jamaica, 1828 ***1640.13*** *p53*
Harper, S.; Quebec, 1856 ***9196.15*** *p6*
Harper, Samuel; Pennsylvania, 1776 ***4629.10*** *p52*
Harper, Samuel 22; Ontario, 1871 ***1823.22*** *p68*
Harper, Sarah 21; Maryland, 1775 ***1220.25*** *p112*
Harper, Stephen; Maryland, 1661 ***2524.55*** *p102*
Harper, Stephen; Maryland, 1665 ***2524.55*** *p102*
Harper, Thomas; Pennsylvania, 1777 ***4629.10*** *p13*
Harper, Thomas 12 *SEE* Harper, Christopher
Harper, Thomas 50; Ontario, 1871 ***1823.22*** *p68*
Harper, William; Maryland, 1666 ***2524.55*** *p102*
Harper, William; Pennsylvania, 1777 ***4629.10*** *p23*
Harper, William 4 *SEE* Harper, Christopher
Harper, William 36; Ontario, 1871 ***1823.15*** *p106*
Harper, William 40; Ontario, 1871 ***1823.22*** *p68*
Harper, Willm.; Maryland, 1658 ***2524.55*** *p102*
Harpf, Johann Nickel; Port uncertain, 1771 ***2856.30*** *p164*
Harpham, Robert 31; Maryland, 1775 ***1220.25*** *p121*
Harpman, Thomas 21; Maryland, 1774 ***1220.25*** *p40*
Harprecht, Elisabeth; Port uncertain, 1775 ***2856.30*** *p164*
Harr, John M.; New York, 1821 ***8197.10*** *p238*
Harr, Michael; America, 1752 ***2856.30*** *p163*
With wife & child
Harr, Michael; America, 1752 ***2856.30*** *p164*
With wife
Harran, Elizabeth; Vermont, 1860-1911 ***5900.10*** *p137*
Harran, Ellen; Vermont, 1848-1880 ***5900.10*** *p135*
Harrass, B. 47; Ontario, 1861 ***2896.28*** *p12*
Harrass, G. 22; Ontario, 1861 ***2896.28*** *p12*
Harrass, H. M. 19; Ontario, 1861 ***2896.28*** *p8*
Harredge, John; Maryland, 1670 ***2524.55*** *p102*
Harrendon, Tristian; New England, 1681 ***1224.1*** *p27*
Harrer, Michael; Port uncertain, 1769 ***2856.30*** *p165*
Harrer, Ursula; Port uncertain, 1751 ***2856.30*** *p165*
Harries, John Hill; Boston, 1778 ***1224.2*** *p52*
Harries, John William; New York, 1824 ***8197.10*** *p239*
Harries, Thomas; New York, 1840 ***8197.10*** *p174*
Harriet, Sister; Maryland, 1910 ***3259.35*** *p19*
Harriet, George 57; Ontario, 1871 ***1823.22*** *p68*
Harrigan, Caroline M. 71; Vermont, 1899 ***5900.10*** *p606*
Harrigan, Daniel; New York, 1837 ***8197.10*** *p90*
Harrigan, Dennis; Vermont, 1853-1881 ***5900.10*** *p365*
Harrigan, Ellen Doherty; Vermont, 1832-1913 ***5900.10*** *p340*
Harrigan, Jeremiah; Vermont, 1836-1902 ***5900.10*** *p340*
Harrigan, John; Vermont, 1849-1867 ***5900.10*** *p365*
Harrigan, John 55; Ontario, 1871 ***1823.22*** *p68*
Harrigan, Mary 70; Vermont, 1894 ***5900.10*** *p590*
Harrigan, Mary Donovan; Vermont, 1845-1898 ***5900.10*** *p365*
Harrigan, Peter 77; Vermont, 1896 ***5900.10*** *p589*
Harrigan, Thomas 70; Ontario, 1871 ***1823.15*** *p106*
Harrigan, Timothy; Vermont, 1845-1923 ***5900.10*** *p365*
Harriman, Edward; New York, 1807 ***8197.10*** *p39*
Harriman, William; New York, New York, 1826 ***1224.3*** *p33*
Harrin, John 40; Maryland, 1775 ***1220.25*** *p100*
Harrington, Ann 73; Vermont, 1911 ***5900.10*** *p408*
Harrington, Anne; Vermont, 1927 ***5900.10*** *p539*
Harrington, Bridget; Vermont, 1843-1932 ***5900.10*** *p161*
Harrington, Bridget 49; Vermont, 1880 ***5900.10*** *p538*
Harrington, Catherine 78; Vermont, n.d. ***5900.10*** *p437*
Harrington, Corneilous 35; Ontario, 1871 ***1823.28*** *p38*
Harrington, Edward S.; Vermont, 1852-1914 ***5900.10*** *p321*
Harrington, Ellen 46; Vermont, 1895 ***5900.10*** *p408*
Harrington, Emma 48; Ontario, 1861 ***2896.25*** *p23*
Harrington, James 21; Vermont, 1864 ***5900.10*** *p359*
Harrington, John; Maryland, 1662 ***2524.55*** *p78*
Harrington, John; New York, 1822 ***8197.10*** *p238*
Harrington, John 27; Ontario, 1871 ***1823.28*** *p38*
Harrington, John 45; Vermont, 1903 ***5900.10*** *p359*
Harrington, Julia A. Jenning; Vermont, 1824-1906 ***5900.10*** *p321*
Harrington, Julia O'Connell 80; Vermont, 1897 ***5900.10*** *p359*
Harrington, Kate; Vermont, 1843-1885 ***5900.10*** *p409*
Harrington, Katherine Gallagher; Vermont, 1858-1909 ***5900.10*** *p595*
Harrington, Margaret; Vermont, 1852-1922 ***5900.10*** *p409*
Harrington, Margaret 50; Vermont, 1872 ***5900.10*** *p283*
Harrington, Mary; Pennsylvania, 1843 ***1224.3*** *p33*
Harrington, Mary; Vermont, 1827-1916 ***5900.10*** *p593*
Harrington, Mary; Vermont, 1840-1910 ***5900.10*** *p551*
Harrington, Mary; Vermont, 1840-1932 ***5900.10*** *p411*
Harrington, Mary 56; Vermont, 1883 ***5900.10*** *p374*
Harrington, Mary Quilty 75; Vermont, 1891 ***5900.10*** *p411*
Harrington, Mathew; Virginia, 1667-1668 ***6212.30*** *p38*
Harrington, Matthias; New York, 1794 ***8197.10*** *p5*
Harrington, Maurice; Vermont, 1847-1925 ***5900.10*** *p595*
Harrington, Maurice 78; Vermont, 1884 ***5900.10*** *p359*
Harrington, Patrick; New York, 1837 ***8197.10*** *p241*
Harrington, Richard; New York, 1840 ***8197.10*** *p173*
Harrington, Sarah; Vermont, 1826-1904 ***5900.10*** *p509*
Harrington, Thomas 80; Vermont, 1894 ***5900.10*** *p411*
Harriott, Jenet 30; Ontario, 1871 ***1823.22*** *p68*
Harris, Master; Quebec, 1858 ***9196.15*** *p34*
Harris, Mr.; Quebec, 1856 ***9196.15*** *p6*
Harris, Mr.; Quebec, 1858 ***9196.15*** *p44*
Harris, Mrs.; Maryland, 1650 ***2524.55*** *p102*
Harris, Mrs.; Maryland, 1651 ***2524.55*** *p102*
Harris, Mrs.; Quebec, 1858 ***9196.15*** *p34*
Harris, Abraham; New York, 1840 ***8197.10*** *p173*
Harris, Abram 42; Ontario, 1871 ***1823.28*** *p38*
Harris, Agnes; New England, 1651 ***1224.1*** *p27*
Harris, Alexander; New York, 1794 ***8197.10*** *p5*
Harris, Alfred 59; Ontario, 1871 ***1823.22*** *p68*
Harris, Alice 6; Ontario, 1861 ***2896.28*** *p32*
Harris, Alise 85; Ontario, 1871 ***1823.15*** *p106*
Harris, Amos 12; Ontario, 1861 ***2896.25*** *p18*
Harris, Anne *SEE* Harris, Elizabeth
Harris, Annie Donnelly; Vermont, 1847-1899 ***5900.10*** *p346*
Harris, Askcott 55; Ontario, 1871 ***1823.15*** *p106*
Harris, Benjamin; Newburyport, Massachusetts, 1779 ***1224.2*** *p52*
Harris, Bridget; Vermont, 1856-1928 ***5900.10*** *p257*
Harris, Cecil 39; Ontario, 1871 ***1823.22*** *p68*
Harris, Charles; Pennsylvania, 1786 ***4629.10*** *p50*
Harris, Charles 9; Ontario, 1861 ***2896.28*** *p32*
Harris, Charles 25; Ontario, 1871 ***1823.15*** *p106*
Harris, Daniel; Jamaica, n.d. ***1224.3*** *p39*
Harris, Daniel; Newport, Rhode Island, 1807 ***1224.3*** *p39*
Harris, David; New York, 1808 ***8197.10*** *p54*
Harris, David; Pennsylvania, 1777 ***4629.10*** *p20*
Harris, Edward; New Jersey, 1827 ***1224.3*** *p34*
Harris, Edward; New York, 1780 ***4629.10*** *p77*
Harris, Edward 37; Maryland, 1775 ***1220.25*** *p113*
Harris, Elizabeth; Maryland, 1667 ***2524.55*** *p102*
Son: Frederick
Child: Anne
Child: Mary
Harris, Elizabeth; Vermont, 1858-1914 ***5900.10*** *p302*
Harris, Elizabeth 10; Ontario, 1861 ***2896.25*** *p18*
Harris, Elizabeth 19; Maryland, 1775 ***1220.25*** *p113*
Harris, Elizabeth 66; Ontario, 1871 ***1823.22*** *p68*
Harris, Ellinor; Maryland, 1681 ***2524.55*** *p102*
Harris, Eve 1; Ontario, 1861 ***2896.25*** *p18*
Harris, Ezekiel 42; Ontario, 1871 ***1823.22*** *p68*
Harris, Francis; Maryland, 1672 ***2524.55*** *p102*
Harris, Francis; Pennsylvania, 1777 ***4629.10*** *p14*
Harris, Frederick *SEE* Harris, Elizabeth
Harris, Genis 7; Ontario, 1861 ***2896.27*** *p25*
Harris, George; Maryland, 1667 ***2524.55*** *p102*
Harris, George; New York, 1822 ***8197.10*** *p238*
Harris, George; New York, 1837 ***8197.10*** *p90*
Harris, George; Virginia, 1665 ***6212.30*** *p19*
Harris, George; Virginia, 1674 ***1224.1*** *p27*
Harris, George 3; Ontario, 1861 ***2896.25*** *p18*
Harris, George 53; Ontario, 1871 ***1823.15*** *p106*
Harris, Guy 11; Ontario, 1861 ***2896.27*** *p25*
Harris, Hannorah Grady 74; Vermont, 1896 ***5900.10*** *p275*
Harris, Henry; Maryland, 1668 ***2524.55*** *p102*
Harris, Henry; Maryland, 1669 ***2524.55*** *p102*
Harris, Henry 44; Ontario, 1871 ***1823.15*** *p106*
Harris, Henry 82; Ontario, 1861 ***2896.27*** *p25*
Harris, Henry G. 5; Ontario, 1861 ***2896.27*** *p25*
Harris, Ida A. 1; Ontario, 1861 ***2896.28*** *p32*
Harris, Isabel; New England, 1700 ***1224.2*** *p52*
Harris, James; Virginia, 1666 ***6212.30*** *p27*
Harris, James 15; Philadelphia, 1774 ***1220.25*** *p67*
Harris, James 20; St. Kitts, 1775 ***1220.25*** *p122*
Harris, James 23; Ontario, 1871 ***1823.28*** *p38*
Harris, James 24; Ontario, 1861 ***2896.27*** *p33*
Harris, James 35; Ontario, 1871 ***1823.15*** *p106*
Harris, James 37; Ontario, 1871 ***1823.15*** *p106*
Harris, Jane 23; Maryland, 1775 ***1220.25*** *p101*
Harris, Jno; Virginia, 1664 ***6212.30*** *p9*
Harris, Jno; Virginia, 1666 ***6212.30*** *p28*
Harris, Jno; Virginia, 1674 ***6212.30*** *p52*
Harris, Jno 27; Ontario, 1861 ***2896.28*** *p6*
Harris, Joanna 41; Ontario, 1861 ***2896.27*** *p25*
Harris, John; Charleston, South Carolina, 1804 ***1224.3*** *p34*
Harris, John; Maryland, 1659 ***2524.55*** *p102*
Harris, John; Maryland, 1682 ***2524.55*** *p102*
Harris, John; New York, 1840 ***8197.10*** *p172*

Harris, John; Virginia, 1666 6212.30 p30
Harris, John; Virginia, 1723 1224.2 p52
Harris, John 26; Ontario, 1871 1823.15 p106
Harris, John 29; Maryland, 1775 1220.25 p112
Harris, John 35; Ontario, 1871 1823.15 p106
Harris, John 38; Ontario, 1871 1823.15 p106
Harris, John 40; Ontario, 1861 2896.27 p25
Harris, John 50; Ontario, 1871 1823.15 p106
Harris, John 50; Ontario, 1871 1823.28 p38
Harris, John 52; Ontario, 1871 1823.15 p106
Harris, John 65; Ontario, 1871 1823.15 p106
Harris, John 69; Ontario, 1871 1823.15 p106
Harris, John 73; Ontario, 1871 1823.22 p68
Harris, John H. 13; Ontario, 1861 2896.25 p18
Harris, John Rennie; Trinidad, 1898 1640.13 p54
Harris, Joseph 15; Philadelphia, 1774 1220.25 p82
Harris, Joseph 30; Ontario, 1871 1823.15 p106
Harris, Julia 28; Ontario, 1871 1823.28 p38
Harris, Katharine; Maryland, 1676 2524.55 p102
Harris, Le B.; Quebec, 1857 9196.15 p15
Harris, Lois Ann 21; Ontario, 1861 2896.27 p33
Harris, Lucinda 30; Ontario, 1861 2896.28 p32
Harris, Margaret; Vermont, 1836-1916 5900.10 p134
Harris, Margaret A. 38; Ontario, 1861 2896.25 p18
Harris, Margaret Gibney; Vermont, 1846-1924 5900.10 p87
Harris, Margaret M.; Vermont, 1855-1917 5900.10 p334
Harris, Martha A. 9; Ontario, 1861 2896.27 p27
Harris, Mary *SEE* Harris, Elizabeth
Harris, Mary; Virginia, 1656 1224.1 p27
Harris, Mary 11; Ontario, 1861 2896.25 p18
Harris, Mary 25; Philadelphia, 1774 1220.25 p27
Harris, Mary 26; Maryland, 1775 1220.25 p105
Harris, Mary 48; Ontario, 1861 2896.27 p27
Harris, Mary Ann 57; Ontario, 1871 1823.15 p106
Harris, Mary H. 41; Ontario, 1861 2896.26 p20
Harris, Milden 64; Ontario, 1871 1823.22 p69
Harris, Moses; Maryland, 1672 2524.55 p102
Harris, Nelson 49; Ontario, 1861 2896.27 p33
Harris, Nelson A. 6; Ontario, 1861 2896.27 p27
Harris, Nicholas; New York, 1836-1838 8197.10 p116
Harris, Patrick 79; Vermont, 1903 5900.10 p275
Harris, Peter 8; Ontario, 1861 2896.25 p18
Harris, Richard; America, 1723 1224.2 p52
Harris, Richard; Maryland, 1653 2524.55 p102
Harris, Richard; New York, 1839 8197.10 p320
Harris, Richard; Pennsylvania, 1701 1224.2 p52
Harris, Richard 16; Maryland, 1775 1220.25 p120
Harris, Richard 29; Virginia, 1774 1220.25 p45
Harris, Richard 35; Virginia, 1773 1220.25 p30
Harris, Robert; Pennsylvania, 1777 4629.10 p24
Harris, Robert; Virginia, 1700 1224.2 p52
Harris, Robert 5; Ontario, 1861 2896.25 p18
Harris, Robert James 23; Ontario, 1871 1823.28 p38
Harris, Samuel; Boston, 1721 1224.2 p52
Harris, Samuel; Maryland, 1655-1656 2524.55 p102
Harris, Samuel 28; Ontario, 1871 1823.15 p106
Harris, Samuel 33; Ontario, 1871 1823.15 p106
Harris, Samuel 56; Ontario, 1861 2896.27 p27
Harris, Sarah 21; Virginia, 1773 1220.25 p30
Harris, Sarah T. 8; Ontario, 1861 2896.27 p33
Harris, Stephen; Maryland or Virginia, 1699 1224.1 p27
Harris, Susanna; New England, 1678 1224.1 p12
Harris, Thomas; Maryland, 1668 2524.55 p102
Harris, Thomas; Maryland, 1671 2524.55 p102
Harris, Thomas; Maryland, 1674 2524.55 p102
Harris, Thomas; Maryland, 1679 2524.55 p102
Harris, Thomas; Virginia, 1666 6212.30 p31
Harris, Thomas 19; Philadelphia, 1774 1220.25 p42
Harris, Thomas 30; Ontario, 1871 1823.22 p69
Harris, Thomas 71; Ontario, 1871 1823.15 p106
Harris, William; Maryland, 1662 2524.55 p85
Harris, William; Maryland, 1675 2524.55 p102
Harris, William; New York, 1807 8197.10 p40
Harris, William; New York, 1836 8197.10 p241
Harris, William; Pennsylvania, 1777 4629.10 p16
Harris, William; Pennsylvania, 1777 4629.10 p22
Harris, William; Virginia, 1666 6212.30 p27
Harris, William 18; Ontario, 1861 2896.26 p20
Harris, William 30; Ontario, 1871 1823.28 p38
Harris, William 35; Ontario, 1871 1823.28 p38
Harris, William 40; Ontario, 1871 1823.15 p106
Harris, William 45; Ontario, 1871 1823.28 p38
Harris, Willison 33; Ontario, 1871 1823.15 p106
Harrise, John; Maryland, 1657 2524.55 p102
Harrise, John; Maryland, 1658 2524.55 p90
Harrise, Mary; Maryland, 1663 2524.55 p103
Harrision, Rose 72; Vermont, 1875 5900.10 p231
Harrison, Miss; Quebec, 1857 9196.15 p14
Harrison, Mr.; Quebec, 1857 9196.15 p24
Harrison, Mr.; Quebec, 1858 9196.15 p34
Harrison, Alfred 40; Ontario, 1871 1823.15 p106
Harrison, Andrew; New York, 1818 8197.10 p237
Harrison, Andrew; New York, 1834 8197.10 p240
Harrison, Ann; Maryland, 1670 2524.55 p103
Harrison, Benjamin; Maryland, 1671 2524.55 p103
Harrison, Benjamin; New York, 1837 8197.10 p91
Harrison, Charles; New Jersey, 1803 1224.3 p34
Harrison, Denise; New York, 1819 1224.3 p34
Harrison, Eleanor 48; Fort Cumberland, Nova Scotia, 1774 1220.25 p18
Harrison, Elizabeth; Maryland, 1658 2524.55 p103
Harrison, Elizabeth; New York, New York, 1821 1224.3 p34
Harrison, Elizabeth 32 *SEE* Harrison, Samuel
Harrison, Ellinore; Maryland, 1663 2524.55 p103
Harrison, Francis; Maryland, 1674 2524.55 p103
Harrison, Francis; Pennsylvania, 1777 4629.10 p15
Harrison, George; New York, 1838 8197.10 p117
Harrison, George; Philadelphia, 1700-1799 1224.2 p52
Harrison, George 32; Ontario, 1871 1823.28 p38
Harrison, George 36; Ontario, 1871 1823.15 p106
Harrison, Gilbert 39; Ontario, 1871 1823.28 p38
Harrison, Henrick; Virginia, 1694 1224.1 p27
Harrison, Henry; New York, 1792-1840 8197.10 p75
Harrison, Jacob; Philadelphia, 1794 4629.10 p80
Harrison, James; New Jersey, 1806 1224.3 p34
Harrison, James; New York, 1794 8197.10 p5
Harrison, James; New York, 1826 8197.10 p337
Harrison, James; Virginia, 1693-1694 6212.30 p60
Harrison, James 19; Maryland, 1774 1220.25 p70
Harrison, Jane 20; Nova Scotia, 1774 1220.25 p14
Harrison, John; New York, 1807 8197.10 p325
Harrison, John; New York, 1826 8197.10 p239
Harrison, John; New York, 1829 8197.10 p65
Harrison, John; Pennsylvania, 1777 4629.10 p15
Harrison, John; South Carolina, 1806 1224.3 p34
Harrison, John 23; Maryland, 1774 1220.25 p59
Harrison, John 24; Maryland, 1774 1220.25 p64
Harrison, John 41; Ontario, 1871 1823.15 p106
Harrison, John 54; Nova Scotia, 1774 1220.25 p136
With wife & 9 children
Harrison, John 67; Ontario, 1871 1823.15 p106
Harrison, John H.; New York, 1807 8197.10 p40
Harrison, Jonas; Savannah, Georgia, 1822 1224.3 p34
Harrison, Joseph; Maryland, 1653 2524.55 p103
Harrison, Joseph; New York, 1829 8197.10 p240
Harrison, Joseph; New York, 1837 8197.10 p91
Harrison, Joseph; Pennsylvania, 1779 4629.10 p40
Harrison, Joseph 42; Ontario, 1871 1823.28 p38
Harrison, Lancelot; Maryland, 1669 2524.55 p103
Harrison, Lother; Carolina, 1720 1224.2 p52
Harrison, Margaret; Vermont, 1830-1902 5900.10 p396
Harrison, Maria 16; Maryland, 1775 1220.25 p21
Harrison, Mary; Maryland, 1681 2524.55 p103
Harrison, Mary 17; Fort Cumberland, Nova Scotia, 1774 1220.25 p16
Harrison, Matthias; Pennsylvania, 1779 4629.10 p40
Harrison, Michall; Virginia, 1665-1666 6212.30 p23
Harrison, Miles; Maryland, 1678 2524.55 p103
Harrison, Nicholas; Virginia, 1653 1224.1 p27
Harrison, Patrick; New York, 1837 8197.10 p91
Harrison, Rebeccah; Maryland, 1681 2524.55 p103
Harrison, Richard; Maryland, 1665 2524.55 p103
Harrison, Richard; New York, 1840 8197.10 p174
Harrison, Richard W.; New York, 1840 8197.10 p173
Harrison, Robert; Augusta, Georgia, 1776 1224.2 p52
Harrison, Robert; Buffalo, New York, 1833 1224.3 p34
Harrison, Robert 38; Savannah, Georgia, 1774 1220.25 p139
Harrison, Samuel; Albany, New York, 1759 1224.2 p53
Harrison, Samuel 41; Philadelphia, 1774 1220.25 p69
Wife: Elizabeth 32
With 4 children
Harrison, Sarah; Maryland, 1673 2524.55 p169
Harrison, Simon 66; Ontario, 1871 1823.22 p69
Harrison, Tho; Virginia, 1690-1691 6212.30 p59
Harrison, Thomas; Maryland, 1671 2524.55 p102
Harrison, Thomas; New England, 1669 1224.1 p27
Harrison, Thomas; New York, 1794 8197.10 p5
Harrison, Thomas; Virginia, 1664-1665 6212.30 p15
Harrison, Thomas 21; Maryland, 1773-1774 1220.25 p33
Harrison, Thomas 21; Maryland, 1775 1220.25 p104
Harrison, Thomas 24; Fort Cumberland, Nova Scotia, 1774 1220.25 p17
Harrison, Thomas 28; Nova Scotia, 1774 1220.25 p15
Harrison, William; New York, 1807 8197.10 p330
Harrison, William; New York, 1818 8197.10 p236
Harrison, William; New York, 1821 8197.10 p238
Harrison, William; New York, 1827 8197.10 p347
Harrison, William 18; Maryland, 1774 1220.25 p39
Harrison, William 21; Maryland, 1775 1220.25 p104
Harrison, William 23; Philadelphia, 1775 1220.25 p107
Harrison, William 30; Ontario, 1871 1823.15 p107
Harrison, William 33; Ontario, 1871 1823.15 p107
Harrison, William 38; Ontario, 1871 1823.15 p107
Harrison, William 39; Maryland, 1774 1220.25 p71
Harrison, William 42; Ontario, 1871 1823.15 p107
Harrison, William Cockworthy; Texas, 1853 1224.3 p34
Harrisson, Patrick; Pennsylvania, 1810 6058.10 p3
Harrod, Daniel; Maryland, 1681 2524.55 p103
Harrod, Henry 30; Maryland, 1774 1220.25 p38
Harrod, John; Virginia, 1666 6212.30 p25
Harrold, Alfred; Philadelphia, 1845 1224.3 p34
Harrold, Richard 48; Ontario, 1871 1823.15 p107
Harrold, Thomas; New York, 1840 8197.10 p174
Harron, Thomas; New York, 1837 8197.10 p80
Harron, Thomas; New York, 1837 8197.10 p90
Harrop, Thomas; New York, 1837 8197.10 p319
Harros, Geo 30; Alaska, 1916 9196.1 p43
Harros, Geo 30; Whitehorse, Yukon, 1916 9196.1 p43
Harrow, Bridget 80; Vermont, 1901 5900.10 p77
Harrower, John 40; Virginia, 1774 1220.25 p45
Harrowes, John 77; Ontario, 1871 1823.15 p107
Harry, John 40; Ontario, 1871 1823.15 p107
Harry, Philip; New York, 1839 8197.10 p241
Harryton, Thomas; Maryland, 1665 2524.55 p103
Harska, Stanislaus; Maryland, 1910 3259.35 p19
Harston, Mary; Maryland, 1656 2524.55 p103
Harstone, John 49; Ontario, 1871 1823.22 p69
Harstone, Mary 40; Ontario, 1871 1823.22 p69
Hart, Miss; Quebec, 1857 9196.15 p24
Hart, Mrs.; Maryland, 1663 2524.55 p103
Hart, Mrs.; Quebec, 1857 9196.15 p24
Hart, Abraham; New York, 1821 8197.10 p238
Hart, Alexander 31; Ontario, 1871 1823.28 p38
Hart, Alfred 25; Ontario, 1871 1823.22 p69
Hart, Alice Moran 52; Vermont, 1844 5900.10 p149
Hart, Alsina 3; Ontario, 1861 2896.28 p63
Hart, Andrew; New York, 1829 8197.10 p352
Hart, Andrew; Virginia, 1723 1224.2 p53
Hart, Ann 50; Ontario, 1871 1823.22 p69
Hart, Archibald 26; Ontario, 1871 1823.28 p38
Hart, Archibald 64; Ontario, 1871 1823.28 p38
Hart, Arthur; Maryland, 1667 2524.55 p103
Hart, Bridget; Vermont, 1840-1915 5900.10 p452
Hart, Catherine 14; New York, New York, 1849 1825.45 p35
Hart, Catherine 21; Philadelphia, 1774 1220.25 p42
Hart, Catherine 32 *SEE* Hart, Michael
Hart, Charles; Charles Town, South Carolina, 1758 1224.2 p53
Hart, Charles; Philadelphia, 1853 1224.3 p34
Hart, Charles; Vermont, 1845-1914 5900.10 p384
Hart, Charles J.; Vermont, 1845-1914 5900.10 p384
Hart, Dominic 84; Vermont, 1888 5900.10 p201
Hart, Edward; Virginia, 1667 6212.30 p36
Hart, Edward 33; Ontario, 1871 1823.15 p107
Hart, Edward 52; Ontario, 1871 1823.22 p69
Hart, Elen J. 30; Vermont, 1888 5900.10 p201
Hart, Elizabeth 76; Vermont, 1885 5900.10 p315
Hart, Ephraim; New York, New York, 1840 1224.3 p34
Hart, Frances 38; Ontario, 1871 1823.22 p69
Hart, George; Newfoundland, 1866 1640.13 p54
Hart, George; Ontario, 1871 1823.22 p69
Hart, George; Vermont, 1850-1919 5900.10 p553
Hart, George; Virginia, 1674-1675 6212.30 p53
Hart, George 33; Ontario, 1871 1823.15 p107
Hart, George 35; Ontario, 1871 1823.22 p69
Hart, George 36; Ontario, 1871 1823.15 p107
Hart, Henry 57; Ontario, 1871 1823.15 p107
Hart, Isaac 23; Maryland, 1774 1220.25 p69
Hart, Jacob; Pennsylvania, 1777 4629.10 p24
Hart, James; Alabama, 1807-1845 1640.10 p77
Hart, James; New York, 1839 8197.10 p242
Hart, James; Vermont, 1808-1873 5900.10 p412
Hart, James; Vermont, 1848-1933 5900.10 p412
Hart, James 23; New York, New York, 1849 1825.45 p35
Hart, James William; San Francisco, 1900 1640.13 p54
Hart, Jane 23; Ontario, 1861 2896.28 p63
Hart, Johann; Port uncertain, 1773 2856.30 p165
Hart, Johanne 57; Vermont, 1865 5900.10 p56
Hart, John; Canada, 1756-1760 4628.40 p45
Hart, John; Long Island, 1784 1224.2 p53
Hart, John; Maryland, 1658 2524.55 p103
Hart, John; Maryland, 1673 2524.55 p103
Hart, John; Maryland, 1775-1781 4628.40 p69
Hart, John; New York, 1836 8197.10 p241
Hart, John; New York, 1839 8197.10 p242
Hart, John; Pennsylvania, 1785 4629.10 p48
Hart, John; Vermont, 1852-1941 5900.10 p201
Hart, John; Virginia, 1671-1672 6212.30 p47
Hart, John; Virginia, 1779 1224.2 p53
Hart, John 1; New York, New York, 1849 1825.45 p35
Hart, John 34; Ontario, 1871 1823.28 p38
Hart, Joseph; New York, 1828 8197.10 p350
Hart, Joseph 21; Maryland, 1774 1220.25 p53
Hart, Kate; Vermont, 1847-1931 5900.10 p137

Hart, Katherine 75; Vermont, 1894 ***5900.10*** *p572*
Hart, Margaret; Halifax, Nova Scotia, 1787 ***1640.13*** *p54*
Hart, Margaret; Vermont, 1853-1916 ***5900.10*** *p251*
Hart, Margarett; Maryland, 1655 ***2524.55*** *p103*
Hart, Mary; Vermont, n.d. ***5900.10*** *p145*
Hart, Mary; Vermont, 1844-1908 ***5900.10*** *p308*
Hart, Mary 8 *SEE* Hart, Michael
Hart, Mary A.; Vermont, 1849-1907 ***5900.10*** *p384*
Hart, Mary Dorsey; Vermont, 1816-1881 ***5900.10*** *p251*
Hart, Mary McCabe; Vermont, 1810-1889 ***5900.10*** *p412*
Hart, Mathew 24; Maryland, 1775 ***1220.25*** *p99*
Hart, Mathew, Jr.; New York, 1840 ***8197.10*** *p301*
Hart, Michael; New York, 1831 ***8197.10*** *p364*
Hart, Michael 17; New York, New York, 1849 ***1825.45*** *p35*
Hart, Michael 36; New York, New York, 1849 ***1825.45*** *p35*
Son: Pat 2
Daughter: Mary 8
Sister: Catherine 32
Hart, Nicholas; Pennsylvania, 1777 ***4629.10*** *p23*
Hart, Nora; Vermont, 1858-1916 ***5900.10*** *p553*
Hart, Pat 2 *SEE* Hart, Michael
Hart, Patrick; New York, 1825-1828 ***8197.10*** *p304*
Hart, Patrick; New York, 1832 ***8197.10*** *p368*
Hart, Peter; Port uncertain, 1774 ***2856.30*** *p165*
Hart, Peter 65; Vermont, 1881 ***5900.10*** *p223*
Hart, Rose; Vermont, 1869-1938 ***5900.10*** *p96*
Hart, Rose Ann T. 32; Vermont, 1872 ***5900.10*** *p509*
Hart, S.; Quebec, 1857 ***9196.15*** *p16*
Hart, Mrs. S.; Quebec, 1857 ***9196.15*** *p16*
Hart, Samuel; New Orleans, 1834 ***1224.3*** *p34*
Hart, Samuel; New York, 1816 ***8197.10*** *p59*
Hart, Samuel 24; Ontario, 1871 ***1823.28*** *p38*
Hart, Samuel 61; Ontario, 1871 ***1823.15*** *p107*
Hart, Sarah Frances; Vermont, 1848-1898 ***5900.10*** *p116*
Hart, Stephen; New England, 1646 ***1224.1*** *p40*
Hart, Steven 32; Ontario, 1871 ***1823.15*** *p107*
Hart, Susannah; Maryland, 1861 ***2524.55*** *p103*
Hart, Thomas; Maryland, 1681 ***2524.55*** *p103*
Hart, Thomas; New York, New York, 1774 ***1224.2*** *p53*
Hart, Thomas; Pennsylvania, 1777 ***4629.10*** *p18*
Hart, Thomas; Vermont, n.d. ***5900.10*** *p251*
Hart, Thomas 16; New York, New York, 1849 ***1825.45*** *p35*
Hart, Thomas 28; Ontario, 1871 ***1823.22*** *p69*
Hart, Ulrich; America, 1740 ***2856.30*** *p165*
Hart, William 22; Jamaica, 1774 ***1220.25*** *p37*
Hart, William 27; Maryland, 1774 ***1220.25*** *p60*
Hart, William S. 1; Ontario, 1861 ***2896.28*** *p63*
Hart, Wm; Virginia, 1667-1668 ***6212.30*** *p38*
Hartcoate, Tho; Virginia, 1664-1665 ***6212.30*** *p16*
Harte, Anna; Vermont, 1886-1960 ***5900.10*** *p578*
Harte, John; Vermont, 1841-1906 ***5900.10*** *p578*
Harte, Mary; Vermont, 1849-1889 ***5900.10*** *p578*
Harte, Sarah; Maryland, 1661 ***2524.55*** *p103*
Harte, Tho.; Maryland, 1681 ***2524.55*** *p103*
Hartel, Theobald; Port uncertain, 1750 ***2856.30*** *p197H*
Hartenstein, Johann; Port uncertain, 1741 ***2856.30*** *p165*
Hartenstein, Michael; New York, 1837 ***8197.10*** *p91*
Harter, Georg; Port uncertain, 1769 ***2856.30*** *p165*
Hartford, Almira 20; Ontario, 1861 ***2896.26*** *p22*
Hartford, John; Virginia, 1663 ***6212.30*** *p1*
Hartford, Obediah 50; Ontario, 1871 ***1823.22*** *p69*
Hartigan, Bridget 70; Vermont, 1903 ***5900.10*** *p379*
Hartigan, Bridget Quirk; Vermont, n.d. ***5900.10*** *p462*
Hartigan, Catherine; Vermont, 1827-1906 ***5900.10*** *p462*
Hartigan, John 59; Vermont, 1893 ***5900.10*** *p462*
Hartigan, Mary Ann; Vermont, 1840-1904 ***5900.10*** *p462*
Hartigan, Michael; Vermont, 1831-1892 ***5900.10*** *p462*
Hartigan, Patrick W. 63; Vermont, 1893 ***5900.10*** *p462*
Harting, John 85; Ontario, 1871 ***1823.28*** *p38*
Hartka, Frank; Maryland, 1910 ***3259.35*** *p19*
Hartle, Tho; Virginia, 1680 ***6212.30*** *p55*
Hartley, Anastasia Ryan; Vermont, 1831-1920 ***5900.10*** *p373*
Hartley, Henrey; Ontario, 1871 ***1823.28*** *p38*
Hartley, James; Pennsylvania, 1777 ***4629.10*** *p25*
Hartley, John 36; Ontario, 1871 ***1823.15*** *p107*
Hartley, Mary 70; Vermont, 1894 ***5900.10*** *p117*
Hartley, Mary Hogan; Vermont, 1790-1874 ***5900.10*** *p364*
Hartley, Philip 57; Vermont, 1884 ***5900.10*** *p373*
Hartley, Stasia; Vermont, 1858-1892 ***5900.10*** *p510*
Hartley, Thomas; Maryland, 1680 ***2524.55*** *p103*
Hartlieb, Apollonia; Port uncertain, 1764 ***2856.30*** *p165*
Hartlieb, Valentin; Port uncertain, 1764 ***2856.30*** *p165*
Hartlings, Phebe; Maryland, 1663 ***2524.55*** *p103*
Hartly, Robert 48; Ontario, 1871 ***1823.28*** *p38*
Hartly, William 35; Ontario, 1871 ***1823.28*** *p38*
Hartman, Abraham; Pennsylvania, 1786 ***4629.10*** *p51*
Hartman, Adam; Pennsylvania, 1841 ***6058.10*** *p17*
Hartman, Franciska; Maryland, 1910 ***3259.35*** *p19*
Hartman, John 43; Ontario, 1871 ***1823.15*** *p107*
Hartman, John 45; Ontario, 1871 ***1823.15*** *p107*
Hartman, Peter; New York, New York, 1832 ***6058.10*** *p15*
Hartman, Simon 39; Ontario, 1871 ***1823.15*** *p107*
Hartman, Simon 62; Ontario, 1871 ***1823.15*** *p107*
Hartmann, . . .; America, 1768 ***2856.30*** *p165*
Hartmann, Mr.; Port uncertain, 1790 ***2856.30*** *p165*
Hartmann, Anna Eva; America, 1776 ***2856.30*** *p165*
Hartmann, Anna Margarete; Port uncertain, 1751 ***2856.30*** *p165*
Hartmann, Georg; Port uncertain, 1767 ***2856.30*** *p165*
Hartmann, Georg Adam; Port uncertain, 1756 ***2856.30*** *p165*
Hartmann, Georg H.; Baltimore, 1889 ***3437.14*** *p156*
Hartmann, Jacob; New York, 1839 ***8197.10*** *p241*
Hartmann, Jacob; Port uncertain, 1791 ***2856.30*** *p165*
Hartmann, Johann Jacob; Port uncertain, 1754 ***2856.30*** *p165*
Hartmann, Johann Martin; Port uncertain, 1729 ***2856.30*** *p165*
Hartmann, Leonard; Port uncertain, 1781 ***2856.30*** *p165*
Hartmann, Margarete; Port uncertain, 1789 ***2856.30*** *p165*
Hartmann, Michael; America, 1738 ***2856.30*** *p165*
Hartmann, Tobias; Port uncertain, 1770 ***2856.30*** *p165*
Hartmann, Ursula; Port uncertain, 1743 ***2856.30*** *p165*
Hartmire, Catherine 48; Ontario, 1871 ***1823.15*** *p107*
Hartnagle, Philip; New York, 1840 ***8197.10*** *p172*
Hartnell, Edward 34; Ontario, 1871 ***1823.22*** *p69*
Hartnell, John 35; Ontario, 1871 ***1823.28*** *p38*
Hartnell, Thomas 21; Ontario, 1871 ***1823.22*** *p69*
Hartnett, Daniel 80; Vermont, 1915 ***5900.10*** *p301*
Hartnett, Hannah Lynch 70; Vermont, 1909 ***5900.10*** *p301*
Hartnett, Hanora Dailey 85; Vermont, 1826 ***5900.10*** *p304*
Hartnett, John; Vermont, 1854-1934 ***5900.10*** *p398*
Hartnett, Maria A.; Vermont, 1859-1920 ***5900.10*** *p398*
Hartnett, Mary 90; Vermont, 1899 ***5900.10*** *p467*
Hartnett, Nellie F.; Vermont, 1859-1905 ***5900.10*** *p467*
Hartnett, Thomas; Vermont, 1829-1909 ***5900.10*** *p304*
Hartney, James 45; Ontario, 1871 ***1823.28*** *p38*
Hartney, Thomas; Vermont, 1841-1872 ***5900.10*** *p427*
Hartnott, Patrick 46; Ontario, 1871 ***1823.22*** *p69*
Hartny, Bridget 60; Ontario, 1871 ***1823.28*** *p38*
Hartny, James 85; Ontario, 1871 ***1823.28*** *p38*
Hartny, John 49; Ontario, 1871 ***1823.28*** *p38*
Hartock, Edward; Maryland, 1665 ***2524.55*** *p103*
Harton, John 60; Ontario, 1871 ***1823.15*** *p107*
Hartrenfft, Christopher; Pennsylvania, 1777 ***4629.10*** *p12*
Hartrenfft, Leonard; Pennsylvania, 1777 ***4629.10*** *p12*
Hartrop, Richard; Maryland, 1663 ***2524.55*** *p103*
Hartshorne, George; Maryland, 1681 ***2524.55*** *p103*
Hartshorne, Hugh; Maryland, 1681 ***2524.55*** *p103*
Hartt, Margaret; Vermont, 1834-1893 ***5900.10*** *p187*
Hartup, Edward 30; Ontario, 1871 ***1823.15*** *p107*
Hartwell, Henry; Virginia, 1699 ***1224.1*** *p28*
Hartwell, Joseph; Maryland, 1656 ***2524.55*** *p103*
Hartwell, Mary; Maryland, 1656 ***2524.55*** *p103*
Hartwell, Mary; Maryland, 1656 ***2524.55*** *p238*
Hartwig, Ambrosius; Port uncertain, 1775 ***2856.30*** *p166*
Hartwig, John Henry 22; Philadelphia, 1774 ***1220.25*** *p42*
Harty, Mr.; Portland, Maine, 1857 ***9196.15*** *p12*
Harty, Anne Connor; Vermont, 1841-1904 ***5900.10*** *p225*
Harty, Bridget; Vermont, 1846-1918 ***5900.10*** *p61*
Harty, Bridget McNamara; Vermont, 1842-1912 ***5900.10*** *p53*
Harty, Cornelius; Vermont, 1802-1877 ***5900.10*** *p63*
Harty, Cornelius, Jr.; Vermont, 1835-1870 ***5900.10*** *p63*
Harty, Margaret; Vermont, 1828-1910 ***5900.10*** *p63*
Harty, Margaret; Vermont, 1858-1913 ***5900.10*** *p63*
Harty, Michael 45; Ontario, 1871 ***1823.28*** *p38*
Harty, Patrick; Vermont, 1846-1924 ***5900.10*** *p53*
Harty, Patrick 33; Ontario, 1871 ***1823.28*** *p38*
Harty, Roger; Vermont, 1835-1931 ***5900.10*** *p225*
Hartz, Ursula; Port uncertain, 1743 ***2856.30*** *p166*
With husband
Harvey, Mr.; Quebec, 1857 ***9196.15*** *p15*
Harvey, Agness 28; Ontario, 1871 ***1823.15*** *p107*
Harvey, Albert 20; Ontario, 1861 ***2896.25*** *p68*
Harvey, Alexander; Pennsylvania, 1787 ***4629.10*** *p50*
Harvey, Alice 18; Maryland, 1775 ***1220.25*** *p109*
Harvey, Ann Kate MacSween *SEE* Harvey, William
Harvey, Austin 4; Ontario, 1861 ***2896.25*** *p25*
Harvey, Bakia; Savannah, Georgia, 1774 ***1640.10*** *p78*
Harvey, Bernard; Vermont, 1809-1888 ***5900.10*** *p602*
Harvey, Bernard 48; Ontario, 1871 ***1823.28*** *p38*
Harvey, Bernerd, Jr. 19; Vermont, 1861 ***5900.10*** *p602*
Harvey, Bridget; Vermont, 1849 ***5900.10*** *p533*
Harvey, Bridget Brady; Vermont, 1863-1951 ***5900.10*** *p398*
Harvey, Catherine; Vermont, 1838-1875 ***5900.10*** *p222*
Harvey, Catherine Shannon; Vermont, 1814-1895 ***5900.10*** *p602*
Harvey, Charles; Illinois, 1853 ***1224.3*** *p34*
Harvey, Charles Arbuthnot; Albany, New York, 1855 ***1224.3*** *p34*
Harvey, Clara; Quebec, 1858 ***9196.15*** *p34*
Harvey, Clara; Vermont, 1872-1873 ***5900.10*** *p190*
Harvey, Daniel 30; Philadelphia, 1774 ***1220.25*** *p26*
Wife: Mary 26
With child 2
Harvey, David; Vermont, 1801-1852 ***5900.10*** *p373*
Harvey, David T.; Vermont, 1857-1938 ***5900.10*** *p548*
Harvey, Edward; New York, 1840 ***8197.10*** *p173*
Harvey, Edward 32; Maryland, 1774 ***1220.25*** *p47*
Harvey, Elizabeth; New York, 1807 ***1224.3*** *p34*
Harvey, Frances *SEE* Harvey, Nicholas
Harvey, Frank 60; Ontario, 1871 ***1823.22*** *p69*
Harvey, George 50; Ontario, 1871 ***1823.15*** *p107*
Harvey, Hannah Truman; Vermont, 1792-1890 ***5900.10*** *p373*
Harvey, Harriet F. 7; Ontario, 1861 ***2896.25*** *p21*
Harvey, J. W.; Vermont, 1856-1936 ***5900.10*** *p548*
Harvey, Jacob; New York, 1829 ***8197.10*** *p299*
Harvey, James; New York, 1839 ***8197.10*** *p242*
Harvey, James; Vermont, 1859-1910 ***5900.10*** *p398*
Harvey, James 17; Vermont, 1862 ***5900.10*** *p529*
Harvey, James 34; Ontario, 1871 ***1823.15*** *p107*
Harvey, James 37; Ontario, 1871 ***1823.15*** *p107*
Harvey, James B. 32; Vermont, 1872 ***5900.10*** *p138*
Harvey, James E. 28; Ontario, 1871 ***1823.22*** *p69*
Harvey, Jane 33; Ontario, 1871 ***1823.28*** *p38*
Harvey, Jane 50; Ontario, 1871 ***1823.22*** *p69*
Harvey, Jemima 44; Ontario, 1871 ***1823.28*** *p38*
Harvey, Jennie Mulcahy; Vermont, 1849-1872 ***5900.10*** *p190*
Harvey, John; America, 1848 ***1224.3*** *p34*
Harvey, John; Maryland, 1667 ***2524.55*** *p103*
Harvey, John; Mexico, n.d. ***1224.3*** *p34*
Harvey, John; Pennsylvania, 1867 ***6058.10*** *p56*
Harvey, John; Vermont, 1843-1934 ***5900.10*** *p533*
Harvey, John; Vermont, 1848-1948 ***5900.10*** *p283*
Harvey, John; Virginia, 1650 ***1224.1*** *p28*
Harvey, John; Virginia, 1665 ***6212.30*** *p19*
Harvey, John 31; Ontario, 1871 ***1823.22*** *p69*
Harvey, John 34; Ontario, 1871 ***1823.22*** *p69*
Harvey, John 35; Maryland, 1775 ***1220.25*** *p96*
Harvey, John 40; Ontario, 1871 ***1823.28*** *p38*
Harvey, John Quilliam; New York, 1838 ***8197.10*** *p378*
Harvey, Joseph; Michigan, 1843 ***1224.3*** *p35*
Harvey, Joseph; New York, 1838 ***8197.10*** *p378*
Harvey, Joseph 18; Philadelphia, 1774 ***1220.25*** *p34*
Harvey, Joseph 46; Ontario, 1871 ***1823.15*** *p107*
Harvey, Julia Ann Deavitt 25; Vermont, 1835 ***5900.10*** *p373*
Harvey, L. E. Colby; Vermont, 1825-1904 ***5900.10*** *p300*
Harvey, L. R.; Vermont, 1823-1898 ***5900.10*** *p300*
Harvey, Lionel 60; Ontario, 1871 ***1823.22*** *p69*
Harvey, Margaret; Vermont, 1822-1889 ***5900.10*** *p540*
Harvey, Margaret; Vermont, 1834-1919 ***5900.10*** *p202*
Harvey, Margaret 25; Vermont, 1865 ***5900.10*** *p602*
Harvey, Maria L.; Vermont, 1822-1880 ***5900.10*** *p548*
Harvey, Mary; Vermont, 1829-1900 ***5900.10*** *p554*
Harvey, Mary 26 *SEE* Harvey, Daniel
Harvey, Mary 30; Ontario, 1871 ***1823.15*** *p107*
Harvey, Mary Ann; Vermont, 1834-1921 ***5900.10*** *p603*
Harvey, Mary E.; Vermont, 1858-1921 ***5900.10*** *p548*
Harvey, Mary Jane 22; Ontario, 1861 ***2896.25*** *p68*
Harvey, Michael; Pennsylvania, 1781 ***4629.10*** *p42*
Harvey, Michaell; Virginia, 1666 ***6212.30*** *p31*
Harvey, Nancy; Vermont, 1828-1909 ***5900.10*** *p283*
Harvey, Nicholas; Albany, New York, 1750 ***1224.2*** *p53*
Harvey, Nicholas; Maryland, 1641 ***2524.55*** *p104*
With wife
Daughter: Frances
Harvey, Peter; New England, 1719 ***1224.2*** *p53*
Harvey, Richard; Maryland, 1670 ***2524.55*** *p104*
Harvey, Richard 50; Ontario, 1871 ***1823.15*** *p107*
Harvey, Robert; New England, 1655 ***1224.1*** *p28*
Harvey, Sarah L. 10; Ontario, 1861 ***2896.25*** *p25*
Harvey, Stephen; Saratoga, New York, 1782 ***1224.2*** *p53*
Harvey, Susanna 65; Ontario, 1871 ***1823.22*** *p69*
Harvey, Susannah 49; Ontario, 1861 ***2896.25*** *p68*
Harvey, Thomas 23; Maryland, 1775 ***1220.25*** *p114*
Harvey, Thomas 75; Ontario, 1871 ***1823.22*** *p69*
Harvey, Thomas R. 45; Ontario, 1871 ***1823.22*** *p69*
Harvey, Timothy; Vermont, 1815-1892 ***5900.10*** *p548*
Harvey, W. S. 30; Ontario, 1871 ***1823.28*** *p38*
Harvey, William; Manitoba, 1888 ***4537.35*** *p65*
Wife: Ann Kate MacSween
Harvey, William; New England, 1648 ***1224.1*** *p13*
Harvey, William; New York, 1839 ***8197.10*** *p132*
Harvey, William Harding; New York, 1840 ***8197.10*** *p242*

Harvey, William S. 36; Ontario, 1871 ***1823.22*** *p69*
Harvey, Wiloughby 38; Maryland, 1775 ***1220.25*** *p111*
Harvie, William 40; Ontario, 1871 ***1823.22*** *p69*
Harvie, William 43; Ontario, 1871 ***1823.22*** *p69*
Harvy, Alice *SEE* Harvy, John
Harvy, David 53; Ontario, 1871 ***1823.22*** *p69*
Harvy, James *SEE* Harvy, John
Harvy, James 47; Ontario, 1861 ***2896.25*** *p40*
Harvy, John *SEE* Harvy, John
Harvy, John; Maryland, 1666 ***2524.55*** *p104*
Wife: Alice
Child: Peter
Child: Alice
Child: John
Child: James
Harvy, Peter *SEE* Harvy, John
Harvye, Henry; Virginia, 1671-1672 ***6212.30*** *p47*
Harwar, Thomas; Virginia, 1704 ***1224.2*** *p53*
Harwer, William; Maryland, 1672 ***2524.55*** *p104*
Harwood, Andrew; Virginia, 1659 ***1224.1*** *p28*
Harwood, Arthur; Virginia, n.d. ***1224.1*** *p28*
Harwood, Edward; New York, 1807 ***8197.10*** *p330*
Harwood, Elizabeth; Maryland, 1665 ***2524.55*** *p104*
Harwood, Elizabeth; New England, 1685 ***1224.1*** *p28*
Harwood, Elizabeth; New York, New York, 1851 ***1224.3*** *p30*
Harwood, Elizabeth; Virginia, 1671 ***6212.30*** *p44*
Harwood, George 41; Ontario, 1871 ***1823.15*** *p107*
Harwood, God; Virginia, 1690-1691 ***6212.30*** *p59*
Harwood, John; Maryland, 1658 ***2524.55*** *p104*
Harwood, John 21; Virginia, 1774 ***1220.25*** *p93*
Harwood, Phillip; Maryland, 1663 ***2524.55*** *p104*
Harwood, Phillip; Maryland, 1665 ***2524.55*** *p104*
Harwood, Thomas; New England, 1685 ***1224.1*** *p28*
Harwood, Thomas 34; Nova Scotia, 1774 ***1220.25*** *p13*
Harwood, Walter 52; Vancouver, British Columbia, 1913 ***9196.1*** *p58*
Harwood, Walter 52; Washington, 1913 ***9196.1*** *p58*
Haryett, William 40; Ontario, 1871 ***1823.28*** *p39*
Harz, Jacob; America, 1751 ***2856.30*** *p166*
Harzkwinski, Anton; Maryland, 1910 ***3259.35*** *p19*
Hasal, Niklas; Port uncertain, 1764 ***2856.30*** *p166*
Hasch, Peter; New York, 1831 ***8197.10*** *p363*
Hasdlick, Mathiss 51; Ontario, 1871 ***1823.28*** *p39*
Hasel, Frederick Augustus; New York, 1837 ***8197.10*** *p241*
Hasel, William 28; Ontario, 1871 ***1823.28*** *p39*
Haselauer, Sebastian; America, 1759 ***2856.30*** *p166*
Haselauer, Sebastian; Port uncertain, 1752 ***2856.30*** *p166*
Haselberger, Philipp; America, 1739 ***2856.30*** *p166*
Haselberger, Philipp; America, 1739 ***2856.30*** *p166*
With wife & 2 children
Haselldowne, Joseph; Maryland, 1660 ***2524.55*** *p104*
Hasely, Lucy 36; Ontario, 1871 ***1823.28*** *p39*
Hasenpflug, Hans Georg; Port uncertain, 1749 ***2856.30*** *p166*
Hasenwandel, Josef; Port uncertain, 1752 ***2856.30*** *p166*
Hasferd, John 55; Ontario, 1871 ***1823.15*** *p107*
Hasfurt, George; Maryland, 1663 ***2524.55*** *p44*
Hasick, Samuel 40; Ontario, 1871 ***1823.15*** *p107*
Hasie, Jacob; Port uncertain, 1751 ***2856.30*** *p166*
With wife & 6 children
Hasin, Catharina; Port uncertain, 1774 ***2856.30*** *p158*
Hasis, Jacob; Port uncertain, 1751 ***2856.30*** *p166*
With wife & 6 children
Hask, Ralph; Maryland, 1658 ***2524.55*** *p104*
Haskard, William 16; Ontario, 1871 ***1823.22*** *p69*
Haskell, William; New York, 1828 ***8197.10*** *p348*
Hasket, John 35; Ontario, 1871 ***1823.15*** *p107*
Haskins, Charles 39; Ontario, 1871 ***1823.28*** *p39*
Haskins, James 13; Philadelphia, 1774 ***1220.25*** *p6*
Haskins, Rachel 65; Ontario, 1871 ***1823.28*** *p39*
Haskins, William 69; Ontario, 1871 ***1823.22*** *p69*
Haslam, Alfred 30; Ontario, 1871 ***1823.15*** *p107*
Haslan, Dr.; Portland, Maine, 1857 ***9196.15*** *p12*
Haslan, George; New York, 1835 ***8197.10*** *p317*
Hasle, James 26; Maryland, 1774 ***1220.25*** *p59*
Haslehurst, Mary; Philadelphia, 1736 ***1224.2*** *p53*
Hasler, Frederick; Pennsylvania, 1777 ***4629.10*** *p28*
Haslett, Joseph; Delaware, 1775-1781 ***4628.40*** *p69*
Haslewood, William; North America, 1759 ***1224.2*** *p53*
Haslinger, Johann; Port uncertain, 1748 ***2856.30*** *p166*
Haslop, Isabella 21; Maryland, 1774 ***1220.25*** *p47*
Haslop, William 22; Philadelphia, 1774 ***1220.25*** *p44*
Hasnitt, Nicholas; Maryland, 1679 ***2524.55*** *p104*
Hason, Ellen; Maryland, 1672 ***2524.55*** *p104*
Hass, August 38; Ontario, 1871 ***1823.28*** *p39*
Hass, Charles 42; Ontario, 1871 ***1823.28*** *p39*
Hass, Diebold; Port uncertain, 1775 ***2856.30*** *p197H*
Hass, Georg; Port uncertain, 1783 ***2856.30*** *p166*
Hass, Gerhard; Port uncertain, 1783 ***2856.30*** *p166*
With wife 3 sons & 4 daughters
Hass, Johann Friedric; Port uncertain, 1783 ***2856.30*** *p166*
Hass, John 43; Kansas, 1891-1910 ***9079.10*** *p40*
Hass, Katie 29; Kansas, 1891-1910 ***9079.10*** *p40*
Hassard, Richard 32; Ontario, 1871 ***1823.15*** *p107*
Hasse, Herman; New York, New York, 1876 ***3437.14*** *p117*
Hassel, Nikolaus; Port uncertain, 1783 ***2856.30*** *p166*
Hasselbach, Anna Margarete; Port uncertain, 1754 ***2856.30*** *p166*
Hasselberger, Samuel; Port uncertain, 1747 ***2856.30*** *p166*
Hasselt, Matthew 33; Ontario, 1871 ***1823.15*** *p107*
Hasselwanger, Johann; America, 1739 ***2856.30*** *p166*
With child
Hassen, Mathew; New York, 1802 ***8197.10*** *p21*
Hassett, Bridget Cloren 62; Vermont, 1903 ***5900.10*** *p136*
Hassett, Catharine; Vermont, 1826-1892 ***5900.10*** *p292*
Hassett, Daniel 72; Vermont, 1880 ***5900.10*** *p345*
Hassett, David; Vermont, 1836-1911 ***5900.10*** *p356*
Hassett, Ellen; Vermont, 1839-1910 ***5900.10*** *p335*
Hassett, Fanny 60; Vermont, 1867 ***5900.10*** *p345*
Hassett, Honora Magner 78; Vermont, 1876 ***5900.10*** *p415*
Hassett, Joanna 34; Vermont, 1880 ***5900.10*** *p345*
Hassett, John; New York, 1837 ***8197.10*** *p90*
Hassett, John 38; Vermont, 1892 ***5900.10*** *p62*
Hassett, Margaret O'Neill; Vermont, 1858-1935 ***5900.10*** *p472*
Hassett, Mary A. Burke; Vermont, 1836-1914 ***5900.10*** *p356*
Hassett, Patrick; Vermont, 1823-1923 ***5900.10*** *p292*
Hassett, Patrick; Vermont, 1856-1900 ***5900.10*** *p472*
Hassett, Patrick 31; Vermont, 1861 ***5900.10*** *p372*
Hassinger, Johann; America, 1748 ***2856.30*** *p167*
With wife & children
Hassland, Michael; Port uncertain, 1623 ***2856.30*** *p167*
With wife 3 sons & daughter
Hassler, Johann; Port uncertain, 1755 ***2856.30*** *p167*
Hasslin, Jeremy; Maryland, 1658 ***2524.55*** *p104*
Hasslinger, Elisabeth; Port uncertain, 1765 ***2856.30*** *p167*
Hassock, George Fisher; Illinois, 1850 ***1224.3*** *p35*
Hast, Gyles; Maryland, 1659 ***2524.55*** *p104*
Haste, Richard 30; New York, 1774 ***1220.25*** *p24*
Hasted, Thomas; Virginia, 1698 ***1224.2*** *p53*
Hasternan, John; Maryland, 1682 ***2524.55*** *p104*
Hastett, Henry; New York, 1838 ***8197.10*** *p241*
Hastie, James 31; Ontario, 1871 ***1823.15*** *p107*
Hastie, William 60; Ontario, 1871 ***1823.15*** *p107*
Hastie, William 65; Ontario, 1871 ***1823.15*** *p108*
Hastier, John; New York, 1794 ***8197.10*** *p5*
Hastin, Richard; Maryland, 1682 ***2524.55*** *p104*
Hasting, Mary 80; Ontario, 1871 ***1823.15*** *p108*
Hastings, Ann; Maryland, 1677 ***2524.55*** *p104*
Hastings, Bridget 35; Vermont, 1876 ***5900.10*** *p147*
Hastings, David 34; Ontario, 1871 ***1823.15*** *p108*
Hastings, George 18; Philadelphia, 1774 ***1220.25*** *p67*
Hastings, John; Virginia, 1707 ***1224.2*** *p53*
Hastings, John 31; Ontario, 1871 ***1823.15*** *p108*
Hastings, John 56; Ontario, 1871 ***1823.15*** *p108*
Hastings, Mary 57; Vermont, 1874 ***5900.10*** *p470*
Hastings, Robert 50; Ontario, 1871 ***1823.15*** *p108*
Hastings, Thomas 40; Ontario, 1871 ***1823.15*** *p108*
Hastings, Thomas 65; Vermont, 1881 ***5900.10*** *p147*
Hastiton, Fanny 73; Ontario, 1871 ***1823.22*** *p69*
Hastwell, Arthur 17; New York, 1774 ***1220.25*** *p141*
Hastwell, Betty 15; New York, 1774 ***1220.25*** *p141*
Hastwell, Edward 1; New York, 1774 ***1220.25*** *p141*
Hastwell, Isabella 4; New York, 1774 ***1220.25*** *p141*
Hastwell, John 23; New York, 1774 ***1220.25*** *p141*
Hastwell, John 46; New York, 1774 ***1220.25*** *p141*
Hastwell, Joseph 21; New York, 1774 ***1220.25*** *p141*
Hastwell, Margaret 5; New York, 1774 ***1220.25*** *p141*
Hastwell, Mary 12; New York, 1774 ***1220.25*** *p141*
Hastwell, Mary 34; New York, 1774 ***1220.25*** *p141*
Hastwell, Richard 7; New York, 1774 ***1220.25*** *p141*
Hastwell, Robert 19; New York, 1774 ***1220.25*** *p141*
Hastwell, Thomas 9; New York, 1774 ***1220.25*** *p141*
Hasty, William 28; Ontario, 1871 ***1823.15*** *p108*
Haswell, John; Virginia, 1682 ***1224.1*** *p28*
Haswell, Sarah; New York, 1829 ***1224.3*** *p35*
Hat, Baptist; New York, 1839 ***8197.10*** *p131*
Hatch, Mrs.; Maryland, 1647 ***2524.55*** *p104*
Hatch, Alice Bradley 54; Vermont, 1872 ***5900.10*** *p249*
Hatch, James; Virginia, 1667 ***6212.30*** *p35*
Hatch, John; Maryland, 1645 ***2524.55*** *p104*
Hatch, Matthew; Georgia, 1765 ***1224.2*** *p53*
Hatch, Nicholas P.; Vermont, 1820-1884 ***5900.10*** *p249*
Hatch, Robert 35; Ontario, 1871 ***1823.28*** *p39*
Hatchett, Mr.; Quebec, 1858 ***9196.15*** *p33*
Hatchman, James; New York, 1834-1838 ***8197.10*** *p117*
Hatchman, John; New York, 1838 ***8197.10*** *p117*
Hatchwell, James 18; Philadelphia, 1774 ***1220.25*** *p4*
Hateley, Robert 50; Ontario, 1871 ***1823.28*** *p39*
Hatfield, Edward 31; Maryland, 1774 ***1220.25*** *p38*
Hatfield, Joshua; Pennsylvania, 1777 ***4629.10*** *p18*
Hatfield, William; New York, 1839 ***8197.10*** *p131*
Hatheway, Job; Pennsylvania, 1786 ***4629.10*** *p54*
Hathgar, H.; Portland, Maine, 1858 ***9196.15*** *p30*
Hathorn, John; New York, 1803 ***8197.10*** *p13*
Hatinger, Sabastian; New York, New York, 1854 ***3437.14*** *p78*
Hatt, Ann; Maryland, 1667 ***2524.55*** *p104*
Hatt, James 36; Ontario, 1871 ***1823.15*** *p108*
Hatt, Thomas; Maryland, 1673 ***2524.55*** *p104*
Hattaff, John H.; New York, 1840 ***8197.10*** *p172*
Hattan, William 45; Ontario, 1871 ***1823.15*** *p108*
Hatter, Abraham; Pennsylvania, 1786 ***4629.10*** *p52*
Hattersley, Josiah 21; Maryland, 1775 ***1220.25*** *p96*
Hattey, Henry; Maryland, 1681 ***2524.55*** *p104*
Hattford, Rich; Virginia, 1667-1668 ***6212.30*** *p39*
Hattich, Friedrich; Port uncertain, 1749 ***2856.30*** *p197H*
Hattley, Wm; Virginia, 1664 ***6212.30*** *p6*
Hatton, Mrs.; Maryland, 1648 ***2524.55*** *p104*
Hatton, Constantine; Maryland, 1656 ***2524.55*** *p104*
Hatton, George; Maryland, 1682 ***2524.55*** *p104*
Hatton, John; Virginia, 1663 ***1224.1*** *p28*
Hatton, William 21; Maryland, 1775 ***1220.25*** *p114*
Hattrick, Peter; New York, 1794 ***8197.10*** *p5*
Hattstein, Catharina; Port uncertain, 1784 ***2856.30*** *p167*
Hatz, Maria Elisabeth; Port uncertain, 1745 ***2856.30*** *p167*
Hauber, Rufina; Port uncertain, 1775 ***2856.30*** *p169*
Hauber, Ursula Elisabet; Port uncertain, 1767 ***2856.30*** *p167*
Haubert, Johann; Port uncertain, 1784 ***2856.30*** *p167*
Haubert, Johann Adam; Port uncertain, 1763 ***2856.30*** *p167*
Haubert, Maria Eulalia; Port uncertain, 1793 ***2856.30*** *p167*
Haubrecht, Johann; Port uncertain, 1740 ***2856.30*** *p167*
Haubrich, Anna Christina; Port uncertain, 1764 ***2856.30*** *p167*
Haubrich, Maria Barbara; Port uncertain, 1775 ***2856.30*** *p167*
Hauch, Jacob; America, 1739 ***2856.30*** *p167*
Hauck, Andreas; Port uncertain, 1775 ***2856.30*** *p167*
Hauck, Anna Maria; America, 1731 ***2856.30*** *p167*
Hauck, Anna Maria; Port uncertain, 1764 ***2856.30*** *p167*
Hauck, Anton; Port uncertain, 1782 ***2856.30*** *p167*
Hauck, Barb. *SEE* Hauck, Johann Peter
Hauck, Bernhard; America, 1749 ***2856.30*** *p167*
Hauck, Blasius; America, 1749 ***2856.30*** *p167*
Hauck, Blasius; America, 1749 ***2856.30*** *p167*
With wife & 2 children
Hauck, Caspar; America, 1743 ***2856.30*** *p168*
Hauck, Catharina; Port uncertain, 1763 ***2856.30*** *p168*
Hauck, Hans Michael; America, 1728 ***2856.30*** *p167*
Hauck, Hans Michael; America, 1749 ***2856.30*** *p167*
Hauck, Jakob; Port uncertain, 1754 ***2856.30*** *p167*
With wife
Hauck, Jakob; Port uncertain, 1764 ***2856.30*** *p167*
Hauck, Jakob; Port uncertain, 1765 ***2856.30*** *p167*
Hauck, Jakob; Port uncertain, 1768 ***2856.30*** *p167*
Hauck, Johann Peter; America, 1764 ***2856.30*** *p168*
Wife: Barb.
With 5 sons & daughter
Hauck, Konrad; Port uncertain, 1764 ***2856.30*** *p167*
Hauck, Margarete; America, 1749 ***2856.30*** *p167*
Hauck, Maria Eva; Port uncertain, 1766 ***2856.30*** *p167*
Hauck, Martin; America, 1752 ***2856.30*** *p167*
With wife & 2 children
Hauck, Paul; Port uncertain, 1764 ***2856.30*** *p167*
Hauck, Peter; America, 1737 ***2856.30*** *p167*
Hauck, Peter; America, 1786 ***2856.30*** *p167*
Hauck, Peter; America, 1789 ***2856.30*** *p167*
Hauck, Peter; Port uncertain, 1736 ***2856.30*** *p167*
Hauckh, Catharina; Port uncertain, 1758 ***2856.30*** *p168*
Hauckh, Georg Anton; Port uncertain, 1747 ***2856.30*** *p168*
Hauckh, Hans Jacob; Port uncertain, 1745 ***2856.30*** *p168*
Hauckh, Jakob; Port uncertain, 1742 ***2856.30*** *p168*
Hauckh, Margarete; Port uncertain, 1765 ***2856.30*** *p168*
Hauckin, Bark; Port uncertain, 1799 ***2856.30*** *p168*
Hauemer, Johann Adam; Port uncertain, 1773 ***2856.30*** *p168*
Hauer, Anton; America, 1750 ***2856.30*** *p168*
With wife & 3 children
Hauer, Anton; America, 1751 ***2856.30*** *p168*
Hauer, Bernhard; America, 1751 ***2856.30*** *p168*
Hauer, Chr; America, 1751 ***2856.30*** *p168*
Hauer, Christof; America, 1751 ***2856.30*** *p168*
With wife & 9 children
Hauer, Friedrich; Port uncertain, 1795 ***2856.30*** *p168*
Hauer, Friedrich; Port uncertain, 1796 ***2856.30*** *p168*
Hauer, Jacob; Port uncertain, 1729 ***2856.30*** *p168*
Hauer, Johann Jacob; Port uncertain, 1727 ***2856.30*** *p168*
Hauer, Michael; America, 1737 ***2856.30*** *p168*
Hauff, Miss; Port uncertain, 1785 ***2856.30*** *p475*

Haufler, Mary; Vermont, 1847-1924 ***5900.10*** *p404*
Haug, . . .; Port uncertain, 1783 ***2856.30*** *p168*
Haug, Antoni; Port uncertain, 1753 ***2856.30*** *p168*
Haug, Barbara; America, 1751 ***2856.30*** *p168*
Haug, Frederick; New York, 1838 ***8197.10*** *p116*
Haug, Hans Adam; Port uncertain, 1747 ***2856.30*** *p168*
Haug, Jacob; Port uncertain, 1771 ***2856.30*** *p168*
Haug, Jacob; Port uncertain, 1794 ***2856.30*** *p168*
Haug, Johann, The Younger; Port uncertain, 1756 ***2856.30*** *p168*
Haug, Johann Georg; Port uncertain, 1783 ***2856.30*** *p168*
Haug, John 50; Ontario, 1871 ***1823.15*** *p108*
Haug, Martin; America, 1752 ***2856.30*** *p168*
Haugen, Sever 44; British Columbia, 1909 ***9196.1*** *p27*
Haugen, Sever 44; Washington, 1909 ***9196.1*** *p27*
Haugh, Catherine McMahon; Vermont, 1843-1900 ***5900.10*** *p270*
Haugh, David 50; Ontario, 1871 ***1823.15*** *p108*
Haugh, Ellen 15; Vermont, 1858 ***5900.10*** *p264*
Haugh, John; Vermont, 1835-1892 ***5900.10*** *p270*
Haugh, Mary 21; Vermont, 1861 ***5900.10*** *p264*
Haugh, Nancy 19; Vermont, 1865 ***5900.10*** *p264*
Haugha, James; Virginia, 1684-1685 ***6212.30*** *p57*
Haughdebaugh, John; Pennsylvania, 1817 ***6058.10*** *p7*
Haughey, John 73; Vermont, 1901 ***5900.10*** *p507*
Haughey, Mary Devaney; Vermont, 1830-1915 ***5900.10*** *p406*
Haughey, Thomas; Vermont, 1840-1912 ***5900.10*** *p406*
Haughian, Bridgid L.; Vermont, 1847-1927 ***5900.10*** *p406*
Haughnau, James; Ontario, 1871 ***1823.28*** *p39*
Haughs, William 40; Vermont, 1864 ***5900.10*** *p364*
Haughton, George; Maryland, 1660 ***2524.55*** *p104*
Haukin, Lawrence; Maryland, 1681 ***2524.55*** *p104*
Haukins, William 35; Ontario, 1871 ***1823.28*** *p39*
Haul, Lawrence 21; Ontario, 1861 ***2896.25*** *p65*
Haul, Mary 27; Ontario, 1861 ***2896.25*** *p65*
Haul, William 28; Ontario, 1861 ***2896.25*** *p65*
Hauman, Mr.; Portland, Maine, 1858 ***9196.15*** *p30*
Haun, Franz Josef; Port uncertain, 1796 ***2856.30*** *p168*
Haun, Joseph 41; Ontario, 1871 ***1823.28*** *p39*
Haunn, Wilhelm; Port uncertain, 1742 ***2856.30*** *p168*
Hauoff, A. 23; Alaska, 1917 ***9196.1*** *p45*
Hauoff, A. 23; Whitehorse, Yukon, 1917 ***9196.1*** *p45*
Haupert, Catharina; Port uncertain, 1785 ***2856.30*** *p168*
Haupert, Frederick; New York, 1840 ***8197.10*** *p174*
Hauprecht, Anna Christina; Port uncertain, 1759 ***2856.30*** *p168*
Hauprecht, Margarete; Port uncertain, 1738 ***2856.30*** *p168*
Haurin, Barbara; Port uncertain, 1747 ***2856.30*** *p169*
Haus, Johann Michael; America, 1751 ***2856.30*** *p169*
Hausa, Christ 46; Ontario, 1871 ***1823.28*** *p39*
Hauser, Anton; America, 1751 ***2856.30*** *p169*
Hauser, Bernard; Port uncertain, 1783 ***2856.30*** *p169*
Hauser, Bernhard; America, 1751 ***2856.30*** *p169*
Hauser, Bernhard; America, 1751 ***2856.30*** *p169*
With wife & 3 children
Hauser, Christof; America, 1751 ***2856.30*** *p169*
Hauser, Emmanuel; New York, 1839 ***8197.10*** *p241*
Hauser, Jacob; Port uncertain, 1769 ***2856.30*** *p197H*
Hauser, Jakob; Port uncertain, 1800 ***2856.30*** *p169*
Hauser, Johann Georg J.; Port uncertain, 1748 ***2856.30*** *p169*
Hauser, Karl; America, 1755 ***2856.30*** *p169*
Hauser, Lorenz; America, 1753 ***2856.30*** *p169*
Hauser, Margarete; America, 1767 ***2856.30*** *p197H*
Hauser, Maria Catharina; Port uncertain, 1782 ***2856.30*** *p169*
With husband & 6 children
Hauser, Maria Catharina; Port uncertain, 1786 ***2856.30*** *p169*
With husband & 6 children
Hauser, Maria Elisabeth; Port uncertain, 1752 ***2856.30*** *p169*
Hauser, Martin; Port uncertain, 1763 ***2856.30*** *p169*
Hauser, Michael; Port uncertain, 1751 ***2856.30*** *p169*
Hauser, Philipp Jacob; Port uncertain, 1752 ***2856.30*** *p197H*
Hauser, Rufina; Port uncertain, 1775 ***2856.30*** *p169*
Hauser, Therese; Port uncertain, 1786 ***2856.30*** *p169*
Hauser, Thomas; Port uncertain, 1764 ***2856.30*** *p169*
Haushalter, Johann; Port uncertain, 1737 ***2856.30*** *p169*
Haushalter, Johann; Port uncertain, 1739 ***2856.30*** *p169*
Haushalter, Johann Adam; America, 1739 ***2856.30*** *p169*
Haushalter, Lorenz; Port uncertain, 1752 ***2856.30*** *p169*
Haushalter, Lorenz; Port uncertain, 1752 ***2856.30*** *p169*
With wife
Haushard, Carl; Maryland, 1910 ***3259.35*** *p19*
Hausler, Johann; Port uncertain, 1796 ***2856.30*** *p197H*
Hausmann, Johann; Port uncertain, 1764 ***2856.30*** *p169*
Hausrath, Johann Michael; Port uncertain, 1772 ***2856.30*** *p169*
Hauss, Adam; Port uncertain, 1785 ***2856.30*** *p169*
Hauss, Johann; America, 1751 ***2856.30*** *p169*
With wife & children
Hauss, Michael; America, 1751 ***2856.30*** *p169*
With wife
Hausser, Adam; Port uncertain, 1737 ***2856.30*** *p197H*
Hausser, Hans Martin; Port uncertain, 1760 ***2856.30*** *p197H*
Hausser, Jakob Thomas; Port uncertain, 1751 ***2856.30*** *p197H*
Hausser, Karl; America, 1755 ***2856.30*** *p197C*
Hausser, Lorenz; Port uncertain, 1752 ***2856.30*** *p197H*
With wife
Hausser, Mathes; Port uncertain, 1732 ***2856.30*** *p170*
With wife
Hausserin, Anna Maria; Port uncertain, 1788 ***2856.30*** *p170*
With husband
Haussler, Christian; Port uncertain, 1741 ***2856.30*** *p197H*
With wife & 4 children
Haussler, Christof; America, 1754 ***2856.30*** *p197H*
Haussler, Christof; Port uncertain, 1754 ***2856.30*** *p197H*
Haussler, Josef; America, 1720 ***2856.30*** *p197H*
Haussler, Philipp Jacob; America, 1772 ***2856.30*** *p197H*
Haussmann, Jakob; Port uncertain, 1785 ***2856.30*** *p170*
With brother
Hausswirt, Michael; Port uncertain, 1785 ***2856.30*** *p170*
Hauswirt, Catharina Kessler; America, 1751 ***2856.30*** *p170*
Hauswirth, Catharina; America, 1751 ***2856.30*** *p170*
With husband & 4 children
Hauswurth, Johann Jakob; America, 1751 ***2856.30*** *p170*
Hauton, George; Pennsylvania, 1777 ***4629.10*** *p22*
Havell, Henry 25; Philadelphia, 1774 ***1220.25*** *p6*
Haven, Rich; Virginia, 1667-1668 ***6212.30*** *p38*
Haverstick, Nicholas; Pennsylvania, 1777 ***4629.10*** *p7*
Haverstick, William; Pennsylvania, 1777 ***4629.10*** *p7*
Haverty, Michael; New York, 1834 ***8197.10*** *p319*
Havey, Mary; Vermont, 1816-1902 ***5900.10*** *p334*
Haviland, Bartholomew; New York, 1823 ***8197.10*** *p238*
Haviland, Bernard; New York, 1823 ***8197.10*** *p238*
Haviland, Jane; New England, 1671 ***1224.1*** *p28*
Haviland, Margaret; New York, New York, 1768 ***1224.2*** *p53*
Haw, Catharina; Port uncertain, 1743 ***2856.30*** *p170*
Haw, Francis 24; Virginia, 1774 ***1220.25*** *p56*
Haw, Georg; Port uncertain, 1623 ***2856.30*** *p170*
Haw, J. H.; Ontario, 1861 ***2896.28*** *p55*
Haw, James 65; Ontario, 1871 ***1823.22*** *p70*
Haw, John 48; Ontario, 1871 ***1823.22*** *p70*
Haward, Wm.; Maryland, 1660 ***2524.55*** *p104*
Hawbridge, Jane 39; New York, 1774 ***1220.25*** *p23*
Hawes, Major; Quebec, 1857 ***9196.15*** *p16*
Hawes, Bridget Leonard 90; Vermont, 1924 ***5900.10*** *p263*
Hawes, John; New York, 1838 ***8197.10*** *p116*
Hawes, John 78; Vermont, 1887 ***5900.10*** *p263*
Hawes, Joshua; Maryland, 1680 ***2524.55*** *p104*
Hawes, Sidney; New York, 1832 ***8197.10*** *p314*
Hawes, William; Virginia, 1735 ***1224.2*** *p53*
Hawford, Elizabeth; Maryland, 1674 ***2524.55*** *p104*
Hawford, John; Maryland, 1675 ***2524.55*** *p104*
Hawford, Mary; Maryland, 1675 ***2524.55*** *p104*
Hawikjy, Margaret 31; Ontario, 1871 ***1823.28*** *p39*
Hawke, Richard; Virginia, 1666 ***6212.30*** *p28*
Hawkens, Victoria 24; Ontario, 1871 ***1823.15*** *p108*
Hawker, Dorothy; Virginia, 1647 ***1224.1*** *p28*
Hawker, Edward; Virginia, 1658 ***1224.1*** *p28*
Hawker, Godfrey; Pennsylvania, 1777 ***4629.10*** *p10*
Hawker, John; New York, 1840 ***8197.10*** *p385*
Hawker, Patience; Maryland, 1663 ***2524.55*** *p104*
Hawker, Philip; Maryland, 1665 ***2524.55*** *p104*
Hawker, Phillip; Maryland, 1680 ***2524.55*** *p104*
Hawkes, John; Norfolk, Virginia, 1790 ***1224.2*** *p54*
Hawkes, Petty; New York, 1831 ***8197.10*** *p354*
Hawkesworth, James; New York, 1834 ***8197.10*** *p240*
Hawkey, John S. 26; Ontario, 1871 ***1823.22*** *p70*
Hawkey, Robert 50; Ontario, 1871 ***1823.22*** *p70*
Hawkin, Nicholas 46; Ontario, 1871 ***1823.22*** *p70*
Hawking, Henry 38; Ontario, 1871 ***1823.15*** *p108*
Hawkins, Mrs.; Maryland, 1640 ***2524.55*** *p104*
Hawkins, A. W. 28; Ontario, 1871 ***1823.22*** *p70*
Hawkins, Ad 5; Ontario, 1861 ***2896.27*** *p8*
Hawkins, Anne; Virginia, 1654 ***1224.1*** *p28*
Hawkins, Charles; New York, 1836 ***8197.10*** *p319*
Hawkins, Elinor *SEE* Hawkins, Henry
Hawkins, Elizabeth 71; Ontario, 1871 ***1823.15*** *p108*
Hawkins, George 45; Ontario, 1871 ***1823.15*** *p108*
Hawkins, George 53; Ontario, 1871 ***1823.22*** *p70*
Hawkins, Henry; Maryland, 1659 ***2524.55*** *p105*
Hawkins, Henry; Maryland, 1666 ***2524.55*** *p104*
Wife: Elinor
Son: John
Hawkins, Henry; Maryland, 1681 ***2524.55*** *p105*
Hawkins, James 40; Ontario, 1871 ***1823.28*** *p39*
Hawkins, James 55; Ontario, 1871 ***1823.15*** *p108*
Hawkins, Jno; Virginia, 1664 ***6212.30*** *p15*
Hawkins, John *SEE* Hawkins, Henry
Hawkins, John; Maryland, 1658 ***2524.55*** *p105*
Hawkins, John; Maryland, 1719 ***1224.2*** *p54*
Hawkins, John; New York, 1767 ***1224.2*** *p54*
Hawkins, John; Virginia, 1666 ***6212.30*** *p30*
Hawkins, John 15; St. John Island, 1775 ***1220.25*** *p121*
Hawkins, John 43; Ontario, 1871 ***1823.15*** *p108*
Hawkins, John 76; Ontario, 1871 ***1823.22*** *p70*
Hawkins, Joseph 56; Ontario, 1871 ***1823.28*** *p39*
Hawkins, Lewis 2; Ontario, 1861 ***2896.27*** *p8*
Hawkins, Mary; Boston, 1721 ***1224.2*** *p54*
Hawkins, Mary; Maryland, 1660 ***2524.55*** *p105*
Hawkins, Mary; Virginia, 1666 ***6212.30*** *p30*
Hawkins, Mary 19; Ontario, 1861 ***2896.27*** *p8*
Hawkins, Mathew 63; Ontario, 1871 ***1823.22*** *p70*
Hawkins, Milard 11; Ontario, 1861 ***2896.27*** *p8*
Hawkins, Peter; Maryland, 1658 ***2524.55*** *p105*
Hawkins, Philip; South Carolina, n.d. ***1224.2*** *p54*
Hawkins, Philip; West Indies, 1782 ***1224.2*** *p54*
Hawkins, Robert 90; Ontario, 1871 ***1823.22*** *p70*
Hawkins, Samuel; Maryland, 1659 ***2524.55*** *p105*
Hawkins, Shel 23; Ontario, 1861 ***2896.27*** *p8*
Hawkins, Sheldon 50; Ontario, 1861 ***2896.27*** *p8*
Hawkins, T.; Ontario, 1861 ***2896.28*** *p61*
Hawkins, Thomas 47; Ontario, 1871 ***1823.15*** *p108*
Hawkins, Truman 14; Ontario, 1861 ***2896.27*** *p8*
Hawkins, W. H. 23; Ontario, 1871 ***1823.28*** *p39*
Hawkins, William; Boston, 1702 ***1224.2*** *p54*
Hawkins, William; New England, 1686 ***1224.1*** *p28*
Hawkins, William 21; Philadelphia, 1775 ***1220.25*** *p122*
Hawkins, William 54; Ontario, 1871 ***1823.15*** *p108*
Hawkins, William 72; Ontario, 1871 ***1823.22*** *p70*
Hawkinson, Henry; Pennsylvania, 1777 ***4629.10*** *p17*
Hawksford, William 21; Maryland, 1775 ***1220.25*** *p115*
Hawkshaw, Robert; Maryland, 1676 ***2524.55*** *p105*
Hawksley, Alfred; Died enroute, 1849 ***1224.3*** *p35*
Hawksworth, John; New York, 1838 ***8197.10*** *p117*
Hawkworth, Adam 34; Nova Scotia, 1774 ***1220.25*** *p135*
With wife & 4 children
Hawky, Regnald; Virginia, 1666 ***6212.30*** *p29*
Hawlay, James 55; Ontario, 1871 ***1823.28*** *p39*
Hawles, Tho; Virginia, 1664 ***6212.30*** *p14*
Hawles, William; Virginia, 1665 ***6212.30*** *p18*
Hawley, Benjamin 30; Ontario, 1861 ***2896.28*** *p49*
Hawley, Enoch 70; Ontario, 1871 ***1823.22*** *p70*
Hawley, Gilbert 67; Ontario, 1871 ***1823.22*** *p70*
Hawley, James; Virginia, 1664 ***6212.30*** *p11*
Hawley, Jeremiah; Maryland, 1651 ***1224.1*** *p28*
Hawley, John 38; Ontario, 1871 ***1823.28*** *p39*
Hawley, Milo 35; Ontario, 1871 ***1823.22*** *p70*
Hawley, Richard 24; Ontario, 1871 ***1823.15*** *p108*
Hawley, William; Boston, 1899 ***1640.13*** *p54*
Hawly, Robert; Maryland, 1649 ***2524.55*** *p105*
Haworth, Richd 29; Ontario, 1871 ***1823.28*** *p39*
Haws, Peter; Pennsylvania, 1777 ***4629.10*** *p17*
Hawtayne, Captain; Quebec, 1857 ***9196.15*** *p17*
Hawthorn, John 30; Ontario, 1871 ***1823.15*** *p108*
Hawthorn, Peter 26; Ontario, 1871 ***1823.15*** *p108*
Hawthorn, Robert 36; Ontario, 1871 ***1823.15*** *p108*
Hawthorn, Robert 73; Ontario, 1871 ***1823.15*** *p108*
Hawthorn, Robt 52; Ontario, 1871 ***1823.28*** *p39*
Hawthorne, Henry 21; Ontario, 1871 ***1823.15*** *p108*
Hawthorne, James 55; Ontario, 1871 ***1823.15*** *p108*
Hawthorne, John 69; Ontario, 1871 ***1823.22*** *p70*
Hawthorne, Thomas 53; Ontario, 1871 ***1823.22*** *p70*
Hawthorne, William 25; Ontario, 1871 ***1823.15*** *p108*
Hawtin, Ann; Maryland, 1664 ***2524.55*** *p105*
Hawtrill, John; Maryland, 1681 ***2524.55*** *p105*
Hawtyn, John; Pennsylvania, 1777 ***4629.10*** *p9*
Haxby, Thomas; New York, 1842 ***1224.3*** *p35*
Haxtrom, John 43; Juneau, Alaska, 1917 ***9196.1*** *p52*
Haxtrom, John 43; Whitehorse, Yukon, 1917 ***9196.1*** *p52*
Hay, Mr.; Quebec, 1857 ***9196.15*** *p14*
Hay, Mr.; Quebec, 1857 ***9196.15*** *p24*
Hay, Rev.; Quebec, 1858 ***9196.15*** *p40*
Hay, Alexander; Charles Town, South Carolina, 1776 ***1224.2*** *p54*
Hay, Alexander 21; Ontario, 1871 ***1823.22*** *p70*
Hay, Andeas 53; Ontario, 1871 ***1823.15*** *p108*
Hay, Andrew; Georgia, 1698 ***1640.13*** *p54*
Hay, Andrew 50; Ontario, 1871 ***1823.22*** *p70*
Hay, Ann 71; Ontario, 1871 ***1823.22*** *p70*
Hay, Arthur; Maryland, 1641 ***2524.55*** *p105*
Hay, Charles; Boston, 1773 ***1224.2*** *p54*
Hay, Charles; Maryland, 1674 ***2524.55*** *p105*
Hay, David 44; Ontario, 1871 ***1823.15*** *p108*
Hay, David 68; Ontario, 1871 ***1823.15*** *p108*
Hay, Duncan; Quebec, 1847 ***1640.13*** *p54*
Hay, Elizabeth 23; Ontario, 1871 ***1823.28*** *p39*

Hay, Hugh; Georgia, 1698 ***1640.13*** *p54*
Hay, James; New Orleans, 1835 ***1640.10*** *p78*
Hay, James; Virginia, 1678 ***1224.1*** *p28*
Hay, James 29; Philadelphia, 1774 ***1220.25*** *p80*
Hay, James 35; Ontario, 1871 ***1823.15*** *p108*
Hay, James 44; Ontario, 1871 ***1823.22*** *p70*
Hay, James, Jr.; New York, 1825 ***8197.10*** *p239*
Hay, Janet; Port uncertain, 1860-1869 ***4537.35*** *p78*
Hay, Jenour; Georgia, 1740 ***1640.10*** *p78*
Hay, John; Georgia, 1698 ***1640.13*** *p54*
Hay, John; Mississippi, 1844 ***1640.10*** *p78*
Hay, John; New York, 1845 ***1224.3*** *p35*
Hay, John 23; Virginia, 1774 ***1220.25*** *p54*
Hay, John 25; Ontario, 1871 ***1823.15*** *p108*
Hay, John 49; Ontario, 1871 ***1823.22*** *p70*
Hay, Margaret; Barbados, 1828 ***1640.13*** *p54*
Hay, Margaret; Mississippi, 1816-1839 ***1640.10*** *p78*
Hay, Mary 72; Ontario, 1871 ***1823.15*** *p108*
Hay, Patrick; Georgia, 1698 ***1640.13*** *p54*
Hay, Peter; New York, 1839 ***8197.10*** *p131*
Hay, Robert; Savannah, Georgia, 1737 ***1640.10*** *p78*
Hay, William; Georgia, 1699 ***1640.13*** *p54*
Hay, William 47; Ontario, 1871 ***1823.22*** *p70*
Hay, William 58; Ontario, 1871 ***1823.28*** *p39*
Hay, William 60; Ontario, 1871 ***1823.15*** *p108*
Haycock, Hamilton; New York, 1826 ***8197.10*** *p239*
Haycroft, John 65; Ontario, 1871 ***1823.15*** *p108*
Hayd, Jacob; America, 1737 ***2856.30*** *p170*
Haydak, Victor; Maryland, 1910 ***3259.35*** *p19*
Hayden, Catherine 62; Vermont, 1890 ***5900.10*** *p564*
Hayden, James; New York, 1839 ***8197.10*** *p382*
Hayden, Jane 77; Ontario, 1871 ***1823.22*** *p70*
Hayden, Jemima; Maine, 1836 ***1224.3*** *p35*
Hayden, John 40; Ontario, 1871 ***1823.22*** *p70*
Hayden, John 58; Ontario, 1871 ***1823.15*** *p108*
Hayden, Joseph 37; Ontario, 1871 ***1823.22*** *p70*
Hayden, Katherine; Vermont, 1845-1917 ***5900.10*** *p46*
Hayden, Laughlin; New York, 1838 ***8197.10*** *p318*
Hayden, Mary 75; Vermont, 1918 ***5900.10*** *p445*
Hayden, Samuel; Maine, 1836 ***1224.3*** *p35*
Haydlauff, Elisabeth; Port uncertain, 1742 ***2856.30*** *p170*
Haydock, Robert; Pennsylvania, 1788 ***4629.10*** *p56*
Haydon, Edward 30; Maryland, 1775 ***1220.25*** *p105*
Haydon, Joseph 18; Baltimore, 1775 ***1220.25*** *p119*
Haye, Margaret 45; Vermont, 1873 ***5900.10*** *p43*
Hayer, Michael; Pennsylvania, 1832 ***6058.10*** *p10*
Hayes, Ann; Vermont, 1841-1920 ***5900.10*** *p166*
Hayes, Ann McGue; Vermont, 1838-1910 ***5900.10*** *p557*
Hayes, Annie; Vermont, 1860-1960 ***5900.10*** *p551*
Hayes, Bid; Vermont, 1858-1933 ***5900.10*** *p133*
Hayes, Bridget 72; Vermont, 1844 ***5900.10*** *p306*
Hayes, Bridget 72; Vermont, 1884 ***5900.10*** *p308*
Hayes, Bridget 75; Vermont, 1883 ***5900.10*** *p59*
Hayes, Bridget Crowley 87; Vermont, 1946 ***5900.10*** *p124*
Hayes, Bridget Kane; Vermont, 1830-1917 ***5900.10*** *p365*
Hayes, Caleb 25; America, 1774 ***1220.25*** *p36*
Hayes, Catherine A.; Vermont, 1855-1915 ***5900.10*** *p339*
Hayes, Charles 14; Ontario, 1861 ***2896.28*** *p37*
Hayes, Cornelius; Vermont, 1824-1885 ***5900.10*** *p260*
Hayes, Cushi 27; Ontario, 1871 ***1823.15*** *p108*
Hayes, Daniel 42; Vermont, 1868 ***5900.10*** *p124*
Hayes, Daniel 85; Vermont, 1908 ***5900.10*** *p302*
Hayes, Daniel, Jr. 68; Vermont, 1929 ***5900.10*** *p124*
Hayes, Dorothy; Maryland, 1659 ***2524.55*** *p51*
Hayes, Mrs. E. T.; Vermont, 1865-1938 ***5900.10*** *p551*
Hayes, Edward; Vermont, 1822-1862 ***5900.10*** *p215*
Hayes, Edward; Vermont, 1856-1927 ***5900.10*** *p215*
Hayes, Eliza Condon; Vermont, 1821-1902 ***5900.10*** *p215*
Hayes, Elizabeth; Vermont, 1856-1929 ***5900.10*** *p179*
Hayes, Elizabeth L.; Vermont, 1853-1937 ***5900.10*** *p128*
Hayes, Ellen 65; Vermont, 1884 ***5900.10*** *p58*
Hayes, Ellen Minogue; Vermont, 1837-1929 ***5900.10*** *p274*
Hayes, Frederick; New York, 1855 ***1224.3*** *p35*
Hayes, George; Maryland, 1674 ***2524.55*** *p105*
Hayes, George; Maryland, 1676 ***2524.55*** *p105*
Hayes, George 17; Ontario, 1861 ***2896.28*** *p37*
Hayes, George 48; Ontario, 1861 ***2896.28*** *p37*
Hayes, Hannora Dugan 72; Vermont, 1891 ***5900.10*** *p327*
Hayes, Hanorah; Vermont, 1810-1895 ***5900.10*** *p166*
Hayes, Helen; New York, 1839 ***8197.10*** *p381*
Hayes, Henrietta 12; Ontario, 1861 ***2896.28*** *p37*
Hayes, Henry H.; New York, 1840 ***8197.10*** *p174*
Hayes, Henry W. 10; Ontario, 1861 ***2896.28*** *p37*
Hayes, J. M.; Vermont, 1862-1915 ***5900.10*** *p551*
Hayes, James; New York, 1827 ***8197.10*** *p240*
Hayes, James; Vermont, n.d. ***5900.10*** *p62*
Hayes, James; Vermont, 1829-1929 ***5900.10*** *p365*
Hayes, James; Vermont, 1854-1863 ***5900.10*** *p173*
Hayes, James; Vermont, 1858-1925 ***5900.10*** *p551*
Hayes, James; Vermont, 1924 ***5900.10*** *p355*
Hayes, James T.; Vermont, 1857 ***5900.10*** *p257*
Hayes, Jennie; Vermont, 1869-1871 ***5900.10*** *p173*
Hayes, John; New York, 1838-1840 ***8197.10*** *p173*
Hayes, John; Vermont, 1837-1911 ***5900.10*** *p557*
Hayes, John; Vermont, 1853-1877 ***5900.10*** *p215*
Hayes, John; Vermont, 1853-1919 ***5900.10*** *p553*
Hayes, John; Virginia, 1672 ***6212.30*** *p49*
Hayes, John 26; Philadelphia, 1774 ***1220.25*** *p35*
Hayes, John 34; Ontario, 1871 ***1823.15*** *p108*
Hayes, John 52; Vermont, 1899 ***5900.10*** *p380*
Hayes, John 78; Vermont, 1908 ***5900.10*** *p306*
Hayes, John 78; Vermont, 1908 ***5900.10*** *p308*
Hayes, Johnf; Vermont, 1818-1899 ***5900.10*** *p249*
Hayes, Johnie 33; Vermont, 1894 ***5900.10*** *p249*
Hayes, Joseph; Virginia, 1678 ***1224.1*** *p28*
Hayes, Joseph L. 3; Ontario, 1861 ***2896.28*** *p37*
Hayes, Julia; Vermont, 1851-1932 ***5900.10*** *p355*
Hayes, Julia; Vermont, 1867-1962 ***5900.10*** *p551*
Hayes, Julia Heffernan; Vermont, 1822-1912 ***5900.10*** *p551*
Hayes, Katherine 69; Vermont, 1890 ***5900.10*** *p173*
Hayes, Lawrence; New York, 1840 ***8197.10*** *p171*
Hayes, Levi 18; Ontario, 1861 ***2896.25*** *p25*
Hayes, Levi 18; Ontario, 1861 ***2896.28*** *p37*
Hayes, Maggie Butler 99; Vermont, 1908 ***5900.10*** *p394*
Hayes, Margaret; Vermont, 1824-1893 ***5900.10*** *p252*
Hayes, Margaret; Vermont, 1837-1910 ***5900.10*** *p63*
Hayes, Martin; Vermont, 1824-1898 ***5900.10*** *p398*
Hayes, Martin 43; Ontario, 1871 ***1823.15*** *p108*
Hayes, Mary; Vermont, 1821-1896 ***5900.10*** *p78*
Hayes, Mary; Vermont, 1837-1894 ***5900.10*** *p582*
Hayes, Mary; Vermont, 1841-1905 ***5900.10*** *p219*
Hayes, Mary; Vermont, 1879-1919 ***5900.10*** *p355*
Hayes, Mary 28; Vermont, 1875 ***5900.10*** *p343*
Hayes, Mary A.; Vermont, 1865-1887 ***5900.10*** *p173*
Hayes, Mary A. Dale; Vermont, 1855-1909 ***5900.10*** *p62*
Hayes, Mary Costello; Vermont, 1851-1912 ***5900.10*** *p69*
Hayes, Mary Dolan 70; Vermont, 1901 ***5900.10*** *p124*
Hayes, Mary Doyle; Vermont, 1825-1913 ***5900.10*** *p302*
Hayes, Mary E. Garvay; Vermont, 1896 ***5900.10*** *p393*
Hayes, Mary Minogue; Vermont, 1856-1915 ***5900.10*** *p257*
Hayes, Mary Quinn 78; Vermont, 1919 ***5900.10*** *p380*
Hayes, Mary Toohey; Vermont, 1828-1903 ***5900.10*** *p260*
Hayes, Michael; Pennsylvania, 1867 ***6058.10*** *p57*
Hayes, Michael; Vermont, 1808-1885 ***5900.10*** *p252*
Hayes, Michael; Vermont, 1808-1885 ***5900.10*** *p398*
Hayes, Michael 48; Vermont, 1875 ***5900.10*** *p58*
Hayes, Nancy A. 40; Vermont, 1879 ***5900.10*** *p372*
Hayes, Nellie L.; Vermont, 1867-1890 ***5900.10*** *p173*
Hayes, Owen; Vermont, 1832-1901 ***5900.10*** *p274*
Hayes, Owen J.; Vermont, 1859-1925 ***5900.10*** *p393*
Hayes, Patrick; Vermont, 1828-1906 ***5900.10*** *p173*
Hayes, Patrick; Vermont, 1847-1931 ***5900.10*** *p551*
Hayes, Patrick; Vermont, 1861-1865 ***5900.10*** *p260*
Hayes, Patrick; Virginia, 1671 ***6212.30*** *p43*
Hayes, Prudence 21; Ontario, 1871 ***1823.15*** *p108*
Hayes, Rebecca; Carolina, 1736 ***1224.2*** *p54*
Hayes, Richard 54; Ontario, 1861 ***2896.25*** *p25*
Hayes, Robert; Virginia, 1666-1667 ***6212.30*** *p32*
Hayes, Robt; Virginia, 1665-1666 ***6212.30*** *p23*
Hayes, Sarah; Maryland, 1663 ***2524.55*** *p105*
Hayes, Sarah White; Vermont, 1821-1908 ***5900.10*** *p249*
Hayes, Thomas; Georgia, 1818 ***1224.3*** *p35*
Hayes, Thomas; New York, 1840 ***8197.10*** *p171*
Hayes, Thomas; Virginia, 1664 ***6212.30*** *p12*
Hayes, William; New York, 1836 ***8197.10*** *p75*
Hayes, William; Vermont, 1821-1903 ***5900.10*** *p551*
Hayes, William; Vermont, 1856-1923 ***5900.10*** *p551*
Hayes, William 15; Philadelphia, 1775 ***1220.25*** *p107*
Hayes, William 21; Maryland, 1774 ***1220.25*** *p73*
Hayes, Mrs. William; Vermont, 1861-1946 ***5900.10*** *p551*
Hayes, William E.; Vermont, 1852-1939 ***5900.10*** *p128*
Hayes, William P.; Vermont, 1888-1948 ***5900.10*** *p560*
Hayes, Winifred; Vermont, 1842-1922 ***5900.10*** *p133*
Hayes, Winifred 74; Vermont, n.d. ***5900.10*** *p58*
Hayesheimer, Michael; America, 1741 ***2856.30*** *p170*
With wife & children
Hayfield, Mary 20; Philadelphia, 1774 ***1220.25*** *p63*
Hayford, Mary Ann Cox; Vermont, 1843-1912 ***5900.10*** *p284*
Hayhurst, James 23; Ontario, 1871 ***1823.22*** *p70*
Hayland, Lawrence; Maryland, 1678 ***2524.55*** *p105*
Hayle, Oliver; Virginia, 1671 ***6212.30*** *p42*
Hayler, Bernhard; America, 1742 ***2856.30*** *p170*
With family
Hayler, Charity; Maryland, 1661-1662 ***2524.55*** *p105*
Son: Henry
Hayler, Henry *SEE* Hayler, Charity
Hayler, Henry; Maryland, 1665 ***2524.55*** *p105*
Hayler, Thomas 35; Philadelphia, 1774 ***1220.25*** *p86*
Hayles, John; Maryland, 1670 ***2524.55*** *p105*
Haylett, Mr.; Quebec, 1858 ***9196.15*** *p33*
Haylett, James; New York, New York, 1841 ***6058.10*** *p30*
Hayley, John 27; Ontario, 1871 ***1823.15*** *p108*
Haylings, Wm.; Maryland, 1681 ***2524.55*** *p105*
Haylock, E. 26; Ontario, 1861 ***2896.28*** *p5*
Haylock, J. 22; Ontario, 1861 ***2896.28*** *p5*
Hayman, Ellenor *SEE* Hayman, Henry
Hayman, Henry; Maryland, 1666 ***2524.55*** *p105*
Relative: Ellenor
Son: Henry, Jr.
Hayman, Henry, Jr. *SEE* Hayman, Henry
Hayman, Jacob; Pennsylvania, 1784 ***4629.10*** *p44*
Hayman, William 22; Philadelphia, 1774 ***1220.25*** *p80*
Hayne, John; New York, 1840 ***8197.10*** *p242*
Hayne, William; New York, 1846 ***1224.3*** *p35*
Haynes, Capt.; Quebec, 1856 ***9196.15*** *p7*
Haynes, Mr.; Quebec, 1856 ***9196.15*** *p5*
Haynes, Mrs.; Quebec, 1856 ***9196.15*** *p7*
Haynes, Edward 48; Ontario, 1871 ***1823.22*** *p70*
Haynes, Elizabeth 22; Maryland, 1774 ***1220.25*** *p76*
Haynes, Fredrick 40; Ontario, 1871 ***1823.22*** *p70*
Haynes, George; Pennsylvania, 1780 ***4629.10*** *p43*
Haynes, Herbert; Virginia, 1737 ***1224.2*** *p54*
Haynes, Jane; Vermont, 1842-1910 ***5900.10*** *p256*
Haynes, John; Philadelphia, 1806 ***1224.3*** *p35*
Haynes, John 22; Philadelphia, 1775 ***1220.25*** *p107*
Haynes, John B. 36; Ontario, 1871 ***1823.22*** *p70*
Haynes, M. D. J.; Quebec, 1856 ***9196.15*** *p11*
Haynes, Mary 89; Ontario, 1871 ***1823.22*** *p70*
Haynes, Richard; America, 1859 ***1640.13*** *p54*
Haynes, Richard 40; Ontario, 1871 ***1823.15*** *p108*
Haynes, Richard 73; Ontario, 1871 ***1823.22*** *p70*
Haynes, Thomas; Maryland, 1663 ***2524.55*** *p105*
Haynes, Thomas; Maryland, 1663 ***2524.55*** *p108*
Haynes, Thomas; Virginia, 1746 ***1224.2*** *p54*
Haynes, William; Maryland, 1659 ***2524.55*** *p105*
Haynes, William 34; Ontario, 1871 ***1823.22*** *p70*
Haynsinger, Philipp; America, 1749 ***2856.30*** *p170*
With wife & 4 children
Hays, Alexander 48; Ontario, 1871 ***1823.22*** *p70*
Hays, Edmund; New York, 1835-1838 ***8197.10*** *p116*
Hays, Edward 40; Ontario, 1871 ***1823.15*** *p109*
Hays, Ellen 73; Ontario, 1871 ***1823.15*** *p109*
Hays, Francis; New York, 1807 ***8197.10*** *p40*
Hays, J. 45; Ontario, 1871 ***1823.15*** *p109*
Hays, James 35; Ontario, 1871 ***1823.15*** *p109*
Hays, James 66; Ontario, 1871 ***1823.28*** *p39*
Hays, Jane; New York, 1833 ***8197.10*** *p358*
Hays, John; Pennsylvania, 1809 ***6058.10*** *p3*
Hays, John; Philadelphia, 1848 ***6058.10*** *p29*
Hays, Margaret; Vermont, 1860-1926 ***5900.10*** *p272*
Hays, Mary; North Carolina, 1744 ***1224.2*** *p97*
Hays, Mary; Vermont, 1852-1918 ***5900.10*** *p42*
Hays, Nathanial; Pennsylvania, 1806 ***6058.10*** *p1*
Hays, Peter 52; Ontario, 1871 ***1823.28*** *p39*
Hays, Richard; Maryland, 1681 ***2524.55*** *p105*
Hays, Robert; Philadelphia, 1850 ***6058.10*** *p37*
Hays, Robert 53; Ontario, 1871 ***1823.15*** *p109*
Hays, Robert 76; Ontario, 1871 ***1823.15*** *p109*
Hays, Sarah; Vermont, 1825-1880 ***5900.10*** *p270*
Hays, Thomas; New York, 1802 ***8197.10*** *p21*
Hays, William; Philadelphia, 1850 ***6058.10*** *p36*
Hayse, William; Maryland, 1665 ***2524.55*** *p105*
Haysham, William; Pennsylvania, 1777 ***4629.10*** *p9*
Hayslop, Alex 61; Ontario, 1871 ***1823.15*** *p109*
Haysman, William; New York, 1838 ***8197.10*** *p117*
Hayt, James; Bridgeport, Connecticut, 1807 ***1224.3*** *p35*
Hayt, Monson; New York, New York, 1807 ***1224.3*** *p35*
Hayter, Elizabeth 60; Ontario, 1871 ***1823.15*** *p109*
Hayton, George 32; Nova Scotia, 1774 ***1220.25*** *p13*
Hayward, Mr.; Quebec, 1857 ***9196.15*** *p24*
Hayward, Mr.; Quebec, 1858 ***9196.15*** *p37*
Hayward, Mrs.; Quebec, 1858 ***9196.15*** *p37*
Hayward, Annie; Vermont, 1855-1877 ***5900.10*** *p451*
Hayward, Caroline 48; Ontario, 1871 ***1823.22*** *p71*
Hayward, Edward 48; Ontario, 1871 ***1823.22*** *p71*
Hayward, Elizabeth; Maryland, 1680 ***2524.55*** *p105*
Hayward, George; New York, 1840 ***8197.10*** *p172*
Hayward, James; New York, 1818 ***8197.10*** *p236*
Hayward, John; Virginia, 1698 ***1224.1*** *p28*
Hayward, Judith; Maryland, 1680 ***2524.55*** *p105*
Hayward, Margaret; New Orleans, 1827 ***1224.3*** *p1*
Hayward, Nicholas; Maryland, 1657 ***2524.55*** *p105*
Hayward, Raphael; Maryland, 1655-1656 ***2524.55*** *p105*
Hayward, Robert 22; Philadelphia, 1775 ***1220.25*** *p107*
Hayward, Stephen; Maryland, 1657 ***2524.55*** *p105*
Hayward, Thomas; New York, 1694 ***1224.1*** *p28*
Hayward, Thomas; Virginia, 1698 ***1224.1*** *p29*
Hayward, Thomisin; Maryland, 1657 ***2524.55*** *p105*
Hayward, William; Maryland, 1661 ***2524.55*** *p105*
Haywood, Colquit 16; Virginia, 1774 ***1220.25*** *p140*
Haywood, Daniell; Virginia, 1671 ***6212.30*** *p42*
Haywood, Elizabeth 25; Maryland, 1775 ***1220.25*** *p98*

Haywood, Francis 24; Virginia, 1774 ***1220.25*** *p53*
Haywood, George 33; Ontario, 1871 ***1823.15*** *p109*
Haywood, John 42; Ontario, 1871 ***1823.15*** *p109*
Haywood, Raphael; Maryland, 1655-1656 ***2524.55*** *p105*
Haywood, Susan *SEE* Haywood, Thomas
Haywood, Thomas; Maryland, 1665 ***2524.55*** *p105*
Relative: Susan
Haywood, Thomas 35; Ontario, 1871 ***1823.15*** *p109*
Haywood, Walter; Maryland, 1665 ***2524.55*** *p106*
Haz, Leonhard; America, 1738 ***2856.30*** *p170*
Hazaldine, Thomas; Portland, Maine, 1858 ***9196.15*** *p29*
Hazard, Ann; Maryland, 1673 ***2524.55*** *p106*
Hazard, Edward; Maryland, 1664 ***2524.55*** *p119*
Hazard, Edward; Maryland, 1682 ***2524.55*** *p106*
Wife: Elizabeth
Hazard, Elizabeth *SEE* Hazard, Edward
Hazard, Hannah M. 11; Ontario, 1861 ***2896.27*** *p16*
Hazard, Joseph 78; Ontario, 1861 ***2896.27*** *p56*
Hazard, Lawren; Pennsylvania, 1793 ***4629.10*** *p64*
Hazard, Lydia E. 12; Ontario, 1861 ***2896.27*** *p16*
Hazard, Mary; New England, 1658 ***1224.1*** *p29*
Hazard, Maturah 41; Ontario, 1861 ***2896.27*** *p16*
Hazard, Miles E. 1; Ontario, 1861 ***2896.27*** *p16*
Hazard, Thomas 16; Ontario, 1861 ***2896.27*** *p16*
Hazard, Wellington 19; Ontario, 1861 ***2896.27*** *p16*
Hazard, William E. 9; Ontario, 1861 ***2896.27*** *p16*
Hazel, Julia 33; Vermont, 1874 ***5900.10*** *p505*
Hazelhurst, Robert; Pennsylvania, 1777 ***4629.10*** *p24*
Hazeltine, Stephen; Vermont, 1829-1888 ***5900.10*** *p616*
Hazelton, Charles; New York, 1838 ***8197.10*** *p116*
Hazelton, Henry; New York, 1838 ***8197.10*** *p116*
Hazelwood, John; Pennsylvania, 1777 ***4629.10*** *p6*
Hazelwood, John 70; Ontario, 1871 ***1823.15*** *p109*
Hazelwood, Thomas; Pennsylvania, 1777 ***4629.10*** *p6*
Hazen, Cornelia M.; Vermont, 1845-1932 ***5900.10*** *p517*
Hazen, Hulda A.; Vermont, 1823-1879 ***5900.10*** *p375*
Hazlet, James; Pennsylvania, 1787 ***4629.10*** *p50*
Hazlet, William; New York, 1840 ***8197.10*** *p171*
Hazletine, Charles 16; Philadelphia, 1774 ***1220.25*** *p43*
Hazleton, Edward; New York, 1821 ***8197.10*** *p237*
Hazleton, Hamilton; Pennsylvania, 1778 ***4629.10*** *p45*
Hazleton, William; Virginia, 1766 ***1224.2*** *p55*
Hazlett, John 28; New York, 1833-1840 ***8197.10*** *p173*
Hazlett, Matthew; New York, 1840 ***8197.10*** *p321*
Hazlewood, George C. 36; Ontario, 1871 ***1823.28*** *p39*
Hazlewood, Robert 25; Maryland, 1774 ***1220.25*** *p46*
Hazlewood, Thomas 16; Philadelphia, 1774 ***1220.25*** *p35*
Hazzard, A. W. 4; Ontario, 1861 ***2896.28*** *p13*
Hazzard, Edna J. Larkin; Vermont, 1857-1914 ***5900.10*** *p492*
Hazzard, Lot 16; Ontario, 1861 ***2896.28*** *p13*
Hea, Charles; Maryland, 1674 ***2524.55*** *p105*
Heaber, Charley 30; Kansas, 1906-1910 ***9079.10*** *p39*
Heaber, Dora 62; Kansas, 1906-1910 ***9079.10*** *p39*
Heabley, Miss; Portland, Maine, 1857 ***9196.15*** *p13*
Heackes, Robert; Virginia, 1667 ***6212.30*** *p37*
Heacock, Peter; Pennsylvania, 1837 ***1224.3*** *p35*
Head, A. 23; Ontario, 1861 ***2896.28*** *p1*
Head, A. M. 1; Ontario, 1861 ***2896.28*** *p1*
Head, George; Philadelphia, 1734 ***1224.2*** *p54*
Head, James; Virginia, 1702 ***6212.30*** *p62*
Head, Jane 22; Ontario, 1861 ***2896.28*** *p38*
Head, Jane 42; Ontario, 1861 ***2896.28*** *p39*
Head, Jno; Virginia, 1665-1666 ***6212.30*** *p22*
Head, John; Maryland, 1668 ***2524.55*** *p106*
Head, John; Pennsylvania, 1779 ***4629.10*** *p38*
Head, John; Virginia, 1666-1667 ***6212.30*** *p32*
Head, John 17; Virginia, 1774 ***1220.25*** *p88*
Head, Joseph; Maryland, 1654 ***2524.55*** *p106*
Head, Margaret 45; Ontario, 1871 ***1823.22*** *p71*
Head, Rich; Virginia, 1664 ***6212.30*** *p13*
Head, Samuel; Pennsylvania, 1777 ***4629.10*** *p29*
Head, Thomas; Maryland, 1649 ***2524.55*** *p106*
Head, William; America, 1834 ***1224.3*** *p35*
Head, William 23; Maryland, 1774 ***1220.25*** *p39*
Headland, John; Maryland, 1664 ***2524.55*** *p106*
Headley, Isabella 38; Ontario, 1871 ***1823.15*** *p109*
Headlund, C. 34; Alaska, 1918 ***9196.1*** *p55*
Headlund, C. 34; Whitehorse, Yukon, 1918 ***9196.1*** *p55*
Headlund, C. 41; Alaska, 1918 ***9196.1*** *p55*
Headlund, C. 41; British Columbia, 1918 ***9196.1*** *p55*
Headrick, Dugal 20; Ontario, 1871 ***1823.28*** *p39*
Headrick, James 61; Ontario, 1871 ***1823.28*** *p39*
Headrick, John 51; Ontario, 1871 ***1823.28*** *p39*
Headrick, William 56; Ontario, 1871 ***1823.28*** *p39*
Heafford, Samuel; New York, 1834 ***8197.10*** *p373*
Heal, Charles; Illinois, 1854 ***1224.3*** *p35*
Heal, James 37; Ontario, 1871 ***1823.22*** *p71*
Heal, Job 77; Ontario, 1871 ***1823.22*** *p71*
Heal, William; Baltimore, 1833 ***1224.3*** *p35*
Heale, George; Rappahannock, Virginia, 1709 ***1224.2*** *p54*
Heale, James 39; Ontario, 1871 ***1823.15*** *p109*
Heale, Mathew; Virginia, 1666-1667 ***6212.30*** *p32*
Healey, . . .; New Hampshire, 1641-1660 ***4628.40*** *p44*
Healey, Ann Bruen; Vermont, 1812-1863 ***5900.10*** *p430*
Healey, Bridget; Vermont, 1828-1916 ***5900.10*** *p430*
Healey, Harriet 38; Vermont, 1859 ***5900.10*** *p598*
Healey, James 40; Ontario, 1871 ***1823.22*** *p71*
Healey, Jeremiah 79; Vermont, 1883 ***5900.10*** *p347*
Healey, John; Vermont, 1811-1888 ***5900.10*** *p430*
Healey, John; Vermont, 1843-1901 ***5900.10*** *p430*
Healey, Margaret; Vermont, 1839-1926 ***5900.10*** *p400*
Healey, Mary 80; Vermont, 1895 ***5900.10*** *p418*
Healey, Nathan; Canada, 1756-1760 ***4628.40*** *p46*
Healey, Patrick; New York, 1827 ***8197.10*** *p240*
Healey, Paul; Nova Scotia, 1745 ***4628.40*** *p45*
Healey, Thomas; Vermont, 1844-1862 ***5900.10*** *p430*
Healey, Thomas 38; Ontario, 1871 ***1823.28*** *p39*
Healy, Anna J.; Vermont, 1857-1884 ***5900.10*** *p82*
Healy, Annie Manion; Vermont, 1861-1910 ***5900.10*** *p588*
Healy, Bridget 50; Ontario, 1871 ***1823.28*** *p39*
Healy, Catherine; Vermont, 1848-1917 ***5900.10*** *p129*
Healy, Dennis; New York, 1802 ***8197.10*** *p21*
Healy, Edward; New York, 1828-1834 ***8197.10*** *p304*
Healy, Edward; Vermont, 1841-1926 ***5900.10*** *p546*
Healy, Ellen; Vermont, 1848-1924 ***5900.10*** *p132*
Healy, James; New York, 1825 ***8197.10*** *p239*
Healy, James; New York, 1828 ***8197.10*** *p64*
Healy, Jeremiah; Vermont, 1830-1903 ***5900.10*** *p427*
Healy, Johannah; Vermont, 1836-1915 ***5900.10*** *p427*
Healy, John; Albany, New York, 1831 ***1224.3*** *p36*
Healy, John; New York, 1837 ***8197.10*** *p90*
Healy, John; Vermont, 1841-1917 ***5900.10*** *p551*
Healy, John 37; Vermont, 1880 ***5900.10*** *p546*
Healy, John M. 79; Vermont, 1918 ***5900.10*** *p89*
Healy, Margaret McGinnis; Vermont, 1843-1911 ***5900.10*** *p546*
Healy, Mary; Vermont, 1793-1881 ***5900.10*** *p83*
Healy, Mary Brennan 88; Vermont, 1881 ***5900.10*** *p89*
Healy, Mary Erwin 79; Vermont, 1915 ***5900.10*** *p89*
Healy, Mary Harrington; Vermont, 1840-1910 ***5900.10*** *p551*
Healy, Owen; New York, 1827 ***8197.10*** *p340*
Healy, Patrick; New York, 1831 ***8197.10*** *p365*
Healy, Patrick; New York, 1831 ***8197.10*** *p370*
Healy, Patrick; Vermont, 1830-1918 ***5900.10*** *p47*
Healy, Patrick; Vermont, 1857-1940 ***5900.10*** *p588*
Healy, Patrick 35; Ontario, 1871 ***1823.28*** *p39*
Healy, Thomas 71; Ontario, 1871 ***1823.15*** *p109*
Healy, William; New York, 1783 ***1224.2*** *p54*
Heaman, Jeremiah 37; Ontario, 1871 ***1823.15*** *p109*
Heaman, William 46; Ontario, 1871 ***1823.15*** *p109*
Heamans, James; Virginia, 1666-1667 ***6212.30*** *p34*
Heanes, James; Pennsylvania, 1777 ***4629.10*** *p20*
Heaney, Patrick 42; Alaska, 1913 ***9196.1*** *p22*
Heaney, Patrick 42; British Columbia, 1913 ***9196.1*** *p22*
Heaney, Thomas; New York, 1838 ***8197.10*** *p117*
Heaney, William; New York, 1825 ***8197.10*** *p239*
Heany, Thomas 43; Ontario, 1871 ***1823.28*** *p39*
Heap, John 15; Philadelphia, 1774 ***1220.25*** *p81*
Heaphy, Bridged; Vermont, 1829-1912 ***5900.10*** *p119*
Heaphy, Catherine Fleming; Vermont, 1840-1895 ***5900.10*** *p116*
Heaphy, Lawrence; Vermont, 1835-1910 ***5900.10*** *p116*
Heapy, John; Philadelphia, 1809 ***1224.3*** *p36*
Heapy, John 31; Ontario, 1871 ***1823.15*** *p109*
Heapy, John 50; Ontario, 1871 ***1823.15*** *p109*
Heapy, William 59; Ontario, 1871 ***1823.15*** *p109*
Heard, James 50; Ontario, 1871 ***1823.15*** *p109*
Heard, John; Alabama, 1823-1845 ***1640.10*** *p78*
Heard, John; Maryland, 1667 ***2524.55*** *p106*
Heard, John; Maryland, 1668 ***2524.55*** *p106*
Heard, John; Pennsylvania, 1779 ***4629.10*** *p41*
Heard, John 21; Maryland, 1774 ***1220.25*** *p77*
Heard, Jos; Virginia, 1672 ***6212.30*** *p50*
Heard, Thomas; Alabama, 1825-1845 ***1640.10*** *p78*
Heard, Thomas; Alabama, 1827-1845 ***1640.10*** *p78*
Heare, Mary; Vermont, 1853-1929 ***5900.10*** *p601*
Hearle, Edw; Virginia, 1666 ***6212.30*** *p30*
Hearle, Francis; Virginia, 1666 ***6212.30*** *p30*
Hearle, Thomas; Virginia, 1666 ***6212.30*** *p28*
Hearn, Anthony; Philadelphia Co., Pennsylvania, 1818 ***1224.3*** *p36*
Hearn, Patrick; New York, 1840 ***8197.10*** *p174*
Hearn, Rose 70; Vermont, 1884 ***5900.10*** *p289*
Hearn, Thomas; New York, 1807 ***8197.10*** *p39*
Hearnden, William 22; Maryland, 1774 ***1220.25*** *p59*
Hearne, Bridget Folliard 72; Vermont, 1909 ***5900.10*** *p605*
Hearne, Dolly Horan 80; Vermont, 1869 ***5900.10*** *p605*
Hearne, John 36; Vermont, 1855 ***5900.10*** *p605*
Hearne, Michael 78; Vermont, 1876 ***5900.10*** *p605*
Hearne, Nicholas; Maine, 1740-1750 ***4628.40*** *p77*
Hearne, Peter; Carolina, 1696 ***1224.1*** *p29*
Hearne, Thomas 42; Vermont, 1862 ***5900.10*** *p605*
Hearns, Michael J.; Vermont, 1826-1913 ***5900.10*** *p468*
Hearns, Winifred D.; Vermont, 1837-1921 ***5900.10*** *p468*
Hearsfield, William; New York, 1805 ***8197.10*** *p29*
Hearsum, Elizabeth; Illinois, 1844 ***1224.3*** *p36*
Hearsum, Mary; Illinois, 1844 ***1224.3*** *p36*
Hearsy, Gerrvis 32; Ontario, 1871 ***1823.28*** *p39*
Heart, John 2; Ontario, 1861 ***2896.25*** *p62*
Heart, John 40; Ontario, 1871 ***1823.15*** *p109*
Heart, Lora 23; Ontario, 1861 ***2896.25*** *p62*
Heart, Mary 57; Ontario, 1861 ***2896.25*** *p62*
Heart, Patrick; New York, 1825-1828 ***8197.10*** *p304*
Heart, William 10; Ontario, 1861 ***2896.25*** *p62*
Heart, William 48; Ontario, 1871 ***1823.28*** *p39*
Hearthe, James Thomas; New York, 1806 ***8197.10*** *p31*
Heartley, Jane 10; Ontario, 1861 ***2896.25*** *p65*
Heartley, Susan 13; Ontario, 1861 ***2896.25*** *p65*
Heartly, Hannah 13; Ontario, 1861 ***2896.25*** *p71*
Heartly, Jane 8; Ontario, 1861 ***2896.25*** *p71*
Heartly, Robert 1; Ontario, 1861 ***2896.25*** *p71*
Heartly, Rose 6; Ontario, 1861 ***2896.25*** *p71*
Heartly, Susan 40; Ontario, 1861 ***2896.25*** *p71*
Hearty, Mr.; Quebec, 1856 ***9196.15*** *p5*
Hearty, Thomas; New York, 1840 ***8197.10*** *p172*
Heaslip, John 55; Ontario, 1871 ***1823.22*** *p71*
Heason, Miss G. H.; Quebec, 1858 ***9196.15*** *p47*
Heast, Daniell; Maryland, 1666 ***2524.55*** *p244*
Heates, Thomas 16; Maryland, 1773-1774 ***1220.25*** *p33*
Heath, Abraham; Virginia, 1664 ***6212.30*** *p6*
Heath, Agness 83; Ontario, 1871 ***1823.22*** *p71*
Heath, Edward; Virginia, 1664 ***6212.30*** *p11*
Heath, Elizabeth; Maryland, 1673 ***2524.55*** *p106*
Heath, Elizabeth 50; Ontario, 1871 ***1823.22*** *p71*
Heath, Francis; Virginia, 1664 ***6212.30*** *p12*
Heath, Henry; Fredericksburg, Virginia, 1772 ***1224.2*** *p54*
Heath, James 27; Vermont, 1864 ***5900.10*** *p202*
Heath, Jane; Maryland, 1677-1681 ***2524.55*** *p106*
Heath, Jno; Virginia, 1664 ***6212.30*** *p12*
Heath, Jno; Virginia, 1665-1666 ***6212.30*** *p22*
Heath, John; Maryland, 1658 ***2524.55*** *p106*
Heath, John; Quebec, 1858 ***9196.15*** *p31*
Heath, John F.; Vermont, 1839-1888 ***5900.10*** *p616*
Heath, Joseph 51; Ontario, 1871 ***1823.28*** *p39*
Heath, Joseph Thomas; Oregon, 1851 ***1224.3*** *p36*
Heath, Rich; Virginia, 1664 ***6212.30*** *p9*
Heath, Richard; Virginia, 1667-1668 ***6212.30*** *p38*
Heath, Robert; Virginia, 1664 ***6212.30*** *p14*
Heath, Robt; Virginia, 1665-1666 ***6212.30*** *p22*
Heath, Robt; Virginia, 1666-1667 ***6212.30*** *p32*
Heath, Sara; Virginia, 1666 ***6212.30*** *p31*
Heath, Thomas; Maryland, 1672 ***2524.55*** *p106*
Heath, Thomas; Maryland, 1677 ***2524.55*** *p106*
Heath, Thomas; Virginia, 1667 ***6212.30*** *p37*
Heath, William; New York, 1839 ***8197.10*** *p132*
Heath, William; New York, New York, 1789 ***1224.2*** *p54*
Heathcoate, Elizabeth; Maryland, 1676 ***2524.55*** *p106*
Heathcoate, Nathaniel; Maryland, 1676 ***2524.55*** *p106*
Heathcot, Nathaniell; Maryland, 1664 ***2524.55*** *p106*
Heathcote, Edward 41; Ontario, 1871 ***1823.22*** *p71*
Heathcote, Elizabeth; New York, 1736 ***1224.2*** *p54*
Heathcote, Emma 31; Ontario, 1871 ***1823.22*** *p71*
Heathcote, Gilbert; New York, 1731 ***1224.2*** *p54*
Heathcote, John; Baltimore, 1814 ***1224.3*** *p36*
Heathcote, Martha; New York, 1731 ***1224.2*** *p54*
Heathcote, Mary; New York, 1731 ***1224.2*** *p54*
Heathcote, Nathaniel; Maryland, 1682 ***1224.1*** *p29*
Heathcote, William; New York, 1723 ***1224.2*** *p54*
Heathcote, William; New York, 1736 ***1224.2*** *p54*
Heathcott, Andrew; Maryland, 1681 ***2524.55*** *p106*
Heathcott, Elizabeth; Maryland, 1676 ***2524.55*** *p106*
Heathcott, Hannah *SEE* Heathcott, Thomas
Heathcott, Johanna; Maryland, 1682 ***2524.55*** *p106*
Heathcott, Nathaniel; Maryland, 1676 ***2524.55*** *p106*
Heathcott, Nathaniell; Maryland, 1664 ***2524.55*** *p106*
Heathcott, Thomas; Maryland, 1663 ***2524.55*** *p106*
Wife: Hannah
Heathcott, William; Maryland, 1682 ***2524.55*** *p106*
Heatherly, Thomas 42; Ontario, 1871 ***1823.22*** *p71*
Heathley, Elizabeth; Maryland, 1681 ***2524.55*** *p106*
Heathman, Anne; Maryland, 1680 ***2524.55*** *p106*
Heatlie, William 39; Ontario, 1871 ***1823.22*** *p71*
Heatly, Edward; San Francisco, 1899 ***1640.13*** *p54*
Heaton, Mr.; Quebec, 1858 ***9196.15*** *p46*
Heaverill, Joseph; Pennsylvania, 1785 ***4629.10*** *p49*
Heavey, Catherine A. Hayes; Vermont, 1855-1915 ***5900.10*** *p339*
Heavey, James 62; Ontario, 1871 ***1823.28*** *p39*
Heavey, William H.; Vermont, 1855-1945 ***5900.10*** *p339*
Heayn, James 32; Ontario, 1871 ***1823.15*** *p109*
Hebblethwait, John 42; Ontario, 1871 ***1823.15*** *p109*
Hebden, Katherine; Maryland, 1631-1685 ***2524.55*** *p106*
Hebden, Thomas; Maryland, 1635 ***2524.55*** *p106*
Hebener, Johann Wendel; Port uncertain, 1751 ***2856.30*** *p170*

Heber, Augustus J.; New York, 1839 8197.10 p242
Hebert, Celesta; Vermont, 1860-1924 5900.10 p108
Hebert, Elizabeth Doon; Vermont, 1858-1912 5900.10 p512
Hebert, John; New York, 1807 8197.10 p40
Hebron, Miss; Quebec, 1858 9196.15 p43
Hechler, Gorg; America, 1754 2856.30 p170
With 5 children
Hechler, Hans George; America, 1754 2856.30 p170
Hecht, Anton; America, 1754 2856.30 p170
Hecht, Anton; Port uncertain, 1754 2856.30 p170
Heck, . . .; Port uncertain, 1771 2856.30 p170
Heck, A. Elis. Barbara; Port uncertain, 1786 2856.30 p170
Heck, Caspar; Port uncertain, 1771 2856.30 p170
Heck, Hiob; Port uncertain, 1735 2856.30 p170
Heck, Marg. Barbara; America, 1783 2856.30 p170
Heck, Philipp; Port uncertain, 1752 2856.30 p170
Heckel, Johann; America, 1752 2856.30 p171
With wife & 2 children
Hecket, Alexander 48; Ontario, 1871 1823.15 p109
Hecket, Andrew 83; Ontario, 1871 1823.15 p109
Heckh, Josef; Port uncertain, 1745 2856.30 p171
Heckie, Jane 46; Ontario, 1871 1823.15 p109
Hecking, James 60; Ontario, 1871 1823.28 p39
Heckmann, Caspar; America, 1751 2856.30 p171
With wife & children
Heckmann, Catharina; America, 1754 2856.30 p171
With 4 children
Heckmann, Catharina; America, 1781 2856.30 p171
Heckmann, Catharina; Port uncertain, 1748 2856.30 p171
Heckmann, Hans Adam; America, 1752 2856.30 p171
Heckmann, Konrad; America, 1765 2856.30 p171
Heckmann, Konrad; America, 1781 2856.30 p171
Heckmann, Konrad; Port uncertain, 1748 2856.30 p171
Heckmann, Konrad; Port uncertain, 1765 2856.30 p171
Heckmann, Niklas; America, 1752 2856.30 p171
Hedden, Samuel 31; Ontario, 1871 1823.15 p109
Hedderwick, John; Georgia, 1698 1640.13 p54
Hedderwick, William; Georgia, 1699 1640.13 p55
Heddle, Mrs.; Quebec, 1856 9196.15 p11
Heddle, Alexander; Savannah, Georgia, 1774 1640.10 p79
Heddle, R.; Quebec, 1856 9196.15 p11
Hedegar, Jacob 35; Ontario, 1871 1823.15 p110
Heden, William 52; Ontario, 1871 1823.15 p110
Hederich, Maria Elisabeth; America, 1789 2856.30 p171
Hedge, Thomas; Maryland, 1671 2524.55 p106
Hedge, Thomas; Maryland, 1676 2524.55 p106
Hedger, Ralph; Virginia, 1666-1667 6212.30 p35
Hedger, William 27; Ontario, 1871 1823.22 p71
Hedges, John; Maryland, 1681 2524.55 p106
Hedges, Richard; Virginia, 1690-1691 6212.30 p59
Hedges, Thomas; Maryland, 1666 2524.55 p179
Hedges, Thomas; Wilmington, North Carolina, 1769 1224.2 p55
Hedican, Edward 40; Ontario, 1871 1823.28 p39
Hedrick, Conrad; New York, 1840 8197.10 p171
Hedwiczarski, Martin; Maryland, 1910 3259.35 p19
Hedzel, Sebastian; Maryland, 1910 3259.35 p20
Heeckmann, Maria Elisabeth; Port uncertain, 1766 2856.30 p171
Heeds, Mary 19; Maryland, 1775 1220.25 p102
Heeger, David; Port uncertain, 1762 2856.30 p171
Heenan, James 39; Ontario, 1871 1823.28 p39
Heenan, Thomas 42; Ontario, 1871 1823.28 p39
Heenan, Thomas 68; Ontario, 1871 1823.22 p71
Heeney, John; Albany, New York, 1833 8197.10 p311
Heeny, John; Pennsylvania, 1786 4629.10 p50
Heer, Michael; Port uncertain, 1770 2856.30 p171
Heere, Richard; Maryland, 1666 2524.55 p106
Heerwagen, Elias G.; New York, 1827-1834 8197.10 p305
Heerwagen, Elias G.; New York, 1831 8197.10 p240
Hees, Wilhelm; Port uncertain, 1845 2856.30 p171
Heese, Elisabeth; Port uncertain, 1750 2856.30 p171
Heet, Edward 42; Ontario, 1871 1823.22 p71
Hefern, Patrick 65; Ontario, 1871 1823.15 p110
Heffel, David 24; Kansas, 1907-1910 9079.10 p18
Heffel, Mollie 23; Kansas, 1907-1910 9079.10 p18
Heffeler, Karl; America, 1737 2856.30 p171
Hefferman, Anne; Portland, Maine, 1858 9196.15 p28
Hefferman, Bridget; Vermont, 1837-1897 5900.10 p380
Heffern, Mr.; Vermont, 1835-1918 5900.10 p254
Heffern, Mrs.; Vermont, 1820-1910 5900.10 p254
Heffern, Ann 62; Vermont, 1906 5900.10 p254
Heffern, Ella; Vermont, 1858-1934 5900.10 p254
Heffern, Michael 76; Vermont, 1915 5900.10 p254
Heffernan, Daniel; Vermont, 1848-1930 5900.10 p444
Heffernan, John; New York, 1803 8197.10 p13
Heffernan, John; New York, 1821 8197.10 p237
Heffernan, Julia; Vermont, 1822-1912 5900.10 p551
Heffernan, Kevin P.; Vermont, 1902-1959 5900.10 p126
Heffernan, Mary A. McCarthy; Vermont, 1854-1928 5900.10 p444
Heffernan, Zita M. Lafayette; Vermont, 1898-1974 5900.10 p126
Heffle, David 65; Kansas, 1906-1910 9079.10 p8
Heffle, Elizabeth 65; Kansas, 1906-1910 9079.10 p8
Heffle, John 20; Kansas, 1906-1910 9079.10 p8
Heffle, Julia 39; Kansas, 1906-1910 9079.10 p8
Heffle, Mike 39; Kansas, 1906-1910 9079.10 p8
Heffle, Molly 18; Kansas, 1907-1910 9079.10 p8
Heffle, Robert 11; Kansas, 1906-1910 9079.10 p8
Heffle, Rosa 13; Kansas, 1906-1910 9079.10 p8
Heffle, Victor 8; Kansas, 1906-1910 9079.10 p8
Heffler, Christopher 78; Ontario, 1871 1823.15 p110
Heffley, Karl; America, 1737 2856.30 p171
Hefford, Charles 13; Ontario, 1871 1823.15 p110
Hefford, Mary Eliz 14; Ontario, 1871 1823.15 p110
Hefford, Sarah 17; Ontario, 1871 1823.15 p110
Heffron, Bridget; Vermont, 1828-1908 5900.10 p107
Heffron, Catherine; Vermont, 1829-1897 5900.10 p116
Heffron, Catherine 70; Vermont, 1907 5900.10 p539
Heffron, Martin 50; Ontario, 1871 1823.22 p71
Heffron, Mary 75; Vermont, 1931 5900.10 p106
Heffron, Robert 68; Vermont, 1885 5900.10 p107
Hefft, Georg; America, 1737 2856.30 p171
Hefft, Georg; America, 1737 2856.30 p171
With wife & children
Hefft, Hans Adam; Port uncertain, 1764 2856.30 p171
With wife & 4 children
Hefft, Michael; Port uncertain, 1764 2856.30 p171
Hefft, Philipp; America, 1737 2856.30 p171
Heflinger, Elisabeth; Port uncertain, 1769 2856.30 p171
Hegan, Martin; New York, 1834 8197.10 p372
Hegarty, Mr.; Quebec, 1858 9196.15 p37
Hegarty, James 41; Ontario, 1861 2896.25 p16
Hegel, Frederick 34; New York, 1827-1838 8197.10 p115
Hegel, Hans Georg; America, 1732 2856.30 p171
Hegel, Jakob; America, 1732 2856.30 p171
Hegen, Anna Maria; Port uncertain, 1744 2856.30 p171
Hegener, Johann Peter; America, 1740 2856.30 p171
Hegener, Peter; Port uncertain, 1764 2856.30 p171
Heger, Georg; Port uncertain, 1756 2856.30 p160
Heger, Georg Adam; Port uncertain, 1753 2856.30 p171
Heger, Valentin; Port uncertain, 1791 2856.30 p171
Heggelbach, Barbara; Port uncertain, 1612 2856.30 p172
With husband
Heggins, John; Maryland, 1681 2524.55 p106
Hegler, Jacob; America, 1752 2856.30 p172
With wife & children
Hegner, Johann Peter; America, 1740 2856.30 p172
Hegner, Peter; Pennsylvania, 1777 4629.10 p8
Heheir, Catherine 75; Vermont, 1903 5900.10 p428
Hehir, Bridget 88; Vermont, n.d. 5900.10 p204
Hehir, Daniel 62; Vermont, 1896 5900.10 p300
Hehir, Margaret; Vermont, 1839-1919 5900.10 p441
Hehir, Mary 57; Vermont, 1890 5900.10 p300
Hehn, Johann Adam; Port uncertain, 1771 2856.30 p172
Hehn, Johann Jacob; America, 1744 2856.30 p172
Hehn, Johann Peter; America, 1741 2856.30 p172
Hehn, Johann Peter; America, 1744 2856.30 p172
Hehn, Matheis; America, 1744 2856.30 p172
Heibes, Elizabeth; Mississippi, 1829-1845 1640.10 p79
Heicks, Edward 24; Ontario, 1871 1823.28 p39
Heid, Johann Jacob; Port uncertain, 1776 2856.30 p172
Heid, Johann Michael; America, 1743-1799 2856.30 p172
Heid, Johann Michael; America, 1753 2856.30 p172
Heid, Maria Sophia; Port uncertain, 1788 2856.30 p172
Heid, Valentin; Port uncertain, 1752 2856.30 p172
Heidecker, Johann; Port uncertain, 1741 2856.30 p172
Heidecker, Johann; Port uncertain, 1771 2856.30 p172
Heidegger, Gustave; New York, 1840 8197.10 p174
Heidele, Johann; Port uncertain, 1751 2856.30 p172
Heiderich, Henrich Nickel; America, 1767 2856.30 p187
Heiderich, Henrich Nickel; America, 1775 2856.30 p187
Heiderich, Henrich Nickel; Port uncertain, 1767 2856.30 p187
Heiderich, Henrich Nickel; Port uncertain, 1787 2856.30 p187
Heiderich, Henrich Nickel; Port uncertain, 1792 2856.30 p187
Heiderich, Maria Elisabeth; Port uncertain, 1783 2856.30 p172
Heiderich, Peter; Port uncertain, 1783 2856.30 p172
With family
Heiderick, Frederick 56; Ontario, 1871 1823.15 p110
Heidlauff, Margarete; Port uncertain, 1614 2856.30 p172
Heidrich, Peter; Port uncertain, 1741 2856.30 p172
With family
Heidrick, Frederick 25; Ontario, 1871 1823.15 p110
Heiffele, Eva 20; Kansas, 1910 9079.10 p51
Heiffele, Reinhardt 22; Kansas, 1910 9079.10 p51
Heiffron, Patrick M.; New York, 1836 8197.10 p77
Heig, Emanuel; America, 1787 2856.30 p172
With family
Heig, Emanuel; Port uncertain, 1763 2856.30 p172
With family
Heigh, Mary *SEE* Heigh, Robert
Heigh, Robert; Maryland, 1659 2524.55 p106
Heigh, Robert; Maryland, 1663 2524.55 p106
Wife: Mary
Height, William; New York, 1840 8197.10 p242
Heighway, John; New Orleans, 1851 1224.3 p36
Heikkela, A. 43; Alaska, 1917 9196.1 p53
Heikkela, A. 43; Whitehorse, Yukon, 1917 9196.1 p53
Heil, Georg; Port uncertain, 1764 2856.30 p172
Heil, Johann; Port uncertain, 1780 2856.30 p173
Heilbronn, Adolph; New York, 1827 8197.10 p240
Heilbronn, Adolph; New York, 1831 8197.10 p67
Heile, Michael; America, 1750 2856.30 p173
Heiler, Frederick; Pennsylvania, 1777 4629.10 p18
Heilmann, Andreas; America, 1736 2856.30 p173
Heilmann, Anna Maria; America, 1744 2856.30 p173
Heilmann, Catharina; Port uncertain, 1764 2856.30 p173
Heilmann, Christoph; Pennsylvania, 1850 6058.10 p26
Heilmann, Kunigunde; Port uncertain, 1764 2856.30 p173
Heilmann, Valentin; America, 1736 2856.30 p173
Heim, . . .; America, 1752 2856.30 p173
Heim, Georg; Port uncertain, 1774 2856.30 p173
Heim, Georg Veit; America, 1736 2856.30 p173
With wife 5 sons & 3 daughters
Heim, Johann Georg; America, 1753 2856.30 p173
With wife & children
Heim, Sus. Catharina; America, 1736 2856.30 p173
With husband 5 sons & 3 daughters
Heim, Theobald; Port uncertain, 1775 2856.30 p173
Heiman, Isaac; New York, New York, 1860 6058.10 p49
Heimbacher, Frederick 44; Ontario, 1871 1823.15 p110
Heimberger, Carl Gustav; New York, 1833 8197.10 p240
Heimberger, Gottfried; Port uncertain, 1788 2856.30 p173
Heimberger, Maria Elisabeth; Port uncertain, 1749 2856.30 p173
Heimberger, Nikolaus; Port uncertain, 1783 2856.30 p173
Heimberger, Nikolaus; Port uncertain, 1788 2856.30 p173
Heimburger, Barbara; Port uncertain, 1796 2856.30 p173
Heimey, John; New York, New York, 1840 3437.14 p47
Heimfahrt, Claudius; Port uncertain, 1768 2856.30 p173
Heimlich, Johann Andreas; America, 1782 2856.30 p173
Hein, Andreas; Port uncertain, 1775 2856.30 p173
Hein, Elisabeth; Port uncertain, 1775 2856.30 p173
Hein, Ernest Henry 37; Ontario, 1871 1823.28 p39
Hein, Ludovika; Port uncertain, 1771 2856.30 p173
Hein, Maria Anna; Port uncertain, 1790 2856.30 p173
Heinberger, Jakob; America, 1751 2856.30 p173
Heindrick, Adam 16; New York, 1775 1220.25 p95
Heine, Hans Michael; Port uncertain, 1781 2856.30 p173
Heine, Ludovika; Port uncertain, 1771 2856.30 p173
Heineman, Alexander; New York, 1838 8197.10 p118
Heinemann, Franz; Port uncertain, 1793 2856.30 p174
Heinemann, Fritz; Port uncertain, 1793 2856.30 p174
Heinemann, Johann Adam; New York, 1836 8197.10 p240
Heinemann, Peter; Port uncertain, 1785 2856.30 p174
With wife
Heiner, Urban; America, 1751 2856.30 p174
With wife
Heiner, Urban; America, 1789 2856.30 p174
Heinig, Miss; America, 1751 2856.30 p38
Heinitz, Anna 69; Kansas, 1907-1910 9079.10 p41
Heinitz, Catharine 47; Kansas, 1910 9079.10 p15
Heinitz, George 33; Kansas, 1907-1910 9079.10 p41
Heinitz, George 47; Kansas, 1891-1910 9079.10 p14
Heinitz, Louise 31; Kansas, 1906-1910 9079.10 p41
Heinitz, Maria 18; Kansas, 1910 9079.10 p15
Heinitze, Amelia 15; Kansas, 1907-1910 9079.10 p16
Heinitze, Anna 20; Kansas, 1907-1910 9079.10 p16
Heinitze, Catherine 44; Kansas, 1907-1910 9079.10 p16
Heinitze, Frederic 17; Kansas, 1907-1910 9079.10 p16
Heinitze, Frederic 45; Kansas, 1907-1910 9079.10 p16
Heinle, Anna 18; Kansas, 1908-1910 9079.10 p18
Heinle, David J. 22; Kansas, 1891-1910 9079.10 p18
Heinle, Michael; America, 1750 2856.30 p173
Heinnich, Maria Barbara; Port uncertain, 1746 2856.30 p174
Heinrich, Andreas; Port uncertain, 1700-1799 2856.30 p174
Heinrich, Catharina; America, 1786 2856.30 p174
Heinrich, Christian; America, 1741 2856.30 p174
Heinrich, Christian; America, 1756 2856.30 p174
Heinrich, Christian; Port uncertain, 1752 2856.30 p174

Heinrich, Christian; Port uncertain, 1755 ***2856.30 p174***
Heinrich, Daniel; Port uncertain, 1792 ***2856.30 p174***
Heinrich, Elisabeth; Port uncertain, 1733 ***2856.30 p174***
Heinrich, Georg; America, 1786 ***2856.30 p174***
Heinrich, Hans; Port uncertain, 1768 ***2856.30 p174***
Heinrich, Jacob; Port uncertain, 1784 ***2856.30 p174***
Heinrich, Johann; America, 1786 ***2856.30 p174***
Heinrich, Johann Jacob; America, 1786 ***2856.30 p174***
Heinrich, Josef; Port uncertain, 1796 ***2856.30 p174***
Heinrich, Maria; America, 1752 ***2856.30 p174***
Heins, Carl 33; Seattle, 1912 ***9196.1 p20***
Heins, Christof; Port uncertain, 1736 ***2856.30 p174***
Heins, Robert 32; Seattle, 1912 ***9196.1 p20***
Heinse, Emil 34; Ontario, 1871 ***1823.28 p39***
Heintz, Anna Maria; Port uncertain, 1742 ***2856.30 p174***
Heintz, Anton Christian; Port uncertain, 1745 ***2856.30 p174***
Heintz, Burkhard; Port uncertain, 1745 ***2856.30 p174***
Heintz, Daniel; Port uncertain, 1732 ***2856.30 p174***
Heintz, Elisabeth; Port uncertain, 1775 ***2856.30 p174***
Heintz, Jacob; America, 1752 ***2856.30 p175***
With wife & 4 children
Heintz, Johann Georg; Port uncertain, 1741 ***2856.30 p175***
Heintz, Johann Nickel; America, 1755 ***2856.30 p175***
Heintz, Johann Nickel; Port uncertain, 1713 ***2856.30 p175***
Heintz, Peter; Port uncertain, 1748 ***2856.30 p175***
With 2 sons
Heintz, Philipp Jacob; Port uncertain, 1784 ***2856.30 p175***
With wife & son
Heintzen, Zetta 34; Alaska, 1914 ***9196.1 p23***
Heinz, Agnes; Port uncertain, 1774 ***2856.30 p175***
Heinz, Franz Anton; Port uncertain, 1783 ***2856.30 p175***
Heinz, Johann Adam; Port uncertain, 1785 ***2856.30 p175***
Heinz, Margarete; Port uncertain, 1796 ***2856.30 p175***
Heinz, Maria Dorothea; Port uncertain, 1777 ***2856.30 p175***
Heinz, Maria Margarete; Port uncertain, 1769 ***2856.30 p175***
Heinz, Maria Sofia; Port uncertain, 1788 ***2856.30 p175***
Heinz, Peter; Port uncertain, 1784 ***2856.30 p175***
Heinz, Sophia; Port uncertain, 1785 ***2856.30 p175***
Heinz, Tobias; Port uncertain, 1786 ***2856.30 p175***
Heinze, Al... 45; Kansas, 1892-1910 ***9079.10 p18***
Heinze, Andrew H. 24; Kansas, 1892-1910 ***9079.10 p15***
Heinze, Catherine 19; Kansas, 1892-1910 ***9079.10 p18***
Heinze, Catherine 27; Kansas, 1910 ***9079.10 p17***
Heinze, Catherine 56; Kansas, 1892-1910 ***9079.10 p15***
Heinze, Christ 20; Kansas, 1906-1910 ***9079.10 p36***
Heinze, Elizabeth 45; Kansas, 1892-1910 ***9079.10 p18***
Heinze, Elizabeth A. 38; Kansas, 1878-1910 ***9079.10 p39***
Heinze, Fred 28; Kansas, 1906-1910 ***9079.10 p9***
Heinze, Fred G. 27; Kansas, 1894-1910 ***9079.10 p17***
Heinze, Frederick 38; Kansas, 1891-1910 ***9079.10 p39***
Heinze, George 4; Kansas, 1906-1910 ***9079.10 p9***
Heinze, George 35; Kansas, 1907-1910 ***9079.10 p17***
Heinze, Katie 25; Kansas, 1906-1910 ***9079.10 p9***
Heinze, Maria 32; Kansas, 1907-1910 ***9079.10 p17***
Heinze, Marie E. 71; Kansas, 1893-1910 ***9079.10 p39***
Heinze, Mary 22; Kansas, 1910 ***9079.10 p51***
Heinze, Mary K. 28; Kansas, 1893-1910 ***9079.10 p37***
Heinze, Mollie 5; Kansas, 1907-1910 ***9079.10 p17***
Heinze, Molly 6; Kansas, 1906-1910 ***9079.10 p9***
Heinze, Peter 55; Kansas, 1875-1910 ***9079.10 p38***
Heinze, Reinhardt 25; Kansas, 1905-1910 ***9079.10 p51***
Heinze, Reinhart 70; Kansas, 1892-1910 ***9079.10 p15***
Heinzel, Andrew 15; Kansas, 1908-1910 ***9079.10 p29***
Heinzel, George Sin 62; Kansas, 1908-1910 ***9079.10 p29***
Heinzel, Mary 60; Kansas, 1908-1910 ***9079.10 p29***
Heinzman, Jacob; New York, New York, 1863 ***3437.14 p83***
Heinzmann, Henry D.; Indiana, 1883-1884 ***3437.14 p195***
Heipel, Paul; America, 1737 ***2856.30 p175***
With family
Heipel, Paul; Port uncertain, 1726 ***2856.30 p175***
With family
Heipel, Paul; Port uncertain, 1727 ***2856.30 p175***
With family
Heipp, Johann Peter; Port uncertain, 1784 ***2856.30 p175***
With wife
Heipp, Peter; Port uncertain, 1741 ***2856.30 p186***
Heipron, John 20; Ontario, 1871 ***1823.22 p71***
Heirer, Eliza; Vermont, 1822-1903 ***5900.10 p200***
Heis, Maria Eulalia; Port uncertain, 1798 ***2856.30 p175***
Heis, Michael; New York, 1836-1838 ***8197.10 p116***
Heiserling, Thomas; Port uncertain, 1764 ***2856.30 p175***
Heiss, Friedrich; Port uncertain, 1796 ***2856.30 p175***
Heisser, Mathes; Canada, 1752 ***2856.30 p175***
With wife & 2 children
Heist, August 32; Ontario, 1871 ***1823.15 p110***
Heist, Henry 16; Ontario, 1871 ***1823.15 p110***
Heist, Jacob 43; Ontario, 1871 ***1823.15 p110***
Heist, Mary Ann 74; Ontario, 1871 ***1823.15 p110***
Heit, Jacob; America, 1751 ***2856.30 p175***
Heit, Johann; Port uncertain, 1793 ***2856.30 p175***
Heiterich, Abraham; America, 1739 ***2856.30 p175***
Heiterich, Johann; America, 1739 ***2856.30 p176***
Heiterich, Johann Michael; America, 1739 ***2856.30 p176***
Heitland, Henry 20; Maryland, 1774 ***1220.25 p58***
Heitz, Diebold; Port uncertain, 1762 ***2856.30 p176***
Heitz, Jakob; America, 1733 ***2856.30 p176***
Heitzman, Christian 63; Ontario, 1871 ***1823.15 p110***
Heitzmann, Jacob; Port uncertain, 1788 ***2856.30 p176***
With father
Heix, Michael; Port uncertain, 1766 ***2856.30 p176***
With children
Heiz, Matthias; Port uncertain, 1763 ***2856.30 p176***
Heiz, Peter; Port uncertain, 1784 ***2856.30 p175***
Hejda, Ignacy; Maryland, 1910 ***3259.35 p20***
Helcott, Matthew; New York, 1783 ***1224.2 p55***
Held, Anna Maria; America, 1764 ***2856.30 p176***
With 2 children
Held, Anna Maria; America, 1765 ***2856.30 p176***
With 2 children
Held, Anna Maria; Port uncertain, 1765 ***2856.30 p176***
Held, Christof; Port uncertain, 1750 ***2856.30 p176***
Held, Henrich; Port uncertain, 1768 ***2856.30 p176***
Held, Johann; America, 1764 ***2856.30 p176***
Held, Johann; America, 1765 ***2856.30 p176***
Held, Maria Elisabeth; Port uncertain, 1765 ***2856.30 p176***
Held, Michael; Port uncertain, 1777 ***2856.30 p176***
With wife
Hele, George; Virginia, 1666 ***6212.30 p28***
Hele, Thomas; Virginia, 1666 ***6212.30 p31***
Hele, Warwick; Pennsylvania, 1711 ***1224.2 p54***
Helerby, George 34; Ontario, 1871 ***1823.15 p110***
Heley, John 40; Ontario, 1871 ***1823.22 p71***
Heley, Richard; New York, 1840 ***8197.10 p242***
Heley, William 54; Ontario, 1871 ***1823.22 p71***
Helfensyng, Michael; America, 1739 ***2856.30 p176***
Helfer, Hinton Rowan; America, 1752 ***2856.30 p176***
Helfer, Johann; Port uncertain, 1794 ***2856.30 p176***
Helfer, Margaret 76; Ontario, 1871 ***1823.15 p110***
Helferich, Barbara; America, 1771 ***2856.30 p176***
Helferich, Georg Jacob; Port uncertain, 1745 ***2856.30 p176***
With wife
Helferich, Jakob; Port uncertain, 1769 ***2856.30 p176***
Helferich, Wilhelm; Port uncertain, 1780 ***2856.30 p176***
Helferty, Dennis 51; Ontario, 1871 ***1823.28 p39***
Helferty, John 35; Ontario, 1871 ***1823.28 p39***
Helferty, Patrick 36; Ontario, 1871 ***1823.28 p39***
Helffenstein, Albert Konrad; America, 1700-1799 ***2856.30 p176***
Helffenstein, Nickel; America, 1739 ***2856.30 p176***
With wife & 4 children
Helfferich, Anna Margarete; Port uncertain, 1748 ***2856.30 p176***
Helfferich, Bernhard; Port uncertain, 1765 ***2856.30 p176***
Helfferich, Elisabeth; Port uncertain, 1763 ***2856.30 p176***
Helfferich, Fritz; Port uncertain, 1790 ***2856.30 p176***
Helfferich, Georg Jacob; Port uncertain, 1745 ***2856.30 p177***
With wife
Helfferich, Georg Jacob; Port uncertain, 1748 ***2856.30 p176***
Helfferich, Georg Jakob; Port uncertain, 1784 ***2856.30 p177***
With wife & 5 children
Helfferich, Georg Marx; Port uncertain, 1743 ***2856.30 p176***
Helfferich, Georg Marx; Port uncertain, 1756 ***2856.30 p176***
Helfferich, Johann; Port uncertain, 1786 ***2856.30 p177***
With wife & children
Helfferich, Marx; Port uncertain, 1755 ***2856.30 p177***
Helffrich, Anna Maria; Port uncertain, 1749 ***2856.30 p177***
Helforty, Hugh 63; Ontario, 1871 ***1823.28 p39***
Helfrich, Mr.; Port uncertain, 1786 ***2856.30 p103***
Helfrich, Catharina; Port uncertain, 1772 ***2856.30 p177***
Helfrich, Dorothea; Port uncertain, 1786 ***2856.30 p177***
Helfrich, Maria Elisabeth; Port uncertain, 1787 ***2856.30 p177***
Helft, Lorenz; Cayenne, 1764 ***2856.30 p177***
With wife & children
Helgore, Robert; Maryland, 1680 ***2524.55 p106***
Helicinski, Peter; Maryland, 1910 ***3259.35 p20***
Helinski, John; Maryland, 1910 ***3259.35 p20***
Helinski, Walter; Maryland, 1910 ***3259.35 p20***
Helkowzk, Alex; Maryland, 1910 ***3259.35 p20***
Hell, Ursula; Port uncertain, 1737 ***2856.30 p177***
With husband
Hellam, Peter; Pennsylvania, 1777 ***4629.10 p13***
Helland, Robert 40; Ontario, 1871 ***1823.15 p110***
Helle, Georg; Port uncertain, 1739 ***2856.30 p177***
Hellebran, Konrad; America, 1732 ***2856.30 p177***
Heller, Abraham; New York, 1797 ***8197.10 p8***
Heller, Anna Elisabeth; Port uncertain, 1757 ***2856.30 p177***
Heller, Elis. Catharina; Port uncertain, 1757 ***2856.30 p177***
Heller, Josef; Port uncertain, 1792 ***2856.30 p177***
Heller, Therese; Port uncertain, 1768 ***2856.30 p177***
Hellewell, Mrs.; Quebec, 1858 ***9196.15 p41***
Helley, Clement; Maryland, 1667 ***2524.55 p106***
Helley, David 21; Maryland, 1774 ***1220.25 p39***
Hellfield, J. D.; Portland, Maine, 1858 ***9196.15 p29***
Hellford, Thomas; Virginia, 1667 ***6212.30 p37***
Hellfrich, Johann Henry; America, 1700-1799 ***2856.30 p177***
Hellmann, . . .; America, 1785 ***2856.30 p177***
Hellmann, Christian; Port uncertain, 1746 ***2856.30 p177***
Hellmann, Jakob; America, 1781 ***2856.30 p177***
Hellmann, Valentin; Port uncertain, 1736 ***2856.30 p177***
Hellmuth, Rev.; Quebec, 1858 ***9196.15 p36***
Hellwein, Maria Barbara; Port uncertain, 1730 ***2856.30 p177***
Hellwig, Karl; America, 1749 ***2856.30 p177***
Hellwig, Karl; Port uncertain, 1749 ***2856.30 p177***
With wife & children
Hellwig, Philipp; Port uncertain, 1784 ***2856.30 p177***
Hellwig, Philipp; Port uncertain, 1785 ***2856.30 p177***
Hellwig, Philipp; Port uncertain, 1788 ***2856.30 p177***
Hellwig, Philipp; Port uncertain, 1794 ***2856.30 p177***
Helly, Clement; Maryland, 1675 ***2524.55 p106***
Helm, A. M. Koch *SEE* Helm, Franz
Helm, Andreas; Port uncertain, 1792 ***2856.30 p177***
Helm, Anna Catharina; America, 1787 ***2856.30 p177***
Helm, Anna Catharina; Port uncertain, 1771 ***2856.30 p177***
Helm, Anna Dorothea; Port uncertain, 1733 ***2856.30 p177***
Helm, Daniel; America, 1768 ***2856.30 p177***
Helm, Dorothea Elisab; Port uncertain, 1788 ***2856.30 p177***
Helm, Franz; America, 1768 ***2856.30 p178***
Wife: A. M. Koch
Helm, Franz Nickel; America, 1787 ***2856.30 p177***
Helm, Franz Nickel; Port uncertain, 1771 ***2856.30 p177***
Helm, Joh. Frz. Daniel; America, 1787 ***2856.30 p177***
Helm, Joh. Frz. Daniel; Port uncertain, 1771 ***2856.30 p177***
Helm, John 83; Ontario, 1871 ***1823.22 p71***
Helm, Jos; Quebec, 1856 ***9196.15 p5***
Helm, Maria Dorothea; America, 1772 ***2856.30 p178***
Helm, Maria Dorothea; Port uncertain, 1773 ***2856.30 p178***
Helm, Maria Elisabeth; America, 1787 ***2856.30 p178***
Helm, Maria Elisabeth; Port uncertain, 1771 ***2856.30 p178***
Helm, Maria Elisabeth; Port uncertain, 1790 ***2856.30 p177***
Helm, Sophia 50; Ontario, 1871 ***1823.22 p71***
Helm, Thomas 37; Ontario, 1871 ***1823.15 p110***
Helme, John; New York, 1800 ***8197.10 p9***
Helmer, Edw; Virginia, 1665-1666 ***6212.30 p22***
Helmle, Nikolaus; America, 1751 ***2856.30 p178***
Helmle, Nikolaus; America, 1768 ***2856.30 p178***
Helmling, Maria Martha Grun; Port uncertain, 1791 ***2856.30 p178***
Helmling, Maria Martha Schober; Port uncertain, 1791 ***2856.30 p178***
Helmstadter, Franz Jakob; Port uncertain, 1781 ***2856.30 p178***
Helmstadter, Franz Jakob; Port uncertain, 1785 ***2856.30 p178***
Helowiz, Peter; Maryland, 1910 ***3259.35 p20***
Helper, Hinton Rowan; America, 1752 ***2856.30 p176***
Helps, Elizabeth 46; Ontario, 1871 ***1823.15 p110***
Helps, Hezakiah 48; Ontario, 1871 ***1823.15 p110***
Helsey, Thomas; Maryland, 1668 ***2524.55 p107***
Helson, Thomas 51; Ontario, 1871 ***1823.22 p71***
Helt, John; Pennsylvania, 1777 ***4629.10 p27***
Heltberg, Charles; New York, 1839 ***8197.10 p131***
Helven, Eve Migary 25; Kansas, 1907-1910 ***9079.10 p46***
Helven, George 30; Kansas, 1907-1910 ***9079.10 p46***
Helwig, Anna Catharina; Port uncertain, 1728 ***2856.30 p178***
Hely, Samuel; Maryland, 1670 ***2524.55 p107***
Helzer, H. P. 31; Kansas, 1910 ***9079.10 p45***
Helzer, Lena 24; Kansas, 1910 ***9079.10 p45***
Heman, Anne; Maryland, 1682 ***2524.55 p107***
Heman, Benjamin; Maryland, 1672 ***2524.55 p107***
Hemard, Peter; Virginia, 1719 ***1224.2 p55***
Hembel, Johann; Port uncertain, 1790 ***2856.30 p178***
Hembel, William; Pennsylvania, 1777 ***4629.10 p30***
Hemberger, Maria Barbara; Port uncertain, 1740 ***2856.30 p178***

Hembrowski, Yan; Maryland, 1910 ***3259.35*** *p20*
Hembs, Anna Maria; Port uncertain, 1751 ***2856.30*** *p178*
Hemelmann, Valentin; Port uncertain, 1749 ***2856.30*** *p178*
With wife & children
Hemens, Robert; Virginia, 1667-1668 ***6212.30*** *p39*
Hemerle, Franz; Port uncertain, 1765 ***2856.30*** *p178*
Hemfford, Christopher; Maryland, 1660 ***2524.55*** *p107*
Heminer, Gertrude 72; Vermont, 1896 ***5900.10*** *p44*
Heminer, John 79; Vermont, 1899 ***5900.10*** *p44*
Hemmell, David 54; Ontario, 1871 ***1823.15*** *p110*
Hemmerlin, Catharina; Port uncertain, 1768 ***2856.30*** *p178*
Hemmerling, Etienne Philipp; New York, 1839 ***8197.10*** *p242*
Hemmerling'sche, . . .; Port uncertain, 1787 ***2856.30*** *p178*
Hemmerling'sche, . . .; Port uncertain, 1788 ***2856.30*** *p178*
Hemming, Miss; Quebec, 1858 ***9196.15*** *p39*
Hemming, Mr.; Quebec, 1858 ***9196.15*** *p39*
Hemming, George; New York, 1853 ***1224.3*** *p36*
Hemming, Wm; Quebec, 1858 ***9196.15*** *p39*
Hemoroski, Frank; Maryland, 1910 ***3259.35*** *p20*
Hemp, Ludwig; Port uncertain, 1769 ***2856.30*** *p178*
Hempel, John William; New York, 1835 ***8197.10*** *p316*
Hemper, Thomas; Maryland, 1660 ***2524.55*** *p107*
Hemperlin, Anton; America, 1736 ***2856.30*** *p178*
Hemperlin, Elisabeth; America, 1751 ***2856.30*** *p178*
Hemphill, Andrew 26; Ontario, 1871 ***1823.15*** *p110*
Hemphill, Thomas; Pennsylvania, 1777 ***4629.10*** *p23*
Hemphill, Thomas; Pennsylvania, 1779 ***4629.10*** *p41*
Hemphill, Thomas 21; Ontario, 1871 ***1823.15*** *p110*
Hempinstall, W. J. 24; Ontario, 1871 ***1823.28*** *p39*
Hemsel, William 31; Nova Scotia, 1774 ***1220.25*** *p136*
With wife & 3 children
Hemsford, Christopher; Maryland, 1660 ***2524.55*** *p107*
Hemsley, Judith *SEE* Hemsley, William
Hemsley, Penelope *SEE* Hemsley, William
Hemsley, William; Baltimore, 1834 ***1224.3*** *p36*
Hemsley, William; Maryland, 1658 ***2524.55*** *p107*
Wife: Judith
Daughter: Penelope
Hemsor, Thomas; Maryland, 1658 ***2524.55*** *p107*
Hemssey, John 60; Ontario, 1871 ***1823.15*** *p110*
Hemsteed, John; Virginia, 1665 ***6212.30*** *p19*
Hemsworth, John; Maryland, 1659 ***2524.55*** *p107*
Hemwell, Robert; Maryland, 1672 ***2524.55*** *p107*
Hemzinger, Christian Gottl; Port uncertain, 1767 ***2856.30*** *p178*
Hemzman, Christian; New York, New York, 1854 ***3437.14*** *p40*
Henaman, Mrs. 23; Ontario, 1861 ***2896.26*** *p30*
Henchie, Margaret 70; Vermont, 1885 ***5900.10*** *p104*
Henckel, Philipp; Port uncertain, 1733 ***2856.30*** *p178*
Henckel, Philipp; Port uncertain, 1748 ***2856.30*** *p178*
Hencken, George; New York, 1825 ***8197.10*** *p239*
Henckenn, Johann; New York, 1826 ***8197.10*** *p239*
Henderman, Hanah 47; Ontario, 1861 ***2896.26*** *p35*
Henderman, James 14; Ontario, 1861 ***2896.26*** *p35*
Henderson, . . .; British Columbia, 1912 ***9196.1*** *p18*
Henderson, Miss; Quebec, 1858 ***9196.15*** *p43*
Henderson, Mr.; Portland, Maine, 1858 ***9196.15*** *p47*
Henderson, Mr.; Quebec, 1856 ***9196.15*** *p5*
Henderson, Mr.; Quebec, 1857 ***9196.15*** *p15*
Henderson, Mr.; Quebec, 1857 ***9196.15*** *p23*
Henderson, Mr. 25; Tobago, West Indies, 1774 ***1220.25*** *p132*
Henderson, Mrs.; Portland, Maine, 1858 ***9196.15*** *p47*
Henderson, Mrs.; Quebec, 1857 ***9196.15*** *p23*
Henderson, Mrs.; Quebec, 1858 ***9196.15*** *p45*
Henderson, Ms. 18; Ontario, 1861 ***2896.28*** *p53*
Henderson, A.; Mobile, Alabama, 1760-1845 ***1640.10*** *p79*
Henderson, Alex 45; Ontario, 1871 ***1823.15*** *p110*
Henderson, Alexander; Pennsylvania, 1777 ***4629.10*** *p7*
Henderson, Andrew 50; Ontario, 1871 ***1823.15*** *p110*
Henderson, Ann 1 *SEE* Henderson, Robert
Henderson, Archibald; Pennsylvania, 1826 ***6058.10*** *p8*
Henderson, Archibald 58; Ontario, 1871 ***1823.28*** *p39*
Henderson, Arthur 31; Ontario, 1871 ***1823.15*** *p110*
Henderson, Bridget O'Brien; Vermont, 1842-1917 ***5900.10*** *p541*
Henderson, Charles; Jamaica, 1850 ***1640.13*** *p55*
Henderson, Charles; Pennsylvania, 1811 ***6058.10*** *p3*
Henderson, Christina 60; Ontario, 1871 ***1823.28*** *p39*
Henderson, D.; Quebec, 1856 ***9196.15*** *p8*
Henderson, Daniel 13; Ontario, 1861 ***2896.28*** *p50*
Henderson, David 9 *SEE* Henderson, Robert
Henderson, David 21; Maryland, 1774 ***1220.25*** *p47*
Henderson, David 45; Ontario, 1871 ***1823.15*** *p110*
Henderson, Donald; Jamaica, 1828 ***1640.13*** *p55*
Henderson, Edward 39; Ontario, 1871 ***1823.22*** *p71*
Henderson, Elizabeth; Vermont, 1823-1898 ***5900.10*** *p326*
Henderson, Elizabeth Dickson; Ontario, 1890 ***1640.13*** *p55*
Henderson, Esebella 70; Ontario, 1871 ***1823.22*** *p71*
Henderson, Francis 56; Ontario, 1871 ***1823.15*** *p110*
Henderson, Francis Hardie; Dominica, 1835 ***1640.13*** *p55*
Henderson, George; New York, 1840 ***8197.10*** *p242*
Henderson, Henry; Long Island, 1782 ***1224.2*** *p55*
Henderson, Henry; Portland, Maine, 1857 ***9196.15*** *p12*
Henderson, Henry; Savannah, Georgia, 1812 ***1640.10*** *p79*
Henderson, Henry; Virginia, 1674 ***1224.1*** *p29*
Henderson, Hester A. 20; Ontario, 1861 ***2896.28*** *p53*
Henderson, J.; Quebec, 1857 ***9196.15*** *p17*
Henderson, J. 15; Ontario, 1861 ***2896.26*** *p10*
Henderson, J. 39; British Columbia, 1912 ***9196.1*** *p18*
Henderson, James; Kingston, Jamaica, 1755 ***1640.13*** *p55*
Henderson, James; New York, 1823 ***8197.10*** *p238*
Henderson, James; New York, New York, 1760 ***1224.2*** *p55*
Henderson, James; New York, New York, 1770 ***1224.2*** *p55*
Henderson, James; New York, New York, 1781 ***1224.2*** *p55*
Henderson, James; Philadelphia, 1772-1794 ***4629.10*** *p80*
Henderson, James; Portland, Maine, 1858 ***9196.15*** *p30*
Henderson, James; Texas, 1853 ***1640.10*** *p79*
Henderson, James 36; Ontario, 1871 ***1823.28*** *p39*
Henderson, James 41; Ontario, 1871 ***1823.15*** *p110*
Henderson, James 45; Ontario, 1871 ***1823.15*** *p110*
Henderson, James 58; Ontario, 1871 ***1823.15*** *p110*
Henderson, James 69; Ontario, 1871 ***1823.15*** *p110*
Henderson, Jane; Jamaica, 1829 ***1640.13*** *p55*
Henderson, Jane 60; Ontario, 1871 ***1823.15*** *p110*
Henderson, Janet 29; Ontario, 1871 ***1823.15*** *p110*
Henderson, John; Georgia, 1787 ***1640.10*** *p79*
Henderson, John; Jamaica, 1755 ***1640.13*** *p55*
Henderson, John; Maryland, 1665 ***2524.55*** *p107*
Henderson, John; Maryland, 1673 ***2524.55*** *p107*
Henderson, John; Portland, Maine, 1857 ***9196.15*** *p12*
Henderson, John 18; Ontario, 1871 ***1823.15*** *p110*
Henderson, John 21; Vancouver, British Columbia, 1913 ***9196.1*** *p57*
Henderson, John 21; Washington, 1913 ***9196.1*** *p57*
Henderson, John 25; Jamaica, 1774 ***1220.25*** *p48*
Henderson, John 25; Ontario, 1871 ***1823.15*** *p110*
Henderson, John 35; Ontario, 1871 ***1823.22*** *p71*
Henderson, John 45; Ontario, 1871 ***1823.15*** *p110*
Henderson, John 62; Ontario, 1871 ***1823.15*** *p110*
Henderson, John 64; Ontario, 1871 ***1823.22*** *p71*
Henderson, Joseph; New York, 1838 ***8197.10*** *p241*
Henderson, Joseph 33; Ontario, 1871 ***1823.28*** *p39*
Henderson, Katherine Gray; Ohio, 1880 ***1640.13*** *p55*
Henderson, Margret 20; Ontario, 1871 ***1823.15*** *p110*
Henderson, Marshal 64; Ontario, 1871 ***1823.28*** *p39*
Henderson, Martha 41; Ontario, 1871 ***1823.22*** *p71*
Henderson, Mary 38; Kansas, 1898-1910 ***9079.10*** *p37*
Henderson, Mary A. 8; Ontario, 1861 ***2896.26*** *p28*
Henderson, Patrick; Maryland, 1663 ***2524.55*** *p212*
Henderson, Peter; Pennsylvania, 1777 ***4629.10*** *p27*
Henderson, Peter; Pennsylvania, 1779 ***4629.10*** *p39*
Henderson, Peter 55; Ontario, 1871 ***1823.15*** *p110*
Henderson, Rebecca 31; Ontario, 1861 ***2896.28*** *p53*
Henderson, Robert; Allegheny Co., Pennsylvania, 1888 ***1640.13*** *p55*
Henderson, Robert; New York, 1838 ***8197.10*** *p241*
Henderson, Robert 6 *SEE* Henderson, Robert
Henderson, Robert 31; Ontario, 1871 ***1823.15*** *p111*
Henderson, Robert 34; New York, 1774 ***1220.25*** *p20*
Wife: Susanna 30
Child: Ann 1
Child: Susanna 4
Child: David 9
Child: Robert 6
Henderson, Robert 45; Ontario, 1871 ***1823.15*** *p111*
Henderson, Robert 52; Ontario, 1871 ***1823.22*** *p71*
Henderson, Robert 54; Ontario, 1871 ***1823.15*** *p111*
Henderson, Robert 66; Ontario, 1871 ***1823.15*** *p111*
Henderson, S. 18; Ontario, 1861 ***2896.28*** *p14*
Henderson, Samuel; New York, 1822 ***8197.10*** *p238*
Henderson, Samuel 31; Ontario, 1861 ***2896.28*** *p53*
Henderson, Stephen; New Orleans, 1831 ***1640.10*** *p79*
Henderson, Susanna 4 *SEE* Henderson, Robert
Henderson, Susanna 30 *SEE* Henderson, Robert
Henderson, T. 41; British Columbia, 1915 ***9196.1*** *p67*
Henderson, T. 41; Washington, 1915 ***9196.1*** *p67*
Henderson, Thomas; New York, 1827 ***8197.10*** *p240*
Henderson, Thomas; New York, 1830 ***8197.10*** *p66*
Henderson, Thomas 33; Ontario, 1871 ***1823.15*** *p111*
Henderson, Thomas 37; Ontario, 1871 ***1823.28*** *p39*
Henderson, Thomas 39; Ontario, 1871 ***1823.15*** *p111*
Henderson, Thomas 43; Ontario, 1871 ***1823.15*** *p111*
Henderson, Thomas 45; Ontario, 1871 ***1823.15*** *p111*
Henderson, Thomas 76; Ontario, 1871 ***1823.22*** *p71*
Henderson, Mrs. W. 29; British Columbia, 1912 ***9196.1*** *p18*
Henderson, W. D.; Quebec, 1857 ***9196.15*** *p13*
Henderson, William; Georgia, 1699 ***1640.13*** *p55*
Henderson, William 28; Maryland, 1774 ***1220.25*** *p5*
Henderson, William 29; Ontario, 1871 ***1823.22*** *p71*
Henderson, William 46; Ontario, 1871 ***1823.15*** *p111*
Henderson, William 49; Ontario, 1871 ***1823.15*** *p111*
Henderson, William 56; Ontario, 1871 ***1823.22*** *p71*
Henderson, William 60; Ontario, 1871 ***1823.15*** *p111*
Henderson, Wm 57; Ontario, 1861 ***2896.28*** *p53*
Hending, Charles; New York, 1840 ***8197.10*** *p174*
Hendnian, Thomas 63; Ontario, 1871 ***1823.15*** *p111*
Hendrak, James 34; Washington, 1915 ***9196.1*** *p67*
Hendren, Patrick 33; Ontario, 1871 ***1823.22*** *p72*
Hendrick, Abraham; America, 1739 ***2856.30*** *p178*
Hendrick, Anthony; Maryland, 1668 ***2524.55*** *p107*
Hendrick, Johann; America, 1739 ***2856.30*** *p178*
Hendrick, Johann Michael; America, 1739 ***2856.30*** *p179*
Hendrick, John; New York, 1839 ***8197.10*** *p131*
Hendrick, William; New York, 1807 ***8197.10*** *p39*
Hendricks, John; New York, 1840 ***8197.10*** *p173*
Hendricksen, William; New York, 1839 ***8197.10*** *p242*
Hendrickson, Anguett Poulson *SEE* Hendrickson, Bartlett
Hendrickson, Bartlett; Maryland, 1664 ***2524.55*** *p107*
Wife: Margarett Anguett
Mother: Anguett Poulson
Hendrickson, Hendrick; Maryland, 1662 ***2524.55*** *p107*
Hendrickson, Margarett Anguett *SEE* Hendrickson, Bartlett
Hendrie, James; Mobile, Alabama, 1808 ***1224.3*** *p36*
Hendriks, Samuel 49; Ontario, 1871 ***1823.15*** *p111*
Hendry, Alexander; Georgia, 1699 ***1640.13*** *p55*
Hendry, Catharine 47; Ontario, 1861 ***2896.27*** *p44*
Hendry, George D. 14; Ontario, 1861 ***2896.27*** *p45*
Hendry, James; Pennsylvania, 1777 ***4629.10*** *p23*
Hendry, James 14; Ontario, 1861 ***2896.28*** *p18*
Hendry, James 40; New York, 1775 ***1220.25*** *p142*
With wife & 3 children
Hendry, James 41; Ontario, 1871 ***1823.15*** *p111*
Hendry, Louisa; Boston, 1893 ***1640.13*** *p55*
Hendry, Mary E. 9; Ontario, 1861 ***2896.27*** *p45*
Hendry, S.; Quebec, 1857 ***9196.15*** *p17*
Hendry, Samuel A. 19; Ontario, 1861 ***2896.27*** *p45*
Hendry, Sophiah 26; Ontario, 1861 ***2896.27*** *p44*
Hendrykowski, Frank; Maryland, 1910 ***3259.35*** *p20*
Hendy, John; Maryland, 1662 ***2524.55*** *p107*
Henebery, Bridget Potter 34; Vermont, 1874 ***5900.10*** *p133*
Heneman, Henry; Pennsylvania, 1777 ***4629.10*** *p26*
Henerich, Susanna Maria; Port uncertain, 1751 ***2856.30*** *p179*
Henery, Alexander 40; Ontario, 1871 ***1823.15*** *p111*
Henery, Louis; New York, 1798-1827 ***8197.10*** *p346*
Henesey, Patrick 28; Ontario, 1871 ***1823.22*** *p72*
Henesey, Samuel; Pennsylvania, 1777 ***4629.10*** *p28*
Henessy, Jeremiah; Pennsylvania, 1863-1866 ***6058.10*** *p56*
Henesy, Abram 6; Ontario, 1861 ***2896.25*** *p59*
Henesy, Arnold 4; Ontario, 1861 ***2896.25*** *p72*
Henesy, Benjamin 18; Ontario, 1861 ***2896.25*** *p59*
Henesy, Catherine 39; Ontario, 1861 ***2896.25*** *p59*
Henesy, George 14; Ontario, 1861 ***2896.25*** *p59*
Henesy, Homer 1; Ontario, 1861 ***2896.25*** *p59*
Henesy, Jane 16; Ontario, 1861 ***2896.25*** *p59*
Henesy, Johanna 63; Ontario, 1871 ***1823.15*** *p111*
Henesy, Kate 47; Vermont, 1882 ***5900.10*** *p482*
Henesy, M. J. 19; Ontario, 1861 ***2896.25*** *p53*
Henesy, Margaret 4; Ontario, 1861 ***2896.25*** *p59*
Henesy, Matilda 19; Ontario, 1861 ***2896.25*** *p59*
Henesy, Peter 2; Ontario, 1861 ***2896.25*** *p59*
Henesy, Ryal 14; Ontario, 1861 ***2896.25*** *p69*
Henesy, Sarah 10; Ontario, 1861 ***2896.25*** *p59*
Henesy, Sarah Ann 33; Ontario, 1861 ***2896.25*** *p72*
Henesy, Sidney 6; Ontario, 1861 ***2896.25*** *p72*
Henesy, Wellington 8; Ontario, 1861 ***2896.25*** *p59*
Henesy, William 12; Ontario, 1861 ***2896.25*** *p59*
Heney, Mary Teresa; Vermont, 1818-1865 ***5900.10*** *p212*
Heney, William Henry; New York, 1839 ***8197.10*** *p131*
Heneyhan, P. 34; Alaska, 1917 ***9196.1*** *p53*
Heneyhan, P. 34; Whitehorse, Yukon, 1917 ***9196.1*** *p53*
Henfrey, Thomas; Maryland, 1668 ***2524.55*** *p107*
Hengler, Franziska; Port uncertain, 1783 ***2856.30*** *p179*
Hengston, Mr.; Quebec, 1858 ***9196.15*** *p41*
Heni, Johann Philipp; America, 1749 ***2856.30*** *p179*
Henich, Maria Barbara; Port uncertain, 1746 ***2856.30*** *p174*
Henie, Jane; Georgia, 1815 ***1640.10*** *p79*
Henie, William; Savannah, Georgia, 1808 ***1640.10*** *p79*
Henig, Adam; Port uncertain, 1793 ***2856.30*** *p179*
Henigan, D. 70; Ontario, 1861 ***2896.28*** *p1*

Henigan, E. 67; Ontario, 1861 ***2896.28*** *p1*
Henigan, M. 37; Ontario, 1861 ***2896.28*** *p1*
Henin, Maria Gertrud; Port uncertain, 1788 ***2856.30*** *p179*
Hening, Frederick 27; Ontario, 1871 ***1823.15*** *p111*
Hening, Jno; Virginia, 1664 ***6212.30*** *p10*
Hening, Mary 26; Ontario, 1871 ***1823.15*** *p111*
Hening, William 25; Maryland, 1775 ***1220.25*** *p120*
Henitage, Thomas 45; Ontario, 1871 ***1823.15*** *p111*
Henitage, William 35; Ontario, 1871 ***1823.15*** *p111*
Henkel, Philipp; New York, 1838 ***8197.10*** *p241*
Henkle, Christopher; Pennsylvania, 1777 ***4629.10*** *p10*
Henle, H.; Portland, Maine, 1857 ***9196.15*** *p13*
Henley, Andrew; Vermont, 1826-1886 ***5900.10*** *p409*
Henley, Andrew; Vermont, 1857-1900 ***5900.10*** *p409*
Henley, Bridget; Vermont, 1854-1898 ***5900.10*** *p182*
Henley, Bridget 77; Vermont, 1903 ***5900.10*** *p182*
Henley, Daniel 22; Vermont, 1864 ***5900.10*** *p172*
Henley, Ellen Egan; Vermont, 1856-1933 ***5900.10*** *p407*
Henley, Ellen Ray; Vermont, 1824-1898 ***5900.10*** *p409*
Henley, Henry; Maryland, 1676 ***2524.55*** *p107*
Henley, John; Maryland, 1669 ***2524.55*** *p22*
Henley, John; Vermont, 1878-1880 ***5900.10*** *p182*
Henley, Mary; Vermont, 1852-1929 ***5900.10*** *p409*
Henley, Patrick 85; Vermont, 1909 ***5900.10*** *p182*
Henley, Patrick, Jr.; Vermont, 1857-1894 ***5900.10*** *p182*
Henley, Peter; North Carolina, 1825 ***1224.3*** *p36*
Henley, Thomas; Vermont, 1851-1929 ***5900.10*** *p407*
Henley, Thomas 77; Vermont, 1894 ***5900.10*** *p182*
Henlin, Jermiah; Pennsylvania, 1852 ***6058.10*** *p30*
Henly, Hen; Virginia, 1666 ***6212.30*** *p31*
Henly, Henry; Virginia, 1700 ***1224.2*** *p55*
Henly, Mary 50; Ontario, 1871 ***1823.15*** *p111*
Henman, Benjamin; Maryland, 1670 ***2524.55*** *p107*
Henn, Miss; Port uncertain, 1793 ***2856.30*** *p179*
Henn, Anna Catharina; Port uncertain, 1754 ***2856.30*** *p179*
Henn, Anna Maria; Port uncertain, 1756 ***2856.30*** *p179*
Henn, Heinrich; Port uncertain, 1763 ***2856.30*** *p179*
Henn, Jeremias; Port uncertain, 1755 ***2856.30*** *p179*
Henn, Johann; America, 1763 ***2856.30*** *p179*
Henn, Johann Georg; America, 1754 ***2856.30*** *p179*
Henn, Johann Jacob; America, 1744 ***2856.30*** *p172*
Henn, Johann Peter; America, 1741 ***2856.30*** *p172*
Henn, Johann Peter; America, 1744 ***2856.30*** *p172*
Henn, Karel; New York, 1839 ***8197.10*** *p241*
Henn, Martin; Port uncertain, 1772 ***2856.30*** *p179*
Henn, Matheis; America, 1744 ***2856.30*** *p172*
Henn, Matthaus; Port uncertain, 1759 ***2856.30*** *p179*
Henn, Peter; New York, 1839 ***8197.10*** *p241*
Henn Family ; America, 1763 ***2856.30*** *p179*
Hennan, Patrick 76; Ontario, 1871 ***1823.22*** *p72*
Hennan, Wibesch 22; Ontario, 1871 ***1823.28*** *p39*
Hennberger, Gottfried; Port uncertain, 1788 ***2856.30*** *p179*
Henneasy, Margaret; Ontario, 1871 ***1823.28*** *p39*
Henneasy, Patrick 35; Ontario, 1871 ***1823.28*** *p39*
Henneberry, Mary; Vermont, 1842-1924 ***5900.10*** *p337*
Hennebery, Bridget; Vermont, 1830-1892 ***5900.10*** *p352*
Hennemann, Philipp; America, 1749 ***2856.30*** *p179*
Hennen, Anna Maria; Port uncertain, 1756 ***2856.30*** *p179*
Hennen, Caroline Louise; New Orleans, 1851 ***1640.10*** *p79*
Henner, Henry 39; Ontario, 1871 ***1823.15*** *p111*
Henners, Magdalyne; Maryland, 1666 ***2524.55*** *p107*
Hennesey, Catherine; Vermont, 1815-1882 ***5900.10*** *p135*
Hennesey, Daniel; Vermont, 1804-1862 ***5900.10*** *p390*
Hennessey, Bridget; Vermont, 1818-1896 ***5900.10*** *p150*
Hennessey, Catherine 70; Vermont, 1899 ***5900.10*** *p475*
Hennessey, Catherine Egab; Vermont, 1843-1909 ***5900.10*** *p382*
Hennessey, Ella M.; Vermont, 1857-1950 ***5900.10*** *p115*
Hennessey, James; Vermont, 1843-1872 ***5900.10*** *p79*
Hennessey, Margaret Foley; Vermont, 1834-1910 ***5900.10*** *p527*
Hennessey, Margaret Tyrell; Vermont, 1845-1918 ***5900.10*** *p79*
Hennessey, Mary Frank; Philadelphia, 1836 ***1224.3*** *p36*
Hennessey, Thomas; Vermont, 1841-1913 ***5900.10*** *p527*
Hennessey, Thomas Jefferson; Vermont, 1833-1904 ***5900.10*** *p382*
Hennessy, Anna Coyle; Vermont, 1842-1923 ***5900.10*** *p444*
Hennessy, Catherine; Vermont, 1823-1891 ***5900.10*** *p435*
Hennessy, John Merritt; Buffalo, New York, 1899 ***3437.14*** *p179*
Hennessy, Mary; Vermont, 1816-1889 ***5900.10*** *p264*
Hennessy, Mary; Vermont, 1826-1900 ***5900.10*** *p79*
Hennessy, Mary; Vermont, 1837-1910 ***5900.10*** *p487*
Hennessy, Mary Phelan; Vermont, 1819-1912 ***5900.10*** *p474*
Hennessy, Matthew; Vermont, 1817-1871 ***5900.10*** *p474*
Hennessy, Patrick; Vermont, 1838-1904 ***5900.10*** *p444*
Hennessy, Philip; New York, 1837 ***8197.10*** *p241*
Hennessy, Thos 50; Ontario, 1871 ***1823.28*** *p39*
Hennesy, Bridget 74; Vermont, 1901 ***5900.10*** *p132*
Hennesy, Cathrine Gallagher; Vermont, 1818-1894 ***5900.10*** *p205*
Hennesy, Dennis 52; Vermont, 1879 ***5900.10*** *p268*
Hennesy, Edward; Pennsylvania, 1862-1868 ***6058.10*** *p66*
Hennesy, Hanora 80; Vermont, 1896 ***5900.10*** *p132*
Hennesy, Jeremiah; Pennsylvania, 1863-1866 ***6058.10*** *p56*
Hennesy, Patrick; New York, 1831 ***8197.10*** *p365*
Hennesy, Thomas 67; Vermont, 1879 ***5900.10*** *p132*
Henney, Dennis; New York, 1804 ***8197.10*** *p27*
Hennigan, Bridget; Vermont, 1859-1938 ***5900.10*** *p176*
Hennigan, Bridget 84; Vermont, 1903 ***5900.10*** *p175*
Hennigan, James 62; Vermont, 1890 ***5900.10*** *p175*
Hennigan, Margaret T. Beirne 76; Vermont, 1936 ***5900.10*** *p176*
Hennigan, Mary 28; Vermont, 1885 ***5900.10*** *p175*
Hennigan, Thomas 33; Vermont, 1894 ***5900.10*** *p176*
Hennin, Magdalena; Port uncertain, 1755 ***2856.30*** *p179*
Hennin, Maria Elisabeth; Port uncertain, 1790 ***2856.30*** *p179*
Henning, Mr.; Quebec, 1858 ***9196.15*** *p41*
Henning, Mrs.; Quebec, 1858 ***9196.15*** *p41*
Henning, James 40; Ontario, 1871 ***1823.15*** *p111*
Henning, James 48; Ontario, 1871 ***1823.15*** *p111*
Henning, John; Maryland, 1665 ***2524.55*** *p80*
Wife: Susanna
Daughter: Mary
Henning, John; Maryland, 1665 ***2524.55*** *p107*
Wife: Susanna
Daughter: Mary
Henning, John; Maryland, 1667 ***2524.55*** *p107*
Wife: Susanna
Daughter: Mary
Henning, Ludwig; New York, 1838 ***8197.10*** *p301*
Henning, Mary *SEE* Henning, John
Henning, Mary 83; Ontario, 1871 ***1823.15*** *p111*
Henning, Susanna *SEE* Henning, John
Henninger, Catharina; Port uncertain, 1748 ***2856.30*** *p179*
Henninger, Magdalena; Port uncertain, 1795 ***2856.30*** *p179*
Henningham, John 38; Ontario, 1871 ***1823.15*** *p111*
Henningson, Christian August; New York, 1827 ***8197.10*** *p338*
Hennish, Henry; Maryland, 1910 ***3259.35*** *p20*
Henny, William 50; Ontario, 1871 ***1823.28*** *p39*
Henrey, Hartley 36; Ontario, 1871 ***1823.28*** *p40*
Henrich, Johann; America, 1751 ***2856.30*** *p180*
Henrich, Johann; Port uncertain, 1747 ***2856.30*** *p179*
Henrich, Johann; Port uncertain, 1767 ***2856.30*** *p180*
With wife & children
Henrich, Johann Adam; Port uncertain, 1763 ***2856.30*** *p179*
Henrich, Johann Adolf; America, 1751 ***2856.30*** *p179*
Henrich, Johann Adolf; Port uncertain, 1736 ***2856.30*** *p179*
Henrich, Johann Christof; Port uncertain, 1751 ***2856.30*** *p180*
With wife & children
Henrich, Johann Nikel; America, 1751 ***2856.30*** *p179*
Henrich, Konrad; Port uncertain, 1741 ***2856.30*** *p180*
Henrich, Martin; America, 1741 ***2856.30*** *p180*
With 5 children
Henrich, Melchior; Port uncertain, 1764 ***2856.30*** *p180*
With wife
Henrich, Nickel; America, 1751 ***2856.30*** *p180*
With wife mother & father
Henrich, Peter; New York, 1839 ***8197.10*** *p131*
Henrich, Velden; Port uncertain, 1751 ***2856.30*** *p180*
With family
Henrich, Wilhelm; America, 1733 ***2856.30*** *p180*
With wife
Henrichs, Johann; America, 1754 ***2856.30*** *p180*
With wife & 3 children
Henrietta, Peter; New York, 1821 ***8197.10*** *p237*
Henrietty, Bernard; New York, 1821 ***8197.10*** *p237*
Henrihan, Patrick 60; Ontario, 1871 ***1823.22*** *p72*
Henriken, Jacob; New York, 1839 ***8197.10*** *p242*
Henring, August 40; Ontario, 1871 ***1823.15*** *p111*
Henring, Christina 72; Ontario, 1871 ***1823.15*** *p111*
Henriques, Abigail; New York, 1836-1838 ***8197.10*** *p116*
Henriques, Abigaile; New York, 1836 ***8197.10*** *p75*
Henriques, David; New York, 1826 ***8197.10*** *p239*
Henriques, David; New York, 1836 ***8197.10*** *p75*
Henriques, Joseph; New York, 1826 ***8197.10*** *p239*
Henriques, Louis B.; New York, 1827 ***8197.10*** *p298*
Henriques, Moses; New York, 1826 ***8197.10*** *p239*
Henriques, Philip; New York, 1802 ***8197.10*** *p21*
Henriques, Sarah; New York, 1836-1838 ***8197.10*** *p116*
Henry, Mr.; Quebec, 1858 ***9196.15*** *p37*
Henry, Mrs.; Quebec, 1858 ***9196.15*** *p37*
Henry, Albert 17; Ontario, 1861 ***2896.28*** *p40*
Henry, Annie 35; Vermont, 1886 ***5900.10*** *p448*
Henry, Archibald; Mississippi, 1837 ***1640.10*** *p79*
Henry, Arthur; New York, New York, 1849 ***6058.10*** *p69*
Henry, Caroline 17; Ontario, 1861 ***2896.28*** *p32*
Henry, Catherine Ryan 64; Vermont, 1884 ***5900.10*** *p167*
Henry, Charles 24; Ontario, 1871 ***1823.15*** *p111*
Henry, Charles 47; Ontario, 1871 ***1823.15*** *p111*
Henry, Edward; New York, 1806 ***8197.10*** *p323*
Henry, Felix; New York, 1831-1838 ***8197.10*** *p117*
Henry, Frank 40; British Columbia, 1910 ***9196.1*** *p29*
Henry, Frank 40; Washington, 1910 ***9196.1*** *p29*
Henry, George 34; Ontario, 1871 ***1823.15*** *p111*
Henry, George 38; Ontario, 1871 ***1823.15*** *p111*
Henry, George 40; Ontario, 1871 ***1823.15*** *p111*
Henry, Jacob; Pennsylvania, 1777 ***4629.10*** *p10*
Henry, James; Pennsylvania, 1815 ***6058.10*** *p5*
Henry, James 18; Ontario, 1871 ***1823.15*** *p111*
Henry, James 65; Vermont, 1873 ***5900.10*** *p167*
Henry, Jane E.; Vermont, 1842-1919 ***5900.10*** *p308*
Henry, John; Richmond, Virginia, 1809 ***1224.3*** *p36*
Henry, John 30; Grenada, 1774 ***1220.25*** *p128*
Henry, John 44; Ontario, 1871 ***1823.15*** *p111*
Henry, John W. 33; Vermont, 1883 ***5900.10*** *p178*
Henry, Johnston 36; Ontario, 1871 ***1823.15*** *p111*
Henry, Joseph 19; Ontario, 1861 ***2896.27*** *p62*
Henry, Louisa Stewart; Boston, 1889 ***1640.13*** *p55*
Henry, Marium 29; Ontario, 1861 ***2896.26*** *p19*
Henry, Martha; Vermont, n.d. ***5900.10*** *p568*
Henry, Martin 51; Ontario, 1861 ***2896.26*** *p27*
Henry, Mary Ann 65; Ontario, 1871 ***1823.15*** *p111*
Henry, Mary J. Kelley; Vermont, 1853-1923 ***5900.10*** *p47*
Henry, N. 11; Ontario, 1861 ***2896.25*** *p8*
Henry, Oscar 25; Ontario, 1861 ***2896.26*** *p19*
Henry, Robert; New York, 1807 ***8197.10*** *p40*
Henry, Robert; Pennsylvania, 1777 ***4629.10*** *p17*
Henry, Robert 36; Maryland, 1774 ***1220.25*** *p85*
Henry, Robert 45; Ontario, 1871 ***1823.15*** *p111*
Henry, Sarah Gilluley 72; Vermont, 1901 ***5900.10*** *p181*
Henry, Simon 45; Ontario, 1871 ***1823.15*** *p111*
Henry, Thomas 64; Vermont, 1887 ***5900.10*** *p181*
Henry, William; Pennsylvania, 1777 ***4629.10*** *p9*
Henry, William H. 1; Ontario, 1861 ***2896.27*** *p68*
Henry, Willis J.; Vermont, 1859-1927 ***5900.10*** *p47*
Henry Family ; Delaware, 1775-1781 ***4628.40*** *p81*
Hensch, Johann; America, 1750 ***2856.30*** *p180*
Henschen, William C.; New York, 1838 ***8197.10*** *p118*
Henseler, Anna Barbara; America, 1751 ***2856.30*** *p180*
With husband
Henseler, Anna Barbara; America, 1786 ***2856.30*** *p180*
With husband
Hensey, George 15; Ontario, 1861 ***2896.27*** *p29*
Hensha, John; Maryland, 1663 ***2524.55*** *p51*
Hensha, John; Maryland, 1663 ***2524.55*** *p107*
Henshaw, Mrs.; Quebec, 1858 ***9196.15*** *p43*
Henshaw, Sarah Richards; New York, New York, 1811 ***1224.3*** *p36*
Henshift, Tho.; Maryland, 1681 ***2524.55*** *p107*
Hensin, Daniel; Port uncertain, 1764 ***2856.30*** *p180*
Hensk, Stanislaw; Maryland, 1910 ***3259.35*** *p20*
Henson, Joseph 35; Maryland, 1775 ***1220.25*** *p101*
Henss, Johann; Port uncertain, 1764 ***2856.30*** *p180*
Hensy, James 21; Vermont, 1855 ***5900.10*** *p606*
Hentig, Mr.; Quebec, 1857 ***9196.15*** *p24*
Henwood, Ella 14; Ontario, 1871 ***1823.28*** *p40*
Henwood, Robert; Maryland, 1680 ***2524.55*** *p107*
Henwood, Roger 57; Ontario, 1871 ***1823.22*** *p72*
Henz, Frederick 30; Ontario, 1871 ***1823.15*** *p111*
Henz, Michael; America, 1752 ***2856.30*** *p180*
Henz, Michael; Port uncertain, 1754 ***2856.30*** *p180*
Henz, Viktor; Port uncertain, 1787 ***2856.30*** *p180*
Henzig, Christ; New York, New York, 1892 ***3437.14*** *p153*
Henzman, Christian; New York, New York, 1854 ***3437.14*** *p40*
Hepburn, Charles; Cape Fear, North Carolina, 1741 ***1640.13*** *p56*
Hepburn, Stacy; Pennsylvania, 1777 ***4629.10*** *p29*
Hepelthorne, Sarah; Maryland, 1681 ***2524.55*** *p107*
Hepelthorne, Sarah; Maryland, 1681 ***2524.55*** *p195*
Hepfinger, Camille French 35; Alaska, 1913 ***9196.1*** *p39*
Hepler, Martin 16; Ontario, 1871 ***1823.15*** *p111*
Hepner, Michael; Maryland, 1910 ***3259.35*** *p20*
Hepp, Henrich; America, 1749 ***2856.30*** *p180*
Hepp, Jacob; New York, 1837 ***8197.10*** *p241*
Hepp, Jakob August; Port uncertain, 1797 ***2856.30*** *p180*
Hepp, Matthaus; Port uncertain, 1697 ***2856.30*** *p180*
Hepp, Phil. Heinrich; Port uncertain, 1791 ***2856.30*** *p180*
Hepp, Sebastian; America, 1741 ***2856.30*** *p180*
Heppe, Georg; Port uncertain, 1782 ***2856.30*** *p180*
Hepworth, Jno; Virginia, 1668-1669 ***6212.30*** *p40*
Her, Anna Sybilla; America, 1764 ***2856.30*** *p180*
With husband
Herald, Mrs.; Quebec, 1857 ***9196.15*** *p26*

Herald, Daniel 38; Ontario, 1871 ***1823.22*** *p72*
Herald, James; Quebec, 1857 ***9196.15*** *p26*
Herald, Lawrence; New York, 1840 ***8197.10*** *p384*
Herault, Elizabeth; Connecticut, 1804 ***1224.3*** *p36*
Herault, John; Charles Town, South Carolina, 1705 ***1224.2*** *p55*
Herb, Elis. Barbara; Port uncertain, 1762 ***2856.30*** *p180*
Herb, Jacob; America, 1768 ***2856.30*** *p180*
Herbach, Johann Peter; America, 1741 ***2856.30*** *p181*
Herbel, Adam; America, 1754 ***2856.30*** *p181*
Herbel, Anna 26; Kansas, 1910 ***9079.10*** *p15*
Herbel, Anna 63; Kansas, 1903-1910 ***9079.10*** *p14*
Herbel, Catharina; Port uncertain, 1771 ***2856.30*** *p181*
Herbel, Catherine 42; Kansas, 1904-1910 ***9079.10*** *p16*
Herbel, Christina 21; Kansas, 1903-1910 ***9079.10*** *p14*
Herbel, David 49; Kansas, 1894-1910 ***9079.10*** *p16*
Herbel, David D. 34; Kansas, 1903-1910 ***9079.10*** *p14*
Herbel, Frederic 44; Kansas, 1904-1910 ***9079.10*** *p16*
Herbel, George 10; Kansas, 1904-1910 ***9079.10*** *p16*
Herbel, Gottfreid 29; Kansas, 1896-1910 ***9079.10*** *p15*
Herbel, Gottfried 17; Kansas, 1904-1910 ***9079.10*** *p16*
Herbel, Johann; America, 1739 ***2856.30*** *p181*
Herbel, Johann; Port uncertain, 1770 ***2856.30*** *p181*
Herbel, Julia 44; Kansas, 1894-1910 ***9079.10*** *p16*
Herben, Anna 17; Kansas, 1902-1910 ***9079.10*** *p28*
Herben, Anna 54; Kansas, 1902-1910 ***9079.10*** *p28*
Herben, Dave 18; Kansas, 1902-1910 ***9079.10*** *p28*
Herben, Fred 33; Kansas, 1904-1910 ***9079.10*** *p28*
Herben, Katie 23; Kansas, 1891-1910 ***9079.10*** *p28*
Herben, Molly 13; Kansas, 1902-1910 ***9079.10*** *p28*
Herben, Reinkandt 28; Kansas, 1902-1910 ***9079.10*** *p28*
Herben, Renkandt 54; Kansas, 1902-1910 ***9079.10*** *p28*
Herber, Adam; Port uncertain, 1750 ***2856.30*** *p181*
Herber, Catharina; Port uncertain, 1755 ***2856.30*** *p181*
Herber, Jacob; Port uncertain, 1750 ***2856.30*** *p181*
Herber, Maria Margarete; Port uncertain, 1750 ***2856.30*** *p181*
Herber, Nickel; Port uncertain, 1750 ***2856.30*** *p181*
Herber, Philipp; Port uncertain, 1750 ***2856.30*** *p181*
With wife & children
Herberer, Annie 11; Kansas, 1910 ***9079.10*** *p51*
Herberer, Annie 48; Kansas, 1910 ***9079.10*** *p51*
Herberer, Conrad 20; Kansas, 1910 ***9079.10*** *p51*
Herberer, Emanuel 14; Kansas, 1910 ***9079.10*** *p51*
Herberer, Henry 18; Kansas, 1910 ***9079.10*** *p51*
Herberer, Martin 57; Kansas, 1900-1910 ***9079.10*** *p51*
Herberer, Thressia 16; Kansas, 1910 ***9079.10*** *p51*
Herberstein, Maria; Port uncertain, 1756 ***2856.30*** *p181*
Herbert, Edw; Virginia, 1665-1666 ***6212.30*** *p23*
Herbert, Ellen Sullivan; Vermont, 1837-1907 ***5900.10*** *p339*
Herbert, George; Maryland, 1673 ***2524.55*** *p107*
Herbert, Henry; New York, 1802 ***8197.10*** *p21*
Herbert, Isaac 23; Savannah, Georgia, 1775 ***1220.25*** *p139*
Herbert, James; Virginia, 1665 ***6212.30*** *p18*
Herbert, James 70; Ontario, 1871 ***1823.22*** *p72*
Herbert, John; Vermont, 1827-1914 ***5900.10*** *p339*
Herbert, Katie B. 17; Vermont, 1889 ***5900.10*** *p550*
Herbert, Margaret Donahue; Vermont, 1851-1914 ***5900.10*** *p583*
Herbert, Margaret Kelty; Vermont, 1833-1911 ***5900.10*** *p550*
Herbert, Mary E. 40; Vermont, 1904 ***5900.10*** *p118*
Herbert, Michael; Vermont, 1841-1909 ***5900.10*** *p583*
Herbert, Patrick; Vermont, 1836-1897 ***5900.10*** *p551*
Herbert, Shilby; Maryland, 1672 ***2524.55*** *p107*
Herbert, Susan; Vermont, 1826-1904 ***5900.10*** *p552*
Herbert, Thomas; Vermont, 1837-1917 ***5900.10*** *p550*
Herbert, Thomas M.; Vermont, 1866-1936 ***5900.10*** *p550*
Herbert, William; Maryland, 1679 ***2524.55*** *p107*
Herbert, William; Philadelphia, 1778 ***1224.2*** *p55*
Herbert, William; Virginia, 1666 ***6212.30*** *p29*
Herbet, Charles 34; Ontario, 1871 ***1823.15*** *p111*
Herbin, Henry; Virginia, 1666-1667 ***6212.30*** *p33*
Herbison, William 45; Ontario, 1871 ***1823.15*** *p111*
Herbit, Michael; New York, 1827 ***8197.10*** *p240*
Herbold, Georg; Port uncertain, 1751 ***2856.30*** *p181*
With wife & 2 children
Herbold, Wilhelm; Port uncertain, 1794 ***2856.30*** *p181*
Herboldt, Mathias; Port uncertain, 1759 ***2856.30*** *p181*
Herbrich, Valentine; New York, 1840 ***8197.10*** *p242*
Herbrt, John 50; Ontario, 1871 ***1823.15*** *p111*
Herbst, Maria Elisabeth; Port uncertain, 1791 ***2856.30*** *p181*
Herbst, Michael; Port uncertain, 1752 ***2856.30*** *p181*
With wife & 3 children
Herbst, Michael; Port uncertain, 1776 ***2856.30*** *p181*
Herbster, Cath. Sabine; Port uncertain, 1767 ***2856.30*** *p181*
Herbster, David; America, 1750 ***2856.30*** *p181*
Herbster, Jacob; America, 1804 ***2856.30*** *p181*
Herbster, Johann Georg; Port uncertain, 1756 ***2856.30*** *p181*
Hercher, Georg; Port uncertain, 1682 ***2856.30*** *p181*
Hercher, Georg; Port uncertain, 1713 ***2856.30*** *p181*
Herchhoff, George; New York, New York, 1856 ***3437.14*** *p21*
Herchoff, George; New York, New York, 1856 ***3437.14*** *p21*
Herd, Walter; Georgia, 1698 ***1640.13*** *p56*
Herd, Welras 41; Ontario, 1871 ***1823.15*** *p111*
Herdel, . . .; America, 1753 ***2856.30*** *p181*
Herdel, Johann Leonard; Port uncertain, 1736 ***2856.30*** *p181*
Herder, A. Elis. *SEE* Herder, Johann Valentin
Herder, Johann Valentin; America, 1752 ***2856.30*** *p181*
Wife: A. Elis.
With 3 children
Herdgvcak, Stanislaw; Maryland, 1910 ***3259.35*** *p20*
Herdi, Philipp; Port uncertain, 1784 ***2856.30*** *p182*
Herdie, James 30; Baltimore, 1775 ***1220.25*** *p118*
Herding, William 39; Ontario, 1871 ***1823.15*** *p112*
Herdlin, Anna Maria; Port uncertain, 1751 ***2856.30*** *p182*
Herdlin, Anna Maria; Port uncertain, 1785 ***2856.30*** *p182*
Herdt, Valentin; America, 1752 ***2856.30*** *p182*
Hereford, Jno.; Virginia, 1667-1668 ***6212.30*** *p39*
Herell, Luccs 30; Ontario, 1871 ***1823.15*** *p112*
Herey, Catherine Carrigan 74; Vermont, 1892 ***5900.10*** *p389*
Herey, Christopher; Vermont, n.d. ***5900.10*** *p389*
Herey, Edward 43; Vermont, 1843 ***5900.10*** *p389*
Herfeld, Johann Dewald; Port uncertain, 1750 ***2856.30*** *p182*
Herford, Henry; New York, 1802 ***8197.10*** *p21*
Herford, John; New York, 1802 ***8197.10*** *p21*
Herg, Christian; Port uncertain, 1791 ***2856.30*** *p182*
Herganreder, Henry; Pennsylvania, 1837 ***6058.10*** *p14*
Hergedt, Johann Peter; America, 1750 ***2856.30*** *p182*
Hergersheimer, Johann Nickel; Port uncertain, 1758 ***2856.30*** *p182*
Hergersheimer, Johann Nickel; Port uncertain, 1763 ***2856.30*** *p182*
Hergert, Johann Peter; America, 1750 ***2856.30*** *p182*
With wife children & son
Hergert, Peter; America, 1751 ***2856.30*** *p182*
Hergesheimer, Anton; America, 1749 ***2856.30*** *p182*
Hergesheimer, Michael; America, 1741 ***2856.30*** *p182*
With wife & 8 children
Herget, Friedrich; America, 1748 ***2856.30*** *p1971*
With wife & 6 children
Herget, Johann Peter; America, 1750 ***2856.30*** *p182*
With wife children & son
Herhel, Margart 75; Ontario, 1871 ***1823.15*** *p112*
Herick, John N. 42; Ontario, 1871 ***1823.15*** *p112*
Hericus, Marcus; Virginia, 1690-1691 ***6212.30*** *p59*
Herig, Eva Margareta; Port uncertain, 1755 ***2856.30*** *p182*
Hering, Andreas; Port uncertain, 1770 ***2856.30*** *p182*
Hering, Hans Jacob; America, 1751 ***2856.30*** *p182*
With wife & 3 children
Hering, Hans Jacob; America, 1753 ***2856.30*** *p182*
Hering, Hans Michael; America, 1769 ***2856.30*** *p182*
Hering, Michael; America, 1775 ***2856.30*** *p182*
Hering, Philipp Ludwig; Port uncertain, 1754 ***2856.30*** *p182*
Herington, Abagail 5; Ontario, 1861 ***2896.25*** *p5*
Herington, Anna A. 13; Ontario, 1861 ***2896.27*** *p20*
Herington, Anna C. 7; Ontario, 1861 ***2896.27*** *p20*
Herington, Anna E. 8; Ontario, 1861 ***2896.25*** *p5*
Herington, Eleanor 17; Ontario, 1861 ***2896.26*** *p32*
Herington, Ellen 20; Ontario, 1861 ***2896.25*** *p5*
Herington, Ervan J. 3; Ontario, 1861 ***2896.27*** *p13*
Herington, George A. 10; Ontario, 1861 ***2896.25*** *p5*
Herington, George W. 30; Ontario, 1861 ***2896.27*** *p13*
Herington, Hariette 30; Ontario, 1861 ***2896.25*** *p5*
Herington, Henrietta A. 6; Ontario, 1861 ***2896.25*** *p5*
Herington, Isaac N. 2; Ontario, 1861 ***2896.25*** *p5*
Herington, Mahaly 28; Ontario, 1861 ***2896.27*** *p13*
Herington, Mary 70; Ontario, 1871 ***1823.28*** *p40*
Herington, Willet 5; Ontario, 1861 ***2896.27*** *p13*
Herken, Edward; New York, 1837 ***8197.10*** *p241*
Herkimer, Nikolaus; America, 1777 ***2856.30*** *p182*
Herkloz, Friedrich; Port uncertain, 1782 ***2856.30*** *p182*
Herknep, George; New York, 1807 ***8197.10*** *p40*
Herlan, Jaque; America, 1750 ***2856.30*** *p182*
With wife & children
Herlan, Jaque; America, 1752 ***2856.30*** *p182*
Herlan, Jaque; Port uncertain, 1752 ***2856.30*** *p182*
With wife & children
Herlemann, George; New York, 1840 ***8197.10*** *p172*
Herley, John F. 63; Vermont, 1913 ***5900.10*** *p122*
Herley, Mary 60; Vermont, 1881 ***5900.10*** *p122*
Herley, Mary A. Galvin 74; Vermont, 1926 ***5900.10*** *p122*
Herlihy, Cornelius; New York, 1831 ***8197.10*** *p314*
Herlihy, M. G.; Vermont, 1857-1909 ***5900.10*** *p339*
Herlihy, Mary J.; Vermont, 1855-1927 ***5900.10*** *p339*
Herlon, Jacob 40; Ontario, 1871 ***1823.28*** *p40*
Herlow, Francis 56; Ontario, 1871 ***1823.15*** *p112*
Herman, Abraham; Maryland, 1663 ***2524.55*** *p107*
Herman, Augustin; Maryland, 1662 ***2524.55*** *p107*
Herman, Augustine; Maryland, 1665 ***2524.55*** *p108*
Wife: Jane
Daughter: Judith
Daughter: Frances
Daughter: Margarita
Son: Epherim Georgius
Son: Caspar
Herman, Caspar *SEE* Herman, Augustine
Herman, Edward 60; Ontario, 1871 ***1823.22*** *p72*
Herman, Ellicia 11; Ontario, 1861 ***2896.25*** *p30*
Herman, Epherim Georgius *SEE* Herman, Augustine
Herman, Frances *SEE* Herman, Augustine
Herman, Francis; Maryland, 1679 ***2524.55*** *p108*
Herman, Francis; Maryland, 1681 ***2524.55*** *p108*
Herman, Jacob; New York, 1834-1838 ***8197.10*** *p117*
Herman, Jane *SEE* Herman, Augustine
Herman, Johann Emmerich; Port uncertain, 1765 ***2856.30*** *p182*
Herman, Johann Emmerich; Port uncertain, 1767 ***2856.30*** *p182*
Herman, John; Baltimore, 1832 ***6058.10*** *p44*
Herman, John; Maryland, 1910 ***3259.35*** *p20*
Herman, Judith *SEE* Herman, Augustine
Herman, Lenora 21; Ontario, 1861 ***2896.25*** *p30*
Herman, Malcolm 6; Ontario, 1861 ***2896.25*** *p71*
Herman, Margarita *SEE* Herman, Augustine
Herman, Martha 27; Ontario, 1861 ***2896.25*** *p71*
Herman, Matthew; Georgia, 1698 ***1640.13*** *p56*
Herman, Rosa 3; Ontario, 1861 ***2896.25*** *p71*
Herman, Sarah 53; Ontario, 1861 ***2896.25*** *p30*
Herman, Suffrona 18; Ontario, 1861 ***2896.25*** *p30*
Herman, Veronica 50; Kansas, 1889-1910 ***9079.10*** *p37*
Herman, Walter S. 16; Ontario, 1861 ***2896.25*** *p30*
Herman, William 55; Kansas, 1889-1910 ***9079.10*** *p37*
Herman, William 59; Ontario, 1861 ***2896.25*** *p30*
Hermann, Anna Barbara; America, 1756 ***2856.30*** *p183*
Hermann, Anna Maria; Port uncertain, 1784 ***2856.30*** *p224*
Hermann, Barbara; Port uncertain, 1693 ***2856.30*** *p183*
With husband & 6 children
Hermann, Bernard; America, 1752 ***2856.30*** *p183*
With wife & 4 children
Hermann, David; America, 1751 ***2856.30*** *p183*
With wife & 4 children
Hermann, David; Port uncertain, 1748 ***2856.30*** *p183*
With wife & 4 children
Hermann, Elisabeth; Port uncertain, 1764 ***2856.30*** *p182*
Hermann, Franz; Port uncertain, 1747 ***2856.30*** *p182*
Hermann, Jacob; Port uncertain, 1764 ***2856.30*** *p182*
Hermann, Jacob; Port uncertain, 1766 ***2856.30*** *p182*
Hermann, Jakob; Port uncertain, 1756 ***2856.30*** *p182*
Hermann, Johann; America, 1752 ***2856.30*** *p182*
Hermann, Johann; America, 1752 ***2856.30*** *p183*
With child
Hermann, Johann; Port uncertain, 1750 ***2856.30*** *p182*
Hermann, Johann Georg; America, 1750 ***2856.30*** *p183*
With wife & 4 children
Hermann, Johann Georg; Port uncertain, 1748 ***2856.30*** *p183*
With wife & 4 children
Hermann, Johann Thiel; America, 1752 ***2856.30*** *p183*
Hermann, Johann Thiel; Port uncertain, 1750 ***2856.30*** *p182*
Hermann, Johann Tiel; America, 1752 ***2856.30*** *p183*
Hermann, Maria Catharina; Port uncertain, 1733 ***2856.30*** *p183*
Hermann, Maria Elisabeth; Port uncertain, 1733 ***2856.30*** *p183*
Hermann, Peter; America, 1783 ***2856.30*** *p183*
Hermann, Peter; Port uncertain, 1799 ***2856.30*** *p183*
Hermann, Simon Heinrich; America, 1752 ***2856.30*** *p183*
Hermanutz, Felicitas; Port uncertain, 1799 ***2856.30*** *p183*
Hermes, Mathes; Port uncertain, 1781 ***2856.30*** *p183*
Hermiston, John 56; Ontario, 1871 ***1823.22*** *p72*
Hermiston, Turnball 60; Ontario, 1871 ***1823.22*** *p72*
Hermitage, Thomas; Maryland, 1666 ***2524.55*** *p108*
Hermon, Anna 57; Kansas, 1906-1910 ***9079.10*** *p11*
Hermon, Elizabeth 12; Kansas, 1906-1910 ***9079.10*** *p11*
Hermon, Henry 18; Kansas, 1906-1910 ***9079.10*** *p11*
Hermon, Jake 28; Kansas, 1906-1910 ***9079.10*** *p11*
Hermon, John 57; Kansas, 1906-1910 ***9079.10*** *p11*
Hermon, John J. 21; Kansas, 1906-1910 ***9079.10*** *p11*
Hermon, Liddy 9; Kansas, 1906-1910 ***9079.10*** *p11*
Hern, A. 38; Alaska, 1914 ***9196.1*** *p41*
Hern, David 60; Ontario, 1871 ***1823.22*** *p72*
Hern, Samul 44; Ontario, 1871 ***1823.15*** *p112*
Hern, Thomas 48; Ontario, 1871 ***1823.15*** *p112*

Hern, William 54; Ontario, 1871 *1823.15 p112*
Herne, Catherine; Maryland, 1658 *2524.55 p108*
Herne, Patrick; New York, 1821 *8197.10 p238*
Herney, John L. 20; Vermont, 1875 *5900.10 p109*
Hernick, George 34; Ontario, 1871 *1823.15 p112*
Herning, Benjamin; Pennsylvania, 1777 *4629.10 p23*
Herold, Friedrich; Port uncertain, 1752 *2856.30 p183*
Herold, Ignaz; Port uncertain, 1768 *2856.30 p183*
Herold, Margarete; Port uncertain, 1765 *2856.30 p183*
Herom, Mrs.; Portland, Maine, 1857 *9196.15 p12*
Herom, J.; Portland, Maine, 1857 *9196.15 p12*
Heron, Alexander; Georgia, 1738 *1640.10 p80*
Heron, Andrew; Augusta, Georgia, 1817 *1224.3 p36*
Heron, Andrew; Augusta, Georgia, 1817 *1640.10 p80*
Heron, Gilbert; Portland, Maine, 1858 *9196.15 p29*
Heron, Margaret; New York, 1764 *1224.2 p80*
Heronimus, Jacob 42; Ontario, 1871 *1823.15 p112*
Heronimus, Wm 49; Ontario, 1871 *1823.15 p112*
Herpel, Johann; America, 1739 *2856.30 p183*
Herr, Joseph 71; Ontario, 1871 *1823.15 p112*
Herr, Philipp Jakob; Port uncertain, 1733 *2856.30 p183*
Herraty, Dennis; New York, 1805 *8197.10 p29*
Herre, Jakob; Port uncertain, 1744 *2856.30 p183*
Herrel, Georg; Port uncertain, 1770 *2856.30 p183*
Herrel, Hans; Port uncertain, 1770 *2856.30 p183*
Herrel, Hans, IV; Port uncertain, 1770 *2856.30 p183*
Herrel-Huster, Hans; Port uncertain, 1770 *2856.30 p183*
Herren, Harriett 67; Vermont, 1857 *5900.10 p556*
Herren, John 73; Vermont, 1854 *5900.10 p556*
Herren, Mary; New York, 1831 *8197.10 p365*
Herren, Robert 42; Ontario, 1871 *1823.22 p72*
Herren, Robert 43; Vermont, 1847 *5900.10 p556*
Herrick, Gershom 33; Ontario, 1871 *1823.28 p40*
Herrick, Michael 40; Ontario, 1871 *1823.28 p40*
Herrick, Thomas W. 44; Ontario, 1871 *1823.28 p40*
Herries, Michael; Georgia, 1751 *1640.10 p80*
Herries, Robert; Florida, 1767 *1640.10 p80*
Herring, Mr.; Quebec, 1857 *9196.15 p15*
Herring, Mrs.; Quebec, 1856 *9196.15 p7*
Herring, Mrs.; Quebec, 1857 *9196.15 p15*
Herring, Ann; Maryland, 1650 *2524.55 p108*
Herring, Arthur; Maryland, 1691 *1224.1 p29*
Herring, Honora Victorine; New York, 1839 *8197.10 p241*
Herring, James; New York, 1830 *1224.3 p36*
Herring, Margaret; Maryland, 1651 *2524.55 p108*
Herring, Michael 37; Georgia, 1774 *1220.25 p47*
Herring, William 27; Virginia, 1775 *1220.25 p95*
Herring, William Edward; Charleston, South Carolina, 1789 *1224.2 p55*
Herrington, A. W. 6; Ontario, 1861 *2896.25 p28*
Herrington, Abigail 74; Ontario, 1861 *2896.25 p47*
Herrington, Allen 4; Ontario, 1861 *2896.25 p40*
Herrington, Augusta 9; Ontario, 1861 *2896.25 p18*
Herrington, B. 14; Ontario, 1861 *2896.25 p28*
Herrington, C. 1; Ontario, 1861 *2896.28 p1*
Herrington, C. 27; Ontario, 1861 *2896.25 p28*
Herrington, C. H. 3; Ontario, 1861 *2896.25 p28*
Herrington, Claracy 26; Ontario, 1861 *2896.25 p40*
Herrington, Clarissa 1; Ontario, 1861 *2896.25 p18*
Herrington, David 7; Ontario, 1861 *2896.25 p18*
Herrington, Emma 19; Ontario, 1861 *2896.25 p18*
Herrington, G. William 7; Ontario, 1861 *2896.28 p1*
Herrington, George 2; Ontario, 1861 *2896.25 p62*
Herrington, George 5; Ontario, 1861 *2896.25 p18*
Herrington, Harriet 4; Ontario, 1861 *2896.25 p62*
Herrington, J. 35; Ontario, 1861 *2896.28 p1*
Herrington, James; Maryland, 1678 *2524.55 p108*
Herrington, Jane 16; Ontario, 1861 *2896.25 p18*
Herrington, Mary 14; Ontario, 1861 *2896.25 p18*
Herrington, Mary Ann 24; Ontario, 1861 *2896.25 p62*
Herrington, Moses 78; Ontario, 1861 *2896.28 p1*
Herrington, N. S. 14; Ontario, 1861 *2896.28 p1*
Herrington, Patrick 68; Ontario, 1871 *1823.22 p72*
Herrington, S. 36; Ontario, 1861 *2896.28 p1*
Herrington, Susannah 6; Ontario, 1861 *2896.25 p62*
Herrington, V. 78; Ontario, 1861 *2896.28 p1*
Herrington, W. S. 1; Ontario, 1861 *2896.25 p28*
Herrington, William 46; Ontario, 1871 *1823.15 p112*
Herrington, William H. 6; Ontario, 1861 *2896.25 p40*
Herrlich, Engelhard; New York, 1837 *8197.10 p91*
Herrman, Christopher Frederick; New York, 1840 *8197.10 p172*
Herrmann, Anna Elisabeth; Port uncertain, 1764 *2856.30 p183*
Herrmann, Anton; America, 1822 *2856.30 p184* With wife & father
Herrmann, Anton; Port uncertain, 1831 *2856.30 p183*
Herrmann, Christopher Frederick; New York, 1838 *8197.10 p241*
Herrmann, Elis. Catharina; Port uncertain, 1763 *2856.30 p183*
Herrmann, Friedrich; America, 1771 *2856.30 p184* With wife & 2 children
Herrmann, Georg; America, 1770 *2856.30 p183*
Herrmann, Georg; Port uncertain, 1770 *2856.30 p184* With family
Herrmann, Gottfried; Port uncertain, 1782 *2856.30 p183*
Herrmann, Heinrich; Port uncertain, 1793 *2856.30 p183*
Herrmann, Johann; Port uncertain, 1769 *2856.30 p183*
Herrmann, Johann; Port uncertain, 1782 *2856.30 p183*
Herrmann, Margarete; Port uncertain, 1752 *2856.30 p183*
Herrmannin, Barbara; America, 1752 *2856.30 p184*
Herron, Bartholomew; Virginia, 1671 *6212.30 p45*
Herron, Elizabeth 88; Vermont, 1887 *5900.10 p556*
Herron, James; Pennsylvania, 1777 *4629.10 p25*
Herron, James 55; Ontario, 1871 *1823.28 p40*
Herron, Maria 45; Ontario, 1871 *1823.22 p72*
Herron, Samuel; Ontario, 1871 *1823.22 p73*
Herron, Thomas 27; Ontario, 1871 *1823.22 p73*
Herrstron, Anton 39; British Columbia, 1917 *9196.1 p52*
Herrstron, Anton 39; Seattle, 1917 *9196.1 p52*
Hertel, Anna Maria; Port uncertain, 1756 *2856.30 p184*
Hertel, Hans Caspar; Port uncertain, 1730 *2856.30 p184*
Herten, Veit; America, 1765 *2856.30 p184*
Hertenell, John 18; Ontario, 1871 *1823.15 p112*
Hertenell, John 40; Ontario, 1871 *1823.15 p112*
Hertenstein, Hans Adam; Port uncertain, 1752 *2856.30 p184*
Hertenstein, Jacob; Port uncertain, 1770 *2856.30 p184*
Hertenstein, Philipp; Port uncertain, 1777 *2856.30 p184* With wife
Herterich, Max; Port uncertain, 1744 *2856.30 p184*
Herterich, Max; Port uncertain, 1764 *2856.30 p184*
Hertge, Michael; Port uncertain, 1731 *2856.30 p184*
Herti, Maria; Port uncertain, 1694 *2856.30 p184*
Hertler, Anna Maria; Port uncertain, 1751 *2856.30 p182*
Hertler, Anna Maria; Port uncertain, 1785 *2856.30 p182*
Hertweck, Georg; Port uncertain, 1766 *2856.30 p184*
Hertz, Jacob; America, 1752 *2856.30 p184* With family
Hertz, Maria Catharina; Port uncertain, 1758 *2856.30 p184*
Hertzel, Henrich; Port uncertain, 1732 *2856.30 p184*
Hertzel, Michael 42; Ontario, 1871 *1823.15 p112*
Hertzel, Michael 77; Ontario, 1871 *1823.15 p112*
Hertzog, Andrew; Pennsylvania, 1777 *4629.10 p13*
Hertzog, Heinrich; Port uncertain, 1755 *2856.30 p184* With wife
Hertzog, Johann; Port uncertain, 1736 *2856.30 p184*
Hertzog, Matthaus; Port uncertain, 1763 *2856.30 p184*
Hervald, Ulrick 40; Ontario, 1871 *1823.15 p112*
Hervig, John; New York, 1804 *8197.10 p27*
Herz, Mr.; Port uncertain, 1771 *2856.30 p185* With wife & children
Herz, Andreas; America, 1749 *2856.30 p185* With wife & children
Herzog, Andreas; America, 1750 *2856.30 p185*
Herzog, Andreas; America, 1773 *2856.30 p185*
Herzog, Andreas; Port uncertain, 1751 *2856.30 p185*
Herzog, Catharina; Port uncertain, 1790 *2856.30 p185*
Herzog, Christian; New York, 1838 *8197.10 p117*
Herzog, Johann Bernhard; America, 1752 *2856.30 p185*
Herzog, Josef; Port uncertain, 1771 *2856.30 p185* With wife & children
Herzog, Michael, America, 1744 *2856.30 p185*
Herzogin, Elis. Catharina; Port uncertain, 1777 *2856.30 p185*
Heseltin, Robert 38; Ontario, 1871 *1823.22 p73*
Heseltine, Delanie; Vermont, 1849-1927 *5900.10 p303*
Heselton, William; Virginia, 1766 *1224.2 p55*
Hesketh, Henry; Sacramento, California, 1856 *1224.3 p36*
Hesketh, Henry 37; Ontario, 1871 *1823.28 p40*
Hesketh, John; New York, 1826 *8197.10 p334*
Hesler, Jakob; Port uncertain, 1753 *2856.30 p186*
Hesler, Peter; New York, 1837 *8197.10 p241*
Hesler, Peter; New York, 1840 *8197.10 p383*
Heslip, William 68; Ontario, 1871 *1823.22 p73*
Hess, Adam; Port uncertain, 1773 *2856.30 p185*
Hess, Andreas; Port uncertain, 1752 *2856.30 p186* With wife
Hess, Andreas; Port uncertain, 1771 *2856.30 p185*
Hess, Andrew 35; Ontario, 1871 *1823.15 p112*
Hess, Anna 70; Ontario, 1871 *1823.15 p112*
Hess, Christian 36; Ontario, 1871 *1823.15 p112*
Hess, Elisabeth; Port uncertain, 1768 *2856.30 p185*
Hess, Frederick 25; Ontario, 1871 *1823.15 p112*
Hess, Georg Ludwig; Port uncertain, 1786 *2856.30 p185*
Hess, George 33; Ontario, 1871 *1823.15 p112*
Hess, George 55; Ontario, 1871 *1823.15 p112*
Hess, Heinrich; Port uncertain, 1781 *2856.30 p185*
Hess, Jacob; Port uncertain, 1789 *2856.30 p185*
Hess, Johann; Port uncertain, 1752 *2856.30 p185*
Hess, Johann Nikolaus; Port uncertain, 1731 *2856.30 p185*
Hess, Johann Nikolaus; Port uncertain, 1770 *2856.30 p185*
Hess, Magdalena; Port uncertain, 1768 *2856.30 p185*
Hess, Maria; Port uncertain, 1736 *2856.30 p185*
Hess, Michael; Port uncertain, 1796 *2856.30 p185*
Hess, Rosina; Port uncertain, 1734 *2856.30 p185*
Hess, Wilhelm; Port uncertain, 1845 *2856.30 p171*
Hess, William 30; Ontario, 1871 *1823.22 p73*
Hesse, Adam; Port uncertain, 1767 *2856.30 p186*
Hesse, Adam 30; Ontario, 1871 *1823.15 p112*
Hessellwood, Mathew 55; Ontario, 1871 *1823.15 p112*
Hesselschwerdt, . . .; Port uncertain, 1792 *2856.30 p186*
Hesser, Adam; New York, 1837 *8197.10 p91*
Hessian, Amos 30; Ontario, 1871 *1823.15 p112*
Hessler, Philipp; Port uncertain, 1783 *2856.30 p186* With wife & children
Hester, Harman 44; Virginia, 1774 *1220.25 p46*
Hester, Jakob; Port uncertain, 1753 *2856.30 p186*
Hester, William; New York, 1840 *8197.10 p385*
Hester, William 40; Ontario, 1871 *1823.28 p40*
Hestler, Charles 25; Ontario, 1871 *1823.15 p112*
Hetchcock, Mary 15; Maryland, 1775 *1220.25 p97*
Hether, Ann; Maryland, 1674 *2524.55 p108*
Hetherington, Christopher 45; New York, 1775 *1220.25 p142* With wife & 7 children
Hetherington, Joseph 35; Ontario, 1871 *1823.15 p112*
Hetherington, Maria 61; Ontario, 1871 *1823.28 p40*
Hetherston, Wm; Virginia, 1671-1672 *6212.30 p47*
Hetlerin, Agnes; Port uncertain, 1792 *2856.30 p186*
Hetmanski, Ben; Maryland, 1910 *3259.35 p20*
Hettel, Michael; Port uncertain, 1787 *2856.30 p186*
Hetteric, Johann; Port uncertain, 1785 *2856.30 p186*
Hettinger, John; New York, 1835 *8197.10 p316*
Hettinger, John; New York, 1837 *8197.10 p91*
Hettland, Owen; Virginia, 1666 *6212.30 p25*
Hettle, John 65; Ontario, 1871 *1823.15 p112*
Hettler, Anna Maria; Port uncertain, 1752 *2856.30 p186*
Hettler, Catharina; Port uncertain, 1769 *2856.30 p186*
Hettler, Hans; Port uncertain, 1759 *2856.30 p186*
Hettlin, Elisabeth; Port uncertain, 1766 *2856.30 p186*
Hettrich, Conrad; New York, 1823 *8197.10 p238*
Hetze1, Charles Francis; New York, 1835 *8197.10 p240*
Hetzel, Adam; Port uncertain, 1762 *2856.30 p186*
Hetzel, Charles Francis; New York, 1837 *8197.10 p91*
Hetzel, Johann Caspar; Port uncertain, 1747 *2856.30 p186*
Hetzel, Johann Christof; Port uncertain, 1733 *2856.30 p186*
Hetzel, Johann Henrich; Port uncertain, 1741 *2856.30 p186*
Hetzel, John Jacob; New York, 1835 *8197.10 p240*
Heu, Johann; Port uncertain, 1791 *2856.30 p186*
Heub, Peter; Port uncertain, 1741 *2856.30 p186*
Heuberger, Hans Georg; Port uncertain, 1761 *2856.30 p186*
Heuberger, Jakob; America, 1769 *2856.30 p186*
Heuberger, Jakob; Canada, 1751 *2856.30 p186*
Heuberger, Jakob; Canada, 1769 *2856.30 p186*
Heuberger, Matthaus; Port uncertain, 1739 *2856.30 p186*
Heuberger, Matthaus; Port uncertain, 1742 *2856.30 p186*
Heuchler, Johann Nickel; America, 1738 *2856.30 p186* With wife & children
Heuger, Franz Carl; America, 1738 *2856.30 p186*
Heugh, Andrew; Maryland, 1771 *1640.13 p56*
Heugham, William; New York, 1840 *8197.10 p172*
Heughes, Edward; Boston, 1818 *6058.10 p37*
Heuley, John 30; Ontario, 1871 *1823.28 p40*
Heup, Johann Peter; Port uncertain, 1784 *2856.30 p175* With wife
Heuschelig, Peter *SEE* Heuschelig, Rosina Catharin
Heuschelig, Rosina Catharin; America, 1732 *2856.30 p186* *Husband:* Peter
Heuse, James; Virginia, 1677 *6212.30 p53*
Heuser, Peter; New York, 1837 *8197.10 p91*
Heusland, Johann; America, 1770 *2856.30 p186*
Heuss, Maria Elisabeth; Port uncertain, 1751 *2856.30 p186*
Heusser, Georg; Port uncertain, 1769 *2856.30 p186*
Heusser, Johann Lenhard; Port uncertain, 1754 *2856.30 p187*
Heuston, Alexander; New York, 1840 *8197.10 p174*
Heuston, George 35; Ontario, 1871 *1823.28 p40*
Hew, John 24; Philadelphia, 1774 *1220.25 p2*
Hewandowski, Albert; Maryland, 1910 *3259.35 p20*
Heward, Mr.; Quebec, 1857 *9196.15 p21*
Hewbanck, Will; Virginia, 1690-1691 *6212.30 p59*
Hewer, Benjamin, Jr.; New York, 1839 *8197.10 p242*
Hewes, Elizabeth; Maryland, 1669 *2524.55 p108*
Hewes, Garret; Pennsylvania, 1786 *4629.10 p54*

Hicks, Daniel 19; Ontario, 1861 ***2896.27*** *p34*
Hicks, Daniel 32; Ontario, 1871 ***1823.15*** *p113*
Hicks, Daniel 46; Ontario, 1871 ***1823.22*** *p73*
Hicks, Daniel 71; Ontario, 1871 ***1823.22*** *p73*
Hicks, Dorothy 66; Ontario, 1871 ***1823.15*** *p113*
Hicks, Mrs. Elyel 57; Ontario, 1871 ***1823.15*** *p113*
Hicks, Emanuel 53; Ontario, 1871 ***1823.22*** *p73*
Hicks, Emily 15; Ontario, 1871 ***1823.15*** *p113*
Hicks, G. 11; Ontario, 1861 ***2896.28*** *p9*
Hicks, George 13; Ontario, 1861 ***2896.27*** *p61*
Hicks, George 13; Ontario, 1861 ***2896.28*** *p64*
Hicks, Harriet 43; Ontario, 1861 ***2896.27*** *p34*
Hicks, Hazelet 19; Ontario, 1861 ***2896.26*** *p36*
Hicks, Jacob; Havana, 1765 ***1224.2*** *p56*
Hicks, Jacob; Portsmouth, 1765 ***1224.2*** *p56*
Hicks, James 39; Ontario, 1871 ***1823.15*** *p113*
Hicks, James 45; Ontario, 1871 ***1823.22*** *p73*
Hicks, James 50; Ontario, 1861 ***2896.26*** *p36*
Hicks, Jane 30; Ontario, 1861 ***2896.27*** *p34*
Hicks, Jane 50; Ontario, 1861 ***2896.26*** *p36*
Hicks, John; Maryland, 1667 ***2524.55*** *p108*
Hicks, John; Maryland, 1669 ***2524.55*** *p108*
Hicks, John; Maryland, 1671 ***2524.55*** *p108*
Hicks, John 37; Ontario, 1871 ***1823.15*** *p113*
Hicks, John, II; Maryland, 1667 ***2524.55*** *p108*
Hicks, John A. 12; Ontario, 1861 ***2896.25*** *p7*
Hicks, Joseph 2; Ontario, 1861 ***2896.28*** *p65*
Hicks, Joseph 73; Ontario, 1871 ***1823.22*** *p73*
Hicks, Lewis W. 17; Ontario, 1861 ***2896.27*** *p61*
Hicks, M. 41; Ontario, 1861 ***2896.28*** *p9*
Hicks, M. J. 26; Ontario, 1861 ***2896.26*** *p12*
Hicks, Mary 15; Ontario, 1861 ***2896.25*** *p7*
Hicks, Mary 61; Ontario, 1861 ***2896.27*** *p34*
Hicks, Mary C. 40; Ontario, 1861 ***2896.25*** *p7*
Hicks, Mary E. 5; Ontario, 1861 ***2896.28*** *p65*
Hicks, Mary E. 21; Ontario, 1861 ***2896.27*** *p34*
Hicks, Minard M. 2; Ontario, 1861 ***2896.27*** *p34*
Hicks, Polly 41; Ontario, 1861 ***2896.27*** *p34*
Hicks, Robert 4; Ontario, 1861 ***2896.28*** *p65*
Hicks, Royal C. 61; Ontario, 1861 ***2896.28*** *p64*
Hicks, S. J.; Ontario, 1861 ***2896.26*** *p4*
Hicks, Samuel; Ontario, 1861 ***2896.28*** *p58*
Hicks, Samuel 25; Ontario, 1861 ***2896.27*** *p61*
Hicks, Samuel 30; Ontario, 1871 ***1823.15*** *p113*
Hicks, Sarah 25; Ontario, 1861 ***2896.28*** *p65*
Hicks, Simon 30; Ontario, 1871 ***1823.15*** *p113*
Hicks, Sylvia; Vermont, 1863-1936 ***5900.10*** *p402*
Hicks, Thomas; Maryland, 1673 ***2524.55*** *p108*
Hicks, Thomas; Maryland, 1680 ***2524.55*** *p108*
Hicks, William; Maryland, 1657 ***2524.55*** *p108*
Hicks, William; Virginia, 1666-1667 ***6212.30*** *p33*
Hicks, William 23; Ontario, 1861 ***2896.27*** *p61*
Hicks, William 58; Ontario, 1871 ***1823.28*** *p40*
Hicksby, Thomas; New York, 1842 ***1224.3*** *p35*
Hickseay, Thomas 69; Ontario, 1871 ***1823.28*** *p40*
Hickson, Margaret MacLease; Vermont, 1819-1901 ***5900.10*** *p595*
Hickson, Richard C.; Vermont, 1809-1883 ***5900.10*** *p595*
Hickton, John George; New York, 1840 ***8197.10*** *p174*
Hicky, John 60; Ontario, 1871 ***1823.22*** *p73*
Hiczkowski, Hadislaus; Maryland, 1910 ***3259.35*** *p20*
Hidden, Daniel 50; Ontario, 1871 ***1823.15*** *p113*
Hiddesheimer, Johann Friedric; Port uncertain, 1751 ***2856.30*** *p188*
Hide, Adam J.; Pennsylvania, 1868 ***6058.10*** *p71*
Hide, Bernard; Virginia, 1664 ***6212.30*** *p15*
Hide, Bernard; Virginia, 1665-1666 ***6212.30*** *p22*
Hide, Bernard; Virginia, 1666-1667 ***6212.30*** *p32*
Hide, Edward; Maryland, 1678 ***2524.55*** *p108*
Hide, Edward; Virginia, 1665 ***6212.30*** *p20*
Hide, James; Virginia, 1664 ***6212.30*** *p12*
Hide, Jean; Philadelphia, 1820 ***1224.3*** *p7*
Hide, Tho; Virginia, 1665-1666 ***6212.30*** *p22*
Hide, William; Maryland, 1659 ***2524.55*** *p108*
Hiderman, Frederick 35; Ontario, 1871 ***1823.28*** *p40*
Hiderman, Menia 39; Ontario, 1871 ***1823.28*** *p40*
Hie, Archibold; Maryland, 1670 ***2524.55*** *p108*
Hieatt, Joseph 18; Philadelphia, 1774 ***1220.25*** *p43*
Hiebers, Johann Caspar; America, 1781 ***2856.30*** *p188*
Hiebers, Johann Caspar; Port uncertain, 1762 ***2856.30*** *p188*
Hiedman, Henry 46; Ontario, 1871 ***1823.28*** *p40*
Hieffner, Johann Adam; Port uncertain, 1760 ***2856.30*** *p188*
Hieman, Isaac; New York, New York, 1860 ***6058.10*** *p49*
Hiengie, Anna 30; Kansas, 1899-1910 ***9079.10*** *p35*
Hieringer, Jacob; Port uncertain, 1751 ***2856.30*** *p188*
With wife & 3 children
Hierninger, Jacob; Port uncertain, 1751 ***2856.30*** *p188*
With wife & 3 children
Hies, Margarete; Port uncertain, 1738 ***2856.30*** *p188*
Hieschmann, A. Marg. Phil. Ina; Port uncertain, 1788 ***2856.30*** *p188*
Hiestand, Maria; Port uncertain, 1770 ***2856.30*** *p188*
Hiforn, John 40; Ontario, 1871 ***1823.15*** *p113*
Hiforn, Juley 70; Ontario, 1871 ***1823.15*** *p113*
Higgans, John; Maryland, 1680 ***2524.55*** *p108*
Higgart, Mormion 50; Ontario, 1871 ***1823.15*** *p113*
Higgatte, Elizabeth; Maryland, 1665 ***2524.55*** *p61*
Higgatte, William; Maryland, 1665 ***2524.55*** *p61*
Higgens, Rachael; Maryland, 1663 ***2524.55*** *p220*
Higgens, Rachell; Maryland, 1663 ***2524.55*** *p109*
Higges, Henry; Maryland, 1681 ***2524.55*** *p109*
Higgeson, Richard; Maryland, 1659 ***2524.55*** *p109*
Higginbotham, Arthur; Baltimore, 1783 ***4629.10*** *p74*
Higgins, Abbie 72; Vermont, 1929 ***5900.10*** *p112*
Higgins, Ann 75; Vermont, 1900 ***5900.10*** *p544*
Higgins, Ann Doolin; Vermont, 1841-1913 ***5900.10*** *p383*
Higgins, Anna 27; Vermont, 1880 ***5900.10*** *p424*
Higgins, Arthur; Pennsylvania, 1777 ***4629.10*** *p16*
Higgins, Barnabas; Pennsylvania, 1777 ***4629.10*** *p22*
Higgins, Benjamin 39; Ontario, 1871 ***1823.15*** *p113*
Higgins, Bernard; New York, New York, 1859 ***6058.10*** *p70*
Higgins, Bernard; Vermont, 1817-1867 ***5900.10*** *p424*
Higgins, Bridget; Vermont, 1837-1930 ***5900.10*** *p439*
Higgins, Catherine Kelly; Vermont, n.d. ***5900.10*** *p424*
Higgins, Christina; Vermont, 1837-1892 ***5900.10*** *p107*
Higgins, Daniel; Vermont, 1826-1897 ***5900.10*** *p53*
Higgins, David; New York, 1840 ***8197.10*** *p171*
Higgins, Ellen; Vermont, 1850-1900 ***5900.10*** *p53*
Higgins, Ellen 71; Vermont, 1908 ***5900.10*** *p108*
Higgins, Fergus; Maine, 1740-1750 ***4628.40*** *p77*
Higgins, Frances 66; Ontario, 1871 ***1823.15*** *p113*
Higgins, George 50; Ontario, 1871 ***1823.15*** *p113*
Higgins, Hugh; New York, 1835 ***8197.10*** *p240*
Higgins, Joanna M. 24; Vermont, 1876 ***5900.10*** *p53*
Higgins, John; New England, 1711 ***1224.2*** *p56*
Higgins, John; New York, 1806 ***8197.10*** *p31*
Higgins, John; Vermont, 1812-1899 ***5900.10*** *p439*
Higgins, John 41; Ontario, 1871 ***1823.22*** *p73*
Higgins, John 50; Ontario, 1871 ***1823.15*** *p113*
Higgins, Joseph 45; Ontario, 1871 ***1823.15*** *p113*
Higgins, Katherine; Vermont, 1849-1901 ***5900.10*** *p53*
Higgins, Katherine Sullivan; Vermont, 1829-1904 ***5900.10*** *p424*
Higgins, Luke 45; Ontario, 1871 ***1823.22*** *p73*
Higgins, Margaret; Vermont, 1855-1924 ***5900.10*** *p428*
Higgins, Martha 53; Ontario, 1861 ***2896.25*** *p42*
Higgins, Mary; Maryland, 1681 ***2524.55*** *p109*
Higgins, Mary; Vermont, n.d. ***5900.10*** *p106*
Higgins, Mary; Vermont, 1813-1896 ***5900.10*** *p422*
Higgins, Mary; Vermont, 1841-1916 ***5900.10*** *p446*
Higgins, Mary 60; Vermont, 1915 ***5900.10*** *p112*
Higgins, Mary Cullinan; Vermont, 1831-1889 ***5900.10*** *p43*
Higgins, Mary E. 20; Vermont, 1876 ***5900.10*** *p53*
Higgins, Mary Griffin 74; Vermont, 1906 ***5900.10*** *p112*
Higgins, Mary O'Leary; Vermont, 1823-1913 ***5900.10*** *p53*
Higgins, Mary Sullivan; Vermont, 1834-1908 ***5900.10*** *p432*
Higgins, Mathew 60; Ontario, 1871 ***1823.22*** *p73*
Higgins, Maurice 22; Maryland, 1774 ***1220.25*** *p39*
Higgins, Michael; New York, 1834 ***8197.10*** *p69*
Higgins, Michael; New York, 1837 ***8197.10*** *p90*
Higgins, Michael; New York, New York, 1853 ***6058.10*** *p36*
Higgins, Michael; Pennsylvania, 1830-1837 ***6058.10*** *p12*
Higgins, Michael; Vermont, 1826-1877 ***5900.10*** *p43*
Higgins, Michael 55; Ontario, 1871 ***1823.22*** *p73*
Higgins, Michael 63; Vermont, 1894 ***5900.10*** *p112*
Higgins, Nellie; Vermont, 1856-1912 ***5900.10*** *p435*
Higgins, Nicholas; Maryland, 1681 ***2524.55*** *p109*
Higgins, Patrick; Vermont, 1833-1913 ***5900.10*** *p383*
Higgins, Patrick 32; Vermont, 1900 ***5900.10*** *p112*
Higgins, Patrick 55; Ontario, 1871 ***1823.28*** *p40*
Higgins, Robert 44; Ontario, 1871 ***1823.22*** *p73*
Higgins, Robert Harpur; Boston, 1776 ***1224.2*** *p56*
Higgins, Rose A.; Vermont, 1856-1936 ***5900.10*** *p167*
Higgins, Sarah A.; Vermont, 1844-1919 ***5900.10*** *p169*
Higgins, Symon; Virginia, 1671-1672 ***6212.30*** *p47*
Higgins, Thomas; New York, 1835-1838 ***8197.10*** *p116*
Higgins, Thomas; Vermont, 1830-1922 ***5900.10*** *p432*
Higgins, Thomas 28; Vermont, 1886 ***5900.10*** *p53*
Higgins, Thomas 82; Vermont, 1882 ***5900.10*** *p424*
Higgins, Thomas, Jr. 56; Vermont, 1903 ***5900.10*** *p424*
Higgins, Timothy; Vermont, 1823-1926 ***5900.10*** *p446*
Higgins, Tully; Maine, 1740-1750 ***4628.40*** *p77*
Higgins, William; New York, 1806 ***8197.10*** *p31*
Higgins, William; New York, New York, 1861 ***6058.10*** *p59*
Higgins, William; Pennsylvania, 1786 ***4629.10*** *p52*
Higgins, William 22; Maryland, 1775 ***1220.25*** *p112*
Higgins, William 24; Ontario, 1871 ***1823.22*** *p73*
Higgins, William 48; Ontario, 1871 ***1823.22*** *p73*
Higgins, William G. 28; Ontario, 1871 ***1823.15*** *p113*
Higginson, Christopher; Virginia, 1666 ***1224.1*** *p29*
Higginson, John; Maryland, 1746 ***1224.2*** *p56*
Higginson, John Henry; New York, 1816 ***8197.10*** *p237*
Higgison, John 51; Ontario, 1871 ***1823.28*** *p40*
Higgons, Jno; Virginia, 1664 ***6212.30*** *p9*
Higgons, John; New England, 1711 ***1224.2*** *p56*
Higgs, Fran; Virginia, 1690-1691 ***6212.30*** *p59*
Higgs, James 54; Ontario, 1871 ***1823.28*** *p40*
Higgs, John; Maryland, 1675 ***2524.55*** *p109*
Higgs, John; Virginia, 1664 ***6212.30*** *p6*
Higgs, Mary; Maryland, 1674 ***2524.55*** *p109*
Higgs, William; New York, 1824 ***8197.10*** *p239*
Higgs, William; Pennsylvania, 1709 ***1224.2*** *p56*
High, Andrea James 79; Ontario, 1871 ***1823.22*** *p73*
High, James 60; Ontario, 1871 ***1823.22*** *p74*
Highet, Robert; New York, 1836 ***8197.10*** *p319*
Highlehoon, Wm.; Maryland, 1681 ***2524.55*** *p109*
Higins, John 41; Ontario, 1871 ***1823.15*** *p113*
Higlin, Anna Maria; Port uncertain, 1751 ***2856.30*** *p188*
Higlin, Friedlin; Port uncertain, 1776 ***2856.30*** *p188*
Higman, Edward 18; Maryland, 1774 ***1220.25*** *p71*
Hignett, Elizabeth *SEE* Hignett, Robert
Hignett, James *SEE* Hignett, Robert
Hignett, Robert; Maryland, 1666 ***2524.55*** *p109*
Relative: Elizabeth
Son: Robert, Jr.
Relative: James
Hignett, Robert, Jr. *SEE* Hignett, Robert
Higson, George 23; New York, 1774 ***1220.25*** *p26*
Hilareth, T. M. F. 62; Ontario, 1871 ***1823.22*** *p74*
Hilbank, Thomas 28; Ontario, 1871 ***1823.22*** *p74*
Hilber, George; New York, 1838 ***8197.10*** *p118*
Hilckert, Miss; Port uncertain, 1736 ***2856.30*** *p188*
Hilckert, Johann Peter; America, 1737 ***2856.30*** *p188*
Hilctowski, Valentine; Maryland, 1910 ***3259.35*** *p20*
Hild, Elisabeth; Port uncertain, 1751 ***2856.30*** *p188*
Hild, Johann Wilhelm; England, 1791 ***2856.30*** *p188*
Hild, Johann Wilhelm; Port uncertain, 1772 ***2856.30*** *p188*
Hildebr, Elisabeth; America, 1732 ***2856.30*** *p218*
Hildebrand, Mr.; America, 1732 ***2856.30*** *p255*
Hildebrand, Friedrich; Port uncertain, 1727 ***2856.30*** *p188*
Hildebrand, Henry; Pennsylvania, 1786 ***4629.10*** *p51*
Hildebrand, John 35; Ontario, 1871 ***1823.15*** *p113*
Hildebrand, Magdalena; Port uncertain, 1727 ***2856.30*** *p188*
Hildebrandt, Elisabeth; America, 1731 ***2856.30*** *p188*
Hildebrandt, Elisabeth; America, 1732 ***2856.30*** *p188*
Hildenbran, Susanna Kundig; America, 1732 ***2856.30*** *p255*
Hildenbrand, Konrad, The Old; America, 1732 ***2856.30*** *p188*
Hildenbrand, Konrad, The Younger; Port uncertain, 1746 ***2856.30*** *p188*
Hildenbrand, Konrad, The Younger; America, 1732 ***2856.30*** *p188*
Hildenbrandt, Johann Adam; Port uncertain, 1788 ***2856.30*** *p188*
Hildersby, Timo; Virginia, 1667 ***6212.30*** *p37*
Hilditch, Rebecca 27; Maryland, 1775 ***1220.25*** *p113*
Hilditch, Wm N. 27; Ontario, 1871 ***1823.28*** *p40*
Hildroth, Heney 45; Ontario, 1871 ***1823.15*** *p113*
Hildwein, John Christoph; New York, 1838 ***8197.10*** *p116*
Hildyard, William; America, 1756 ***1224.2*** *p56*
Hileman, Christoph; Pennsylvania, 1850 ***6058.10*** *p26*
Hiles, William 45; Ontario, 1871 ***1823.15*** *p113*
Hilfferich, Georg Jacob; Port uncertain, 1743 ***2856.30*** *p188*
Hilgard, Theodore; New York, 1833 ***8197.10*** *p240*
Hilgenberg, Amelia 44; Kansas, 1876-1910 ***9079.10*** *p19*
Hilgenberg, Chris 49; Kansas, 1874-1910 ***9079.10*** *p19*
Hilgenberg, David 48; Kansas, 1876-1910 ***9079.10*** *p39*
Hilgert, Johann Christof; Port uncertain, 1747 ***2856.30*** *p189*
With 8 children
Hilgert, Johann Franz; Port uncertain, 1751 ***2856.30*** *p189*
Hilgert, Matheis; Port uncertain, 1794 ***2856.30*** *p189*
Hilgerth, Philipp; Port uncertain, 1747 ***2856.30*** *p189*
With wife & children
Hiliewicz, Stanislausa; Maryland, 1910 ***3259.35*** *p20*
Hiliky, John 33; Ontario, 1861 ***2896.25*** *p24*
Hilint, Elizabeth 21; Maryland, 1774 ***1220.25*** *p85*
Hiliwicz, Austin; Maryland, 1910 ***3259.35*** *p20*
Hill, . . .; Boston, 1765 ***4628.40*** *p114*
Hill, Miss; Quebec, 1858 ***9196.15*** *p40*
Hill, Mr.; Quebec, 1857 ***9196.15*** *p14*
Hill, Mr.; Quebec, 1857 ***9196.15*** *p21*
Hill, Mr.; Quebec, 1857 ***9196.15*** *p24*
Hill, Abell; Maryland, 1675 ***2524.55*** *p109*
Hill, Adam; Maryland, 1768 ***1224.2*** *p56*

Hill, Alice *SEE* Hill, John
Hill, Alice; Maryland, 1678 ***2524.55*** *p109*
Hill, Allen; Virginia, 1726 ***1224.2*** *p56*
Hill, Amos *SEE* Hill, Thomas
Hill, Andrew; Virginia, 1664 ***6212.30*** *p12*
Hill, Ann *SEE* Hill, William
Hill, Ann; Maryland, 1677 ***2524.55*** *p109*
Hill, Ann 21; Philadelphia, 1774 ***1220.25*** *p63*
Hill, Ann 24; Carolina, 1775 ***1220.25*** *p123*
Hill, Annie; Vermont, 1826-1898 ***5900.10*** *p83*
Hill, Anthony 57; Nova Scotia, 1774 ***1220.25*** *p13*
Hill, Archibald; Iroquois Co., Illinois, 1858 ***1640.13*** *p56*
Hill, Bridget 38; Vermont, 1876 ***5900.10*** *p214*
Hill, C. 23; Alaska, 1912 ***9196.1*** *p39*
Hill, C. 23; Yukon, 1912 ***9196.1*** *p39*
Hill, Casper 46; Ontario, 1871 ***1823.15*** *p113*
Hill, Charles; Georgia, 1700 ***1640.13*** *p56*
Hill, Charles; New York, 1807 ***8197.10*** *p332*
Hill, Charles 16; Maryland, 1773-1774 ***1220.25*** *p33*
Hill, Christian *SEE* Hill, Thomas
Hill, Clement; Maryland, 1675 ***2524.55*** *p109*
Hill, D. B. 63; Ontario, 1861 ***2896.27*** *p9*
Hill, David *SEE* Hill, Thomas
Hill, David; Pennsylvania, 1779 ***4629.10*** *p41*
Hill, David 45; Ontario, 1871 ***1823.15*** *p113*
Hill, Dorothy; Maryland, 1666 ***2524.55*** *p115*
Hill, Edward; Virginia, 1677 ***1224.1*** *p31*
Hill, Elizabeth *SEE* Hill, John
Hill, Elizabeth *SEE* Hill, William
Hill, Elizabeth 2 *SEE* Hill, John
Hill, Elizabeth 38; Ontario, 1871 ***1823.22*** *p74*
Hill, Ellinor *SEE* Hill, William
Hill, Francis; Maryland, 1665 ***2524.55*** *p109*
Hill, Francis; Maryland, 1666 ***2524.55*** *p109*
Hill, Francis 66; Ontario, 1871 ***1823.15*** *p113*
Hill, George; Boston, 1879 ***1640.13*** *p56*
Hill, George 25; Ontario, 1871 ***1823.22*** *p74*
Hill, George 45; Ontario, 1871 ***1823.15*** *p113*
Hill, George 50; Ontario, 1871 ***1823.22*** *p74*
Hill, Hans Adam; America, 1727 ***2856.30*** *p189*
Hill, Harriett 36; Ontario, 1871 ***1823.22*** *p74*
Hill, Hassadia *SEE* Hill, Thomas
Hill, Henry; Pennsylvania, 1777 ***4629.10*** *p11*
Hill, Henry 38; Maryland, 1774 ***1220.25*** *p52*
Hill, Henry 46; Ontario, 1871 ***1823.28*** *p40*
Hill, Hugh; Pennsylvania, 1848 ***6058.10*** *p25*
Hill, Hugh; Vermont, 1836-1909 ***5900.10*** *p423*
Hill, Hugh 49; Ontario, 1871 ***1823.15*** *p113*
Hill, Isaac; New York, 1815 ***8197.10*** *p236*
Hill, Isaac 44; Ontario, 1871 ***1823.15*** *p113*
Hill, Isic 18; Ontario, 1861 ***2896.27*** *p8*
Hill, J. 20; Ontario, 1861 ***2896.26*** *p9*
Hill, Jacob; Maryland, 1680 ***2524.55*** *p109*
Hill, Jame 36; Ontario, 1871 ***1823.15*** *p113*
Hill, James; Chicago, 1853 ***1224.3*** *p37*
Hill, James; New York, 1839 ***8197.10*** *p241*
Hill, James; Virginia, 1664 ***6212.30*** *p7*
Hill, James 29; Ontario, 1871 ***1823.15*** *p113*
Hill, James 52; Ontario, 1871 ***1823.22*** *p74*
Hill, James H.; New York, 1838 ***8197.10*** *p241*
Hill, James Spackman; Cincinnati, 1830 ***1224.3*** *p37*
Hill, Jane; Maryland, 1659 ***2524.55*** *p109*
Hill, Jane; Virginia, 1666 ***6212.30*** *p27*
Hill, Jane 28 *SEE* Hill, John
Hill, Jane 46; Ontario, 1871 ***1823.22*** *p74*
Hill, Joan; Virginia, 1665-1666 ***6212.30*** *p24*
Hill, Johann; Port uncertain, 1786 ***2856.30*** *p189*
Hill, Johann; Port uncertain, 1787 ***2856.30*** *p189*
Hill, John; Maryland, 1658 ***2524.55*** *p109*
Sister: Mary
Hill, John; Maryland, 1666 ***2524.55*** *p178*
Hill, John; Maryland, 1669 ***2524.55*** *p109*
Wife: Alice
Child: Jude
Child: Elizabeth
Hill, John; Maryland, 1678 ***2524.55*** *p109*
Hill, John; New York, 1807 ***8197.10*** *p40*
Hill, John; New York, 1838 ***8197.10*** *p116*
Hill, John; Quebec, 1858 ***9196.15*** *p37*
Hill, John; Virginia, 1666-1667 ***6212.30*** *p34*
Hill, John 24; Virginia, 1773 ***1220.25*** *p28*
Hill, John 25; Fort Cumberland, Nova Scotia, 1774 ***1220.25*** *p17*
Wife: Jane 28
Child: Mary 1
Child: Elizabeth 2
Child: Thomas 2
Hill, John 26; Ontario, 1871 ***1823.28*** *p40*
Hill, John 30; Ontario, 1871 ***1823.15*** *p113*
Hill, John 45; Ontario, 1871 ***1823.15*** *p113*
Hill, John 47; Ontario, 1871 ***1823.28*** *p40*
Hill, John 56; Ontario, 1871 ***1823.28*** *p40*
Hill, John 70; Ontario, 1871 ***1823.15*** *p113*
Hill, John, Sr. 66; Ontario, 1871 ***1823.28*** *p40*
Hill, Mrs. John; Quebec, 1858 ***9196.15*** *p37*
Hill, John Leacock; Pennsylvania, 1784 ***4629.10*** *p45*
Hill, Joseph *SEE* Hill, Thomas
Hill, Joseph; New York, 1805 ***8197.10*** *p29*
Hill, Joseph 21; Maryland, 1775 ***1220.25*** *p120*
Hill, Judath 60; Ontario, 1871 ***1823.15*** *p113*
Hill, Jude *SEE* Hill, John
Hill, Littleton; South Carolina, 1752 ***1224.2*** *p56*
Hill, M. 15; Ontario, 1861 ***2896.26*** *p9*
Hill, M. 17; Ontario, 1861 ***2896.26*** *p9*
Hill, M. 22; Ontario, 1861 ***2896.26*** *p9*
Hill, Margaret; Maryland, 1654 ***2524.55*** *p110*
Hill, Marget 16; Ontario, 1861 ***2896.27*** *p8*
Hill, Margret; Virginia, 1678 ***6212.30*** *p54*
Hill, Margret 96; Ontario, 1871 ***1823.15*** *p113*
Hill, Marion; Montreal, 1891 ***1640.13*** *p56*
Hill, Martha; Virginia, 1778 ***1224.2*** *p56*
Hill, Mary *SEE* Hill, John
Hill, Mary; Charles Town, South Carolina, 1749 ***1224.2*** *p9*
Hill, Mary; Maryland, 1680 ***2524.55*** *p109*
Hill, Mary; New England, 1680 ***1224.1*** *p58*
Hill, Mary; New Orleans, 1842 ***1224.3*** *p45*
Hill, Mary; Vermont, 1869-1945 ***5900.10*** *p607*
Hill, Mary 1 *SEE* Hill, John
Hill, Mathew; Maryland, 1650 ***2524.55*** *p109*
Hill, Michaell; Virginia, 1666 ***6212.30*** *p27*
Hill, Missall Stodart; Boston, 1878 ***1640.13*** *p56*
Hill, Niel 41; Ontario, 1871 ***1823.15*** *p114*
Hill, Peter; Port uncertain, 1741 ***2856.30*** *p189*
Hill, R. 38; Ontario, 1861 ***2896.27*** *p9*
Hill, Rich; Virginia, 1693-1694 ***6212.30*** *p60*
Hill, Richard; Maryland, 1672 ***2524.55*** *p109*
Hill, Richard; Died enroute, 1635 ***1224.1*** *p29*
Hill, Richard 24; Ontario, 1861 ***2896.28*** *p54*
Hill, Richard 24; Philadelphia, 1774 ***1220.25*** *p66*
Hill, Richard 37; Maryland, 1774 ***1220.25*** *p57*
Hill, Robert 32; Ontario, 1871 ***1823.22*** *p74*
Hill, Robert 46; Ontario, 1871 ***1823.15*** *p114*
Hill, Robert B. 28; Ontario, 1871 ***1823.28*** *p40*
Hill, Ruth *SEE* Hill, Thomas
Hill, S. 2; Ontario, 1861 ***2896.26*** *p9*
Hill, S. 5; Ontario, 1861 ***2896.26*** *p9*
Hill, Samuel *SEE* Hill, William
Hill, Samuel; Charles Town, South Carolina, 1787 ***1224.2*** *p56*
Hill, Samuel; Maryland, 1660 ***2524.55*** *p109*
Hill, Samuel; New York, 1826 ***8197.10*** *p336*
Hill, Samuel; Virginia, 1695 ***1224.1*** *p29*
Hill, Sarah Nugent; Vermont, 1843-1913 ***5900.10*** *p424*
Hill, Simon; Pennsylvania, 1842 ***6058.10*** *p18*
Hill, Simon 64; Ontario, 1871 ***1823.15*** *p114*
Hill, Stephen 64; Ontario, 1871 ***1823.15*** *p114*
Hill, Thomas *SEE* Hill, Thomas
Hill, Thomas; Canada, 1869 ***1640.13*** *p56*
Hill, Thomas; Maryland, 1652 ***2524.55*** *p109*
Child: Ruth
Child: Hassadia
Child: Thomas
Wife: Christian
Child: Joseph
Child: David
Child: Amos
Hill, Thomas; Maryland, 1658 ***2524.55*** *p109*
Hill, Thomas 2 *SEE* Hill, John
Hill, Thomas 22; Maryland, 1774 ***1220.25*** *p59*
Hill, Thomas 35; Ontario, 1871 ***1823.15*** *p114*
Hill, Thomas 35; Virginia, 1773 ***1220.25*** *p30*
Hill, Thomas 36; Ontario, 1871 ***1823.28*** *p40*
Hill, Thomas 37; Ontario, 1871 ***1823.15*** *p114*
Hill, Thomas 47; Ontario, 1871 ***1823.22*** *p74*
Hill, Thomas 50; Ontario, 1871 ***1823.15*** *p114*
Hill, Thomas 55; Ontario, 1871 ***1823.28*** *p40*
Hill, Thomas 56; Ontario, 1871 ***1823.15*** *p114*
Hill, Thomas 57; Ontario, 1871 ***1823.28*** *p40*
Hill, Thomas 77; Vermont, 1908 ***5900.10*** *p214*
Hill, Valentine; Maryland, 1675 ***2524.55*** *p109*
Hill, Valentine; New England, 1688 ***1224.1*** *p29*
Hill, Walter 33; Ontario, 1871 ***1823.15*** *p114*
Hill, William *SEE* Hill, William
Hill, William; Maryland, 1658 ***2524.55*** *p110*
Hill, William; Maryland, 1667 ***2524.55*** *p109*
Wife: Ann
Daughter: Elizabeth
Son: William
Daughter: Ellinor
Son: Samuel
Hill, William; Maryland, 1669 ***2524.55*** *p110*
Hill, William; New England, 1665 ***1224.1*** *p24*
Hill, William; New Orleans, 1826 ***1640.10*** *p80*
Hill, William; Nova Scotia, 1804 ***1224.3*** *p37*
Hill, William; Ontario, 1871 ***1823.22*** *p74*
Hill, William; Pennsylvania, 1779 ***4629.10*** *p41*
Hill, William; Pennsylvania, 1807 ***6058.10*** *p1*
Hill, William 20; Ontario, 1861 ***2896.27*** *p19*
Hill, William 26; Ontario, 1871 ***1823.15*** *p114*
Hill, William 29; Ontario, 1871 ***1823.15*** *p114*
Hill, William 31; Ontario, 1871 ***1823.22*** *p74*
Hill, William 41; Ontario, 1871 ***1823.22*** *p74*
Hill, William 45; Ontario, 1871 ***1823.28*** *p40*
Hill, William 46; Ontario, 1871 ***1823.15*** *p114*
Hill, William 50; Ontario, 1871 ***1823.15*** *p114*
Hill, William 50; Ontario, 1871 ***1823.22*** *p74*
Hill, William 58; Ontario, 1871 ***1823.28*** *p40*
Hill, Willoughby; Virginia, 1703 ***1224.2*** *p56*
Hilla, John J.; Maryland, 1910 ***3259.35*** *p20*
Hillard, Flora 32; Alaska, 1914 ***9196.1*** *p25*
Hillard, Flora 32; British Columbia, 1914 ***9196.1*** *p25*
Hillard, Fred 35; Alaska, 1914 ***9196.1*** *p25*
Hillard, Fred 35; British Columbia, 1914 ***9196.1*** *p25*
Hillard, Mrs. S. 29; Alaska, 1913 ***9196.1*** *p22*
Hillard, Mrs. S. 29; British Columbia, 1913 ***9196.1*** *p22*
Hillary, Thomas; Maryland, 1666 ***2524.55*** *p110*
Hillbank, George 33; Ontario, 1871 ***1823.22*** *p74*
Hillbank, Peter 54; Ontario, 1871 ***1823.22*** *p74*
Hillbibern, Christian; Port uncertain, 1758 ***2856.30*** *p189*
Hillegas, Georg Albrecht; America, 1746 ***2856.30*** *p189*
Hillegas, Michael; America, 1729-1799 ***2856.30*** *p189*
Hillegass, Albrecht; America, 1769 ***2856.30*** *p189*
Hillen, John; Maryland, 1665 ***2524.55*** *p110*
Hiller, Johannes; New York, 1837 ***8197.10*** *p90*
Hiller, John Michial 23; Ontario, 1871 ***1823.15*** *p114*
Hiller, Richard 21; Virginia, 1773 ***1220.25*** *p29*
Hillert, Franz Anton; Port uncertain, 1770 ***2856.30*** *p189*
Hilliar, Frederick 27; Virginia, 1774 ***1220.25*** *p38*
Hilliar, John 31; Ontario, 1871 ***1823.15*** *p114*
Hilliar, Luisa 70; Ontario, 1871 ***1823.15*** *p114*
Hilliard, Edm; Virginia, 1664 ***6212.30*** *p7*
Hilliard, Isaace; Maryland, 1671 ***2524.55*** *p110*
Hilliard, John 80; Ontario, 1871 ***1823.15*** *p114*
Hilliard, John, Sr.; Maryland, 1665 ***2524.55*** *p110*
Relative: Mary
Son: John, Jr.
Hilliard, John, Jr. *SEE* Hilliard, John, Sr.
Hilliard, Mary *SEE* Hilliard, John, Sr.
Hilliard, Mary; Maryland, 1681 ***2524.55*** *p110*
Hilliard, Mary 68; Vermont, 1879 ***5900.10*** *p269*
Hilliard, Thomas 36; Ontario, 1871 ***1823.28*** *p40*
Hillier, Charles 40; Ontario, 1871 ***1823.15*** *p114*
Hillier, David 30; Philadelphia, 1774 ***1220.25*** *p66*
Hillier, Isaac; Virginia, 1664-1665 ***6212.30*** *p16*
Hillier, James 26; Maryland, 1774 ***1220.25*** *p70*
Hillier, Joseph; Pennsylvania, 1821-1835 ***6058.10*** *p19*
Hillier, Samuel; Pennsylvania, 1844 ***6058.10*** *p19*
Hillier, William 32; Ontario, 1871 ***1823.15*** *p114*
Hilliher, Elizabeth 32; Vermont, 1815 ***5900.10*** *p606*
Hilliker, James; New York, 1840 ***8197.10*** *p242*
Hilling, Thomas J. 47; Alaska, 1917 ***9196.1*** *p8*
Hilling, Thomas J. 47; Yukon, 1917 ***9196.1*** *p8*
Hillman, Ann 70; Ontario, 1871 ***1823.15*** *p114*
Hillman, Charles 18; Ontario, 1871 ***1823.15*** *p114*
Hillmann, Miss; America, 1752 ***2856.30*** *p189*
With sister
Hills, Blanch E. 31; Ontario, 1861 ***2896.28*** *p29*
Hills, James; Savannah, Georgia, 1804 ***1640.10*** *p80*
Hills, Robert 6; Ontario, 1861 ***2896.28*** *p29*
Hills, William; Maryland, 1655 ***2524.55*** *p110*
Hills, William; Maryland, 1657 ***2524.55*** *p110*
Hillsburgh, Charles; New York, 1827 ***8197.10*** *p240*
Hillsburgh, Charles; New York, 1827 ***8197.10*** *p342*
Hillton, Robert; Virginia, 1665 ***6212.30*** *p20*
Hilly, John; Virginia, 1698 ***6212.30*** *p61*
Hillyard, William 60; Ontario, 1871 ***1823.15*** *p114*
Hillyer, William 21; Virginia, 1774 ***1220.25*** *p87*
Hilowoich, John; Maryland, 1910 ***3259.35*** *p20*
Hilpert, Eva Elisabeth; Port uncertain, 1733 ***2856.30*** *p189*
Hilsch, Gabriel; Port uncertain, 1784 ***2856.30*** *p189*
Hilson, George; Virginia, 1679 ***1224.1*** *p29*
Hiltenbrandt, Adam; America, 1750 ***2856.30*** *p189*
Hilton, Benjamin; New York, New York, 1834 ***1224.3*** *p37*
Hilton, John; Maryland, 1675 ***2524.55*** *p110*
Hilton, John; New York, 1833 ***8197.10*** *p358*
Hilton, John 28; Ontario, 1871 ***1823.22*** *p74*
Hilton, Nowell; Charlestown, Massachusetts, 1689 ***1224.1*** *p29*
Hilton, Simson 76; Ontario, 1871 ***1823.22*** *p74*
Hilton, William; New York, 1840 ***8197.10*** *p174*
Hiltzheimer, Jacob; America, 1729-1799 ***2856.30*** *p189*
Hiltzheimer, Robert; Pennsylvania, 1786 ***4629.10*** *p53*
Hilz, Peter; America, 1764 ***2856.30*** *p189*
Himan, Isaac; New York, New York, 1860 ***6058.10*** *p49*
Himer, Louis 24; Ontario, 1871 ***1823.28*** *p40*
Himes, Henry 36; Ontario, 1871 ***1823.15*** *p114*

Himler, A. M. Kress *SEE* Himler, Heinrich
Himler, H.; America, 1748 ***2856.30*** *p245*
Himler, Heinrich; America, 1748 ***2856.30*** *p189*
With wife
Himler, Heinrich; America, 1748 ***2856.30*** *p189*
Wife: A. M. Kress
Himler, Thomas 34; Virginia, 1774 ***1220.25*** *p88*
Himmel, Christmann; Port uncertain, 1697 ***2856.30*** *p189*
Himmel, Hans Georg; Port uncertain, 1758 ***2856.30*** *p189*
Himmel, Matthaus; Port uncertain, 1768 ***2856.30*** *p189*
Himmelberger, Georg; America, 1749 ***2856.30*** *p189*
Himmele, Marianna; Port uncertain, 1784 ***2856.30*** *p189*
Himmelmann, Philipp; America, 1752 ***2856.30*** *p189*
With wife & 10 children
Himmelspacher, Caspar; Port uncertain, 1737 ***2856.30*** *p189*
Himmelspacher, Caspar; Port uncertain, 1782 ***2856.30*** *p189*
Himmlin, Catharina; Port uncertain, 1770 ***2856.30*** *p189*
Himperler, Anton; America, 1737 ***2856.30*** *p189*
Himtey, Mary; Maryland, 1671 ***2524.55*** *p110*
Hinan, John 22; Philadelphia, 1774 ***1220.25*** *p66*
Hinch, Sarah 21; Philadelphia, 1774 ***1220.25*** *p63*
Hinch, William; New York, New York, 1834 ***6058.10*** *p32*
Hinchey, Hannah; Vermont, 1812-1901 ***5900.10*** *p272*
Hinchey, Hanora Quirk; Vermont, 1844-1904 ***5900.10*** *p414*
Hinchey, James; Vermont, 1845-1925 ***5900.10*** *p414*
Hinchey, James; Vermont, 1886 ***5900.10*** *p272*
Hinchey, Nathan 60; Ontario, 1871 ***1823.22*** *p74*
Hinchey, Nora 75; Vermont, 1905 ***5900.10*** *p591*
Hinchey, Sarah; Vermont, 1803-1895 ***5900.10*** *p415*
Hinchey, Thomas; Vermont, 1828-1928 ***5900.10*** *p591*
Hinchley, Sarah; Maryland, 1665 ***2524.55*** *p110*
Hinchman, John; New Jersey, 1790 ***1224.2*** *p56*
Hinckel, Christian; America, 1740 ***2856.30*** *p189*
Hinckel, Christian; America, 1741 ***2856.30*** *p189*
Hinckel, Johann; Port uncertain, 1770 ***2856.30*** *p189*
Hinckel, Konrad; Port uncertain, 1732 ***2856.30*** *p189*
Hinckelin, Maria Margarete; Port uncertain, 1770 ***2856.30*** *p190*
With husband
Hinckey, Annie 62; Vermont, 1888 ***5900.10*** *p590*
Hinckhel, Konrad; America, 1748 ***2856.30*** *p190*
Hinckhel, Konrad; Port uncertain, 1748 ***2856.30*** *p190*
With wife & 4 children
Hinckley, William; Florida, 1850 ***1224.3*** *p37*
Hincks, Arthur; Virginia, 1664 ***6212.30*** *p12*
Hincks, Dorothy; Maryland, 1668 ***2524.55*** *p110*
Hincks, James; Vermont, 1849-1920 ***5900.10*** *p318*
Hincks, Mary Smith; Vermont, 1852-1911 ***5900.10*** *p318*
Hind, Ann 65; Ontario, 1871 ***1823.15*** *p114*
Hind, Anna 20; Ontario, 1871 ***1823.15*** *p114*
Hind, Edward; Maryland, 1665 ***2524.55*** *p110*
Hind, George 37; Ontario, 1871 ***1823.15*** *p114*
Hind, Isaac 32; Maryland, 1774 ***1220.25*** *p60*
Hind, Jane 52; Ontario, 1871 ***1823.22*** *p74*
Hind, John 21; Maryland, 1774 ***1220.25*** *p70*
Hind, John 40; Ontario, 1871 ***1823.15*** *p114*
Hind, John 40; Philadelphia, 1774 ***1220.25*** *p43*
Hind, Robert 36; Ontario, 1871 ***1823.15*** *p114*
Hind, Thomas; New York, 1833-1838 ***8197.10*** *p116*
Hind, William; Virginia, 1673 ***1224.1*** *p29*
Hind, William 45; Ontario, 1871 ***1823.15*** *p114*
Hinde, Elizabeth; Maryland, 1674 ***2524.55*** *p110*
Hinde, Mary; Maryland, 1674 ***2524.55*** *p110*
Hinderhuber, Johann; Port uncertain, 1752 ***2856.30*** *p190*
Hinders, Richard; Maryland, 1669 ***2524.55*** *p110*
Hinderschid, Wilhelm; America, 1749 ***2856.30*** *p190*
With wife & 2 children
Hinderson, Alice *SEE* Hinderson, James
Hinderson, Bertrett; Maryland, 1661 ***2524.55*** *p110*
Relative: Sindricke
Hinderson, James; Maryland, 1668 ***2524.55*** *p110*
Wife: Alice
Child: John
Child: Jeane
Child: William
Hinderson, Jeane *SEE* Hinderson, James
Hinderson, John *SEE* Hinderson, James
Hinderson, Sindricke *SEE* Hinderson, Bertrett
Hinderson, William *SEE* Hinderson, James
Hindhaugh, William; New York, 1839 ***8197.10*** *p241*
Hindinarch, Michael 35; Ontario, 1871 ***1823.28*** *p40*
Hindle, Mr.; Quebec, 1856 ***9196.15*** *p8*
Hindle, Mrs.; Quebec, 1856 ***9196.15*** *p8*
Hindman, Susan 3; Ontario, 1871 ***1823.15*** *p114*
Hinds, Christopher 68; Ontario, 1871 ***1823.22*** *p74*
Hinds, David; New York, 1839 ***8197.10*** *p242*
Hinds, James; New York, 1839 ***8197.10*** *p242*
Hinds, Jane 67; Ontario, 1871 ***1823.22*** *p74*
Hine, Edgar; Virginia, 1663 ***6212.30*** *p1*
Hine, Thomas; New Orleans, 1845 ***1224.3*** *p37*
Hine, William; Virginia, 1666 ***6212.30*** *p27*
Hine, William 50; Ontario, 1871 ***1823.15*** *p114*
Hine, Wm.; Maryland, 1670 ***2524.55*** *p110*
Hineditee, William 43; Ontario, 1871 ***1823.15*** *p114*
Hiner, Heinrich; America, 1764 ***2856.30*** *p190*
Hines, Catherine; Vermont, 1851-1916 ***5900.10*** *p90*
Hines, Hannah Fitzgerald; Vermont, 1832-1914 ***5900.10*** *p126*
Hines, Jane; Vermont, 1852-1921 ***5900.10*** *p558*
Hines, M. 52; Ontario, 1861 ***2896.28*** *p9*
Hines, Margaret Brennan 27; Vermont, 1877 ***5900.10*** *p557*
Hines, Margaret Brennan 27; Vermont, 1877 ***5900.10*** *p569*
Hines, Martin; Vermont, 1840-1925 ***5900.10*** *p557*
Hines, Martin; Vermont, 1840-1925 ***5900.10*** *p569*
Hines, Mary; Vermont, 1846-1919 ***5900.10*** *p253*
Hines, Mary 65; Vermont, 1870 ***5900.10*** *p526*
Hines, Patrick; Vermont, 1847-1905 ***5900.10*** *p558*
Hines, R. 64; Ontario, 1861 ***2896.28*** *p9*
Hines, Richard 78; Vermont, 1872 ***5900.10*** *p526*
Hines, Richard Johnston; New Orleans, 1850 ***1224.3*** *p37*
Hines, William; Pennsylvania, 1846 ***6058.10*** *p22*
Hines, William; Vermont, 1833-1910 ***5900.10*** *p126*
Hines, William 40; Ontario, 1871 ***1823.15*** *p114*
Hiney, Godfrey; Pennsylvania, 1777 ***4629.10*** *p12*
Hingh, James; Virginia, 1666-1667 ***6212.30*** *p32*
Hingston, Mr.; Quebec, 1857 ***9196.15*** *p18*
Hingston, W. G. 63; Ontario, 1871 ***1823.15*** *p114*
Hinkley, Mary A. 5; Vermont, 1858 ***5900.10*** *p152*
Hinkley, Sarah; Maryland, 1631-1685 ***2524.55*** *p110*
Hinkley, Silas 48; Vermont, 1859 ***5900.10*** *p152*
Hinkley, Thomas; New York, New York, 1816 ***6058.10*** *p33*
Hinks, Harvey 55; Ontario, 1871 ***1823.15*** *p114*
Hinman, Ja; Virginia, 1665-1666 ***6212.30*** *p22*
Hinman, Thomas; Virginia, 1664 ***6212.30*** *p13*
Hinnenschied, Gertrud; Port uncertain, 1792 ***2856.30*** *p190*
Hinrichs, Carl Ernst Louis; New York, 1838 ***8197.10*** *p241*
Hinrichs, Charles F. A.; New York, 1840 ***8197.10*** *p242*
Hinritz, John; New York, 1838 ***8197.10*** *p117*
Hinsall, Thomas; Maryland, 1666 ***2524.55*** *p110*
Hinson, Ann *SEE* Hinson, Thomas
Hinson, Grace *SEE* Hinson, Thomas
Hinson, John *SEE* Hinson, Thomas
Hinson, John; Maryland, 1666 ***2524.55*** *p110*
Hinson, Rachiell; Maryland, 1666 ***2524.55*** *p110*
Hinson, Thomas; Maryland, 1651 ***2524.55*** *p110*
With wife
Child: Ann
Child: Grace
Child: John
Hinson, Thomas; Maryland, 1667 ***2524.55*** *p119*
With wife
Hinstandt, Jakob; America, 1752 ***2856.30*** *p190*
Hinton, Mrs.; Maryland, 1665 ***2524.55*** *p110*
Hinton, Anne; Virginia, 1635 ***1224.1*** *p23*
Hinton, Christopher; Maryland, 1667 ***2524.55*** *p110*
Hinton, James 23; Maryland, 1774 ***1220.25*** *p64*
Hinton, Joane *SEE* Hinton, Thomas
Hinton, John; New York, 1803 ***8197.10*** *p13*
Hinton, Louis E. 19; Ontario, 1871 ***1823.28*** *p40*
Hinton, Samuel; Maryland, 1671 ***2524.55*** *p110*
Hinton, Samuel 21; Ontario, 1871 ***1823.28*** *p40*
Hinton, Thomas; Maryland, 1662 ***2524.55*** *p110*
Wife: Joane
Hinton, William; Maryland, 1681 ***2524.55*** *p110*
Hintz, Alexander; New York, 1838 ***8197.10*** *p117*
Hiorne, William 26; Maryland, 1774 ***1220.25*** *p54*
Hiorns, William; Philadelphia, n.d. ***1224.2*** *p56*
Hipert, Paul; Port uncertain, 1790 ***2856.30*** *p190*
Hipert, Philipp; Port uncertain, 1790 ***2856.30*** *p190*
Hipkins, Paris; Georgia, 1855 ***1224.3*** *p37*
Hipkis, Peter; Maryland, 1656 ***2524.55*** *p110*
Hipp, Adam; Port uncertain, 1790 ***2856.30*** *p190*
Hipp, Michael; Port uncertain, 1790 ***2856.30*** *p190*
Hipper, John; New York, 1807 ***8197.10*** *p40*
Hippert, Paul; Port uncertain, 1790 ***2856.30*** *p190*
Hippert, Philipp; Port uncertain, 1790 ***2856.30*** *p190*
Hippert, Philipp; Port uncertain, 1793 ***2856.30*** *p190*
Hippesley, Joseph 16; Maryland, 1774 ***1220.25*** *p61*
Hippesty, Thomas; Maryland, 1649 ***2524.55*** *p180*
Hipples, James 40; Ontario, 1871 ***1823.15*** *p114*
Hippmann, Matthaus; Port uncertain, 1734 ***2856.30*** *p190*
With wife & 4 children
Hipwell, Abraham; New York, 1815 ***8197.10*** *p56*
Hirce, Michel 31; Ontario, 1861 ***2896.27*** *p20*
Hirce, Rose 23; Ontario, 1861 ***2896.27*** *p20*
Hirle, Michael; Port uncertain, 1772 ***2856.30*** *p190*
Hirlemann, George; New York, 1836 ***8197.10*** *p241*
Hirren, Thomas 66; Ontario, 1871 ***1823.22*** *p74*
Hirrly, Ellen 25; Ontario, 1871 ***1823.15*** *p114*
Hirrly, John 58; Ontario, 1871 ***1823.15*** *p115*
Hirrly, Margaret 29; Ontario, 1871 ***1823.15*** *p115*
Hirrly, William 11; Ontario, 1871 ***1823.15*** *p115*
Hirsch, Anna Maria; Port uncertain, 1745 ***2856.30*** *p190*
Hirsch, Barbara; Port uncertain, 1767 ***2856.30*** *p190*
Hirsch, Charles 35; Ontario, 1871 ***1823.28*** *p40*
Hirsch, Christian; Port uncertain, 1750 ***2856.30*** *p190*
Hirsch, Hans Georg; Port uncertain, 1733 ***2856.30*** *p190*
Hirsch, Hans Georg; Port uncertain, 1771 ***2856.30*** *p190*
Hirsch, Jacob; Port uncertain, 1764 ***2856.30*** *p190*
With wife & 4 children
Hirsch, Johann; Port uncertain, 1771 ***2856.30*** *p190*
Hirsch, Nikolaus; Port uncertain, 1771 ***2856.30*** *p190*
Hirsch, Peter; Port uncertain, 1755 ***2856.30*** *p190*
Hirsch, Philipp; America, 1774 ***2856.30*** *p190*
Hirsch, Philipp; America, 1774 ***2856.30*** *p190*
With wife
Hirsch, Philipp; Port uncertain, 1773 ***2856.30*** *p190*
Hirsch, Susanna; Port uncertain, 1746 ***2856.30*** *p190*
With husband
Hirschberger, Henrich; America, 1768 ***2856.30*** *p190*
Hirschel, Miss; Port uncertain, 1785 ***2856.30*** *p305*
Hirschel, Niklas; Port uncertain, 1725 ***2856.30*** *p190*
Hirschelmann, Nikol; Port uncertain, 1774 ***2856.30*** *p190*
Hirschfeld, Christof; Port uncertain, 1788 ***2856.30*** *p190*
Hirschfeld, J. F.; America, 1764 ***2856.30*** *p323*
Hirschfeld, Johann Friedric; America, 1764 ***2856.30*** *p191*
With wife & 3 children
Hirschman, Mr.; America, 1751 ***2856.30*** *p340*
Hirschman, Mr.; America, 1757 ***2856.30*** *p340*
Hirschmann, Johann Georg; America, 1751 ***2856.30*** *p191*
With wife
Hirschmann, Johann Georg; America, 1757 ***2856.30*** *p191*
With wife
Hirschs'sche, Miss; Port uncertain, 1751 ***2856.30*** *p191*
With sister
Hirt, Anna Elisabeth; Port uncertain, 1784 ***2856.30*** *p191*
With husband
Hirt, Hans Georg; Port uncertain, 1760 ***2856.30*** *p191*
With wife
Hirth, Anton; Port uncertain, 1753 ***2856.30*** *p191*
Hirth, Benedikt; Port uncertain, 1773 ***2856.30*** *p191*
Hirth, John; Indiana, 1881-1886 ***3437.14*** *p193*
Hirth, Michael; America, 1737 ***2856.30*** *p191*
Hirth, Peter; America, 1764 ***2856.30*** *p191*
Hirz, Andreas; Port uncertain, 1759 ***2856.30*** *p191*
Hirzler, Catharina; Port uncertain, 1745 ***2856.30*** *p191*
With husband
Hiscocks, Robert 49; Ontario, 1871 ***1823.15*** *p115*
Hiscox, Richard; New York, 1840 ***8197.10*** *p242*
Hiskius, Johann; Port uncertain, 1755 ***2856.30*** *p191*
Hislop, Adam 47; Ontario, 1871 ***1823.15*** *p115*
Hislop, Alexander 40; Ontario, 1871 ***1823.15*** *p115*
Hislop, Andrew; New York, 1835 ***8197.10*** *p240*
Hislop, Andrew; New York, 1838 ***8197.10*** *p118*
Hislop, Andrew 37; Ontario, 1871 ***1823.15*** *p115*
Hislop, Elizabeth W. 71; Ontario, 1871 ***1823.15*** *p115*
Hislop, George 38; Ontario, 1871 ***1823.15*** *p115*
Hislop, James 32; Ontario, 1871 ***1823.15*** *p115*
Hislop, James 39; Ontario, 1871 ***1823.15*** *p115*
Hislop, James 72; Ontario, 1871 ***1823.15*** *p115*
Hislop, John 47; Ontario, 1871 ***1823.15*** *p115*
Hislop, John 74; Ontario, 1871 ***1823.15*** *p115*
Hislop, Mary; Georgia, 1735 ***1640.10*** *p80*
Hislop, Thomas 37; Ontario, 1871 ***1823.15*** *p115*
Hislop, Thomas 55; Ontario, 1871 ***1823.15*** *p115*
Hislop, William 45; Ontario, 1871 ***1823.15*** *p115*
Hisme, Andrew 30; Jamaica, 1774 ***1220.25*** *p72*
Hissey, Wm; Quebec, 1857 ***9196.15*** *p13*
Hisure, Peter; Maryland, 1681 ***2524.55*** *p111*
Hitchboone, Richard; Maryland, 1664 ***2524.55*** *p115*
Hitchcoake, Christopher; Maryland, 1673 ***2524.55*** *p111*
Hitchcock, Miss; Quebec, 1857 ***9196.15*** *p19*
Hitchcock, Mr.; Quebec, 1857 ***9196.15*** *p19*
Hitchcock, Miss C.; Quebec, 1857 ***9196.15*** *p19*
Hitchcock, Elizabeth Wigmore; New York, New York, 1840 ***1224.3*** *p37*
Hitchcock, James; New York, 1840 ***8197.10*** *p174*
Hitchcock, William G.; New York, 1826 ***8197.10*** *p348*
Hitchcox, Christopher; Maryland, 1673 ***2524.55*** *p111*
Hitchen, Fredrick 47; Ontario, 1871 ***1823.22*** *p74*
Hitchens, Philip; New York, 1806 ***8197.10*** *p31*
Hitchens, William 65; Ontario, 1871 ***1823.22*** *p74*
Hitchin, John 21; Maryland, 1774 ***1220.25*** *p70*
Hitchins, Daniel; New England, 1679 ***1224.1*** *p30*
Hitchins, Joseph; New England, 1679 ***1224.1*** *p30*
Hitchins, Thomas; South Carolina, 1749 ***1224.2*** *p56*
Hitley, Phillip; Virginia, 1664 ***6212.30*** *p13*

Hiton, Richard 22; New York, 1774 ***1220.25*** *p24*
Hitsch, Gabriel; Port uncertain, 1784 ***2856.30*** *p189*
Hitschler, Anna Maria; Port uncertain, 1754 ***2856.30*** *p191*
With 2 children
Hitschler, Anna Maria; Port uncertain, 1759 ***2856.30*** *p191*
Hittshaw, Margarite; Maryland, 1665 ***2524.55*** *p111*
Hitz, Andreas; Port uncertain, 1759 ***2856.30*** *p191*
Hitzfeld, Michael; Port uncertain, 1791 ***2856.30*** *p191*
Hix, Samuel 16; Philadelphia, 1774 ***1220.25*** *p42*
Hjertuick, A. 27; Alaska, 1918 ***9196.1*** *p54*
Hjertuick, A. 27; Whitehorse, Yukon, 1918 ***9196.1*** *p54*
Hlatbrink, Wm 43; Washington, 1909 ***9196.1*** *p25*
Hlisczefski, Joseph; Maryland, 1910 ***3259.35*** *p20*
Hmielewski, Adam; Maryland, 1910 ***3259.35*** *p20*
Hoage, Mary; Vermont, 1844-1914 ***5900.10*** *p458*
Hoar, Mary; Vermont, 1853-1901 ***5900.10*** *p193*
Hoard, Mary; Virginia, 1672 ***6212.30*** *p50*
Hoare, Mr.; Quebec, 1858 ***9196.15*** *p40*
Hoare, Bridget 8 *SEE* Hoare, Michael
Hoare, David; Maryland, 1681 ***2524.55*** *p111*
Hoare, George 25; Ontario, 1871 ***1823.28*** *p40*
Hoare, James; New York, 1840 ***8197.10*** *p242*
Hoare, James 5 *SEE* Hoare, Michael
Hoare, John 7 *SEE* Hoare, Michael
Hoare, John 22; Maryland, 1775 ***1220.25*** *p103*
Hoare, Mary 11 *SEE* Hoare, Michael
Hoare, Mary 30 *SEE* Hoare, Michael
Hoare, Michael 35; New York, New York, 1848 ***1825.45*** *p16*
Wife: Mary 30
Daughter: Mary 11
Daughter: Bridget 8
Son: James 5
Son: John 7
Son: Thomas 2
Hoare, Thomas; Virginia, 1665-1666 ***6212.30*** *p25*
Hoare, Thomas 2 *SEE* Hoare, Michael
Hoare, Thomas 50; Ontario, 1871 ***1823.15*** *p115*
Hobach, Dieter; America, 1742 ***2856.30*** *p191*
Hobart, Mathew T. 50; Ontario, 1871 ***1823.22*** *p74*
Hobbard, Elizabeth; Maryland, 1673 ***2524.55*** *p111*
Hobbes, Mr.; Quebec, 1858 ***9196.15*** *p44*
Hobbes, Mrs.; Quebec, 1858 ***9196.15*** *p44*
Hobbs, Mr.; Quebec, 1856 ***9196.15*** *p7*
Hobbs, Mr.; Quebec, 1857 ***9196.15*** *p22*
Hobbs, Ann *SEE* Hobbs, Richard
Hobbs, Elizabeth; Middlesex Co., Virginia, 1698 ***1224.1*** *p30*
Hobbs, George; Maryland, 1653 ***2524.55*** *p111*
Hobbs, Gervis; Maryland, 1656 ***2524.55*** *p111*
Hobbs, James 41; Ontario, 1871 ***1823.15*** *p115*
Hobbs, Joseph; New England, 1697 ***1224.1*** *p30*
Hobbs, Joye; Maryland, 1677 ***2524.55*** *p111*
Hobbs, Richard 33; St. Christopher, 1773 ***1220.25*** *p127*
Sister: Ann
Hobbs, Sarah 82; Ontario, 1871 ***1823.28*** *p40*
Hobbs, Thomas; Virginia, 1667 ***6212.30*** *p37*
Hobby, Charles; Boston, n.d. ***1224.2*** *p56*
Hobday, Edward; New York, 1830 ***8197.10*** *p312*
Hobdey, Mary; Maryland, 1667 ***2524.55*** *p111*
Hobec, Thomas 20; Maryland, 1775 ***1220.25*** *p116*
Hober, William; New York, New York, 1854 ***6058.10*** *p73*
Hobison, Mary 91; Ontario, 1871 ***1823.15*** *p115*
Hobkirk, George 47; Ontario, 1871 ***1823.15*** *p115*
Hobkirk, John; New York, New York, 1780 ***1224.2*** *p57*
Hobkirk, Robert 45; Ontario, 1871 ***1823.15*** *p115*
Hobler, Frederick; Pennsylvania, 1836 ***6058.10*** *p12*
Hoblin, Thomas; Virginia, 1666 ***6212.30*** *p27*
Hoblin, Thomas; Virginia, 1666 ***6212.30*** *p28*
Hobson, Arthur; Virginia, 1667-1668 ***6212.30*** *p39*
Hobson, Jonathan; New York, 1794 ***8197.10*** *p5*
Hobson, Joshua; Maryland, 1680 ***2524.55*** *p111*
Hobson, Martha; Maryland, 1673 ***2524.55*** *p111*
Hobson, Roger; Maryland, 1668 ***2524.55*** *p115*
Hobson, Thomas; Maryland, 1673 ***2524.55*** *p111*
Hobtaile, Wm; Virginia, 1690-1691 ***6212.30*** *p59*
Hoch, Georg; America, 1738 ***2856.30*** *p191*
Hoch, Jakob; America, 1738 ***2856.30*** *p191*
With wife & 9 children
Hoch, Johann Jakob; Port uncertain, 1750 ***2856.30*** *p191*
Hoch, John; New York, 1838 ***8197.10*** *p117*
Hoch, Martin; America, 1753 ***2856.30*** *p191*
With wife & 2 children
Hocher, Catharina; Port uncertain, 1765 ***2856.30*** *p192*
Hochmuth, Mrs. Ernst; Port uncertain, 1791 ***2856.30*** *p192*
Hochreither, Margarete; Port uncertain, 1766 ***2856.30*** *p192*
Hochreuter, Jacob; Port uncertain, 1786 ***2856.30*** *p192*
Hochreuther, Balthasar; Port uncertain, 1786 ***2856.30*** *p192*
Hochstrasser, Miss; America, 1763 ***2856.30*** *p192*
Hochstrasser, Paul; America, 1753 ***2856.30*** *p192*
Hochstrasser, Paul; America, 1764 ***2856.30*** *p192*
Hochwieler, Mathias; America, 1749 ***2856.30*** *p192*
Hock, Andreas; America, 1754 ***2856.30*** *p192*
With wife & children
Hock, Hans Georg; America, 1737 ***2856.30*** *p192*
Hock, Johann Daniel; America, 1740 ***2856.30*** *p192*
Hockenhull, Richard; South Carolina, 1733 ***1224.2*** *p57*
Hockin, Eva; Port uncertain, 1755 ***2856.30*** *p192*
Hocking, John; Ontario, 1855 ***1224.3*** *p37*
Hockley, Thomas; Philadelphia, 1781 ***1224.2*** *p57*
Hockley, William Branson; Philadelphia, 1796 ***1224.2*** *p57*
Hocky, Henry 67; Ontario, 1871 ***1823.15*** *p115*
Hoctor, Bridget 46; Vermont, 1878 ***5900.10*** *p215*
Hoctor, Harriet Baker; Vermont, 1810-1882 ***5900.10*** *p221*
Hoctor, Timothy; Vermont, 1807-1890 ***5900.10*** *p221*
Hodd, Thomas; Virginia, 1797 ***1224.2*** *p57*
Hoddard, William; Maryland, 1677-1678 ***2524.55*** *p111*
Hodder, Charles; New York, 1837 ***8197.10*** *p91*
Hodder, Simon 55; Ontario, 1871 ***1823.15*** *p115*
Hodet, Joseph M. 63; Vermont, 1902 ***5900.10*** *p585*
Hodge, Mrs.; Quebec, 1856 ***9196.15*** *p7*
Hodge, A. 56; Ontario, 1871 ***1823.15*** *p115*
Hodge, A. G. 23; Ontario, 1871 ***1823.15*** *p115*
Hodge, Andrew; Pennsylvania, 1777 ***4629.10*** *p8*
Hodge, David; New Orleans, 1819 ***1640.10*** *p80*
Hodge, David 65; Ontario, 1871 ***1823.15*** *p115*
Hodge, Elizabeth; Kingston, Jamaica, 1845 ***1640.13*** *p56*
Hodge, Hugh; Pennsylvania, 1777 ***4629.10*** *p11*
Hodge, Hugh, Jr.; Pennsylvania, 1777 ***4629.10*** *p14*
Hodge, John; Ontario, 1871 ***1823.22*** *p74*
Hodge, Joseph 37; Carolina, 1775 ***1220.25*** *p123*
Hodge, Robert Bickford; New Jersey, 1845 ***1224.3*** *p37*
Hodge, Roger; Virginia, 1668-1669 ***6212.30*** *p40*
Hodge, Samuel 34; Ontario, 1871 ***1823.22*** *p74*
Hodge, Sarah 46; Ontario, 1871 ***1823.15*** *p115*
Hodge, William; New York, 1829-1838 ***8197.10*** *p115*
Hodgens, John 29; Ontario, 1871 ***1823.15*** *p115*
Hodgens, Joseph 31; Ontario, 1871 ***1823.15*** *p115*
Hodgent, Andrew 52; Ontario, 1871 ***1823.15*** *p115*
Hodgent, Anges 82; Ontario, 1871 ***1823.15*** *p115*
Hodgent, Archibald 43; Ontario, 1871 ***1823.15*** *p115*
Hodger, John 50; Ontario, 1871 ***1823.15*** *p115*
Hodges, Charles 39; Ontario, 1871 ***1823.28*** *p40*
Hodges, Edmund 35; Ontario, 1871 ***1823.22*** *p74*
Hodges, Elizabeth 74; Vermont, 1916 ***5900.10*** *p317*
Hodges, Frederick Downer; New York, New York, 1845 ***1224.3*** *p37*
Hodges, George J.; Vermont, 1846-1924 ***5900.10*** *p317*
Hodges, Giles 28; America, 1774 ***1220.25*** *p36*
Hodges, John N. 26; Ontario, 1871 ***1823.15*** *p115*
Hodges, Julia; Vermont, 1869-1952 ***5900.10*** *p163*
Hodges, Mary; Vermont, 1866-1940 ***5900.10*** *p163*
Hodges, Nathaniel; America, 1748 ***1224.2*** *p57*
Hodges, Peter; New Jersey, 1697 ***1224.1*** *p30*
Hodges, Rachael Grant; Vermont, 1849-1919 ***5900.10*** *p317*
Hodges, Richard 22; Virginia, 1774 ***1220.25*** *p90*
Hodges, Samuel 35; Philadelphia, 1774 ***1220.25*** *p69*
Hodges, Sander; Maryland, 1665 ***2524.55*** *p237*
Hodges, Thomas; Maryland, 1666 ***2524.55*** *p111*
Hodges, Thomas 24; Virginia, 1775 ***1220.25*** *p95*
Hodges, Thomas 25; Jamaica, 1775 ***1220.25*** *p96*
Hodges, William; Maryland, 1669 ***2524.55*** *p111*
Hodgeson, Elizabeth *SEE* Hodgeson, Elizabeth
Hodgeson, Elizabeth; Maryland, 1671 ***2524.55*** *p111*
Son: Joshua
Son: Job
Daughter: Elizabeth
Hodgeson, Job *SEE* Hodgeson, Elizabeth
Hodgeson, John; Maryland, 1668 ***2524.55*** *p111*
Hodgeson, John; Maryland, 1669 ***2524.55*** *p111*
Hodgeson, Joshua *SEE* Hodgeson, Elizabeth
Hodgeson, Richard; Maryland, 1631-1685 ***2524.55*** *p111*
Hodgett, Joanna 30; Ontario, 1871 ***1823.15*** *p115*
Hodgins, George 18; Ontario, 1871 ***1823.15*** *p115*
Hodgins, George 52; Ontario, 1871 ***1823.15*** *p115*
Hodgins, James; New York, 1824 ***8197.10*** *p238*
Hodgins, James 35; Ontario, 1871 ***1823.15*** *p115*
Hodgins, John 71; Ontario, 1871 ***1823.15*** *p115*
Hodgins, John W. 36; Ontario, 1871 ***1823.28*** *p40*
Hodgins, Mathew 74; Ontario, 1871 ***1823.28*** *p40*
Hodgins, Thomas 35; Ontario, 1871 ***1823.15*** *p116*
Hodgins, William 40; Ontario, 1871 ***1823.28*** *p40*
Hodgkin, John; Maryland, 1651 ***2524.55*** *p111*
Relative: Mary
Hodgkin, Mary *SEE* Hodgkin, John
Hodgkin, Mary; Maryland, 1658 ***2524.55*** *p111*
Hodgkins, Ja; Virginia, 1666-1667 ***6212.30*** *p32*
Hodgkins, James; Virginia, 1665-1666 ***6212.30*** *p23*
Hodgkins, Thomas; Virginia, 1691 ***6212.30*** *p59*
Hodgkinson, Mr.; Portland, Maine, 1857 ***9196.15*** *p13*
Hodgkinson, Anthony; Pennsylvania, 1777 ***4629.10*** *p14*
Hodgkinson, Bethana; Pennsylvania, 1777 ***4629.10*** *p12*
Hodgskinson, Christopher; Virginia, 1718 ***1224.2*** *p57*
Hodgson, Catherine 40 *SEE* Hodgson, Thomas
Hodgson, David 40; Ontario, 1871 ***1823.28*** *p40*
Hodgson, Mrs. E. 60; Ontario, 1871 ***1823.15*** *p116*
Hodgson, Edward; Maryland, 1663 ***2524.55*** *p111*
Hodgson, Edward; Maryland, 1673 ***2524.55*** *p111*
Hodgson, J.; Quebec, 1857 ***9196.15*** *p19*
Hodgson, J. C. 43; Ontario, 1871 ***1823.28*** *p40*
Hodgson, John; Pennsylvania, 1777 ***4629.10*** *p15*
Hodgson, John; Portland, Maine, 1858 ***9196.15*** *p29*
Hodgson, John 26; Maryland, 1775 ***1220.25*** *p120*
Hodgson, John 30; Philadelphia, 1774 ***1220.25*** *p68*
Hodgson, John 38; British Columbia, 1910 ***9196.1*** *p30*
Hodgson, John 38; Seattle, 1910 ***9196.1*** *p30*
Hodgson, Richard; Maryland, 1631-1685 ***2524.55*** *p111*
Hodgson, Samuel; Pennsylvania, 1779 ***4629.10*** *p37*
Hodgson, T.; Quebec, 1856 ***9196.15*** *p7*
Hodgson, Thomas; New York, 1838 ***8197.10*** *p117*
Hodgson, Thomas 38; Nova Scotia, 1774 ***1220.25*** *p136*
Hodgson, Thomas 39; Philadelphia, 1774 ***1220.25*** *p68*
Wife: Catherine 40
With child
Hodgson, William 22; Nova Scotia, 1774 ***1220.25*** *p13*
Hodkeson, Elizabeth; Maryland, 1681 ***2524.55*** *p111*
Hodleys, John; Maryland, 1667 ***2524.55*** *p111*
Hodnett, Ellen; Vermont, 1814-1902 ***5900.10*** *p418*
Hodoff, I. 28; Alaska, 1917 ***9196.1*** *p49*
Hodoff, I. 28; Whitehorse, Yukon, 1917 ***9196.1*** *p49*
Hodrus, Matthias; Port uncertain, 1748 ***2856.30*** *p192*
Hodson, Mr.; Quebec, 1858 ***9196.15*** *p39*
Hodson, Edward; Maryland, 1664 ***2524.55*** *p111*
Hodson, William 15; Philadelphia, 1774 ***1220.25*** *p81*
Hody, John; Virginia, 1663 ***6212.30*** *p4*
Hodzek, Michael; Maryland, 1910 ***3259.35*** *p20*
Hoefle, Johannes; New York, 1837 ***8197.10*** *p91*
Hoegy, Henry 48; Ontario, 1871 ***1823.15*** *p116*
Hoegy, Lewis 24; Ontario, 1871 ***1823.15*** *p116*
Hoegy, Margaret 73; Ontario, 1871 ***1823.15*** *p116*
Hoegy, Peter 44; Ontario, 1871 ***1823.15*** *p116*
Hoehn, Friedrich; Port uncertain, 1783 ***2856.30*** *p192*
Hoehn, George; New York, New York, 1856 ***3437.14*** *p22*
Hoehn, John; New York, New York, 1856 ***3437.14*** *p11*
Hoel, John 28; Alaska, 1917 ***9196.1*** *p45*
Hoel, John 28; Whitehorse, Yukon, 1917 ***9196.1*** *p45*
Hoenig, Johann Peter; Port uncertain, 1771 ***2856.30*** *p192*
Hoenig, Johann Peter; Port uncertain, 1783 ***2856.30*** *p192*
Hoenig, Johann Peter; Port uncertain, 1786 ***2856.30*** *p192*
Hoerthler, Georg Adam; America, 1754 ***2856.30*** *p197B*
Hoey, Elizabeth J.; Vermont, 1865-1949 ***5900.10*** *p452*
Hoey, Frank; Castleton, Vermont, 1825 ***5900.10*** *p7*
Hoey, John 56; Ontario, 1871 ***1823.22*** *p75*
Hoey, Mary A. Laffey; Vermont, 1856-1887 ***5900.10*** *p476*
Hoey, Mary Boland; Vermont, 1835-1930 ***5900.10*** *p452*
Hoey, William F.; Vermont, 1848-1904 ***5900.10*** *p476*
Hoeyer, Franz Carl; America, 1738 ***2856.30*** *p192*
Hof, Johann Konrad; America, 1764 ***2856.30*** *p192*
Hofacker, Peter; Port uncertain, 1791 ***2856.30*** *p192*
Hofacker, Peter; Port uncertain, 1792 ***2856.30*** *p192*
Hofelich, Matthaus; Port uncertain, 1786 ***2856.30*** *p192*
Hofer, Therese; Port uncertain, 1755 ***2856.30*** *p192*
Hofer, Victor; New York, 1825-1834 ***8197.10*** *p308*
Hoferin, Hans; Port uncertain, 1766 ***2856.30*** *p197H*
Hoff, Johann; America, 1730 ***2856.30*** *p193*
With wife
Hoff, Johann Atam; America, 1730 ***2856.30*** *p193*
Hoff, John; America, 1730 ***2856.30*** *p193*
Hoff, Lorenz; America, 1749 ***2856.30*** *p193*
Hoffahrt, Michael; Port uncertain, 1761 ***2856.30*** *p193*
Hoffecker, Henrich; America, 1793 ***2856.30*** *p193*
Hoffer, Johann Michael; Port uncertain, 1750 ***2856.30*** *p193*
Hoffgartner, Anton; Port uncertain, 1748 ***2856.30*** *p193*
Hoffgartner, Anton; Port uncertain, 1796 ***2856.30*** *p193*
Hoffheinz, Konrad; America, 1740 ***2856.30*** *p193*
Hoffman, Adam; Pennsylvania, 1777 ***4629.10*** *p12*
Hoffman, Charles 22; Texas, 1914 ***9196.1*** *p64*
Hoffman, Charles Frederick; New York, 1840 ***8197.10*** *p173*
Hoffman, Ernst 61; Ontario, 1871 ***1823.15*** *p116*
Hoffman, Frederick; Pennsylvania, 1777 ***4629.10*** *p14*
Hoffman, Henry 40; Ontario, 1871 ***1823.15*** *p116*
Hoffman, John; New York, 1830 ***8197.10*** *p360*
Hoffman, John; Pennsylvania, 1777 ***4629.10*** *p10*
Hoffman, John; Pennsylvania, 1777 ***4629.10*** *p13*
Hoffman, Joseph 64; Ontario, 1871 ***1823.15*** *p116*

Hoffman, Michael; New York, 1836 ***8197.10*** *p75*
Hoffman, Michael; Port uncertain, 1747 ***2856.30*** *p194*
Hoffman, Peter 45; Ontario, 1871 ***1823.15*** *p116*
Hoffman, Sophia; Maryland, 1910 ***3259.35*** *p20*
Hoffmann, Mr.; America, 1749 ***2856.30*** *p195*
With wife & children
Hoffmann, Adam Henrich; America, 1752 ***2856.30*** *p193*
Hoffmann, Adam Henrich; America, 1761 ***2856.30*** *p193*
Hoffmann, Adam Henrich; Port uncertain, 1751 ***2856.30*** *p193*
Hoffmann, Andreas; America, 1762 ***2856.30*** *p194*
Hoffmann, Anna Catharina; Port uncertain, 1748 ***2856.30*** *p193*
Hoffmann, Anna Catharina; Port uncertain, 1762 ***2856.30*** *p193*
Hoffmann, Anna Maria; America, 1765 ***2856.30*** *p193*
Hoffmann, Anna Maria; Port uncertain, 1794 ***2856.30*** *p193*
Hoffmann, Apollonia; Port uncertain, 1751 ***2856.30*** *p193*
Hoffmann, Catharina; Port uncertain, 1732 ***2856.30*** *p193*
Hoffmann, Catharina Clara; America, 1785 ***2856.30*** *p193*
Hoffmann, Catharina Clara; Port uncertain, 1759 ***2856.30*** *p193*
Hoffmann, Daniel; America, 1739 ***2856.30*** *p193*
Hoffmann, Daniel; America, 1748 ***2856.30*** *p193*
Hoffmann, Dietrich; America, 1762 ***2856.30*** *p194*
Hoffmann, Egidius; America, 1736 ***2856.30*** *p195*
With wife 2 sons & daughter
Hoffmann, Egidius; America, 1737 ***2856.30*** *p195*
Hoffmann, Erhard; America, 1738 ***2856.30*** *p193*
Hoffmann, Eva Catharina; Port uncertain, 1777 ***2856.30*** *p193*
Hoffmann, Friedrich; America, 1749 ***2856.30*** *p195*
With wife & child
Hoffmann, Georg; America, 1738 ***2856.30*** *p195*
With wife & children
Hoffmann, Georg; America, 1764 ***2856.30*** *p195*
With wife
Hoffmann, Gertrud; Port uncertain, 1765 ***2856.30*** *p193*
Hoffmann, Heinrich; America, 1762 ***2856.30*** *p194*
Hoffmann, Henerick; America, 1727 ***2856.30*** *p193*
Hoffmann, Henrich; Port uncertain, 1764 ***2856.30*** *p193*
Hoffmann, Henrich; Port uncertain, 1765 ***2856.30*** *p193*
Hoffmann, Henrich; Port uncertain, 1789 ***2856.30*** *p193*
Hoffmann, Henrich; Port uncertain, 1791 ***2856.30*** *p193*
Hoffmann, Henrich Adam; America, 1753 ***2856.30*** *p193*
Hoffmann, Jakob; America, 1743 ***2856.30*** *p193*
Hoffmann, Jakob; America, 1749 ***2856.30*** *p195*
With wife & child
Hoffmann, Jakob; America, 1754 ***2856.30*** *p193*
Hoffmann, Jakob; America, 1762 ***2856.30*** *p193*
Hoffmann, Jakob; Port uncertain, 1749 ***2856.30*** *p195*
With wife & child
Hoffmann, Mrs. Jakob; Port uncertain, 1752 ***2856.30*** *p193*
Hoffmann, Johann; America, 1739 ***2856.30*** *p193*
Hoffmann, Johann; Canada, 1752 ***2856.30*** *p195*
Hoffmann, Johann; Port uncertain, 1741 ***2856.30*** *p193*
Hoffmann, Johann; Port uncertain, 1748 ***2856.30*** *p193*
Hoffmann, Johann Georg; Port uncertain, 1754 ***2856.30*** *p193*
Hoffmann, Johann Henrich; Port uncertain, 1727 ***2856.30*** *p194*
Hoffmann, Johann Michael; Port uncertain, 1768 ***2856.30*** *p194*
Hoffmann, Johann Peter; America, 1739 ***2856.30*** *p194*
Hoffmann, Johann Valentin; America, 1751 ***2856.30*** *p194*
Hoffmann, Johann Wilhelm; America, 1741 ***2856.30*** *p194*
Hoffmann, Jorg; Port uncertain, 1752 ***2856.30*** *p194*
Hoffmann, Karl Henrich; England, 1765 ***2856.30*** *p194*
With 4 children
Hoffmann, Margarete; America, 1786 ***2856.30*** *p194*
Hoffmann, Margarete; America, 1789 ***2856.30*** *p194*
Hoffmann, Maria Barbara; Port uncertain, 1755 ***2856.30*** *p194*
Hoffmann, Maria Barbara; Port uncertain, 1756 ***2856.30*** *p194*
Hoffmann, Maria Catharina; Port uncertain, 1763 ***2856.30*** *p194*
Hoffmann, Maria Elisabeth; Port uncertain, 1751 ***2856.30*** *p194*
Hoffmann, Maria Elisabeth; Port uncertain, 1755 ***2856.30*** *p194*
Hoffmann, Maria Eva; Port uncertain, 1754 ***2856.30*** *p194*
Hoffmann, Maria Ursula; Port uncertain, 1745 ***2856.30*** *p194*
Hoffmann, Martin; America, 1739 ***2856.30*** *p194*
Hoffmann, Martin; America, 1749 ***2856.30*** *p194*
Hoffmann, Matthaus; Port uncertain, 1728 ***2856.30*** *p194*
Hoffmann, Michael; America, 1747 ***2856.30*** *p194*
Hoffmann, Michael; New York, 1839 ***8197.10*** *p241*
Hoffmann, Michael; Port uncertain, 1752 ***2856.30*** *p195*
With wife & 3 children
Hoffmann, Niklas; Port uncertain, 1765 ***2856.30*** *p194*
Hoffmann, Peter; America, 1738 ***2856.30*** *p194*
Hoffmann, Peter; America, 1741 ***2856.30*** *p194*
Hoffmann, Philipp; America, 1741 ***2856.30*** *p194*
Hoffmann, Philipp; America, 1752 ***2856.30*** *p194*
Hoffmann, Philipp; America, 1784 ***2856.30*** *p194*
Hoffmann, Philipp; Port uncertain, 1768 ***2856.30*** *p194*
Hoffmann, Philipp; Port uncertain, 1772 ***2856.30*** *p194*
Hoffmann, Regina; Port uncertain, 1766 ***2856.30*** *p194*
Hoffmann, Reinhard; Port uncertain, 1749 ***2856.30*** *p195*
With wife & children
Hoffmann, Richard; America, 1749 ***2856.30*** *p195*
With wife & children
Hoffmann, Valentin; America, 1751 ***2856.30*** *p194*
Hoffmann, Valentin; Port uncertain, 1763 ***2856.30*** *p194*
Hoffmann, Velthen; America, 1753 ***2856.30*** *p194*
Hoffmann, Wilhelm; Port uncertain, 1764 ***2856.30*** *p195*
With wife & child
Hoffmannin, Christiane; Port uncertain, 1754 ***2856.30*** *p195*
Hoffmannin, Maria Margarete; Port uncertain, 1728 ***2856.30*** *p195*
Hoffmannin, Maria Margarete; Port uncertain, 1728 ***2856.30*** *p283*
Hoffmur, John 74; Ontario, 1871 ***1823.15*** *p116*
Hoffner, Henry; Pennsylvania, 1777 ***4629.10*** *p45*
Hoffnung, Miss; Portland, Maine, 1858 ***9196.15*** *p27*
Hoffnung, Mr.; Portland, Maine, 1858 ***9196.15*** *p27*
Hoffnung, Mr., Jr.; Portland, Maine, 1858 ***9196.15*** *p27*
Hoffstattler, Jorg Theobald; America, 1749 ***2856.30*** *p195*
Hoffstetter, Andreas; Port uncertain, 1782 ***2856.30*** *p195*
Hoffstrom, Alexander; New York, 1837 ***8197.10*** *p241*
Hofheintz, Georg; America, 1751 ***2856.30*** *p195*
Hofheintz, Georg; America, 1761 ***2856.30*** *p195*
Hofheinz, Mrs. Hermann; America, 1770 ***2856.30*** *p195*
With children
Hofley, Rebeck 24; Ontario, 1871 ***1823.15*** *p116*
Hoflin, Mathias; Port uncertain, 1749 ***2856.30*** *p197H*
Hofman, Christopher 76; Ontario, 1871 ***1823.15*** *p116*
Hofmann, Andreas; Port uncertain, 1788 ***2856.30*** *p195*
Hofmann, Andreas; Port uncertain, 1790 ***2856.30*** *p195*
Hofmann, Anna Barbara; Port uncertain, 1731 ***2856.30*** *p196*
Hofmann, Anna Elisabeth; Port uncertain, 1731 ***2856.30*** *p196*
Hofmann, Catharina; Port uncertain, 1735 ***2856.30*** *p195*
Hofmann, Elisabeth; America, 1758 ***2856.30*** *p196*
Husband: Schmidt
Hofmann, Georg; Port uncertain, 1756 ***2856.30*** *p195*
Hofmann, Georg Michael; Port uncertain, 1790 ***2856.30*** *p195*
Hofmann, Georg Peter; Port uncertain, 1775 ***2856.30*** *p195*
Hofmann, Johann Peter; Port uncertain, 1793 ***2856.30*** *p195*
Hofmann, Margarete Garner; Port uncertain, 1752 ***2856.30*** *p196*
Hofmann, Maria Helene; Port uncertain, 1793 ***2856.30*** *p195*
Hofmann, Maria Magdalena; America, 1758 ***2856.30*** *p196*
Husband: Naegele
Hofmann, Maria Margarete; Port uncertain, 1772 ***2856.30*** *p195*
Hofmann, Martin; America, 1764 ***2856.30*** *p196*
With wife & 6 children
Hofmann, Naegele *SEE* Hofmann, Maria Magdalena
Hofmann, Nickel; America, 1754 ***2856.30*** *p196*
Hofmann, Nickel; America, 1754 ***2856.30*** *p196*
With wife & 3 children
Hofmann, Paul; America, 1764 ***2856.30*** *p196*
With wife & 5 children
Hofmann, Peter; Port uncertain, 1792 ***2856.30*** *p196*
Hofmann, Philipp; America, 1752 ***2856.30*** *p196*
Hofmann, Philipp; Port uncertain, 1786 ***2856.30*** *p196*
Hofmann, Philipp Karl; Port uncertain, 1788 ***2856.30*** *p196*
Hofmann, Philipp Nikel; America, 1761 ***2856.30*** *p196*
Hofmann, Schmidt *SEE* Hofmann, Elisabeth
Hofmann, Valentin; America, 1754 ***2856.30*** *p196*
Hofmann, Velthen; America, 1753 ***2856.30*** *p196*
Hofmann, Wendel; Port uncertain, 1786 ***2856.30*** *p196*
Hofmannin, Cath. Barbara; Port uncertain, 1755 ***2856.30*** *p196*
With husband
Hofmannin, Maria Elisabeth; Port uncertain, 1734 ***2856.30*** *p196*
Hofmeister, Anna Margarete; Port uncertain, 1737 ***2856.30*** *p196*
Hogan, Rev.; Quebec, 1856 ***9196.15*** *p8*
Hogan, Adelade E.; Vermont, 1845-1924 ***5900.10*** *p376*
Hogan, Ann; Vermont, 1837-1910 ***5900.10*** *p162*
Hogan, Ann 68; Vermont, 1892 ***5900.10*** *p97*
Hogan, Anna; Vermont, 1850-1908 ***5900.10*** *p147*
Hogan, Anna Dolan; Vermont, 1862-1944 ***5900.10*** *p394*
Hogan, Anthony; Vermont, 1825-1890 ***5900.10*** *p447*
Hogan, Bridget; Vermont, 1812-1868 ***5900.10*** *p42*
Hogan, Bridget; Vermont, 1859-1916 ***5900.10*** *p274*
Hogan, Bridget 33; Vermont, 1881 ***5900.10*** *p270*
Hogan, Bridget 45; Vermont, 1867 ***5900.10*** *p260*
Hogan, Bridget 76; Vermont, 1895 ***5900.10*** *p177*
Hogan, Bridget 76; Vermont, 1908 ***5900.10*** *p506*
Hogan, Bridget Fitzgerald; Vermont, 1846-1928 ***5900.10*** *p167*
Hogan, Bridget Gleason; Vermont, 1845-1910 ***5900.10*** *p442*
Hogan, Bridget Meehen; Vermont, 1874 ***5900.10*** *p63*
Hogan, Bridget O'Day; Vermont, n.d. ***5900.10*** *p87*
Hogan, Bridget O'Hare; Vermont, 1825-1896 ***5900.10*** *p54*
Hogan, Catherine 1; Vermont, 1879 ***5900.10*** *p576*
Hogan, Catherine 49; Vermont, 1891 ***5900.10*** *p396*
Hogan, Catherine Hines; Vermont, 1851-1916 ***5900.10*** *p90*
Hogan, Catherine M.; Vermont, 1851-1910 ***5900.10*** *p54*
Hogan, Charles P.; Vermont, 1843-1915 ***5900.10*** *p455*
Hogan, Daniel 78; Vermont, 1891 ***5900.10*** *p264*
Hogan, David; Vermont, 1854-1923 ***5900.10*** *p167*
Hogan, Dennis; Vermont, 1849-1913 ***5900.10*** *p258*
Hogan, Dennis 26; Vermont, 1869 ***5900.10*** *p87*
Hogan, Dennis 52; Vermont, 1867 ***5900.10*** *p260*
Hogan, Dennis 87; Vermont, 1869 ***5900.10*** *p264*
Hogan, Edmund 43; Ontario, 1871 ***1823.15*** *p116*
Hogan, Edward; Vermont, 1826-1912 ***5900.10*** *p54*
Hogan, Elizabeth; Vermont, 1835-1905 ***5900.10*** *p125*
Hogan, Elizabeth Meehan; Vermont, 1857-1889 ***5900.10*** *p136*
Hogan, Ellen; Vermont, 1831-1902 ***5900.10*** *p509*
Hogan, Ellen; Vermont, 1848-1888 ***5900.10*** *p349*
Hogan, Ellen 49; Vermont, 1900 ***5900.10*** *p114*
Hogan, Ellen O'Dea; Vermont, 1850-1936 ***5900.10*** *p81*
Hogan, Hannah; Vermont, 1847-1917 ***5900.10*** *p187*
Hogan, Hanora; Vermont, 1830-1910 ***5900.10*** *p393*
Hogan, Henry; Vermont, 1842-1930 ***5900.10*** *p356*
Hogan, Hugh; Vermont, 1870-1910 ***5900.10*** *p54*
Hogan, Isabelle Duggen; Vermont, 1822-1857 ***5900.10*** *p372*
Hogan, James; Vermont, 1853-1936 ***5900.10*** *p394*
Hogan, James 40; Ontario, 1871 ***1823.28*** *p41*
Hogan, James 45; Ontario, 1871 ***1823.28*** *p41*
Hogan, James 60; Ontario, 1871 ***1823.28*** *p40*
Hogan, James 84; Vermont, 1884 ***5900.10*** *p73*
Hogan, James D. 44; Vermont, 1899 ***5900.10*** *p473*
Hogan, Jane Dolan; Vermont, 1849-1926 ***5900.10*** *p258*
Hogan, Jeremiah; Vermont, 1815-1906 ***5900.10*** *p42*
Hogan, Jeremiah; Vermont, 1851-1929 ***5900.10*** *p67*
Hogan, Johanna McNamara; Vermont, 1804-1882 ***5900.10*** *p125*
Hogan, Johannah 60; Vermont, 1894 ***5900.10*** *p264*
Hogan, Johannah 77; Vermont, 1863 ***5900.10*** *p264*
Hogan, Johannah Coleman; Vermont, 1808-1891 ***5900.10*** *p348*
Hogan, John; New England, 1775-1781 ***4628.40*** *p68*
Hogan, John; Vermont, n.d. ***5900.10*** *p249*
Hogan, John; Vermont, 1802-1885 ***5900.10*** *p348*
Hogan, John; Vermont, 1816-1902 ***5900.10*** *p274*
Hogan, John; Vermont, 1865-1888 ***5900.10*** *p349*
Hogan, John 28; Ontario, 1871 ***1823.15*** *p116*
Hogan, John 60; Ontario, 1871 ***1823.15*** *p116*
Hogan, John 68; Vermont, 1890 ***5900.10*** *p97*
Hogan, John 72; Vermont, 1894 ***5900.10*** *p264*
Hogan, John Edward; Vermont, 1853-1914 ***5900.10*** *p136*
Hogan, John Edward 10; Vermont, 1843 ***5900.10*** *p529*
Hogan, Julia; Vermont, 1864-1900 ***5900.10*** *p425*
Hogan, Julia 82; Vermont, 1884 ***5900.10*** *p207*
Hogan, Katherine; Vermont, 1851-1929 ***5900.10*** *p537*
Hogan, Margaret; Vermont, 1828-1901 ***5900.10*** *p125*
Hogan, Margaret; Vermont, 1846-1935 ***5900.10*** *p139*
Hogan, Margaret; Vermont, 1846-1935 ***5900.10*** *p169*
Hogan, Margaret 24; Vermont, 1870 ***5900.10*** *p245*
Hogan, Margaret 38; Vermont, 1857 ***5900.10*** *p577*
Hogan, Margaret 60; Vermont, 1888 ***5900.10*** *p73*
Hogan, Margaret Casey; Vermont, 1813-1878 ***5900.10*** *p537*
Hogan, Margaret Foley; Vermont, 1833-1871 ***5900.10*** *p447*
Hogan, Margaret L. 47; Vermont, 1892 ***5900.10*** *p497*
Hogan, Margaret Mahar; Vermont, 1853-1911 ***5900.10*** *p434*
Hogan, Maria; Vermont, 1826-1904 ***5900.10*** *p152*
Hogan, Maria; Vermont, 1826-1904 ***5900.10*** *p182*
Hogan, Maria; Vermont, 1845-1922 ***5900.10*** *p42*

Hogan, Maria; Vermont, 1851-1894 ***5900.10*** *p128*
Hogan, Maria; Vermont, 1862-1927 ***5900.10*** *p425*
Hogan, Martin 1; Vermont, 1869 ***5900.10*** *p576*
Hogan, Mary; Vermont, 1790-1874 ***5900.10*** *p364*
Hogan, Mary; Vermont, 1832-1860 ***5900.10*** *p156*
Hogan, Mary; Vermont, 1835-1910 ***5900.10*** *p297*
Hogan, Mary 1; Vermont, 1862 ***5900.10*** *p576*
Hogan, Mary 33; Vermont, 1865 ***5900.10*** *p264*
Hogan, Mary 40; Ontario, 1871 ***1823.28*** *p41*
Hogan, Mary 74; Vermont, 1877 ***5900.10*** *p453*
Hogan, Mary A.; Vermont, 1841-1903 ***5900.10*** *p339*
Hogan, Mary A.; Vermont, 1857-1923 ***5900.10*** *p69*
Hogan, Mary A. Murphy 83; Vermont, 1937 ***5900.10*** *p473*
Hogan, Mary Ann 4; Vermont, 1858 ***5900.10*** *p348*
Hogan, Mary Cray; Vermont, 1854-1919 ***5900.10*** *p67*
Hogan, Mary Dwyer 80; Vermont, 1897 ***5900.10*** *p177*
Hogan, Mary Grace; Vermont, 1845-1930 ***5900.10*** *p255*
Hogan, Mary J. 48; Vermont, 1887 ***5900.10*** *p453*
Hogan, Mary Mee; Vermont, 1848-1866 ***5900.10*** *p349*
Hogan, Mary Rush; Vermont, 1868-1954 ***5900.10*** *p136*
Hogan, Mary Susanna; Cincinnati, 1887 ***1640.13*** *p56*
Hogan, Mary Tehan; Vermont, 1841-1914 ***5900.10*** *p356*
Hogan, Mary White; Vermont, 1816-1909 ***5900.10*** *p274*
Hogan, Mathew 50; Vermont, 1890 ***5900.10*** *p396*
Hogan, Matthew; New York, 1804 ***8197.10*** *p27*
Hogan, Matthias 25; Ontario, 1871 ***1823.28*** *p41*
Hogan, Michael; New York, 1808 ***8197.10*** *p236*
Hogan, Michael; New York, 1811 ***8197.10*** *p57*
Hogan, Michael; New York, 1835 ***1224.3*** *p37*
Hogan, Michael; Vermont, n.d. ***5900.10*** *p87*
Hogan, Michael; Vermont, 1792-1883 ***5900.10*** *p125*
Hogan, Michael; Vermont, 1848-1912 ***5900.10*** *p434*
Hogan, Michael 40; Ontario, 1871 ***1823.22*** *p75*
Hogan, Michael 55; Ontario, 1871 ***1823.22*** *p75*
Hogan, Michael 65; Ontario, 1871 ***1823.15*** *p116*
Hogan, Michael 96; Vermont, 1895 ***5900.10*** *p372*
Hogan, Michael J.; Vermont, 1844-1902 ***5900.10*** *p442*
Hogan, Michael P.; Vermont, 1854-1948 ***5900.10*** *p90*
Hogan, Nancy 42; Vermont, 1870 ***5900.10*** *p207*
Hogan, Patrick; Pennsylvania, 1777 ***4629.10*** *p25*
Hogan, Patrick; Pennsylvania, 1779 ***4629.10*** *p40*
Hogan, Patrick; Portland, Maine, 1860 ***6058.10*** *p64*
Hogan, Patrick; Vermont, 1843-1903 ***5900.10*** *p81*
Hogan, Patrick; Vermont, 1848-1916 ***5900.10*** *p138*
Hogan, Patrick; Vermont, 1848-1916 ***5900.10*** *p169*
Hogan, Patrick 30; Ontario, 1871 ***1823.15*** *p116*
Hogan, Patrick 56; Ontario, 1871 ***1823.15*** *p116*
Hogan, Patrick 56; Ontario, 1871 ***1823.22*** *p75*
Hogan, Patrick 76; Vermont, 1875 ***5900.10*** *p176*
Hogan, Patrick 90; Vermont, 1889 ***5900.10*** *p87*
Hogan, Robert 79; Vermont, 1875 ***5900.10*** *p453*
Hogan, Sadie L.; Vermont, 1880-1966 ***5900.10*** *p480*
Hogan, Sarah; Vermont, 1835-1920 ***5900.10*** *p453*
Hogan, Sarah; Vermont, 1859-1937 ***5900.10*** *p59*
Hogan, Sarah 66; Vermont, 1872 ***5900.10*** *p434*
Hogan, Sarah Carroll 70; Vermont, 1902 ***5900.10*** *p249*
Hogan, Stephan; Vermont, 1826-1894 ***5900.10*** *p348*
Hogan, Susan M. Boyle; Vermont, 1846-1905 ***5900.10*** *p127*
Hogan, Tarty; Maryland, 1678 ***2524.55*** *p111*
Hogan, Thirza Maynard; Vermont, 1847-1926 ***5900.10*** *p455*
Hogan, Thomas; New York, 1840 ***8197.10*** *p171*
Hogan, Thomas; New York, 1840 ***8197.10*** *p174*
Hogan, Thomas; Vermont, 1844-1930 ***5900.10*** *p255*
Hogan, Thomas 57; Ontario, 1871 ***1823.15*** *p116*
Hogan, Timothy 60; Ontario, 1871 ***1823.22*** *p75*
Hogan, William; Maryland, 1682 ***2524.55*** *p111*
Hogan, William; Vermont, 1840-1913 ***5900.10*** *p356*
Hogan, William 31; Ontario, 1871 ***1823.15*** *p116*
Hogan, William 55; Vermont, 1875 ***5900.10*** *p203*
Hogan, William D.; Vermont, 1842-1896 ***5900.10*** *p127*
Hogan, William T.; Vermont, 1854-1911 ***5900.10*** *p69*
Hogan, Winnifred 87; Vermont, 1890 ***5900.10*** *p87*
Hogarth, George; Baltimore, 1844 ***1224.3*** *p38*
Hogarth, James; Victoria, British Columbia, 1900 ***1640.13*** *p56*
Hogarth, Robert 32; Ontario, 1871 ***1823.15*** *p116*
Hogarth, Septemas 46; Ontario, 1871 ***1823.15*** *p116*
Hogden, John 49; Philadelphia, 1774 ***1220.25*** *p66*
Hogel, Miss; America, 1738 ***2856.30*** *p197H*
With sister
Hogel, Jakob; America, 1738 ***2856.30*** *p197H*
Hogel, Johann; America, 1738 ***2856.30*** *p197H*
Hogeland, Benjamin; Pennsylvania, 1777 ***4629.10*** *p7*
Hogg, Christian; Maryland, 1657 ***2524.55*** *p111*
Hogg, David 24; Ontario, 1871 ***1823.15*** *p116*
Hogg, George; New York, 1833 ***8197.10*** *p70*
Hogg, George 36; Ontario, 1871 ***1823.22*** *p75*
Hogg, George 46; Ontario, 1871 ***1823.22*** *p75*
Hogg, Hugh 31; Ontario, 1871 ***1823.28*** *p41*
Hogg, James 35; Ontario, 1871 ***1823.15*** *p116*
Hogg, James 44; Ontario, 1871 ***1823.15*** *p116*
Hogg, James 57; Ontario, 1871 ***1823.15*** *p116*
Hogg, John 47; Ontario, 1871 ***1823.22*** *p75*
Hogg, Joseph 60; Ontario, 1871 ***1823.15*** *p116*
Hogg, Mark; Georgia, 1699 ***1640.13*** *p56*
Hogg, Richard 15; Philadelphia, 1775 ***1220.25*** *p122*
Hogg, Robert; Pennsylvania, 1779 ***4629.10*** *p39*
Hogg, Robert 28; Maryland, 1774 ***1220.25*** *p53*
Hogg, Robert 36; Ontario, 1871 ***1823.15*** *p116*
Hogg, Robert 73; Ontario, 1871 ***1823.15*** *p116*
Hogg, Thomas; New York, 1839 ***8197.10*** *p131*
Hogg, William; America, 1809 ***1224.3*** *p38*
Hogg, William 26; Ontario, 1871 ***1823.15*** *p116*
Hogg, William 35; Ontario, 1871 ***1823.15*** *p116*
Hogg, William 57; Ontario, 1871 ***1823.22*** *p75*
Hoggan, William; New York, 1803 ***8197.10*** *p13*
Hoggart, Robert 21; Virginia, 1773 ***1220.25*** *p28*
Hogge, Michaell; Virginia, 1666-1667 ***6212.30*** *p34*
Hoggett, Eliza 36; Ontario, 1871 ***1823.15*** *p117*
Hoggett, Michael 47; Ontario, 1871 ***1823.15*** *p117*
Hoggins, Anne; Maryland, 1681 ***2524.55*** *p111*
Hoggon, William; Maryland, 1673 ***2524.55*** *p111*
Hogin, Anna Barbara; Port uncertain, 1750 ***2856.30*** *p197H*
Hogins, John 35; Ontario, 1871 ***1823.15*** *p117*
Hogins, Thomas 39; Ontario, 1871 ***1823.15*** *p117*
Hoglebaugher, John; Pennsylvania, 1829 ***6058.10*** *p9*
Hogstaffe, Samuel; Maryland, 1663 ***2524.55*** *p137*
Hoguet, Anthony; New York, 1832-1838 ***8197.10*** *p118*
Hogward, John; Virginia, 1664 ***6212.30*** *p8*
Hohbusch, St; Port uncertain, 1700-1799 ***2856.30*** *p197*
With wife & 4 children
Hohbusch, Stefan; Port uncertain, 1770 ***2856.30*** *p197a*
With wife & 4 children
Hohe, Jacob; Port uncertain, 1765 ***2856.30*** *p197H*
Hohin, Maria Elisabeth; Port uncertain, 1766 ***2856.30*** *p197H*
Hohl, Henrich; America, 1752 ***2856.30*** *p197a*
With wife & children
Hohl, Henrich; Port uncertain, 1751 ***2856.30*** *p197a*
With wife & children
Hohl, Jakob; Port uncertain, 1768 ***2856.30*** *p197a*
Hohl, Martin; Port uncertain, 1768 ***2856.30*** *p197a*
Hohl, Valentin; America, 1753 ***2856.30*** *p197H*
Hohlbein, Malehior; Baltimore, 1848 ***6058.10*** *p27*
Hohle, Niklas; Port uncertain, 1719 ***2856.30*** *p197A*
With 5 children
Hohman, Valanh 45; Ontario, 1871 ***1823.15*** *p117*
Hohn, Johann; Port uncertain, 1773 ***2856.30*** *p197H*
Hohne, Mrs. Jakob; America, 1746 ***2856.30*** *p197H*
Hohner, Jacob 38; Ontario, 1871 ***1823.15*** *p117*
Hohner, Mathias 46; Ontario, 1871 ***1823.15*** *p117*
Hohrn, Johann Martin; Port uncertain, 1754 ***2856.30*** *p197B*
Hohschied, Mattaus; Port uncertain, 1781 ***2856.30*** *p197a*
With wife & 5 children
Hoile, John; Virginia, 1666-1667 ***6212.30*** *p35*
Hoiles, Agnes 27; Ontario, 1871 ***1823.15*** *p117*
Hojnacki, Joseph; Maryland, 1910 ***3259.35*** *p20*
Hojnoski, William; Maryland, 1910 ***3259.35*** *p20*
Hokins, John; Virginia, 1671-1672 ***6212.30*** *p45*
Hokworski, John; Maryland, 1910 ***3259.35*** *p20*
Holajda, Thomas; Maryland, 1910 ***3259.35*** *p20*
Holbarg, Reyer; New York, 1833-1838 ***8197.10*** *p116*
Holbein, Charles 28; Ontario, 1871 ***1823.15*** *p117*
Holberg, John; Pennsylvania, 1786 ***4629.10*** *p54*
Holbrook, Deidama; America, 1853 ***1640.13*** *p56*
Holbrook, Eleanor; America, 1853 ***1640.13*** *p56*
Holbrook, Joan; Virginia, 1667 ***6212.30*** *p37*
Holbrook, John 12; Philadelphia, 1775 ***1220.25*** *p8*
Holbrook, Mary Jane 45; Vermont, 1864 ***5900.10*** *p295*
Holbrook, Samll; Virginia, 1667 ***6212.30*** *p37*
Holcombe, Florence E.; Vermont, 1852-1891 ***5900.10*** *p286*
Holcombe, John; New Jersey, 1670 ***1224.1*** *p30*
Holcroft, George; New Jersey, 1666 ***1224.1*** *p30*
Hold, Michael; Port uncertain, 1777 ***2856.30*** *p176*
With wife
Holdcroft, Thomas 60; Ontario, 1871 ***1823.28*** *p41*
Holden, Mrs.; Quebec, 1856 ***9196.15*** *p7*
Holden, Abraham 37; Maryland, 1775 ***1220.25*** *p103*
Holden, Arthur; Portland, Maine, 1858 ***9196.15*** *p31*
Holden, Edward Henry Strange; New York, 1838 ***8197.10*** *p116*
Holden, Ellen; Vermont, 1844-1894 ***5900.10*** *p61*
Holden, James 52; Ontario, 1871 ***1823.15*** *p117*
Holden, John; New York, 1829 ***8197.10*** *p359*
Holden, John 32; Ontario, 1871 ***1823.28*** *p41*
Holden, Patrick; New York, 1837 ***8197.10*** *p90*
Holden, Ralph 24; Maryland, 1774 ***1220.25*** *p73*
Holden, Roger; Maryland, 1666 ***2524.55*** *p111*
Holden, Thomas 27; Maryland, 1775 ***1220.25*** *p104*
Holden, William 40; Ontario, 1871 ***1823.28*** *p41*
Holdenbeck, Ralph 29; Ontario, 1871 ***1823.28*** *p41*
Holdenriedt, Ignaz; America, 1720 ***2856.30*** *p197a*
Holder, Emanuel 40; Ontario, 1871 ***1823.15*** *p117*
Holder, John; New York, 1840 ***8197.10*** *p173*
Holder, William; New York, 1840 ***8197.10*** *p173*
Holdermann, Jacob; America, 1759 ***2856.30*** *p197a*
With wife
Holderness, William; Boston, 1775 ***4629.10*** *p80*
Holding, Edward; Boston, 1751 ***1224.2*** *p57*
Holding, John 26; Maryland, 1774 ***1220.25*** *p2*
Holding, Peter; New England, 1693 ***1224.1*** *p30*
Holditch, James; Carolina, 1702 ***1224.2*** *p57*
Holditch, Samuel 72; Ontario, 1871 ***1823.28*** *p41*
Holdman, Mr.; Jamaica, 1775 ***1220.25*** *p132*
Holdman, Louis 56; Ontario, 1871 ***1823.15*** *p117*
Holdman, Tho; Virginia, 1672 ***6212.30*** *p50*
Holdstock, Joseph; Pennsylvania, 1777 ***4629.10*** *p28*
Holdsworth, Colonel; Quebec, 1858 ***9196.15*** *p31*
Holdsworth, Francis 62; Ontario, 1871 ***1823.22*** *p75*
Holdsworth, Samuel; Maryland, 1678 ***2524.55*** *p111*
Holebrook, Mary; Maryland, 1670 ***2524.55*** *p111*
Holebrook, Thomas; Maryland, 1681 ***2524.55*** *p111*
Holeman, Abraham; Maryland, 1649 ***2524.55*** *p111*
Holeman, William; Maryland, 1649 ***2524.55*** *p38*
Holeman, William; Maryland, 1658 ***2524.55*** *p111*
Holems, Robert 64; Ontario, 1871 ***1823.15*** *p117*
Holenback, George Leonard; New York, New York, 1856 ***3437.14*** *p10*
Holenbeck, George 35; Ontario, 1871 ***1823.15*** *p117*
Holengren, P. A. 25; Alaska, 1918 ***9196.1*** *p55*
Holengren, P. A. 25; Yukon, 1918 ***9196.1*** *p55*
Holenzyeski, Sylvester; Maryland, 1910 ***3259.35*** *p20*
Holesworth, Miss; Quebec, 1857 ***9196.15*** *p18*
Holewinski, Stanislaw; Maryland, 1910 ***3259.35*** *p20*
Holford, James; New York, 1833-1838 ***8197.10*** *p117*
Holford, James; New York, 1839 ***8197.10*** *p131*
Holiday, John 46; Nova Scotia, 1774 ***1220.25*** *p136*
With wife & 5 children
Holiday, Sarah 22; Virginia, 1775 ***1220.25*** *p95*
Holiday, Thomas 35; Ontario, 1871 ***1823.28*** *p41*
Holiday, Thomas 59; Ontario, 1871 ***1823.15*** *p117*
Holiday, William; South Carolina, 1810 ***1224.3*** *p38*
Holin, Catharina; Port uncertain, 1723 ***2856.30*** *p197H*
Holines, Francis; Maryland, 1681 ***2524.55*** *p112*
Holines, Robt.; Maryland, 1650 ***2524.55*** *p112*
Holinshed, William 28; Ontario, 1871 ***1823.28*** *p41*
Holioke, Elizar; New England, 1662 ***1224.1*** *p47*
Holkirk, William 19; Maryland, 1774 ***1220.25*** *p53*
Holl, Abraham; America, 1738 ***2856.30*** *p197a*
Holl, Andreas; America, 1738 ***2856.30*** *p197a*
Holl, Anton; Port uncertain, 1753 ***2856.30*** *p197I*
Holl, Dieterich; Port uncertain, 1751 ***2856.30*** *p197I*
Holl, Henrich; America, 1752 ***2856.30*** *p197a*
With wife & children
Holl, Henrich; Port uncertain, 1751 ***2856.30*** *p197a*
With wife & children
Holl, Johann Georg; Port uncertain, 1787 ***2856.30*** *p197a*
Holl, Johann Nicolas; Port uncertain, 1755 ***2856.30*** *p197a*
Holl, John; New York, 1838 ***8197.10*** *p116*
Holl, Nickel; America, 1738 ***2856.30*** *p197a*
Holl, Philipp; America, 1727 ***2856.30*** *p197I*
Holl, Rosina; Port uncertain, 1741 ***2856.30*** *p197I*
Hollamby, James; New York, New York, 1780 ***1224.2*** *p57*
Hollan, George; Maryland, 1668 ***2524.55*** *p112*
Holland, Mr.; Quebec, 1856 ***9196.15*** *p9*
Holland, Mrs.; Quebec, 1857 ***9196.15*** *p18*
Holland, Abigail 76; Vermont, 1899 ***5900.10*** *p54*
Holland, Addie M. Witherell; Vermont, 1867-1929 ***5900.10*** *p402*
Holland, Anthony 39; Ontario, 1871 ***1823.15*** *p117*
Holland, Bridget; Vermont, 1851-1889 ***5900.10*** *p359*
Holland, C.; Quebec, 1856 ***9196.15*** *p10*
Holland, Mrs. C.; Quebec, 1856 ***9196.15*** *p10*
Holland, Catherine; Vermont, 1855-1937 ***5900.10*** *p69*
Holland, Charles 35; Ontario, 1871 ***1823.28*** *p41*
Holland, Cornelius; New York, 1840 ***8197.10*** *p173*
Holland, Daniel; Maryland, 1668 ***2524.55*** *p112*
Holland, Daniel; Maryland, 1671 ***2524.55*** *p112*
Holland, Dennice; Maryland, 1678 ***2524.55*** *p112*
Holland, Dennis; Maryland, 1668 ***2524.55*** *p112*
Holland, Dennis; Vermont, 1855-1943 ***5900.10*** *p402*
Holland, Dennis 80; Vermont, 1897 ***5900.10*** *p366*
Holland, Edward 7; Vermont, 1859 ***5900.10*** *p362*
Holland, Elizabeth; Pennsylvania, 1690 ***1224.1*** *p30*
Holland, Elizabeth; Virginia, 1658 ***1224.1*** *p30*
Holland, Ellen Lane; Vermont, 1824-1909 ***5900.10*** *p395*
Holland, Francis *SEE* Holland, Francis
Holland, Francis; Maryland, 1661 ***2524.55*** *p112*
Wife: Mary
Son: Francis
Holland, George; Maryland, 1668 ***2524.55*** *p112*

Holland, George; Maryland, 1670 ***2524.55*** *p112*
Holland, George 79; Ontario, 1871 ***1823.15*** *p117*
Holland, H.; Quebec, 1856 ***9196.15*** *p10*
Holland, Mrs. H.; Quebec, 1856 ***9196.15*** *p10*
Holland, Hanora; Vermont, 1837-1924 ***5900.10*** *p359*
Holland, Henry 60; Ontario, 1871 ***1823.15*** *p117*
Holland, James; Virginia, 1667 ***6212.30*** *p35*
Holland, James 41; Ontario, 1871 ***1823.15*** *p117*
Holland, James 58; Ontario, 1871 ***1823.15*** *p117*
Holland, Jeremiah 30; Ontario, 1871 ***1823.28*** *p41*
Holland, John; Maryland, 1680 ***2524.55*** *p112*
Holland, John; Vermont, 1811-1901 ***5900.10*** *p395*
Holland, John 30; Ontario, 1871 ***1823.28*** *p41*
Holland, John 41; Ontario, 1871 ***1823.15*** *p117*
Holland, John 54; Vermont, 1872 ***5900.10*** *p366*
Holland, Marcus 46; Vermont, 1901 ***5900.10*** *p289*
Holland, Margaret; Vermont, 1853-1930 ***5900.10*** *p393*
Holland, Margaret; Vermont, 1857-1936 ***5900.10*** *p394*
Holland, Margaret Boughen 80; Vermont, 1898 ***5900.10*** *p366*
Holland, Margaret Mulcahy; Vermont, 1838-1914 ***5900.10*** *p356*
Holland, Margaret Rairdon 75; Vermont, 1864 ***5900.10*** *p366*
Holland, Margaret Sweeney; Vermont, 1839-1914 ***5900.10*** *p366*
Holland, Mary *SEE* Holland, Francis
Holland, Mary; Vermont, 1855-1955 ***5900.10*** *p426*
Holland, Mary; Vermont, 1856-1941 ***5900.10*** *p393*
Holland, Mary 39; Vermont, 1871 ***5900.10*** *p373*
Holland, Mary Cotter 30; Vermont, 1865 ***5900.10*** *p366*
Holland, Mary Lane; Vermont, 1832-1911 ***5900.10*** *p393*
Holland, Michael; Vermont, 1850-1924 ***5900.10*** *p394*
Holland, Michael 54; Ontario, 1871 ***1823.15*** *p117*
Holland, Nathaniel; New England, 1658 ***1224.1*** *p30*
Holland, Nellie M. Halloran; Vermont, 1862-1917 ***5900.10*** *p609*
Holland, Nicholas J.; Vermont, 1864-1905 ***5900.10*** *p609*
Holland, Peter; Vermont, 1813-1895 ***5900.10*** *p393*
Holland, Richard; Virginia, 1664 ***6212.30*** *p6*
Holland, Samuel; Virginia, 1658 ***1224.1*** *p30*
Holland, T.; Quebec, 1857 ***9196.15*** *p25*
Holland, Thomas 20; Virginia, 1775 ***1220.25*** *p110*
Holland, Thomas 54; Ontario, 1871 ***1823.15*** *p117*
Holland, Timothy 87; Vermont, 1918 ***5900.10*** *p372*
Holland, William; Georgia, 1699 ***1640.13*** *p57*
Holland, William 24; Ontario, 1871 ***1823.15*** *p117*
Holland, William 37; Ontario, 1871 ***1823.28*** *p41*
Holland, William 55; Ontario, 1871 ***1823.22*** *p75*
Holland, William 62; Ontario, 1871 ***1823.15*** *p117*
Holland, William P.; New York, 1831-1840 ***8197.10*** *p174*
Hollander, Georg; Port uncertain, 1747 ***2856.30*** *p197a* With wife & children
Hollander, Heinrich; Port uncertain, 1767 ***2856.30*** *p197a*
Hollander, Jacob; Port uncertain, 1774 ***2856.30*** *p197a*
Hollander, Peter; Port uncertain, 1764 ***2856.30*** *p197a* With wife & children
Hollands, Walter; New York, 1839 ***8197.10*** *p131*
Hollandsworth, Elisa 23; Ontario, 1861 ***2896.27*** *p31*
Hollemake, Mr.; Quebec, 1856 ***9196.15*** *p8*
Hollenbach, Hiskias; Port uncertain, 1754 ***2856.30*** *p197a*
Hollenback, William 25; Ontario, 1871 ***1823.22*** *p75*
Holleran, Bridget; Vermont, 1840-1906 ***5900.10*** *p427*
Holleran, Bridget; Vermont, 1859-1943 ***5900.10*** *p578*
Holleran, Bridget 76; Vermont, 1877 ***5900.10*** *p248*
Holleran, Margaret; Vermont, 1854-1893 ***5900.10*** *p574*
Holleran, Margaret; Vermont, 1855-1902 ***5900.10*** *p275*
Holleran, Margaret 61; Vermont, 1895 ***5900.10*** *p248*
Holleran, Margaret 74; Vermont, 1905 ***5900.10*** *p275*
Holleran, Maria; Vermont, 1844-1932 ***5900.10*** *p557*
Holleran, Matthew 64; Vermont, 1888 ***5900.10*** *p275*
Holley, Ann; Vermont, 1848-1922 ***5900.10*** *p609*
Holley, Isaac 20; Ontario, 1861 ***2896.28*** *p27*
Holley, Susan 26; Ontario, 1861 ***2896.28*** *p27*
Hollibone, Edward; Maryland, 1673 ***2524.55*** *p112*
Hollibrooke, Henry; Virginia, 1668-1669 ***6212.30*** *p41*
Holliday, Arthur; New York, 1807 ***8197.10*** *p40*
Holliday, Edward; Philadelphia, 1789 ***4629.10*** *p58* *Wife:* Elizabeth
Holliday, Elizabeth *SEE* Holliday, Edward
Holliday, Jane; Virginia, 1681-1682 ***6212.30*** *p56*
Holliday, John 40; Nova Scotia, 1774 ***1220.25*** *p136*
Holliday, Peter 21; Philadelphia, 1789 ***4629.10*** *p58*
Holliday, Robert 30; New York, 1775 ***1220.25*** *p94*
Holliday, William 66; Ontario, 1871 ***1823.28*** *p41*
Hollidge, Thomas; New York, New York, 1802 ***8197.10*** *p131*
Holliger, Philip; Maryland, 1666 ***2524.55*** *p112*
Hollinge, Laughlin; Maryland, 1653 ***2524.55*** *p112*
Hollinger, Jakob; America, 1736 ***2856.30*** *p197a* With wife & child
Hollinger, Jakob; America, 1737 ***2856.30*** *p197a*
Hollings, James; Virginia, 1665-1666 ***6212.30*** *p24*
Hollings, Luke; Virginia, 1665-1666 ***6212.30*** *p23*
Hollings, Luke; Virginia, 1666-1667 ***6212.30*** *p32*
Hollingsby, Jeffry; Virginia, 1667 ***6212.30*** *p37*
Hollingsworth, John; Maryland, 1658 ***2524.55*** *p112*
Hollingsworth, Levi; Pennsylvania, 1779 ***4629.10*** *p40*
Hollingsworth, Levy; Pennsylvania, 1777 ***4629.10*** *p22*
Hollingworth, George 21; Maryland, 1775 ***1220.25*** *p107*
Hollingworth, John 41; Ontario, 1871 ***1823.28*** *p41*
Hollis, Barbary; Virginia, 1666-1667 ***6212.30*** *p35*
Hollis, Daniel 24; Philadelphia, 1775 ***1220.25*** *p9*
Hollis, Edm; Virginia, 1667 ***6212.30*** *p37*
Hollis, John; Maryland, 1648 ***2524.55*** *p112*
Hollis, John, Jr.; New York, 1840 ***8197.10*** *p173*
Hollis, Lawrence M.; New York, 1836 ***8197.10*** *p241*
Hollis, Nicholas; Virginia, 1666-1667 ***6212.30*** *p35*
Hollis, Thomas Frederick; Dominica, 1834 ***1224.3*** *p38*
Hollis, Thomas Pelham; New York, 1834 ***1224.3*** *p38*
Hollis, William; Maryland, 1682 ***2524.55*** *p112*
Hollister, George; Boston, 1693 ***1224.1*** *p30*
Holliwell, John; Maryland, 1663 ***2524.55*** *p112*
Holloran, Bridget 75; Vermont, 1893 ***5900.10*** *p248*
Holloran, Matthew 58; Vermont, 1872 ***5900.10*** *p248*
Holloren, Hanora 65; Vermont, 1897 ***5900.10*** *p66*
Holloren, John 65; Vermont, 1904 ***5900.10*** *p66*
Holloren, Nora 70; Vermont, 1904 ***5900.10*** *p467*
Hollornan, Michael; Pennsylvania, 1868 ***6058.10*** *p73*
Hollow, John 65; Ontario, 1871 ***1823.15*** *p117*
Hollow, William; Maryland, 1674 ***2524.55*** *p112*
Holloway, Charles; Virginia, 1664 ***6212.30*** *p12*
Holloway, Thomas 32; Ontario, 1871 ***1823.15*** *p117*
Holloway, William 21; Maryland, 1775 ***1220.25*** *p101*
Hollowell, Israel; Pennsylvania, 1779 ***4629.10*** *p40*
Hollowell, John; Philadelphia, 1779 ***1224.2*** *p57*
Hollowell, Rebecca; Virginia, 1688 ***6212.30*** *p57*
Hollric, Elis. Catharina; Port uncertain, 1770 ***2856.30*** *p462*
Hollstein, Konrad; Port uncertain, 1783 ***2856.30*** *p197l*
Hollstein, Magdalena; Port uncertain, 1796 ***2856.30*** *p197l*
Holly, Mrs. 70; Ontario, 1871 ***1823.28*** *p41*
Holly, Bernard; Maryland, 1658 ***2524.55*** *p112*
Holly, Elies 38; Ontario, 1871 ***1823.15*** *p117*
Holly, Elizabeth; Maryland, 1680 ***2524.55*** *p112*
Holly, Patrick 35; Ontario, 1871 ***1823.28*** *p41*
Holly, Timothy 28; Ontario, 1871 ***1823.28*** *p41*
Holly, William 41; Ontario, 1871 ***1823.28*** *p41*
Hollyoake, Mr.; Quebec, 1856 ***9196.15*** *p10*
Hollywood, Patrick; New York, 1834 ***8197.10*** *p240*
Holm, Eli; Maryland, 1672 ***2524.55*** *p112*
Holm, Hans Broun; New York, 1834 ***8197.10*** *p69*
Holman, G. W.; Quebec, 1857 ***9196.15*** *p25*
Holman, Mary; New York, 1851 ***1224.3*** *p70*
Holman, William 29; Ontario, 1871 ***1823.15*** *p117*
Holmann, J. 22; Alaska, 1912 ***9196.1*** *p39*
Holmann, J. 22; Whitehorse, Yukon, 1912 ***9196.1*** *p39*
Holmberg, A. 20; British Columbia, 1910 ***9196.1*** *p15*
Holmden, John; New York, New York, 1827 ***6058.10*** *p31*
Holmden, Rich; Virginia, 1664 ***6212.30*** *p7*
Holmden, Thomas; Pennsylvania, 1846 ***6058.10*** *p21*
Holmden, Walter; New York, New York, 1827 ***6058.10*** *p31*
Holme, John; Maryland, 1662 ***2524.55*** *p112*
Holmes, . . .; Boston, 1765 ***4628.40*** *p114*
Holmes, Mr.; Quebec, 1857 ***9196.15*** *p17*
Holmes, Mr.; Quebec, 1858 ***9196.15*** *p34*
Holmes, Mr.; Quebec, 1858 ***9196.15*** *p44*
Holmes, Mr.; Quebec, 1858 ***9196.15*** *p47*
Holmes, Mrs.; Quebec, 1858 ***9196.15*** *p47*
Holmes, Adam 44; Ontario, 1871 ***1823.22*** *p75*
Holmes, Alexander; Pennsylvania, 1777 ***4629.10*** *p28*
Holmes, Ann Quinn 81; Vermont, 1895 ***5900.10*** *p483*
Holmes, Arthur 43; Ontario, 1871 ***1823.22*** *p75*
Holmes, Barbara 50; Ontario, 1871 ***1823.28*** *p41*
Holmes, Benjaman 40; Ontario, 1871 ***1823.15*** *p117*
Holmes, Edmond 47; Ontario, 1871 ***1823.15*** *p117*
Holmes, Elizabeth; Maryland, 1671 ***2524.55*** *p112*
Holmes, George 36; Ontario, 1871 ***1823.22*** *p75*
Holmes, George 37; Ontario, 1871 ***1823.28*** *p41*
Holmes, Gervas 45; Ontario, 1871 ***1823.22*** *p75*
Holmes, Godfrey 41; Ontario, 1871 ***1823.15*** *p118*
Holmes, Grace; Maryland, 1681 ***2524.55*** *p112*
Holmes, Henry 40; Ontario, 1871 ***1823.15*** *p118*
Holmes, Henry 41; Ontario, 1871 ***1823.28*** *p41*
Holmes, James; New York, 1834 ***8197.10*** *p316*
Holmes, James; Quebec, 1858 ***9196.15*** *p32*
Holmes, James; Virginia, 1709 ***1224.2*** *p57*
Holmes, James 21; Maryland, 1774 ***1220.25*** *p61*
Holmes, James 60; Ontario, 1871 ***1823.28*** *p41*
Holmes, John; Pennsylvania, 1777 ***4629.10*** *p18*
Holmes, John; Pennsylvania, 1779 ***4629.10*** *p36*
Holmes, John 32; Virginia, 1773 ***1220.25*** *p31*
Holmes, John 50; Ontario, 1871 ***1823.15*** *p118*
Holmes, John 60; Ontario, 1871 ***1823.15*** *p118*
Holmes, John 65; Ontario, 1871 ***1823.28*** *p41*
Holmes, John J.; Connecticut, 1888 ***1640.13*** *p57*
Holmes, John L.; Vermont, 1856-1932 ***5900.10*** *p416*
Holmes, Joseph 30; Ontario, 1871 ***1823.28*** *p41*
Holmes, Joseph 51; Ontario, 1871 ***1823.15*** *p118*
Holmes, Margaret 80; Ontario, 1871 ***1823.15*** *p118*
Holmes, Mary 67; Ontario, 1871 ***1823.28*** *p41*
Holmes, Mary 74; Ontario, 1871 ***1823.15*** *p118*
Holmes, Mary A. Caden; Vermont, 1850-1924 ***5900.10*** *p416*
Holmes, Muriel 45; Ontario, 1871 ***1823.15*** *p118*
Holmes, Nathaniel 56; Ontario, 1871 ***1823.15*** *p118*
Holmes, Ole Saml 53; Alaska, 1916 ***9196.1*** *p6*
Holmes, Ole Saml 53; Yukon, 1916 ***9196.1*** *p6*
Holmes, Richard 45; Ontario, 1871 ***1823.15*** *p118*
Holmes, Robert 34; Ontario, 1871 ***1823.15*** *p118*
Holmes, Robert 36; Ontario, 1871 ***1823.28*** *p41*
Holmes, Samuel 30; Ontario, 1871 ***1823.15*** *p118*
Holmes, Samuel 33; Ontario, 1871 ***1823.15*** *p118*
Holmes, Samuel 63; Ontario, 1871 ***1823.15*** *p118*
Holmes, Thomas; Maryland, 1663 ***2524.55*** *p112*
Holmes, Thomas; Maryland, 1673 ***2524.55*** *p112*
Holmes, Thomas; Maryland, 1674 ***2524.55*** *p112*
Holmes, Thomas; Maryland, 1675 ***2524.55*** *p112*
Holmes, Thomas 29; Maryland, 1774 ***1220.25*** *p39*
Holmes, Thomas 31; New York, 1775 ***1220.25*** *p94*
Holmes, Thomas 47; Ontario, 1871 ***1823.15*** *p118*
Holmes, William; America, 1649 ***1224.1*** *p30*
Holmes, William 17; Maryland, 1774 ***1220.25*** *p77*
Holmes, William 32; Ontario, 1871 ***1823.15*** *p118*
Holmes, William 36; Ontario, 1871 ***1823.22*** *p75*
Holmes, William 40; Ontario, 1871 ***1823.15*** *p118*
Holmes, William 48; Ontario, 1871 ***1823.28*** *p41*
Holmes, William C.; New York, 1840 ***8197.10*** *p172*
Holminiak, Vincenty; Maryland, 1910 ***3259.35*** *p20*
Holmodel, Falintine 39; Ontario, 1871 ***1823.15*** *p118*
Holmquist, Cornelius; New York, 1840 ***8197.10*** *p173*
Holmsted, Francis 28; Ontario, 1871 ***1823.15*** *p118*
Holmwood, Milleson; Maryland, 1650 ***2524.55*** *p113*
Holmwood, Thomas; Maryland, 1631-1685 ***2524.55*** *p113*
Holnan, James 80; Ontario, 1861 ***2896.27*** *p66*
Holoday, Andrew 42; Ontario, 1871 ***1823.28*** *p41*
Hologhan, Mary 60; Ontario, 1871 ***1823.15*** *p118*
Hologhan, Patrick 30; Ontario, 1871 ***1823.15*** *p118*
Hologhan, Thomas 30; Ontario, 1871 ***1823.15*** *p118*
Hologhan, Thomas 73; Ontario, 1871 ***1823.15*** *p118*
Hololski, John; Maryland, 1910 ***3259.35*** *p20*
Holopicki, John; Maryland, 1910 ***3259.35*** *p20*
Holotz, George; New York, New York, 1849 ***3437.14*** *p34*
Holron, Bridget; Vermont, 1854 ***5900.10*** *p248*
Holron, Kate McCreary; Vermont, 1894 ***5900.10*** *p248*
Holron, Patrick; Vermont, 1826-1899 ***5900.10*** *p248*
Holst, Volmar; British Columbia, 1915 ***9196.1*** *p56*
Holst, Volmar; Seattle, 1915 ***9196.1*** *p56*
Holstead, John; Virginia, 1671 ***6212.30*** *p44*
Holstead, William; Virginia, 1671 ***6212.30*** *p44*
Holstein, Mrs. Martin; Port uncertain, 1768 ***2856.30*** *p197l*
Holt, Mrs.; Maryland, 1646 ***2524.55*** *p112*
Holt, Anne; Maryland, 1658 ***2524.55*** *p112*
Holt, Anthony 35; Ontario, 1871 ***1823.15*** *p118*
Holt, Catherine 50; Ontario, 1861 ***2896.27*** *p36*
Holt, E.; Quebec, 1856 ***9196.15*** *p6*
Holt, Edm; Virginia, 1667 ***6212.30*** *p37*
Holt, Eliza.; Maryland, 1678 ***2524.55*** *p116*
Holt, Elizabeth; Washington, District of Columbia, 1809 ***1224.3*** *p38*
Holt, Emily J. 24; Ontario, 1861 ***2896.27*** *p37*
Holt, Henry; Maryland, 1672 ***2524.55*** *p112*
Holt, Henry 17; Ontario, 1861 ***2896.27*** *p36*
Holt, James; Maryland, 1682 ***2524.55*** *p112*
Holt, James; Virginia, 1667 ***6212.30*** *p35*
Holt, Jno; Virginia, 1664 ***6212.30*** *p9*
Holt, John; Virginia, 1665-1666 ***6212.30*** *p20*
Holt, John 15; Ontario, 1861 ***2896.27*** *p36*
Holt, Mary; Virginia, 1666 ***6212.30*** *p27*
Holt, Nath; Virginia, 1667 ***6212.30*** *p37*
Holt, Nehemiah; Virginia, 1667-1668 ***6212.30*** *p38*
Holt, Richard; Virginia, 1665 ***6212.30*** *p19*
Holt, Robert; Virginia, 1666-1667 ***6212.30*** *p32*
Holt, Robt; Virginia, 1664 ***6212.30*** *p14*
Holt, Robt; Virginia, 1665-1666 ***6212.30*** *p23*
Holt, Roger; Virginia, 1666 ***6212.30*** *p26*
Holt, Tho; Virginia, 1665-1666 ***6212.30*** *p23*
Holt, Tho; Virginia, 1667 ***6212.30*** *p35*
Holt, Thomas; Virginia, 1666-1667 ***6212.30*** *p32*
Holt, William; Maryland, 1681 ***2524.55*** *p112*
Holt, William 25; Ontario, 1871 ***1823.15*** *p118*
Holt, William 52; Ontario, 1871 ***1823.15*** *p118*
Holt, Wm; Quebec, 1856 ***9196.15*** *p5*

Holte, John; Maryland, 1674 2524.55 p112
Holten, Richard 26; Ontario, 1871 1823.28 p41
Holthour, John 40; Ontario, 1871 1823.15 p118
Holton, Ann McGuire 78; Vermont, 1897 5900.10 p565
Holton, George 21; America, 1774 1220.25 p37
Holton, Jacob; Pennsylvania, 1777 4629.10 p18
Holton, Johanna M.; Vermont, 1877-1950 5900.10 p551
Holton, John; Maryland, 1697 1224.1 p30
Holton, Robert; Maryland, 1658 2524.55 p115
Holton, Thomas; Maryland, 1668 2524.55 p112
Holton, William; New York, 1828 8197.10 p240
Holtzbacher, Johann; Port uncertain, 1747 2856.30 p197a
Holtzer, Christian; Port uncertain, 1755 2856.30 p197a
Holtzer, Johann; Port uncertain, 1758 2856.30 p197a
Holtzer, Ursula; Port uncertain, 1720 2856.30 p197a
Holtzwarth, Caspar; America, 1751 2856.30 p197a
Holyoak, Mr.; Quebec, 1858 9196.15 p47
Holz, John 38; Ontario, 1871 1823.15 p118
Holzbaur, Johann; Port uncertain, 1741 2856.30 p197A
Holzhauer, Barbara; Port uncertain, 1766 2856.30 p197A
Holzhauser, Abraham; Port uncertain, 1754 2856.30 p197A
Holzhauser, Diederich; Port uncertain, 1754 2856.30 p197A
Holzle, Michael; Port uncertain, 1752 2856.30 p197I
Holzman, Geo 45; Ontario, 1871 1823.15 p118
Holzschuh, Johann Michael; Port uncertain, 1738 2856.30 p197A
Holzwart, Hans Jacob; Port uncertain, 1777 2856.30 p197A
Homan, Herbert; Maryland, 1673 2524.55 p112
Homberger, Christian; Port uncertain, 1741 2856.30 p197A
Home, Charles; New York, 1748 1224.2 p57
Home, Edward; Pennsylvania, 1779 4629.10 p40
Home, Francis; New York, 1831 8197.10 p366
Home, Franz; Port uncertain, 1749 2856.30 p197A
Home, J. W.; Portland, Maine, 1858 9196.15 p30
Home, J. W.; Quebec, 1858 9196.15 p42
Home, James; Jamaica, 1785 1640.13 p57
Home, William; New York, 1892 1640.13 p57
Homer, Joseph; New York, 1834-1838 8197.10 p117
Homes, Ellen 21; Ontario, 1861 2896.28 p33
Homes, Sarah; Maryland, 1665 2524.55 p63
Homewood, James; Maryland, 1649 2524.55 p112
Homewood, James; Maryland, 1663 2524.55 p113
Homewood, John; Maryland, 1649 2524.55 p113
Homewood, Milleson *SEE* Homewood, Thomas
Homewood, Milleson; Maryland, 1650 2524.55 p113
Homewood, Milleson; Maryland, 1665 2524.55 p113
Homewood, Thomas; Maryland, 1631-1685 2524.55 p113
Homewood, Thomas; Maryland, 1663 2524.55 p113
Homewood, Thomas; Maryland, 1665 2524.55 p113
Wife: Milleson
Homewth, Frederick 41; Ontario, 1871 1823.28 p41
Homeyer, John Henry; New York, 1807 8197.10 p39
Homfeld, Henry; New York, 1807 8197.10 p40
Homfray, Jeston; New Jersey, 1803 1224.3 p38
Homfray, Thomas; Maryland, 1681 2524.55 p117
Hommell, Frank 46; Ontario, 1871 1823.15 p118
Homuth, Charles 60; Ontario, 1871 1823.15 p118
Homuth, William 32; Ontario, 1871 1823.15 p118
Hon, George; New York, 1837 8197.10 p92
Honan, Ann; Vermont, 1817-1909 5900.10 p548
Honan, Martin; Vermont, 1824-1902 5900.10 p548
Honan, Nora J.; Vermont, 1866-1947 5900.10 p548
Honeck, Johann Michael; Port uncertain, 1746 2856.30 p197A
Honecker, Michael; Port uncertain, 1774 2856.30 p197A
Honey, Edward 54; Ontario, 1871 1823.22 p75
Honey, George; Pennsylvania, 1777 4629.10 p13
Honey, James 37; Ontario, 1871 1823.22 p75
Honey, John 35; Ontario, 1871 1823.15 p118
Honey, John 60; Ontario, 1871 1823.22 p75
Honey, William; Mississippi, 1798-1845 1640.10 p80
Honeywood, Arthur 22; Maryland, 1774 1220.25 p77
Honich, Jacob; America, 1764 2856.30 p197I
Honig, Anna Margarete; Port uncertain, 1743 2856.30 p197I
Honig, Dietrich; Port uncertain, 1743 2856.30 p197I
Honig, Jacob; America, 1750 2856.30 p197I
With wife & 2 children
Honig, Jacob; America, 1752 2856.30 p197I
With wife & 2 children
Honigan, Patrick; Pennsylvania, 1866 6058.10 p51
Honing, Maria Catharina; Port uncertain, 1750 2856.30 p197I
Honiton, Samuel 45; Ontario, 1871 1823.15 p118
Honn, Franz; Port uncertain, 1749 2856.30 p197A
Honn, Maria Elisabeth; Port uncertain, 1755 2856.30 p197A
Honner, James; New York, 1837 8197.10 p91
Honon, Thomas 30; Ontario, 1871 1823.22 p75
Honoret, Rev.; Quebec, 1856 9196.15 p9
Honsburgh, John 50; Ontario, 1871 1823.22 p75
Honsdon, Henry 21; Virginia, 1774 1220.25 p87
Honson, James 43; Ontario, 1871 1823.15 p118
Honywood, John; America, 1639 1224.1 p30
Hood, Charles 19; Ontario, 1871 1823.15 p118
Hood, David; America, 1860 1640.13 p57
Hood, Elizabeth; Maryland, 1665 2524.55 p113
Hood, Elizabeth 30; Maryland, 1775 1220.25 p112
Hood, Fredrick 39; Ontario, 1871 1823.15 p118
Hood, George 45; Ontario, 1871 1823.15 p118
Hood, John; Pennsylvania, 1777 4629.10 p21
Hood, John; Pennsylvania, 1779 4629.10 p36
Hood, Joseph 58; Ontario, 1871 1823.15 p118
Hood, Matthew; Tobago, West Indies, 1824 1640.13 p57
Hood, Thomas; Pennsylvania, 1786 4629.10 p49
Hood, Thomas 47; Ontario, 1871 1823.15 p118
Hood, William; Charleston, South Carolina, 1837 1224.3 p38
Hood, William 29; Virginia, 1774 1220.25 p45
Hoodell, Nathaniel; Maryland, 1661 2524.55 p113
Hooden, Jno; Virginia, 1665-1666 6212.30 p23
Hoodless, William R.; New York, 1831 8197.10 p367
Hoods, Mary; Maryland, 1674 2524.55 p115
Hoodson, Henry; Maryland, 1668 2524.55 p113
Wife: Ledda
Daughter: Ledda
Hoodson, Ledda *SEE* Hoodson, Henry
Hooey, Edward 26; Ontario, 1871 1823.28 p41
Hooey, John; New York, 1807 8197.10 p40
Hooey, Stewart 50; Ontario, 1871 1823.22 p75
Hooey, Wm 26; Ontario, 1871 1823.28 p41
Hoofman, William 33; Ontario, 1871 1823.28 p41
Hoog, Josef, The Younger; America, 1826 2856.30 p197A
Hook, Joseph; Maryland, 1680 2524.55 p113
Hook, Samuel 38; Philadelphia, 1774 1220.25 p82
Hookamer, Jacob; New England, 1709 1224.2 p118
Hooke, Ann; Maryland, 1680 2524.55 p113
Hooke, Edward; Maryland, 1662 2524.55 p200
Hooke, Edward; Maryland, 1672 2524.55 p113
Hooke, Ellenor; Virginia, 1663 6212.30 p3
Hooke, Humphry; Virginia, 1666 6212.30 p25
Hooke, James; Virginia, 1667-1668 6212.30 p38
Hooke, Jeremiah; Maryland, 1680 2524.55 p113
Hooke, John; New York, 1802 8197.10 p21
Hooke, Mary; Maryland, 1680 2524.55 p113
Hooke, Roger; Maryland, 1680 2524.55 p113
Hooke, Samuel; Pennsylvania, 1777 4629.10 p12
Hooke, Thomas; Maryland, 1672 2524.55 p113
Hooker, Charles 50; Ontario, 1871 1823.15 p118
Hooker, Joane *SEE* Hooker, Thomas
Hooker, John 29; Ontario, 1871 1823.22 p75
Hooker, Martin; Maryland, 1660 2524.55 p113
Hooker, Mary; New England, 1651 1224.1 p30
Hooker, Mary; Virginia, 1682 1224.1 p30
Hooker, Peter; Died enroute, 1639 1224.1 p30
Hooker, Ralph; Barbados, 1665 1224.1 p30
Hooker, Samuel; New England, 1655 1224.1 p30
Hooker, Stephen; New York, 1840 8197.10 p242
Hooker, Thomas; Maryland, 1653 2524.55 p113
Wife: Joane
Hooker, Thomas 15; Maryland, 1774 1220.25 p62
Hooker, William; New York, New York, 1749 1224.2 p57
Hooker, William; Pensacola, Florida, 1767 1224.2 p57
Hookerage, Janet 42; Ontario, 1871 1823.15 p119
Hoolihan, Patrick; Ontario, 1871 1823.28 p41
Hoons, Mary 18; Maryland, 1775 1220.25 p102
Hooper, Anabella 11; Ontario, 1871 1823.22 p75
Hooper, Ann *SEE* Hooper, Maximillian
Hooper, Charles 10; Ontario, 1871 1823.22 p75
Hooper, Charles 48; Ontario, 1871 1823.15 p119
Hooper, David 47; Ontario, 1871 1823.28 p41
Hooper, Dinah 7; Ontario, 1871 1823.22 p75
Hooper, Elizabeth *SEE* Hooper, Henry
Hooper, Ellinor *SEE* Hooper, Maximillian
Hooper, Francis; Maryland, 1654 2524.55 p113
Hooper, Geo.; Maryland, 1662 2524.55 p113
Hooper, George; Maryland, 1680 2524.55 p113
Hooper, George; New York, 1807 8197.10 p40
Hooper, H. 28; British Columbia, 1913 9196.1 p62
Hooper, H. 28; Washington, 1913 9196.1 p62
Hooper, Henry *SEE* Hooper, Henry
Hooper, Henry; Maryland, 1658 2524.55 p113
With wife
Child: Henry
Child: Elizabeth
Child: Mary
Child: Sarah
Child: Richard
Hooper, James; Virginia, 1667-1668 6212.30 p38
Hooper, James 22; Philadelphia, 1774 1220.25 p81
Hooper, James 40; Ontario, 1871 1823.15 p119
Hooper, Jane *SEE* Hooper, Thomas
Hooper, Jane; Maryland, 1680 2524.55 p113
Hooper, Jeremiah 39; Maryland, 1774 1220.25 p41
Hooper, Joanna 50; Ontario, 1871 1823.15 p119
Hooper, John 54; Ontario, 1871 1823.15 p119
Hooper, Jonathan 14; Ontario, 1871 1823.22 p75
Hooper, Joseph *SEE* Hooper, Maximillian
Hooper, Mary *SEE* Hooper, Henry
Hooper, Mary 18; Virginia, 1774 1220.25 p87
Hooper, Maximillian *SEE* Hooper, Maximillian
Hooper, Maximillian; Maryland, 1666 2524.55 p113
Daughter-In-Law: Ellinor
Brother: Joseph
Son: Joseph
Daughter: Suzan
Daughter: Ann
Son: Maximillian
Hooper, Richard *SEE* Hooper, Henry
Hooper, Robert; Maryland, 1668 2524.55 p113
Hooper, Robert 22; Maryland, 1774 1220.25 p53
Hooper, Sarah *SEE* Hooper, Henry
Hooper, Susan; Virginia, 1666 6212.30 p31
Hooper, Susanna 27; Ontario, 1871 1823.22 p76
Hooper, Suzan *SEE* Hooper, Maximillian
Hooper, Thomas; Maryland, 1658 2524.55 p113
Wife: Jane
Hooper, Thomas; New York, 1851 1224.3 p38
Hooper, Thomas 16; Ontario, 1871 1823.22 p76
Hooper, William 19; Ontario, 1871 1823.22 p76
Hooper, William 36; Ontario, 1871 1823.15 p119
Hooper, William 52; Ontario, 1871 1823.22 p76
Hoople, Charles M.; New York, 1840 8197.10 p172
Hoorosky, Casmer; Maryland, 1910 3259.35 p20
Hooton, George; New York, 1851 1224.3 p38
Hooton, John; New Jersey, 1805 1224.3 p38
Hooton, Mary *SEE* Hooton, Thomas
Hooton, Sarah *SEE* Hooton, Thomas
Hooton, Thomas; Maryland, 1665 2524.55 p113
Wife: Mary
Daughter: Sarah
Hoover, Archibald 35; Ontario, 1861 2896.27 p21
Hoover, Elizabeth 35; Ontario, 1861 2896.27 p23
Hoover, Georgina 8; Ontario, 1861 2896.27 p23
Hoover, Ida Jane 3; Ontario, 1861 2896.27 p23
Hoover, Isaac 6; Ontario, 1861 2896.27 p23
Hoover, Jacob; America, 1738 2856.30 p197A
Hoover, Jacob 70; Ontario, 1861 2896.27 p21
Hoover, John 29; Ontario, 1861 2896.28 p64
Hoover, John 85; Ontario, 1871 1823.15 p119
Hoover, Margaret 69; Ontario, 1861 2896.27 p21
Hopa, Anna; Maryland, 1910 3259.35 p20
Hope, Mrs.; Portland, Maine, 1857 9196.15 p12
Hope, Abraham; Maryland, 1651 2524.55 p113
Hope, Charles Cowan; Montreal, 1900 1640.13 p57
Hope, Cornelius; New York, 1821 8197.10 p237
Hope, Frank; Vermont, 1845-1890 5900.10 p392
Hope, Frederick; New York, 1840 8197.10 p173
Hope, Henry; North Carolina, 1738 1224.2 p57
Hope, John; Georgia, 1734 1640.10 p80
Hope, John; New York, 1830 8197.10 p240
Hope, John; Quebec, 1858 9196.15 p32
Hope, Mathew 70; Ontario, 1871 1823.22 p76
Hope, Thomas; Jamaica, 1699 1640.13 p57
Hope, William; Maryland, 1660 2524.55 p113
Hopes, Samuel 36; Ontario, 1871 1823.28 p41
Hopewell, Ann; Maryland, 1649 2524.55 p114
Hopfner, Aloys; Port uncertain, 1788 2856.30 p197I
Hopkins, Mr.; Quebec, 1856 9196.15 p7
Hopkins, Mr.; Quebec, 1856 9196.15 p9
Hopkins, Mr.; Quebec, 1858 9196.15 p34
Hopkins, Mr., Jr.; Quebec, 1858 9196.15 p34
Hopkins, Mrs.; Maryland, 1666 2524.55 p114
Hopkins, Mrs.; Quebec, 1858 9196.15 p42
Hopkins, Mrs. 40; Ontario, 1871 1823.15 p119
Hopkins, Mrs. 82; Ontario, 1861 2896.28 p8
Hopkins, Ann 29; Baltimore, 1775 1220.25 p116
Hopkins, Ann 33 *SEE* Hopkins, William
Hopkins, Anne 62; Vermont, 1870 5900.10 p246
Hopkins, Annie Manning; Vermont, 1856-1918 5900.10 p114
Hopkins, Benjamin; New York, 1807 8197.10 p40
Hopkins, Benjamin 48; Ontario, 1871 1823.22 p76
Hopkins, Catherine 6; Ontario, 1861 2896.25 p40
Hopkins, Charles 65; Ontario, 1871 1823.22 p76
Hopkins, Daniel; Maryland, 1682 2524.55 p114
Hopkins, Elizabeth 18; Philadelphia, 1774 1220.25 p42
Hopkins, Garrett; Maryland, 1658 2524.55 p38
Hopkins, George 37; Ontario, 1871 1823.22 p76
Hopkins, Hannah *SEE* Hopkins, Samuel
Hopkins, Hugh 50; Ontario, 1871 1823.15 p119

Hopkins, James 42; Ontario, 1871 ***1823.15*** *p119*
Hopkins, James 77; Vermont, 1875 ***5900.10*** *p575*
Hopkins, Jean; Virginia, 1664 ***6212.30*** *p11*
Hopkins, Jno; Virginia, 1664 ***6212.30*** *p7*
Hopkins, Job; New York, 1807 ***8197.10*** *p330*
Hopkins, John; Maryland, 1669 ***2524.55*** *p114*
Hopkins, John; New York, 1821 ***8197.10*** *p238*
Hopkins, John; Philadelphia, 1850 ***1224.3*** *p38*
Hopkins, John 19; Maryland, 1775 ***1220.25*** *p112*
Hopkins, Jonas; Maryland, 1682 ***2524.55*** *p114*
Hopkins, Joseph; Maryland, 1664 ***2524.55*** *p114*
Hopkins, Joseph; Maryland, 1667 ***2524.55*** *p114*
With wife
Hopkins, Joseph 42; Ontario, 1861 ***2896.25*** *p5*
Hopkins, Joseph 56; Ontario, 1871 ***1823.22*** *p76*
Hopkins, Margaret 41; Ontario, 1861 ***2896.25*** *p5*
Hopkins, Mary; Vermont, 1846-1906 ***5900.10*** *p504*
Hopkins, Matthew; New York, 1839 ***8197.10*** *p132*
Hopkins, Michael; Pennsylvania, 1777 ***4629.10*** *p20*
Hopkins, Michael; Vermont, 1847-1904 ***5900.10*** *p114*
Hopkins, Nathan *SEE* Hopkins, Samuel
Hopkins, Owen; Virginia, 1663 ***6212.30*** *p2*
Hopkins, Patrick 25; Maryland, 1774 ***1220.25*** *p77*
Hopkins, Peter; Virginia, 1666-1667 ***6212.30*** *p33*
Hopkins, Robert; Maryland, 1652 ***2524.55*** *p114*
Hopkins, Robert; Pennsylvania, 1777 ***4629.10*** *p16*
Hopkins, Robert; Pennsylvania, 1788 ***4629.10*** *p56*
Hopkins, Robert 45; Ontario, 1871 ***1823.28*** *p41*
Hopkins, Samuel *SEE* Hopkins, Samuel
Hopkins, Samuel; Maryland, 1680 ***2524.55*** *p114*
Wife: Hannah
Child: Hannah
Child: Temperance
Child: Samuel
Child: Nathan
Hopkins, Sarah 15; Ontario, 1861 ***2896.25*** *p5*
Hopkins, Temperance *SEE* Hopkins, Samuel
Hopkins, Thomas; Maryland, 1659 ***2524.55*** *p114*
Hopkins, Thomas; Maryland, 1681 ***2524.55*** *p114*
Hopkins, Thomas 42; Vermont, 1848 ***5900.10*** *p246*
Hopkins, William; Virginia, 1735 ***1224.2*** *p57*
Hopkins, William 33; America, 1774 ***1220.25*** *p36*
Wife: Ann 33
Hopkins, Wm; Virginia, 1664 ***6212.30*** *p8*
Hopkinson, Daniel; Virginia, 1637 ***1224.1*** *p30*
Hopkinson, Elizabeth; Maryland, 1666 ***2524.55*** *p114*
Hopkinson, Francis; Pennsylvania, 1777 ***4629.10*** *p14*
Hople, William 43; Ontario, 1871 ***1823.15*** *p119*
Hoppa, Thomas; Maryland, 1910 ***3259.35*** *p20*
Hopper, Anthony 19; Maryland, 1775 ***1220.25*** *p109*
Hopper, Dorothy *SEE* Hopper, John
Hopper, Edward 46; Ontario, 1871 ***1823.15*** *p119*
Hopper, John; Maryland, 1665 ***2524.55*** *p114*
Wife: Dorothy
Hopper, John 23; Nova Scotia, 1774 ***1220.25*** *p135*
Hopper, Robert; Maryland, 1666 ***2524.55*** *p114*
Hopper, S.; Quebec, 1856 ***9196.15*** *p6*
Hopper, Thomas 32; Maryland, 1774 ***1220.25*** *p72*
Hopper, Thomas 32; Maryland, 1774 ***1220.25*** *p77*
Hopper, William 42; Ontario, 1871 ***1823.22*** *p76*
Hoppermill, John 45; Ontario, 1871 ***1823.15*** *p119*
Hopson, John 65; Ontario, 1871 ***1823.15*** *p119*
Hopton, Mr.; Quebec, 1858 ***9196.15*** *p36*
Hopton, Mrs.; Quebec, 1857 ***9196.15*** *p25*
Hopton, Mrs.; Quebec, 1858 ***9196.15*** *p36*
Hopton, Rich; Virginia, 1665-1666 ***6212.30*** *p23*
Hopton, William; Charles Town, South Carolina, 1788 ***1224.2*** *p58*
Hopton, Wm; Virginia, 1665-1666 ***6212.30*** *p21*
Hopwood, Jemima; New York, 1844 ***1224.3*** *p67*
Hopwood, Thomas; Virginia, 1671-1672 ***6212.30*** *p47*
Hopworth, Jno.; Maryland, 1680 ***2524.55*** *p114*
Hor, Anna Dorothea; Port uncertain, 1793 ***2856.30*** *p197I*
Horagievic, Alexander; Maryland, 1910 ***3259.35*** *p20*
Horan, Ann 7 *SEE* Horan, Patrick
Horan, Anne 34 *SEE* Horan, Michael
Horan, Bridget; Vermont, 1853-1906 ***5900.10*** *p218*
Horan, Bridget King; Vermont, 1831-1905 ***5900.10*** *p554*
Horan, Catherine 4 *SEE* Horan, Michael
Horan, Catherine 5 *SEE* Horan, Patrick
Horan, Catherine 29 *SEE* Horan, Patrick
Horan, Dolly 80; Vermont, 1869 ***5900.10*** *p605*
Horan, Eliza 16; New York, New York, 1848 ***1825.45*** *p35*
Horan, Elizabeth; Vermont, 1867-1918 ***5900.10*** *p596*
Horan, Elizabeth 70; Vermont, 1882 ***5900.10*** *p268*
Horan, Ellen; Vermont, 1845-1945 ***5900.10*** *p220*
Horan, James; New York, 1837 ***8197.10*** *p90*
Horan, James; Vermont, 1846-1922 ***5900.10*** *p213*
Horan, John; Vermont, 1847-1902 ***5900.10*** *p218*
Horan, John 3 *SEE* Horan, Patrick
Horan, John 48; Vermont, 1881-1900 ***5900.10*** *p306*
Horan, John 51; Ontario, 1871 ***1823.15*** *p119*
Horan, John F.; Vermont, 1859-1949 ***5900.10*** *p554*
Horan, John L.; Vermont, 1830-1903 ***5900.10*** *p554*
Horan, Margaret 12 *SEE* Horan, Patrick
Horan, Marie Condon; Vermont, 1847-1947 ***5900.10*** *p213*
Horan, Martin; Vermont, 1831-1912 ***5900.10*** *p334*
Horan, Mary; Vermont, 1815-1890 ***5900.10*** *p213*
Horan, Mary 10 *SEE* Horan, Patrick
Horan, Mary McMahon; Vermont, 1846-1917 ***5900.10*** *p334*
Horan, Melvina 40; Vermont, 1896 ***5900.10*** *p307*
Horan, Michael 6 *SEE* Horan, Michael
Horan, Michael 38; New York, New York, 1848 ***1825.45*** *p35*
Wife: Anne 34
Son: Michael 6
Daughter: Catherine 4
Son: Thomas 2
Horan, Nellie 15; Vermont, 1871 ***5900.10*** *p107*
Horan, Patrick 30; New York, New York, 1852 ***1825.45*** *p58*
Wife: Catherine 29
Daughter: Ann 7
Daughter: Margaret 12
Daughter: Mary 10
Daughter: Catherine 5
Son: John 3
Horan, Peter 52; Vermont, 1870 ***5900.10*** *p207*
Horan, Theresa R.; Vermont, 1866-1925 ***5900.10*** *p554*
Horan, Thomas 2 *SEE* Horan, Michael
Horan, Thomas 40; Ontario, 1871 ***1823.15*** *p119*
Horbach, Anna Catharina; Port uncertain, 1786 ***2856.30*** *p197A*
Horbach, Anna Ottilia; Port uncertain, 1757 ***2856.30*** *p197A*
Horbach, Jacob; Port uncertain, 1777 ***2856.30*** *p197A*
Horbach, Johann Peter; America, 1741 ***2856.30*** *p197A*
With wife & child
Horbach, Konrad; Port uncertain, 1749 ***2856.30*** *p197A*
Horbach, Konrad; Port uncertain, 1757 ***2856.30*** *p197A*
Horbach, Maria Margarete; Port uncertain, 1751 ***2856.30*** *p197A*
Horbach, Maria Margarete; Port uncertain, 1752 ***2856.30*** *p197A*
Horbach, Peter; Port uncertain, 1751 ***2856.30*** *p197A*
Horbagh, Johann Peter; America, 1741 ***2856.30*** *p197A*
Horbelt, George Dietrich; New York, 1834-1838 ***8197.10*** *p117*
Horbelt, John L.; New York, 1838 ***8197.10*** *p117*
Hordan, Alexander; Alabama, 1822-1845 ***1640.10*** *p80*
Wife: Margaret
Hordan, Margaret *SEE* Hordan, Alexander
Hordt, Valentin; America, 1752 ***2856.30*** *p182*
Hordt, Veit; America, 1764 ***2856.30*** *p197I*
Hore, Francis; Virginia, 1664 ***6212.30*** *p12*
Hore, James; New York, 1837 ***8197.10*** *p91*
Hore, Matthew; New York, 1806 ***8197.10*** *p324*
Hore, Robert 88; Ontario, 1871 ***1823.28*** *p41*
Hore, William 41; Ontario, 1871 ***1823.22*** *p76*
Hore, William 71; Ontario, 1871 ***1823.22*** *p76*
Horeing, Jon; Virginia, 1674-1675 ***6212.30*** *p53*
Horey, Annie; Vermont, 1848-1926 ***5900.10*** *p353*
Horigan, Catherine 70; Vermont, 1892 ***5900.10*** *p551*
Horigan, Denice 24; Ontario, 1861 ***2896.27*** *p60*
Horigan, Patrick; Pennsylvania, 1866 ***6058.10*** *p51*
Horis, Mrs. Michael; America, 1749 ***2856.30*** *p197I*
Horle, Niklas; Port uncertain, 1719 ***2856.30*** *p197A*
With 5 children
Horlemann, Elisabeth; Port uncertain, 1781 ***2856.30*** *p197I*
Horley, John; Charles Town, South Carolina, 1804 ***1224.3*** *p38*
Horley, William; Charles Town, South Carolina, 1804 ***1224.3*** *p38*
Horlock, Joseph; Charleston, South Carolina, 1803 ***1224.3*** *p38*
Horman, Henry; Maryland, 1679 ***2524.55*** *p114*
Hormann, Jacob; Port uncertain, 1752 ***2856.30*** *p197I*
Hormann, Johanna; Port uncertain, 1793 ***2856.30*** *p197A*
Horn, Apollonia; Port uncertain, 1751 ***2856.30*** *p197A*
Horn, Charles E.; New York, 1838 ***8197.10*** *p241*
Horn, Christian; New York, 1837 ***8197.10*** *p90*
Horn, Christina 47; Ontario, 1871 ***1823.15*** *p119*
Horn, Edward; Maryland, 1654-1655 ***2524.55*** *p114*
Horn, Edward; Maryland, 1658 ***2524.55*** *p114*
Horn, Fridrich; Port uncertain, 1764 ***2856.30*** *p197A*
Horn, Georg Peter; America, 1752 ***2856.30*** *p197B*
With wife
Horn, Janet; Savannah, Georgia, 1775 ***1640.10*** *p81*
Horn, Johann Martin; Port uncertain, 1754 ***2856.30*** *p197B*
Horn, John; New York, 1838 ***8197.10*** *p377*
Horn, Stephen 52; Ontario, 1871 ***1823.28*** *p41*
Horn, William 51; Ontario, 1871 ***1823.15*** *p119*
Hornbach, Catharina; Cayenne, 1764 ***2856.30*** *p197B*
Hornbe, Robert; Virginia, 1704 ***1224.2*** *p58*
Hornbeck, Gardner 37; Ontario, 1871 ***1823.22*** *p76*
Hornbeck, Peter 60; Ontario, 1871 ***1823.22*** *p76*
Hornberger, Jacob; America, 1749 ***2856.30*** *p197B*
With wife
Hornberger, Jakob; America, 1740 ***2856.30*** *p197B*
Hornberger, Stefan; America, 1760 ***2856.30*** *p197B*
With wife
Hornblower, Ebenezer; New York, 1815 ***8197.10*** *p236*
Hornbrook, Bridget D.; Vermont, 1848-1900 ***5900.10*** *p344*
Hornbrook, Catherine; Vermont, 1843-1934 ***5900.10*** *p344*
Hornbrook, Catherine McCarty; Vermont, 1813-1879 ***5900.10*** *p344*
Hornbrook, Daniel; Vermont, 1840-1860 ***5900.10*** *p344*
Hornbrook, Ellen; Vermont, 1849-1872 ***5900.10*** *p344*
Hornbrook, Henry; Vermont, 1850-1877 ***5900.10*** *p344*
Hornbrook, John; Vermont, 1836-1929 ***5900.10*** *p344*
Hornbrook, Nancy; Vermont, 1841-1858 ***5900.10*** *p344*
Hornbrook, Timothy; Vermont, 1842-1874 ***5900.10*** *p344*
Hornbrook, William; Vermont, 1810-1872 ***5900.10*** *p343*
Hornbrooke, Mary McCarron; Vermont, 1843-1927 ***5900.10*** *p333*
Hornbrooke, William; Vermont, 1839-1919 ***5900.10*** *p332*
Hornby, Frederick; New York, 1838 ***8197.10*** *p115*
Hornby, James; New York, 1838 ***8197.10*** *p115*
Hornby, William; New York, 1828-1834 ***8197.10*** *p308*
Horne, Mr. 26; St. Kitts, 1773-1774 ***1220.25*** *p131*
Horne, Edward; Maryland, 1665 ***2524.55*** *p114*
Horne, Edward; Maryland, 1678 ***2524.55*** *p114*
Horne, George; Pennsylvania, 1777 ***4629.10*** *p26*
Horne, George; Pennsylvania, 1779 ***4629.10*** *p40*
Horne, Henry 22; Maryland, 1774 ***1220.25*** *p70*
Horne, Johann; Port uncertain, 1794 ***2856.30*** *p197B*
Horne, Margaret; Maryland, 1674 ***2524.55*** *p114*
Horne, Richard; Maryland, 1673 ***2524.55*** *p114*
Horne, Thomas; Maryland, 1663 ***2524.55*** *p114*
Horne, Thomas B. 33; Ontario, 1871 ***1823.22*** *p76*
Horne, Winifred; Maryland, 1665 ***2524.55*** *p114*
Hornek, Frank; Maryland, 1910 ***3259.35*** *p20*
Horner, Miss; Quebec, 1858 ***9196.15*** *p42*
Horner, Elizabeth; Maryland, 1663 ***2524.55*** *p114*
Horner, Georg Friedrich; Port uncertain, 1712 ***2856.30*** *p197B*
Horner, Henrich; America, 1750 ***2856.30*** *p197I*
Horner, James; New York, 1806 ***8197.10*** *p322*
Horner, Joel 65; Ontario, 1871 ***1823.15*** *p119*
Horner, John 60; Ontario, 1871 ***1823.15*** *p119*
Horner, Michael; Port uncertain, 1752 ***2856.30*** *p197I*
Horner, Michael; Port uncertain, 1752 ***2856.30*** *p197I*
With wife & 5 children
Horner, Michael; Port uncertain, 1766 ***2856.30*** *p197I*
Horner, Michael; Port uncertain, 1794 ***2856.30*** *p197I*
Horney, Henry 34; Ontario, 1871 ***1823.15*** *p119*
Horney, Henry 66; Ontario, 1871 ***1823.15*** *p119*
Horney, James 32; Ontario, 1871 ***1823.15*** *p119*
Hornidge, Catherine; Vermont, 1840-1891 ***5900.10*** *p583*
Hornidge, James; Vermont, 1840-1901 ***5900.10*** *p583*
Hornsby, Mr.; Quebec, 1858 ***9196.15*** *p34*
Hornsby, Thomas; Philadelphia, 1790 ***4629.10*** *p60*
Hornsinger, Johann; America, 1738 ***2856.30*** *p197B*
Hornstein, Josef; Port uncertain, 1720 ***2856.30*** *p197B*
Hornung, Anna Maria; Port uncertain, 1763 ***2856.30*** *p197B*
Hornung, Maria Eva; Port uncertain, 1759 ***2856.30*** *p197B*
Hornung, Michael; Port uncertain, 1751 ***2856.30*** *p197B*
Hornung, Peter; Port uncertain, 1748 ***2856.30*** *p197B*
Hornung, Stefan; Port uncertain, 1764 ***2856.30*** *p197B*
Hornung, Stefan; Port uncertain, 1791 ***2856.30*** *p197B*
Horpel, Johann; America, 1733 ***2856.30*** *p197I*
With wife
Horpel, Johann; America, 1739 ***2856.30*** *p197I*
Horrabin, Edward 22; Maryland, 1775 ***1220.25*** *p113*
Horrell, Francis 14; Philadelphia, 1775 ***1220.25*** *p8*
Horrell, Thomas Armstrong; Texas, 1841 ***1224.3*** *p38*
Horrmann, Jacob; Port uncertain, 1752 ***2856.30*** *p197I*
With family
Horrmann, Josef; Port uncertain, 1753 ***2856.30*** *p197I*
Horrocks, J.; Quebec, 1856 ***9196.15*** *p8*
Horrocks, J.; Quebec, 1858 ***9196.15*** *p36*
Horrocks, James; New York, 1840 ***8197.10*** *p173*
Horrocks, James; Virginia, 1772 ***1224.2*** *p58*
Horrocks, Richard; New York, 1828 ***8197.10*** *p240*
Hor.san, Edward; Maryland, 1661 ***2524.55*** *p130*
Horsch, . . .; America, 1766 ***2856.30*** *p197B*
Horscroft, Ambrose 35; Ontario, 1861 ***2896.27*** *p39*
Horscroft, Eleanor 27; Ontario, 1861 ***2896.27*** *p39*
Horscroft, Lucy Ann 1; Ontario, 1861 ***2896.27*** *p39*

Horscroft, Thomas 7; Ontario, 1861 ***2896.27*** *p39*
Horscroft, William H. 4; Ontario, 1861 ***2896.27*** *p39*
Horsedowne, William; Virginia, 1668-1669 ***6212.30*** *p41*
Horseey, Joseph; Maryland, 1665 ***2524.55*** *p114*
Horseley, Joseph; Maryland, 1665 ***2524.55*** *p114*
Horseman, Jane; Maryland, 1682 ***2524.55*** *p114*
Horseman, Robert; New York, 1799 ***1640.13*** *p57*
Horseman, Thomas; Maryland, 1682 ***2524.55*** *p114*
Horsey, Abigall *SEE* Horsey, Stephen
Horsey, John *SEE* Horsey, Stephen
Horsey, Mary *SEE* Horsey, Stephen
Horsey, Rose; Maryland, 1665 ***2524.55*** *p114*
Horsey, Samuel *SEE* Horsey, Stephen
Horsey, Sarah *SEE* Horsey, Stephen
Horsey, Stephen; Maryland, 1661 ***2524.55*** *p114*
Wife: Sarah
Relative: John
Relative: Mary
Relative: Abigall
Relative: Samuel
Son: Stephen, Jr.
Horsey, Stephen, Jr. *SEE* Horsey, Stephen
Horsfield, Joseph 24; Maryland, 1774 ***1220.25*** *p71*
Horsfield, Luke 36; Maryland, 1774 ***1220.25*** *p71*
Horsford, George; Maryland, 1665 ***2524.55*** *p138*
Horsford, Harriet; Vermont, 1852-1922 ***5900.10*** *p79*
Horsin, Peter; New York, 1840 ***8197.10*** *p242*
Horsingham, Henry; Virginia, 1663 ***6212.30*** *p1*
Horsington, Jno; Virginia, 1667 ***6212.30*** *p37*
Horsley, Derum; Maryland, 1673 ***2524.55*** *p114*
Horsley, Edmond; Maryland, 1673 ***2524.55*** *p101*
Horsley, William 62; Ontario, 1871 ***1823.22*** *p76*
Horsly, Derum; Maryland, 1673 ***2524.55*** *p114*
Horsly, John; Virginia, 1667 ***6212.30*** *p35*
Horsman, Christopher 27; Fort Cumberland, Nova Scotia, 1775 ***1220.25*** *p21*
Horsman, Jno; Virginia, 1665-1666 ***6212.30*** *p22*
Horsman, Jno; Virginia, 1666-1667 ***6212.30*** *p32*
Horsmanden, Daniel; New York, New York, 1786 ***1224.2*** *p58*
Horssel, Johann; America, 1739 ***2856.30*** *p197I*
Horst, . . .; America, 1766 ***2856.30*** *p197B*
Horst, George J. 46; Kansas, 1877-1910 ***9079.10*** *p21*
Horst, Mary C. 40; Kansas, 1877-1910 ***9079.10*** *p21*
Horte, Samuell; Maryland, 1660 ***2524.55*** *p114*
Horter, . . .; America, 1782 ***2856.30*** *p197I*
Horter, A. M.; America, 1764 ***2856.30*** *p504*
Horter, Anna Maria; America, 1765 ***2856.30*** *p197B*
With husband
Horter, Anna Maria; Port uncertain, 1756 ***2856.30*** *p197B*
With husband
Horter, Anna Maria; Port uncertain, 1764 ***2856.30*** *p197B*
With husband
Horter, Barb.; America, 1765 ***2856.30*** *p504*
Horter, Georg Adam; America, 1754 ***2856.30*** *p197B*
Horter, Georg Adam; Port uncertain, 1756 ***2856.30*** *p197B*
Horter, Hans Jacob; Port uncertain, 1733 ***2856.30*** *p197I*
Horter, Hans Jacob; Port uncertain, 1763 ***2856.30*** *p197I*
Horter, Johann Georg; America, 1775 ***2856.30*** *p197B*
Horter, Matthaus; Port uncertain, 1733 ***2856.30*** *p197I*
Horter, Matthaus; Port uncertain, 1763 ***2856.30*** *p197I*
Horter, Peter; Port uncertain, 1733 ***2856.30*** *p197I*
Horter, Peter; Port uncertain, 1763 ***2856.30*** *p197I*
Horter, Valtin; America, 1765 ***2856.30*** *p197B*
Horth, Friedrich; America, 1748 ***2856.30*** *p197I*
With wife & 6 children
Horthler, Georg; America, 1754 ***2856.30*** *p197I*
Horti, Philipp; Port uncertain, 1784 ***2856.30*** *p197I*
Hortley, Elizabeth 15; Ontario, 1861 ***2896.25*** *p40*
Horton, Ann 55; Ontario, 1871 ***1823.15*** *p119*
Horton, Edward; Maryland, 1666 ***2524.55*** *p114*
Horton, Elizabeth; Maryland, 1681 ***2524.55*** *p115*
Horton, Fanny E. 24; Ontario, 1871 ***1823.22*** *p76*
Horton, Francis E.; Vermont, 1860-1907 ***5900.10*** *p353*
Horton, Henry 42; Ontario, 1871 ***1823.15*** *p119*
Horton, Henry 76; Ontario, 1871 ***1823.15*** *p119*
Horton, Hillery 49; Ontario, 1871 ***1823.15*** *p119*
Horton, Horace 47; Ontario, 1871 ***1823.15*** *p119*
Horton, James; Vermont, 1845-1914 ***5900.10*** *p353*
Horton, Jeremiah; Pennsylvania, 1777 ***4629.10*** *p30*
Horton, Katherine J. Tracey; Vermont, 1855-1913 ***5900.10*** *p353*
Horton, Mary E.; Vermont, 1843-1904 ***5900.10*** *p385*
Horton, N.; Quebec, 1858 ***9196.15*** *p45*
Horton, Robert; Virginia, 1665-1666 ***6212.30*** *p25*
Horton, Roger; Virginia, 1667-1668 ***6212.30*** *p39*
Horton, Walter; Virginia, 1666 ***6212.30*** *p29*
Horty, James; New York, 1840 ***8197.10*** *p173*
Horty, Radger 34; Ontario, 1871 ***1823.28*** *p41*
Horusby, F. 41; Fairbanks, Alaska, 1910 ***9196.1*** *p10*
Horusby, F. 41; Yukon, 1910 ***9196.1*** *p10*
Horwarth, Franz; Port uncertain, 1762 ***2856.30*** *p197B*
With 2 children
Horwood, Edward; Maryland, 1654 ***2524.55*** *p115*
Horwood, Joel; Boston, 1697 ***1224.1*** *p30*
Hos, Mrs. Jakob; Port uncertain, 1769 ***2856.30*** *p197J*
With 3 daughters
Hose, John Jacob 80; Ontario, 1861 ***2896.25*** *p50*
Hoseman, Jos 30; Washington, 1914 ***9196.1*** *p64*
Hosier, William; Milwaukee, 1857 ***1224.3*** *p38*
Hosker, Benjamin; Maryland, 1681 ***2524.55*** *p115*
Hosker, Edward 45; Ontario, 1871 ***1823.15*** *p119*
Hoskin, Edward W.; New York, 1834 ***8197.10*** *p69*
Hoskin, Henry 49; Ontario, 1871 ***1823.22*** *p76*
Hoskin, William 45; Ontario, 1871 ***1823.22*** *p76*
Hosking, Joseph 39; Ontario, 1871 ***1823.28*** *p41*
Hosking, William 33; Ontario, 1871 ***1823.28*** *p41*
Hoskins, Alexander 30; Ontario, 1871 ***1823.22*** *p76*
Hoskins, Bennett; Maryland, 1654 ***2524.55*** *p115*
Hoskins, John; Maryland, 1681 ***2524.55*** *p115*
Hoskins, John; Virginia, 1666-1667 ***6212.30*** *p33*
Hoskins, John 21; Virginia, 1774 ***1220.25*** *p74*
Hoskins, Phill; Maryland, 1672 ***2524.55*** *p115*
Hoskins, Richard; Pennsylvania, 1701 ***1224.2*** *p58*
Hoskins, Thomas 25; Maryland, 1774 ***1220.25*** *p39*
Hoskins, Thomas 51; Ontario, 1871 ***1823.22*** *p76*
Hoskins, William 36; Ontario, 1871 ***1823.22*** *p76*
Hoslins, Philip; Maryland, 1676 ***2524.55*** *p115*
Hoss, Eva; Port uncertain, 1764 ***2856.30*** *p197B*
Hoss, Johann; Port uncertain, 1749 ***2856.30*** *p197B*
Hossack, Donald 70; Ontario, 1871 ***1823.22*** *p76*
Hossack, James 42; Ontario, 1871 ***1823.22*** *p76*
Hossack, James 62; Ontario, 1871 ***1823.22*** *p76*
Hosser, Rebecca 16; Maryland, 1775 ***1220.25*** *p109*
Hossermann, Johann; Canada, 1752 ***2856.30*** *p195*
Hossly, Derum; Maryland, 1666 ***2524.55*** *p101*
Hostane, Lawrence; Maryland, 1681 ***2524.55*** *p115*
Hosted, Rachel; Virginia, 1681 ***6212.30*** *p55*
Hoster, Caspar; Port uncertain, 1729 ***2856.30*** *p197B*
Hoster, Johann; America, 1741 ***2856.30*** *p197B*
Hostler, Chesman 63; Ontario, 1871 ***1823.15*** *p120*
Hostler, Sarah 61; Ontario, 1871 ***1823.15*** *p120*
Hostler, Thomas 40; Ontario, 1871 ***1823.22*** *p76*
Hotcbono, Richard; Maryland, 1664 ***2524.55*** *p115*
Hotchens, Richard; Maryland, 1663 ***2524.55*** *p115*
Hotchkis, William 31; Maryland, 1775 ***1220.25*** *p97*
Hotham, Richard 40; Philadelphia, 1774 ***1220.25*** *p55*
Hottirman, Ferdinand 42; Ontario, 1871 ***1823.28*** *p41*
Hottler, Christof; Port uncertain, 1796 ***2856.30*** *p197C*
Hottum, Margarete; Port uncertain, 1764 ***2856.30*** *p197C*
Hotzel, Johann Christof; Port uncertain, 1742 ***2856.30*** *p197J*
Hotzler, Elis. Catharina; Port uncertain, 1747 ***2856.30*** *p197J*
Houber, Michael; Port uncertain, 1784 ***2856.30*** *p197C*
With wife
Houchen, Sarah 26; Maryland, 1775 ***1220.25*** *p98*
Houchen, Susanna 30; Maryland, 1775 ***1220.25*** *p98*
Houds, Mary; Maryland, 1674 ***2524.55*** *p115*
Houffington, Rich; Virginia, 1672 ***6212.30*** *p48*
Houg, David; America, 1739 ***2856.30*** *p197C*
Hough, Jacob; America, 1739 ***2856.30*** *p197C*
Houghton, Frank 26; Ontario, 1871 ***1823.28*** *p41*
Houghton, George 58; Ontario, 1871 ***1823.15*** *p120*
Houghton, Jane; New York, New York, 1854 ***1224.3*** *p38*
Houghton, John; Charles Town, South Carolina, 1751 ***1224.2*** *p58*
Houghton, Margaret Monaghan; Vermont, 1845-1929 ***5900.10*** *p48*
Houghton, Mary; New England, 1653 ***1224.1*** *p31*
Houghton, Nathaniel; Pennsylvania, 1780 ***4629.10*** *p43*
Houghton, Rich; Virginia, 1665-1666 ***6212.30*** *p24*
Houghton, Thomas; Vermont, 1839-1916 ***5900.10*** *p48*
Houghton, Truman 24; Ontario, 1871 ***1823.22*** *p76*
Houk, Jerik Adam; America, 1733 ***2856.30*** *p197C*
Houlahan, Michael 56; Ontario, 1871 ***1823.22*** *p76*
Houlcratt, William; Virginia, 1666-1667 ***6212.30*** *p33*
Houlden, Alice; Maryland, 1677 ***2524.55*** *p115*
Houlden, Joseph; Maryland, 1677 ***2524.55*** *p115*
Houlden, Joshua; Maryland, 1681 ***2524.55*** *p115*
Houlding, Alice; Maryland, 1677 ***2524.55*** *p115*
Houlding, Joseph; Maryland, 1677 ***2524.55*** *p115*
Houlditch, Mr.; Quebec, 1857 ***9196.15*** *p23*
Houlditch, Mrs.; Quebec, 1857 ***9196.15*** *p23*
Houldsworth, Michael; Jamaica, 1706 ***1224.2*** *p57*
Houldsworth, Michael; New York, 1706 ***1224.2*** *p57*
Houlhan, Mary 22; Ontario, 1871 ***1823.28*** *p41*
Houlihan, Hanora; Vermont, 1842-1911 ***5900.10*** *p169*
Houlihan, James; Vermont, 1810-1897 ***5900.10*** *p218*
Houlihan, Mary; Vermont, 1855-1923 ***5900.10*** *p212*
Houlihan, Mary Touhey; Vermont, 1810-1897 ***5900.10*** *p218*
Houliston, Thomas; Canada, 1889 ***1640.13*** *p57*
Hoult, John 26; Virginia, 1774 ***1220.25*** *p93*
Houlton, Robert; Maryland, 1658 ***2524.55*** *p115*
Hounsby, John 30; Jamaica, 1775 ***1220.25*** *p144*
Hounsby, John 30; St. Christopher, 1775 ***1220.25*** *p144*
Hounslow, Mary Ann; Philadelphia Co., Pennsylvania, 1828 ***1224.3*** *p38*
Hounsly, Mathew; Virginia, 1666-1667 ***6212.30*** *p34*
Houragan, John 88; Vermont, 1877 ***5900.10*** *p209*
Hourd, Roderick 60; Ontario, 1871 ***1823.22*** *p76*
House, Anne; Virginia, 1663 ***6212.30*** *p4*
House, James 17; Jamaica, 1774 ***1220.25*** *p92*
House, John 32; Ontario, 1871 ***1823.22*** *p76*
House, Rowland; Virginia, 1667 ***6212.30*** *p37*
House, Samuel; Pennsylvania, 1784 ***4629.10*** *p44*
Houseal, Frances; South Carolina, 1810 ***1224.3*** *p39*
Housely, Alfred 32; Ontario, 1871 ***1823.22*** *p76*
Houseman, Mrs.; Portland, Maine, 1858 ***9196.15*** *p47*
Houseman, Rev.; Portland, Maine, 1858 ***9196.15*** *p47*
Houseman, Heinrich; New York, 1807 ***8197.10*** *p40*
Houser, Jacob; Pennsylvania, 1777 ***4629.10*** *p12*
Housley, Charles 25; Ontario, 1871 ***1823.22*** *p76*
Housman, George Jacob; Pennsylvania, 1777 ***4629.10*** *p15*
Houson, H.; Portland, Maine, 1858 ***9196.15*** *p28*
Housser, Karl; America, 1755 ***2856.30*** *p197C*
Houst, Joseph; Maryland, 1674 ***2524.55*** *p115*
Houston, . . .; South Carolina, 1750-1770 ***4628.40*** *p98*
Houston, Ann; Georgia, 1818 ***1640.10*** *p81*
Houston, Anna; Vermont, 1849-1930 ***5900.10*** *p224*
Houston, Catharine 42; Vermont, 1875 ***5900.10*** *p223*
Houston, George; Pennsylvania, 1777 ***4629.10*** *p9*
Houston, George; Vermont, 1852-1939 ***5900.10*** *p223*
Houston, George 3; Vermont, 1844 ***5900.10*** *p237*
Houston, George 32; Ontario, 1871 ***1823.28*** *p41*
Houston, George 48; Ontario, 1871 ***1823.15*** *p120*
Houston, Grace *SEE* Houston, Robert
Houston, Hugh 62; Ontario, 1871 ***1823.22*** *p76*
Houston, Isabella 45; Ontario, 1861 ***2896.25*** *p58*
Houston, James; Vermont, 1854-1931 ***5900.10*** *p223*
Houston, James 52; Ontario, 1871 ***1823.15*** *p120*
Houston, James 54; Ontario, 1871 ***1823.15*** *p120*
Houston, John; Georgia, 1775-1781 ***4628.40*** *p69*
Houston, Margret 40; Ontario, 1871 ***1823.28*** *p41*
Houston, Mary; Vermont, 1835-1905 ***5900.10*** *p223*
Houston, Mary A. Woods; Vermont, 1857-1926 ***5900.10*** *p223*
Houston, Patrick, Sr.; Vermont, 1784-1876 ***5900.10*** *p237*
Houston, Robert; Maryland, 1668 ***2524.55*** *p115*
Wife: Grace
Houston, Robert; New York, New York, 1850 ***6058.10*** *p37*
Houston, Sally; Vermont, 1846 ***5900.10*** *p237*
Houston, Sarah; Vermont, 1844-1857 ***5900.10*** *p237*
Houston, Susan 65; Vermont, 1881 ***5900.10*** *p223*
Houston, Thomas 60; Ontario, 1871 ***1823.15*** *p120*
Houston, William; Georgia, 1732 ***1640.10*** *p82*
Houstone, Grace *SEE* Houstone, Robert
Houstone, Robert; Maryland, 1668 ***2524.55*** *p115*
Wife: Grace
Houstoun, Agnes; Jamaica, 1853 ***1640.13*** *p57*
Houstoun, George; Georgia, 1756 ***1640.10*** *p81*
Houstoun, Helen; Illinois, 1894 ***1640.13*** *p57*
Houstoun, James; Georgia, 1733 ***1640.10*** *p81*
Houstoun, James; Georgia, 1738 ***1640.10*** *p81*
Houstoun, John; Georgia, 1796 ***1640.10*** *p81*
Houstoun, Patrick; Georgia, 1733 ***1640.10*** *p81*
Houstoun, Robert; Georgia, 1760 ***1640.10*** *p82*
Houstoun, William; Georgia, 1699 ***1640.13*** *p57*
Houstoun, William; Grenada, 1843 ***1640.13*** *p57*
Houstown, Alexander 22; Grenada, 1776 ***1220.25*** *p129*
Hoveington, Richd; Virginia, 1690-1691 ***6212.30*** *p58*
Hovey, Charles 30; Ontario, 1871 ***1823.15*** *p120*
How, Mr.; Jamaica, 1775 ***1220.25*** *p133*
How, Charles A. 8; Ontario, 1861 ***2896.28*** *p57*
How, Francis 30; Maryland, 1774 ***1220.25*** *p2*
How, George J. 6; Ontario, 1861 ***2896.28*** *p57*
How, Isaac 24; Virginia, 1773 ***1220.25*** *p29*
How, Isabella 2; Ontario, 1861 ***2896.28*** *p57*
How, J. H.; Ontario, 1861 ***2896.28*** *p57*
How, John; Virginia, 1681 ***6212.30*** *p55*
How, John 2; Ontario, 1861 ***2896.28*** *p57*
How, Mary 5; Ontario, 1861 ***2896.28*** *p57*
How, Mary 30; Ontario, 1861 ***2896.28*** *p56*
How, Mary 33; Ontario, 1861 ***2896.25*** *p57*
How, Rebecca 10; Ontario, 1861 ***2896.28*** *p56*
How, Richard; Virginia, 1664 ***6212.30*** *p15*
How, Richard; Virginia, 1665 ***6212.30*** *p17*
How, William; Pennsylvania, 1777 ***4629.10*** *p13*
How, William H. 4; Ontario, 1861 ***2896.28*** *p57*
Howall, James 40; Ontario, 1871 ***1823.15*** *p120*
Howan, James 27; Ontario, 1871 ***1823.15*** *p120*
Howan, John 24; Ontario, 1871 ***1823.15*** *p120*
Howan, Richard 22; Ontario, 1871 ***1823.15*** *p120*
Howard, Mr.; Quebec, 1856 ***9196.15*** *p6*

Hoyt, Julia Scammon; Vermont, 1850-1899 ***5900.10*** *p175*
Hoyt, Julia Sherman; Vermont, 1834-1905 ***5900.10*** *p175*
Hoyt, Mary 47; Vermont, 1891 ***5900.10*** *p280*
Hoyt, Stephen; New York, 1810 ***1224.3*** *p39*
Hoyt, William H.; Vermont, 1813-1883 ***5900.10*** *p175*
Hoyt, William H., Jr.; Vermont, 1851-1914 ***5900.10*** *p174*
Hoz, Martin; Port uncertain, 1766 ***2856.30*** *p197C*
Hrobocensky, Joseph; Maryland, 1910 ***3259.35*** *p20*
Hua, Paul; Quebec, 1858 ***9196.15*** *p31*
Hua, Mrs. Paul; Quebec, 1858 ***9196.15*** *p31*
Hubanck, Hen; Virginia, 1684-1685 ***6212.30*** *p57*
Hubard, John; Virginia, 1665-1666 ***6212.30*** *p25*
Hubbard, Mrs.; Quebec, 1857 ***9196.15*** *p23*
Hubbard, Abraham; Pennsylvania, 1786 ***4629.10*** *p50*
Hubbard, Humphry; Maryland, 1672 ***2524.55*** *p116*
Hubbard, John 20; Maryland, 1774 ***1220.25*** *p46*
Hubbard, Luccy Susana 73; Ontario, 1871 ***1823.15*** *p120*
Hubbard, Margaret Murphy; Vermont, 1814-1895 ***5900.10*** *p61*
Hubbard, Nathaniel; Havana, 1763 ***1224.2*** *p58*
Hubbard, Nathaniel; New Haven, Connecticut, 1763 ***1224.2*** *p58*
Hubbard, Patrick 86; Vermont, 1895 ***5900.10*** *p61*
Hubbard, Tadius 32; Ontario, 1871 ***1823.28*** *p42*
Hubbard, Thomas; Virginia, 1697 ***1224.1*** *p31*
Hubbard, Thomas 32; Ontario, 1871 ***1823.15*** *p120*
Hubbard, William; Pennsylvania, 1786 ***4629.10*** *p47*
Hubbart, Joseph 40; Maryland, 1774 ***1220.25*** *p37*
Hubbell, Martin 80; Ontario, 1871 ***1823.22*** *p77*
Hubber, Isaack; Maryland, 1659 ***2524.55*** *p116*
Hubbert, Adber; Maryland, 1667 ***2524.55*** *p116*
Hubbert, Garrit 71; Ontario, 1871 ***1823.15*** *p120*
Hubbert, Miles; Virginia, 1672 ***6212.30*** *p49*
Hubbert, William; Maryland, 1664 ***2524.55*** *p116*
Hubborton, Myles; Maryland, 1651 ***2524.55*** *p116*
Hubbs, Abigail 64; Ontario, 1861 ***2896.26*** *p5*
Hubbs, Abram 70; Ontario, 1861 ***2896.28*** *p25*
Hubbs, Agnes 18; Ontario, 1861 ***2896.27*** *p72*
Hubbs, Allen 17; Ontario, 1861 ***2896.28*** *p26*
Hubbs, Amos 64; Ontario, 1861 ***2896.26*** *p5*
Hubbs, Andrew 21; Ontario, 1861 ***2896.28*** *p26*
Hubbs, Angeline 32; Ontario, 1861 ***2896.27*** *p30*
Hubbs, Arnet 15; Ontario, 1861 ***2896.28*** *p26*
Hubbs, Aurelia 17; Ontario, 1861 ***2896.28*** *p25*
Hubbs, B. A. 36; Ontario, 1861 ***2896.26*** *p5*
Hubbs, B. H. 45; Ontario, 1861 ***2896.27*** *p72*
Hubbs, Benjamin 13; Ontario, 1861 ***2896.28*** *p25*
Hubbs, Benjamin W. 11; Ontario, 1861 ***2896.27*** *p62*
Hubbs, C. B. 11; Ontario, 1861 ***2896.28*** *p57*
Hubbs, Caleb 21; Ontario, 1861 ***2896.25*** *p68*
Hubbs, Caleb P. 21; Ontario, 1861 ***2896.28*** *p57*
Hubbs, Charles 19; Ontario, 1861 ***2896.28*** *p26*
Hubbs, Cornelius 20; Ontario, 1861 ***2896.28*** *p25*
Hubbs, Elisa A. 41; Ontario, 1861 ***2896.27*** *p62*
Hubbs, Emily 31; Ontario, 1861 ***2896.27*** *p25*
Hubbs, Enid J. 14; Ontario, 1861 ***2896.27*** *p62*
Hubbs, Eustatia 40; Ontario, 1861 ***2896.28*** *p25*
Hubbs, George L. 7; Ontario, 1861 ***2896.27*** *p62*
Hubbs, H. 13; Ontario, 1861 ***2896.27*** *p69*
Hubbs, Hannah E. 12; Ontario, 1861 ***2896.27*** *p64*
Hubbs, Hannah E. 13; Ontario, 1861 ***2896.28*** *p57*
Hubbs, Haveland, Sr. 67; Ontario, 1861 ***2896.27*** *p36*
Hubbs, Henry A. 16; Ontario, 1861 ***2896.27*** *p62*
Hubbs, J. 18; Ontario, 1861 ***2896.28*** *p57*
Hubbs, James 7; Ontario, 1861 ***2896.28*** *p26*
Hubbs, Jemima 15; Ontario, 1861 ***2896.28*** *p45*
Hubbs, Jemima 22; Ontario, 1861 ***2896.28*** *p26*
Hubbs, John 20; Ontario, 1861 ***2896.28*** *p26*
Hubbs, John H. 9; Ontario, 1861 ***2896.27*** *p62*
Hubbs, Lavinia 1; Ontario, 1861 ***2896.27*** *p40*
Hubbs, Liddy 22; Ontario, 1861 ***2896.28*** *p26*
Hubbs, Lyda J. 14; Ontario, 1861 ***2896.27*** *p62*
Hubbs, Lydia 32; Ontario, 1861 ***2896.26*** *p5*
Hubbs, Mahetable 40; Ontario, 1861 ***2896.28*** *p25*
Hubbs, Margaret 3; Ontario, 1861 ***2896.28*** *p26*
Hubbs, Margaret 24; Ontario, 1861 ***2896.28*** *p57*
Hubbs, Margaret J. 30; Ontario, 1861 ***2896.27*** *p40*
Hubbs, Martha 20; Ontario, 1861 ***2896.27*** *p69*
Hubbs, Martha 60; Ontario, 1861 ***2896.27*** *p36*
Hubbs, Martha J. 9; Ontario, 1861 ***2896.27*** *p30*
Hubbs, Martha M. 5; Ontario, 1861 ***2896.27*** *p62*
Hubbs, Mary 36; Ontario, 1861 ***2896.28*** *p26*
Hubbs, Mary 47; Ontario, 1861 ***2896.28*** *p57*
Hubbs, Mary A. 7; Ontario, 1861 ***2896.27*** *p62*
Hubbs, Mary J. 40; Ontario, 1861 ***2896.27*** *p72*
Hubbs, Mary M. 14; Ontario, 1861 ***2896.27*** *p72*
Hubbs, Matilda 40; Ontario, 1861 ***2896.27*** *p62*
Hubbs, Nancy 10; Ontario, 1861 ***2896.26*** *p5*
Hubbs, Paul 18; Ontario, 1861 ***2896.28*** *p25*
Hubbs, Phebe 21; Ontario, 1861 ***2896.27*** *p65*
Hubbs, Phebe 22; Ontario, 1861 ***2896.28*** *p57*
Hubbs, Phila A. 16; Ontario, 1861 ***2896.27*** *p62*
Hubbs, Philip 4; Ontario, 1861 ***2896.28*** *p26*
Hubbs, R. B. 16; Ontario, 1861 ***2896.28*** *p57*
Hubbs, Rebecca 16; Ontario, 1861 ***2896.27*** *p31*
Hubbs, Rhoda E. 13; Ontario, 1861 ***2896.27*** *p30*
Hubbs, Richard H. 9; Ontario, 1861 ***2896.27*** *p25*
Hubbs, Robert; Ontario, 1861 ***2896.28*** *p25*
Hubbs, Robert 11; Ontario, 1861 ***2896.28*** *p25*
Hubbs, Robert 19; Ontario, 1861 ***2896.28*** *p26*
Hubbs, Robert B. 6; Ontario, 1861 ***2896.27*** *p25*
Hubbs, S. Alva; Ontario, 1861 ***2896.28*** *p57*
Hubbs, Sarah 43; Ontario, 1861 ***2896.28*** *p26*
Hubbs, Sarah J. 3; Ontario, 1861 ***2896.27*** *p25*
Hubbs, Stephen 19; Ontario, 1861 ***2896.28*** *p25*
Hubbs, Thomas 17; Ontario, 1861 ***2896.27*** *p69*
Hubbs, Thomas L. 10; Ontario, 1861 ***2896.28*** *p26*
Hubbs, Willet 5; Ontario, 1861 ***2896.27*** *p40*
Hubbs, William 9; Ontario, 1861 ***2896.28*** *p25*
Hubbs, William E. 13; Ontario, 1861 ***2896.27*** *p62*
Hubbs, William W. 9; Ontario, 1861 ***2896.28*** *p57*
Hubele, Ulrich; Canada, 1751 ***2856.30*** *p197C*
Huber, Andy 38; British Columbia, 1914 ***9196.1*** *p23*
Huber, Andy 38; Oregon, 1914 ***9196.1*** *p23*
Huber, Anna; Port uncertain, 1748 ***2856.30*** *p197C*
Huber, Anna Elisabeth; Port uncertain, 1744 ***2856.30*** *p197C*
Huber, Anna Maria; Port uncertain, 1795 ***2856.30*** *p197C*
Huber, Balthasar; Port uncertain, 1786 ***2856.30*** *p197C*
Huber, Eva Barbara; America, 1787 ***2856.30*** *p197C*
Huber, Georg; America, 1768 ***2856.30*** *p197C*
Huber, Georg; Port uncertain, 1761 ***2856.30*** *p197F*
Huber, Georg; Port uncertain, 1784 ***2856.30*** *p197C*
Huber, George; Pennsylvania, 1778 ***4629.10*** *p32*
Huber, Gorg; America, 1743 ***2856.30*** *p197C*
Huber, Hans; America, 1735 ***2856.30*** *p197C*
Huber, Hans; Port uncertain, 1732 ***2856.30*** *p197C*
Huber, Hans Adam; America, 1738 ***2856.30*** *p197C*
Huber, Hans Jerg; Port uncertain, 1737 ***2856.30*** *p197C*
Huber, Henrich; America, 1744 ***2856.30*** *p197C*
Huber, Henrich; America, 1747 ***2856.30*** *p197C*
Huber, Jacob; America, 1750 ***2856.30*** *p197F*
With wife & 2 children
Huber, Jacob; America, 1751 ***2856.30*** *p197C*
Huber, Jacob; Port uncertain, 1784 ***2856.30*** *p197C*
Huber, Johann; Port uncertain, 1785 ***2856.30*** *p197C*
Huber, Johann; Port uncertain, 1795 ***2856.30*** *p197C*
Huber, Johann; Port uncertain, 1796 ***2856.30*** *p197C*
Huber, Johann Georg; America, 1750 ***2856.30*** *p197C*
Huber, Johann Georg; Port uncertain, 1754 ***2856.30*** *p197C*
Huber, Johann Peter; Port uncertain, 1784 ***2856.30*** *p197C*
Huber, Jorg; America, 1743 ***2856.30*** *p197C*
Huber, Margarete; Port uncertain, 1774 ***2856.30*** *p197C*
Huber, Margarete; Port uncertain, 1784 ***2856.30*** *p197C*
Huber, Maria Catharina; Port uncertain, 1775 ***2856.30*** *p515*
Huber, Maria Margarete; Port uncertain, 1762 ***2856.30*** *p197C*
Huber, Michael; America, 1752 ***2856.30*** *p197D*
With daughter
Huber, Michael; America, 1763 ***2856.30*** *p197C*
Huber, Michael; Port uncertain, 1763 ***2856.30*** *p197C*
Huber, Michael; Port uncertain, 1770 ***2856.30*** *p197C*
Huber, Peter; Port uncertain, 1749 ***2856.30*** *p197D*
With wife & 4 children
Huber, Philipp; Port uncertain, 1780 ***2856.30*** *p197C*
Huber, William; New York, New York, 1854 ***6058.10*** *p73*
Huberg, Simon; New York, 1837 ***8197.10*** *p91*
Hubert, Charles; Maryland, 1910 ***3259.35*** *p20*
Hubert, Georg; Port uncertain, 1782 ***2856.30*** *p197D*
Hubertley, Mary; Maryland, 1674 ***2524.55*** *p116*
Hubertsley, Mary; Maryland, 1674 ***2524.55*** *p116*
Hubgen, Margarete; Port uncertain, 1759 ***2856.30*** *p197F*
Hubgen, Margarete; Port uncertain, 1761 ***2856.30*** *p197F*
Hubgen, Maria Elisabeth; Port uncertain, 1755 ***2856.30*** *p197F*
Hubgen, Matheiss; America, 1741 ***2856.30*** *p197F*
Hubley, Adam; Pennsylvania, 1777 ***4629.10*** *p24*
Hubley, Joseph; Pennsylvania, 1777 ***4629.10*** *p8*
Hubner, Anna Margarete; America, 1740 ***2856.30*** *p197G*
Hubner, Elis. Barbara; America, 1740 ***2856.30*** *p197G*
Hubner, Fredrick 34; Ontario, 1871 ***1823.28*** *p42*
Hubner, Johann Jakob; America, 1740 ***2856.30*** *p197G*
Hubscher, Matthaus; America, 1751 ***2856.30*** *p197G*
Hubscher, Ulrich; Port uncertain, 1737 ***2856.30*** *p197G*
Hubser, Ulrich; America, 1738 ***2856.30*** *p225*
Huckabone, Mary 70; Ontario, 1871 ***1823.28*** *p42*
Huckh, Anton; Port uncertain, 1770 ***2856.30*** *p197D*
With wife & children
Huckh, Georg; Port uncertain, 1740 ***2856.30*** *p197D*
Huckh, Ignaz; Port uncertain, 1752 ***2856.30*** *p197D*
Huckh, Johann; Port uncertain, 1762 ***2856.30*** *p197D*
Huckh, Johann Daniel; Port uncertain, 1746 ***2856.30*** *p197D*
Huckh, Josef; Port uncertain, 1769 ***2856.30*** *p197D*
Huckh, Maria Magdalena; Port uncertain, 1752 ***2856.30*** *p197D*
Huckher, Johann; Port uncertain, 1762 ***2856.30*** *p197D*
Huckmann, Abraham; America, 1770 ***2856.30*** *p197D*
Huckmann, Anna Maria; America, 1770 ***2856.30*** *p197D*
Huckmann, Henrich; America, 1770 ***2856.30*** *p197D*
Huckstep, Samuel; Virginia, 1696 ***1224.1*** *p31*
Huckstep, Thos 38; Ontario, 1871 ***1823.15*** *p120*
Huctable, Thomas 40; Ontario, 1871 ***1823.15*** *p120*
Hudack, Philip; Maryland, 1910 ***3259.35*** *p20*
Hudd, Thomas 22; Philadelphia, 1774 ***1220.25*** *p43*
Hudden, Peyace; Maryland, 1681 ***2524.55*** *p116*
Hudden, Richard; Maryland, 1681 ***2524.55*** *p116*
Huddle, Joseph; Pennsylvania, 1777 ***4629.10*** *p26*
Huddleston, Hugh; Jamaica, 1763 ***1640.13*** *p58*
Huddock, Thomas; Maryland, 1679 ***2524.55*** *p116*
Hudgins, Mrs. 42; Ontario, 1861 ***2896.26*** *p25*
Hudgins, C. 1; Ontario, 1861 ***2896.26*** *p10*
Hudgins, E. 2; Ontario, 1861 ***2896.26*** *p10*
Hudgins, E. 20; Ontario, 1861 ***2896.26*** *p10*
Hudgins, Em 19; Ontario, 1861 ***2896.26*** *p10*
Hudgins, H. 38; Ontario, 1861 ***2896.26*** *p10*
Hudgins, Hellen 2; Ontario, 1861 ***2896.26*** *p25*
Hudgins, J. 7; Ontario, 1861 ***2896.26*** *p10*
Hudgins, L. 16; Ontario, 1861 ***2896.26*** *p10*
Hudgins, R. 9; Ontario, 1861 ***2896.26*** *p10*
Hudgins, R. 19; Ontario, 1861 ***2896.26*** *p10*
Hudie, William 65; Ontario, 1871 ***1823.15*** *p120*
Huditz, Peter; Port uncertain, 1762 ***2856.30*** *p197D*
Hudla, Andy; Maryland, 1910 ***3259.35*** *p20*
Hudle, John; Pennsylvania, 1777 ***4629.10*** *p13*
Hudleston, Thomas 18; Maryland, 1775 ***1220.25*** *p119*
Hudleston, Wm; Virginia, 1666 ***6212.30*** *p30*
Hudly, William; Virginia, 1665 ***6212.30*** *p18*
Hudon, E.; Portland, Maine, 1858 ***9196.15*** *p29*
Hudon, Masses 28; Ontario, 1871 ***1823.28*** *p42*
Hudon, Thomas 46; Vermont, 1885 ***5900.10*** *p482*
Hudson, Major; Quebec, 1857 ***9196.15*** *p14*
Hudson, Abednego; New Bern, North Carolina, 1787 ***1224.2*** *p58*
Hudson, C. 1; Ontario, 1861 ***2896.28*** *p2*
Hudson, Charles 60; Ontario, 1871 ***1823.22*** *p77*
Hudson, Elizabeth; Maryland, 1664 ***2524.55*** *p116*
Hudson, Elizabeth; Maryland, 1665 ***2524.55*** *p116*
Hudson, George 42; Ontario, 1871 ***1823.15*** *p120*
Hudson, Henry; Maryland, 1662 ***2524.55*** *p116*
With wife
Relative: Juliana
Relative: Mary
Relative: Neptuina
Hudson, Henry; Maryland, 1668 ***2524.55*** *p113*
Wife: Ledda
Daughter: Ledda
Hudson, Henry; Maryland, 1671 ***2524.55*** *p116*
Wife: Lydia
Daughter: Lydia
Hudson, Henry; New York, 1840 ***8197.10*** *p172*
Hudson, Isaac 30; Ontario, 1871 ***1823.15*** *p120*
Hudson, Isabella 52; Ontario, 1871 ***1823.28*** *p42*
Hudson, James; New York, 1840 ***8197.10*** *p242*
Hudson, James 16; Baltimore, 1775 ***1220.25*** *p119*
Hudson, John; Boston, 1702 ***1224.2*** *p58*
Hudson, John; New York, 1840 ***8197.10*** *p174*
Hudson, John 20; Maryland, 1774 ***1220.25*** *p39*
Hudson, Juliana *SEE* Hudson, Henry
Hudson, Ledda *SEE* Hudson, Henry
Hudson, Lydia *SEE* Hudson, Henry
Hudson, Lydia; Maryland, 1671 ***2524.55*** *p116*
Hudson, M. J. 25; Ontario, 1861 ***2896.28*** *p2*
Hudson, Mary *SEE* Hudson, Henry
Hudson, Mary 22; Baltimore, 1775 ***1220.25*** *p119*
Hudson, Mary 32; Ontario, 1871 ***1823.22*** *p77*
Hudson, Morris 37; Ontario, 1871 ***1823.15*** *p120*
Hudson, Neptuina *SEE* Hudson, Henry
Hudson, Ralph 37; Ontario, 1871 ***1823.15*** *p121*
Hudson, Rowland; Virginia, 1665 ***6212.30*** *p17*
Hudson, Samuel; Pennsylvania, 1777 ***4629.10*** *p23*
Hudson, Samuel; Pennsylvania, 1779 ***4629.10*** *p38*
Hudson, Sarah 67; Ontario, 1871 ***1823.15*** *p121*
Hudson, Susanna 22; Philadelphia, 1774 ***1220.25*** *p63*
Hudson, Thomas; New York, 1834 ***8197.10*** *p240*
Hudson, Thomas; New York, 1840 ***8197.10*** *p174*
Hudson, Thomas 22; Maryland, 1774 ***1220.25*** *p39*
Hudson, Thomas 22; Virginia, 1774 ***1220.25*** *p55*
Hudson, Thomas 51; Ontario, 1871 ***1823.28*** *p42*
Hudson, William; Maryland, 1659 ***2524.55*** *p116*
Hudson, William; Pennsylvania, 1777 ***4629.10*** *p10*
Hudson, William 20; Virginia, 1774 ***1220.25*** *p46*
Hudson, William 25; Maryland, 1775 ***1220.25*** *p96*
Hudson, William 32; Maryland, 1775 ***1220.25*** *p98*

Hueber, Josef; Port uncertain, 1739 ***2856.30*** *p197D*
Hueber, Lorenz; Port uncertain, 1754 ***2856.30*** *p197D*
Hueber, Margarete; Port uncertain, 1623 ***2856.30*** *p197D*
Hueber, Michael; Port uncertain, 1784 ***2856.30*** *p197D*
With wife
Huekill, Daniell; Maryland, 1666 ***2524.55*** *p116*
Huenmondir, John; New York, 1837 ***8197.10*** *p92*
Huertis, James; New York, New York, 1824 ***1224.3*** *p40*
Hues, Atlanta; Virginia, 1663 ***6212.30*** *p1*
Hues, Edwd; Virginia, 1690-1691 ***6212.30*** *p58*
Hues, Frances; Maryland, 1662 ***2524.55*** *p116*
Hues, John; Virginia, 1698 ***6212.30*** *p61*
Hues, Mary; Virginia, 1668-1669 ***6212.30*** *p40*
Hues, Sarah; Virginia, 1668-1669 ***6212.30*** *p40*
Hueson, Edward Henzell; New York, 1838 ***8197.10*** *p318*
Huest, Johann Barthel; Port uncertain, 1751 ***2856.30*** *p197D*
Hueston, John 57; Ontario, 1871 ***1823.28*** *p42*
Hueston, William 48; Ontario, 1871 ***1823.15*** *p121*
Huff, Adda 13; Ontario, 1871 ***1823.22*** *p77*
Huff, Albert 24; Ontario, 1861 ***2896.25*** *p65*
Huff, Alger 22; Ontario, 1861 ***2896.25*** *p65*
Huff, Ann 70; Ontario, 1861 ***2896.26*** *p22*
Huff, Anthelia 27; Ontario, 1861 ***2896.26*** *p22*
Huff, Bathena S. 6; Ontario, 1861 ***2896.26*** *p22*
Huff, Catharine 54; Ontario, 1861 ***2896.27*** *p44*
Huff, Catharine L. 14; Ontario, 1861 ***2896.27*** *p44*
Huff, Charles 10; Ontario, 1861 ***2896.26*** *p21*
Huff, Charlotte 17; Ontario, 1861 ***2896.26*** *p22*
Huff, Cinda R. 12; Ontario, 1861 ***2896.27*** *p44*
Huff, Delilah 2; Ontario, 1861 ***2896.26*** *p22*
Huff, Elisha A. 10; Ontario, 1861 ***2896.27*** *p44*
Huff, Elizabeth G. 23; Ontario, 1861 ***2896.27*** *p44*
Huff, Emily 19; Ontario, 1861 ***2896.25*** *p65*
Huff, Gilbert 28; Ontario, 1861 ***2896.25*** *p65*
Huff, Henry 39; Alaska, 1917 ***9196.1*** *p7*
Huff, Henry 39; Yukon, 1917 ***9196.1*** *p7*
Huff, Henryetta 8; Ontario, 1861 ***2896.26*** *p21*
Huff, Hosea 5; Ontario, 1861 ***2896.26*** *p22*
Huff, Ines L. 1; Ontario, 1861 ***2896.27*** *p42*
Huff, Isaac 38; Ontario, 1861 ***2896.27*** *p58*
Huff, James 8; Ontario, 1861 ***2896.25*** *p39*
Huff, James 16; Ontario, 1861 ***2896.27*** *p44*
Huff, James E. 15; Ontario, 1861 ***2896.27*** *p43*
Huff, Joanna 21; Ontario, 1861 ***2896.27*** *p44*
Huff, Julia 50; Ontario, 1861 ***2896.25*** *p65*
Huff, Lisander F. 8; Ontario, 1861 ***2896.27*** *p44*
Huff, Louisa 26; Ontario, 1861 ***2896.25*** *p65*
Huff, Lucy E. 12; Ontario, 1861 ***2896.27*** *p43*
Huff, Lucy E. 54; Ontario, 1861 ***2896.27*** *p43*
Huff, Lydia J. 22; Ontario, 1861 ***2896.27*** *p42*
Huff, Margaret 4; Ontario, 1861 ***2896.26*** *p22*
Huff, Margaret 58; Ontario, 1861 ***2896.25*** *p3*
Huff, Mary 22; Ontario, 1861 ***2896.25*** *p39*
Huff, Mary A. 31; Ontario, 1861 ***2896.26*** *p21*
Huff, Peter, Jr. 28; Ontario, 1861 ***2896.25*** *p65*
Huff, R.; Ontario, 1861 ***2896.28*** *p64*
Huff, Rachel 30; Ontario, 1861 ***2896.27*** *p46*
Huff, Robert 17; Ontario, 1861 ***2896.25*** *p70*
Huff, Robert James 6; Ontario, 1861 ***2896.27*** *p46*
Huff, S. 89; Ontario, 1861 ***2896.25*** *p28*
Huff, Sarah 18; Ontario, 1861 ***2896.27*** *p44*
Huff, William 15; Ontario, 1861 ***2896.25*** *p65*
Huff, Zilfy 25; Ontario, 1861 ***2896.26*** *p22*
Huffin, Barbara; Port uncertain, 1732 ***2856.30*** *p197G*
Huffman, Almira 39; Ontario, 1861 ***2896.28*** *p35*
Huffman, Sarah E. 14; Ontario, 1861 ***2896.28*** *p35*
Huffman, Thomas 12; Ontario, 1861 ***2896.28*** *p35*
Huffner, Albert; Port uncertain, 1764 ***2856.30*** *p159*
Hufschmidt, Mr.; Port uncertain, 1771 ***2856.30*** *p197D*
With wife
Huftale, Mary E.; Ontario, 1861 ***2896.25*** *p4*
Hufty, Jonathan; Pennsylvania, 1777 ***4629.10*** *p17*
Hug, Anna Maria; Port uncertain, 1750 ***2856.30*** *p197D*
Hug, Christian; Port uncertain, 1794 ***2856.30*** *p197D*
Hug, Franz; Port uncertain, 1741 ***2856.30*** *p197D*
Hug, Johann Anton; Port uncertain, 1789 ***2856.30*** *p197D*
With wife
Hug, Michael; America, 1749 ***2856.30*** *p197D*
Hugains, Richard; Maryland, 1649 ***2524.55*** *p116*
Hugate, Mary; Maryland, 1660 ***2524.55*** *p116*
Hugel, Cath.; Port uncertain, 1769 ***2856.30*** *p118*
Hugel, Franz Carl; America, 1738 ***2856.30*** *p197G*
Hugelmann, Jacob, The Old; Port uncertain, 1759 ***2856.30*** *p197D*
With wife & children
Huger, Daniel; South Carolina, 1756 ***1224.2*** *p58*
Huges, Edward; Virginia, 1676 ***6212.30*** *p53*
Huges, Patrick 55; Ontario, 1871 ***1823.15*** *p121*
Hugeson, John; Maryland, 1663 ***2524.55*** *p116*
Hugeson, Wm; Virginia, 1664 ***6212.30*** *p14*
Hugeson, Wm; Virginia, 1665-1666 ***6212.30*** *p22*
Hugesson, Captain; Quebec, 1857 ***9196.15*** *p26*
Hugesson, Mrs.; Quebec, 1857 ***9196.15*** *p26*
Huget, Johann Adam; Port uncertain, 1791 ***2856.30*** *p197E*
Huget, Johann Karl; Port uncertain, 1791 ***2856.30*** *p197E*
Huggard, Richard 53; Ontario, 1871 ***1823.28*** *p42*
Huggeson, John; Maryland, 1673 ***2524.55*** *p116*
Hugget, Peter; America, 1737 ***2856.30*** *p197E*
Huggin, Thomas; Maryland, 1662 ***2524.55*** *p116*
Huggin, William 30; Maryland, 1775 ***1220.25*** *p105*
Huggins, Henry; America, 1887 ***1640.13*** *p58*
Huggins, Richard; Maryland, 1649 ***2524.55*** *p116*
Huggins, Richard; Maryland, 1671 ***2524.55*** *p133*
Huggins, Robert; Carolina, 1677 ***1224.1*** *p31*
Huggins, Thomas; Pennsylvania, 1777 ***4629.10*** *p10*
Hugh, Hamilton 28; Ontario, 1871 ***1823.15*** *p121*
Hughes, Mr.; Quebec, 1857 ***9196.15*** *p21*
Hughes, Mr.; Quebec, 1858 ***9196.15*** *p36*
Hughes, Mr.; Quebec, 1858 ***9196.15*** *p37*
Hughes, Mrs.; Quebec, 1857 ***9196.15*** *p15*
Hughes, Mrs.; Quebec, 1857 ***9196.15*** *p26*
Hughes, Rev.; Quebec, 1857 ***9196.15*** *p15*
Hughes, Albert 24; Ontario, 1871 ***1823.15*** *p121*
Hughes, Anna; Maryland, 1910 ***3259.35*** *p20*
Hughes, Anne; Maryland, 1659 ***2524.55*** *p116*
Hughes, Arthur 17; Virginia, 1775 ***1220.25*** *p110*
Hughes, Betty 21; America, 1774 ***1220.25*** *p36*
Hughes, Bridget 57; Vermont, 1891 ***5900.10*** *p246*
Hughes, Bridget McCanna 64; Vermont, 1898 ***5900.10*** *p591*
Hughes, Catherine 18; Ontario, 1861 ***2896.27*** *p34*
Hughes, Catherine Glynn; Vermont, 1844-1878 ***5900.10*** *p204*
Hughes, Charles; Virginia, 1809 ***1224.3*** *p39*
Hughes, Charles 12; Ontario, 1861 ***2896.27*** *p26*
Hughes, Daniel; New York, 1828-1832 ***8197.10*** *p308*
Hughes, Daniel; New York, 1839 ***8197.10*** *p380*
Hughes, Daniel 37; Ontario, 1871 ***1823.28*** *p42*
Hughes, David; New York, 1840 ***8197.10*** *p174*
Hughes, David; Pennsylvania, 1772 ***1224.2*** *p58*
Hughes, Diana 26; Maryland, 1774 ***1220.25*** *p61*
Hughes, Edward; Boston, 1818 ***6058.10*** *p37*
Hughes, Edward; New York, 1837 ***8197.10*** *p90*
Hughes, Edward; New York, 1837 ***8197.10*** *p241*
Hughes, Edward; New York, 1840 ***8197.10*** *p242*
Hughes, Edward; Vermont, 1845-1917 ***5900.10*** *p217*
Hughes, Elisha 51; Ontario, 1871 ***1823.15*** *p121*
Hughes, Ellen; Vermont, 1857-1930 ***5900.10*** *p591*
Hughes, Esther Clark; Vermont, 1861-1917 ***5900.10*** *p206*
Hughes, Ferdinand; Portland, Maine, 1828 ***8197.10*** *p116*
Hughes, Francis 73; Vermont, 1868 ***5900.10*** *p368*
Hughes, Francis Jones 40; Ontario, 1871 ***1823.28*** *p42*
Hughes, George; Pennsylvania, 1781 ***4629.10*** *p43*
Hughes, George 36; Ontario, 1871 ***1823.15*** *p121*
Hughes, Griffith; Maryland, 1671 ***2524.55*** *p116*
Hughes, Henry 18; Maryland, 1774 ***1220.25*** *p76*
Hughes, Ida L.; Vermont, 1865-1926 ***5900.10*** *p187*
Hughes, Issiac 54; Ontario, 1871 ***1823.28*** *p42*
Hughes, J. B.; Quebec, 1856 ***9196.15*** *p7*
Hughes, James; New York, 1834-1838 ***8197.10*** *p116*
Hughes, James; New York, 1839 ***8197.10*** *p242*
Hughes, James 62; Ontario, 1871 ***1823.22*** *p77*
Hughes, James 80; Vermont, 1902 ***5900.10*** *p246*
Hughes, James B.; Vermont, 1842-1912 ***5900.10*** *p316*
Hughes, John; New York, 1807 ***8197.10*** *p39*
Hughes, John; New York, 1823 ***8197.10*** *p238*
Hughes, John; New York, 1840 ***8197.10*** *p171*
Hughes, John; New York, 1840 ***8197.10*** *p174*
Hughes, John; Vermont, 1845-1933 ***5900.10*** *p204*
Hughes, John 45; Maryland, 1774 ***1220.25*** *p46*
Hughes, John Stokes; New Orleans, 1856 ***1224.3*** *p39*
Hughes, Jone *SEE* Hughes, Thomas
Hughes, Joseph; Maryland, 1668 ***2524.55*** *p117*
Hughes, Kate Brown; Vermont, 1847-1928 ***5900.10*** *p204*
Hughes, Katherine McMahon; Vermont, 1850-1912 ***5900.10*** *p316*
Hughes, Mary; Maryland, 1659 ***2524.55*** *p117*
Hughes, Mary; Vermont, 1810-1906 ***5900.10*** *p265*
Hughes, Mary; Vermont, 1835-1911 ***5900.10*** *p420*
Hughes, Mary 15; Maryland, 1775 ***1220.25*** *p112*
Hughes, Mary 59; Vermont, 1881 ***5900.10*** *p252*
Hughes, Mary 65; Vermont, 1881 ***5900.10*** *p398*
Hughes, Mary Sweeney; Vermont, 1848 ***5900.10*** *p217*
Hughes, Mary Williams 50; Vermont, 1879 ***5900.10*** *p194*
Hughes, Michl 29; Ontario, 1871 ***1823.28*** *p42*
Hughes, Owen; New York, 1836 ***8197.10*** *p75*
Hughes, P.; Quebec, 1856 ***9196.15*** *p11*
Hughes, Patrick; New York, 1834 ***8197.10*** *p69*
Hughes, Patrick 57; Ontario, 1871 ***1823.28*** *p42*
Hughes, Peter 26; Ontario, 1871 ***1823.28*** *p42*
Hughes, Philip; New York, 1818 ***8197.10*** *p237*
Hughes, Philip; New York, 1821 ***8197.10*** *p238*
Hughes, Rich; Virginia, 1672 ***6212.30*** *p48*
Hughes, Richard; Georgia, 1763 ***1224.2*** *p58*
Hughes, Richard W.; New York, 1840 ***8197.10*** *p172*
Hughes, Robert; Virginia, 1727 ***1224.2*** *p59*
Hughes, Samuel 19; Maryland, 1774 ***1220.25*** *p6*
Hughes, Sarah *SEE* Hughes, Thomas
Hughes, Stephen 33; Maryland, 1774 ***1220.25*** *p39*
Hughes, Thomas *SEE* Hughes, Thomas
Hughes, Thomas; Maryland, 1665 ***2524.55*** *p117*
Wife: Jone
Hughes, Thomas; Maryland, 1665 ***2524.55*** *p117*
Wife: Sarah
Son: Thomas
Hughes, Thomas; Pennsylvania, 1868 ***6058.10*** *p73*
Hughes, Thomas 21; Georgia, 1774 ***1220.25*** *p48*
Hughes, Thomas 21; Maryland, 1774 ***1220.25*** *p62*
Hughes, Timothy; Vermont, 1855-1892 ***5900.10*** *p206*
Hughes, William; Boston, 1731 ***1224.2*** *p59*
Hughes, William; New York, 1807 ***8197.10*** *p40*
Hughes, William; New York, 1837 ***8197.10*** *p91*
Hughes, William; Pennsylvania, 1777 ***4629.10*** *p20*
Hughes, William 18; Ontario, 1861 ***2896.27*** *p26*
Hughes, William 34; Maryland, 1774 ***1220.25*** *p73*
Hughes, William 59; Ontario, 1871 ***1823.15*** *p121*
Hughey, John 31; Ontario, 1871 ***1823.28*** *p42*
Hughey, Susanah 22; Ontario, 1871 ***1823.28*** *p42*
Hughs, Edward; Boston, 1818 ***6058.10*** *p37*
Hughs, Elizabeth 20; Ontario, 1871 ***1823.15*** *p121*
Hughs, Francis; Virginia, 1664 ***6212.30*** *p9*
Hughs, John; Ontario, 1726 ***1224.2*** *p58*
Hughs, John 56; Ontario, 1871 ***1823.15*** *p121*
Hughs, Patrick 54; Ontario, 1871 ***1823.28*** *p42*
Hughs, William; New York, 1825 ***8197.10*** *p239*
Hughson, George 46; Ontario, 1871 ***1823.28*** *p42*
Hughton, Joyce; Maryland, 1669 ***2524.55*** *p117*
Hugill, Elizabeth 77; Ontario, 1871 ***1823.15*** *p121*
Hugill, John 52; Ontario, 1871 ***1823.15*** *p121*
Hugill, Joseph H. 37; Ontario, 1871 ***1823.15*** *p121*
Hugill, William 41; Ontario, 1871 ***1823.15*** *p121*
Hugin, Anna Margarete; Port uncertain, 1751 ***2856.30*** *p160*
Hugin, Anna Maria; Port uncertain, 1750 ***2856.30*** *p197D*
Hugin, Johann; Port uncertain, 1769 ***2856.30*** *p197G*
Hugins, Albert 29; Ontario, 1861 ***2896.27*** *p70*
Hugler, Margarete; Port uncertain, 1783 ***2856.30*** *p197E*
Huglin, Simon; Port uncertain, 1788 ***2856.30*** *p197G*
Hugo, James; Baltimore, 1819 ***6058.10*** *p47*
Huhn, Jakob; Port uncertain, 1789 ***2856.30*** *p197E*
Huhner, Jacob; America, 1738 ***2856.30*** *p197G*
With wife & child
Huichy, Patrick 47; Ontario, 1871 ***1823.22*** *p78*
Huie, James; Virginia, 1816 ***1640.13*** *p58*
Huight, James 55; Ontario, 1871 ***1823.15*** *p121*
Huisman, Abraham; New York, New York, 1748 ***1224.2*** *p59*
Hujet, Michael; America, 1749 ***2856.30*** *p197E*
With wife & 4 children
Hujet, Peter; America, 1737 ***2856.30*** *p197E*
Hujet, Sof.; America, 1741 ***2856.30*** *p320*
Hujet, Sof.; America, 1741 ***2856.30*** *p328*
Hujet, Sofie; America, 1742 ***2856.30*** *p197E*
Hujet, Sofie; America, 1742 ***2856.30*** *p328*
Hujethin, Maria Sydonia; Port uncertain, 1745 ***2856.30*** *p197E*
Hukaszewicz, Anthony; Maryland, 1910 ***3259.35*** *p20*
Huker, Nicolaus; Port uncertain, 1751 ***2856.30*** *p197E*
With wife & 2 children
Hukh, Anna Margarete; Port uncertain, 1737 ***2856.30*** *p197E*
Hukmann, Andreas; America, 1742 ***2856.30*** *p197E*
With wife & 3 children
Hukmann, Konrad; America, 1749 ***2856.30*** *p197E*
Hukmann, Leonhard; Port uncertain, 1754 ***2856.30*** *p197E*
Hukmann, Peter; Port uncertain, 1748 ***2856.30*** *p197E*
With wife & 3 children
Hulbert, Edward; Maryland, 1682 ***2524.55*** *p117*
Hulbert, William; Pennsylvania, 1785 ***4629.10*** *p48*
Hulbret, William 55; Ontario, 1871 ***1823.15*** *p121*
Hulburt, Royal 46; Ontario, 1871 ***1823.22*** *p78*
Hulcen, Michael; New York, 1840 ***8197.10*** *p242*
Hulett, Joseph; Virginia, 1668-1669 ***6212.30*** *p40*
Hulick, Peter; Pennsylvania, 1777 ***4629.10*** *p18*
Hulihan, Catherine; Vermont, 1842-1922 ***5900.10*** *p69*
Hulihan, John 65; Vermont, 1888 ***5900.10*** *p73*
Hulihan, Mary Leonard 70; Vermont, 1899 ***5900.10*** *p73*
Hulihan, Patrick 45; Ontario, 1871 ***1823.28*** *p42*
Huling, Alexander; New York, 1711 ***1224.2*** *p59*
Huliston, Rololert 35; Ontario, 1871 ***1823.15*** *p121*
Hull, Barbara; Port uncertain, 1731 ***2856.30*** *p197G*
Hull, Edward; Maryland, 1663 ***2524.55*** *p117*
Wife: Margarett
Daughter: Margarett
Son: John

Hunter, C. 56; British Columbia, 1914 ***9196.1*** *p24*
Hunter, C. 56; New Mexico, 1914 ***9196.1*** *p24*
Hunter, Daniel; Wilmington, North Carolina, 1831 ***1224.3*** *p39*
Hunter, Daniel 65; Ontario, 1861 ***2896.27*** *p55*
Hunter, David 82; Vermont, 1898 ***5900.10*** *p283*
Hunter, Elizabeth 51; Ontario, 1871 ***1823.15*** *p122*
Hunter, Fenwick 24; Ontario, 1871 ***1823.15*** *p122*
Hunter, Flora A.; Vermont, 1843-1911 ***5900.10*** *p455*
Hunter, George; Vermont, 1825-1885 ***5900.10*** *p194*
Hunter, George 40; Fort Cumberland, Nova Scotia, 1774 ***1220.25*** *p17*
Hunter, George 45; Ontario, 1871 ***1823.28*** *p42*
Hunter, Hamilton; New York, 1806 ***8197.10*** *p31*
Hunter, Henry 45; Ontario, 1871 ***1823.15*** *p122*
Hunter, Henry J.; New York, 1839 ***8197.10*** *p242*
Hunter, Hugh; Pennsylvania, 1847 ***6058.10*** *p23*
Hunter, Isaac; Maryland, 1662 ***2524.55*** *p118*
Hunter, Isaac; Maryland, 1665 ***2524.55*** *p118*
Hunter, James; New York, 1827 ***8197.10*** *p239*
Hunter, James; New York, 1839 ***8197.10*** *p131*
Hunter, James; Pennsylvania, 1777 ***4629.10*** *p23*
Hunter, James; Pennsylvania, 1778 ***4629.10*** *p34*
Hunter, James 23; Ontario, 1871 ***1823.28*** *p42*
Hunter, James 29; Ontario, 1861 ***2896.25*** *p47*
Hunter, James 29; Ontario, 1871 ***1823.15*** *p122*
Hunter, James 61; Ontario, 1871 ***1823.15*** *p122*
Hunter, James S. 64; Ontario, 1871 ***1823.22*** *p78*
Hunter, James W. 40; Ontario, 1871 ***1823.15*** *p122*
Hunter, John; Montreal, 1892 ***1640.13*** *p58*
Hunter, John; Norfolk, Virginia, 1783 ***1224.2*** *p59*
Hunter, John; Virginia, n.d. ***1224.2*** *p59*
Hunter, John 40; Ontario, 1871 ***1823.15*** *p122*
Hunter, John 46; Ontario, 1871 ***1823.15*** *p122*
Hunter, John 48; Ontario, 1871 ***1823.15*** *p122*
Hunter, John 55; Ontario, 1871 ***1823.15*** *p122*
Hunter, John 56; Ontario, 1871 ***1823.15*** *p122*
Hunter, John 57; Ontario, 1871 ***1823.15*** *p122*
Hunter, John 67; Ontario, 1871 ***1823.22*** *p78*
Hunter, Joseph; Pennsylvania, 1777 ***4629.10*** *p25*
Hunter, Joseph 27; Ontario, 1871 ***1823.28*** *p42*
Hunter, Kenneth 60; Ontario, 1871 ***1823.15*** *p122*
Hunter, Leonard 44; Ontario, 1871 ***1823.15*** *p122*
Hunter, Margaret; Jamaica, 1847 ***1640.13*** *p58*
Hunter, Mathew 20; New York, 1774 ***1220.25*** *p24*
Hunter, Moore 32; Ontario, 1871 ***1823.28*** *p42*
Hunter, Nelly 61; Ontario, 1861 ***2896.27*** *p55*
Hunter, Patrick; Savannah, Georgia, 1738 ***1640.10*** *p83*
Hunter, R. 19; Ontario, 1861 ***2896.27*** *p1*
Hunter, Richard 53; Ontario, 1871 ***1823.15*** *p122*
Hunter, Robert; Georgia, 1703 ***1640.13*** *p58*
Hunter, Robert; New York, 1836-1838 ***8197.10*** *p116*
Hunter, Robert; New York, 1840 ***8197.10*** *p172*
Hunter, Robert 55; Ontario, 1871 ***1823.15*** *p122*
Hunter, Robert 62; Ontario, 1871 ***1823.15*** *p122*
Hunter, Robert Cathcart; Montreal, 1834 ***1640.13*** *p58*
Hunter, Samuel 20; Nevis, 1773 ***1220.25*** *p30*
Hunter, Septimus Hewgill; New Orleans, 1848 ***1224.3*** *p39*
Hunter, Septimus Howgill; New York, 1840 ***8197.10*** *p172*
Hunter, Simon 84; Ontario, 1871 ***1823.15*** *p122*
Hunter, Thomas; Virginia, 1884 ***1640.13*** *p58*
Hunter, Thomas 29; Ontario, 1871 ***1823.28*** *p42*
Hunter, Thomas 55; Ontario, 1871 ***1823.15*** *p122*
Hunter, William; New York, 1830 ***8197.10*** *p303*
Hunter, William; New York, 1830 ***8197.10*** *p313*
Hunter, William; Pennsylvania, 1777 ***4629.10*** *p17*
Hunter, William; Philadelphia, 1796 ***1224.2*** *p59*
Hunter, William; Savannah, Georgia, 1802 ***1640.10*** *p83*
Hunter, William; Savannah, Georgia, 1804 ***1640.10*** *p84*
Hunter, William 63; Ontario, 1871 ***1823.22*** *p78*
Hunter, William 75; Ontario, 1871 ***1823.15*** *p122*
Hunter, Wm 53; Ontario, 1871 ***1823.15*** *p122*
Hunters, Simon 25; Ontario, 1871 ***1823.15*** *p122*
Huntington, Erastus 55; Ontario, 1871 ***1823.28*** *p42*
Huntington, George 60; Ontario, 1871 ***1823.22*** *p78*
Huntington, Henry; New York, New York, 1832 ***1224.3*** *p39*
Huntington, Henry 33; Ontario, 1871 ***1823.22*** *p78*
Huntington, S. A. 58; Ontario, 1871 ***1823.28*** *p42*
Huntington, Sarah Morgan; Hartford, Connecticut, 1850 ***1224.3*** *p39*
Huntington, Thomas; New York, 1801 ***1224.3*** *p40*
Huntley, Christopher; Maryland, 1657 ***2524.55*** *p118*
Huntley, Miss E.; Portland, Maine, 1857 ***9196.15*** *p13*
Huntley, Richard; New York, New York, 1829 ***1224.3*** *p40*
Huntley, Thomas; Maryland, 1665 ***2524.55*** *p114*
Huntlong, Hugh 27; Philadelphia, 1774 ***1220.25*** *p63*
Huntly, James; Virginia, 1665-1666 ***6212.30*** *p24*
Huntly, Joab; Virginia, 1666-1667 ***6212.30*** *p35*
Huntly, Thomas; Maryland, 1672 ***2524.55*** *p118*
Hunton, Mr.; Quebec, 1857 ***9196.15*** *p20*
Hunton, Benjamin; Maryland, 1668 ***2524.55*** *p118*
Hunton, Rebecca; Virginia, 1671 ***6212.30*** *p43*
Huntzicker, Daniel; America, 1754 ***2856.30*** *p197E*
Huntzicker, Thomas; America, 1754 ***2856.30*** *p197E*
Huntzicker, Thomas; America, 1754 ***2856.30*** *p197F*
With wife & 8 children
Huntzinger, Johann; America, 1738 ***2856.30*** *p197F*
Hunzelmann, Georg; Port uncertain, 1790 ***2856.30*** *p197F*
With family
Huot, James 78; Ontario, 1871 ***1823.28*** *p42*
Hupeden, Augustus William; New York, 1819 ***8197.10*** *p237*
Hupeden, Augustus William; New York, 1825 ***8197.10*** *p297*
Huper, Hans Jacob; America, 1738 ***2856.30*** *p197F*
Hupfer, Sebastan 48; Ontario, 1871 ***1823.15*** *p122*
Huppert, Jakob; Port uncertain, 1764 ***2856.30*** *p197F*
Hupsin, Ulrich; America, 1738 ***2856.30*** *p225*
Hurbucka, Emilia; Maryland, 1910 ***3259.35*** *p21*
Hurd, Ellen 30; Vermont, 1877 ***5900.10*** *p111*
Hurd, John 14; Maryland, 1775 ***1220.25*** *p10*
Hurd, Thomas 38; Ontario, 1871 ***1823.15*** *p122*
Hurd, William 54; Ontario, 1871 ***1823.22*** *p78*
Hurdon, W. H.; Quebec, 1857 ***9196.15*** *p25*
Hurdy, Jane 16; Fort Cumberland, Nova Scotia, 1775 ***1220.25*** *p21*
Hurford, John; New York, 1821 ***8197.10*** *p237*
Hurlbut, Emaline A. McGowan 68; Vermont, 1881 ***5900.10*** *p377*
Hurle, Augustine; Virginia, 1667 ***6212.30*** *p35*
Hurle, Thomas; Maryland, 1668 ***2524.55*** *p118*
Hurley, Anna Cornelia; Vermont, 1897-1981 ***5900.10*** *p360*
Hurley, Anne Chadwick; Vermont, 1841-1921 ***5900.10*** *p508*
Hurley, Bridget 28; Vermont, 1869 ***5900.10*** *p139*
Hurley, C. E.; Vermont, 1849-1911 ***5900.10*** *p484*
Hurley, Catherine; Vermont, 1894 ***5900.10*** *p331*
Hurley, Catherine 31; Ontario, 1871 ***1823.15*** *p122*
Hurley, Catherine D. 14; Vermont, 1865 ***5900.10*** *p260*
Hurley, Cornelius; Vermont, 1828-1871 ***5900.10*** *p364*
Hurley, Cornelius 33; Vermont, 1867 ***5900.10*** *p360*
Hurley, Cornelius 33; Vermont, 1898 ***5900.10*** *p360*
Hurley, Daniel 21; Maryland, 1774 ***1220.25*** *p74*
Hurley, Daniel G.; Vermont, 1819-1870 ***5900.10*** *p508*
Hurley, Dennis 53; Vermont, 1905 ***5900.10*** *p197*
Hurley, Edward Timothy; Vermont, 1895-1965 ***5900.10*** *p360*
Hurley, Elizabeth; Vermont, 1828-1901 ***5900.10*** *p489*
Hurley, Elizabeth; Vermont, 1849-1936 ***5900.10*** *p458*
Hurley, Ellen; Vermont, 1843-1889 ***5900.10*** *p339*
Hurley, Ellen; Vermont, 1847-1922 ***5900.10*** *p332*
Hurley, Ellen N.; Vermont, 1848-1917 ***5900.10*** *p440*
Hurley, Hannah Corcoran; Vermont, 1860-1942 ***5900.10*** *p231*
Hurley, James; New York, 1838 ***8197.10*** *p241*
Hurley, James; Vermont, 1859-1898 ***5900.10*** *p231*
Hurley, James 22; Vermont, 1883 ***5900.10*** *p360*
Hurley, James 37; Vermont, 1879 ***5900.10*** *p366*
Hurley, James 47; Vermont, 1882 ***5900.10*** *p260*
Hurley, James Cornelius; Vermont, 1890-1896 ***5900.10*** *p360*
Hurley, John; New York, 1802 ***8197.10*** *p21*
Hurley, John; Vermont, 1818-1884 ***5900.10*** *p90*
Hurley, John; Vermont, 1857-1924 ***5900.10*** *p483*
Hurley, John 47; Ontario, 1871 ***1823.15*** *p122*
Hurley, John 50; Ontario, 1871 ***1823.15*** *p122*
Hurley, John 63; Ontario, 1871 ***1823.22*** *p78*
Hurley, John 70; Vermont, 1876 ***5900.10*** *p366*
Hurley, John 80; Vermont, 1902 ***5900.10*** *p72*
Hurley, John, Jr.; Vermont, 1850-1884 ***5900.10*** *p90*
Hurley, John C.; Vermont, 1861-1909 ***5900.10*** *p360*
Hurley, John Gregory; Vermont, 1893-1962 ***5900.10*** *p360*
Hurley, John S.; Boston, 1833 ***8197.10*** *p131*
Hurley, Julia S.; Vermont, 1820-1886 ***5900.10*** *p90*
Hurley, Katherine Moriarty; Vermont, 1854-1914 ***5900.10*** *p339*
Hurley, Margaret; Vermont, 1866-1926 ***5900.10*** *p483*
Hurley, Margaret Dacey 74; Vermont, 1894 ***5900.10*** *p484*
Hurley, Mary; Vermont, n.d. ***5900.10*** *p74*
Hurley, Mary; Vermont, 1851-1925 ***5900.10*** *p365*
Hurley, Mary; Vermont, 1864-1898 ***5900.10*** *p504*
Hurley, Mary; Vermont, 1919 ***5900.10*** *p331*
Hurley, Mary 53; Vermont, 1885 ***5900.10*** *p338*
Hurley, Mary Catherine; Vermont, 1894 ***5900.10*** *p483*
Hurley, Mary Dorothy; Vermont, 1887-1972 ***5900.10*** *p360*
Hurley, Mary L. O'Leary; Vermont, 1816-1913 ***5900.10*** *p364*
Hurley, Mary O'Donahue; Vermont, 1863-1940 ***5900.10*** *p360*
Hurley, Mary O'Neil 82; Vermont, 1888 ***5900.10*** *p366*
Hurley, Michael; New York, 1840 ***8197.10*** *p243*
Hurley, Michael; Vermont, 1793-1883 ***5900.10*** *p365*
Hurley, Michael 26; Ontario, 1871 ***1823.22*** *p78*
Hurley, Michael 63; Vermont, 1891 ***5900.10*** *p81*
Hurley, Michael D.; Vermont, 1854-1894 ***5900.10*** *p339*
Hurley, Michail 16; Vermont, 1865 ***5900.10*** *p360*
Hurley, Patrick; New York, 1837 ***8197.10*** *p91*
Hurley, Patrick; New York, 1840 ***8197.10*** *p243*
Hurley, Patrick; Vermont, 1847-1903 ***5900.10*** *p88*
Hurley, Paul 48; Maryland, 1775 ***1220.25*** *p108*
Hurley, Paul O'Donahue; Vermont, 1900-1964 ***5900.10*** *p360*
Hurley, Sarah; Vermont, 1826-1911 ***5900.10*** *p538*
Hurley, Sarah 28; Vermont, 1874 ***5900.10*** *p366*
Hurley, Sarah J.; Vermont, 1854-1942 ***5900.10*** *p115*
Hurley, Thomas; New York, 1840 ***8197.10*** *p243*
Hurley, Thomas 86; Vermont, 1896 ***5900.10*** *p81*
Hurley, William; New York, 1818 ***8197.10*** *p236*
Hurlocke, George; Maryland, 1668 ***2524.55*** *p118*
Hurly, John; New York, 1831 ***8197.10*** *p313*
Hurmann, . . .; America, 1786 ***2856.30*** *p197F*
Hurn, Mrs.; Quebec, 1857 ***9196.15*** *p15*
Hurnissin, Magdalena; Port uncertain, 1729 ***2856.30*** *p197G*
Huron, Lawrence; Philadelphia, 1785 ***4629.10*** *p62*
Hurry, Jean *SEE* Hurry, John
Hurry, John; Savannah, Georgia, 1774 ***1640.10*** *p84*
Wife: Jean
Child: Jean
Child: William
Hurry, Samuel; Philadelphia, 1824 ***1224.3*** *p40*
Hurry, William *SEE* Hurry, John
Hursch, Margarete; Port uncertain, 1752 ***2856.30*** *p197G*
Hurson, Alice; Vermont, 1949 ***5900.10*** *p168*
Hurson, Anne; Vermont, 1906 ***5900.10*** *p168*
Hurson, Bridget; Vermont, n.d. ***5900.10*** *p533*
Hurson, Ellen; Vermont, 1884 ***5900.10*** *p168*
Hurson, Ellen Donahue; Vermont, 1853-1916 ***5900.10*** *p130*
Hurson, Frank; Vermont, 1869-1890 ***5900.10*** *p168*
Hurson, James; Vermont, 1909 ***5900.10*** *p533*
Hurson, John; Vermont, 1805-1869 ***5900.10*** *p168*
Hurson, Mary E.; Vermont, 1871-1887 ***5900.10*** *p533*
Hurson, Mary Jane; Vermont, 1943 ***5900.10*** *p168*
Hurson, Patrick J.; Vermont, 1839-1915 ***5900.10*** *p130*
Hurst, Mr.; America, 1764 ***2856.30*** *p197F*
With wife
Hurst, Alice *SEE* Hurst, John
Hurst, Ann 21; Philadelphia, 1774 ***1220.25*** *p63*
Hurst, Charles; Pennsylvania, 1777 ***4629.10*** *p23*
Hurst, Jacob; Port uncertain, 1774 ***2856.30*** *p197F*
With wife
Hurst, Joane *SEE* Hurst, John
Hurst, John; Maryland, 1681 ***2524.55*** *p118*
Wife: Alice
Stepchild: Martha
Daughter: Joane
Stepchild: Robert
Hurst, Marianna; Port uncertain, 1758 ***2856.30*** *p197F*
Hurst, Martha *SEE* Hurst, John
Hurst, Mary Ann 73; Ontario, 1871 ***1823.28*** *p42*
Hurst, Robert *SEE* Hurst, John
Hurst, Robert 26; Ontario, 1871 ***1823.28*** *p42*
Hurst, Robert 30; Philadelphia, 1774 ***1220.25*** *p6*
Hurst, Stephen 15; Virginia, 1774 ***1220.25*** *p53*
Hurst, Theodore 64; Ontario, 1871 ***1823.15*** *p122*
Hurster, David; Port uncertain, 1783 ***2856.30*** *p197G*
Hurster, Johann; Port uncertain, 1764 ***2856.30*** *p197F*
Hurtel, Peter; New York, 1803 ***8197.10*** *p13*
Hurth, Bernhard; Port uncertain, 1745 ***2856.30*** *p197G*
Hurth, Johann; Port uncertain, 1742 ***2856.30*** *p197G*
Hurth, Magdalena; Port uncertain, 1766 ***2856.30*** *p197G*
Hurzyamski, Miecylas; Maryland, 1910 ***3259.35*** *p21*
Husband, A. 27; Ontario, 1871 ***1823.28*** *p42*
Husband, Mary J. Hogan 48; Vermont, 1887 ***5900.10*** *p453*
Husband, Sarah 65; Vermont, 1888 ***5900.10*** *p453*
Husband, Thomas Craskell; Jamaica, n.d. ***1224.3*** *p40*
Husband, Thomas Craskell; Trenton, New Jersey, 1838 ***1224.3*** *p40*
Husbands, Richard; Maryland, 1659 ***2524.55*** *p118*
Husbands, Richd.; Maryland, 1658 ***2524.55*** *p118*
Husbands, Richd; Virginia, 1671 ***6212.30*** *p42*
Husking, Mary *SEE* Husking, William
Husking, William; Maryland, 1673 ***2524.55*** *p118*
Wife: Mary
Huskula, Jane; Maryland, 1671 ***2524.55*** *p118*
Huson, John 40; Ontario, 1871 ***1823.28*** *p42*
Hussay, William 41; Ontario, 1871 ***1823.28*** *p42*
Hussburne, Joseph; Pennsylvania, 1779 ***4629.10*** *p33*

Hussey, Lt.; Quebec, 1857 ***9196.15*** *p16*
Hussey, Miss; Quebec, 1857 ***9196.15*** *p21*
Hussey, Ammeill; Nantucket, Massachusetts, 1808 ***1224.3*** *p40*
Hussey, James; Maryland, 1666 ***2524.55*** *p118*
Hussey, John; Maryland, 1662 ***2524.55*** *p118*
Hussey, John; North America, 1760 ***1224.2*** *p59*
Hussey, Naverall; Maryland, 1660 ***2524.55*** *p118*
Hussey, Peter; Virginia, 1664 ***6212.30*** *p8*
Hussey, Sam; Virginia, 1672-1673 ***6212.30*** *p51*
Hussey, Thomas; Maryland, 1667 ***2524.55*** *p118*
Hussey, William 56; Ontario, 1871 ***1823.15*** *p122*
Hussie, Michael; Georgia, 1698 ***1640.13*** *p58*
Hussie, Naverall; Maryland, 1660 ***2524.55*** *p118*
Hussner, Catharina; Port uncertain, 1763 ***2856.30*** *p197F*
Husson, Balthasar; America, 1739 ***2856.30*** *p197F*
Husson, Joseph; New York, 1819 ***8197.10*** *p237*
Hussoy, Mary 75; Ontario, 1871 ***1823.15*** *p122*
Hussoy, Patrick 60; Ontario, 1871 ***1823.15*** *p122*
Husst, Johann Georg; America, 1740 ***2856.30*** *p197F*
Hussy, George; Virginia, 1666-1667 ***6212.30*** *p33*
Hussy, James; Virginia, 1666-1667 ***6212.30*** *p34*
Hussy, Thomas 86; Ontario, 1871 ***1823.15*** *p122*
Hust, Ann; Maryland, 1671 ***2524.55*** *p118*
Hust, Elizabeth; Maryland, 1660 ***2524.55*** *p118*
Hust, John; Maryland, 1671 ***2524.55*** *p118*
Husten, James; Maryland, 1663 ***2524.55*** *p118*
Huster, Catharina; Port uncertain, 1763 ***2856.30*** *p197F*
Huster, Susanna Maria; Port uncertain, 1745 ***2856.30*** *p197F*
Hustin, John Wilson; Pennsylvania, 1777 ***4629.10*** *p19*
Hustis, James; New York, New York, 1824 ***1224.3*** *p40*
Huston, Catherine 79; Ontario, 1871 ***1823.15*** *p122*
Huston, James 40; Ontario, 1871 ***1823.28*** *p42*
Huston, Robert; Pennsylvania, 1810 ***6058.10*** *p3*
Huston, William 43; Ontario, 1871 ***1823.15*** *p122*
Hutchens, Mathew; Maryland, 1680 ***2524.55*** *p118*
Hutchens, Thomas; Pennsylvania, 1781 ***4629.10*** *p43*
Hutcheson, Alexander Gordon; Hawaii, 1896 ***1640.13*** *p58*
Hutcheson, Andrew 16; Ontario, 1861 ***2896.28*** *p50*
Hutcheson, Charity 6; Ontario, 1861 ***2896.28*** *p50*
Hutcheson, Gilbert 25; Ontario, 1861 ***2896.28*** *p50*
Hutcheson, John; New York, 1829 ***8197.10*** *p312*
Hutcheson, Jonathan 51; Ontario, 1861 ***2896.28*** *p50*
Hutcheson, Mary 10; Ontario, 1861 ***2896.28*** *p50*
Hutchin, Frederick; Virginia, 1727 ***1224.2*** *p60*
Hutchings, Noy Willey; Charles Town, South Carolina, 1792 ***1224.2*** *p60*
Hutchings, Richard; Charles Town, South Carolina, 1791 ***1224.2*** *p60*
Hutchins, Charles; Maryland, 1701 ***1224.2*** *p60*
Hutchins, Ebonezer 39; Ontario, 1871 ***1823.28*** *p42*
Hutchins, Elizabeth; Maryland, 1669 ***2524.55*** *p118*
Hutchins, Frances; Philadelphia, 1819 ***1224.3*** *p33*
Hutchins, George 25; Ontario, 1871 ***1823.28*** *p42*
Hutchins, John; New York, 1777 ***1224.2*** *p60*
Hutchins, Nancie J.; Vermont, 1858-1932 ***5900.10*** *p555*
Hutchins, Richard; Maryland, 1651 ***2524.55*** *p118*
Hutchins, Richard; Maryland, 1673 ***2524.55*** *p118*
Hutchins, Sarah; Vermont, 1857-1937 ***5900.10*** *p375*
Hutchins, Thomas; New York, 1840 ***8197.10*** *p174*
Hutchins, William; Savannah, Georgia, 1821 ***1640.10*** *p84*
Hutchins, Zacharia; Pennsylvania, 1777 ***4629.10*** *p8*
Hutchinson, . . .; Boston, 1765 ***4628.40*** *p114*
Hutchinson, Miss; Quebec, 1857 ***9196.15*** *p21*
Hutchinson, A. 9; Ontario, 1861 ***2896.28*** *p1*
Hutchinson, Abraham; Virginia, 1687 ***1224.1*** *p31*
Hutchinson, Alexander; Alabama, 1829-1845 ***1640.10*** *p84*
Hutchinson, Alexander; New York, 1838 ***8197.10*** *p241*
Hutchinson, Angeline 22; Ontario, 1861 ***2896.27*** *p66*
Hutchinson, Ann 2; New York, 1774 ***1220.25*** *p24*
Hutchinson, Ann 44; Ontario, 1871 ***1823.28*** *p42*
Hutchinson, Anthony John; Arkansas, 1850 ***1224.3*** *p40*
Hutchinson, Daniel 21; Virginia, 1774 ***1220.25*** *p75*
Hutchinson, E. 33; Ontario, 1861 ***2896.28*** *p13*
Hutchinson, E. H. 23; Ontario, 1861 ***2896.28*** *p13*
Hutchinson, F. 30; Ontario, 1861 ***2896.28*** *p2*
Hutchinson, F. J. 2; Ontario, 1861 ***2896.28*** *p2*
Hutchinson, Francis 10; New York, 1774 ***1220.25*** *p23*
Hutchinson, George 42; Ontario, 1871 ***1823.15*** *p122*
Hutchinson, George 55; Ontario, 1871 ***1823.15*** *p122*
Hutchinson, Gordon F. 1; Ontario, 1861 ***2896.27*** *p66*
Hutchinson, H. 17; Ontario, 1861 ***2896.28*** *p14*
Hutchinson, Hanah 13; Ontario, 1861 ***2896.28*** *p26*
Hutchinson, J. 7; Ontario, 1861 ***2896.28*** *p13*
Hutchinson, James; Virginia, 1698 ***6212.30*** *p61*
Hutchinson, James 39; Ontario, 1871 ***1823.22*** *p78*
Hutchinson, Jamima 65; Ontario, 1861 ***2896.28*** *p52*
Hutchinson, John; New York, 1794 ***8197.10*** *p5*
Hutchinson, John; Virginia, 1666 ***6212.30*** *p26*
Hutchinson, John 22; Halifax, Nova Scotia, 1774 ***1220.25*** *p138*
Hutchinson, Joseph 27; Virginia, 1774 ***1220.25*** *p56*
Hutchinson, M. 8; Ontario, 1861 ***2896.28*** *p13*
Hutchinson, M. 16; Ontario, 1861 ***2896.28*** *p1*
Hutchinson, M. 19; Ontario, 1861 ***2896.28*** *p4*
Hutchinson, M. 20; Ontario, 1861 ***2896.28*** *p1*
Hutchinson, M. 30; Ontario, 1861 ***2896.28*** *p2*
Hutchinson, M. E. 3; Ontario, 1861 ***2896.28*** *p2*
Hutchinson, Major 9; New York, 1774 ***1220.25*** *p24*
Hutchinson, Margaret 8; New York, 1774 ***1220.25*** *p24*
Hutchinson, Margaret 30; New York, 1774 ***1220.25*** *p23*
Hutchinson, P. A. 1; Ontario, 1861 ***2896.28*** *p2*
Hutchinson, R.; Quebec, 1856 ***9196.15*** *p6*
Hutchinson, R.; Quebec, 1858 ***9196.15*** *p42*
Hutchinson, Ralph 7; New York, 1774 ***1220.25*** *p24*
Hutchinson, Richard 38; Ontario, 1871 ***1823.28*** *p42*
Hutchinson, Robert; Virginia, 1650 ***1224.1*** *p31*
Hutchinson, Robt; Virginia, 1665 ***6212.30*** *p17*
Hutchinson, S. 14; Ontario, 1861 ***2896.28*** *p1*
Hutchinson, S. 61; Ontario, 1861 ***2896.28*** *p13*
Hutchinson, S. E. 1; Ontario, 1861 ***2896.28*** *p13*
Hutchinson, S. M. 4; Ontario, 1861 ***2896.28*** *p13*
Hutchinson, Samuel 24; Maryland, 1775 ***1220.25*** *p121*
Hutchinson, Sarah 40; Ontario, 1871 ***1823.28*** *p42*
Hutchinson, T. 4; Ontario, 1861 ***2896.28*** *p2*
Hutchinson, William; Alabama, 1800-1845 ***1640.10*** *p84*
Hutchinson, William; New York, 1840 ***8197.10*** *p242*
Hutchinson, William 46; Ontario, 1871 ***1823.15*** *p122*
Hutchison, Mrs. 50; Ontario, 1871 ***1823.15*** *p123*
Hutchison, Alexander; Georgia, 1699 ***1640.13*** *p58*
Hutchison, Ann 49; Ontario, 1871 ***1823.22*** *p78*
Hutchison, David; Chicago, 1854 ***1640.13*** *p59*
Hutchison, David; New York, 1837 ***8197.10*** *p90*
Hutchison, David 54; Ontario, 1871 ***1823.22*** *p77*
Hutchison, James; Honduras, 1790-1796 ***1640.13*** *p59*
Hutchison, James 14; Ontario, 1871 ***1823.22*** *p78*
Hutchison, James 40; New York, 1775 ***1220.25*** *p143*
With wife & 4 children
Hutchison, James 46; Ontario, 1871 ***1823.15*** *p123*
Hutchison, John 49; Ontario, 1871 ***1823.22*** *p78*
Hutchison, John 56; Ontario, 1871 ***1823.22*** *p78*
Hutchison, Joseph; Pennsylvania, 1777 ***4629.10*** *p31*
Hutchison, Margret 51; Ontario, 1871 ***1823.15*** *p123*
Hutchison, Mary 21; Ontario, 1871 ***1823.22*** *p78*
Hutchison, Mary C. *SEE* Hutchison, Peter
Hutchison, Peter *SEE* Hutchison, Peter
Hutchison, Peter; Mobile, Alabama, 1823-1845 ***1640.10*** *p84*
Wife: Mary C.
Son: Peter
Son: William M.
Hutchison, Thomas 55; Ontario, 1871 ***1823.22*** *p78*
Hutchison, W. G. 49; Ontario, 1871 ***1823.22*** *p78*
Hutchison, William M. *SEE* Hutchison, Peter
Huterer, Matthias; Port uncertain, 1770 ***2856.30*** *p197F*
Huth, Jakob; Port uncertain, 1743 ***2856.30*** *p197F*
Huth, Martin; America, 1754 ***2856.30*** *p197F*
Hutler, Lorenz; America, 1740 ***2856.30*** *p197G*
Hutmacher, Elias; Port uncertain, 1736 ***2856.30*** *p197F*
Hutmacher, Melchior; America, 1738 ***2856.30*** *p197F*
Hutmacher, Melchior; America, 1738 ***2856.30*** *p197F*
With wife & 3 children
Hutson, Andrew 42; Ontario, 1871 ***1823.28*** *p42*
Hutson, George Stoddart 25; Ontario, 1871 ***1823.28*** *p42*
Hutson, James 43; Ontario, 1871 ***1823.28*** *p42*
Hutson, John 32; Ontario, 1871 ***1823.28*** *p42*
Hutson, John 35; Ontario, 1871 ***1823.15*** *p123*
Hutt, Christian; Port uncertain, 1616 ***2856.30*** *p197G*
With wife & 2 sons
Huttard, Jno; Virginia, 1672 ***6212.30*** *p50*
Hutten, Christian; Port uncertain, 1616 ***2856.30*** *p197G*
With wife & 2 sons
Huttenberger, Karl; Port uncertain, 1741 ***2856.30*** *p197F*
Huttenloch, Josef; Port uncertain, 1794 ***2856.30*** *p197F*
Hutter, Hans Georg; Port uncertain, 1767 ***2856.30*** *p197F*
Hutter, Peter; Port uncertain, 1781 ***2856.30*** *p197G*
Hutterson, Robert 25; Ontario, 1871 ***1823.15*** *p123*
Hutton, Mr.; Quebec, 1857 ***9196.15*** *p15*
Hutton, Mr.; Quebec, 1858 ***9196.15*** *p33*
Hutton, Andrew; Virginia, 1668-1669 ***6212.30*** *p40*
Hutton, Andrew 73; Ontario, 1871 ***1823.28*** *p43*
Hutton, Arthur 35; Ontario, 1871 ***1823.28*** *p43*
Hutton, Charles; Virginia, 1722 ***1224.2*** *p60*
Hutton, Christopher 24; Maryland, 1774 ***1220.25*** *p71*
Hutton, Geo; Virginia, 1666-1667 ***6212.30*** *p32*
Hutton, George; Virginia, 1664 ***6212.30*** *p15*
Hutton, George; Virginia, 1665-1666 ***6212.30*** *p22*
Hutton, George 54; Ontario, 1871 ***1823.15*** *p123*
Hutton, James; Georgia, 1698 ***1640.13*** *p59*
Hutton, James 15; Halifax, Nova Scotia, 1775 ***1220.25*** *p22*
Hutton, John; Georgia, 1698 ***1640.13*** *p59*
Hutton, John; New York, 1840 ***8197.10*** *p172*
Hutton, John 22; Ontario, 1871 ***1823.15*** *p123*
Hutton, John 45; Ontario, 1871 ***1823.22*** *p78*
Hutton, John 45; Ontario, 1871 ***1823.28*** *p43*
Hutton, Joseph; New York, 1840 ***8197.10*** *p384*
Hutton, Pat 64; Alaska, 1917 ***9196.1*** *p52*
Hutton, Pat 64; British Columbia, 1917 ***9196.1*** *p52*
Hutton, Robert; New York, 1825 ***8197.10*** *p239*
Hutton, Robert; Virginia, 1703 ***1224.2*** *p60*
Hutton, Sarah 59; Ontario, 1871 ***1823.22*** *p78*
Hutton, Thomas 53; Ontario, 1871 ***1823.22*** *p78*
Hutton, William 34; Ontario, 1871 ***1823.15*** *p123*
Hutton, William 45; Ontario, 1871 ***1823.15*** *p123*
Hutton, William Dalgleish; Iowa, 1899 ***1640.13*** *p59*
Huttson, Henry 21; Nova Scotia, 1774 ***1220.25*** *p135*
Hutz, Ignaz; Port uncertain, 1755 ***2856.30*** *p197F*
Hutz, Ignaz; Port uncertain, 1805 ***2856.30*** *p197F*
Huv, Maria Catharina; Port uncertain, 1782 ***2856.30*** *p197F*
Huvin, Maria Catharina; Port uncertain, 1782 ***2856.30*** *p197F*
Huxtable, Ann 60; Ontario, 1871 ***1823.15*** *p123*
Huxtable, John 44; Ontario, 1871 ***1823.15*** *p123*
Huxtable, John 83; Ontario, 1871 ***1823.15*** *p123*
Huyck, Adaline A. 11; Ontario, 1861 ***2896.28*** *p24*
Huyck, Caroline 53; Ontario, 1861 ***2896.27*** *p56*
Huyck, Cornelius 31; Ontario, 1861 ***2896.25*** *p5*
Huyck, D. 66; Ontario, 1861 ***2896.28*** *p3*
Huyck, Eliza 19; Ontario, 1861 ***2896.25*** *p5*
Huyck, George 16; Ontario, 1861 ***2896.28*** *p21*
Huyck, Hannah 50; Ontario, 1861 ***2896.28*** *p24*
Huyck, Henry 67; Ontario, 1861 ***2896.25*** *p5*
Huyck, Jane E. 23; Ontario, 1861 ***2896.27*** *p45*
Huyck, Jane M. 31; Ontario, 1861 ***2896.27*** *p28*
Huyck, John W. 6; Ontario, 1861 ***2896.28*** *p19*
Huyck, Margaret E. 9; Ontario, 1861 ***2896.28*** *p19*
Huyck, Martha J. 4; Ontario, 1861 ***2896.27*** *p28*
Huyck, Mary E. 1; Ontario, 1861 ***2896.27*** *p45*
Huyck, Mary J. 17; Ontario, 1861 ***2896.28*** *p19*
Huyck, Mary M. 12; Ontario, 1861 ***2896.25*** *p5*
Huyck, Patience 36; Ontario, 1861 ***2896.28*** *p21*
Huyck, Permila 21; Ontario, 1861 ***2896.28*** *p19*
Huyck, Phebe Ann 14; Ontario, 1861 ***2896.28*** *p24*
Huyck, Phebe Ann 29; Ontario, 1861 ***2896.28*** *p19*
Huyck, Platt 51; Ontario, 1861 ***2896.28*** *p24*
Huyck, Rachel 37; Ontario, 1861 ***2896.25*** *p5*
Huyck, Sarah A. 9; Ontario, 1861 ***2896.25*** *p5*
Huyck, Sarah V. 1; Ontario, 1861 ***2896.25*** *p5*
Huycke, Cornelius A. 66; Ontario, 1861 ***2896.28*** *p41*
Huycke, E. 42; Ontario, 1861 ***2896.28*** *p2*
Huycke, Eliza 26; Ontario, 1861 ***2896.28*** *p40*
Huycke, Emmerilla 35; Ontario, 1861 ***2896.28*** *p35*
Huycke, H. 21; Ontario, 1861 ***2896.26*** *p12*
Huycke, James 24; Ontario, 1861 ***2896.25*** *p2*
Huycke, Janet 25; Ontario, 1861 ***2896.25*** *p1*
Huycke, Josephine 2; Ontario, 1861 ***2896.28*** *p35*
Huycke, Mary E. 21; Ontario, 1861 ***2896.28*** *p41*
Huycke, Richard A. 19; Ontario, 1861 ***2896.28*** *p41*
Huycke, Sarah 36; Ontario, 1861 ***2896.28*** *p41*
Huycke, Sylva 22; Ontario, 1861 ***2896.28*** *p40*
Huycke, William 23; Ontario, 1861 ***2896.28*** *p41*
Huycke, William 25; Ontario, 1861 ***2896.28*** *p40*
Huycke, William A. 64; Ontario, 1861 ***2896.28*** *p40*
Huyke, Mrs. 24; Ontario, 1861 ***2896.26*** *p27*
Huyke, Elonis 24; Ontario, 1861 ***2896.26*** *p27*
Huyke, J. D. 2; Ontario, 1861 ***2896.26*** *p27*
Huyke, Peter 4; Ontario, 1861 ***2896.26*** *p27*
Huyke, S. H. Hamilton 1; Ontario, 1861 ***2896.26*** *p27*
Hyam, Joseph 17; Grenada, 1775-1776 ***1220.25*** *p126*
Hyatt, Aaron 2; Ontario, 1861 ***2896.27*** *p60*
Hyatt, Abraham 7; Ontario, 1861 ***2896.27*** *p60*
Hyatt, Caleb 73; Ontario, 1861 ***2896.28*** *p3*
Hyatt, Charles 4; Ontario, 1861 ***2896.27*** *p60*
Hyatt, E. 4; Ontario, 1861 ***2896.28*** *p12*
Hyatt, Edgar 9; Ontario, 1861 ***2896.27*** *p60*
Hyatt, Elizabeth 22; Ontario, 1861 ***2896.27*** *p26*
Hyatt, Fidelia 18; Ontario, 1861 ***2896.27*** *p27*
Hyatt, George 4; Ontario, 1861 ***2896.27*** *p26*
Hyatt, James; New York, 1831 ***8197.10*** *p314*
Hyatt, James; New York, 1831-1836 ***8197.10*** *p310*
Hyatt, Jane 59; Ontario, 1861 ***2896.27*** *p26*
Hyatt, John 5; Ontario, 1861 ***2896.27*** *p60*
Hyatt, John 16; Ontario, 1861 ***2896.27*** *p26*
Hyatt, John J. 1; Ontario, 1861 ***2896.27*** *p26*
Hyatt, Lydia J. 25; Ontario, 1861 ***2896.27*** *p26*
Hyatt, M. 31; Ontario, 1861 ***2896.28*** *p12*
Hyatt, M. 63; Ontario, 1861 ***2896.28*** *p3*
Hyatt, Mary 33; Ontario, 1861 ***2896.27*** *p60*
Hyatt, O. 11; Ontario, 1861 ***2896.28*** *p12*
Hyatt, Robert 7; Ontario, 1861 ***2896.27*** *p26*
Hyatt, S. 9; Ontario, 1861 ***2896.28*** *p12*
Hyatt, Susan 61; Ontario, 1861 ***2896.27*** *p26*
Hyatt, Susanna 19; Ontario, 1861 ***2896.27*** *p26*

Hyatt, William 7; Ontario, 1861 ***2896.28*** *p12*
Hyatt, William 22; Ontario, 1861 ***2896.27*** *p26*
Hybzinski, Michael; Maryland, 1910 ***3259.35*** *p21*
Hychla, Szszepan; Maryland, 1910 ***3259.35*** *p21*
Hyde, A. W.; Vermont, 1786-1847 ***5900.10*** *p150*
Hyde, Abner 70; Ontario, 1871 ***1823.22*** *p79*
Hyde, Charlotte; Baltimore, 1805 ***1224.3*** *p88*
Hyde, Daniell; Maryland, 1663 ***2524.55*** *p77*
Hyde, Eliza; Vermont, 1821-1915 ***5900.10*** *p278*
Hyde, Henry; New York, 1708 ***1224.2*** *p60*
Hyde, James; Pennsylvania, 1866 ***6058.10*** *p52*
Hyde, James; Vermont, n.d. ***5900.10*** *p57*
Hyde, John; New York, 1794 ***8197.10*** *p5*
Hyde, John; New York, 1840 ***8197.10*** *p242*
Hyde, Josiah 66; Ontario, 1871 ***1823.22*** *p79*
Hyde, Thomas W.; New York, 1839 ***8197.10*** *p131*
Hyde, William; Maryland, 1659 ***2524.55*** *p118*
Hyderick, Abraham; America, 1739 ***2856.30*** *p197F*
Hyderick, Johann; America, 1739 ***2856.30*** *p197F*
Hyderick, Johann Michael; America, 1739 ***2856.30*** *p197F*
Hye, Archibald; Maryland, 1673 ***2524.55*** *p118*
Hyett, Almiry 39; Ontario, 1861 ***2896.26*** *p33*
Hyett, Catherine 10; Ontario, 1861 ***2896.26*** *p33*
Hyett, Charles L. 4; Ontario, 1861 ***2896.26*** *p33*
Hyett, Freeman 8; Ontario, 1861 ***2896.26*** *p33*
Hyett, Galasper 40; Ontario, 1861 ***2896.26*** *p33*
Hyett, John; Maryland, 1656 ***2524.55*** *p118*
Hyett, John; Maryland, 1663 ***2524.55*** *p118*
Hyett, John 4; Ontario, 1861 ***2896.26*** *p33*
Hyett, Mary; Maryland, 1663 ***2524.55*** *p119*
Hyett, Mary Ann 16; Ontario, 1861 ***2896.26*** *p33*
Hyett, Richard; Virginia, 1671-1672 ***6212.30*** *p47*
Hyett, Sharlett 8; Ontario, 1861 ***2896.26*** *p33*
Hyett, William 10; Ontario, 1861 ***2896.26*** *p33*
Hygate, Michael; Maryland, 1664 ***2524.55*** *p119*
Hyglendowski, Thomas K.; Maryland, 1910 ***3259.35*** *p21*
Hyland, Anna; Vermont, 1858-1937 ***5900.10*** *p184*
Hyland, Elizabeth; Vermont, 1856-1933 ***5900.10*** *p171*
Hyland, Hannah Quinn; Vermont, 1820-1915 ***5900.10*** *p185*
Hyland, Margaret; Vermont, 1841-1929 ***5900.10*** *p185*
Hyland, Mark; New York, 1802 ***8197.10*** *p21*
Hyland, Mary; Maryland, 1665 ***2524.55*** *p119*
Hyland, Mary; Vermont, 1848-1918 ***5900.10*** *p185*
Hyland, Michael; Vermont, 1852-1928 ***5900.10*** *p185*
Hyland, Patrick; Vermont, 1807-1873 ***5900.10*** *p185*
Hyland, William; New York, 1830 ***8197.10*** *p240*
Hylen, Nicholas; New York, 1821 ***8197.10*** *p237*
Hylen, Nicholas; New York, 1827 ***8197.10*** *p341*
Hyndes, Michael; New York, 1838 ***8197.10*** *p318*
Hyndham, J. B.; Quebec, 1858 ***9196.15*** *p36*
Hyndman, Mr.; Quebec, 1858 ***9196.15*** *p42*
Hyndman, Mrs.; Quebec, 1858 ***9196.15*** *p41*
Hyndman, Ann Lousia 43; Ontario, 1871 ***1823.15*** *p123*
Hyndman, Campbell 42; Ontario, 1871 ***1823.15*** *p123*
Hyndman, John 41; Ontario, 1871 ***1823.15*** *p123*
Hyndman, Samuel 44; Ontario, 1871 ***1823.15*** *p123*
Hynds, Bridget 70; Vermont, 1903 ***5900.10*** *p589*
Hyne, Charles 38; Ontario, 1871 ***1823.28*** *p43*
Hyne, Joseph William; New York, 1839 ***8197.10*** *p131*
Hyne, William; Maryland, 1669 ***2524.55*** *p119*
Hyne, William 28; Ontario, 1871 ***1823.28*** *p43*
Hyne, William 45; Ontario, 1871 ***1823.22*** *p79*
Hynes, Alexander 23; Maryland, 1774 ***1220.25*** *p71*
Hynes, Andrew 48; Ontario, 1871 ***1823.28*** *p43*
Hynes, Ann; Vermont, 1817-1898 ***5900.10*** *p136*
Hynes, Anna Kinsella; Vermont, 1855-1993 ***5900.10*** *p273*
Hynes, Catherine E.; Vermont, 1858-1935 ***5900.10*** *p598*
Hynes, Daniel; New York, 1837 ***8197.10*** *p90*
Hynes, Edward; Vermont, 1854-1922 ***5900.10*** *p185*
Hynes, Edward 22; Maryland, 1775 ***1220.25*** *p112*
Hynes, Ellen W. Walsh 58; Vermont, 1892 ***5900.10*** *p419*
Hynes, Henry; Vermont, 1852-1910 ***5900.10*** *p273*
Hynes, James; New York, 1864 ***6058.10*** *p67*
Hynes, John R. 68; Vermont, 1899 ***5900.10*** *p419*
Hynes, Julia C. Crowley; Vermont, 1854-1939 ***5900.10*** *p185*
Hynes, Mary A.; Vermont, 1856-1926 ***5900.10*** *p419*
Hynes, Mary G.; Vermont, 1843-1897 ***5900.10*** *p195*
Hynes, Michael; Vermont, 1836-1893 ***5900.10*** *p195*
Hynes, William 28; Vermont, 1879 ***5900.10*** *p261*
Hynie, Hester; Maryland, 1665 ***2524.55*** *p119*
Hynson, Thomas; Maryland, 1667 ***2524.55*** *p119*
With wife
Hyop, Lawrence; Maryland, 1664 ***2524.55*** *p119*
Hypinor, Walenty; Maryland, 1910 ***3259.35*** *p21*
Hyslop, Mrs.; Quebec, 1858 ***9196.15*** *p44*
Hyslop, Agnso 81; Ontario, 1871 ***1823.15*** *p123*
Hyslop, Charles; New York, 1807 ***8197.10*** *p40*
Hyslop, Gilbert; New York, 1808 ***8197.10*** *p54*
Hyslop, Gilbert, Jr.; New York, 1807 ***8197.10*** *p40*
Hyslop, Jean; Jamaica, 1811 ***1640.13*** *p59*
Hyslop, John 50; Ontario, 1871 ***1823.15*** *p123*
Hyslop, Robert 40; Ontario, 1871 ***1823.15*** *p123*
Hyslop, Thomas 29; Ontario, 1871 ***1823.15*** *p123*
Hyslop, William 41; Ontario, 1871 ***1823.15*** *p123*

I

Ibach, Jacob; Port uncertain, 1765 ***2856.30*** *p198*
Ibach, Matthaus; Port uncertain, 1774 ***2856.30*** *p198*
Ibbotson, Henry; New York, 1836 ***8197.10*** *p76*
Ibel, Hans Georg; Port uncertain, 1737 ***2856.30*** *p198*
Ibig, Henrich; Port uncertain, 1792 ***2856.30*** *p198*
Ibinger, Adam; America, 1752 ***2856.30*** *p198*
With 6 children
Ibright, Jacob; Maryland, 1665 ***2524.55*** *p119*
Icacff, Kim 27; Washington, 1914 ***9196.1*** *p66*
Icard, Jean Baptist; Philadelphia, 1793 ***4629.10*** *p76*
Icoeff, P. 27; Alaska, 1916 ***9196.1*** *p42*
Icoeff, P. 27; Whitehorse, Yukon, 1916 ***9196.1*** *p42*
Igar, Veronim; Maryland, 1910 ***3259.35*** *p21*
Igel, . . .; Port uncertain, 1787 ***2856.30*** *p198*
Ignalb, John; Maryland, 1910 ***3259.35*** *p21*
Ignanowska, Captuder; Maryland, 1910 ***3259.35*** *p21*
Ignatowski, Apolimary; Maryland, 1910 ***3259.35*** *p21*
Ignatowski, Stanislaw; Maryland, 1910 ***3259.35*** *p21*
Ignatrus, Main 60; Ontario, 1871 ***1823.15*** *p123*
Igo, Catherine Geelen 58; Vermont, 1880 ***5900.10*** *p270*
Igoe, Bridget; Vermont, 1837-1912 ***5900.10*** *p217*
Ihle, Johann Georg; America, 1754 ***2856.30*** *p198*
Ihle, Johann Georg; Port uncertain, 1754 ***2856.30*** *p198*
Ihlinger, Michael; Port uncertain, 1740 ***2856.30*** *p198*
Ihringer, Philipp; America, 1751 ***2856.30*** *p198*
Iichcombe, William; Maryland, 1668 ***2524.55*** *p219*
Ilch, Hans; Port uncertain, 1770 ***2856.30*** *p198*
Ilch, Paul; Port uncertain, 1770 ***2856.30*** *p198*
Iles, Edward 28; Ontario, 1871 ***1823.22*** *p79*
Iles, Richard; Maryland, 1682 ***2524.55*** *p119*
Ilges, Johann Peter; Port uncertain, 1737 ***2856.30*** *p198*
Iliad, Mary; Maryland, 1679 ***2524.55*** *p119*
Iling, Georg; Port uncertain, 1751 ***2856.30*** *p198*
Illes, John; Virginia, 1663 ***6212.30*** *p4*
Illford, Tho; Virginia, 1666 ***6212.30*** *p25*
Illig, Christof; Port uncertain, 1781 ***2856.30*** *p198*
Illig, Johann; Port uncertain, 1754 ***2856.30*** *p198*
Illing, Francis; Maryland, 1661 ***2524.55*** *p119*
Illinois, Mary 45; Ontario, 1871 ***1823.28*** *p43*
Illinworth, Richard; Maryland, 1667 ***2524.55*** *p119*
Illion, Heinrich; Port uncertain, 1773 ***2856.30*** *p198*
Illy, Johann Peter; Port uncertain, 1784 ***2856.30*** *p198*
With wife
Ilsch, Theobald; Port uncertain, 1723 ***2856.30*** *p198*
Ilsic, Henry 31; Ontario, 1871 ***1823.15*** *p123*
Ilsic, Ludwig 70; Ontario, 1871 ***1823.15*** *p123*
Ilsley, Randal 17; New York, 1775 ***1220.25*** *p94*
Ilvery, Mr.; Quebec, 1857 ***9196.15*** *p24*
Ily, Johann Georg; Port uncertain, 1726 ***2856.30*** *p198*
Imbert, Frederick; New York, 1807 ***8197.10*** *p51*
Imboden, Konrad; Port uncertain, 1731 ***2856.30*** *p198*
Imbodin, Maria Elisabeth; Port uncertain, 1751 ***2856.30*** *p198*
Imbold, Maria Catharina; Port uncertain, 1763 ***2856.30*** *p198*
Imbott, Maria Catharina; Port uncertain, 1763 ***2856.30*** *p198*
Imbrecht, Georg Ludwig; Port uncertain, 1733 ***2856.30*** *p198*
Imer, Abraham; South Carolina, 1775 ***1224.2*** *p60*
Imhof, Jakob; Port uncertain, 1723 ***2856.30*** *p198*
Imhoff, Catharina; America, 1764 ***2856.30*** *p198*
Imhoff, Henry; Pennsylvania, 1827 ***6058.10*** *p9*
Imhoff, Titus; New York, 1807 ***8197.10*** *p41*
Imich, Jakob; Port uncertain, 1770 ***2856.30*** *p198*
Immel, Jacob; Port uncertain, 1790 ***2856.30*** *p198*
Immel, Michael; Pennsylvania, 1777 ***4629.10*** *p9*
Immensee, Josef; Port uncertain, 1780 ***2856.30*** *p198*
Immer, Rosino; Port uncertain, 1746 ***2856.30*** *p198*
Immesberger, Anna Maria; Port uncertain, 1779 ***2856.30*** *p198*
Immich, Anna Catharina; Port uncertain, 1751 ***2856.30*** *p198*
Immig, Anna Margarete; Port uncertain, 1767 ***2856.30*** *p198*
Immig, Georg; Port uncertain, 1779 ***2856.30*** *p198*
Impfinger, Anna Elisabeth; America, 1752 ***2856.30*** *p199*
With husband & 7 children
Impfinger, Johann Werner; America, 1752 ***2856.30*** *p199*
With wife & 7 children
Imrie, Duncan; St. Augustine, Florida, 1754-1782 ***1640.10*** *p84*
Imrie, Duncan; St. Augustine, Florida, 1782 ***1640.13*** *p60*
Imrie, John; St. Augustine, Florida, 1782 ***1640.10*** *p84*
Imrie, William Beck; Quebec, 1876 ***1640.13*** *p60*
Inata, John; Maryland, 1910 ***3259.35*** *p21*
Ince, George; New York, 1830 ***8197.10*** *p243*
Ince, James; Pennsylvania, 1785 ***4629.10*** *p48*
Inch, Nathaniel; New York, 1837 ***8197.10*** *p92*
Inch, William 35; Ontario, 1871 ***1823.28*** *p43*
Inch, William 38; Ontario, 1871 ***1823.28*** *p43*
Inchboard, Jno.; Maryland, 1669 ***2524.55*** *p119*
Inchboard, William; Maryland, 1680 ***2524.55*** *p119*
Inches, Andrew; Fredericton, New Brunswick, 1898 ***1640.13*** *p60*
Inck, Georg Jakob; America, 1749 ***2856.30*** *p199*
In Craf, Denis; Maryland, 1678 ***2524.55*** *p119*
In Craff, Denis; Maryland, 1678 ***2524.55*** *p119*
Indian, Ahbetahkezhikch 80; Ontario, 1871 ***1823.28*** *p43*
Indian, Ahwonebahgooqua 70; Ontario, 1871 ***1823.28*** *p43*
Indian, Angelic 52; Ontario, 1871 ***1823.28*** *p43*
Indian, Anninnece 39; Ontario, 1871 ***1823.28*** *p43*
Indian, Arkmaqua 2; Ontario, 1871 ***1823.28*** *p43*
Indian, Columbus 62; Ontario, 1871 ***1823.28*** *p43*
Indian, Columbus 67; Ontario, 1871 ***1823.28*** *p43*
Indian, Ence 67; Ontario, 1871 ***1823.28*** *p43*
Indian, Galigalikewai 52; Ontario, 1871 ***1823.28*** *p44*
Indian, Ishkemah 50; Ontario, 1871 ***1823.28*** *p44*
Indian, Jocko 54; Ontario, 1871 ***1823.28*** *p44*
Indian, Kakige 72; Ontario, 1871 ***1823.28*** *p44*
Indian, Katherine; Maryland, 1661 ***2524.55*** *p119*
Indian, Kewaigahbossequ 52; Ontario, 1871 ***1823.28*** *p44*
Indian, Kinewahbai 42; Ontario, 1871 ***1823.28*** *p44*
Indian, Macknoot 25; Ontario, 1871 ***1823.28*** *p44*
Indian, Maitwaiqwab 50; Ontario, 1871 ***1823.28*** *p44*
Indian, Margrette 50; Ontario, 1871 ***1823.28*** *p44*
Indian, Misquahkezhik 5; Ontario, 1871 ***1823.28*** *p45*
Indian, Mocositance 38; Ontario, 1871 ***1823.28*** *p45*
Indian, Mocotabin 52; Ontario, 1871 ***1823.28*** *p45*
Indian, Nabakainu 62; Ontario, 1871 ***1823.28*** *p45*
Indian, Nebumsqua 16; Ontario, 1871 ***1823.28*** *p45*
Indian, Negonoquoum 12; Ontario, 1871 ***1823.28*** *p45*
Indian, Nindoquesoquc; Ontario, 1871 ***1823.28*** *p45*
Indian, Ojamance 30; Ontario, 1871 ***1823.28*** *p46*
Indian, Okewah 30; Ontario, 1871 ***1823.28*** *p46*
Indian, Onizenahsqutciw 62; Ontario, 1871 ***1823.28*** *p46*
Indian, Osawanimiki 42; Ontario, 1871 ***1823.28*** *p46*
Indian, Osowquonn 67; Ontario, 1871 ***1823.28*** *p46*
Indian, Paishahbunoquai 30; Ontario, 1871 ***1823.28*** *p46*
Indian, Patahwonoquetoq 20; Ontario, 1871 ***1823.28*** *p46*
Indian, Penessewekezhik 55; Ontario, 1871 ***1823.28*** *p46*
Indian, Pindunwan 52; Ontario, 1871 ***1823.28*** *p46*
Indian, Sahkewenaibe 67; Ontario, 1871 ***1823.28*** *p46*
Indian, Showwondai 60; Ontario, 1871 ***1823.28*** *p47*
Indian, Tenasa 55; Ontario, 1871 ***1823.28*** *p47*
Indian, Thomas; New England, 1695 ***1224.1*** *p31*
Indian, Wabosaqua 40; Ontario, 1871 ***1823.28*** *p47*
Indian, Wahsahg 52; Ontario, 1871 ***1823.28*** *p47*
Indian, Wahsquonaikezhi 35; Ontario, 1871 ***1823.28*** *p47*
Indian, Waimegwance 62; Ontario, 1871 ***1823.28*** *p47*
Indian, Waiudegooquai 57; Ontario, 1871 ***1823.28*** *p47*
Indian, Washeskinnie 30; Ontario, 1871 ***1823.28*** *p47*
Indian, Wattappe 50; Ontario, 1871 ***1823.28*** *p47*
Indian, Wawdahbunoquai 30; Ontario, 1871 ***1823.28*** *p47*
Indian, White 32; Ontario, 1871 ***1823.28*** *p47*
Indos, Aaron 53; Ontario, 1871 ***1823.15*** *p123*
Ingalls, Alfred 31; Ontario, 1871 ***1823.22*** *p79*
Ingalls, Mary 35; Ontario, 1871 ***1823.15*** *p123*
Ingalls, Mary 73; Ontario, 1871 ***1823.15*** *p123*
Ingate, Anne; New York, New York, 1847 ***1224.3*** *p40*
Ingelfinger, Reinmuth; Port uncertain, 1792 ***2856.30*** *p199*
Ingenheimer, Johann; Port uncertain, 1766 ***2856.30*** *p199*
Ingersell, Jared; Pennsylvania, 1778 ***4629.10*** *p43*
Ingersol, Henry 71; Ontario, 1871 ***1823.22*** *p79*
Ingersoll, Jared; New Haven, Connecticut, 1783 ***1224.2*** *p60*
Ingham, Samuel 45; Ontario, 1871 ***1823.22*** *p79*
Ingham, Thomas; New York, 1819 ***8197.10*** *p243*
Ingham, Thomas, Jr.; New York, 1821 ***8197.10*** *p243*
Ingles, George 60; Ontario, 1871 ***1823.22*** *p79*
Ingles, James; New York, 1840 ***8197.10*** *p176*
Ingles, James 56; Ontario, 1871 ***1823.22*** *p79*
Ingles, John 29; Ontario, 1871 ***1823.15*** *p123*
Ingles, Joseph 46; Ontario, 1871 ***1823.15*** *p123*
Ingles, Robert 45; Ontario, 1871 ***1823.15*** *p123*
Ingles, Thomas; Pennsylvania, 1777 ***4629.10*** *p11*
Inglesby, Edw; Virginia, 1666 ***6212.30*** *p25*
Inglesby, John; New York, 1807 ***8197.10*** *p41*
Ingless, Georgy 22; Ontario, 1871 ***1823.28*** *p48*
Inglinger, Maria Margarete; Port uncertain, 1784 ***2856.30*** *p199*
Inglis, Alexander; St. Kitts, 1752 ***1640.13*** *p60*
Inglis, Andrew; Savannah, Georgia, 1770 ***1640.10*** *p84*
Inglis, Andrew 61; Ontario, 1871 ***1823.22*** *p79*
Inglis, Charles; Georgia, 1698 ***1640.13*** *p60*
Inglis, George; Maryland, 1664 ***2524.55*** *p76*
Relative: Mary
Son: George, Jr.
Inglis, George, Jr. *SEE* Inglis, George
Inglis, Henry; Georgia, 1698 ***1640.13*** *p60*
Inglis, Henry; New York, New York, 1844 ***6058.10*** *p24*
Inglis, James; Georgia, 1699 ***1640.13*** *p60*
Inglis, James; Louisiana, 1836 ***1640.10*** *p84*
Inglis, James; Maryland, 1785 ***1640.13*** *p60*
Inglis, John; Savannah, Georgia, 1772 ***1640.10*** *p85*
Inglis, John 42; Ontario, 1871 ***1823.28*** *p48*
Inglis, John 53; Ontario, 1871 ***1823.22*** *p79*
Inglis, John 56; Ontario, 1871 ***1823.15*** *p123*
Inglis, Mary *SEE* Inglis, George
Inglis, Peter 43; Ontario, 1871 ***1823.22*** *p79*
Inglis, Robert; Georgia, 1699 ***1640.13*** *p60*
Inglis, Samuel; Pennsylvania, 1777 ***4629.10*** *p22*
Inglis, Thomas; Charles Town, South Carolina, n.d. ***1224.2*** *p60*
Inglis, Thomas; Jamaica, 1788 ***1224.2*** *p60*
Inglis, William 77; Ontario, 1871 ***1823.28*** *p48*
Inglish, Ann; Maryland, 1677 ***2524.55*** *p119*
Inglish, John 32; Ontario, 1871 ***1823.15*** *p123*
Ingold, Jacob 65; Ontario, 1871 ***1823.15*** *p123*
Ingoldsby, Richard; New York, 1719 ***1224.2*** *p60*
Ingraham, George; New England, 1764 ***1224.2*** *p60*
Ingram, Alexander 49; Ontario, 1871 ***1823.15*** *p123*

Ingram, Alexander 60; Ontario, 1871 ***1823.15*** *p123*
Ingram, Ann; Virginia, 1693-1694 ***6212.30*** *p60*
Ingram, Anne *SEE* Ingram, Robert
Ingram, Bridget; Vermont, n.d. ***5900.10*** *p498*
Ingram, Dora 19; Ontario, 1871 ***1823.15*** *p123*
Ingram, George; Pennsylvania, 1777 ***4629.10*** *p13*
Ingram, Isaac; America, 1874 ***1640.13*** *p60*
Ingram, Isabella 51; Ontario, 1871 ***1823.22*** *p79*
Ingram, James *SEE* Ingram, Robert
Ingram, John *SEE* Ingram, Robert
Ingram, John; Maryland, 1665 ***2524.55*** *p119*
Ingram, John 72; Ontario, 1871 ***1823.22*** *p79*
Ingram, Joseph; Died enroute, 1653 ***1224.1*** *p31*
Ingram, Richard; Virginia, 1663 ***6212.30*** *p3*
Ingram, Robert; Maryland, 1664 ***2524.55*** *p119*
Relative: Anne
Relative: James
Relative: John
Ingram, Roger; Maryland, 1663 ***2524.55*** *p119*
Ingram, Thomas; Maryland, 1670 ***2524.55*** *p119*
Ingram, Thomas; Maryland, 1717 ***1224.2*** *p60*
Ingram, W. H. 41; Ontario, 1871 ***1823.28*** *p48*
Ingram, William; New York, 1837 ***8197.10*** *p92*
Ingram, William 22; Maryland, 1774 ***1220.25*** *p70*
Ingram, William Alexander; Chicago, 1900 ***1640.13*** *p60*
Inkson, Richard; Pennsylvania, 1777 ***4629.10*** *p15*
Inloes, Henry; Maryland, 1661 ***2524.55*** *p119*
With wife
In Mahon, Edm.; Maryland, 1678 ***2524.55*** *p119*
Inman, Essey 17; Ontario, 1871 ***1823.15*** *p123*
Inman, Mary; South Carolina, 1769 ***1224.2*** *p60*
Inman, Robert; Boston, 1712 ***1224.2*** *p60*
Inman, Roger; Maryland, 1679 ***2524.55*** *p119*
Innerarity, Eliza J. *SEE* Innerarity, Frances
Innerarity, Frances; Alabama, 1818-1845 ***1640.10*** *p85*
Child: J. W. G.
Child: Louisa
Child: Eliza J.
Innerarity, J. W. G. *SEE* Innerarity, Frances
Innerarity, James; Florida, 1796 ***1640.10*** *p85*
Innerarity, John; Pensacola, Florida, 1792 ***1640.10*** *p85*
Innerarity, John; Savannah, Georgia, 1805 ***1224.3*** *p40*
Innerarity, Louisa *SEE* Innerarity, Frances
Innes, Alexander; Georgia, 1698 ***1640.13*** *p60*
Innes, Isabella 30; Ontario, 1871 ***1823.22*** *p79*
Innes, James 33; Ontario, 1871 ***1823.22*** *p79*
Innes, John 67; Ontario, 1871 ***1823.15*** *p123*
Innes, John L. 55; Ontario, 1871 ***1823.22*** *p79*
Innes, Stephen 42; Ontario, 1871 ***1823.22*** *p79*
Innes, William 38; Ontario, 1871 ***1823.22*** *p79*
Inness, Henry; New York, 1794 ***8197.10*** *p5*
Innis, Ann *SEE* Innis, Thomas
Innis, Ann; Maryland, 1651 ***2524.55*** *p119*
Innis, George 40; Ontario, 1871 ***1823.22*** *p79*
Innis, James; Maryland, 1659 ***2524.55*** *p119*
Innis, John 60; Ontario, 1871 ***1823.28*** *p48*
Innis, Robert 23; Virginia, 1774 ***1220.25*** *p45*
Innis, Sharlotte 60; Ontario, 1871 ***1823.22*** *p79*
Innis, Simon 40; Maryland, 1774 ***1220.25*** *p70*
Innis, Thomas; Maryland, 1659 ***2524.55*** *p119*
Wife: Ann
Innis, William; Maryland, 1680 ***2524.55*** *p119*
In Owen, James; Maryland, 1678 ***2524.55*** *p119*
Insh, Joan; Maryland, 1651 ***2524.55*** *p119*
Inshaw, Joseph; New York, 1838 ***8197.10*** *p243*
Inslee, William; New Jersey, 1898 ***1640.13*** *p60*
Insley, A. 12; Ontario, 1861 ***2896.26*** *p15*
Insley, A. 20; Ontario, 1861 ***2896.26*** *p15*
Insley, Ada E. 3; Ontario, 1861 ***2896.27*** *p56*
Insley, Andrew; Maryland, 1663 ***2524.55*** *p119*
Insley, Calvin P. 3; Ontario, 1861 ***2896.27*** *p25*
Insley, Daniel C. 17; Ontario, 1861 ***2896.27*** *p25*
Insley, Eliza 22; Ontario, 1861 ***2896.27*** *p56*
Insley, Elmira 28; Ontario, 1861 ***2896.27*** *p56*
Insley, Henry 61; Ontario, 1861 ***2896.27*** *p56*
Insley, Isiah 9; Ontario, 1861 ***2896.27*** *p25*
Insley, J. 31; Ontario, 1861 ***2896.26*** *p15*
Insley, J. 60; Ontario, 1861 ***2896.26*** *p15*
Insley, L. 1; Ontario, 1861 ***2896.26*** *p15*
Insley, L. 25; Ontario, 1861 ***2896.26*** *p15*
Insley, M. 19; Ontario, 1861 ***2896.26*** *p11*
Insley, M. 23; Ontario, 1861 ***2896.26*** *p15*
Insley, M. 62; Ontario, 1861 ***2896.26*** *p15*
Insley, Mary 38; Ontario, 1861 ***2896.27*** *p25*
Insley, Mary E. 9; Ontario, 1861 ***2896.27*** *p56*
Insley, Orine 11; Ontario, 1861 ***2896.27*** *p25*
Insley, Ruliff G. 4; Ontario, 1861 ***2896.27*** *p56*
Insley, Sarah E. 1; Ontario, 1861 ***2896.27*** *p25*
Insley, Walter 8; Ontario, 1861 ***2896.27*** *p56*
Insley, William H. 1; Ontario, 1861 ***2896.27*** *p56*
Insley, William H. 5; Ontario, 1861 ***2896.27*** *p25*
Inverarity, James; Florida, 1796 ***1640.10*** *p85*
Inverarity, John; Pensacola, Florida, 1792 ***1640.10*** *p85*
Inverdale, Chas; Portland, Maine, 1858 ***9196.15*** *p28*
Invines, Thomas 30; Ontario, 1871 ***1823.22*** *p79*
Inwood, John Payne; Savannah, Georgia, 1847 ***1224.3*** *p40*
Inwood, Joshua 45; Ontario, 1871 ***1823.15*** *p124*
Inwoon, John 30; Ontario, 1871 ***1823.15*** *p124*
Inxge, Elizabeth 71; Ontario, 1871 ***1823.15*** *p124*
Inxoe, Aeron 26; Ontario, 1871 ***1823.15*** *p124*
Ioaden, Joseph 57; Ontario, 1871 ***1823.15*** *p124*
Ioneoff, M. 23; Alaska, 1917 ***9196.1*** *p45*
Ioneoff, M. 23; Whitehorse, Yukon, 1917 ***9196.1*** *p45*
Irbis, Sidney 36; Ontario, 1871 ***1823.28*** *p48*
Irby, Walter; Virginia, 1652 ***1224.1*** *p32*
Ire, William; Virginia, 1664 ***6212.30*** *p8*
Ireland, Mr.; Quebec, 1858 ***9196.15*** *p42*
Ireland, Allan 59; Ontario, 1871 ***1823.15*** *p124*
Ireland, Amos; Philadelphia, 1789 ***4629.10*** *p57*
Wife: Sarah
Ireland, Amos 29; Philadelphia, 1789 ***4629.10*** *p57*
Ireland, David; Virginia, 1817 ***1640.10*** *p85*
Ireland, David 31; Ontario, 1871 ***1823.22*** *p79*
Ireland, Elizabeth; Maryland, 1677 ***2524.55*** *p120*
Ireland, George 43; Ontario, 1871 ***1823.15*** *p124*
Ireland, Henry; New York, 1830 ***8197.10*** *p66*
Ireland, Henry 66; Ontario, 1871 ***1823.15*** *p124*
Ireland, James 28; Ontario, 1871 ***1823.15*** *p124*
Ireland, James 60; Ontario, 1871 ***1823.15*** *p124*
Ireland, John; Boston, 1699 ***1224.1*** *p32*
Ireland, Michael 73; Ontario, 1871 ***1823.22*** *p79*
Ireland, Richard 66; Ontario, 1871 ***1823.22*** *p80*
Ireland, Robert 36; Ontario, 1871 ***1823.15*** *p124*
Ireland, Robert 40; Ontario, 1871 ***1823.22*** *p80*
Ireland, Robt; Virginia, 1665-1666 ***6212.30*** *p23*
Ireland, Sarah *SEE* Ireland, Amos
Ireland, Thomas 17; Maryland, 1774 ***1220.25*** *p73*
Ireland, Thomas 40; Ontario, 1871 ***1823.22*** *p80*
Ireland, William; Maryland, 1665 ***2524.55*** *p120*
Ireland, William 35; Ontario, 1871 ***1823.22*** *p80*
Ireland, William M.; New York, 1826-1834 ***8197.10*** *p305*
Ireland, William M.; New York, 1828 ***8197.10*** *p243*
Iress, Isaac 49; Ontario, 1871 ***1823.28*** *p48*
Irgrain, Gairh 43; Ontario, 1871 ***1823.15*** *p124*
Irick, Christopher; Pennsylvania, 1786 ***4629.10*** *p49*
Irion, Philipp Jakob; America, 1759 ***2856.30*** *p199*
With wife
Irish, Charles; New York, 1812 ***8197.10*** *p243*
Irish, Charles; New York, 1815 ***8197.10*** *p56*
Irish, Eldridge 35; Ontario, 1871 ***1823.22*** *p80*
Irish, G. N. F. 60; Ontario, 1871 ***1823.22*** *p80*
Irish, John; Virginia, 1688 ***6212.30*** *p57*
Irish, William Augustus; New York, 1818 ***8197.10*** *p243*
Irishman, William; Maryland, 1655-1656 ***2524.55*** *p120*
Irneman, George Moon 47; Ontario, 1871 ***1823.15*** *p124*
Iron, Nicholas; Virginia, 1659 ***1224.1*** *p29*
Ironman, Joseph 61; Oregon, 1914 ***9196.1*** *p66*
Ironmonger, Corderoy; Virginia, 1681 ***1224.1*** *p32*
Irons, George; Alabama, 1836-1845 ***1640.10*** *p85*
Irons, James; Alabama, 1836-1845 ***1640.10*** *p85*
Ironside, James; Virginia, 1666-1667 ***6212.30*** *p33*
Irrewynski, Jan; Maryland, 1910 ***3259.35*** *p21*
Irvan, William 36; Ontario, 1871 ***1823.15*** *p124*
Irvin, Andrew; Savannah, Georgia, 1762 ***1640.10*** *p85*
Irvin, Elizabeth 2; Ontario, 1861 ***2896.28*** *p63*
Irvin, Elizabeth 33; Ontario, 1861 ***2896.28*** *p63*
Irvin, George 72; Ontario, 1871 ***1823.15*** *p124*
Irvin, Hariet 3; Ontario, 1861 ***2896.28*** *p63*
Irvin, James; New York, 1830 ***8197.10*** *p243*
Irvin, James; New York, 1833 ***8197.10*** *p243*
Irvin, James; Pennsylvania, 1786 ***4629.10*** *p47*
Irvin, Margaret 8; Ontario, 1861 ***2896.28*** *p63*
Irvin, Martha 5; Ontario, 1861 ***2896.28*** *p63*
Irvin, Mary E. 13; Ontario, 1861 ***2896.28*** *p63*
Irvin, Richard; New York, 1829 ***8197.10*** *p243*
Irvin, Richard; New York, 1834 ***8197.10*** *p72*
Irvin, Robert 6; Ontario, 1861 ***2896.28*** *p63*
Irvin, Robert 40; Ontario, 1861 ***2896.28*** *p63*
Irvin, Robert 51; Ontario, 1871 ***1823.15*** *p124*
Irvin, Samuel 11; Ontario, 1861 ***2896.28*** *p63*
Irvine, Adam 38; Quebec, 1775 ***1220.25*** *p108*
Wife: Elizabeth 36
With 3 children
Irvine, Charles; Tobago, West Indies, 1798 ***1640.13*** *p60*
Irvine, Christopher 37; Ontario, 1871 ***1823.15*** *p124*
Irvine, D. A.; Quebec, 1856 ***9196.15*** *p7*
Irvine, Elizabeth 36 *SEE* Irvine, Adam
Irvine, Elizabeth 37; Ontario, 1861 ***2896.27*** *p23*
Irvine, George 6; Ontario, 1861 ***2896.27*** *p23*
Irvine, Gerrard 40; Ontario, 1871 ***1823.15*** *p124*
Irvine, James; Savannah, Georgia, 1775 ***1640.10*** *p85*
Irvine, James 35; Ontario, 1871 ***1823.15*** *p124*
Irvine, Joanna 3; Ontario, 1861 ***2896.27*** *p23*
Irvine, John; Georgia, 1771 ***1640.10*** *p86*
Irvine, John; Savannah, Georgia, 1774 ***1640.10*** *p86*
Irvine, John; Savannah, Georgia, 1808 ***1640.10*** *p86*
Irvine, John 9; Ontario, 1861 ***2896.27*** *p23*
Irvine, John 35; Ontario, 1861 ***2896.27*** *p20*
Irvine, John 38; Ontario, 1871 ***1823.15*** *p124*
Irvine, John 45; Ontario, 1871 ***1823.15*** *p124*
Irvine, John 90; Ontario, 1871 ***1823.15*** *p124*
Irvine, Joseph 7; Ontario, 1861 ***2896.27*** *p23*
Irvine, Margaret; Georgia, 1775 ***1640.10*** *p154*
Irvine, Robert 44; Ontario, 1871 ***1823.15*** *p124*
Irvine, Thomas Washington; New York, 1825 ***8197.10*** *p243*
Irvine, Walter; Tobago, West Indies, 1825 ***1640.13*** *p61*
Irvine, William; New England, 1775-1781 ***4628.40*** *p68*
Irvine, William 44; Ontario, 1871 ***1823.22*** *p80*
Irvine, William 62; Ontario, 1871 ***1823.28*** *p48*
Irving, David; Portland, Maine, 1858 ***9196.15*** *p30*
Irving, John; Bahamas, 1840 ***1640.13*** *p61*
Irving, William 72; Ontario, 1871 ***1823.15*** *p124*
Irwin, Mr.; Quebec, 1858 ***9196.15*** *p31*
Irwin, Archibald 46; Ontario, 1871 ***1823.28*** *p48*
Irwin, Catherine *SEE* Irwin, Jane
Irwin, David 60; Ontario, 1871 ***1823.15*** *p124*
Irwin, Elisabeth 52; Ontario, 1871 ***1823.15*** *p124*
Irwin, Elizabeth 36; Vermont, 1848 ***5900.10*** *p471*
Irwin, Henry 30; Ontario, 1861 ***2896.27*** *p17*
Irwin, James 22; Antigua (Antego), 1773-1774 ***1220.25*** *p32*
Irwin, James 34; Ontario, 1871 ***1823.28*** *p48*
Irwin, James 39; Ontario, 1871 ***1823.15*** *p124*
Irwin, Jane; Alabama, 1833 ***1640.10*** *p86*
Daughter: Margaret
Daughter: Catherine
Irwin, Jaret; Pennsylvania, 1847 ***6058.10*** *p20*
Irwin, John 47; Ontario, 1871 ***1823.15*** *p124*
Irwin, John 60; Ontario, 1871 ***1823.15*** *p124*
Irwin, John 82; Ontario, 1871 ***1823.15*** *p124*
Irwin, Margaret *SEE* Irwin, Jane
Irwin, Mary 12; Ontario, 1861 ***2896.27*** *p17*
Irwin, Mary 92; Vermont, 1880 ***5900.10*** *p471*
Irwin, Matthew; Pennsylvania, 1777 ***4629.10*** *p9*
Irwin, Richard; New York, 1807 ***8197.10*** *p41*
Irwin, Richard 32; Ontario, 1871 ***1823.28*** *p48*
Irwin, Richard 50; Ontario, 1871 ***1823.15*** *p124*
Irwin, Thomas; Georgia, 1762 ***1640.10*** *p86*
Irwin, Thomas 41; Ontario, 1871 ***1823.15*** *p124*
Irwin, Thomas 49; Ontario, 1871 ***1823.28*** *p48*
Irwin, W. Francis 50; Ontario, 1871 ***1823.15*** *p124*
Irwin, William; Alabama, 1837-1845 ***1640.10*** *p86*
Irwin, William; New York, 1803 ***8197.10*** *p13*
Irwin, William; Savannah, Georgia, 1765 ***1640.10*** *p86*
Irwin, William 29; Ontario, 1871 ***1823.28*** *p48*
Irwin, William 52; Ontario, 1871 ***1823.15*** *p124*
Irwin, William 58; Ontario, 1871 ***1823.15*** *p124*
Irwin, William 70; Ontario, 1871 ***1823.15*** *p124*
Irwin, William 75; Vermont, 1876 ***5900.10*** *p471*
Irwine, Arthur 60; Ontario, 1871 ***1823.28*** *p48*
Irwine, Christ.; Pennsylvania, 1779 ***4629.10*** *p38*
Irwine, James 37; Ontario, 1871 ***1823.22*** *p80*
Irwine, James 60; Ontario, 1871 ***1823.15*** *p124*
Irwine, Thomas; Pennsylvania, 1779 ***4629.10*** *p38*
Isaac, Alexander; Georgia, 1698 ***1640.13*** *p61*
Isaac, Caroline 5; Ontario, 1861 ***2896.26*** *p17*
Isaac, Elizabeth 11; Ontario, 1861 ***2896.26*** *p17*
Isaac, George 60; Ontario, 1871 ***1823.22*** *p80*
Isaac, Grace 41; Ontario, 1861 ***2896.26*** *p17*
Isaac, Henry 25; Ontario, 1871 ***1823.15*** *p124*
Isaac, Henry 48; Ontario, 1871 ***1823.22*** *p80*
Isaac, James; New York, 1827 ***8197.10*** *p243*
Isaac, James; New York, 1830 ***8197.10*** *p66*
Isaac, John W. 9; Ontario, 1861 ***2896.26*** *p17*
Isaac, Joseph 19; Virginia, 1773 ***1220.25*** *p30*
Isaac, Mary A. 14; Ontario, 1861 ***2896.26*** *p17*
Isaac, Orinda 2; Ontario, 1861 ***2896.26*** *p17*
Isaac, Robert; Savannah, Georgia, 1801 ***1640.10*** *p86*
Isaac, Salina 12; Ontario, 1861 ***2896.26*** *p17*
Isaac, Samuel 51; Ontario, 1871 ***1823.15*** *p124*
Isaac, Simon; New York, 1840 ***8197.10*** *p176*
Isaac, Thomas 63; Ontario, 1871 ***1823.15*** *p124*
Isaac, William 22; Grenada, 1776 ***1220.25*** *p129*
Isaac, William 43; Ontario, 1861 ***2896.26*** *p17*
Isaac, William, Sr. 84; Ontario, 1871 ***1823.22*** *p80*
Isaac, William, Jr. 58; Ontario, 1871 ***1823.22*** *p80*
Isaacs, Miss; Quebec, 1857 ***9196.15*** *p21*
Isaacs, Jonas; New York, 1839 ***8197.10*** *p133*
Isaacs, Moses; New York, 1840 ***8197.10*** *p243*
Isaacs, Samuel 21; Baltimore, 1775 ***1220.25*** *p118*
Isaacs, William 53; Ontario, 1871 ***1823.22*** *p80*
Isabel, Isabel Ines 10; Ontario, 1871 ***1823.15*** *p124*
Isafford, Samuel 36; Ontario, 1871 ***1823.15*** *p124*
Isarvey, William 40; Ontario, 1871 ***1823.15*** *p124*
Isbister, Hugh; Savannah, Georgia, 1775 ***1640.10*** *p86*
Isbister, Thomas 26; Ontario, 1871 ***1823.15*** *p124*

J

Jabas, Abraham Lewis; New York, 1837 ***8197.10*** *p92*
Jabas, George William; New York, 1837 ***8197.10*** *p92*
Jablonski, Julia; Maryland, 1910 ***3259.35*** *p21*
Jablonsky, John; Maryland, 1910 ***3259.35*** *p21*
Jabloski, Jacob; Maryland, 1910 ***3259.35*** *p21*
Jabson, Elinor; Maryland, 1675 ***2524.55*** *p120*
Jachelski, Felix; Maryland, 1910 ***3259.35*** *p21*
Jachimsen, Louis; New York, 1832 ***8197.10*** *p244*
Jachowski, Joseph F.; Maryland, 1910 ***3259.35*** *p21*
Jachowski, Julian B.; Maryland, 1910 ***3259.35*** *p21*
Jack, Adam; America, 1752 ***2856.30*** *p208*
With wife & son
Jack, Francis; Pennsylvania, 1787 ***4629.10*** *p51*
Jack, James 48; Ontario, 1871 ***1823.28*** *p48*
Jack, John; Pennsylvania, 1777 ***4629.10*** *p31*
Jack, John W. 60; Ontario, 1871 ***1823.28*** *p48*
Jack, Margarete; Port uncertain, 1786 ***2856.30*** *p200*
Jack, Mary; Montreal, 1890 ***1640.13*** *p62*
Jackall, W.; Quebec, 1856 ***9196.15*** *p10*
Jackawitz, Katarsyna; Maryland, 1910 ***3259.35*** *p21*
Jacke, Michael; Port uncertain, 1751 ***2856.30*** *p200*
Jackes, Lancelott; Virginia, 1679-1680 ***6212.30*** *p54*
Jackhelski, Joseph; Maryland, 1910 ***3259.35*** *p21*
Jackiewicz, Jacob; Maryland, 1910 ***3259.35*** *p21*
Jacklin, Robinson 52; Ontario, 1871 ***1823.28*** *p48*
Jacklin, Thomas; Port uncertain, 1744 ***2856.30*** *p208*
Jackman, Barbara 69; Ontario, 1871 ***1823.15*** *p125*
Jackman, Joseph John; Virginia, 1714 ***1224.2*** *p61*
Jackman, Moses 65; Ontario, 1871 ***1823.15*** *p125*
Jackner, Charles; Maryland, 1668 ***2524.55*** *p120*
Jackowiak, Valentine; Maryland, 1910 ***3259.35*** *p21*
Jackowitz, Michael; Maryland, 1910 ***3259.35*** *p21*
Jackowski, Maryana; Maryland, 1910 ***3259.35*** *p21*
Jackowsky, Vicenty; Maryland, 1910 ***3259.35*** *p21*
Jacks, James 19; Maryland, 1774 ***1220.25*** *p57*
Jackson, Mr.; Quebec, 1857 ***9196.15*** *p13*
Jackson, Mr.; Quebec, 1857 ***9196.15*** *p26*
Jackson, Mr.; Quebec, 1858 ***9196.15*** *p46*
Jackson, A. 35; Ontario, 1861 ***2896.28*** *p1*
Jackson, A. H. W.; Vermont, 1816-1889 ***5900.10*** *p376*
Jackson, Alberta Jane 4; Ontario, 1861 ***2896.27*** *p35*
Jackson, Alexander 60; Ontario, 1871 ***1823.15*** *p125*
Jackson, Alva 20; Ontario, 1861 ***2896.27*** *p33*
Jackson, Andrew; Charleston, South Carolina, 1765 ***4628.40*** *p98*
With wife & 2 sons
Jackson, Angeline 37; Ontario, 1861 ***2896.27*** *p41*
Jackson, Ann; Maryland, 1651 ***2524.55*** *p218*
Jackson, Anne E. 11; Ontario, 1861 ***2896.27*** *p41*
Jackson, Archibald 43; Ontario, 1871 ***1823.15*** *p125*
Jackson, Arthur; Virginia, 1712 ***1224.2*** *p61*
Jackson, Benjamin 40; Nova Scotia, 1774 ***1220.25*** *p136*
With wife & 3 sons
Jackson, Bridget Owens; Vermont, 1850-1928 ***5900.10*** *p442*
Jackson, Caroline 7; Ontario, 1861 ***2896.27*** *p41*
Jackson, Catherine 22; Ontario, 1861 ***2896.27*** *p33*
Jackson, Charles 40; Ontario, 1871 ***1823.28*** *p48*
Jackson, Charlotte 8; Ontario, 1861 ***2896.25*** *p5*
Jackson, David; Pennsylvania, 1777 ***4629.10*** *p7*
Jackson, David 29; Ontario, 1871 ***1823.15*** *p125*
Jackson, David 35; Ontario, 1871 ***1823.28*** *p48*
Jackson, E. 20; Ontario, 1861 ***2896.28*** *p8*
Jackson, Miss E.; Quebec, 1858 ***9196.15*** *p43*
Jackson, Edgar 19; Ontario, 1861 ***2896.27*** *p33*
Jackson, Edward; Boston, 1763 ***1224.2*** *p61*
Jackson, Edward; Maryland, 1659 ***2524.55*** *p120*
Jackson, Edward; New England, 1668 ***1224.1*** *p41*
Jackson, Edward; Quebec, 1856 ***9196.15*** *p10*
Jackson, Edward 15; Georgia, 1775 ***1220.25*** *p124*
Jackson, Edward 22; Philadelphia, 1775 ***1220.25*** *p10*
Jackson, Elgin 6; Ontario, 1861 ***2896.27*** *p33*
Jackson, Eliza; Virginia, 1663 ***6212.30*** *p4*
Jackson, Elizabeth; Maryland, 1682 ***2524.55*** *p120*
Jackson, Elizabeth 60; Ontario, 1861 ***2896.27*** *p33*
Jackson, Elizabeth J. 10; Ontario, 1861 ***2896.25*** *p24*
Jackson, Ellen 83; Ontario, 1871 ***1823.15*** *p125*
Jackson, Ellen 83; Ontario, 1871 ***1823.22*** *p80*
Jackson, Ellinor; Virginia, 1663 ***6212.30*** *p3*
Jackson, Emily J. 9; Ontario, 1861 ***2896.27*** *p41*
Jackson, Emma A. 3; Ontario, 1861 ***2896.27*** *p34*
Jackson, Erastus 11; Ontario, 1861 ***2896.27*** *p35*
Jackson, Francis; Maryland, 1662 ***2524.55*** *p120*
Jackson, Francis Blower; New York, 1833 ***8197.10*** *p244*
Jackson, Fred 26; British Columbia, 1914 ***9196.1*** *p66*
Jackson, Fred 26; San Francisco, 1914 ***9196.1*** *p66*
Jackson, G. 25; Ontario, 1861 ***2896.28*** *p8*
Jackson, George; Charleston, South Carolina, 1866 ***1640.13*** *p62*
Jackson, George; Pennsylvania, 1777 ***4629.10*** *p11*
Jackson, George 38; Ontario, 1871 ***1823.15*** *p125*
Jackson, George 41; Ontario, 1861 ***2896.25*** *p24*
Jackson, George 45; Ontario, 1871 ***1823.22*** *p80*
Jackson, George Knowil; Boston, 1824 ***1224.3*** *p41*
Jackson, George T. 12; Ontario, 1861 ***2896.25*** *p24*
Jackson, Harriet 31; Ontario, 1861 ***2896.27*** *p34*
Jackson, Harry; Philadelphia, 1797 ***1224.2*** *p61*
Jackson, Heman; Vermont, 1838-1923 ***5900.10*** *p442*
Jackson, Henrey 26; Ontario, 1871 ***1823.28*** *p48*
Jackson, Henry; New York, 1837 ***8197.10*** *p92*
Jackson, Henry 28; Ontario, 1871 ***1823.28*** *p48*
Jackson, Henry 35; Ontario, 1861 ***2896.25*** *p5*
Jackson, Henry 35; Ontario, 1871 ***1823.15*** *p125*
Jackson, Henry 47; Ontario, 1871 ***1823.22*** *p80*
Jackson, Hial 14; Ontario, 1861 ***2896.27*** *p41*
Jackson, Hugh 30; Ontario, 1871 ***1823.28*** *p48*
Jackson, Ida M. 2; Ontario, 1861 ***2896.27*** *p35*
Jackson, Irvin 21; Ontario, 1871 ***1823.15*** *p125*
Jackson, Isaac; Jamaica, 1856 ***1640.13*** *p62*
Jackson, Isaac; Pennsylvania, 1863 ***6058.10*** *p48*
Jackson, Isaac 40; Ontario, 1871 ***1823.15*** *p125*
Jackson, Isabella 25; Virginia, 1774 ***1220.25*** *p23*
Jackson, J. 22; Ontario, 1861 ***2896.28*** *p9*
Jackson, Jacob 30; Ontario, 1871 ***1823.15*** *p125*
Jackson, Jacob S. 15; Ontario, 1861 ***2896.27*** *p33*
Jackson, James; Georgia, 1699 ***1640.13*** *p62*
Jackson, James; New York, 1797 ***8197.10*** *p8*
Jackson, James; New York, 1840 ***8197.10*** *p175*
Jackson, James; New York, 1840 ***8197.10*** *p321*
Jackson, James; New York, 1840 ***8197.10*** *p386*
Jackson, James 19; Maryland, 1775 ***1220.25*** *p112*
Jackson, James 26; Ontario, 1871 ***1823.28*** *p48*
Jackson, James 38; Ontario, 1861 ***2896.25*** *p52*
Jackson, Jane; Boston, 1824 ***1224.3*** *p41*
Jackson, Jane 22; Ontario, 1861 ***2896.27*** *p34*
Jackson, Jane 34; Ontario, 1871 ***1823.28*** *p48*
Jackson, Jas H. 55; Ontario, 1871 ***1823.28*** *p48*
Jackson, John; Boston, 1783 ***1224.2*** *p61*
Jackson, John; Maryland, 1673 ***2524.55*** *p120*
Jackson, John; Minnesota, 1885 ***1640.13*** *p62*
Jackson, John; New York, 1806 ***8197.10*** *p31*
Jackson, John; New York, 1807 ***8197.10*** *p41*
Jackson, John; New York, 1823 ***8197.10*** *p244*
Jackson, John; Pennsylvania, 1777 ***4629.10*** *p11*
Jackson, John 29; Maryland, 1775 ***1220.25*** *p105*
Jackson, John 32; Philadelphia, 1774 ***1220.25*** *p67*
Jackson, John 36; Ontario, 1871 ***1823.28*** *p48*
Jackson, John 37; Ontario, 1871 ***1823.28*** *p48*
Jackson, John 43; Ontario, 1871 ***1823.15*** *p125*
Jackson, John 44; Ontario, 1871 ***1823.28*** *p48*
Jackson, John 48; Ontario, 1871 ***1823.15*** *p125*
Jackson, John 51; Ontario, 1871 ***1823.15*** *p125*
Jackson, John 70; Ontario, 1871 ***1823.15*** *p125*
Jackson, John, Sr.; New York, 1834 ***8197.10*** *p73*
Jackson, John A.; New York, 1824 ***8197.10*** *p244*
Jackson, Joseph 35; Ontario, 1871 ***1823.15*** *p125*
Jackson, Joseph Condon; New York, 1840 ***8197.10*** *p175*
Jackson, Julia; Vermont, 1839-1910 ***5900.10*** *p46*
Jackson, M. E. 1; Ontario, 1861 ***2896.28*** *p8*
Jackson, Margaret 48; Ontario, 1871 ***1823.28*** *p48*
Jackson, Margarett; Maryland, 1657 ***2524.55*** *p120*
Jackson, Maria L. McGowan; Vermont, 1827-1908 ***5900.10*** *p376*
Jackson, Mary; Boston, 1646 ***1224.1*** *p32*
Jackson, Mary C. 8; Ontario, 1861 ***2896.25*** *p24*
Jackson, Michael 39; Maryland, 1775 ***1220.25*** *p102*
Jackson, Michael 65; Ontario, 1871 ***1823.22*** *p80*
Jackson, Nicholas; Maryland, 1657 ***2524.55*** *p120*
Jackson, Norman 30; Ontario, 1871 ***1823.22*** *p80*
Jackson, Peter; Savannah, Georgia, 1809 ***1640.10*** *p86*
Jackson, Phoebe 2; Ontario, 1861 ***2896.27*** *p33*
Jackson, Rebecca 23; Ontario, 1861 ***2896.27*** *p35*
Jackson, Richard; Maryland, 1659 ***2524.55*** *p120*
Jackson, Richard; Maryland, 1673 ***2524.55*** *p120*
Jackson, Richard; Maryland, 1674 ***2524.55*** *p120*
Jackson, Robert; New York, 1829-1834 ***8197.10*** *p308*
Jackson, Robert 37; Ontario, 1871 ***1823.28*** *p48*
Jackson, Robert 39; Nova Scotia, 1774 ***1220.25*** *p135*
With wife & 3 children
Jackson, Robert 48; Nova Scotia, 1774 ***1220.25*** *p135*
With wife & 3 children
Jackson, Robert 49; Ontario, 1871 ***1823.28*** *p48*
Jackson, Robert 57; Ontario, 1861 ***2896.25*** *p24*
Jackson, Sam.; Maryland, 1661 ***2524.55*** *p51*
Jackson, Samuel; New England, 1693 ***1224.1*** *p32*
Jackson, Samuel; New York, 1825-1834 ***8197.10*** *p308*
Jackson, Samuel; New York, 1839 ***8197.10*** *p133*
Jackson, Samuel; Pennsylvania, 1779 ***4629.10*** *p40*
Jackson, Samuel 29; Ontario, 1871 ***1823.15*** *p125*
Jackson, Samuell; Maryland, 1663 ***2524.55*** *p51*
Jackson, Sarah 28; Maryland, 1775 ***1220.25*** *p105*
Jackson, Sarah A. 7; Ontario, 1861 ***2896.27*** *p34*
Jackson, Sarah A. 13; Ontario, 1861 ***2896.27*** *p35*
Jackson, Sarah Jane 13; Ontario, 1861 ***2896.28*** *p24*
Jackson, Sarah M. 5; Ontario, 1861 ***2896.27*** *p41*
Jackson, Stephen; Maryland, 1775 ***1220.25*** *p113*
Jackson, Stephen 22; Ontario, 1861 ***2896.27*** *p33*
Jackson, Susan 27; Ontario, 1861 ***2896.27*** *p34*
Jackson, Susanna 11; Quebec, 1775 ***1220.25*** *p106*
Jackson, Theodore; Boston, 1824 ***1224.3*** *p41*
Jackson, Thomas 21; Maryland, 1774 ***1220.25*** *p78*
Jackson, Thomas 23; Maryland, 1775 ***1220.25*** *p100*
Jackson, Thomas 26; Philadelphia, 1774 ***1220.25*** *p69*
Jackson, Thomas 32; Ontario, 1871 ***1823.15*** *p125*
Jackson, Thomas 35; Ontario, 1871 ***1823.15*** *p125*
Jackson, Thomas 36; Ontario, 1871 ***1823.15*** *p125*
Jackson, Thomas 38; Ontario, 1871 ***1823.15*** *p125*
Jackson, Thomas 48; Philadelphia, 1774 ***1220.25*** *p66*
Jackson, Thomas 73; Ontario, 1871 ***1823.15*** *p125*
Jackson, Thos 42; Ontario, 1871 ***1823.28*** *p48*
Jackson, W. H. 8; Ontario, 1861 ***2896.28*** *p8*
Jackson, Willet 70; Ontario, 1861 ***2896.27*** *p33*
Jackson, William; Maryland, 1660 ***2524.55*** *p120*
Jackson, William; New York, 1807 ***8197.10*** *p41*

Jackson, William; Pennsylvania, 1841 ***1224.3*** *p41*
Jackson, William 16; Georgia, 1775 ***1220.25*** *p126*
Jackson, William 24; Maryland, 1775 ***1220.25*** *p114*
Jackson, William 30; Virginia, 1774 ***1220.25*** *p90*
Jackson, William 34; Ontario, 1871 ***1823.15*** *p125*
Jackson, William 40; Ontario, 1871 ***1823.28*** *p48*
Jackson, William 57; Ontario, 1871 ***1823.15*** *p125*
Jackson, William 79; Ontario, 1871 ***1823.22*** *p81*
Jackson, William B. 1; Ontario, 1861 ***2896.27*** *p34*
Jackson, Xpter; Virginia, 1672 ***6212.30*** *p50*
Jackston, John; Pennsylvania, 1777 ***4629.10*** *p18*
Jackyna, Anna Elisabeth; Port uncertain, 1749 ***2856.30*** *p200*
Jaclard, Sebastian; New York, 1834-1838 ***8197.10*** *p120*
Jaclard, Sebastien; New York, 1834 ***8197.10*** *p244*
Jaclson, David; New York, 1792-1840 ***8197.10*** *p344*
Jacob, Anna Wall; New England, 1673 ***1224.1*** *p60*
Jacob, Anton; Port uncertain, 1782 ***2856.30*** *p200*
Jacob, Augustus; New York, 1838 ***8197.10*** *p244*
Jacob, Frederick; New York, 1839 ***8197.10*** *p244*
Jacob, G. A.; America, 1764 ***2856.30*** *p146*
Jacob, Gabriell; Virginia, 1671-1672 ***6212.30*** *p46*
Jacob, Georg; Port uncertain, 1749 ***2856.30*** *p200*
Jacob, Georg Abraham; America, 1764 ***2856.30*** *p200*
With wife & 4 children
Jacob, Hans Jakob; America, 1738 ***2856.30*** *p200*
Jacob, Johann Adam; Port uncertain, 1764 ***2856.30*** *p200*
With son & 2 daughters
Jacob, Johann Georg; Port uncertain, 1756 ***2856.30*** *p200*
Jacob, John; New York, 1838 ***8197.10*** *p244*
Jacob, John; Pennsylvania, 1777 ***4629.10*** *p13*
Jacob, John; Virginia, 1666 ***6212.30*** *p32*
Jacob, Maria Elisabeth; Port uncertain, 1752 ***2856.30*** *p200*
Jacob, Marx; Port uncertain, 1739 ***2856.30*** *p200*
Jacob, Michael; New York, 1837 ***8197.10*** *p244*
Jacob, Philipp; America, 1738 ***2856.30*** *p200*
Jacob, Richard; Maryland, 1655-1656 ***2524.55*** *p120*
Jacob, Samuel 20; Maryland, 1774 ***1220.25*** *p52*
Jacob, Tobias; Pennsylvania, 1785 ***4629.10*** *p44*
Jacob, William; Virginia, 1682 ***1224.1*** *p32*
Jacobi, Adam; America, 1750 ***2856.30*** *p200*
Jacobi, Adam; America, 1751 ***2856.30*** *p200*
Jacobi, Adam; Port uncertain, 1773 ***2856.30*** *p200*
Jacobi, Anna Catharina; Port uncertain, 1773 ***2856.30*** *p200*
Jacobi, Anna Maria; Port uncertain, 1733 ***2856.30*** *p200*
Jacobi, Anna Maria; Port uncertain, 1762 ***2856.30*** *p200*
Jacobi, Catharina; Port uncertain, 1765 ***2856.30*** *p200*
Jacobi, Elisabeth; Port uncertain, 1734 ***2856.30*** *p200*
Jacobi, Jakob; America, 1750 ***2856.30*** *p200*
Jacobi, Jakob; Port uncertain, 1750 ***2856.30*** *p200*
With wife & 3 children
Jacobi, Johann Adam; America, 1751 ***2856.30*** *p200*
Jacobi, Johann Michael; Port uncertain, 1752 ***2856.30*** *p200*
Jacobi, Johann Nickel; Port uncertain, 1766 ***2856.30*** *p200*
Jacobi, Jost; America, 1750 ***2856.30*** *p200*
With wife & 7 children
Jacobi, Jost; Port uncertain, 1748 ***2856.30*** *p200*
Jacobi, Konrad; Port uncertain, 1775 ***2856.30*** *p200*
Jacobi, Mathes; America, 1750 ***2856.30*** *p200*
Jacobi, Peter; America, 1750 ***2856.30*** *p200*
Jacobi, Sebastian; America, 1739 ***2856.30*** *p200*
With wife
Jacobi, Simon; Port uncertain, 1773 ***2856.30*** *p200*
Jacobin, Anna Elisabeth; America, 1753 ***2856.30*** *p201*
With 3 children
Jacobin, Anna Sophia; Port uncertain, 1773 ***2856.30*** *p200*
Jacobin, Maria Catharina; Port uncertain, 1777 ***2856.30*** *p200*
Jacobin, Maria Elisabeth; Port uncertain, 1784 ***2856.30*** *p201*
Jacobs, Angel; New York, 1824-1834 ***8197.10*** *p369*
Jacobs, Ann 67; Ontario, 1871 ***1823.15*** *p125*
Jacobs, Benjamin; New York, 1807 ***8197.10*** *p41*
Jacobs, Catharina; America, 1739 ***2856.30*** *p238*
Jacobs, Christoffer; New York, 1807 ***8197.10*** *p41*
Jacobs, Israel B.; New York, 1805 ***8197.10*** *p29*
Jacobs, Jacob; New York, 1838 ***8197.10*** *p244*
Jacobs, James 36; Ontario, 1871 ***1823.22*** *p81*
Jacobs, Johann Adam; Port uncertain, 1771 ***2856.30*** *p201*
Jacobs, John; New York, 1822 ***8197.10*** *p244*
Jacobs, John; New York, 1840 ***8197.10*** *p175*
Jacobs, John; Pennsylvania, 1785 ***4629.10*** *p44*
Jacobs, Joseph 25; Ontario, 1871 ***1823.15*** *p125*
Jacobs, Moses 22; Philadelphia, 1775 ***1220.25*** *p107*
Jacobs, Samuel; New York, 1807 ***8197.10*** *p41*
Jacobs, Thomas 25; Maryland, 1774 ***1220.25*** *p73*
Jacobs, Thomas 46; Ontario, 1871 ***1823.22*** *p81*
Jacobs, William H.; New York, 1830 ***8197.10*** *p361*
Jacobson, Abm; Virginia, 1673 ***6212.30*** *p51*
Jacobson, Alicia *SEE* Jacobson, Peter
Jacobson, Anna *SEE* Jacobson, Peter
Jacobson, J. 30; Alaska, 1911 ***9196.1*** *p16*
Jacobson, J. 30; British Columbia, 1911 ***9196.1*** *p16*
Jacobson, John; Maryland, 1661 ***2524.55*** *p120*
Jacobson, Peter; Maryland, 1658 ***2524.55*** *p120*
Wife: Alicia
Son: Sifray
Daughter: Anna
Jacobson, Sifray *SEE* Jacobson, Peter
Jacobson, Swansea; Philadelphia, 1844 ***1224.3*** *p41*
Jacobus, Julius; New York, 1840 ***8197.10*** *p175*
Jacoby, John 40; Ontario, 1871 ***1823.15*** *p125*
Jacoby, William; Nicaragua, 1882 ***1640.13*** *p62*
Jacomella, Peter; New York, 1840 ***8197.10*** *p245*
Jacon, Christian; New York, 1839 ***8197.10*** *p244*
Jacorbson, Aaron; Maryland, 1666 ***2524.55*** *p120*
Jacosson, Aaron; Maryland, 1666 ***2524.55*** *p120*
Jacquard, Daniel; Port uncertain, 1785 ***2856.30*** *p201*
With wife
Jacque, William 25; Maryland, 1774 ***1220.25*** *p52*
Jacquelin, Francis 21; Maryland, 1774 ***1220.25*** *p62*
Jacquelin, John Michael; New York, 1823 ***8197.10*** *p63*
Jacques, Eleanor 28 *SEE* Jacques, Joseph
Jacques, Henry; Maryland, 1658 ***2524.55*** *p120*
Jacques, Joseph 28; Fort Cumberland, Nova Scotia, 1774 ***1220.25*** *p19*
Wife: Eleanor 28
Jacusfskie, Stonaslouce; Maryland, 1910 ***3259.35*** *p21*
Jaczebowski, Stanislaw; Maryland, 1910 ***3259.35*** *p21*
Jaczycky, Valentin; Maryland, 1910 ***3259.35*** *p21*
Jadworalski, Adam J.; Maryland, 1910 ***3259.35*** *p21*
Jaeger, Franz; Port uncertain, 1786 ***2856.30*** *p201*
With wife & children
Jaeger, Friedrich; Port uncertain, 1781 ***2856.30*** *p201*
Jaeger, Henrich; Port uncertain, 1774 ***2856.30*** *p201*
Jaffers, Hugh; New York, 1838 ***8197.10*** *p377*
Jaffins, S. Ila 48; Ontario, 1871 ***1823.15*** *p125*
Jaffords, Maurice; New York, 1830 ***8197.10*** *p313*
Jaffords, Michael; New York, 1830 ***8197.10*** *p313*
Jaffray, Alexander; Savannah, Georgia, 1810 ***1640.10*** *p87*
Jager, Andreas; Port uncertain, 1768 ***2856.30*** *p208*
Jager, Catharina; Port uncertain, 1724 ***2856.30*** *p208*
Jager, Georg; Port uncertain, 1786 ***2856.30*** *p208*
Jager, Hans Georg; Port uncertain, 1759 ***2856.30*** *p208*
Jager, Jacob; Port uncertain, 1772 ***2856.30*** *p208*
Jager, Jacob; Port uncertain, 1783 ***2856.30*** *p208*
Jager, Johann; Port uncertain, 1755 ***2856.30*** *p208*
Jager, Johann Christia; Port uncertain, 1759 ***2856.30*** *p208*
Jager, Johann Michael; Port uncertain, 1772 ***2856.30*** *p208*
Jager, Johann Nikolaus; Port uncertain, 1745 ***2856.30*** *p208*
Jager, Johann Philipp; Port uncertain, 1772 ***2856.30*** *p208*
Jager, Magdalena; Port uncertain, 1768 ***2856.30*** *p208*
Jager, Matthaus; Port uncertain, 1790 ***2856.30*** *p208*
Jager, Nikolaus; America, 1749 ***2856.30*** *p208*
Jager, Peter; New York, 1840 ***8197.10*** *p194*
Jager, Peter; Port uncertain, 1714 ***2856.30*** *p208*
Jager, Peter; Port uncertain, 1765 ***2856.30*** *p208*
Jagerin, Anna Barbara; Port uncertain, 1751 ***2856.30*** *p208*
Jagerin, Philippina; Port uncertain, 1734 ***2856.30*** *p208*
Jagler, Maria; Port uncertain, 1760 ***2856.30*** *p209*
Jago, John; Virginia, 1739 ***1224.2*** *p61*
Jagoda, Andrew; Maryland, 1910 ***3259.35*** *p21*
Jagodsinski, Jaikadeny; Maryland, 1910 ***3259.35*** *p21*
Jagodzinski, Joseph; Maryland, 1910 ***3259.35*** *p21*
Jagodzynsky, Michael; Maryland, 1910 ***3259.35*** *p21*
Jagschinski, Jicuy; Maryland, 1910 ***3259.35*** *p21*
Jahnecke, Frederick; New York, 1817 ***8197.10*** *p60*
Jahraus, Friedrich; Port uncertain, 1764 ***2856.30*** *p201*
Jahraus, Georg Adam; America, 1786 ***2856.30*** *p201*
Jahraus, Johann Georg; Port uncertain, 1764 ***2856.30*** *p201*
Jakes, Lancelot; Virginia, 1684-1685 ***6212.30*** *p57*
Jakes, William 51; Ontario, 1871 ***1823.22*** *p81*
Jakowski, John; Maryland, 1910 ***3259.35*** *p21*
Jakrygowski, Jacob; Maryland, 1910 ***3259.35*** *p21*
Jakubowski, John; Maryland, 1910 ***3259.35*** *p21*
Jakubowski, Joseph; Maryland, 1910 ***3259.35*** *p21*
Jaleski, Adam; Maryland, 1910 ***3259.35*** *p21*
Jalland, John; Baltimore, 1810 ***1224.3*** *p41*
Jaloskie, John; Maryland, 1910 ***3259.35*** *p21*
Jameison, Alexander 54; Ontario, 1871 ***1823.22*** *p81*
James, Miss; Quebec, 1857 ***9196.15*** *p20*
James, Mr.; Quebec, 1858 ***9196.15*** *p47*
James, Mrs.; Quebec, 1857 ***9196.15*** *p15*
James, Mrs.; Quebec, 1857 ***9196.15*** *p20*
James, A.; Quebec, 1857 ***9196.15*** *p20*
James, Ann *SEE* James, William
James, Ann 21; Maryland, 1774 ***1220.25*** *p61*
James, Anne; Maryland, 1682 ***2524.55*** *p120*
James, Anthony; New York, 1840 ***8197.10*** *p175*
James, B. W.; Pennsylvania, 1861 ***6058.10*** *p74*
James, Benjamin; Illinois, 1829 ***1224.3*** *p41*
James, Bonsall; Pennsylvania, 1786 ***4629.10*** *p49*
James, Catherine; Alabama, 1834-1845 ***1640.10*** *p87*
James, Charles; Maryland, 1661 ***2524.55*** *p120*
Brother: John
James, Daniel 22; Maryland, 1775 ***1220.25*** *p96*
James, David 17; Ontario, 1871 ***1823.22*** *p81*
James, Edward; Maryland, 1673 ***2524.55*** *p120*
James, Edward; Virginia, 1659 ***1224.1*** *p32*
James, Elisha; Virginia, 1706 ***1224.2*** *p61*
James, Eliza.; Virginia, 1663 ***6212.30*** *p2*
James, Eliza 65; Ontario, 1871 ***1823.28*** *p48*
James, Elizabeth; Georgia, 1734 ***1640.10*** *p87*
James, Elizabeth 23; Ontario, 1871 ***1823.22*** *p81*
James, Elizabeth 74; Ontario, 1871 ***1823.15*** *p125*
James, Ellinor; Maryland, 1669 ***2524.55*** *p120*
James, Evan 22; Maryland, 1775 ***1220.25*** *p99*
James, Francis; Maryland, 1910 ***3259.35*** *p21*
James, George; Pennsylvania, 1777 ***4629.10*** *p22*
James, George 18; Philadelphia, 1774 ***1220.25*** *p6*
James, Henrietta 18; Maryland, 1775 ***1220.25*** *p115*
James, Henry 40; Ontario, 1871 ***1823.28*** *p48*
James, Hugh 73; Ontario, 1871 ***1823.28*** *p48*
James, J. E.; Quebec, 1857 ***9196.15*** *p15*
James, Jacob; New York, 1807 ***8197.10*** *p326*
James, James; New York, 1823 ***8197.10*** *p244*
James, Jenkin; Maryland, 1669 ***2524.55*** *p120*
James, Joane; Maryland, 1675 ***2524.55*** *p86*
James, John *SEE* James, Charles
James, John *SEE* James, William
James, John; Maryland, 1668 ***2524.55*** *p120*
James, John; New York, 1807 ***8197.10*** *p41*
James, John; Virginia, 1663 ***6212.30*** *p1*
James, John; Virginia, 1668-1669 ***6212.30*** *p40*
James, John; Virginia, 1693-1694 ***6212.30*** *p60*
James, John 55; Ontario, 1871 ***1823.22*** *p81*
James, Joseph; Maryland, 1664 ***2524.55*** *p120*
James, Josiah; Pennsylvania, 1777 ***4629.10*** *p9*
James, Katharine; Maryland, 1681 ***2524.55*** *p120*
James, Levi 64; Ontario, 1871 ***1823.22*** *p81*
James, Margaret 30; Ontario, 1861 ***2896.27*** *p32*
James, Maude C. Casey; Vermont, 1890-1950 ***5900.10*** *p520*
James, Michael 65; Vermont, 1850 ***5900.10*** *p612*
James, Nathaniel 73; Ontario, 1871 ***1823.28*** *p48*
James, Norman; Portland, Maine, 1858 ***9196.15*** *p30*
James, Mrs. Norman; Portland, Maine, 1858 ***9196.15*** *p30*
James, Philip 33; Ontario, 1871 ***1823.15*** *p126*
James, Richard; Maryland, 1665 ***2524.55*** *p36*
James, Richard 38; Ontario, 1871 ***1823.15*** *p126*
James, Richard 66; Ontario, 1871 ***1823.28*** *p48*
James, Robert; Maryland, 1673 ***2524.55*** *p120*
James, Robert 16; Ontario, 1871 ***1823.15*** *p126*
James, Samuel 27; Ontario, 1871 ***1823.22*** *p81*
James, Sarah 21; Ontario, 1871 ***1823.22*** *p81*
James, Stephen 25; Ontario, 1871 ***1823.22*** *p81*
James, Theophilus; Maryland, 1658 ***2524.55*** *p121*
James, Thomas; Charles Town, South Carolina, 1759 ***1224.2*** *p61*
James, Thomas; Maryland, 1672 ***2524.55*** *p121*
James, Thomas 43; Alaska, 1911 ***9196.1*** *p12*
James, Thomas 43; British Columbia, 1911 ***9196.1*** *p12*
James, Thomas 43; Ontario, 1871 ***1823.15*** *p126*
James, Thomas 45; Ontario, 1871 ***1823.28*** *p48*
James, William; Maryland, 1650 ***2524.55*** *p121*
James, William; Maryland, 1658 ***2524.55*** *p121*
Wife: Ann
Son: John
James, William; Maryland, 1665 ***2524.55*** *p129*
James, William; New York, 1807 ***8197.10*** *p41*
James, William; New York, 1827 ***8197.10*** *p347*
James, William; Philadelphia, 1848 ***6058.10*** *p31*
James, William 46; Ontario, 1871 ***1823.15*** *p126*
Jamesom, William 27; Ontario, 1871 ***1823.28*** *p48*
Jameson, Alexander 32; Ontario, 1871 ***1823.15*** *p126*
Jameson, Allamd 48; Ontario, 1871 ***1823.28*** *p48*
Jameson, David C.; Pennsylvania, 1864 ***6058.10*** *p68*
Jameson, George 52; Ontario, 1871 ***1823.22*** *p81*
Jameson, James 21; Virginia, 1773 ***1220.25*** *p30*
Jameson, John 23; Virginia, 1775 ***1220.25*** *p95*
Jameson, Mary Ann 27; Ontario, 1861 ***2896.27*** *p36*
Jameson, Robert; New York, 1794 ***8197.10*** *p5*
Jameson, Robert 27; Ontario, 1861 ***2896.27*** *p36*
Jamieson, Alex 22; Ontario, 1871 ***1823.15*** *p126*
Jamieson, Alexander 50; Ontario, 1871 ***1823.15*** *p126*
Jamieson, Cassillis; New York, New York, 1836 ***6058.10*** *p20*
Jamieson, E. L. 42; Vermont, 1892 ***5900.10*** *p243*

Jamieson, James; Georgia, 1698 ***1640.13*** *p62*
Jamieson, James; New York, 1807 ***8197.10*** *p328*
Jamieson, James; Tobago, West Indies, 1783 ***1640.13*** *p62*
Jamieson, James 26; Ontario, 1871 ***1823.22*** *p81*
Jamieson, James Ferguson; Trinidad, 1868 ***1640.13*** *p62*
Jamieson, John; Montreal, 1848 ***1640.13*** *p62*
Jamieson, John; Savannah, Georgia, 1768 ***1640.10*** *p87*
Jamieson, John 30; Ontario, 1871 ***1823.15*** *p126*
Jamieson, John 38; Ontario, 1871 ***1823.22*** *p81*
Jamieson, John 57; Ontario, 1871 ***1823.28*** *p48*
Jamieson, Mary 50; Ontario, 1871 ***1823.22*** *p81*
Jamieson, Quintin; Pennsylvania, 1837 ***6058.10*** *p13*
Jamieson, Thomas 45; Ontario, 1871 ***1823.15*** *p126*
Jamieson, Thomas Henry; Buffalo, New York, 1891 ***1640.13*** *p62*
Jamieson, William; New York, 1834 ***8197.10*** *p359*
Jamieson, William 19; Ontario, 1871 ***1823.15*** *p126*
Jamieson, William 24; Ontario, 1871 ***1823.22*** *p81*
Jamieson, William 53; Ontario, 1871 ***1823.22*** *p81*
Jamieson, William 54; Ontario, 1871 ***1823.28*** *p48*
Jamison, Alexander 34; Ontario, 1871 ***1823.22*** *p81*
Jamison, And'w; Pennsylvania, 1784 ***4629.10*** *p44*
Jamison, Cassillis; New York, New York, 1836 ***6058.10*** *p20*
Jamison, David C.; Pennsylvania, 1864 ***6058.10*** *p68*
Jamison, Gilbert; New York, New York, 1838 ***6058.10*** *p44*
Jamison, James 28; Ontario, 1871 ***1823.15*** *p126*
Jamison, John; Pennsylvania, 1777 ***4629.10*** *p31*
Jamison, John; Pennsylvania, 1836 ***6058.10*** *p14*
Jamison, Marmaduke; Pennsylvania, 1778 ***4629.10*** *p32*
Jamison, Quintin; Pennsylvania, 1837 ***6058.10*** *p13*
Jamison, Robert; Pennsylvania, 1777 ***4629.10*** *p31*
Jamison, Robert 20; Ontario, 1871 ***1823.15*** *p126*
Jamison, Robert 31; Ontario, 1871 ***1823.15*** *p126*
Jamison, Thomas 62; Ontario, 1871 ***1823.15*** *p126*
Jamison, William 62; Ontario, 1871 ***1823.15*** *p126*
Janbick, Stefan; Maryland, 1910 ***3259.35*** *p21*
Jancock, Jno; Virginia, 1664 ***6212.30*** *p9*
Jancynski, Walter; Maryland, 1910 ***3259.35*** *p21*
Jand, Johann; Port uncertain, 1750 ***2856.30*** *p201*
Janes, Alice McCummings; Vermont, 1855-1911 ***5900.10*** *p518*
Janes, Cyrus 79; Vermont, 1889 ***5900.10*** *p556*
Janes, Elizabeth Ryan 64; Vermont, 1885 ***5900.10*** *p556*
Janes, Joane; Maryland, 1667 ***2524.55*** *p121*
Janes, Judson; Vermont, 1847-1908 ***5900.10*** *p518*
Janetzka, Matthais; Maryland, 1910 ***3259.35*** *p21*
Janetzka, William; Maryland, 1910 ***3259.35*** *p21*
Janicky, Pawel; Maryland, 1910 ***3259.35*** *p21*
Janis, Elizabeth 60; Ontario, 1871 ***1823.15*** *p126*
Janisinski, Maria; Maryland, 1910 ***3259.35*** *p21*
Janka, Anton; Maryland, 1910 ***3259.35*** *p21*
Janka, John; Maryland, 1910 ***3259.35*** *p22*
Janke, Fredrick; Ontario, 1871 ***1823.28*** *p48*
Jankewiak, James; Maryland, 1910 ***3259.35*** *p22*
Jankiewicz, Frank; Maryland, 1910 ***3259.35*** *p22*
Jankiewicz, Henry; Maryland, 1910 ***3259.35*** *p22*
Jankiewicz, Stanislaw; Maryland, 1910 ***3259.35*** *p22*
Jankoski, Annie; Maryland, 1910 ***3259.35*** *p22*
Jankowiak, Anthony; Maryland, 1910 ***3259.35*** *p22*
Jankowiak, John; Maryland, 1910 ***3259.35*** *p22*
Jankowski, Francis; Maryland, 1910 ***3259.35*** *p22*
Jankowski, Jakup; Maryland, 1910 ***3259.35*** *p22*
Jankowski, James; Maryland, 1910 ***3259.35*** *p22*
Jankowski, John; Maryland, 1910 ***3259.35*** *p22*
Jankowski, Joseph; Maryland, 1910 ***3259.35*** *p22*
Jankowski, Stanislaw; Maryland, 1910 ***3259.35*** *p22*
Jankowski, William; Maryland, 1910 ***3259.35*** *p22*
Janoka, Wroh; Maryland, 1910 ***3259.35*** *p22*
Janowiak, John; Maryland, 1910 ***3259.35*** *p22*
Janowiak, Sophia; Maryland, 1910 ***3259.35*** *p22*
Janowski, Andrew; Maryland, 1910 ***3259.35*** *p22*
Janowski, Kostenty; Maryland, 1910 ***3259.35*** *p22*
Janowski, Wojciech; Maryland, 1910 ***3259.35*** *p22*
Janowsky, Antonie; Maryland, 1910 ***3259.35*** *p22*
Jansen, A. 26; British Columbia, 1913 ***9196.1*** *p62*
Jansen, A. 26; Washington, 1913 ***9196.1*** *p62*
Jansin, Anna Gertrud; Port uncertain, 1723 ***2856.30*** *p201*
Janski, John; Maryland, 1910 ***3259.35*** *p22*
Janson, Franz; Port uncertain, 1766 ***2856.30*** *p201*
Janson, Johann Adam; Port uncertain, 1743 ***2856.30*** *p201*
Janson, Johann Georg; Port uncertain, 1764 ***2856.30*** *p201*
Janson, Peter; Georgia, 1698 ***1640.13*** *p62*
Janthe, Jakob; Port uncertain, 1741 ***2856.30*** *p202*
Jantowegeska, John; Maryland, 1910 ***3259.35*** *p22*
Jantz, Sebastian; Port uncertain, 1764 ***2856.30*** *p202*
January, Benjamin; Pennsylvania, 1777 ***4629.10*** *p7*
Janus, Anna; Maryland, 1910 ***3259.35*** *p22*
Januskowski, John; Maryland, 1910 ***3259.35*** *p22*
Januszuski, Annie; Maryland, 1910 ***3259.35*** *p22*
Januszuski, John; Maryland, 1910 ***3259.35*** *p22*
Janyska, Valentine; Maryland, 1910 ***3259.35*** *p22*
Janz, Georg; Port uncertain, 1765 ***2856.30*** *p202*
Janz, Johann; Port uncertain, 1765 ***2856.30*** *p202*
Japali, Charles; Maryland, 1910 ***3259.35*** *p22*
Japkowski, Joseph; Maryland, 1910 ***3259.35*** *p22*
Jaques, Mrs. Adam; America, 1754 ***2856.30*** *p202*
Jaques, Benjamin 45; Ontario, 1871 ***1823.22*** *p81*
Jaques, Christopher 59; Ontario, 1871 ***1823.22*** *p81*
Jaques, Clark 16; Ontario, 1861 ***2896.28*** *p38*
Jaques, Edmond; Maryland, 1640 ***2524.55*** *p121*
Jaques, Eliza 3; Ontario, 1861 ***2896.28*** *p38*
Jaques, Emily 16; Ontario, 1861 ***2896.26*** *p35*
Jaques, Eugenia 7; Ontario, 1861 ***2896.28*** *p38*
Jaques, Hanah 13; Ontario, 1861 ***2896.26*** *p35*
Jaques, James 58; Ontario, 1861 ***2896.28*** *p38*
Jaques, John 21; Ontario, 1861 ***2896.26*** *p35*
Jaques, John 26; Nova Scotia, 1774 ***1220.25*** *p135*
With wife & 3 children
Jaques, John 66; Ontario, 1871 ***1823.22*** *p81*
Jaques, Joseph 50; Ontario, 1871 ***1823.22*** *p81*
Jaques, Josephine 9; Ontario, 1861 ***2896.28*** *p38*
Jaques, William 13; Ontario, 1861 ***2896.28*** *p38*
Jaran, Charles; Maryland, 1910 ***3259.35*** *p22*
Jaras, Joseph; Maryland, 1910 ***3259.35*** *p22*
Jaras, Mareu; Maryland, 1910 ***3259.35*** *p22*
Jardine, John; Ontario, 1884 ***1640.13*** *p62*
Jardine, Robert S.; Virginia, 1815 ***1224.3*** *p41*
Jardly, Thomas; Maryland, 1660-1661 ***2524.55*** *p121*
Jardly, Thomas; Maryland, 1660-1661 ***2524.55*** *p247*
Jargeneson, John; Maryland, 1661 ***2524.55*** *p121*
Jarlinger, Christiana; Port uncertain, 1791 ***2856.30*** *p202*
Jarmain, Wm; Virginia, 1681-1682 ***6212.30*** *p56*
Jarockowicz, Mary; Maryland, 1910 ***3259.35*** *p22*
Jaronczyl, Tolafila; Maryland, 1910 ***3259.35*** *p22*
Jaroszewsky, Jacob; Maryland, 1910 ***3259.35*** *p22*
Jaroszynski, John; Maryland, 1910 ***3259.35*** *p22*
Jarowski, Ignady; Maryland, 1910 ***3259.35*** *p22*
Jarowski, John; Maryland, 1910 ***3259.35*** *p22*
Jarowsky, Stefan; Maryland, 1910 ***3259.35*** *p22*
Jarrard, Alexander 33; Ontario, 1871 ***1823.15*** *p126*
Jarratt, Joseph; New York, 1834 ***8197.10*** *p244*
Jarratt, Thomas 17; Ontario, 1861 ***2896.27*** *p29*
Jarratt, William 40; Nova Scotia, 1774 ***1220.25*** *p136*
Jarrett, Elizabeth 16; Maryland, 1775 ***1220.25*** *p97*
Jarrod, Mary 28; Maryland, 1775 ***1220.25*** *p115*
Jarrott, James 42; Ontario, 1871 ***1823.15*** *p126*
Jarshniski, Alexandar; Maryland, 1910 ***3259.35*** *p22*
Jarsinski, Henry; Maryland, 1910 ***3259.35*** *p22*
Jarvie, David; Georgia, 1734 ***1640.10*** *p87*
Jarvis, Miss; Quebec, 1858 ***9196.15*** *p46*
Jarvis, Mr.; Quebec, 1856 ***9196.15*** *p10*
Jarvis, Mr.; Quebec, 1857 ***9196.15*** *p14*
Jarvis, Edward; Rhode Island, 1722 ***1224.2*** *p61*
Jarvis, Edward; Virginia, 1665 ***6212.30*** *p19*
Jarvis, Emma 31; Ontario, 1871 ***1823.15*** *p126*
Jarvis, George 21; Virginia, 1775 ***1220.25*** *p110*
Jarvis, Harriet; Vermont, 1855-1908 ***5900.10*** *p339*
Jarvis, J. M.; Quebec, 1857 ***9196.15*** *p13*
Jarvis, Jno; Virginia, 1664 ***6212.30*** *p14*
Jarvis, John; Maryland, 1673 ***2524.55*** *p121*
Jarvis, John; Pennsylvania, 1777 ***4629.10*** *p15*
Jarvis, John 31; Ontario, 1871 ***1823.15*** *p126*
Jarvis, Mathew; New York, 1794 ***8197.10*** *p5*
Jarvis, T. H.; Quebec, 1858 ***9196.15*** *p40*
Jarvis, Thomas; Maryland, 1659 ***2524.55*** *p121*
Jarvis, Thomas; New York, 1838 ***8197.10*** *p120*
Jarvis, Thomas; Virginia, 1684 ***1224.1*** *p32*
Jarvis, Walter; New York, 1839 ***8197.10*** *p134*
Jarzynski, James; Maryland, 1910 ***3259.35*** *p22*
Jasanski, Peter; Maryland, 1910 ***3259.35*** *p22*
Jasauska, Matthais; Maryland, 1910 ***3259.35*** *p22*
Jasckoo, Ed; Virginia, 1683 ***6212.30*** *p56*
Jasienski, Sophia; Maryland, 1910 ***3259.35*** *p22*
Jasik, Joseph; Maryland, 1910 ***3259.35*** *p22*
Jasinski, Teokadia; Maryland, 1910 ***3259.35*** *p22*
Jasinski, Wladislaus; Maryland, 1910 ***3259.35*** *p23*
Jasinsky, John; Maryland, 1910 ***3259.35*** *p23*
Jaskolsky, Wincent; Maryland, 1910 ***3259.35*** *p23*
Jasomik, Wolenty; Maryland, 1910 ***3259.35*** *p23*
Jasonowski, Charles; Maryland, 1910 ***3259.35*** *p23*
Jasper, Jno; Virginia, 1674 ***6212.30*** *p52*
Jassenski, Joseph; Maryland, 1910 ***3259.35*** *p23*
Jaswmincska, Abbina; Maryland, 1910 ***3259.35*** *p23*
Jaszynoki, Wladystaw; Maryland, 1910 ***3259.35*** *p23*
Jaszynski, Mary; Maryland, 1910 ***3259.35*** *p23*
Jauch, Agathe; Port uncertain, 1702 ***2856.30*** *p202*
Jauch, Therese; Port uncertain, 1758 ***2856.30*** *p202*
Jauncey, James; New York, New York, n.d. ***1224.2*** *p61*
Jauncey, Mary; New York, New York, 1822 ***1224.3*** *p41*
Jauncey, William; New York, New York, 1829 ***1224.3*** *p41*
Jauter, Jacob; America, 1750 ***2856.30*** *p202*
With wife & 4 children
Javes, William 41; Baltimore, 1775 ***1220.25*** *p118*
Jawadny, Frank; Maryland, 1910 ***3259.35*** *p23*
Jawan, Jean Bte 39; Ontario, 1871 ***1823.28*** *p48*
Jawan, Pierre 40; Ontario, 1871 ***1823.28*** *p48*
Jawan, Therese 66; Ontario, 1871 ***1823.28*** *p48*
Jawananakwat, Jacques 62; Ontario, 1871 ***1823.28*** *p48*
Jawananakwat, Pierre 35; Ontario, 1871 ***1823.28*** *p48*
Jawanebin, Louis 57; Ontario, 1871 ***1823.28*** *p48*
Jawinsky, Peter; Maryland, 1910 ***3259.35*** *p23*
Jaworski, Joseph; Maryland, 1910 ***3259.35*** *p23*
Jaworski, Michael; Maryland, 1910 ***3259.35*** *p23*
Jaworsky, Frank; Maryland, 1910 ***3259.35*** *p23*
Jaworsky, George; Maryland, 1910 ***3259.35*** *p23*
Jaworsky, Henry J.; Maryland, 1910 ***3259.35*** *p23*
Jaworsky, Ignatz; Maryland, 1910 ***3259.35*** *p23*
Jaworsky, Leokady; Maryland, 1910 ***3259.35*** *p23*
Jaworsky, Michael; Maryland, 1910 ***3259.35*** *p23*
Jay, Edgar 36; Ontario, 1871 ***1823.28*** *p48*
Jay, Peter; New York, 1785 ***1224.2*** *p61*
Jazdowski, Jessie; Winnipeg, Manitoba, 1884 ***1640.13*** *p62*
Jazdzyk, Casmer; Maryland, 1910 ***3259.35*** *p23*
Jeames, Sarah; Maryland, 1680 ***2524.55*** *p121*
Jeane, John; Brunswick, North Carolina, 1752 ***1224.2*** *p61*
Jeannotat, Francis Xavier; New York, 1840 ***8197.10*** *p175*
Jeans, John; New York, 1839 ***8197.10*** *p133*
Jeay, John 45; Ontario, 1871 ***1823.28*** *p48*
Jeckel, Miss; America, 1741 ***2856.30*** *p497*
Jeckel, Johann Jakob; America, 1752 ***2856.30*** *p202*
Jeckel, Maria Sara; America, 1741 ***2856.30*** *p202*
With husband
Jeckell, John; New York, 1783 ***1224.2*** *p61*
Jeckh, Max; Port uncertain, 1740 ***2856.30*** *p202*
Jecques, Thomas 60; Ontario, 1871 ***1823.15*** *p126*
Jecton, Roger; Virginia, 1690-1691 ***6212.30*** *p59*
Jedmoralsky, Stanislaus; Maryland, 1910 ***3259.35*** *p23*
Jeehell, William 37; Ontario, 1871 ***1823.15*** *p126*
Jefcott, Daniell; Maryland, 1664 ***2524.55*** *p121*
Jeferds, Ephraim 40; Ontario, 1871 ***1823.15*** *p126*
Jeferson, Isabella 40; Ontario, 1871 ***1823.15*** *p126*
Jefert, John; New York, 1840 ***8197.10*** *p175*
Jefferies, John; New York, 1806 ***8197.10*** *p323*
Jefferies, John; North Carolina, 1777 ***1224.2*** *p61*
Jefferis, Richard; Virginia, 1664 ***6212.30*** *p10*
Jeffers, Mrs.; Quebec, 1858 ***9196.15*** *p44*
Jeffers, John 91; Vermont, 1910 ***5900.10*** *p503*
Jeffers, Margaret Mitchell 49; Vermont, 1868 ***5900.10*** *p503*
Jeffers, Patrick; New York, 1807 ***8197.10*** *p41*
Jeffers, William; New York, 1840 ***8197.10*** *p175*
Jeffers, William F.; New York, 1836 ***8197.10*** *p244*
Jefferson, Georgina; Chicago, 1892 ***1640.13*** *p62*
Jefferson, John *SEE* Jefferson, Richard
Jefferson, Margarett *SEE* Jefferson, Richard
Jefferson, Richard; Maryland, 1682 ***2524.55*** *p121*
Wife: Margarett
Son: John
Son: Thomas
Jefferson, Robert 24; Nova Scotia, 1774 ***1220.25*** *p136*
Jefferson, Robert 38; Philadelphia, 1774 ***1220.25*** *p63*
Jefferson, Susanna 36; Ontario, 1871 ***1823.15*** *p126*
Jefferson, Thomas *SEE* Jefferson, Richard
Jeffery, James 21; Philadelphia, 1774 ***1220.25*** *p67*
Jeffery, John; New York, 1818 ***8197.10*** *p243*
Jeffery, John 86; Ontario, 1871 ***1823.15*** *p126*
Jeffery, Richard 42; Ontario, 1871 ***1823.28*** *p48*
Jeffery, Sarah; Virginia, 1671-1672 ***6212.30*** *p46*
Jeffery, William 61; Ontario, 1871 ***1823.15*** *p126*
Jefferyes, Ellinor; Maryland, 1667 ***2524.55*** *p121*
Jefferyes, Richard; Virginia, 1671-1672 ***6212.30*** *p46*
Jefferys, Elizabeth; Maryland, 1667 ***2524.55*** *p174*
Jefferys, Ellinor; Maryland, 1667 ***2524.55*** *p174*
Jefferys, Michael; New York, 1821 ***8197.10*** *p243*
Jefferys, Nicholas; New York, 1807 ***8197.10*** *p41*
Jefferys, Samuel; Pennsylvania, 1777 ***4629.10*** *p23*
Jefferys, Samuel; Pennsylvania, 1779 ***4629.10*** *p40*
Jefferys, William; Virginia, 1715 ***1224.2*** *p61*
Jefferys, William 15; Philadelphia, 1774 ***1220.25*** *p42*
Jeffrey, Master; Quebec, 1857 ***9196.15*** *p17*
Jeffrey, Mr.; Quebec, 1858 ***9196.15*** *p38*
Jeffrey, A.; Quebec, 1856 ***9196.15*** *p7*
Jeffrey, H.; Quebec, 1856 ***9196.15*** *p7*
Jeffrey, Joseph; New York, 1779 ***1224.2*** *p61*
Jeffrey, Joseph 23; Ontario, 1871 ***1823.28*** *p48*
Jeffrey, Samuel 26; Ontario, 1871 ***1823.28*** *p48*
Jeffrey, Samuel 48; Ontario, 1871 ***1823.28*** *p48*
Jeffreys, Herbert; Virginia, 1679 ***1224.1*** *p32*
Jeffreys, James; Pennsylvania, 1777 ***4629.10*** *p28*
Jeffreys, Peter; Maryland, 1733 ***1224.2*** *p61*

Jock, Johann Martin; Port uncertain, 1754 ***2856.30*** *p203*
Jock, Martin; Port uncertain, 1737 ***2856.30*** *p209*
Jockel, Johann; Port uncertain, 1756 ***2856.30*** *p203*
Jockin, Elisabeth; America, 1753 ***2856.30*** *p203*
Jockin, Elisabeth; America, 1769 ***2856.30*** *p203*
Joddrell, William; Virginia, 1692 ***1224.1*** *p33*
Joessen, Adam; Port uncertain, 1774 ***2856.30*** *p203*
  With wife
Joest, Adam; Port uncertain, 1774 ***2856.30*** *p203*
  With wife
Johann, Elisabeth; Port uncertain, 1741 ***2856.30*** *p203*
  With husband
Johann, Nicolaus; Port uncertain, 1754 ***2856.30*** *p203*
Johanson, Osan 25; Whitehorse, Yukon, 1917 ***9196.1*** *p52*
Johes, Edward; Maryland, 1675 ***2524.55*** *p122*
Johes, John 34; Ontario, 1871 ***1823.28*** *p49*
John, David; New York, 1807 ***8197.10*** *p41*
John, Margarett; Maryland, 1668 ***2524.55*** *p122*
John, New; Virginia, 1671 ***6212.30*** *p43*
John, Thomas; Maryland, 1682 ***2524.55*** *p126*
John, Tom 35; Alaska, 1914 ***9196.1*** *p24*
Johnas, Annie; Maryland, 1910 ***3259.35*** *p23*
Johnes, Hugh 24; Ontario, 1871 ***1823.28*** *p49*
Johns, Mr.; Quebec, 1858 ***9196.15*** *p31*
Johns, Anne; Maryland, 1681 ***2524.55*** *p122*
Johns, Charles 29; Ontario, 1871 ***1823.22*** *p82*
Johns, Charles 56; Ontario, 1871 ***1823.22*** *p82*
Johns, David 78; Ontario, 1871 ***1823.15*** *p127*
Johns, Elizabeth 23; Ontario, 1871 ***1823.15*** *p127*
Johns, George 62; Ontario, 1871 ***1823.22*** *p82*
Johns, James 21; Maryland, 1774 ***1220.25*** *p74*
Johns, James 42; Ontario, 1871 ***1823.15*** *p127*
Johns, James 47; Ontario, 1871 ***1823.15*** *p127*
Johns, John; Carolina, 1700 ***1224.2*** *p62*
Johns, John 24; Maryland, 1774 ***1220.25*** *p76*
Johns, Mary 20; Ontario, 1871 ***1823.15*** *p127*
Johns, Mary 33; Ontario, 1871 ***1823.15*** *p127*
Johns, Matthew; Pennsylvania, 1777 ***4629.10*** *p26*
Johns, Richard; Maryland, 1672 ***2524.55*** *p122*
Johns, Richard; Maryland, 1672 ***2524.55*** *p125*
Johns, Richard 48; Ontario, 1871 ***1823.15*** *p127*
Johns, Richard B. 12; Ontario, 1861 ***2896.27*** *p29*
Johns, Robert 66; Ontario, 1871 ***1823.15*** *p127*
Johns, Robt Kimber 36; Ontario, 1871 ***1823.28*** *p49*
Johns, Thomas 43; Ontario, 1871 ***1823.15*** *p127*
Johns, Thomas 56; Ontario, 1871 ***1823.22*** *p82*
Johns, Thomas 60; Ontario, 1871 ***1823.22*** *p82*
Johns, Thomas 73; Ontario, 1871 ***1823.15*** *p127*
Johns, William 37; Ontario, 1871 ***1823.15*** *p127*
Johns, William 40; Ontario, 1871 ***1823.15*** *p127*
Johns, William 45; Ontario, 1871 ***1823.15*** *p127*
Johns, William 49; Ontario, 1871 ***1823.22*** *p82*
Johns, William 69; Ontario, 1871 ***1823.15*** *p127*
Johns, William 80; Ontario, 1871 ***1823.15*** *p127*
Johnsen, John; New York, 1807 ***8197.10*** *p327*
Johnson, Mr.; Portland, Maine, 1858 ***9196.15*** *p30*
Johnson, Mr. 22; Jamaica, 1775 ***1220.25*** *p132*
Johnson, Mrs.; Maryland, 1651 ***2524.55*** *p122*
Johnson, Mrs.; Portland, Maine, 1858 ***9196.15*** *p30*
Johnson, Mrs. 36; Ontario, 1861 ***2896.26*** *p26*
Johnson, Mrs. 39; Ontario, 1861 ***2896.26*** *p25*
Johnson, Mrs. 58; Ontario, 1861 ***2896.26*** *p29*
Johnson, Abell; Maryland, 1682 ***2524.55*** *p122*
Johnson, Abraham; Maryland, 1701 ***1224.2*** *p62*
Johnson, AEmilia; Maryland, 1658 ***2524.55*** *p122*
Johnson, Agnetta *SEE* Johnson, Paul
Johnson, Albert; Maryland, 1665 ***2524.55*** *p122*
  Child: John
  Wife: Venemey
  Child: Katherine
Johnson, Albert; Maryland, 1666 ***2524.55*** *p122*
  Wife: Fene
  Child: Mary
  Child: Hendrick
Johnson, Alexander; Alabama, 1815-1845 ***1640.10*** *p87*
Johnson, Alexander 31; Ontario, 1871 ***1823.15*** *p127*
Johnson, Alfred 24; British Columbia, 1910 ***9196.1*** *p29*
Johnson, Alfred 24; Washington, 1910 ***9196.1*** *p29*
Johnson, Alice; Maryland, 1674 ***2524.55*** *p122*
Johnson, Alice 9; Ontario, 1861 ***2896.27*** *p33*
Johnson, Amond; New York, 1807 ***8197.10*** *p41*
Johnson, Amy 38; Ontario, 1861 ***2896.27*** *p38*
Johnson, Andreas *SEE* Johnson, Paul
Johnson, Andrew; Virginia, 1708 ***1224.2*** *p62*
Johnson, Andrew 22; Alaska, 1912 ***9196.1*** *p19*
Johnson, Andrew 22; British Columbia, 1912 ***9196.1*** *p19*
Johnson, Ann *SEE* Johnson, David
Johnson, Ann *SEE* Johnson, Peter
Johnson, Ann; Virginia, 1686-1687 ***6212.30*** *p57*
Johnson, Ann 31; Ontario, 1861 ***2896.28*** *p53*
Johnson, Anna Katherine; Maryland, 1664 ***2524.55*** *p122*
Johnson, Annakin *SEE* Johnson, Paul
Johnson, Anne; Virginia, 1664 ***6212.30*** *p10*
Johnson, Axel 33; Alaska, 1913 ***9196.1*** *p23*
Johnson, Axel 33; British Columbia, 1913 ***9196.1*** *p23*
Johnson, B. Jane 9; Ontario, 1861 ***2896.26*** *p26*
Johnson, B. S. 16; Ontario, 1861 ***2896.26*** *p25*
Johnson, Barnes; Maryland, 1651-1652 ***2524.55*** *p89*
Johnson, Barnes; Maryland, 1658 ***2524.55*** *p122*
Johnson, Bartle; Maryland, 1665 ***2524.55*** *p122*
Johnson, Bela 75; Ontario, 1861 ***2896.27*** *p33*
Johnson, Benjamin H. 53; Ontario, 1871 ***1823.28*** *p49*
Johnson, Bernard; Maryland, 1680 ***2524.55*** *p122*
Johnson, Billa; Maryland, 1664 ***2524.55*** *p123*
Johnson, C. A. 7; Ontario, 1861 ***2896.25*** *p32*
Johnson, Carl 27; Alaska, 1914 ***9196.1*** *p24*
Johnson, Catharine 19; Ontario, 1861 ***2896.26*** *p29*
Johnson, Catherine 1; Ontario, 1861 ***2896.28*** *p36*
Johnson, Catherine 11; Ontario, 1861 ***2896.25*** *p42*
Johnson, Catherine Murphy; Vermont, 1861 ***5900.10*** *p446*
Johnson, Charles; Maryland, 1682 ***2524.55*** *p123*
Johnson, Charles; New Castle, Delaware, 1827 ***1224.3*** *p41*
Johnson, Charles; Ontario, 1861 ***2896.25*** *p67*
Johnson, Charles 21; Maryland, 1774 ***1220.25*** *p65*
Johnson, Charles 26; Ontario, 1861 ***2896.25*** *p66*
Johnson, Charles 40; Ontario, 1871 ***1823.28*** *p49*
Johnson, Chris 32; Washington, 1914 ***9196.1*** *p65*
Johnson, Christen *SEE* Johnson, Paul
Johnson, Christian; Maryland, 1673 ***2524.55*** *p123*
Johnson, Christopher; Maryland, 1668 ***2524.55*** *p123*
Johnson, Cornelius; Maryland, 1667 ***2524.55*** *p123*
Johnson, Cynthia 12; Ontario, 1861 ***2896.26*** *p25*
Johnson, Daniel; Maryland, 1658 ***2524.55*** *p123*
Johnson, Daniel; New England, 1696 ***1224.1*** *p33*
Johnson, Daniel 41; Ontario, 1871 ***1823.22*** *p82*
Johnson, David *SEE* Johnson, David
Johnson, David; Maryland, 1666 ***2524.55*** *p123*
  Wife: Ann
  Son: David
Johnson, David 43; Ontario, 1871 ***1823.22*** *p82*
Johnson, David 48; Maryland, 1775 ***1220.25*** *p115*
Johnson, Delia Carroll 56; Vermont, 1872 ***5900.10*** *p438*
Johnson, Dell; Vermont, 1863-1919 ***5900.10*** *p457*
Johnson, Derick; Virginia, 1672 ***6212.30*** *p51*
Johnson, E. 30; Alaska, 1912 ***9196.1*** *p38*
Johnson, E. 30; Whitehorse, Yukon, 1912 ***9196.1*** *p38*
Johnson, Edith; Portland, Maine, 1858 ***9196.15*** *p30*
Johnson, Edward; Maryland, 1672 ***2524.55*** *p123*
Johnson, Edward; Maryland, 1673 ***2524.55*** *p123*
Johnson, Edward; New York, 1838 ***8197.10*** *p378*
Johnson, Edward; New York, 1840 ***8197.10*** *p175*
Johnson, Edward; Vermont, 1781-1860 ***5900.10*** *p178*
Johnson, Edward 18; Ontario, 1861 ***2896.27*** *p17*
Johnson, Edward 20; Maryland, 1774 ***1220.25*** *p59*
Johnson, Edward 22; Maryland, 1774 ***1220.25*** *p70*
Johnson, Edward 30; Maryland, 1774 ***1220.25*** *p58*
Johnson, Edward 45; Ontario, 1871 ***1823.15*** *p128*
Johnson, Elgin B. 8; Ontario, 1861 ***2896.27*** *p38*
Johnson, Elias; Virginia, 1671 ***6212.30*** *p43*
Johnson, Elijah 50; Ontario, 1871 ***1823.22*** *p82*
Johnson, Eliza; Portland, Maine, 1858 ***9196.15*** *p30*
Johnson, Eliza 14; Ontario, 1861 ***2896.26*** *p26*
Johnson, Eliza 32; Ontario, 1861 ***2896.28*** *p54*
Johnson, Eliza J. Lavery; Vermont, 1849-1910 ***5900.10*** *p606*
Johnson, Elizabeth *SEE* Johnson, John
Johnson, Elizabeth; Maryland, 1663 ***2524.55*** *p123*
Johnson, Elizabeth; Maryland, 1665 ***2524.55*** *p236*
Johnson, Elizabeth; Maryland, 1677 ***2524.55*** *p123*
Johnson, Elizabeth; Maryland, 1681 ***2524.55*** *p123*
Johnson, Elizabeth 68; Ontario, 1871 ***1823.22*** *p82*
Johnson, Ella Jane; Vermont, 1879-1920 ***5900.10*** *p121*
Johnson, Ellen 21; Ontario, 1861 ***2896.25*** *p66*
Johnson, Ellen 30; Alaska, 1918 ***9196.1*** *p55*
Johnson, Ellen 30; British Columbia, 1918 ***9196.1*** *p55*
Johnson, Ellinor; Virginia, 1663 ***6212.30*** *p4*
Johnson, Emanuel 16 *SEE* Johnson, William
Johnson, Enoch 29; Ontario, 1861 ***2896.28*** *p26*
Johnson, Fanny; Portland, Maine, 1858 ***9196.15*** *p30*
Johnson, Fene *SEE* Johnson, Albert
Johnson, Frances; Maryland, 1677 ***2524.55*** *p67*
Johnson, Francis; Maryland, 1660 ***2524.55*** *p248*
Johnson, Francis; Maryland, 1664 ***2524.55*** *p123*
  Wife: Katherine
Johnson, Francis; New York, 1840 ***8197.10*** *p175*
Johnson, Frank 42; British Columbia, 1911 ***9196.1*** *p34*
Johnson, Frank 42; Washington, 1911 ***9196.1*** *p34*
Johnson, Fred 24; Washington, 1914 ***9196.1*** *p66*
Johnson, Fred 47; British Columbia, 1913 ***9196.1*** *p21*
Johnson, Fred 47; Washington, 1913 ***9196.1*** *p21*
Johnson, G. 40; Alaska, 1913 ***9196.1*** *p23*
Johnson, G. 40; British Columbia, 1913 ***9196.1*** *p23*
Johnson, George; Georgia, 1734 ***1640.10*** *p87*
Johnson, George; Maryland, 1663 ***2524.55*** *p123*
Johnson, George; New York, 1835 ***8197.10*** *p70*
Johnson, George; Vermont, 1782-1864 ***5900.10*** *p470*
Johnson, George; Vermont, 1853-1928 ***5900.10*** *p438*
Johnson, George 15; Jamaica, 1773 ***1220.25*** *p30*
Johnson, George 24; Maryland, 1775 ***1220.25*** *p97*
Johnson, George 25; Baltimore, 1775 ***1220.25*** *p118*
Johnson, George 26 *SEE* Johnson, William
Johnson, George H. 28; Ontario, 1871 ***1823.15*** *p128*
Johnson, George W.; Vermont, 1852-1945 ***5900.10*** *p606*
Johnson, Gilbert 4; Ontario, 1861 ***2896.28*** *p36*
Johnson, Giles; Virginia, 1673 ***6212.30*** *p51*
Johnson, Gus 26; Washington, 1914 ***9196.1*** *p66*
Johnson, Hariette 9; Ontario, 1861 ***2896.25*** *p13*
Johnson, Hendrick *SEE* Johnson, Albert
Johnson, Hendrick; Virginia, 1672 ***6212.30*** *p50*
Johnson, Henery 48; Ontario, 1871 ***1823.28*** *p49*
Johnson, Henrich *SEE* Johnson, Paul
Johnson, Henry; Maryland, 1667 ***2524.55*** *p123*
Johnson, Henry; Maryland, 1674 ***2524.55*** *p123*
Johnson, Henry; Maryland, 1681 ***2524.55*** *p123*
Johnson, Henry; New York, 1840 ***8197.10*** *p175*
Johnson, Henry 32; Ontario, 1871 ***1823.28*** *p49*
Johnson, Henry 62; Ontario, 1871 ***1823.15*** *p128*
Johnson, Herbert M. 11; Ontario, 1861 ***2896.27*** *p38*
Johnson, Hersford 21; Maryland, 1774 ***1220.25*** *p77*
Johnson, Hezekiah 22; Jamaica, 1774 ***1220.25*** *p79*
Johnson, Hugh; Maryland, 1658 ***2524.55*** *p123*
Johnson, Hugh; Maryland, 1658 ***2524.55*** *p207*
Johnson, Hugh 52; Ontario, 1871 ***1823.15*** *p128*
Johnson, Mrs. I. 50; British Columbia, 1915 ***9196.1*** *p68*
Johnson, Mrs. I. 50; Washington, 1915 ***9196.1*** *p68*
Johnson, Ida 2; Ontario, 1861 ***2896.28*** *p59*
Johnson, Is...; Maryland, 1666 ***2524.55*** *p123*
Johnson, Isaac; Pennsylvania, 1787 ***4629.10*** *p55*
Johnson, Isaack; Maryland, 1661 ***2524.55*** *p123*
Johnson, Isabella; Maryland, 1674 ***2524.55*** *p123*
Johnson, J. H. 42; Alaska, 1917 ***9196.1*** *p49*
Johnson, J. H. 42; Yukon, 1917 ***9196.1*** *p49*
Johnson, J. H. 43; Alaska, 1917 ***9196.1*** *p44*
Johnson, J. H. 43; British Columbia, 1917 ***9196.1*** *p44*
Johnson, Jacob; Maryland, 1673 ***2524.55*** *p123*
Johnson, Jacob; Maryland, 1675 ***2524.55*** *p123*
Johnson, Jacob; New York, 1807 ***8197.10*** *p41*
Johnson, Jacob; Pennsylvania, 1777 ***4629.10*** *p27*
Johnson, Jacob 18; Maryland, 1774 ***1220.25*** *p69*
Johnson, Jacob H. 13; Ontario, 1861 ***2896.27*** *p38*
Johnson, James *SEE* Johnson, Peter
Johnson, James; Georgia, 1751 ***1640.10*** *p87*
Johnson, James; Maryland, 1680 ***2524.55*** *p123*
  Wife: Rachell
  Son: William
Johnson, James; New York, 1824-1832 ***8197.10*** *p308*
Johnson, James; New York, 1831-1838 ***8197.10*** *p120*
Johnson, James 40; Ontario, 1871 ***1823.28*** *p49*
Johnson, James 42; Virginia, 1774 ***1220.25*** *p89*
Johnson, James 48; Vermont, 1882 ***5900.10*** *p92*
Johnson, James 60; Ontario, 1871 ***1823.15*** *p128*
Johnson, James A. 15; Ontario, 1861 ***2896.25*** *p12*
Johnson, Jane; Maryland, 1681 ***2524.55*** *p123*
Johnson, Jane 78; Ontario, 1861 ***2896.25*** *p42*
Johnson, Jane A.; Ontario, 1861 ***2896.28*** *p57*
Johnson, Jane Ann 29; Ontario, 1861 ***2896.25*** *p66*
Johnson, Jannet 60; Ontario, 1871 ***1823.28*** *p49*
Johnson, Jas 47; Ontario, 1871 ***1823.22*** *p82*
Johnson, Jay M. 7; Ontario, 1861 ***2896.27*** *p38*
Johnson, Johanna 43; British Columbia, 1915 ***9196.1*** *p16*
Johnson, Johanna 43; Washington, 1915 ***9196.1*** *p16*
Johnson, John *SEE* Johnson, Albert
Johnson, John; Boston, 1903 ***3437.14*** *p137*
Johnson, John; Maryland, 1658 ***2524.55*** *p123*
Johnson, John; Maryland, 1663 ***2524.55*** *p123*
Johnson, John; Maryland, 1666 ***2524.55*** *p123*
  Relative: Elizabeth
Johnson, John; Maryland, 1681 ***2524.55*** *p123*
Johnson, John; New York, 1797 ***8197.10*** *p8*
Johnson, John; New York, 1838 ***8197.10*** *p120*
Johnson, John; New York, 1840 ***8197.10*** *p175*
Johnson, John; Pennsylvania, 1777 ***4629.10*** *p14*
Johnson, John; Pennsylvania, 1786 ***4629.10*** *p53*
Johnson, John; Pennsylvania, 1827 ***1224.3*** *p41*
Johnson, John; Virginia, 1682 ***1224.1*** *p33*
Johnson, John; Virginia, 1688 ***1224.1*** *p33*
Johnson, John; Virginia, 1703-1704 ***6212.30*** *p62*
Johnson, John 20; Nova Scotia, 1774 ***1220.25*** *p135*
Johnson, John 22; Maryland, 1775 ***1220.25*** *p96*
Johnson, John 23; Maryland, 1775 ***1220.25*** *p105*
Johnson, John 25; Quebec, 1774 ***1220.25*** *p62*
Johnson, John 27; Fort Cumberland, Nova Scotia, 1774 ***1220.25*** *p18*
  Wife: Martha 23
  Child: William 1
Johnson, John 34; Ontario, 1871 ***1823.15*** *p128*

Johnson, John 44; Ontario, 1871 1823.15 p128
Johnson, John 45; Maryland, 1775 1220.25 p108
Johnson, John 47; Ontario, 1871 1823.15 p128
Johnson, John 50; Ontario, 1871 1823.15 p128
Johnson, John 52; British Columbia, 1915 9196.1 p68
Johnson, John 52; Washington, 1915 9196.1 p68
Johnson, John 56; Ontario, 1871 1823.22 p82
Johnson, John 60; Ontario, 1871 1823.28 p49
Johnson, John 66; Ontario, 1861 2896.28 p26
Johnson, John 76; Ontario, 1861 2896.28 p53
Johnson, John 77; Ontario, 1871 1823.15 p128
Johnson, John, II; Maryland, 1663 2524.55 p123
Johnson, John B. 46; British Columbia, 1917 9196.1 p16
Johnson, John B. 46; Washington, 1917 9196.1 p16
Johnson, John G. 14; Ontario, 1861 2896.25 p42
Johnson, John H. 2; Ontario, 1861 2896.27 p38
Johnson, John N. 4; Ontario, 1861 2896.28 p54
Johnson, Joseph 14 *SEE* Johnson, William
Johnson, Joseph 14; Jamaica, 1774 1220.25 p72
Johnson, Joshua; Washington, District of Columbia, 1805 1224.3 p41
Johnson, Kate Gallagher 49; Vermont, 1894 5900.10 p205
Johnson, Katherine *SEE* Johnson, Albert
Johnson, Katherine *SEE* Johnson, Francis
Johnson, L. 26; Alaska, 1917 9196.1 p45
Johnson, L. 26; Whitehorse, Yukon, 1917 9196.1 p45
Johnson, Lucy A. 22; Ontario, 1861 2896.25 p12
Johnson, Luke; Virginia, 1659 1224.1 p33
Johnson, Lyman 59; Ontario, 1861 2896.25 p66
Johnson, M. 42; Ontario, 1861 2896.25 p32
Johnson, M. E. 1; Ontario, 1861 2896.26 p26
Johnson, Maidy 14; British Columbia, 1915 9196.1 p16
Johnson, Maidy 14; Washington, 1915 9196.1 p16
Johnson, Malissa 24; Ontario, 1861 2896.25 p66
Johnson, Margaret; New York, New York, 1823 1224.3 p6
Johnson, Margaret 48 *SEE* Johnson, William
Johnson, Margaret 49; Vermont, 1890 5900.10 p438
Johnson, Margaret A. 17; Ontario, 1861 2896.25 p42
Johnson, Margaret Maloney; Vermont, 1856-1939 5900.10 p277
Johnson, Margaretta *SEE* Johnson, Paul
Johnson, Marget 61; Ontario, 1871 1823.15 p128
Johnson, Marshall 19; Ontario, 1861 2896.25 p42
Johnson, Martha 23 *SEE* Johnson, John
Johnson, Martha A.; Ontario, 1861 2896.25 p13
Johnson, Martin; New York, 1838 8197.10 p120
Johnson, Martin J.; Vermont, 1848-1938 5900.10 p277
Johnson, Mary *SEE* Johnson, Albert
Johnson, Mary *SEE* Johnson, Peter
Johnson, Mary; Maryland, 1658 2524.55 p123
Johnson, Mary; Maryland, 1665 2524.55 p124
Johnson, Mary; Portland, Maine, 1858 9196.15 p30
Johnson, Mary; Vermont, 1829-1898 5900.10 p145
Johnson, Mary; Vermont, 1838-1929 5900.10 p204
Johnson, Mary; Virginia, 1668-1669 6212.30 p41
Johnson, Mary; Virginia, 1669-1670 6212.30 p41
Johnson, Mary; Virginia, 1672 6212.30 p49
Johnson, Mary 13; Ontario, 1861 2896.25 p32
Johnson, Mary 20; New York, 1774 1220.25 p141
Johnson, Mary 24; Ontario, 1871 1823.22 p82
Johnson, Mary 42; Ontario, 1861 2896.25 p12
Johnson, Mary 57; Ontario, 1871 1823.15 p128
Johnson, Mary 60; Ontario, 1871 1823.15 p128
Johnson, Mary 70; Ontario, 1871 1823.15 p128
Johnson, Mary 84; Ontario, 1871 1823.22 p82
Johnson, Mary Ann 54; Ontario, 1871 1823.15 p128
Johnson, Mary E. 12; Ontario, 1861 2896.25 p12
Johnson, Mary E. Sullivan; Vermont, 1858-1921 5900.10 p158
Johnson, Mary Hazard; New England, 1658 1224.1 p29
Johnson, Mary J.; Vermont, 1856-1934 5900.10 p282
Johnson, Mary J. Gallagher; Vermont, 1851-1923 5900.10 p277
Johnson, Mathew; Virginia, 1664-1665 6212.30 p16
Johnson, Mathew 40; Ontario, 1871 1823.15 p128
Johnson, Matilda 21; Ontario, 1861 2896.25 p42
Johnson, Matthew 48; Ontario, 1871 1823.15 p128
Johnson, Michael; Canada, 1756-1760 4628.40 p45
Johnson, Michael; Maryland, 1674 2524.55 p124
Johnson, Michael 55; Ontario, 1871 1823.22 p82
Johnson, Nathan 60; Ontario, 1871 1823.15 p128
Johnson, Nathaniel; Carolina, 1701 1224.2 p62
Johnson, Nathaniel; New York, 1837 8197.10 p92
Johnson, Nicholas; New York, 1802 8197.10 p21
Johnson, Nicholas; New York, 1840 8197.10 p175
Johnson, Nicholas; Virginia, 1663 1224.1 p33
Johnson, Oliver 18; Ontario, 1861 2896.25 p66
Johnson, P. 28; Ontario, 1861 2896.26 p14
Johnson, Paul; Maryland, 1661 2524.55 p124
Wife: Agnetta
Daughter: Margaretta
Daughter: Annakin
Daughter: Christen
Son: Henrich
Son: Andreas
Johnson, Peter *SEE* Johnson, Peter
Johnson, Peter; Maryland, 1651 2524.55 p124
Wife: Ann
Relative: Mary
Relative: James
Relative: Peter
Johnson, Peter; Maryland, 1651 2524.55 p124
With wife
Son: James
Johnson, Peter; Virginia, 1666-1667 6212.30 p34
Johnson, Peter; Virginia, 1693 1224.1 p33
Johnson, Rachel 29; Ontario, 1861 2896.28 p36
Johnson, Rachell *SEE* Johnson, James
Johnson, Ranselor 23; Ontario, 1861 2896.25 p66
Johnson, Rebecca 26; Ontario, 1861 2896.27 p33
Johnson, Rebecca 69; Ontario, 1861 2896.27 p33
Johnson, Richard 58; Ontario, 1871 1823.22 p82
Johnson, Richard 76; Vermont, 1885 5900.10 p438
Johnson, Richd.; Maryland, 1652-1653 2524.55 p124
Johnson, Robert; South Carolina, 1735 1224.2 p62
Johnson, Robert 27; Ontario, 1871 1823.15 p128
Johnson, Robert 41; Maryland, 1774 1220.25 p52
Johnson, Robert 47; Vermont, n.d. 5900.10 p446
Johnson, Roger; Virginia, 1664 6212.30 p5
Johnson, Rose; Vermont, 1831-1911 5900.10 p479
Johnson, S. 22; Alaska, 1913 9196.1 p40
Johnson, S. J. 10; Ontario, 1861 2896.25 p32
Johnson, Samuel; Georgia, 1820 1640.10 p87
Johnson, Samuel; New York, 1840 8197.10 p175
Johnson, Samuel 21; America, 1774 1220.25 p35
Johnson, Samuel 38; Ontario, 1871 1823.15 p128
Johnson, Sanford 12; Ontario, 1861 2896.26 p26
Johnson, Sarah; Charleston, South Carolina, 1838 1224.3 p41
Johnson, Sarah 16; British Columbia, 1915 9196.1 p16
Johnson, Sarah 16; Washington, 1915 9196.1 p16
Johnson, Sarah 19; Ontario, 1861 2896.28 p59
Johnson, Sarah E. 18; Ontario, 1861 2896.25 p12
Johnson, Sary Ann 29; Ontario, 1861 2896.25 p63
Johnson, Simon; New York, New York, 1823 1224.3 p41
Johnson, Stephen 75; Vermont, 1910 5900.10 p605
Johnson, Susan 15; Ontario, 1861 2896.25 p66
Johnson, Susan McKenna; Vermont, 1783-1867 5900.10 p178
Johnson, Susanna Duncombe; Virginia, 1694 1224.1 p33
Johnson, Suzan; Maryland, 1665 2524.55 p124
Johnson, Mrs. Svenborg Erickson 30; British Columbia, 1917 9196.1 p16
Johnson, Mrs. Svenborg Erickson 30; Washington, 1917 9196.1 p16
Johnson, Tanyah Bartle; Maryland, 1665 2524.55 p124
Johnson, Tho.; Maryland, 1681 2524.55 p124
Johnson, Thomas; New York, 1839 8197.10 p133
Johnson, Thomas; New York, 1840 8197.10 p175
Johnson, Thomas; Savannah, Georgia, 1808 1224.3 p42
Johnson, Thomas; Vermont, 1827-1908 5900.10 p179
Johnson, Thomas; Virginia, 1690-1691 6212.30 p59
Johnson, Thomas 16; Maryland, 1774 1220.25 p7
Johnson, Thomas 23; New York, 1774 1220.25 p25
Johnson, Thomas 30; Ontario, 1871 1823.28 p49
Johnson, Thomas 55; Ontario, 1871 1823.15 p128
Johnson, Thomas 62; Ontario, 1871 1823.15 p128
Johnson, Thomas 79; Ontario, 1871 1823.15 p128
Johnson, Thomas P. 52; Vermont, 1892 5900.10 p205
Johnson, Thomas Wm 35; Ontario, 1871 1823.15 p128
Johnson, Thos N. 34; British Columbia, 1913 9196.1 p21
Johnson, Uzal; New Jersey, 1828 1224.3 p42
Johnson, V. 26; Alaska, 1916 9196.1 p43
Johnson, V. 26; Whitehorse, Yukon, 1916 9196.1 p43
Johnson, Venemey *SEE* Johnson, Albert
Johnson, W. A. 7; Ontario, 1861 2896.26 p26
Johnson, W. E. 23; British Columbia, 1915 9196.1 p67
Johnson, W. E. 23; Washington, 1915 9196.1 p67
Johnson, W. R. 9; Ontario, 1861 2896.25 p42
Johnson, Walter; Maryland, 1681 2524.55 p124
Johnson, William *SEE* Johnson, James
Johnson, William; Maryland, 1665 2524.55 p124
Johnson, William; Maryland, 1669 2524.55 p14
Johnson, William; Maryland, 1673 2524.55 p124
Johnson, William; New York, 1766 4628.40 p113
Johnson, William; New York, 1776 1224.2 p62
Johnson, William; New York, 1804 8197.10 p27
Johnson, William; New York, 1834 8197.10 p319
Johnson, William; Ontario, 1861 2896.25 p13
Johnson, William; Vermont, 1855-1927 5900.10 p158
Johnson, William 1 *SEE* Johnson, John
Johnson, William 16; Maryland, 1774 1220.25 p62
Johnson, William 20; Ontario, 1871 1823.22 p82
Johnson, William 22; Nova Scotia, 1774 1220.25 p135
Johnson, William 23 *SEE* Johnson, William
Johnson, William 28; Fort Cumberland, Nova Scotia, 1775 1220.25 p21
Johnson, William 30; Baltimore, 1775 1220.25 p118
Johnson, William 33; Ontario, 1871 1823.15 p128
Johnson, William 36; Ontario, 1871 1823.28 p49
Johnson, William 40; America, 1774 1220.25 p36
Johnson, William 48; Ontario, 1871 1823.15 p128
Johnson, William 49; Halifax, Nova Scotia, 1775 1220.25 p22
Wife: Margaret 48
Child: Emanuel 16
Child: Joseph 14
Child: William 23
Child: George 26
Johnson, William 50; Ontario, 1871 1823.28 p49
Johnson, William 65; Ontario, 1871 1823.15 p128
Johnson, William 70; Ontario, 1871 1823.15 p128
Johnson, William A. 3; Ontario, 1861 2896.25 p32
Johnson, William A. 52; Ontario, 1861 2896.25 p42
Johnson, William Cecil; New York, 1823 8197.10 p63
Johnson, William Edward 25; Ontario, 1871 1823.15 p128
Johnson, Winifred McDonough; Vermont, 1855-1902 5900.10 p438
Johnson, Wm 22; Alaska, 1917 9196.1 p53
Johnson, Wm 22; Whitehorse, Yukon, 1917 9196.1 p53
Johnson, Wm 38; Washington, 1914 9196.1 p65
Johnson, Z. M. 7; Ontario, 1861 2896.25 p32
Johnsons, George; Albany, New York, 1817 1224.3 p42
Johnston, Sarah *SEE* Johnston, Neil
Johnston, Miss; Quebec, 1857 9196.15 p22
Johnston, Mr.; Quebec, 1858 9196.15 p41
Johnston, Absolem; Pennsylvania, 1779 4629.10 p36
Johnston, Adam; Jamaica, 1795 1640.13 p63
Johnston, Adam 38; Ontario, 1871 1823.22 p82
Johnston, Adam 45; Ontario, 1871 1823.28 p49
Johnston, Agness 60; Ontario, 1871 1823.28 p49
Johnston, Alexander *SEE* Johnston, Angus
Johnston, Alexander *SEE* Johnston, Neil
Johnston, Alexander *SEE* Johnston, Roderick
Johnston, Alexander; Georgia, 1699 1640.13 p63
Johnston, Alexander; New York, 1836-1839 8197.10 p133
Johnston, Alexander 24; Ontario, 1871 1823.15 p129
Johnston, Alexander 35; Ontario, 1871 1823.15 p129
Johnston, Alexander 40; Ontario, 1871 1823.15 p129
Johnston, Andrew; Augusta, Georgia, 1779 1640.10 p88
Johnston, Andrew; Georgia, 1763 1640.10 p88
Johnston, Andrew; New York, 1807 8197.10 p329
Johnston, Andrew 45; Ontario, 1871 1823.15 p129
Johnston, Andrew 55; Ontario, 1871 1823.28 p49
Johnston, Andrew 66; Ontario, 1871 1823.22 p82
Johnston, Angus *SEE* Johnston, Roderick
Johnston, Angus; Port uncertain, 1850-1859 4537.37 p107
Wife: Kirsty Munro
Child: Murdo
Child: Margaret
Child: Donald
Child: Alexander
Child: Roderick
Child: Archie
Child: Mary
Child: John
Johnston, Angus; Port uncertain, 1850-1859 4537.37 p107
Wife: Mary
Child: Kate
Child: John
Child: Alexander
Child: Margaret
Child: Donald
Johnston, Ann *SEE* Johnston, Donald
Johnston, Ann *SEE* Johnston, Neil
Johnston, Ann; Michigan, 1882 4537.37 p88
Johnston, Ann; Savannah, Georgia, 1774 1640.10 p88
Johnston, Ann MacLeod *SEE* Johnston, James
Johnston, Anne 35; Ontario, 1861 2896.27 p3
Johnston, Archibald 45; Ontario, 1871 1823.22 p82
Johnston, Archibald 46; Ontario, 1871 1823.22 p82
Johnston, Archibald 76; Ontario, 1871 1823.22 p82
Johnston, Archie *SEE* Johnston, Angus
Johnston, Arthur 30; Ontario, 1871 1823.28 p49
Johnston, Catherine *SEE* Johnston, James
Johnston, Catherine *SEE* Johnston, John
Johnston, Catherine; Port uncertain, 1840-1849 4537.37 p111
Johnston, Catherine MacDonald *SEE* Johnston, Neil
Johnston, Charles; New York, 1837 8197.10 p92
Johnston, Charles; New York, New York, 1864 6058.10 p58

Johnston, Charles; Pennsylvania, 1779 ***4629.10*** *p33*
Johnston, Charlotte 23; Ontario, 1871 ***1823.15*** *p129*
Johnston, Christopher 75; Ontario, 1871 ***1823.15*** *p129*
Johnston, Cornelius; Pennsylvania, 1866 ***6058.10*** *p51*
Johnston, D. 67; Ontario, 1861 ***2896.25*** *p4*
Johnston, David; Savannah, Georgia, 1820 ***1640.10*** *p88*
Johnston, David; Savannah, Georgia, 1821 ***1640.10*** *p88*
Johnston, David 27; Ontario, 1871 ***1823.15*** *p129*
Johnston, David 37; Ontario, 1871 ***1823.15*** *p129*
Johnston, Donald *SEE* Johnston, Angus
Johnston, Donald *SEE* Johnston, John
Johnston, Donald *SEE* Johnston, Murdo
Johnston, Donald *SEE* Johnston, Neil
Johnston, Donald; Ontario, 1849 ***4537.37*** *p35*
Child: Neil
Child: Kirsty
Child: John
Wife: Margaret
Child: Ann
Child: Murdo
Johnston, Donald; Port uncertain, 1840-1849 ***4537.37*** *p107*
Wife: Marion
Johnston, Edward 21; Ontario, 1871 ***1823.15*** *p129*
Johnston, Edward 22; Ontario, 1871 ***1823.15*** *p129*
Johnston, Edward 36; Ontario, 1871 ***1823.15*** *p129*
Johnston, Effie *SEE* Johnston, Neil
Johnston, Effie *SEE* Johnston, Roderick
Johnston, Elisabeth 38; Ontario, 1871 ***1823.28*** *p49*
Johnston, Elizabeth 49; Ontario, 1871 ***1823.15*** *p129*
Johnston, Elliott 60; Ontario, 1871 ***1823.28*** *p49*
Johnston, Flora; Port uncertain, 1850-1859 ***4537.37*** *p132*
Johnston, Flora MacQuarrie *SEE* Johnston, John
Johnston, Francis; Philadelphia, 1778 ***1224.2*** *p62*
Johnston, Francis 30; Ontario, 1871 ***1823.22*** *p83*
Johnston, Francis 48; Ontario, 1871 ***1823.22*** *p83*
Johnston, Gabriel; North Carolina, 1753 ***1224.2*** *p62*
Johnston, George; Augusta, Georgia, 1756 ***1640.10*** *p88*
Johnston, George 22; Ontario, 1861 ***2896.25*** *p2*
Johnston, George 35; Ontario, 1871 ***1823.22*** *p83*
Johnston, George 41; Ontario, 1861 ***2896.27*** *p3*
Johnston, George Milligan; Georgia, 1735-1799 ***1640.10*** *p88*
Johnston, Gus 29; British Columbia, 1909 ***9196.1*** *p28*
Johnston, Gus 29; Washington, 1909 ***9196.1*** *p28*
Johnston, Henery 47; Ontario, 1871 ***1823.15*** *p129*
Johnston, Henry 40; Ontario, 1871 ***1823.28*** *p49*
Johnston, Hugh 56; Ontario, 1871 ***1823.28*** *p49*
Johnston, Isibela 65; Ontario, 1871 ***1823.15*** *p129*
Johnston, Isobel Flett *SEE* Johnston, Nicol
Johnston, James *SEE* Johnston, Roderick
Johnston, James; Georgia, 1698 ***1640.13*** *p63*
Johnston, James; Georgia, 1750 ***1640.10*** *p88*
Johnston, James; Georgia, 1763 ***1640.10*** *p89*
Johnston, James; New York, 1803 ***8197.10*** *p13*
Johnston, James; New York, 1840 ***8197.10*** *p175*
Johnston, James; Nova Scotia, 1840-1849 ***4537.37*** *p9*
Wife: Ann MacLeod
Child: Catherine
Child: Mary
Johnston, James; Pennsylvania, 1777 ***4629.10*** *p8*
Johnston, James; Quebec, 1856 ***9196.15*** *p10*
Johnston, James; Vermont, 1836-1936 ***5900.10*** *p425*
Johnston, James 24; Ontario, 1871 ***1823.15*** *p129*
Johnston, James 30; Ontario, 1871 ***1823.28*** *p49*
Johnston, James 32; Ontario, 1871 ***1823.15*** *p129*
Johnston, James 34; Ontario, 1871 ***1823.15*** *p129*
Johnston, James 36; Ontario, 1871 ***1823.15*** *p129*
Johnston, James 36; Ontario, 1871 ***1823.28*** *p49*
Johnston, James 43; Ontario, 1871 ***1823.28*** *p49*
Johnston, James 45; Ontario, 1871 ***1823.15*** *p129*
Johnston, James 45; Ontario, 1871 ***1823.28*** *p49*
Johnston, James 47; Ontario, 1871 ***1823.28*** *p49*
Johnston, James 54; Ontario, 1871 ***1823.15*** *p129*
Johnston, James 55; Ontario, 1871 ***1823.15*** *p129*
Johnston, James 60; Ontario, 1871 ***1823.15*** *p129*
Johnston, James 60; Ontario, 1871 ***1823.28*** *p49*
Johnston, James 64; Ontario, 1871 ***1823.28*** *p49*
Johnston, James 68; Ontario, 1871 ***1823.15*** *p129*
Johnston, James 73; Ontario, 1871 ***1823.22*** *p83*
Johnston, James Wm 49; Ontario, 1871 ***1823.28*** *p49*
Johnston, Janet *SEE* Johnston, Nicol
Johnston, Janet; Savannah, Georgia, 1775 ***1640.10*** *p89*
Johnston, Janet 59; Ontario, 1871 ***1823.15*** *p129*
Johnston, Jeremiah; Pennsylvania, 1777 ***4629.10*** *p17*
Johnston, Johanna; Philadelphia, 1839 ***1224.3*** *p42*
Johnston, John *SEE* Johnston, Angus
Johnston, John *SEE* Johnston, Donald
Johnston, John *SEE* Johnston, John
Johnston, John *SEE* Johnston, Murdo
Johnston, John *SEE* Johnston, Neil
Johnston, John *SEE* Johnston, Roderick
Johnston, John; Florida, 1767 ***1640.10*** *p89*
Johnston, John; Georgia, 1699 ***1640.13*** *p63*
Johnston, John; Mississippi, 1845 ***1640.10*** *p89*
Wife: Catherine
Johnston, John; New York, 1807 ***8197.10*** *p325*
Johnston, John; Ontario, 1849 ***4537.32*** *p11*
Wife: Kirsty
Child: Sam
Child: Donald
Child: Ranald
Child: John
Child: Mary
Johnston, John; Ontario, 1849 ***4537.37*** *p36*
Wife: Flora MacQuarrie
Child: Margaret
Child: Donald
Child: Roderick
Johnston, John; Ontario, 1850-1859 ***4537.37*** *p36*
Wife: Kirsty
Child: Ranald
Child: Donald
Child: Sam
Child: John
Child: Mary
Johnston, John; Pennsylvania, 1777 ***4629.10*** *p27*
Johnston, John; Pennsylvania, 1866 ***6058.10*** *p51*
Johnston, John; Portland, Maine, 1857 ***9196.15*** *p12*
Johnston, John 21; Ontario, 1871 ***1823.15*** *p129*
Johnston, John 24; Ontario, 1871 ***1823.15*** *p129*
Johnston, John 27; Ontario, 1871 ***1823.15*** *p129*
Johnston, John 29; Ontario, 1871 ***1823.28*** *p49*
Johnston, John 30; Ontario, 1871 ***1823.28*** *p49*
Johnston, John 34; Ontario, 1871 ***1823.15*** *p129*
Johnston, John 35; Ontario, 1871 ***1823.15*** *p129*
Johnston, John 36; Ontario, 1871 ***1823.15*** *p129*
Johnston, John 38; Ontario, 1871 ***1823.22*** *p83*
Johnston, John 40; Ontario, 1871 ***1823.15*** *p130*
Johnston, John 41; Ontario, 1871 ***1823.15*** *p129*
Johnston, John 44; Ontario, 1871 ***1823.15*** *p129*
Johnston, John 44; Ontario, 1871 ***1823.22*** *p83*
Johnston, John 46; Ontario, 1871 ***1823.15*** *p129*
Johnston, John 52; Ontario, 1871 ***1823.28*** *p49*
Johnston, John 61; Ontario, 1871 ***1823.22*** *p83*
Johnston, John 68; Ontario, 1871 ***1823.28*** *p49*
Johnston, John 70; Ontario, 1871 ***1823.15*** *p130*
Johnston, John Natross; New York, 1839 ***8197.10*** *p244*
Johnston, Joseph; Pennsylvania, 1777 ***4629.10*** *p8*
Johnston, Kate *SEE* Johnston, Angus
Johnston, Kate *SEE* Johnston, Neil
Johnston, Kirsty *SEE* Johnston, Donald
Johnston, Kirsty *SEE* Johnston, John
Johnston, Kirsty Munro *SEE* Johnston, Angus
Johnston, Lane 47; Ontario, 1871 ***1823.28*** *p49*
Johnston, Lawrence; Pennsylvania, 1777 ***4629.10*** *p27*
Johnston, Lewis; Georgia, 1756 ***1640.10*** *p89*
Johnston, Lewis; Georgia, 1798 ***1224.2*** *p63*
Johnston, Lewis; St. Kitts, 1756 ***1640.10*** *p89*
Johnston, Margaret *SEE* Johnston, Angus
Johnston, Margaret *SEE* Johnston, Donald
Johnston, Margaret *SEE* Johnston, John
Johnston, Margaret *SEE* Johnston, Roderick
Johnston, Margaret 58; Ontario, 1871 ***1823.15*** *p130*
Johnston, Margaret 70; Ontario, 1871 ***1823.22*** *p83*
Johnston, Marion *SEE* Johnston, Donald
Johnston, Marion; Port uncertain, 1840-1849 ***4537.37*** *p116*
Johnston, Marion MacDonald *SEE* Johnston, Roderick
Johnston, Martha 60; Ontario, 1871 ***1823.15*** *p130*
Johnston, Mary *SEE* Johnston, Angus
Johnston, Mary *SEE* Johnston, James
Johnston, Mary *SEE* Johnston, John
Johnston, Mary; Ontario, 1840-1849 ***4537.37*** *p68*
Johnston, Mary 18; Ontario, 1871 ***1823.15*** *p130*
Johnston, Mary 55; Ontario, 1871 ***1823.15*** *p130*
Johnston, Mary 56; Ontario, 1871 ***1823.22*** *p83*
Johnston, Mary 69; Ontario, 1871 ***1823.15*** *p130*
Johnston, Mary MacDougall *SEE* Johnston, Murdo
Johnston, Murdo *SEE* Johnston, Angus
Johnston, Murdo *SEE* Johnston, Donald
Johnston, Murdo; Ontario, 1849 ***4537.37*** *p36*
Wife: Mary MacDougall
Child: Donald
Child: John
Johnston, Neil *SEE* Johnston, Donald
Johnston, Neil; Nova Scotia, 1840-1849 ***4537.37*** *p10*
Wife: Catherine MacDonald
Child: John
Child: Ann
Child: Donald
Child: Kate
Child: Sarah
Child: Effie
Child: Ranald
Child: Sam
Child: Alexander
Johnston, Nicol; Savannah, Georgia, 1775 ***1640.10*** *p89*
Wife: Isobel Flett
Daughter: Janet
Johnston, Niviro 43; Ontario, 1871 ***1823.15*** *p130*
Johnston, Noble 38; Ontario, 1871 ***1823.15*** *p130*
Johnston, Phebe 67; Ontario, 1861 ***2896.25*** *p2*
Johnston, Ranald *SEE* Johnston, John
Johnston, Ranald *SEE* Johnston, Neil
Johnston, Ranald *SEE* Johnston, Roderick
Johnston, Richard; Pennsylvania, 1777 ***4629.10*** *p15*
Johnston, Richard 54; Ontario, 1871 ***1823.15*** *p130*
Johnston, Robert; Florida, 1767 ***1640.10*** *p90*
Johnston, Robert; Georgia, 1732 ***1640.10*** *p89*
Johnston, Robert; New York, 1821 ***8197.10*** *p244*
Johnston, Robert; New York, 1837 ***8197.10*** *p92*
Johnston, Robert; Virginia, n.d. ***1224.2*** *p63*
Johnston, Robert 36; Ontario, 1871 ***1823.15*** *p130*
Johnston, Robert 40; Ontario, 1871 ***1823.22*** *p83*
Johnston, Robert 45; Ontario, 1871 ***1823.22*** *p83*
Johnston, Robert 67; Ontario, 1871 ***1823.15*** *p130*
Johnston, Robert 70; Ontario, 1871 ***1823.15*** *p130*
Johnston, Roderick *SEE* Johnston, Angus
Johnston, Roderick *SEE* Johnston, John
Johnston, Roderick; Port uncertain, 1840-1849 ***4537.37*** *p108*
Wife: Marion MacDonald
Child: Margaret
Child: Effie
Child: Angus
Child: Ranald
Child: Alexander
Child: James
Child: John
Johnston, Sam *SEE* Johnston, John
Johnston, Sam *SEE* Johnston, Neil
Johnston, Saml 42; Ontario, 1871 ***1823.28*** *p49*
Johnston, Samuel; New York, 1839 ***8197.10*** *p133*
Johnston, Samuel; New York, 1840 ***8197.10*** *p175*
Johnston, Samuel; Pennsylvania, 1786 ***4629.10*** *p49*
Johnston, Samuel 29; Ontario, 1871 ***1823.28*** *p49*
Johnston, Samuel 30; Ontario, 1871 ***1823.15*** *p130*
Johnston, Samuel 50; Ontario, 1871 ***1823.15*** *p130*
Johnston, Susan 50; Ontario, 1871 ***1823.28*** *p49*
Johnston, Thomas; New Orleans, 1866 ***1640.13*** *p63*
Johnston, Thomas; New York, 1840 ***8197.10*** *p321*
Johnston, Thomas 20; Ontario, 1871 ***1823.28*** *p50*
Johnston, Thomas 25; Ontario, 1871 ***1823.15*** *p130*
Johnston, Thomas 30; Ontario, 1871 ***1823.28*** *p49*
Johnston, Thomas 40; Ontario, 1871 ***1823.15*** *p130*
Johnston, Thomas 41; Ontario, 1871 ***1823.15*** *p130*
Johnston, Thomas 55; Ontario, 1871 ***1823.15*** *p130*
Johnston, Thomas 58; Ontario, 1871 ***1823.15*** *p130*
Johnston, Thomas Ridout; Florida, 1767 ***1640.10*** *p90*
Johnston, Thos 55; Ontario, 1871 ***1823.15*** *p130*
Johnston, Walter; Georgia, 1699 ***1640.13*** *p63*
Johnston, William; New York, 1802 ***8197.10*** *p21*
Johnston, William; New York, 1821 ***8197.10*** *p244*
Johnston, William; Pennsylvania, 1786 ***4629.10*** *p49*
Johnston, William 24; Ontario, 1871 ***1823.15*** *p130*
Johnston, William 26; Philadelphia, 1774 ***1220.25*** *p81*
Johnston, William 30; Ontario, 1871 ***1823.15*** *p130*
Johnston, William 32; Ontario, 1871 ***1823.15*** *p130*
Johnston, William 35; Ontario, 1871 ***1823.15*** *p130*
Johnston, William 37; Ontario, 1871 ***1823.15*** *p130*
Johnston, William 40; Ontario, 1871 ***1823.15*** *p130*
Johnston, William 44; Ontario, 1871 ***1823.15*** *p130*
Johnston, William 45; Ontario, 1871 ***1823.22*** *p83*
Johnston, William 47; Ontario, 1871 ***1823.15*** *p130*
Johnston, William 50; Ontario, 1871 ***1823.15*** *p130*
Johnston, William 51; Ontario, 1871 ***1823.15*** *p130*
Johnston, William 53; Ontario, 1871 ***1823.15*** *p130*
Johnston, William 70; Ontario, 1871 ***1823.15*** *p130*
Johnston, William 71; Ontario, 1871 ***1823.15*** *p130*
Johnston, William 75; Ontario, 1871 ***1823.28*** *p50*
Johnston, William 77; Ontario, 1871 ***1823.15*** *p130*
Johnston, William John; New York, 1805 ***8197.10*** *p243*
Johnstone, Mr.; Quebec, 1856 ***9196.15*** *p6*
Johnstone, Andrew; Petersburg, Virginia, 1788 ***1640.13*** *p63*
Johnstone, Charles; New York, New York, 1864 ***6058.10*** *p58*
Johnstone, Christopher 50; Ontario, 1871 ***1823.15*** *p130*
Johnstone, David C. 74; Ontario, 1871 ***1823.22*** *p83*
Johnstone, George; Florida, 1764-1783 ***1640.10*** *p88*
Johnstone, George; Pensacola, Florida, 1766 ***1640.10*** *p88*
Johnstone, George 13; Ontario, 1871 ***1823.15*** *p130*
Johnstone, Hugh; Antigua (Antego), 1862 ***1640.13*** *p63*
Johnstone, James 37; Ontario, 1871 ***1823.22*** *p83*
Johnstone, James 38; Ontario, 1871 ***1823.15*** *p130*
Johnstone, James 39; Ontario, 1871 ***1823.15*** *p131*
Johnstone, James 46; Ontario, 1871 ***1823.15*** *p131*

Johnstone, James 56; Ontario, 1871 ***1823.15*** *p130*
Johnstone, Jessie; New Orleans, 1892 ***1640.13*** *p63*
Johnstone, John; Kingston, Jamaica, 1828 ***1640.13*** *p63*
Johnstone, John; New York, 1839 ***8197.10*** *p133*
Johnstone, John; Washington, 1856 ***1224.3*** *p42*
Johnstone, John 23; Ontario, 1871 ***1823.15*** *p131*
Johnstone, John 27; Ontario, 1871 ***1823.15*** *p131*
Johnstone, John 36; Ontario, 1871 ***1823.15*** *p131*
Johnstone, John 41; Ontario, 1871 ***1823.15*** *p131*
Johnstone, John 60; Ontario, 1871 ***1823.15*** *p131*
Johnstone, Joseph 79; Ontario, 1871 ***1823.22*** *p83*
Johnstone, Margaret Elizabeth; British Columbia, 1900 ***1640.13*** *p63*
Johnstone, Mary 46; Ontario, 1871 ***1823.15*** *p131*
Johnstone, Robert 18; Ontario, 1871 ***1823.15*** *p131*
Johnstone, Robert 34; Ontario, 1871 ***1823.15*** *p131*
Johnstone, Thomas; Jamaica, 1830 ***1640.13*** *p63*
Johnstone, Walter; America, 1887 ***1640.13*** *p63*
Johnstone, William 36; Ontario, 1871 ***1823.15*** *p131*
Johnstone, William 63; Ontario, 1871 ***1823.15*** *p131*
Joho, Hans Michael; Port uncertain, 1740 ***2856.30*** *p203*
Joho, Martin; Port uncertain, 1740 ***2856.30*** *p203*
Johren, Mrs. Johann; Port uncertain, 1750 ***2856.30*** *p203*
Johusky, Stanislau; Maryland, 1910 ***3259.35*** *p23*
Joice, George 22; Ontario, 1871 ***1823.22*** *p83*
Joice, Mary 63; Vermont, 1863 ***5900.10*** *p525*
Joine, Margrett; Maryland, 1678 ***2524.55*** *p124*
Joint, Thomas 65; Ontario, 1871 ***1823.28*** *p50*
Joiorns, Katherine; Maryland, 1679 ***2524.55*** *p124*
Jolcham, James 40; Ontario, 1871 ***1823.22*** *p83*
Jolicoeur, Nancie; Ontario, 1871 ***1823.28*** *p50*
Joliffe, Tho; Virginia, 1664 ***6212.30*** *p9*
Jolland, Charles; Rhode Island, 1780 ***1224.2*** *p63*
Joller, John; New York, 1833-1838 ***8197.10*** *p120*
Jolley, Ja; Virginia, 1663 ***6212.30*** *p4*
Jolley, William; Maryland, 1666 ***2524.55*** *p124*
Jolliff, John; New York, 1840 ***8197.10*** *p245*
Jolliffe, Mary; Georgia, 1741 ***1640.10*** *p90*
Jolly, Mr.; Florida, 1775 ***1640.10*** *p90*
Jolly, Mr.; St. Augustine, Florida, 1775 ***1640.10*** *p90*
Jolly, Eliza *SEE* Jolly, James
Jolly, Elizabeth *SEE* Jolly, James
Jolly, James; Maryland, 1655 ***2524.55*** *p124*
Wife: Elizabeth
Son: William
Jolly, James; Virginia, 1665-1666 ***6212.30*** *p20*
Wife: Eliza
Daughter: Eliza
Jolly, James 40; Maryland, 1775 ***1220.25*** *p101*
Jolly, Jessie; Quebec, 1858 ***9196.15*** *p37*
Jolly, John; New York, 1833-1838 ***8197.10*** *p120*
Jolly, Martin; Florida, 1767 ***1640.10*** *p90*
Jolly, Martin 22; St. Vincent, 1775 ***1220.25*** *p129*
Jolly, Thomas; New York, 1830 ***8197.10*** *p361*
Jolly, Thos; Quebec, 1856 ***9196.15*** *p11*
Jolly, Walter; New York, 1830 ***8197.10*** *p360*
Jolly, William *SEE* Jolly, James
Joly, Mr.; Quebec, 1858 ***9196.15*** *p41*
Jome, Allen 45; Ontario, 1871 ***1823.28*** *p50*
Jomkiewia, Joseph; Maryland, 1910 ***3259.35*** *p23*
Jonas, Henry; Pennsylvania, 1777 ***4629.10*** *p13*
Jonas, James; New York, 1827 ***8197.10*** *p244*
Jonas, Philip; New York, 1807 ***8197.10*** *p41*
Jonason, O. 25; British Columbia, 1909 ***9196.1*** *p27*
Jonason, O. 25; Washington, 1909 ***9196.1*** *p27*
Jone, Francis Joseph; New York, 1836 ***8197.10*** *p244*
Jones, Miss; Quebec, 1857 ***9196.15*** *p26*
Jones, Miss; Quebec, 1858 ***9196.15*** *p45*
Jones, Mr., Jr.; Quebec, 1857 ***9196.15*** *p17*
Jones, Mrs.; Maryland, 1665 ***2524.55*** *p124*
Jones, Mrs.; Maryland, 1668 ***2524.55*** *p124*
Jones, Mrs.; Maryland, 1682 ***2524.55*** *p124*
Jones, Mrs.; Philadelphia, 1774 ***1220.25*** *p55*
Jones, Ab.; Pennsylvania, 1784 ***4629.10*** *p43*
Jones, Abraham; Maryland, 1658 ***2524.55*** *p124*
Jones, Abraham; New York, 1839 ***8197.10*** *p133*
Jones, Allen; Virginia, 1792 ***1224.2*** *p63*
Jones, Amanda 10; Ontario, 1861 ***2896.28*** *p45*
Jones, Ann; Maryland, 1665 ***2524.55*** *p124*
Jones, Ann; Maryland, 1674 ***2524.55*** *p124*
Jones, Ann; New England, 1661 ***1224.1*** *p38*
Jones, Anne *SEE* Jones, Samuel
Jones, Anne; Maryland, 1631-1685 ***2524.55*** *p124*
Jones, Anne; Maryland, 1663 ***2524.55*** *p49*
Jones, Anne; Maryland, 1676 ***2524.55*** *p124*
Jones, Anne 3; Ontario, 1861 ***2896.28*** *p51*
Jones, Anne 49; Ontario, 1871 ***1823.15*** *p131*
Jones, Annis; Maryland, 1658 ***2524.55*** *p124*
Jones, Anthony; New York, 1807 ***8197.10*** *p41*
Jones, Barbarah; Maryland, 1658 ***2524.55*** *p124*
Jones, Benjamin; Maryland, 1681 ***2524.55*** *p124*
Jones, Benjamin; Pennsylvania, 1786 ***4629.10*** *p49*
Jones, Blathwaite; Pennsylvania, 1777 ***4629.10*** *p11*
Jones, Bridget; Vermont, 1822-1905 ***5900.10*** *p335*
Jones, C. E.; Quebec, 1858 ***9196.15*** *p45*
Jones, Mrs. C. E.; Quebec, 1858 ***9196.15*** *p45*
Jones, Catharine 23; Ontario, 1861 ***2896.28*** *p47*
Jones, Catherine 32; Ontario, 1871 ***1823.15*** *p131*
Jones, Catherine 37; Ontario, 1871 ***1823.22*** *p83*
Jones, Catherine 41; Vermont, 1886 ***5900.10*** *p475*
Jones, Cecilia A. 6; Ontario, 1861 ***2896.28*** *p42*
Jones, Charles *SEE* Jones, John
Jones, Charles 20; Maryland, 1774 ***1220.25*** *p64*
Jones, Charles 25; Maryland, 1775 ***1220.25*** *p10*
Jones, Charles 50; Ontario, 1871 ***1823.28*** *p50*
Jones, Charles 54; Ontario, 1871 ***1823.28*** *p50*
Jones, Charles 55; Ontario, 1871 ***1823.28*** *p50*
Jones, Christopher; New York, New York, 1852 ***1224.3*** *p42*
Jones, Christopher 28; Ontario, 1871 ***1823.22*** *p83*
Jones, Corintha 10; Ontario, 1861 ***2896.28*** *p26*
Jones, Cornelia 16; Ontario, 1861 ***2896.28*** *p45*
Jones, Daniel 48; Ontario, 1871 ***1823.15*** *p131*
Jones, David; Maryland, 1662 ***2524.55*** *p124*
Jones, David; New York, 1825 ***8197.10*** *p244*
Jones, David; New York, 1839 ***8197.10*** *p383*
Jones, David; New York, 1840 ***8197.10*** *p384*
Jones, David 25; Virginia, 1774 ***1220.25*** *p55*
Jones, Dean; Pennsylvania, 1779 ***4629.10*** *p37*
Jones, Dorothy 67; Ontario, 1871 ***1823.22*** *p83*
Jones, E.; Quebec, 1857 ***9196.15*** *p24*
Jones, Eden Henry; New York, 1853 ***1224.3*** *p42*
Jones, Edgar; Virginia, 1664-1665 ***6212.30*** *p16*
Jones, Edgar; Virginia, 1667 ***6212.30*** *p36*
Jones, Edw; Virginia, 1672-1673 ***6212.30*** *p51*
Jones, Edw; Virginia, 1674 ***6212.30*** *p52*
Jones, Edward; Maryland, 1663 ***2524.55*** *p124*
Jones, Edward 21; Maryland, 1774 ***1220.25*** *p78*
Jones, Edward 29; Ontario, 1871 ***1823.15*** *p131*
Jones, Edward 47; Ontario, 1871 ***1823.28*** *p50*
Jones, Edwd; Virginia, 1702 ***6212.30*** *p62*
Jones, Elen J. 23; Ontario, 1861 ***2896.28*** *p51*
Jones, Eliz; Virginia, 1690-1691 ***6212.30*** *p58*
Jones, Eliza 54; Ontario, 1871 ***1823.28*** *p50*
Jones, Elizabeth *SEE* Jones, John
Jones, Elizabeth; Maryland, 1662 ***2524.55*** *p85*
Jones, Elizabeth; Maryland, 1665 ***2524.55*** *p124*
Jones, Elizabeth 20; Ontario, 1861 ***2896.28*** *p29*
Jones, Elizabeth 22; Ontario, 1861 ***2896.28*** *p51*
Jones, Elizabeth 23; Philadelphia, 1774 ***1220.25*** *p43*
Jones, Ellis; New York, 1807 ***8197.10*** *p41*
Jones, Ellis 23; Philadelphia, 1774 ***1220.25*** *p66*
Jones, Evan; Virginia, 1667 ***6212.30*** *p35*
Jones, Even; Virginia, 1663 ***6212.30*** *p1*
Jones, Florence 2; Ontario, 1861 ***2896.28*** *p47*
Jones, Frances; Maryland, 1661 ***2524.55*** *p124*
Jones, Frances 5; Ontario, 1861 ***2896.28*** *p51*
Jones, Frances H. 13; Ontario, 1861 ***2896.28*** *p55*
Jones, Francis; Maryland, 1665 ***2524.55*** *p96*
Jones, Francis; Virginia, 1666 ***6212.30*** *p28*
Jones, Francis P. 60; Ontario, 1861 ***2896.28*** *p51*
Jones, Franklin 16; Ontario, 1861 ***2896.28*** *p18*
Jones, George; New York, 1817 ***8197.10*** *p243*
Jones, George; New York, 1818 ***8197.10*** *p243*
Jones, George; Philadelphia, 1752 ***1224.2*** *p63*
Jones, George 7; Ontario, 1861 ***2896.28*** *p45*
Jones, George 21; Ontario, 1861 ***2896.28*** *p55*
Jones, George 21; Philadelphia, 1774 ***1220.25*** *p80*
Jones, George 24; Ontario, 1871 ***1823.15*** *p131*
Jones, George 51; Ontario, 1861 ***2896.28*** *p45*
Jones, George 73; Ontario, 1871 ***1823.15*** *p131*
Jones, Griffith; Pennsylvania, 1777 ***4629.10*** *p6*
Jones, Griffith; Pennsylvania, 1777 ***4629.10*** *p25*
Jones, Hannah 20; Ontario, 1861 ***2896.28*** *p35*
Jones, Hariet 8; Ontario, 1861 ***2896.28*** *p55*
Jones, Hariet 15; Ontario, 1861 ***2896.28*** *p51*
Jones, Hariet 51; Ontario, 1861 ***2896.28*** *p55*
Jones, Harry 75; Ontario, 1871 ***1823.28*** *p50*
Jones, Henry; Charleston, South Carolina, 1815 ***1224.3*** *p42*
Jones, Henry; Maryland, 1657 ***2524.55*** *p125*
Jones, Henry; New York, 1838 ***8197.10*** *p120*
Jones, Henry; Pennsylvania, 1777 ***4629.10*** *p10*
Jones, Henry; Virginia, 1666 ***6212.30*** *p27*
Jones, Henry 21; Philadelphia, 1774 ***1220.25*** *p44*
Jones, Henry 23; Baltimore, 1775 ***1220.25*** *p119*
Jones, Henry 27; Ontario, 1871 ***1823.22*** *p83*
Jones, Hugh; Maryland, 1704 ***1224.2*** *p63*
Jones, Hugh; New York, 1807 ***8197.10*** *p41*
Jones, Hugh; Virginia, 1683 ***6212.30*** *p56*
Jones, Hugh 25; America, 1774 ***1220.25*** *p36*
Jones, Humphry; Virginia, 1672 ***6212.30*** *p48*
Jones, Isaac; Pennsylvania, 1777 ***4629.10*** *p17*
Jones, Isaac; Pennsylvania, 1777 ***4629.10*** *p28*
Jones, Isaac 64; Ontario, 1871 ***1823.15*** *p131*
Jones, Isabella; Maryland, 1667 ***2524.55*** *p125*
Jones, J.; Quebec, 1856 ***9196.15*** *p11*
Jones, James; New York, 1827 ***8197.10*** *p346*
Jones, James; Vermont, 1820-1860 ***5900.10*** *p335*
Jones, James 4; Ontario, 1861 ***2896.28*** *p55*
Jones, James 24; Philadelphia, 1775 ***1220.25*** *p9*
Jones, James 27; Ontario, 1871 ***1823.15*** *p131*
Jones, James 57; Ontario, 1871 ***1823.15*** *p131*
Jones, James 65; Ontario, 1861 ***2896.28*** *p28*
Jones, James 75; Ontario, 1871 ***1823.22*** *p83*
Jones, James A.; New York, 1837 ***8197.10*** *p92*
Jones, James F. 3; Ontario, 1861 ***2896.28*** *p18*
Jones, Jane; Maryland, 1681 ***1224.1*** *p60*
Jones, Jane 30; Ontario, 1861 ***2896.28*** *p42*
Jones, Jane 43; Ontario, 1861 ***2896.25*** *p53*
Jones, Jane 48; Ontario, 1861 ***2896.28*** *p45*
Jones, Jenkin; Maryland, 1669 ***2524.55*** *p120*
Jones, Jesper; Virginia, 1663 ***6212.30*** *p2*
Jones, Jesse; Pennsylvania, 1777 ***4629.10*** *p22*
Jones, Jno; Virginia, 1681-1682 ***6212.30*** *p56*
Jones, Jno; Virginia, 1690-1691 ***6212.30*** *p59*
Jones, John *SEE* Jones, Samuel
Jones, John; Maryland, 1649 ***2524.55*** *p125*
Jones, John; Maryland, 1661 ***2524.55*** *p125*
Son: Charles
Jones, John; Maryland, 1665 ***2524.55*** *p125*
Relative: Charles
Relative: Winifred
Relative: Richard
Jones, John; Maryland, 1665 ***2524.55*** *p163*
Jones, John; Maryland, 1668 ***2524.55*** *p125*
Jones, John; Maryland, 1674 ***2524.55*** *p125*
Wife: Sarah
Daughter: Elizabeth
Jones, John; Maryland, 1674 ***2524.55*** *p125*
Jones, John; Maryland, 1675 ***2524.55*** *p125*
Jones, John; Maryland, 1676 ***2524.55*** *p125*
Wife: Sarah
Daughter: Elizabeth
Jones, John; Maryland, 1681 ***2524.55*** *p125*
Jones, John; Mobile, Alabama, 1793-1845 ***1640.10*** *p90*
Jones, John; New York, 1790 ***1224.2*** *p63*
Jones, John; New York, 1803 ***8197.10*** *p13*
Jones, John; New York, 1835-1838 ***8197.10*** *p120*
Jones, John; New York, 1837 ***8197.10*** *p318*
Jones, John; New York, 1838 ***8197.10*** *p375*
Jones, John; New York, 1839 ***8197.10*** *p133*
Jones, John; New York, 1840 ***8197.10*** *p245*
Jones, John; New York, New York, 1849 ***1224.3*** *p42*
Jones, John; Pennsylvania, 1723 ***1224.2*** *p63*
Jones, John; Pennsylvania, 1777 ***4629.10*** *p21*
Jones, John; Pennsylvania, 1786 ***4629.10*** *p53*
Jones, John; South Carolina, 1754 ***1224.2*** *p63*
Jones, John; Virginia, 1663 ***6212.30*** *p1*
Jones, John; Virginia, 1663 ***6212.30*** *p3*
Jones, John; Virginia, 1663-1664 ***6212.30*** *p5*
Jones, John; Virginia, 1664 ***6212.30*** *p6*
Jones, John; Virginia, 1664 ***6212.30*** *p8*
Jones, John; Virginia, 1672 ***6212.30*** *p48*
Jones, John; Virginia, 1681 ***1224.1*** *p33*
Jones, John 2; Ontario, 1861 ***2896.28*** *p51*
Jones, John 15; New York, 1775 ***1220.25*** *p94*
Jones, John 19; Maryland, 1775 ***1220.25*** *p120*
Jones, John 19; Ontario, 1861 ***2896.28*** *p51*
Jones, John 26; Virginia, 1774 ***1220.25*** *p93*
Jones, John 27; Philadelphia, 1774 ***1220.25*** *p27*
Jones, John 27; Virginia, 1774 ***1220.25*** *p54*
Jones, John 31; Maryland, 1774 ***1220.25*** *p47*
Jones, John 36; Maryland, 1775 ***1220.25*** *p102*
Jones, John 38; Ontario, 1871 ***1823.15*** *p131*
Jones, John 51; Ontario, 1871 ***1823.15*** *p131*
Jones, John 66; Ontario, 1861 ***2896.27*** *p20*
Jones, John 80; Ontario, 1871 ***1823.28*** *p50*
Jones, John Coffin; Boston, 1838 ***1224.3*** *p42*
Jones, John J.; New York, 1839 ***8197.10*** *p133*
Jones, John M.; New York, 1834-1838 ***8197.10*** *p121*
Jones, John R.; New York, 1838 ***8197.10*** *p244*
Jones, Jonas 84; Ontario, 1871 ***1823.22*** *p83*
Jones, Jonathan; Maryland, 1649 ***2524.55*** *p125*
Jones, Jonathan; Maryland, 1663 ***2524.55*** *p125*
Jones, Jonathan; Maryland, 1666 ***2524.55*** *p125*
Jones, Jonn 59; Ontario, 1871 ***1823.15*** *p131*
Jones, Joseph; New York, 1839 ***8197.10*** *p133*
Jones, Joseph 21; Ontario, 1871 ***1823.28*** *p50*
Jones, Joseph 35; America, 1774 ***1220.25*** *p36*
Jones, Joseph 36; Alaska, 1916 ***9196.1*** *p43*
Jones, Joseph 36; Yukon, 1916 ***9196.1*** *p43*
Jones, Josias; Virginia, 1686 ***1224.1*** *p33*
Jones, Lavisa 17; Ontario, 1861 ***2896.28*** *p29*
Jones, Lewis; Maryland, 1675 ***2524.55*** *p125*
Jones, Lewis; South Carolina, 1748 ***1224.2*** *p63*
Jones, Lewis; Virginia, 1667 ***6212.30*** *p37*
Jones, Losco; California, 1829 ***1224.3*** *p42*
Jones, Louis J.; Maryland, 1910 ***3259.35*** *p23*

Jones, Louisa; Ohio, 1852 ***1224.3*** *p42*
Jones, Louisa; Toronto, n.d. ***1224.3*** *p42*
Jones, Lydia J. 12; Ontario, 1861 ***2896.28*** *p51*
Jones, Margaret; Vermont, 1858-1932 ***5900.10*** *p353*
Jones, Margaret 17; Ontario, 1861 ***2896.28*** *p55*
Jones, Margarett *SEE* Jones, Will.
Jones, Margrett; Virginia, 1674 ***6212.30*** *p52*
Jones, Maria 66; Ontario, 1861 ***2896.28*** *p45*
Jones, Martha; Virginia, 1664 ***6212.30*** *p14*
Jones, Mary *SEE* Jones, Samuel
Jones, Mary; Maryland, 1631-1685 ***2524.55*** *p125*
Jones, Mary; Maryland, 1650 ***2524.55*** *p125*
Jones, Mary; Maryland, 1653 ***2524.55*** *p125*
Jones, Mary; Maryland, 1674 ***2524.55*** *p125*
Jones, Mary; Maryland, 1678 ***2524.55*** *p125*
Jones, Mary; Vermont, 1850-1921 ***5900.10*** *p354*
Jones, Mary; Virginia, 1664 ***6212.30*** *p6*
Jones, Mary; Virginia, 1666 ***6212.30*** *p25*
Jones, Mary; Virginia, 1698 ***6212.30*** *p61*
Jones, Mary 4; Ontario, 1861 ***2896.28*** *p51*
Jones, Mary 21; Maryland, 1775 ***1220.25*** *p115*
Jones, Mary 22; Virginia, 1774 ***1220.25*** *p88*
Jones, Mary 56; Ontario, 1871 ***1823.22*** *p83*
Jones, Mary 68; Ontario, 1871 ***1823.22*** *p83*
Jones, Mary 82; Ontario, 1861 ***2896.28*** *p26*
Jones, Mary Ann; Boston, 1791 ***1224.2*** *p63*
Jones, Mary E. 12; Ontario, 1861 ***2896.28*** *p45*
Jones, Mary E. 14; Ontario, 1861 ***2896.28*** *p18*
Jones, Mary M. 30; Ontario, 1861 ***2896.28*** *p35*
Jones, Melissa 25; Ontario, 1861 ***2896.28*** *p51*
Jones, Melissa J. 9; Ontario, 1861 ***2896.28*** *p18*
Jones, Meredith; Virginia, 1667-1668 ***6212.30*** *p38*
Jones, Michael; New York, New York, 1866 ***3437.14*** *p120*
Jones, Minerva J. 11; Ontario, 1861 ***2896.27*** *p29*
Jones, Morgan; Maryland, 1667 ***2524.55*** *p125*
Jones, Morgan; Virginia, 1667-1668 ***6212.30*** *p39*
Jones, Morris; Maryland, 1664 ***2524.55*** *p125*
Jones, Morris; Maryland, 1666 ***2524.55*** *p125*
Jones, Morris; Virginia, 1667 ***6212.30*** *p37*
Jones, Moses 18; Maryland, 1774 ***1220.25*** *p41*
Jones, Nancy 11; Ontario, 1861 ***2896.28*** *p55*
Jones, Nathan; Pennsylvania, 1777 ***4629.10*** *p13*
Jones, Nicholas; Maryland, 1682 ***2524.55*** *p125*
Jones, Owen; Maryland, 1665 ***2524.55*** *p10*
Jones, Owen; Maryland, 1668 ***2524.55*** *p125*
With wife
Jones, Owen; New York, 1698 ***1224.1*** *p33*
Jones, Owen 50; Ontario, 1871 ***1823.15*** *p131*
Jones, Peter; New York, 1807 ***8197.10*** *p325*
Jones, Phebe A. 15; Ontario, 1861 ***2896.28*** *p55*
Jones, Philip; Maryland, 1674 ***2524.55*** *p125*
Jones, Philip 27; Maryland, 1775 ***1220.25*** *p104*
Jones, Phillip; Maryland, 1661 ***2524.55*** *p177*
Jones, R.; Quebec, 1857 ***9196.15*** *p17*
Jones, Mrs. R.; Quebec, 1857 ***9196.15*** *p17*
Jones, Rees; New York, New York, 1848 ***6058.10*** *p35*
Jones, Rich; Virginia, 1665-1666 ***6212.30*** *p21*
Jones, Richard *SEE* Jones, John
Jones, Richard; Maryland, 1671 ***2524.55*** *p125*
Jones, Richard; Maryland, 1672 ***2524.55*** *p125*
Jones, Richard; Maryland, 1675 ***2524.55*** *p125*
Jones, Richard; New York, 1807 ***8197.10*** *p41*
Jones, Richard; New York, 1827 ***8197.10*** *p340*
Jones, Richard; Virginia, 1659 ***1224.1*** *p33*
Jones, Richard; Virginia, 1667-1668 ***6212.30*** *p38*
Jones, Richard; Virginia, 1669-1670 ***6212.30*** *p41*
Jones, Richard 17; America, 1774 ***1220.25*** *p35*
Jones, Richard 21; Philadelphia, 1774 ***1220.25*** *p80*
Jones, Richard 23; Maryland, 1774 ***1220.25*** *p74*
Jones, Richard 50; Ontario, 1871 ***1823.15*** *p131*
Jones, Richard S.; New York, 1838 ***8197.10*** *p120*
Jones, Robert; Maryland, 1658 ***2524.55*** *p126*
Jones, Robert; Maryland, 1665 ***2524.55*** *p126*
Jones, Robert; Maryland, 1680 ***2524.55*** *p126*
Jones, Robert; Maryland, 1682 ***2524.55*** *p126*
Jones, Robert; New York, 1807 ***8197.10*** *p41*
Jones, Robert; Pennsylvania, 1777 ***4629.10*** *p12*
Jones, Robert; Virginia, 1771 ***1224.2*** *p63*
Jones, Robert 22; Maryland, 1774 ***1220.25*** *p39*
Jones, Robert 22; Philadelphia, 1774 ***1220.25*** *p81*
Jones, Robert 23; Ontario, 1861 ***2896.28*** *p51*
Jones, Robert 24; Ontario, 1861 ***2896.28*** *p42*
Jones, Robert 38; Ontario, 1861 ***2896.28*** *p26*
Jones, Robert 50; Ontario, 1871 ***1823.15*** *p131*
Jones, Robert 51; Ontario, 1871 ***1823.22*** *p84*
Jones, Robert 60; Ontario, 1871 ***1823.15*** *p131*
Jones, Robert, Sr. 82; Ontario, 1861 ***2896.28*** *p26*
Jones, Robert H. 10; Ontario, 1861 ***2896.28*** *p33*
Jones, Robert M.; New York, 1836 ***8197.10*** *p319*
Jones, Robert Nelson 5; Ontario, 1861 ***2896.28*** *p18*
Jones, Robert Strettle; Pennsylvania, 1777 ***4629.10*** *p23*
Jones, Robt; Virginia, 1665-1666 ***6212.30*** *p23*
Jones, Robt; Virginia, 1666 ***6212.30*** *p26*
Jones, Robt; Virginia, 1666-1667 ***6212.30*** *p32*
Jones, Rodorick; Maryland, 1676 ***2524.55*** *p126*
Jones, Roger; Virginia, 1664-1665 ***6212.30*** *p16*
Jones, Rowland; Maryland, 1670 ***2524.55*** *p232*
Jones, Samll, Jr.; Virginia, 1664 ***6212.30*** *p6*
Jones, Samuel *SEE* Jones, Samuel
Jones, Samuel; Maryland, 1662 ***2524.55*** *p126*
Wife: Mary
Son: Samuel
Son: John
Jones, Samuel; Maryland, 1682 ***2524.55*** *p126*
Wife: Mary
Child: Anne
Child: Mary
Child: John
Jones, Samuel; New England, 1673 ***1224.1*** *p33*
Jones, Samuel; New York, 1834 ***8197.10*** *p73*
Jones, Samuel; Pennsylvania, 1779 ***4629.10*** *p40*
Jones, Samuel; Pennsylvania, 1786 ***4629.10*** *p54*
Jones, Samuel; Died enroute, 1693 ***1224.1*** *p33*
Jones, Samuel 17; Ontario, 1871 ***1823.15*** *p131*
Jones, Samuel 18; Philadelphia, 1775 ***1220.25*** *p8*
Jones, Samuel 30; Ontario, 1871 ***1823.15*** *p131*
Jones, Samuel 40; Ontario, 1871 ***1823.15*** *p131*
Jones, Samuel 44; Ontario, 1861 ***2896.28*** *p18*
Jones, Samuel 63; Ontario, 1871 ***1823.15*** *p131*
Jones, Samuel B.; New York, 1839 ***8197.10*** *p134*
Jones, Samuel J. 7; Ontario, 1861 ***2896.28*** *p18*
Jones, Samuell; Maryland, 1663 ***2524.55*** *p51*
Jones, Samuell; Maryland, 1678 ***2524.55*** *p126*
Jones, Samuell; Virginia, 1664 ***6212.30*** *p6*
Jones, Sarah *SEE* Jones, John
Jones, Sarah; Maryland, 1665 ***2524.55*** *p126*
Jones, Sarah; Maryland, 1676 ***2524.55*** *p126*
Jones, Sarah; Virginia, 1672 ***6212.30*** *p48*
Jones, Sarah; Virginia, 1703-1704 ***6212.30*** *p62*
Jones, Sarah 67; Ontario, 1871 ***1823.15*** *p131*
Jones, Scriven 22; Maryland, 1775 ***1220.25*** *p98*
Jones, Simon; Maryland, 1776 ***1224.2*** *p63*
Jones, Stephen 50; Ontario, 1871 ***1823.15*** *p131*
Jones, Susanna; Maryland, 1682 ***2524.55*** *p126*
Jones, Susanna; New York, 1829 ***8197.10*** *p351*
Jones, Susanna; Virginia, 1672 ***6212.30*** *p48*
Jones, Susanna 13; Ontario, 1861 ***2896.28*** *p26*
Jones, Susanna 31; Ontario, 1871 ***1823.15*** *p131*
Jones, Susannah A. 11; Ontario, 1861 ***2896.28*** *p18*
Jones, Tho.; Maryland, 1681 ***2524.55*** *p126*
Jones, Tho; Virginia, 1672 ***6212.30*** *p48*
Jones, Thomas; Maryland, 1649-1658 ***2524.55*** *p126*
Jones, Thomas; Maryland, 1655 ***2524.55*** *p126*
Jones, Thomas; Maryland, 1665 ***2524.55*** *p78*
Jones, Thomas; Maryland, 1666 ***2524.55*** *p126*
Jones, Thomas; Maryland, 1672 ***2524.55*** *p126*
Jones, Thomas; Maryland, 1676 ***2524.55*** *p126*
Jones, Thomas; Maryland, 1678 ***2524.55*** *p138*
Jones, Thomas; Maryland, 1681 ***2524.55*** *p126*
Jones, Thomas; New York, n.d. ***1224.2*** *p63*
Jones, Thomas; New York, 1838 ***8197.10*** *p120*
Jones, Thomas; New York, 1840 ***8197.10*** *p175*
Jones, Thomas; Pennsylvania, 1777 ***4629.10*** *p10*
Jones, Thomas; Pennsylvania, 1851 ***6058.10*** *p29*
Jones, Thomas; Virginia, 1626 ***1224.1*** *p33*
Jones, Thomas; Virginia, 1663 ***6212.30*** *p3*
Jones, Thomas; Virginia, 1664 ***6212.30*** *p5*
Jones, Thomas; Virginia, 1664 ***6212.30*** *p11*
Jones, Thomas; Virginia, 1664 ***6212.30*** *p12*
Jones, Thomas; Virginia, 1671 ***6212.30*** *p42*
Jones, Thomas; Virginia, 1671-1672 ***6212.30*** *p47*
Jones, Thomas; Virginia, 1698 ***1224.1*** *p33*
Jones, Thomas; Virginia, 1703-1704 ***6212.30*** *p62*
Jones, Thomas; Virginia, 1724 ***1224.2*** *p63*
Jones, Thomas 13; Philadelphia, 1774 ***1220.25*** *p4*
Jones, Thomas 17; Maryland, 1775 ***1220.25*** *p109*
Jones, Thomas 18; Philadelphia, 1774 ***1220.25*** *p4*
Jones, Thomas 21; Maryland, 1774 ***1220.25*** *p73*
Jones, Thomas 21; Maryland, 1775 ***1220.25*** *p105*
Jones, Thomas 22; Maryland, 1774 ***1220.25*** *p41*
Jones, Thomas 22; Maryland, 1775 ***1220.25*** *p98*
Jones, Thomas 22; Maryland, 1775 ***1220.25*** *p116*
Jones, Thomas 22; Ontario, 1871 ***1823.15*** *p131*
Jones, Thomas 27; Maryland, 1775 ***1220.25*** *p109*
Jones, Thomas 29; Philadelphia, 1774 ***1220.25*** *p23*
Jones, Thomas 35; Ontario, 1871 ***1823.28*** *p50*
Jones, Thomas 83; Ontario, 1871 ***1823.28*** *p50*
Jones, Thos; Portland, Maine, 1858 ***9196.15*** *p28*
Jones, Tom 21; Washington, 1914 ***9196.1*** *p64*
Jones, Walter; Maryland, 1673 ***2524.55*** *p126*
Jones, Whitworth; Quebec, 1858 ***9196.15*** *p45*
Jones, Will.; Maryland, 1665 ***2524.55*** *p126*
Wife: Margarett
Jones, William; Alabama, 1789-1845 ***1640.10*** *p90*
Jones, William; Charles Town, South Carolina, n.d. ***1224.2*** *p63*
Jones, William; Maryland, 1658 ***2524.55*** *p126*
Jones, William; Maryland, 1659 ***2524.55*** *p126*
Jones, William; Maryland, 1662 ***2524.55*** *p126*
Jones, William; Maryland, 1663 ***2524.55*** *p126*
Jones, William; Maryland, 1670 ***2524.55*** *p126*
Jones, William; Maryland, 1673 ***2524.55*** *p126*
Jones, William; Maryland, 1674 ***2524.55*** *p126*
Jones, William; Maryland, 1681 ***2524.55*** *p126*
Jones, William; New York, 1765 ***1224.2*** *p63*
Jones, William; New York, 1802 ***8197.10*** *p21*
Jones, William; New York, 1807 ***8197.10*** *p41*
Jones, William; New York, 1834 ***8197.10*** *p244*
Jones, William; New York, 1836 ***8197.10*** *p319*
Jones, William; New York, 1840 ***8197.10*** *p175*
Jones, William; Pennsylvania, 1777 ***4629.10*** *p11*
Jones, William; Philadelphia, 1735 ***1224.2*** *p63*
Jones, William; Savannah, Georgia, 1809 ***1640.10*** *p90*
Jones, William; Texas, 1848 ***1224.3*** *p42*
Jones, William; Virginia, 1663 ***6212.30*** *p2*
Jones, William; Virginia, 1665-1666 ***6212.30*** *p20*
Jones, William; Virginia, 1718 ***1224.2*** *p63*
Jones, William 15; Maryland, 1775 ***1220.25*** *p113*
Jones, William 18; Virginia, 1774 ***1220.25*** *p55*
Jones, William 21; Maryland, 1775 ***1220.25*** *p115*
Jones, William 22; Maryland, 1774 ***1220.25*** *p70*
Jones, William 22; Virginia, 1774 ***1220.25*** *p92*
Jones, William 23; Maryland, 1775 ***1220.25*** *p103*
Jones, William 24; Maryland, 1775 ***1220.25*** *p112*
Jones, William 25; Maryland, 1775 ***1220.25*** *p114*
Jones, William 35; Ontario, 1871 ***1823.15*** *p132*
Jones, William 38; Philadelphia, 1774 ***1220.25*** *p80*
Jones, William 39; Ontario, 1871 ***1823.15*** *p132*
Jones, William 47; Ontario, 1871 ***1823.15*** *p132*
Jones, William B. 15; Ontario, 1861 ***2896.28*** *p33*
Jones, Willm; Maryland, 1673 ***2524.55*** *p126*
Jones, Winifred *SEE* Jones, John
Jones, Winifred; Maryland, 1664 ***2524.55*** *p197*
Jones, Wm; Virginia, 1679-1680 ***6212.30*** *p54*
Jones, Wm Henry 30; Ontario, 1871 ***1823.28*** *p50*
Jones Gibb, Mrs.; Quebec, 1856 ***9196.15*** *p11*
Jones Gibb, J.; Quebec, 1856 ***9196.15*** *p11*
Joneson, Geo 38; British Columbia, 1909 ***9196.1*** *p28*
Joneson, Geo 38; Seattle, 1909 ***9196.1*** *p28*
Jonin, Anna; Port uncertain, 1734 ***2856.30*** *p203*
Jonston, Michael 63; Ontario, 1871 ***1823.22*** *p84*
Jope, Priscilla; Pittsburgh, 1837 ***1224.3*** *p4*
Jope, Sarah; Pittsburgh, 1852 ***1224.3*** *p85*
Joplin, Garthorn John 18; Ontario, 1871 ***1823.22*** *p84*
Joplin, William 55; Ontario, 1871 ***1823.22*** *p84*
Jopp, Hugh 22; Maryland, 1774 ***1220.25*** *p58*
Jopp, Jost; Port uncertain, 1729 ***2856.30*** *p203*
Joran, Martin; Maryland, 1910 ***3259.35*** *p23*
Jordaine, Jonas; Maryland, 1663 ***2524.55*** *p126*
Jordan, Mr.; Portland, Maine, 1858 ***9196.15*** *p27*
Jordan, Anton; Port uncertain, 1769 ***2856.30*** *p203*
Jordan, Anton; Port uncertain, 1770 ***2856.30*** *p203*
Jordan, Edward 70; Vermont, 1898 ***5900.10*** *p609*
Jordan, Elizabeth 30; Ontario, 1861 ***2896.27*** *p62*
Jordan, Francis; New York, 1839 ***8197.10*** *p244*
Jordan, Francis 35; Ontario, 1871 ***1823.15*** *p132*
Jordan, Godfred 43; Ontario, 1871 ***1823.28*** *p50*
Jordan, James 65; Ontario, 1871 ***1823.28*** *p50*
Jordan, Jane; Virginia, 1792 ***1224.2*** *p64*
Jordan, Jno; Virginia, 1664 ***6212.30*** *p15*
Jordan, John; Maryland, 1682 ***2524.55*** *p126*
Jordan, John; New York, 1834-1838 ***8197.10*** *p120*
Jordan, John 34; Ontario, 1871 ***1823.15*** *p132*
Jordan, John 45; Ontario, 1861 ***2896.27*** *p61*
Jordan, Josef; Port uncertain, 1741 ***2856.30*** *p203*
With 3 children
Jordan, Lewis; Vermont, 1838-1910 ***5900.10*** *p194*
Jordan, Mary; Ontario, 1861 ***2896.27*** *p61*
Jordan, Mary E. Lepp; Vermont, 1847-1938 ***5900.10*** *p194*
Jordan, Mary M.; Vermont, 1861-1939 ***5900.10*** *p526*
Jordan, Patrick; New York, 1834-1838 ***8197.10*** *p120*
Jordan, Patrick 40; Ontario, 1871 ***1823.28*** *p50*
Jordan, Robert; Virginia, 1668 ***1224.1*** *p33*
Jordan, Samuel 15; Philadelphia, 1775 ***1220.25*** *p8*
Jordan, Samuel 62; Ontario, 1871 ***1823.28*** *p50*
Jordan, Susanna 21; Philadelphia, 1775 ***1220.25*** *p122*
Jordan, Thomas 17; Maryland, 1775 ***1220.25*** *p114*
Jordan, Thomas 25; Ontario, 1871 ***1823.15*** *p132*
Jordan, Thomas 64; Ontario, 1871 ***1823.15*** *p132*
Jordan, William M. 21; Ontario, 1871 ***1823.15*** *p132*
Jorden, Alexander; Maryland, 1663 ***2524.55*** *p127*
Jorden, Susanna; Maryland, 1672 ***2524.55*** *p127*
Jorenson, Mrs.; Maryland, 1664 ***2524.55*** *p127*
Jorg, Johann Niklas; Port uncertain, 1784 ***2856.30*** *p209*
Jorger, Marianna; Port uncertain, 1796 ***2856.30*** *p209*
Jorginson, Mr.; Quebec, 1858 ***9196.15*** *p33*

Jorins, Margrett; Maryland, 1679 ***2524.55*** *p127*
Jorningham, Ellinor; Maryland, 1654 ***2524.55*** *p127*
Jorrington, Mrs.; Quebec, 1857 ***9196.15*** *p27*
Jortan, Richard; Maryland, 1673 ***2524.55*** *p127*
Jorton, Richard; Maryland, 1671 ***2524.55*** *p127*
Jory, James 61; Ontario, 1871 ***1823.15*** *p132*
Jos, Valentin; Port uncertain, 1772 ***2856.30*** *p203*
Jos, Valentin; Port uncertain, 1802 ***2856.30*** *p203*
Jose, John; Boston, 1706 ***1224.2*** *p64*
Joseph, Adam; New York, 1840 ***8197.10*** *p245*
Joseph, Andreas; Port uncertain, 1789 ***2856.30*** *p203*
Joseph, Benedictus; New York, 1851 ***1224.3*** *p42*
Joseph, Eliza; New York, 1853 ***1224.3*** *p42*
Joseph, John; Quebec, 1856 ***9196.15*** *p5*
Joseph, Samuel; Cincinnati, 1827 ***1224.3*** *p42*
Josephson, Manuel; Pennsylvania, 1777 ***4629.10*** *p14*
Joshulska, Michael; Maryland, 1910 ***3259.35*** *p23*
Josiah, James; Pennsylvania, 1777 ***4629.10*** *p8*
Joslin, John 38; Ontario, 1871 ***1823.15*** *p132*
Josling, Henry 50; Ontario, 1871 ***1823.15*** *p132*
Josop, Joseph; Maryland, 1671 ***2524.55*** *p127*
Joss, Jakob; Port uncertain, 1764 ***2856.30*** *p204*
Josslen, Anna Catharina; Port uncertain, 1750 ***2856.30*** *p209*
Jost, Andreas; New York, 1840 ***8197.10*** *p175*
Jost, Anna Margarete; Port uncertain, 1774 ***2856.30*** *p204*
Jost, Anna Maria; Port uncertain, 1766 ***2856.30*** *p204*
Jost, Christof; America, 1818 ***2856.30*** *p204*
Jost, Ernst Ludwig; Port uncertain, 1762 ***2856.30*** *p204*
Jost, J. Felix Martin; Port uncertain, 1761 ***2856.30*** *p204*
Jost, Jakob; America, 1739 ***2856.30*** *p204*
Jost, Jakob; Port uncertain, 1728 ***2856.30*** *p204*
Jost, Jakob; Port uncertain, 1764 ***2856.30*** *p204*
Jost, Jakob; Port uncertain, 1766 ***2856.30*** *p204*
Jost, Joanna; America, 1818 ***2856.30*** *p204*
Jost, Johann; America, 1738 ***2856.30*** *p204*
Jost, Johann; Port uncertain, 1749 ***2856.30*** *p204*
Jost, Johann Konrad; Port uncertain, 1755 ***2856.30*** *p204*
Jost, Johann Nickel; Port uncertain, 1740 ***2856.30*** *p204*
Jost, Johann Philipp; Port uncertain, 1765 ***2856.30*** *p204*
Jost, Leopold; America, 1738 ***2856.30*** *p204*
Jost, Leopold; Port uncertain, 1737 ***2856.30*** *p204*
Jost, Margarete; Port uncertain, 1790 ***2856.30*** *p204*
Jost, Maria; Port uncertain, 1794 ***2856.30*** *p204*
Jost, Peter; America, 1738 ***2856.30*** *p204*
Jost, Philipp; Port uncertain, 1752 ***2856.30*** *p204*
Jost, Wilhelm; Port uncertain, 1784 ***2856.30*** *p204*
Jouan, Auguste; New York, 1827 ***8197.10*** *p347*
Jouet, John Troup; New Jersey, 1794 ***1224.2*** *p64*
Jouett, Daniel Troop; Philadelphia, 1814 ***1224.3*** *p42*
Joughin, Margaret; New York, 1819 ***8197.10*** *p61*
Jourdaine, Elizabeth *SEE* Jourdaine, John
Jourdaine, Elizabeth; Maryland, 1682 ***2524.55*** *p127*
Jourdaine, John; Maryland, 1670 ***2524.55*** *p127*
Wife: Elizabeth
Jourdon, Edward 40; Ontario, 1871 ***1823.28*** *p50*
Journ, John 16; Virginia, 1774 ***1220.25*** *p94*
Jouski, J. 25; Alaska, 1912 ***9196.1*** *p39*
Jouski, J. 25; Whitehorse, Yukon, 1912 ***9196.1*** *p39*
Jouski, R. 26; Alaska, 1912 ***9196.1*** *p39*
Jouski, R. 26; Whitehorse, Yukon, 1912 ***9196.1*** *p39*
Jouy, Peter Louis; New York, 1821 ***8197.10*** *p243*
Joy, Ann 48; Ontario, 1871 ***1823.15*** *p132*
Joy, Erasmus; Virginia, 1682 ***1224.1*** *p33*
Joy, George; Boston, 1680 ***1224.1*** *p33*
Joy, George; Virginia, 1664 ***6212.30*** *p9*
Joy, Henry 21; Ontario, 1871 ***1823.15*** *p132*
Joy, James 23; Maryland, 1774 ***1220.25*** *p62*
Joy, James 33; Ontario, 1871 ***1823.15*** *p132*
Joy, Margarett; Maryland, 1649 ***2524.55*** *p127*
Joy, Mary; Maryland, 1670 ***2524.55*** *p127*
Joy, Thomas; Virginia, 1665 ***6212.30*** *p18*
Joyce, . . .; Maryland, 1631-1685 ***2524.55*** *p127*
Joyce, David; New York, 1830 ***8197.10*** *p244*
Joyce, Dorothy Cotchett; New England, 1658 ***1224.1*** *p15*
Joyce, Elizabeth *SEE* Joyce, John
Joyce, Elizabeth; Maryland, 1661 ***2524.55*** *p46*
Joyce, Elizabeth; Vermont, 1854-1932 ***5900.10*** *p193*
Joyce, John *SEE* Joyce, John
Joyce, John; Maryland, 1653 ***2524.55*** *p127*
Wife: Elizabeth
Child: John
Child: Mary
Joyce, John; New York, 1840 ***8197.10*** *p175*
Joyce, John 76; Vermont, 1901 ***5900.10*** *p218*
Joyce, Mary *SEE* Joyce, John
Joyce, Mary Hanley 72; Vermont, 1899 ***5900.10*** *p218*
Joyce, Patrick; New York, 1837 ***8197.10*** *p92*
Joyce, Patrick 42; Vermont, 1877 ***5900.10*** *p163*
Joyce, Wm; Virginia, 1664 ***6212.30*** *p9*
Joye, George; Virginia, 1664 ***6212.30*** *p14*
Joye, Peter; Maryland, 1665 ***2524.55*** *p127*
Joye, Thomas; Virginia, 1664 ***6212.30*** *p15*
Joyner, Thomas; Virginia, 1675 ***1224.1*** *p34*
Joyner, William; Maryland, 1669 ***2524.55*** *p127*
Jozchuski, Brnfrez; Maryland, 1910 ***3259.35*** *p23*
Jozefa, Marek; Maryland, 1910 ***3259.35*** *p23*
Jre, Samuell; Virginia, 1664 ***6212.30*** *p14*
Jsansinzki, Martin; Maryland, 1910 ***3259.35*** *p23*
Jsksas, Julius; Maryland, 1910 ***3259.35*** *p23*
Jub, Thomas; Maryland, 1668 ***2524.55*** *p223*
Jubal, Martin; Maryland, 1910 ***3259.35*** *p23*
Jubery, Mary J. 37; Vermont, 1887 ***5900.10*** *p602*
Jubick, Agness; Maryland, 1910 ***3259.35*** *p23*
Jubin, John M.; New York, 1807 ***8197.10*** *p41*
Jubkouski, Mike; Maryland, 1910 ***3259.35*** *p23*
Juby, Febe 81; Ontario, 1871 ***1823.22*** *p84*
Juby, William 22; Ontario, 1871 ***1823.28*** *p50*
Juckes, Edward; South Carolina, 1715 ***1224.2*** *p64*
Judah, Eleazor; Pennsylvania, 1779 ***4629.10*** *p36*
Judah, Elizabeth; New York, 1832 ***8197.10*** *p356*
Judah, Moses; Pennsylvania, 1777 ***4629.10*** *p30*
Judah, Samuel; Pennsylvania, 1777 ***4629.10*** *p28*
Judd, Fredrick 27; Ontario, 1871 ***1823.28*** *p50*
Judd, James; Cincinnati, 1851 ***1224.3*** *p43*
Judd, Margaret M. Carroll; Vermont, 1834-1909 ***5900.10*** *p465*
Judd, Sylvester; Vermont, 1842-1924 ***5900.10*** *p465*
Judd, Sylvester; Vermont, 1842-1924 ***5900.10*** *p466*
Judge, Ann E. Conlon 52; Vermont, 1904 ***5900.10*** *p414*
Judge, Bryan 55; Vermont, 1898 ***5900.10*** *p414*
Judge, Hanora McCormack 56; Vermont, 1894 ***5900.10*** *p115*
Judge, Mary McCaffrey; Vermont, 1847-1929 ***5900.10*** *p509*
Judge, Patrick 63; Ontario, 1871 ***1823.15*** *p132*
Judge, Thomas; New York, 1839 ***8197.10*** *p381*
Judge, Thomas 87; Vermont, 1898 ***5900.10*** *p115*
Judith, Maria; America, 1750 ***2856.30*** *p204*
With children
Judson, Thomas 19; Maryland, 1774 ***1220.25*** *p72*
Juell, John; Virginia, 1663 ***6212.30*** *p2*
Jues, James; Maryland, 1668 ***2524.55*** *p127*
Jugelewicz, Frank; Maryland, 1910 ***3259.35*** *p23*
Jugierski, Michael; Maryland, 1910 ***3259.35*** *p24*
Jugley, John; New York, 1807 ***8197.10*** *p41*
Jugold, Eliz; Virginia, 1671-1672 ***6212.30*** *p47*
Jukes, David 23; Nova Scotia, 1774 ***1220.25*** *p135*
Jules, John; Virginia, 1672 ***6212.30*** *p50*
Juletto, Frank 41; Washington, 1911 ***9196.1*** *p33*
Julg, Johann Georg; Port uncertain, 1737 ***2856.30*** *p208*
Julin, Carls; America, 1760 ***1224.2*** *p64*
Julis, Ettiennio 24; Alaska, 1913 ***9196.1*** *p23*
Julius, George Henry; New York, 1835 ***8197.10*** *p317*
Julor, Elizabeth; Maryland, 1678 ***2524.55*** *p127*
Jump, William; Maryland, 1665 ***2524.55*** *p10*
Junck, Luisa; Port uncertain, 1774 ***2856.30*** *p204*
Junck, Maria Catharina; Port uncertain, 1785 ***2856.30*** *p204*
Junck, Maria Margarete; Port uncertain, 1774 ***2856.30*** *p204*
Junck, Maria Margarete; Port uncertain, 1785 ***2856.30*** *p204*
Junckel, Johann Georg; Port uncertain, 1738 ***2856.30*** *p204*
Juncker, Daniel; Port uncertain, 1729 ***2856.30*** *p204*
Juncker, Friedrich; Port uncertain, 1764 ***2856.30*** *p204*
Juncker, Jakob; Port uncertain, 1741 ***2856.30*** *p205*
With wife & 3 children
Juncker, Maria Margarete; Port uncertain, 1785 ***2856.30*** *p204*
Junckh, Elisabeth; Port uncertain, 1747 ***2856.30*** *p205*
Junckh, Heinrich; Port uncertain, 1747 ***2856.30*** *p205*
Junckher, Anna Christina; Port uncertain, 1750 ***2856.30*** *p205*
Junckhin, Maria Catharina; Port uncertain, 1746 ***2856.30*** *p205*
Junes, Thomas; St. Augustine, Florida, 1786 ***1640.10*** *p90*
Jung, Abraham; America, 1751 ***2856.30*** *p205*
Jung, Anna Barbara; Port uncertain, 1786 ***2856.30*** *p205*
Jung, Anna Catharina; Port uncertain, 1759 ***2856.30*** *p205*
Jung, Anna Elisabeth; America, 1754 ***2856.30*** *p205*
Jung, Anna Margarete; Port uncertain, 1752 ***2856.30*** *p205*
Jung, Anna Margarete; Port uncertain, 1758 ***2856.30*** *p205*
Jung, Anna Ursula; Port uncertain, 1776 ***2856.30*** *p205*
Jung, Barbara; Port uncertain, 1753 ***2856.30*** *p205*
Jung, Barbara; Port uncertain, 1754 ***2856.30*** *p205*
Jung, Bernhard; America, 1753 ***2856.30*** *p205*
Jung, Bernhard; Port uncertain, 1753 ***2856.30*** *p207*
With wife & child
Jung, Catharina; America, 1753 ***2856.30*** *p205*
Jung, Catharina; Port uncertain, 1769 ***2856.30*** *p205*
Jung, Christian; Port uncertain, 1800 ***2856.30*** *p205*
Jung, Christina; Port uncertain, 1786 ***2856.30*** *p207*
With husband
Jung, Gabriel; America, 1741 ***2856.30*** *p205*
Jung, Hans; Port uncertain, 1762 ***2856.30*** *p205*
Jung, Henrich; America, 1744 ***2856.30*** *p205*
Jung, Henrich; Port uncertain, 1785 ***2856.30*** *p206*
Jung, Jacob; America, 1771 ***2856.30*** *p205*
Jung, Jakob; America, 1751 ***2856.30*** *p205*
Jung, Jakob; America, 1752 ***2856.30*** *p207*
With wife & 2 children
Jung, Jakob; Port uncertain, 1741 ***2856.30*** *p205*
Jung, Jakob; Port uncertain, 1753 ***2856.30*** *p206*
With 2 children
Jung, Jakob; Port uncertain, 1791 ***2856.30*** *p205*
Jung, Johann; Port uncertain, 1757 ***2856.30*** *p207*
With wife & 4 children
Jung, Johann; Port uncertain, 1762 ***2856.30*** *p208*
Jung, Johann; Port uncertain, 1764 ***2856.30*** *p205*
Jung, Johann; Port uncertain, 1788 ***2856.30*** *p205*
Jung, Mrs. Johann; America, 1744 ***2856.30*** *p206*
With 4 children
Jung, Johann Adam; America, 1749 ***2856.30*** *p206*
Jung, Johann Adam; America, 1762 ***2856.30*** *p206*
Jung, Johann Georg; America, 1768 ***2856.30*** *p205*
Jung, Johann Georg; America, 1772 ***2856.30*** *p205*
Jung, Johann Jacob; America, 1755 ***2856.30*** *p206*
Jung, Johann Jacob; America, 1764 ***2856.30*** *p206*
Jung, Johann Jacob; Port uncertain, 1784 ***2856.30*** *p206*
Jung, Johann Jacob; Port uncertain, 1786 ***2856.30*** *p205*
Jung, Johann Michael; Port uncertain, 1788 ***2856.30*** *p205*
Jung, Johann Niklas; Port uncertain, 1764 ***2856.30*** *p205*
Jung, Johann Peter; America, 1749 ***2856.30*** *p206*
Jung, Johann Wendel; Port uncertain, 1749 ***2856.30*** *p205*
Jung, John; New York, 1835 ***8197.10*** *p310*
Jung, Karl; America, 1741 ***2856.30*** *p205*
Jung, Konrad; Port uncertain, 1796 ***2856.30*** *p205*
Jung, Magdalena; Port uncertain, 1752 ***2856.30*** *p205*
Jung, Maria Catharina; America, 1762 ***2856.30*** *p206*
Jung, Maria Catharina; Port uncertain, 1758 ***2856.30*** *p205*
Jung, Maria Elisabeth; Port uncertain, 1785 ***2856.30*** *p206*
Jung, Maria Magdalena; Port uncertain, 1750 ***2856.30*** *p206*
Jung, Maria Margarete; Port uncertain, 1748 ***2856.30*** *p207*
Jung, Melchior; America, 1751 ***2856.30*** *p206*
Jung, Niklas; Port uncertain, 1778 ***2856.30*** *p206*
Jung, Peter; Port uncertain, 1746 ***2856.30*** *p206*
Jung, Peter; Port uncertain, 1760 ***2856.30*** *p206*
Jung, Peter Christian; Port uncertain, 1769 ***2856.30*** *p206*
Jung, Philipp; America, 1744 ***2856.30*** *p207*
With wife & 8 children
Jung, Sebastian; England, 1783 ***2856.30*** *p206*
Jung, Theobald; New York, 1831 ***8197.10*** *p365*
Jung, Theobald; New York, 1831 ***8197.10*** *p369*
Jung, Thomas; Port uncertain, 1746 ***2856.30*** *p206*
Jung, Valentin; America, 1742 ***2856.30*** *p206*
Jung, Valentin; America, 1744 ***2856.30*** *p206*
Jung, Wenzel; Port uncertain, 1785 ***2856.30*** *p206*
Jungbluth, Jakob; Port uncertain, 1733 ***2856.30*** *p207*
Jungbluth, Jakob; Port uncertain, 1775 ***2856.30*** *p207*
Jungbluth, Johann; Port uncertain, 1774 ***2856.30*** *p207*
Jungbluth, Kilian; Port uncertain, 1736 ***2856.30*** *p207*
Jungbluth, Kilian; Port uncertain, 1775 ***2856.30*** *p207*
Jungbluth, Peter; Port uncertain, 1732 ***2856.30*** *p207*
Jungel, Johann Georg; Port uncertain, 1727 ***2856.30*** *p208*
Jungerich, John; New York, 1807 ***8197.10*** *p42*
Junghuth, Christof; Port uncertain, 1753 ***2856.30*** *p207*
Junginger, Anna; America, 1751 ***2856.30*** *p207*
Jungk, Margarete; Port uncertain, 1785 ***2856.30*** *p207*
Jungk, Maria Catharina; Port uncertain, 1790 ***2856.30*** *p207*
Jungk, Maria Elisabeth; Port uncertain, 1748 ***2856.30*** *p207*
Jungk, Quirin; Port uncertain, 1750 ***2856.30*** *p207*
With wife & 2 children
Jungkh, Johann Nickel; Port uncertain, 1750 ***2856.30*** *p207*
Jungling, Franz Josef; Port uncertain, 1780 ***2856.30*** *p208*
Jungling, Franz Josef; Port uncertain, 1781 ***2856.30*** *p208*
Jungmann, Johann Georg; America, 1731 ***2856.30*** *p207*
Jungmann, Johann Georg; America, 1808 ***2856.30*** *p207*
Jungmann, Karl; Port uncertain, 1764 ***2856.30*** *p207*
Jungs, Johann; Port uncertain, 1762 ***2856.30*** *p208*
Junier, Kenneth; Savannah, Georgia, 1807 ***1640.10*** *p90*
Junop, Martin 25; Ontario, 1871 ***1823.28*** *p50*
Junor, Donald 46; Ontario, 1871 ***1823.15*** *p132*
Junor, John 28; Ontario, 1871 ***1823.15*** *p132*
Junor, John 42; Ontario, 1871 ***1823.22*** *p84*
Juntilla, Gus; Alaska, 1916 ***9196.1*** *p6*
Juntilla, Gus; Yukon, 1916 ***9196.1*** *p6*

Jurak, Henry; Maryland, 1910 ***3259.35*** *p24*
Juravich, M. 30; Alaska, 1917 ***9196.1*** *p48*
Juravich, M. 30; Whitehorse, Yukon, 1917 ***9196.1*** *p48*
Jurcher, Francis Louis; New York, New York, 1856 ***3437.14*** *p59*
Jurden, Sian; New York, 1837 ***8197.10*** *p92*
Jurgens, Henry; New York, 1836 ***8197.10*** *p319*
Jurich, G. 37; Alaska, 1912 ***9196.1*** *p38*
Jurich, G. 37; Yukon, 1912 ***9196.1*** *p38*
Juris, John; Maryland, 1910 ***3259.35*** *p24*
Juris, Kazmierz; Maryland, 1910 ***3259.35*** *p24*
Juris, Martin; Maryland, 1910 ***3259.35*** *p24*
Jurovich, M. 34; Alaska, 1917 ***9196.1*** *p46*
Jurovich, M. 34; Whitehorse, Yukon, 1917 ***9196.1*** *p46*
Just, Andreas; New York, 1840 ***8197.10*** *p175*
Just, Maria Magdalena; Port uncertain, 1762 ***2856.30*** *p208*
Justice, George; Pennsylvania, 1777 ***4629.10*** *p12*
Justice, George, Jr.; Pennsylvania, 1779 ***4629.10*** *p40*
Justice, Ralph; Virginia, 1668-1669 ***6212.30*** *p40*
Justis, Ralph; Virginia, 1672 ***6212.30*** *p49*
Juszczewski, Raymond; Maryland, 1910 ***3259.35*** *p24*
Jutowski, Boleslaw; Maryland, 1910 ***3259.35*** *p24*
Jutz, Valentin; America, 1737 ***2856.30*** *p208*
With wife & 5 children
Jutzky, Anna Margarete; America, 1762 ***2856.30*** *p208*
Jutzky, Anna Margarete; America, 1768 ***2856.30*** *p208*
Juwkowski, Jacob; Maryland, 1910 ***3259.35*** *p24*
Juxon, William; Virginia, 1672 ***1224.1*** *p34*
Juzi, Cornelius; Port uncertain, 1784 ***2856.30*** *p208*
Jzebowski, John; Maryland, 1910 ***3259.35*** *p24*
Jzikowski, Edward; Maryland, 1910 ***3259.35*** *p24*

K

Kabbawsa, George 19; Ontario, 1871 ***1823.28*** *p50*
Kablin, Jno.; Maryland, 1679 ***2524.55*** *p127*
Kabrensky, Antony; Maryland, 1910 ***3259.35*** *p24*
Kach, Caspar; Port uncertain, 1754 ***2856.30*** *p210*
Kacher, Ludwig; Pennsylvania, 1777 ***4629.10*** *p9*
Kacholozki, Martin; Maryland, 1910 ***3259.35*** *p24*
Kacsinski, Joseph; Maryland, 1910 ***3259.35*** *p24*
Kaczmarek, Mary; Maryland, 1910 ***3259.35*** *p24*
Kaczorowski, John; Maryland, 1910 ***3259.35*** *p24*
Kaczynski, Jacob; Maryland, 1910 ***3259.35*** *p24*
Kaddatz, Augustus 54; Ontario, 1871 ***1823.28*** *p50*
Kadel, Peter; Port uncertain, 1749 ***2856.30*** *p210*
Kadger, Thomas; Maryland, 1650 ***2524.55*** *p127*
Kadlubowski, Ignatya; Maryland, 1910 ***3259.35*** *p24*
Kadzimierack, Joseph; Maryland, 1910 ***3259.35*** *p24*
Kaemmerle, Jacob; New York, 1838 ***8197.10*** *p121*
Kaenecke, John; Maryland, 1910 ***3259.35*** *p24*
Kaercher, Michael; Port uncertain, 1778 ***2856.30*** *p210*
Kaezorowska, Joseph; Maryland, 1910 ***3259.35*** *p24*
Kafel, John; Maryland, 1910 ***3259.35*** *p24*
Kafska, Sylvester; Maryland, 1910 ***3259.35*** *p24*
Kag, Johanna; Port uncertain, 1749 ***2856.30*** *p210*
Kagan, John 31; Ontario, 1871 ***1823.22*** *p84*
Kahler, Katie; Maryland, 1910 ***3259.35*** *p24*
Kahn, Charles; New York, 1832 ***8197.10*** *p316*
Kahn, Isaac; New York, 1840 ***8197.10*** *p247*
Kaight, Tena; Maryland, 1910 ***3259.35*** *p24*
Kain, Andrew 67; Ontario, 1871 ***1823.15*** *p132*
Kain, Anne; Vermont, 1873-1874 ***5900.10*** *p325*
Kain, Elizabeth 67; Ontario, 1871 ***1823.15*** *p132*
Kain, Ellen Plunkett; Vermont, 1840-1912 ***5900.10*** *p325*
Kain, Francis C.; Vermont, 1889-1896 ***5900.10*** *p325*
Kain, George H.; Vermont, 1884-1898 ***5900.10*** *p325*
Kain, John; Vermont, 1838 ***5900.10*** *p325*
Kain, John 40; Ontario, 1871 ***1823.15*** *p132*
Kain, Margaret 60; Vermont, 1907 ***5900.10*** *p580*
Kain, Peter; New York, 1837 ***8197.10*** *p93*
Kain, Quinton; New York, 1836 ***8197.10*** *p79*
Kaine, . . .; Boston, 1662 ***1224.1*** *p34*
Kaine, Bridget Moran 71; Vermont, 1925 ***5900.10*** *p115*
Kaine, Ellen Burns 85; Vermont, 1902 ***5900.10*** *p103*
Kaine, John 80; Vermont, 1902 ***5900.10*** *p103*
Kaine, John T.; Vermont, 1858-1951 ***5900.10*** *p115*
Kainmuska, John; Maryland, 1910 ***3259.35*** *p24*
Kair, Thomas 25; Jamaica, 1774 ***1220.25*** *p60*
Kaiser, Friedrich; Port uncertain, 1761 ***2856.30*** *p210*
Kaiser, Henry; Baltimore, 1847 ***6058.10*** *p38*
Kaiser, Ignaz; Port uncertain, 1765 ***2856.30*** *p210*
Kaiser, John; New York, New York, 1848 ***3437.14*** *p110*
Kaiser, Thomas; Maryland, 1910 ***3259.35*** *p24*
Kaiske, Frances; Maryland, 1910 ***3259.35*** *p24*
Kaison, James 40; Ontario, 1871 ***1823.22*** *p84*
Kajduk, Mary; Maryland, 1910 ***3259.35*** *p24*
Kakowski, Sadie; Maryland, 1910 ***3259.35*** *p24*
Kalber, Magdalena; Port uncertain, 1744 ***2856.30*** *p255*
Kalber, Martin; America, 1744 ***2856.30*** *p255*
With wife & children
Kalberin, Margarete; Port uncertain, 1747 ***2856.30*** *p255*
Kalbfleisch, Johann Georg; Port uncertain, 1749 ***2856.30*** *p210*
Kalbfleisch, John 28; Ontario, 1871 ***1823.15*** *p132*
Kalbfleisch, John 37; Ontario, 1871 ***1823.15*** *p132*
Kalbfleisch, Martin; New York, 1831 ***8197.10*** *p246*
Kalbfleish, Anna 62; Ontario, 1871 ***1823.15*** *p132*
Kalbfleish, Henry 38; Ontario, 1871 ***1823.15*** *p132*
Kalbfuss, Friedrich; America, 1788 ***2856.30*** *p210*
Kalblen, Johann Georg; America, 1752 ***2856.30*** *p255*
Kalblen, Johann Georg; Philadelphia, 1752 ***2856.30*** *p255*
Kalbler, Michael; Port uncertain, 1771 ***2856.30*** *p255*
Kalbsfuess, Jakob; America, 1741 ***2856.30*** *p210*
Kaldin, Anna Maria; Port uncertain, 1763 ***2856.30*** *p210*
Kale, John 61; Ontario, 1871 ***1823.15*** *p132*
Kaleen, Michael; Pennsylvania, 1867 ***6058.10*** *p59*
Kalendik, Felix; Maryland, 1910 ***3259.35*** *p24*
Kaler, Gutlib 37; Ontario, 1871 ***1823.15*** *p132*
Kaley, Mary Ann 48; Ontario, 1871 ***1823.22*** *p84*
Kalies, Albert 38; Ontario, 1871 ***1823.28*** *p50*
Kalin, Thomas 24; Halifax, Nova Scotia, 1775 ***1220.25*** *p22*
Kalinowski, Joseph; Maryland, 1910 ***3259.35*** *p24*
Kalinowski, Stanislaw; Maryland, 1910 ***3259.35*** *p24*
Kalinowsky, Alexander; Maryland, 1910 ***3259.35*** *p24*
Kalinowsky, Stephen; Maryland, 1910 ***3259.35*** *p24*
Kalinsak, George; Maryland, 1910 ***3259.35*** *p24*
Kalinski, John; Maryland, 1910 ***3259.35*** *p24*
Kalkowski, Victor; Maryland, 1910 ***3259.35*** *p24*
Kallbach, Philipp; America, 1741 ***2856.30*** *p210*
Kalnak, John; Maryland, 1910 ***3259.35*** *p24*
Kalscypiski, Anthony; Maryland, 1910 ***3259.35*** *p24*
Kalsczynski, Tom; Maryland, 1910 ***3259.35*** *p24*
Kalsing, Josef; Port uncertain, 1790 ***2856.30*** *p210*
Kalska, Maria; Maryland, 1910 ***3259.35*** *p24*
Kalt, Anna Maria; Port uncertain, 1763 ***2856.30*** *p210*
Kalt, Hans Georg; America, 1765 ***2856.30*** *p210*
Kalt, Jacob; Port uncertain, 1796 ***2856.30*** *p210*
Kalt, Johann; Port uncertain, 1764 ***2856.30*** *p210*
Kalt, Josef; Port uncertain, 1759 ***2856.30*** *p210*
Kalt, Maria; Port uncertain, 1796 ***2856.30*** *p210*
Kalt, Maria Anna; Port uncertain, 1741 ***2856.30*** *p210*
Kaltenbacher, Friedrich; America, 1737 ***2856.30*** *p210*
Kalty, Ella; Vermont, 1865-1900 ***5900.10*** *p549*
Kalty, John; Vermont, 1837-1913 ***5900.10*** *p549*
Kalty, Nancy McMullen; Vermont, 1830-1890 ***5900.10*** *p549*
Kalty, Sarah A.; Vermont, 1867-1879 ***5900.10*** *p549*
Kalwa, Bronislaw; Maryland, 1910 ***3259.35*** *p24*
Kalz, John; New York, 1840 ***8197.10*** *p177*
Kamda, Anton; Maryland, 1910 ***3259.35*** *p24*
Kamerle, Hans Georg; Port uncertain, 1735 ***2856.30*** *p211*
Kamey, Lawrence 23; Philadelphia, 1774 ***1220.25*** *p82*
Kamiansky, Wladislow; Maryland, 1910 ***3259.35*** *p24*
Kamienski, John; Maryland, 1910 ***3259.35*** *p24*
Kaminski, Piotr; Maryland, 1910 ***3259.35*** *p24*
Kaminski, Stanislaus; New York, 1840 ***8197.10*** *p247*
Kaminsky, Henry; Maryland, 1910 ***3259.35*** *p24*
Kaminsky, Leon; Maryland, 1910 ***3259.35*** *p24*
Kamisky, Stanislaw; Maryland, 1910 ***3259.35*** *p24*
Kamm, Bernhard; Port uncertain, 1790 ***2856.30*** *p211*
Kammer, Gertrud; America, 1763 ***2856.30*** *p211*
Kammer, Gertrud; Port uncertain, 1774 ***2856.30*** *p211*
Kammerer, Johann; America, 1752 ***2856.30*** *p211*
With family
Kammerer, Johann; Port uncertain, 1752 ***2856.30*** *p211*
With family
Kammerer, Johann Jakob; Port uncertain, 1751 ***2856.30*** *p255*
Kammey, Francis; New York, 1837 ***8197.10*** *p92*
Kammuller, Andreas; Port uncertain, 1739 ***2856.30*** *p211*
Kampf, Christian; America, 1750 ***2856.30*** *p255*
Kampf, Christian; Port uncertain, 1750 ***2856.30*** *p255*
Kamyowski, John; Maryland, 1910 ***3259.35*** *p25*
Kamzeski, John; Maryland, 1910 ***3259.35*** *p25*
Kanada, William 21; Ontario, 1861 ***2896.28*** *p16*
Kanaley, Edward; Vermont, 1828-1910 ***5900.10*** *p93*
Kanaley, Margaret Meehan; Vermont, 1837-1918 ***5900.10*** *p93*
Kandy, Joseph; Maryland, 1910 ***3259.35*** *p25*
Kane, . . .; New Hampshire, 1641-1660 ***4628.40*** *p44*
Kane, Ann S.; Vermont, 1854-1925 ***5900.10*** *p338*
Kane, Anna; Vermont, 1845-1928 ***5900.10*** *p119*
Kane, Barney; New York, 1840 ***8197.10*** *p247*
Kane, Bridget; Vermont, 1830-1917 ***5900.10*** *p365*
Kane, Bridget; Vermont, 1832-1888 ***5900.10*** *p336*
Kane, Bridget; Vermont, 1833-1869 ***5900.10*** *p263*
Kane, Bridget; Vermont, 1835-1901 ***5900.10*** *p311*
Kane, Bridget 34; Vermont, 1887 ***5900.10*** *p447*
Kane, Elizabeth; Vermont, 1820-1920 ***5900.10*** *p289*
Kane, Ellen; Vermont, 1844-1906 ***5900.10*** *p288*
Kane, Ellen; Vermont, 1848-1948 ***5900.10*** *p162*
Kane, Ellen 11 months; Vermont, 1853 ***5900.10*** *p498*
Kane, Ellen 20; Vermont, 1872 ***5900.10*** *p525*
Kane, James; New York, 1821 ***8197.10*** *p245*
Kane, James; Pennsylvania, 1866 ***6058.10*** *p55*
Kane, James 38; Ontario, 1871 ***1823.15*** *p132*
Kane, John; New York, 1819 ***8197.10*** *p245*
Kane, John; New York, 1840 ***8197.10*** *p247*
Kane, John; New York, New York, 1822 ***1224.3*** *p43*
Kane, John 9 months; Vermont, 1835 ***5900.10*** *p152*
Kane, John 40; Ontario, 1871 ***1823.28*** *p50*
Kane, John 90; Vermont, 1906 ***5900.10*** *p225*
Kane, John P.; Vermont, 1850-1937 ***5900.10*** *p171*
Kane, Margaret; Vermont, 1842-1911 ***5900.10*** *p85*
Kane, Maria; Vermont, 1831-1899 ***5900.10*** *p338*
Kane, Mary 19; Vermont, 1850 ***5900.10*** *p498*
Kane, Mary 42; Vermont, 1860 ***5900.10*** *p263*
Kane, Mary Ann; Vermont, 1833-1906 ***5900.10*** *p180*
Kane, Michael 22; Vermont, 1870-1879 ***5900.10*** *p263*
Kane, Michal 50; Ontario, 1871 ***1823.22*** *p84*
Kane, Norah; Vermont, 1901 ***5900.10*** *p127*
Kane, Patrick; Vermont, 1824 ***5900.10*** *p338*
Kane, Patrick; Vermont, 1848-1924 ***5900.10*** *p119*
Kane, Patrick 50; Ontario, 1871 ***1823.28*** *p50*
Kane, Peter; Vermont, 1841-1930 ***5900.10*** *p288*
Kane, Thomas; New York, 1828 ***8197.10*** *p65*
Kane, Thomas; Pennsylvania, 1777 ***4629.10*** *p12*
Kane, William 54; Vermont, 1855 ***5900.10*** *p613*
Kanechiak, Mary; Maryland, 1910 ***3259.35*** *p25*
Kanecki, Wawzynk; Maryland, 1910 ***3259.35*** *p25*
Kaneczky, Walenty; Maryland, 1910 ***3259.35*** *p25*
Kanieck, Konstenty; Maryland, 1910 ***3259.35*** *p25*
Kaniecki, Frank; Maryland, 1910 ***3259.35*** *p25*
Kankaras, T. 28; Alaska, 1917 ***9196.1*** *p47*
Kankaras, T. 28; Yukon, 1917 ***9196.1*** *p47*
Kanlinski, Jacob; Maryland, 1910 ***3259.35*** *p25*
Kannengieser, George; New York, 1840 ***8197.10*** *p247*
Kannesky, Wadyslaw; Maryland, 1910 ***3259.35*** *p25*
Kannon, Bridget; Vermont, 1895 ***5900.10*** *p536*
Kanosh, Jollineau 60; Ontario, 1871 ***1823.28*** *p50*
Kansinska, Rosalie; Maryland, 1910 ***3259.35*** *p25*
Kanster, Rienhardt 35; Kansas, 1879-1910 ***9079.10*** *p34*
Kant, Charles 28; Ontario, 1871 ***1823.28*** *p50*
Kant, Ferdinand 31; Ontario, 1871 ***1823.28*** *p50*
Kant, John 32; Ontario, 1871 ***1823.28*** *p50*
Kantorski, John; Maryland, 1910 ***3259.35*** *p25*
Kanva, Vincent; Maryland, 1910 ***3259.35*** *p25*
Kaogome, Joseph 52; Ontario, 1871 ***1823.28*** *p50*
Kaough, Edward; New York, 1840 ***8197.10*** *p177*
Kapa, Joseph; Maryland, 1910 ***3259.35*** *p25*
Kapich, Geo 30; Alaska, 1916 ***9196.1*** *p44*
Kapich, Geo 30; Whitehorse, Yukon, 1916 ***9196.1*** *p44*
Kapisjak, John; Maryland, 1910 ***3259.35*** *p25*
Kappes, Bartel; Port uncertain, 1752 ***2856.30*** *p211*

Kappes, Jakob; America, 1792 ***2856.30*** *p211*
Kappes, Martin; America, 1754 ***2856.30*** *p211*
Kappes, Mrs. Mathes; America, 1754 ***2856.30*** *p211*
Kappes, Philipp; America, 1792 ***2856.30*** *p211*
Kappis, Hans Georg; Port uncertain, 1751 ***2856.30*** *p211*
With wife & children
Kapriryk, Thomas; Maryland, 1910 ***3259.35*** *p25*
Kaprisorenski, Michael; Maryland, 1910 ***3259.35*** *p25*
Kaps, Hans; Port uncertain, 1790 ***2856.30*** *p211*
Karaban, Anton; Maryland, 1910 ***3259.35*** *p25*
Karaczewski, Frank; Maryland, 1910 ***3259.35*** *p25*
Karans, John; New York, 1826 ***8197.10*** *p246*
Karas, Sophia; Maryland, 1910 ***3259.35*** *p25*
Karbe, Elizabeth; Maryland, 1658 ***2524.55*** *p127*
Karch, Anna Margarete; Port uncertain, 1790 ***2856.30*** *p211*
Karch, Georg; Port uncertain, 1764 ***2856.30*** *p211*
Karch, Hans; Port uncertain, 1770 ***2856.30*** *p211*
Karch, Heinrich; Port uncertain, 1750 ***2856.30*** *p212*
Karch, Sebastian; Port uncertain, 1711 ***2856.30*** *p211*
Karcher, Andreas; Port uncertain, 1759 ***2856.30*** *p211*
Karcher, Andreas; Port uncertain, 1760 ***2856.30*** *p211*
Karcher, Anna Maria; Port uncertain, 1725 ***2856.30*** *p211*
Karcher, Anton; Port uncertain, 1790 ***2856.30*** *p211*
Karcher, Elisabeth; Port uncertain, 1796 ***2856.30*** *p211*
Karcher, Franziska; Port uncertain, 1773 ***2856.30*** *p211*
Karcher, Josef; Port uncertain, 1780 ***2856.30*** *p211*
Karcher, Leonard; Port uncertain, 1781 ***2856.30*** *p255*
Karcher, Margarete; Port uncertain, 1748 ***2856.30*** *p211*
Karcher, Maria Magdalena; Port uncertain, 1755 ***2856.30*** *p211*
Karcher, Matthaus; Port uncertain, 1790 ***2856.30*** *p211*
Karcher, Matthias; New York, 1838 ***8197.10*** *p113*
Karcher, Michael; Port uncertain, 1772 ***2856.30*** *p211*
Karcher, Philipp Jacob; Port uncertain, 1762 ***2856.30*** *p211*
Karchthaler, Eva; Port uncertain, 1789 ***2856.30*** *p211*
Karck, Ferdinand; New York, 1839 ***8197.10*** *p320*
Karcnewska, Anton; Maryland, 1910 ***3259.35*** *p25*
Karcz, Franciszek; Maryland, 1910 ***3259.35*** *p25*
Karczski, Leon; Maryland, 1910 ***3259.35*** *p25*
Kardas, John; Maryland, 1910 ***3259.35*** *p25*
Kardecka, Josephine; Maryland, 1910 ***3259.35*** *p25*
Karel, Friedrich; Port uncertain, 1774 ***2856.30*** *p212*
Karer, Hans Georg; Port uncertain, 1730 ***2856.30*** *p212*
Kares, Andrew; Maryland, 1910 ***3259.35*** *p25*
Karezeswski, Joseph; Maryland, 1910 ***3259.35*** *p25*
Karg, Heinrich; Port uncertain, 1750 ***2856.30*** *p212*
Karg, Konrad; Port uncertain, 1741 ***2856.30*** *p212*
Kargin, John 35; Alaska, 1914 ***9196.1*** *p24*
Karginow, B. 37; Alaska, 1916 ***9196.1*** *p42*
Karginow, B. 37; Whitehorse, Yukon, 1916 ***9196.1*** *p42*
Kargis, Andrew 64; Ontario, 1871 ***1823.15*** *p132*
Karichnewski, Martin; Maryland, 1910 ***3259.35*** *p25*
Karigan, Thomas; New York, 1821 ***8197.10*** *p64*
Karkowska, Katerzyna; Maryland, 1910 ***3259.35*** *p25*
Karls, Adam; Maryland, 1910 ***3259.35*** *p25*
Karls, Elisabeth Weber; Port uncertain, 1784 ***2856.30*** *p212*
Karlsin, Elisabeth; Port uncertain, 1763 ***2856.30*** *p481*
Karlsin, Elisabeth Weber; Port uncertain, 1784 ***2856.30*** *p212*
Karlson, H. 29; British Columbia, 1910 ***9196.1*** *p15*
Karmann, Peter; Port uncertain, 1784 ***2856.30*** *p212*
Karn, Konrad; Port uncertain, 1766 ***2856.30*** *p212*
With wife & 3 children
Karney, Ann 14 *SEE* Karney, Patrick
Karney, Ann 37 *SEE* Karney, Patrick
Karney, Arthur 5; Ontario, 1861 ***2896.27*** *p5*
Karney, James 35; Ontario, 1861 ***2896.27*** *p5*
Karney, Joseph 11 *SEE* Karney, Patrick
Karney, Mary 21 *SEE* Karney, Patrick
Karney, Pat 18 *SEE* Karney, Patrick
Karney, Patrick 45; New York, New York, 1852 ***1825.45*** *p58*
Wife: Ann 37
Son: Pat 18
Son: Thomas 16
Son: William 8
Daughter: Mary 21
Daughter: Ann 14
Son: Joseph 11
Karney, Peter; Pennsylvania, 1867 ***6058.10*** *p60*
Karney, Susan 34; Ontario, 1861 ***2896.27*** *p5*
Karney, Thomas 16 *SEE* Karney, Patrick
Karney, Vic A. 2; Ontario, 1861 ***2896.27*** *p5*
Karney, William 8 *SEE* Karney, Patrick
Karnlis, Gerhaza; Maryland, 1910 ***3259.35*** *p25*
Karnoska, Franciska; Maryland, 1910 ***3259.35*** *p25*
Karny, Arthur 65; Ontario, 1871 ***1823.15*** *p132*
Karolski, Frank; Maryland, 1910 ***3259.35*** *p25*
Karotschi, Franziska; Port uncertain, 1793 ***2856.30*** *p212*
Karoz, Kazmiess; Maryland, 1910 ***3259.35*** *p25*
Karp, Anna Eva; Port uncertain, 1765 ***2856.30*** *p212*
Karp, Peter; Port uncertain, 1768 ***2856.30*** *p212*
Karpansak, Alexander; Maryland, 1910 ***3259.35*** *p25*
Karpf, Johann Nickel; America, 1773 ***2856.30*** *p164*
Karpf, Johann Nickel; America, 1774 ***2856.30*** *p164*
Karpinski, Alexander; Maryland, 1910 ***3259.35*** *p25*
Karpinski, John L.; Maryland, 1910 ***3259.35*** *p25*
Karpinsky, Frank; Maryland, 1910 ***3259.35*** *p25*
Karpomez, Peter; Maryland, 1910 ***3259.35*** *p25*
Karpp, Josef; Port uncertain, 1752 ***2856.30*** *p212*
Karr, Andrew; New York, 1826 ***8197.10*** *p333*
Karr, George 28; Ontario, 1871 ***1823.15*** *p132*
Karr, James 81; Ontario, 1871 ***1823.22*** *p84*
Karr, John; Pennsylvania, 1785 ***4629.10*** *p48*
Karr, William; Pennsylvania, 1777 ***4629.10*** *p26*
Karrer, Christian; Port uncertain, 1712 ***2856.30*** *p212*
Karrer, Marianna; Port uncertain, 1742 ***2856.30*** *p212*
Karsch, Johann Adam; Port uncertain, 1784 ***2856.30*** *p212*
Karsick, Jacob; Maryland, 1910 ***3259.35*** *p25*
Karst, Catherina 54; Kansas, 1876-1910 ***9079.10*** *p23*
Karst, Elis. Margarete; Port uncertain, 1774 ***2856.30*** *p212*
Karst, Georg; Port uncertain, 1750 ***2856.30*** *p212*
Karst, Johann; America, 1744 ***2856.30*** *p212*
Karst, Michael; Port uncertain, 1752 ***2856.30*** *p212*
Karst, Reinhart 35; Kansas, 1876-1910 ***9079.10*** *p23*
Karst, Reinhart 58; Kansas, 1876-1910 ***9079.10*** *p23*
Karsten, Johann; Port uncertain, 1787 ***2856.30*** *p212*
Karta, Anna; Maryland, 1910 ***3259.35*** *p25*
Karvorski, Joseph, Sr.; Maryland, 1910 ***3259.35*** *p25*
Karwacka, Michael; Maryland, 1910 ***3259.35*** *p25*
Karwacka, Walynty; Maryland, 1910 ***3259.35*** *p25*
Karwacki, John F.; Maryland, 1910 ***3259.35*** *p25*
Kasewitz, Frank; Maryland, 1910 ***3259.35*** *p25*
Kasey, James; Maryland, 1671 ***2524.55*** *p127*
Kasey, John; New York, 1833 ***8197.10*** *p303*
Kasfby, Albert; Maryland, 1910 ***3259.35*** *p25*
Kashak, Joseph; Maryland, 1910 ***3259.35*** *p25*
Kasimierski, Nicolas; Maryland, 1910 ***3259.35*** *p25*
Kasinski, Stanaslaus; Maryland, 1910 ***3259.35*** *p25*
Kasner, Barnet; San Francisco, 1851 ***1224.3*** *p43*
Kasner, Christian 26; Ontario, 1871 ***1823.15*** *p132*
Kaspar, Sophia; Maryland, 1910 ***3259.35*** *p26*
Kasper, Martin; Maryland, 1910 ***3259.35*** *p26*
Kasper, Wilhelm; America, 1747 ***2856.30*** *p212*
Kasprowicz, Frank; Maryland, 1910 ***3259.35*** *p26*
Kass, Ernest; New York, 1813 ***8197.10*** *p245*
Kass, Ernest; New York, 1816 ***8197.10*** *p59*
Kassberger, Johann; America, 1752 ***2856.30*** *p212*
With wife & 3 children
Kassel, Adam; New York, 1837-1838 ***8197.10*** *p121*
Kassmeyer, Matthaus; Port uncertain, 1766 ***2856.30*** *p255*
Kast, Franz; Port uncertain, 1753 ***2856.30*** *p212*
Kast, Hans Georg; America, 1749 ***2856.30*** *p212*
Kast, Hans Georg; America, 1750 ***2856.30*** *p212*
Kast, Johann; Port uncertain, 1787 ***2856.30*** *p212*
Kastask, Peter; Maryland, 1910 ***3259.35*** *p26*
Kaster, Maria Catharina; Port uncertain, 1791 ***2856.30*** *p255*
Kastner, Mrs. Christian; America, 1750 ***2856.30*** *p256*
Kastner, Christina; Port uncertain, 1793 ***2856.30*** *p213*
Kastner, Georg Adam; America, 1748 ***2856.30*** *p213*
Kastner, Johann Georg; Port uncertain, 1788 ***2856.30*** *p213*
Kastner, Margarete; Port uncertain, 1765 ***2856.30*** *p213*
Kaszubinsky, Frank; Maryland, 1910 ***3259.35*** *p26*
Kaszubinsky, John; Maryland, 1910 ***3259.35*** *p26*
Kaszubski, Marian; Maryland, 1910 ***3259.35*** *p26*
Kaszuzak, James; Maryland, 1910 ***3259.35*** *p26*
Katcher, Robert; Virginia, 1668-1669 ***6212.30*** *p40*
Kate, Louise 24; Vermont, 1885 ***5900.10*** *p605*
Kate, William; Maryland, 1664 ***2524.55*** *p127*
Katecei, Ignacy; Maryland, 1910 ***3259.35*** *p26*
Katen, Mary 50; Vermont, 1842 ***5900.10*** *p612*
Katherin, Rose; Maryland, 1682 ***2524.55*** *p127*
Katowicz, Charles R.; Maryland, 1910 ***3259.35*** *p26*
Kattenhorn, John; New York, 1839 ***8197.10*** *p247*
Kattile, John 46; Ontario, 1871 ***1823.28*** *p50*
Kattyle, Thomas 38; Ontario, 1871 ***1823.28*** *p50*
Katz, Georg; Port uncertain, 1795 ***2856.30*** *p213*
Katz, Georg; Port uncertain, 1796 ***2856.30*** *p213*
Katzenberger, Adam; Port uncertain, 1764 ***2856.30*** *p213*
With family
Katzenberger, Maria Johanna; America, 1774 ***2856.30*** *p213*
Katzinski, Adam; Maryland, 1910 ***3259.35*** *p26*
Kau, Cath. Elisabeth; Port uncertain, 1756 ***2856.30*** *p213*
Kaub, Maria Ottilia; Port uncertain, 1756 ***2856.30*** *p213*
Kaucher, Jacob, Jr.; America, 1751 ***2856.30*** *p213*
Kaucher, Jacob, Jr.; America, 1751 ***2856.30*** *p213*
With wife & children
Kaucher, Jacob Friedrich; America, 1751 ***2856.30*** *p213*
Kaucher, Jacob Friedrich; Port uncertain, 1751 ***2856.30*** *p213*
Kaucher, Michael; America, 1751 ***2856.30*** *p213*
Kauck, Georg Balthasar; America, 1762 ***2856.30*** *p213*
Kauck, Georg Balthasar; Port uncertain, 1769 ***2856.30*** *p213*
Kauck, Georg Balthasar; Port uncertain, 1788 ***2856.30*** *p213*
Kaufel, Margareth 13; Ontario, 1871 ***1823.15*** *p132*
Kaufer, Peter; Port uncertain, 1784 ***2856.30*** *p256*
Kauffer, Barbara; America, 1786 ***2856.30*** *p256*
Husband: Peter
Kauffer, Georg Jakob; America, 1757 ***2856.30*** *p256*
Kauffer, Peter *SEE* Kauffer, Barbara
Kauffer, Peter; America, 1752 ***2856.30*** *p256*
Kauffer, Peter; America, 1786 ***2856.30*** *p256*
Kauffler, Theobald; Port uncertain, 1770 ***2856.30*** *p256*
Kauffler, Theobald; Port uncertain, 1773 ***2856.30*** *p256*
Kauffmann, Elisabeth; America, 1754 ***2856.30*** *p213*
Kauffmann, Georg; Port uncertain, 1748 ***2856.30*** *p213*
Kauffmann, Hans Adam; America, 1747 ***2856.30*** *p213*
Kauffmann, Hans Adam; America, 1747 ***2856.30*** *p213*
With wife
Kauffmann, J. Baptist Anton; Port uncertain, 1745 ***2856.30*** *p213*
With wife
Kauffmann, Johann; America, 1754 ***2856.30*** *p213*
Kauffmann, Johann, Jr.; America, 1754 ***2856.30*** *p213*
Kauffmann, Johann Adam; America, 1753 ***2856.30*** *p213*
Kauffmann, Ludwig; Port uncertain, 1770 ***2856.30*** *p213*
Kauffmann, Ludwig; Port uncertain, 1774 ***2856.30*** *p213*
Kauffmann, Ludwig; Port uncertain, 1775 ***2856.30*** *p213*
Kaufman, Henry; Pennsylvania, 1856 ***6058.10*** *p36*
Kaufmann, Heinrich; America, 1779 ***2856.30*** *p213*
Kaufmann, Peter; Port uncertain, 1769 ***2856.30*** *p213*
Kaufmann, Susanna Cath.; Port uncertain, 1794 ***2856.30*** *p214*
Kaufmeyer, Felicitas; America, 1751 ***2856.30*** *p214*
Kaugho, Morris 25; Maryland, 1774 ***1220.25*** *p59*
Kaul, Anna Elisabeth; Port uncertain, 1793 ***2856.30*** *p214*
Kaul, Catharina; Port uncertain, 1792 ***2856.30*** *p214*
Kaul, Johannetta Cath; Port uncertain, 1790 ***2856.30*** *p214*
Kaul, Judith; Port uncertain, 1738 ***2856.30*** *p214*
Kaul, Juliana; Port uncertain, 1785 ***2856.30*** *p214*
Kaul, Peter; Port uncertain, 1792 ***2856.30*** *p214*
Kaupel, Ann 16; Ontario, 1871 ***1823.15*** *p132*
Kaupinski, Alexander; Maryland, 1910 ***3259.35*** *p26*
Kauschmann, Caspar; America, 1748 ***2856.30*** *p214*
Kaussmann, Hans Adam; Port uncertain, 1747 ***2856.30*** *p214*
With wife & 3 children
Kauter, Bernhard; Port uncertain, 1785 ***2856.30*** *p214*
Kauth, Elisabeth; Port uncertain, 1736 ***2856.30*** *p214*
Kautuska, James; Maryland, 1910 ***3259.35*** *p26*
Kautz, Jacob, Jr.; America, 1752 ***2856.30*** *p214*
Kautz, Jacob, Sr.; America, 1749 ***2856.30*** *p214*
Kautz, Johann Georg; America, 1745 ***2856.30*** *p214*
Kautz, Johann Georg; America, 1752 ***2856.30*** *p214*
Kautz, Martin; America, 1749 ***2856.30*** *p214*
With wife & child
Kautz, Michael; America, 1749 ***2856.30*** *p214*
Kautz, Philipp; Port uncertain, 1726 ***2856.30*** *p214*
Kauz, Caspar; America, 1744 ***2856.30*** *p214*
With wife & 4 children
Kauz, Christof; America, 1744 ***2856.30*** *p214*
With wife & children
Kavada, Joseph 16; Ontario, 1871 ***1823.15*** *p132*
Kavalefsky, Steve J.; Maryland, 1910 ***3259.35*** *p26*
Kavanagh, Ann Breen 51; Vermont, 1850 ***5900.10*** *p524*
Kavanagh, James; Maine, 1780 ***4628.40*** *p77*
Kavanagh, John; New York, 1837 ***8197.10*** *p246*
Kavanagh, Margt 20; Ontario, 1871 ***1823.28*** *p50*
Kavanagh Family ; Maine, 1775-1781 ***4628.40*** *p81*
Kavanaugh, Bridget O'Connor; Vermont, 1846-1918 ***5900.10*** *p109*
Kavanaugh, Daniel; Vermont, 1836-1911 ***5900.10*** *p109*
Kavanaugh, Ellen; Vermont, 1843-1873 ***5900.10*** *p409*
Kavaunaught, Anisstasia 56; Ontario, 1871 ***1823.22*** *p84*
Kaveny, John 66; Vermont, 1895 ***5900.10*** *p586*
Kaveny, Margaret 66; Vermont, 1893 ***5900.10*** *p587*
Kavernyski, Andrew; Maryland, 1910 ***3259.35*** *p26*
Kawa, Tekla; Maryland, 1910 ***3259.35*** *p26*
Kawacjki, Walenty; Maryland, 1910 ***3259.35*** *p26*
Kawalefsky, John; Maryland, 1910 ***3259.35*** *p26*
Kawecki, Jacob; Maryland, 1910 ***3259.35*** *p26*
Kawelusky, Warren; Maryland, 1910 ***3259.35*** *p26*
Kawicki, Walter; Maryland, 1910 ***3259.35*** *p26*
Kawsen, Peter; Maryland, 1679 ***2524.55*** *p127*
Kay, Miss; Quebec, 1857 ***9196.15*** *p25*
Kay, Mr.; Portland, Maine, 1858 ***9196.15*** *p30*
Kay, Ann 9 *SEE* Kay, Bryan

Kay, Brian 20; Fort Cumberland, Nova Scotia, 1774 ***1220.25*** *p17*
Kay, Bryan 38; Fort Cumberland, Nova Scotia, 1774 ***1220.25*** *p16*
Wife: Dorothy 42
Child: Hannah 14
Child: Elizabeth 16
Child: Jane 7
Child: Ann 9
Child: Sarah 12
Brother: Robert 42
Kay, Catherine 53; Ontario, 1871 ***1823.15*** *p132*
Kay, Dorothy 42 *SEE* Kay, Bryan
Kay, Elizabeth 16 *SEE* Kay, Bryan
Kay, Hannah 14 *SEE* Kay, Bryan
Kay, James 56; Ontario, 1871 ***1823.28*** *p50*
Kay, Jane 7 *SEE* Kay, Bryan
Kay, Jas; Quebec, 1858 ***9196.15*** *p38*
Kay, John 49; Ontario, 1871 ***1823.15*** *p132*
Kay, Robert 42 *SEE* Kay, Bryan
Kay, Sarah 12 *SEE* Kay, Bryan
Kay, Thomas M. 36; Ontario, 1871 ***1823.15*** *p132*
Kay, William; Jamaica, 1841 ***1640.13*** *p64*
Kay, William; New York, 1807 ***8197.10*** *p43*
Kay, William 20; Fort Cumberland, Nova Scotia, 1774 ***1220.25*** *p16*
Kay, William 60; Ontario, 1871 ***1823.15*** *p132*
Kaye, Charles 30; Maryland, 1774 ***1220.25*** *p72*
Kaye, Charles 45; Ontario, 1871 ***1823.28*** *p50*
Kaye, James 28; Ontario, 1871 ***1823.28*** *p50*
Kayffer, Johann; Port uncertain, 1752 ***2856.30*** *p214*
Kayler, Frederick; New York, 1802 ***8197.10*** *p22*
Kays, Richard 42; Ontario, 1871 ***1823.28*** *p50*
Kayser, Adam; Port uncertain, 1766 ***2856.30*** *p214*
Kayser, Agnes; Port uncertain, 1736 ***2856.30*** *p214*
Kayser, Balthasar; Port uncertain, 1766 ***2856.30*** *p214*
Kayser, C. Graafin *SEE* Kayser, Johann Martin
Kayser, Friedrich; America, 1754 ***2856.30*** *p214*
Kayser, Friedrich; Port uncertain, 1754 ***2856.30*** *p214*
Kayser, Henrich; Port uncertain, 1783 ***2856.30*** *p214*
Kayser, Jacob; Port uncertain, 1763 ***2856.30*** *p214*
Kayser, Johann; Port uncertain, 1737 ***2856.30*** *p214*
Kayser, Johann Martin; America, 1763 ***2856.30*** *p215*
Wife: C. Graafin
Kayser, Johann Peter; Port uncertain, 1781 ***2856.30*** *p214*
Kayser, Ulrich; America, 1731 ***2856.30*** *p214*
Kaysser, Johann; Port uncertain, 1750 ***2856.30*** *p215*
Kaysser, Johann Adam; Port uncertain, 1753 ***2856.30*** *p215*
Kaysser, Johann Michael; Port uncertain, 1747 ***2856.30*** *p215*
Kaysser, Josef; Port uncertain, 1768 ***2856.30*** *p215*
Kayssner, Georg; America, 1764 ***2856.30*** *p215*
With wife & 6 children
Kazemarck, John; Maryland, 1910 ***3259.35*** *p26*
Kazmayer, Anna; Port uncertain, 1616 ***2856.30*** *p215*
With husband & 2 children
Kazmayer, Elisabeth; Port uncertain, 1619 ***2856.30*** *p215*
With husband & son
Kazmierczak, Joseph; Maryland, 1910 ***3259.35*** *p26*
Keable, Edward 28; Ontario, 1871 ***1823.22*** *p84*
Keag, Andrew 21; Ontario, 1871 ***1823.15*** *p132*
Keag, James 21; Ontario, 1871 ***1823.15*** *p132*
Keag, Jane 20; Ontario, 1871 ***1823.15*** *p133*
Keahoe, Agness Sinnott; Vermont, 1850-1909 ***5900.10*** *p50*
Keahoe, John 62; Vermont, 1884 ***5900.10*** *p50*
Kealey, James; New York, 1838 ***8197.10*** *p247*
Kealey, James; New York, 1840 ***8197.10*** *p176*
Keall, Thomas 60; Ontario, 1871 ***1823.28*** *p50*
Keam, John; New York, 1840 ***8197.10*** *p176*
Keam, Samuel 27; Ontario, 1871 ***1823.22*** *p84*
Kean, Daniel 49; Ontario, 1871 ***1823.22*** *p84*
Kean, John 37; Ontario, 1871 ***1823.22*** *p84*
Kean, Reynold; Pennsylvania, 1779 ***4629.10*** *p39*
Kean, Sarah; Canada, 1880 ***1640.13*** *p64*
Keanan, William; New York, 1840 ***8197.10*** *p177*
Keane, Ellen; Vermont, 1819-1891 ***5900.10*** *p439*
Keane, John; Maryland, 1675 ***2524.55*** *p127*
Keane, John 27; Ontario, 1871 ***1823.22*** *p84*
Keane, Mary; Vermont, 1842-1912 ***5900.10*** *p53*
Keane, Mary Agnes 35; Vermont, 1891 ***5900.10*** *p60*
Keane, Nathaniel; Pennsylvania, 1786 ***4629.10*** *p50*
Keane, Patrick A.; New York, 1840 ***8197.10*** *p302*
Keanes, George 60; Ontario, 1871 ***1823.15*** *p133*
Kearigan, Ann 34; Vermont, 1866 ***5900.10*** *p209*
Kearn, Bridget 65; Ontario, 1871 ***1823.22*** *p84*
Kearn, Carlotte 58; Ontario, 1871 ***1823.22*** *p84*
Kearnan, Michael; New York, 1821 ***8197.10*** *p245*
Kearnan, Miles; New York, 1839 ***8197.10*** *p380*
Kearney, Ann 14 *SEE* Kearney, Patrick
Kearney, Ann 37 *SEE* Kearney, Patrick
Kearney, Ann Dougherty; Vermont, 1854-1931 ***5900.10*** *p304*
Kearney, Bernard F.; Vermont, 1852-1923 ***5900.10*** *p304*
Kearney, Bridget 26; Ontario, 1871 ***1823.28*** *p50*
Kearney, Felix; New York, 1837 ***8197.10*** *p93*
Kearney, Joseph 11 *SEE* Kearney, Patrick
Kearney, Julia Louisa; New York, 1857 ***1224.3*** *p54*
Kearney, Lawrence; New York, 1834-1838 ***8197.10*** *p121*
Kearney, Lillian; Vermont, 1875-1958 ***5900.10*** *p225*
Kearney, Margaret 19; Vermont, 1858 ***5900.10*** *p575*
Kearney, Mary 21 *SEE* Kearney, Patrick
Kearney, Michael R.; Vermont, 1856-1938 ***5900.10*** *p225*
Kearney, Pat 18 *SEE* Kearney, Patrick
Kearney, Patrick; New York, 1804 ***8197.10*** *p27*
Kearney, Patrick 45; New York, New York, 1852 ***1825.45*** *p58*
Wife: Ann 37
Daughter: Mary 21
Son: Joseph 11
Son: Thomas 16
Son: William 8
Daughter: Ann 14
Son: Pat 18
Kearney, Peter; Pennsylvania, 1867 ***6058.10*** *p60*
Kearney, Peter 58; Ontario, 1871 ***1823.15*** *p133*
Kearney, Samuel; Pennsylvania, 1784 ***4629.10*** *p44*
Kearney, Susan; New Jersey, 1851 ***1224.3*** *p43*
Kearney, Thomas 16 *SEE* Kearney, Patrick
Kearney, William 8 *SEE* Kearney, Patrick
Kearns, Ann 47; Ontario, 1871 ***1823.28*** *p50*
Kearns, Charles; New York, 1818 ***8197.10*** *p245*
Kearns, Mary Donovan 32; Vermont, 1873 ***5900.10*** *p213*
Kearny, James; New York, 1833-1838 ***8197.10*** *p121*
Kearny, Michael; New York, 1836 ***8197.10*** *p79*
Kearny, Michael James 41; Ontario, 1871 ***1823.28*** *p50*
Kearny, Philip; Perth Amboy, New Jersey, 1783 ***1224.2*** *p64*
Kearny, Susannah; Perth Amboy, New Jersey, 1746 ***1224.2*** *p64*
Kearsing, John; New York, 1820 ***8197.10*** *p245*
Kearsing, John; New York, 1825 ***8197.10*** *p246*
Kearsley, James; New York, 1838 ***8197.10*** *p247*
Kearsley, James; New York, 1840 ***8197.10*** *p176*
Kearsley, Margaret; Philadelphia, 1779 ***1224.2*** *p64*
Kearwin, Mary; Vermont, 1861-1901 ***5900.10*** *p45*
Keasey, John; New York, 1831 ***8197.10*** *p314*
Keasey, John; New York, 1833 ***8197.10*** *p303*
Keater, William 29; Maryland, 1774 ***1220.25*** *p6*
Keates, William; Pennsylvania, 1777 ***4629.10*** *p10*
Keating, Mr.; Quebec, 1857 ***9196.15*** *p14*
Keating, Bridget Grant; Vermont, 1834-1913 ***5900.10*** *p308*
Keating, Bridget Leonard; Vermont, 1843-1927 ***5900.10*** *p309*
Keating, Daniel; Vermont, 1833-1904 ***5900.10*** *p308*
Keating, Daniel J.; Vermont, 1839-1916 ***5900.10*** *p309*
Keating, Eliza; Vermont, 1822-1906 ***5900.10*** *p59*
Keating, James 45; Ontario, 1871 ***1823.15*** *p133*
Keating, James 60; Ontario, 1871 ***1823.22*** *p84*
Keating, John; Vermont, 1829-1892 ***5900.10*** *p219*
Keating, John; Vermont, 1852-1923 ***5900.10*** *p307*
Keating, John; Vermont, 1860-1929 ***5900.10*** *p592*
Keating, John 61; Vermont, 1875 ***5900.10*** *p309*
Keating, John 86; Vermont, 1918 ***5900.10*** *p207*
Keating, Julia 48; Vermont, 1895 ***5900.10*** *p309*
Keating, Kate Connor 47; Vermont, 1882 ***5900.10*** *p207*
Keating, Margaret 86; Vermont, 1896 ***5900.10*** *p309*
Keating, Margaret J.; Vermont, 1853-1941 ***5900.10*** *p307*
Keating, Maria Sheridan; Vermont, 1844-1900 ***5900.10*** *p219*
Keating, Mary; Vermont, 1853-1945 ***5900.10*** *p48*
Keating, Mary Cronan; Vermont, 1853-1940 ***5900.10*** *p307*
Keating, Mary Hickey; Vermont, 1866-1912 ***5900.10*** *p592*
Keating, Nancy; Vermont, 1821-1905 ***5900.10*** *p380*
Keating, Patrick 42; Ontario, 1871 ***1823.15*** *p133*
Keating, Patrick H.; Vermont, 1850-1940 ***5900.10*** *p307*
Keating, Richard; New York, 1818 ***8197.10*** *p245*
Keating, Stephen; New York, 1837 ***8197.10*** *p92*
Keating, Stephen 60; Ontario, 1871 ***1823.15*** *p133*
Keating, Thomas; New York, 1837 ***8197.10*** *p93*
Keating, Walter 28; Ontario, 1871 ***1823.15*** *p133*
Keaton, James 25; Philadelphia, 1775 ***1220.25*** *p9*
Keaveny, John; New York, 1840 ***8197.10*** *p177*
Keavney, Bridget Battles; Vermont, 1849-1937 ***5900.10*** *p572*
Keavney, Patrick; Vermont, 1844-1919 ***5900.10*** *p572*
Keay, Wm; Virginia, 1671 ***6212.30*** *p44*
Kebassin, David 35; Ontario, 1871 ***1823.28*** *p50*
Kebble, Edward; Maryland, 1664 ***2524.55*** *p127*
Kebby, Henry; New England, 1642 ***1224.1*** *p34*
Keberich, Georg; Port uncertain, 1748 ***2856.30*** *p215*
Kebeshkany, Louis 54; Ontario, 1871 ***1823.28*** *p50*
Keble, John; Pennsylvania, 1777 ***4629.10*** *p21*
Keble, Peter; Virginia, 1664 ***6212.30*** *p9*
Kech, John Wendling; New York, 1840 ***8197.10*** *p177*
Kech, Matthias; New York, 1840 ***8197.10*** *p247*
Kech, Nikolaus; Port uncertain, 1733 ***2856.30*** *p215*
Kechine, J. W. 30; Ontario, 1871 ***1823.28*** *p51*
Kechlein, Peter; America, 1751 ***2856.30*** *p215*
Kechler, Christof; America, 1751 ***2856.30*** *p215*
Keck, Michael; Port uncertain, 1770 ***2856.30*** *p215*
Keckeissen, Francis; New York, 1840 ***8197.10*** *p177*
Keckh, Joachim; Port uncertain, 1748 ***2856.30*** *p215*
Keckh, Joachim; Port uncertain, 1777 ***2856.30*** *p215*
Keddie, Alexander 60; Ontario, 1871 ***1823.28*** *p51*
Keddy, Elizabeth 61; Ontario, 1871 ***1823.15*** *p133*
Kedezejewski, William; Maryland, 1910 ***3259.35*** *p26*
Kedger, Robert; Maryland, 1641 ***2524.55*** *p127*
With wife
Kedger, Robert; Maryland, 1663 ***2524.55*** *p127*
Kedman, Thomas 28; Maryland, 1775 ***1220.25*** *p101*
Kedring, John; Maryland, 1910 ***3259.35*** *p26*
Kedring, Stanistaw; Maryland, 1910 ***3259.35*** *p26*
Kedsley, Francis 47; Ontario, 1871 ***1823.15*** *p133*
Kedslie, John; Washington, 1847 ***1640.13*** *p64*
Kedton, William 19; Maryland, 1774 ***1220.25*** *p71*
Kedziererski, Josef; Maryland, 1910 ***3259.35*** *p26*
Keeble, Henry 27; Maryland, 1775 ***1220.25*** *p103*
Keech, Simon; Virginia, 1688 ***1224.1*** *p34*
Keech, Thomas; Maryland, 1717 ***1224.2*** *p64*
Keef, Charles; Vermont, n.d. ***5900.10*** *p164*
Keef, Cumiliary 70; Ontario, 1871 ***1823.15*** *p133*
Keef, David; Vermont, n.d. ***5900.10*** *p164*
Keef, Elen 27; Ontario, 1861 ***2896.27*** *p55*
Keef, Ellis; Maryland, 1678 ***2524.55*** *p127*
Keef, Timothy 24; Ontario, 1861 ***2896.27*** *p55*
Keefe, Alexander 84; Vermont, 1909 ***5900.10*** *p426*
Keefe, Barney E.; Vermont, 1856-1920 ***5900.10*** *p407*
Keefe, Bridget; Vermont, 1855-1904 ***5900.10*** *p159*
Keefe, Charles; Vermont, 1811-1873 ***5900.10*** *p412*
Keefe, Charles; Vermont, 1850-1911 ***5900.10*** *p407*
Keefe, David; Vermont, 1834-1919 ***5900.10*** *p553*
Keefe, David 69; Ontario, 1871 ***1823.15*** *p133*
Keefe, Elizabeth 71; Vermont, 1879 ***5900.10*** *p156*
Keefe, Ellen; Maryland, 1682 ***2524.55*** *p127*
Keefe, Ellen; Vermont, 1840-1920 ***5900.10*** *p70*
Keefe, Ellen; Vermont, 1841-1910 ***5900.10*** *p395*
Keefe, Ellen; Vermont, 1842-1910 ***5900.10*** *p90*
Keefe, Ellen; Vermont, 1849-1929 ***5900.10*** *p56*
Keefe, Ellen Drislane 76; Vermont, 1912 ***5900.10*** *p426*
Keefe, Ellen Howrigan; Vermont, 1863-1923 ***5900.10*** *p407*
Keefe, George L.; New York, 1839 ***8197.10*** *p320*
Keefe, George N.; Vermont, 1855-1910 ***5900.10*** *p401*
Keefe, Hannah M. 72; Vermont, 1922 ***5900.10*** *p62*
Keefe, Hattie A.; Vermont, 1869-1931 ***5900.10*** *p401*
Keefe, James E.; Vermont, 1857-1930 ***5900.10*** *p553*
Keefe, Jane O'Connell; Vermont, 1865-1928 ***5900.10*** *p59*
Keefe, Jane Troy; Vermont, 1823-1917 ***5900.10*** *p57*
Keefe, Jeremiah; Vermont, 1857-1927 ***5900.10*** *p59*
Keefe, Jeremiah 79; Vermont, 1886 ***5900.10*** *p55*
Keefe, Johanna; Vermont, 1848-1900 ***5900.10*** *p427*
Keefe, John N.; Vermont, 1847-1916 ***5900.10*** *p59*
Keefe, John T.; Vermont, 1856-1929 ***5900.10*** *p66*
Keefe, Julia A. 78; Vermont, 1941 ***5900.10*** *p65*
Keefe, Julia Brown 75; Vermont, 1894 ***5900.10*** *p65*
Keefe, Katherine Flavin; Vermont, 1855-1929 ***5900.10*** *p66*
Keefe, Katherine Murphy; Vermont, 1850-1922 ***5900.10*** *p59*
Keefe, Margaret 35; Vermont, 1878 ***5900.10*** *p569*
Keefe, Margaret T. Kennedy; Vermont, 1833-1918 ***5900.10*** *p553*
Keefe, Martin 24; Vermont, 1847 ***5900.10*** *p156*
Keefe, Mary 46; Vermont, 1886 ***5900.10*** *p59*
Keefe, Mary A.; Vermont, 1858-1925 ***5900.10*** *p444*
Keefe, Mary Brown 53; Vermont, 1871 ***5900.10*** *p56*
Keefe, Mary Drislane 89; Vermont, 1908 ***5900.10*** *p55*
Keefe, Mary E.; Vermont, 1867-1936 ***5900.10*** *p553*
Keefe, Mary McBryne 82; Vermont, 1896 ***5900.10*** *p412*
Keefe, Michael; New York, 1821 ***8197.10*** *p245*
Keefe, Nora; Vermont, 1837-1918 ***5900.10*** *p56*
Keefe, Nora 55; Vermont, 1901 ***5900.10*** *p62*
Keefe, Owen 27; Virginia, 1774 ***1220.25*** *p87*
Keefe, Owen 38; Vermont, 1862 ***5900.10*** *p57*
Keefe, Patrick; New York, 1840 ***8197.10*** *p177*
Keefe, Patrick; Vermont, 1842-1914 ***5900.10*** *p427*
Keeffe, Eugene 17 *SEE* Keeffe, Margaret
Keeffe, Hanora 19 *SEE* Keeffe, John
Keeffe, Jeane 13 *SEE* Keeffe, Margaret
Keeffe, Johanna 21 *SEE* Keeffe, Margaret
Keeffe, John 25; New York, New York, 1850 ***1825.45*** *p50*
Sister: Hanora 19

Keeffe, John 35; Ontario, 1871 ***1823.28*** *p51*
Keeffe, Margaret 50; New York, New York, 1849 ***1825.45*** *p50*
Son: Eugene 17
Daughter: Jeane 13
Daughter: Johanna 21
Daughter: Nano 23
Keeffe, Nano 23 *SEE* Keeffe, Margaret
Keeffer, Daniel; America, 1741 ***2856.30*** *p215*
Keegan, Catherine; Vermont, 1849-1918 ***5900.10*** *p84*
Keegan, James; New York, 1840 ***8197.10*** *p177*
Keegan, Mary; Vermont, 1824-1907 ***5900.10*** *p561*
Keelan, James; New York, 1818 ***8197.10*** *p245*
Keelan, Michael; New York, 1826 ***8197.10*** *p335*
Keelan, Thomas; New York, 1831 ***8197.10*** *p365*
Keele, John; Maryland, 1652 ***2524.55*** *p127*
Keelee, Jno; Maryland, 1671 ***2524.55*** *p127*
Keeleln, James; New York, New York, 1857 ***3437.14*** *p56*
Keeler, George; New York, 1827 ***8197.10*** *p246*
Keeler, James 30; Ontario, 1871 ***1823.22*** *p84*
Keeler, Martin 70; Ontario, 1871 ***1823.22*** *p84*
Keeler, Timothy; New York, 1837 ***8197.10*** *p93*
Keeley, Annie E.; Vermont, 1857-1935 ***5900.10*** *p451*
Keeley, John; Vermont, n.d. ***5900.10*** *p190*
Keeley, Mary E.; Vermont, 1837-1895 ***5900.10*** *p440*
Keeling, Charles; New York, New York, 1787 ***1224.2*** *p64*
Keeling, Mathew 25; Maryland, 1775 ***1220.25*** *p105*
Keeling, William; New York, 1823 ***1224.3*** *p43*
Keelty, James 74; Vermont, 1872 ***5900.10*** *p344*
Keelty, Thomas 73; Vermont, 1872 ***5900.10*** *p346*
Keely, Mary Ann 45; Ontario, 1871 ***1823.28*** *p51*
Keen, Edward 23; Baltimore, 1775 ***1220.25*** *p117*
Keen, James 22; Maryland, 1774 ***1220.25*** *p76*
Keen, Mary *SEE* Keen, William
Keen, Mary; New Orleans, 1854 ***1224.3*** *p43*
Keen, Phillip 42; Ontario, 1871 ***1823.15*** *p133*
Keen, Tobias; Pennsylvania, 1777 ***4629.10*** *p9*
Keen, William; Maryland, 1667 ***2524.55*** *p128*
Wife: Mary
Keen, William; Maryland, 1670 ***2524.55*** *p128*
Keenaghan, Wm 54; Ontario, 1871 ***1823.15*** *p133*
Keenan, Aaron; Vermont, 1852-1908 ***5900.10*** *p517*
Keenan, Anna; Vermont, 1869-1928 ***5900.10*** *p420*
Keenan, Anna Peggs; Vermont, 1856-1935 ***5900.10*** *p518*
Keenan, Annie M.; Vermont, 1852-1938 ***5900.10*** *p517*
Keenan, Barnard; New York, 1803 ***8197.10*** *p13*
Keenan, Bridget; Vermont, 1823-1861 ***5900.10*** *p235*
Keenan, Catharine 62; Vermont, 1899 ***5900.10*** *p512*
Keenan, Catherine; Vermont, 1831-1893 ***5900.10*** *p517*
Keenan, Catherine 86; Vermont, 1880 ***5900.10*** *p477*
Keenan, Catherine McCaffrey; Vermont, 1842-1906 ***5900.10*** *p89*
Keenan, Catherine McGue 59; Vermont, 1893 ***5900.10*** *p594*
Keenan, Charles; Vermont, 1827-1910 ***5900.10*** *p518*
Keenan, Charles H. 61; Vermont, 1913 ***5900.10*** *p278*
Keenan, Elenor A. Burke; Vermont, 1835-1905 ***5900.10*** *p262*
Keenan, Eliza Hyde; Vermont, 1821-1915 ***5900.10*** *p278*
Keenan, Francis; Vermont, 1872-1889 ***5900.10*** *p262*
Keenan, Isabella; Vermont, 1854-1872 ***5900.10*** *p262*
Keenan, J. C.; Vermont, 1837-1903 ***5900.10*** *p420*
Keenan, James; New York, 1839 ***8197.10*** *p379*
Keenan, James; Vermont, 1831-1907 ***5900.10*** *p262*
Keenan, James; Vermont, 1837-1910 ***5900.10*** *p486*
Keenan, James; Vermont, 1850-1923 ***5900.10*** *p497*
Keenan, James, Jr.; Vermont, 1864-1900 ***5900.10*** *p262*
Keenan, John; Vermont, 1830-1901 ***5900.10*** *p89*
Keenan, John; Vermont, 1837-1906 ***5900.10*** *p389*
Keenan, John P. 36; Vermont, 1900 ***5900.10*** *p263*
Keenan, Margaret; Vermont, 1843-1912 ***5900.10*** *p512*
Keenan, Margaret; Vermont, 1856-1861 ***5900.10*** *p262*
Keenan, Margaret Daly 78; Vermont, 1876 ***5900.10*** *p262*
Keenan, Margaret Kennedy; Vermont, 1836-1911 ***5900.10*** *p263*
Keenan, Martin; Vermont, 1829-1861 ***5900.10*** *p517*
Keenan, Mary; Vermont, 1836-1916 ***5900.10*** *p48*
Keenan, Mary A. 13; Vermont, 1868 ***5900.10*** *p262*
Keenan, Mary A. Moore; Vermont, 1835-1893 ***5900.10*** *p471*
Keenan, Mary Ann Casey; Vermont, 1833-1903 ***5900.10*** *p486*
Keenan, Mary Ellen; Vermont, 1862-1863 ***5900.10*** *p262*
Keenan, Mary Flanagan; Vermont, 1858-1939 ***5900.10*** *p268*
Keenan, Mary Hughes; Vermont, 1835-1911 ***5900.10*** *p420*
Keenan, Mary J. 39; Vermont, 1890 ***5900.10*** *p435*
Keenan, Mary J. Ryan 40; Vermont, 1897 ***5900.10*** *p259*
Keenan, Mary Quigley; Vermont, 1820-1931 ***5900.10*** *p272*
Keenan, Mary Smith; Vermont, 1839-1906 ***5900.10*** *p486*
Keenan, Michael; New York, 1837 ***8197.10*** *p92*
Keenan, Michael; New York, 1837 ***8197.10*** *p93*
Keenan, Michael 74; Vermont, 1903 ***5900.10*** *p262*
Keenan, Nancy Dowling; Vermont, 1840-1920 ***5900.10*** *p389*
Keenan, Patrick; Vermont, 1820-1891 ***5900.10*** *p272*
Keenan, Patrick H.; Vermont, 1853-1913 ***5900.10*** *p268*
Keenan, Peter H.; Vermont, 1828-1906 ***5900.10*** *p486*
Keenan, Rosa 74; Vermont, 1877 ***5900.10*** *p516*
Keenan, Rosa Keenan 74; Vermont, 1877 ***5900.10*** *p516*
Keenan, Rose 88; Vermont, 1893 ***5900.10*** *p435*
Keenan, Sarah Ann; Vermont, 1853-1934 ***5900.10*** *p281*
Keenan, Thomas J.; Vermont, 1832-1891 ***5900.10*** *p471*
Keene, Edward *SEE* Keene, Henry
Keene, Francis; Maryland, 1680 ***2524.55*** *p128*
Keene, Francis; Maryland, 1681 ***2524.55*** *p128*
Keene, Henry; Maryland, 1653 ***2524.55*** *p129*
Brother: Richard
Brother: Edward
Keene, Katherine; Maryland, 1679 ***2524.55*** *p129*
Keene, Mary *SEE* Keene, William
Keene, Richard *SEE* Keene, Henry
Keene, William; Maryland, 1667 ***2524.55*** *p128*
Wife: Mary
Keene, William; Maryland, 1670 ***2524.55*** *p128*
Keene, William 34; Maryland, 1774 ***1220.25*** *p7*
Keenen, Catherine; Vermont, 1876 ***5900.10*** *p516*
Keenen, John; New York, 1840 ***8197.10*** *p247*
Keenen, Paul 71; Vermont, 1866 ***5900.10*** *p513*
Keener, Christian 57; Ontario, 1871 ***1823.15*** *p133*
Keenin, James 40; Ontario, 1871 ***1823.22*** *p84*
Keennan, Peter 65; Ontario, 1871 ***1823.22*** *p84*
Keenser, Johann Nikolaus; America, 1738 ***2856.30*** *p215*
Keeny, Rose; Maryland, 1680 ***2524.55*** *p128*
Keep, James 19; Virginia, 1774 ***1220.25*** *p94*
Keep, Lancelot; Maryland, 1646 ***2524.55*** *p128*
Keernin, Bernard; New York, 1828 ***8197.10*** *p312*
Keernin, Bernard; New York, 1828 ***8197.10*** *p313*
Kees, David 34; Ontario, 1871 ***1823.15*** *p133*
Kees, Samuel 80; Ontario, 1871 ***1823.15*** *p133*
Keese, John; Maryland, 1665 ***2524.55*** *p128*
Keeshan, Sarah 77; Vermont, 1908 ***5900.10*** *p260*
Keesler, Charles; Pennsylvania, 1779 ***4629.10*** *p39*
Keetch, James; Maryland, 1672 ***2524.55*** *p128*
Keettle, Frances 32; Ontario, 1871 ***1823.15*** *p133*
Keettle, Robert 68; Ontario, 1871 ***1823.15*** *p133*
Keevlan, James 79; Vermont, 1913 ***5900.10*** *p254*
Keevlan, Mary Carvey; Vermont, 1831-1926 ***5900.10*** *p258*
Keevlan, Mary McCann 53; Vermont, 1898 ***5900.10*** *p254*
Keevlan, Thomas; Vermont, 1832-1906 ***5900.10*** *p258*
Keffler, Anna Maria; Port uncertain, 1753 ***2856.30*** *p215*
Kegel, John Christian; Philadelphia, 1791-1792 ***4629.10*** *p65*
Keger, Powel 21; Ontario, 1871 ***1823.15*** *p133*
Kegge, Michael; America, 1765 ***2856.30*** *p215*
Kegikwagiwe, Joseph 72; Ontario, 1871 ***1823.28*** *p51*
Kegikwagiwe, Joseph, Jr. 42; Ontario, 1871 ***1823.28*** *p51*
Kehl, Anna Elisabeth; Port uncertain, 1784 ***2856.30*** *p215*
Kehl, Gotlip 42; Ontario, 1871 ***1823.28*** *p51*
Kehl, Maria Elisabeth; Port uncertain, 1762 ***2856.30*** *p215*
Kehler, Anna Elisabeth; Port uncertain, 1768 ***2856.30*** *p215*
Kehler, Johann Peter; America, 1748 ***2856.30*** *p215*
Kehler, Peter; Port uncertain, 1749 ***2856.30*** *p215*
Kehlin, Anna Margarete; Port uncertain, 1731 ***2856.30*** *p215*
Keho, James 36; Ontario, 1871 ***1823.15*** *p133*
Keho, John 36; Ontario, 1871 ***1823.28*** *p51*
Kehoe, Ann Harrington 73; Vermont, 1911 ***5900.10*** *p408*
Kehoe, Ann Lacey 68; Vermont, 1884 ***5900.10*** *p410*
Kehoe, Bridget 62; Vermont, 1903 ***5900.10*** *p408*
Kehoe, Bridget 82; Vermont, 1880 ***5900.10*** *p199*
Kehoe, Edward 62; Vermont, 1894 ***5900.10*** *p408*
Kehoe, James 68; Vermont, 1904 ***5900.10*** *p408*
Kehoe, James 80; Vermont, 1872 ***5900.10*** *p408*
Kehoe, John; New York, 1806 ***8197.10*** *p31*
Kehoe, John 39; Vermont, 1873 ***5900.10*** *p199*
Kehoe, John E.; Vermont, 1857-1873 ***5900.10*** *p408*
Kehoe, Joseph 20; Vermont, 1864 ***5900.10*** *p199*
Kehoe, Lizzie; Vermont, 1867-1951 ***5900.10*** *p408*
Kehoe, Margaret 66; Ontario, 1871 ***1823.22*** *p84*
Kehoe, Margaret 75; Vermont, 1896 ***5900.10*** *p408*
Kehoe, Mary; Vermont, 1834-1908 ***5900.10*** *p408*
Kehoe, Mary 75; Vermont, 1873 ***5900.10*** *p408*
Kehoe, Mary Kennedy; Vermont, 1832-1915 ***5900.10*** *p408*
Kehoe, Michael; New York, 1831 ***8197.10*** *p366*
Kehoe, Michael; Vermont, 1823-1899 ***5900.10*** *p408*
Kehoe, Michael 31; Vermont, 1863 ***5900.10*** *p199*
Kehoe, Miles 60; Vermont, 1886 ***5900.10*** *p408*
Kehoe, Patrick 76; Vermont, 1873 ***5900.10*** *p199*
Kehoe, Philhip 68; Ontario, 1871 ***1823.15*** *p133*
Kehr, Anna Maria; America, 1748 ***2856.30*** *p505*
Kehr, Georg; America, 1752 ***2856.30*** *p215*
With wife & 2 children
Kehrt, Johann Valentin; America, 1751 ***2856.30*** *p215*
Kehrt, Johann Valentin; America, 1757 ***2856.30*** *p215*
Kehrt, Johann Valentin; Port uncertain, 1748 ***2856.30*** *p215*
Keiblin, Barbara; Port uncertain, 1759 ***2856.30*** *p215*
Keich, Simon; Virginia, 1655 ***1224.1*** *p34*
Keidel, Wilhelm; Port uncertain, 1775 ***2856.30*** *p216*
Keifer, George 39; Ontario, 1871 ***1823.15*** *p133*
Keiffer, Jacob; New York, 1838 ***8197.10*** *p121*
Keighly, Katherine; Maryland, 1678 ***2524.55*** *p128*
Keightly, Sarah 58; Ontario, 1871 ***1823.22*** *p84*
Keil, Catherine E. 36; Kansas, 1901-1910 ***9079.10*** *p21*
Keil, David 9; Kansas, 1901-1910 ***9079.10*** *p21*
Keil, Fred 56; Kansas, 1910 ***9079.10*** *p44*
Keil, Georg; America, 1752 ***2856.30*** *p216*
Keil, George 37; Kansas, 1901-1910 ***9079.10*** *p21*
Keil, Mary 56; Kansas, 1910 ***9079.10*** *p44*
Keilack, Andreas; Port uncertain, 1799 ***2856.30*** *p216*
Keiler, Ludwig; Port uncertain, 1724 ***2856.30*** *p216*
Keiley, James; New York, 1837 ***8197.10*** *p92*
Keilhauer, Gertrud; Port uncertain, 1776 ***2856.30*** *p216*
Keilhauer, Margarete; Port uncertain, 1790 ***2856.30*** *p232*
Keilhauer, Margarete Kling; Port uncertain, 1790 ***2856.30*** *p216*
Keilhauer, Niklas; Port uncertain, 1783 ***2856.30*** *p216*
Keilly, . . .; New Hampshire, 1641-1660 ***4628.40*** *p44*
Kein, George 25; Ontario, 1871 ***1823.22*** *p84*
Keinan, William 50; Ontario, 1871 ***1823.15*** *p133*
Keinath, Catherine 46; Ontario, 1871 ***1823.15*** *p133*
Keines, Katharine; Maryland, 1681 ***2524.55*** *p128*
Keipert, Hans Adam; Port uncertain, 1736 ***2856.30*** *p216*
Keipert, Hans Adam; Port uncertain, 1737 ***2856.30*** *p216*
Keipert, Maria Agnesa; Port uncertain, 1736 ***2856.30*** *p216*
Keipert, Maria Agnesa; Port uncertain, 1737 ***2856.30*** *p216*
Keippel, Philipp; Port uncertain, 1780 ***2856.30*** *p216*
Keir, Jean; Philadelphia, 1831 ***1640.13*** *p64*
Keir, John 47; Ontario, 1871 ***1823.22*** *p84*
Keirnin, Bernard; New York, 1831 ***8197.10*** *p303*
Keiser, Henry; Baltimore, 1847 ***6058.10*** *p38*
Keiser, John; Pennsylvania, 1785 ***4629.10*** *p48*
Keiser, Michael; America, 1763 ***2856.30*** *p216*
Keissner, Henrich; Port uncertain, 1781 ***2856.30*** *p216*
Keitch, Jane; Maryland, 1674 ***2524.55*** *p128*
Keitel, Jakob; America, 1787 ***2856.30*** *p216*
Keitel, Wilhelm; Port uncertain, 1775 ***2856.30*** *p216*
Keith, Mr.; Quebec, 1857 ***9196.15*** *p24*
Keith, Mrs.; Quebec, 1857 ***9196.15*** *p24*
Keith, Ann; Georgia, 1807 ***1224.3*** *p48*
Keith, Ann; Georgia, 1807 ***1640.10*** *p91*
Keith, Charles; Georgia, 1818 ***1224.3*** *p43*
Keith, Charles; Georgia, 1818 ***1640.10*** *p91*
Keith, Charles 84; Ontario, 1871 ***1823.15*** *p133*
Keith, Charlotte; Charles Town, South Carolina, 1807 ***1224.3*** *p4*
Keith, Duncan 30; Baltimore, 1775 ***1220.25*** *p118*
Keith, James; Charles Town, South Carolina, n.d. ***1224.2*** *p64*
Keith, James; Charles Town, South Carolina, n.d. ***1224.3*** *p43*
Keith, James 24; Maryland, 1774 ***1220.25*** *p77*
Keith, Jean; Boston, 1893 ***1640.13*** *p64*
Keith, John 50; Ontario, 1871 ***1823.22*** *p84*
Keith, Mary; South Carolina, 1807 ***1224.3*** *p43*
Keith, Reten 80; Ontario, 1871 ***1823.22*** *p84*
Keith, Robert; Georgia, 1699 ***1640.13*** *p64*
Keith, Thomas 53; Ontario, 1871 ***1823.22*** *p84*
Kelagher, Terrence; New York, 1834 ***8197.10*** *p373*
Kelan, Wojciech; Maryland, 1910 ***3259.35*** *p26*
Kelby, William 35; Ontario, 1871 ***1823.28*** *p51*
Keleher, John; Vermont, 1859-1935 ***5900.10*** *p405*
Keleher, Mary J. Armstrong; Vermont, 1869-1939 ***5900.10*** *p405*
Keleher, Mary Sullivan; Vermont, 1837-1907 ***5900.10*** *p405*
Keleher, Peter; Vermont, 1829-1883 ***5900.10*** *p405*
Keley, Daniell; Virginia, 1703-1704 ***6212.30*** *p62*
Kelhcher, James; Pennsylvania, 1787 ***4629.10*** *p50*
Keliher, John; New York, 1834 ***8197.10*** *p372*
Kell, Catherine J.; Vermont, 1851-1910 ***5900.10*** *p401*
Kell, Isabella; Maryland, 1675 ***2524.55*** *p128*
Kell, James A.; Vermont, 1850-1895 ***5900.10*** *p401*
Kellam, John; Virginia, 1666 ***6212.30*** *p31*
Kellan, Mary Ann 35; Ontario, 1871 ***1823.15*** *p133*
Kelland, Matthew 42; Ontario, 1871 ***1823.15*** *p133*
Kelland, William 49; Ontario, 1871 ***1823.22*** *p85*
Kellaway, Robert 36; Ontario, 1871 ***1823.15*** *p133*

Kelle, Richd; Virginia, 1671 ***6212.30*** *p42*
Kelleher, Charlotte Livingston; Vermont, 1854-1915 ***5900.10*** *p333*
Kelleher, Dan 29 *SEE* Kelleher, Daniel
Kelleher, Daniel 69; New York, New York, 1849 ***1825.45*** *p50*
Son: Dan 29
Nephew: John 36
Daughter-In-Law: Kitty 26
Grandson: Tade 2
Daughter: Mary 21
Granddaughter: Kitty 3
Kelleher, John; Vermont, 1831-1901 ***5900.10*** *p218*
Kelleher, John 36 *SEE* Kelleher, Daniel
Kelleher, Kitty 3 *SEE* Kelleher, Daniel
Kelleher, Kitty 26 *SEE* Kelleher, Daniel
Kelleher, Mary 21 *SEE* Kelleher, Daniel
Kelleher, Mary Duggan; Vermont, 1850-1928 ***5900.10*** *p333*
Kelleher, Michael; Vermont, 1847-1899 ***5900.10*** *p333*
Kelleher, Patrick 65; Ontario, 1871 ***1823.22*** *p85*
Kelleher, Rose Cosgrove; Vermont, 1839-1915 ***5900.10*** *p218*
Kelleher, Tade 2 *SEE* Kelleher, Daniel
Kelleher, Thomas 20; Ontario, 1871 ***1823.22*** *p85*
Kelleher, Timothy J.; Vermont, 1854-1905 ***5900.10*** *p333*
Kellehor, William; New York, 1837 ***8197.10*** *p92*
Keller, Adam; Port uncertain, 1756 ***2856.30*** *p218*
Keller, Aloys; New York, 1839 ***8197.10*** *p247*
Keller, Amelia 48; Kansas, 1906-1910 ***9079.10*** *p16*
Keller, Anna Elisabeth; Port uncertain, 1752 ***2856.30*** *p216*
Keller, Anna Maria; Port uncertain, 1789 ***2856.30*** *p216*
Keller, Antoni; America, 1740 ***2856.30*** *p216*
Keller, Antoni; America, 1740 ***2856.30*** *p218*
With wife & children
Keller, Bernhard; America, 1751 ***2856.30*** *p216*
Keller, Catharina; Port uncertain, 1768 ***2856.30*** *p216*
Keller, Catharina; Port uncertain, 1791 ***2856.30*** *p216*
Keller, Catharina; Port uncertain, 1793 ***2856.30*** *p216*
Keller, Christina; Port uncertain, 1795 ***2856.30*** *p216*
Keller, Christof; Port uncertain, 1746 ***2856.30*** *p216*
Keller, David 11; Kansas, 1908-1910 ***9079.10*** *p18*
Keller, David 32; Kansas, 1909-1910 ***9079.10*** *p36*
Keller, David 33; Kansas, 1903-1910 ***9079.10*** *p18*
Keller, Elisabeth Hildebr; America, 1732 ***2856.30*** *p218*
With 10 children
Keller, Eva; Port uncertain, 1752 ***2856.30*** *p216*
Keller, Eva; Port uncertain, 1765 ***2856.30*** *p218*
With husband
Keller, Franz Josef; Port uncertain, 1784 ***2856.30*** *p216*
Keller, Franziska; Port uncertain, 1785 ***2856.30*** *p216*
Keller, Franziska; Port uncertain, 1786 ***2856.30*** *p216*
Keller, Friedrich; Port uncertain, 1752 ***2856.30*** *p216*
Keller, Friedrich; Port uncertain, 1784 ***2856.30*** *p216*
Keller, Gabriel; Port uncertain, 1758 ***2856.30*** *p217*
Keller, George; New York, 1839 ***8197.10*** *p247*
Keller, Hans Adam; Port uncertain, 1767 ***2856.30*** *p217*
Keller, Hans Georg; Port uncertain, 1758 ***2856.30*** *p217*
Keller, Hans Georg; Port uncertain, 1769 ***2856.30*** *p217*
Keller, Heinrich; Port uncertain, 1795 ***2856.30*** *p217*
Keller, Heinrich; Port uncertain, 1796 ***2856.30*** *p217*
Keller, Henrich; Port uncertain, 1785 ***2856.30*** *p217*
Keller, Jacob; America, 1738 ***2856.30*** *p217*
Keller, Jacob; Port uncertain, 1737 ***2856.30*** *p217*
Keller, Mrs. Jakob; Port uncertain, 1766 ***2856.30*** *p217*
Keller, James 13; Ontario, 1861 ***2896.28*** *p57*
Keller, Jarrich; America, 1732 ***2856.30*** *p217*
Keller, Joh. Heinrich; America, 1738 ***2856.30*** *p217*
Keller, Joh. Heinrich; America, 1738 ***2856.30*** *p218*
With wife & children
Keller, Johann; America, 1732 ***2856.30*** *p217*
Keller, Johann; America, 1753 ***2856.30*** *p217*
Keller, Johann; America, 1764 ***2856.30*** *p217*
Keller, Johann; America, 1776 ***2856.30*** *p217*
Keller, Johann Bartel; Port uncertain, 1753 ***2856.30*** *p217*
Keller, Johann Daniel; Port uncertain, 1738 ***2856.30*** *p218*
With wife & children
Keller, Johann Nickel; Port uncertain, 1791 ***2856.30*** *p217*
Keller, Johann Thiel; Port uncertain, 1763 ***2856.30*** *p217*
Keller, Josef; America, 1736 ***2856.30*** *p218*
With wife & 3 sons
Keller, Josef; America, 1737 ***2856.30*** *p222*
Keller, Josef; Port uncertain, 1736 ***2856.30*** *p217*
Keller, Julia 30; Kansas, 1907-1910 ***9079.10*** *p18*
Keller, Kilian; Canada, 1749 ***2856.30*** *p218*
With wife & children
Keller, Lewis; Pennsylvania, 1779 ***4629.10*** *p39*
Keller, Maria Angela; Port uncertain, 1753 ***2856.30*** *p217*
Keller, Maria Catharina Weeber; Port uncertain, 1753 ***2856.30*** *p483*
Keller, Maria Elisabeth; Port uncertain, 1775 ***2856.30*** *p217*
Keller, Maria Magdalena; Port uncertain, 1740 ***2856.30*** *p217*
Keller, Maria Magdalena; Port uncertain, 1755 ***2856.30*** *p217*
Keller, Maria Magdalena; Port uncertain, 1757 ***2856.30*** *p217*
Keller, Maria Magdalena; Port uncertain, 1758 ***2856.30*** *p217*
Keller, Maria Margarete; Port uncertain, 1777 ***2856.30*** *p217*
Keller, Maria Margareth Loscher; America, 1732 ***2856.30*** *p218*
With 6 children
Keller, Marie 7; Kansas, 1909-1910 ***9079.10*** *p36*
Keller, Marie 25; Kansas, 1909-1910 ***9079.10*** *p36*
Keller, Martin; New York, 1837 ***8197.10*** *p93*
Keller, Michael; America, 1744 ***2856.30*** *p217*
Keller, Michael 40; Ontario, 1871 ***1823.15*** *p133*
Keller, Nikolaus; Port uncertain, 1743 ***2856.30*** *p217*
Keller, Paul; Pennsylvania, 1779 ***4629.10*** *p40*
Keller, Peter 20; Ontario, 1861 ***2896.26*** *p37*
Keller, Reinhart 48; Kansas, 1899-1910 ***9079.10*** *p16*
Keller, Susanna; Port uncertain, 1730 ***2856.30*** *p217*
Keller, Susanna; Port uncertain, 1779 ***2856.30*** *p217*
Keller, Ulrich; Port uncertain, 1751 ***2856.30*** *p218*
Keller, Ursula; Port uncertain, 1753 ***2856.30*** *p218*
Keller, Wendel; America, 1749 ***2856.30*** *p218*
Keller, Wilhelm; Port uncertain, 1777 ***2856.30*** *p218*
Kellerman, Catrine 49; Ontario, 1871 ***1823.15*** *p133*
Kellerman, Leonhardt 56; Ontario, 1871 ***1823.15*** *p133*
Kellermann, Anna Ottilia; Port uncertain, 1745 ***2856.30*** *p218*
Kellermann, Bonaventura; Port uncertain, 1779 ***2856.30*** *p218*
Kellermann, Johann Adam; Port uncertain, 1741 ***2856.30*** *p218*
Kellermann, Johann Wolfgang; America, 1743 ***2856.30*** *p218*
Kellett, Harris; New York, 1807 ***8197.10*** *p330*
Kellett, Robert; New York, 1807 ***8197.10*** *p330*
Kellett, Sarah A. 57; Vermont, 1900-1909 ***5900.10*** *p310*
Kelley, Agnes B.; Vermont, 1926 ***5900.10*** *p127*
Kelley, Allice 36; Vermont, 1873 ***5900.10*** *p476*
Kelley, Andrew; Vermont, 1827-1914 ***5900.10*** *p235*
Kelley, Ann 49; Vermont, 1866 ***5900.10*** *p448*
Kelley, Ann 84; Vermont, 1917 ***5900.10*** *p471*
Kelley, Ann Donahue; Vermont, 1835-1926 ***5900.10*** *p355*
Kelley, Ann Foley 62; Vermont, 1892 ***5900.10*** *p564*
Kelley, Anne; Vermont, 1832-1908 ***5900.10*** *p431*
Kelley, Annie Mangan 33; Vermont, 1887 ***5900.10*** *p417*
Kelley, Barney; Vermont, 1847-1915 ***5900.10*** *p471*
Kelley, Bridget; Vermont, 1826-1900 ***5900.10*** *p440*
Kelley, Bridget; Vermont, 1853-1931 ***5900.10*** *p161*
Kelley, Bridget 13; Vermont, 1862 ***5900.10*** *p229*
Kelley, Bridget 17; Vermont, 1868 ***5900.10*** *p429*
Kelley, Bridget 45; Vermont, 1880 ***5900.10*** *p413*
Kelley, Bridget 70; Vermont, 1871 ***5900.10*** *p450*
Kelley, Bridget Skeane 70; Vermont, 1875 ***5900.10*** *p615*
Kelley, Call 70; Vermont, 1883 ***5900.10*** *p530*
Kelley, Catharine 70; Vermont, 1878 ***5900.10*** *p471*
Kelley, Catharine Kennedy; Vermont, 1846-1919 ***5900.10*** *p186*
Kelley, Catherine; Vermont, 1841-1918 ***5900.10*** *p83*
Kelley, Catherine; Vermont, 1863-1936 ***5900.10*** *p458*
Kelley, Catherine 40; Vermont, 1862 ***5900.10*** *p245*
Kelley, Catherine A.; Vermont, 1856-1925 ***5900.10*** *p516*
Kelley, Cathern Howley; Vermont, 1854-1893 ***5900.10*** *p425*
Kelley, Charles E.; Vermont, 1870-1887 ***5900.10*** *p168*
Kelley, Daniel 66; Vermont, 1870 ***5900.10*** *p450*
Kelley, Daniel 70; Vermont, 1869 ***5900.10*** *p411*
Kelley, Edward; Vermont, 1853-1917 ***5900.10*** *p476*
Kelley, Edward 45; Vermont, 1900 ***5900.10*** *p265*
Kelley, Edward 50; Ontario, 1871 ***1823.28*** *p51*
Kelley, Edward 79; Vermont, 1876 ***5900.10*** *p615*
Kelley, Edw'd; Vermont, n.d. ***5900.10*** *p100*
Kelley, Eliza Ann; Vermont, 1848-1910 ***5900.10*** *p497*
Kelley, Elizabeth; Vermont, 1855-1894 ***5900.10*** *p355*
Kelley, Elizabeth 69; Vermont, 1911 ***5900.10*** *p471*
Kelley, Elizabeth C.; Vermont, 1862-1962 ***5900.10*** *p284*
Kelley, Elizabeth Cline; Vermont, 1810-1878 ***5900.10*** *p214*
Kelley, Ella J.; Vermont, 1861-1929 ***5900.10*** *p519*
Kelley, Ellen; Vermont, n.d. ***5900.10*** *p152*
Kelley, Ellen; Vermont, 1839-1882 ***5900.10*** *p538*
Kelley, Ellen; Vermont, 1860-1938 ***5900.10*** *p141*
Kelley, Ellen 73; Vermont, 1870 ***5900.10*** *p202*
Kelley, Ellen Daly 31; Vermont, 1868 ***5900.10*** *p235*
Kelley, Ellen Gaffany; Vermont, 1830-1904 ***5900.10*** *p201*
Kelley, Ellen Garvey; Vermont, 1903 ***5900.10*** *p168*
Kelley, Ellen Mullen 80; Vermont, 1901 ***5900.10*** *p297*
Kelley, Ellen Todd; Vermont, 1835-1914 ***5900.10*** *p511*
Kelley, Francis 50; Vermont, 1868 ***5900.10*** *p150*
Kelley, Frank; Vermont, 1794-1886 ***5900.10*** *p429*
Kelley, Frank 33; Vermont, 1850 ***5900.10*** *p342*
Kelley, George; Vermont, 1903 ***5900.10*** *p168*
Kelley, Hannah O'Grady; Vermont, 1824-1899 ***5900.10*** *p302*
Kelley, Hugh 72; Vermont, 1901 ***5900.10*** *p445*
Kelley, James; Vermont, 1817-1898 ***5900.10*** *p47*
Kelley, James; Vermont, 1820-1880 ***5900.10*** *p438*
Kelley, James; Vermont, 1821-1909 ***5900.10*** *p459*
Kelley, James; Vermont, 1842-1903 ***5900.10*** *p578*
Kelley, James 65; Vermont, 1899 ***5900.10*** *p471*
Kelley, James 74; Vermont, 1870 ***5900.10*** *p471*
Kelley, James B.; Vermont, 1858-1908 ***5900.10*** *p141*
Kelley, James P.; Vermont, 1863-1963 ***5900.10*** *p284*
Kelley, Jane 89; Ontario, 1871 ***1823.22*** *p85*
Kelley, Jane Ann; Vermont, 1846-1891 ***5900.10*** *p538*
Kelley, Jedson 22 months; Vermont, 1856 ***5900.10*** *p373*
Kelley, Jeremiah; Vermont, 1832-1864 ***5900.10*** *p355*
Kelley, Johanna; Vermont, 1864 ***5900.10*** *p356*
Kelley, John; Newbury, Massachusetts, 1635 ***4628.40*** *p75*
Kelley, John; Vermont, 1836-1905 ***5900.10*** *p186*
Kelley, John; Vermont, 1840-1917 ***5900.10*** *p152*
Kelley, John; Vermont, 1858-1916 ***5900.10*** *p355*
Kelley, John; Vermont, 1904 ***5900.10*** *p168*
Kelley, John 45; Ontario, 1871 ***1823.22*** *p85*
Kelley, John 64; Ontario, 1871 ***1823.15*** *p133*
Kelley, John 66; Vermont, 1888 ***5900.10*** *p265*
Kelley, Joseph; Vermont, 1849-1934 ***5900.10*** *p463*
Kelley, Joseph 25; Ontario, 1871 ***1823.15*** *p133*
Kelley, Julia 58; Vermont, 1889 ***5900.10*** *p235*
Kelley, Julia A. Lobdell; Vermont, 1850-1938 ***5900.10*** *p321*
Kelley, Katharine; Vermont, 1850-1920 ***5900.10*** *p45*
Kelley, Katie 1; Vermont, 1869 ***5900.10*** *p429*
Kelley, Lawrence; Vermont, n.d. ***5900.10*** *p164*
Kelley, Lawrence; Vermont, 1867 ***5900.10*** *p152*
Kelley, Luke; Vermont, 1832-1917 ***5900.10*** *p431*
Kelley, Margaret; Vermont, 1823-1904 ***5900.10*** *p505*
Kelley, Margaret; Vermont, 1842-1909 ***5900.10*** *p510*
Kelley, Margaret 4; Vermont, 1847 ***5900.10*** *p522*
Kelley, Margaret 65; Vermont, 1894 ***5900.10*** *p265*
Kelley, Margaret 72; Vermont, 1884 ***5900.10*** *p229*
Kelley, Margaret Baldwin; Vermont, 1900 ***5900.10*** *p127*
Kelley, Margaret McPhilomy; Vermont, 1843-1897 ***5900.10*** *p578*
Kelley, Maria H.; Vermont, 1828-1899 ***5900.10*** *p47*
Kelley, Mary; Vermont, 1823-1893 ***5900.10*** *p438*
Kelley, Mary; Vermont, 1840-1911 ***5900.10*** *p265*
Kelley, Mary; Vermont, 1851-1933 ***5900.10*** *p429*
Kelley, Mary; Vermont, 1852-1918 ***5900.10*** *p553*
Kelley, Mary; Vermont, 1860-1863 ***5900.10*** *p284*
Kelley, Mary 44; Vermont, 1867 ***5900.10*** *p265*
Kelley, Mary 46; Vermont, 1885 ***5900.10*** *p300*
Kelley, Mary 50; Vermont, 1880 ***5900.10*** *p150*
Kelley, Mary 55; Vermont, 1884 ***5900.10*** *p338*
Kelley, Mary 55; Vermont, 1926 ***5900.10*** *p214*
Kelley, Mary 70; Vermont, 1896 ***5900.10*** *p505*
Kelley, Mary A.; Vermont, 1845-1917 ***5900.10*** *p448*
Kelley, Mary A.; Vermont, 1854-1886 ***5900.10*** *p148*
Kelley, Mary J.; Vermont, 1853-1923 ***5900.10*** *p47*
Kelley, Mary L.; Vermont, 1836-1905 ***5900.10*** *p286*
Kelley, Mary O'Donnell 50; Vermont, 1861 ***5900.10*** *p445*
Kelley, Mary Waters; Vermont, 1834-1904 ***5900.10*** *p429*
Kelley, Maryett 23; Vermont, 1849 ***5900.10*** *p194*
Kelley, Michael; New York, 1834 ***8197.10*** *p71*
Kelley, Michael J. 31; Vermont, 1888 ***5900.10*** *p429*
Kelley, Nancy; Vermont, 1851-1889 ***5900.10*** *p218*
Kelley, Nancy A. McSorley 31; Vermont, 1879 ***5900.10*** *p471*
Kelley, Patrick; Pennsylvania, 1867 ***6058.10*** *p57*
Kelley, Patrick; Vermont, 1806-1876 ***5900.10*** *p214*
Kelley, Patrick; Vermont, 1830-1900 ***5900.10*** *p284*
Kelley, Patrick; Vermont, 1839-1894 ***5900.10*** *p425*
Kelley, Patrick 23; Vermont, 1869 ***5900.10*** *p448*
Kelley, Patrick 50; Vermont, 1874 ***5900.10*** *p297*
Kelley, Patrick 71; Ontario, 1871 ***1823.15*** *p133*
Kelley, Patrick 73; Vermont, 1875 ***5900.10*** *p229*
Kelley, Patrick 79; Ontario, 1871 ***1823.22*** *p85*
Kelley, Paul 18; Vermont, 1872 ***5900.10*** *p530*
Kelley, Peter 80; Vermont, 1917 ***5900.10*** *p234*
Kelley, Robert W.; Vermont, 1861-1925 ***5900.10*** *p356*
Kelley, Rosa Kirk; Vermont, 1838-1917 ***5900.10*** *p284*
Kelley, Samuel T.; Vermont, 1847-1921 ***5900.10*** *p321*
Kelley, Sarah J.; Vermont, 1854-1889 ***5900.10*** *p168*
Kelley, Thomas; Vermont, 1839-1897 ***5900.10*** *p538*
Kelley, Thomas; Vermont, 1852-1936 ***5900.10*** *p438*
Kelley, Thomas 34; Vermont, 1885 ***5900.10*** *p417*
Kelley, Thomas 42; Vermont, 1882 ***5900.10*** *p214*
Kelley, Thomas 83; Vermont, 1907 ***5900.10*** *p619*
Kelley, Thomas E. 79; Vermont, 1906 ***5900.10*** *p564*

Kelley, Thomas F.; Vermont, 1856-1926 ***5900.10*** *p516*
Kelley, Timothy 49; Vermont, 1859 ***5900.10*** *p448*
Kelley, W. H.; Vermont, 1920 ***5900.10*** *p127*
Kelley, William; Vermont, 1913 ***5900.10*** *p511*
Kelley, William 4 weeks; Vermont, 1845 ***5900.10*** *p457*
Kelley, William 35; Vermont, 1891 ***5900.10*** *p110*
Kelley, William 67; Vermont, 1907 ***5900.10*** *p250*
Kelley, William 68; Vermont, 1879 ***5900.10*** *p215*
Kelley, William D. 48; Vermont, 1875 ***5900.10*** *p201*
Kellie, James 55; Ontario, 1871 ***1823.22*** *p85*
Kellihan, John; New York, 1837 ***8197.10*** *p246*
Kelliher, Dennis; Vermont, 1815-1895 ***5900.10*** *p418*
Kelliher, Ellen Hodnett; Vermont, 1814-1902 ***5900.10*** *p418*
Kellingsworth, James; Virginia, 1667 ***6212.30*** *p36*
Kellington, Mathew 31; Ontario, 1871 ***1823.15*** *p133*
Kellner, Joseph 53; Ontario, 1871 ***1823.15*** *p133*
Kello, George 67; Ontario, 1871 ***1823.28*** *p51*
Kello, John 40; Ontario, 1871 ***1823.28*** *p51*
Kellock, George; New York, 1838 ***8197.10*** *p122*
Kellogg, James 72; Ontario, 1871 ***1823.22*** *p85*
Kellond, Thomas; Boston, 1679 ***1224.1*** *p34*
Kellt, Margaret; Vermont, 1862-1912 ***5900.10*** *p430*
Kellum, John; Virginia, 1664 ***6212.30*** *p6*
Kelly, . . .; New Hampshire, 1641-1660 ***4628.40*** *p44*
Kelly, . . .; Vermont, 1847 ***5900.10*** *p26*
Kelly, Miss; Quebec, 1858 ***9196.15*** *p44*
Kelly, Alice 50; Ontario, 1871 ***1823.28*** *p51*
Kelly, Andrew; New York, 1794 ***8197.10*** *p6*
Kelly, Ann; New Jersey, 1891 ***1640.13*** *p64*
Kelly, Ann; Vermont, 1843-1905 ***5900.10*** *p219*
Kelly, Ann; Vermont, 1885 ***5900.10*** *p91*
Kelly, Ann 17 *SEE* Kelly, John, Sr.
Kelly, Ann 28; Ontario, 1871 ***1823.15*** *p133*
Kelly, Ann 51; Ontario, 1871 ***1823.22*** *p85*
Kelly, Ann E. 6; Ontario, 1861 ***2896.26*** *p32*
Kelly, Ann Holley; Vermont, 1848-1922 ***5900.10*** *p609*
Kelly, Ann Quinn; Vermont, 1839-1907 ***5900.10*** *p151*
Kelly, Anna; Maryland, 1910 ***3259.35*** *p26*
Kelly, Anne 10 *SEE* Kelly, Pat
Kelly, Anne 12 *SEE* Kelly, James
Kelly, Anne 19; Vermont, 1875 ***5900.10*** *p363*
Kelly, Anne 94; Ontario, 1871 ***1823.15*** *p133*
Kelly, Arthur; New York, 1830 ***8197.10*** *p361*
Kelly, B. 26; Philadelphia, 1774 ***1220.25*** *p6*
Kelly, Barney 21 *SEE* Kelly, John, Sr.
Kelly, Barney 60; Ontario, 1871 ***1823.28*** *p51*
Kelly, Betsey; Vermont, 1831-1925 ***5900.10*** *p446*
Kelly, Bridget; Vermont, 1836-1914 ***5900.10*** *p432*
Kelly, Bridget; Vermont, 1838-1870 ***5900.10*** *p113*
Kelly, Bridget 1 *SEE* Kelly, Pat
Kelly, Bridget 2; Vermont, 1856 ***5900.10*** *p189*
Kelly, Bridget 8 *SEE* Kelly, John, Sr.
Kelly, Bridget 14; Vermont, 1863 ***5900.10*** *p169*
Kelly, Bridget 22; Ontario, 1871 ***1823.28*** *p51*
Kelly, Bridget 65; Vermont, 1872 ***5900.10*** *p211*
Kelly, Bridget Elwood; Vermont, 1816-1902 ***5900.10*** *p376*
Kelly, Bridget L.; Vermont, 1857-1917 ***5900.10*** *p350*
Kelly, Bryan 21; New York, New York, 1848 ***1825.45*** *p35*
Kelly, Caroline 11; Ontario, 1861 ***2896.26*** *p18*
Kelly, Catharine 46; Ontario, 1871 ***1823.15*** *p133*
Kelly, Catharine 88; Vermont, 1869 ***5900.10*** *p479*
Kelly, Catherine; Vermont, n.d. ***5900.10*** *p424*
Kelly, Catherine; Vermont, 1819-1896 ***5900.10*** *p189*
Kelly, Catherine; Vermont, 1826-1903 ***5900.10*** *p363*
Kelly, Catherine 9 *SEE* Kelly, Margaret
Kelly, Catherine 14 *SEE* Kelly, James
Kelly, Catherine 21; New York, New York, 1849 ***1825.45*** *p35*
Kelly, Catherine 35; Vermont, 1868 ***5900.10*** *p169*
Kelly, Catherine 72; Vermont, 1890 ***5900.10*** *p244*
Kelly, Charles; New York, 1837 ***8197.10*** *p93*
Kelly, Christopher 50; Ontario, 1871 ***1823.28*** *p51*
Kelly, Cornelius 30; Vermont, 1865 ***5900.10*** *p618*
Kelly, Daniel; Canada, 1756-1760 ***4628.40*** *p45*
Kelly, Daniel; New York, 1816 ***8197.10*** *p59*
Kelly, Daniel; Nova Scotia, 1745 ***4628.40*** *p44*
Kelly, Daniel 30; Ontario, 1871 ***1823.15*** *p133*
Kelly, Daniel 37; Ontario, 1871 ***1823.28*** *p51*
Kelly, Daniel, Sr. 66; Ontario, 1861 ***2896.26*** *p18*
Kelly, Daniel, Jr. 22; Ontario, 1861 ***2896.26*** *p18*
Kelly, Darby; Canada, 1756-1760 ***4628.40*** *p45*
Kelly, David 5; Ontario, 1861 ***2896.26*** *p18*
Kelly, David 24; Ontario, 1861 ***2896.27*** *p22*
Kelly, David C. 6 months; Vermont, 1856 ***5900.10*** *p189*
Kelly, Edmond; Baltimore, 1794 ***1224.2*** *p64*
Kelly, Edw. C.; Vermont, 1846-1891 ***5900.10*** *p434*
Kelly, Edward 18 *SEE* Kelly, James
Kelly, Edward 21; Maryland, 1774 ***1220.25*** *p70*
Kelly, Edward 36; America, 1774 ***1220.25*** *p36*
Kelly, Eleanor; Vermont, 1842-1923 ***5900.10*** *p425*
Kelly, Eleanor 29; Ontario, 1861 ***2896.26*** *p32*
Kelly, Eliza 10 *SEE* Kelly, James
Kelly, Eliza 36 *SEE* Kelly, Pat
Kelly, Eliza A. 66; Vermont, 1889 ***5900.10*** *p539*
Kelly, Elizabeth; Vermont, 1856-1894 ***5900.10*** *p486*
Kelly, Elizabeth 50; Ontario, 1871 ***1823.15*** *p134*
Kelly, Elizabeth 65; Vermont, 1882 ***5900.10*** *p580*
Kelly, Ellen 7 *SEE* Kelly, James
Kelly, Ellen 21; Ontario, 1871 ***1823.22*** *p85*
Kelly, Ellen 49; Vermont, 1878 ***5900.10*** *p367*
Kelly, Felix; New York, 1827 ***8197.10*** *p341*
Kelly, Francis 36; Ontario, 1871 ***1823.15*** *p134*
Kelly, George; Pennsylvania, 1779 ***4629.10*** *p35*
Kelly, George 15; Ontario, 1861 ***2896.26*** *p18*
Kelly, George 36; Ontario, 1871 ***1823.15*** *p134*
Kelly, George C. 7; Ontario, 1861 ***2896.26*** *p17*
Kelly, Gregory; New York, 1821 ***8197.10*** *p245*
Kelly, Hanora; Vermont, 1838-1906 ***5900.10*** *p86*
Kelly, Hanora; Vermont, 1839-1879 ***5900.10*** *p266*
Kelly, Henry; New York, 1840 ***8197.10*** *p177*
Kelly, Herbert 1; Ontario, 1861 ***2896.26*** *p18*
Kelly, Honora 49; Vermont, 1852 ***5900.10*** *p189*
Kelly, Honora Gordon; Vermont, 1859-1926 ***5900.10*** *p54*
Kelly, Hugh; New York, 1838 ***8197.10*** *p377*
Kelly, Isaac; Pennsylvania, 1777 ***4629.10*** *p24*
Kelly, James; Canada, 1756-1760 ***4628.40*** *p45*
Kelly, James; Maryland, 1682 ***2524.55*** *p128*
Kelly, James; New York, 1820-1831 ***8197.10*** *p369*
Kelly, James; New York, 1839 ***8197.10*** *p247*
Kelly, James; Rhode Island, 1778 ***1224.2*** *p64*
Kelly, James; Vermont, 1826-1889 ***5900.10*** *p218*
Kelly, James 16 *SEE* Kelly, James
Kelly, James 24; Ontario, 1861 ***2896.26*** *p32*
Kelly, James 25; Virginia, 1774 ***1220.25*** *p93*
Kelly, James 26; Ontario, 1871 ***1823.28*** *p51*
Kelly, James 30; Ontario, 1871 ***1823.15*** *p134*
Kelly, James 44; Ontario, 1871 ***1823.15*** *p134*
Kelly, James 45; New York, New York, 1848 ***1825.45*** *p16*
Wife: Mary 40
Son: John 2
Daughter: Catherine 14
Daughter: Ellen 7
Daughter: Mary 20
Daughter: Eliza 10
Daughter: Anne 12
Son: James 16
Son: Edward 18
Kelly, James 64; Ontario, 1871 ***1823.28*** *p51*
Kelly, James W.; Vermont, 1864 ***5900.10*** *p238*
Kelly, Jane 26; Ontario, 1871 ***1823.15*** *p134*
Kelly, Jemima 28; Ontario, 1861 ***2896.26*** *p18*
Kelly, Jemima 30; Ontario, 1861 ***2896.26*** *p17*
Kelly, Jeremiah; New York, 1820 ***8197.10*** *p245*
Kelly, Jeremiah; New York, 1837 ***8197.10*** *p93*
Kelly, Joanna 14; Vermont, 1865 ***5900.10*** *p539*
Kelly, Johanna 46; Vermont, 1872 ***5900.10*** *p266*
Kelly, John; Canada, 1756-1760 ***4628.40*** *p45*
Kelly, John; New York, 1802 ***8197.10*** *p21*
Kelly, John; New York, 1815 ***8197.10*** *p56*
Kelly, John; New York, 1831-1838 ***8197.10*** *p121*
Kelly, John; New York, 1838 ***8197.10*** *p247*
Kelly, John; New York, 1839 ***8197.10*** *p139*
Kelly, John; New York, 1840 ***8197.10*** *p247*
Kelly, John; Pennsylvania, 1821 ***6058.10*** *p6*
Kelly, John; Pennsylvania, 1823 ***6058.10*** *p8*
Kelly, John; Pennsylvania, 1866 ***6058.10*** *p55*
Kelly, John; Vermont, n.d. ***5900.10*** *p107*
Kelly, John; Virginia, 1666 ***6212.30*** *p31*
Kelly, John 2 *SEE* Kelly, James
Kelly, John 22; New York, 1832-1838 ***8197.10*** *p121*
Kelly, John 25; New York, 1831-1840 ***8197.10*** *p177*
Kelly, John 26; Vermont, 1863 ***5900.10*** *p211*
Kelly, John 28; Ontario, 1871 ***1823.15*** *p134*
Kelly, John 29; Vermont, 1875 ***5900.10*** *p107*
Kelly, John 30; Ontario, 1861 ***2896.25*** *p50*
Kelly, John 32; Washington, 1914 ***9196.1*** *p64*
Kelly, John 35; Ontario, 1871 ***1823.28*** *p51*
Kelly, John 36; Ontario, 1871 ***1823.15*** *p134*
Kelly, John 38; Ontario, 1871 ***1823.28*** *p51*
Kelly, John 40; Ontario, 1871 ***1823.15*** *p134*
Kelly, John 40; Ontario, 1871 ***1823.28*** *p51*
Kelly, John 42; Ontario, 1871 ***1823.22*** *p85*
Kelly, John 45; Ontario, 1871 ***1823.15*** *p134*
Kelly, John 46; Ontario, 1871 ***1823.15*** *p134*
Kelly, John 56; Ontario, 1871 ***1823.28*** *p51*
Kelly, John 62; Ontario, 1871 ***1823.28*** *p51*
Kelly, John 63; Ontario, 1871 ***1823.28*** *p51*
Kelly, John 75; Ontario, 1871 ***1823.15*** *p134*
Kelly, John 85; Vermont, 1866 ***5900.10*** *p619*
Kelly, John, Sr. 52; New York, New York, 1849 ***1825.45*** *p36*
Son: Barney 21
Son: Thomas 19
Daughter: Bridget 8
Daughter: Mary 11
Daughter: Ann 17
Son: Michael 18
Son: John, Jr. 24
Kelly, John, Jr. 36; Ontario, 1871 ***1823.28*** *p51*
Kelly, John, Jr. 24 *SEE* Kelly, John, Sr.
Kelly, John E.; Vermont, 1825-1893 ***5900.10*** *p187*
Kelly, John F.; Vermont, 1850-1920 ***5900.10*** *p142*
Kelly, John H.; New York, 1840 ***8197.10*** *p176*
Kelly, John J.; Vermont, 1848-1896 ***5900.10*** *p169*
Kelly, John M. 8; Ontario, 1861 ***2896.26*** *p17*
Kelly, John P. 19; Vermont, 1862 ***5900.10*** *p286*
Kelly, Joseph 7; Ontario, 1871 ***1823.15*** *p134*
Kelly, Julie; Maryland, 1682 ***2524.55*** *p128*
Kelly, Katherine M. Flannery; Vermont, 1847-1903 ***5900.10*** *p434*
Kelly, Katie S. 25; Vermont, 1882 ***5900.10*** *p590*
Kelly, Lakey 25; Philadelphia, 1774 ***1220.25*** *p81*
Kelly, Lawrance 39; Baltimore, 1775 ***1220.25*** *p118*
Kelly, Lawrence; Pennsylvania, 1786 ***4629.10*** *p50*
Kelly, Luke 62; Ontario, 1871 ***1823.15*** *p134*
Kelly, Maggie E. 5; Vermont, 1866 ***5900.10*** *p189*
Kelly, Margaret; Vermont, 1845-1910 ***5900.10*** *p218*
Kelly, Margaret 7 *SEE* Kelly, Margaret
Kelly, Margaret 18; Ontario, 1861 ***2896.27*** *p13*
Kelly, Margaret 35; New York, New York, 1849 ***1825.45*** *p36*
Daughter: Catherine 9
Daughter: Margaret 7
Kelly, Margaret 35; Ontario, 1871 ***1823.22*** *p85*
Kelly, Margaret Cannan 66; Vermont, 1897 ***5900.10*** *p369*
Kelly, Margaret Hartt; Vermont, 1834-1893 ***5900.10*** *p187*
Kelly, Margaret J.; Vermont, 1856-1919 ***5900.10*** *p246*
Kelly, Maria 14 *SEE* Kelly, Pat
Kelly, Mary; Vermont, 1833-1912 ***5900.10*** *p492*
Kelly, Mary; Vermont, 1837-1903 ***5900.10*** *p219*
Kelly, Mary; Vermont, 1856-1901 ***5900.10*** *p274*
Kelly, Mary 11 *SEE* Kelly, John, Sr.
Kelly, Mary 20 *SEE* Kelly, James
Kelly, Mary 32; Vermont, 1874 ***5900.10*** *p62*
Kelly, Mary 40 *SEE* Kelly, James
Kelly, Mary 42; Ontario, 1871 ***1823.15*** *p134*
Kelly, Mary 56; Ontario, 1871 ***1823.22*** *p85*
Kelly, Mary 66; Vermont, 1866 ***5900.10*** *p449*
Kelly, Mary A.; Vermont, 1933 ***5900.10*** *p266*
Kelly, Mary E. 1; Ontario, 1861 ***2896.26*** *p17*
Kelly, Mary E. 8; Ontario, 1861 ***2896.26*** *p32*
Kelly, Mary E. 44; Vermont, 1892 ***5900.10*** *p107*
Kelly, Mary M. 9; Ontario, 1861 ***2896.26*** *p18*
Kelly, Mary Walsh; Vermont, 1800-1849 ***5900.10*** *p187*
Kelly, Mathew 67; Ontario, 1871 ***1823.15*** *p134*
Kelly, Mathias; Pennsylvania, 1777 ***4629.10*** *p16*
Kelly, Matilda 6; Ontario, 1861 ***2896.26*** *p18*
Kelly, Michael; Vermont, n.d. ***5900.10*** *p110*
Kelly, Michael; Vermont, 1786-1861 ***5900.10*** *p187*
Kelly, Michael; Vermont, 1815-1886 ***5900.10*** *p189*
Kelly, Michael; Vermont, 1819-1894 ***5900.10*** *p302*
Kelly, Michael; Vermont, 1858-1932 ***5900.10*** *p54*
Kelly, Michael 18 *SEE* Kelly, John, Sr.
Kelly, Michael 30; Ontario, 1871 ***1823.28*** *p51*
Kelly, Michael 35; Ontario, 1871 ***1823.28*** *p51*
Kelly, Michael 75; Vermont, 1889 ***5900.10*** *p244*
Kelly, Michael C.; New York, 1837 ***8197.10*** *p319*
Kelly, Michael D. 14; Vermont, 1868 ***5900.10*** *p539*
Kelly, Michael F.; Vermont, 1835-1912 ***5900.10*** *p151*
Kelly, Morris; New York, 1838 ***8197.10*** *p121*
Kelly, Moses 60; Ontario, 1871 ***1823.28*** *p51*
Kelly, Nancy A. 5; Ontario, 1861 ***2896.26*** *p17*
Kelly, Nansey 64; Ontario, 1871 ***1823.22*** *p85*
Kelly, Owen; New York, 1840 ***8197.10*** *p247*
Kelly, Pat 40; New York, New York, 1848 ***1825.45*** *p16*
Wife: Eliza 36
Daughter: Bridget 1
Daughter: Maria 14
Daughter: Anne 10
Son: Thomas 12
Son: William 8
Kelly, Patrick; Maryland, 1682 ***2524.55*** *p128*
Kelly, Patrick; New York, 1804 ***8197.10*** *p28*
Kelly, Patrick; New York, 1807 ***8197.10*** *p43*
Kelly, Patrick; New York, 1825-1834 ***8197.10*** *p305*
Kelly, Patrick; New York, 1827 ***8197.10*** *p341*
Kelly, Patrick; New York, 1828 ***8197.10*** *p246*
Kelly, Patrick; New York, 1837 ***8197.10*** *p93*
Kelly, Patrick; New York, 1838 ***8197.10*** *p121*
Kelly, Patrick; New York, 1840 ***8197.10*** *p177*
Kelly, Patrick; Ontario, 1871 ***1823.28*** *p51*
Kelly, Patrick; Pennsylvania, 1867 ***6058.10*** *p57*

Kelly, Patrick; Vermont, 1826-1910 5900.10 p446
Kelly, Patrick; Vermont, 1834-1904 5900.10 p86
Kelly, Patrick; Vermont, 1853-1898 5900.10 p363
Kelly, Patrick 34; Ontario, 1861 2896.26 p32
Kelly, Patrick 40; Ontario, 1871 1823.15 p134
Kelly, Patrick 45; Ontario, 1871 1823.28 p51
Kelly, Patrick 58; Ontario, 1871 1823.28 p51
Kelly, Patrick 67; Vermont, 1885 5900.10 p369
Kelly, Patrick 72; Vermont, 1870 5900.10 p169
Kelly, Patrick J.; Vermont, 1814-1877 5900.10 p246
Kelly, Peter; New York, 1834 8197.10 p79
Kelly, Peter; New York, 1839 8197.10 p381
Kelly, Philip; Canada, 1756-1760 4628.40 p46
Kelly, Richard; New York, 1836-1838 8197.10 p122
Kelly, Richard; Vermont, 1926 5900.10 p266
Kelly, Robert; New York, 1803 8197.10 p13
Kelly, Robert 35; Ontario, 1871 1823.15 p134
Kelly, Roger; Maryland, 1675 2524.55 p128
Kelly, Rosette 58; Vermont, 1905 5900.10 p297
Kelly, Samuel R.; Vermont, 1849-1933 5900.10 p597
Kelly, Sarah A. Higgins; Vermont, 1844-1919 5900.10 p169
Kelly, Sarah Alia; Vermont, 1859-1907 5900.10 p246
Kelly, Sarah J. 3; Ontario, 1861 2896.26 p17
Kelly, Sarah M. 75; Vermont, 1888 5900.10 p590
Kelly, Sarah McCarthy; Vermont, 1826-1907 5900.10 p246
Kelly, Sarahann 25; Ontario, 1861 2896.26 p18
Kelly, Sinon 36; Ontario, 1871 1823.28 p51
Kelly, Sophiah 18; Ontario, 1861 2896.26 p18
Kelly, Susanna 19; Ontario, 1861 2896.26 p18
Kelly, Susie M.; Vermont, 1863-1943 5900.10 p597
Kelly, Thomas; New York, 1840 8197.10 p176
Kelly, Thomas; Vermont, 1842-1919 5900.10 p609
Kelly, Thomas 10; Ontario, 1861 2896.26 p32
Kelly, Thomas 12 *SEE* Kelly, Pat
Kelly, Thomas 19 *SEE* Kelly, John, Sr.
Kelly, Thomas 43; Ontario, 1871 1823.15 p134
Kelly, Thomas 48; Ontario, 1871 1823.15 p134
Kelly, Thomas 50; Ontario, 1871 1823.15 p134
Kelly, Thomas F.; Vermont, n.d. 5900.10 p107
Kelly, William; Canada, 1756-1760 4628.40 p45
Kelly, William; Georgia, 1848 1640.10 p91
Kelly, William; New York, 1821 8197.10 p245
Kelly, William; New York, 1833 8197.10 p246
Kelly, William; Vermont, 1822-1900 5900.10 p363
Kelly, William 8 *SEE* Kelly, Pat
Kelly, William 22; Ontario, 1871 1823.22 p85
Kelly, William 50; Ontario, 1871 1823.15 p134
Kelly, William 70; Ontario, 1871 1823.28 p51
Kelly, Wm.; Nova Scotia, 1745 4628.40 p45
Kellye, Edmund; Virginia, 1671 6212.30 p42
Kelma, Wm.; New York, New York, 1853 6058.10 p39
Kelminiak, Joseph J.; Maryland, 1910 3259.35 p26
Kelner, Clara 32; Ontario, 1861 2896.28 p61
Kelner, Constanty; Maryland, 1910 3259.35 p26
Kelner, Victoria 11; Ontario, 1861 2896.28 p61
Kelner, Wellington 5; Ontario, 1861 2896.28 p61
Kelner, Zilpa 3; Ontario, 1861 2896.28 p61
Kelow, William 9; Ontario, 1871 1823.28 p51
Kelsall, Robert; Georgia, 1780 1640.10 p91
Kelsch, Johann Nicolas; Port uncertain, 1770 2856.30 p218
With wife
Kelsey, Benjamin 16; Maryland, 1775 1220.25 p111
Kelsey, Mary; Maryland, 1681 2524.55 p128
Kelsey, Mary; Maryland, 1682 2524.55 p128
Kelsey, Samuel; Pennsylvania, 1777 4629.10 p23
Kelso, Archibald; Georgia, 1698 1640.13 p64
Kelso, George; Pennsylvania, 1777 4629.10 p9
Kelso, J.; Quebec, 1858 9196.15 p44
Kelso, James; New York, 1803 8197.10 p13
Kelson, Charles 60; Ontario, 1871 1823.28 p51
Kelsy, Darby; Maryland, 1682 2524.55 p128
Kelsy, William; Maryland, 1677-1681 2524.55 p128
Keltsch, Anna Eva; Port uncertain, 1765 2856.30 p218
Kelty, Ann; Vermont, 1838-1925 5900.10 p296
Kelty, Bridget; Vermont, 1834-1871 5900.10 p554
Kelty, Bridget; Vermont, 1836-1909 5900.10 p298
Kelty, Bridget 32; Vermont, 1871 5900.10 p346
Kelty, Bridget 56; Vermont, 1872 5900.10 p368
Kelty, Ellen F.; Vermont, 1835-1910 5900.10 p548
Kelty, Honora; Vermont, 1858-1958 5900.10 p554
Kelty, John; Vermont, 1804-1880 5900.10 p368
Kelty, M.; Vermont, 1826-1926 5900.10 p334
Kelty, Margaret; Vermont, 1833-1911 5900.10 p550
Kelty, Mary; Vermont, 1846-1884 5900.10 p550
Kelty, Mary 85; Vermont, 1891 5900.10 p344
Kelty, Nancy; Vermont, 1841-1922 5900.10 p553
Kelty, Nancy Teresa 33; Vermont, 1863 5900.10 p346
Kelty, Patrick; Vermont, 1836-1950 5900.10 p548
Kelty, Winifred S.; Vermont, 1836-1914 5900.10 p552
Kelway, Margaret; New England, 1651 1224.1 p34
Kelway, Mary; New England, 1651 1224.1 p34
Kelway, Melcas; New England, 1651 1224.1 p34
Kely, Joshua S. 21; Vermont, 1854 5900.10 p303
Kelzer, Mgdl. Geberz *SEE* Kelzer, Peter
Kelzer, Peter; Port uncertain, 1764 2856.30 p218
Kelzer, Peter; Port uncertain, 1785 2856.30 p218
Wife: Mgdl. Geberz
Kemady, Margret; Virginia, 1690-1691 6212.30 p59
Kembe, Thomas; Virginia, 1665 1224.1 p34
Kember, Martin; Port uncertain, 1785 2856.30 p218
Kemberg, Hans Michael; Port uncertain, 1748 2856.30 p218
Kemble, Grace; Virginia, 1695 1224.1 p25
Kemeter, Johann; Port uncertain, 1783 2856.30 p218
Kemick, Edward 35; Ontario, 1871 1823.15 p134
Keminz, Stefan; Port uncertain, 1747 2856.30 p218
With wife & children
Kemm, Caspar; Port uncertain, 1765 2856.30 p218
With wife & child
Kemmer, Hans Nickel; America, 1749 2856.30 p218
With wife & 2 children
Kemp, Alzada 11; Ontario, 1861 2896.25 p4
Kemp, Amos 5; Ontario, 1861 2896.25 p14
Kemp, Anna 61; Ontario, 1861 2896.25 p4
Kemp, Anson L. 1; Ontario, 1861 2896.25 p14
Kemp, Cornelius 28; Ontario, 1861 2896.25 p4
Kemp, Elizabeth 33; Ontario, 1861 2896.25 p4
Kemp, George; Bahamas, 1789 1224.2 p64
Kemp, George; Florida, n.d. 1224.2 p64
Kemp, George; Florida, 1789 1640.10 p91
Kemp, George; Pennsylvania, 1788 4629.10 p56
Kemp, George 39; Ontario, 1871 1823.22 p85
Kemp, Henry 18; Ontario, 1871 1823.28 p51
Kemp, James; New York, 1837 8197.10 p93
Kemp, James A. 15; Ontario, 1861 2896.25 p4
Kemp, Jane 51; Ontario, 1861 2896.25 p4
Kemp, Jeremiah 18; Ontario, 1861 2896.25 p4
Kemp, John; New Orleans, 1847 1640.10 p91
Kemp, John; New York, 1840 8197.10 p177
Kemp, John 56; Ontario, 1871 1823.15 p134
Kemp, John, Jr. 29; Ontario, 1871 1823.15 p134
Kemp, Joshua C. 19; Ontario, 1861 2896.25 p4
Kemp, Mary 27; Ontario, 1861 2896.25 p14
Kemp, Phebe J. 10; Ontario, 1861 2896.25 p4
Kemp, Ransalier 7; Ontario, 1861 2896.25 p14
Kemp, Robert; Virginia, 1666-1667 6212.30 p33
Kemp, Samuel; Maryland, 1682 2524.55 p128
Kemp, Sarah 13; Ontario, 1861 2896.25 p4
Kemp, Sarah M. 3; Ontario, 1861 2896.25 p14
Kemp, Sarah S. 19; Ontario, 1861 2896.25 p33
Kemp, Thos; Quebec, 1856 9196.15 p10
Kemp, Townson 23; Ontario, 1861 2896.25 p4
Kemp, W. H.; Portland, Maine, 1858 9196.15 p31
Kemp, William; Maryland, 1660 2524.55 p128
Kemp, William; Pennsylvania, 1786 4629.10 p47
Kemp, Wm; Virginia, 1671-1672 6212.30 p47
Kempe, Ann; Maryland, 1668 2524.55 p128
Child: John
Child: William
Kempe, J. J. 32; Alaska, 1917 9196.1 p46
Kempe, J. J. 32; Whitehorse, Yukon, 1917 9196.1 p46
Kempe, John *SEE* Kempe, Ann
Kempe, Richard; Virginia, 1656 1224.1 p34
Kempe, Thomas; Maryland, 1656 2524.55 p128
Kempe, William *SEE* Kempe, Ann
Kemper, Andreas; Port uncertain, 1784 2856.30 p219
Kemperling, Philipp; Port uncertain, 1768 2856.30 p219
Kempf, Bernhard; Port uncertain, 1754 2856.30 p219
Kempff, Johann Georg; Port uncertain, 1735 2856.30 p219
Kempff, Johann Georg; Port uncertain, 1742 2856.30 p219
With wife & children
Kempka, Pawel; Maryland, 1910 3259.35 p26
Kempton, Thomas 64; Ontario, 1871 1823.15 p134
Kemys, Samuel 14; Philadelphia, 1775 1220.25 p8
Kenady, Alex 43; Ontario, 1871 1823.22 p86
Kenan, Michael; New York, 1839 8197.10 p381
Kenan, Moses 60; Ontario, 1871 1823.15 p134
Kenastone, Edw; Virginia, 1664 6212.30 p12
Kendal, Ann 21; Maryland, 1775 1220.25 p105
Kendall, Bernard; Virginia, 1666 6212.30 p30
Kendall, George; Maryland, 1681 2524.55 p128
Kendall, Herbert; Virginia, 1664 6212.30 p14
Kendall, Herbert; Virginia, 1665-1666 6212.30 p22
Kendall, Jo.; Maryland, 1681 2524.55 p128
Kendall, Jone; Maryland, 1666 2524.55 p205
Kendall, Thomas; New York, New York, 1829 8197.10 p177
Kendall, Walter; Virginia, 1666 6212.30 p27
Kendell, George 26; Ontario, 1871 1823.28 p51
Kendell, John 43; Ontario, 1871 1823.22 p86
Kender, William; Maryland, 1910 3259.35 p26
Kendrick, Mr.; Quebec, 1857 9196.15 p17
Kendrick, Elizabeth; Virginia, 1701 6212.30 p61
Kendy, Bridget 83; Vermont, 1872 5900.10 p109
Kendzierski, Adam J.; Maryland, 1910 3259.35 p26
Kendziersky, Martin; Maryland, 1910 3259.35 p26
Kendzieski, Michael; Maryland, 1910 3259.35 p26
Keneda, Adam 44; Ontario, 1871 1823.28 p51
Keneda, William 82; Ontario, 1871 1823.28 p51
Keneday, Jane; Virginia, 1673 6212.30 p51
Keneday, William; Maryland, 1665 2524.55 p138
Kenedy, Angus 46; Ontario, 1871 1823.15 p134
Kenedy, Duncan 36; Ontario, 1871 1823.15 p134
Kenedy, John 15 *SEE* Kenedy, Peggy
Kenedy, John 32; Ontario, 1871 1823.28 p51
Kenedy, Mathew 67; Ontario, 1871 1823.22 p86
Kenedy, Michel 57; Ontario, 1871 1823.15 p134
Kenedy, Mikle 27; Ontario, 1861 2896.27 p13
Kenedy, Peggy 40; New York, New York, 1849 1825.45 p31
Son: John 15
Son: Thomas 7
Kenedy, Thomas 7 *SEE* Kenedy, Peggy
Kenedy, William 48; Ontario, 1871 1823.22 p86
Kenefick, Catherine Connor; Vermont, 1852-1904 5900.10 p598
Kenefick, Michael; Vermont, 1843-1922 5900.10 p598
Kenehan, Ann 8 *SEE* Kenehan, John
Kenehan, Jeremiah 16 *SEE* Kenehan, John
Kenehan, John 12 *SEE* Kenehan, John
Kenehan, John 45; New York, New York, 1852 1825.45 p58
Wife: Mary 37
Daughter: Ann 8
Son: Jeremiah 16
Son: John 12
Son: William 6
Son: Matthew 18
Kenehan, Mary 37 *SEE* Kenehan, John
Kenehan, Matthew 18 *SEE* Kenehan, John
Kenehan, William 6 *SEE* Kenehan, John
Kenian, Catherine 67; Vermont, 1878 5900.10 p163
Kenion, Roger; Virginia, 1665-1666 6212.30 p22
Keniry, Catherine; Vermont, 1815-1892 5900.10 p220
Kenison, Rogier; Virginia, 1666-1667 6212.30 p32
Kenly, William; Pennsylvania, 1777 4629.10 p12
Kenn, James 65; Ontario, 1871 1823.15 p134
Kenn, William M.; Mississippi, 1827-1845 1640.10 p91
Kenna, Ellen 37; Vermont, 1872 5900.10 p164
Kenna, Hugh 45; Vermont, 1874 5900.10 p45
Kenna, John 24; Vermont, 1870-1879 5900.10 p164
Kenna, Sarah; Vermont, 1838-1912 5900.10 p172
Kennada, Thomas 55; Ontario, 1871 1823.28 p51
Kennady, John; Maryland, 1681 2524.55 p128
Kennady, Joseph 51; Ontario, 1871 1823.28 p51
Kennag, Sarah; Maryland, 1680 2524.55 p128
Kennailly, Thomas 60; Ontario, 1871 1823.22 p86
Kennan, William; Richmond, Virginia, 1768 1640.13 p64
Kennan, William; Virginia, 1765 1224.2 p64
Kennas, Sarah; Maryland, 1678 2524.55 p128
Kennas, Sarah; Maryland, 1680 2524.55 p128
Kenneda, James 40; Ontario, 1871 1823.15 p134
Kenneday, Alexander 38; Virginia, 1774 1220.25 p46
Kenneday, John 26; Philadelphia, 1774 1220.25 p6
Kenneday, Mary 21; Maryland, 1774 1220.25 p65
Kenneday, Michael 33; Maryland, 1774 1220.25 p2
Kenneday, R. 21; Ontario, 1871 1823.28 p51
Kenneday, Thomas 23; Maryland, 1773-1774 1220.25 p34
Kenneday, Timothy 21; Virginia, 1774 1220.25 p92
Kennedy, . . .; Vermont, n.d. 5900.10 p222
Kennedy, Miss; Quebec, 1856 9196.15 p8
Kennedy, Miss; Quebec, 1857 9196.15 p16
Kennedy, Mr.; Quebec, 1857 9196.15 p20
Kennedy, Mr.; Quebec, 1858 9196.15 p41
Kennedy, Mr.; Vermont, 1839-1920 5900.10 p583
Kennedy, Mrs.; Quebec, 1856 9196.15 p8
Kennedy, Mrs.; Vermont, 1838-1923 5900.10 p583
Kennedy, Mrs. 33; New York, New York, 1849 1825.45 p37
Kennedy, A. S. R.; Quebec, 1856 9196.15 p8
Kennedy, Abel S. 49; Ontario, 1871 1823.22 p86
Kennedy, Adam; Antigua (Antego), 1698 1224.1 p34
Kennedy, Alexander 30; Ontario, 1871 1823.15 p134
Kennedy, Alice E.; Vermont, 1835-1904 5900.10 p129
Kennedy, Alicia 71; Ontario, 1871 1823.22 p86
Kennedy, Andrew; New York, 1834 8197.10 p72
Kennedy, Angus; New York, 1807 8197.10 p43
Kennedy, Ann 14 *SEE* Kennedy, Pat
Kennedy, Ann 15; New York, New York, 1849 1825.45 p37
Kennedy, Ann Hagan 73; Vermont, 1891 5900.10 p345
Kennedy, Ann McGinn; Vermont, 1850-1935 5900.10 p50

Kennedy, Annabella; Saskatchewan, 1884 ***4537.37*** *p104*
Kennedy, Anne 24 *SEE* Kennedy, Pat
Kennedy, Anne T. 58; Vermont, 1903 ***5900.10*** *p164*
Kennedy, Biddy 16 *SEE* Kennedy, Pat
Kennedy, Biddy 20 *SEE* Kennedy, Thomas
Kennedy, Bridget; Vermont, 1821-1911 ***5900.10*** *p50*
Kennedy, Bridget; Vermont, 1823-1899 ***5900.10*** *p180*
Kennedy, Bridget; Vermont, 1854-1921 ***5900.10*** *p138*
Kennedy, Bridget 9; New York, New York, 1849 ***1825.45*** *p37*
Kennedy, Bridget 20 *SEE* Kennedy, Pat
Kennedy, Bridget 24 *SEE* Kennedy, Pat
Kennedy, Bridget 56; Ontario, 1871 ***1823.22*** *p86*
Kennedy, Bridget 67; Vermont, 1909 ***5900.10*** *p571*
Kennedy, Bridget 70; Vermont, 1873 ***5900.10*** *p591*
Kennedy, Bridget Kane 34; Vermont, 1887 ***5900.10*** *p447*
Kennedy, Catharine; Vermont, 1846-1919 ***5900.10*** *p186*
Kennedy, Catherine; Vermont, 1843-1918 ***5900.10*** *p142*
Kennedy, Catherine; Vermont, 1844-1877 ***5900.10*** *p110*
Kennedy, Catherine; Vermont, 1845-1919 ***5900.10*** *p222*
Kennedy, Catherine 9; New York, New York, 1849 ***1825.45*** *p37*
Kennedy, Catherine 18 *SEE* Kennedy, Pat
Kennedy, Catherine 19 *SEE* Kennedy, Pat
Kennedy, Catherine 21; Ontario, 1861 ***2896.28*** *p7*
Kennedy, Catherine 46; Ontario, 1871 ***1823.28*** *p51*
Kennedy, Catherine 68; Vermont, 1902 ***5900.10*** *p165*
Kennedy, Catherine Howrigan; Vermont, 1848-1935 ***5900.10*** *p476*
Kennedy, Catherine Knirk; Vermont, 1803-1864 ***5900.10*** *p164*
Kennedy, Cecelia; Vermont, 1940 ***5900.10*** *p323*
Kennedy, Charlotte; Vermont, 1846-1934 ***5900.10*** *p489*
Kennedy, Clara J.; Vermont, 1882-1967 ***5900.10*** *p355*
Kennedy, Clarisa J.; Vermont, 1881-1954 ***5900.10*** *p355*
Kennedy, Cornelius; Maryland, 1659 ***2524.55*** *p128*
Kennedy, Cornelius E.; Vermont, 1939 ***5900.10*** *p169*
Kennedy, Daniel; Georgia, 1761 ***1640.10*** *p91*
Kennedy, Daniel; Vermont, 1873-1874 ***5900.10*** *p110*
Kennedy, Daniel 18; New York, New York, 1849 ***1825.45*** *p37*
Kennedy, Daniel 52; Ontario, 1871 ***1823.15*** *p134*
Kennedy, Dennis; Maryland, 1656 ***2524.55*** *p128*
Kennedy, Dominick; New York, 1840 ***8197.10*** *p177*
Kennedy, Donald; Georgia, 1743 ***1640.10*** *p91*
Kennedy, Donald; Georgia, 1757 ***1640.10*** *p91*
Kennedy, Duncan; Georgia, 1743 ***1640.10*** *p91*
Kennedy, Duncan 29; Ontario, 1871 ***1823.15*** *p134*
Kennedy, Edward; New York, 1830-1838 ***8197.10*** *p121*
Kennedy, Elizabeth; Vermont, 1838-1894 ***5900.10*** *p472*
Kennedy, Ellen; Vermont, 1834-1873 ***5900.10*** *p476*
Kennedy, Ellen 3; New York, New York, 1849 ***1825.45*** *p36*
Kennedy, Ellen Doharty 42; Vermont, 1863 ***5900.10*** *p611*
Kennedy, Ellen Flinn; Vermont, 1837-1917 ***5900.10*** *p477*
Kennedy, Ellen Hahar; Vermont, 1815-1898 ***5900.10*** *p578*
Kennedy, Ellen Keefe; Vermont, 1841-1910 ***5900.10*** *p395*
Kennedy, Ellon 62; Ontario, 1871 ***1823.15*** *p134*
Kennedy, Emerson Michael; Vermont, 1848-1930 ***5900.10*** *p323*
Kennedy, F.; Quebec, 1856 ***9196.15*** *p8*
Kennedy, F., Jr.; Quebec, 1856 ***9196.15*** *p8*
Kennedy, Francis; New York, 1837 ***8197.10*** *p93*
Kennedy, Frank E.; Vermont, 1887 ***5900.10*** *p355*
Kennedy, George 48; Ontario, 1871 ***1823.22*** *p86*
Kennedy, George 52; Ontario, 1871 ***1823.22*** *p86*
Kennedy, Hannah; Vermont, 1836-1913 ***5900.10*** *p164*
Kennedy, Hannah 12 *SEE* Kennedy, Pat
Kennedy, Helen; Vermont, 1958 ***5900.10*** *p169*
Kennedy, Helen F.; Vermont, 1859-1898 ***5900.10*** *p186*
Kennedy, Honoria 18 *SEE* Kennedy, Thomas
Kennedy, Hugh; Georgia, 1757 ***1640.10*** *p91*
Kennedy, James; Pennsylvania, 1777 ***4629.10*** *p20*
Kennedy, James; Pennsylvania, 1832 ***6058.10*** *p17*
Kennedy, James; Vermont, n.d. ***5900.10*** *p249*
Kennedy, James; Vermont, 1850-1918 ***5900.10*** *p138*
Kennedy, James; Vermont, 1867 ***5900.10*** *p77*
Kennedy, James 38; Ontario, 1871 ***1823.15*** *p134*
Kennedy, James 38; Vermont, 1883 ***5900.10*** *p470*
Kennedy, James 44; Ontario, 1871 ***1823.22*** *p86*
Kennedy, James 52; Vermont, 1887 ***5900.10*** *p447*
Kennedy, James 64; Ontario, 1871 ***1823.22*** *p86*
Kennedy, James L.; Vermont, 1877-1905 ***5900.10*** *p355*
Kennedy, Jane; Florida, 1818 ***1640.10*** *p92*
Kennedy, Jane; Vermont, 1870-1873 ***5900.10*** *p110*
Kennedy, Jane 72; Ontario, 1871 ***1823.15*** *p135*
Kennedy, Johanna Bagley; Vermont, 1836-1919 ***5900.10*** *p442*
Kennedy, Johanna C.; Vermont, 1856-1931 ***5900.10*** *p119*
Kennedy, John; Florida, n.d. ***1224.3*** *p43*
Kennedy, John; Florida, 1777 ***1640.10*** *p92*
Kennedy, John; Georgia, 1761 ***1640.10*** *p92*
Kennedy, John; New York, 1828-1834 ***8197.10*** *p308*
Kennedy, John; New York, 1829 ***8197.10*** *p65*
Kennedy, John; New York, 1831 ***8197.10*** *p303*
Kennedy, John; New York, 1834 ***8197.10*** *p373*
Kennedy, John; New York, New York, 1818 ***8197.10*** *p336*
Kennedy, John; Pennsylvania, 1885 ***1640.13*** *p64*
Kennedy, John; Vermont, 1804-1891 ***5900.10*** *p470*
Kennedy, John; Vermont, 1820-1893 ***5900.10*** *p156*
Kennedy, John; Vermont, 1829-1904 ***5900.10*** *p442*
Kennedy, John; Vermont, 1830-1903 ***5900.10*** *p50*
Kennedy, John; Vermont, 1856-1920 ***5900.10*** *p301*
Kennedy, John 16 *SEE* Kennedy, Pat
Kennedy, John 25; Ontario, 1861 ***2896.28*** *p7*
Kennedy, John 35; Ontario, 1871 ***1823.15*** *p135*
Kennedy, John 37; Vermont, 1899 ***5900.10*** *p118*
Kennedy, John 54; Ontario, 1871 ***1823.28*** *p51*
Kennedy, John 71; Vermont, 1892 ***5900.10*** *p507*
Kennedy, John 80; Ontario, 1871 ***1823.15*** *p135*
Kennedy, John E.; Vermont, 1856-1935 ***5900.10*** *p407*
Kennedy, John J.; Vermont, 1832-1916 ***5900.10*** *p168*
Kennedy, John J.; Vermont, 1837-1916 ***5900.10*** *p171*
Kennedy, John J.; Vermont, 1870-1932 ***5900.10*** *p169*
Kennedy, John M.; Vermont, 1874-1881 ***5900.10*** *p257*
Kennedy, John P.; Vermont, 1885-1896 ***5900.10*** *p355*
Kennedy, Julia Duggan; Vermont, 1831-1904 ***5900.10*** *p301*
Kennedy, Julian 48; Ontario, 1871 ***1823.22*** *p86*
Kennedy, Katherine; Vermont, 1827-1924 ***5900.10*** *p131*
Kennedy, Kenneth; New Orleans, 1812 ***1640.10*** *p92*
Kennedy, Laughlin 77; Ontario, 1871 ***1823.15*** *p135*
Kennedy, Lawrence; Vermont, 1852-1933 ***5900.10*** *p50*
Kennedy, Mamie 2 months; Vermont, 1882 ***5900.10*** *p449*
Kennedy, Margaret; Vermont, 1813-1871 ***5900.10*** *p583*
Kennedy, Margaret; Vermont, 1836-1911 ***5900.10*** *p263*
Kennedy, Margaret; Vermont, 1840-1908 ***5900.10*** *p392*
Kennedy, Margaret 65; Vermont, 1866 ***5900.10*** *p231*
Kennedy, Margaret 90; Ontario, 1871 ***1823.15*** *p135*
Kennedy, Margaret Halloran 58; Vermont, 1900 ***5900.10*** *p128*
Kennedy, Margaret Sullivan; Vermont, 1835-1906 ***5900.10*** *p156*
Kennedy, Margaret T.; Vermont, 1833-1918 ***5900.10*** *p553*
Kennedy, Maria 66; Vermont, 1923 ***5900.10*** *p421*
Kennedy, Martha; Vermont, 1795-1882 ***5900.10*** *p146*
Kennedy, Mary; Nova Scotia, 1840-1849 ***4537.35*** *p33*
Kennedy, Mary; Vermont, 1832-1915 ***5900.10*** *p408*
Kennedy, Mary; Vermont, 1832-1919 ***5900.10*** *p156*
Kennedy, Mary; Vermont, 1833-1903 ***5900.10*** *p257*
Kennedy, Mary; Vermont, 1836-1902 ***5900.10*** *p168*
Kennedy, Mary; Vermont, 1841-1910 ***5900.10*** *p164*
Kennedy, Mary; Vermont, 1853-1898 ***5900.10*** *p117*
Kennedy, Mary; Vermont, 1856-1934 ***5900.10*** *p102*
Kennedy, Mary; Vermont, 1902-1936 ***5900.10*** *p171*
Kennedy, Mary 10 *SEE* Kennedy, Pat
Kennedy, Mary 24; New York, New York, 1849 ***1825.45*** *p36*
Kennedy, Mary 40 *SEE* Kennedy, Pat
Kennedy, Mary 50 *SEE* Kennedy, Peter
Kennedy, Mary 60; Vermont, 1885 ***5900.10*** *p457*
Kennedy, Mary 67; Vermont, 1913 ***5900.10*** *p445*
Kennedy, Mary 71; Ontario, 1871 ***1823.22*** *p86*
Kennedy, Mary 72; Vermont, 1867 ***5900.10*** *p618*
Kennedy, Mary 80; Vermont, 1906 ***5900.10*** *p247*
Kennedy, Mary A.; Vermont, 1854-1919 ***5900.10*** *p594*
Kennedy, Mary A. 67; Vermont, 1922 ***5900.10*** *p165*
Kennedy, Mary A. Russell; Vermont, 1856-1919 ***5900.10*** *p407*
Kennedy, Mary Ann 6; New York, New York, 1849 ***1825.45*** *p37*
Kennedy, Mary E.; Vermont, 1874-1956 ***5900.10*** *p257*
Kennedy, Mary Fitzgerald; Vermont, 1861-1904 ***5900.10*** *p355*
Kennedy, Mary Flynn; Vermont, 1851-1946 ***5900.10*** *p323*
Kennedy, Mary Hogan; Vermont, 1832-1860 ***5900.10*** *p156*
Kennedy, Mary O'Brien; Vermont, 1806-1889 ***5900.10*** *p470*
Kennedy, Mary Treahey; Vermont, 1851-1924 ***5900.10*** *p257*
Kennedy, Mary White; Vermont, 1845-1910 ***5900.10*** *p442*
Kennedy, Maurice 86; Vermont, 1897 ***5900.10*** *p117*
Kennedy, Michael; Vermont, 1849-1911 ***5900.10*** *p257*
Kennedy, Michael 17; New York, New York, 1849 ***1825.45*** *p37*
Kennedy, Michael 35; Ontario, 1871 ***1823.28*** *p51*
Kennedy, Michael E.; Vermont, 1867-1889 ***5900.10*** *p169*
Kennedy, Nancy 59; Vermont, 1879 ***5900.10*** *p109*
Kennedy, Nancy Rooney; Vermont, 1840-1916 ***5900.10*** *p276*
Kennedy, Nora W.; Vermont, 1867-1942 ***5900.10*** *p166*
Kennedy, Pat 10; New York, New York, 1848 ***1825.45*** *p36*
Kennedy, Pat 12; New York, New York, 1849 ***1825.45*** *p37*
Kennedy, Pat 28; New York, New York, 1848 ***1825.45*** *p36*
Wife: Anne 24
Sister: Bridget 24
Sister: Catherine 19
Kennedy, Pat 48; New York, New York, 1848 ***1825.45*** *p36*
Daughter: Biddy 16
Daughter: Bridget 20
Son: Thomas 6
Son: John 16
Wife: Mary 40
Daughter: Hannah 12
Daughter: Catherine 18
Daughter: Peggy 4
Daughter: Ann 14
Daughter: Mary 10
Kennedy, Patrick; New York, 1807 ***8197.10*** *p330*
Kennedy, Patrick; New York, 1839 ***8197.10*** *p139*
Kennedy, Patrick; Vermont, 1812-1854 ***5900.10*** *p583*
Kennedy, Patrick; Vermont, 1830-1900 ***5900.10*** *p578*
Kennedy, Patrick; Vermont, 1847-1919 ***5900.10*** *p276*
Kennedy, Patrick 40; Ontario, 1871 ***1823.28*** *p51*
Kennedy, Patrick P. 53; Vermont, 1900 ***5900.10*** *p185*
Kennedy, Pearce; New York, 1831-1837 ***8197.10*** *p311*
Kennedy, Peggy 4 *SEE* Kennedy, Pat
Kennedy, Peggy 17 *SEE* Kennedy, Thomas
Kennedy, Peter; Vermont, 1851-1909 ***5900.10*** *p510*
Kennedy, Peter 63; New York, New York, 1852 ***1825.45*** *p59*
Wife: Mary 50
Kennedy, Richard; Vermont, 1848-1916 ***5900.10*** *p355*
Kennedy, Richard W.; Vermont, 1880 ***5900.10*** *p355*
Kennedy, Robert; Canada, 1876 ***1640.13*** *p64*
Kennedy, Robert 49; Ontario, 1871 ***1823.15*** *p135*
Kennedy, Samuel 35; Ontario, 1871 ***1823.22*** *p86*
Kennedy, Sarah; Vermont, 1817-1905 ***5900.10*** *p309*
Kennedy, Sarah A.; Vermont, 1823-1902 ***5900.10*** *p146*
Kennedy, Sarah Ann; Vermont, 1858-1864 ***5900.10*** *p301*
Kennedy, Sophia M. 83; Vermont, 1882 ***5900.10*** *p499*
Kennedy, Stasia Hartley; Vermont, 1858-1892 ***5900.10*** *p510*
Kennedy, Th. R.; Pennsylvania, 1784 ***4629.10*** *p44*
Kennedy, Thomas; Canada, 1756-1760 ***4628.40*** *p45*
Kennedy, Thomas; New York, 1840 ***8197.10*** *p176*
Kennedy, Thomas; Vermont, 1794-1840 ***5900.10*** *p146*
Kennedy, Thomas; Vermont, 1795-1875 ***5900.10*** *p476*
Kennedy, Thomas; Vermont, 1839-1913 ***5900.10*** *p441*
Kennedy, Thomas 6 *SEE* Kennedy, Pat
Kennedy, Thomas 30; New York, New York, 1849 ***1825.45*** *p36*
Sister: Biddy 20
Sister: Honoria 18
Sister: Peggy 17
Kennedy, Thomas B.; Vermont, 1838-1903 ***5900.10*** *p475*
Kennedy, Thomas C.; Vermont, 1878-1944 ***5900.10*** *p355*
Kennedy, Thomas F. 27; Vermont, 1884 ***5900.10*** *p448*
Kennedy, Thomas H.; New York, 1803 ***8197.10*** *p13*
Kennedy, Timothy; Vermont, 1827-1874 ***5900.10*** *p301*
Kennedy, Timothy E.; Vermont, 1866-1931 ***5900.10*** *p301*
Kennedy, William; Georgia, 1736 ***1640.10*** *p92*
Kennedy, William; Georgia, 1743 ***1640.10*** *p92*
Kennedy, William; Georgia, 1757 ***1640.10*** *p92*
Kennedy, William; New York, 1838 ***8197.10*** *p375*
Kennedy, William; Pennsylvania, 1777 ***4629.10*** *p21*
Kennedy, William; Savannah, Georgia, 1799 ***1640.10*** *p92*
Kennedy, William; Vermont, 1837-1908 ***5900.10*** *p395*
Kennedy, William 25; South Carolina, 1774 ***1220.25*** *p83*
Kennedy, William 29; Ontario, 1871 ***1823.28*** *p51*
Kennedy, William 37; Ontario, 1871 ***1823.28*** *p51*
Kennedy, William 45; Ontario, 1871 ***1823.22*** *p86*
Kennell, Cornelius; Maryland, 1658 ***2524.55*** *p128*
Kennelly, Edward 40; Ontario, 1871 ***1823.28*** *p51*
Kennelly, Hannah 66; Vermont, 1905 ***5900.10*** *p167*
Kennelly, John 21; Virginia, 1774 ***1220.25*** *p45*
Kennelly, Martin 40; Ontario, 1871 ***1823.28*** *p51*
Kennelly, Martin 50; Ontario, 1871 ***1823.28*** *p51*
Kennemont, Hugh; Maryland, 1663 ***2524.55*** *p49*
Kennesy, Patrick; New York, 1831 ***8197.10*** *p369*
Kennet, Elizabeth *SEE* Kennet, William
Kennet, Martha *SEE* Kennet, William
Kennet, Mary *SEE* Kennet, William

Kennet, Susannah *SEE* Kennet, William
Kennet, Susannah; Maryland, 1682 ***2524.55*** *p129*
Kennet, William; Maryland, 1682 ***2524.55*** *p129*
Wife: Elizabeth
Child: Mary
Child: Susannah
Child: Elizabeth
Child: Martha
Kenney, Ann 60; Ontario, 1861 ***2896.28*** *p43*
Kenney, Ann 74; Vermont, 1892 ***5900.10*** *p200*
Kenney, Anne 50; Ontario, 1871 ***1823.28*** *p51*
Kenney, James; Vermont, 1851-1922 ***5900.10*** *p503*
Kenney, James 15; Ontario, 1861 ***2896.28*** *p43*
Kenney, John 26; Vermont, 1857 ***5900.10*** *p611*
Kenney, John 71; Vermont, 1892 ***5900.10*** *p503*
Kenney, Marion Lonergan; Vermont, 1859-1923 ***5900.10*** *p503*
Kenney, William 58; Ontario, 1871 ***1823.22*** *p86*
Kennick, Edward; Maryland, 1910 ***3259.35*** *p26*
Kennilly, Patrick 60; Ontario, 1871 ***1823.15*** *p135*
Kennimount, Anne *SEE* Kennimount, John
Kennimount, John *SEE* Kennimount, John
Kennimount, John; Maryland, 1654 ***2524.55*** *p129*
Wife: Anne
Son: Patrick
Son: John
Kennimount, Patrick *SEE* Kennimount, John
Kenniston, Thomas; Maryland, 1672 ***2524.55*** *p129*
Kennnedy, Edward; Vermont, 1842-1912 ***5900.10*** *p43*
Kennon, John; New York, 1837 ***8197.10*** *p93*
Kennpek, Charles 30; Ontario, 1871 ***1823.28*** *p51*
Kenny, Andrew 66; Ontario, 1871 ***1823.22*** *p86*
Kenny, Ann 60; Ontario, 1861 ***2896.25*** *p64*
Kenny, Dennis; New York, 1807 ***8197.10*** *p330*
Kenny, Edward 1; Ontario, 1861 ***2896.28*** *p39*
Kenny, J.; Portland, Maine, 1858 ***9196.15*** *p30*
Kenny, James 70; Ontario, 1871 ***1823.15*** *p135*
Kenny, John; Canada, 1756-1760 ***4628.40*** *p45*
Kenny, John 31; Ontario, 1871 ***1823.28*** *p51*
Kenny, John 89; Vermont, 1899 ***5900.10*** *p559*
Kenny, Joseph 39; Ontario, 1871 ***1823.15*** *p135*
Kenny, Margaret 80; Vermont, 1890 ***5900.10*** *p616*
Kenny, Margret 59; Ontario, 1871 ***1823.28*** *p51*
Kenny, Mary Howard 82; Vermont, 1903 ***5900.10*** *p581*
Kenny, Michael; Maryland, 1910 ***3259.35*** *p26*
Kenny, Michael; New York, 1806 ***8197.10*** *p31*
Kenny, Michael; New York, 1821 ***8197.10*** *p245*
Kenny, Michael; Vermont, 1875 ***5900.10*** *p266*
Kenny, Miles 60; Ontario, 1871 ***1823.15*** *p135*
Kenny, Patrick; New York, 1837 ***8197.10*** *p92*
Kenny, Patrick 78; Vermont, 1896 ***5900.10*** *p581*
Kenny, Paul 35; Ontario, 1871 ***1823.15*** *p135*
Kenny, Richard; Nova Scotia, 1745 ***4628.40*** *p45*
Kenny, Richard 16; Philadelphia, 1774 ***1220.25*** *p34*
Kenny, Samuel; Canada, 1756-1760 ***4628.40*** *p46*
Kenny, Sarah 76; Vermont, 1912 ***5900.10*** *p559*
Kenny, Stephen; Canada, 1756-1760 ***4628.40*** *p46*
Kenny, Thomas 18; Ontario, 1861 ***2896.25*** *p63*
Kenny, Thomas 29; Ontario, 1871 ***1823.22*** *p86*
Kenny, William 25; Ontario, 1861 ***2896.28*** *p39*
Kenny, William 73; Ontario, 1871 ***1823.15*** *p135*
Kennymont, Anne; Maryland, 1654 ***2524.55*** *p129*
Kennymont, John; Maryland, 1654 ***2524.55*** *p129*
Kennymont, Patrick; Maryland, 1654 ***2524.55*** *p129*
Kenop, David; Maryland, 1666 ***2524.55*** *p129*
Kensela, James 52; Ontario, 1871 ***1823.15*** *p135*
Kensela, Thomas 16; Ontario, 1871 ***1823.15*** *p135*
Kensey, Philip; Pennsylvania, 1779 ***4629.10*** *p37*
Kensicki, Joseph; Maryland, 1910 ***3259.35*** *p26*
Kensley, Paul 49; Ontario, 1871 ***1823.28*** *p51*
Kent, Anne *SEE* Kent, William
Kent, David H.; Vermont, 1849-1919 ***5900.10*** *p272*
Kent, Edward 21; Baltimore, 1775 ***1220.25*** *p118*
Kent, Francis; Maryland, 1682 ***2524.55*** *p129*
Kent, George 54; Ontario, 1871 ***1823.22*** *p86*
Kent, Henry *SEE* Kent, Henry, I
Kent, Henry 25; Maryland, 1774 ***1220.25*** *p46*
Kent, Henry, I; Maryland, 1665 ***2524.55*** *p129*
Relative: Thomeson
Relative: John
Relative: Thomas
Relative: Henry
Relative: John
Kent, Jno; Virginia, 1664 ***6212.30*** *p15*
Kent, John *SEE* Kent, Henry, I
Kent, John; New York, 1827 ***8197.10*** *p341*
Kent, John 30; Ontario, 1871 ***1823.15*** *p135*
Kent, John D.; New York, 1832 ***8197.10*** *p357*
Kent, Mary Ellen 38; Vermont, 1889 ***5900.10*** *p272*
Kent, Richard; New England, 1648 ***1224.1*** *p8*
Kent, Sextus 48; Ontario, 1871 ***1823.15*** *p135*
Kent, Thomas *SEE* Kent, Henry, I
Kent, Thomas; Virginia, 1665 ***6212.30*** *p17*
Kent, Thomeson *SEE* Kent, Henry, I
Kent, Will; Maryland, 1663 ***2524.55*** *p129*
Kent, William; Maryland, 1666 ***2524.55*** *p129*
Wife: Anne
Kent, William Ralph; Ottawa, 1876 ***1640.13*** *p64*
Kent, Wm; Virginia, 1664 ***6212.30*** *p15*
Kentish, Ann 17; Philadelphia, 1775 ***1220.25*** *p122*
Kentish, Richard; Maryland, 1673 ***2524.55*** *p129*
Kenton, Joseph; Maryland, 1682 ***2524.55*** *p129*
Kentrzgewski, Robert; Maryland, 1910 ***3259.35*** *p26*
Kenward, William 25; Ontario, 1871 ***1823.28*** *p51*
Kenwick, Mr.; Quebec, 1856 ***9196.15*** *p7*
Kenworthy, Bridget Riley 78; Vermont, 1903 ***5900.10*** *p301*
Kenworthy, John; New York, 1840 ***8197.10*** *p177*
Kenworthy, Joseph 49; Vermont, 1883 ***5900.10*** *p301*
Kenygen, Margarett; Maryland, 1682 ***2524.55*** *p129*
Kenyon, Henry; Boston, 1855 ***1640.13*** *p64*
Kenythorpe, Elizabeth; Virginia, 1629 ***1224.1*** *p18*
Kenzie, Patrick 44; Ontario, 1871 ***1823.22*** *p86*
Keogan, Bartholomew; New York, 1825-1828 ***8197.10*** *p308*
Keogan, Dennis 75; Ontario, 1871 ***1823.22*** *p86*
Keogan, James; New York, 1831 ***8197.10*** *p67*
Keogan, Patrick 45; Ontario, 1871 ***1823.22*** *p86*
Keogan, Philip; New York, 1837 ***8197.10*** *p93*
Keogh, Bridget; Vermont, 1840-1897 ***5900.10*** *p537*
Keogh, Bridget 71; Vermont, 1868 ***5900.10*** *p367*
Keogh, John; Vermont, 1843-1931 ***5900.10*** *p385*
Keogh, Martin; New York, 1824 ***8197.10*** *p246*
Keogh, Mary; Vermont, 1820-1892 ***5900.10*** *p315*
Keogh, Michael 38; Ontario, 1871 ***1823.15*** *p135*
Keon, Dennis 78; Ontario, 1871 ***1823.22*** *p86*
Keon, John 66; Ontario, 1871 ***1823.22*** *p86*
Keoper, Frederick; Baltimore, 1858 ***3437.14*** *p62*
Keopsel, William 24; Ontario, 1871 ***1823.28*** *p51*
Keough, Anna Stachia Murry; Vermont, 1828-1890 ***5900.10*** *p46*
Keough, Bridget; Vermont, 1833-1919 ***5900.10*** *p363*
Keough, Bridget Flynn 91; Vermont, 1897 ***5900.10*** *p342*
Keough, George 57; Ontario, 1871 ***1823.15*** *p135*
Keough, Hanora Cannan; Vermont, 1836-1910 ***5900.10*** *p355*
Keough, John; Vermont, 1829-1920 ***5900.10*** *p355*
Keough, Malachi 92; Vermont, 1885 ***5900.10*** *p342*
Keough, Margaret 55; Vermont, 1865 ***5900.10*** *p252*
Keough, Patrick; Vermont, 1820-1900 ***5900.10*** *p46*
Keough, Patrick; Vermont, 1831-1919 ***5900.10*** *p276*
Keough, Peter 35; Ontario, 1871 ***1823.22*** *p86*
Keough, Thomas S. 47; Ontario, 1871 ***1823.22*** *p86*
Kepec, Wojcisch; Maryland, 1910 ***3259.35*** *p26*
Kepler, Adam; America, 1791 ***2856.30*** *p219*
Kepler, Sim; America, 1794 ***2856.30*** *p219*
Kepler, Simon; America, 1787 ***2856.30*** *p219*
Kepler, Simon; America, 1791 ***2856.30*** *p219*
Keppel, Ellen Corkery 27; Vermont, 1883 ***5900.10*** *p106*
Keppeler, Friedrich; Port uncertain, 1745 ***2856.30*** *p219*
Keppeler, Josef; Port uncertain, 1724 ***2856.30*** *p219*
Keppeler, Josef; Port uncertain, 1744 ***2856.30*** *p219*
Keppler, Simon; America, 1773 ***2856.30*** *p219*
Kerassy, Thomas; New York, 1829 ***8197.10*** *p352*
Keravin, Bartholomew 40; Ontario, 1871 ***1823.28*** *p51*
Keravin, James 65; Ontario, 1871 ***1823.28*** *p52*
Keravin, Thomas 30; Ontario, 1871 ***1823.28*** *p52*
Kerbel, J. Helm. Fried., America, 1741 ***2856.30*** *p219*
With wife & children
Kerbel, Johann Jakob; Port uncertain, 1781 ***2856.30*** *p219*
Kerby, Nicholas; New York, 1837 ***8197.10*** *p93*
Kerby, William; Maryland, 1666 ***2524.55*** *p179*
Kerby, William; Maryland, 1674 ***2524.55*** *p129*
Kerch, Samuel; America, 1749 ***2856.30*** *p219*
Kerche, Catherine 33; Ontario, 1871 ***1823.15*** *p135*
Kercher, Anna Catharina Brunner; America, 1785 ***2856.30*** *p219*
Kercher, Jacob; America, 1750 ***2856.30*** *p219*
Kercher, Jacob 44; Ontario, 1871 ***1823.15*** *p135*
Kercher, Margereth 78; Ontario, 1871 ***1823.15*** *p135*
Kercher, Michael; Port uncertain, 1793 ***2856.30*** *p219*
Kercherd, Liniherd; America, 1740 ***2856.30*** *p219*
Kere, Michael; America, 1768 ***2856.30*** *p219*
Kereal, Andrew; Maryland, 1910 ***3259.35*** *p26*
Keregan, Daniel; New York, 1840 ***8197.10*** *p177*
Kerie, John Julius; Philadelphia, 1847 ***1224.3*** *p43*
Kerigan, Dennis; New York, 1837 ***8197.10*** *p92*
Kerigan, James; New York, 1834 ***8197.10*** *p71*
Kerigan, Patrick; New York, 1840 ***8197.10*** *p176*
Kerin, Austin; Vermont, 1828-1904 ***5900.10*** *p335*
Kerin, Ellen Hassett; Vermont, 1839-1910 ***5900.10*** *p335*
Kerin, Honora; Vermont, 1830-1875 ***5900.10*** *p337*
Kerin, Inez M.; Vermont, 1861-1925 ***5900.10*** *p552*
Kerin, Mary; Vermont, 1798-1879 ***5900.10*** *p337*
Kerin, Mortimer; Vermont, 1860-1886 ***5900.10*** *p335*
Kerin, Morty; Vermont, 1796-1876 ***5900.10*** *p337*
Kerin, Nancy; Vermont, 1839-1881 ***5900.10*** *p331*
Kerin, Nora; Vermont, 1879-1882 ***5900.10*** *p335*
Kerin, Patrick 40; Ontario, 1871 ***1823.22*** *p86*
Kerin, Patrick H.; Vermont, 1845-1924 ***5900.10*** *p552*
Kerin, Thomas; Vermont, 1874-1912 ***5900.10*** *p335*
Kerins, John 42; Vermont, 1859 ***5900.10*** *p373*
Kerito, S. 52; Seattle, 1913 ***9196.1*** *p22*
Kerkem, Wm.; Maryland, 1664 ***2524.55*** *p129*
Kerkler, Aurel; Port uncertain, 1704 ***2856.30*** *p219*
Kerkler, Aurel; Port uncertain, 1744 ***2856.30*** *p219*
Kerkler, Josef; Port uncertain, 1702 ***2856.30*** *p219*
Kerkler, Josef; Port uncertain, 1742 ***2856.30*** *p219*
Kerksick, John; Maryland, 1669 ***2524.55*** *p129*
Wife: Martha
Kerksick, Martha *SEE* Kerksick, John
Kerkwood, James; Maryland, 1680 ***2524.55*** *p129*
Kerler, Jakob; America, 1752 ***2856.30*** *p219*
With wife & children
Kerley, Mary 61; Vermont, 1876 ***5900.10*** *p242*
Kerley, Michael 65; Vermont, 1848 ***5900.10*** *p604*
Kerlin, William; Pennsylvania, 1777 ***4629.10*** *p11*
Kerling, Henry; Virginia, 1665 ***6212.30*** *p18*
Kermer, Elisbeath 22; Ontario, 1871 ***1823.28*** *p52*
Kermet, Barbara 21; Maryland, 1775 ***1220.25*** *p102*
Kern, Balthasar; America, 1752 ***2856.30*** *p220*
With wife & 3 children
Kern, Caspar; Port uncertain, 1768 ***2856.30*** *p219*
Kern, Christian; Port uncertain, 1771 ***2856.30*** *p219*
Kern, Dominik; Port uncertain, 1774 ***2856.30*** *p219*
Kern, Friedrich; America, 1747 ***2856.30*** *p220*
With children
Kern, Friedrich; New York, 1837 ***8197.10*** *p92*
Kern, Georg; America, 1737 ***2856.30*** *p220*
With wife & children
Kern, Georg; America, 1738 ***2856.30*** *p220*
Kern, Georg; Port uncertain, 1737 ***2856.30*** *p219*
Kern, Hans Georg; America, 1749 ***2856.30*** *p220*
Kern, Hans Georg; Port uncertain, 1745 ***2856.30*** *p220*
Kern, Hans Georg; Port uncertain, 1746 ***2856.30*** *p220*
With wife & 6 children
Kern, Hans Georg; Port uncertain, 1780 ***2856.30*** *p220*
Kern, Henrich; America, 1752 ***2856.30*** *p220*
With wife & 3 children
Kern, Jacob; America, 1754 ***2856.30*** *p220*
Kern, Jacob; Port uncertain, 1754 ***2856.30*** *p220*
Kern, Jacob; Port uncertain, 1771 ***2856.30*** *p220*
Kern, Mrs. Jacob; America, 1752 ***2856.30*** *p220*
With 5 children
Kern, Jakob; Port uncertain, 1774 ***2856.30*** *p220*
Kern, Mrs. Jakob; America, 1752 ***2856.30*** *p220*
Kern, Johann Heinrich; Port uncertain, 1755 ***2856.30*** *p220*
Kern, John; New York, 1839 ***8197.10*** *p139*
Kern, Ludwig; America, 1752 ***2856.30*** *p220*
With wife & 3 children
Kern, Margaret; Vermont, 1810-1867 ***5900.10*** *p326*
Kern, Mathias; America, 1747 ***2856.30*** *p220*
With 2 children
Kern, Matthaus; America, 1754 ***2856.30*** *p220*
Kern, Matthaus; Port uncertain, 1796 ***2856.30*** *p220*
Kern, Regina; Port uncertain, 1761 ***2856.30*** *p220*
Kern, Sophia Catharin; Port uncertain, 1769 ***2856.30*** *p220*
Kernaghan, David 40; Ontario, 1871 ***1823.22*** *p86*
Kernaghan, Jane 43; Ontario, 1871 ***1823.22*** *p86*
Kernaghan, William 48; Ontario, 1871 ***1823.22*** *p86*
Kernaghan, William 93; Ontario, 1871 ***1823.22*** *p86*
Kernahan, Ellen 16; Ontario, 1871 ***1823.15*** *p135*
Kernan, Frank 80; Vermont, 1894 ***5900.10*** *p618*
Kernan, Jane 55; Vermont, 1888 ***5900.10*** *p618*
Kerne, Katherine; Maryland, 1679 ***2524.55*** *p129*
Kerner, Barbara; Port uncertain, 1763 ***2856.30*** *p220*
Kerney, Richard; Virginia, 1671-1672 ***6212.30*** *p47*
Kerns, Thomas 56; Ontario, 1871 ***1823.15*** *p135*
Kerpen, Nikolaus; England, 1725 ***2856.30*** *p220*
Kerr, Alexander *SEE* Kerr, Donald
Kerr, Alexander *SEE* Kerr, John
Kerr, Alexander *SEE* Kerr, Roderick
Kerr, Alexander; Philadelphia, 1802 ***1224.3*** *p43*
Kerr, Alexander 35; Ontario, 1871 ***1823.15*** *p135*
Kerr, Andrew 30; Ontario, 1871 ***1823.22*** *p86*
Kerr, Andrew 37; Ontario, 1871 ***1823.28*** *p52*
Kerr, Andrew A. 62; Ontario, 1871 ***1823.28*** *p52*
Kerr, Angus *SEE* Kerr, John
Kerr, Ann; Saskatchewan, 1880-1889 ***4537.35*** *p68*
Kerr, Catherine *SEE* Kerr, Donald
Kerr, Catherine *SEE* Kerr, Peter
Kerr, Christopher; New Orleans, 1805 ***1640.10*** *p92*
Kerr, David 30; Jamaica, 1775 ***1220.25*** *p133*
Kerr, David 54; Ontario, 1871 ***1823.22*** *p86*
Kerr, Donald *SEE* Kerr, Peter

Keverline, George; Baltimore, 1842 ***6058.10*** *p27*
Keverline, Michael; New York, New York, 1849 ***6058.10*** *p32*
Keverline, Nicholas; Baltimore, 1842 ***6058.10*** *p25*
Kevlan, Michael; New York, 1840 ***8197.10*** *p177*
Kevny, Patrick; New York, 1826 ***8197.10*** *p246*
Kevsinski, Adam; Maryland, 1910 ***3259.35*** *p26*
Kewbrell, Dennis; Maryland, 1681 ***2524.55*** *p129*
Kewen, James 63; Ontario, 1871 ***1823.22*** *p87*
Kewin, Terance 67; Ontario, 1871 ***1823.22*** *p87*
Key, Alfred; Quebec, 1858 ***9196.15*** *p37*
Key, Dorothy; Virginia, 1688 ***6212.30*** *p58*
Key, Isaac; Virginia, 1680 ***1224.1*** *p34*
Key, James; Maryland, 1681 ***2524.55*** *p129*
Key, W. J.; Quebec, 1856 ***9196.15*** *p9*
Keydel, Anna Maria; America, 1739 ***2856.30*** *p222*
Keyes, Alice; Virginia, 1678 ***6212.30*** *p54*
Keyes, Harriett Emily 53; Ontario, 1871 ***1823.22*** *p87*
Keyes, Jane 65; Ontario, 1871 ***1823.15*** *p136*
Keyes, William 70; Ontario, 1871 ***1823.15*** *p136*
Keyffert, Leonard; Port uncertain, 1734 ***2856.30*** *p222*
KeyJare, Joseph T.; Maryland, 1910 ***3259.35*** *p26*
Keyl, Jakob; Port uncertain, 1730 ***2856.30*** *p222*
Keyl, Johann Peter; Port uncertain, 1759 ***2856.30*** *p222*
With wife
Keyler, Josef; America, 1737 ***2856.30*** *p222*
Keylock, Anthony; New England, 1711 ***1224.2*** *p65*
Keymer, William 32; Maryland, 1774 ***1220.25*** *p60*
Keymester, John 39; Maryland, 1774 ***1220.25*** *p71*
Keyne, Edward *SEE* Keyne, Henry
Keyne, Henry; Maryland, 1653 ***2524.55*** *p129*
Brother: Richard
Brother: Edward
Keyne, Richard *SEE* Keyne, Henry
Keyogh, Thomas; New York, 1840 ***8197.10*** *p177*
Keypper, Johann Jacob; Port uncertain, 1786 ***2856.30*** *p222*
Keypperer, Johann Jacob; Port uncertain, 1786 ***2856.30*** *p222*
Keyrnes, Michael; New York, 1840 ***8197.10*** *p176*
Keys, Christopher; New York, 1822 ***8197.10*** *p246*
Keys, Edward; New York, 1838 ***8197.10*** *p122*
Keys, Hugh 68; Ontario, 1871 ***1823.15*** *p136*
Keys, Jemima 22; America, 1774 ***1220.25*** *p37*
Keys, John 58; Ontario, 1871 ***1823.15*** *p136*
Keys, Joseph 51; Ontario, 1871 ***1823.28*** *p52*
Keys, Mathias 23; America, 1774 ***1220.25*** *p37*
Keys, Susan 12; Ontario, 1871 ***1823.28*** *p52*
Keys, Thos 50; Ontario, 1871 ***1823.28*** *p52*
Keysar, Edmond; Maryland, 1677 ***2524.55*** *p129*
Keysar, Edmund; Maryland, 1671 ***2524.55*** *p130*
Keysar, Edward; Maryland, 1671 ***2524.55*** *p130*
Keyser, F. G. L. 24; British Columbia, 1909 ***9196.1*** *p27*
Keyser, F. G. L. 24; Washington, 1909 ***9196.1*** *p27*
Keyting, Nicholas; Maryland, 1649 ***2524.55*** *p130*
Kezejewska, Mary; Maryland, 1910 ***3259.35*** *p26*
Kezes, James 45; Ontario, 1871 ***1823.15*** *p136*
Kezes, Robert 41; Ontario, 1871 ***1823.15*** *p136*
Kezes, Thomas 36; Ontario, 1871 ***1823.15*** *p136*
Kezes, Thomas 50; Ontario, 1871 ***1823.15*** *p136*
Kezhick, Peter 33; Ontario, 1871 ***1823.28*** *p52*
Kezmier, Michael; Maryland, 1910 ***3259.35*** *p26*
Khratt, Hans; Port uncertain, 1624 ***2856.30*** *p222*
With wife & 6 children
Kibble, Stephen; New York, New York, 1782 ***1224.2*** *p65*
Kibblethwaite, Susan; Maryland, 1655 ***2524.55*** *p175*
Kibblewhite, Susan; Maryland, 1658 ***2524.55*** *p130*
Kibele, Franz Josef; Port uncertain, 1765 ***2856.30*** *p222*
Kibich, Peter; Port uncertain, 1747 ***2856.30*** *p222*
Kibler, Johann Georg; Port uncertain, 1770 ***2856.30*** *p222*
Kibler, Johann Georg; Port uncertain, 1794 ***2856.30*** *p222*
Kiblr, Ursula; Port uncertain, 1730 ***2856.30*** *p222*
Kibuski, Thomas; Maryland, 1910 ***3259.35*** *p26*
Kic, Peter; Maryland, 1910 ***3259.35*** *p26*
Kichlam, James 58; Vermont, 1905 ***5900.10*** *p253*
Kichlam, Margaret 39; Vermont, 1886 ***5900.10*** *p253*
Kichlein, Peter; America, 1776 ***2856.30*** *p222*
Kichler, Johann; America, 1740 ***2856.30*** *p222*
Kicialewski, Czaclav; Maryland, 1910 ***3259.35*** *p26*
Kicialewski, Joseph; Maryland, 1910 ***3259.35*** *p26*
Kickbush, William 35; Ontario, 1871 ***1823.28*** *p52*
Kicksbaugh, Jno.; Maryland, 1680 ***2524.55*** *p130*
Kid, George 45; Ontario, 1871 ***1823.28*** *p52*
Kid, William; New York, 1803 ***8197.10*** *p13*
Kidby, John; Virginia, 1655 ***1224.1*** *p34*
Kidd, Mr.; Quebec, 1857 ***9196.15*** *p25*
Kidd, Mrs.; Quebec, 1857 ***9196.15*** *p25*
Kidd, Elizabeth 16; Ontario, 1871 ***1823.15*** *p136*
Kidd, G.; Georgia, 1764 ***1640.10*** *p93*
Kidd, J.; Portland, Maine, 1857 ***9196.15*** *p13*
Kidd, John 36; Ontario, 1871 ***1823.15*** *p136*
Kidd, Joseph 45; Ontario, 1871 ***1823.15*** *p136*
Kidd, Mary Adeline; Connecticut, 1826 ***1224.3*** *p43*
Kidd, Thomas 39; Ontario, 1871 ***1823.15*** *p136*
Kidd, Whitten; New York, 1838 ***8197.10*** *p379*
Kidder, Benjamin 15; Baltimore, 1775 ***1220.25*** *p118*
Kidder, William 20; Maryland, 1774 ***1220.25*** *p78*
Kiddi, A. 50; Alaska, 1917 ***9196.1*** *p51*
Kiddi, A. 50; Yukon, 1917 ***9196.1*** *p51*
Kiddle, Andrew 34; Ontario, 1871 ***1823.15*** *p136*
Kidesejeski, Frank; Maryland, 1910 ***3259.35*** *p27*
Kidgell, Nicholas; America, 1727 ***1224.2*** *p65*
Kidley, Jno; Virginia, 1665-1666 ***6212.30*** *p23*
Kidman, Thomas 27; Maryland, 1775 ***1220.25*** *p97*
Kidner, Mr.; Quebec, 1857 ***9196.15*** *p13*
Kidner, Mrs.; Quebec, 1857 ***9196.15*** *p13*
Kidney, William 85; Vermont, 1885 ***5900.10*** *p108*
Kidsley, . . .; Mississippi, 1815-1845 ***1640.10*** *p93*
Kidson, Joseph; New York, 1807 ***8197.10*** *p328*
Kidwell, Jane; Maryland, 1665 ***2524.55*** *p130*
Kidwell, Patrick 34; Vermont, 1832 ***5900.10*** *p516*
Kiebiger, Friedrich; Port uncertain, 1790 ***2856.30*** *p222*
Kiebler, Anton; Port uncertain, 1734 ***2856.30*** *p222*
Kiebler, Anton; Port uncertain, 1764 ***2856.30*** *p222*
Kieckhoefer, Adolphus T.; New York, 1839 ***8197.10*** *p139*
Kieckhofer, Adolphus T.; New York, 1837 ***8197.10*** *p79*
Kieczal, Jacob; Maryland, 1910 ***3259.35*** *p27*
Kiefe, Anna L.; Vermont, 1869-1937 ***5900.10*** *p609*
Kiefer, Anna Maria; Port uncertain, 1746 ***2856.30*** *p222*
Kiefer, Bernhard; Port uncertain, 1755 ***2856.30*** *p222*
Kiefer, Catharina; Port uncertain, 1739 ***2856.30*** *p222*
Kiefer, Catharina; Port uncertain, 1761 ***2856.30*** *p222*
Kiefer, Christian; Port uncertain, 1783 ***2856.30*** *p222*
Kiefer, Francis; New York, 1840 ***8197.10*** *p176*
Kiefer, Hans Michael; America, 1733 ***2856.30*** *p223*
With wife & children
Kiefer, Heinrich Jacob; Port uncertain, 1766 ***2856.30*** *p222*
Kiefer, Henrich; America, 1749 ***2856.30*** *p222*
Kiefer, Henrich; Port uncertain, 1749 ***2856.30*** *p222*
Kiefer, Jacob; New York, 1836-1838 ***8197.10*** *p121*
Kiefer, Johann; Port uncertain, 1784 ***2856.30*** *p223*
With family
Kiefer, Lorrenz; New York, 1837 ***8197.10*** *p93*
Kiefer, Marx; America, 1744 ***2856.30*** *p223*
Kiefer, Marx; America, 1766 ***2856.30*** *p223*
Kiefer, Marx; Port uncertain, 1744 ***2856.30*** *p223*
Kiefer, Peter; Port uncertain, 1764 ***2856.30*** *p223*
Kiefer, Peter; Port uncertain, 1780 ***2856.30*** *p223*
Kiefer, Peter; Port uncertain, 1782 ***2856.30*** *p223*
With wife & children
Kiefer, Theodor; Port uncertain, 1754 ***2856.30*** *p223*
Kiefer, Valentin; America, 1736 ***2856.30*** *p223*
Kiefer, Valentin; America, 1737 ***2856.30*** *p223*
Kieffer, Abraham; America, 1748 ***2856.30*** *p223*
Kieffer, Abraham; America, 1748 ***2856.30*** *p223*
With wife & 5 children
Kieffer, Abraham, Jr.; America, 1748 ***2856.30*** *p223*
Kieffer, Anna Barbara; Port uncertain, 1748 ***2856.30*** *p223*
Kieffer, Anna Rosina; Port uncertain, 1751 ***2856.30*** *p223*
Kieffer, Caspar; America, 1748 ***2856.30*** *p223*
Kieffer, Caspar; America, 1748 ***2856.30*** *p224*
With wife & 5 children
Kieffer, Cath. Franziska; Port uncertain, 1746 ***2856.30*** *p223*
Kieffer, Christina; Port uncertain, 1759 ***2856.30*** *p223*
Kieffer, Daniel; America, 1737 ***2856.30*** *p223*
With wife & children
Kieffer, Daniel; America, 1741 ***2856.30*** *p223*
Kieffer, Friedrich; America, 1737 ***2856.30*** *p223*
Kieffer, Jacob; America, 1741 ***2856.30*** *p223*
Kieffer, Jacob; America, 1769 ***2856.30*** *p223*
Kieffer, Joahnn Wendel; America, 1748 ***2856.30*** *p223*
Kieffer, Johann; Port uncertain, 1775 ***2856.30*** *p223*
Kieffer, Johann Jacob; Port uncertain, 1753 ***2856.30*** *p223*
Kieffer, Josef Ulrich; Port uncertain, 1740 ***2856.30*** *p223*
Kieffer, Maria Barbara; America, 1750 ***2856.30*** *p223*
Kieffer, Michael; Port uncertain, 1775 ***2856.30*** *p223*
Kieffer, Paul; Port uncertain, 1761 ***2856.30*** *p223*
Kieffer, Peter; America, 1741 ***2856.30*** *p223*
Kieffer, Peter; Port uncertain, 1741 ***2856.30*** *p224*
With wife & 5 children
Kieffer, Theobald; America, 1737 ***2856.30*** *p223*
With wife & children
Kieffer, Theobald; Port uncertain, 1745 ***2856.30*** *p223*
With wife & children
Kieffner, Jacob; America, 1738 ***2856.30*** *p224*
Kieghler, Johann; America, 1740 ***2856.30*** *p222*
Kiehl, Jakob; America, 1742 ***2856.30*** *p224*
Kiel, George J. 68; Kansas, 1876-1910 ***9079.10*** *p22*
Kiel, Mary; Maryland, 1910 ***3259.35*** *p27*
Kiel, Rinehart 44; Kansas, 1878-1910 ***9079.10*** *p11*
Kiel, Sophia 70; Ontario, 1871 ***1823.28*** *p52*
Kieley, Ellen; Vermont, 1852-1903 ***5900.10*** *p424*
Kielty, Thomas; New York, 1839 ***8197.10*** *p383*
Kiely, Anna; Vermont, 1863-1955 ***5900.10*** *p317*
Kiely, Catherine; Vermont, 1858-1950 ***5900.10*** *p397*
Kiely, Eugene; Vermont, 1846-1921 ***5900.10*** *p397*
Kiely, Francis 65; Ontario, 1871 ***1823.28*** *p52*
Kiely, Joanna; Vermont, 1845-1914 ***5900.10*** *p403*
Kiely, John; New York, 1837 ***8197.10*** *p92*
Kiely, John 40; Ontario, 1871 ***1823.28*** *p52*
Kiely, John 80; Ontario, 1871 ***1823.28*** *p52*
Kiely, Margaret; Vermont, 1828-1889 ***5900.10*** *p397*
Kiely, Mary; Vermont, 1852-1933 ***5900.10*** *p397*
Kiely, Patrick 28; Ontario, 1871 ***1823.28*** *p52*
Kiely, Timothy; Vermont, 1814-1887 ***5900.10*** *p397*
Kienberger, Barbara; Port uncertain, 1760 ***2856.30*** *p224*
Kienzler, Johann; Port uncertain, 1737 ***2856.30*** *p224*
Kienzler, Johann; Port uncertain, 1767 ***2856.30*** *p224*
Kierans, Thomas; New York, 1827 ***8197.10*** *p345*
Kierce, Susan; Vermont, 1835-1894 ***5900.10*** *p45*
Kierman, James; Philadelphia, 1790 ***4629.10*** *p60*
Kiernan, Cornelius; New York, 1838 ***8197.10*** *p120*
Kiernan, Ellen; Vermont, 1853-1910 ***5900.10*** *p185*
Kiernan, Francis; New York, 1827 ***8197.10*** *p246*
Kiernan, Francis; New York, 1840 ***8197.10*** *p176*
Kiernan, John; New York, 1838 ***8197.10*** *p301*
Kiernan, Joseph; New York, 1840 ***8197.10*** *p176*
Kiernan, Julia; Vermont, 1818-1896 ***5900.10*** *p307*
Kiernan, Lawrence; Vermont, 1850-1914 ***5900.10*** *p307*
Kiernan, Mathew; Vermont, 1857-1936 ***5900.10*** *p307*
Kiernan, Michael; New York, 1837 ***8197.10*** *p92*
Kiernan, Patrick; New York, 1836 ***8197.10*** *p79*
Kiernan, Patrick; Vermont, 1821-1909 ***5900.10*** *p307*
Kiernan, Patrick, Jr.; Vermont, 1853-1932 ***5900.10*** *p307*
Kiernan, Peter; New York, 1828 ***8197.10*** *p65*
Kiernan, Robert; New York, 1837 ***8197.10*** *p93*
Kierny, John 60; Ontario, 1871 ***1823.22*** *p87*
Kierpko, Wojdacek; Maryland, 1910 ***3259.35*** *p27*
Kiersey, Hanora Welch; Vermont, 1855-1933 ***5900.10*** *p80*
Kiesinger, Jakob; America, 1726 ***2856.30*** *p224*
Kiewogloski, James; Maryland, 1910 ***3259.35*** *p27*
Kiffe, Thomas; Maryland, 1668 ***2524.55*** *p130*
Kifrelelain, Peter; Philadelphia, 1793 ***4629.10*** *p83*
Kihl, Maria Elisabeth; Port uncertain, 1784 ***2856.30*** *p224*
Kihn, Johann Jakob; Port uncertain, 1745 ***2856.30*** *p224*
Kilb, Johann Nickel; Port uncertain, 1775 ***2856.30*** *p224*
Kilb, M. Philippine; Port uncertain, 1789 ***2856.30*** *p224*
Kilbourn, Julia; Vermont, 1846-1941 ***5900.10*** *p321*
Kilbourne, Thomas; Maryland, 1681 ***2524.55*** *p130*
Kilbride, Ann 50; Vermont, 1868 ***5900.10*** *p298*
Kilburn, Isaac 21; Maryland, 1774 ***1220.25*** *p77*
Kilby, Thomas 62; Ontario, 1871 ***1823.28*** *p52*
Kilcannon, Anthony 17; New York, New York, 1848 ***1825.45*** *p37*
Kilcey, Gus; Maryland, 1910 ***3259.35*** *p27*
Kildall, M. 87; Alaska, 1917 ***9196.1*** *p70*
Kildall, M. 87; Vancouver, British Columbia, 1917 ***9196.1*** *p70*
Kildell, Robert; Maryland, 1664 ***2524.55*** *p130*
Kile, Jno; Virginia, 1673 ***6212.30*** *p51*
Kilenski, Adam; Maryland, 1910 ***3259.35*** *p27*
Kiles, Richard; New York, 1839 ***8197.10*** *p371*
Kiley, Ada; Vermont, 1874-1943 ***5900.10*** *p496*
Kiley, Bridget; Vermont, 1823-1911 ***5900.10*** *p489*
Kiley, Catherine 56; Vermont, 1870 ***5900.10*** *p369*
Kiley, Ellen Power 32; Vermont, 1857 ***5900.10*** *p368*
Kiley, Mary; Vermont, 1826-1904 ***5900.10*** *p268*
Kiley, William 58; Vermont, 1868 ***5900.10*** *p368*
Kilfoil, William; New York, 1840 ***8197.10*** *p177*
Kilfoy, Ellen 30; Ontario, 1871 ***1823.28*** *p52*
Kilfoy, James 40; Ontario, 1871 ***1823.28*** *p52*
Kilgalan, Bridget; Vermont, 1830-1902 ***5900.10*** *p205*
Kilgallen, John; Vermont, 1835-1901 ***5900.10*** *p204*
Kilgallen, Mary Johnson; Vermont, 1838-1929 ***5900.10*** *p204*
Kilgallen, Mary Ryan; Vermont, 1859-1946 ***5900.10*** *p204*
Kilgallen, Patrick; Vermont, 1861-1938 ***5900.10*** *p204*
Kilgallen, Patrick 76; Vermont, 1900 ***5900.10*** *p204*
Kilgallen, Winneford 28; Vermont, 1871 ***5900.10*** *p206*
Kilgarlan, Catherine Barnicle 71; Vermont, 1887 ***5900.10*** *p206*
Kilgarlan, John; Vermont, 1815-1898 ***5900.10*** *p206*
Kilgarlan, Mary Comer; Vermont, 1820-1920 ***5900.10*** *p206*
Kilgarlan, Thomas; Vermont, n.d. ***5900.10*** *p206*
Kilgore, James; Pennsylvania, 1821 ***6058.10*** *p6*
Kilgore, James; Pennsylvania, 1837 ***6058.10*** *p13*
Kilgore, John; Pennsylvania, 1777 ***4629.10*** *p31*
Kilgore, John; Pennsylvania, 1837 ***6058.10*** *p13*
Kilgore, William 42; Ontario, 1871 ***1823.28*** *p52*
Kilgour, Alexander; Georgia, 1698 ***1640.13*** *p65*
Kilian, Ignaz; Port uncertain, 1791 ***2856.30*** *p224*

Kilian, Jacob; Port uncertain, 1792 ***2856.30*** *p224*
Kilius, . . .; Port uncertain, 1749 ***2856.30*** *p224*
Kilkowski, Frank; Maryland, 1910 ***3259.35*** *p27*
Kilkowski, Martin; Maryland, 1910 ***3259.35*** *p27*
Kilkowsky, Maryan; Maryland, 1910 ***3259.35*** *p27*
Kill, Jakob; America, 1752 ***2856.30*** *p224*
With wife & 4 children
Killalea, Abegail 27; New York, New York, 1849 ***1825.45*** *p37*
Sister: Biddy 25
Sister: Ellen 17
Sister: Catherine 20
Killalea, Ann 20 *SEE* Killalea, Catherine
Killalea, Biddy 25 *SEE* Killalea, Abegail
Killalea, Bridget 9 *SEE* Killalea, Darby
Killalea, Bridget 16; New York, New York, 1848 ***1825.45*** *p37*
Killalea, Bridget 35; New York, New York, 1848 ***1825.45*** *p37*
Son: John 8
Daughter: Mary 11
Son: Mark 1
Daughter: Margaret 7
Killalea, Catherine 7 *SEE* Killalea, Catherine
Killalea, Catherine 20 *SEE* Killalea, Abegail
Killalea, Catherine 45; New York, New York, 1849 ***1825.45*** *p37*
Daughter: Ann 20
Daughter: Margaret 15
Daughter: Catherine 7
Killalea, Darby 46; New York, New York, 1848 ***1825.45*** *p37*
Wife: Margaret 44
Daughter: Mary 16
Daughter: Bridget 9
Son: John 15
Killalea, Ellen 17 *SEE* Killalea, Abegail
Killalea, John 8 *SEE* Killalea, Bridget
Killalea, John 15 *SEE* Killalea, Darby
Killalea, John 19; New York, New York, 1848 ***1825.45*** *p37*
Killalea, Lawrence 8 *SEE* Killalea, Mathias
Killalea, Margaret 7 *SEE* Killalea, Bridget
Killalea, Margaret 15 *SEE* Killalea, Catherine
Killalea, Margaret 44 *SEE* Killalea, Darby
Killalea, Mark 1 *SEE* Killalea, Bridget
Killalea, Mary 11 *SEE* Killalea, Bridget
Killalea, Mary 16 *SEE* Killalea, Darby
Killalea, Mathias 10 *SEE* Killalea, Mathias
Killalea, Mathias 45; New York, New York, 1848 ***1825.45*** *p37*
Wife: Sally 40
Son: Lawrence 8
Son: Michael 19
Son: Thomas 14
Daughter: Peggy 16
Son: Mathias 10
Killalea, Michael 19 *SEE* Killalea, Mathias
Killalea, Patrick 17 *SEE* Killalea, Patrick, Sr.
Killalea, Patrick, Sr. 42; New York, New York, 1848 ***1825.45*** *p37*
Son: Patrick 17
Killalea, Peggy 16 *SEE* Killalea, Mathias
Killalea, Sally 40 *SEE* Killalea, Mathias
Killalea, Thomas 14 *SEE* Killalea, Mathias
Killaly, Miss; Quebec, 1858 ***9196.15*** *p36*
Killam, Sarah; Vermont, 1851-1873 ***5900.10*** *p455*
Killam, Sarah E. Moody; Vermont, 1825-1879 ***5900.10*** *p455*
Killam, Tho.; Maryland, 1678 ***2524.55*** *p130*
Killam, William M.; Vermont, 1826-1906 ***5900.10*** *p455*
Killann, Daniel 24; Ontario, 1871 ***1823.28*** *p52*
Kille, Karl; New York, 1806 ***8197.10*** *p324*
Killeen, Catherine A. McMahon 27; Vermont, 1867 ***5900.10*** *p329*
Killen, Catherine Logan 70; Vermont, 1859 ***5900.10*** *p152*
Killen, Mary 69; Vermont, 1901 ***5900.10*** *p297*
Killen, Nicholas 66; Vermont, 1857 ***5900.10*** *p152*
Killen, Sarah; Vermont, 1839-1908 ***5900.10*** *p240*
Killen, William 61; Ontario, 1871 ***1823.15*** *p137*
Killeoran, Michael 38; Ontario, 1871 ***1823.28*** *p52*
Killgallen, Ann; Vermont, 1821-1877 ***5900.10*** *p205*
Killian, Anna Maria Hermann; Port uncertain, 1784 ***2856.30*** *p224*
Killian, Cornelius 71; Ontario, 1871 ***1823.22*** *p87*
Killian, Elizabeth 39; Kansas, 1910 ***9079.10*** *p42*
Killian, Justus 40; Kansas, 1910 ***9079.10*** *p42*
Killick, Sarah; Rochester, New York, 1838 ***1224.3*** *p43*
Killick, Wickens; New York, 1839 ***8197.10*** *p139*
Killigrew, John; Virginia, 1666 ***6212.30*** *p28*
Killin, Eliza; Vermont, 1827-1904 ***5900.10*** *p133*
Killin, Furrus 60; Ontario, 1871 ***1823.22*** *p87*
Killin, James; New York, 1821 ***8197.10*** *p245*
Killin, Luke 71; Ontario, 1871 ***1823.22*** *p87*
Killin, Michael; Vermont, 1828-1878 ***5900.10*** *p133*
Killin, Patrick; New York, 1821 ***8197.10*** *p245*
Killin, Patrick; New York, 1828 ***8197.10*** *p65*
Killin, Patrick 45; Ontario, 1871 ***1823.22*** *p87*
Killinger, Christina 36; Ontario, 1871 ***1823.15*** *p137*
Killion, Mary Colton; Vermont, 1854-1930 ***5900.10*** *p44*
Killion, Michael; Vermont, 1852-1925 ***5900.10*** *p44*
Killip, Clark 11; Ontario, 1861 ***2896.28*** *p38*
Killip, Eliza 9; Ontario, 1861 ***2896.28*** *p38*
Killip, Jane 15; Ontario, 1861 ***2896.28*** *p38*
Killip, Mary E. 49; Ontario, 1861 ***2896.28*** *p38*
Killip, Thomas 50; Ontario, 1861 ***2896.28*** *p38*
Killius, Anna Maria; Port uncertain, 1793 ***2856.30*** *p224*
Killius, Christian; Port uncertain, 1790 ***2856.30*** *p224*
Killman, Judith *SEE* Killman, William
Killman, Margery *SEE* Killman, William
Killman, William; Maryland, 1665 ***2524.55*** *p130*
Wife: Judith
Daughter: Margery
Killmer, William; Baltimore, 1852 ***6058.10*** *p32*
Killoran, Dominick 76; Ontario, 1871 ***1823.28*** *p52*
Killoran, John 39; Ontario, 1871 ***1823.15*** *p137*
Killoran, Mary 56; Ontario, 1871 ***1823.28*** *p52*
Killorne, James 27; Ontario, 1871 ***1823.28*** *p52*
Killorne, Margaret 26; Ontario, 1871 ***1823.28*** *p52*
Killpatrick, Henry 48; Ontario, 1871 ***1823.22*** *p87*
Killy, Nancy 101; Vermont, 1867 ***5900.10*** *p226*
Killy, R. H.; Quebec, 1858 ***9196.15*** *p37*
Kilman, William 23; Virginia, 1773 ***1220.25*** *p30*
Kilp, Eva Elisabeth; Port uncertain, 1791 ***2856.30*** *p224*
Kilp, Maria; Port uncertain, 1733 ***2856.30*** *p224*
Kilpatrick, Alexander; New York, 1807 ***8197.10*** *p43*
Kilpatrick, George; Louisville, Kentucky, 1869 ***1640.13*** *p65*
Kilpatrick, George 62; Ontario, 1871 ***1823.15*** *p137*
Kilpatrick, Helen 77; Vermont, 1907 ***5900.10*** *p289*
Kilpatrick, J. E.; Quebec, 1856 ***9196.15*** *p6*
Kilpatrick, John 22; Vermont, 1877 ***5900.10*** *p289*
Kilpatrick, John 40; Ontario, 1871 ***1823.15*** *p137*
Kilpatrick, Joseph 27; Ontario, 1871 ***1823.15*** *p137*
Kilpatrick, Mary 65; Ontario, 1871 ***1823.15*** *p137*
Kilpatrick, Mary A. 16; Vermont, 1877 ***5900.10*** *p289*
Kilpatrick, Rasple 37; Ontario, 1871 ***1823.15*** *p137*
Kilpatrick, Robert 42; Vermont, 1876 ***5900.10*** *p289*
Kilpatrick, Robert 72; Ontario, 1871 ***1823.15*** *p137*
Kilpatrick, Samuel 24; Ontario, 1871 ***1823.15*** *p137*
Kilpatrick, W.; Quebec, 1856 ***9196.15*** *p5*
Kilpatrick, Mrs. W.; Quebec, 1856 ***9196.15*** *p5*
Kilpatrick, William; Pennsylvania, 1826 ***6058.10*** *p9*
Kilpatrick, William 30; Ontario, 1871 ***1823.15*** *p137*
Kilpeck, Ellen Leddy; Vermont, 1847-1947 ***5900.10*** *p535*
Kilpeck, James; Vermont, 1847-1952 ***5900.10*** *p535*
Kilpin, William; Virginia, 1716 ***1224.2*** *p65*
Kilpp, Heinrich; Port uncertain, 1775 ***2856.30*** *p224*
Kilsch, Jacob; Port uncertain, 1770 ***2856.30*** *p224*
Kilson, Cutbert; Maryland, 1663 ***2524.55*** *p130*
Kiltener, Simon 75; Ontario, 1871 ***1823.22*** *p87*
Kilving, Jno; Virginia, 1664 ***6212.30*** *p9*
Kim, Mary 30; Ontario, 1871 ***1823.28*** *p52*
Kim, Philipp; Port uncertain, 1754 ***2856.30*** *p224*
Kimball, Eliza Ann Kelley; Vermont, 1848-1910 ***5900.10*** *p497*
Kimble, Hezekiah; Pennsylvania, 1777 ***4629.10*** *p18*
Kimily, A. 18; Ontario, 1861 ***2896.25*** *p28*
Kimily, M. 15; Ontario, 1861 ***2896.25*** *p28*
Kimley, George; Pennsylvania, 1777 ***4629.10*** *p19*
Kimm, Johann; America, 1738 ***2856.30*** *p251*
Kimmel, Mrs. Chr.; Port uncertain, 1764 ***2856.30*** *p224*
Kimmel, Philipp; Port uncertain, 1755 ***2856.30*** *p224*
Kimmer, James 23; Ontario, 1871 ***1823.28*** *p52*
Kimmins, Annie; Vermont, 1838-1904 ***5900.10*** *p545*
Kimp, John 74; Ontario, 1871 ***1823.15*** *p137*
Kimpel, Rosina; Port uncertain, 1764 ***2856.30*** *p224*
Kimpton, John 37; Ontario, 1871 ***1823.28*** *p52*
Kinahan, Robert W. 36; Ontario, 1871 ***1823.15*** *p137*
Kinard, Jane 40; Ontario, 1871 ***1823.15*** *p137*
Kincaid, George; Georgia, n.d. ***1224.2*** *p65*
Kincaid, George; Georgia, 1791 ***1640.10*** *p93*
Kincaid, Samuel 86; Vermont, 1902 ***5900.10*** *p374*
Kinch, William; New York, 1826 ***8197.10*** *p334*
Kinch, Wm 21; Ontario, 1871 ***1823.28*** *p52*
Kinchin, Nathaniel; Maryland, 1659 ***2524.55*** *p130*
Kincreton, Thomas; Maryland, 1680 ***2524.55*** *p130*
Kind, George; New York, 1839 ***8197.10*** *p139*
Kinder, John; Pennsylvania, 1864 ***6058.10*** *p48*
Kinder, Josef; Port uncertain, 1785 ***2856.30*** *p224*
Kinder, Joseph 39; Ontario, 1871 ***1823.28*** *p52*
Kinder, Mgdl.; Port uncertain, 1784 ***2856.30*** *p236*
Kinder, Mgdl.; Port uncertain, 1784 ***2856.30*** *p240*
Kinder, Mgdl.; Port uncertain, 1784 ***2856.30*** *p241*
Kindigh, Martin; America, 1727 ***2856.30*** *p224*
Kindle, Abigail 4; Ontario, 1861 ***2896.27*** *p14*
Kindle, Andreas; Port uncertain, 1790 ***2856.30*** *p224*
Kindle, James 14; Ontario, 1861 ***2896.27*** *p3*
Kindle, James 35; Ontario, 1861 ***2896.27*** *p3*
Kindle, James 35; Ontario, 1861 ***2896.27*** *p14*
Kindle, Joseph 6; Ontario, 1861 ***2896.27*** *p3*
Kindle, M. 10; Ontario, 1861 ***2896.27*** *p3*
Kindle, William 70; Ontario, 1861 ***2896.27*** *p22*
Kindler, Johann; Port uncertain, 1751 ***2856.30*** *p225*
Kindon, John Augusta 21; Virginia, 1774 ***1220.25*** *p55*
Kindsey, Elizabeth; Maryland, 1661 ***2524.55*** *p130*
Kindsey, Hugh; Maryland, 1661 ***2524.55*** *p130*
Kindsey, Paul; Maryland, 1661 ***2524.55*** *p130*
Kindt, Martin; Port uncertain, 1749 ***2856.30*** *p225*
Kine, Darby; New York, 1807 ***8197.10*** *p328*
Kine, Mary; Virginia, 1664 ***6212.30*** *p6*
Kiner, Richard; Maryland, 1678 ***2524.55*** *p130*
Kines, Joshua 75; Ontario, 1871 ***1823.22*** *p87*
Kiney, Charles 63; Ontario, 1871 ***1823.22*** *p87*
Kiney, Joseph 11; Ontario, 1861 ***2896.26*** *p34*
King, Capt.; Quebec, 1857 ***9196.15*** *p20*
King, Dr.; Quebec, 1857 ***9196.15*** *p22*
King, Miss; Quebec, 1857 ***9196.15*** *p16*
King, Miss; Quebec, 1858 ***9196.15*** *p39*
King, Mr.; Quebec, 1857 ***9196.15*** *p17*
King, Mrs.; Quebec, 1858 ***9196.15*** *p47*
King, Abraham 25; Philadelphia, 1774 ***1220.25*** *p67*
King, Adam 53; Ontario, 1871 ***1823.22*** *p87*
King, Andrew 49; Ontario, 1871 ***1823.22*** *p87*
King, Ann 82; Vermont, 1919 ***5900.10*** *p237*
King, Ann 93; Ontario, 1871 ***1823.15*** *p137*
King, Anna Houston; Vermont, 1849-1930 ***5900.10*** *p224*
King, Anna M.; Vermont, 1862-1899 ***5900.10*** *p64*
King, Anne; South Carolina, 1740 ***1224.2*** *p65*
King, Anthony; New York, 1838 ***8197.10*** *p121*
King, Armina A.; Vermont, 1844-1929 ***5900.10*** *p244*
King, Arnold 37; Ontario, 1871 ***1823.15*** *p137*
King, Benjamin; Pennsylvania, 1777 ***4629.10*** *p14*
King, Benjamin Owen 56; Ontario, 1871 ***1823.22*** *p87*
King, Bridget; Vermont, 1831-1905 ***5900.10*** *p554*
King, Bridget; Vermont, 1847-1873 ***5900.10*** *p227*
King, Bridget 81; Vermont, 1888 ***5900.10*** *p549*
King, Catherine Albin; Charleston, South Carolina, 1854 ***1224.3*** *p44*
King, Catherine Nelon 47; Vermont, 1867 ***5900.10*** *p64*
King, Chancy 11; Ontario, 1861 ***2896.27*** *p6*
King, Charles; New York, 1826 ***8197.10*** *p246*
King, Charles 21; Virginia, 1774 ***1220.25*** *p87*
King, Charles G. 25; Ontario, 1871 ***1823.28*** *p52*
King, Christopher 21; Baltimore, 1775 ***1220.25*** *p118*
King, Cynthia 8; Ontario, 1861 ***2896.27*** *p6*
King, Mrs. D.; Quebec, 1856 ***9196.15*** *p8*
King, Daniel; Annapolis, Maryland, 1725 ***1224.2*** *p65*
King, Daniel; Pennsylvania, 1777 ***4629.10*** *p15*
King, David; Pennsylvania, 1826 ***6058.10*** *p8*
King, David 45; Ontario, 1871 ***1823.28*** *p52*
King, Duncan 50; Ontario, 1871 ***1823.15*** *p137*
King, Edward; Virginia, 1688 ***1224.1*** *p34*
King, Edward 24; Philadelphia, 1774 ***1220.25*** *p63*
King, Edward 35; Ontario, 1871 ***1823.28*** *p52*
King, Edward P.; New York, 1838 ***8197.10*** *p247*
King, Elias; Maryland, 1682 ***2524.55*** *p130*
King, Elinor; Maryland, 1673 ***2524.55*** *p130*
King, Elizabeth 62; Ontario, 1871 ***1823.28*** *p52*
King, Ellen; Vermont, 1842-1915 ***5900.10*** *p549*
King, Ellen; Vermont, 1845-1884 ***5900.10*** *p227*
King, Ellen Dooley 74; Vermont, 1885 ***5900.10*** *p237*
King, Esther Eustace; Vermont, 1843-1907 ***5900.10*** *p324*
King, Eusebius; Virginia, 1711 ***1224.2*** *p65*
King, F.; Quebec, 1857 ***9196.15*** *p24*
King, F. E. 5; Ontario, 1861 ***2896.28*** *p2*
King, Francis; Maryland, 1681 ***2524.55*** *p130*
King, George; Maryland, 1663 ***2524.55*** *p49*
King, George 21; Maryland, 1775 ***1220.25*** *p97*
King, George 35; Virginia, 1774 ***1220.25*** *p89*
King, George 37; Ontario, 1861 ***2896.28*** *p2*
King, George 60; Ontario, 1871 ***1823.22*** *p87*
King, George 61; Ontario, 1871 ***1823.15*** *p137*
King, George B., Jr.; New York, 1817-1834 ***8197.10*** *p308*
King, George W.; New York, 1840 ***8197.10*** *p177*
King, Gilbert; Pennsylvania, 1779 ***4629.10*** *p37*
King, Hannah 57; Ontario, 1871 ***1823.15*** *p137*
King, Horatio; Washington, District of Columbia, 1898 ***1640.13*** *p65*
King, Hugh; Jamaica, 1740 ***1640.13*** *p65*
King, Hugh 31; Ontario, 1871 ***1823.28*** *p52*
King, James; New York, 1834 ***8197.10*** *p372*
King, James; New York, 1839 ***8197.10*** *p139*
King, James; Pennsylvania, 1777 ***4629.10*** *p28*
King, James; Virginia, 1666-1667 ***6212.30*** *p35*
King, James 21; Philadelphia, 1774 ***1220.25*** *p35*
King, James 22; Maryland, 1775 ***1220.25*** *p114*

King, James 42; Vermont, 1852 5900.10 p383
King, James 92; Ontario, 1871 1823.28 p52
King, Jane *SEE* King, John
King, Jno; Maryland, 1679 2524.55 p130
King, Jno; Virginia, 1666 6212.30 p26
King, Johanna; Vermont, n.d. 5900.10 p58
King, Johanna 26; Vermont, 1881 5900.10 p56
King, John *SEE* King, John
King, John; Baltimore, 1805 1224.3 p44
King, John; Martinique, 1787 1640.13 p65
King, John; Martinique, 1799 1640.13 p65
King, John; Maryland, 1649 2524.55 p77
King, John; Maryland, 1666 2524.55 p130
Relative: Jane
Relative: John
Relative: Mary
King, John; New Jersey, 1831 1224.3 p44
King, John; New York, 1805 8197.10 p29
King, John; New York, 1821 8197.10 p246
King, John; New York, 1821-1834 8197.10 p304
King, John; New York, 1823 8197.10 p246
King, John; New York, 1828-1833 8197.10 p308
King, John; New York, 1832 8197.10 p368
King, John; Pennsylvania, 1777 4629.10 p8
King, John; Pennsylvania, 1786 4629.10 p49
King, John; Pennsylvania, 1868 6058.10 p76
King, John; Vermont, 1845-1926 5900.10 p223
King, John; Vermont, 1847-1909 5900.10 p56
King, John 17; Philadelphia, 1774 1220.25 p34
King, John 21; Maryland, 1774 1220.25 p61
King, John 21; Ontario, 1871 1823.15 p137
King, John 24; Maryland, 1775 1220.25 p113
King, John 43; Ontario, 1871 1823.28 p52
King, John 60; Ontario, 1871 1823.15 p137
King, John 78; Vermont, 1881 5900.10 p326
King, John, Jr.; Maryland, 1666 2524.55 p130
King, John, II; Maryland, 1663 2524.55 p130
King, John Curle; Virginia, 1763 1224.2 p65
King, John J.; Vermont, 1848-1920 5900.10 p549
King, Joseph; New York, 1803 8197.10 p13
King, Joseph; New York, 1840 8197.10 p176
King, Joseph 38; Ontario, 1871 1823.15 p137
King, Joseph 50; Ontario, 1871 1823.15 p137
King, Josiah; Connecticut, 1764 1224.2 p65
King, Julia 40; Vermont, 1852 5900.10 p383
King, M. Belle; Vermont, 1929 5900.10 p549
King, Manheim; New York, 1839 8197.10 p139
King, Margaret; Vermont, 1839-1916 5900.10 p241
King, Margaret; Vermont, 1850-1927 5900.10 p56
King, Margaret 48; Ontario, 1871 1823.22 p87
King, Margret M. 67; Ontario, 1871 1823.22 p87
King, Mark Joseph; New York, 1839 8197.10 p139
King, Mary *SEE* King, John
King, Mary *SEE* King, Robert
King, Mary 18; Vermont, 1861 5900.10 p178
King, Mary 34; Vermont, 1866 5900.10 p87
King, Mary 45; Ontario, 1861 2896.27 p6
King, Mary A.; Vermont, 1858-1938 5900.10 p67
King, Mary E.; Vermont, 1831-1905 5900.10 p334
King, Michael 23; Vermont, 1870 5900.10 p549
King, Michael 50; Ontario, 1871 1823.15 p137
King, Nathaniel; Boston, 1747 1224.2 p65
King, Patience; Maryland, 1681 2524.55 p130
King, Patrick; Vermont, 1827-1878 5900.10 p67
King, Patrick 74; Vermont, 1870 5900.10 p237
King, Peter; New York, New York, 1866 3437.14 p93
King, Peter; Pennsylvania, 1868 6058.10 p63
King, Peter; Vermont, 1839-1900 5900.10 p324
King, Peter, Sr. 50; Ontario, 1871 1823.28 p52
King, Richard 39; Ontario, 1871 1823.28 p52
King, Robert; Maryland, 1666 2524.55 p130
Wife: Suzanna
Daughter: Mary
King, Robert 13; Ontario, 1861 2896.27 p6
King, Robert 23; Maryland, 1775 1220.25 p21
King, Robert 58; Ontario, 1871 1823.28 p52
King, Ruth; Maryland, 1665 2524.55 p10
King, S. 35; Ontario, 1861 2896.28 p2
King, Samuel; Virginia, 1745 1224.2 p65
King, Samuel 24; Jamaica, 1775 1220.25 p144
King, Sarah 74; Ontario, 1871 1823.22 p87
King, Seth; Havana, 1764 1224.2 p65
King, Stephen 45; Ontario, 1871 1823.15 p137
King, Suzanna *SEE* King, Robert
King, Sydney 6; Ontario, 1861 2896.27 p6
King, Thomas; Charles Town, South Carolina, 1810 1224.3 p44
King, Thomas; Maryland, 1652 2524.55 p130
King, Thomas; Maryland, 1670 2524.55 p130
King, Thomas; New England, 1658 1224.1 p34
King, Thomas; New York, 1807 8197.10 p43
King, Thomas; New York, 1840 8197.10 p176
King, Thomas; Virginia, 1663 6212.30 p4
King, Thomas; Virginia, 1666-1667 6212.30 p34
King, Thomas 21; Fort Cumberland, Nova Scotia, 1775 1220.25 p21
King, Thomas 28; America, 1774 1220.25 p36
King, Thomas 66; Ontario, 1871 1823.22 p87
King, Thomas Long; New York, 1840 8197.10 p176
King, William; Maryland, 1732 1224.2 p65
King, William; Pennsylvania, 1868 6058.10 p73
King, William; Philadelphia, 1795 1224.2 p65
King, William 15; Ontario, 1861 2896.27 p6
King, William 40; Ontario, 1871 1823.15 p137
King, William 47; Vermont, 1867 5900.10 p64
King, William 48; Ontario, 1871 1823.15 p137
King, William H. 7; Ontario, 1861 2896.28 p2
King, William Simpson; New York, 1900 1640.13 p65
King, Willm; Virginia, 1703 6212.30 p62
Kingdom, George 66; Ontario, 1871 1823.15 p137
Kinge, Joane Slany; New England, 1649 1224.1 p53
Kingford, Philip 23; Maryland, 1775 1220.25 p112
Kingham, Thomas; Maryland, 1673 2524.55 p130
Kinghine, Ann 34; Ontario, 1871 1823.28 p52
Kings, Daniel, Jr.; Pennsylvania, 1788 4629.10 p56
Kingsberry, Edward *SEE* Kingsberry, Robert
Kingsberry, Elizabeth *SEE* Kingsberry, Robert
Kingsberry, Mary *SEE* Kingsberry, Robert
Kingsberry, Robert; Maryland, 1652 2524.55 p130
Wife: Mary
Stepchild: Edward
Stepchild: Elizabeth
Kingsbury, C. A. 47; Ontario, 1861 2896.28 p65
Kingsbury, Edward *SEE* Kingsbury, Robert
Kingsbury, Eliza 33; Ontario, 1861 2896.28 p65
Kingsbury, Elizabeth *SEE* Kingsbury, Robert
Kingsbury, Eva E. 3; Ontario, 1861 2896.28 p65
Kingsbury, Jane 11; Ontario, 1861 2896.28 p65
Kingsbury, Jonathan; Massachusetts, 1807 1224.3 p44
Kingsbury, Mary *SEE* Kingsbury, Robert
Kingsbury, Robert; Maryland, 1652 2524.55 p130
Wife: Mary
Stepchild: Edward
Stepchild: Elizabeth
Kingsbury, Rosetta 9; Ontario, 1861 2896.28 p65
Kingsbury, Sarah 7; Ontario, 1861 2896.28 p65
Kingshott, James 59; Ontario, 1871 1823.28 p52
Kingsley, A. B. 3; Ontario, 1861 2896.27 p4
Kingsley, Bridget Kelley; Vermont, 1826-1900 5900.10 p440
Kingsley, Bridget R.; Vermont, 1791-1861 5900.10 p440
Kingsley, Daniel; Vermont, 1853-1920 5900.10 p592
Kingsley, Dennis; Vermont, 1828-1909 5900.10 p430
Kingsley, Edward; Vermont, 1850-1931 5900.10 p486
Kingsley, Elizabeth McDonnell; Vermont, 1853-1931 5900.10 p592
Kingsley, Ellen; Vermont, 1838-1926 5900.10 p440
Kingsley, Ellen 80; Vermont, 1921 5900.10 p430
Kingsley, Fred 1; Ontario, 1861 2896.27 p4
Kingsley, James; Vermont, 1839-1896 5900.10 p440
Kingsley, Jane 38; Ontario, 1861 2896.27 p4
Kingsley, Jennie; Vermont, 1859-1941 5900.10 p375
Kingsley, Lawrence 52; Vermont, 1892 5900.10 p430
Kingsley, M. M. 10; Ontario, 1861 2896.27 p4
Kingsley, Mary E. Duffy; Vermont, 1857-1921 5900.10 p487
Kingsley, Michael; Vermont, 1826-1858 5900.10 p440
Kingsley, N. T. 5; Ontario, 1861 2896.27 p4
Kingsley, P. J. 14; Ontario, 1861 2896.27 p4
Kingsley, Robert 60; Ontario, 1871 1823.22 p87
Kingsley, Rose A. Duffy; Vermont, 1858-1891 5900.10 p486
Kingsley, S. A. 17; Ontario, 1861 2896.27 p4
Kingsley, W. H. 13; Ontario, 1861 2896.27 p4
Kingston, Mrs.; Quebec, 1858 9196.15 p36
Kingston, Professor; Quebec, 1858 9196.15 p36
Kingston, Elener 50; Ontario, 1861 2896.27 p21
Kingston, John; Vermont, 1822-1900 5900.10 p47
Kingston, John 48; Ontario, 1861 2896.27 p21
Kingston, John, Sr.; Vermont, 1826-1900 5900.10 p356
Kingston, John, Jr.; Vermont, 1851-1920 5900.10 p356
Kingston, Joseph 10; Ontario, 1861 2896.27 p21
Kingston, Martyn; Maryland, 1659 2524.55 p130
Kingston, Mary; Vermont, 1826-1898 5900.10 p47
Kingston, Mary; Vermont, 1826-1898 5900.10 p356
Kingston, Mary McDonough; Vermont, 1859-1922 5900.10 p356
Kingston, Nancy 64; Vermont, 1876 5900.10 p362
Kingston, Sarah 13; Ontario, 1861 2896.27 p21
Kingston, Thomas 32; Ontario, 1871 1823.28 p52
Kingston, William; Vermont, 1840-1910 5900.10 p356
Kingston, William 62; Ontario, 1871 1823.22 p87
Kingstone, Mr.; Quebec, 1858 9196.15 p38
Kinhel, Konrad; Port uncertain, 1769 2856.30 p235
Kiniry, Bartholomew; Vermont, 1832-1907 5900.10 p64
Kiniry, Bridget Callahan 43; Vermont, 1884 5900.10 p53
Kiniry, Daniel 49; Vermont, 1880 5900.10 p65
Kiniry, Ellen; Vermont, 1837-1921 5900.10 p64
Kiniry, Ellen R.; Vermont, 1851-1921 5900.10 p55
Kiniry, Johannah Gallaran; Vermont, 1867 5900.10 p63
Kiniry, M. Driscol 66; Vermont, 1868 5900.10 p64
Kiniry, Mary 47; Vermont, 1881 5900.10 p66
Kiniry, Nancy; Vermont, 1840-1914 5900.10 p64
Kiniry, Nora; Vermont, 1858-1937 5900.10 p64
Kiniry, Thomas 59; Vermont, 1896 5900.10 p53
Kiniry, William 78; Vermont, 1876 5900.10 p64
Kinlan, Henry; New York, 1837 8197.10 p93
Kinloch, James; New York, 1838 8197.10 p247
Kinly, Richard; Pennsylvania, 1777 4629.10 p12
Kinmond, Miss; Quebec, 1857 9196.15 p26
Kinmond, Mr.; Quebec, 1857 9196.15 p26
Kinnacher, Leopold; Port uncertain, 1785 2856.30 p225
Kinnaird, David; Georgia, 1734 1640.10 p93
Kinnaley, Norah 70; Vermont, 1891 5900.10 p80
Kinnally, Margaret 102; Vermont, 1893 5900.10 p430
Kinnally, Patrick 63; Vermont, 1906 5900.10 p430
Kinnard, William; Pennsylvania, 1786 4629.10 p52
Kinnealy, James; Vermont, 1866 5900.10 p566
Kinnealy, John; Vermont, 1865 5900.10 p566
Kinnealy, Michael; Vermont, 1860 5900.10 p566
Kinnear, James; Tennessee, 1853 1640.10 p93
Kinnear, Robert; Pennsylvania, 1817 6058.10 p5
Kinnear, William; Pennsylvania, 1787 4629.10 p56
Kinneir, Alexander; Georgia, 1698 1640.13 p65
Kinnell, William; Georgia, 1698 1640.13 p65
Kinnelly, Daniel 63; Ontario, 1871 1823.28 p52
Kinnelly, John 35; Ontario, 1871 1823.28 p53
Kinnelly, Martin 68; Ontario, 1871 1823.28 p53
Kinnelly, Michael 30; Ontario, 1871 1823.28 p53
Kinnelly, Patrick 34; Ontario, 1871 1823.28 p53
Kinnen, John; New York, 1839 8197.10 p139
Kinnersley, William; Philadelphia, 1714 1224.2 p65
Kinney, Mrs. 55; Ontario, 1861 2896.26 p31
Kinney, Ann 11; Ontario, 1861 2896.27 p10
Kinney, Ann 22; Ontario, 1861 2896.28 p46
Kinney, Bedy 7; Ontario, 1861 2896.27 p10
Kinney, Christiana 20; Ontario, 1861 2896.26 p31
Kinney, Elen 13; Ontario, 1861 2896.27 p10
Kinney, Elen 41; Ontario, 1861 2896.27 p10
Kinney, Ellen Scully 76; Vermont, 1907 5900.10 p79
Kinney, James 1; Ontario, 1861 2896.27 p10
Kinney, Jer 5; Ontario, 1861 2896.27 p10
Kinney, John; New York, 1822 8197.10 p370
Kinney, John; New York, 1834 8197.10 p372
Kinney, John 18; Ontario, 1861 2896.26 p31
Kinney, John 30; Ontario, 1871 1823.22 p87
Kinney, Margaret Bowe; Vermont, 1830-1915 5900.10 p611
Kinney, Mary; Vermont, 1824-1892 5900.10 p74
Kinney, Mary; Vermont, 1824-1892 5900.10 p79
Kinney, Mary 7; Ontario, 1861 2896.26 p31
Kinney, Mary 7; Ontario, 1861 2896.27 p11
Kinney, Mary 16; Ontario, 1861 2896.27 p10
Kinney, Mary 70; Ontario, 1861 2896.28 p46
Kinney, Mary B. 66; Vermont, 1868 5900.10 p463
Kinney, Michael 20; Ontario, 1861 2896.28 p44
Kinney, Patric 51; Ontario, 1861 2896.27 p10
Kinney, Peter 4; Ontario, 1861 2896.28 p46
Kinney, Robert 22; Ontario, 1861 2896.26 p31
Kinney, Terry 34; Ontario, 1871 1823.28 p53
Kinney, Thomas; Vermont, 1815-1880 5900.10 p611
Kinney, Thomas 14; Ontario, 1861 2896.26 p31
Kinney, Thomas 24; Ontario, 1861 2896.28 p46
Kinney, Thomas 84; Vermont, 1914 5900.10 p79
Kinney, William 50; Ontario, 1861 2896.26 p31
Kinniar, Alexander 24; Ontario, 1871 1823.15 p137
Kinnich, Patrick 35; Alaska, 1917 9196.1 p7
Kinnich, Patrick 35; Yukon, 1917 9196.1 p7
Kinnicutt, Edward; Providence, Rhode Island, 1754 1224.2 p65
Kinniff, Thomas; Philadelphia, 1836 6058.10 p18
Kinny, Peter 80; Ontario, 1871 1823.15 p137
Kinschler, Johann; Port uncertain, 1768 2856.30 p225
Kinsel, Martin; Pennsylvania, 1784 4629.10 p44
Kinsella, Ann; Vermont, 1838-1900 5900.10 p158
Kinsella, Anna; Vermont, 1855-1993 5900.10 p273
Kinsella, Annie 17; Ontario, 1871 1823.28 p53
Kinsella, Ellen Burke; Vermont, 1834-1906 5900.10 p261
Kinsella, Laurence; Vermont, 1829-1907 5900.10 p261
Kinsella, Margaret; Vermont, 1850-1896 5900.10 p158
Kinsella, Martha; Vermont, 1845-1920 5900.10 p552
Kinsella, Mary Donovan; Vermont, 1830-1881 5900.10 p441
Kinsella, Michael; Vermont, 1826-1893 5900.10 p440
Kinsella, Patrick 28; Vermont, 1871 5900.10 p271
Kinsey, Evan; New York, 1807 8197.10 p43
Kinsey, Margarett; Maryland, 1661 2524.55 p130
Kinshilan, Patrick 30; Ontario, 1871 1823.15 p137

Kinshman, Alex.; Virginia, 1663 ***6212.30*** *p2*
Kinsilla, Anne 52; Ontario, 1871 ***1823.15*** *p137*
Kinsilla, Mary 20; Ontario, 1871 ***1823.15*** *p137*
Kinskoff, Abrahart 45; Ontario, 1871 ***1823.15*** *p139*
Kinsler, Henrich; America, 1712 ***2856.30*** *p225*
Kinsley, Ann Starr 70; Vermont, 1892 ***5900.10*** *p361*
Kinsley, Christian; Pennsylvania, 1777 ***4629.10*** *p9*
Kinsley, Dinnes; Vermont, 1869 ***5900.10*** *p361*
Kinsley, John; Vermont, 1849-1929 ***5900.10*** *p357*
Kinsley, Kate 16; Ontario, 1871 ***1823.28*** *p53*
Kinsley, Mary A.; Vermont, 1855-1935 ***5900.10*** *p357*
Kinsley, Michael; Vermont, 1842-1932 ***5900.10*** *p357*
Kinsley, Michael 20; Vermont, 1877 ***5900.10*** *p361*
Kinsley, Michael 44; Vermont, 1870 ***5900.10*** *p361*
Kinsley, Sarah Fischer; Vermont, 1863-1936 ***5900.10*** *p357*
Kinsley, Sarah Malany 78; Vermont, 1884 ***5900.10*** *p360*
Kinsley, Thomas 82; Vermont, 1899 ***5900.10*** *p360*
Kinslow, Thomas 25; Maryland, 1775 ***1220.25*** *p101*
Kinsly, Frazer; Pennsylvania, 1777 ***4629.10*** *p6*
Kinsly, John; Pennsylvania, 1777 ***4629.10*** *p16*
Kinsman, Richard 62; Ontario, 1871 ***1823.22*** *p87*
Kinstry, Thomas; New York, 1839 ***8197.10*** *p139*
Kinsvater, Frederick 2; Kansas, 1910 ***9079.10*** *p46*
Kinsvater, Fredrick 2; Kansas, 1910 ***9079.10*** *p5*
Kinsvater, Jacob 36; Kansas, 1907-1910 ***9079.10*** *p5*
Kinsvater, Jacob 36; Kansas, 1907-1910 ***9079.10*** *p46*
Kinsvater, Katie 33; Kansas, 1910 ***9079.10*** *p5*
Kinsvater, Katie 33; Kansas, 1910 ***9079.10*** *p46*
Kinsvater, Marie 7; Kansas, 1910 ***9079.10*** *p5*
Kinsvater, Marie 7; Kansas, 1910 ***9079.10*** *p46*
Kintinsky, Frank; Maryland, 1910 ***3259.35*** *p27*
Kintscher, Friedrich; Port uncertain, 1769 ***2856.30*** *p225*
Kintzing, William D. 24; Ontario, 1871 ***1823.28*** *p53*
Kinward, Thomas 55; Ontario, 1871 ***1823.15*** *p137*
Kinzel, Christof; America, 1738 ***2856.30*** *p153*
With wife
Kinzer, Johann Nikolaus; America, 1738 ***2856.30*** *p225*
Kinzler, Johann Jacob; America, 1738 ***2856.30*** *p225*
Kioshk, Benoit 39; Ontario, 1871 ***1823.28*** *p53*
Kioshk, Pierre 32; Ontario, 1871 ***1823.28*** *p53*
Kiper, Thomas; Maryland, 1910 ***3259.35*** *p27*
Kipling, Ann 60; Ontario, 1871 ***1823.28*** *p53*
Kippar, R.; Quebec, 1857 ***9196.15*** *p19*
Kippax, William; New York, 1840 ***8197.10*** *p177*
Kippean, Hanna 30; Ontario, 1871 ***1823.28*** *p53*
Kippen, Andrew 58; Ontario, 1871 ***1823.28*** *p53*
Kippenhahn, Ulrich; Port uncertain, 1791 ***2856.30*** *p225*
Kippenhahn, Ulrich; Port uncertain, 1793 ***2856.30*** *p225*
Kippenhan, Ulrich; Port uncertain, 1791 ***2856.30*** *p225*
Kippenhan, Ulrich; Port uncertain, 1793 ***2856.30*** *p225*
Kipper, Elisabeth; Port uncertain, 1790 ***2856.30*** *p225*
Kipper, Franz; Port uncertain, 1790 ***2856.30*** *p225*
Kipper, Maria Barbara; Port uncertain, 1772 ***2856.30*** *p225*
Kipper, Michael; Port uncertain, 1759 ***2856.30*** *p225*
Kipphan, Philipp; America, 1749 ***2856.30*** *p225*
With wife & children
Kipple, John; Pennsylvania, 1777 ***4629.10*** *p30*
Kipshaven, Elizabeth; Maryland, 1673 ***2524.55*** *p131*
Kipshaven, Margery; Maryland, 1673 ***2524.55*** *p131*
Kipsier, Ulrich; America, 1738 ***2856.30*** *p225*
Kipsier, Ulrich; Port uncertain, 1738 ***2856.30*** *p225*
Kirbee, Elizabeth 55; Vermont, 1904 ***5900.10*** *p163*
Kirby, Agnes J.; Vermont, 1856-1892 ***5900.10*** *p163*
Kirby, Catherine; Vermont, 1808-1888 ***5900.10*** *p549*
Kirby, Christopher 21; Maryland, 1774 ***1220.25*** *p70*
Kirby, Edward; Pennsylvania, 1777 ***4629.10*** *p28*
Kirby, Elizabeth McWilliams; Vermont, 1830-1877 ***5900.10*** *p163*
Kirby, Elizabeth Thompson; Vermont, 1832-1901 ***5900.10*** *p168*
Kirby, Ellen; Vermont, 1847-1885 ***5900.10*** *p193*
Kirby, George; Maryland, 1661 ***2524.55*** *p131*
Kirby, George 34; Ontario, 1871 ***1823.28*** *p53*
Kirby, J. Henry; Vermont, 1826-1890 ***5900.10*** *p168*
Kirby, James; Richmond, Virginia, 1815 ***1224.3*** *p44*
Kirby, James; Vermont, 1834-1917 ***5900.10*** *p166*
Kirby, Jane; Vermont, 1906 ***5900.10*** *p86*
Kirby, John; Maryland, 1661 ***2524.55*** *p131*
Kirby, Johnnie; Vermont, 1853-1865 ***5900.10*** *p163*
Kirby, Nathaniel 49; Ontario, 1871 ***1823.28*** *p53*
Kirby, Rich; Virginia, 1665-1666 ***6212.30*** *p24*
Kirby, Timothy; Vermont, 1903 ***5900.10*** *p86*
Kirby, Valentine 16; Philadelphia, 1775 ***1220.25*** *p107*
Kirby, William; Maryland, 1666 ***2524.55*** *p131*
Kirby, William; New York, 1822 ***8197.10*** *p246*
Kirbyson, Nicholas 68; Ontario, 1871 ***1823.28*** *p53*
Kirch, Anton; Port uncertain, 1784 ***2856.30*** *p225*
Kirch, Lambert; Port uncertain, 1784 ***2856.30*** *p225*
Kirchberg, Josef; America, 1761 ***2856.30*** *p225*
Kirchenbauer, Michael; America, 1754 ***2856.30*** *p225*
With 2 daughters
Kirchner, Christof; Port uncertain, 1795 ***2856.30*** *p225*
Kirchner, Johann; Port uncertain, 1742 ***2856.30*** *p225*
Kirchner, Johann; Port uncertain, 1749 ***2856.30*** *p225*
Kirdonski, Michael; Maryland, 1910 ***3259.35*** *p27*
Kirek, John Diossy; New York, 1807 ***8197.10*** *p43*
Kirger, Chr. Jacob; America, 1753 ***2856.30*** *p225*
Kirk, Aceneith K.; Vermont, 1845-1901 ***5900.10*** *p497*
Kirk, Agnes 15; Ontario, 1861 ***2896.28*** *p54*
Kirk, Ann, Sr. 96; Vermont, 1844 ***5900.10*** *p235*
Kirk, Ann, Jr. 11 days; Vermont, 1832 ***5900.10*** *p235*
Kirk, Anne; Vermont, 1849-1920 ***5900.10*** *p285*
Kirk, Charles; Portland, Maine, 1858 ***9196.15*** *p30*
Kirk, Charles 44; Ontario, 1861 ***2896.28*** *p54*
Kirk, David; Mississippi, 1820-1845 ***1640.10*** *p93*
Kirk, David 48; Ontario, 1871 ***1823.22*** *p87*
Kirk, David 57; Ontario, 1871 ***1823.15*** *p138*
Kirk, Elizabeth; Vermont, 1854-1940 ***5900.10*** *p605*
Kirk, Ellen Burns; Vermont, 1851-1937 ***5900.10*** *p217*
Kirk, Emelie Doud; Vermont, 1837-1915 ***5900.10*** *p608*
Kirk, Francis; Vermont, 1833-1907 ***5900.10*** *p608*
Kirk, George 52; Ontario, 1871 ***1823.22*** *p87*
Kirk, James 26; Ontario, 1871 ***1823.22*** *p87*
Kirk, James 47; Ontario, 1871 ***1823.15*** *p138*
Kirk, James H. 16; Ontario, 1861 ***2896.28*** *p54*
Kirk, John; Vermont, 1862-1945 ***5900.10*** *p605*
Kirk, John 50; Ontario, 1871 ***1823.28*** *p53*
Kirk, John 51; Ontario, 1871 ***1823.22*** *p87*
Kirk, John 55; Ontario, 1871 ***1823.15*** *p138*
Kirk, John Bartholomew; Vermont, 1847-1916 ***5900.10*** *p217*
Kirk, John G.; New York, 1833-1838 ***8197.10*** *p122*
Kirk, Julia; Vermont, 1868-1935 ***5900.10*** *p588*
Kirk, Julia 62; Vermont, 1890 ***5900.10*** *p476*
Kirk, Lawrence 70; Vermont, 1869 ***5900.10*** *p232*
Kirk, Lewis 53; Ontario, 1871 ***1823.15*** *p138*
Kirk, Luecta J. 13; Ontario, 1861 ***2896.28*** *p54*
Kirk, Martin; Maryland, 1646 ***2524.55*** *p131*
With wife
Kirk, Mary; Vermont, 1804-1877 ***5900.10*** *p325*
Kirk, Mary 4 months; Vermont, 1823 ***5900.10*** *p606*
Kirk, Mary Flanagan 57; Vermont, 1876 ***5900.10*** *p601*
Kirk, Mary Jane 6 months; Vermont, 1860 ***5900.10*** *p605*
Kirk, Mary Sharkey 68; Vermont, 1879 ***5900.10*** *p232*
Kirk, O. R.; Vermont, 1846-1893 ***5900.10*** *p497*
Kirk, Peter; Vermont, 1853-1915 ***5900.10*** *p605*
Kirk, Peter 57; Vermont, 1884 ***5900.10*** *p476*
Kirk, Robert; New York, 1830 ***8197.10*** *p354*
Kirk, Robert 60; Ontario, 1871 ***1823.15*** *p138*
Kirk, Rosa; Vermont, 1838-1917 ***5900.10*** *p284*
Kirk, Rosie Murphy; Vermont, 1826-1899 ***5900.10*** *p605*
Kirk, Sarah; Vermont, 1842-1930 ***5900.10*** *p600*
Kirk, Terrience; Vermont, 1812-1898 ***5900.10*** *p605*
Kirk, Thomas; Rochester, New York, 1893 ***1640.13*** *p65*
Kirk, Thomas; Virginia, 1741 ***1224.2*** *p65*
Kirk, Thomas 80; Vermont, 1891 ***5900.10*** *p600*
Kirk, Walter 63; Ontario, 1871 ***1823.28*** *p53*
Kirk, William; New York, 1792-1840 ***8197.10*** *p360*
Kirk, William 25; Ontario, 1871 ***1823.28*** *p53*
Kirkbey, William 43; Ontario, 1871 ***1823.15*** *p138*
Kirkbride, Alx 46; Ontario, 1871 ***1823.15*** *p138*
Kirkby, Ann 4 *SEE* Kirkby, John
Kirkby, Ann 24 *SEE* Kirkby, John
Kirkby, Francis; Maryland, 1659 ***2524.55*** *p131*
Kirkby, John 2 *SEE* Kirkby, John
Kirkby, John 29; New York, 1774 ***1220.25*** *p24*
Wife: Ann 24
Child: Ann 4
Child: John 2
Kirke, Jo; Virginia, 1673 ***6212.30*** *p51*
Kirke, Joane *SEE* Kirke, John
Kirke, John; Maryland, 1669 ***2524.55*** *p131*
Wife: Joane
Daughter: Sarah
Kirke, John; Virginia, 1664 ***6212.30*** *p10*
Kirke, Martyn; Maryland, 1659 ***2524.55*** *p131*
With wife
Kirke, Sarah *SEE* Kirke, John
Kirkeby, Sarah; Virginia, 1673 ***6212.30*** *p51*
Kirkehame, Rose; Maryland, 1678 ***2524.55*** *p131*
Kirkhaldie, David; New York, 1807 ***8197.10*** *p43*
Kirkham, Edward 22; Maryland, 1773-1774 ***1220.25*** *p34*
Kirkham, John; New York, 1839 ***8197.10*** *p139*
Kirkhason, Herman; Maryland, 1681 ***2524.55*** *p131*
Kirkland, Alex 1; Ontario, 1861 ***2896.28*** *p38*
Kirkland, Derwent 6; Ontario, 1861 ***2896.28*** *p38*
Kirkland, Gavin 8; Ontario, 1861 ***2896.28*** *p38*
Kirkland, James 10; Ontario, 1861 ***2896.28*** *p38*
Kirkland, James 51; Ontario, 1861 ***2896.28*** *p38*
Kirkland, Jessie 40; Ontario, 1861 ***2896.28*** *p38*
Kirkland, Mary 23; Ontario, 1861 ***2896.28*** *p36*
Kirkland, Moses; Jamaica, 1789 ***1224.2*** *p66*
Kirkland, Moses; South Carolina, 1789 ***1224.2*** *p66*
Kirkland, R. 1; Ontario, 1861 ***2896.25*** *p1*
Kirkland, Tho; Virginia, 1666-1667 ***6212.30*** *p32*
Kirkland, William 40; Ontario, 1861 ***2896.25*** *p1*
Kirkley, Thomas; Maryland, 1665 ***2524.55*** *p131*
Kirkling, Thomas 42; Ontario, 1871 ***1823.28*** *p53*
Kirkman, C. W.; Portland, Maine, 1858 ***9196.15*** *p29*
Kirkman, Melcher; Maryland, 1664 ***2524.55*** *p131*
Kirkman, Robert; New York, 1834-1838 ***8197.10*** *p121*
Kirkman, Robert Francis 44; Ontario, 1871 ***1823.28*** *p53*
Kirkman, Thomas; Nashville, Tennessee, 1815 ***1224.3*** *p44*
Kirkman, Thomas; Nashville, Tennessee, 1828 ***1224.3*** *p44*
Kirkner, Kaspar; New York, 1840 ***8197.10*** *p385*
Kirkness, Mary 48; Ontario, 1871 ***1823.15*** *p138*
Kirkness, Thomas 30; Ontario, 1871 ***1823.28*** *p53*
Kirkpaterick, John 35; Ontario, 1871 ***1823.15*** *p138*
Kirkpatrick, Mr.; Quebec, 1857 ***9196.15*** *p18*
Kirkpatrick, Mrs.; Quebec, 1856 ***9196.15*** *p6*
Kirkpatrick, Mrs.; Quebec, 1857 ***9196.15*** *p18*
Kirkpatrick, Alexander 42; Ontario, 1871 ***1823.15*** *p138*
Kirkpatrick, Ann 33; Ontario, 1871 ***1823.15*** *p138*
Kirkpatrick, Edward 83; Ontario, 1871 ***1823.15*** *p138*
Kirkpatrick, James; Pennsylvania, 1777 ***4629.10*** *p19*
Kirkpatrick, James 40; Ontario, 1871 ***1823.22*** *p87*
Kirkpatrick, John; Georgia, 1699 ***1640.13*** *p65*
Kirkpatrick, John 43; Ontario, 1871 ***1823.15*** *p138*
Kirkpatrick, Mary 32; Ontario, 1871 ***1823.22*** *p87*
Kirkpatrick, Sarah Slattery 40; Vermont, 1915 ***5900.10*** *p450*
Kirkpatrick, William; Mississippi, 1825-1845 ***1640.10*** *p93*
Kirkpatrick, William; New York, 1834 ***8197.10*** *p71*
Kirkpatrick, William 31; Ontario, 1871 ***1823.28*** *p53*
Kirkpatrick, William 32; Ontario, 1871 ***1823.15*** *p138*
Kirkup, Mr.; Quebec, 1858 ***9196.15*** *p34*
Kirkwood, Mr.; Quebec, 1858 ***9196.15*** *p43*
Kirkwood, James; Maryland, 1678 ***2524.55*** *p131*
Kirkwood, Jane 22; Ontario, 1871 ***1823.22*** *p88*
Kirl, Heinrich; Port uncertain, 1784 ***2856.30*** *p225*
Kirlan, Bridget; Vermont, n.d. ***5900.10*** *p237*
Kirland, Tho; Virginia, 1665-1666 ***6212.30*** *p22*
Kirle, John; Virginia, 1666-1667 ***6212.30*** *p34*
Kirley, Bridget 84; Vermont, 1886 ***5900.10*** *p236*
Kirley, Catherine; Vermont, 1837-1914 ***5900.10*** *p456*
Kirley, Edward 74; Vermont, 1876 ***5900.10*** *p236*
Kirley, Elizabeth A.; Vermont, 1846-1874 ***5900.10*** *p236*
Kirley, Margaret; Vermont, 1839-1927 ***5900.10*** *p236*
Kirley, Margaret King; Vermont, 1839-1916 ***5900.10*** *p241*
Kirley, Thomas; Vermont, 1835-1911 ***5900.10*** *p241*
Kirsch, Johann; America, 1744 ***2856.30*** *p226*
Kirsch, Johann Georg; America, 1744 ***2856.30*** *p226*
With wife & 2 children
Kirsch, Johann Konrad; America, 1752 ***2856.30*** *p226*
Kirsch, Konrad; America, 1744 ***2856.30*** *p226*
Kirschberg, Georg; America, 1819 ***2856.30*** *p226*
Kirschner, Daniel; America, 1771 ***2856.30*** *p226*
Kirschner, John; New York, New York, 1853 ***3437.14*** *p7*
Kirshner, Johann George; America, 1748 ***2856.30*** *p226*
Kirst, Anna Maria; Port uncertain, 1747 ***2856.30*** *p226*
Kirton, James 52; Ontario, 1871 ***1823.15*** *p138*
Kirton, Joseph; New York, 1819 ***8197.10*** *p245*
Kirwan, Jane 80; Vermont, 1862 ***5900.10*** *p345*
Kirwin, Bridget 77; Vermont, 1889 ***5900.10*** *p309*
Kirwood, John; Chicago, 1872 ***1640.13*** *p65*
Kish, Matthes; America, 1739 ***2856.30*** *p226*
Kishmura, M. 24; Washington, 1913 ***9196.1*** *p60*
Kisielewsky, Seraryn; Maryland, 1910 ***3259.35*** *p27*
Kisner, Joseph; Maryland, 1910 ***3259.35*** *p27*
Kissack, Daniel; New York, 1840 ***8197.10*** *p321*
Kissinger, Daniel; Port uncertain, 1783 ***2856.30*** *p226*
Kissnagel, Matthaus; Port uncertain, 1783 ***2856.30*** *p226*
Kist, Friedrich; Port uncertain, 1774 ***2856.30*** *p226*
Kiste, Thomas; Maryland, 1670 ***2524.55*** *p131*
Kister, Johann Martin; Port uncertain, 1752 ***2856.30*** *p226*
Kistler, Georg; America, 1818 ***2856.30*** *p226*
With wife
Kistler, Hans Jacob; Port uncertain, 1756 ***2856.30*** *p226*
Kistler, Johann; America, 1737 ***2856.30*** *p226*
Kistler, Johann; Port uncertain, 1737 ***2856.30*** *p226*
With 3 sons
Kistner, Joseph; Indiana, 1883-1884 ***3437.14*** *p197*
Kistner, Michael; Port uncertain, 1695 ***2856.30*** *p226*
Kistonn, Jarvis; Maryland, 1668 ***2524.55*** *p131*
Kitchekakake, Cecil 52; Ontario, 1871 ***1823.28*** *p53*
Kitchen, John 26; Ontario, 1871 ***1823.28*** *p53*
Kitcher, Richard 36; Maryland, 1775 ***1220.25*** *p99*
Kitchibatiss, Charles 75; Ontario, 1871 ***1823.28*** *p53*
Kitchibatiss, J. Bte 41; Ontario, 1871 ***1823.28*** *p53*
Kitchin, John 40; Ontario, 1871 ***1823.15*** *p138*
Kitching, Ritchard 45; Ontario, 1871 ***1823.28*** *p53*

Klingender, Frederick; New Orleans, 1836 ***1224.3*** *p44*
Klinger, Anton; America, 1749 ***2856.30*** *p232*
Klinger, Maria Barbara; Port uncertain, 1738 ***2856.30*** *p232*
Klinger, Maria Catharina; Port uncertain, 1752 ***2856.30*** *p232*
Klinghamer, Claudius; Port uncertain, 1785 ***2856.30*** *p232*
Klingler, Andreas; Port uncertain, 1750 ***2856.30*** *p232*
Klingler, George Michael Christian; New York, 1834-1838 ***8197.10*** *p121*
Klingler, Thomas; Port uncertain, 1765 ***2856.30*** *p232*
Klinglin, Margarete; Port uncertain, 1760 ***2856.30*** *p232*
Klinglisin, Magdalena; Port uncertain, 1769 ***2856.30*** *p232*
Klinouski, Henry; Maryland, 1910 ***3259.35*** *p27*
Klinowski, Frank; Maryland, 1910 ***3259.35*** *p27*
Klionofski, Joseph; Maryland, 1910 ***3259.35*** *p27*
Klippel, Miss; Port uncertain, 1758 ***2856.30*** *p232*
Klippel, Johann Georg; Port uncertain, 1745 ***2856.30*** *p232*
Klippel, Johann Peter; Port uncertain, 1765 ***2856.30*** *p232*
Klippel, Maria Apollonia; Port uncertain, 1751 ***2856.30*** *p232*
Klippel, Peter; Port uncertain, 1788 ***2856.30*** *p232*
Klippel, Philipp; Port uncertain, 1788 ***2856.30*** *p232*
Klipplin, Maria Margarete; Port uncertain, 1786 ***2856.30*** *p232*
Kloc, Michel; Maryland, 1910 ***3259.35*** *p27*
Klock, . . .; Port uncertain, 1784 ***2856.30*** *p232*
Klock, Engelhard; America, 1752 ***2856.30*** *p232*
Klock, Engelhard; Port uncertain, 1751 ***2856.30*** *p232*
Klokoski, Andrew; Maryland, 1910 ***3259.35*** *p27*
Kloniger, Johann; Port uncertain, 1756 ***2856.30*** *p232*
Klonowski, Adam; Maryland, 1910 ***3259.35*** *p27*
Klonowski, Joseph; Maryland, 1910 ***3259.35*** *p27*
Klopf, Anton; America, 1751 ***2856.30*** *p232*
With wife & 3 children
Klopfer, Georg; Port uncertain, 1765 ***2856.30*** *p233*
With 4 children
Klopfer, Georg Adam; America, 1756 ***2856.30*** *p234*
Klopfer, Georg Adam; America, 1758 ***2856.30*** *p234*
Klopp, Veronika Becker; America, 1790 ***2856.30*** *p233*
Kloppey, Friedrich; America, 1750 ***2856.30*** *p233*
Kloppeyer, Friedrich; America, 1750 ***2856.30*** *p233*
Kloppeyn, Friedrich; America, 1751 ***2856.30*** *p233*
Klor, Johann; Port uncertain, 1794 ***2856.30*** *p233*
With family
Klorin, Maria Magdalena; America, 1749 ***2856.30*** *p234*
With 2 children
Klos, Anna Maria; Port uncertain, 1762 ***2856.30*** *p233*
Klos, Stanislaus; Maryland, 1910 ***3259.35*** *p27*
Klosinska, Walenty; Maryland, 1910 ***3259.35*** *p27*
Kloss, Anton; Port uncertain, 1731 ***2856.30*** *p233*
Kloss, Johann; Port uncertain, 1740 ***2856.30*** *p233*
Kloss, Melchior; America, 1738 ***2856.30*** *p233*
With wife & children
Klother, Jacob; America, 1738 ***2856.30*** *p233*
With wife & children
Klotz, Anna Maria; Port uncertain, 1762 ***2856.30*** *p233*
Klotz, George; New York, New York, 1849 ***3437.14*** *p34*
Klotz, Jacob; America, 1738 ***2856.30*** *p233*
Klotz, Johann Martin; Port uncertain, 1764 ***2856.30*** *p233*
Kluchinski, John; Maryland, 1910 ***3259.35*** *p27*
Kluck, Peter; America, 1748 ***2856.30*** *p233*
With child
Klucznik, Hilno; Maryland, 1910 ***3259.35*** *p27*
Kluczyk, Constance; Maryland, 1910 ***3259.35*** *p27*
Klugshertz, Anna Maria; Port uncertain, 1753 ***2856.30*** *p233*
Klugshertz, Elisabeth; Port uncertain, 1750 ***2856.30*** *p171*
Klugshertz, Elisabeth; Port uncertain, 1750 ***2856.30*** *p233*
Klugshertz, Elisabeth Haase; Port uncertain, 1750 ***2856.30*** *p233*
Klumb, Anna Sophia; Port uncertain, 1765 ***2856.30*** *p233*
Klumb, Maria Clara; Port uncertain, 1756 ***2856.30*** *p233*
Klumbt, Hieronymus; Port uncertain, 1747 ***2856.30*** *p233*
With wife & children
Klumbt, Philipp; Port uncertain, 1747 ***2856.30*** *p233*
With wife & children
Klump, Dorothea; Port uncertain, 1785 ***2856.30*** *p233*
Klump, Maria Magdalena; Port uncertain, 1764 ***2856.30*** *p233*
Husband: Melchior
Klump, Maria Rosina; Port uncertain, 1758 ***2856.30*** *p233*
Klump, Marianna; Port uncertain, 1745 ***2856.30*** *p233*
Klump, Melchior *SEE* Klump, Maria Magdalena
Klumpp, Georg; Port uncertain, 1749 ***2856.30*** *p233*
Klumpp, John 36; Ontario, 1871 ***1823.15*** *p138*
Klunck, Friedrich; Port uncertain, 1770 ***2856.30*** *p233*
Klunckh, Anna Elisabeth; Port uncertain, 1745 ***2856.30*** *p233*
Klusicki, Michael; Maryland, 1910 ***3259.35*** *p27*
Klymonuski, Michael; Maryland, 1910 ***3259.35*** *p27*
Klyn, Hans Adam; America, 1743 ***2856.30*** *p229*
Klyski, Henry; Maryland, 1910 ***3259.35*** *p27*
Klyusziuth, Wilhelm; Maryland, 1910 ***3259.35*** *p27*
Klywszundt, John; Maryland, 1910 ***3259.35*** *p27*
Klywszundt, Michael; Maryland, 1910 ***3259.35*** *p27*
Kmieriak, George; Maryland, 1910 ***3259.35*** *p27*
Knab, Marianna; Port uncertain, 1766 ***2856.30*** *p234*
Knab, Vinzenz; Port uncertain, 1741 ***2856.30*** *p234*
Knab, Vinzenz; Port uncertain, 1771 ***2856.30*** *p234*
Knabe, Joseph; Maryland, 1910 ***3259.35*** *p27*
Knaese, Warner; New York, 1807 ***8197.10*** *p43*
Knafik, Stanislaus; Maryland, 1910 ***3259.35*** *p27*
Knap, AEmilia *SEE* Knap, Robert
Knap, Johann; Port uncertain, 1764 ***2856.30*** *p234*
Knap, Peter; Port uncertain, 1785 ***2856.30*** *p234*
Knap, Robert; Maryland, 1658 ***2524.55*** *p131*
Daughter: Susanna
Wife: AEmilia
Knap, Susanna *SEE* Knap, Robert
Knapheade, Hermann; New York, 1839 ***8197.10*** *p247*
Knapp, Mrs.; Maryland, 1651 ***2524.55*** *p131*
Knapp, Alpheus 68; Ontario, 1871 ***1823.22*** *p88*
Knapp, Anna Maria; Port uncertain, 1757 ***2856.30*** *p234*
Knapp, Catharina; Port uncertain, 1764 ***2856.30*** *p234*
Knapp, Henry 22; Ontario, 1861 ***2896.28*** *p18*
Knapp, Jakob; Port uncertain, 1777 ***2856.30*** *p234*
With wife & children
Knapp, Jerg Wilhelm; Port uncertain, 1776 ***2856.30*** *p234*
Knapp, Johann Christia; Port uncertain, 1784 ***2856.30*** *p234*
Knapp, Jonathan; Connecticut, 1763 ***1224.2*** *p66*
Knapp, Jonathan; Havana, 1763 ***1224.2*** *p66*
Knapp, Ludwig; Port uncertain, 1775 ***2856.30*** *p234*
Knapp, Valentin; Port uncertain, 1778 ***2856.30*** *p234*
Knapp, Wilhelm; Port uncertain, 1782 ***2856.30*** *p234*
Knapper, Jacob; New York, 1807 ***8197.10*** *p43*
Knapstus, Christof; Port uncertain, 1680 ***2856.30*** *p234*
Knapton, Albin; Carolina, 1708 ***1224.2*** *p66*
Knarr, John Jacob; Indiana, 1843-1900 ***3437.14*** *p205*
Knasiak, Jacob; Maryland, 1910 ***3259.35*** *p27*
Knatchbull, Jno; Virginia, 1665-1666 ***6212.30*** *p24*
Knauber, Heinrich; Port uncertain, 1770 ***2856.30*** *p234*
Knauber, Heinrich; Port uncertain, 1771 ***2856.30*** *p234*
Knauf, Sebastian; New York, New York, 1857 ***6058.10*** *p49*
Knaus, Godfrey; New York, 1839 ***8197.10*** *p139*
Knaut, Laura 12; Ontario, 1871 ***1823.28*** *p53*
Knay, Sebastian; Port uncertain, 1770 ***2856.30*** *p234*
Knear, Jane; Vermont, n.d. ***5900.10*** *p320*
Kneas, Christopher; Pennsylvania, 1777 ***4629.10*** *p13*
Kneawse, Mary; Maryland, 1910 ***3259.35*** *p27*
Knebel, Henrick; New York, 1831 ***8197.10*** *p67*
Knebel, John Jacob; New York, 1806 ***8197.10*** *p31*
Knecht, Catharina; Port uncertain, 1745 ***2856.30*** *p234*
Knecht, Johann; America, 1740 ***2856.30*** *p234*
Knecht, Johann; America, 1747 ***2856.30*** *p235*
With wife
Knecht, Johann; America, 1748 ***2856.30*** *p234*
Knecht, Johann; America, 1748 ***2856.30*** *p235*
Knecht, Johann; America, 1792 ***2856.30*** *p234*
Knecht, Johann; Port uncertain, 1789 ***2856.30*** *p234*
Knecht, Konrad; Port uncertain, 1783 ***2856.30*** *p234*
Knechtel, Daniel 38; Ontario, 1871 ***1823.15*** *p138*
Knee, Mrs.; Quebec, 1858 ***9196.15*** *p37*
Kneebel, Henrich; New York, 1829 ***8197.10*** *p246*
Kneedsen, Andrew 36; Alaska, 1917 ***9196.1*** *p54*
Kneedsen, Andrew 36; Whitehorse, Yukon, 1917 ***9196.1*** *p54*
Kneeland, Ann Eliza Boynton; Vermont, 1850-1872 ***5900.10*** *p303*
Kneeland, Charles H.; Vermont, 1844-1875 ***5900.10*** *p303*
Kneeshaw, Miss; Quebec, 1858 ***9196.15*** *p35*
Kneeshaw, Anne 61; Ontario, 1871 ***1823.15*** *p138*
Kneib, Anton; Port uncertain, 1781 ***2856.30*** *p235*
Kneip, Michael; Port uncertain, 1784 ***2856.30*** *p235*
Kneis, John; Pennsylvania, 1777 ***4629.10*** *p7*
Knell, Johann; Port uncertain, 1765 ***2856.30*** *p235*
Knell, Peter; America, 1791 ***2856.30*** *p235*
Knell, Sabine Frizin; America, 1791 ***2856.30*** *p123*
Knepper, Konrad; Port uncertain, 1749 ***2856.30*** *p235*
With wife & 2 children
Kneringer, John; New York, 1808 ***8197.10*** *p54*
Knestler, Barbara; Port uncertain, 1742 ***2856.30*** *p235*
Knet, Francis 15; Maryland, 1775 ***1220.25*** *p102*
Knewshaw, Wm 44; Ontario, 1871 ***1823.28*** *p53*
Knezavich, M. 39; Alaska, 1916 ***9196.1*** *p42*
Knezavich, M. 39; Whitehorse, Yukon, 1916 ***9196.1*** *p42*
Knichel, Catharina; Port uncertain, 1778 ***2856.30*** *p235*
Knichel, Konrad; Port uncertain, 1769 ***2856.30*** *p235*
Kniebas, Christian; New York, 1840 ***8197.10*** *p247*
Knier, Christian; Port uncertain, 1777 ***2856.30*** *p235*
Kniewizel, Catharina; Port uncertain, 1751 ***2856.30*** *p235*
Kniff, Michael; New York, 1835 ***8197.10*** *p316*
Knight, Abram; New York, 1812 ***8197.10*** *p245*
Knight, Alfred 61; Ontario, 1871 ***1823.15*** *p139*
Knight, Charles; New York, 1839 ***8197.10*** *p247*
Knight, Charles; Philadelphia, 1839 ***1224.3*** *p44*
Knight, Daniel; New York, 1828 ***8197.10*** *p246*
Knight, Edward; Maryland, 1681 ***2524.55*** *p131*
Wife: Joane
Daughter: Elizabeth
Knight, Elizabeth *SEE* Knight, Edward
Knight, Gabriel 47; Ontario, 1871 ***1823.28*** *p53*
Knight, George; Virginia, 1684 ***1224.1*** *p35*
Knight, Griffin 26; Maryland, 1774 ***1220.25*** *p74*
Knight, Hannah; New England, 1657 ***1224.1*** *p59*
Knight, Henry; Maryland, 1675 ***1224.1*** *p35*
Knight, Henry; Virginia, 1668-1669 ***6212.30*** *p40*
Knight, Herbert 1; Ontario, 1861 ***2896.28*** *p59*
Knight, Jacob 21; Maryland, 1774 ***1220.25*** *p57*
Knight, James 29; Ontario, 1871 ***1823.28*** *p53*
Knight, James 55; Ontario, 1871 ***1823.15*** *p139*
Knight, Joane *SEE* Knight, Edward
Knight, Johann; America, 1748 ***2856.30*** *p235*
Knight, John; Maryland, 1681 ***2524.55*** *p131*
Knight, John; Maryland, 1682 ***2524.55*** *p131*
Knight, John; New York, 1839 ***8197.10*** *p139*
Knight, John; Pennsylvania, 1777 ***4629.10*** *p13*
Knight, John; Pennsylvania, 1793 ***1224.2*** *p66*
Knight, John 16; Maryland, 1774 ***1220.25*** *p8*
Knight, John 19; Maryland, 1774 ***1220.25*** *p7*
Knight, John 25; Ontario, 1871 ***1823.28*** *p53*
Knight, John 25; Virginia, 1774 ***1220.25*** *p55*
Knight, John 26; Maryland, 1774 ***1220.25*** *p37*
Knight, John 44; Ontario, 1871 ***1823.15*** *p139*
Knight, John 48; Ontario, 1871 ***1823.28*** *p53*
Knight, John 59; Ontario, 1871 ***1823.22*** *p88*
Knight, John 60; Ontario, 1871 ***1823.15*** *p139*
Knight, Jonathan; Virginia, 1668-1669 ***6212.30*** *p41*
Knight, Joseph; Maryland, 1682 ***2524.55*** *p131*
Knight, Margarett; Maryland, 1660 ***2524.55*** *p131*
Knight, Mary; Virginia, 1664 ***6212.30*** *p10*
Knight, Mary; Virginia, 1672 ***6212.30*** *p50*
Knight, Mary; Virginia, 1685 ***1224.1*** *p35*
Knight, Mary; Virginia, 1703-1704 ***6212.30*** *p62*
Knight, Nathaniel; Jamestown, Virginia, 1678 ***1224.1*** *p35*
Knight, Richard; Maryland, 1675 ***2524.55*** *p131*
Knight, Richard; Norfolk, Virginia, 1771 ***1224.2*** *p66*
Knight, Richard 47; Ontario, 1871 ***1823.22*** *p88*
Knight, Robert 25; Philadelphia, 1775 ***1220.25*** *p9*
Knight, Robert 26; Carolina, 1774 ***1220.25*** *p38*
Knight, Thomas 29; Ontario, 1871 ***1823.28*** *p53*
Knight, Thomas 81; Ontario, 1871 ***1823.28*** *p53*
Knight, Toby; New England, 1660 ***1224.1*** *p35*
Knight, William; New York, 1838 ***8197.10*** *p121*
Knight, William; Norfolk, Virginia, 1771 ***1224.2*** *p66*
Knight, William; Virginia, 1671-1672 ***6212.30*** *p47*
Knight, Wm; Virginia, 1671-1672 ***6212.30*** *p47*
Knightel, John 47; Ontario, 1871 ***1823.15*** *p139*
Knightly, John 60; Ontario, 1871 ***1823.15*** *p139*
Knighton, John; Maryland, 1720 ***1224.2*** *p66*
Knighton, Thomas; Maryland, 1670 ***2524.55*** *p131*
Kninski, Alexander; Maryland, 1910 ***3259.35*** *p27*
Knipe, James; New York, 1839 ***8197.10*** *p139*
Knipe, William; New England, 1750 ***1224.2*** *p66*
Knipenberger, Wilhelm; Port uncertain, 1764 ***2856.30*** *p235*
Knippenberger, Caspar; Port uncertain, 1796 ***2856.30*** *p235*
Knirk, Catherine; Vermont, 1803-1864 ***5900.10*** *p164*
Knittel, Franz; Port uncertain, 1737 ***2856.30*** *p235*
Kniveton, Mathew; Maryland, 1662 ***2524.55*** *p131*
Knjsiak, Joseph; Maryland, 1910 ***3259.35*** *p27*
Knobel, Jakob; Port uncertain, 1745 ***2856.30*** *p236*
Knobel, Johann Nikolaus; Port uncertain, 1764 ***2856.30*** *p236*
Knobler, Josef; Port uncertain, 1729 ***2856.30*** *p236*
Knoblin, Maria Elisabeth; Port uncertain, 1762 ***2856.30*** *p236*
Knobloch, Jacob; America, 1738 ***2856.30*** *p235*
Knobloch, Jacob; Port uncertain, 1738 ***2856.30*** *p235*
Knobloch, Johann Georg; Port uncertain, 1753 ***2856.30*** *p235*
Knobloch, Maria; Port uncertain, 1746 ***2856.30*** *p235*
Knobloch, Nikolaus; Port uncertain, 1754 ***2856.30*** *p235*
Knochenmann, David; America, 1740 ***2856.30*** *p235*
Knodel, Daniel; America, 1770 ***2856.30*** *p235*
Knodel, Johann George; New York, 1837 ***8197.10*** *p93*
Knodlin, Margarete; Port uncertain, 1796 ***2856.30*** *p236*
Knolber, Johan Philip; New York, 1836 ***8197.10*** *p246*
Knoll, Anna 39; Kansas, 1908-1910 ***9079.10*** *p10*
Knoll, Anton; Port uncertain, 1797 ***2856.30*** *p235*
Knoll, Balthasar; Port uncertain, 1732 ***2856.30*** *p235*
Knoll, Catherine 14; Kansas, 1908-1910 ***9079.10*** *p10*

Kohler, Wendel; America, 1741 2856.30 p256
With wife & child
Kohlin, Catharina; Port uncertain, 1766 2856.30 p256
Kohlmann, Sebastian; America, 1737 2856.30 p239
Kohn, Frederick 45; Ontario, 1871 1823.28 p53
Kohnin, Catharina; America, 1752 2856.30 p239
Kohwazk, Annie; Maryland, 1910 3259.35 p28
Koinovick, Frank; Maryland, 1910 3259.35 p28
Kokanterfer, Charles; Pennsylvania, 1777 4629.10 p11
Kolachowski, Audney; Maryland, 1910 3259.35 p28
Kolacz, Thomas; Maryland, 1910 3259.35 p28
Kolakavitch, Frank; Maryland, 1910 3259.35 p28
Kolakowski, Joseph; Maryland, 1910 3259.35 p28
Kolb, Andreas; America, 1763 2856.30 p239
With family
Kolb, Antoni; Port uncertain, 1762 2856.30 p239
Kolb, Georg Josef; America, 1806 2856.30 p239
Kolb, Georg Josef; America, 1816 2856.30 p239
Kolb, Henry; New York, 1839 8197.10 p320
Kolb, Jacob; New York, 1838 8197.10 p121
Kolb, Johan; New York, 1840 8197.10 p176
Kolb, Johann; Port uncertain, 1751 2856.30 p239
Kolb, Johann; Port uncertain, 1766 2856.30 p239
Kolb, Johann Andreas; Philadelphia, 1764 2856.30 p239
Kolb, John; Maryland, 1910 3259.35 p28
Kolb, Michael; Port uncertain, 1764 2856.30 p239
With wife & 4 children
Kolb, Nikolaus; Port uncertain, 1696 2856.30 p239
Kolb, Valentin; Port uncertain, 1783 2856.30 p239
With wife son & daughter
Kolblin, Jacob; Port uncertain, 1762 2856.30 p256
Kolbun, Johan; New York, 1807 8197.10 p43
Koler, Elis. Catharina; Port uncertain, 1793 2856.30 p256
Koler, Jacob; Port uncertain, 1790 2856.30 p239
Kolf, Johan; New York, 1840 8197.10 p176
Kolinewa, Mary; Maryland, 1910 3259.35 p28
Kolinski, George; Maryland, 1910 3259.35 p28
Kolisiskie, Frank; Maryland, 1910 3259.35 p28
Kolkowski, Joseph; Maryland, 1910 3259.35 p28
Kollarz, Charles; Maryland, 1910 3259.35 p28
Kolleanwicki, Katherine; Maryland, 1910 3259.35 p28
Koller, Miss; Port uncertain, 1793 2856.30 p256
Koller, Adolph 44; British Columbia, 1914 9196.1 p24
Koller, Adolph 44; Mississippi, 1914 9196.1 p24
Kollhaus, Peter; Port uncertain, 1784 2856.30 p239
Kolodsyski, Michael; Maryland, 1910 3259.35 p28
Kolokosski, Joseph; Maryland, 1910 3259.35 p28
Kolovinski, Mary; Maryland, 1910 3259.35 p28
Kolozy, John; Maryland, 1910 3259.35 p28
Kolsch, Elisabeth; Port uncertain, 1765 2856.30 p256
Kolski, Alexander; Maryland, 1910 3259.35 p28
Kolsmidt, Carl 45; Ontario, 1871 1823.28 p53
Kolub, Alexander; Maryland, 1910 3259.35 p28
Kolup, James; Maryland, 1910 3259.35 p28
Kolvaleski, John; Maryland, 1910 3259.35 p28
Kolwilski, James; Maryland, 1910 3259.35 p28
Komelsky, John; Maryland, 1910 3259.35 p29
Komjunz, Johann; Port uncertain, 1726 2856.30 p239
Komjunz, Johann; Port uncertain, 1748 2856.30 p239
Komle, Sebastian; Port uncertain, 1795 2856.30 p257
Komle, Sebastian; Port uncertain, 1796 2856.30 p257
Kompflieb, Hermann; America, 1741 2856.30 p240
Konarzofski, Frank; Maryland, 1910 3259.35 p29
Koneszna, John; Maryland, 1910 3259.35 p29
Konielski, Joseph; Maryland, 1910 3259.35 p29
Konig, Abraham; America, 1751 2856.30 p257
Konig, Abraham; America, 1751 2856.30 p257
With family
Konig, Anna Maria Stuhler; Port uncertain, 1784 2856.30 p257
Konig, Balthasar; America, 1751 2856.30 p257
Konig, Georg Friedrich; America, 1738 2856.30 p257
Konig, Georg Jacob; Port uncertain, 1781 2856.30 p257
Konig, Georg Michael; Port uncertain, 1737 2856.30 p257
Konig, Georg Peter; Port uncertain, 1764 2856.30 p257
Konig, Gottfried; America, 1752 2856.30 p257
Konig, Gottfried; Port uncertain, 1737 2856.30 p257
With wife 2 sons & 2 daughters
Konig, Jacob; America, 1744 2856.30 p257
Konig, Jakob; Port uncertain, 1764 2856.30 p257
Konig, Johann; Port uncertain, 1752 2856.30 p257
Konig, Josef; Port uncertain, 1725 2856.30 p257
Konig, Konrad; Port uncertain, 1764 2856.30 p257
Konig, Maria; Port uncertain, 1737 2856.30 p257
Konig, Maria Catharina; America, 1749 2856.30 p257
Konig, Michael; America, 1748 2856.30 p257
Konig, Michael; America, 1749 2856.30 p257
Konig, Nickel; America, 1749 2856.30 p257
Konig, Niklas; America, 1752 2856.30 p257
Konig, Niklas; America, 1752 2856.30 p257
With wife & 2 children
Konig, Niklas; Port uncertain, 1730 2856.30 p257
Konig, Peter; America, 1752 2856.30 p257
Konig, Peter; Port uncertain, 1756 2856.30 p257
Konig, Therese; Port uncertain, 1762 2856.30 p257
Konig, Thomas; Port uncertain, 1741 2856.30 p257
Konig, Wilhelm; Port uncertain, 1749 2856.30 p257
Konofska, Joseph; Maryland, 1910 3259.35 p29
Konofska, Teopl; Maryland, 1910 3259.35 p29
Konopacka, Blazej; Maryland, 1910 3259.35 p29
Konrad, Eva Maria Schneider; Port uncertain, 1700-1799 2856.30 p406
Konrad, John; New York, 1840 8197.10 p247
Konrad, Mathias; Port uncertain, 1789 2856.30 p240
Kontzsky, George; Maryland, 1910 3259.35 p29
Koockhart, Sebastian; America, 1739 2856.30 p240
Kopcszinski, Lizzie; Maryland, 1910 3259.35 p29
Kope, William; Pennsylvania, 1777 4629.10 p13
Koper, Frederick; Baltimore, 1858 3437.14 p62
Kopera, Joseph; Maryland, 1910 3259.35 p29
Kopera, Kazmer; Maryland, 1910 3259.35 p29
Kopf, Anna Catharina; America, 1752 2856.30 p240
Kopf, George William; New York, 1839 8197.10 p247
Kopf, Johann; Port uncertain, 1784 2856.30 p240
Wife: Mgdl. Kinder
Kopf, Melchior; Port uncertain, 1744 2856.30 p240
Kopf, Mgdl. Kinder *SEE* Kopf, Johann
Kopieczyk, Joseph; Maryland, 1910 3259.35 p29
Kopinska, Josephine; Maryland, 1910 3259.35 p29
Kopinski, Frank; Maryland, 1910 3259.35 p29
Kopitch, Joseph; Maryland, 1910 3259.35 p29
Kopka, William 43; Ontario, 1871 1823.28 p53
Koplanczk, Joseph; Maryland, 1910 3259.35 p29
Kopland, Frederick; Baltimore, 1848 6058.10 p42
Koplin, Gotlip 50; Ontario, 1871 1823.28 p53
Koplin, Henretia 50; Ontario, 1871 1823.28 p53
Kopman, Frederick; Baltimore, 1848 6058.10 p42
Kopp, Catharina; Port uncertain, 1747 2856.30 p240
Kopp, Christian; Port uncertain, 1800 2856.30 p240
Kopp, Daniel; Port uncertain, 1784 2856.30 p240
Kopp, Franz; Port uncertain, 1776 2856.30 p240
Kopp, Friedrich; Port uncertain, 1782 2856.30 p240
Kopp, Jacob; Pennsylvania, 1777 4629.10 p7
Kopp, Johann; Port uncertain, 1787 2856.30 p240
Kopp, Johann; Port uncertain, 1794 2856.30 p240
Kopp, Johann Georg; Port uncertain, 1764 2856.30 p240
Kopp, Johann Wilhelm; Port uncertain, 1762 2856.30 p240
Kopp, Matheis; Port uncertain, 1756 2856.30 p240
Kopp, Nikolaus; Port uncertain, 1762 2856.30 p240
Kopp, Otto H.; New York, 1840 8197.10 p177
Koppe, Friedrich; Port uncertain, 1797 2856.30 p241
Koppe, Johann; Port uncertain, 1784 2856.30 p241
Wife: Mgdl. Kinder
Koppe, Mgdl. Kinder *SEE* Koppe, Johann
Koppen, Mrs. Jacob; Port uncertain, 1771 2856.30 p241
Koppen, Magdalena; Port uncertain, 1771 2856.30 p241
Kopperich, Anna Maria; Port uncertain, 1754 2856.30 p241
Koprowski, Joseph; Maryland, 1910 3259.35 p29
Kopycinski, Theodore; Maryland, 1910 3259.35 p29
Korans, Samuel 20; Kansas, 1907-1910 9079.10 p16
Korb, Sebastian; Port uncertain, 1789 2856.30 p241
Korb, Sebastian; Port uncertain, 1790 2856.30 p241
Korber, Anna Elisabeth; America, 1751 2856.30 p257
Korber, Johann Michael; America, 1738 2856.30 p257
Korber, Konrad; America, 1751 2856.30 p257
Kordas, Joseph; Maryland, 1910 3259.35 p29
Kordonski, Josef; Maryland, 1910 3259.35 p29
Kordonski, Joseph; Maryland, 1910 3259.35 p29
Kordonski, Walenty; Maryland, 1910 3259.35 p29
Kordovski, Wawszyn; Maryland, 1910 3259.35 p29
Koretkowsky, Vladislow; Maryland, 1910 3259.35 p29
Korling, Mattheis; Port uncertain, 1739 2856.30 p258
Korlowska, James; Maryland, 1910 3259.35 p29
Korman, John 32; Ontario, 1871 1823.15 p139
Kormann, Anna Barbara; Port uncertain, 1749 2856.30 p241
Korn, Augustus; New York, 1839 8197.10 p247
Korn, Johann; Port uncertain, 1770 2856.30 p241
Korn, Martin; America, 1772 2856.30 p241
Korn, Martin; America, 1783 2856.30 p241
Korn, Mathias; Port uncertain, 1772 2856.30 p241
Korn, Valentin; America, 1763 2856.30 p241
Korn, Valentin; Port uncertain, 1772 2856.30 p241
Korn, Valentin Simon; America, 1764 2856.30 p241
Korner, Jakob; America, 1750 2856.30 p258
Kornhas, Johann; America, 1784 2856.30 p241
Kornhas, Johann; Port uncertain, 1783 2856.30 p241
Kororowski, Michael; Maryland, 1910 3259.35 p29
Koroveski, Joseph; Maryland, 1910 3259.35 p29
Korowkowski, Stanislaw; Maryland, 1910 3259.35 p29
Korprowski, Frank; Maryland, 1910 3259.35 p29
Korrenberg, Johann; America, 1783 2856.30 p241
Kortoske, Mr.; Quebec, 1856 9196.15 p7
Kortoske, Mrs.; Quebec, 1856 9196.15 p7
Korttman, Samuel 24; Ontario, 1871 1823.15 p139
Koryasyewski, Frank; Maryland, 1910 3259.35 p29
Korycki, John; Maryland, 1910 3259.35 p29
Korytowski, Christian; Maryland, 1910 3259.35 p29
Korzinska, Pelgra; Maryland, 1910 3259.35 p29
Korzynowsky, Cerin; Maryland, 1910 3259.35 p29
Kosajchski, Francia; Maryland, 1910 3259.35 p29
Kosakowski, Joseph; Maryland, 1910 3259.35 p29
Kosakowsky, Leon; Maryland, 1910 3259.35 p29
Kosalowsky, Naopol; Maryland, 1910 3259.35 p29
Koscinsky, Wincenty; Maryland, 1910 3259.35 p29
Koserski, Julius; Maryland, 1910 3259.35 p29
Koshiskie, Joseph; Maryland, 1910 3259.35 p29
Kosiba, Wojcich; Maryland, 1910 3259.35 p29
Kosie, Henry 40; Ontario, 1871 1823.15 p139
Kosinski, Felix; Maryland, 1910 3259.35 p29
Kosinskie, August; Maryland, 1910 3259.35 p29
Koski, A. 34; Alaska, 1917 9196.1 p46
Koski, A. 34; Whitehorse, Yukon, 1917 9196.1 p46
Koslofskie, Joseph; Maryland, 1910 3259.35 p29
Koslovski, August; Maryland, 1910 3259.35 p29
Kosmack, Ferdinand 38; Ontario, 1871 1823.28 p53
Kosoff, George 22; Alaska, 1917 9196.1 p47
Kosoff, George 22; Whitehorse, Yukon, 1917 9196.1 p47
Kossi, L.; Quebec, 1856 9196.15 p5
Kost, Franz; America, 1753 2856.30 p241
With wife & 4 children
Koster, Eleonore Cath.; America, 1747 2856.30 p258
Koster, Jerg; America, 1749 2856.30 p241
Koster, John; New York, 1803 8197.10 p13
Kostoski, James; Maryland, 1910 3259.35 p29
Kostowski, John; Maryland, 1910 3259.35 p29
Kosycki, Stephen; Maryland, 1910 3259.35 p29
Kosyki, Adam; Maryland, 1910 3259.35 p29
Kot, Mary; Maryland, 1910 3259.35 p30
Kotowschski, Alex; Maryland, 1910 3259.35 p30
Kotowsky, Boleslaw; Maryland, 1910 3259.35 p30
Kotsdrachtski, Boroly; Maryland, 1910 3259.35 p30
Kottler, Anton; America, 1744 2856.30 p241
Kottler, Anton; America, 1746 2856.30 p241
Kottmann, Christopher 52; Ontario, 1871 1823.28 p53
Kotz, Anna Elisabeth; Port uncertain, 1748 2856.30 p258
Kotz, Johann David; Port uncertain, 1785 2856.30 p258
Kouloneis, S. 28; Alaska, 1917 9196.1 p46
Kouloneis, S. 28; Whitehorse, Yukon, 1917 9196.1 p46
Kouski, James; Maryland, 1910 3259.35 p30
Kovalewski, Stansilaus; Maryland, 1910 3259.35 p30
Kovalske, Mike; Maryland, 1910 3259.35 p30
Kovieczny, Wojciech; Maryland, 1910 3259.35 p30
Kovjack, Henry; Maryland, 1910 3259.35 p30
Kowalauski, Martin; Maryland, 1910 3259.35 p30
Kowaleski, Joseph H.; Maryland, 1910 3259.35 p30
Kowalewski, Andrew; Maryland, 1910 3259.35 p30
Kowalewski, Jacob; Maryland, 1910 3259.35 p30
Kowalewski, John W.; Maryland, 1910 3259.35 p30
Kowalewski, Martin; Maryland, 1910 3259.35 p30
Kowalewski, Stanislau; Maryland, 1910 3259.35 p30
Kowaloska, Kamila; Maryland, 1910 3259.35 p30
Kowalowski, Stanislaus; Maryland, 1910 3259.35 p30
Kowalska, Frank; Maryland, 1910 3259.35 p30
Kowalski, Anna; Maryland, 1910 3259.35 p30
Kowalski, Anton; Maryland, 1910 3259.35 p30
Kowalski, Elizabeth; Maryland, 1910 3259.35 p30
Kowalski, Frank; Maryland, 1910 3259.35 p30
Kowalski, Frank B.; Maryland, 1910 3259.35 p30
Kowalski, Jacob; Maryland, 1910 3259.35 p30
Kowalski, John; Maryland, 1910 3259.35 p30
Kowalski, Joseph; Maryland, 1910 3259.35 p30
Kowalski, Rose P.; Maryland, 1910 3259.35 p30
Kowalski, Stanislaus; Maryland, 1910 3259.35 p30
Kowalski, Stanislaw; Maryland, 1910 3259.35 p30
Kowalski, Stephen; Maryland, 1910 3259.35 p30
Kowalski, Stevan; Maryland, 1910 3259.35 p30
Kowalsky, Antony; Maryland, 1910 3259.35 p30
Kowartksa, John; Maryland, 1910 3259.35 p30
Kowinski, George; Maryland, 1910 3259.35 p30
Kowlowski, John; Maryland, 1910 3259.35 p30
Kowlsfki, Peter; Maryland, 1910 3259.35 p30
Koz, Nikol; Port uncertain, 1793 2856.30 p258
Kozak, Joseph; Maryland, 1910 3259.35 p30
Kozepka, Peter; Maryland, 1910 3259.35 p30
Kozepsky, Kazimer; Maryland, 1910 3259.35 p30
Kozera, Alexander; Maryland, 1910 3259.35 p30
Kozews, Walter; Maryland, 1910 3259.35 p30
Kozierski, Stanislaw; Maryland, 1910 3259.35 p30
Kozlawski, Adam; Maryland, 1910 3259.35 p30
Kozloska, Joseph; Maryland, 1910 3259.35 p30
Kozlowski, John; Maryland, 1910 3259.35 p30
Kozlowski, John; Maryland, 1910 3259.35 p31
Kozlowski, Joseph; Maryland, 1910 3259.35 p31
Kozlowski, Stanislaus; Maryland, 1910 3259.35 p31
Kozlowsky, Antony; Maryland, 1910 3259.35 p31

Kozlowsky, Michael; Maryland, 1910 *3259.35 p31*
Kozlowsky, Tomas; Maryland, 1910 *3259.35 p31*
Kozlsoski, Joseph; Maryland, 1910 *3259.35 p31*
Kozniersky, Michael; Maryland, 1910 *3259.35 p31*
Kozowski, James; Maryland, 1910 *3259.35 p31*
Koztowski, Anthony; Maryland, 1910 *3259.35 p31*
Kraehmer, Anna Margarete; Port uncertain, 1766 *2856.30 p241*
Kraehmer, Henrich; Port uncertain, 1771 *2856.30 p241*
Kraehmer, Johann Philipp; Port uncertain, 1784 *2856.30 p242*
Kraemer, A. M. Roetz *SEE* Kraemer, Wendelin
Kraemer, Gottlieb; Port uncertain, 1765 *2856.30 p241*
Kraemer, Johann Philipp; Port uncertain, 1784 *2856.30 p242*
Kraemer, Josef; Port uncertain, 1791 *2856.30 p241*
Kraemer, Margarete; Port uncertain, 1765 *2856.30 p242*
Kraemer, Margarete; Port uncertain, 1777 *2856.30 p242*
Kraemer, Mrs. Peter; Port uncertain, 1764 *2856.30 p242*
Kraemer, Wendelin; America, 1764 *2856.30 p242*
Wife: A. M. Roetz
Krafft, Andreas; Port uncertain, 1771 *2856.30 p242*
Krafft, Anna Catharina; Port uncertain, 1736 *2856.30 p242*
Krafft, Christina; Port uncertain, 1769 *2856.30 p242*
Krafft, Ignaz; Port uncertain, 1794 *2856.30 p242*
Krafft, Johann; Port uncertain, 1764 *2856.30 p242*
Krafft, Johann; Port uncertain, 1767 *2856.30 p242*
Krafft, Johann; Port uncertain, 1790 *2856.30 p242*
Krafft, Johann Valentin; America, 1742 *2856.30 p242*
Krafft, Paul; Port uncertain, 1752 *2856.30 p242*
Krafft, Philipp; Port uncertain, 1785 *2856.30 p242*
Krafft, Philipp Ludwig; Port uncertain, 1764 *2856.30 p242*
Kraft, Miss; Port uncertain, 1762 *2856.30 p126*
Kraft, Anna Maria; America, 1764 *2856.30 p126*
Kraft, Dave 24; Kansas, 1892-1910 *9079.10 p12*
Kraft, Henry 28; Ontario, 1871 *1823.15 p139*
Kraft, Jacob 55; Kansas, 1892-1910 *9079.10 p12*
Kraft, John; New York, 1838 *8197.10 p121*
Kraft, John 19; Ontario, 1871 *1823.15 p139*
Kraft, Nicolaus; Port uncertain, 1732 *2856.30 p242*
Kraft, Nicolaus; Port uncertain, 1748 *2856.30 p242*
Kraft, Scharoletta 52; Kansas, 1892-1910 *9079.10 p12*
Krag, Ludvig; New York, 1831 *8197.10 p246*
Krahe, Caspar; America, 1744 *2856.30 p247*
With wife & children
Krahmann, Anna Barbara; Port uncertain, 1751 *2856.30 p247*
Krahmer, Barthel; Port uncertain, 1754 *2856.30 p242*
Krahmer, Christof; America, 1738 *2856.30 p248*
Krahmer, Eitel Albrecht; America, 1789 *2856.30 p242*
Krahmer, Gertrud; Port uncertain, 1770 *2856.30 p247*
Krahmer, Hans Martin; America, 1738 *2856.30 p248*
Krahmer, Martin; Port uncertain, 1785 *2856.30 p248*
With wife
Krahmer, Samuel; Port uncertain, 1764 *2856.30 p248*
Krahmerin, Anna Catharina; Port uncertain, 1737 *2856.30 p248*
Krahnin, Magdalena; Port uncertain, 1774 *2856.30 p242*
Kraiger, Tina; Maryland, 1910 *3259.35 p31*
Kralik, Tomacz; Maryland, 1910 *3259.35 p31*
Kramb, Johanna; Port uncertain, 1762 *2856.30 p242*
Kramer, Adam; Port uncertain, 1761 *2856.30 p248*
Kramer, Anna Maria; Port uncertain, 1783 *2856.30 p242*
Kramer, Catharina; Port uncertain, 1755 *2856.30 p248*
Kramer, Christian 9; Kansas, 1909-1910 *9079.10 p26*
Kramer, Christian 31; Kansas, 1909-1910 *9079.10 p26*
Kramer, Francis; New York, 1807 *8197.10 p37*
Kramer, Franz; Port uncertain, 1785 *2856.30 p248*
Kramer, Georg; America, 1779 *2856.30 p242*
Kramer, Georg; America, 1781 *2856.30 p242*
Kramer, Georg; Port uncertain, 1784 *2856.30 p243*
With wife & 2 children
Kramer, Georg; Port uncertain, 1784 *2856.30 p248*
With wife & 2 children
Kramer, Henrich; Port uncertain, 1720 *2856.30 p242*
Kramer, Issak; Port uncertain, 1804 *2856.30 p242*
With family
Kramer, Jacob; Port uncertain, 1776 *2856.30 p242*
Kramer, Jacob; Port uncertain, 1795 *2856.30 p242*
Kramer, Jacob; Port uncertain, 1796 *2856.30 p242*
Kramer, Jadwiga J.; Maryland, 1910 *3259.35 p31*
Kramer, Jakob; Port uncertain, 1753 *2856.30 p248*
Kramer, Johann; Port uncertain, 1753 *2856.30 p248*
Kramer, Johann; Port uncertain, 1764 *2856.30 p248*
Kramer, Johann Adam; Port uncertain, 1783 *2856.30 p248*
Kramer, Johann Georg; America, 1769 *2856.30 p248*
Kramer, John; New York, 1838 *8197.10 p121*
Kramer, Karolina; Port uncertain, 1790 *2856.30 p248*
Kramer, Ludwig; America, 1791 *2856.30 p242*
Kramer, Martin, Sr.; America, 1779 *2856.30 p242*
Kramer, Martin, Jr.; America, 1779 *2856.30 p242*
Kramer, Martin, Sr.; America, 1781 *2856.30 p242*
Kramer, Martin, Jr.; America, 1781 *2856.30 p242*
Kramer, Michael; America, 1750 *2856.30 p248*
With wife
Kramer, Michael; Port uncertain, 1770 *2856.30 p242*
Kramer, Philipp; Port uncertain, 1802 *2856.30 p248*
Kramer, Philipp Henrich; Port uncertain, 1787 *2856.30 p248*
Kramer, Sophia 26; Kansas, 1909-1910 *9079.10 p26*
Krammer, Joseph; New York, 1835 *8197.10 p310*
Kramp, Johanna; Port uncertain, 1762 *2856.30 p242*
Kranckel, Peter; Port uncertain, 1729 *2856.30 p248*
Krandler, Christof; America, 1750 *2856.30 p248*
With wife & child
Krankel, Adam; Port uncertain, 1780 *2856.30 p248*
Krans, Paul; Maryland, 1910 *3259.35 p31*
Krantzmann, Johann Georg; Port uncertain, 1754 *2856.30 p243*
Kranz, Catherine 40; Ontario, 1871 *1823.28 p53*
Kranz, Nicholos 37; Ontario, 1871 *1823.28 p53*
Kraslia, John; Maryland, 1910 *3259.35 p31*
Krassin, Catharina; America, 1744 *2856.30 p248*
Kratz, Anna Margarete; Port uncertain, 1786 *2856.30 p144*
Kratz, Charles; Maryland, 1910 *3259.35 p31*
Kratz, Johann; Port uncertain, 1722 *2856.30 p243*
Kratz, John; New York, 1839 *8197.10 p247*
Kratzert, Anna Elisabeth; Port uncertain, 1750 *2856.30 p144*
Kratzert, Eva Elisabeth; Port uncertain, 1750 *2856.30 p144*
Kratzert, Johann Adam; Port uncertain, 1774 *2856.30 p243*
Kratzmann, Johann Georg; Port uncertain, 1753 *2856.30 p243*
Kratzmann, Johann Georg; Port uncertain, 1754 *2856.30 p243*
Kraus, Christina Barba; Port uncertain, 1751 *2856.30 p243*
Kraus, Franz Philipp; Port uncertain, 1769 *2856.30 p243*
Kraus, Georg; America, 1751 *2856.30 p243*
With wife & 2 children
Kraus, Johann Georg; America, 1751 *2856.30 p243*
With wife & child
Kraus, Lillian; Maryland, 1910 *3259.35 p31*
Kraus, Michael; America, 1750 *2856.30 p243*
Krause, Anna Maria; America, 1765 *2856.30 p243*
With husband
Kraushaar, Nicolas; Port uncertain, 1783 *2856.30 p243*
Kraushaar, Nicolas; Port uncertain, 1783 *2856.30 p243*
With wife 4 sons & 2 daughters
Krauska, Agnes; Maryland, 1910 *3259.35 p31*
Krauss, Anton; Port uncertain, 1792 *2856.30 p243*
Krauss, Catharina; Port uncertain, 1783 *2856.30 p243*
Krauss, Franz Xaver; Port uncertain, 1774 *2856.30 p243*
Krauss, Jakob; America, 1749 *2856.30 p243*
Krauss, Johann; Port uncertain, 1787 *2856.30 p243*
Krauss, Johann Georg; America, 1749 *2856.30 p243*
Krauss, Johann Georg; America, 1754 *2856.30 p149*
Krauss, Johann Georg; America, 1754 *2856.30 p243*
With wife & children
Krauss, Johann Niklas; America, 1749 *2856.30 p243*
Krauss, Philipp Jakob; Port uncertain, 1749 *2856.30 p243*
With wife & 5 children
Krauss, Simon; America, 1749 *2856.30 p243*
Krauss, Wilzum; New York, 1838 *8197.10 p122*
Krauter, Balthasar; Port uncertain, 1760 *2856.30 p248*
Krauter, Elisabeth; Port uncertain, 1767 *2856.30 p248*
Krauth, Catharina; Port uncertain, 1768 *2856.30 p244*
Krauth, Jacob Friedrich; Port uncertain, 1781 *2856.30 p244*
Krauth, Ludwig; Port uncertain, 1782 *2856.30 p244*
Krawczynski, George; Maryland, 1910 *3259.35 p31*
Krawzyk, Anthony; Maryland, 1910 *3259.35 p31*
Kraz, Anna Margarete; Port uncertain, 1781 *2856.30 p244*
Kraz, Martin; Maryland, 1910 *3259.35 p31*
Krazer, Anna Maria; Port uncertain, 1795 *2856.30 p244*
Krazinski, Walenty; Maryland, 1910 *3259.35 p31*
Krebber, Jakob; America, 1755 *2856.30 p244*
Krebber, Jakob; America, 1791 *2856.30 p244*
Krebil, Christian; America, 1744 *2856.30 p244*
Krebin, Maria Barbara; Port uncertain, 1775 *2856.30 p244*
Krebs, Anna Maria; Port uncertain, 1762 *2856.30 p244*
Krebs, Anna Maria; Port uncertain, 1763 *2856.30 p244*
Krebs, Christian; Port uncertain, 1753 *2856.30 p244*
Krebs, Georg; Port uncertain, 1769 *2856.30 p244*
Krebs, Henrich; Port uncertain, 1779 *2856.30 p244*
Krebs, Mrs. Jacob; Port uncertain, 1737 *2856.30 p244*
Krebs, Johann Jakob; Port uncertain, 1752 *2856.30 p244*
Krebs, Marianna; Port uncertain, 1762 *2856.30 p244*
Krebs, Marianna; Port uncertain, 1763 *2856.30 p244*
Krebs, Philipp; America, 1751 *2856.30 p244*
Krebuhl, Johann; America, 1733 *2856.30 p244*
Krechtler, Catharina; Port uncertain, 1789 *2856.30 p244*
Kreeger, Frederic 26; Ontario, 1871 *1823.28 p53*
Krefka, Anthony; Maryland, 1910 *3259.35 p31*
Krehbuhl, Jacob; America, 1738 *2856.30 p244*
Krehbuhl, Jacob; America, 1788 *2856.30 p244*
Krehbuhl, Michael; America, 1793 *2856.30 p244*
Krehbuhl, Peter; America, 1739 *2856.30 p244*
Krehebuhl, Johann; America, 1744 *2856.30 p244*
Krehebuhl, Johann; America, 1744 *2856.30 p244*
With wife & 3 children
Kreher, Anna Margarete; America, 1752 *2856.30 p244*
With child
Kreim, Henrich; Port uncertain, 1782 *2856.30 p245*
Krein, John 50; Ontario, 1871 *1823.15 p139*
Kreis, Philipp; Port uncertain, 1764 *2856.30 p245*
Kreischer, Heinrich; Port uncertain, 1745 *2856.30 p245*
Kreischer, Johann; Port uncertain, 1739 *2856.30 p245*
Kreischer, Johann Jost; America, 1749 *2856.30 p245*
Kreischer, Johann Niklas; America, 1749 *2856.30 p245*
Kreischer, Philipp; America, 1749 *2856.30 p245*
Kreiter, George; New York, 1840 *8197.10 p247*
Kreiter, Philip; New York, 1840 *8197.10 p247*
Krekorich, Julius 30; Alaska, 1914 *9196.1 p24*
Krelinski, Mary; Maryland, 1910 *3259.35 p31*
Kremer, Barbara; Port uncertain, 1736 *2856.30 p245*
Kremer, Georg; Port uncertain, 1691 *2856.30 p245*
Kremer, Johann Georg; Port uncertain, 1755 *2856.30 p245*
Kremer, Michael; Pennsylvania, 1777 *4629.10 p12*
Kremer, Peter; America, 1749 *2856.30 p245*
Kremer, Peter; Port uncertain, 1749 *2856.30 p245*
Kremnau, Maria; Port uncertain, 1744 *2856.30 p245*
Kremski, Joseph; Maryland, 1910 *3259.35 p31*
Krener, Jacob; Pennsylvania, 1786 *4629.10 p51*
Krenkel, Andreas; Port uncertain, 1764 *2856.30 p245*
Krenkel, Matthaus; Port uncertain, 1784 *2856.30 p245*
Krentel, Nicolaus; Port uncertain, 1779 *2856.30 p245*
Krenzler, Kunigunda; Port uncertain, 1761 *2856.30 p245*
Krepp, Crego; New York, New York, 1856 *6058.10 p46*
Kreps, Adam; America, 1738 *2856.30 p245*
Kreps, Philipp; America, 1753 *2856.30 p245*
Kresler, Philipp; America, 1732 *2856.30 p70*
Kress, A. M.; America, 1748 *2856.30 p189*
Kress, Anna Margarete; America, 1748 *2856.30 p245*
With husband
Kress, Jakob; America, 1741 *2856.30 p245*
With wife & child
Kresser, Niklas; Port uncertain, 1783 *2856.30 p245*
Kressler, Adam 36; Ontario, 1871 *1823.15 p139*
Kretsch, Johann Lambert; Port uncertain, 1785 *2856.30 p245*
Kretts, Henrick; Georgia, 1698 *1640.13 p66*
Kretts, Paul; Georgia, 1698 *1640.13 p66*
Kretzschmann, Henry; New York, 1838 *8197.10 p247*
Kreuger, Mary; Ontario, 1871 *1823.28 p53*
Kreuscher, Philipp; Port uncertain, 1749 *2856.30 p246*
With wife & children
Kreuser, Wilhelm; Port uncertain, 1745 *2856.30 p246*
Kreuser, Wilhelm; Port uncertain, 1788 *2856.30 p246*
Kreusser, Christof; America, 1752 *2856.30 p245*
Kreutzer, Maria Elisabeth; Port uncertain, 1789 *2856.30 p245*
Kreutzer, Niclas; Port uncertain, 1734 *2856.30 p245*
Kreuzbauer, . . .; America, 1774 *2856.30 p246*
Krewet, Charles; Vermont, 1876-1961 *5900.10 p172*
Krewet, Conrad; New York, 1840 *8197.10 p176*
Krewet, Delia; Vermont, 1876-1953 *5900.10 p172*
Krey, Hans; Port uncertain, 1750 *2856.30 p246*
Kreyder, Johann Jacob; Port uncertain, 1746 *2856.30 p246*
Kreyn, David; Port uncertain, 1733 *2856.30 p246*
Kreys, Catharina; Port uncertain, 1773 *2856.30 p246*
Krez, Zacharias; Port uncertain, 1773 *2856.30 p246*
Kric, John; Maryland, 1910 *3259.35 p31*
Kriechbaum, Johann Konrad; America, 1752 *2856.30 p226*
Krieg, Franz Josef; Port uncertain, 1763 *2856.30 p246*
Krieg, Johann; Port uncertain, 1746 *2856.30 p246*
Krieg, Marianna; Port uncertain, 1766 *2856.30 p246*
Krieg, Sophie; America, 1757 *2856.30 p246*
With husband & 4 children
Krieger, Caspar; Port uncertain, 1783 *2856.30 p246*
Krieger, Christof; Port uncertain, 1792 *2856.30 p246*
Krieger, Elisabeth; Port uncertain, 1757 *2856.30 p246*
Krieger, Gorg; America, 1740 *2856.30 p246*
Krieger, Jacob; Port uncertain, 1797 *2856.30 p246*
Krieger, John E.; Maryland, 1910 *3259.35 p31*
Krieger, Peter; Port uncertain, 1828 *2856.30 p246*

Krieger, Philipp Daniel; Port uncertain, 1778 ***2856.30*** *p246*
Kriehofer, Reimund; Port uncertain, 1755 ***2856.30*** *p246*
Kriehofer, Reimund; Port uncertain, 1785 ***2856.30*** *p246*
Krier, Frederick 38; Ontario, 1871 ***1823.28*** *p53*
Krier, Johanna 56; Ontario, 1871 ***1823.28*** *p53*
Krier, Martin; New York, 1836-1838 ***8197.10*** *p121*
Krigbaum, Magdalena; Port uncertain, 1765 ***2856.30*** *p246*
Krigner, Christian 34; Ontario, 1871 ***1823.15*** *p139*
Krim, Erasmus; America, 1741 ***2856.30*** *p246*
Krim, Feltin; America, 1740 ***2856.30*** *p246*
Krim, Johann; America, 1738 ***2856.30*** *p246*
Krim, Martin; America, 1738 ***2856.30*** *p246*
Krim, Wendel; America, 1754 ***2856.30*** *p246*
Krimling, Josef; Port uncertain, 1781 ***2856.30*** *p246*
Krimus, Jaque; America, 1737 ***2856.30*** *p70*
Kring, Clark 39; Ontario, 1871 ***1823.22*** *p88*
Kring, Mary 4; Ontario, 1871 ***1823.22*** *p88*
Kriniciak, John; Maryland, 1910 ***3259.35*** *p31*
Kriniciak, Joseph; Maryland, 1910 ***3259.35*** *p31*
Krishofka, Katharine; Maryland, 1910 ***3259.35*** *p31*
Kristiansen, M. 28; British Columbia, 1912 ***9196.1*** *p15*
Kristiansen, M. 28; San Francisco, 1912 ***9196.1*** *p15*
Kristianson, Albin; Boston, 1903 ***3437.14*** *p135*
Kristineck, Wladislaw; Maryland, 1910 ***3259.35*** *p31*
Kristinson, P. E. 49; British Columbia, 1912 ***9196.1*** *p15*
Kristkievicz, Stanislaw; Maryland, 1910 ***3259.35*** *p31*
Krjiskowski, Michael; Maryland, 1910 ***3259.35*** *p31*
Krmarra, Frank; Maryland, 1910 ***3259.35*** *p31*
Kroasen, Francis; Pennsylvania, 1777 ***4629.10*** *p26*
Kroasen, Francis; Pennsylvania, 1779 ***4629.10*** *p36*
Krob, Catharina; Port uncertain, 1759 ***2856.30*** *p147*
Krob, Catharina; Port uncertain, 1759 ***2856.30*** *p247*
Krober, Valentin; Port uncertain, 1791 ***2856.30*** *p248*
Krohl, Charolotte 25; Kansas, 1910 ***9079.10*** *p46*
Krohl, George 30; Kansas, 1907-1910 ***9079.10*** *p46*
Krohn, Josef; Port uncertain, 1752 ***2856.30*** *p247*
With wife & 2 children
Krohner, Adam; Port uncertain, 1741 ***2856.30*** *p248*
Krohner, Anna Maria; Port uncertain, 1788 ***2856.30*** *p248*
Krohner, Joh. Jacob, Jr.; America, 1751 ***2856.30*** *p248*
Krohner, Joh. Jacob, Jr.; Port uncertain, 1751 ***2856.30*** *p248*
Krol, James; Maryland, 1910 ***3259.35*** *p31*
Krol, John; Maryland, 1910 ***3259.35*** *p31*
Krol, Katherina; Maryland, 1910 ***3259.35*** *p31*
Krolcarek, Marcin; Maryland, 1910 ***3259.35*** *p31*
Krolezyk, Peter; Maryland, 1910 ***3259.35*** *p31*
Kroll, Martin; America, 1754 ***2856.30*** *p247*
Kromak, Joseph; Maryland, 1910 ***3259.35*** *p31*
Kromer, Anna Maria; Port uncertain, 1783 ***2856.30*** *p242*
Kron, Hubert; Port uncertain, 1781 ***2856.30*** *p247*
Kron, Konrad; Port uncertain, 1784 ***2856.30*** *p147*
Kronauer, Agathe; Port uncertain, 1786 ***2856.30*** *p247*
Kroner, Hans Georg; Port uncertain, 1753 ***2856.30*** *p248*
Kroner, Jacob, Jr.; America, 1751 ***2856.30*** *p151*
Kroner, Joseph; Pennsylvania, 1834 ***6058.10*** *p11*
Kronnenberger, Magnus; Port uncertain, 1784 ***2856.30*** *p247*
Kronner, Philipp; Port uncertain, 1802 ***2856.30*** *p248*
Krook, August; New York, 1826 ***8197.10*** *p336*
Krop, Dorathe 70; Ontario, 1871 ***1823.28*** *p53*
Kropf, Catharina; Port uncertain, 1746 ***2856.30*** *p247*
Kropp, Felix; Maryland, 1910 ***3259.35*** *p31*
Kropp, Frank; Maryland, 1910 ***3259.35*** *p31*
Kroskowski, Frank; Maryland, 1910 ***3259.35*** *p31*
Krotz, Franz Anton; Port uncertain, 1806 ***2856.30*** *p247*
Krotz, Konrad; America, 1753 ***2856.30*** *p247*
Krouchuski, Jacob; Maryland, 1910 ***3259.35*** *p31*
Krouchuski, William; Maryland, 1910 ***3259.35*** *p31*
Krouse, Amaudas 32; Ontario, 1871 ***1823.15*** *p139*
Krowkowski, Carl; Maryland, 1910 ***3259.35*** *p31*
Krowszyk, Stanislaus; Maryland, 1910 ***3259.35*** *p31*
Kru, Alex 22; Kansas, 1910 ***9079.10*** *p47*
Kru, Henry 23; Kansas, 1908-1910 ***9079.10*** *p53*
Kru, Jacob 35; Kansas, 1906-1910 ***9079.10*** *p46*
Kru, Margaret 33; Kansas, 1910 ***9079.10*** *p46*
Kru, Mary 20; Kansas, 1910 ***9079.10*** *p53*
Krub, Henrich; Port uncertain, 1770 ***2856.30*** *p247*
Krue, Joseph; Maryland, 1910 ***3259.35*** *p31*
Kruer, Fredrick 66; Ontario, 1871 ***1823.28*** *p53*
Kruer, Fredricka 66; Ontario, 1871 ***1823.28*** *p53*
Kruer, John 64; Ontario, 1871 ***1823.28*** *p53*
Krug, Adam 34; Kansas, 1876-1910 ***9079.10*** *p31*
Krug, Alex 30; Kansas, 1900-1910 ***9079.10*** *p49*
Krug, Alexander 10; Kansas, 1900-1910 ***9079.10*** *p36*
Krug, Anna 39; Kansas, 1900-1910 ***9079.10*** *p35*
Krug, Anna 54; Kansas, 1875-1910 ***9079.10*** *p26*
Krug, Anna E. 19; Kansas, 1892-1910 ***9079.10*** *p21*
Krug, Catherina 59; Kansas, 1899-1910 ***9079.10*** *p21*
Krug, Frederic 22; Kansas, 1899-1910 ***9079.10*** *p21*
Krug, G. J. 51; Kansas, 1890-1910 ***9079.10*** *p44*
Krug, George 14; Kansas, 1900-1910 ***9079.10*** *p35*
Krug, George 64; Kansas, 1899-1910 ***9079.10*** *p21*
Krug, George, Jr. 38; Kansas, 1900-1910 ***9079.10*** *p35*
Krug, George Jacob 29; Kansas, 1898-1910 ***9079.10*** *p49*
Krug, Henry 24; Kansas, 1910 ***9079.10*** *p45*
Krug, Henry 32; Kansas, 1910 ***9079.10*** *p42*
Krug, Henry 61; Kansas, 1876-1910 ***9079.10*** *p48*
Krug, Henry, Jr. 27; Kansas, 1910 ***9079.10*** *p51*
Krug, Jacob 87; Kansas, 1890-1910 ***9079.10*** *p44*
Krug, Jacob A. 36; Kansas, 1876-1910 ***9079.10*** *p35*
Krug, John Henry 57; Kansas, 1892-1910 ***9079.10*** *p51*
Krug, John J. 55; Kansas, 1875-1910 ***9079.10*** *p26*
Krug, Katherine 60; Kansas, 1910 ***9079.10*** *p48*
Krug, Katie 13; Kansas, 1900-1910 ***9079.10*** *p35*
Krug, Martha 28; Kansas, 1910 ***9079.10*** *p49*
Krug, Mary 19; Kansas, 1910 ***9079.10*** *p26*
Krug, Mary 28; Kansas, 1910 ***9079.10*** *p49*
Krug, Mary 30; Kansas, 1900-1910 ***9079.10*** *p35*
Krug, Mary 46; Kansas, 1910 ***9079.10*** *p51*
Krug, Mary 51; Kansas, 1910 ***9079.10*** *p44*
Krug, Matilda 31; Kansas, 1910 ***9079.10*** *p44*
Krug, Mollie 25; Kansas, 1910 ***9079.10*** *p42*
Krug, Peter 24; Kansas, 1899-1910 ***9079.10*** *p21*
Krug, Philip 26; Kansas, 1899-1910 ***9079.10*** *p21*
Krug, Sophia 18; Kansas, 1899-1910 ***9079.10*** *p21*
Krug, Victor P. 5; Kansas, 1910 ***9079.10*** *p35*
Kruger, Mr.; Port uncertain, 1790 ***2856.30*** *p247*
Kruger, Charles 45; Ontario, 1871 ***1823.15*** *p139*
Kruger, George William; New York, 1840 ***8197.10*** *p247*
Kruger, James; Maryland, 1910 ***3259.35*** *p31*
Kruger, John 46; Ontario, 1871 ***1823.15*** *p139*
Kruger, Ludwig; Port uncertain, 1783 ***2856.30*** *p248*
Kruger, Roman; Maryland, 1910 ***3259.35*** *p32*
Krugiski, Martin; Maryland, 1910 ***3259.35*** *p32*
Kruk, John; Maryland, 1910 ***3259.35*** *p32*
Krukenberger, Adam; Port uncertain, 1751 ***2856.30*** *p247*
Krulikowski, Josef; Maryland, 1910 ***3259.35*** *p32*
Krum, Philipp; America, 1741 ***2856.30*** *p247*
Krumbach, Jakob; Port uncertain, 1749 ***2856.30*** *p247*
Krumer, Jacob; Port uncertain, 1768 ***2856.30*** *p247*
Krumm, Georg; Port uncertain, 1769 ***2856.30*** *p54*
Krumm, Konrad; New York, 1838 ***8197.10*** *p121*
Krummenauer, Maria Elisabeth; Port uncertain, 1792 ***2856.30*** *p247*
Krunsky, Andrew 67; Ontario, 1871 ***1823.28*** *p53*
Krup, Anna Maria; Port uncertain, 1754 ***2856.30*** *p247*
Krupensick, Michael; Maryland, 1910 ***3259.35*** *p32*
Krupp, Greyor; New York, New York, 1856 ***6058.10*** *p46*
Kruse, August 30; Ontario, 1871 ***1823.15*** *p139*
Kruse, August 66; Ontario, 1871 ***1823.15*** *p139*
Kruse, Claus 48; Ontario, 1871 ***1823.15*** *p139*
Krusheck, Stanislow; Maryland, 1910 ***3259.35*** *p32*
Krusinski, Casimar; Maryland, 1910 ***3259.35*** *p32*
Krusniewski, Benjamin; Maryland, 1910 ***3259.35*** *p32*
Krutz, Minie 15; Ontario, 1871 ***1823.28*** *p53*
Kruzla, Peter; Maryland, 1910 ***3259.35*** *p32*
Krygier, Joseph; Maryland, 1910 ***3259.35*** *p32*
Krymski, Pawel; Maryland, 1910 ***3259.35*** *p32*
Krymski, Stanislaus; Maryland, 1910 ***3259.35*** *p32*
Krysiak, Stephan; Maryland, 1910 ***3259.35*** *p32*
Kryvoch, Julia; Maryland, 1910 ***3259.35*** *p32*
Ksiazck, Anna; Maryland, 1910 ***3259.35*** *p32*
Ksiczogsolska, John; Maryland, 1910 ***3259.35*** *p32*
Ksiniski, Andy; Maryland, 1910 ***3259.35*** *p32*
Kuava, Wadwaf; Maryland, 1910 ***3259.35*** *p32*
Kubeck, Johann; Port uncertain, 1764 ***2856.30*** *p253*
Kubel, Jakob; Port uncertain, 1749 ***2856.30*** *p248*
Kubel, Johann; Port uncertain, 1750 ***2856.30*** *p253*
Kubenich, Konrad; Port uncertain, 1772 ***2856.30*** *p253*
Kuber, Henrich; Port uncertain, 1786 ***2856.30*** *p248*
Kubisky, Felix; Maryland, 1910 ***3259.35*** *p32*
Kubler, Anton; Port uncertain, 1746 ***2856.30*** *p253*
Kubler, Elisabeth; Port uncertain, 1792 ***2856.30*** *p253*
Kubli, Ms.; Port uncertain, 1795 ***2856.30*** *p253*
Kublin, Barbara; Port uncertain, 1759 ***2856.30*** *p253*
Kubrvik, Mary; Maryland, 1910 ***3259.35*** *p32*
Kuc, Henry; Maryland, 1910 ***3259.35*** *p32*
Kuc, John; Maryland, 1910 ***3259.35*** *p32*
Kuc, Joseph; Maryland, 1910 ***3259.35*** *p32*
Kuc, Michael; Maryland, 1910 ***3259.35*** *p32*
Kuc, Samuel; Maryland, 1910 ***3259.35*** *p32*
Kuc, Stephen; Maryland, 1910 ***3259.35*** *p32*
Kuchanski, Welenty; Maryland, 1910 ***3259.35*** *p32*
Kucharski, John; Maryland, 1910 ***3259.35*** *p32*
Kuchenmeister, Christopher 72; Ontario, 1871 ***1823.15*** *p139*
Kuchenthal, Henry Philip; Pennsylvania, 1853 ***1224.3*** *p44*
Kuchlen, Jacob; Port uncertain, 1740 ***2856.30*** *p253*
With 3 children
Kuchler, Hugo; Port uncertain, 1741 ***2856.30*** *p253*
Kuchler, Johann; America, 1737 ***2856.30*** *p253*
Kuchler, Johann; Port uncertain, 1736 ***2856.30*** *p254*
With wife 2 sons & 4 daughters
Kuchler, Johann; Port uncertain, 1753 ***2856.30*** *p249*
Kuchler, Josef; America, 1740 ***2856.30*** *p253*
Kuchler, Michael; Port uncertain, 1741 ***2856.30*** *p253*
Kuchlin, Michael; Port uncertain, 1762 ***2856.30*** *p254*
Kuchta, Anton; Maryland, 1910 ***3259.35*** *p32*
Kuchta, John; Maryland, 1910 ***3259.35*** *p32*
Kuckhart, Daniel; America, 1739 ***2856.30*** *p210*
Kuczarski, John; Maryland, 1910 ***3259.35*** *p32*
Kuczewski, Joseph; Maryland, 1910 ***3259.35*** *p32*
Kuczewski, Kasmier; Maryland, 1910 ***3259.35*** *p32*
Kuczewsky, Stanislaw; Maryland, 1910 ***3259.35*** *p32*
Kuczynski, Antony; Maryland, 1910 ***3259.35*** *p32*
Kuczynski, Constant; Maryland, 1910 ***3259.35*** *p32*
Kuczynski, Paul; Maryland, 1910 ***3259.35*** *p32*
Kudak, Peter; Maryland, 1910 ***3259.35*** *p32*
Kuderer, Hans Wendel; Port uncertain, 1694 ***2856.30*** *p249*
Kuderer, Johann; Port uncertain, 1770 ***2856.30*** *p249*
Kuderer, Simon; Port uncertain, 1792 ***2856.30*** *p249*
Kuderin, Marianna; Port uncertain, 1763 ***2856.30*** *p249*
Kudges, Janus; Maryland, 1910 ***3259.35*** *p32*
Kudlok, Frank; Maryland, 1910 ***3259.35*** *p32*
Kuebler, Monika; Port uncertain, 1755 ***2856.30*** *p254*
Kuellwater, Judeth; Maryland, 1668 ***2524.55*** *p131*
Kuenin, Maria; Port uncertain, 1745 ***2856.30*** *p254*
Kuetziny, Alexander Emil 15; Ontario, 1871 ***1823.28*** *p53*
Kugel, Hans Martin; Port uncertain, 1744 ***2856.30*** *p249*
Kugele, Josef; Port uncertain, 1750 ***2856.30*** *p254*
Kugele, Josef; Port uncertain, 1780 ***2856.30*** *p254*
Kuger, Frederick 46; Ontario, 1871 ***1823.15*** *p139*
Kughta, Stefan; Maryland, 1910 ***3259.35*** *p32*
Kugowski, Waditas; Maryland, 1910 ***3259.35*** *p32*
Kuhekopf, Maria Anna; Port uncertain, 1766 ***2856.30*** *p249*
Kuhl, Anna Elisabeth; Port uncertain, 1784 ***2856.30*** *p215*
Kuhle, Johann; America, 1737 ***2856.30*** *p253*
Kuhle, Johann; Port uncertain, 1736 ***2856.30*** *p254*
With wife 2 sons & 4 daughters
Kuhlke, Casper H.; New York, 1840 ***8197.10*** *p176*
Kuhlwein, Johann Michael; Port uncertain, 1746 ***2856.30*** *p254*
Kuhn, Mr.; Port uncertain, 1749 ***2856.30*** *p288*
Kuhn, Mr.; Port uncertain, 1764 ***2856.30*** *p254*
With 2 brothers
Kuhn, Anna Barbara; America, 1774 ***2856.30*** *p374*
Kuhn, Anna Barbara; Port uncertain, 1769 ***2856.30*** *p374*
Kuhn, Anna Barbara Romich; America, 1769 ***2856.30*** *p250*
Kuhn, Anna Elisabeth; America, 1741 ***2856.30*** *p250*
With 2 sons
Kuhn, Anna Eva Massmann; Port uncertain, 1749 ***2856.30*** *p250*
With 2 children
Kuhn, Caspar; Port uncertain, 1764 ***2856.30*** *p254*
Kuhn, Catharina; Port uncertain, 1769 ***2856.30*** *p249*
Kuhn, Christina; America, 1796 ***2856.30*** *p250*
Kuhn, Christof; Port uncertain, 1785 ***2856.30*** *p254*
Kuhn, Elias; Port uncertain, 1749 ***2856.30*** *p250*
With 3 children
Kuhn, Elisabeth; America, 1793 ***2856.30*** *p254*
Kuhn, Franz Adam; Port uncertain, 1766 ***2856.30*** *p249*
Kuhn, Friedrich; Port uncertain, 1790 ***2856.30*** *p249*
Kuhn, Friedrich; Port uncertain, 1791 ***2856.30*** *p249*
Kuhn, Georg; Port uncertain, 1750 ***2856.30*** *p250*
Kuhn, George; New York, 1840 ***8197.10*** *p176*
Kuhn, Hans Gorg; America, 1752 ***2856.30*** *p249*
Kuhn, Henrich; Port uncertain, 1763 ***2856.30*** *p249*
Kuhn, Hermann; Port uncertain, 1779 ***2856.30*** *p249*
Kuhn, Jacob; Port uncertain, 1785 ***2856.30*** *p254*
Kuhn, Jakob; Port uncertain, 1741 ***2856.30*** *p250*
With wife & 3 sons
Kuhn, Johan; Port uncertain, 1750 ***2856.30*** *p250*
Kuhn, Johann; Port uncertain, 1735 ***2856.30*** *p249*
Kuhn, Johann; Port uncertain, 1742 ***2856.30*** *p249*
Kuhn, Johann; Port uncertain, 1751 ***2856.30*** *p249*
Kuhn, Johann; Port uncertain, 1788 ***2856.30*** *p249*
Kuhn, Johann Georg; America, 1753 ***2856.30*** *p249*
Kuhn, Johann Heinrich; America, 1766 ***2856.30*** *p254*
Kuhn, Johann Michael; Port uncertain, 1770 ***2856.30*** *p249*
Kuhn, Johann Peter; America, 1764 ***2856.30*** *p250*
With father
Kuhn, Johann Peter; America, 1764 ***2856.30*** *p254*
Kuhn, Johann Peter; Port uncertain, 1764 ***2856.30*** *p254*
Kuhn, Johann Wilhelm; Port uncertain, 1767 ***2856.30*** *p249*
Kuhn, Johann Wilhelm; Port uncertain, 1769 ***2856.30*** *p249*
Kuhn, John 50; Ontario, 1871 ***1823.15*** *p139*

Kuhn, Leonard; Port uncertain, 1773 ***2856.30*** *p249*
Kuhn, Ludwig; Pennsylvania, 1777 ***4629.10*** *p11*
Kuhn, Ludwig Konrad; America, 1763 ***2856.30*** *p249*
Kuhn, Margarete; America, 1752 ***2856.30*** *p249*
Kuhn, Margarete; America, 1770 ***2856.30*** *p249*
Kuhn, Margarete; America, 1786 ***2856.30*** *p249*
Kuhn, Maria; Port uncertain, 1769 ***2856.30*** *p254*
Kuhn, Maria Catharina; Port uncertain, 1757 ***2856.30*** *p249*
Kuhn, Maria Margarete; Port uncertain, 1783 ***2856.30*** *p254*
Kuhn, Martin; New York, 1838 ***8197.10*** *p121*
Kuhn, Matthaus; Port uncertain, 1759 ***2856.30*** *p249*
Kuhn, Peter; Port uncertain, 1748 ***2856.30*** *p250*
Kuhn, Peter; Port uncertain, 1764 ***2856.30*** *p250*
Kuhn, Veltin; Port uncertain, 1764 ***2856.30*** *p250*
Kuhn, Vinzenz; America, 1764 ***2856.30*** *p250*
With father
Kuhn, Vinzenz; America, 1764 ***2856.30*** *p254*
Kuhn, Vinzenz; Port uncertain, 1764 ***2856.30*** *p254*
Kuhnberger, Martin; Port uncertain, 1772 ***2856.30*** *p254*
Kuhnel, Martin; Port uncertain, 1730 ***2856.30*** *p254*
Kuhnel, Martin; Port uncertain, 1765 ***2856.30*** *p254*
Kuhnen, Elias; Port uncertain, 1749 ***2856.30*** *p250*
With 3 children
Kuhner, Christof; Port uncertain, 1776 ***2856.30*** *p250*
Kuhner, Christof; Port uncertain, 1790 ***2856.30*** *p250*
Kuhner, Johann Adam; America, 1738 ***2856.30*** *p254*
Kuhner, Johann Georg; Port uncertain, 1745 ***2856.30*** *p250*
Kuhner, Johann Michael; Port uncertain, 1739 ***2856.30*** *p254*
Kuhner, Margarete; Port uncertain, 1761 ***2856.30*** *p254*
Kuhner, Michael; Port uncertain, 1768 ***2856.30*** *p250*
Kuhni, Martin; Port uncertain, 1790 ***2856.30*** *p250*
Kuhnin, Christina; America, 1796 ***2856.30*** *p250*
Kuhnlen, Mrs. Johann; Port uncertain, 1764 ***2856.30*** *p254*
Kuinowsky, Wladislow; Maryland, 1910 ***3259.35*** *p32*
Kujawa, Antone; Maryland, 1910 ***3259.35*** *p32*
Kujtineak, Wojciech; Maryland, 1910 ***3259.35*** *p32*
Kukan, Alexander 35; Dominica, 1774 ***1220.25*** *p127*
Kulack, Joseph; Maryland, 1910 ***3259.35*** *p32*
Kulacki, Ludwik; Maryland, 1910 ***3259.35*** *p32*
Kulacky, Lukasz; Maryland, 1910 ***3259.35*** *p32*
Kulcinski, John; Maryland, 1910 ***3259.35*** *p32*
Kulecs, Frank; Maryland, 1910 ***3259.35*** *p33*
Kulesa, John; Maryland, 1910 ***3259.35*** *p33*
Kulicinic, Anton; Maryland, 1910 ***3259.35*** *p33*
Kuliczwicz, Antonie; Maryland, 1910 ***3259.35*** *p33*
Kulinski, Michael; Maryland, 1910 ***3259.35*** *p33*
Kulinski, Walter; Maryland, 1910 ***3259.35*** *p33*
Kuliszewski, Edward; Maryland, 1910 ***3259.35*** *p33*
Kullman, Maria Elisabeth; Port uncertain, 1786 ***2856.30*** *p76*
Kullman, Maria Elisabeth; Port uncertain, 1788 ***2856.30*** *p76*
Kullmann, Miss; America, 1760 ***2856.30*** *p250*
Kullmann, Catharina; Port uncertain, 1784 ***2856.30*** *p254*
Kullmann, Christof; Port uncertain, 1783 ***2856.30*** *p250*
Kullmann, Christof; Port uncertain, 1786 ***2856.30*** *p250*
Kullmann, Christof; Port uncertain, 1788 ***2856.30*** *p250*
Kullmann, Friedrich; Port uncertain, 1783 ***2856.30*** *p250*
Kullmann, Friedrich; Port uncertain, 1784 ***2856.30*** *p250*
Kullmann, Jacob; America, 1761 ***2856.30*** *p250*
Kullmann, Jacob; America, 1768 ***2856.30*** *p250*
Kullmann, Johann; Port uncertain, 1784 ***2856.30*** *p254*
Kullmann, Johann; Port uncertain, 1785 ***2856.30*** *p250*
Kullmann, M. Christiana; America, 1760 ***2856.30*** *p250*
Kullmann, Niclas; America, 1768 ***2856.30*** *p250*
Kullmann, Peter; Port uncertain, 1784 ***2856.30*** *p255*
Kullmann, Wilhelm; Port uncertain, 1785 ***2856.30*** *p250*
Kulsch, Daniel; Port uncertain, 1765 ***2856.30*** *p251*
Kulsch, Daniel; Port uncertain, 1765 ***2856.30*** *p255*
Kulski, Antonie W.; Maryland, 1910 ***3259.35*** *p33*
Kulsonski, Anton; Maryland, 1910 ***3259.35*** *p33*
Kultz, Konrad; America, 1738 ***2856.30*** *p255*
With wife & 4 children
Kulus, Bacher 55; Ontario, 1871 ***1823.28*** *p53*
Kulz, J. Georg Wilhelm; Port uncertain, 1774 ***2856.30*** *p255*
Kum, Johann; America, 1738 ***2856.30*** *p251*
Kumendros, G. 48; Alaska, 1918 ***9196.1*** *p56*
Kumendros, G. 48; British Columbia, 1918 ***9196.1*** *p56*
Kumforth, Leonhard; Port uncertain, 1743 ***2856.30*** *p251*
With wife & children
Kumlert, Martin; Virginia, 1775 ***1220.25*** *p123*
Kumlin, Miss; America, 1764 ***2856.30*** *p195*
Kumm, Johann; America, 1739 ***2856.30*** *p251*
Kummel, Jakob; Port uncertain, 1751 ***2856.30*** *p255*
Kummel, Johann; Port uncertain, 1754 ***2856.30*** *p255*
With wife
Kummer, Barbara; Port uncertain, 1694 ***2856.30*** *p251*
Kummer, Barbara; Port uncertain, 1694 ***2856.30*** *p255*
Kummerer, Michael; Port uncertain, 1745 ***2856.30*** *p251*
Kummerlin, Anna Catharina; Port uncertain, 1793 ***2856.30*** *p255*
Kummerlin, Jacob; Port uncertain, 1796 ***2856.30*** *p255*
Kumner, Jonsica; Maryland, 1910 ***3259.35*** *p33*
Kumpff, Georg; America, 1749 ***2856.30*** *p251*
Kun, Elisabeth; Port uncertain, 1792 ***2856.30*** *p251*
Kun, Gottfried; Port uncertain, 1732 ***2856.30*** *p251*
Kunber, William 18; Maryland, 1774 ***1220.25*** *p41*
Kunckel, Anna Catharina; Port uncertain, 1765 ***2856.30*** *p251*
Kunckel, William; Pennsylvania, 1784 ***4629.10*** *p44*
Kundig, Susanna; America, 1732 ***2856.30*** *p255*
With husband
Kundig, Susanna; America, 1732 ***2856.30*** *p255*
Kunkal, John H.; Baltimore, 1847 ***6058.10*** *p26*
Kunkel, Christian; Pennsylvania, 1777 ***4629.10*** *p17*
Kunkel, John H.; Baltimore, 1847 ***6058.10*** *p26*
Kunkelmann, Jacob Charles; New York, 1837 ***8197.10*** *p247*
Kunkle, John H.; Baltimore, 1847 ***6058.10*** *p26*
Kunst, Johann; America, 1738 ***2856.30*** *p251*
Kunst, Peter Jost; America, 1738 ***2856.30*** *p251*
Kunts, Johann; America, 1738 ***2856.30*** *p251*
Kunts, Peter Jost; America, 1738 ***2856.30*** *p251*
Kuntz, Anna Catharina; America, 1740 ***2856.30*** *p251*
Kuntz, Anna Elisabeth; America, 1750 ***2856.30*** *p251*
Kuntz, Catharina; Port uncertain, 1773 ***2856.30*** *p251*
Kuntz, Elisabeth; Port uncertain, 1734 ***2856.30*** *p251*
Kuntz, Eva; Port uncertain, 1767 ***2856.30*** *p251*
Kuntz, Franz; America, 1750 ***2856.30*** *p251*
Kuntz, Jacob; Port uncertain, 1758 ***2856.30*** *p251*
Kuntz, Johann; America, 1738 ***2856.30*** *p251*
Kuntz, Johann Georg; Port uncertain, 1750 ***2856.30*** *p251*
Kuntz, Johann Jacob; America, 1750 ***2856.30*** *p251*
Kuntz, Johann Nickel; America, 1740 ***2856.30*** *p251*
Kuntz, Johann Nicolaus; Port uncertain, 1786 ***2856.30*** *p251*
Kuntz, Michael; Port uncertain, 1753 ***2856.30*** *p251*
Kuntz, Peter; Port uncertain, 1752 ***2856.30*** *p251*
Kuntz, Peter; Port uncertain, 1753 ***2856.30*** *p251*
With wife & 4 children
Kuntz, Peter Jost; America, 1738 ***2856.30*** *p251*
Kuntz, Veronika; Port uncertain, 1757 ***2856.30*** *p251*
Kuntzer, Johann Jacob; America, 1738 ***2856.30*** *p251*
Kuntzer, Nickel; America, 1754 ***2856.30*** *p251*
Kuntzler, Catharina; Port uncertain, 1761 ***2856.30*** *p255*
Kuntzler, Christof; Port uncertain, 1737 ***2856.30*** *p255*
Kuntzmann, Margarete; Port uncertain, 1796 ***2856.30*** *p252*
Kunz, A. M. Wiser *SEE* Kunz, Johann
Kunz, Anna Catharina; Port uncertain, 1777 ***2856.30*** *p252*
Kunz, Anna Margarete; Port uncertain, 1787 ***2856.30*** *p252*
Kunz, Anna Maria; Port uncertain, 1785 ***2856.30*** *p252*
Kunz, Catharina; Port uncertain, 1766 ***2856.30*** *p252*
Kunz, Catharina; Port uncertain, 1789 ***2856.30*** *p252*
Kunz, Elisabeth; Port uncertain, 1740 ***2856.30*** *p252*
Kunz, Franz; New York, 1839 ***8197.10*** *p65*
Kunz, Georg; America, 1754 ***2856.30*** *p252*
With wife & 3 children
Kunz, Gertrud; Port uncertain, 1765 ***2856.30*** *p252*
Kunz, Jakob; Port uncertain, 1783 ***2856.30*** *p252*
Kunz, Jakob; Port uncertain, 1784 ***2856.30*** *p252*
Kunz, Johann; America, 1754 ***2856.30*** *p252*
Wife: A. M. Wiser
Kunz, Johann Theobald; Port uncertain, 1738 ***2856.30*** *p252*
Kunz, John George; New York, 1839 ***8197.10*** *p139*
Kunz, Magdalena; Port uncertain, 1788 ***2856.30*** *p252*
Kunz, Maria Catharina; Port uncertain, 1790 ***2856.30*** *p252*
Kunz, Maria Elisabeth; Port uncertain, 1770 ***2856.30*** *p252*
Kunz, Martin; Port uncertain, 1795 ***2856.30*** *p252*
Kunz, Peter; America, 1747 ***2856.30*** *p253*
With 2 sons
Kunz, Peter; Port uncertain, 1791 ***2856.30*** *p252*
Kunz, Ursula; Port uncertain, 1762 ***2856.30*** *p252*
Kunzer, Georg; Port uncertain, 1766 ***2856.30*** *p252*
Kupeczki, Wallace; Maryland, 1910 ***3259.35*** *p33*
Kuper, Heinrich George; Baltimore, 1857 ***1224.3*** *p44*
Kupfer, Erhard; Port uncertain, 1764 ***2856.30*** *p252*
Kupferle, Josef; Port uncertain, 1783 ***2856.30*** *p255*
Kupferlin, Rufina; Port uncertain, 1763 ***2856.30*** *p255*
Kupper, Georg; Port uncertain, 1752 ***2856.30*** *p252*
Kurak, Thomas; Maryland, 1910 ***3259.35*** *p33*
Kurcab, Antoni; Maryland, 1910 ***3259.35*** *p33*
Kurek, Agnes; Maryland, 1910 ***3259.35*** *p33*
Kurek, Franciska; Maryland, 1910 ***3259.35*** *p33*
Kurek, John; Maryland, 1910 ***3259.35*** *p33*
Kurkey, Antoine 45; Ontario, 1871 ***1823.28*** *p53*
Kurowski, Frank; Maryland, 1910 ***3259.35*** *p33*
Kurowski, Jacob; Maryland, 1910 ***3259.35*** *p33*
Kurowski, Joseph J.; Maryland, 1910 ***3259.35*** *p33*
Kurowski, Michael; Maryland, 1910 ***3259.35*** *p33*
Kurowsky, Joseph; Maryland, 1910 ***3259.35*** *p33*
Kursheedt, Israel B.; New York, 1803 ***8197.10*** *p13*
Kursinger, Hans Georg; Port uncertain, 1728 ***2856.30*** *p255*
Kurth, Carl 85; Ontario, 1871 ***1823.28*** *p53*
Kurtz, Anna Elisabeth; America, 1739 ***2856.30*** *p252*
Kurtz, Anna Maria; Port uncertain, 1763 ***2856.30*** *p253*
Kurtz, Anna Maria; Port uncertain, 1765 ***2856.30*** *p253*
Kurtz, Barbara; Port uncertain, 1763 ***2856.30*** *p253*
Kurtz, Barbara; Port uncertain, 1765 ***2856.30*** *p253*
Kurtz, Friedrich; Port uncertain, 1783 ***2856.30*** *p253*
Kurtz, Henry; Pennsylvania, 1777 ***4629.10*** *p12*
Kurtz, Henry; Pennsylvania, 1777 ***4629.10*** *p24*
Kurtz, Johann Georg; America, 1753 ***2856.30*** *p253*
With wife & 3 children
Kurtz, Johann Peter; Port uncertain, 1740 ***2856.30*** *p252*
Kurtz, Josef; Port uncertain, 1763 ***2856.30*** *p253*
Kurtz, Josef; Port uncertain, 1765 ***2856.30*** *p253*
Kurtz, Josef; Port uncertain, 1770 ***2856.30*** *p252*
Kurtz, Peter; Pennsylvania, 1777 ***4629.10*** *p22*
Kurz, . . .; America, 1749 ***2856.30*** *p253*
Kurz, Benedikt; Port uncertain, 1762 ***2856.30*** *p253*
Kurz, Georg; Port uncertain, 1750 ***2856.30*** *p253*
With wife & 5 children
Kurz, Hans Georg; Port uncertain, 1748 ***2856.30*** *p253*
With wife 2 sons & 3 daughters
Kurz, Peter; America, 1747 ***2856.30*** *p253*
With 2 sons
Kurz, Philipp; Port uncertain, 1764 ***2856.30*** *p253*
Kurz, Philipp; Port uncertain, 1781 ***2856.30*** *p253*
Kus, Joseph; Maryland, 1910 ***3259.35*** *p33*
Kusch, Georg; Port uncertain, 1770 ***2856.30*** *p253*
Kusel, Christopher H.; New York, 1826 ***8197.10*** *p334*
Kusick, James; New York, 1839 ***8197.10*** *p247*
Kuss, Hans Georg; Port uncertain, 1763 ***2856.30*** *p255*
Kusser, Maria Sybilla Bohler; America, 1774 ***2856.30*** *p253*
Kussler, Jakob; Port uncertain, 1785 ***2856.30*** *p253*
Kussmanl, Johannes; New York, 1839 ***8197.10*** *p139*
Kussmaul, Christof; Port uncertain, 1780 ***2856.30*** *p253*
Kussmaul, Jacob; America, 1746 ***2856.30*** *p253*
Kussmaul, Jacob; Port uncertain, 1746 ***2856.30*** *p253*
Kustner, Catharina; Port uncertain, 1766 ***2856.30*** *p255*
Kustner, Josef; Port uncertain, 1769 ***2856.30*** *p255*
Kustudiga, V. 28; Alaska, 1916 ***9196.1*** *p43*
Kustudiga, V. 28; Whitehorse, Yukon, 1916 ***9196.1*** *p43*
Kutscher, Michael; Port uncertain, 1795 ***2856.30*** *p253*
Kutz, Frank; Maryland, 1910 ***3259.35*** *p33*
Kutz, Joseph; Maryland, 1910 ***3259.35*** *p33*
Kutz, Stanislaus; Maryland, 1910 ***3259.35*** *p33*
Kutzmann, Anna Eva; Port uncertain, 1742 ***2856.30*** *p253*
Kuyawa, Albert G.; Maryland, 1910 ***3259.35*** *p33*
Kuyawa, Francis; Maryland, 1910 ***3259.35*** *p33*
Kuyawa, Magdeline; Maryland, 1910 ***3259.35*** *p33*
Kuz, Johann; Port uncertain, 1745 ***2856.30*** *p253*
Kuzinski, Lears; Maryland, 1910 ***3259.35*** *p33*
Kuzma, Michael; Maryland, 1910 ***3259.35*** *p33*
Kuzmarski, Joseph; Maryland, 1910 ***3259.35*** *p33*
Kuzyski, Stanislaw; Maryland, 1910 ***3259.35*** *p33*
Kuzzlau, John; Maryland, 1910 ***3259.35*** *p33*
Kvernuik, C. 25; Alaska, 1917 ***9196.1*** *p48*
Kvernuik, C. 25; Whitehorse, Yukon, 1917 ***9196.1*** *p48*
Kwaksnik, John; Maryland, 1910 ***3259.35*** *p33*
Kwasink, Stephen; Maryland, 1910 ***3259.35*** *p33*
Kwasnieski, Andy; Maryland, 1910 ***3259.35*** *p33*
Kwasnink, Joseph; Maryland, 1910 ***3259.35*** *p33*
Kwercinski, Wladyslaw; Maryland, 1910 ***3259.35*** *p33*
Kwiakouski, Casimi; Maryland, 1910 ***3259.35*** *p33*
Kwiatkowska, Valeria; Maryland, 1910 ***3259.35*** *p33*
Kwiatkowski, Andrew; Maryland, 1910 ***3259.35*** *p33*
Kwiatkowski, John; Maryland, 1910 ***3259.35*** *p33*
Kwiatkowski, Lizzie; Maryland, 1910 ***3259.35*** *p33*
Kwiatkowski, Martin; Maryland, 1910 ***3259.35*** *p33*
Kwiatkowski, Michael; Maryland, 1910 ***3259.35*** *p33*
Kwiatkowski, Vincent; Maryland, 1910 ***3259.35*** *p33*
Kwiatkowsky, Henryk; Maryland, 1910 ***3259.35*** *p33*
Kwiocki, Ignatius; Maryland, 1910 ***3259.35*** *p33*
Kwiwis, Mrs. 72; Ontario, 1871 ***1823.28*** *p53*
Kwizkowski, Joseph; Maryland, 1910 ***3259.35*** *p33*
Kworta, Agata; Maryland, 1910 ***3259.35*** *p33*
Kyd, William; Montreal, 1865 ***1640.13*** *p66*
Kydd, John 25; Ontario, 1871 ***1823.15*** *p139*
Kydd, John 55; Ontario, 1871 ***1823.15*** *p139*
Kydd, Robert 30; Ontario, 1871 ***1823.15*** *p139*
Kyle, Alexander 47; Ontario, 1871 ***1823.15*** *p139*
Kyle, Catherine Seymore; Vermont, 1846-1919 ***5900.10*** *p318*

L

Laabs, Henry 32; Ontario, 1871 ***1823.28*** *p53*
Laader, Mr.; Quebec, 1857 ***9196.15*** *p26*
Laaman, M. 27; Alaska, 1917 ***9196.1*** *p46*
Laaman, M. 27; Whitehorse, Yukon, 1917 ***9196.1*** *p46*
Laarin, Anna Margarete; Port uncertain, 1744 ***2856.30*** *p259*
Labared, Mrs.; Quebec, 1858 ***9196.15*** *p42*
La Barre, Joseph; New York, 1794 ***8197.10*** *p6*
Labatt, Edward; New York, 1838 ***8197.10*** *p251*
Labatut, Jean Marie Joseph; New York, 1806 ***8197.10*** *p31*
Labawan, Martin; New York, 1807 ***8197.10*** *p330*
Labhart, John W.; New York, 1807 ***8197.10*** *p44*
La Boissier, Armand Gabriel Francois Paparel; Philadelphia, 1793 ***4629.10*** *p71*
LaBonte, Mary E. Cooley; Vermont, 1852-1902 ***5900.10*** *p349*
Labory, Pierre Joseph; New York, 1815 ***8197.10*** *p56*
Labougiski, Ignatius; Maryland, 1910 ***3259.35*** *p34*
Lacey, Ann 68; Vermont, 1884 ***5900.10*** *p410*
Lacey, Catherine; Vermont, 1863-1949 ***5900.10*** *p186*
Lacey, Catherine 72; Vermont, 1883 ***5900.10*** *p410*
Lacey, Dennis 77; Vermont, 1889 ***5900.10*** *p410*
Lacey, Ellen 47; Ontario, 1871 ***1823.22*** *p88*
Lacey, James 58; Ontario, 1871 ***1823.22*** *p88*
Lacey, Jane; Virginia, 1679-1680 ***6212.30*** *p54*
Lacey, Margaret; Vermont, 1845-1904 ***5900.10*** *p410*
Lacey, Mary; Vermont, 1847-1921 ***5900.10*** *p193*
Lacey, William 56; Ontario, 1871 ***1823.22*** *p88*
Lachance, Francis 52; Ontario, 1871 ***1823.28*** *p54*
Lachayze, Elias V.; New York, 1816 ***8197.10*** *p59*
Lacher, Anna Maria; Port uncertain, 1768 ***2856.30*** *p259*
Lacher, Anthony; Virginia, 1671-1672 ***6212.30*** *p46*
Lacher, Georg; Port uncertain, 1795 ***2856.30*** *p280*
Lacher, Georg; Port uncertain, 1796 ***2856.30*** *p280*
Lacher, Jacobina; Port uncertain, 1744 ***2856.30*** *p259*
Lacher, Josef; Port uncertain, 1735 ***2856.30*** *p259*
Lacher, Josef; Port uncertain, 1765 ***2856.30*** *p259*
Lacher, Josef; Port uncertain, 1778 ***2856.30*** *p259*
Lacher, Maria; Port uncertain, 1762 ***2856.30*** *p259*
Lacher, Maria Catharina; Port uncertain, 1740 ***2856.30*** *p259*
Lacher, Michael; Port uncertain, 1790 ***2856.30*** *p259*
Lachman, Mark 26; Maryland, 1774 ***1220.25*** *p73*
Lachnane, Ellon 40; Ontario, 1871 ***1823.28*** *p54*
Lack, John 21; Baltimore, 1775 ***1220.25*** *p119*
Lackey, Anna Campbell 57; Vermont, 1893 ***5900.10*** *p71*
Lackey, Robert 24; Ontario, 1871 ***1823.22*** *p88*
Lackey, Robert 60; Ontario, 1871 ***1823.15*** *p140*
Lackey, William 70; Vermont, 1894 ***5900.10*** *p71*
Lackie, John; New York, 1827 ***8197.10*** *p250*
Lackland, Miles; Virginia, 1665-1666 ***6212.30*** *p25*
Laclair, Rose Shatney 38; Vermont, 1877 ***5900.10*** *p203*
Lacock, James; Pennsylvania, 1866 ***6058.10*** *p56*
Lacombe, Joseph; Philadelphia, 1793 ***4629.10*** *p71*
Lacoste, Anne Mary; New York, 1831 ***8197.10*** *p356*
Lacostte, John; New York, 1807 ***8197.10*** *p331*
La Cross, Mrs.; Quebec, 1856 ***9196.15*** *p8*
Lacton, John; Virginia, 1664 ***6212.30*** *p14*
Lacy, Capt.; Quebec, 1856 ***9196.15*** *p5*
Lacy, Mrs.; Quebec, 1856 ***9196.15*** *p5*
Lacy, David; Virginia, 1664 ***6212.30*** *p11*
Lacy, Elizabeth Riley 56; Vermont, 1889 ***5900.10*** *p135*
Lacy, James 30; Vermont, 1847 ***5900.10*** *p611*
Lacy, James 32; Ontario, 1871 ***1823.15*** *p140*
Lacy, John 35; Ontario, 1871 ***1823.28*** *p54*
Lacy, John 40; Ontario, 1871 ***1823.15*** *p140*
Lacy, John 52; Ontario, 1871 ***1823.22*** *p88*
Lacy, Patrick; Virginia, 1700 ***1224.2*** *p67*
Lacy, Philip; Pennsylvania, 1777 ***4629.10*** *p19*
Lacy, Philip 21; Vermont, 1846 ***5900.10*** *p611*
Lacy, Thomas 53; Ontario, 1871 ***1823.15*** *p140*
Ladam, Bridget; Vermont, 1895 ***5900.10*** *p149*
Ladbrook, Richd; Virginia, 1671 ***6212.30*** *p42*
Ladd, Alexander Morrison; Oregon, 1893 ***1640.13*** *p67*
Laddauer, Rudolph; New York, 1840 ***8197.10*** *p321*
Laddret, Master; Quebec, 1858 ***9196.15*** *p40*
Ladds, Jane *SEE* Ladds, William
Ladds, Joseph; New York, 1840 ***8197.10*** *p187*
Ladds, William; Maryland, 1664 ***2524.55*** *p217*
Wife: Jane
Ladeau, Caroline Seymour; Vermont, 1840-1921 ***5900.10*** *p533*
Ladeau, Frank; Vermont, 1838-1922 ***5900.10*** *p533*
Ladell, Caroline 18; Ontario, 1871 ***1823.28*** *p54*
Ladell, G. H. 48; Ontario, 1871 ***1823.28*** *p54*
Laden, Lucy Lavery 41; Vermont, 1891 ***5900.10*** *p223*
Laden, Margaret Holleran 61; Vermont, 1895 ***5900.10*** *p248*
Laden, Michael 61; Vermont, 1879 ***5900.10*** *p223*
Laden, Michael J.; Vermont, 1849-1918 ***5900.10*** *p224*
Laden, Patrick; New York, 1834 ***8197.10*** *p72*
Laden, Thomas E. 52; Vermont, 1885 ***5900.10*** *p248*
Laderin, Ursula; Port uncertain, 1762 ***2856.30*** *p259*
Ladger, Thomas; Maryland, 1650 ***2524.55*** *p127*
Ladislas, Progin 41; Washington, 1913 ***9196.1*** *p59*
Ladna, Ignatius; Maryland, 1910 ***3259.35*** *p34*
Lado, Charles 20; Ontario, 1861 ***2896.25*** *p46*
Ladon, Mary 67; Vermont, 1877 ***5900.10*** *p614*
Ladstone, William; Virginia, 1709 ***1224.2*** *p67*
Laduke, Catherine; Vermont, 1824-1895 ***5900.10*** *p361*
Lafar, Aurelia; Vermont, 1852-1920 ***5900.10*** *p513*
Lafar, Joseph 21; Philadelphia, 1774 ***1220.25*** *p69*
Lafaurie, Jean Baptiste de Mauret; Philadelphia, 1793 ***4629.10*** *p70*
Lafayette, Zita M.; Vermont, 1898-1974 ***5900.10*** *p126*
Laferre, Georg; Port uncertain, 1759 ***2856.30*** *p259*
Laferre, Margarete; Port uncertain, 1759 ***2856.30*** *p259*
Laferre, Maria Elisabeth; Port uncertain, 1759 ***2856.30*** *p259*
Laferty, Art 26; Idaho, 1914 ***9196.1*** *p64*
Lafevre, Johann; Port uncertain, 1753 ***2856.30*** *p259*
Lafferty, Dennis; New York, 1840 ***8197.10*** *p252*
Laffette, Mary; South Carolina, 1752 ***1224.2*** *p67*
Laffey, Mary A.; Vermont, 1856-1887 ***5900.10*** *p476*
Laflame, George; Indiana, 1867-1903 ***3437.14*** *p139*
Lafley, Christopher 68; Vermont, 1886 ***5900.10*** *p222*
Lafley, Henry; Vermont, 1853-1905 ***5900.10*** *p357*
Lafley, Margaret Longey 41; Vermont, 1874 ***5900.10*** *p222*
Lafley, Mary Dolan; Vermont, 1862-1944 ***5900.10*** *p357*
Laforen, Hipolite; New York, 1805 ***8197.10*** *p29*
Lafricain, Mr.; Quebec, 1858 ***9196.15*** *p41*
Lagam, William 47; Ontario, 1871 ***1823.28*** *p54*
Lagas, Franz Henry; New York, 1840 ***8197.10*** *p186*
Lague, Barthelemy; New York, 1796 ***8197.10*** *p7*
Lagunski, John; Maryland, 1910 ***3259.35*** *p34*
Lahey, Mary 68; Vermont, 1900 ***5900.10*** *p337*
Lahm, Johann Konrad; America, 1746 ***2856.30*** *p259*
Lahm, Johann Konrad; Port uncertain, 1741 ***2856.30*** *p259*
Lahm, Konrad; America, 1741 ***2856.30*** *p260*
Lahm, Maria Catharina; America, 1741 ***2856.30*** *p259*
Lahm, Maria Margarete; Port uncertain, 1747 ***2856.30*** *p259*
Lahm, Nickel; America, 1741 ***2856.30*** *p259*
Lahm, Nikolaus; America, 1741 ***2856.30*** *p259*
Lahm, Susanna; Port uncertain, 1747 ***2856.30*** *p259*
Lahr, Balthasar; America, 1721 ***2856.30*** *p259*
Lahr, Balthasar; Port uncertain, 1744 ***2856.30*** *p259*
Lahr, Georg; America, 1721 ***2856.30*** *p259*
Lahr, Georg; Port uncertain, 1744 ***2856.30*** *p259*
Lahti, R. 36; Alaska, 1917 ***9196.1*** *p53*
Lahti, R. 36; Whitehorse, Yukon, 1917 ***9196.1*** *p53*
Lahy, Mary Bowler 25; Vermont, 1873 ***5900.10*** *p108*
Laibet, Michael; Port uncertain, 1727 ***2856.30*** *p259*
Laible, Catharina; Port uncertain, 1745 ***2856.30*** *p260*
Laidlaw, Catherine 21; Ontario, 1871 ***1823.15*** *p140*
Laidlaw, Catherine 60; Ontario, 1871 ***1823.15*** *p140*
Laidlaw, Christian; Baltimore, 1847 ***1640.13*** *p67*
Laidlaw, James 30; Ontario, 1871 ***1823.15*** *p140*
Laidlaw, James 42; Ontario, 1871 ***1823.15*** *p140*
Laidlaw, John; New York, 1820 ***8197.10*** *p248*
Laidlaw, John 40; Ontario, 1871 ***1823.15*** *p140*
Laidlaw, Robert 37; Ontario, 1871 ***1823.15*** *p140*
Laidlaw, Robert 39; Ontario, 1871 ***1823.15*** *p140*
Laidlaw, Thomas 35; Ontario, 1871 ***1823.15*** *p140*
Laidlaw, William; Halifax, Nova Scotia, 1827 ***1640.13*** *p67*
Laidlaw, William 66; Ontario, 1871 ***1823.15*** *p140*
Laight, Edward; Virginia, 1679 ***1224.1*** *p35*
Laikie, Archibald 24; Maryland, 1774 ***1220.25*** *p77*
Laine, David; New York, 1821 ***8197.10*** *p249*
Laing, Alexander Morrison; Kingston, Jamaica, 1894 ***1640.13*** *p67*
Laing, Andrew *SEE* Laing, Donald
Laing, Ann *SEE* Laing, Donald
Laing, Barthoamew 31; Ontario, 1871 ***1823.15*** *p140*
Laing, Catherine; Ontario, 1851 ***4537.32*** *p14*
Laing, Donald *SEE* Laing, John
Laing, Donald; Nova Scotia, 1843 ***4537.37*** *p10*
Wife: Kirsty MacPhail
Child: Andrew
Child: Flora
Child: Marion
Child: Ann
Child: John
Laing, Flora *SEE* Laing, Donald
Laing, George; Ontario, 1872 ***1640.13*** *p67*
Laing, James; Jamaica, 1827 ***1640.13*** *p67*
Laing, John *SEE* Laing, Donald
Laing, John; Nova Scotia, 1843 ***4537.37*** *p10*
Wife: Marion MacDonald
Child: Donald
Laing, John; Virgin Islands, 1851 ***1640.13*** *p67*
Laing, John 35; Ontario, 1871 ***1823.15*** *p140*
Laing, John 43; Ontario, 1871 ***1823.22*** *p88*
Laing, John 66; Ontario, 1871 ***1823.15*** *p140*
Laing, Kirsty; Nova Scotia, 1840-1849 ***4537.37*** *p9*
Laing, Kirsty MacPhail *SEE* Laing, Donald
Laing, Marion *SEE* Laing, Donald
Laing, Marion MacDonald *SEE* Laing, John
Laing, William; New Jersey, 1738 ***1640.13*** *p67*
Lainz, Joseph; New York, 1807 ***8197.10*** *p43*
Laird, Mr.; Quebec, 1858 ***9196.15*** *p38*
Laird, Mrs.; Quebec, 1858 ***9196.15*** *p38*
Laird, Alexander 28; Ontario, 1871 ***1823.15*** *p140*
Laird, C. A.; Mobile, Alabama, 1820-1845 ***1640.10*** *p94*
Laird, Calvin 3; Ontario, 1861 ***2896.25*** *p15*
Laird, Cladus 31; Ontario, 1871 ***1823.15*** *p140*
Laird, Delia 15; Ontario, 1861 ***2896.25*** *p15*
Laird, Eliza 38; Ontario, 1861 ***2896.27*** *p1*
Laird, George 39; Ontario, 1861 ***2896.27*** *p1*
Laird, H. A. 45; Ontario, 1861 ***2896.25*** *p15*

Laird, Horatio 12; Ontario, 1861 ***2896.25*** *p15*
Laird, James; Pennsylvania, 1777 ***4629.10*** *p18*
Laird, James 20; Ontario, 1861 ***2896.25*** *p15*
Laird, James 47; Ontario, 1871 ***1823.15*** *p140*
Laird, John 5; Ontario, 1861 ***2896.25*** *p15*
Laird, John 12; Ontario, 1861 ***2896.27*** *p1*
Laird, Mary; Mobile, Alabama, 1858 ***1640.10*** *p94*
Laird, Reuben 7; Ontario, 1861 ***2896.25*** *p15*
Laird, Robert; Mobile, Alabama, 1814-1845 ***1640.10*** *p94*
Laird, Thomas 9; Ontario, 1861 ***2896.25*** *p15*
Laird, William; Mobile, Alabama, 1849 ***1640.10*** *p94*
Laird, William 17; Maryland, 1774 ***1220.25*** *p46*
Laird, William C. 14; Ontario, 1861 ***2896.25*** *p15*
Laisne, Jean Baptiste Hypolite; New York, 1823 ***8197.10*** *p63*
Laithwaite, Mary 68; Ontario, 1871 ***1823.15*** *p140*
Laitlin, Hans Georg; Port uncertain, 1756 ***2856.30*** *p260*
Lake, Capt.; Quebec, 1856 ***9196.15*** *p8*
Lake, Mrs.; Quebec, 1856 ***9196.15*** *p8*
Lake, Charles; Maryland, 1765 ***1224.2*** *p67*
Lake, Charles 46; Maryland, 1774 ***1220.25*** *p59*
Lake, Elizabeth 17; Ontario, 1871 ***1823.15*** *p140*
Lake, Jno; Virginia, 1664 ***6212.30*** *p13*
Lake, John 47; Ontario, 1871 ***1823.15*** *p140*
Lake, Margaret; Ontario, 1871 ***1823.22*** *p88*
Lake, Richard; Maryland, 1661 ***2524.55*** *p132*
Lake, Tho; Virginia, 1665-1666 ***6212.30*** *p22*
Lake, Thomas; Pennsylvania, 1777 ***4629.10*** *p23*
Lake, William Walton; New York, 1838 ***1224.3*** *p45*
Lakeman, Daniel 22; Virginia, 1774 ***1220.25*** *p45*
Laker, Johann Wilhelm; Port uncertain, 1797 ***2856.30*** *p260*
Lakowski, Constantine; Maryland, 1910 ***3259.35*** *p34*
Lakuis, Faderesz; Maryland, 1910 ***3259.35*** *p34*
Lalas, Edward 60; Ontario, 1871 ***1823.28*** *p54*
Lalement, Anna Margarete; America, 1759 ***2856.30*** *p260*
Lalicki, Michael; Maryland, 1910 ***3259.35*** *p34*
Lalley, Michael; New York, 1840 ***8197.10*** *p321*
Lallo, Catheryn; Maryland, 1659 ***2524.55*** *p132*
Lally, Catherine; Vermont, 1814-1899 ***5900.10*** *p601*
Lalone, David 17; Ontario, 1861 ***2896.27*** *p18*
Lalor, Edward; Vermont, 1854-1920 ***5900.10*** *p421*
Lalor, Edward 56; Vermont, 1872 ***5900.10*** *p420*
Lalor, Emma; Vermont, 1863-1939 ***5900.10*** *p420*
Lalor, Henry; Pennsylvania, 1777 ***4629.10*** *p28*
Lalor, Henry; Pennsylvania, 1779 ***4629.10*** *p40*
Lalor, Jennie E. Simonds 34; Vermont, 1885 ***5900.10*** *p431*
Lalor, Mary E. Coffey; Vermont, 1864-1940 ***5900.10*** *p421*
Lalor, Mary O'Halloran 52; Vermont, 1880 ***5900.10*** *p420*
La Lougel, James Charles 32; Ontario, 1871 ***1823.15*** *p140*
Lamarch, . . .; Port uncertain, 1731 ***2856.30*** *p260*
Lamard, Steph; Virginia, 1665-1666 ***6212.30*** *p22*
Lamb, Andrew E. 37; Vermont, 1894 ***5900.10*** *p288*
Lamb, Bryan 21; Baltimore, 1775 ***1220.25*** *p118*
Lamb, Christian; Port uncertain, 1785 ***2856.30*** *p260*
Lamb, David 60; Ontario, 1871 ***1823.15*** *p140*
Lamb, Dorothy; Virginia, 1663 ***6212.30*** *p4*
Lamb, Edward 55; Ontario, 1871 ***1823.15*** *p140*
Lamb, Francis; Maryland, 1667 ***2524.55*** *p132*
Lamb, Henry; Virginia, 1666-1667 ***6212.30*** *p33*
Lamb, James; Maryland, 1668 ***2524.55*** *p132*
Lamb, James 19; Ontario, 1871 ***1823.22*** *p88*
Lamb, Job 35; Ontario, 1871 ***1823.28*** *p54*
Lamb, John; Virginia, 1664 ***6212.30*** *p12*
Lamb, John 12; Ontario, 1861 ***2896.27*** *p71*
Lamb, John 21; Nova Scotia, 1774 ***1220.25*** *p135*
Lamb, John 39; Philadelphia, 1774 ***1220.25*** *p66*
Lamb, Joseph 21; Maryland, 1775 ***1220.25*** *p102*
Lamb, Margaret; Vermont, 1830-1910 ***5900.10*** *p291*
Lamb, Margaret 46; Ontario, 1871 ***1823.15*** *p140*
Lamb, Margaret 50; Ontario, 1861 ***2896.27*** *p71*
Lamb, Maria Ann; New York, 1824 ***8197.10*** *p250*
Lamb, Martin; America, 1741 ***2856.30*** *p260*
Lamb, Mary 19; Ontario, 1861 ***2896.27*** *p71*
Lamb, Owen 17; Ontario, 1861 ***2896.27*** *p71*
Lamb, Patrick 24; Ontario, 1861 ***2896.27*** *p71*
Lamb, Stephen; Long Island, 1778 ***1224.2*** *p67*
Lamb, Thomas; New York, 1838 ***8197.10*** *p122*
Lamb, Thomas 11; Ontario, 1861 ***2896.27*** *p71*
Lamb, Thomas 63; Ontario, 1871 ***1823.15*** *p141*
Lamb, William 15; Ontario, 1861 ***2896.27*** *p71*
Lamb, William 21; Jamaica, 1774 ***1220.25*** *p79*
Lamb, William 29; Ontario, 1871 ***1823.22*** *p88*
Lamb, William 60; Ontario, 1861 ***2896.27*** *p71*
Lamb, William 74; Ontario, 1871 ***1823.15*** *p141*
Lambacher, Therese; Port uncertain, 1771 ***2856.30*** *p260*
Lambaert, Herman J.; Pennsylvania, 1785 ***4629.10*** *p44*
Lambert, . . . 40; Grenada, 1774 ***1220.25*** *p127*
Lambert, Mr.; Quebec, 1858 ***9196.15*** *p35*
Lambert, Amey; Maryland, 1663 ***2524.55*** *p132*
Lambert, Andreas; America, 1772 ***2856.30*** *p260*
Lambert, Ann *SEE* Lambert, Josias
Lambert, Anna Elisabeth; Port uncertain, 1752 ***2856.30*** *p260*
Lambert, Anthony 36; Maryland, 1775 ***1220.25*** *p97*
Lambert, Anthony 36; Maryland, 1775 ***1220.25*** *p102*
Lambert, Balthasar; America, 1739 ***2856.30*** *p260*
Lambert, Balthasar; Port uncertain, 1740 ***2856.30*** *p260*
Lambert, C. 54; Ontario, 1861 ***2896.25*** *p29*
Lambert, Catherine 5; Ontario, 1861 ***2896.28*** *p63*
Lambert, Charles A.; New York, 1838 ***8197.10*** *p251*
Lambert, D.; New York, 1838 ***8197.10*** *p318*
Lambert, David 2; Ontario, 1861 ***2896.28*** *p63*
Lambert, E. 8; Ontario, 1861 ***2896.26*** *p13*
Lambert, Edward 36; Ontario, 1871 ***1823.28*** *p54*
Lambert, Emma 13; Ontario, 1861 ***2896.28*** *p63*
Lambert, George 25; Virginia, 1773 ***1220.25*** *p29*
Lambert, H. 59; Ontario, 1861 ***2896.26*** *p15*
Lambert, J. C. 3; Ontario, 1861 ***2896.26*** *p13*
Lambert, James 21; Virginia, 1773 ***1220.25*** *p29*
Lambert, Jane 35; Ontario, 1861 ***2896.28*** *p63*
Lambert, John; New York, 1819 ***8197.10*** *p248*
Lambert, John 23; British Columbia, 1910 ***9196.1*** *p32*
Lambert, John 23; Seattle, 1910 ***9196.1*** *p32*
Lambert, John 39; Ontario, 1871 ***1823.28*** *p54*
Lambert, Jonathan; Boston, 1711 ***1224.2*** *p67*
Lambert, Josias; Maryland, 1664 ***2524.55*** *p132*
Wife: Ann
Lambert, Katherine; Vermont, 1840-1912 ***5900.10*** *p168*
Lambert, M. 14; Ontario, 1861 ***2896.25*** *p29*
Lambert, Margarete; Port uncertain, 1762 ***2856.30*** *p260*
Lambert, Maria Juliana; Port uncertain, 1755 ***2856.30*** *p260*
Lambert, Martin 21; Ontario, 1861 ***2896.28*** *p10*
Lambert, Peter; America, 1772 ***2856.30*** *p260*
Lambert, Richard; Maryland, 1673 ***2524.55*** *p132*
Lambert, Robert; New York, 1838 ***8197.10*** *p122*
Lambert, Robt; Virginia, 1690-1691 ***6212.30*** *p59*
Lambert, S. 11; Ontario, 1861 ***2896.25*** *p29*
Lambert, Tho; Virginia, 1664 ***6212.30*** *p15*
Lambert, Tho; Virginia, 1666-1667 ***6212.30*** *p32*
Lambert, Thomas; Maryland, 1654 ***2524.55*** *p132*
Lambert, Thomas; Virginia, 1664 ***6212.30*** *p12*
Lambert, Thomas; Virginia, 1665-1666 ***6212.30*** *p22*
Lambert, Vincent; Maryland, 1703 ***1224.2*** *p67*
Lambert, Walter; New Orleans, 1821 ***1224.3*** *p45*
Lambert, William; Boston, 1750 ***1224.2*** *p67*
Lambert, William; Maryland, 1665-1666 ***2524.55*** *p132*
Lambert, William 21; Philadelphia, 1774 ***1220.25*** *p66*
Lamberti, Peter; America, 1770 ***2856.30*** *p260*
Lamberton, James; Pennsylvania, 1841 ***6058.10*** *p17*
Lamberton, James G.; Pennsylvania, 1844 ***6058.10*** *p19*
Lamberton, Robert; Pennsylvania, 1830 ***6058.10*** *p9*
Lamberton, William; Philadelphia, 1845 ***6058.10*** *p29*
Lambeth, Jonathan; Maryland, 1680 ***2524.55*** *p132*
Lambey, John 44; Ontario, 1871 ***1823.15*** *p141*
Lambie, Elisabeth Dundas; Jamaica, 1821 ***1640.13*** *p67*
Lambie, Florence J. 2; Ontario, 1861 ***2896.27*** *p52*
Lambie, Rebecca 32; Ontario, 1861 ***2896.27*** *p52*
Lambie, Rebecca M. 14; Ontario, 1861 ***2896.27*** *p52*
Lambie, Salona 8; Ontario, 1861 ***2896.27*** *p52*
Lambie, William A. 5; Ontario, 1861 ***2896.27*** *p52*
Lambkin, Leonard 46; Ontario, 1871 ***1823.15*** *p141*
Lambking, George 38; Ontario, 1871 ***1823.15*** *p141*
Lambrecht, Anton; Port uncertain, 1755 ***2856.30*** *p260*
Lambrecht, Antoni; Port uncertain, 1754 ***2856.30*** *p260*
Lambrecht, Mrs. Karl; America, 1752 ***2856.30*** *p260*
With 2 children
Lambrook, Henry 38; Ontario, 1871 ***1823.15*** *p141*
Lambseed, Fran.; Maryland, 1678 ***2524.55*** *p132*
Lameneck, Johann Jakob; America, 1740 ***2856.30*** *p260*
Lamenski, James L.; Maryland, 1910 ***3259.35*** *p34*
Lamenski, Michael; Maryland, 1910 ***3259.35*** *p34*
Lamer, Mary; Maryland, 1666 ***2524.55*** *p132*
Lamer, Thomas; Maryland, 1666 ***2524.55*** *p132*
Lamey, Thomas 5; Ontario, 1871 ***1823.22*** *p88*
Lamey, William 54; Ontario, 1871 ***1823.22*** *p89*
Laming, John 36; Ontario, 1871 ***1823.28*** *p54*
Laminski, Frank; Maryland, 1910 ***3259.35*** *p34*
Lamm, Konrad; America, 1741 ***2856.30*** *p260*
Lammer, Joseph; New York, 1828 ***8197.10*** *p348*
Lammers, Peter; Port uncertain, 1783 ***2856.30*** *p260*
Lammers, Peter; Port uncertain, 1783 ***2856.30*** *p260*
With wife son & 3 daughters
Lammi, J. G.; Port uncertain, 1709 ***2856.30*** *p334*
Lammi, Johann Georg; Port uncertain, 1724 ***2856.30*** *p260*
With wife
Lammi, Johann Georg; Port uncertain, 1724 ***2856.30*** *p261*
With wife
Lammie, William 59; Ontario, 1871 ***1823.15*** *p141*
Lamon, Isabella; Alabama, 1864 ***1640.10*** *p94*
Lamond, John; Georgia, 1698 ***1640.13*** *p67*
Lamont, Mrs. 63; Ontario, 1871 ***1823.15*** *p141*
Lamont, Angus 30; Ontario, 1871 ***1823.15*** *p141*
Lamont, Archiebald 29; Ontario, 1871 ***1823.15*** *p141*
Lamont, Boyden; Trinidad, 1837 ***1640.13*** *p67*
Lamont, Donald 32; Ontario, 1871 ***1823.28*** *p54*
Lamont, Donald 66; Ontario, 1871 ***1823.15*** *p141*
Lamont, Fletcher; St. Louis, 1875 ***1640.13*** *p67*
Lamont, George 27; Ontario, 1871 ***1823.28*** *p54*
Lamont, Hugh 33; Ontario, 1871 ***1823.15*** *p141*
Lamont, Hugh 59; Ontario, 1871 ***1823.28*** *p54*
Lamont, James 30; Ontario, 1871 ***1823.15*** *p141*
Lamont, John 37; Ontario, 1871 ***1823.15*** *p141*
Lamont, John 57; Ontario, 1871 ***1823.15*** *p141*
Lamont, John 75; Ontario, 1871 ***1823.15*** *p141*
Lamont, Malcom 45; Ontario, 1871 ***1823.15*** *p141*
Lamont, Margaret 52; Ontario, 1871 ***1823.15*** *p141*
Lamont of Benmore, John; Trinidad, 1850 ***1640.13*** *p67*
Lamorandier, Alixis 64; Ontario, 1871 ***1823.28*** *p54*
Lamorandiere, Chs 53; Ontario, 1871 ***1823.28*** *p54*
Lamore, Peter; Maryland, 1665 ***2524.55*** *p132*
Lamothe, John Bertrand; New York, 1823 ***8197.10*** *p250*
Lamotte, William Henry; New York, 1857 ***1224.3*** *p45*
Lamouk, S. 32; British Columbia, 1910 ***9196.1*** *p28*
Lamouk, S. 32; Washington, 1910 ***9196.1*** *p28*
Lamp, Anna Justina; Port uncertain, 1792 ***2856.30*** *p261*
Lamp, Martin; America, 1741 ***2856.30*** *p261*
Lamparske, John; Maryland, 1910 ***3259.35*** *p34*
Lampart, Georg; Port uncertain, 1771 ***2856.30*** *p261*
With wife & 4 children
Lampe, Johann Henrich; Port uncertain, 1766 ***2856.30*** *p261*
Lampen, Mathew 23; Maryland, 1775 ***1220.25*** *p104*
Lampert, Margarete; Port uncertain, 1733 ***2856.30*** *p261*
Lamphart, Georg; Port uncertain, 1764 ***2856.30*** *p261*
Lamphigh, John; Virginia, 1666 ***6212.30*** *p30*
Lamphire, Thomas 81; Ontario, 1871 ***1823.28*** *p54*
Lampin, Anna Bella; Maryland, 1673 ***2524.55*** *p132*
Lampin, Elizabeth; Maryland, 1673 ***2524.55*** *p132*
Lampin, Thomas; Maryland, 1667 ***2524.55*** *p132*
Lampkey, John 56; Ontario, 1871 ***1823.28*** *p54*
Lampkey, Luey 40; Ontario, 1871 ***1823.28*** *p54*
Lampman, Celia E.; Vermont, 1847-1918 ***5900.10*** *p518*
Lamport, Edward 46; Ontario, 1871 ***1823.15*** *p141*
Lamport, Joseph 75; Ontario, 1871 ***1823.15*** *p141*
Lampre, Martin 23; Ontario, 1871 ***1823.15*** *p141*
Lampson, Charles G. 15; Ontario, 1861 ***2896.25*** *p25*
Lampson, Elizabeth J. 35; Ontario, 1861 ***2896.25*** *p25*
Lampson, Marrietta 5; Ontario, 1861 ***2896.25*** *p25*
Lampson, Rosilla A. 13; Ontario, 1861 ***2896.25*** *p25*
Lampson, William Elgin 9; Ontario, 1861 ***2896.25*** *p25*
L'Amy, Johann Georg; Port uncertain, 1724 ***2856.30*** *p260*
With wife
Lamy, Michael 65; Ontario, 1871 ***1823.22*** *p89*
Lanagan, John; New York, 1838 ***8197.10*** *p376*
Lanan, Bridget 84; Vermont, 1920 ***5900.10*** *p584*
Lancaster, Mrs.; Portland, Maine, 1858 ***9196.15*** *p27*
Lancaster, Daniel 53; Ontario, 1871 ***1823.22*** *p89*
Lancaster, Edward L. 40; Ontario, 1871 ***1823.28*** *p54*
Lancaster, Elisha; Virginia, 1694 ***1224.1*** *p35*
Lancaster, George; Maryland, 1673 ***2524.55*** *p132*
Lancaster, James; New York, 1837 ***8197.10*** *p95*
Lancaster, John 16; Maryland, 1774 ***1220.25*** *p65*
Lancaster, John 55; Ontario, 1871 ***1823.22*** *p89*
Lancaster, Robert; Virginia, 1685 ***1224.1*** *p35*
Lance, Charles 50; Ontario, 1871 ***1823.28*** *p54*
Lance, Richard 37; Ontario, 1871 ***1823.28*** *p55*
Lanchester, Robert 39; Ontario, 1871 ***1823.28*** *p55*
Lanchfield, Francis; Maryland, 1659 ***2524.55*** *p132*
Lanckeman, Dietrich; New York, 1807 ***8197.10*** *p44*
Lanckenau, Alexander; New York, 1807 ***8197.10*** *p44*
Lancovski, Theresa; Maryland, 1910 ***3259.35*** *p34*
Land, Henry; Pennsylvania, 1784 ***4629.10*** *p43*
Land, Priscilla; Maryland, 1649 ***2524.55*** *p132*
Landall, James; Maryland, 1681 ***2524.55*** *p132*
Landau, Christopher; New York, 1825 ***8197.10*** *p250*
Lande, Alice; Virginia, 1671 ***6212.30*** *p42*
Landeis, Barbara; Port uncertain, 1781 ***2856.30*** *p261*
Landeis, Magdalena; Port uncertain, 1781 ***2856.30*** *p261*
Landele, Philipp; Port uncertain, 1781 ***2856.30*** *p261*
Landell, John; New York, 1794 ***8197.10*** *p6*
Landen, Henry; Maryland, 1737 ***1224.2*** *p67*
Lander, Miss; Quebec, 1857 ***9196.15*** *p16*
Lander, Joanna 28; Maryland, 1775 ***1220.25*** *p114*
Lander, Johann Jakob; Port uncertain, 1760 ***2856.30*** *p261*
Lander, John 19; Philadelphia, 1774 ***1220.25*** *p82*
Lander, John 41; Ontario, 1861 ***2896.25*** *p60*
Lander, Kate; Vermont, 1850-1917 ***5900.10*** *p390*
Lander, William 3; Ontario, 1861 ***2896.25*** *p60*
Landerberger, Mathias; Pennsylvania, 1777 ***4629.10*** *p16*

Landerfin, Mary Devine; Vermont, 1837-1920 ***5900.10*** *p113*
Landeri, Anna Maria; Port uncertain, 1766 ***2856.30*** *p261*
Landers, Bartholomew; Vermont, 1854-1929 ***5900.10*** *p94*
Landers, Cuthbert; Pennsylvania, 1777 ***4629.10*** *p10*
Landers, John 28; Maryland, 1774 ***1220.25*** *p53*
Landers, John 40; Ontario, 1871 ***1823.28*** *p55*
Landers, John 77; Vermont, 1892 ***5900.10*** *p94*
Landers, Samuel 25; Maryland, 1774 ***1220.25*** *p77*
Landes, Friedrich; America, 1749 ***2856.30*** *p263*
Landes, Henrich; America, 1749 ***2856.30*** *p261*
With wife & 2 children
Landes, Rudolf Christia; America, 1749 ***2856.30*** *p263*
Landidge, Mary; Maryland, 1681 ***2524.55*** *p132*
Landifield, William; Boston, 1776 ***1224.2*** *p67*
Landis, Rich; Virginia, 1665-1666 ***6212.30*** *p22*
Landmesser, Jacob; America, 1770 ***2856.30*** *p261*
With wife
Landmesser, Jacob; Port uncertain, 1770 ***2856.30*** *p261*
With wife
Landon, Car 32; Ontario, 1861 ***2896.27*** *p7*
Landon, Gard 3; Ontario, 1861 ***2896.27*** *p6*
Landon, George 9; Ontario, 1861 ***2896.27*** *p6*
Landon, H. 5; Ontario, 1861 ***2896.27*** *p6*
Landon, John 40; Ontario, 1861 ***2896.27*** *p6*
Landon, Mary 67; Ontario, 1861 ***2896.27*** *p7*
Landon, Norman 71; Ontario, 1861 ***2896.27*** *p7*
Landon, Thomas 24; Maryland, 1775 ***1220.25*** *p107*
Landon, W.; Ontario, 1861 ***2896.27*** *p6*
Landon, William 11; Ontario, 1861 ***2896.27*** *p6*
Landreth, Katherine; Grenada, 1848 ***1640.13*** *p67*
Landrun, Francis; Maryland, 1676 ***2524.55*** *p132*
Landry, Edith 63; Vermont, 1899 ***5900.10*** *p616*
Landsboro, John 57; Ontario, 1871 ***1823.15*** *p141*
Landsboro, Samuel 51; Ontario, 1871 ***1823.15*** *p141*
Landsborogh, James 42; Ontario, 1871 ***1823.15*** *p141*
Landsborough, Jane 86; Ontario, 1871 ***1823.15*** *p141*
Landsborough, Robert 53; Ontario, 1871 ***1823.15*** *p141*
Landsmann, Jakob; America, 1738 ***2856.30*** *p261*
Landt, Johann Peter; Port uncertain, 1773 ***2856.30*** *p261*
Landy, John; New York, 1837 ***8197.10*** *p94*
Lane, Mrs.; Maryland, 1680 ***2524.55*** *p132*
Lane, Mrs.; Quebec, 1858 ***9196.15*** *p46*
Lane, Ann 44; Ontario, 1871 ***1823.28*** *p55*
Lane, Ann 65; Vermont, 1884 ***5900.10*** *p305*
Lane, Anne; Maryland, 1650 ***2524.55*** *p132*
Lane, Anne; Maryland, 1662 ***2524.55*** *p231*
Lane, Anne; Virginia, 1671-1672 ***6212.30*** *p47*
Lane, Bridget L.; Vermont, 1850-1918 ***5900.10*** *p300*
Lane, Catharine 76; Vermont, 1900 ***5900.10*** *p370*
Lane, Charles C. 17; Ontario, 1861 ***2896.28*** *p25*
Lane, David A. 15; Ontario, 1861 ***2896.28*** *p25*
Lane, Elizabeth; Maryland, 1672 ***2524.55*** *p132*
Lane, Ellen; Vermont, 1824-1909 ***5900.10*** *p395*
Lane, Ennis 45; Vermont, 1888 ***5900.10*** *p54*
Lane, Frencis R. 20; Ontario, 1861 ***2896.28*** *p25*
Lane, George; Maryland, 1662 ***2524.55*** *p28*
Lane, George A. 10; Ontario, 1861 ***2896.28*** *p25*
Lane, Gideon 29; Ontario, 1861 ***2896.28*** *p10*
Lane, Hanora Sullivan 72; Vermont, 1913 ***5900.10*** *p54*
Lane, Henry; Vermont, 1846-1907 ***5900.10*** *p256*
Lane, Henry 30; Ontario, 1871 ***1823.15*** *p141*
Lane, James 30; Ontario, 1871 ***1823.15*** *p141*
Lane, James A.; Vermont, 1833-1910 ***5900.10*** *p278*
Lane, James T. 25; Ontario, 1861 ***2896.28*** *p25*
Lane, Jeremiah 49; Ontario, 1871 ***1823.28*** *p55*
Lane, Jesper; Maryland, 1680 ***2524.55*** *p132*
Lane, John; Maryland, 1662 ***2524.55*** *p132*
Lane, John; Maryland, 1667 ***2524.55*** *p133*
Lane, John; North Carolina, 1748 ***1224.2*** *p67*
Lane, John; Vermont, 1818-1905 ***5900.10*** *p489*
Lane, John 17; Maryland, 1774 ***1220.25*** *p7*
Lane, John 17; Maryland, 1774 ***1220.25*** *p8*
Lane, John 28; Barbados, 1773-1774 ***1220.25*** *p32*
Lane, John 28; Ontario, 1871 ***1823.15*** *p141*
Lane, John 29; Ontario, 1871 ***1823.28*** *p55*
Lane, John 50; Ontario, 1871 ***1823.28*** *p55*
Lane, John F. 22; Ontario, 1861 ***2896.28*** *p25*
Lane, K. 20; Ontario, 1861 ***2896.28*** *p7*
Lane, Katherine; Vermont, 1855-1923 ***5900.10*** *p588*
Lane, Lydia B. 49; Ontario, 1861 ***2896.28*** *p25*
Lane, Lydia M. 19; Ontario, 1861 ***2896.28*** *p25*
Lane, Margaret 78; Vermont, 1871 ***5900.10*** *p305*
Lane, Margaret Foley; Vermont, 1827-1915 ***5900.10*** *p489*
Lane, Margaret M. Beaulac; Vermont, 1845-1945 ***5900.10*** *p278*
Lane, Martha; North Carolina, 1756 ***1224.2*** *p67*
Lane, Martha Davenport 68; Vermont, 1892 ***5900.10*** *p303*
Lane, Mary; Vermont, 1832-1911 ***5900.10*** *p393*
Lane, Mary Kelway; New England, 1651 ***1224.1*** *p34*
Lane, Michael; Vermont, 1844-1932 ***5900.10*** *p300*
Lane, Minerva A. 8; Ontario, 1861 ***2896.28*** *p25*
Lane, Patrick 80; Vermont, 1885 ***5900.10*** *p303*
Lane, Peter; Maryland, 1680 ***2524.55*** *p133*
Lane, Priscilla; Maryland, 1649 ***2524.55*** *p133*
Lane, Richard 32; Ontario, 1871 ***1823.22*** *p89*
Lane, Richard S.; New York, 1840 ***8197.10*** *p384*
Lane, Samuel W. 26; Ontario, 1871 ***1823.22*** *p89*
Lane, Sarah 21; Ontario, 1861 ***2896.25*** *p30*
Lane, Symon; Virginia, 1671-1672 ***6212.30*** *p47*
Lane, Thomas; Maryland, 1681 ***2524.55*** *p133*
Lane, Thomas; New York, 1839 ***8197.10*** *p252*
Lane, Thomas; Virginia, 1677 ***1224.1*** *p35*
Lane, Thomas 49; Ontario, 1871 ***1823.15*** *p141*
Lane, Thomas 58; Ontario, 1871 ***1823.28*** *p55*
Lane, Walter; Maryland, 1672 ***2524.55*** *p133*
Lane, Willet 18; Ontario, 1861 ***2896.27*** *p59*
Lane, William 19; Maryland, 1774 ***1220.25*** *p7*
Lane, William 46; Ontario, 1871 ***1823.28*** *p55*
Lane, William 58; Ontario, 1871 ***1823.15*** *p141*
Lane, William H. 5; Ontario, 1861 ***2896.28*** *p25*
Lanes, John; Virginia, 1670 ***6212.30*** *p42*
Laney, Thomas; Canada, 1756-1760 ***4628.40*** *p45*
Lanfear, Mary Hill; New Orleans, 1842 ***1224.3*** *p45*
Lang, Mr.; Quebec, 1858 ***9196.15*** *p35*
Lang, Agnes; Maryland, 1910 ***3259.35*** *p34*
Lang, Alexander; Port uncertain, 1775 ***2856.30*** *p261*
Lang, Ann 26; Vermont, 1876 ***5900.10*** *p537*
Lang, Anna Apollonia; Port uncertain, 1750 ***2856.30*** *p261*
Lang, Anna Barbara; Port uncertain, 1768 ***2856.30*** *p261*
Lang, Anna Elisabeth; America, 1749 ***2856.30*** *p261*
Lang, Anna Elisabeth; America, 1749 ***2856.30*** *p263*
With husband
Lang, Anna Maria; Port uncertain, 1729 ***2856.30*** *p261*
Lang, Anna Maria; Port uncertain, 1766 ***2856.30*** *p261*
Lang, August 49; Ontario, 1871 ***1823.28*** *p55*
Lang, B. B.; Vermont, 1848-1908 ***5900.10*** *p153*
Lang, Barbara *SEE* Lang, Hans Adam
Lang, Benjamin; New England, 1750 ***1224.2*** *p67*
Lang, Bridget Mary; Vermont, 1848-1903 ***5900.10*** *p181*
Lang, Catharina; America, 1752 ***2856.30*** *p261*
Lang, Catharina; Port uncertain, 1773 ***2856.30*** *p261*
Lang, Catherine 24; Vermont, 1876 ***5900.10*** *p153*
Lang, Christian; Port uncertain, 1769 ***2856.30*** *p261*
Lang, Christian; Port uncertain, 1770 ***2856.30*** *p261*
Lang, Christina; Port uncertain, 1751 ***2856.30*** *p261*
Lang, Daniel; Port uncertain, 1760 ***2856.30*** *p261*
Lang, Eliza 21; Vermont, 1876 ***5900.10*** *p537*
Lang, Ellen 25; Vermont, 1880 ***5900.10*** *p537*
Lang, Friedrich; Port uncertain, 1732 ***2856.30*** *p261*
Lang, George 26; Ontario, 1871 ***1823.22*** *p89*
Lang, Hans Adam; America, 1739 ***2856.30*** *p263*
Wife: Barbara
Lang, Hans Georg; Port uncertain, 1752 ***2856.30*** *p261*
Lang, Hans Jacob; America, 1752 ***2856.30*** *p261*
Lang, Hans Michael; America, 1752 ***2856.30*** *p263*
With wife & 2 children
Lang, Jacob; America, 1754 ***2856.30*** *p261*
Lang, Jacob; Port uncertain, 1753 ***2856.30*** *p261*
Lang, Jacob; Port uncertain, 1766 ***2856.30*** *p262*
Lang, Jacob; Port uncertain, 1769 ***2856.30*** *p261*
Lang, Jakob; America, 1737 ***2856.30*** *p262*
Lang, Jakob; Port uncertain, 1737 ***2856.30*** *p262*
Lang, Jakob; Port uncertain, 1767 ***2856.30*** *p262*
Lang, James; Vermont, 1817-1902 ***5900.10*** *p153*
Lang, James; Vermont, 1854-1924 ***5900.10*** *p153*
Lang, Jerg; America, 1752 ***2856.30*** *p262*
Lang, Johann; Port uncertain, 1795 ***2856.30*** *p262*
Lang, Johann; Port uncertain, 1796 ***2856.30*** *p262*
Lang, Johann Daniel; Port uncertain, 1784 ***2856.30*** *p262*
Lang, Johann Jacob; America, 1733 ***2856.30*** *p262*
Lang, Johann Jakob; Port uncertain, 1744 ***2856.30*** *p262*
Lang, Johann Jakob; Port uncertain, 1749 ***2856.30*** *p262*
Lang, Johann Martin; Port uncertain, 1764 ***2856.30*** *p262*
Lang, Johann Nickel; America, 1736 ***2856.30*** *p262*
Lang, Johann Nickel; America, 1736 ***2856.30*** *p263*
With wife & children
Lang, Johann Peter; Port uncertain, 1751 ***2856.30*** *p263*
With wife & children
Lang, Johann Valtin; America, 1737 ***2856.30*** *p262*
Lang, John; Pennsylvania, 1858 ***6058.10*** *p40*
Lang, Konrad; America, 1744 ***2856.30*** *p263*
With wife & 4 children
Lang, Konrad; America, 1752 ***2856.30*** *p262*
Lang, Konrad; Port uncertain, 1784 ***2856.30*** *p262*
Lang, Leonhart; America, 1749 ***2856.30*** *p262*
Lang, Lothar; Port uncertain, 1769 ***2856.30*** *p262*
Lang, Margaret; Vermont, 1769-1878 ***5900.10*** *p612*
Lang, Margaret 70; Ontario, 1871 ***1823.22*** *p89*
Lang, Maria Apollonia; Port uncertain, 1753 ***2856.30*** *p262*
Lang, Maria Catharina; Port uncertain, 1750 ***2856.30*** *p262*
Lang, Maria Christina; America, 1765 ***2856.30*** *p262*
Lang, Martin; Port uncertain, 1737 ***2856.30*** *p262*
Lang, Mary 5; Vermont, 1854 ***5900.10*** *p153*
Lang, Mary Cassidy 72; Vermont, 1894 ***5900.10*** *p153*
Lang, Mary Jane 22; Vermont, 1874 ***5900.10*** *p537*
Lang, Michael; New York, 1837 ***8197.10*** *p95*
Lang, Michael; Port uncertain, 1753 ***2856.30*** *p262*
Lang, Michael; Port uncertain, 1754 ***2856.30*** *p262*
Lang, Michael 46; Ontario, 1871 ***1823.28*** *p55*
Lang, Nickel; Port uncertain, 1767 ***2856.30*** *p262*
Lang, Nickhel; Port uncertain, 1756 ***2856.30*** *p262*
Lang, Patrick Henry; Vermont, 1852-1923 ***5900.10*** *p153*
Lang, Peter 54; Ontario, 1871 ***1823.22*** *p89*
Lang, Philipp; Port uncertain, 1794 ***2856.30*** *p262*
Lang, Philipp Adam; Port uncertain, 1764 ***2856.30*** *p262*
Lang, Philipp Jakob; Port uncertain, 1777 ***2856.30*** *p262*
Lang, Sarah 80; Vermont, 1893 ***5900.10*** *p537*
Lang, Sebastian; Port uncertain, 1766 ***2856.30*** *p262*
Lang, Therese; Port uncertain, 1764 ***2856.30*** *p262*
Lang, Thomas; Port uncertain, 1766 ***2856.30*** *p262*
Lang, Veit; Port uncertain, 1612 ***2856.30*** *p262*
Lang, William Giltenan; Boston, 1856 ***1224.3*** *p45*
Lang, Winifred; Vermont, 1834-1907 ***5900.10*** *p138*
Langan, Catherine A.; Vermont, 1832-1900 ***5900.10*** *p186*
Langan, James; New York, 1839 ***8197.10*** *p252*
Langan, Mathew 26; Ontario, 1871 ***1823.28*** *p55*
Langan, Thomas; New York, 1837 ***8197.10*** *p95*
Langbridge, Mr.; Quebec, 1856 ***9196.15*** *p6*
Langdale, Mr.; Quebec, 1858 ***9196.15*** *p34*
Langdale, William 51; Ontario, 1871 ***1823.15*** *p141*
Langdell, Anne; Maryland, 1676 ***2524.55*** *p133*
Langdon, Emily Jane 28; Ontario, 1871 ***1823.28*** *p55*
Langdon, James; New York, 1831 ***8197.10*** *p366*
Langdon, John 18; Maryland, 1775 ***1220.25*** *p102*
Langdon, Walter; Virginia, 1666 ***6212.30*** *p28*
Langdon, William; New York, 1842 ***1224.3*** *p45*
Langdon, William 59; Ontario, 1871 ***1823.22*** *p89*
Lange, Elizabeth; Virginia, 1669-1670 ***6212.30*** *p41*
Lange, Elizabeth; Virginia, 1681-1682 ***6212.30*** *p55*
Lange, Frederick; New York, 1840 ***8197.10*** *p252*
Lange, Hen; Virginia, 1672 ***6212.30*** *p50*
Lange, Maria Margaretha; New York, 1840 ***8197.10*** *p385*
Lange, Otto; Indiana, 1879-1884 ***3437.14*** *p199*
Langegger, Josef; Port uncertain, 1745 ***2856.30*** *p263*
Langen, James; New York, 1837 ***8197.10*** *p94*
Langenbach, Christina; Port uncertain, 1782 ***2856.30*** *p263*
Langenbach, Christina; Port uncertain, 1784 ***2856.30*** *p263*
Langendorf, Catharina; Port uncertain, 1768 ***2856.30*** *p263*
Langendorfer, . . .; Port uncertain, 1771 ***2856.30*** *p263*
Langenfeld, Lucia; Port uncertain, 1764 ***2856.30*** *p263*
Husband: Maladin
Langenfeld, Maladin *SEE* Langenfeld, Lucia
Langester, John 29; Philadelphia, 1774 ***1220.25*** *p67*
Langfeild, Obadiath; Virginia, 1667-1668 ***6212.30*** *p38*
Langfield, Mr.; Quebec, 1858 ***9196.15*** *p42*
Langfield, Francis; Maryland, 1653 ***2524.55*** *p82*
Langford, Edward; Maryland, 1644 ***2524.55*** *p133*
Langford, Humphry; Virginia, 1671-1672 ***6212.30*** *p47*
Langford, Isaac 50; Ontario, 1871 ***1823.28*** *p55*
Langford, John; Maryland, 1658 ***2524.55*** *p133*
Langford, John 62; Ontario, 1871 ***1823.22*** *p89*
Langford, Manuel 34; Ontario, 1871 ***1823.22*** *p89*
Langford, Thomas 50; Ontario, 1871 ***1823.28*** *p55*
Langford, William 32; Maryland, 1774 ***1220.25*** *p70*
Langhafe, Amalia 28; Kansas, 1897-1910 ***9079.10*** *p37*
Langhafe, David 40; Kansas, 1892-1910 ***9079.10*** *p37*
Langhen, Anne; Virginia, 1667 ***6212.30*** *p35*
Langherrer, Owin; Virginia, 1664-1665 ***6212.30*** *p16*
Langhom, James; Virginia, 1690-1691 ***6212.30*** *p59*
Langhorne, Daniel; Maryland, 1681 ***2524.55*** *p133*
Langhorne, Thomas; Pennsylvania, 1689 ***1224.1*** *p35*
Langhorne, William; Maryland, 1716 ***1224.2*** *p67*
Langler, Johann Nikolaus; Port uncertain, 1745 ***2856.30*** *p280*
Langley, George; Maryland, 1671 ***2524.55*** *p133*
Langley, Henry; Maryland, 1671 ***2524.55*** *p133*
Langley, James; New York, 1806 ***8197.10*** *p322*
Langley, John 27; Philadelphia, 1774 ***1220.25*** *p67*
Langley, Josiah 25; Philadelphia, 1774 ***1220.25*** *p67*
Langley, Margaret; Maryland, 1699 ***1224.1*** *p35*
Langley, Mathew; Virginia, 1664 ***6212.30*** *p11*
Langley, Thomas; Maryland, 1665 ***2524.55*** *p133*
Langley, Timothy 22; Philadelphia, 1774 ***1220.25*** *p67*
Langley, William; Maryland, 1657 ***2524.55*** *p133*
Langlois, Charles; New York, 1824 ***8197.10*** *p250*
Langlois, J.; Quebec, 1857 ***9196.15*** *p23*

Langly, Tho; Virginia, 1666 6212.30 p28
Langoski, John; Maryland, 1910 3259.35 p34
Langridge, Levi; New York, 1828 8197.10 p65
Langsaver, Johnathan; Baltimore, 1852 6058.10 p38
Langsdaile, Jno; Virginia, 1681-1682 6212.30 p56
Langstader, Bernard; New York, 1840 8197.10 p252
Langstea, John; Pennsylvania, 1779 4629.10 p36
Langsten, Archibald C., Jr.; New York, 1837 8197.10 p107
Langston, Mrs.; Maryland, 1682 2524.55 p133
Langston, William; Maryland, 1682 2524.55 p133
Langston, William; Virginia, 1659 1224.1 p35
Langton, Alfred 32; Ontario, 1871 1823.28 p55
Langton, Edward; Maryland, 1679 2524.55 p133
Langton, Jane *SEE* Langton, Walter
Langton, Joseph J.; Vermont, 1846-1922 5900.10 p491
Langton, Mary; Vermont, 1846-1925 5900.10 p491
Langton, Walter *SEE* Langton, Walter
Langton, Walter; Maryland, 1667 2524.55 p133
Wife: Jane
Child: Walter
Child: Jane
Langton, Wenman 39; Ontario, 1871 1823.28 p55
Langtree, Jas 28; Ontario, 1871 1823.28 p55
Languishe, William 30; New York, 1833-1837 8197.10 p94
Langwill, Jessie; New York, 1899 1640.13 p67
Langworth, James; Maryland, 1635-1641 2524.55 p133
Langworth, James; Maryland, 1647 2524.55 p133
Lanigan, Cornelius 71; Vermont, 1894 5900.10 p260
Lanigan, James 17; Vermont, 1873 5900.10 p325
Lanigan, Peter 28; Vermont, 1882 5900.10 p325
Lanigan, Sarah Keeshan 77; Vermont, 1908 5900.10 p260
Laninger, Balthasar; Port uncertain, 1763 2856.30 p263
Lanman, William; Boston, 1726 1224.2 p67
Lannaier, Augustine; New York, 1802 8197.10 p22
Lannen, James 31; Ontario, 1871 1823.15 p142
Lanner, Lawrence; Pennsylvania, 1825 6058.10 p8
Lannigan, Richard; New York, 1840 8197.10 p252
Lannock, Martha; Maryland, 1653 2524.55 p133
Lannon, John 40; Ontario, 1871 1823.28 p55
Lannon, Patrick 37; Ontario, 1871 1823.22 p89
Lannsur, Augustine; New York, 1802 8197.10 p22
Lannuier, Augustus; New York, 1809 8197.10 p55
Lanphier, Silas A. 69; Ontario, 1871 1823.22 p89
Lansanski, John; Maryland, 1910 3259.35 p34
Lansford, Mary; Maryland, 1668 2524.55 p133
Lant, Miss; Quebec, 1857 9196.15 p16
Lant, Mr.; Quebec, 1857 9196.15 p16
Lant, Miles; Maryland, 1668 2524.55 p133
Lantes, Friedrich; America, 1749 2856.30 p263
Lantes, Rudolf Christia; America, 1749 2856.30 p263
Lantherne, Will; Maryland, 1664 2524.55 p133
Lantry, Thomas; New York, 1837 8197.10 p94
Lantz, Anna Maria; Port uncertain, 1739 2856.30 p263
Lantz, Hans Peter; America, 1738 2856.30 p263
Lantz, Jakob; America, 1738 2856.30 p263
Lantz, Johann; Port uncertain, 1739 2856.30 p263
Lantz, Leonard; Port uncertain, 1726 2856.30 p263
With wife & children
Lantz, Michael; America, 1738 2856.30 p263
Lanus, Peter; New York, 1807 8197.10 p44
Lanwehr, Friedrich; Port uncertain, 1799 2856.30 p263
Lanxman, Johann Georg; New York, 1838 8197.10 p122
Lanz, Mrs. Michael; America, 1738 2856.30 p263
Lanzenberger, Marianna; Port uncertain, 1768 2856.30 p263
With husband & 6 children
Lapan, Mary 75; Vermont, 1910 5900.10 p485
Lapham, Joel; Pennsylvania, 1866 6058.10 p51
Lapier, John 49; Ontario, 1871 1823.15 p142
Lapier, Mary 70; Ontario, 1871 1823.15 p142
Lapierre, Azilda; Vermont, 1855-1919 5900.10 p85
Lapierre, Josephine; Vermont, 1854 5900.10 p193
Laporete, Joseph Polyxene; Windward Islands, 1837 1640.13 p68
Lapp, Samuel 81; Ontario, 1871 1823.22 p89
Lapp, Sarah 19; Ontario, 1861 2896.27 p56
Lappage, Edward; Maryland, 1681 2524.55 p133
Lappon, William; New York, 1795 8197.10 p7
Lapsley, David; Pennsylvania, 1777 4629.10 p25
Lapslu, Elizabeth 55; Ontario, 1871 1823.15 p142
Lapthone, Petr; Virginia, 1672 6212.30 p50
Laque, Georg; Port uncertain, 1764 2856.30 p263
Larabee, John; New England, 1694 1224.1 p35
Laragne, R. Lachicotte 34; Pennsylvania, 1794 4629.10 p63
Laraman, Wm; Virginia, 1664 6212.30 p15
Laranceson, Job 16; Ontario, 1861 2896.28 p60
Laraneson, Margaret; Maryland, 1674 2524.55 p134
Lard, Hester; Maryland, 1660 2524.55 p133
Larding, Jesper; Maryland, 1651 2524.55 p133
Lardois, Jean; Virginia, 1664 6212.30 p5
Larelle, Joseph; Philadelphia, 1794 4629.10 p81
Laremore, Alexander; Maryland, 1658 2524.55 p133
Larence, Charles 15; Ontario, 1861 2896.27 p14
Larford, Tho; Virginia, 1667 6212.30 p36
Large, Alfred; New York, 1840 8197.10 p252
Large, William 53; Ontario, 1871 1823.15 p142
Largery, John; New York, 1827 8197.10 p343
Largish, Thomas; Maryland, 1663 2524.55 p133
Larichi, P. F. 32; Ontario, 1871 1823.22 p89
Larimar, George 60; Ontario, 1871 1823.15 p142
Larinan, Michael; New York, 1838 8197.10 p122
Larise, P. 30; Alaska, 1917 9196.1 p53
Larise, P. 30; Whitehorse, Yukon, 1917 9196.1 p53
Larke, Rowland; Virginia, 1666 6212.30 p25
Larkey, Nicholas; Maryland, 1659 2524.55 p133
Larkey, Nocholas; Maryland, 1659 2524.55 p12
Larkie, Nicholas; Maryland, 1661 2524.55 p133
With wife
Larkin, Ann; Vermont, n.d. 5900.10 p594
Larkin, Anna 68; Vermont, 1887 5900.10 p467
Larkin, Catherine; Vermont, 1824-1898 5900.10 p392
Larkin, Catherine L.; Vermont, 1835-1915 5900.10 p594
Larkin, Charles; Vermont, 1875-1912 5900.10 p392
Larkin, Edna J.; Vermont, 1857-1914 5900.10 p492
Larkin, Elizabeth; Vermont, 1866 5900.10 p157
Larkin, James; New York, 1840 8197.10 p187
Larkin, James; Vermont, 1822-1888 5900.10 p392
Larkin, James; Vermont, 1860-1924 5900.10 p392
Larkin, James 74; Ontario, 1861 2896.27 p31
Larkin, Julia 58; Vermont, 1908 5900.10 p395
Larkin, Margaret; Vermont, n.d. 5900.10 p199
Larkin, Maria; Vermont, 1856-1936 5900.10 p392
Larkin, Mary; Vermont, 1840-1922 5900.10 p157
Larkin, Michael; New York, 1840 8197.10 p186
Larkin, Neil; New York, 1839 8197.10 p320
Larkin, Patrick; New York, 1840 8197.10 p186
Larkin, Patrick; Vermont, 1848-1932 5900.10 p395
Larkin, Peter; New York, 1840 8197.10 p185
Larkin, Peter 40; Vermont, 1896 5900.10 p91
Larkin, Rosa; Vermont, 1862-1937 5900.10 p91
Larkin, Thomas 47; Vermont, 1872 5900.10 p248
Larkins, Mr.; Quebec, 1858 9196.15 p39
Larkins, James; New York, 1697 1224.1 p35
Larkins, Thomas; San Francisco, 1850 1224.3 p45
Larmang, Samuel 68; Ontario, 1871 1823.22 p89
Larmay, Frederick 51; Ontario, 1871 1823.15 p142
Larmay, Lucy 38; Vermont, 1875 5900.10 p202
Larmont, Thomas 40; Ontario, 1871 1823.15 p142
Larmoth, Thom.; Maryland, 1682 2524.55 p133
Larmount, John; Boston, 1720 1224.2 p67
Larmy, Louisa 88; Vermont, 1931 5900.10 p202
Larmy, Peter 77; Vermont, 1914 5900.10 p202
Larn, Anna; Ontario, 1861 2896.28 p63
Larn, Joseph; Ontario, 1861 2896.28 p63
Larner, . . .; Albany, New York, 1758 1224.2 p67
Larner, Kate Burke; Vermont, 1855-1904 5900.10 p159
Larner, Margaret O.; Vermont, 1894 5900.10 p409
Larner, Maria Barry; Vermont, 1851-1887 5900.10 p315
Larner, Mark W.; Vermont, 1855-1886 5900.10 p409
Larner, Michael; Vermont, 1879-1933 5900.10 p315
Larner, Michael; Vermont, 1890 5900.10 p409
Larner, Thomas; Vermont, 1857-1930 5900.10 p159
Larner, William; Vermont, 1848-1888 5900.10 p315
Larney, James; New York, 1839 8197.10 p320
Larney, Michael; New York, 1837 8197.10 p94
LaRoche, James; Maryland, 1670 2524.55 p127
Larose, Frank 61; Ontario, 1871 1823.28 p55
Larot, Peter; Pennsylvania, 1777 4629.10 p29
Larramore, Alexander; Maryland, 1658 2524.55 p133
Larramore, Edward *SEE* Larramore, Roger
Larramore, Rachell *SEE* Larramore, Roger
Larramore, Roger; Maryland, 1661 2524.55 p133
Wife: Rachell
Son: Edward
Larramore, Roger; Maryland, 1663 2524.55 p134
Larrance, George 72; Ontario, 1871 1823.22 p89
Larrance, Mary; Maryland, 1666 2524.55 p134
Larrance, William; Maryland, 1665 2524.55 p134
Larrence, Charles; Boston, 1687 1224.1 p35
Larrett, Fanny 38; Ontario, 1871 1823.28 p55
Larsen, A. 53; Alaska, 1918 9196.1 p54
Larsen, A. 53; Whitehorse, Yukon, 1918 9196.1 p54
Larsen, C. 28; Alaska, 1916 9196.1 p42
Larsen, C. 28; Whitehorse, Yukon, 1916 9196.1 p42
Larsen, Hans; New York, New York, 1889 3437.14 p140
Larsen, John 27; British Columbia, 1914 9196.1 p65
Larsen, John 27; Washington, 1914 9196.1 p65
Larsen, Ole 23; British Columbia, 1912 9196.1 p15
Larsen, Ole 23; San Francisco, 1912 9196.1 p15
Larson, Alex 23; Alaska, 1915 9196.1 p42
Larson, Eric 34; British Columbia, 1913 9196.1 p21
Larson, Eric 34; Seattle, 1913 9196.1 p21
Larson, Godfrey; New York, New York, 1902 3437.14 p132
Larson, Gus 30; British Columbia, 1909 9196.1 p28
Larson, Gus 30; Seattle, 1909 9196.1 p28
Larson, Gust 42; British Columbia, 1909 9196.1 p27
Larson, Gust 42; Seattle, 1909 9196.1 p27
Larson, Marie 24; Seattle, 1917 9196.1 p52
Larson, Marie 24; Yukon, 1917 9196.1 p52
Larson, Ole 21; Seattle, 1917 9196.1 p51
Larson, Ole 21; Yukon, 1917 9196.1 p51
La Rue, Mr.; Portland, Maine, 1857 9196.15 p12
Larue, Mr.; Quebec, 1858 9196.15 p32
La Rue, Joseph Henry; New York, 1803 8197.10 p9
Larue, Peter 60; Ontario, 1861 2896.25 p39
Larus, Charles 42; Ontario, 1871 1823.22 p89
Larwill, Abraham; New York, 1820 8197.10 p249
Lasage, Madiline 80; Ontario, 1871 1823.28 p55
Lasak, Francis W.; New York, 1828 8197.10 p65
Lasavich, E. 40; Alaska, 1917 9196.1 p50
Lasavich, E. 40; British Columbia, 1917 9196.1 p50
Laselle, Emma W.; Vermont, 1854-1926 5900.10 p500
Lasey, John 27; Maryland, 1774 1220.25 p47
Lash, Mrs.; Quebec, 1858 9196.15 p42
Lasham, John 29; Ontario, 1871 1823.15 p142
Lasher, Will.; Maryland, 1652 2524.55 p134
Lashley, Lauchlin; North Carolina, 1801 1640.10 p94
Lasier, Batsheba 11; Ontario, 1861 2896.27 p29
Lasing, Anne; Virginia, 1667-1668 6212.30 p39
Lasingby, Robt; Virginia, 1666-1667 6212.30 p35
Lasingby, Thomas; Virginia, 1667-1668 6212.30 p39
Lasinn, Anna Maria Schmutzig; Port uncertain, 1784 2856.30 p280
Lasinsky, Dominik; Maryland, 1910 3259.35 p34
Laskowski, Antony; Maryland, 1910 3259.35 p34
Lasome, William 32; Ontario, 1871 1823.15 p142
Lass, Johann Philipp; America, 1746 2856.30 p263
With wife & 5 children
Lass, Johann Valentin; America, 1754 2856.30 p263
Lassam, William 32; Ontario, 1871 1823.28 p55
Lassells, Jarvis; Maryland, 1682 2524.55 p134
Lassingby, Roger; Virginia, 1664-1665 6212.30 p16
Lassmeyer, Matthaus; Port uncertain, 1761 2856.30 p280
Last, Harry 56; Ontario, 1871 1823.28 p55
Latchett, Robert; Maryland, 1682 2524.55 p134
Latchfeild, Nich; Virginia, 1668-1669 6212.30 p40
Latchvin, George; Maryland, 1677 2524.55 p134
Latchwin, George; Maryland, 1677 2524.55 p134
Lateur, Benjamin 22; Ontario, 1861 2896.25 p11
Lateur, Deborah 55; Ontario, 1861 2896.25 p11
Lateur, Lewis 19; Ontario, 1861 2896.25 p11
Lateur, Lucy M. 10; Ontario, 1861 2896.25 p11
Latewood, William 21; Maryland, 1775 1220.25 p120
Latham, Carey; New England, 1680 1224.1 p34
Latham, John 16; Virginia, 1774 1220.25 p91
Latham, John 32; Halifax, Nova Scotia, 1774 1220.25 p138
Latham, Mary 20; Grenada, 1774 1220.25 p127
Latham, Nathaniel; New York, 1818 8197.10 p248
Latham, Samuel; New York, 1839 8197.10 p136
Latham, Stephen; Maryland, 1660 2524.55 p134
Latham, Thomas 20; Maryland, 1774 1220.25 p60
Latham, William; Maryland, 1662 2524.55 p134
Latham, William Henry; New York, 1844 1224.3 p45
Lathanski, M.; Maryland, 1910 3259.35 p34
Lathbarey, John; Virginia, 1703-1704 6212.30 p62
Lathbury, John; Virginia, 1655 1224.1 p35
Latheme, William; Maryland, 1662 2524.55 p134
Lather, William; Maryland, 1659 2524.55 p134
Lathorn, Edward; Maryland, 1681 2524.55 p134
Lathum, Deborah; Virginia, 1690 6212.30 p58
Lathur, Hermann; America, 1749 2856.30 p263
Latimen, Annie 24; Ontario, 1871 1823.15 p142
Latimen, Edward 20; Ontario, 1871 1823.15 p142
Latimen, John 22; Ontario, 1871 1823.15 p142
Latimen, Mary 58; Ontario, 1871 1823.15 p142
Latimen, Sarah 18; Ontario, 1871 1823.15 p142
Latimen, Thomas 26; Ontario, 1871 1823.15 p142
Latimer, George; Pennsylvania, 1777 4629.10 p31
Latimer, Henry 62; Ontario, 1871 1823.15 p142
Latimer, John; New York, 1839 8197.10 p136
Latimer, Robert 60; Ontario, 1871 1823.15 p142
Latimor, James 25; Ontario, 1871 1823.22 p90
Latimore, Amey; Maryland, 1672 2524.55 p134
Latoes, Clement; Maryland, 1661 2524.55 p134
Laton, Cristop; Virginia, 1666 6212.30 p29
Laton, Henry; Virginia, 1671 6212.30 p42
Laton, William; Virginia, 1703-1704 6212.30 p62
Latremouille, Julia Joanna; Vermont, 1796-1822 5900.10 p321
Latroyes, Elizabeth *SEE* Latroyes, Peter
Latroyes, Peter; Maryland, 1669 2524.55 p134
Wife: Elizabeth
Latroys, Elizabeth *SEE* Latroys, Peter

Latroys, Peter; Maryland, 1669 2524.55 p134
Wife: Elizabeth
Latsendis, Nick 20; Washington, 1913 9196.1 p61
Latta, James Douglas; Texas, 1896 1640.13 p68
Latta, Robert; New York, 1838 8197.10 p123
Lattan, Lewis; New York, 1834 8197.10 p72
Lattig, Johann Georg; America, 1738 2856.30 p264
Lattimer, Marg 74; Ontario, 1871 1823.22 p90
Lattimes, Levi 30; Ontario, 1871 1823.15 p142
Lattin, Nicholas; Maryland, 1681 2524.55 p134
Lattner, Franziska; Port uncertain, 1716 2856.30 p264
With child
Lattner, Gotthard; Port uncertain, 1746 2856.30 p264
Lattner, Joachim; Port uncertain, 1714 2856.30 p264
Lattoton, James 39; Ontario, 1871 1823.15 p142
Laub, Catharina; America, 1732 2856.30 p264
Laub, Catharina; Port uncertain, 1621 2856.30 p264
Laub, Catharina; Port uncertain, 1757 2856.30 p264
With 6 children
Laub, Catharina; Port uncertain, 1765 2856.30 p264
With 6 children
Laub, Fridrich; Port uncertain, 1727 2856.30 p264
Laub, John; New York, 1834 8197.10 p72
Laubach, Christian; Port uncertain, 1784 2856.30 p264
Laubach, Christian; Port uncertain, 1785 2856.30 p264
Laubban, Alex 26; Kansas, 1909-1910 9079.10 p46
Laubban, Marie 25; Kansas, 1910 9079.10 p46
Laube, Catharina; Port uncertain, 1757 2856.30 p264
With 6 children
Laube, Catharina; Port uncertain, 1765 2856.30 p264
With 6 children
Laubenbach, Mrs. Andreas; America, 1738 2856.30 p264
With 2 daughters
Laubenberger, Anna Maria; Port uncertain, 1746 2856.30 p264
Laubenstein, Johann; Port uncertain, 1783 2856.30 p264
With wife & children
Laubenstein, Johann Peter; America, 1764 2856.30 p264
Laubenstein, Maria Elisabeth; America, 1782 2856.30 p264
With daughter
Laubenstein, Maria Elisabeth; America, 1787 2856.30 p264
With daughter
Laubenstein, Maria Elisabeth; Port uncertain, 1767 2856.30 p264
With daughter
Laubenstein, Peter; America, 1764 2856.30 p264
Laubenstein, Philipp; Port uncertain, 1781 2856.30 p264
Laucher, Josef; Port uncertain, 1738 2856.30 p264
Lauchinski, Andy; Maryland, 1910 3259.35 p34
Lauck, David; Pennsylvania, 1786 4629.10 p51
Laudan, Charles P.; New York, 1834 8197.10 p72
Laudenberger, Fred 31; Ontario, 1871 1823.28 p55
Lauder, Christian; Jamaica, 1802 1640.13 p68
Lauder, David 65; Ontario, 1861 2896.27 p39
Lauder, George; Jamaica, 1802 1640.13 p68
Lauder, Jane; Savannah, Georgia, 1823 1640.10 p94
Lauder, Margaret 70; Ontario, 1871 1823.22 p90
Lauder, Mary; Augusta, Georgia, 1797 1640.10 p95
Lauder, Mary; Georgia, 1797 1640.13 p68
Lauder, Robert Seaton; Jamaica, 1802 1640.13 p68
Lauder, Thomas; Maryland, 1681 2524.55 p134
Lauder, William; Jamaica, 1802 1640.13 p68
Lauder, William 43; Ontario, 1871 1823.22 p90
Lauders, John 44; Ontario, 1871 1823.15 p142
Laudmild, Francis; Maryland, 1671 2524.55 p134
Laudum, Francis; Maryland, 1671 2524.55 p134
Lauenschneider, Peter; Port uncertain, 1786 2856.30 p264
Lauer, Anna Maria; Port uncertain, 1783 2856.30 p265
Lauer, Barbara; Port uncertain, 1696 2856.30 p265
Lauer, Barbara; Port uncertain, 1717 2856.30 p265
Lauer, Catharina; Port uncertain, 1788 2856.30 p264
Lauer, Christian; America, 1733 2856.30 p264
Lauer, Christian; America, 1739 2856.30 p264
Lauer, Christina; America, 1769 2856.30 p264
Lauer, Jakob; America, 1737 2856.30 p264
Lauer, Johann Michael; Port uncertain, 1740 2856.30 p264
Lauer, Johann Michael; Port uncertain, 1749 2856.30 p264
Lauer, Ludwig; Port uncertain, 1792 2856.30 p264
Lauer, Michael; America, 1737 2856.30 p264
Lauermann, Josef; Port uncertain, 1766 2856.30 p265
Laufer, Christian; America, 1754 2856.30 p265
Laufer, Christian; Port uncertain, 1728 2856.30 p265
Laufer, Johann Peter; Port uncertain, 1784 2856.30 p265
Laufer, Johann Peter; Port uncertain, 1790 2856.30 p265
Laufer, Lorenz; America, 1754 2856.30 p265
Laufer, Lorenz; Port uncertain, 1728 2856.30 p265
Lauff, Charlotte; Port uncertain, 1749 2856.30 p265
Lauff, Johann Konrad; Port uncertain, 1746 2856.30 p265
Lauff, Philip L.; New York, 1802 8197.10 p9
Lauger, Sara; Port uncertain, 1796 2856.30 p265
Laughan, George; Maryland, 1652-1658 2524.55 p134
Laugher, Elizabeth; Hartford, Connecticut, n.d. 1224.3 p87
Laughlen, Peter; New York, 1837 8197.10 p94
Laughlin, Catherine 76; Vermont, 1907 5900.10 p539
Laughlin, George; New York, 1831-1838 8197.10 p122
Laughlin, J. D. 77; Vermont, 1900 5900.10 p498
Laughlin, James 21; New York, 1836-1840 8197.10 p186
Laughlin, Patrick 40; Ontario, 1871 1823.15 p142
Laughlin, Samuel; Pennsylvania, 1846 6058.10 p22
Laughlin, Thomas 45; Ontario, 1871 1823.22 p90
Laughlin, Timothy; New York, 1835-1838 8197.10 p122
Laughorn, Charles Frederick; New York, 1839 8197.10 p136
Laughran, Edward; New York, 1836 8197.10 p76
Laughrin, John 50; Ontario, 1871 1823.28 p55
Laughry, Matthew; New York, 1840 8197.10 p185
Laughton, Patrick; Georgia, 1698 1640.13 p68
Lauinger, Michael; Port uncertain, 1752 2856.30 p265
With wife & children
Launay, Augustus; New York, 1834 8197.10 p72
Laundon, Margaretta; Ohio, 1855 1224.3 p45
Laundre, Paul; New York, 1822 8197.10 p249
Laundy, Edward 31; Ontario, 1871 1823.15 p142
Laundy, Henry 62; Ontario, 1871 1823.15 p142
Laur, A. 24; Ontario, 1861 2896.28 p15
Laur, C. M. 12; Ontario, 1861 2896.28 p15
Laur, J. 30; Ontario, 1861 2896.28 p15
Laur, James T. 66; Ontario, 1861 2896.28 p15
Laur, M. 16; Ontario, 1861 2896.28 p15
Laur, M. 18; Ontario, 1861 2896.28 p10
Laur, M. 33; Ontario, 1861 2896.28 p15
Laur, Susanna Marg.; America, 1748 2856.30 p265
Laurance, Rich; Virginia, 1668-1669 6212.30 p40
Laurance, Robert; Virginia, 1666-1667 6212.30 p33
Laurence, James; Virginia, 1694 1224.1 p35
Laurence, Louis 34; Ontario, 1871 1823.28 p55
Laurence, William 50; Ontario, 1871 1823.15 p142
Laurenson, Peter; Illinois, 1866 1640.13 p68
Laurent, Mr.; Quebec, 1857 9196.15 p13
Laurent, Arndee; Belize, 1873 1640.13 p68
Laurent, Jos; Quebec, 1858 9196.15 p34
Laurer, Georg; Port uncertain, 1763 2856.30 p265
Laurie, Archibald; Quebec, 1886 1640.13 p68
Laurie, David; Mississippi, 1837 1640.10 p95
Wife: Isabel
Child: Isabel
Laurie, Duncan 40; Ontario, 1871 1823.28 p55
Laurie, Francis; Quebec, 1886 1640.13 p68
Laurie, Isabel SEE Laurie, David
Laurie, William; New York, 1807 8197.10 p44
Laurin, Barbara; Port uncertain, 1696 2856.30 p265
Laurin, Barbara; Port uncertain, 1717 2856.30 p265
Laurin, Susanna Marg.; America, 1748 2856.30 p265
Laurison, Joseph 76; Ontario, 1871 1823.15 p142
Laurison, Nathanial 71; Ontario, 1871 1823.15 p142
Laurison, William C. 80; Ontario, 1871 1823.15 p142
Lausch, Gabriel; America, 1744 2856.30 p265
With wife & children
Lausch, Gabriel; America, 1753 2856.30 p265
Lausch, Hans Adam; Port uncertain, 1753 2856.30 p265
Lausen, A. 31; British Columbia, 1912 9196.1 p15
Lauson, William; Georgia, 1699 1640.13 p68
Laust, Martin; Port uncertain, 1749 2856.30 p265
Laut, James 81; Ontario, 1871 1823.15 p142
Laut, John 47; Ontario, 1871 1823.15 p142
Lauter, Jost; Port uncertain, 1764 2856.30 p265
Lauter, Nicol; Port uncertain, 1792 2856.30 p265
Lauterbach, Franziska; Port uncertain, 1748 2856.30 p265
Lauterbach, Juliana; Port uncertain, 1748 2856.30 p265
Lauterbach, Justina; Port uncertain, 1748 2856.30 p265
Lautermann, Heinrich; America, 1790 2856.30 p265
With children
Lautermann, Heinrich; Port uncertain, 1762 2856.30 p265
With children
Lautermann, Peter; America, 1764 2856.30 p265
Lautermann, Peter; America, 1767 2856.30 p265
Lauther, Johann; Port uncertain, 1713 2856.30 p265
Lauttenbach, Peter; Port uncertain, 1764 2856.30 p265
Lautz, Elis. Catharina; Port uncertain, 1741 2856.30 p265
Lautzenhauser, David; Port uncertain, 1764 2856.30 p265
Lautzenhauser, Heinrich; America, 1764 2856.30 p265
Lautzenhauser, Heinz David; Port uncertain, 1764 2856.30 p265
Lautzenhauser, Jacob; America, 1764 2856.30 p266
Lautzenhauser, Jakob; Port uncertain, 1764 2856.30 p265
Lautzenhauser, Peter; America, 1764 2856.30 p266
Lauucre, Patrick 70; Ontario, 1871 1823.15 p142
Laux, Anna Maria; Port uncertain, 1755 2856.30 p266
Laux, Barbara; Port uncertain, 1756 2856.30 p266
Laux, Joh. Christian; Port uncertain, 1775 2856.30 p266
Laux, Maria Catharina; Port uncertain, 1775 2856.30 p266
Lauzon, Ann Cavanaugh; Vermont, 1842-1914 5900.10 p184
Lauzon, Joseph; Vermont, 1830-1909 5900.10 p184
Lavall, Johann Michael; America, 1749 2856.30 p266
With wife & 4 children
Lavalley, Matilda; Vermont, 1861-1938 5900.10 p141
Lavardo, A. 38; Alaska, 1914 9196.1 p41
Lavell, Ann Dolan; Vermont, 1833-1907 5900.10 p132
Lavell, Ellen; Vermont, 1868-1936 5900.10 p132
Lavell, John; Vermont, 1821-1890 5900.10 p132
Lavell, John 24; America, 1774 1220.25 p36
Lavell, John E.; Vermont, 1858-1926 5900.10 p132
Lavell, Peter J.; Vermont, 1856-1909 5900.10 p132
Lavelle, Austin; Vermont, 1812-1884 5900.10 p190
Lavelle, Austin 45; Ontario, 1871 1823.28 p56
Lavelle, Bridget Coggins; Vermont, 1810-1898 5900.10 p190
Lavelle, Ellen Ward; Vermont, 1838-1907 5900.10 p140
Lavelle, John 42; Vermont, 1893 5900.10 p185
Lavelle, Mary; Vermont, 1794-1884 5900.10 p137
Lavelle, Mary; Vermont, 1848-1924 5900.10 p129
Lavelle, Mary Ann Murphy 85; Vermont, 1943 5900.10 p185
Lavelle, Patrick; Vermont, 1840-1909 5900.10 p140
Lavelle, Patrick 30; Ontario, 1871 1823.28 p56
Laven, Thomas 40; Ontario, 1871 1823.15 p142
Lavender, Mr.; Quebec, 1857 9196.15 p23
Lavender, George; New York, 1840 8197.10 p186
Lavender, John; New York, 1840 8197.10 p186
Lavender, John 27; Maryland, 1774 1220.25 p38
Lavender, William; New York, 1840 8197.10 p252
Laver, Mr.; Quebec, 1858 9196.15 p36
Laverlocher, John Nicker 57; Ontario, 1871 1823.28 p56
Lavermore, John; New York, 1807 8197.10 p43
Lavers, James; Pennsylvania, 1777 4629.10 p14
Lavery, Ann Jane Snider; Vermont, 1830-1910 5900.10 p603
Lavery, Bridget; Vermont, 1803-1888 5900.10 p381
Lavery, C. Edwin; Vermont, 1856-1945 5900.10 p602
Lavery, Catherine; Vermont, 1820-1900 5900.10 p381
Lavery, Eliza J.; Vermont, 1849-1910 5900.10 p606
Lavery, Ellen 64; Vermont, 1906 5900.10 p379
Lavery, Ellen M.; Vermont, 1844-1914 5900.10 p379
Lavery, Hannah J. Doherty; Vermont, 1859-1943 5900.10 p602
Lavery, Hugh 43; Ontario, 1871 1823.22 p90
Lavery, Joseph 67; Vermont, 1911 5900.10 p602
Lavery, Lucretia; Vermont, 1833-1895 5900.10 p603
Lavery, Mary Ann Harvey; Vermont, 1834-1921 5900.10 p603
Lavery, Mary Ayers 51; Vermont, 1854 5900.10 p602
Lavery, Mary J. Jubery 37; Vermont, 1887 5900.10 p602
Lavery, Peter J.; Vermont, 1831-1902 5900.10 p603
Lavery, Richard; Vermont, 1840-1911 5900.10 p275
Lavery, Sara A. O'Brien; Vermont, 1850-1932 5900.10 p275
Lavery, William 30; Ontario, 1871 1823.22 p90
Lavery, William 96; Vermont, 1878 5900.10 p602
Lavery, William J.; Vermont, 1828-1915 5900.10 p603
Lavett, Manuel; New York, 1834 8197.10 p372
Lavey, Mary 86; Vermont, 1897 5900.10 p200
Lavicka, Michel; Maryland, 1910 3259.35 p34
Lavie, Joseph M.; New York, 1817 8197.10 p248
Lavigne, Harriett; Vermont, 1822-1882 5900.10 p375
Lavin, Catherine 30; Ontario, 1871 1823.15 p142
Lavin, John 60; Ontario, 1871 1823.15 p142
Lavin, Lawrence; New York, 1829 8197.10 p352
Lavin, Thomas; New York, 1838 8197.10 p251
Lavin, Thomas 33; Ontario, 1871 1823.15 p142
Lavine, Catherine 47; Ontario, 1871 1823.28 p56
Lavington, Stephen; South Carolina, 1759 1224.2 p67
Lavinour, Robert 73; Ontario, 1871 1823.22 p90
Lavort, William 47; Ontario, 1871 1823.15 p142
Law, Mrs. 59; Ontario, 1871 1823.28 p56
Law, Andrew 27; Maryland, 1774 1220.25 p57
Law, Ann 74; Ontario, 1861 2896.25 p57
Law, David, Jr.; New York, 1807 8197.10 p44
Law, Elizabeth T. Murphy; Vermont, 1847-1906 5900.10 p52
Law, George N.; New York, 1838 8197.10 p123
Law, Hugh; Pennsylvania, 1777 4629.10 p28
Law, James B.; Vermont, 1843-1908 5900.10 p52
Law, John; New Orleans, 1802-1812 1640.10 p95
Law, John; New York, 1840 8197.10 p186

Law, John 18; Vermont, 1864 ***5900.10*** *p232*
Law, Joseph; Georgia, 1674-1845 ***1640.10*** *p95*
Law, Joseph 21; Maryland, 1774 ***1220.25*** *p79*
Law, Mary A.; Vermont, 1854-1912 ***5900.10*** *p49*
Law, Patrick; Vermont, 1850-1924 ***5900.10*** *p49*
Law, Robert 55; Ontario, 1871 ***1823.28*** *p56*
Law, Thomas 26; Maryland, 1775 ***1220.25*** *p105*
Law, William; Belize, 1878 ***1640.13*** *p68*
Law, William; Georgia, 1698 ***1640.13*** *p68*
Law, Wm 50; Ontario, 1871 ***1823.28*** *p56*
Lawconlav, Antoine 40; Ontario, 1871 ***1823.28*** *p56*
Lawder, J. 70; Ontario, 1861 ***2896.25*** *p47*
Lawder, James 17; Ontario, 1861 ***2896.25*** *p57*
Lawder, John 39; Ontario, 1871 ***1823.22*** *p90*
Lawence, Minnie; Maryland, 1910 ***3259.35*** *p34*
Lawes, Charles 42; Ontario, 1871 ***1823.22*** *p90*
Lawes, Nicholas; Maryland, 1658 ***2524.55*** *p134*
Lawford, J.; Quebec, 1856 ***9196.15*** *p9*
Lawford, Susannah Josephine; Indiana, 1850 ***1224.3*** *p45*
Lawinsky, Vincent; Maryland, 1910 ***3259.35*** *p34*
Lawish, James 42; Ontario, 1871 ***1823.15*** *p142*
Lawland, Gus Adolph; Alaska, 1915 ***9196.1*** *p11*
Lawland, Gus Adolph; British Columbia, 1915 ***9196.1*** *p11*
Lawlar, John 48; Ontario, 1871 ***1823.22*** *p90*
Lawler, Alex'der; Philadelphia, 1790 ***4629.10*** *p83*
Lawler, Catharine Dupont; Vermont, 1834-1896 ***5900.10*** *p265*
Lawler, Catherine McAnaney 60; Vermont, 1892 ***5900.10*** *p436*
Lawler, Cathrine Cassidy; Vermont, 1850-1920 ***5900.10*** *p219*
Lawler, Hanora; Vermont, 1822-1888 ***5900.10*** *p329*
Lawler, James; New York, 1840 ***8197.10*** *p186*
Lawler, James; Vermont, 1838-1915 ***5900.10*** *p219*
Lawler, James 27; Vermont, 1870 ***5900.10*** *p265*
Lawler, James 65; Ontario, 1871 ***1823.22*** *p90*
Lawler, Joanna 67; Vermont, 1876 ***5900.10*** *p226*
Lawler, John 52; Vermont, 1886 ***5900.10*** *p219*
Lawler, Mary 20; Maryland, 1774 ***1220.25*** *p59*
Lawler, Michael; New York, 1824 ***8197.10*** *p250*
Lawler, Michael; New York, 1840 ***8197.10*** *p187*
Lawler, Patrick; New York, 1839 ***8197.10*** *p382*
Lawless, Miss; Portland, Maine, 1857 ***9196.15*** *p12*
Lawless, John 38; Ontario, 1871 ***1823.22*** *p90*
Lawless, Patrick 61; Ontario, 1871 ***1823.28*** *p56*
Lawley, Francis; Virginia, 1664 ***6212.30*** *p11*
Lawlor, Annie 36; Ontario, 1871 ***1823.22*** *p90*
Lawlor, Catherine; Vermont, 1846-1912 ***5900.10*** *p442*
Lawlor, Catherine Hulihan; Vermont, 1842-1922 ***5900.10*** *p69*
Lawlor, Celia Doyle; Vermont, 1833-1904 ***5900.10*** *p476*
Lawlor, Eliza 77; Vermont, 1908 ***5900.10*** *p485*
Lawlor, Ellen 58; Vermont, 1886 ***5900.10*** *p480*
Lawlor, Ellen 78; Vermont, 1908 ***5900.10*** *p55*
Lawlor, Hannora 47; Vermont, 1875 ***5900.10*** *p360*
Lawlor, Jane 70; Ontario, 1871 ***1823.15*** *p142*
Lawlor, Joanna 76; Vermont, 1909 ***5900.10*** *p61*
Lawlor, John; Vermont, 1835-1914 ***5900.10*** *p69*
Lawlor, Julia 80; Vermont, 1909 ***5900.10*** *p480*
Lawlor, Julia Stapleton; Vermont, 1797-1863 ***5900.10*** *p480*
Lawlor, Lawrence; Pennsylvania, 1777 ***4629.10*** *p8*
Lawlor, Mary 73; Vermont, 1896 ***5900.10*** *p480*
Lawlor, Mary Woods; Vermont, 1830-1900 ***5900.10*** *p473*
Lawlor, Mathew; Vermont, 1837-1906 ***5900.10*** *p473*
Lawlor, Michael; New York, 1840 ***8197.10*** *p252*
Lawlor, Michael 72; Vermont, 1885 ***5900.10*** *p61*
Lawne, A.; Quebec, 1858 ***9196.15*** *p33*
Lawne, Christopher; Virginia, 1620 ***1224.1*** *p36*
Lawrance, Edward 41; Virginia, 1774 ***1220.25*** *p45*
Lawrance, Henry 61; Ontario, 1871 ***1823.15*** *p143*
Lawrance, John; Maryland, 1658 ***2524.55*** *p134*
Daughter: Mary
Lawrance, John; New York, New York, 1856 ***3437.14*** *p77*
Lawrance, Mary *SEE* Lawrance, John
Lawrance, Morrisey 70; Ontario, 1871 ***1823.15*** *p143*
Lawrance, Phillip; Maryland, 1673 ***2524.55*** *p134*
Lawrance, Richard; Maryland, 1631-1685 ***2524.55*** *p134*
Lawrance, Sarah Ann 22; Maryland, 1774 ***1220.25*** *p59*
Lawrance, Thomas 17; Maryland, 1774 ***1220.25*** *p5*
Lawrance, Thomas 20; Maryland, 1774 ***1220.25*** *p64*
Lawrance, Thomas 33; Maryland, 1774 ***1220.25*** *p52*
Lawrance, Thomas 39; Ontario, 1871 ***1823.15*** *p143*
Lawrance, Treacy 40; Ontario, 1871 ***1823.15*** *p143*
Lawremore, Roger; Maryland, 1663 ***2524.55*** *p134*
Lawrence, Mrs.; Maryland, 1680 ***2524.55*** *p134*
Lawrence, Alfred 23; Ontario, 1871 ***1823.15*** *p143*
Lawrence, Andrew 11; Ontario, 1861 ***2896.25*** *p37*
Lawrence, Anne; Maryland, 1681 ***2524.55*** *p134*
Lawrence, Anthony 36; Virginia, 1773 ***1220.25*** *p30*
Lawrence, Archibald 23; Ontario, 1861 ***2896.25*** *p37*
Lawrence, Catharine Scully 60; Vermont, 1871 ***5900.10*** *p591*
Lawrence, Catherine 27; Vermont, 1879 ***5900.10*** *p114*
Lawrence, Charles Kane; New York, 1809 ***8197.10*** *p55*
Lawrence, Daniell; Maryland, 1673 ***2524.55*** *p134*
Lawrence, David 93; Vermont, 1903 ***5900.10*** *p224*
Lawrence, Eliza White 55; Vermont, 1892 ***5900.10*** *p604*
Lawrence, Frank; Maryland, 1910 ***3259.35*** *p34*
Lawrence, Henry; Maryland, 1660 ***2524.55*** *p134*
Lawrence, Henry; Maryland, 1680 ***2524.55*** *p134*
Lawrence, Henry; Maryland, 1681 ***2524.55*** *p134*
Lawrence, Henry; New York, 1818 ***8197.10*** *p248*
Lawrence, Hester A. 20; Ontario, 1861 ***2896.28*** *p30*
Lawrence, Isaac 44; Ontario, 1871 ***1823.22*** *p90*
Lawrence, James 25; Ontario, 1871 ***1823.15*** *p143*
Lawrence, John; Maryland, 1681 ***2524.55*** *p134*
Lawrence, John; Norfolk, Virginia, 1828 ***1224.3*** *p45*
Lawrence, John; Pennsylvania, 1777 ***4629.10*** *p21*
Lawrence, John; Pennsylvania, 1777 ***4629.10*** *p23*
Lawrence, John; Philadelphia, 1857 ***1224.3*** *p45*
Lawrence, John 42; Ontario, 1871 ***1823.22*** *p90*
Lawrence, John 60; Ontario, 1871 ***1823.15*** *p143*
Lawrence, Margarett; Maryland, 1668 ***2524.55*** *p134*
Lawrence, Mark; New York, 1832 ***8197.10*** *p368*
Lawrence, Martha 17; Ontario, 1861 ***2896.25*** *p37*
Lawrence, Mary; Boston, 1742 ***1224.2*** *p68*
Lawrence, Mary; Vermont, 1825-1898 ***5900.10*** *p50*
Lawrence, Mary 49; Ontario, 1861 ***2896.25*** *p37*
Lawrence, Mary Shelley; Vermont, 1852-1919 ***5900.10*** *p50*
Lawrence, Mordecai; Pennsylvania, 1779 ***4629.10*** *p41*
Lawrence, Rebecca 26; Ontario, 1861 ***2896.25*** *p31*
Lawrence, Samuel 28; Ontario, 1861 ***2896.25*** *p31*
Lawrence, Sarah Jane; Long Island, 1893 ***1640.13*** *p69*
Lawrence, Staats; Pennsylvania, 1779 ***4629.10*** *p39*
Lawrence, Stephen; New York, 1807 ***8197.10*** *p330*
Lawrence, Thomas; Maryland, 1649 ***2524.55*** *p134*
Lawrence, Thomas; Pennsylvania, 1777 ***4629.10*** *p16*
Lawrence, Thomas 18; New York, 1775 ***1220.25*** *p94*
Lawrence, William; Pennsylvania, 1777 ***4629.10*** *p23*
Lawrence, William; Pennsylvania, 1861-1864 ***6058.10*** *p49*
Lawrence, William; Virginia, 1674 ***6212.30*** *p52*
Lawrence, Wm M. 50; Ontario, 1871 ***1823.28*** *p56*
Lawrenceson, Margaret; Maryland, 1674 ***2524.55*** *p134*
Lawrey, Thomas 18; Ontario, 1871 ***1823.15*** *p143*
Lawrie, Agnes 72; Ontario, 1871 ***1823.28*** *p56*
Lawrie, Gawen; East New Jersey, 1697 ***1224.1*** *p36*
Lawrie, James 28; Maryland, 1774 ***1220.25*** *p57*
Lawrie, Jane 30; Ontario, 1871 ***1823.15*** *p143*
Lawrie, John; Ontario, 1855 ***1640.13*** *p69*
Lawrie, Robert; St. Vincent, 1770 ***1640.13*** *p69*
Lawrie, Robert Black; Florida, 1822-1838 ***1640.10*** *p95*
Lawrie, William 61; Ontario, 1871 ***1823.15*** *p143*
Lawry, William 53; Ontario, 1871 ***1823.15*** *p143*
Laws, John; New York, 1827 ***8197.10*** *p344*
Laws, Jonathan; Virginia, 1666 ***6212.30*** *p27*
Laws, Simmons; New York, 1827 ***8197.10*** *p344*
Laws, William 22; Maryland, 1774 ***1220.25*** *p51*
Lawsin, Rankin 26; Ontario, 1871 ***1823.28*** *p56*
Lawska, John; Maryland, 1910 ***3259.35*** *p34*
Lawson, Miss; Quebec, 1856 ***9196.15*** *p7*
Lawson, Miss; Quebec, 1858 ***9196.15*** *p35*
Lawson, Mr.; Quebec, 1858 ***9196.15*** *p35*
Lawson, Mr.; Quebec, 1858 ***9196.15*** *p44*
Lawson, Mr., Jr.; Quebec, 1858 ***9196.15*** *p35*
Lawson, Mrs.; Maryland, 1650-1651 ***2524.55*** *p134*
Lawson, Mrs.; Quebec, 1858 ***9196.15*** *p35*
Lawson, Mrs.; Quebec, 1858 ***9196.15*** *p44*
Lawson, A.; Fairbanks, Alaska, 1909 ***9196.1*** *p8*
Lawson, A.; Yukon, 1909 ***9196.1*** *p8*
Lawson, A... 50; Seattle, 1917 ***9196.1*** *p52*
Lawson, A... 50; Yukon, 1917 ***9196.1*** *p52*
Lawson, Adlina 18; Ontario, 1861 ***2896.28*** *p19*
Lawson, Affa 39; Ontario, 1861 ***2896.25*** *p20*
Lawson, Alexander 42; Ontario, 1871 ***1823.15*** *p143*
Lawson, Alexander 48; Ontario, 1871 ***1823.28*** *p56*
Lawson, Alfaretta 9; Ontario, 1861 ***2896.25*** *p20*
Lawson, Anthony 50; Ontario, 1871 ***1823.15*** *p143*
Lawson, Clark 16; Ontario, 1861 ***2896.28*** *p22*
Lawson, Eliza; Virginia, 1666 ***6212.30*** *p29*
Lawson, George 36; Ontario, 1871 ***1823.15*** *p143*
Lawson, Henry; New York, 1836 ***8197.10*** *p76*
Lawson, Henry 32; Maryland, 1775 ***1220.25*** *p106*
Lawson, Isabella; West Indies, 1881 ***1640.13*** *p69*
Lawson, J. M. 75; Ontario, 1871 ***1823.22*** *p90*
Lawson, John; Georgia, 1760 ***1640.10*** *p95*
Lawson, John; New Orleans, 1822 ***1640.10*** *p95*
Lawson, John; New York, 1807 ***8197.10*** *p44*
Lawson, John 30; Ontario, 1871 ***1823.15*** *p143*
Lawson, John 83; Ontario, 1871 ***1823.22*** *p90*
Lawson, John Cook 95; Ontario, 1871 ***1823.22*** *p90*
Lawson, Malissa 16; Ontario, 1861 ***2896.25*** *p20*
Lawson, Mariah 52; Ontario, 1861 ***2896.28*** *p44*
Lawson, Mes D. 61; Ontario, 1871 ***1823.15*** *p143*
Lawson, Peter 58; Ontario, 1871 ***1823.22*** *p90*
Lawson, Phebe J. 24; Ontario, 1861 ***2896.28*** *p31*
Lawson, Robert; Maryland, 1714 ***1224.2*** *p68*
Lawson, Sarah J. 9; Ontario, 1861 ***2896.28*** *p33*
Lawson, William 61; Ontario, 1871 ***1823.22*** *p90*
Lawson, William 62; Ontario, 1871 ***1823.15*** *p143*
Lawter, James; Maryland, 1679 ***2524.55*** *p134*
Lawton, Charles; Pennsylvania, 1777 ***4629.10*** *p13*
Lawton, Hanora 50; Vermont, 1866 ***5900.10*** *p577*
Lawton, Joseph; Charleston, South Carolina, 1855 ***1224.3*** *p45*
Lawton, Joseph 30; Maryland, 1774 ***1220.25*** *p84*
Lawton, Timothy; New York, 1840 ***8197.10*** *p252*
Lax, Thomas; New York, 1807 ***8197.10*** *p44*
Laxgang, Lorenz; America, 1750 ***2856.30*** *p266*
With wife & children
Laxon, Thomas; Long Island, 1784 ***1224.2*** *p68*
Laxton, Catherine; Cincinnati, 1845 ***1224.3*** *p84*
Lay, Anna Maria; Port uncertain, 1777 ***2856.30*** *p266*
Lay, Benjamin; Pennsylvania, 1760 ***1224.2*** *p68*
Lay, James 52; Ontario, 1871 ***1823.22*** *p90*
Lay, Konrad; Port uncertain, 1791 ***2856.30*** *p266*
Lay, Konrad; Port uncertain, 1792 ***2856.30*** *p266*
Lay, Mathias; Port uncertain, 1784 ***2856.30*** *p266*
Lay, Mathias; Port uncertain, 1784 ***2856.30*** *p266*
With wife
Layden, Luke; New York, 1834 ***8197.10*** *p72*
Laydon, Patrick 40; Ontario, 1871 ***1823.15*** *p143*
Layer, Anna Barbara; America, 1759 ***2856.30*** *p266*
Layland, William; New York, 1837 ***8197.10*** *p94*
Layman, Christy 33; Ontario, 1871 ***1823.28*** *p56*
Layman, Martin 33; Ontario, 1871 ***1823.28*** *p56*
Layman, Matthe 44; Ontario, 1871 ***1823.28*** *p56*
Layton, Miss; Portland, Maine, 1858 ***9196.15*** *p30*
Layton, Elizabeth 26 *SEE* Layton, Francis
Layton, Francis 18 months *SEE* Layton, Francis
Layton, Francis 29; Nova Scotia, 1774 ***1220.25*** *p13*
Wife: Elizabeth 26
Son: Francis 18 months
Layton, John 22; Nova Scotia, 1774 ***1220.25*** *p13*
Layton, Susannah; Illinois, 1842 ***1224.3*** *p45*
Layton, Thomas 32; Jamaica, 1774 ***1220.25*** *p20*
Layton, William; Virginia, 1663 ***6212.30*** *p3*
Layton, Wm.; Maryland, 1670 ***2524.55*** *p232*
Lazarwiz, Rosa; Maryland, 1910 ***3259.35*** *p34*
Lazenby, John Birks; New York, 1818 ***8197.10*** *p248*
Lazeski, Felix; Maryland, 1910 ***3259.35*** *p34*
Lazier, Ada 31; Ontario, 1861 ***2896.27*** *p19*
Lazier, Amealia 16; Ontario, 1861 ***2896.27*** *p50*
Lazier, George 25; Ontario, 1861 ***2896.27*** *p19*
Lazier, H. 6; Ontario, 1861 ***2896.27*** *p19*
Lazier, Henry 4; Ontario, 1861 ***2896.27*** *p19*
Lazier, Peter 75; Ontario, 1861 ***2896.27*** *p19*
Lazier, Sarah 46; Ontario, 1861 ***2896.27*** *p19*
Lazier, Waddeson 19; Ontario, 1861 ***2896.27*** *p19*
Laziere, Bathsheba 12; Ontario, 1861 ***2896.27*** *p13*
Laziere, Dorland B. 18; Ontario, 1861 ***2896.27*** *p13*
Laziere, Jane 53; Ontario, 1861 ***2896.27*** *p17*
Laziere, Leonora 8; Ontario, 1861 ***2896.27*** *p13*
Laziere, Maribeth 78; Ontario, 1861 ***2896.27*** *p13*
Laziere, Mary 51; Ontario, 1861 ***2896.27*** *p13*
Laziere, Nicholas 59; Ontario, 1861 ***2896.27*** *p13*
Laziere, Sophia 21; Ontario, 1861 ***2896.27*** *p13*
Lazinby, William 21; Maryland, 1774 ***1220.25*** *p78*
Lazorek, Wojcheck; Maryland, 1910 ***3259.35*** *p34*
Lea, Thomas; Virginia, 1627 ***1224.1*** *p45*
Lea, Thomas 50; Ontario, 1871 ***1823.28*** *p56*
Lea, William; Philadelphia, 1749 ***1224.2*** *p68*
Lea, William 60; Ontario, 1871 ***1823.15*** *p143*
Leaboyteaus, John; Pennsylvania, 1777 ***4629.10*** *p6*
Leach, Mr.; Quebec, 1857 ***9196.15*** *p13*
Leach, Ann 75; Ontario, 1871 ***1823.22*** *p90*
Leach, George 29; Ontario, 1871 ***1823.28*** *p56*
Leach, George 32; Ontario, 1871 ***1823.15*** *p143*
Leach, George 51; Ontario, 1871 ***1823.22*** *p90*
Leach, Henry C.; Vermont, 1850-1924 ***5900.10*** *p50*
Leach, James 27; Nova Scotia, 1774 ***1220.25*** *p13*
Leach, James 32; Ontario, 1871 ***1823.22*** *p90*
Leach, John; New England, 1722 ***1224.2*** *p68*
Leach, John 17; Virginia, 1774 ***1220.25*** *p88*
Leach, Joseph 47; Ontario, 1871 ***1823.22*** *p90*
Leach, Joseph 54; Ontario, 1871 ***1823.15*** *p143*
Leach, Mable J.; Vermont, 1875-1924 ***5900.10*** *p120*
Leach, Margaret 47; Ontario, 1871 ***1823.22*** *p90*
Leach, Mary 21; Philadelphia, 1774 ***1220.25*** *p63*
Leach, Maryann 32; Vermont, 1871 ***5900.10*** *p232*
Leach, Sairyam 26; Ontario, 1871 ***1823.15*** *p143*
Leach, Thomas 40; Ontario, 1871 ***1823.15*** *p143*
Leacock, Samuel; Pennsylvania, 1777 ***4629.10*** *p16*
Leacy, Mary 24; Ontario, 1871 ***1823.28*** *p56*

Leddy, Michael; Vermont, 1849-1916 ***5900.10*** *p531*
Leddy, Michael 85; Vermont, 1865 ***5900.10*** *p526*
Leddy, Peter J.; Vermont, 1853-1928 ***5900.10*** *p533*
Leddy, Thomas 70; Ontario, 1871 ***1823.15*** *p144*
Ledergerber, Sebastian; Port uncertain, 1733 ***2856.30*** *p267*
Ledergerber, Sebastian; Port uncertain, 1766 ***2856.30*** *p267*
Lederhaas, Peter; America, 1764 ***2856.30*** *p267*
Lederlin, Anna Barbara; Port uncertain, 1765 ***2856.30*** *p267*
Ledermann, Marianna; Port uncertain, 1770 ***2856.30*** *p267*
Ledet, Isaiah Lewis; New York, 1794 ***8197.10*** *p6*
Ledet, Joseph M.; New York, 1797 ***8197.10*** *p9*
Ledeyman, Mary; Maryland, 1666 ***2524.55*** *p135*
Ledger, John; Virginia, 1779 ***1224.2*** *p68*
Ledger, Matthew; California, 1852 ***1224.3*** *p45*
Ledgerwood, Hance 30; Ontario, 1871 ***1823.28*** *p56*
Ledingham, John; St. Johns, Newfoundland, 1898 ***1640.13*** *p69*
Ledlie, John; New York, 1829 ***8197.10*** *p312*
Ledru, John; Pennsylvania, 1777 ***4629.10*** *p19*
Ledrue, Joseph; Pennsylvania, 1777 ***4629.10*** *p22*
Leduc, Francis 50; Ontario, 1871 ***1823.28*** *p56*
Ledwidge, John; Virginia, 1703 ***1224.2*** *p68*
Ledwith, James William; New York, 1839 ***8197.10*** *p252*
Ledwith, Richard F.; New York, 1830 ***8197.10*** *p251*
Ledwith, Richard F.; New York, 1838 ***8197.10*** *p123*
Ledyard, Mr.; Quebec, 1856 ***9196.15*** *p6*
Lee, . . .; Boston, 1765 ***4628.40*** *p114*
Lee, Alexander 21; Virginia, 1774 ***1220.25*** *p93*
Lee, Alice; New Jersey, 1785 ***1224.2*** *p68*
Lee, Allen; New York, 1817 ***8197.10*** *p248*
Lee, Ann Casey 65; Vermont, 1912 ***5900.10*** *p72*
Lee, Anna Stacey 45; Vermont, 1896 ***5900.10*** *p101*
Lee, Bridget Donovan; Vermont, 1836-1889 ***5900.10*** *p78*
Lee, Catherine A.; Vermont, 1850 ***5900.10*** *p342*
Lee, Catherine McNiff; Vermont, 1844-1906 ***5900.10*** *p154*
Lee, Catherine Reynolds; Vermont, 1811-1901 ***5900.10*** *p342*
Lee, Charles; Virginia, 1785 ***1224.2*** *p68*
Lee, Christian; Philadelphia, 1789 ***4629.10*** *p58*
Wife: Olena
Lee, Christopher; New York, 1810-1834 ***8197.10*** *p309*
Lee, Christopher 23; Philadelphia, 1789 ***4629.10*** *p58*
Lee, Deborah; Maryland, 1653 ***2524.55*** *p135*
Lee, Edward; Maryland, 1663 ***2524.55*** *p219*
Lee, Edward; Vermont, 1862-1925 ***5900.10*** *p554*
Lee, Edward M.; Vermont, 1853-1879 ***5900.10*** *p154*
Lee, Elizabeth; Maryland, 1659 ***2524.55*** *p135*
Lee, Ellen; Vermont, 1830-1882 ***5900.10*** *p159*
Lee, Francis 62; Vermont, 1854 ***5900.10*** *p342*
Lee, Francis Ryan 43; Vermont, 1867 ***5900.10*** *p143*
Lee, Grace; Maryland, 1653 ***2524.55*** *p135*
Lee, Hannah; Maryland, 1662 ***2524.55*** *p135*
Lee, Hannah 27; Vermont, 1861 ***5900.10*** *p576*
Lee, Hanora; Vermont, 1851-1852 ***5900.10*** *p154*
Lee, Hattie L. Brown; Vermont, 1851-1885 ***5900.10*** *p348*
Lee, Henry; Maryland, 1659 ***2524.55*** *p51*
Lee, Henry; Maryland, 1664 ***2524.55*** *p135*
Lee, Henry; Pennsylvania, 1777 ***4629.10*** *p12*
Lee, Henry; Virginia, 1664 ***6212.30*** *p12*
Lee, Honora; Vermont, 1824-1898 ***5900.10*** *p154*
Lee, Honora Kelty; Vermont, 1858-1958 ***5900.10*** *p554*
Lee, Hugh; Maryland, 1662 ***2524.55*** *p135*
Lee, Hugh; Pennsylvania, 1832 ***6058.10*** *p10*
Lee, Hugh 46; Vermont, 1864 ***5900.10*** *p72*
Lee, Humphry; Maryland, 1657 ***2524.55*** *p135*
Lee, Isaac; Virginia, 1727 ***1224.2*** *p68*
Lee, James; Maryland, 1658 ***2524.55*** *p135*
Lee, James; New Jersey, 1763 ***1224.2*** *p68*
Lee, James; Vermont, 1812-1895 ***5900.10*** *p154*
Lee, James; Vermont, 1821-1894 ***5900.10*** *p214*
Lee, James; Vermont, 1866-1868 ***5900.10*** *p154*
Lee, James; Virginia, 1703-1704 ***6212.30*** *p62*
Lee, James 26; Philadelphia, 1774 ***1220.25*** *p80*
Lee, James B.; Vermont, 1853 ***5900.10*** *p342*
Lee, James B.; Vermont, 1853-1919 ***5900.10*** *p62*
Lee, Jane S.; Vermont, 1844-1865 ***5900.10*** *p342*
Lee, Janet 36; Ontario, 1871 ***1823.15*** *p144*
Lee, Jeremiah; Vermont, 1849-1899 ***5900.10*** *p154*
Lee, John; Boston, 1840 ***1224.3*** *p46*
Lee, John; Maryland, 1658 ***2524.55*** *p135*
Lee, John; Maryland, 1658 ***2524.55*** *p135*
Wife: Mary
Lee, John; New England, 1692 ***1224.1*** *p36*
Lee, John; South Carolina, 1833 ***1224.3*** *p46*
Lee, John; Vermont, 1838-1909 ***5900.10*** *p78*
Lee, John; Virginia, 1656 ***1224.1*** *p38*
Lee, John 16; Philadelphia, 1774 ***1220.25*** *p81*
Lee, John 35; Maryland, 1774 ***1220.25*** *p41*
Lee, John 45; Ontario, 1871 ***1823.15*** *p144*
Lee, John 47; Ontario, 1871 ***1823.28*** *p56*
Lee, John 54; Vermont, 1870 ***5900.10*** *p72*
Lee, John 69; Ontario, 1871 ***1823.15*** *p144*
Lee, John F.; Vermont, 1846 ***5900.10*** *p342*
Lee, John F.; Vermont, 1846-1916 ***5900.10*** *p348*
Lee, Joseph; Cambridge, Massachusetts, 1803 ***1224.3*** *p46*
Lee, Julia; Vermont, 1830-1927 ***5900.10*** *p583*
Lee, Katie; Vermont, 1861-1862 ***5900.10*** *p154*
Lee, Kieth 32; Ontario, 1871 ***1823.15*** *p144*
Lee, Maggie; Vermont, 1857-1861 ***5900.10*** *p154*
Lee, Margaret; Vermont, 1791-1881 ***5900.10*** *p159*
Lee, Margaret 75; Vermont, 1891 ***5900.10*** *p369*
Lee, Margret; Maryland, 1668 ***2524.55*** *p135*
Lee, Martin; Vermont, 1839-1903 ***5900.10*** *p287*
Lee, Mary *SEE* Lee, John
Lee, Mary; Vermont, 1848-1926 ***5900.10*** *p287*
Lee, Mary; Virginia, 1671 ***6212.30*** *p45*
Lee, Mary A.; Vermont, 1862-1863 ***5900.10*** *p154*
Lee, Mary A. Lowlor 59; Vermont, 1882 ***5900.10*** *p214*
Lee, Mary Ann; Vermont, 1840-1860 ***5900.10*** *p342*
Lee, Michael; Vermont, 1835-1858 ***5900.10*** *p342*
Lee, Michael 72; Vermont, 1885 ***5900.10*** *p369*
Lee, Nellie; Vermont, 1858-1873 ***5900.10*** *p159*
Lee, Olena *SEE* Lee, Christian
Lee, P.; Vermont, 1831-1916 ***5900.10*** *p159*
Lee, Peter; Vermont, 1806-1890 ***5900.10*** *p342*
Lee, Peter B., Jr.; Vermont, 1856-1885 ***5900.10*** *p342*
Lee, Philomeleo 79; Ontario, 1871 ***1823.22*** *p91*
Lee, R. F.; Vermont, 1854-1954 ***5900.10*** *p159*
Lee, Richard; Vermont, 1799-1875 ***5900.10*** *p159*
Lee, Richard; Virginia, 1665 ***1224.1*** *p36*
Lee, Richard, Jr.; New York, 1804 ***8197.10*** *p27*
Lee, Richard, Jr.; New York, 1805 ***8197.10*** *p29*
Lee, Robert; Maryland, 1681 ***2524.55*** *p135*
Lee, Robert; Maryland, 1682 ***2524.55*** *p135*
Lee, Robert; Philadelphia, 1793 ***4629.10*** *p83*
Lee, Robert 22; Virginia, 1774 ***1220.25*** *p92*
Lee, Robert 85; Ontario, 1871 ***1823.15*** *p144*
Lee, Roger 46; Ontario, 1871 ***1823.15*** *p144*
Lee, Roseanna 67; Vermont, 1896 ***5900.10*** *p75*
Lee, Samuel; Maryland, 1666 ***2524.55*** *p135*
Lee, Samuel 32; Maryland, 1774 ***1220.25*** *p60*
Lee, Sarah; Boston, 1850 ***1224.3*** *p46*
Lee, Sarah; Virginia, 1703-1704 ***6212.30*** *p62*
Lee, Thomas; Maryland, 1659 ***2524.55*** *p135*
Lee, Thomas; Maryland, 1678 ***2524.55*** *p218*
Lee, Thomas; Vermont, 1837-1865 ***5900.10*** *p342*
Lee, Thomas 42; Ontario, 1871 ***1823.15*** *p144*
Lee, Thomas 60; Ontario, 1871 ***1823.28*** *p56*
Lee, William; Maryland, 1681 ***2524.55*** *p135*
Lee, William; New York, 1840 ***8197.10*** *p186*
Lee, William; North Carolina, 1761 ***1224.2*** *p69*
Lee, William; Pennsylvania, 1786 ***4629.10*** *p49*
Lee, William; Philadelphia, 1778 ***1224.2*** *p69*
Lee, William; Vermont, 1827-1905 ***5900.10*** *p458*
Lee, William 21; Maryland, 1775 ***1220.25*** *p105*
Lee, William 25; Virginia, 1774 ***1220.25*** *p87*
Lee, William 26; Maryland, 1774 ***1220.25*** *p72*
Lee, William 35; Ontario, 1871 ***1823.28*** *p56*
Lee, Wm; Virginia, 1666 ***6212.30*** *p26*
Lear, Philipp; America, 1754 ***2856.30*** *p267*
Leech, Hanah; Virginia, 1668-1669 ***6212.30*** *p40*
Leech, Hannah; Virginia, 1672 ***6212.30*** *p49*
Leech, James 52; Ontario, 1871 ***1823.28*** *p56*
Leech, John; New York, 1840 ***8197.10*** *p187*
Leech, John; Pennsylvania, 1777 ***4629.10*** *p28*
Leech, John, Sr.; Pennsylvania, 1776 ***4629.10*** *p52*
Leech, Peter 58; Ontario, 1871 ***1823.28*** *p56*
Leech, Sarah B. 18; Ontario, 1871 ***1823.15*** *p144*
Leech, Thomas; Pennsylvania, 1777 ***4629.10*** *p20*
Leech, William; Maryland, 1675 ***2524.55*** *p135*
Leech, William; Mississippi, 1831 ***1640.10*** *p95*
Leech, William; Pennsylvania, 1779 ***4629.10*** *p37*
Leeck, Wm; Virginia, 1665-1666 ***6212.30*** *p22*
Leed, Mike 26; Washington, 1912 ***9196.1*** *p36*
Leeds, John; Canada, 1854 ***1224.3*** *p46*
Leeds, Robert; Maryland, 1665 ***2524.55*** *p135*
Leefe, Edward Benjamin; New York, 1839 ***8197.10*** *p252*
Leehaffer, Fredric 46; Ontario, 1871 ***1823.28*** *p56*
Leehinger, George; New York, 1840 ***8197.10*** *p185*
Leeht, Michael; Pennsylvania, 1861 ***6058.10*** *p45*
Leek, John 17; Virginia, 1773 ***1220.25*** *p29*
Leeks, Abraham; Virginia, 1666-1667 ***6212.30*** *p35*
Leeks, Thomas 30; Ontario, 1871 ***1823.22*** *p91*
Leeman, William; New York, 1838 ***8197.10*** *p122*
Leeming, Mrs.; Quebec, 1857 ***9196.15*** *p18*
Leeming, David 55; Ontario, 1871 ***1823.22*** *p91*
Leeming, James; Quebec, 1858 ***9196.15*** *p42*
Leeming, John 42; Ontario, 1871 ***1823.15*** *p144*
Leen, Mary Cray; Vermont, 1845-1929 ***5900.10*** *p71*
Leen, Patrick B.; Vermont, 1860-1939 ***5900.10*** *p71*
Leenard, Jakob; Port uncertain, 1734 ***2856.30*** *p267*
Leene, John; Vermont, 1858-1941 ***5900.10*** *p70*
Leene, Mary Finn; Vermont, 1856-1940 ***5900.10*** *p70*
Leenwarden, Moses Jacob; New York, 1835-1838 ***8197.10*** *p123*
Leep, William; New York, 1834 ***8197.10*** *p251*
Leepe, William; New York, 1821 ***8197.10*** *p249*
Leeper, Adam 2; Ontario, 1861 ***2896.26*** *p34*
Leeper, Esabella 13; Ontario, 1861 ***2896.26*** *p34*
Leeper, James; New York, 1832 ***8197.10*** *p368*
Leeper, Jane 40; Ontario, 1861 ***2896.26*** *p34*
Leeper, Mary Ann 7; Ontario, 1861 ***2896.26*** *p34*
Leeper, Robert 11; Ontario, 1861 ***2896.26*** *p34*
Leeper, Samuel 9; Ontario, 1861 ***2896.26*** *p34*
Leeper, Sarah 5; Ontario, 1861 ***2896.26*** *p34*
Leeper, Thomas 9; Ontario, 1861 ***2896.26*** *p34*
Leer, Philipp; America, 1754 ***2856.30*** *p267*
Lees, Jane; Canada, 1891 ***1640.13*** *p69*
Lees, John; New York, 1894 ***1640.13*** *p69*
Lees, Peter 33; Vancouver, British Columbia, 1913 ***9196.1*** *p58*
Lees, Peter 33; Washington, 1913 ***9196.1*** *p58*
Lees, Richard; Pennsylvania, 1777 ***4629.10*** *p18*
Lees, Robert 36; Ontario, 1871 ***1823.15*** *p144*
Leeson, Henry 60; Ontario, 1871 ***1823.22*** *p91*
Leeson, Samuel 31; Ontario, 1871 ***1823.22*** *p91*
Leeth, Thomas; Virginia, 1711 ***1224.2*** *p69*
Lefebre, Mr.; Quebec, 1858 ***9196.15*** *p39*
Lefebre, John; New York, 1840 ***8197.10*** *p187*
LeFeirure, John; Maryland, 1675 ***2524.55*** *p135*
Lefevre, Mr.; Quebec, 1857 ***9196.15*** *p15*
Lefevre, Mr.; Quebec, 1858 ***9196.15*** *p36*
Lefevre, Francis 49; Pennsylvania, 1794 ***4629.10*** *p63*
Lefevre, Victor 57; Ontario, 1871 ***1823.28*** *p57*
Leffers, Anthony; New York, 1836 ***8197.10*** *p319*
Lefkiewicz, Dominic; Maryland, 1910 ***3259.35*** *p34*
Lefleur, Francquis 68; Ontario, 1871 ***1823.28*** *p57*
Le Fort, John; New York, 1796 ***8197.10*** *p7*
Le Fount, Mary 19; Maryland, 1774 ***1220.25*** *p83*
Le Frang, Magdalena; Port uncertain, 1795 ***2856.30*** *p266*
Lefray, Anthony 60; Ontario, 1871 ***1823.15*** *p144*
Le French, George; New York, 1804 ***8197.10*** *p27*
Lefroy, Mr.; Quebec, 1858 ***9196.15*** *p32*
Lefroy, Mrs.; Quebec, 1858 ***9196.15*** *p32*
Leftwich, Ellinor; Virginia, 1663 ***6212.30*** *p3*
Legal, Joseph; New York, 1823 ***8197.10*** *p249*
Legaratte, Joseph 34; Ontario, 1871 ***1823.28*** *p57*
Legard, Joseph 21; Maryland, 1774 ***1220.25*** *p73*
Legare, Cyril; Portland, Maine, 1858 ***9196.15*** *p27*
Legay, Louis Andre; New York, 1836 ***8197.10*** *p317*
Legear, Robert 40; Ontario, 1871 ***1823.15*** *p144*
Legener, Leopold; Port uncertain, 1727 ***2856.30*** *p266*
Leger, Claudius; New York, 1829 ***8197.10*** *p351*
Leger, Daniel; New York, 1809 ***8197.10*** *p55*
Legestawa, Tina; Maryland, 1910 ***3259.35*** *p34*
Leget, Samuel 52; Ontario, 1871 ***1823.15*** *p144*
Legg, Mr.; Quebec, 1858 ***9196.15*** *p36*
Legg, Charles 70; Ontario, 1871 ***1823.28*** *p57*
Legg, John; Jamaica, 1776 ***1640.13*** *p69*
Legg, John 40; Ontario, 1871 ***1823.28*** *p57*
Legg, Rodey 40; Ontario, 1871 ***1823.28*** *p57*
Legg, Thomas 28; Ontario, 1871 ***1823.28*** *p57*
Leggett, William; Massachusetts, 1823 ***1224.3*** *p46*
Legier, Antoine; New York, 1835 ***8197.10*** *p251*
Le Graet, Pierre; New York, 1815 ***8197.10*** *p56*
Legram, Peter; Port uncertain, 1785 ***2856.30*** *p267*
Legrand, Anna Maria; Port uncertain, 1789 ***2856.30*** *p267*
Le Grand, Francois; New York, 1816 ***8197.10*** *p59*
Le Grand, Peter; New York, 1839 ***8197.10*** *p136*
Legrand, Peter; Port uncertain, 1785 ***2856.30*** *p267*
Legrice, James 47; Ontario, 1871 ***1823.15*** *p144*
Legron, Lorenz; America, 1752 ***2856.30*** *p267*
With wife & 8 children
Legron, Lorenz; Port uncertain, 1745 ***2856.30*** *p267*
With wife & children
Legron, Tobias; America, 1752 ***2856.30*** *p267*
With wife & 2 children
Legrum, Peter; Port uncertain, 1785 ***2856.30*** *p267*
Lehanke, Joseph; New York, 1837 ***8197.10*** *p94*
Lehchek, Alexander; Maryland, 1910 ***3259.35*** *p34*
Lehe, Wendel; Port uncertain, 1752 ***2856.30*** *p267*
Lehea, Thomas; Maryland, 1678 ***2524.55*** *p135*
Lehemann, Antoni; Port uncertain, 1759 ***2856.30*** *p267*
With family
Lehemann, Michael; America, 1750 ***2856.30*** *p267*
Lehemann, Michael; Port uncertain, 1749 ***2856.30*** *p267*
Lehemann, Michael; Port uncertain, 1750 ***2856.30*** *p267*
Lehenmann, Lorenz; Port uncertain, 1695 ***2856.30*** *p267*
Lehenmann, Lorenz; Port uncertain, 1696 ***2856.30*** *p267*
Lehmann, Albert 35; Ontario, 1871 ***1823.28*** *p57*
Lehmann, Christian; America, 1755 ***2856.30*** *p267*
Lehmann, Gustave 39; Ontario, 1871 ***1823.28*** *p57*

Lehmann, Jacob; America, 1750 ***2856.30*** *p267*
With wife & 4 children
Lehmann, Jacob; America, 1751 ***2856.30*** *p267*
Lehmann, Jacob; New York, 1840 ***8197.10*** *p185*
Lehmann, Lorenz; Port uncertain, 1695 ***2856.30*** *p267*
Lehmann, Lorenz; Port uncertain, 1696 ***2856.30*** *p267*
Lehmann, Philipp Jakob; America, 1752 ***2856.30*** *p267*
Lehn, Jakob; Port uncertain, 1742 ***2856.30*** *p267*
Lehnard, Christof; Port uncertain, 1770 ***2856.30*** *p267*
Lehnen, John; Vermont, n.d. ***5900.10*** *p200*
Lehniss, Barbara; Port uncertain, 1791 ***2856.30*** *p267*
Lehr, Maria Catharina; Port uncertain, 1757 ***2856.30*** *p267*
Lehr, Rudolph; Pennsylvania, 1777 ***4629.10*** *p12*
Lehr, Wilhelm; Port uncertain, 1749 ***2856.30*** *p267*
Leiayate, John 50; Ontario, 1871 ***1823.15*** *p144*
Leib, George; Pennsylvania, 1778 ***4629.10*** *p34*
Leib, Johann; America, 1727 ***2856.30*** *p268*
Leibel, Andreas; Port uncertain, 1788 ***2856.30*** *p268*
Leibenzeter, Jacob; Pennsylvania, 1777 ***4629.10*** *p30*
Leible, Franz; Port uncertain, 1784 ***2856.30*** *p268*
Leible, Johann; Port uncertain, 1766 ***2856.30*** *p268*
Leiblen, Nicol; Port uncertain, 1773 ***2856.30*** *p268*
Leich, William; Pennsylvania, 1777 ***4629.10*** *p26*
Leichner, Mrs. Georg; America, 1744 ***2856.30*** *p268*
With son
Leicht, Adam; Port uncertain, 1773 ***2856.30*** *p268*
Leicht, Johann; Port uncertain, 1770 ***2856.30*** *p268*
Leicht, Maria; Port uncertain, 1781 ***2856.30*** *p268*
Leichter, Balthasar; Port uncertain, 1766 ***2856.30*** *p268*
Leichtweis, Leonard; Port uncertain, 1769 ***2856.30*** *p268*
Leiffer, Emanuel; Port uncertain, 1749 ***2856.30*** *p268*
Leige, Richard; Virginia, 1666-1667 ***6212.30*** *p32*
Leige, Righ; Virginia, 1665-1666 ***6212.30*** *p23*
Leigh, Mr.; Quebec, 1857 ***9196.15*** *p15*
Leigh, Alice; Maryland, 1665 ***2524.55*** *p135*
Leigh, Humphrey; Died enroute, 1663 ***1224.1*** *p36*
Leigh, Martain 38; Ontario, 1871 ***1823.15*** *p144*
Leigh, Rich; Virginia, 1664 ***6212.30*** *p13*
Leight, Ja; Virginia, 1665-1666 ***6212.30*** *p23*
Leight, James; Virginia, 1666-1667 ***6212.30*** *p32*
Leight, Jno; Virginia, 1665-1666 ***6212.30*** *p22*
Leight, Jno; Virginia, 1666-1667 ***6212.30*** *p32*
Leighton, Robert; Virginia, 1664 ***6212.30*** *p11*
Leighton, William 27; Ontario, 1871 ***1823.28*** *p57*
Leighton, William 48; Ontario, 1871 ***1823.15*** *p144*
Leigme, Michaell; Virginia, 1668-1669 ***6212.30*** *p41*
Leimbacher, Georg; America, 1744 ***2856.30*** *p268*
With wife & 5 children
Leimenstoll, Hans Jerg; Port uncertain, 1762 ***2856.30*** *p268*
Lein, John Ludowick; New York, 1840 ***8197.10*** *p186*
Leiner, Nickel; America, 1738 ***2856.30*** *p268*
Leinig, Johann; New York, 1807 ***8197.10*** *p44*
Leininger, Ana Barbara; Port uncertain, 1769 ***2856.30*** *p268*
Leininger, Christian; Port uncertain, 1744 ***2856.30*** *p268*
Leininger, Georg; Port uncertain, 1780 ***2856.30*** *p268*
Leininger, Georg; Port uncertain, 1792 ***2856.30*** *p268*
Leiper, Andrew; Pennsylvania, 1777 ***4629.10*** *p16*
Leiper, John; Manitoba, 1887 ***1640.13*** *p69*
Leiper, Thomas; Pennsylvania, 1777 ***4629.10*** *p13*
Leipholt, Frederick 70; Ontario, 1871 ***1823.15*** *p144*
Leipholt, Henry 31; Ontario, 1871 ***1823.15*** *p144*
Leir, Parick 45; Ontario, 1871 ***1823.28*** *p57*
Leird, Andrew; New York, 1821 ***8197.10*** *p249*
Leiretz, John C.; New York, 1807 ***8197.10*** *p43*
Leiser, Anna Elisabeth; Port uncertain, 1793 ***2856.30*** *p268*
Leiser, Elisabeth; Port uncertain, 1785 ***2856.30*** *p268*
Leiser, John; Pennsylvania, 1777 ***4629.10*** *p16*
Leiser, Nickel; America, 1738 ***2856.30*** *p268*
Leiser, Philipp; Port uncertain, 1754 ***2856.30*** *p268*
With 6 children
Leishman, Alex H. 30; British Columbia, 1915 ***9196.1*** *p67*
Leishman, Alex H. 30; Washington, 1915 ***9196.1*** *p67*
Leishman, John 49; Ontario, 1871 ***1823.15*** *p144*
Leishman, Richard 27; Ontario, 1871 ***1823.15*** *p144*
Leiss, Jakob; Port uncertain, 1752 ***2856.30*** *p268*
Leist, Catharina; Port uncertain, 1762 ***2856.30*** *p268*
Leist, Maria Margarete; Port uncertain, 1750 ***2856.30*** *p268*
Leister, Dorothy; Maryland, 1658 ***2524.55*** *p135*
Leister, Philipp; Port uncertain, 1775 ***2856.30*** *p268*
Leister, Samuel; Maryland, 1658 ***2524.55*** *p135*
Leitch, Mr.; Quebec, 1858 ***9196.15*** *p35*
Leitch, Ann; Port uncertain, 1850-1859 ***4537.37*** *p127*
Leitch, George; North America, 1811 ***1640.13*** *p69*
Leitch, James 30; Ontario, 1871 ***1823.28*** *p57*
Leitch, James, Sr. 68; Ontario, 1871 ***1823.28*** *p57*
Leitch, Mary Ann 22; Ontario, 1871 ***1823.28*** *p57*
Leitch, Robert 38; Ontario, 1871 ***1823.28*** *p57*
Leitch, William; Maryland, 1675 ***2524.55*** *p135*
Leitch, William; Ontario, 1864 ***1640.13*** *p70*
Leitch, William Trotter; New York, 1834-1838 ***8197.10*** *p123*
Leith, Alexander; Philadelphia, 1750 ***1640.13*** *p69*
Leith, David; Jamaica, 1841 ***1640.13*** *p69*
Leith, David 59; Ontario, 1871 ***1823.28*** *p57*
Leith, Hamilton 52; Ontario, 1871 ***1823.15*** *p144*
Leith, Jane 62; Ontario, 1871 ***1823.22*** *p91*
Leith, John; Kingston, Jamaica, 1800 ***1640.13*** *p69*
Leith, Mary; Vermont, 1852-1904 ***5900.10*** *p505*
Leith, Portuas; Vermont, 1841-1915 ***5900.10*** *p505*
Leith, William 45; Ontario, 1871 ***1823.22*** *p91*
Leitner, Konrad; Port uncertain, 1786 ***2856.30*** *p271*
Leiwilski, Josephine; Maryland, 1910 ***3259.35*** *p34*
Leiz, Regina; Port uncertain, 1739 ***2856.30*** *p268*
Leizin, Regina; Port uncertain, 1739 ***2856.30*** *p268*
Lekich, V. 46; Alaska, 1917 ***9196.1*** *p47*
Lekich, V. 46; Whitehorse, Yukon, 1917 ***9196.1*** *p47*
Lekrand, Anna Maria; Port uncertain, 1789 ***2856.30*** *p269*
Leland, Thomas; Pennsylvania, 1777 ***4629.10*** *p11*
Lelerand, Anna Maria; Port uncertain, 1789 ***2856.30*** *p269*
Lellbach, Balthasar; Port uncertain, 1778 ***2856.30*** *p269*
Lellbach, Balthasar; Port uncertain, 1780 ***2856.30*** *p269*
Lelli, Aaim; New York, 1840 ***8197.10*** *p252*
Lelong, Martin; New York, 1838 ***8197.10*** *p122*
Lemaire, Ellen B.; Vermont, 1854-1932 ***5900.10*** *p167*
Lemaire, John; New York, 1840 ***8197.10*** *p187*
Leman, Hickford; Maryland, 1732 ***1224.2*** *p69*
Lembert, Peter; Port uncertain, 1785 ***2856.30*** *p269*
Lembsch, Antoni; Port uncertain, 1737 ***2856.30*** *p269*
Lemerand, Xavier 48; Ontario, 1871 ***1823.28*** *p57*
Lemery, Josephine; Vermont, 1849-1907 ***5900.10*** *p335*
Le Mesurier, Miss; Quebec, 1857 ***9196.15*** *p14*
Lemesurier, Mr.; Quebec, 1857 ***9196.15*** *p13*
Le Mesurier, Mr.; Quebec, 1858 ***9196.15*** *p32*
Leming, Robert 51; Fort Cumberland, Nova Scotia, 1774 ***1220.25*** *p18*
Leming, Robert, Jr. 17; Fort Cumberland, Nova Scotia, 1774 ***1220.25*** *p18*
Leming, Thomas 27; Jamaica, 1773 ***1220.25*** *p31*
Leminger, Mr.; America, 1764 ***2856.30*** *p269*
With wife
Leminger, N.; America, 1764 ***2856.30*** *p514*
Lemka, William 38; Ontario, 1871 ***1823.28*** *p57*
Lemman, Edward; Virginia, 1671 ***6212.30*** *p44*
Lemmon, Ann 38; Ontario, 1871 ***1823.15*** *p144*
Lemmy, Johann Georg; Port uncertain, 1724 ***2856.30*** *p261*
With wife
Lemo, Joe 35; California, 1914 ***9196.1*** *p64*
Lemon, Bently 29; Ontario, 1861 ***2896.25*** *p30*
Lemorre, John Baptist; Pennsylvania, 1779 ***4629.10*** *p41*
Lemoy, I.; Quebec, 1856 ***9196.15*** *p8*
Le Moyne, Adolph; New York, 1831 ***8197.10*** *p251*
Le Moyne, Adolphe; New York, New York, 1828 ***8197.10*** *p305*
Lempton, Robert; Maryland, 1672 ***2524.55*** *p135*
Lenardo, Victor 40; Seattle, 1910 ***9196.1*** *p29*
Lenart, Maria; Maryland, 1910 ***3259.35*** *p34*
Lender, Peter; New York, 1819 ***8197.10*** *p248*
Lender, Peter 22; New York, 1824 ***8197.10*** *p63*
Lendrum, James; New York, New York, 1848 ***6058.10*** *p34*
Lendrum, John; New York, New York, 1848 ***6058.10*** *p34*
Lendz, Joseph; Maryland, 1910 ***3259.35*** *p34*
Le Neve, Michael; Maryland, 1707 ***1224.2*** *p69*
Leneveu, Lewis 26; Maryland, 1774 ***1220.25*** *p64*
Lengenfeld, Lucia; Port uncertain, 1764 ***2856.30*** *p269*
Husband: Malatin
Lengenfeld, Lucia; Port uncertain, 1764 ***2856.30*** *p284*
Lengenfeld, Lucia; Port uncertain, 1765 ***2856.30*** *p284*
Lengenfeld, Malatin *SEE* Lengenfeld, Lucia
Lengenfeld, Margarete; Port uncertain, 1755 ***2856.30*** *p269*
Lenhard, Adam; Port uncertain, 1751 ***2856.30*** *p269*
With wife & 5 children
Lenhard, Christina; Port uncertain, 1736 ***2856.30*** *p269*
Lenihan, Dennis J.; Vermont, 1842-1905 ***5900.10*** *p565*
Lenihan, Mary Crowley; Vermont, 1840-1906 ***5900.10*** *p565*
Lennart, John; New York, 1840 ***8197.10*** *p187*
Lennen, John 44; Ontario, 1871 ***1823.15*** *p144*
Lennen, Thomas 60; Ontario, 1871 ***1823.15*** *p144*
Lennig, Hans Peter; Port uncertain, 1676 ***2856.30*** *p269*
With wife & children
Lennon, Bridget; Vermont, 1852-1926 ***5900.10*** *p400*
Lennon, James; New York, 1840 ***8197.10*** *p185*
Lennon, John; New York, 1832 ***8197.10*** *p368*
Lennon, John; New York, 1839 ***8197.10*** *p381*
Lennon, Joseph; New York, 1823 ***8197.10*** *p250*
Lennon, Joseph 57; Ontario, 1871 ***1823.15*** *p144*
Lennon, Patrick; New York, 1844 ***8197.10*** *p10*
Lennox, Miss; Quebec, 1857 ***9196.15*** *p25*
Lennox, Patrick 77; Vermont, 1869 ***5900.10*** *p513*
Lennox, Rose Doon; Vermont, 1795-1877 ***5900.10*** *p513*
Lennox, Thos 54; Ontario, 1871 ***1823.28*** *p57*
Lenox, Anthony; New York, 1828-1831 ***8197.10*** *p369*
Lenox, David; Pennsylvania, 1777 ***4629.10*** *p25*
Lenox, James; New York, 1794 ***8197.10*** *p6*
Lenox, John 46; Ontario, 1871 ***1823.22*** *p91*
Lenox, Margaret; Ontario, 1861 ***2896.25*** *p64*
Lenox, Robert; Ontario, 1861 ***2896.25*** *p64*
Lensher, John; Maryland, 1677 ***2524.55*** *p135*
Lensinger, Hans; Port uncertain, 1738 ***2856.30*** *p269*
Lenthall, Edward; Virginia, 1664 ***6212.30*** *p11*
Lenthall, Phillip; Philadelphia, 1724 ***1224.2*** *p69*
Lenthall, Richard; Maryland, 1665 ***2524.55*** *p135*
Lenthall, Richard; Virginia, 1664 ***6212.30*** *p8*
Lentithon, Anthony; New York, 1831 ***8197.10*** *p299*
Lentz, Adam; Port uncertain, 1780 ***2856.30*** *p269*
Lentz, Anna Elisabeth; Port uncertain, 1756 ***2856.30*** *p269*
Lentz, Catharina; Port uncertain, 1764 ***2856.30*** *p269*
Lentz, David; New York, 1838 ***8197.10*** *p122*
Lentz, Henry; Pennsylvania, 1777 ***4629.10*** *p26*
Lentz, Henry; Pennsylvania, 1787 ***4629.10*** *p55*
Lentz, Henry F.; New York, 1831 ***8197.10*** *p251*
Lentz, Jacob; Port uncertain, 1764 ***2856.30*** *p269*
Lentz, John; Maryland, 1910 ***3259.35*** *p34*
Lentz, Martin; Maryland, 1910 ***3259.35*** *p34*
Lentz, Philipp; America, 1739 ***2856.30*** *p269*
With 3 daughters
Lentz, Tobias; New York, 1838 ***8197.10*** *p122*
Lentzin, Anna Elisabeth; Port uncertain, 1756 ***2856.30*** *p269*
Lentzinger, Hans; Port uncertain, 1738 ***2856.30*** *p269*
Lenz, Andreas; Port uncertain, 1761 ***2856.30*** *p269*
Lenz, Georg, The Younger; Port uncertain, 1752 ***2856.30*** *p269*
Lenz, Jakob; Port uncertain, 1752 ***2856.30*** *p269*
Lenz, Jakob; Port uncertain, 1788 ***2856.30*** *p269*
Lenz, Johann; America, 1754 ***2856.30*** *p269*
Lenz, Johann Adam; America, 1754 ***2856.30*** *p269*
Lenz, Josef; Cayenne, 1764 ***2856.30*** *p270*
With wife son & 2 daughters
Lenz, Joseph 38; Ontario, 1871 ***1823.15*** *p144*
Lenz, Maria Catharina; Port uncertain, 1758 ***2856.30*** *p269*
Lenz, Philipp, The Older; Port uncertain, 1767 ***2856.30*** *p269*
Leoffler, August Charles Frederic; New York, 1793 ***8197.10*** *p6*
Leonard, A. J.; Vermont, 1815-1893 ***5900.10*** *p322*
Leonard, Abigail Caswell; Vermont, 1817-1899 ***5900.10*** *p322*
Leonard, Adell; Vermont, 1853-1920 ***5900.10*** *p193*
Leonard, Alice; Vermont, 1810-1894 ***5900.10*** *p565*
Leonard, Alice E. Farwell; Vermont, 1848-1926 ***5900.10*** *p322*
Leonard, Allie; Vermont, 1863-1875 ***5900.10*** *p322*
Leonard, Ann; Vermont, 1829-1904 ***5900.10*** *p588*
Leonard, Bernard M.; Vermont, 1847-1901 ***5900.10*** *p302*
Leonard, Betsey 83; Vermont, 1893 ***5900.10*** *p66*
Leonard, Bridget; Vermont, 1814-1883 ***5900.10*** *p302*
Leonard, Bridget; Vermont, 1843-1927 ***5900.10*** *p309*
Leonard, Bridget; Vermont, 1897-1971 ***5900.10*** *p353*
Leonard, Bridget 24; Vermont, 1873 ***5900.10*** *p179*
Leonard, Bridget 45; Vermont, 1869 ***5900.10*** *p75*
Leonard, Bridget 90; Vermont, 1924 ***5900.10*** *p263*
Leonard, Bridget C.; Vermont, 1835-1918 ***5900.10*** *p353*
Leonard, Bridget Dwyer; Vermont, 1844-1924 ***5900.10*** *p257*
Leonard, Bridget Harris; Vermont, 1856-1928 ***5900.10*** *p257*
Leonard, Bridget Hogan 76; Vermont, 1908 ***5900.10*** *p506*
Leonard, Bridget Shahen; Vermont, 1858-1940 ***5900.10*** *p176*
Leonard, Calvin; Vermont, 1811-1867 ***5900.10*** *p322*
Leonard, Catherine 90; Vermont, 1932 ***5900.10*** *p462*
Leonard, Catherine Barrett; Vermont, 1840-1921 ***5900.10*** *p181*
Leonard, Catherine Dillon 73; Vermont, 1892 ***5900.10*** *p540*
Leonard, Christian; America, 1738 ***2856.30*** *p270*
With 2 children
Leonard, David; Vermont, 1835-1922 ***5900.10*** *p353*
Leonard, Dennis 25; Vermont, 1867 ***5900.10*** *p261*
Leonard, Dennis 64; Vermont, 1880 ***5900.10*** *p580*
Leonard, Edward; New York, 1817 ***8197.10*** *p248*
Leonard, Edward; Vermont, 1844-1917 ***5900.10*** *p257*
Leonard, Edward; Vermont, 1857-1935 ***5900.10*** *p599*

Leonard, Ellen; Vermont, 1847-1911 ***5900.10*** *p461*
Leonard, Ellen; Vermont, 1854-1940 ***5900.10*** *p126*
Leonard, Ellen MacDonald; Vermont, 1844-1909 ***5900.10*** *p446*
Leonard, Ellen Mattimore; Vermont, 1852-1925 ***5900.10*** *p127*
Leonard, Ellen O'Connell; Vermont, 1812-1889 ***5900.10*** *p460*
Leonard, Emmett; Vermont, 1846-1919 ***5900.10*** *p322*
Leonard, Esther Mosley; Vermont, 1819-1874 ***5900.10*** *p322*
Leonard, Eugene; Vermont, 1845-1921 ***5900.10*** *p460*
Leonard, Frances; Vermont, 1842-1854 ***5900.10*** *p322*
Leonard, Francis J.; New York, 1840 ***8197.10*** *p187*
Leonard, Georg; Port uncertain, 1764 ***2856.30*** *p270*
Leonard, Hannah 27; Vermont, 1869 ***5900.10*** *p460*
Leonard, Hanora 50; Ontario, 1871 ***1823.22*** *p91*
Leonard, Harriett Bashaw; Vermont, 1861-1936 ***5900.10*** *p462*
Leonard, Harry; Vermont, 1862-1929 ***5900.10*** *p176*
Leonard, Henry; Vermont, 1844-1908 ***5900.10*** *p193*
Leonard, James; Vermont, 1856-1928 ***5900.10*** *p353*
Leonard, James 34; Ontario, 1871 ***1823.22*** *p91*
Leonard, James 45; Ontario, 1871 ***1823.22*** *p91*
Leonard, James A. 27; Vermont, 1881 ***5900.10*** *p462*
Leonard, James C.; Pennsylvania, 1866 ***6058.10*** *p52*
Leonard, James E.; Vermont, 1856-1907 ***5900.10*** *p127*
Leonard, Jane 65; Vermont, 1872 ***5900.10*** *p247*
Leonard, Johann; America, 1738 ***2856.30*** *p270*
With wife & children
Leonard, Johanna; Vermont, 1846-1929 ***5900.10*** *p126*
Leonard, Johannah; Vermont, 1842-1869 ***5900.10*** *p460*
Leonard, Johannah 86; Vermont, 1888 ***5900.10*** *p247*
Leonard, Johannah Fitzgerald; Vermont, 1858-1908 ***5900.10*** *p353*
Leonard, John; New York, 1826 ***8197.10*** *p250*
Leonard, John; Vermont, 1842-1912 ***5900.10*** *p257*
Leonard, John; Vermont, 1858-1918 ***5900.10*** *p353*
Leonard, John 22; Ontario, 1871 ***1823.28*** *p57*
Leonard, John J.; Vermont, 1852-1903 ***5900.10*** *p462*
Leonard, John S. 74; Vermont, 1899 ***5900.10*** *p462*
Leonard, Joseph T.; Vermont, 1846-1920 ***5900.10*** *p90*
Leonard, Julia; Vermont, 1856-1945 ***5900.10*** *p302*
Leonard, Julie Sausville; Vermont, 1850-1936 ***5900.10*** *p90*
Leonard, Katherine; Vermont, 1831-1914 ***5900.10*** *p391*
Leonard, Katherine; Vermont, 1833-1910 ***5900.10*** *p241*
Leonard, Katherine; Vermont, 1833-1910 ***5900.10*** *p460*
Leonard, Katherine; Vermont, 1861-1902 ***5900.10*** *p505*
Leonard, Mary; Vermont, 1825-1893 ***5900.10*** *p88*
Leonard, Mary; Vermont, 1849-1931 ***5900.10*** *p460*
Leonard, Mary 70; Vermont, 1899 ***5900.10*** *p73*
Leonard, Mary 78; Vermont, 1892 ***5900.10*** *p580*
Leonard, Mary Ann; Vermont, 1858-1932 ***5900.10*** *p505*
Leonard, Mary Dowling; Vermont, 1830-1893 ***5900.10*** *p85*
Leonard, Mary Griffin; Vermont, 1830-1902 ***5900.10*** *p73*
Leonard, Mary Harrington; Vermont, 1840-1932 ***5900.10*** *p411*
Leonard, Matthew; Vermont, 1828-1875 ***5900.10*** *p73*
Leonard, Michael; Vermont, 1831-1903 ***5900.10*** *p85*
Leonard, Michael; Vermont, 1842-1888 ***5900.10*** *p446*
Leonard, Mitchell; Vermont, 1855-1927 ***5900.10*** *p48*
Leonard, Nettie; Vermont, 1858-1861 ***5900.10*** *p322*
Leonard, Owen; New York, 1846 ***3437.14*** *p105*
Leonard, Owen; Vermont, 1805-1893 ***5900.10*** *p460*
Leonard, Owen 64; Ontario, 1871 ***1823.22*** *p91*
Leonard, Patrick 75; Vermont, 1894 ***5900.10*** *p540*
Leonard, Patrick 75; Vermont, 1910 ***5900.10*** *p506*
Leonard, Peggy 23; New York, New York, 1849 ***1825.45*** *p33*
Leonard, Rosa 86; Ontario, 1871 ***1823.22*** *p91*
Leonard, Terrence; New York, 1838 ***8197.10*** *p122*
Leonard, Thomas; Vermont, 1820-1909 ***5900.10*** *p398*
Leonard, Thomas; Vermont, 1830-1902 ***5900.10*** *p181*
Leonard, Thomas; Vermont, 1831-1912 ***5900.10*** *p411*
Leonard, Thomas; Vermont, 1873 ***5900.10*** *p179*
Leonard, Thomas 58; Vermont, 1862 ***5900.10*** *p75*
Leonard, W. E. 45; Ontario, 1871 ***1823.15*** *p144*
Leonard, William 15; Philadelphia, 1774 ***1220.25*** *p81*
Leonard, William 36; Ontario, 1871 ***1823.15*** *p145*
Leonard, William 52; Ontario, 1871 ***1823.22*** *p91*
Leonard, Wm; Virginia, 1664 ***6212.30*** *p14*
Leonard, Wm; Virginia, 1665-1666 ***6212.30*** *p22*
Leonard, Wm; Virginia, 1666-1667 ***6212.30*** *p32*
Leongasella, Geo 35; Seattle, 1911 ***9196.1*** *p33*
Leonhard, Adelheid; Port uncertain, 1775 ***2856.30*** *p270*
Leonhard, Christian; Pennsylvania, 1777 ***4629.10*** *p8*
Leonhard, Eva; Port uncertain, 1773 ***2856.30*** *p270*
Leonhard, Georg Christof; America, 1737 ***2856.30*** *p270*
Leonhard, Jeremias; Port uncertain, 1730 ***2856.30*** *p270*
Leonhard, Joachim; Port uncertain, 1793 ***2856.30*** *p270*
Leonhard, Johann; Port uncertain, 1747 ***2856.30*** *p270*
Leonhard, Johann; Port uncertain, 1764 ***2856.30*** *p270*
Leonhard, Johann Wilhelm; America, 1752 ***2856.30*** *p270*
Leonhard, Josef; Port uncertain, 1729 ***2856.30*** *p270*
Leonhard, Josef; Port uncertain, 1735 ***2856.30*** *p270*
Leonhard, Niklas; America, 1752 ***2856.30*** *p270*
Leonhard, Niklas; Port uncertain, 1749 ***2856.30*** *p270*
Leonhard, Ottilia; Port uncertain, 1786 ***2856.30*** *p270*
Leonhard, Peter; Port uncertain, 1784 ***2856.30*** *p270*
Leonhardin, Ottilia; Port uncertain, 1786 ***2856.30*** *p270*
Leonhardt, Maria Anna; Port uncertain, 1757 ***2856.30*** *p270*
Leopold, Georg Adam; Port uncertain, 1754 ***2856.30*** *p270*
With wife
Leo-Wolf, Morris; New York, 1829 ***8197.10*** *p294*
Leo-Wolf, William; New York, 1829 ***8197.10*** *p294*
Lepell, George 33; Ontario, 1871 ***1823.28*** *p57*
Lepenotiere, Mr.; Quebec, 1858 ***9196.15*** *p37*
Leper, James 50; Ontario, 1871 ***1823.22*** *p91*
Leper, William; New York, 1837 ***8197.10*** *p94*
Le Pilletere, Jean Louis; Philadelphia, 1793 ***4629.10*** *p71*
Lepo, John 30; Maryland, 1775 ***1220.25*** *p98*
Lepp, Margarete; Port uncertain, 1772 ***2856.30*** *p270*
Lepp, Mary E.; Vermont, 1847-1938 ***5900.10*** *p194*
Leppar, William 55; Ontario, 1871 ***1823.15*** *p145*
Leppert, Miss; Port uncertain, 1781 ***2856.30*** *p270*
Leppert, Miss; Port uncertain, 1792 ***2856.30*** *p270*
Leppert, Jacob; Port uncertain, 1791 ***2856.30*** *p270*
Leppert, Johann; Port uncertain, 1760 ***2856.30*** *p270*
Leppert, Michael; Port uncertain, 1738 ***2856.30*** *p270*
Leppig, Johann Georg; America, 1765 ***2856.30*** *p270*
Leppington, Edward 38; Ontario, 1871 ***1823.15*** *p145*
Lepszuwna, Olszula; Maryland, 1910 ***3259.35*** *p34*
Leptka, William 37; Ontario, 1871 ***1823.28*** *p57*
Ler, Constantine; Virginia, 1665-1666 ***6212.30*** *p24*
Leray, Peter Lewis; New York, 1807 ***8197.10*** *p44*
Lerch, Daniel; Port uncertain, 1754 ***2856.30*** *p270*
Lerch, Melchior; Port uncertain, 1752 ***2856.30*** *p270*
Lercher, Gottfred; New York, 1840 ***8197.10*** *p186*
Leremore, Thomas; Maryland, 1650 ***2524.55*** *p136*
Le Reux, Peeter; Virginia, 1654 ***1224.1*** *p36*
Leristeyn, Hans Martin; America, 1727 ***2856.30*** *p270*
Leristeyn, Jan Barned; America, 1727 ***2856.30*** *p270*
Lerkley, Thomas; Maryland, 1671 ***2524.55*** *p136*
Lerner, Catharina; Port uncertain, 1760 ***2856.30*** *p270*
Lerner, Heinrich; Port uncertain, 1759 ***2856.30*** *p270*
Lerner, Johann Georg; Port uncertain, 1792 ***2856.30*** *p270*
Lerner, Johann Heinrich; Port uncertain, 1759 ***2856.30*** *p271*
Lero, George 21; Ontario, 1871 ***1823.28*** *p57*
Lero, Peter 23; Ontario, 1871 ***1823.28*** *p57*
LeRoche, Charles; Maryland, 1669 ***2524.55*** *p136*
Lerort, Gnaz Anton; Port uncertain, 1786 ***2856.30*** *p271*
Lersch, Franz; Port uncertain, 1785 ***2856.30*** *p271*
Lersch, P.; America, 1746 ***2856.30*** *p197H*
Lertill, Sarah; Virginia, 1671-1672 ***6212.30*** *p46*
Lerwck, Wladislawa; Maryland, 1910 ***3259.35*** *p34*
Lesauge, Louis 19; Ontario, 1871 ***1823.28*** *p57*
Lesby, Robert; Maryland, 1671 ***2524.55*** *p136*
Lesch, Peter; America, 1749 ***2856.30*** *p271*
Leschinsky, Hermana; Maryland, 1910 ***3259.35*** *p34*
L'Escott, Frances; Charles Town, South Carolina, 1753 ***1224.2*** *p69*
Leseiur, John; Maryland, 1666 ***2524.55*** *p136*
Leshay, John; Pennsylvania, 1777 ***4629.10*** *p20*
Lesher, George; Pennsylvania, 1777 ***4629.10*** *p12*
Leshowa, Julian S.; Maryland, 1910 ***3259.35*** *p34*
Lesiak, Franciszek; Maryland, 1910 ***3259.35*** *p34*
Lesiecki, Jacob; Maryland, 1910 ***3259.35*** *p34*
Lesig, Billy 26; Alaska, 1908 ***9196.1*** *p37*
Lesinewski, Antonie; Maryland, 1910 ***3259.35*** *p34*
Leski, Mary; Maryland, 1910 ***3259.35*** *p34*
Lesle, John 35; Ontario, 1871 ***1823.15*** *p145*
Leslee, John; Richmond, Virginia, 1820 ***1224.3*** *p46*
Lesley, James 36; Ontario, 1871 ***1823.22*** *p91*
Lesley, Robert; Georgia, 1774 ***1640.10*** *p96*
Lesley, William 70; Ontario, 1871 ***1823.22*** *p91*
Leslie, Alexander; New York, 1838 ***8197.10*** *p251*
Leslie, Alexander; New York, 1840 ***8197.10*** *p186*
Leslie, Alex'r; Ontario, 1861 ***2896.28*** *p45*
Leslie, Ann Young 63; Ontario, 1861 ***2896.28*** *p7*
Leslie, Charles 37; Virginia, 1774 ***1220.25*** *p46*
Leslie, Colin 66; Ontario, 1871 ***1823.22*** *p91*
Leslie, Isabella Young 49; Ontario, 1861 ***2896.28*** *p7*
Leslie, John; Alabama, 1815-1845 ***1640.10*** *p96*
Leslie, John; Florida, 1782 ***1640.10*** *p95*
Leslie, John; Norfolk, Virginia, 1831 ***1224.3*** *p46*
Leslie, John; Richmond, Virginia, 1820 ***1224.3*** *p46*
Leslie, John 32; Ontario, 1871 ***1823.15*** *p145*
Leslie, John Alexander; Toronto, 1889 ***1640.13*** *p70*
Leslie, Margaret Young 53; Ontario, 1861 ***2896.28*** *p7*
Leslie, Peter; Savannah, Georgia, 1805 ***1640.10*** *p96*
Leslie, Robert; California, 1890 ***1640.13*** *p70*
Leslie, Robert; Florida, 1792 ***1640.10*** *p96*
Leslie, William 63; Ontario, 1871 ***1823.15*** *p145*
Leslin, Anna Margarete; America, 1750 ***2856.30*** *p271*
With 3 sons
Lesly, Robert; Maryland, 1671 ***2524.55*** *p136*
Lessey, George; Maryland, 1910 ***3259.35*** *p34*
Lessing, Meyer; New York, 1838 ***8197.10*** *p251*
Lessing, Meyer; New York, 1840 ***8197.10*** *p185*
Lessle, Valentin; Port uncertain, 1761 ***2856.30*** *p271*
Lessley, David 24; New York, 1774 ***1220.25*** *p20*
Lessley, Robert 17; Georgia, 1774 ***1220.25*** *p48*
Lesslie, Margaret; Vermont, 1826-1912 ***5900.10*** *p509*
Lesson, James; Maryland, 1663 ***2524.55*** *p66*
Lessor, Elizabeth Preston; Vermont, 1846-1915 ***5900.10*** *p93*
Lessor, Henry J.; Vermont, 1841-1920 ***5900.10*** *p93*
Lest, Anna Elisabeth; America, 1750 ***2856.30*** *p271*
With 3 sons
Lested, Margaret; Maryland, 1674 ***2524.55*** *p136*
Lester, Mr.; Quebec, 1858 ***9196.15*** *p37*
Lester, Charles 21; Maryland, 1774 ***1220.25*** *p47*
Lester, Daniel; Pennsylvania, 1777 ***4629.10*** *p25*
Lester, Francis 18; Maryland, 1774 ***1220.25*** *p78*
Lester, George; New York, 1811-1834 ***8197.10*** *p304*
Lester, Wm; Virginia, 1674-1675 ***6212.30*** *p53*
Lestin, Anna Elisabeth; America, 1750 ***2856.30*** *p271*
With 3 sons
Lestin, Anna Margarete; America, 1750 ***2856.30*** *p271*
With 3 sons
Lestourgeon, Susannah Mary; Illinois, 1857 ***1224.3*** *p70*
Lestrade, M. A. L. Depeyre; New York, 1830 ***8197.10*** *p251*
Lestrange, Peter; New York, 1836-1838 ***8197.10*** *p122*
Letchcock, Tho; Virginia, 1671-1672 ***6212.30*** *p47*
Letchworth, George; Maryland, 1659-1660 ***2524.55*** *p136*
Letchworth, Thomas; Maryland, 1658 ***2524.55*** *p136*
With wife
Letchworth, Thomas; Virginia, 1657 ***1224.1*** *p36*
Letelier, Peter; Pennsylvania, 1777 ***4629.10*** *p10*
Letregue, Anthony 81; Ontario, 1871 ***1823.15*** *p145*
Letrush, Mary Ann 50; Ontario, 1871 ***1823.22*** *p91*
Lett, Ralph 46; Ontario, 1871 ***1823.28*** *p57*
Lett, Ralph W. 50; Ontario, 1871 ***1823.28*** *p57*
Lett, Thomas 36; Ontario, 1871 ***1823.28*** *p57*
Lett, Thos Ben 41; Ontario, 1871 ***1823.28*** *p57*
Letter, Bridget Finnegan; Vermont, 1831-1916 ***5900.10*** *p288*
Letter, Flavia; Vermont, 1839-1892 ***5900.10*** *p288*
Letter, Grave; Maryland, 1668 ***2524.55*** *p136*
Letters, Adar 61; Vermont, 1878 ***5900.10*** *p290*
Lettle, James S. 49; Ontario, 1871 ***1823.15*** *p145*
Leuck, Simon; America, 1755 ***2856.30*** *p271*
Leuck, Simon; Port uncertain, 1713 ***2856.30*** *p271*
Leuenberg, Jacob; Port uncertain, 1755 ***2856.30*** *p271*
Leuger, Friedrich; Port uncertain, 1754 ***2856.30*** *p271*
Leuloff, Ferdinand 26; Ontario, 1871 ***1823.28*** *p57*
Leuloff, Fredrick 31; Ontario, 1871 ***1823.28*** *p57*
Leuloff, William 45; Ontario, 1871 ***1823.28*** *p57*
Leur, Johann Peter; America, 1754 ***2856.30*** *p271*
Leutner, Konrad; Port uncertain, 1786 ***2856.30*** *p271*
Leuz, Leonard; Port uncertain, 1751 ***2856.30*** *p271*
Levan, Samuel; Pennsylvania, 1777 ***4629.10*** *p6*
Levandovski, Walter; Maryland, 1910 ***3259.35*** *p34*
Levanduski, Joseph; Maryland, 1910 ***3259.35*** *p34*
Levarock, Wm; Virginia, 1671 ***6212.30*** *p44*
Levaten, A.; Quebec, 1856 ***9196.15*** *p7*
Levee, Francis; New York, 1826 ***8197.10*** *p333*
Levely, Charles 12; Ontario, 1861 ***2896.25*** *p70*
Levenstyn, Jacob; New York, 1839 ***8197.10*** *p136*
Lever, Adam 39; Ontario, 1871 ***1823.22*** *p92*
Lever, Ashton 21; Maryland, 1775 ***1220.25*** *p112*
Levering, Griffith; Pennsylvania, 1777 ***4629.10*** *p19*
Leverston, Ann 22; Virginia, 1774 ***1220.25*** *p88*
Leverton, Martha; Maryland, 1680 ***2524.55*** *p136*
Levett, Elizabeth; Maryland, 1730 ***1224.2*** *p69*
Levett, Francis; St. Augustine, Florida, 1786 ***1224.2*** *p69*
Levett, William; Maryland, 1672 ***2524.55*** *p136*
Levi, Mr.; Quebec, 1858 ***9196.15*** *p40*
Levi, Hester 18; Jamaica, 1774 ***1220.25*** *p68*
Levi, Sylvester; New York, 1838 ***8197.10*** *p122*
Levick, George; New York, 1851 ***1224.3*** *p46*
Levin, Thomas C.; New York, 1835 ***8197.10*** *p251*
Levine, Amelia 30; Ontario, 1871 ***1823.28*** *p57*
Levine, Bridget; Vermont, 1851-1922 ***5900.10*** *p75*
Levine, John 46; Ontario, 1871 ***1823.28*** *p57*
Levine, Joseph; Vermont, 1846-1920 ***5900.10*** *p75*
Levingston, Elizabeth 55; Ontario, 1871 ***1823.28*** *p57*
Levingston, James 67; Ontario, 1871 ***1823.28*** *p57*
Levingstone, Chloe 27; Philadelphia, 1774 ***1220.25*** *p43*

Lidget, Charles; Boston, n.d. ***1224.1*** *p36*
Lidgett, Charles; Boston, 1701 ***1224.2*** *p69*
Lidsey, James; Maryland, 1675 ***2524.55*** *p137*
Lidtky, William 39; Ontario, 1871 ***1823.28*** *p58*
Lieb, Arnold; Port uncertain, 1746 ***2856.30*** *p272*
Lieb, J. Mich.; Port uncertain, 1725 ***2856.30*** *p514*
Liebel, Maria Eva; Port uncertain, 1754 ***2856.30*** *p272*
Liebelin, Maria Eva; Port uncertain, 1754 ***2856.30*** *p272*
Liebenstein, Bernhard; America, 1727 ***2856.30*** *p272*
Liebenstein, Bernhard; America, 1756 ***2856.30*** *p272*
Liebenstein, Bernhard; Port uncertain, 1737 ***2856.30*** *p272*
Liebenstein, Bernhard; Port uncertain, 1751 ***2856.30*** *p272*
Liebenstein, Hans Martin; America, 1727 ***2856.30*** *p272*
Liebenstein, Jan Barned; America, 1727 ***2856.30*** *p272*
Liebenstein, Magdalena Garn; America, 1756 ***2856.30*** *p272*
Liebenstein, Magdalena Garn; Port uncertain, 1751 ***2856.30*** *p272*
Liebenstein, Magdalena Garn; Port uncertain, 1752 ***2856.30*** *p272*
Liebenstein, Magdalena Garn; Port uncertain, 1754 ***2856.30*** *p272*
Liebenstein, Maria Magdalena; America, 1727 ***2856.30*** *p272*
Liebenstein, Maria Magdalena; America, 1750 ***2856.30*** *p272*
Liebenstein, Maria Magdalena; Port uncertain, 1737 ***2856.30*** *p272*
Liebenstein, Martin; America, 1727 ***2856.30*** *p272*
Liebenstein, Martin; America, 1750 ***2856.30*** *p272*
Liebenstein, Martin; Port uncertain, 1737 ***2856.30*** *p272*
Liebenstein, Martin; Port uncertain, 1751 ***2856.30*** *p272*
Liebich, Ignaz; Port uncertain, 1772 ***2856.30*** *p272*
Liebich, Matheis; Port uncertain, 1790 ***2856.30*** *p272*
Liebich, Simon; Port uncertain, 1768 ***2856.30*** *p272*
Liedke, William; Ontario, 1871 ***1823.28*** *p58*
Liedster, Thomas; Maryland, 1681 ***2524.55*** *p137*
Liefchild, Mr.; Quebec, 1858 ***9196.15*** *p40*
Lies, Anna Maria; Port uncertain, 1738 ***2856.30*** *p272*
Lies, Felicitas; Port uncertain, 1741 ***2856.30*** *p272*
Lies, Johann; Port uncertain, 1738 ***2856.30*** *p272*
Lies, Lorenz; Port uncertain, 1741 ***2856.30*** *p272*
With wife
Liesenfeld, Christof; Port uncertain, 1774 ***2856.30*** *p273*
Lieser, Paul; Port uncertain, 1764 ***2856.30*** *p273*
Liesk, Matthew 33; Ontario, 1871 ***1823.28*** *p58*
Liez, Georg; Port uncertain, 1740 ***2856.30*** *p273*
Liez, Johann Georg; Port uncertain, 1749 ***2856.30*** *p275*
Lifsk, Martin 35; Ontario, 1871 ***1823.28*** *p58*
Liftchild, Timothy; New York, 1838 ***8197.10*** *p123*
Liger, Nickel; America, 1738 ***2856.30*** *p273*
Liggins, Thomas 34; Maryland, 1774 ***1220.25*** *p60*
Light, Alexander; Virginia, 1664 ***6212.30*** *p15*
Light, Christopher; New York, 1840 ***8197.10*** *p252*
Light, Frances; Maryland, 1663 ***2524.55*** *p137*
Light, Frances; Maryland, 1665 ***2524.55*** *p137*
Light, Frances; Maryland, 1665 ***2524.55*** *p240*
Light, John; Pennsylvania, 1777 ***4629.10*** *p12*
Light, Rowland; Virginia, 1665-1666 ***6212.30*** *p24*
Lightfoot, Frances; Newport, Rhode Island, 1800 ***1224.3*** *p46*
Lightfoot, Sarah 18; New York, 1774 ***1220.25*** *p20*
Lightle, Goveneer 50; Ontario, 1871 ***1823.22*** *p92*
Lightlee, Mary; Virginia, 1703-1704 ***6212.30*** *p62*
Lighton, Patrick; Georgia, 1699 ***1640.13*** *p70*
Ligings, John; Maryland, 1670 ***2524.55*** *p28*
Lignowska, Anna; Maryland, 1910 ***3259.35*** *p35*
Lihinoffyz, Rosalia; Maryland, 1910 ***3259.35*** *p35*
Lijewski, John; Maryland, 1910 ***3259.35*** *p35*
Likely, Mr.; Quebec, 1857 ***9196.15*** *p25*
Likely, Mrs.; Quebec, 1857 ***9196.15*** *p25*
Likorski, Peter; Maryland, 1910 ***3259.35*** *p35*
Lilby, John 19; Ontario, 1861 ***2896.27*** *p29*
Lile, James; Maryland, 1677 ***2524.55*** *p137*
Lile, John; Maryland, 1663-1664 ***2524.55*** *p137*
Lill, Joshua 46; Ontario, 1871 ***1823.22*** *p92*
Lilley, James 23; Virginia, 1774 ***1220.25*** *p93*
Lilley, James 37; Virginia, 1774 ***1220.25*** *p93*
Lilley, Jane; Jamaica, 1750 ***1224.2*** *p106*
Lilley, Jane; Philadelphia, 1750 ***1224.2*** *p106*
Lilley, Joseph 16; Maryland, 1775 ***1220.25*** *p104*
Lilley, William; Maryland, 1679 ***2524.55*** *p137*
Lillibridge, Alice *SEE* Lillibridge, Robert
Lillibridge, Robert; Philadelphia, 1789 ***4629.10*** *p57*
Wife: Alice
Lillibridge, Thomas 26; Philadelphia, 1789 ***4629.10*** *p57*
Lillingstone, Mary Ann; Maryland, 1721 ***1224.2*** *p69*
Lillis, Bridget Flannagan 63; Vermont, 1896 ***5900.10*** *p104*
Lillis, Catharine 59; Vermont, 1900 ***5900.10*** *p108*
Lillis, Ellen Collins 65; Vermont, 1895 ***5900.10*** *p102*
Lillis, Hannah; Vermont, 1845-1904 ***5900.10*** *p105*
Lillis, John 25; Vermont, 1864 ***5900.10*** *p102*
Lillis, Margaret 72; Vermont, 1889 ***5900.10*** *p573*
Lillis, Mary 65; Vermont, 1874 ***5900.10*** *p105*
Lillis, Mary A. 51; Vermont, 1882 ***5900.10*** *p104*
Lillis, Mary Mortal 77; Vermont, 1883 ***5900.10*** *p102*
Lillis, Michael 80; Vermont, 1897 ***5900.10*** *p104*
Lillis, Michael 80; Vermont, 1909 ***5900.10*** *p104*
Lillis, Patrick 72; Vermont, 1904 ***5900.10*** *p102*
Lillis, Thomas 69; Ontario, 1871 ***1823.22*** *p92*
Lilly, Barnard 49; Ontario, 1871 ***1823.22*** *p92*
Lilly, Mark; Virginia, 1666 ***6212.30*** *p27*
Lilly, Mary 50; Ontario, 1871 ***1823.22*** *p92*
Lilly, Mary 87; Ontario, 1871 ***1823.22*** *p92*
Lilly, William 30; Maryland, 1774 ***1220.25*** *p73*
Lillystone, John; Philadelphia, 1751 ***1224.2*** *p69*
Limbach, Henrich Wilhelm; Port uncertain, 1766 ***2856.30*** *p273*
Limbach, Michael; Port uncertain, 1774 ***2856.30*** *p273*
With wife & 3 daughters
Limbe, Giles; Virginia, 1672-1673 ***6212.30*** *p51*
Limberger, Jakob; Port uncertain, 1764 ***2856.30*** *p273*
Limberger, Johann; Port uncertain, 1753 ***2856.30*** *p273*
Limbridge, Elizabeth; Virginia, 1703-1704 ***6212.30*** *p63*
Lime, Jno; Virginia, 1674 ***6212.30*** *p52*
Limes, Emmanuel; Philadelphia, 1792 ***4629.10*** *p69*
Limes, Joan; Virginia, 1665-1666 ***6212.30*** *p25*
Limford, Elizabeth 21; Maryland, 1775 ***1220.25*** *p105*
Limington, James 80; Ontario, 1871 ***1823.28*** *p58*
Limmer, Heinr. Valentin; America, 1767 ***2856.30*** *p273*
Limmons, Arthur 23; Ontario, 1871 ***1823.28*** *p58*
Limonoch, Wojciech; Maryland, 1910 ***3259.35*** *p35*
Linacre, James; New York, 1796 ***8197.10*** *p7*
Linahan, Cornelius 18; Ontario, 1861 ***2896.27*** *p71*
Linahan, Cornelius 50; Ontario, 1861 ***2896.27*** *p71*
Linahan, Ellen 50; Ontario, 1861 ***2896.27*** *p71*
Linaker, Joseph; Virginia, 1672 ***6212.30*** *p49*
Linard, Hans Adam; Port uncertain, 1745 ***2856.30*** *p273*
With wife & 2 children
Linay, Ann *SEE* Linay, John
Linay, Isobel *SEE* Linay, John
Linay, James *SEE* Linay, John
Linay, John; Georgia, 1774 ***1640.10*** *p96*
Wife: Isobel
Child: Ann
Child: James
Lincecombe, William; Maryland, 1678 ***2524.55*** *p137*
Linch, Daniel 22; Maryland, 1775 ***1220.25*** *p102*
Linch, Fanny 17; Ontario, 1861 ***2896.28*** *p48*
Linch, John; New York, New York, 1778 ***1224.2*** *p72*
Linch, Nicholas 26; Philadelphia, 1775 ***1220.25*** *p9*
Linch, Timothy 40; Ontario, 1871 ***1823.15*** *p145*
Linch, William; Vermont, 1819-1894 ***5900.10*** *p460*
Linck, Anna Margarete; America, 1752 ***2856.30*** *p273*
Linck, Jakob; Port uncertain, 1770 ***2856.30*** *p273*
Linck, Johann Leonard; Port uncertain, 1781 ***2856.30*** *p273*
With wife & children
Linck, Peter; New York, 1807 ***8197.10*** *p44*
Linckh, Catharina; Port uncertain, 1769 ***2856.30*** *p273*
Linckh, Melchior; Port uncertain, 1702 ***2856.30*** *p273*
Lincolinl, Garet; Maryland, 1678 ***2524.55*** *p137*
Lincoln, John 39; Ontario, 1871 ***1823.15*** *p145*
Lincolne, Ann; Maryland, 1674 ***2524.55*** *p137*
Lincolne, Jonathan; Maryland, 1662 ***2524.55*** *p137*
Lincolne, Jonathan; Maryland, 1674 ***2524.55*** *p137*
Lincott, Thomas; Maryland, 1680 ***2524.55*** *p137*
Lind, Eva Elisabeth; America, 1750 ***2856.30*** *p273*
Lind, George 20; Maryland, 1774 ***1220.25*** *p59*
Lind, Johann; Port uncertain, 1754 ***2856.30*** *p273*
With wife & 5 children
Lind, Margarete; America, 1750 ***2856.30*** *p273*
Lind, Thomas 32; Ontario, 1871 ***1823.15*** *p145*
Lindebaum, Miss; Port uncertain, 1783 ***2856.30*** *p273*
With sister
Lindeman, Jan; New York, 1807 ***8197.10*** *p44*
Lindemann, . . .; Port uncertain, 1771 ***2856.30*** *p273*
Lindemann, Adam; Port uncertain, 1753 ***2856.30*** *p273*
Lindemann, Benjamin; Port uncertain, 1742 ***2856.30*** *p273*
Lindemann, Burkhardt; America, 1753 ***2856.30*** *p273*
Lindemann, Burkhardt; America, 1753 ***2856.30*** *p274*
With wife & 7 children
Lindemann, Friedrich; Port uncertain, 1776 ***2856.30*** *p273*
Lindemann, Georg; Port uncertain, 1795 ***2856.30*** *p273*
Lindemann, Georg; Port uncertain, 1796 ***2856.30*** *p273*
Lindemann, Henrich; America, 1740 ***2856.30*** *p273*
Lindemann, Jakob; America, 1740 ***2856.30*** *p273*
Lindemann, Justus; America, 1740 ***2856.30*** *p273*
Lindemann, Magdalena; Port uncertain, 1794 ***2856.30*** *p273*
Lindemann, Mardalena; Port uncertain, 1795 ***2856.30*** *p273*
Lindemann, Margarete; Port uncertain, 1753 ***2856.30*** *p273*
Lindemann, Sebastian; Port uncertain, 1752 ***2856.30*** *p274*
Lindemer, John; Pennsylvania, 1786 ***4629.10*** *p53*
Linden, Ann 50; Ontario, 1871 ***1823.22*** *p92*
Linden, Conrad; New York, 1840 ***8197.10*** *p187*
Linden, Hugh 70; Ontario, 1871 ***1823.22*** *p92*
Linden, John 60; Ontario, 1871 ***1823.22*** *p92*
Linden, Maria Magdalena; Port uncertain, 1755 ***2856.30*** *p274*
Lindener, Johann; Port uncertain, 1776 ***2856.30*** *p274*
Lindenfeld, Charles 37; Ontario, 1871 ***1823.15*** *p145*
Lindenfelser, Georg; Port uncertain, 1764 ***2856.30*** *p274*
Linder, Johann Georg; Port uncertain, 1783 ***2856.30*** *p274*
Linder, Martin; Port uncertain, 1784 ***2856.30*** *p274*
With wife
Linderman, William 49; Ontario, 1871 ***1823.28*** *p58*
Lindesay, John; New York, 1753 ***1224.2*** *p69*
Lindesey, James; Maryland, 1647 ***2524.55*** *p137*
Lindgren, J. 47; Alaska, 1912 ***9196.1*** *p38*
Lindley, Anne 27; Ontario, 1871 ***1823.28*** *p58*
Lindley, James; New York, 1838 ***8197.10*** *p251*
Lindmark, John; New York, 1839 ***8197.10*** *p65*
Lindner, Elisabeth; Port uncertain, 1766 ***2856.30*** *p274*
Lindo, Abraham; Philadelphia, 1792 ***4629.10*** *p66*
Lindon, Fanny 3; Ontario, 1861 ***2896.27*** *p24*
Lindon, George 31; Ontario, 1861 ***2896.27*** *p24*
Lindon, Hyatt 2; Ontario, 1861 ***2896.27*** *p24*
Lindon, Nappy 5; Ontario, 1861 ***2896.27*** *p24*
Lindon, Patrick; New York, 1839 ***8197.10*** *p252*
Lindrum, James; New York, New York, 1848 ***6058.10*** *p34*
Lindsay, Miss; Quebec, 1857 ***9196.15*** *p17*
Lindsay, Mr.; Quebec, 1857 ***9196.15*** *p19*
Lindsay, Mr.; Quebec, 1858 ***9196.15*** *p31*
Lindsay, Charles Philip; New York, New York, 1855 ***1224.3*** *p47*
Lindsay, Elizabeth 70; Ontario, 1871 ***1823.22*** *p92*
Lindsay, George, Jr.; New York, 1829 ***8197.10*** *p352*
Lindsay, James; New Orleans, 1822 ***1640.10*** *p97*
Lindsay, James 46; Ontario, 1871 ***1823.28*** *p58*
Lindsay, John; New York, 1840 ***8197.10*** *p186*
Lindsay, John 35; Ontario, 1871 ***1823.28*** *p58*
Lindsay, John 54; Ontario, 1871 ***1823.28*** *p58*
Lindsay, Mary *SEE* Lindsay, Thomas
Lindsay, Thomas; Philadelphia, 1789 ***4629.10*** *p57*
Wife: Mary
Lindsay, Thomas 36; Philadelphia, 1789 ***4629.10*** *p57*
Lindsay, Thomas 42; Ontario, 1871 ***1823.28*** *p58*
Lindsay, William; New York, 1807 ***8197.10*** *p43*
Lindsay, William 34; Ontario, 1871 ***1823.28*** *p58*
Lindsay, William 50; Ontario, 1871 ***1823.28*** *p58*
Lindsey, Christopher 63; Ontario, 1871 ***1823.15*** *p145*
Lindsey, David; New York, 1803 ***8197.10*** *p14*
Lindsey, Edmond; Maryland, 1650 ***2524.55*** *p137*
Lindsey, Edmond; Maryland, 1656 ***2524.55*** *p137*
Lindsey, Edmond; Maryland, 1663 ***2524.55*** *p137*
Relative: Elinour
Lindsey, Elinour *SEE* Lindsey, Edmond
Lindsey, George; New York, 1807 ***8197.10*** *p43*
Lindsey, Isabella 14; Ontario, 1871 ***1823.15*** *p145*
Lindsey, James; Maryland, 1647 ***2524.55*** *p137*
Lindsey, James; Maryland, 1648 ***2524.55*** *p137*
Lindsey, James 18; Ontario, 1871 ***1823.15*** *p145*
Lindsey, John; Maryland, 1650 ***2524.55*** *p137*
Lindsey, John; Maryland, 1672 ***2524.55*** *p137*
Lindsey, John 23; Jamaica, 1774 ***1220.25*** *p79*
Lindsey, Margarett; Maryland, 1652 ***2524.55*** *p137*
Lindsey, Thomas; Maryland, 1674 ***2524.55*** *p137*
Lindsey, William 16; Ontario, 1871 ***1823.15*** *p145*
Lindsie, John; Maryland, 1650 ***2524.55*** *p137*
Lindsy, James 34; Ontario, 1871 ***1823.15*** *p145*
Lindt, Johann; America, 1749 ***2856.30*** *p274*
With family
Lindvist, Karl 25; Washington, 1913 ***9196.1*** *p59*
Lindy, Nicholas; New York, 1832-1840 ***8197.10*** *p186*
Line, Ann; Maryland, 1682 ***2524.55*** *p137*
Line, Wm; Virginia, 1666 ***6212.30*** *p26*
Linegar, Joseph; Virginia, 1668-1669 ***6212.30*** *p40*
Lineger, John; Maryland, 1682 ***2524.55*** *p137*
Linehan, Catherine 35; Vermont, 1876 ***5900.10*** *p101*
Linehan, Daniel; New York, 1840 ***8197.10*** *p186*
Linehan, Dennis; New York, 1802 ***8197.10*** *p22*
Linehan, Dennis 71; Vermont, 1876 ***5900.10*** *p101*
Linehan, Johana 52; Vermont, 1866 ***5900.10*** *p101*
Linehan, John; Vermont, 1832-1920 ***5900.10*** *p290*
Linehan, Mary Ellen Roache 57; Vermont, 1889 ***5900.10*** *p290*
Linen, George; New York, 1807 ***8197.10*** *p43*

Lines, Henry 41; Ontario, 1871 ***1823.15*** *p145*
Lines, Margaret; Maryland, 1674 ***2524.55*** *p137*
Lines, Philip; Maryland, 1674 ***2524.55*** *p137*
Lines, Phillip; Maryland, 1668 ***2524.55*** *p137*
Lines, Robert; Maryland, 1681 ***2524.55*** *p137*
Linesay, James H. 34; Ontario, 1871 ***1823.15*** *p145*
Linesay, John 72; Ontario, 1871 ***1823.15*** *p145*
Linety, Wladislaus; Maryland, 1910 ***3259.35*** *p35*
Ling, Bridget Hale; Vermont, 1861-1928 ***5900.10*** *p503*
Ling, Edward; Vermont, 1851-1922 ***5900.10*** *p503*
Ling, Mathew 21; Maryland, 1774 ***1220.25*** *p47*
Ling, Philip; Pennsylvania, 1777 ***4629.10*** *p25*
Ling, Philip; Pennsylvania, 1779 ***4629.10*** *p40*
Linga, Chas 35; Alaska, 1917 ***9196.1*** *p48*
Linga, Chas 35; Whitehorse, Yukon, 1917 ***9196.1*** *p48*
Lingan, Ann; Maryland, 1674 ***2524.55*** *p137*
Lingan, George; Maryland, 1664 ***2524.55*** *p137*
Linge, Anna 48; Ontario, 1871 ***1823.15*** *p145*
Linge, Robert; Virginia, 1666-1667 ***6212.30*** *p34*
Lingen, Edward; Virginia, 1665-1666 ***6212.30*** *p20*
Lingenfelder, Georg Valentin; America, 1765 ***2856.30*** *p274*
Lingenfelder, Johann; America, 1738 ***2856.30*** *p274*
Lingenfelder, Johann; America, 1762 ***2856.30*** *p274*
Lingenfelder, Maria Barbara; Port uncertain, 1790 ***2856.30*** *p274*
Lingeredler, Johann; America, 1738 ***2856.30*** *p274*
Lingh, Samuell; Virginia, 1666 ***6212.30*** *p30*
Lingsly, Michaell; Virginia, 1665-1666 ***6212.30*** *p24*
Lingworth, William 29; Ontario, 1871 ***1823.15*** *p145*
Lingworth, William 37; Ontario, 1871 ***1823.15*** *p145*
Linhan, Bryan; Maryland, 1682 ***2524.55*** *p137*
Linian, Bridget 35; Ontario, 1861 ***2896.27*** *p73*
Linian, Michael 1; Ontario, 1861 ***2896.27*** *p73*
Linian, William 40; Ontario, 1861 ***2896.27*** *p73*
Link, Elizabeth 21; Ontario, 1871 ***1823.28*** *p58*
Link, Fredrick 19; Ontario, 1871 ***1823.28*** *p58*
Link, Jacob 30; Ontario, 1871 ***1823.15*** *p145*
Link, John 62; Ontario, 1871 ***1823.15*** *p145*
Link, Konrad; Port uncertain, 1783 ***2856.30*** *p274*
Link, Leonhard; Port uncertain, 1786 ***2856.30*** *p274*
Link, Martin 28; Ontario, 1871 ***1823.15*** *p145*
Linkehorne, William; Maryland, 1660 ***2524.55*** *p137*
Linkenhenner, Michael; Port uncertain, 1780 ***2856.30*** *p274*
Linkhauer, Elisabeth; Port uncertain, 1750 ***2856.30*** *p274*
Linkhorne, William; Maryland, 1660 ***2524.55*** *p137*
Linklater, James 72; Ontario, 1871 ***1823.15*** *p145*
Linklater, Thomas 40; Ontario, 1871 ***1823.28*** *p58*
Linkleather, Andrew 30; Ontario, 1871 ***1823.15*** *p145*
Linkleather, John 43; Ontario, 1871 ***1823.15*** *p145*
Linkleather, John 93; Ontario, 1871 ***1823.15*** *p145*
Linkleather, Magnes 48; Ontario, 1871 ***1823.15*** *p145*
Linkleather, Peter 28; Ontario, 1871 ***1823.15*** *p145*
Linkleather, William 41; Ontario, 1871 ***1823.15*** *p145*
Linkletter, Thomas 32; Ontario, 1871 ***1823.15*** *p146*
Links, Georg; New York, 1838 ***8197.10*** *p123*
Linley, Luke 21; Maryland, 1775 ***1220.25*** *p113*
Linn, Charles; New York, 1840 ***8197.10*** *p187*
Linn, Edward M.; New York, 1822 ***8197.10*** *p62*
Linn, Johann Niklas; America, 1753 ***2856.30*** *p274*
Linn, Patrick; New York, 1825 ***8197.10*** *p250*
Linn, Peter; America, 1739 ***2856.30*** *p274*
Linn, Phil. Henrich; America, 1753 ***2856.30*** *p274*
Linn, Phil. Henrich, America, 1761 ***2856.30*** *p274*
Linn, Richard 40; Ontario, 1871 ***1823.28*** *p58*
Linn, Thomas; Virginia, 1667-1668 ***6212.30*** *p39*
Linn, William; Charles Town, South Carolina, 1735 ***1224.2*** *p72*
Linnehan, Daniel; New York, 1840 ***8197.10*** *p186*
Linnenbach, Johann; America, 1750 ***2856.30*** *p274*
With wife & daughter
Linnihan, Catherine Kirby; Vermont, 1808-1888 ***5900.10*** *p549*
Linnihan, Dinnis; Vermont, 1851-1868 ***5900.10*** *p549*
Linnihan, Ellen; Vermont, 1921 ***5900.10*** *p549*
Linnihan, James; Vermont, 1810-1876 ***5900.10*** *p549*
Linnihan, James; Vermont, 1855-1872 ***5900.10*** *p549*
Linnon, William; Georgia, 1775 ***1640.10*** *p97*
Linnon, William 19; Georgia, 1775 ***1220.25*** *p124*
Linoges, Mr.; Quebec, 1858 ***9196.15*** *p38*
Lins, Christof; Brazil, 1529 ***2856.30*** *p275*
Linsen, Jacob; Port uncertain, 1775 ***2856.30*** *p275*
Linsey, Mary; Maryland, 1659 ***2524.55*** *p137*
Linsingberg, Frederick L.; New York, New York, 1853 ***6058.10*** *p48*
Linskeys, Eva; Maryland, 1910 ***3259.35*** *p35*
Linsley, John; Maryland, 1675 ***2524.55*** *p137*
Lintifelt, Jake 28; Ontario, 1871 ***1823.15*** *p146*
Lintin, William 67; Ontario, 1871 ***1823.22*** *p92*
Linton, Ann; Philadelphia, 1785 ***1224.2*** *p70*
Linton, Elizabeth 7; Ontario, 1871 ***1823.22*** *p92*
Linton, Elizabeth 67; Ontario, 1871 ***1823.22*** *p92*
Linton, George 21; Maryland, 1775 ***1220.25*** *p109*
Linton, John 28; Nova Scotia, 1774 ***1220.25*** *p14*
Linton, John 70; Ontario, 1871 ***1823.22*** *p92*
Linton, Mary 40; Ontario, 1871 ***1823.22*** *p92*
Linton, William 21; Maryland, 1774 ***1220.25*** *p77*
Linton, William 48; Ontario, 1871 ***1823.22*** *p92*
Lintz, Frederick; New York, 1796 ***8197.10*** *p7*
Lintz, Hans Georg; America, 1749 ***2856.30*** *p275*
Lintz, Hans Georg; Port uncertain, 1750 ***2856.30*** *p275*
Lintz, Jerg; America, 1749 ***2856.30*** *p275*
Lintz, Marianna; Port uncertain, 1768 ***2856.30*** *p275*
Linwood, Faith; Virginia, 1690-1691 ***6212.30*** *p59*
Linz, Andreas; Port uncertain, 1764 ***2856.30*** *p275*
Linz, Christof; Brazil, 1529 ***2856.30*** *p275*
Linz, Georg; Port uncertain, 1740 ***2856.30*** *p273*
Linz, Johann Georg; Port uncertain, 1749 ***2856.30*** *p275*
Linzee, John; Massachusetts, 1799 ***1224.2*** *p70*
Lions, William 26; Ontario, 1871 ***1823.15*** *p146*
Lipcombe, James 35; Maryland, 1775 ***1220.25*** *p108*
Lipdry, Jacob 30; Maryland, 1774 ***1220.25*** *p51*
Lipinski, Albert; Maryland, 1910 ***3259.35*** *p35*
Lipinski, Josephine; Maryland, 1910 ***3259.35*** *p35*
Lipinski, Madislaw; Maryland, 1910 ***3259.35*** *p35*
Lipka, Adalbert; Maryland, 1910 ***3259.35*** *p35*
Lipka, Martin; Maryland, 1910 ***3259.35*** *p35*
Lipka, Woricek; Maryland, 1910 ***3259.35*** *p35*
Lipkey, John 33; Ontario, 1871 ***1823.28*** *p58*
Lipp, Bernard; Port uncertain, 1800 ***2856.30*** *p275*
Lipp, Jacob; Pennsylvania, 1785 ***4629.10*** *p48*
Lipp, Johp; Pennsylvania, 1776 ***4629.10*** *p52*
Lippatt, Henry 60; Ontario, 1871 ***1823.15*** *p146*
Lippert, Henry 25; Ontario, 1871 ***1823.15*** *p146*
Lippert, Johann Georg; Port uncertain, 1753 ***2856.30*** *p275*
Lippurger, Georg; Port uncertain, 1751 ***2856.30*** *p275*
Lipscomb, James; Virginia, 1665 ***6212.30*** *p17*
Lipset, John 64; Ontario, 1871 ***1823.28*** *p58*
Lipset, Robert 70; Ontario, 1871 ***1823.28*** *p58*
Lipski, John; Maryland, 1910 ***3259.35*** *p35*
Lipsky, Helena; Maryland, 1910 ***3259.35*** *p35*
Lirich, Frederick; Pennsylvania, 1777 ***4629.10*** *p9*
Lirich, John Frederick; Pennsylvania, 1777 ***4629.10*** *p9*
Lischinsky, Alexander; Maryland, 1910 ***3259.35*** *p35*
Lisco, Mary Manny; Vermont, 1793-1873 ***5900.10*** *p320*
Liscum, Adolphus 64; Ontario, 1871 ***1823.22*** *p92*
Liscum, George 37; Ontario, 1871 ***1823.22*** *p92*
Lisek, Bartholomew; Maryland, 1910 ***3259.35*** *p35*
Lisenfeld, Anton; Port uncertain, 1765 ***2856.30*** *p275*
Lish, John 21; Maryland, 1774 ***1220.25*** *p64*
Lishe, Barbara 48; Ontario, 1871 ***1823.28*** *p58*
Lishman, John 35; Maryland, 1775 ***1220.25*** *p108*
Lisicki, Joseph; Maryland, 1910 ***3259.35*** *p35*
Lisiecki, Ignacy; Maryland, 1910 ***3259.35*** *p35*
Lisiezki, Ludwig; Maryland, 1910 ***3259.35*** *p35*
Lisle, Bridget; New England, 1689 ***1224.1*** *p36*
Lisle, John 45; Ontario, 1871 ***1823.22*** *p93*
Lisle, Margaret Warren; New Haven, Connecticut, 1827 ***1224.3*** *p47*
Lisper, Henry 38; Philadelphia, 1775 ***1220.25*** *p100*
Liss, Johann; Port uncertain, 1784 ***2856.30*** *p275*
With wife & 2 sons
Lisson, James; Maryland, 1663 ***2524.55*** *p66*
Lissout, Wm.; Maryland, 1680 ***2524.55*** *p138*
Lister, Emmanuel; New York, 1840 ***8197.10*** *p186*
Lister, Farrol 23; Maryland, 1775 ***1220.25*** *p100*
Lister, James; Maryland, 1658 ***2524.55*** *p138*
Lister, John Smith; Pennsylvania, 1785 ***4629.10*** *p45*
Lister, Joseph; New York, 1830 ***8197.10*** *p363*
Lister, Richard; Virginia, 1664 ***6212.30*** *p12*
Liston, John; Fishkill, New York, 1852 ***1640.13*** *p70*
Liston, Morris; Maryland, 1666 ***2524.55*** *p123*
Liston, Robert Henry; Montreal, 1841 ***1640.13*** *p70*
Liston, Robert Ramage; Maryland, 1825 ***1640.13*** *p70*
Litch, William 43; Ontario, 1871 ***1823.15*** *p146*
Litchfeild, Wm; Virginia, 1668-1669 ***6212.30*** *p40*
Litchfeild, Wm; Virginia, 1672 ***6212.30*** *p49*
Litchfield, Dolly 50; Ontario, 1871 ***1823.22*** *p93*
Litchfield, John 21; Virginia, 1775 ***1220.25*** *p100*
Literski, Adam F.; Maryland, 1910 ***3259.35*** *p35*
Literski, Anton; Maryland, 1910 ***3259.35*** *p35*
Lithcow, Andrew 11 *SEE* Lithcow, Andrew
Lithcow, Andrew 37; Georgia, 1775 ***1220.25*** *p125*
Wife: Elizabeth 35
Child: Robert 4
Child: Jane 1
Child: Elizabeth 2
Child: Andrew 11
Lithcow, Elizabeth 2 *SEE* Lithcow, Andrew
Lithcow, Elizabeth 35 *SEE* Lithcow, Andrew
Lithcow, Jane 1 *SEE* Lithcow, Andrew
Lithcow, Robert 4 *SEE* Lithcow, Andrew
Lithgoe, Mary; Maryland, 1681 ***2524.55*** *p138*
Lithgone, James; New York, 1837 ***8197.10*** *p94*
Lithgow, Mr. 34; Grenada, 1774-1775 ***1220.25*** *p129*
Lithgow, Robert; Georgia, 1775 ***1640.10*** *p97*
Lithgow, William; Wilmington, North Carolina, 1754 ***1224.2*** *p70*
Lithman, Catharine 18; Virginia, 1775 ***1220.25*** *p95*
Litinski, Mary; Maryland, 1910 ***3259.35*** *p35*
Litle, Barbera 29; Ontario, 1871 ***1823.28*** *p58*
Litle, Elenor 38; Ontario, 1871 ***1823.28*** *p58*
Litle, John 46; Ontario, 1871 ***1823.28*** *p58*
Litle, Margret 64; Ontario, 1871 ***1823.28*** *p58*
Litster, Hugh; Georgia, 1699 ***1640.13*** *p70*
Litster, William 40; Ontario, 1871 ***1823.22*** *p93*
Litston, Peter 54; Ontario, 1871 ***1823.22*** *p93*
Litteaur, Mr.; Quebec, 1858 ***9196.15*** *p31*
Littel, Robert 66; Ontario, 1871 ***1823.15*** *p146*
Litteringe, Fran; Virginia, 1672 ***6212.30*** *p50*
Littfield, Richard; Maryland, 1681 ***2524.55*** *p138*
Littich, Anna Margarete Ackermann; America, 1766 ***2856.30*** *p275*
Littiger, Franz Leonard; Port uncertain, 1751 ***2856.30*** *p275*
With wife & children
Little, . . .; Boston, 1737 ***4628.40*** *p114*
Little, Mr.; Quebec, 1857 ***9196.15*** *p20*
Little, Ann 24 *SEE* Little, Thomas
Little, Ann Jane 35; Ontario, 1871 ***1823.28*** *p58*
Little, Basill; Virginia, 1658 ***1224.1*** *p36*
Little, Benjamin; Maryland, 1681 ***2524.55*** *p138*
Little, Benjamin 41; Ontario, 1871 ***1823.28*** *p58*
Little, Chas 26; Washington, 1913 ***9196.1*** *p60*
Little, Christopher; Maryland, 1673 ***2524.55*** *p138*
Little, Edw; Virginia, 1668-1669 ***6212.30*** *p40*
Little, Francis 44; Ontario, 1871 ***1823.15*** *p146*
Little, George 40; Ontario, 1871 ***1823.15*** *p146*
Little, H. A.; Quebec, 1857 ***9196.15*** *p19*
Little, Henry 23; Ontario, 1871 ***1823.22*** *p93*
Little, J.; Mississippi, 1805-1845 ***1640.10*** *p97*
Little, James; New York, 1839 ***8197.10*** *p136*
Little, James; Pennsylvania, 1777 ***4629.10*** *p13*
Little, James 16; Virginia, 1775 ***1220.25*** *p110*
Little, James 42; Ontario, 1871 ***1823.28*** *p58*
Little, Joane; Maryland, 1673 ***2524.55*** *p138*
Little, John; Maryland, 1652-1658 ***2524.55*** *p138*
Wife: Mary
Little, John; New York, 1825 ***8197.10*** *p250*
Little, John; Pennsylvania, 1777 ***4629.10*** *p9*
Little, John 30; Virginia, 1774 ***1220.25*** *p92*
Little, John 48; Ontario, 1871 ***1823.15*** *p146*
Little, John 63; Ontario, 1871 ***1823.22*** *p93*
Little, John 64; Ontario, 1871 ***1823.22*** *p93*
Little, John 72; Ontario, 1871 ***1823.22*** *p93*
Little, Joseph 47; Ontario, 1871 ***1823.15*** *p146*
Little, Mary *SEE* Little, John
Little, Mary 72; Ontario, 1871 ***1823.15*** *p146*
Little, Mary Ann Miles; Vermont, 1852-1923 ***5900.10*** *p485*
Little, Michael; New York, 1794 ***8197.10*** *p6*
Little, Michael; New York, 1828 ***8197.10*** *p350*
Little, Michael; New York, 1828-1831 ***8197.10*** *p369*
Little, Peter; Vermont, 1846-1932 ***5900.10*** *p485*
Little, Peter, Sr.; Vermont, 1850-1890 ***5900.10*** *p485*
Little, Richard 21; Maryland, 1774 ***1220.25*** *p57*
Little, Robert; New York, 1837 ***8197.10*** *p94*
Little, Robert 43; Ontario, 1871 ***1823.22*** *p93*
Little, Robert 62; Ontario, 1871 ***1823.28*** *p58*
Little, Simon 50, Ontario, 1871 ***1823.15*** *p146*
Little, Stewart 40; Ontario, 1871 ***1823.28*** *p58*
Little, Thomas 27; Fort Cumberland, Nova Scotia, 1774 ***1220.25*** *p19*
Wife: Ann 24
Little, Thomas 46; Ontario, 1871 ***1823.15*** *p146*
Little, Thomas 71; Ontario, 1871 ***1823.15*** *p146*
Little, Thomas Patrick; New York, 1840 ***8197.10*** *p187*
Little, W. C.; Quebec, 1857 ***9196.15*** *p16*
Little, William; New York, 1813 ***1640.10*** *p97*
Little, William 20; St. Kitts, 1774 ***1220.25*** *p44*
Little, William 40; Ontario, 1871 ***1823.15*** *p146*
Little, William 44; Ontario, 1871 ***1823.15*** *p146*
Little, William 51; Ontario, 1871 ***1823.15*** *p146*
Littleboy, Laurence; Virginia, 1653 ***1224.1*** *p36*
Littledale, Johnson; Chicago, 1863 ***1640.13*** *p70*
Littlefair, Edward 29; Ontario, 1871 ***1823.15*** *p146*
Littlefair, Emerson 35; Ontario, 1871 ***1823.15*** *p146*
Littlefair, Margery 63; Ontario, 1871 ***1823.15*** *p146*
Littlefair, William 65; Ontario, 1871 ***1823.15*** *p146*
Littlejohn, James; Pennsylvania, 1786 ***4629.10*** *p53*
Littler, William; Boston, 1765 ***1224.2*** *p70*
Littleton, Gabriel; Virginia, 1665 ***6212.30*** *p17*
Littleton, Southy; Virginia, 1666 ***6212.30*** *p27*
Littlewood, Miss; Quebec, 1857 ***9196.15*** *p21*
Littlewood, Benjamin 21; Philadelphia, 1774 ***1220.25*** *p73*
Litwonska, John J.; Maryland, 1910 ***3259.35*** *p35*

Litzenberger, Anna Catharina; Port uncertain, 1776 ***2856.30*** *p275*
Litzenberger, George; Pennsylvania, 1777 ***4629.10*** *p22*
Liveller, Alice; Maryland, 1651 ***2524.55*** *p138*
Livingston, Anne Ash; Charles Town, South Carolina, 1721 ***1224.2*** *p70*
Livingston, Archibald Charles; America, 1879 ***1640.13*** *p70*
Livingston, Charlotte; Vermont, 1854-1915 ***5900.10*** *p333*
Livingston, Gilbert Robert; New York, 1817 ***1224.3*** *p47*
Livingston, Hezekia; Vermont, 1837-1923 ***5900.10*** *p518*
Livingston, John; New London, Connecticut, 1720 ***1224.2*** *p70*
Livingston, John 45; Ontario, 1871 ***1823.28*** *p58*
Livingston, Lydia; Vermont, 1841-1915 ***5900.10*** *p518*
Livingston, Mortimer; New York, New York, 1858 ***1224.3*** *p47*
Livingston, Neil 50; Ontario, 1871 ***1823.28*** *p58*
Livingston, Robert 23; Ontario, 1871 ***1823.15*** *p146*
Livingston, Susan 45; Ontario, 1871 ***1823.28*** *p58*
Livingston, Thomas 46; Ontario, 1871 ***1823.15*** *p146*
Livingston, William Hardie; New Jersey, 1892 ***1640.13*** *p70*
Livingstone, A.; Mississippi, 1814-1845 ***1640.10*** *p97*
Livingstone, A. C.; Florida, 1735-1845 ***1640.10*** *p97*
Livingstone, Duncan 37; Ontario, 1871 ***1823.15*** *p146*
Livingstone, Henry; New York, 1786 ***1224.2*** *p70*
Livingstone, Hugh; Georgia, 1741 ***1640.10*** *p97*
Livingstone, Hugh 54; Ontario, 1871 ***1823.28*** *p58*
Livingstone, Isabella 70; Ontario, 1871 ***1823.15*** *p146*
Livingstone, John; New York, New York, 1786 ***1224.2*** *p70*
Livingstone, N. M. 36; Ontario, 1871 ***1823.15*** *p146*
Livingstone, William; South Carolina, n.d. ***1224.2*** *p70*
Livingstone, William 71; Ontario, 1871 ***1823.28*** *p58*
Liydd, Jane 85; Ontario, 1871 ***1823.15*** *p146*
Liydd, Robert 52; Ontario, 1871 ***1823.15*** *p146*
Liydd, William 28; Ontario, 1871 ***1823.15*** *p146*
Lizard, David 35; Ontario, 1871 ***1823.15*** *p146*
Lizinger, Johann; Port uncertain, 1749 ***2856.30*** *p275*
Llemon, John 42; Ontario, 1871 ***1823.15*** *p146*
Llewellin, John; Maryland, 1681 ***2524.55*** *p138*
Llong, Nicholas; Virginia, 1666 ***6212.30*** *p28*
Lloyd, Alexander; Virginia, 1679 ***1224.1*** *p36*
Lloyd, Anne; Vermont, 1846-1926 ***5900.10*** *p562*
Lloyd, Annie 53; Ontario, 1871 ***1823.28*** *p58*
Lloyd, Catherine 56; Vermont, 1862 ***5900.10*** *p574*
Lloyd, Daniel; New York, 1840 ***1224.3*** *p47*
Lloyd, David 32; Ontario, 1871 ***1823.22*** *p93*
Lloyd, Edward; Maryland, n.d. ***1224.1*** *p36*
Lloyd, Elizabeth; Virginia, 1657 ***1224.1*** *p36*
Lloyd, Elizabeth Carter; Virginia, 1694 ***1224.1*** *p36*
Lloyd, G.; Quebec, 1858 ***9196.15*** *p33*
Lloyd, Hanora Dwyer; Vermont, 1826-1906 ***5900.10*** *p422*
Lloyd, Hanora Maloney; Vermont, 1831-1899 ***5900.10*** *p438*
Lloyd, Henrietta Maria; Maryland, 1697 ***1224.1*** *p36*
Lloyd, Henry; Boston, n.d. ***1224.2*** *p70*
Lloyd, James; Boston, 1696 ***1224.1*** *p36*
Lloyd, Jehue; Pennsylvania, 1779 ***4629.10*** *p41*
Lloyd, John; Pennsylvania, 1779 ***4629.10*** *p41*
Lloyd, John; South Carolina, 1746 ***1224.2*** *p70*
Lloyd, John; Vermont, 1822-1907 ***5900.10*** *p422*
Lloyd, John 40; Ontario, 1871 ***1823.28*** *p58*
Lloyd, John 62; Ontario, 1871 ***1823.28*** *p58*
Lloyd, Lucy 20; Maryland, 1773-1774 ***1220.25*** *p33*
Lloyd, Margaret; New Orleans, 1838 ***1224.3*** *p47*
Lloyd, Mary 40; Vermont, 1867 ***5900.10*** *p566*
Lloyd, Mary B.; New York, 1837 ***8197.10*** *p94*
Lloyd, Richard; Maryland, 1665 ***2524.55*** *p138*
Lloyd, Richard; Vermont, 1824-1909 ***5900.10*** *p438*
Lloyd, Sarah; South Carolina, 1760 ***1224.2*** *p121*
Lloyd, Serah 61; Ontario, 1871 ***1823.28*** *p58*
Lloyd, Simon; Virginia, 1657 ***1224.1*** *p36*
Lloyd, Thomas; Maryland, 1679 ***2524.55*** *p138*
Lloyd, Thomas; New York, 1838 ***8197.10*** *p251*
Lloyd, Thomas 27; Maryland, 1775 ***1220.25*** *p104*
Lloyd, William; Pennsylvania, 1786 ***4629.10*** *p55*
Lloyd, William; Virginia, 1678 ***1224.1*** *p37*
Lloyd, William 27; Ontario, 1871 ***1823.28*** *p58*
Lloyde, Henry; Maryland, 1664 ***2524.55*** *p138*
Lloyde, John; Virginia, 1653 ***1224.1*** *p36*
Loach, Thomas; Virginia, 1667 ***6212.30*** *p37*
Loader, William; Maryland, 1642 ***2524.55*** *p138*
Loadman, James 41; Ontario, 1871 ***1823.15*** *p146*
Loane, Anna Hoye 43; Vermont, 1880 ***5900.10*** *p503*
Loane, Betty Ramsey 85; Vermont, 1875 ***5900.10*** *p503*
Loane, Eliza C. 53; Vermont, 1891 ***5900.10*** *p501*
Loane, James 68; Vermont, 1895 ***5900.10*** *p503*
Loane, Peter 85; Vermont, 1881 ***5900.10*** *p503*
Loane, Robert 56; Vermont, 1892 ***5900.10*** *p503*
Loard, John 64; Ontario, 1871 ***1823.22*** *p93*
Loaz, Johann; America, 1733 ***2856.30*** *p278*
Lob, Heinrich; Port uncertain, 1752 ***2856.30*** *p280*
Lobb, George 57; Ontario, 1871 ***1823.15*** *p146*
Lobb, Samuel 45; Ontario, 1871 ***1823.28*** *p58*
Lobb, William 62; Ontario, 1871 ***1823.22*** *p93*
Lobby, Edward 55; Ontario, 1871 ***1823.15*** *p148*
Lobdell, Julia A.; Vermont, 1850-1938 ***5900.10*** *p321*
Loberetyesin, Lasser; Maryland, 1910 ***3259.35*** *p35*
Lobescher, Martin; Port uncertain, 1779 ***2856.30*** *p275*
With 3 children
Lobescher, Martin; Port uncertain, 1784 ***2856.30*** *p275*
With 3 children
Loble, Georg; America, 1751 ***2856.30*** *p280*
With wife
Lobler, Magdalena; Port uncertain, 1734 ***2856.30*** *p280*
Loch, George; Maryland, 1910 ***3259.35*** *p35*
Loch, Mrs. Lorenz; America, 1749 ***2856.30*** *p275*
With 5 children
Loch, Thomas; Georgia, 1741 ***1640.10*** *p97*
Loch, William; Jamaica, 1815 ***1640.13*** *p71*
Lochbaum, Justus; Port uncertain, 1764 ***2856.30*** *p276*
Lochead, Samuel 37; Ontario, 1871 ***1823.15*** *p146*
Locher, Johann Jakob; America, 1765 ***2856.30*** *p276*
Lochery, William; Pennsylvania, 1778 ***4629.10*** *p32*
Lochhead, James; Mississippi, 1810-1845 ***1640.10*** *p98*
Lochle, Ignaz; Port uncertain, 1741 ***2856.30*** *p281*
Lochle, Ignaz; Port uncertain, 1771 ***2856.30*** *p281*
Lochner, Christopher; Pennsylvania, 1777 ***4629.10*** *p15*
Locie, Alice M. 14; Ontario, 1861 ***2896.28*** *p34*
Locie, Betsy 55; Ontario, 1861 ***2896.28*** *p34*
Locie, Daniel J. 12; Ontario, 1861 ***2896.28*** *p41*
Locie, Elizabeth 22; Ontario, 1861 ***2896.28*** *p34*
Locie, Florence A. 1; Ontario, 1861 ***2896.28*** *p34*
Locie, Randolph 24; Ontario, 1861 ***2896.28*** *p40*
Locie, Reuben 19; Ontario, 1861 ***2896.28*** *p40*
Locie, Sarah A. 32; Ontario, 1861 ***2896.28*** *p41*
Locie, Susan A. 32; Ontario, 1861 ***2896.28*** *p34*
Locie, Walter B. 2; Ontario, 1861 ***2896.28*** *p41*
Lock, Frank; Maryland, 1910 ***3259.35*** *p35*
Lock, Jane 27; Ontario, 1871 ***1823.22*** *p93*
Lock, John; America, 1725 ***1224.2*** *p70*
Lock, Joseph 38; British Columbia, 1911 ***9196.1*** *p34*
Lock, Joseph 38; Washington, 1911 ***9196.1*** *p34*
Lock, Thomas; Maryland, 1673 ***2524.55*** *p138*
Lock, William 74; Ontario, 1871 ***1823.22*** *p93*
Lockart, George 40; Ontario, 1871 ***1823.15*** *p146*
Lockart, William 52; Ontario, 1871 ***1823.22*** *p93*
Locke, Joan; Virginia, 1671-1672 ***6212.30*** *p47*
Locke, Julia B.; Vermont, 1822-1849 ***5900.10*** *p300*
Lockely, Nich; Virginia, 1684-1685 ***6212.30*** *p57*
Locker, James; Virginia, 1722 ***1224.2*** *p70*
Locker, Mary; Maryland, 1667 ***2524.55*** *p138*
Locker, Thomas; Virginia, 1671-1672 ***6212.30*** *p46*
Locketh, Elizabeth; Maryland, 1657 ***2524.55*** *p138*
Lockett, Miss; Quebec, 1858 ***9196.15*** *p33*
Lockett, Mr.; Quebec, 1858 ***9196.15*** *p33*
Lockett, Mr., Jr.; Quebec, 1858 ***9196.15*** *p33*
Lockett, Mrs.; Quebec, 1858 ***9196.15*** *p33*
Lockett, Elizabeth; Maryland, 1658 ***2524.55*** *p138*
Lockett, Marke; Maryland, 1675 ***2524.55*** *p138*
Lockey, William; Maryland, 1681 ***2524.55*** *p138*
Lockhard, Richard 39; Ontario, 1871 ***1823.15*** *p147*
Lockhart, Alexander; New York, 1899 ***1640.13*** *p71*
Lockhart, John; Georgia, 1699 ***1640.13*** *p71*
Lockhart, Robert 40; Ontario, 1871 ***1823.22*** *p93*
Lockhart, William; New York, 1827 ***8197.10*** *p344*
Lockhead, Charles; Pennsylvania, 1868 ***6058.10*** *p76*
Lockhead, Henry; Pennsylvania, 1777 ***4629.10*** *p28*
Lockheed, Thomas 28; Ontario, 1871 ***1823.28*** *p58*
Lockice, Tho; Virginia, 1674-1675 ***6212.30*** *p53*
Lockie, Alexander 31; Ontario, 1871 ***1823.15*** *p147*
Lockie, Alexander 36; Ontario, 1871 ***1823.22*** *p93*
Lockie, Thomas Oman; Toronto, 1868 ***1640.13*** *p71*
Lockier, George; Maryland, 1678 ***2524.55*** *p138*
Lockier, George; Maryland, 1680 ***2524.55*** *p138*
Locking, Alexander 29; Ontario, 1871 ***1823.15*** *p147*
Locklin, Lawrence 50; Ontario, 1871 ***1823.22*** *p93*
Lockman, Ann; Maryland, 1673 ***2524.55*** *p138*
Lockovich, Geo 34; Alaska, 1916 ***9196.1*** *p43*
Lockovich, Geo 34; Whitehorse, Yukon, 1916 ***9196.1*** *p43*
Lockridge, Samuel 48; Ontario, 1871 ***1823.15*** *p147*
Lockwar, Samuel 17; New York, 1775 ***1220.25*** *p94*
Lockwood, Mr.; Quebec, 1857 ***9196.15*** *p13*
Lockwood, John 32; Ontario, 1871 ***1823.15*** *p147*
Lockwood, Joseph 84; Ontario, 1871 ***1823.22*** *p93*
Lockwood, Thomas R.; New York, 1840 ***8197.10*** *p185*
Lockwood, Thomas S.; New York, 1837 ***8197.10*** *p94*
Lockwood, William; New York, 1834 ***8197.10*** *p315*
Lockwood, William; New York, 1838 ***8197.10*** *p251*
Lockwood, William; New York, 1839 ***8197.10*** *p136*
Lockwood, William; New York, 1840 ***8197.10*** *p186*
Locky, Edward; Virginia, 1667 ***1224.1*** *p37*
Lockyer, Cornelius C.; New York, 1840 ***8197.10*** *p187*
Lockyer, Thomas; New York, 1836-1838 ***8197.10*** *p123*
Lodecka, Ernie; Maryland, 1910 ***3259.35*** *p35*
Loderer, . . .; Port uncertain, 1769 ***2856.30*** *p276*
Lodg, Alis; Maryland, 1652 ***2524.55*** *p138*
Lodge, Edward; Maryland, 1700 ***1224.2*** *p70*
Lodge, Mathew 20; Fort Cumberland, Nova Scotia, 1775 ***1220.25*** *p21*
Lodge, Philip; New York, 1821 ***8197.10*** *p249*
Lodge, William; New York, 1839 ***8197.10*** *p136*
Lodges, John; Maryland, 1679 ***2524.55*** *p138*
Loe, Agnes; Virginia, 1664 ***6212.30*** *p15*
Loe, Augustin; Virginia, 1666-1667 ***6212.30*** *p34*
Loe, Margery; Maryland, 1661 ***2524.55*** *p138*
Loe, Maxamillion; Virginia, 1664 ***6212.30*** *p14*
Loe, Richard; Maryland, 1641 ***2524.55*** *p138*
Loe, Robt; Virginia, 1668-1669 ***6212.30*** *p40*
Loe, Robt; Virginia, 1703 ***6212.30*** *p62*
Loek, Yan; Maryland, 1910 ***3259.35*** *p35*
Loesch, Anna Margarete; Port uncertain, 1774 ***2856.30*** *p276*
Loesch, Philipp Adam; Port uncertain, 1778 ***2856.30*** *p276*
Loffel, Balthasar; America, 1750 ***2856.30*** *p281*
With wife
Loffler, Dietrich; America, 1751 ***2856.30*** *p281*
Loffler, Dietrich; America, 1751 ***2856.30*** *p281*
With wife & 4 children
Loffler, Franziska; Port uncertain, 1752 ***2856.30*** *p281*
Lofftis, Rich; Virginia, 1664 ***6212.30*** *p9*
Loft, George Frederick 27; Ontario, 1871 ***1823.15*** *p147*
Loft, William 61; Ontario, 1871 ***1823.15*** *p147*
Lofthoug, Mary; Maryland, 1674 ***2524.55*** *p138*
Lofthouse, Alvara; St. Augustine, Florida, 1778 ***1224.2*** *p71*
Loftis, Robert; Maryland, 1661 ***2524.55*** *p138*
Loftman, Benjamin 16; Maryland, 1774 ***1220.25*** *p78*
Loftus, Biddy 9 *SEE* Loftus, Biddy
Loftus, Biddy 40; New York, New York, 1848 ***1825.45*** *p38*
Son: John 15
Daughter: Mary Ann 16
Daughter: Mary 22
Son: Michael 15
Son: Thomas 6
Daughter: Ellen 3
Daughter: Biddy 9
Loftus, David; New York, 1839 ***8197.10*** *p252*
Loftus, Ellen 3 *SEE* Loftus, Biddy
Loftus, James; New York, 1834 ***8197.10*** *p74*
Loftus, John 15 *SEE* Loftus, Biddy
Loftus, Kate Caden; Vermont, 1840-1914 ***5900.10*** *p436*
Loftus, Mary 22 *SEE* Loftus, Biddy
Loftus, Mary Ann 16 *SEE* Loftus, Biddy
Loftus, Michael 15 *SEE* Loftus, Biddy
Loftus, Patrick 41; Vermont, 1882 ***5900.10*** *p436*
Loftus, Thomas; New York, 1839 ***8197.10*** *p252*
Loftus, Thomas 6 *SEE* Loftus, Biddy
Logan, Adam; New York, 1802 ***8197.10*** *p22*
Logan, Adam; New York, 1812 ***8197.10*** *p57*
Logan, Agness 58; Ontario, 1871 ***1823.15*** *p147*
Logan, Andrew; Nova Scotia, 1745 ***4628.40*** *p44*
Logan, Arnslor 36; Ontario, 1871 ***1823.15*** *p147*
Logan, Catherine 70; Vermont, 1859 ***5900.10*** *p152*
Logan, Charles 51; Ontario, 1871 ***1823.15*** *p147*
Logan, David; New York, 1806 ***8197.10*** *p31*
Logan, David 76; Ontario, 1871 ***1823.15*** *p147*
Logan, Edward; Canada, 1756-1760 ***4628.40*** *p45*
Logan, Francis; New York, 1831 ***8197.10*** *p365*
Logan, Francis 85; Vermont, 1877 ***5900.10*** *p151*
Logan, George; New York, 1840 ***8197.10*** *p186*
Logan, George; Virginia, 1781 ***1224.2*** *p71*
Logan, James; Pennsylvania, 1775-1781 ***4628.40*** *p69*
Logan, James 27; Maryland, 1774 ***1220.25*** *p61*
Logan, James 43; Ontario, 1871 ***1823.15*** *p147*
Logan, Jean 75; Ontario, 1871 ***1823.15*** *p147*
Logan, John; Canada, 1756-1760 ***4628.40*** *p45*
Logan, John; New York, 1822 ***8197.10*** *p249*
Logan, John; Nova Scotia, 1745 ***4628.40*** *p44*
Logan, John; Savannah, Georgia, 1810-1812 ***1640.10*** *p98*
Logan, John 19; Philadelphia, 1775 ***1220.25*** *p107*
Logan, John 40; Ontario, 1871 ***1823.15*** *p147*
Logan, John 63; Alaska, 1918 ***9196.1*** *p8*
Logan, John 63; Yukon, 1918 ***9196.1*** *p8*
Logan, Margaret; South Carolina, 1791 ***1224.2*** *p71*
Logan, Margaret Haley; Vermont, 1820-1863 ***5900.10*** *p562*
Logan, Patrick 60; Ontario, 1871 ***1823.22*** *p93*
Logan, Robert; Pennsylvania, 1777 ***4629.10*** *p8*
Logan, Robt; Virginia, 1701-1702 ***6212.30*** *p61*
Logan, Sara; Virginia, 1701-1702 ***6212.30*** *p61*
Logan, Sarah 75; Ontario, 1871 ***1823.15*** *p147*
Logan, Thomas; New York, 1828 ***8197.10*** *p251*

Logan, Thomas 39; Ontario, 1871 ***1823.15*** *p147*
Logan, W. E.; Canada, 1875 ***1640.13*** *p71*
Logan, William; Charleston, South Carolina, 1802 ***1224.3*** *p47*
Logan, William; New York, 1831 ***8197.10*** *p366*
Logan, William; New York, 1838 ***8197.10*** *p251*
Logan, William; Philadelphia, 1780 ***1224.2*** *p71*
Logan, William 45; Ontario, 1871 ***1823.15*** *p147*
Logan, William 49; Ontario, 1871 ***1823.22*** *p93*
Logan, William 52; Ontario, 1871 ***1823.15*** *p147*
Loge, Abraham; Havana, 1765 ***1224.2*** *p70*
Loge, Abraham; Rhode Island, 1765 ***1224.2*** *p70*
Logg, Robert 60; Ontario, 1871 ***1823.15*** *p147*
Loggat, John; Philadelphia, 1785 ***1640.13*** *p71*
Loghan, Michael 32; Ontario, 1871 ***1823.15*** *p147*
Loghan, Thomas 66; Ontario, 1871 ***1823.15*** *p147*
Logie, James; Oregon, 1854 ***1640.13*** *p71*
Logie, Thomas 46; Ontario, 1871 ***1823.15*** *p147*
Logie, Walter 44; Ontario, 1871 ***1823.15*** *p147*
Logie, William 51; Ontario, 1871 ***1823.15*** *p147*
Logue, Edward; New York, 1821 ***8197.10*** *p249*
Logue, James; New York, 1840 ***8197.10*** *p321*
Logue, James 75; Vermont, 1869 ***5900.10*** *p324*
Logue, Owen; New York, 1828-1840 ***8197.10*** *p185*
Logue, William; New York, 1823 ***8197.10*** *p250*
Lohinski, William; Maryland, 1910 ***3259.35*** *p36*
Lohmann, Heinrich; Port uncertain, 1751 ***2856.30*** *p276*
Lohmayer, Mrs. Josef; Port uncertain, 1790 ***2856.30*** *p276*
Lohmuller, Georg; America, 1756 ***2856.30*** *p276*
Lohmuller, Johann; America, 1752 ***2856.30*** *p276*
Lohmuller, Johann Heinrich; America, 1752 ***2856.30*** *p276*
Lohmuller, Michael; America, 1756 ***2856.30*** *p276*
Lohn, Louisa; Maryland, 1910 ***3259.35*** *p36*
Lohodziski, Stanislau; Maryland, 1910 ***3259.35*** *p36*
Lohrer, Maria Magdalena; Port uncertain, 1785 ***2856.30*** *p276*
Lohrman, George; Pennsylvania, 1777 ***4629.10*** *p9*
Lohrmann, David; America, 1752 ***2856.30*** *p276*
With wife & 4 children
Lohrmann, Hans; America, 1752 ***2856.30*** *p276*
Lohrmann, Matthaus; America, 1752 ***2856.30*** *p276*
Lohrs, Henrich; Port uncertain, 1764 ***2856.30*** *p281*
Lohse, Frederick A.; New York, 1823 ***8197.10*** *p249*
Loir, Christian 42; Ontario, 1871 ***1823.15*** *p147*
Lokke, L. 45; Alaska, 1917 ***9196.1*** *p7*
Lokke, L. 45; Yukon, 1917 ***9196.1*** *p7*
Lollbach, Balthasar; Port uncertain, 1778 ***2856.30*** *p269*
Lollbach, Balthasar; Port uncertain, 1780 ***2856.30*** *p269*
Lolley, Gilbert; Maryland, 1667 ***2524.55*** *p138*
Lolly, Gilbert; Maryland, 1673 ***2524.55*** *p138*
Loly, Gilbert; Maryland, 1673 ***2524.55*** *p138*
Loman, Ava E. 51; Kansas, 1877-1910 ***9079.10*** *p23*
Loman, John 49; Kansas, 1878-1910 ***9079.10*** *p23*
Lomas, John; Annapolis, Maryland, 1757 ***1224.2*** *p71*
Lomas, William 33; Jamaica, 1774 ***1220.25*** *p72*
Lomax, Joshua; Virginia, 1665-1666 ***6212.30*** *p21*
Lomax, Thomas; Maryland, 1664 ***2524.55*** *p138*
Lombard, James; New York, 1840 ***8197.10*** *p186*
Lombart, John Baptist Ann Marie; New York, 1795 ***8197.10*** *p7*
Lombart, Nicholas; New York, 1839 ***8197.10*** *p136*
Lomes, Richard 21; Philadelphia, 1774 ***1220.25*** *p63*
Lomisky, John; Maryland, 1910 ***3259.35*** *p36*
Lomovich, J. 26; Alaska, 1917 ***9196.1*** *p47*
Lomovich, J. 26; Whitehorse, Yukon, 1917 ***9196.1*** *p47*
Lonagan, Nancy 78; Ontario, 1871 ***1823.22*** *p93*
Lonagan, Patrick; New York, 1837 ***8197.10*** *p94*
Lonague, Thomas; New York, 1837 ***8197.10*** *p95*
Londe, Adolphe; New York, 1831 ***8197.10*** *p367*
London, Abigall *SEE* London, Ambroze
London, Ambroze; Maryland, 1665 ***2524.55*** *p138*
Wife: Mary
Child: Abigall
Child: Mary, Jr.
Child: Ruth
London, Anna 30; Kansas, 1892-1910 ***9079.10*** *p25*
London, Mary *SEE* London, Ambroze
London, Mary, Jr. *SEE* London, Ambroze
London, Ruth *SEE* London, Ambroze
Lone, Elizabeth 21; Virginia, 1774 ***1220.25*** *p91*
Lone, Frank; Vermont, 1833-1907 ***5900.10*** *p310*
Lone, Sarah; Vermont, 1845-1927 ***5900.10*** *p310*
Lonegrove, Rich; Virginia, 1672 ***6212.30*** *p51*
Lonek, Agnes; Maryland, 1910 ***3259.35*** *p36*
Lonergan, Bridget; Vermont, n.d. ***5900.10*** *p153*
Lonergan, Catherine; Vermont, n.d. ***5900.10*** *p153*
Lonergan, Edward W.; Vermont, 1853-1929 ***5900.10*** *p80*
Lonergan, Ellen 41; Vermont, 1874 ***5900.10*** *p53*
Lonergan, Johanna; Vermont, 1825-1872 ***5900.10*** *p80*
Lonergan, John; Vermont, 1822-1895 ***5900.10*** *p80*
Lonergan, John; Vermont, 1838-1902 ***5900.10*** *p153*
Lonergan, John 21; Vermont, 1860 ***5900.10*** *p561*
Lonergan, John 75; Vermont, 1891 ***5900.10*** *p571*
Lonergan, Julia C. Daly 28; Vermont, 1861 ***5900.10*** *p502*
Lonergan, Margaret Dwyer 48; Vermont, 1877 ***5900.10*** *p571*
Lonergan, Margaret G.; Vermont, 1856-1895 ***5900.10*** *p80*
Lonergan, Marion; Vermont, 1859-1923 ***5900.10*** *p503*
Lonergan, Mary; Vermont, 1865-1941 ***5900.10*** *p129*
Lonergan, Mary Peters; Vermont, 1857-1930 ***5900.10*** *p89*
Lonergan, Maty Dwyer 36; Vermont, 1846 ***5900.10*** *p64*
Lonergan, Michael; Vermont, 1855-1906 ***5900.10*** *p89*
Lonergan, Michael 24; Vermont, 1865 ***5900.10*** *p153*
Lonergan, Patrick; New York, 1839 ***8197.10*** *p252*
Lonergan, Patrick 51; Vermont, 1853 ***5900.10*** *p64*
Lonergan, Peter P. 53; Vermont, 1880 ***5900.10*** *p502*
Lonergan, Sarah McMahon 37; Vermont, 1881 ***5900.10*** *p153*
Lonergan, Thomas 74; Vermont, 1906 ***5900.10*** *p53*
Lonergan, W. W.; Vermont, 1830-1873 ***5900.10*** *p80*
Lones, Johann Georg; Port uncertain, 1751 ***2856.30*** *p276*
With wife & 4 sons
Lonex, Thomas; Maryland, 1910 ***3259.35*** *p36*
Loney, William; Pennsylvania, 1850 ***6058.10*** *p27*
Long, Mr.; Quebec, 1858 ***9196.15*** *p46*
Long, Mrs.; Quebec, 1858 ***9196.15*** *p46*
Long, Benjamin 34; Ontario, 1871 ***1823.15*** *p147*
Long, Benjamin 52; Ontario, 1871 ***1823.28*** *p58*
Long, Bridget Doyle; Vermont, 1830-1914 ***5900.10*** *p103*
Long, Catherine 25; Ontario, 1871 ***1823.15*** *p147*
Long, Catherine 87; Vermont, 1897 ***5900.10*** *p114*
Long, Daniel; Vermont, 1824-1900 ***5900.10*** *p103*
Long, David; Maryland, 1678 ***2524.55*** *p138*
Wife: Elizabeth
Child: John
Child: Thomas
Child: Mary
Long, Dennis; Vermont, 1835-1929 ***5900.10*** *p429*
Long, Edward; Virginia, 1665-1666 ***6212.30*** *p25*
Long, Edward 40; Ontario, 1871 ***1823.22*** *p93*
Long, Elizabeth *SEE* Long, David
Long, Elizabeth *SEE* Long, William
Long, Elizabeth; Maryland, 1658 ***2524.55*** *p138*
Long, Elizabeth 22; Maryland, 1775 ***1220.25*** *p105*
Long, Elizabeth Burgh; Virginia, 1827 ***1224.3*** *p47*
Long, Ellen Costine 47; Vermont, 1902 ***5900.10*** *p70*
Long, George 22; Maryland, 1774 ***1220.25*** *p47*
Long, Henry 23; Virginia, 1774 ***1220.25*** *p56*
Long, Honora Austin 73; Vermont, 1913 ***5900.10*** *p101*
Long, James; Philadelphia, 1793 ***4629.10*** *p79*
Long, James 43; Ontario, 1871 ***1823.28*** *p58*
Long, James Page; New York, 1834 ***8197.10*** *p251*
Long, James Page; New York, 1839 ***8197.10*** *p136*
Long, Job; Vermont, 1838-1919 ***5900.10*** *p122*
Long, Johannah Donahue 65; Vermont, 1914 ***5900.10*** *p426*
Long, John *SEE* Long, David
Long, John; Pennsylvania, 1779 ***4629.10*** *p38*
Long, John; Vermont, 1850-1915 ***5900.10*** *p491*
Long, John; Virginia, 1665 ***6212.30*** *p19*
Long, John; Virginia, 1666-1667 ***6212.30*** *p35*
Long, John; Virginia, 1667-1668 ***6212.30*** *p38*
Long, John 23; Maryland, 1774 ***1220.25*** *p78*
Long, John 48; Ontario, 1871 ***1823.15*** *p147*
Long, John 50; Ontario, 1871 ***1823.15*** *p147*
Long, John 60; Vermont, 1860-1869 ***5900.10*** *p114*
Long, John 76; Ontario, 1871 ***1823.15*** *p147*
Long, Joseph 36; Ontario, 1871 ***1823.15*** *p147*
Long, Lettice; Virginia, 1666 ***6212.30*** *p26*
Long, Mary *SEE* Long, David
Long, Mary *SEE* Long, William
Long, Mary; Maryland, 1658 ***2524.55*** *p139*
Long, Mary; Vermont, 1847-1918 ***5900.10*** *p491*
Long, Mary 46; Vermont, 1865 ***5900.10*** *p113*
Long, Mary A. 97; Vermont, 1938 ***5900.10*** *p114*
Long, Mary Hannifin; Vermont, n.d. ***5900.10*** *p122*
Long, Mary Walsh; Vermont, 1846-1924 ***5900.10*** *p429*
Long, Matthew 30; Ontario, 1871 ***1823.15*** *p147*
Long, Michaell; Virginia, 1666 ***6212.30*** *p25*
Long, Nathaniel; New York, 1837 ***8197.10*** *p95*
Long, Nicholas 46; Ontario, 1871 ***1823.15*** *p147*
Long, Nicholas 50; Ontario, 1871 ***1823.15*** *p147*
Long, Oliver; New York, 1825 ***8197.10*** *p250*
Long, Patrick 65; Ontario, 1871 ***1823.15*** *p147*
Long, Patrick R. 76; Vermont, 1912 ***5900.10*** *p426*
Long, Rebecca; Virginia, 1666-1667 ***6212.30*** *p34*
Long, Rebecca; Virginia, 1667-1668 ***6212.30*** *p39*
Long, Rich; Virginia, 1664 ***6212.30*** *p14*
Long, Richard; Maryland, 1665 ***2524.55*** *p139*
Long, Richard; South Carolina, 1719 ***1224.2*** *p71*
Long, Robert; Texas, 1849 ***1224.3*** *p47*
Long, Robert; Virginia, 1666 ***6212.30*** *p28*
Long, Robert 21; Maryland, 1774 ***1220.25*** *p51*
Long, Robert 60; Ontario, 1871 ***1823.15*** *p147*
Long, Samuel; New York, 1807 ***8197.10*** *p325*
Long, Samuel 28; Maryland, 1774 ***1220.25*** *p71*
Long, Samuel 35; Ontario, 1871 ***1823.22*** *p93*
Long, Samuell; Maryland, 1665 ***2524.55*** *p110*
Long, Thomas *SEE* Long, David
Long, Thomas; Maryland, 1665 ***2524.55*** *p139*
Long, Thomas; Virginia, 1665-1666 ***6212.30*** *p23*
Long, Thomas; Virginia, 1666-1667 ***6212.30*** *p32*
Long, William; Maryland, 1658 ***2524.55*** *p139*
Wife: Elizabeth
Daughter: Mary
Long, William; New York, 1834-1838 ***8197.10*** *p122*
Long, William; New York, 1840 ***8197.10*** *p186*
Long, William; Pennsylvania, 1786 ***4629.10*** *p49*
Long, William; Virginia, 1666-1667 ***6212.30*** *p32*
Long, William 43; Ontario, 1871 ***1823.15*** *p147*
Long, William 49; Ontario, 1871 ***1823.28*** *p58*
Long, Wm.; Maryland, 1670 ***2524.55*** *p28*
Long, Zacharias; Pennsylvania, 1779 ***4629.10*** *p40*
Longbotham, Reuben; Maryland, 1677 ***2524.55*** *p139*
Longbotham, Reuben; Maryland, 1680 ***2524.55*** *p139*
Longchamp, Ignacius P.; New York, 1797 ***8197.10*** *p9*
Longdon, Martha 35; Ontario, 1861 ***2896.25*** *p39*
Longdon, Mary 12; Ontario, 1861 ***2896.25*** *p39*
Longe, Jno; Virginia, 1664 ***6212.30*** *p15*
Longe, Richard; Virginia, 1664 ***6212.30*** *p9*
Longe, Theodorick; Virginia, 1664 ***6212.30*** *p5*
Longest, Daniel 40; Maryland, 1775 ***1220.25*** *p103*
Longet, Antoine; New York, 1823 ***8197.10*** *p250*
Longey, Margaret 41; Vermont, 1874 ***5900.10*** *p222*
Longfield, Thomas; New York, 1819 ***8197.10*** *p248*
Longford, John; Pennsylvania, 1779 ***4629.10*** *p38*
Longham, George; New York, 1840 ***8197.10*** *p252*
Longhead, James; Pennsylvania, 1777 ***4629.10*** *p7*
Longhead, Robert; Pennsylvania, 1779 ***4629.10*** *p41*
Longhover, John 24; Kansas, 1898-1910 ***9079.10*** *p16*
Longhover, Laura 19; Kansas, 1892-1910 ***9079.10*** *p16*
Longhurst, William; New York, 1805 ***8197.10*** *p322*
Longking, Joseph; New York, 1839 ***8197.10*** *p136*
Longland, John; Albany, New York, 1758 ***1224.2*** *p71*
Longley, Robert Benjamin; Boston, 1792 ***1224.2*** *p71*
Longman, James 48; Ontario, 1871 ***1823.15*** *p147*
Longman, Richard; Virginia, 1679 ***1224.1*** *p37*
Longman, Robert; New York, 1835 ***8197.10*** *p251*
Longmuir, James 40; Ontario, 1871 ***1823.22*** *p94*
Longraver, Janathan; Baltimore, 1852 ***6058.10*** *p38*
Longsdon, William; Maryland, 1678 ***2524.55*** *p139*
Longue, Thomas; New York, 1837 ***8197.10*** *p95*
Longust, Reuben 35; Virginia, 1774 ***1220.25*** *p89*
Longwood, William 23; Philadelphia, 1775 ***1220.25*** *p107*
Longworth, Benjamin 70; Ontario, 1871 ***1823.15*** *p147*
Longworth, John 84; Ontario, 1871 ***1823.15*** *p147*
Longworth, William 55; Ontario, 1871 ***1823.15*** *p147*
Lonigan, Patrick; New York, 1837 ***8197.10*** *p94*
Lonne, John; Maryland, 1663 ***2524.55*** *p139*
Lonner, Joseph; Virginia, 1671-1672 ***6212.30*** *p46*
Lonsberry, David 44; Ontario, 1871 ***1823.22*** *p94*
Lont, Mary 31; Ontario, 1861 ***2896.25*** *p24*
Lont, Mary J. 11; Ontario, 1861 ***2896.25*** *p24*
Lont, Mary M. 24; Ontario, 1861 ***2896.25*** *p24*
Lont, William A. 10; Ontario, 1861 ***2896.25*** *p24*
Lont, William E. 1; Ontario, 1861 ***2896.25*** *p24*
Looby, John 15; New York, New York, 1849 ***1825.45*** *p38*
Looker, Benjamin 24; Maryland, 1774 ***1220.25*** *p61*
Lookup, Alexander; Texas, 1849 ***1640.10*** *p98*
Looney, Daniel 60; Ontario, 1871 ***1823.15*** *p148*
Looney, John 59; Vermont, 1914 ***5900.10*** *p304*
Looney, John 77; Vermont, 1905 ***5900.10*** *p467*
Looney, Mary 52; Vermont, 1885 ***5900.10*** *p467*
Looney, Orilla 67; Vermont, 1928 ***5900.10*** *p304*
Looney, Simeon; Philadelphia, 1825-1826 ***6058.10*** *p27*
Looney, William; Pennsylvania, 1850 ***6058.10*** *p27*
Loose, Johann Jakob; America, 1788 ***2856.30*** *p276*
Looser, Johann; Port uncertain, 1777 ***2856.30*** *p276*
With wife
Looses, William; Maryland, 1681 ***2524.55*** *p139*
Looworthy, Samuel 65; Ontario, 1871 ***1823.15*** *p148*
Lope, Richard; Maryland, 1637 ***2524.55*** *p139*
Lopes, Louis; New York, 1796 ***8197.10*** *p7*
Lopinski, William; Maryland, 1910 ***3259.35*** *p36*
Lops, Ambrose 26; Maryland, 1775 ***1220.25*** *p101*
Loraine, Tony 21; British Columbia, 1909 ***9196.1*** *p27*
Loraine, Tony 21; Seattle, 1909 ***9196.1*** *p27*
Lorance, John 25; Vermont, 1879 ***5900.10*** *p287*
Lorch, Elisabeth; Port uncertain, 1746 ***2856.30*** *p281*
Lorch, Hans; Port uncertain, 1746 ***2856.30*** *p281*
Lorch, Johann; Port uncertain, 1760 ***2856.30*** *p276*
Lorch, Johann; Port uncertain, 1789 ***2856.30*** *p276*
Lorch, Martin; Port uncertain, 1779 ***2856.30*** *p276*

Lovell, James; Maryland, 1673 2524.55 p139
Lovell, John 47; Ontario, 1861 2896.27 p12
Lovell, Laurance 41; Ontario, 1871 1823.15 p148
Lovell, Linas 16; Ontario, 1861 2896.27 p12
Lovell, Margaret 36; Ontario, 1861 2896.27 p16
Lovell, Mary; Virginia, 1701-1702 6212.30 p61
Lovell, Mary 39; Ontario, 1861 2896.27 p12
Lovell, Sarah; Virginia, 1688 1224.1 p43
Lovell, Sintha M. 9; Ontario, 1861 2896.27 p12
Lovell, Thomas 17; Ontario, 1861 2896.27 p16
Lovell, William 34; America, 1774 1220.25 p36
Lovell, William King; Long Island, 1776 1224.2 p71
Lovelock, John; Virginia, 1667-1668 6212.30 p39
Lovely, Deliverance; Maryland, 1658 2524.55 p139
Lovely, Patrick 52; Ontario, 1871 1823.28 p59
Loven, Melcher; Pennsylvania, 1777 4629.10 p15
Lover, James 15; Philadelphia, 1775 1220.25 p107
Lovern, Emma L.; Vermont, 1855-1925 5900.10 p539
Lovet, William; Maryland, 1674 2524.55 p139
Lovett, Charles 56; Ontario, 1871 1823.15 p148
Lovett, Fred 24; Washington, 1914 9196.1 p65
Lovett, John; New York, 1802 8197.10 p22
Lovett, Patrick; Vermont, 1829-1929 5900.10 p220
Lovett, Thomas; Virginia, 1709 1224.2 p71
Lovett, William 56; Ontario, 1871 1823.22 p94
Lovgren, O. 34; British Columbia, 1917 9196.1 p51
Lovgren, O. 34; Seattle, 1917 9196.1 p51
Lovine, George; Maryland, 1910 3259.35 p36
Low, Mr.; Quebec, 1857 9196.15 p26
Low, Alexander; Savannah, Georgia, 1816 1640.10 p99
Low, Ann 37; Ontario, 1861 2896.25 p72
Low, Anna Eva; Port uncertain, 1744 2856.30 p281
Low, Francis 54; Ontario, 1871 1823.22 p94
Low, George; Virginia, 1664 6212.30 p15
Low, George 40; Ontario, 1871 1823.15 p148
Low, Grace Shaw; Montreal, 1882 1640.13 p71
Low, Hugh 10; Ontario, 1861 2896.25 p70
Low, James; Georgia, 1735-1819 1640.10 p99
Low, John; Virginia, 1665 6212.30 p17
Low, John; Virginia, 1666-1667 6212.30 p34
Low, John 14; Ontario, 1861 2896.25 p70
Low, John 19; Maryland, 1774 1220.25 p51
Low, John 23; Virginia, 1773 1220.25 p28
Low, John 23; Virginia, 1774 1220.25 p53
Low, John 43; Ontario, 1871 1823.22 p94
Low, John 75; Ontario, 1871 1823.15 p148
Low, Martha 18; Ontario, 1861 2896.25 p70
Low, Mary; Maryland, 1681 2524.55 p139
Low, Mary 43; Ontario, 1861 2896.25 p70
Low, Mathias; Port uncertain, 1784 2856.30 p266
Low, Mathias; Port uncertain, 1784 2856.30 p266
With wife
Low, Richard; Maryland, 1663 2524.55 p139
Low, Richard; Virginia, 1655 1224.1 p37
Low, Robert 12; Ontario, 1861 2896.25 p70
Low, Sarah 17; Ontario, 1861 2896.25 p72
Low, Thomas; New York, 1825 8197.10 p250
Low, Thomas 17; Virginia, 1774 1220.25 p45
Low, William; Georgia, 1698 1640.13 p72
Low, William 17; Ontario, 1861 2896.25 p70
Low, William David; Virginia, 1881 1640.13 p72
Low, Wm; Virginia, 1664 6212.30 p15
Lowbell, Mark; Virginia, 1666-1667 6212.30 p34
Lowd, John; Canada, 1756-1760 4628.40 p46
Lowden, James; Maryland, 1668 2524.55 p55
Lowder, Ann; Maryland, 1673 2524.55 p139
Lowder, David 15; Ontario, 1861 2896.25 p67
Lowder, Edward; Maryland, 1673 2524.55 p139
Lowder, Euphemia 33; Ontario, 1861 2896.25 p67
Lowder, Francis 38; Ontario, 1861 2896.25 p67
Lowder, Jane 36; Ontario, 1861 2896.25 p67
Lowder, Jone; Maryland, 1673 2524.55 p140
Lowder, Margaret 73; Ontario, 1861 2896.25 p67
Lowder, Mary; Maryland, 1682 2524.55 p140
Lowder, Mary; Virginia, 1666-1667 6212.30 p34
Lowder, Sarah 9; Ontario, 1861 2896.25 p67
Lowder, Thomas; Virginia, 1667-1668 6212.30 p38
Lowder, Thomas 45; Ontario, 1861 2896.25 p67
Lowder, William 71; Ontario, 1861 2896.25 p67
Lowdin, John; New York, 1840 8197.10 p252
Lowdrell, Edgar; Virginia, 1667-1668 6212.30 p39
Lowe, Miss; Quebec, 1858 9196.15 p46
Lowe, Mr.; Quebec, 1856 9196.15 p9
Lowe, Charles; Maryland, 1682 2524.55 p140
Lowe, David 44; Ontario, 1871 1823.28 p59
Lowe, H.; Quebec, 1856 9196.15 p7
Lowe, Henry; Maryland, 1731 1224.2 p71
Lowe, John; New York, 1834 8197.10 p372
Lowe, John 22; Ontario, 1871 1823.28 p59
Lowe, John 29; Ontario, 1871 1823.22 p94
Lowe, John 51; Ontario, 1871 1823.28 p59
Lowe, Joshua; New York, 1834 8197.10 p251
Lowe, Mary 58; Ontario, 1871 1823.28 p59
Lowe, Robt; Virginia, 1672 6212.30 p49
Lowe, Samuel; New York, 1820 8197.10 p248
Lowe, Samuel J.; New York, 1826 8197.10 p333
Lowe, Samuel James; New York, 1821 8197.10 p249
Lowe, Sarah 29; Virginia, 1774 1220.25 p89
Lowe, Thomas; New York, New York, 1782 1224.2 p71
Lowe, Thomas 30; Ontario, 1871 1823.28 p59
Lowe, Timothy; Virginia, 1663 6212.30 p2
Lowe, William; Maryland, 1658 2524.55 p140
Lowe, William 19; Ontario, 1871 1823.28 p59
Lowe, William 55; Ontario, 1871 1823.28 p59
Lowee, C. 15; Ontario, 1861 2896.26 p9
Lowee, P. 17; Ontario, 1861 2896.26 p9
Lowee, S. 1; Ontario, 1861 2896.26 p9
Lowee, S. 19; Ontario, 1861 2896.26 p9
Lowell, Edward; Maryland, 1669 2524.55 p140
Lowell, Edward; Maryland, 1676 2524.55 p140
Lowenberg, Maria Margarete; Canada, 1759 2856.30 p281
Lowenberg, Philipp; Port uncertain, 1788 2856.30 p281
Lowenbruckh, Sebastian; Port uncertain, 1738 2856.30 p281
Lowenich, Michael; Port uncertain, 1764 2856.30 p281
Lowentzon, Martin L. 48; Alaska, 1912 9196.1 p19
Lowentzon, Martin L. 48; British Columbia, 1912 9196.1 p19
Lower, Johann; America, 1737 2856.30 p278
Lowers, Ralph; Maryland, 1673 2524.55 p140
Lowerson, Mary 27; Fort Cumberland, Nova Scotia, 1775 1220.25 p21
Lowerson, Richard 32; Fort Cumberland, Nova Scotia, 1774 1220.25 p17
Lowery, David; New York, 1822 8197.10 p249
Lowery, Hugh 65; Ontario, 1871 1823.15 p148
Lowery, James 34; Ontario, 1871 1823.22 p94
Lowery, John; New York, 1831 8197.10 p67
Lowery, Peter; Pennsylvania, 1777 4629.10 p16
Lowery, Samuel; New York, 1830 8197.10 p66
Lowery, Samuel; Pennsylvania, 1777 4629.10 p13
Lowery, Stephen; Pennsylvania, 1777 4629.10 p17
Lowery, William 50; Ontario, 1871 1823.28 p59
Lowes, David 46; Ontario, 1871 1823.15 p148
Lowes, Elizabeth; Maryland, 1664 2524.55 p140
Lowes, Gedion 50; Ontario, 1871 1823.15 p148
Lowes, John; Virginia, 1671 6212.30 p45
Lowey, Arthur; New York, 1794 8197.10 p6
Lowey, J. 14; Ontario, 1861 2896.26 p10
Lowfield, Miss; Quebec, 1857 9196.15 p15
Lowger, Henry; Virginia, 1690-1691 6212.30 p59
Lowick, John; Maryland, 1668 2524.55 p140
Lowin, Samuel 56; Ontario, 1871 1823.28 p59
Lowland, Timothy; Virginia, 1666-1667 6212.30 p35
Lowlor, Mary A. 59; Vermont, 1882 5900.10 p214
Lowman, Mr.; Quebec, 1857 9196.15 p15
Lowndee, Henry; Jamaica, 1854 1640.13 p72
Lowndes, Mr.; Quebec, 1856 9196.15 p11
Lowndes, Roger; South Carolina, 1735 1224.2 p71
Lowne, John; Virginia, 1667 6212.30 p37
Lownes, John; Pennsylvania, 1776 4629.10 p53
Lowns, Thomas; Virginia, 1667-1668 6212.30 p38
Lowr, Agnes 62; Ontario, 1871 1823.15 p148
Lowrey, Eliza *SEE* Lowrey, William
Lowrey, John; New York, 1838 8197.10 p122
Lowrey, Sarah; Maryland, 1682 2524.55 p140
Lowrey, William; Maryland, 1653 2524.55 p140
Wife: Eliza
Lowrie, Charles 50; Ontario, 1871 1823.15 p148
Lowrie, James 32; Ontario, 1871 1823.15 p148
Lowry, Miss; Quebec, 1856 9196.15 p7
Lowry, Ann 12 *SEE* Lowry, Patrick
Lowry, Ann 43 *SEE* Lowry, Patrick
Lowry, Charles 28; Ontario, 1871 1823.15 p148
Lowry, Elizabeth *SEE* Lowry, William
Lowry, James 32; Ontario, 1871 1823.15 p149
Lowry, Jean; Virginia, 1666-1667 6212.30 p35
Lowry, John 20 *SEE* Lowry, Patrick
Lowry, Mary 27; Fort Cumberland, Nova Scotia, 1775 1220.25 p21
Lowry, Patrick 40; New York, New York, 1852 1825.45 p59
Wife: Ann 43
Son: John 20
Daughter: Ann 12
Daughter: Sarah 17
Lowry, Robert; New York, 1822 8197.10 p249
Lowry, Robert 30; Ontario, 1871 1823.15 p149
Lowry, Samuel 52; Ontario, 1871 1823.15 p149
Lowry, Sarah 17 *SEE* Lowry, Patrick
Lowry, William; Maryland, 1664 2524.55 p140
Wife: Elizabeth
Lowry, William; New York, 1835 8197.10 p251
Lowry, William; New York, 1838 8197.10 p123
Lowry, William 94; Ontario, 1871 1823.15 p149
Lowth, Marcella; Vermont, 1780-1848 5900.10 p383
Lowth, Marcella; Vermont, 1850-1931 5900.10 p383
Lowther, Mary 21; Fort Cumberland, Nova Scotia, 1774 1220.25 p19
Lowy, Arthur; New York, 1794 8197.10 p6
Loyd, Edward; Maryland, 1673 2524.55 p201
Loyd, Edward; Maryland, 1679 2524.55 p140
Loyd, Eliza 18; Ontario, 1871 1823.15 p149
Loyd, Fred; Vermont, 1843-1898 5900.10 p459
Loyd, John; Virginia, 1663 6212.30 p2
Loyd, John; Virginia, 1664 6212.30 p8
Loyd, Margret; Virginia, 1668-1669 6212.30 p41
Loyd, Owen; Virginia, 1666-1667 6212.30 p34
Loyd, Philemon; Maryland, 1659 2524.55 p140
Loyd, Thomas 28; Maryland, 1774 1220.25 p78
Loynes, Margaret Duoney 48; Vermont, 1854 5900.10 p74
Loz, Johann; America, 1733 2856.30 p278
Lozanski, Wladyslaw; Maryland, 1910 3259.35 p36
Lozbeier, Johann Peter; Port uncertain, 1790 2856.30 p281
Lozo, Paul 23; Ontario, 1871 1823.22 p94
Lozum, Charles 15; Philadelphia, 1774 1220.25 p43
Lrevah, B. 26; Alaska, 1914 9196.1 p41
Luard, Mr.; Quebec, 1858 9196.15 p32
Luard, Mrs.; Quebec, 1858 9196.15 p32
Luato, A. 30; Alaska, 1917 9196.1 p46
Luato, A. 30; Whitehorse, Yukon, 1917 9196.1 p46
Lubava, Anna; Maryland, 1910 3259.35 p36
Lubbish, Henry; Maryland, 1910 3259.35 p36
Lubey, John 15; New York, New York, 1849 1825.45 p38
Lubey, Mary; Maryland, 1670 2524.55 p196
Lubinski, Barbara C.; Maryland, 1910 3259.35 p36
Lubinsky, Stanislaw; Maryland, 1910 3259.35 p36
Lubor, Nathanll; Virginia, 1671-1672 6212.30 p46
Luby, John 15; New York, New York, 1849 1825.45 p38
Luby, John 60; Ontario, 1871 1823.15 p149
Luby, Mary; Maryland, 1670 2524.55 p196
Lucar, Thomas; Virginia, 1671 6212.30 p44
Lucas, Mrs.; Maryland, 1651 2524.55 p140
Lucas, Mrs.; Quebec, 1857 9196.15 p20
Lucas, Adam 23; Ontario, 1871 1823.15 p149
Lucas, Ann *SEE* Lucas, Peter
Lucas, Anna Margarete; Port uncertain, 1788 2856.30 p278
Lucas, Charles; Maryland, 1722 1224.2 p71
Lucas, Charles August; Vermont, 1850-1929 5900.10 p300
Lucas, David; Virginia, 1665 6212.30 p17
Lucas, Elisabeth; Port uncertain, 1778 2856.30 p278
Lucas, F. R.; Quebec, 1857 9196.15 p20
Lucas, Hewill 23; Maryland, 1774 1220.25 p3
Lucas, James 47; Ontario, 1871 1823.28 p59
Lucas, Johann; Port uncertain, 1753 2856.30 p278
Lucas, John; New York, 1835 8197.10 p251
Lucas, John; New York, 1840 8197.10 p187
Lucas, John; Pennsylvania, 1781 4629.10 p42
Lucas, John 23; Maryland, 1774 1220.25 p79
Lucas, John 45; Ontario, 1871 1823.15 p149
Lucas, Jonathan; Charleston, South Carolina, 1822 1224.3 p47
Lucas, Margarette Sullivan; Vermont, 1811-1901 5900.10 p300
Lucas, Mary Ann Donnelly; Vermont, 1854-1894 5900.10 p300
Lucas, Michael; Vermont, n.d. 5900.10 p300
Lucas, Nellie; Vermont, 1858-1917 5900.10 p300
Lucas, Peter; Maryland, 1668 2524.55 p140
Wife: Ann
Lucas, Peter; Virginia, 1693 1224.1 p37
Lucas, Samuel; New York, 1813 8197.10 p58
Lucas, Thomas; Virginia, 1675 1224.1 p37
Lucas, William; Virginia, 1738 1224.2 p71
Lucass, Catharina; America, 1749 2856.30 p278
Luccardt, Johann Georg; Port uncertain, 1750 2856.30 p278
Luce, Benjiman 11; Ontario, 1871 1823.28 p59
Luce, Joanna McMahon; Vermont, 1863-1945 5900.10 p130
Luce, Johanna M. Holton; Vermont, 1877-1950 5900.10 p551
Luce, Lawrence C.; Vermont, 1883-1952 5900.10 p551
Luce, Orlo; Vermont, 1859-1937 5900.10 p130
Lucett, Maurice; New York, New York, 1856 3437.14 p44
Luchs, Hans; Port uncertain, 1770 2856.30 p278
Lucich, N. 28; Alaska, 1917 9196.1 p49
Lucich, N. 28; Yukon, 1917 9196.1 p49
Lucitt, Maurice; New York, New York, 1856 3437.14 p44
Luck, Edward 22; Maryland, 1775 1220.25 p96
Luck, Paul 37; Ontario, 1871 1823.15 p149

Lucker, Georg; Port uncertain, 1751 ***2856.30*** *p278*
Lucker, Johann Georg; America, 1754 ***2856.30*** *p272*
Luckey, Loviday 74; Ontario, 1871 ***1823.22*** *p94*
Luckins, John; Virginia, 1666-1667 ***6212.30*** *p34*
Luckman, James 37; Maryland, 1775 ***1220.25*** *p105*
Luckman, John; Maryland, 1665 ***2524.55*** *p140*
Luckowska, Joseph; Maryland, 1910 ***3259.35*** *p36*
Lucky, Theophilus; New York, 1832 ***8197.10*** *p357*
Lucus, Charles; Maryland, 1665 ***2524.55*** *p140*
Lucus, Ellinor; Virginia, 1663 ***6212.30*** *p4*
Lucus, William; Maryland, 1652 ***2524.55*** *p140*
With wife
Lucy, Jeremiah 60; Ontario, 1871 ***1823.22*** *p94*
Lucy, Robert V.; New York, 1840 ***8197.10*** *p185*
Lucy, William; New York, 1802 ***8197.10*** *p22*
Luczensky, Stanislaw; Maryland, 1910 ***3259.35*** *p36*
Luczkowski, James; Maryland, 1910 ***3259.35*** *p36*
Ludby, John; New York, 1819 ***8197.10*** *p248*
Ludby, John; New York, 1821 ***8197.10*** *p249*
Ludby, John; New York, 1822 ***8197.10*** *p249*
Luddy, Ellen; Vermont, 1837-1899 ***5900.10*** *p425*
Luder, Anna Barbara; Port uncertain, 1775 ***2856.30*** *p280*
Luder, Jakob; Port uncertain, 1784 ***2856.30*** *p278*
Luderell, James; Maryland, 1671 ***2524.55*** *p140*
Luders, Johann Michael; Port uncertain, 1775 ***2856.30*** *p280*
Ludescher, . . .; Port uncertain, 1801 ***2856.30*** *p278*
Ludford, Arthur; Maryland, 1673 ***2524.55*** *p140*
Ludgate, Alexander 45; Ontario, 1871 ***1823.22*** *p94*
Ludgate, Antony 44; Ontario, 1871 ***1823.28*** *p59*
Ludgate, John 45; Ontario, 1871 ***1823.28*** *p59*
Ludgate, Michael 32; Ontario, 1871 ***1823.28*** *p59*
Ludham, Edmund; Virginia, 1655 ***1224.1*** *p37*
Ludi, Peter; America, 1741 ***2856.30*** *p278*
Ludlam, Anne; South Carolina, 1729 ***1224.2*** *p72*
Ludlam, Harriet L.; Vermont, 1849-1916 ***5900.10*** *p598*
Ludlam, William; Vermont, 1843-1910 ***5900.10*** *p598*
Ludley, Eleanor 35; Maryland, 1775 ***1220.25*** *p114*
Ludley, John; New York, 1821 ***8197.10*** *p249*
Ludley, John; New York, 1822 ***8197.10*** *p249*
Ludlow, Edward; Virginia, 1664-1665 ***6212.30*** *p16*
Ludlow, Francis; Virginia, 1671 ***1224.1*** *p37*
Ludlow, Gabriel Gabriel; New Brunswick, 1809 ***1224.3*** *p47*
Ludlow, Geo; Virginia, 1664 ***6212.30*** *p12*
Ludlow, George; York, Virginia, 1656 ***1224.1*** *p37*
Ludlow, Gulian; New York, 1848 ***1224.3*** *p47*
Ludlow, John; Virginia, 1664 ***1224.1*** *p37*
Ludlowe, George; Virginia, 1683 ***1224.1*** *p37*
Ludly, John; New York, 1819 ***8197.10*** *p248*
Ludly, John; New York, 1830 ***8197.10*** *p66*
Ludman, Mary *SEE* Ludman, Thomas
Ludman, Thomas; Maryland, 1666 ***2524.55*** *p140*
Wife: Mary
Ludovich, Geo 40; Seattle, 1911 ***9196.1*** *p33*
Ludvisken, Paul 27; Alaska, 1914 ***9196.1*** *p23*
Ludwell, James; Maryland, 1676 ***2524.55*** *p140*
Ludwell, Thomas; Virginia, 1679 ***1224.1*** *p37*
Ludwig, Mrs.; Quebec, 1858 ***9196.15*** *p42*
Ludwig, Abraham; Port uncertain, 1767 ***2856.30*** *p278*
Ludwig, Anna Barbara; Port uncertain, 1760 ***2856.30*** *p278*
Ludwig, Anton; Port uncertain, 1730 ***2856.30*** *p278*
Ludwig, Anton; Port uncertain, 1768 ***2856.30*** *p278*
Ludwig, Christina; Port uncertain, 1795 ***2856.30*** *p278*
Ludwig, Christof; America, 1749 ***2856.30*** *p278*
Ludwig, Hans Adam; America, 1749 ***2856.30*** *p278*
Ludwig, Jakob; America, 1749 ***2856.30*** *p278*
Ludwig, Johann; Port uncertain, 1764 ***2856.30*** *p279*
With wife & 3 children
Ludwig, Mrs. Johann; America, 1749 ***2856.30*** *p279*
With son
Ludwig, Johann Georg; America, 1750 ***2856.30*** *p279*
Wife: Marg.
Ludwig, Johann Peter; America, 1749 ***2856.30*** *p278*
Ludwig, Leonard; Port uncertain, 1767 ***2856.30*** *p278*
Ludwig, Lorenz, Jr.; Port uncertain, 1790 ***2856.30*** *p278*
Ludwig, Marg. *SEE* Ludwig, Johann Georg
Ludwig, Margarete; Port uncertain, 1776 ***2856.30*** *p278*
Ludwig, Maria Magdalena; Port uncertain, 1783 ***2856.30*** *p279*
Ludwig, Maria Margarete; America, 1738 ***2856.30*** *p279*
Ludwig, Maria Margarete; Port uncertain, 1755 ***2856.30*** *p279*
Ludwig, Martin; Port uncertain, 1781 ***2856.30*** *p279*
With wife & 5 children
Ludwig, Marx; America, 1744 ***2856.30*** *p279*
Ludwig, Philip; New York, 1837 ***8197.10*** *p95*
Ludwigin, Eva Catharina; Port uncertain, 1739 ***2856.30*** *p279*
Ludwin, Hans Peter; Port uncertain, 1795 ***2856.30*** *p279*
With wife & 3 children
Luellyn, James; Virginia, 1664-1665 ***6212.30*** *p16*
Luetz, Stephen; New York, 1837 ***8197.10*** *p94*
Luff, John N.; New York, 1803 ***8197.10*** *p13*
Luff, Valentine; New York, 1802 ***8197.10*** *p22*
Luffman, William; Maryland, 1660 ***2524.55*** *p140*
Luffman, William; Maryland, 1672 ***2524.55*** *p140*
Lufft, Christof; Port uncertain, 1744 ***2856.30*** *p279*
Lufman, Frances 8; Ontario, 1861 ***2896.27*** *p71*
Lufman, Larnnen 15; Ontario, 1861 ***2896.27*** *p71*
Lufman, Lucy 45; Ontario, 1861 ***2896.27*** *p71*
Lufman, William 3; Ontario, 1861 ***2896.27*** *p71*
Lufman, William 55; Ontario, 1861 ***2896.27*** *p71*
Lufsky, George; New York, 1807 ***8197.10*** *p44*
Lugden, William 58; Ontario, 1871 ***1823.15*** *p149*
Luger, John; Pennsylvania, 1777 ***4629.10*** *p18*
Lugger, Nath; Virginia, 1666 ***6212.30*** *p30*
Lugow, Frances 16; Ontario, 1871 ***1823.28*** *p59*
Lugsden, Master; Quebec, 1858 ***9196.15*** *p33*
Lugsden, Miss; Quebec, 1858 ***9196.15*** *p33*
Lugsden, James; Quebec, 1858 ***9196.15*** *p33*
Lugsden, Mrs. James; Quebec, 1858 ***9196.15*** *p33*
Luhring, Henry; New York, 1832 ***8197.10*** *p368*
Luhrs, Berend; New York, 1840 ***8197.10*** *p386*
Luib, Jacob; Port uncertain, 1770 ***2856.30*** *p279*
Luickardt, Josef; Port uncertain, 1712 ***2856.30*** *p279*
Luickardt, Josef; Port uncertain, 1740 ***2856.30*** *p279*
Luis, Ferdinand; New York, 1840 ***8197.10*** *p252*
Luis, Samuel; Pennsylvania, 1778 ***4629.10*** *p32*
Luiscom, Richd.; Maryland, 1680 ***2524.55*** *p140*
Luja, Joseph; Maryland, 1910 ***3259.35*** *p36*
Lukaszewiks, Frank; Maryland, 1910 ***3259.35*** *p36*
Lukaszoraski, John; Maryland, 1910 ***3259.35*** *p36*
Luke, Benjamin 47; Ontario, 1871 ***1823.22*** *p94*
Luke, Benjeman 67; Ontario, 1871 ***1823.28*** *p59*
Luke, John; Virginia, 1672 ***6212.30*** *p50*
Luke, John 23; Ontario, 1871 ***1823.28*** *p59*
Luke, Wm; Virginia, 1665 ***6212.30*** *p18*
Lukens, David; Pennsylvania, 1787 ***4629.10*** *p55*
Lukens, Jacob; Pennsylvania, 1786 ***4629.10*** *p51*
Luker, John 49; Ontario, 1871 ***1823.15*** *p149*
Luker, Richard 75; Ontario, 1871 ***1823.15*** *p149*
Lukes, William 42; Ontario, 1871 ***1823.15*** *p149*
Lukesazny, Joseph; Maryland, 1910 ***3259.35*** *p36*
Lukey, Sampson 34; Ontario, 1871 ***1823.22*** *p94*
Luking, Ann 39 *SEE* Luking, Joshua
Luking, Joshua 41; Halifax, Nova Scotia, 1774 ***1220.25*** *p138*
Wife: Ann 39
With child 11
Lukowski, Biguneto; Maryland, 1910 ***3259.35*** *p36*
Luloff, John 43; Ontario, 1871 ***1823.28*** *p59*
Lulsfelder, Solomon Lob; New York, 1840 ***8197.10*** *p321*
Lum, Hannah *SEE* Lum, John
Lum, John; Philadelphia, 1789 ***4629.10*** *p58*
Wife: Hannah
Lum, John 22; Philadelphia, 1789 ***4629.10*** *p58*
Lumbard, Mrs.; Maryland, 1659 ***2524.55*** *p140*
Lumbard, Francis; Maryland, 1650 ***2524.55*** *p140*
Lumbard, Francis; Maryland, 1664 ***2524.55*** *p140*
Lumbert, Ann; Maryland, 1663 ***2524.55*** *p140*
Lumbrozo, Elizabeth; Maryland, 1662 ***2524.55*** *p140*
Lumbrozo, Jacob; Maryland, 1656 ***2524.55*** *p140*
Lumby, Christopher 40; Ontario, 1871 ***1823.22*** *p94*
Lumley, Miss; Quebec, 1856 ***9196.15*** *p7*
Lumley, Diana 14 *SEE* Lumley, Thomas
Lumley, John 6 *SEE* Lumley, Thomas
Lumley, John 23; Nova Scotia, 1774 ***1220.25*** *p14*
Lumley, Ruth 44 *SEE* Lumley, Thomas
Lumley, Thomas 45; Fort Cumberland, Nova Scotia, 1774 ***1220.25*** *p17*
Wife: Ruth 44
Child: John 6
Child: Diana 14
Lummerton, George W.; Indiana, 1870-1884 ***3437.14*** *p196*
Lumpey, Ambrose 26; Maryland, 1775 ***1220.25*** *p98*
Lumpp, Catharina; Port uncertain, 1757 ***2856.30*** *p279*
Lumsdel, Samuel 50; Ontario, 1871 ***1823.15*** *p149*
Lumsden, James 22; Virginia, 1774 ***1220.25*** *p56*
Lumsden, James 54; Ontario, 1871 ***1823.28*** *p59*
Lunan, Francis; Florida, 1767 ***1640.10*** *p99*
Lunard, Lieut.; Quebec, 1857 ***9196.15*** *p14*
Lund, Andrew 36; Alaska, 1913 ***9196.1*** *p22*
Lund, Andrew 36; British Columbia, 1913 ***9196.1*** *p22*
Lunday, Alford 20; Ontario, 1861 ***2896.25*** *p69*
Lundberg, A. 27; Alaska, 1917 ***9196.1*** *p49*
Lundberg, A. 27; Whitehorse, Yukon, 1917 ***9196.1*** *p49*
Lundberg, Jonas Augustus; New York, 1836 ***8197.10*** *p76*
Lundergan, Margaret 57; Vermont, 1893 ***5900.10*** *p78*
Lundgren, David 36; Kansas, 1901-1910 ***9079.10*** *p35*
Lundgren, Mary 30; Kansas, 1901-1910 ***9079.10*** *p35*
Lundie, Archibald; Savannah, Georgia, 1776 ***1640.10*** *p99*
Lundley, Miss; Quebec, 1856 ***9196.15*** *p7*
Lundragan, Timothy; Vermont, 1817-1901 ***5900.10*** *p579*
Lundragen, Bridget McMahon; Vermont, 1830-1914 ***5900.10*** *p579*
Lundrigan, Edmund; Vermont, 1843-1912 ***5900.10*** *p97*
Lundrigan, Hanna; Vermont, 1850-1937 ***5900.10*** *p97*
Lundy, Miss; Quebec, 1858 ***9196.15*** *p47*
Lundy, Rev.; Quebec, 1858 ***9196.15*** *p47*
Lundy, R. 25; Vancouver, British Columbia, 1910 ***9196.1*** *p15*
Lundy, Thomas; New York, 1839 ***8197.10*** *p136*
Lung, Adam; America, 1750 ***2856.30*** *p279*
With wife
Lung, Adam; America, 1751 ***2856.30*** *p279*
Lung, Adam; Port uncertain, 1751 ***2856.30*** *p279*
With wife
Lungley, Thomas; Virginia, 1834 ***1224.3*** *p47*
Luniley, George 45; Ontario, 1871 ***1823.22*** *p94*
Lunn, Mr.; Quebec, 1858 ***9196.15*** *p42*
Lunn, Mrs.; Quebec, 1858 ***9196.15*** *p42*
Lunn, J. H. 45; Alaska, 1917 ***9196.1*** *p48*
Lunn, J. H. 45; Whitehorse, Yukon, 1917 ***9196.1*** *p48*
Lunn, James 44; Ontario, 1871 ***1823.15*** *p149*
Lunn, William 64; Ontario, 1871 ***1823.22*** *p94*
Lunne, Richard 50; Ontario, 1871 ***1823.28*** *p59*
Lunny, Edward; New York, 1807 ***8197.10*** *p328*
Lunny, Edward; New York, 1807 ***8197.10*** *p331*
Lunny, Mary 80; Vermont, 1911 ***5900.10*** *p559*
Lunny, Patrick; New York, 1807 ***8197.10*** *p328*
Lunoy, Mr.; Quebec, 1858 ***9196.15*** *p41*
Lunt, Mr.; Portland, Maine, 1858 ***9196.15*** *p30*
Lupnin, Adyann 10; Ontario, 1861 ***2896.27*** *p73*
Lupton, Miss; Portland, Maine, 1858 ***9196.15*** *p47*
Lupton, Mrs.; Portland, Maine, 1858 ***9196.15*** *p47*
Lurck, Maria; America, 1764 ***2856.30*** *p279*
Lurton, Henry; Virginia, 1665 ***6212.30*** *p17*
Lusby, Dorothy *SEE* Lusby, Robert
Lusby, Elizabeth *SEE* Lusby, Robert
Lusby, Henry 23; Maryland, 1774 ***1220.25*** *p52*
Lusby, Jacob *SEE* Lusby, Robert
Lusby, Rebecca *SEE* Lusby, Robert
Lusby, Robert; Maryland, 1662 ***2524.55*** *p140*
Wife: Dorothy
Child: Rebecca
Child: Sarah
Child: Jacob
Child: Elizabeth
Lusby, Robert 21; Maryland, 1774 ***1220.25*** *p52*
Lusby, Sarah *SEE* Lusby, Robert
Lusby, Thomas 16; Philadelphia, 1774 ***1220.25*** *p35*
Luscombe, Richard 60; Ontario, 1871 ***1823.22*** *p94*
Luscombe, Thomas; Boston, 1699 ***1224.1*** *p37*
Luscombe, Thomas; Boston, 1700 ***1224.2*** *p72*
Luscombe, William 16; Maryland, 1773-1774 ***1220.25*** *p33*
Luscton, William 26; Ontario, 1871 ***1823.15*** *p149*
Lush, John; New York, 1840 ***8197.10*** *p185*
Lush, Thomas Ryall; New York, 1840 ***8197.10*** *p187*
Lushefski, Peter; Maryland, 1910 ***3259.35*** *p36*
Lusher, Francis; Pennsylvania, 1777 ***4629.10*** *p14*
Lusher, John 23; Maryland, 1775 ***1220.25*** *p113*
Lushet, John; Pennsylvania, 1777 ***4629.10*** *p11*
Lusk, John; New York, 1889 ***1640.13*** *p72*
Lusk, Thomas 40; Ontario, 1871 ***1823.15*** *p149*
Luskischuski, Viech; Maryland, 1910 ***3259.35*** *p36*
Luskowski, Henry; Maryland, 1910 ***3259.35*** *p36*
Lusner, Charles 58; Ontario, 1871 ***1823.15*** *p149*
Lussan, Julien; Grenada, 1826 ***1640.13*** *p72*
Lussle, Jacob; Port uncertain, 1764 ***2856.30*** *p280*
Lust, Anna 4; Kansas, 1910 ***9079.10*** *p47*
Lust, Henry 30; Kansas, 1908-1910 ***9079.10*** *p47*
Lust, Mary 29; Kansas, 1910 ***9079.10*** *p47*
Lutela, Sam 20; British Columbia, 1909 ***9196.1*** *p27*
Lutela, Sam 20; Seattle, 1909 ***9196.1*** *p27*
Luteral, Jane 40; Ontario, 1871 ***1823.15*** *p149*
Lutes, Charles 45; Ontario, 1871 ***1823.28*** *p59*
Luteth, Magnes 55; Ontario, 1871 ***1823.15*** *p149*
Luttens, Herman; Georgia, 1698 ***1640.13*** *p72*
Lutter, Elisabeth; Port uncertain, 1790 ***2856.30*** *p279*
Lutter, Jacob; New York, 1838 ***8197.10*** *p123*
Luttit, William; Maryland, 1681 ***2524.55*** *p140*
Lutton, John 17; Philadelphia, 1774 ***1220.25*** *p4*
Lutton, William; Maryland, 1669 ***2524.55*** *p140*
Lutz, . . .; America, 1729 ***2856.30*** *p279*
Lutz, Miss; America, 1753 ***2856.30*** *p364*
Lutz, Daniel; Port uncertain, 1784 ***2856.30*** *p279*
Lutz, El. Barb. Dick *SEE* Lutz, Philipp
Lutz, Frederick; Pennsylvania, 1777 ***4629.10*** *p9*
Lutz, Hans Martin; Port uncertain, 1747 ***2856.30*** *p279*
Lutz, Jacob; America, 1744 ***2856.30*** *p279*
Lutz, Jacob; America, 1744 ***2856.30*** *p280*
With wife & children
Lutz, Johann; Port uncertain, 1752 ***2856.30*** *p279*
Lutz, Johannes; New York, 1837 ***8197.10*** *p95*

Lutz, John George; New York, 1840 **8197.10** *p185*
Lutz, Leonard; Pennsylvania, 1777 **4629.10** *p12*
Lutz, Mathias; Port uncertain, 1751 **2856.30** *p279*
Lutz, Michael; America, 1727 **2856.30** *p279*
Lutz, Peter; New York, 1836-1838 **8197.10** *p123*
Lutz, Philipp; Port uncertain, 1784 **2856.30** *p280*
Wife: El. Barb. Dick
Lutz, Valentin; Port uncertain, 1737 **2856.30** *p280*
With wife
Lutzenberger, Johann Adam; America, 1740 **2856.30** *p280*
Luue, Johan Georg; New York, 1839 **8197.10** *p252*
Lux, Henry; New York, 1838 **8197.10** *p251*
Luxton, Bailey 47; Ontario, 1871 **1823.15** *p149*
Luxton, George; New York, 1837 **8197.10** *p94*
Luxton, George 33; Ontario, 1871 **1823.15** *p149*
Luxton, Henry 30; Ontario, 1871 **1823.15** *p149*
Luxton, John 66; Ontario, 1871 **1823.15** *p149*
Luxton, Thomas 67; Ontario, 1871 **1823.22** *p94*
Luxton, William 41; Ontario, 1871 **1823.15** *p149*
Luysmunski, August; Maryland, 1910 **3259.35** *p36*
Luyster, Mary; New York, 1829 **8197.10** *p351*
Luz, Eva; Port uncertain, 1788 **2856.30** *p280*
Luz, Johann; America, 1733 **2856.30** *p280*
With wife & 3 children
Luz, Johann; Port uncertain, 1732 **2856.30** *p280*
With wife & 3 children
Luz, Johann; Port uncertain, 1733 **2856.30** *p280*
With wife & 3 children
Luz, Maria Magdalena; Port uncertain, 1749 **2856.30** *p280*
Luz, Peter; America, 1744 **2856.30** *p280*
With wife & 2 children
Luzel, Johann Ludwig; Port uncertain, 1785 **2856.30** *p280*
Luzelberger, Johann Michael; Port uncertain, 1747 **2856.30** *p280*
Luzelberger, Nickel; Port uncertain, 1792 **2856.30** *p280*
Luzenberger, Margarete; Port uncertain, 1777 **2856.30** *p280*
Luzenberger, Maria Elisabeth; Port uncertain, 1786 **2856.30** *p280*
Luzenberger, Peter; Port uncertain, 1783 **2856.30** *p280*
Lvosdof, Lawrence; Maryland, 1910 **3259.35** *p36*
Lyall, James Mitchell; Boston, 1874 **1640.13** *p72*
Lyall, John; New York, 1807 **8197.10** *p43*
Lyall, William David; Boston, 1891 **1640.13** *p72*
Lyaodocka, Mary; Maryland, 1910 **3259.35** *p36*
Lyardocka, Yojcek; Maryland, 1910 **3259.35** *p36*
Lycett, William; New York, 1778 **1224.2** *p72*
Lydall, Isabell; Maryland, 1678 **2524.55** *p141*
Lyddall, George; Virginia, 1667 **1224.1** *p44*
Lyde, Byfield; Boston, 1777 **1224.2** *p72*
Lyde, Byfield; Halifax, Nova Scotia, 1777 **1224.2** *p72*
Lydich, Jacob; Pennsylvania, 1778 **4629.10** *p32*
Lye, William 18; Philadelphia, 1774 **1220.25** *p81*
Lyell, Mrs.; Maryland, 1663 **2524.55** *p141*
Lyell, John; Texas, 1898 **1640.13** *p72*
Lyell, Wiliam; Pennsylvania, 1777 **4629.10** *p18*
Lyghtle, Christopher 82; Ontario, 1871 **1823.22** *p94*
Lyghtle, David 52; Ontario, 1871 **1823.22** *p94*
Lyle, George 5; Ontario, 1861 **2896.27** *p1*
Lyle, James 34; Ontario, 1871 **1823.28** *p59*
Lyle, William 37; Ontario, 1871 **1823.22** *p95*
Lylewski, George; Maryland, 1910 **3259.35** *p36*
Lymbrie, George; Virginia, 1637 **1224.1** *p37*
Lymburner, Matthew; Massachusetts, 1789 **1224.2** *p72*
Lymburner, Matthew; New Brunswick, n.d. **1224.2** *p72*
Lymhen, Isaac 25; Ontario, 1871 **1823.15** *p149*
Lyn, Daniel 46; Ontario, 1871 **1823.28** *p59*
Lyn, Hugh 41; Ontario, 1871 **1823.28** *p59*
Lynam, Edward; Pennsylvania, 1841 **6058.10** *p18*
Lynam, Patrick; New York, 1837 **8197.10** *p94*
Lynam, William; Quebec, 1833 **6058.10** *p17*
Lynar, Anthony; New York, 1819 **8197.10** *p248*
Lynar, David; New York, 1821 **8197.10** *p249*
Lynaugh, Anna; Vermont, 1843-1905 **5900.10** *p429*
Lynch, Abigail Holland 76; Vermont, 1899 **5900.10** *p54*
Lynch, Alexander; New York, 1840 **8197.10** *p187*
Lynch, Alice M. 25; Vermont, 1892 **5900.10** *p303*
Lynch, Ann 48; Vermont, 1883 **5900.10** *p426*
Lynch, Ann Bradshaw; Vermont, 1805-1896 **5900.10** *p396*
Lynch, Ann O'Connor 79; Vermont, 1908 **5900.10** *p63*
Lynch, Anne 50; Ontario, 1871 **1823.15** *p149*
Lynch, Anne Charlotte; Vermont, n.d. **5900.10** *p3*
Lynch, Annie M.; Vermont, 1858-1930 **5900.10** *p508*
Lynch, Barney; New York, 1839 **8197.10** *p380*
Lynch, Bernard; New York, 1839 **8197.10** *p381*
Lynch, Bridget; Vermont, 1848-1932 **5900.10** *p80*
Lynch, Bridget; Vermont, 1851-1881 **5900.10** *p76*
Lynch, Bridget; Vermont, 1855-1934 **5900.10** *p398*
Lynch, Bridget; Vermont, 1857-1883 **5900.10** *p149*
Lynch, Bridget 50; Ontario, 1871 **1823.22** *p95*
Lynch, Bridget 57; Vermont, 1892 **5900.10** *p591*
Lynch, Bridget A. Callahan; Vermont, 1861-1934 **5900.10** *p192*
Lynch, Bridget A. Reynolds; Vermont, 1925 **5900.10** *p94*
Lynch, Bridget F.; Vermont, 1841-1900 **5900.10** *p122*
Lynch, Bridget McGuire; Vermont, 1840-1914 **5900.10** *p82*
Lynch, Catherine; Vermont, 1826-1888 **5900.10** *p149*
Lynch, Catherine; Vermont, 1858-1953 **5900.10** *p361*
Lynch, Catherine 25; Ontario, 1871 **1823.15** *p149*
Lynch, Catherine 50; Ontario, 1871 **1823.28** *p59*
Lynch, Catherine Splain; Vermont, 1863-1935 **5900.10** *p161*
Lynch, Daniel; Vermont, 1853-1933 **5900.10** *p508*
Lynch, Daniel 40; Ontario, 1871 **1823.22** *p95*
Lynch, Daniel 70; Ontario, 1871 **1823.22** *p95*
Lynch, David 63; Vermont, 1917 **5900.10** *p63*
Lynch, Dennis; New York, 1821 **8197.10** *p249*
Lynch, Dennis; New York, 1838 **8197.10** *p251*
Lynch, Dennis; New York, 1840 **8197.10** *p187*
Lynch, Dennis 62; Ontario, 1871 **1823.28** *p59*
Lynch, Dominick; New York, n.d. **1224.3** *p47*
Lynch, E.; Pennsylvania, 1868 **6058.10** *p74*
Lynch, Edward; Vermont, 1821-1886 **5900.10** *p149*
Lynch, Edward 60; Ontario, 1871 **1823.22** *p95*
Lynch, Edward R.; Vermont, 1853-1933 **5900.10** *p161*
Lynch, Eliza; Vermont, 1849-1902 **5900.10** *p395*
Lynch, Elizabeth; Vermont, 1858-1923 **5900.10** *p533*
Lynch, Ellen; Vermont, 1851-1900 **5900.10** *p135*
Lynch, Ellen; Vermont, 1853-1899 **5900.10** *p130*
Lynch, Ellen 48; Vermont, 1889 **5900.10** *p589*
Lynch, Ellen 53; Vermont, 1875 **5900.10** *p100*
Lynch, Ellen Prior; Vermont, 1830-1905 **5900.10** *p506*
Lynch, Francis James 41; Ontario, 1871 **1823.22** *p95*
Lynch, Guy; New York, 1838 **8197.10** *p123*
Lynch, Hannah 50; Vermont, 1891 **5900.10** *p616*
Lynch, Hannah 70; Vermont, 1909 **5900.10** *p301*
Lynch, Hannora 53; Vermont, 1890 **5900.10** *p396*
Lynch, Helen Murphy; Vermont, 1889-1916 **5900.10** *p131*
Lynch, Hugh; New York, 1834-1838 **8197.10** *p123*
Lynch, Hugh; New York, 1837 **8197.10** *p95*
Lynch, Ieiawiah 40; Ontario, 1871 **1823.15** *p149*
Lynch, James; New York, 1834 **8197.10** *p74*
Lynch, James; New York, 1840 **8197.10** *p187*
Lynch, James; Vermont, 1882 **5900.10** *p305*
Lynch, James 24; Maryland, 1774 **1220.25** *p46*
Lynch, James 60; Ontario, 1871 **1823.28** *p59*
Lynch, James 65; Ontario, 1871 **1823.22** *p95*
Lynch, James P. 27; Vermont, 1885 **5900.10** *p301*
Lynch, Jane H.; Vermont, 1837-1902 **5900.10** *p332*
Lynch, Jeramiah 55; Ontario, 1871 **1823.28** *p59*
Lynch, Jeremiah; New York, 1839 **8197.10** *p136*
Lynch, Joanna 29; Vermont, 1893 **5900.10** *p63*
Lynch, Johanah; Vermont, 1861-1896 **5900.10** *p361*
Lynch, Johanna; Vermont, 1808-1903 **5900.10** *p356*
Lynch, Johanna 52; Vermont, 1895 **5900.10** *p396*
Lynch, Johanna Costello; Vermont, 1847-1916 **5900.10** *p70*
Lynch, Johannah; Vermont, 1861-1896 **5900.10** *p358*
Lynch, John; New York, 1827 **8197.10** *p250*
Lynch, John; New York, 1833-1838 **8197.10** *p122*
Lynch, John; New York, 1837 **8197.10** *p94*
Lynch, John; New York, 1837 **8197.10** *p95*
Lynch, John; Vermont, 1847-1934 **5900.10** *p110*
Lynch, John; Vermont, 1857-1924 **5900.10** *p361*
Lynch, John; Vermont, 1863-1888 **5900.10** *p358*
Lynch, John; Vermont, 1863-1888 **5900.10** *p361*
Lynch, John; Vermont, 1867 **5900.10** *p77*
Lynch, John 16; Maryland, 1774 **1220.25** *p76*
Lynch, John 24; Ontario, 1871 **1823.15** *p149*
Lynch, John 29; Seattle, 1913 **9196.1** *p60*
Lynch, John 56; Ontario, 1871 **1823.28** *p59*
Lynch, John 66; Vermont, 1893 **5900.10** *p426*
Lynch, John 76; Vermont, 1915 **5900.10** *p467*
Lynch, John, Sr.; Vermont, 1802-1867 **5900.10** *p396*
Lynch, Josephine Beauregard 67; Vermont, 1929 **5900.10** *p162*
Lynch, Kate Francis 22; Vermont, 1880 **5900.10** *p63*
Lynch, Lucy; Vermont, 1851-1934 **5900.10** *p429*
Lynch, Margaret; Vermont, 1833-1907 **5900.10** *p566*
Lynch, Margaret; Vermont, 1833-1913 **5900.10** *p562*
Lynch, Margaret; Vermont, 1834-1909 **5900.10** *p303*
Lynch, Margaret A. 26; Vermont, 1893 **5900.10** *p467*
Lynch, Margaret Curran; Vermont, 1836-1906 **5900.10** *p110*
Lynch, Margaret Harrington; Vermont, 1852-1922 **5900.10** *p409*
Lynch, Margaret McCarty; Vermont, 1822-1903 **5900.10** *p361*
Lynch, Maria; Vermont, 1847-1875 **5900.10** *p536*
Lynch, Maria; Vermont, 1847-1928 **5900.10** *p415*
Lynch, Martin 17; Vermont, 1873 **5900.10** *p530*
Lynch, Mary; Vermont, 1831-1870 **5900.10** *p508*
Lynch, Mary; Vermont, 1851-1927 **5900.10** *p334*
Lynch, Mary; Vermont, 1860-1919 **5900.10** *p96*
Lynch, Mary 51; Vermont, 1879 **5900.10** *p82*
Lynch, Mary 65; Vermont, 1903 **5900.10** *p467*
Lynch, Mary 78; Vermont, 1937 **5900.10** *p438*
Lynch, Mary 86; Vermont, 1917 **5900.10** *p396*
Lynch, Mary A. Donegan; Vermont, 1848-1920 **5900.10** *p563*
Lynch, Mary Carrigan; Vermont, 1827-1900 **5900.10** *p332*
Lynch, Mary Dougharty 52; Vermont, 1827 **5900.10** *p511*
Lynch, Mary Griffin; Vermont, 1848-1914 **5900.10** *p101*
Lynch, Mary Moore; Vermont, 1863-1917 **5900.10** *p130*
Lynch, Mary Ryan; Vermont, 1854-1928 **5900.10** *p396*
Lynch, Mathew 23; Ontario, 1871 **1823.15** *p149*
Lynch, Michael; Vermont, 1811-1903 **5900.10** *p361*
Lynch, Michael; Vermont, 1826-1884 **5900.10** *p332*
Lynch, Michael; Vermont, 1849-1932 **5900.10** *p396*
Lynch, Michael; Vermont, 1855-1920 **5900.10** *p361*
Lynch, Michael; Vermont, 1861-1931 **5900.10** *p149*
Lynch, Michael 21; Vermont, n.d. **5900.10** *p305*
Lynch, Michael 36; Ontario, 1871 **1823.22** *p95*
Lynch, Michael 44; Ontario, 1871 **1823.22** *p95*
Lynch, Michael 53; Vermont, 1900 **5900.10** *p616*
Lynch, Michael 60; Ontario, 1871 **1823.22** *p95*
Lynch, Michael 70; Vermont, 1874 **5900.10** *p100*
Lynch, Nellie E.; Vermont, 1863-1929 **5900.10** *p429*
Lynch, Patrick; New York, 1802 **8197.10** *p22*
Lynch, Patrick; New York, 1837 **8197.10** *p94*
Lynch, Patrick; New York, 1838 **8197.10** *p251*
Lynch, Patrick; Vermont, n.d. **5900.10** *p148*
Lynch, Patrick; Vermont, 1803 **5900.10** *p3*
Lynch, Patrick; Vermont, 1816-1886 **5900.10** *p82*
Lynch, Patrick; Vermont, 1819-1883 **5900.10** *p332*
Lynch, Patrick; Vermont, 1826-1874 **5900.10** *p101*
Lynch, Patrick; Vermont, 1830-1903 **5900.10** *p566*
Lynch, Patrick; Vermont, 1833-1905 **5900.10** *p424*
Lynch, Patrick 80; Vermont, 1880 **5900.10** *p301*
Lynch, Patrick J.; Vermont, 1865-1916 **5900.10** *p130*
Lynch, Peter; Vermont, 1824-1889 **5900.10** *p562*
Lynch, Peter; Vermont, 1859-1927 **5900.10** *p192*
Lynch, Richard 45; Vermont, 1881 **5900.10** *p591*
Lynch, Richd; Virginia, 1671 **6212.30** *p42*
Lynch, Thomas; New York, 1827 **8197.10** *p250*
Lynch, Thomas; South Carolina, n.d. **4628.40** *p48*
Lynch, Thomas; Vermont, n.d. **5900.10** *p305*
Lynch, Thomas; Vermont, 1839-1903 **5900.10** *p563*
Lynch, Thomas; Vermont, 1864-1936 **5900.10** *p458*
Lynch, Thomas; Vermont, 1917 **5900.10** *p122*
Lynch, Thomas 55; Ontario, 1871 **1823.15** *p149*
Lynch, Thomas 66; Vermont, 1896 **5900.10** *p62*
Lynch, Thomas 76; Vermont, 1916 **5900.10** *p54*
Lynch, Thomas E. 61; Vermont, 1912 **5900.10** *p162*
Lynch, Thomas J.; Vermont, 1850-1935 **5900.10** *p409*
Lynch, Timothy; Vermont, 1853 **5900.10** *p335*
Lynch, Timothy; Vermont, 1853-1896 **5900.10** *p94*
Lynch, Timothy 38; Ontario, 1871 **1823.28** *p59*
Lynch, William; Maryland, 1681 **2524.55** *p141*
Lynch, William; New York, 1840 **8197.10** *p187*
Lynch, William; Vermont, 1817-1873 **5900.10** *p506*
Lynch, William H.; Vermont, 1839-1895 **5900.10** *p303*
Lynch Family ; South Carolina, 1775-1781 **4628.40** *p81*
Lynd, William 28; Ontario, 1861 **2896.27** *p21*
Lyndall, Joseph; Pennsylvania, 1777 **4629.10** *p26*
Lyndell, Timothy; Maryland, 1664 **2524.55** *p141*
Lynden, Hulda 28; Seattle, 1917 **9196.1** *p52*
Lynden, Hulda 28; Yukon, 1917 **9196.1** *p52*
Lyndon, Augustine; Boston, 1699 **1224.1** *p37*
Lyne, Joseph; Virginia, 1701 **1224.2** *p72*
Lynell, Richard; Pennsylvania, 1777 **4629.10** *p26*
Lynes, Mr.; Quebec, 1858 **9196.15** *p34*
Lynes, John; Maryland, 1663 **2524.55** *p141*
Lynes, Phillip; Maryland, 1668 **2524.55** *p137*
Lynham, George; New York, 1809 **8197.10** *p55*
Lynn, Dan.; Maryland, 1671 **2524.55** *p141*
Lynn, George; Maryland, 1665 **2524.55** *p24*
Lynn, Henery; America, 1753 **2856.30** *p280*
Lynn, James 20; Philadelphia, 1774 **1220.25** *p6*
Lynn, James 42; Ontario, 1871 **1823.15** *p149*
Lynn, James 98; Ontario, 1871 **1823.15** *p149*
Lynn, Joseph; Pennsylvania, 1779 **4629.10** *p38*
Lynn, Patrick 49; Ontario, 1871 **1823.15** *p149*
Lynn, Samuel Goodenough 55; Ontario, 1871 **1823.28** *p59*
Lynn, Thomas 17; Maryland, 1774 **1220.25** *p5*
Lynn, Thomas 34; Ontario, 1871 **1823.15** *p149*
Lynn, William 45; Ontario, 1871 **1823.15** *p149*
Lynskey, Bridget 25; New York, New York, 1848 **1825.45** *p38*
Lynskey, Catherine 10 *SEE* Lynskey, Michael

M

Maag, George Adam; New York, 1834 ***8197.10*** *p319*
Maag, Jakob; America, 1737 ***2856.30*** *p282*
Maag, John; Pennsylvania, 1784 ***4629.10*** *p44*
Maag, John Baptiste; New York, 1832 ***8197.10*** *p263*
Maap, Christian 43; Ontario, 1871 ***1823.28*** *p59*
Maap, Gustav 47; Ontario, 1871 ***1823.28*** *p59*
Maas, Charles 57; Ontario, 1871 ***1823.28*** *p59*
Maas, Hannah 62; Ontario, 1871 ***1823.28*** *p59*
Maas, Jacob; America, 1752 ***2856.30*** *p282*
Maas, Jakob; America, 1752 ***2856.30*** *p282*
Maas, Peter; New York, 1837 ***8197.10*** *p100*
Maass, Georg; America, 1732 ***2856.30*** *p282*
Maass, Johann Adam; Port uncertain, 1747 ***2856.30*** *p282*
With wife & children
Mabbatt, Samuel; New York, 1803 ***8197.10*** *p14*
Mabbs, George; Maryland, 1657 ***2524.55*** *p141*
Mabee, Loisie 23; Ontario, 1861 ***2896.28*** *p64*
Mabert, Edward; New York, 1838 ***8197.10*** *p264*
Mable, Ellen Fitzgerald; Vermont, 1851-1898 ***5900.10*** *p535*
Mable, George W.; Vermont, 1850-1941 ***5900.10*** *p535*
Mable, Katherine Hogan; Vermont, 1851-1929 ***5900.10*** *p537*
Mabletuft, Samuel 21; Maryland, 1774 ***1220.25*** *p40*
Maby, G. E. 10; Ontario, 1861 ***2896.26*** *p13*
Maby, J. 36; Ontario, 1861 ***2896.26*** *p13*
Maby, M. E. 12; Ontario, 1861 ***2896.26*** *p13*
Maby, M. J. 4; Ontario, 1861 ***2896.26*** *p13*
Maby, P. A. 19; Ontario, 1861 ***2896.26*** *p13*
Maby, S. E. 8; Ontario, 1861 ***2896.26*** *p13*
Maby, W. C. 16; Ontario, 1861 ***2896.26*** *p13*
Macaire, Francis; Charles Town, South Carolina, 1691 ***1224.1*** *p38*
Macalester, James; Louisiana, 1797 ***1640.10*** *p99*
MacAlister, Elizabeth 77; Ontario, 1871 ***1823.15*** *p150*
MacAlister, John 47; Ontario, 1871 ***1823.15*** *p150*
MacAlister, Robert 42; Ontario, 1871 ***1823.15*** *p150*
Macall, John; Maryland, 1681 ***2524.55*** *p141*
MacAllister, Alex L. 50; Ontario, 1871 ***1823.15*** *p150*
Macan, Roger; Virginia, 1668-1669 ***6212.30*** *p40*
MacArthur, Angus; Ontario, 1851 ***4537.32*** *p11*
Wife: Isabella MacAulay
Child: John
Child: Isabella
Child: Effie
Child: Mary
Child: Kirsty
MacArthur, Ann *SEE* MacArthur, John
MacArthur, Catherine *SEE* MacArthur, John
MacArthur, Effie *SEE* MacArthur, Angus
MacArthur, Effie; Ontario, 1851 ***4537.32*** *p44*
MacArthur, Isabella *SEE* MacArthur, Angus
MacArthur, Isabella MacAulay *SEE* MacArthur, Angus
MacArthur, John *SEE* MacArthur, Angus
MacArthur, John *SEE* MacArthur, John
MacArthur, John; Ontario, 1851 ***4537.32*** *p11*
Wife: Kirsty MacDonald
Child: Ann
Child: John
Child: Catherine
Child: Neil
MacArthur, Kirsty *SEE* MacArthur, Angus
MacArthur, Kirsty MacDonald *SEE* MacArthur, John
MacArthur, Mary *SEE* MacArthur, Angus
MacArthur, Neil *SEE* MacArthur, John
Macarthy, Maurice 25; Ontario, 1871 ***1823.28*** *p59*
Macartney, Lady; Grenada, 1776 ***1220.25*** *p129*
Macartney, George 34; Grenada, 1776 ***1220.25*** *p129*
Macartney, William; New York, 1837 ***8197.10*** *p263*
Macartney, William; New York, 1839 ***8197.10*** *p141*
Macarty, Darby; Maryland, 1672 ***2524.55*** *p141*
MacAskill, Alexander *SEE* MacAskill, John
MacAskill, Alexander *SEE* MacAskill, Michael
MacAskill, Alexander *SEE* MacAskill, Norman
MacAskill, Allan *SEE* MacAskill, John
MacAskill, Allan; Nova Scotia, 1828 ***4537.35*** *p12*
Wife: Rachel
Child: Donald
Child: Mary
Child: Malcolm
Child: Kenneth
Child: Catherine
Child: John
Child: Sarah
MacAskill, Allan; Port uncertain, 1850-1859 ***4537.37*** *p108*
Child: Mary
Child: Margaret
Wife: Mary MacKellaig
Child: Archie
Child: John
MacAskill, Angus *SEE* MacAskill, John
MacAskill, Angus *SEE* MacAskill, Norman
MacAskill, Angus; Ontario, 1860-1869 ***4537.35*** *p56*
Wife: Mary MacLeod
Child: Catherine
Child: Donald
Child: Murdo
Child: Hugh
Child: Mary
MacAskill, Angus; Ontario, 1863 ***4537.32*** *p12*
Wife: Mary MacLeod
Child: Catherine
Child: Neil
Child: Mary
MacAskill, Angus; Port uncertain, 1850-1859 ***4537.35*** *p79*
Wife: Marion
Child: John
Child: Mary
Child: Donald
MacAskill, Ann *SEE* MacAskill, Donald
MacAskill, Ann *SEE* MacAskill, John
MacAskill, Ann *SEE* MacAskill, Malcolm
MacAskill, Ann *SEE* MacAskill, Murdo
MacAskill, Ann; Ontario, 1851 ***4537.32*** *p76*
MacAskill, Ann MacLeod *SEE* MacAskill, Malcolm
MacAskill, Archie *SEE* MacAskill, Allan
MacAskill, Barbara; Port uncertain, 1850-1859 ***4537.37*** *p118*
MacAskill, Bennington *SEE* MacAskill, Ewen
MacAskill, Catherine *SEE* MacAskill, Allan
MacAskill, Catherine *SEE* MacAskill, Angus
MacAskill, Catherine *SEE* MacAskill, Donald
MacAskill, Catherine *SEE* MacAskill, Ewen
MacAskill, Catherine *SEE* MacAskill, John
MacAskill, Catherine *SEE* MacAskill, Michael
MacAskill, Catherine *SEE* MacAskill, Norman
MacAskill, Catherine; Nova Scotia, 1825 ***4537.35*** *p28*
MacAskill, Catherine; Ontario, 1855 ***4537.32*** *p34*
MacAskill, Catherine; Port uncertain, 1860-1869 ***4537.35*** *p85*
MacAskill, Donald *SEE* MacAskill, Allan
MacAskill, Donald *SEE* MacAskill, Angus
MacAskill, Donald *SEE* MacAskill, Donald
MacAskill, Donald *SEE* MacAskill, John
MacAskill, Donald *SEE* MacAskill, Murdo
MacAskill, Donald *SEE* MacAskill, Norman
MacAskill, Donald *SEE* MacAskill, Roderick
MacAskill, Donald; Nova Scotia, 1840-1849 ***4537.35*** *p13*
Wife: Ann
Child: Mary
Child: Ann
Child: Kenneth
Child: Neil
MacAskill, Donald; Nova Scotia, 1845 ***4537.35*** *p13*
Wife: Rachel
Child: John
Child: Catherine
Child: Marion
Child: Mary
MacAskill, Donald; Ontario, 1850-1859 ***4537.37*** *p36*
Wife: Mary MacInnes
Child: James
Child: Donald
Child: Effie
Child: Catherine
Child: Roderick
MacAskill, Donald; Ontario, 1851 ***4537.32*** *p12*
Wife: Mary MacInnes
Child: Catherine
Child: Effie
MacAskill, Effie *SEE* MacAskill, Donald
MacAskill, Effie *SEE* MacAskill, John
MacAskill, Ewen; Nova Scotia, 1830-1839 ***4537.35*** *p13*
Wife: Margaret MacLeod
Child: Catherine
Child: Bennington
MacAskill, Finlay *SEE* MacAskill, John
MacAskill, Gormelia; Ontario, 1851 ***4537.32*** *p66*
MacAskill, Helen; Nova Scotia, 1840-1849 ***4537.35*** *p25*
MacAskill, Hugh *SEE* MacAskill, Angus
MacAskill, Isabella *SEE* MacAskill, Michael
MacAskill, Isabella; Ontario, 1870-1879 ***4537.32*** *p70*
MacAskill, James *SEE* MacAskill, Donald
MacAskill, Jessie *SEE* MacAskill, Malcolm
MacAskill, Jessie MacLachlan *SEE* MacAskill, John
MacAskill, John *SEE* MacAskill, Allan
MacAskill, John *SEE* MacAskill, Angus
MacAskill, John *SEE* MacAskill, Donald
MacAskill, John *SEE* MacAskill, John
MacAskill, John *SEE* MacAskill, Norman
MacAskill, John *SEE* MacAskill, Roderick
MacAskill, John; America, 1870-1879 ***4537.35*** *p74*
Child: Margaret
Wife: Jessie MacLachlan
MacAskill, John; Nova Scotia, 1828 ***4537.35*** *p13*
Wife: Marion MacDonald
Child: Donald
Child: Finlay
Child: John
Child: Norman
Child: Sarah
MacAskill, John; Nova Scotia, 1840-1849 ***4537.35*** *p13*
Wife: Mary Campbell
Child: Kenneth
Child: Catherine
Child: Murdo
Child: Norman
MacAskill, John; Saskatchewan, 1890 ***4537.35*** *p65*
Wife: Mary Morrison
Child: Marion
Child: Margaret
Child: Roderick

Child: Catherine
Child: Mary
Child: Kirsty
Child: Neil
MacAskill, John; Port uncertain, 1840-1849 ***4537.35*** *p79*
Wife: Kirsty
Child: Catherine
Child: Roderick
Child: Angus
Child: Ann
MacAskill, John; Port uncertain, 1840-1849 ***4537.35*** *p79*
Wife: Mary
Child: Norman
Child: Kirsty
Child: Donald
Child: Marion
Child: John
Child: Finlay
MacAskill, John; Port uncertain, 1850-1859 ***4537.37*** *p108*
Wife: Marion O'Henley
Child: Alexander
Child: Mary
Child: Marion
Child: Allan
Child: Kirsty
Child: Effie
Child: Ann
MacAskill, Kenneth *SEE* MacAskill, Allan
MacAskill, Kenneth *SEE* MacAskill, Donald
MacAskill, Kenneth *SEE* MacAskill, John
MacAskill, Kenneth *SEE* MacAskill, Roderick
MacAskill, Kenneth; Nova Scotia, 1820-1829 ***4537.35*** *p14*
MacAskill, Kirsty *SEE* MacAskill, John
MacAskill, Kirsty *SEE* MacAskill, Murdo
MacAskill, Kirsty *SEE* MacAskill, Norman
MacAskill, Kirsty Campbell *SEE* MacAskill, Norman
MacAskill, Malcolm *SEE* MacAskill, Allan
MacAskill, Malcolm *SEE* MacAskill, Malcolm
MacAskill, Malcolm; Nova Scotia, 1840-1849 ***4537.35*** *p14*
Wife: Ann MacLeod
Child: Norman
Son: Malcolm
Child: Murdo
Child: Mary
Child: Sarah
Child: Jessie
Child: Ann
MacAskill, Margaret *SEE* MacAskill, Allan
MacAskill, Margaret *SEE* MacAskill, John
MacAskill, Margaret; Nova Scotia, 1840-1849 ***4537.35*** *p18*
MacAskill, Margaret MacLeod *SEE* MacAskill, Ewen
MacAskill, Marion *SEE* MacAskill, Angus
MacAskill, Marion *SEE* MacAskill, Donald
MacAskill, Marion *SEE* MacAskill, John
MacAskill, Marion *SEE* MacAskill, Michael
MacAskill, Marion MacDonald *SEE* MacAskill, John
MacAskill, Marion O'Henley *SEE* MacAskill, John
MacAskill, Mary *SEE* MacAskill, Allan
MacAskill, Mary *SEE* MacAskill, Angus
MacAskill, Mary *SEE* MacAskill, Donald
MacAskill, Mary *SEE* MacAskill, John
MacAskill, Mary *SEE* MacAskill, Malcolm
MacAskill, Mary *SEE* MacAskill, Michael
MacAskill, Mary *SEE* MacAskill, Murdo
MacAskill, Mary *SEE* MacAskill, Norman
MacAskill, Mary; Nova Scotia, 1828 ***4537.35*** *p29*
MacAskill, Mary; Nova Scotia, 1830-1839 ***4537.35*** *p36*
MacAskill, Mary; Port uncertain, 1850-1859 ***4537.37*** *p118*
MacAskill, Mary Campbell *SEE* MacAskill, John
MacAskill, Mary MacInnes *SEE* MacAskill, Donald
MacAskill, Mary MacKellaig *SEE* MacAskill, Allan
MacAskill, Mary MacLeod *SEE* MacAskill, Angus
MacAskill, Mary Morrison *SEE* MacAskill, John
MacAskill, Michael; Nova Scotia, 1840-1849 ***4537.35*** *p14*
Wife: Catherine
Child: Marion
Child: Alexander
Child: Neil
Child: Mary
Child: Isabella
MacAskill, Murdo *SEE* MacAskill, Angus
MacAskill, Murdo *SEE* MacAskill, John
MacAskill, Murdo *SEE* MacAskill, Malcolm
MacAskill, Murdo; Nova Scotia, 1840-1849 ***4537.35*** *p14*
Wife: Mary
Child: Roderick
Child: Kirsty
Child: Donald
Child: Ann
MacAskill, Neil *SEE* MacAskill, Angus
MacAskill, Neil *SEE* MacAskill, Donald
MacAskill, Neil *SEE* MacAskill, John
MacAskill, Neil *SEE* MacAskill, Michael
MacAskill, Norman *SEE* MacAskill, John
MacAskill, Norman *SEE* MacAskill, Malcolm
MacAskill, Norman; Nova Scotia, 1830-1839 ***4537.35*** *p14*
Wife: Kirsty Campbell
Child: Catherine
Child: Donald
Child: Alexander
Child: Kirsty
Child: Angus
Child: John
Child: Mary
MacAskill, Norman; Nova Scotia, 1840-1849 ***4537.35*** *p15*
Child: Roderick
Child: Kirsty
Wife: Rachel
Child: Donald
Child: Catherine
MacAskill, Norman; Nova Scotia, 1870-1879 ***4537.35*** *p15*
MacAskill, Rachel *SEE* MacAskill, Allan
MacAskill, Rachel *SEE* MacAskill, Donald
MacAskill, Rachel *SEE* MacAskill, Norman
MacAskill, Rachel; Ontario, 1860-1869 ***4537.32*** *p7*
MacAskill, Rachel; Ontario, 1860-1869 ***4537.35*** *p56*
MacAskill, Roderick *SEE* MacAskill, Donald
MacAskill, Roderick *SEE* MacAskill, John
MacAskill, Roderick *SEE* MacAskill, Murdo
MacAskill, Roderick *SEE* MacAskill, Norman
MacAskill, Roderick; Nova Scotia, 1830-1839 ***4537.35*** *p15*
Wife: Sarah MacAuley
Child: Kenneth
Child: Donald
Child: John
MacAskill, Sarah *SEE* MacAskill, Allan
MacAskill, Sarah *SEE* MacAskill, John
MacAskill, Sarah *SEE* MacAskill, Malcolm
MacAskill, Sarah MacAuley *SEE* MacAskill, Roderick
MacAulay, Alexander *SEE* MacAulay, Donald
MacAulay, Alexander; Ontario, 1849 ***4537.32*** *p12*
Wife: Kirsty MacLean
Child: Allan
Child: Archie
Child: Ann
Child: Neil
MacAulay, Allan *SEE* MacAulay, Alexander
MacAulay, Allan; Ontario, 1848 ***4537.32*** *p13*
Wife: Catherine MacLellan
MacAulay, Angus *SEE* MacAulay, Angus
MacAulay, Angus *SEE* MacAulay, Donald
MacAulay, Angus *SEE* MacAulay, John
MacAulay, Angus *SEE* MacAulay, Murdo
MacAulay, Angus; Ontario, 1849 ***4537.32*** *p13*
Child: Mary
Child: Marion
Child: Archie
Wife: Margaret MacDonald
MacAulay, Angus; Ontario, 1863 ***4537.32*** *p13*
Wife: Marion MacLeod
Child: Angus
Child: Malcolm
Child: John
Child: Ann
Child: George
MacAulay, Angus; Ontario, 1870 ***4537.32*** *p13*
Wife: Mary MacLean
MacAulay, Angus; Port uncertain, 1840-1849 ***4537.37*** *p108*
Wife: Ann MacPherson
Child: Mary
Child: Archie
Child: Donald
Child: Catherine
MacAulay, Ann *SEE* MacAulay, Alexander
MacAulay, Ann *SEE* MacAulay, Angus
MacAulay, Ann *SEE* MacAulay, Donald
MacAulay, Ann *SEE* MacAulay, George
MacAulay, Ann *SEE* MacAulay, John
MacAulay, Ann *SEE* MacAulay, Murdo
MacAulay, Ann; Ontario, 1855 ***4537.32*** *p93*
MacAulay, Ann; Prince Edward Island, 1848 ***4537.37*** *p25*
MacAulay, Ann MacDonald *SEE* MacAulay, Donald
MacAulay, Ann MacPherson *SEE* MacAulay, Angus
MacAulay, Archie *SEE* MacAulay, Alexander
MacAulay, Archie *SEE* MacAulay, Angus
MacAulay, Archie *SEE* MacAulay, Catherine
MacAulay, Archie *SEE* MacAulay, Mary
MacAulay, Archie *SEE* MacAulay, Neil
MacAulay, Archie; Nova Scotia, 1848 ***4537.37*** *p10*
Wife: Catherine Nicolson
Mother: Effie
MacAulay, Betsy *SEE* MacAulay, Robert
MacAulay, Catherine *SEE* MacAulay, Angus
MacAulay, Catherine *SEE* MacAulay, Donald
MacAulay, Catherine *SEE* MacAulay, John
MacAulay, Catherine *SEE* MacAulay, Murdo
MacAulay, Catherine; Ontario, 1840-1849 ***4537.37*** *p77*
MacAulay, Catherine; Ontario, 1850 ***4537.37*** *p48*
MacAulay, Catherine; Port uncertain, 1840-1849 ***4537.37*** *p108*
Child: Hugh
Child: Archie
MacAulay, Catherine; Port uncertain, 1840-1849 ***4537.37*** *p111*
MacAulay, Catherine Laing *SEE* MacAulay, Donald
MacAulay, Catherine MacLellan *SEE* MacAulay, Allan
MacAulay, Catherine Nicolson *SEE* MacAulay, Archie
Macaulay, Daniel; America, 1770 ***1224.2*** *p72*
Macaulay, Daniel; Charleston, South Carolina, n.d. ***1224.3*** *p48*
MacAulay, Donald *SEE* MacAulay, Angus
MacAulay, Donald *SEE* MacAulay, Donald
MacAulay, Donald *SEE* MacAulay, John
MacAulay, Donald *SEE* MacAulay, Murdo
MacAulay, Donald; Canada, 1860-1869 ***4537.35*** *p71*
Wife: Ann MacDonald
Sister: Marion
Sister: Ann
Child: Alexander
Child: Angus
MacAulay, Donald; Ontario, 1840-1849 ***4537.32*** *p14*
Wife: Ann
Child: Angus
Child: Janet
Child: Kirsty
Child: Donald
Child: Murdo
Child: Margaret
MacAulay, Donald; Ontario, 1850-1859 ***4537.37*** *p37*
Child: Francis
Wife: Mary MacDonald
Child: Flora
Child: Catherine
Child: John
Child: Margaret
Child: Mary
Child: Angus
Child: Kate
Child: Ann
MacAulay, Donald; Ontario, 1851 ***4537.32*** *p14*
Wife: Catherine Laing
Child: John
Child: Kenneth
Child: Ranald
Child: Margaret
Child: John
MacAulay, Donald; Ontario, 1855 ***4537.32*** *p14*
Wife: Margaret MacDonald
Child: Neil
Child: Angus
Child: Ann
Child: Norman
Child: Dougal
Child: John
Child: George
Child: Donald
Child: Mary
MacAulay, Donald; Ontario, 1855 ***4537.32*** *p15*
Wife: Mary MacLeod
Child: Mary
Child: Catherine
Child: Murdo
MacAulay, Donald; Prince Edward Island, 1840-1843 ***4537.37*** *p23*
Wife: Sarah MacPherson
Child: Malcolm
Child: Ranald
Child: Effie
Child: Catherine
MacAulay, Donald; Port uncertain, 1840-1849 ***4537.37*** *p108*
Wife: Margaret MacDonald
Child: Donald
Child: Lachlan

MacCormick, Ann *SEE* MacCormick, Donald
MacCormick, Ann *SEE* MacCormick, Lachlan
MacCormick, Ann *SEE* MacCormick, Malcolm
MacCormick, Ann; Nova Scotia, 1840-1849 ***4537.37*** *p15*
MacCormick, Ann; Ontario, 1848 ***4537.37*** *p43*
MacCormick, Ann; Ontario, 1848 ***4537.37*** *p81*
MacCormick, Ann; Ontario, 1849 ***4537.32*** *p85*
MacCormick, Ann; Ontario, 1849 ***4537.37*** *p86*
MacCormick, Ann; Port uncertain, 1840-1849 ***4537.37*** *p112*
MacCormick, Ann; Port uncertain, 1840-1849 ***4537.37*** *p121*
MacCormick, Ann Currie *SEE* MacCormick, Neil
MacCormick, Ann MacDonald *SEE* MacCormick, Donald
MacCormick, Ann MacIsaac *SEE* MacCormick, Donald
MacCormick, Ann MacMillan *SEE* MacCormick, Donald
MacCormick, Ann MacPherson *SEE* MacCormick, Lachlan
MacCormick, Archie *SEE* MacCormick, Archie
MacCormick, Archie *SEE* MacCormick, Neil
MacCormick, Archie; Ontario, 1850-1859 ***4537.37*** *p38*
Wife: Mary MacPhee
Child: Malcolm
Child: Ann
Child: Donald
Child: Archie
Child: John
Child: Marion
Child: Lachlan
Child: Mary
MacCormick, Archie; Ontario, 1851 ***4537.32*** *p17*
Wife: Mary MacPhee
Child: Malcolm
Child: Flora
Child: Marion
Child: Mary
Child: Archie
Child: Lachlan
Child: John
MacCormick, Catherine *SEE* MacCormick, Andrew
MacCormick, Catherine *SEE* MacCormick, Catherine MacDonald
MacCormick, Catherine *SEE* MacCormick, Donald
MacCormick, Catherine *SEE* MacCormick, Duncan
MacCormick, Catherine *SEE* MacCormick, John
MacCormick, Catherine *SEE* MacCormick, Lachlan
MacCormick, Catherine *SEE* MacCormick, Ranald
MacCormick, Catherine; Ontario, 1847-1849 ***4537.37*** *p63*
MacCormick, Catherine; Ontario, 1849 ***4537.32*** *p40*
MacCormick, Catherine; Ontario, 1850-1859 ***4537.37*** *p64*
MacCormick, Catherine; Ontario, 1851 ***4537.32*** *p41*
MacCormick, Catherine; Ontario, 1851 ***4537.37*** *p82*
MacCormick, Catherine; Saskatchewan, 1884 ***4537.37*** *p97*
MacCormick, Catherine; Port uncertain, 1840-1849 ***4537.37*** *p123*
MacCormick, Catherine MacDonald; Ontario, 1847-1849 ***4537.37*** *p40*
Child: Angus
Child: Donald
Child: John
Child: Neil
Child: Catherine
MacCormick, Catherine MacDonald; Ontario, 1849 ***4537.32*** *p18*
Child: Angus
Child: John
Child: Neil
Child: Catherine
Child: Donald
MacCormick, Catherine MacPherson *SEE* MacCormick, Malcolm
MacCormick, Donald *SEE* MacCormick, Andrew
MacCormick, Donald *SEE* MacCormick, Archie
MacCormick, Donald *SEE* MacCormick, Catherine MacDonald
MacCormick, Donald *SEE* MacCormick, Donald
MacCormick, Donald *SEE* MacCormick, John
MacCormick, Donald *SEE* MacCormick, Malcolm
MacCormick, Donald *SEE* MacCormick, Neil
MacCormick, Donald; Ontario, 1840-1849 ***4537.37*** *p38*
Child: Sarah
Child: Ewen
Child: Norman
Wife: Ann MacMillan
Child: Catherine
MacCormick, Donald; Ontario, 1840-1849 ***4537.37*** *p39*
Wife: Mary MacDonald
MacCormick, Donald; Ontario, 1848 ***4537.37*** *p38*
Wife: Ann MacIsaac
Child: Mary
MacCormick, Donald; Ontario, 1849 ***4537.37*** *p39*
Wife: Mary MacLeod
Child: Catherine
Child: Margaret
MacCormick, Donald; Ontario, 1850-1859 ***4537.37*** *p39*
Wife: Marion Walker
Child: Catherine
Child: Ewen
Child: Neil
Child: Mary
MacCormick, Donald; Ontario, 1850-1859 ***4537.37*** *p39*
Wife: Mary MacDonald
Child: Kirsty
Child: John
Child: Angus
Child: Margaret
Child: James
MacCormick, Donald; Ontario, 1850-1859 ***4537.37*** *p39*
Wife: Mary MacDonald
Child: John
Child: Angus
Child: James
Child: Kirsty
Child: Catherine
Child: Margaret
MacCormick, Donald; Ontario, 1851 ***4537.32*** *p18*
Wife: Mary MacDonald
Child: Angus
Child: Margaret
Child: Kirsty
Child: James
Child: John
Child: Catherine
MacCormick, Donald; Saskatchewan, 1884 ***4537.37*** *p91*
Wife: Ann MacDonald
Child: Marion
MacCormick, Donald; Port uncertain, 1840-1849 ***4537.37*** *p109*
Wife: Mary MacRury
Child: Lachlan
Child: John
Child: Ann
Child: Catherine
Child: Donald
Child: Angus
MacCormick, Duncan; Ontario, 1850-1859 ***4537.37*** *p40*
Wife: Mary MacDonald
Child: Catherine
Child: Hugh
Child: Neil
Child: Angus
MacCormick, Duncan; Ontario, 1851 ***4537.32*** *p18*
Wife: Mary MacDonald
Child: Neil
Child: Catherine
Child: Hugh
Child: Angus
MacCormick, Effie *SEE* MacCormick, Andrew
MacCormick, Effie *SEE* MacCormick, Lachlan
MacCormick, Effie; Ontario, 1851 ***4537.37*** *p59*
MacCormick, Ewen *SEE* MacCormick, Alexander
MacCormick, Ewen *SEE* MacCormick, Donald
MacCormick, Ewen *SEE* MacCormick, Lachlan
MacCormick, Flora *SEE* MacCormick, Archie
MacCormick, Flora; Ontario, 1840-1849 ***4537.37*** *p75*
MacCormick, Flora; Ontario, 1849 ***4537.32*** *p74*
MacCormick, Hugh *SEE* MacCormick, Duncan
MacCormick, James *SEE* MacCormick, Donald
MacCormick, John *SEE* MacCormick, Alexander
MacCormick, John *SEE* MacCormick, Andrew
MacCormick, John *SEE* MacCormick, Angus
MacCormick, John *SEE* MacCormick, Archie
MacCormick, John *SEE* MacCormick, Catherine MacDonald
MacCormick, John *SEE* MacCormick, Donald
MacCormick, John *SEE* MacCormick, Malcolm
MacCormick, John *SEE* MacCormick, Neil
MacCormick, John *SEE* MacCormick, Peter
MacCormick, John; Saskatchewan, 1884 ***4537.37*** *p91*
Wife: Mary MacDonald
Child: Marion
Child: Donald
Child: Kate
Child: Alexander
Child: Catherine
MacCormick, Kate *SEE* MacCormick, John
MacCormick, Kirsty *SEE* MacCormick, Alexander
MacCormick, Kirsty *SEE* MacCormick, Andrew
MacCormick, Kirsty *SEE* MacCormick, Angus
MacCormick, Kirsty *SEE* MacCormick, Donald
MacCormick, Kirsty *SEE* MacCormick, Malcolm
MacCormick, Kirsty *SEE* MacCormick, Peter
MacCormick, Lachlan *SEE* MacCormick, Archie
MacCormick, Lachlan *SEE* MacCormick, Donald
MacCormick, Lachlan; Nova Scotia, 1847-1849 ***4537.37*** *p11*
Wife: Ann MacPherson
Child: Ewen
Child: Ann
Child: Mary
Child: Effie
Child: Catherine
MacCormick, Malcolm *SEE* MacCormick, Archie
MacCormick, Malcolm; Nova Scotia, 1840-1849 ***4537.37*** *p11*
Wife: Catherine MacPherson
Child: Roderick
Child: Kirsty
Child: John
Child: Donald
Child: Ann
MacCormick, Margaret *SEE* MacCormick, Andrew
MacCormick, Margaret *SEE* MacCormick, Donald
MacCormick, Marion *SEE* MacCormick, Andrew
MacCormick, Marion *SEE* MacCormick, Archie
MacCormick, Marion *SEE* MacCormick, Donald
MacCormick, Marion *SEE* MacCormick, John
MacCormick, Marion *SEE* MacCormick, Neil
MacCormick, Marion *SEE* MacCormick, Ranald
MacCormick, Marion; Port uncertain, 1850-1859 ***4537.37*** *p124*
MacCormick, Marion MacDonald *SEE* MacCormick, Angus
MacCormick, Marion Walker *SEE* MacCormick, Andrew
MacCormick, Marion Walker *SEE* MacCormick, Donald
MacCormick, Mary *SEE* MacCormick, Alexander
MacCormick, Mary *SEE* MacCormick, Andrew
MacCormick, Mary *SEE* MacCormick, Archie
MacCormick, Mary *SEE* MacCormick, Donald
MacCormick, Mary *SEE* MacCormick, Lachlan
MacCormick, Mary *SEE* MacCormick, Neil
MacCormick, Mary *SEE* MacCormick, Ranald
MacCormick, Mary; Ontario, 1849 ***4537.37*** *p56*
MacCormick, Mary; Ontario, 1849 ***4537.37*** *p67*
MacCormick, Mary; Saskatchewan, 1884 ***4537.37*** *p92*
MacCormick, Mary MacAulay *SEE* MacCormick, Neil
MacCormick, Mary MacCormick *SEE* MacCormick, Ranald
MacCormick, Mary MacDonald *SEE* MacCormick, Donald
MacCormick, Mary MacDonald *SEE* MacCormick, Duncan
MacCormick, Mary MacDonald *SEE* MacCormick, John
MacCormick, Mary MacLeod *SEE* MacCormick, Donald
MacCormick, Mary MacPhee *SEE* MacCormick, Archie
MacCormick, Mary MacRury *SEE* MacCormick, Donald
MacCormick, Mary Morrison *SEE* MacCormick, Neil
MacCormick, Mary O'Henley *SEE* MacCormick, Andrew
MacCormick, Matilda *SEE* MacCormick, Neil
MacCormick, Matilda; Ontario, 1840-1849 ***4537.37*** *p62*
MacCormick, Neil *SEE* MacCormick, Catherine MacDonald
MacCormick, Neil *SEE* MacCormick, Donald
MacCormick, Neil *SEE* MacCormick, Duncan
MacCormick, Neil; Nova Scotia, 1848 ***4537.37*** *p11*
Wife: Mary MacAulay
Child: Donald
MacCormick, Neil; Ontario, 1849 ***4537.37*** *p40*
Wife: Mary Morrison
Child: Mary
Child: Marion
Child: Sarah
Child: Archie
Child: Donald
Child: Matilda
MacCormick, Neil; Ontario, 1850-1859 ***4537.37*** *p40*
Wife: Ann Currie
Child: John
Child: Mary
Child: Donald
Child: Alexander
Child: Sarah
MacCormick, Neil; Ontario, 1851 ***4537.32*** *p18*
Wife: Ann Currie
Child: Alexander
Child: Donald
MacCormick, Norman *SEE* MacCormick, Donald
MacCormick, Peter *SEE* MacCormick, Angus
MacCormick, Peter *SEE* MacCormick, Ranald

MacCormick, Peter; Ontario, 1848 ***4537.37*** *p41*
Child: John
Child: Alexander
Wife: Kirsty
MacCormick, Ranald; Saskatchewan, 1884 ***4537.37*** *p92*
Child: Roderick
Child: Marion
Child: Mary
Child: Catherine
Wife: Mary MacCormick
Child: Peter
Child: Angus
MacCormick, Roderick *SEE* MacCormick, Andrew
MacCormick, Roderick *SEE* MacCormick, Malcolm
MacCormick, Roderick *SEE* MacCormick, Ranald
MacCormick, Sarah *SEE* MacCormick, Donald
MacCormick, Sarah *SEE* MacCormick, Neil
MacCorqudale, Alexander *SEE* MacCorqudale, Angus
MacCorqudale, Angus; Ontario, 1850-1859 ***4537.37*** *p41*
Wife: Janet MacEachan
Child: Margaret
Child: Donald
Child: Lachlan
Child: Kate
Child: Alexander
MacCorqudale, Donald *SEE* MacCorqudale, Angus
MacCorqudale, Janet MacEachan *SEE* MacCorqudale, Angus
MacCorqudale, Kate *SEE* MacCorqudale, Angus
MacCorqudale, Lachlan *SEE* MacCorqudale, Angus
MacCorqudale, Margaret *SEE* MacCorqudale, Angus
MacCoull, Alexander; Georgia, 1736 ***1640.10*** *p104*
Maccubin, John; Maryland, 1649 ***2524.55*** *p141*
MacCuish, Ann MacKenzie *SEE* MacCuish, John
MacCuish, Catherine *SEE* MacCuish, John
MacCuish, Catherine; Saskatchewan, 1889 ***4537.35*** *p70*
MacCuish, Donald *SEE* MacCuish, Margaret
MacCuish, Effie; Nova Scotia, 1820-1829 ***4537.35*** *p16*
MacCuish, Finlay *SEE* MacCuish, John
MacCuish, Flora; Nova Scotia, 1826-1829 ***4537.35*** *p16*
MacCuish, John *SEE* MacCuish, John
MacCuish, John *SEE* MacCuish, Margaret
MacCuish, John; Port uncertain, 1880-1889 ***4537.35*** *p79*
Wife: Ann MacKenzie
Child: John
Child: Catherine
Child: Finlay
Child: Mary
MacCuish, Margaret; Port uncertain, 1840-1849 ***4537.37*** *p109*
Child: Donald
Child: John
MacCuish, Marion; Ontario, 1860-1869 ***4537.35*** *p60*
MacCuish, Marion; Ontario, 1862 ***4537.32*** *p70*
MacCuish, Mary *SEE* MacCuish, John
MacCusbic, Angus *SEE* MacCusbic, Donald
MacCusbic, Angus; Nova Scotia, 1820-1829 ***4537.35*** *p15*
Wife: Kirsty MacLeod
Child: Malcolm
MacCusbic, Ann MacKillop *SEE* MacCusbic, Malcolm
MacCusbic, Catherine *SEE* MacCusbic, Malcolm
MacCusbic, Catherine *SEE* MacCusbic, Roderick
MacCusbic, Catherine; Nova Scotia, 1850-1859 ***4537.35*** *p37*
MacCusbic, Donald *SEE* MacCusbic, Malcolm
MacCusbic, Donald; Nova Scotia, 1840-1849 ***4537.35*** *p15*
Wife: Mary MacLeod
Child: John
Child: Murdo
Child: Angus
Child: Mary
Child: Flora
MacCusbic, Effie *SEE* MacCusbic, Roderick
MacCusbic, Effie MacCuish *SEE* MacCusbic, John
MacCusbic, Finlay *SEE* MacCusbic, John
MacCusbic, Finlay *SEE* MacCusbic, Malcolm
MacCusbic, Flora *SEE* MacCusbic, Donald
MacCusbic, Flora MacCuish *SEE* MacCusbic, John
MacCusbic, Hannah *SEE* MacCusbic, Roderick
MacCusbic, Janet *SEE* MacCusbic, Malcolm
MacCusbic, Jessie; Nova Scotia, 1820-1829 ***4537.35*** *p24*
MacCusbic, John *SEE* MacCusbic, Donald
MacCusbic, John; Nova Scotia, 1820-1829 ***4537.35*** *p16*
Wife: Effie MacCuish
MacCusbic, John; Nova Scotia, 1826-1829 ***4537.35*** *p16*
Wife: Flora MacCuish
Child: Kirsty
Child: Finlay
Child: Mary
MacCusbic, Kirsty *SEE* MacCusbic, John
MacCusbic, Kirsty; Nova Scotia, 1840-1849 ***4537.35*** *p38*
MacCusbic, Kirsty Campbell *SEE* MacCusbic, Roderick
MacCusbic, Kirsty MacLeod *SEE* MacCusbic, Angus
MacCusbic, Malcolm *SEE* MacCusbic, Angus
MacCusbic, Malcolm; Nova Scotia, 1840-1849 ***4537.35*** *p16*
Wife: Ann MacKillop
Child: Catherine
Child: Donald
Child: Finlay
Child: Margaret
Child: Janet
MacCusbic, Margaret *SEE* MacCusbic, Malcolm
MacCusbic, Margaret; Nova Scotia, 1840-1849 ***4537.35*** *p34*
MacCusbic, Mary *SEE* MacCusbic, Donald
MacCusbic, Mary *SEE* MacCusbic, John
MacCusbic, Mary MacLeod *SEE* MacCusbic, Donald
MacCusbic, Murdo *SEE* MacCusbic, Donald
MacCusbic, Peter *SEE* MacCusbic, Roderick
MacCusbic, Roderick; Port uncertain, 1860-1869 ***4537.35*** *p79*
Wife: Kirsty Campbell
Child: Catherine
Child: Effie
Child: Hannah
Child: Peter
MacDermid, Alexander *SEE* MacDermid, Donald
MacDermid, Alexander *SEE* MacDermid, Kenneth
MacDermid, Angus *SEE* MacDermid, Donald
MacDermid, Angus *SEE* MacDermid, John
MacDermid, Angus *SEE* MacDermid, Kenneth
MacDermid, Angus *SEE* MacDermid, Murdo
MacDermid, Angus; Port uncertain, 1840-1849 ***4537.35*** *p79*
Wife: Ann
Child: Hannah
Child: Donald
MacDermid, Ann *SEE* MacDermid, Angus
MacDermid, Ann *SEE* MacDermid, Donald
MacDermid, Ann *SEE* MacDermid, Finlay
MacDermid, Ann *SEE* MacDermid, John
MacDermid, Ann *SEE* MacDermid, William
MacDermid, Ann; Nova Scotia, n.d. ***4537.35*** *p16*
MacDermid, Ann; Nova Scotia, 1840-1849 ***4537.35*** *p17*
Child: Donald
Child: John
Child: Archie
Child: Hannah
MacDermid, Archie *SEE* MacDermid, Ann
MacDermid, Archie *SEE* MacDermid, Murdo
MacDermid, Betsy *SEE* MacDermid, Finlay
MacDermid, Catherine *SEE* MacDermid, Finlay
MacDermid, Catherine *SEE* MacDermid, John
MacDermid, Catherine *SEE* MacDermid, Kenneth
MacDermid, Catherine; Nova Scotia, 1840-1849 ***4537.35*** *p22*
MacDermid, Catherine; Port uncertain, 1860-1869 ***4537.35*** *p81*
MacDermid, Catherine Campbell *SEE* MacDermid, Donald
MacDermid, Catherine MacDonald *SEE* MacDermid, Kenneth
MacDermid, Catherine MacLeod *SEE* MacDermid, John
MacDermid, Donald *SEE* MacDermid, Angus
MacDermid, Donald *SEE* MacDermid, Ann
MacDermid, Donald *SEE* MacDermid, Donald
MacDermid, Donald *SEE* MacDermid, Finlay
MacDermid, Donald *SEE* MacDermid, John
MacDermid, Donald; Nova Scotia, 1840-1849 ***4537.35*** *p16*
Wife: Sarah
Child: Malcolm
Child: Donald
Child: Una
Child: Margaret
Child: Ann
MacDermid, Donald; Ontario, 1860-1869 ***4537.32*** *p19*
Wife: Catherine Campbell
Child: Angus
Child: Alexander
Child: Rachel
MacDermid, Donald; Port uncertain, 1860-1869 ***4537.35*** *p79*
Wife: Catherine Campbell
Child: Alexander
Child: Rachel
MacDermid, Donald J. *SEE* MacDermid, William
MacDermid, Effie *SEE* MacDermid, Finlay
MacDermid, Effie *SEE* MacDermid, John
MacDermid, Effie *SEE* MacDermid, Murdo
MacDermid, Finlay; Nova Scotia, 1840-1849 ***4537.35*** *p16*
Wife: Catherine
Child: John
Child: Betsy
Child: Sarah
Child: Roderick
Child: Effie
Child: Mary
Child: Donald
Child: Ann
Child: Norman
Child: Catherine
MacDermid, Flora *SEE* MacDermid, John
MacDermid, Hannah *SEE* MacDermid, Angus
MacDermid, Hannah *SEE* MacDermid, Ann
MacDermid, Isabella *SEE* MacDermid, Kenneth
MacDermid, Isabella *SEE* MacDermid, William
MacDermid, James *SEE* MacDermid, John
MacDermid, James; Canada, 1850-1859 ***4537.35*** *p71*
MacDermid, Janet; Ontario, 1860-1869 ***4537.32*** *p19*
MacDermid, Jessie *SEE* MacDermid, William
MacDermid, John *SEE* MacDermid, Ann
MacDermid, John *SEE* MacDermid, Finlay
MacDermid, John *SEE* MacDermid, John
MacDermid, John *SEE* MacDermid, Murdo
MacDermid, John *SEE* MacDermid, William
MacDermid, John; Canada, 1860-1869 ***4537.35*** *p72*
Wife: Catherine MacLeod
Child: Catherine
Child: Margaret
Child: Roderick
Child: Flora
Child: William
Child: Malcolm
MacDermid, John; Canada, 1860-1869 ***4537.35*** *p72*
Wife: Margaret MacKinnon
Child: Angus
MacDermid, John; Nova Scotia, 1840-1849 ***4537.35*** *p17*
Wife: Mary Morrison
Child: Effie
Child: John
Child: Donald
Child: Ann
Child: James
MacDermid, John; Port uncertain, 1860-1869 ***4537.35*** *p79*
Wife: Margaret MacKinnon
Child: Angus
Child: Catherine
MacDermid, Kenneth; Ontario, 1860-1869 ***4537.32*** *p19*
Wife: Catherine MacDonald
Child: Mary
Child: Norman
Child: Alexander
Child: Catherine
Child: Angus
Child: Kirsty
Child: Isabella
Child: Rachel
MacDermid, Kenneth; Ontario, 1860-1869 ***4537.35*** *p56*
Wife: Catherine MacDonald
Child: Mary
Child: Alexander
Child: Norman
Child: Rachel
Child: Angus
Child: Isabella
Child: Kirsty
Child: Catherine
MacDermid, Kirsty *SEE* MacDermid, Kenneth
MacDermid, Kirsty *SEE* MacDermid, William
MacDermid, Kirsty; Nova Scotia, 1820-1829 ***4537.35*** *p12*
MacDermid, Kirsty; Nova Scotia, 1840-1849 ***4537.35*** *p12*
MacDermid, Kirsty Shaw *SEE* MacDermid, William
MacDermid, Louisa *SEE* MacDermid, Murdo
MacDermid, Malcolm *SEE* MacDermid, Donald
MacDermid, Malcolm *SEE* MacDermid, John
MacDermid, Margaret *SEE* MacDermid, Donald
MacDermid, Margaret *SEE* MacDermid, John
MacDermid, Margaret *SEE* MacDermid, Murdo
MacDermid, Margaret MacKinnon *SEE* MacDermid, John
MacDermid, Marion *SEE* MacDermid, Murdo
MacDermid, Marion; Nova Scotia, 1844 ***4537.35*** *p34*
MacDermid, Marion; Port uncertain, 1860-1869 ***4537.35*** *p80*
MacDermid, Mary *SEE* MacDermid, Finlay
MacDermid, Mary *SEE* MacDermid, Kenneth
MacDermid, Mary Morrison *SEE* MacDermid, John

MacDermid, Murdo; Nova Scotia, 1840-1849 ***4537.35*** *p17*
Wife: Effie
Child: Marion
Child: John
Child: Angus
Child: Archie
MacDermid, Murdo; Port uncertain, 1840-1849 ***4537.35*** *p79*
Wife: Louisa
Child: Archie
Child: Margaret
Child: Sally
MacDermid, Norman *SEE* MacDermid, Finlay
MacDermid, Norman *SEE* MacDermid, Kenneth
MacDermid, Rachel *SEE* MacDermid, Donald
MacDermid, Rachel *SEE* MacDermid, Kenneth
MacDermid, Roderick *SEE* MacDermid, Finlay
MacDermid, Roderick *SEE* MacDermid, John
MacDermid, Sally *SEE* MacDermid, Murdo
MacDermid, Sarah *SEE* MacDermid, Donald
MacDermid, Sarah *SEE* MacDermid, Finlay
MacDermid, Sarah *SEE* MacDermid, William
MacDermid, Una *SEE* MacDermid, Donald
MacDermid, William *SEE* MacDermid, John
MacDermid, William; Nova Scotia, 1840-1849 ***4537.35*** *p17*
Wife: Kirsty Shaw
Child: Ann
Child: John
Child: Donald J.
Child: Jessie
Child: Sarah
Child: Kirsty
Child: Isabella
MacDermot, H. 45; Ontario, 1871 ***1823.15*** *p150*
MacDiarmid, Donald; Saskatchewan, 1883 ***4537.37*** *p92*
MacDonald, Agnes *SEE* MacDonald, Donald
MacDonald, Alex *SEE* MacDonald, Angus
MacDonald, Alex *SEE* MacDonald, Ann
MacDonald, Alexander *SEE* MacDonald, Alexander
MacDonald, Alexander *SEE* MacDonald, Allan
MacDonald, Alexander *SEE* MacDonald, Angus
MacDonald, Alexander *SEE* MacDonald, Donald
MacDonald, Alexander *SEE* MacDonald, Ewen
MacDonald, Alexander *SEE* MacDonald, Isabella
MacDonald, Alexander *SEE* MacDonald, Janet
MacDonald, Alexander *SEE* MacDonald, John
MacDonald, Alexander *SEE* MacDonald, Kirsty MacPhee
MacDonald, Alexander *SEE* MacDonald, Lachlan
MacDonald, Alexander *SEE* MacDonald, Malcolm
MacDonald, Alexander *SEE* MacDonald, Marion
MacDonald, Alexander *SEE* MacDonald, Marion MacLeod
MacDonald, Alexander *SEE* MacDonald, Mary
MacDonald, Alexander *SEE* MacDonald, Mary MacFarlane
MacDonald, Alexander *SEE* MacDonald, Mary MacKay
MacDonald, Alexander *SEE* MacDonald, Mary Morrison
MacDonald, Alexander *SEE* MacDonald, Michael
MacDonald, Alexander *SEE* MacDonald, Murdo
MacDonald, Alexander *SEE* MacDonald, Neil
MacDonald, Alexander *SEE* MacDonald, Norman
MacDonald, Alexander *SEE* MacDonald, Ranald
MacDonald, Alexander *SEE* MacDonald, Roderick
MacDonald, Alexander *SEE* MacDonald, Sam
Macdonald, Alexander; Georgia, 1741 ***1640.10*** *p107*
Macdonald, Alexander; North Carolina, n.d. ***1224.2*** *p73*
MacDonald, Alexander; Nova Scotia, 1840 ***4537.35*** *p17*
Wife: Catherine
Child: John
MacDonald, Alexander; Nova Scotia, 1840-1849 ***4537.37*** *p11*
Wife: Catherine
Child: Norman
Child: Mary
Child: Lachlan
Child: William
MacDonald, Alexander; Nova Scotia, 1850-1859 ***4537.37*** *p12*
Wife: Catherine
Child: Kirsty
Child: Malcolm
Child: Ann
Child: Allan
Child: Ranald
MacDonald, Alexander; Ontario, 1840-1849 ***4537.37*** *p41*
Wife: Catherine MacEachan
Child: Ranald
Child: John
Child: Mary
MacDonald, Alexander; Ontario, 1840-1849 ***4537.37*** *p42*
Wife: Margaret MacKinnon
Child: Margaret
Child: Alexander
MacDonald, Alexander; Ontario, 1840-1849 ***4537.37*** *p42*
Wife: Marion Campbell
Child: Kirsty
Child: Catherine
Child: Marion
Child: Donald
Child: Angus
Child: Alexander
Child: Mary
Child: Flora
MacDonald, Alexander; Ontario, 1849 ***4537.37*** *p42*
Child: John
Child: Catherine
Child: Ranald
Wife: Catherine MacIsaac
Child: Marion
Child: Allan
MacDonald, Alexander; Ontario, 1850 ***4537.37*** *p42*
Wife: Marion MacPhee
Child: Marion
Child: Neil
Child: Effie
Child: John
Child: Kirsty
Child: Lachlan
Child: Ann
MacDonald, Alexander; Ontario, 1850-1859 ***4537.37*** *p43*
Wife: Penny MacEachan
Child: Ann
Child: Angus
Child: Catherine
Child: Eliza
Child: Ranald
Child: Margaret
Child: Sally
MacDonald, Alexander; Ontario, 1851 ***4537.32*** *p19*
Wife: Kate
Child: Sarah
Child: Kirsty
Child: Ranald
Child: William
Child: John
Child: Archie
Child: Marion
MacDonald, Alexander; Ontario, 1851 ***4537.37*** *p41*
Child: Ranald
Child: Archie
Child: Kirsty
Child: Marion
Wife: Kate
MacDonald, Alexander; Saskatchewan, 1883 ***4537.37*** *p92*
Wife: Catherine MacPhee
MacDonald, Alexander; Saskatchewan, 1884 ***4537.37*** *p92*
Wife: Marion MacDonald
Child: Isabella
Child: Flora
Child: Ranald
MacDonald, Alexander; Port uncertain, 1840-1849 ***4537.37*** *p109*
Wife: Marion
Child: Marion
Child: Kirsty
MacDonald, Alexander; Port uncertain, 1840-1849 ***4537.37*** *p109*
Wife: Mary MacLellan
Child: Archie
Child: Penny
Child: Marion
Child: John
MacDonald, Alexander; Port uncertain, 1840-1849 ***4537.37*** *p109*
Child: Ann
Child: Roderick
Child: Ranald
Child: Donald
Wife: Mary MacLeod
MacDonald, Alexander; Port uncertain, 1840-1849 ***4537.37*** *p109*
Wife: Mary
Child: Ranald
Child: John
MacDonald, Alexander; Port uncertain, 1840-1849 ***4537.37*** *p109*
Child: Archie
Child: Marion
MacDonald, Alexander; Port uncertain, 1840-1849 ***4537.37*** *p110*
Sibling: Marion
Sibling: Mary
Sibling: Ranald
MacDonald, Alexander; Port uncertain, 1850-1859 ***4537.37*** *p109*
Wife: Janet
MacDonald, Alexander; Port uncertain, 1850-1859 ***4537.37*** *p109*
Wife: Janet Grieve
Child: Mary
Child: Archie
Child: William
Child: Ann
MacDonald, Alexander; Port uncertain, 1850-1859 ***4537.37*** *p109*
Sibling: Kate
Sibling: Ann
MacDonald, Allan *SEE* MacDonald, Alexander
MacDonald, Allan *SEE* MacDonald, Angus
MacDonald, Allan *SEE* MacDonald, Donald
MacDonald, Allan *SEE* MacDonald, Hector
MacDonald, Allan *SEE* MacDonald, John
MacDonald, Allan; Ontario, 1840-1849 ***4537.37*** *p43*
Wife: Margaret MacIntyre
Child: Marion
Child: Lachlan
Child: Donald
MacDonald, Allan; Ontario, 1849 ***4537.32*** *p20*
Child: Alexander
Child: Marion
Child: Lachlan
Child: Donald
Wife: Margaret MacIntyre
MacDonald, Allan; Ontario, 1851 ***4537.32*** *p20*
Wife: Ann MacEachan
Child: Lachlan
Child: Hugh
Child: Effie
Child: Marion
Child: Donald
Child: John
Child: Roderick
MacDonald, Allan; Port uncertain, 1850-1859 ***4537.37*** *p109*
Wife: Ann MacEachan
Child: Lachlan
Child: Hugh
Child: John
Child: Effie
Child: Donald
Child: Marion
Child: Roderick
MacDonald, Amelia *SEE* MacDonald, Donald
MacDonald, Andrew *SEE* MacDonald, Donald
MacDonald, Angus *SEE* MacDonald, Alexander
MacDonald, Angus *SEE* MacDonald, Angus
MacDonald, Angus *SEE* MacDonald, Catherine Campbell
MacDonald, Angus *SEE* MacDonald, Catherine Johnston
MacDonald, Angus *SEE* MacDonald, Catherine MacKinnon
MacDonald, Angus *SEE* MacDonald, Catherine MacLean
MacDonald, Angus *SEE* MacDonald, Donald
MacDonald, Angus *SEE* MacDonald, Duncan
MacDonald, Angus *SEE* MacDonald, John
MacDonald, Angus *SEE* MacDonald, Kirsty MacPhee
MacDonald, Angus *SEE* MacDonald, Lachlan
MacDonald, Angus *SEE* MacDonald, Malcolm
MacDonald, Angus *SEE* MacDonald, Marion Cunningham
MacDonald, Angus *SEE* MacDonald, Marion MacLeod
MacDonald, Angus *SEE* MacDonald, Mary MacFarlane
MacDonald, Angus *SEE* MacDonald, Michael
MacDonald, Angus *SEE* MacDonald, Murdo
MacDonald, Angus *SEE* MacDonald, Neil
MacDonald, Angus *SEE* MacDonald, Norman
MacDonald, Angus *SEE* MacDonald, Ranald
MacDonald, Angus *SEE* MacDonald, Roderick
MacDonald, Angus *SEE* MacDonald, Slaine
MacDonald, Angus *SEE* MacDonald, William
MacDonald, Angus; Falkland Islands, 1870-1879 ***4537.35*** *p74*
Wife: Kirsty Morrison
Child: Mary
Child: Murdo
MacDonald, Angus; Nova Scotia, 1841 ***4537.37*** *p12*
Wife: Mary MacIsaac
Child: Marion
Child: Roderick
Child: John
Child: Ranald

Child: Donald
Child: Lachlan
Child: Kate
MacDonald, Angus; Ontario, 1848 ***4537.37*** *p43*
Wife: Ann Bowie
Child: Allan
Child: Marion
Child: Archie
MacDonald, Angus; Ontario, 1848 ***4537.37*** *p43*
Wife: Ann MacCormick
Child: John
Child: Mary
Child: John
Child: Ranald
MacDonald, Angus; Ontario, 1851 ***4537.32*** *p21*
Wife: Catherine Smith
Child: Peggy
Child: John
Child: Malcolm
Child: Donald
Child: Murdo
MacDonald, Angus; Ontario, 1851 ***4537.32*** *p21*
Wife: Mary
Child: Alexander
Child: Margaret
MacDonald, Angus; Ontario, 1851 ***4537.37*** *p44*
With wife
Child: Donald
Child: James
Child: Alex
MacDonald, Angus; Ontario, 1855 ***4537.32*** *p21*
Wife: Ann MacLeod
Child: Mary
Child: Norman
Child: Kenneth
Child: Angus
Child: Jane
Child: Donald
Child: William
Child: Catherine
Child: John
MacDonald, Angus; Ontario, 1860-1869 ***4537.32*** *p20*
Wife: Ann MacLeod
Child: Mary
Child: John
Child: Margaret
Child: Alexander
Child: Malcolm
Child: Donald
Child: James
MacDonald, Angus; Ontario, 1860-1869 ***4537.35*** *p57*
Wife: Ann MacLeod
Child: Alexander
Child: Mary
Child: James
Child: Donald
Child: Malcolm
Child: John
MacDonald, Angus; Port uncertain, 1840-1849 ***4537.35*** *p80*
With wife
Child: Kirsty
Child: Janet
MacDonald, Angus; Port uncertain, 1840-1849 ***4537.37*** *p110*
Wife: Kate
Child: Malcolm
Child: Neil
Child: Donald
Child: John
Child: Mary
MacDonald, Angus; Port uncertain, 1840-1849 ***4537.37*** *p110*
Wife: Effie MacMillan
Child: Roderick
Child: Margaret
Child: James
MacDonald, Angus; Port uncertain, 1840-1849 ***4537.37*** *p110*
Wife: Marion
Child: Donald
Child: Effie
MacDonald, Angus; Port uncertain, 1840-1849 ***4537.37*** *p110*
Wife: Marion
Child: Kate
Child: Angus
MacDonald, Angus; Port uncertain, 1840-1849 ***4537.37*** *p110*
Child: Mary
Child: Donald
Child: Isabella
Child: Penny
MacDonald, Angus; Port uncertain, 1850-1859 ***4537.35*** *p80*
Child: Marion
Wife: Mary Morrison
Child: John
Child: Roderick
Child: Kirsty
MacDonald, Angus; Port uncertain, 1850-1859 ***4537.37*** *p110*
Wife: Ann O'Henley
Child: Flora
Child: Malcolm
Child: Ann
Child: Ranald
MacDonald, Angus; Port uncertain, 1850-1859 ***4537.37*** *p110*
Wife: Ann Cumming
Child: Marion
Child: Malcolm
Child: Peggy
Child: Sally
Child: Donald
Child: Mary
MacDonald, Angus; Port uncertain, 1850-1859 ***4537.37*** *p110*
Wife: Kirsty
Child: Mary
Child: Donald
Child: Janet
Child: Effie
MacDonald, Ann *SEE* MacDonald, Alexander
MacDonald, Ann *SEE* MacDonald, Angus
MacDonald, Ann *SEE* MacDonald, Ann
MacDonald, Ann *SEE* MacDonald, Archie
MacDonald, Ann *SEE* MacDonald, Catherine Johnston
MacDonald, Ann *SEE* MacDonald, Donald
MacDonald, Ann *SEE* MacDonald, Effie
MacDonald, Ann *SEE* MacDonald, Ewen
MacDonald, Ann *SEE* MacDonald, John
MacDonald, Ann *SEE* MacDonald, Kenneth
MacDonald, Ann *SEE* MacDonald, Kirsty
MacDonald, Ann *SEE* MacDonald, Lachlan
MacDonald, Ann *SEE* MacDonald, Malcolm
MacDonald, Ann *SEE* MacDonald, Marion
MacDonald, Ann *SEE* MacDonald, Marion MacKay
MacDonald, Ann *SEE* MacDonald, Mary MacFarlane
MacDonald, Ann *SEE* MacDonald, Mary MacKay
MacDonald, Ann *SEE* MacDonald, Mary Morrison
MacDonald, Ann *SEE* MacDonald, Michael
MacDonald, Ann *SEE* MacDonald, Norman
MacDonald, Ann *SEE* MacDonald, Ranald
MacDonald, Ann *SEE* MacDonald, Roderick
MacDonald, Ann *SEE* MacDonald, Sam
MacDonald, Ann *SEE* MacDonald, Sarah MacLellan
MacDonald, Ann *SEE* MacDonald, William
MacDonald, Ann; Canada, 1860-1869 ***4537.35*** *p71*
MacDonald, Ann; Nova Scotia, 1820-1829 ***4537.35*** *p35*
MacDonald, Ann; Nova Scotia, 1840-1849 ***4537.35*** *p18*
Sibling: John
Sibling: Peter
Sibling: Catherine
MacDonald, Ann; Ontario, 1850-1859 ***4537.37*** *p32*
MacDonald, Ann; Ontario, 1851 ***4537.32*** *p5*
MacDonald, Ann; Ontario, 1851 ***4537.32*** *p58*
MacDonald, Ann; Ontario, 1851 ***4537.32*** *p65*
MacDonald, Ann; Ontario, 1855 ***4537.32*** *p58*
MacDonald, Ann; Ontario, 1860-1869 ***4537.35*** *p58*
MacDonald, Ann; Ontario, 1862 ***4537.32*** *p48*
MacDonald, Ann; Quebec, 1870-1879 ***4537.35*** *p64*
MacDonald, Ann; Saskatchewan, 1884 ***4537.37*** *p91*
MacDonald, Ann; Port uncertain, 1840-1849 ***4537.37*** *p114*
Child: Donald
Child: Effie
Child: Alex
MacDonald, Ann; Port uncertain, 1840-1849 ***4537.37*** *p125*
MacDonald, Ann; Port uncertain, 1840-1849 ***4537.37*** *p126*
MacDonald, Ann; Port uncertain, 1840-1849 ***4537.37*** *p130*
MacDonald, Ann; Port uncertain, 1850-1859 ***4537.37*** *p114*
Child: Margaret
Child: Donald
Child: Marion
MacDonald, Ann; Port uncertain, 1850-1859 ***4537.37*** *p114*
Child: Lachlan
Child: Ann
Child: Kate
Child: Kirsty
MacDonald, Ann; Port uncertain, 1862-1869 ***4537.35*** *p80*
Child: Donald
Child: Mary
Child: Marion
Child: Roderick
MacDonald, Ann Bowie *SEE* MacDonald, Angus
MacDonald, Ann Cumming *SEE* MacDonald, Angus
MacDonald, Ann Johnston *SEE* MacDonald, Donald
MacDonald, Ann MacCormick *SEE* MacDonald, Angus
MacDonald, Ann MacCormick *SEE* MacDonald, John
MacDonald, Ann MacDougall *SEE* MacDonald, Ranald
MacDonald, Ann MacEachan *SEE* MacDonald, Allan
MacDonald, Ann MacInnes *SEE* MacDonald, Ranald
MacDonald, Ann MacKinnon *SEE* MacDonald, John
MacDonald, Ann MacKinnon; Ontario, 1862 ***4537.32*** *p32*
Child: John
Child: Margaret
Child: Neil
Child: Kirsty
Child: Mary
Child: Marion
MacDonald, Ann MacLeod *SEE* MacDonald, Angus
MacDonald, Ann MacLeod *SEE* MacDonald, Donald
MacDonald, Ann MacLeod *SEE* MacDonald, John
MacDonald, Ann MacLeod; Saskatchewan, 1884 ***4537.37*** *p93*
Child: Archie
Child: Donald
Child: Roderick
Child: Kirsty
MacDonald, Ann MacPhee *SEE* MacDonald, John
MacDonald, Ann Matheson *SEE* MacDonald, John
MacDonald, Ann O'Henley *SEE* MacDonald, Angus
MacDonald, Ann Walker *SEE* MacDonald, John
MacDonald, Archaa 40; Ontario, 1871 ***1823.15*** *p150*
Macdonald, Archibald; Georgia, 1737 ***1640.10*** *p107*
MacDonald, Archibald; New York, 1817 ***1224.3*** *p48*
MacDonald, Archibald; Vermont, 1841-1908 ***5900.10*** *p518*
MacDonald, Archie *SEE* MacDonald, Alexander
MacDonald, Archie *SEE* MacDonald, Angus
MacDonald, Archie *SEE* MacDonald, Ann MacLeod
MacDonald, Archie *SEE* MacDonald, Catherine Johnston
MacDonald, Archie *SEE* MacDonald, Donald
MacDonald, Archie *SEE* MacDonald, John
MacDonald, Archie *SEE* MacDonald, Marion
MacDonald, Archie *SEE* MacDonald, Neil
MacDonald, Archie *SEE* MacDonald, Sarah MacLellan
MacDonald, Archie; Ontario, 1850-1859 ***4537.37*** *p44*
Wife: Kirsty Monk
Child: Marion
Child: Neil
Child: Malcolm
Child: Margaret
Child: Catherine
Child: Godfrey
Child: Mary
MacDonald, Archie; Ontario, 1851 ***4537.32*** *p22*
Wife: Kirsty Monk
Child: Marion
Child: Neil
Child: Margaret
Child: Catherine
Child: Mary
Child: Godfrey
MacDonald, Archie; Saskatchewan, 1883 ***4537.37*** *p93*
MacDonald, Archie; Port uncertain, 1840-1849 ***4537.37*** *p110*
Wife: Effie MacPherson
Child: Ann
Child: John
MacDonald, Archie; Port uncertain, 1840-1849 ***4537.37*** *p110*
Child: Catherine
Child: Donald
Child: Marion
Child: Mary
Wife: Kirsty
MacDonald, Archie K. *SEE* MacDonald, Marion
MacDonald, Archie N. *SEE* MacDonald, John
MacDonald, Catherine *SEE* MacDonald, Alexander
MacDonald, Catherine *SEE* MacDonald, Angus
MacDonald, Catherine *SEE* MacDonald, Ann
MacDonald, Catherine *SEE* MacDonald, Archie
MacDonald, Catherine *SEE* MacDonald, Donald
MacDonald, Catherine *SEE* MacDonald, Duncan
MacDonald, Catherine *SEE* MacDonald, Effie Morrison
MacDonald, Catherine *SEE* MacDonald, Evander
MacDonald, Catherine *SEE* MacDonald, Ewen
MacDonald, Catherine *SEE* MacDonald, John
MacDonald, Catherine *SEE* MacDonald, Kenneth

MacDonald, Catherine *SEE* MacDonald, Kirsty
MacDonald, Catherine *SEE* MacDonald, Lachlan
MacDonald, Catherine *SEE* MacDonald, Malcolm
MacDonald, Catherine *SEE* MacDonald, Marion MacKay
MacDonald, Catherine *SEE* MacDonald, Murdo
MacDonald, Catherine *SEE* MacDonald, Neil
Macdonald, Catherine *SEE* Macdonald, Norman
MacDonald, Catherine *SEE* MacDonald, Norman
MacDonald, Catherine *SEE* MacDonald, Ranald
MacDonald, Catherine *SEE* MacDonald, Roderick
MacDonald, Catherine *SEE* MacDonald, William
MacDonald, Catherine; Maryland, 1888 ***4537.35*** *p68*
MacDonald, Catherine; North Carolina, 1774 ***4537.35*** *p9*
MacDonald, Catherine; Nova Scotia, 1840-1849 ***4537.37*** *p10*
MacDonald, Catherine; Nova Scotia, 1847-1849 ***4537.37*** *p17*
MacDonald, Catherine; Ontario, 1847-1849 ***4537.37*** *p40*
MacDonald, Catherine; Ontario, 1849 ***4537.32*** *p18*
MacDonald, Catherine; Ontario, 1849 ***4537.37*** *p60*
MacDonald, Catherine; Ontario, 1851 ***4537.32*** *p37*
MacDonald, Catherine; Ontario, 1851 ***4537.32*** *p55*
MacDonald, Catherine; Ontario, 1851 ***4537.32*** *p58*
MacDonald, Catherine; Ontario, 1860-1869 ***4537.32*** *p19*
MacDonald, Catherine; Ontario, 1860-1869 ***4537.35*** *p56*
MacDonald, Catherine; Ontario, 1860-1869 ***4537.35*** *p58*
MacDonald, Catherine; Ontario, 1862 ***4537.32*** *p60*
MacDonald, Catherine; Ontario, 1863 ***4537.32*** *p9*
MacDonald, Catherine; Prince Edward Island, 1848 ***4537.37*** *p25*
MacDonald, Catherine; Quebec, 1850-1859 ***4537.32*** *p10*
MacDonald, Catherine; Saskatchewan, 1884 ***4537.37*** *p102*
MacDonald, Catherine; Port uncertain, 1840-1849 ***4537.37*** *p106*
MacDonald, Catherine; Port uncertain, 1840-1849 ***4537.37*** *p107*
MacDonald, Catherine; Port uncertain, 1840-1849 ***4537.37*** *p114*
Child: Jessie
Child: Neil
MacDonald, Catherine; Port uncertain, 1850-1859 ***4537.37*** *p132*
MacDonald, Catherine; Port uncertain, 1860-1869 ***4537.35*** *p78*
MacDonald, Catherine Campbell; Port uncertain, 1850-1859 ***4537.37*** *p112*
Child: Kirsty
Child: Marion
Child: John
Child: Angus
MacDonald, Catherine Currie *SEE* MacDonald, Hector
MacDonald, Catherine Johnston; Port uncertain, 1840-1849 ***4537.37*** *p111*
Child: John
Child: Ewen
Child: Mary
Child: Janet
Child: Archie
Child: Angus
Child: Ann
Child: Marion
Child: Kirsty
MacDonald, Catherine MacAskill *SEE* MacDonald, Roderick
MacDonald, Catherine MacAulay *SEE* MacDonald, Donald
MacDonald, Catherine MacAulay *SEE* MacDonald, Lachlan
MacDonald, Catherine MacDermid *SEE* MacDonald, Kenneth
MacDonald, Catherine MacEachan *SEE* MacDonald, Alexander
MacDonald, Catherine MacIntyre *SEE* MacDonald, Donald
MacDonald, Catherine MacIntyre *SEE* MacDonald, Ranald
MacDonald, Catherine MacIsaac *SEE* MacDonald, Alexander
MacDonald, Catherine MacKinnon; Port uncertain, 1860-1869 ***4537.35*** *p80*
Child: Kirsty
Child: Kenneth
Child: Angus
Child: Donald
Child: John
MacDonald, Catherine MacLean *SEE* MacDonald, John
MacDonald, Catherine MacLean; Ontario, 1851 ***4537.32*** *p21*
Child: Finlay
Child: John
Child: William
Child: Malcolm
Child: Donald
Child: Angus
MacDonald, Catherine MacLellan *SEE* MacDonald, John
MacDonald, Catherine MacLennan *SEE* MacDonald, John
MacDonald, Catherine MacMillan *SEE* MacDonald, Donald
MacDonald, Catherine MacMillan *SEE* MacDonald, Lachlan
MacDonald, Catherine MacPhee *SEE* MacDonald, Alexander
MacDonald, Catherine MacQueen *SEE* MacDonald, Donald
MacDonald, Catherine Morrison *SEE* MacDonald, Donald
MacDonald, Catherine Morrison *SEE* MacDonald, Roderick
MacDonald, Catherine Smith *SEE* MacDonald, Angus
MacDonald, Charles *SEE* MacDonald, Donald
MacDonald, Charles *SEE* MacDonald, Hector
Macdonald, Christian; Georgia, 1738 ***1640.10*** *p108*
MacDonald, Christy 27; Ontario, 1871 ***1823.15*** *p150*
MacDonald, Colin *SEE* MacDonald, Donald
MacDonald, Colin *SEE* MacDonald, John
MacDonald, Colin *SEE* MacDonald, Murdo
MacDonald, Colin; Port uncertain, 1840-1849 ***4537.37*** *p110*
Sibling: Sarah
Sibling: Jane
Sibling: Donald
MacDonald, David *SEE* MacDonald, Ewen
MacDonald, Donald *SEE* MacDonald, Alexander
MacDonald, Donald *SEE* MacDonald, Allan
MacDonald, Donald *SEE* MacDonald, Angus
MacDonald, Donald *SEE* MacDonald, Ann
MacDonald, Donald *SEE* MacDonald, Ann MacLeod
MacDonald, Donald *SEE* MacDonald, Archie
MacDonald, Donald *SEE* MacDonald, Catherine MacKinnon
MacDonald, Donald *SEE* MacDonald, Catherine MacLean
MacDonald, Donald *SEE* MacDonald, Colin
MacDonald, Donald *SEE* MacDonald, Donald
MacDonald, Donald *SEE* MacDonald, Duncan
MacDonald, Donald *SEE* MacDonald, John
MacDonald, Donald *SEE* MacDonald, Lachlan
MacDonald, Donald *SEE* MacDonald, Malcolm
MacDonald, Donald *SEE* MacDonald, Marion
MacDonald, Donald *SEE* MacDonald, Marion MacKay
MacDonald, Donald *SEE* MacDonald, Mary Morrison
MacDonald, Donald *SEE* MacDonald, Michael
MacDonald, Donald *SEE* MacDonald, Murdo
MacDonald, Donald *SEE* MacDonald, Neil
MacDonald, Donald *SEE* MacDonald, Norman
MacDonald, Donald *SEE* MacDonald, Ranald
MacDonald, Donald *SEE* MacDonald, Roderick
Macdonald, Donald; Florida, 1841 ***1640.10*** *p108*
Macdonald, Donald; Georgia, 1736 ***1640.10*** *p108*
Macdonald, Donald; Georgia, 1737 ***1640.10*** *p108*
Macdonald, Donald; Georgia, 1757 ***1640.10*** *p108*
Macdonald, Donald; Georgia, 1834 ***1640.10*** *p108*
MacDonald, Donald; Michigan, 1882 ***4537.37*** *p88*
Wife: Ann Johnston
Child: Alexander
Child: Archie
Child: Margaret
Child: Roderick
Child: John
Child: Flora Jane
Child: Flora
MacDonald, Donald; Nova Scotia, 1840-1849 ***4537.35*** *p18*
Child: John
Child: Hector
Child: Kirsty
Wife: Margaret MacAskill
Child: Catherine
Child: Neil
MacDonald, Donald; Nova Scotia, 1840-1849 ***4537.35*** *p18*
Wife: Mary MacDonald
Child: Ann
Child: John
Child: Catherine
MacDonald, Donald; Nova Scotia, 1840-1849 ***4537.37*** *p12*
Wife: Catherine Morrison
Child: Alexander
Child: Neil
Child: Allan
Child: John
Child: Angus
Child: James
Child: Catherine
Child: Michael
MacDonald, Donald; Ontario, 1840-1849 ***4537.37*** *p44*
Wife: Fanny
Child: Sarah
Child: Flora
Child: Margaret
Child: Alexander
MacDonald, Donald; Ontario, 1840-1849 ***4537.37*** *p45*
Wife: Marion Morrison
Child: Catherine
Child: Neil
Child: Donald
Child: Mary
Child: John
Child: James
Child: Sarah
Child: Archie
MacDonald, Donald; Ontario, 1849 ***4537.32*** *p26*
Wife: Marion Morrison
Child: Archie
Child: Mary
Child: Donald
Child: Neil
Child: Catherine
Child: Sarah
Child: John
Child: James
MacDonald, Donald; Ontario, 1849 ***4537.37*** *p44*
Child: Alexander
Child: Kate
Child: Ann
Wife: Flora MacIsaac
Child: Flora
Child: Donald
Child: Ranald
Child: Angus
MacDonald, Donald; Ontario, 1850-1859 ***4537.37*** *p45*
Wife: Mary MacPhee
Child: Mary
Child: Archie
Child: Margaret
Child: Alexander
MacDonald, Donald; Ontario, 1851 ***4537.32*** *p22*
Wife: Ann
Child: Kirsty
Child: Margaret
Child: Norman
Child: Angus
Child: John
Child: Ann
MacDonald, Donald; Ontario, 1851 ***4537.32*** *p22*
Wife: Catherine
Child: Effie
Child: John
Child: Ann
Child: Margaret
MacDonald, Donald; Ontario, 1851 ***4537.32*** *p23*
Wife: Flora Nicolson
Child: Donald
Child: Ann
Child: Alexander
Child: Jessie
Child: Angus
Child: Marion
Child: John
Child: Malcolm
Child: Una
Child: Archie
MacDonald, Donald; Ontario, 1851 ***4537.32*** *p23*
Child: Malcolm
Child: Kirsty
Child: Ann
Wife: Kirsty MacAulay
Child: Angus
MacDonald, Donald; Ontario, 1851 ***4537.32*** *p24*
Wife: Kirsty MacLeod
Child: Donald
Child: Kirsty
MacDonald, Donald; Ontario, 1851 ***4537.32*** *p24*
Wife: Margaret
Child: Margaret
Child: Catherine
Child: John
Child: Murdo
MacDonald, Donald; Ontario, 1851 ***4537.32*** *p25*
Wife: Marion
Child: John
Child: Norman
Child: Margaret
MacDonald, Donald; Ontario, 1851 ***4537.32*** *p25*
Wife: Marion
Child: Charles

MacDonald, Finlay; Ontario, 1863 ***4537.32*** *p27*
Wife: Margaret MacLennan
Child: Malcolm
Child: Marion
Child: Roderick
Child: John
MacDonald, Flora *SEE* MacDonald, Alexander
MacDonald, Flora *SEE* MacDonald, Angus
MacDonald, Flora *SEE* MacDonald, Donald
MacDonald, Flora *SEE* MacDonald, John
MacDonald, Flora *SEE* MacDonald, Johnnie
MacDonald, Flora *SEE* MacDonald, Kirsty
MacDonald, Flora *SEE* MacDonald, Kirsty MacPhee
MacDonald, Flora *SEE* MacDonald, Lachlan
MacDonald, Flora *SEE* MacDonald, Marion
MacDonald, Flora *SEE* MacDonald, Marion Cunningham
MacDonald, Flora *SEE* MacDonald, Michael
MacDonald, Flora *SEE* MacDonald, Neil
MacDonald, Flora *SEE* MacDonald, Norman
MacDonald, Flora *SEE* MacDonald, Ranald
MacDonald, Flora *SEE* MacDonald, Roderick
MacDonald, Flora; Nova Scotia, 1868 ***4537.37*** *p18*
MacDonald, Flora; Ontario, 1849 ***4537.37*** *p74*
MacDonald, Flora; Ontario, 1851 ***4537.32*** *p8*
MacDonald, Flora; Port uncertain, 1840-1849 ***4537.37*** *p129*
MacDonald, Flora; Port uncertain, 1850-1859 ***4537.37*** *p116*
MacDonald, Flora Corbett; Ontario, 1851 ***4537.32*** *p31*
MacDonald, Flora Jane *SEE* MacDonald, Donald
MacDonald, Flora MacIsaac *SEE* MacDonald, Donald
MacDonald, Flora Nicolson *SEE* MacDonald, Donald
Macdonald, Florenica; Georgia, 1738 ***1640.10*** *p109*
MacDonald, Francis *SEE* MacDonald, Murdo
Macdonald, George; Georgia, 1736 ***1640.10*** *p109*
Macdonald, George; Georgia, 1741 ***1640.10*** *p109*
MacDonald, Godfrey *SEE* MacDonald, Archie
MacDonald, Hector *SEE* MacDonald, Donald
MacDonald, Hector *SEE* MacDonald, Murdo
MacDonald, Hector; Port uncertain, 1840-1849 ***4537.37*** *p112*
Wife: Catherine Currie
Child: Charles
Child: Allan
MacDonald, Hezekia Livingston; Vermont, 1837-1923 ***5900.10*** *p518*
MacDonald, Hugh *SEE* MacDonald, Allan
MacDonald, Hugh *SEE* MacDonald, Duncan
MacDonald, Hugh *SEE* MacDonald, John
Macdonald, Hugh; Georgia, 1736 ***1640.10*** *p109*
MacDonald, Isabella *SEE* MacDonald, Alexander
MacDonald, Isabella *SEE* MacDonald, Angus
MacDonald, Isabella *SEE* MacDonald, John
MacDonald, Isabella *SEE* MacDonald, Murdo
MacDonald, Isabella *SEE* MacDonald, Ranald
MacDonald, Isabella *SEE* MacDonald, Roderick
MacDonald, Isabella; Ontario, 1851 ***4537.32*** *p42*
MacDonald, Isabella; Port uncertain, 1840-1849 ***4537.37*** *p114*
Child: Slaine
Child: Murdo
Child: Alexander
Child: Marion
Child: William
MacDonald, Isabella; Port uncertain, 1850-1859 ***4537.37*** *p132*
MacDonald, Isabella MacIntyre *SEE* MacDonald, John
MacDonald, Isabella Martin *SEE* MacDonald, Roderick
MacDonald, Isabella Murray *SEE* MacDonald, Duncan
MacDonald, James *SEE* MacDonald, Angus
MacDonald, James *SEE* MacDonald, Donald
MacDonald, James *SEE* MacDonald, John
MacDonald, James *SEE* MacDonald, Roderick
MacDonald, James; Ontario, 1847-1849 ***4537.37*** *p46*
Wife: Sarah
MacDonald, James; Ontario, 1849 ***4537.32*** *p27*
Wife: Sarah
MacDonald, James; Port uncertain, 1840-1849 ***4537.37*** *p112*
Wife: Kirsty
Child: Lexy
MacDonald, Jane *SEE* MacDonald, Angus
MacDonald, Jane *SEE* MacDonald, Colin
MacDonald, Jane *SEE* MacDonald, Janet
MacDonald, Jane *SEE* MacDonald, John
MacDonald, Jane *SEE* MacDonald, Roderick
MacDonald, Jane; Ontario, 1851 ***4537.32*** *p56*
MacDonald, Janet *SEE* MacDonald, Alexander
MacDonald, Janet *SEE* MacDonald, Angus
MacDonald, Janet *SEE* MacDonald, Catherine Johnston
MacDonald, Janet *SEE* MacDonald, Donald
MacDonald, Janet *SEE* MacDonald, John
MacDonald, Janet *SEE* MacDonald, Kirsty MacPhee
MacDonald, Janet *SEE* MacDonald, Malcolm
MacDonald, Janet *SEE* MacDonald, Murdo
MacDonald, Janet *SEE* MacDonald, Norman
MacDonald, Janet *SEE* MacDonald, Ranald
MacDonald, Janet; Ontario, 1850-1859 ***4537.37*** *p82*
MacDonald, Janet; Ontario, 1851 ***4537.32*** *p15*
MacDonald, Janet; Ontario, 1851 ***4537.32*** *p90*
MacDonald, Janet; Prince Edward Island, 1848 ***4537.37*** *p25*
MacDonald, Janet; Saskatchewan, 1884 ***4537.37*** *p93*
Child: Mary
Child: Jane
Child: Lexy
Child: Alexander
MacDonald, Janet Grieve *SEE* MacDonald, Alexander
MacDonald, Janet MacIsaac *SEE* MacDonald, John
MacDonald, Jessie *SEE* MacDonald, Catherine
MacDonald, Jessie *SEE* MacDonald, Donald
MacDonald, Jessie *SEE* MacDonald, John
MacDonald, Jessie *SEE* MacDonald, Ranald
MacDonald, Jessie *SEE* MacDonald, Roderick
MacDonald, Joan *SEE* MacDonald, Donald
MacDonald, Joan *SEE* MacDonald, Duncan
MacDonald, John *SEE* MacDonald, Alexander
MacDonald, John *SEE* MacDonald, Allan
MacDonald, John *SEE* MacDonald, Angus
MacDonald, John *SEE* MacDonald, Ann
MacDonald, John *SEE* MacDonald, Ann MacKinnon
MacDonald, John *SEE* MacDonald, Archie
MacDonald, John *SEE* MacDonald, Catherine Campbell
MacDonald, John *SEE* MacDonald, Catherine Johnston
MacDonald, John *SEE* MacDonald, Catherine MacKinnon
MacDonald, John *SEE* MacDonald, Catherine MacLean
MacDonald, John *SEE* MacDonald, Donald
MacDonald, John *SEE* MacDonald, Duncan
MacDonald, John *SEE* MacDonald, Evander
MacDonald, John *SEE* MacDonald, Finlay
MacDonald, John *SEE* MacDonald, John
MacDonald, John *SEE* MacDonald, Kenneth
MacDonald, John *SEE* MacDonald, Kirsty
MacDonald, John *SEE* MacDonald, Lachlan
MacDonald, John *SEE* MacDonald, Malcolm
MacDonald, John *SEE* MacDonald, Marion
MacDonald, John *SEE* MacDonald, Mary Morrison
MacDonald, John *SEE* MacDonald, Michael
MacDonald, John *SEE* MacDonald, Murdo
Macdonald, John *SEE* Macdonald, Norman
MacDonald, John *SEE* MacDonald, Norman
MacDonald, John *SEE* MacDonald, Rachel
MacDonald, John *SEE* MacDonald, Ranald
MacDonald, John *SEE* MacDonald, Roderick
MacDonald, John *SEE* MacDonald, Slaine
MacDonald, John *SEE* MacDonald, William
Macdonald, John; Georgia, 1741 ***1640.10*** *p110*
MacDonald, John; Manitoba, 1888 ***4537.35*** *p65*
Wife: Kirsty MacLeod
Child: Catherine
Child: Donald
Child: William Harvey
MacDonald, John; Manitoba, 1888 ***4537.35*** *p66*
Wife: Mary Shaw
Child: Marion
Child: Neil
Child: Alexander
Child: Catherine
Child: Duncan
Child: Archie N.
Child: John
Child: Norman
MacDonald, John; Nova Scotia, 1834 ***4537.35*** *p18*
Wife: Ann MacLeod
Child: Sarah
Child: Norman
Child: Murdo
MacDonald, John; Nova Scotia, 1840-1849 ***4537.37*** *p12*
Wife: Mary
Child: Angus
Child: John
Child: Colin
Child: Kirsty
Child: Allan
MacDonald, John; Ontario, 1840-1849 ***4537.37*** *p46*
Wife: Ann
Child: Kirsty
Child: Mary
Child: Donald
Child: John
MacDonald, John; Ontario, 1840-1849 ***4537.37*** *p46*
Wife: Ann Walker
Child: Mary
Child: Angus
Child: Alexander
Child: Ann
Child: Donald
MacDonald, John; Ontario, 1840-1849 ***4537.37*** *p47*
Wife: Janet MacIsaac
Child: Rachel
Child: Effie
Child: John
Child: Roderick
Child: Jessie
Child: Donald
MacDonald, John; Ontario, 1840-1849 ***4537.37*** *p47*
Wife: Marion MacEachan
Child: Janet
Child: Ann
Child: Catherine
MacDonald, John; Ontario, 1840-1849 ***4537.37*** *p47*
Child: John
Child: Angus
Child: Ewen
Child: Donald
Child: Catherine
Wife: Marion MacIntyre
Child: Mary
MacDonald, John; Ontario, 1840-1849 ***4537.37*** *p48*
Wife: Mary MacPhee
Child: Kate
Child: John
Child: Dougal
Child: Mary
MacDonald, John; Ontario, 1840-1849 ***4537.37*** *p48*
Wife: Penny MacPhee
Child: Ann
Child: Donald
Child: Angus
Child: Kirsty
Child: Mary
MacDonald, John; Ontario, 1849 ***4537.32*** *p30*
Wife: Mary MacPhee
Child: John
Child: Dougal
Child: Kate
Child: Mary
MacDonald, John; Ontario, 1849 ***4537.32*** *p30*
Wife: Penny MacPhee
Child: Ann
Child: Kirsty
Child: Mary
Child: Donald
Child: Angus
MacDonald, John; Ontario, 1850-1859 ***4537.37*** *p46*
Wife: Catherine MacLellan
Child: Marion
Child: Alexander
Child: Kirsty
Child: Mary
Child: Angus
Child: Margaret
MacDonald, John; Ontario, 1850-1859 ***4537.37*** *p47*
Wife: Mary MacDougall
Child: Mary
Child: Alexander
Child: Archie
Child: Duncan
Child: Janet
MacDonald, John; Ontario, 1851 ***4537.32*** *p27*
Wife: Ann
Child: Margaret
MacDonald, John; Ontario, 1851 ***4537.32*** *p28*
Wife: Catherine MacLellan
Child: Margaret
Child: Alexander
Child: Kirsty
Child: Mary
Child: Marion
Child: Angus
MacDonald, John; Ontario, 1851 ***4537.32*** *p28*
Child: Ann
Child: Angus
Wife: Ann Matheson
Stepchild: Mary
Stepchild: Margaret
Child: John
Child: Flora
Stepchild: Ann
Stepchild: Isabella
Child: Margaret
Child: Catherine
MacDonald, John; Ontario, 1851 ***4537.32*** *p29*
Wife: Kirsty
MacDonald, John; Ontario, 1851 ***4537.32*** *p29*
Wife: Mary MacDougall
Child: Duncan
Child: Alexander

MacDonald, Mary; Ontario, 1850-1859 ***4537.37*** *p37*
MacDonald, Mary; Ontario, 1850-1859 ***4537.37*** *p39*
MacDonald, Mary; Ontario, 1850-1859 ***4537.37*** *p40*
MacDonald, Mary; Ontario, 1850-1859 ***4537.37*** *p66*
MacDonald, Mary; Ontario, 1850-1859 ***4537.37*** *p74*
MacDonald, Mary; Ontario, 1851 ***4537.32*** *p18*
MacDonald, Mary; Ontario, 1851 ***4537.32*** *p53*
MacDonald, Mary; Ontario, 1851 ***4537.32*** *p74*
MacDonald, Mary; Ontario, 1851 ***4537.32*** *p78*
MacDonald, Mary; Ontario, 1851 ***4537.32*** *p87*
MacDonald, Mary; Ontario, 1860-1869 ***4537.35*** *p62*
MacDonald, Mary; Ontario, 1862 ***4537.32*** *p85*
MacDonald, Mary; Ontario, 1863 ***4537.32*** *p9*
MacDonald, Mary; Ontario, 1863 ***4537.32*** *p46*
MacDonald, Mary; Ontario, 1863 ***4537.32*** *p87*
MacDonald, Mary; Quebec, 1855 ***4537.32*** *p59*
MacDonald, Mary; Saskatchewan, 1884 ***4537.37*** *p91*
MacDonald, Mary; Port uncertain, 1840-1849 ***4537.35*** *p81*
Child: Murdo
Child: Malcolm
Child: Marion
Child: Mary
Child: Alexander
MacDonald, Mary; Port uncertain, 1840-1849 ***4537.37*** *p120*
MacDonald, Mary; Port uncertain, 1840-1849 ***4537.37*** *p127*
MacDonald, Mary; Port uncertain, 1840-1849 ***4537.37*** *p129*
MacDonald, Mary; Port uncertain, 1850-1859 ***4537.37*** *p106*
MacDonald, Mary; Port uncertain, 1850-1859 ***4537.37*** *p118*
MacDonald, Mary Ann *SEE* MacDonald, Duncan
MacDonald, Mary Ann *SEE* MacDonald, John
MacDonald, Mary Ann *SEE* MacDonald, Lachlan
MacDonald, Mary Ann *SEE* MacDonald, Murdo
MacDonald, Mary Beaton *SEE* MacDonald, Ranald
MacDonald, Mary Belle *SEE* MacDonald, John
MacDonald, Mary Gillies *SEE* MacDonald, Roderick
MacDonald, Mary Lexy *SEE* MacDonald, Roderick
MacDonald, Mary M. *SEE* MacDonald, Johnnie
MacDonald, Mary MacDonald *SEE* MacDonald, Donald
MacDonald, Mary MacDougall *SEE* MacDonald, John
MacDonald, Mary MacFarlane; Ontario, 1855 ***4537.32*** *p32*
Child: Mary
Child: Alexander
Child: Ann
Child: Angus
Child: Margaret
Child: Murdo
MacDonald, Mary MacIsaac *SEE* MacDonald, Angus
MacDonald, Mary MacKay; Port uncertain, 1860-1869 ***4537.35*** *p81*
Child: Ann
Child: Thomas
Child: William
Child: Alexander
MacDonald, Mary MacLellan *SEE* MacDonald, Alexander
MacDonald, Mary MacLennan *SEE* MacDonald, John
MacDonald, Mary MacLeod *SEE* MacDonald, Alexander
MacDonald, Mary MacLeod *SEE* MacDonald, Donald
MacDonald, Mary MacPhee *SEE* MacDonald, Donald
MacDonald, Mary MacPhee *SEE* MacDonald, John
MacDonald, Mary MacPherson *SEE* MacDonald, John
MacDonald, Mary MacPherson *SEE* MacDonald, Peter
MacDonald, Mary MacRury *SEE* MacDonald, Roderick
MacDonald, Mary Martin *SEE* MacDonald, Murdo
MacDonald, Mary Matheson *SEE* MacDonald, Murdo
MacDonald, Mary Morrison *SEE* MacDonald, Angus
MacDonald, Mary Morrison; Saskatchewan, 1889 ***4537.35*** *p66*
Child: Donald
Child: Alexander
Child: Kirsty
Child: Ann
Child: John
MacDonald, Mary Ross *SEE* MacDonald, John
MacDonald, Mary Sarah *SEE* MacDonald, Duncan
MacDonald, Mary Shaw *SEE* MacDonald, John
MacDonald, Michael *SEE* MacDonald, Donald
MacDonald, Michael; Nova Scotia, 1840-1849 ***4537.37*** *p13*
Wife: Margaret
Child: John
Child: Flora
Child: Donald
Child: Mary
Child: Angus
Child: Alexander
Child: Ann
MacDonald, Morgana *SEE* MacDonald, Sam
MacDonald, Murdo *SEE* MacDonald, Angus
MacDonald, Murdo *SEE* MacDonald, Donald
MacDonald, Murdo *SEE* MacDonald, Duncan
MacDonald, Murdo *SEE* MacDonald, Finlay
MacDonald, Murdo *SEE* MacDonald, Isabella
MacDonald, Murdo *SEE* MacDonald, John
MacDonald, Murdo *SEE* MacDonald, Kenneth
MacDonald, Murdo *SEE* MacDonald, Mary
MacDonald, Murdo *SEE* MacDonald, Mary MacFarlane
MacDonald, Murdo *SEE* MacDonald, Murdo
MacDonald, Murdo *SEE* MacDonald, Neil
MacDonald, Murdo *SEE* MacDonald, Roderick
MacDonald, Murdo; Ontario, 1850-1859 ***4537.32*** *p32*
Wife: Mary Martin
Child: Nathaniel
Child: Murdo
Child: Donald
Child: Mary Ann
Child: Margaret
Child: Catherine
Child: Janet
Child: Francis
Child: Alexander
MacDonald, Murdo; Ontario, 1863 ***4537.32*** *p33*
Wife: Mary Matheson
Child: Mary
Child: Colin
Child: Donald
MacDonald, Murdo; Quebec, 1860-1869 ***4537.35*** *p63*
Wife: Kirsty Campbell
Child: Mary
Child: Catherine
Child: Finlay
Child: Roderick
Child: Effie
Child: Alexander
MacDonald, Murdo; Port uncertain, 1840-1849 ***4537.35*** *p81*
Wife: Catherine
Child: Donald
Child: Angus
Child: Mary
Child: John
Child: Peter
MacDonald, Murdo; Port uncertain, 1840-1849 ***4537.37*** *p113*
Wife: Margaret
Child: Hector
Child: Catherine
Child: Mary
MacDonald, Murdo; Port uncertain, 1840-1849 ***4537.37*** *p113*
Wife: Mary
Child: Donald
Child: Mary
Child: Marion
Child: Isabella
MacDonald, Murdock 79; Ontario, 1871 ***1823.15*** *p150*
MacDonald, Nathaniel *SEE* MacDonald, Murdo
MacDonald, Neil *SEE* MacDonald, Alexander
MacDonald, Neil *SEE* MacDonald, Angus
MacDonald, Neil *SEE* MacDonald, Ann MacKinnon
MacDonald, Neil *SEE* MacDonald, Archie
MacDonald, Neil *SEE* MacDonald, Catherine
MacDonald, Neil *SEE* MacDonald, Donald
MacDonald, Neil *SEE* MacDonald, John
MacDonald, Neil *SEE* MacDonald, Neil
MacDonald, Neil *SEE* MacDonald, Ranald
MacDonald, Neil *SEE* MacDonald, William
MacDonald, Neil; Nova Scotia, 1820-1829 ***4537.35*** *p19*
Wife: Rachel
Child: Roderick
Child: Norman
Child: Neil
MacDonald, Neil; Nova Scotia, 1840-1849 ***4537.35*** *p18*
Wife: Mary
Child: Angus
Child: Catherine
Child: Donald
MacDonald, Neil; Nova Scotia, 1842 ***4537.37*** *p13*
Wife: Flora
Child: Donald
Child: Catherine
Child: Mary
Child: Margaret
Child: Archie
Child: Angus
MacDonald, Neil; Ontario, 1860-1869 ***4537.35*** *p57*
Wife: Margaret
Child: Rachel
Child: Sarah
Child: Murdo
Child: Kirsty
Child: Alexander
MacDonald, Neil; Ontario, 1862 ***4537.32*** *p33*
Wife: Margaret
Child: Alexander
Child: Rachel
MacDonald, Neil; Port uncertain, 1850-1859 ***4537.37*** *p113*
Relative: Marion
Child: Mary
Child: Lachlan
Child: Catherine
Child: Angus
Child: Donald
MacDonald, Norman *SEE* MacDonald, Alexander
MacDonald, Norman *SEE* MacDonald, Angus
MacDonald, Norman *SEE* MacDonald, Donald
MacDonald, Norman *SEE* MacDonald, John
MacDonald, Norman *SEE* MacDonald, John Donn
MacDonald, Norman *SEE* MacDonald, Marion Cunningham
MacDonald, Norman *SEE* MacDonald, Neil
MacDonald, Norman *SEE* MacDonald, Roderick
Macdonald, Norman; Georgia, 1741 ***1640.10*** *p111*
Wife: Elizabeth Mackay
Child: John
Child: Catherine
MacDonald, Norman; Ontario, 1855 ***4537.32*** *p33*
Wife: Margaret Matheson
MacDonald, Norman; Saskatchewan, 1884 ***4537.37*** *p96*
Wife: Kirsty MacAulay
Child: Mary
Child: Angus
MacDonald, Norman; Port uncertain, 1840-1849 ***4537.35*** *p81*
Wife: Catherine
Child: Ann
Child: Donald
Child: Alexander
Child: Roderick
Child: Catherine
Child: Effie
Child: Flora
MacDonald, Norman; Port uncertain, 1840-1849 ***4537.37*** *p113*
Wife: Janet
Child: Catherine
Child: Angus
Child: Ann
Child: John
MacDonald, Norman; Port uncertain, 1850-1859 ***4537.37*** *p113*
Wife: Ann
Child: Marion
Child: Donald
Child: Lexy
Child: Catherine
Child: Angus
Child: Kirsty
MacDonald, Patrick; Jamaica, 1772 ***1640.13*** *p85*
MacDonald, Peggy *SEE* MacDonald, Angus
MacDonald, Peggy *SEE* MacDonald, John
MacDonald, Peggy *SEE* MacDonald, Lachlan
MacDonald, Penny *SEE* MacDonald, Alexander
MacDonald, Penny *SEE* MacDonald, Angus
MacDonald, Penny; Port uncertain, 1850-1859 ***4537.37*** *p120*
MacDonald, Penny MacEachan *SEE* MacDonald, Alexander
MacDonald, Penny MacPhee *SEE* MacDonald, John
MacDonald, Peter *SEE* MacDonald, Ann
MacDonald, Peter *SEE* MacDonald, Donald
MacDonald, Peter *SEE* MacDonald, Murdo
MacDonald, Peter; Port uncertain, 1840-1849 ***4537.37*** *p113*
Wife: Mary MacPherson
Child: Malcolm
Child: Mary
MacDonald, Rachel *SEE* MacDonald, John
MacDonald, Rachel *SEE* MacDonald, Marion Cunningham
MacDonald, Rachel *SEE* MacDonald, Marion MacKay
MacDonald, Rachel *SEE* MacDonald, Neil
MacDonald, Rachel *SEE* MacDonald, Roderick
Macdonald, Rachel; Georgia, 1738 ***1640.10*** *p111*
MacDonald, Rachel; Port uncertain, 1840-1849 ***4537.37*** *p115*
Child: Roderick
Child: John
MacDonald, Rachel; Port uncertain, 1860-1869 ***4537.37*** *p123*

MacDougall, John *SEE* MacDougall, Angus
MacDougall, John *SEE* MacDougall, Archie
MacDougall, John; Saskatchewan, 1884 ***4537.37*** *p97*
Wife: Catherine MacCormick
MacDougall, John L. *SEE* MacDougall, Donald
MacDougall, Julia; Port uncertain, 1840-1849 ***4537.37*** *p107*
MacDougall, Malcolm *SEE* MacDougall, Angus
MacDougall, Margaret *SEE* MacDougall, Angus
MacDougall, Margaret *SEE* MacDougall, Archie
MacDougall, Margaret *SEE* MacDougall, Norman
MacDougall, Margaret MacSween *SEE* MacDougall, Donald
MacDougall, Mary; Ontario, 1849 ***4537.37*** *p36*
MacDougall, Mary; Ontario, 1850-1859 ***4537.37*** *p47*
MacDougall, Mary; Ontario, 1851 ***4537.32*** *p29*
MacDougall, Mary; Port uncertain, 1850-1859 ***4537.37*** *p119*
MacDougall, Norman; Port uncertain, 1840-1849 ***4537.37*** *p115*
Sibling: Margaret
Sibling: Jane
MacDowell, Mary; Maryland, 1658 ***2524.55*** *p141*
MacDowell, Willm.; Maryland, 1658 ***2524.55*** *p141*
Mace, Rowland; Maryland, 1643 ***2524.55*** *p141*
Mace, Sandford; Georgia, 1745 ***1224.2*** *p75*
Mace, Thomas; New York, 1815 ***8197.10*** *p56*
MacEachan, Alexander *SEE* MacEachan, Donald
MacEachan, Alexander *SEE* MacEachan, John
MacEachan, Alexander *SEE* MacEachan, Malcolm
MacEachan, Alexander *SEE* MacEachan, Roderick
MacEachan, Alexander; Ontario, 1840-1849 ***4537.37*** *p50*
Wife: Mary MacKinnon
Child: Lachlan
Child: Angus
Child: Mary
Child: Ann
Child: Donald
Child: Catherine
Child: John
MacEachan, Allan *SEE* MacEachan, Donald
MacEachan, Angus *SEE* MacEachan, Alexander
MacEachan, Angus *SEE* MacEachan, Angus
MacEachan, Angus *SEE* MacEachan, Donald
MacEachan, Angus *SEE* MacEachan, John
MacEachan, Angus; Port uncertain, 1850-1859 ***4537.37*** *p115*
Child: Catherine
Child: Angus
Child: Margaret
Wife: Mary MacIsaac
Child: John
MacEachan, Ann *SEE* MacEachan, Alexander
MacEachan, Ann *SEE* MacEachan, Charles
MacEachan, Ann *SEE* MacEachan, Malcolm
MacEachan, Ann *SEE* MacEachan, Neil
MacEachan, Ann *SEE* MacEachan, Roderick
MacEachan, Ann; Ontario, 1851 ***4537.32*** *p20*
MacEachan, Ann; Pictou, Nova Scotia, 1848 ***4537.37*** *p29*
MacEachan, Ann; Port uncertain, 1850-1859 ***4537.37*** *p109*
MacEachan, Catherine *SEE* MacEachan, Alexander
MacEachan, Catherine *SEE* MacEachan, Angus
MacEachan, Catherine *SEE* MacEachan, John
MacEachan, Catherine *SEE* MacEachan, Malcolm
MacEachan, Catherine *SEE* MacEachan, Neil
MacEachan, Catherine; Ontario, 1840-1849 ***4537.37*** *p41*
MacEachan, Catherine; Ontario, 1840-1849 ***4537.37*** *p53*
MacEachan, Catherine MacIntyre *SEE* MacEachan, Neil
MacEachan, Catherine MacIsaac *SEE* MacEachan, Donald
MacEachan, Catherine O'Henley *SEE* MacEachan, John
MacEachan, Charles; Nova Scotia, 1840-1849 ***4537.37*** *p14*
Wife: Marion Morrison
Child: Donald
Child: Marion
Child: Margaret
Child: Ann
MacEachan, Donald *SEE* MacEachan, Alexander
MacEachan, Donald *SEE* MacEachan, Charles
MacEachan, Donald *SEE* MacEachan, John
MacEachan, Donald *SEE* MacEachan, Neil
MacEachan, Donald *SEE* MacEachan, Ranald
MacEachan, Donald; Ontario, 1849 ***4537.37*** *p50*
Wife: Catherine MacIsaac
Child: Mary
Sister: Mary
MacEachan, Donald; Ontario, 1850-1859 ***4537.37*** *p51*
Child: Ranald
Child: Allan
Child: John
Wife: Kirsty MacInnes
Child: Mary
Child: Duncan
Child: Marion
MacEachan, Donald; Ontario, 1850-1859 ***4537.37*** *p51*
Wife: Margaret MacDonald
Child: Angus
Child: Sarah
Child: Alexander
Child: Mary
Child: Effie
MacEachan, Donald; Ontario, 1851 ***4537.32*** *p36*
Wife: Kirsty MacInnes
Child: John
Child: Marion
Child: Mary
Child: Allan
Child: Ranald
Child: Duncan
MacEachan, Duncan *SEE* MacEachan, Donald
MacEachan, Effie *SEE* MacEachan, Donald
MacEachan, Effie *SEE* MacEachan, John
MacEachan, Effie *SEE* MacEachan, Roderick
MacEachan, Effie; Ontario, 1840-1849 ***4537.37*** *p75*
MacEachan, Eliza; Ontario, 1850-1859 ***4537.37*** *p34*
MacEachan, Eliza; Ontario, 1851 ***4537.32*** *p8*
MacEachan, Emily Ferguson *SEE* MacEachan, Neil
MacEachan, Ewen *SEE* MacEachan, John
MacEachan, Flora *SEE* MacEachan, Neil
MacEachan, Flora; Ontario, 1848 ***4537.37*** *p61*
MacEachan, Flora; Port uncertain, 1840-1849 ***4537.37*** *p119*
MacEachan, Hector *SEE* MacEachan, Malcolm
MacEachan, Hector *SEE* MacEachan, Neil
MacEachan, Jane *SEE* MacEachan, Malcolm
MacEachan, Janet *SEE* MacEachan, John
MacEachan, Janet *SEE* MacEachan, Neil
MacEachan, Janet; Ontario, 1840-1849 ***4537.37*** *p56*
MacEachan, Janet; Ontario, 1850-1859 ***4537.37*** *p41*
MacEachan, Janet; Ontario, 1851 ***4537.37*** *p63*
MacEachan, John *SEE* MacEachan, Alexander
MacEachan, John *SEE* MacEachan, Angus
MacEachan, John *SEE* MacEachan, Donald
MacEachan, John *SEE* MacEachan, John
MacEachan, John *SEE* MacEachan, Neil
MacEachan, John *SEE* MacEachan, Ranald
MacEachan, John; Port uncertain, 1840-1849 ***4537.37*** *p115*
Wife: Catherine
MacEachan, John; Port uncertain, 1840-1849 ***4537.37*** *p115*
Wife: Catherine O'Henley
Child: John
Child: Neil
Child: Margaret
Child: Ewen
Child: Janet
MacEachan, John; Port uncertain, 1840-1849 ***4537.37*** *p115*
Wife: Effie
Child: Marion
Child: Angus
Child: Donald
MacEachan, John; Port uncertain, 1840-1849 ***4537.37*** *p115*
Wife: Marion MacDonald
Child: Catherine
Child: Alexander
Child: Ranald
Child: John
Child: Mary
MacEachan, Kate *SEE* MacEachan, Neil
MacEachan, Kirsty *SEE* MacEachan, Malcolm
MacEachan, Kirsty *SEE* MacEachan, Roderick
MacEachan, Kirsty; Ontario, 1848 ***4537.37*** *p59*
MacEachan, Kirsty MacInnes *SEE* MacEachan, Donald
MacEachan, Kirsty MacIntyre *SEE* MacEachan, Neil
MacEachan, Lachlan *SEE* MacEachan, Alexander
MacEachan, Malcolm; Ontario, 1840-1849 ***4537.37*** *p51*
Wife: Mary MacInnes
Child: Marion
Child: Jane
Child: Kirsty
Child: Hector
Child: Alexander
Child: Catherine
Child: Ann
MacEachan, Margaret *SEE* MacEachan, Angus
MacEachan, Margaret *SEE* MacEachan, Charles
MacEachan, Margaret *SEE* MacEachan, John
MacEachan, Margaret *SEE* MacEachan, Roderick
MacEachan, Margaret; Ontario, 1849 ***4537.37*** *p84*
MacEachan, Margaret; Port uncertain, 1840-1849 ***4537.37*** *p114*
MacEachan, Margaret MacDonald *SEE* MacEachan, Donald
MacEachan, Margaret O'Henley *SEE* MacEachan, Ranald
MacEachan, Marion *SEE* MacEachan, Charles
MacEachan, Marion *SEE* MacEachan, Donald
MacEachan, Marion *SEE* MacEachan, John
MacEachan, Marion *SEE* MacEachan, Malcolm
MacEachan, Marion *SEE* MacEachan, Neil
MacEachan, Marion *SEE* MacEachan, Roderick
MacEachan, Marion; Ontario, 1840-1849 ***4537.37*** *p47*
MacEachan, Marion; Ontario, 1851 ***4537.32*** *p38*
MacEachan, Marion; Ontario, 1851 ***4537.37*** *p55*
MacEachan, Marion MacDonald *SEE* MacEachan, John
MacEachan, Marion MacLeod *SEE* MacEachan, Roderick
MacEachan, Marion Morrison *SEE* MacEachan, Charles
MacEachan, Mary *SEE* MacEachan, Alexander
MacEachan, Mary *SEE* MacEachan, Donald
MacEachan, Mary *SEE* MacEachan, John
MacEachan, Mary *SEE* MacEachan, Neil
MacEachan, Mary *SEE* MacEachan, Roderick
MacEachan, Mary; Ontario, 1850-1859 ***4537.37*** *p64*
MacEachan, Mary; Ontario, 1851 ***4537.37*** *p61*
MacEachan, Mary; Prince Edward Island, 1848 ***4537.37*** *p24*
MacEachan, Mary Campbell *SEE* MacEachan, Neil
MacEachan, Mary Currie *SEE* MacEachan, Ranald
MacEachan, Mary MacInnes *SEE* MacEachan, Malcolm
MacEachan, Mary MacIsaac *SEE* MacEachan, Angus
MacEachan, Mary MacKinnon *SEE* MacEachan, Alexander
MacEachan, Neil *SEE* MacEachan, John
MacEachan, Neil *SEE* MacEachan, Neil
MacEachan, Neil; Ontario, 1849 ***4537.37*** *p51*
Wife: Catherine MacIntyre
MacEachan, Neil; Ontario, 1849 ***4537.37*** *p52*
Wife: Emily Ferguson
Child: Marion
Child: John
Child: Flora
Child: Norman
Child: Janet
Child: Catherine
Child: Neil
MacEachan, Neil; Ontario, 1849 ***4537.37*** *p52*
Wife: Kirsty MacIntyre
Child: Marion
Child: Neil
Child: Donald
Child: Mary
Child: Catherine
Child: Roderick
Child: John
MacEachan, Neil; Port uncertain, 1840-1849 ***4537.37*** *p115*
Wife: Mary Campbell
Child: Hector
Child: John
Child: Donald
Child: Mary
Child: Ann
Child: Kate
MacEachan, Norman *SEE* MacEachan, Neil
MacEachan, Penny; Nova Scotia, 1840-1849 ***4537.37*** *p21*
MacEachan, Penny; Ontario, 1850-1859 ***4537.37*** *p43*
MacEachan, Penny; Prince Edward Island, 1841 ***4537.37*** *p24*
MacEachan, Ranald *SEE* MacEachan, Donald
MacEachan, Ranald *SEE* MacEachan, John
MacEachan, Ranald; Saskatchewan, 1884 ***4537.37*** *p97*
Wife: Margaret O'Henley
Child: Donald
MacEachan, Ranald; Port uncertain, 1850-1859 ***4537.37*** *p115*
Wife: Mary Currie
Child: John
MacEachan, Ranald; Port uncertain, 1850-1859 ***4537.37*** *p116*
Wife: Sarah MacPhee
MacEachan, Roderick *SEE* MacEachan, Neil
MacEachan, Roderick; Ontario, 1851 ***4537.37*** *p52*
Wife: Marion MacLeod
Child: Kirsty
Child: Margaret
Child: Alexander
Child: Marion
Child: Ann
Child: Mary
Child: Effie

MacEachan, Sarah *SEE* MacEachan, Donald
MacEachan, Sarah MacPhee *SEE* MacEachan, Ranald
MacEachnie, Samuel; Tobago, West Indies, 1840 ***1640.13*** *p85*
Maceever, Evander; Georgia, 1737 ***1640.10*** *p113*
Maceever, Roderick; Georgia, 1738 ***1640.10*** *p113*
Macek, Frances; Maryland, 1910 ***3259.35*** *p36*
Macek, Miela; Maryland, 1910 ***3259.35*** *p36*
Macer, Alexander; Georgia, 1740 ***1640.10*** *p148*
MacEwan, George William; Toronto, 1881 ***1640.13*** *p85*
Macfarlan, Frederick, Jr.; New York, 1827 ***8197.10*** *p345*
Macfarlan, Thomas; New York, 1827 ***8197.10*** *p345*
MacFarland, Susan 75; Vermont, 1879 ***5900.10*** *p455*
MacFarlane, Angus *SEE* MacFarlane, John
MacFarlane, Angus; Ontario, 1851 ***4537.32*** *p36*
Wife: Kirsty Murray
Child: Mary
MacFarlane, Ann MacIver *SEE* MacFarlane, John
Macfarlane, Duncan; Georgia, 1734 ***1640.10*** *p113*
MacFarlane, Flora; Port uncertain, 1870-1879 ***4537.35*** *p85*
MacFarlane, Isabella; Ontario, 1863 ***4537.32*** *p55*
MacFarlane, Jessie Gillies; Ontario, 1851 ***4537.32*** *p36*
Macfarlane, John; New York, 1839 ***8197.10*** *p141*
MacFarlane, John; Ontario, 1851 ***4537.32*** *p36*
Wife: Ann MacIver
Child: Murdo
Child: Malcolm
Child: Margaret
Child: Angus
MacFarlane, Kirsty Murray *SEE* MacFarlane, Angus
MacFarlane, Malcolm *SEE* MacFarlane, John
MacFarlane, Malcolm; Ontario, 1851 ***4537.32*** *p37*
Wife: Marion MacLeod
MacFarlane, Margaret *SEE* MacFarlane, John
MacFarlane, Marion MacLeod *SEE* MacFarlane, Malcolm
MacFarlane, Mary *SEE* MacFarlane, Angus
MacFarlane, Mary; Ontario, 1855 ***4537.32*** *p32*
MacFarlane, Murdo *SEE* MacFarlane, John
MacFaull, John; New York, 1806 ***8197.10*** *p322*
Macfie, James 44; Ontario, 1871 ***1823.28*** *p59*
Macfrary, James; Georgia, 1757 ***1640.10*** *p113*
MacGregor, Alexander; Ontario, 1855 ***4537.32*** *p37*
Wife: Kirsty MacKay
Child: John
Child: Murdo
Child: Margaret
MacGregor, Angus *SEE* MacGregor, Donald
MacGregor, Ann *SEE* MacGregor, Donald
MacGregor, Catherine MacDonald *SEE* MacGregor, Donald
MacGregor, Coll; New York, 1793 ***8197.10*** *p1*
MacGregor, Donald *SEE* MacGregor, Malcolm
MacGregor, Donald; Ontario, 1851 ***4537.32*** *p37*
Wife: Catherine MacDonald
Child: Angus
Child: Murdo
Child: John
Child: Ann
Child: Margaret
MacGregor, Duncan *SEE* MacGregor, Malcolm
Macgregor, Gregory; Georgia, 1738 ***1640.10*** *p116*
Macgregor, Jane; Georgia, 1734 ***1640.10*** *p116*
MacGregor, John *SEE* MacGregor, Alexander
MacGregor, John *SEE* MacGregor, Donald
MacGregor, Kirsty *SEE* MacGregor, Malcolm
MacGregor, Kirsty MacKay *SEE* MacGregor, Alexander
MacGregor, Kirsty MacKay *SEE* MacGregor, Malcolm
MacGregor, Malcolm; Ontario, 1851 ***4537.32*** *p37*
Wife: Kirsty MacKay
Child: Mary
Child: Kirsty
Child: Donald
Child: Duncan
MacGregor, Margaret *SEE* MacGregor, Alexander
MacGregor, Margaret *SEE* MacGregor, Donald
MacGregor, Mary *SEE* MacGregor, Malcolm
MacGregor, Murdo *SEE* MacGregor, Alexander
MacGregor, Murdo *SEE* MacGregor, Donald
Macgregor, William; Georgia, 1759 ***1640.10*** *p116*
Macguire, Peter 17; Maryland, 1775 ***1220.25*** *p120*
Mach, Frank; Maryland, 1910 ***3259.35*** *p36*
Mach, Marian; Maryland, 1910 ***3259.35*** *p36*
Macha, Joseph; Maryland, 1910 ***3259.35*** *p36*
Machalak, Lucy; Maryland, 1910 ***3259.35*** *p36*
Machan, Robert 27; Ontario, 1871 ***1823.15*** *p150*
Machan, William 33; Ontario, 1871 ***1823.15*** *p150*
Machanich, Nicholas; New York, New York, 1888 ***3437.14*** *p144*
Machanicher, Nicholas; New York, New York, 1888 ***3437.14*** *p144*
Machattie, Mr.; Quebec, 1857 ***9196.15*** *p26*
Machay, Robert; Maryland, 1682 ***2524.55*** *p141*
Machelder, Alexander; Maryland, 1671 ***2524.55*** *p141*
Machen, Jno; Virginia, 1664 ***6212.30*** *p11*
Macher, Peter; Maryland, 1910 ***3259.35*** *p36*
Machin, Owen; New York, 1839 ***8197.10*** *p264*
Machjeski, Marian; Maryland, 1910 ***3259.35*** *p36*
Machku, Andrew; Maryland, 1910 ***3259.35*** *p36*
Machlin, Edward; New York, 1830 ***8197.10*** *p312*
Machmer, Wilhelm; Port uncertain, 1764 ***2856.30*** *p282*
Machnaik, Antonie; Maryland, 1910 ***3259.35*** *p36*
Machoney, Teage; Maryland, 1671 ***2524.55*** *p141*
Machor, Matthew 40; Ontario, 1871 ***1823.28*** *p59*
Machrie, James; New York, 1832 ***8197.10*** *p357*
Machsynski, Alex; Maryland, 1910 ***3259.35*** *p36*
Maciewjewski, Henry J.; Maryland, 1910 ***3259.35*** *p36*
MacInnes, Agnes *SEE* MacInnes, Archie
MacInnes, Alexander *SEE* MacInnes, Donald
MacInnes, Alexander *SEE* MacInnes, James
MacInnes, Alexander *SEE* MacInnes, Neil
MacInnes, Alexander; Ontario, 1840-1849 ***4537.37*** *p52*
Wife: Mary
Child: Effie
Child: Peter
Child: Donald
Child: Kate
MacInnes, Alexander; Port uncertain, 1840-1849 ***4537.37*** *p116*
Wife: Catherine
Child: Kate
Child: Donald
Child: John
Child: Peter
MacInnes, Alexander; Port uncertain, 1840-1849 ***4537.37*** *p116*
Wife: Effie
Child: Margaret
Child: Jessie
Child: John
MacInnes, Alexander; Port uncertain, 1850-1859 ***4537.37*** *p116*
Wife: Effie
Child: Janet
Child: John
MacInnes, Allan *SEE* MacInnes, Angus
MacInnes, Allan *SEE* MacInnes, Malcolm
MacInnes, Allan *SEE* MacInnes, Neil
MacInnes, Allan *SEE* MacInnes, Ranald
MacInnes, Angus *SEE* MacInnes, Malcolm
MacInnes, Angus *SEE* MacInnes, Ranald
MacInnes, Angus; Ontario, 1840-1849 ***4537.37*** *p53*
Wife: Catherine Morrison
Child: Effie
Child: Donald
Child: Allan
Child: Marion
Child: Eliza
Child: John
Child: Margaret
MacInnes, Angus; Port uncertain, 1840-1849 ***4537.37*** *p116*
Wife: Catherine Walker
Child: John
Child: Roderick
Child: Catherine
MacInnes, Ann *SEE* MacInnes, Donald
MacInnes, Ann *SEE* MacInnes, Finlay
MacInnes, Ann *SEE* MacInnes, Malcolm
MacInnes, Ann *SEE* MacInnes, Neil
MacInnes, Ann *SEE* MacInnes, Peter
MacInnes, Ann; Ontario, 1840-1849 ***4537.37*** *p73*
MacInnes, Ann; Ontario, 1850-1859 ***4537.37*** *p49*
MacInnes, Ann; Ontario, 1851 ***4537.32*** *p33*
MacInnes, Ann; Ontario, 1851 ***4537.32*** *p65*
MacInnes, Ann; Port uncertain, 1850-1859 ***4537.37*** *p124*
MacInnes, Ann MacLean *SEE* MacInnes, Donald
MacInnes, Archie *SEE* MacInnes, Archie
MacInnes, Archie *SEE* MacInnes, Donald
MacInnes, Archie *SEE* MacInnes, Lachlan
MacInnes, Archie *SEE* MacInnes, Peter
MacInnes, Archie; Nova Scotia, 1840-1849 ***4537.37*** *p14*
Wife: Margaret
Child: Jane
Child: John
Child: Archie
Child: Agnes
Child: Dougal
MacInnes, Catherine *SEE* MacInnes, Alexander
MacInnes, Catherine *SEE* MacInnes, Angus
MacInnes, Catherine *SEE* MacInnes, Donald
MacInnes, Catherine *SEE* MacInnes, Effie
MacInnes, Catherine *SEE* MacInnes, John
MacInnes, Catherine *SEE* MacInnes, Malcolm
MacInnes, Catherine *SEE* MacInnes, Neil
MacInnes, Catherine *SEE* MacInnes, Peter
MacInnes, Catherine; Canada, 1890-1899 ***4537.35*** *p73*
MacInnes, Catherine; Nova Scotia, 1850-1859 ***4537.37*** *p18*
MacInnes, Catherine; Ontario, 1849 ***4537.37*** *p57*
MacInnes, Catherine; Ontario, 1851 ***4537.32*** *p73*
MacInnes, Catherine; Port uncertain, 1840-1849 ***4537.37*** *p128*
MacInnes, Catherine; Port uncertain, 1840-1849 ***4537.37*** *p133*
MacInnes, Catherine; Port uncertain, 1850-1859 ***4537.37*** *p118*
MacInnes, Catherine Campbell *SEE* MacInnes, Donald
MacInnes, Catherine MacEachan; Ontario, 1840-1849 ***4537.37*** *p53*
MacInnes, Catherine MacIntyre *SEE* MacInnes, Donald
MacInnes, Catherine MacMillan *SEE* MacInnes, Neil
MacInnes, Catherine Morrison *SEE* MacInnes, Angus
MacInnes, Catherine Smith *SEE* MacInnes, John
MacInnes, Catherine Walker *SEE* MacInnes, Angus
MacInnes, Colin *SEE* MacInnes, Donald
MacInnes, Donald *SEE* MacInnes, Alexander
MacInnes, Donald *SEE* MacInnes, Angus
MacInnes, Donald *SEE* MacInnes, Donald
MacInnes, Donald *SEE* MacInnes, Finlay
MacInnes, Donald *SEE* MacInnes, Malcolm
MacInnes, Donald *SEE* MacInnes, Neil
MacInnes, Donald *SEE* MacInnes, Ranald
MacInnes, Donald; Nova Scotia, 1840-1849 ***4537.37*** *p14*
Wife: Mary
Child: Alexander
Child: Donald
Child: Mary
Child: John
Child: Hugh
MacInnes, Donald; Ontario, 1849 ***4537.37*** *p53*
Child: Kirsty
Child: Finlay
Wife: Marion O'Henley
MacInnes, Donald; Ontario, 1851 ***4537.37*** *p53*
Wife: Margaret Morrison
Child: Catherine
Child: Colin
Child: Neil
Child: Margaret
Child: John
Child: Malcolm
Child: Marion
MacInnes, Donald; Saskatchewan, 1884 ***4537.37*** *p97*
Wife: Mary MacKenzie
Child: Mary
Child: Flora
Child: Kirsty
Child: Margaret
MacInnes, Donald; Port uncertain, 1840-1849 ***4537.37*** *p116*
Wife: Ann MacLean
Child: Donald
Child: Catherine
Child: Effie
Child: Archie
Child: Margaret
MacInnes, Donald; Port uncertain, 1840-1849 ***4537.37*** *p116*
Wife: Marion Johnston
Child: John
Child: Mary
Child: Ann
Child: Alexander
Child: Malcolm
Child: James
MacInnes, Donald; Port uncertain, 1840-1849 ***4537.37*** *p116*
Wife: Mary Gordon
Child: Kenneth
Child: Dougal
MacInnes, Donald; Port uncertain, 1850-1859 ***4537.37*** *p116*
Child: Malcolm
Child: Roderick
Child: Duncan
Child: John
Child: Marion
Child: Flora
Wife: Catherine Campbell
MacInnes, Donald; Port uncertain, 1850-1859 ***4537.37*** *p116*
Wife: Catherine MacIntyre
Child: Mary
MacInnes, Dougal *SEE* MacInnes, Archie
MacInnes, Dougal *SEE* MacInnes, Donald
MacInnes, Duncan *SEE* MacInnes, Donald
MacInnes, Duncan *SEE* MacInnes, John

MacInnes, Effie *SEE* MacInnes, Alexander
MacInnes, Effie *SEE* MacInnes, Angus
MacInnes, Effie *SEE* MacInnes, Donald
MacInnes, Effie; Port uncertain, 1840-1849 ***4537.37*** *p117*
Child: Kirsty
Child: Catherine
Child: Mary
MacInnes, Eliza *SEE* MacInnes, Angus
MacInnes, Evander *SEE* MacInnes, Finlay
MacInnes, Ewen *SEE* MacInnes, Malcolm
MacInnes, Finlay *SEE* MacInnes, Donald
MacInnes, Finlay *SEE* MacInnes, Lachlan
MacInnes, Finlay *SEE* MacInnes, Neil
MacInnes, Finlay; Port uncertain, 1840-1849 ***4537.35*** *p81*
With wife
Child: John
Child: Donald
Child: Ann
MacInnes, Finlay; Port uncertain, 1860-1869 ***4537.35*** *p81*
Wife: Marion Kerr
Child: Peter
Child: Margaret
Child: Evander
MacInnes, Flora *SEE* MacInnes, Donald
MacInnes, Flora *SEE* MacInnes, Ranald
MacInnes, Flora MacDonald *SEE* MacInnes, John
MacInnes, Hugh *SEE* MacInnes, Donald
MacInnes, James *SEE* MacInnes, Donald
MacInnes, James *SEE* MacInnes, John
MacInnes, James *SEE* MacInnes, Lachlan
MacInnes, James; Port uncertain, 1840-1849 ***4537.37*** *p116*
Wife: Marion MacDonald
Child: John
Child: Mary
Child: Alexander
MacInnes, Jane *SEE* MacInnes, Archie
MacInnes, Janet *SEE* MacInnes, Alexander
MacInnes, Janet; Port uncertain, 1850-1859 ***4537.37*** *p132*
MacInnes, Jessie *SEE* MacInnes, Alexander
MacInnes, John *SEE* MacInnes, Alexander
MacInnes, John *SEE* MacInnes, Angus
MacInnes, John *SEE* MacInnes, Archie
MacInnes, John *SEE* MacInnes, Donald
MacInnes, John *SEE* MacInnes, Finlay
MacInnes, John *SEE* MacInnes, James
MacInnes, John *SEE* MacInnes, John
MacInnes, John *SEE* MacInnes, Malcolm
MacInnes, John *SEE* MacInnes, Neil
MacInnes, John; Ontario, 1851 ***4537.37*** *p54*
Wife: Catherine Smith
Child: Margaret
Child: John
Child: Malcolm
MacInnes, John; Port uncertain, 1840-1849 ***4537.37*** *p117*
Wife: Margaret Morrison
MacInnes, John; Port uncertain, 1850-1859 ***4537.37*** *p116*
Wife: Flora MacDonald
Child: John
Child: Catherine
MacInnes, John; Port uncertain, 1850-1859 ***4537.37*** *p117*
Wife: Marion MacDonald
Child: James
Child: Malcolm
Child: Duncan
MacInnes, Kate *SEE* MacInnes, Alexander
MacInnes, Kate Munro *SEE* MacInnes, Neil
MacInnes, Kenneth *SEE* MacInnes, Donald
MacInnes, Kenneth *SEE* MacInnes, Neil
MacInnes, Kirsty *SEE* MacInnes, Donald
MacInnes, Kirsty *SEE* MacInnes, Effie
MacInnes, Kirsty; Ontario, 1850-1859 ***4537.37*** *p51*
MacInnes, Kirsty; Ontario, 1851 ***4537.32*** *p36*
MacInnes, Lachlan; Ontario, 1850-1859 ***4537.37*** *p54*
Wife: Mary
Child: Finlay
Child: Archie
Child: James
MacInnes, Malcolm *SEE* MacInnes, Donald
MacInnes, Malcolm *SEE* MacInnes, John
MacInnes, Malcolm *SEE* MacInnes, Neil
MacInnes, Malcolm; Nova Scotia, 1840-1849 ***4537.37*** *p14*
Wife: Rachel
Child: Catherine
Child: Allan
Child: Ewen
Child: Mary
Child: Margaret
Child: Ann
Child: Angus
Child: Donald
Child: John
MacInnes, Margaret *SEE* MacInnes, Alexander
MacInnes, Margaret *SEE* MacInnes, Angus
MacInnes, Margaret *SEE* MacInnes, Archie
MacInnes, Margaret *SEE* MacInnes, Donald
MacInnes, Margaret *SEE* MacInnes, Finlay
MacInnes, Margaret *SEE* MacInnes, John
MacInnes, Margaret *SEE* MacInnes, Malcolm
MacInnes, Margaret *SEE* MacInnes, Neil
MacInnes, Margaret; Ontario, 1850-1859 ***4537.37*** *p65*
MacInnes, Margaret; Ontario, 1851 ***4537.32*** *p53*
MacInnes, Margaret Morrison *SEE* MacInnes, Donald
MacInnes, Margaret Morrison *SEE* MacInnes, John
MacInnes, Margaret Steele *SEE* MacInnes, Ranald
MacInnes, Marion *SEE* MacInnes, Angus
MacInnes, Marion *SEE* MacInnes, Donald
MacInnes, Marion; Port uncertain, 1850-1859 ***4537.37*** *p131*
MacInnes, Marion Johnston *SEE* MacInnes, Donald
MacInnes, Marion Kerr *SEE* MacInnes, Finlay
MacInnes, Marion MacDonald *SEE* MacInnes, James
MacInnes, Marion MacDonald *SEE* MacInnes, John
MacInnes, Marion O'Henley *SEE* MacInnes, Donald
MacInnes, Marjory *SEE* MacInnes, Peter
MacInnes, Mary *SEE* MacInnes, Donald
MacInnes, Mary *SEE* MacInnes, Effie
MacInnes, Mary *SEE* MacInnes, James
MacInnes, Mary *SEE* MacInnes, Lachlan
MacInnes, Mary *SEE* MacInnes, Malcolm
MacInnes, Mary *SEE* MacInnes, Neil
MacInnes, Mary; Ontario, 1840-1849 ***4537.37*** *p51*
MacInnes, Mary; Ontario, 1850-1859 ***4537.37*** *p33*
MacInnes, Mary; Ontario, 1850-1859 ***4537.37*** *p36*
MacInnes, Mary; Ontario, 1851 ***4537.32*** *p5*
MacInnes, Mary; Ontario, 1851 ***4537.32*** *p12*
MacInnes, Mary; Port uncertain, 1850-1859 ***4537.37*** *p118*
MacInnes, Mary; Port uncertain, 1860-1869 ***4537.35*** *p82*
MacInnes, Mary Gordon *SEE* MacInnes, Donald
MacInnes, Mary MacDonald *SEE* MacInnes, Peter
MacInnes, Mary *SEE* MacInnes, Alexander
MacInnes, Mary MacIntyre *SEE* MacInnes, Neil
MacInnes, Mary MacKenzie *SEE* MacInnes, Donald
MacInnes, Murdo *SEE* MacInnes, Neil
MacInnes, Neil *SEE* MacInnes, Donald
MacInnes, Neil; Ontario, 1851 ***4537.37*** *p54*
Wife: Kate Munro
Child: John
Child: Kenneth
Child: Murdo
Child: Roderick
Child: Catherine
Child: Finlay
Brother: Murdo
Child: Malcolm
MacInnes, Neil; Pictou, Nova Scotia, 1848 ***4537.37*** *p29*
Child: Finlay
Child: Donald
Wife: Penny
MacInnes, Neil; Port uncertain, 1840-1849 ***4537.37*** *p117*
Wife: Catherine MacMillan
Child: Catherine
Child: Donald
Child: Ann
Child: Mary
MacInnes, Neil; Port uncertain, 1840-1849 ***4537.37*** *p117*
Wife: Mary MacIntyre
Child: Margaret
Child: John
Child: Alexander
Child: Allan
Child: Mary
MacInnes, Penny *SEE* MacInnes, Neil
MacInnes, Peter *SEE* MacInnes, Alexander
MacInnes, Peter *SEE* MacInnes, Finlay
MacInnes, Peter; Ontario, 1840-1849 ***4537.37*** *p54*
Wife: Mary MacDonald
Child: Marjory
MacInnes, Peter; Port uncertain, 1840-1849 ***4537.37*** *p117*
Wife: Catherine
Child: Archie
Child: Ann
MacInnes, Rachel *SEE* MacInnes, Malcolm
MacInnes, Ranald; Ontario, 1850-1859 ***4537.37*** *p55*
Wife: Margaret Steele
Child: Donald
Child: Flora
Child: Allan
Child: Angus
MacInnes, Ranald; Ontario, 1851 ***4537.32*** *p38*
Wife: Margaret Steele
Child: Donald
Child: Flora
Child: Allan
Child: Angus
MacInnes, Roderick *SEE* MacInnes, Angus
MacInnes, Roderick *SEE* MacInnes, Donald
MacInnes, Roderick *SEE* MacInnes, Neil
Macintosh, Mr.; Quebec, 1858 ***9196.15*** *p42*
Macintosh, Mrs.; Quebec, 1858 ***9196.15*** *p42*
Macintosh, Ms.; Georgia, 1738 ***1640.10*** *p123*
Macintosh, Adam; Georgia, 1736 ***1640.10*** *p118*
Macintosh, Aeneas; Georgia, 1738 ***1640.10*** *p118*
MacIntosh, Allan; Port uncertain, 1840-1849 ***4537.37*** *p117*
Sibling: Jessie
Sibling: Flora
Sibling: Angus
Sibling: Donald
Sibling: Lachlan
MacIntosh, Angus *SEE* MacIntosh, Allan
MacIntosh, Angus *SEE* MacIntosh, Duncan
MacIntosh, Angus *SEE* MacIntosh, Effie MacLellan
MacIntosh, Angus *SEE* MacIntosh, Finlay
MacIntosh, Angus *SEE* MacIntosh, John
MacIntosh, Angus; Ontario, 1849 ***4537.37*** *p55*
Wife: Marion Morrison
Child: John
Child: Mary
MacIntosh, Angus; Ontario, 1849 ***4537.37*** *p55*
Wife: Mary MacPhee
Child: Dougal
Child: Neil
Child: Lachlan
Child: Marion
Child: Donald
Child: Sarah
MacIntosh, Angus; Ontario, 1851 ***4537.32*** *p38*
Wife: Marion MacEachan
Child: John
Child: Ann
Child: Flora
Child: Mary
MacIntosh, Angus; Ontario, 1851 ***4537.37*** *p55*
Wife: Marion MacEachan
Child: John
Child: Ann
MacIntosh, Ann *SEE* MacIntosh, Angus
MacIntosh, Ann *SEE* MacIntosh, Donald
MacIntosh, Ann *SEE* MacIntosh, Neil
Macintosh, Ann; Georgia, 1759 ***1640.10*** *p118*
Macintosh, Benjamin; Georgia, 1736 ***1640.10*** *p118*
MacIntosh, Catherine *SEE* MacIntosh, Catherine
MacIntosh, Catherine *SEE* MacIntosh, Donald
MacIntosh, Catherine; Port uncertain, 1840-1849 ***4537.37*** *p117*
Child: Mary
Child: Catherine
Child: John
Macintosh, Catherine Munro; Georgia, 1736 ***1640.10*** *p118*
MacIntosh, Donald *SEE* MacIntosh, Allan
MacIntosh, Donald *SEE* MacIntosh, Angus
MacIntosh, Donald *SEE* MacIntosh, Donald
MacIntosh, Donald *SEE* MacIntosh, Ewen
MacIntosh, Donald *SEE* MacIntosh, Neil
Macintosh, Donald; Georgia, 1736 ***1640.10*** *p119*
Macintosh, Donald; Georgia, 1737 ***1640.10*** *p119*
Macintosh, Donald; Georgia, 1741 ***1640.10*** *p119*
Macintosh, Donald; Georgia, 1757 ***1640.10*** *p119*
MacIntosh, Donald; Ontario, 1849 ***4537.37*** *p56*
Wife: Mary MacCormick
Child: Marion
Child: Dougal
Child: Neil
Child: John
Child: Donald
Child: Ewen
Child: Mary
Child: Malcolm
MacIntosh, Donald; Port uncertain, 1840-1849 ***4537.37*** *p117*
Wife: Mary Morrison
Child: Ann
Child: Catherine
Child: Donald
MacIntosh, Dougal *SEE* MacIntosh, Angus
MacIntosh, Dougal *SEE* MacIntosh, Donald
MacIntosh, Dougal *SEE* MacIntosh, Effie MacLellan
MacIntosh, Dougal *SEE* MacIntosh, Neil

MacIntosh, Dougal; Port uncertain, 1840-1849 ***4537.37*** *p117*
Wife: Janet MacLellan
MacIntosh, Duncan; Port uncertain, 1850-1859 ***4537.37*** *p117*
Wife: Marion MacLellan
Child: Neil
Child: Marion
Child: Angus
Child: Flora
MacIntosh, Effie MacLellan; Ontario, 1844-1849 ***4537.37*** *p56*
Child: Marion
Child: Kirsty
Child: Angus
Child: Margaret
Child: Dougal
Child: John
MacIntosh, Ewen *SEE* MacIntosh, Donald
MacIntosh, Ewen; Port uncertain, 1840-1849 ***4537.37*** *p117*
Wife: Mary MacMillan
Child: Marion
Child: Michael
Child: Donald
Child: Mary
Child: Flora
MacIntosh, Finlay; Saskatchewan, 1884 ***4537.37*** *p98*
Wife: Margaret MacDonald
Child: Angus
Child: Margaret
Child: Flora
MacIntosh, Flora *SEE* MacIntosh, Allan
MacIntosh, Flora *SEE* MacIntosh, Angus
MacIntosh, Flora *SEE* MacIntosh, Duncan
MacIntosh, Flora *SEE* MacIntosh, Ewen
MacIntosh, Flora *SEE* MacIntosh, Finlay
Macintosh, George; Georgia, 1757 ***1640.10*** *p119*
Macintosh, Gregor; Havana, 1765 ***1224.2*** *p73*
Macintosh, Isabel; Georgia, 1738 ***1640.10*** *p119*
MacIntosh, Isabella *SEE* MacIntosh, Malcolm
Macintosh, James; Florida, 1787 ***1640.10*** *p119*
MacIntosh, Janet MacEachan *SEE* MacIntosh, Malcolm
MacIntosh, Janet MacLellan *SEE* MacIntosh, Dougal
MacIntosh, Jessie *SEE* MacIntosh, Allan
MacIntosh, John *SEE* MacIntosh, Angus
MacIntosh, John *SEE* MacIntosh, Catherine
MacIntosh, John *SEE* MacIntosh, Donald
MacIntosh, John *SEE* MacIntosh, Effie MacLellan
Macintosh, John *SEE* Macintosh, John
MacIntosh, John *SEE* MacIntosh, John
MacIntosh, John *SEE* MacIntosh, Neil
Macintosh, John; Georgia, 1736 ***1640.10*** *p119*
Wife: Margory Fraser
Child: William
Child: John
Child: Lachlan
Macintosh, John; Georgia, 1736 ***1640.10*** *p120*
Macintosh, John; Georgia, 1737 ***1640.10*** *p120*
Macintosh, John; Georgia, 1759 ***1640.10*** *p120*
Macintosh, John; Georgia, 1760 ***1640.10*** *p120*
Macintosh, John; Georgia, 1775 ***1640.10*** *p121*
MacIntosh, John; Ontario, 1849 ***4537.37*** *p56*
With wife
Child: Angus
Child: John
MacIntosh, John 36; Ontario, 1871 ***1823.15*** *p150*
MacIntosh, Kirsty *SEE* MacIntosh, Effie MacLellan
MacIntosh, Kirsty; Port uncertain, 1840-1849 ***4537.37*** *p125*
MacIntosh, Lachlan *SEE* MacIntosh, Allan
MacIntosh, Lachlan *SEE* MacIntosh, Angus
Macintosh, Lachlan *SEE* Macintosh, John
Macintosh, Lachlan; Augusta, Georgia, 1756 ***1640.10*** *p121*
Macintosh, Lachlan; Georgia, 1736 ***1640.10*** *p121*
Macintosh, Lachlan; Georgia, 1740 ***1640.10*** *p121*
Macintosh, Lachlan; Georgia, 1757 ***1640.10*** *p121*
Macintosh, Lachlan; Georgia, 1774 ***1640.10*** *p121*
Macintosh, Lachlan; Savannah, Georgia, 1740 ***1640.10*** *p121*
Macintosh, Lachlan; Savannah, Georgia, 1791 ***1640.10*** *p121*
MacIntosh, Malcolm *SEE* MacIntosh, Donald
MacIntosh, Malcolm; Ontario, 1840-1849 ***4537.37*** *p56*
Wife: Janet MacEachan
Child: Isabella
Child: Mary
MacIntosh, Margaret *SEE* MacIntosh, Effie MacLellan
MacIntosh, Margaret *SEE* MacIntosh, Finlay
MacIntosh, Margaret MacDonald *SEE* MacIntosh, Finlay
Macintosh, Margory Fraser *SEE* Macintosh, John
MacIntosh, Marion *SEE* MacIntosh, Angus
MacIntosh, Marion *SEE* MacIntosh, Donald
MacIntosh, Marion *SEE* MacIntosh, Duncan
MacIntosh, Marion *SEE* MacIntosh, Effie MacLellan
MacIntosh, Marion *SEE* MacIntosh, Ewen
MacIntosh, Marion MacEachan *SEE* MacIntosh, Angus
MacIntosh, Marion MacLellan *SEE* MacIntosh, Duncan
MacIntosh, Marion Morrison *SEE* MacIntosh, Angus
MacIntosh, Mary *SEE* MacIntosh, Angus
MacIntosh, Mary *SEE* MacIntosh, Catherine
MacIntosh, Mary *SEE* MacIntosh, Donald
MacIntosh, Mary *SEE* MacIntosh, Ewen
MacIntosh, Mary *SEE* MacIntosh, Malcolm
MacIntosh, Mary *SEE* MacIntosh, Neil
Macintosh, Mary; Georgia, 1738 ***1640.10*** *p122*
MacIntosh, Mary MacCormick *SEE* MacIntosh, Donald
MacIntosh, Mary MacMillan *SEE* MacIntosh, Ewen
MacIntosh, Mary MacPhee *SEE* MacIntosh, Angus
MacIntosh, Mary MacPhee *SEE* MacIntosh, Neil
MacIntosh, Mary Morrison *SEE* MacIntosh, Donald
MacIntosh, Michael *SEE* MacIntosh, Ewen
MacIntosh, Neil *SEE* MacIntosh, Angus
MacIntosh, Neil *SEE* MacIntosh, Donald
MacIntosh, Neil *SEE* MacIntosh, Duncan
MacIntosh, Neil; Ontario, 1840-1849 ***4537.37*** *p57*
Wife: Mary MacPhee
Child: Mary
Child: John
Child: Donald
Child: Dougal
Child: Ann
Child: Stephen
Macintosh, Robert; Georgia, 1736 ***1640.10*** *p122*
Macintosh, Roderick; Georgia, 1736 ***1640.10*** *p122*
Macintosh, Roderick; Georgia, 1759 ***1640.10*** *p122*
MacIntosh, Sarah *SEE* MacIntosh, Angus
Macintosh, Sarah; Georgia, 1740 ***1640.10*** *p122*
MacIntosh, Stephen *SEE* MacIntosh, Neil
Macintosh, William *SEE* Macintosh, John
Macintosh, William; Georgia, 1736 ***1640.10*** *p122*
Macintyre, Mr.; Quebec, 1858 ***9196.15*** *p42*
MacIntyre, Alexander *SEE* MacIntyre, Donald
MacIntyre, Alexander *SEE* MacIntyre, Duncan
MacIntyre, Alexander *SEE* MacIntyre, Ewen
MacIntyre, Alexander *SEE* MacIntyre, James
MacIntyre, Alexander *SEE* MacIntyre, John
MacIntyre, Alexander; Ontario, 1850-1859 ***4537.37*** *p57*
Child: Donald
Child: Jessie
Wife: Ann O'Henley
Child: Mary
MacIntyre, Alexander; Ontario, 1851 ***4537.32*** *p38*
Wife: Ann O'Henley
Child: Mary
Child: Donald
MacIntyre, Allan *SEE* MacIntyre, Ewen
MacIntyre, Allan *SEE* MacIntyre, James
MacIntyre, Andrew; Nova Scotia, 1840-1849 ***4537.37*** *p15*
Wife: Ann MacCormick
Child: Kirsty
Child: Hugh
Child: Penny
Child: Norman
Child: Donald
MacIntyre, Angus *SEE* MacIntyre, Angus
MacIntyre, Angus *SEE* MacIntyre, Ann Morrison
MacIntyre, Angus *SEE* MacIntyre, Donald
MacIntyre, Angus *SEE* MacIntyre, Duncan
MacIntyre, Angus *SEE* MacIntyre, Flora MacIsaac
MacIntyre, Angus *SEE* MacIntyre, Gormelia Campbell
MacIntyre, Angus *SEE* MacIntyre, Hector
MacIntyre, Angus *SEE* MacIntyre, John
MacIntyre, Angus *SEE* MacIntyre, Lachlan
MacIntyre, Angus *SEE* MacIntyre, Malcolm
MacIntyre, Angus *SEE* MacIntyre, Neil
MacIntyre, Angus *SEE* MacIntyre, Ranald
MacIntyre, Angus *SEE* MacIntyre, Roderick
MacIntyre, Angus *SEE* MacIntyre, Stephen
MacIntyre, Angus; Nova Scotia, 1828 ***4537.35*** *p19*
Wife: Margaret Morrison
Child: Catherine
Child: Norman
MacIntyre, Angus; Ontario, 1849 ***4537.37*** *p57*
Wife: Catherine MacInnes
Child: John
Child: Effie
Child: Malcolm
Child: Angus
Child: Matilda
Child: Mary
Child: Marion
Child: Finlay
MacIntyre, Angus; Port uncertain, 1850-1859 ***4537.37*** *p117*
Child: Donald
Wife: Catherine Currie
MacIntyre, Angus; Port uncertain, 1850-1859 ***4537.37*** *p118*
Wife: Margaret
Child: John
Child: Mary
Child: Flora
Child: Ann
MacIntyre, Angus; Port uncertain, 1850-1859 ***4537.37*** *p118*
Wife: Mary MacInnes
Child: Ann
Child: Mary
Child: Donald
Child: Margaret
MacIntyre, Angus; Port uncertain, 1850-1859 ***4537.37*** *p118*
Wife: Mary MacLeod
Child: Catherine
MacIntyre, Ann *SEE* MacIntyre, Angus
MacIntyre, Ann *SEE* MacIntyre, Ann Morrison
MacIntyre, Ann *SEE* MacIntyre, Donald
MacIntyre, Ann *SEE* MacIntyre, Duncan
MacIntyre, Ann *SEE* MacIntyre, Gormelia Campbell
MacIntyre, Ann *SEE* MacIntyre, James
MacIntyre, Ann *SEE* MacIntyre, John
MacIntyre, Ann *SEE* MacIntyre, Lachlan
MacIntyre, Ann *SEE* MacIntyre, Neil
MacIntyre, Ann *SEE* MacIntyre, Stephen
MacIntyre, Ann; Prince Edward Island, 1848 ***4537.37*** *p26*
MacIntyre, Ann MacCormick *SEE* MacIntyre, Andrew
MacIntyre, Ann MacLeod *SEE* MacIntyre, John
MacIntyre, Ann Morrison *SEE* MacIntyre, John
MacIntyre, Ann Morrison *SEE* MacIntyre, Malcolm
MacIntyre, Ann Morrison; Ontario, 1851 ***4537.32*** *p39*
Child: Marion
Child: Catherine
Child: Malcolm
Child: Ann
Child: Angus
Child: John
MacIntyre, Ann O'Henley *SEE* MacIntyre, Alexander
MacIntyre, Archie *SEE* MacIntyre, John
MacIntyre, Archie *SEE* MacIntyre, Roderick
MacIntyre, Barbara MacAskill *SEE* MacIntyre, Donald
MacIntyre, Catherine *SEE* MacIntyre, Angus
MacIntyre, Catherine *SEE* MacIntyre, Ann Morrison
MacIntyre, Catherine *SEE* MacIntyre, Donald
MacIntyre, Catherine *SEE* MacIntyre, Duncan
MacIntyre, Catherine MacInnes *SEE* MacIntyre, James
MacIntyre, Catherine *SEE* MacIntyre, John
MacIntyre, Catherine *SEE* MacIntyre, Malcolm
MacIntyre, Catherine *SEE* MacIntyre, Neil
MacIntyre, Catherine *SEE* MacIntyre, Ranald
MacIntyre, Catherine; Ontario, 1840-1849 ***4537.37*** *p62*
MacIntyre, Catherine; Ontario, 1849 ***4537.32*** *p72*
MacIntyre, Catherine; Ontario, 1849 ***4537.37*** *p49*
MacIntyre, Catherine; Ontario, 1849 ***4537.37*** *p51*
MacIntyre, Catherine; Quebec, 1840-1849 ***4537.37*** *p72*
MacIntyre, Catherine; Port uncertain, 1840-1849 ***4537.37*** *p111*
MacIntyre, Catherine; Port uncertain, 1850-1859 ***4537.37*** *p105*
MacIntyre, Catherine; Port uncertain, 1850-1859 ***4537.37*** *p116*
MacIntyre, Catherine; Port uncertain, 1870-1879 ***4537.37*** *p105*
MacIntyre, Catherine Bowie *SEE* MacIntyre, James
MacIntyre, Catherine Currie *SEE* MacIntyre, Angus
MacIntyre, Catherine Ferguson *SEE* MacIntyre, Ewen
MacIntyre, Catherine MacDonald *SEE* MacIntyre, John
MacIntyre, Catherine MacDonald *SEE* MacIntyre, Neil
MacIntyre, Catherine MacInnes *SEE* MacIntyre, Angus
MacIntyre, Catherine MacIsaac *SEE* MacIntyre, John
MacIntyre, Catherine MacPhee *SEE* MacIntyre, Hector
MacIntyre, Catherine Robertson *SEE* MacIntyre, Lachlan
MacIntyre, Catherine Steele *SEE* MacIntyre, John
MacIntyre, Charles *SEE* MacIntyre, John
MacIntyre, Donald *SEE* MacIntyre, Alexander
MacIntyre, Donald *SEE* MacIntyre, Andrew
MacIntyre, Donald *SEE* MacIntyre, Angus
MacIntyre, Donald *SEE* MacIntyre, Donald
MacIntyre, Donald *SEE* MacIntyre, Duncan
MacIntyre, Donald *SEE* MacIntyre, Ewen
MacIntyre, Donald *SEE* MacIntyre, Gormelia Campbell
MacIntyre, Donald *SEE* MacIntyre, James
MacIntyre, Donald *SEE* MacIntyre, John
MacIntyre, Donald *SEE* MacIntyre, Lachlan
MacIntyre, Donald *SEE* MacIntyre, Malcolm

MacIntyre, John; Port uncertain, 1850-1859 ***4537.37*** *p119*
Wife: Kirsty MacLellan
Child: Catherine
Child: James
MacIntyre, Kate *SEE* MacIntyre, John
MacIntyre, Kirsty *SEE* MacIntyre, Andrew
MacIntyre, Kirsty *SEE* MacIntyre, Donald
MacIntyre, Kirsty *SEE* MacIntyre, John
MacIntyre, Kirsty *SEE* MacIntyre, Malcolm
MacIntyre, Kirsty *SEE* MacIntyre, Mary
MacIntyre, Kirsty *SEE* MacIntyre, Roderick
MacIntyre, Kirsty; Ontario, 1849 ***4537.37*** *p52*
MacIntyre, Kirsty Campbell *SEE* MacIntyre, Neil
MacIntyre, Kirsty MacEachan *SEE* MacIntyre, John
MacIntyre, Kirsty MacLellan *SEE* MacIntyre, Duncan
MacIntyre, Kirsty MacLellan *SEE* MacIntyre, John
MacIntyre, Kirsty Steele *SEE* MacIntyre, Hector
MacIntyre, Lachlan *SEE* MacIntyre, James
MacIntyre, Lachlan *SEE* MacIntyre, John
MacIntyre, Lachlan; Nova Scotia, 1840-1849 ***4537.37*** *p15*
Wife: Catherine Robertson
Child: Duncan
Child: Marion
Child: Ann
Child: Hector
Child: Sally
Child: Donald
MacIntyre, Lachlan; Port uncertain, 1850-1859 ***4537.37*** *p119*
Wife: Margaret Bowie
Child: John
Child: Angus
Child: Duncan
Child: Hector
MacIntyre, Lachlan *SEE* MacIntyre, John
MacIntyre, Malcolm *SEE* MacIntyre, Angus
MacIntyre, Malcolm *SEE* MacIntyre, Ann Morrison
MacIntyre, Malcolm *SEE* MacIntyre, John
MacIntyre, Malcolm *SEE* MacIntyre, Roderick
MacIntyre, Malcolm; Ontario, 1850-1859 ***4537.37*** *p60*
Wife: Ann Morrison
Child: John
Child: Angus
Child: Donald
MacIntyre, Malcolm; Ontario, 1851 ***4537.32*** *p39*
Wife: Ann Morrison
Child: Angus
Child: John
Child: Donald
MacIntyre, Malcolm; Port uncertain, 1840-1849 ***4537.37*** *p119*
Wife: Catherine
Child: Ewen
Child: Mary
Child: Kirsty
MacIntyre, Malcom; New York, 1796 ***8197.10*** *p8*
MacIntyre, Margaret *SEE* MacIntyre, Angus
MacIntyre, Margaret *SEE* MacIntyre, Donald
MacIntyre, Margaret *SEE* MacIntyre, Ewen
MacIntyre, Margaret *SEE* MacIntyre, Gormelia Campbell
MacIntyre, Margaret *SEE* MacIntyre, James
MacIntyre, Margaret *SEE* MacIntyre, John
MacIntyre, Margaret; Ontario, 1840-1849 ***4537.37*** *p43*
MacIntyre, Margaret; Ontario, 1849 ***4537.32*** *p20*
MacIntyre, Margaret; Ontario, 1849 ***4537.37*** *p70*
MacIntyre, Margaret; Ontario, 1851 ***4537.37*** *p62*
MacIntyre, Margaret; Port uncertain, 1850-1859 ***4537.37*** *p131*
MacIntyre, Margaret Beaton *SEE* MacIntyre, John
MacIntyre, Margaret Bowie *SEE* MacIntyre, Lachlan
MacIntyre, Margaret Morrison *SEE* MacIntyre, Angus
MacIntyre, Margaret Munro *SEE* MacIntyre, Neil
MacIntyre, Marion *SEE* MacIntyre, Angus
MacIntyre, Marion *SEE* MacIntyre, Ann Morrison
MacIntyre, Marion *SEE* MacIntyre, Donald
MacIntyre, Marion *SEE* MacIntyre, John
MacIntyre, Marion *SEE* MacIntyre, Lachlan
MacIntyre, Marion *SEE* MacIntyre, Mary MacLeod
MacIntyre, Marion *SEE* MacIntyre, Neil
MacIntyre, Marion *SEE* MacIntyre, Roderick
MacIntyre, Marion; Ontario, 1840-1849 ***4537.37*** *p47*
MacIntyre, Marion; Ontario, 1851 ***4537.37*** *p35*
MacIntyre, Marion MacDonald *SEE* MacIntyre, John
MacIntyre, Marion MacDonald *SEE* MacIntyre, Stephen
MacIntyre, Marion MacKinnon *SEE* MacIntyre, John
MacIntyre, Marion MacLeod *SEE* MacIntyre, Duncan
MacIntyre, Marion Morrison *SEE* MacIntyre, Donald
MacIntyre, Mary *SEE* MacIntyre, Alexander
MacIntyre, Mary *SEE* MacIntyre, Angus
MacIntyre, Mary *SEE* MacIntyre, Donald
MacIntyre, Mary *SEE* MacIntyre, Duncan
MacIntyre, Mary *SEE* MacIntyre, Flora MacIsaac
MacIntyre, Mary *SEE* MacIntyre, James
MacIntyre, Mary *SEE* MacIntyre, John
MacIntyre, Mary *SEE* MacIntyre, Malcolm
MacIntyre, Mary *SEE* MacIntyre, Neil
MacIntyre, Mary *SEE* MacIntyre, Roderick
MacIntyre, Mary; Nova Scotia, 1840-1849 ***4537.37*** *p19*
MacIntyre, Mary; Ontario, 1848 ***4537.37*** *p83*
MacIntyre, Mary; Ontario, 1849 ***4537.37*** *p76*
MacIntyre, Mary; Ontario, 1851 ***4537.37*** *p67*
MacIntyre, Mary; Prince Edward Island, 1848 ***4537.37*** *p24*
Sister: Kirsty
Sister: Effie
MacIntyre, Mary; Port uncertain, 1840-1849 ***4537.37*** *p117*
MacIntyre, Mary; Port uncertain, 1840-1849 ***4537.37*** *p120*
Child: Ranald
MacIntyre, Mary; Port uncertain, 1850-1859 ***4537.37*** *p105*
MacIntyre, Mary Ann *SEE* MacIntyre, John
MacIntyre, Mary Currie *SEE* MacIntyre, John
MacIntyre, Mary Davidson *SEE* MacIntyre, Roderick
MacIntyre, Mary MacAskill *SEE* MacIntyre, Donald
MacIntyre, Mary MacDonald *SEE* MacIntyre, Donald
MacIntyre, Mary MacDougall *SEE* MacIntyre, Ranald
MacIntyre, Mary MacEachan *SEE* MacIntyre, Duncan
MacIntyre, Mary MacEachan *SEE* MacIntyre, Neil
MacIntyre, Mary MacInnes *SEE* MacIntyre, Angus
MacIntyre, Mary MacLeod *SEE* MacIntyre, Angus
MacIntyre, Mary MacLeod; Port uncertain, 1840-1849 ***4537.37*** *p119*
Child: James
Child: Marion
Child: Peggy
MacIntyre, Mary MacPhee *SEE* MacIntyre, Roderick
MacIntyre, Matilda *SEE* MacIntyre, Angus
MacIntyre, Matthew *SEE* MacIntyre, John
MacIntyre, Michael *SEE* MacIntyre, Donald
MacIntyre, Michael *SEE* MacIntyre, Flora MacIsaac
MacIntyre, Michael *SEE* MacIntyre, John
MacIntyre, Neil *SEE* MacIntyre, Donald
MacIntyre, Neil *SEE* MacIntyre, Duncan
MacIntyre, Neil *SEE* MacIntyre, Hector
MacIntyre, Neil; Ontario, 1848 ***4537.37*** *p61*
Wife: Flora MacEachan
Child: Donald
MacIntyre, Neil; Ontario, 1849 ***4537.37*** *p60*
Wife: Catherine MacDonald
Child: Ann
Child: John
Child: Catherine
Child: Mary
Child: Angus
MacIntyre, Neil; Ontario, 1850-1859 ***4537.37*** *p61*
Wife: Margaret Munro
Child: Marion
Child: Ann
Child: Donald
Child: Angus
Child: Flora
MacIntyre, Neil; Ontario, 1851 ***4537.37*** *p61*
Wife: Mary MacEachan
Child: Hector
Child: Angus
Child: Ranald
MacIntyre, Neil; Port uncertain, 1850-1859 ***4537.37*** *p119*
Wife: Kirsty Campbell
Child: Hector
Child: Marion
Child: Mary
MacIntyre, Norman *SEE* MacIntyre, Andrew
MacIntyre, Norman *SEE* MacIntyre, Angus
MacIntyre, Norman *SEE* MacIntyre, Duncan
MacIntyre, Peggy *SEE* MacIntyre, Mary MacLeod
MacIntyre, Peggy Currie *SEE* MacIntyre, John
MacIntyre, Penny *SEE* MacIntyre, Andrew
MacIntyre, Penny MacDonald *SEE* MacIntyre, Roderick
MacIntyre, Peter *SEE* MacIntyre, Gormelia Campbell
MacIntyre, Peter; Saskatchewan, 1884 ***4537.37*** *p98*
Wife: Flora Steele
Child: Donald
Child: Ranald
MacIntyre, Rachel *SEE* MacIntyre, Hector
MacIntyre, Ranald *SEE* MacIntyre, Donald
MacIntyre, Ranald *SEE* MacIntyre, James
MacIntyre, Ranald *SEE* MacIntyre, Mary
MacIntyre, Ranald *SEE* MacIntyre, Neil
MacIntyre, Ranald *SEE* MacIntyre, Peter
MacIntyre, Ranald *SEE* MacIntyre, Roderick
MacIntyre, Ranald; Port uncertain, 1850-1859 ***4537.37*** *p119*
Wife: Mary MacDougall
Child: Angus
Child: Eliza
Child: Catherine
MacIntyre, Roderick *SEE* MacIntyre, Donald
MacIntyre, Roderick *SEE* MacIntyre, Ewen
MacIntyre, Roderick *SEE* MacIntyre, John
MacIntyre, Roderick *SEE* MacIntyre, Roderick
MacIntyre, Roderick; Ontario, 1851 ***4537.37*** *p61*
Wife: Mary MacPhee
Child: Angus
Child: John
Child: Donald
Child: Roderick
MacIntyre, Roderick; Port uncertain, 1840-1849 ***4537.37*** *p119*
Wife: Flora MacEachan
Child: Kirsty
Child: Marion
MacIntyre, Roderick; Port uncertain, 1850-1859 ***4537.37*** *p120*
Child: Angus
Child: Donald
Wife: Mary Davidson
MacIntyre, Roderick; Port uncertain, 1850-1859 ***4537.37*** *p120*
Wife: Penny MacDonald
Child: Marion
Child: Archie
Child: Flora
Child: Mary
Child: Ranald
Child: Roderick
Child: Malcolm
MacIntyre, Sally *SEE* MacIntyre, Lachlan
MacIntyre, Sally; Ontario, 1840-1849 ***4537.37*** *p63*
MacIntyre, Stephen; Port uncertain, 1850-1859 ***4537.37*** *p120*
Wife: Marion MacDonald
Child: Ann
Child: Angus
MacIntyre, Una; Ontario, 1840-1849 ***4537.37*** *p76*
MacIsaac, Alexander *SEE* MacIsaac, Angus
MacIsaac, Alexander *SEE* MacIsaac, Donald
MacIsaac, Alexander *SEE* MacIsaac, John
MacIsaac, Alexander; Nova Scotia, 1840-1843 ***4537.37*** *p15*
Wife: Mary MacPhee
Child: Mary
Child: Archie
Child: Donald
MacIsaac, Angus *SEE* MacIsaac, Angus
MacIsaac, Angus *SEE* MacIsaac, Donald
MacIsaac, Angus *SEE* MacIsaac, John
MacIsaac, Angus *SEE* MacIsaac, Murdo
MacIsaac, Angus *SEE* MacIsaac, Neil
MacIsaac, Angus *SEE* MacIsaac, Peter
MacIsaac, Angus; Nova Scotia, 1840-1849 ***4537.37*** *p15*
Wife: Kirsty Martin
Child: Mary
Child: Roderick
Child: Donald
Child: John
Child: Alexander
MacIsaac, Angus; Ontario, 1851 ***4537.37*** *p62*
Wife: Margaret MacIntyre
Child: Donald
Child: Margaret
Child: Hector
Child: Archie
Child: Neil
Child: Marion
Child: Angus
MacIsaac, Angus; Port uncertain, 1840-1849 ***4537.37*** *p120*
Wife: Margaret MacDonald
Child: Jane
Child: Angus
Child: John
Child: Ann
MacIsaac, Ann *SEE* MacIsaac, Angus
MacIsaac, Ann *SEE* MacIsaac, Ann Steele
MacIsaac, Ann *SEE* MacIsaac, Donald
MacIsaac, Ann *SEE* MacIsaac, John
MacIsaac, Ann *SEE* MacIsaac, Neil
MacIsaac, Ann *SEE* MacIsaac, Peter
MacIsaac, Ann; Ontario, 1848 ***4537.37*** *p38*
MacIsaac, Ann Steele *SEE* MacIsaac, Donald
MacIsaac, Ann Steele; Ontario, 1849 ***4537.32*** *p40*
Child: John
Child: Flora

Child: Malcolm
Child: Ann
MacIsaac, Archie *SEE* MacIsaac, Alexander
MacIsaac, Archie *SEE* MacIsaac, Angus
MacIsaac, Archie *SEE* MacIsaac, Donald
MacIsaac, Archie; Ontario, 1840-1849 ***4537.37*** *p62*
Wife: Catherine MacIntyre
Child: Mary
Child: Neil
MacIsaac, Catherine *SEE* MacIsaac, Hector
MacIsaac, Catherine *SEE* MacIsaac, John
MacIsaac, Catherine *SEE* MacIsaac, Neil
MacIsaac, Catherine; Ontario, 1840-1849 ***4537.37*** *p84*
MacIsaac, Catherine; Ontario, 1849 ***4537.32*** *p95*
MacIsaac, Catherine; Ontario, 1849 ***4537.37*** *p42*
MacIsaac, Catherine; Ontario, 1849 ***4537.37*** *p50*
MacIsaac, Catherine; Ontario, 1849 ***4537.37*** *p67*
MacIsaac, Catherine; Ontario, 1850-1859 ***4537.37*** *p58*
MacIsaac, Catherine Campbell *SEE* MacIsaac, Neil
MacIsaac, Catherine Campbell *SEE* MacIsaac, Ranald
MacIsaac, Catherine MacCormick *SEE* MacIsaac, John
MacIsaac, Catherine MacCormick *SEE* MacIsaac, Peter
MacIsaac, Catherine MacIntyre *SEE* MacIsaac, Archie
MacIsaac, Catherine MacLean *SEE* MacIsaac, Neil
MacIsaac, Catherine MacPhee *SEE* MacIsaac, Neil
MacIsaac, Donald *SEE* MacIsaac, Alexander
MacIsaac, Donald *SEE* MacIsaac, Angus
MacIsaac, Donald *SEE* MacIsaac, John
MacIsaac, Donald *SEE* MacIsaac, Kirsty
MacIsaac, Donald *SEE* MacIsaac, Mary
MacIsaac, Donald *SEE* MacIsaac, Murdo
MacIsaac, Donald *SEE* MacIsaac, Neil
MacIsaac, Donald *SEE* MacIsaac, Ranald
MacIsaac, Donald; Ontario, 1789-1900 ***4537.37*** *p62*
Wife: Ann Steele
Child: Malcolm
Child: Flora
Child: John
Child: Ann
MacIsaac, Donald; Ontario, 1840-1849 ***4537.37*** *p62*
Wife: Matilda MacCormick
Child: Mary
Brother: Archie
Child: Angus
Child: John
Child: Marion
Child: Dougal
Child: Neil
MacIsaac, Donald; Ontario, 1840-1849 ***4537.37*** *p63*
Wife: Sally MacIntyre
Child: Sally
Child: Mary
Child: Kate
Child: Angus
Child: Alexander
Child: John
MacIsaac, Dougal *SEE* MacIsaac, Donald
MacIsaac, Effie *SEE* MacIsaac, John
MacIsaac, Effie *SEE* MacIsaac, Murdo
MacIsaac, Effie Buchanan *SEE* MacIsaac, Murdo
MacIsaac, Eliza *SEE* MacIsaac, John
MacIsaac, Ewen *SEE* MacIsaac, John
MacIsaac, Finlay *SEE* MacIsaac, Neil
MacIsaac, Flora *SEE* MacIsaac, Ann Steele
MacIsaac, Flora *SEE* MacIsaac, Donald
MacIsaac, Flora *SEE* MacIsaac, John
MacIsaac, Flora *SEE* MacIsaac, Neil
MacIsaac, Flora *SEE* MacIsaac, Ranald
MacIsaac, Flora; Ontario, 1849 ***4537.37*** *p44*
MacIsaac, Flora; Saskatchewan, 1884 ***4537.37*** *p98*
MacIsaac, Hector *SEE* MacIsaac, Angus
MacIsaac, Hector; Port uncertain, 1840-1849 ***4537.37*** *p120*
Wife: Catherine
Child: Mary
Child: Roderick
MacIsaac, James *SEE* MacIsaac, Kirsty
MacIsaac, Jane *SEE* MacIsaac, Angus
MacIsaac, Janet; Ontario, 1840-1849 ***4537.37*** *p47*
MacIsaac, Janet MacEachan *SEE* MacIsaac, John
MacIsaac, John *SEE* MacIsaac, Angus
MacIsaac, John *SEE* MacIsaac, Ann Steele
MacIsaac, John *SEE* MacIsaac, Donald
MacIsaac, John *SEE* MacIsaac, John
MacIsaac, John *SEE* MacIsaac, Kirsty
MacIsaac, John *SEE* MacIsaac, Murdo
MacIsaac, John *SEE* MacIsaac, Neil
MacIsaac, John *SEE* MacIsaac, Peter
MacIsaac, John *SEE* MacIsaac, Ranald
MacIsaac, John; Nova Scotia, 1840-1845 ***4537.37*** *p16*
Wife: Mary MacDonald
Child: Mary
Child: Flora
Child: Kate
MacIsaac, John; Ontario, 1840-1849 ***4537.37*** *p63*
Wife: Mary MacMillan
Child: Angus
Child: Donald
MacIsaac, John; Ontario, 1847-1849 ***4537.37*** *p63*
Child: Kirsty
Child: Flora
Child: Donald
Child: Eliza
Child: Catherine
Wife: Catherine MacCormick
Child: Effie
Child: Ann
Child: Alexander
MacIsaac, John; Ontario, 1849 ***4537.32*** *p40*
Wife: Catherine MacCormick
Child: Catherine
Child: Eliza
Child: Flora
Child: Effie
Child: Alexander
Child: Kirsty
Child: Ann
Child: Donald
MacIsaac, John; Ontario, 1851 ***4537.37*** *p63*
Wife: Janet MacEachan
Brother: John
Child: Catherine
Child: Mary
MacIsaac, John; Port uncertain, 1840-1849 ***4537.37*** *p120*
Wife: Mary MacDonald
Child: Catherine
Child: Flora
MacIsaac, John; Port uncertain, 1850-1859 ***4537.37*** *p120*
Wife: Margaret MacLeod
Child: Ewen
Child: Catherine
Child: Mary
Child: Angus
MacIsaac, Kate *SEE* MacIsaac, Donald
MacIsaac, Kate *SEE* MacIsaac, John
MacIsaac, Kate *SEE* MacIsaac, Kirsty
MacIsaac, Kirsty *SEE* MacIsaac, John
MacIsaac, Kirsty *SEE* MacIsaac, Neil
MacIsaac, Kirsty *SEE* MacIsaac, Peter
MacIsaac, Kirsty; Port uncertain, 1840-1849 ***4537.37*** *p120*
Child: Kate
Child: James
Child: John
Child: Donald
MacIsaac, Kirsty Martin *SEE* MacIsaac, Angus
MacIsaac, Lachlan; Port uncertain, 1840-1849 ***4537.37*** *p120*
Child: Mary
Child: Neil
MacIsaac, Malcolm *SEE* MacIsaac, Ann Steele
MacIsaac, Malcolm *SEE* MacIsaac, Donald
MacIsaac, Margaret *SEE* MacIsaac, Angus
MacIsaac, Margaret; Nova Scotia, 1830-1839 ***4537.35*** *p29*
MacIsaac, Margaret MacDonald *SEE* MacIsaac, Angus
MacIsaac, Margaret MacIntyre *SEE* MacIsaac, Angus
MacIsaac, Margaret MacLeod *SEE* MacIsaac, John
MacIsaac, Marion *SEE* MacIsaac, Angus
MacIsaac, Marion *SEE* MacIsaac, Donald
MacIsaac, Marion *SEE* MacIsaac, Neil
MacIsaac, Marion *SEE* MacIsaac, Ranald
MacIsaac, Marion; Port uncertain, 1840-1849 ***4537.37*** *p112*
MacIsaac, Mary *SEE* MacIsaac, Alexander
MacIsaac, Mary *SEE* MacIsaac, Angus
MacIsaac, Mary *SEE* MacIsaac, Archie
MacIsaac, Mary *SEE* MacIsaac, Donald
MacIsaac, Mary *SEE* MacIsaac, Hector
MacIsaac, Mary *SEE* MacIsaac, John
MacIsaac, Mary *SEE* MacIsaac, Lachlan
MacIsaac, Mary *SEE* MacIsaac, Murdo
MacIsaac, Mary *SEE* MacIsaac, Neil
MacIsaac, Mary *SEE* MacIsaac, Peter
MacIsaac, Mary; Nova Scotia, 1840-1843 ***4537.37*** *p18*
MacIsaac, Mary; Nova Scotia, 1840-1849 ***4537.37*** *p21*
MacIsaac, Mary; Nova Scotia, 1841 ***4537.37*** *p12*
MacIsaac, Mary; Ontario, 1848 ***4537.37*** *p85*
MacIsaac, Mary; Ontario, 1849 ***4537.32*** *p95*
MacIsaac, Mary; Ontario, 1849 ***4537.37*** *p75*
MacIsaac, Mary; Port uncertain, 1840-1849 ***4537.37*** *p106*
MacIsaac, Mary; Port uncertain, 1840-1849 ***4537.37*** *p121*
Child: Donald
MacIsaac, Mary; Port uncertain, 1850-1859 ***4537.37*** *p115*
MacIsaac, Mary MacDonald *SEE* MacIsaac, John
MacIsaac, Mary MacEachan *SEE* MacIsaac, Neil
MacIsaac, Mary MacMillan *SEE* MacIsaac, John
MacIsaac, Mary MacPhee *SEE* MacIsaac, Alexander
MacIsaac, Matilda MacCormick *SEE* MacIsaac, Donald
MacIsaac, Murdo; Ontario, 1850-1859 ***4537.37*** *p64*
Wife: Effie Buchanan
Child: Effie
Child: Angus
Child: Donald
Child: John
Child: Mary
Child: Neil
MacIsaac, Murdo; Ontario, 1851 ***4537.32*** *p40*
Wife: Effie Buchanan
Child: Effie
Child: Angus
Child: Donald
Child: John
Child: Neil
Child: Mary
MacIsaac, Neil *SEE* MacIsaac, Angus
MacIsaac, Neil *SEE* MacIsaac, Archie
MacIsaac, Neil *SEE* MacIsaac, Donald
MacIsaac, Neil *SEE* MacIsaac, Lachlan
MacIsaac, Neil *SEE* MacIsaac, Murdo
MacIsaac, Neil *SEE* MacIsaac, Neil
MacIsaac, Neil; Ontario, 1849 ***4537.37*** *p64*
Wife: Catherine MacLean
Child: Mary
Child: Catherine
Child: Kirsty
Child: John
Child: Marion
Child: Donald
Child: Finlay
MacIsaac, Neil; Ontario, 1850-1859 ***4537.37*** *p64*
Wife: Mary MacEachan
Child: Ann
Child: Donald
Child: Flora
Child: Marion
Child: Angus
MacIsaac, Neil; Port uncertain, 1840-1849 ***4537.37*** *p120*
Wife: Catherine Campbell
Child: Donald
MacIsaac, Neil; Port uncertain, 1840-1849 ***4537.37*** *p120*
Wife: Catherine MacPhee
Child: Neil
Child: Flora
Child: John
Child: Donald
Child: Mary
MacIsaac, Peggy *SEE* MacIsaac, Peter
MacIsaac, Peter; Ontario, 1850-1859 ***4537.37*** *p64*
Wife: Catherine MacCormick
Child: Mary
Child: Ranald
Child: Kirsty
Child: Angus
Child: Peggy
Child: John
Child: Ann
MacIsaac, Peter; Ontario, 1851 ***4537.32*** *p41*
Wife: Catherine MacCormick
Child: Kirsty
Child: Angus
Child: Peggy
Child: Mary
Child: John
Child: Ann
Child: Ranald
MacIsaac, Ranald *SEE* MacIsaac, Peter
MacIsaac, Ranald; Port uncertain, 1840-1849 ***4537.37*** *p120*
Wife: Catherine Campbell
Child: Donald
Child: John
Child: Marion
Child: Flora
MacIsaac, Roderick *SEE* MacIsaac, Angus
MacIsaac, Roderick *SEE* MacIsaac, Hector
MacIsaac, Roderick; Saskatchewan, 1884 ***4537.37*** *p98*
MacIsaac, Sally *SEE* MacIsaac, Donald
MacIsaac, Sally MacIntyre *SEE* MacIsaac, Donald
Macittrick, John; Maryland, 1665 ***2524.55*** *p141*
MacIver, Alexander *SEE* MacIver, James
MacIver, Allan; Ontario, 1855 ***4537.32*** *p41*
Wife: Catherine MacLeod
Child: Malcolm
Child: John

MacIver, Angus *SEE* MacIver, James
MacIver, Angus *SEE* MacIver, Malcolm
MacIver, Angus *SEE* MacIver, Murdo
MacIver, Angus; Ontario, 1855 ***4537.32*** *p41*
Wife: Catherine MacKay
Child: Kirsty
Child: Mary
Child: Annabella
Child: Colin
MacIver, Ann *SEE* MacIver, Donald
MacIver, Ann *SEE* MacIver, John
MacIver, Ann *SEE* MacIver, Kenneth
MacIver, Ann *SEE* MacIver, Malcolm
MacIver, Ann *SEE* MacIver, Norman
MacIver, Ann; Ontario, 1851 ***4537.32*** *p36*
MacIver, Ann MacKenzie *SEE* MacIver, James
MacIver, Ann MacLeod *SEE* MacIver, Duncan
MacIver, Ann Matheson *SEE* MacIver, Malcolm
MacIver, Ann Murray *SEE* MacIver, Donald
MacIver, Ann Smith *SEE* MacIver, John
MacIver, Ann Smith *SEE* MacIver, Norman
MacIver, Annabella *SEE* MacIver, Angus
MacIver, Betsy *SEE* MacIver, John
MacIver, Betsy; Ontario, 1851 ***4537.32*** *p70*
MacIver, Catherine *SEE* MacIver, Duncan
MacIver, Catherine *SEE* MacIver, John
MacIver, Catherine *SEE* MacIver, Margaret MacDonald
MacIver, Catherine *SEE* MacIver, Norman
MacIver, Catherine; Ontario, 1855 ***4537.32*** *p76*
MacIver, Catherine; Ontario, 1855 ***4537.32*** *p79*
MacIver, Catherine MacKay *SEE* MacIver, Angus
MacIver, Catherine MacLean *SEE* MacIver, John
MacIver, Catherine MacLeod *SEE* MacIver, Allan
MacIver, Colin *SEE* MacIver, Angus
MacIver, Donald *SEE* MacIver, Duncan
MacIver, Donald *SEE* MacIver, James
MacIver, Donald *SEE* MacIver, John
MacIver, Donald *SEE* MacIver, Kenneth
MacIver, Donald *SEE* MacIver, Malcolm
MacIver, Donald *SEE* MacIver, Murdo
MacIver, Donald; Augusta, Georgia, 1817 ***1224.3*** *p49*
MacIver, Donald; Ontario, 1851 ***4537.32*** *p42*
Wife: Isabella MacDonald
Child: Isabella
Child: Malcolm
MacIver, Donald; Ontario, 1863 ***4537.32*** *p42*
Wife: Ann Murray
Child: Ann
Child: Kirsty
Child: Margaret
Child: Mary
MacIver, Donald; Ontario, 1863 ***4537.32*** *p42*
Wife: Mary Smith
MacIver, Duncan; Ontario, 1863 ***4537.32*** *p43*
Child: Donald
Child: John
Child: Mary Ann
Child: Hannah
Wife: Ann MacLeod
Child: Catherine
MacIver, Effie *SEE* MacIver, John
MacIver, Effie MacArthur *SEE* MacIver, John
MacIver, Hannah *SEE* MacIver, Duncan
MacIver, Isabella *SEE* MacIver, Donald
MacIver, Isabella *SEE* MacIver, John
MacIver, Isabella *SEE* MacIver, Kenneth
MacIver, Isabella MacDonald *SEE* MacIver, Donald
MacIver, Isabella MacKay *SEE* MacIver, Malcolm
MacIver, James; Ontario, 1851 ***4537.32*** *p43*
Wife: Ann MacKenzie
Child: Margaret
Child: Angus
Child: Alexander
Child: Murdo
Child: Donald
Child: Malcolm
Child: John
MacIver, Joan *SEE* MacIver, John
MacIver, John *SEE* MacIver, Allan
MacIver, John *SEE* MacIver, Duncan
MacIver, John *SEE* MacIver, James
MacIver, John *SEE* MacIver, John
MacIver, John *SEE* MacIver, Kenneth
MacIver, John *SEE* MacIver, Malcolm
MacIver, John *SEE* MacIver, Murdo
MacIver, John; Ontario, 1851 ***4537.32*** *p44*
Wife: Effie MacArthur
Child: Norman
Child: Isabella
Child: John
Child: Malcolm
Child: Donald
MacIver, John; Ontario, 1863 ***4537.32*** *p43*
Child: Kirsty
Child: John
Child: Catherine
Child: Ann
Wife: Catherine MacLean
Child: Donald
Child: Betsy
Child: Murdo
Child: Margaret
MacIver, John; Ontario, 1880-1889 ***4537.32*** *p44*
Wife: Ann Smith
Child: Joan
Child: Effie
MacIver, Kenneth *SEE* MacIver, Murdo
MacIver, Kenneth; Ontario, 1863 ***4537.32*** *p44*
Wife: Mary MacLean
Child: John
Child: Ann
Child: Magdalene
Child: Mary
Child: Isabella
Child: Donald
MacIver, Kirsty *SEE* MacIver, Angus
MacIver, Kirsty *SEE* MacIver, Donald
MacIver, Kirsty *SEE* MacIver, John
MacIver, Kirsty *SEE* MacIver, Malcolm
MacIver, Kirsty *SEE* MacIver, Murdo
MacIver, Kirsty; Ontario, 1855 ***4537.32*** *p23*
MacIver, Kirsty Ann *SEE* MacIver, Malcolm
MacIver, Kirsty MacDonald *SEE* MacIver, Malcolm
MacIver, Kirsty Morrison *SEE* MacIver, Murdo
MacIver, Kirsty Smith; Ontario, 1851 ***4537.32*** *p44*
MacIver, Magdalene *SEE* MacIver, Kenneth
MacIver, Malcolm *SEE* MacIver, Allan
MacIver, Malcolm *SEE* MacIver, Donald
MacIver, Malcolm *SEE* MacIver, James
MacIver, Malcolm *SEE* MacIver, John
MacIver, Malcolm *SEE* MacIver, Malcolm
MacIver, Malcolm; Ontario, 1851 ***4537.32*** *p45*
Wife: Ann Matheson
Child: Donald
Child: John
Child: Kirsty Ann
Child: Ann
Child: Kirsty
MacIver, Malcolm; Ontario, 1851 ***4537.32*** *p46*
MacIver, Malcolm; Ontario, 1851 ***4537.32*** *p46*
Wife: Margaret Graham
Child: Margaret
MacIver, Malcolm; Ontario, 1855 ***4537.32*** *p45*
Wife: Isabella MacKay
Child: Ann
Child: Malcolm
Child: Mary Ann
Child: Donald
MacIver, Malcolm; Ontario, 1855 ***4537.32*** *p46*
Wife: Kirsty MacDonald
Child: Angus
Child: Margaret
MacIver, Malcolm; Ontario, 1860-1869 ***4537.32*** *p45*
MacIver, Margaret *SEE* MacIver, Donald
MacIver, Margaret *SEE* MacIver, James
MacIver, Margaret *SEE* MacIver, John
MacIver, Margaret *SEE* MacIver, Malcolm
MacIver, Margaret *SEE* MacIver, Murdo
MacIver, Margaret; Ontario, 1851 ***4537.32*** *p88*
MacIver, Margaret; Ontario, 1855 ***4537.32*** *p94*
MacIver, Margaret; Ontario, 1863 ***4537.32*** *p67*
MacIver, Margaret Graham *SEE* MacIver, Malcolm
MacIver, Margaret MacDonald; Ontario, 1855 ***4537.32*** *p41*
Child: Catherine
Child: Murdo
MacIver, Mary *SEE* MacIver, Angus
MacIver, Mary *SEE* MacIver, Donald
MacIver, Mary *SEE* MacIver, Kenneth
MacIver, Mary *SEE* MacIver, Murdo
MacIver, Mary Ann *SEE* MacIver, Duncan
MacIver, Mary Ann *SEE* MacIver, Malcolm
MacIver, Mary MacDonald *SEE* MacIver, Murdo
MacIver, Mary MacLean *SEE* MacIver, Kenneth
MacIver, Mary Smith *SEE* MacIver, Donald
MacIver, Murdo *SEE* MacIver, James
MacIver, Murdo *SEE* MacIver, John
MacIver, Murdo *SEE* MacIver, Margaret MacDonald
MacIver, Murdo; Ontario, 1855 ***4537.32*** *p47*
Wife: Kirsty Morrison
Child: Mary
Child: Donald
Child: Margaret
Child: William
Child: Kirsty
Child: Angus
Child: John
MacIver, Murdo; Ontario, 1863 ***4537.32*** *p46*
Child: Kenneth
Wife: Mary MacDonald
MacIver, Norman *SEE* MacIver, John
MacIver, Norman; Ontario, 1863 ***4537.32*** *p47*
Wife: Ann Smith
Child: Catherine
Child: Ann
MacIver, William *SEE* MacIver, Murdo
Mack, . . .; Vermont, n.d. ***5900.10*** *p314*
Mack, Alexander; America, 1729 ***2856.30*** *p282*
Mack, Andreas; America, 1752 ***2856.30*** *p282*
Mack, Anna Beane; Vermont, 1855-1940 ***5900.10*** *p126*
Mack, Anna Maria; America, 1751 ***2856.30*** *p282*
Mack, Balthasar; America, 1752 ***2856.30*** *p282*
With wife & child
Mack, Barcy 38; Ontario, 1861 ***2896.26*** *p35*
Mack, Bridget Mary Cairns; Vermont, 1840-1921 ***5900.10*** *p392*
Mack, Bridget Mary Nester; Vermont, 1816-1897 ***5900.10*** *p314*
Mack, Charles; Vermont, 1847-1929 ***5900.10*** *p126*
Mack, David 54; Ontario, 1871 ***1823.15*** *p150*
Mack, Ellen Cronin; Vermont, 1844-1925 ***5900.10*** *p120*
Mack, Ellen M.; Vermont, 1850-1932 ***5900.10*** *p118*
Mack, Ellen Welch 98; Vermont, 1901 ***5900.10*** *p116*
Mack, Fannie; Vermont, 1866-1885 ***5900.10*** *p314*
Mack, Francis; New York, 1839 ***8197.10*** *p264*
Mack, Hanora 37; Vermont, 1861 ***5900.10*** *p361*
Mack, Jakob; America, 1752 ***2856.30*** *p282*
With wife & 3 children
Mack, Mrs. Jakob; America, 1738 ***2856.30*** *p282*
Mack, James; Vermont, 1853-1932 ***5900.10*** *p111*
Mack, James, Sr. 85; Vermont, 1892 ***5900.10*** *p116*
Mack, Johann; America, 1752 ***2856.30*** *p282*
Mack, John; Maryland, 1659 ***2524.55*** *p141*
Mack, John; Vermont, 1840-1911 ***5900.10*** *p120*
Mack, Katherine; Vermont, 1862-1938 ***5900.10*** *p314*
Mack, M.; Mobile, Alabama, 1810-1845 ***1640.10*** *p148*
Mack, Margaret Kennedy; Vermont, 1840-1908 ***5900.10*** *p392*
Mack, Margarete; America, 1769 ***2856.30*** *p282*
Mack, Mary; Vermont, 1840-1912 ***5900.10*** *p316*
Mack, Mary Fitts; Vermont, 1858-1923 ***5900.10*** *p314*
Mack, Mathes; Port uncertain, 1786 ***2856.30*** *p282*
Mack, Michael; Vermont, 1812-1865 ***5900.10*** *p314*
Mack, Michael; Vermont, 1824-1904 ***5900.10*** *p391*
Mack, Michael; Vermont, 1856-1915 ***5900.10*** *p314*
Mack, Nora Baker; Vermont, 1855-1914 ***5900.10*** *p111*
Mack, Patrick; Vermont, 1832-1895 ***5900.10*** *p392*
Mack, Peiter; America, 1752 ***2856.30*** *p282*
Mack, Philipp Jakob; America, 1752 ***2856.30*** *p282*
Mack, Theobald; Port uncertain, 1786 ***2856.30*** *p282*
Mack, Thomas 21; Philadelphia, 1774 ***1220.25*** *p67*
Mack, William; Vermont, 1853-1865 ***5900.10*** *p314*
Mackaness, Thomas Thornton M.; New York, 1805 ***8197.10*** *p29*
Mackanit, Tho; Virginia, 1698 ***6212.30*** *p61*
Mackany, Robert; Maryland, 1675 ***2524.55*** *p141*
Mackany, Roderick; Georgia, 1738 ***1640.10*** *p124*
Mackara, Owen; Maryland, 1665 ***2524.55*** *p141*
Mackarmey, Joan; Maryland, 1680 ***2524.55*** *p141*
Mackartie, Jno; Virginia, 1688 ***6212.30*** *p58*
Mackasay, Patrick 46; Ontario, 1871 ***1823.15*** *p150*
Mackavoy, A. 20; Ontario, 1861 ***2896.26*** *p14*
Mackay, Mr.; Georgia, 1736 ***1640.10*** *p131*
MacKay, Mr.; Ontario, 1830-1839 ***4537.32*** *p50*
With wife
Mackay, Mr.; Quebec, 1856 ***9196.15*** *p10*
Mackay, Mr.; Quebec, 1857 ***9196.15*** *p21*
MacKay, Alexander *SEE* MacKay, Angus
MacKay, Alexander *SEE* MacKay, Donald
Mackay, Alexander; Georgia, 1736 ***1640.10*** *p125*
MacKay, Alexander; Port uncertain, 1840-1849 ***4537.37*** *p121*
Wife: Marion
Child: Angus
Child: Donald
MacKay, Angus *SEE* MacKay, Alexander
MacKay, Angus *SEE* MacKay, Angus
MacKay, Angus *SEE* MacKay, Donald
MacKay, Angus *SEE* MacKay, Duncan
MacKay, Angus *SEE* MacKay, John
MacKay, Angus *SEE* MacKay, Malcolm
Mackay, Angus; Georgia, 1736 ***1640.10*** *p125*
Mackay, Angus; Georgia, 1741 ***1640.10*** *p125*
Mackay, Angus; Georgia, 1757 ***1640.10*** *p125*
MacKay, Angus; Nova Scotia, 1840-1849 ***4537.37*** *p16*
Wife: Catherine
Child: Mary

Child: Charles
Child: Donald
MacKay, Angus; Ontario, 1851 ***4537.32*** *p48*
Uncle: John
MacKay, Angus; Ontario, 1851 ***4537.32*** *p48*
Child: Catherine
Child: Effie
Child: Malcolm
Wife: Marion MacLennan
Child: John
Child: Alexander
Child: Mary
Child: Kirsty
MacKay, Angus; Ontario, 1860-1869 ***4537.35*** *p58*
Wife: Flora
Child: Ann
Child: John
Child: Finlay
MacKay, Angus; Ontario, 1862 ***4537.32*** *p47*
Wife: Flora
Child: Finlay
Child: Ann
Child: John
MacKay, Angus; Ontario, 1863 ***4537.32*** *p47*
Wife: Kirsty Morrison
Child: John
Child: Ann
Child: Kirsty
Child: Malcolm
Child: Catherine
Child: Murdo
MacKay, Angus; Ontario, 1863 ***4537.32*** *p48*
Wife: Margaret MacKenzie
Child: Alexander
Child: Donald
Child: Norman
Child: Kirsty
Child: Angus
Child: John
Child: Malcolm
Mackay, Angus 28; Ontario, 1871 ***1823.15*** *p150*
Mackay, Angus 61; Ontario, 1871 ***1823.15*** *p150*
MacKay, Ann *SEE* MacKay, Angus
MacKay, Ann *SEE* MacKay, Donald
MacKay, Ann *SEE* MacKay, Duncan
MacKay, Ann *SEE* MacKay, John
MacKay, Ann *SEE* MacKay, Neil
MacKay, Ann; Ontario, 1851 ***4537.32*** *p78*
MacKay, Ann; Ontario, 1863 ***4537.32*** *p93*
MacKay, Ann MacDonald *SEE* MacKay, Donald
Mackay, Anne; Georgia, 1741 ***1640.10*** *p31*
MacKay, Betsy MacKiggan *SEE* MacKay, Donald
Mackay, C. A. 55; Alaska, 1916 ***9196.1*** *p44*
Mackay, C. A. 55; Yukon, 1916 ***9196.1*** *p44*
MacKay, Catherine *SEE* MacKay, Angus
MacKay, Catherine *SEE* MacKay, John
MacKay, Catherine *SEE* MacKay, Malcolm
MacKay, Catherine *SEE* MacKay, Mary
MacKay, Catherine *SEE* MacKay, Neil
Mackay, Catherine; Georgia, 1741 ***1640.10*** *p125*
MacKay, Catherine; Ontario, 1851 ***4537.32*** *p68*
MacKay, Catherine; Ontario, 1855 ***4537.32*** *p41*
MacKay, Catherine MacLeod *SEE* MacKay, Malcolm
MacKay, Charles *SEE* MacKay, Angus
Mackay, Charles; Georgia, 1736 ***1640.10*** *p125*
Mackay, Chris 40; Ontario, 1871 ***1823.15*** *p150*
Mackay, Christian; Georgia, 1741 ***1640.10*** *p98*
Daughter: Katherine
Mackay, Daniel; Georgia, 1758 ***1640.10*** *p125*
Mackay, Daniel; Georgia, 1759 ***1640.10*** *p126*
Mackay, Daniel; Georgia, 1761 ***1640.10*** *p126*
MacKay, Donald *SEE* MacKay, Alexander
MacKay, Donald *SEE* MacKay, Angus
MacKay, Donald *SEE* MacKay, Donald
MacKay, Donald *SEE* MacKay, Ewen
MacKay, Donald *SEE* MacKay, Finlay
MacKay, Donald *SEE* MacKay, John
MacKay, Donald *SEE* MacKay, Malcolm
Mackay, Donald; Georgia, 1741 ***1640.10*** *p126*
Son: James
Daughter: Margaret
Mackay, Donald; Georgia, 1741 ***1640.10*** *p126*
Mackay, Donald; Georgia, 1757 ***1640.10*** *p126*
Mackay, Donald; Georgia, 1768 ***1640.10*** *p126*
MacKay, Donald; Ontario, 1840-1849 ***4537.37*** *p65*
Wife: Betsy MacKiggan
Child: Angus
MacKay, Donald; Ontario, 1860-1869 ***4537.35*** *p58*
Wife: Ann MacDonald
Child: Alexander
Child: Rachel
Child: Neil
Child: Malcolm
Child: Murdo
Child: Donald
Child: Peter
Child: Kirsty
Child: Kenneth
MacKay, Donald; Ontario, 1862 ***4537.32*** *p48*
Wife: Ann MacDonald
Child: Rachel
Child: Malcolm
Child: Marion
Child: Neil
Child: Murdo
Child: Kirsty
Child: Kenneth
Child: Alexander
Child: Donald
Child: Peter
MacKay, Donald; Ontario, 1863 ***4537.32*** *p49*
Wife: Kirsty Graham
MacKay, Donald; Ontario, 1863 ***4537.32*** *p49*
Wife: Margaret MacLean
Child: Ann
MacKay, Donald; Saskatchewan, 1865-1900 ***4537.37*** *p98*
Mackay, Donald Bain; Georgia, 1741 ***1640.10*** *p126*
MacKay, Dougal *SEE* MacKay, Malcolm
MacKay, Duncan; Nova Scotia, 1840-1849 ***4537.35*** *p19*
Wife: Kirsty MacLeod
Child: Gregor
Child: Mary
Child: Kirsty
Child: Angus
Sister: Ann
Child: Roderick
Child: Neil
Child: Rachel
Child: Ann
MacKay, Effie *SEE* MacKay, Angus
MacKay, Effie *SEE* MacKay, Finlay
MacKay, Effie *SEE* MacKay, John
MacKay, Effie MacLean *SEE* MacKay, John
Mackay, Elizabeth *SEE* Mackay, John
Mackay, Elizabeth; Georgia, 1741 ***1640.10*** *p111*
Mackay, Elizabeth; Georgia, 1741 ***1640.10*** *p126*
Mackay, Elizabeth Ann; Georgia, 1775 ***1640.10*** *p127*
MacKay, Ewen; Saskatchewan, 1889 ***4537.35*** *p66*
Wife: Kirsty Morrison
Child: Mary
Child: John
Child: Donald
MacKay, Finlay *SEE* MacKay, Angus
MacKay, Finlay; Ontario, 1860-1869 ***4537.35*** *p58*
Wife: Marion MacDonald
Child: Neil
Child: Donald
Child: Margaret
Child: Margaret
Child: John
Child: John
Child: Murdo
Child: Rachel
Child: Effie
Child: Kenneth
MacKay, Finlay; Ontario, 1862 ***4537.32*** *p49*
Wife: Marion MacDonald
Child: Effie
Child: Neil
Child: Donald
Child: Margaret
Child: John
Child: Kenneth
Child: Murdo
Child: Rachel
MacKay, Flora *SEE* MacKay, Angus
Mackay, Francis; New York, 1838 ***8197.10*** *p263*
Mackay, George; Georgia, 1741 ***1640.10*** *p127*
Mackay, George; Trinidad, 1837 ***1640.13*** *p87*
Mackay, George Grant; Vancouver, British Columbia, 1893 ***1640.13*** *p87*
MacKay, Gregor *SEE* MacKay, Duncan
Mackay, H.; Quebec, 1858 ***9196.15*** *p32*
Mackay, Hugh *SEE* Mackay, John
Mackay, Hugh; Georgia, 1735 ***1640.10*** *p127*
Mackay, Hugh; Georgia, 1736 ***1640.10*** *p127*
Mackay, Hugh; Georgia, 1742 ***1640.10*** *p127*
MacKay, Isabella *SEE* MacKay, Neil
MacKay, Isabella; Ontario, 1855 ***4537.32*** *p45*
MacKay, Isabella MacLennan *SEE* MacKay, John
MacKay, Isabella Murray *SEE* MacKay, Malcolm
Mackay, Isobel; Georgia, 1741 ***1640.10*** *p127*
Mackay, James *SEE* Mackay, Donald
Mackay, James; Georgia, 1735 ***1640.10*** *p127*
Mackay, James; Georgia, 1736 ***1640.10*** *p128*
Mackay, James; Georgia, 1739 ***1640.10*** *p127*
Mackay, James; Georgia, 1756 ***1640.10*** *p128*
Mackay, James; Jamaica, 1798 ***1640.13*** *p87*
Mackay, Janet *SEE* Mackay, John
MacKay, John *SEE* MacKay, Angus
MacKay, John *SEE* MacKay, Ewen
MacKay, John *SEE* MacKay, Finlay
Mackay, John *SEE* Mackay, John
MacKay, John *SEE* MacKay, John
MacKay, John *SEE* MacKay, Malcolm
MacKay, John *SEE* MacKay, Murdo
MacKay, John *SEE* MacKay, Roderick
Mackay, John; Georgia, 1733 ***1640.10*** *p128*
Mackay, John; Georgia, 1733 ***1640.10*** *p129*
Mackay, John; Georgia, 1736 ***1640.10*** *p128*
Wife: Janet
Child: Hugh
Child: Mary
Child: William
Child: John
Child: Elizabeth
Mackay, John; Georgia, 1736 ***1640.10*** *p128*
Mackay, John; Georgia, 1736 ***1640.10*** *p129*
Mackay, John; Georgia, 1753 ***1640.10*** *p129*
Mackay, John; Georgia, 1761 ***1640.10*** *p129*
MacKay, John; Manitoba, 1888 ***4537.35*** *p66*
With brother-in-law
Mackay, John; New York, 1838 ***8197.10*** *p264*
MacKay, John; Ontario, 1851 ***4537.32*** *p50*
Wife: Kirsty
Child: John
Child: Murdo
Child: Norman
Child: Angus
Child: Margaret
Child: Donald
Child: Catherine
Child: Malcolm
MacKay, John; Ontario, 1851 ***4537.32*** *p50*
Uncle: John
MacKay, John; Ontario, 1863 ***4537.32*** *p49*
Wife: Effie MacLean
Child: Effie
Child: Margaret
Child: Angus
Child: Ann
MacKay, John; Saskatchewan, 1889 ***4537.35*** *p66*
Wife: Isabella MacLennan
Child: Rachel
Child: Mary
Child: Malcolm
Mackay, John 15; Philadelphia, 1774 ***1220.25*** *p34*
Mackay, John 25; Philadelphia, 1774 ***1220.25*** *p67*
Mackay, John Alexander 18; Maryland, 1774 ***1220.25*** *p54*
Mackay, Joseph; New York, 1840 ***8197.10*** *p178*
Mackay, Katherine *SEE* Mackay, Christian
MacKay, Kenneth *SEE* MacKay, Donald
MacKay, Kenneth *SEE* MacKay, Finlay
MacKay, Kenneth *SEE* MacKay, Mary
MacKay, Kirsty *SEE* MacKay, Angus
MacKay, Kirsty *SEE* MacKay, Donald
MacKay, Kirsty *SEE* MacKay, Duncan
MacKay, Kirsty *SEE* MacKay, John
MacKay, Kirsty *SEE* MacKay, Malcolm
MacKay, Kirsty *SEE* MacKay, Murdo
MacKay, Kirsty; Canada, 1860-1869 ***4537.35*** *p72*
MacKay, Kirsty; Ontario, 1851 ***4537.32*** *p37*
MacKay, Kirsty; Ontario, 1855 ***4537.32*** *p37*
MacKay, Kirsty Graham *SEE* MacKay, Donald
MacKay, Kirsty MacKinnon *SEE* MacKay, Roderick
MacKay, Kirsty MacLeod *SEE* MacKay, Duncan
MacKay, Kirsty Morrison *SEE* MacKay, Angus
MacKay, Kirsty Morrison *SEE* MacKay, Ewen
MacKay, Lexy; Quebec, 1887 ***4537.35*** *p64*
MacKay, Malcolm *SEE* MacKay, Angus
MacKay, Malcolm *SEE* MacKay, Donald
MacKay, Malcolm *SEE* MacKay, John
MacKay, Malcolm *SEE* MacKay, Murdo
MacKay, Malcolm; Ontario, 1863 ***4537.32*** *p50*
Wife: Isabella Murray
Child: Catherine
MacKay, Malcolm; Ontario, 1863 ***4537.32*** *p51*
Wife: Kirsty
Child: John
MacKay, Malcolm; Saskatchewan, 1889 ***4537.35*** *p67*
Wife: Catherine MacLeod
Child: Dougal
Child: Marjory
Child: Neil
Child: Donald
Child: Roderick
Child: Angus
Child: Mary

Mackay, Malcolm 45; Ontario, 1871 ***1823.15*** *p150*
Mackay, Margaret *SEE* Mackay, Donald
MacKay, Margaret *SEE* MacKay, Finlay
MacKay, Margaret *SEE* MacKay, John
MacKay, Margaret *SEE* MacKay, Murdo
MacKay, Margaret; Ontario, 1860-1869 ***4537.35*** *p57*
MacKay, Margaret; Ontario, 1862 ***4537.32*** *p29*
MacKay, Margaret MacKenzie *SEE* MacKay, Angus
MacKay, Margaret MacLean *SEE* MacKay, Donald
Mackay, Marian; Georgia, 1741 ***1640.10*** *p129*
MacKay, Marion *SEE* MacKay, Alexander
MacKay, Marion *SEE* MacKay, Donald
MacKay, Marion *SEE* MacKay, Murdo
MacKay, Marion *SEE* MacKay, Roderick
MacKay, Marion; Port uncertain, 1861-1869 ***4537.35*** *p80*
MacKay, Marion MacDonald *SEE* MacKay, Finlay
MacKay, Marion MacLennan *SEE* MacKay, Angus
MacKay, Marion MacLennan *SEE* MacKay, Ranald
MacKay, Marion Smith *SEE* MacKay, Neil
MacKay, Marjory *SEE* MacKay, Malcolm
MacKay, Mary *SEE* MacKay, Angus
MacKay, Mary *SEE* MacKay, Duncan
MacKay, Mary *SEE* MacKay, Ewen
Mackay, Mary *SEE* Mackay, John
MacKay, Mary *SEE* MacKay, John
MacKay, Mary *SEE* MacKay, Malcolm
MacKay, Mary *SEE* MacKay, Neil
MacKay, Mary; Manitoba, 1888 ***4537.35*** *p67*
Mackay, Mary; Vermont, 1841-1896 ***5900.10*** *p327*
MacKay, Mary; Port uncertain, 1840-1849 ***4537.35*** *p81*
Child: Kenneth
Child: Catherine
MacKay, Mary; Port uncertain, 1860-1869 ***4537.35*** *p81*
MacKay, Mary; Port uncertain, 1860-1869 ***4537.35*** *p82*
MacKay, Mary; Port uncertain, 1860-1869 ***4537.35*** *p86*
MacKay, Murdo *SEE* MacKay, Angus
MacKay, Murdo *SEE* MacKay, Donald
MacKay, Murdo *SEE* MacKay, Finlay
MacKay, Murdo *SEE* MacKay, John
MacKay, Murdo; Ontario, 1863 ***4537.32*** *p51*
Wife: Marion
Child: Kirsty
Child: Margaret
Child: John
Child: Malcolm
Mackay, Murdoch; Savannah, Georgia, 1775 ***1640.10*** *p129*
MacKay, Neil *SEE* MacKay, Donald
MacKay, Neil *SEE* MacKay, Duncan
MacKay, Neil *SEE* MacKay, Finlay
MacKay, Neil *SEE* MacKay, Malcolm
Mackay, Neil; Georgia, 1736 ***1640.10*** *p129*
MacKay, Neil; Ontario, 1855 ***4537.32*** *p51*
Wife: Marion Smith
Child: Catherine
Child: Mary
Child: Ann
Child: Isabella
Mackay, Neil 56; Ontario, 1871 ***1823.15*** *p150*
MacKay, Norman *SEE* MacKay, Angus
MacKay, Norman *SEE* MacKay, John
Mackay, Patrick; Georgia, 1732 ***1640.10*** *p129*
Mackay, Patrick; Georgia, 1755 ***1640.10*** *p130*
Mackay, Patrick; Savannah, Georgia, 1764 ***1640.10*** *p130*
Mackay, Paul; Alabama, 1822-1845 ***1640.10*** *p131*
MacKay, Peter *SEE* MacKay, Donald
Mackay, Peter; New York, 1838 ***8197.10*** *p376*
Mackay, Peter 64; Ontario, 1871 ***1823.15*** *p150*
Mackay, R.; Quebec, 1858 ***9196.15*** *p38*
MacKay, Rachel *SEE* MacKay, Donald
MacKay, Rachel *SEE* MacKay, Duncan
MacKay, Rachel *SEE* MacKay, Finlay
MacKay, Rachel *SEE* MacKay, John
MacKay, Rachel; Nova Scotia, 1840-1849 ***4537.35*** *p33*
MacKay, Ranald; Manitoba, 1888 ***4537.35*** *p67*
Wife: Marion MacLennan
Mackay, Robert; California, 1881 ***1640.13*** *p87*
Mackay, Robert; Georgia, 1737 ***1640.10*** *p130*
Mackay, Robert; Virginia, 1772 ***1224.2*** *p74*
Mackay, Robert 84; Ontario, 1871 ***1823.22*** *p95*
MacKay, Roderick *SEE* MacKay, Duncan
MacKay, Roderick *SEE* MacKay, Malcolm
MacKay, Roderick; Manitoba, 1888 ***4537.35*** *p67*
Wife: Kirsty MacKinnon
Child: John
Child: Marion
Father: John
Mackay, Samuel; Georgia, 1742 ***1640.10*** *p130*
MacKay, Sarah; Nova Scotia, 1820-1829 ***4537.35*** *p27*
Mackay, William *SEE* Mackay, John
Mackay, William; Georgia, 1733 ***1640.10*** *p130*
MacKay, William; Georgia, 1736 ***1640.10*** *p131*
Mackay, William; Georgia, 1737 ***1640.10*** *p131*
Mackay, William; Georgia, 1740 ***1640.10*** *p131*
Mackay, William; Georgia, 1741 ***1640.10*** *p130*
Mackay, William; Georgia, 1741-1845 ***1640.10*** *p131*
Mackay, William; Georgia, 1762 ***1640.10*** *p131*
Mackay, William 54; Ontario, 1871 ***1823.15*** *p150*
Mackcay, Daniell; Maryland, 1665 ***2524.55*** *p141*
Mackclang, Woney; Virginia, 1703-1704 ***6212.30*** *p62*
Mackcramy, Aurit; Virginia, 1703-1704 ***6212.30*** *p62*
MackDaniell, Daniel; Maryland, 1682 ***2524.55*** *p141*
MackDannel, Redman; Maryland, 1681 ***2524.55*** *p141*
Mackdovell, Ennis; Maryland, 1674 ***2524.55*** *p141*
Mackeile, John; Maryland, 1673 ***2524.55*** *p141*
Mackeles, Jean; America, 1752 ***2856.30*** *p282*
With wife
Mackelgar, Daniell; Maryland, 1674 ***2524.55*** *p141*
Mackell, James; New York, 1834 ***8197.10*** *p71*
MacKellaig, Mary; Port uncertain, 1850-1859 ***4537.37*** *p108*
MacKellar, Dugald; St. Johns, Newfoundland, 1847 ***1640.13*** *p87*
Macken, James; New York, 1831 ***8197.10*** *p367*
Mackennie, Francis; Virginia, 1692-1693 ***6212.30*** *p59*
Mackenny, Margarett *SEE* Mackenny, Martin
Mackenny, Martin; Maryland, 1663 ***2524.55*** *p141*
Wife: Margarett
MacKensie, John 32; Alaska, 1917 ***9196.1*** *p7*
MacKensie, John 32; Yukon, 1917 ***9196.1*** *p7*
Mackenzie, Miss; Quebec, 1858 ***9196.15*** *p44*
Mackenzie, Mr.; Quebec, 1857 ***9196.15*** *p24*
Mackenzie, Mr.; Quebec, 1858 ***9196.15*** *p36*
MacKenzie, Alex 40; Ontario, 1871 ***1823.15*** *p150*
MacKenzie, Alexander *SEE* MacKenzie, Alexander
MacKenzie, Alexander *SEE* MacKenzie, John
MacKenzie, Alexander; Ontario, 1851 ***4537.32*** *p51*
MacKenzie, Alexander; Port uncertain, 1840-1849 ***4537.35*** *p81*
Wife: Mary
Child: Kirsty
Child: Alexander
Child: Murdo
Child: Duncan
Child: Francis
Mackenzie, Andrew; Georgia, 1738 ***1640.10*** *p132*
MacKenzie, Angus; Port uncertain, 1850-1859 ***4537.37*** *p121*
Wife: Sheila
Child: Peggy
Child: Mary
Child: Catherine
Child: Archie
MacKenzie, Ann *SEE* MacKenzie, Donald
MacKenzie, Ann *SEE* MacKenzie, Dougal
MacKenzie, Ann *SEE* MacKenzie, John
MacKenzie, Ann *SEE* MacKenzie, Kenneth
MacKenzie, Ann; Ontario, 1851 ***4537.32*** *p43*
MacKenzie, Ann; Port uncertain, 1880-1889 ***4537.35*** *p79*
MacKenzie, Annabella Gillies *SEE* MacKenzie, Kenneth
MacKenzie, Archie *SEE* MacKenzie, Angus
MacKenzie, C. J. M.; Vermont, 1846-1900 ***5900.10*** *p598*
MacKenzie, Catherine *SEE* MacKenzie, Angus
MacKenzie, Catherine *SEE* MacKenzie, Donald
Mackenzie, Catherine; Georgia, 1740 ***1640.10*** *p132*
Mackenzie, Christina; Alabama, 1790-1845 ***1640.10*** *p132*
Mackenzie, Colin Nicolson; America, 1872 ***1640.13*** *p88*
MacKenzie, David; America, 1776 ***1640.13*** *p88*
MacKenzie, Donald *SEE* MacKenzie, Dougal
MacKenzie, Donald *SEE* MacKenzie, Kenneth
MacKenzie, Donald *SEE* MacKenzie, Malcolm
MacKenzie, Donald *SEE* MacKenzie, Mary
Mackenzie, Donald; Georgia, 1738 ***1640.10*** *p132*
MacKenzie, Donald; Ontario, 1860-1869 ***4537.35*** *p58*
Wife: Kirsty MacLennan
Child: Kirsty
Child: Sarah
Child: Donald W.
Child: Mary
Child: Duncan
Child: Murdo
Child: Marion
Child: Margaret
Child: Catherine
Child: Ann
MacKenzie, Donald; Ontario, 1862 ***4537.32*** *p52*
Wife: Kirsty MacLennan
Child: Murdo
Child: Catherine
Child: Margaret
Child: Marion
Child: Ann
Child: Duncan
MacKenzie, Donald W. *SEE* MacKenzie, Donald
MacKenzie, Dougal *SEE* MacKenzie, Dougal
MacKenzie, Dougal; Manitoba, 1888 ***4537.35*** *p67*
Child: Malcolm
Child: John
Wife: Mary MacKay
Child: Finlay
Child: Ann
Brother: Donald
Child: Dougal
Mackenzie, Douglas; Grenada, 1854 ***1640.13*** *p88*
MacKenzie, Duncan *SEE* MacKenzie, Alexander
MacKenzie, Duncan *SEE* MacKenzie, Donald
MacKenzie, Duncan *SEE* MacKenzie, John
MacKenzie, Duncan *SEE* MacKenzie, Malcolm
Mackenzie, Duncan; New York, 1736 ***1224.2*** *p73*
Mackenzie, Duncan; New York, 1736 ***1224.2*** *p74*
MacKenzie, Ewen *SEE* MacKenzie, Malcolm
MacKenzie, Finlay *SEE* MacKenzie, Dougal
MacKenzie, Flora *SEE* MacKenzie, John
MacKenzie, Francis *SEE* MacKenzie, Alexander
Mackenzie, Hector; New York, n.d. ***1224.3*** *p49*
Mackenzie, Hector; Trinidad, 1808 ***1224.3*** *p49*
MacKenzie, Hugh *SEE* MacKenzie, John
MacKenzie, Isabella *SEE* MacKenzie, Kenneth
Mackenzie, J. O.; Quebec, 1858 ***9196.15*** *p36*
Mackenzie, Joanna; Wisconsin, 1882 ***1640.13*** *p88*
MacKenzie, John *SEE* MacKenzie, Dougal
MacKenzie, John *SEE* MacKenzie, John
MacKenzie, John *SEE* MacKenzie, Kenneth
Mackenzie, John; Georgia, 1737 ***1640.10*** *p132*
MacKenzie, John; Jamaica, 1785 ***1640.13*** *p88*
MacKenzie, John; Nova Scotia, 1843-1847 ***4537.37*** *p16*
Wife: Rachel
Child: Duncan
Child: Alexander
Child: Margaret
Child: Flora
Child: Hugh
Child: John
MacKenzie, John; Ontario, 1840-1849 ***4537.37*** *p65*
Sister: Ann
Sister: Kate
Mackenzie, John; San Francisco, 1886 ***1640.13*** *p88*
Mackenzie, John 16; Carolina, 1774 ***1220.25*** *p91*
MacKenzie, Kate *SEE* MacKenzie, John
MacKenzie, Kate *SEE* MacKenzie, Mary
MacKenzie, Kenneth; Ontario, 1855 ***4537.32*** *p52*
Child: Isabella
Wife: Annabella Gillies
Child: Ann
Child: John
Child: Kirsty
Child: Donald
Child: John
MacKenzie, Kirsty *SEE* MacKenzie, Alexander
MacKenzie, Kirsty *SEE* MacKenzie, Donald
MacKenzie, Kirsty *SEE* MacKenzie, Kenneth
MacKenzie, Kirsty; Ontario, 1855 ***4537.32*** *p92*
MacKenzie, Kirsty; Port uncertain, 1850-1859 ***4537.37*** *p108*
MacKenzie, Kirsty MacLennan *SEE* MacKenzie, Donald
MacKenzie, L. J. M.; Vermont, 1816-1889 ***5900.10*** *p598*
MacKenzie, L. J. M.; Vermont, 1848-1902 ***5900.10*** *p598*
MacKenzie, Lachlan *SEE* MacKenzie, Mary
MacKenzie, M. D. M.; Vermont, 1815-1898 ***5900.10*** *p598*
MacKenzie, Malcolm *SEE* MacKenzie, Dougal
MacKenzie, Malcolm; Port uncertain, 1840-1849 ***4537.37*** *p121*
Wife: Margaret
Child: Duncan
Child: Ewen
Child: Donald
MacKenzie, Margaret *SEE* MacKenzie, Donald
MacKenzie, Margaret *SEE* MacKenzie, John
MacKenzie, Margaret *SEE* MacKenzie, Malcolm
MacKenzie, Margaret; Ontario, 1863 ***4537.32*** *p48*
MacKenzie, Marion *SEE* MacKenzie, Donald
MacKenzie, Mary *SEE* MacKenzie, Alexander
MacKenzie, Mary *SEE* MacKenzie, Angus
MacKenzie, Mary *SEE* MacKenzie, Donald
MacKenzie, Mary; Saskatchewan, 1884 ***4537.37*** *p97*
MacKenzie, Mary; Port uncertain, 1840-1849 ***4537.37*** *p121*
Child: Kate
Child: Donald
Child: Lachlan
MacKenzie, Mary MacKay *SEE* MacKenzie, Dougal
MacKenzie, Murdo *SEE* MacKenzie, Alexander
MacKenzie, Murdo *SEE* MacKenzie, Donald
Mackenzie, Patrick Mitchell; Tobago, West Indies, 1875 ***1640.13*** *p88*
MacKenzie, Peggy *SEE* MacKenzie, Angus
MacKenzie, Peter; Saskatchewan, 1883 ***4537.37*** *p99*

Child: Donald
Child: James N.
Child: Peter
Child: Sarah
Child: Ann
MacKinnon, Donald; Saskatchewan, 1884 ***4537.37*** *p99*
Wife: Sarah MacDonald
Child: Alexander
Child: Marion
Child: Ranald
Child: Ewen
Child: John
Child: Donald
Child: Catherine
Child: Neil
MacKinnon, Donald; Port uncertain, 1850-1859 ***4537.35*** *p82*
Wife: Kirsty Morrison
Child: Ann
MacKinnon, Donald; Port uncertain, 1860-1869 ***4537.35*** *p82*
Wife: Una MacLeod
Child: Catherine
Child: Kirsty
Child: Mary
Child: John
MacKinnon, Donald John *SEE* MacKinnon, Hector
MacKinnon, Effie *SEE* MacKinnon, Malcolm
MacKinnon, Effie; Nova Scotia, 1840-1849 ***4537.35*** *p31*
MacKinnon, Ewen *SEE* MacKinnon, Donald
MacKinnon, Ewen; Saskatchewan, 1883 ***4537.37*** *p99*
Sister: Mary
MacKinnon, Ewen; Port uncertain, 1840-1849 ***4537.37*** *p121*
Wife: Marion Walker
Child: Mary
Child: Margaret
Child: Donald
Child: Neil
Child: Alexander
MacKinnon, Flora *SEE* MacKinnon, Donald
MacKinnon, Flora *SEE* MacKinnon, John
MacKinnon, Flora *SEE* MacKinnon, Rachel
MacKinnon, Francis *SEE* MacKinnon, Norman
MacKinnon, George *SEE* MacKinnon, Bannatyne
MacKinnon, Hector; Nova Scotia, 1828 ***4537.35*** *p21*
With wife
Child: Norman
Child: Catherine
Child: Margaret
Child: Hugh
MacKinnon, Hector; Saskatchewan, 1884 ***4537.37*** *p100*
Child: Donald
Child: Lachlan
Wife: Marion MacDonald
Child: Jane
Child: Mary
Child: Neil
Child: John
Child: Donald John
Child: Mary Ann
MacKinnon, Hector; Port uncertain, 1840-1849 ***4537.37*** *p121*
Wife: Ann MacCormick
Child: Angus
Child: John
Child: Donald
Child: Peggy
Child: Neil
Child: Mary
Child: Kate
MacKinnon, Hector; Port uncertain, 1840-1849 ***4537.37*** *p121*
Wife: Margaret Morrison
Child: Alexander
Child: John
Child: Rachel
Child: Ann
MacKinnon, Hugh *SEE* MacKinnon, Hector
MacKinnon, James; Nova Scotia, 1840-1849 ***4537.37*** *p16*
Wife: Kirsty Martin
Child: Angus
Child: Marion
Child: Lachlan
Child: Penny
Child: Mary
Child: John
MacKinnon, James N. *SEE* MacKinnon, Donald
MacKinnon, Jane *SEE* MacKinnon, Hector
MacKinnon, Janet *SEE* MacKinnon, Angus
MacKinnon, Janet *SEE* MacKinnon, John
MacKinnon, Joan *SEE* MacKinnon, Catherine MacDonald
MacKinnon, John *SEE* MacKinnon, Alexander
MacKinnon, John *SEE* MacKinnon, Angus
MacKinnon, John *SEE* MacKinnon, Bannatyne
MacKinnon, John *SEE* MacKinnon, Catherine MacDonald
MacKinnon, John *SEE* MacKinnon, Donald
MacKinnon, John *SEE* MacKinnon, Hector
MacKinnon, John *SEE* MacKinnon, James
MacKinnon, John *SEE* MacKinnon, John
MacKinnon, John *SEE* MacKinnon, Malcolm
MacKinnon, John *SEE* MacKinnon, Neil
MacKinnon, John *SEE* MacKinnon, Norman
MacKinnon, John *SEE* MacKinnon, Rachel MacLeod
MacKinnon, John *SEE* MacKinnon, William
MacKinnon, John; Ontario, 1850-1859 ***4537.37*** *p66*
Child: Janet
Child: Mary
Child: Angus
Child: Peggy
Child: John
Wife: Mary MacDonald
Child: Donald
MacKinnon, John; Ontario, 1851 ***4537.32*** *p53*
Wife: Mary MacDonald
Child: Peggy
Child: Donald
Child: Janet
Child: Mary
Child: Angus
Child: John
MacKinnon, John; Ontario, 1851 ***4537.37*** *p66*
Wife: Ann MacLellan
Child: Murdo
Child: Norman
Child: Malcolm
Child: Alexander
Child: Neil
MacKinnon, John; Port uncertain, 1840-1849 ***4537.37*** *p121*
Wife: Flora
Child: Catherine
MacKinnon, Kate *SEE* MacKinnon, Hector
MacKinnon, Kate MacDonald *SEE* MacKinnon, Angus
MacKinnon, Kenneth *SEE* MacKinnon, Catherine MacDonald
MacKinnon, Kirsty *SEE* MacKinnon, Donald
MacKinnon, Kirsty *SEE* MacKinnon, Malcolm
MacKinnon, Kirsty *SEE* MacKinnon, Murdo
MacKinnon, Kirsty *SEE* MacKinnon, Norman
MacKinnon, Kirsty; Manitoba, 1888 ***4537.35*** *p67*
MacKinnon, Kirsty; Port uncertain, 1850-1859 ***4537.35*** *p80*
MacKinnon, Kirsty Martin *SEE* MacKinnon, James
MacKinnon, Kirsty Morrison *SEE* MacKinnon, Donald
MacKinnon, Lachlan *SEE* MacKinnon, Donald
MacKinnon, Lachlan *SEE* MacKinnon, Hector
MacKinnon, Lachlan *SEE* MacKinnon, James
MacKinnon, Malcolm *SEE* MacKinnon, John
MacKinnon, Malcolm *SEE* MacKinnon, Norman
MacKinnon, Malcolm *SEE* MacKinnon, William
MacKinnon, Malcolm; Canada, 1860-1869 ***4537.35*** *p72*
Wife: Marion Cunningham MacDonald
Child: John
Child: Kirsty
MacKinnon, Malcolm; Nova Scotia, 1840-1849 ***4537.35*** *p21*
Wife: Kirsty
Child: Donald
Child: Kirsty
Child: Effie
Child: John
Child: William
Child: Norman
MacKinnon, Margaret *SEE* MacKinnon, Angus
MacKinnon, Margaret *SEE* MacKinnon, Bannatyne
MacKinnon, Margaret *SEE* MacKinnon, Donald
MacKinnon, Margaret *SEE* MacKinnon, Ewen
MacKinnon, Margaret *SEE* MacKinnon, Hector
MacKinnon, Margaret *SEE* MacKinnon, Rachel
MacKinnon, Margaret *SEE* MacKinnon, William
MacKinnon, Margaret; Canada, 1860-1869 ***4537.35*** *p72*
MacKinnon, Margaret; Ontario, 1840-1849 ***4537.37*** *p42*
MacKinnon, Margaret; Port uncertain, 1860-1869 ***4537.35*** *p79*
MacKinnon, Margaret MacInnes *SEE* MacKinnon, Donald
MacKinnon, Margaret Morrison *SEE* MacKinnon, Hector
MacKinnon, Marion *SEE* MacKinnon, Bannatyne
MacKinnon, Marion *SEE* MacKinnon, Catherine MacDonald
MacKinnon, Marion *SEE* MacKinnon, Donald
MacKinnon, Marion *SEE* MacKinnon, James
MacKinnon, Marion; Nova Scotia, 1840-1849 ***4537.37*** *p21*
MacKinnon, Marion; Port uncertain, 1840-1849 ***4537.37*** *p119*
MacKinnon, Marion; Port uncertain, 1860-1869 ***4537.35*** *p80*
MacKinnon, Marion Cunningham MacDonald *SEE* MacKinnon, Malcolm
MacKinnon, Marion MacDonald *SEE* MacKinnon, Hector
MacKinnon, Marion Walker *SEE* MacKinnon, Ewen
MacKinnon, Mary *SEE* MacKinnon, Angus
MacKinnon, Mary *SEE* MacKinnon, Catherine MacDonald
MacKinnon, Mary *SEE* MacKinnon, Donald
MacKinnon, Mary *SEE* MacKinnon, Ewen
MacKinnon, Mary *SEE* MacKinnon, Hector
MacKinnon, Mary *SEE* MacKinnon, James
MacKinnon, Mary *SEE* MacKinnon, John
MacKinnon, Mary *SEE* MacKinnon, Murdo
MacKinnon, Mary *SEE* MacKinnon, Rachel
MacKinnon, Mary; Ontario, 1840-1849 ***4537.37*** *p50*
MacKinnon, Mary; Ontario, 1849 ***4537.32*** *p54*
MacKinnon, Mary; Ontario, 1850-1859 ***4537.37*** *p66*
MacKinnon, Mary Ann *SEE* MacKinnon, Catherine MacDonald
MacKinnon, Mary Ann *SEE* MacKinnon, Hector
MacKinnon, Mary Ann *SEE* MacKinnon, Rachel MacLeod
MacKinnon, Mary MacDonald *SEE* MacKinnon, John
MacKinnon, Mary MacPherson *SEE* MacKinnon, Neil
MacKinnon, Mary Morrison *SEE* MacKinnon, Alexander
MacKinnon, Murdo *SEE* MacKinnon, Angus
MacKinnon, Murdo *SEE* MacKinnon, Donald
MacKinnon, Murdo *SEE* MacKinnon, John
MacKinnon, Murdo; Nova Scotia, 1850-1859 ***4537.35*** *p21*
Wife: Mary
Child: Mary
Child: Kirsty
MacKinnon, Neil *SEE* MacKinnon, Donald
MacKinnon, Neil *SEE* MacKinnon, Ewen
MacKinnon, Neil *SEE* MacKinnon, Hector
MacKinnon, Neil *SEE* MacKinnon, John
MacKinnon, Neil *SEE* MacKinnon, Rachel
MacKinnon, Neil; Ontario, 1840-1849 ***4537.37*** *p66*
Wife: Mary MacPherson
Child: Ann
Child: Roderick
Child: Catherine
Child: John
Child: Donald
MacKinnon, Norman *SEE* MacKinnon, Bannatyne
MacKinnon, Norman *SEE* MacKinnon, Donald
MacKinnon, Norman *SEE* MacKinnon, Hector
MacKinnon, Norman *SEE* MacKinnon, John
MacKinnon, Norman *SEE* MacKinnon, Malcolm
MacKinnon, Norman *SEE* MacKinnon, William
MacKinnon, Norman; Nova Scotia, 1840-1849 ***4537.35*** *p22*
Wife: Rachel Campbell
Child: Malcolm
Child: John
Child: Francis
Child: Kirsty
MacKinnon, Peggy *SEE* MacKinnon, Angus
MacKinnon, Peggy *SEE* MacKinnon, Hector
MacKinnon, Peggy *SEE* MacKinnon, John
MacKinnon, Penny *SEE* MacKinnon, James
MacKinnon, Peter *SEE* MacKinnon, Donald
MacKinnon, Rachel *SEE* MacKinnon, Bannatyne
MacKinnon, Rachel *SEE* MacKinnon, Hector
MacKinnon, Rachel; America, 1860-1869 ***4537.35*** *p74*
MacKinnon, Rachel; Port uncertain, 1850-1859 ***4537.37*** *p121*
Child: Mary
Child: Margaret
Child: Donald
Child: Flora
Child: Neil
MacKinnon, Rachel Campbell *SEE* MacKinnon, Norman
MacKinnon, Rachel MacLeod; Port uncertain, 1860-1869 ***4537.35*** *p82*
Child: Mary Ann
Child: John
MacKinnon, Ranald *SEE* MacKinnon, Donald
MacKinnon, Roderick *SEE* MacKinnon, Alexander
MacKinnon, Roderick *SEE* MacKinnon, Angus
MacKinnon, Roderick *SEE* MacKinnon, Neil
MacKinnon, Sarah *SEE* MacKinnon, Donald
MacKinnon, Sarah MacDonald *SEE* MacKinnon, Donald
MacKinnon, Una MacLeod *SEE* MacKinnon, Donald

MacKinnon, William *SEE* MacKinnon, Bannatyne
MacKinnon, William *SEE* MacKinnon, Malcolm
MacKinnon, William; Nova Scotia, 1840-1849 ***4537.35*** *p22*
Wife: Margaret
Child: Norman
Child: John
Child: Malcolm
Mackinson, Thomas; New York, 1839 ***8197.10*** *p380*
Mackintosh, Charles; New York, 1749 ***1224.2*** *p73*
MacKintosh, Elizabeth Herron 88; Vermont, 1887 ***5900.10*** *p556*
Mackintosh, James; Florida, n.d. ***1224.2*** *p73*
MacKintosh, John 72; Vermont, 1860 ***5900.10*** *p556*
Mackintosh, Lachlan; Charleston, South Carolina, 1789 ***1224.2*** *p73*
Mackintosh, Robert; New York, New York, 1782 ***1224.2*** *p73*
Mackintosh, Robert; Tortola, 1782 ***1224.2*** *p73*
Mackit, Thomas; Maryland, 1682 ***2524.55*** *p141*
Macklam, George 41; Ontario, 1871 ***1823.28*** *p59*
Macklarne, Nicholas; Maryland, 1682 ***2524.55*** *p141*
Macklaughlan, Daniell; Maryland, 1682 ***2524.55*** *p141*
Macklin, Edmind 33; Ontario, 1871 ***1823.22*** *p95*
Macklin, Edward; New York, 1828-1834 ***8197.10*** *p309*
Macklin, Edward 48; Ontario, 1871 ***1823.22*** *p95*
Macklin, Edwin 37; Ontario, 1871 ***1823.22*** *p95*
Macklin, James 65; Ontario, 1871 ***1823.22*** *p95*
Macklin, John; New York, 1837 ***8197.10*** *p263*
Macklin, John 24; Carolina, 1774 ***1220.25*** *p50*
Wife: Mary 23
Macklin, Mary 23 *SEE* Macklin, John
Macklin, Robert; Maryland, 1658 ***2524.55*** *p141*
Macklin, Robert 46; Ontario, 1871 ***1823.22*** *p95*
Macklin, Samuel 60; Ontario, 1871 ***1823.22*** *p95*
Macklin, Sarah; New York, 1839 ***8197.10*** *p264*
Macklin, William 43; Ontario, 1871 ***1823.22*** *p95*
Macknamery, John; Maryland, 1675 ***2524.55*** *p142*
Macknemarra, Cover; Maryland, 1682 ***2524.55*** *p142*
Macknemarrough, Timothy; Maryland, 1664 ***2524.55*** *p142*
Macknin, James; Maryland, 1675 ***2524.55*** *p142*
Mackowiak, Mary; Maryland, 1910 ***3259.35*** *p36*
Mackowiak, Stefan; Maryland, 1910 ***3259.35*** *p37*
Mackoy, Daniel; Maryland, 1675 ***2524.55*** *p142*
Mackrel, Margaret 90; Vermont, 1929 ***5900.10*** *p405*
Mackrell, Edward 25; Virginia, 1775 ***1220.25*** *p95*
Mackrell, James 21; Virginia, 1775 ***1220.25*** *p95*
Mackrell, Thomas; Maryland, 1682 ***2524.55*** *p142*
Mackrell, Thomas; Virginia, 1665-1666 ***6212.30*** *p25*
Mackrey, Jeffry; Maryland, 1675 ***2524.55*** *p142*
Mackrue, Owen; Maryland, 1665 ***2524.55*** *p142*
Macksey, Ellen; Vermont, 1845-1900 ***5900.10*** *p358*
Macksey, Mary Ann; Vermont, 1847-1885 ***5900.10*** *p81*
Mackton, John; Virginia, 1663 ***6212.30*** *p2*
Mackworth, Francis; Virginia, 1664 ***6212.30*** *p12*
Mackworth, Joslin; Virginia, 1664 ***6212.30*** *p7*
Mackwrath, Lancelot; Virginia, 1690-1691 ***6212.30*** *p59*
Macky, Catharine 61; Ontario, 1871 ***1823.28*** *p59*
Macky, John 51; Ontario, 1871 ***1823.28*** *p59*
Macky, Joseph; New York, 1807 ***8197.10*** *p44*
Macky, Laurance 57; Ontario, 1871 ***1823.28*** *p59*
MacLachlan, Jessie; America, 1870-1879 ***4537.35*** *p74*
Maclean, Miss; Quebec, 1857 ***9196.15*** *p23*
Maclean, Mr.; Quebec, 1857 ***9196.15*** *p23*
MacLean, Alexander *SEE* MacLean, Donald
MacLean, Alexander *SEE* MacLean, Duncan
MacLean, Alexander *SEE* MacLean, John
Maclean, Alexander; Georgia, 1736 ***1640.10*** *p136*
Maclean, Alexander; Georgia, 1737 ***1640.10*** *p136*
MacLean, Alexander; Port uncertain, 1850-1859 ***4537.37*** *p122*
Wife: Margaret MacDonald
Child: Donald
Child: Ewen
Child: Neil
Child: Mary
Child: James
MacLean, Allan *SEE* MacLean, Angus
Maclean, Allan; Georgia, 1736 ***1640.10*** *p136*
MacLean, Angus *SEE* MacLean, Donald
MacLean, Angus *SEE* MacLean, Isabella MacAulay
MacLean, Angus *SEE* MacLean, John
MacLean, Angus *SEE* MacLean, Kenneth
MacLean, Angus *SEE* MacLean, Neil
MacLean, Angus *SEE* MacLean, Norman
MacLean, Angus; Ontario, 1851 ***4537.32*** *p54*
Wife: Marion MacDonald
Child: Catherine
Child: Hector
Child: Ann
Child: Donald
Child: Kirsty
Child: Allan
MacLean, Angus; Ontario, 1855 ***4537.32*** *p54*
Wife: Margaret Morrison
Child: Kirsty
Child: Isabella
Child: Ann
Child: Marion
Child: Donald
Child: Norman
Child: Malcolm
Child: Margaret
MacLean, Angus; Port uncertain, 1840-1849 ***4537.37*** *p122*
Sibling: Ann
Sibling: Janet
MacLean, Ann *SEE* MacLean, Angus
MacLean, Ann *SEE* MacLean, Donald
MacLean, Ann *SEE* MacLean, Hugh
MacLean, Ann *SEE* MacLean, John
MacLean, Ann *SEE* MacLean, Norman
MacLean, Ann; Ontario, 1863 ***4537.32*** *p79*
MacLean, Ann; Ontario, 1885 ***4537.32*** *p80*
MacLean, Ann; Port uncertain, 1840-1849 ***4537.35*** *p82*
Child: Lachlan
Child: Catherine
MacLean, Ann; Port uncertain, 1840-1849 ***4537.37*** *p116*
MacLean, Ann Campbell *SEE* MacLean, John
MacLean, Archie *SEE* MacLean, Archie
MacLean, Archie *SEE* MacLean, Kenneth
MacLean, Archie; Port uncertain, 1850-1859 ***4537.37*** *p122*
Wife: Penny Steele
Child: Archie
Child: Margaret
MacLean, Can 17; Ontario, 1871 ***1823.15*** *p150*
MacLean, Catherine *SEE* MacLean, Angus
MacLean, Catherine *SEE* MacLean, Ann
MacLean, Catherine *SEE* MacLean, Donald
MacLean, Catherine *SEE* MacLean, Ewen
MacLean, Catherine *SEE* MacLean, John
MacLean, Catherine *SEE* MacLean, Kenneth
MacLean, Catherine *SEE* MacLean, Malcolm
MacLean, Catherine *SEE* MacLean, Neil
MacLean, Catherine *SEE* MacLean, Norman
MacLean, Catherine; Maryland, 1888 ***4537.35*** *p70*
MacLean, Catherine; Nova Scotia, 1840-1849 ***4537.37*** *p17*
MacLean, Catherine; Ontario, 1849 ***4537.37*** *p64*
MacLean, Catherine; Ontario, 1851 ***4537.32*** *p21*
MacLean, Catherine; Ontario, 1863 ***4537.32*** *p43*
MacLean, Catherine; Port uncertain, 1850-1859 ***4537.37*** *p112*
MacLean, Catherine MacDonald *SEE* MacLean, John
MacLean, Charles *SEE* MacLean, John
MacLean, Donald *SEE* MacLean, Alexander
MacLean, Donald *SEE* MacLean, Angus
MacLean, Donald *SEE* MacLean, Donald
MacLean, Donald *SEE* MacLean, Duncan
MacLean, Donald *SEE* MacLean, Ewen
MacLean, Donald *SEE* MacLean, John
MacLean, Donald *SEE* MacLean, Malcolm
MacLean, Donald *SEE* MacLean, Neil
MacLean, Donald *SEE* MacLean, Norman
Maclean, Donald; Florida, 1778 ***1640.10*** *p136*
MacLean, Donald; Ontario, 1849 ***4537.32*** *p54*
Wife: Mary MacKinnon
Child: Hector
Child: Catherine
MacLean, Donald; Ontario, 1850-1859 ***4537.37*** *p66*
Wife: Mary MacKinnon
Child: Catherine
Child: Margaret
Child: Kirsty
Child: Hector
MacLean, Donald; Ontario, 1850-1859 ***4537.37*** *p67*
Wife: Sarah MacDonald
Child: James
Child: Ann
Child: Margaret
Child: John
Child: Catherine
Child: Sarah
Child: Donald
MacLean, Donald; Port uncertain, 1840-1849 ***4537.37*** *p122*
Wife: Catherine
Child: James
Child: Flora
Child: John
Child: Alexander
Child: Angus
Child: Ewen
Child: Hector
MacLean, Duncan; Port uncertain, 1850-1859 ***4537.37*** *p122*
Child: John
Child: Kirsty
Child: Alexander
Child: Donald
Child: Mary
Child: Ewen
MacLean, Effie *SEE* MacLean, Ewen
MacLean, Effie *SEE* MacLean, Malcolm
MacLean, Effie; Ontario, 1863 ***4537.32*** *p49*
MacLean, Effie MacDonald *SEE* MacLean, Norman
MacLean, Ewen *SEE* MacLean, Alexander
MacLean, Ewen *SEE* MacLean, Donald
MacLean, Ewen *SEE* MacLean, Duncan
MacLean, Ewen; Prince Edward Island, 1848 ***4537.37*** *p25*
Wife: Janet MacDonald
Child: Effie
Child: Donald
Child: Mary
Child: Catherine
Child: Marion
MacLean, Flora *SEE* MacLean, Donald
MacLean, George *SEE* MacLean, John
Maclean, George; Georgia, 1736 ***1640.10*** *p137*
MacLean, Hector *SEE* MacLean, Angus
MacLean, Hector *SEE* MacLean, Donald
MacLean, Hector *SEE* MacLean, John
MacLean, Hector *SEE* MacLean, Neil
Maclean, Henry Clinton; New York, 1834 ***8197.10*** *p316*
MacLean, Hugh; Port uncertain, 1840-1849 ***4537.37*** *p122*
Child: Marion
Child: Lachlan
Child: Ann
Child: Jessie
MacLean, Isabella *SEE* MacLean, Angus
MacLean, Isabella *SEE* MacLean, Malcolm
MacLean, Isabella *SEE* MacLean, Neil
Maclean, Isabella 36; Ontario, 1871 ***1823.22*** *p95*
MacLean, Isabella MacAulay; Ontario, 1855 ***4537.32*** *p53*
Child: Mary
Child: Margaret
Child: John
Child: Angus
Child: Norman
MacLean, Isabella MacFarlane *SEE* MacLean, Kenneth
MacLean, James *SEE* MacLean, Alexander
MacLean, James *SEE* MacLean, Donald
MacLean, Jane *SEE* MacLean, Norman
MacLean, Jane MacDonald *SEE* MacLean, Malcolm
MacLean, Janet *SEE* MacLean, Angus
MacLean, Janet *SEE* MacLean, Kenneth
MacLean, Janet; Port uncertain, 1840-1849 ***4537.37*** *p130*
MacLean, Janet MacDonald *SEE* MacLean, Ewen
MacLean, Janet Morrison *SEE* MacLean, Norman
MacLean, Jessie *SEE* MacLean, Hugh
MacLean, Jessie *SEE* MacLean, John
MacLean, John *SEE* MacLean, Donald
MacLean, John *SEE* MacLean, Duncan
MacLean, John *SEE* MacLean, Isabella MacAulay
MacLean, John *SEE* MacLean, John
MacLean, John *SEE* MacLean, Kenneth
MacLean, John *SEE* MacLean, Neil
MacLean, John *SEE* MacLean, Norman
Maclean, John; Georgia, 1736 ***1640.10*** *p137*
Maclean, John; Georgia, 1738 ***1640.10*** *p137*
Maclean, John; Georgia, 1741 ***1640.10*** *p137*
MacLean, John; Ontario, 1851 ***4537.32*** *p55*
Wife: Catherine MacDonald
Child: Murdo
Child: John
Child: Margaret
Child: Donald
MacLean, John; Ontario, 1855 ***4537.32*** *p55*
Wife: Margaret Stewart
Child: John
Child: George
Child: Alexander
Child: Donald
Child: Ann
MacLean, John; Port uncertain, 1840-1849 ***4537.35*** *p82*
Wife: Mary
Child: Catherine
Child: Alexander
MacLean, John; Port uncertain, 1840-1849 ***4537.37*** *p122*
Wife: Catherine
Child: John
Child: Angus

MacLean, John; Port uncertain, 1840-1849 ***4537.37*** *p122*
Child: Mary
Child: Ranald
Child: Malcolm
Child: Marion
Child: Hector
Wife: Jessie
MacLean, John; Port uncertain, 1840-1849 ***4537.37*** *p122*
Wife: Mary MacNeil
Child: Donald
Child: Penny
Child: Ann
Child: Charles
Child: Malcolm
MacLean, John; Port uncertain, 1850-1859 ***4537.37*** *p122*
Wife: Ann Campbell
Child: Catherine
Child: Donald
Child: Marion
Child: Kirsty
Child: Mary
Child: John
MacLean, Kate *SEE* MacLean, Roderick
MacLean, Kenneth; Ontario, 1863 ***4537.32*** *p55*
Wife: Isabella MacFarlane
Child: Kirsty
Child: John
Child: Angus
Child: Catherine
Child: Margaret
Child: Janet
MacLean, Kenneth; Port uncertain, 1840-1849 ***4537.37*** *p122*
Wife: Una
Child: Archie
MacLean, Kirsty *SEE* MacLean, Angus
MacLean, Kirsty *SEE* MacLean, Donald
MacLean, Kirsty *SEE* MacLean, Duncan
MacLean, Kirsty *SEE* MacLean, John
MacLean, Kirsty *SEE* MacLean, Kenneth
MacLean, Kirsty *SEE* MacLean, Neil
MacLean, Kirsty; Ontario, 1849 ***4537.32*** *p12*
MacLean, Kirsty; Ontario, 1870-1879 ***4537.32*** *p24*
MacLean, Lachlan *SEE* MacLean, Ann
MacLean, Lachlan *SEE* MacLean, Hugh
MacLean, Lexy; Ontario, 1863 ***4537.32*** *p82*
MacLean, Malcolm *SEE* MacLean, Angus
MacLean, Malcolm *SEE* MacLean, John
MacLean, Malcolm; Ontario, 1851 ***4537.32*** *p56*
Wife: Jane MacDonald
Child: Isabella
MacLean, Malcolm; Ontario, 1863 ***4537.32*** *p56*
Child: Effie
Wife: Margaret MacLeod
Child: Donald
Child: Catherine
MacLean, Margaret *SEE* MacLean, Angus
MacLean, Margaret *SEE* MacLean, Archie
MacLean, Margaret *SEE* MacLean, Donald
MacLean, Margaret *SEE* MacLean, Isabella MacAulay
MacLean, Margaret *SEE* MacLean, John
MacLean, Margaret *SEE* MacLean, Kenneth
MacLean, Margaret *SEE* MacLean, Neil
MacLean, Margaret *SEE* MacLean, Norman
MacLean, Margaret *SEE* MacLean, Roderick
MacLean, Margaret; Ontario, 1851 ***4537.32*** *p80*
MacLean, Margaret; Ontario, 1863 ***4537.32*** *p49*
MacLean, Margaret MacDonald *SEE* MacLean, Alexander
MacLean, Margaret MacLeod *SEE* MacLean, Malcolm
MacLean, Margaret Morrison *SEE* MacLean, Angus
MacLean, Margaret Stewart *SEE* MacLean, John
MacLean, Marion *SEE* MacLean, Angus
MacLean, Marion *SEE* MacLean, Ewen
MacLean, Marion *SEE* MacLean, Hugh
MacLean, Marion *SEE* MacLean, John
MacLean, Marion *SEE* MacLean, Neil
MacLean, Marion; Saskatchewan, 1884 ***4537.37*** *p90*
MacLean, Marion MacDonald *SEE* MacLean, Angus
MacLean, Mary *SEE* MacLean, Alexander
MacLean, Mary *SEE* MacLean, Duncan
MacLean, Mary *SEE* MacLean, Ewen
MacLean, Mary *SEE* MacLean, Isabella MacAulay
MacLean, Mary *SEE* MacLean, John
MacLean, Mary *SEE* MacLean, Neil
MacLean, Mary *SEE* MacLean, Norman
MacLean, Mary *SEE* MacLean, Roderick
MacLean, Mary; Nova Scotia, 1828 ***4537.35*** *p27*
MacLean, Mary; Ontario, 1811-1847 ***4537.37*** *p73*
MacLean, Mary; Ontario, 1849 ***4537.32*** *p73*
MacLean, Mary; Ontario, 1850-1859 ***4537.37*** *p73*
MacLean, Mary; Ontario, 1860-1869 ***4537.32*** *p87*
MacLean, Mary; Ontario, 1863 ***4537.32*** *p44*
MacLean, Mary; Ontario, 1870 ***4537.32*** *p13*
MacLean, Mary MacKinnon *SEE* MacLean, Donald
MacLean, Mary MacLeod *SEE* MacLean, Norman
MacLean, Mary MacNeil *SEE* MacLean, John
MacLean, Murdo *SEE* MacLean, John
MacLean, Murdo *SEE* MacLean, Norman
MacLean, Murdo; Ontario, 1851 ***4537.32*** *p56*
MacLean, Murdoch; West Indies, 1797 ***1640.13*** *p90*
MacLean, Neil *SEE* MacLean, Alexander
MacLean, Neil; Nova Scotia, 1830-1839 ***4537.35*** *p22*
With wife
Child: Rachel
Child: John
Child: Donald
MacLean, Neil; Port uncertain, 1840-1849 ***4537.37*** *p122*
Wife: Catherine
Child: Hector
Child: Margaret
Child: Mary
Child: Donald
Child: Angus
MacLean, Neil; Port uncertain, 1850-1859 ***4537.37*** *p123*
Wife: Marion
Child: Isabella
Child: Norman
Child: Kirsty
Child: Margaret
Child: Donald
MacLean, Norman *SEE* MacLean, Angus
MacLean, Norman *SEE* MacLean, Isabella MacAulay
MacLean, Norman *SEE* MacLean, Neil
MacLean, Norman *SEE* MacLean, Roderick
MacLean, Norman; Ontario, 1851 ***4537.32*** *p57*
Wife: Effie MacDonald
Child: Catherine
MacLean, Norman; Ontario, 1855 ***4537.32*** *p57*
Wife: Janet Morrison
Child: Angus
Child: Margaret
MacLean, Norman; Ontario, 1855 ***4537.32*** *p57*
Wife: Mary MacLeod
Child: John
Child: Donald
Child: Ann
Child: Catherine
Child: Murdo
MacLean, Norman; Port uncertain, 1840-1849 ***4537.37*** *p123*
Wife: Mary
Child: Jane
Child: Donald
Child: Catherine
Child: Mary
MacLean, Penny *SEE* MacLean, John
MacLean, Penny Steele *SEE* MacLean, Archie
MacLean, Rachel *SEE* MacLean, Neil
MacLean, Ranald *SEE* MacLean, John
MacLean, Richmond *SEE* MacLean, Roderick
MacLean, Roderick; Port uncertain, 1840-1849 ***4537.35*** *p82*
Wife: Mary
Child: Margaret
Child: Norman
Child: Richmond
Child: William
Child: Kate
MacLean, Sarah *SEE* MacLean, Donald
MacLean, Sarah MacDonald *SEE* MacLean, Donald
Maclean, Simon; Georgia, 1740 ***1640.10*** *p138*
MacLean, Una *SEE* MacLean, Kenneth
MacLean, William *SEE* MacLean, Roderick
MacLease, Margaret; Vermont, 1819-1901 ***5900.10*** *p595*
MacLeay, Allan *SEE* MacLeay, John
MacLeay, Allan *SEE* MacLeay, Kenneth
MacLeay, Allan; Ontario, 1851 ***4537.32*** *p58*
Wife: Ann MacDonald
Child: Ann
Child: John
MacLeay, Allan; Ontario, 1851 ***4537.32*** *p58*
Wife: Catherine MacDonald
Child: Catherine
Child: Janet
Child: John
MacLeay, Ann *SEE* MacLeay, Allan
MacLeay, Ann *SEE* MacLeay, John
MacLeay, Ann *SEE* MacLeay, Roderick
MacLeay, Ann MacDonald *SEE* MacLeay, Allan
MacLeay, Ann MacDonald *SEE* MacLeay, John
MacLeay, Catherine *SEE* MacLeay, Allan
MacLeay, Catherine *SEE* MacLeay, Kenneth
MacLeay, Catherine *SEE* MacLeay, Roderick
MacLeay, Catherine MacDonald *SEE* MacLeay, Allan
MacLeay, Donald *SEE* MacLeay, John
MacLeay, Donald *SEE* MacLeay, Kenneth
MacLeay, Donald *SEE* MacLeay, Roderick
MacLeay, Effie *SEE* MacLeay, John
MacLeay, Effie; Ontario, 1851 ***4537.32*** *p35*
MacLeay, George *SEE* MacLeay, John
MacLeay, Janet *SEE* MacLeay, Allan
MacLeay, John *SEE* MacLeay, Allan
MacLeay, John *SEE* MacLeay, John
MacLeay, John *SEE* MacLeay, Kenneth
MacLeay, John *SEE* MacLeay, Roderick
MacLeay, John; Ontario, 1855 ***4537.32*** *p58*
Wife: Ann MacDonald
Child: Kirsty
Child: Ann
Child: Mary
Child: John
Child: George
Child: Effie
Child: Donald
Child: Allan
MacLeay, Kenneth *SEE* MacLeay, Kenneth
MacLeay, Kenneth; Quebec, 1855 ***4537.32*** *p59*
Wife: Mary MacDonald
Child: John
Child: Murdo
Child: Kenneth
Child: Catherine
Child: Malcolm
Child: Kirsty
Child: Allan
Child: Donald
MacLeay, Kirsty *SEE* MacLeay, John
MacLeay, Kirsty *SEE* MacLeay, Kenneth
MacLeay, Malcolm *SEE* MacLeay, Kenneth
MacLeay, Margaret MacDonald; Ontario, 1816-1880 ***4537.32*** *p58*
MacLeay, Margaret Smith *SEE* MacLeay, Roderick
MacLeay, Mary *SEE* MacLeay, John
MacLeay, Mary MacDonald *SEE* MacLeay, Kenneth
MacLeay, Murdo *SEE* MacLeay, Kenneth
MacLeay, Murdo *SEE* MacLeay, Roderick
MacLeay, Roderick; Ontario, 1855 ***4537.32*** *p59*
Wife: Margaret Smith
Child: Ann
Child: Murdo
Child: Catherine
Child: Donald
Child: John
Maclehose, James; Kingston, Jamaica, 1812 ***1640.13*** *p90*
Maclellan, . . .; Florida, 1769 ***1640.10*** *p138*
MacLellan, Alexander *SEE* MacLellan, Finlay
MacLellan, Allan *SEE* MacLellan, Ranald
MacLellan, Angus *SEE* MacLellan, Angus
MacLellan, Angus *SEE* MacLellan, Archie
MacLellan, Angus *SEE* MacLellan, John
MacLellan, Angus *SEE* MacLellan, Kirsty
MacLellan, Angus *SEE* MacLellan, Roderick
MacLellan, Angus; Ontario, 1849 ***4537.37*** *p67*
Wife: Catherine MacIsaac
Child: Catherine
Child: Penny
Child: Donald
Child: John
Child: Flora
Child: Neil
Child: Ranald
Child: Kirsty
MacLellan, Angus; Ontario, 1849 ***4537.37*** *p67*
Wife: Mary MacCormick
Child: Marion
Child: Mary
Child: Matilda
Child: Angus
MacLellan, Angus; Port uncertain, 1840-1849 ***4537.37*** *p123*
Wife: Catherine MacCormick
Child: Mary
Child: Paul
Child: Malcolm
Child: Ann
Child: John
Child: Donald
MacLellan, Angus; Port uncertain, 1850-1859 ***4537.37*** *p123*
Child: Mary
Child: Marion
Child: Donald
Wife: Jane MacAulay
Child: Michael
Child: John

MacLellan, Angus; Port uncertain, 1860-1869 ***4537.37*** *p123*
Wife: Rachel MacDonald
Child: Donald
Child: Archie
MacLellan, Ann *SEE* MacLellan, Angus
MacLellan, Ann *SEE* MacLellan, Donald
MacLellan, Ann *SEE* MacLellan, John
MacLellan, Ann *SEE* MacLellan, Margaret
MacLellan, Ann; Ontario, 1850-1859 ***4537.37*** *p70*
MacLellan, Ann; Ontario, 1851 ***4537.32*** *p65*
MacLellan, Ann; Ontario, 1851 ***4537.37*** *p66*
MacLellan, Ann Campbell *SEE* MacLellan, Donald
MacLellan, Ann MacAulay *SEE* MacLellan, John
MacLellan, Ann MacLeod *SEE* MacLellan, John
MacLellan, Archie *SEE* MacLellan, Angus
MacLellan, Archie *SEE* MacLellan, Archie
MacLellan, Archie *SEE* MacLellan, Donald
MacLellan, Archie *SEE* MacLellan, John
MacLellan, Archie; Ontario, 1851 ***4537.32*** *p59*
Wife: Marion MacLeod
Child: John
Child: Donald
Child: Catherine
Child: Malcolm
Child: Angus
Child: Kirsty
Child: Flora
MacLellan, Archie; Ontario, 1851 ***4537.37*** *p67*
Wife: Mary MacIntyre
Child: Mary
Child: John
Child: Margaret
Child: Archie
MacLellan, Archie; Port uncertain, 1850-1859 ***4537.37*** *p123*
Wife: Marion MacLeod
Child: Malcolm
Child: Angus
Child: Catherine
Child: Donald
Child: John
Child: Kirsty
Child: Flora
MacLellan, Catherine *SEE* MacLellan, Angus
MacLellan, Catherine *SEE* MacLellan, Archie
MacLellan, Catherine *SEE* MacLellan, Donald
MacLellan, Catherine *SEE* MacLellan, John
MacLellan, Catherine *SEE* MacLellan, Kirsty
MacLellan, Catherine; Ontario, 1848 ***4537.32*** *p13*
MacLellan, Catherine; Ontario, 1850-1859 ***4537.37*** *p46*
MacLellan, Catherine; Ontario, 1851 ***4537.32*** *p28*
MacLellan, Catherine; Port uncertain, 1850-1859 ***4537.37*** *p105*
MacLellan, Catherine; Port uncertain, 1850-1859 ***4537.37*** *p132*
MacLellan, Catherine MacCormick *SEE* MacLellan, Angus
MacLellan, Catherine MacIsaac *SEE* MacLellan, Angus
MacLellan, Catherine MacQuarrie *SEE* MacLellan, John
MacLellan, Donald *SEE* MacLellan, Angus
MacLellan, Donald *SEE* MacLellan, Archie
MacLellan, Donald *SEE* MacLellan, Donald
MacLellan, Donald *SEE* MacLellan, Finlay
MacLellan, Donald *SEE* MacLellan, Hector
MacLellan, Donald *SEE* MacLellan, John
MacLellan, Donald *SEE* MacLellan, Margaret
MacLellan, Donald *SEE* MacLellan, Roderick
MacLellan, Donald; Ontario, 1840-1849 ***4537.37*** *p68*
Wife: Mary MacAulay
Child: Catherine
Child: John
Child: Effie
Child: Rachel
Child: Flora
Child: Ann
MacLellan, Donald; Ontario, 1849 ***4537.32*** *p60*
Wife: Mary MacAulay
Child: Rachel
Child: Flora
Child: Catherine
Child: John
Child: Effie
Child: Ann
MacLellan, Donald; Ontario, 1851 ***4537.37*** *p68*
Child: Margaret
Child: James
Child: Donald
Child: Archie
Wife: Ann Campbell
Child: Murdo
Child: Mary
Child: John
MacLellan, Donald; Port uncertain, 1850-1859 ***4537.37*** *p123*
Wife: Margaret MacRae
Child: Marion
Child: George
Child: John
MacLellan, Donald; Port uncertain, 1850-1859 ***4537.37*** *p123*
Child: Catherine
Child: John
Child: Malcolm
Wife: Marjory Ferguson
Child: Kirsty
MacLellan, Effie *SEE* MacLellan, Donald
MacLellan, Effie *SEE* MacLellan, Hector
MacLellan, Effie; Ontario, 1844-1849 ***4537.37*** *p56*
MacLellan, Effie; Port uncertain, 1850-1859 ***4537.37*** *p105*
MacLellan, Ewen *SEE* MacLellan, Roderick
MacLellan, Ewen; Prince Edward Island, 1848 ***4537.37*** *p25*
Wife: Kirsty MacLeod
Child: Roderick
MacLellan, Finlay *SEE* MacLellan, John
MacLellan, Finlay; Port uncertain, 1840-1849 ***4537.37*** *p123*
Wife: Isabella
Child: Alexander
Child: Donald
Child: John
Child: Jessie
Child: Kirsty
MacLellan, Flora *SEE* MacLellan, Angus
MacLellan, Flora *SEE* MacLellan, Archie
MacLellan, Flora *SEE* MacLellan, Donald
MacLellan, Flora *SEE* MacLellan, John
MacLellan, Flora Crawford; Port uncertain, 1870-1879 ***4537.37*** *p123*
Child: James
Child: Mary
Child: Margaret
MacLellan, Flora MacMillan *SEE* MacLellan, Roderick
MacLellan, George *SEE* MacLellan, Donald
MacLellan, Hector; Ontario, 1851 ***4537.32*** *p60*
Wife: Mary Currie
Child: Effie
Child: Donald
MacLellan, Hector; Ontario, 1851 ***4537.37*** *p68*
Wife: Mary Currie
Child: Effie
Child: Donald
MacLellan, Isabella *SEE* MacLellan, Finlay
MacLellan, Isabella; Ontario, 1850-1859 ***4537.37*** *p76*
MacLellan, James *SEE* MacLellan, Donald
MacLellan, James *SEE* MacLellan, Flora Crawford
MacLellan, Jane MacAulay *SEE* MacLellan, Angus
MacLellan, Janet; Port uncertain, 1840-1849 ***4537.37*** *p117*
MacLellan, Jessie *SEE* MacLellan, Finlay
MacLellan, Jessie; Ontario, 1840-1849 ***4537.37*** *p73*
MacLellan, John *SEE* MacLellan, Angus
MacLellan, John *SEE* MacLellan, Archie
MacLellan, John *SEE* MacLellan, Donald
MacLellan, John *SEE* MacLellan, Finlay
MacLellan, John *SEE* MacLellan, John
MacLellan, John *SEE* MacLellan, Ranald
MacLellan, John *SEE* MacLellan, Roderick
MacLellan, John; Ontario, 1840-1849 ***4537.37*** *p68*
Wife: Mary Johnston
Child: Ann
Child: Finlay
Child: Neil
Child: Mary
Child: Donald
MacLellan, John; Prince Edward Island, 1848 ***4537.37*** *p25*
Wife: Ann MacAulay
Child: Donald
Child: Penny
Child: Flora
Child: Malcolm
Child: Marion
MacLellan, John; Port uncertain, 1840-1849 ***4537.37*** *p124*
Wife: Catherine MacQuarrie
Child: Donald
Child: Ann
Child: Marion
Child: Margaret
Child: Mary
MacLellan, John; Port uncertain, 1850-1859 ***4537.37*** *p123*
Wife: Ann MacLeod
Child: Donald
Child: Archie
Child: Neil
Child: Angus
Child: John
Child: Mary
Child: Catherine
MacLellan, John; Port uncertain, 1850-1859 ***4537.37*** *p124*
Wife: Kirsty MacMillan
Child: John
Child: Ann
Child: Angus
Child: Mary
MacLellan, Kate *SEE* MacLellan, Roderick
MacLellan, Kirsty *SEE* MacLellan, Angus
MacLellan, Kirsty *SEE* MacLellan, Archie
MacLellan, Kirsty *SEE* MacLellan, Donald
MacLellan, Kirsty *SEE* MacLellan, Finlay
MacLellan, Kirsty *SEE* MacLellan, Roderick
MacLellan, Kirsty; Ontario, 1840-1849 ***4537.37*** *p58*
MacLellan, Kirsty; Ontario, 1840-1849 ***4537.37*** *p82*
MacLellan, Kirsty; Ontario, 1849 ***4537.32*** *p39*
MacLellan, Kirsty; Port uncertain, 1840-1849 ***4537.37*** *p124*
Child: Marion
Child: Catherine
Child: Angus
MacLellan, Kirsty; Port uncertain, 1840-1849 ***4537.37*** *p132*
MacLellan, Kirsty; Port uncertain, 1850-1859 ***4537.37*** *p119*
MacLellan, Kirsty MacLeod *SEE* MacLellan, Ewen
MacLellan, Kirsty MacMillan *SEE* MacLellan, John
MacLellan, Malcolm *SEE* MacLellan, Angus
MacLellan, Malcolm *SEE* MacLellan, Archie
MacLellan, Malcolm *SEE* MacLellan, Donald
MacLellan, Malcolm *SEE* MacLellan, John
MacLellan, Margaret *SEE* MacLellan, Archie
MacLellan, Margaret *SEE* MacLellan, Donald
MacLellan, Margaret *SEE* MacLellan, Flora Crawford
MacLellan, Margaret *SEE* MacLellan, John
MacLellan, Margaret *SEE* MacLellan, Ranald
MacLellan, Margaret *SEE* MacLellan, Roderick
MacLellan, Margaret; Saskatchewan, 1884 ***4537.37*** *p100*
MacLellan, Margaret; Port uncertain, 1840-1849 ***4537.37*** *p123*
Child: Ann
Child: Robert
Child: Una
Child: Mary
Child: Donald
MacLellan, Margaret; Port uncertain, 1850-1859 ***4537.37*** *p132*
MacLellan, Margaret MacRae *SEE* MacLellan, Donald
MacLellan, Marion *SEE* MacLellan, Angus
MacLellan, Marion *SEE* MacLellan, Donald
MacLellan, Marion *SEE* MacLellan, John
MacLellan, Marion *SEE* MacLellan, Kirsty
MacLellan, Marion; Prince Edward Island, 1848 ***4537.37*** *p27*
MacLellan, Marion; Port uncertain, 1850-1859 ***4537.37*** *p111*
MacLellan, Marion; Port uncertain, 1850-1859 ***4537.37*** *p117*
MacLellan, Marion MacCormick *SEE* MacLellan, Roderick
MacLellan, Marion MacLeod *SEE* MacLellan, Archie
MacLellan, Marjory Ferguson *SEE* MacLellan, Donald
MacLellan, Mary *SEE* MacLellan, Angus
MacLellan, Mary *SEE* MacLellan, Archie
MacLellan, Mary *SEE* MacLellan, Donald
MacLellan, Mary *SEE* MacLellan, Flora Crawford
MacLellan, Mary *SEE* MacLellan, John
MacLellan, Mary *SEE* MacLellan, Margaret
MacLellan, Mary *SEE* MacLellan, Roderick
MacLellan, Mary; Ontario, 1840-1849 ***4537.37*** *p70*
MacLellan, Mary; Port uncertain, 1840-1849 ***4537.37*** *p106*
MacLellan, Mary; Port uncertain, 1840-1849 ***4537.37*** *p109*
MacLellan, Mary; Port uncertain, 1850-1859 ***4537.37*** *p130*
MacLellan, Mary Currie *SEE* MacLellan, Hector
MacLellan, Mary Johnston *SEE* MacLellan, John
MacLellan, Mary MacAulay *SEE* MacLellan, Donald
MacLellan, Mary MacCormick *SEE* MacLellan, Angus
MacLellan, Mary MacIntyre *SEE* MacLellan, Archie
MacLellan, Matilda *SEE* MacLellan, Angus
MacLellan, Michael *SEE* MacLellan, Angus

MacLellan, Murdo *SEE* MacLellan, Donald
MacLellan, Neil *SEE* MacLellan, Angus
MacLellan, Neil *SEE* MacLellan, John
MacLellan, Paul *SEE* MacLellan, Angus
MacLellan, Penny *SEE* MacLellan, Angus
MacLellan, Penny *SEE* MacLellan, John
MacLellan, Rachel *SEE* MacLellan, Donald
MacLellan, Rachel; Port uncertain, 1850-1859 ***4537.37*** *p107*
MacLellan, Rachel MacDonald *SEE* MacLellan, Angus
MacLellan, Ranald *SEE* MacLellan, Angus
MacLellan, Ranald; Port uncertain, 1850-1859 ***4537.37*** *p124*
Wife: Margaret
Child: John
Child: Allan
MacLellan, Robert *SEE* MacLellan, Margaret
MacLellan, Roderick *SEE* MacLellan, Ewen
MacLellan, Roderick; Prince Edward Island, 1848 ***4537.37*** *p26*
Wife: Flora MacMillan
Child: Margaret
Child: Mary
Child: Donald
Child: Ewen
MacLellan, Roderick; Port uncertain, 1850-1859 ***4537.37*** *p124*
Wife: Marion MacCormick
Child: John
Child: Angus
Child: Kate
Child: Donald
Child: Kirsty
Child: Margaret
Child: Mary
MacLellan, Sarah; Port uncertain, 1840-1849 ***4537.37*** *p113*
MacLellan, Una *SEE* MacLellan, Margaret
MacLennan, Alex *SEE* MacLennan, Donald
MacLennan, Alexander *SEE* MacLennan, Ann
MacLennan, Alexander *SEE* MacLennan, Donald
MacLennan, Alexander *SEE* MacLennan, Duncan
MacLennan, Alexander *SEE* MacLennan, Marion MacLeod
MacLennan, Alexander; Port uncertain, 1860-1869 ***4537.35*** *p82*
Wife: Mary MacInnes
Child: Donald
Child: John
Child: Murdo
Child: Helen
Child: Malcolm
Child: Louisa
Child: William
MacLennan, Angus *SEE* MacLennan, Murdo
MacLennan, Ann *SEE* MacLennan, Donald
MacLennan, Ann *SEE* MacLennan, Janet Martin
MacLennan, Ann *SEE* MacLennan, Malcolm
MacLennan, Ann *SEE* MacLennan, Marion MacLeod
MacLennan, Ann; Ontario, 1862 ***4537.32*** *p62*
Sibling: Lexy
Sibling: Janet
Sibling: Alexander
Sibling: Hannah
MacLennan, Ann MacLeod *SEE* MacLennan, Duncan
MacLennan, Bess MacLeod *SEE* MacLennan, Kenneth
MacLennan, Catherine *SEE* MacLennan, Janet Martin
MacLennan, Catherine *SEE* MacLennan, Murdo
MacLennan, Catherine *SEE* MacLennan, Neil
MacLennan, Catherine; Nova Scotia, 1828 ***4537.35*** *p26*
MacLennan, Catherine; Port uncertain, 1840-1849 ***4537.35*** *p80*
MacLennan, Catherine MacDermid *SEE* MacLennan, Murdo
MacLennan, Catherine MacDonald *SEE* MacLennan, Donald
MacLennan, Donald *SEE* MacLennan, Alexander
MacLennan, Donald *SEE* MacLennan, Duncan
MacLennan, Donald *SEE* MacLennan, Malcolm
MacLennan, Donald *SEE* MacLennan, Murdo
MacLennan, Donald *SEE* MacLennan, Neil
MacLennan, Donald; Ontario, 1850-1859 ***4537.32*** *p60*
Child: Isabella
Wife: Marion
Child: Mary
Child: Alex
Child: Kirsty
Child: Murdo
Child: Peggy
Child: John
Child: William
MacLennan, Donald; Ontario, 1860-1869 ***4537.35*** *p58*
Wife: Catherine MacDonald
Child: Sarah
Child: Neil
Child: Alexander
Child: Ann
MacLennan, Donald; Ontario, 1862 ***4537.32*** *p60*
Wife: Catherine MacDonald
Child: Alexander
Child: Ann
MacLennan, Duncan; Ontario, 1851 ***4537.32*** *p61*
Wife: Ann MacLeod
Child: Alexander
Child: Neil
Child: Mary
Child: John
Child: Donald
MacLennan, Effie *SEE* MacLennan, Murdo
MacLennan, Eliza *SEE* MacLennan, Murdo
MacLennan, Flora *SEE* MacLennan, Janet Martin
MacLennan, Hannah *SEE* MacLennan, Ann
MacLennan, Hannah *SEE* MacLennan, Marion MacLeod
MacLennan, Helen *SEE* MacLennan, Alexander
MacLennan, Isabella *SEE* MacLennan, Donald
MacLennan, Isabella; Saskatchewan, 1889 ***4537.35*** *p66*
MacLennan, Janet *SEE* MacLennan, Ann
MacLennan, Janet *SEE* MacLennan, Marion MacLeod
MacLennan, Janet Martin; Ontario, 1851 ***4537.32*** *p61*
Child: Catherine
Child: Flora
Child: Kirsty
Child: Roderick
Child: Ann
Child: Margaret
MacLennan, John *SEE* MacLennan, Alexander
MacLennan, John *SEE* MacLennan, Donald
MacLennan, John *SEE* MacLennan, Duncan
MacLennan, John *SEE* MacLennan, Mary MacKay
MacLennan, John *SEE* MacLennan, Neil
MacLennan, Kenneth; Canada, 1890-1899 ***4537.35*** *p72*
Wife: Bess MacLeod
MacLennan, Kenneth; Maryland, 1880-1889 ***4537.35*** *p68*
MacLennan, Kirsty *SEE* MacLennan, Donald
MacLennan, Kirsty *SEE* MacLennan, Janet Martin
MacLennan, Kirsty *SEE* MacLennan, Murdo
MacLennan, Kirsty; Ontario, 1860-1869 ***4537.35*** *p58*
MacLennan, Kirsty; Ontario, 1862 ***4537.32*** *p52*
MacLennan, Kirsty MacKay *SEE* MacLennan, Neil
MacLennan, Lexy *SEE* MacLennan, Ann
MacLennan, Lexy *SEE* MacLennan, Marion MacLeod
MacLennan, Louisa *SEE* MacLennan, Alexander
MacLennan, Malcolm *SEE* MacLennan, Alexander
MacLennan, Malcolm *SEE* MacLennan, Malcolm
MacLennan, Malcolm; Nova Scotia, 1830-1839 ***4537.32*** *p61*
Wife: Mary Matheson
Child: Ann
Child: Donald
Child: Malcolm
MacLennan, Margaret *SEE* MacLennan, Janet Martin
MacLennan, Margaret *SEE* MacLennan, Neil
MacLennan, Margaret; Ontario, 1851 ***4537.32*** *p75*
MacLennan, Margaret; Ontario, 1860-1869 ***4537.35*** *p57*
MacLennan, Margaret; Ontario, 1863 ***4537.32*** *p27*
MacLennan, Marion *SEE* MacLennan, Donald
MacLennan, Marion; Manitoba, 1888 ***4537.35*** *p67*
MacLennan, Marion; Ontario, 1851 ***4537.32*** *p48*
MacLennan, Marion MacLeod; Ontario, 1862-1869 ***4537.35*** *p59*
Child: Ann
Child: Janet
Child: Hannah
Child: Alexander
Child: Lexy
MacLennan, Mary *SEE* MacLennan, Donald
MacLennan, Mary *SEE* MacLennan, Duncan
MacLennan, Mary *SEE* MacLennan, Murdo
MacLennan, Mary; Nova Scotia, 1820-1829 ***4537.35*** *p30*
MacLennan, Mary; Ontario, 1851 ***4537.32*** *p29*
MacLennan, Mary; Ontario, 1863 ***4537.32*** *p81*
MacLennan, Mary Ann *SEE* MacLennan, Neil
MacLennan, Mary MacInnes *SEE* MacLennan, Alexander
MacLennan, Mary MacKay; Port uncertain, 1860-1869 ***4537.35*** *p82*
Child: John
With family
MacLennan, Mary Matheson *SEE* MacLennan, Malcolm
MacLennan, Murdo *SEE* MacLennan, Alexander
MacLennan, Murdo *SEE* MacLennan, Donald
MacLennan, Murdo *SEE* MacLennan, Murdo
MacLennan, Murdo; Nova Scotia, 1840-1849 ***4537.35*** *p22*
Wife: Catherine MacDermid
Child: Angus
Child: Catherine
Child: Eliza
Child: Mary
Child: Effie
Child: Kirsty
MacLennan, Murdo; Ontario, 1851 ***4537.32*** *p61*
Wife: Catherine
Child: Donald
Child: Murdo
MacLennan, Neil *SEE* MacLennan, Donald
MacLennan, Neil *SEE* MacLennan, Duncan
MacLennan, Neil; Canada, 1860-1869 ***4537.35*** *p72*
Wife: Kirsty MacKay
Child: Catherine
Child: John
Child: Mary Ann
Child: Norman
Child: Margaret
Child: Donald
MacLennan, Norman *SEE* MacLennan, Neil
MacLennan, Peggy *SEE* MacLennan, Donald
MacLennan, Roderick *SEE* MacLennan, Janet Martin
MacLennan, Sarah *SEE* MacLennan, Donald
MacLennan, William *SEE* MacLennan, Alexander
MacLennan, William *SEE* MacLennan, Donald
MacLeod, Alex *SEE* MacLeod, John
MacLeod, Alexander *SEE* MacLeod, Alexander
MacLeod, Alexander *SEE* MacLeod, Donald
MacLeod, Alexander *SEE* MacLeod, John
MacLeod, Alexander *SEE* MacLeod, Kenneth
MacLeod, Alexander *SEE* MacLeod, Kirsty MacKillop
MacLeod, Alexander *SEE* MacLeod, Malcolm
MacLeod, Alexander *SEE* MacLeod, Margaret
MacLeod, Alexander *SEE* MacLeod, Mary
MacLeod, Alexander *SEE* MacLeod, Murdo
MacLeod, Alexander *SEE* MacLeod, Neil
MacLeod, Alexander *SEE* MacLeod, Norman
MacLeod, Alexander *SEE* MacLeod, Roderick
MacLeod, Alexander; California, 1860-1869 ***4537.35*** *p75*
Wife: Catherine Morrison
Child: Norman
Child: Donald J.
MacLeod, Alexander; Falkland Islands, 1880-1889 ***4537.35*** *p75*
MacLeod, Alexander; Nova Scotia, 1826-1829 ***4537.35*** *p23*
With wife
Child: Margaret
Child: Catherine
Child: Kirsty
Child: Mary
Child: John
Child: Roderick
MacLeod, Alexander; Nova Scotia, 1830-1839 ***4537.35*** *p22*
Wife: Ann
Child: Norman
Child: Neil
With daughter
Child: Donald
Child: Kirsty
Child: Ann
MacLeod, Alexander; Nova Scotia, 1840-1849 ***4537.35*** *p23*
Wife: Flora
Child: Alexander
Child: Roderick
Son: Malcolm
MacLeod, Alexander; Ontario, 1855 ***4537.32*** *p62*
Wife: Betty
Child: Norman
Child: Catherine
Child: Ann
Child: Donald
MacLeod, Alexander; Ontario, 1860-1869 ***4537.35*** *p59*
Wife: Marion Kerr
Child: Salvia
Child: William
Child: Roderick
Child: Kirsty
Child: Marion
Child: Mary
Child: John
Child: Angus
MacLeod, Alexander; Ontario, 1880-1889 ***4537.32*** *p62*
Child: Donald
Child: Mary Ann
Child: Norman

MacLeod, Alexander; Port uncertain, 1840-1849 ***4537.35*** *p82*
Wife: Effie MacMillan
Child: Catherine
Child: John
Child: Donald
Child: Jessie
Child: Norman
MacLeod, Alexander; Port uncertain, 1840-1849 ***4537.35*** *p82*
Wife: Flora
Child: William
Child: Mary
Child: Duncan
Child: Margaret
Child: Ann
Child: John
MacLeod, Alexander; Port uncertain, 1840-1849 ***4537.35*** *p82*
Wife: Margaret
Child: Mary
MacLeod, Alexander; Port uncertain, 1840-1849 ***4537.35*** *p82*
With wife
Child: Roderick
MacLeod, Alexander; Port uncertain, 1860-1869 ***4537.35*** *p82*
Wife: Marion
Child: Norman
Child: Margaret
MacLeod, Allan *SEE* MacLeod, Donald
MacLeod, Allan *SEE* MacLeod, John
MacLeod, Allan *SEE* MacLeod, Murdo
MacLeod, Allan *SEE* MacLeod, Roderick
MacLeod, Andrew *SEE* MacLeod, Kenneth
MacLeod, Angus *SEE* MacLeod, Alexander
MacLeod, Angus *SEE* MacLeod, Donald
MacLeod, Angus *SEE* MacLeod, Ewen
MacLeod, Angus *SEE* MacLeod, John
MacLeod, Angus *SEE* MacLeod, Margaret
MacLeod, Angus *SEE* MacLeod, Mary
MacLeod, Angus *SEE* MacLeod, Murdo
MacLeod, Angus *SEE* MacLeod, Norman
MacLeod, Angus; Maryland, 1888 ***4537.35*** *p68*
Wife: Mary Nicolson
Child: Effie
MacLeod, Angus; Nova Scotia, 1820-1829 ***4537.35*** *p23*
Wife: Ann Shaw
Child: Malcolm
Child: John
MacLeod, Angus; Nova Scotia, 1840-1849 ***4537.35*** *p23*
Child: Roderick
Wife: Mary Shaw
Child: Catherine
Child: Margaret
Child: Mary
Child: John
Child: Neil
MacLeod, Angus; Nova Scotia, 1840-1849 ***4537.35*** *p23*
Wife: Mary
Child: Isabella
Child: Margaret
Child: John
Child: Ann
Child: Roderick
MacLeod, Angus; Ontario, 1840-1849 ***4537.37*** *p69*
Child: John
Child: Archie
Wife: Ann Beaton
MacLeod, Angus; Ontario, 1860-1869 ***4537.35*** *p59*
Wife: Catherine MacPhee
Child: Mary
Child: Malcolm
Child: Fanny
MacLeod, Angus; Ontario, 1862 ***4537.32*** *p62*
Wife: Catherine MacPhee
Child: Fanny
Child: Malcolm
Child: Mary
MacLeod, Angus; Quebec, 1860-1869 ***4537.35*** *p63*
Wife: Kirsty MacDonald
Child: Marion
Child: Dougal
Child: Margaret
Child: Kirsty
Child: Donald
Child: Mary
MacLeod, Angus; Port uncertain, 1840-1849 ***4537.35*** *p83*
Wife: Margaret
Child: Donald
MacLeod, Angus; Port uncertain, 1840-1849 ***4537.37*** *p124*
Wife: Effie
Child: Mary
Child: Roderick
MacLeod, Angus; Port uncertain, 1840-1849 ***4537.37*** *p124*
Wife: Marion
Child: Marion
Child: Ann
MacLeod, Ann *SEE* MacLeod, Alexander
MacLeod, Ann *SEE* MacLeod, Angus
MacLeod, Ann *SEE* MacLeod, Bannatyne
MacLeod, Ann *SEE* MacLeod, Donald
MacLeod, Ann *SEE* MacLeod, Duncan
MacLeod, Ann *SEE* MacLeod, John
MacLeod, Ann *SEE* MacLeod, Kenneth
MacLeod, Ann *SEE* MacLeod, Malcolm
MacLeod, Ann *SEE* MacLeod, Murdo
MacLeod, Ann *SEE* MacLeod, Norman
MacLeod, Ann *SEE* MacLeod, Roderick
MacLeod, Ann *SEE* MacLeod, William
MacLeod, Ann; Nova Scotia, 1830-1839 ***4537.35*** *p34*
MacLeod, Ann; Nova Scotia, 1834 ***4537.35*** *p18*
MacLeod, Ann; Nova Scotia, 1840-1849 ***4537.35*** *p14*
MacLeod, Ann; Nova Scotia, 1840-1849 ***4537.35*** *p36*
MacLeod, Ann; Nova Scotia, 1840-1849 ***4537.37*** *p9*
MacLeod, Ann; Ontario, 1851 ***4537.32*** *p61*
MacLeod, Ann; Ontario, 1855 ***4537.32*** *p21*
MacLeod, Ann; Ontario, 1860-1869 ***4537.32*** *p20*
MacLeod, Ann; Ontario, 1860-1869 ***4537.35*** *p57*
MacLeod, Ann; Ontario, 1860-1869 ***4537.35*** *p62*
MacLeod, Ann; Ontario, 1862 ***4537.32*** *p84*
MacLeod, Ann; Ontario, 1863 ***4537.32*** *p43*
MacLeod, Ann; Saskatchewan, 1884 ***4537.37*** *p93*
MacLeod, Ann; Port uncertain, 1840-1849 ***4537.37*** *p110*
MacLeod, Ann; Port uncertain, 1850-1859 ***4537.37*** *p119*
MacLeod, Ann; Port uncertain, 1850-1859 ***4537.37*** *p123*
MacLeod, Ann Beaton *SEE* MacLeod, Angus
MacLeod, Ann Gillies *SEE* MacLeod, John
MacLeod, Ann MacDonald *SEE* MacLeod, Duncan
MacLeod, Ann MacInnes *SEE* MacLeod, John
MacLeod, Ann MacKinnon *SEE* MacLeod, Donald
MacLeod, Ann MacLellan *SEE* MacLeod, John
MacLeod, Ann Matheson *SEE* MacLeod, John
MacLeod, Ann Morrison *SEE* MacLeod, John
MacLeod, Ann Murray *SEE* MacLeod, Murdo
MacLeod, Ann Shaw *SEE* MacLeod, Angus
MacLeod, Annabella *SEE* MacLeod, Donald
MacLeod, Archie *SEE* MacLeod, Angus
MacLeod, Archie *SEE* MacLeod, Donald
MacLeod, Archie *SEE* MacLeod, Hector
MacLeod, Archie *SEE* MacLeod, Neil
MacLeod, Bannatyne; Saskatchewan, 1880-1889 ***4537.35*** *p69*
Wife: Ann
Child: William
Child: John
Child: Catherine
MacLeod, Bella *SEE* MacLeod, John
MacLeod, Bess; Canada, 1890-1899 ***4537.35*** *p72*
MacLeod, Betsy *SEE* MacLeod, Charles
MacLeod, Betsy *SEE* MacLeod, Donald
MacLeod, Betsy *SEE* MacLeod, Murdo
MacLeod, Betsy MacIver *SEE* MacLeod, William
MacLeod, Betty *SEE* MacLeod, Alexander
MacLeod, Bridget *SEE* MacLeod, Kenneth
MacLeod, Caroline Gauld *SEE* MacLeod, John
MacLeod, Catherine *SEE* MacLeod, Alexander
MacLeod, Catherine *SEE* MacLeod, Angus
MacLeod, Catherine *SEE* MacLeod, Bannatyne
MacLeod, Catherine *SEE* MacLeod, Donald
MacLeod, Catherine *SEE* MacLeod, John
MacLeod, Catherine *SEE* MacLeod, Malcolm
MacLeod, Catherine *SEE* MacLeod, Margaret
MacLeod, Catherine *SEE* MacLeod, Murdo
MacLeod, Catherine *SEE* MacLeod, Norman
MacLeod, Catherine *SEE* MacLeod, Roderick
MacLeod, Catherine; Canada, 1860-1869 ***4537.35*** *p72*
MacLeod, Catherine; Ontario, 1850-1859 ***4537.37*** *p32*
MacLeod, Catherine; Ontario, 1851 ***4537.32*** *p9*
MacLeod, Catherine; Ontario, 1855 ***4537.32*** *p41*
MacLeod, Catherine; Ontario, 1863 ***4537.32*** *p93*
MacLeod, Catherine; Saskatchewan, 1884 ***4537.37*** *p103*
MacLeod, Catherine; Saskatchewan, 1889 ***4537.35*** *p67*
MacLeod, Catherine Campbell *SEE* MacLeod, John
MacLeod, Catherine MacAskill *SEE* MacLeod, Roderick
MacLeod, Catherine MacInnes *SEE* MacLeod, Donald
MacLeod, Catherine MacKay *SEE* MacLeod, Malcolm
MacLeod, Catherine MacLean *SEE* MacLeod, Donald
MacLeod, Catherine MacLennan *SEE* MacLeod, Malcolm
MacLeod, Catherine MacPhee *SEE* MacLeod, Angus
MacLeod, Catherine Morrison *SEE* MacLeod, Alexander
MacLeod, Charles *SEE* MacLeod, Murdo
MacLeod, Charles; South America, 1890-1899 ***4537.35*** *p75*
Wife: Margaret MacAulay
Child: Mary
Child: Finlay
Child: Robert
Child: John
Child: Rachel
Child: Donald John
Child: Betsy
Child: Murdo
Child: Margaret
MacLeod, Christopher *SEE* MacLeod, John
MacLeod, David *SEE* MacLeod, Malcolm
MacLeod, Donald *SEE* MacLeod, Alexander
MacLeod, Donald *SEE* MacLeod, Angus
MacLeod, Donald *SEE* MacLeod, Donald
MacLeod, Donald *SEE* MacLeod, Duncan
MacLeod, Donald *SEE* MacLeod, Ewen
MacLeod, Donald *SEE* MacLeod, John
MacLeod, Donald *SEE* MacLeod, Kenneth
MacLeod, Donald *SEE* MacLeod, Kirsty
MacLeod, Donald *SEE* MacLeod, Kirsty MacKillop
MacLeod, Donald *SEE* MacLeod, Malcolm
MacLeod, Donald *SEE* MacLeod, Mary
MacLeod, Donald *SEE* MacLeod, Murdo
MacLeod, Donald *SEE* MacLeod, Neil
MacLeod, Donald *SEE* MacLeod, Norman
MacLeod, Donald *SEE* MacLeod, Peter
MacLeod, Donald *SEE* MacLeod, Roderick
MacLeod, Donald; Canada, 1850-1859 ***4537.35*** *p69*
MacLeod, Donald; Canada, 1890-1899 ***4537.35*** *p73*
Wife: Catherine MacInnes
MacLeod, Donald; Nova Scotia, 1820-1829 ***4537.35*** *p24*
Wife: Jessie MacCusbic
Child: Alexander
Child: Betsy
Child: Sarah
Child: Flora
MacLeod, Donald; Nova Scotia, 1836-1839 ***4537.35*** *p24*
Wife: Catherine
Child: Annabella
Child: Donald
Child: Murdo
Child: Norman
Child: Rachel
Child: Catherine
MacLeod, Donald; Nova Scotia, 1838 ***4537.35*** *p24*
Wife: Mary Morrison
Child: Ann
Child: Alexander
Child: Peggy
Child: Kirsty
Child: Catherine
MacLeod, Donald; Nova Scotia, 1840-1849 ***4537.35*** *p24*
Wife: Kirsty
Child: Alexander
Child: Donald
Child: Rachel
Child: John
Child: Mary
MacLeod, Donald; Nova Scotia, 1840-1849 ***4537.37*** *p17*
Wife: Catherine MacLean
Child: Marion
Child: Ranald
Child: Murdo
Child: Alexander
Child: Julia
MacLeod, Donald; Nova Scotia, 1840-1849 ***4537.37*** *p17*
Wife: Kirsty
Child: Hector
Child: Duncan
MacLeod, Donald; Ontario, 1840-1849 ***4537.37*** *p69*
Wife: Flora MacPherson
Child: Margaret
Child: Archie
Child: Hector
Child: Kenneth
Child: Angus
Child: Kirsty
Child: Ranald
MacLeod, Donald; Ontario, 1840-1849 ***4537.37*** *p69*
Wife: Mary
Child: Norman
Child: Roderick
Child: John
Child: Angus
Child: Ann
MacLeod, Donald; Ontario, 1851 ***4537.32*** *p63*
Wife: Effie
Child: Kirsty

MacLeod, John; Nova Scotia, 1828 ***4537.35*** *p26*
Wife: Lexy Campbell
Child: Alexander
Child: Kenneth
MacLeod, John; Nova Scotia, 1840-1849 ***4537.35*** *p25*
Wife: Ann Gillies
Child: Murdo
Child: Isabella
Child: Ann
Child: John
Child: Alexander
Child: Roderick
MacLeod, John; Nova Scotia, 1840-1849 ***4537.35*** *p25*
Wife: Ann Morrison
Child: John
Child: Ann
Child: Roderick
Child: Allan
Child: Kirsty
MacLeod, John; Ontario, 1850-1859 ***4537.37*** *p70*
Wife: Ann MacLellan
Child: Harriet
Child: Marion
Child: Catherine
Child: Angus
Child: Neil
MacLeod, John; Ontario, 1850-1859 ***4537.37*** *p70*
Wife: Flora MacAulay
Child: Catherine
Child: Alexander
MacLeod, John; Ontario, 1851 ***4537.32*** *p65*
Wife: Ann MacInnes
Child: Ranald
Child: Marion
Child: Mary
Child: Lexy
Child: Ewen
Child: Kirsty
MacLeod, John; Ontario, 1851 ***4537.32*** *p65*
Wife: Ann MacLellan
Child: Neil
MacLeod, John; Ontario, 1851 ***4537.32*** *p66*
Wife: Flora MacAulay
Child: Alex
MacLeod, John; Ontario, 1851 ***4537.32*** *p66*
Wife: Gormelia MacAskill
Child: Catherine
Child: Donald
Child: Alexander
Child: Margaret
Child: Ann
Child: Murdo
MacLeod, John; Ontario, 1851 ***4537.32*** *p67*
Wife: Marion Morrison
Child: John
Child: Angus
Child: Kenneth
Child: Malcolm
Child: Donald
Child: Duncan
MacLeod, John; Ontario, 1851 ***4537.32*** *p68*
Wife: Mary
Child: Catherine
Child: Kirsty
Child: Ann
Child: Mary Ann
Child: Donald
Child: Jane
Child: Malcolm
Child: John
MacLeod, John; Ontario, 1855 ***4537.32*** *p66*
Wife: Isabella
Child: Kenneth
Child: Murdo
Child: Norman
Child: Donald
Child: Catherine
MacLeod, John; Ontario, 1855 ***4537.32*** *p67*
Wife: Lily MacRae
Child: Effie
Child: John
Child: George
Child: William
Child: Ann
Child: Murdo
MacLeod, John; Ontario, 1863 ***4537.32*** *p66*
Wife: Ann Matheson
Child: Effie
Child: Donald
Child: Marion
Child: Mary
Child: Angus
Child: Catherine
MacLeod, John; Ontario, 1863 ***4537.32*** *p67*
Wife: Margaret MacIver
Child: John
Child: Kenneth
Child: Catherine
MacLeod, John; Ontario, 1863 ***4537.32*** *p67*
Child: Donald
Child: Catherine
Child: Ann
Child: George
Child: Bella
MacLeod, John; Prince Edward Island, 1840 ***4537.35*** *p39*
Wife: Marion MacDonald
MacLeod, John; Prince Edward Island, 1892 ***4537.35*** *p39*
Wife: Caroline Gauld
MacLeod, John; Port uncertain, 1840-1849 ***4537.35*** *p83*
Wife: Effie
Child: John
Child: Duncan
Child: Marion
Child: Mary
MacLeod, John; Port uncertain, 1840-1849 ***4537.35*** *p83*
Wife: Kirsty
Child: Angus
Child: Marion
Child: Roderick
Child: Margaret
MacLeod, John; Port uncertain, 1840-1849 ***4537.37*** *p124*
Wife: Flora
Child: Marion
Child: Murdo
Child: Isabella
Child: John
Child: Catherine
MacLeod, John; Port uncertain, 1840-1849 ***4537.37*** *p125*
Wife: Marion
Child: Neil
Child: Kate
Child: Donald
Child: Ann
Child: Kirsty
MacLeod, John; Port uncertain, 1840-1849 ***4537.37*** *p125*
Wife: Marion
Child: Mary
Child: Donald
Child: Kenneth
Child: Neil
Child: Kirsty
MacLeod, John; Port uncertain, 1840-1849 ***4537.37*** *p125*
Sibling: Kenneth
Sibling: Alexander
Sibling: Donald
MacLeod, John; Port uncertain, 1850-1859 ***4537.35*** *p83*
Wife: Rachel
Child: Donald
Child: Murdo
Child: Norman
MacLeod, John; Port uncertain, 1850-1859 ***4537.37*** *p124*
Child: Lexy
Child: Marion
Child: Mary
Child: Ranald
Wife: Ann MacInnes
Child: Kirsty
Child: Ewen
MacLeod, John; Port uncertain, 1850-1859 ***4537.37*** *p124*
Wife: Kate
Child: Kate
MacLeod, John; Port uncertain, 1860-1869 ***4537.35*** *p83*
Wife: Catherine
Child: Alexander
Child: Donald
MacLeod, John; Port uncertain, 1880-1889 ***4537.35*** *p83*
Child: Roderick
Child: John
Wife: Effie Morrison
MacLeod, John D. *SEE* MacLeod, Donald
MacLeod, John Neil; Ontario, 1866 ***4537.35*** *p60*
Wife: Jessie Fleming
Child: Henry
Child: John
Child: Jessie
Child: James
Child: Harriet
MacLeod, Julia *SEE* MacLeod, Donald
MacLeod, Julia *SEE* MacLeod, Norman
MacLeod, Kate *SEE* MacLeod, Donald
MacLeod, Kate *SEE* MacLeod, John
MacLeod, Kenneth *SEE* MacLeod, Donald
MacLeod, Kenneth *SEE* MacLeod, John
MacLeod, Kenneth *SEE* MacLeod, Margaret
MacLeod, Kenneth *SEE* MacLeod, Marion
MacLeod, Kenneth *SEE* MacLeod, Norman
MacLeod, Kenneth *SEE* MacLeod, Roderick
MacLeod, Kenneth; Maryland, 1888 ***4537.35*** *p69*
Wife: Lexy MacDonald
Child: Rachel
Child: Flora
Child: Marion
Child: Alexander
Child: Kirsty
MacLeod, Kenneth; Ontario, 1850-1859 ***4537.32*** *p68*
MacLeod, Kenneth; Ontario, 1863 ***4537.32*** *p68*
Child: Donald
Child: Ann
Child: Norman
Child: Murdo
Child: George
Wife: Ann
Child: John
MacLeod, Kenneth; Port uncertain, 1840-1849 ***4537.35*** *p83*
Wife: Kirsty
Child: Mary
MacLeod, Kenneth; Port uncertain, 1840-1849 ***4537.35*** *p83*
Wife: Mary Morrison
Child: Kirsty
Child: Rachel
Child: Effie
Child: Andrew
MacLeod, Kenneth; Port uncertain, 1850-1859 ***4537.37*** *p125*
Wife: Mary Maxwell
Child: Ann
Child: Malcolm
Child: Bridget
Child: Hugh
MacLeod, Kirsty *SEE* MacLeod, Alexander
MacLeod, Kirsty *SEE* MacLeod, Angus
MacLeod, Kirsty *SEE* MacLeod, Donald
MacLeod, Kirsty *SEE* MacLeod, Hector
MacLeod, Kirsty *SEE* MacLeod, John
MacLeod, Kirsty *SEE* MacLeod, Kenneth
MacLeod, Kirsty *SEE* MacLeod, Mary
MacLeod, Kirsty *SEE* MacLeod, Murdo
MacLeod, Kirsty *SEE* MacLeod, Neil
MacLeod, Kirsty *SEE* MacLeod, Norman
MacLeod, Kirsty; Falkland Islands, 1870-1879 ***4537.35*** *p76*
MacLeod, Kirsty; Manitoba, 1888 ***4537.35*** *p65*
MacLeod, Kirsty; Maryland, 1888 ***4537.35*** *p70*
MacLeod, Kirsty; Nova Scotia, 1820-1829 ***4537.35*** *p15*
MacLeod, Kirsty; Nova Scotia, 1840-1849 ***4537.35*** *p19*
MacLeod, Kirsty; Ontario, 1850-1859 ***4537.32*** *p83*
MacLeod, Kirsty; Ontario, 1851 ***4537.32*** *p24*
MacLeod, Kirsty; Ontario, 1851 ***4537.32*** *p71*
Child: Murdo
Child: John
Child: Donald
MacLeod, Kirsty; Ontario, 1860-1869 ***4537.35*** *p61*
MacLeod, Kirsty; Ontario, 1863 ***4537.32*** *p7*
MacLeod, Kirsty; Ontario, 1863 ***4537.32*** *p83*
MacLeod, Kirsty; Prince Edward Island, 1848 ***4537.37*** *p25*
MacLeod, Kirsty Beaton *SEE* MacLeod, John
MacLeod, Kirsty MacDonald *SEE* MacLeod, Angus
MacLeod, Kirsty MacDonald *SEE* MacLeod, Murdo
MacLeod, Kirsty MacKillop; Port uncertain, 1860-1869 ***4537.35*** *p84*
Child: Alexander
Child: Mary
Child: John
Child: Donald
Child: Mary
MacLeod, Lexy *SEE* MacLeod, John
MacLeod, Lexy *SEE* MacLeod, Malcolm
MacLeod, Lexy Campbell *SEE* MacLeod, John
MacLeod, Lexy MacDonald *SEE* MacLeod, Kenneth
MacLeod, Lily MacRae *SEE* MacLeod, John
MacLeod, Malcolm *SEE* MacLeod, Alexander
MacLeod, Malcolm *SEE* MacLeod, Angus
MacLeod, Malcolm *SEE* MacLeod, Donald
MacLeod, Malcolm *SEE* MacLeod, John
MacLeod, Malcolm *SEE* MacLeod, Kenneth
MacLeod, Malcolm *SEE* MacLeod, Mary Morrison
MacLeod, Malcolm *SEE* MacLeod, Murdo
MacLeod, Malcolm *SEE* MacLeod, Norman
MacLeod, Malcolm; Nova Scotia, 1828 ***4537.35*** *p26*
Wife: Catherine MacLennan
Child: Norman
Daughter: Catherine
MacLeod, Malcolm; Ontario, 1851 ***4537.32*** *p68*
Wife: Catherine MacKay
Child: David

MacLeod, Malcolm; Ontario, 1860-1869 ***4537.35*** *p60*
Wife: Catherine
Child: Alexander
Child: Roderick
Child: Effie
Child: John
Child: Donald
Child: Margaret
MacLeod, Malcolm; Ontario, 1862 ***4537.32*** *p69*
Wife: Catherine
Child: Donald
Child: Margaret
Child: John
MacLeod, Malcolm; Port uncertain, 1840-1849 ***4537.35*** *p84*
Wife: Catherine
Child: Finlay
MacLeod, Malcolm; Port uncertain, 1840-1849 ***4537.37*** *p125*
Wife: Ann
Child: Ann
Child: Roderick
Child: Lexy
Child: Ewen
Child: Norman
Child: Marion
Child: Catherine
Child: William
MacLeod, Malcolm; Port uncertain, 1850-1859 ***4537.35*** *p83*
Wife: Ann
Child: Jane
Child: Margaret
MacLeod, Margaret *SEE* MacLeod, Alexander
MacLeod, Margaret *SEE* MacLeod, Angus
MacLeod, Margaret *SEE* MacLeod, Charles
MacLeod, Margaret *SEE* MacLeod, Donald
MacLeod, Margaret *SEE* MacLeod, James
MacLeod, Margaret *SEE* MacLeod, John
MacLeod, Margaret *SEE* MacLeod, Malcolm
MacLeod, Margaret *SEE* MacLeod, Margaret
MacLeod, Margaret *SEE* MacLeod, Murdo
MacLeod, Margaret *SEE* MacLeod, Neil
MacLeod, Margaret *SEE* MacLeod, Norman
MacLeod, Margaret *SEE* MacLeod, Roderick
MacLeod, Margaret *SEE* MacLeod, William
MacLeod, Margaret; America, 1850-1859 ***4537.35*** *p77*
MacLeod, Margaret; America, 1862 ***4537.32*** *p86*
MacLeod, Margaret; Canada, 1890-1899 ***4537.35*** *p71*
MacLeod, Margaret; Nova Scotia, 1830-1839 ***4537.35*** *p13*
MacLeod, Margaret; Nova Scotia, 1838 ***4537.35*** *p26*
MacLeod, Margaret; Nova Scotia, 1840-1849 ***4537.35*** *p28*
Child: James
Child: Catherine
Child: Margaret
MacLeod, Margaret; Nova Scotia, 1840-1849 ***4537.35*** *p37*
MacLeod, Margaret; Ontario, 1850-1859 ***4537.37*** *p87*
MacLeod, Margaret; Ontario, 1851 ***4537.32*** *p76*
MacLeod, Margaret; Ontario, 1851 ***4537.32*** *p91*
MacLeod, Margaret; Ontario, 1851 ***4537.32*** *p96*
MacLeod, Margaret; Ontario, 1855 ***4537.32*** *p80*
MacLeod, Margaret; Ontario, 1863 ***4537.32*** *p56*
MacLeod, Margaret; Port uncertain, 1840-1849 ***4537.35*** *p84*
Child: Angus
Child: Kenneth
MacLeod, Margaret; Port uncertain, 1840-1849 ***4537.37*** *p125*
Child: Alexander
Child: Murdo
Child: John
Child: Effie
Child: Catherine
Child: Angus
MacLeod, Margaret; Port uncertain, 1850-1859 ***4537.37*** *p120*
MacLeod, Margaret Campbell *SEE* MacLeod, Murdo
MacLeod, Margaret Ferguson *SEE* MacLeod, Peter
MacLeod, Margaret MacAulay *SEE* MacLeod, Charles
MacLeod, Margaret MacIver *SEE* MacLeod, John
MacLeod, Margaret MacLeod *SEE* MacLeod, Neil
MacLeod, Marion *SEE* MacLeod, Alexander
MacLeod, Marion *SEE* MacLeod, Angus
MacLeod, Marion *SEE* MacLeod, Donald
MacLeod, Marion *SEE* MacLeod, Hector
MacLeod, Marion *SEE* MacLeod, John
MacLeod, Marion *SEE* MacLeod, Kenneth
MacLeod, Marion *SEE* MacLeod, Malcolm
MacLeod, Marion *SEE* MacLeod, Mary
MacLeod, Marion *SEE* MacLeod, Mary Morrison
MacLeod, Marion *SEE* MacLeod, Murdo
MacLeod, Marion *SEE* MacLeod, Norman
MacLeod, Marion *SEE* MacLeod, Roderick
MacLeod, Marion; Ontario, 1851 ***4537.32*** *p37*
MacLeod, Marion; Ontario, 1851 ***4537.32*** *p59*
MacLeod, Marion; Ontario, 1851 ***4537.37*** *p52*
MacLeod, Marion; Ontario, 1855 ***4537.32*** *p16*
MacLeod, Marion; Ontario, 1862-1869 ***4537.35*** *p59*
MacLeod, Marion; Ontario, 1863 ***4537.32*** *p13*
MacLeod, Marion; Ontario, 1863 ***4537.32*** *p25*
MacLeod, Marion; Port uncertain, 1840-1849 ***4537.37*** *p131*
MacLeod, Marion; Port uncertain, 1850-1859 ***4537.37*** *p118*
MacLeod, Marion; Port uncertain, 1850-1859 ***4537.37*** *p123*
MacLeod, Marion; Port uncertain, 1860-1869 ***4537.35*** *p81*
MacLeod, Marion; Port uncertain, 1860-1869 ***4537.35*** *p82*
Child: Kenneth
Child: Roderick
MacLeod, Marion Kerr *SEE* MacLeod, Alexander
MacLeod, Marion MacCuish *SEE* MacLeod, Murdo
MacLeod, Marion MacDonald *SEE* MacLeod, Hector
MacLeod, Marion MacDonald *SEE* MacLeod, John
MacLeod, Marion Morrison *SEE* MacLeod, John
MacLeod, Mary *SEE* MacLeod, Alexander
MacLeod, Mary *SEE* MacLeod, Angus
MacLeod, Mary *SEE* MacLeod, Charles
MacLeod, Mary *SEE* MacLeod, Donald
MacLeod, Mary *SEE* MacLeod, Ewen
MacLeod, Mary *SEE* MacLeod, James
MacLeod, Mary *SEE* MacLeod, John
MacLeod, Mary *SEE* MacLeod, Kenneth
MacLeod, Mary *SEE* MacLeod, Kirsty MacKillop
MacLeod, Mary *SEE* MacLeod, Mary
MacLeod, Mary *SEE* MacLeod, Murdo
MacLeod, Mary *SEE* MacLeod, Norman
MacLeod, Mary *SEE* MacLeod, Roderick
MacLeod, Mary *SEE* MacLeod, William
Macleod, Mary; Georgia, 1740 ***1640.10*** *p140*
Macleod, Mary; North Carolina, 1793 ***1224.2*** *p74*
MacLeod, Mary; Nova Scotia, 1820-1829 ***4537.35*** *p38*
MacLeod, Mary; Nova Scotia, 1828 ***4537.35*** *p33*
MacLeod, Mary; Nova Scotia, 1840-1849 ***4537.35*** *p12*
MacLeod, Mary; Nova Scotia, 1840-1849 ***4537.35*** *p15*
MacLeod, Mary; Nova Scotia, 1865 ***4537.35*** *p20*
MacLeod, Mary; Ontario, 1849 ***4537.37*** *p39*
MacLeod, Mary; Ontario, 1851 ***4537.32*** *p88*
MacLeod, Mary; Ontario, 1855 ***4537.32*** *p15*
MacLeod, Mary; Ontario, 1855 ***4537.32*** *p57*
MacLeod, Mary; Ontario, 1855 ***4537.32*** *p73*
MacLeod, Mary; Ontario, 1860-1869 ***4537.35*** *p56*
MacLeod, Mary; Ontario, 1863 ***4537.32*** *p12*
MacLeod, Mary; Prince Edward Island, 1848 ***4537.37*** *p23*
MacLeod, Mary; Saskatchewan, 1884 ***4537.37*** *p101*
MacLeod, Mary; Saskatchewan, 1889 ***4537.35*** *p65*
MacLeod, Mary; Port uncertain, 1840-1849 ***4537.35*** *p84*
Child: Alexander
Child: Donald
Child: Angus
Child: Jessie
MacLeod, Mary; Port uncertain, 1840-1849 ***4537.37*** *p109*
MacLeod, Mary; Port uncertain, 1840-1849 ***4537.37*** *p119*
MacLeod, Mary; Port uncertain, 1840-1849 ***4537.37*** *p125*
Child: William
Child: Rachel
Child: Kirsty
Child: Alexander
MacLeod, Mary; Port uncertain, 1840-1849 ***4537.37*** *p128*
MacLeod, Mary; Port uncertain, 1850-1859 ***4537.35*** *p84*
Child: Mary
Child: Marion
Child: Murdo
MacLeod, Mary; Port uncertain, 1850-1859 ***4537.37*** *p118*
MacLeod, Mary; Port uncertain, 1860-1869 ***4537.35*** *p78*
MacLeod, Mary Ann *SEE* MacLeod, Alexander
MacLeod, Mary Ann *SEE* MacLeod, Donald
MacLeod, Mary Ann *SEE* MacLeod, John
MacLeod, Mary Ann *SEE* MacLeod, Murdo
MacLeod, Mary MacLean *SEE* MacLeod, Norman
MacLeod, Mary Maxwell *SEE* MacLeod, Kenneth
MacLeod, Mary Morrison *SEE* MacLeod, Donald
MacLeod, Mary Morrison *SEE* MacLeod, Kenneth
MacLeod, Mary Morrison; Ontario, 1850-1859 ***4537.32*** *p65*
Child: Marion
Child: John
Child: Malcolm
MacLeod, Mary Morrison; Ontario, 1850-1859 ***4537.35*** *p59*
Child: Marion
Child: John
Child: Malcolm
MacLeod, Mary Nicolson *SEE* MacLeod, Angus
MacLeod, Mary Ross *SEE* MacLeod, Norman
MacLeod, Mary Shaw *SEE* MacLeod, Angus
MacLeod, Murchison *SEE* MacLeod, Donald
MacLeod, Murdo *SEE* MacLeod, Charles
MacLeod, Murdo *SEE* MacLeod, Donald
MacLeod, Murdo *SEE* MacLeod, Hector
MacLeod, Murdo *SEE* MacLeod, John
MacLeod, Murdo *SEE* MacLeod, Kenneth
MacLeod, Murdo *SEE* MacLeod, Kirsty
MacLeod, Murdo *SEE* MacLeod, Margaret
MacLeod, Murdo *SEE* MacLeod, Mary
MacLeod, Murdo *SEE* MacLeod, Norman
MacLeod, Murdo; Nova Scotia, 1840-1849 ***4537.35*** *p26*
Wife: Effie
Child: Marion
Child: Jessie
Child: Donald
Child: Mary
Child: John
MacLeod, Murdo; Ontario, 1851 ***4537.32*** *p69*
Wife: Ann Murray
Child: Kirsty
Child: Catherine
Child: Mary
Child: Angus
Child: Allan
Child: Marion
Child: John
Child: Margaret
MacLeod, Murdo; Ontario, 1851 ***4537.32*** *p69*
Wife: Kirsty MacDonald
Child: Catherine
Child: Alexander
MacLeod, Murdo; Ontario, 1860-1869 ***4537.35*** *p60*
Wife: Margaret Campbell
Child: Margaret
Child: Norman
Child: Marion
Child: Hannah
MacLeod, Murdo; Ontario, 1860-1869 ***4537.35*** *p60*
Wife: Marion MacCuish
Child: John
Child: Marion
Child: Mary Ann
Child: Charles
Child: Alexander
MacLeod, Murdo; Ontario, 1862 ***4537.32*** *p70*
Wife: Margaret Campbell
Child: Hannah
Child: Norman
Child: Margaret
Child: Marion
MacLeod, Murdo; Ontario, 1862 ***4537.32*** *p70*
Wife: Marion MacCuish
Child: Marion
Child: Charles
Child: Alexander
Child: John
MacLeod, Murdo; Pictou, Nova Scotia, 1848 ***4537.37*** *p30*
Wife: Catherine
Child: Allan
Child: Mary
Child: Ann
Child: Margaret
MacLeod, Murdo; Port uncertain, 1840-1849 ***4537.35*** *p84*
Wife: Marion
Child: Ann
Child: Margaret
Child: Kirsty
Child: Catherine
Child: John
MacLeod, Murdo; Port uncertain, 1840-1849 ***4537.35*** *p84*
Child: John
Child: Malcolm
Child: Marion
Child: Donald
Child: Angus
Wife: Mary
Child: Ann

MacLeod, Murdo; Port uncertain, 1840-1849 ***4537.35*** *p84*
Wife: Rachel
Child: Betsy
MacLeod, Murdo; Port uncertain, 1850-1859 ***4537.35*** *p84*
Child: Mary
Child: Effie
MacLeod, Neil *SEE* MacLeod, Alexander
MacLeod, Neil *SEE* MacLeod, Angus
MacLeod, Neil *SEE* MacLeod, Donald
MacLeod, Neil *SEE* MacLeod, Ewen
MacLeod, Neil *SEE* MacLeod, John
MacLeod, Neil *SEE* MacLeod, Norman
MacLeod, Neil *SEE* MacLeod, Peter
MacLeod, Neil; Nova Scotia, 1838 ***4537.35*** *p26*
Wife: Margaret MacLeod
Child: Roderick N.
Child: Norman
Child: Margaret
MacLeod, Neil; Philippines, 1750-1900 ***4537.35*** *p76*
Brother: Alexander
MacLeod, Neil; Port uncertain, 1840-1849 ***4537.35*** *p84*
Wife: Rachel Morrison
Child: Peter
Child: John
Child: Duncan
Child: Kirsty
Child: Donald
Child: Roderick
Child: Archie
MacLeod, Norman *SEE* MacLeod, Alexander
MacLeod, Norman *SEE* MacLeod, Donald
MacLeod, Norman *SEE* MacLeod, Duncan
MacLeod, Norman *SEE* MacLeod, John
MacLeod, Norman *SEE* MacLeod, Kenneth
MacLeod, Norman *SEE* MacLeod, Malcolm
MacLeod, Norman *SEE* MacLeod, Murdo
MacLeod, Norman *SEE* MacLeod, Neil
MacLeod, Norman *SEE* MacLeod, Norman
MacLeod, Norman; Canada, 1880-1889 ***4537.35*** *p73*
Sister: Una
MacLeod, Norman; Falkland Islands, 1880-1889 ***4537.35*** *p76*
Wife: Mary Ross
MacLeod, Norman; Nova Scotia, 1820-1829 ***4537.35*** *p27*
Wife: Sarah MacKay
Child: Donald
Child: John
Child: Ann
Child: Flora
Child: Kenneth
Child: Mary
Child: Kirsty
MacLeod, Norman; Nova Scotia, 1828 ***4537.35*** *p27*
Wife: Mary MacLean
Child: Malcolm
Child: Donald
Child: Angus
Father: Malcolm
MacLeod, Norman; Nova Scotia, 1828 ***4537.35*** *p27*
With wife
Child: John
Child: Margaret
Child: Mary
Child: Kenneth
MacLeod, Norman; Nova Scotia, 1840-1849 ***4537.35*** *p27*
Wife: Julia
Child: Margaret
Child: Donald
Child: Kirsty
Child: Neil
Child: Roderick
MacLeod, Norman; Ontario, 1870-1879 ***4537.32*** *p70*
Wife: Isabella MacAskill
Child: Mary
Child: Donald
Child: Catherine
Child: Malcolm
Child: Effie
Child: John
MacLeod, Norman; Port uncertain, 1840-1849 ***4537.35*** *p84*
Wife: Marion
Child: Kirsty
MacLeod, Norman; Port uncertain, 1840-1849 ***4537.37*** *p125*
Wife: Effie
Child: Murdo
Child: Alexander
MacLeod, Norman; Port uncertain, 1850-1859 ***4537.35*** *p84*
Wife: Catherine
Child: Norman
Child: Neil
Child: Murdo
Child: Donald
Child: Margaret
Child: Ann
Child: Finlay
MacLeod, Peggy *SEE* MacLeod, Donald
MacLeod, Peggy *SEE* MacLeod, John
MacLeod, Penny *SEE* MacLeod, Hector
MacLeod, Peter *SEE* MacLeod, Neil
MacLeod, Peter; Nova Scotia, 1840-1849 ***4537.35*** *p28*
Wife: Margaret Ferguson
Child: Neil
Child: Donald
Child: Effie
Child: Ewen
MacLeod, Rachel *SEE* MacLeod, Charles
MacLeod, Rachel *SEE* MacLeod, Donald
MacLeod, Rachel *SEE* MacLeod, Duncan
MacLeod, Rachel *SEE* MacLeod, John
MacLeod, Rachel *SEE* MacLeod, Kenneth
MacLeod, Rachel *SEE* MacLeod, Mary
MacLeod, Rachel *SEE* MacLeod, Murdo
MacLeod, Rachel; Port uncertain, 1860-1869 ***4537.35*** *p82*
MacLeod, Rachel Morrison *SEE* MacLeod, Neil
MacLeod, Ranald *SEE* MacLeod, Donald
MacLeod, Ranald *SEE* MacLeod, John
MacLeod, Robert *SEE* MacLeod, Charles
MacLeod, Roderick *SEE* MacLeod, Alexander
MacLeod, Roderick *SEE* MacLeod, Angus
MacLeod, Roderick *SEE* MacLeod, Donald
MacLeod, Roderick *SEE* MacLeod, Ewen
MacLeod, Roderick *SEE* MacLeod, John
MacLeod, Roderick *SEE* MacLeod, Malcolm
MacLeod, Roderick *SEE* MacLeod, Marion
MacLeod, Roderick *SEE* MacLeod, Neil
MacLeod, Roderick *SEE* MacLeod, Norman
MacLeod, Roderick; Nova Scotia, 1825 ***4537.35*** *p28*
Wife: Catherine MacAskill
Child: Mary
Child: Allan
Child: Kenneth
MacLeod, Roderick; Nova Scotia, 1830-1839 ***4537.35*** *p28*
Wife: Sarah
Child: John
Child: Donald
Child: Alexander
Child: Ann
MacLeod, Roderick; Ontario, 1870-1879 ***4537.32*** *p68*
With relative
MacLeod, Roderick; Port uncertain, 1850-1859 ***4537.35*** *p84*
Wife: Marion
Child: Effie
Child: Catherine
Child: Isabella
MacLeod, Roderick; Port uncertain, 1850-1859 ***4537.37*** *p125*
Wife: Margaret
Child: Isabella
MacLeod, Roderick N. *SEE* MacLeod, Neil
MacLeod, Salvia *SEE* MacLeod, Alexander
MacLeod, Sarah *SEE* MacLeod, Donald
MacLeod, Sarah *SEE* MacLeod, John
MacLeod, Sarah *SEE* MacLeod, Roderick
MacLeod, Sarah; Nova Scotia, 1865 ***4537.35*** *p20*
MacLeod, Sarah MacKay *SEE* MacLeod, Norman
MacLeod, Una *SEE* MacLeod, Norman
MacLeod, Una; Port uncertain, 1860-1869 ***4537.35*** *p82*
MacLeod, William *SEE* MacLeod, Alexander
MacLeod, William *SEE* MacLeod, Bannatyne
MacLeod, William *SEE* MacLeod, Donald
MacLeod, William *SEE* MacLeod, John
MacLeod, William *SEE* MacLeod, Malcolm
MacLeod, William *SEE* MacLeod, Mary
MacLeod, William; Maryland, 1888 ***4537.35*** *p69*
With brother-in-law
MacLeod, William; Ontario, 1851 ***4537.32*** *p70*
Wife: Betsy MacIver
Child: Ann
Child: Gormelia
Child: Margaret
Child: Mary
Maclin, John 80; Ontario, 1871 ***1823.22*** *p95*
Maclure, William; Indiana, 1845 ***1224.3*** *p50*
Macly, Waclau; Maryland, 1910 ***3259.35*** *p37*
MacMillan, Alexander *SEE* MacMillan, Alexander
MacMillan, Alexander *SEE* MacMillan, Angus
MacMillan, Alexander *SEE* MacMillan, John
MacMillan, Alexander *SEE* MacMillan, Michael
MacMillan, Alexander; Ontario, 1840-1849 ***4537.37*** *p70*
Wife: Mary MacLellan
Child: Catherine
Child: Kirsty
MacMillan, Alexander; Ontario, 1849 ***4537.37*** *p70*
Wife: Margaret MacIntyre
Child: Alexander
Child: Neil
Child: Michael
Child: Flora
Child: Mary
Child: Donald
Child: John
Child: Catherine
MacMillan, Alexander; Port uncertain, 1840-1849 ***4537.37*** *p125*
Wife: Mary Currie
Child: Marion
Child: John
Child: Allan
Child: Catherine
Child: Michael
Child: Donald
Child: Alexander
MacMillan, Allan *SEE* MacMillan, Alexander
MacMillan, Andrew *SEE* MacMillan, Donald
MacMillan, Angus *SEE* MacMillan, Angus
MacMillan, Angus *SEE* MacMillan, John
MacMillan, Angus; Nova Scotia, 1820-1829 ***4537.35*** *p28*
With wife
MacMillan, Angus; Nova Scotia, 1840-1849 ***4537.37*** *p17*
Wife: Ann
Child: Flora
Child: Roderick
Child: Joan
Child: Ann
MacMillan, Angus; Ontario, 1880-1889 ***4537.32*** *p71*
Child: John
Child: Malcolm
Child: William
Child: Angus
Wife: Ann MacKinnon
Child: Mary
Child: Alexander
MacMillan, Angus; Ontario, 1880-1889 ***4537.35*** *p60*
Wife: Ann MacKinnon
Child: Angus
Child: Malcolm
Child: John
Child: Alexander
Child: William
MacMillan, Angus; Quebec, 1840-1849 ***4537.37*** *p71*
Wife: Flora
Child: Donald
Child: John
MacMillan, Angus; Quebec, 1849 ***4537.32*** *p71*
Wife: Flora
Child: Donald
Child: John
MacMillan, Angus; Port uncertain, 1840-1849 ***4537.37*** *p125*
Wife: Ann MacDonald
Child: Alexander
Child: Catherine
MacMillan, Ann *SEE* MacMillan, Angus
MacMillan, Ann *SEE* MacMillan, Donald
MacMillan, Ann *SEE* MacMillan, John
MacMillan, Ann *SEE* MacMillan, Malcolm
MacMillan, Ann *SEE* MacMillan, Marion
MacMillan, Ann *SEE* MacMillan, Peter
MacMillan, Ann; Ontario, 1840-1849 ***4537.37*** *p38*
MacMillan, Ann; Ontario, 1840-1849 ***4537.37*** *p85*
MacMillan, Ann; Ontario, 1849 ***4537.32*** *p95*
MacMillan, Ann Ferguson *SEE* MacMillan, Peter
MacMillan, Ann MacDonald *SEE* MacMillan, Angus
MacMillan, Ann MacDonald *SEE* MacMillan, John
MacMillan, Ann MacKinnon *SEE* MacMillan, Angus
MacMillan, Ann MacKinnon *SEE* MacMillan, Kenneth
MacMillan, Archie; Ontario, 1849 ***4537.37*** *p71*
Wife: Catherine Morrison
Child: Julia
Child: Janet
Child: Margaret
Child: Kirsty
Child: Lachlan
MacMillan, Catherine *SEE* MacMillan, Alexander
MacMillan, Catherine *SEE* MacMillan, Angus
MacMillan, Catherine *SEE* MacMillan, Donald
MacMillan, Catherine *SEE* MacMillan, John
MacMillan, Catherine *SEE* MacMillan, Malcolm

MacNeil, John; Ontario, 1851 ***4537.32*** *p72*
Wife: Mary
Child: Murdo
Child: Flora
Child: Michael
Child: Catherine
Child: Mary
Child: Finlay
MacNeil, Kate *SEE* MacNeil, Janet
MacNeil, Kirsty *SEE* MacNeil, John
MacNeil, Mary *SEE* MacNeil, John
MacNeil, Mary; Vermont, n.d. ***5900.10*** *p321*
MacNeil, Mary; Port uncertain, 1840-1849 ***4537.37*** *p122*
MacNeil, Michael *SEE* MacNeil, John
MacNeil, Murdo *SEE* MacNeil, John
MacNeil, Neil; Charleston, South Carolina, 1824 ***1224.3*** *p50*
MacNeill, Donald; Nova Scotia, 1830-1839 ***4537.35*** *p29*
Wife: Margaret MacIsaac
Child: Roderick
MacNeill, Hector *SEE* MacNeill, Norman
MacNeill, Margaret MacIsaac *SEE* MacNeill, Donald
MacNeill, Mary *SEE* MacNeill, Norman
MacNeill, Mary MacKillop *SEE* MacNeill, Norman
MacNeill, Norman; Nova Scotia, 1820-1829 ***4537.35*** *p29*
Child: Hector
Child: Mary
Wife: Mary MacKillop
MacNeill, Roderick *SEE* MacNeill, Donald
MacNicol, John; Florida, 1894 ***1640.13*** *p92*
Macniven, Allan; Savannah, Georgia, 1805 ***1640.10*** *p144*
Macoben, John; Maryland, 1649 ***2524.55*** *p142*
Macoby, Mortegh; Maryland, 1679 ***2524.55*** *p142*
Macom, Jno; Virginia, 1668-1669 ***6212.30*** *p41*
Macom, Katherine *SEE* Macom, Thomas
Macom, Thomas; Maryland, 1665 ***2524.55*** *p142*
Wife: Katherine
Macombe, James; New York, 1797 ***1224.2*** *p74*
Macomber, Sarah A. 69; Vermont, 1922 ***5900.10*** *p377*
Maconachie, William; Maryland, 1743 ***1640.13*** *p84*
Macoun, Frederic 42; Ontario, 1871 ***1823.22*** *p95*
Macoy, Alexander; Vermont, 1816-1849 ***5900.10*** *p198*
Macoy, Mary R. Farr; Vermont, 1816-1897 ***5900.10*** *p198*
MacPhail, Angus *SEE* MacPhail, Angus
MacPhail, Angus *SEE* MacPhail, Donald
MacPhail, Angus *SEE* MacPhail, John
MacPhail, Angus; Nova Scotia, 1820-1829 ***4537.35*** *p29*
Wife: Margaret MacDonald
Child: Donald
Child: William
With 2 daughters
Child: Angus
Child: John Roderick
Child: James
MacPhail, Ann *SEE* MacPhail, Donald
MacPhail, Archie *SEE* MacPhail, Donald
MacPhail, Archie *SEE* MacPhail, John
MacPhail, Catherine *SEE* MacPhail, Donald
MacPhail, Donald *SEE* MacPhail, Angus
MacPhail, Donald *SEE* MacPhail, Donald
MacPhail, Donald *SEE* MacPhail, John
MacPhail, Donald; Nova Scotia, 1828 ***4537.35*** *p29*
Wife: Mary MacAskill
Child: Angus
Child: Archie
Child: Effie
Child: Kirsty
Child: Mary
Child: Sarah
Child: John
Child: Finlay
MacPhail, Donald; Ontario, 1855 ***4537.32*** *p73*
Wife: Mary MacLeod
Child: Catherine
Child: Ann
Child: Norman
Child: Mary
Child: Malcolm
Child: Donald
MacPhail, Effie *SEE* MacPhail, Donald
MacPhail, Finlay *SEE* MacPhail, Donald
MacPhail, James *SEE* MacPhail, Angus
MacPhail, John *SEE* MacPhail, Donald
MacPhail, John *SEE* MacPhail, John
MacPhail, John; Nova Scotia, 1820-1829 ***4537.35*** *p30*
Wife: Mary MacLennan
Son: Donald
Son: Archie
Son: John
Son: Angus
Son: Neil
MacPhail, John Roderick *SEE* MacPhail, Angus
MacPhail, Kirsty *SEE* MacPhail, Donald
MacPhail, Kirsty; Nova Scotia, 1843 ***4537.37*** *p10*
MacPhail, Malcolm *SEE* MacPhail, Donald
MacPhail, Margaret MacDonald *SEE* MacPhail, Angus
MacPhail, Mary *SEE* MacPhail, Donald
MacPhail, Mary MacAskill *SEE* MacPhail, Donald
MacPhail, Mary MacLennan *SEE* MacPhail, John
MacPhail, Mary MacLeod *SEE* MacPhail, Donald
MacPhail, Neil *SEE* MacPhail, John
MacPhail, Norman *SEE* MacPhail, Donald
MacPhail, Sarah *SEE* MacPhail, Donald
MacPhail, William *SEE* MacPhail, Angus
MacPhee, Alexander *SEE* MacPhee, Murdo
MacPhee, Alexander; Port uncertain, 1850-1859 ***4537.37*** *p127*
Child: Archie
Child: Marion
Child: Flora
Child: Isabella
Child: Ann
Child: Lexy
Wife: Catherine MacNash
Child: Effie
MacPhee, Alexander; Port uncertain, 1850-1859 ***4537.37*** *p127*
Wife: Effie MacNeil
Child: Kirsty
Child: Angus
Child: Donald
Child: Effie
Child: Mary
Child: John
Child: Catherine
MacPhee, Angus *SEE* MacPhee, Alexander
MacPhee, Angus *SEE* MacPhee, Angus
MacPhee, Angus *SEE* MacPhee, Archie
MacPhee, Angus *SEE* MacPhee, Donald
MacPhee, Angus *SEE* MacPhee, Francis
MacPhee, Angus *SEE* MacPhee, Hector
MacPhee, Angus *SEE* MacPhee, John
MacPhee, Angus *SEE* MacPhee, Lachlan
MacPhee, Angus *SEE* MacPhee, Mary MacIntyre
MacPhee, Angus *SEE* MacPhee, Neil
MacPhee, Angus *SEE* MacPhee, Ranald
MacPhee, Angus; Nova Scotia, 1848 ***4537.37*** *p18*
Wife: Sarah MacDonald
Child: Angus
Child: Kirsty
Child: Ranald
MacPhee, Angus; Ontario, 1811-1847 ***4537.37*** *p73*
Wife: Mary MacLean
Child: Lachlan
Child: Sarah
Child: Ann
Child: Margaret
Child: Mary
Child: Catherine
Child: Marion
MacPhee, Angus; Ontario, 1849 ***4537.32*** *p73*
Wife: Mary MacLean
Child: Mary
Child: Margaret
Child: Ann
Child: Sarah
Child: Lachlan
Child: Marion
Child: Catherine
MacPhee, Angus; Ontario, 1850-1859 ***4537.37*** *p73*
Wife: Mary MacLean
Child: Mary
Child: Michael
Child: Marion
Child: Donald
Child: Catherine
Child: Hector
Child: Neil
MacPhee, Angus; Saskatchewan, 1884 ***4537.37*** *p100*
Nephew: Lachlan
Child: Catherine
Child: Lachlan
Child: Mary
MacPhee, Angus; Port uncertain, 1840-1849 ***4537.37*** *p127*
Wife: Ann Steele
Child: Donald
Child: Catherine
MacPhee, Ann *SEE* MacPhee, Alexander
MacPhee, Ann *SEE* MacPhee, Angus
MacPhee, Ann *SEE* MacPhee, Archie
MacPhee, Ann *SEE* MacPhee, Donald
MacPhee, Ann *SEE* MacPhee, Hugh
MacPhee, Ann *SEE* MacPhee, John
MacPhee, Ann *SEE* MacPhee, Mary MacDonald
MacPhee, Ann *SEE* MacPhee, Neil
MacPhee, Ann *SEE* MacPhee, Roderick
MacPhee, Ann; Port uncertain, 1840-1849 ***4537.37*** *p112*
MacPhee, Ann Leitch *SEE* MacPhee, John
MacPhee, Ann MacInnes *SEE* MacPhee, Archie
MacPhee, Ann Steele *SEE* MacPhee, Angus
MacPhee, Annabella *SEE* MacPhee, Mary MacIntyre
MacPhee, Archie *SEE* MacPhee, Alexander
MacPhee, Archie *SEE* MacPhee, Francis
MacPhee, Archie *SEE* MacPhee, John
MacPhee, Archie *SEE* MacPhee, Sarah
MacPhee, Archie; Nova Scotia, 1850-1859 ***4537.37*** *p18*
Wife: Catherine MacInnes
Child: Malcolm
Child: Mary
Child: Ranald
Child: Flora
Child: Dougal
MacPhee, Archie; Ontario, 1840-1849 ***4537.37*** *p73*
Wife: Ann MacInnes
Child: Malcolm
Child: Neil
Child: Mary
MacPhee, Archie; Ontario, 1849 ***4537.37*** *p74*
Wife: Flora MacDonald
MacPhee, Archie; Ontario, 1851 ***4537.32*** *p73*
Wife: Catherine MacInnes
Child: Flora
Child: Malcolm
Child: Dougal
Child: Ranald
Child: Mary
MacPhee, Archie; Ontario, 1851 ***4537.32*** *p74*
Wife: Mary MacDonald
Child: Catherine
Child: Sarah
Child: Margaret
Child: Ann
Child: Neil
Child: Francis
MacPhee, Archie; Saskatchewan, 1884 ***4537.37*** *p100*
Wife: Margaret MacLellan
Child: Mary Ann
Child: Angus
Child: Malcolm
Child: Mary
Child: Catherine
MacPhee, Archie; Port uncertain, 1840-1849 ***4537.37*** *p127*
Wife: Kirsty
MacPhee, Catherine *SEE* MacPhee, Alexander
MacPhee, Catherine *SEE* MacPhee, Angus
MacPhee, Catherine *SEE* MacPhee, Archie
MacPhee, Catherine *SEE* MacPhee, Donald
MacPhee, Catherine *SEE* MacPhee, Hugh
MacPhee, Catherine *SEE* MacPhee, John
MacPhee, Catherine *SEE* MacPhee, Mary MacDonald
MacPhee, Catherine *SEE* MacPhee, Murdo
MacPhee, Catherine *SEE* MacPhee, Neil
MacPhee, Catherine; Ontario, 1840-1849 ***4537.37*** *p58*
MacPhee, Catherine; Ontario, 1860-1869 ***4537.35*** *p59*
MacPhee, Catherine; Ontario, 1862 ***4537.32*** *p62*
MacPhee, Catherine; Saskatchewan, 1883 ***4537.37*** *p92*
MacPhee, Catherine; Saskatchewan, 1884 ***4537.37*** *p99*
MacPhee, Catherine; Port uncertain, 1840-1849 ***4537.37*** *p120*
MacPhee, Catherine MacInnes *SEE* MacPhee, Archie
MacPhee, Catherine MacInnes *SEE* MacPhee, Neil
MacPhee, Catherine MacNash *SEE* MacPhee, Alexander
MacPhee, Donald *SEE* MacPhee, Alexander
MacPhee, Donald *SEE* MacPhee, Angus
MacPhee, Donald *SEE* MacPhee, Donald
MacPhee, Donald *SEE* MacPhee, John
MacPhee, Donald *SEE* MacPhee, Lachlan
MacPhee, Donald *SEE* MacPhee, Mary MacIntyre
MacPhee, Donald *SEE* MacPhee, Neil
MacPhee, Donald; Nova Scotia, 1840-1843 ***4537.37*** *p18*
Wife: Mary MacIsaac
Child: Donald
MacPhee, Donald; Ontario, 1849 ***4537.37*** *p75*
Wife: Mary MacIsaac
Child: Catherine
Child: Donald
Child: Angus
MacPhee, Donald; Ontario, 1851 ***4537.32*** *p74*
Wife: Jessie Currie
Child: Donald
Child: Isabella
Child: Donald
Child: Mary
Child: Margaret
Child: Ann

MacPhee, Neil; Port uncertain, 1840-1849 ***4537.37*** *p128*
Wife: Mary
Child: Margaret
Child: Angus
Child: John
Child: James
MacPhee, Penny; Ontario, 1840-1849 ***4537.37*** *p48*
MacPhee, Penny; Ontario, 1849 ***4537.32*** *p30*
MacPhee, Ranald *SEE* MacPhee, Angus
MacPhee, Ranald *SEE* MacPhee, Archie
MacPhee, Ranald *SEE* MacPhee, Murdo
MacPhee, Ranald; Saskatchewan, 1884 ***4537.37*** *p101*
Child: Mary
Child: Murdo
Child: Angus
Child: Neil
MacPhee, Roderick *SEE* MacPhee, Francis
MacPhee, Roderick *SEE* MacPhee, Neil
MacPhee, Roderick; Ontario, 1849 ***4537.37*** *p76*
Wife: Mary
Child: Mary
Child: Ann
Child: Flora
MacPhee, Sarah *SEE* MacPhee, Angus
MacPhee, Sarah *SEE* MacPhee, Archie
MacPhee, Sarah *SEE* MacPhee, Donald
MacPhee, Sarah *SEE* MacPhee, John
MacPhee, Sarah *SEE* MacPhee, Mary MacDonald
MacPhee, Sarah; Port uncertain, 1840-1849 ***4537.37*** *p128*
Child: Margaret
Child: Archie
MacPhee, Sarah; Port uncertain, 1840-1849 ***4537.37*** *p131*
MacPhee, Sarah; Port uncertain, 1850-1859 ***4537.37*** *p116*
MacPhee, Sarah MacDonald *SEE* MacPhee, Angus
MacPhee, Una MacIntyre *SEE* MacPhee, Lachlan
MacPherson, Alexander *SEE* MacPherson, Donald
Macpherson, Alexander; Florida, 1771 ***1640.10*** *p144*
MacPherson, Alexander; Saskatchewan, 1883 ***4537.37*** *p101*
Wife: Effie MacMillan
Child: Malcolm
MacPherson, Alexander; Port uncertain, 1840-1849 ***4537.37*** *p128*
Wife: Catherine
Child: Janet
Child: Donald
Child: Angus
Child: Catherine
MacPherson, Angus *SEE* MacPherson, Alexander
MacPherson, Angus *SEE* MacPherson, Angus
MacPherson, Angus *SEE* MacPherson, John
MacPherson, Angus *SEE* MacPherson, Neil
MacPherson, Angus; Ontario, 1850-1859 ***4537.37*** *p77*
Wife: Catherine Black
Child: Mary
Child: Kirsty
Child: Marion
Child: Angus
Child: Catherine
Child: Ann
Child: Ranald
MacPherson, Angus; Ontario, 1851 ***4537.32*** *p75*
Wife: Catherine Black
Child: Mary
Child: Kirsty
Child: Marion
Child: Angus
Child: Catherine
Child: Ann
Child: Ranald
MacPherson, Angus; Port uncertain, 1840-1849 ***4537.37*** *p128*
Wife: Mary MacLeod
Child: Malcolm
Child: Neil
Child: Ann
Child: Archie
Child: Mary
MacPherson, Ann *SEE* MacPherson, Angus
MacPherson, Ann *SEE* MacPherson, Donald
MacPherson, Ann *SEE* MacPherson, John
MacPherson, Ann *SEE* MacPherson, Murdo
MacPherson, Ann *SEE* MacPherson, Roderick
MacPherson, Ann; Nova Scotia, 1847-1849 ***4537.37*** *p11*
MacPherson, Ann; Ontario, 1851 ***4537.32*** *p75*
MacPherson, Ann; Port uncertain, 1840-1849 ***4537.37*** *p108*
MacPherson, Ann; Port uncertain, 1840-1849 ***4537.37*** *p133*
MacPherson, Ann Morrison *SEE* MacPherson, Donald
MacPherson, Annabella *SEE* MacPherson, John
MacPherson, Archie *SEE* MacPherson, Angus
MacPherson, Archie; Port uncertain, 1840-1849 ***4537.37*** *p128*
Wife: Mary
Child: John
Child: Ewen
Child: Lachlan
Child: Kirsty
MacPherson, Cathellus *SEE* MacPherson, John
MacPherson, Catherine *SEE* MacPherson, Alexander
MacPherson, Catherine *SEE* MacPherson, Angus
MacPherson, Catherine *SEE* MacPherson, Donald
MacPherson, Catherine *SEE* MacPherson, John
MacPherson, Catherine *SEE* MacPherson, Neil
MacPherson, Catherine; Nova Scotia, 1840-1849 ***4537.37*** *p11*
MacPherson, Catherine Black *SEE* MacPherson, Angus
MacPherson, Catherine MacAulay *SEE* MacPherson, John
MacPherson, Catherine MacDonald *SEE* MacPherson, John
MacPherson, Dan *SEE* MacPherson, Donald
MacPherson, Donald *SEE* MacPherson, Alexander
MacPherson, Donald *SEE* MacPherson, John
MacPherson, Donald *SEE* MacPherson, Murdo
MacPherson, Donald *SEE* MacPherson, Neil
MacPherson, Donald *SEE* MacPherson, Roderick
Macpherson, Donald; Florida, 1771 ***1640.10*** *p144*
MacPherson, Donald; Saskatchewan, 1884 ***4537.37*** *p102*
Wife: Ann Morrison
Child: Donald J.
Child: Neil
Child: Dan
Child: Kirsty
Child: Alexander
Child: Mary
Child: Catherine
MacPherson, Donald; Port uncertain, 1840-1849 ***4537.37*** *p128*
Child: Catherine
Wife: Ann
MacPherson, Donald; Port uncertain, 1840-1849 ***4537.37*** *p128*
Wife: Mary Gillies
Child: William
Child: John
Child: Flora
Child: Isabella
MacPherson, Donald; Port uncertain, 1840-1849 ***4537.37*** *p128*
Wife: Mary
Child: John
Child: William
Child: Flora
MacPherson, Donald A. *SEE* MacPherson, Lachlan
MacPherson, Donald J. *SEE* MacPherson, Donald
MacPherson, Effie *SEE* MacPherson, John
MacPherson, Effie *SEE* MacPherson, Murdo
MacPherson, Effie; Saskatchewan, 1884 ***4537.37*** *p95*
MacPherson, Effie; Port uncertain, 1840-1849 ***4537.37*** *p110*
MacPherson, Effie MacMillan *SEE* MacPherson, Alexander
MacPherson, Ewen *SEE* MacPherson, Archie
MacPherson, Fergus *SEE* MacPherson, Neil
MacPherson, Flora *SEE* MacPherson, Donald
MacPherson, Flora *SEE* MacPherson, John
MacPherson, Flora *SEE* MacPherson, Roderick
MacPherson, Flora; Ontario, 1840-1849 ***4537.37*** *p69*
MacPherson, Flora; Port uncertain, 1850-1859 ***4537.37*** *p131*
MacPherson, Isabella *SEE* MacPherson, Donald
Macpherson, James; Florida, 1764 ***1640.10*** *p144*
Macpherson, James; Georgia, 1733 ***1640.10*** *p144*
MacPherson, Janet *SEE* MacPherson, Alexander
MacPherson, Janet Ferguson *SEE* MacPherson, Neil
MacPherson, John *SEE* MacPherson, Archie
MacPherson, John *SEE* MacPherson, Donald
MacPherson, John *SEE* MacPherson, John
MacPherson, John *SEE* MacPherson, Neil
MacPherson, John *SEE* MacPherson, Roderick
Macpherson, John; Georgia, 1737 ***1640.10*** *p145*
Macpherson, John; Georgia, 1759 ***1640.10*** *p145*
MacPherson, John; Nova Scotia, 1840-1849 ***4537.37*** *p19*
Wife: Kirsty
Child: John
Child: Donald
Child: Neil
Child: Mary
Child: Effie
Child: Kirsty
MacPherson, John; Ontario, 1840-1849 ***4537.37*** *p77*
Wife: Catherine MacAulay
Child: John
Child: Sam
Child: Margaret
MacPherson, John; Ontario, 1850-1859 ***4537.37*** *p77*
Wife: Mary MacVicar
Child: Cathellus
Child: Donald
Child: Margaret
Child: Angus
Child: Catherine
Child: Rachel
Child: John
MacPherson, John; Ontario, 1851 ***4537.32*** *p75*
Wife: Mary MacVicar
Child: Angus
Child: Catherine
Child: Marion
Child: Mary
Child: Cathellus
Child: Rachel
Child: Margaret
Child: John
Child: Donald
MacPherson, John; Saskatchewan, 1884 ***4537.37*** *p102*
Wife: Catherine MacDonald
Child: Flora
Child: Mary
Child: Ann
Child: Angus
Child: Mary Ann
Child: Annabella
MacPherson, John; Port uncertain, 1840-1849 ***4537.37*** *p128*
Wife: Catherine
Child: Catherine
Child: John
Child: Roderick
Child: Donald
MacPherson, John; Port uncertain, 1840-1849 ***4537.37*** *p128*
Wife: Marion
Child: Neil
Child: Angus
Child: Kirsty
MacPherson, John; Port uncertain, 1840-1849 ***4537.37*** *p129*
Wife: Mary MacDonald
Child: Kirsty
Child: John
Child: Marion
Child: Donald
Child: Catherine
MacPherson, John; Port uncertain, 1850-1859 ***4537.37*** *p129*
Wife: Mary Burke
Child: Flora
Child: Donald
Child: Mary
Child: Ann
MacPherson, John K. *SEE* MacPherson, Lachlan
MacPherson, Kate; Port uncertain, 1840-1849 ***4537.37*** *p127*
MacPherson, Kirsty *SEE* MacPherson, Angus
MacPherson, Kirsty *SEE* MacPherson, Archie
MacPherson, Kirsty *SEE* MacPherson, Donald
MacPherson, Kirsty *SEE* MacPherson, John
MacPherson, Kirsty; Port uncertain, 1840-1849 ***4537.37*** *p129*
Child: Rachel
Child: Roderick
MacPherson, Kirsty Nicolson *SEE* MacPherson, Lachlan
MacPherson, Lachlan *SEE* MacPherson, Archie
MacPherson, Lachlan; Saskatchewan, 1883 ***4537.37*** *p102*
Child: Donald A.
Child: John K.
Child: Mary
Child: Peggy
Wife: Kirsty Nicolson
MacPherson, Malcolm *SEE* MacPherson, Alexander
MacPherson, Malcolm *SEE* MacPherson, Angus
MacPherson, Margaret *SEE* MacPherson, John
MacPherson, Margaret *SEE* MacPherson, Murdo
MacPherson, Margaret *SEE* MacPherson, Roderick
MacPherson, Margaret; Ontario, 1850-1859 ***4537.37*** *p81*
MacPherson, Margaret; Ontario, 1851 ***4537.32*** *p84*
MacPherson, Marion *SEE* MacPherson, Angus
MacPherson, Marion *SEE* MacPherson, John
MacPherson, Marion *SEE* MacPherson, Neil
MacPherson, Marion *SEE* MacPherson, Roderick
MacPherson, Marion MacRury *SEE* MacPherson, William

Child: Mary
Child: Malcolm
MacRitchie, Kirsty *SEE* MacRitchie, John
MacRitchie, Kirsty *SEE* MacRitchie, Murdo
MacRitchie, Malcolm *SEE* MacRitchie, John
MacRitchie, Margaret *SEE* MacRitchie, John
MacRitchie, Margaret *SEE* MacRitchie, Murdo
MacRitchie, Margaret MacLeod; Ontario, 1851 ***4537.32*** *p76*
MacRitchie, Marion *SEE* MacRitchie, John
MacRitchie, Mary *SEE* MacRitchie, John
MacRitchie, Mary; Ontario, 1851 ***4537.32*** *p92*
MacRitchie, Murdo *SEE* MacRitchie, John
MacRitchie, Murdo; Ontario, 1851 ***4537.32*** *p76*
Wife: Ann MacAskill
Child: Margaret
Child: Donald
Child: Kirsty
Child: Catherine
Child: Charles
MacRitchie, Thomas Elder; Kansas, 1876 ***1640.13*** *p92*
MacRury, Angus *SEE* MacRury, Malcolm
MacRury, Angus; Saskatchewan, 1884 ***4537.37*** *p103*
MacRury, Angus; Port uncertain, 1840-1849 ***4537.37*** *p129*
Wife: Ann
Child: Norman
Child: Penny
Child: Archie
MacRury, Ann *SEE* MacRury, Angus
MacRury, Archie *SEE* MacRury, Angus
MacRury, Catherine *SEE* MacRury, Malcolm
MacRury, Flora *SEE* MacRury, Malcolm
MacRury, Joan *SEE* MacRury, Malcolm
MacRury, Kirsty; Saskatchewan, 1883 ***4537.37*** *p95*
MacRury, Kirsty; Saskatchewan, 1884 ***4537.37*** *p89*
MacRury, Malcolm; Saskatchewan, 1884 ***4537.37*** *p103*
Wife: Margaret
Cousin: Catherine
Child: Mary Ann
Child: Joan
Cousin: Flora
Child: Angus
MacRury, Margaret *SEE* MacRury, Malcolm
MacRury, Marion; Saskatchewan, 1883 ***4537.37*** *p102*
MacRury, Mary; Saskatchewan, 1883 ***4537.37*** *p96*
MacRury, Mary; Port uncertain, 1840-1849 ***4537.37*** *p109*
MacRury, Mary Ann *SEE* MacRury, Malcolm
MacRury, Norman *SEE* MacRury, Angus
MacRury, Penny *SEE* MacRury, Angus
Macrznak, Lawrence; Maryland, 1910 ***3259.35*** *p37*
MacSherry, Margerat 76; Ontario, 1871 ***1823.15*** *p151*
MacSherry, Wilson 37; Ontario, 1871 ***1823.15*** *p151*
MacSween, Angus *SEE* MacSween, Malcolm
MacSween, Ann *SEE* MacSween, Torlach
MacSween, Ann Kate; Manitoba, 1888 ***4537.35*** *p65*
MacSween, Catherine MacCuish *SEE* MacSween, Torlach
MacSween, Catherine Nicolson *SEE* MacSween, John
MacSween, Effie *SEE* MacSween, Malcolm
MacSween, Effie *SEE* MacSween, Murdo
MacSween, Effie; Ontario, 1860-1912 ***4537.35*** *p61*
MacSween, John *SEE* MacSween, Malcolm
MacSween, John; Ontario, 1855 ***4537.32*** *p77*
Wife: Catherine Nicolson
Child: Kenneth
Child: Kirsty
Child: Margaret
Child: Malcolm
Child: Murdo
Child: Peter
Child: Roderick
MacSween, Kenneth *SEE* MacSween, John
MacSween, Kirsty *SEE* MacSween, John
MacSween, Kirsty *SEE* MacSween, Malcolm
MacSween, Malcolm *SEE* MacSween, John
MacSween, Malcolm *SEE* MacSween, Malcolm
MacSween, Malcolm; Ontario, 1860-1869 ***4537.35*** *p61*
Wife: Rachel Morrison
Child: Kirsty
Child: Roderick
Child: John
Child: Angus
Child: Effie
Child: Marion
MacSween, Malcolm; Ontario, 1862 ***4537.32*** *p77*
Child: Marion
Child: Malcolm
Child: Kirsty
Child: John
Child: Marion
Child: Effie
Child: Angus
Wife: Rachel Morrison
Child: Roderick
MacSween, Margaret *SEE* MacSween, John
MacSween, Margaret; Saskatchewan, 1884 ***4537.37*** *p97*
MacSween, Marion *SEE* MacSween, Malcolm
MacSween, Marion *SEE* MacSween, Torlach
MacSween, Mary *SEE* MacSween, Murdo
MacSween, Mary; Nova Scotia, 1820-1829 ***4537.35*** *p35*
MacSween, Murdo *SEE* MacSween, John
MacSween, Murdo; Port uncertain, 1840-1849 ***4537.35*** *p85*
Wife: Mary
Child: Effie
MacSween, Neil *SEE* MacSween, Torlach
MacSween, Peter *SEE* MacSween, John
MacSween, Rachel Morrison *SEE* MacSween, Malcolm
MacSween, Roderick *SEE* MacSween, John
MacSween, Roderick *SEE* MacSween, Malcolm
MacSween, Torlach; Saskatchewan, 1889 ***4537.35*** *p70*
Brother: Neil
Sister: Ann
Sister: Marion
Wife: Catherine MacCuish
Macully, James F.; New York, 1839 ***8197.10*** *p264*
Maculski, Charles; Maryland, 1910 ***3259.35*** *p37*
MacVicar, Angus *SEE* MacVicar, Duncan
MacVicar, Ann *SEE* MacVicar, James
MacVicar, Catherine *SEE* MacVicar, Duncan
MacVicar, Catherine *SEE* MacVicar, James
MacVicar, Donald *SEE* MacVicar, James
MacVicar, Duncan; Ontario, 1840-1849 ***4537.37*** *p78*
Wife: Mary
Child: Catherine
Child: Kirsty
Child: Angus
MacVicar, Duncan; Ontario, 1849 ***4537.32*** *p77*
Wife: Mary
Child: Catherine
Child: Angus
Child: Kirsty
MacVicar, Effie *SEE* MacVicar, James
MacVicar, Ewen *SEE* MacVicar, James
MacVicar, James; Port uncertain, 1850-1859 ***4537.37*** *p129*
Wife: Catherine
Child: Catherine
Child: Ann
Child: John
Child: Donald
Child: Ewen
Child: Effie
MacVicar, John *SEE* MacVicar, James
MacVicar, Kirsty *SEE* MacVicar, Duncan
MacVicar, Mary *SEE* MacVicar, Duncan
MacVicar, Mary; Ontario, 1850-1859 ***4537.37*** *p77*
MacVicar, Mary; Ontario, 1851 ***4537.32*** *p75*
Macwell, William 33; Georgia, 1775 ***1220.25*** *p126*
Macy, Henry; Maryland, 1671 ***2524.55*** *p142*
Macylander, John; Maryland, 1664 ***2524.55*** *p142*
Maczeinniec, Konstanti; Maryland, 1910 ***3259.35*** *p37*
Maczewitz, Michael; Maryland, 1910 ***3259.35*** *p37*
Maczka, Walenty; Maryland, 1910 ***3259.35*** *p37*
Madagan, Patrick 45; Ontario, 1871 ***1823.22*** *p95*
Maday, John; Maryland, 1910 ***3259.35*** *p37*
Madbery, John; Maryland, 1658 ***2524.55*** *p142*
Madden, Abbie; Vermont, 1852-1889 ***5900.10*** *p228*
Madden, Catherine 16 *SEE* Madden, Mary
Madden, George; Canada, 1756-1760 ***4628.40*** *p45*
Madden, Helen 70; Vermont, 1879 ***5900.10*** *p162*
Madden, James; New York, 1840 ***8197.10*** *p264*
Madden, John; Vermont, n.d. ***5900.10*** *p110*
Madden, John; Vermont, 1802-1868 ***5900.10*** *p78*
Madden, John 17; Virginia, 1775 ***1220.25*** *p109*
Madden, John 21; Vermont, 1864 ***5900.10*** *p162*
Madden, John 27; Ontario, 1871 ***1823.15*** *p151*
Madden, John 79; Vermont, 1891 ***5900.10*** *p86*
Madden, Julia C. 19; Vermont, 1870 ***5900.10*** *p162*
Madden, Margaret; Vermont, n.d. ***5900.10*** *p110*
Madden, Margaret Claffery; Vermont, n.d. ***5900.10*** *p110*
Madden, Maria; Vermont, 1852-1889 ***5900.10*** *p89*
Madden, Mark 19; Vermont, 1864 ***5900.10*** *p566*
Madden, Martin; Vermont, n.d. ***5900.10*** *p110*
Madden, Mary; Vermont, n.d. ***5900.10*** *p110*
Madden, Mary 32; Vermont, 1877 ***5900.10*** *p162*
Madden, Mary 46; New York, New York, 1848 ***1825.45*** *p18*
Son: Thomas 13
Daughter: Catherine 16
Madden, Mary 66; Vermont, 1886 ***5900.10*** *p86*
Madden, Mary 80; Vermont, 1905 ***5900.10*** *p79*
Madden, Mary Hayes; Vermont, 1821-1896 ***5900.10*** *p78*
Madden, Patrick; New York, 1838 ***8197.10*** *p124*
Madden, Patrick; Pennsylvania, 1868 ***6058.10*** *p74*
Madden, Patrick 74; Vermont, 1883 ***5900.10*** *p162*
Madden, Roseanna Lee 67; Vermont, 1896 ***5900.10*** *p75*
Madden, Thomas 13 *SEE* Madden, Mary
Madden, Thomas 80; Vermont, 1909 ***5900.10*** *p75*
Maddigan, Martin 56; Vermont, 1867 ***5900.10*** *p328*
Maddin, Mary J.; Vermont, 1817-1897 ***5900.10*** *p365*
Maddisore, Jno; Virginia, 1666 ***6212.30*** *p25*
Maddock, Thomas; Maryland, 1651 ***2524.55*** *p142*
Maddocke, Thomas; Maryland, 1664 ***2524.55*** *p142*
Maddocks, Bonus; Maryland, 1662 ***2524.55*** *p142*
Maddocks, Henry; Maryland, 1682 ***2524.55*** *p142*
Maddon, Chris H. 41; Ontario, 1871 ***1823.28*** *p59*
Maddone, Edmund; Maryland, 1681 ***2524.55*** *p142*
Maddox, Ann; Maryland, 1669 ***2524.55*** *p148*
Maddox, Jonathan; New York, 1779 ***1224.2*** *p75*
Maddox, William; Virginia, 1665-1666 ***6212.30*** *p24*
Made, Adam; Port uncertain, 1771 ***2856.30*** *p282*
Madeare, Dennis; Maryland, 1657 ***2524.55*** *p142*
Madel, Ulrich; Port uncertain, 1755 ***2856.30*** *p318*
Madelle, John 58; Ontario, 1871 ***1823.28*** *p59*
Maden, John; Pennsylvania, 1868 ***6058.10*** *p72*
Maden, Thomas 47; Ontario, 1871 ***1823.28*** *p59*
Mader, Bernhard; America, 1743 ***2856.30*** *p282*
Mader, Jakob; Port uncertain, 1771 ***2856.30*** *p282*
Mader, Josef; Port uncertain, 1764 ***2856.30*** *p318*
Madery, George; Pennsylvania, 1777 ***4629.10*** *p20*
Madge, Walter 58; Ontario, 1871 ***1823.15*** *p151*
Madgwick, Martha; New York, 1839 ***1224.3*** *p76*
Madha, Nicholas; Baltimore, 1846 ***6058.10*** *p26*
Madich, Geo 20; Washington, 1911 ***9196.1*** *p33*
Madich, Paderan 55; Washington, 1911 ***9196.1*** *p33*
Madigan, Bridget; Vermont, 1910 ***5900.10*** *p466*
Madigan, Bridget Baker; Vermont, 1916 ***5900.10*** *p134*
Madigan, Bridget McElroy; Vermont, 1838-1923 ***5900.10*** *p134*
Madigan, Dennis 56; Ontario, 1871 ***1823.28*** *p59*
Madigan, Ellen; Vermont, 1847-1917 ***5900.10*** *p584*
Madigan, James; Vermont, 1815-1895 ***5900.10*** *p131*
Madigan, James; Vermont, 1839-1922 ***5900.10*** *p134*
Madigan, James 42; Ontario, 1871 ***1823.22*** *p95*
Madigan, John; New York, 1828 ***8197.10*** *p298*
Madigan, John; Pennsylvania, 1868 ***6058.10*** *p75*
Madigan, John 31; Ontario, 1871 ***1823.15*** *p151*
Madigan, John 52; Vermont, 1896 ***5900.10*** *p134*
Madigan, Julia Crimmins; Vermont, 1856-1884 ***5900.10*** *p134*
Madigan, Katherine Kennedy; Vermont, 1827-1924 ***5900.10*** *p131*
Madigan, Mary; Vermont, 1857-1946 ***5900.10*** *p131*
Madigan, Mary 34; Ontario, 1871 ***1823.28*** *p59*
Madigan, Mary J. 34; Vermont, 1885 ***5900.10*** *p316*
Madigan, Michael 36; Ontario, 1871 ***1823.15*** *p151*
Madigan, Patrick; Vermont, 1847-1886 ***5900.10*** *p134*
Madigan, Susan 35; Vermont, 1862 ***5900.10*** *p561*
Madigan, Thomas 35; Vermont, 1874 ***5900.10*** *p416*
Madigan, Thomas 59; Ontario, 1871 ***1823.28*** *p59*
Madill, Ann 35; Ontario, 1871 ***1823.15*** *p151*
Madison, John 60; Ontario, 1871 ***1823.15*** *p151*
Madison, Sam 27; British Columbia, 1909 ***9196.1*** *p27*
Madison, Sam 27; Seattle, 1909 ***9196.1*** *p27*
Madox, Wm; Virginia, 1664 ***6212.30*** *p14*
Madra, Polin E.; Maryland, 1910 ***3259.35*** *p37*
Maduro, John 40; Seattle, 1911 ***9196.1*** *p33*
Madyski, Joseph; Maryland, 1910 ***3259.35*** *p37*
Maenle, Mathias; Port uncertain, 1765 ***2856.30*** *p282*
Maentle, Mathias; Port uncertain, 1765 ***2856.30*** *p282*
Maenzysski, Peter; Maryland, 1910 ***3259.35*** *p37*
Maer, Francis; New York, 1840 ***8197.10*** *p265*
Maesner, Anna 29; Kansas, 1910 ***9079.10*** *p47*
Maesner, Carl 2; Kansas, 1910 ***9079.10*** *p47*
Maesner, Henry 33; Kansas, 1908-1910 ***9079.10*** *p47*
Maesner, Leda 4; Kansas, 1910 ***9079.10*** *p47*
Mafebanski, George; Maryland, 1910 ***3259.35*** *p37*
Maffet, Robert; Pennsylvania, 1777 ***4629.10*** *p14*
Magahan, Gerry; Pennsylvania, 1866 ***6058.10*** *p54*
Magan, Anne 28 *SEE* Magan, John
Magan, Catherine 24 *SEE* Magan, John
Magan, Ellen 26 *SEE* Magan, John
Magan, John 34; New York, New York, 1847 ***1825.45*** *p18*
Sister: Anne 28
Sister: Ellen 26
Sister: Catherine 24
Brother: Patrick 22
Magan, Patrick 22 *SEE* Magan, John
Maganty, Patrick; New York, 1834 ***8197.10*** *p263*
Maganty, Patrick; New York, 1836 ***8197.10*** *p79*
Magarge, Patrick; Pennsylvania, 1777 ***4629.10*** *p25*
Magarvey, Jane 33; Ontario, 1871 ***1823.15*** *p151*
Magasch, Heinrich; America, 1749 ***2856.30*** *p282*
Magatsch, Heinrich; America, 1749 ***2856.30*** *p282*
Magee, Bernard 25; Philadelphia, 1789 ***4629.10*** *p59*

Magee, Catharine; Vermont, 1845-1926 ***5900.10*** *p337*
Magee, Dennis; Philadelphia, 1789 ***4629.10*** *p59*
Wife: Mary
Magee, Edward; Vermont, 1833-1907 ***5900.10*** *p88*
Magee, Ellenor Coffey; Vermont, 1826-1890 ***5900.10*** *p88*
Magee, George; Maryland, 1682 ***2524.55*** *p142*
Magee, James; New York, 1803 ***8197.10*** *p14*
Magee, James 43; Ontario, 1871 ***1823.15*** *p151*
Magee, James 64; Ontario, 1871 ***1823.15*** *p151*
Magee, John; New York, 1807 ***8197.10*** *p44*
Magee, John; Pennsylvania, 1779 ***4629.10*** *p40*
Magee, John; Vermont, n.d. ***5900.10*** *p337*
Magee, John 72; Ontario, 1871 ***1823.15*** *p151*
Magee, Katherine; Vermont, 1854-1943 ***5900.10*** *p119*
Magee, Mary *SEE* Magee, Dennis
Magee, Matthias; New York, 1834 ***8197.10*** *p316*
Magee, Peter 44; Ontario, 1871 ***1823.15*** *p151*
Mageen, Robert; Vermont, 1828-1915 ***5900.10*** *p439*
Mageivy, Patrick 35; Ontario, 1871 ***1823.15*** *p151*
Magemei, Johann; Port uncertain, 1766 ***2856.30*** *p282*
Magemei, Philipp; Port uncertain, 1766 ***2856.30*** *p282*
Magenis, Arthur; New York, 1817 ***8197.10*** *p258*
Mager, A. El.; Port uncertain, 1791 ***2856.30*** *p494*
Mager, Josef; Port uncertain, 1766 ***2856.30*** *p282*
Magerer, Susanna; Port uncertain, 1764 ***2856.30*** *p283*
Magerowic, Dora; Maryland, 1910 ***3259.35*** *p37*
Magg, Henry; Pennsylvania, 1777 ***4629.10*** *p10*
Magg, Josef; Port uncertain, 1736 ***2856.30*** *p283*
Magg, Josef; Port uncertain, 1766 ***2856.30*** *p283*
Magguire, Elizabeth 17; Maryland, 1774 ***1220.25*** *p83*
Maghan, Thomas; New York, 1807 ***8197.10*** *p44*
Magher, Patrick; New York, 1839 ***8197.10*** *p264*
Maghie, Robert 57; Ontario, 1871 ***1823.22*** *p95*
Maghond, Desmond; Maryland, 1671 ***2524.55*** *p142*
Magiff, Daniel; Vermont, 1817-1874 ***5900.10*** *p490*
Magiff, Ellen; Vermont, 1821-1908 ***5900.10*** *p491*
Magiff, Frances Mann; Vermont, 1851-1931 ***5900.10*** *p490*
Magiff, Michael; Vermont, 1852-1935 ***5900.10*** *p490*
Magill, Bryall; Maryland, 1681 ***2524.55*** *p142*
Magill, Ellen 59; Ontario, 1871 ***1823.22*** *p95*
Magill, Henry 57; Ontario, 1871 ***1823.15*** *p151*
Magill, James 43; Ontario, 1871 ***1823.15*** *p151*
Magill, Jane 63; Ontario, 1871 ***1823.22*** *p95*
Magill, Sarah 23; Ontario, 1871 ***1823.22*** *p95*
Magill, Thomas 26; Ontario, 1871 ***1823.22*** *p95*
Maginn, Catharine; Vermont, 1822-1894 ***5900.10*** *p50*
Maginn, Hugh; Vermont, 1814-1890 ***5900.10*** *p50*
Maginn, John; New York, 1821 ***8197.10*** *p259*
Maginn, William; Pennsylvania, 1866 ***6058.10*** *p56*
Maginnis, Edward; New York, 1826 ***8197.10*** *p333*
Maginnis, William; New York, 1834 ***8197.10*** *p74*
Magle, John; New York, 1840 ***8197.10*** *p178*
Maglency, Michael 30; Ontario, 1871 ***1823.28*** *p60*
Magner, Ellen; Vermont, 1841-1915 ***5900.10*** *p484*
Magner, Ellen 74; Vermont, 1906 ***5900.10*** *p108*
Magner, Ellen 83; Vermont, 1913 ***5900.10*** *p433*
Magner, Honora; Vermont, 1827-1866 ***5900.10*** *p113*
Magner, Honora; Vermont, 1867 ***5900.10*** *p113*
Magner, Honora 78; Vermont, 1876 ***5900.10*** *p415*
Magner, James, Jr.; Vermont, 1836-1869 ***5900.10*** *p113*
Magner, Mrs. James; Vermont, 1798-1885 ***5900.10*** *p113*
Magner, William; Vermont, 1870-1891 ***5900.10*** *p113*
Magnett, Charles; Maryland, 1637 ***2524.55*** *p142*
Magnin, John; New York, 1831 ***8197.10*** *p366*
Magnus, Hubert; Port uncertain, 1733 ***2856.30*** *p283*
Magnusson, Levi Joseph; New York, 1834 ***8197.10*** *p263*
Magoffin, Alexander 78; Ontario, 1871 ***1823.15*** *p151*
Magoffin, Elizabeth 57; Ontario, 1871 ***1823.15*** *p151*
Magone, Mr.; Quebec, 1858 ***9196.15*** *p33*
Magor, William 58; Ontario, 1871 ***1823.28*** *p60*
Magouvran, Patrick; New York, 1821 ***8197.10*** *p260*
Magowan, Louisa O. 27; Vermont, 1853 ***5900.10*** *p454*
Magowan, Susan D.; Vermont, 1835-1916 ***5900.10*** *p282*
Magragh, James 50; Ontario, 1871 ***1823.22*** *p96*
Magraht, Bridjit 45; Ontario, 1871 ***1823.22*** *p96*
Magraht, James 49; Ontario, 1871 ***1823.22*** *p96*
Magranel, Hugh; New York, 1834 ***8197.10*** *p373*
Magrath, Catherine 3; Ontario, 1861 ***2896.25*** *p37*
Magrath, Daniel 40; Ontario, 1871 ***1823.28*** *p60*
Magrath, George; New York, 1840 ***8197.10*** *p179*
Magrath, John 11; Ontario, 1861 ***2896.25*** *p37*
Magrath, M. A. 13; Ontario, 1861 ***2896.25*** *p37*
Magrath, Michael; New York, 1840 ***8197.10*** *p179*
Magrath, Owen; New York, 1840 ***8197.10*** *p181*
Magrath, Owen 41; Ontario, 1861 ***2896.25*** *p37*
Magrath, William 32; Ontario, 1871 ***1823.28*** *p60*
Magrath, William E. 7; Ontario, 1861 ***2896.25*** *p37*
Magraugh, Owen; New York, 1840 ***8197.10*** *p181*
Magraw, Terrence; New York, 1837 ***8197.10*** *p98*
Magregor, Hugh; Maryland, 1673 ***2524.55*** *p142*
Magregor, James; Maryland, 1673 ***2524.55*** *p142*
Magregor, Malcom 54; Ontario, 1871 ***1823.15*** *p151*
Maguire, Abbie Griffin; Vermont, 1856-1925 ***5900.10*** *p108*
Maguire, Ann; Vermont, 1833-1889 ***5900.10*** *p618*
Maguire, Anne; Vermont, 1858-1940 ***5900.10*** *p440*
Maguire, Bridget; Vermont, 1831-1909 ***5900.10*** *p596*
Maguire, Edward; New York, 1834 ***8197.10*** *p74*
Maguire, James; New York, 1836-1838 ***8197.10*** *p123*
Maguire, James H.; Vermont, 1849-1919 ***5900.10*** *p443*
Maguire, James H. 3; Ontario, 1861 ***2896.27*** *p57*
Maguire, John; Vermont, 1806-1888 ***5900.10*** *p212*
Maguire, John 1; Ontario, 1861 ***2896.27*** *p57*
Maguire, John 30; New York, New York, 1847 ***1825.45*** *p18*
Wife: Mary 30
Daughter: Mary 3
Son: Patrick 5
Maguire, John 42; Ontario, 1871 ***1823.22*** *p96*
Maguire, John 42; Ontario, 1871 ***1823.28*** *p60*
Maguire, John H.; Vermont, 1849-1883 ***5900.10*** *p108*
Maguire, Kate; Vermont, 1830-1865 ***5900.10*** *p440*
Maguire, Lydia D. 8; Ontario, 1861 ***2896.27*** *p57*
Maguire, Margaret 79; Vermont, 1887 ***5900.10*** *p589*
Maguire, Mary; Vermont, 1837-1883 ***5900.10*** *p504*
Maguire, Mary 3 *SEE* Maguire, John
Maguire, Mary 11; Ontario, 1861 ***2896.27*** *p57*
Maguire, Mary 30 *SEE* Maguire, John
Maguire, Mary 62; Vermont, 1877 ***5900.10*** *p618*
Maguire, Mary E. Keeley; Vermont, 1837-1895 ***5900.10*** *p440*
Maguire, Mary Eveline; Vermont, 1846-1913 ***5900.10*** *p447*
Maguire, Mary J. Moloney; Vermont, 1849-1921 ***5900.10*** *p443*
Maguire, Mary Teresa Heney; Vermont, 1818-1865 ***5900.10*** *p212*
Maguire, Mathew 19; Vermont, 1864 ***5900.10*** *p203*
Maguire, Mathew 77; Vermont, 1877 ***5900.10*** *p203*
Maguire, Michael; New York, 1827 ***8197.10*** *p342*
Maguire, Michael; New York, 1834 ***8197.10*** *p74*
Maguire, Patrick; Vermont, 1827-1904 ***5900.10*** *p440*
Maguire, Patrick 5 *SEE* Maguire, John
Maguire, Patrick 39; Ontario, 1861 ***2896.27*** *p57*
Maguire, Philip; Pennsylvania, 1777 ***4629.10*** *p19*
Maguire, Robert 40; Ontario, 1871 ***1823.22*** *p96*
Magwood, Charles 69; Ontario, 1871 ***1823.15*** *p151*
Magwyer, Cornelius; Maryland, 1658 ***2524.55*** *p142*
Mahaffy, Francis; New York, 1834 ***8197.10*** *p263*
Mahaffy, Francis; New York, 1838 ***8197.10*** *p124*
Mahain, Roger 28; Ontario, 1871 ***1823.28*** *p60*
Mahaine, Darby; Maryland, 1682 ***2524.55*** *p142*
Mahaloone, Dermott; Maryland, 1658 ***2524.55*** *p142*
Mahalski, Alex; Maryland, 1910 ***3259.35*** *p37*
Mahan, James 55; Ontario, 1871 ***1823.28*** *p60*
Mahan, Jane; Alabama, 1805-1845 ***1640.10*** *p148*
Mahan, John 51; Ontario, 1871 ***1823.28*** *p60*
Mahan, Margaret 78; Vermont, 1905 ***5900.10*** *p78*
Mahan, Margret 25; Ontario, 1871 ***1823.28*** *p60*
Mahan, Patrick; New York, 1822 ***8197.10*** *p260*
Mahan, William 67; Ontario, 1871 ***1823.28*** *p60*
Mahaney, Catherine 60; Vermont, 1889 ***5900.10*** *p466*
Mahaney, Honora 60; Vermont, 1884 ***5900.10*** *p336*
Mahany, Daniel; Pennsylvania, 1867 ***6058.10*** *p56*
Mahany, Dennis 27; Baltimore, 1775 ***1220.25*** *p117*
Mahany, John; Pennsylvania, 1850 ***6058.10*** *p28*
Mahar, Anna Ryan; Vermont, 1849-1931 ***5900.10*** *p245*
Mahar, Bridget 52; Vermont, 1896 ***5900.10*** *p254*
Mahar, Dennis; Vermont, 1857-1881 ***5900.10*** *p259*
Mahar, Johanna; Vermont, 1856-1956 ***5900.10*** *p582*
Mahar, John; Vermont, 1855 ***5900.10*** *p259*
Mahar, John 24; Vermont, 1893 ***5900.10*** *p260*
Mahar, John D.; Vermont, 1846-1903 ***5900.10*** *p245*
Mahar, John S.; Vermont, 1815-1893 ***5900.10*** *p259*
Mahar, Julia; Vermont, 1853-1941 ***5900.10*** *p256*
Mahar, Julia 37; Vermont, 1863 ***5900.10*** *p260*
Mahar, Julia Minogue; Vermont, 1825-1898 ***5900.10*** *p259*
Mahar, Margaret; Vermont, 1853-1911 ***5900.10*** *p434*
Mahar, Mary; Vermont, 1835-1899 ***5900.10*** *p395*
Mahar, Mary; Vermont, 1843-1923 ***5900.10*** *p251*
Mahar, Mary; Vermont, 1850-1909 ***5900.10*** *p267*
Mahar, Mary 60; Ontario, 1871 ***1823.28*** *p60*
Mahar, Mary A.; Vermont, 1857-1933 ***5900.10*** *p464*
Mahar, Michael; Vermont, 1848-1849 ***5900.10*** *p259*
Mahar, Michael 27; Vermont, 1881 ***5900.10*** *p260*
Mahar, Patrick; Vermont, 1869 ***5900.10*** *p259*
Mahar, Patrick 60; Vermont, 1917 ***5900.10*** *p256*
Mahar, Thomas; Vermont, 1858 ***5900.10*** *p259*
Mahar, Thomas 68; Vermont, 1893 ***5900.10*** *p260*
Mahar, William; Vermont, 1855 ***5900.10*** *p259*
Mahasky, Joseph; Maryland, 1910 ***3259.35*** *p37*
Maher, Catherine 76; Vermont, 1892 ***5900.10*** *p330*
Maher, Elizabeth; Vermont, 1838-1897 ***5900.10*** *p74*
Maher, Ellen 26; Vermont, 1877 ***5900.10*** *p587*
Maher, Ellen 86; Vermont, 1902 ***5900.10*** *p545*
Maher, Ellen Moore; Vermont, 1862-1903 ***5900.10*** *p464*
Maher, James 48; Ontario, 1871 ***1823.28*** *p60*
Maher, John; New York, 1839 ***8197.10*** *p264*
Maher, John; Vermont, 1859-1949 ***5900.10*** *p464*
Maher, John 62; Vermont, 1905 ***5900.10*** *p545*
Maher, John 74; Vermont, 1922 ***5900.10*** *p587*
Maher, John R.; Vermont, n.d. ***5900.10*** *p149*
Maher, Maria Margarete; Port uncertain, 1728 ***2856.30*** *p283*
Maher, Mary; Vermont, 1852-1928 ***5900.10*** *p429*
Maher, Mary Hogan 33; Vermont, 1865 ***5900.10*** *p264*
Maher, Mary Walsh; Vermont, 1862-1905 ***5900.10*** *p444*
Maher, Mathew; Vermont, 1830-1878 ***5900.10*** *p74*
Maher, Michael; Vermont, 1854-1913 ***5900.10*** *p90*
Maher, Michael 76; Vermont, 1891 ***5900.10*** *p545*
Maher, Nancy Starr 97; Vermont, 1914 ***5900.10*** *p587*
Maher, Patrick; New York, 1802 ***8197.10*** *p22*
Maher, Patrick; New York, 1840 ***8197.10*** *p180*
Maher, Patrick 33; Ontario, 1871 ***1823.22*** *p96*
Maher, Perce 24; Pennsylvania, 1794 ***4629.10*** *p63*
Maher, Robert; Vermont, 1845-1940 ***5900.10*** *p444*
Mahier, Richard; New England, 1721 ***1224.2*** *p75*
Mahiney, Wm 37; Ontario, 1871 ***1823.28*** *p60*
Mahl, Christof; America, 1753 ***2856.30*** *p283*
Mahlecker, Barbara; Port uncertain, 1766 ***2856.30*** *p283*
Mahler, Ernst; America, 1740 ***2856.30*** *p283*
Mahler, Maria; Port uncertain, 1757 ***2856.30*** *p283*
Mahlin, Ursula; Port uncertain, 1774 ***2856.30*** *p318*
Mahn, Morgan; Virginia, 1663 ***6212.30*** *p1*
Mahom, Teag; Maryland, 1671 ***2524.55*** *p142*
Mahon, Catharine 42; Vermont, 1874 ***5900.10*** *p514*
Mahon, Con; New York, 1828 ***8197.10*** *p262*
Mahon, Delanie Heseltine; Vermont, 1849-1927 ***5900.10*** *p303*
Mahon, Jennie; Vermont, 1845-1913 ***5900.10*** *p243*
Mahon, John; Vermont, 1841-1905 ***5900.10*** *p303*
Mahon, Mary 61; Vermont, 1867 ***5900.10*** *p514*
Mahon, Patrick; New York, 1839 ***8197.10*** *p264*
Mahon, William 75; Ontario, 1871 ***1823.15*** *p151*
Mahonbey, Mary Ann; Vermont, 1829-1906 ***5900.10*** *p324*
Mahone, Jeremiah; Maryland, 1671 ***2524.55*** *p142*
Mahoney, Annie; Vermont, 1852-1935 ***5900.10*** *p503*
Mahoney, C.; Vermont, 1850-1950 ***5900.10*** *p158*
Mahoney, Catharine; Vermont, n.d. ***5900.10*** *p608*
Mahoney, Catharine 56; Vermont, 1883 ***5900.10*** *p110*
Mahoney, Catherine; Vermont, n.d. ***5900.10*** *p340*
Mahoney, Daniel; Vermont, 1823-1903 ***5900.10*** *p425*
Mahoney, Daniel 50; Vermont, 1872 ***5900.10*** *p110*
Mahoney, Dennis 38; Ontario, 1871 ***1823.15*** *p151*
Mahoney, Eliza; Vermont, 1856-1935 ***5900.10*** *p464*
Mahoney, Elizabeth; Vermont, 1833-1905 ***5900.10*** *p327*
Mahoney, Elizabeth; Vermont, 1834-1899 ***5900.10*** *p425*
Mahoney, Ellen; Vermont, 1831-1847 ***5900.10*** *p327*
Mahoney, Ellen Finn; Vermont, 1843-1901 ***5900.10*** *p327*
Mahoney, Ellen Spillane 37; Vermont, 1893 ***5900.10*** *p180*
Mahoney, George D.; Vermont, 1846-1870 ***5900.10*** *p482*
Mahoney, James 55; Ontario, 1871 ***1823.28*** *p60*
Mahoney, Jeremiah; Vermont, 1824-1887 ***5900.10*** *p410*
Mahoney, Jeremiah; Vermont, 1836-1919 ***5900.10*** *p327*
Mahoney, Jeremiah 50; Ontario, 1871 ***1823.15*** *p151*
Mahoney, Joanna; Vermont, 1853-1953 ***5900.10*** *p158*
Mahoney, John; Vermont, 1805-1870 ***5900.10*** *p327*
Mahoney, John; Vermont, 1840-1843 ***5900.10*** *p327*
Mahoney, John 60; Ontario, 1871 ***1823.15*** *p151*
Mahoney, Julia; Vermont, 1838-1843 ***5900.10*** *p327*
Mahoney, Julia A.; Vermont, 1844-1861 ***5900.10*** *p327*
Mahoney, Julia McCarthy; Vermont, 1807-1874 ***5900.10*** *p327*
Mahoney, Katherine 63; Vermont, 1875 ***5900.10*** *p105*
Mahoney, Katherine McGee; Vermont, 1865-1923 ***5900.10*** *p482*
Mahoney, Margaret; Vermont, 1855-1926 ***5900.10*** *p536*
Mahoney, Margaret 69; Ontario, 1871 ***1823.15*** *p151*
Mahoney, Margaret 74; Vermont, 1904 ***5900.10*** *p200*
Mahoney, Mary; Vermont, n.d. ***5900.10*** *p340*
Mahoney, Mary; Vermont, 1835-1857 ***5900.10*** *p327*
Mahoney, Mary 80; Ontario, 1871 ***1823.22*** *p96*
Mahoney, Mary Foran; Vermont, 1832-1914 ***5900.10*** *p340*
Mahoney, Mary Kelley; Vermont, 1840-1911 ***5900.10*** *p265*
Mahoney, Matthew; Pennsylvania, 1850 ***6058.10*** *p26*
Mahoney, Michael; New York, 1839 ***8197.10*** *p264*
Mahoney, Michael; Vermont, 1842-1871 ***5900.10*** *p265*
Mahoney, Michael 26; Ontario, 1871 ***1823.28*** *p60*
Mahoney, Nancy; Vermont, 1836 ***5900.10*** *p410*
Mahoney, Patrick; New York, 1837 ***8197.10*** *p100*
Mahoney, Patrick; Pennsylvania, 1850 ***6058.10*** *p26*
Mahoney, Patrick; Vermont, 1840-1908 ***5900.10*** *p265*

Mahoney, S. D.; Vermont, n.d. ***5900.10*** *p340*
Mahoney, Sylvester; Vermont, n.d. ***5900.10*** *p340*
Mahoney, Thomas A.; Vermont, 1846-1903 ***5900.10*** *p327*
Mahoney, William 45; Ontario, 1871 ***1823.15*** *p151*
Mahoney, William 68; Vermont, 1872 ***5900.10*** *p105*
Mahoney, William H.; Vermont, 1850-1929 ***5900.10*** *p482*
Mahony, Bartholomew; New York, 1806 ***8197.10*** *p32*
Mahony, Charles; New York, 1802 ***8197.10*** *p22*
Mahony, Cornelius; New York, 1838 ***8197.10*** *p376*
Mahony, Dan 18 *SEE* Mahony, Mary
Mahony, Dennis; New York, 1837 ***8197.10*** *p99*
Mahony, Edward 23; Virginia, 1774 ***1220.25*** *p93*
Mahony, Edward 35; Ontario, 1871 ***1823.15*** *p151*
Mahony, Ellen 26 *SEE* Mahony, Mary
Mahony, Ellin; Maryland, 1678 ***2524.55*** *p142*
Mahony, Francis; Pennsylvania, 1777 ***4629.10*** *p28*
Mahony, Jasper 16; Maryland, 1775 ***1220.25*** *p97*
Mahony, Jeremiah; New York, 1820 ***8197.10*** *p259*
Mahony, Jeremiah; New York, 1827 ***8197.10*** *p341*
Mahony, Johanna 21 *SEE* Mahony, Mary
Mahony, John; New York, 1807 ***8197.10*** *p327*
Mahony, John; New York, 1831 ***8197.10*** *p365*
Mahony, John; New York, 1837 ***6058.10*** *p25*
Mahony, John 20; Ontario, 1871 ***1823.28*** *p60*
Mahony, Joseph 23; Virginia, 1774 ***1220.25*** *p93*
Mahony, Mary 55; New York, New York, 1850 ***1825.45*** *p52*
Son: Dan 18
Daughter: Ellen 26
Daughter: Johanna 21
Daughter: Norry 12
Son: Tade 14
Mahony, Norry 12 *SEE* Mahony, Mary
Mahony, Patrick; Pennsylvania, 1850 ***6058.10*** *p26*
Mahony, Peter; New York, 1837 ***8197.10*** *p100*
Mahony, Tade 14 *SEE* Mahony, Mary
Mahony, Timothy 43; Ontario, 1871 ***1823.15*** *p151*
Mahood, John 82; Ontario, 1871 ***1823.15*** *p151*
Mahood, Joseph 37; Ontario, 1871 ***1823.15*** *p151*
Mahood, Robert 40; Ontario, 1871 ***1823.15*** *p151*
Mahvavish, S. 45; Alaska, 1914 ***9196.1*** *p41*
Mahwen, Jno; Virginia, 1666 ***6212.30*** *p28*
Mai, Adam, Sr. 65; Kansas, 1889-1910 ***9079.10*** *p48*
Mai, Adam, Jr. 35; Kansas, 1895-1910 ***9079.10*** *p33*
Mai, Adam B. 31; Kansas, 1902-1910 ***9079.10*** *p7*
Mai, Adam G. 24; Kansas, 1890-1910 ***9079.10*** *p44*
Mai, Catherine 42; Kansas, 1906-1910 ***9079.10*** *p27*
Mai, Catherine 57; Kansas, 1891-1910 ***9079.10*** *p29*
Mai, Clara 64; Kansas, 1910 ***9079.10*** *p48*
Mai, Dollie 6; Kansas, 1907-1910 ***9079.10*** *p29*
Mai, Emma 37; Kansas, 1898-1910 ***9079.10*** *p7*
Mai, George 26; Kansas, 1891-1910 ***9079.10*** *p6*
Mai, George 44; Kansas, 1876-1910 ***9079.10*** *p27*
Mai, Henry, Jr. 28; Kansas, 1910 ***9079.10*** *p43*
Mai, John G. 59; Kansas, 1891-1910 ***9079.10*** *p29*
Mai, John Henry 34; Kansas, 1910 ***9079.10*** *p48*
Mai, John P. 33; Kansas, 1907-1910 ***9079.10*** *p29*
Mai, Lizzie 31; Kansas, 1910 ***9079.10*** *p43*
Mai, Lyda 14; Kansas, 1898-1910 ***9079.10*** *p7*
Mai, Mary 27; Kansas, 1907-1910 ***9079.10*** *p29*
Mai, Mollie 27; Kansas, 1910 ***9079.10*** *p48*
Mai, Peter 12; Kansas, 1898-1910 ***9079.10*** *p7*
Mai, Peter 40; Kansas, 1898-1910 ***9079.10*** *p7*
Maiangowi, Louis 52; Ontario, 1871 ***1823.28*** *p60*
Maich, Mrs. Hans Jerg; America, 1753 ***2856.30*** *p283*
Maichkavitz, Joseph; Maryland, 1910 ***3259.35*** *p37*
Maiden, Ann 71; Ontario, 1871 ***1823.22*** *p96*
Maiden, Catherine V. 6; Ontario, 1861 ***2896.25*** *p16*
Maiden, Charles 40; Ontario, 1871 ***1823.22*** *p96*
Maiden, Charles T. 4; Ontario, 1861 ***2896.25*** *p16*
Maiden, Eliza M. 7; Ontario, 1861 ***2896.25*** *p16*
Maiden, Harriet 12; Ontario, 1861 ***2896.25*** *p16*
Maiden, Nancy 1; Ontario, 1861 ***2896.25*** *p16*
Maiden, Phebe E. 10; Ontario, 1861 ***2896.25*** *p16*
Maiden, Robert 37; Ontario, 1861 ***2896.25*** *p16*
Maiden, Victoria 7; Ontario, 1861 ***2896.25*** *p18*
Maiden, William; Philadelphia, 1756 ***1224.2*** *p75*
Maidens, Jane 46; Ontario, 1861 ***2896.27*** *p49*
Maidens, John 39; Ontario, 1861 ***2896.27*** *p49*
Maidens, John C. 12; Ontario, 1861 ***2896.27*** *p49*
Maides, John; Maryland, 1667 ***2524.55*** *p142*
Maidmont, Mathew 39; Ontario, 1871 ***1823.22*** *p96*
Maien, John 40; Ontario, 1871 ***1823.15*** *p151*
Maier, Elisabeth; America, 1764 ***2856.30*** *p283*
With husband
Maigrot, Lewis; New York, 1835 ***8197.10*** *p317*
Mailes, Christian; America, 1753 ***2856.30*** *p283*
Mailhouse, Mr.; Quebec, 1858 ***9196.15*** *p34*
Mailhouse, Mrs.; Quebec, 1858 ***9196.15*** *p34*
Mailins, Margrit; Virginia, 1666-1667 ***6212.30*** *p35*
Mailley, Miss; Quebec, 1858 ***9196.15*** *p46*
Mailley, I. Abbe; Quebec, 1858 ***9196.15*** *p46*
Maime, Ezekiel; Maryland, 1659 ***2524.55*** *p142*
Maimsley, Miss; Quebec, 1857 ***9196.15*** *p17*
Main, George; Georgia, 1736 ***1640.10*** *p148*
Main, Helen; Nova Scotia, 1886 ***1640.13*** *p73*
Main, James; New York, 1807 ***8197.10*** *p45*
Main, John; New York, 1806 ***8197.10*** *p324*
Main, John 54; Ontario, 1871 ***1823.22*** *p96*
Main, Maria; Mississippi, 1822-1839 ***1640.10*** *p148*
Main, William; Pennsylvania, 1777 ***4629.10*** *p12*
Mainhard, Joachim; Port uncertain, 1764 ***2856.30*** *p283*
Mainprize, John 67; Ontario, 1871 ***1823.15*** *p151*
Mains, George 67; Ontario, 1871 ***1823.15*** *p151*
Mains, William 38; Ontario, 1871 ***1823.15*** *p152*
Maintain, Anthony D.; Long Island, 1806 ***8197.10*** *p259*
Mainwaring, William; Virginia, 1764 ***1224.2*** *p75*
Mainzer, Johann Friedric; Port uncertain, 1765 ***2856.30*** *p283*
Maiock, Thomas; Maryland, 1672 ***2524.55*** *p142*
Maiow, Cahill 71; Ontario, 1871 ***1823.15*** *p152*
Mair, Geo 35; Alaska, 1913 ***9196.1*** *p20*
Mair, Geo 35; British Columbia, 1913 ***9196.1*** *p20*
Mair, George 35; Ontario, 1871 ***1823.15*** *p152*
Mair, Jacob 61; Kansas, 1876-1910 ***9079.10*** *p27*
Mair, John 43; Ontario, 1871 ***1823.15*** *p152*
Mair, Mary E. 60; Kansas, 1876-1910 ***9079.10*** *p27*
Mair, Peter 35; America, 1774 ***1220.25*** *p36*
Mair, William 46; Ontario, 1871 ***1823.15*** *p152*
Mairet, Henri; New York, 1837 ***8197.10*** *p100*
Mairn, Barbra 28; Ontario, 1871 ***1823.15*** *p152*
Mairn, Peter 43; Ontario, 1871 ***1823.15*** *p152*
Maisch, Ignaz; Port uncertain, 1796 ***2856.30*** *p283*
Maisenbacher, Adam; Port uncertain, 1788 ***2856.30*** *p283*
Maisey, Arthur 19; Ontario, 1871 ***1823.15*** *p152*
Maitland, Mr.; Quebec, 1858 ***9196.15*** *p35*
Maitland, Mr.; Quebec, 1858 ***9196.15*** *p42*
Maitland, Mr.; Quebec, 1858 ***9196.15*** *p47*
Maitland, Mrs.; Quebec, 1858 ***9196.15*** *p47*
Maitland, David; New York, 1824 ***8197.10*** *p259*
Maitland, Henry 65; Ontario, 1871 ***1823.22*** *p96*
Maitland, John; New York, 1840 ***8197.10*** *p385*
Maitland, John; Ontario, 1839 ***1640.13*** *p73*
Maitland, Joseph; New York, 1823 ***8197.10*** *p262*
Maitland, Lionel 16; Ontario, 1871 ***1823.22*** *p96*
Maitland, Richard; New York, New York, 1773 ***1224.2*** *p75*
Maitland, William; Georgia, 1698 ***1640.13*** *p73*
Maittaur, Mr.; Quebec, 1857 ***9196.15*** *p19*
Maize, James 56; Ontario, 1871 ***1823.15*** *p152*
Maize, John 46; Ontario, 1871 ***1823.15*** *p152*
Maize, William 38; Ontario, 1871 ***1823.15*** *p152*
Majcharz, Kazimer; Maryland, 1910 ***3259.35*** *p37*
Majchrak, John; Maryland, 1910 ***3259.35*** *p37*
Majeheyki, Joe; Maryland, 1910 ***3259.35*** *p37*
Majer, Christian; America, 1754 ***2856.30*** *p283*
Majer, Friedrich; America, 1788 ***2856.30*** *p283*
Majer, Stefan; America, 1752 ***2856.30*** *p283*
Majer, Stefan; America, 1781 ***2856.30*** *p283*
Majer, Stefan; America, 1787 ***2856.30*** *p283*
Majewsky, Alexander; Maryland, 1910 ***3259.35*** *p37*
Majka, Ignac; Maryland, 1910 ***3259.35*** *p37*
Majka, Jacenty; Maryland, 1910 ***3259.35*** *p37*
Majka, John; Maryland, 1910 ***3259.35*** *p37*
Majka, Peter; Maryland, 1910 ***3259.35*** *p37*
Major, Amalia 32; Kansas, 1898-1910 ***9079.10*** *p38*
Major, Fredrick 67; Kansas, 1878-1910 ***9079.10*** *p38*
Major, George P. 40; Kansas, 1878-1910 ***9079.10*** *p37*
Major, Henry; Philadelphia, 1793 ***4629.10*** *p72*
Major, Henry 21; Kansas, 1892-1910 ***9079.10*** *p38*
Major, Henry 48; Kansas, 1892-1910 ***9079.10*** *p15*
Major, Hugo 27; Alaska, 1916 ***9196.1*** *p6*
Major, Hugo 27; Yukon, 1916 ***9196.1*** *p6*
Major, Jacob F. 33; Kansas, 1879-1910 ***9079.10*** *p16*
Major, Jacop P. 53; Kansas, 1892-1910 ***9079.10*** *p38*
Major, James 27; Virginia, 1773 ***1220.25*** *p29*
Major, John; New York, 1839 ***8197.10*** *p264*
Major, Margaret 47; Kansas, 1892-1910 ***9079.10*** *p15*
Major, Mary 61; Kansas, 1878-1910 ***9079.10*** *p38*
Major, Richard; New York, 1839 ***8197.10*** *p141*
Major, Sizzie 52; Kansas, 1892-1910 ***9079.10*** *p38*
Mak, . . .; America, 1752 ***2856.30*** *p283*
With 5 siblings
Mak, Wolfgang; America, 1751 ***2856.30*** *p183*
With 6 children
Mak, Wolfgang; America, 1751 ***2856.30*** *p283*
With 6 children
Makacke, Frank 32; Alaska, 1908 ***9196.1*** *p37*
Makar, James 25; Maryland, 1775 ***1220.25*** *p101*
Makaski, John; Maryland, 1910 ***3259.35*** *p37*
Makateotawa, Louis 32; Ontario, 1871 ***1823.28*** *p60*
Makateotawa, Pierre 61; Ontario, 1871 ***1823.28*** *p60*
Makateotawa, Pierre, Jr. 34; Ontario, 1871 ***1823.28*** *p60*
Make, M. 31; Alaska, 1914 ***9196.1*** *p41*
Makeil, Elizabeth *SEE* Makeil, John
Makeil, Ellen *SEE* Makeil, John
Makeil, Isabell *SEE* Makeil, John
Makeil, John *SEE* Makeil, John
Makeil, John; Maryland, 1669 ***2524.55*** *p143*
Wife: Ellen
Child: Mary
Child: Elizabeth
Child: John
Child: Isabell
Makeil, Mary *SEE* Makeil, John
Makeill, Elizabeth *SEE* Makeill, John
Makeill, Ellen *SEE* Makeill, John
Makeill, Isabell *SEE* Makeill, John
Makeill, John *SEE* Makeill, John
Makeill, John; Maryland, 1669 ***2524.55*** *p143*
Wife: Ellen
Child: Isabell
Child: Mary
Child: Elizabeth
Child: John
Makeill, Mary *SEE* Makeill, John
Makenney, Charles; Vermont, 1829-1863 ***5900.10*** *p282*
Makens, Mark 52; Ontario, 1871 ***1823.15*** *p152*
Makenzie, Thomas 60; Ontario, 1871 ***1823.15*** *p152*
Makernish, Anguish; Maryland, 1664 ***2524.55*** *p143*
Makery, Daniell; Maryland, 1665 ***2524.55*** *p141*
Wife: Homar
Son: Richard
Makery, Homar *SEE* Makery, Daniell
Makery, Richard *SEE* Makery, Daniell
Makey, Willm.; Maryland, 1666 ***2524.55*** *p143*
Makiney, Walter 25; Vermont, 1853 ***5900.10*** *p283*
Making, Elias 30; Maryland, 1774 ***1220.25*** *p78*
Makins, John; Chicago, 1857 ***1224.3*** *p50*
Makins, Thomas; New England, 1672 ***1224.1*** *p6*
Makins, William; Maryland, 1670 ***2524.55*** *p143*
Makitt, John; Maryland, 1666 ***2524.55*** *p143*
Makowiecki, Wincent; Maryland, 1910 ***3259.35*** *p37*
Makowski, Annie; Maryland, 1910 ***3259.35*** *p37*
Makowski, John; Maryland, 1910 ***3259.35*** *p37*
Makraska, Maryanna; Maryland, 1910 ***3259.35*** *p37*
Makrina, Mary; Maryland, 1910 ***3259.35*** *p37*
Malach, Henrich; Port uncertain, 1741 ***2856.30*** *p283*
Malachowsky, Frank; Maryland, 1910 ***3259.35*** *p37*
Malacki, Joseph; Maryland, 1910 ***3259.35*** *p37*
Maladin, Mr.; Port uncertain, 1764 ***2856.30*** *p263*
Malana, Catherine; Vermont, 1832-1915 ***5900.10*** *p126*
Malaniff, Mary 57; Vermont, 1879 ***5900.10*** *p528*
Malanowski, Joseph; Maryland, 1910 ***3259.35*** *p37*
Malany, Sarah 78; Vermont, 1884 ***5900.10*** *p360*
Malatin, Mr.; Port uncertain, 1764 ***2856.30*** *p269*
Malberger, Henry 24; Kansas, 1887-1910 ***9079.10*** *p6*
Malberger, Jacob 21; Kansas, 1910 ***9079.10*** *p52*
Malberger, Jacob 54; Kansas, 1892-1910 ***9079.10*** *p52*
Malberger, Maggie 52; Kansas, 1910 ***9079.10*** *p52*
Malberger, Molly 24; Kansas, 1892-1910 ***9079.10*** *p6*
Malboro, Margaret 38; Vermont, 1874 ***5900.10*** *p53*
Malcamronne, Miss; Quebec, 1858 ***9196.15*** *p37*
Malcamronne, Mrs.; Quebec, 1858 ***9196.15*** *p37*
Malcolm, . . .; Boston, 1765 ***4628.40*** *p114*
Malcolm, Farquhar; Georgia, n.d. ***1224.2*** *p75*
Malcolm, Farquhar; Georgia, 1791 ***1640.10*** *p148*
Malcolm, Jane; Georgia, 1734 ***1640.10*** *p148*
Malcolm, John; Missouri, 1888 ***1640.13*** *p73*
Malcolm, John; North America, 1793 ***1224.2*** *p75*
Malcolm, Quintin; New England, 1752 ***1640.13*** *p73*
Malcomson, Sutherland 29; Ontario, 1871 ***1823.15*** *p152*
Malcon, William 46; Ontario, 1871 ***1823.15*** *p152*
Malder, John; Philadelphia, 1794 ***4629.10*** *p82*
Malders, William F.; Maryland, 1910 ***3259.35*** *p37*
Maldet, Caspar; Port uncertain, 1787 ***2856.30*** *p283*
With 2 sons & 2 daughters
Maldin, Rowland; Virginia, 1666 ***6212.30*** *p26*
Male, Ambrose 60; Ontario, 1871 ***1823.22*** *p96*
Male, John 55; Ontario, 1871 ***1823.22*** *p96*
Malecki, Michel; Maryland, 1910 ***3259.35*** *p37*
Maleska, Piolo; Maryland, 1910 ***3259.35*** *p37*
Maleski, Martin; Maryland, 1910 ***3259.35*** *p37*
Malet, Edwin; Virginia, 1665 ***6212.30*** *p17*
Maletzka, Frank; Maryland, 1910 ***3259.35*** *p37*
Maley, Ellen O'Hallerin 66; Vermont, 1892 ***5900.10*** *p249*
Maley, James 60; Ontario, 1871 ***1823.28*** *p60*
Maley, John 75; Vermont, 1895 ***5900.10*** *p249*
Maley, Michael 47; Ontario, 1871 ***1823.15*** *p152*
Malezski, Walter; Maryland, 1910 ***3259.35*** *p37*
Mali, Henry W.; New York, 1828 ***8197.10*** *p262*
Mali, Henry W. T.; New York, 1826-1834 ***8197.10*** *p306*
Malibran, Eugene; New York, 1817 ***8197.10*** *p60*
Malicke, James; Maryland, 1910 ***3259.35*** *p37*
Malicki, Valenty; Maryland, 1910 ***3259.35*** *p37*
Malikowsky, John; Maryland, 1910 ***3259.35*** *p37*

Malin, David; Pennsylvania, 1777 4629.10 p45
Malin, John; Pennsylvania, 1777 4629.10 p45
Malingre, Lewis; New York, 1797 8197.10 p8
Malinoski, Joseph; Maryland, 1910 3259.35 p37
Malinowski, Adam; Maryland, 1910 3259.35 p37
Malinowski, Antonie; Maryland, 1910 3259.35 p37
Malinowski, Julian; Maryland, 1910 3259.35 p37
Malinowski, Kazimer; Maryland, 1910 3259.35 p37
Malinowski, Michall; Maryland, 1910 3259.35 p37
Malinowski, Peter; Maryland, 1910 3259.35 p37
Malinowski, Stanislaw; Maryland, 1910 3259.35 p38
Malinowski, Wincenty; Maryland, 1910 3259.35 p38
Malinowsky, Alexander; Maryland, 1910 3259.35 p38
Malinski, John; Maryland, 1910 3259.35 p38
Maliserki, Francis; Maryland, 1910 3259.35 p38
Mall, Christof Ludwig; Port uncertain, 1753 2856.30 p284
With wife & son
Mall, Friedrich; Port uncertain, 1753 2856.30 p284
With wife & son
Mall, Jacob; Port uncertain, 1744 2856.30 p284
Mall, Nehemiah; Pennsylvania, 1777 4629.10 p18
Mallam, Joseph; New York, 1840 8197.10 p181
Mallard, David 58; Ontario, 1871 1823.28 p60
Mallard, Margret 97; Ontario, 1871 1823.28 p60
Mallard, Thomas; Maryland, 1660-1661 2524.55 p143
Mallatin, Lucia Lengenfeld; Port uncertain, 1764 2856.30 p284
Mallatin, Lucia Lengenfeld; Port uncertain, 1765 2856.30 p284
Mallen, Patrick; New York, 1840 8197.10 p265
Mallet, Joseph 18; Ontario, 1871 1823.22 p96
Mallett, Jenkin; Maryland, 1656 2524.55 p143
Mallett, Richard 27; Ontario, 1871 1823.22 p96
Mallett, Winifred Wolseley; Maryland, 1697 1224.1 p38
Mallin, J. 15; Ontario, 1861 2896.27 p6
Mallison, Charles; New York, 1840 8197.10 p265
Mallisson, Daniel; New York, 1840 8197.10 p181
Mallisson, Mathew; New York, 1840 8197.10 p181
Malloburn, Tho; Virginia, 1674-1675 6212.30 p53
Malloch, Mr.; Quebec, 1856 9196.15 p11
Malloch, Edward; Ottawa, 1872 1640.13 p73
Malloch, Edward; Texas, 1819-1845 1640.10 p148
Malloch, James; Montreal, 1898 1640.13 p73
Malloch, John; Georgia, 1698 1640.13 p73
Malloch, William; Colorado, 1896 1640.13 p73
Mallock, John; New York, 1837 8197.10 p99
Mallond, Thomas; Maryland, 1660-1661 2524.55 p143
Malloney, John; Virginia, 1681-1682 6212.30 p55
Mallortie, David; South Carolina, 1736 1224.2 p75
Mallory, Albert 13; Ontario, 1861 2896.27 p29
Mallory, David 15; Ontario, 1861 2896.27 p29
Mallory, Evy E. 45; Ontario, 1871 1823.22 p96
Mallory, Florisabella; Virginia, 1769 1224.2 p75
Mallory, Phillip; Virginia, 1661 1224.1 p38
Mallory, Smith 12; Ontario, 1861 2896.27 p29
Mallory, Truman J.; Vermont, 1851-1940 5900.10 p90
Mallory, William; Virginia, 1769 1224.2 p75
Mallough, John 52; Ontario, 1871 1823.15 p152
Mallough, Joseph 40; Ontario, 1871 1823.15 p152
Mallough, William 51; Ontario, 1871 1823.15 p152
Mallowes, John; Virginia, 1663 6212.30 p1
Malloy, Annie 3; Vermont, 1867 5900.10 p209
Malloy, Catherine Rafferty; Vermont, 1851-1925 5900.10 p127
Malloy, Edward A.; New York, 1840 8197.10 p181
Malloy, John; New York, 1834 8197.10 p179
Malloy, Mary 75; Vermont, 1873 5900.10 p614
Malloy, Mary J.; Vermont, 1853-1901 5900.10 p483
Malloy, Mary M.; Vermont, 1890-1911 5900.10 p483
Malloy, Michael; Vermont, 1847-1894 5900.10 p127
Malloy, Patrick H.; Vermont, 1845-1912 5900.10 p483
Mally, Daniel; New York, 1840 8197.10 p179
Malm, Andrew 23; Maryland, 1773-1774 1220.25 p33
Malonay, James 75; Vermont, 1887 5900.10 p610
Malone, . . .; New Hampshire, 1641-1660 4628.40 p44
Malone, Barney; Vermont, 1842-1925 5900.10 p455
Malone, Bernard 20; Ontario, 1871 1823.28 p60
Malone, Bernard 26; Ontario, 1871 1823.28 p60
Malone, Bridget 33; Ontario, 1871 1823.22 p96
Malone, Bridget 83; Vermont, 1904 5900.10 p381
Malone, Catherine; Vermont, 1863-1919 5900.10 p443
Malone, Catherine 65; Vermont, 1887 5900.10 p410
Malone, Catherine Ryan; Vermont, 1846-1915 5900.10 p273
Malone, Charles 76; Vermont, 1891 5900.10 p381
Malone, Charles, Jr. 27; Vermont, 1880 5900.10 p381
Malone, Edward 35; Ontario, 1871 1823.28 p60
Malone, Flora A. Hunter; Vermont, 1843-1911 5900.10 p455
Malone, Francis; New York, 1821 8197.10 p260
Malone, George 36; Ontario, 1871 1823.28 p60
Malone, Henry; Nova Scotia, 1745 4628.40 p45
Malone, James 36; Ontario, 1871 1823.28 p60
Malone, Jermiah; Vermont, 1846-1934 5900.10 p273
Malone, John; Canada, 1756-1760 4628.40 p45
Malone, John; New York, 1832 8197.10 p368
Malone, John; Vermont, 1838-1919 5900.10 p257
Malone, John; Virginia, 1669-1670 6212.30 p41
Malone, John 30; Maryland, 1775 1220.25 p106
Malone, John 45; Ontario, 1871 1823.15 p152
Malone, John 50; Vermont, 1876 5900.10 p410
Malone, Jonathan; Canada, 1756-1760 4628.40 p45
Malone, Julia 68; Vermont, 1876 5900.10 p227
Malone, Lawrence; New York, 1840 8197.10 p178
Malone, Margaret; Vermont, 1837-1920 5900.10 p455
Malone, Margaret Barrett; Vermont, 1836-1926 5900.10 p257
Malone, Margrett 76; Vermont, 1883 5900.10 p525
Malone, Mark 27; Maryland, 1774 1220.25 p54
Malone, Mary; Vermont, 1827-1906 5900.10 p241
Malone, Mary 47; Vermont, 1895 5900.10 p381
Malone, Mary 65; Ontario, 1871 1823.22 p96
Malone, Mary Kennedy; Vermont, 1833-1903 5900.10 p257
Malone, Mary Maguire 62; Vermont, 1877 5900.10 p618
Malone, Michael 25; Vermont, 1870 5900.10 p449
Malone, Patrick; Vermont, 1823-1875 5900.10 p378
Malone, Patrick; Vermont, 1832-1909 5900.10 p257
Malone, Patrick 25; Ontario, 1871 1823.28 p60
Malone, Penelope; Vermont, 1843-1903 5900.10 p273
Malone, Phillip 30; Ontario, 1871 1823.28 p60
Malone, R. C.; Vermont, 1861-1904 5900.10 p381
Malone, Richard; New York, 1836 8197.10 p263
Malone, Richard; Nova Scotia, 1745 4628.40 p45
Malone, William; Pennsylvania, 1777 4629.10 p12
Maloney, Ann 4; Vermont, 1850 5900.10 p279
Maloney, Ann 61; Vermont, 1886 5900.10 p299
Maloney, Anna L.; Vermont, 1868-1915 5900.10 p278
Maloney, Anne; Vermont, 1829-1912 5900.10 p436
Maloney, Bridget; Vermont, 1827-1895 5900.10 p476
Maloney, Bridget Cain 32; Vermont, 1857 5900.10 p428
Maloney, Catherine; Vermont, 1853-1918 5900.10 p477
Maloney, Catherine Heheir 75; Vermont, 1903 5900.10 p428
Maloney, Daniel; Pennsylvania, 1777 4629.10 p15
Maloney, Daniel; Vermont, 1834-1916 5900.10 p441
Maloney, Daniel 76; Vermont, n.d. 5900.10 p279
Maloney, Elizabeth 5; Vermont, 1863 5900.10 p361
Maloney, Elizabeth Worrall; Vermont, 1840-1900 5900.10 p417
Maloney, Ellen 75; Vermont, 1886 5900.10 p60
Maloney, Ellen Kelley; Vermont, n.d. 5900.10 p152
Maloney, Hanora; Vermont, 1831-1899 5900.10 p438
Maloney, Hanora Mack 37; Vermont, 1861 5900.10 p361
Maloney, Hanorah; Vermont, 1811-1898 5900.10 p369
Maloney, James 78; Vermont, 1890 5900.10 p212
Maloney, James S.; Vermont, 1837-1905 5900.10 p391
Maloney, John; New York, 1837 6058.10 p19
Maloney, John; Pennsylvania, 1868 6058.10 p66
Maloney, John; Vermont, 1799-1853 5900.10 p242
Maloney, John; Vermont, 1831-1907 5900.10 p284
Maloney, John; Vermont, 1839-1919 5900.10 p391
Maloney, John 9; Vermont, 1865 5900.10 p210
Maloney, John 31; Ontario, 1871 1823.15 p152
Maloney, Julia C. Sullivan; Vermont, 1842-1919 5900.10 p298
Maloney, Katherine Leonard; Vermont, 1831-1914 5900.10 p391
Maloney, Margaret; Vermont, 1843-1914 5900.10 p247
Maloney, Margaret; Vermont, 1856-1939 5900.10 p277
Maloney, Margaret Hehir; Vermont, 1839-1919 5900.10 p441
Maloney, Mary; Vermont, 1811-1887 5900.10 p242
Maloney, Mary; Vermont, 1834-1911 5900.10 p303
Maloney, Mary 57; Vermont, 1881 5900.10 p501
Maloney, Mary 70; Ontario, 1871 1823.15 p152
Maloney, Mary 84; Vermont, 1919 5900.10 p428
Maloney, Mary A. 47; Vermont, 1896 5900.10 p239
Maloney, Mary King 34; Vermont, 1866 5900.10 p87
Maloney, Mary McNamara 81; Vermont, 1899 5900.10 p392
Maloney, Mary Rourke 68; Vermont, 1888 5900.10 p212
Maloney, Michael; Vermont, 1826 5900.10 p417
Maloney, Michael 74; Vermont, 1901 5900.10 p87
Maloney, Nora Holloren 70; Vermont, 1904 5900.10 p467
Maloney, Patrick; Vermont, n.d. 5900.10 p152
Maloney, Patrick; Vermont, 1833-1853 5900.10 p242
Maloney, Patrick 45; Ontario, 1871 1823.28 p60
Maloney, Patrick 90; Vermont, 1909 5900.10 p428
Maloney, Rebecca 3 months; Vermont, 1861 5900.10 p361
Maloney, Richard; Vermont, 1840-1905 5900.10 p242
Maloney, Sarah 71; Vermont, 1894 5900.10 p454
Maloney, Sarah Noland; Vermont, 1842-1905 5900.10 p284
Maloney, Simon; Vermont, 1818-1882 5900.10 p476
Maloney, Thomas; Vermont, 1843-1904 5900.10 p242
Maloney, Thomas 75; Vermont, 1912 5900.10 p467
Maloney, Timothy 1; Vermont, 1856 5900.10 p361
Maloney, Timothy 60; Vermont, 1870 5900.10 p361
Maloney, W. J.; Vermont, 1842-1917 5900.10 p298
Maloney, William; Vermont, 1837-1861 5900.10 p242
Malony, Anne 65; Ontario, 1871 1823.15 p152
Malony, James 72; Vermont, 1886 5900.10 p402
Malony, Joseph; Vermont, 1851-1910 5900.10 p402
Malony, Margaret 60; Vermont, 1919 5900.10 p402
Malony, Mary 78; Vermont, 1921 5900.10 p402
Malony, Mary Moylan 64; Vermont, 1887 5900.10 p402
Malony, Michael 44; Vermont, 1898 5900.10 p402
Malony, Nellie E. 56; Vermont, 1920 5900.10 p402
Malony, William 41; Vermont, 1907 5900.10 p402
Maloon, Ebenezar; Canada, 1756-1760 4628.40 p45
Malowney, Michael 40; Ontario, 1871 1823.15 p152
Maloy, Edward; New York, 1804 8197.10 p26
Maloy, Margaret 85; Vermont, 1926 5900.10 p364
Maloy, Mary 77; Vermont, 1889 5900.10 p279
Maloy, Michael 25; Vermont, 1871 5900.10 p364
Maloy, Patrick 45; Ontario, 1871 1823.28 p60
Maloy, Thomas 58; Ontario, 1871 1823.15 p152
Malpas, Edward W. 25; Ontario, 1871 1823.28 p60
Malsewski, Lippert; Maryland, 1910 3259.35 p38
Malstrom, Hilda 55; British Columbia, 1914 9196.1 p11
Malstrom, Hilda 55; Washington, 1914 9196.1 p11
Maltby, Charles; Philadelphia, 1808 1224.3 p50
Maltby, George; Baltimore, 1808 1224.3 p50
Maltman, John; New York, 1838 8197.10 p124
Maltman, William; New York, 1830 8197.10 p262
Malton, Thomas; Maryland, 1655 2524.55 p143
Malvitch, Zofia; Maryland, 1910 3259.35 p38
Malyshiski, Casimir; Maryland, 1910 3259.35 p38
Mam, Peter; Maryland, 1910 3259.35 p38
Mamon, Thomas; Maryland, 1676 2524.55 p143
Man, Lieutenant; Grenada, 1775 1220.25 p133
Man, Catherin; Maryland, 1670 2524.55 p143
Man, Edward; New York, 1707 1224.2 p75
Man, Elizabeth; Maryland, 1663 2524.55 p143
Man, James; Maryland, 1661 2524.55 p143
Man, Mary 60; Ontario, 1871 1823.22 p96
Man, Wm; Virginia, 1665-1666 6212.30 p24
Manae, William; Ontario, 1871 1823.15 p152
Managan, James 15; Maryland, 1775 1220.25 p102
Managhan, Edward; New York, 1803 8197.10 p14
Managhan, Hugh 42; Ontario, 1871 1823.15 p152
Manahan, Anthony 20; New York, New York, 1849 1825.45 p39
Manahan, Bridget Kiley; Vermont, 1823-1911 5900.10 p489
Manahan, Daniel; Vermont, 1845-1896 5900.10 p489
Manahan, Edna Brenmer; Vermont, 1871-1908 5900.10 p278
Manahan, John; Vermont, 1852-1910 5900.10 p278
Manahan, John; Vermont, 1852-1910 5900.10 p489
Manahan, Mary A.; Vermont, 1845 5900.10 p519
Manahan, Mary A.; Vermont, 1846-1928 5900.10 p472
Manahan, Timothy; Vermont, 1820-1895 5900.10 p489
Manasse, Caspar; Port uncertain, 1729 2856.30 p284
Manby, Aaron; Kingston, Jamaica, 1780 1224.2 p75
Manby, Aaron; Savannah, Georgia, 1780 1224.2 p75
Mancary, James 75; Ontario, 1871 1823.15 p152
Mancaster, John; Maryland, 1675 2524.55 p143
Mancer, Charles 36; Ontario, 1871 1823.15 p152
Manden, Jno; Virginia, 1664 6212.30 p14
Mander, William; New York, New York, 1849 1224.3 p50
Manders, Mary 23; Ontario, 1871 1823.28 p60
Mandevile, Miss 25; Barbados, 1774 1220.25 p131
Mandevill, Anna 7; Ontario, 1861 2896.27 p73
Mandevill, Edwin 11; Ontario, 1861 2896.27 p73
Mandevill, F. W. 45; Ontario, 1861 2896.27 p73
Mandevill, Henry 9; Ontario, 1861 2896.27 p73
Mandevill, M. A. 50; Ontario, 1861 2896.27 p73
Mandser, Mary; Maryland, 1661 2524.55 p143
Mane, Margaret 27; Vermont, 1874 5900.10 p247
Manery, Thomas 36; Ontario, 1871 1823.15 p152
Manes, Ann 60; Ontario, 1871 1823.22 p96
Manes, William 24; Ontario, 1871 1823.15 p152
Maney, Margaret Rohan; Vermont, 1796-1878 5900.10 p504
Maney, Mary; Vermont, 1824-1893 5900.10 p504
Maney, Morris 23; Virginia, 1774 1220.25 p93
Maney, Pat 55; Ontario, 1871 1823.28 p60
Manfan, Edward; Maryland, 1654 2524.55 p143
Manfan, Rebecca; Maryland, 1654 2524.55 p143
Manfield, George; Virginia, 1670 1224.1 p38
Mang, John; Pennsylvania, 1858 6058.10 p40
Mang, Valentin; Port uncertain, 1749 2856.30 p284

Mangan, Andrew; Vermont, n.d. ***5900.10*** *p84*
Mangan, Andrew; Vermont, 1833-1894 ***5900.10*** *p435*
Mangan, Ann Toohey; Vermont, 1843-1907 ***5900.10*** *p420*
Mangan, Anne Maloney; Vermont, 1829-1912 ***5900.10*** *p436*
Mangan, Annie 33; Vermont, 1887 ***5900.10*** *p417*
Mangan, Bridget; Vermont, 1800-1875 ***5900.10*** *p420*
Mangan, Bridget Egan; Vermont, 1825-1894 ***5900.10*** *p435*
Mangan, Catherine; Vermont, 1834-1872 ***5900.10*** *p434*
Mangan, Catherine; Vermont, 1837-1903 ***5900.10*** *p416*
Mangan, Charles 4; Ontario, 1871 ***1823.28*** *p60*
Mangan, Francis; Vermont, 1826-1890 ***5900.10*** *p434*
Mangan, Harold; Vermont, n.d. ***5900.10*** *p84*
Mangan, James; New York, 1837 ***8197.10*** *p99*
Mangan, John; New York, 1840 ***8197.10*** *p265*
Mangan, John 63; Vermont, 1891 ***5900.10*** *p416*
Mangan, Katherine; Vermont, n.d. ***5900.10*** *p84*
Mangan, Martin 32; Ontario, 1871 ***1823.28*** *p60*
Mangan, Mary; Vermont, n.d. ***5900.10*** *p84*
Mangan, Mary 28; Ontario, 1871 ***1823.28*** *p60*
Mangan, Mary A.; Vermont, 1855-1920 ***5900.10*** *p434*
Mangan, Mary Ganey; Vermont, 1835-1897 ***5900.10*** *p135*
Mangan, Mary Murtaugh; Vermont, 1833-1913 ***5900.10*** *p427*
Mangan, Mathew 2; Ontario, 1871 ***1823.28*** *p60*
Mangan, Mathew 28; Ontario, 1871 ***1823.28*** *p60*
Mangan, Nellie Higgins; Vermont, 1856-1912 ***5900.10*** *p435*
Mangan, Owen; Vermont, 1812-1890 ***5900.10*** *p436*
Mangan, Patrick; Vermont, 1834-1879 ***5900.10*** *p420*
Mangan, Patrick 42; Ontario, 1871 ***1823.28*** *p60*
Mangan, Patrick 45; Ontario, 1871 ***1823.28*** *p60*
Mangan, Mrs. Patrick; Vermont, 1827-1896 ***5900.10*** *p435*
Mangan, Patrick A.; Vermont, 1859-1942 ***5900.10*** *p435*
Mangan, Paul; Vermont, n.d. ***5900.10*** *p84*
Mangan, Thomas F.; Vermont, 1833-1901 ***5900.10*** *p427*
Mangan, William; Vermont, 1826-1896 ***5900.10*** *p135*
Mangane, John 31; Ontario, 1871 ***1823.28*** *p60*
Mangart, Jakob; America, 1741 ***2856.30*** *p284*
With family
Mangay, Miss; Quebec, 1856 ***9196.15*** *p5*
Mangen, Catherine 56; Ontario, 1861 ***2896.27*** *p5*
Mangen, John 37; Ontario, 1871 ***1823.28*** *p60*
Manger, Maria Elisabeth; America, 1755 ***2856.30*** *p284*
Manger, Maria Elisabeth; America, 1770 ***2856.30*** *p284*
Manger, Wilhelm; America, 1749 ***2856.30*** *p284*
With sister
Manghir, August 13; Ontario, 1871 ***1823.28*** *p60*
Manghir, Henry 8; Ontario, 1871 ***1823.28*** *p60*
Mangin, Ann; Vermont, 1831-1886 ***5900.10*** *p399*
Mangin, Catherine 67; Vermont, 1887 ***5900.10*** *p165*
Mangin, James; New York, 1837 ***8197.10*** *p99*
Mangle, Maria; Alabama, 1812-1845 ***1640.10*** *p148*
Mangles, Fabian; New York, 1831 ***8197.10*** *p366*
Mangles, John; New York, 1840 ***8197.10*** *p265*
Mangold, Anna Maria; Port uncertain, 1773 ***2856.30*** *p284*
Mangold, Catharina Waldmann; America, 1744 ***2856.30*** *p284*
Mangold, Josef; Port uncertain, 1724 ***2856.30*** *p284*
Mangold, Josef; Port uncertain, 1754 ***2856.30*** *p284*
Mangold, Justina; Port uncertain, 1794 ***2856.30*** *p284*
Maniates, Nicholas; New York, 1828-1834 ***8197.10*** *p309*
Maniewski, Peter; Maryland, 1910 ***3259.35*** *p38*
Manifold, Mrs.; Quebec, 1857 ***9196.15*** *p20*
Manigault, Gabriel; South Carolina, 1784 ***1224.2*** *p75*
Manigold, Peter; New York, 1830 ***8197.10*** *p262*
Maning, Edw; Virginia, 1664 ***6212.30*** *p14*
Maning, Giles; Virginia, 1665 ***6212.30*** *p20*
Maning, Johannah; Virginia, 1703-1704 ***6212.30*** *p63*
Manington, Edmond 36; Ontario, 1871 ***1823.28*** *p60*
Manington, Wm.; Virginia, 1664 ***6212.30*** *p7*
Manion, Annie; Vermont, 1861-1910 ***5900.10*** *p588*
Manion, Ellen 50; Vermont, 1879 ***5900.10*** *p586*
Manion, Martin, Sr. 67; Ontario, 1871 ***1823.28*** *p60*
Manion, Thomas; New York, 1840 ***8197.10*** *p321*
Manion, Thomas 68; Vermont, 1897 ***5900.10*** *p586*
Manitowabi, Louis 60; Ontario, 1871 ***1823.28*** *p60*
Manitowabi, Pierre 30; Ontario, 1871 ***1823.28*** *p60*
Manitowabi, Simon 24; Ontario, 1871 ***1823.28*** *p60*
Manksiswitz, Marting; Maryland, 1910 ***3259.35*** *p38*
Manley, Catherine; Vermont, 1830-1913 ***5900.10*** *p504*
Manley, Henry 24; Ontario, 1871 ***1823.22*** *p96*
Manley, Henry Chorley; Charles Town, South Carolina, 1800 ***1224.3*** *p50*
Manley, John; Buffalo, New York, 1857 ***6058.10*** *p55*
Manley, Mark 40; Ontario, 1871 ***1823.22*** *p96*
Manley, Mary L.; Vermont, 1837-1920 ***5900.10*** *p495*
Manley, Nellie 44; Vermont, 1899 ***5900.10*** *p579*
Manley, Rich; Virginia, 1664 ***6212.30*** *p14*
Manley, Tho; Virginia, 1664 ***6212.30*** *p14*
Manley, Tho; Virginia, 1665-1666 ***6212.30*** *p24*
Manley, William 23; Ontario, 1871 ***1823.22*** *p96*
Manley, William 31; Philadelphia, 1775 ***1220.25*** *p9*
Manloe, Elizabeth; Maryland, 1672 ***2524.55*** *p143*
Manlove, Ann *SEE* Manlove, Marke
Manlove, Christopher *SEE* Manlove, Marke
Manlove, Elizabeth *SEE* Manlove, Marke
Manlove, George *SEE* Manlove, Marke
Manlove, Hannah *SEE* Manlove, Marke
Manlove, John *SEE* Manlove, Marke
Manlove, Marke; Maryland, 1665 ***2524.55*** *p143*
Relative: George
Relative: William
Relative: Marke, Jr.
Relative: Ann
Relative: John
Relative: Elizabeth
Relative: Perce
Relative: Thomas
Relative: Hannah
Relative: Christopher
Manlove, Marke, Jr. *SEE* Manlove, Marke
Manlove, Perce *SEE* Manlove, Marke
Manlove, Thomas *SEE* Manlove, Marke
Manlove, William *SEE* Manlove, Marke
Manlow, Elizabeth; Maryland, 1673 ***2524.55*** *p143*
Manlow, John; Maryland, 1631-1685 ***2524.55*** *p143*
Manlufmore, Mary 15; Philadelphia, 1774 ***1220.25*** *p63*
Manly, Anthony 63; Ontario, 1871 ***1823.15*** *p152*
Manly, Bridget 16 *SEE* Manly, Richard
Manly, Bridget 40 *SEE* Manly, Richard
Manly, David 48; Ontario, 1871 ***1823.28*** *p60*
Manly, Ellen 18 *SEE* Manly, Richard
Manly, Henry; Pennsylvania, 1785 ***4629.10*** *p48*
Manly, James; New York, 1794 ***8197.10*** *p6*
Manly, James 9 *SEE* Manly, Richard
Manly, John; Buffalo, New York, 1857 ***6058.10*** *p55*
Manly, John 12 *SEE* Manly, Richard
Manly, Joseph 65; Ontario, 1871 ***1823.22*** *p96*
Manly, Mary 14 *SEE* Manly, Richard
Manly, Rich; Virginia, 1665-1666 ***6212.30*** *p21*
Manly, Richard 3 *SEE* Manly, Richard
Manly, Richard 48; New York, New York, 1848 ***1825.45*** *p39*
Wife: Bridget 40
Daughter: Mary 14
Son: James 9
Son: Richard 3
Daughter: Bridget 16
Daughter: Ellen 18
Son: John 12
Mann, Mr.; Quebec, 1857 ***9196.15*** *p20*
Mann, Adam; Port uncertain, 1783 ***2856.30*** *p284*
Mann, Anna; America, 1752 ***2856.30*** *p284*
Mann, Anna Margaretha; America, 1752 ***2856.30*** *p285*
With 6 children
Mann, Bernard; America, 1732 ***2856.30*** *p284*
Mann, Bridget; Vermont, 1851-1934 ***5900.10*** *p44*
Mann, Bridget 16; Vermont, 1853 ***5900.10*** *p546*
Mann, Christof; America, 1741 ***2856.30*** *p285*
With wife & son
Mann, Christof; Port uncertain, 1736 ***2856.30*** *p284*
Mann, David; America, 1752 ***2856.30*** *p284*
Mann, David 41; Ontario, 1871 ***1823.15*** *p152*
Mann, Eliza 55; Ontario, 1871 ***1823.22*** *p96*
Mann, Ellen; Vermont, 1857-1945 ***5900.10*** *p43*
Mann, Frances; Vermont, 1851-1931 ***5900.10*** *p490*
Mann, Francis; New York, 1821-1833 ***8197.10*** *p304*
Mann, Francis; New York, 1831 ***8197.10*** *p313*
Mann, Francis; New York, 1831 ***8197.10*** *p315*
Mann, G. H.; Vermont, 1845-1916 ***5900.10*** *p555*
Mann, Georg; America, 1752 ***2856.30*** *p284*
Mann, Georg Bernard; Port uncertain, 1700-1799 ***2856.30*** *p284*
Mann, George 21; Maryland, 1774 ***1220.25*** *p71*
Mann, George 30; Ontario, 1871 ***1823.15*** *p152*
Mann, Godfrey; New York, 1839 ***8197.10*** *p141*
Mann, Jacob; America, 1738 ***2856.30*** *p284*
Mann, Jakob; America, 1738 ***2856.30*** *p285*
With mother
Mann, Jakob; America, 1749 ***2856.30*** *p284*
Mann, James; Vermont, 1848-1880 ***5900.10*** *p43*
Mann, James 25; Ontario, 1871 ***1823.15*** *p152*
Mann, James 31; Maryland, 1775 ***1220.25*** *p97*
Mann, Jane M.; Vermont, 1856-1905 ***5900.10*** *p556*
Mann, Johann Georg; America, 1752 ***2856.30*** *p284*
Mann, John; Vermont, 1803-1855 ***5900.10*** *p546*
Mann, John 30; Philadelphia, 1774 ***1220.25*** *p66*
Mann, Konrad; America, 1752 ***2856.30*** *p284*
Mann, Louisa S. Powers; Vermont, 1852-1922 ***5900.10*** *p555*
Mann, Margaret; Vermont, 1836-1908 ***5900.10*** *p135*
Mann, Margaret 66; Vermont, 1898 ***5900.10*** *p594*
Mann, Margaret Morrissey; Vermont, 1850-1948 ***5900.10*** *p43*
Mann, Maria Barbara; Port uncertain, 1750 ***2856.30*** *p284*
Mann, Mary; Massachusetts, 1803 ***1224.3*** *p50*
Mann, Mary 31; Vermont, 1892 ***5900.10*** *p596*
Mann, Math; America, 1752 ***2856.30*** *p284*
Mann, Michael; America, 1752 ***2856.30*** *p284*
Mann, Patrick 69; Vermont, 1896 ***5900.10*** *p593*
Mann, Peter; America, 1750 ***2856.30*** *p285*
With wife & 2 children
Mann, R.; Quebec, 1856 ***9196.15*** *p5*
Mann, Mrs. R.; Quebec, 1856 ***9196.15*** *p5*
Mann, Robert 60; Ontario, 1871 ***1823.15*** *p152*
Mann, Sarah; Vermont, 1849-1944 ***5900.10*** *p43*
Mann, Thomas; Vermont, 1838-1920 ***5900.10*** *p135*
Mann, Thomas, Sr.; Vermont, 1854-1940 ***5900.10*** *p43*
Mann, William; Jamaica, n.d. ***1224.2*** *p75*
Mann, William; Pensacola, Florida, 1781 ***1224.2*** *p75*
Mann, William; Pensacola, Florida, 1781 ***1640.10*** *p148*
Mann, William 51; Ontario, 1871 ***1823.22*** *p96*
Mannahan, Patrick 65; Ontario, 1871 ***1823.22*** *p96*
Mannbach, Nicolaus; Port uncertain, 1740 ***2856.30*** *p285*
Mannders, Thomas 29; Ontario, 1871 ***1823.15*** *p152*
Mannel, Catharina; Port uncertain, 1771 ***2856.30*** *p319*
Mannering, George; New York, 1839 ***8197.10*** *p142*
Manners, Rebeccah; Maryland, 1670 ***2524.55*** *p143*
Manney, Bridget Kelty; Vermont, 1834-1871 ***5900.10*** *p554*
Manney, Patrick 60; Vermont, 1887 ***5900.10*** *p554*
Mannheimer, Andreas; Port uncertain, 1744 ***2856.30*** *p285*
Mannherz, Miss; America, 1785 ***2856.30*** *p285*
Mannherz, Hans; Port uncertain, 1628 ***2856.30*** *p285*
Mannherz, Heinrich; America, 1785 ***2856.30*** *p285*
Mannherz, Heinrich; Port uncertain, 1785 ***2856.30*** *p285*
Mannig, August Friedric; Port uncertain, 1748 ***2856.30*** *p319*
Manniiherz, Hans; Port uncertain, 1628 ***2856.30*** *p285*
Manning, Anna; Vermont, 1848-1888 ***5900.10*** *p302*
Manning, Annie; Vermont, 1856-1918 ***5900.10*** *p114*
Manning, Bridget 55; Ontario, 1871 ***1823.28*** *p60*
Manning, Bridget O'Conner 70; Vermont, 1896 ***5900.10*** *p109*
Manning, Daniel; New York, 1840 ***8197.10*** *p179*
Manning, Daniel 48; Vermont, 1884 ***5900.10*** *p108*
Manning, Daniel 80; Vermont, 1902 ***5900.10*** *p336*
Manning, Daniel V.; Vermont, 1854-1929 ***5900.10*** *p119*
Manning, David; Vermont, 1855-1940 ***5900.10*** *p555*
Manning, Dennis 30; Vermont, 1882 ***5900.10*** *p109*
Manning, Edmund 35; Ontario, 1871 ***1823.15*** *p153*
Manning, Edward 64; Ontario, 1871 ***1823.15*** *p153*
Manning, Elizabeth; Maryland, 1674 ***2524.55*** *p143*
Manning, Ellen 42; Vermont, 1872 ***5900.10*** *p111*
Manning, Ellen 79; Vermont, 1885 ***5900.10*** *p109*
Manning, Ellen D.; Vermont, 1844-1929 ***5900.10*** *p284*
Manning, Ellen Higgins 71; Vermont, 1908 ***5900.10*** *p108*
Manning, Francis; Charles Town, South Carolina, 1826 ***1224.3*** *p50*
Manning, Francis 51; Ontario, 1871 ***1823.15*** *p153*
Manning, George 63; Ontario, 1871 ***1823.22*** *p96*
Manning, Grace *SEE* Manning, Thomas
Manning, Honora Curry; Vermont, 1874-1949 ***5900.10*** *p117*
Manning, Honora Mahaney 60; Vermont, 1884 ***5900.10*** *p336*
Manning, James 12; Vermont, 1864 ***5900.10*** *p109*
Manning, James 47; Ontario, 1871 ***1823.15*** *p153*
Manning, Jane Newman 39; Vermont, 1870 ***5900.10*** *p140*
Manning, John *SEE* Manning, Thomas
Manning, John; New York, 1840 ***8197.10*** *p181*
Manning, John 18; Vermont, 1862 ***5900.10*** *p109*
Manning, John 20; Vermont, 1867 ***5900.10*** *p336*
Manning, Lawrence 45; Ontario, 1871 ***1823.15*** *p153*
Manning, Martha J. Colebrook; Vermont, 1863-1933 ***5900.10*** *p119*
Manning, Mary 15; Vermont, 1867 ***5900.10*** *p336*
Manning, Mary 56; Vermont, 1879 ***5900.10*** *p105*
Manning, Mary F.; Vermont, 1861-1930 ***5900.10*** *p555*
Manning, Mary Kennedy; Vermont, 1853-1898 ***5900.10*** *p117*
Manning, Michael; Vermont, 1841-1919 ***5900.10*** *p284*
Manning, Michael W.; Vermont, 1851-1902 ***5900.10*** *p119*
Manning, Mitchell; New York, 1840 ***8197.10*** *p181*
Manning, Nora C. Doyle; Vermont, 1864-1916 ***5900.10*** *p119*
Manning, Patrick; Vermont, 1845-1909 ***5900.10*** *p47*
Manning, Patrick; Vermont, 1858-1926 ***5900.10*** *p117*
Manning, Rebecca 52; Ontario, 1871 ***1823.22*** *p96*

Manning, Richard 47; Ontario, 1871 1823.15 p153
Manning, Robert 31; Maryland, 1775 1220.25 p114
Manning, Samuell 49; Ontario, 1871 1823.15 p153
Manning, Thomas *SEE* Manning, Thomas
Manning, Thomas; Maryland, 1659 2524.55 p143
Relative: Grace
Son: John
Son: Thomas
Manning, Thomas 30; Jamaica, 1775 1220.25 p144
Manning, Thomas 30; St. Christopher, 1775 1220.25 p144
Manning, Thomas 36; Ontario, 1871 1823.15 p153
Manning, Thomas 48; Vermont, 1871 5900.10 p105
Manning, Thomas 56; Vermont, 1866 5900.10 p109
Manning, Thomas 68; Vermont, 1888 5900.10 p109
Manning, William 16; Philadelphia, 1774 1220.25 p80
Manning, William 30; Ontario, 1871 1823.15 p153
Manning, William 51; Ontario, 1871 1823.15 p153
Manning, William John; Ontario, 1871 1823.15 p153
Manninge, Grace *SEE* Manninge, Thomas
Manninge, John *SEE* Manninge, Thomas
Manninge, Thomas *SEE* Manninge, Thomas
Manninge, Thomas; Maryland, 1659 2524.55 p143
Relative: Grace
Son: John
Son: Thomas
Mannion, John 17 *SEE* Mannion, Pat
Mannion, Malachy 10 *SEE* Mannion, Pat
Mannion, Mary 5 *SEE* Mannion, Pat
Mannion, Pat 13 *SEE* Mannion, Pat
Mannion, Pat 38; New York, New York, 1849 1825.45 p39
Wife: Peggy 40
Daughter: Mary 5
Son: John 17
Son: Malachy 10
Son: Thomas 8
Son: Pat 13
Mannion, Peggy 40 *SEE* Mannion, Pat
Mannion, Thomas 8 *SEE* Mannion, Pat
Mannix, Bella Taggart; Vermont, 1844-1926 5900.10 p403
Mannix, James; Vermont, 1843-1915 5900.10 p403
Mannlin, Catharina; Port uncertain, 1763 2856.30 p319
Mannlin, Marianna; Port uncertain, 1795 2856.30 p285
Mannocks, Elizabeth; Maryland, 1679 2524.55 p143
Mannocks, Hugh; Maryland, 1679 2524.55 p143
Mannocks, Jno.; Maryland, 1679 2524.55 p143
Mannocks, Katherine; Maryland, 1679 2524.55 p143
Mannocks, Margaret; Maryland, 1679 2524.55 p144
Manns, Frederick 46; Ontario, 1871 1823.15 p153
Manns, Johann Michael; America, 1756 2856.30 p285
Manny, Anne; Vermont, 1816-1859 5900.10 p321
Manny, Daniel; Vermont, 1785-1865 5900.10 p321
Manny, Elizabeth; Vermont, 1830-1849 5900.10 p321
Manny, Hugh; Vermont, 1801-1802 5900.10 p321
Manny, Isabella; Vermont, n.d. 5900.10 p320
Manny, Jane; Vermont, n.d. 5900.10 p320
Manny, Jane Knear; Vermont, n.d. 5900.10 p320
Manny, Margaret; Vermont, 1834-1849 5900.10 p321
Manny, Mary; Vermont, 1793-1873 5900.10 p320
Manny, Mary MacNeil; Vermont, n.d. 5900.10 p321
Manny, Nancy; Vermont, n.d. 5900.10 p320
Manny, Robert; Vermont, n.d. 5900.10 p321
Manny, Robert K.; Vermont, 1826-1849 5900.10 p321
Manny, William; Vermont, n.d. 5900.10 p320
Manny, William; Vermont, 1795-1871 5900.10 p321
Mano, Tom 30; British Columbia, 1909 9196.1 p27
Mano, Tom 30; Seattle, 1909 9196.1 p27
Manor, Jennie E.; Vermont, 1861-1919 5900.10 p318
Manqunsae, P. 30; British Columbia, 1912 9196.1 p15
Mansard, Louis Nicholas; Philadelphia, 1792 4629.10 p75
Mansel, Godfried; New York, 1803 8197.10 p14
Mansell, John; Maryland, 1637 2524.55 p144
Mansfeild, Henry; Virginia, 1668-1669 6212.30 p41
Mansfield, Elizabeth 20; Maryland, 1774 1220.25 p59
Mansfield, John; Vermont, n.d. 5900.10 p61
Mansfield, John 23; Maryland, 1775 1220.25 p99
Mansfield, Richard; New York, 1839 8197.10 p264
Mansfield, Walter; Maryland, 1651 2524.55 p144
Mansfield, William 60; Ontario, 1871 1823.15 p153
Manship, Elizabeth *SEE* Manship, Richard
Manship, Mary *SEE* Manship, Richard
Manship, Rachel *SEE* Manship, Richard
Manship, Richard *SEE* Manship, Richard
Manship, Richard; Maryland, 1652-1653 2524.55 p144
With wife
Child: Mary
Child: Elizabeth
Child: Richard
Child: Rachel
Manship, Richard; Maryland, 1658 2524.55 p144
Child: Rachel
Child: Richard
Wife: Elizabeth
Child: Elizabeth
Child: Mary
Manski, Joseph; Maryland, 1910 3259.35 p38
Manson, Capt.; Quebec, 1856 9196.15 p9
Manson, Mrs.; Maryland, 1661 2524.55 p144
Manson, Alexander 30; Ontario, 1871 1823.15 p153
Manson, Andrew; America, 1809 1640.10 p148
Manson, Anna 25; Ontario, 1861 2896.27 p74
Manson, Barbara; Georgia, 1775 1640.10 p149
Manson, Barbara 23; Georgia, 1775 1220.25 p126
Manson, Charles 34; Ontario, 1861 2896.27 p74
Manson, David 44; Ontario, 1871 1823.15 p153
Manson, Elizabeth; Georgia, 1775 1640.10 p149
Manson, Elizabeth 9; Georgia, 1775 1220.25 p126
Manson, Elizabeth 26; Georgia, 1775 1220.25 p126
Manson, Janet; Savannah, Georgia, 1775 1640.10 p149
Manson, John 30; Ontario, 1871 1823.28 p60
Manson, John 45; Ontario, 1871 1823.15 p153
Manson, John 55; Ontario, 1871 1823.15 p153
Manson, Margaret; Georgia, 1775 1640.10 p149
Manson, Margaret 25; Georgia, 1775 1220.25 p126
Manson, Mary 24; Ontario, 1871 1823.15 p153
Manson, Mary E. 19; Ontario, 1861 2896.27 p74
Manson, Thomas; Georgia, 1775 1640.10 p149
Manson, Thomas; New York, 1831 8197.10 p354
Manson, Thomas 16; Georgia, 1775 1220.25 p126
Manson, William; Augusta, Georgia, 1780 1640.10 p149
Manson, William; Savannah, Georgia, 1775 1640.10 p149
Manstidge, Robert; Virginia, 1630 1224.1 p38
Mansur, Alvah; St. Louis, 1898 1640.13 p73
Mantel, Johann; Port uncertain, 1722 2856.30 p296
Mantel, Johann; Port uncertain, 1762 2856.30 p296
Mantell, George 12; Ontario, 1871 1823.15 p153
Mantifle, Chas 60; Ontario, 1871 1823.28 p60
Mantik, Frank; Maryland, 1910 3259.35 p38
Mantik, William; Maryland, 1910 3259.35 p38
Mantom, Priscilla; Maryland, 1665 2524.55 p144
Mantom, Sarah; Maryland, 1665 2524.55 p144
Manton, Henry 37; Ontario, 1871 1823.15 p153
Mantona, Bernard; New York, 1831 8197.10 p364
Mants, Mathias 24; Kansas, 1904-1910 9079.10 p23
Mantz, Andreas; Port uncertain, 1759 2856.30 p285
With wife
Mantz, Franz; Port uncertain, 1768 2856.30 p285
Mantz, Marx; America, 1744 2856.30 p285
Mantz, Mathes; Port uncertain, 1745 2856.30 p285
With wife
Manum, Jno; Virginia, 1664 6212.30 p14
Manvell, John; New York, 1834 8197.10 p263
Manwaring, John; New York, 1836 8197.10 p371
Manwaring, Margerett; Maryland, 1658 2524.55 p144
Many, Laurence 42; Ontario, 1871 1823.28 p60
Manye, Ellen 32; Vermont, 1870 5900.10 p63
Manying, Maria; Vermont, 1810-1860 5900.10 p160
Manyor, Patrick 27; America, 1774 1220.25 p36
Manyott, John; Maryland, 1664 2524.55 p144
Manythorpe, Thomas; Maryland, 1672 2524.55 p144
Manyweathers, James; Maryland, 1682 2524.55 p144
Manz, Anna Margarete; Port uncertain, 1746 2856.30 p285
Manz, Caspar; Port uncertain, 1773 2856.30 p285
Manz, Eva; Port uncertain, 1769 2856.30 p285
Manz, Hans Adam; Port uncertain, 1784 2856.30 p285
Manz, Michel; New York, 1837 8197.10 p100
Manzanedo, Jose; New York, 1840 8197.10 p181
Manzanedo, Joseph; New York, 1838 8197.10 p264
Maoney, Patrick; Maryland, 1666 2524.55 p148
Mapieralski, Lucy; Maryland, 1910 3259.35 p38
Maplet, Mary; New England, 1647 1224.1 p38
Mapson, Susanna; New England, 1660 1224.1 p38
Maquillen, John 27; Ontario, 1871 1823.28 p60
Maquire, Benjamin 56; Ontario, 1871 1823.15 p153
Mar, Martin; Maryland, 1665 2524.55 p144
Mara, Francis 23; Virginia, 1774 1220.25 p54
Marache, Napoleon; New York, 1840 8197.10 p178
Marato, L. 26; Washington, 1913 9196.1 p60
Maraya, James; Pennsylvania, 1868 6058.10 p73
Marbeck, Ludwig; Port uncertain, 1770 2856.30 p285
Marbin, Dorothea; Port uncertain, 1798 2856.30 p285
With husband
Marbin, Thomas; Maryland, 1713 1224.2 p76
Marcain, John *SEE* Marcain, John
Marcain, John; Maryland, 1662 2524.55 p144
Son: John
Marcam, John *SEE* Marcam, John
Marcam, John; Maryland, 1662 2524.55 p144
Father: John
Marcella, Edward 13; Ontario, 1871 1823.28 p60
Marcella, George 30; Ontario, 1871 1823.28 p60
Marcellin, Anthony; New York, 1807 8197.10 p45
March, Benjamin 29; Virginia, 1774 1220.25 p87
March, Jane 72; Ontario, 1871 1823.28 p61
March, Joseph 21; Virginia, 1774 1220.25 p87
Marchand, Charles Laurent Marie; New York, 1830 1224.3 p50
Marchant, Frederick; New York, 1807 8197.10 p45
Marchant, John; New York, 1840 8197.10 p178
Marchant, Martha; Maryland, 1669 2524.55 p144
Marchant, Wm.; Maryland, 1670 2524.55 p144
Marche, Sarah Ann 14; Ontario, 1871 1823.22 p96
Marchinski, John; Maryland, 1910 3259.35 p38
Marchlewicz, John; Maryland, 1910 3259.35 p38
Marcinki, Paul; Maryland, 1910 3259.35 p38
Marcinkow, Anna; Maryland, 1910 3259.35 p38
Marcinkowski, Stefan; Maryland, 1910 3259.35 p38
Marcker, Frdr. Sebastian; America, 1787 2856.30 p285
Marcker, Friedrich Seb.; America, 1771 2856.30 p285
Marcker, Johann Philipp; Port uncertain, 1781 2856.30 p285
Marcker, Peter; America, 1739 2856.30 p285
Marckh, Jacob; Port uncertain, 1748 2856.30 p285
Marckhin, Therese; Port uncertain, 1749 2856.30 p285
Marckstaler, Michael; Port uncertain, 1775 2856.30 p286
Marco, John 56; Ontario, 1871 1823.15 p153
Marco, Mary 78; Ontario, 1871 1823.15 p153
Marcorelle, Anthony; New York, 1798 8197.10 p9
Marcoski, Eva; Maryland, 1910 3259.35 p38
Marcus, Martin 38; Ontario, 1871 1823.28 p61
Mardah, Robert; Maryland, 1672 2524.55 p144
Mardah, Robert; Maryland, 1673 2524.55 p144
Marding, Jasper; Virginia, 1667 6212.30 p37
Mare, Luke; Maryland, 1664 2524.55 p144
Marecka, Theofila; Maryland, 1910 3259.35 p38
Marecki, Stanislaum; Maryland, 1910 3259.35 p38
Mareene, Milleson; Maryland, 1655 2524.55 p144
Marek, Jan; Maryland, 1910 3259.35 p38
Marengo, Katherine Foley; Vermont, 1857-1937 5900.10 p132
Marengo, Peter E.; Vermont, 1854-1923 5900.10 p132
Mareski, Wilko; Maryland, 1910 3259.35 p38
Maret, Arthur; New York, New York, 1899 3437.14 p174
Marfilius, Wilhelm; New York, 1837 8197.10 p99
Margaret, Lake 85; Ontario, 1871 1823.22 p96
Margaritel, Giovan; New York, 1840 8197.10 p265
Marghiem, Mollie 19; Kansas, 1910 9079.10 p49
Margritts, John; Virginia, 1666 6212.30 p26
Margunek, Marcelia; Maryland, 1910 3259.35 p38
Marigan, Patrick; Vermont, 1824-1898 5900.10 p459
Marigaw, Anne 9; Ontario, 1861 2896.27 p19
Marigaw, Bridget 43; Ontario, 1861 2896.27 p19
Marigaw, James 6; Ontario, 1861 2896.27 p19
Marigaw, James 43; Ontario, 1861 2896.27 p19
Marigaw, Mary 10; Ontario, 1861 2896.27 p19
Marigaw, Patrick 13; Ontario, 1861 2896.27 p19
Marilley, Richard 15; Maryland, 1774 1220.25 p61
Marinan, Honora Doyle 35; Vermont, 1878 5900.10 p138
Marines, Mary; Maryland, 1910 3259.35 p38
Marino, Nicholas 47; Ontario, 1871 1823.15 p153
Marion, Mr.; Quebec, 1858 9196.15 p41
Marion, Amedee Jean; New York, 1832-1837 8197.10 p311
Marion, Jas 44; British Columbia, 1911 9196.1 p33
Marion, Jas 44; Seattle, 1911 9196.1 p33
Marion, John 40; British Columbia, 1910 9196.1 p31
Marion, John 40; Seattle, 1910 9196.1 p31
Mariott, George; Maryland, 1682 2524.55 p144
Maris, William; Pennsylvania, 1777 4629.10 p13
Marishshin, Wm.; Maryland, 1681 2524.55 p144
Marjewski, Frank; Maryland, 1910 3259.35 p38
Marjoribanks, Joseph; Georgia, 1698 1640.13 p73
Mark, Ann; Vermont, 1748-1824 5900.10 p620
Mark, Deborah 5 *SEE* Mark, Thomas
Mark, Elizabeth 9 *SEE* Mark, Thomas
Mark, Isaac 16 *SEE* Mark, Thomas
Mark, John; Vermont, 1746-1832 5900.10 p620
Mark, John 22; Maryland, 1774 1220.25 p3
Mark, Kenward 35; Ontario, 1871 1823.22 p96
Mark, Louis; New York, 1806 8197.10 p32
Mark, Mary 18 *SEE* Mark, Thomas
Mark, Philip 21; Philadelphia, 1774 1220.25 p4
Mark, Robert 39; Ontario, 1871 1823.22 p96
Mark, Sarah 14 *SEE* Mark, Thomas
Mark, Sarah 46 *SEE* Mark, Thomas
Mark, Thomas 45; New York, 1774 1220.25 p140
Wife: Sarah 46
Child: Isaac 16
Child: Elizabeth 9
Child: Deborah 5

Marshall, James; Charles Town, South Carolina, 1767 ***1224.2*** *p76*
Marshall, James 24; Barbados, 1774 ***1220.25*** *p62*
With wife 22
Marshall, James 46; Ontario, 1871 ***1823.15*** *p154*
Marshall, Jane 60; Ontario, 1871 ***1823.22*** *p97*
Marshall, John; Maryland, 1717 ***1224.2*** *p76*
Marshall, John; New York, 1813 ***8197.10*** *p58*
Marshall, John; New York, 1829-1831 ***8197.10*** *p369*
Marshall, John; Pennsylvania, 1777 ***4629.10*** *p22*
Marshall, John; Pennsylvania, 1777 ***4629.10*** *p28*
Marshall, John; Pennsylvania, 1785 ***4629.10*** *p48*
Marshall, John; Vermont, 1814-1894 ***5900.10*** *p460*
Marshall, John; Virginia, 1671-1672 ***6212.30*** *p46*
Marshall, John; Virginia, 1793 ***1224.2*** *p76*
Marshall, John 25; Ontario, 1861 ***2896.27*** *p9*
Marshall, John 50; Ontario, 1871 ***1823.15*** *p154*
Marshall, John 65; Ontario, 1871 ***1823.22*** *p97*
Marshall, Joseph; New York, 1796 ***8197.10*** *p8*
Marshall, Joseph; New York, 1821 ***8197.10*** *p260*
Marshall, Joseph 40; Ontario, 1871 ***1823.15*** *p154*
Marshall, Katherine; Maryland, 1631-1685 ***2524.55*** *p145*
Marshall, Margaret 35; Vermont, 1879 ***5900.10*** *p540*
Marshall, Martha M. Dunn; Vermont, 1879-1944 ***5900.10*** *p392*
Marshall, Mary; Vermont, 1839-1911 ***5900.10*** *p328*
Marshall, Mary 32; Vermont, 1861 ***5900.10*** *p369*
Marshall, Mary 80; Vermont, 1895 ***5900.10*** *p540*
Marshall, Michael; Maryland, 1910 ***3259.35*** *p38*
Marshall, Michael 19; Vermont, 1864 ***5900.10*** *p540*
Marshall, Peter; Maryland, 1667 ***2524.55*** *p145*
Marshall, Richard 20; Vermont, 1861 ***5900.10*** *p540*
Marshall, Robert; New York, 1828 ***8197.10*** *p262*
Marshall, Robert; New York, 1832 ***8197.10*** *p356*
Marshall, Robert; Pennsylvania, 1778 ***4629.10*** *p32*
Marshall, Robert; Philadelphia, 1790 ***4629.10*** *p61*
Marshall, Robert 18; Ontario, 1871 ***1823.15*** *p154*
Marshall, Robert 52; Ontario, 1871 ***1823.28*** *p61*
Marshall, S. A. 21; Ontario, 1861 ***2896.26*** *p3*
Marshall, Samuel; New England, 1694 ***1224.1*** *p38*
Marshall, Thomas *SEE* Marshall, Thomas
Marshall, Thomas; Maryland, 1664 ***2524.55*** *p145*
Marshall, Thomas; Maryland, 1680 ***2524.55*** *p145*
Son: William
Son: Thomas
Marshall, Thomas; Philadelphia, 1849 ***6058.10*** *p25*
Marshall, Thomas 44; Ontario, 1871 ***1823.15*** *p154*
Marshall, Thomas George 49; Ontario, 1871 ***1823.28*** *p61*
Marshall, William *SEE* Marshall, Thomas
Marshall, William; Baton Rouge, Louisiana, 1804 ***1224.3*** *p51*
Marshall, William; Jamaica, 1796 ***1640.13*** *p74*
Marshall, William; Maryland, 1672 ***2524.55*** *p145*
Marshall, William; Mississippi, 1794 ***1640.10*** *p150*
Marshall, William; New Orleans, 1803 ***1640.10*** *p150*
Marshall, William; Pennsylvania, 1777 ***4629.10*** *p7*
Marshall, William; Tobago, West Indies, 1790 ***1640.13*** *p73*
Marshall, William; Vermont, 1822-1864 ***5900.10*** *p328*
Marshall, William 50; Maryland, 1774 ***1220.25*** *p37*
With wife & 10 children
Marshall, Wm 25; Ontario, 1871 ***1823.28*** *p61*
Marsham, Jno; Virginia, 1664 ***6212.30*** *p12*
Marsham, Katherine; Maryland, 1664 ***2524.55*** *p145*
Marshel, Henry 30; Ontario, 1871 ***1823.15*** *p154*
Marshel, John 34; Ontario, 1871 ***1823.15*** *p154*
Marshell, John 50; Ontario, 1871 ***1823.15*** *p154*
Marsh't, Martha; Maryland, 1664 ***2524.55*** *p145*
Marsi, Martin; New York, 1836 ***8197.10*** *p263*
Marski, Antone J.; Maryland, 1910 ***3259.35*** *p38*
Marski, John T.; Maryland, 1910 ***3259.35*** *p38*
Marski, Joseph; Maryland, 1910 ***3259.35*** *p38*
Marski, Joseph A.; Maryland, 1910 ***3259.35*** *p38*
Marski, Justina; Maryland, 1910 ***3259.35*** *p38*
Marski, Michael; Maryland, 1910 ***3259.35*** *p38*
Marskotka, Peter; Maryland, 1910 ***3259.35*** *p38*
Marsleland, John; Quebec, 1858 ***9196.15*** *p33*
Marson, Catharine 26; Ontario, 1861 ***2896.28*** *p59*
Marson, Catharine 28; Ontario, 1861 ***2896.28*** *p59*
Marson, David 17; Ontario, 1861 ***2896.28*** *p59*
Marson, Gabrill; Maryland, 1668 ***2524.55*** *p145*
Marson, Lanor 57; Ontario, 1861 ***2896.28*** *p59*
Marson, Susan 22; Ontario, 1861 ***2896.28*** *p59*
Marsters, Silas W.; New York, 1839 ***8197.10*** *p141*
Marston, Richard; Maryland, 1676 ***2524.55*** *p145*
Marston, Robert; Maryland, 1655-1656 ***2524.55*** *p145*
Marston, Robert; New York, 1840 ***8197.10*** *p179*
Marston, Thomas; New York, New York, 1814 ***1224.3*** *p51*
Marston, Wm; Virginia, 1665-1666 ***6212.30*** *p21*
Marstone, Robert; Maryland, 1655-1656 ***2524.55*** *p145*
Martans, John 32; Seattle, 1911 ***9196.1*** *p34*
Martauski, Frank; Maryland, 1910 ***3259.35*** *p38*
Martell, Abraham 24; Ontario, 1871 ***1823.28*** *p61*
Martell, William 70; Ontario, 1871 ***1823.22*** *p97*
Marten, G. 28; Alaska, 1908 ***9196.1*** *p36*
Marter, Cristine 36; Ontario, 1871 ***1823.15*** *p154*
Marthin, Joerg; America, 1753 ***2856.30*** *p286*
Martin, . . .; New Hampshire, 1641-1660 ***4628.40*** *p44*
Martin, Miss; Quebec, 1858 ***9196.15*** *p36*
Martin, Miss; Port uncertain, 1793 ***2856.30*** *p286*
With sister
Martin, Mr.; America, 1756 ***2856.30*** *p397*
Martin, Mr.; Quebec, 1858 ***9196.15*** *p32*
Martin, Mr.; Quebec, 1858 ***9196.15*** *p45*
Martin, Mrs.; America, 1751 ***2856.30*** *p287*
With husband
Martin, Mrs.; Maryland, 1655 ***2524.55*** *p145*
Martin, Mrs.; Maryland, 1661 ***2524.55*** *p145*
Martin, Mrs.; Quebec, 1858 ***9196.15*** *p32*
Martin, Mrs. 32; Ontario, 1871 ***1823.15*** *p155*
Martin, Sister 45; Ontario, 1871 ***1823.28*** *p61*
Martin, A. El. *SEE* Martin, Johann Nikolaus
Martin, Abel 49; Ontario, 1871 ***1823.15*** *p154*
Martin, Abla 83; Ontario, 1871 ***1823.15*** *p154*
Martin, Adam; Pennsylvania, 1777 ***4629.10*** *p18*
Martin, Alex; Toronto, 1882 ***1640.13*** *p74*
Martin, Alexander *SEE* Martin, Donald
Martin, Alexander *SEE* Martin, Ranald
Martin, Alexander 32; Ontario, 1871 ***1823.15*** *p154*
Martin, Alexander 52; Ontario, 1871 ***1823.22*** *p97*
Martin, Alice; Vermont, 1860-1960 ***5900.10*** *p122*
Martin, Amos 46; Ontario, 1871 ***1823.15*** *p154*
Martin, Andrew; Pennsylvania, 1786 ***4629.10*** *p52*
Martin, Andrew 34; Ontario, 1871 ***1823.22*** *p97*
Martin, Angus *SEE* Martin, John
Martin, Angus *SEE* Martin, Margaret
Martin, Angus *SEE* Martin, Mary
Martin, Angus *SEE* Martin, Neil
Martin, Angus *SEE* Martin, Ranald
Martin, Angus; Port uncertain, 1840-1849 ***4537.35*** *p85*
With wife
Child: John
Child: Roderick
Child: Kirsty
Child: Mary
Child: Jessie
Martin, Ann *SEE* Martin, Catherine MacDonald
Martin, Ann *SEE* Martin, Donald
Martin, Ann *SEE* Martin, John
Martin, Ann *SEE* Martin, Margaret
Martin, Ann; Ontario, 1871 ***1823.15*** *p154*
Martin, Ann MacKay *SEE* Martin, Donald
Martin, Ann Morrison; Port uncertain, 1840-1849 ***4537.37*** *p129*
Child: Mary
Child: Effie
Child: Catherine
Child: Betsy
Child: John
Martin, Anna; Vermont, 1879-1912 ***5900.10*** *p553*
Martin, Anna Maria; Port uncertain, 1756 ***2856.30*** *p286*
Martin, Apollonia; Port uncertain, 1612 ***2856.30*** *p287*
With 2 sons & 4 daughters
Martin, Archie *SEE* Martin, John
Martin, Archie; Port uncertain, 1840-1849 ***4537.35*** *p85*
Wife: Mary
Child: Mary
Martin, Aurilla Ducharme 68; Vermont, 1892 ***5900.10*** *p298*
Martin, Bernard; Pennsylvania, 1814 ***6058.10*** *p4*
Martin, Betsy *SEE* Martin, Ann Morrison
Martin, Bridget 56; Ontario, 1871 ***1823.28*** *p61*
Martin, C. 30; Ontario, 1861 ***2896.26*** *p11*
Martin, Catharine; New York, 1838 ***8197.10*** *p318*
Martin, Catherine *SEE* Martin, Ann Morrison
Martin, Catherine *SEE* Martin, Flora MacDonald
Martin, Catherine *SEE* Martin, John
Martin, Catherine *SEE* Martin, Neil
Martin, Catherine; Milwaukee, 1899 ***1640.13*** *p74*
Martin, Catherine; Vermont, 1822-1886 ***5900.10*** *p122*
Martin, Catherine; Vermont, 1850-1938 ***5900.10*** *p156*
Martin, Catherine 82; Vermont, 1917 ***5900.10*** *p102*
Martin, Catherine 85; Vermont, 1895 ***5900.10*** *p101*
Martin, Catherine MacAskill *SEE* Martin, Finlay
Martin, Catherine MacDonald; Maryland, 1888 ***4537.35*** *p68*
Child: Donald
Child: Mary
Child: Ann
Child: Mary Ann
Child: John
Child: Joan
Child: Marion
Child: Kenneth
Martin, Catherine Morrison *SEE* Martin, John
Martin, Charles; New York, 1840 ***8197.10*** *p182*
Martin, Charles; Pennsylvania, 1837 ***6058.10*** *p14*
Martin, Charles; Pennsylvania, 1861 ***6058.10*** *p45*
Martin, Charles 19; New York, 1816-1828 ***8197.10*** *p298*
Martin, Charles 35; Ontario, 1871 ***1823.28*** *p61*
Martin, Charles 40; Ontario, 1871 ***1823.15*** *p154*
Martin, Charles 50; Ontario, 1871 ***1823.22*** *p97*
Martin, Christein 64; Ontario, 1871 ***1823.28*** *p61*
Martin, Christina; Port uncertain, 1750 ***2856.30*** *p286*
Martin, Christopher; Maryland, 1634 ***2524.55*** *p145*
Martin, Christopher; Pennsylvania, 1777 ***4629.10*** *p13*
Martin, Christopher 24; Ontario, 1871 ***1823.28*** *p61*
Martin, Christopher 70; Ontario, 1871 ***1823.28*** *p61*
Martin, Conrad; New York, 1839 ***8197.10*** *p264*
Martin, Damaras *SEE* Martin, Robert
Martin, Daniel; Georgia, 1823 ***1640.10*** *p150*
Martin, Daniel; New York, 1827 ***8197.10*** *p344*
Martin, David *SEE* Martin, John
Martin, David 44; Ontario, 1871 ***1823.15*** *p154*
Martin, Dietrich; Port uncertain, 1741 ***2856.30*** *p287*
With wife & 5 children
Martin, Dominic *SEE* Martin, John
Martin, Donald *SEE* Martin, Catherine MacDonald
Martin, Donald *SEE* Martin, Donald
Martin, Donald *SEE* Martin, Finlay
Martin, Donald *SEE* Martin, Flora MacDonald
Martin, Donald *SEE* Martin, John
Martin, Donald *SEE* Martin, Margaret
Martin, Donald *SEE* Martin, Mary
Martin, Donald *SEE* Martin, Neil
Martin, Donald *SEE* Martin, Ranald
Martin, Donald; Ontario, 1851 ***4537.32*** *p78*
Child: Malcolm
Child: Margaret
Wife: Ann MacKay
Child: Kirsty
Child: Murdo
Child: Norman
Child: Ann
Martin, Donald; Ontario, 1851 ***4537.32*** *p78*
Wife: Mary MacDonald
Child: Donald
Child: Alexander
Child: John
Child: Margaret
Child: Mary
Child: Murdo
Martin, Donald; Port uncertain, 1840-1849 ***4537.35*** *p85*
Wife: Margaret
Child: Margaret
Child: Mary
Child: John
Martin, Donald 69; Ontario, 1871 ***1823.15*** *p154*
Martin, Duncan *SEE* Martin, Flora MacDonald
Martin, Edmund 55; Ontario, 1871 ***1823.22*** *p97*
Martin, Edw; Virginia, 1701-1702 ***6212.30*** *p61*
Martin, Edward; New York, 1839 ***8197.10*** *p141*
Martin, Effie *SEE* Martin, Margaret
Martin, Effie *SEE* Martin, Ann Morrison
Martin, Effie *SEE* Martin, John
Martin, Elis. Catharina; Port uncertain, 1789 ***2856.30*** *p286*
Martin, Elisa 26; Ontario, 1861 ***2896.26*** *p37*
Martin, Elisabeth; Port uncertain, 1749 ***2856.30*** *p286*
Martin, Elisha 60; Ontario, 1871 ***1823.15*** *p154*
Martin, Eliza L. 62; Vermont, 1885 ***5900.10*** *p98*
Martin, Elizabeth *SEE* Martin, John
Martin, Elizabeth *SEE* Martin, Robert
Martin, Elizabeth; Vermont, n.d. ***5900.10*** *p122*
Martin, Elizabeth; Vermont, 1868 ***5900.10*** *p122*
Martin, Elizabeth 67; Vermont, 1889 ***5900.10*** *p585*
Martin, Elizabeth 67; Vermont, 1889 ***5900.10*** *p589*
Martin, Elizabeth, Jr. *SEE* Martin, Robert
Martin, Ella Flynn; Vermont, 1852-1925 ***5900.10*** *p244*
Martin, Ellen; Virginia, 1703-1704 ***6212.30*** *p63*
Martin, Ellen B. Lemaire; Vermont, 1854-1932 ***5900.10*** *p167*
Martin, Ellen Elizabeth 31; Vermont, 1871 ***5900.10*** *p114*
Martin, Eluah 49; Ontario, 1871 ***1823.15*** *p154*
Martin, Ema 2; Ontario, 1861 ***2896.26*** *p37*
Martin, F.; Quebec, 1858 ***9196.15*** *p36*
Martin, Felix 38; Vermont, 1898 ***5900.10*** *p297*
Martin, Finlay; Port uncertain, 1860-1869 ***4537.35*** *p85*
Wife: Catherine MacAskill
Child: Mary Jessie
Child: Donald
Child: Kenneth
Child: Kate
Child: Kirsty
Martin, Flora *SEE* Martin, Flora MacDonald
Martin, Flora *SEE* Martin, John
Martin, Flora *SEE* Martin, Neil

Martin, Flora MacDonald; Port uncertain, 1840-1849 ***4537.37*** *p129*
Child: Mary
Child: Catherine
Child: Duncan
Child: Flora
Child: Donald
Martin, Frances *SEE* Martin, Francis
Martin, Francis; Maryland, 1649 ***2524.55*** *p146*
With wife
Child: Frances
Child: William
Child: Lodowicke
Martin, Francis; Maryland, 1672 ***2524.55*** *p146*
Martin, Francis; Maryland, 1674 ***2524.55*** *p146*
Martin, Francis 81; Ontario, 1871 ***1823.15*** *p154*
Martin, Frank; Pennsylvania, 1867 ***6058.10*** *p60*
Martin, Georg; America, 1753 ***2856.30*** *p287*
With wife & 3 children
Martin, Georg; Port uncertain, 1751 ***2856.30*** *p286*
Martin, Georg Adam; America, 1765 ***2856.30*** *p286*
Martin, George; Maryland, 1653 ***2524.55*** *p146*
Martin, George; Maryland, 1663 ***2524.55*** *p49*
Martin, George; New York, 1807 ***8197.10*** *p45*
Martin, George; New York, 1821 ***8197.10*** *p260*
Martin, George; Pennsylvania, 1815-1845 ***1640.10*** *p150*
Martin, George 50; Ontario, 1871 ***1823.28*** *p61*
Martin, George 60; Ontario, 1871 ***1823.22*** *p97*
Martin, Godfry; Virginia, 1665-1666 ***6212.30*** *p24*
Martin, Grizel; America, 1770 ***1640.13*** *p74*
Martin, Guion; New York, 1825 ***8197.10*** *p63*
Wife: Margaret
Martin, Hannah *SEE* Martin, John
Martin, Hannah *SEE* Martin, Thomas
Martin, Hannah; Maryland, 1681 ***2524.55*** *p146*
Martin, Hans; America, 1735 ***2856.30*** *p286*
Martin, Hans; Port uncertain, 1752 ***2856.30*** *p286*
Martin, Hans Adam; Port uncertain, 1793 ***2856.30*** *p286*
Martin, Hans Stefan; America, 1751 ***2856.30*** *p286*
Martin, Heinrich; New York, 1836 ***8197.10*** *p79*
Martin, Henry; New York, 1840 ***8197.10*** *p182*
Martin, Henry; Pennsylvania, 1777 ***4629.10*** *p8*
Martin, Hugh 72; Vermont, 1881 ***5900.10*** *p589*
Martin, Hugh 79; Vermont, 1881 ***5900.10*** *p585*
Martin, Isaac; Georgia, 1755 ***1640.10*** *p150*
Martin, Isaac 22; Maryland, 1775 ***1220.25*** *p101*
Martin, Isabella; Ontario, 1855 ***4537.32*** *p35*
Martin, Isabella 48; Ontario, 1871 ***1823.28*** *p61*
Martin, J. G. 28; Alaska, 1910 ***9196.1*** *p9*
Martin, J. G. 28; Whitehorse, Yukon, 1910 ***9196.1*** *p9*
Martin, J. J. 2; Ontario, 1861 ***2896.26*** *p11*
Martin, Jacob; New York, 1838 ***8197.10*** *p124*
Martin, Jacob; Pennsylvania, 1777 ***4629.10*** *p11*
Martin, James; Charleston, South Carolina, 1771 ***1640.10*** *p150*
Martin, James; Georgia, 1699 ***1640.13*** *p74*
Martin, James; Maryland, 1660 ***2524.55*** *p146*
Martin, James; New York, 1829 ***8197.10*** *p352*
Martin, James; New York, 1838 ***8197.10*** *p124*
Martin, James; New York, 1840 ***8197.10*** *p265*
Martin, James; Pennsylvania, 1777 ***4629.10*** *p31*
Martin, James; Pennsylvania, 1808 ***6058.10*** *p2*
Martin, James 18; Ontario, 1871 ***1823.28*** *p61*
Martin, James 25; Ontario, 1871 ***1823.28*** *p61*
Martin, James 34; Ontario, 1871 ***1823.28*** *p61*
Martin, James 36; Ontario, 1871 ***1823.15*** *p154*
Martin, James 37; Ontario, 1871 ***1823.28*** *p61*
Martin, James 67; Ontario, 1871 ***1823.15*** *p154*
Martin, James J. 48; Ontario, 1871 ***1823.22*** *p97*
Martin, Jane 18; Ontario, 1861 ***2896.26*** *p34*
Martin, Jane 26; Ontario, 1871 ***1823.15*** *p154*
Martin, Jane 30; Carolina, 1775 ***1220.25*** *p123*
Martin, Jane 60; Ontario, 1861 ***2896.26*** *p34*
Martin, Janet; Ontario, 1851 ***4537.32*** *p61*
Martin, Jean; America, 1771 ***2856.30*** *p287*
With wife & 2 children
Martin, Jennet 50; Ontario, 1871 ***1823.28*** *p61*
Martin, Jennie; Vermont, 1859-1914 ***5900.10*** *p407*
Martin, Jessie *SEE* Martin, Angus
Martin, Jno; Virginia, 1674 ***6212.30*** *p52*
Martin, Joan *SEE* Martin, Catherine MacDonald
Martin, Johann; Port uncertain, 1740 ***2856.30*** *p287*
With wife & children
Martin, Johann; Port uncertain, 1763 ***2856.30*** *p286*
Martin, Johann; Port uncertain, 1779 ***2856.30*** *p286*
Martin, Johann; Port uncertain, 1785 ***2856.30*** *p287*
With wife & children
Martin, Johann Friedric; America, 1749 ***2856.30*** *p287*
Martin, Johann Georg; Port uncertain, 1783 ***2856.30*** *p287*
Martin, Johann Nikolaus; America, 1756 ***2856.30*** *p287*
Wife: A. El.
With son & daughter
Martin, Johann Nikolaus; America, 1766 ***2856.30*** *p287*
Wife: A. El.
With son & daughter
Martin, Johann Peter; America, 1751 ***2856.30*** *p287*
Martin, Johann Peter; America, 1770 ***2856.30*** *p287*
Martin, Johann Peter; Port uncertain, 1772 ***2856.30*** *p287*
Martin, Johann Peter; Port uncertain, 1773 ***2856.30*** *p287*
Martin, Johann Stefan; America, 1761 ***2856.30*** *p287*
Martin, John *SEE* Martin, Angus
Martin, John *SEE* Martin, Ann Morrison
Martin, John *SEE* Martin, Catherine MacDonald
Martin, John *SEE* Martin, Donald
Martin, John *SEE* Martin, John
Martin, John *SEE* Martin, Mary
Martin, John *SEE* Martin, Ranald
Martin, John; Georgia, 1738 ***1640.10*** *p150*
Martin, John; Georgia, 1775-1781 ***4628.40*** *p69*
Martin, John; Maryland, 1670 ***2524.55*** *p146*
Wife: Ann
Child: Mary
Child: Hannah
Child: Elizabeth
Son: John
Martin, John; Maryland, 1681 ***2524.55*** *p146*
Martin, John; Maryland, 1682 ***2524.55*** *p146*
Martin, John; New England, 1674 ***1224.1*** *p38*
Martin, John; New York, 1821 ***8197.10*** *p259*
Martin, John; New York, 1829 ***8197.10*** *p65*
Martin, John; New York, 1838 ***8197.10*** *p124*
Martin, John; New York, 1839 ***8197.10*** *p264*
Martin, John; New York, 1840 ***8197.10*** *p178*
Martin, John; New York, 1840 ***8197.10*** *p182*
Martin, John; North Carolina, 1793 ***1224.2*** *p76*
Martin, John; Ontario, 1851 ***4537.32*** *p78*
Wife: Catherine Morrison
Child: Angus
Child: Norman
Child: John
Child: David
Child: Flora
Child: Donald
Martin, John; Pennsylvania, 1777 ***4629.10*** *p19*
Martin, John; Pennsylvania, 1777 ***4629.10*** *p21*
Martin, John; Vermont, n.d. ***5900.10*** *p122*
Martin, John; Vermont, 1842-1923 ***5900.10*** *p299*
Martin, John; Virginia, 1666 ***6212.30*** *p31*
Martin, John; Port uncertain, 1850-1859 ***4537.37*** *p130*
Wife: Kate MacQuarrie
Child: Angus
Child: Archie
Child: Effie
Child: Catherine
Child: Ann
Child: Dominic
Child: Flora
Martin, John 35; Ontario, 1871 ***1823.15*** *p154*
Martin, John 35; Ontario, 1871 ***1823.28*** *p61*
Martin, John 42; Ontario, 1871 ***1823.15*** *p154*
Martin, John 46; Ontario, 1871 ***1823.15*** *p154*
Martin, John 48; Ontario, 1871 ***1823.28*** *p61*
Martin, John 50; Ontario, 1871 ***1823.22*** *p97*
Martin, John 53; Ontario, 1871 ***1823.15*** *p154*
Martin, John 53; Ontario, 1871 ***1823.22*** *p97*
Martin, John 60; Ontario, 1871 ***1823.28*** *p61*
Martin, John, Sr. 77; Ontario, 1871 ***1823.15*** *p154*
Martin, John A.; Vermont, 1848-1902 ***5900.10*** *p298*
Martin, John B.; New York, 1819-1834 ***8197.10*** *p304*
Martin, John B.; Vermont, 1854-1925 ***5900.10*** *p167*
Martin, Joseph; New York, 1805 ***8197.10*** *p29*
Martin, Joseph; Pennsylvania, 1786 ***4629.10*** *p54*
Martin, Joseph; Virginia, 1667 ***1224.1*** *p38*
Martin, Joseph 16; Maryland, 1774 ***1220.25*** *p73*
Martin, Joseph 24; Maryland, 1775 ***1220.25*** *p104*
Martin, Joseph 30; Maryland, 1774 ***1220.25*** *p64*
Martin, Joseph 56; Ontario, 1861 ***2896.26*** *p34*
Martin, Julia 74; Vermont, 1896 ***5900.10*** *p206*
Martin, Kate *SEE* Martin, Finlay
Martin, Kate MacQuarrie *SEE* Martin, John
Martin, Kenneth *SEE* Martin, Catherine MacDonald
Martin, Kenneth *SEE* Martin, Finlay
Martin, Kenneth *SEE* Martin, Neil
Martin, Kirsty *SEE* Martin, Angus
Martin, Kirsty *SEE* Martin, Donald
Martin, Kirsty *SEE* Martin, Finlay
Martin, Kirsty *SEE* Martin, Neil
Martin, Kirsty; Nova Scotia, 1840-1849 ***4537.37*** *p15*
Martin, Kirsty; Nova Scotia, 1840-1849 ***4537.37*** *p16*
Martin, Lewis 34; Philadelphia, 1774 ***1220.25*** *p43*
Martin, Lodowicke *SEE* Martin, Francis
Martin, Malcolm *SEE* Martin, Donald
Martin, Marg; Virginia, 1672 ***6212.30*** *p50*
Martin, Margaret *SEE* Martin, Donald
Martin, Margaret *SEE* Martin, Guion
Martin, Margaret *SEE* Martin, Neil
Martin, Margaret; Montreal, 1884 ***1640.13*** *p74*
Martin, Margaret; New York, 1831 ***8197.10*** *p356*
Martin, Margaret; Port uncertain, 1840-1849 ***4537.37*** *p130*
Child: Donald
Child: Angus
Child: Marion
Child: Effie
Child: Ann
Martin, Margaret; Port uncertain, 1840-1849 ***4537.37*** *p130*
Martin, Margaret Santos; Vermont, 1844-1896 ***5900.10*** *p378*
Martin, Margaret Wyld; Virginia, 1691 ***1224.1*** *p65*
Martin, Margret Johnson 20; Ontario, 1871 ***1823.15*** *p155*
Martin, Maria; Port uncertain, 1739 ***2856.30*** *p287*
With husband
Martin, Maria Elisabeth; Port uncertain, 1792 ***2856.30*** *p287*
Martin, Marion *SEE* Martin, Catherine MacDonald
Martin, Marion *SEE* Martin, Margaret
Martin, Marion *SEE* Martin, Neil
Martin, Marion; Ontario, 1851 ***4537.32*** *p31*
Martin, Marion MacDonald *SEE* Martin, Ranald
Martin, Martin *SEE* Martin, Mary
Martin, Martin; Vermont, 1792-1890 ***5900.10*** *p101*
Martin, Mary *SEE* Martin, Angus
Martin, Mary *SEE* Martin, Ann Morrison
Martin, Mary *SEE* Martin, Archie
Martin, Mary *SEE* Martin, Catherine MacDonald
Martin, Mary *SEE* Martin, Donald
Martin, Mary *SEE* Martin, Flora MacDonald
Martin, Mary *SEE* Martin, John
Martin, Mary *SEE* Martin, Mary
Martin, Mary *SEE* Martin, Neil
Martin, Mary *SEE* Martin, Robert
Martin, Mary; Maryland, 1674 ***2524.55*** *p146*
Martin, Mary; Nova Scotia, 1840-1849 ***4537.37*** *p19*
Child: Donald
Child: John
Child: Martin
Child: Mary
Child: Angus
Child: Michael
Martin, Mary; Ontario, 1850-1859 ***4537.32*** *p32*
Martin, Mary; Vermont, 1841-1923 ***5900.10*** *p119*
Martin, Mary 53; Ontario, 1871 ***1823.15*** *p155*
Martin, Mary 90; Ontario, 1871 ***1823.15*** *p155*
Martin, Mary A.; Vermont, 1846-1916 ***5900.10*** *p119*
Martin, Mary A. Mackin 52; Vermont, 1887 ***5900.10*** *p234*
Martin, Mary Ann *SEE* Martin, Catherine MacDonald
Martin, Mary Ann McGlynn; Vermont, 1848-1918 ***5900.10*** *p299*
Martin, Mary Green; Vermont, 1885 ***5900.10*** *p298*
Martin, Mary Jessie *SEE* Martin, Finlay
Martin, Mary MacDonald *SEE* Martin, Donald
Martin, Mathew 30; Ontario, 1871 ***1823.28*** *p61*
Martin, Mathias; America, 1751 ***2856.30*** *p18*
With wife
Martin, Matthias; Port uncertain, 1741 ***2856.30*** *p287*
Martin, Michael *SEE* Martin, Mary
Martin, Michael; Boston, 1701 ***1224.2*** *p76*
Martin, Michael; Pennsylvania, 1868 ***6058.10*** *p72*
Martin, Michael 74; Vermont, 1911 ***5900.10*** *p88*
Martin, Michel; New York, 1837 ***8197.10*** *p100*
Martin, Murdo *SEE* Martin, Donald
Martin, Narciso de Francisco; New York, 1833 ***8197.10*** *p358*
Martin, Neil; Nova Scotia, 1840-1849 ***4537.37*** *p20*
Child: Margaret
Child: Donald
Child: Kirsty
Child: Flora
Child: Ranald
Child: Mary
Child: Catherine
Child: Roderick
Wife: Catherine
Martin, Neil; Port uncertain, 1850-1859 ***4537.37*** *p130*
Wife: Mary
Child: Kenneth
Child: Marion
Child: Angus
Child: Mary
Child: Flora
Martin, Norman *SEE* Martin, Donald
Martin, Norman *SEE* Martin, John
Martin, Patrick; New York, 1824 ***8197.10*** *p262*
Martin, Patrick; New York, 1835 ***8197.10*** *p70*
Martin, Patrick; New York, 1837 ***8197.10*** *p99*

Martin, Patrick; Pennsylvania, 1777 ***4629.10*** *p26*
Martin, Patrick 40; Ontario, 1871 ***1823.15*** *p155*
Martin, Patrick 64; Ontario, 1871 ***1823.22*** *p97*
Martin, Peter; New York, 1807 ***8197.10*** *p45*
Martin, Peter; New York, 1838 ***8197.10*** *p123*
Martin, Peter; New York, 1840 ***8197.10*** *p265*
Martin, Peter; Vermont, 1820-1917 ***5900.10*** *p298*
Martin, Peter; Vermont, 1823-1903 ***5900.10*** *p378*
Martin, Peter; Virginia, 1666 ***6212.30*** *p25*
Martin, Peter; Port uncertain, 1773 ***2856.30*** *p287*
Martin, Peter 35; Virginia, 1774 ***1220.25*** *p90*
Martin, Philip; New York, 1837 ***8197.10*** *p318*
Martin, Philip; New York, 1838 ***8197.10*** *p264*
Martin, Polly; Georgia, 1760-1845 ***1640.10*** *p150*
Martin, Rachel; Jamaica, 1844 ***1640.13*** *p74*
Martin, Ranald *SEE* Martin, Neil
Martin, Ranald; Port uncertain, 1850-1859 ***4537.37*** *p130*
Wife: Marion MacDonald
Child: Donald
Child: Alexander
Child: Angus
Child: John
Martin, Rice; Virginia, 1666 ***6212.30*** *p26*
Martin, Richard; Maryland, 1665 ***2524.55*** *p146*
Martin, Richard; New England, 1659 ***1224.1*** *p38*
Martin, Richard; Virginia, 1721 ***1224.2*** *p76*
Martin, Robert; Georgia, 1775 ***1640.10*** *p150*
Martin, Robert; Maryland, 1649 ***2524.55*** *p146*
Martin, Robert; Maryland, 1649 ***2524.55*** *p146*
Wife: Elizabeth
Child: Sarah
Child: Mary
Child: Damaras
Child: Robt., Jr.
Child: Elizabeth, Jr.
Martin, Robert; New Orleans, 1834 ***1224.3*** *p51*
Martin, Robert; New York, 1827 ***8197.10*** *p345*
Martin, Robert; New York, 1834 ***8197.10*** *p71*
Martin, Robert; Ohio, 1894 ***1640.13*** *p74*
Martin, Robert 21; Maryland, 1774 ***1220.25*** *p69*
Martin, Robert 23; Antigua (Antego), 1774 ***1220.25*** *p86*
Martin, Robert 26; Georgia, 1775 ***1220.25*** *p125*
Martin, Robert 46; Ontario, 1871 ***1823.28*** *p61*
Martin, Robert Anthony; Louisiana, 1857 ***1224.3*** *p51*
Martin, Robt., Jr. *SEE* Martin, Robert
Martin, Roderick *SEE* Martin, Angus
Martin, Roderick *SEE* Martin, Neil
Martin, Rose Clark; Vermont, 1854-1928 ***5900.10*** *p564*
Martin, S. N. 4; Ontario, 1861 ***2896.26*** *p11*
Martin, Samuel; Hempstead, New York, 1806 ***1224.3*** *p51*
Martin, Samuel; New York, 1824-1828 ***8197.10*** *p309*
Martin, Samuel E.; New York, 1807 ***8197.10*** *p45*
Martin, Sarah *SEE* Martin, Robert
Martin, Sarah 16; Ontario, 1861 ***2896.26*** *p34*
Martin, Stephen 72; Ontario, 1871 ***1823.15*** *p155*
Martin, Susan; Virginia, 1674 ***6212.30*** *p52*
Martin, Theodore; Portland, Maine, 1858 ***9196.15*** *p30*
Martin, Thomas; Maryland, 1682 ***2524.55*** *p146*
Wife: Hannah
Son: William
Martin, Thomas; New York, 1830 ***8197.10*** *p361*
Martin, Thomas; New York, 1836-1838 ***8197.10*** *p123*
Martin, Thomas; New York, 1838 ***8197.10*** *p124*
Martin, Thomas 23; Philadelphia, 1775 ***1220.25*** *p107*
Martin, Thomas 55; Ontario, 1871 ***1823.15*** *p155*
Martin, Thomas 65; Ontario, 1871 ***1823.28*** *p61*
Martin, Thomas B. 35; Ontario, 1871 ***1823.15*** *p155*
Martin, Thomas C.; Pennsylvania, 1868 ***6058.10*** *p65*
Martin, Valentin; America, 1758 ***2856.30*** *p287*
With wife & daughter
Martin, Valentin; Port uncertain, 1765 ***2856.30*** *p287*
Martin, W. 27; Alaska, 1917 ***9196.1*** *p48*
Martin, W. 27; Whitehorse, Yukon, 1917 ***9196.1*** *p48*
Martin, W. A. 48; British Columbia, 1909 ***9196.1*** *p26*
Martin, W. A. 48; Washington, 1909 ***9196.1*** *p26*
Martin, William *SEE* Martin, Francis
Martin, William *SEE* Martin, Thomas
Martin, William; Baltimore, 1800 ***1224.3*** *p51*
Martin, William; Maryland, 1681 ***2524.55*** *p146*
Martin, William; New York, 1836-1838 ***8197.10*** *p123*
Martin, William; New York, 1839 ***8197.10*** *p264*
Martin, William; Pennsylvania, 1777 ***4629.10*** *p8*
Martin, William; Vermont, 1839-1924 ***5900.10*** *p119*
Martin, William 21; Maryland, 1774 ***1220.25*** *p73*
Martin, William 27; Ontario, 1871 ***1823.22*** *p97*
Martin, William 30; Ontario, 1871 ***1823.28*** *p61*
Martin, William 35; Ontario, 1871 ***1823.15*** *p155*
Martin, William 36; Maryland, 1774 ***1220.25*** *p57*
Martin, William 41; Ontario, 1871 ***1823.15*** *p155*
Martin, William 48; Ontario, 1871 ***1823.15*** *p155*
Martin, William 50; Ontario, 1871 ***1823.15*** *p155*
Martin, William 54; Ontario, 1871 ***1823.15*** *p155*
Martin, William 69; Ontario, 1871 ***1823.15*** *p155*
Martin, William 72; Ontario, 1871 ***1823.15*** *p155*
Martin, William A.; Vermont, 1842-1894 ***5900.10*** *p244*
Martin, William E.; Vermont, 1860-1960 ***5900.10*** *p122*
Martin, Wm 35; Ontario, 1871 ***1823.28*** *p61*
Martindale, Jonathan; Long Island, 1782 ***1224.2*** *p76*
Martine, Ann; Maryland, 1671 ***2524.55*** *p146*
Martineau, Matthew; Philadelphia, 1799 ***1224.2*** *p77*
Martineaux, Martha *SEE* Martineaux, Peter
Martineaux, Matthew 34; Philadelphia, 1789 ***4629.10*** *p57*
Martineaux, Peter; Philadelphia, 1789 ***4629.10*** *p57*
Wife: Martha
Martini, . . .; America, 1790 ***2856.30*** *p287*
Martini, Johann Peter; America, 1770 ***2856.30*** *p287*
Martini, Johann Peter; America, 1773 ***2856.30*** *p287*
Martinin, Maria; Port uncertain, 1739 ***2856.30*** *p287*
With husband
Martinin, Maria Elisabeth; Port uncertain, 1792 ***2856.30*** *p287*
Martins, Ferdinand 24; Ontario, 1871 ***1823.28*** *p61*
Marton, Alexander 42; Ontario, 1871 ***1823.15*** *p155*
Marton, John; Pennsylvania, 1778 ***4629.10*** *p45*
Martskin, Bronislow; Maryland, 1910 ***3259.35*** *p38*
Martyn, Mrs.; Maryland, 1659 ***2524.55*** *p146*
Martyn, Henry; Boston, 1849 ***1224.3*** *p51*
Martyn, Jo.; Maryland, 1681 ***2524.55*** *p146*
Martyn, Nicholas; Virginia, 1656 ***1224.1*** *p38*
Martyn, Richard; Portsmouth, New Hampshire, 1737 ***1224.2*** *p76*
Martyn, Robert; Maryland, 1659 ***2524.55*** *p146*
With wife & 5 children
Martyn, Samuel; Charles Town, South Carolina, 1734 ***1224.2*** *p76*
Martyn, Thomas 41; Ontario, 1871 ***1823.28*** *p61*
Maruv, John; Maryland, 1910 ***3259.35*** *p38*
Marvin, Amos 12; Ontario, 1861 ***2896.25*** *p72*
Marvin, Amy 34; Ontario, 1861 ***2896.25*** *p72*
Marvin, Burnet 69; Ontario, 1861 ***2896.25*** *p72*
Marvin, Daniel 73; Ontario, 1861 ***2896.25*** *p72*
Marvin, Jesse 6; Ontario, 1861 ***2896.25*** *p72*
Marvin, John 1; Ontario, 1861 ***2896.25*** *p72*
Marvin, Ruamy 10; Ontario, 1861 ***2896.25*** *p72*
Marvin, Ruanny 31; Ontario, 1861 ***2896.25*** *p72*
Marvin, Steven 8; Ontario, 1861 ***2896.25*** *p72*
Marvine, George; Pennsylvania, 1786 ***4629.10*** *p50*
Marvuott, William 28; Ontario, 1871 ***1823.15*** *p155*
Marwich, John 24; Alaska, 1908 ***9196.1*** *p37*
Marwick, John 39; Ontario, 1871 ***1823.15*** *p155*
Marwood, John 46; Ontario, 1871 ***1823.15*** *p155*
Marwood, Matt 67; Ontario, 1871 ***1823.15*** *p155*
Marx, Anna Maria; Port uncertain, 1746 ***2856.30*** *p288*
Marx, Catharina; Port uncertain, 1779 ***2856.30*** *p288*
Marx, Catharina; Port uncertain, 1791 ***2856.30*** *p287*
Marx, Georg Thomas; America, 1754 ***2856.30*** *p287*
Marx, Georg Thomas; Port uncertain, 1754 ***2856.30*** *p287*
Marx, Jacob; Port uncertain, 1781 ***2856.30*** *p287*
Marx, Maria Elisabeth; Port uncertain, 1767 ***2856.30*** *p287*
Marx, Maria Elisabth; Port uncertain, 1786 ***2856.30*** *p287*
Marx, Michael; Port uncertain, 1762 ***2856.30*** *p287*
Marx, Philipp; Port uncertain, 1749 ***2856.30*** *p288*
Marx, Wilhelm; Port uncertain, 1740 ***2856.30*** *p288*
With wife & 2 children
Marxer, Marianna; Port uncertain, 1759 ***2856.30*** *p288*
Marxin, Anna Maria; Port uncertain, 1746 ***2856.30*** *p288*
Marxin, Catharina; Port uncertain, 1779 ***2856.30*** *p288*
Mary, Grate; Virginia, 1671 ***6212.30*** *p43*
Marylander, John; Maryland, 1664 ***2524.55*** *p142*
Marzceki, Francis; Maryland, 1910 ***3259.35*** *p38*
Marzulis, Joseph; Maryland, 1910 ***3259.35*** *p38*
Mascall, Joane; Maryland, 1677 ***2524.55*** *p146*
Mascall, Richard; Maryland, 1671 ***2524.55*** *p146*
Mascall, Stephen; Maryland, 1668 ***2524.55*** *p146*
Masenhunmet, Adam 45; Ontario, 1871 ***1823.28*** *p61*
Mash, Thomas; New York, 1822 ***8197.10*** *p261*
Mashinska, Frances; Maryland, 1910 ***3259.35*** *p38*
Mashman, Samuel 36; Maryland, 1774 ***1220.25*** *p84*
Masholder, John; America, 1767 ***2856.30*** *p288*
Masicke, Judith; Maryland, 1659 ***2524.55*** *p146*
Maskal, Henry 19; Carolina, 1774 ***1220.25*** *p38*
Maskill, Teodor; Maryland, 1910 ***3259.35*** *p39*
Maskimming, John 27; Ontario, 1871 ***1823.28*** *p61*
Maskimming, Thomas 54; Ontario, 1871 ***1823.28*** *p61*
Maskll, Joseph; Maryland, 1910 ***3259.35*** *p39*
Maslin, Henry; Virginia, 1665-1666 ***6212.30*** *p25*
Maslowski, Wojciech; Maryland, 1910 ***3259.35*** *p39*
Masohlder, Jacob; America, 1764 ***2856.30*** *p288*
Mason, Miss; Quebec, 1857 ***9196.15*** *p23*
Mason, Miss; Quebec, 1857 ***9196.15*** *p26*
Mason, Mr.; Quebec, 1857 ***9196.15*** *p23*
Mason, Mrs.; Quebec, 1857 ***9196.15*** *p23*
Mason, Abraham; Pennsylvania, 1777 ***4629.10*** *p15*
Mason, Abraham 43; Nova Scotia, 1774 ***1220.25*** *p14*
Mason, Alex; St. Vincent, 1820 ***1640.13*** *p74*
Mason, Alexander 51; Ontario, 1871 ***1823.22*** *p97*
Mason, Anne Pecke; New England, 1658 ***1224.1*** *p44*
Mason, Arthur; New England, 1718 ***1224.2*** *p77*
Mason, Benj'n; Pennsylvania, 1785 ***4629.10*** *p44*
Mason, Caleb; New York, 1851 ***1224.3*** *p51*
Mason, Charles 30; Ontario, 1871 ***1823.15*** *p155*
Mason, Charles 37; Ontario, 1871 ***1823.15*** *p155*
Mason, Charles 60; Ontario, 1871 ***1823.15*** *p155*
Mason, Charlet 37; Ontario, 1861 ***2896.25*** *p39*
Mason, Daniel; New York, 1795 ***8197.10*** *p7*
Mason, Daniel 37; Ontario, 1871 ***1823.15*** *p155*
Mason, Edward; Maryland, 1682 ***2524.55*** *p147*
Mason, Edward 19; Ontario, 1861 ***2896.25*** *p38*
Mason, Edward 62; Ontario, 1871 ***1823.15*** *p155*
Mason, Eliza 12; Ontario, 1861 ***2896.25*** *p39*
Mason, Eliza 69; Ontario, 1871 ***1823.22*** *p97*
Mason, Francis 33; Nova Scotia, 1774 ***1220.25*** *p136*
Mason, George; Portland, Maine, 1857 ***9196.15*** *p12*
Mason, George; Virginia, 1667-1668 ***6212.30*** *p38*
Mason, Henry 51; Ontario, 1871 ***1823.22*** *p97*
Mason, Hester; Watertown, Massachusetts, 1702 ***1224.2*** *p77*
Mason, Hugh; Watertown, Massachusetts, 1702 ***1224.2*** *p77*
Mason, James; New York, 1797 ***8197.10*** *p8*
Mason, James; Pennsylvania, 1811 ***6058.10*** *p4*
Mason, James 37; Ontario, 1871 ***1823.22*** *p97*
Mason, James 38; Ontario, 1871 ***1823.22*** *p97*
Mason, Jane; New England, 1658 ***1224.1*** *p51*
Mason, Jane 25; Maryland, 1775 ***1220.25*** *p103*
Mason, Janet; New York, 1850 ***1640.13*** *p74*
Mason, Jno; Virginia, 1665-1666 ***6212.30*** *p21*
Mason, John; Georgia, 1698 ***1640.13*** *p74*
Mason, John; Maryland, 1659-1660 ***2524.55*** *p147*
Mason, John; Pennsylvania, 1777 ***4629.10*** *p8*
Mason, John 21; Philadelphia, 1774 ***1220.25*** *p80*
Mason, John 33; Ontario, 1871 ***1823.28*** *p61*
Mason, John 40; Ontario, 1871 ***1823.15*** *p155*
Mason, John 44; Ontario, 1871 ***1823.22*** *p97*
Mason, John 75; Ontario, 1871 ***1823.15*** *p155*
Mason, Joseph 67; Ontario, 1871 ***1823.15*** *p155*
Mason, Julia; Quebec, 1858 ***9196.15*** *p34*
Mason, Kathrine; Maryland, 1662 ***2524.55*** *p147*
Mason, Lemuel; Virginia, 1680 ***1224.1*** *p13*
Mason, Margery; Maryland, 1682 ***2524.55*** *p147*
Mason, Marmaduke 22; Virginia, 1774 ***1220.25*** *p91*
Mason, Martha 58; Ontario, 1871 ***1823.22*** *p97*
Mason, Mary A. McAllister 39; Vermont, 1878 ***5900.10*** *p281*
Mason, Michael; Maryland, 1659 ***2524.55*** *p147*
Mason, Peter; Virginia, 1751 ***1224.2*** *p77*
Mason, Peter 30; Ontario, 1871 ***1823.28*** *p61*
Mason, Rachaell; Maryland, 1662 ***2524.55*** *p147*
Mason, Rachell; Maryland, 1678 ***2524.55*** *p154*
Mason, Richard; Pennsylvania, 1777 ***4629.10*** *p20*
Mason, Richard 15; Maryland, 1775 ***1220.25*** *p102*
Mason, Robert; Maryland, 1663 ***2524.55*** *p147*
Mason, Robert; Maryland, 1664 ***2524.55*** *p147*
Mason, Robert; Virginia, 1670 ***6212.30*** *p42*
Mason, Robert 17; Virginia, 1775 ***1220.25*** *p95*
Mason, Rose 23; Maryland, 1775 ***1220.25*** *p105*
Mason, Samuel; New York, 1840 ***8197.10*** *p384*
Mason, Samuel 39; Ontario, 1871 ***1823.28*** *p61*
Mason, Samuel 61; Ontario, 1871 ***1823.28*** *p61*
Mason, Thomas; Maryland, 1667 ***2524.55*** *p114*
Mason, Thomas; Maryland, 1732 ***1224.2*** *p77*
Mason, Thomas; Virginia, 1675 ***1224.1*** *p39*
Mason, Thomas 40; Ontario, 1871 ***1823.15*** *p155*
Mason, William; Maryland, 1682 ***2524.55*** *p147*
Mason, William; New York, 1849 ***1640.13*** *p74*
Mason, William; Pennsylvania, 1777 ***4629.10*** *p8*
Mason, William 37; Ontario, 1871 ***1823.22*** *p97*
Mason, William 59; Ontario, 1871 ***1823.15*** *p155*
Mason, William 65; Ontario, 1871 ***1823.28*** *p61*
Mason, William S. 5; Ontario, 1861 ***2896.25*** *p39*
Masoner, Jacob; Pennsylvania, 1777 ***4629.10*** *p8*
Masowa, Alexander; Maryland, 1910 ***3259.35*** *p39*
Maspoole, James; New York, 1834 ***8197.10*** *p73*
Mass, Christian 66; Ontario, 1871 ***1823.15*** *p155*
Mass, Georg; America, 1749 ***2856.30*** *p288*
Mass, Martin; Port uncertain, 1754 ***2856.30*** *p288*
Mass, Michael; Port uncertain, 1697 ***2856.30*** *p288*
Masseau, Alexander; New York, 1807 ***8197.10*** *p44*
Masser, Sofia; Port uncertain, 1778 ***2856.30*** *p288*
Masserback, Felix; Virginia, 1775 ***1220.25*** *p122*
Masserin, Sofia; Port uncertain, 1778 ***2856.30*** *p288*
Massey, Catherine 9; Ontario, 1861 ***2896.25*** *p21*
Massey, Charles; Pennsylvania, 1777 ***4629.10*** *p11*
Massey, George 37; Ontario, 1871 ***1823.28*** *p61*
Massey, Henry; Maryland, 1673 ***2524.55*** *p147*
Massey, Henry 49; Ontario, 1861 ***2896.25*** *p21*

Massey, Margaret 18; Ontario, 1861 *2896.25 p1*
Massey, Mary E. 4; Ontario, 1861 *2896.25 p21*
Massey, Ralph; Virginia, 1664-1665 *6212.30 p16*
Massey, Samuel; Pennsylvania, 1777 *4629.10 p9*
Massey, William; Detroit, 1839 *6058.10 p35*
Massey, William 2; Ontario, 1861 *2896.25 p21*
Massholder, Jakob; America, 1767 *2856.30 p288*
Massias, Abraham; New York, 1795 *8197.10 p7*
Massie, Charles 44; Ontario, 1871 *1823.22 p97*
Massie, John 37; Ontario, 1871 *1823.22 p98*
Massie, John 50; Ontario, 1871 *1823.22 p98*
Massie, T.; Quebec, 1856 *9196.15 p6*
Massing, Niklas; Port uncertain, 1792 *2856.30 p288*
With wife & 10 children
Massing, Niklas; Port uncertain, 1793 *2856.30 p288*
With wife & 6 children
Massingberd, . . .; Quebec, 1857 *9196.15 p17*
Massmann, Anna Eva; Port uncertain, 1749 *2856.30 p250*
Massmann, Anna Eva; Port uncertain, 1749 *2856.30 p288*
With husband & 2 children
Massmann, Kuhn; Port uncertain, 1749 *2856.30 p288*
Massner, Paul 49; Ontario, 1871 *1823.15 p155*
Masson, Mr.; Quebec, 1856 *9196.15 p11*
Masson, Mr.; Quebec, 1857 *9196.15 p27*
Masson, Rev.; Quebec, 1856 *9196.15 p11*
Masson, Bridget 26; Ontario, 1871 *1823.28 p61*
Masson, J. B. Louis; New York, New York, 1835 *6058.10 p20*
Masson, James 65; Ontario, 1871 *1823.22 p98*
Masson, Thomas 55; Ontario, 1871 *1823.22 p98*
Masson, William 72; Ontario, 1871 *1823.22 p98*
Masstin, Robert 28; Maryland, 1774 *1220.25 p62*
Mast, Dorothy; Maryland, 1660 *2524.55 p147*
Master, Edw; Virginia, 1665-1666 *6212.30 p21*
Master, Edw; Virginia, 1665-1666 *6212.30 p22*
Master, Edward; Virginia, 1664 *6212.30 p13*
Master, Robert; Savannah, Georgia, 1798 *1224.2 p77*
Masterer, Abraham; Maryland, 1673 *2524.55 p147*
Masters, Mrs.; Quebec, 1857 *9196.15 p18*
Masters, Ann 40; Ontario, 1861 *2896.25 p52*
Masters, Chauncey 28; Ontario, 1861 *2896.25 p52*
Masters, E. 18; Ontario, 1861 *2896.28 p15*
Masters, George 21; Ontario, 1861 *2896.25 p52*
Masters, J. C. 6; Ontario, 1861 *2896.25 p51*
Masters, Jacob 24; Ontario, 1861 *2896.25 p52*
Masters, James W. 2; Ontario, 1861 *2896.25 p52*
Masters, Jane 6; Ontario, 1861 *2896.25 p52*
Masters, John; Maryland, 1669 *2524.55 p147*
Masters, Rich; Virginia, 1665-1666 *6212.30 p21*
Masters, Richard; Virginia, 1664 *6212.30 p13*
Masters, Robt; Virginia, 1663 *6212.30 p4*
Masters, Storey J. C. 8; Ontario, 1861 *2896.25 p51*
Masters, Susan 25; Ontario, 1861 *2896.25 p68*
Masters, Susannah 71; Ontario, 1871 *1823.22 p98*
Masters, Thomas; Maryland, 1657 *2524.55 p147*
Masters, William; Pennsylvania, 1778 *4629.10 p34*
Masters, William 42; Ontario, 1861 *2896.25 p52*
Masterson, James 36; Maryland, 1774 *1220.25 p84*
Masterson, Michael; Philadelphia, 1825 *8197.10 p369*
Masterson, Patrick; New York, 1836 *8197.10 p317*
Masterson, Patrick 58; Ontario, 1871 *1823.22 p98*
Masterson, Thomas; Georgia, 1740 *1640.10 p151*
Masterton, A. K.; Portland, Maine, 1858 *9196.15 p30*
Masterton, Adam; New York, 1794 *8197.10 p2*
Masterton, Alex; Georgia, 1698 *1640.13 p74*
Masterton, Alexander; New York, 1829 *8197.10 p65*
Masterton, David; Baltimore, 1833 *1640.13 p74*
Masterton, John; New York, 1840 *8197.10 p383*
Mastin, Alonzo 1; Ontario, 1861 *2896.27 p27*
Mastin, Arnold 9; Ontario, 1861 *2896.27 p28*
Mastin, Bernard 57; Ontario, 1861 *2896.28 p41*
Mastin, Bethena 1; Ontario, 1861 *2896.27 p34*
Mastin, Betsy E. 30; Ontario, 1861 *2896.27 p25*
Mastin, Catherine 14; Ontario, 1861 *2896.27 p35*
Mastin, Catherine 30; Ontario, 1861 *2896.25 p10*
Mastin, Catherine 31; Ontario, 1861 *2896.27 p34*
Mastin, Dexter 22; Ontario, 1861 *2896.27 p26*
Mastin, E. C. 1; Ontario, 1861 *2896.25 p10*
Mastin, Elicta 53; Ontario, 1861 *2896.25 p11*
Mastin, Elisa 25; Ontario, 1861 *2896.27 p25*
Mastin, Elisa 39; Ontario, 1861 *2896.27 p25*
Mastin, Eliza 26; Ontario, 1861 *2896.27 p26*
Mastin, Elizabeth 34; Ontario, 1861 *2896.27 p26*
Mastin, Elizabeth 53; Ontario, 1861 *2896.27 p26*
Mastin, Elizabeth Jane 9; Ontario, 1861 *2896.27 p34*
Mastin, Enrietta 18; Ontario, 1861 *2896.27 p26*
Mastin, Fidelia 4; Ontario, 1861 *2896.27 p25*
Mastin, Florance C. 1; Ontario, 1861 *2896.27 p26*
Mastin, G. 9; Ontario, 1861 *2896.27 p9*
Mastin, George F. 10; Ontario, 1861 *2896.27 p25*
Mastin, Gilbert E. 12; Ontario, 1861 *2896.27 p35*
Mastin, Guy 20; Ontario, 1861 *2896.27 p35*
Mastin, H. 10; Ontario, 1861 *2896.28 p2*
Mastin, H. 30; Ontario, 1861 *2896.28 p2*
Mastin, Harriet 25; Ontario, 1861 *2896.27 p34*
Mastin, Helen 48; Ontario, 1861 *2896.27 p35*
Mastin, Isaiah 2; Ontario, 1861 *2896.27 p28*
Mastin, Jane 15; Ontario, 1861 *2896.27 p34*
Mastin, John 4; Ontario, 1861 *2896.27 p28*
Mastin, John, Sr. 67; Ontario, 1861 *2896.27 p26*
Mastin, John N. 8; Ontario, 1861 *2896.27 p26*
Mastin, Johnathan 65; Ontario, 1861 *2896.27 p46*
Mastin, L. 18; Ontario, 1861 *2896.28 p54*
Mastin, Lydia 19; Ontario, 1861 *2896.27 p46*
Mastin, M. 34; Ontario, 1861 *2896.27 p9*
Mastin, Margaret A. 1; Ontario, 1861 *2896.25 p10*
Mastin, Marshall 4; Ontario, 1861 *2896.27 p26*
Mastin, Martha Ann 5; Ontario, 1861 *2896.27 p28*
Mastin, Mary 33; Ontario, 1861 *2896.27 p28*
Mastin, Mary E. 8; Ontario, 1861 *2896.25 p10*
Mastin, Mary E. 22; Ontario, 1861 *2896.27 p46*
Mastin, Mary J. 23; Ontario, 1861 *2896.25 p10*
Mastin, Mary Susan 3; Ontario, 1861 *2896.27 p27*
Mastin, Matilda 24; Ontario, 1861 *2896.27 p28*
Mastin, Matury J. 2; Ontario, 1861 *2896.27 p26*
Mastin, Minerva 14; Ontario, 1861 *2896.27 p25*
Mastin, Ophelia 8; Ontario, 1861 *2896.27 p28*
Mastin, Phebe Jane 27; Ontario, 1861 *2896.27 p27*
Mastin, Rachel E. 8; Ontario, 1861 *2896.27 p25*
Mastin, Reuben B. 14; Ontario, 1861 *2896.27 p46*
Mastin, S. 3; Ontario, 1861 *2896.27 p9*
Mastin, Samuel 3; Ontario, 1861 *2896.27 p34*
Mastin, Sarah Ann 20; Ontario, 1861 *2896.27 p26*
Mastin, Sarah E. 5; Ontario, 1861 *2896.25 p10*
Mastin, Sarah M. 6; Ontario, 1861 *2896.27 p27*
Mastin, Stephen 26; Ontario, 1861 *2896.28 p54*
Mastin, Stephen B. 27; Ontario, 1861 *2896.27 p46*
Mastin, Susan 33; Ontario, 1861 *2896.27 p46*
Mastin, Theodore S. 4; Ontario, 1861 *2896.27 p28*
Mastin, Titus 5; Ontario, 1861 *2896.27 p34*
Mastin, Ustatia 10; Ontario, 1861 *2896.27 p26*
Mastin, William 20; Ontario, 1861 *2896.25 p11*
Mastin, William A. 5; Ontario, 1861 *2896.27 p26*
Mastin, William H. 3; Ontario, 1861 *2896.25 p10*
Mastin, William P. 7; Ontario, 1861 *2896.27 p28*
Maston, Alexander 40; Ontario, 1871 *1823.15 p155*
Maston, J. 75; Ontario, 1861 *2896.26 p14*
Maston, John; New York, 1802 *8197.10 p22*
Maston, S. 40; Ontario, 1861 *2896.26 p14*
Maston, W. 12; Ontario, 1861 *2896.26 p14*
Maston, William 30; Ontario, 1871 *1823.15 p155*
Mastre, Rev.; Quebec, 1856 *9196.15 p9*
Mastris, Sarah J. 17; Ontario, 1861 *2896.28 p42*
Mastris, Thomas; Maryland, 1657 *2524.55 p147*
Masurer, Philip; New York, 1702 *1224.2 p77*
Matanoski, Anton; Maryland, 1910 *3259.35 p39*
Matassek, Julian; Maryland, 1910 *3259.35 p39*
Matchet, Isaac 37; Ontario, 1871 *1823.28 p61*
Matchiiwita, Onesime 52; Ontario, 1871 *1823.28 p61*
Matcovich, Antonio; New York, 1839 *8197.10 p264*
Matecki, John; Maryland, 1910 *3259.35 p39*
Matek, Frank; Maryland, 1910 *3259.35 p39*
Mater, Charles 26; Virginia, 1774 *1220.25 p55*
Materacki, Joseph; Maryland, 1910 *3259.35 p39*
Matern, Johann Georg; America, 1751 *2856.30 p288*
Matern, Michael; Canada, 1751 *2856.30 p288*
Matershaw, Jeffrey; Maryland, 1672 *2524.55 p147*
Mateuszek, Felex; Maryland, 1910 *3259.35 p39*
Matfeld, Gustavus A.; New York, 1837 *8197.10 p318*
Matha, Nicholas; Baltimore, 1846 *6058.10 p26*
Matha, Nicholas; Baltimore, 1848 *6058.10 p46*
Mathason, Alexander 27; Philadelphia, 1774 *1220.25 p66*
Matheis, Andreas; America, 1764 *2856.30 p288*
Matheis, Franz Xaver; Port uncertain, 1789 *2856.30 p289*
Matheiss, Magdalena; Port uncertain, 1753 *2856.30 p289*
Mather, Arthur Gilmour; Nashville, Tennessee, 1896 *1640.13 p74*
Mather, Edward Edmund; Philadelphia, 1899 *1640.13 p74*
Mather, Eliza 25; Philadelphia, 1774 *1220.25 p63*
Mather, Gilbert; Virginia, 1668 *1224.1 p39*
Mather, Hannah E. McGowan 45; Vermont, 1873 *5900.10 p281*
Mather, R. H.; Quebec, 1856 *9196.15 p6*
Mather, Ralph; New York, 1792 *4629.10 p82*
Mather, Richard; Pittsburgh, 1763 *1224.2 p77*
Mather, Samuel; Massachusetts, 1816 *1224.3 p51*
Mather, Sarah; Virginia, 1671-1672 *6212.30 p46*
Mather, Thomas; Died enroute, 1687 *1224.1 p39*
Mather, Thomas 33; Ontario, 1871 *1823.22 p98*
Mathers, Mr.; Quebec, 1857 *9196.15 p21*
Mathers, Mrs.; Quebec, 1857 *9196.15 p21*
Mathers, Henry 54; Ontario, 1871 *1823.15 p155*
Mathers, James; Pennsylvania, 1777 *4629.10 p12*
Mathers, John; Maryland, 1681 *2524.55 p147*
Mathers, Joseph; New York, New York, 1843 *1224.3 p51*
Mathershaw, Joseph 21; Virginia, 1774 *1220.25 p89*
Mathes, Adolph 36; Ontario, 1871 *1823.15 p155*
Mathes, Anna Margarete; Port uncertain, 1751 *2856.30 p289*
Mathes, Anselm 70; Ontario, 1871 *1823.15 p155*
Mathes, Christof; Port uncertain, 1764 *2856.30 p289*
Mathes, Eva; Port uncertain, 1764 *2856.30 p289*
Mathes, Johann Henrich; Port uncertain, 1728 *2856.30 p289*
Mathes, Johann Michael; America, 1738 *2856.30 p289*
Mathes, Johann Michael; Port uncertain, 1737 *2856.30 p289*
Mathes, Maria Catharina; Port uncertain, 1764 *2856.30 p289*
Mathes, Maria Elisabeth; Port uncertain, 1764 *2856.30 p289*
Mathes, Nicol; Port uncertain, 1781 *2856.30 p289*
Mathes, William 31; Ontario, 1871 *1823.15 p155*
Matheson, Alexander *SEE* Matheson, Donald
Matheson, Angus *SEE* Matheson, Donald
Matheson, Ann *SEE* Matheson, Donald
Matheson, Ann *SEE* Matheson, John
Matheson, Ann *SEE* Matheson, Murdo
Matheson, Ann *SEE* Matheson, Neil
Matheson, Ann *SEE* Matheson, William
Matheson, Ann; Ontario, 1851 *4537.32 p28*
Matheson, Ann; Ontario, 1851 *4537.32 p45*
Matheson, Ann; Ontario, 1855 *4537.32 p93*
Matheson, Ann; Ontario, 1863 *4537.32 p66*
Matheson, Ann MacLean *SEE* Matheson, John
Matheson, Ann MacLean *SEE* Matheson, Malcolm
Matheson, Ann Morrison *SEE* Matheson, Donald
Matheson, Annabella *SEE* Matheson, Murdo
Matheson, Archibald 40; Ontario, 1871 *1823.15 p155*
Matheson, Catherine *SEE* Matheson, Donald
Matheson, Catherine *SEE* Matheson, John
Matheson, Catherine *SEE* Matheson, Neil
Matheson, Catherine *SEE* Matheson, William
Matheson, Catherine MacIver *SEE* Matheson, Donald
Matheson, Donald *SEE* Matheson, John
Matheson, Donald *SEE* Matheson, Malcolm
Matheson, Donald *SEE* Matheson, Murdo
Matheson, Donald *SEE* Matheson, Neil
Matheson, Donald; Ontario, 1851 *4537.32 p79*
Wife: Ann Morrison
Child: Catherine
Matheson, Donald; Ontario, 1855 *4537.32 p79*
Wife: Catherine MacIver
Child: Ann
Child: Kirsty
Child: Angus
Child: Alexander
Matheson, Donald 52; Ontario, 1871 *1823.15 p155*
Matheson, Dorothy *SEE* Matheson, Neil
Matheson, Dougal 55; Ontario, 1871 *1823.15 p156*
Matheson, Duncan *SEE* Matheson, Neil
Matheson, Duncan; Augusta, Georgia, 1806-1812 *1640.10 p151*
Matheson, Flora *SEE* Matheson, Murdo
Matheson, Hugh *SEE* Matheson, William
Matheson, Hugh; Port uncertain, 1840-1849 *4537.37 p130*
Wife: Janet MacLean
Matheson, James 53; Ontario, 1871 *1823.22 p98*
Matheson, Janet MacLean *SEE* Matheson, Hugh
Matheson, John *SEE* Matheson, John
Matheson, John *SEE* Matheson, Murdo
Matheson, John *SEE* Matheson, Neil
Matheson, John; Ontario, 1855 *4537.32 p80*
Wife: Margaret MacLeod
Child: Donald
Child: John
Child: Norman
Child: Kenneth
Child: Murdo
Child: Mary
Child: Margaret
Child: Ann
Matheson, John; Ontario, 1863 *4537.32 p79*
Wife: Ann MacLean
Child: John
Child: Neil
Child: Margaret
Child: Murdo
Child: Malcolm
Child: Donald
Matheson, John; Port uncertain, 1850-1859 *4537.37 p130*
Wife: Mary MacLellan
Child: Kirsty

Mattingly, Thomas; Maryland, 1665 ***2524.55*** *p147*
Wife: Elizabeth
Child: Thomas
Child: Elizabeth
Child: Casar
Child: Judeth
Mattinly, Casar *SEE* Mattinly, Thomas
Mattinly, Elizabeth *SEE* Mattinly, Thomas
Mattinly, Judeth *SEE* Mattinly, Thomas
Mattinly, Thomas *SEE* Mattinly, Thomas
Mattinly, Thomas; Maryland, 1665 ***2524.55*** *p147*
Wife: Elizabeth
Child: Elizabeth
Child: Judeth
Child: Casar
Child: Thomas
Mattio, G. L. 34; Alaska, 1915 ***9196.1*** *p42*
Mattis, Cornelia 85; Ontario, 1861 ***2896.27*** *p69*
Mattis, Isaac 85; Ontario, 1861 ***2896.27*** *p69*
Mattison, Eva; Vermont, 1855-1909 ***5900.10*** *p77*
Mattison, Mary; Boston, 1750 ***1224.2*** *p77*
Mattmann, Philibert; Port uncertain, 1740 ***2856.30*** *p290*
Mattmuller, Josef; Port uncertain, 1781 ***2856.30*** *p290*
Mattox, Ann; Maryland, 1669 ***2524.55*** *p148*
Mattox, Wm; Virginia, 1674-1675 ***6212.30*** *p53*
Matts, Jonas; Virginia, 1674 ***6212.30*** *p52*
Matts, Robt; Virginia, 1667-1668 ***6212.30*** *p38*
Mattson, Andrew; Maryland, 1673 ***2524.55*** *p148*
Matushefsky, Frank; Maryland, 1910 ***3259.35*** *p39*
Matusky, Emerick; Maryland, 1910 ***3259.35*** *p39*
Matussewski, James; Maryland, 1910 ***3259.35*** *p39*
Matuszek, Jan; Maryland, 1910 ***3259.35*** *p39*
Matzen, Mrs. Lorenz; Port uncertain, 1752 ***2856.30*** *p290*
Matzinger, Jacob; America, 1735 ***2856.30*** *p290*
Matzinger, Jacob; Port uncertain, 1737 ***2856.30*** *p290*
With wife & 8 children
Mau, Michael 50; Ontario, 1871 ***1823.28*** *p62*
Maucher, Elisabeth; Port uncertain, 1775 ***2856.30*** *p290*
Maucher, Hans Georg; Port uncertain, 1749 ***2856.30*** *p290*
Maucher, Hans Georg; Port uncertain, 1771 ***2856.30*** *p290*
Maucher, Xaver; Port uncertain, 1764 ***2856.30*** *p290*
Mauchler, Johann Christof; America, 1784 ***2856.30*** *p290*
Mauckert, Johann; America, 1738 ***2856.30*** *p290*
With wife & 2 children
Maud, H. B. 3; Ontario, 1861 ***2896.27*** *p71*
Maude, Francis C. 42; Ontario, 1871 ***1823.28*** *p62*
Mauduit, William; Maryland, 1750 ***1224.2*** *p77*
Mauduit, William; Maryland, 1786 ***1224.2*** *p78*
Mauer, Clara; Port uncertain, 1790 ***2856.30*** *p290*
With husband
Mauerin, Marianna; Port uncertain, 1765 ***2856.30*** *p290*
Mauger, Charles; New York, 1834 ***8197.10*** *p71*
Mauger, Daniel; New York, 1834 ***8197.10*** *p71*
Mauger, Isaac; Massachusetts, 1807 ***1224.3*** *p53*
Maughan, Ann Brenan; Vermont, 1811-1893 ***5900.10*** *p569*
Maughan, Bridget; Vermont, 1843-1904 ***5900.10*** *p557*
Maughan, Thomas; Vermont, 1801-1868 ***5900.10*** *p569*
Maughone, Desmond; Maryland, 1668 ***2524.55*** *p148*
Maughone, Jerman; Maryland, 1668 ***2524.55*** *p148*
Maugier, Thomas 40; Ontario, 1871 ***1823.28*** *p62*
Maul, George; New York, 1834-1840 ***8197.10*** *p300*
Maule, Thomas, Jr.; New York, 1803 ***8197.10*** *p14*
Maull, John 43; Ontario, 1871 ***1823.15*** *p156*
Maulsby, William; Pennsylvania, 1778 ***4629.10*** *p45*
Maultis, Katherine; Maryland, 1671 ***2524.55*** *p148*
Maun, Anna G.; Vermont, 1858-1928 ***5900.10*** *p491*
Maun, Edward; Vermont, 1829-1911 ***5900.10*** *p491*
Maun, Ellen S.; Vermont, 1859-1945 ***5900.10*** *p491*
Maun, Joanna Tobin; Vermont, 1829-1912 ***5900.10*** *p491*
Maun, John E.; Vermont, 1855-1924 ***5900.10*** *p491*
Maunders, Thomas 33; Maryland, 1775 ***1220.25*** *p107*
Maunelon, John; Virginia, 1672 ***6212.30*** *p49*
Mauoney, Patrick; Maryland, 1666 ***2524.55*** *p148*
Maurer, Adam; America, 1740 ***2856.30*** *p290*
With wife & children
Maurer, Beda; Port uncertain, 1776 ***2856.30*** *p290*
Maurer, Catharina; America, 1764 ***2856.30*** *p422*
Maurer, Christof; Port uncertain, 1781 ***2856.30*** *p290*
Maurer, Eva; Port uncertain, 1764 ***2856.30*** *p290*
Maurer, Georg Michael; Port uncertain, 1764 ***2856.30*** *p290*
With wife & 4 children
Maurer, Johann; America, 1741 ***2856.30*** *p290*
Maurer, Johann Adam; America, 1740 ***2856.30*** *p290*
Maurer, Peter; Port uncertain, 1790 ***2856.30*** *p290*
Maurice, Benjamin; New York, 1794 ***8197.10*** *p2*
Maurice, Elizabeth; Maryland, 1654 ***2524.55*** *p148*
Maurice, Jno; Virginia, 1702 ***6212.30*** *p62*
Maurice, John; Maryland, 1658 ***2524.55*** *p148*
Maurice, Thomas; New York, 1796 ***8197.10*** *p8*
Maurice, William; New York, 1794 ***8197.10*** *p2*
Mauroumet, John; Havana, 1775 ***1224.2*** *p78*
Mauroumet, John; New York, n.d. ***1224.2*** *p78*
Maus, Charlotte Cath.; Port uncertain, 1774 ***2856.30*** *p290*
Maus, Franz Karl; Port uncertain, 1774 ***2856.30*** *p291*
Maus, Franz Klar; America, 1781 ***2856.30*** *p291*
Maus, Georg Jakob; America, 1774 ***2856.30*** *p291*
Maus, Georg Jakob; Port uncertain, 1768 ***2856.30*** *p291*
Maus, Jakob; America, 1768 ***2856.30*** *p291*
Maus, Maria Angelika; Port uncertain, 1778 ***2856.30*** *p291*
Maus, Maria Barbara; Port uncertain, 1785 ***2856.30*** *p291*
Mauser, Joseph 70; Ontario, 1871 ***1823.22*** *p98*
Maushuk, A. 31; Alaska, 1916 ***9196.1*** *p43*
Maushuk, A. 31; Whitehorse, Yukon, 1916 ***9196.1*** *p43*
Mauslin, Anna Maria; Port uncertain, 1773 ***2856.30*** *p291*
Mauson, Alexander 30; Ontario, 1871 ***1823.15*** *p156*
Mauss, Fritz; Port uncertain, 1776 ***2856.30*** *p291*
Mauss, Maria; Port uncertain, 1772 ***2856.30*** *p291*
Mavell, Richard; Virginia, 1678 ***1224.1*** *p39*
Maves, August 32; Ontario, 1871 ***1823.28*** *p62*
Maves, Fredrick 52; Ontario, 1871 ***1823.28*** *p62*
Maw, Henrietta 19; Ontario, 1871 ***1823.22*** *p98*
Mawberry, William; Maryland, 1671 ***2524.55*** *p148*
Mawbey, William; New York, 1838 ***8197.10*** *p125*
Mawer, George; Virginia, 1682 ***1224.1*** *p39*
Mawhaney, John 50; Ontario, 1871 ***1823.28*** *p62*
Mawhiney, George 43; Ontario, 1871 ***1823.15*** *p156*
Mawhiney, John; Pennsylvania, 1838 ***6058.10*** *p15*
Mawhinney, Isaiah 42; Ontario, 1871 ***1823.15*** *p156*
Mawhinney, John 45; Ontario, 1871 ***1823.15*** *p156*
Maxfield, James; Maryland, 1682 ***2524.55*** *p148*
Maxfield, Jeremiah; Bristol, Rhode Island, 1753 ***1224.2*** *p78*
Maxfield, Mary; Maryland, 1681 ***2524.55*** *p148*
Maxon, Anthony 12; Ontario, 1861 ***2896.25*** *p54*
Maxon, E. 3; Ontario, 1861 ***2896.25*** *p54*
Maxon, Edward 14; Ontario, 1861 ***2896.25*** *p54*
Maxon, J. C. 10; Ontario, 1861 ***2896.25*** *p54*
Maxon, M. 1; Ontario, 1861 ***2896.25*** *p54*
Maxon, M. J. 8; Ontario, 1861 ***2896.25*** *p54*
Maxon, Maria 39; Ontario, 1861 ***2896.25*** *p54*
Maxon, Matilda 16; Ontario, 1861 ***2896.25*** *p54*
Maxton, Andrew; Georgia, 1759 ***1640.10*** *p151*
Maxwell, Mrs.; Quebec, 1858 ***9196.15*** *p47*
Maxwell, Alexander; Pennsylvania, 1777 ***4629.10*** *p31*
Maxwell, Alexr 65; Ontario, 1871 ***1823.28*** *p62*
Maxwell, Audley; Georgia, 1756 ***1640.10*** *p151*
Maxwell, Audley, Jr.; Georgia, 1756 ***1640.10*** *p151*
Maxwell, David 19; Georgia, 1775 ***1220.25*** *p125*
Maxwell, David 25; Pennsylvania, 1832-1856 ***6058.10*** *p37*
Maxwell, David 62; Ontario, 1871 ***1823.15*** *p156*
Maxwell, Eliza 59; Ontario, 1871 ***1823.15*** *p156*
Maxwell, George 47; Ontario, 1871 ***1823.15*** *p156*
Maxwell, George T.; New York, 1840 ***8197.10*** *p181*
Maxwell, James; Georgia, 1767 ***1640.10*** *p151*
Maxwell, James; Maryland, 1658 ***2524.55*** *p148*
Maxwell, James 55; Ontario, 1871 ***1823.15*** *p156*
Maxwell, James, Jr.; Georgia, 1768 ***1640.10*** *p151*
Maxwell, Jared 34; Ontario, 1871 ***1823.15*** *p156*
Maxwell, John; Georgia, 1763 ***1640.10*** *p151*
Maxwell, John; Georgia, 1767 ***1640.10*** *p151*
Maxwell, John; Maryland, 1667 ***2524.55*** *p148*
Maxwell, John 25; Maryland, 1775 ***1220.25*** *p115*
Maxwell, John 34; Ontario, 1871 ***1823.15*** *p156*
Maxwell, Joseph William; Georgia, 1803-1845 ***1640.10*** *p151*
Maxwell, Mary; Maryland, 1659 ***2524.55*** *p148*
Maxwell, Mary; Port uncertain, 1850-1859 ***4537.37*** *p125*
Maxwell, Patrick J.; Vermont, 1872 ***5900.10*** *p178*
Maxwell, Primrose; Georgia, 1741 ***1640.10*** *p152*
Maxwell, Robert; Mississippi, 1831-1845 ***1640.10*** *p152*
Maxwell, Robert 18; Carolina, 1774 ***1220.25*** *p83*
Maxwell, Robert 36; Ontario, 1871 ***1823.15*** *p156*
Maxwell, Samuel; Vermont, 1833 ***6058.10*** *p37*
Maxwell, Thomas; Georgia, 1762 ***1640.10*** *p152*
Maxwell, Thomas; New York, 1837 ***8197.10*** *p99*
Maxwell, Thomas; New York, 1840 ***8197.10*** *p178*
Maxwell, Thomas; New York, 1840 ***8197.10*** *p180*
Maxwell, Thomas 37; Ontario, 1871 ***1823.15*** *p156*
Maxwell, Thos 41; Ontario, 1871 ***1823.22*** *p98*
Maxwell, William; Georgia, 1767 ***1640.10*** *p152*
Maxwell, William; Georgia, 1775 ***1640.10*** *p152*
Maxwell, William; New England, 1775-1781 ***4628.40*** *p68*
Maxwell, William 20; Ontario, 1861 ***2896.27*** *p13*
Maxwell, William 40; Ontario, 1871 ***1823.22*** *p98*
Maxwell, William H.; New York, 1840 ***8197.10*** *p179*
May, Mr.; Portland, Maine, 1857 ***9196.15*** *p12*
May, Mr.; Port uncertain, 1725 ***2856.30*** *p291*
May, Mrs.; Portland, Maine, 1858 ***9196.15*** *p29*
May, Mrs.; Quebec, 1857 ***9196.15*** *p14*
May, Mrs.; Quebec, 1858 ***9196.15*** *p32*
May, Ann 31; Ontario, 1871 ***1823.15*** *p156*
May, Anna; Port uncertain, 1697 ***2856.30*** *p291*
May, Anna Catharina; America, 1749 ***2856.30*** *p291*
With husband
May, Anna Elisabeth; Port uncertain, 1744 ***2856.30*** *p291*
May, Anna Sophia; Port uncertain, 1755 ***2856.30*** *p291*
May, Anne 65; Ontario, 1871 ***1823.28*** *p62*
May, Anthony 35; Ontario, 1871 ***1823.22*** *p98*
May, Antoine; New York, 1839 ***8197.10*** *p264*
May, Benjamin 68; Ontario, 1871 ***1823.22*** *p98*
May, Charles 22; Virginia, 1774 ***1220.25*** *p86*
May, Edw; Virginia, 1664 ***6212.30*** *p9*
May, Edward 35; Philadelphia, 1774 ***1220.25*** *p68*
May, Francis 21; Philadelphia, 1774 ***1220.25*** *p82*
May, Geo; Virginia, 1665-1666 ***6212.30*** *p21*
May, George; Virginia, 1664 ***6212.30*** *p13*
May, George 23; Ontario, 1871 ***1823.15*** *p156*
May, George 41; Ontario, 1871 ***1823.28*** *p62*
May, Gregor; Port uncertain, 1764 ***2856.30*** *p291*
May, Henrich; Port uncertain, 1737 ***2856.30*** *p291*
May, Henry 24; Ontario, 1871 ***1823.28*** *p62*
May, J.; Quebec, 1856 ***9196.15*** *p6*
May, Jakob; Port uncertain, 1764 ***2856.30*** *p291*
May, James; Maryland, 1679 ***2524.55*** *p148*
May, James 29; Ontario, 1871 ***1823.15*** *p156*
May, James 40; Ontario, 1871 ***1823.22*** *p98*
May, John; Virginia, 1664 ***6212.30*** *p9*
May, John 37; Virginia, 1774 ***1220.25*** *p93*
May, John 48; Ontario, 1871 ***1823.15*** *p156*
May, John 55; Ontario, 1871 ***1823.22*** *p98*
May, John 68; Ontario, 1871 ***1823.22*** *p98*
May, Joseph; Maryland, 1910 ***3259.35*** *p39*
May, Konrad; Port uncertain, 1749 ***2856.30*** *p291*
May, Margaret 60; Ontario, 1871 ***1823.15*** *p157*
May, Maria Catharina; Port uncertain, 1778 ***2856.30*** *p291*
May, Mary; Maryland, 1663 ***2524.55*** *p148*
May, Mary; Maryland, 1666 ***2524.55*** *p148*
May, Philipp; America, 1750 ***2856.30*** *p291*
With children
May, Richard 46; Ontario, 1871 ***1823.22*** *p98*
May, Richard 47; Ontario, 1871 ***1823.15*** *p157*
May, Samuel 47; Ontario, 1871 ***1823.22*** *p98*
May, Samuel 59; Ontario, 1871 ***1823.22*** *p98*
May, T.; Quebec, 1858 ***9196.15*** *p42*
May, Mrs. T.; Quebec, 1858 ***9196.15*** *p42*
May, T. K.; Quebec, 1858 ***9196.15*** *p32*
May, Thomas; Virginia, 1665-1666 ***6212.30*** *p25*
May, Thomas; Virginia, 1700 ***1224.2*** *p78*
May, Thomas 34; Ontario, 1871 ***1823.15*** *p157*
May, Thomas 44; Ontario, 1871 ***1823.15*** *p157*
May, Thomas 62; Ontario, 1871 ***1823.28*** *p62*
May, Thomas P.; New York, 1839 ***8197.10*** *p264*
May, William; Maryland, 1654 ***2524.55*** *p148*
May, William; South Carolina, 1739 ***1224.2*** *p78*
May, William 20; Ontario, 1871 ***1823.15*** *p157*
May, William 35; Ontario, 1871 ***1823.28*** *p62*
May, William 39; Ontario, 1871 ***1823.22*** *p98*
May, William 67; Ontario, 1871 ***1823.22*** *p98*
May, William 74; Ontario, 1871 ***1823.15*** *p157*
May, William Henry 47; Ontario, 1871 ***1823.15*** *p157*
Maybank, David; South Carolina, 1725 ***1224.2*** *p78*
Maybank, Susan; South Carolina, 1725 ***1224.2*** *p78*
Maybee, Benjamin 81; Ontario, 1871 ***1823.22*** *p99*
Maybee, Byron 2; Ontario, 1861 ***2896.25*** *p56*
Maybee, Cecilia 1; Ontario, 1861 ***2896.25*** *p56*
Maybee, Eliza Jane 9; Ontario, 1861 ***2896.25*** *p22*
Maybee, H. M. 21; Ontario, 1861 ***2896.25*** *p39*
Maybee, Hanson 56; Ontario, 1871 ***1823.22*** *p99*
Maybee, Hellen 64; Ontario, 1861 ***2896.25*** *p56*
Maybee, Henry 82; Ontario, 1861 ***2896.25*** *p34*
Maybee, Mary 64; Ontario, 1861 ***2896.25*** *p60*
Maybee, Newton 3; Ontario, 1861 ***2896.25*** *p56*
Maybee, Peter 70; Ontario, 1861 ***2896.26*** *p26*
Maybee, Phebe Ann 28; Ontario, 1861 ***2896.25*** *p56*
Maybee, Saphrona 15; Ontario, 1861 ***2896.25*** *p22*
Maybee, William R. 15; Ontario, 1861 ***2896.25*** *p22*
Mayberry, Andrew 63; Ontario, 1871 ***1823.15*** *p157*
Mayberry, Henry; New York, 1840 ***8197.10*** *p178*
Mayberry, Margaret 61; Ontario, 1871 ***1823.15*** *p157*
Maybery, Charles; Tennessee, 1843 ***1224.3*** *p51*
Mayden, John; Maryland, 1668 ***2524.55*** *p148*
Mayden, John; Maryland, 1673 ***2524.55*** *p148*
Maye, Cornelius; Virginia, 1636 ***1224.1*** *p39*
Mayeliski, Walenty; Maryland, 1910 ***3259.35*** *p39*
Mayell, William; New York, 1797 ***8197.10*** *p9*
Mayenschein, Johann Friedric; America, 1763 ***2856.30*** *p291*
With wife & 4 children
Mayer, . . .; America, 1761 ***2856.30*** *p292*
Mayer, A. M. Schalit *SEE* Mayer, Peter

McAllister, John; Vermont, 1850-1909 ***5900.10*** *p496*
McAllister, John 42; Ontario, 1871 ***1823.22*** *p99*
McAllister, John 51; Ontario, 1871 ***1823.15*** *p157*
McAllister, Mary A. 39; Vermont, 1878 ***5900.10*** *p281*
McAllister, Mary Hale 63; Vermont, 1883 ***5900.10*** *p494*
McAllister, Mary Trueland 83; Vermont, 1892 ***5900.10*** *p297*
McAllister, Nellie; Vermont, 1844-1926 ***5900.10*** *p298*
McAllister, Robert 48; Ontario, 1871 ***1823.15*** *p157*
McAllister, Robert 60; Vermont, 1870 ***5900.10*** *p494*
McAllister, Robt 40; Ontario, 1871 ***1823.15*** *p157*
McAllister, Rosette Kelly 58; Vermont, 1905 ***5900.10*** *p297*
McAllister, William; New York, 1840 ***8197.10*** *p184*
McAllister, William 35; Ontario, 1871 ***1823.15*** *p157*
McAllister, Wm 56; Ontario, 1871 ***1823.15*** *p157*
McAllum, Maryann; North Carolina, 1790-1845 ***1640.10*** *p99*
McAlpin, Alexander; South Carolina, 1760-1769 ***1640.10*** *p99*
McAlpin, Archibald; South Carolina, 1776-1822 ***1640.10*** *p100*
McAlpin, Donald; Georgia, 1743 ***1640.10*** *p100*
McAlpin, Helen McInnes *SEE* McAlpin, Henry
McAlpin, Henry; Georgia, 1804-1812 ***1640.10*** *p100*
Wife: Helen McInnes
McAlpin, John 30; Ontario, 1871 ***1823.28*** *p62*
McAlpin, Patrick; New York, 1837 ***8197.10*** *p97*
McAlpin, William; New York, 1807 ***8197.10*** *p46*
McAlpine, James 35; Ontario, 1871 ***1823.22*** *p99*
McAlpine, Walter; Pennsylvania, 1779 ***4629.10*** *p41*
McAnaley, Martin; New York, 1803 ***8197.10*** *p14*
McAnally, Daniel; New York, 1830 ***8197.10*** *p363*
McAnally, Lawrence; New York, 1840 ***8197.10*** *p185*
McAnaney, Annie; Vermont, 1844-1887 ***5900.10*** *p436*
McAnaney, Bridget; Vermont, 1846-1904 ***5900.10*** *p436*
McAnaney, Catherine 60; Vermont, 1892 ***5900.10*** *p436*
McAnaney, Catherine 86; Vermont, 1907 ***5900.10*** *p615*
McAnaney, Mary 56; Vermont, 1890 ***5900.10*** *p436*
McAndrew, Alexander; Georgia, 1775 ***1640.10*** *p100*
McAndrew, Alexander 18; Georgia, 1775 ***1220.25*** *p126*
McAndrew, John 48; Ontario, 1871 ***1823.28*** *p62*
McAnly, Anne 22; Ontario, 1871 ***1823.15*** *p157*
McAnly, Kenneth 25; Ontario, 1871 ***1823.15*** *p157*
McAnly, Neil 30; Ontario, 1871 ***1823.15*** *p157*
McAnly, Norman 30; Ontario, 1871 ***1823.15*** *p157*
McAnnally, Mrs. 37; Ontario, 1861 ***2896.26*** *p27*
McAnnally, James; New York, 1839 ***8197.10*** *p138*
McAnnally, Mary 2; Ontario, 1861 ***2896.26*** *p27*
McAnnally, Michael 12; Ontario, 1861 ***2896.26*** *p27*
McAnnally, Owen 51; Ontario, 1861 ***2896.26*** *p27*
McAnnally, Peter 11; Ontario, 1861 ***2896.26*** *p27*
McAnnulla, Isabella 67; Vermont, 1874 ***5900.10*** *p314*
McAnnulla, James 88; Vermont, 1883 ***5900.10*** *p314*
McArdell, Francis; New York, 1840 ***8197.10*** *p185*
McArdle, Catherine; Vermont, 1829-1890 ***5900.10*** *p617*
McArdle, Henry 62; Ontario, 1871 ***1823.15*** *p157*
McArdle, Joseph; New York, 1839 ***8197.10*** *p138*
McArdle, Michael 28; Ontario, 1871 ***1823.15*** *p157*
McArdle, Owen; New York, 1840 ***8197.10*** *p183*
McArdle, Patrick; New York, 1804 ***8197.10*** *p27*
McArdle, Thomas; Vermont, 1816-1881 ***5900.10*** *p617*
McArter, John 43; Ontario, 1871 ***1823.15*** *p157*
McArtha, Nella 71; Vermont, 1849 ***5900.10*** *p612*
McArthur, Alexander 35; Ontario, 1871 ***1823.15*** *p157*
McArthur, Alexander 65; Ontario, 1871 ***1823.22*** *p99*
McArthur, Archy 55; Ontario, 1871 ***1823.15*** *p157*
McArthur, Duncan 26; Ontario, 1871 ***1823.15*** *p157*
McArthur, Elizabeth; Georgia, 1805-1845 ***1640.10*** *p100*
McArthur, Evangeline Wilkins; Vermont, 1854-1915 ***5900.10*** *p494*
McArthur, Helen; St. Vincent, 1838 ***1640.13*** *p82*
McArthur, Hugh 64; Ontario, 1871 ***1823.22*** *p99*
McArthur, Isabella; Canada, 1892 ***1640.13*** *p83*
McArthur, James 45; Ontario, 1871 ***1823.28*** *p62*
McArthur, John; Grenada, 1834 ***1640.13*** *p83*
McArthur, John 32; Ontario, 1871 ***1823.15*** *p157*
McArthur, John 35; Ontario, 1871 ***1823.15*** *p157*
McArthur, John 57; Ontario, 1871 ***1823.15*** *p157*
McArthur, John 62; Ontario, 1871 ***1823.15*** *p157*
McArthur, John 72; Ontario, 1871 ***1823.22*** *p99*
McArthur, Louise; Vermont, 1863-1955 ***5900.10*** *p310*
McArthur, Neil; Alabama, 1829 ***1640.10*** *p100*
McArthur, Peter 70; Ontario, 1871 ***1823.15*** *p157*
McArthur, William 29; Ontario, 1871 ***1823.15*** *p157*
McArthur, William W.; Vermont, 1848-1897 ***5900.10*** *p494*
McArtney, Joseph 62; Ontario, 1871 ***1823.15*** *p157*
McArty, Catharine Callan 23; Vermont, 1865 ***5900.10*** *p478*
McAsh, John 52; Ontario, 1871 ***1823.15*** *p157*
McAulay, Robert; Georgia, 1699 ***1640.13*** *p83*
McAuley, Alexander 50; Ontario, 1871 ***1823.22*** *p99*
McAuley, Catherine 71; Ontario, 1871 ***1823.22*** *p99*
McAuley, James 55; Ontario, 1871 ***1823.22*** *p99*
McAuley, Katherine; Vermont, 1845-1916 ***5900.10*** *p379*
McAuley, Thomas; New York, 1839 ***8197.10*** *p258*
McAuley, Thomas 35; Ontario, 1871 ***1823.22*** *p99*
McAuliff, Ellen O'Reilley 24; Vermont, 1894 ***5900.10*** *p240*
McAuliff, M.; Vermont, 1837-1915 ***5900.10*** *p458*
McAuliff, Mary A. Maloney 47; Vermont, 1896 ***5900.10*** *p239*
McAuliff, P. 42; Alaska, 1917 ***9196.1*** *p53*
McAuliff, P. 42; Whitehorse, Yukon, 1917 ***9196.1*** *p53*
McAuliff, Patrick 55; Vermont, 1853 ***5900.10*** *p611*
McAuliffe, Anna; Vermont, 1857-1929 ***5900.10*** *p144*
McAuliffe, Bridget Sullivan; Vermont, 1841-1873 ***5900.10*** *p371*
McAuliffe, Daniel; Vermont, 1834-1886 ***5900.10*** *p234*
McAuliffe, Daniel; Vermont, 1845-1900 ***5900.10*** *p66*
McAuliffe, David; Vermont, 1833-1886 ***5900.10*** *p144*
McAuliffe, Denis 28; New York, New York, 1849 ***1825.45*** *p51*
Brother: Michael 22
Sister: Johanna 24
Brother: Robert 17
McAuliffe, Ellen Powers; Vermont, 1841-1904 ***5900.10*** *p144*
McAuliffe, Henry J.; Vermont, 1880-1942 ***5900.10*** *p144*
McAuliffe, James; Vermont, 1867-1868 ***5900.10*** *p144*
McAuliffe, Johanna 24 *SEE* McAuliffe, Denis
McAuliffe, John; Vermont, 1842-1904 ***5900.10*** *p70*
McAuliffe, Julia F.; Vermont, 1842-1915 ***5900.10*** *p234*
McAuliffe, Linus; Vermont, n.d. ***5900.10*** *p234*
McAuliffe, Lucy; Vermont, n.d. ***5900.10*** *p234*
McAuliffe, Martha; Vermont, 1865-1868 ***5900.10*** *p144*
McAuliffe, Mary; Vermont, n.d. ***5900.10*** *p234*
McAuliffe, Mary; Vermont, 1860-1866 ***5900.10*** *p144*
McAuliffe, Mary Supple; Vermont, 1844-1919 ***5900.10*** *p70*
McAuliffe, Michael; Vermont, n.d. ***5900.10*** *p234*
McAuliffe, Michael 22 *SEE* McAuliffe, Denis
McAuliffe, Robert; Vermont, 1869-1870 ***5900.10*** *p144*
McAuliffe, Robert 17 *SEE* McAuliffe, Denis
McAuliffe, William; Vermont, 1838-1916 ***5900.10*** *p371*
McAuliffe, William H.; Vermont, 1858-1937 ***5900.10*** *p144*
McAulley, William; New York, 1807 ***8197.10*** *p46*
McAuly, Charles 60; Ontario, 1871 ***1823.22*** *p99*
McAuly, Jane 52; Ontario, 1871 ***1823.22*** *p100*
McAuly, John 48; Ontario, 1871 ***1823.28*** *p62*
McAvela, James 30; Ontario, 1871 ***1823.22*** *p100*
McAvoy, Ann; Vermont, 1905 ***5900.10*** *p178*
McAvoy, Ann Eliza; Vermont, 1867-1881 ***5900.10*** *p330*
McAvoy, Barnard 43; Ontario, 1861 ***2896.27*** *p5*
McAvoy, Bridget; Vermont, 1817-1886 ***5900.10*** *p179*
McAvoy, Bridget; Vermont, 1862-1888 ***5900.10*** *p179*
McAvoy, Bridget McGrath; Vermont, 1834-1879 ***5900.10*** *p330*
McAvoy, Daniel; Vermont, 1818-1901 ***5900.10*** *p179*
McAvoy, Daniel 66; Ontario, 1861 ***2896.27*** *p5*
McAvoy, Edward; Vermont, 1837-1921 ***5900.10*** *p128*
McAvoy, Elen 12; Ontario, 1861 ***2896.27*** *p5*
McAvoy, Elen 41; Ontario, 1861 ***2896.27*** *p5*
McAvoy, Esther 10; Ontario, 1861 ***2896.27*** *p5*
McAvoy, James 65; Ontario, 1871 ***1823.22*** *p100*
McAvoy, Jno 25; Ontario, 1871 ***1823.15*** *p157*
McAvoy, John; Vermont, 1835-1897 ***5900.10*** *p330*
McAvoy, John 1; Ontario, 1861 ***2896.27*** *p5*
McAvoy, John E.; Vermont, 1851-1887 ***5900.10*** *p179*
McAvoy, Margaret; Vermont, 1833-1894 ***5900.10*** *p186*
McAvoy, Margaret Finnessy; Vermont, 1850-1934 ***5900.10*** *p129*
McAvoy, Mary; Vermont, n.d. ***5900.10*** *p128*
McAvoy, Mary 15; Ontario, 1861 ***2896.27*** *p5*
McAvoy, Patrick 26; Ontario, 1871 ***1823.22*** *p100*
McAvoy, Therressy 4; Ontario, 1861 ***2896.27*** *p5*
McAvoy, Thomas H.; Vermont, 1840-1893 ***5900.10*** *p129*
McAwly, Peter; New York, 1825 ***8197.10*** *p255*
McBane, John 48; Ontario, 1871 ***1823.28*** *p62*
McBean, D.; Mississippi, 1816-1845 ***1640.10*** *p101*
McBean, David; Mississippi, 1830-1845 ***1640.10*** *p101*
McBean, James; Mississippi, 1824-1845 ***1640.10*** *p101*
McBean, John *SEE* McBean, Lauchlan
McBean, John; Georgia, 1757 ***1640.10*** *p101*
McBean, John McWillie; Georgia, 1736 ***1640.10*** *p101*
McBean, Lauchlan; Augusta, Georgia, 1756 ***1640.10*** *p101*
Son: William
Son: John
McBean, William *SEE* McBean, Lauchlan
McBean, William; Florida, 1767 ***1640.10*** *p102*
McBeath, George; Savannah, Georgia, 1775 ***1640.10*** *p102*
McBeath, James; New York, 1806 ***8197.10*** *p31*
McBerney, Samuell 48; Ontario, 1871 ***1823.15*** *p157*
McBeth, Alexander; New York, 1802 ***8197.10*** *p23*
McBeth, Alexander 24; Ontario, 1871 ***1823.15*** *p157*
McBeth, Christian 55; Ontario, 1871 ***1823.15*** *p158*
McBeth, Duncan 20; Ontario, 1871 ***1823.15*** *p158*
McBeth, James 53; Ontario, 1871 ***1823.15*** *p158*
McBeth, Janet 22; Ontario, 1871 ***1823.15*** *p158*
McBeth, John 52; Ontario, 1871 ***1823.15*** *p158*
McBeth, Walter 17; Ontario, 1871 ***1823.15*** *p158*
McBlain, Robert; New York, 1828 ***8197.10*** *p256*
McBlain, Robert; New York, 1830 ***8197.10*** *p66*
McBlane, Aleck 26; Ontario, 1871 ***1823.28*** *p62*
McBone, Thomas 26; Maryland, 1775 ***1220.25*** *p111*
McBowen, James 50; Ontario, 1871 ***1823.28*** *p62*
McBrearty, James; New York, 1839 ***8197.10*** *p320*
McBrian, David 45; Ontario, 1871 ***1823.15*** *p158*
McBrian, Margery 70; Ontario, 1871 ***1823.22*** *p100*
McBride, Ada Bell 83; Vermont, 1930 ***5900.10*** *p374*
McBride, Alexander 70; Ontario, 1871 ***1823.22*** *p100*
McBride, Alvira; Vermont, 1855-1904 ***5900.10*** *p375*
McBride, Andrew; New York, 1807 ***8197.10*** *p328*
McBride, Andrew; New York, 1837 ***8197.10*** *p97*
McBride, Ann 60; Ontario, 1871 ***1823.15*** *p158*
McBride, Antony; Georgia, 1734 ***1640.10*** *p102*
McBride, Archibald 33; Ontario, 1871 ***1823.28*** *p62*
McBride, Bridget 36; Ontario, 1871 ***1823.15*** *p158*
McBride, Calvin 56; Vermont, 1893 ***5900.10*** *p463*
McBride, Catherine Agan; Vermont, 1817-1900 ***5900.10*** *p220*
McBride, Clement; Mississippi, 1819-1845 ***1640.10*** *p102*
McBride, Dougald 31; Ontario, 1871 ***1823.22*** *p100*
McBride, Ella M. 5; Vermont, 1874 ***5900.10*** *p374*
McBride, Ellen; Vermont, 1844-1944 ***5900.10*** *p220*
McBride, Emily 2; Vermont, 1852 ***5900.10*** *p374*
McBride, Emma E. 3; Vermont, 1862 ***5900.10*** *p374*
McBride, Emma Phelps; Vermont, 1860-1952 ***5900.10*** *p463*
McBride, Henry; Georgia, 1734 ***1640.10*** *p102*
McBride, Hugh; New York, 1826 ***8197.10*** *p255*
McBride, Hugh; New York, 1830 ***8197.10*** *p66*
McBride, James; Kentucky, 1743 ***4628.40*** *p78*
McBride, James; New York, 1802 ***8197.10*** *p23*
McBride, James; New York, 1818 ***8197.10*** *p63*
McBride, James; New York, 1837 ***8197.10*** *p97*
McBride, James; Vermont, 1818-1906 ***5900.10*** *p217*
McBride, James 21; Ontario, 1871 ***1823.22*** *p100*
McBride, James 30; Ontario, 1871 ***1823.28*** *p62*
McBride, James 62; Vermont, 1884 ***5900.10*** *p374*
McBride, James E. 48; Vermont, 1894 ***5900.10*** *p374*
McBride, James F.; Pennsylvania, 1830 ***6058.10*** *p26*
McBride, James Franklin; Vermont, 1849-1915 ***5900.10*** *p463*
McBride, Jane 32; Vermont, 1870 ***5900.10*** *p220*
McBride, John; New York, 1802 ***8197.10*** *p23*
McBride, John; New York, 1834 ***8197.10*** *p315*
McBride, Joseph; Vermont, 1844-1892 ***5900.10*** *p220*
McBride, Julia Gordon 44; Vermont, 1883 ***5900.10*** *p463*
McBride, Malcom 5; Vermont, 1858 ***5900.10*** *p374*
McBride, Martha 16; Baltimore, 1775 ***1220.25*** *p119*
McBride, Mary; Vermont, 1852-1926 ***5900.10*** *p216*
McBride, Mary; Vermont, 1857-1928 ***5900.10*** *p373*
McBride, Mary Ann 41; Vermont, 1885 ***5900.10*** *p220*
McBride, Mary McDevitt; Vermont, 1827-1911 ***5900.10*** *p217*
McBride, Michael; New York, 1824 ***8197.10*** *p255*
McBride, Michael; Vermont, 1839-1904 ***5900.10*** *p220*
McBride, Nancy 43; Vermont, 1891 ***5900.10*** *p374*
McBride, Neil 35; Vermont, 1876 ***5900.10*** *p582*
McBride, Patrick; New York, 1837 ***8197.10*** *p96*
McBride, Patrick; Pennsylvania, 1868 ***6058.10*** *p74*
McBride, Richard 32; Ontario, 1871 ***1823.22*** *p100*
McBride, Robert; New York, 1840 ***8197.10*** *p184*
McBride, Rose; Vermont, 1825-1892 ***5900.10*** *p486*
McBride, Ruth McNeil 70; Vermont, 1895 ***5900.10*** *p374*
McBride, Sarah Jane 26; Vermont, 1882 ***5900.10*** *p314*
McBride, Stephen 61; Ontario, 1871 ***1823.22*** *p100*
McBride, Susan Black 73; Vermont, 1877 ***5900.10*** *p463*
McBride, Thomas; New York, 1821 ***8197.10*** *p253*
McBride, Thomas; Pennsylvania, 1785 ***4629.10*** *p48*
McBride, Thomas 35; Ontario, 1871 ***1823.28*** *p62*
McBride, Thomas 50; Ontario, 1871 ***1823.15*** *p158*
McBride, Thomas 60; Ontario, 1871 ***1823.22*** *p100*
McBride, Thomas 70; Ontario, 1871 ***1823.15*** *p158*
McBride, Thomas 72; Vermont, 1868 ***5900.10*** *p463*
McBride, William; Pennsylvania, 1830 ***6058.10*** *p26*
McBride, William; Vermont, 1847-1913 ***5900.10*** *p216*
McBride, William 32; Ontario, 1871 ***1823.28*** *p62*
McBride, William 39; Ontario, 1871 ***1823.15*** *p158*
McBride, William 46; Ontario, 1871 ***1823.22*** *p100*
McBridge, Cornelia; Vermont, 1836-1917 ***5900.10*** *p598*
McBrien, Ann 52; Ontario, 1871 ***1823.15*** *p158*
McBrien, Hugh 45; Ontario, 1871 ***1823.15*** *p158*
McBrien, Jeremiah 37; Ontario, 1871 ***1823.15*** *p158*

McBrien, Jonathan 40; Ontario, 1871 1823.15 p158
McBrien, Mary 82; Ontario, 1871 1823.15 p158
McBrien, Mary 90; Ontario, 1871 1823.15 p158
McBrien, Moses 46; Ontario, 1871 1823.15 p158
McBrien, Robert 50; Ontario, 1871 1823.15 p158
McBrien, Simon Lewis 57; Ontario, 1871 1823.22 p100
McBrien, William 40; Ontario, 1871 1823.15 p158
McBrierty, Patrick; New York, 1806 8197.10 p324
McBrine, James; Vermont, 1771-1850 5900.10 p150
McBrine, Robert 51; Ontario, 1871 1823.22 p100
McBryde, John; Georgia, 1735-1845 1640.10 p102
McBryde, Thomas; Charles Town, South Carolina, 1795 1224.2 p72
McBryne, Mary 82; Vermont, 1896 5900.10 p412
McBurney, Alexander; New York, 1830 8197.10 p257
McBurney, Alexander; New York, 1833 8197.10 p68
McBurney, Cad.; New York, 1803 8197.10 p14
McBurney, John 36; Ontario, 1871 1823.15 p158
McBurney, John 65; Ontario, 1871 1823.15 p158
McBurney, Margaret 70; Ontario, 1871 1823.15 p158
McBurney, Thomas; New York, 1822 8197.10 p254
McBurney, Thomas; New York, 1839 8197.10 p379
McBurnie, David 28; Ontario, 1861 2896.27 p28
McBurnie, James 26; Ontario, 1861 2896.27 p38
McBurnie, Jane 24; Ontario, 1861 2896.27 p38
McBurnie, Jane 50; Ontario, 1861 2896.27 p30
McBurnie, Joseph 30; Ontario, 1871 1823.15 p158
McBurnie, Margaret 22; Ontario, 1861 2896.27 p28
McBurny, Hugh 27; Ontario, 1871 1823.15 p158
McCaa, Andrew 58; Ontario, 1871 1823.15 p158
McCabe, Albert 24; Washington, 1913 9196.1 p60
McCabe, Alexander; Vermont, n.d. 5900.10 p409
McCabe, Bernard; New York, 1839 8197.10 p379
McCabe, Bernard; Vermont, 1839-1910 5900.10 p587
McCabe, Bernard; Vermont, 1839-1910 5900.10 p592
McCabe, Bernard 72; Ontario, 1871 1823.15 p158
McCabe, Catherine 67; Vermont, 1905 5900.10 p465
McCabe, Catherine Clark; Vermont, 1859-1902 5900.10 p409
McCabe, Edward; New York, 1822 8197.10 p62
McCabe, Edward 47; Ontario, 1871 1823.28 p62
McCabe, Ellen Donelly 43; Vermont, 1899 5900.10 p536
McCabe, Ellen Donnelly; Vermont, 1856-1899 5900.10 p536
McCabe, Francis; New York, 1840 8197.10 p184
McCabe, George; Pennsylvania, 1840 6058.10 p19
McCabe, George 72; Ontario, 1871 1823.15 p158
McCabe, Hugh; New York, 1838 8197.10 p119
McCabe, Hugh; New York, 1838 8197.10 p126
McCabe, Hugh 46; Ontario, 1871 1823.22 p100
McCabe, Hugh 78; Ontario, 1871 1823.15 p158
McCabe, James; Vermont, n.d. 5900.10 p167
McCabe, James; Vermont, 1840-1904 5900.10 p409
McCabe, James 55; Ontario, 1871 1823.28 p62
McCabe, James 67; Ontario, 1871 1823.22 p100
McCabe, John; New York, 1837 8197.10 p374
McCabe, John 50; Ontario, 1871 1823.28 p62
McCabe, Kate Connelly; Vermont, 1840-1885 5900.10 p587
McCabe, Katie Connolly; Vermont, 1840-1885 5900.10 p592
McCabe, Mary; Vermont, 1810-1889 5900.10 p412
McCabe, Mary Bannagan 80; Vermont, 1910 5900.10 p588
McCabe, Mary Mooney; Vermont, 1799-1891 5900.10 p587
McCabe, Mary Mooney; Vermont, 1799-1891 5900.10 p592
McCabe, Michael 40; Ontario, 1871 1823.15 p158
McCabe, Miles; Pennsylvania, 1817 6058.10 p5
McCabe, Owen; New York, 1818 8197.10 p60
McCabe, Owen; Vermont, 1794-1873 5900.10 p587
McCabe, Owen; Vermont, 1794-1873 5900.10 p592
McCabe, Owen; Vermont, 1847-1902 5900.10 p587
McCabe, Patrick; New York, 1830 8197.10 p257
McCabe, Patrick; New York, 1837 8197.10 p95
McCabe, Peter; Vermont, 1837-1909 5900.10 p592
McCabe, Thomas 66; Ontario, 1871 1823.28 p62
McCabe, William 50; Ontario, 1871 1823.15 p158
McCabe, Wm H.; Vermont, 1853-1926 5900.10 p536
McCachran, William 40; Ontario, 1871 1823.28 p62
McCadam, Owen; New York, 1840 8197.10 p321
McCaddin, Henry; New York, 1831 8197.10 p366
McCae, Alexander 50; Ontario, 1871 1823.15 p158
McCae, William 52; Ontario, 1871 1823.15 p158
McCaffrey, Andrew 16; Vermont, 1870 5900.10 p205
McCaffrey, Bridget; Vermont, 1831-1870 5900.10 p80
McCaffrey, Catherine; Vermont, 1842-1906 5900.10 p89
McCaffrey, Elizabeth; Vermont, 1835-1920 5900.10 p601
McCaffrey, Ellen McGrath; Vermont, 1854-1907 5900.10 p142
McCaffrey, Ellen Ryan; Vermont, 1853-1898 5900.10 p204
McCaffrey, Emma McDonald; Vermont, n.d. 5900.10 p183
McCaffrey, Hugh; New York, 1825 8197.10 p255
McCaffrey, Hugh; New York, 1840 8197.10 p258
McCaffrey, J. 31; Ontario, 1861 2896.25 p29
McCaffrey, J. H.; Vermont, 1857-1929 5900.10 p183
McCaffrey, James; Vermont, 1834-1898 5900.10 p186
McCaffrey, John; Vermont, 1859-1928 5900.10 p142
McCaffrey, Katherine Cavanagh; Vermont, 1843-1929 5900.10 p186
McCaffrey, Mary; Vermont, 1847-1929 5900.10 p509
McCaffrey, Mary A.; Vermont, 1855-1936 5900.10 p205
McCaffrey, Mary Cassidy; Vermont, 1824-1898 5900.10 p205
McCaffrey, Mathew; Vermont, 1835-1909 5900.10 p552
McCaffrey, Patrick; Vermont, 1823-1901 5900.10 p205
McCaffrey, Phillip; Vermont, 1882 5900.10 p148
McCaffrey, Sarah; Vermont, 1825-1888 5900.10 p135
McCaffrey, Susan; Vermont, 1830-1897 5900.10 p142
McCaffrey, Susan Baird; Vermont, 1908 5900.10 p148
McCaffrey, Thomas 46; Vermont, 1903 5900.10 p205
McCaffrey, William J.; Vermont, 1849 5900.10 p204
McCaffry, James; New York, 1827 8197.10 p341
McCagherty, Eliza 56; Ontario, 1871 1823.28 p62
McCagherty, Patrick 60; Ontario, 1871 1823.28 p62
McCague, James 44; Ontario, 1871 1823.15 p158
McCaig, Danial 80; Ontario, 1871 1823.15 p158
McCaig, William 51; Ontario, 1871 1823.15 p158
McCaigue, James 60; Ontario, 1871 1823.15 p158
McCail, Catherine J. 26; Vermont, 1880 5900.10 p384
McCail, John 76; Vermont, 1874 5900.10 p384
McCail, Mary 68; Vermont, 1895 5900.10 p384
McCail, William B. 28; Vermont, 1893 5900.10 p384
McCain, Arthur 40; Ontario, 1871 1823.15 p158
McCale, Bridget; Vermont, 1842-1900 5900.10 p159
McCale, Francis H.; Vermont, 1856-1918 5900.10 p141
McCale, Jennie A. McGuire; Vermont, 1869-1969 5900.10 p141
McCale, John; New York, 1807 8197.10 p325
McCale, John 21; Ontario, 1871 1823.28 p62
McCale, John 38; Ontario, 1871 1823.22 p100
McCall, Mr.; Quebec, 1857 9196.15 p18
McCall, Mr.; Quebec, 1858 9196.15 p44
McCall, Alexander 27; Ontario, 1871 1823.15 p158
McCall, Ann 70; Ontario, 1871 1823.15 p158
McCall, Archibald; Pennsylvania, 1777 4629.10 p22
McCall, Bryan; New York, 1826 8197.10 p256
McCall, Catharine Flood; Washington, District of Columbia, 1831 1224.3 p48
McCall, Catherine Diffley 79; Vermont, 1892 5900.10 p92
McCall, Donald S. 54; Ontario, 1871 1823.22 p100
McCall, Dougall 60; Ontario, 1871 1823.15 p159
McCall, Francis; New York, 1840 8197.10 p185
McCall, George; New York, 1832 8197.10 p357
McCall, George 30; Ontario, 1871 1823.15 p159
McCall, Henry; New York, 1807 8197.10 p46
McCall, Honour; Vermont, 1820-1880 5900.10 p436
McCall, Hugh; New York, 1839 8197.10 p379
McCall, James; New York, 1794 8197.10 p2
McCall, John; New York, 1840 8197.10 p182
McCall, John; Tobago, West Indies, 1886 1640.13 p83
McCall, John 60; Ontario, 1871 1823.15 p159
McCall, Robert 45; Ontario, 1871 1823.15 p159
McCall, Samuel; Pennsylvania, 1839 6058.10 p15
McCall, William; New York, 1837 8197.10 p97
McCall, William 36; Ontario, 1871 1823.15 p159
McCallam, John 42; Ontario, 1871 1823.28 p62
McCallister, James 34; Ontario, 1871 1823.22 p100
McCallister, Jane; Vermont, 1840-1928 5900.10 p208
McCallum, A. C. 35; Ontario, 1871 1823.28 p62
McCallum, Archibald 28; New York, 1823-1824 8197.10 p309
McCallum, Duncan 75; Ontario, 1871 1823.28 p62
McCallum, Elizabeth 26; Ontario, 1871 1823.28 p62
McCallum, H.; Quebec, 1858 9196.15 p32
McCallum, James 39; Ontario, 1871 1823.15 p159
McCallum, John 40; Ontario, 1871 1823.15 p159
McCallum, John 43; Ontario, 1871 1823.15 p159
McCallum, John 51; Ontario, 1871 1823.15 p159
McCallum, M.; New York, 1876 1640.13 p83
McCallum, Margaret; Washington, District of Columbia, 1888 1640.13 p83
McCallum, Mary 50; Ontario, 1871 1823.15 p159
McCallum, Neil; Jamaica, 1835 1640.13 p83
McCallum, Peter; Alabama, 1769-1845 1640.10 p103
McCallum, Peter 64; Ontario, 1871 1823.22 p100
McCallum, Robert; Minnesota, 1876 1640.13 p83
McCallum, William 15; Ontario, 1861 2896.28 p9
McCallum, Zachariah; New York, 1806 8197.10 p32
McCallum, Zachery 54; Ontario, 1871 1823.15 p159
McCally, Norman; Pennsylvania, 1786 4629.10 p46
McCalum, Mary 70; Ontario, 1871 1823.15 p159
McCambrage, James 54; Ontario, 1871 1823.22 p100
McCambrage, Thomas 36; Ontario, 1871 1823.28 p63
McCammon, Mark; New York, 1794 8197.10 p2
McCan, James 60; Ontario, 1871 1823.22 p100
McCan, Peter 34; Ontario, 1871 1823.15 p159
McCana, Nancy; Vermont, 1824-1901 5900.10 p227
McCance, James 64; Ontario, 1871 1823.15 p159
McCandless, James; Mississippi, 1817-1845 1640.10 p103
McCandless, John; New York, 1839 8197.10 p139
McCandlish, Grizel; America, 1770 1640.13 p83
McCane, James 38; Ontario, 1871 1823.22 p100
McCane, Thomas; New York, New York, 1860 6058.10 p55
McCanir, Richard 68; Ontario, 1871 1823.15 p159
McCann, Abram 37; Ontario, 1871 1823.22 p100
McCann, Andrew; New York, 1834-1838 8197.10 p119
McCann, Andrew; New York, 1838 8197.10 p126
McCann, Ann McInlear 72; Vermont, n.d. 5900.10 p545
McCann, Arthur; New York, 1838 8197.10 p376
McCann, Arthur 47; Ontario, 1871 1823.22 p100
McCann, Bridget 84; Vermont, 1907 5900.10 p318
McCann, David; New York, 1838 8197.10 p376
McCann, Edward; New York, 1821 8197.10 p253
McCann, Edward 31; Ontario, 1871 1823.28 p63
McCann, Edward J.; Vermont, 1856-1932 5900.10 p195
McCann, George 60; Ontario, 1871 1823.15 p159
McCann, Hannah Sullivan; Vermont, 1860-1952 5900.10 p304
McCann, Helen O'Conner 30; Vermont, 1863 5900.10 p502
McCann, Hugh; New York, 1826 8197.10 p255
McCann, Hugh; New York, 1840 8197.10 p185
McCann, John; Vermont, 1855-1908 5900.10 p311
McCann, John 20; Vermont, 1868 5900.10 p545
McCann, John 67; Ontario, 1871 1823.22 p100
McCann, John 81; Ontario, 1871 1823.22 p100
McCann, John 84; Vermont, 1897 5900.10 p545
McCann, Margaret; Vermont, 1853-1933 5900.10 p311
McCann, Mary; Vermont, 1857-1925 5900.10 p195
McCann, Mary 53; Vermont, 1898 5900.10 p254
McCann, Mary Fitzgerald 81; Vermont, 1910 5900.10 p503
McCann, Michael 56; Vermont, 1880 5900.10 p502
McCann, Nancy 43; Vermont, 1864 5900.10 p545
McCann, Owen; New York, New York, 1863 6058.10 p59
McCann, Patrick; New York, 1837 8197.10 p97
McCann, Patrick; New York, 1838 8197.10 p376
McCann, Patrick; Pennsylvania, 1864-1867 6058.10 p59
McCann, Philip; New York, 1826 8197.10 p256
McCann, William; Vermont, 1857-1931 5900.10 p304
McCann, William 43; Vermont, 1868 5900.10 p503
McCann, Wilson 62; Ontario, 1871 1823.15 p159
McCanna, Bridget 64; Vermont, 1898 5900.10 p591
McCanna, John; New York, 1836 8197.10 p77
McCanna, John; New York, 1839 8197.10 p258
McCanna, Patrick 40; Ontario, 1871 1823.15 p159
McCannal, Ann 16; Ontario, 1861 2896.27 p20
McCannal, Bridget 1; Ontario, 1861 2896.27 p20
McCannal, Eleanor 36; Ontario, 1861 2896.27 p20
McCannal, Thomas 5; Ontario, 1861 2896.27 p20
McCans, Hugh 43; Ontario, 1871 1823.28 p63
McCanse, Mary I.; Vermont, 1846-1928 5900.10 p481
McCaracher, Daniel; Pennsylvania, 1777 4629.10 p18
McCarcher, William 43; Ontario, 1871 1823.15 p159
McCardell, Philip; Pennsylvania, 1777 4629.10 p26
McCarey, Patrick; New York, 1832 8197.10 p314
McCarey, Patrick; New York, 1832 8197.10 p316
McCarl, Edward T.; Vermont, 1866-1939 5900.10 p122
McCarl, Margaret; Vermont, 1862-1957 5900.10 p123
McCarra, John 50; Ontario, 1871 1823.15 p159
McCarragher, Mary A.; Vermont, 1854-1938 5900.10 p461
McCarrill, John; Canada, 1756-1760 4628.40 p45
McCarroll, Mr.; Vermont, 1793-1862 5900.10 p493
McCarroll, Mrs.; Vermont, 1799-1887 5900.10 p493
McCarroll, Charles H.; Vermont, 1838-1914 5900.10 p496
McCarroll, John B.; Vermont, 1831-1874 5900.10 p493
McCarroll, Mary 18; Vermont, 1867 5900.10 p161
McCarroll, Sarah A. Green; Vermont, 1851-1912 5900.10 p496
McCarroll, Thomas; Vermont, 1827-1890 5900.10 p493
McCarron, David 51; Ontario, 1871 1823.15 p159
McCarron, James 84; Ontario, 1871 1823.15 p159
McCarron, Mary; Vermont, 1843-1927 5900.10 p333
McCarron, Mary 45; Ontario, 1871 1823.15 p159
McCartan, James; New York, 1807 8197.10 p332
McCarter, David 34; Ontario, 1871 1823.28 p63
McCarter, Henry 73; Ontario, 1871 1823.15 p159

McCarter, James; Utah, 1883 ***1640.13*** *p83*
McCarter, John; Pennsylvania, 1785 ***4629.10*** *p44*
McCartey, John; Pennsylvania, 1777 ***4629.10*** *p12*
McCarthey, E. A. 27; Ontario, 1861 ***2896.28*** *p15*
McCarthey, Felix 60; Ontario, 1871 ***1823.28*** *p63*
McCarthey, G. M. 3; Ontario, 1861 ***2896.28*** *p15*
McCarthur, Daniel 54; Ontario, 1871 ***1823.15*** *p159*
McCarthy, Alice 68; Vermont, 1860 ***5900.10*** *p56*
McCarthy, Alice Brown; Vermont, 1845-1945 ***5900.10*** *p614*
McCarthy, Andrew J.; Vermont, 1841-1921 ***5900.10*** *p64*
McCarthy, Ann 2; New York, New York, 1848 ***1825.45*** *p29*
McCarthy, Ann Doran 66; Vermont, 1896 ***5900.10*** *p484*
McCarthy, Anna B.; Vermont, 1853-1932 ***5900.10*** *p176*
McCarthy, Bridget 55 *SEE* McCarthy, John
McCarthy, Bridget Delligan; Vermont, 1859-1935 ***5900.10*** *p490*
McCarthy, Bridget Powers; Vermont, 1841-1903 ***5900.10*** *p563*
McCarthy, Catharine O'Day; Vermont, n.d. ***5900.10*** *p344*
McCarthy, Catherine 70; Vermont, 1875 ***5900.10*** *p574*
McCarthy, Charles 49; Ontario, 1871 ***1823.15*** *p159*
McCarthy, Cornelius; Vermont, 1849-1929 ***5900.10*** *p88*
McCarthy, Cornelius 82; Vermont, 1914 ***5900.10*** *p484*
McCarthy, Daniel; New York, 1837 ***8197.10*** *p95*
McCarthy, Daniel; New York, 1838 ***8197.10*** *p125*
McCarthy, Daniel; New York, 1839 ***8197.10*** *p258*
McCarthy, Daniel; New York, New York, 1861 ***6058.10*** *p55*
McCarthy, Daniel; Vermont, n.d. ***5900.10*** *p79*
McCarthy, Daniel; Vermont, 1858-1901 ***5900.10*** *p59*
McCarthy, David 75; Ontario, 1871 ***1823.15*** *p159*
McCarthy, Dennis; Vermont, 1825-1910 ***5900.10*** *p73*
McCarthy, Dennis; Vermont, 1825-1910 ***5900.10*** *p79*
McCarthy, Donald 65; Vermont, 1877 ***5900.10*** *p574*
McCarthy, Edward 12 *SEE* McCarthy, John
McCarthy, Eliza; New York, 1831 ***8197.10*** *p354*
McCarthy, Eliza Keating; Vermont, 1822-1906 ***5900.10*** *p59*
McCarthy, Ellen; Vermont, 1836-1906 ***5900.10*** *p586*
McCarthy, Ellen 73; Vermont, 1891 ***5900.10*** *p586*
McCarthy, Ellen A.; Vermont, 1857-1928 ***5900.10*** *p159*
McCarthy, Ellen Bowen; Vermont, n.d. ***5900.10*** *p79*
McCarthy, Ellen Donovan; Vermont, 1804-1873 ***5900.10*** *p73*
McCarthy, Ellen Donovan; Vermont, 1834-1873 ***5900.10*** *p79*
McCarthy, Ellen E.; Vermont, 1837-1913 ***5900.10*** *p447*
McCarthy, Fanny 77; Vermont, 1875 ***5900.10*** *p63*
McCarthy, Felix E.; Vermont, 1861-1932 ***5900.10*** *p355*
McCarthy, Florence; Boston, 1827 ***8197.10*** *p301*
McCarthy, Florence 45; Vermont, 1896 ***5900.10*** *p563*
McCarthy, Florence 61; Ontario, 1871 ***1823.28*** *p63*
McCarthy, Frank; Vermont, 1847-1908 ***5900.10*** *p585*
McCarthy, G.; Portland, Maine, 1857 ***9196.15*** *p12*
McCarthy, Hanna 36; Vermont, 1847 ***5900.10*** *p146*
McCarthy, Hannorah 84; Vermont, 1907 ***5900.10*** *p362*
McCarthy, Hannorah 84; Vermont, 1907 ***5900.10*** *p366*
McCarthy, Honora; Vermont, 1790-1905 ***5900.10*** *p79*
McCarthy, Honora; Vermont, 1833-1863 ***5900.10*** *p432*
McCarthy, Honora 77; Vermont, 1894 ***5900.10*** *p477*
McCarthy, James; New York, 1839 ***8197.10*** *p258*
McCarthy, James 17; Vermont, 1869 ***5900.10*** *p65*
McCarthy, James 55; Vermont, 1899 ***5900.10*** *p614*
McCarthy, James D.; Vermont, 1851-1926 ***5900.10*** *p176*
McCarthy, Jeremiah; Vermont, 1857-1921 ***5900.10*** *p356*
McCarthy, Jeremiah; Vermont, 1858-1945 ***5900.10*** *p355*
McCarthy, Jerry C.; Vermont, 1856-1935 ***5900.10*** *p484*
McCarthy, Johanna 60; Ontario, 1871 ***1823.15*** *p159*
McCarthy, John; New York, 1821 ***8197.10*** *p254*
McCarthy, John; New York, 1835 ***8197.10*** *p257*
McCarthy, John; New York, 1837 ***8197.10*** *p97*
McCarthy, John; New York, 1840 ***8197.10*** *p183*
McCarthy, John; New York, New York, 1848 ***1825.45*** *p56*
With mother & sister
McCarthy, John; Pennsylvania, 1779 ***4629.10*** *p38*
McCarthy, John; Vermont, 1822-1872 ***5900.10*** *p58*
McCarthy, John; Vermont, 1843 ***5900.10*** *p149*
McCarthy, John 33; Vermont, 1861 ***5900.10*** *p362*
McCarthy, John 33; Vermont, 1861 ***5900.10*** *p366*
McCarthy, John 50; Ontario, 1871 ***1823.28*** *p63*
McCarthy, John 60; New York, New York, 1848 ***1825.45*** *p29*
Wife: Bridget 55
Son: Martin 15
Son: Thomas 14
Daughter: Peggy 21
Daughter: Mary 25
Son: Peter 10
Son: Edward 12
McCarthy, John 84; Vermont, 1886 ***5900.10*** *p586*
McCarthy, Joseph; Canada, 1756-1760 ***4628.40*** *p46*
McCarthy, Julia; Vermont, 1807-1874 ***5900.10*** *p327*
McCarthy, Julia A. Barry; Vermont, 1868-1940 ***5900.10*** *p484*
McCarthy, Katherine Crimmins; Vermont, 1832-1913 ***5900.10*** *p356*
McCarthy, Lucy A.; Vermont, 1856-1923 ***5900.10*** *p548*
McCarthy, Margaret 22; New York, New York, 1849 ***1825.45*** *p51*
McCarthy, Margaret O'Connell; Vermont, 1852-1925 ***5900.10*** *p352*
McCarthy, Martin 15 *SEE* McCarthy, John
McCarthy, Mary; Vermont, 1839-1919 ***5900.10*** *p88*
McCarthy, Mary 25 *SEE* McCarthy, John
McCarthy, Mary 83; Vermont, 1890 ***5900.10*** *p569*
McCarthy, Mary 88; Vermont, 1902 ***5900.10*** *p85*
McCarthy, Mary A.; Vermont, 1854-1928 ***5900.10*** *p444*
McCarthy, Mary Ann; Vermont, 1854-1900 ***5900.10*** *p485*
McCarthy, Mary Corbett; Vermont, 1852-1920 ***5900.10*** *p585*
McCarthy, Mary Crowley 95; Vermont, 1879 ***5900.10*** *p585*
McCarthy, Mary E.; Vermont, 1855-1904 ***5900.10*** *p353*
McCarthy, Mary E. Sullivan 48; Vermont, 1909 ***5900.10*** *p563*
McCarthy, Mary McGinley; Vermont, 1848-1917 ***5900.10*** *p195*
McCarthy, Mary O'Mara; Vermont, 1837-1906 ***5900.10*** *p80*
McCarthy, Mary O'Neill; Vermont, 1855-1925 ***5900.10*** *p356*
McCarthy, Mary Y.; Vermont, 1853-1903 ***5900.10*** *p483*
McCarthy, Michael; Vermont, 1833-1858 ***5900.10*** *p59*
McCarthy, Michael 39; Ontario, 1871 ***1823.15*** *p159*
McCarthy, Nancy Kiniry; Vermont, 1840-1914 ***5900.10*** *p64*
McCarthy, Nealy 1; Vermont, 1864 ***5900.10*** *p484*
McCarthy, Owen; Vermont, 1840-1913 ***5900.10*** *p563*
McCarthy, Patrick; New York, 1838 ***8197.10*** *p125*
McCarthy, Patrick; Vermont, 1840-1914 ***5900.10*** *p597*
McCarthy, Patrick; Vermont, 1847-1921 ***5900.10*** *p352*
McCarthy, Patrick; Vermont, 1849-1937 ***5900.10*** *p195*
McCarthy, Patrick; Vermont, 1854-1904 ***5900.10*** *p59*
McCarthy, Patrick 40; Vermont, 1866 ***5900.10*** *p371*
McCarthy, Patrick 45; Ontario, 1871 ***1823.15*** *p159*
McCarthy, Patrick 57; Ontario, 1871 ***1823.28*** *p63*
McCarthy, Patrick 70; Ontario, 1871 ***1823.22*** *p100*
McCarthy, Peggy 21 *SEE* McCarthy, John
McCarthy, Peter 10 *SEE* McCarthy, John
McCarthy, Richard; New York, 1828 ***8197.10*** *p256*
McCarthy, Rosa 9; Vermont, 1875 ***5900.10*** *p484*
McCarthy, Rose E. Dolan; Vermont, 1872-1939 ***5900.10*** *p355*
McCarthy, Sarah; Vermont, 1826-1907 ***5900.10*** *p246*
McCarthy, Susan Walker; Vermont, 1840-1915 ***5900.10*** *p597*
McCarthy, Thomas 14 *SEE* McCarthy, John
McCarthy, Thomas 28; Ontario, 1871 ***1823.15*** *p159*
McCarthy, Thomas 97; Vermont, 1885 ***5900.10*** *p344*
McCarthy, Thomas R.; Vermont, 1857-1924 ***5900.10*** *p490*
McCarthy, Timothy; New York, 1839 ***8197.10*** *p138*
McCarthy, Timothy; Vermont, 1849-1917 ***5900.10*** *p353*
McCarthy, Timothy 65; Ontario, 1871 ***1823.15*** *p159*
McCarthy, William; Vermont, 1840-1925 ***5900.10*** *p80*
McCarthy, William; Vermont, 1855-1928 ***5900.10*** *p282*
McCarthy, William C.; Vermont, 1898-1952 ***5900.10*** *p355*
McCartin, Charles; New York, 1822 ***8197.10*** *p255*
McCartney, Alexander 25; Ontario, 1871 ***1823.15*** *p159*
McCartney, Eliza; Alabama, 1829 ***1224.3*** *p48*
McCartney, Eliza 47; Ontario, 1861 ***2896.28*** *p20*
McCartney, Eliz'th 67; Ontario, 1861 ***2896.26*** *p32*
McCartney, George 41; Ontario, 1871 ***1823.15*** *p159*
McCartney, Hannah 22; Ontario, 1861 ***2896.28*** *p20*
McCartney, Henrietta J. 12; Ontario, 1861 ***2896.28*** *p20*
McCartney, John; New York, 1837 ***8197.10*** *p97*
McCartney, John 41; Ontario, 1871 ***1823.15*** *p160*
McCartney, Nancy J. 16; Ontario, 1861 ***2896.28*** *p20*
McCartney, Robert 67; Ontario, 1871 ***1823.15*** *p160*
McCartney, Sarah E. 18; Ontario, 1861 ***2896.28*** *p20*
McCartney, Thomas 72; Ontario, 1861 ***2896.28*** *p20*
McCartney, Umphry; Pennsylvania, 1840 ***6058.10*** *p23*
McCartney, William 20; Ontario, 1861 ***2896.28*** *p20*
McCartny, Anne 70; Ontario, 1871 ***1823.15*** *p160*
McCarton, James; New York, 1840 ***8197.10*** *p183*
McCarty, Alice 59; Ontario, 1871 ***1823.28*** *p63*
McCarty, Ann 56; Vermont, 1902 ***5900.10*** *p281*
McCarty, Ann Starr; Vermont, 1823-1907 ***5900.10*** *p393*
McCarty, Annie; Vermont, n.d. ***5900.10*** *p348*
McCarty, Annie 73; Ontario, 1871 ***1823.28*** *p63*
McCarty, Catherine; Vermont, 1813-1879 ***5900.10*** *p344*
McCarty, Catherine 65; Vermont, 1880 ***5900.10*** *p237*
McCarty, Catherine 72; Vermont, 1890 ***5900.10*** *p116*
McCarty, Catherine Cain 80; Vermont, 1894 ***5900.10*** *p614*
McCarty, Charles 60; Ontario, 1871 ***1823.22*** *p100*
McCarty, Clara; Vermont, n.d. ***5900.10*** *p348*
McCarty, Cornelius 15; Vermont, 1858 ***5900.10*** *p347*
McCarty, Daniel 40; Ontario, 1871 ***1823.15*** *p160*
McCarty, Elennor 81; Vermont, 1913 ***5900.10*** *p367*
McCarty, Eliza M. 15; Vermont, 1874 ***5900.10*** *p481*
McCarty, Elizabeth; Vermont, 1850-1923 ***5900.10*** *p143*
McCarty, Elizabeth 79; Vermont, 1893 ***5900.10*** *p595*
McCarty, Elizabeth Hilliher 32; Vermont, 1815 ***5900.10*** *p606*
McCarty, Ellen; Vermont, n.d. ***5900.10*** *p347*
McCarty, Ellen; Vermont, 1826-1891 ***5900.10*** *p205*
McCarty, Ellen; Vermont, 1845-1914 ***5900.10*** *p225*
McCarty, Ellen; Vermont, 1852-1889 ***5900.10*** *p481*
McCarty, Ellen; Vermont, 1854-1923 ***5900.10*** *p594*
McCarty, Ellen; Vermont, 1886 ***5900.10*** *p549*
McCarty, Ellen Healy; Vermont, 1848-1924 ***5900.10*** *p132*
McCarty, Ellenor; Vermont, n.d. ***5900.10*** *p366*
McCarty, Euganie 27; Ontario, 1871 ***1823.28*** *p63*
McCarty, Eugene; Vermont, n.d. ***5900.10*** *p347*
McCarty, Felix 30; Ontario, 1871 ***1823.28*** *p63*
McCarty, Florance 13 days; Vermont, 1854 ***5900.10*** *p367*
McCarty, Florance 2; Vermont, 1855 ***5900.10*** *p367*
McCarty, Florance 22; Ontario, 1871 ***1823.28*** *p63*
McCarty, Hannah; Vermont, n.d. ***5900.10*** *p396*
McCarty, Hannah Crowley; Vermont, 1892 ***5900.10*** *p481*
McCarty, Hannah E.; Vermont, 1826-1906 ***5900.10*** *p207*
McCarty, Henry; New York, 1837 ***8197.10*** *p375*
McCarty, Jane A. Donlin; Vermont, 1859 ***5900.10*** *p158*
McCarty, Jane F. O'Hagan; Vermont, 1860-1916 ***5900.10*** *p341*
McCarty, Jane McCallister; Vermont, 1840-1928 ***5900.10*** *p208*
McCarty, Jeremiah 27; Ontario, 1871 ***1823.22*** *p100*
McCarty, Jeremiah 32; Ontario, 1871 ***1823.28*** *p63*
McCarty, Johanna 62; Vermont, 1890 ***5900.10*** *p476*
McCarty, John; Vermont, 1796-1874 ***5900.10*** *p207*
McCarty, John; Vermont, 1845-1896 ***5900.10*** *p132*
McCarty, John; Vermont, 1853-1909 ***5900.10*** *p594*
McCarty, John; Vermont, 1858-1911 ***5900.10*** *p366*
McCarty, John; Vermont, 1882 ***5900.10*** *p481*
McCarty, John 6; Vermont, 1868 ***5900.10*** *p104*
McCarty, John 30; Ontario, 1871 ***1823.22*** *p100*
McCarty, John 37; Vermont, 1813 ***5900.10*** *p606*
McCarty, John 45; Ontario, 1871 ***1823.28*** *p63*
McCarty, John 52; Ontario, 1871 ***1823.22*** *p100*
McCarty, John 66; Vermont, 1888 ***5900.10*** *p366*
McCarty, John 82; Ontario, 1871 ***1823.22*** *p100*
McCarty, Julia; Vermont, n.d. ***5900.10*** *p366*
McCarty, Kate; Vermont, n.d. ***5900.10*** *p348*
McCarty, Katherine Sears 67; Vermont, 1894 ***5900.10*** *p595*
McCarty, Katie Downes; Vermont, 1864-1892 ***5900.10*** *p258*
McCarty, Margaret; Vermont, n.d. ***5900.10*** *p347*
McCarty, Margaret; Vermont, n.d. ***5900.10*** *p348*
McCarty, Margaret; Vermont, n.d. ***5900.10*** *p366*
McCarty, Margaret; Vermont, 1804-1879 ***5900.10*** *p143*
McCarty, Margaret; Vermont, 1822-1903 ***5900.10*** *p361*
McCarty, Margaret; Vermont, 1857-1929 ***5900.10*** *p395*
McCarty, Margaret 57; Ontario, 1871 ***1823.22*** *p101*
McCarty, Mary; Vermont, 1845-1913 ***5900.10*** *p484*
McCarty, Mary; Vermont, 1852-1925 ***5900.10*** *p278*
McCarty, Mary; Vermont, 1864-1921 ***5900.10*** *p143*
McCarty, Mary 23; Vermont, 1888 ***5900.10*** *p366*
McCarty, Mary 30; Vermont, 1864 ***5900.10*** *p245*
McCarty, Mary A. Kennedy; Vermont, 1854-1919 ***5900.10*** *p594*
McCarty, Mary Ann 25; Vermont, 1875 ***5900.10*** *p480*
McCarty, Mary L. Manley; Vermont, 1837-1920 ***5900.10*** *p495*
McCarty, Michael; New York, 1834 ***8197.10*** *p315*
McCarty, Michael; New York, 1837 ***8197.10*** *p97*
McCarty, Michael; New York, 1837 ***8197.10*** *p318*
McCarty, Michael; Vermont, 1830-1914 ***5900.10*** *p595*
McCarty, Michael; Vermont, 1836-1908 ***5900.10*** *p486*
McCarty, Michael 12 days; Vermont, 1859 ***5900.10*** *p367*
McCarty, Nora; Vermont, 1868-1915 ***5900.10*** *p143*
McCarty, Norman; Vermont, 1832-1916 ***5900.10*** *p208*
McCarty, Orland 47; Vermont, 1882 ***5900.10*** *p207*
McCarty, Patrick; New York, 1807 ***8197.10*** *p328*
McCarty, Patrick; Vermont, 1848-1923 ***5900.10*** *p341*
McCarty, Patrick 40; Vermont, 1866 ***5900.10*** *p359*
McCarty, Patrick 82; Vermont, 1893 ***5900.10*** *p480*

McCarty, Patrick, Jr. 26; Vermont, 1879 ***5900.10*** *p480*
McCarty, Sally Coburn; Vermont, 1799-1892 ***5900.10*** *p207*
McCarty, Thomas; Vermont, 1805-1887 ***5900.10*** *p143*
McCarty, Thomas 22; Maryland, 1774 ***1220.25*** *p37*
McCarty, Thomas 60; Ontario, 1871 ***1823.22*** *p101*
McCarty, Thomas, Jr.; Vermont, 1842-1901 ***5900.10*** *p143*
McCarty, Timothy; Vermont, 1850-1934 ***5900.10*** *p281*
McCarty, Timothy 73; Vermont, 1876 ***5900.10*** *p614*
McCarty, William; Vermont, 1837-1901 ***5900.10*** *p495*
McCarty, William 9; Vermont, 1860 ***5900.10*** *p347*
McCarty, William B.; Vermont, 1858-1914 ***5900.10*** *p158*
McCarty, William E.; Vermont, 1852-1939 ***5900.10*** *p594*
McCary, Thomas 63; Ontario, 1871 ***1823.22*** *p101*
McCasdy, John 37; Ontario, 1871 ***1823.15*** *p160*
McCaskel, Finlay 61; Ontario, 1871 ***1823.28*** *p63*
McCaskie, James; Dominican Republic, 1798 ***1640.13*** *p83*
McCaskill, Daniel; America, 1760-1770 ***1640.10*** *p103*
McCaskill, Finley; Florida, 1796-1845 ***1640.10*** *p103*
McCaskill, Isabel; Florida, 1820 ***1640.10*** *p103*
McCaskill, Kenneth 90; Ontario, 1871 ***1823.28*** *p63*
McCaslin, Arthur 72; Ontario, 1871 ***1823.15*** *p160*
McCauchie, Francis 36; Ontario, 1871 ***1823.15*** *p160*
McCaughay, John 39; Ontario, 1871 ***1823.15*** *p160*
McCaughern, Daniel 57; Vermont, 1873 ***5900.10*** *p103*
McCaughern, Nancy Dimond; Vermont, 1830-1914 ***5900.10*** *p103*
McCaughern, Robert 18; Vermont, 1873 ***5900.10*** *p103*
McCaughey, James 49; Ontario, 1871 ***1823.15*** *p160*
McCaughey, John 33; Ontario, 1871 ***1823.22*** *p101*
McCaughey, William 40; Ontario, 1871 ***1823.22*** *p101*
McCaul, John 73; Ontario, 1871 ***1823.15*** *p160*
McCaulay, Robert; New York, 1840 ***8197.10*** *p321*
McCaulay, Thomas 50; Ontario, 1871 ***1823.22*** *p101*
McCauley, Cornelius 45; Vermont, 1873 ***5900.10*** *p220*
McCauley, John; New York, 1830 ***8197.10*** *p256*
McCauley, John 26; Ontario, 1871 ***1823.28*** *p63*
McCauley, Margaret Gartland; Vermont, 1833-1895 ***5900.10*** *p311*
McCauley, Mary Ann McBride 41; Vermont, 1885 ***5900.10*** *p220*
McCauley, Mary McDonough; Vermont, 1837-1906 ***5900.10*** *p558*
McCauley, Owen; New York, 1839 ***8197.10*** *p258*
McCauley, Patrick, Sr. 59; Ontario, 1871 ***1823.22*** *p101*
McCauley, Terrance; Vermont, 1835-1917 ***5900.10*** *p558*
McCauley, William; Vermont, 1830-1893 ***5900.10*** *p311*
McCauliff, Patrick 44; Vermont, 1877 ***5900.10*** *p63*
McCauly, Elizabeth H.; Vermont, 1852-1952 ***5900.10*** *p597*
McCauly, Francis 60; Ontario, 1871 ***1823.22*** *p101*
McCaun, Patrick 70; Ontario, 1871 ***1823.15*** *p160*
McCausland, James; Pennsylvania, 1824 ***6058.10*** *p8*
McCausland, James, Sr.; New York, 1832 ***8197.10*** *p357*
McCausland, John; New York, 1838 ***8197.10*** *p125*
McCausland, William; New York, 1828 ***8197.10*** *p349*
McCavet, Ellen McDermott; Vermont, 1845-1933 ***5900.10*** *p419*
McCavet, James 3; Vermont, 1872 ***5900.10*** *p99*
McCavet, John; Vermont, 1837-1900 ***5900.10*** *p419*
McCavitt, John; New York, 1824 ***8197.10*** *p255*
McCaw, E. 3; Ontario, 1861 ***2896.26*** *p13*
McCaw, James; Virginia, 1791 ***1640.13*** *p83*
McCaw, L. S. 6; Ontario, 1861 ***2896.26*** *p13*
McCaw, M. E. 15; Ontario, 1861 ***2896.26*** *p13*
McCaw, W. 41; Ontario, 1861 ***2896.26*** *p13*
McCaw, W. W. 13; Ontario, 1861 ***2896.26*** *p13*
McCawley, John; New York, 1840 ***8197.10*** *p183*
McCawley, John 39; Ontario, 1871 ***1823.28*** *p63*
McCawley, Mary; Vermont, 1840-1915 ***5900.10*** *p384*
McCawley, Patrick 45; Ontario, 1871 ***1823.28*** *p63*
McCay, Anne 60; Ontario, 1871 ***1823.15*** *p160*
McCay, J. S.; Alabama, 1839-1845 ***1640.10*** *p103*
McCay, John; Savannah, Georgia, 1810-1812 ***1640.10*** *p103*
With wife & 2 children
McCeaver, Peter; New York, 1809 ***8197.10*** *p55*
McCelland, John 90; Ontario, 1871 ***1823.15*** *p160*
McCelvy, Maren 59; Ontario, 1871 ***1823.15*** *p160*
McCeun, Capt. 30; New York, 1774 ***1220.25*** *p49*
McChesney, Eliza 75; Vermont, 1883 ***5900.10*** *p493*
McChesney, Hugh 22; Ontario, 1871 ***1823.22*** *p101*
McClain, Allen 60; Ontario, 1871 ***1823.22*** *p101*
McClain, Andrew; Mobile, Alabama, 1826-1845 ***1640.10*** *p103*
McClain, Hugh *SEE* McClain, Laughlin
McClain, Jacob; Pennsylvania, 1777 ***4629.10*** *p31*
McClain, Laughlin 14; Philadelphia, 1782 ***4629.10*** *p74*
Father: Hugh
McClain, Samuel; Pennsylvania, 1777 ***4629.10*** *p19*
McClaine, James; New York, 1802 ***8197.10*** *p23*
McClane, Mary Riley; Vermont, 1885 ***5900.10*** *p191*
McClaren, Isabella 60; Ontario, 1871 ***1823.28*** *p63*
McClarin, Ms. M.; Mississippi, 1790-1820 ***1640.10*** *p103*
McClarty, Dugal 50; Ontario, 1871 ***1823.15*** *p160*
McClary, . . .; New Hampshire, 1641-1660 ***4628.40*** *p44*
McClary, Alexander; Canada, 1756-1760 ***4628.40*** *p45*
McClary, Andrew; Nova Scotia, 1745 ***4628.40*** *p45*
McClary, John; Nova Scotia, 1745 ***4628.40*** *p45*
McClay, Emma M.; Vermont, 1856-1929 ***5900.10*** *p597*
McClay, Eva B.; Vermont, 1853-1914 ***5900.10*** *p597*
McClay, Gustavus; Vermont, 1826-1912 ***5900.10*** *p597*
McClay, Rosina Shaw; Vermont, 1828-1914 ***5900.10*** *p597*
McClean, Mrs. 56; Ontario, 1871 ***1823.15*** *p160*
McClean, Alexander 42; Ontario, 1871 ***1823.15*** *p160*
McClean, Archiebald 34; Ontario, 1871 ***1823.15*** *p160*
McClean, Barkle; Philadelphia, 1793 ***4629.10*** *p67*
McClean, Bernard 58; Vermont, 1892 ***5900.10*** *p125*
McClean, Grace 15; Ontario, 1861 ***2896.28*** *p27*
McClean, Isabell 60; Ontario, 1871 ***1823.15*** *p160*
McClean, Jane Manny; Vermont, n.d. ***5900.10*** *p320*
McClean, John; New York, 1810 ***8197.10*** *p252*
McClean, John 63; Ontario, 1871 ***1823.15*** *p160*
McClean, Own 66; Vermont, 1870-1879 ***5900.10*** *p125*
McClearen, James; Pennsylvania, 1777 ***4629.10*** *p24*
McCleary, Archibald; New York, 1830 ***8197.10*** *p363*
McCleery, James; New York, 1821 ***8197.10*** *p254*
McCleester, John; New York, 1840 ***8197.10*** *p182*
McClegmont, William 60; Ontario, 1871 ***1823.15*** *p160*
McClegmont, William 80; Ontario, 1871 ***1823.15*** *p160*
McClellan, Catherine D.; Vermont, 1855-1948 ***5900.10*** *p140*
McClellan, Robt 52; Ontario, 1871 ***1823.28*** *p63*
McClelland, Archie 25; Ontario, 1871 ***1823.22*** *p101*
McClelland, David 41; Ontario, 1871 ***1823.28*** *p63*
McClelland, Hugh; Pennsylvania, 1819 ***6058.10*** *p6*
McClelland, Hugh 73; Ontario, 1871 ***1823.28*** *p63*
McClelland, John; Georgia, 1757 ***1640.10*** *p104*
McClelland, John; Guatemala, 1832 ***1640.13*** *p83*
McClelland, John 25; Ontario, 1871 ***1823.28*** *p63*
McClelland, Mary; Georgia, 1762 ***1640.10*** *p104*
McClelland, Mary; Vermont, 1840-1918 ***5900.10*** *p321*
McClelland, Moses 38; Ontario, 1871 ***1823.28*** *p63*
McClelland, William 40; Ontario, 1871 ***1823.22*** *p101*
McClement, Ferguson 40; Ontario, 1871 ***1823.15*** *p160*
McClemhay, Mary 73; Ontario, 1871 ***1823.15*** *p160*
McClemhay, Robert 73; Ontario, 1871 ***1823.15*** *p160*
McClenachan, Blair; Pennsylvania, 1777 ***4629.10*** *p15*
McClenaghan, Andrew Thomson; St. Vincent, 1881 ***1640.13*** *p83*
McClenathan, . . . 2; Vermont, 1859 ***5900.10*** *p293*
McClenchey, Henry 44; Ontario, 1871 ***1823.15*** *p160*
McClenchy, Bridget 32; Ontario, 1871 ***1823.15*** *p160*
McClennan, John; Canada, 1756-1760 ***4628.40*** *p45*
McClennan, John 68; Ontario, 1871 ***1823.28*** *p63*
McClennan, Wm 43; Ontario, 1871 ***1823.28*** *p63*
McClentock, Alexander; New England, 1753 ***1224.2*** *p72*
McClentock, William; New England, 1753 ***1224.2*** *p72*
McCleod, Roderick 52; Ontario, 1871 ***1823.15*** *p160*
McClinchy, Matthew 37; Ontario, 1871 ***1823.15*** *p160*
McClinin, John; New York, 1838 ***8197.10*** *p126*
McClinton, Jane; Vermont, 1818-1905 ***5900.10*** *p595*
McClinton, Jane Tracy; Vermont, 1837-1895 ***5900.10*** *p595*
McClinton, John 43; Ontario, 1871 ***1823.15*** *p160*
McClinton, Joseph; Vermont, 1831-1913 ***5900.10*** *p595*
McClister, Francis; Pennsylvania, 1777 ***4629.10*** *p13*
McClocklin, David 59; Ontario, 1871 ***1823.15*** *p160*
McClocklin, David 90; Ontario, 1871 ***1823.15*** *p160*
McClocklin, Samuel 19; Ontario, 1871 ***1823.15*** *p160*
McClocklin, Thomas 35; Ontario, 1871 ***1823.15*** *p160*
McClory, John 56; Ontario, 1871 ***1823.15*** *p160*
McCloskey, Francis; New York, 1840 ***8197.10*** *p386*
McClosky, Daniel; New York, 1827 ***8197.10*** *p343*
McCloud, D. 18; Ontario, 1861 ***2896.28*** *p14*
McCloud, John; New York, 1765 ***1224.2*** *p72*
McCloud, John 28; Virginia, 1773 ***1220.25*** *p29*
McCloud, Kennith 44; Ontario, 1871 ***1823.15*** *p161*
McCloud, Roderick 17; Tobago, West Indies, 1775 ***1220.25*** *p96*
McCloud, Rodrick 20; Ontario, 1871 ***1823.15*** *p161*
McCloughlin, Margaret McKeon 37; Vermont, 1885 ***5900.10*** *p580*
McCloy, Archibald 51; Ontario, 1871 ***1823.15*** *p161*
McCloy, Margaret 78; Ontario, 1871 ***1823.15*** *p161*
McCluer, James 87; Vermont, 1865 ***5900.10*** *p457*
McCluer, Rebecca 69; Vermont, 1850 ***5900.10*** *p457*
McCluer, William 19; Ontario, 1871 ***1823.22*** *p101*
McClune, James; Philadelphia, 1854 ***6058.10*** *p47*
McClune, Robert; New York, New York, 1853 ***6058.10*** *p32*
McClunnan, Thomas 35; Ontario, 1871 ***1823.15*** *p161*
McClure, Miss; Quebec, 1858 ***9196.15*** *p36*
McClure, Addie McKinney; Vermont, 1848-1929 ***5900.10*** *p282*
McClure, Adelia 17; Vermont, 1863 ***5900.10*** *p500*
McClure, Alexander; Charles Town, South Carolina, 1812 ***1224.3*** *p48*
McClure, Donald 75; Ontario, 1871 ***1823.15*** *p161*
McClure, Hugh 37; Ontario, 1871 ***1823.15*** *p161*
McClure, James; Pennsylvania, 1787 ***4629.10*** *p56*
McClure, Jane E. Austin; Vermont, 1846-1884 ***5900.10*** *p282*
McClure, John; New York, 1807 ***8197.10*** *p46*
McClure, John; New York, 1836-1838 ***8197.10*** *p120*
McClure, John; New York, 1838 ***8197.10*** *p126*
McClure, John; Pennsylvania, 1839 ***6058.10*** *p22*
McClure, John; Vermont, 1838-1909 ***5900.10*** *p282*
McClure, Margret 19; Ontario, 1871 ***1823.22*** *p101*
McClure, Mary 66; Ontario, 1871 ***1823.15*** *p161*
McClure, Mary Aseltyne 69; Vermont, 1874 ***5900.10*** *p500*
McClure, Mary Stewart; Vermont, 1872-1930 ***5900.10*** *p282*
McClure, Ransom D.; Vermont, 1842-1912 ***5900.10*** *p282*
McClure, Samuel; Pennsylvania, 1777 ***4629.10*** *p12*
McCluskey, Barnard 33; Vermont, 1876 ***5900.10*** *p513*
McCluskey, Catharine 43; Vermont, 1869 ***5900.10*** *p513*
McCluskey, Ellen 15; Vermont, 1865 ***5900.10*** *p513*
McCluskey, Hugh 54; Vermont, 1870 ***5900.10*** *p513*
McCluskey, James; Vermont, 1846-1904 ***5900.10*** *p513*
McCluskey, John; New York, 1836 ***8197.10*** *p77*
McCluskey, Lydia; Vermont, 1852-1944 ***5900.10*** *p496*
McCluskey, Mary A.; Vermont, 1840-1903 ***5900.10*** *p513*
McCluskey, Richard; New York, 1838 ***8197.10*** *p125*
McClusky, Bernard; New York, 1840 ***8197.10*** *p258*
McClusky, Oren 60; Ontario, 1861 ***2896.26*** *p24*
McClusky, William; New York, 1826 ***8197.10*** *p332*
McCobb, James; Pennsylvania, 1779 ***4629.10*** *p38*
McCoid, Hugh 19; Ontario, 1861 ***2896.25*** *p9*
McCoid, John 21; Ontario, 1861 ***2896.26*** *p1*
McCoid, M. A. 16; Ontario, 1861 ***2896.25*** *p9*
McCoid, Margaret 9; Ontario, 1861 ***2896.25*** *p9*
McCoid, Mary A. 52; Ontario, 1861 ***2896.25*** *p9*
McCoid, William 61; Ontario, 1861 ***2896.25*** *p9*
McCoig, John; South Carolina, 1828 ***1640.10*** *p104*
McColgan, James; New York, 1830 ***8197.10*** *p362*
McColgan, Michael; New York, 1834 ***8197.10*** *p372*
McColgan, Patrick; New York, 1840 ***8197.10*** *p184*
McColl, Alexander 66; Ontario, 1871 ***1823.22*** *p101*
McColl, Archibald 58; Ontario, 1871 ***1823.22*** *p101*
McColl, Duncan 39; Ontario, 1871 ***1823.22*** *p101*
McColl, Hugh; New York, 1876 ***1640.13*** *p83*
McColl, Hugh 49; Ontario, 1871 ***1823.22*** *p101*
McColl, John 63; Ontario, 1871 ***1823.22*** *p101*
McColl, John S. 53; Ontario, 1871 ***1823.22*** *p101*
McColl, Nancy 52; Ontario, 1871 ***1823.22*** *p101*
McColl, William 37; Maryland, 1774 ***1220.25*** *p83*
McCollam, J.; Quebec, 1857 ***9196.15*** *p17*
McColley, Benjamin 33; Maryland, 1774 ***1220.25*** *p57*
McColliff, W. M.; Vermont, n.d. ***5900.10*** *p498*
McCollogh, William; Pennsylvania, 1779 ***4629.10*** *p41*
McCollom, John; Pennsylvania, 1786 ***4629.10*** *p49*
McCollom, Marion Deering; Vermont, 1841-1915 ***5900.10*** *p597*
McCollom, Mary 14; Vermont, 1852 ***5900.10*** *p304*
McCollom, William; Vermont, 1831-1909 ***5900.10*** *p597*
McCollough, Barbara 25; Ontario, 1861 ***2896.25*** *p62*
McCollough, Don 63; Ontario, 1861 ***2896.25*** *p62*
McCollough, George 27; Ontario, 1861 ***2896.25*** *p62*
McCollough, Henry 3; Ontario, 1861 ***2896.25*** *p64*
McCollough, Henry 24; Ontario, 1861 ***2896.25*** *p62*
McCollough, Hugh; New York, New York, 1848 ***6058.10*** *p31*
McCollough, Mary 4; Ontario, 1861 ***2896.25*** *p62*
McCollough, Patrick 21; New York, 1824-1827 ***8197.10*** *p309*
McCollough, William; Pennsylvania, 1855 ***6058.10*** *p34*
McCollum, Allen; Pennsylvania, 1777 ***4629.10*** *p13*
McCollum, Archable 46; Ontario, 1871 ***1823.28*** *p63*
McCollum, Archibald; North Carolina, 1820 ***1640.10*** *p104*
McCollum, John; Georgia, 1757 ***1640.10*** *p104*
McCollum, Margaret 60; Vermont, 1806 ***5900.10*** *p304*
McCollum, Sarah A. 68; Vermont, 1887 ***5900.10*** *p301*
McColly, John; New York, 1840 ***8197.10*** *p184*
McColm, Quintin; New England, 1746 ***1640.13*** *p83*
McColough, William; Pennsylvania, 1777 ***4629.10*** *p10*
McComb, Alexander; New York, 1831 ***8197.10*** *p367*
McComb, Ann 27; Ontario, 1861 ***2896.28*** *p47*
McComb, Hannah 3; Ontario, 1861 ***2896.28*** *p47*
McComb, James 1; Ontario, 1861 ***2896.28*** *p47*
McComb, James 30; Ontario, 1861 ***2896.28*** *p47*

McCunn, John 22; Philadelphia, 1775 ***1220.25*** *p107*
McCunn, Mathew 15; Philadelphia, 1774 ***1220.25*** *p4*
McCurdie, William 54; Ontario, 1871 ***1823.28*** *p64*
McCurdy, Archabald 52; Ontario, 1871 ***1823.15*** *p163*
McCurdy, James 59; Ontario, 1871 ***1823.15*** *p163*
McCurdy, James 78; Vermont, 1896 ***5900.10*** *p212*
McCurdy, Jane Green 63; Vermont, 1891 ***5900.10*** *p212*
McCurdy, John 35; Ontario, 1871 ***1823.15*** *p163*
McCurdy, Samuel 46; Ontario, 1871 ***1823.15*** *p163*
McCurdy, Thomas 25; Ontario, 1871 ***1823.15*** *p163*
McCurdy, William; Pennsylvania, 1781 ***4629.10*** *p42*
McCurrie, Andrew; Georgia, 1761 ***1640.10*** *p105*
McCurtis, William 38; Ontario, 1871 ***1823.15*** *p163*
McCutcheon, Hugh 47; Ontario, 1871 ***1823.22*** *p102*
McCutcheon, James 31; Ontario, 1871 ***1823.15*** *p163*
McCutcheon, John 50; Ontario, 1871 ***1823.15*** *p163*
McCutcheon, John 58; Ontario, 1871 ***1823.15*** *p163*
McCutcheon, Joseph 27; Ontario, 1871 ***1823.15*** *p163*
McCutcheon, Robert 30; Ontario, 1871 ***1823.15*** *p163*
McCutchin, Robert; New York, 1837 ***8197.10*** *p97*
McCutchon, David; Scott Co., Iowa, 1852 ***1224.3*** *p48*
McCutchon, Thomas 40; Ontario, 1871 ***1823.22*** *p102*
McCutheon, Francis 37; Ontario, 1871 ***1823.15*** *p163*
McDade, Robert; New York, 1840 ***8197.10*** *p184*
McDane, Julia 5; Vermont, 1855 ***5900.10*** *p161*
McDaniel, Alexander 26; Virginia, 1774 ***1220.25*** *p87*
McDaniel, Angus; Florida, 1831 ***1640.10*** *p105*
McDaniel, Catherine; North Carolina, 1820 ***1640.10*** *p106*
McDaniel, John; Florida, 1790-1845 ***1640.10*** *p106*
McDaniel, John R.; Florida, 1805-1845 ***1640.10*** *p106*
McDaniel, Lewis 33; Ontario, 1871 ***1823.28*** *p64*
McDaniel, Margaret; Florida, 1790-1845 ***1640.10*** *p106*
McDaniel, Peter; Florida, 1828 ***1640.10*** *p106*
McDaniel, Peter; Florida, 1829 ***1640.10*** *p106*
McDaniel, Robert 34; Ontario, 1871 ***1823.28*** *p64*
McDaniels, James 30; Ontario, 1871 ***1823.28*** *p64*
McDavid, Michael; Pennsylvania, 1850 ***6058.10*** *p26*
McDeade, Robert; New York, 1840 ***8197.10*** *p184*
McDearmont, Mathew 60; Ontario, 1871 ***1823.15*** *p163*
McDeirmed, James 50; Ontario, 1871 ***1823.28*** *p64*
McDermid, James 65; Ontario, 1871 ***1823.15*** *p163*
McDermid, John 34; Ontario, 1871 ***1823.28*** *p64*
McDermid, Mary; Georgia, 1790-1845 ***1640.10*** *p107*
McDermid, Peter 38; Ontario, 1871 ***1823.28*** *p64*
McDermit, John; New York, 1827 ***8197.10*** *p344*
McDermot, Anna S.; Vermont, 1816-1892 ***5900.10*** *p451*
McDermot, Archibald; Pennsylvania, 1777 ***4629.10*** *p27*
McDermot, Charles; New York, 1821 ***8197.10*** *p254*
McDermot, Henry 66; Ontario, 1871 ***1823.28*** *p64*
McDermot, Joseph 27; Ontario, 1871 ***1823.15*** *p163*
McDermott, Adeline; Vermont, 1849-1933 ***5900.10*** *p224*
McDermott, Angus 40; Ontario, 1871 ***1823.15*** *p163*
McDermott, Anne 8 *SEE* McDermott, Michael
McDermott, Anne 25 *SEE* McDermott, Hugh
McDermott, Annie; Vermont, 1816-1884 ***5900.10*** *p543*
McDermott, Annie 7 months; Vermont, 1877 ***5900.10*** *p449*
McDermott, Annie M. Genty; Vermont, 1861-1920 ***5900.10*** *p584*
McDermott, Bernard 28 *SEE* McDermott, Hugh
McDermott, Bessy 20 *SEE* McDermott, Hugh
McDermott, Betty 14 *SEE* McDermott, Michael
McDermott, Bridget; Vermont, 1806-1899 ***5900.10*** *p542*
McDermott, Bridget 11 *SEE* McDermott, Mary
McDermott, Bridget 70; Vermont, 1912 ***5900.10*** *p273*
McDermott, Bridget Reynolds; Vermont, 1831-1884 ***5900.10*** *p426*
McDermott, Catherine 80; Vermont, 1916 ***5900.10*** *p542*
McDermott, Cornelius; New York, 1840 ***8197.10*** *p320*
McDermott, Edward; Pennsylvania, 1779 ***4629.10*** *p38*
McDermott, Eliza 48 *SEE* McDermott, Hugh
McDermott, Ellen; Vermont, 1845-1933 ***5900.10*** *p419*
McDermott, Ellen 10 *SEE* McDermott, Michael
McDermott, Ellen 13 *SEE* McDermott, Hugh
McDermott, Ellen 20 *SEE* McDermott, Mary
McDermott, Ellen 40 *SEE* McDermott, Michael
McDermott, Francis; New York, 1838 ***8197.10*** *p257*
McDermott, Henry; Vermont, 1819-1912 ***5900.10*** *p490*
McDermott, Hugh 12 *SEE* McDermott, Hugh
McDermott, Hugh 50; New York, New York, 1847 ***1825.45*** *p17*
Wife: Eliza 48
Daughter: Anne 25
Daughter: Ellen 13
Daughter: Bessy 20
Daughter: Susan 22
Daughter: Rosanna 14
Son: William 18
Son: Bernard 28
Son: Hugh 12
Son: John 24
Son: James 26
McDermott, J. A.; Quebec, 1857 ***9196.15*** *p14*
McDermott, James; Vermont, 1837-1914 ***5900.10*** *p304*
McDermott, James; Vermont, 1852-1936 ***5900.10*** *p490*
McDermott, James 26 *SEE* McDermott, Hugh
McDermott, James 31; Ontario, 1871 ***1823.28*** *p64*
McDermott, Janet 36; Ontario, 1871 ***1823.15*** *p163*
McDermott, John; New York, 1840 ***8197.10*** *p183*
McDermott, John; Vermont, 1845-1889 ***5900.10*** *p78*
McDermott, John 13 *SEE* McDermott, Mary
McDermott, John 20; Ontario, 1871 ***1823.15*** *p163*
McDermott, John 24 *SEE* McDermott, Hugh
McDermott, John 24; Ontario, 1871 ***1823.15*** *p163*
McDermott, John 55; Vermont, 1889 ***5900.10*** *p440*
McDermott, John 59; Ontario, 1871 ***1823.15*** *p163*
McDermott, Joseph; New York, 1840 ***8197.10*** *p183*
McDermott, Katherine Davin; Vermont, 1860-1890 ***5900.10*** *p584*
McDermott, Katherine Owens 60; Vermont, 1905 ***5900.10*** *p440*
McDermott, Kenneth 58; Ontario, 1871 ***1823.15*** *p163*
McDermott, Margaret; Vermont, 1842-1916 ***5900.10*** *p307*
McDermott, Margaret; Vermont, 1884-1978 ***5900.10*** *p606*
McDermott, Margaret 73; Vermont, 1922 ***5900.10*** *p422*
McDermott, Margaret Richards; Vermont, 1827-1910 ***5900.10*** *p490*
McDermott, Maria 12 *SEE* McDermott, Michael
McDermott, Mary; Vermont, 1844-1910 ***5900.10*** *p560*
McDermott, Mary; Vermont, 1866-1940 ***5900.10*** *p273*
McDermott, Mary 17 *SEE* McDermott, Mary
McDermott, Mary 44; New York, New York, 1847 ***1825.45*** *p17*
Son: John 13
Daughter: Bridget 11
Daughter: Ellen 20
Daughter: Mary 17
Son: Thomas 15
McDermott, Mary 44; Ontario, 1871 ***1823.28*** *p64*
McDermott, Mary A.; Vermont, 1855-1942 ***5900.10*** *p426*
McDermott, Mary H. Crosby; Vermont, 1850-1914 ***5900.10*** *p304*
McDermott, Matilda 60; Vermont, 1904 ***5900.10*** *p483*
McDermott, Michael; New York, 1827 ***8197.10*** *p256*
McDermott, Michael; New York, 1833 ***8197.10*** *p257*
McDermott, Michael; New York, 1834 ***8197.10*** *p74*
McDermott, Michael; Vermont, 1804-1878 ***5900.10*** *p542*
McDermott, Michael 16 *SEE* McDermott, Michael
McDermott, Michael 44; New York, New York, 1847 ***1825.45*** *p17*
Wife: Ellen 40
Daughter: Maria 12
Daughter: Ellen 10
Son: Michael 16
Daughter: Anne 8
Daughter: Betty 14
McDermott, Michael 47; Vermont, 1883 ***5900.10*** *p390*
McDermott, Mitchell; Vermont, 1833-1932 ***5900.10*** *p224*
McDermott, Norman 15; Ontario, 1871 ***1823.15*** *p163*
McDermott, Patrick; New York, 1838 ***8197.10*** *p125*
McDermott, Patrick; Vermont, 1854-1935 ***5900.10*** *p584*
McDermott, Patrick 58; Vermont, 1880 ***5900.10*** *p273*
McDermott, Patrick 76; Vermont, 1872 ***5900.10*** *p542*
McDermott, Peter; New York, 1827 ***8197.10*** *p314*
McDermott, Peter; New York, 1832 ***8197.10*** *p303*
McDermott, Rosanna 14 *SEE* McDermott, Hugh
McDermott, Susan 22 *SEE* McDermott, Hugh
McDermott, Thomas; New York, 1837 ***8197.10*** *p95*
McDermott, Thomas; Vermont, 1822-1881 ***5900.10*** *p426*
McDermott, Thomas; Vermont, 1854-1914 ***5900.10*** *p426*
McDermott, Thomas 15 *SEE* McDermott, Mary
McDermott, William 18 *SEE* McDermott, Hugh
McDeurmaid, Donald 48; Ontario, 1871 ***1823.15*** *p163*
McDevit, Margaret 1 month; Vermont, 1874 ***5900.10*** *p208*
McDevit, Mary Jane 6 months; Vermont, 1875 ***5900.10*** *p208*
McDevitt, Andrew 41; Vermont, 1879 ***5900.10*** *p560*
McDevitt, Ann; Vermont, 1879-1913 ***5900.10*** *p214*
McDevitt, Anne; Vermont, 1843-1923 ***5900.10*** *p221*
McDevitt, Charles; New York, 1839 ***8197.10*** *p138*
McDevitt, David; Vermont, 1831-1897 ***5900.10*** *p570*
McDevitt, Ellen McGuigen; Vermont, 1846-1927 ***5900.10*** *p221*
McDevitt, H. D.; Mobile, Alabama, 1822-1845 ***1640.10*** *p107*
McDevitt, James K.; Vermont, 1854-1932 ***5900.10*** *p568*
McDevitt, James M.; Vermont, 1838-1886 ***5900.10*** *p221*
McDevitt, Jane; Vermont, 1826-1901 ***5900.10*** *p217*
McDevitt, John; Vermont, 1826-1889 ***5900.10*** *p214*
McDevitt, John; Vermont, 1833-1913 ***5900.10*** *p217*
McDevitt, John; Vermont, 1849-1919 ***5900.10*** *p221*
McDevitt, John 90; Vermont, 1916 ***5900.10*** *p562*
McDevitt, Margaret 41; Vermont, 1895 ***5900.10*** *p221*
McDevitt, Margaret Fitzpatrick 65; Vermont, 1898 ***5900.10*** *p560*
McDevitt, Margaret Hanley; Vermont, 1862-1919 ***5900.10*** *p568*
McDevitt, Margaret Stuart; Vermont, 1824-1861 ***5900.10*** *p213*
McDevitt, Mary; Vermont, 1827-1911 ***5900.10*** *p217*
McDevitt, Mary Corey; Vermont, 1818-1906 ***5900.10*** *p570*
McDevitt, Mary E.; Vermont, 1863-1940 ***5900.10*** *p386*
McDevitt, Mary Perkinson; Vermont, 1822-1907 ***5900.10*** *p213*
McDevitt, Matthew; Vermont, 1825-1902 ***5900.10*** *p212*
McDevitt, Patrick; Vermont, n.d. ***5900.10*** *p571*
McDevitt, Patrick; Vermont, 1855-1928 ***5900.10*** *p386*
McDevitt, Rebecca McPhilmny; Vermont, 1841-1879 ***5900.10*** *p214*
McDevitt, Sarah McLaughlin; Vermont, 1858-1904 ***5900.10*** *p386*
McDevitt, Susan; Vermont, 1840-1920 ***5900.10*** *p220*
McDevitt, Susan Gallagher 72; Vermont, 1905 ***5900.10*** *p562*
McDiamid, Arichabald 42; Ontario, 1871 ***1823.15*** *p163*
McDiarmid, John 80; Ontario, 1871 ***1823.28*** *p64*
McDirmid, George; Ontario, 1871 ***1823.15*** *p163*
McDixon, Daniel; Vermont, 1839-1903 ***5900.10*** *p376*
McDixon, Esther Robinson; Vermont, 1844 ***5900.10*** *p376*
McDonagh, Francis; New York, 1832 ***8197.10*** *p257*
McDonagh, James; New York, 1795 ***8197.10*** *p1*
McDonagh, James; New York, 1795 ***8197.10*** *p6*
McDonagh, John 45; Ontario, 1871 ***1823.15*** *p163*
McDonagh, William 41; Ontario, 1871 ***1823.15*** *p163*
McDonal, Catharine; Vermont, 1847-1882 ***5900.10*** *p142*
McDonal, James 37; Ontario, 1871 ***1823.28*** *p64*
McDonald, Miss; Quebec, 1857 ***9196.15*** *p25*
McDonald, Mr.; Portland, Maine, 1857 ***9196.15*** *p13*
McDonald, Mr.; Portland, Maine, 1858 ***9196.15*** *p28*
McDonald, Mr.; Quebec, 1858 ***9196.15*** *p34*
McDonald, Mrs.; Portland, Maine, 1857 ***9196.15*** *p13*
McDonald, Mrs.; Portland, Maine, 1858 ***9196.15*** *p28*
McDonald, Rev.; Quebec, 1858 ***9196.15*** *p47*
McDonald, A. C.; Quebec, 1856 ***9196.15*** *p5*
McDonald, Aaron G. 9; Ontario, 1861 ***2896.27*** *p50*
McDonald, Adelaide 14; Ontario, 1861 ***2896.27*** *p32*
McDonald, Adeline 14; Ontario, 1861 ***2896.27*** *p26*
McDonald, Adeline 30; Ontario, 1861 ***2896.27*** *p26*
McDonald, Albert 13; Ontario, 1861 ***2896.27*** *p33*
McDonald, Albert 18; Ontario, 1861 ***2896.27*** *p72*
McDonald, Alex 2; Ontario, 1861 ***2896.28*** *p37*
McDonald, Alex 30; Ontario, 1871 ***1823.15*** *p163*
McDonald, Alex 68; Ontario, 1871 ***1823.15*** *p163*
McDonald, Alexander; Florida, n.d. ***1224.3*** *p48*
McDonald, Alexander; Florida, 1782 ***1640.10*** *p107*
McDonald, Alexander; Georgia, 1737 ***1640.10*** *p107*
McDonald, Alexander; Georgia, 1758 ***1640.10*** *p107*
McDonald, Alexander; Louisiana, 1811-1845 ***1640.10*** *p107*
McDonald, Alexander; Montreal, 1860 ***1640.13*** *p84*
McDonald, Alexander; New York, 1794 ***8197.10*** *p1*
McDonald, Alexander; New York, 1807 ***8197.10*** *p46*
McDonald, Alexander; Ontario, 1871 ***1823.28*** *p64*
McDonald, Alexander; Pennsylvania, 1808 ***6058.10*** *p2*
McDonald, Alexander 27; Ontario, 1871 ***1823.15*** *p164*
McDonald, Alexander 30; Ontario, 1871 ***1823.15*** *p164*
McDonald, Alexander 32; Ontario, 1871 ***1823.28*** *p64*
McDonald, Alexander 35; Ontario, 1871 ***1823.22*** *p102*
McDonald, Alexander 40; Ontario, 1871 ***1823.15*** *p164*
McDonald, Alexander 44; Ontario, 1871 ***1823.22*** *p102*
McDonald, Alexander 50; Ontario, 1871 ***1823.15*** *p164*
McDonald, Alexander 50; Ontario, 1871 ***1823.28*** *p64*
McDonald, Alexander 51; Ontario, 1871 ***1823.28*** *p64*
McDonald, Alexander 57; Vermont, 1870 ***5900.10*** *p309*
McDonald, Alexander 60; Ontario, 1871 ***1823.15*** *p164*
McDonald, Alexander 68; Ontario, 1871 ***1823.15*** *p163*
McDonald, Alexander 79; Ontario, 1871 ***1823.15*** *p164*
McDonald, Alexander 81; Ontario, 1871 ***1823.22*** *p102*
McDonald, Alexd 76; Ontario, 1871 ***1823.28*** *p64*
McDonald, Alice 12; Ontario, 1861 ***2896.27*** *p72*
McDonald, Allan 37; Ontario, 1871 ***1823.15*** *p164*
McDonald, Allen 12; Ontario, 1861 ***2896.27*** *p60*
McDonald, Allen 71; Ontario, 1871 ***1823.15*** *p164*
McDonald, Allen M. 2; Ontario, 1861 ***2896.27*** *p26*
McDonald, Almira 36; Ontario, 1861 ***2896.27*** *p27*
McDonald, Alwilda 11; Ontario, 1861 ***2896.27*** *p50*
McDonald, Alxd 25; Ontario, 1871 ***1823.28*** *p64*
McDonald, Amanda 3; Ontario, 1861 ***2896.27*** *p50*
McDonald, Andrew; Vermont, 1861-1941 ***5900.10*** *p216*
McDonald, Angus 31; Ontario, 1871 ***1823.15*** *p164*
McDonald, Angus 36; Ontario, 1871 ***1823.28*** *p64*
McDonald, Angus 50; Ontario, 1871 ***1823.15*** *p164*
McDonald, Angus 55; Ontario, 1871 ***1823.15*** *p164*

McDonald, Angus 60; Ontario, 1871 ***1823.15*** *p164*
McDonald, Angus 60; Ontario, 1871 ***1823.28*** *p64*
McDonald, Ann; North Carolina, 1803 ***1224.3*** *p48*
McDonald, Ann 35; Ontario, 1871 ***1823.15*** *p164*
McDonald, Ann 64; Ontario, 1871 ***1823.15*** *p164*
McDonald, Anna 24; Ontario, 1861 ***2896.25*** *p12*
McDonald, Anna 52; Vermont, 1890 ***5900.10*** *p511*
McDonald, Anne 58; Ontario, 1871 ***1823.15*** *p164*
McDonald, Archibald; New York, 1828 ***8197.10*** *p348*
McDonald, Archibald 24; Ontario, 1871 ***1823.15*** *p164*
McDonald, Archibald 35; Ontario, 1871 ***1823.15*** *p164*
McDonald, Archibald 41; Ontario, 1871 ***1823.15*** *p164*
McDonald, Archibald 50; Ontario, 1871 ***1823.15*** *p164*
McDonald, Archibald 52; Ontario, 1871 ***1823.28*** *p64*
McDonald, Archibald 60; Ontario, 1871 ***1823.15*** *p164*
McDonald, Archibald 69; Ontario, 1871 ***1823.15*** *p164*
McDonald, Archibald 83; Ontario, 1871 ***1823.22*** *p102*
McDonald, Archy 38; Ontario, 1871 ***1823.28*** *p64*
McDonald, Archy 55; Ontario, 1871 ***1823.28*** *p64*
McDonald, Barbara; Georgia, 1767-1845 ***1640.10*** *p108*
McDonald, Barnard 44; Ontario, 1871 ***1823.22*** *p103*
McDonald, Benjamin 17; Ontario, 1861 ***2896.27*** *p60*
McDonald, Benjamin 18; Ontario, 1861 ***2896.27*** *p60*
McDonald, Bridget 41; Ontario, 1871 ***1823.22*** *p103*
McDonald, Bridget Diffley; Vermont, 1865-1932 ***5900.10*** *p216*
McDonald, Bridget Kirwin 77; Vermont, 1889 ***5900.10*** *p309*
McDonald, Carrie B.; Vermont, 1867-1954 ***5900.10*** *p304*
McDonald, Catherine; Vermont, 1859-1887 ***5900.10*** *p212*
McDonald, Catherine 15; Ontario, 1861 ***2896.28*** *p50*
McDonald, Catherine 35; Ontario, 1861 ***2896.27*** *p33*
McDonald, Catherine 50; Ontario, 1871 ***1823.15*** *p164*
McDonald, Catherine 63; Ontario, 1861 ***2896.27*** *p26*
McDonald, Catherine 80; Ontario, 1871 ***1823.15*** *p164*
McDonald, Celestia 10; Ontario, 1861 ***2896.27*** *p27*
McDonald, Chales 37; Ontario, 1871 ***1823.15*** *p164*
McDonald, Charles 18; Ontario, 1861 ***2896.25*** *p16*
McDonald, Charles 65; Ontario, 1861 ***2896.27*** *p71*
McDonald, Charles 70; Ontario, 1871 ***1823.15*** *p164*
McDonald, Christy 60; Ontario, 1871 ***1823.15*** *p164*
McDonald, Christy 70; Ontario, 1871 ***1823.15*** *p164*
McDonald, Cinthia E. 6; Ontario, 1861 ***2896.27*** *p27*
McDonald, Cornelius 7; Ontario, 1861 ***2896.27*** *p67*
McDonald, D.; Mississippi, 1825-1845 ***1640.10*** *p109*
McDonald, D. 20; Ontario, 1861 ***2896.25*** *p33*
McDonald, Daniel 21; Ontario, 1861 ***2896.27*** *p27*
McDonald, Daniel 50; Ontario, 1871 ***1823.15*** *p164*
McDonald, David; Georgia, 1699 ***1640.13*** *p84*
McDonald, David 10; Ontario, 1861 ***2896.27*** *p26*
McDonald, David 40; British Columbia, 1910 ***9196.1*** *p29*
McDonald, David 40; Washington, 1910 ***9196.1*** *p29*
McDonald, David 66; Ontario, 1861 ***2896.28*** *p31*
McDonald, Dennis; New York, 1796 ***8197.10*** *p8*
McDonald, Dennis; Vermont, 1823-1902 ***5900.10*** *p200*
McDonald, Donald; America, n.d. ***1224.2*** *p73*
McDonald, Donald; New York, 1807 ***8197.10*** *p46*
McDonald, Donald 20; Ontario, 1871 ***1823.15*** *p164*
McDonald, Donald 22; Ontario, 1871 ***1823.15*** *p164*
McDonald, Donald 25; Ontario, 1871 ***1823.15*** *p164*
McDonald, Donald 26; Ontario, 1871 ***1823.28*** *p64*
McDonald, Donald 28; Ontario, 1871 ***1823.15*** *p164*
McDonald, Donald 35; Ontario, 1871 ***1823.15*** *p164*
McDonald, Donald 36; Ontario, 1871 ***1823.15*** *p164*
McDonald, Donald 45; Ontario, 1871 ***1823.15*** *p164*
McDonald, Donald 50; Ontario, 1871 ***1823.15*** *p164*
McDonald, Donald 52; Ontario, 1871 ***1823.15*** *p164*
McDonald, Donald 52; Ontario, 1871 ***1823.28*** *p64*
McDonald, Donald 55; Ontario, 1871 ***1823.15*** *p164*
McDonald, Donald 60; Ontario, 1871 ***1823.15*** *p164*
McDonald, Donald 75; Ontario, 1871 ***1823.15*** *p164*
McDonald, Donald J. 46; Ontario, 1871 ***1823.15*** *p164*
McDonald, Dongald 29; Ontario, 1871 ***1823.15*** *p165*
McDonald, Duncan; Georgia, 1737 ***1640.10*** *p108*
McDonald, Duncan 28; Maryland, 1774 ***1220.25*** *p52*
McDonald, Duncan 38; Ontario, 1871 ***1823.15*** *p165*
McDonald, Duncan 43; Ontario, 1871 ***1823.15*** *p165*
McDonald, Duncan 59; Ontario, 1871 ***1823.15*** *p165*
McDonald, Duncan 65; Ontario, 1871 ***1823.15*** *p165*
McDonald, Duncan 71; Ontario, 1871 ***1823.15*** *p165*
McDonald, E. 2; Ontario, 1861 ***2896.28*** *p16*
McDonald, E. Triphena 4; Ontario, 1861 ***2896.27*** *p50*
McDonald, Edward 42; Ontario, 1871 ***1823.28*** *p64*
McDonald, Elgin 8; Ontario, 1861 ***2896.27*** *p33*
McDonald, Eliza 2; Ontario, 1861 ***2896.28*** *p49*
McDonald, Eliza A. 20; Ontario, 1861 ***2896.28*** *p37*
McDonald, Eliza Heirer; Vermont, 1822-1903 ***5900.10*** *p200*
McDonald, Elizabeth 24; Ontario, 1861 ***2896.28*** *p49*
McDonald, Elizabeth 32; Ontario, 1861 ***2896.27*** *p72*
McDonald, Elizabeth 38; Ontario, 1871 ***1823.22*** *p103*
McDonald, Elizabeth E. 4; Ontario, 1861 ***2896.27*** *p64*
McDonald, Elizabeth Walsh; Vermont, 1855-1928 ***5900.10*** *p452*
McDonald, Ellen; Vermont, 1841-1921 ***5900.10*** *p263*
McDonald, Emilia 6; Ontario, 1861 ***2896.27*** *p60*
McDonald, Emma; Vermont, n.d. ***5900.10*** *p183*
McDonald, Emma 3; Ontario, 1861 ***2896.28*** *p49*
McDonald, Eustatin 19; Ontario, 1861 ***2896.27*** *p60*
McDonald, Evan; Charles Town, South Carolina, 1764 ***1224.2*** *p73*
McDonald, F. B. 33; Maryland, 1775 ***1220.25*** *p108*
McDonald, F. C. 39; Ontario, 1871 ***1823.22*** *p103*
McDonald, Finley 37; Ontario, 1871 ***1823.15*** *p165*
McDonald, Flora; Georgia, 1857 ***1640.10*** *p109*
McDonald, Florence 2; Ontario, 1861 ***2896.27*** *p64*
McDonald, Francis 14; Ontario, 1861 ***2896.27*** *p50*
McDonald, Franklin 5; Ontario, 1861 ***2896.27*** *p64*
McDonald, George; Georgia, 1763 ***1640.10*** *p109*
McDonald, George; Georgia, 1786 ***1640.10*** *p109*
McDonald, George 6; Ontario, 1861 ***2896.27*** *p72*
McDonald, George 18; Ontario, 1861 ***2896.27*** *p60*
McDonald, George 28; Ontario, 1871 ***1823.15*** *p165*
McDonald, George 71; Ontario, 1871 ***1823.28*** *p64*
McDonald, George N. 45; Ontario, 1871 ***1823.22*** *p103*
McDonald, Gilbert 19; Ontario, 1861 ***2896.27*** *p27*
McDonald, Grace; Nova Scotia, 1887 ***1640.13*** *p84*
McDonald, Griman 14; Ontario, 1861 ***2896.27*** *p67*
McDonald, H. 5; Ontario, 1861 ***2896.28*** *p16*
McDonald, H. 58; Ontario, 1861 ***2896.28*** *p6*
McDonald, Hannah Elizabeth 17; Ontario, 1861 ***2896.27*** *p64*
McDonald, Harriet 8; Ontario, 1861 ***2896.28*** *p31*
McDonald, Harriet 14; Ontario, 1861 ***2896.27*** *p60*
McDonald, Helen 60; Ontario, 1871 ***1823.15*** *p165*
McDonald, Henry 11; Ontario, 1861 ***2896.27*** *p67*
McDonald, Herbert 3; Ontario, 1861 ***2896.27*** *p33*
McDonald, Hugh 44; Ontario, 1871 ***1823.15*** *p165*
McDonald, Hugh 55; Ontario, 1871 ***1823.15*** *p165*
McDonald, Hugh 60; Ontario, 1871 ***1823.15*** *p165*
McDonald, Hugh 61; Ontario, 1871 ***1823.15*** *p165*
McDonald, Ida M. Gibson; Vermont, 1865-1958 ***5900.10*** *p402*
McDonald, Isaac P. 3; Ontario, 1861 ***2896.27*** *p27*
McDonald, Isabella 65; Ontario, 1871 ***1823.22*** *p103*
McDonald, James; Georgia, 1734 ***1640.10*** *p109*
McDonald, James; New York, 1806 ***8197.10*** *p325*
McDonald, James; New York, 1820-1834 ***8197.10*** *p304*
McDonald, James; New York, 1840 ***8197.10*** *p184*
McDonald, James; Savannah, Georgia, 1811 ***1640.10*** *p110*
McDonald, James 17; Ontario, 1861 ***2896.27*** *p62*
McDonald, James 18; Ontario, 1871 ***1823.15*** *p165*
McDonald, James 19; Ontario, 1861 ***2896.27*** *p68*
McDonald, James 25; Ontario, 1871 ***1823.15*** *p165*
McDonald, James 28; Ontario, 1871 ***1823.15*** *p165*
McDonald, James 35; Ontario, 1871 ***1823.15*** *p165*
McDonald, James 40; Ontario, 1871 ***1823.15*** *p165*
McDonald, James 42; Ontario, 1871 ***1823.15*** *p165*
McDonald, James 50; Ontario, 1871 ***1823.15*** *p165*
McDonald, James 56; Ontario, 1871 ***1823.15*** *p165*
McDonald, James 76; Ontario, 1871 ***1823.15*** *p165*
McDonald, James H.; New York, New York, 1838 ***6058.10*** *p46*
McDonald, James H.; Vermont, 1855-1931 ***5900.10*** *p69*
McDonald, Jane 29; Ontario, 1861 ***2896.27*** *p64*
McDonald, Jane 52; Ontario, 1871 ***1823.28*** *p64*
McDonald, Jane Byrne 84; Vermont, 1905 ***5900.10*** *p57*
McDonald, Jansan; Ontario, 1871 ***1823.15*** *p165*
McDonald, Jennette 6; Ontario, 1861 ***2896.28*** *p31*
McDonald, John; Alabama, 1800-1845 ***1640.10*** *p110*
McDonald, John; Georgia, 1734 ***1640.10*** *p110*
McDonald, John; Georgia, 1739 ***1640.10*** *p110*
McDonald, John; Georgia, 1740 ***1640.10*** *p110*
McDonald, John; Georgia, 1743 ***1640.10*** *p110*
McDonald, John; Georgia, 1821 ***1640.10*** *p110*
McDonald, John; Kingston, Jamaica, 1899 ***1640.13*** *p84*
McDonald, John; Mobile, Alabama, 1826-1845 ***1640.10*** *p110*
McDonald, John; Montreal, 1891 ***1640.13*** *p84*
McDonald, John; New York, 1807 ***8197.10*** *p331*
McDonald, John; New York, 1823 ***8197.10*** *p255*
McDonald, John; Vermont, 1833-1914 ***5900.10*** *p511*
McDonald, John; Vermont, 1863-1888 ***5900.10*** *p216*
McDonald, John 17; Ontario, 1861 ***2896.28*** *p31*
McDonald, John 22; Maryland, 1774 ***1220.25*** *p74*
McDonald, John 26; Ontario, 1871 ***1823.15*** *p165*
McDonald, John 28; Ontario, 1871 ***1823.15*** *p165*
McDonald, John 30; Ontario, 1871 ***1823.15*** *p165*
McDonald, John 32; Ontario, 1871 ***1823.15*** *p165*
McDonald, John 34; Ontario, 1871 ***1823.15*** *p165*
McDonald, John 35; Ontario, 1871 ***1823.15*** *p165*
McDonald, John 36; Ontario, 1871 ***1823.28*** *p64*
McDonald, John 37; Ontario, 1871 ***1823.28*** *p64*
McDonald, John 39; Ontario, 1871 ***1823.28*** *p64*
McDonald, John 40; Ontario, 1871 ***1823.15*** *p165*
McDonald, John 42; Ontario, 1871 ***1823.15*** *p165*
McDonald, John 45; Ontario, 1871 ***1823.28*** *p64*
McDonald, John 47; Ontario, 1871 ***1823.28*** *p64*
McDonald, John 49; Ontario, 1871 ***1823.28*** *p64*
McDonald, John 50; Ontario, 1871 ***1823.15*** *p165*
McDonald, John 50; Ontario, 1871 ***1823.22*** *p103*
McDonald, John 57; Ontario, 1871 ***1823.22*** *p103*
McDonald, John 58; Vermont, 1892 ***5900.10*** *p511*
McDonald, John 59; Ontario, 1871 ***1823.15*** *p165*
McDonald, John 65; Ontario, 1871 ***1823.28*** *p64*
McDonald, John 68; Ontario, 1871 ***1823.15*** *p165*
McDonald, John 77; Ontario, 1871 ***1823.15*** *p165*
McDonald, John K.; Vermont, 1853-1914 ***5900.10*** *p402*
McDonald, John N. 13; Ontario, 1861 ***2896.25*** *p21*
McDonald, John S.; New York, 1837 ***8197.10*** *p375*
McDonald, Jonathon 61; Ontario, 1871 ***1823.28*** *p64*
McDonald, Joseph E. 16; Ontario, 1861 ***2896.25*** *p21*
McDonald, Jul 24; Ontario, 1861 ***2896.27*** *p60*
McDonald, Katherine; Vermont, 1845-1903 ***5900.10*** *p395*
McDonald, Kenith 42; Ontario, 1871 ***1823.15*** *p166*
McDonald, Koary 48; Ontario, 1871 ***1823.15*** *p166*
McDonald, L. 40; Ontario, 1861 ***2896.28*** *p6*
McDonald, L. J. 40; Ontario, 1861 ***2896.26*** *p2*
McDonald, Laughlan 22; Ontario, 1871 ***1823.15*** *p166*
McDonald, Laughlin; Nova Scotia, 1869 ***1640.13*** *p84*
McDonald, Lesy 45; Ontario, 1871 ***1823.15*** *p166*
McDonald, Lewis 36; Ontario, 1871 ***1823.15*** *p166*
McDonald, Louisa J. 3; Ontario, 1861 ***2896.27*** *p26*
McDonald, Lydd 10; Ontario, 1861 ***2896.27*** *p60*
McDonald, Lydd 50; Ontario, 1861 ***2896.27*** *p60*
McDonald, Lydia J. 22; Ontario, 1861 ***2896.27*** *p26*
McDonald, M. 24; Ontario, 1861 ***2896.28*** *p16*
McDonald, M. 41; Ontario, 1861 ***2896.28*** *p16*
McDonald, M. J. 13; Ontario, 1861 ***2896.27*** *p26*
McDonald, M. J. 22; Ontario, 1861 ***2896.26*** *p2*
McDonald, Malcolm 18; Ontario, 1871 ***1823.15*** *p166*
McDonald, Margaret; Vermont, 1862 ***5900.10*** *p148*
McDonald, Margaret 5; Ontario, 1861 ***2896.28*** *p49*
McDonald, Margaret 36; Ontario, 1861 ***2896.28*** *p31*
McDonald, Margaret 55; Ontario, 1861 ***2896.27*** *p62*
McDonald, Margaret 60; Ontario, 1871 ***1823.28*** *p64*
McDonald, Margaret 65; Ontario, 1871 ***1823.15*** *p166*
McDonald, Margret 21; Ontario, 1871 ***1823.15*** *p166*
McDonald, Margret 46; Ontario, 1871 ***1823.15*** *p166*
McDonald, Margret 58; Ontario, 1871 ***1823.28*** *p64*
McDonald, Margret 78; Ontario, 1871 ***1823.15*** *p166*
McDonald, Martin 37; Ontario, 1871 ***1823.28*** *p64*
McDonald, Mary; St. Louis, 1893 ***1640.13*** *p85*
McDonald, Mary; Vermont, 1826-1911 ***5900.10*** *p164*
McDonald, Mary; Vermont, 1827-1906 ***5900.10*** *p241*
McDonald, Mary; Vermont, 1840-1922 ***5900.10*** *p241*
McDonald, Mary; Vermont, 1855-1931 ***5900.10*** *p452*
McDonald, Mary 14; Ontario, 1861 ***2896.27*** *p27*
McDonald, Mary 21; Ontario, 1871 ***1823.22*** *p103*
McDonald, Mary 24; Ontario, 1861 ***2896.25*** *p56*
McDonald, Mary 24; Ontario, 1861 ***2896.27*** *p68*
McDonald, Mary 45; Ontario, 1871 ***1823.22*** *p103*
McDonald, Mary 66; Ontario, 1861 ***2896.27*** *p71*
McDonald, Mary 70; Ontario, 1871 ***1823.15*** *p166*
McDonald, Mary 74; Ontario, 1871 ***1823.15*** *p166*
McDonald, Mary 75; Ontario, 1871 ***1823.15*** *p166*
McDonald, Mary 80; Ontario, 1871 ***1823.15*** *p166*
McDonald, Mary A. 19; Ontario, 1861 ***2896.27*** *p71*
McDonald, Mary A. Murphy; Vermont, 1857-1934 ***5900.10*** *p69*
McDonald, Mary Ann; Vermont, 1859-1940 ***5900.10*** *p474*
McDonald, Mary C. Collen 38; Vermont, 1906 ***5900.10*** *p229*
McDonald, Mary E. 35; Ontario, 1861 ***2896.25*** *p21*
McDonald, Mary Fitzgerald; Vermont, 1841-1913 ***5900.10*** *p511*
McDonald, Mathew; New York, 1823 ***8197.10*** *p255*
McDonald, Mehetabel 37; Ontario, 1861 ***2896.27*** *p50*
McDonald, Michael; Ontario, 1871 ***1823.22*** *p103*
McDonald, Michael 21; Philadelphia, 1774 ***1220.25*** *p82*
McDonald, Minard 17; Ontario, 1861 ***2896.27*** *p27*
McDonald, Murdock 65; Ontario, 1871 ***1823.28*** *p64*
McDonald, Nancy 12; Ontario, 1861 ***2896.27*** *p50*
McDonald, Nancy 15; Ontario, 1861 ***2896.27*** *p68*
McDonald, Nancy 23; Ontario, 1871 ***1823.22*** *p103*
McDonald, Neil 24; Ontario, 1871 ***1823.15*** *p166*
McDonald, Norman 72; Ontario, 1871 ***1823.15*** *p166*
McDonald, Owen 53; Ontario, 1871 ***1823.22*** *p103*
McDonald, P. M. 17; Ontario, 1861 ***2896.28*** *p6*
McDonald, Pat 33; Ontario, 1871 ***1823.28*** *p64*
McDonald, Pat 42; British Columbia, 1913 ***9196.1*** *p58*
McDonald, Pat 42; Seattle, 1913 ***9196.1*** *p58*
McDonald, Patrick; New York, 1830 ***8197.10*** *p312*
McDonald, Patrick; Philadelphia, 1793 ***4629.10*** *p74*

McGloan, Farrel; New York, 1829 ***8197.10*** *p353*
McGloan, Patrick; New York, 1838 ***8197.10*** *p257*
McGlocklin, Owen; Pennsylvania, 1785 ***4629.10*** *p48*
McGloin, Patrick; New York, 1839 ***8197.10*** *p257*
McGlone, Henry G.; New York, New York, 1865 ***3437.14*** *p90*
McGloughlin, James 35; Ontario, 1871 ***1823.22*** *p104*
McGloughlyn, Mary J.; Vermont, 1847-1899 ***5900.10*** *p266*
McGluichy, Mr.; Portland, Maine, 1858 ***9196.15*** *p30*
McGlynn, Bridget; Vermont, 1822-1892 ***5900.10*** *p143*
McGlynn, Margaret; Vermont, n.d. ***5900.10*** *p602*
McGlynn, Mary 26; Vermont, 1856 ***5900.10*** *p522*
McGlynn, Mary Ann; Vermont, 1848-1918 ***5900.10*** *p299*
McGonagle, James, Jr.; Philadelphia, 1815-1818 ***8197.10*** *p304*
McGonegal, Andrew 45; Ontario, 1871 ***1823.28*** *p66*
McGonegal, Jerome B. 36; Ontario, 1871 ***1823.22*** *p104*
McGonigal, Felix; New York, 1807 ***8197.10*** *p46*
McGonnigle, Francis; Philadelphia, 1793 ***4629.10*** *p77*
McGooden, Mr. 12; Ontario, 1861 ***2896.26*** *p7*
McGooden, Mrs. 56; Ontario, 1861 ***2896.26*** *p27*
McGooden, Mrs. 62; Ontario, 1861 ***2896.26*** *p26*
McGooden, Ann 9; Ontario, 1861 ***2896.26*** *p27*
McGooden, Bridgett 24; Ontario, 1861 ***2896.26*** *p26*
McGooden, E. 77; Ontario, 1861 ***2896.26*** *p7*
McGooden, George 17; Ontario, 1861 ***2896.26*** *p27*
McGooden, H. 18; Ontario, 1861 ***2896.26*** *p7*
McGooden, Hannah 13; Ontario, 1861 ***2896.26*** *p27*
McGooden, Henry 20; Ontario, 1861 ***2896.26*** *p26*
McGooden, Henry 71; Ontario, 1861 ***2896.26*** *p26*
McGooden, J. 10; Ontario, 1861 ***2896.26*** *p7*
McGooden, J. 57; Ontario, 1861 ***2896.26*** *p7*
McGooden, John 52; Ontario, 1861 ***2896.26*** *p27*
McGooden, M. 15; Ontario, 1861 ***2896.26*** *p7*
McGooden, M. 49; Ontario, 1861 ***2896.26*** *p7*
McGooden, Martha 19; Ontario, 1861 ***2896.26*** *p27*
McGooden, R. 22; Ontario, 1861 ***2896.26*** *p26*
McGooden, Robert 11; Ontario, 1861 ***2896.26*** *p27*
McGooden, Sarah 15; Ontario, 1861 ***2896.26*** *p27*
McGooden, W. H. 7; Ontario, 1861 ***2896.26*** *p27*
McGookin, Barney 28; Vermont, 1862 ***5900.10*** *p52*
McGookin, Catherine; Vermont, 1825-1907 ***5900.10*** *p52*
McGookin, Hannah 62; Vermont, 1885 ***5900.10*** *p52*
McGookin, Margaret; Vermont, 1854-1926 ***5900.10*** *p492*
McGookin, Rodney 45; Vermont, 1866 ***5900.10*** *p235*
McGorory, James; Philadelphia, 1849 ***6058.10*** *p41*
McGorty, Elizabeth E.; Vermont, 1844-1916 ***5900.10*** *p298*
McGorty, Frank; Vermont, 1844-1879 ***5900.10*** *p298*
McGotorick, John 47; Ontario, 1871 ***1823.22*** *p104*
McGough, Catherine; Vermont, 1842-1932 ***5900.10*** *p587*
McGough, John; New York, 1838 ***8197.10*** *p257*
McGough, John; Vermont, 1838-1915 ***5900.10*** *p157*
McGough, Mary 67; Vermont, 1874 ***5900.10*** *p470*
McGough, Mary Larkin; Vermont, 1840-1922 ***5900.10*** *p157*
McGourty, Ann 30; Vermont, 1867 ***5900.10*** *p510*
McGourty, Bridget McGlinn 69; Vermont, 1868 ***5900.10*** *p296*
McGourty, Patrick 33; Ontario, 1871 ***1823.22*** *p104*
McGourty, Phillip 40; Ontario, 1871 ***1823.22*** *p104*
McGourty, Rosa 87; Vermont, 1914 ***5900.10*** *p296*
McGoven, John J.; Vermont, 1843-1912 ***5900.10*** *p410*
McGoven, Mary C. Doyle; Vermont, 1848-1913 ***5900.10*** *p410*
McGovern, Andrew 41; Vermont, 1885 ***5900.10*** *p410*
McGovern, Ann; Vermont, 1811-1895 ***5900.10*** *p533*
McGovern, Anna E.; Vermont, 1858-1918 ***5900.10*** *p47*
McGovern, Catherine; Vermont, 1850-1922 ***5900.10*** *p193*
McGovern, Charles; Vermont, 1836-1918 ***5900.10*** *p504*
McGovern, D. T.; Vermont, 1841-1902 ***5900.10*** *p335*
McGovern, Daniel; Vermont, 1803-1887 ***5900.10*** *p533*
McGovern, Elizabeth Bulger; Vermont, 1844-1914 ***5900.10*** *p335*
McGovern, Elizabeth Farrell; Vermont, 1836-1910 ***5900.10*** *p504*
McGovern, Ellen; Vermont, 1841-1890 ***5900.10*** *p534*
McGovern, Hugh; New York, 1827 ***8197.10*** *p256*
McGovern, Hugh; New York, 1831 ***8197.10*** *p367*
McGovern, James; New York, 1821 ***8197.10*** *p254*
McGovern, Jane; Vermont, 1847-1893 ***5900.10*** *p534*
McGovern, Julia L.; Vermont, 1856-1929 ***5900.10*** *p410*
McGovern, Margaret; Vermont, 1852-1921 ***5900.10*** *p351*
McGovern, Mark; Vermont, 1850-1921 ***5900.10*** *p351*
McGovern, Michael; Vermont, 1858 ***5900.10*** *p603*
McGovern, Myles 45; Ontario, 1871 ***1823.22*** *p104*
McGovern, Patrick 81; Vermont, 1926 ***5900.10*** *p410*
McGovery, Marthy 5; Ontario, 1861 ***2896.26*** *p36*
McGovery, Mary 8; Ontario, 1861 ***2896.26*** *p36*
McGovery, Mary 30; Ontario, 1861 ***2896.26*** *p36*
McGowan, . . .; New Hampshire, 1641-1660 ***4628.40*** *p44*
McGowan, Alexander; New Hampshire, 1710 ***4628.40*** *p44*
McGowan, Anna 64; Vermont, 1867 ***5900.10*** *p501*
McGowan, Bartholomy; New York, 1827 ***8197.10*** *p340*
McGowan, Bartley; New York, 1840 ***8197.10*** *p258*
McGowan, Caroline; Vermont, 1821-1883 ***5900.10*** *p377*
McGowan, Edward; Vermont, 1836-1908 ***5900.10*** *p560*
McGowan, Eliza; Vermont, 1813-1875 ***5900.10*** *p377*
McGowan, Elizabeth F.; Vermont, 1789-1863 ***5900.10*** *p377*
McGowan, Ellen Keefe; Vermont, 1840-1920 ***5900.10*** *p70*
McGowan, Emaline A. 68; Vermont, 1881 ***5900.10*** *p377*
McGowan, Emma; Vermont, 1884 ***5900.10*** *p199*
McGowan, Francis; New York, 1837 ***8197.10*** *p97*
McGowan, George; Vermont, 1828-1912 ***5900.10*** *p494*
McGowan, George 21; Ontario, 1871 ***1823.15*** *p170*
McGowan, Hannah E. 45; Vermont, 1873 ***5900.10*** *p281*
McGowan, Hannah Robinson 44; Vermont, 1871 ***5900.10*** *p377*
McGowan, Hugh 26; Vermont, 1873 ***5900.10*** *p529*
McGowan, James; New York, 1803 ***8197.10*** *p15*
McGowan, James; New York, 1806 ***8197.10*** *p324*
McGowan, James; New York, 1823 ***8197.10*** *p255*
McGowan, James; Vermont, 1829-1901 ***5900.10*** *p70*
McGowan, James E.; Vermont, 1815-1901 ***5900.10*** *p377*
McGowan, Jane; Vermont, 1839-1909 ***5900.10*** *p571*
McGowan, Jane 19; Ontario, 1871 ***1823.15*** *p170*
McGowan, Jane 47; Ontario, 1871 ***1823.15*** *p170*
McGowan, Jannet 23; Ontario, 1871 ***1823.15*** *p170*
McGowan, John; Canada, 1756-1760 ***4628.40*** *p45*
McGowan, John; Canada, 1756-1760 ***4628.40*** *p46*
McGowan, John; New Hampshire, 1724 ***4628.40*** *p44*
McGowan, John; New York, 1807 ***8197.10*** *p329*
McGowan, John; New York, 1829 ***8197.10*** *p353*
McGowan, John; Vermont, n.d. ***5900.10*** *p307*
McGowan, John 33; Vermont, 1870 ***5900.10*** *p501*
McGowan, John 63; Vermont, 1894 ***5900.10*** *p502*
McGowan, John P.; New York, 1826 ***8197.10*** *p334*
McGowan, Jos.; Nova Scotia, 1745 ***4628.40*** *p45*
McGowan, Laura; Vermont, 1829-1876 ***5900.10*** *p377*
McGowan, Margaret; Vermont, 1836-1903 ***5900.10*** *p565*
McGowan, Maria L.; Vermont, 1827-1908 ***5900.10*** *p376*
McGowan, Mark 60; Ontario, 1871 ***1823.22*** *p104*
McGowan, Martin; New York, 1831 ***8197.10*** *p355*
McGowan, Mary; Manitoba, 1899 ***1640.13*** *p86*
McGowan, Mary 25; Vermont, 1878 ***5900.10*** *p169*
McGowan, Mary A.; Vermont, 1835-1914 ***5900.10*** *p494*
McGowan, Matthew; New York, 1837 ***8197.10*** *p97*
McGowan, Michael; New York, 1821 ***8197.10*** *p254*
McGowan, Michael; New York, 1822 ***8197.10*** *p254*
McGowan, Michael; New York, 1827 ***8197.10*** *p340*
McGowan, Michael; New York, 1839 ***8197.10*** *p258*
McGowan, Michael 40; Ontario, 1861 ***2896.25*** *p21*
McGowan, Michael 67; Ontario, 1871 ***1823.15*** *p170*
McGowan, Patrick; New York, 1816 ***8197.10*** *p59*
McGowan, Patrick; New York, 1822 ***8197.10*** *p254*
McGowan, Patrick; New York, 1827 ***8197.10*** *p340*
McGowan, Patrick; New York, 1838 ***8197.10*** *p257*
McGowan, Peter; New York, 1821 ***8197.10*** *p254*
McGowan, Robert; New Orleans, 1807-1812 ***1640.10*** *p115*
McGowan, Robert 72; Ontario, 1871 ***1823.15*** *p170*
McGowan, Robert 79; Vermont, 1870 ***5900.10*** *p377*
McGowan, Samuel; Canada, 1756-1760 ***4628.40*** *p46*
McGowan, Samuel; New York, 1834 ***8197.10*** *p74*
McGowan, Thomas; New York, 1838 ***8197.10*** *p257*
McGowan, Thomas 42; Ontario, 1871 ***1823.28*** *p66*
McGowan, William C.; Vermont, 1825-1897 ***5900.10*** *p377*
McGowen, Amanda; Vermont, 1810-1851 ***5900.10*** *p377*
McGowen, Bridget 80; Vermont, 1898 ***5900.10*** *p280*
McGowen, George; Vermont, 1818-1871 ***5900.10*** *p377*
McGowen, John A.; Vermont, 1848-1919 ***5900.10*** *p280*
McGowen, Libbie Callan 39; Vermont, 1886 ***5900.10*** *p280*
McGowen, Patrick; Vermont, 1858 ***5900.10*** *p529*
McGowen, Thomas; Vermont, 1853-1930 ***5900.10*** *p280*
McGowen, Thomas; Vermont, 1881 ***5900.10*** *p561*
McGowin, John; New York, 1807 ***8197.10*** *p329*
McGown, Bartly; New York, 1828-1831 ***8197.10*** *p369*
McGown, Farrel; New York, 1828 ***8197.10*** *p350*
McGown, John; New York, 1828 ***8197.10*** *p349*
McGown, Sarah 85; Ontario, 1871 ***1823.22*** *p104*
McGown, William; New York, 1828-1831 ***8197.10*** *p369*
McGowran, Peter; Georgia, 1734 ***1640.10*** *p115*
McGrady, Andrew; Canada, 1756-1760 ***4628.40*** *p46*
McGragh, Catharine 57; Ontario, 1871 ***1823.22*** *p104*
McGrail, Austin; Vermont, 1854-1935 ***5900.10*** *p52*
McGrail, Esther Walker; Vermont, 1856-1937 ***5900.10*** *p52*
McGrain, James; New York, 1839 ***8197.10*** *p139*
McGrain, John 22; New York, 1833-1840 ***8197.10*** *p185*
McGram, John; New York, 1840 ***8197.10*** *p184*
McGranaghan, James; New York, 1838 ***8197.10*** *p377*
McGrath, Mr.; Vermont, 1841-1915 ***5900.10*** *p487*
McGrath, Mrs.; Vermont, 1842-1919 ***5900.10*** *p487*
McGrath, Allen 16; Ontario, 1861 ***2896.28*** *p25*
McGrath, Ann; Vermont, 1833-1908 ***5900.10*** *p80*
McGrath, Ann McGarry 56; Vermont, 1878 ***5900.10*** *p604*
McGrath, Anna; Vermont, 1846-1902 ***5900.10*** *p426*
McGrath, Bedelia Monan 72; Vermont, 1904 ***5900.10*** *p600*
McGrath, Bridget; Vermont, 1834-1879 ***5900.10*** *p330*
McGrath, Bridget; Vermont, 1841-1915 ***5900.10*** *p353*
McGrath, Bridget; Vermont, 1851-1925 ***5900.10*** *p555*
McGrath, Bridget; Vermont, 1861-1942 ***5900.10*** *p128*
McGrath, Bridget 18; Vermont, 1862 ***5900.10*** *p168*
McGrath, Bridget 20; Vermont, 1872 ***5900.10*** *p326*
McGrath, Bridget 60; Vermont, 1872 ***5900.10*** *p167*
McGrath, Bridget 76; Vermont, 1884 ***5900.10*** *p168*
McGrath, Bridget E.; Vermont, n.d. ***5900.10*** *p604*
McGrath, Bridget Green; Vermont, 1846-1929 ***5900.10*** *p538*
McGrath, Catharine 21; Vermont, 1878 ***5900.10*** *p604*
McGrath, Catherine; Vermont, 1850-1922 ***5900.10*** *p143*
McGrath, Catherine 23; Vermont, 1869 ***5900.10*** *p526*
McGrath, Catherine Raven; Vermont, n.d. ***5900.10*** *p604*
McGrath, Daniel; Vermont, 1818-1893 ***5900.10*** *p369*
McGrath, Daniel; Vermont, 1818-1893 ***5900.10*** *p370*
McGrath, Dennis 60; Vermont, 1899 ***5900.10*** *p307*
McGrath, Eddie; Vermont, 1876-1878 ***5900.10*** *p413*
McGrath, Edward; Vermont, 1846-1923 ***5900.10*** *p395*
McGrath, Edward; Vermont, 1864 ***5900.10*** *p167*
McGrath, Edward; Vermont, 1869-1870 ***5900.10*** *p559*
McGrath, Edward 34; Ontario, 1871 ***1823.28*** *p66*
McGrath, Elizabeth 29; Vermont, 1888 ***5900.10*** *p289*
McGrath, Ellen; Vermont, 1847-1929 ***5900.10*** *p605*
McGrath, Ellen; Vermont, 1854-1907 ***5900.10*** *p142*
McGrath, Ellen; Vermont, 1873-1874 ***5900.10*** *p413*
McGrath, Ellen 28; Vermont, 1882 ***5900.10*** *p604*
McGrath, Ellen 33; Vermont, 1865 ***5900.10*** *p605*
McGrath, Ellen Burke; Vermont, 1856-1911 ***5900.10*** *p485*
McGrath, Ellen Corbett 64; Vermont, 1886 ***5900.10*** *p551*
McGrath, Fred 2; Ontario, 1861 ***2896.25*** *p1*
McGrath, Henry 50; Ontario, 1871 ***1823.22*** *p105*
McGrath, James; New York, 1840 ***8197.10*** *p258*
McGrath, James 36; Ontario, 1871 ***1823.22*** *p105*
McGrath, James 70; Ontario, 1871 ***1823.22*** *p105*
McGrath, James 73; Vermont, 1883 ***5900.10*** *p604*
McGrath, John; New York, 1807 ***8197.10*** *p46*
McGrath, John; New York, 1821 ***8197.10*** *p254*
McGrath, John; New York, 1840 ***8197.10*** *p182*
McGrath, John; New York, 1840 ***8197.10*** *p183*
McGrath, John; Vermont, 1857-1920 ***5900.10*** *p370*
McGrath, John 33; Ontario, 1871 ***1823.28*** *p66*
McGrath, John 34; Ontario, 1871 ***1823.22*** *p105*
McGrath, John 86; Vermont, 1901 ***5900.10*** *p604*
McGrath, John B. 77; Vermont, 1929 ***5900.10*** *p604*
McGrath, Julia 64; Vermont, 1878 ***5900.10*** *p268*
McGrath, Julia A. 29; Vermont, 1892 ***5900.10*** *p604*
McGrath, Julia Barry; Vermont, 1852-1911 ***5900.10*** *p395*
McGrath, Julia Burns 35; Vermont, 1883 ***5900.10*** *p604*
McGrath, Katherine McDonald; Vermont, 1845-1903 ***5900.10*** *p395*
McGrath, Lawrence; New York, 1837 ***8197.10*** *p98*
McGrath, Margaret; Vermont, 1835-1897 ***5900.10*** *p452*
McGrath, Margaret 27; Ontario, 1861 ***2896.25*** *p1*
McGrath, Margaret 27; Vermont, 1865 ***5900.10*** *p526*
McGrath, Margaret 30; Ontario, 1871 ***1823.22*** *p105*
McGrath, Margaret 45; Vermont, 1875 ***5900.10*** *p605*
McGrath, Margaret Garvey; Vermont, 1828-1895 ***5900.10*** *p176*
McGrath, Margaret Ready; Vermont, 1845-1877 ***5900.10*** *p138*
McGrath, Margaret Ready; Vermont, 1845-1877 ***5900.10*** *p170*
McGrath, Martin 95; Vermont, 1882 ***5900.10*** *p526*
McGrath, Mary; Vermont, 1818-1898 ***5900.10*** *p88*
McGrath, Mary; Vermont, 1828-1903 ***5900.10*** *p559*
McGrath, Mary; Vermont, 1829-1881 ***5900.10*** *p330*
McGrath, Mary; Vermont, 1850-1895 ***5900.10*** *p604*
McGrath, Mary; Vermont, 1856-1935 ***5900.10*** *p370*
McGrath, Mary 22; Vermont, 1866 ***5900.10*** *p526*
McGrath, Mary 36; Vermont, 1890 ***5900.10*** *p258*
McGrath, Mary 66; Vermont, 1901 ***5900.10*** *p307*
McGrath, Mary 70; Vermont, 1894 ***5900.10*** *p369*
McGrath, Mary 70; Vermont, 1894 ***5900.10*** *p370*
McGrath, Mary 88; Vermont, 1893 ***5900.10*** *p258*
McGrath, Mary 90; Vermont, 1891 ***5900.10*** *p526*

McGrath, Mary E. Murphy; Vermont, 1864-1941 ***5900.10*** *p129*
McGrath, Mary Mahar; Vermont, 1843-1923 ***5900.10*** *p251*
McGrath, Mary McMullen; Vermont, 1852-1938 ***5900.10*** *p326*
McGrath, Mary Tuberty; Vermont, 1819-1899 ***5900.10*** *p326*
McGrath, Michael; New York, 1840 ***8197.10*** *p184*
McGrath, Michael; New York, 1840 ***8197.10*** *p185*
McGrath, Michael; Vermont, 1842-1917 ***5900.10*** *p326*
McGrath, Michael; Vermont, 1850-1889 ***5900.10*** *p485*
McGrath, Michael 37; Ontario, 1871 ***1823.15*** *p170*
McGrath, Michael 60; Ontario, 1871 ***1823.28*** *p66*
McGrath, Nancy; Vermont, 1834-1887 ***5900.10*** *p551*
McGrath, Patrick; New York, 1835 ***8197.10*** *p257*
McGrath, Patrick; Vermont, 1810-1892 ***5900.10*** *p326*
McGrath, Patrick; Vermont, 1827-1900 ***5900.10*** *p176*
McGrath, Patrick; Vermont, 1834-1914 ***5900.10*** *p138*
McGrath, Patrick; Vermont, 1834-1914 ***5900.10*** *p170*
McGrath, Patrick; Vermont, 1842-1901 ***5900.10*** *p251*
McGrath, Patrick; Vermont, 1843-1925 ***5900.10*** *p538*
McGrath, Patrick 21; Vermont, 1873 ***5900.10*** *p326*
McGrath, Patrick 89; Vermont, 1887 ***5900.10*** *p258*
McGrath, Peter 53; Ontario, 1871 ***1823.28*** *p66*
McGrath, Richard D.; Vermont, 1845-1911 ***5900.10*** *p394*
McGrath, S. T. G. 5; Ontario, 1861 ***2896.25*** *p1*
McGrath, Sarah Emily; Vermont, n.d. ***5900.10*** *p604*
McGrath, Stephen; New York, 1828 ***8197.10*** *p256*
McGrath, Susan; Vermont, 1851-1858 ***5900.10*** *p559*
McGrath, Thomas; New York, 1807 ***8197.10*** *p45*
McGrath, Thomas; New York, 1834 ***8197.10*** *p372*
McGrath, Thomas; Vermont, 1824-1896 ***5900.10*** *p551*
McGrath, Thomas 57; Vermont, 1886 ***5900.10*** *p212*
McGrath, Thomas 65; Ontario, 1871 ***1823.28*** *p66*
McGrath, Thomas 65; Vermont, 1886 ***5900.10*** *p600*
McGrath, Timothy 34; Vermont, 1850 ***5900.10*** *p349*
McGrath, William; Vermont, 1860-1865 ***5900.10*** *p559*
McGrath, William; Vermont, 1864-1937 ***5900.10*** *p128*
McGrath, William H. 25; Ontario, 1861 ***2896.25*** *p1*
McGratten, Hugh 40; Ontario, 1871 ***1823.15*** *p170*
McGratten, Nelly 60; Ontario, 1871 ***1823.15*** *p170*
McGratton, John 30; Ontario, 1871 ***1823.15*** *p170*
McGratton, William 33; Ontario, 1871 ***1823.15*** *p170*
McGraw, Barney 30; Ontario, 1871 ***1823.22*** *p105*
McGraw, Eliza Mahoney; Vermont, 1856-1935 ***5900.10*** *p464*
McGraw, James; Vermont, 1851-1926 ***5900.10*** *p464*
McGraw, John 19; Ontario, 1871 ***1823.22*** *p105*
McGraw, Katie 23; Vermont, 1876 ***5900.10*** *p81*
McGraw, Michael; New York, 1832 ***8197.10*** *p357*
McGraw, Owen; New York, 1836 ***8197.10*** *p77*
McGrayne, Charles 44; Ontario, 1871 ***1823.22*** *p105*
McGreen, Alice; Vermont, 1825-1892 ***5900.10*** *p59*
McGreen, Joseph; Vermont, 1857-1924 ***5900.10*** *p54*
McGreen, Nora Savage; Vermont, 1866-1929 ***5900.10*** *p54*
McGreen, Thomas; Vermont, 1823-1846 ***5900.10*** *p59*
McGreery, James 54; Ontario, 1871 ***1823.28*** *p66*
McGreevy, Ann; Vermont, 1831-1901 ***5900.10*** *p191*
McGreevy, Jane A.; Vermont, 1852-1932 ***5900.10*** *p181*
McGreevy, John 61; Vermont, 1877 ***5900.10*** *p192*
McGreevy, Margaret C.; Vermont, 1830-1915 ***5900.10*** *p181*
McGreevy, Margaret E.; Vermont, 1849-1883 ***5900.10*** *p182*
McGreevy, Michael; New York, New York, 1859 ***6058.10*** *p62*
McGreevy, Patrick; Vermont, 1851-1923 ***5900.10*** *p182*
McGreevy, Peter; New York, New York, 1852 ***1224.3*** *p49*
McGreggor, John; Pennsylvania, 1785 ***4629.10*** *p48*
McGregor, Mrs.; Quebec, 1858 ***9196.15*** *p33*
McGregor, Alescander 40; Ontario, 1871 ***1823.15*** *p170*
McGregor, Alex 40; Ontario, 1871 ***1823.22*** *p105*
McGregor, Alex 50; Ontario, 1871 ***1823.28*** *p66*
McGregor, Alex 74; Ontario, 1871 ***1823.22*** *p105*
McGregor, Alexander 40; Ontario, 1871 ***1823.22*** *p105*
McGregor, Archibald 32; Ontario, 1871 ***1823.15*** *p170*
McGregor, Archibald 70; Ontario, 1871 ***1823.15*** *p170*
McGregor, Celia E. Lampman; Vermont, 1847-1918 ***5900.10*** *p518*
McGregor, Charles; New York, 1807 ***8197.10*** *p326*
McGregor, Charles 42; Ontario, 1871 ***1823.22*** *p105*
McGregor, Charles 57; Ontario, 1871 ***1823.15*** *p170*
McGregor, Colin 54; Ontario, 1871 ***1823.28*** *p66*
McGregor, Daniel; Georgia, 1699 ***1640.13*** *p86*
McGregor, Daniel 44; Ontario, 1871 ***1823.28*** *p66*
McGregor, Daniel 60; Ontario, 1871 ***1823.15*** *p170*
McGregor, David 28; Ontario, 1871 ***1823.22*** *p105*
McGregor, Duncan; North Carolina, 1784-1845 ***1640.10*** *p115*
McGregor, Duncan 29; Ontario, 1871 ***1823.15*** *p170*
McGregor, Duncan 30; Ontario, 1871 ***1823.15*** *p170*
McGregor, Duncan 49; Ontario, 1871 ***1823.28*** *p66*
McGregor, Ella J. Kelley; Vermont, 1861-1929 ***5900.10*** *p519*
McGregor, Elspeth 26; Ontario, 1871 ***1823.22*** *p105*
McGregor, Fanny; New York, 1835 ***8197.10*** *p257*
McGregor, George 30; Ontario, 1871 ***1823.28*** *p66*
McGregor, George 48; Ontario, 1871 ***1823.22*** *p105*
McGregor, Hector 50; Ontario, 1871 ***1823.15*** *p170*
McGregor, Henry C.; Vermont, 1845-1914 ***5900.10*** *p518*
McGregor, James 50; Ontario, 1871 ***1823.15*** *p170*
McGregor, James 61; Ontario, 1871 ***1823.28*** *p66*
McGregor, Jane 30; Ontario, 1871 ***1823.15*** *p170*
McGregor, Jane A. 45; Ontario, 1871 ***1823.15*** *p170*
McGregor, Janet 48; Ontario, 1871 ***1823.28*** *p66*
McGregor, John; California, 1876 ***1640.13*** *p86*
McGregor, John; Charlottetown, Prince Edward Island, 1808 ***1640.10*** *p116*
McGregor, John; Mississippi, 1790-1845 ***1640.10*** *p116*
McGregor, John 30; Ontario, 1871 ***1823.15*** *p170*
McGregor, John 37; Ontario, 1871 ***1823.15*** *p170*
McGregor, John 45; Ontario, 1871 ***1823.15*** *p170*
McGregor, John 57; Ontario, 1871 ***1823.28*** *p66*
McGregor, John 70; Ontario, 1871 ***1823.28*** *p66*
McGregor, John, Sr.; Georgia, 1743 ***1640.10*** *p116*
McGregor, John, Jr.; Georgia, 1743 ***1640.10*** *p116*
McGregor, John Atholl; Tortola, 1851 ***1640.13*** *p86*
McGregor, Kenith 61; Ontario, 1871 ***1823.15*** *p170*
McGregor, Malcolm 63; Ontario, 1871 ***1823.15*** *p170*
McGregor, Malcom 61; Ontario, 1871 ***1823.15*** *p170*
McGregor, Margaret 77; Ontario, 1871 ***1823.15*** *p170*
McGregor, Mary J.; Vermont, 1845-1922 ***5900.10*** *p401*
McGregor, Murdouch 40; Ontario, 1871 ***1823.15*** *p170*
McGregor, Neil; Jamaica, 1798 ***1640.13*** *p86*
McGregor, Oscar; Vermont, 1848-1927 ***5900.10*** *p519*
McGregor, Patrick; Jamaica, 1823 ***1640.13*** *p86*
McGregor, Peter 53; Vermont, 1849 ***5900.10*** *p59*
McGregor, Peter B.; Pennsylvania, 1868 ***6058.10*** *p64*
McGregor, Robert; Vermont, 1842-1905 ***5900.10*** *p401*
McGregor, Thomas 48; Ontario, 1871 ***1823.28*** *p66*
McGregor, William; Havana, 1766 ***1224.2*** *p73*
McGrewery, Arthur 28; Ontario, 1871 ***1823.15*** *p170*
McGrigor, Ann 87; Ontario, 1871 ***1823.15*** *p170*
McGrigor, Donald 55; Ontario, 1871 ***1823.15*** *p170*
McGrigor, Grigor 50; Ontario, 1871 ***1823.15*** *p171*
McGrigor, Heugh 58; Ontario, 1871 ***1823.15*** *p171*
McGrigor, John 50; Ontario, 1871 ***1823.15*** *p171*
McGriskin, Patrick; Pennsylvania, 1866 ***6058.10*** *p51*
McGroaty, Bridget; Vermont, 1840-1906 ***5900.10*** *p85*
McGroety, John; New York, 1838 ***8197.10*** *p378*
McGrogen, Felise 47; Ontario, 1871 ***1823.15*** *p171*
McGroray, Patrick 52; Vermont, 1867 ***5900.10*** *p512*
McGrorty, William B.; Vermont, 1905 ***5900.10*** *p196*
McGrory, Robert 30; Ontario, 1871 ***1823.15*** *p171*
McGrory, William 26; Ontario, 1871 ***1823.15*** *p171*
McGruer, Alexander; Georgia, 1737 ***1640.10*** *p116*
McGruer, Anne; Georgia, 1738 ***1640.10*** *p116*
McGruer, John; Georgia, 1737 ***1640.10*** *p117*
McGuchan, Catherine 68; Ontario, 1871 ***1823.28*** *p66*
McGuchan, John 70; Ontario, 1871 ***1823.28*** *p66*
McGuckien, Mary 66; Vermont, 1877 ***5900.10*** *p155*
McGuckin, William; New York, 1828 ***8197.10*** *p256*
McGuckin, William M.; New York, 1831 ***8197.10*** *p303*
McGue, Ann; Vermont, 1838-1910 ***5900.10*** *p557*
McGue, Anna E. McGovern; Vermont, 1858-1918 ***5900.10*** *p47*
McGue, Bridget McCool; Vermont, 1833-1918 ***5900.10*** *p446*
McGue, Catherine 49; Vermont, 1866 ***5900.10*** *p328*
McGue, Catherine 59; Vermont, 1893 ***5900.10*** *p594*
McGue, Edward; Vermont, 1838-1913 ***5900.10*** *p446*
McGue, James; Vermont, 1845-1905 ***5900.10*** *p47*
McGue, John 71; Vermont, 1879 ***5900.10*** *p328*
McGue, John 76; Vermont, 1908 ***5900.10*** *p581*
McGue, Lawrence 68; Vermont, 1897 ***5900.10*** *p238*
McGue, Margaret; Vermont, 1844-1890 ***5900.10*** *p568*
McGue, Margaret 68; Vermont, 1908 ***5900.10*** *p581*
McGue, Mary Tynan; Vermont, 1833-1918 ***5900.10*** *p238*
McGue, Peter 37; Vermont, 1880 ***5900.10*** *p472*
McGue, Rosa; Vermont, 1860-1954 ***5900.10*** *p278*
McGue, Thomas 33; Vermont, 1863 ***5900.10*** *p328*
McGuffie, Margaret Farrall 23; Vermont, 1867 ***5900.10*** *p328*
McGuigan, Alice; Vermont, 1803-1875 ***5900.10*** *p440*
McGuigan, James; Vermont, 1848-1899 ***5900.10*** *p208*
McGuigan, Margaret Daily 55; Vermont, 1871 ***5900.10*** *p208*
McGuigan, Michael 77; Vermont, 1891 ***5900.10*** *p208*
McGuigen, Ellen; Vermont, 1846-1927 ***5900.10*** *p221*
McGuigen, Mary; Vermont, 1807 ***5900.10*** *p212*
McGuin, Isa 40; Ontario, 1861 ***2896.27*** *p2*
McGuin, Schery 10; Ontario, 1861 ***2896.27*** *p2*
McGuiness, Chitiana 66; Ontario, 1871 ***1823.15*** *p171*
McGuiness, Daniel 24; Ontario, 1871 ***1823.15*** *p171*
McGuiness, Donald 70; Ontario, 1871 ***1823.15*** *p171*
McGuiness, James; Vermont, 1846-1897 ***5900.10*** *p265*
McGuiness, John 50; Ontario, 1871 ***1823.15*** *p171*
McGuiness, Malcome 29; Ontario, 1871 ***1823.15*** *p171*
McGuiness, Margaret; Vermont, 1845-1920 ***5900.10*** *p265*
McGuiness, Neill 22; Ontario, 1871 ***1823.15*** *p171*
McGuiness, Roary 48; Ontario, 1871 ***1823.15*** *p171*
McGuiness, Roary 93; Ontario, 1871 ***1823.15*** *p171*
McGuiness, Sarah 25; Ontario, 1871 ***1823.15*** *p171*
McGuiness, Thomas 26; Vermont, 1886 ***5900.10*** *p448*
McGuinness, Bridget; Vermont, 1813 ***5900.10*** *p363*
McGuinness, Margaret 6 months; Vermont, 1856 ***5900.10*** *p363*
McGuinness, Peter; Vermont, 1818-1894 ***5900.10*** *p363*
McGuire, Andrew; New York, 1827 ***8197.10*** *p256*
McGuire, Andrew 52; Ontario, 1871 ***1823.22*** *p105*
McGuire, Ann; Vermont, 1835-1935 ***5900.10*** *p73*
McGuire, Ann; Vermont, 1848-1875 ***5900.10*** *p581*
McGuire, Ann 56; Vermont, 1873 ***5900.10*** *p616*
McGuire, Ann 78; Vermont, 1897 ***5900.10*** *p565*
McGuire, Ann Cox 62; Vermont, 1900 ***5900.10*** *p558*
McGuire, Anthony 62; Ontario, 1871 ***1823.22*** *p105*
McGuire, Arthur 46; Ontario, 1871 ***1823.15*** *p171*
McGuire, Bernard; New York, 1837 ***8197.10*** *p97*
McGuire, Bridget; Vermont, 1840-1914 ***5900.10*** *p82*
McGuire, Bridget 69; Ontario, 1871 ***1823.22*** *p105*
McGuire, Bridget Flannigan 34; Vermont, 1872 ***5900.10*** *p568*
McGuire, Bridget Mulligan; Vermont, 1834-1893 ***5900.10*** *p89*
McGuire, Catherine; Vermont, 1842-1907 ***5900.10*** *p288*
McGuire, Catherine 47; Ontario, 1871 ***1823.15*** *p171*
McGuire, Charles; Vermont, 1837-1909 ***5900.10*** *p89*
McGuire, Charles 35; Ontario, 1871 ***1823.15*** *p171*
McGuire, Charles 56; Ontario, 1871 ***1823.28*** *p66*
McGuire, Charles 64; Vermont, 1928 ***5900.10*** *p314*
McGuire, Christine 35; Ontario, 1871 ***1823.15*** *p171*
McGuire, Daniel 22; Philadelphia, 1774 ***1220.25*** *p66*
McGuire, Daniel 84; Vermont, 1884 ***5900.10*** *p559*
McGuire, Daniel A. 84; Vermont, 1884 ***5900.10*** *p568*
McGuire, Edward; Georgia, 1759 ***1640.10*** *p117*
McGuire, Edward 63; Ontario, 1871 ***1823.22*** *p105*
McGuire, Eliza 24; Ontario, 1871 ***1823.22*** *p105*
McGuire, Elizabeth; Vermont, 1815-1900 ***5900.10*** *p419*
McGuire, Elizabeth; Vermont, 1851-1921 ***5900.10*** *p95*
McGuire, Ellen; Vermont, 1860-1894 ***5900.10*** *p351*
McGuire, Ellen 43; Ontario, 1871 ***1823.28*** *p66*
McGuire, Ellen Scanlon 74; Vermont, 1877 ***5900.10*** *p72*
McGuire, Francis; New York, 1834 ***8197.10*** *p373*
McGuire, Francis 29; Ontario, 1871 ***1823.22*** *p105*
McGuire, Francis 40; Ontario, 1871 ***1823.22*** *p105*
McGuire, Francis R. 49; Ontario, 1871 ***1823.22*** *p105*
McGuire, George 45; Ontario, 1871 ***1823.15*** *p171*
McGuire, Hugh; New York, 1837 ***8197.10*** *p99*
McGuire, Hugh 83; Ontario, 1871 ***1823.28*** *p66*
McGuire, James; New York, 1833-1838 ***8197.10*** *p119*
McGuire, James; New York, 1838 ***8197.10*** *p125*
McGuire, James; New York, 1839 ***8197.10*** *p138*
McGuire, James; Pennsylvania, 1777 ***4629.10*** *p17*
McGuire, James; Vermont, 1829-1892 ***5900.10*** *p74*
McGuire, James; Vermont, 1837-1925 ***5900.10*** *p558*
McGuire, James 27; Ontario, 1871 ***1823.15*** *p171*
McGuire, James 28; Ontario, 1871 ***1823.22*** *p105*
McGuire, James 38; Ontario, 1871 ***1823.22*** *p105*
McGuire, James 38; Ontario, 1871 ***1823.28*** *p66*
McGuire, James 50; Ontario, 1871 ***1823.22*** *p105*
McGuire, James 52; Vermont, 1861 ***5900.10*** *p72*
McGuire, James 62; Ontario, 1871 ***1823.28*** *p66*
McGuire, James 68; Ontario, 1871 ***1823.22*** *p105*
McGuire, James 73; Vermont, 1892 ***5900.10*** *p417*
McGuire, Jane 70; Ontario, 1871 ***1823.28*** *p66*
McGuire, Jennie A.; Vermont, 1869-1969 ***5900.10*** *p141*
McGuire, John; New York, 1831 ***8197.10*** *p364*
McGuire, John; New York, 1838 ***8197.10*** *p257*
McGuire, John; Pennsylvania, 1866 ***6058.10*** *p56*
McGuire, John 24; Ontario, 1861 ***2896.25*** *p68*
McGuire, John 63; Ontario, 1871 ***1823.22*** *p105*
McGuire, John 66; Ontario, 1871 ***1823.22*** *p105*
McGuire, John C.; Vermont, 1866-1904 ***5900.10*** *p266*
McGuire, Joseph; Georgia, 1760 ***1640.10*** *p117*
McGuire, Joseph; New York, 1838 ***8197.10*** *p257*
McGuire, Joseph; New York, 1840 ***8197.10*** *p184*
McGuire, Joseph; Vermont, 1871-1872 ***5900.10*** *p266*
McGuire, Kate 45; Vermont, 1885 ***5900.10*** *p313*
McGuire, Lauchlane McQuarry; New York, 1783 ***1640.13*** *p86*
McGuire, Luke 54; Ontario, 1871 ***1823.22*** *p105*
McGuire, Margaret 50; Ontario, 1871 ***1823.15*** *p171*
McGuire, Martin; New York, 1837 ***8197.10*** *p98*
McGuire, Mary; Vermont, 1805-1878 ***5900.10*** *p444*

McGuire, Mary; Vermont, 1822-1882 ***5900.10*** *p75*
McGuire, Mary 38; Ontario, 1861 ***2896.27*** *p2*
McGuire, Mary A. 46; Vermont, 1894 ***5900.10*** *p95*
McGuire, Mary E.; Vermont, 1863-1918 ***5900.10*** *p266*
McGuire, Mary J. McGloughlyn; Vermont, 1847-1899 ***5900.10*** *p266*
McGuire, Matthias; New York, 1837 ***8197.10*** *p97*
McGuire, Michael; New York, 1837 ***8197.10*** *p99*
McGuire, Michael; Vermont, 1887 ***5900.10*** *p85*
McGuire, Michael 29; Ontario, 1871 ***1823.22*** *p105*
McGuire, Michael 35; Ontario, 1871 ***1823.22*** *p105*
McGuire, Michael 46; Ontario, 1871 ***1823.28*** *p66*
McGuire, Nancy Winters 63; Vermont, 1874 ***5900.10*** *p559*
McGuire, Nancy Winters 63; Vermont, 1874 ***5900.10*** *p568*
McGuire, Patrick; New York, 1826-1834 ***8197.10*** *p306*
McGuire, Patrick; New York, 1827-1831 ***8197.10*** *p369*
McGuire, Patrick; New York, 1828 ***8197.10*** *p256*
McGuire, Patrick; New York, 1838 ***8197.10*** *p301*
McGuire, Patrick; New York, 1838 ***8197.10*** *p378*
McGuire, Patrick; New York, 1840 ***8197.10*** *p182*
McGuire, Patrick; Vermont, 1835-1935 ***5900.10*** *p73*
McGuire, Patrick 33; Ontario, 1871 ***1823.22*** *p105*
McGuire, Patrick 35; Ontario, 1871 ***1823.15*** *p171*
McGuire, Patrick 47; Ontario, 1871 ***1823.22*** *p105*
McGuire, Patrick 50; Ontario, 1871 ***1823.22*** *p105*
McGuire, Patrick 55; Ontario, 1871 ***1823.15*** *p171*
McGuire, Patrick 58; Vermont, 1895 ***5900.10*** *p163*
McGuire, Patrick 69; Ontario, 1871 ***1823.22*** *p106*
McGuire, Peter; New York, 1828 ***8197.10*** *p256*
McGuire, Peter; New York, 1834 ***8197.10*** *p74*
McGuire, Peter 56; Ontario, 1871 ***1823.22*** *p106*
McGuire, Philip; New York, 1840 ***8197.10*** *p387*
McGuire, Rose 45; Ontario, 1871 ***1823.15*** *p171*
McGuire, Rose 50; Ontario, 1871 ***1823.22*** *p106*
McGuire, Sarah Davis; Vermont, 1836-1871 ***5900.10*** *p74*
McGuire, Susan 25; Ontario, 1871 ***1823.22*** *p106*
McGuire, Thomas; New York, 1836 ***8197.10*** *p77*
McGuire, Thomas; Vermont, 1804-1889 ***5900.10*** *p613*
McGuire, Thomas; Vermont, 1837-1913 ***5900.10*** *p266*
McGuire, Thomas 31; Ontario, 1871 ***1823.22*** *p106*
McGuire, Thomas 66; Vermont, 1900 ***5900.10*** *p313*
McGuire, Timothy; New York, 1830 ***8197.10*** *p257*
McGuirk, Alice Dooley; Vermont, 1834-1926 ***5900.10*** *p423*
McGuirk, Ann Powderly 88; Vermont, 1922 ***5900.10*** *p434*
McGuirk, Charles W.; Vermont, 1858-1938 ***5900.10*** *p420*
McGuirk, Honor Reilley 89; Vermont, 1876 ***5900.10*** *p450*
McGuirk, Honora; Vermont, 1827-1886 ***5900.10*** *p441*
McGuirk, James; Vermont, 1852-1911 ***5900.10*** *p443*
McGuirk, Jane; Vermont, 1833 ***5900.10*** *p450*
McGuirk, John; Vermont, 1831-1918 ***5900.10*** *p423*
McGuirk, Katherine A. Corcoran; Vermont, 1856-1925 ***5900.10*** *p443*
McGuirk, Margaret; Vermont, 1850-1916 ***5900.10*** *p382*
McGuirk, Matthew 71; Vermont, 1899 ***5900.10*** *p434*
McGuirk, Matthew 84; Vermont, 1871 ***5900.10*** *p450*
McGuirk, Nora A. Saunders; Vermont, 1857-1923 ***5900.10*** *p420*
McGuirk, Patrick 47; Vermont, 1864 ***5900.10*** *p450*
McGuiry, Laughlin; New York, 1750 ***1224.2*** *p73*
McGuoen, Patrick; New York, 1836 ***8197.10*** *p77*
McGurn, Patrick 56; Vermont, 1882 ***5900.10*** *p78*
McGuyre, Bridget 20; Vermont, 1856 ***5900.10*** *p157*
McGuyre, Catharine; Vermont, n.d. ***5900.10*** *p157*
McGuyre, Catherine 80; Vermont, 1889 ***5900.10*** *p157*
McGuyre, James 15; Vermont, 1855 ***5900.10*** *p157*
McGuyre, John; Vermont, n.d. ***5900.10*** *p157*
McGuyre, John 40; Vermont, 1881 ***5900.10*** *p203*
McGwan, Thomas 45; Ontario, 1871 ***1823.22*** *p106*
McHardy, Duncan 48; Ontario, 1871 ***1823.15*** *p171*
McHardy, John 80; Ontario, 1871 ***1823.15*** *p171*
McHardy, Norman 35; Ontario, 1871 ***1823.15*** *p171*
McHardy, Robert 46; Ontario, 1871 ***1823.15*** *p171*
McHardy, William; Savannah, Georgia, 1820 ***1640.10*** *p117*
McHarley, Bridget *SEE* McHarley, Cecilia
McHarley, Cecilia; Alabama, 1800-1845 ***1640.10*** *p117*
Husband: Thomas
Daughter: Bridget
McHarley, Thomas *SEE* McHarley, Cecilia
McHarry, John 52; Ontario, 1871 ***1823.22*** *p106*
McHean, Maria 23 *SEE* McHean, Stewart
McHean, Stewart 30; Philadelphia, 1774 ***1220.25*** *p68*
Wife: Maria 23
McHee, John; Pennsylvania, 1778 ***4629.10*** *p32*
McHendry, Isaac; Pennsylvania, 1777 ***4629.10*** *p31*
McHendry, Micham; Pennsylvania, 1778 ***4629.10*** *p32*
McHenry, James; Georgia, 1760 ***1640.10*** *p117*
McHenry, James; Savannah, Georgia, 1806-1812 ***1640.10*** *p117*
McHenry, John 60; Ontario, 1871 ***1823.15*** *p171*
McHenry, Marion; Georgia, 1795-1822 ***1640.10*** *p117*
McHenry, Matthew; Pensacola, Florida, 1768 ***1640.10*** *p118*
McHenry, Robert; Georgia, 1822 ***1640.10*** *p118*
McHoats, Catherine 50; Kansas, 1877-1910 ***9079.10*** *p2*
McHoats, Cristian 88; Kansas, 1877-1910 ***9079.10*** *p2*
McHoffie, William 35; Ontario, 1871 ***1823.15*** *p171*
McHolm, James 40; Ontario, 1871 ***1823.22*** *p106*
McHrath, David; Pennsylvania, 1852 ***6058.10*** *p30*
McHugh, Catherine; Vermont, n.d. ***5900.10*** *p316*
McHugh, Catherine; Vermont, 1848-1923 ***5900.10*** *p145*
McHugh, Catherine Ann; Vermont, 1862-1916 ***5900.10*** *p527*
McHugh, Charles Peter; Vermont, 1870-1872 ***5900.10*** *p527*
McHugh, Dennis; Vermont, 1832-1922 ***5900.10*** *p316*
McHugh, Edward; New York, 1835-1838 ***8197.10*** *p119*
McHugh, Edward; New York, 1838 ***8197.10*** *p126*
McHugh, Elizabeth; Vermont, 1847-1912 ***5900.10*** *p316*
McHugh, Francis; Vermont, 1865-1932 ***5900.10*** *p527*
McHugh, George; Vermont, n.d. ***5900.10*** *p316*
McHugh, James; Vermont, n.d. ***5900.10*** *p135*
McHugh, James 36; Ontario, 1871 ***1823.28*** *p66*
McHugh, James 47; Ontario, 1871 ***1823.22*** *p106*
McHugh, Jane; Vermont, 1824-1907 ***5900.10*** *p568*
McHugh, John; Vermont, 1814-1903 ***5900.10*** *p568*
McHugh, John 50; Ontario, 1871 ***1823.28*** *p66*
McHugh, John 58; Ontario, 1871 ***1823.28*** *p66*
McHugh, Margret 35; Ontario, 1871 ***1823.22*** *p106*
McHugh, Mary; Vermont, n.d. ***5900.10*** *p135*
McHugh, Mary McGettrick; Vermont, 1838-1921 ***5900.10*** *p527*
McHugh, Matthew; Pennsylvania, 1777 ***4629.10*** *p21*
McHugh, Matthew; Pennsylvania, 1779 ***4629.10*** *p41*
McHugh, Michael; Vermont, 1829-1913 ***5900.10*** *p527*
McHugh, Michael 45; Ontario, 1871 ***1823.28*** *p66*
McHugh, Patrick; Pennsylvania, 1867 ***6058.10*** *p58*
McHugh, Patrick 35; Ontario, 1871 ***1823.28*** *p66*
McHugh, Sarah A.; Vermont, 1859-1882 ***5900.10*** *p135*
McHugh, Sarah McCaffrey; Vermont, 1825-1888 ***5900.10*** *p135*
McHugh, Terrance; Vermont, 1815-1889 ***5900.10*** *p135*
McHugh, Thomas; New York, 1834 ***8197.10*** *p257*
McHugh, Thomas; New York, 1839 ***8197.10*** *p381*
McHugh, Thomas 60; Ontario, 1871 ***1823.15*** *p171*
McHugh, William H.; Vermont, 1866-1889 ***5900.10*** *p135*
McHugo, Bridget; Vermont, 1866-1895 ***5900.10*** *p178*
McHugo, Ellen A.; Vermont, 1864-1953 ***5900.10*** *p178*
McHugo, John; Vermont, 1824-1887 ***5900.10*** *p178*
McHugo, Margaret; Vermont, 1851-1919 ***5900.10*** *p178*
McHugo, Thomas; Vermont, 1856-1893 ***5900.10*** *p178*
McHugo, Winnifred Ward; Vermont, 1825-1911 ***5900.10*** *p178*
McHutchinson, Rev.; Quebec, 1856 ***9196.15*** *p9*
McIbbon, Heinry 55; Ontario, 1871 ***1823.28*** *p66*
McIbbon, James 43; Ontario, 1871 ***1823.28*** *p66*
McIbbon, Joseph 39; Ontario, 1871 ***1823.28*** *p66*
McIbbon, Joseph 49; Ontario, 1871 ***1823.28*** *p66*
McIbbon, Sarah 55; Ontario, 1871 ***1823.28*** *p66*
McIlhinny, William; Pennsylvania, 1777 ***4629.10*** *p9*
McIllroy, William 39; Ontario, 1871 ***1823.15*** *p171*
McIlroy, William; Pennsylvania, 1785 ***4629.10*** *p48*
McIlroy, William 25; Ontario, 1871 ***1823.28*** *p66*
McIlwain, Agness 55; Ontario, 1871 ***1823.15*** *p171*
McIlwain, David 48; Ontario, 1871 ***1823.15*** *p171*
McIlwain, John 25; Ontario, 1871 ***1823.15*** *p171*
McIlwain, John 34; Ontario, 1871 ***1823.15*** *p171*
McIlwain, William 50; Ontario, 1871 ***1823.15*** *p171*
McIlwraith, Mrs.; Quebec, 1858 ***9196.15*** *p44*
McInarny, Michael 54; Ontario, 1871 ***1823.15*** *p171*
McIndoe, William; New York, 1838 ***8197.10*** *p257*
McInerney, John; Vermont, 1843-1932 ***5900.10*** *p394*
McInerney, Julia Minouge; Vermont, 1854-1924 ***5900.10*** *p394*
McInerney, Margaret; Vermont, 1847-1902 ***5900.10*** *p252*
McInerny, John 8; Vermont, 1861 ***5900.10*** *p259*
McInerny, John 57; Vermont, 1865 ***5900.10*** *p259*
McInesny, Dennis 50; Ontario, 1871 ***1823.28*** *p66*
McIniry, James 50; Ontario, 1871 ***1823.28*** *p66*
McInis, Christy 45; Ontario, 1871 ***1823.15*** *p171*
McInis, Flora 40; Ontario, 1871 ***1823.15*** *p171*
McInis, Kenith 18; Ontario, 1871 ***1823.15*** *p171*
McInis, Mary 20; Ontario, 1871 ***1823.15*** *p171*
McInlear, Ann 72; Vermont, n.d. ***5900.10*** *p545*
McInlear, Katherine; Vermont, 1850-1885 ***5900.10*** *p545*
McInnerny, Thomas 68; Ontario, 1871 ***1823.28*** *p66*
McInnes, Andrew; Canada, 1891 ***1640.13*** *p86*
McInnes, Angus 44; Ontario, 1871 ***1823.28*** *p66*
McInnes, Angus 62; Ontario, 1871 ***1823.28*** *p66*
McInnes, Archibald 44; Ontario, 1871 ***1823.15*** *p171*
McInnes, Archibald 75; Ontario, 1871 ***1823.15*** *p171*
McInnes, Catherine 65; Ontario, 1871 ***1823.15*** *p172*
McInnes, Helen; Georgia, 1804-1812 ***1640.10*** *p100*
McInnes, John 39; Ontario, 1871 ***1823.15*** *p172*
McInnes, John 79; Ontario, 1871 ***1823.28*** *p66*
McInnes, William 43; Ontario, 1871 ***1823.15*** *p172*
McInnes, William 56; Ontario, 1871 ***1823.15*** *p172*
McInnis, Ann 23; Ontario, 1871 ***1823.15*** *p172*
McInnis, Catherine 78; Ontario, 1871 ***1823.15*** *p172*
McInnis, Donald 42; Ontario, 1871 ***1823.15*** *p172*
McInnis, John 40; Ontario, 1871 ***1823.15*** *p172*
McIntere, Jane 90; Ontario, 1871 ***1823.28*** *p66*
McIntire, Donald 28; Ontario, 1871 ***1823.15*** *p172*
McIntire, George; Pennsylvania, 1866 ***6058.10*** *p53*
McIntire, James; New York, New York, 1852 ***6058.10*** *p39*
McIntire, John; New York, New York, 1854 ***6058.10*** *p39*
McIntire, John 25; Ontario, 1871 ***1823.28*** *p66*
McIntire, Robert; Pennsylvania, 1856 ***6058.10*** *p37*
McIntire, Thomas 50; Ontario, 1871 ***1823.15*** *p172*
McIntire, William; New York, 1803 ***8197.10*** *p14*
McIntomney, Luke 60; Ontario, 1871 ***1823.28*** *p66*
McIntosh, Mr.; Georgia, 1763 ***1640.10*** *p123*
McIntosh, Mr.; Quebec, 1856 ***9196.15*** *p9*
McIntosh, Mr.; Quebec, 1857 ***9196.15*** *p14*
McIntosh, A.; Quebec, 1856 ***9196.15*** *p8*
McIntosh, Alexander; Charles Town, South Carolina, 1772 ***1224.2*** *p73*
McIntosh, Alexander; Pennsylvania, 1867 ***6058.10*** *p56*
McIntosh, Alexr 34; Ontario, 1871 ***1823.22*** *p106*
McIntosh, Alice C.; Vermont, 1844-1910 ***5900.10*** *p500*
McIntosh, Allan; New York, 1814 ***8197.10*** *p58*
McIntosh, Angus; Georgia, 1743 ***1640.10*** *p118*
McIntosh, Archibald; Mobile, Alabama, 1815-1845 ***1640.10*** *p118*
McIntosh, Charles 41; Ontario, 1871 ***1823.15*** *p172*
McIntosh, Daniel; Savannah, Georgia, 1807 ***1640.10*** *p119*
McIntosh, David 45; Ontario, 1871 ***1823.22*** *p106*
McIntosh, Donald 50; Ontario, 1871 ***1823.15*** *p172*
McIntosh, Donald 66; Ontario, 1871 ***1823.15*** *p172*
McIntosh, Donald 70; Ontario, 1871 ***1823.15*** *p172*
McIntosh, Duncan; Jamaica, 1744 ***1640.13*** *p86*
McIntosh, Duncan 41; Ontario, 1871 ***1823.15*** *p172*
McIntosh, George 42; Ontario, 1871 ***1823.15*** *p172*
McIntosh, Hugh 59; Ontario, 1871 ***1823.15*** *p172*
McIntosh, Isabella 52; Ontario, 1871 ***1823.22*** *p106*
McIntosh, Isabella 67; Ontario, 1871 ***1823.22*** *p106*
McIntosh, Jacklin 67; Ontario, 1871 ***1823.15*** *p172*
McIntosh, James 24; Ontario, 1871 ***1823.22*** *p106*
McIntosh, James 60; Ontario, 1871 ***1823.15*** *p172*
McIntosh, Jane 50; Ontario, 1871 ***1823.15*** *p172*
McIntosh, Jane 64; Ontario, 1871 ***1823.15*** *p172*
McIntosh, Jane 75; Ontario, 1871 ***1823.22*** *p106*
McIntosh, Jane Mitchell 64; Vermont, 1876 ***5900.10*** *p499*
McIntosh, John; Mexico, 1900 ***1640.13*** *p87*
McIntosh, John; Mobile, Alabama, 1764 ***1640.10*** *p121*
McIntosh, John; New York, New York, 1865 ***3437.14*** *p86*
McIntosh, John; Savannah, Georgia, 1810 ***1640.10*** *p121*
McIntosh, John 32; Georgia, 1775 ***1220.25*** *p125*
McIntosh, John 40; Ontario, 1871 ***1823.15*** *p172*
McIntosh, John 42; Ontario, 1871 ***1823.22*** *p106*
McIntosh, John 50; Ontario, 1871 ***1823.15*** *p172*
McIntosh, John 52; Ontario, 1871 ***1823.15*** *p172*
McIntosh, John 60; Ontario, 1871 ***1823.15*** *p172*
McIntosh, John F. 69; Vermont, 1890 ***5900.10*** *p499*
McIntosh, Lachlan; Ontario, 1854 ***1640.13*** *p87*
McIntosh, Margret 38; Ontario, 1871 ***1823.15*** *p172*
McIntosh, Martha 76; Ontario, 1871 ***1823.15*** *p172*
McIntosh, Mary; North Carolina, 1770-1845 ***1640.10*** *p122*
McIntosh, Mary 86; Ontario, 1871 ***1823.15*** *p172*
McIntosh, Nicholas 35; New York, 1775 ***1220.25*** *p142*
McIntosh, Peter 37; Ontario, 1871 ***1823.15*** *p172*
McIntosh, Peter 65; Ontario, 1871 ***1823.28*** *p67*
McIntosh, Philip 48; Ontario, 1871 ***1823.15*** *p172*
McIntosh, Robert; New York, 1838 ***8197.10*** *p376*
McIntosh, Robert 42; Ontario, 1871 ***1823.15*** *p172*
McIntosh, Thomas 45; Ontario, 1871 ***1823.28*** *p67*
McIntosh, William; Georgia, 1759 ***1640.10*** *p123*
McIntosh, William; Washington, 1892 ***1640.13*** *p87*
McIntosh, William 47; Ontario, 1871 ***1823.15*** *p172*
McIntosh, William 48; Ontario, 1871 ***1823.28*** *p67*
McIntosh, William 65; Ontario, 1871 ***1823.15*** *p172*
McIntrye, Mr.; Quebec, 1857 ***9196.15*** *p20*
McIntyre, . . .; Ontario, 1861 ***2896.28*** *p41*
McIntyre, Mr.; Georgia, 1738 ***1640.10*** *p124*
McIntyre, A. C.; Savannah, Georgia, 1807-1812 ***1640.10*** *p123*

McKerrall, William; Dallas, 1874 1640.13 p89
McKetrick, Robt 46; Ontario, 1871 1823.28 p68
McKever, Donald 42; Ontario, 1871 1823.15 p176
McKever, Mary Elizabeth; Vermont, 1876 5900.10 p481
McKey, Adam 45; Ontario, 1871 1823.15 p176
McKey, Catherine 92; Ontario, 1871 1823.15 p176
McKey, Elisabeth 47; Ontario, 1871 1823.15 p176
McKey, George 63; Ontario, 1871 1823.15 p176
McKey, Samuel 26; Ontario, 1871 1823.15 p176
McKey, Sutherland 53; Ontario, 1871 1823.28 p68
McKey, William 50; Ontario, 1871 1823.28 p68
McKezsie, Rose A. Higgins; Vermont, 1856-1936 5900.10 p167
McKibbin, Mrs. 43; Ontario, 1861 2896.26 p28
McKibbin, Emma 6; Ontario, 1861 2896.26 p28
McKibbin, John 53; Ontario, 1861 2896.26 p28
McKibbin, John S.; New York, 1821 8197.10 p254
McKibbin, John W. 3; Ontario, 1861 2896.26 p28
McKibbin, Joseph; New York, 1802 8197.10 p23
McKibbin, Lorinda 8; Ontario, 1861 2896.26 p28
McKibbin, Maryann 20; Ontario, 1861 2896.26 p28
McKibbin, Phillip 13; Ontario, 1861 2896.26 p28
McKibbin, R. H. 18; Ontario, 1861 2896.26 p28
McKibbin, Sharlott 16; Ontario, 1861 2896.26 p28
McKibbon, Andrew 45; Ontario, 1871 1823.15 p176
McKibbon, Archibald 13; Ontario, 1861 2896.26 p37
McKibbon, Daniel 9; Ontario, 1861 2896.26 p36
McKibbon, Elisa 8; Ontario, 1861 2896.26 p36
McKibbon, Ellen 13; Ontario, 1861 2896.26 p36
McKibbon, Henry 48; Ontario, 1861 2896.26 p36
McKibbon, Jacob 8; Ontario, 1861 2896.26 p37
McKibbon, James 11; Ontario, 1861 2896.26 p36
McKibbon, Jane 38; Ontario, 1861 2896.26 p36
McKibbon, John H. 15; Ontario, 1861 2896.26 p36
McKibbon, Lenord 6; Ontario, 1861 2896.26 p37
McKibbon, Martha 32; Ontario, 1861 2896.26 p36
McKibbon, Mary 5; Ontario, 1861 2896.26 p36
McKibbon, Mary 10; Ontario, 1861 2896.26 p37
McKibbon, Mary J. 17; Ontario, 1861 2896.26 p36
McKibbon, Nancy 10; Ontario, 1861 2896.26 p36
McKibbon, Nancy 38; Ontario, 1861 2896.26 p37
McKibbon, Stephen 4; Ontario, 1861 2896.26 p36
McKibbon, Thomas 7; Ontario, 1861 2896.26 p36
McKibbon, Thomas 44; Ontario, 1861 2896.26 p37
McKibbon, William 14; Ontario, 1861 2896.26 p37
McKidd, Mrs.; Quebec, 1857 9196.15 p25
McKie, John; Augusta, Georgia, 1810-1812 1640.10 p134
McKie, John; New York, 1823 8197.10 p255
McKie, Peter; Augusta, Georgia, 1811 1640.10 p134
McKiernan, Charles 40; Ontario, 1871 1823.28 p68
McKiernan, Cornelius; New York, 1838 8197.10 p126
McKiernan, James 51; Ontario, 1871 1823.28 p68
McKiernan, John 46; Ontario, 1871 1823.28 p68
McKiggin, John; New York, 1821 8197.10 p254
McKill, Robert; Tobago, West Indies, 1821 1640.13 p89
McKillop, Alexander 21; Ontario, 1871 1823.28 p68
McKillop, Caroline Hadley; Vermont, 1849-1920 5900.10 p500
McKillop, James; Vermont, 1826-1906 5900.10 p509
McKillop, Janet 74; Ontario, 1871 1823.22 p107
McKillop, Margaret Lesslie; Vermont, 1826-1912 5900.10 p509
McKillop, Nancy; Vermont, 1836-1901 5900.10 p510
McKillop, Patrick; Vermont, 1841-1914 5900.10 p510
McKim, . . .; Ontario, 1871 1823.15 p176
McKim, David 40; Ontario, 1871 1823.15 p176
McKim, George 38; Ontario, 1871 1823.15 p176
McKim, Matilda 18; Ontario, 1861 2896.27 p56
McKim, Rebecca 75; Ontario, 1871 1823.15 p176
McKimmie, Alexander; Georgia, 1736 1640.10 p134
McKindley, Andrew 45; Ontario, 1861 2896.26 p37
McKindley, Archibald 15; Ontario, 1861 2896.26 p37
McKindley, Jane 12; Ontario, 1861 2896.26 p37
McKindley, Margret 1; Ontario, 1861 2896.26 p34
McKindley, Mary 40; Ontario, 1861 2896.26 p37
McKindley, Sarah 6; Ontario, 1861 2896.26 p34
McKindley, Thomas 4; Ontario, 1861 2896.26 p34
McKindley, William 2; Ontario, 1861 2896.26 p34
McKiney, Caroline 31; Vermont, 1867 5900.10 p281
McKiney, Emiley 5; Vermont, 1845 5900.10 p281
McKiney, Hannah 55; Vermont, 1865 5900.10 p281
McKiney, William 69; Vermont, 1869 5900.10 p281
McKinlay, John 55; Ontario, 1871 1823.22 p107
McKinley, Alexander; Pennsylvania, 1786 4629.10 p52
McKinley, Ann 51; Vermont, 1886 5900.10 p290
McKinley, Archibald 45; Ontario, 1871 1823.28 p68
McKinley, Gilbert; New York, New York, 1846 6058.10 p33
McKinley, Jane 37; Ontario, 1871 1823.15 p176
McKinley, John; Delaware, 1775-1781 4628.40 p69
McKinley, John; New York, 1803 8197.10 p15
McKinley, John; New York, 1831 8197.10 p355
McKinley, John; New York, New York, 1826 8197.10 p125
McKinley, John; New York, New York, 1847 6058.10 p33
McKinley, John 35; Ontario, 1871 1823.28 p68
McKinley, John 47; Ontario, 1871 1823.15 p176
McKinley, Margret 45; Ontario, 1871 1823.28 p68
McKinley, Mary 77; Ontario, 1871 1823.15 p176
McKinley, Peter 36; Ontario, 1871 1823.28 p68
McKinley, Robert; New York, 1802 8197.10 p23
McKinley, William; Pennsylvania, 1847 6058.10 p20
McKinn, Margaret; Vermont, 1840-1924 5900.10 p539
McKinna, John; Jamaica, 1766 1640.13 p89
McKinna, Michael; New York, 1840 8197.10 p182
McKinnay, John; Pennsylvania, 1777 4629.10 p12
McKinnel, John; New York, 1784 1640.13 p89
McKinnell, Robert; Ontario, 1894 1640.13 p89
McKinnen, Robert; Pensacola, Florida, 1767 1640.10 p135
McKinney, . . .; New York, 1837 8197.10 p375
McKinney, Addie; Vermont, 1848-1929 5900.10 p282
McKinney, Barney; Pennsylvania, 1812 6058.10 p4
McKinney, Daniel 43; Ontario, 1861 2896.28 p20
McKinney, Edward; New York, 1828-1831 8197.10 p369
McKinney, Jane; Vermont, 1833-1905 5900.10 p517
McKinney, John; Pennsylvania, 1777 4629.10 p15
McKinney, John; Pennsylvania, 1808 6058.10 p2
McKinney, Martha; Vermont, 1845-1892 5900.10 p282
McKinnon, Mr.; Quebec, 1858 9196.15 p44
McKinnon, Alexander 65; Ontario, 1871 1823.15 p176
McKinnon, Angus 47; Ontario, 1871 1823.15 p176
McKinnon, Ann 57; Ontario, 1871 1823.15 p176
McKinnon, Archibald; Georgia, 1775 1640.10 p134
McKinnon, Catherine *SEE* McKinnon, John
McKinnon, Catherine; Florida, 1768-1845 1640.10 p134
McKinnon, Charles 42; Ontario, 1871 1823.15 p176
McKinnon, Charles William; Georgia, 1771 1640.10 p134
McKinnon, Christian; Florida, 1760-1845 1640.10 p134
McKinnon, Daniel 22; Ontario, 1871 1823.15 p177
McKinnon, Daniel 30; Ontario, 1871 1823.15 p176
McKinnon, Daniel 33; Ontario, 1871 1823.15 p176
McKinnon, Daniel 75; Ontario, 1871 1823.15 p177
McKinnon, Donald; North Carolina, 1803 1224.3 p49
McKinnon, Donald 35; Ontario, 1871 1823.28 p68
McKinnon, Donald 43; Ontario, 1871 1823.15 p177
McKinnon, Duncan 34; Ontario, 1871 1823.15 p177
McKinnon, Hugh 26; Ontario, 1871 1823.15 p177
McKinnon, Hugh 30; Ontario, 1871 1823.15 p177
McKinnon, Isabella; Canada, 1895 1640.13 p89
McKinnon, James 39; Ontario, 1871 1823.15 p177
McKinnon, John; Georgia, 1775 1640.10 p134
McKinnon, John; North Carolina, 1801-1829 1640.10 p134
Wife: Catherine
McKinnon, John; Savannah, Georgia, 1825 1640.10 p134
McKinnon, John 30; Ontario, 1871 1823.15 p177
McKinnon, John 47; Ontario, 1871 1823.15 p177
McKinnon, Joseph 40; Ontario, 1871 1823.15 p177
McKinnon, Margaret 76; Ontario, 1871 1823.15 p177
McKinnon, Mary 80; Ontario, 1871 1823.15 p177
McKinnon, Neal 44; Ontario, 1871 1823.15 p177
McKinnon, William 61; Ontario, 1871 1823.22 p107
McKinnon, Wm 61; Ontario, 1871 1823.15 p177
McKinon, Alexander 50; Ontario, 1871 1823.15 p177
McKinon, Donald 50; Ontario, 1871 1823.15 p177
McKinon, Duncan 38; Ontario, 1871 1823.15 p177
McKinon, Murdoch 30; Ontario, 1871 1823.15 p177
McKinstry, William; Concord, New Hampshire, 1824 1224.3 p49
McKinzie, John 39; Ontario, 1871 1823.22 p107
McKinzie, Peter 60; Ontario, 1871 1823.28 p68
McKirdy, Mr.; Quebec, 1858 9196.15 p40
McKirdy, Mrs.; Quebec, 1858 9196.15 p40
McKirdy, Jane 85; Ontario, 1871 1823.15 p177
McKirriwin, Christina 61; Ontario, 1871 1823.15 p177
McKittrick, Thomas; New York, 1802 8197.10 p252
McKiver, Alice 46; Ontario, 1871 1823.15 p177
McKiver, John 18; Ontario, 1871 1823.15 p177
McKiver, John 48; Ontario, 1871 1823.28 p68
McKiver, Mary 60; Ontario, 1871 1823.15 p177
McKnally, Michael 18; Philadelphia, 1774 1220.25 p44
McKnight, Bridget E. McNally; Vermont, 1857-1896 5900.10 p127
McKnight, Dorothey 65; Ontario, 1871 1823.15 p177
McKnight, Edward W.; Vermont, 1855-1910 5900.10 p127
McKnight, James 57; Ontario, 1871 1823.22 p107
McKnight, Jane 82; Ontario, 1871 1823.15 p177
McKnight, John; New York, 1840 8197.10 p183
McKnight, Michael; New York, 1838 8197.10 p125
McKnight, Robert; New York, 1839 8197.10 p380
McKnight, Robert; Pennsylvania, 1777 4629.10 p8
McKnight, Thomas; New Jersey, 1900 1640.13 p89
McKnight, William 36; Ontario, 1871 1823.15 p177
McKoin, Thomas 28; Virginia, 1773 1220.25 p29
McKoone, John; Virginia, 1672 6212.30 p49
McKough, Mary; Vermont, n.d. 5900.10 p59
McKouskey, John 40; Ontario, 1871 1823.28 p68
McKow, Margaret *SEE* McKow, William
McKow, Robert *SEE* McKow, William
McKow, William *SEE* McKow, William
McKow, William; Alabama, 1821-1845 1640.10 p135
Wife: Margaret
Son: William
Son: Robert
McKowan, James; New York, 1818-1834 8197.10 p309
McKoy, Thomas; New York, 1807 8197.10 p46
McKune, James; New York, 1836 8197.10 p257
McKyes, Clarisa 71; Ontario, 1871 1823.22 p107
McLachlan, Daniel; Georgia, 1737 1640.10 p135
McLachlan, George; British Columbia, 1895 1640.13 p89
McLachlan, James 55; Ontario, 1871 1823.28 p68
McLachlan, Lachlan; Georgia, 1737 1640.10 p135
McLachlane, John Alexander; Wisconsin, 1857 1640.13 p89
McLachlin, John 40; Ontario, 1871 1823.15 p177
McLachlin, Margaret 67; Ontario, 1871 1823.15 p177
McLachline, Patrick 70; Ontario, 1871 1823.15 p177
McLagan, Alexander 47; Ontario, 1871 1823.15 p177
McLagan, John 51; Ontario, 1871 1823.15 p177
McLaghlan, James; New York, 1802 8197.10 p23
McLain, A.; Alabama, 1804-1845 1640.10 p135
McLain, John 30; Ontario, 1871 1823.28 p68
McLaine, Julia A.; Vermont, 1853-1918 5900.10 p532
McLane, Archibald 23; Vermont, 1864 5900.10 p493
McLane, Ellen Dixon 76; Vermont, 1876 5900.10 p411
McLane, James 72; Vermont, 1870 5900.10 p411
McLane, James W.; Vermont, 1852-1909 5900.10 p531
McLane, Jennie F. McKenna 39; Vermont, 1885 5900.10 p142
McLane, John; Vermont, 1821-1898 5900.10 p534
McLane, John 34; Vermont, 1872 5900.10 p411
McLane, Mary Mullin; Vermont, 1828-1882 5900.10 p534
McLane, Nancy; Vermont, 1831-1908 5900.10 p145
McLane, Nancy Duffy; Vermont, 1846-1921 5900.10 p531
McLane, Sarah; Vermont, 1833-1913 5900.10 p225
McLaran, Duncan 62; Ontario, 1871 1823.15 p177
McLaren, Aless 61; Ontario, 1871 1823.28 p68
McLaren, Alex 44; Ontario, 1871 1823.15 p177
McLaren, Alexander; St. Kitts, 1868 1640.13 p89
McLaren, Ann 84; Ontario, 1871 1823.28 p68
McLaren, Archabald 37; Ontario, 1871 1823.15 p177
McLaren, Catherine 33; Ontario, 1871 1823.15 p177
McLaren, Catherine 73; Ontario, 1871 1823.15 p177
McLaren, Daniel; New York, 1796 8197.10 p8
McLaren, Finlay; New York, 1796 8197.10 p8
McLaren, J.; Quebec, 1858 9196.15 p33
McLaren, James 34; Ontario, 1871 1823.15 p177
McLaren, James 59; Ontario, 1871 1823.28 p68
McLaren, John 62; Ontario, 1871 1823.28 p68
McLaren, John 63; Ontario, 1871 1823.28 p68
McLaren, M.; New York, 1876 1640.13 p89
McLaren, Malcolm 65; Ontario, 1871 1823.28 p68
McLaren, Mary 35; Ontario, 1871 1823.15 p178
McLaren, Peter 50; Ontario, 1871 1823.28 p68
McLaren, Robert 40; Ontario, 1871 1823.28 p68
McLaren, Robert John Robertson 44; Ontario, 1871 1823.28 p68
McLaren, William 58; Ontario, 1871 1823.28 p68
McLaren, William R. 56; Ontario, 1871 1823.28 p68
McLarne, Mary 50; Ontario, 1871 1823.28 p68
McLarney, Michael; New York, 1836 8197.10 p317
McLarney, Thomas; New York, 1836 8197.10 p77
McLarty, Charles; Jamaica, 1812 1640.13 p89
McLarty, John 28; Ontario, 1871 1823.28 p68
McLary, John 61; Ontario, 1871 1823.22 p107
McLatchie, Charles; Florida, 1774 1640.10 p135
McLatchie, Charles; Florida, 1796 1224.2 p74
McLatchie, Elizabeth; Florida, 1774 1640.10 p135
McLatchie, Robert; Savannah, Georgia, 1766 1640.10 p135
McLauchlan, D. James 39; Ontario, 1871 1823.28 p68
McLauchlan, Duncan 64; Ontario, 1871 1823.28 p68
McLauchlan, James 58; Ontario, 1871 1823.28 p68
McLauchlan, John 63; Ontario, 1871 1823.28 p68
McLauchlan, Thomas 65; Ontario, 1871 1823.28 p68
McLauchlin, Daniel; North Carolina, 1795-1825 1640.10 p135
Relative: Margaret
McLauchlin, Margaret *SEE* McLauchlin, Daniel
McLauchlin, Margaret; Georgia, 1790-1842 1640.10 p193

McLauchlin, Margaret; Georgia, 1790-1845 ***1640.10*** *p135*
McLaughlan, Alexander 40; Ontario, 1871 ***1823.28*** *p68*
McLaughlan, Dennis; Nova Scotia, 1745 ***4628.40*** *p45*
McLaughlan, James; Canada, 1756-1760 ***4628.40*** *p45*
McLaughlan, John; Canada, 1756-1760 ***4628.40*** *p45*
McLaughlan, John 42; Ontario, 1871 ***1823.15*** *p178*
McLaughlan, Robert; Maine, 1740-1750 ***4628.40*** *p77*
McLaughlan, Thomas; Nova Scotia, 1745 ***4628.40*** *p45*
McLaughlan, William; Maine, 1740-1750 ***4628.40*** *p77*
McLaughlen, Robert 51; Ontario, 1871 ***1823.28*** *p68*
McLaughlin, Alice 32; Vermont, 1860 ***5900.10*** *p559*
McLaughlin, Andrew; Vermont, 1818-1881 ***5900.10*** *p561*
McLaughlin, Andrew; Vermont, 1864-1867 ***5900.10*** *p208*
McLaughlin, Ann McNiff; Vermont, 1840-1905 ***5900.10*** *p433*
McLaughlin, Ann Tully; Vermont, 1833-1927 ***5900.10*** *p217*
McLaughlin, Anna Payne; Vermont, 1854-1954 ***5900.10*** *p186*
McLaughlin, Annie Mahoney; Vermont, 1852-1935 ***5900.10*** *p503*
McLaughlin, Arthur; New York, 1837 ***8197.10*** *p95*
McLaughlin, Barbara A.; Vermont, 1795-1872 ***5900.10*** *p437*
McLaughlin, Barbara A.; Vermont, 1849-1928 ***5900.10*** *p434*
McLaughlin, Barney; New York, 1807 ***8197.10*** *p46*
McLaughlin, Barney; New York, 1834 ***8197.10*** *p373*
McLaughlin, Barney; New York, 1839 ***8197.10*** *p380*
McLaughlin, Benjamin; Pennsylvania, 1835 ***6058.10*** *p11*
McLaughlin, Bernard; Vermont, 1855-1925 ***5900.10*** *p562*
McLaughlin, Bernard 6; Vermont, 1860 ***5900.10*** *p210*
McLaughlin, Bridget; Vermont, 1834-1909 ***5900.10*** *p415*
McLaughlin, Bridget; Vermont, 1834-1909 ***5900.10*** *p432*
McLaughlin, Bridget 75; Vermont, 1876 ***5900.10*** *p251*
McLaughlin, Bridget O'Rourke; Vermont, 1813-1878 ***5900.10*** *p415*
McLaughlin, Bridget Walsh; Vermont, 1836-1913 ***5900.10*** *p415*
McLaughlin, Catherine; Vermont, 1844-1873 ***5900.10*** *p416*
McLaughlin, Catherine Carney; Vermont, 1824-1899 ***5900.10*** *p220*
McLaughlin, Catherine Leddy; Vermont, 1845-1925 ***5900.10*** *p537*
McLaughlin, Charles; New York, 1839 ***8197.10*** *p138*
McLaughlin, Charles 42; Ontario, 1871 ***1823.15*** *p178*
McLaughlin, Charles 46; Ontario, 1871 ***1823.15*** *p178*
McLaughlin, Daniel; New York, 1838 ***8197.10*** *p376*
McLaughlin, Daniel; New York, 1840 ***8197.10*** *p183*
McLaughlin, Dennis; New York, 1834 ***8197.10*** *p373*
McLaughlin, Elizabeth Butler; Vermont, 1839-1913 ***5900.10*** *p605*
McLaughlin, Elizabeth McGuire; Vermont, 1815-1900 ***5900.10*** *p419*
McLaughlin, Elizabeth Tiernan; Vermont, 1864-1933 ***5900.10*** *p398*
McLaughlin, Ellen; Vermont, 1838-1912 ***5900.10*** *p419*
McLaughlin, Ellen 75; Vermont, 1890 ***5900.10*** *p434*
McLaughlin, Ellen Keane; Vermont, 1819-1891 ***5900.10*** *p439*
McLaughlin, Henry; New York, 1837 ***8197.10*** *p96*
McLaughlin, Isabella 55; Ontario, 1871 ***1823.15*** *p178*
McLaughlin, James; Indiana, 1852-1884 ***3437.14*** *p202*
McLaughlin, James; New York, 1821 ***8197.10*** *p254*
McLaughlin, James; New York, 1840 ***8197.10*** *p384*
McLaughlin, James; Pennsylvania, 1835 ***6058.10*** *p12*
McLaughlin, James; Vermont, 1805-1871 ***5900.10*** *p178*
McLaughlin, James; Vermont, 1828-1914 ***5900.10*** *p605*
McLaughlin, James; Vermont, 1839-1918 ***5900.10*** *p503*
McLaughlin, James; Vermont, 1859-1921 ***5900.10*** *p537*
McLaughlin, James 43; Ontario, 1871 ***1823.22*** *p107*
McLaughlin, James 45; Ontario, 1871 ***1823.15*** *p178*
McLaughlin, James 80; Vermont, 1903 ***5900.10*** *p415*
McLaughlin, James, Jr.; Vermont, 1843-1865 ***5900.10*** *p178*
McLaughlin, Jane McDurmond 52; Vermont, 1890 ***5900.10*** *p182*
McLaughlin, Jennie E.; Vermont, 1851-1909 ***5900.10*** *p444*
McLaughlin, John; New York, 1824 ***8197.10*** *p255*
McLaughlin, John; New York, 1837 ***8197.10*** *p97*
McLaughlin, John; Vermont, 1815-1897 ***5900.10*** *p419*
McLaughlin, John; Vermont, 1842-1918 ***5900.10*** *p537*
McLaughlin, John; Vermont, 1854-1900 ***5900.10*** *p398*
McLaughlin, John 47; Ontario, 1871 ***1823.28*** *p68*
McLaughlin, John 55; Ontario, 1871 ***1823.28*** *p68*
McLaughlin, John C.; Vermont, 1845-1928 ***5900.10*** *p178*
McLaughlin, John C., Jr.; Vermont, 1849-1924 ***5900.10*** *p419*
McLaughlin, John J.; Vermont, 1855-1933 ***5900.10*** *p186*
McLaughlin, John K.; Vermont, 1824-1890 ***5900.10*** *p437*
McLaughlin, Katherine McGinley; Vermont, 1859-1916 ***5900.10*** *p562*
McLaughlin, Kerin; Vermont, 1821-1899 ***5900.10*** *p220*
McLaughlin, Louise Kate 24; Vermont, 1885 ***5900.10*** *p605*
McLaughlin, Malcolm 55; Ontario, 1871 ***1823.22*** *p107*
McLaughlin, Margaret; Georgia, 1800 ***1640.10*** *p136*
McLaughlin, Margaret; New York, 1839 ***8197.10*** *p381*
McLaughlin, Margaret; Vermont, 1861-1918 ***5900.10*** *p419*
McLaughlin, Margaret; Vermont, 1906 ***5900.10*** *p178*
McLaughlin, Margaret McGrath 45; Vermont, 1875 ***5900.10*** *p605*
McLaughlin, Margaret Rigney; Vermont, 1828-1906 ***5900.10*** *p212*
McLaughlin, Mark; New York, 1807 ***8197.10*** *p332*
McLaughlin, Martin; Vermont, 1832-1918 ***5900.10*** *p217*
McLaughlin, Mary; Vermont, 1809-1902 ***5900.10*** *p438*
McLaughlin, Mary; Vermont, 1840-1912 ***5900.10*** *p445*
McLaughlin, Mary 43; Vermont, 1895 ***5900.10*** *p580*
McLaughlin, Mary 48; Vermont, 1863 ***5900.10*** *p572*
McLaughlin, Mary 67; Vermont, 1896 ***5900.10*** *p573*
McLaughlin, Mary 78; Vermont, 1881 ***5900.10*** *p242*
McLaughlin, Mary A.; Vermont, 1899 ***5900.10*** *p178*
McLaughlin, Mary Burke 85; Vermont, 1872 ***5900.10*** *p434*
McLaughlin, Mary Carol 79; Vermont, 1900 ***5900.10*** *p204*
McLaughlin, Mary E. 25; Vermont, 1882 ***5900.10*** *p605*
McLaughlin, Mary E. Colligan; Vermont, 1854-1940 ***5900.10*** *p558*
McLaughlin, Mary Keegan; Vermont, 1824-1907 ***5900.10*** *p561*
McLaughlin, Mary McNulla 39; Vermont, 1885 ***5900.10*** *p313*
McLaughlin, Mary Stewart; Vermont, 1834-1910 ***5900.10*** *p437*
McLaughlin, Mathew 5; Vermont, 1860 ***5900.10*** *p210*
McLaughlin, Matilda Gallagher; Vermont, 1849-1919 ***5900.10*** *p576*
McLaughlin, Michael; New York, 1839 ***8197.10*** *p138*
McLaughlin, Michael; Vermont, 1823-1903 ***5900.10*** *p433*
McLaughlin, Michael; Vermont, 1850-1918 ***5900.10*** *p558*
McLaughlin, Nancy; Vermont, 1832-1884 ***5900.10*** *p546*
McLaughlin, Nellie M.; Vermont, 1855-1881 ***5900.10*** *p437*
McLaughlin, Owen; New York, 1821 ***8197.10*** *p253*
McLaughlin, Owen; New York, New York, 1847 ***6058.10*** *p42*
McLaughlin, Patrick; New York, 1819 ***8197.10*** *p253*
McLaughlin, Patrick; New York, 1821 ***8197.10*** *p254*
McLaughlin, Patrick; New York, 1827 ***8197.10*** *p346*
McLaughlin, Patrick; New York, 1837 ***8197.10*** *p98*
McLaughlin, Patrick; New York, 1838 ***8197.10*** *p125*
McLaughlin, Patrick; New York, 1840 ***8197.10*** *p182*
McLaughlin, Patrick; Vermont, 1808-1883 ***5900.10*** *p415*
McLaughlin, Patrick; Vermont, 1832-1908 ***5900.10*** *p415*
McLaughlin, Patrick; Vermont, 1832-1908 ***5900.10*** *p432*
McLaughlin, Patrick; Vermont, 1841-1904 ***5900.10*** *p576*
McLaughlin, Patrick; Vermont, 1853-1928 ***5900.10*** *p419*
McLaughlin, Patrick 27; Vermont, 1883 ***5900.10*** *p537*
McLaughlin, Patrick 78; Vermont, 1886 ***5900.10*** *p434*
McLaughlin, Patrick J.; Vermont, 1849-1928 ***5900.10*** *p444*
McLaughlin, Peter; New York, 1826 ***8197.10*** *p336*
McLaughlin, Peter 42; Ontario, 1871 ***1823.15*** *p178*
McLaughlin, Richard; New York, 1835 ***8197.10*** *p257*
McLaughlin, Robert 62; Ontario, 1871 ***1823.15*** *p178*
McLaughlin, Robert 75; Vermont, 1907 ***5900.10*** *p182*
McLaughlin, Robert T.; Vermont, 1852-1911 ***5900.10*** *p432*
McLaughlin, Rose Anna; Vermont, 1858-1869 ***5900.10*** *p208*
McLaughlin, Sarah; Vermont, 1858-1904 ***5900.10*** *p386*
McLaughlin, Stewart; New York, 1840 ***8197.10*** *p183*
McLaughlin, Terrance; Vermont, 1847-1927 ***5900.10*** *p605*
McLaughlin, Thomas; New York, 1840 ***8197.10*** *p182*
McLaughlin, Thomas; Vermont, 1818-1887 ***5900.10*** *p210*
McLaughlin, Thomas; Vermont, 1818-1887 ***5900.10*** *p212*
McLaughlin, Thomas; Vermont, 1862-1867 ***5900.10*** *p208*
McLaughlin, William; New York, 1826 ***8197.10*** *p335*
McLaughlin, William; Vermont, 1814-1894 ***5900.10*** *p251*
McLaughlin, William; Vermont, 1866-1867 ***5900.10*** *p208*
McLaughlin, William 38; Ontario, 1871 ***1823.15*** *p178*
McLaughlin, William 56; Ontario, 1871 ***1823.15*** *p178*
McLaughllin, Ann; Vermont, 1813-1865 ***5900.10*** *p178*
McLaws, Jane; Salt Lake City, 1895 ***1640.13*** *p89*
McLay, Alex 28; Ontario, 1871 ***1823.28*** *p68*
McLay, Alexander 30; Ontario, 1871 ***1823.28*** *p68*
McLay, Mary 24; Ontario, 1871 ***1823.28*** *p68*
McLay, William 24; Ontario, 1871 ***1823.28*** *p68*
McLea, Archibald; New Orleans, 1819 ***1640.10*** *p136*
McLea, William; Augusta, Georgia, 1811-1812 ***1640.10*** *p136*
McLean, Miss; Quebec, 1858 ***9196.15*** *p41*
McLean, A. P. 33; Ontario, 1871 ***1823.15*** *p178*
McLean, Agnes; San Francisco, 1887 ***1640.13*** *p90*
McLean, Alex 30; Ontario, 1871 ***1823.15*** *p178*
McLean, Alexander; New York, 1821 ***8197.10*** *p253*
McLean, Amanda 25; Ontario, 1861 ***2896.25*** *p16*
McLean, Angus 27; Ontario, 1871 ***1823.28*** *p68*
McLean, Angus 58; Ontario, 1871 ***1823.15*** *p178*
McLean, Angus 69; Ontario, 1871 ***1823.15*** *p178*
McLean, Ann 36; Ontario, 1871 ***1823.15*** *p178*
McLean, Ann 53; Ontario, 1871 ***1823.15*** *p178*
McLean, Ann 60; Ontario, 1871 ***1823.22*** *p107*
McLean, Archable 38; Ontario, 1871 ***1823.28*** *p68*
McLean, Archibald 52; Ontario, 1871 ***1823.15*** *p178*
McLean, Archibald 59; Ontario, 1871 ***1823.15*** *p178*
McLean, Arthur 30; Ontario, 1871 ***1823.15*** *p178*
McLean, Catherine 23; Ontario, 1871 ***1823.15*** *p178*
McLean, Catherine 48; Ontario, 1871 ***1823.15*** *p178*
McLean, Catherine 77; Ontario, 1871 ***1823.15*** *p178*
McLean, Charles; Jamaica, 1804 ***1640.13*** *p90*
McLean, Charles 35; Ontario, 1871 ***1823.15*** *p178*
McLean, Daniel; North Carolina, 1775-1811 ***1640.10*** *p136*
Relative: Florida
McLean, Daniel M.; New York, 1822 ***8197.10*** *p62*
McLean, Donal; Florida, 1769-1845 ***1640.10*** *p137*
McLean, Donald; Florida, 1769 ***1640.10*** *p136*
McLean, Donald; St. Augustine, Florida, 1778 ***1640.13*** *p90*
McLean, Donald 27; Ontario, 1871 ***1823.15*** *p178*
McLean, Donald 32; Ontario, 1871 ***1823.15*** *p178*
McLean, Donald 56; Ontario, 1871 ***1823.15*** *p178*
McLean, Donald 56; Ontario, 1871 ***1823.28*** *p68*
McLean, Donald 63; Ontario, 1871 ***1823.28*** *p68*
McLean, Duncan; West Indies, 1825 ***1640.13*** *p90*
McLean, Duncan 21; Maryland, 1775 ***1220.25*** *p104*
McLean, Duncan 36; Ontario, 1871 ***1823.15*** *p178*
McLean, Duncan 63; Ontario, 1871 ***1823.28*** *p68*
McLean, Ewan; New York, 1877 ***1640.13*** *p90*
McLean, Florida *SEE* McLean, Daniel
McLean, George 27; Ontario, 1871 ***1823.15*** *p178*
McLean, George 35; Ontario, 1871 ***1823.15*** *p178*
McLean, George 39; Ontario, 1871 ***1823.28*** *p68*
McLean, George Duncan; Jamaica, 1859 ***1640.13*** *p90*
McLean, Hector 21; Ontario, 1871 ***1823.15*** *p178*
McLean, Hector 33; Ontario, 1871 ***1823.15*** *p178*
McLean, Hector 50; Ontario, 1871 ***1823.15*** *p178*
McLean, Hugh; Jamaica, 1846 ***1640.13*** *p90*
McLean, J.; Quebec, 1858 ***9196.15*** *p37*
McLean, J. L. 38; Ontario, 1871 ***1823.28*** *p69*
McLean, James; Jamaica, 1804 ***1640.13*** *p90*
McLean, James; North Carolina, 1808-1816 ***1640.10*** *p137*
McLean, James; Pennsylvania, 1886 ***3437.14*** *p128*
McLean, James 55; Ontario, 1871 ***1823.15*** *p178*
McLean, John; Georgia, 1743 ***1640.10*** *p137*
McLean, John; Georgia, 1774 ***1640.10*** *p137*
McLean, John 18; Ontario, 1871 ***1823.15*** *p179*
McLean, John 32; Ontario, 1871 ***1823.15*** *p179*
McLean, John 45; Ontario, 1871 ***1823.28*** *p69*
McLean, John 51; Ontario, 1871 ***1823.28*** *p69*
McLean, John 69; Ontario, 1871 ***1823.15*** *p179*
McLean, John 79; Ontario, 1871 ***1823.22*** *p107*
McLean, John 82; Ontario, 1871 ***1823.28*** *p69*
McLean, Lachlan 53; Ontario, 1871 ***1823.28*** *p69*
McLean, Lauchlan; Pennsylvania, 1777 ***4629.10*** *p6*
McLean, Malcom 42; Ontario, 1871 ***1823.28*** *p69*
McLean, Malcomb 57; Ontario, 1871 ***1823.15*** *p179*
McLean, Margaret 87; Ontario, 1871 ***1823.15*** *p179*
McLean, Mary 22; Ontario, 1861 ***2896.25*** *p15*
McLean, Mary 58; Ontario, 1871 ***1823.15*** *p179*
McLean, Mary 60; Ontario, 1871 ***1823.15*** *p179*
McLean, Murdock 37; Ontario, 1871 ***1823.15*** *p179*
McLean, Neal 50; Ontario, 1871 ***1823.15*** *p179*
McLean, Niel 42; Ontario, 1871 ***1823.28*** *p69*
McLean, Paul; New York, 1806 ***8197.10*** *p31*
McLean, Peter 40; Ontario, 1871 ***1823.28*** *p69*
McLean, R.; Alabama, 1818-1845 ***1640.10*** *p138*

McLean, Robert 54; Ontario, 1871 ***1823.15*** *p179*
McLean, Robert 64; Ontario, 1871 ***1823.15*** *p179*
McLean, Robert 75; Ontario, 1871 ***1823.28*** *p69*
McLean, Samuel 42; Ontario, 1871 ***1823.15*** *p179*
McLean, Samuel 51; Ontario, 1871 ***1823.28*** *p69*
McLean, Sarah 60; Ontario, 1871 ***1823.15*** *p179*
McLean, Sarah 65; Ontario, 1871 ***1823.15*** *p179*
McLean, T.; Georgia, 1764 ***1640.10*** *p138*
McLean, William; New York, 1840 ***8197.10*** *p258*
McLean, William 16; Ontario, 1871 ***1823.15*** *p179*
McLean, William 31; Ontario, 1871 ***1823.15*** *p179*
McLean, William 40; Ontario, 1871 ***1823.28*** *p69*
McLear, Ann O'Neill 82; Vermont, 1903 ***5900.10*** *p295*
McLearn, Peter 36; Ontario, 1871 ***1823.15*** *p179*
McLeay, Donald; Portland, Oregon, 1898 ***1640.13*** *p90*
McLeay, Richard; New York, 1839 ***8197.10*** *p139*
McLeay, Thomas; New York, 1839 ***8197.10*** *p258*
McLeece, William 50; Ontario, 1871 ***1823.28*** *p69*
McLeese, Daniel 37; Ontario, 1871 ***1823.28*** *p69*
McLeester, John; New York, 1831 ***8197.10*** *p365*
McLeish, Agnes; Savannah, Georgia, 1817 ***1640.10*** *p138*
McLeish, John; Georgia, 1743 ***1640.10*** *p138*
McLelan, Adam 27; Ontario, 1871 ***1823.28*** *p69*
McLelan, Margaret 30; Ontario, 1871 ***1823.15*** *p179*
McLellan, Archibald 52; Ontario, 1871 ***1823.28*** *p69*
McLellan, Charles; New York, 1840 ***8197.10*** *p184*
McLellan, Dougall 44; Ontario, 1871 ***1823.28*** *p69*
McLellan, George 53; Ontario, 1871 ***1823.28*** *p69*
McLellan, Hector 50; Ontario, 1871 ***1823.15*** *p179*
McLellan, James; Grenada, 1788 ***1640.13*** *p90*
McLellan, John 32; Ontario, 1871 ***1823.28*** *p69*
McLellan, John 60; Ontario, 1871 ***1823.28*** *p69*
McLellan, John 67; Ontario, 1871 ***1823.28*** *p69*
McLellan, Sarah 20; Ontario, 1871 ***1823.28*** *p69*
McLellen, William 48; Ontario, 1871 ***1823.22*** *p107*
McLenathan, Willard 75; Vermont, 1878 ***5900.10*** *p293*
McLeneehan, James; Nova Scotia, 1745 ***4628.40*** *p45*
McLennan, F. 27; Ontario, 1871 ***1823.28*** *p69*
McLennan, John 38; Ontario, 1871 ***1823.15*** *p179*
McLennan, John 39; Ontario, 1871 ***1823.15*** *p179*
McLennan, Jurley 65; Ontario, 1871 ***1823.15*** *p179*
McLennan, Malcom 37; Ontario, 1871 ***1823.15*** *p179*
McLennan, Martin 60; Ontario, 1871 ***1823.15*** *p179*
McLennan, Sarah 18; Ontario, 1871 ***1823.22*** *p107*
McLennan, William 58; Ontario, 1871 ***1823.15*** *p179*
McLennon, Catherine 36; Ontario, 1871 ***1823.15*** *p179*
McLennon, Duncan 50; Ontario, 1871 ***1823.15*** *p179*
McLennon, Jessie 45; Ontario, 1871 ***1823.15*** *p179*
McLennon, John 50; Ontario, 1871 ***1823.28*** *p69*
McLeod, Mr.; Quebec, 1857 ***9196.15*** *p22*
McLeod, Mrs.; Quebec, 1857 ***9196.15*** *p22*
McLeod, A. Mary 23; Ontario, 1871 ***1823.15*** *p179*
McLeod, Alexander *SEE* McLeod, Mary
McLeod, Alexander; Dominica, 1790-1799 ***1640.13*** *p90*
McLeod, Alexander; Georgia, 1738 ***1640.10*** *p138*
McLeod, Alexander 28; Ontario, 1871 ***1823.15*** *p179*
McLeod, Alexander 32; Ontario, 1871 ***1823.15*** *p179*
McLeod, Alexander 47; Ontario, 1871 ***1823.28*** *p69*
McLeod, Alick 40; Ontario, 1871 ***1823.15*** *p179*
McLeod, Angus; Georgia, 1736 ***1640.10*** *p138*
McLeod, Angus 35; Ontario, 1871 ***1823.15*** *p179*
McLeod, Angus 60; Ontario, 1871 ***1823.22*** *p107*
McLeod, Ann 76; Ontario, 1871 ***1823.15*** *p179*
McLeod, Ann McCarty 56; Vermont, 1902 ***5900.10*** *p281*
McLeod, Catherine; Georgia, 1738 ***1640.10*** *p138*
McLeod, Christa 60; Ontario, 1871 ***1823.15*** *p180*
McLeod, Christie 50; Ontario, 1871 ***1823.15*** *p180*
McLeod, Christina 75; Ontario, 1871 ***1823.15*** *p180*
McLeod, Daniel; New York, 1840 ***8197.10*** *p185*
McLeod, Daniel 25; Ontario, 1871 ***1823.15*** *p180*
McLeod, Daniel 35; Ontario, 1871 ***1823.15*** *p180*
McLeod, David; New York, 1840 ***8197.10*** *p184*
McLeod, Donald; Georgia, 1736 ***1640.10*** *p139*
McLeod, Donald; Georgia, 1779 ***1640.10*** *p139*
McLeod, Donald 23; Ontario, 1871 ***1823.15*** *p180*
McLeod, Donald 46; Ontario, 1871 ***1823.15*** *p180*
McLeod, Donald 50; Ontario, 1871 ***1823.28*** *p69*
McLeod, Elizabeth 50; Ontario, 1871 ***1823.15*** *p180*
McLeod, Emma 16; Ontario, 1871 ***1823.15*** *p180*
McLeod, Evan; Georgia, 1737 ***1640.10*** *p139*
McLeod, George; Georgia, 1736 ***1640.10*** *p139*
McLeod, George; New York, 1794 ***8197.10*** *p6*
McLeod, George 54; Ontario, 1871 ***1823.15*** *p180*
McLeod, George 75; Ontario, 1871 ***1823.15*** *p180*
McLeod, Georgie E. Thompson; Vermont, 1866-1944 ***5900.10*** *p455*
McLeod, Hector; New York, 1822 ***1224.3*** *p50*
McLeod, Hugh; Georgia, 1736 ***1640.10*** *p139*
McLeod, Hugh 34; Ontario, 1871 ***1823.15*** *p180*
McLeod, Hugh 50; Ontario, 1871 ***1823.15*** *p180*
McLeod, Ida 5; Ontario, 1871 ***1823.15*** *p180*
McLeod, James; New York, 1821 ***8197.10*** *p254*
McLeod, James; New York, 1827 ***8197.10*** *p343*
McLeod, James 45; Ontario, 1871 ***1823.28*** *p69*
McLeod, Janet; Georgia, 1741 ***1640.10*** *p162*
McLeod, John; Georgia, 1737 ***1640.10*** *p139*
McLeod, John; Georgia, 1760 ***1640.10*** *p140*
McLeod, John 28; Ontario, 1871 ***1823.15*** *p180*
McLeod, John 33; Ontario, 1871 ***1823.28*** *p69*
McLeod, John 40; Ontario, 1871 ***1823.15*** *p180*
McLeod, John 42; Ontario, 1871 ***1823.15*** *p180*
McLeod, John 44; Ontario, 1871 ***1823.22*** *p107*
McLeod, John 63; Ontario, 1871 ***1823.15*** *p180*
McLeod, John 66; Ontario, 1871 ***1823.22*** *p107*
McLeod, John 84; Ontario, 1871 ***1823.15*** *p180*
McLeod, Julia; Vermont, 1845-1899 ***5900.10*** *p516*
McLeod, Loughling 65; Ontario, 1871 ***1823.15*** *p180*
McLeod, Malchon 30; Ontario, 1871 ***1823.15*** *p180*
McLeod, Malchon 45; Ontario, 1871 ***1823.15*** *p180*
McLeod, Malcolm 45; Ontario, 1871 ***1823.28*** *p69*
McLeod, Margaret 65; Ontario, 1871 ***1823.15*** *p180*
McLeod, Mary; Florida, 1808-1831 ***1640.10*** *p140*
Relative: Alexander
Relative: Sarah
McLeod, Mary; North Carolina, 1782-1818 ***1640.10*** *p140*
McLeod, Mary 19; Ontario, 1871 ***1823.15*** *p180*
McLeod, Murdoch; Georgia, 1758 ***1640.10*** *p140*
McLeod, Murdoch; Ontario, 1873 ***1640.13*** *p90*
McLeod, Murdoch; Savannah, Georgia, 1823 ***1640.10*** *p140*
McLeod, Murdoch 46; Ontario, 1871 ***1823.15*** *p180*
McLeod, Murdock 21; Ontario, 1871 ***1823.15*** *p180*
McLeod, Murdock 64; Ontario, 1871 ***1823.15*** *p180*
McLeod, Norman 42; Ontario, 1871 ***1823.28*** *p69*
McLeod, Robert; Vermont, 1840-1921 ***5900.10*** *p455*
McLeod, Robert 60; Ontario, 1871 ***1823.15*** *p180*
McLeod, Roderick; Alabama, 1788-1824 ***1640.10*** *p141*
McLeod, Roderick; Georgia, 1737 ***1640.10*** *p140*
McLeod, Roderick; Georgia, 1737 ***1640.10*** *p141*
McLeod, Roderick; Georgia, 1767 ***1640.10*** *p141*
McLeod, Roderick; Savannah, Georgia, 1807-1812 ***1640.10*** *p141*
McLeod, Roderick 25; Ontario, 1871 ***1823.28*** *p69*
McLeod, Roderick 27; Ontario, 1871 ***1823.15*** *p180*
McLeod, Sarah *SEE* McLeod, Mary
McLeod, Susannah; New York, 1822 ***1224.3*** *p50*
McLeod, Thomas 56; Ontario, 1871 ***1823.15*** *p180*
McLeod, William; South Carolina, 1792-1824 ***1640.10*** *p141*
McLimont, Mr.; Quebec, 1858 ***9196.15*** *p33*
McLimont, Mrs.; Quebec, 1858 ***9196.15*** *p33*
McLinchey, James 36; Ontario, 1871 ***1823.15*** *p180*
McLinden, Daniel 54; Ontario, 1871 ***1823.28*** *p69*
McLinzey, Murray; Pensacola, Florida, 1774 ***1640.10*** *p141*
McLinzey, Murray 28; Pensacola, Florida, 1774 ***1220.25*** *p75*
McLodd, John 28; Ontario, 1871 ***1823.15*** *p180*
McLogan, Mr.; Quebec, 1856 ***9196.15*** *p5*
McLoud, Archibald 52; Ontario, 1871 ***1823.15*** *p180*
McLoud, Jane 66; Ontario, 1871 ***1823.15*** *p180*
McLoud, Murdock 36; Ontario, 1871 ***1823.15*** *p180*
McLoud, Roderich 33; Ontario, 1871 ***1823.15*** *p180*
McLoughlan, James; Nova Scotia, 1745 ***4628.40*** *p45*
McLoughlan, John; Nova Scotia, 1745 ***4628.40*** *p45*
McLoughlin, Anna 43; Vermont, 1885 ***5900.10*** *p253*
McLoughlin, Bridget 4 *SEE* McLoughlin, Thomas
McLoughlin, Catherine 1 *SEE* McLoughlin, Thomas
McLoughlin, Ellen 35 *SEE* McLoughlin, Thomas
McLoughlin, James 84; Ontario, 1871 ***1823.22*** *p107*
McLoughlin, Julia Kilbourn; Vermont, 1846-1941 ***5900.10*** *p321*
McLoughlin, Margaret; Vermont, 1840-1924 ***5900.10*** *p572*
McLoughlin, Patrick 43; Ontario, 1871 ***1823.22*** *p107*
McLoughlin, Peter; New York, 1827 ***8197.10*** *p341*
McLoughlin, Thomas 37; New York, New York, 1849 ***1825.45*** *p38*
Wife: Ellen 35
Daughter: Bridget 4
Daughter: Catherine 1
McLoughlin, Thomas S.; Vermont, 1847-1930 ***5900.10*** *p321*
McLoughlin, Timothy; Vermont, 1911 ***5900.10*** *p253*
McLourley, Hugh; New York, 1828-1834 ***8197.10*** *p305*
McLoy, David 23; Ontario, 1871 ***1823.15*** *p181*
McLoy, Edward 50; Ontario, 1871 ***1823.28*** *p69*
McLoy, John 25; Ontario, 1871 ***1823.15*** *p181*
McLure, Amaretta 72; Vermont, 1889 ***5900.10*** *p457*
McLure, John B. 57; Vermont, 1904 ***5900.10*** *p310*
McLure, Mary; Vermont, 1839-1899 ***5900.10*** *p350*
McLure, Nathaniel 76; Vermont, 1893 ***5900.10*** *p457*
McLure, William; Vermont, 1832-1854 ***5900.10*** *p349*
McLuskey, Joseph 40; Ontario, 1871 ***1823.15*** *p181*
McMahan, Alice 75; Vermont, 1883 ***5900.10*** *p232*
McMahan, Ann 87; Vermont, 1896 ***5900.10*** *p572*
McMahan, Bridget; Vermont, 1840-1881 ***5900.10*** *p51*
McMahan, John; Vermont, 1823-1868 ***5900.10*** *p64*
McMahan, John 43; Ontario, 1871 ***1823.22*** *p107*
McMahan, John 45; Ontario, 1871 ***1823.28*** *p69*
McMahan, John 48; Ontario, 1871 ***1823.28*** *p69*
McMahan, John 52; Ontario, 1871 ***1823.28*** *p69*
McMahan, Mary 70; Vermont, 1883 ***5900.10*** *p468*
McMahan, Mary Ellen 27; Vermont, 1868 ***5900.10*** *p64*
McMahan, Maurice 46; Ontario, 1871 ***1823.28*** *p69*
McMahan, Michael 24; Ontario, 1871 ***1823.22*** *p107*
McMahan, Patrick 85; Vermont, 1879 ***5900.10*** *p232*
McMahan, Timothy 67; Vermont, 1878 ***5900.10*** *p468*
McMahan, Timothy 76; Ontario, 1871 ***1823.22*** *p108*
McMahon, . . .; Vermont, 1830 ***5900.10*** *p26*
McMahon, Ann; Vermont, 1819-1876 ***5900.10*** *p270*
McMahon, Ann; Vermont, 1848-1925 ***5900.10*** *p351*
McMahon, Ann 60; Vermont, 1876 ***5900.10*** *p269*
McMahon, Ann 87; Vermont, 1896 ***5900.10*** *p581*
McMahon, Ann Clifford 65; Vermont, 1890 ***5900.10*** *p418*
McMahon, Ann Foley; Vermont, 1828-1909 ***5900.10*** *p542*
McMahon, Ann Owens 85; Vermont, 1883 ***5900.10*** *p51*
McMahon, Anne C.; Vermont, 1860-1920 ***5900.10*** *p550*
McMahon, Bridget; Vermont, 1830-1914 ***5900.10*** *p579*
McMahon, Bridget; Vermont, 1831-1891 ***5900.10*** *p550*
McMahon, Bridget 20; Ontario, 1861 ***2896.25*** *p21*
McMahon, Bridget 45; Vermont, 1863 ***5900.10*** *p571*
McMahon, Bridget 60; Vermont, 1884 ***5900.10*** *p301*
McMahon, Bridget 68; Vermont, 1885 ***5900.10*** *p332*
McMahon, Catherine; Vermont, 1838-1925 ***5900.10*** *p329*
McMahon, Catherine; Vermont, 1843-1900 ***5900.10*** *p270*
McMahon, Catherine 26; Ontario, 1861 ***2896.27*** *p74*
McMahon, Catherine 40; Vermont, 1884 ***5900.10*** *p466*
McMahon, Catherine 66; Vermont, 1893 ***5900.10*** *p269*
McMahon, Catherine A. 27; Vermont, 1867 ***5900.10*** *p329*
McMahon, Catherine Doherty; Vermont, 1828-1902 ***5900.10*** *p129*
McMahon, Catherine McNaney; Vermont, 1849-1924 ***5900.10*** *p51*
McMahon, Catherine Shanley; Vermont, 1856-1922 ***5900.10*** *p151*
McMahon, Charles; New York, 1838 ***8197.10*** *p257*
McMahon, Charlotte 2; Ontario, 1861 ***2896.27*** *p24*
McMahon, Cornelius L.; Vermont, 1853-1924 ***5900.10*** *p129*
McMahon, Daniel 21; Vermont, 1881 ***5900.10*** *p64*
McMahon, Edward; New York, 1838 ***8197.10*** *p376*
McMahon, Edward F.; Vermont, 1876-1955 ***5900.10*** *p550*
McMahon, Elizabeth; Vermont, 1838-1892 ***5900.10*** *p488*
McMahon, Elizabeth 54; Vermont, 1846 ***5900.10*** *p240*
McMahon, Elizabeth 55; Vermont, 1877 ***5900.10*** *p477*
McMahon, Ellen; Vermont, 1836-1916 ***5900.10*** *p409*
McMahon, Ellen; Vermont, 1861-1889 ***5900.10*** *p331*
McMahon, Ellen 23; Vermont, 1873 ***5900.10*** *p330*
McMahon, Ellen Broderick 60; Vermont, 1898 ***5900.10*** *p74*
McMahon, Ellen Fleming; Vermont, 1839-1901 ***5900.10*** *p76*
McMahon, Ellen Gill 36; Vermont, 1899 ***5900.10*** *p313*
McMahon, Emily A. Halen; Vermont, 1848-1929 ***5900.10*** *p197*
McMahon, Emma C. Gardner; Vermont, 1855-1923 ***5900.10*** *p189*
McMahon, Frances 32; Vermont, 1844 ***5900.10*** *p237*
McMahon, Francis; Illinois, 1890 ***3437.14*** *p158*
McMahon, Henry C.; Vermont, 1860-1920 ***5900.10*** *p129*
McMahon, Honora; Vermont, 1874-1883 ***5900.10*** *p329*
McMahon, Honora McGuirk; Vermont, 1827-1886 ***5900.10*** *p441*
McMahon, Hugh 62; Vermont, 1874 ***5900.10*** *p51*
McMahon, Hugh 94; Ontario, 1871 ***1823.22*** *p108*
McMahon, James; Canada, 1756-1760 ***4628.40*** *p45*
McMahon, James; New York, 1802 ***8197.10*** *p252*
McMahon, James; New York, 1837 ***8197.10*** *p97*
McMahon, James; New York, 1837 ***8197.10*** *p257*
McMahon, James; Vermont, 1842-1933 ***5900.10*** *p241*
McMahon, James; Vermont, 1856-1923 ***5900.10*** *p550*
McMahon, James 58; Ontario, 1871 ***1823.28*** *p69*
McMahon, James J.; Vermont, 1851-1922 ***5900.10*** *p197*
McMahon, James J.; Vermont, 1876-1920 ***5900.10*** *p329*
McMahon, Jane; Vermont, 1856-1896 ***5900.10*** *p46*
McMahon, Jane 71; Vermont, 1903 ***5900.10*** *p261*
McMahon, Joanna; Vermont, 1863-1945 ***5900.10*** *p130*
McMahon, Joanna E.; Vermont, 1863-1945 ***5900.10*** *p129*
McMahon, Joanna F. Sullivan; Vermont, 1851-1888 ***5900.10*** *p170*
McMahon, Johanna F.; Vermont, 1851-1883 ***5900.10*** *p138*
McMahon, John; Canada, 1756-1760 ***4628.40*** *p45*

McMahon, John; New York, 1823 ***8197.10*** *p255*
McMahon, John; New York, 1838 ***8197.10*** *p376*
McMahon, John; Vermont, 1827-1904 ***5900.10*** *p550*
McMahon, John; Vermont, 1830-1897 ***5900.10*** *p76*
McMahon, John; Vermont, 1841-1911 ***5900.10*** *p51*
McMahon, John; Vermont, 1847-1888 ***5900.10*** *p351*
McMahon, John; Vermont, 1849-1920 ***5900.10*** *p334*
McMahon, John 27; Ontario, 1871 ***1823.22*** *p108*
McMahon, John 36; Vermont, 1901 ***5900.10*** *p64*
McMahon, John 45; Ontario, 1871 ***1823.15*** *p181*
McMahon, John 70; Vermont, 1898 ***5900.10*** *p418*
McMahon, John, Jr.; New York, 1840 ***8197.10*** *p183*
McMahon, John, Jr.; New York, 1840 ***8197.10*** *p184*
McMahon, John B.; Vermont, 1840-1910 ***5900.10*** *p422*
McMahon, John F.; Vermont, 1864-1900 ***5900.10*** *p550*
McMahon, John P.; Vermont, 1878-1917 ***5900.10*** *p329*
McMahon, Katherine; Vermont, 1850-1912 ***5900.10*** *p316*
McMahon, Louis J.; Vermont, 1853-1921 ***5900.10*** *p189*
McMahon, Lucy; Vermont, 1858-1940 ***5900.10*** *p299*
McMahon, Margaret; Vermont, 1815-1895 ***5900.10*** *p351*
McMahon, Margaret; Vermont, 1866-1944 ***5900.10*** *p130*
McMahon, Margaret; Vermont, 1870-1970 ***5900.10*** *p334*
McMahon, Margaret 54; Vermont, 1872 ***5900.10*** *p429*
McMahon, Margaret 58; Vermont, 1894 ***5900.10*** *p279*
McMahon, Margaret 60; Vermont, 1874 ***5900.10*** *p53*
McMahon, Margaret A.; Vermont, 1866-1944 ***5900.10*** *p129*
McMahon, Martin; Vermont, 1840-1912 ***5900.10*** *p441*
McMahon, Mary; Vermont, 1838-1912 ***5900.10*** *p351*
McMahon, Mary; Vermont, 1846-1917 ***5900.10*** *p334*
McMahon, Mary; Vermont, 1847-1929 ***5900.10*** *p141*
McMahon, Mary 23; Ontario, 1861 ***2896.27*** *p24*
McMahon, Mary 74; Vermont, 1894 ***5900.10*** *p138*
McMahon, Mary 74; Vermont, 1894 ***5900.10*** *p170*
McMahon, Mary A.; Vermont, n.d. ***5900.10*** *p129*
McMahon, Mary A. 91; Vermont, 1934 ***5900.10*** *p316*
McMahon, Mary D.; Vermont, 1850-1928 ***5900.10*** *p333*
McMahon, Mary Hastings 57; Vermont, 1874 ***5900.10*** *p470*
McMahon, Mary J. McEnaney; Vermont, 1840-1926 ***5900.10*** *p241*
McMahon, Mary L.; Vermont, 1862 ***5900.10*** *p550*
McMahon, Mary Lonergan; Vermont, 1865-1941 ***5900.10*** *p129*
McMahon, Mary Neenan; Vermont, 1848-1948 ***5900.10*** *p334*
McMahon, Mary Ruane 80; Vermont, 1874 ***5900.10*** *p465*
McMahon, Michael; New York, 1803 ***8197.10*** *p14*
McMahon, Michael; Vermont, 1823-1876 ***5900.10*** *p542*
McMahon, Michael; Vermont, 1872-1924 ***5900.10*** *p329*
McMahon, Michael 30; Vermont, 1874 ***5900.10*** *p329*
McMahon, Michael 50; Ontario, 1871 ***1823.28*** *p69*
McMahon, Michael 55; Ontario, 1871 ***1823.28*** *p69*
McMahon, Michael 58; Ontario, 1871 ***1823.28*** *p69*
McMahon, Michael 72; Vermont, 1896 ***5900.10*** *p138*
McMahon, Michael 72; Vermont, 1896 ***5900.10*** *p170*
McMahon, Michael 100; Vermont, 1893 ***5900.10*** *p279*
McMahon, Michael D.; Vermont, 1858-1935 ***5900.10*** *p129*
McMahon, Nancy Hanna 74; Vermont, 1862 ***5900.10*** *p279*
McMahon, Patrick; New York, 1807 ***8197.10*** *p325*
McMahon, Patrick; New York, 1828 ***8197.10*** *p350*
McMahon, Patrick; New York, 1838 ***8197.10*** *p125*
McMahon, Patrick; Vermont, 1822-1878 ***5900.10*** *p129*
McMahon, Patrick; Vermont, 1828-1917 ***5900.10*** *p329*
McMahon, Patrick; Vermont, 1843-1915 ***5900.10*** *p568*
McMahon, Patrick; Vermont, 1854-1911 ***5900.10*** *p151*
McMahon, Patrick 57; Vermont, 1887 ***5900.10*** *p332*
McMahon, Patrick W.; Vermont, n.d. ***5900.10*** *p129*
McMahon, Peter 33; Ontario, 1871 ***1823.28*** *p69*
McMahon, Phillip; New York, 1839 ***8197.10*** *p379*
McMahon, Roger; Nova Scotia, 1745 ***4628.40*** *p44*
McMahon, Roseanna; Vermont, 1897 ***5900.10*** *p422*
McMahon, Sarah; Vermont, 1844-1926 ***5900.10*** *p328*
McMahon, Sarah 37; Vermont, 1881 ***5900.10*** *p153*
McMahon, Sarah 85; Vermont, 1895 ***5900.10*** *p153*
McMahon, Thomas; Vermont, 1844-1924 ***5900.10*** *p51*
McMahon, Thomas 35; Ontario, 1871 ***1823.22*** *p108*
McMahon, Thomas 39; Vermont, 1873 ***5900.10*** *p74*
McMahon, Thomas 79; Vermont, 1893 ***5900.10*** *p429*
McMahon, Thomas 84; Vermont, 1885 ***5900.10*** *p301*
McMahon, Thomas E.; Vermont, 1839-1920 ***5900.10*** *p333*
McMahon, Thomas F.; Vermont, 1853-1874 ***5900.10*** *p138*
McMahon, Thomas F.; Vermont, 1853-1899 ***5900.10*** *p170*
McMahon, Thomas F.; Vermont, 1879-1927 ***5900.10*** *p329*
McMahon, Timothy 74; Ontario, 1871 ***1823.28*** *p69*
McMahon, William; New York, 1837 ***8197.10*** *p95*
McMan, George 45; Ontario, 1871 ***1823.15*** *p181*
McManas, Ann 40; Ontario, 1871 ***1823.28*** *p69*
McManas, Bernard 65; Ontario, 1871 ***1823.22*** *p108*
McManas, John 40; Ontario, 1871 ***1823.28*** *p69*
McManas, Mary 20; Ontario, 1871 ***1823.28*** *p69*
McManas, Patrick 24; Ontario, 1871 ***1823.28*** *p69*
McManimon, George H. 23; Vermont, 1879 ***5900.10*** *p556*
McManimon, Jemima 71; Vermont, 1880 ***5900.10*** *p556*
McManimon, William 91; Vermont, 1893 ***5900.10*** *p556*
McManis, Barney; Vermont, 1859-1935 ***5900.10*** *p553*
McManis, Jennie Breen; Vermont, 1852-1923 ***5900.10*** *p553*
McManis, John 42; Ontario, 1871 ***1823.22*** *p108*
McMann, Bridget 48; Ontario, 1871 ***1823.22*** *p108*
McMann, Mary 65; Ontario, 1871 ***1823.22*** *p108*
McMann, Timothy 33; Ontario, 1871 ***1823.22*** *p108*
McMannaman, Edward 65; Ontario, 1871 ***1823.22*** *p108*
McMannis, Aurilla Nichols 62; Vermont, 1870 ***5900.10*** *p528*
McMannis, John 37; Vermont, 1874 ***5900.10*** *p528*
McMannis, Mary 57; Vermont, 1878 ***5900.10*** *p527*
McMannis, Patrick 73; Vermont, 1872 ***5900.10*** *p528*
McMannis, Sarah; Vermont, 1836-1916 ***5900.10*** *p340*
McMannus, Bernard 55; Ontario, 1871 ***1823.15*** *p181*
McMannus, James 50; Ontario, 1871 ***1823.15*** *p181*
McMannus, Thomas 73; Ontario, 1871 ***1823.22*** *p108*
McManus, Captain; Quebec, 1857 ***9196.15*** *p18*
McManus, Andrew; New York, 1821 ***8197.10*** *p254*
McManus, Andrew; New York, 1826 ***8197.10*** *p336*
McManus, Andrew 21 *SEE* McManus, Thomas
McManus, Cath 28; Ontario, 1871 ***1823.15*** *p181*
McManus, Catherine 4; Ontario, 1871 ***1823.22*** *p108*
McManus, Catherine 49; Ontario, 1871 ***1823.15*** *p181*
McManus, Charle 66; Ontario, 1871 ***1823.15*** *p181*
McManus, Ellen; Vermont, 1857-1932 ***5900.10*** *p128*
McManus, Felix 77; Vermont, 1884 ***5900.10*** *p619*
McManus, Fred 7; Ontario, 1871 ***1823.22*** *p108*
McManus, Henry; New York, 1834 ***8197.10*** *p257*
McManus, Henry; New York, 1840 ***8197.10*** *p185*
McManus, James; New York, 1824 ***8197.10*** *p255*
McManus, James; New York, 1828 ***8197.10*** *p256*
McManus, James 20 *SEE* McManus, Thomas
McManus, James 37; Ontario, 1871 ***1823.22*** *p108*
McManus, Jane; Vermont, 1844-1880 ***5900.10*** *p510*
McManus, John; New York, 1838 ***8197.10*** *p125*
McManus, John; New York, 1838 ***8197.10*** *p257*
McManus, John 60; Ontario, 1871 ***1823.28*** *p69*
McManus, John 72; Ontario, 1871 ***1823.28*** *p69*
McManus, Margaret Mullaney; Vermont, 1835-1908 ***5900.10*** *p436*
McManus, Martin; Vermont, n.d. ***5900.10*** *p450*
McManus, Mary 18 *SEE* McManus, Thomas
McManus, Mary 23; British Columbia, 1910 ***9196.1*** *p12*
McManus, Mary 23; Seattle, 1910 ***9196.1*** *p12*
McManus, Michael; New York, 1838 ***8197.10*** *p125*
McManus, Pat 23 *SEE* McManus, Thomas
McManus, Patrick; New York, 1837 ***8197.10*** *p97*
McManus, Peter; Vermont, 1837-1919 ***5900.10*** *p436*
McManus, Philip; New York, 1826 ***8197.10*** *p255*
McManus, Philip; New York, 1839 ***8197.10*** *p380*
McManus, Redmond; New York, 1829 ***8197.10*** *p256*
McManus, Redmond; New York, 1832 ***8197.10*** *p68*
McManus, Rosa 68; Vermont, 1887 ***5900.10*** *p527*
McManus, Rose; Vermont, 1849-1927 ***5900.10*** *p596*
McManus, Susannah 3; Vermont, 1866 ***5900.10*** *p522*
McManus, Terrance 71; Ontario, 1871 ***1823.28*** *p69*
McManus, Thomas 24; New York, New York, 1848 ***1825.45*** *p18*
Brother: Andrew 21
Brother: Pat 23
Brother: Mary 18
McManus, Thomas 29; New York, New York, 1848 ***1825.45*** *p18*
Brother: James 20
McManus, Timothy 46; Ontario, 1871 ***1823.28*** *p69*
McMariam, Thomas 35; Ontario, 1871 ***1823.15*** *p181*
McMartin, Duncan 79; Ontario, 1871 ***1823.15*** *p181*
McMartin, John 55; Ontario, 1871 ***1823.28*** *p69*
McMaster, James 30; Ontario, 1871 ***1823.22*** *p108*
McMaster, John; Wiscasset, 1824 ***1224.3*** *p50*
McMaster, John 31; Vermont, 1811 ***5900.10*** *p376*
McMaster, John K. 3; Vermont, 1815 ***5900.10*** *p376*
McMaster, Samuel; New Orleans, 1807-1812 ***1640.10*** *p141*
McMaster, Thomas 28; Ontario, 1871 ***1823.22*** *p108*
McMaster, Thomas 50; Ontario, 1871 ***1823.28*** *p69*
McMaster, William; Canada, 1756-1760 ***4628.40*** *p45*
McMaster, William; Massachusetts, 1815 ***1224.3*** *p50*
McMasters, Stephen B.; New York, 1839 ***8197.10*** *p383*
McMasters, William; Georgia, 1826 ***1640.10*** *p141*
McMath, Eliza 81; Ontario, 1871 ***1823.15*** *p181*
McMath, Hugh 51; Ontario, 1871 ***1823.15*** *p181*
McMath, Samuel 58; Ontario, 1871 ***1823.15*** *p181*
McMath, William 46; Ontario, 1871 ***1823.15*** *p181*
McMeahan, Mr.; Quebec, 1857 ***9196.15*** *p16*
McMeekin, Matty E.; Vermont, 1817-1894 ***5900.10*** *p456*
McMenamen, Daniel; Pennsylvania, 1777 ***4629.10*** *p14*
McMenimen, Mr.; Vermont, 1835-1907 ***5900.10*** *p111*
McMenimen, Mrs.; Vermont, 1836-1881 ***5900.10*** *p111*
McMenimen, Catharine; Vermont, 1863-1924 ***5900.10*** *p111*
McMenimen, Catharine Colden; Vermont, 1864-1865 ***5900.10*** *p111*
McMenimen, Henry C.; Vermont, 1855-1877 ***5900.10*** *p111*
McMenimen, Mary; Vermont, 1869-1870 ***5900.10*** *p111*
McMenomin, Michael; New York, 1830 ***8197.10*** *p361*
McMenomy, Edward; New York, 1838 ***8197.10*** *p302*
McMenomy, Patrick; New York, 1836 ***8197.10*** *p257*
McMichael, Archibald 40; Ontario, 1871 ***1823.15*** *p181*
McMichael, Gilbert 54; Ontario, 1871 ***1823.15*** *p181*
McMichael, Robert 37; Ontario, 1871 ***1823.15*** *p181*
McMichael, Robert 78; Ontario, 1871 ***1823.15*** *p181*
McMichael, William 36; Ontario, 1871 ***1823.15*** *p181*
McMichail, Alexr 34; Ontario, 1871 ***1823.28*** *p69*
McMichal, James 47; Ontario, 1871 ***1823.15*** *p181*
McMichal, Mary 47; Ontario, 1871 ***1823.15*** *p181*
McMichal, Thomas 50; Ontario, 1871 ***1823.15*** *p181*
McMicken, Miss; Quebec, 1858 ***9196.15*** *p33*
McMicken, Mrs.; Quebec, 1858 ***9196.15*** *p33*
McMicken, John 28; Ontario, 1871 ***1823.28*** *p69*
McMillan, Lieut.; Canada, 1756-1760 ***4628.40*** *p46*
McMillan, A. P.; Mississippi, 1846 ***1640.10*** *p142*
Wife: Jane
McMillan, Agness 23; Ontario, 1871 ***1823.15*** *p181*
McMillan, Alexander; Pittston, Pennsylvania, 1859 ***1640.13*** *p90*
McMillan, Betty; North Carolina, 1818 ***1224.3*** *p50*
McMillan, Bridget 40; Ontario, 1871 ***1823.15*** *p181*
McMillan, David; Alabama, 1842 ***1640.10*** *p142*
McMillan, David 32; Ontario, 1871 ***1823.28*** *p69*
McMillan, Donald 49; Ontario, 1871 ***1823.28*** *p69*
McMillan, Duncan 32; Ontario, 1871 ***1823.15*** *p181*
McMillan, Duncan 50; Ontario, 1871 ***1823.28*** *p69*
McMillan, Elizabeth 87; Ontario, 1871 ***1823.15*** *p181*
McMillan, Hugh 40; Ontario, 1871 ***1823.15*** *p181*
McMillan, Isabella 39; Ontario, 1871 ***1823.15*** *p181*
McMillan, James; New York, 1837 ***8197.10*** *p95*
McMillan, Jane *SEE* McMillan, A. P.
McMillan, John; Georgia, 1743 ***1640.10*** *p142*
McMillan, John; New York, 1840 ***8197.10*** *p386*
McMillan, John 28; Ontario, 1871 ***1823.15*** *p181*
McMillan, John 47; Ontario, 1871 ***1823.15*** *p181*
McMillan, John 48; Ontario, 1871 ***1823.28*** *p69*
McMillan, John 57; Ontario, 1871 ***1823.15*** *p181*
McMillan, John 58; Ontario, 1871 ***1823.15*** *p181*
McMillan, Margaret 36; Vermont, 1886 ***5900.10*** *p329*
McMillan, Mary; Georgia, 1779-1845 ***1640.10*** *p142*
McMillan, Mary 80; Ontario, 1871 ***1823.15*** *p181*
McMillan, Mavy 47; Ontario, 1871 ***1823.15*** *p181*
McMillan, Miles 26; Ontario, 1871 ***1823.15*** *p181*
McMillan, N.; Alabama, 1815-1845 ***1640.10*** *p142*
McMillan, Neil; St. Vincent, 1842 ***1640.13*** *p91*
McMillan, Peter 40; Ontario, 1871 ***1823.28*** *p69*
McMillan, Peter 73; Ontario, 1871 ***1823.28*** *p69*
McMillan, Robert 46; Ontario, 1871 ***1823.22*** *p108*
McMillan, Robert 49; Ontario, 1871 ***1823.15*** *p181*
McMillan, Thomas; South Carolina, 1804-1845 ***1640.10*** *p142*
McMillan, Thomas 91; Ontario, 1871 ***1823.22*** *p108*
McMillan, William; New York, 1837 ***8197.10*** *p95*
McMillan, William 36; Ontario, 1871 ***1823.15*** *p181*
McMillen, Archibald 30; Ontario, 1871 ***1823.15*** *p182*
McMillen, Bertha 35; Ontario, 1871 ***1823.15*** *p182*
McMillen, John; New York, New York, 1840 ***6058.10*** *p70*
McMillen, John 33; Ontario, 1871 ***1823.15*** *p182*
McMillen, John 38; Ontario, 1871 ***1823.15*** *p182*
McMillen, John 44; Ontario, 1871 ***1823.15*** *p182*
McMillen, John 53; Ontario, 1871 ***1823.22*** *p108*
McMillen, Malcom 40; Ontario, 1871 ***1823.15*** *p182*
McMillen, Neil 50; Ontario, 1871 ***1823.15*** *p182*
McMillen, Robert 27; Ontario, 1871 ***1823.15*** *p182*
McMillen, Robert 31; Ontario, 1871 ***1823.15*** *p182*
McMillian, Robert 17; Ontario, 1871 ***1823.15*** *p182*
McMillian, William 59; Ontario, 1871 ***1823.15*** *p182*
McMillin, James; New York, 1802 ***8197.10*** *p23*
McMinn, James 55; Ontario, 1871 ***1823.15*** *p182*
McMinn, John; Pennsylvania, 1785 ***4629.10*** *p49*
McMordie, Ann 62; Ontario, 1871 ***1823.15*** *p182*
McMordie, Henry 39; Ontario, 1871 ***1823.15*** *p182*
McMordie, Robert 32; Ontario, 1871 ***1823.15*** *p182*
McMorrow, John; Vermont, 1820-1905 ***5900.10*** *p395*

McMorrow, Margaret Rooney; Vermont, 1828-1910 ***5900.10*** *p395*
McMorrow, Michael; Vermont, 1818-1904 ***5900.10*** *p391*
McMulkin, James 32; Ontario, 1871 ***1823.15*** *p182*
McMullen, . . .; New Hampshire, 1641-1660 ***4628.40*** *p44*
McMullen, Alexander; Vermont, 1862-1923 ***5900.10*** *p326*
McMullen, Alexander 61; Ontario, 1871 ***1823.28*** *p70*
McMullen, Daniel; New York, 1827 ***8197.10*** *p256*
McMullen, Eliza McNally; Vermont, 1864-1905 ***5900.10*** *p326*
McMullen, Elizabeth Henderson; Vermont, 1823-1898 ***5900.10*** *p326*
McMullen, Francis; Vermont, 1812-1909 ***5900.10*** *p326*
McMullen, Francis, Jr.; Vermont, 1858-1904 ***5900.10*** *p326*
McMullen, Isobel; St. Augustine, Florida, 1786 ***1640.10*** *p142*
McMullen, James; New York, 1836 ***8197.10*** *p77*
McMullen, James; Vermont, 1804-1896 ***5900.10*** *p196*
McMullen, James; Vermont, 1866-1884 ***5900.10*** *p326*
McMullen, James 78; Ontario, 1861 ***2896.27*** *p1*
McMullen, James H.; Vermont, 1836-1918 ***5900.10*** *p196*
McMullen, Jane 60; Ontario, 1861 ***2896.27*** *p1*
McMullen, John; New York, 1823 ***8197.10*** *p255*
McMullen, John; Pennsylvania, 1826 ***6058.10*** *p8*
McMullen, John; Vermont, 1856-1927 ***5900.10*** *p326*
McMullen, John 43; Ontario, 1871 ***1823.22*** *p108*
McMullen, Joseph; Vermont, 1853-1941 ***5900.10*** *p323*
McMullen, Katie Crosby; Vermont, 1853-1934 ***5900.10*** *p554*
McMullen, Linda S. Smith; Vermont, 1870-1926 ***5900.10*** *p326*
McMullen, Luke; New York, 1840 ***8197.10*** *p178*
McMullen, Margaret Sherry; Vermont, 1859-1917 ***5900.10*** *p323*
McMullen, Mary; Vermont, 1852-1938 ***5900.10*** *p326*
McMullen, Mary 55; Ontario, 1871 ***1823.15*** *p182*
McMullen, Mary D.; Vermont, 1843-1894 ***5900.10*** *p196*
McMullen, Mary J.; Vermont, 1856-1926 ***5900.10*** *p554*
McMullen, Mary Jane; Vermont, 1814-1861 ***5900.10*** *p196*
McMullen, Mary Jane; Vermont, 1836-1906 ***5900.10*** *p196*
McMullen, Michael 25; Ontario, 1871 ***1823.15*** *p182*
McMullen, Nancy; Vermont, 1830-1890 ***5900.10*** *p549*
McMullen, Ro 18; Ontario, 1861 ***2896.27*** *p1*
McMullen, Robert; Pennsylvania, 1777 ***4629.10*** *p17*
McMullen, Robert J.; Vermont, 1846-1904 ***5900.10*** *p554*
McMullen, Sarah; Vermont, 1864-1866 ***5900.10*** *p326*
McMullen, Stiles; Vermont, 1797-1904 ***5900.10*** *p458*
McMullen, Thomas; Vermont, 1862-1949 ***5900.10*** *p323*
McMullen, William; New York, 1822 ***8197.10*** *p255*
McMullen, William 20; Ontario, 1861 ***2896.27*** *p1*
McMullen, William 50; Ontario, 1871 ***1823.28*** *p70*
McMullin, Angus 56; Ontario, 1871 ***1823.15*** *p182*
McMullin, Charles 30; Ontario, 1871 ***1823.15*** *p182*
McMullin, John; Virginia, 1783 ***1224.2*** *p74*
McMullin, John 56; Ontario, 1871 ***1823.15*** *p182*
McMullin, Thomas 36; Ontario, 1871 ***1823.22*** *p108*
McMullin, William; Savannah, Georgia, 1735-1737 ***1640.10*** *p142*
McMullin, William 50; Ontario, 1871 ***1823.28*** *p70*
McMurphy, Angus 35; British Columbia, 1910 ***9196.1*** *p31*
McMurphy, Angus 35; Washington, 1910 ***9196.1*** *p31*
McMurphy, James; Canada, 1756-1760 ***4628.40*** *p46*
McMurphy, John; Nova Scotia, 1745 ***4628.40*** *p45*
McMurray, Bridget Ann; Vermont, 1848-1869 ***5900.10*** *p558*
McMurray, Catherine 69; Vermont, 1890 ***5900.10*** *p558*
McMurray, Francis; New York, 1821 ***8197.10*** *p253*
McMurray, George; New York, 1807 ***8197.10*** *p45*
McMurray, James 37; Ontario, 1871 ***1823.22*** *p108*
McMurray, Joseph; New York, 1826 ***8197.10*** *p255*
McMurray, Joseph; New York, 1830 ***8197.10*** *p66*
McMurray, Mary; Vermont, 1851-1885 ***5900.10*** *p558*
McMurray, Michael 84; Vermont, 1892 ***5900.10*** *p558*
McMurray, Michael E.; Vermont, 1858-1860 ***5900.10*** *p558*
McMurray, Robert; New York, 1840 ***8197.10*** *p258*
McMurray, Thomas; New York, 1828 ***8197.10*** *p256*
McMurray, Thomas 40; Ontario, 1871 ***1823.28*** *p70*
McMurray, William 50; Ontario, 1871 ***1823.15*** *p182*
McMurrich, John; Toronto, 1886 ***1640.13*** *p91*
McMurry, Ann; Vermont, 1840-1911 ***5900.10*** *p416*
McMurry, Arthur 35; Ontario, 1871 ***1823.22*** *p108*
McMurry, Bernard 84; Vermont, 1886 ***5900.10*** *p416*
McMurry, John 64; Ontario, 1871 ***1823.22*** *p108*
McMurry, Joseph 28; Ontario, 1871 ***1823.22*** *p108*
McMurry, Robert 36; Ontario, 1871 ***1823.28*** *p70*
McMurter, G. 2; Ontario, 1861 ***2896.25*** *p47*
McMurter, J. H. 4; Ontario, 1861 ***2896.25*** *p47*
McMurter, M. J. 32; Ontario, 1861 ***2896.25*** *p47*
McMurter, Reuben 7; Ontario, 1861 ***2896.25*** *p47*
McMurter, S. A. 10; Ontario, 1861 ***2896.25*** *p47*
McMurtrey, Thomas 53; Ontario, 1871 ***1823.22*** *p108*
McMurtrie, John 50; Ontario, 1871 ***1823.15*** *p182*
McMurtrie, William; New York, 1832 ***8197.10*** *p356*
McMurtrie, William; Pennsylvania, 1777 ***4629.10*** *p21*
McMurtry, Mrs. 49; Ontario, 1871 ***1823.22*** *p108*
McMurtry, Ellen 35; Ontario, 1871 ***1823.22*** *p108*
McMurtry, Samuel G.; New York, New York, 1849 ***3437.14*** *p8*
McMyler, James Jos 45; Alaska, 1916 ***9196.1*** *p6*
McMyler, James Jos 45; Yukon, 1916 ***9196.1*** *p6*
McNab, . . .; Mobile, Alabama, 1767 ***1640.10*** *p142*
McNab, Miss; Quebec, 1857 ***9196.15*** *p26*
McNab, Mr.; Quebec, 1858 ***9196.15*** *p35*
McNab, Alexander 58; Ontario, 1871 ***1823.28*** *p70*
McNab, Allan 51; Ontario, 1871 ***1823.28*** *p70*
McNab, Archibald; New York, 1767 ***1224.2*** *p74*
McNab, Archibald 55; Ontario, 1871 ***1823.28*** *p70*
McNab, Catharine 42; Ontario, 1871 ***1823.28*** *p70*
McNab, Collan 40; Ontario, 1871 ***1823.28*** *p70*
McNab, Dougald Campbell 49; Ontario, 1871 ***1823.28*** *p70*
McNab, Duncan 41; Ontario, 1871 ***1823.28*** *p70*
McNab, Duncan 82; Ontario, 1871 ***1823.28*** *p70*
McNab, Isabella 78; Ontario, 1871 ***1823.28*** *p70*
McNab, James; New York, 1794 ***8197.10*** *p1*
McNab, John; New York, 1797 ***8197.10*** *p9*
McNab, John 50; Ontario, 1871 ***1823.28*** *p70*
McNab, John 51; Ontario, 1871 ***1823.28*** *p70*
McNab, John 52; Ontario, 1871 ***1823.15*** *p182*
McNab, John 73; Ontario, 1871 ***1823.28*** *p70*
McNab, John Duncan 49; Ontario, 1871 ***1823.28*** *p70*
McNab, Peter 36; Ontario, 1871 ***1823.15*** *p182*
McNabb, Alex 45; Ontario, 1871 ***1823.28*** *p70*
McNabb, Alice 46; Ontario, 1871 ***1823.22*** *p109*
McNabb, Allen 45; Ontario, 1871 ***1823.28*** *p70*
McNabb, James 57; Ontario, 1871 ***1823.15*** *p182*
McNabb, John; New York, 1802 ***8197.10*** *p23*
McNabb, Samuel 44; Ontario, 1871 ***1823.28*** *p70*
McNabb, William 36; Ontario, 1871 ***1823.28*** *p70*
McNaboe, Elizabeth 79; Vermont, 1893 ***5900.10*** *p468*
McNaboe, Mary Kelly; Vermont, 1837-1903 ***5900.10*** *p219*
McNaboe, Owen; Vermont, 1823-1896 ***5900.10*** *p219*
McNaff, Daniel; Pennsylvania, 1777 ***4629.10*** *p27*
McNair, Alexander 37; Ontario, 1871 ***1823.15*** *p182*
McNair, Donald 62; Ontario, 1871 ***1823.15*** *p182*
McNair, Duncan 36; Ontario, 1871 ***1823.15*** *p182*
McNair, Flora 59; Ontario, 1871 ***1823.15*** *p182*
McNair, George 52; Ontario, 1871 ***1823.15*** *p182*
McNair, Hugh; New Orleans, 1844 ***1640.10*** *p142*
McNair, Hugh; New Orleans, 1844 ***1640.13*** *p91*
McNair, Isabella 88; Ontario, 1871 ***1823.15*** *p182*
McNair, James; New Orleans, 1807-1843 ***1640.10*** *p143*
McNair, James; New Orleans, 1824 ***1640.10*** *p143*
McNair, James; New Orleans, 1843 ***1640.13*** *p91*
McNair, James 41; Ontario, 1871 ***1823.15*** *p182*
McNair, James 46; Ontario, 1871 ***1823.15*** *p182*
McNair, John 54; Ontario, 1871 ***1823.15*** *p182*
McNair, Margaret 60; Ontario, 1871 ***1823.15*** *p182*
McNair, Neil 73; Ontario, 1871 ***1823.15*** *p182*
McNair, Robert; Georgia, 1698 ***1640.13*** *p91*
McNair, Robert; Pennsylvania, 1777 ***4629.10*** *p24*
McNairnay, Hugh Chas 50; Ontario, 1871 ***1823.28*** *p70*
McNairne, Hannah; America, 1785 ***1640.13*** *p91*
McNairy, . . .; South Carolina, 1750-1770 ***4628.40*** *p98*
McNalley, Catherine 93; Vermont, 1866 ***5900.10*** *p604*
McNally, Angeline Donaldson; Vermont, 1845-1914 ***5900.10*** *p513*
McNally, Arthur; Vermont, 1836-1919 ***5900.10*** *p512*
McNally, Bridget E.; Vermont, 1857-1896 ***5900.10*** *p127*
McNally, Catharine Ford; Vermont, 1830-1923 ***5900.10*** *p489*
McNally, Catherine 21; Vermont, 1865 ***5900.10*** *p516*
McNally, Eliza; Vermont, 1864-1905 ***5900.10*** *p326*
McNally, Ellen O'Kane; Vermont, 1847-1914 ***5900.10*** *p514*
McNally, Francis; Vermont, 1839-1888 ***5900.10*** *p514*
McNally, Henry; Vermont, 1853-1906 ***5900.10*** *p514*
McNally, Henry 24; Vermont, 1847 ***5900.10*** *p498*
McNally, James 32; Vermont, 1865 ***5900.10*** *p516*
McNally, James 51; Vermont, 1847 ***5900.10*** *p498*
McNally, John; New Orleans, 1886 ***1640.13*** *p91*
McNally, John; New York, 1837 ***8197.10*** *p98*
McNally, John; Vermont, 1830-1914 ***5900.10*** *p514*
McNally, John; Vermont, 1838-1912 ***5900.10*** *p513*
McNally, Mary 56; Vermont, 1852 ***5900.10*** *p498*
McNally, Mary Dunning; Vermont, 1837-1912 ***5900.10*** *p512*
McNally, Mary O'Kane; Vermont, 1839-1919 ***5900.10*** *p514*
McNally, Michael; New York, 1840 ***8197.10*** *p183*
McNally, Sarah 3; Ontario, 1871 ***1823.22*** *p109*
McNally, Terene; Vermont, 1832-1912 ***5900.10*** *p458*
McNally, Terrence; New York, 1827 ***8197.10*** *p347*
McNalty, Terrence; New York, 1806 ***8197.10*** *p324*
McNama, Michal 74; Ontario, 1871 ***1823.22*** *p109*
McNamara, Alice; Vermont, 1861-1863 ***5900.10*** *p358*
McNamara, Alice; Vermont, 1872-1931 ***5900.10*** *p358*
McNamara, Alice Elliot; Vermont, 1830-1901 ***5900.10*** *p358*
McNamara, Andrew; Pennsylvania, 1850 ***6058.10*** *p26*
McNamara, Andrew; Pennsylvania, 1868 ***6058.10*** *p75*
McNamara, Ann; Vermont, 1826-1917 ***5900.10*** *p585*
McNamara, Ann; Vermont, 1836-1910 ***5900.10*** *p609*
McNamara, Ann Coyne 89; Vermont, 1922 ***5900.10*** *p591*
McNamara, Arthur 67; Vermont, 1885 ***5900.10*** *p102*
McNamara, Bridget; Vermont, 1820-1892 ***5900.10*** *p430*
McNamara, Bridget; Vermont, 1837-1918 ***5900.10*** *p468*
McNamara, Bridget; Vermont, 1838-1915 ***5900.10*** *p87*
McNamara, Bridget; Vermont, 1842-1912 ***5900.10*** *p53*
McNamara, Bridget; Vermont, 1857-1881 ***5900.10*** *p331*
McNamara, Catherine; Vermont, 1832-1919 ***5900.10*** *p590*
McNamara, Catherine; Vermont, 1853-1922 ***5900.10*** *p169*
McNamara, Catherine; Vermont, 1882 ***5900.10*** *p426*
McNamara, Catherine McMahon 66; Vermont, 1893 ***5900.10*** *p269*
McNamara, Daniel; Vermont, 1822-1893 ***5900.10*** *p546*
McNamara, Daniel 38; Vermont, 1882 ***5900.10*** *p414*
McNamara, Darby; New York, 1838 ***8197.10*** *p126*
McNamara, David 19; Vermont, 1887 ***5900.10*** *p211*
McNamara, Denis 50; Ontario, 1871 ***1823.28*** *p70*
McNamara, Dennis; New York, 1840 ***8197.10*** *p182*
McNamara, Dennis 70; Vermont, 1896 ***5900.10*** *p269*
McNamara, Eliza Campbell; Vermont, 1839-1897 ***5900.10*** *p259*
McNamara, Elizabeth McCue; Vermont, 1865-1931 ***5900.10*** *p592*
McNamara, Hannah; Vermont, 1856-1929 ***5900.10*** *p592*
McNamara, Hanora; Vermont, n.d. ***5900.10*** *p250*
McNamara, Hanora Egan 99; Vermont, 1881 ***5900.10*** *p591*
McNamara, James; Vermont, 1814-1868 ***5900.10*** *p430*
McNamara, James; Vermont, 1858-1890 ***5900.10*** *p53*
McNamara, Jane Meehan 78; Vermont, 1888 ***5900.10*** *p66*
McNamara, Johanna; Vermont, 1804-1882 ***5900.10*** *p125*
McNamara, John; Vermont, 1820-1898 ***5900.10*** *p554*
McNamara, John; Vermont, 1831-1883 ***5900.10*** *p431*
McNamara, John; Vermont, 1867-1890 ***5900.10*** *p211*
McNamara, John; Vermont, 1892 ***5900.10*** *p53*
McNamara, John; Vermont, 1899 ***5900.10*** *p331*
McNamara, John 29; Ontario, 1871 ***1823.28*** *p70*
McNamara, John H.; Vermont, 1858-1929 ***5900.10*** *p358*
McNamara, Julia; Vermont, 1853-1872 ***5900.10*** *p358*
McNamara, Julia; Vermont, 1861-1911 ***5900.10*** *p216*
McNamara, Julia Burke; Vermont, 1893 ***5900.10*** *p53*
McNamara, Kate; Vermont, 1858-1905 ***5900.10*** *p391*
McNamara, Margaret; Vermont, 1845-1909 ***5900.10*** *p589*
McNamara, Margaret Fahey 87; Vermont, 1901 ***5900.10*** *p590*
McNamara, Margaret Neville 52; Vermont, 1872 ***5900.10*** *p197*
McNamara, Martin 60; Ontario, 1871 ***1823.28*** *p70*
McNamara, Mary; Vermont, 1834-1914 ***5900.10*** *p576*
McNamara, Mary 1; Vermont, 1859 ***5900.10*** *p198*
McNamara, Mary 81; Vermont, 1899 ***5900.10*** *p392*
McNamara, Mary Ann; Vermont, 1848-1936 ***5900.10*** *p435*
McNamara, Mary Ann 42; Vermont, 1879 ***5900.10*** *p211*
McNamara, Mary Carroll 70; Vermont, 1910 ***5900.10*** *p102*
McNamara, Mary Gannon 58; Vermont, 1883 ***5900.10*** *p546*
McNamara, Mary Harvey; Vermont, 1829-1900 ***5900.10*** *p554*
McNamara, Mary Walsh; Vermont, 1836-1883 ***5900.10*** *p431*
McNamara, Michael; New York, 1820-1834 ***8197.10*** *p309*
McNamara, Michael; Vermont, 1822-1887 ***5900.10*** *p554*
McNamara, Michael; Vermont, 1842-1902 ***5900.10*** *p87*
McNamara, Michael; Vermont, 1853-1929 ***5900.10*** *p592*
McNamara, Michael; Vermont, 1867-1887 ***5900.10*** *p53*
McNamara, Michael 41; Vermont, 1863 ***5900.10*** *p259*
McNamara, Morris; Vermont, 1861-1883 ***5900.10*** *p53*
McNamara, Nellie; Vermont, 1864-1939 ***5900.10*** *p432*
McNamara, Patrick; New York, 1838 ***8197.10*** *p120*

McNamara, Patrick; New York, 1838 8197.10 p126
McNamara, Patrick; New York, 1838 8197.10 p257
McNamara, Patrick; Vermont, n.d. 5900.10 p250
McNamara, Patrick; Vermont, 1817-1908 5900.10 p358
McNamara, Patrick; Vermont, 1890-1899 5900.10 p591
McNamara, Patrick 29; Ontario, 1871 1823.28 p70
McNamara, Patrick 34; Ontario, 1871 1823.28 p70
McNamara, Patrick 73; Vermont, 1902 5900.10 p609
McNamara, Peter; New York, 1807 8197.10 p46
McNamara, Richard; Vermont, 1869-1890 5900.10 p211
McNamara, Richard 55; Vermont, 1881 5900.10 p211
McNamara, Roger 21; Vermont, 1859 5900.10 p198
McNamara, Sarah Collins; Vermont, 1822-1895 5900.10 p592
McNamara, Thomas 35; Ontario, 1871 1823.28 p70
McNamara, Thomas 62; Vermont, 1879 5900.10 p269
McNamara, Thomas 89; Vermont, 1900 5900.10 p590
McNamara, Timothy 63; Vermont, 1897 5900.10 p591
McNamara, William; Vermont, 1837-1891 5900.10 p259
McNamara, William; Vermont, 1857-1914 5900.10 p259
McNamara, William 10; Vermont, 1864 5900.10 p211
McNamarra, Darby; New York, 1838 8197.10 p120
McNamee, Alice 68; Vermont, 1890 5900.10 p619
McNamee, Bernard 78; Vermont, 1896 5900.10 p619
McNamee, Charles 35; Ontario, 1871 1823.28 p70
McNamee, James; New York, 1834 8197.10 p373
McNamee, Michael; New York, 1840 8197.10 p184
McNaney, . . . 91; Vermont, 1859 5900.10 p454
McNaney, Anna 51; Vermont, 1896 5900.10 p49
McNaney, Barnard 22; Vermont, 1881 5900.10 p454
McNaney, Barney 26; Vermont, 1884 5900.10 p49
McNaney, Catherine; Vermont, 1849-1924 5900.10 p51
McNaney, Edward 34; Vermont, 1882 5900.10 p454
McNaney, Ellen 9 months; Vermont, 1856 5900.10 p49
McNaney, George A.; Vermont, 1850-1907 5900.10 p48
McNaney, J. E.; Vermont, 1850-1921 5900.10 p454
McNaney, James 43; Vermont, 1865 5900.10 p454
McNaney, James R. 22; Vermont, 1887 5900.10 p454
McNaney, Lizzie 22; Vermont, 1889 5900.10 p49
McNaney, Margaret 74; Vermont, 1899 5900.10 p49
McNaney, Mary 2; Vermont, 1856 5900.10 p49
McNaney, Mary Roark; Vermont, 1852-1923 5900.10 p48
McNaney, Sarah Maloney 71; Vermont, 1894 5900.10 p454
McNann, David 50; Ontario, 1871 1823.15 p182
McNannis, Margaret; Vermont, 1853-1883 5900.10 p338
McNannis, William J. 25; Vermont, 1865 5900.10 p338
McNanny, Rose 25; Vermont, 1842 5900.10 p146
McNany, Barney 62; Vermont, 1887 5900.10 p236
McNany, Delia A. 34; Vermont, 1891 5900.10 p49
McNany, Jas; Vermont, n.d. 5900.10 p50
McNarmarn, Patrick 41; Ontario, 1871 1823.15 p182
McNas, Alexander 22; Ontario, 1871 1823.15 p182
McNassar, Catherine Hanley; Vermont, 1829-1893 5900.10 p535
McNassar, Peter; Vermont, n.d. 5900.10 p535
McNassor, Ellen; Vermont, 1924-1955 5900.10 p535
McNattan, Alex; Pennsylvania, 1809 6058.10 p3
McNaught, A.; Quebec, 1857 9196.15 p19
McNaught, Charles Henry; Pennsylvania, 1866 1640.13 p91
McNaught, David 29; Ontario, 1871 1823.15 p182
McNaught, David George; Montreal, 1889 1640.13 p91
McNaught, John 59; Ontario, 1871 1823.15 p182
McNaughten, Donald; New York, 1807 8197.10 p46
McNaughton, Alex; Pennsylvania, 1809 6058.10 p3
McNaughton, Alexander 40; Ontario, 1871 1823.22 p109
McNaughton, Donald 77; Ontario, 1871 1823.28 p70
McNaughton, John; New York, 1837 8197.10 p98
McNaughton, John 29; Ontario, 1871 1823.28 p70
McNaughton, John 50; Ontario, 1871 1823.15 p182
McNaughton, John 55; Ontario, 1871 1823.22 p109
McNaughton, John 55; Ontario, 1871 1823.28 p70
McNaughton, John 58; Ontario, 1871 1823.15 p182
McNaughton, Margaret 32; Ontario, 1871 1823.15 p182
McNaughton, Mary 24; Ontario, 1871 1823.28 p70
McNaughton, Peter 41; Ontario, 1871 1823.15 p183
McNaughton, Peter Edward; New York, 1836-1838 8197.10 p120
McNaughton, Peter Edward; New York, 1838 8197.10 p126
McNaughton, Robert 55; Ontario, 1871 1823.15 p183
McNaugton, Duncan 50; Ontario, 1871 1823.15 p183
McNay, William 36; Ontario, 1871 1823.15 p183
McNeal, Ann 40; Vermont, 1864 5900.10 p578
McNeal, Archy 45; Ontario, 1871 1823.28 p70
McNeal, Bridget 31; Vermont, 1887 5900.10 p578
McNeal, Duncan 48; Ontario, 1871 1823.15 p183
McNeal, Patrick; New York, 1802 8197.10 p23
McNeal, Patrick 50; Vermont, 1862 5900.10 p578
McNeally, Sarah 20; Ontario, 1871 1823.15 p183
McNeany, Patrick; New York, 1824 8197.10 p255
McNee, Duncan 65; Ontario, 1871 1823.28 p70
McNee, Duncan 71; Ontario, 1871 1823.15 p183
McNee, James 38; Ontario, 1871 1823.28 p70
McNee, James 59; Ontario, 1871 1823.28 p70
McNee, Robert 62; Ontario, 1871 1823.28 p70
McNeely, Isaac; New York, 1807 8197.10 p46
McNeil, Mr.; Quebec, 1857 9196.15 p17
McNeil, Ann; Vermont, 1845-1906 5900.10 p579
McNeil, Archibald 47; Ontario, 1871 1823.15 p183
McNeil, Catharine 56; Ontario, 1871 1823.22 p109
McNeil, Donald 36; Ontario, 1871 1823.28 p70
McNeil, Donald 76; Ontario, 1871 1823.15 p183
McNeil, Duncan 47; Ontario, 1871 1823.15 p183
McNeil, Emma Ransom; Vermont, 1857-1922 5900.10 p243
McNeil, Hugh; Savannah, Georgia, 1826 1640.10 p143
McNeil, James; New York, 1838 8197.10 p125
McNeil, James; Nova Scotia, 1745 4628.40 p44
McNeil, James; Vermont, 1841-1912 5900.10 p349
McNeil, James 32; Ontario, 1871 1823.28 p70
McNeil, James 59; Ontario, 1871 1823.15 p183
McNeil, Jane; Vermont, 1915 5900.10 p244
McNeil, Jane Haley; Vermont, 1842-1925 5900.10 p349
McNeil, John; Mobile, Alabama, 1831-1845 1640.10 p143
McNeil, John; Nova Scotia, 1745 4628.40 p45
McNeil, John; St. Johns, Newfoundland, 1898 1640.13 p91
McNeil, John; Vermont, 1832-1905 5900.10 p243
McNeil, John 30; Ontario, 1871 1823.28 p70
McNeil, John I. 33; Ontario, 1871 1823.15 p183
McNeil, Joseph; Vermont, 1844-1910 5900.10 p243
McNeil, Marion 57; Ontario, 1871 1823.15 p183
McNeil, Mary; Vermont, 1806-1893 5900.10 p243
McNeil, Mary J. 71; Vermont, 1928 5900.10 p568
McNeil, Neil 24; Ontario, 1871 1823.28 p70
McNeil, Reuben; Vermont, 1849-1870 5900.10 p244
McNeil, Robert; Vermont, 1810-1887 5900.10 p243
McNeil, Ruth 70; Vermont, 1895 5900.10 p374
McNeil, Sarah A. Ward 54; Vermont, 1907 5900.10 p560
McNeil, Thomas; South Carolina, n.d. 1224.2 p74
McNeil, William; Vermont, 1846-1875 5900.10 p244
McNeil, William John 40; Ontario, 1871 1823.28 p70
McNeile, J.; Quebec, 1857 9196.15 p20
McNeill, Catherine 24; Ontario, 1871 1823.15 p183
McNeill, Charles, Jr.; New York, 1808 8197.10 p54
McNeill, Flora 20; Ontario, 1871 1823.15 p183
McNeill, Hannah; Vermont, 1796-1887 5900.10 p401
McNeill, Hugh 27; Ontario, 1871 1823.22 p109
McNeill, John; Canada, 1873 1640.13 p91
McNeill, John; New York, 1810 8197.10 p57
McNeill, John 45; Ontario, 1871 1823.15 p183
McNeill, Malcolm; Jamaica, 1785 1640.13 p91
McNeill, Mary 22; Ontario, 1871 1823.15 p183
McNeill, Mary 99; Ontario, 1871 1823.15 p183
McNeill, Mary J. 78; Ontario, 1871 1823.22 p109
McNeill, Michael 28; Ontario, 1871 1823.15 p183
McNeill, Neill; Georgia, 1699 1640.13 p91
McNeill, Philip 30; Ontario, 1871 1823.15 p183
McNeily, David 50; Ontario, 1871 1823.15 p183
McNeish, John; New York, 1828 8197.10 p298
McNeish, Thomas; Michigan, 1888 1640.13 p92
McNelly, John 50; Ontario, 1871 1823.28 p70
McNemara, Patrick; New York, 1807 8197.10 p327
McNeran, Malcolm; Philadelphia, 1806 1640.13 p92
McNerny, Mary; Vermont, 1843-1905 5900.10 p608
McNertney, . . .; Vermont, n.d. 5900.10 p314
McNery, Mary 79; Vermont, 1882 5900.10 p543
McNery, Simon 80; Vermont, 1888 5900.10 p543
McNeven, Alex 60; Ontario, 1871 1823.28 p70
McNevin, Donald 50; Ontario, 1871 1823.15 p183
McNevin, William James; New York, 1806 8197.10 p252
McNichol, Abraham 30; Ontario, 1871 1823.15 p183
McNichol, James, Sr. 73; Ontario, 1871 1823.28 p70
McNichols, Hugh 62; Vermont, 1864 5900.10 p227
McNichols, Jane L. Tunney; Vermont, 1850-1934 5900.10 p535
McNichols, John W. 65; Vermont, 1905 5900.10 p535
McNichols, Mary 71; Vermont, 1880 5900.10 p227
McNickle, Arthur; New York, 1807 8197.10 p329
McNicol, Colin; Perth Amboy, New Jersey, 1764 1224.2 p74
McNicol, John; Kingston, Jamaica, 1816 1640.13 p92
McNicol, Malcolm 45; Ontario, 1871 1823.15 p183
McNicol, Nicol; Georgia, 1743 1640.10 p143
McNicol, Norman 58; Ontario, 1871 1823.15 p183
McNider, Mr.; Quebec, 1858 9196.15 p46
McNider, Mrs.; Quebec, 1858 9196.15 p46
McNie, Alex 55; Ontario, 1871 1823.28 p70
McNiece, Sarah 80; Vermont, 1877 5900.10 p473
McNiel, Neil 30; Ontario, 1871 1823.15 p183
McNiel, Patrick; New York, 1802 8197.10 p23
McNiel, Robert 65; Ontario, 1871 1823.28 p70
McNiell, Thomas; New York, 1838 8197.10 p378
McNiff, Ann; Vermont, 1840-1905 5900.10 p433
McNiff, Bridget; Vermont, 1836-1913 5900.10 p426
McNiff, Catherine; Vermont, 1844-1906 5900.10 p154
McNiff, Ellen 65; Vermont, 1892 5900.10 p432
McNiff, James 87; Vermont, 1911 5900.10 p432
McNiff, Mary; Vermont, 1853-1935 5900.10 p432
McNiff, Michael 33; Ontario, 1871 1823.15 p183
McNight, James 59; Ontario, 1871 1823.15 p183
McNight, Margaret 24; Ontario, 1871 1823.15 p183
McNight, William 32; Ontario, 1871 1823.15 p183
McNish, John; Savannah, Georgia, 1803-1812 1640.10 p143
McNiven, Alexander 56; Ontario, 1871 1823.28 p70
McNiven, Alexander 84; Ontario, 1871 1823.28 p70
McNiven, Archibald; New York, 1802 8197.10 p23
McNulla, Bridget 70; Vermont, 1895 5900.10 p313
McNulla, Bridget 78; Vermont, 1933 5900.10 p313
McNulla, Ellen 23; Vermont, 1879 5900.10 p313
McNulla, John 21; Vermont, 1878 5900.10 p313
McNulla, Mary 39; Vermont, 1885 5900.10 p313
McNulla, Michael 55; Vermont, 1867 5900.10 p313
McNulty, Alexander; Vermont, 1857-1901 5900.10 p609
McNulty, Barney 62; Vermont, 1880 5900.10 p528
McNulty, Catherine J.; Vermont, 1866-1954 5900.10 p609
McNulty, Charles; New York, 1840 8197.10 p258
McNulty, Domnick 80; Ontario, 1871 1823.28 p70
McNulty, Ellen Casey 53; Vermont, 1870 5900.10 p528
McNulty, Felix; New York, 1827 8197.10 p256
McNulty, Henry; Vermont, 1824-1908 5900.10 p532
McNulty, James; New York, 1828 8197.10 p350
McNulty, John 2; Vermont, 1852 5900.10 p521
McNulty, John 36; Ontario, 1871 1823.28 p70
McNulty, John 40; Ontario, 1871 1823.28 p70
McNulty, John W.; Vermont, 1856-1924 5900.10 p402
McNulty, M. J. 27; British Columbia, 1915 9196.1 p68
McNulty, M. J. 27; Washington, 1915 9196.1 p68
McNulty, Margaret 17; Vermont, 1866 5900.10 p509
McNulty, Margaret 73; Vermont, 1908 5900.10 p532
McNulty, Margaret Trudden; Vermont, 1829-1909 5900.10 p311
McNulty, Martin 30; Ontario, 1871 1823.28 p70
McNulty, Mary Saultry; Vermont, 1817-1902 5900.10 p532
McNulty, Michael 20; Ontario, 1871 1823.28 p70
McNulty, Patrick; New York, 1839 8197.10 p138
McNulty, Patrick 40; Ontario, 1871 1823.28 p70
McNulty, Patrick 65; Ontario, 1871 1823.28 p70
McNulty, Susie; Vermont, 1857-1918 5900.10 p401
McNulty, Sylvia Hicks; Vermont, 1863-1936 5900.10 p402
McNutt, A. M. 37; Ontario, 1871 1823.22 p109
McOmish, John; New Orleans, 1830 1640.10 p144
McOnnel, James 39; Ontario, 1871 1823.22 p109
McOok, David 39; Ontario, 1871 1823.22 p109
McOult, Frederick; San Francisco, 1915 9196.1 p57
McPack, Patrick; New York, 1840 8197.10 p183
McPeach, Henry 49; Ontario, 1871 1823.28 p70
McPeach, John 45; Ontario, 1871 1823.28 p70
McPeach, Patrick 60; Ontario, 1871 1823.28 p70
McPeak, James 45; Ontario, 1871 1823.15 p183
McPeck, John; Vermont, 1852-1917 5900.10 p475
McPeke, John; New York, 1830 8197.10 p360
McPhaedris, . . .; New Hampshire, 1641-1660 4628.40 p44
McPhail, Alexander; Pennsylvania, 1785 4629.10 p48
McPhail, Archy 45; Ontario, 1871 1823.15 p183
McPhail, Donald 28; Ontario, 1871 1823.15 p183
McPhail, Duncan 56; Ontario, 1871 1823.15 p183
McPhail, Hugh 42; Ontario, 1871 1823.15 p183
McPhail, Hugh 50; Ontario, 1871 1823.22 p109
McPhail, John; Pennsylvania, 1785 4629.10 p48
McPhail, John 46; Ontario, 1871 1823.15 p183
McPhail, John 52; Ontario, 1871 1823.15 p183
McPhail, Margaret 71; Ontario, 1871 1823.22 p109
McPhail, Peter 62; Ontario, 1871 1823.15 p184
McPhail, Ronald 48; Ontario, 1871 1823.15 p184
McPhail, William; Pennsylvania, 1785 4629.10 p48
McPharson, John; Pennsylvania, 1777 4629.10 p14
McPhaul, Archibald 12; Ontario, 1861 2896.27 p71
McPhaul, Eliza 39; Ontario, 1861 2896.27 p71
McPhaul, Ellen 6; Ontario, 1861 2896.27 p71
McPhaul, Karry 4; Ontario, 1861 2896.27 p71
McPhaul, Maud 2; Ontario, 1861 2896.27 p71
McPhaul, Thomas 10; Ontario, 1861 2896.27 p71
McPhearson, Ann; New York, 1765 1224.2 p74
McPhearson, Colin; New York, 1765 1224.2 p74
McPhee, Christif 60; Ontario, 1871 1823.15 p184
McPhee, Daniel 21; Maryland, 1775 1220.25 p112
McPhee, Duncan 56; Ontario, 1871 1823.15 p184
McPhee, Hugh 55; Ontario, 1871 1823.15 p184
McPhee, John 61; Ontario, 1871 1823.15 p184

McPhee, Mary 40; Ontario, 1871 ***1823.15*** *p184*
McPhelin, Margaret; Vermont, 1825-1915 ***5900.10*** *p126*
McPhenson, Robert 40; Ontario, 1871 ***1823.15*** *p184*
McPherson, Mr.; Georgia, 1738 ***1640.10*** *p145*
McPherson, Mrs.; Quebec, 1858 ***9196.15*** *p35*
McPherson, A.; Quebec, 1857 ***9196.15*** *p17*
McPherson, Adam; New York, 1830 ***8197.10*** *p354*
McPherson, Alexander 27; Ontario, 1871 ***1823.28*** *p70*
McPherson, Alexander 39; Ontario, 1871 ***1823.28*** *p71*
McPherson, Alexander 63; Ontario, 1871 ***1823.15*** *p184*
McPherson, Alexander, Sr.; Georgia, 1743 ***1640.10*** *p144*
McPherson, Andrew; New York, 1840 ***8197.10*** *p182*
McPherson, Andrew; Tobago, West Indies, 1857 ***1640.13*** *p92*
McPherson, Angus, Jr.; Georgia, 1743 ***1640.10*** *p144*
McPherson, Barbara; Washington, 1864 ***1640.13*** *p92*
McPherson, Catharine 68; Ontario, 1871 ***1823.15*** *p184*
McPherson, Colin 61; Ontario, 1871 ***1823.28*** *p71*
McPherson, Donald 30; Ontario, 1871 ***1823.28*** *p71*
McPherson, Donald 55; Ontario, 1871 ***1823.15*** *p184*
McPherson, Donald 60; Ontario, 1871 ***1823.15*** *p184*
McPherson, Duncan 50; Ontario, 1871 ***1823.15*** *p184*
McPherson, Duncan 73; Ontario, 1871 ***1823.22*** *p109*
McPherson, Elizabeth 63; Ontario, 1871 ***1823.28*** *p71*
McPherson, Emma Jessie; Tobago, West Indies, 1891 ***1640.13*** *p92*
McPherson, George; Mississippi, 1735-1848 ***1640.10*** *p144*
McPherson, Hugh 36; Ontario, 1871 ***1823.15*** *p184*
McPherson, J. A.; Quebec, 1856 ***9196.15*** *p9*
McPherson, James; Georgia, 1743 ***1640.10*** *p144*
McPherson, James 40; Ontario, 1871 ***1823.15*** *p184*
McPherson, John; Boston, 1873 ***1640.13*** *p92*
McPherson, John; Georgia, 1743 ***1640.10*** *p145*
McPherson, John; Jamaica, 1800 ***1640.13*** *p92*
McPherson, John 22; Ontario, 1871 ***1823.15*** *p184*
McPherson, John 45; Ontario, 1871 ***1823.15*** *p184*
McPherson, Leach 40; Ontario, 1871 ***1823.15*** *p184*
McPherson, Malcom 48; Ontario, 1871 ***1823.28*** *p71*
McPherson, Mary; New York, n.d. ***1224.2*** *p75*
McPherson, Mary; Quebec, 1792 ***1224.2*** *p75*
McPherson, Paul; Georgia, 1743 ***1640.10*** *p145*
McPherson, Peter 60; Ontario, 1871 ***1823.15*** *p184*
McPherson, Peter 63; Ontario, 1871 ***1823.22*** *p109*
McPherson, Robert J.; Pennsylvania, 1865 ***6058.10*** *p49*
McPherson, Samuel 28; Ontario, 1871 ***1823.15*** *p184*
McPherson, William; Jamaica, 1798 ***1640.13*** *p92*
McPherson, William 22; Philadelphia, 1774 ***1220.25*** *p55*
McPherson, William 44; Ontario, 1871 ***1823.15*** *p184*
McPherson, William 44; Ontario, 1871 ***1823.28*** *p71*
McPhilemy, William 45; Ontario, 1871 ***1823.28*** *p71*
McPhilimy, Susan 3; Vermont, 1868 ***5900.10*** *p208*
McPhillip, George 59; Ontario, 1871 ***1823.15*** *p184*
McPhillips, Patrick 55; Ontario, 1871 ***1823.15*** *p184*
McPhilmny, Rebecca; Vermont, 1841-1879 ***5900.10*** *p214*
McPhilmy, Sarah 62; Vermont, 1901 ***5900.10*** *p570*
McPhilomy, Ann McDevitt; Vermont, 1879-1913 ***5900.10*** *p214*
McPhilomy, John 46; Vermont, 1879 ***5900.10*** *p214*
McPhilomy, Margaret; Vermont, 1843-1897 ***5900.10*** *p578*
McPhin, Matthew; New York, 1840 ***8197.10*** *p184*
McPhun, Matthew; New York, 1840 ***8197.10*** *p184*
McPontony, Louis 31; Ontario, 1871 ***1823.28*** *p71*
McQaid, Mary 68; Ontario, 1871 ***1823.15*** *p184*
McQuade, Hugh; New York, 1839 ***8197.10*** *p258*
McQuade, James; Vermont, 1829-1906 ***5900.10*** *p565*
McQuade, James 30; Ontario, 1871 ***1823.15*** *p184*
McQuade, James 71; Ontario, 1871 ***1823.15*** *p184*
McQuade, John; New York, 1824 ***8197.10*** *p255*
McQuade, Maria 80; Ontario, 1871 ***1823.28*** *p71*
McQuade, Mary Munday; Vermont, 1834-1916 ***5900.10*** *p565*
McQuade, Michael 39; Ontario, 1871 ***1823.15*** *p184*
McQuaid, Elizabeth 63; Ontario, 1871 ***1823.15*** *p184*
McQuaid, John; New York, 1807 ***8197.10*** *p46*
McQuaig, Hannah Ann 8; Ontario, 1861 ***2896.27*** *p38*
McQuaig, John; North Carolina, 1780-1845 ***1640.10*** *p146*
McQuarrie, Ellin 30; Ontario, 1871 ***1823.15*** *p184*
McQuarrie, Malcom 65; Ontario, 1871 ***1823.15*** *p184*
McQuarry, Hugh 35; Ontario, 1871 ***1823.15*** *p184*
McQuay, Andrew 25; Ontario, 1861 ***2896.25*** *p3*
McQuay, Eliza J. 6; Ontario, 1861 ***2896.25*** *p3*
McQuay, Prudence 27; Ontario, 1861 ***2896.25*** *p3*
McQuay, Sarah 2; Ontario, 1861 ***2896.25*** *p3*
McQuay, William 4; Ontario, 1861 ***2896.25*** *p3*
McQueen, Allan 38; Ontario, 1871 ***1823.15*** *p185*
McQueen, Anne; Savannah, Georgia, 1809 ***1640.10*** *p146*
McQueen, James; Georgia, 1739 ***1640.10*** *p146*
McQueen, James 50; Ontario, 1871 ***1823.15*** *p185*
McQueen, Jannet 83; Ontario, 1871 ***1823.15*** *p185*
McQueen, John; North Carolina, 1773-1821 ***1640.10*** *p146*
McQueen, John; Savannah, Georgia, 1822 ***1640.10*** *p146*
McQueen, John 60; Ontario, 1871 ***1823.15*** *p185*
McQueen, Mary 65; Ontario, 1871 ***1823.15*** *p185*
McQueen, Peter; New York, 1830 ***8197.10*** *p354*
McQueen, Peter 49; Ontario, 1871 ***1823.15*** *p185*
McQueen, Robert; New York, 1803 ***8197.10*** *p14*
McQueen, Robert 47; Ontario, 1871 ***1823.15*** *p185*
McQueen, Thomas 35; Ontario, 1871 ***1823.15*** *p185*
McQueen, William; Jamaica, 1804 ***1640.13*** *p92*
McQueen, William 50; Ontario, 1871 ***1823.15*** *p185*
McQueeney, Catherine; Vermont, 1820-1886 ***5900.10*** *p230*
McQueeney, Charles; Vermont, 1846-1879 ***5900.10*** *p240*
McQueeney, Ella; Vermont, 1863-1925 ***5900.10*** *p478*
McQueeney, John; Vermont, 1833-1916 ***5900.10*** *p478*
McQueeney, Michael; Vermont, 1820-1876 ***5900.10*** *p230*
McQuestein, James 66; Ontario, 1871 ***1823.28*** *p71*
McQuestion, Ellen McCarty; Vermont, 1852-1889 ***5900.10*** *p481*
McQueston, Anthony; Pennsylvania, 1777 ***4629.10*** *p16*
McQuigin, Christopher; New York, 1840 ***8197.10*** *p258*
McQuillam, Ann 65; Ontario, 1871 ***1823.22*** *p109*
McQuillen, Patrick; New York, 1840 ***8197.10*** *p258*
McQuillian, Bridget 78; Vermont, 1890 ***5900.10*** *p279*
McQuillin, Edward 45; Ontario, 1871 ***1823.15*** *p185*
McQuillin, Wm 41; Ontario, 1871 ***1823.15*** *p185*
McQuin, John; Augusta, Georgia, 1804-1812 ***1640.10*** *p146*
McQuin, Peter; New York, 1839 ***8197.10*** *p258*
McQuinn, John; New York, 1794 ***8197.10*** *p1*
McQuiod, C. 9; Ontario, 1861 ***2896.26*** *p12*
McQuiod, C. 16; Ontario, 1861 ***2896.26*** *p12*
McQuiod, H. B. 6; Ontario, 1861 ***2896.26*** *p12*
McQuiod, J. 21; Ontario, 1861 ***2896.26*** *p12*
McQuiod, M. J. 15; Ontario, 1861 ***2896.26*** *p12*
McQuiod, R. 45; Ontario, 1861 ***2896.26*** *p12*
McQuiod, S. 13; Ontario, 1861 ***2896.26*** *p12*
McQuiod, S. M. 23; Ontario, 1861 ***2896.26*** *p12*
McQuiod, William 19; Ontario, 1861 ***2896.26*** *p12*
McQuire, Margaret 77; Vermont, 1886 ***5900.10*** *p570*
McQuirk, James; New York, 1837 ***8197.10*** *p98*
McQuisten, Mr.; Portland, Maine, 1858 ***9196.15*** *p27*
McQuiston, James; Pennsylvania, 1777 ***4629.10*** *p31*
McQuitty, David 59; Ontario, 1871 ***1823.28*** *p71*
McQuitty, Joseph 62; Ontario, 1871 ***1823.28*** *p71*
McQuitty, Phebe 58; Ontario, 1871 ***1823.28*** *p71*
McQuoid, George Henry 5; Ontario, 1861 ***2896.27*** *p70*
McQuoid, Hing 1; Ontario, 1861 ***2896.27*** *p70*
McQuoid, Hiram 25; Ontario, 1861 ***2896.27*** *p70*
McQuoid, James W. 3; Ontario, 1861 ***2896.27*** *p70*
McQuoid, Mary M. J. 20; Ontario, 1861 ***2896.27*** *p70*
McQuoid, Rachel 24; Ontario, 1861 ***2896.27*** *p70*
McQuoid, William; Ontario, 1861 ***2896.26*** *p27*
McRae, Alexander 30; Ontario, 1871 ***1823.15*** *p185*
McRae, Arthur 28; Ontario, 1871 ***1823.15*** *p185*
McRae, Catherine; South Carolina, 1766-1806 ***1640.10*** *p146*
McRae, Catherine; Wilmington, North Carolina, 1770 ***1640.10*** *p146*
McRae, Christopher; Georgia, 1821 ***1640.10*** *p147*
McRae, Daniel; Georgia, 1766-1845 ***1640.10*** *p147*
McRae, Donald 71; Ontario, 1871 ***1823.22*** *p109*
McRae, Duncan 28; Ontario, 1871 ***1823.15*** *p185*
McRae, John; Jamaica, 1837 ***1640.13*** *p92*
McRae, John 40; Alaska, 1911 ***9196.1*** *p16*
McRae, John 40; British Columbia, 1911 ***9196.1*** *p16*
McRae, John 65; Ontario, 1871 ***1823.28*** *p71*
McRae, Kenneth; Charleston, South Carolina, 1826 ***1640.10*** *p147*
McRae, Kennith 55; Ontario, 1871 ***1823.15*** *p185*
McRael, Thomas 19; Maryland, 1775 ***1220.25*** *p108*
McRagne, George 23; Ontario, 1861 ***2896.27*** *p29*
McRavy, Jennie; Vermont, 1847-1907 ***5900.10*** *p131*
McRay, Duncan 30; Ontario, 1871 ***1823.28*** *p71*
McRay, Sarah; North Carolina, 1790-1810 ***1640.10*** *p147*
McRea, Donald 33; Ontario, 1871 ***1823.15*** *p185*
McRea, Donald 35; Ontario, 1871 ***1823.28*** *p71*
McRea, Hugh; Georgia, 1761-1845 ***1640.10*** *p147*
McRea, James 45; Ontario, 1871 ***1823.28*** *p71*
McRea, Margret 30; Ontario, 1871 ***1823.28*** *p71*
McRea, Richard 28; Ontario, 1871 ***1823.15*** *p185*
McRea, Richard 50; Ontario, 1871 ***1823.28*** *p71*
McRea, William 37; Ontario, 1871 ***1823.15*** *p185*
McRea, William 38; Ontario, 1871 ***1823.15*** *p185*
McReadie, William 37; Ontario, 1871 ***1823.28*** *p71*
McReally, Gilson 21; Ontario, 1871 ***1823.22*** *p109*
McRnney, Archibald 63; Ontario, 1871 ***1823.15*** *p185*
McRobbie, William; Canada, 1894 ***1640.13*** *p92*
McRoberts, James 62; Ontario, 1871 ***1823.22*** *p109*
McShane, Anna; Vermont, 1856-1925 ***5900.10*** *p126*
McShane, Barnabas; Pennsylvania, 1779 ***4629.10*** *p37*
McShane, John; Pennsylvania, 1779 ***4629.10*** *p39*
McShane, Owen J.; Vermont, 1853-1933 ***5900.10*** *p126*
McShane, Terence; New York, 1837 ***8197.10*** *p257*
McShannock, Duncan 41; Ontario, 1871 ***1823.15*** *p185*
McShannock, Isabella 46; Ontario, 1871 ***1823.15*** *p185*
McSherry, James 80; Ontario, 1871 ***1823.15*** *p185*
McSherry, Mary; Vermont, 1825-1907 ***5900.10*** *p130*
McSorley, Mary; Vermont, 1808-1892 ***5900.10*** *p475*
McSorley, Mary J.; Vermont, 1850-1909 ***5900.10*** *p475*
McSorley, Nancy A. 31; Vermont, 1879 ***5900.10*** *p471*
McSorley, Patrick; New York, 1840 ***8197.10*** *p183*
McSorley, William 60; Vermont, 1876 ***5900.10*** *p602*
McSourley, Hugh; New York, 1832 ***8197.10*** *p314*
McSourley, Thos 60; Ontario, 1871 ***1823.28*** *p71*
McSourley, Wm 60; Ontario, 1871 ***1823.28*** *p71*
McSourly, John 54; Ontario, 1871 ***1823.28*** *p71*
McStay, Catherine McGough; Vermont, 1842-1932 ***5900.10*** *p587*
McSvein, Malcolm; Florida, 1775-1845 ***1640.10*** *p147*
McSwan, John 26; Ontario, 1871 ***1823.15*** *p185*
McSwan, Robt 58; Ontario, 1871 ***1823.15*** *p185*
McSweeney, Abbie; Vermont, 1838-1926 ***5900.10*** *p116*
McSweeney, Margaret 99; Vermont, 1937 ***5900.10*** *p186*
McSweeney, Margaret McMahon; Vermont, 1866-1944 ***5900.10*** *p130*
McSweeney, Patrick E.; Vermont, 1862-1938 ***5900.10*** *p130*
McSweeny, Bryan; Canada, 1756-1760 ***4628.40*** *p45*
McSweeny, John; New York, 1837 ***8197.10*** *p97*
McTaggart, Donald 39; Ontario, 1871 ***1823.15*** *p185*
McTaggart, James 63; Ontario, 1871 ***1823.15*** *p185*
McTaggart, Malcom 51; Ontario, 1871 ***1823.15*** *p185*
McTaggart, Stephen 19; Ontario, 1861 ***2896.27*** *p29*
McTague, Ann 80; Vermont, 1897 ***5900.10*** *p286*
McTavish, Donald 48; Ontario, 1871 ***1823.15*** *p185*
McTavish, Donald 59; Ontario, 1871 ***1823.15*** *p185*
McTavish, Douglas 40; Ontario, 1871 ***1823.15*** *p185*
McTavish, Duncan 48; Ontario, 1871 ***1823.15*** *p186*
McTavish, Hugh George; Virginia, 1873 ***1640.13*** *p92*
McTavish, John 48; Ontario, 1871 ***1823.15*** *p186*
McTavish, John 59; Ontario, 1871 ***1823.15*** *p186*
McTavish, Neal 60; Ontario, 1871 ***1823.15*** *p186*
McTavish, Peter 50; Ontario, 1871 ***1823.15*** *p186*
McTierney, Alice McLaughlin 32; Vermont, 1860 ***5900.10*** *p559*
McTierney, Bryan 63; Vermont, 1880 ***5900.10*** *p559*
McTierney, John; Vermont, 1854-1918 ***5900.10*** *p448*
McTierney, Lizzie A. Rourke 32; Vermont, 1885 ***5900.10*** *p559*
McTierney, Mary 38; Vermont, 1884 ***5900.10*** *p523*
McVain, John; Georgia, 1828 ***1640.10*** *p147*
McVair, Archibald; Philadelphia, 1794 ***4629.10*** *p84*
McVaney, John; New York, 1831 ***8197.10*** *p365*
McVay, John 52; Vermont, 1886 ***5900.10*** *p362*
McVay, John 52; Vermont, 1886 ***5900.10*** *p365*
McVay, John 52; Vermont, 1886 ***5900.10*** *p369*
McVay, Margaret 63; Ontario, 1871 ***1823.15*** *p186*
McVean, Cecilia A. 9; Ontario, 1861 ***2896.27*** *p16*
McVean, David H. 4; Ontario, 1861 ***2896.27*** *p16*
McVean, Mary 35; Ontario, 1861 ***2896.27*** *p16*
McVean, Maryalveretta 5; Ontario, 1861 ***2896.27*** *p16*
McVeeters, Samuel 35; Ontario, 1871 ***1823.28*** *p71*
McVeeters, Samuel 63; Ontario, 1871 ***1823.28*** *p71*
McVeeters, William 40; Ontario, 1871 ***1823.28*** *p71*
McVety, George 44; Ontario, 1871 ***1823.22*** *p109*
McVety, Isabella 35; Ontario, 1871 ***1823.22*** *p109*
McVety, Thomas 43; Ontario, 1871 ***1823.15*** *p186*
McVey, Bridget; Vermont, 1835-1910 ***5900.10*** *p538*
McVey, Catharine; Vermont, 1873 ***5900.10*** *p527*
McVey, Daniel; Vermont, 1830-1888 ***5900.10*** *p538*
McVey, James; New York, 1840 ***8197.10*** *p182*
McVey, John; Boston, 1832 ***8197.10*** *p126*
McVey, John; Boston, 1835 ***8197.10*** *p120*
McVey, Patrick; New York, 1834-1838 ***8197.10*** *p120*
McVey, Patrick; New York, 1838 ***8197.10*** *p126*
McVey, Patrick 64; Vermont, 1840 ***5900.10*** *p148*
McVicar, Archibald; Jamaica, 1763 ***1640.13*** *p92*
McVicar, Barnabas 22; Virginia, 1775 ***1220.25*** *p110*
McVicar, Christina 61; Ontario, 1871 ***1823.28*** *p71*
McVicar, Marjory; Kingston, Jamaica, 1827 ***1640.13*** *p93*
McVicars, Christie; Savannah, Georgia, 1804 ***1640.10*** *p147*
McVicer, Adam 53; Ontario, 1871 ***1823.15*** *p186*
McVickar, James; New York, 1802 ***8197.10*** *p23*
McVied, James 62; Ontario, 1871 ***1823.15*** *p186*
McVittie, Simon 62; Ontario, 1871 ***1823.15*** *p186*
McVittie, Simon, Jr. 37; Ontario, 1871 ***1823.15*** *p186*
McWade, James 30; Ontario, 1871 ***1823.15*** *p186*
McWain, Jennie R.; Vermont, 1852-1910 ***5900.10*** *p308*
McWhan, Thomas; New Orleans, 1848 ***1640.10*** *p148*
McWhannel, Thomas Douglas; America, 1877 ***1640.13*** *p93*

McWhiney, Andrew 33; Ontario, 1871 *1823.15 p186*
McWhiney, John 55; Ontario, 1871 *1823.15 p186*
McWhinney, A.; Quebec, 1856 *9196.15 p8*
McWhinnie, Peter; New York, 1834 *8197.10 p74*
McWhirk, Felix; Vermont, 1866-1929 *5900.10 p277*
McWhirk, Samuel; Vermont, 1857-1930 *5900.10 p277*
McWhirter, Thomas; New York, 1833 *8197.10 p257*
McWhirter, William 45; Ontario, 1871 *1823.28 p71*
McWhorter, . . .; South Carolina, 1750-1770 *4628.40 p98*
McWhorter, Alexander; New York, 1821 *8197.10 p254*
McWhorter, Alexander; New York, 1826 *8197.10 p334*
McWillam, John 70; Ontario, 1871 *1823.15 p186*
McWillam, Margret 68; Ontario, 1871 *1823.15 p186*
McWilliam, Bridget Millen; Vermont, 1894 *5900.10 p179*
McWilliam, Helen; Ontario, 1887 *1640.13 p93*
McWilliam, Hugh 65; Ontario, 1871 *1823.15 p186*
McWilliam, John; Grenada, 1826 *1640.13 p93*
McWilliam, William 33; Ontario, 1871 *1823.22 p109*
McWilliams, Andrew 20; Vermont, 1848 *5900.10 p156*
McWilliams, David; New York, 1837 *8197.10 p97*
McWilliams, Elizabeth; Vermont, 1830-1877 *5900.10 p163*
McWilliams, Hugh 33; Vermont, 1870 *5900.10 p156*
McWilliams, Isabelle 85; Vermont, 1905 *5900.10 p313*
McWilliams, James; New York, 1839 *8197.10 p257*
McWilliams, John 40; Ontario, 1861 *2896.25 p9*
McWilliams, John E.; Vermont, n.d. *5900.10 p156*
McWilliams, Joseph; Vermont, n.d. *5900.10 p156*
McWilliams, M. E. 12; Ontario, 1861 *2896.25 p9*
McWilliams, Margaret 11 months; Vermont, n.d. *5900.10 p156*
McWilliams, Mary 73; Vermont, 1882 *5900.10 p156*
McWilliams, Mary Quinn 51; Vermont, 1871 *5900.10 p600*
McWilliams, Mathew 44; Vermont, 1847 *5900.10 p156*
McWilliams, Minnie 73; Vermont, 1882 *5900.10 p156*
McWilliams, Patrick 77; Vermont, 1872 *5900.10 p156*
Mdigan, Simon 50; Ontario, 1871 *1823.28 p71*
Meacham, Alexander 17; Ontario, 1861 *2896.25 p36*
Meacham, Ann E. 22; Ontario, 1861 *2896.25 p36*
Meacham, Harriet 9; Ontario, 1861 *2896.25 p36*
Meacham, James H. 12; Ontario, 1861 *2896.25 p36*
Meacham, S. E. 44; Ontario, 1861 *2896.25 p36*
Meacham, Sophia E. 24; Ontario, 1861 *2896.25 p36*
Meacham, Thomas 14; Ontario, 1861 *2896.25 p36*
Meacham, Walter 20; Ontario, 1861 *2896.25 p36*
Meacher, Henry; New York, 1834 *8197.10 p73*
Mead, Alice A. 20; Vermont, 1876 *5900.10 p283*
Mead, Catherine; Vermont, 1819-1899 *5900.10 p165*
Mead, Henry; New York, 1827 *8197.10 p340*
Mead, James 27; Maryland, 1775 *1220.25 p99*
Mead, John 17; Virginia, 1774 *1220.25 p92*
Mead, John 39; Philadelphia, 1774 *1220.25 p66*
Mead, Joseph 37; Maryland, 1774 *1220.25 p78*
Mead, Sanders; Virginia, 1665-1666 *6212.30 p21*
Mead, William; New York, 1827 *8197.10 p339*
Mead, William 15; Baltimore, 1775 *1220.25 p117*
Meade, Wm 22; Washington, 1915 *9196.1 p67*
Meadle, Godfrew 54; Ontario, 1871 *1823.15 p186*
Meadows, James 52; Ontario, 1871 *1823.22 p110*
Meager, Thomas B.; Pennsylvania, 1818-1836 *6058.10 p12*
Meagher, Bridget; Vermont, 1837-1910 *5900.10 p581*
Meagher, Bridget Harney 98; Vermont, 1910 *5900.10 p253*
Meagher, Bridget Hennebery; Vermont, 1830-1892 *5900.10 p352*
Meagher, Catherine; Vermont, 1858-1932 *5900.10 p352*
Meagher, Catherine; Vermont, 1871-1965 *5900.10 p166*
Meagher, Edward; Vermont, 1868-1894 *5900.10 p352*
Meagher, James; Vermont, 1873-1926 *5900.10 p352*
Meagher, Jane Ryan; Vermont, 1853-1932 *5900.10 p249*
Meagher, John 23; Vermont, 1880 *5900.10 p166*
Meagher, John Henry; Vermont, 1859-1892 *5900.10 p352*
Meagher, Margaret; Vermont, 1865-1939 *5900.10 p352*
Meagher, Martin 82; Vermont, 1933 *5900.10 p166*
Meagher, Mary; Vermont, 1854-1913 *5900.10 p352*
Meagher, Mary 75; Vermont, 1907 *5900.10 p166*
Meagher, Michael; Vermont, 1849-1918 *5900.10 p249*
Meagher, Michael 84; Vermont, 1893 *5900.10 p253*
Meagher, Patrick; Vermont, 1858-1929 *5900.10 p352*
Meagher, Philip 32; Vermont, 1882 *5900.10 p166*
Meagher, Richard; Vermont, 1867-1933 *5900.10 p352*
Meagher, Thomas 75; Vermont, 1884 *5900.10 p166*
Meagher, Thomas, Jr. 24; Vermont, 1879 *5900.10 p166*
Meagher, William; Vermont, 1821-1906 *5900.10 p352*
Meagher, William; Vermont, 1865-1921 *5900.10 p352*
Meaka, John; Maryland, 1679 *2524.55 p148*
Meaker, Travy; Maryland, 1678 *2524.55 p148*
Meaker, Tready; Maryland, 1679 *2524.55 p148*
Meakes, Guy; Maryland, 1662 *2524.55 p149*
Meakin, George; New York, 1840 *8197.10 p180*
Meakins, Samuel 29; Maryland, 1774 *1220.25 p41*
Meakins, William; Maryland, 1671 *2524.55 p149*
Meaks, John; Maryland, 1662 *2524.55 p149*
Mealey, Martin 25; Virginia, 1774 *1220.25 p93*
Mealnek, Annie; Maryland, 1910 *3259.35 p39*
Mean, Mr.; Quebec, 1857 *9196.15 p15*
Mean, Hopkin; Maryland, 1681 *2524.55 p149*
Means, Hugh; Pennsylvania, 1777 *4629.10 p7*
Means, Thomas; New York, 1838 *8197.10 p124*
Meany, Mr.; Vermont, 1871 *5900.10 p346*
Meany, Anastasia 40; Vermont, 1880 *5900.10 p466*
Meany, Bridget Kelty 32; Vermont, 1871 *5900.10 p346*
Meany, John; New York, 1840 *8197.10 p265*
Meany, Michael 72; Vermont, 1900 *5900.10 p466*
Meare, John; Maryland, 1658 *2524.55 p149*
Meares, Ann; Virginia, 1677 *6212.30 p53*
Meares, Elizabeth *SEE* Meares, John
Meares, Elizabeth *SEE* Meares, William
Meares, John *SEE* Meares, Thomas
Meares, John; Maryland, 1660 *2524.55 p149*
Meares, John; Maryland, 1682 *2524.55 p149*
Wife: Mary
Daughter: Elizabeth
Meares, Margarett *SEE* Meares, Thomas
Meares, Mary *SEE* Meares, John
Meares, Mary; Maryland, 1681 *2524.55 p149*
Meares, Morris; Virginia, 1666-1667 *6212.30 p34*
Meares, Thomas *SEE* Meares, Thomas
Meares, Thomas; Maryland, 1659 *2524.55 p149*
Wife: Margarett
Son: John
Son: Thomas
Meares, Thomas; Maryland, 1672 *2524.55 p149*
Wife: Margarett
Son: Thomas
Son: John
Meares, William; Maryland, 1665 *2524.55 p149*
Wife: Elizabeth
Mearns, Andrew; Savannah, Georgia, 1820 *1640.10 p152*
Mears, John; Pittsburgh, 1818 *1224.3 p51*
Mears, Richard 50; Ontario, 1871 *1823.28 p71*
Mears, Walter Hunter; Baton Rouge, Louisiana, 1839 *1224.3 p51*
Mears, William; Pittsburgh, 1828 *1224.3 p51*
Mease, Edward; Pensacola, Florida, 1781 *1224.2 p78*
Mease, James; Pennsylvania, 1777 *4629.10 p7*
Mease, James; Pennsylvania, 1786 *4629.10 p55*
Mease, John; Pennsylvania, 1777 *4629.10 p8*
Mease, Matthew; Pennsylvania, 1781 *4629.10 p42*
Meath, Henry; New York, 1807 *8197.10 p45*
Meave, Fort; Maryland, 1665 *2524.55 p149*
Mecarte, Darby; Virginia, 1703-1704 *6212.30 p63*
Mechell, Thomas; Maryland, 1661 *2524.55 p149*
Mechin, Rene; New York, 1840 *8197.10 p179*
Mechlinski, Adam J.; Maryland, 1910 *3259.35 p39*
Mechlinski, Zacheuer; Maryland, 1910 *3259.35 p39*
Mechtel, Barbara; Cayenne, 1764 *2856.30 p294*
Mecker, Johann; Port uncertain, 1771 *2856.30 p294*
Mecker, Johann; Port uncertain, 1773 *2856.30 p294*
MeCrow, John; Virginia, 1658 *1224.1 p38*
Mecum, Martha; Virginia, 1667-1668 *6212.30 p39*
Medard, Catharina; America, 1753 *2856.30 p294*
Medard, Catharina; America, 1758 *2856.30 p294*
Medard, Catharina; America, 1769 *2856.30 p294*
Medard, Elisabeth; Port uncertain, 1700-1799 *2856.30 p294*
Medard, Karl; America, 1753 *2856.30 p294*
Medard, Karl; America, 1758 *2856.30 p294*
Medard, Karl; America, 1769 *2856.30 p294*
Medard, Valentin; America, 1753 *2856.30 p294*
Medard, Valentin; America, 1758 *2856.30 p294*
Medard, Valentin; America, 1769 *2856.30 p294*
Medborough, Elizabeth; Maryland, 1682 *2524.55 p149*
Medborough, John; Maryland, 1658 *2524.55 p149*
Medcalf, Henry; New York, 1806 *8197.10 p32*
Medcalf, William 64; Ontario, 1871 *1823.22 p110*
Medcalfe, Jno; Virginia, 1671-1672 *6212.30 p47*
Medcalfe, John; Maryland, 1673 *2524.55 p18*
Medd, Henry 49; Ontario, 1871 *1823.15 p186*
Medd, Robert 38; Ontario, 1871 *1823.15 p186*
Meder, Leonard; America, 1765 *2856.30 p294*
Meder, Leonard; Canada, 1752 *2856.30 p294*
Meder, Ulrich; America, 1752 *2856.30 p294*
With wife & 2 children
Meder, Ulrich; Canada, 1752 *2856.30 p294*
With wife & 2 children
Medert, Mathias; Port uncertain, 1786 *2856.30 p294*
Medget, Joseph 16; Philadelphia, 1774 *1220.25 p81*
Medhurst, Thomas; Virginia, 1713 *1224.2 p78*
Mediecki, Simon; Maryland, 1910 *3259.35 p39*
Medland, Jane; New York, New York, 1856 *1224.3 p23*
Medlar, Mary; Vermont, 1855-1942 *5900.10 p340*
Medlicott, Edmund; Charles Town, South Carolina, 1717 *1224.2 p78*
Medly, John; Maryland, 1641-1647 *2524.55 p149*
With wife
Medston, John; Maryland, 1656 *2524.55 p149*
Medway, Elizabeth 8 *SEE* Medway, Robert
Medway, Lydia 5 *SEE* Medway, Robert
Medway, Lydia 33 *SEE* Medway, Robert
Medway, Robert 2 *SEE* Medway, Robert
Medway, Robert 35; Norfolk, Virginia, 1774 *1220.25 p19*
Wife: Lydia 33
Child: Lydia 5
Child: Robert 2
Child: Elizabeth 8
Child: Susanna 10
Medway, Susanna 10 *SEE* Medway, Robert
Mee, Ann; Vermont, 1851-1930 *5900.10 p334*
Mee, Catherine *SEE* Mee, George
Mee, Edward James; Philadelphia, 1848 *1224.3 p51*
Mee, Elizabeth; Vermont, 1852-1948 *5900.10 p332*
Mee, George; Maryland, 1651 *2524.55 p149*
Wife: Catherine
Stepchild: John
Mee, George 27; Ontario, 1871 *1823.15 p186*
Mee, John *SEE* Mee, George
Mee, John; Vermont, 1814-1900 *5900.10 p334*
Mee, John G.; Vermont, 1841-1893 *5900.10 p339*
Mee, Joseph 32; Ontario, 1871 *1823.15 p186*
Mee, Luke; Vermont, 1818-1893 *5900.10 p340*
Mee, Margaret; Vermont, 1854-1935 *5900.10 p340*
Mee, Martin; Vermont, 1853-1912 *5900.10 p334*
Mee, Mary; Vermont, 1848-1866 *5900.10 p349*
Mee, Mary A. Hogan; Vermont, 1841-1903 *5900.10 p339*
Mee, Mary Canty; Vermont, 1863-1916 *5900.10 p334*
Mee, Mary Havey; Vermont, 1816-1902 *5900.10 p334*
Mee, Thomas; New York, 1828-1832 *8197.10 p304*
Mee, William 24; Baltimore, 1775 *1220.25 p118*
Mee, Winefred Fallan; Vermont, 1817-1896 *5900.10 p340*
Meech, John; Maryland, 1664 *2524.55 p149*
Meech, John 17; Philadelphia, 1774 *1220.25 p80*
Meech, Thomas; Maryland, 1663 *2524.55 p149*
Meeds, John; Maryland, 1656 *2524.55 p149*
Meegin, Thomas; Virginia, 1703-1704 *6212.30 p63*
Meehan, Ann Moylan; Vermont, n.d. *5900.10 p558*
Meehan, Anne Fitzgerald; Vermont, 1822-1903 *5900.10 p227*
Meehan, Betsey Leonard 83; Vermont, 1893 *5900.10 p66*
Meehan, Bridget 68; Vermont, 1879 *5900.10 p314*
Meehan, Bridget 74; Vermont, 1905 *5900.10 p465*
Meehan, Bridget Gorman; Vermont, 1856-1937 *5900.10 p461*
Meehan, Cornelius; Vermont, 1815-1898 *5900.10 p382*
Meehan, Edward 88; Vermont, 1903 *5900.10 p130*
Meehan, Elizabeth; Vermont, 1857-1889 *5900.10 p136*
Meehan, Francis; New York, 1837 *8197.10 p98*
Meehan, Honora 55; Vermont, 1875 *5900.10 p382*
Meehan, James; New York, 1834 *8197.10 p73*
Meehan, James 84; Vermont, 1913 *5900.10 p291*
Meehan, Jane 78; Vermont, 1888 *5900.10 p66*
Meehan, John; New York, 1837 *8197.10 p99*
Meehan, John; Vermont, 1839-1915 *5900.10 p558*
Meehan, Kate; Vermont, 1842-1920 *5900.10 p464*
Meehan, Katherine; Vermont, 1836-1914 *5900.10 p357*
Meehan, Margaret; Vermont, 1837-1918 *5900.10 p93*
Meehan, Margaret 35; Vermont, 1869 *5900.10 p335*
Meehan, Margaret 68; Vermont, 1901 *5900.10 p66*
Meehan, Martin; Vermont, 1835-1893 *5900.10 p303*
Meehan, Mary; Vermont, 1820-1911 *5900.10 p382*
Meehan, Mary 60; Vermont, 1864 *5900.10 p571*
Meehan, Mary A. Moylan 27; Vermont, 1884 *5900.10 p561*
Meehan, Mary Butler; Vermont, 1860-1940 *5900.10 p126*
Meehan, Mary Maloney; Vermont, 1834-1911 *5900.10 p303*
Meehan, Michael; Vermont, 1858-1919 *5900.10 p126*
Meehan, Michael 72; Ontario, 1871 *1823.22 p110*
Meehan, Patrick 50; Ontario, 1871 *1823.22 p110*
Meehan, Patrick 81; Vermont, 1885 *5900.10 p66*
Meehan, Patrick J.; Vermont, 1849-1918 *5900.10 p461*
Meehan, Thomas; New York, 1823 *8197.10 p262*
Meehan, William; Vermont, 1820-1898 *5900.10 p227*
Meehen, Bridget; Vermont, 1874 *5900.10 p63*
Meek, Eduard; New York, 1802 *8197.10 p23*
Meeke, James; Maryland, 1681 *2524.55 p149*
Meeken, Michael 60; Ontario, 1871 *1823.28 p71*
Meekes, John; Maryland, 1662 *2524.55 p149*
Meekes, John; Maryland, 1662 *2524.55 p150*
Meekes, John; Virginia, 1674 *6212.30 p52*
Meekes, William; New York, 1839 *8197.10 p141*

Meekham, Samuel 15; Philadelphia, 1774 ***1220.25*** *p80*
Meekin, Andrew; Maryland, 1673 ***2524.55*** *p150*
Meekins, Richard; Maryland, 1676 ***2524.55*** *p150*
Meekins, William; Maryland, 1671 ***2524.55*** *p150*
Meeks, John; Maryland, 1662 ***2524.55*** *p150*
Meeks, Thomas; New York, 1802 ***8197.10*** *p22*
Meelles, Thomas; Maryland, 1657 ***2524.55*** *p150*
Meenan, Daniel; New York, 1836 ***8197.10*** *p79*
Meerbrei, Adam; America, 1819 ***2856.30*** *p294*
Meeres, Hannah; Maryland, 1659 ***2524.55*** *p143*
Meeres, Hugh; Virginia, 1665 ***6212.30*** *p17*
Meeres, Mary; Virginia, 1671-1672 ***6212.30*** *p48*
Meeres, Rowland; Virginia, 1666 ***6212.30*** *p25*
Meeres, Stephen; Boston, 1689 ***1224.1*** *p39*
Meers, Anne; Virginia, 1684-1685 ***6212.30*** *p57*
Meers, Anne 85; Vermont, 1905 ***5900.10*** *p249*
Meers, Dennis; Vermont, 1871 ***5900.10*** *p249*
Meers, Hannah; Maryland, 1658 ***2524.55*** *p150*
Meers, Rowland; Virginia, 1667 ***6212.30*** *p36*
Meerstetter, Jacob; Port uncertain, 1783 ***2856.30*** *p294*
Meert, Joseph Michael; New York, 1822 ***8197.10*** *p260*
Mees, Heinrich; Port uncertain, 1724 ***2856.30*** *p294*
Mees, Jakob; America, 1752 ***2856.30*** *p282*
Mees, Jakob; Port uncertain, 1746 ***2856.30*** *p294*
Meet, Fanny; Maryland, 1910 ***3259.35*** *p39*
Meetcalf, Lewis 35; Ontario, 1871 ***1823.15*** *p186*
Meetcalf, Robert 38; Ontario, 1871 ***1823.15*** *p186*
Meets, Thomas; Maryland, 1657 ***2524.55*** *p150*
Mefert, Adam; Port uncertain, 1783 ***2856.30*** *p295*
Megan, Samuel 50; Ontario, 1871 ***1823.15*** *p186*
Megar, Patrick; New York, 1836 ***8197.10*** *p263*
Megar, Philip; Pennsylvania, 1777 ***4629.10*** *p10*
Megarry, Annie 22; Vermont, 1834 ***5900.10*** *p607*
Megee, Ammon 73; Vermont, 1868 ***5900.10*** *p519*
Megee, Dolly A.; Vermont, 1818-1893 ***5900.10*** *p282*
Megee, Elisha; Vermont, n.d. ***5900.10*** *p519*
Megee, George 74; Ontario, 1871 ***1823.15*** *p186*
Megee, Mary 25; Ontario, 1871 ***1823.15*** *p186*
Megettegen, James; Pennsylvania, 1777 ***4629.10*** *p26*
Meggison, William D. 37; Ontario, 1871 ***1823.28*** *p71*
Meghan, Henry; New York, 1827 ***8197.10*** *p341*
Megiberen, Ann 40; Ontario, 1861 ***2896.27*** *p55*
Megiberen, Anne 6; Ontario, 1861 ***2896.27*** *p55*
Megiberen, Catherine 10; Ontario, 1861 ***2896.27*** *p55*
Megiberen, Flere 5; Ontario, 1861 ***2896.27*** *p55*
Megiberen, John 45; Ontario, 1861 ***2896.27*** *p55*
Megiberen, Margaret 8; Ontario, 1861 ***2896.27*** *p55*
Megiberen, Mary 14; Ontario, 1861 ***2896.27*** *p55*
Megiberen, Teressa 3; Ontario, 1861 ***2896.27*** *p55*
Megintes, James 32; Ontario, 1861 ***2896.25*** *p65*
Meglynn, Helen Spears 62; Vermont, 1890 ***5900.10*** *p533*
Megone, Mr.; Quebec, 1857 ***9196.15*** *p13*
Megorock, Hugh; Maryland, 1663 ***2524.55*** *p150*
Megram, Edward; New York, 1832 ***8197.10*** *p369*
Megson, Robert; New York, 1807 ***8197.10*** *p328*
Megt, Anthony; New York, 1837 ***8197.10*** *p99*
Megwonnubbe, Andrew 40; Ontario, 1871 ***1823.28*** *p71*
Mehan, Charles; New York, 1840 ***8197.10*** *p179*
Mehan, Edward 3; Vermont, 1852 ***5900.10*** *p319*
Mehan, Edward 50; Vermont, 1885 ***5900.10*** *p474*
Mehan, Lizzie 18; Vermont, 1862 ***5900.10*** *p66*
Mehan, Michael 67; Vermont, 1847 ***5900.10*** *p319*
Mehan, Thomas 32; Ontario, 1871 ***1823.22*** *p110*
Mehe, Maria Barbara; America, 1737 ***2856.30*** *p295*
Mehegan, John; New York, 1840 ***8197.10*** *p301*
Mehl, Justice; Pennsylvania, 1831 ***6058.10*** *p10*
Mehl, Margarete; Port uncertain, 1761 ***2856.30*** *p295*
Mehler, John 25; Kansas, 1910 ***9079.10*** *p44*
Mehler, Philipp; Port uncertain, 1776 ***2856.30*** *p295*
Meiblo, James; Georgia, 1698 ***1640.13*** *p75*
Meickhart, Peter; Mississippi, 1724 ***2856.30*** *p295*
With family
Meidervriski, Joseph; Maryland, 1910 ***3259.35*** *p39*
Meidinger, Jacob 44; Ontario, 1871 ***1823.15*** *p186*
Meier, A. C.; Port uncertain, 1786 ***2856.30*** *p295*
Meier, Anna 15; Kansas, 1905-1910 ***9079.10*** *p34*
Meier, Casper; New York, 1803 ***8197.10*** *p14*
Meier, Cathie 17; Kansas, 1905-1910 ***9079.10*** *p34*
Meier, Elizabeth 29; Kansas, 1905-1910 ***9079.10*** *p35*
Meier, Fredrick 18; Kansas, 1898-1910 ***9079.10*** *p41*
Meier, Fredrick 45; Kansas, 1898-1910 ***9079.10*** *p41*
Meier, George 25; Kansas, 1905-1910 ***9079.10*** *p34*
Meier, George 54; Kansas, 1905-1910 ***9079.10*** *p34*
Meier, Gotfred 5; Kansas, 1905-1910 ***9079.10*** *p34*
Meier, Gotfred 10; Kansas, 1905-1910 ***9079.10*** *p34*
Meier, Henry 36; Ontario, 1871 ***1823.15*** *p186*
Meier, Jacob 32; Kansas, 1905-1910 ***9079.10*** *p35*
Meier, John Hardenbergh; New York, 1820 ***1224.3*** *p52*
Meier, Mary 7; Kansas, 1905-1910 ***9079.10*** *p35*
Meier, Mary 16; Kansas, 1898-1910 ***9079.10*** *p41*
Meier, Mary 32; Kansas, 1903-1910 ***9079.10*** *p41*
Meier, Mary C. 52; Kansas, 1905-1910 ***9079.10*** *p34*
Meier, Mollie 23; Kansas, 1905-1910 ***9079.10*** *p34*
Meier, Philipp; Port uncertain, 1790 ***2856.30*** *p295*
Meier, Rachel; New York, 1820 ***1224.3*** *p52*
Meier, Sebastian; Port uncertain, 1766 ***2856.30*** *p295*
Meighan, Andrew; New York, 1807 ***8197.10*** *p325*
Meighan, Cathrine 62; Vermont, 1869 ***5900.10*** *p233*
Meighan, Francis; New York, 1837 ***8197.10*** *p100*
Meighan, Philip; New York, 1840 ***8197.10*** *p384*
Meighan, Sarah; Vermont, 1819-1886 ***5900.10*** *p342*
Meigher, Josephine; Vermont, 1865-1949 ***5900.10*** *p195*
Meik, William; Georgia, 1699 ***1640.13*** *p75*
Meikle, Agnes 41; Ontario, 1871 ***1823.28*** *p71*
Meikle, Isabella; Canada, 1892 ***1640.13*** *p76*
Meiklejohn, Thomas; Georgia, 1700 ***1640.13*** *p75*
Mein, Robert; New York, 1888 ***1640.13*** *p75*
Meinel, George; New York, 1798 ***8197.10*** *p9*
Meinhard, Johann; Port uncertain, 1768 ***2856.30*** *p295*
Meinhard, Johann Niklas; America, 1763 ***2856.30*** *p295*
Meinhard, Johann Peter; America, 1763 ***2856.30*** *p295*
Meinhard, Maria Elisabeth; Port uncertain, 1791 ***2856.30*** *p295*
Meinicke, Henry; Maryland, 1910 ***3259.35*** *p39*
Meintzer, Anna Catharina; Port uncertain, 1750 ***2856.30*** *p295*
Meintzer, Johann Georg; America, 1736 ***2856.30*** *p295*
Meintzer, Johann Georg; America, 1736 ***2856.30*** *p295*
With family
Meintzer, Johann Georg; America, 1737 ***2856.30*** *p295*
Meinzer, Ernst Friedrich; Port uncertain, 1755 ***2856.30*** *p295*
With wife
Meinzer, Johann; America, 1738 ***2856.30*** *p295*
Meinzer, Johann, Sr.; America, 1751 ***2856.30*** *p295*
Meinzer, Johann, Sr.; Port uncertain, 1751 ***2856.30*** *p295*
Meinzer, Johann, Jr.; America, 1751 ***2856.30*** *p295*
Meinzer, Johann, Jr.; America, 1751 ***2856.30*** *p295*
With wife & 2 children
Meinzer, Johann, Jr.; Port uncertain, 1751 ***2856.30*** *p295*
Meinzer, Lorenz, Sr.; Port uncertain, 1737 ***2856.30*** *p295*
Meinzer, Martin; America, 1751 ***2856.30*** *p295*
Meinzer, Martin; America, 1751 ***2856.30*** *p295*
With wife & 2 children
Meinzer, Peter; Port uncertain, 1737 ***2856.30*** *p295*
Meir, George Jacob 48; Kansas, 1910 ***9079.10*** *p42*
Meir, Jacob 22; Kansas, 1910 ***9079.10*** *p42*
Meir, Katie 16; Kansas, 1910 ***9079.10*** *p42*
Meir, Katie 47; Kansas, 1910 ***9079.10*** *p42*
Meir, Mary 13; Kansas, 1910 ***9079.10*** *p42*
Meircraft, John; Maryland, 1666 ***2524.55*** *p155*
Meisch, Maria Gertrud; Port uncertain, 1770 ***2856.30*** *p295*
Meiss, Angelika; America, 1728 ***2856.30*** *p295*
Meiss, Angelika; Port uncertain, 1728 ***2856.30*** *p295*
Meiss, Maria Kunigunda; America, 1728 ***2856.30*** *p295*
Meiss, Maria Kunigunda; Port uncertain, 1728 ***2856.30*** *p295*
Meiss, Susanna Cath.; Port uncertain, 1769 ***2856.30*** *p295*
Meister, Mrs. Jakob; Port uncertain, 1764 ***2856.30*** *p296*
With son
Meister, Philipp Jacob; Port uncertain, 1755 ***2856.30*** *p295*
Meister, Veit; America, 1751 ***2856.30*** *p295*
Meister, Veit; America, 1765 ***2856.30*** *p295*
Meistner, Friedr. Gottlieb; Port uncertain, 1771 ***2856.30*** *p296*
With wife
Meitzel, Andreas; America, 1720 ***2856.30*** *p296*
Meixel, Anton; Port uncertain, 1796 ***2856.30*** *p296*
Meixel, Ignaz; Port uncertain, 1792 ***2856.30*** *p296*
Mejake, Etienne 34; Ontario, 1871 ***1823.28*** *p71*
Meka, John; Maryland, 1679 ***2524.55*** *p148*
Mekemson, James; Pennsylvania, 1777 ***4629.10*** *p7*
Mel, John; New York, 1815-1834 ***8197.10*** *p304*
Mel, John; New York, 1833 ***8197.10*** *p263*
Melady, Bridget 75; Vermont, 1912 ***5900.10*** *p565*
Melady, Bridget 78; Vermont, 1864 ***5900.10*** *p72*
Melady, Thomas 84; Vermont, 1916 ***5900.10*** *p565*
Melaney, William 17; Vermont, 1864 ***5900.10*** *p58*
Melauen, Mary 54; Vermont, 1876 ***5900.10*** *p51*
Melaven, Alice Howrigan; Vermont, 1849-1921 ***5900.10*** *p324*
Melaven, Eugene E.; Vermont, 1857-1888 ***5900.10*** *p324*
Melaven, Frances M.; Vermont, 1869-1893 ***5900.10*** *p324*
Melaven, James H.; Vermont, 1832-1917 ***5900.10*** *p324*
Melch, Anton; America, 1764 ***2856.30*** *p296*
Melch, Anton; Canada, 1764 ***2856.30*** *p296*
Melcher, Andreas; Port uncertain, 1768 ***2856.30*** *p296*
Melcher, Johann; Port uncertain, 1762 ***2856.30*** *p296*
Melcher, Johann Georg; Port uncertain, 1768 ***2856.30*** *p296*
Melcher, Josef; America, 1764 ***2856.30*** *p296*
Melcher, Maria; Port uncertain, 1680 ***2856.30*** *p296*
Melcher, Maria; Port uncertain, 1726 ***2856.30*** *p296*
Melchior, Mr.; Port uncertain, 1764 ***2856.30*** *p233*
Melchior, Catharina; Port uncertain, 1738 ***2856.30*** *p296*
Melchiore, F. 33; Seattle, 1912 ***9196.1*** *p20*
Melczyn, Robert; Maryland, 1910 ***3259.35*** *p39*
Meldon, Patrick 39; Vermont, 1864 ***5900.10*** *p430*
Meldrew, John 46; Ontario, 1871 ***1823.15*** *p186*
Meldrin, James; New York, 1807 ***8197.10*** *p45*
Meldrum, Miss; Georgia, 1804 ***1640.10*** *p152*
Meldrum, Rev.; Portland, Maine, 1857 ***9196.15*** *p12*
Meldrum, Andrew 12; Ontario, 1871 ***1823.15*** *p186*
Meldrum, Christina 11; Ontario, 1871 ***1823.15*** *p186*
Meldrum, George 15; Ontario, 1871 ***1823.15*** *p186*
Meldrun, Wm R.; Portland, Maine, 1858 ***9196.15*** *p28*
Meleady, Catherine Battles 45; Vermont, 1899 ***5900.10*** *p562*
Meleady, Michael; Vermont, 1848-1932 ***5900.10*** *p562*
Melenko, Steaf; Maryland, 1910 ***3259.35*** *p39*
Melerski, Anna; Maryland, 1910 ***3259.35*** *p39*
Meletta, Charles Conrad; New York, 1840 ***8197.10*** *p264*
Melhaff, Wilhelm; America, 1764 ***2856.30*** *p296*
Melinder, C. 25; Alaska, 1913 ***9196.1*** *p39*
Melinder, C. 25; Yukon, 1913 ***9196.1*** *p39*
Melinder, V. 26; Alaska, 1913 ***9196.1*** *p39*
Melinder, V. 26; Yukon, 1913 ***9196.1*** *p39*
Mell, Samuel; Maryland, 1681 ***2524.55*** *p150*
Mellahane, Durman; Maryland, 1654 ***2524.55*** *p209*
Mellan, Bernard 66; Ontario, 1871 ***1823.28*** *p71*
Mellan, John 67; Vermont, 1846 ***5900.10*** *p519*
Melledy, Ann 70; Vermont, 1898 ***5900.10*** *p190*
Melledy, Edward 84; Vermont, 1870-1879 ***5900.10*** *p164*
Mellen, Ann 40; Vermont, 1867 ***5900.10*** *p232*
Mellen, Bridget 75; Vermont, 1866 ***5900.10*** *p234*
Mellendy, Mary 77; Vermont, 1902 ***5900.10*** *p188*
Melleous, George; New York, 1829 ***8197.10*** *p303*
Meller, John; Maryland, 1664 ***2524.55*** *p76*
Mellers, George 21; Virginia, 1774 ***1220.25*** *p54*
Mellers, James 28; Maryland, 1774 ***1220.25*** *p54*
Mellert, Johann Georg; Port uncertain, 1784 ***2856.30*** *p296*
Melleson, James; Maryland, 1650 ***2524.55*** *p150*
Melley, John 54; Ontario, 1871 ***1823.28*** *p71*
Mellichops, Nicholas; Virginia, 1668-1669 ***6212.30*** *p40*
Mellin, David; Pennsylvania, 1777 ***4629.10*** *p24*
Mellin, Henry 41; Ontario, 1871 ***1823.15*** *p187*
Mellis, Samuel; New York, 1795 ***8197.10*** *p6*
Mellis, William; Georgia, 1811 ***1640.10*** *p152*
Mellis, William 55; Ontario, 1871 ***1823.22*** *p110*
Mellish, Lucy 35; Ontario, 1871 ***1823.15*** *p187*
Mello, John 61; Ontario, 1871 ***1823.15*** *p187*
Mellord, David; Georgia, 1775 ***1640.10*** *p152*
Mellord, Isabella; Georgia, 1775 ***1640.10*** *p152*
Mellot, Peter; Port uncertain, 1712 ***2856.30*** *p296*
Mellowes, Hannah; New England, 1651 ***1224.1*** *p53*
Melloy, Daniel; New York, 1840 ***8197.10*** *p179*
Melloy, Henry; New York, 1803 ***8197.10*** *p14*
Melody, Jane; Vermont, 1847-1904 ***5900.10*** *p167*
Meloman, Duncan 65; Ontario, 1871 ***1823.15*** *p187*
Meloniz, Frank; Maryland, 1910 ***3259.35*** *p39*
Melovich, Jaage 21; Alaska, 1908 ***9196.1*** *p37*
Melson, Elizabeth; Maryland, 1672 ***2524.55*** *p150*
Melson, John; Maryland, 1672 ***2524.55*** *p184*
Melson, William 24; Virginia, 1774 ***1220.25*** *p89*
Melter, Mr.; America, 1771 ***2856.30*** *p67*
Melter, Mr.; America, 1772 ***2856.30*** *p67*
Melton, John; Maryland, 1667 ***2524.55*** *p150*
Meltone, Chas 20; Ontario, 1871 ***1823.15*** *p187*
Melvil, James 29; Philadelphia, 1774 ***1220.25*** *p5*
Melvill, Alexander; New York, 1839 ***8197.10*** *p142*
Melvill, George S.; New York, 1834 ***8197.10*** *p71*
Melville, Andrew 56; Ontario, 1871 ***1823.28*** *p71*
Melville, Frances 50; Ontario, 1871 ***1823.28*** *p71*
Melville, John; Georgia, 1699 ***1640.13*** *p75*
Melville, John; North Dakota, 1886 ***1640.13*** *p75*
Melville, John 70; Ontario, 1871 ***1823.28*** *p71*
Melville, Suirance 50; Ontario, 1871 ***1823.15*** *p187*
Melville, William; Austin, Texas, 1735-1845 ***1640.10*** *p153*
Melville, William 56; Ontario, 1871 ***1823.22*** *p110*
Melvin, James; Savannah, Georgia, 1808 ***1640.10*** *p153*
Melvin, James J.; Vermont, 1845-1904 ***5900.10*** *p443*
Melvin, John; Montreal, 1889 ***1640.13*** *p75*
Melvin, Mary; Vermont, 1825-1906 ***5900.10*** *p395*
Memmes, Julius; Maryland, 1910 ***3259.35*** *p39*
Men, . . .; Maryland, 1668 ***2524.55*** *p150*
Men, Ann; Maryland, 1668 ***2524.55*** *p150*
With child
Menck, William; New York, 1836 ***8197.10*** *p263*
Menck, William; New York, 1838 ***8197.10*** *p124*
Menckin, Susanna Marg.; Port uncertain, 1732 ***2856.30*** *p296*
Mendel, Friedrich; Port uncertain, 1786 ***2856.30*** *p296*
Mendel, Johann; Port uncertain, 1722 ***2856.30*** *p296*
Mendel, Johann; Port uncertain, 1762 ***2856.30*** *p296*
Mendenhall, Thomas; Pennsylvania, 1777 ***4629.10*** *p24*

Mendes, Isaac; Pensacola, Florida, 1769 1224.2 p78
Mendia, Joseph; New York, 1824 8197.10 p262
Mendorfelth, John; Pennsylvania, 1777 4629.10 p24
Mendoza, J. M. 24; Alaska, 1914 9196.1 p41
Menefie, George; Virginia, 1647 1224.1 p39
Menertie, Daniel; Pennsylvania, 1777 4629.10 p11
Meney, Thomas 33; Ontario, 1871 1823.22 p110
Meng, . . .; America, 1776 2856.30 p296
Meng, Gertrud; America, 1796 2856.30 p296
With 2 children & mother
Meng, Johann Christop; America, 1728 2856.30 p296
Meng, Lorenz; America, 1739 2856.30 p296
With wife & 2 children
Meng, Lorenz; Port uncertain, 1730 2856.30 p296
Meng, William; Pennsylvania, 1778 4629.10 p34
Meng, Wollery; Pennsylvania, 1777 4629.10 p10
Mengel, Friedrich; America, 1742 2856.30 p296
Mengel, Wilhelm; America, 1753 2856.30 p296
Mengel, Wilhelm; America, 1753 2856.30 p296
With wife & children
Menges, Hieronimus; America, 1739 2856.30 p296
Menges, Maria Elisabeth; Port uncertain, 1790 2856.30 p296
Menges, Maria Margarete; Port uncertain, 1738 2856.30 p297
Menges, Ottilia; Port uncertain, 1739 2856.30 p297
Mengin, Gertrud; America, 1796 2856.30 p296
With 2 children & mother
Menik, Anna; Port uncertain, 1739 2856.30 p297
Menikin, Anna; Port uncertain, 1739 2856.30 p297
Menine, M. 35; Alaska, 1908 9196.1 p36
Menine, M. 35; Alaska, 1908 9196.1 p37
Mennard, George 21; Nova Scotia, 1774 1220.25 p136
With wife & child
Mennard, Robert 27; Nova Scotia, 1774 1220.25 p136
Menne, Michael; Port uncertain, 1741 2856.30 p297
Mennel, John 49; Ontario, 1871 1823.15 p187
Mennell, William 60; Ontario, 1871 1823.15 p187
Mennin, Anna Maria; Port uncertain, 1791 2856.30 p297
Menns, John; Virginia, 1665-1666 6212.30 p22
Mensch, Anna Margarete; Port uncertain, 1741 2856.30 p297
Mensch, Christina; Port uncertain, 1786 2856.30 p297
Mensch, Frederick Augustus; New York, 1825 8197.10 p261
Mensch, Frederick Augustus; New York, 1830 8197.10 p66
Mensch, Karl; Port uncertain, 1783 2856.30 p297
Mensch, Margarete; Port uncertain, 1738 2856.30 p297
Mensch, Maria Margarete; Port uncertain, 1791 2856.30 p297
Menschin, Christina; Port uncertain, 1786 2856.30 p297
Mentiale, Anne SEE Mentiale, Jeffery
Mentiale, Francis SEE Mentiale, Jeffery
Mentiale, Jane SEE Mentiale, Jeffery
Mentiale, Jeffery SEE Mentiale, Jeffery
Mentiale, Jeffery; Maryland, 1666 2524.55 p150
Daughter: Francis
Daughter: Anne
Daughter: Jane
Son: Randall
Son: Jeffery
Daughter: Mary
Mentiale, Mary SEE Mentiale, Jeffery
Mentiale, Randall SEE Mentiale, Jeffery
Mentin, Michael; New York, 1807 8197.10 p45
Mentony, Jakob; Port uncertain, 1783 2856.30 p297
Menzar, Henry; New York, 1838 8197.10 p124
Menzes, John; Pennsylvania, 1787 4629.10 p50
Menzies, Capt.; Quebec, 1858 9196.15 p34
Menzies, Mrs.; Quebec, 1858 9196.15 p34
Menzies, George H. 34; Ontario, 1871 1823.28 p71
Menzies, Jane 38; Ontario, 1871 1823.28 p71
Menzies, Jessie 22; Ontario, 1871 1823.15 p187
Menzies, John; Jamaica, 1768 1640.13 p75
Menzies, John 29; Ontario, 1871 1823.15 p187
Menzies, John 32; Ontario, 1871 1823.15 p187
Menzies, Ninian; Richmond, Virginia, 1780 1640.13 p75
Menzies, Robert 50; Ontario, 1871 1823.28 p71
Menzies, Sarah; New York, 1818 1224.3 p52
Menzies, W. C.; Quebec, 1857 9196.15 p13
Menzies, William 40; Ontario, 1871 1823.15 p187
Menzinger, Leonard; Port uncertain, 1751 2856.30 p297
Menzinger, Magdalena; Port uncertain, 1751 2856.30 p297
Meorry, William 50; Ontario, 1871 1823.15 p187
Merad, Marianna; Port uncertain, 1788 2856.30 p297
Mercer, Major; Portland, Maine, 1857 9196.15 p12
Mercer, A. O. 12; Ontario, 1861 2896.25 p33
Mercer, Burrandine; Virginia, 1654 1224.1 p39
Mercer, C. M. 15; Ontario, 1861 2896.25 p33
Mercer, Gabriel; Maryland, 1681 2524.55 p150
Mercer, George 22; Maryland, 1775 1220.25 p102
Mercer, James; Albany, New York, 1759 1224.2 p78
Mercer, James; New York, 1838 8197.10 p263
Mercer, James Francis; Oswego, New York, 1760 1224.2 p78
Mercer, Joana Neilson; Idaho, 1897 1640.13 p75
Mercer, John; Savannah, Georgia, 1810 1640.10 p153
Mercer, Richard; Charles Town, South Carolina, 1788 1224.2 p78
Mercer, Rowland; Virginia, 1665-1666 6212.30 p25
Mercer, Samuel; Georgia, 1738 1640.10 p153
Mercer, Sarah 33; Ontario, 1861 2896.25 p33
Merchant, Annie O'Brien; Vermont, 1849-1916 5900.10 p593
Merchant, William; Barbados, 1756 1224.2 p78
Merchant, William; Boston, 1756 1224.2 p78
Merchant, William; Maryland, 1669 2524.55 p150
Merchant, William; Vermont, 1849-1909 5900.10 p593
Merchiston, Robert; Georgia, 1698 1640.13 p75
Merch't, Martha; Maryland, 1664 2524.55 p145
Mercier, Francis; New York, 1840 8197.10 p178
Mercier, James 62; Ontario, 1871 1823.28 p71
Mercier, Thomas; America, 1759 1224.2 p78
Merck, Apollonia; America, 1752 2856.30 p297
Merckel, Peter; Pennsylvania, 1777 4629.10 p18
Merckel, Wilhelm; Port uncertain, 1784 2856.30 p297
Mercker, Christian; Port uncertain, 1757 2856.30 p297
Mercker, Franz; Port uncertain, 1771 2856.30 p297
Mercker, Maria Elisabeth; Port uncertain, 1776 2856.30 p297
Mercker, Peter; America, 1739 2856.30 p297
Mercker, Peter; Port uncertain, 1785 2856.30 p297
Merckh, Hans Georg; Port uncertain, 1740 2856.30 p297
Merckh, Peter; Port uncertain, 1760 2856.30 p297
Merckhel, David; Port uncertain, 1748 2856.30 p297
Merckher, Anna Margarete; Port uncertain, 1733 2856.30 p297
Merckher, Jakob; Port uncertain, 1757 2856.30 p297
Merckher, Maria Elisabeth; Port uncertain, 1758 2856.30 p297
Merckhin, Elisabeth; Port uncertain, 1746 2856.30 p297
Merckhin, Ursula; Port uncertain, 1722 2856.30 p297
Merckhlin, Catharina; Port uncertain, 1760 2856.30 p297
Merckler, Barbara; Port uncertain, 1759 2856.30 p297
Merckler, Christof; Port uncertain, 1742 2856.30 p297
Mercklin, Christof; Port uncertain, 1744 2856.30 p297
Mercklin, Eva; Port uncertain, 1775 2856.30 p297
Mercklin, Jacob; America, 1750 2856.30 p297
Mercklin, Jacob; America, 1750 2856.30 p298
With wife & children
Mercklin, Konrad; America, 1751 2856.30 p297
Mercklin, Konrad; Port uncertain, 1754 2856.30 p298
Mercklin, Simon; America, 1750 2856.30 p298
Mercklin, Simon; America, 1750 2856.30 p298
With wife & children
Mercy, George 28; Maryland, 1774 1220.25 p64
Merdiff, H. 40; Ontario, 1861 2896.27 p6
Mere, James 45; Ontario, 1871 1823.15 p187
Merecraft, James; Virginia, 1663 6212.30 p1
Meredith, James; Virginia, 1671-1672 6212.30 p47
Meredith, Jonathan; Pennsylvania, 1777 4629.10 p21
Meredith, Jonathan; Pennsylvania, 1779 4629.10 p40
Meredith, Love; Virginia, 1660 1224.1 p60
Meredith, Mary; Maryland, 1681 2524.55 p150
Meredith, Reese; Pennsylvania, 1777 4629.10 p21
Meredith, Samuel; Pennsylvania, 1777 4629.10 p18
Meredith, Thomas; Pennsylvania, 1777 4629.10 p23
Meredith, William; Pennsylvania, 1777 4629.10 p25
Merefield, Edward; Germantown, Pennsylvania, 1768 1224.2 p79
Meret, Charles 50; Ontario, 1871 1823.28 p71
Merett, Robert; Maryland, 1663 2524.55 p150
Merg, Heinrich; Port uncertain, 1737 2856.30 p298
Merger, Marianna; Port uncertain, 1769 2856.30 p298
Merian, Mr.; Port uncertain, 1784 2856.30 p298
With wife & children
Merian, John J.; New York, 1835 8197.10 p263
Merian, John J.; New York, 1840 8197.10 p181
Meridath, Ellinor; Virginia, 1665 6212.30 p17
Meridath, Jno; Virginia, 1665-1666 6212.30 p22
Meridath, Wm; Virginia, 1664 6212.30 p14
Merideth, Henry 56; Ontario, 1871 1823.22 p110
Meridith, Mary 76; Ontario, 1871 1823.22 p110
Merigan, Catherine 30; Ontario, 1871 1823.28 p71
Merigan, James 56; Ontario, 1871 1823.28 p71
Meriman, . . .; New England, 1656 1224.1 p39
Merin, Anna Maria; Port uncertain, 1791 2856.30 p298
Meriton, John; Maryland, 1682 2524.55 p150
Meriton, Joshua; Virginia, 1674 1224.1 p39
Merkely, George; Pennsylvania, 1776 4629.10 p53
Merker, Frederick; Pennsylvania, 1777 4629.10 p12
Merker, Georg Nikolaus; Port uncertain, 1767 2856.30 p298
Merker, Maria Magdalena; Port uncertain, 1769 2856.30 p298
Merkie, James; Maryland, 1910 3259.35 p39
Merkin, Johann Nickel; Port uncertain, 1752 2856.30 p298
Merlin, Ralph; Virginia, 1667 6212.30 p35
Mermiss, Anton A. 42; Kansas, 1876-1910 9079.10 p7
Mermiss, Brumehida 18; Kansas, 1900-1910 9079.10 p8
Mermiss, Catherine E. 38; Kansas, 1875-1910 9079.10 p7
Mermiss, Elizabeth 64; Kansas, 1896-1910 9079.10 p8
Mermiss, Linton 65; Kansas, 1896-1910 9079.10 p8
Merner, Gottlieb 39; Ontario, 1871 1823.15 p187
Mernia, Conrad 35; Kansas, 1877-1910 9079.10 p7
Mernia, Pauline 34; Kansas, 1877-1910 9079.10 p7
Merordit, Lewis; Maryland, 1676 2524.55 p150
Merraday, Susannah; Virginia, 1703-1704 6212.30 p63
Merrall, Richard; New York, 1840 8197.10 p178
Merrefield, Robt; Virginia, 1674-1675 6212.30 p53
Merrekin, Christian; Maryland, 1659 2524.55 p151
Relative: John, Sr.
Relative: William
Relative: Joshua
Relative: Mary
Relative: Hugh
Relative: John, Jr.
Merrekin, Hugh SEE Merrekin, Christian
Merrekin, John, Sr. SEE Merrekin, Christian
Merrekin, John, Jr. SEE Merrekin, Christian
Merrekin, Joshua SEE Merrekin, Christian
Merrekin, Mary SEE Merrekin, Christian
Merrekin, William SEE Merrekin, Christian
Merrer, Thomas; Virginia, 1666-1667 6212.30 p35
Merriam, Margery 47; Ontario, 1871 1823.22 p110
Merriam, Samuel 42; Ontario, 1871 1823.22 p110
Merrian, Samuel; Pennsylvania, 1785 4629.10 p44
Merriben, Joseph; Maryland, 1910 3259.35 p39
Merrichurch, Thomas; Maryland, 1671 2524.55 p151
Merrick, Dennis; Pennsylvania, 1702 1224.2 p79
Merrick, Patrick; New York, 1828-1831 8197.10 p309
Merrick, Philip M.; New York, 1834 8197.10 p372
Merrick, Thomas 21; Baltimore, 1775 1220.25 p118
Merrick, Thomas 22; Maryland, 1775 1220.25 p103
Merriday, Love; Maryland, 1661 2524.55 p74
Merrideth, Mankins 42; Ontario, 1871 1823.15 p187
Merridith, Riochard; Maryland, 1661 2524.55 p130
Merriken, Hugh; Maryland, 1698 1224.1 p39
Merrill, Mr.; Quebec, 1857 9196.15 p20
Merrill, Elizabeth; Maryland, 1682 2524.55 p151
Merrill, John 36; Maryland, 1775 1220.25 p120
Merrill, William; Maryland, 1668 2524.55 p241
Merrill, William; Maryland, 1682 2524.55 p151
Merrils, Catherine 8; Ontario, 1861 2896.27 p59
Merrils, Lovina 30; Ontario, 1861 2896.27 p59
Merrils, M. A. 10; Ontario, 1861 2896.27 p59
Merrils, P. M. 3; Ontario, 1861 2896.27 p59
Merrils, Roda A. 17; Ontario, 1861 2896.27 p59
Merriman, Michael 25; Ontario, 1871 1823.28 p71
Merriott, Midleton 20; Maryland, 1775 1220.25 p97
Merritt, Ann 20; Virginia, 1775 1220.25 p95
Merritt, Elizabeth; Maryland, 1681 2524.55 p151
Merritt, Richard; Virginia, 1692 1224.1 p39
Merruliess, Mr.; Quebec, 1857 9196.15 p26
Merry, Edward; New York, 1807 8197.10 p45
Merry, James 62; Ontario, 1871 1823.15 p187
Merry, William 75; Ontario, 1871 1823.15 p187
Merryfield, John 19; Virginia, 1774 1220.25 p56
Merryfield, John 74; Ontario, 1871 1823.22 p110
Merryfield, Robert 15; Philadelphia, 1774 1220.25 p81
Merrylees, James; Savannah, Georgia, 1790 1640.10 p153
Mersch, Elis. Catharina; Port uncertain, 1763 2856.30 p319
Mersch, Jost; Port uncertain, 1751 2856.30 p298
With wife & 2 children
Mersch, Maria Sophia; Port uncertain, 1791 2856.30 p298
Mersch, Peter; Port uncertain, 1774 2856.30 p298
Merschheimer, Henrich; America, 1764 2856.30 p298
Merschheimer, Henrich; Port uncertain, 1764 2856.30 p298
Merssey, William 23; Virginia, 1773 1220.25 p29
Merston, John; Georgia, 1699 1640.13 p75
Mertens, C. Schwarz SEE Mertens, Johann
Mertens, Catharina Schwarz; America, 1742 2856.30 p418
Mertens, Johann; America, 1742 2856.30 p298
Wife: C. Schwarz
Mertey, Steven; Maryland, 1673 2524.55 p151
Mertin, Hans Nickel; Port uncertain, 1762 2856.30 p298
Mertov, M. 27; Alaska, 1917 9196.1 p50
Mertov, M. 27; Yukon, 1917 9196.1 p50
Mertz, Jakob; America, 1732 2856.30 p298

Mertz, Marianna; Port uncertain, 1750 ***2856.30*** *p298*
Merx, Xaver; Port uncertain, 1796 ***2856.30*** *p298*
With wife & 2 children
Merz, Anna Sabine; Port uncertain, 1783 ***2856.30*** *p298*
Merz, Johann Jakob; Port uncertain, 1778 ***2856.30*** *p298*
Merz, Niklas; America, 1744 ***2856.30*** *p298*
Merz, Philipp; America, 1749 ***2856.30*** *p298*
With wife
Merzer, George M. 45; Ontario, 1871 ***1823.15*** *p187*
Merzin, Anna Sabine; Port uncertain, 1783 ***2856.30*** *p298*
Mesersmith, John Andrew; Pennsylvania, 1779 ***4629.10*** *p35*
Meshemahkenahge, Mrs. 60; Ontario, 1871 ***1823.28*** *p71*
Mesheminonaquah, Jean Baptiste 62; Ontario, 1871 ***1823.28*** *p72*
Meshinini, Pierre 74; Ontario, 1871 ***1823.28*** *p72*
Mesick, Mary; New York, 1836 ***1224.3*** *p52*
Mesick, Peter Henry; New York, 1836 ***1224.3*** *p52*
Meskill, George 28; Ontario, 1871 ***1823.28*** *p72*
Mesklosky, Thomas; Maryland, 1910 ***3259.35*** *p39*
Messella, John; New Orleans, 1852 ***3437.14*** *p75*
Messemer, Johann Michael; America, 1749 ***2856.30*** *p299*
Messemer, Johann Michael; Port uncertain, 1749 ***2856.30*** *p299*
With wife & 4 children
Messenger, James; Virginia, 1857 ***1224.3*** *p52*
Messenger, John 12; Ontario, 1861 ***2896.28*** *p59*
Messenger, L. 18; Ontario, 1861 ***2896.25*** *p35*
Messenger, Sarah 14; Ontario, 1861 ***2896.25*** *p37*
Messenger, Sarah 46; Ontario, 1861 ***2896.25*** *p35*
Messenger, Thomas; New York, 1839 ***8197.10*** *p381*
Messenger, Thomas; Virginia, 1663 ***6212.30*** *p1*
Messer, John 45; Ontario, 1871 ***1823.15*** *p187*
Messer, Nikol; America, 1737 ***2856.30*** *p299*
Messer, William 35; Ontario, 1871 ***1823.15*** *p187*
Messerly, John; New Orleans, 1852 ***3437.14*** *p46*
Messerschmidt, Jakob; Port uncertain, 1732 ***2856.30*** *p299*
Messerschmitt, Christina; Port uncertain, 1782 ***2856.30*** *p299*
Messersmith, Henry 31; Ontario, 1871 ***1823.15*** *p187*
Messersmith, John Andrew, Jr.; Pennsylvania, 1777 ***4629.10*** *p22*
Messler, C. 40; Ontario, 1861 ***2896.26*** *p15*
Messler, C. G. 16; Ontario, 1861 ***2896.26*** *p15*
Messler, E. 16; Ontario, 1861 ***2896.26*** *p15*
Messler, J. H. 8; Ontario, 1861 ***2896.26*** *p15*
Messler, M. 36; Ontario, 1861 ***2896.26*** *p15*
Messler, Peter; Port uncertain, 1783 ***2856.30*** *p299*
Messner, Catharina; Port uncertain, 1752 ***2856.30*** *p299*
With husband
Messner, Paul; Pennsylvania, 1864 ***6058.10*** *p67*
Messnerin, Catharina; Port uncertain, 1752 ***2856.30*** *p299*
With husband
Metcalf, Miss; Quebec, 1858 ***9196.15*** *p47*
Metcalf, Mr.; Quebec, 1858 ***9196.15*** *p36*
Metcalf, Mr.; Quebec, 1858 ***9196.15*** *p45*
Metcalf, Mrs.; Quebec, 1858 ***9196.15*** *p36*
Metcalf, Mrs.; Quebec, 1858 ***9196.15*** *p47*
Metcalf, Cyrus; New York, 1819-1834 ***8197.10*** *p306*
Metcalf, Inez O.; Vermont, 1848-1919 ***5900.10*** *p598*
Metcalf, Samuel W.; New York, 1822-1834 ***8197.10*** *p306*
Metcalf, Thomas; Maryland, 1680 ***2524.55*** *p151*
Metcalf, William 16; New York, 1774 ***1220.25*** *p24*
Metcalf, William 25; Virginia, 1775 ***1220.25*** *p100*
Metcalfe, Bernard; New York, 1797 ***8197.10*** *p9*
Metcalfe, John; New York, 1840 ***8197.10*** *p180*
Metcalfe, John; Virginia, 1762 ***1224.2*** *p79*
Metcalfe, Richard; Pennsylvania, 1763 ***1224.2*** *p79*
Metcalfe, Robert; Maryland, 1666 ***2524.55*** *p151*
Metcalfe, Simon; New York, 1797 ***1224.2*** *p79*
Metford, Bulmer; Maryland, 1664 ***2524.55*** *p151*
Wife: Fortune
Son: Thomas
Metford, Fortune *SEE* Metford, Bulmer
Metford, Francis; New York, 1835 ***8197.10*** *p263*
Metford, Thomas *SEE* Metford, Bulmer
Metford, William 36; Ontario, 1871 ***1823.15*** *p187*
Metherelly, James 23; Ontario, 1871 ***1823.22*** *p110*
Methven, Charles Caithness; Jamaica, 1845 ***1640.13*** *p75*
Methwin, Paul; Virginia, 1664 ***6212.30*** *p9*
Metice, Solloman 90; Ontario, 1871 ***1823.15*** *p187*
Metoch, Wolffgang; Pennsylvania, 1787 ***4629.10*** *p55*
Metossage, Francois 55; Ontario, 1871 ***1823.28*** *p72*
Metsinger, Henry; New York, 1840 ***8197.10*** *p178*
Metsol, Sam 22; Washington, 1913 ***9196.1*** *p59*
Metter, Mrs. Haupert; Port uncertain, 1725 ***2856.30*** *p299*
With 4 children
Mettfort, Anthony; Maryland, 1665 ***2524.55*** *p151*
Mettleship, Elizabeth *SEE* Mettleship, Robert
Mettleship, Robert; Maryland, 1680 ***2524.55*** *p151*
Wife: Elizabeth
Relative: Roger, Jr.
Mettleship, Roger, Jr. *SEE* Mettleship, Robert
Metweiashi, Mrs. 58; Ontario, 1871 ***1823.28*** *p72*
Metweiashi, William 34; Ontario, 1871 ***1823.28*** *p72*
Metz, . . .; Port uncertain, 1787 ***2856.30*** *p299*
With 3 siblings
Metz, Christof; Port uncertain, 1766 ***2856.30*** *p299*
Metz, Johann Hermann; America, 1749 ***2856.30*** *p299*
Metz, Johann Hermann; America, 1749 ***2856.30*** *p299*
With family
Metz, Johann Jakob; America, 1749 ***2856.30*** *p299*
Metz, Martin; Port uncertain, 1762 ***2856.30*** *p299*
With children
Metz, Valentin; America, 1764 ***2856.30*** *p299*
Metzendorff, Henry D. A.; New York, 1837 ***8197.10*** *p100*
Metzer, Michael; New York, 1837 ***8197.10*** *p100*
Metzger, Franz; Port uncertain, 1764 ***2856.30*** *p300*
With wife & 3 children
Metzger, Georg; Port uncertain, 1764 ***2856.30*** *p299*
With family
Metzger, Georg Valentin; America, 1749 ***2856.30*** *p299*
With wife & 2 children
Metzger, Jakob; Port uncertain, 1765 ***2856.30*** *p299*
Metzger, Johann Jakob; America, 1742 ***2856.30*** *p300*
With wife & 4 children
Metzger, John Joachim; New York, 1836 ***8197.10*** *p317*
Metzger, Ludwig; America, 1742 ***2856.30*** *p299*
With wife & child
Metzger, Michael; America, 1764 ***2856.30*** *p299*
Metzger, Michael; Port uncertain, 1764 ***2856.30*** *p299*
Metzger, Philipp; Port uncertain, 1752 ***2856.30*** *p299*
Metzinger, Peter; New York, 1839 ***8197.10*** *p141*
Metzler, Georg Michael; Port uncertain, 1762 ***2856.30*** *p300*
Metzler, Georg Michael; Port uncertain, 1791 ***2856.30*** *p300*
Metzler, Mrs. J.; British Columbia, 1909 ***9196.1*** *p8*
Metzler, Mrs. J.; Fairbanks, Alaska, 1909 ***9196.1*** *p8*
Metzler, Josef; Port uncertain, 1783 ***2856.30*** *p300*
Metzler, Josef; Port uncertain, 1784 ***2856.30*** *p300*
Meucci, Anthonio; New York, 1826 ***8197.10*** *p333*
Meurer, Philipp; America, 1742 ***2856.30*** *p300*
Meurer, Philipp; America, 1771 ***2856.30*** *p300*
Meurer, Philipp Jakob; America, 1787 ***2856.30*** *p300*
Meuret, Arthur; New York, New York, 1899 ***3437.14*** *p174*
Mever, Christopher; America, 1889 ***1640.13*** *p75*
Mew, . . .; Maryland, 1668 ***2524.55*** *p150*
Mew, Ann; Maryland, 1668 ***2524.55*** *p150*
With child
Mew, Ellis; New England, 1671 ***1224.1*** *p39*
Mew, Noel; Rhode Island, 1700 ***1224.2*** *p79*
Mew, Sarah; New England, 1671 ***1224.1*** *p39*
Mew, Zachary; Maryland, 1672 ***2524.55*** *p151*
Mewanes, Henry; Virginia, 1679-1680 ***6212.30*** *p54*
Mey, Anna Margarete; America, 1748 ***2856.30*** *p300*
Mey, Daniel; America, 1743 ***2856.30*** *p300*
Mey, Daniel; America, 1748 ***2856.30*** *p300*
Mey, Franz Peter; America, 1748 ***2856.30*** *p300*
Mey, Friedrich; America, 1749 ***2856.30*** *p300*
With wife & 3 children
Mey, Johann Philpp; Port uncertain, 1729 ***2856.30*** *p300*
Mey, Leonhard; America, 1748 ***2856.30*** *p300*
Mey, Maria Catharina; America, 1748 ***2856.30*** *p300*
Mey, Maria Elisabeth; America, 1748 ***2856.30*** *p300*
Mey, Philipp Friedr.; America, 1743 ***2856.30*** *p300*
Meyer, Mr.; Port uncertain, 1755 ***2856.30*** *p392*
Meyer, Adolph 68; Ontario, 1871 ***1823.15*** *p187*
Meyer, Andreas; Port uncertain, 1752 ***2856.30*** *p300*
Meyer, Angelika; America, 1752 ***2856.30*** *p300*
Meyer, Angelika; Port uncertain, 1759 ***2856.30*** *p301*
Meyer, Ann Charlotte; New York, 1840 ***8197.10*** *p265*
Meyer, Anna Barbara; Port uncertain, 1751 ***2856.30*** *p300*
Meyer, Anna M. 27; Kansas, 1906-1910 ***9079.10*** *p21*
Meyer, Barbara; Port uncertain, 1786 ***2856.30*** *p300*
Meyer, Catharine 48; Kansas, 1891-1910 ***9079.10*** *p19*
Meyer, Catherine 7; Kansas, 1906-1910 ***9079.10*** *p21*
Meyer, Christian; Port uncertain, 1784 ***2856.30*** *p300*
Meyer, Christian; Port uncertain, 1785 ***2856.30*** *p301*
Meyer, Christian E.; New York, 1840 ***8197.10*** *p182*
Meyer, Mrs. Christof; Port uncertain, 1761 ***2856.30*** *p300*
Meyer, Conrad; America, 1749 ***2856.30*** *p300*
Meyer, Daniel; Port uncertain, 1751 ***2856.30*** *p300*
Meyer, Diederich; Port uncertain, 1745 ***2856.30*** *p301*
With wife & 4 children
Meyer, Elisabeth; Port uncertain, 1773 ***2856.30*** *p300*
Meyer, Elizabeth 16; Kansas, 1900-1910 ***9079.10*** *p21*
Meyer, Franz Simon; Port uncertain, 1770 ***2856.30*** *p301*
With wife
Meyer, Friedrich; America, 1741 ***2856.30*** *p300*
Meyer, Fritz; New York, New York, 1854 ***6058.10*** *p65*
Meyer, Georg; Port uncertain, 1741 ***2856.30*** *p300*
Meyer, George 40; Ontario, 1871 ***1823.15*** *p187*
Meyer, Gotfried 49; Kansas, 1891-1910 ***9079.10*** *p19*
Meyer, Gottfreid 20; Kansas, 1891-1910 ***9079.10*** *p19*
Meyer, Hans; Port uncertain, 1742 ***2856.30*** *p300*
Meyer, Hans Georg; America, 1751 ***2856.30*** *p301*
Meyer, Hans Georg; America, 1751 ***2856.30*** *p301*
With wife & 4 children
Meyer, Hans Jacob; America, 1749 ***2856.30*** *p300*
Meyer, Heinrich; Port uncertain, 1765 ***2856.30*** *p300*
Meyer, Heinrich; Port uncertain, 1770 ***2856.30*** *p300*
Meyer, Henry; New York, 1807 ***8197.10*** *p327*
Meyer, Henry 38; Kansas, 1900-1910 ***9079.10*** *p21*
Meyer, Jacob; America, 1727 ***2856.30*** *p300*
Meyer, Jacob 32; Ontario, 1871 ***1823.15*** *p187*
Meyer, Jacob Friedrich; America, 1769 ***2856.30*** *p300*
Meyer, Jakob; America, 1749 ***2856.30*** *p301*
With wife & 5 children
Meyer, Jakob; Port uncertain, 1750 ***2856.30*** *p301*
Meyer, Jakob; Port uncertain, 1751 ***2856.30*** *p301*
Meyer, Johann; America, 1764 ***2856.30*** *p301*
Meyer, John Jacob; New York, 1839 ***8197.10*** *p141*
Meyer, Julius; America, 1764 ***2856.30*** *p301*
Meyer, Kattie 16; Kansas, 1900-1910 ***9079.10*** *p21*
Meyer, Konrad; America, 1752 ***2856.30*** *p301*
With wife
Meyer, Leonhard; America, 1738 ***2856.30*** *p301*
Meyer, Leonhard; Port uncertain, 1738 ***2856.30*** *p300*
Meyer, Leopolt; New York, 1831 ***8197.10*** *p263*
Meyer, Leopolt; New York, 1832 ***8197.10*** *p368*
Meyer, Lewis; New York, 1839 ***8197.10*** *p141*
Meyer, Lewis Henry; New York, 1840 ***8197.10*** *p265*
Meyer, Ludwig 61; Ontario, 1871 ***1823.15*** *p187*
Meyer, Marianna; Port uncertain, 1765 ***2856.30*** *p301*
Meyer, Martin; Port uncertain, 1767 ***2856.30*** *p301*
Meyer, Matthaus; Port uncertain, 1741 ***2856.30*** *p301*
Meyer, Michael; America, 1741 ***2856.30*** *p301*
Meyer, Michael; America, 1741 ***2856.30*** *p301*
With wife & 6 children
Meyer, Michael; America, 1751 ***2856.30*** *p301*
Meyer, Michael; America, 1751 ***2856.30*** *p301*
With wife & children
Meyer, Michael; Port uncertain, 1744 ***2856.30*** *p301*
Meyer, Peter; America, 1744 ***2856.30*** *p301*
Meyer, Peter; Port uncertain, 1747 ***2856.30*** *p301*
Meyer, Philipp; Port uncertain, 1775 ***2856.30*** *p301*
Meyer, Philipp; Port uncertain, 1775 ***2856.30*** *p324*
Meyer, Simon; America, 1741 ***2856.30*** *p301*
Meyer, Susanna; America, 1742 ***2856.30*** *p301*
Meyer, Walledine; America, 1754 ***2856.30*** *p301*
Meyer, Wilhelm; Port uncertain, 1772 ***2856.30*** *p301*
Meyer, Wilhelm; Port uncertain, 1774 ***2856.30*** *p301*
With wife & children
Meyerdorff, Anna Barbara; Port uncertain, 1752 ***2856.30*** *p301*
Meyerin, Angelika; Port uncertain, 1759 ***2856.30*** *p301*
Meyerly, Conrad; Pennsylvania, 1777 ***4629.10*** *p9*
Meyers, Benjamin; Pennsylvania, 1777 ***4629.10*** *p23*
Meyers, Christopher; Pennsylvania, 1778 ***4629.10*** *p43*
Meyers, George; Pennsylvania, 1777 ***4629.10*** *p19*
Meyers, George; Pennsylvania, 1779 ***4629.10*** *p36*
Meyers, Jacob; Pennsylvania, 1777 ***4629.10*** *p15*
Meyers, Mary; Vermont, 1830-1916 ***5900.10*** *p594*
Meyhchkya, Walter; Maryland, 1910 ***3259.35*** *p39*
Meynard, Charles Cosme Marie 33; Pennsylvania, 1793 ***4629.10*** *p64*
Meyo, John; Maryland, 1662 ***2524.55*** *p151*
Meyss, Heinrich; Port uncertain, 1741 ***2856.30*** *p301*
Mezeck, Jewell; Virginia, 1664-1665 ***6212.30*** *p16*
Mezer, Franz; Port uncertain, 1770 ***2856.30*** *p301*
With 3 daughters
Mezger, Abraham; Port uncertain, 1749 ***2856.30*** *p302*
Mezger, Hans Michel; America, 1752 ***2856.30*** *p302*
Mezger, Hans Michel; Port uncertain, 1738 ***2856.30*** *p302*
Mezger, Philippine; Port uncertain, 1790 ***2856.30*** *p302*
Mezgerin, Philippine; Port uncertain, 1790 ***2856.30*** *p302*
Mezies, George 25; Ontario, 1871 ***1823.28*** *p72*
Mezies, George 34; Ontario, 1871 ***1823.28*** *p72*
Mezler, Hans Georg; Port uncertain, 1759 ***2856.30*** *p302*
Mezler, Hans Georg; Port uncertain, 1762 ***2856.30*** *p302*
Mezler, Jacob; Port uncertain, 1759 ***2856.30*** *p302*
Mezler, Jacob; Port uncertain, 1762 ***2856.30*** *p302*
Mge, Jane; Maryland, 1664 ***2524.55*** *p151*
Mgrarek, Thomas; Maryland, 1910 ***3259.35*** *p39*
Mibross, Jane 30; Georgia, 1775 ***1220.25*** *p126*
Michael, Mr. 31; Ontario, 1861 ***2896.26*** *p13*
Michael, B. 41; Juneau, Alaska, 1917 ***9196.1*** *p45*
Michael, B. 41; Whitehorse, Yukon, 1917 ***9196.1*** *p45*
Michael, George 16; Kansas, 1910 ***9079.10*** *p26*
Michael, Jacob; New York, 1837 ***8197.10*** *p100*
Michael, James 62; Ontario, 1871 ***1823.22*** *p111*
Michaelies, Ferd 35; Ontario, 1871 ***1823.28*** *p72*

Michaelis, August 26; Ontario, 1871 ***1823.28*** *p72*
Michaelis, Earnest 30; Ontario, 1871 ***1823.28*** *p72*
Michaelis, Edward 28; Ontario, 1871 ***1823.28*** *p72*
Michaelis, Frederick 36; Ontario, 1871 ***1823.28*** *p72*
Michaelis, J. Henry 32; Kansas, 1880-1910 ***9079.10*** *p21*
Michaelis, Paulina 22; Kansas, 1906-1910 ***9079.10*** *p21*
Michaell, Elizabeth; Virginia, 1674 ***6212.30*** *p52*
Michaels, Charles 22; Ontario, 1871 ***1823.28*** *p72*
Michaelson, Jacob; Maryland, 1661 ***2524.55*** *p151*
Michaleau, Henry 32; Kansas, 1910 ***9079.10*** *p44*
Michaleau, Lyddia 34; Kansas, 1910 ***9079.10*** *p44*
Michaless, John 29; Kansas, 1910 ***9079.10*** *p45*
Michaletti, Luigi; New York, 1830 ***8197.10*** *p362*
Michalewski, Sigmund; Maryland, 1910 ***3259.35*** *p39*
Michall, Conrad 36; Ontario, 1871 ***1823.15*** *p187*
Michalovski, Kazmer; Maryland, 1910 ***3259.35*** *p39*
Michalski, Frank; Maryland, 1910 ***3259.35*** *p39*
Michalski, Michalina; Maryland, 1910 ***3259.35*** *p39*
Michalski, Stefan; Maryland, 1910 ***3259.35*** *p39*
Michalsky, Frank; Maryland, 1910 ***3259.35*** *p40*
Michalsky, John; Maryland, 1910 ***3259.35*** *p40*
Michaud, Catherine Rogan; Vermont, 1811-1904 ***5900.10*** *p146*
Michaud, Stephen; Vermont, 1811-1847 ***5900.10*** *p146*
Micheal, Frederick 40; Kansas, 1891-1910 ***9079.10*** *p26*
Micheal, Mary 40; Kansas, 1891-1910 ***9079.10*** *p26*
Micheal, May 18; Kansas, 1891-1910 ***9079.10*** *p26*
Michealis, Catherine 56; Kansas, 1877-1910 ***9079.10*** *p20*
Michealis, Catherine 69; Kansas, 1892-1910 ***9079.10*** *p24*
Michealis, Cristian 88; Kansas, 1877-1910 ***9079.10*** *p20*
Michealis, Elizabeth 25; Kansas, 1907-1910 ***9079.10*** *p20*
Michealis, Georg H. 29; Kansas, 1907-1910 ***9079.10*** *p20*
Michealis, George H. 44; Kansas, 1879-1910 ***9079.10*** *p21*
Michealis, George H. 69; Kansas, 1892-1910 ***9079.10*** *p24*
Michealis, J. J., Sr. 73; Kansas, 1870-1910 ***9079.10*** *p24*
Michealis, John J. 31; Kansas, 1879-1910 ***9079.10*** *p21*
Michealis, Lena 33; Kansas, 1892-1910 ***9079.10*** *p21*
Michealis, Mary E. 39; Kansas, 1878-1910 ***9079.10*** *p21*
Michealis, S. George 27; Kansas, 1893-1910 ***9079.10*** *p20*
Michel, Anna Elisabeth; Port uncertain, 1756 ***2856.30*** *p302*
Michel, Anna Maria; Port uncertain, 1786 ***2856.30*** *p302*
Michel, Catharina; America, 1750 ***2856.30*** *p302*
Michel, Christof; America, 1749 ***2856.30*** *p302*
With 2 children
Michel, Georg; America, 1749 ***2856.30*** *p302*
With 2 children
Michel, Johann Andreas; Port uncertain, 1760 ***2856.30*** *p302*
Michel, Johann Philipp; Port uncertain, 1767 ***2856.30*** *p302*
Michel, Ludwig; Port uncertain, 1741 ***2856.30*** *p302*
With wife
Michel, Nickel; Port uncertain, 1768 ***2856.30*** *p302*
Michel, Nikolaus; Port uncertain, 1768 ***2856.30*** *p302*
Michel, Mrs. Paul; Port uncertain, 1764 ***2856.30*** *p302*
With 3 children
Michel, Peter; Port uncertain, 1741 ***2856.30*** *p302*
Michel, Peter; Port uncertain, 1752 ***2856.30*** *p302*
Michel, Peter; Port uncertain, 1755 ***2856.30*** *p302*
Michel, Peter; Port uncertain, 1783 ***2856.30*** *p302*
Michel, Philipp Adam; Port uncertain, 1752 ***2856.30*** *p302*
Michel, Sarah 36; Ontario, 1861 ***2896.27*** *p53*
Michel, Sebastian; America, 1762 ***2856.30*** *p302*
With wife & 4 children
Michel, Valentin; Port uncertain, 1764 ***2856.30*** *p302*
Michel, Mrs. Valentin; America, 1793 ***2856.30*** *p302*
Michelberger, Joachim; Port uncertain, 1612 ***2856.30*** *p302*
Michelin, Anna Elisabeth; Port uncertain, 1756 ***2856.30*** *p302*
Michell, Mrs.; Maryland, 1648 ***2524.55*** *p151*
Michell, Alexander; Maryland, 1673 ***2524.55*** *p151*
Michell, Henry; Virginia, 1663 ***6212.30*** *p3*
Michell, Joane Townsend; Virginia, 1661 ***1224.1*** *p39*
Michell, John; Virginia, 1666-1667 ***6212.30*** *p33*
Michell, Richard; Maryland, 1681 ***2524.55*** *p153*
Michell, Tho; Virginia, 1668-1669 ***6212.30*** *p40*
Michelle, Piccimin 24; British Columbia, 1913 ***9196.1*** *p21*
Michelmann, Christian; Port uncertain, 1755 ***2856.30*** *p302*
Michelmann, Christian; Port uncertain, 1795 ***2856.30*** *p302*
Michels, Anna Margarete; Port uncertain, 1738 ***2856.30*** *p302*
Michels, Charles; New York, New York, 1882 ***3437.14*** *p122*
Michels, Friedrich; America, 1744 ***2856.30*** *p302*
Michels, Henry 50; Ontario, 1871 ***1823.22*** *p111*
Michelson, Alexander; Maryland, 1671 ***2524.55*** *p151*
Michelwain, John; Pennsylvania, 1777 ***4629.10*** *p10*
Michener, Absalem; Pennsylvania, 1786 ***4629.10*** *p51*
Michenfelder, Johann Caspar; Philadelphia, 1773 ***2856.30*** *p303*
Michenfelder, Johann Caspar; Port uncertain, 1768 ***2856.30*** *p302*
Michiall, Ludwick 48; Ontario, 1871 ***1823.15*** *p187*
Michibyaski, Mary; Maryland, 1910 ***3259.35*** *p40*
Michie, Ann 70; Ontario, 1871 ***1823.22*** *p111*
Michie, Duncan 42; Alaska, 1916 ***9196.1*** *p6*
Michie, Duncan 42; Yukon, 1916 ***9196.1*** *p6*
Michie, John 36; Ontario, 1871 ***1823.22*** *p111*
Michie, William 43; Ontario, 1871 ***1823.15*** *p187*
Michiel, Gustave 36; Ontario, 1871 ***1823.28*** *p72*
Michiewicz, Pelagia; Maryland, 1910 ***3259.35*** *p40*
Michikelinese, David 50; Ontario, 1871 ***1823.28*** *p72*
Michill, William; Maryland, 1665 ***2524.55*** *p151*
Michler, Peter; Port uncertain, 1748 ***2856.30*** *p303*
Michlinski, Joseph; Maryland, 1910 ***3259.35*** *p40*
Micho, Wm.; Maryland, 1675 ***2524.55*** *p151*
Micholak, Martin; Maryland, 1910 ***3259.35*** *p40*
Micholls, James; New York, 1839 ***8197.10*** *p141*
Mick, Daniel 45; Ontario, 1871 ***1823.28*** *p72*
Mick, George 56; Ontario, 1871 ***1823.28*** *p72*
Mick, John; Maryland, 1910 ***3259.35*** *p40*
Mick, John 54; Ontario, 1871 ***1823.28*** *p72*
Mick, Mountefer 35; Ontario, 1871 ***1823.28*** *p72*
Mick, Peter 45; Ontario, 1871 ***1823.28*** *p72*
Micke, Lewis; Pennsylvania, 1777 ***4629.10*** *p26*
Micke, Lewis; Pennsylvania, 1779 ***4629.10*** *p39*
Mickell, Alex; Maryland, 1670 ***2524.55*** *p151*
Mickell, Ephraim Christian 34; Maryland, 1774 ***1220.25*** *p78*
Mickenhauser, Johann Adam; Port uncertain, 1765 ***2856.30*** *p303*
Mickens, Henery 35; Ontario, 1871 ***1823.15*** *p187*
Mickle, James; New York, 1795 ***8197.10*** *p7*
Micklejohn, David 45; Ontario, 1871 ***1823.22*** *p111*
Mickleson, August 28; Ontario, 1871 ***1823.28*** *p72*
Mickleson, Enos 18; British Columbia, 1917 ***9196.1*** *p69*
Mickleson, Enos 18; Washington, 1917 ***9196.1*** *p69*
Mickley, Isaack; Maryland, 1680 ***2524.55*** *p151*
Mickols, Jane; Virginia, 1671 ***6212.30*** *p44*
Mickowski, Rudolph; Maryland, 1910 ***3259.35*** *p40*
Miczhski, James; Maryland, 1910 ***3259.35*** *p40*
Miczynski, John; Maryland, 1910 ***3259.35*** *p40*
Middaugh, George; Pennsylvania, 1777 ***4629.10*** *p14*
Middelton, Emily 21; Ontario, 1871 ***1823.15*** *p187*
Middlemiss, Elizabeth 60; Ontario, 1871 ***1823.15*** *p187*
Middlemiss, James; St. Vincent, 1823 ***1640.13*** *p76*
Middleton, Miss; Quebec, 1857 ***9196.15*** *p25*
Middleton, Amy; Maryland, 1681 ***2524.55*** *p151*
Middleton, Arthur; South Carolina, 1740 ***1224.2*** *p79*
Middleton, Charle 61; Ontario, 1871 ***1823.15*** *p187*
Middleton, Elizabeth; Maryland, 1663 ***2524.55*** *p151*
Middleton, Geo; Virginia, 1665-1666 ***6212.30*** *p21*
Middleton, Hannah; New England, 1650 ***1224.1*** *p39*
Middleton, James; Philadelphia, 1746 ***1224.2*** *p79*
Middleton, Jon; Virginia, 1674-1675 ***6212.30*** *p53*
Middleton, Mary; Maryland, 1681 ***2524.55*** *p151*
Middleton, Mary Helen; Philadelphia, 1857 ***1224.3*** *p52*
Middleton, Robert; Virginia, 1627 ***1224.1*** *p39*
Middleton, Sarah 57; Ontario, 1871 ***1823.15*** *p188*
Middleton, Thomas; Charles Town, South Carolina, 1799 ***1224.2*** *p79*
Middleton, Thomas; Charleston, South Carolina, 1799 ***1224.3*** *p52*
Middleton, Thomas; Virginia, 1663 ***6212.30*** *p3*
Middleton, Thomas; Virginia, 1664 ***6212.30*** *p8*
Middleton, W. E.; Portland, Maine, 1858 ***9196.15*** *p28*
Middleton, William 21; Maryland, 1775 ***1220.25*** *p120*
Middleton, William 23; Jamaica, 1774 ***1220.25*** *p79*
Middleton, William Thomas; Cincinnati, 1839 ***1224.3*** *p52*
Middole, Samuel; New York, 1840 ***8197.10*** *p384*
Midellemess, Andrew; New York, 1806 ***8197.10*** *p32*
Midford, Elizabeth; Virginia, 1667-1668 ***6212.30*** *p39*
Midford, William; Charles Town, South Carolina, 1746 ***1224.2*** *p79*
Midgely, Thomas; Maryland, 1680 ***2524.55*** *p151*
Midgley, Mr.; Quebec, 1856 ***9196.15*** *p7*
Midgley, Mrs.; Quebec, 1856 ***9196.15*** *p7*
Midgley, Edward J.; New York, 1827 ***8197.10*** *p337*
Midmer, William 41; Ontario, 1861 ***2896.27*** *p67*
Midwood, James, Jr.; New York, 1828 ***8197.10*** *p262*
Midy, Touissant; New York, 1821 ***8197.10*** *p260*
Mieduszewski, Bronislaw; Maryland, 1910 ***3259.35*** *p40*
Miedzianswoka, Joseph A.; Maryland, 1910 ***3259.35*** *p40*
Miege, Pierre Auguste; New York, 1831 ***8197.10*** *p367*
Miekles, Hermond 25; Ontario, 1871 ***1823.28*** *p72*
Miencikowski, Stanislaus; Maryland, 1910 ***3259.35*** *p40*
Mier, Barney; Pennsylvania, 1786 ***4629.10*** *p55*
Mier, Joseph Marquis; New York, 1839 ***8197.10*** *p264*
Mieregaes, Otto Heinrich; New York, 1831 ***8197.10*** *p368*
Miero, Stephen; Maryland, 1682 ***2524.55*** *p151*
Miers, Frederic E. 3; Ontario, 1861 ***2896.27*** *p32*
Miers, Melvill A. 5; Ontario, 1861 ***2896.27*** *p32*
Mierzwicki, George; Maryland, 1910 ***3259.35*** *p40*
Miewiadony, Philip; Maryland, 1910 ***3259.35*** *p40*
Mifflin, Benjamin, Jr.; Pennsylvania, 1779 ***4629.10*** *p41*
Mifflin, George; Pennsylvania, 1777 ***4629.10*** *p27*
Mifflin, John; Pennsylvania, 1777 ***4629.10*** *p23*
Mifflin, John F.; Pennsylvania, 1778 ***4629.10*** *p34*
Mifflin, Thomas; Pennsylvania, 1777 ***4629.10*** *p28*
Migakwat, Louis 38; Ontario, 1871 ***1823.28*** *p72*
Migent, Michael 22; Virginia, 1774 ***1220.25*** *p89*
Migeot, Johann; America, 1744 ***2856.30*** *p303*
Migert, Johann; America, 1744 ***2856.30*** *p303*
Miggleston, Thomas; Georgia, 1699 ***1640.13*** *p76*
Might, E. 28; Ontario, 1861 ***2896.28*** *p8*
Might, F. W. 6; Ontario, 1861 ***2896.28*** *p8*
Might, G. 3; Ontario, 1861 ***2896.28*** *p8*
Migliore, Nicolo; New York, 1840 ***8197.10*** *p265*
Mihalak, Antonina; Maryland, 1910 ***3259.35*** *p40*
Mihan, Frank 60; Ontario, 1871 ***1823.22*** *p111*
Miire, Geo 26; Seattle, 1913 ***9196.1*** *p59*
Mik, Andrew; Maryland, 1910 ***3259.35*** *p40*
Mik, Isidor; Maryland, 1910 ***3259.35*** *p40*
Mike, Tony 23; Alaska, 1914 ***9196.1*** *p11*
Mikell, H. C. 10; Ontario, 1861 ***2896.25*** *p8*
Mikell, Jane 30; Ontario, 1861 ***2896.25*** *p8*
Mikell, W. R. 14; Ontario, 1861 ***2896.25*** *p8*
Mikle, Abigal 49; Ontario, 1861 ***2896.25*** *p22*
Mikle, Alfred 17; Ontario, 1861 ***2896.25*** *p22*
Mikle, Catherine 11; Ontario, 1861 ***2896.25*** *p22*
Mikle, Charles 7; Ontario, 1861 ***2896.25*** *p22*
Mikle, Donall 14; Ontario, 1861 ***2896.25*** *p22*
Mikle, Eliza 17; Ontario, 1861 ***2896.25*** *p17*
Mikle, Ellen 12; Ontario, 1861 ***2896.25*** *p17*
Mikle, Emily 3; Ontario, 1861 ***2896.25*** *p17*
Mikle, George E. 1; Ontario, 1861 ***2896.25*** *p17*
Mikle, Gillard 10; Ontario, 1861 ***2896.25*** *p17*
Mikle, Hannah 19; Ontario, 1861 ***2896.25*** *p17*
Mikle, James 22; Ontario, 1861 ***2896.25*** *p17*
Mikle, Josephine 3; Ontario, 1861 ***2896.25*** *p15*
Mikle, Lucinda 14; Ontario, 1861 ***2896.25*** *p17*
Mikle, Margy Ann 25; Ontario, 1861 ***2896.25*** *p15*
Mikle, Mary M. 20; Ontario, 1861 ***2896.25*** *p22*
Mikle, Parcina 8; Ontario, 1861 ***2896.25*** *p17*
Mikle, Robert 5; Ontario, 1861 ***2896.25*** *p15*
Mikle, Sarah 19; Ontario, 1861 ***2896.25*** *p17*
Mikle, Sarah Ann 44; Ontario, 1861 ***2896.25*** *p17*
Mikle, Sarah C. 7; Ontario, 1861 ***2896.25*** *p15*
Mikle, Stephen 15; Ontario, 1861 ***2896.25*** *p22*
Mikle, Unis Jane 9; Ontario, 1861 ***2896.25*** *p22*
Mikle, William 21; Ontario, 1861 ***2896.25*** *p22*
Mikle, William 24; Ontario, 1861 ***2896.25*** *p17*
Mikolazko, Jan M.; Maryland, 1910 ***3259.35*** *p40*
Mikulska, Josef; Maryland, 1910 ***3259.35*** *p40*
Milam, John; Virginia, 1701 ***1224.2*** *p83*
Milar, Dan 45; Alaska, 1915 ***9196.1*** *p42*
Milay, John; New York, 1839 ***8197.10*** *p382*
Milberger, Eulah 52; Kansas, 1910 ***9079.10*** *p42*
Milberger, Ferdinand 57; Kansas, 1890-1910 ***9079.10*** *p42*
Milberger, Fred 33; Kansas, 1910 ***9079.10*** *p42*
Milberger, Henry 24; Kansas, 1910 ***9079.10*** *p42*
Milberger, Justine 21; Kansas, 1910 ***9079.10*** *p42*
Milberger, Pauline 32; Kansas, 1910 ***9079.10*** *p42*
Milborn, Andrew 7; Carolina, 1774 ***1220.25*** *p91*
Milborn, Christopher 2; Carolina, 1774 ***1220.25*** *p91*
Milburn, Elizabeth; Georgia, 1775 ***1640.10*** *p153*
Milburn, Elizabeth 20; Georgia, 1775 ***1220.25*** *p126*
Milburn, John; New York, 1838 ***8197.10*** *p125*
Milby, Benjamin; New York, 1830 ***8197.10*** *p313*
Milch, Johann; America, 1808 ***2856.30*** *p303*
Milcholwska, Adam; Maryland, 1910 ***3259.35*** *p40*
Mildenberger, Elis. Margarete; Port uncertain, 1786 ***2856.30*** *p303*
Mildenberger, Jakob; Port uncertain, 1764 ***2856.30*** *p303*
Milder, Hans Adam; America, 1727 ***2856.30*** *p303*
Mildner, Friedrich; Port uncertain, 1733 ***2856.30*** *p303*
Mildner, Johann Georg; Port uncertain, 1790 ***2856.30*** *p303*
Mildon, Elizabeth 25; Ontario, 1861 ***2896.27*** *p1*
Miler, Edward; New York, 1807 ***8197.10*** *p332*
Miles, Captain; Quebec, 1857 ***9196.15*** *p24*
Miles, Mr.; Quebec, 1857 ***9196.15*** *p24*
Miles, Mrs.; Quebec, 1857 ***9196.15*** *p24*
Miles, Alexander 59; Ontario, 1871 ***1823.28*** *p72*
Miles, Ann; Virginia, 1666 ***6212.30*** *p26*
Miles, Benjamin 21; Maryland, 1775 ***1220.25*** *p99*
Miles, Bridget 4; Vermont, 1859 ***5900.10*** *p241*
Miles, Caroline; Vermont, 1840-1940 ***5900.10*** *p193*

Miller, James; New York, 1821 ***8197.10*** *p259*
Miller, James; Portland, Maine, 1857 ***9196.15*** *p12*
Miller, James; Saskatchewan, 1884 ***4537.37*** *p104*
Child: William
Child: Mary Ann
Child: John
Child: Thomas
Child: George
Child: Mary
Child: Ann
Wife: Mary Ann Black
Child: Jenny
Child: James
Miller, James; Savannah, Georgia, 1807 ***1640.10*** *p154*
Miller, James; Virginia, 1666-1667 ***6212.30*** *p33*
Miller, James 15; Baltimore, 1775 ***1220.25*** *p119*
Miller, James 43; Ontario, 1871 ***1823.28*** *p72*
Miller, James 45; Ontario, 1871 ***1823.15*** *p188*
Miller, James 50; Ontario, 1871 ***1823.15*** *p188*
Miller, James 55; Ontario, 1871 ***1823.15*** *p188*
Miller, James Broom; Ontario, 1881 ***1640.13*** *p76*
Miller, James H. 5; Ontario, 1861 ***2896.25*** *p38*
Miller, Jane 25; Halifax, Nova Scotia, 1774 ***1220.25*** *p138*
Miller, Jenny *SEE* Miller, James
Miller, Jesse 19; Ontario, 1861 ***2896.27*** *p36*
Miller, Mrs. Joh. Engelhart; America, 1796 ***2856.30*** *p304*
Miller, Johann; America, 1738 ***2856.30*** *p303*
Miller, Johann; America, 1739 ***2856.30*** *p303*
Miller, John *SEE* Miller, James
Miller, John *SEE* Miller, William
Miller, John; Georgia, 1698 ***1640.13*** *p76*
Miller, John; Maryland, 1661 ***2524.55*** *p196*
Miller, John; Maryland, 1667 ***2524.55*** *p152*
Miller, John; Maryland, 1672 ***2524.55*** *p152*
Miller, John; Maryland, 1681 ***2524.55*** *p152*
Miller, John; Maryland, 1910 ***3259.35*** *p40*
Miller, John; New Jersey, 1816 ***1224.3*** *p52*
Miller, John; New York, 1794 ***8197.10*** *p2*
Miller, John; New York, 1802 ***8197.10*** *p22*
Miller, John; New York, 1825 ***8197.10*** *p261*
Miller, John; New York, 1834 ***8197.10*** *p319*
Miller, John; New York, 1840 ***8197.10*** *p181*
Miller, John; Pennsylvania, 1777 ***4629.10*** *p24*
Miller, John; Pennsylvania, 1779 ***4629.10*** *p39*
Miller, John; Pennsylvania, 1868 ***1640.13*** *p77*
Miller, John; Savannah, Georgia, 1807 ***1640.10*** *p154*
Miller, John 13; Ontario, 1861 ***2896.25*** *p37*
Miller, John 18; Kansas, 1905-1910 ***9079.10*** *p20*
Miller, John 21; Maryland, 1774 ***1220.25*** *p65*
Miller, John 22; Ontario, 1871 ***1823.15*** *p188*
Miller, John 26; Maryland, 1774 ***1220.25*** *p59*
Miller, John 27; Ontario, 1871 ***1823.15*** *p189*
Miller, John 33; Ontario, 1871 ***1823.15*** *p188*
Miller, John 33; Ontario, 1871 ***1823.22*** *p111*
Miller, John 38; Ontario, 1871 ***1823.22*** *p111*
Miller, John 41; Ontario, 1861 ***2896.27*** *p36*
Miller, John 46; Ontario, 1871 ***1823.15*** *p189*
Miller, John 50; Ontario, 1871 ***1823.15*** *p188*
Miller, John 52; Ontario, 1871 ***1823.28*** *p72*
Miller, John 60; Ontario, 1871 ***1823.15*** *p188*
Miller, John 65; Ontario, 1871 ***1823.22*** *p111*
Miller, John, Jr.; Pennsylvania, 1786 ***4629.10*** *p50*
Miller, John A. 47; Kansas, 1880-1910 ***9079.10*** *p4*
Miller, John G.; New York, New York, 1848 ***6058.10*** *p33*
Miller, John Philip; Pennsylvania, 1777 ***4629.10*** *p23*
Miller, John R. 29; Ontario, 1871 ***1823.15*** *p189*
Miller, Josef; Port uncertain, 1689 ***2856.30*** *p303*
Miller, Josef; Port uncertain, 1727 ***2856.30*** *p303*
Miller, Josef; Port uncertain, 1761 ***2856.30*** *p303*
Miller, Joseph; New York, 1838 ***8197.10*** *p378*
Miller, Joseph; New York, 1839 ***8197.10*** *p10*
Miller, Joseph 29; Maryland, 1775 ***1220.25*** *p114*
Miller, Julie; Maryland, 1910 ***3259.35*** *p40*
Miller, Kasimir; Port uncertain, 1742 ***2856.30*** *p303*
Miller, Katie 21; Kansas, 1906-1910 ***9079.10*** *p4*
Miller, Katie 21; Kansas, 1906-1910 ***9079.10*** *p41*
Miller, Katie 30; Kansas, 1910 ***9079.10*** *p5*
Miller, Katie 30; Kansas, 1910 ***9079.10*** *p50*
Miller, Katie 56; Kansas, 1906-1910 ***9079.10*** *p4*
Miller, Katie 56; Kansas, 1906-1910 ***9079.10*** *p41*
Miller, Leandria 21; Ontario, 1861 ***2896.26*** *p3*
Miller, Leonard 22; Maryland, 1775 ***1220.25*** *p100*
Miller, Lizzie 35; Kansas, 1905-1910 ***9079.10*** *p4*
Miller, Lizzie 35; Kansas, 1905-1910 ***9079.10*** *p40*
Miller, Lydia 41; Ontario, 1861 ***2896.26*** *p3*
Miller, Mahala 23; Ontario, 1861 ***2896.26*** *p18*
Miller, Malcolm; Georgia, 1698 ***1640.13*** *p77*
Miller, Margaret; Halifax, Nova Scotia, 1823 ***1224.3*** *p52*
Miller, Margaret 50; Ontario, 1871 ***1823.15*** *p189*
Miller, Margaret Irvine *SEE* Miller, William
Miller, Margarete; America, 1728 ***2856.30*** *p303*
Miller, Marget 63; Ontario, 1871 ***1823.15*** *p189*
Miller, Marshall 10; Ontario, 1861 ***2896.25*** *p38*
Miller, Martin 14; Kansas, 1905-1910 ***9079.10*** *p4*
Miller, Martin 14; Kansas, 1905-1910 ***9079.10*** *p40*
Miller, Martin 44; Ontario, 1861 ***2896.25*** *p7*
Miller, Mary *SEE* Miller, James
Miller, Mary; St. Louis, 1893 ***1640.13*** *p77*
Miller, Mary; Vermont, 1847-1926 ***5900.10*** *p225*
Miller, Mary 7; Kansas, 1905-1910 ***9079.10*** *p4*
Miller, Mary 7; Kansas, 1910 ***9079.10*** *p40*
Miller, Mary 19; Kansas, 1910 ***9079.10*** *p5*
Miller, Mary 70; Ontario, 1871 ***1823.15*** *p189*
Miller, Mary Ann *SEE* Miller, James
Miller, Mary Ann Black *SEE* Miller, James
Miller, Mary E. 20; Ontario, 1861 ***2896.25*** *p7*
Miller, Matilda 14; Ontario, 1861 ***2896.26*** *p22*
Miller, Michael; America, 1741 ***2856.30*** *p303*
Miller, Michael; America, 1741 ***2856.30*** *p304*
With wife & 5 children
Miller, Michael; Maryland, 1670 ***2524.55*** *p152*
Miller, Michael; Maryland, 1910 ***3259.35*** *p40*
Miller, Neil; Mississippi, 1801-1845 ***1640.10*** *p154*
Miller, Nicholas 34; Maryland, 1775 ***1220.25*** *p109*
Miller, Norris; Ontario, 1861 ***2896.28*** *p52*
Miller, Oliver 42; Ontario, 1871 ***1823.22*** *p111*
Miller, Peter; Pennsylvania, 1779 ***4629.10*** *p40*
Miller, Peter; Tennessee, 1787-1845 ***1640.10*** *p154*
Miller, Peter; Port uncertain, 1720 ***2856.30*** *p303*
Miller, Phebe 2; Ontario, 1861 ***2896.25*** *p37*
Miller, Phebe 83; Ontario, 1861 ***2896.25*** *p37*
Miller, Philip 9; Kansas, 1905-1910 ***9079.10*** *p4*
Miller, Philip 9; Kansas, 1905-1910 ***9079.10*** *p40*
Miller, Philip 35; Kansas, 1905-1910 ***9079.10*** *p4*
Miller, Philip 35; Kansas, 1905-1910 ***9079.10*** *p40*
Miller, R.; Quebec, 1858 ***9196.15*** *p41*
Miller, Rachel 42; Ontario, 1861 ***2896.26*** *p19*
Miller, Richard; Virginia, 1664 ***6212.30*** *p12*
Miller, Richard 26; Philadelphia, 1774 ***1220.25*** *p67*
Miller, Richard 52; Ontario, 1861 ***2896.26*** *p20*
Miller, Richard 70; Ontario, 1871 ***1823.15*** *p189*
Miller, Rob.; Maryland, 1652 ***2524.55*** *p152*
Miller, Robert; New Orleans, 1850 ***1640.10*** *p154*
Miller, Robert 26; Ontario, 1871 ***1823.28*** *p72*
Miller, Robert 29; Ontario, 1871 ***1823.15*** *p189*
Miller, Robert 40; Ontario, 1871 ***1823.15*** *p189*
Miller, Robert 60; Ontario, 1871 ***1823.15*** *p189*
Miller, Robt; Virginia, 1663 ***6212.30*** *p1*
Miller, Rose 60; Ontario, 1871 ***1823.15*** *p189*
Miller, Ruth; Ontario, 1861 ***2896.28*** *p52*
Miller, Samuel 36; Ontario, 1871 ***1823.15*** *p189*
Miller, Samuel 50; Ontario, 1871 ***1823.22*** *p111*
Miller, Sarah 36; Ontario, 1861 ***2896.25*** *p37*
Miller, Stephen 9; Ontario, 1861 ***2896.25*** *p37*
Miller, T. T. 58; Kansas, 1910 ***9079.10*** *p5*
Miller, Theodore 20; Ontario, 1861 ***2896.26*** *p22*
Miller, Thomas *SEE* Miller, James
Miller, Thomas; Maryland, 1658 ***2524.55*** *p179*
Miller, Thomas; Maryland, 1672 ***2524.55*** *p152*
Miller, Thomas; Maryland, 1673 ***2524.55*** *p152*
Miller, Thomas; Maryland, 1674 ***2524.55*** *p152*
Miller, Thomas; Maryland, 1675 ***2524.55*** *p152*
Miller, Valentine; New York, 1840 ***8197.10*** *p180*
Miller, Veronika; Port uncertain, 1774 ***2856.30*** *p304*
Miller, Walter 18; Ontario, 1861 ***2896.26*** *p3*
Miller, Wilburn 6; Ontario, 1861 ***2896.26*** *p19*
Miller, William *SEE* Miller, James
Miller, William *SEE* Miller, William
Miller, William; America, 1871 ***1640.13*** *p77*
Miller, William; Georgia, 1775 ***1640.10*** *p154*
Child: Hugh
Child: John
Child: William
Child: Isobel
Wife: Margaret Irvine
Miller, William; New York, 1821 ***8197.10*** *p260*
Miller, William; New York, 1829 ***8197.10*** *p351*
Miller, William; New York, 1830 ***1640.10*** *p155*
Miller, William; Pennsylvania, 1777 ***4629.10*** *p9*
Miller, William; Wilmington, North Carolina, 1781 ***1640.13*** *p77*
Miller, William 24; Maryland, 1774 ***1220.25*** *p61*
Miller, William 27; Ontario, 1871 ***1823.15*** *p189*
Miller, William 29; Maryland, 1774 ***1220.25*** *p78*
Miller, William 32; Ontario, 1871 ***1823.15*** *p189*
Miller, William 34; Ontario, 1871 ***1823.15*** *p189*
Miller, William 47; Ontario, 1871 ***1823.28*** *p72*
Miller, William 65; Ontario, 1871 ***1823.15*** *p189*
Miller, Zachariah; New York, 1806 ***8197.10*** *p32*
Millerd, Thomas; Maryland, 1671 ***2524.55*** *p152*
Milles, Charles; Maryland, 1682 ***2524.55*** *p152*
Milles, Dorothy; Maryland, 1682 ***2524.55*** *p152*
Milles, Rich; Virginia, 1663 ***6212.30*** *p4*
Milles, Roger; Virginia, 1667 ***6212.30*** *p37*
Millford, Martha; Virginia, 1663 ***6212.30*** *p1*
Milligan, Andrew 50; Ontario, 1871 ***1823.22*** *p111*
Milligan, Elgin 3; Ontario, 1861 ***2896.28*** *p64*
Milligan, Elizabeth 27; Ontario, 1861 ***2896.28*** *p64*
Milligan, George 65; Ontario, 1871 ***1823.22*** *p111*
Milligan, Hiram 9; Ontario, 1861 ***2896.28*** *p64*
Milligan, John; New York, New York, 1837 ***6058.10*** *p31*
Milligan, John 57; Ontario, 1871 ***1823.15*** *p189*
Milligan, Mary 1; Ontario, 1861 ***2896.28*** *p64*
Milligan, Richard 30; Ontario, 1871 ***1823.15*** *p189*
Milligan, Royal 11; Ontario, 1861 ***2896.28*** *p64*
Milligan, Thomas G. 40; Ontario, 1871 ***1823.22*** *p111*
Milligan, Wellington 5; Ontario, 1861 ***2896.28*** *p64*
Milligan, William; Charleston, South Carolina, 1811 ***1224.3*** *p52*
Milligan, William; Mobile, Alabama, 1844 ***1640.10*** *p155*
Milligan, William; Mobile, Alabama, 1844 ***1640.13*** *p77*
Milligan, William; New York, 1802 ***8197.10*** *p22*
Milliken, Andrew 48; Ontario, 1871 ***1823.15*** *p189*
Milliken, John 28; Ontario, 1871 ***1823.15*** *p189*
Millin, Catherine 57; Ontario, 1871 ***1823.15*** *p189*
Milliner, Francis 31; Maryland, 1774 ***1220.25*** *p51*
Millington, Mary; New York, 1856 ***1224.3*** *p52*
Millington, Nathaniel 23; Maryland, 1774 ***1220.25*** *p59*
Millington, Ruth; Maryland, 1670 ***2524.55*** *p152*
Million, James 42; Ontario, 1871 ***1823.15*** *p189*
Million, John *SEE* Million, John
Million, John; Maryland, 1682 ***2524.55*** *p152*
Wife: Katherine
Son: John
Daughter: Katherine
Million, John 53; Ontario, 1871 ***1823.15*** *p189*
Million, Katherine *SEE* Million, John
Million, Patrick 62; Ontario, 1871 ***1823.15*** *p189*
Millman, Thomas; Maryland, 1681 ***2524.55*** *p153*
Millner, Mathew; Maryland, 1663 ***2524.55*** *p153*
Millner, William; New York, 1794 ***8197.10*** *p2*
Millonas, John 34; Juneau, Alaska, 1917 ***9196.1*** *p45*
Millonas, John 34; Whitehorse, Yukon, 1917 ***9196.1*** *p45*
Mills, Mr.; Quebec, 1858 ***9196.15*** *p31*
Mills, Alfred 41; Ontario, 1861 ***2896.27*** *p53*
Mills, Andrew; New York, 1750 ***1224.2*** *p79*
Mills, Andrew; Savannah, Georgia, 1811 ***1640.10*** *p155*
Mills, Ann; Maryland, 1650-1651 ***2524.55*** *p153*
Mills, Ann; Maryland, 1664 ***2524.55*** *p153*
Mills, Ann 67; Ontario, 1861 ***2896.27*** *p56*
Mills, Anna 18; Ontario, 1861 ***2896.27*** *p30*
Mills, Anne M. 27; Ontario, 1861 ***2896.27*** *p57*
Mills, Catherine Dwyer 40; Vermont, 1872 ***5900.10*** *p200*
Mills, Charles 46; Ontario, 1861 ***2896.27*** *p57*
Mills, Charles, Jr. 16; Ontario, 1861 ***2896.27*** *p57*
Mills, David 30; Ontario, 1871 ***1823.15*** *p189*
Mills, E. Amelia 3; Ontario, 1861 ***2896.27*** *p54*
Mills, Eliza 45; Ontario, 1861 ***2896.27*** *p54*
Mills, Elizabeth 49; Ontario, 1861 ***2896.27*** *p57*
Mills, Elizabeth, Jr. 18; Ontario, 1861 ***2896.27*** *p57*
Mills, Elizabeth Hayes; Vermont, 1856-1929 ***5900.10*** *p179*
Mills, Emily 8; Ontario, 1861 ***2896.27*** *p54*
Mills, Esther 23; Maryland, 1774 ***1220.25*** *p59*
Mills, Fortune; Virginia, 1673 ***6212.30*** *p51*
Mills, George; New York, 1840 ***8197.10*** *p178*
Mills, George; Virginia, 1712 ***1224.2*** *p79*
Mills, George 11; Ontario, 1861 ***2896.27*** *p57*
Mills, George 28; Ontario, 1861 ***2896.26*** *p4*
Mills, George 45; Ontario, 1871 ***1823.28*** *p72*
Mills, George 67; Ontario, 1871 ***1823.15*** *p189*
Mills, Henry; New York, 1840 ***8197.10*** *p179*
Mills, Humphry; Maryland, 1682 ***2524.55*** *p153*
Mills, Idy; Maryland, 1650-1651 ***2524.55*** *p153*
Mills, Isaac 44; Ontario, 1871 ***1823.28*** *p72*
Mills, James; New York, 1794 ***8197.10*** *p2*
Mills, James; Virginia, 1673 ***6212.30*** *p51*
Mills, James 44; Ontario, 1871 ***1823.15*** *p189*
Mills, Joan; Virginia, 1663 ***6212.30*** *p1*
Mills, Joan; Virginia, 1663 ***6212.30*** *p2*
Mills, John; Alexandria, Virginia, 1786 ***1224.2*** *p79*
Mills, John; Alexandria, Virginia, 1847 ***1224.3*** *p52*
Mills, John; Maryland, 1670 ***2524.55*** *p153*
Mills, John; Maryland, 1676 ***2524.55*** *p153*
Mills, John 37; Ontario, 1871 ***1823.15*** *p189*
Mills, John, Jr.; New York, 1804 ***8197.10*** *p29*
Mills, Joseph 21; Ontario, 1861 ***2896.27*** *p57*
Mills, Joseph 76; Ontario, 1861 ***2896.27*** *p56*
Mills, Louisa 23; Ontario, 1861 ***2896.26*** *p4*
Mills, Mary; Maryland, 1665 ***2524.55*** *p153*
Mills, Mary; Maryland, 1665 ***2524.55*** *p198*
Mills, Mary; Maryland, 1668 ***2524.55*** *p153*
Mills, Mary; Maryland, 1677 ***2524.55*** *p153*
Mills, Mary 55; Ontario, 1871 ***1823.15*** *p189*
Mills, Mary A. 80; Ontario, 1871 ***1823.15*** *p189*
Mills, Maten 22; Virginia, 1774 ***1220.25*** *p86*
Mills, Patrick D.; Vermont, 1861-1932 ***5900.10*** *p179*

Mills, Phebe 35; Ontario, 1861 ***2896.25*** *p4*
Mills, Ralph; Virginia, 1664 ***6212.30*** *p5*
Mills, Rebecca 27; Ontario, 1861 ***2896.27*** *p56*
Mills, Richard; Maryland, 1663 ***2524.55*** *p51*
Mills, Richard; Virginia, 1664 ***6212.30*** *p9*
Mills, Richard 13; Ontario, 1861 ***2896.27*** *p57*
Mills, Richard 23; Philadelphia, 1774 ***1220.25*** *p68*
Mills, Richard 24; Ontario, 1871 ***1823.28*** *p72*
Mills, Robert; Ontario, 1861 ***2896.25*** *p9*
Mills, Robert 22; Maryland, 1774 ***1220.25*** *p71*
Mills, Samuel; Maryland, 1679 ***2524.55*** *p153*
Mills, Samuel; Pennsylvania, 1845 ***6058.10*** *p21*
Mills, Sarah; Virginia, 1672 ***6212.30*** *p48*
Mills, Thomas; Maryland, 1663 ***2524.55*** *p153*
Mills, Thomas 18; Maryland, 1774 ***1220.25*** *p64*
Mills, Thomas 22; Maryland, 1775 ***1220.25*** *p105*
Mills, Thomas 25; Ontario, 1861 ***2896.27*** *p56*
Mills, Thomas 28; Jamaica, 1774 ***1220.25*** *p40*
Mills, William; New York, 1834 ***8197.10*** *p315*
Mills, William; Savannah, Georgia, 1805 ***1640.10*** *p155*
Mills, William; Virginia, 1653 ***1224.1*** *p40*
Mills, William 30; Ontario, 1861 ***2896.27*** *p57*
Mills, William 37; Ontario, 1871 ***1823.15*** *p190*
Mills, William 63; Ontario, 1871 ***1823.15*** *p190*
Mills, William Henry; Bahamas, 1790 ***1224.2*** *p80*
Mills, William Henry; South Carolina, n.d. ***1224.2*** *p80*
Millson, John; New York, 1796 ***8197.10*** *p8*
Millson, Robert 31; Ontario, 1871 ***1823.28*** *p72*
Millward, H.; Quebec, 1858 ***9196.15*** *p38*
Millward, John; Virginia, 1666 ***6212.30*** *p29*
Milne, Alexander; Connecticut, 1889 ***1640.13*** *p77*
Milne, Alexander; New Orleans, 1838 ***1640.10*** *p155*
Milne, Alexander; New York, 1836 ***8197.10*** *p263*
Milne, Alexander 48; Ontario, 1871 ***1823.15*** *p190*
Milne, Alexander Panton; New York, 1898 ***1640.13*** *p77*
Milne, Andrew; New Orleans, 1806-1812 ***1640.10*** *p155*
Milne, Andrew 45; Ontario, 1871 ***1823.22*** *p111*
Milne, Andrew 63; Ontario, 1871 ***1823.28*** *p72*
Milne, George 33; Ontario, 1871 ***1823.28*** *p72*
Milne, George 39; Ontario, 1871 ***1823.28*** *p72*
Milne, George 53; Ontario, 1871 ***1823.22*** *p112*
Milne, Isabella 53; Ontario, 1871 ***1823.15*** *p190*
Milne, James; Pittsburgh, 1765 ***1224.2*** *p80*
Milne, James 22; Ontario, 1871 ***1823.15*** *p190*
Milne, James 54; Ontario, 1871 ***1823.22*** *p112*
Milne, James 64; Ontario, 1871 ***1823.15*** *p190*
Milne, Jessie; Winnipeg, Manitoba, 1884 ***1640.13*** *p77*
Milne, John; Savannah, Georgia, 1783 ***1640.10*** *p155*
Milne, John Radcliffe; Honduras, 1827 ***1640.13*** *p77*
Milne, William; Jamaica, 1850 ***1640.13*** *p77*
Milner, Elizabeth 30; Nova Scotia, 1774 ***1220.25*** *p137*
Milner, Elizabeth 50; Nova Scotia, 1774 ***1220.25*** *p137*
Milner, Jonathan 26; Nova Scotia, 1774 ***1220.25*** *p137*
Milner, Robert 33; Nova Scotia, 1774 ***1220.25*** *p137*
Milner, Thomas; Maryland, 1653 ***2524.55*** *p153*
Milner, William; Boston, 1713 ***1224.2*** *p80*
Milnor, William; Pennsylvania, 1777 ***4629.10*** *p8*
Milns, Henry; New York, 1839 ***8197.10*** *p142*
Milon, Sarah Gayers 84; Vermont, 1878 ***5900.10*** *p580*
Milroy, David; Bermuda, 1865 ***1640.13*** *p77*
Milsteed, John 22; Virginia, 1774 ***1220.25*** *p56*
Milteberger, Martin; Port uncertain, 1744 ***2856.30*** *p304*
Miltenberger, Anna Catharina; Port uncertain, 1711 ***2856.30*** *p304*
Milton, George 22; Baltimore, 1775 ***1220.25*** *p117*
Milton, Jno; Virginia, 1664 ***6212.30*** *p15*
Milton, R.; Quebec, 1857 ***9196.15*** *p14*
Milton, Sally 66; Ontario, 1861 ***2896.28*** *p45*
Milton, Samuel 81; Ontario, 1861 ***2896.28*** *p45*
Milton, Thomas 28; Baltimore, 1775 ***1220.25*** *p117*
Miltone, Alfred; New York, 1838 ***8197.10*** *p123*
Milward, Robert; Virginia, 1718 ***1224.2*** *p80*
Mimczyk, John; Maryland, 1910 ***3259.35*** *p40*
Minacker, Mrs. 46; Ontario, 1861 ***2896.26*** *p29*
Minacker, Dann 12; Ontario, 1861 ***2896.26*** *p29*
Minacker, Emma 8; Ontario, 1861 ***2896.26*** *p29*
Minacker, Isaac 14; Ontario, 1861 ***2896.26*** *p29*
Minacker, John 4; Ontario, 1861 ***2896.26*** *p29*
Minacker, Maud 6; Ontario, 1861 ***2896.26*** *p29*
Minacker, Sanford 17; Ontario, 1861 ***2896.26*** *p29*
Minacker, Sarah 18; Ontario, 1861 ***2896.26*** *p29*
Minahan, Bridget Butler 69; Vermont, 1898 ***5900.10*** *p124*
Minahan, James 84; Vermont, 1905 ***5900.10*** *p124*
Minahan, Katherine M.; Vermont, 1863-1907 ***5900.10*** *p130*
Minakwat, Paul 56; Ontario, 1871 ***1823.28*** *p72*
Minas, Darias E. 11; Ontario, 1861 ***2896.28*** *p53*
Minas, George E. 6; Ontario, 1861 ***2896.28*** *p53*
Minas, James 41; Ontario, 1861 ***2896.28*** *p53*
Minas, William W. 3; Ontario, 1861 ***2896.28*** *p53*
Minckel, Georg Adam; Port uncertain, 1785 ***2856.30*** *p304*
Minehan, Biddy 41; New York, New York, 1851 ***1825.45*** *p51*
Son: John 15
Son: Patrick 12
Minehan, Dennis 59; Vermont, 1898 ***5900.10*** *p337*
Minehan, John 15 *SEE* Minehan, Biddy
Minehan, Mary Lahey 68; Vermont, 1900 ***5900.10*** *p337*
Minehan, Patrick 12 *SEE* Minehan, Biddy
Miner, Catherine; Vermont, 1842-1920 ***5900.10*** *p284*
Miner, Daniel; Vermont, n.d. ***5900.10*** *p492*
Miner, Electa 58; Ontario, 1871 ***1823.28*** *p72*
Miner, Elizabeth; Vermont, 1844-1925 ***5900.10*** *p492*
Miner, Henry L.; Vermont, 1823-1910 ***5900.10*** *p194*
Miner, Mary T.; Vermont, 1858-1877 ***5900.10*** *p535*
Miner, Matilda Gates; Vermont, 1845-1923 ***5900.10*** *p194*
Miner, Patrick 90; Vermont, 1881 ***5900.10*** *p236*
Miner, Samuell; Maryland, 1661 ***2524.55*** *p153*
Miner, Willie L. 5; Vermont, 1862 ***5900.10*** *p535*
Minerabi, Samuel; New York, 1840 ***8197.10*** *p182*
Minerbi, Samuel; New York, 1835 ***8197.10*** *p263*
Miners, James 35; Ontario, 1871 ***1823.28*** *p72*
Miners, William 49; Ontario, 1871 ***1823.15*** *p190*
Minett, Charles James 29; Ontario, 1871 ***1823.28*** *p72*
Ming, Henry 54; Ontario, 1871 ***1823.22*** *p112*
Ming, Lorenz; America, 1739 ***2856.30*** *p304*
Mingam, Robert; New York, 1821 ***8197.10*** *p259*
Mingan, Robert; New York, 1821 ***8197.10*** *p259*
Mingay, John 44; Philadelphia, 1774 ***1220.25*** *p82*
Minges, Valentin; Port uncertain, 1779 ***2856.30*** *p304*
Minges, Valentin; Port uncertain, 1780 ***2856.30*** *p304*
Minhold, Martin; Pennsylvania, 1777 ***4629.10*** *p13*
Minich, Christian; Pennsylvania, 1777 ***4629.10*** *p25*
Minich, Hans Georg; America, 1754 ***2856.30*** *p304*
Minich, Philipp; America, 1754 ***2856.30*** *p304*
Minithorpe, Thomas; Maryland, 1666 ***2524.55*** *p153*
Mink, Apollonia; America, 1846 ***2856.30*** *p304*
With husband & children
Minking, Charles 45; Ontario, 1871 ***1823.28*** *p72*
Minn, Anna Catharina; Port uncertain, 1790 ***2856.30*** *p304*
Minnett, John; Maryland, 1658-1663 ***2524.55*** *p20*
Minnick, Christian; Pennsylvania, 1786 ***1224.2*** *p80*
Minniker, John; Maryland, 1659 ***2524.55*** *p153*
Minnis, Jane 70; Ontario, 1861 ***2896.28*** *p35*
Minns, James 50; Ontario, 1871 ***1823.22*** *p112*
Minns, James 60; Boston, 1774 ***1220.25*** *p58*
Minns, James, Jr. 30; Boston, 1774 ***1220.25*** *p58*
Minns, Katherine A. Delligan 40; Vermont, 1902 ***5900.10*** *p513*
Minogue, Annie 38; Vermont, 1897 ***5900.10*** *p262*
Minogue, Bridget Quigley; Vermont, 1841-1934 ***5900.10*** *p272*
Minogue, Ellen; Vermont, 1837-1929 ***5900.10*** *p274*
Minogue, James 34; Vermont, 1862 ***5900.10*** *p262*
Minogue, James 77; Vermont, 1868 ***5900.10*** *p262*
Minogue, John; Vermont, 1859-1880 ***5900.10*** *p262*
Minogue, Julia; Vermont, 1825-1898 ***5900.10*** *p259*
Minogue, Julia 50; Vermont, 1882 ***5900.10*** *p262*
Minogue, Mary; Vermont, 1856-1915 ***5900.10*** *p257*
Minogue, Mary 2 months; Vermont, 1854 ***5900.10*** *p262*
Minogue, Michael; Vermont, 1842-1889 ***5900.10*** *p272*
Minogue, Michael 22; Vermont, 1865 ***5900.10*** *p261*
Minogue, Patrick 35; Vermont, 1858 ***5900.10*** *p269*
Minogue, Patrick 44; Vermont, 1869 ***5900.10*** *p262*
Minogue, Winefred 55; Vermont, 1878 ***5900.10*** *p269*
Minor, Charles; Maryland, 1637 ***2524.55*** *p148*
Minor, Charles; Maryland, 1637-1640 ***2524.55*** *p153*
Minor, Francis 89; Vermont, 1894 ***5900.10*** *p292*
Minor, John 82; Vermont, 1872 ***5900.10*** *p279*
Minor, Margaret 83; Vermont, 1892 ***5900.10*** *p292*
Minor, Mary L. 67; Vermont, 1857 ***5900.10*** *p279*
Minor, Samuell; Maryland, 1661 ***2524.55*** *p153*
Minor, Sarah J.; Vermont, 1863-1921 ***5900.10*** *p243*
Minott, Theophilus; Boston, 1705 ***1224.2*** *p80*
Minouge, Julia; Vermont, 1854-1924 ***5900.10*** *p394*
Minphey, Samuel 15; Maryland, 1775 ***1220.25*** *p104*
Minshen, William 22; Ontario, 1861 ***2896.25*** *p23*
Minshull, John 46; Ontario, 1871 ***1823.15*** *p190*
Minter, Albert; New York, New York, 1867 ***3437.14*** *p103*
Minter, Harmann; New York, New York, 1860 ***3437.14*** *p82*
Minter, John; Maryland, 1668 ***2524.55*** *p153*
Minterne, John; Virginia, 1619 ***1224.1*** *p40*
Minthard, Robert; Virginia, 1665 ***6212.30*** *p19*
Minto, Alison 50; Ontario, 1871 ***1823.22*** *p112*
Minto, George 41; Ontario, 1871 ***1823.22*** *p112*
Minton, Jane 66; Ontario, 1871 ***1823.15*** *p190*
Minty, William; Louisiana, 1735-1845 ***1640.10*** *p155*
Mirandoli, Edward; New York, 1839 ***8197.10*** *p320*
Mirfield, Mary 52; Ontario, 1871 ***1823.22*** *p112*
Mirfield, Samuel 28; Ontario, 1871 ***1823.22*** *p112*
Mirie, Frank 38; Alaska, 1914 ***9196.1*** *p24*
Miriski, Frank; Maryland, 1910 ***3259.35*** *p40*
Mirkin, Richard; Maryland, 1662 ***2524.55*** *p153*
Mirton, Jane 74; Ontario, 1871 ***1823.15*** *p190*
Mirus, Adam; Maryland, 1910 ***3259.35*** *p40*
Mischott, Friedrich; New York, 1807 ***8197.10*** *p327*
Miscimiesky, Antony; Maryland, 1910 ***3259.35*** *p40*
Misel, Abraham; Port uncertain, 1744 ***2856.30*** *p304*
With wife & child
Misental, Georg; Port uncertain, 1764 ***2856.30*** *p304*
Mishawas, Thomas 53; Ontario, 1871 ***1823.28*** *p72*
Mishibiniguna, Daniel 54; Ontario, 1871 ***1823.28*** *p72*
Mishibiniguna, Moyse 64; Ontario, 1871 ***1823.28*** *p73*
Mishkryski, Stanislay; Maryland, 1910 ***3259.35*** *p40*
Mishnak, Carrie; Maryland, 1910 ***3259.35*** *p40*
Mishon, Willm; Maryland, 1673 ***2524.55*** *p153*
Misiora, Joseph; Maryland, 1910 ***3259.35*** *p40*
Miske, Michael 24; Ontario, 1871 ***1823.28*** *p73*
Miskelley, James 34; Ontario, 1871 ***1823.28*** *p73*
Miskin, Sarah 69; Ontario, 1861 ***2896.25*** *p23*
Miskowitz, Victoria; Maryland, 1910 ***3259.35*** *p40*
Mislinski, John; Maryland, 1910 ***3259.35*** *p40*
Miss, David 36; Kansas, 1888-1910 ***9079.10*** *p40*
Miss, Mary 34; Kansas, 1878-1910 ***9079.10*** *p40*
Missisangwe, Michel 39; Ontario, 1871 ***1823.28*** *p73*
Mississance, Michelle 65; Ontario, 1871 ***1823.28*** *p73*
Mistelmuller, Wendel; Port uncertain, 1752 ***2856.30*** *p304*
Mistmann, Mr.; Port uncertain, 1785 ***2856.30*** *p304*
With wife
Mitchal, Robert W. 38; Ontario, 1871 ***1823.15*** *p190*
Mitcham, Christopher 25; Maryland, 1775 ***1220.25*** *p121*
Mitchel, Allan 35; Ontario, 1871 ***1823.15*** *p190*
Mitchel, Andrew 45; Ontario, 1871 ***1823.15*** *p190*
Mitchel, Bridget 50; Ontario, 1871 ***1823.28*** *p73*
Mitchel, Catherine 58; Ontario, 1871 ***1823.15*** *p190*
Mitchel, James 25; Ontario, 1871 ***1823.15*** *p190*
Mitchel, John; Canada, 1756-1760 ***4628.40*** *p45*
Mitchel, John 21; Maryland, 1775 ***1220.25*** *p105*
Mitchel, John 23; Virginia, 1774 ***1220.25*** *p46*
Mitchel, John 40; Ontario, 1871 ***1823.15*** *p190*
Mitchel, John 60; Ontario, 1871 ***1823.28*** *p73*
Mitchel, John 69; Ontario, 1871 ***1823.15*** *p190*
Mitchel, Joseph; America, 1790 ***4628.40*** *p29*
Mitchel, Samuel 24; Virginia, 1774 ***1220.25*** *p46*
Mitchel, Samuel 59; Ontario, 1871 ***1823.15*** *p190*
Mitchel, Thomas; Maryland, 1910 ***3259.35*** *p40*
Mitchel, Thomas 31; Ontario, 1871 ***1823.15*** *p190*
Mitchel, W. C. 36; Ontario, 1871 ***1823.28*** *p73*
Mitchell, Abraham 44; Ontario, 1871 ***1823.28*** *p73*
Mitchell, Alexander; Maryland, 1673 ***2524.55*** *p153*
Mitchell, Alexander; New York, 1807 ***8197.10*** *p45*
Mitchell, Alexander; New York, 1825 ***8197.10*** *p262*
Mitchell, Alexander; Savannah, Georgia, 1798 ***1640.10*** *p155*
Mitchell, Alexander 58; Ontario, 1871 ***1823.15*** *p190*
Mitchell, Alexander; Jamaica, 1799 ***1640.13*** *p77*
Mitchell, Alice; Vermont, 1852-1878 ***5900.10*** *p349*
Mitchell, Alice; Virginia, 1666 ***6212.30*** *p26*
Mitchell, Andrew; Georgia, 1739 ***1640.10*** *p155*
Mitchell, Andrew 36; Ontario, 1871 ***1823.15*** *p190*
Mitchell, Anne 43; Ontario, 1871 ***1823.22*** *p112*
Mitchell, Arthur 54; Ontario, 1871 ***1823.15*** *p190*
Mitchell, Benjamin; New York, 1761 ***1224.2*** *p80*
Mitchell, Bridget; Vermont, 1834-1899 ***5900.10*** *p435*
Mitchell, C. 25; Alaska, 1912 ***9196.1*** *p38*
Mitchell, C. 25; Yukon, 1912 ***9196.1*** *p38*
Mitchell, Catherine 13; Ontario, 1871 ***1823.15*** *p190*
Mitchell, Catherine 58; Ontario, 1871 ***1823.22*** *p112*
Mitchell, Charles; New York, 1837 ***8197.10*** *p100*
Mitchell, Charles; New York, 1838 ***8197.10*** *p125*
Mitchell, Charles 34; Ontario, 1861 ***2896.28*** *p32*
Mitchell, David; New York, 1803 ***8197.10*** *p14*
Mitchell, David; New York, 1835-1838 ***8197.10*** *p123*
Mitchell, David; Oregon, 1874 ***1640.13*** *p78*
Mitchell, David 72; Ontario, 1871 ***1823.15*** *p190*
Mitchell, David Brydie; America, 1783 ***1640.10*** *p155*
Mitchell, Donald; California, 1889 ***1640.13*** *p78*
Mitchell, Donald 40; Ontario, 1871 ***1823.28*** *p73*
Mitchell, E. 21; Ontario, 1861 ***2896.28*** *p3*
Mitchell, E. 36; Ontario, 1861 ***2896.28*** *p3*
Mitchell, Eliza 73; Ontario, 1871 ***1823.22*** *p112*
Mitchell, Eliza M. 10; Ontario, 1861 ***2896.27*** *p37*
Mitchell, Elizabeth; New Orleans, 1790 ***1640.10*** *p160*
Mitchell, Elizabeth 43; Ontario, 1861 ***2896.27*** *p37*
Mitchell, Ellen 73; Vermont, 1916 ***5900.10*** *p123*
Mitchell, F. J. 18; Ontario, 1861 ***2896.28*** *p3*
Mitchell, F. N. 2; Ontario, 1861 ***2896.28*** *p3*
Mitchell, G. A. 12; Ontario, 1861 ***2896.28*** *p3*
Mitchell, George; New York, 1823 ***8197.10*** *p262*
Mitchell, George 16; Ontario, 1861 ***2896.27*** *p37*
Mitchell, George 28; Ontario, 1871 ***1823.15*** *p190*
Mitchell, George 48; Ontario, 1871 ***1823.22*** *p112*

Mitchell, George 64; Ontario, 1871 **1823.22** *p112*
Mitchell, George 70; Ontario, 1871 **1823.22** *p112*
Mitchell, George Abercromby; England, 1861 **1640.13** *p78*
Mitchell, H. L. 16; Ontario, 1861 **2896.28** *p3*
Mitchell, Henry; Maryland, 1681 **2524.55** *p153*
Mitchell, Henry; New York, 1807 **8197.10** *p331*
Mitchell, Henry; New York, 1832 **8197.10** *p263*
Mitchell, Humphry; Maryland, 1664 **2524.55** *p153*
Mitchell, Isaac 45; Ontario, 1871 **1823.22** *p112*
Mitchell, J. A. 6; Ontario, 1861 **2896.28** *p3*
Mitchell, Jacob; Maryland, 1910 **3259.35** *p40*
Mitchell, James; Georgia, 1699 **1640.13** *p78*
Mitchell, James; New York, 1822 **8197.10** *p260*
Mitchell, James; Pennsylvania, 1777 **4629.10** *p18*
Mitchell, James; Pennsylvania, 1861-1868 **6058.10** *p67*
Mitchell, James; Rhode Island, 1781 **1224.2** *p80*
Mitchell, James 6; Ontario, 1861 **2896.27** *p37*
Mitchell, James 42; Ontario, 1871 **1823.15** *p191*
Mitchell, James 43; Ontario, 1871 **1823.15** *p191*
Mitchell, James 45; Ontario, 1871 **1823.28** *p73*
Mitchell, James 51; Ontario, 1871 **1823.15** *p191*
Mitchell, James 53; Ontario, 1871 **1823.15** *p191*
Mitchell, James 54; Ontario, 1871 **1823.22** *p112*
Mitchell, James Alexander; New Orleans, 1845 **1640.10** *p156*
Mitchell, James McNair; Newfoundland, 1894 **1640.13** *p78*
Mitchell, Jane 17; Ontario, 1871 **1823.15** *p191*
Mitchell, Jane 64; Vermont, 1876 **5900.10** *p499*
Mitchell, Jessie 27; Ontario, 1871 **1823.22** *p112*
Mitchell, Jno 70; Ontario, 1861 **2896.28** *p3*
Mitchell, John; Florida, 1776 **1640.10** *p156*
Mitchell, John; Georgia, 1761 **1640.10** *p156*
Mitchell, John; Jamaica, 1824 **1640.13** *p78*
Mitchell, John; Maryland, 1672 **2524.55** *p153*
Mitchell, John; Maryland, 1673 **2524.55** *p153*
Mitchell, John; Maryland, 1680 **2524.55** *p153*
Mitchell, John; New York, 1836-1840 **8197.10** *p302*
Mitchell, John; Pennsylvania, 1777 **4629.10** *p7*
Mitchell, John; Pennsylvania, 1785 **4629.10** *p49*
Mitchell, John; St. Johns, Newfoundland, 1879 **1640.13** *p78*
Mitchell, John; Vermont, 1824-1897 **5900.10** *p349*
Mitchell, John 10; Ontario, 1871 **1823.15** *p191*
Mitchell, John 30; Ontario, 1871 **1823.15** *p191*
Mitchell, John 36; Ontario, 1871 **1823.15** *p191*
Mitchell, John 41; Ontario, 1871 **1823.15** *p191*
Mitchell, John 54; Ontario, 1871 **1823.15** *p191*
Mitchell, John 58; Ontario, 1871 **1823.15** *p191*
Mitchell, John 62; Ontario, 1871 **1823.22** *p112*
Mitchell, John 66; Ontario, 1871 **1823.22** *p112*
Mitchell, John 68; Ontario, 1871 **1823.22** *p112*
Mitchell, John 73; Ontario, 1871 **1823.15** *p191*
Mitchell, Joseph; Pennsylvania, 1777 **4629.10** *p29*
Mitchell, Joseph; Virginia, 1710 **1224.2** *p80*
Mitchell, Kate D.; Vermont, 1848-1931 **5900.10** *p351*
Mitchell, M. E. 10; Ontario, 1861 **2896.28** *p3*
Mitchell, Margaret; Quebec, 1841 **1640.13** *p78*
Mitchell, Margaret 22; Ontario, 1871 **1823.15** *p191*
Mitchell, Margaret 49; Vermont, 1868 **5900.10** *p503*
Mitchell, Mark; Maryland, 1681 **2524.55** *p153*
Mitchell, Mark 19; Virginia, 1774 **1220.25** *p45*
Mitchell, Mary 19, Ontario, 1871 **1823.15** *p191*
Mitchell, Mary 30; Ontario, 1861 **2896.28** *p32*
Mitchell, Mary Ann 16; Ontario, 1861 **2896.27** *p34*
Mitchell, Nancy Dwyer; Vermont, 1869-1900 **5900.10** *p332*
Mitchell, Nora; Vermont, 1828-1901 **5900.10** *p349*
Mitchell, Owen 45; Ontario, 1871 **1823.15** *p191*
Mitchell, P. C. 14; Ontario, 1861 **2896.28** *p3*
Mitchell, Rachell; Maryland, 1664 **2524.55** *p153*
Mitchell, Richard; Maryland, 1681 **2524.55** *p153*
Mitchell, Richard 15; Philadelphia, 1774 **1220.25** *p80*
Mitchell, Robert; New York, 1803 **8197.10** *p14*
Mitchell, Robert; Savannah, Georgia, 1830 **1640.10** *p156*
Mitchell, Robert; Savannah, Georgia, 1846 **1224.3** *p52*
Mitchell, Robert 8; Ontario, 1861 **2896.27** *p37*
Mitchell, Robert 45; Ontario, 1861 **2896.27** *p37*
Mitchell, Robert, Sr. 74; Ontario, 1871 **1823.22** *p112*
Mitchell, S. E. 34; Ontario, 1871 **1823.28** *p73*
Mitchell, Samll; Virginia, 1666 **6212.30** *p26*
Mitchell, Sarah J. 3; Ontario, 1861 **2896.27** *p37*
Mitchell, Shedrick 32; Ontario, 1871 **1823.22** *p112*
Mitchell, Thomas; Maryland, 1648 **2524.55** *p153*
With wife & 2 children
Mitchell, Thomas; Vermont, 1834-1915 **5900.10** *p69*
Mitchell, Thomas 23; Dominica, 1773 **1220.25** *p31*
Mitchell, Thomas 25; Ontario, 1871 **1823.15** *p191*
Mitchell, Thomas 32; Ontario, 1871 **1823.22** *p112*
Mitchell, Thomas 40; Ontario, 1871 **1823.15** *p191*
Mitchell, Thomas 47; Ontario, 1871 **1823.15** *p191*
Mitchell, Thomas R. 24; Ontario, 1871 **1823.15** *p191*
Mitchell, Thomas Reeves; Mississippi, 1846 **1640.10** *p156*
Mitchell, Thompson; New York, 1840 **8197.10** *p264*
Mitchell, Timothy; Vermont, 1851-1882 **5900.10** *p349*
Mitchell, W. H.; Vermont, 1841-1934 **5900.10** *p514*
Mitchell, Walter; Georgia, 1698 **1640.13** *p78*
Mitchell, Walter; New York, 1802 **8197.10** *p22*
Mitchell, William; New York, 1825 **8197.10** *p297*
Mitchell, William; Vermont, 1842-1915 **5900.10** *p351*
Mitchell, William 21; Philadelphia, 1775 **1220.25** *p107*
Mitchell, William 28; Maryland, 1773-1774 **1220.25** *p33*
Mitchell, William 40; Ontario, 1871 **1823.15** *p191*
Mitchell, William 51; Ontario, 1871 **1823.15** *p191*
Mitchell, William 55; Ontario, 1871 **1823.15** *p191*
Mitchell, Wm.; New York, 1840 **8197.10** *p180*
Mitchell, Wm; Virginia, 1672 **6212.30** *p49*
Mitchell, Zeb 35; Vermont, 1874 **5900.10** *p169*
Mitchelson, John 60; Ontario, 1871 **1823.15** *p191*
Mitchene, Mary 74; Vermont, 1900 **5900.10** *p316*
Mitchinson, William 30; Norfolk, Virginia, 1774 **1220.25** *p20*
Mithovich, Mich 25; Alaska, 1912 **9196.1** *p20*
Mithovich, Mich 25; British Columbia, 1912 **9196.1** *p20*
Mitick, John; Virginia, 1663 **6212.30** *p3*
Mitner, Robert 20; Philadelphia, 1774 **1220.25** *p20*
Mitschel, Josef; Port uncertain, 1745 **2856.30** *p304*
Mitson, John 21; Virginia, 1774 **1220.25** *p93*
Mittag, Maria Elisabeth; Port uncertain, 1748 **2856.30** *p304*
Mitten, Margaret; Vermont, 1872 **5900.10** *p181*
Mittenmuller, Catharina; America, 1751 **2856.30** *p304*
With husband
Mitteregger, Jacob; New York, 1829 **8197.10** *p312*
Mittermuller, Barbara; Port uncertain, 1755 **2856.30** *p304*
Mittford, Anthony; Maryland, 1664 **2524.55** *p153*
Mittin, James; Virginia, 1667-1668 **6212.30** *p39*
Mitton, John 22; Nova Scotia, 1774 **1220.25** *p135*
Mityiche, Mr.; Quebec, 1858 **9196.15** *p36*
Mitzel, Johann; Port uncertain, 1751 **2856.30** *p304*
Mitzenroth, Jakob; Port uncertain, 1730 **2856.30** *p304*
Miubay, Peter 55; Ontario, 1871 **1823.15** *p191*
Miziah, John 61; Ontario, 1871 **1823.28** *p73*
Mizigon, Antoine 50; Ontario, 1871 **1823.28** *p73*
Mizigon, Joselle 20; Ontario, 1871 **1823.28** *p73*
Mizigon, Micheal 50; Ontario, 1871 **1823.28** *p73*
Mizigon, Susan 3; Ontario, 1871 **1823.28** *p73*
Mlaughlin, James; Pennsylvania, 1835 **6058.10** *p12*
Mlynawyk, Stanislaw; Maryland, 1910 **3259.35** *p40*
M Mahony, Edm.; Maryland, 1678 **2524.55** *p119*
Moan, Alexander 42; Ontario, 1871 **1823.22** *p112*
Moan, Mary 72; Vermont, 1877 **5900.10** *p530*
Moan, Patrick; New York, 1804 **8197.10** *p27*
Moasley, Thomas; Maryland, 1673 **2524.55** *p153*
Moat, Alexander; Savannah, Georgia, 1775 **1640.10** *p156*
Moaz, George 30; Ontario, 1871 **1823.15** *p191*
Mobach, Margarete; Port uncertain, 1762 **2856.30** *p304*
Moch, Hugh; Pennsylvania, 1827 **6058.10** *p9*
Mochl, Henry; Pennsylvania, 1827 **6058.10** *p9*
Mock, Johann; Port uncertain, 1785 **2856.30** *p305*
With wife
Mock, Johann Adam; Port uncertain, 1748 **2856.30** *p305*
Mockh, Catharina; Port uncertain, 1700 **2856.30** *p305*
Mocosik, Joseph 55; Ontario, 1871 **1823.28** *p73*
Mocotabin, Bob 35; Ontario, 1871 **1823.28** *p73*
Mocotaikwoshk, Louis 38; Ontario, 1871 **1823.28** *p73*
Mode, Adam; Port uncertain, 1771 **2856.30** *p282*
Modiford, Francis; Maryland, 1669 **2524.55** *p157*
Modland, John 46; Ontario, 1871 **1823.15** *p191*
Modrak, John; Maryland, 1910 **3259.35** *p40*
Modry, Mrs. Joh.; Port uncertain, 1806 **2856.30** *p515*
Moehauski, William; Maryland, 1910 **3259.35** *p40*
Moehring, Gotthilf; New York, 1827 **8197.10** *p262*
Moeller, Phallender; New York, 1840 **8197.10** *p181*
Moen, A. R.; New York, 1840 **8197.10** *p181*
Moers, Franz; Port uncertain, 1766 **2856.30** *p305*
Moessnerin, Magdalena; Port uncertain, 1789 **2856.30** *p305*
Moffat, Alexander 69; Ontario, 1871 **1823.28** *p73*
Moffat, Alexr, Jr. 41; Ontario, 1871 **1823.28** *p73*
Moffat, David 56; Ontario, 1871 **1823.15** *p191*
Moffat, David 69; Ontario, 1871 **1823.15** *p191*
Moffat, George 40; Ontario, 1871 **1823.15** *p191*
Moffat, Henry 48; Ontario, 1871 **1823.28** *p73*
Moffat, James; Georgia, 1699 **1640.13** *p78*
Moffat, Jas P. 43; Ontario, 1871 **1823.28** *p73*
Moffat, John; New York, 1839 **8197.10** *p142*
Moffat, John 38; Ontario, 1871 **1823.15** *p191*
Moffat, John 71; Ontario, 1871 **1823.15** *p191*
Moffat, Thomas 36; Ontario, 1871 **1823.22** *p112*
Moffat, Walter 38; Ontario, 1871 **1823.15** *p191*
Moffat, William 40; Ontario, 1871 **1823.15** *p191*
Moffat, William 45; Ontario, 1871 **1823.28** *p73*
Moffatt, Anna Ward; Vermont, 1858-1926 **5900.10** *p496*
Moffatt, Arthur; Vermont, 1866-1950 **5900.10** *p460*
Moffatt, Mrs. B.; Mississippi, 1735-1845 **1640.10** *p156*
Moffatt, Charles 88; Ontario, 1871 **1823.22** *p113*
Moffatt, Elizabeth 60; Ontario, 1871 **1823.15** *p191*
Moffatt, George 40; Ontario, 1871 **1823.15** *p191*
Moffatt, Isabella 30; Ontario, 1871 **1823.15** *p191*
Moffatt, J.; Quebec, 1857 **9196.15** *p26*
Moffatt, John; New York, 1803 **8197.10** *p14*
Moffatt, Martha 51; Ontario, 1871 **1823.22** *p113*
Moffatt, Mary Ann Quine 32; Vermont, 1875 **5900.10** *p287*
Moffatt, R. D.; South Carolina, 1816-1845 **1640.10** *p156*
Moffatt, Richard; Ontario, 1871 **1823.22** *p113*
Moffatt, Robert 45; Ontario, 1871 **1823.15** *p191*
Moffatt, William 28; Ontario, 1871 **1823.15** *p191*
Moffatt, William 41; Ontario, 1871 **1823.15** *p191*
Moffatt, William W.; Vermont, 1858-1918 **5900.10** *p496*
Moffatt, Willie 2 days; Vermont, 1888 **5900.10** *p601*
Moffett, Bridget; Vermont, 1835-1900 **5900.10** *p187*
Moffett, John; Vermont, 1881 **5900.10** *p290*
Moffett, Joseph; Vermont, 1842-1913 **5900.10** *p288*
Moffett, Mary Ann McElroy; Vermont, 1838-1900 **5900.10** *p288*
Moffett, William; Maryland, 1667 **2524.55** *p153*
Moffit, Isabell 68; Ontario, 1871 **1823.22** *p113*
Moffit, William 39; Ontario, 1871 **1823.22** *p113*
Mog, Daniel; America, 1752 **2856.30** *p305*
Mog, Hans Georg; Port uncertain, 1752 **2856.30** *p305*
Mog, Matthaus; America, 1832 **2856.30** *p305*
Mogasin, Benjamin 55; Ontario, 1871 **1823.22** *p113*
Moger, Isaac; Massachusetts, 1807 **1224.3** *p53*
Mogg, John 20; Ontario, 1871 **1823.15** *p191*
Mogg, John 39; Ontario, 1871 **1823.15** *p191*
Mogridge, Alexander Augustus Perry; New Orleans, 1856 **1224.3** *p53*
Mohaghan, Michael; Pennsylvania, 1867 **6058.10** *p58*
Mohan, Hannah 50; Ontario, 1871 **1823.22** *p113*
Mohan, Margaret; Vermont, n.d. **5900.10** *p230*
Mohan, Thomas; Vermont, 1853-1885 **5900.10** *p98*
Moher, Robert; Vermont, 1845-1940 **5900.10** *p444*
Mohk, Johann; Port uncertain, 1785 **2856.30** *p305*
With wife
Mohl, Henrich; America, 1751 **2856.30** *p319*
With wife & children
Mohl, Henrich; America, 1752 **2856.30** *p319*
With wife & children
Mohlin, Friedrich; Port uncertain, 1744 **2856.30** *p319*
Mohlin, Friedrich; Port uncertain, 1745 **2856.30** *p319*
Mohlin, Michael; Port uncertain, 1703 **2856.30** *p319*
Mohlin, Michael; Port uncertain, 1745 **2856.30** *p319*
Mohnkern, Conrad; Pennsylvania, 1841 **6058.10** *p17*
Mohnkern, Henry; Pennsylvania, 1839 **6058.10** *p17*
Mohns, Agustus 39; Ontario, 1871 **1823.28** *p73*
Mohone, John; Maryland, 1676 **2524.55** *p154*
Mohr, Barbara; Port uncertain, 1748 **2856.30** *p305*
Mohr, Catharina; Port uncertain, 1774 **2856.30** *p305*
Mohr, Gabriel; Port uncertain, 1746 **2856.30** *p305*
Mohr, Gabriel; Port uncertain, 1756 **2856.30** *p305*
With 4 children
Mohr, Georg; Port uncertain, 1764 **2856.30** *p305*
Mohr, Hans; Port uncertain, 1722 **2856.30** *p305*
Mohr, Jakob; America, 1749 **2856.30** *p305*
Mohr, Johan George; Virginia, 1775 **1220.25** *p123*
Mohr, Johann; Port uncertain, 1722 **2856.30** *p305*
Mohr, Johann; Port uncertain, 1764 **2856.30** *p305*
With wife & 3 children
Mohr, Johann, The Old; Port uncertain, 1744 **2856.30** *p305*
Mohr, Johann Georg; Port uncertain, 1740 **2856.30** *p305*
Mohr, Johann Nikolaus; Port uncertain, 1759 **2856.30** *p305*
Mohr, Konrad; America, 1752 **2856.30** *p305*
With wife & 2 children
Mohr, Konrad; Port uncertain, 1759 **2856.30** *p305*
Mohr, Leonard; Port uncertain, 1740 **2856.30** *p305*
Mohr, Margarete; Port uncertain, 1738 **2856.30** *p305*
Mohr, Margarete; Port uncertain, 1787 **2856.30** *p305*
Mohr, Maria Barbara; Port uncertain, 1756 **2856.30** *p305*
Mohr, Mathes Wilhelm; Port uncertain, 1773 **2856.30** *p305*
Mohr, Michael; Port uncertain, 1746 **2856.30** *p305*
Mohr, Michael; Port uncertain, 1809 **2856.30** *p305*
With wife & son
Mohr, Peter; America, 1739 **2856.30** *p305*
Mohr, Peter; Port uncertain, 1789 **2856.30** *p305*
Mohra, Balthasar; Port uncertain, 1777 **2856.30** *p306*
Mohrer, Andreas; Port uncertain, 1754 **2856.30** *p306*
Mohun, Mr.; Quebec, 1857 **9196.15** *p24*
Mohun, Nath; Virginia, 1666 **6212.30** *p28*
Mohus, William; Maryland, 1659 **2524.55** *p154*
Moile, Jno; Virginia, 1666 **6212.30** *p28*
Moiles, James 77; Vermont, 1870 **5900.10** *p325*

Moiles, Thomas; Vermont, 1841-1905 ***5900.10*** *p452*
Moine, Alexandre; New York, New York, 1898 ***3437.14*** *p169*
Moine, Claude; Indiana, 1901 ***3437.14*** *p142*
Moir, Mr.; Quebec, 1856 ***9196.15*** *p6*
Moir, Alexander 49; Ontario, 1871 ***1823.15*** *p192*
Moir, Andrew 21; Maryland, 1774 ***1220.25*** *p53*
Moir, Andrew 45; Ontario, 1871 ***1823.15*** *p192*
Moir, George 51; Ontario, 1871 ***1823.15*** *p192*
Moir, George 55; Ontario, 1871 ***1823.15*** *p192*
Moir, Jacob 60; Ontario, 1871 ***1823.15*** *p192*
Moir, James 22; Maryland, 1774 ***1220.25*** *p53*
Moir, James 46; Ontario, 1871 ***1823.15*** *p192*
Moir, John; New York, 1807 ***8197.10*** *p45*
Moir, John; New York, 1840 ***8197.10*** *p265*
Moir, John 20; Ontario, 1871 ***1823.15*** *p192*
Moir, Peter 38; Ontario, 1871 ***1823.15*** *p192*
Moir, Robert 47; Ontario, 1871 ***1823.15*** *p192*
Moir, Thomas 34; Ontario, 1871 ***1823.15*** *p192*
Moir, William; New York, 1840 ***8197.10*** *p179*
Moir, William 32; Ontario, 1871 ***1823.15*** *p192*
Moirarty, James 28; Ontario, 1871 ***1823.28*** *p73*
Moirarty, Patrick 55; Ontario, 1871 ***1823.28*** *p73*
Moirce, Claude; Indiana, 1901 ***3437.14*** *p142*
Mokejwski, Teofril; Maryland, 1910 ***3259.35*** *p40*
Mokrajk, James; Maryland, 1910 ***3259.35*** *p40*
Mokram, Nancy 41; Ontario, 1871 ***1823.15*** *p192*
Molan, James 17; Maryland, 1774 ***1220.25*** *p60*
Moland, William; Pennsylvania, 1777 ***4629.10*** *p27*
Moland, William 21; Maryland, 1774 ***1220.25*** *p73*
Molcto, Fra.; Maryland, 1633 ***2524.55*** *p154*
Molder, Elis. Margarete; Port uncertain, 1807 ***2856.30*** *p306*
Molder, Robert; Maryland, 1673 ***2524.55*** *p154*
Mole, Zacharias; New York, 1807 ***8197.10*** *p45*
Moledore, Adam; Pennsylvania, 1777 ***4629.10*** *p12*
Molesworth, Thos 48; Ontario, 1871 ***1823.15*** *p192*
Molineaux, Mary; Vermont, 1853-1912 ***5900.10*** *p349*
Molineux, Wm.; New York, 1840 ***8197.10*** *p182*
Molinex, Jno; Virginia, 1665 ***6212.30*** *p22*
Molins, William; Maryland, 1659 ***2524.55*** *p154*
Molius, Johann; America, 1769 ***2856.30*** *p306*
Moll, Diebold; Port uncertain, 1771 ***2856.30*** *p306*
Moll, Henrich; America, 1751 ***2856.30*** *p319*
With wife & children
Moll, Henrich; America, 1752 ***2856.30*** *p319*
With wife & children
Moll, J. H.; America, 1752 ***2856.30*** *p482*
Moll, Jan; New York, 1806 ***8197.10*** *p32*
Moll, Johann Georg; Port uncertain, 1780 ***2856.30*** *p306*
Moll, Johann Heinrich; America, 1752 ***2856.30*** *p319*
Wife: M. C. Wedel
With 3 daughters
Moll, Johann Valentin; America, 1752 ***2856.30*** *p319*
Moll, M. C. Wedel *SEE* Moll, Johann Heinrich
Moll, Michael; America, 1750 ***2856.30*** *p306*
With wife
Moll, Simon; Port uncertain, 1719 ***2856.30*** *p306*
Mollard, Charles 40; Ontario, 1871 ***1823.15*** *p192*
Mollard, Emma 30; Ontario, 1871 ***1823.15*** *p192*
Mollard, James 41; Ontario, 1871 ***1823.15*** *p192*
Mollard, Thomas 32; Ontario, 1871 ***1823.15*** *p192*
Mollard, William 36; Ontario, 1871 ***1823.15*** *p192*
Moller, Frederick; New York, 1838 ***8197.10*** *p124*
Mollet, Elizabeth 21; Philadelphia, 1774 ***1220.25*** *p63*
Molley, Mrs. 30; Carolina, 1774 ***1220.25*** *p66*
Molling, William 19; Virginia, 1774 ***1220.25*** *p88*
Mollins, John; Virginia, 1671-1672 ***6212.30*** *p47*
Molloy, Edward; Vermont, 1824-1915 ***5900.10*** *p217*
Molloy, James; Canada, 1756-1760 ***4628.40*** *p45*
Molloy, John; Vermont, 1821-1848 ***5900.10*** *p478*
Molloy, John; Virginia, 1722 ***1224.2*** *p80*
Molloy, Katherine Murrey; Vermont, 1824-1847 ***5900.10*** *p478*
Molloy, Lawrence 3; Vermont, 1872 ***5900.10*** *p208*
Molloy, Lawrence 82; Vermont, 1871 ***5900.10*** *p209*
Molloy, Margaret 96; Vermont, 1886 ***5900.10*** *p209*
Molloy, Mary; Vermont, 1826-1915 ***5900.10*** *p217*
Molloy, Mary E. 10; Vermont, 1872 ***5900.10*** *p208*
Molloy, Mary E. McDonough; Vermont, 1837-1910 ***5900.10*** *p478*
Molloy, Moses; Vermont, 1825-1906 ***5900.10*** *p478*
Molloy, Patrick; New York, 1838 ***8197.10*** *p124*
Molloy, Patrick J.; New York, 1839 ***8197.10*** *p264*
Molloy, Susan 53; Ontario, 1871 ***1823.28*** *p73*
Mollrone, Cornelius; Maryland, 1659 ***2524.55*** *p154*
Molnar, George; Pennsylvania, 1868 ***6058.10*** *p65*
Molnaus, Frank; Maryland, 1910 ***3259.35*** *p40*
Moloney, B. J. 46; Vermont, 1902 ***5900.10*** *p583*
Moloney, Bryan; Vermont, 1835-1919 ***5900.10*** *p584*
Moloney, Catherine Teelon; Vermont, 1839-1899 ***5900.10*** *p584*
Moloney, James; Canada, 1756-1760 ***4628.40*** *p45*
Moloney, James; Nova Scotia, 1745 ***4628.40*** *p45*
Moloney, John; Canada, 1756-1760 ***4628.40*** *p45*
Moloney, John 1; Vermont, 1864 ***5900.10*** *p361*
Moloney, John 45; Vermont, 1865 ***5900.10*** *p361*
Moloney, John 55; Ontario, 1871 ***1823.28*** *p73*
Moloney, Joseph; Canada, 1756-1760 ***4628.40*** *p46*
Moloney, Margaret; Vermont, 1825-1896 ***5900.10*** *p254*
Moloney, Margaret Davine; Vermont, 1830-1893 ***5900.10*** *p563*
Moloney, Martin; Vermont, 1823-1896 ***5900.10*** *p563*
Moloney, Martin 57; Vermont, 1876 ***5900.10*** *p240*
Moloney, Mary Helen; Vermont, 1852-1914 ***5900.10*** *p391*
Moloney, Mary J.; Vermont, 1849-1921 ***5900.10*** *p443*
Moloney, Mary Ryan 80; Vermont, 1910 ***5900.10*** *p557*
Moloney, Michael 60; Ontario, 1871 ***1823.28*** *p73*
Moloney, Michael 84; Vermont, 1901 ***5900.10*** *p557*
Moloney, Patrick 55; Ontario, 1871 ***1823.28*** *p73*
Moloney, Sarah Star 86; Vermont, 1912 ***5900.10*** *p361*
Molony, Catharine 74; Vermont, 1865 ***5900.10*** *p236*
Molony, John; New York, 1840 ***8197.10*** *p264*
Molony, John 30; Ontario, 1871 ***1823.15*** *p192*
Molony, John 70; Ontario, 1871 ***1823.15*** *p192*
Molony, Patrick; New York, 1830 ***8197.10*** *p353*
Molony, Thomas 81; Vermont, 1853 ***5900.10*** *p236*
Molson, Miss; Quebec, 1856 ***9196.15*** *p9*
Molson, Mr.; Quebec, 1856 ***9196.15*** *p9*
Molson, Mr.; Quebec, 1858 ***9196.15*** *p46*
Molson, Mrs.; Quebec, 1858 ***9196.15*** *p46*
Molson, A.; Quebec, 1857 ***9196.15*** *p18*
Molson, J.; Quebec, 1857 ***9196.15*** *p18*
Molson, Mrs. J.; Quebec, 1857 ***9196.15*** *p18*
Molter, Bernard; Port uncertain, 1752 ***2856.30*** *p306*
Molter, Jakob; Port uncertain, 1772 ***2856.30*** *p306*
Molter, Peter; America, 1771 ***2856.30*** *p306*
With wife
Molter, Peter; America, 1772 ***2856.30*** *p306*
With wife
Molyneaux, William 39; Ontario, 1871 ***1823.15*** *p192*
Molyneux, Anthony Lancaster; Georgia, 1852 ***1224.3*** *p53*
Molys, William; Maryland, 1659 ***2524.55*** *p154*
Molz, Friedrich; Port uncertain, 1785 ***2856.30*** *p306*
With wife & children
Molz, Johann Leonard; Port uncertain, 1778 ***2856.30*** *p306*
Molzberger, Johann; America, 1751 ***2856.30*** *p306*
With family
Mombauer, Johann Nikolaus; America, 1739 ***2856.30*** *p306*
Mombauer, Nickel; America, 1739 ***2856.30*** *p306*
With wife & 5 children
Mombauer, Nikolaus; America, 1739 ***2856.30*** *p306*
Mombauer, Peter; America, 1739 ***2856.30*** *p306*
With father 2 wives & 6 children
Momford, Stephen; Maryland, 1668 ***2524.55*** *p154*
Momford, Steven; Maryland, 1659 ***2524.55*** *p154*
Mon, B. Mathias 24; Kansas, 1909-1910 ***9079.10*** *p2*
Monachan, Sarah 35; Ontario, 1871 ***1823.15*** *p192*
Monag, Virginia; Vermont, 1863-1961 ***5900.10*** *p541*
Monaghan, Amy; Vermont, 1850-1934 ***5900.10*** *p607*
Monaghan, Ann Mundy; Vermont, 1915 ***5900.10*** *p580*
Monaghan, Anthony 20; New York, New York, 1849 ***1825.45*** *p39*
Monaghan, Bridget 63; Vermont, 1919 ***5900.10*** *p607*
Monaghan, Charles 31; Vermont, 1865 ***5900.10*** *p602*
Monaghan, Elizabeth McGrath 29; Vermont, 1888 ***5900.10*** *p289*
Monaghan, Helen 72; Vermont, 1864 ***5900.10*** *p502*
Monaghan, Hugh 48; Ontario, 1871 ***1823.28*** *p73*
Monaghan, Hugh 75; Vermont, 1916 ***5900.10*** *p607*
Monaghan, James; Vermont, 1825-1903 ***5900.10*** *p289*
Monaghan, John; New York, 1834 ***8197.10*** *p315*
Monaghan, John 11; Vermont, 1866 ***5900.10*** *p289*
Monaghan, John 38; Ontario, 1871 ***1823.28*** *p73*
Monaghan, Margaret; Vermont, 1845-1929 ***5900.10*** *p48*
Monaghan, Margaret J. B. 44; Vermont, 1881 ***5900.10*** *p289*
Monaghan, Mary 74; Vermont, 1919 ***5900.10*** *p607*
Monaghan, Patrick; New York, 1807 ***8197.10*** *p328*
Monaghan, Thomas; Vermont, 1911 ***5900.10*** *p580*
Monaghan, William; New York, 1838 ***8197.10*** *p124*
Monahan, Anna; Vermont, 1856-1935 ***5900.10*** *p419*
Monahan, Bridget; Vermont, 1829-1905 ***5900.10*** *p336*
Monahan, Catharine 90; Vermont, 1880 ***5900.10*** *p201*
Monahan, Catherine; Vermont, 1849-1924 ***5900.10*** *p131*
Monahan, Catherine Doran; Vermont, 1848-1918 ***5900.10*** *p170*
Monahan, Catherine McNamara; Vermont, 1882 ***5900.10*** *p426*
Monahan, Fanny; Vermont, 1795-1876 ***5900.10*** *p583*
Monahan, George 7; Ontario, 1861 ***2896.28*** *p49*
Monahan, Hugh 36; Ontario, 1861 ***2896.28*** *p49*
Monahan, John; Vermont, 1905 ***5900.10*** *p426*
Monahan, John 2; Ontario, 1861 ***2896.28*** *p49*
Monahan, John J.; Vermont, 1852-1885 ***5900.10*** *p557*
Monahan, Julia Ann Graham; Vermont, 1856-1889 ***5900.10*** *p419*
Monahan, Katherine; Vermont, 1831-1904 ***5900.10*** *p583*
Monahan, Letty 4; Ontario, 1861 ***2896.28*** *p49*
Monahan, Margaret; Vermont, 1853-1856 ***5900.10*** *p557*
Monahan, Margaret 78; Vermont, 1889 ***5900.10*** *p423*
Monahan, Margaret O'Leary 30; Vermont, 1881 ***5900.10*** *p423*
Monahan, Mary; Vermont, 1828-1879 ***5900.10*** *p539*
Monahan, Mary; Vermont, 1858-1944 ***5900.10*** *p582*
Monahan, Mary Conlin; Vermont, 1829-1906 ***5900.10*** *p557*
Monahan, Mary McCarthy 83; Vermont, 1890 ***5900.10*** *p569*
Monahan, Nancy 34; Ontario, 1861 ***2896.28*** *p49*
Monahan, Owen; New York, 1839 ***8197.10*** *p380*
Monahan, Owen; Vermont, 1848-1925 ***5900.10*** *p419*
Monahan, Patrick; New York, 1839 ***8197.10*** *p141*
Monahan, Patrick, Sr. 84; Vermont, 1883 ***5900.10*** *p423*
Monahan, Richard; New York, 1829 ***8197.10*** *p353*
Monahan, Robert; Vermont, 1827-1904 ***5900.10*** *p557*
Monahan, Thomas; Vermont, 1846-1917 ***5900.10*** *p170*
Monahan, Thomas 60; Vermont, 1862 ***5900.10*** *p569*
Monahan, William 9; Ontario, 1861 ***2896.28*** *p49*
Monan, Bedelia 72; Vermont, 1904 ***5900.10*** *p600*
Monas, John; New York, 1840 ***8197.10*** *p178*
Monax, James; Virginia, 1665 ***6212.30*** *p18*
Monazynski, Leo; Maryland, 1910 ***3259.35*** *p40*
Monbert, J. J.; Portland, Maine, 1858 ***9196.15*** *p28*
Monbray, Hugh 36; Ontario, 1871 ***1823.15*** *p192*
Monch, Simon; Port uncertain, 1727 ***2856.30*** *p319*
Monck, Edward; South Carolina, 1713 ***1224.2*** *p80*
Monck, Hanah; Maryland, 1673 ***2524.55*** *p154*
Monck, James; Maryland, 1673 ***2524.55*** *p154*
Moncrief, Alexander; New York, 1835 ***8197.10*** *p263*
Moncrief, Robert; New York, 1807 ***8197.10*** *p45*
Moncrief, William; New York, 1790 ***1224.2*** *p80*
Moncrieff, Alexander; New York, 1840 ***8197.10*** *p179*
Moncrieff, Archibald; Maryland, 1803 ***1640.13*** *p78*
Moncrieff, David; Georgia, 1699 ***1640.13*** *p78*
Moncrieff, George; Georgia, 1699 ***1640.13*** *p78*
Moncrieff, Isabella; Florida, 1779 ***1640.10*** *p156*
Moncrieff, Isabella; St. Augustine, Florida, 1779 ***1224.2*** *p80*
Moncrieff, James; Florida, 1763 ***1640.10*** *p157*
Moncrieffe, Margaret Heron; New York, 1764 ***1224.2*** *p80*
Moncrieffe, Thomas; New York, 1792 ***1224.2*** *p80*
Mond, Edw; Virginia, 1664 ***6212.30*** *p10*
Monday, David 35; Ontario, 1871 ***1823.22*** *p113*
Mondindale, William 20; Maryland, 1774 ***1220.25*** *p51*
Mondy, Richard 22; Maryland, 1775 ***1220.25*** *p111*
Mone, Andrew 31; Ontario, 1871 ***1823.15*** *p192*
Mone, Francis 54; Ontario, 1871 ***1823.28*** *p73*
Mone, Hugh 30; Ontario, 1871 ***1823.28*** *p73*
Monehan, Patrick 63; Ontario, 1871 ***1823.22*** *p113*
Monehen, John; New York, 1833 ***8197.10*** *p315*
Moneley, Ann; Maryland, 1679 ***2524.55*** *p154*
Moneley, Mary; Maryland, 1679 ***2524.55*** *p154*
Mones, Mark 23; Maryland, 1775 ***1220.25*** *p109*
Money, Ann 24; Baltimore, 1775 ***1220.25*** *p117*
Money, John; North Carolina, 1781 ***1224.2*** *p80*
Moneyey, William; Savannah, Georgia, 1819 ***1640.10*** *p157*
Moneyman, John; Maryland, 1651 ***2524.55*** *p154*
Moneypenny, Miss; Quebec, 1856 ***9196.15*** *p7*
Moneypenny, Miss; Quebec, 1858 ***9196.15*** *p37*
Moneypenny, Mr.; Quebec, 1858 ***9196.15*** *p37*
Moneypenny, Mrs.; Quebec, 1858 ***9196.15*** *p37*
Moneypenny, Mary; New York, 1831 ***8197.10*** *p67*
Mong, John; Pennsylvania, 1858 ***6058.10*** *p40*
Monger, I. P. 27; Ontario, 1871 ***1823.28*** *p73*
Mongomery, John 27; Ontario, 1871 ***1823.22*** *p113*
Monhouse, George 31; Ontario, 1871 ***1823.28*** *p73*
Monig, Johann; Port uncertain, 1725 ***2856.30*** *p306*
Monig, Johann; Port uncertain, 1756 ***2856.30*** *p306*
Monins, Edw; Virginia, 1665-1666 ***6212.30*** *p22*
Monk, Catherine *SEE* Monk, Ranald
Monk, Donald *SEE* Monk, Ranald
Monk, Effie *SEE* Monk, Ranald
Monk, Effie; Ontario, 1849 ***4537.32*** *p72*
Monk, Jane 48; Ontario, 1871 ***1823.15*** *p192*
Monk, John; Charles Town, South Carolina, 1789 ***1224.2*** *p80*
Monk, Kirsty; Ontario, 1850-1859 ***4537.37*** *p44*
Monk, Kirsty; Ontario, 1851 ***4537.32*** *p22*
Monk, Malcolm *SEE* Monk, Ranald
Monk, Marion MacMillan *SEE* Monk, Ranald
Monk, Neil *SEE* Monk, Ranald

Mooney, Margaret 79; Vermont, 1901 5900.10 p609
Mooney, Mary; Vermont, 1799-1891 5900.10 p587
Mooney, Mary; Vermont, 1799-1891 5900.10 p592
Mooney, Mary; Vermont, 1845-1912 5900.10 p593
Mooney, Mary; Vermont, 1851-1930 5900.10 p397
Mooney, Mary; Vermont, 1856-1931 5900.10 p352
Mooney, Mary; Vermont, 1861-1905 5900.10 p199
Mooney, Mary 34; Vermont, 1872 5900.10 p571
Mooney, Mary A.; Vermont, 1860-1907 5900.10 p383
Mooney, Mary A.; Vermont, 1866-1925 5900.10 p385
Mooney, Mary Ann; Vermont, 1863-1929 5900.10 p136
Mooney, Mary Ann 78; Vermont, 1916 5900.10 p376
Mooney, Mary B. Kinney 66; Vermont, 1868 5900.10 p463
Mooney, Mary Breakey; Vermont, 1816-1904 5900.10 p495
Mooney, Mary Conlin 79; Vermont, 1903 5900.10 p386
Mooney, Mary Jane 23; Vermont, 1855 5900.10 p463
Mooney, Mary Kennedy; Vermont, 1832-1919 5900.10 p156
Mooney, Mary McGinn; Vermont, 1848-1922 5900.10 p392
Mooney, Mathew 73; Ontario, 1871 1823.15 p193
Mooney, Michael 59; Vermont, 1894 5900.10 p392
Mooney, Nancy; Vermont, 1842-1917 5900.10 p47
Mooney, Nellie Pickett; Vermont, 1859-1919 5900.10 p351
Mooney, P. C. 65; Vermont, 1879 5900.10 p196
Mooney, Patrick; New York, 1827 8197.10 p261
Mooney, Patrick; New York, 1840 8197.10 p265
Mooney, Patrick; Vermont, 1812-1892 5900.10 p495
Mooney, Patrick 58; Ontario, 1871 1823.28 p73
Mooney, Richard; Vermont, 1857-1957 5900.10 p385
Mooney, Richard 51; Vermont, 1879 5900.10 p386
Mooney, Sarah 16; Vermont, 1833 5900.10 p494
Mooney, Sarah A.; Vermont, 1841-1904 5900.10 p496
Mooney, Thomas; New York, 1806 8197.10 p32
Mooney, Thomas; New York, 1816 8197.10 p59
Mooney, Thomas 56; Vermont, 1812 5900.10 p493
Mooney, William; Vermont, 1829-1882 5900.10 p384
Mooney, William 60; Ontario, 1871 1823.15 p193
Mooney, William 65; Ontario, 1871 1823.15 p193
Mooney, William H.; Vermont, 1849-1930 5900.10 p495
Moonteith, Charles 40; Ontario, 1871 1823.15 p193
Moor, Alsina 5; Ontario, 1861 2896.26 p17
Moor, Ann *SEE* Moor, Richard
Moor, Ann 37; Ontario, 1861 2896.26 p17
Moor, Anne 24; Ontario, 1871 1823.28 p73
Moor, Cecilia A. 9; Ontario, 1861 2896.25 p25
Moor, D. W. C. 2; Ontario, 1861 2896.25 p25
Moor, David 7; Ontario, 1861 2896.26 p17
Moor, David 64; Ontario, 1871 1823.28 p73
Moor, David 67; Ontario, 1861 2896.26 p17
Moor, Edwin R. 2; Ontario, 1861 2896.26 p17
Moor, Eliza Ann 27; Ontario, 1861 2896.25 p25
Moor, Ferguson; Philadelphia, 1798 1224.2 p81
Moor, George W. 7; Ontario, 1861 2896.25 p25
Moor, Isaih 35; Ontario, 1871 1823.15 p193
Moor, Jane *SEE* Moor, Richard
Moor, Jane; Maryland, 1658 2524.55 p154
Moor, John 21; Philadelphia, 1774 1220.25 p44
Moor, John 24; New York, 1775 1220.25 p142
With wife & child
Moor, John 28; Vermont, 1880 5900.10 p106
Moor, John 30; Ontario, 1871 1823.15 p193
Moor, Loisa 2; Ontario, 1861 2896.26 p17
Moor, Margaret; Ontario, 1861 2896.25 p63
Moor, Martha 36; Ontario, 1871 1823.28 p73
Moor, Mary *SEE* Moor, Richard
Moor, Mathew 22; Maryland, 1774 1220.25 p71
Moor, Matthias 45; Ontario, 1871 1823.28 p73
Moor, Richard; Maryland, 1652 2524.55 p154
Daughter: Temperance
Daughter: Mary
Daughter: Ann
Wife: Jane
Moor, Robert 36; Ontario, 1871 1823.15 p193
Moor, Samuel 38; Maryland, 1774 1220.25 p78
Moor, Stephen 50; Ontario, 1871 1823.28 p73
Moor, Stephen 95; Ontario, 1871 1823.28 p73
Moor, Temperance *SEE* Moor, Richard
Moor, Walter 25; Ontario, 1871 1823.15 p193
Moor, William 16; Ontario, 1861 2896.26 p17
Moor, William 20; Ontario, 1871 1823.15 p193
Moor, William C. 5; Ontario, 1861 2896.25 p25
Moore, . . .; Boston, 1737 4628.40 p114
Moore, Mr.; Quebec, 1856 9196.15 p7
Moore, Mr.; Quebec, 1857 9196.15 p23
Moore, Mrs.; Ontario, 1861 2896.25 p1
Moore, Mrs.; Quebec, 1856 9196.15 p7
Moore, Mrs. 30; Ontario, 1861 2896.26 p24
Moore, Alexander; Boston, 1794 1224.2 p81
Moore, Andrew; Maryland, 1658 2524.55 p156
Moore, Angenette 10; Ontario, 1861 2896.28 p38
Moore, Anguish; Maryland, 1682 2524.55 p154
Moore, Ann; Maryland, 1662 2524.55 p99
Moore, Ann 50; Ontario, 1871 1823.15 p193
Moore, Anna; Vermont, 1806-1869 5900.10 p336
Moore, Anne *SEE* Moore, William
Moore, Anne Connell 66; Vermont, 1921 5900.10 p423
Moore, Arabella; Maryland, 1681 2524.55 p154
Moore, Arch'd 12; Ontario, 1861 2896.26 p36
Moore, Arthur 32; Ontario, 1871 1823.15 p193
Moore, Austin; Virginia, 1667-1668 6212.30 p38
Moore, Barbery; Ontario, 1861 2896.25 p1
Moore, Bridget *SEE* Moore, Maurice
Moore, Bridget 21; Vermont, 1871 5900.10 p99
Moore, Bridget English; Vermont, 1826-1879 5900.10 p173
Moore, Caroline 5; Ontario, 1861 2896.25 p65
Moore, Catharine Charles; Philadelphia Co., Pennsylvania, 1837 1224.3 p53
Moore, Catherine 14; Ontario, 1861 2896.26 p33
Moore, Catherine 46; Ontario, 1871 1823.15 p193
Moore, Catherine 69; Vermont, 1897 5900.10 p597
Moore, Catherine McCarty 72; Vermont, 1890 5900.10 p116
Moore, Cathrin 44; Vermont, 1880 5900.10 p214
Moore, Charles; New York, 1840 8197.10 p180
Moore, Charles; Pennsylvania, 1777 4629.10 p16
Moore, Charles 26; Ontario, 1871 1823.28 p73
Moore, Charles C. 45; Ontario, 1871 1823.22 p113
Moore, Chas; Portland, Maine, 1858 9196.15 p28
Moore, Clarissa 31; Ontario, 1861 2896.27 p22
Moore, Daniel; Canada, 1756-1760 4628.40 p45
Moore, Daniel; Maryland, 1661 2524.55 p68
Moore, David 62; Ontario, 1871 1823.15 p193
Moore, David W. 7; Ontario, 1861 2896.26 p36
Moore, E. A. 2; Ontario, 1861 2896.27 p22
Moore, Edward; Pennsylvania, 1777 4629.10 p22
Moore, Edward J. 30; Ontario, 1871 1823.15 p193
Moore, Eligan 52; Ontario, 1871 1823.15 p193
Moore, Eliza; Virginia, 1664 6212.30 p10
Moore, Elizabeth; Maryland, 1658-1663 2524.55 p20
Moore, Elizabeth; Maryland, 1681 2524.55 p154
Moore, Elizabeth; Virginia, 1664 6212.30 p14
Moore, Elizabeth; Virginia, 1674 6212.30 p52
Moore, Elizabeth; Virginia, 1789 1224.2 p94
Moore, Elizabeth 18; Vermont, 1860 5900.10 p471
Moore, Elizabeth 58; Ontario, 1871 1823.15 p193
Moore, Elizabeth Irwin 36; Vermont, 1848 5900.10 p471
Moore, Ellen; Vermont, 1840-1882 5900.10 p81
Moore, Ellen; Vermont, 1840-1912 5900.10 p471
Moore, Ellen; Vermont, 1852-1873 5900.10 p173
Moore, Ellen; Vermont, 1857-1939 5900.10 p193
Moore, Ellen; Vermont, 1862-1903 5900.10 p464
Moore, Ellen 33; Vermont, 1854 5900.10 p228
Moore, Ellen 60; Ontario, 1861 2896.26 p33
Moore, Ellen Dower; Vermont, 1850-1920 5900.10 p174
Moore, Ellen Lynch; Vermont, 1853-1899 5900.10 p130
Moore, Ellen Sammon; Vermont, 1855-1929 5900.10 p274
Moore, Emma; Ontario, 1861 2896.25 p1
Moore, Emma 77; Ontario, 1871 1823.28 p74
Moore, Fanny 60; Ontario, 1861 2896.27 p39
Moore, Francis; Pennsylvania, 1786 4629.10 p47
Moore, George; New York, 1834 8197.10 p71
Moore, George; New York, 1837 8197.10 p99
Moore, George; Pennsylvania, 1778 4629.10 p34
Moore, George 16; Virginia, 1774 1220.25 p53
Moore, George 33; Ontario, 1871 1823.15 p193
Moore, Georgent 23; Ontario, 1871 1823.15 p193
Moore, Hannah M. 10; Ontario, 1861 2896.27 p22
Moore, Harmen 70; Ontario, 1871 1823.28 p74
Moore, Harriet J. 5; Ontario, 1861 2896.27 p22
Moore, Henry; Maryland, 1659 2524.55 p154
Moore, Henry; New York, 1770 1224.2 p81
Moore, Henry; Virginia, 1665-1666 6212.30 p24
Moore, Henry C.; Vermont, 1850-1901 5900.10 p274
Moore, J. B. 38; Ontario, 1861 2896.25 p50
Moore, James; Maryland, 1661 2524.55 p154
Moore, James; New England, 1775-1781 4628.40 p68
Moore, James; New York, 1806 8197.10 p32
Moore, James; New York, 1807 8197.10 p329
Moore, James; New York, 1818 8197.10 p258
Moore, James; New York, 1821 8197.10 p259
Moore, James; New York, 1832 8197.10 p314
Moore, James; New York, 1834 8197.10 p71
Moore, James; Nova Scotia, 1745 4628.40 p45
Moore, James; South Carolina, 1775-1781 4628.40 p69
Moore, James; Vermont, 1853-1873 5900.10 p173
Moore, James; Virginia, 1665 6212.30 p20
Moore, James 29; Maryland, 1774 1220.25 p52
Moore, James 35; Ontario, 1861 2896.26 p34
Moore, James 36; Ontario, 1871 1823.15 p193
Moore, James 40; Ontario, 1871 1823.15 p193
Moore, James 60; Ontario, 1871 1823.28 p74
Moore, James 85; Ontario, 1871 1823.22 p113
Moore, Jane; Maryland, 1662 2524.55 p99
Moore, Jane; Pennsylvania, 1846 1224.3 p53
Moore, Jeffery; Virginia, 1663 6212.30 p2
Moore, Jno.; Nova Scotia, 1745 4628.40 p45
Moore, Jno; Virginia, 1674 6212.30 p51
Moore, Joan E.; Vermont, 1858-1902 5900.10 p233
Moore, Johanna E. Wright; Vermont, 1828-1908 5900.10 p228
Moore, John *SEE* Moore, John
Moore, John *SEE* Moore, Maurice
Moore, John; Canada, 1756-1760 4628.40 p45
Moore, John; Kentucky, 1852 1224.3 p53
Moore, John; Maryland, 1652-1658 2524.55 p154
Moore, John; Maryland, 1667 2524.55 p154
Moore, John; Maryland, 1669 2524.55 p154
Wife: Mary
Child: Mary
Child: John
Moore, John; New York, 1840 8197.10 p180
Moore, John; New York, 1840 8197.10 p181
Moore, John; Pennsylvania, 1777 4629.10 p31
Moore, John; Vermont, 1799-1890 5900.10 p214
Moore, John; Vermont, 1857-1892 5900.10 p130
Moore, John; Virginia, 1664 6212.30 p6
Moore, John; Virginia, 1664-1665 6212.30 p16
Moore, John; Virginia, 1667-1668 6212.30 p39
Moore, John 14; Ontario, 1861 2896.26 p24
Moore, John 15; Maryland, 1775 1220.25 p103
Moore, John 16; Baltimore, 1775 1220.25 p117
Moore, John 21; Virginia, 1774 1220.25 p55
Moore, John 22; Ontario, 1871 1823.15 p193
Moore, John 23; Virginia, 1775 1220.25 p95
Moore, John 25; Baltimore, 1775 1220.25 p117
Moore, John 30; Ontario, 1861 2896.26 p24
Moore, John 30; Ontario, 1871 1823.28 p74
Moore, John 32; Maryland, 1774 1220.25 p51
Moore, John 33; Ontario, 1871 1823.22 p113
Moore, John 40; Ontario, 1871 1823.28 p74
Moore, John 41; Ontario, 1871 1823.28 p74
Moore, John 60; Ontario, 1861 2896.27 p39
Moore, John 62; Ontario, 1871 1823.15 p193
Moore, John 72; Ontario, 1871 1823.15 p193
Moore, John 77; Vermont, 1897 5900.10 p597
Moore, John A.; Vermont, 1857-1943 5900.10 p597
Moore, John B.; New York, 1840 8197.10 p265
Moore, John Mitchell; Jamaica, 1794 1640.13 p79
Moore, John W. 14; Ontario, 1861 2896.27 p22
Moore, Joseph; Vermont, 1861-1885 5900.10 p173
Moore, Joseph 27; Virginia, 1774 1220.25 p93
Moore, Joseph 36; Ontario, 1861 2896.27 p22
Moore, Joseph A. 1; Ontario, 1861 2896.27 p22
Moore, Julia *SEE* Moore, Maurice
Moore, Julia 75; Ontario, 1871 1823.15 p193
Moore, Julia A.; Vermont, 1801-1892 5900.10 p214
Moore, Julia M. 45; Vermont, 1884 5900.10 p529
Moore, Lambert; New York, New York, 1808 1224.3 p53
Moore, Lauson 27; Ontario, 1871 1823.15 p193
Moore, Margaret *SEE* Moore, Martin
Moore, Margaret *SEE* Moore, Maurice
Moore, Margaret; Vermont, 1827-1862 5900.10 p173
Moore, Margaret 21; America, 1774 1220.25 p35
Moore, Margaret 21; New York, 1775 1220.25 p142
Moore, Margaret 22; Vermont, 1869 5900.10 p471
Moore, Margaret Howard 88; Vermont, 1924 5900.10 p219
Moore, Marmeduke; Virginia, 1664 6212.30 p7
Moore, Martha 68; Ontario, 1871 1823.15 p193
Moore, Martin; Maryland, 1666 2524.55 p244
Moore, Martin; Maryland, 1672 2524.55 p154
Wife: Margaret
Daughter: Mary
Moore, Mary *SEE* Moore, John
Moore, Mary *SEE* Moore, Martin
Moore, Mary *SEE* Moore, Maurice
Moore, Mary *SEE* Moore, William
Moore, Mary; Maryland, 1662 2524.55 p99
Moore, Mary; New York, 1784 1224.2 p81
Moore, Mary; Vermont, 1863-1917 5900.10 p130
Moore, Mary 24; Ontario, 1871 1823.15 p194
Moore, Mary 42; Vermont, 1908 5900.10 p562
Moore, Mary 78; Vermont, 1883 5900.10 p97
Moore, Mary A.; Vermont, 1835-1893 5900.10 p471
Moore, Mary A. 27; Vermont, 1888 5900.10 p228
Moore, Mary E. 12; Ontario, 1861 2896.27 p22
Moore, Maurice *SEE* Moore, Maurice
Moore, Maurice; New York, 1849 1224.3 p53
Child: Mary
Child: Margaret
Child: Julia
Child: Maurice

More, Catherine 50; Ontario, 1871 ***1823.22*** *p114*
More, Daniel; Maryland, 1667 ***2524.55*** *p155*
More, David 50; Ontario, 1861 ***2896.27*** *p28*
More, Edward; Maryland, 1672 ***2524.55*** *p155*
More, Elizabeth *SEE* More, John
More, Elizabeth *SEE* More, Thomas
More, Elizabeth; Maryland, 1672 ***2524.55*** *p155*
More, George 17; Ontario, 1861 ***2896.28*** *p24*
More, Henry; Maryland, 1663 ***2524.55*** *p155*
More, James; New York, 1807 ***8197.10*** *p46*
More, Jere; New York, 1802 ***8197.10*** *p22*
More, John; Maryland, 1667 ***2524.55*** *p154*
More, John; Maryland, 1672 ***2524.55*** *p155*
Wife: Elizabeth
Daughter: Mary
More, John 19; Ontario, 1861 ***2896.28*** *p24*
More, John 50; Ontario, 1861 ***2896.28*** *p24*
More, Lucinda 15; Ontario, 1861 ***2896.28*** *p24*
More, Margaret *SEE* More, Martin
More, Margaret 20; Ontario, 1861 ***2896.28*** *p59*
More, Martin; Maryland, 1672 ***2524.55*** *p154*
Wife: Margaret
Daughter: Mary
More, Mary *SEE* More, John
More, Mary *SEE* More, Martin
More, Mary; Maryland, 1672 ***2524.55*** *p155*
More, Sarah; Florida, 1810-1837 ***1640.10*** *p160*
More, Sarah; Virginia, 1693-1694 ***6212.30*** *p60*
More, Susan 45; Ontario, 1861 ***2896.28*** *p24*
More, Thomas; Maryland, 1667 ***2524.55*** *p155*
Wife: Elizabeth
More, William; Maryland, 1672 ***2524.55*** *p155*
More, Wm; Virginia, 1681-1682 ***6212.30*** *p56*
Morecraft, Ann; Virginia, 1666 ***6212.30*** *p30*
Morecraft, Hen; Virginia, 1666 ***6212.30*** *p25*
Morecraft, John; Maryland, 1666 ***2524.55*** *p155*
Morecroft, Edmund; Virginia, 1639 ***1224.1*** *p40*
Morehead, William; Pennsylvania, 1808 ***6058.10*** *p2*
Morehouse, Ann Turner; South Carolina, 1817 ***1224.3*** *p81*
Morel, John; Pennsylvania, 1777 ***4629.10*** *p11*
Morel, Tryphena Dunbar; Savannah, Georgia, 1810 ***1224.3*** *p53*
Moreland, Rachel 40; Ontario, 1871 ***1823.15*** *p194*
Morell, Henrich; Port uncertain, 1756 ***2856.30*** *p307*
Moreman, Allise; Maryland, 1637 ***2524.55*** *p155*
Moren, Bridget 36; Vermont, 1878 ***5900.10*** *p148*
Moren, Margaret Degnan 52; Vermont, 1862 ***5900.10*** *p149*
Moren, Mary 61; Vermont, 1877 ***5900.10*** *p326*
Morenze, Henry D. 20; Ontario, 1871 ***1823.15*** *p194*
Moreran, William 21; Baltimore, 1775 ***1220.25*** *p117*
Moretast, Mary; Maryland, 1662 ***2524.55*** *p155*
Moreton, Anthony; Georgia, 1749 ***1224.2*** *p82*
Moreton, George; New York, 1834 ***8197.10*** *p73*
Morewood, Thomas; New York, 1794 ***8197.10*** *p2*
Morey, Miss; Quebec, 1858 ***9196.15*** *p42*
Morey, Mr.; Quebec, 1858 ***9196.15*** *p42*
Morey, John; New York, 1818 ***8197.10*** *p259*
Morfett, Hannah 14 *SEE* Morfett, William
Morfett, Mary 9 *SEE* Morfett, William
Morfett, Mary 48 *SEE* Morfett, William
Morfett, William 12 *SEE* Morfett, William
Morfett, William 44; Norfolk, Virginia, 1774 ***1220.25*** *p19*
Wife: Mary 48
Child: Hannah 14
Child: William 12
Child: Mary 9
Morgan, . . .; Virginia, 1674-1675 ***6212.30*** *p53*
Morgan, Miss; Quebec, 1856 ***9196.15*** *p10*
Morgan, Mr.; Quebec, 1858 ***9196.15*** *p31*
Morgan, Mr.; Vermont, 1848-1908 ***5900.10*** *p250*
Morgan, Mrs.; Maryland, 1649 ***2524.55*** *p155*
Morgan, Mrs.; Maryland, 1661 ***2524.55*** *p155*
Morgan, Mrs.; Vermont, 1844-1916 ***5900.10*** *p250*
Morgan, Abigail 47; Ontario, 1861 ***2896.26*** *p5*
Morgan, Alice; Maryland, 1667 ***2524.55*** *p246*
Husband: William
Morgan, Ann; Illinois, 1847 ***1224.3*** *p54*
Morgan, Ann; Maryland, 1670 ***2524.55*** *p155*
Morgan, Anne; Massachusetts, 1849 ***1224.3*** *p54*
Morgan, Benjamin; Pennsylvania, 1777 ***4629.10*** *p22*
Morgan, Bernard; New York, 1839 ***8197.10*** *p264*
Morgan, Catherine 53; Vermont, 1879 ***5900.10*** *p591*
Morgan, Catherine Thompson; Vermont, 1851-1900 ***5900.10*** *p423*
Morgan, Charles 31; Philadelphia, 1775 ***1220.25*** *p9*
Morgan, D.; Quebec, 1858 ***9196.15*** *p41*
Morgan, Daniel; Georgia, 1839-1866 ***1640.10*** *p160*
Morgan, Daniel; New England, 1775-1781 ***4628.40*** *p68*
Morgan, David 71; Ontario, 1871 ***1823.15*** *p194*
Morgan, David B.; New York, 1840 ***8197.10*** *p178*
Morgan, Edward *SEE* Morgan, Jenkin
Morgan, Edward; New York, 1838 ***8197.10*** *p264*
Morgan, Edward 36; Ontario, 1871 ***1823.28*** *p74*
Morgan, Eliza 46; Ontario, 1861 ***2896.26*** *p2*
Morgan, Elizabeth *SEE* Morgan, Jenkin
Morgan, Elizabeth; Maryland, 1631-1685 ***2524.55*** *p155*
Morgan, Elizabeth; Maryland, 1659 ***2524.55*** *p155*
Morgan, Elizabeth; Maryland, 1668 ***2524.55*** *p111*
Morgan, Elizabeth 22; Baltimore, 1775 ***1220.25*** *p119*
Morgan, Elizabeth 70; Ontario, 1861 ***2896.27*** *p32*
Morgan, Emily 21; Ontario, 1861 ***2896.27*** *p35*
Morgan, Francis; New London, Connecticut, 1849 ***1224.3*** *p54*
Morgan, George; Maryland, 1681 ***2524.55*** *p155*
Morgan, George; New York, 1837 ***8197.10*** *p100*
Morgan, George; Virginia, 1669 ***1224.1*** *p40*
Morgan, George Cadogan; Massachusetts, 1848 ***1224.3*** *p54*
Morgan, Griffith; New York, 1839 ***8197.10*** *p141*
Morgan, Harriet; New London, Connecticut, 1839 ***1224.3*** *p54*
Morgan, Harry; New York, New York, 1899 ***3437.14*** *p184*
Morgan, Henry *SEE* Morgan, Jenkin
Morgan, Henry; Maryland, 1637 ***2524.55*** *p155*
Morgan, Henry; Virginia, 1666 ***6212.30*** *p26*
Morgan, Howell; New York, 1807 ***8197.10*** *p45*
Morgan, J.; Quebec, 1858 ***9196.15*** *p31*
Morgan, Ja; Virginia, 1664 ***6212.30*** *p7*
Morgan, James; New York, 1837 ***8197.10*** *p263*
Morgan, James 48; Ontario, 1871 ***1823.28*** *p74*
Morgan, James 56; Ontario, 1871 ***1823.22*** *p114*
Morgan, James 75; Ontario, 1871 ***1823.28*** *p74*
Morgan, Jarvis; Maryland, 1667 ***2524.55*** *p155*
Morgan, Jenken; Virginia, 1663 ***6212.30*** *p4*
Morgan, Jenkin; Maryland, 1661 ***2524.55*** *p155*
Wife: Rebecca
Child: Henry
Child: Edward
Child: Elizabeth
Child: William
Morgan, John; Georgia, 1698 ***1640.13*** *p79*
Morgan, John; Maryland, 1663 ***2524.55*** *p242*
Morgan, John; Maryland, 1665 ***2524.55*** *p155*
Wife: Katherine
Morgan, John; Maryland, 1666 ***2524.55*** *p171*
Morgan, John; New York, 1803 ***8197.10*** *p14*
Morgan, John 12; Ontario, 1861 ***2896.26*** *p2*
Morgan, John 36; Ontario, 1871 ***1823.15*** *p194*
Morgan, John 38; Ontario, 1871 ***1823.28*** *p74*
Morgan, John 58; Ontario, 1871 ***1823.22*** *p114*
Morgan, John 60; Ontario, 1861 ***2896.26*** *p2*
Morgan, John, Jr.; Maryland, 1658 ***2524.55*** *p155*
Morgan, John Pierre; Philadelphia, 1794 ***4629.10*** *p81*
Morgan, John Sextus; Massachusetts, 1848 ***1224.3*** *p54*
Morgan, Jude; Virginia, 1661 ***1224.1*** *p40*
Morgan, Katherine *SEE* Morgan, John
Morgan, Lawrence; Pennsylvania, 1831 ***6058.10*** *p10*
Morgan, Lewis 15; Maryland, 1775 ***1220.25*** *p98*
Morgan, Luke Ashburner; Massachusetts, 1848 ***1224.3*** *p54*
Morgan, Lydia 48; Ontario, 1861 ***2896.27*** *p51*
Morgan, Mary; Virginia, 1667 ***6212.30*** *p36*
Morgan, Mary 50; Ontario, 1871 ***1823.15*** *p194*
Morgan, Mary Jane 56; Ontario, 1871 ***1823.28*** *p74*
Morgan, Mathew 56; Ontario, 1871 ***1823.22*** *p114*
Morgan, Matilda 10; Ontario, 1861 ***2896.26*** *p2*
Morgan, Owin; Virginia, 1666 ***6212.30*** *p25*
Morgan, Patrick; New Orleans, 1806 ***1224.3*** *p54*
Morgan, Peter; Pennsylvania, 1777 ***4629.10*** *p7*
Morgan, Phillip; Maryland, 1658 ***2524.55*** *p155*
Morgan, Rebecca *SEE* Morgan, Jenkin
Morgan, Rice; Maryland, 1676 ***2524.55*** *p155*
Morgan, Richard; New York, 1796 ***8197.10*** *p8*
Morgan, Richard 54; Ontario, 1861 ***2896.27*** *p51*
Morgan, Richard 66; Vermont, 1852 ***5900.10*** *p293*
Morgan, Robert; Colorado, 1896 ***1640.13*** *p79*
Morgan, Robt 35; Ontario, 1871 ***1823.28*** *p74*
Morgan, Samuel; Maryland, 1662 ***2524.55*** *p92*
Morgan, Samuel; Pennsylvania, 1861 ***6058.10*** *p45*
Morgan, Sarah; Hartford, Connecticut, 1850 ***1224.3*** *p39*
Morgan, Sarah 20; Ontario, 1861 ***2896.27*** *p35*
Morgan, Sarah E. 16; Ontario, 1861 ***2896.27*** *p51*
Morgan, Susanna; Maryland, 1681 ***2524.55*** *p155*
Morgan, T. 5; Ontario, 1861 ***2896.26*** *p2*
Morgan, Thomas; Illinois, 1851 ***1224.3*** *p54*
Morgan, Thomas; Maryland, 1680 ***2524.55*** *p155*
Morgan, Thomas; New York, 1836 ***1224.3*** *p54*
Morgan, Thomas; Pennsylvania, 1777 ***4629.10*** *p14*
Morgan, Thomas; Virginia, 1666-1667 ***6212.30*** *p33*
Morgan, Thomas 16; Maryland, 1775 ***1220.25*** *p112*
Morgan, Thomas 25; Baltimore, 1775 ***1220.25*** *p118*
Morgan, Thomas 27; Maryland, 1774 ***1220.25*** *p83*
Morgan, Thomas 81; Ontario, 1861 ***2896.27*** *p32*
Morgan, Walter 53; Ontario, 1871 ***1823.28*** *p74*
Morgan, William *SEE* Morgan, Alice
Morgan, William *SEE* Morgan, Jenkin
Morgan, William; Maryland, 1661 ***2524.55*** *p133*
Morgan, William; Maryland, 1663 ***2524.55*** *p155*
Morgan, William; Maryland, 1669 ***2524.55*** *p156*
Morgan, William; Maryland, 1672 ***2524.55*** *p155*
Morgan, William; Maryland, 1681 ***2524.55*** *p156*
Morgan, William 21; Maryland, 1774 ***1220.25*** *p52*
Morgan, William 31; Virginia, 1773 ***1220.25*** *p28*
Morgan, William 37; Ontario, 1871 ***1823.15*** *p194*
Morgan, Wm; Virginia, 1672 ***6212.30*** *p48*
Morganie, William; Maryland, 1655 ***2524.55*** *p156*
Morgans, Morgan; New York, 1807 ***8197.10*** *p45*
Morganstein, Samuel 27; Kansas, 1910 ***9079.10*** *p44*
Morganstern, Magdalene 40; Kansas, 1885-1910 ***9079.10*** *p13*
Morganstern, William 49; Kansas, 1878-1910 ***9079.10*** *p13*
Morgantholler, Mordart; New York, 1840 ***8197.10*** *p180*
Morgenstern, Catherine E. 34; Kansas, 1878-1910 ***9079.10*** *p12*
Morgenstern, Engel; America, 1793 ***2856.30*** *p307*
Morgenstern, Engel; America, 1795 ***2856.30*** *p307*
Morgenstern, Fred W. 36; Kansas, 1878-1910 ***9079.10*** *p12*
Morgenstern, Johann Nikolaus; Port uncertain, 1781 ***2856.30*** *p307*
Morgenstern, Samuel 51; Kansas, 1878-1910 ***9079.10*** *p12*
Morgenstern, Walkelmena 44; Kansas, 1879-1910 ***9079.10*** *p12*
Morgin, Anne; Virginia, 1663 ***6212.30*** *p4*
Morgin, Eliz; Virginia, 1681-1682 ***6212.30*** *p56*
Morhardt, Anna Maria; Port uncertain, 1765 ***2856.30*** *p307*
Mori, Susanna; Port uncertain, 1754 ***2856.30*** *p307*
Moriarity, Daniel; Vermont, 1832-1903 ***5900.10*** *p118*
Moriarity, Edward; Vermont, 1860-1932 ***5900.10*** *p548*
Moriarity, Ellen 50; Vermont, 1862 ***5900.10*** *p112*
Moriarity, Joana Prendiville 43; Vermont, 1883 ***5900.10*** *p329*
Moriarity, Johanna Fitzgerald 55; Vermont, 1875 ***5900.10*** *p112*
Moriarity, M.; Vermont, 1834-1915 ***5900.10*** *p554*
Moriarity, Margaret Ryan; Vermont, 1829-1902 ***5900.10*** *p548*
Moriarity, Peter; Vermont, 1827-1923 ***5900.10*** *p548*
Moriartney, Sarah 32; Ontario, 1871 ***1823.28*** *p74*
Moriarty, Annie T.; Vermont, 1867-1920 ***5900.10*** *p552*
Moriarty, Bridget 40; Vermont, 1866 ***5900.10*** *p372*
Moriarty, Daniel; Vermont, 1835-1899 ***5900.10*** *p552*
Moriarty, Daniel 25; Ontario, 1871 ***1823.28*** *p74*
Moriarty, Daniel 88; Ontario, 1871 ***1823.28*** *p74*
Moriarty, Frank H.; Vermont, 1852-1922 ***5900.10*** *p70*
Moriarty, Hanora Lawler; Vermont, 1822-1888 ***5900.10*** *p329*
Moriarty, Harry E.; Vermont, 1878-1927 ***5900.10*** *p358*
Moriarty, Jennie M.; Vermont, 1866-1945 ***5900.10*** *p358*
Moriarty, Johanna E. Leary; Vermont, 1867-1947 ***5900.10*** *p70*
Moriarty, Johanna O'Connor 71; Vermont, 1885 ***5900.10*** *p54*
Moriarty, John; Vermont, 1820-1890 ***5900.10*** *p329*
Moriarty, John; Vermont, 1839-1914 ***5900.10*** *p358*
Moriarty, John; Vermont, 1852-1916 ***5900.10*** *p444*
Moriarty, John H. 74; Vermont, 1892 ***5900.10*** *p54*
Moriarty, Katharine Dooley; Vermont, 1848-1914 ***5900.10*** *p358*
Moriarty, Katherine; Vermont, 1854-1914 ***5900.10*** *p339*
Moriarty, Margaret; Vermont, 1850-1926 ***5900.10*** *p349*
Moriarty, Margaret Reardon; Vermont, 1853-1910 ***5900.10*** *p338*
Moriarty, Mary; Vermont, 1817-1884 ***5900.10*** *p343*
Moriarty, Mary Boyle; Vermont, 1853-1933 ***5900.10*** *p444*
Moriarty, Michael 65; Vermont, 1886 ***5900.10*** *p338*
Moriarty, Nancy 65; Vermont, 1871 ***5900.10*** *p367*
Moriarty, Patrick 27; Ontario, 1871 ***1823.28*** *p74*
Moriarty, Patrick 70; Ontario, 1871 ***1823.28*** *p74*
Moriarty, Patrick 98; Vermont, 1890 ***5900.10*** *p367*
Moriarty, Peter; America, 1790 ***4628.40*** *p29*
Moriarty, Thomas 68; Vermont, 1901 ***5900.10*** *p329*
Moriarty, Winifred S. Kelty; Vermont, 1836-1914 ***5900.10*** *p552*
Moriarty, Winston P. 36; Vermont, 1887 ***5900.10*** *p54*
Morien, John 23; Maryland, 1773-1774 ***1220.25*** *p33*
Morierty, Catherine Qualters 70; Vermont, 1922 ***5900.10*** *p62*
Morierty, Michael; Vermont, n.d. ***5900.10*** *p62*
Morigan, Hugh 40; Ontario, 1871 ***1823.28*** *p74*
Morin, Andrew; New York, 1836 ***8197.10*** *p263*

Morin, David 69; Ontario, 1871 ***1823.22*** *p114*
Moring, Nichelas 47; Ontario, 1871 ***1823.15*** *p194*
Morinski, Michael; Maryland, 1910 ***3259.35*** *p41*
Moris, Benjamin 24; Ontario, 1871 ***1823.22*** *p114*
Moriseite, John; Georgia, 1698 ***1640.13*** *p79*
Morisey, Mary 74; Vermont, 1868 ***5900.10*** *p506*
Morison, Angus 40; Ontario, 1871 ***1823.15*** *p194*
Morison, Isabela 70; Ontario, 1871 ***1823.15*** *p194*
Morison, James, Sr.; New York, 1832 ***8197.10*** *p357*
Morison, Jemima; Charleston, South Carolina, 1804 ***1640.13*** *p79*
Morison, John; Jamaica, n.d. ***1224.3*** *p54*
Morison, John; Mexico, 1853 ***1640.13*** *p79*
Morison, John; Ohio, 1840 ***1224.3*** *p54*
Morison, Malcolm; Annapolis, Nova Scotia, 1790 ***1224.2*** *p82*
Morison, Malcolm; New York, n.d. ***1224.2*** *p82*
Morison, Samuel; New York, 1808 ***8197.10*** *p54*
Morison, Thomas; Haiti, 1876 ***1640.13*** *p79*
Morison, William 25; Ontario, 1871 ***1823.15*** *p194*
Morison, William 76; Ontario, 1871 ***1823.15*** *p194*
Morison, William Gray; Quebec, 1884 ***1640.13*** *p79*
Morissey, Richard; Pennsylvania, 1866 ***6058.10*** *p51*
Moritz, Dietrich; Port uncertain, 1754 ***2856.30*** *p307*
Moritzki, Thomas; Maryland, 1910 ***3259.35*** *p41*
Morkeski, Cazmir; Maryland, 1910 ***3259.35*** *p41*
Morland, Michael 17; New York, 1833-1840 ***8197.10*** *p181*
Morley, Anne; Maryland, 1673 ***2524.55*** *p156*
Husband: Thomas
Morley, Benjamin 30; Ontario, 1871 ***1823.15*** *p194*
Morley, Charles 25; Ontario, 1871 ***1823.28*** *p74*
Morley, David; North Carolina, 1752 ***1224.2*** *p81*
Morley, Henery 65; Ontario, 1871 ***1823.15*** *p194*
Morley, Isaac 35; Ontario, 1871 ***1823.15*** *p194*
Morley, James 45; Ontario, 1871 ***1823.15*** *p194*
Morley, John; New England, 1661 ***1224.1*** *p10*
Morley, John; Virginia, 1664 ***6212.30*** *p8*
Morley, John 60; Ontario, 1871 ***1823.28*** *p74*
Morley, Robert; Virginia, 1667-1668 ***6212.30*** *p38*
Morley, Thomas *SEE* Morley, Anne
Morley, Timothy; New York, 1840 ***8197.10*** *p179*
Morlock, Mr.; Port uncertain, 1775 ***2856.30*** *p307*
With wife
Morlock, Andreas; Port uncertain, 1744 ***2856.30*** *p307*
Morlock, Matthew 43; Ontario, 1871 ***1823.15*** *p194*
Morlock, Michael; America, 1767 ***2856.30*** *p307*
Morlock, Michael; Port uncertain, 1766 ***2856.30*** *p307*
Morlock, Michel, Sr.; Port uncertain, 1775 ***2856.30*** *p307*
Morlot, Robert; New York, 1831 ***8197.10*** *p364*
Morly, Anne; Maryland, 1673 ***2524.55*** *p156*
Husband: Thomas
Morly, Joseph; Virginia, 1667 ***6212.30*** *p37*
Morly, Thomas *SEE* Morly, Anne
Mormann, Hans Georg; Port uncertain, 1758 ***2856.30*** *p319*
Mormann, Ursula; Port uncertain, 1765 ***2856.30*** *p307*
Morn, John; Savannah, Georgia, 1775 ***1640.10*** *p160*
Mornoch, John; Jamaica, 1818 ***1640.13*** *p73*
Moro, Gaetano; New York, 1831 ***8197.10*** *p354*
Morolds, Robert 64; Ontario, 1871 ***1823.15*** *p194*
Moroney, James; New York, 1840 ***8197.10*** *p178*
Moroney, James 29; Vermont, 1875 ***5900.10*** *p558*
Moroney, John 29; Vermont, 1875 ***5900.10*** *p569*
Moroney, John 52; Vermont, 1892 ***5900.10*** *p562*
Moroney, Kate Nagle 78; Vermont, 1924 ***5900.10*** *p558*
Moroney, Margaret Collins 56; Vermont, 1884 ***5900.10*** *p465*
Moroney, Margaret Sammon; Vermont, 1844-1914 ***5900.10*** *p562*
Moroney, Mary; Vermont, 1872 ***5900.10*** *p319*
Moroney, Mary O'Donnell; Vermont, 1938 ***5900.10*** *p427*
Moroney, Patrick 68; Vermont, 1886 ***5900.10*** *p465*
Moroney, Thomas F.; Vermont, 1927 ***5900.10*** *p427*
Moroski, Joseph; Maryland, 1910 ***3259.35*** *p41*
Morowski, Victoria; Maryland, 1910 ***3259.35*** *p41*
Morpeth, Thomas 15; Philadelphia, 1774 ***1220.25*** *p43*
Morr, Andreas; Port uncertain, 1751 ***2856.30*** *p307*
Morr, Michael; Port uncertain, 1781 ***2856.30*** *p307*
Morra, Andrew; Maryland, 1658 ***2524.55*** *p156*
Morrah, Francis 38; Ontario, 1871 ***1823.28*** *p74*
Morrant, John; Long Island, 1780 ***1224.2*** *p81*
Morrarta, Teage; Virginia, 1663 ***6212.30*** *p2*
Morrell, Mrs.; Quebec, 1858 ***9196.15*** *p41*
Morrell, John; New Jersey, 1823 ***1224.3*** *p54*
Morrell, Mary Crawley; New Jersey, 1823 ***1224.3*** *p54*
Morrell, Thomas; New York, 1828 ***8197.10*** *p349*
Morrell, William; Pennsylvania, 1777 ***4629.10*** *p24*
Morres, John 30; Virginia, 1774 ***1220.25*** *p87*
Morresy, Lawrence 58; Ontario, 1871 ***1823.28*** *p74*
Morrey, Anne; Philadelphia, 1749 ***1224.2*** *p81*
Morrey, Richard; Philadelphia, 1756 ***1224.2*** *p81*
Morrey, Sarah; Philadelphia, 1756 ***1224.2*** *p81*
Morrice, Henry; Maryland, 1651 ***2524.55*** *p156*
Morrice, L.; Portland, Maine, 1858 ***9196.15*** *p27*
Morrice, Robert; Maryland, 1659 ***2524.55*** *p156*
Morrice, Robt.; Maryland, 1658 ***2524.55*** *p156*
Morrill, John H.; Vermont, 1853-1929 ***5900.10*** *p451*
Morrill, Mary Molineaux; Vermont, 1853-1912 ***5900.10*** *p349*
Morrill, Peter; Vermont, 1854-1903 ***5900.10*** *p349*
Morrill, Rosana; Vermont, 1865-1963 ***5900.10*** *p451*
Morrine, William; Savannah, Georgia, 1805 ***1640.10*** *p160*
Morriott, Mr.; Quebec, 1858 ***9196.15*** *p36*
Morris, Miss; Portland, Maine, 1858 ***9196.15*** *p28*
Morris, Miss; Quebec, 1858 ***9196.15*** *p41*
Morris, Mr.; Quebec, 1857 ***9196.15*** *p20*
Morris, Mr.; Quebec, 1857 ***9196.15*** *p26*
Morris, Mr.; Quebec, 1858 ***9196.15*** *p37*
Morris, Mr.; Quebec, 1858 ***9196.15*** *p41*
Morris, Mr.; Quebec, 1858 ***9196.15*** *p47*
Morris, Mrs.; Quebec, 1856 ***9196.15*** *p8*
Morris, Mrs.; Quebec, 1857 ***9196.15*** *p26*
Morris, Mrs.; Quebec, 1858 ***9196.15*** *p41*
Morris, A. P.; Quebec, 1856 ***9196.15*** *p8*
Morris, Alexander; Toronto, 1890 ***1640.13*** *p79*
Morris, Alexander 50; Ontario, 1871 ***1823.15*** *p195*
Morris, Alfred 50; Ontario, 1871 ***1823.15*** *p195*
Morris, Ann *SEE* Morris, Richard
Morris, Ann; Maryland, 1665 ***2524.55*** *p156*
Morris, Ann; Vermont, 1818-1910 ***5900.10*** *p339*
Morris, Ann; Virginia, 1664 ***6212.30*** *p12*
Morris, Ann 40; Ontario, 1871 ***1823.15*** *p195*
Morris, Ann 68; Vermont, 1898 ***5900.10*** *p468*
Morris, Ann Gallagher 52; Vermont, 1904 ***5900.10*** *p441*
Morris, Anna; Philadelphia, 1801 ***1224.3*** *p54*
Morris, Anne; Maryland, 1668 ***2524.55*** *p55*
Morris, Arthur 36; Maryland, 1775 ***1220.25*** *p102*
Morris, Bernard; New York, 1839 ***8197.10*** *p264*
Morris, Bridget; Vermont, 1829-1884 ***5900.10*** *p467*
Morris, Bridget T.; Vermont, 1847-1874 ***5900.10*** *p436*
Morris, Cadwallader; Pennsylvania, 1777 ***4629.10*** *p29*
Morris, Cadwallader; Pennsylvania, 1779 ***4629.10*** *p41*
Morris, Charles 28; Ontario, 1871 ***1823.22*** *p114*
Morris, Charles Hughes; New York, 1836 ***8197.10*** *p317*
Morris, Charlotte 81; Ontario, 1871 ***1823.15*** *p195*
Morris, Christopher 22; Baltimore, 1775 ***1220.25*** *p116*
Morris, Cornelius; New York, 1807 ***8197.10*** *p45*
Morris, Cornelius; Virginia, 1666 ***6212.30*** *p26*
Morris, David; America, 1819 ***1640.13*** *p80*
Morris, Dennis; Virginia, 1663 ***6212.30*** *p4*
Morris, Edw; Virginia, 1663 ***6212.30*** *p4*
Morris, Edw; Virginia, 1672 ***6212.30*** *p48*
Morris, Edward; Maryland, 1681 ***2524.55*** *p156*
Morris, Edward 49; Ontario, 1871 ***1823.22*** *p114*
Morris, Eliza 28; Ontario, 1871 ***1823.22*** *p114*
Morris, Elizabeth *SEE* Morris, John
Morris, Elizabeth *SEE* Morris, Manasseth
Morris, Elizabeth *SEE* Morris, William
Morris, Elizabeth; Alabama, 1797-1845 ***1640.10*** *p160*
Morris, Elizabeth; Maryland, 1673 ***2524.55*** *p156*
Morris, Elizabeth; Maryland, 1682 ***2524.55*** *p156*
Morris, Elizabeth; Vermont, 1851-1915 ***5900.10*** *p492*
Morris, Elizabeth 16; Maryland, 1774 ***1220.25*** *p59*
Morris, Elizabeth 22; Philadelphia, 1774 ***1220.25*** *p55*
Morris, Elizabeth 54; Vermont, 1897 ***5900.10*** *p526*
Morris, Elizabeth Duffey; Vermont, 1837 ***5900.10*** *p528*
Morris, Ellen; Vermont, 1833-1910 ***5900.10*** *p493*
Morris, George 23; Virginia, 1774 ***1220.25*** *p89*
Morris, George 69; Ontario, 1871 ***1823.15*** *p195*
Morris, Gilbert 74; Vermont, 1914 ***5900.10*** *p441*
Morris, Hannah; Maryland, 1666 ***2524.55*** *p156*
Morris, Henry 27; Virginia, 1774 ***1220.25*** *p54*
Morris, Hopkin; Virginia, 1664 ***6212.30*** *p5*
Morris, Isabella; Alabama, 1838 ***1640.10*** *p160*
Morris, Israel; Pennsylvania, 1785 ***4629.10*** *p47*
Morris, James; New York, 1825 ***8197.10*** *p262*
Morris, James; Vermont, 1831 ***5900.10*** *p528*
Morris, James 21; Maryland, 1775 ***1220.25*** *p102*
Morris, James 53; Ontario, 1871 ***1823.28*** *p74*
Morris, Jane; Virginia, 1666 ***6212.30*** *p26*
Morris, Jenckin; Maryland, 1672 ***2524.55*** *p156*
Morris, John; Charles Town, South Carolina, 1778 ***1224.2*** *p81*
Morris, John; Kingston, Jamaica, 1778 ***1224.2*** *p81*
Morris, John; Maryland, 1631-1685 ***2524.55*** *p156*
Wife: Elizabeth
Morris, John; New Jersey, 1797 ***1224.2*** *p81*
Morris, John; New York, 1840 ***8197.10*** *p178*
Morris, John; New York, 1840 ***8197.10*** *p180*
Morris, John; New York, 1840 ***8197.10*** *p387*
Morris, John; Pennsylvania, 1779 ***4629.10*** *p40*
Morris, John; Virginia, 1698 ***6212.30*** *p61*
Morris, John; Virginia, 1703 ***6212.30*** *p62*
Morris, John 60; Ontario, 1871 ***1823.15*** *p195*
Morris, John C. 7; Ontario, 1871 ***1823.28*** *p74*
Morris, Joseph; Pennsylvania, 1777 ***4629.10*** *p25*
Morris, Joseph; Philadelphia, 1790 ***4629.10*** *p83*
Morris, Joseph Handford; Cleveland, Ohio, 1849 ***1224.3*** *p54*
Morris, Julia Louisa Kearney; New York, 1857 ***1224.3*** *p54*
Morris, Katharine; Maryland, 1682 ***2524.55*** *p156*
Morris, Katherine; Maryland, 1678 ***2524.55*** *p156*
Morris, Lewis; Virginia, 1666 ***6212.30*** *p26*
Morris, Louis C.; Vermont, 1837-1913 ***5900.10*** *p539*
Morris, M.; Quebec, 1858 ***9196.15*** *p32*
Morris, Manasseth; Maryland, 1682 ***2524.55*** *p156*
Wife: Elizabeth
Morris, Margaret McKinn; Vermont, 1840-1924 ***5900.10*** *p539*
Morris, Margarett; Maryland, 1672 ***2524.55*** *p156*
Morris, Maria 54; Vermont, 1905 ***5900.10*** *p506*
Morris, Martha; Virginia, 1665-1666 ***6212.30*** *p24*
Morris, Martin 60; Newfoundland, 1774 ***1220.25*** *p1*
Morris, Mary *SEE* Morris, William
Morris, Mary 52; Vermont, 1884 ***5900.10*** *p378*
Morris, Mary 83; Vermont, 1903 ***5900.10*** *p504*
Morris, Mary Burke; Vermont, 1827-1881 ***5900.10*** *p52*
Morris, Mary J. Maddin; Vermont, 1817-1897 ***5900.10*** *p365*
Morris, Matthew 63; Ontario, 1871 ***1823.15*** *p195*
Morris, Nellie F. Hartnett; Vermont, 1859-1905 ***5900.10*** *p467*
Morris, Nicholas; New York, 1803 ***8197.10*** *p14*
Morris, Owen; Virginia, 1668-1669 ***6212.30*** *p41*
Morris, Owin; Virginia, 1665-1666 ***6212.30*** *p25*
Morris, Patrick 70; Vermont, 1892 ***5900.10*** *p468*
Morris, Peter; New York, 1839 ***8197.10*** *p264*
Morris, Peter; Vermont, 1815-1895 ***5900.10*** *p365*
Morris, Philip; Maryland, 1674 ***2524.55*** *p156*
Morris, Prince 63; Ontario, 1871 ***1823.15*** *p195*
Morris, Rachael; Maryland, 1797 ***1224.2*** *p122*
Morris, Rebecca *SEE* Morris, William
Morris, Richard; Maryland, 1668 ***2524.55*** *p156*
Relative: Ann
Morris, Richard; Maryland, 1670 ***2524.55*** *p156*
Morris, Richard; Richmond, Virginia, 1809 ***1224.3*** *p54*
Morris, Robert; Maryland, 1659 ***2524.55*** *p156*
Morris, Robert; New York, 1802 ***8197.10*** *p22*
Morris, Robert; New York, 1821 ***8197.10*** *p260*
Morris, Robert; New York, 1827 ***8197.10*** *p261*
Morris, Robert; Pennsylvania, 1777 ***4629.10*** *p8*
Morris, Robert; Pennsylvania, 1777 ***4629.10*** *p20*
Morris, Robt.; Maryland, 1658 ***2524.55*** *p156*
Morris, Rolland H. 56; Oregon, 1913 ***9196.1*** *p60*
Morris, Sam'l Cadwallader; Pennsylvania, 1777 ***4629.10*** *p29*
Morris, Samuel; Pennsylvania, 1779 ***4629.10*** *p36*
Morris, Samuel 55; Ontario, 1871 ***1823.15*** *p195*
Morris, Samuel C.; Pennsylvania, 1779 ***4629.10*** *p35*
Morris, Samuell *SEE* Morris, William
Morris, Sarah *SEE* Morris, William
Morris, Sarah 84; Vermont, 1931 ***5900.10*** *p61*
Morris, Stephen 36; Maryland, 1775 ***1220.25*** *p99*
Morris, Thom; Maryland, 1665 ***2524.55*** *p156*
Morris, Thomas; Florida, 1797 ***1224.2*** *p81*
Morris, Thomas; Pennsylvania, 1779 ***4629.10*** *p35*
Morris, Thomas; Vermont, 1817-1906 ***5900.10*** *p52*
Morris, Thomas; Virginia, 1671-1672 ***6212.30*** *p48*
Morris, Thomas; Virginia, 1687 ***1224.1*** *p40*
Morris, Thomas 26; Ontario, 1871 ***1823.15*** *p195*
Morris, Thomas 41; Ontario, 1871 ***1823.28*** *p74*
Morris, W. B.; Portland, Maine, 1858 ***9196.15*** *p28*
Morris, William; Maryland, 1680 ***2524.55*** *p156*
Daughter: Sarah
Wife: Rebecca
Daughter: Elizabeth
Daughter: Mary
Son: Samuell
Daughter: Rebecca
Morris, William; Maryland, 1793 ***1224.2*** *p81*
Morris, William; New York, 1830 ***8197.10*** *p66*
Morris, William; New York, New York, 1893 ***3437.14*** *p164*
Morris, William; Pennsylvania, 1777 ***4629.10*** *p14*
Morris, William; Pennsylvania, 1777 ***4629.10*** *p26*
Morris, William; Pennsylvania, 1778 ***4629.10*** *p34*
Morris, William 17; Maryland, 1775 ***1220.25*** *p102*
Morris, William 40; Ontario, 1871 ***1823.15*** *p195*
Morris, William 53; Ontario, 1871 ***1823.15*** *p195*
Morris, William 80; Ontario, 1871 ***1823.15*** *p195*
Morris, Wm; Virginia, 1664 ***6212.30*** *p5*
Morris, Woolaston 21; Maryland, 1774 ***1220.25*** *p62*
Morrisay, Richard; Pennsylvania, 1866 ***6058.10*** *p51*
Morrisee, Ellen 11; Vermont, 1864 ***5900.10*** *p347*
Morrisey, Ellen 45; Vermont, 1860 ***5900.10*** *p305*
Morrisey, John; New York, 1752 ***1224.2*** *p82*

Morrisey, Julia 59; Vermont, 1905 ***5900.10*** *p394*
Morrisey, Michael; Vermont, 1841-1921 ***5900.10*** *p42*
Morrisey, William; Vermont, 1810-1899 ***5900.10*** *p304*
Morrish, Charles 32; Ontario, 1871 ***1823.15*** *p195*
Morrish, Nicholas 48; Ontario, 1871 ***1823.15*** *p195*
Morrish, Thomas 41; Ontario, 1871 ***1823.15*** *p195*
Morrish, Thomas 75; Ontario, 1871 ***1823.15*** *p195*
Morrison, Mr.; Quebec, 1856 ***9196.15*** *p9*
Morrison, Mr.; Quebec, 1857 ***9196.15*** *p23*
Morrison, Agnes *SEE* Morrison, Murdo
Morrison, Alexander *SEE* Morrison, Donald
Morrison, Alexander *SEE* Morrison, Ewen
Morrison, Alexander *SEE* Morrison, John
Morrison, Alexander *SEE* Morrison, Neil
Morrison, Alexander *SEE* Morrison, Ranald
Morrison, Alexander *SEE* Morrison, Roderick
Morrison, Alexander; America, 1880-1889 ***4537.35*** *p76*
Brother: Kenneth
Morrison, Alexander; Nova Scotia, 1820-1829 ***4537.35*** *p30*
Wife: Sophia
Child: Roderick
Child: Donald
Morrison, Alexander; Nova Scotia, 1830-1839 ***4537.35*** *p30*
Wife: Mary
Child: Neil
Child: John
Morrison, Alexander; Ontario, 1849 ***4537.37*** *p79*
Wife: Margaret Stewart
Child: Donald
Child: Ann
Morrison, Alexander; Pennsylvania, 1777 ***4629.10*** *p23*
Morrison, Alexander; Vermont, 1856-1919 ***5900.10*** *p141*
Morrison, Alexander; Port uncertain, 1840-1849 ***4537.37*** *p130*
Wife: Margaret Martin
Child: Archie
Child: Neil
Morrison, Alick 50; Ontario, 1871 ***1823.15*** *p195*
Morrison, Allan *SEE* Morrison, Angus
Morrison, Allan *SEE* Morrison, Ann MacIntyre
Morrison, Allan *SEE* Morrison, Donald
Morrison, Allan *SEE* Morrison, Lachlan
Morrison, Allan *SEE* Morrison, William
Morrison, Allan; Nova Scotia, 1826 ***4537.35*** *p30*
Wife: Mary
Child: Kenneth
Child: Roderick
Child: Effie
Child: Mary
Child: Catherine
Child: Malcolm
Morrison, Allan; Port uncertain, 1850-1859 ***4537.37*** *p130*
Wife: Effie MacNeil
Child: Janet
Child: Ann
Child: John
Child: Angus
Child: Neil
Morrison, Andrew 37; Ontario, 1871 ***1823.15*** *p195*
Morrison, Andrew 70; Ontario, 1871 ***1823.22*** *p114*
Morrison, Angus *SEE* Morrison, Allan
Morrison, Angus *SEE* Morrison, Angus
Morrison, Angus *SEE* Morrison, Donald
Morrison, Angus *SEE* Morrison, Ewen
Morrison, Angus *SEE* Morrison, John
Morrison, Angus *SEE* Morrison, Kenneth
Morrison, Angus *SEE* Morrison, Malcolm
Morrison, Angus *SEE* Morrison, Michael
Morrison, Angus *SEE* Morrison, Norman
Morrison, Angus *SEE* Morrison, Peter
Morrison, Angus *SEE* Morrison, Ranald
Morrison, Angus; Maryland, 1888 ***4537.35*** *p70*
Wife: Catherine MacLean
Child: Mary
Child: Murdo
Child: Malcolm
Child: Kate
Child: Norman
Child: Bess
Child: Archie
Morrison, Angus; Nova Scotia, 1820-1829 ***4537.35*** *p31*
Wife: Martha Catherine MacKillop
Child: Roderick
Child: Donald
Child: Duncan
Child: John
Morrison, Angus; Ontario, 1840-1849 ***4537.37*** *p79*
Wife: Mary Steele
Child: Donald
Child: Marion
Morrison, Angus; Ontario, 1849 ***4537.32*** *p82*
Wife: Mary Steele
Child: Donald
Child: Marion
Morrison, Angus; Ontario, 1849 ***4537.37*** *p79*
Wife: Catherine
Morrison, Angus; Ontario, 1849 ***4537.37*** *p79*
Wife: Janet Walker
Child: Angus
Child: John
Morrison, Angus; Ontario, 1862 ***4537.32*** *p81*
Wife: Lexy Ross
Child: Mary
Child: Margaret
Child: Kirsty
Child: Neil
Morrison, Angus; Ontario, 1863 ***4537.32*** *p81*
Wife: Jane Murray
Child: Kirsty
Morrison, Angus; Ontario, 1863 ***4537.35*** *p61*
Wife: Lexy Ross
Child: Kirsty
Child: Margaret
Child: Neil
Child: Mary
Morrison, Angus; Port uncertain, 1840-1849 ***4537.37*** *p130*
Wife: Kate MacPhee
Child: Marion
Child: Kate
Child: Allan
Child: Angus
Child: John
Morrison, Angus; Port uncertain, 1860-1869 ***4537.35*** *p85*
Wife: Effie MacLeod
Child: Effie
Child: Catherine
Child: Margaret Ann
Child: Mary
Child: Marion
Morrison, Angus 40; Ontario, 1871 ***1823.15*** *p195*
Morrison, Angus 41; Ontario, 1871 ***1823.15*** *p195*
Morrison, Ann *SEE* Morrison, Alexander
Morrison, Ann *SEE* Morrison, Allan
Morrison, Ann *SEE* Morrison, Ann MacIntyre
Morrison, Ann *SEE* Morrison, Donald
Morrison, Ann *SEE* Morrison, Ewen
Morrison, Ann *SEE* Morrison, John
Morrison, Ann *SEE* Morrison, Kenneth
Morrison, Ann *SEE* Morrison, Malcolm
Morrison, Ann *SEE* Morrison, Michael
Morrison, Ann *SEE* Morrison, Murdo
Morrison, Ann *SEE* Morrison, Neil
Morrison, Ann *SEE* Morrison, Norman
Morrison, Ann *SEE* Morrison, Peter
Morrison, Ann *SEE* Morrison, Ranald
Morrison, Ann *SEE* Morrison, Roderick
Morrison, Ann; Nova Scotia, 1840-1849 ***4537.35*** *p25*
Morrison, Ann; Ontario, 1840-1849 ***4537.37*** *p31*
Morrison, Ann; Ontario, 1849 ***4537.32*** *p4*
Morrison, Ann; Ontario, 1850 ***4537.37*** *p59*
Morrison, Ann; Ontario, 1850-1859 ***4537.37*** *p60*
Morrison, Ann; Ontario, 1850-1859 ***4537.37*** *p78*
Morrison, Ann; Ontario, 1851 ***4537.32*** *p39*
Morrison, Ann; Ontario, 1851 ***4537.32*** *p79*
Morrison, Ann; Saskatchewan, 1884 ***4537.37*** *p102*
Morrison, Ann; Port uncertain, 1840-1849 ***4537.37*** *p129*
Morrison, Ann; Port uncertain, 1850-1859 ***4537.37*** *p133*
Morrison, Ann MacCormick *SEE* Morrison, Neil
Morrison, Ann MacDonald *SEE* Morrison, Neil
Morrison, Ann MacDonald; Port uncertain, 1840-1849 ***4537.37*** *p130*
Child: Catherine
Child: Donald
Child: John
Morrison, Ann MacIntyre; Prince Edward Island, 1848 ***4537.37*** *p26*
Child: Ann
Child: Allan
Child: Mary
Child: James
Child: Neil
Morrison, Ann MacKinnon *SEE* Morrison, John
Morrison, Ann MacLeod *SEE* Morrison, Kenneth
Morrison, Ann MacLeod *SEE* Morrison, Peter
Morrison, Ann Shaw *SEE* Morrison, Neil
Morrison, Ann Tulley 54; Vermont, 1889 ***5900.10*** *p573*
Morrison, Ann Walker *SEE* Morrison, John
Morrison, Archie *SEE* Morrison, Alexander
Morrison, Archie *SEE* Morrison, Angus
Morrison, Archie *SEE* Morrison, Donald
Morrison, Archie *SEE* Morrison, Norman
Morrison, Bannatyne *SEE* Morrison, John
Morrison, Barbara *SEE* Morrison, Roderick
Morrison, Bella Gillies *SEE* Morrison, John
Morrison, Bess *SEE* Morrison, Angus
Morrison, Bess *SEE* Morrison, Ewen
Morrison, Catherine *SEE* Morrison, Allan
Morrison, Catherine *SEE* Morrison, Angus
Morrison, Catherine *SEE* Morrison, Ann MacDonald
Morrison, Catherine *SEE* Morrison, Donald
Morrison, Catherine *SEE* Morrison, John
Morrison, Catherine *SEE* Morrison, Kenneth
Morrison, Catherine *SEE* Morrison, Lachlan
Morrison, Catherine *SEE* Morrison, Malcolm
Morrison, Catherine *SEE* Morrison, Neil
Morrison, Catherine *SEE* Morrison, Norman
Morrison, Catherine; California, 1860-1869 ***4537.35*** *p75*
Morrison, Catherine; Georgia, 1736 ***1640.10*** *p160*
Morrison, Catherine; Nova Scotia, 1840-1849 ***4537.35*** *p36*
Child: Donald
Child: William
Morrison, Catherine; Nova Scotia, 1840-1849 ***4537.37*** *p12*
Morrison, Catherine; Ontario, 1840-1849 ***4537.37*** *p53*
Morrison, Catherine; Ontario, 1848 ***4537.37*** *p83*
Morrison, Catherine; Ontario, 1849 ***4537.37*** *p71*
Morrison, Catherine; Ontario, 1849 ***4537.37*** *p84*
Morrison, Catherine; Ontario, 1850 ***4537.37*** *p50*
Morrison, Catherine; Ontario, 1851 ***4537.32*** *p78*
Morrison, Catherine; Ontario, 1851 ***4537.37*** *p85*
Morrison, Catherine MacCormick *SEE* Morrison, Norman
Morrison, Catherine MacLean *SEE* Morrison, Angus
Morrison, Catherine Paterson *SEE* Morrison, Donald
Morrison, Charles; Vermont, 1845-1930 ***5900.10*** *p296*
Morrison, Charles 4; Ontario, 1861 ***2896.28*** *p37*
Morrison, Charles H.; Vermont, 1838-1914 ***5900.10*** *p496*
Morrison, Christopher; Georgia, 1699 ***1640.13*** *p80*
Morrison, Constance *SEE* Morrison, John
Morrison, David *SEE* Morrison, John
Morrison, David; New Orleans, 1790 ***1640.10*** *p160*
Wife: Elizabeth Mitchell
Morrison, David 64; Vermont, 1883 ***5900.10*** *p573*
Morrison, Donald *SEE* Morrison, Alexander
Morrison, Donald *SEE* Morrison, Angus
Morrison, Donald *SEE* Morrison, Ann MacDonald
Morrison, Donald *SEE* Morrison, Catherine
Morrison, Donald *SEE* Morrison, Donald
Morrison, Donald *SEE* Morrison, Ewen
Morrison, Donald *SEE* Morrison, Finlay
Morrison, Donald *SEE* Morrison, John
Morrison, Donald *SEE* Morrison, Kenneth
Morrison, Donald *SEE* Morrison, Malcolm
Morrison, Donald *SEE* Morrison, Mary MacAulay
Morrison, Donald *SEE* Morrison, Mary MacAuley
Morrison, Donald *SEE* Morrison, Michael
Morrison, Donald *SEE* Morrison, Neil
Morrison, Donald *SEE* Morrison, Norman
Morrison, Donald *SEE* Morrison, Peter
Morrison, Donald *SEE* Morrison, Ranald
Morrison, Donald *SEE* Morrison, Roderick
Morrison, Donald *SEE* Morrison, William
Morrison, Donald; Nova Scotia, 1820-1829 ***4537.35*** *p31*
Sister: Margaret
Sister: Mary
Morrison, Donald; Nova Scotia, 1820-1829 ***4537.35*** *p32*
Brother: Neil
Morrison, Donald; Nova Scotia, 1828 ***4537.35*** *p32*
Wife: Margaret
Child: Catherine
Child: Kirsty
Child: Archie
Morrison, Donald; Nova Scotia, 1834 ***4537.35*** *p32*
Wife: Margaret
Child: Angus
Child: Kirsty
Morrison, Donald; Nova Scotia, 1840-1849 ***4537.35*** *p31*
Wife: Ann
Child: Donald
Child: John
Child: Effie
Child: Kirsty
Child: Flora
Child: Isabella
Child: Jessie
Morrison, Donald; Nova Scotia, 1840-1849 ***4537.35*** *p31*
Wife: Catherine Paterson
Child: Catherine
Child: Norman
Child: Angus
Child: Alexander

Morrison, Donald; Nova Scotia, 1840-1849 ***4537.35*** *p31*
Wife: Effie MacKinnon
Child: Catherine
Child: Malcolm
Child: Mary
Child: Roderick
Child: Kirsty
Child: John
Morrison, Donald; Nova Scotia, 1840-1849 ***4537.35*** *p32*
Child: Roderick
Child: Ann
Child: Sandford
Child: Murdo
Child: Mary
Wife: Kirsty Ferguson
Morrison, Donald; Ontario, 1849 ***4537.37*** *p80*
Wife: Mary MacDonald
Child: Alexander
Child: Ann
Child: Kirsty
Child: Flora
Child: Catherine
Child: Ewen
Child: Mary
Child: Margaret
Child: Donald
Morrison, Donald; Ontario, 1863 ***4537.32*** *p82*
Child: Angus
Child: Kirsty
Child: Alexander
Wife: Lexy MacLean
Child: Allan
Child: Catherine
Child: Effie
Child: Ann
Morrison, Donald; Ontario, 1880-1889 ***4537.32*** *p82*
Morrison, Donald; Quebec, 1887 ***4537.35*** *p63*
Son: Ewen
Son: Sorley
Daughter: Marion
Morrison, Donald; Port uncertain, 1840-1849 ***4537.35*** *p85*
Wife: Effie
Child: Rachel
Child: Marion
Child: Kenneth
Child: Roderick
Child: John
Morrison, Donald; Port uncertain, 1840-1849 ***4537.37*** *p130*
Wife: Flora
Child: Kate
Child: Kenneth
Child: Mary
Child: Jane
Morrison, Donald; Port uncertain, 1840-1849 ***4537.37*** *p131*
Wife: Marion MacLeod
Child: Catherine
Child: John
Child: Mary
Morrison, Donald; Port uncertain, 1840-1849 ***4537.37*** *p131*
Wife: Sarah
Child: Archie
Child: Sarah
Child: Mary
Child: Catherine
Child: John
Morrison, Donald; Port uncertain, 1850-1859 ***4537.37*** *p131*
Child: Alexander
Child: Catherine
Wife: Isabella MacRae
Child: Mary
Child: Rachel
Child: Margaret
Morrison, Donald; Port uncertain, 1870-1879 ***4537.35*** *p85*
Wife: Flora MacFarlane
Child: John
Child: Alexander
Child: Catherine
Child: Archie
Morrison, Dougal *SEE* Morrison, Neil
Morrison, Duncan *SEE* Morrison, Angus
Morrison, Effie *SEE* Morrison, Allan
Morrison, Effie *SEE* Morrison, Angus
Morrison, Effie *SEE* Morrison, Donald
Morrison, Effie *SEE* Morrison, Finlay
Morrison, Effie *SEE* Morrison, John
Morrison, Effie *SEE* Morrison, Malcolm
Morrison, Effie *SEE* Morrison, Neil
Morrison, Effie *SEE* Morrison, Norman
Morrison, Effie; Ontario, 1851 ***4537.32*** *p31*
Morrison, Effie; Saskatchewan, 1883 ***4537.37*** *p94*
Morrison, Effie; Port uncertain, 1870-1879 ***4537.35*** *p80*
Morrison, Effie; Port uncertain, 1880-1889 ***4537.35*** *p83*
Morrison, Effie Campbell *SEE* Morrison, Norman
Morrison, Effie MacAulay *SEE* Morrison, Finlay
Morrison, Effie MacKinnon *SEE* Morrison, Donald
Morrison, Effie MacLeod *SEE* Morrison, Angus
Morrison, Effie MacNeil *SEE* Morrison, Allan
Morrison, Effie MacSween *SEE* Morrison, John
Morrison, Effie Smith *SEE* Morrison, Norman
Morrison, Eliza Finch; Antigua (Antego), 1867 ***1640.13*** *p80*
Morrison, Elizabeth Mitchell *SEE* Morrison, David
Morrison, Ellen; Vermont, 1839-1922 ***5900.10*** *p131*
Morrison, Emily J. 21; Ontario, 1861 ***2896.28*** *p37*
Morrison, Ewen *SEE* Morrison, Donald
Morrison, Ewen *SEE* Morrison, Finlay
Morrison, Ewen *SEE* Morrison, John
Morrison, Ewen; Falkland Islands, 1870-1879 ***4537.35*** *p76*
Wife: Kirsty MacLeod
Child: Hector
Child: John
Child: Donald
Child: Margaret
Child: Mary
Morrison, Ewen; Quebec, 1880-1889 ***4537.35*** *p63*
Wife: Bess
Child: Roderick
Child: Malcolm
Child: Angus
Child: Donald
Child: John
Morrison, Ewen; Port uncertain, 1840-1849 ***4537.35*** *p85*
With wife
Child: Kenneth
Child: John
Morrison, Ewen; Port uncertain, 1850-1859 ***4537.37*** *p131*
Wife: Sophia MacMillan
Child: Donald
Child: Alexander
Child: Kirsty
Child: Isabella
Child: John
Child: Marion
Child: Ann
Child: Mary
Morrison, Finlay *SEE* Morrison, Peter
Morrison, Finlay; Nova Scotia, 1828 ***4537.35*** *p32*
With wife
Child: John
Child: Kenneth
Child: Donald
Morrison, Finlay; Nova Scotia, 1840-1849 ***4537.35*** *p32*
Wife: Effie MacAulay
Child: Ewen
Child: Kirsty
Child: Morris
Child: John
Child: Margaret
Morrison, Finlay; South America, 1880-1889 ***4537.35*** *p76*
Morrison, Finlay; Port uncertain, 1840-1849 ***4537.35*** *p85*
Wife: Effie
Child: Kirsty
Child: Malcolm
Child: Mary
Child: John
Morrison, Flora *SEE* Morrison, Donald
Morrison, Flora *SEE* Morrison, John
Morrison, Flora *SEE* Morrison, Kenneth
Morrison, Flora *SEE* Morrison, Neil
Morrison, Flora; Ontario, 1840-1849 ***4537.37*** *p72*
Morrison, Flora MacFarlane *SEE* Morrison, Donald
Morrison, Flora MacLeod *SEE* Morrison, Murdo
Morrison, Flora MacPherson *SEE* Morrison, Michael
Morrison, Francis; New York, 1833 ***8197.10*** *p315*
Morrison, Francis; New York, 1833-1838 ***8197.10*** *p311*
Morrison, Hannah *SEE* Morrison, John
Morrison, Hector *SEE* Morrison, Ewen
Morrison, Helen *SEE* Morrison, Kenneth
Morrison, Hugh *SEE* Morrison, Norman
Morrison, Hugh; Georgia, 1736 ***1640.10*** *p160*
Morrison, Hugh; Georgia, 1736 ***1640.10*** *p161*
Morrison, Hugh; Maryland, 1888 ***4537.35*** *p70*
Morrison, Hugh; New York, 1827 ***8197.10*** *p261*
Morrison, Hugh 35; Ontario, 1871 ***1823.28*** *p74*
Morrison, Hugh 39; Ontario, 1871 ***1823.15*** *p195*
Morrison, Isabella *SEE* Morrison, Donald
Morrison, Isabella *SEE* Morrison, Ewen
Morrison, Isabella *SEE* Morrison, John
Morrison, Isabella *SEE* Morrison, Lachlan
Morrison, Isabella *SEE* Morrison, Malcolm
Morrison, Isabella *SEE* Morrison, Norman
Morrison, Isabella; Nova Scotia, 1833-1837 ***4537.35*** *p30*
Morrison, Isabella MacRae *SEE* Morrison, Donald
Morrison, J.; Quebec, 1858 ***9196.15*** *p46*
Morrison, James *SEE* Morrison, Ann MacIntyre
Morrison, James *SEE* Morrison, John
Morrison, James *SEE* Morrison, Lachlan
Morrison, James; New York, 1802 ***8197.10*** *p22*
Morrison, James; New York, 1827 ***8197.10*** *p262*
Morrison, James; Pennsylvania, 1777 ***4629.10*** *p8*
Morrison, James; Vermont, n.d. ***5900.10*** *p139*
Morrison, James; Vermont, n.d. ***5900.10*** *p169*
Morrison, James 33; Ontario, 1871 ***1823.22*** *p114*
Morrison, James 40; Ontario, 1871 ***1823.15*** *p195*
Morrison, James 53; Ontario, 1871 ***1823.22*** *p114*
Morrison, James 68; Ontario, 1871 ***1823.15*** *p195*
Morrison, Jane *SEE* Morrison, Donald
Morrison, Jane *SEE* Morrison, Norman
Morrison, Jane *SEE* Morrison, Ranald
Morrison, Jane 38; Ontario, 1871 ***1823.15*** *p195*
Morrison, Jane Murray *SEE* Morrison, Angus
Morrison, Janet *SEE* Morrison, Allan
Morrison, Janet *SEE* Morrison, John
Morrison, Janet *SEE* Morrison, Michael
Morrison, Janet; Ontario, 1855 ***4537.32*** *p57*
Morrison, Janet; Ontario, 1863 ***4537.32*** *p91*
Morrison, Janet Walker *SEE* Morrison, Angus
Morrison, Jessie *SEE* Morrison, Donald
Morrison, Jessie *SEE* Morrison, John
Morrison, Joan *SEE* Morrison, John
Morrison, John *SEE* Morrison, Alexander
Morrison, John *SEE* Morrison, Allan
Morrison, John *SEE* Morrison, Angus
Morrison, John *SEE* Morrison, Ann MacDonald
Morrison, John *SEE* Morrison, Donald
Morrison, John *SEE* Morrison, Ewen
Morrison, John *SEE* Morrison, Finlay
Morrison, John *SEE* Morrison, John
Morrison, John *SEE* Morrison, Kenneth
Morrison, John *SEE* Morrison, Malcolm
Morrison, John *SEE* Morrison, Mary MacAulay
Morrison, John *SEE* Morrison, Mary MacAuley
Morrison, John *SEE* Morrison, Michael
Morrison, John *SEE* Morrison, Neil
Morrison, John *SEE* Morrison, Norman
Morrison, John *SEE* Morrison, Peter
Morrison, John *SEE* Morrison, Ranald
Morrison, John; Canada, 1870-1889 ***4537.35*** *p73*
Sibling: Mary
Sibling: Constance
Sibling: Ewen
Sibling: Norman
Sibling: Donald
Sibling: Catherine
Morrison, John; Georgia, 1743 ***1640.10*** *p161*
Morrison, John; New York, 1807 ***8197.10*** *p45*
Morrison, John; New York, 1830 ***8197.10*** *p353*
Morrison, John; Nova Scotia, 1820-1829 ***4537.35*** *p34*
Wife: Rachel
Child: Alexander
Child: Angus
Child: Kirsty
Morrison, John; Nova Scotia, 1828 ***4537.35*** *p33*
Wife: Mary MacLeod
Child: John
Child: Murdo
Morrison, John; Nova Scotia, 1838 ***4537.35*** *p33*
Wife: Catherine
Child: Donald
Morrison, John; Nova Scotia, 1840-1849 ***4537.35*** *p33*
Wife: Ann
Child: Sam
Child: Kirsty
Morrison, John; Nova Scotia, 1840-1849 ***4537.35*** *p33*
Wife: Mary Kennedy
Child: Hannah
Child: John
Child: William
Child: Donald
Child: Murdo
Morrison, John; Nova Scotia, 1840-1849 ***4537.35*** *p33*
Wife: Rachel MacKay
Child: Ann
Child: John
Child: Effie
Child: Kenneth
Child: Donald
Child: Murdo

Morrison, John; Nova Scotia, 1845 ***4537.35*** *p33*
Wife: Kirsty
Child: Catherine
Child: Ann
Morrison, John; Ontario, 1849 ***4537.37*** *p80*
Wife: Ann
Child: Effie
Child: Malcolm
Child: Flora
Child: Kirsty
Child: Catherine
Child: Mary
Child: Ranald
Child: Donald
Morrison, John; Ontario, 1849 ***4537.37*** *p80*
Wife: Kirsty O'Henley
Child: Catherine
Morrison, John; Ontario, 1850-1859 ***4537.32*** *p83*
Wife: Kirsty MacLeod
Child: Angus
Child: Marion
Child: Mary
Child: Bannatyne
Morrison, John; Ontario, 1850-1859 ***4537.37*** *p80*
Sister: Janet
Morrison, John; Ontario, 1850-1859 ***4537.37*** *p81*
Wife: Margaret MacPherson
Child: Margaret
Child: Donald
Child: Ann
Child: Flora
Child: Mary
Morrison, John; Ontario, 1850-1859 ***4537.37*** *p81*
Wife: Marion MacDonald
Child: Michael
Child: Ranald
Child: John
Morrison, John; Ontario, 1851 ***4537.32*** *p83*
Sister: Janet
Morrison, John; Ontario, 1851 ***4537.32*** *p84*
Wife: Margaret MacPherson
Child: Donald
Child: Margaret
Child: Flora
Child: Mary
Child: Ann
Morrison, John; Ontario, 1860-1869 ***4537.35*** *p61*
Wife: Kirsty MacLeod
Child: Alexander
Child: Bannatyne
Child: Mary
Child: Marion
Child: Roderick
Child: Angus
Morrison, John; Ontario, 1860-1912 ***4537.35*** *p61*
Wife: Effie MacSween
Child: David
Child: Margaret
Child: Mary
Child: John
Child: Ann
Morrison, John; Ontario, 1863 ***4537.32*** *p82*
Morrison, John; Ontario, 1863 ***4537.32*** *p83*
Wife: Kirsty MacLeod
Child: Kirsty
Child: Catherine
Child: Angus
Child: Mary
Child: Margaret
Morrison, John; Pictou, Nova Scotia, 1848 ***4537.37*** *p30*
Wife: Bella Gillies
Child: Ann
Child: Angus
Morrison, John; Quebec, 1870-1879 ***4537.35*** *p64*
Wife: Mary Campbell
Child: Roderick
Child: Mary Ann
Child: Kirsty Ann
Child: Joan
Child: Kenneth
Child: Margaret
Child: Marion
Child: Catherine
Morrison, John; Vermont, 1894 ***5900.10*** *p139*
Morrison, John; Vermont, 1894 ***5900.10*** *p169*
Morrison, John; Virginia, 1703-1704 ***6212.30*** *p63*
Morrison, John; Port uncertain, 1840-1849 ***4537.35*** *p86*
Wife: Isabella
Child: Margaret
Morrison, John; Port uncertain, 1840-1849 ***4537.35*** *p86*
Wife: Kirsty
Child: James
Child: Kirsty
Child: Jessie
Child: Marion
Morrison, John; Port uncertain, 1840-1849 ***4537.35*** *p86*
Wife: Kirsty
Child: Neil
Child: Mary
Morrison, John; Port uncertain, 1840-1849 ***4537.37*** *p131*
Wife: Ann Walker
Child: Marion
Morrison, John; Port uncertain, 1840-1849 ***4537.37*** *p131*
Wife: Sarah MacPhee
Child: Donald
Child: John
Child: Sarah
Child: Margaret
Child: Angus
Morrison, John; Port uncertain, 1850-1859 ***4537.37*** *p131*
Wife: Catherine
Child: Margaret
Morrison, John; Port uncertain, 1850-1859 ***4537.37*** *p131*
Wife: Marion MacInnes
Child: Marion
Child: Ranald
Child: Angus
Morrison, John; Port uncertain, 1850-1859 ***4537.37*** *p131*
Wife: Margaret
Child: Catherine
Morrison, John; Port uncertain, 1860-1869 ***4537.35*** *p86*
Wife: Ann MacKinnon
Child: Murdo
Child: Angus
Child: Marion
Morrison, John 16; Vermont, 1868 ***5900.10*** *p296*
Morrison, John 32; Ontario, 1871 ***1823.15*** *p195*
Morrison, John 55; Ontario, 1871 ***1823.15*** *p195*
Morrison, John 55; Ontario, 1871 ***1823.28*** *p74*
Morrison, John 72; Ontario, 1871 ***1823.22*** *p114*
Morrison, John B. *SEE* Morrison, Ranald
Morrison, John H.; New York, New York, 1848 ***6058.10*** *p45*
Morrison, Joseph; Pennsylvania, 1868 ***6058.10*** *p71*
Morrison, Kate *SEE* Morrison, Angus
Morrison, Kate *SEE* Morrison, Donald
Morrison, Kate MacPhee *SEE* Morrison, Angus
Morrison, Kenneth *SEE* Morrison, Alexander
Morrison, Kenneth *SEE* Morrison, Allan
Morrison, Kenneth *SEE* Morrison, Donald
Morrison, Kenneth *SEE* Morrison, Ewen
Morrison, Kenneth *SEE* Morrison, Finlay
Morrison, Kenneth *SEE* Morrison, John
Morrison, Kenneth *SEE* Morrison, Peter
Morrison, Kenneth *SEE* Morrison, Philip
Morrison, Kenneth *SEE* Morrison, William
Morrison, Kenneth; Falkland Islands, 1880-1889 ***4537.35*** *p76*
Morrison, Kenneth; Nova Scotia, 1820-1829 ***4537.35*** *p35*
Child: Donald
Child: Angus
Child: Catherine
Child: Margaret
Child: Sarah
Wife: Mary MacSween
Child: John
Morrison, Kenneth; Nova Scotia, 1830-1839 ***4537.35*** *p34*
Wife: Ann MacLeod
Child: Kirsty
Child: Sarah
Child: Donald
Child: Angus
Morrison, Kenneth; Nova Scotia, 1840-1849 ***4537.35*** *p34*
Wife: Margaret MacCusbic
Child: Flora
Son: Roderick
Child: Donald
Son: Murdo
Child: John
Morrison, Kenneth; Nova Scotia, 1844 ***4537.35*** *p34*
Wife: Marion MacDermid
Child: Mary
Morrison, Kenneth; Ontario, 1860-1869 ***4537.35*** *p62*
Wife: Ann MacLeod
Child: John
Child: Donald
Child: Mary
Child: Norman
Child: Helen
Child: Margaret
Child: Kirsty
Morrison, Kenneth; Ontario, 1862 ***4537.32*** *p84*
Wife: Ann MacLeod
Child: Kirsty
Child: Margaret
Child: Helen
Child: Norman
Child: Mary
Child: Donald
Child: John
Morrison, Kenneth; Port uncertain, 1860-1869 ***4537.35*** *p86*
Wife: Mary MacKay
Child: Murdo
Child: Ann
Child: Margaret
Child: Marion
Morrison, Kirsty *SEE* Morrison, Angus
Morrison, Kirsty *SEE* Morrison, Donald
Morrison, Kirsty *SEE* Morrison, Ewen
Morrison, Kirsty *SEE* Morrison, Finlay
Morrison, Kirsty *SEE* Morrison, John
Morrison, Kirsty *SEE* Morrison, Kenneth
Morrison, Kirsty *SEE* Morrison, Malcolm
Morrison, Kirsty *SEE* Morrison, Murdo
Morrison, Kirsty *SEE* Morrison, Norman
Morrison, Kirsty *SEE* Morrison, Peter
Morrison, Kirsty *SEE* Morrison, Philip
Morrison, Kirsty; Falkland Islands, 1870-1879 ***4537.35*** *p74*
Morrison, Kirsty; Nova Scotia, 1825 ***4537.35*** *p38*
Morrison, Kirsty; Ontario, 1855 ***4537.32*** *p47*
Morrison, Kirsty; Ontario, 1863 ***4537.32*** *p47*
Morrison, Kirsty; Saskatchewan, 1889 ***4537.35*** *p66*
Morrison, Kirsty; Port uncertain, 1850-1859 ***4537.35*** *p82*
Morrison, Kirsty Ann *SEE* Morrison, John
Morrison, Kirsty Ferguson *SEE* Morrison, Donald
Morrison, Kirsty Graham *SEE* Morrison, Malcolm
Morrison, Kirsty MacLeod *SEE* Morrison, Ewen
Morrison, Kirsty MacLeod *SEE* Morrison, John
Morrison, Kirsty O'Henley *SEE* Morrison, John
Morrison, Lachlan; Port uncertain, 1850-1859 ***4537.37*** *p131*
Wife: Margaret MacIntyre
Child: Allan
Child: Mary
Child: James
Child: Isabella
Child: Catherine
Morrison, Lexy MacKay *SEE* Morrison, Sorley
Morrison, Lexy MacLean *SEE* Morrison, Donald
Morrison, Lexy Ross *SEE* Morrison, Angus
Morrison, Louisia E. Marie 22; Ontario, 1871 ***1823.15*** *p195*
Morrison, MacIntosh *SEE* Morrison, Mary MacAulay
Morrison, MacIntosh *SEE* Morrison, Mary MacAuley
Morrison, Malcolm *SEE* Morrison, Allan
Morrison, Malcolm *SEE* Morrison, Angus
Morrison, Malcolm *SEE* Morrison, Donald
Morrison, Malcolm *SEE* Morrison, Ewen
Morrison, Malcolm *SEE* Morrison, Finlay
Morrison, Malcolm *SEE* Morrison, John
Morrison, Malcolm *SEE* Morrison, Malcolm
Morrison, Malcolm *SEE* Morrison, Roderick
Morrison, Malcolm; Alaska, 1890-1899 ***4537.35*** *p76*
Morrison, Malcolm; Nova Scotia, 1820-1829 ***4537.35*** *p35*
Wife: Effie
Child: Murdo
Morrison, Malcolm; Ontario, 1863 ***4537.32*** *p85*
Child: Roderick
Child: Mary
Child: Isabella
Child: Angus
Child: Margaret
Child: Ann
Child: Donald
Child: Marion
Wife: Kirsty Graham
Child: John
Morrison, Malcolm; Port uncertain, 1840-1849 ***4537.35*** *p86*
Child: Catherine
Child: Angus
Child: Kirsty
Child: Mary
Child: Effie
Child: Malcolm
With wife
Child: Marion
Morrison, Malcolm 62; Ontario, 1871 ***1823.15*** *p195*
Morrison, Malcom 40; Ontario, 1871 ***1823.28*** *p74*
Morrison, Malcom 67; Ontario, 1871 ***1823.15*** *p195*
Morrison, Margaret *SEE* Morrison, Angus

Morrison, Margaret *SEE* Morrison, Donald
Morrison, Margaret *SEE* Morrison, Ewen
Morrison, Margaret *SEE* Morrison, Finlay
Morrison, Margaret *SEE* Morrison, John
Morrison, Margaret *SEE* Morrison, Kenneth
Morrison, Margaret *SEE* Morrison, Malcolm
Morrison, Margaret *SEE* Morrison, Mary MacAulay
Morrison, Margaret *SEE* Morrison, Mary MacAuley
Morrison, Margaret *SEE* Morrison, Murdo
Morrison, Margaret *SEE* Morrison, Neil
Morrison, Margaret *SEE* Morrison, Norman
Morrison, Margaret *SEE* Morrison, Roderick
Morrison, Margaret *SEE* Morrison, William
Morrison, Margaret; Nova Scotia, 1828 ***4537.35*** *p11*
Morrison, Margaret; Nova Scotia, 1828 ***4537.35*** *p19*
Morrison, Margaret; Ontario, 1850-1859 ***4537.32*** *p84*
Morrison, Margaret; Ontario, 1851 ***4537.37*** *p53*
Morrison, Margaret; Ontario, 1855 ***4537.32*** *p54*
Morrison, Margaret; Ontario, 1864 ***4537.32*** *p6*
Morrison, Margaret; Ontario, 1864 ***4537.35*** *p56*
Morrison, Margaret; Port uncertain, 1840-1849 ***4537.37*** *p117*
Morrison, Margaret; Port uncertain, 1840-1849 ***4537.37*** *p121*
Morrison, Margaret Ann *SEE* Morrison, Angus
Morrison, Margaret MacCusbic *SEE* Morrison, Kenneth
Morrison, Margaret MacIntyre *SEE* Morrison, Lachlan
Morrison, Margaret MacLeod; America, 1862 ***4537.32*** *p86*
Morrison, Margaret MacPherson *SEE* Morrison, John
Morrison, Margaret MacRae *SEE* Morrison, Roderick
Morrison, Margaret Martin *SEE* Morrison, Alexander
Morrison, Margaret Stewart *SEE* Morrison, Alexander
Morrison, Marion *SEE* Morrison, Angus
Morrison, Marion *SEE* Morrison, Donald
Morrison, Marion *SEE* Morrison, Ewen
Morrison, Marion *SEE* Morrison, John
Morrison, Marion *SEE* Morrison, Kenneth
Morrison, Marion *SEE* Morrison, Malcolm
Morrison, Marion *SEE* Morrison, Neil
Morrison, Marion *SEE* Morrison, Norman
Morrison, Marion *SEE* Morrison, Ranald
Morrison, Marion; Nova Scotia, 1840-1849 ***4537.37*** *p14*
Morrison, Marion; Ontario, 1840-1849 ***4537.37*** *p45*
Morrison, Marion; Ontario, 1849 ***4537.32*** *p26*
Morrison, Marion; Ontario, 1849 ***4537.37*** *p55*
Morrison, Marion; Ontario, 1851 ***4537.32*** *p67*
Morrison, Marion; Ontario, 1851 ***4537.32*** *p74*
Morrison, Marion; Ontario, 1851 ***4537.37*** *p74*
Morrison, Marion; Quebec, 1880-1889 ***4537.35*** *p64*
Morrison, Marion; Port uncertain, 1850-1859 ***4537.37*** *p118*
Morrison, Marion MacDermid *SEE* Morrison, Kenneth
Morrison, Marion MacDonald *SEE* Morrison, John
Morrison, Marion MacInnes *SEE* Morrison, John
Morrison, Marion MacLeod *SEE* Morrison, Donald
Morrison, Marion Paterson *SEE* Morrison, Norman
Morrison, Marjory *SEE* Morrison, William
Morrison, Marshall 13; Ontario, 1861 ***2896.28*** *p37*
Morrison, Martha Catherine MacKillop *SEE* Morrison, Angus
Morrison, Mary *SEE* Morrison, Alexander
Morrison, Mary *SEE* Morrison, Allan
Morrison, Mary *SEE* Morrison, Angus
Morrison, Mary *SEE* Morrison, Ann MacIntyre
Morrison, Mary *SEE* Morrison, Donald
Morrison, Mary *SEE* Morrison, Ewen
Morrison, Mary *SEE* Morrison, Finlay
Morrison, Mary *SEE* Morrison, John
Morrison, Mary *SEE* Morrison, Kenneth
Morrison, Mary *SEE* Morrison, Lachlan
Morrison, Mary *SEE* Morrison, Malcolm
Morrison, Mary *SEE* Morrison, Mary MacAuley
Morrison, Mary *SEE* Morrison, Michael
Morrison, Mary *SEE* Morrison, Neil
Morrison, Mary *SEE* Morrison, Norman
Morrison, Mary *SEE* Morrison, Peter
Morrison, Mary *SEE* Morrison, Ranald
Morrison, Mary *SEE* Morrison, Roderick
Morrison, Mary *SEE* Morrison, Sorley
Morrison, Mary; Nova Scotia, 1838 ***4537.35*** *p24*
Morrison, Mary; Nova Scotia, 1840-1849 ***4537.35*** *p11*
Morrison, Mary; Nova Scotia, 1840-1849 ***4537.35*** *p17*
Morrison, Mary; Nova Scotia, 1840-1849 ***4537.35*** *p21*
Morrison, Mary; Ontario, 1849 ***4537.37*** *p40*
Morrison, Mary; Ontario, 1850-1859 ***4537.32*** *p65*
Morrison, Mary; Ontario, 1850-1859 ***4537.35*** *p59*
Morrison, Mary; Ontario, 1880-1889 ***4537.32*** *p15*
Morrison, Mary; Saskatchewan, 1889 ***4537.35*** *p66*
Morrison, Mary; Saskatchewan, 1890 ***4537.35*** *p65*
Morrison, Mary; Port uncertain, 1840-1849 ***4537.35*** *p83*
Morrison, Mary; Port uncertain, 1840-1849 ***4537.37*** *p117*
Morrison, Mary; Port uncertain, 1850-1859 ***4537.35*** *p80*
Morrison, Mary 24; Ontario, 1871 ***1823.15*** *p195*
Morrison, Mary 66; Ontario, 1871 ***1823.15*** *p195*
Morrison, Mary 92; Vermont, 1873 ***5900.10*** *p295*
Morrison, Mary Ann *SEE* Morrison, John
Morrison, Mary Ann *SEE* Morrison, Sorley
Morrison, Mary Campbell *SEE* Morrison, John
Morrison, Mary Campbell *SEE* Morrison, Murdo
Morrison, Mary J. Driscoll; Vermont, 1851-1927 ***5900.10*** *p243*
Morrison, Mary Jane 45; Vermont, 1864 ***5900.10*** *p295*
Morrison, Mary Jane Holbrook 45; Vermont, 1864 ***5900.10*** *p295*
Morrison, Mary Kennedy *SEE* Morrison, John
Morrison, Mary MacAskill *SEE* Morrison, William
Morrison, Mary MacAulay; Ontario, 1850-1859 ***4537.32*** *p84*
  Child: John
  Child: William
  Child: MacIntosh
  Child: Donald
  Child: Margaret
  Child: Roderick
Morrison, Mary MacAuley; Ontario, 1850-1859 ***4537.35*** *p62*
  Child: Donald
  Child: MacIntosh
  Child: Margaret
  Child: Roderick
  Child: John
  Stepchild: Margaret
  Stepchild: Mary
  Child: William
Morrison, Mary MacDonald *SEE* Morrison, Donald
Morrison, Mary MacDonald *SEE* Morrison, Murdo
Morrison, Mary MacKay *SEE* Morrison, Kenneth
Morrison, Mary MacLeod *SEE* Morrison, John
Morrison, Mary MacSween *SEE* Morrison, Kenneth
Morrison, Mary Matheson *SEE* Morrison, Norman
Morrison, Mary Steele *SEE* Morrison, Angus
Morrison, Matthew; New York, 1827 ***8197.10*** *p338*
Morrison, Matthew 43; Ontario, 1871 ***1823.15*** *p195*
Morrison, Matthew 88; Ontario, 1871 ***1823.15*** *p195*
Morrison, Michael *SEE* Morrison, John
Morrison, Michael *SEE* Morrison, Norman
Morrison, Michael; Port uncertain, 1850-1859 ***4537.37*** *p131*
  Wife: Flora MacPherson
  Child: Janet
  Child: Angus
  Child: Mary
  Child: Donald
  Child: John
  Child: Ann
Morrison, Michael 42; Ontario, 1871 ***1823.22*** *p114*
Morrison, Michael 43; Ontario, 1871 ***1823.28*** *p74*
Morrison, Morris *SEE* Morrison, Finlay
Morrison, Morris 25; Baltimore, 1775 ***1220.25*** *p118*
Morrison, Murdo *SEE* Morrison, Angus
Morrison, Murdo *SEE* Morrison, Donald
Morrison, Murdo *SEE* Morrison, John
Morrison, Murdo *SEE* Morrison, Kenneth
Morrison, Murdo *SEE* Morrison, Malcolm
Morrison, Murdo *SEE* Morrison, Norman
Morrison, Murdo; Chile, 1880-1889 ***4537.35*** *p77*
  Wife: Mary Campbell
Morrison, Murdo; Nova Scotia, 1836-1839 ***4537.35*** *p35*
  Wife: Flora MacLeod
  Child: Norman
Morrison, Murdo; Ontario, 1860-1869 ***4537.35*** *p62*
  Wife: Mary MacDonald
  Child: Rachel
  Child: Ann
  Child: Agnes
  Child: Margaret
  Child: Kirsty
Morrison, Murdo; Ontario, 1862 ***4537.32*** *p85*
  Wife: Mary MacDonald
  Child: Kirsty
  Child: Margaret
  Child: Rachel
  Child: Ann
Morrison, Murdo 29; Ontario, 1871 ***1823.28*** *p74*
Morrison, Murdock 45; Ontario, 1871 ***1823.28*** *p75*
Morrison, Nancy 48; Ontario, 1871 ***1823.22*** *p114*
Morrison, Neil *SEE* Morrison, Alexander
Morrison, Neil *SEE* Morrison, Allan
Morrison, Neil *SEE* Morrison, Angus
Morrison, Neil *SEE* Morrison, Ann MacIntyre
Morrison, Neil *SEE* Morrison, Donald
Morrison, Neil *SEE* Morrison, John
Morrison, Neil *SEE* Morrison, Neil
Morrison, Neil *SEE* Morrison, Norman
Morrison, Neil *SEE* Morrison, William
Morrison, Neil; Nova Scotia, 1820-1829 ***4537.35*** *p35*
  Wife: Ann MacDonald
  Child: Mary
  Child: Donald
Morrison, Neil; Nova Scotia, 1820-1829 ***4537.35*** *p35*
  Wife: Mary
  Brother: Roderick
  Brother: Donald
  Child: John
  Child: Catherine
  Child: Neil
Morrison, Neil; Nova Scotia, 1826-1829 ***4537.35*** *p36*
  Wife: Rachel Shaw
  Child: Roderick
  Child: Sarah
  Child: Alexander
  Child: Ann
Morrison, Neil; Nova Scotia, 1840-1849 ***4537.35*** *p35*
  Wife: Ann Shaw
  Child: John
  Child: Mary
  Child: Donald
Morrison, Neil; Ontario, 1848 ***4537.37*** *p81*
  Wife: Ann MacCormick
  Child: Effie
  Child: Marion
  Child: Donald
Morrison, Neil; Ontario, 1849 ***4537.32*** *p85*
  Wife: Ann MacCormick
  Child: John
  Child: Effie
  Child: Marion
  Child: Donald
Morrison, Neil; Ontario, 1850-1859 ***4537.37*** *p81*
  Wife: Mary
  Child: Mary
  Child: Margaret
  Child: Dougal
  Child: Flora
  Child: John
Morrison, Neil; Ontario, 1851 ***4537.32*** *p85*
  Wife: Mary
  Child: Mary
  Child: Margaret
  Child: Flora
  Child: John
Morrison, Neil; Port uncertain, 1840-1849 ***4537.35*** *p86*
  Brother: Alexander
  Brother: John
  Sister: Marion
  Sister: Ann
Morrison, Nicholas; New York, 1837 ***8197.10*** *p99*
Morrison, Norman *SEE* Morrison, Angus
Morrison, Norman *SEE* Morrison, Donald
Morrison, Norman *SEE* Morrison, John
Morrison, Norman *SEE* Morrison, Kenneth
Morrison, Norman *SEE* Morrison, Murdo
Morrison, Norman; America, 1860-1869 ***4537.35*** *p62*
  Wife: Ann
  Child: John
  Child: Neil
  Child: Mary
  Child: Murdo
Morrison, Norman; America, 1862 ***4537.32*** *p86*
  Wife: Ann
  Child: Neil
  Child: Mary
Morrison, Norman; Nova Scotia, 1828 ***4537.35*** *p36*
  Wife: Marion Paterson
  Child: Catherine
  Child: Peggy
  Child: Mary
  Child: Archie
Morrison, Norman; Ontario, 1851 ***4537.37*** *p82*
  Wife: Catherine MacCormick
  Child: Mary
  Child: Catherine
  Brother: John
  Child: Michael
Morrison, Norman; Ontario, 1855 ***4537.32*** *p86*
  Wife: Effie Campbell
  Child: Catherine
  Child: Kirsty
  Child: William
  Child: Angus
  Child: Isabella
  Child: Effie
  Child: Donald
Morrison, Norman; Ontario, 1860-1869 ***4537.35*** *p62*
  Wife: Ann
  Child: Mary
  Child: Murdo

Child: John
Child: Neil
Morrison, Norman; Ontario, 1863 ***4537.32*** *p86*
Wife: Effie Smith
Child: Jane
Child: Margaret
Child: Thomas
Child: Catherine
Child: Ann
Child: William
Morrison, Norman; Ontario, 1863 ***4537.32*** *p87*
Wife: Mary Matheson
Child: Donald
Child: Catherine
Child: Murdo
Morrison, Norman; Port uncertain, 1840-1849 ***4537.35*** *p86*
Wife: Effie
Child: Marion
Child: Hugh
Morrison, Patrick 34; Ontario, 1871 ***1823.28*** *p75*
Morrison, Patrick 50; Ontario, 1871 ***1823.15*** *p195*
Morrison, Peggy *SEE* Morrison, Norman
Morrison, Peter; Manitoba, 1845-1889 ***4537.35*** *p63*
Sister: Kirsty
Morrison, Peter; Nova Scotia, 1840-1849 ***4537.35*** *p36*
Wife: Ann MacLeod
Child: John
Child: Angus
Child: Donald
Child: Ann
Morrison, Peter; Saskatchewan, 1889 ***4537.35*** *p70*
Child: Roderick
Child: Mary
Child: Finlay
Child: Donald
Wife: Mary
Child: Kenneth
Morrison, Philip; Nova Scotia, 1830-1839 ***4537.35*** *p36*
With wife
Child: Kenneth
Child: Kirsty
Morrison, Rachel *SEE* Morrison, Donald
Morrison, Rachel *SEE* Morrison, John
Morrison, Rachel *SEE* Morrison, Murdo
Morrison, Rachel *SEE* Morrison, Roderick
Morrison, Rachel; Ontario, 1860-1869 ***4537.35*** *p61*
Morrison, Rachel; Ontario, 1862 ***4537.32*** *p77*
Morrison, Rachel; Port uncertain, 1840-1849 ***4537.35*** *p84*
Morrison, Rachel MacKay *SEE* Morrison, John
Morrison, Rachel Shaw *SEE* Morrison, Neil
Morrison, Ranald *SEE* Morrison, John
Morrison, Ranald; Saskatchewan, 1884 ***4537.37*** *p104*
Wife: Ann
Child: John
Child: Donald
Child: Marion
Child: Alexander
Child: Jane
Child: Mary
Child: John B.
Child: Angus
Morrison, Rebecca 45; Ontario, 1871 ***1823.15*** *p195*
Morrison, Robert; Georgia, 1737 ***1640.10*** *p130*
Morrison, Robert 46; Ontario, 1871 ***1823.15*** *p195*
Morrison, Robert 49; Ontario, 1871 ***1823.15*** *p195*
Morrison, Robert 75; Vermont, 1853 ***5900.10*** *p295*
Morrison, Roderick *SEE* Morrison, Alexander
Morrison, Roderick *SEE* Morrison, Allan
Morrison, Roderick *SEE* Morrison, Angus
Morrison, Roderick *SEE* Morrison, Donald
Morrison, Roderick *SEE* Morrison, Ewen
Morrison, Roderick *SEE* Morrison, John
Morrison, Roderick *SEE* Morrison, Kenneth
Morrison, Roderick *SEE* Morrison, Malcolm
Morrison, Roderick *SEE* Morrison, Mary MacAulay
Morrison, Roderick *SEE* Morrison, Mary MacAuley
Morrison, Roderick *SEE* Morrison, Neil
Morrison, Roderick *SEE* Morrison, Peter
Morrison, Roderick *SEE* Morrison, William
Morrison, Roderick; Mississippi, 1838 ***1640.10*** *p161*
Morrison, Roderick; Quebec, 1873 ***4537.35*** *p64*
Wife: Margaret MacRae
Child: Mary
Child: Malcolm
Child: Donald
Child: Barbara
Morrison, Roderick; Port uncertain, 1840-1849 ***4537.35*** *p86*
Wife: Rachel
Child: Alexander
Child: Margaret
Child: Ann
Child: Donald
Child: Mary
Morrison, Sam *SEE* Morrison, John
Morrison, Sandford *SEE* Morrison, Donald
Morrison, Sarah *SEE* Morrison, Donald
Morrison, Sarah *SEE* Morrison, John
Morrison, Sarah *SEE* Morrison, Kenneth
Morrison, Sarah *SEE* Morrison, Neil
Morrison, Sarah; Vermont, 1832-1901 ***5900.10*** *p496*
Morrison, Sarah 10; Ontario, 1861 ***2896.28*** *p37*
Morrison, Sarah 44; Ontario, 1861 ***2896.28*** *p37*
Morrison, Sarah Cosgrove; Vermont, 1855-1953 ***5900.10*** *p141*
Morrison, Sarah MacPhee *SEE* Morrison, John
Morrison, Sophia *SEE* Morrison, Alexander
Morrison, Sophia MacMillan *SEE* Morrison, Ewen
Morrison, Sorley *SEE* Morrison, Donald
Morrison, Sorley; Quebec, 1887 ***4537.35*** *p64*
Wife: Lexy MacKay
Child: Mary Ann
Child: Mary
Morrison, Susan 15; Ontario, 1861 ***2896.28*** *p37*
Morrison, Thomas *SEE* Morrison, Norman
Morrison, Thomas; New York, 1837 ***8197.10*** *p99*
Morrison, Thomas 27; Philadelphia, 1774 ***1220.25*** *p66*
Morrison, Thomson 56; Ontario, 1871 ***1823.15*** *p195*
Morrison, Wadden; Maryland, 1649 ***2524.55*** *p156*
Morrison, Wesley 23; Ontario, 1861 ***2896.28*** *p37*
Morrison, William *SEE* Morrison, Catherine
Morrison, William *SEE* Morrison, John
Morrison, William *SEE* Morrison, Mary MacAulay
Morrison, William *SEE* Morrison, Mary MacAuley
Morrison, William *SEE* Morrison, Norman
Morrison, William; Jamaica, 1854 ***1640.13*** *p80*
Morrison, William; Massachusetts, 1889 ***1640.13*** *p80*
Morrison, William; New York, 1807 ***8197.10*** *p44*
Morrison, William; New York, 1840 ***8197.10*** *p181*
Morrison, William; Nova Scotia, 1830-1839 ***4537.35*** *p36*
Wife: Mary MacAskill
Child: Kenneth
Child: Neil
Child: Roderick
Child: Donald
Child: Marjory
Child: Allan
Child: Margaret
Morrison, William 26; Maryland, 1774 ***1220.25*** *p72*
Morrison, William 35; Ontario, 1871 ***1823.15*** *p196*
Morrison, William 55; Ontario, 1871 ***1823.28*** *p75*
Morrison, William John; Vermont, 1850-1916 ***5900.10*** *p243*
Morriss, Henry; New York, 1839 ***8197.10*** *p264*
Morrissey, Anne S. 80; Vermont, 1887 ***5900.10*** *p45*
Morrissey, Bridget; Vermont, 1850-1950 ***5900.10*** *p427*
Morrissey, Bridget 2 *SEE* Morrissey, John
Morrissey, Bridget 6 *SEE* Morrissey, Thomas
Morrissey, Bridget McGrath; Vermont, 1841-1915 ***5900.10*** *p353*
Morrissey, Catherine 4 *SEE* Morrissey, John
Morrissey, Ellen; Vermont, n.d. ***5900.10*** *p43*
Morrissey, Ellen; Vermont, 1832-1887 ***5900.10*** *p42*
Morrissey, Ellen; Vermont, 1833-1895 ***5900.10*** *p76*
Morrissey, Ellen 11 *SEE* Morrissey, John
Morrissey, Hannah 33 *SEE* Morrissey, John
Morrissey, Hannora; Vermont, 1828-1909 ***5900.10*** *p76*
Morrissey, James P.; Vermont, 1840-1917 ***5900.10*** *p353*
Morrissey, John; Vermont, 1849-1929 ***5900.10*** *p43*
Morrissey, John 12 *SEE* Morrissey, Thomas
Morrissey, John 40; New York, New York, 1848 ***1825.45*** *p39*
Wife: Hannah 33
Daughter: Ellen 11
Daughter: Maria 10
Daughter: Catherine 4
Son: Pat 3
Daughter: Bridget 2
Morrissey, John 77; Vermont, 1890 ***5900.10*** *p45*
Morrissey, John N.; Vermont, 1825-1889 ***5900.10*** *p76*
Morrissey, Margaret; Vermont, 1795-1884 ***5900.10*** *p226*
Morrissey, Margaret; Vermont, 1827 ***5900.10*** *p46*
Morrissey, Margaret; Vermont, 1831-1885 ***5900.10*** *p43*
Morrissey, Margaret; Vermont, 1850-1948 ***5900.10*** *p43*
Morrissey, Margaret Haye 45; Vermont, 1873 ***5900.10*** *p43*
Morrissey, Maria 10 *SEE* Morrissey, John
Morrissey, Maria Hogan; Vermont, 1845-1922 ***5900.10*** *p42*
Morrissey, Mary 8 *SEE* Morrissey, Thomas
Morrissey, Mary 80; Vermont, 1928 ***5900.10*** *p70*
Morrissey, Mary E.; Vermont, 1853-1883 ***5900.10*** *p43*
Morrissey, Michael; Vermont, 1835-1905 ***5900.10*** *p45*
Morrissey, Pat 3 *SEE* Morrissey, John
Morrissey, Patrick; Vermont, 1827-1888 ***5900.10*** *p46*
Morrissey, Peggy 36 *SEE* Morrissey, Thomas
Morrissey, Sarah Mann; Vermont, 1849-1944 ***5900.10*** *p43*
Morrissey, Susan Kierce; Vermont, 1835-1894 ***5900.10*** *p45*
Morrissey, Thomas 37; New York, New York, 1848 ***1825.45*** *p39*
Son: John 12
Daughter: Bridget 6
Daughter: Mary 8
Wife: Peggy 36
Morrissey, William 41; Vermont, 1868 ***5900.10*** *p43*
Morrisson, Catherine; Vermont, 1826-1926 ***5900.10*** *p617*
Morrisson, Edward; Vermont, 1822-1900 ***5900.10*** *p616*
Morrisson, John 30; Ontario, 1871 ***1823.15*** *p196*
Morrisson, Martin 83; Vermont, 1881 ***5900.10*** *p616*
Morrisson, Mary C. 82; Vermont, 1889 ***5900.10*** *p616*
Morrisson, Maurice; New York, 1834 ***8197.10*** *p73*
Morrough, Nicholas 21; Maryland, 1775 ***1220.25*** *p120*
Morrough, Richard 50; Ontario, 1871 ***1823.15*** *p196*
Morrow, Alexander 33; Ontario, 1871 ***1823.22*** *p114*
Morrow, Andrew; New York, 1839 ***8197.10*** *p141*
Morrow, Bridget; Vermont, 1839-1923 ***5900.10*** *p553*
Morrow, Cristen 15; Ontario, 1861 ***2896.25*** *p6*
Morrow, David; New York, New York, 1847 ***6058.10*** *p41*
Morrow, James 40; Ontario, 1871 ***1823.22*** *p114*
Morrow, James 60; Ontario, 1861 ***2896.25*** *p6*
Morrow, John 34; Ontario, 1871 ***1823.28*** *p75*
Morrow, John 40; Ontario, 1871 ***1823.15*** *p196*
Morrow, John 47; Ontario, 1871 ***1823.15*** *p196*
Morrow, John 53; Ontario, 1871 ***1823.22*** *p114*
Morrow, Louisa 69; Ontario, 1871 ***1823.15*** *p196*
Morrow, Margaret 19; Ontario, 1861 ***2896.25*** *p6*
Morrow, Margaret A. 20; Ontario, 1861 ***2896.28*** *p53*
Morrow, Mary Suppll 79; Vermont, 1903 ***5900.10*** *p337*
Morrow, Richard 46; Ontario, 1871 ***1823.28*** *p75*
Morrow, Robert 37; Ontario, 1871 ***1823.15*** *p196*
Morrow, Robert 42; Ontario, 1871 ***1823.22*** *p114*
Morrow, Sarah 40; Ontario, 1861 ***2896.25*** *p6*
Morrow, Sarah 56; Ontario, 1871 ***1823.15*** *p196*
Morrow, Thomas 45; Ontario, 1871 ***1823.22*** *p114*
Morrow, William; New York, 1804 ***8197.10*** *p27*
Morrow, William 50; Ontario, 1871 ***1823.15*** *p196*
Morrow, William 70; Ontario, 1871 ***1823.28*** *p75*
Morrsion, Mary; Ontario, 1850-1859 ***4537.32*** *p84*
Mors, Jakobina; Port uncertain, 1761 ***2856.30*** *p307*
Morsch, Elis. Catharina; Port uncertain, 1763 ***2856.30*** *p319*
Morsch, Maria Catharina; Port uncertain, 1767 ***2856.30*** *p319*
Morsch, Peter; Port uncertain, 1783 ***2856.30*** *p319*
Morschheimer, Johann Nikolas; Port uncertain, 1756 ***2856.30*** *p307*
Morse, Mr.; Quebec, 1857 ***9196.15*** *p26*
Morse, Mrs.; Quebec, 1857 ***9196.15*** *p26*
Morse, A. 63; Alaska, 1918 ***9196.1*** *p54*
Morse, A. 63; Whitehorse, Yukon, 1918 ***9196.1*** *p54*
Morse, Henry; Virginia, 1775 ***1224.2*** *p82*
Morse, J. S.; Quebec, 1857 ***9196.15*** *p19*
Morse, John; New York, 1828 ***8197.10*** *p262*
Morse, Lucas; Vermont, 1833-1911 ***5900.10*** *p554*
Morse, Mary; Vermont, 1857-1911 ***5900.10*** *p593*
Morse, Mary Child; Ohio, 1829 ***1224.3*** *p54*
Morse, Mary F. Crosby; Vermont, 1836-1912 ***5900.10*** *p554*
Morse, Minnie; Vermont, 1858-1943 ***5900.10*** *p593*
Morsey, Edmond; Maryland, 1675 ***2524.55*** *p157*
Morson, Mrs.; Portland, Maine, 1858 ***9196.15*** *p27*
Mortal, Mary 77; Vermont, 1883 ***5900.10*** *p102*
Mortemoore, Henry; Maryland, 1652 ***2524.55*** *p157*
Mortemore, Joice; Maryland, 1663 ***2524.55*** *p157*
Morten, Wm; Virginia, 1664 ***6212.30*** *p9*
Mortier, Abraham; New York, New York, 1785 ***1224.2*** *p82*
Mortimer, . . .; Boston, 1737 ***4628.40*** *p114*
Mortimer, Miss; Quebec, 1857 ***9196.15*** *p18*
Mortimer, Asa S. 4; Ontario, 1861 ***2896.27*** *p37*
Mortimer, Deborah 36; Ontario, 1861 ***2896.27*** *p37*
Mortimer, F. 39; British Columbia, 1918 ***9196.1*** *p72*
Mortimer, F. 39; Washington, 1918 ***9196.1*** *p72*
Mortimer, George; New York, 1818 ***8197.10*** *p258*
Mortimer, John; New York, 1820 ***8197.10*** *p259*
Mortimer, John, Jr.; New York, 1821 ***8197.10*** *p260*
Mortimer, Martha E. 1; Ontario, 1861 ***2896.27*** *p37*
Mortimer, Mary; New York, 1834 ***8197.10*** *p373*
Mortimer, Mary J. 6; Ontario, 1861 ***2896.27*** *p37*
Mortimer, May 34; British Columbia, 1918 ***9196.1*** *p72*
Mortimer, May 34; Washington, 1918 ***9196.1*** *p72*
Mortimer, Richard; New York, 1824 ***8197.10*** *p64*
Mortimer, Sangar 15; Ontario, 1861 ***2896.27*** *p37*
Mortimer, Thomas; New York, 1834 ***8197.10*** *p263*

Morton, . . .; Boston, 1765 4628.40 p114
Morton, Mr.; Portland, Maine, 1857 9196.15 p12
Morton, Mr.; Quebec, 1858 9196.15 p37
Morton, Mrs.; Quebec, 1858 9196.15 p37
Morton, Andrew; New York, 1804 8197.10 p27
Morton, George; New York, 1821 8197.10 p260
Morton, Hugh 12; Ontario, 1861 2896.27 p56
Morton, James; Pennsylvania, 1777 4629.10 p22
Morton, James 25; America, 1774 1220.25 p35
Morton, James 43; Ontario, 1871 1823.22 p114
Morton, Jane 63; Ontario, 1871 1823.28 p75
Morton, John; Carolina, 1699 1224.1 p40
Morton, John; Carolina, 1706 1224.2 p82
Morton, John; Mobile, Alabama, 1828-1845 1640.10 p161
Morton, John; New York, 1803 8197.10 p14
Morton, John; Virginia, 1666 6212.30 p31
Morton, Joseph; Carolina, 1706 1224.2 p82
Morton, Joseph; New York, 1821 8197.10 p260
Morton, Joseph; New York, 1834 8197.10 p73
Morton, Joshue 29; Ontario, 1871 1823.28 p75
Morton, Margaret; Chicago, 1872 1640.13 p80
Morton, Mark 42; Savannah, Georgia, 1775 1220.25 p139
With wife & 3 children
Morton, Mary; Maryland, 1665 2524.55 p157
Morton, Mary; Maryland, 1673 2524.55 p157
Morton, Mary; Virginia, 1666-1667 6212.30 p34
Morton, Patrick; New York, 1834 8197.10 p372
Morton, R. J. 32; Ontario, 1861 2896.25 p40
Morton, Richard; Virginia, 1663 1224.1 p40
Morton, Robert; New York, 1828 8197.10 p350
Morton, Robert; Pennsylvania, 1777 4629.10 p22
Morton, Thomas; New England, 1660 1224.1 p40
Morton, Thomas; New York, 1821 8197.10 p260
Morton, Walter; New York, 1802 8197.10 p22
Morton, Walter; Virginia, 1663 6212.30 p4
Morton, William; New York, 1857 1224.3 p55
Morton, William H.; New York, 1806 8197.10 p32
Morton, Wm; Virginia, 1664 6212.30 p12
Morvik, Tom 20; Alaska, 1913 9196.1 p22
Morvik, Tom 20; British Columbia, 1913 9196.1 p22
Morzuska, Michael; Maryland, 1910 3259.35 p41
Moscrip, Mrs. R. 80; Ontario, 1871 1823.22 p114
Mosel, Konrad; Port uncertain, 1759 2856.30 p307
Moseley, Henry; Virginia, 1664 6212.30 p6
Mosely, Mr.; Quebec, 1858 9196.15 p37
Mosely, Edward; Virginia, 1665-1666 6212.30 p24
Mosely, Jean; Virginia, 1667 6212.30 p37
Mosely, Nich; Virginia, 1665-1666 6212.30 p23
Mosely, Susan; Maryland, 1671 2524.55 p157
Mosely, Thomas; Maryland, 1666 2524.55 p157
Mosenberger, Martin; Port uncertain, 1759 2856.30 p308
Mosenheimer, Jakob; Port uncertain, 1784 2856.30 p308
Moser, Anna Margarete; Port uncertain, 1791 2856.30 p308
Moser, Catharina; America, 1744 2856.30 p308
Moser, David; Port uncertain, 1752 2856.30 p308
Moser, Elias; New York, 1837 8197.10 p100
Moser, Elisabeth; Port uncertain, 1773 2856.30 p308
Moser, Johann; America, 1766 2856.30 p308
Moser, Johann Georg; America, 1766 2856.30 p308
Moser, Johann Georg; America, 1790 2856.30 p308
Moser, Johann Georg; America, 1793 2856.30 p308
Moser, Johann Michael; Port uncertain, 1749 2856.30 p308
Moser, Johann Michael; Port uncertain, 1772 2856.30 p308
Moser, Johanna; Port uncertain, 1779 2856.30 p308
Moser, Josef; Port uncertain, 1746 2856.30 p308
Moser, Maria Elisabeth; Port uncertain, 1780 2856.30 p308
Moser, Nikol; America, 1737 2856.30 p299
Moser, Philip; Pennsylvania, 1777 4629.10 p7
Moser, Regina; America, 1752 2856.30 p308
Moses, Christian; America, 1749 2856.30 p308
Moses, Christian; Port uncertain, 1764 2856.30 p308
Moses, Christian; Port uncertain, 1765 2856.30 p308
Moses, Cristop; Virginia, 1663 6212.30 p2
Moses, Isaac; Pennsylvania, 1777 4629.10 p8
Moses, Joseph; Charleston, South Carolina, 1803 1224.3 p55
Moses, Lyon 24; Philadelphia, 1774 1220.25 p63
Moses, Mathew 65; Ontario, 1871 1823.15 p196
Moses, Moses; Pennsylvania, 1777 4629.10 p18
Moses, William; New York, 1807 8197.10 p45
Mosey, William 39; Ontario, 1871 1823.28 p75
Mosgop, Thomas 47; Ontario, 1871 1823.15 p196
Mosgrove, James 41; Ontario, 1871 1823.15 p196
Mosgrove, John 55; Ontario, 1871 1823.15 p196
Mosgrove, Thomas 50; Ontario, 1871 1823.15 p196
Moshnikowski, Stanislawa; Maryland, 1910 3259.35 p41
Moshnikowsky, Michael; Maryland, 1910 3259.35 p41
Mosler, Elias; New York, 1837 8197.10 p100
Mosler, Johann; Port uncertain, 1729 2856.30 p319
With wife & 2 children
Mosley, Elizabeth 20; Maryland, 1773-1774 1220.25 p33
Mosley, Esther; Vermont, 1819-1874 5900.10 p322
Mosley, John 67; Ontario, 1871 1823.15 p196
Mosley, Thomas; Maryland, 1673 2524.55 p153
Mosner, Andreas; Port uncertain, 1765 2856.30 p319
Mosoane, John; Maryland, 1674 2524.55 p157
Mosovski, Michael; Maryland, 1910 3259.35 p41
Moss, Benja 80; Ontario, 1871 1823.15 p196
Moss, Henry; New York, 1838 8197.10 p124
Moss, Jacob; Port uncertain, 1685 2856.30 p319
Moss, John 54; Ontario, 1871 1823.15 p196
Moss, Joseph 21; Virginia, 1775 1220.25 p95
Moss, Mary 74; Vermont, 1891 5900.10 p486
Moss, Richard; Maryland, 1649 2524.55 p157
Moss, Robert 40; Maryland, 1775 1220.25 p101
Moss, Sarah 45; Ontario, 1871 1823.15 p196
Moss, Thomas; New York, 1837 8197.10 p99
Moss, William 42; Ontario, 1871 1823.15 p196
Mosse, Ann; Maryland, 1661 2524.55 p157
Mosse, Elizabeth; Maryland, 1631-1685 2524.55 p157
Mosse, Margery; Virginia, 1667-1668 6212.30 p39
Mosser, . . .; Port uncertain, 1760 2856.30 p308
Mosser, Johann; Port uncertain, 1733 2856.30 p308
Mosser, Maria Anna; Port uncertain, 1771 2856.30 p308
Mosser, Martin; America, 1751 2856.30 p308
Mosserin, Margarete; Port uncertain, 1749 2856.30 p308
Mossey, Jennie Mahon; Vermont, 1845-1913 5900.10 p243
Mossey, John B.; Vermont, 1841-1904 5900.10 p243
Mossey, Rose; Vermont, 1866-1931 5900.10 p513
Mossher, Hans Georg; Port uncertain, 1768 2856.30 p308
Mossher, Peter; Port uncertain, 1768 2856.30 p308
Mossher, Therese; Port uncertain, 1768 2856.30 p308
Mossinger, Jacob; America, 1752 2856.30 p319
Mossinger, Jacob; Port uncertain, 1752 2856.30 p319
With family
Mossinger, Jacob; Port uncertain, 1753 2856.30 p319
With family
Mossinger, Jacob; Port uncertain, 1769 2856.30 p319
Mossinger, Marg. Barbara; Port uncertain, 1769 2856.30 p319
Mosslang, Therese; Port uncertain, 1776 2856.30 p319
Mosslin, Magdalene; America, 1752 2856.30 p319
With daughter
Mossmann, Johann Friedric; Port uncertain, 1754 2856.30 p308
Mossner, Mrs. Anton; Port uncertain, 1776 2856.30 p319
With 5 children
Mossner, Caspar; America, 1744 2856.30 p319
Mossner, Catharina; Port uncertain, 1795 2856.30 p319
Mossner, Ernst; Port uncertain, 1754 2856.30 p319
Mossner, Ernst; Port uncertain, 1771 2856.30 p319
Mossner, Georg Adam; Port uncertain, 1775 2856.30 p319
Mossner, Martin; Port uncertain, 1786 2856.30 p319
Mossner, Michael; America, 1738 2856.30 p319
Mossner, Michael; Port uncertain, 1737 2856.30 p319
Mossy, Ann 86; Ontario, 1861 2896.25 p63
Mossy, William 82; Ontario, 1861 2896.25 p63
Most, John; New York, 1840 8197.10 p179
Moste, Edward; Virginia, 1666-1667 6212.30 p35
Mostgoove, Stewart 35; Ontario, 1871 1823.15 p196
Mostler, John Christian; New York, 1837 8197.10 p100
Moteley, James 65; Ontario, 1871 1823.15 p196
Mothersell, William 91; Ontario, 1871 1823.22 p114
Motley, . . .; Boston, 1765 4628.40 p114
Motral, Thomas 26; Jamaica, 1775 1220.25 p113
Motsch, Johann Jakob; Port uncertain, 1764 2856.30 p308
With wife son & 2 daughters
Motsch, Johannes; New York, 1839 8197.10 p264
Motschski, Peter; Maryland, 1910 3259.35 p41
Mott, Bridget Mullen; Vermont, 1855-1913 5900.10 p126
Mott, Edmund; New York, 1705 1224.2 p82
Mott, George; Vermont, 1852-1915 5900.10 p126
Mott, Jenkin; Maryland, 1658 2524.55 p157
Mott, John Prescott; Nova Scotia, 1897 1640.13 p80
Mott, Richard; New York, 1839 8197.10 p141
Motteux, Benjamin; South Carolina, 1725 1224.2 p82
Motton, Susan; Canada, 1885 1640.13 p80
Motz, Jacob 54; Ontario, 1871 1823.15 p196
Motz, Jakob; Port uncertain, 1748 2856.30 p308
With wife & 4 children
Motz, Jakob; Port uncertain, 1750 2856.30 p308
Moubray, Ralph; New York, 1827 8197.10 p342
Moubrey, Thomas; New York, 1837 8197.10 p99
Moudiford, Francis; Maryland, 1669 2524.55 p157
Mouere, Adam; America, 1740 2856.30 p308
Mouggish, Alexander 52; Ontario, 1871 1823.15 p196
Moughan, Michael; New York, 1823 8197.10 p261
Moughoon, Joane; Maryland, 1681 2524.55 p157
Mould, Charles; New York, 1821 8197.10 p259
Mould, John; Maryland, 1667 2524.55 p157
Mould, Martin; Maryland, 1657 2524.55 p157
Mould, Robert; Virginia, 1666-1667 6212.30 p34
Moulder, Joseph; Pennsylvania, 1777 4629.10 p6
Moulder, Robt.; Maryland, 1671 2524.55 p157
Mouldy, Iasac 39; Ontario, 1871 1823.22 p114
Moulins, Mr.; Quebec, 1858 9196.15 p36
Moulson, Foulke; Virginia, 1674 1224.1 p40
Moulston, Ann; Maryland, 1671 2524.55 p157
Moulston, Thomas; Maryland, 1671 2524.55 p157
Moulsworth, Ja; Virginia, 1667-1668 6212.30 p38
Moulsworth, Jno; Virginia, 1666 6212.30 p28
Moult, William; Virginia, 1657 1224.1 p40
Moulton, Foulk; Virginia, 1679 1224.1 p40
Moultrie, Cecilia; Florida, 1781 1640.10 p161
Moultrie, Cecilia; St. Augustine, Florida, 1781 1224.2 p82
Moultrie, James; Florida, 1763 1640.10 p161
Moultrie, Walter; Georgia, 1698 1640.13 p80
Moumbar, Peter; America, 1739 2856.30 p308
Moundee, Alexander; Maryland, 1665 2524.55 p125
Mounsfor, Mrs.; Maryland, 1664 2524.55 p157
Mountague, Jane; Maryland, 1659 2524.55 p157
Mountague, Margaret Kelway; New England, 1651 1224.1 p34
Mountague, Samll; Virginia, 1665 6212.30 p18
Mountague, Stephen; Maryland, 1655-1656 2524.55 p157
Mountain, Mr.; Quebec, 1857 9196.15 p24
Mountain, Thomas 52; Ontario, 1871 1823.15 p196
Mountair, Dorothy 26; New York, 1774 1220.25 p141
Mountair, Francis 25; New York, 1774 1220.25 p141
Mountayne, William; Maryland, 1673 2524.55 p157
Mountcastle, John; Ohio, 1833 1224.3 p55
Mountcastle, S. H. 69; Ontario, 1871 1823.15 p196
Mountege, Jame; Maryland, 1664 2524.55 p157
Mountegue, Cornelius; Maryland, 1672 2524.55 p157
Mountfort, Edwin; Virginia, 1663 6212.30 p1
Mountfort, Sara; Virginia, 1664 6212.30 p14
Mountgomery, James; Virginia, 1697 1224.1 p40
Mountjoy, Mary Noyes; New England, 1699 1224.1 p42
Mountly, John; Virginia, 1666-1667 6212.30 p34
Mountney, Andrew 59; Ontario, 1871 1823.22 p115
Mountshort, John; Maryland, 1679 2524.55 p157
Mourth, John; Maryland, 1652 2524.55 p157
Mourton, Mary; Maryland, 1674 2524.55 p157
Mous, Philip; Pennsylvania, 1777 4629.10 p12
Mouse, Thomas; Virginia, 1665-1666 6212.30 p24
Mouton, August; New York, New York, 1856 3437.14 p48
Movish, John; Maryland, 1910 3259.35 p41
Mowat, Elizabeth; Savannah, Georgia, 1774 1640.10 p161
Mowat, James; Savannah, Georgia, 1774 1640.10 p161
Mowat, John; Savannah, Georgia, 1774 1640.10 p162
Mowate, Alexander; Philadelphia, 1717 1224.2 p82
Mowatt, George 13; Ontario, 1871 1823.22 p115
Mowbray, Hugh; New York, 1804 8197.10 p27
Mowbray, James 24; Ontario, 1871 1823.15 p196
Mowbray, John 40; Ontario, 1871 1823.15 p196
Mowbray, Joseph 56; Ontario, 1871 1823.15 p196
Mowbray, Richard; Ottawa, 1858 1640.13 p80
Mowbray, Robert 29; Ontario, 1871 1823.15 p197
Mowbray, Thomas 43; Ontario, 1871 1823.28 p75
Mowrer, Adam; America, 1740 2856.30 p309
Moxam, Susan 36; Ontario, 1871 1823.28 p75
Moxley, William; Maryland, 1659 2524.55 p157
Moxon, Martha; New York, 1831 1224.3 p55
Moy, Elizabeth *SEE* Moy, Richard
Moy, Richard; Maryland, 1665 2524.55 p157
Wife: Elizabeth
Daughter: Elizabeth
Moyan, Johanna C. Kennedy; Vermont, 1856-1931 5900.10 p119
Moyan, Michael J.; Vermont, 1851-1921 5900.10 p118
Moydes, James; Pennsylvania, 1777 4629.10 p18
Moye, John; Virginia, 1658 1224.1 p63
Moye, Richard; Virginia, 1658 1224.1 p63
Moyen, Mr.; Quebec, 1858 9196.15 p47
Moyes, James; Georgia, 1698 1640.13 p80
Moylan, . . .; New England, 1775-1781 4628.40 p81
Moylan, Ann; Vermont, n.d. 5900.10 p558
Moylan, James; New York, 1839 8197.10 p141
Moylan, John; Vermont, 1919 5900.10 p185
Moylan, Joseph; Canada, 1756-1760 4628.40 p45
Moylan, Margaret; Vermont, 1846-1914 5900.10 p579
Moylan, Margaret; Vermont, 1908 5900.10 p185
Moylan, Mary; Vermont, 1837-1871 5900.10 p564
Moylan, Mary; Vermont, 1911 5900.10 p185
Moylan, Mary 45; Ontario, 1871 1823.15 p197

Moylan, Mary 64; Vermont, 1887 ***5900.10*** *p402*
Moylan, Mary A. 27; Vermont, 1884 ***5900.10*** *p561*
Moylan, Mary Cain; Vermont, 1790-1877 ***5900.10*** *p558*
Moylan, Michael; Vermont, 1831-1906 ***5900.10*** *p579*
Moylan, Patrick; New York, 1840 ***8197.10*** *p179*
Moylan, Patrick 52; Ontario, 1871 ***1823.15*** *p197*
Moylan, Stephen; New England, 1775-1781 ***4628.40*** *p68*
Moyle, David; Virginia, 1666 ***6212.30*** *p30*
Moynagh, Philip; Pennsylvania, 1779 ***4629.10*** *p40*
Moynahan, Rodger 18; Vermont, 1880 ***5900.10*** *p360*
Moynehan, Dan 18 *SEE* Moynehan, Mary
Moynehan, Denis 33; New York, New York, 1850 ***1825.45*** *p51*
Wife: Johanna 28
Son: John 2
Daughter: Johanna 5
Moynehan, Ellen 26 *SEE* Moynehan, Mary
Moynehan, Johanna 5 *SEE* Moynehan, Denis
Moynehan, Johanna 21 *SEE* Moynehan, Mary
Moynehan, Johanna 28 *SEE* Moynehan, Denis
Moynehan, John 2 *SEE* Moynehan, Denis
Moynehan, Mary 55; New York, New York, 1850 ***1825.45*** *p52*
Son: Dan 18
Daughter: Norry 12
Son: Tade 14
Daughter: Ellen 26
Daughter: Johanna 21
Moynehan, Norry 12 *SEE* Moynehan, Mary
Moynehan, Tade 14 *SEE* Moynehan, Mary
Moynihan, Biddy 41; New York, New York, 1851 ***1825.45*** *p51*
Son: John 15
Son: Patrick 12
Moynihan, Catharine 59; Vermont, 1886 ***5900.10*** *p106*
Moynihan, Catherine Gaffney 69; Vermont, 1899 ***5900.10*** *p507*
Moynihan, Denis 33; New York, New York, 1850 ***1825.45*** *p51*
Wife: Johanna 28
Daughter: Johanna 5
Son: John 2
Moynihan, Ellen 75; Vermont, 1897 ***5900.10*** *p117*
Moynihan, Eugene; Pennsylvania, 1868 ***6058.10*** *p61*
Moynihan, Honora 75; Vermont, 1898 ***5900.10*** *p104*
Moynihan, Humphrey; Vermont, 1854-1894 ***5900.10*** *p104*
Moynihan, Johanna 5 *SEE* Moynihan, Denis
Moynihan, Johanna 28 *SEE* Moynihan, Denis
Moynihan, John 2 *SEE* Moynihan, Denis
Moynihan, John 15 *SEE* Moynihan, Biddy
Moynihan, Margaret 70; Vermont, 1895 ***5900.10*** *p104*
Moynihan, Mary; Vermont, 1854-1917 ***5900.10*** *p129*
Moynihan, Mary 69; Vermont, 1888 ***5900.10*** *p105*
Moynihan, Mary O'Connor; Vermont, 1876 ***5900.10*** *p104*
Moynihan, Mary T.; Vermont, 1866-1886 ***5900.10*** *p104*
Moynihan, Patrick 12 *SEE* Moynihan, Biddy
Moynihan, Timothy 47; Ontario, 1871 ***1823.28*** *p75*
Moynihan, Timothy 66; Vermont, 1877 ***5900.10*** *p104*
Moynihan, Timothy W.; Vermont, 1854-1904 ***5900.10*** *p47*
Moynough, John H.; Indiana, 1896 ***3437.14*** *p168*
Moys, Mr.; America, 1774 ***2856.30*** *p309*
With 2 brothers
Moys, Mr.; Port uncertain, 1744 ***2856.30*** *p309*
With 2 brothers
Moyse, Jane 46; Ontario, 1871 ***1823.22*** *p115*
Moyse, Joseph; New England, 1650 ***1224.1*** *p55*
Moysney, Mr.; Quebec, 1857 ***9196.15*** *p23*
Mraka, Romem; Maryland, 1910 ***3259.35*** *p41*
Mrkoich, Jul 30; Alaska, 1914 ***9196.1*** *p11*
Mrosinski, Dominick; Maryland, 1910 ***3259.35*** *p41*
Mrowczynski, William; Maryland, 1910 ***3259.35*** *p41*
Mroz, John; Maryland, 1910 ***3259.35*** *p41*
Mrozewski, John; Maryland, 1910 ***3259.35*** *p41*
Mrozinski, Franczek; Maryland, 1910 ***3259.35*** *p41*
Mrozinski, Michael; Maryland, 1910 ***3259.35*** *p41*
Mroznski, Barbara; Maryland, 1910 ***3259.35*** *p41*
Much, Jeremiah; Pennsylvania, 1777 ***4629.10*** *p13*
Muchall, Frederick 38; Ontario, 1871 ***1823.22*** *p115*
Muck, Wm; Virginia, 1664 ***6212.30*** *p10*
Muckenbrod, Therese; Port uncertain, 1766 ***2856.30*** *p309*
Muckleston, Miss; Quebec, 1858 ***9196.15*** *p44*
Muckleston, Mrs.; Quebec, 1858 ***9196.15*** *p44*
Muckley, Giles; Maryland, 1658 ***2524.55*** *p157*
Mucklin, Friedrich; Port uncertain, 1783 ***2856.30*** *p310*
Muddey, Thomas 58; Ontario, 1871 ***1823.15*** *p197*
Muddigan, Timothy 35; Ontario, 1871 ***1823.15*** *p197*
Mudge, George 52; Ontario, 1871 ***1823.28*** *p75*
Mudge, Henry 19; Ontario, 1871 ***1823.28*** *p75*
Mudge, James 15; Ontario, 1871 ***1823.28*** *p75*
Mudgett, Ellen O'Neill; Vermont, 1855-1912 ***5900.10*** *p532*
Mudgett, Eugene P.; Vermont, 1854 ***5900.10*** *p532*
Mueller, Mr.; America, 1757 ***2856.30*** *p246*
Mueller, Arthur; New York, 1837 ***8197.10*** *p99*
Mueller, Jacquer 28; Kansas, 1910 ***9079.10*** *p4*
Mueller, Normie 3; Kansas, 1910 ***9079.10*** *p4*
Muen, John; Maryland, 1661 ***2524.55*** *p187*
Muffel, Johann Bernhard; Port uncertain, 1738 ***2856.30*** *p309*
Muffetts, John; Maryland, 1674 ***2524.55*** *p157*
Mugridge, Thomas 37; Ontario, 1871 ***1823.15*** *p197*
Muhl, Maria Magdalena; America, 1754 ***2856.30*** *p310*
Muhlberger, Bernhard; Port uncertain, 1746 ***2856.30*** *p310*
Muhlburger, Anna Catharina; Port uncertain, 1758 ***2856.30*** *p310*
Muhldrymer, Johann; Port uncertain, 1747 ***2856.30*** *p310*
Muhleiser, Michael; Port uncertain, 1764 ***2856.30*** *p310*
With wife & 2 children
Muhleiss, Johann Nikolaus; Port uncertain, 1754 ***2856.30*** *p310*
Muhler, Joseph; Pennsylvania, 1786 ***4629.10*** *p49*
Muhlhauser, Ms.; America, 1737 ***2856.30*** *p310*
With husband
Muhlhauser, Georg; America, 1746 ***2856.30*** *p310*
With family
Muhlhauser, Johann; Port uncertain, 1745 ***2856.30*** *p310*
Muhlhoffer, Johann Friedric; Port uncertain, 1749 ***2856.30*** *p310*
Muhlin, Maria Magdalena; America, 1754 ***2856.30*** *p310*
Muhlschlager, Anna Maria; Port uncertain, 1770 ***2856.30*** *p310*
Muhlschlegel, Andreas; America, 1750 ***2856.30*** *p310*
Muir, Alexander; Georgia, 1699 ***1640.13*** *p80*
Muir, Alexander 21; Virginia, 1773 ***1220.25*** *p29*
Muir, Andrew 55; Ontario, 1871 ***1823.15*** *p197*
Muir, Augusta; St. Johns, Newfoundland, 1878 ***1640.13*** *p80*
Muir, Ebenezer; New York, 1840 ***8197.10*** *p178*
Muir, Elizabeth; Ontario, 1891 ***1640.13*** *p81*
Muir, Ellen *SEE* Muir, James
Muir, George *SEE* Muir, James
Muir, Isabella 76; Ontario, 1871 ***1823.15*** *p197*
Muir, James; Georgia, 1732 ***1640.10*** *p162*
Wife: Ellen
Son: John
Son: George
Muir, James; Jamaica, 1850 ***1640.13*** *p81*
Muir, James; New Brunswick, 1846 ***1640.13*** *p81*
Muir, John *SEE* Muir, James
Muir, John; Jamaica, 1816 ***1640.13*** *p81*
Muir, John; Kingston, Jamaica, 1849 ***1640.13*** *p81*
Muir, John; Savannah, Georgia, 1759 ***1640.10*** *p162*
Muir, R.; Quebec, 1858 ***9196.15*** *p42*
Muir, Mrs. R.; Quebec, 1858 ***9196.15*** *p42*
Muir, Thomas 38; Ontario, 1871 ***1823.28*** *p75*
Muir, W.; Quebec, 1858 ***9196.15*** *p35*
Muir, William; Georgia, 1698 ***1640.13*** *p81*
Muir, William; Missouri, 1889 ***1640.13*** *p81*
Muir, William; New York, 1829 ***8197.10*** *p312*
Muir, William; New York, 1840 ***8197.10*** *p179*
Muir, William; Philadelphia, 1793 ***4629.10*** *p68*
Muir, William 61; Ontario, 1871 ***1823.15*** *p197*
Muire, James; Virginia, 1689 ***1224.1*** *p41*
Muire, Jannet 21; Ontario, 1871 ***1823.15*** *p197*
Muirhead, John 57; Ontario, 1871 ***1823.22*** *p115*
Muirhead, W.; Quebec, 1856 ***9196.15*** *p5*
Muirhead, Wm 31; Alaska, 1911 ***9196.1*** *p12*
Muirhead, Wm 31; British Columbia, 1911 ***9196.1*** *p12*
Mukel, Christian; America, 1749 ***2856.30*** *p309*
With wife & children
Mukersal, Jane 19; Ontario, 1861 ***2896.25*** *p48*
Mulane, Patrick; New York, 1840 ***8197.10*** *p265*
Mulcachey, Michael 55; Ontario, 1871 ***1823.28*** *p75*
Mulcahey, Cathrine Donovan; Vermont, 1844-1906 ***5900.10*** *p489*
Mulcahey, John F.; Vermont, 1836-1901 ***5900.10*** *p577*
Mulcahey, Margaret; Vermont, 1814-1902 ***5900.10*** *p190*
Mulcahey, Michael; Vermont, 1833-1910 ***5900.10*** *p353*
Mulcahey, Nora Collins; Vermont, 1857-1909 ***5900.10*** *p353*
Mulcahey, William; Vermont, 1840-1915 ***5900.10*** *p489*
Mulcahy, Andrew; New York, 1840 ***8197.10*** *p264*
Mulcahy, Bridget H. 38; Vermont, 1893 ***5900.10*** *p94*
Mulcahy, Elizabeth McGuire; Vermont, 1851-1921 ***5900.10*** *p95*
Mulcahy, Ellen B. 90; Vermont, 1905 ***5900.10*** *p94*
Mulcahy, Ellen E.; Vermont, 1849-1913 ***5900.10*** *p442*
Mulcahy, James; Vermont, 1810-1881 ***5900.10*** *p190*
Mulcahy, Jennie; Vermont, 1849-1872 ***5900.10*** *p190*
Mulcahy, Margaret; Vermont, 1838-1914 ***5900.10*** *p356*
Mulcahy, Mary; Vermont, 1818-1907 ***5900.10*** *p160*
Mulcahy, Patrick; New York, 1840 ***8197.10*** *p264*
Mulcahy, Patrick 89; Vermont, 1898 ***5900.10*** *p94*
Mulcahy, Patrick J.; Vermont, 1852-1938 ***5900.10*** *p95*
Mulcaster, Edward 66; Ontario, 1871 ***1823.15*** *p197*
Mulcoher, Daniel; Maryland, 1681 ***2524.55*** *p157*
Muldoon, Catherine Donnelly 46; Vermont, 1858 ***5900.10*** *p74*
Muldoon, Charles; New York, 1834 ***8197.10*** *p71*
Muldoon, Christopher 47; Ontario, 1871 ***1823.15*** *p197*
Muldoon, Henry; Vermont, 1851-1917 ***5900.10*** *p492*
Muldoon, James 46; Ontario, 1871 ***1823.15*** *p197*
Muldoon, John 30; Pennsylvania, 1815-1817 ***8197.10*** *p347*
Muldoon, John 45; Ontario, 1871 ***1823.15*** *p197*
Muldoon, Margaret 73; Ontario, 1871 ***1823.15*** *p197*
Muldoon, Mary; Vermont, 1820-1899 ***5900.10*** *p75*
Muldoon, Mary Ann; Vermont, 1863-1954 ***5900.10*** *p492*
Muldoon, Patrick; New York, 1840 ***8197.10*** *p321*
Muldoon, Patrick 40; Ontario, 1871 ***1823.28*** *p75*
Mulenhore, William 50; Ontario, 1871 ***1823.28*** *p75*
Mulera, James 22; New York, New York, 1847 ***1825.45*** *p18*
Brother: Thomas 20
Mulera, Thomas 20 *SEE* Mulera, James
Mulere, Catherine 30; New York, New York, 1847 ***1825.45*** *p18*
Mulhall, James 40; Ontario, 1871 ***1823.22*** *p115*
Mulhall, Mary; Vermont, 1795-1882 ***5900.10*** *p474*
Mulhallond, Richard; New York, 1836 ***8197.10*** *p263*
Mulharn, Catherine; Vermont, 1834-1900 ***5900.10*** *p426*
Mulhearn, Ann McKeone 59; Vermont, 1887 ***5900.10*** *p570*
Mulhearn, Martin 63; Vermont, 1885 ***5900.10*** *p570*
Mulheran, John; New York, 1804 ***8197.10*** *p27*
Mulheran, Peter; New York, 1828 ***8197.10*** *p349*
Mulhern, Catherine; Vermont, 1840-1913 ***5900.10*** *p584*
Mulhern, Jane McGowan; Vermont, 1839-1909 ***5900.10*** *p571*
Mulhern, Mary 101; Vermont, 1904 ***5900.10*** *p584*
Mulhern, Mathew 73; Ontario, 1871 ***1823.22*** *p115*
Mulhern, Thomas; Vermont, 1828-1896 ***5900.10*** *p571*
Mulheron, Catharine; Vermont, n.d. ***5900.10*** *p238*
Mulheron, Sarah M. Mattimore; Vermont, 1854-1926 ***5900.10*** *p186*
Mulheron, Susan; Vermont, 1852-1915 ***5900.10*** *p186*
Mulheron, Thomas F.; Vermont, 1852-1929 ***5900.10*** *p186*
Mulherron, John; Pennsylvania, 1837 ***6058.10*** *p14*
Mulhol, Kate 36; Ontario, 1871 ***1823.22*** *p115*
Mulhol, Micheal 37; Ontario, 1871 ***1823.22*** *p115*
Mulholand, John 20; Ontario, 1871 ***1823.15*** *p197*
Mulhollan, Bernard; New York, 1804 ***8197.10*** *p27*
Mulholland, Andrew 22; Ontario, 1861 ***2896.27*** *p5*
Mulholland, David 19; Ontario, 1861 ***2896.27*** *p5*
Mulholland, Elizabeth 54; Ontario, 1861 ***2896.27*** *p5*
Mulholland, James; New York, 1840 ***8197.10*** *p180*
Mulholland, James 50; Ontario, 1871 ***1823.15*** *p197*
Mulholland, John 60; Ontario, 1871 ***1823.22*** *p115*
Mulholland, Margaret 27; Ontario, 1861 ***2896.27*** *p5*
Mulholland, Mary 20; Ontario, 1861 ***2896.27*** *p5*
Mulholland, Matthew 16; Ontario, 1861 ***2896.27*** *p5*
Mulholland, Richard; New York, 1839 ***8197.10*** *p142*
Mulholland, Thomas 24; Ontario, 1861 ***2896.27*** *p5*
MulHolland, William; Buffalo, New York, 1834 ***6058.10*** *p35*
Mulholland, William; New York, 1840 ***8197.10*** *p181*
Mulhollands, Hugh; New York, 1837 ***8197.10*** *p99*
Mulich, Johann; Port uncertain, 1765 ***2856.30*** *p310*
Muligan, Ann 30; Ontario, 1861 ***2896.27*** *p3*
Muligan, James 40; Ontario, 1861 ***2896.27*** *p3*
Muligan, John 50; Ontario, 1861 ***2896.27*** *p3*
Mulihan, Margaret 60; Vermont, 1883 ***5900.10*** *p433*
Mulihan, Patrick 71; Vermont, 1899 ***5900.10*** *p433*
Mulinhill, John; Baltimore, 1850 ***6058.10*** *p63*
Mull, Valentin; Port uncertain, 1770 ***2856.30*** *p310*
Mullally, Richard; New York, 1826 ***8197.10*** *p261*
Mullaly, James; Vermont, 1854-1929 ***5900.10*** *p96*
Mullaly, Mary J. Markham; Vermont, 1859-1949 ***5900.10*** *p96*
Mullaly, Patrick; New York, 1840 ***8197.10*** *p385*
Mullaly, Patrick; Vermont, 1844-1893 ***5900.10*** *p462*
Mullan, Miss; Quebec, 1857 ***9196.15*** *p22*
Mullan, Michael; New York, 1840 ***8197.10*** *p265*
Mullan, Stuart; New York, 1804 ***8197.10*** *p27*
Mullan, William; New York, 1827 ***8197.10*** *p341*
Mullaney, Betsey; Vermont, 1865 ***5900.10*** *p436*
Mullaney, Bridget; Vermont, 1852-1930 ***5900.10*** *p204*
Mullaney, John; Vermont, 1847-1923 ***5900.10*** *p204*
Mullaney, Louisa; Vermont, 1870-1957 ***5900.10*** *p204*
Mullaney, Margaret; Vermont, 1835-1908 ***5900.10*** *p436*
Mullaney, Mary; Vermont, 1827-1910 ***5900.10*** *p436*
Mullaney, Mary; Vermont, 1905 ***5900.10*** *p436*

Muller, Johann Adam; America, 1765 ***2856.30*** *p312*
Muller, Johann Adam; Port uncertain, 1738 ***2856.30*** *p309*
Muller, Johann Adam; Port uncertain, 1750 ***2856.30*** *p312*
Muller, Johann Adam; Port uncertain, 1776 ***2856.30*** *p312*
Muller, Johann Erhard; Port uncertain, 1727 ***2856.30*** *p312*
Muller, Johann Friedric; America, 1750 ***2856.30*** *p312*
Muller, Johann Georg; America, 1754 ***2856.30*** *p317*
With wife & 3 children
Muller, Johann Jakob; Port uncertain, 1771 ***2856.30*** *p313*
Muller, Johann Jakob; Port uncertain, 1789 ***2856.30*** *p313*
Muller, Johann Karl; Port uncertain, 1733 ***2856.30*** *p313*
Muller, Johann Michael; America, 1749 ***2856.30*** *p317*
With wife & 3 children
Muller, Johann Nickel; America, 1748 ***2856.30*** *p317*
With wife & 2 children
Muller, Johann Nicolaus; Port uncertain, 1747 ***2856.30*** *p313*
Muller, Johann Niklas; Port uncertain, 1764 ***2856.30*** *p313*
Muller, Johann Nikol; Port uncertain, 1700-1799 ***2856.30*** *p313*
Muller, Johann Nikolaus; America, 1749 ***2856.30*** *p313*
Muller, Johann Nikolaus; Port uncertain, 1766 ***2856.30*** *p313*
Muller, Johann Peter; America, 1741 ***2856.30*** *p316*
With wife & children
Muller, Johann Peter; Port uncertain, 1740 ***2856.30*** *p313*
Muller, Johann Peter; Port uncertain, 1749 ***2856.30*** *p309*
Muller, Johann Philipp; Port uncertain, 1754 ***2856.30*** *p314*
Muller, Johann Walter; Port uncertain, 1754 ***2856.30*** *p314*
Muller, Johann Wilhelm; Port uncertain, 1755 ***2856.30*** *p313*
Muller, John; New York, 1840 ***8197.10*** *p181*
Muller, John; New York, 1840 ***8197.10*** *p265*
Muller, John U.; New York, 1832 ***8197.10*** *p299*
Muller, Josef; Port uncertain, 1745 ***2856.30*** *p313*
Muller, Josef; Port uncertain, 1795 ***2856.30*** *p313*
Muller, Josef; Port uncertain, 1796 ***2856.30*** *p313*
Muller, Jost; Port uncertain, 1792 ***2856.30*** *p313*
Muller, Karl; Port uncertain, 1768 ***2856.30*** *p313*
Muller, Karl; Port uncertain, 1777 ***2856.30*** *p313*
Muller, Konrad; Port uncertain, 1754 ***2856.30*** *p314*
Muller, Konrad; Port uncertain, 1784 ***2856.30*** *p313*
Muller, Leonhard; America, 1744 ***2856.30*** *p313*
Muller, Lorenz; Port uncertain, 1783 ***2856.30*** *p317*
With wife & son
Muller, Louis 27; Ontario, 1871 ***1823.15*** *p197*
Muller, Ludwig; Port uncertain, 1768 ***2856.30*** *p313*
Muller, Ludwig; Port uncertain, 1789 ***2856.30*** *p313*
Muller, Magdalena; Port uncertain, 1759 ***2856.30*** *p313*
Muller, Marg. Zimmer *SEE* Muller, Jakob
Muller, Margarete; America, 1727 ***2856.30*** *p313*
Muller, Margarete; America, 1780 ***2856.30*** *p313*
Muller, Margarete; Port uncertain, 1740 ***2856.30*** *p313*
Muller, Margarete; Port uncertain, 1769 ***2856.30*** *p313*
Muller, Maria; Port uncertain, 1723 ***2856.30*** *p313*
Muller, Maria Agnes; Port uncertain, 1785 ***2856.30*** *p313*
Muller, Maria Barbara; Port uncertain, 1760 ***2856.30*** *p317*
Muller, Maria Christina; Port uncertain, 1750 ***2856.30*** *p313*
Muller, Maria Elisabeth; America, 1758 ***2856.30*** *p313*
Muller, Maria Elisabeth; Port uncertain, 1754 ***2856.30*** *p313*
Muller, Maria Elisabeth; Port uncertain, 1783 ***2856.30*** *p313*
Muller, Maria Franziska; Port uncertain, 1737 ***2856.30*** *p313*
Muller, Maria Loretta; Port uncertain, 1749 ***2856.30*** *p313*
Muller, Maria Margarete; Port uncertain, 1775 ***2856.30*** *p313*
Muller, Maria Margarete; Port uncertain, 1785 ***2856.30*** *p313*
Muller, Martin; America, 1752 ***2856.30*** *p317*
With wife & 4 children
Muller, Martin; Port uncertain, 1749 ***2856.30*** *p317*
With wife & 4 children
Muller, Martin; Port uncertain, 1783 ***2856.30*** *p313*
Muller, Mrs. Martin; Port uncertain, 1775 ***2856.30*** *p315*
With child
Muller, Matheis; America, 1749 ***2856.30*** *p316*
With wife
Muller, Mathias; Port uncertain, 1753 ***2856.30*** *p316*
With wife & children
Muller, Matthias; America, 1749 ***2856.30*** *p313*
Muller, Michael; America, 1738 ***2856.30*** *p314*
Muller, Michael; America, 1739 ***2856.30*** *p317*
With wife & 7 children
Muller, Michael; America, 1741 ***2856.30*** *p304*
With wife & 5 children
Muller, Michael; Port uncertain, 1613 ***2856.30*** *p317*
With wife son & daughter
Muller, Michael; Port uncertain, 1749 ***2856.30*** *p313*
Muller, Michael; Port uncertain, 1753 ***2856.30*** *p316*
With wife
Muller, Michael; Port uncertain, 1783 ***2856.30*** *p317*
Wife: C. Anstatt
Muller, Michael; Port uncertain, 1791 ***2856.30*** *p313*
Muller, Nickel; America, 1738 ***2856.30*** *p314*
Muller, Nickel; Port uncertain, 1756 ***2856.30*** *p314*
Muller, Nickel; Port uncertain, 1758 ***2856.30*** *p314*
Muller, Nicol; Port uncertain, 1775 ***2856.30*** *p314*
Muller, Niklas; America, 1738 ***2856.30*** *p314*
Muller, Niklas; Port uncertain, 1763 ***2856.30*** *p314*
Muller, Nikolaus; America, 1741 ***2856.30*** *p314*
Muller, Nikolaus; Port uncertain, 1741 ***2856.30*** *p314*
Muller, Peter; America, 1766 ***2856.30*** *p314*
Muller, Peter; America, 1767 ***2856.30*** *p314*
Muller, Peter; America, 1768 ***2856.30*** *p314*
Muller, Peter; America, 1772 ***2856.30*** *p314*
Muller, Peter; New York, 1830 ***8197.10*** *p262*
Muller, Peter; Port uncertain, 1749 ***2856.30*** *p314*
Muller, Peter; Port uncertain, 1751 ***2856.30*** *p314*
Muller, Peter; Port uncertain, 1764 ***2856.30*** *p316*
With wife
Muller, Peter; Port uncertain, 1784 ***2856.30*** *p314*
Muller, Peter Thomas; America, 1738 ***2856.30*** *p314*
Muller, Philip; New York, 1840 ***8197.10*** *p265*
Muller, Philipp; America, 1749 ***2856.30*** *p314*
Muller, Philipp; Canada, 1751 ***2856.30*** *p314*
Muller, Philipp; Port uncertain, 1749 ***2856.30*** *p316*
With wife & children
Muller, Philipp; Port uncertain, 1754 ***2856.30*** *p314*
Muller, Philipp; Port uncertain, 1767 ***2856.30*** *p314*
Muller, Philipp Georg; America, 1749 ***2856.30*** *p317*
With wife & 2 children
Muller, Philipp Jakob; Port uncertain, 1730 ***2856.30*** *p314*
Muller, Pips Gorg; America, 1749 ***2856.30*** *p314*
Muller, Rahel; America, 1751 ***2856.30*** *p314*
Muller, Rembertus; New York, 1812 ***8197.10*** *p57*
Muller, Robert 39; Ontario, 1871 ***1823.15*** *p197*
Muller, Sebastian; Port uncertain, 1774 ***2856.30*** *p314*
Muller, Simon; Port uncertain, 1783 ***2856.30*** *p317*
With wife son & daughter
Muller, Sophia Heinz; Port uncertain, 1785 ***2856.30*** *p175*
Muller, Valentin; Port uncertain, 1783 ***2856.30*** *p314*
Muller, Valentine; New York, 1840 ***8197.10*** *p181*
Muller, Wendel; America, 1748 ***2856.30*** *p314*
Muller, Wilhelm; America, 1744 ***2856.30*** *p314*
Muller, Wilhelm; America, 1748 ***2856.30*** *p314*
Muller, William 34; Ontario, 1871 ***1823.28*** *p75*
Muller, Zacharias; America, 1754 ***2856.30*** *p314*
Mullera, Anne 2 *SEE* Mullera, Thomas
Mullera, Anne 9 *SEE* Mullera, James
Mullera, Anne 25; New York, New York, 1848 ***1825.45*** *p18*
Mullera, Bridget 10 *SEE* Mullera, James
Mullera, Bridget 50 *SEE* Mullera, James
Mullera, Bridget 55 *SEE* Mullera, Thomas
Mullera, Catherine 30; New York, New York, 1847 ***1825.45*** *p18*
Mullera, Denis 12 *SEE* Mullera, James
Mullera, Francis 6 *SEE* Mullera, John
Mullera, James 4 *SEE* Mullera, John
Mullera, James 22; New York, New York, 1847 ***1825.45*** *p18*
Brother: Thomas 20
Mullera, James 50; New York, New York, 1847 ***1825.45*** *p18*
Wife: Bridget 50
Daughter: Anne 9
Daughter: Bridget 10
Son: Denis 12
Mullera, John 8 *SEE* Mullera, John
Mullera, John 35; New York, New York, 1848 ***1825.45*** *p19*
Wife: Sarah 30
Son: James 4
Son: John 8
Son: Patrick 12
Brother: Pat 25
Son: Thomas 10
Son: Francis 6
Mullera, Mary 30 *SEE* Mullera, Thomas
Mullera, Pat 25 *SEE* Mullera, John
Mullera, Pat 29; New York, New York, 1848 ***1825.45*** *p18*
Mullera, Patrick 12 *SEE* Mullera, John
Mullera, Sarah 30 *SEE* Mullera, John
Mullera, Thomas 6 *SEE* Mullera, Thomas
Mullera, Thomas 10 *SEE* Mullera, John
Mullera, Thomas 20 *SEE* Mullera, James
Mullera, Thomas 36; New York, New York, 1848 ***1825.45*** *p19*
Wife: Mary 30
Son: Thomas 6
Mother: Bridget 55
Daughter: Anne 2
Mullerea, Catherine 30; New York, New York, 1847 ***1825.45*** *p18*
Mullerin, Maria Barbara; Port uncertain, 1755 ***2856.30*** *p317*
Mullerin, Maria Barbara; Port uncertain, 1760 ***2856.30*** *p317*
Mullet, William 93; Ontario, 1861 ***2896.27*** *p41*
Mullett, George 14; Ontario, 1861 ***2896.27*** *p29*
Mullick, Lawrence; Maryland, 1664 ***2524.55*** *p173*
Mulligan, Rev.; Quebec, 1856 ***9196.15*** *p11*
Mulligan, Anne C.; Vermont, 1883-1927 ***5900.10*** *p313*
Mulligan, Azilda Lapierre; Vermont, 1855-1919 ***5900.10*** *p85*
Mulligan, Bernard; New York, 1837 ***8197.10*** *p100*
Mulligan, Bridget; Vermont, 1834-1893 ***5900.10*** *p89*
Mulligan, Catherine J.; Vermont, 1872-1887 ***5900.10*** *p313*
Mulligan, Charles; New York, 1827 ***8197.10*** *p343*
Mulligan, Danial 50; Ontario, 1871 ***1823.28*** *p75*
Mulligan, James; New York, 1837 ***8197.10*** *p263*
Mulligan, James; New York, 1840 ***8197.10*** *p180*
Mulligan, James; Vermont, 1834-1913 ***5900.10*** *p465*
Mulligan, Jane; Vermont, 1831-1911 ***5900.10*** *p313*
Mulligan, Jerome B.; Vermont, 1864-1910 ***5900.10*** *p313*
Mulligan, John; New York, 1838 ***8197.10*** *p124*
Mulligan, John; Vermont, 1850-1914 ***5900.10*** *p85*
Mulligan, John P.; Vermont, 1877-1907 ***5900.10*** *p313*
Mulligan, Maria; Vermont, 1837-1909 ***5900.10*** *p465*
Mulligan, Mary A.; Vermont, 1859-1909 ***5900.10*** *p84*
Mulligan, Mary A.; Vermont, 1868-1951 ***5900.10*** *p313*
Mulligan, Mary Bowen 66; Vermont, 1885 ***5900.10*** *p84*
Mulligan, Mary L. Haley; Vermont, 1840-1914 ***5900.10*** *p313*
Mulligan, Mary McCawley; Vermont, 1840-1915 ***5900.10*** *p384*
Mulligan, Matthew; New York, 1837 ***8197.10*** *p263*
Mulligan, Matthew; Vermont, 1834-1880 ***5900.10*** *p384*
Mulligan, Michael; New York, 1834 ***8197.10*** *p263*
Mulligan, Michael 71; Ontario, 1871 ***1823.28*** *p75*
Mulligan, Michael 80; Vermont, 1912 ***5900.10*** *p84*
Mulligan, Patrick; Vermont, 1829-1912 ***5900.10*** *p313*
Mulligan, Samuel; New York, 1839 ***8197.10*** *p264*
Mulligan, Thomas; New York, 1838 ***8197.10*** *p379*
Mulligen, David 44; Ontario, 1871 ***1823.28*** *p75*
Mullika, Andreas; Maryland, 1661 ***2524.55*** *p110*
Mullikin, Mary; Maryland, 1659 ***2524.55*** *p158*
Mullin, Ann; Vermont, 1826-1900 ***5900.10*** *p568*
Mullin, Anna; Vermont, 1844-1938 ***5900.10*** *p388*
Mullin, Arthur 82; Vermont, 1887 ***5900.10*** *p382*
Mullin, Arthur, Jr.; Vermont, 1848-1927 ***5900.10*** *p382*
Mullin, Ellen Magner 74; Vermont, 1906 ***5900.10*** *p108*
Mullin, Francis 24; Vermont, 1877 ***5900.10*** *p382*
Mullin, James 40; Ontario, 1871 ***1823.15*** *p197*
Mullin, John; New York, 1825 ***8197.10*** *p261*
Mullin, John; New York, 1840 ***8197.10*** *p181*
Mullin, John; Vermont, 1846-1908 ***5900.10*** *p382*
Mullin, John 14 *SEE* Mullin, Mary
Mullin, John H.; Vermont, 1865-1901 ***5900.10*** *p382*
Mullin, Kate White; Vermont, 1858-1908 ***5900.10*** *p383*
Mullin, Katie; Vermont, 1863-1891 ***5900.10*** *p382*
Mullin, Margaret McGue; Vermont, 1844-1890 ***5900.10*** *p568*
Mullin, Margaret McGuirk; Vermont, 1850-1916 ***5900.10*** *p382*
Mullin, Mary; Vermont, 1828-1882 ***5900.10*** *p534*
Mullin, Mary 45; New York, New York, 1848 ***1825.45*** *p39*
Son: John 14
Mullin, Mary A. Tiernay; Vermont, 1849-1911 ***5900.10*** *p382*
Mullin, Mary Ann Riley; Vermont, 1843-1923 ***5900.10*** *p382*
Mullin, Mary McGee 72; Vermont, 1888 ***5900.10*** *p382*
Mullin, Mary O'Brien; Vermont, 1858-1945 ***5900.10*** *p120*
Mullin, Mary O'Neil 28; Vermont, 1886 ***5900.10*** *p584*
Mullin, Michael; Vermont, 1834-1912 ***5900.10*** *p568*
Mullin, Michael; Vermont, 1842-1928 ***5900.10*** *p382*
Mullin, Patrick; Vermont, 1829-1897 ***5900.10*** *p568*
Mullin, Patrick; Vermont, 1836-1905 ***5900.10*** *p382*
Mullin, Patrick; Vermont, 1856-1859 ***5900.10*** *p382*
Mullin, Thomas; Vermont, 1855-1924 ***5900.10*** *p120*
Mullin, Thomas 28; Vermont, 1868 ***5900.10*** *p382*
Mullin, Thomas 74; Vermont, 1892 ***5900.10*** *p108*

Mulliner, Samuel; New York, 1839 ***8197.10*** *p264*
Mullings, Mary A. 41; Vermont, 1915 ***5900.10*** *p126*
Mullings, William 22; Ontario, 1871 ***1823.15*** *p197*
Mullins, Catherine; Vermont, 1841-1912 ***5900.10*** *p135*
Mullins, Catherine 30; Ontario, 1871 ***1823.28*** *p75*
Mullins, Catherine Hennesey; Vermont, 1815-1882 ***5900.10*** *p135*
Mullins, Dennis; Vermont, 1850-1875 ***5900.10*** *p135*
Mullins, Honora; Vermont, 1847-1916 ***5900.10*** *p135*
Mullins, Isaac 24; Ontario, 1871 ***1823.15*** *p197*
Mullins, John; Vermont, n.d. ***5900.10*** *p156*
Mullins, John 60; Ontario, 1871 ***1823.28*** *p75*
Mullins, Mary A.; Vermont, 1848-1916 ***5900.10*** *p147*
Mullins, Simon; Virginia, 1671-1672 ***6212.30*** *p46*
Mullins, Stephen 35; Ontario, 1871 ***1823.28*** *p75*
Mullins, William; Virginia, 1621 ***1224.1*** *p41*
Mullony, John; Philadelphia, 1800 ***1224.3*** *p55*
Mullony, William; New York, 1827 ***8197.10*** *p344*
Mulloy, James; Vermont, 1840-1893 ***5900.10*** *p307*
Mulloy, Margaret McDermott; Vermont, 1842-1916 ***5900.10*** *p307*
Mullraine, Cornelius; Maryland, 1681 ***2524.55*** *p158*
Mullunly, Margdin 25; Maryland, 1774 ***1220.25*** *p78*
Mullvihill, Dominic; New York, 1838 ***8197.10*** *p377*
Muloney, Elizabeth; Vermont, 1858-1941 ***5900.10*** *p121*
Muloy, John 40; Ontario, 1871 ***1823.28*** *p75*
Mulper, Maria; Port uncertain, 1733 ***2856.30*** *p317*
Mulqueen, Ann McAvoy; Vermont, 1905 ***5900.10*** *p178*
Mulqueen, Ann Purcell; Vermont, 1841-1899 ***5900.10*** *p74*
Mulqueen, Bridget Farrell 69; Vermont, 1903 ***5900.10*** *p135*
Mulqueen, Daniel; Vermont, 1826-1914 ***5900.10*** *p547*
Mulqueen, Dennis 54; Vermont, 1882 ***5900.10*** *p135*
Mulqueen, Ellen 22; Vermont, 1880 ***5900.10*** *p135*
Mulqueen, John; Vermont, 1845-1906 ***5900.10*** *p74*
Mulqueen, John; Vermont, 1857-1932 ***5900.10*** *p186*
Mulqueen, John 37; Vermont, 1892 ***5900.10*** *p135*
Mulqueen, Margaret 75; Vermont, 1889 ***5900.10*** *p98*
Mulqueen, Mary; Vermont, 1858-1921 ***5900.10*** *p193*
Mulqueen, Mary; Vermont, 1862-1936 ***5900.10*** *p547*
Mulqueen, Mary E. Donahue; Vermont, 1857-1908 ***5900.10*** *p186*
Mulqueen, Mary F.; Vermont, 1838-1916 ***5900.10*** *p547*
Mulqueen, Michael; Vermont, 1876 ***5900.10*** *p178*
Mulqueen, Nora 54; Vermont, 1871 ***5900.10*** *p98*
Mulqueen, Patrick 52; Vermont, 1867 ***5900.10*** *p98*
Mulqueene, Catherine Powers 55; Vermont, 1879 ***5900.10*** *p170*
Mulqueene, Patrick; Vermont, 1823-1878 ***5900.10*** *p170*
Mulrady, Thomas; New York, 1840 ***8197.10*** *p182*
Mulraine, Alexander; Maryland, 1669 ***2524.55*** *p158*
Mulrang, Neil 52; Ontario, 1871 ***1823.28*** *p75*
Mulrean, Helena; Maryland, 1678 ***2524.55*** *p158*
Mulrooney, Michael; New York, 1839 ***8197.10*** *p383*
Mulroy, John 48; Ontario, 1871 ***1823.15*** *p197*
Mulroy, Michael 59; Ontario, 1871 ***1823.28*** *p75*
Mulson, Edward; New York, 1831 ***8197.10*** *p366*
Mulvaney, Barclay 52; Ontario, 1871 ***1823.22*** *p115*
Mulvaney, Bridget; Vermont, 1836-1914 ***5900.10*** *p475*
Mulvaney, Peter 46; Ontario, 1871 ***1823.22*** *p115*
Mulvany, Patrick 62; Vermont, 1896 ***5900.10*** *p345*
Mulveny, James; New York, 1831 ***8197.10*** *p365*
Mulvey, Allice 24; Vermont, 1857 ***5900.10*** *p560*
Mulvey, Bridget Hanley; Vermont, 1846-1917 ***5900.10*** *p266*
Mulvey, Jeremiah; Vermont, 1846-1918 ***5900.10*** *p266*
Mulvey, John; New York, 1839 ***8197.10*** *p141*
Mulvey, Mary Meehan 60; Vermont, 1864 ***5900.10*** *p571*
Mulvey, Patrick 26; Vermont, 1851 ***5900.10*** *p560*
Mulvey, Patrick 38; Vermont, 1844 ***5900.10*** *p611*
Mulvey, Peter; New York, 1839 ***8197.10*** *p141*
Mulvey, Roger; New York, 1816 ***8197.10*** *p59*
Mulvey, Thomas 65; Vermont, 1866 ***5900.10*** *p571*
Mulvihill, Daniel 90; Ontario, 1871 ***1823.28*** *p75*
Mulvihill, Ellen 60; Ontario, 1871 ***1823.28*** *p75*
Mulvihill, John; New York, 1838 ***8197.10*** *p376*
Mulvihill, Martin 40; Ontario, 1871 ***1823.28*** *p75*
Mulvihill, Martin 50; Ontario, 1871 ***1823.28*** *p75*
Mulvihill, Martin 60; Ontario, 1871 ***1823.28*** *p75*
Mulvihill, Michael 50; Ontario, 1871 ***1823.28*** *p75*
Mulvihill, Michael 54; Ontario, 1871 ***1823.28*** *p75*
Mulvihill, Thomas 60; Ontario, 1871 ***1823.28*** *p75*
Mulville, John; Baltimore, 1850 ***6058.10*** *p63*
Mulvyhill, Michael 40; Ontario, 1871 ***1823.28*** *p75*
Mumbac, Miss; America, 1754 ***2856.30*** *p442*
Mumbac, Miss; Port uncertain, 1767 ***2856.30*** *p442*
Mumbach, Agnes; America, 1767 ***2856.30*** *p309*
With husband
Mumford, Ann McGuire; Vermont, 1848-1875 ***5900.10*** *p581*
Mumford, Ann McNeil; Vermont, 1845-1906 ***5900.10*** *p579*
Mumford, Anna; Vermont, 1848 ***5900.10*** *p581*
Mumford, Brenton; Rhode Island, 1817 ***1224.3*** *p55*
Mumford, Bridget Difley; Vermont, 1844-1875 ***5900.10*** *p583*
Mumford, C.; Portland, Maine, 1858 ***9196.15*** *p29*
Mumford, Catherine; Vermont, n.d. ***5900.10*** *p565*
Mumford, Charles; Vermont, 1840-1906 ***5900.10*** *p581*
Mumford, Ellen Gaffney; Vermont, 1857-1899 ***5900.10*** *p562*
Mumford, George; Vermont, 1834-1899 ***5900.10*** *p583*
Mumford, James; Castleton, Vermont, 1833 ***5900.10*** *p7*
With wife
Mumford, John 40; Ontario, 1871 ***1823.22*** *p115*
Mumford, Margaret 54; Vermont, 1863 ***5900.10*** *p565*
Mumford, Mary; Vermont, 1851-1880 ***5900.10*** *p560*
Mumford, Patrick; Vermont, 1848-1922 ***5900.10*** *p562*
Mumford, Thomas; Maryland, 1662 ***2524.55*** *p158*
Mumford, Thomas J.; Vermont, 1841-1912 ***5900.10*** *p579*
Mumforth, Mary; Maryland, 1681 ***2524.55*** *p158*
Mun, Andrew 55; Ontario, 1871 ***1823.15*** *p197*
Mun, John; Maryland, 1665 ***2524.55*** *p158*
Muncaster, John 31; Ontario, 1871 ***1823.28*** *p75*
Muncey, Lancelott 58; Ontario, 1871 ***1823.22*** *p115*
Munch, Adam; Port uncertain, 1740 ***2856.30*** *p317*
Munch, Mrs. Dietrich; America, 1749 ***2856.30*** *p317*
Munch, Franziska; Port uncertain, 1784 ***2856.30*** *p318*
Munch, Georg; Port uncertain, 1734 ***2856.30*** *p317*
Munch, Georg; Port uncertain, 1736 ***2856.30*** *p318*
Munch, Georg; Port uncertain, 1784 ***2856.30*** *p318*
Munch, Georg Elias; Port uncertain, 1792 ***2856.30*** *p318*
With wife
Munch, Hans Georg; America, 1754 ***2856.30*** *p318*
Munch, J.; America, 1777 ***2856.30*** *p289*
Munch, J.; Port uncertain, 1762 ***2856.30*** *p289*
Munch, Jacob; Port uncertain, 1766 ***2856.30*** *p318*
Munch, Johann; Port uncertain, 1726 ***2856.30*** *p318*
Munch, Johann Henrich; Canada, 1751 ***2856.30*** *p318*
Munch, Johann Leonhard; Port uncertain, 1754 ***2856.30*** *p318*
Munch, Johann Peter; Port uncertain, 1785 ***2856.30*** *p318*
Munch, Magdalena; Port uncertain, 1729 ***2856.30*** *p318*
Munch, Maria Eva; Port uncertain, 1793 ***2856.30*** *p318*
Munch, Mathes; Port uncertain, 1774 ***2856.30*** *p318*
Munch, Peter; Port uncertain, 1753 ***2856.30*** *p318*
Munch, Philipp; America, 1754 ***2856.30*** *p318*
Munch, Simon; Port uncertain, 1764 ***2856.30*** *p318*
With family
Munch, Theodor; Port uncertain, 1775 ***2856.30*** *p318*
Munch, Theodor; Port uncertain, 1785 ***2856.30*** *p318*
Muncisryniski, Antonia; Maryland, 1910 ***3259.35*** *p41*
Muncke, Jno; Virginia, 1672 ***6212.30*** *p50*
Munckel, Johann Adam; Port uncertain, 1764 ***2856.30*** *p318*
Mund, Martha; Maryland, 1667 ***2524.55*** *p174*
Mundalla, Mr.; Quebec, 1857 ***9196.15*** *p27*
Munday, Alice Leonard; Vermont, 1810-1894 ***5900.10*** *p565*
Munday, Jane; Maryland, 1668 ***2524.55*** *p42*
Munday, John F.; Vermont, 1852-1904 ***5900.10*** *p565*
Munday, Joseph; Virginia, 1702 ***1224.2*** *p82*
Munday, Margaret A.; Vermont, 1849-1928 ***5900.10*** *p557*
Munday, Mary; Maryland, 1651 ***2524.55*** *p158*
Munday, Mary; Vermont, 1834-1916 ***5900.10*** *p565*
Munday, Richard; Virginia, 1738 ***1224.2*** *p82*
Munday, Thomas; Vermont, 1798-1892 ***5900.10*** *p565*
Munday, Will'm 26; Ontario, 1871 ***1823.28*** *p75*
Mundel, Bartel; Port uncertain, 1781 ***2856.30*** *p318*
Mundell, John; Pennsylvania, 1697 ***1224.1*** *p41*
Mundell, Stewart 41; Ontario, 1871 ***1823.15*** *p197*
Mundell, William 88; Ontario, 1871 ***1823.15*** *p197*
Mundell, William A.; New York, 1839 ***8197.10*** *p382*
Mundey, John; Virginia, 1666 ***6212.30*** *p29*
Mundle, John 76; Ontario, 1871 ***1823.28*** *p75*
Mundle, Samuel 55; Ontario, 1871 ***1823.22*** *p115*
Mundle, William 34; Ontario, 1871 ***1823.15*** *p197*
Mundy, Ann; Long Island, 1851 ***1224.3*** *p55*
Mundy, Ann; Vermont, 1915 ***5900.10*** *p580*
Mundy, Henry; New England, 1653 ***1224.1*** *p53*
Munford, Edward; Maryland, 1681 ***2524.55*** *p158*
Munford, William; Virginia, 1678 ***1224.1*** *p41*
Munich, Hans Georg; America, 1754 ***2856.30*** *p309*
Munich, Philipp; America, 1754 ***2856.30*** *p309*
Muniewsky, Pawel; Maryland, 1910 ***3259.35*** *p41*
Munly, Ann 30; Ontario, 1871 ***1823.22*** *p115*
Munn, Archibald; Newfoundland, 1877 ***1640.13*** *p81*
Munn, Duncan; Newfoundland, 1855 ***1640.13*** *p81*
Munn, Ellen; Vermont, 1839-1912 ***5900.10*** *p553*
Munn, Ira; Vermont, 1842-1913 ***5900.10*** *p553*
Munn, Jno; Virginia, 1665-1666 ***6212.30*** *p22*
Munn, John 21; Maryland, 1774 ***1220.25*** *p74*
Munn, John 57; Ontario, 1871 ***1823.15*** *p198*
Munn, Thomas; New York, 1838 ***8197.10*** *p124*
Munn, William; New York, New York, 1852 ***1224.3*** *p55*
Munnes, John; Maryland, 1653 ***2524.55*** *p158*
Munning, Benjamin 40; Ontario, 1871 ***1823.15*** *p198*
Munnings, George Garnett Husk; New York, 1855 ***1224.3*** *p55*
Munro, Mrs.; Quebec, 1857 ***9196.15*** *p14*
Munro, Alexander; Georgia, 1739 ***1640.10*** *p162*
Munro, Angus *SEE* Munro, John
Munro, Ann *SEE* Munro, John
Munro, Ann 56; Ontario, 1871 ***1823.15*** *p198*
Munro, Archie *SEE* Munro, John
Munro, Catherine *SEE* Munro, Donald
Munro, Catherine *SEE* Munro, John
Munro, Colin; Jamaica, 1800 ***1640.13*** *p81*
Munro, David; Mississippi, 1792 ***1640.10*** *p162*
Munro, Donald *SEE* Munro, John
Munro, Donald; Port uncertain, 1840-1849 ***4537.37*** *p131*
Wife: Nancy
Child: Catherine
Child: Mary
Munro, Ellen 52; Ontario, 1871 ***1823.22*** *p115*
Munro, George 48; Ontario, 1871 ***1823.28*** *p75*
Munro, Hugh; New York, 1805 ***8197.10*** *p29*
Munro, James; Georgia, 1741 ***1640.10*** *p162*
Wife: Janet McLeod
Munro, Janet McLeod *SEE* Munro, James
Munro, Jessie 60; Ontario, 1871 ***1823.22*** *p115*
Munro, Jno; Virginia, 1672 ***6212.30*** *p50*
Munro, John *SEE* Munro, John
Munro, John; Grenada, 1831 ***1640.13*** *p81*
Munro, John; New York, 1884 ***1640.13*** *p81*
Munro, John; Ontario, 1860-1869 ***4537.32*** *p87*
Wife: Mary MacLean
Child: Angus
Child: Archie
Child: Roderick
Child: Kirsty
Child: Ann
Child: Donald
Munro, John; Quebec, 1856 ***9196.15*** *p6*
Munro, John; Port uncertain, 1850-1859 ***4537.37*** *p132*
Wife: Margaret MacLellan
Child: Mary
Child: John
Child: Catherine
Munro, John 50; Ontario, 1871 ***1823.15*** *p198*
Munro, John 54; Ontario, 1871 ***1823.22*** *p115*
Munro, John 62; Ontario, 1871 ***1823.15*** *p198*
Munro, John 84; Ontario, 1871 ***1823.22*** *p115*
Munro, Kate; Ontario, 1851 ***4537.37*** *p54*
Munro, Kirsty *SEE* Munro, John
Munro, Kirsty; Port uncertain, 1850-1859 ***4537.35*** *p86*
Child: Rachel
Child: Mary
Munro, Kirsty; Port uncertain, 1850-1859 ***4537.37*** *p107*
Munro, Kristy; Ontario, 1870-1879 ***4537.32*** *p68*
Munro, Lilly 90; Ontario, 1871 ***1823.22*** *p115*
Munro, Malcom; Long Island, 1766 ***1224.2*** *p82*
Munro, Margaret; Ontario, 1850-1859 ***4537.37*** *p61*
Munro, Margaret Arnott; Nova Scotia, 1895 ***1640.13*** *p81*
Munro, Margaret MacLellan *SEE* Munro, John
Munro, Mary *SEE* Munro, Donald
Munro, Mary *SEE* Munro, John
Munro, Mary *SEE* Munro, Kirsty
Munro, Mary A. 31; Ontario, 1861 ***2896.25*** *p47*
Munro, Mary MacLean *SEE* Munro, John
Munro, Moses; St. Johns, Newfoundland, 1897 ***1640.13*** *p81*
Munro, Nancy *SEE* Munro, Donald
Munro, Neil 42; Ontario, 1871 ***1823.15*** *p198*
Munro, Rachel *SEE* Munro, Kirsty
Munro, Robert; Jamaica, 1829 ***1640.13*** *p81*
Munro, Roderick *SEE* Munro, John
Munro, Rupert 61; Ontario, 1871 ***1823.15*** *p198*
Munro, Simon; Georgia, 1763 ***1640.10*** *p162*
Munro, Simon 64; Ontario, 1871 ***1823.15*** *p198*
Munro, Susan 16; Ontario, 1861 ***2896.25*** *p19*
Munro, Sutherland 44; Ontario, 1871 ***1823.15*** *p198*
Munro, Thomas 64; Ontario, 1871 ***1823.15*** *p198*
Munro, William; Georgia, 1739 ***1640.10*** *p162*
Munro, William 40; Ontario, 1871 ***1823.15*** *p198*
Munroe, Alex 24; British Columbia, 1910 ***9196.1*** *p31*
Munroe, Alex 24; Seattle, 1910 ***9196.1*** *p31*
Munroe, Alexr 36; Ontario, 1871 ***1823.15*** *p198*
Munroe, Collin 65; Ontario, 1871 ***1823.15*** *p198*
Munroe, Elizabeth 36; Ontario, 1861 ***2896.25*** *p25*
Munroe, George W. 7; Ontario, 1861 ***2896.25*** *p25*
Munroe, James 26; Ontario, 1871 ***1823.15*** *p198*
Munroe, John 63; Ontario, 1871 ***1823.28*** *p75*
Munroe, John A. 9; Ontario, 1861 ***2896.25*** *p25*
Munroe, Martha A. 1; Ontario, 1861 ***2896.25*** *p25*
Munroe, Mary E. 3; Ontario, 1861 ***2896.25*** *p25*
Munroe, Neil 38; Ontario, 1871 ***1823.15*** *p198*

Munroe, Roderick 40; Ontario, 1871 ***1823.15*** *p198*
Munroe, Thomas; Virginia, 1815 ***1640.10*** *p162*
Munroe, William; Florida, 1819-1845 ***1640.10*** *p163*
Munroe, William 5; Ontario, 1861 ***2896.25*** *p25*
Munrow, Rodrick 22; Ontario, 1871 ***1823.22*** *p115*
Munrow, William 23; Ontario, 1861 ***2896.26*** *p35*
Munsey, Joseph 63; Ontario, 1871 ***1823.22*** *p115*
Munslin, Richard 50; Ontario, 1871 ***1823.22*** *p115*
Munson, Alfred E. 46; Ontario, 1871 ***1823.22*** *p115*
Munson, George; Ontario, 1871 ***1823.28*** *p75*
Munson, Hannah 66; Ontario, 1871 ***1823.22*** *p115*
Munsteiner, Johann Nikolaus; Port uncertain, 1773 ***2856.30*** *p318*
Munster, Catharina; Port uncertain, 1787 ***2856.30*** *p318*
Munster, Nikol; Port uncertain, 1783 ***2856.30*** *p318*
Munton, William 21; Maryland, 1775 ***1220.25*** *p115*
Muntz, Peter; Port uncertain, 1751 ***2856.30*** *p318*
Muntzer, Michael; Port uncertain, 1764 ***2856.30*** *p318*
Munz, Christof; America, 1752 ***2856.30*** *p318*
Munz, Michael; America, 1752 ***2856.30*** *p309*
Munzer, Johann Philipp; Port uncertain, 1714 ***2856.30*** *p318*
Munzer, Johann Philipp; Port uncertain, 1716 ***2856.30*** *p318*
Munzinger, Chatharina; Port uncertain, 1777 ***2856.30*** *p309*
Muquo, Mary 60; Ontario, 1871 ***1823.28*** *p75*
Muratrsky, Andrew; Maryland, 1910 ***3259.35*** *p41*
Murawski, Anna; Maryland, 1910 ***3259.35*** *p41*
Murchenson, Murdock 52; Ontario, 1871 ***1823.15*** *p198*
Murcheson, Danail 34; Ontario, 1871 ***1823.15*** *p198*
Murcheson, Donald 40; Ontario, 1871 ***1823.15*** *p198*
Murchie, Alexander 51; Ontario, 1871 ***1823.15*** *p198*
Murchie, Charles 54; Ontario, 1871 ***1823.15*** *p198*
Murchison, Alex 23; British Columbia, 1910 ***9196.1*** *p30*
Murchison, Alex 23; Seattle, 1910 ***9196.1*** *p30*
Murchison, Alexander *SEE* Murchison, Malcolm
Murchison, Catherine *SEE* Murchison, Malcolm
Murchison, Donald *SEE* Murchison, John
Murchison, Donald *SEE* Murchison, Malcolm
Murchison, Donald; Alabama, 1816-1819 ***1640.10*** *p163*
Murchison, Hugh *SEE* Murchison, John
Murchison, Jessie *SEE* Murchison, Malcolm
Murchison, John; Georgia, 1736 ***1640.10*** *p163*
Murchison, John; Port uncertain, 1840-1849 ***4537.37*** *p132*
Wife: Kirsty MacLellan
Child: Murdo
Child: Hugh
Child: Donald
Child: Margaret
Murchison, Kirsty MacLellan *SEE* Murchison, John
Murchison, Malcolm; Port uncertain, 1850-1859 ***4537.37*** *p132*
Child: Alexander
Child: Jessie
Child: Mary
Wife: Catherine
Child: Donald
Murchison, Margaret *SEE* Murchison, John
Murchison, Mary *SEE* Murchison, Malcolm
Murchison, Murdo *SEE* Murchison, John
Murchison, Murdoch 48; Ontario, 1871 ***1823.15*** *p198*
Murdie, Andrew 57; Ontario, 1871 ***1823.15*** *p198*
Murdiff, Alvin 14; Ontario, 1861 ***2896.27*** *p7*
Murdoch, Mr.; Quebec, 1856 ***9196.15*** *p8*
Murdoch, Alexander 40; Ontario, 1871 ***1823.15*** *p198*
Murdoch, Barbara 20; Ontario, 1871 ***1823.15*** *p198*
Murdoch, David Ritchie; Montreal, 1895 ***1640.13*** *p81*
Murdoch, Miss J.; Quebec, 1857 ***9196.15*** *p19*
Murdoch, James 37; Ontario, 1871 ***1823.15*** *p198*
Murdoch, James 47; Ontario, 1871 ***1823.28*** *p75*
Murdoch, John; America, 1844 ***1640.13*** *p82*
Murdoch, John; New York, 1806 ***8197.10*** *p325*
Murdoch, John 45; Ontario, 1871 ***1823.15*** *p198*
Murdoch, Miss M.; Quebec, 1857 ***9196.15*** *p19*
Murdoch, Mary 60; Ontario, 1871 ***1823.15*** *p198*
Murdoch, Robert; North America, 1759 ***1224.2*** *p82*
Murdoch, William 41; Ontario, 1871 ***1823.15*** *p198*
Murdock, Alexander; New York, 1839 ***8197.10*** *p264*
Murdock, Amelia 29; Ontario, 1861 ***2896.25*** *p15*
Murdock, Andrew; New York, 1812 ***1224.3*** *p55*
Murdock, Ann; Vermont, 1843-1922 ***5900.10*** *p161*
Murdock, Elizabeth 40; Ontario, 1871 ***1823.28*** *p75*
Murdock, George 52; Ontario, 1871 ***1823.15*** *p198*
Murdock, Green 29; Ontario, 1861 ***2896.25*** *p15*
Murdock, John; Pennsylvania, 1777 ***4629.10*** *p17*
Murdock, John 21; Virginia, 1774 ***1220.25*** *p141*
Murdock, Mary 34; Vermont, 1864 ***5900.10*** *p203*
Murdock, Mary McClelland; Vermont, 1840-1918 ***5900.10*** *p321*
Murdock, Robert; North America, 1759 ***1224.2*** *p82*
Murdock, Robert 41; Ontario, 1871 ***1823.22*** *p115*
Murdock, Samuel; Pennsylvania, 1777 ***4629.10*** *p22*
Murdock, Samuel; Pennsylvania, 1779 ***4629.10*** *p40*
Murdock, Samuel 19; Virginia, 1774 ***1220.25*** *p141*
Murdock, Thomas; New York, 1838 ***8197.10*** *p378*
Murdock, Thomas; Vermont, 1833-1908 ***5900.10*** *p321*
Murdock, Thomas 17; Virginia, 1774 ***1220.25*** *p141*
Murdough, John; New York, 1821 ***8197.10*** *p260*
Murdough, John; New York, 1826 ***8197.10*** *p336*
Murdy, Michael 34; Ontario, 1871 ***1823.15*** *p198*
Mure, James; California, 1892 ***1640.13*** *p82*
Mure, John; New Orleans, 1735-1845 ***1640.10*** *p163*
Murefort, Wm; Virginia, 1672-1673 ***6212.30*** *p51*
Murey, John 34; Ontario, 1871 ***1823.28*** *p75*
Murfy, Kate 57; Vermont, 1889 ***5900.10*** *p537*
Murgarnski, Andrew; Maryland, 1910 ***3259.35*** *p41*
Murgatroyd, Thomas; Pennsylvania, 1777 ***4629.10*** *p21*
Murgatroyd, Thomas; Pennsylvania, 1779 ***4629.10*** *p41*
Muriel, Ygnacio; Mexico, 1859 ***1640.13*** *p82*
Murley, Robert 27; Ontario, 1871 ***1823.15*** *p198*
Murly, John 49; Ontario, 1871 ***1823.15*** *p198*
Murly, Thomas; Virginia, 1666-1667 ***6212.30*** *p35*
Murnane, Ellen; Vermont, 1817-1913 ***5900.10*** *p115*
Murney, Miss; Quebec, 1856 ***9196.15*** *p9*
Murney, Miss; Quebec, 1857 ***9196.15*** *p25*
Murney, Mr.; Quebec, 1857 ***9196.15*** *p25*
Murney, Mrs.; Quebec, 1857 ***9196.15*** *p25*
Murney, E. S. 14; Ontario, 1861 ***2896.27*** *p7*
Murney, G. H. 25; Ontario, 1861 ***2896.27*** *p7*
Murney, George H. 6; Ontario, 1861 ***2896.25*** *p20*
Murney, John G. 2; Ontario, 1861 ***2896.25*** *p20*
Murney, L. 20; Ontario, 1861 ***2896.27*** *p7*
Murney, M. 27; Ontario, 1861 ***2896.27*** *p7*
Murney, M. J. 22; Ontario, 1861 ***2896.25*** *p46*
Murney, Peter J. 9; Ontario, 1861 ***2896.25*** *p20*
Murney, Sarah 51; Ontario, 1861 ***2896.27*** *p7*
Murney, Sarah M. 30; Ontario, 1861 ***2896.25*** *p20*
Murney, William R. 5; Ontario, 1861 ***2896.25*** *p20*
Muro, Margery 32; Ontario, 1871 ***1823.22*** *p115*
Muroock, James 54; Ontario, 1871 ***1823.15*** *p198*
Murphey, Dennis 62; Ontario, 1871 ***1823.15*** *p198*
Murphey, Ellen; Vermont, n.d. ***5900.10*** *p68*
Murphey, Hannah; Vermont, 1866-1950 ***5900.10*** *p122*
Murphey, Honora; Maryland, 1678 ***2524.55*** *p158*
Murphey, James 26; Ontario, 1871 ***1823.28*** *p75*
Murphey, Jno; Virginia, 1668-1669 ***6212.30*** *p40*
Murphey, John; Maryland, 1682 ***2524.55*** *p158*
Murphey, John; Virginia, 1672 ***6212.30*** *p49*
Murphey, Owen; Virginia, 1668-1669 ***6212.30*** *p40*
Murphey, Richard 33; Ontario, 1871 ***1823.28*** *p75*
Murphey, Susan M. Shannon 28; Vermont, 1879 ***5900.10*** *p289*
Murphy, . . .; New Hampshire, 1641-1660 ***4628.40*** *p44*
Murphy, Mr.; Quebec, 1856 ***9196.15*** *p6*
Murphy, Mr.; Quebec, 1858 ***9196.15*** *p32*
Murphy, Mr.; Vermont, n.d. ***5900.10*** *p476*
Murphy, Mrs.; Quebec, 1858 ***9196.15*** *p32*
Murphy, Mrs.; Vermont, n.d. ***5900.10*** *p476*
Murphy, Alice; Vermont, 1829-1912 ***5900.10*** *p531*
Murphy, Alice; Vermont, 1851-1930 ***5900.10*** *p472*
Murphy, Alice E. Finnegan; Vermont, 1856-1919 ***5900.10*** *p187*
Murphy, Angaline 31; Ontario, 1861 ***2896.25*** *p11*
Murphy, Ann; Vermont, 1823-1896 ***5900.10*** *p472*
Murphy, Ann 48; Vermont, 1892 ***5900.10*** *p239*
Murphy, Ann 62; Vermont, 1887 ***5900.10*** *p485*
Murphy, Ann 74; Vermont, 1887 ***5900.10*** *p165*
Murphy, Ann Hogan; Vermont, 1837-1910 ***5900.10*** *p162*
Murphy, Ann R.; Vermont, 1916 ***5900.10*** *p183*
Murphy, Anna; Vermont, 1870-1958 ***5900.10*** *p202*
Murphy, Anna K. 77; Vermont, 1922 ***5900.10*** *p445*
Murphy, Anna M.; Vermont, 1853-1933 ***5900.10*** *p131*
Murphy, Anna Regan; Vermont, 1869-1960 ***5900.10*** *p391*
Murphy, Annie; Vermont, 1851-1872 ***5900.10*** *p86*
Murphy, Annie 35; Vermont, 1889 ***5900.10*** *p94*
Murphy, Annie 74; Vermont, 1906 ***5900.10*** *p42*
Murphy, Annie Horey; Vermont, 1848-1926 ***5900.10*** *p353*
Murphy, Anthony 2; Ontario, 1861 ***2896.28*** *p36*
Murphy, Archibald 45; Ontario, 1871 ***1823.15*** *p198*
Murphy, B. 26; Maryland, 1774 ***1220.25*** *p7*
Murphy, Bartley; New York, 1840 ***8197.10*** *p178*
Murphy, Bertha M. Nutting; Vermont, 1874-1924 ***5900.10*** *p406*
Murphy, Bridget; Vermont, 1816-1880 ***5900.10*** *p268*
Murphy, Bridget; Vermont, 1829-1914 ***5900.10*** *p486*
Murphy, Bridget; Vermont, 1835-1911 ***5900.10*** *p248*
Murphy, Bridget; Vermont, 1846-1885 ***5900.10*** *p539*
Murphy, Bridget; Vermont, 1862-1936 ***5900.10*** *p439*
Murphy, Bridget; Vermont, 1898 ***5900.10*** *p541*
Murphy, Bridget; Vermont, 1914 ***5900.10*** *p447*
Murphy, Bridget 30; Ontario, 1871 ***1823.22*** *p115*
Murphy, Bridget McGrath; Vermont, 1861-1942 ***5900.10*** *p128*
Murphy, Bridget Sullivan; Vermont, 1856-1918 ***5900.10*** *p327*
Murphy, Bryan; Maryland, 1682 ***2524.55*** *p158*
Murphy, Caroline M. 2; Ontario, 1861 ***2896.25*** *p11*
Murphy, Catharine E.; Vermont, 1841-1865 ***5900.10*** *p480*
Murphy, Catharine Kelly 88; Vermont, 1869 ***5900.10*** *p479*
Murphy, Catharine Quinn; Vermont, 1810-1884 ***5900.10*** *p480*
Murphy, Catherine; Vermont, 1826-1905 ***5900.10*** *p475*
Murphy, Catherine; Vermont, 1851-1913 ***5900.10*** *p120*
Murphy, Catherine; Vermont, 1861 ***5900.10*** *p446*
Murphy, Catherine; Vermont, 1869-1927 ***5900.10*** *p255*
Murphy, Catherine 38; Vermont, 1885 ***5900.10*** *p163*
Murphy, Catherine 69; Ontario, 1871 ***1823.22*** *p115*
Murphy, Catherine 70; Vermont, 1870 ***5900.10*** *p163*
Murphy, Catherine 83; Vermont, 1910 ***5900.10*** *p540*
Murphy, Catherine Cain 45; Vermont, 1870 ***5900.10*** *p573*
Murphy, Catherine Dwyer; Vermont, 1896 ***5900.10*** *p116*
Murphy, Catherine H. Flynn; Vermont, 1854-1917 ***5900.10*** *p563*
Murphy, Catherine Monahan; Vermont, 1849-1924 ***5900.10*** *p131*
Murphy, Charles 27; Maryland, 1775 ***1220.25*** *p96*
Murphy, Christopher 67; Ontario, 1871 ***1823.28*** *p75*
Murphy, Cornelius; Vermont, 1817-1897 ***5900.10*** *p619*
Murphy, Daniel; Canada, 1756-1760 ***4628.40*** *p45*
Murphy, Daniel; Maryland, 1681 ***2524.55*** *p158*
Murphy, Daniel; New York, 1840 ***8197.10*** *p180*
Murphy, Daniel 6; Vermont, 1868 ***5900.10*** *p364*
Murphy, Daniel 70; Vermont, 1869 ***5900.10*** *p341*
Murphy, Daniel, II; Canada, 1756-1760 ***4628.40*** *p46*
Murphy, Daniel E.; Vermont, 1866-1949 ***5900.10*** *p406*
Murphy, Daniell; Maryland, 1680 ***2524.55*** *p158*
Murphy, David; Vermont, 1861-1901 ***5900.10*** *p459*
Murphy, David 44; Ontario, 1861 ***2896.27*** *p66*
Murphy, Davis 20; Ontario, 1861 ***2896.25*** *p11*
Murphy, Deborah; Ontario, 1861 ***2896.27*** *p66*
Murphy, Deborah 12; Ontario, 1861 ***2896.25*** *p11*
Murphy, Deborah 19; Ontario, 1861 ***2896.27*** *p64*
Murphy, Denis 45; Ontario, 1861 ***2896.28*** *p9*
Murphy, Dennis; New York, 1837 ***8197.10*** *p99*
Murphy, Dennis M. 43; Vermont, 1893 ***5900.10*** *p131*
Murphy, Dewey; Vermont, 1901 ***5900.10*** *p459*
Murphy, Edward; Maryland, 1681 ***2524.55*** *p158*
Murphy, Edward; Vermont, 1885-1960 ***5900.10*** *p255*
Murphy, Edward 36; Vermont, 1874 ***5900.10*** *p163*
Murphy, Edward 67; Vermont, 1883 ***5900.10*** *p298*
Murphy, Edward 70; Vermont, 1893 ***5900.10*** *p350*
Murphy, Edward 71; Vermont, 1893 ***5900.10*** *p387*
Murphy, Edward D. 40; Vermont, 1885 ***5900.10*** *p61*
Murphy, Edward F. 21; Vermont, 1882 ***5900.10*** *p298*
Murphy, Edward J.; Vermont, 1824-1910 ***5900.10*** *p89*
Murphy, Edward Patrick; Vermont, 1898-1936 ***5900.10*** *p256*
Murphy, Eliza; Vermont, 1843-1903 ***5900.10*** *p274*
Murphy, Eliza; Vermont, 1843-1927 ***5900.10*** *p348*
Murphy, Eliza 2; Vermont, 1872 ***5900.10*** *p486*
Murphy, Eliza 50; Vermont, 1893 ***5900.10*** *p131*
Murphy, Elizabeth; Vermont, n.d. ***5900.10*** *p266*
Murphy, Elizabeth; Vermont, 1866-1873 ***5900.10*** *p531*
Murphy, Elizabeth 30; Ontario, 1871 ***1823.15*** *p198*
Murphy, Elizabeth 65; Vermont, 1909 ***5900.10*** *p152*
Murphy, Elizabeth Brearton; Vermont, 1867-1942 ***5900.10*** *p256*
Murphy, Elizabeth Finnessy 87; Vermont, 1920 ***5900.10*** *p141*
Murphy, Elizabeth T.; Vermont, 1847-1906 ***5900.10*** *p52*
Murphy, Ellen; Quebec, 1858 ***9196.15*** *p32*
Murphy, Ellen; Vermont, n.d. ***5900.10*** *p266*
Murphy, Ellen; Vermont, 1821-1879 ***5900.10*** *p63*
Murphy, Ellen; Vermont, 1859-1935 ***5900.10*** *p95*
Murphy, Ellen 50; Vermont, 1882 ***5900.10*** *p345*
Murphy, Ellen 74; Vermont, 1919 ***5900.10*** *p464*
Murphy, Ellen 82; Vermont, 1913 ***5900.10*** *p204*
Murphy, Ellen Bethel; Vermont, 1854-1928 ***5900.10*** *p397*
Murphy, Ellen Bunney; Vermont, n.d. ***5900.10*** *p266*
Murphy, Ellen G. Smith; Vermont, 1859-1937 ***5900.10*** *p452*
Murphy, Ellen Harrington 46; Vermont, 1895 ***5900.10*** *p408*
Murphy, Ellen Rourke; Vermont, 1847-1930 ***5900.10*** *p82*
Murphy, Ellen Sullivan; Vermont, 1850-1942 ***5900.10*** *p115*
Murphy, Ellen Walsh; Vermont, 1852-1948 ***5900.10*** *p277*
Murphy, Emily; Vermont, n.d. ***5900.10*** *p60*

Murphy, Eurila A. 7; Ontario, 1861 ***2896.25*** *p11*
Murphy, Florence Foster; Vermont, 1878-1927 ***5900.10*** *p255*
Murphy, Francis; Vermont, 1832-1906 ***5900.10*** *p299*
Murphy, Francis H.; Vermont, 1856-1877 ***5900.10*** *p619*
Murphy, Francis T.; Vermont, 1853-1944 ***5900.10*** *p299*
Murphy, Frank J.; Vermont, 1875-1968 ***5900.10*** *p490*
Murphy, Frederick 11 months; Vermont, n.d. ***5900.10*** *p115*
Murphy, George T.; Vermont, 1887-1934 ***5900.10*** *p256*
Murphy, H. 35; Ontario, 1861 ***2896.27*** *p1*
Murphy, Hail; Quebec, 1858 ***9196.15*** *p32*
Murphy, Hannah; Vermont, 1842-1926 ***5900.10*** *p586*
Murphy, Hannorah 24; Vermont, 1869 ***5900.10*** *p345*
Murphy, Hanora; Vermont, 1841-1892 ***5900.10*** *p592*
Murphy, Hanora Cashman; Vermont, 1828-1908 ***5900.10*** *p590*
Murphy, Harriet Rose; Vermont, 1832-1909 ***5900.10*** *p89*
Murphy, Helen; Vermont, 1889-1916 ***5900.10*** *p131*
Murphy, Helen M.; Vermont, 1885-1946 ***5900.10*** *p256*
Murphy, Helena; Vermont, n.d. ***5900.10*** *p476*
Murphy, Henry 29; Vermont, 1887 ***5900.10*** *p297*
Murphy, Henry F.; Vermont, 1899-1965 ***5900.10*** *p256*
Murphy, Hercules 56; Ontario, 1871 ***1823.28*** *p75*
Murphy, Honor; Maryland, 1682 ***2524.55*** *p158*
Murphy, Hugh; Vermont, 1826 ***5900.10*** *p13*
Murphy, J.; Portland, Maine, 1858 ***9196.15*** *p30*
Murphy, J. B. 41; Vermont, 1895 ***5900.10*** *p434*
Murphy, James; New York, 1821 ***8197.10*** *p259*
Murphy, James; New York, 1837 ***8197.10*** *p263*
Murphy, James; New York, 1840 ***8197.10*** *p180*
Murphy, James; Quebec, 1858 ***9196.15*** *p32*
Murphy, James; Vermont, 1813-1897 ***5900.10*** *p531*
Murphy, James; Vermont, 1822-1868 ***5900.10*** *p72*
Murphy, James; Vermont, 1825-1901 ***5900.10*** *p297*
Murphy, James; Vermont, 1860-1924 ***5900.10*** *p452*
Murphy, James; Vermont, 1864-1900 ***5900.10*** *p273*
Murphy, James; Vermont, 1870-1934 ***5900.10*** *p163*
Murphy, James 24; Ontario, 1871 ***1823.28*** *p75*
Murphy, James 25; Philadelphia, 1774 ***1220.25*** *p23*
Murphy, James 30; Ontario, 1871 ***1823.15*** *p198*
Murphy, James 38; Ontario, 1871 ***1823.22*** *p115*
Murphy, James 45; Ontario, 1871 ***1823.28*** *p75*
Murphy, James 50; Ontario, 1871 ***1823.28*** *p75*
Murphy, James 68; Vermont, 1885 ***5900.10*** *p619*
Murphy, James 75; Vermont, 1870 ***5900.10*** *p514*
Murphy, James 88; Vermont, 1912 ***5900.10*** *p434*
Murphy, James, Sr. 50; Ontario, 1871 ***1823.28*** *p75*
Murphy, James C. 31; Vermont, 1886 ***5900.10*** *p364*
Murphy, James M.; Vermont, 1874-1935 ***5900.10*** *p490*
Murphy, James P.; Vermont, 1856-1913 ***5900.10*** *p397*
Murphy, James P.; Vermont, 1862 ***5900.10*** *p125*
Murphy, Jane; Quebec, 1858 ***9196.15*** *p32*
Murphy, Jane; Vermont, 1863-1949 ***5900.10*** *p185*
Murphy, Jane 20; New York, New York, 1850 ***1825.45*** *p52*
Murphy, Jennie 27; Vermont, 1896 ***5900.10*** *p297*
Murphy, Jeremiah 23; Virginia, 1774 ***1220.25*** *p89*
Murphy, Jeremiah J.; Vermont, 1850-1912 ***5900.10*** *p447*
Murphy, Johanna; Vermont, 1829-1911 ***5900.10*** *p348*
Murphy, Johanna; Vermont, 1856-1919 ***5900.10*** *p120*
Murphy, Johanna 20; New York, New York, 1850 ***1825.45*** *p52*
Murphy, Johanna 60; Vermont, 1876 ***5900.10*** *p337*
Murphy, Johanna 85; Vermont, 1876 ***5900.10*** *p57*
Murphy, Johanna 85; Vermont, 1935 ***5900.10*** *p116*
Murphy, John; Boston, 1833 ***8197.10*** *p124*
Murphy, John; Maryland, 1682 ***2524.55*** *p158*
Murphy, John; New York, 1804 ***8197.10*** *p27*
Murphy, John; New York, 1818 ***8197.10*** *p259*
Murphy, John; New York, 1821 ***8197.10*** *p259*
Murphy, John; New York, 1826 ***8197.10*** *p336*
Murphy, John; New York, 1827-1831 ***8197.10*** *p309*
Murphy, John; New York, 1838 ***8197.10*** *p124*
Murphy, John; New York, 1838 ***8197.10*** *p263*
Murphy, John; New York, 1840 ***8197.10*** *p179*
Murphy, John; New York, 1840 ***8197.10*** *p265*
Murphy, John; New York, New York, 1853 ***3437.14*** *p112*
Murphy, John; New York, New York, 1857 ***3437.14*** *p57*
Murphy, John; Quebec, 1858 ***9196.15*** *p32*
Murphy, John; Vermont, n.d. ***5900.10*** *p476*
Murphy, John; Vermont, 1756-1841 ***5900.10*** *p606*
Murphy, John; Vermont, 1845-1945 ***5900.10*** *p586*
Murphy, John; Vermont, 1848-1921 ***5900.10*** *p277*
Murphy, John; Vermont, 1849-1927 ***5900.10*** *p333*
Murphy, John; Vermont, 1855-1872 ***5900.10*** *p531*
Murphy, John; Vermont, 1855-1907 ***5900.10*** *p275*
Murphy, John; Vermont, 1883 ***5900.10*** *p337*
Murphy, John; Vermont, 1894-1994 ***5900.10*** *p254*
Murphy, John 1; Ontario, 1861 ***2896.28*** *p36*
Murphy, John 8; Vermont, 1847 ***5900.10*** *p499*
Murphy, John 26; Ontario, 1871 ***1823.15*** *p198*
Murphy, John 35; Ontario, 1871 ***1823.28*** *p75*
Murphy, John 35; Vermont, 1880 ***5900.10*** *p204*
Murphy, John 40; Vermont, 1888 ***5900.10*** *p116*
Murphy, John 43; Vermont, 1883 ***5900.10*** *p288*
Murphy, John 45; Ontario, 1871 ***1823.22*** *p115*
Murphy, John 49; Ontario, 1861 ***2896.25*** *p11*
Murphy, John 53; Ontario, 1871 ***1823.28*** *p75*
Murphy, John 54; Vermont, 1886 ***5900.10*** *p486*
Murphy, John 55; Vermont, 1860 ***5900.10*** *p575*
Murphy, John 60; Ontario, 1871 ***1823.28*** *p75*
Murphy, John 71; Vermont, 1886 ***5900.10*** *p590*
Murphy, John 73; Vermont, 1900 ***5900.10*** *p573*
Murphy, John 77; Vermont, 1894 ***5900.10*** *p540*
Murphy, John 82; Vermont, 1924 ***5900.10*** *p590*
Murphy, John C.; Vermont, n.d. ***5900.10*** *p60*
Murphy, John C.; Vermont, 1867-1940 ***5900.10*** *p120*
Murphy, John D. 4; Ontario, 1861 ***2896.25*** *p11*
Murphy, John H.; Vermont, 1846-1941 ***5900.10*** *p291*
Murphy, John J.; Vermont, 1855-1927 ***5900.10*** *p69*
Murphy, John L.; Vermont, 1861-1940 ***5900.10*** *p128*
Murphy, John P.; Vermont, 1857-1916 ***5900.10*** *p90*
Murphy, John S. 68; Vermont, 1903 ***5900.10*** *p183*
Murphy, John W.; Vermont, 1860-1922 ***5900.10*** *p391*
Murphy, Jonathan 8; Ontario, 1861 ***2896.27*** *p64*
Murphy, Joseph; Vermont, 1867-1913 ***5900.10*** *p348*
Murphy, Joseph 45; Alaska, 1912 ***9196.1*** *p19*
Murphy, Joseph 45; British Columbia, 1912 ***9196.1*** *p19*
Murphy, Joseph M.; Vermont, 1872-1946 ***5900.10*** *p354*
Murphy, Josephine; Quebec, 1858 ***9196.15*** *p32*
Murphy, Josephine E.; Vermont, 1876-1956 ***5900.10*** *p116*
Murphy, Josiah 13; Ontario, 1861 ***2896.27*** *p64*
Murphy, Julia; Vermont, 1829-1896 ***5900.10*** *p300*
Murphy, Julia 11; Vermont, 1868 ***5900.10*** *p364*
Murphy, Julia 89; Vermont, 1905 ***5900.10*** *p602*
Murphy, Julia A.; Vermont, 1849-1921 ***5900.10*** *p510*
Murphy, Julia Butler; Vermont, 1889 ***5900.10*** *p273*
Murphy, Julia Hodges; Vermont, 1869-1952 ***5900.10*** *p163*
Murphy, Julia M.; Vermont, 1896-1975 ***5900.10*** *p256*
Murphy, Julia Poule 76; Vermont, 1896 ***5900.10*** *p434*
Murphy, Julie 39; Vermont, 1858 ***5900.10*** *p44*
Murphy, Kate McNamara; Vermont, 1858-1905 ***5900.10*** *p391*
Murphy, Katherine; Vermont, 1850-1922 ***5900.10*** *p59*
Murphy, Katherine A.; Vermont, 1881-1939 ***5900.10*** *p116*
Murphy, Katherine Walton 50; Vermont, 1895 ***5900.10*** *p108*
Murphy, Katie 7; Vermont, 1872 ***5900.10*** *p486*
Murphy, Katie 24; Vermont, 1879 ***5900.10*** *p204*
Murphy, Kattie; Vermont, 1879 ***5900.10*** *p222*
Murphy, Laurance C. 31; Vermont, 1862 ***5900.10*** *p518*
Murphy, Lizzie C. 50; Vermont, 1890 ***5900.10*** *p364*
Murphy, Lolita J. Moody; Vermont, 1885-1933 ***5900.10*** *p490*
Murphy, Mable J. Leach; Vermont, 1875-1924 ***5900.10*** *p120*
Murphy, Margaret; Vermont, n.d. ***5900.10*** *p266*
Murphy, Margaret; Vermont, 1814-1895 ***5900.10*** *p61*
Murphy, Margaret; Vermont, 1831-1894 ***5900.10*** *p46*
Murphy, Margaret; Vermont, 1835-1926 ***5900.10*** *p299*
Murphy, Margaret; Vermont, 1868-1949 ***5900.10*** *p531*
Murphy, Margaret 24; Vermont, 1875 ***5900.10*** *p345*
Murphy, Margaret 45; Vermont, 1877 ***5900.10*** *p471*
Murphy, Margaret 69; Vermont, 1902 ***5900.10*** *p350*
Murphy, Margaret 76; Vermont, 1905 ***5900.10*** *p364*
Murphy, Margaret 85; Vermont, 1898 ***5900.10*** *p139*
Murphy, Margaret 96; Vermont, 1885 ***5900.10*** *p350*
Murphy, Margaret Barron; Vermont, 1868-1946 ***5900.10*** *p256*
Murphy, Margaret Callaghan 62; Vermont, 1887 ***5900.10*** *p619*
Murphy, Margaret E.; Vermont, 1859-1917 ***5900.10*** *p542*
Murphy, Margaret E.; Vermont, 1872-1910 ***5900.10*** *p481*
Murphy, Margaret E.; Vermont, 1873-1949 ***5900.10*** *p116*
Murphy, Margaret Hannan; Vermont, 1861-1923 ***5900.10*** *p125*
Murphy, Margaret O'Brine 77; Vermont, 1915 ***5900.10*** *p587*
Murphy, Margaret O'Connor; Vermont, 1817-1849 ***5900.10*** *p606*
Murphy, Margaret S.; Vermont, 1852-1928 ***5900.10*** *p447*
Murphy, Margaret T.; Vermont, 1833-1897 ***5900.10*** *p83*
Murphy, Marguerite; Vermont, 1902 ***5900.10*** *p256*
Murphy, Mariah 42; Ontario, 1861 ***2896.27*** *p62*
Murphy, Martin; New York, 1840 ***8197.10*** *p181*
Murphy, Martin A.; Vermont, 1850-1924 ***5900.10*** *p419*
Murphy, Martin T.; Vermont, 1863-1935 ***5900.10*** *p120*
Murphy, Mary; Maryland, 1681 ***2524.55*** *p158*
Murphy, Mary; Vermont, n.d. ***5900.10*** *p476*
Murphy, Mary; Vermont, n.d. ***5900.10*** *p481*
Murphy, Mary; Vermont, 1821-1902 ***5900.10*** *p279*
Murphy, Mary; Vermont, 1838-1919 ***5900.10*** *p221*
Murphy, Mary; Vermont, 1846-1904 ***5900.10*** *p609*
Murphy, Mary; Vermont, 1853-1870 ***5900.10*** *p86*
Murphy, Mary; Vermont, 1858-1875 ***5900.10*** *p268*
Murphy, Mary; Vermont, 1858-1938 ***5900.10*** *p119*
Murphy, Mary; Vermont, 1861-1919 ***5900.10*** *p274*
Murphy, Mary; Vermont, 1877-1899 ***5900.10*** *p459*
Murphy, Mary; Vermont, 1893 ***5900.10*** *p459*
Murphy, Mary; Vermont, 1900-1977 ***5900.10*** *p351*
Murphy, Mary 25; Ontario, 1871 ***1823.15*** *p199*
Murphy, Mary 32; Vermont, 1847 ***5900.10*** *p610*
Murphy, Mary 40; Ontario, 1871 ***1823.28*** *p76*
Murphy, Mary 40; Vermont, 1876 ***5900.10*** *p470*
Murphy, Mary 40; Vermont, 1886 ***5900.10*** *p389*
Murphy, Mary 60; Vermont, 1901 ***5900.10*** *p589*
Murphy, Mary 65; Vermont, 1888 ***5900.10*** *p447*
Murphy, Mary 75; Vermont, 1890 ***5900.10*** *p176*
Murphy, Mary 76; Vermont, 1885 ***5900.10*** *p341*
Murphy, Mary 86; Vermont, 1890 ***5900.10*** *p341*
Murphy, Mary 96; Vermont, 1915 ***5900.10*** *p92*
Murphy, Mary A.; Vermont, 1857-1934 ***5900.10*** *p69*
Murphy, Mary A.; Vermont, 1859-1935 ***5900.10*** *p419*
Murphy, Mary A.; Vermont, 1861-1899 ***5900.10*** *p162*
Murphy, Mary A.; Vermont, 1861-1933 ***5900.10*** *p90*
Murphy, Mary A.; Vermont, 1864-1921 ***5900.10*** *p158*
Murphy, Mary A.; Vermont, 1876-1933 ***5900.10*** *p489*
Murphy, Mary A. 8; Ontario, 1861 ***2896.25*** *p11*
Murphy, Mary A. 20; Ontario, 1861 ***2896.28*** *p36*
Murphy, Mary A. 41; Vermont, 1902 ***5900.10*** *p364*
Murphy, Mary A. 83; Vermont, 1937 ***5900.10*** *p473*
Murphy, Mary A. Smith; Vermont, 1861-1944 ***5900.10*** *p292*
Murphy, Mary Ann 25; Vermont, 1858 ***5900.10*** *p479*
Murphy, Mary Ann 85; Vermont, 1943 ***5900.10*** *p185*
Murphy, Mary Ann Mullen; Vermont, 1856-1920 ***5900.10*** *p224*
Murphy, Mary Connor; Vermont, n.d. ***5900.10*** *p350*
Murphy, Mary Cummings; Vermont, 1930-1999 ***5900.10*** *p254*
Murphy, Mary E.; Vermont, 1864-1941 ***5900.10*** *p129*
Murphy, Mary E.; Vermont, 1879-1891 ***5900.10*** *p222*
Murphy, Mary E. O'Brien; Vermont, 1854-1943 ***5900.10*** *p420*
Murphy, Mary E. Powers; Vermont, 1874-1953 ***5900.10*** *p354*
Murphy, Mary E. Rivers; Vermont, 1861-1902 ***5900.10*** *p126*
Murphy, Mary Flood; Vermont, 1831-1888 ***5900.10*** *p83*
Murphy, Mary Glynn 82; Vermont, 1907 ***5900.10*** *p94*
Murphy, Mary Hogan; Vermont, 1835-1910 ***5900.10*** *p297*
Murphy, Mary J.; Vermont, 1856-1919 ***5900.10*** *p490*
Murphy, Mary J. Hickey; Vermont, 1851-1911 ***5900.10*** *p299*
Murphy, Mary McDermott; Vermont, 1866-1940 ***5900.10*** *p273*
Murphy, Mary Muldoon; Vermont, 1820-1899 ***5900.10*** *p75*
Murphy, Mary Nolan; Vermont, 1825-1888 ***5900.10*** *p86*
Murphy, Mary S. 1; Vermont, n.d. ***5900.10*** *p119*
Murphy, Mary Tully; Vermont, n.d. ***5900.10*** *p119*
Murphy, Mary Vaughn; Vermont, 1819-1913 ***5900.10*** *p619*
Murphy, Mary Whalen 52; Vermont, 1894 ***5900.10*** *p348*
Murphy, Matthew 45; Ontario, 1871 ***1823.28*** *p76*
Murphy, Maurice; Maryland, 1682 ***2524.55*** *p158*
Murphy, Michael; New York, 1830 ***8197.10*** *p262*
Murphy, Michael; New York, 1833 ***8197.10*** *p358*
Murphy, Michael; New York, 1837 ***8197.10*** *p99*
Murphy, Michael; New York, 1840 ***8197.10*** *p179*
Murphy, Michael; Pennsylvania, 1868 ***6058.10*** *p77*
Murphy, Michael; Vermont, n.d. ***5900.10*** *p207*
Murphy, Michael; Vermont, 1831-1907 ***5900.10*** *p83*
Murphy, Michael; Vermont, 1834-1882 ***5900.10*** *p75*
Murphy, Michael; Vermont, 1853-1936 ***5900.10*** *p408*
Murphy, Michael; Vermont, 1857-1922 ***5900.10*** *p224*
Murphy, Michael 22; Maryland, 1775 ***1220.25*** *p121*
Murphy, Michael 43; Vermont, 1865 ***5900.10*** *p541*
Murphy, Michael 49; Ontario, 1871 ***1823.22*** *p115*
Murphy, Michael 50; Ontario, 1871 ***1823.15*** *p199*
Murphy, Michael 58; Ontario, 1871 ***1823.15*** *p199*
Murphy, Michael C.; Vermont, 1857-1888 ***5900.10*** *p563*
Murphy, Michael H.; New York, 1836 ***8197.10*** *p79*
Murphy, Michael J. 33; Vermont, 1873 ***5900.10*** *p152*
Murphy, Michael T. 34; Vermont, 1880 ***5900.10*** *p82*
Murphy, Minnie; Vermont, n.d. ***5900.10*** *p194*
Murphy, Morris; Maryland, 1682 ***2524.55*** *p158*
Murphy, Moses 83; Vermont, 1884 ***5900.10*** *p163*
Murphy, Nellie O'Brien; Vermont, 1858-1922 ***5900.10*** *p275*

Murphy, Nellie Riordan 73; Vermont, 1882 5900.10 p593
Murphy, Nora W. Kennedy; Vermont, 1867-1942 5900.10 p166
Murphy, Owen; New York, 1836 8197.10 p263
Murphy, Owen; Vermont, 1804-1885 5900.10 p268
Murphy, Owen A.; Vermont, 1832-1881 5900.10 p479
Murphy, Owen H.; Vermont, 1879-1918 5900.10 p479
Murphy, Owen L.; Vermont, 1830-1908 5900.10 p69
Murphy, Owny; Maryland, 1682 2524.55 p158
Murphy, Patrick; Maryland, 1682 2524.55 p158
Murphy, Patrick; New York, 1835 8197.10 p263
Murphy, Patrick; New York, 1840 8197.10 p178
Murphy, Patrick; New York, 1840 8197.10 p180
Murphy, Patrick; Vermont, 1833-1898 5900.10 p162
Murphy, Patrick 12; Vermont, 1887 5900.10 p141
Murphy, Patrick 25; Ontario, 1871 1823.15 p199
Murphy, Patrick 35; Vermont, 1885 5900.10 p108
Murphy, Patrick 38; Ontario, 1871 1823.22 p115
Murphy, Patrick 55; Ontario, 1871 1823.28 p76
Murphy, Patrick 56; Ontario, 1861 2896.27 p62
Murphy, Patrick 62; Vermont, 1889 5900.10 p116
Murphy, Patrick 74; Vermont, 1891 5900.10 p94
Murphy, Patrick 77; Vermont, 1897 5900.10 p296
Murphy, Patrick H.; Vermont, 1861-1904 5900.10 p162
Murphy, Patrick J.; Vermont, 1856-1939 5900.10 p69
Murphy, Perry; Vermont, 1810-1876 5900.10 p86
Murphy, Peter; New York, 1840 8197.10 p178
Murphy, Peter 25; Ontario, 1871 1823.28 p76
Murphy, Peter 63; Ontario, 1871 1823.15 p199
Murphy, Peter 88; Vermont, 1890 5900.10 p434
Murphy, Peter H.; Vermont, 1840-1863 5900.10 p480
Murphy, Phebe 17; Ontario, 1861 2896.27 p64
Murphy, Philip; Vermont, 1822-1907 5900.10 p442
Murphy, Philip; Vermont, 1857-1926 5900.10 p268
Murphy, Richard; Vermont, n.d. 5900.10 p266
Murphy, Richard; Vermont, 1857-1907 5900.10 p253
Murphy, Richard 50; Ontario, 1861 2896.27 p64
Murphy, Richard 50; Ontario, 1871 1823.22 p116
Murphy, Richard J. 16; Ontario, 1861 2896.27 p64
Murphy, Rosa McGourty 87; Vermont, 1914 5900.10 p296
Murphy, Rosannah; Ontario, 1861 2896.27 p66
Murphy, Rosannah 15; Ontario, 1861 2896.25 p11
Murphy, Rose; Vermont, 1858-1939 5900.10 p531
Murphy, Rosie; Vermont, 1826-1899 5900.10 p605
Murphy, Sally B. Dunbar 41; Vermont, 1839 5900.10 p518
Murphy, Sally Louisa 3 months; Vermont, 1831 5900.10 p518
Murphy, Sarah 11 months; Vermont, 1867 5900.10 p486
Murphy, Sarah 19; Ontario, 1871 1823.15 p199
Murphy, Sarah 50; Ontario, 1871 1823.15 p199
Murphy, Sarah 65; Vermont, 1901 5900.10 p479
Murphy, Sarah 69; Vermont, 1872 5900.10 p545
Murphy, Sarah A.; Vermont, 1832-1906 5900.10 p481
Murphy, Sarah A.; Vermont, 1853-1926 5900.10 p479
Murphy, Sarah Egan; Vermont, 1828-1910 5900.10 p442
Murphy, Sarah Gettings; Vermont, 1856-1919 5900.10 p253
Murphy, Sarah M. 9; Ontario, 1861 2896.25 p11
Murphy, Sarah McFarlin; Vermont, 1839-1918 5900.10 p288
Murphy, Shrine; Quebec, 1858 9196.15 p32
Murphy, Simon 82; Vermont, 1885 5900.10 p139
Murphy, Sophia Donahue; Vermont, 1856-1936 5900.10 p333
Murphy, Stephen; New York, 1840 8197.10 p265
Murphy, Susan 90; Vermont, 1894 5900.10 p601
Murphy, Susannah 47; Ontario, 1861 2896.25 p11
Murphy, Thomas; New York, 1827 8197.10 p261
Murphy, Thomas; New York, 1827 8197.10 p262
Murphy, Thomas; New York, 1837 8197.10 p99
Murphy, Thomas; Pennsylvania, 1868 6058.10 p73
Murphy, Thomas; Vermont, 1831-1926 5900.10 p131
Murphy, Thomas; Vermont, 1860-1933 5900.10 p86
Murphy, Thomas; Vermont, 1862-1919 5900.10 p120
Murphy, Thomas; Vermont, 1892 5900.10 p272
Murphy, Thomas 27; Maryland, 1774 1220.25 p52
Murphy, Thomas 28; Ontario, 1871 1823.15 p199
Murphy, Thomas 28; Ontario, 1871 1823.22 p116
Murphy, Thomas 40; Ontario, 1871 1823.28 p76
Murphy, Thomas 56; Ontario, 1871 1823.22 p116
Murphy, Thomas 64; Ontario, 1871 1823.22 p116
Murphy, Thomas 75; Vermont, 1926 5900.10 p470
Murphy, Thomas 76; Ontario, 1871 1823.28 p76
Murphy, Thomas A.; Vermont, 1851-1918 5900.10 p115
Murphy, Thomas H.; Vermont, 1859-1917 5900.10 p158
Murphy, Thomas J.; Vermont, 1867-1938 5900.10 p256
Murphy, Thomas J.; Vermont, 1873-1939 5900.10 p163
Murphy, Timothy; Vermont, 1821-1880 5900.10 p348
Murphy, Timothy 50; Ontario, 1871 1823.28 p76
Murphy, Timothy 75; Vermont, 1888 5900.10 p593
Murphy, Timothy J.; Vermont, 1855-1926 5900.10 p420
Murphy, Timothy J.; Vermont, 1864-1921 5900.10 p256
Murphy, Walter; New York, 1821 8197.10 p260
Murphy, Walter 25; Ontario, 1871 1823.15 p199
Murphy, Walter M. 68; Vermont, n.d. 5900.10 p119
Murphy, William; New York, 1838 8197.10 p124
Murphy, William; New York, 1840 8197.10 p265
Murphy, William; Vermont, 1794-1874 5900.10 p606
Murphy, William; Vermont, 1811-1851 5900.10 p43
Murphy, William; Vermont, 1855-1902 5900.10 p187
Murphy, William 21; Ontario, 1861 2896.27 p64
Murphy, William 33; Ontario, 1871 1823.15 p199
Murphy, William 40; Ontario, 1871 1823.15 p199
Murphy, William 45; Vermont, 1862 5900.10 p364
Murphy, William 48; Ontario, 1871 1823.28 p76
Murphy, William 65; Vermont, 1867 5900.10 p152
Murphy, William H.; Vermont, 1847-1929 5900.10 p353
Murphy, William H. 27; Ontario, 1861 2896.25 p11
Murphy, William J.; Vermont, 1864-1909 5900.10 p166
Murphy, William M.; Vermont, 1848 5900.10 p327
Murphy, William T. 66; Vermont, 1892 5900.10 p587
Murphy, Willie; Vermont, 1868 5900.10 p207
Murphy, Winifred 60; Vermont, 1897 5900.10 p563
Murr, Michael; America, 1771 2856.30 p309
Murray, Mr.; Quebec, 1858 9196.15 p44
Murray, Mrs.; Augusta, Georgia, 1807 1640.10 p165
Murray, Mrs.; Quebec, 1858 9196.15 p44
Murray, Adam 45; Ontario, 1871 1823.15 p199
Murray, Alexander; Georgia, 1736 1640.10 p163
Murray, Alexander; Georgia, 1743 1640.10 p163
Murray, Alexander; New Orleans, 1854 1640.10 p163
Murray, Alexander; Ontario, 1851 4537.32 p87
Wife: Mary MacDonald
Child: Kenneth
Child: Angus
Murray, Alexander; Philadelphia, 1795 1224.2 p82
Murray, Alexander; Providence, Rhode Island, 1880 1640.13 p82
Murray, Alexander 40; Ontario, 1871 1823.22 p116
Murray, Alexander 45; Ontario, 1871 1823.15 p199
Murray, Alexander McGrigor; Maryland, 1856 1640.13 p82
Murray, Allan *SEE* Murray, Ann Graham
Murray, Allan; Ontario, 1863 4537.32 p87
Wife: Mary MacDonald
Child: Kirsty
Murray, Allan 40; Ontario, 1871 1823.15 p199
Murray, Andrew; Galveston, Texas, 1858 1640.10 p164
Murray, Andrew; Jamaica, 1844 1640.13 p82
Murray, Andrew J.; Vermont, 1848-1879 5900.10 p341
Murray, Angus *SEE* Murray, Alexander
Murray, Angus *SEE* Murray, John
Murray, Angus; Ontario, 1851 4537.32 p88
Wife: Margaret MacIver
Child: Kirsty
Child: Norman
Child: Isabella
Murray, Ann *SEE* Murray, William
Murray, Ann; Georgia, 1741 1640.10 p164
Murray, Ann; Ontario, 1851 4537.32 p69
Murray, Ann; Ontario, 1863 4537.32 p42
Murray, Ann; Vermont, n.d. 5900.10 p188
Murray, Ann 69; Vermont, 1899 5900.10 p77
Murray, Ann Graham; Ontario, 1863 4537.32 p88
Child: Allan
Child: Jane
Murray, Annabelle; Vermont, 1838-1924 5900.10 p443
Murray, Bridget; Vermont, 1838-1916 5900.10 p76
Murray, Bridget; Vermont, 1850-1903 5900.10 p437
Murray, Catherine *SEE* Murray, George
Murray, Catherine *SEE* Murray, John
Murray, Catherine 68; Ontario, 1871 1823.15 p199
Murray, Catherine 90; Vermont, 1919 5900.10 p194
Murray, Catherine Gillies *SEE* Murray, Neil
Murray, Catherine Meagher; Vermont, 1871-1965 5900.10 p166
Murray, Charles; America, 1700 1224.2 p82
Murray, Charles; Louisiana, 1853 1640.10 p164
Murray, Charles S.; Vermont, 1848-1892 5900.10 p191
Murray, Christian; Georgia, 1738 1640.10 p164
Murray, Christie 41; Ontario, 1871 1823.15 p199
Murray, Christien 35; Ontario, 1871 1823.15 p199
Murray, Colin *SEE* Murray, Neil
Murray, David; Savannah, Georgia, 1771 1640.10 p164
Murray, David; Savannah, Georgia, 1775 1640.10 p164
Murray, David 23; Georgia, 1775 1220.25 p125
Murray, David 25; Ontario, 1871 1823.15 p199
Murray, David 65; Ontario, 1871 1823.15 p199
Murray, Delia; Vermont, 1844-1911 5900.10 p317
Murray, Donald 70; Ontario, 1871 1823.15 p199
Murray, Edward 78; Vermont, 1889 5900.10 p77
Murray, Edward F.; Vermont, 1868-1947 5900.10 p166
Murray, Eliza 35; Ontario, 1861 2896.25 p39
Murray, Ellen Kirby; Vermont, 1847-1885 5900.10 p193
Murray, Francis 40; Ontario, 1871 1823.28 p76
Murray, Francis S. 28; Vermont, n.d. 5900.10 p193
Murray, Gabriel; Augusta, Georgia, 1832 1640.10 p164
Murray, Gabriel; Augusta, Georgia, 1832 1640.13 p82
Murray, Garrett 68; Vermont, 1893 5900.10 p147
Murray, George; Georgia, 1802-1812 1640.10 p165
Murray, George; Mobile, Alabama, 1838-1845 1640.10 p165
Wife: Catherine
Daughter: Catherine
Murray, George; New York, 1840 8197.10 p178
Murray, George 39; Ontario, 1871 1823.15 p199
Murray, Helen Catarecy; Vermont, 1841-1909 5900.10 p322
Murray, Henry; New York, 1836 8197.10 p79
Murray, Henry 2; Ontario, 1861 2896.25 p39
Murray, Hugh; New York, 1840 8197.10 p182
Murray, Hugh, Sr. 54; Ontario, 1871 1823.22 p116
Murray, Hugh R.; New York, 1802 8197.10 p22
Murray, Irvin J.; Vermont, 1847-1930 5900.10 p125
Murray, Isabella *SEE* Murray, Angus
Murray, Isabella; Ontario, 1863 4537.32 p26
Murray, Isabella; Ontario, 1863 4537.32 p50
Murray, James; New Jersey, 1810 1224.3 p55
Murray, James; New York, 1829 8197.10 p359
Murray, James; New York, 1831 8197.10 p366
Murray, James; New York, 1833 8197.10 p315
Murray, James; New York, 1837 8197.10 p100
Murray, James; New York, 1840 8197.10 p180
Murray, James; Pennsylvania, 1868 6058.10 p73
Murray, James; St. Louis, 1848 1640.13 p82
Murray, James; Vermont, 1841-1888 5900.10 p347
Murray, James 11; Ontario, 1861 2896.25 p39
Murray, James 27; Ontario, 1871 1823.28 p76
Murray, James 39; Ontario, 1871 1823.22 p116
Murray, James 40; Ontario, 1871 1823.28 p76
Murray, James 62; Ontario, 1871 1823.15 p199
Murray, James 80; Ontario, 1871 1823.15 p199
Murray, James H.; Vermont, 1823-1892 5900.10 p182
Murray, James R.; Vermont, 1849-1921 5900.10 p432
Murray, Jane *SEE* Murray, Ann Graham
Murray, Jane; Ontario, 1863 4537.32 p81
Murray, Jane 89; Ontario, 1871 1823.28 p76
Murray, Janet 71; Ontario, 1871 1823.15 p199
Murray, Jean; Charleston, South Carolina, 1783 1640.13 p82
Murray, John *SEE* Murray, Neil
Murray, John; Buffalo, New York, 1817 1224.3 p55
Murray, John; Florida, 1766 1640.10 p165
Murray, John; Georgia, 1736 1640.10 p165
Murray, John; New Brunswick, 1795 1224.2 p83
Murray, John; New York, 1802 8197.10 p22
Murray, John; New York, 1807 8197.10 p45
Murray, John; New York, 1824 8197.10 p302
Murray, John; New York, 1827 8197.10 p261
Murray, John; New York, 1839 8197.10 p264
Murray, John; New York, 1839 8197.10 p382
Murray, John; North America, 1759 1224.2 p82
Murray, John; Ontario, 1851 4537.32 p88
Wife: Mary MacLeod
Child: Kenneth
Child: Catherine
Child: Angus
Murray, John; Rutland, Massachusetts, n.d. 1224.2 p83
Murray, John; Vermont, 1839-1914 5900.10 p322
Murray, John 30; British Columbia, 1910 9196.1 p29
Murray, John 30; Washington, 1910 9196.1 p29
Murray, John 38; Ontario, 1871 1823.15 p199
Murray, John 42; Ontario, 1871 1823.15 p199
Murray, John 48; Vermont, 1876 5900.10 p296
Murray, John 60; Ontario, 1871 1823.15 p199
Murray, John 75; Ontario, 1871 1823.15 p199
Murray, John Dods; Quebec, 1857 9196.15 p22
Murray, John William Boyles; New York, 1817 1224.3 p55
Murray, Joseph; Vermont, 1840-1928 5900.10 p317
Murray, Joseph 36; Ontario, 1871 1823.15 p199
Murray, Katherine Welch; Vermont, 1850-1923 5900.10 p125
Murray, Kenneth *SEE* Murray, Alexander
Murray, Kenneth *SEE* Murray, John
Murray, Kenneth 25; Ontario, 1871 1823.15 p199
Murray, Kirsty *SEE* Murray, Allan
Murray, Kirsty *SEE* Murray, Angus
Murray, Kirsty *SEE* Murray, William
Murray, Kirsty; Ontario, 1851 4537.32 p36
Murray, Malcom 23; Ontario, 1871 1823.15 p199
Murray, Margaret *SEE* Murray, William
Murray, Margaret; Milwaukee, 1897 1640.13 p82
Murray, Margaret 5; Ontario, 1861 2896.25 p39
Murray, Margaret 63; Vermont, 1897 5900.10 p427
Murray, Margaret MacIver *SEE* Murray, Angus

N

Naterlow, Joseph 16; Virginia, 1775 ***1220.25*** *p106*
Naters, Thomas; Long Island, n.d. ***1224.3*** *p56*
Naters, Thomas; Quebec, n.d. ***1224.3*** *p56*
Nathan, Bridget; Vermont, 1836-1914 ***5900.10*** *p335*
Nathan, Catherine; Vermont, 1838-1911 ***5900.10*** *p335*
Nathan, James; New York, 1840 ***8197.10*** *p302*
Nathan, Lawrence 44; Ontario, 1871 ***1823.22*** *p116*
Nathan, Thomas 53; Ontario, 1871 ***1823.22*** *p116*
Nation, James; New York, 1840 ***8197.10*** *p191*
Nations, Thomas; Maryland, 1681 ***2524.55*** *p159*
Naton, F. 43; Ontario, 1861 ***2896.25*** *p53*
Naton, J. 40; Ontario, 1861 ***2896.25*** *p28*
Naton, M. 10; Ontario, 1861 ***2896.25*** *p53*
Naton, M. 29; Ontario, 1861 ***2896.25*** *p28*
Naton, M. 40; Ontario, 1861 ***2896.25*** *p53*
Naton, M. A. 7; Ontario, 1861 ***2896.25*** *p28*
Natts, James; Virginia, 1675 ***6212.30*** *p53*
Nau, . . .; America, 1763 ***2856.30*** *p321*
Nau, . . .; America, 1790 ***2856.30*** *p321*
Nau, Anton; America, 1740 ***2856.30*** *p321*
Nau, Jacob; America, 1740 ***2856.30*** *p321*
Nau, Johann Adam; Port uncertain, 1791 ***2856.30*** *p321*
Nauderhald, Oswald; Pennsylvania, 1777 ***4629.10*** *p7*
Naudin, Stephen Nicholas; New York, 1835 ***8197.10*** *p266*
Nauer, Wilhelm; Port uncertain, 1760 ***2856.30*** *p321*
Naufin, William; Maryland, 1637 ***2524.55*** *p159*
Naughton, Catherine 26; New York, New York, 1848 ***1825.45*** *p39*
Naughton, Catherine 50; Ontario, 1871 ***1823.28*** *p76*
Naumann, Michael; Port uncertain, 1724 ***2856.30*** *p321*
With wife & 4 children
Nauricki, Josephine; Maryland, 1910 ***3259.35*** *p42*
Navar, Francis; New York, 1815 ***8197.10*** *p56*
Navel, Bridget 79; Vermont, 1892 ***5900.10*** *p145*
Navel, Lawrence 88; Vermont, 1885 ***5900.10*** *p145*
Naven, Annie 29; Vermont, 1882 ***5900.10*** *p448*
Naven, Julia 26; Ontario, 1871 ***1823.28*** *p76*
Naven, Susan Smith; Vermont, 1852-1878 ***5900.10*** *p544*
Navin, Annie Curlane; Vermont, 1843-1894 ***5900.10*** *p220*
Navin, Hanora 30; Vermont, 1866 ***5900.10*** *p618*
Navin, Patrick; Vermont, 1840-1911 ***5900.10*** *p220*
Navins, Catherine 42; Vermont, 1864 ***5900.10*** *p232*
Nawashkesk, Alex 35; Ontario, 1871 ***1823.28*** *p76*
Nawoakwegijy, Michael 51; Ontario, 1871 ***1823.28*** *p76*
Naworski, Stephen; Maryland, 1910 ***3259.35*** *p42*
Nawracki, Andrew; Maryland, 1910 ***3259.35*** *p42*
Nawrozki, Joseph; Maryland, 1910 ***3259.35*** *p42*
Nay, John; Canada, 1875 ***1640.13*** *p94*
Nay, Samuel 30; Ontario, 1871 ***1823.15*** *p201*
Nayler, Abram; Virginia, 1671-1672 ***6212.30*** *p47*
Nayler, Rich; Virginia, 1665-1666 ***6212.30*** *p21*
Naylon, Mr.; Vermont, 1846-1918 ***5900.10*** *p385*
Naylon, Mrs.; Vermont, 1842-1989 ***5900.10*** *p386*
Naylon, Ellen 23; Vermont, 1877 ***5900.10*** *p199*
Naylon, Margaret 69; Vermont, 1889 ***5900.10*** *p199*
Naylon, Michael 76; Vermont, 1887 ***5900.10*** *p199*
Naylor, Benjamin 54; Ontario, 1871 ***1823.15*** *p201*
Naylor, Christopr.; Maryland, 1659 ***2524.55*** *p159*
Naylor, Eliza 70; Ontario, 1871 ***1823.22*** *p116*
Naylor, Elizabeth 12; Philadelphia, 1775 ***1220.25*** *p27*
Naylor, Henry; Pennsylvania, 1868 ***6058.10*** *p62*
Naylor, Sarah; Virginia, 1663 ***6212.30*** *p3*
Naylour, Abraham; Maryland, 1672 ***2524.55*** *p159*
Naymon, Josephine; Maryland, 1910 ***3259.35*** *p42*
Neagle, Catherine 69; Vermont, 1885 ***5900.10*** *p289*
Neagle, James 34; Ontario, 1871 ***1823.15*** *p201*
Neagle, John 25; Ontario, 1871 ***1823.22*** *p116*
Neagle, Mary 69; Vermont, 1894 ***5900.10*** *p309*
Neagle, Michael; New York, 1840 ***8197.10*** *p266*
Neal, . . .; Boston, 1737 ***4628.40*** *p114*
Neal, . . .; New Hampshire, 1641-1660 ***4628.40*** *p44*
Neal, Ellen; Vermont, 1843-1925 ***5900.10*** *p496*
Neal, George; New York, 1838 ***8197.10*** *p127*
Neal, James; Canada, 1756-1760 ***4628.40*** *p45*
Neal, John; Maryland, 1658 ***2524.55*** *p159*
Neale, Caleb; Maryland, 1660 ***2524.55*** *p159*
Neale, Charles; New York, 1837 ***8197.10*** *p96*
Neale, Elinor; Maryland, 1674 ***2524.55*** *p159*
Child: Susanna
Child: Jacob, Jr.
Neale, Francis; Maryland, 1673 ***2524.55*** *p159*
Neale, Giles; Maryland, 1681 ***2524.55*** *p159*
Neale, Henry; Maryland, 1668 ***2524.55*** *p159*
Neale, Jacob, Jr. *SEE* Neale, Elinor
Neale, James; Maryland, 1654 ***2524.55*** *p159*
Neale, John; Virginia, 1682 ***1224.1*** *p41*
Neale, Margarett; Maryland, 1676 ***2524.55*** *p159*
Neale, Mary; Maryland, 1675 ***2524.55*** *p159*
Neale, Owen; Virginia, 1664 ***6212.30*** *p5*
Neale, Robert; Maryland, 1653 ***2524.55*** *p159*
Neale, Sarah 17; Maryland, 1775 ***1220.25*** *p109*
Neale, Susanna *SEE* Neale, Elinor
Neale, Thomas; Georgia, 1738 ***1640.10*** *p165*
Neale, Thomas; Maryland, 1675 ***1224.1*** *p41*
Neale, Thomas 18; Philadelphia, 1774 ***1220.25*** *p43*
Neale, Walter; Virginia, 1665 ***6212.30*** *p20*
Neale, William; Maryland, 1651 ***2524.55*** *p169*
Neale, William; Maryland, 1654 ***2524.55*** *p159*
Neale, William; Maryland, 1666 ***2524.55*** *p159*
Nealett, Margarett; Maryland, 1654 ***2524.55*** *p159*
Nealis, John; New York, 1826 ***8197.10*** *p266*
Nealis, Peter; New York, 1840 ***8197.10*** *p190*
Nealon, Ann Lane 65; Vermont, 1884 ***5900.10*** *p305*
Nealon, Bridget Dailey; Vermont, 1857-1930 ***5900.10*** *p305*
Nealon, Eva M. Pond 41; Vermont, 1890 ***5900.10*** *p305*
Nealon, Michael 76; Vermont, 1880 ***5900.10*** *p305*
Nealon, Patrick; Vermont, 1847-1923 ***5900.10*** *p305*
Nealon, William 56; Ontario, 1871 ***1823.22*** *p116*
Nealson, James 65; Ontario, 1871 ***1823.22*** *p116*
Near, Philipp; America, 1741 ***2856.30*** *p321*
Neary, Anne 7 *SEE* Neary, Mary
Neary, Bridget 1 *SEE* Neary, Patrick
Neary, Bridget 14 *SEE* Neary, Mary
Neary, Catherine 24 *SEE* Neary, Mary
Neary, Ellen; Vermont, 1833-1897 ***5900.10*** *p424*
Neary, James 3 *SEE* Neary, Mary
Neary, John 16 *SEE* Neary, Mary
Neary, Mary; Vermont, 1828-1894 ***5900.10*** *p424*
Neary, Mary 28 *SEE* Neary, Patrick
Neary, Mary 35; New York, New York, 1847 ***1825.45*** *p19*
Son: James 3
Brother-In-Law: John 16
Sister-In-Law: Bridget 14
Sister-In-Law: Catherine 24
Daughter: Anne 7
Neary, Michael; New York, 1837 ***8197.10*** *p96*
Neary, Patrick 40; New York, New York, 1847 ***1825.45*** *p19*
Wife: Mary 28
Daughter: Bridget 1
Nease, Fredric H. 11; Ontario, 1861 ***2896.28*** *p18*
Nease, George 40; Ontario, 1861 ***2896.28*** *p18*
Nease, George S. 4; Ontario, 1861 ***2896.28*** *p18*
Nease, Gilbert H. 6; Ontario, 1861 ***2896.28*** *p18*
Nease, Sophia 42; Ontario, 1861 ***2896.28*** *p18*
Neatherwood, Joseph 19; Jamaica, 1774 ***1220.25*** *p68*
Neats, William; New York, 1840 ***8197.10*** *p191*
Neave, John 25; Maryland, 1774 ***1220.25*** *p79*
Neave, Robert; Maryland, 1653 ***2524.55*** *p159*
Neaves, George 57; Ontario, 1871 ***1823.15*** *p201*
Nebarl, Conrad 31; Ontario, 1871 ***1823.15*** *p201*
Neboddy, Mrs. 66; Ontario, 1861 ***2896.26*** *p30*
Nebolich, S. 32; Alaska, 1917 ***9196.1*** *p49*
Nebolich, S. 32; Whitehorse, Yukon, 1917 ***9196.1*** *p49*
Nech, Danll; Virginia, 1663 ***6212.30*** *p4*
Neckerauer, Anna Margarete Bois; America, 1766 ***2856.30*** *p321*
Necum, Niklas; America, 1749 ***2856.30*** *p321*
Nedham, James; Virginia, 1677 ***1224.1*** *p41*
Nedham, Thomas; Maryland, 1649 ***2524.55*** *p159*
Needham, Christopher; Maryland, 1651 ***2524.55*** *p160*
With wife
Son: Edward
Son: Thomas
Needham, Dorothy *SEE* Needham, Henry
Needham, Edward *SEE* Needham, Christopher
Needham, Henry; Maryland, 1659 ***2524.55*** *p160*
Wife: Patience
Child: Martha
Child: Dorothy
Child: Margarett
Needham, Jno; Virginia, 1664 ***6212.30*** *p15*
Needham, John; Pennsylvania, 1868 ***6058.10*** *p65*
Needham, Margarett *SEE* Needham, Henry
Needham, Martha *SEE* Needham, Henry
Needham, Patience *SEE* Needham, Henry
Needham, Thomas *SEE* Needham, Christopher
Needham, Thomas; New York, 1807 ***8197.10*** *p46*
Needham, William; Maryland, 1826 ***1224.3*** *p56*
Needham, William; Pennsylvania, 1868 ***6058.10*** *p65*
Needs, James 21; Maryland, 1774 ***1220.25*** *p47*
Neelands, John 24; Ontario, 1871 ***1823.15*** *p201*
Neele, John; Pennsylvania, 1779 ***4629.10*** *p32*
Neely, Francis; New York, 1840 ***8197.10*** *p191*
Neenan, John 75; Vermont, 1897 ***5900.10*** *p474*
Neenan, Mary; Vermont, 1848-1948 ***5900.10*** *p334*
Neenan, Mary A.; Vermont, 1856-1925 ***5900.10*** *p326*
Neenan, Mary Powers 70; Vermont, 1893 ***5900.10*** *p192*
Neenan, Michael; New York, 1832 ***8197.10*** *p314*
Nees, Andreas; Port uncertain, 1771 ***2856.30*** *p321*
Nees, Maria Margarete; Port uncertain, 1794 ***2856.30*** *p321*
Neeson, Dennis; New York, 1834 ***8197.10*** *p315*
Neeson, Dennis; New York, 1836 ***8197.10*** *p77*
Neeson, James; New York, 1834 ***8197.10*** *p315*
Neeson, James; New York, 1836 ***8197.10*** *p77*
Neess, Johann Adam; America, 1749 ***2856.30*** *p321*
With wife & 4 children
Neess, Johann Michael; America, 1737 ***2856.30*** *p321*
Neess, Jorg Andreas; America, 1750 ***2856.30*** *p321*
With wife & 2 children
Neeve, Fort; Maryland, 1662 ***2524.55*** *p160*
Neeve, Mary; Virginia, 1674 ***1224.1*** *p41*
Neff, Andreas; America, 1744 ***2856.30*** *p321*
With wife 2 children & mother
Neff, Andreas; America, 1747 ***2856.30*** *p321*
Neff, Anna Maria; America, 1744 ***2856.30*** *p321*
Neff, Georg; America, 1738 ***2856.30*** *p321*
With wife & 2 children
Neff, Jakob; America, 1785 ***2856.30*** *p321*
Neff, Jakob; America, 1789 ***2856.30*** *p321*
Neff, Jakob; Port uncertain, 1786 ***2856.30*** *p321*
Neff, Michael; America, 1748 ***2856.30*** *p321*
Neff, Sebastian; America, 1744 ***2856.30*** *p321*
Nefian, Jakob; Port uncertain, 1786 ***2856.30*** *p321*
Nefian, Maria Margarete; Port uncertain, 1786 ***2856.30*** *p322*
Negele, Andreas; America, 1785 ***2856.30*** *p322*
Negele, Jacob 45; Kansas, 1883-1910 ***9079.10*** *p12*
Negele, Mary 17; Kansas, 1893-1910 ***9079.10*** *p12*
Negele, Mary 45; Kansas, 1893-1910 ***9079.10*** *p12*
Negelie, Johann; America, 1738 ***2856.30*** *p322*
Negeninik, C. 22; Alaska, 1908 ***9196.1*** *p36*
Neger, Michael; Port uncertain, 1788 ***2856.30*** *p322*
Neglee, Jacob; Pennsylvania, 1777 ***4629.10*** *p24*
Neglee, John; Pennsylvania, 1777 ***4629.10*** *p15*
Negonekezhik, Peter 40; Ontario, 1871 ***1823.28*** *p76*
Negus, Thomas 21; Philadelphia, 1774 ***1220.25*** *p66*
Neher, John; Vermont, 1841-1931 ***5900.10*** *p89*
Neher, Kathrine Ott; Vermont, 1848-1917 ***5900.10*** *p89*
Neick, Nickel; America, 1742 ***2856.30*** *p322*
Neidens, John, Jr. 37; Kansas, 1891-1910 ***9079.10*** *p20*
Neidens, Mary 30; Kansas, 1891-1910 ***9079.10*** *p20*
Neidenthal, Kate 37; Kansas, 1877-1910 ***9079.10*** *p6*
Neidenthal, Mike 46; Kansas, 1892-1910 ***9079.10*** *p6*
Neidig, Barbara; Port uncertain, 1764 ***2856.30*** *p322*
Neife, Mrs.; Maryland, 1666 ***2524.55*** *p160*
Neil, Mr.; Quebec, 1857 ***9196.15*** *p13*
Neil, Edwin 24; Ontario, 1871 ***1823.28*** *p76*
Neil, George 31; Ontario, 1871 ***1823.15*** *p201*
Neil, Henry; Pennsylvania, 1777 ***4629.10*** *p14*
Neil, John; Canada, 1756-1760 ***4628.40*** *p46*
Neil, John; New York, 1807 ***8197.10*** *p47*
Neil, Robert; Barbados, 1853 ***1640.13*** *p94*
Neil, Robert 60; Ontario, 1871 ***1823.22*** *p116*
Neil, Samueil 26; Ontario, 1871 ***1823.15*** *p201*
Neil, Samuel 53; Ontario, 1871 ***1823.15*** *p201*
Neil, Sebastian; Pennsylvania, 1777 ***4629.10*** *p27*
Neil, Thomas; Trinidad, 1843 ***1640.13*** *p94*
Neilan, Bridget; Vermont, 1883 ***5900.10*** *p54*
Neilan, Catherine; Vermont, 1839-1928 ***5900.10*** *p55*
Neilan, Michael; Vermont, 1800-1871 ***5900.10*** *p55*
Neilands, Thomas 35; Ontario, 1871 ***1823.15*** *p201*
Neild, Mr.; Quebec, 1857 ***9196.15*** *p17*
Neild, Mr.; Quebec, 1858 ***9196.15*** *p40*
Neile, Herege; Maryland, 1659 ***2524.55*** *p164*
Neile, Hugh; Maryland, 1659 ***2524.55*** *p164*
Neill, Charles 54; Ontario, 1871 ***1823.22*** *p116*
Neill, Francis 50; Ontario, 1871 ***1823.28*** *p76*
Neill, Jane 85; Ontario, 1871 ***1823.22*** *p116*
Neill, Samuel; Mississippi, 1809 ***1224.3*** *p56*
Neill, Thomas; New York, 1838 ***8197.10*** *p127*
Neill, Thomas 22; Maryland, 1774 ***1220.25*** *p3*
Neillands, Robert; Montreal, 1840 ***1640.13*** *p94*
Neilson, A. 30; Alaska, 1917 ***9196.1*** *p49*
Neilson, A. 30; Whitehorse, Yukon, 1917 ***9196.1*** *p49*
Neilson, E. George 37; Ontario, 1871 ***1823.28*** *p76*
Neilson, Regina 39; Seattle, 1916 ***9196.1*** *p6*
Neilson, Regina 39; Yukon, 1916 ***9196.1*** *p6*
Neilson, Richard; Carolina, 1743 ***1224.2*** *p83*
Neilson, Thomas; Georgia, 1698 ***1640.13*** *p94*
Neits, Frederick 33; Ontario, 1871 ***1823.28*** *p76*
Neiv, Mr.; Quebec, 1858 ***9196.15*** *p39*
Nekolich, L. 27; Alaska, 1916 ***9196.1*** *p44*
Nekolich, L. 27; Whitehorse, Yukon, 1916 ***9196.1*** *p44*
Nelan, Isebella 36; Ontario, 1871 ***1823.28*** *p76*
Nelan, Margaret 55; Ontario, 1871 ***1823.28*** *p76*
Nelas, Francis; New York, 1839 ***8197.10*** *p136*
Nelden, John 58; Ontario, 1871 ***1823.28*** *p76*
Nelgren, George 32; British Columbia, 1911 ***9196.1*** *p34*
Nelgren, George 32; Washington, 1911 ***9196.1*** *p34*
Nelka, John M.; Maryland, 1910 ***3259.35*** *p42*
Nelka, Maruna; Maryland, 1910 ***3259.35*** *p42*
Nell, James 32; Ontario, 1871 ***1823.15*** *p201*
Nell, Oscar 31; British Columbia, 1909 ***9196.1*** *p27*

Nevins, Jerome; Vermont, 1832-1901 ***5900.10*** *p232*
Nevins, Johanna; Vermont, 1839-1908 ***5900.10*** *p491*
Nevins, John; Maine, 1829 ***1224.3*** *p56*
Nevins, John 20; Vermont, 1848 ***5900.10*** *p232*
Nevins, John 41; Ontario, 1871 ***1823.22*** *p117*
Nevins, John 56; Ontario, 1871 ***1823.15*** *p201*
Nevins, Joseph 44; Ontario, 1871 ***1823.22*** *p117*
Nevins, Margaret 64; Vermont, 1873 ***5900.10*** *p232*
Nevins, Mary; Vermont, 1800-1883 ***5900.10*** *p239*
Nevins, Mary; Vermont, 1832-1899 ***5900.10*** *p232*
Nevins, Mary Ann; Vermont, 1849-1881 ***5900.10*** *p239*
Nevins, Patrick; Vermont, 1841-1909 ***5900.10*** *p239*
New, James 40; Ontario, 1871 ***1823.28*** *p77*
New, Joseph 54; Ontario, 1871 ***1823.28*** *p77*
New, Martin 38; Virginia, 1774 ***1220.25*** *p55*
New, Richard; Maryland, 1678 ***2524.55*** *p160*
New, Thomas; Pennsylvania, 1732 ***1224.2*** *p83*
New, Thomas 50; Ontario, 1871 ***1823.28*** *p77*
New, William 38; Ontario, 1871 ***1823.28*** *p77*
New, Young 47; Ontario, 1871 ***1823.28*** *p77*
Newal, Charles 17; Ontario, 1871 ***1823.15*** *p201*
Newall, Cunningham; Savannah, Georgia, 1807 ***1640.10*** *p166*
Newall, John; North Carolina, 1772 ***1224.2*** *p83*
Newall, John 43; Ontario, 1871 ***1823.15*** *p201*
Newan, Alice; Vermont, 1847-1888 ***5900.10*** *p379*
Newark, Mr.; Quebec, 1858 ***9196.15*** *p34*
Newark, Mrs.; Quebec, 1858 ***9196.15*** *p34*
Newbaur, M. 53; Alaska, 1916 ***9196.1*** *p44*
Newbaur, M. 53; Whitehorse, Yukon, 1916 ***9196.1*** *p44*
Newberry, Elinor; Maryland, 1663 ***2524.55*** *p160*
Newberry, J.; Quebec, 1857 ***9196.15*** *p20*
Newberry, John 19; New York, 1775 ***1220.25*** *p94*
Newberry, Roger; New England, 1744 ***1224.2*** *p83*
Newberry, Roger; West Indies, 1744 ***1224.2*** *p83*
Newbey, Ellinor; Maryland, 1663 ***2524.55*** *p160*
Newbigging, David; Ontario, 1853 ***1640.13*** *p94*
Newbigging, Hugh; Pennsylvania, 1785 ***4629.10*** *p48*
Newble, Thomas; New York, 1837 ***8197.10*** *p374*
Newbould, Samuel; New York, 1818 ***8197.10*** *p265*
Newburry, Peter 34; Ontario, 1871 ***1823.28*** *p77*
Newby, Samuel; New York, 1837 ***8197.10*** *p96*
Newcastle, John; Maryland, 1680-1681 ***2524.55*** *p160*
Newchatel, Peter; Philadelphia, 1793 ***4629.10*** *p67*
Newcomb, Ann 76; Ontario, 1871 ***1823.22*** *p117*
Newcomb, James 45; Ontario, 1871 ***1823.15*** *p202*
Newcomb, John; New York, 1802-1834 ***8197.10*** *p306*
Newcomb, John 45; Ontario, 1871 ***1823.15*** *p202*
Newcomb, Octavine 23; Ontario, 1871 ***1823.28*** *p77*
Newcomb, Thomas 45; Ontario, 1871 ***1823.22*** *p117*
Newcombe, Master; Quebec, 1857 ***9196.15*** *p17*
Newcombe, Miss; Quebec, 1857 ***9196.15*** *p17*
Newcombe, Henry; Quebec, 1857 ***9196.15*** *p17*
Newcombe, James; Quebec, 1857 ***9196.15*** *p17*
Newcombe, Richard; New Castle, Delaware, 1848 ***1224.3*** *p56*
Newcombe, Mrs. S.; Quebec, 1857 ***9196.15*** *p17*
Newcombe, William 36; Ontario, 1871 ***1823.15*** *p202*
Newcombe, Wm; Quebec, 1857 ***9196.15*** *p17*
Newcombe, Mrs. Wm; Quebec, 1857 ***9196.15*** *p17*
Newcome, William 18; Maryland, 1774 ***1220.25*** *p57*
Newcomen, Samuel; Charles Town, South Carolina, 1792 ***1224.2*** *p83*
Newdigate, Nathaniel; Rhode Island, 1750 ***1224.2*** *p83*
Newell, Edwin 25; Ontario, 1871 ***1823.28*** *p77*
Newell, Emma 13; Ontario, 1871 ***1823.15*** *p202*
Newell, James; Maryland, 1663 ***2524.55*** *p160*
Newell, John; New York, 1729 ***1224.2*** *p83*
Newell, John 51; Ontario, 1871 ***1823.28*** *p77*
Newell, Jonathan; Virginia, 1675 ***1224.1*** *p41*
Newell, William 45; Ontario, 1871 ***1823.15*** *p202*
Newens, Harriet; New York, 1846 ***1224.3*** *p56*
Newett, Wm; Portland, Maine, 1858 ***9196.15*** *p28*
Newfeild, Jeffry; Virginia, 1667-1668 ***6212.30*** *p39*
Newham, William Stobbs; New York, 1840 ***8197.10*** *p191*
Newheal, High 40; Ontario, 1871 ***1823.22*** *p117*
Newington, Jeffry; Virginia, 1667 ***6212.30*** *p36*
Newitt, Elizabeth; Maryland, 1665 ***2524.55*** *p160*
Newland, Henry 22; Virginia, 1774 ***1220.25*** *p46*
Newland, John 21; Maryland, 1774 ***1220.25*** *p61*
Newland, Thomas 32; Maryland, 1775 ***1220.25*** *p99*
Newlove, Stephen 48; Ontario, 1871 ***1823.15*** *p202*
Newly, Mary; Maryland, 1665 ***2524.55*** *p114*
Newman, Mr.; Quebec, 1857 ***9196.15*** *p26*
Newman, Mrs.; Quebec, 1857 ***9196.15*** *p26*
Newman, Abraham; Maryland, 1673 ***2524.55*** *p160*
Newman, Adam 13; Ontario, 1871 ***1823.15*** *p202*
Newman, Ann; Maryland, 1670 ***2524.55*** *p160*
Newman, C. F. 24; Maryland, 1775 ***1220.25*** *p99*
Newman, Catherine 15; Ontario, 1871 ***1823.15*** *p202*
Newman, Charles; New York, New York, 1829 ***8197.10*** *p127*
Newman, Charles 22; Ontario, 1871 ***1823.15*** *p202*
Newman, Charles 30; Ontario, 1871 ***1823.15*** *p202*
Newman, Edward; Virginia, 1672 ***1224.1*** *p32*
Newman, Edward 19; Georgia, 1774 ***1220.25*** *p48*
Newman, Elizabeth; Maryland, 1681 ***2524.55*** *p160*
Newman, Ellinor; Maryland, 1673 ***2524.55*** *p160*
Newman, Francis; Maryland, 1820 ***1224.3*** *p56*
Newman, Geo; Virginia, 1664 ***6212.30*** *p14*
Newman, Geo; Virginia, 1665-1666 ***6212.30*** *p22*
Newman, George; Maryland, 1651 ***2524.55*** *p160*
Newman, Henry; Maryland, 1671 ***2524.55*** *p160*
Newman, Henry 32; Ontario, 1871 ***1823.15*** *p202*
Newman, James; Virginia, 1665-1666 ***6212.30*** *p21*
Newman, Jane; Maryland, 1667 ***2524.55*** *p160*
Newman, Jane 39; Vermont, 1870 ***5900.10*** *p140*
Newman, John; Maryland, 1666 ***2524.55*** *p160*
Newman, John; Maryland, 1682 ***2524.55*** *p160*
Newman, John; New England, 1739 ***1224.2*** *p84*
Newman, John; New York, 1744 ***1224.2*** *p84*
Newman, John; New York, 1826 ***8197.10*** *p336*
Newman, John; New York, 1828 ***8197.10*** *p266*
Newman, John; Pennsylvania, 1777 ***4629.10*** *p16*
Newman, John 31; Ontario, 1871 ***1823.28*** *p77*
Newman, John Pearse; New York, 1808 ***8197.10*** *p265*
Newman, Jone; Maryland, 1666 ***2524.55*** *p161*
Newman, Lawrens; New York, 1834 ***8197.10*** *p72*
Newman, Louisa 55; Ontario, 1871 ***1823.15*** *p202*
Newman, Martha 23; Baltimore, 1775 ***1220.25*** *p119*
Newman, Mary; Vermont, 1815-1869 ***5900.10*** *p140*
Newman, Mary 19; Ontario, 1871 ***1823.15*** *p202*
Newman, Michael; New York, 1840 ***8197.10*** *p385*
Newman, Nicholas; Maryland, 1674 ***2524.55*** *p161*
Newman, Nicholas; Virginia, 1671 ***6212.30*** *p44*
Newman, Pain; Pennsylvania, 1777 ***4629.10*** *p19*
Newman, Richard; Virginia, 1666-1667 ***6212.30*** *p33*
Newman, Robert; New York, 1783 ***1224.2*** *p84*
Newman, Roger; Maryland, 1704 ***1224.2*** *p84*
Newman, Samuel; Boston, 1696 ***1224.1*** *p41*
Newman, Samuel; New York, 1803 ***8197.10*** *p15*
Newman, Samuel 24; Philadelphia, 1774 ***1220.25*** *p3*
Newman, Samuel 56; Ontario, 1871 ***1823.22*** *p117*
Newman, Thomas; Maryland, 1666 ***2524.55*** *p161*
Newman, Thomas 16; Virginia, 1774 ***1220.25*** *p89*
Newman, Timothy; Pennsylvania, 1777 ***4629.10*** *p8*
Newman, William 25; Philadelphia, 1775 ***1220.25*** *p122*
Newman, William 46; Ontario, 1871 ***1823.22*** *p117*
Newman, Wingate; Pennsylvania, 1777 ***4629.10*** *p7*
Newmar, Thomas; Maryland, 1661 ***2524.55*** *p161*
Newmarch, Robert 43; Ontario, 1871 ***1823.15*** *p202*
Newon, Thos H. 17; Ontario, 1871 ***1823.15*** *p202*
Newport, Mr.; Quebec, 1858 ***9196.15*** *p34*
Newport, George; New York, 1812 ***8197.10*** *p265*
Newport, James 19; Maryland, 1775 ***1220.25*** *p10*
Newport, William; Maryland, 1672 ***2524.55*** *p161*
Newport, William; Maryland, 1673 ***2524.55*** *p161*
News, Edward; New York, 1827 ***8197.10*** *p345*
Newsent, Dave 10; Kansas, 1905-1910 ***9079.10*** *p28*
Newsent, George 35; Kansas, 1905-1910 ***9079.10*** *p28*
Newsent, Kate 8; Kansas, 1905-1910 ***9079.10*** *p28*
Newsent, Mary 31; Kansas, 1905-1910 ***9079.10*** *p28*
Newsham, Robert; New York, 1794 ***8197.10*** *p5*
Newsom, Eli; New York, 1834 ***8197.10*** *p266*
Newsome, Henry 56; Ontario, 1871 ***1823.28*** *p77*
Newsome, Henry F. 26; Ontario, 1871 ***1823.28*** *p77*
Newsome, Mark 25; Maryland, 1774 ***1220.25*** *p64*
Newson, Eli; New York, 1839 ***8197.10*** *p136*
Newson, Richard 19; Virginia, 1774 ***1220.25*** *p55*
Newson, Robert 39; Ontario, 1871 ***1823.22*** *p117*
Newson, William 47; Ontario, 1871 ***1823.15*** *p202*
Newstead, Robert 28; Jamaica, 1775 ***1220.25*** *p144*
Newter, John 21; Virginia, 1774 ***1220.25*** *p87*
Newth, Samuel 23; Maryland, 1775 ***1220.25*** *p101*
Newton, Mr.; Portland, Maine, 1858 ***9196.15*** *p30*
Newton, Ambrose; Pittsburgh, 1772 ***1224.2*** *p84*
Newton, Ann; Missouri, 1898 ***1640.13*** *p94*
Newton, Anthony; New England, 1647 ***1224.1*** *p42*
Newton, Caroline 61; Ontario, 1871 ***1823.15*** *p202*
Newton, Catherine; Virginia, 1788 ***1640.13*** *p94*
Newton, Christopher; Maryland, 1681 ***2524.55*** *p161*
Newton, Edward; Maryland, 1725 ***1224.2*** *p84*
Newton, Elizabeth; New Orleans, 1853 ***1224.3*** *p56*
Newton, Ellen Lynch; Vermont, 1851-1900 ***5900.10*** *p135*
Newton, Fanny 60; Ontario, 1871 ***1823.15*** *p202*
Newton, Fergus 24; America, 1774 ***1220.25*** *p36*
Newton, Francis; Died enroute, 1662 ***1224.1*** *p42*
Newton, Frederick 23; Ontario, 1871 ***1823.15*** *p202*
Newton, George 51; Ontario, 1871 ***1823.15*** *p202*
Newton, Henry 48; Ontario, 1871 ***1823.15*** *p202*
Newton, James; New York, 1807 ***8197.10*** *p47*
Newton, James S.; New York, 1828-1831 ***8197.10*** *p370*
Newton, Jennie; Vermont, 1859-1892 ***5900.10*** *p147*
Newton, Joane; New England, 1647 ***1224.1*** *p42*
Newton, John; Maryland, 1673 ***2524.55*** *p161*
Newton, John; Maryland, 1681 ***2524.55*** *p161*
Newton, John; Virginia, 1664 ***6212.30*** *p13*
Newton, John; Virginia, 1666-1667 ***6212.30*** *p34*
Newton, John 37; Ontario, 1871 ***1823.15*** *p202*
Newton, John 56; Ontario, 1871 ***1823.22*** *p117*
Newton, John W. 27; Ontario, 1871 ***1823.22*** *p117*
Newton, Joseph; Died enroute, 1694 ***1224.1*** *p42*
Newton, Mary; Maryland, 1682 ***2524.55*** *p161*
Newton, Mary 21; Maryland, 1775 ***1220.25*** *p111*
Newton, Matthew 30; Halifax, Nova Scotia, 1775 ***1220.25*** *p124*
Newton, Robert; New York, 1840 ***8197.10*** *p190*
Newton, Robert 50; Ontario, 1871 ***1823.15*** *p202*
Newton, Rosa Burns; Vermont, 1856-1880 ***5900.10*** *p135*
Newton, Rose; Vermont, 1839 ***5900.10*** *p147*
Newton, Samuel; New York, 1802 ***8197.10*** *p23*
Newton, Thomas 49; Ontario, 1871 ***1823.15*** *p202*
Newton, William; New York, New York, n.d. ***1224.2*** *p84*
Newton, William; Vermont, 1829-1907 ***5900.10*** *p147*
Newton, William; Vermont, 1854-1954 ***5900.10*** *p135*
Newton, William 42; Ontario, 1871 ***1823.28*** *p77*
New-worth, Wm; Virginia, 1663 ***6212.30*** *p2*
Nexford, Rowland; Virginia, 1666-1667 ***6212.30*** *p34*
Ney, Anna Elisabeth; Port uncertain, 1746 ***2856.30*** *p324*
Ney, John 22; Ontario, 1871 ***1823.28*** *p77*
Ney, Robert 26; Ontario, 1871 ***1823.28*** *p77*
Neydlinger, Matthias; America, 1753 ***2856.30*** *p324*
Neyer, Philipp; Port uncertain, 1775 ***2856.30*** *p301*
Neyer, Philipp; Port uncertain, 1775 ***2856.30*** *p324*
Neyle, Edgar; Pennsylvania, 1864-1865 ***6058.10*** *p50*
Neyss, Johann Michael; America, 1737 ***2856.30*** *p324*
Nezyarino, W. 37; Alaska, 1914 ***9196.1*** *p40*
Nibergal, Conrad 52; Ontario, 1871 ***1823.15*** *p202*
Niblet, Ed John 50; Ontario, 1871 ***1823.28*** *p77*
Niblett, Rich; Virginia, 1672 ***6212.30*** *p50*
Niblo, William; New York, 1838 ***8197.10*** *p127*
Nichell, Samuel; Maryland, 1670 ***2524.55*** *p161*
Nichoel, Christopher 36; Ontario, 1871 ***1823.28*** *p77*
Nichol, Mr.; Quebec, 1857 ***9196.15*** *p13*
Nichol, Alexander 36; Ontario, 1871 ***1823.15*** *p202*
Nichol, David 50; Ontario, 1871 ***1823.28*** *p77*
Nichol, Edward 51; Ontario, 1871 ***1823.15*** *p202*
Nichol, James 40; Ontario, 1871 ***1823.15*** *p202*
Nichol, James 44; Ontario, 1871 ***1823.15*** *p202*
Nichol, James 44; Ontario, 1871 ***1823.22*** *p117*
Nichol, James 50; Ontario, 1871 ***1823.15*** *p202*
Nichol, John 75; Ontario, 1871 ***1823.28*** *p77*
Nichol, Robert 22; Ontario, 1871 ***1823.15*** *p202*
Nichol, Simon 74; Ontario, 1871 ***1823.22*** *p117*
Nichol, Thomas 43; Ontario, 1871 ***1823.28*** *p77*
Nichola, Lewis; Pennsylvania, 1779 ***4629.10*** *p36*
Nicholas, Charles 40; Ontario, 1871 ***1823.22*** *p117*
Nicholas, Edw.; Virginia, 1664 ***6212.30*** *p15*
Nicholas, Francis 55; Ontario, 1871 ***1823.22*** *p117*
Nicholas, John 56; Ontario, 1871 ***1823.28*** *p77*
Nicholas, Mary; New England, 1687 ***1224.1*** *p10*
Nicholas, Michael; Philadelphia, 1791 ***4629.10*** *p80*
Nicholas, Richard 22; Maryland, 1774 ***1220.25*** *p77*
Nicholas, Samuel; Pennsylvania, 1777 ***4629.10*** *p16*
Nicholas, Thomas; Maryland, 1665 ***2524.55*** *p161*
Nicholas, William; Virginia, 1734 ***1224.2*** *p84*
Nicholason, Ronald 68; Ontario, 1871 ***1823.15*** *p202*
Nicholason, William; Pennsylvania, 1777 ***4629.10*** *p17*
Nicholes, Richard 26; Ontario, 1871 ***1823.28*** *p77*
Nicholl, Margaret 60; Ontario, 1871 ***1823.22*** *p117*
Nicholl, William; North America, 1787 ***1224.2*** *p84*
Nicholle, Walter 38; Ontario, 1871 ***1823.15*** *p202*
Nicholls, Anthony Edward; New York, 1813 ***8197.10*** *p265*
Nicholls, Francis *SEE* Nicholls, William
Nicholls, Francis; Maryland, 1680 ***2524.55*** *p161*
Nicholls, George; Maryland, 1667 ***2524.55*** *p161*
Nicholls, Humphry; Maryland, 1667 ***2524.55*** *p161*
Nicholls, James; Maryland, 1681 ***2524.55*** *p161*
Nicholls, John; Maryland, 1648 ***2524.55*** *p161*
With wife & children
Nicholls, John; Maryland, 1673 ***2524.55*** *p161*
Nicholls, John; Maryland, 1682 ***2524.55*** *p161*
Nicholls, John; Philadelphia, 1751 ***1224.2*** *p84*
Nicholls, John; Virginia, 1666 ***6212.30*** *p28*
Nicholls, John 48; Ontario, 1871 ***1823.28*** *p77*
Nicholls, John Henry 24; Ontario, 1871 ***1823.28*** *p77*
Nicholls, Joseph 41; Ontario, 1871 ***1823.15*** *p202*
Nicholls, Mary 60; Ontario, 1871 ***1823.22*** *p117*
Nicholls, Richard; New York, New York, 1783 ***1224.2*** *p84*
Nicholls, Richard; Virginia, 1692 ***1224.1*** *p42*
Nicholls, William; Maryland, 1666 ***2524.55*** *p161*
Wife: Francis
Nicholls, William; Pennsylvania, 1700 ***1224.2*** *p84*
Nicholos, George; Virginia, 1671-1672 ***6212.30*** *p45*
Nichols, Aurilla 62; Vermont, 1870 ***5900.10*** *p528*
Nichols, Catherine 50; Vermont, 1876 ***5900.10*** *p155*

Niles, Frances M. 3; Ontario, 1861 ***2896.28*** *p26*
Niles, Mary 33; Ontario, 1861 ***2896.28*** *p26*
Niles, Richard 56; Ontario, 1871 ***1823.22*** *p117*
Niles, Thomas 45; Ontario, 1871 ***1823.22*** *p117*
Niles, William 30; Ontario, 1871 ***1823.22*** *p117*
Niles, William T. 11; Ontario, 1861 ***2896.28*** *p26*
Niley, Mrs. E.; Quebec, 1856 ***9196.15*** *p9*
Nilius, Johann; Port uncertain, 1752 ***2856.30*** *p326*
Nilka, Thomas; Maryland, 1910 ***3259.35*** *p42*
Nilkey, Julious 28; Ontario, 1871 ***1823.28*** *p77*
Nilly, Francis; Virginia, 1671 ***6212.30*** *p42*
Nilva, George 44; Alaska, 1917 ***9196.1*** *p48*
Nilva, George 44; Whitehorse, Yukon, 1917 ***9196.1*** *p48*
Niman, Charles 32; Ontario, 1871 ***1823.28*** *p77*
Niman, Frederick 33; Ontario, 1871 ***1823.28*** *p77*
Niman, Frederick 36; Ontario, 1871 ***1823.28*** *p77*
Niman, Ludwick 65; Ontario, 1871 ***1823.28*** *p77*
Niman, Richard 55; Ontario, 1871 ***1823.28*** *p77*
Nimdell, Richard; Maryland, 1672 ***2524.55*** *p161*
Nimmo, Andrew; Georgia, 1698 ***1640.13*** *p95*
Nimmo, James 3; Ontario, 1871 ***1823.15*** *p203*
Nimms, Mr.; Quebec, 1858 ***9196.15*** *p46*
Nimms, Mrs.; Quebec, 1858 ***9196.15*** *p46*
Nina, Phillip; Quebec, 1858 ***9196.15*** *p31*
Niniminus, George 32; Ontario, 1871 ***1823.15*** *p203*
Niordan, Daniel 48; Ontario, 1871 ***1823.28*** *p77*
Nipp, Ferdinand; Port uncertain, 1790 ***2856.30*** *p326*
Nisbet, Alexander; Augusta, Georgia, 1809-1812 ***1640.10*** *p166*
Nisbet, George; Jamaica, 1895 ***1640.13*** *p95*
Nisbet, George 33; Ontario, 1871 ***1823.15*** *p203*
Nisbet, Robert; Nevis, 1743 ***1640.13*** *p95*
Nisbet, Robert 43; Ontario, 1871 ***1823.15*** *p203*
Nisbet, William; New York, 1827 ***8197.10*** *p343*
Nisbit, Elizabeth; South Carolina, 1762 ***1224.2*** *p120*
Nisbit, Matilda 11; Ontario, 1871 ***1823.15*** *p203*
Nitka, Baltuni; Maryland, 1910 ***3259.35*** *p42*
Nitschkowski, Eugene; Maryland, 1910 ***3259.35*** *p42*
Nittel, Barbara; Port uncertain, 1775 ***2856.30*** *p326*
Nittel, Hans Michael; America, 1744 ***2856.30*** *p326*
Nittlefield, James 23; Ontario, 1871 ***1823.15*** *p203*
Nittlefield, John 60; Ontario, 1871 ***1823.15*** *p203*
Nittlefield, William 37; Ontario, 1871 ***1823.15*** *p203*
Nitzel, William 31; Ontario, 1871 ***1823.28*** *p77*
Nival, William 21; Ontario, 1871 ***1823.28*** *p77*
Niven, Mr.; Quebec, 1858 ***9196.15*** *p33*
Niven, George; New York, 1807 ***8197.10*** *p331*
Niven, John; New Jersey, 1843 ***1224.3*** *p57*
Niven, John Paterson; New Jersey, 1840 ***1640.13*** *p95*
Niven, William; Montana, 1895 ***1640.13*** *p95*
Niver, Katherine; Maryland, 1671 ***2524.55*** *p161*
Nivin, Margaret 40; Ontario, 1871 ***1823.22*** *p118*
Nix, A. L. 20; Ontario, 1861 ***2896.25*** *p46*
Nix, Charles H. 9; Ontario, 1861 ***2896.25*** *p13*
Nix, Charlotte; Ontario, 1861 ***2896.25*** *p11*
Nix, Charlotte 28; Ontario, 1861 ***2896.25*** *p11*
Nix, Georg; Port uncertain, 1765 ***2856.30*** *p326*
Nix, Hannah 30; Ontario, 1861 ***2896.25*** *p13*
Nix, Jesse 21; Ontario, 1861 ***2896.25*** *p52*
Nix, Lewis 1; Ontario, 1861 ***2896.25*** *p11*
Nix, M. A. 10; Ontario, 1861 ***2896.25*** *p46*
Nix, M. A. 40; Ontario, 1861 ***2896.25*** *p46*
Nix, Martha A. 1; Ontario, 1861 ***2896.25*** *p13*
Nix, Osker 5; Ontario, 1861 ***2896.25*** *p13*
Nix, P. R. 7; Ontario, 1861 ***2896.25*** *p46*
Nix, Peter H. 61; Ontario, 1861 ***2896.25*** *p46*
Nix, S. 3; Ontario, 1861 ***2896.25*** *p11*
Nix, S. C. 18; Ontario, 1861 ***2896.25*** *p46*
Nix, S. L. 16; Ontario, 1861 ***2896.25*** *p46*
Nix, S. M. 10; Ontario, 1861 ***2896.25*** *p46*
Nix, William H. 28; Ontario, 1861 ***2896.25*** *p46*
Nix, William M. 2; Ontario, 1861 ***2896.25*** *p13*
Nixon, Allan 60; Ontario, 1871 ***1823.15*** *p203*
Nixon, Catherine 28; Ontario, 1871 ***1823.22*** *p118*
Nixon, Ellen; Vermont, 1895 ***5900.10*** *p494*
Nixon, George; New York, 1805 ***8197.10*** *p30*
Nixon, George 40; Ontario, 1871 ***1823.15*** *p203*
Nixon, Hugh 30; Ontario, 1871 ***1823.15*** *p203*
Nixon, James; New York, 1813 ***8197.10*** *p265*
Nixon, James; Pennsylvania, 1867 ***6058.10*** *p59*
Nixon, John; Pennsylvania, 1777 ***4629.10*** *p9*
Nixon, John 44; Ontario, 1871 ***1823.15*** *p203*
Nixon, John 104; Ontario, 1871 ***1823.15*** *p203*
Nixon, John B.; New York, 1830 ***8197.10*** *p362*
Nixon, John J.; Vermont, 1823-1908 ***5900.10*** *p596*
Nixon, Margaret 32; Ontario, 1871 ***1823.15*** *p203*
Nixon, Margaret 75; Ontario, 1871 ***1823.15*** *p203*
Nixon, Maria 72; Ontario, 1871 ***1823.22*** *p118*
Nixon, Ralph 30; Ontario, 1871 ***1823.15*** *p203*
Nixon, Richard 25; New York, 1775 ***1220.25*** *p142*
With wife
Nixon, Robert 52; Ontario, 1871 ***1823.22*** *p118*
Nixon, Sarah Ann; Vermont, 1832-1932 ***5900.10*** *p596*
Nixon, Serah Jane 27; Ontario, 1871 ***1823.22*** *p118*
Nixon, Thomas; Virginia, 1668-1669 ***6212.30*** *p41*
Nixon, William 26; Ontario, 1871 ***1823.28*** *p77*
Noah, Samuel; Pennsylvania, 1785 ***4629.10*** *p44*
Noak, Christe 26; Ontario, 1871 ***1823.28*** *p77*
Noak, Marten 42; Ontario, 1871 ***1823.28*** *p77*
Noakes, George; Maryland, 1670 ***2524.55*** *p161*
Noark, Mattk 35; Ontario, 1871 ***1823.28*** *p77*
Nobbs, Mary *SEE* Nobbs, Thomas
Nobbs, Mary; Maryland, 1631-1685 ***2524.55*** *p161*
Nobbs, Thomas; Maryland, 1637 ***2524.55*** *p161*
With wife
Daughter: Mary
Nobels, Irven 35; Ontario, 1861 ***2896.27*** *p2*
Nobels, Mary 7; Ontario, 1861 ***2896.27*** *p2*
Nobels, Sarah 75; Ontario, 1861 ***2896.27*** *p2*
Nober, Jakob; Port uncertain, 1765 ***2856.30*** *p326*
With wife & 3 children
Noble, . . .; Boston, 1737 ***4628.40*** *p114*
Noble, Alexander 81; Ontario, 1871 ***1823.22*** *p118*
Noble, Archibald; New York, 1807 ***8197.10*** *p331*
Noble, Barbara 39; Ontario, 1871 ***1823.22*** *p118*
Noble, Charles 35; Ontario, 1871 ***1823.15*** *p203*
Noble, Duncan; Florida, 1786 ***1640.10*** *p166*
Noble, Edward 44; Ontario, 1871 ***1823.28*** *p77*
Noble, Fanny 83; Ontario, 1871 ***1823.22*** *p118*
Noble, Francis; New York, 1807 ***8197.10*** *p330*
Noble, George 23; Ontario, 1861 ***2896.25*** *p72*
Noble, Isaack; Maryland, 1672 ***2524.55*** *p161*
Noble, Jane 50; Ontario, 1871 ***1823.22*** *p118*
Noble, Jerod 30; Ontario, 1871 ***1823.15*** *p204*
Noble, Joab 59; Ontario, 1871 ***1823.22*** *p118*
Noble, John; Georgia, 1743 ***1640.10*** *p167*
Noble, John; Maryland, 1682 ***2524.55*** *p161*
Noble, John 56; Ontario, 1871 ***1823.22*** *p118*
Noble, John 66; Ontario, 1871 ***1823.15*** *p204*
Noble, Joseph 26; Ontario, 1871 ***1823.15*** *p204*
Noble, Joseph 54; Ontario, 1871 ***1823.22*** *p118*
Noble, Margaret 35; Ontario, 1871 ***1823.15*** *p204*
Noble, Mark; Maryland, 1673 ***2524.55*** *p162*
Noble, Mark 48; Ontario, 1871 ***1823.22*** *p118*
Noble, Nevill; New York, 1787 ***1224.2*** *p85*
Noble, Robert; New York, 1839 ***8197.10*** *p136*
Noble, Robert 63; Ontario, 1871 ***1823.22*** *p118*
Noble, Samuel 50; Ontario, 1871 ***1823.15*** *p204*
Noble, Thomas 26; Ontario, 1871 ***1823.15*** *p204*
Noble, W. 49; Alaska, 1917 ***9196.1*** *p49*
Noble, W. 49; Whitehorse, Yukon, 1917 ***9196.1*** *p49*
Noble, William; New York, 1840 ***8197.10*** *p266*
Noble, William 1; Ontario, 1861 ***2896.25*** *p72*
Nobles, C. 25; Ontario, 1861 ***2896.26*** *p12*
Nobles, D. 20; Ontario, 1861 ***2896.26*** *p7*
Nobles, D. K. 15; Ontario, 1861 ***2896.26*** *p7*
Nobles, E. 51; Ontario, 1861 ***2896.26*** *p7*
Nobles, George 9; Ontario, 1861 ***2896.25*** *p61*
Nobles, Hannah 17; Ontario, 1861 ***2896.25*** *p61*
Nobles, James 7; Ontario, 1861 ***2896.25*** *p61*
Nobles, Lavina 21; Ontario, 1861 ***2896.28*** *p64*
Nobles, Lavina 22; Ontario, 1861 ***2896.25*** *p61*
Nobles, M. E. 12; Ontario, 1861 ***2896.26*** *p7*
Nobles, M. J. 4; Ontario, 1861 ***2896.26*** *p7*
Nobles, Mary *SEE* Nobles, Thomas
Nobles, Peter 11; Ontario, 1861 ***2896.25*** *p61*
Nobles, T. 8; Ontario, 1861 ***2896.26*** *p7*
Nobles, Thomas; Maryland, 1637 ***2524.55*** *p162*
With wife
Daughter: Mary
Nobles, Thomas 47; Ontario, 1861 ***2896.26*** *p7*
Nock, David; Pennsylvania, 1844 ***6058.10*** *p19*
Nock, Edward; New York, New York, 1836 ***6058.10*** *p18*
Nock, Eliza; Virginia, 1667 ***6212.30*** *p37*
Nock, Henry; Pennsylvania, 1844 ***6058.10*** *p19*
Nock, William; Virginia, 1667 ***6212.30*** *p37*
Nockold, Samuel; New York, 1719 ***1224.2*** *p85*
Noddin, Michael; Nova Scotia, 1774 ***1220.25*** *p137*
Nodel, Daniel; Pennsylvania, 1777 ***4629.10*** *p11*
Nodes, Edw; Virginia, 1698 ***6212.30*** *p60*
Nodolny, Adam; Maryland, 1910 ***3259.35*** *p42*
Nodolsky, Peter; Maryland, 1910 ***3259.35*** *p42*
Noe, Christof; Canada, 1763 ***2856.30*** *p327*
Noe, Christof; Port uncertain, 1764 ***2856.30*** *p326*
Noel, Elizabeth; New York, New York, n.d. ***1224.3*** *p57*
Noel, Henry C.; Alabama, 1837 ***1224.3*** *p57*
Noell, Edw; Virginia, 1665-1666 ***6212.30*** *p23*
Noell, James; Maryland, 1659 ***2524.55*** *p162*
Noell, Thos.; Maryland, 1658 ***2524.55*** *p162*
Nogel, Anna 27; Kansas, 1910 ***9079.10*** *p49*
Nogel, Catherina 26; Kansas, 1910 ***9079.10*** *p48*
Nogel, Jacob 26; Kansas, 1908-1910 ***9079.10*** *p48*
Nogel, Jacob 31; Kansas, 1900-1910 ***9079.10*** *p49*
Noglen, Leonard; New York, New York, 1850 ***6058.10*** *p44*
Nogler, Leonard; New York, New York, 1850 ***6058.10*** *p44*
Nogra, Christian 48; Ontario, 1871 ***1823.28*** *p77*
Noice, Charles 51; Ontario, 1871 ***1823.28*** *p77*
Noice, Thomas 53; Ontario, 1871 ***1823.15*** *p204*
Nojekam, J. Bte 42; Ontario, 1871 ***1823.28*** *p77*
Noke, William; Maryland, 1783 ***1224.2*** *p85*
Nolan, Mrs. 52; Ontario, 1871 ***1823.28*** *p77*
Nolan, Ada B. Cross; Vermont, 1864-1926 ***5900.10*** *p499*
Nolan, Amelia St. Pierre; Vermont, 1862-1937 ***5900.10*** *p225*
Nolan, Catharine Cassidy; Vermont, 1837-1937 ***5900.10*** *p510*
Nolan, Catherine Powers; Vermont, n.d. ***5900.10*** *p139*
Nolan, Edward; Vermont, 1854-1932 ***5900.10*** *p225*
Nolan, George 26; Ontario, 1871 ***1823.28*** *p77*
Nolan, Henry 25; Ontario, 1871 ***1823.15*** *p204*
Nolan, James 30; Ontario, 1871 ***1823.22*** *p118*
Nolan, John; Vermont, 1831-1931 ***5900.10*** *p510*
Nolan, John; Vermont, 1838-1905 ***5900.10*** *p139*
Nolan, Margret 40; Ontario, 1871 ***1823.22*** *p118*
Nolan, Martin 64; Vermont, 1893 ***5900.10*** *p249*
Nolan, Mary; Vermont, 1825-1888 ***5900.10*** *p86*
Nolan, Mary; Vermont, 1855-1955 ***5900.10*** *p291*
Nolan, Mary 40; Ontario, 1871 ***1823.22*** *p118*
Nolan, Mary 73; Vermont, 1883 ***5900.10*** *p480*
Nolan, Mary 74; Vermont, 1911 ***5900.10*** *p249*
Nolan, Patrick 75; Ontario, 1871 ***1823.22*** *p118*
Nolan, Peter 48; Ontario, 1871 ***1823.15*** *p204*
Nolan, Sarah; Vermont, 1836-1905 ***5900.10*** *p322*
Nolan, Sophie; Vermont, 1821-1867 ***5900.10*** *p384*
Nolan, Thomas 28; Vermont, 1908 ***5900.10*** *p249*
Nolan, Thomas Flood; New York, 1838 ***8197.10*** *p126*
Nolan, William 30; Ontario, 1871 ***1823.28*** *p77*
Nolan, William P.; Vermont, 1855-1926 ***5900.10*** *p499*
Noland, Bridget Kirlan; Vermont, n.d. ***5900.10*** *p237*
Noland, Hannah Donley 32; Vermont, 1880 ***5900.10*** *p237*
Noland, John 78; Vermont, 1871 ***5900.10*** *p237*
Noland, Mary A.; Vermont, 1828-1913 ***5900.10*** *p237*
Noland, Sarah; Vermont, 1842-1905 ***5900.10*** *p284*
Nolastek, Martin F.; Maryland, 1910 ***3259.35*** *p42*
Nolbrow, William 28; Maryland, 1774 ***1220.25*** *p71*
Nold, Josef; Port uncertain, 1754 ***2856.30*** *p326*
Nold, Josef; Port uncertain, 1787 ***2856.30*** *p326*
Nolen, James; New York, 1839 ***8197.10*** *p382*
Nolen, James 35; Ontario, 1871 ***1823.15*** *p204*
Nolin, Ellen Conroy; Vermont, 1853-1925 ***5900.10*** *p513*
Nolin, Louis; Vermont, 1845-1904 ***5900.10*** *p513*
Noll, Diebold; Port uncertain, 1771 ***2856.30*** *p306*
Noll, Sebastian; Port uncertain, 1764 ***2856.30*** *p326*
With wife & 2 children
Noll, William 27; Philadelphia, 1774 ***1220.25*** *p80*
Nolonier, Mr. 40; Grenada, 1774-1775 ***1220.25*** *p129*
Nolten, Henry 38; Ontario, 1871 ***1823.28*** *p77*
Nolton, Jacob; New York, 1807 ***8197.10*** *p47*
Nonamaker, Andrew; Pennsylvania, 1786 ***4629.10*** *p49*
Nonis, George 23; Philadelphia, 1775 ***1220.25*** *p122*
Nonius, Karl; Port uncertain, 1740 ***2856.30*** *p326*
Nonn, Emer; New York, 1806 ***8197.10*** *p323*
Nonnenmacher, Benedikt; Port uncertain, 1786 ***2856.30*** *p326*
Nonnenmacher, Konrad; Port uncertain, 1791 ***2856.30*** *p326*
Nonnweyler, Elis. Margarete; Port uncertain, 1733 ***2856.30*** *p326*
Nonnweyler, Franz; Port uncertain, 1755 ***2856.30*** *p326*
Nonoter, Jacob; Pennsylvania, 1778 ***4629.10*** *p34*
Noonan, Anna Casey; Vermont, 1865-1934 ***5900.10*** *p128*
Noonan, Catherine 68; Vermont, 1878 ***5900.10*** *p269*
Noonan, Daniel 60; Ontario, 1871 ***1823.22*** *p118*
Noonan, Dennis; Vermont, 1805-1885 ***5900.10*** *p167*
Noonan, Edward; Vermont, 1855-1900 ***5900.10*** *p128*
Noonan, Elizabeth; Vermont, 1836-1899 ***5900.10*** *p511*
Noonan, James; New York, New York, 1827 ***8197.10*** *p191*
Noonan, James P.; Vermont, n.d. ***5900.10*** *p399*
Noonan, Jeremiah 62; Vermont, 1901 ***5900.10*** *p176*
Noonan, Jno; Vermont, n.d. ***5900.10*** *p143*
Noonan, John 62; Vermont, 1889 ***5900.10*** *p155*
Noonan, John 83; Vermont, 1897 ***5900.10*** *p615*
Noonan, John W.; Vermont, 1856-1925 ***5900.10*** *p451*
Noonan, Kate I. 59; Vermont, 1926 ***5900.10*** *p452*
Noonan, Kate Purcell; Vermont, 1865-1949 ***5900.10*** *p451*
Noonan, Katherine Spellman 76; Vermont, 1890 ***5900.10*** *p615*
Noonan, Margaret Clarey; Vermont, 1847-1932 ***5900.10*** *p176*
Noonan, Martha; Vermont, n.d. ***5900.10*** *p399*
Noonan, Mary 63; Vermont, 1888 ***5900.10*** *p571*
Noonan, Mary Donovan; Vermont, 1825-1895 ***5900.10*** *p168*

Noonan, Mary McKenzie; Vermont, 1827-1915 ***5900.10*** *p155*
Noonan, Mary O'Leary; Vermont, 1833-1878 ***5900.10*** *p177*
Noonan, Michael R.; Vermont, n.d. ***5900.10*** *p399*
Noonan, Patrick; Vermont, 1840-1884 ***5900.10*** *p511*
Noonan, Patrick W.; Vermont, n.d. ***5900.10*** *p399*
Noonan, Thomas J.; Vermont, n.d. ***5900.10*** *p399*
Noonan, Timothy; Vermont, n.d. ***5900.10*** *p399*
Noone, Mary; Vermont, 1845-1924 ***5900.10*** *p393*
Noonen, Cornelius; New York, 1838 ***8197.10*** *p266*
Nooney, Helen; Illinois, 1894 ***1640.13*** *p95*
Noore, John; Died enroute, 1693 ***1224.1*** *p42*
Noparstek, Dora; Maryland, 1910 ***3259.35*** *p42*
Nopel, Anton; Port uncertain, 1736 ***2856.30*** *p327*
Nopel, Anton; Port uncertain, 1737 ***2856.30*** *p327*
Nopp, Josef; Port uncertain, 1764 ***2856.30*** *p327*
Norbel, Valentin; Port uncertain, 1725 ***2856.30*** *p328*
Norcuski, Antone; Maryland, 1910 ***3259.35*** *p42*
Nordblad, Gustav; New York, 1840 ***8197.10*** *p191*
Nordell, John; Virginia, 1665 ***6212.30*** *p18*
Nordige, Katherin; Virginia, 1671-1672 ***6212.30*** *p45*
Nordon, John; Pennsylvania, 1777 ***4629.10*** *p19*
Nordonski, James; Maryland, 1910 ***3259.35*** *p42*
Norgal, John; Maryland, 1910 ***3259.35*** *p42*
Norgrove, Nathaniel; Pennsylvania, 1777 ***4629.10*** *p13*
Norie, Catharine; Portsmouth, New Hampshire, 1804 ***1224.3*** *p49*
Noris, Hugh 30; Ontario, 1871 ***1823.15*** *p204*
Norisic, Peter; Maryland, 1910 ***3259.35*** *p42*
Norlee, James; Virginia, 1681-1682 ***6212.30*** *p56*
Norleigh, Henry; Virginia, 1666-1667 ***6212.30*** *p32*
Norlin, Johan 27; British Columbia, 1911 ***9196.1*** *p15*
Norlin, Johan 27; San Francisco, 1911 ***9196.1*** *p15*
Norman, Mrs.; Maryland, 1650 ***2524.55*** *p162*
Norman, Mrs.; Maryland, 1658 ***2524.55*** *p162*
Norman, Mrs.; Quebec, 1857 ***9196.15*** *p23*
Norman, Agnes; Maryland, 1658 ***2524.55*** *p162*
Norman, Charles 60; Ontario, 1871 ***1823.15*** *p204*
Norman, Edward; Maryland, 1672 ***2524.55*** *p162*
Norman, Jane; Maryland, 1664 ***2524.55*** *p162*
Norman, Jno; Virginia, 1681-1682 ***6212.30*** *p56*
Norman, John; Charles Town, South Carolina, 1813 ***1224.3*** *p57*
Norman, John; Maryland, 1667 ***2524.55*** *p162*
Norman, John 18; Maryland, 1774 ***1220.25*** *p69*
Norman, John 22; Philadelphia, 1774 ***1220.25*** *p67*
Norman, John Moore; New York, 1835-1840 ***8197.10*** *p302*
Norman, Joseph; Pennsylvania, 1777 ***4629.10*** *p29*
Norman, Rebecca; Maryland, 1676 ***2524.55*** *p162*
Norman, Thomas; New York, 1826-1834 ***8197.10*** *p305*
Norman, William; New York, 1802 ***8197.10*** *p23*
Norman, William; New York, 1809 ***8197.10*** *p55*
Norman, William 26; Ontario, 1871 ***1823.28*** *p77*
Norman, William 60; Ontario, 1871 ***1823.15*** *p204*
Normand, A.; Quebec, 1858 ***9196.15*** *p35*
Normand, John; Maryland, 1650 ***2524.55*** *p162*
Normann, Henry H.; New York, 1806 ***8197.10*** *p32*
Normard, Mr.; Quebec, 1858 ***9196.15*** *p36*
Normile, Bridget; Vermont, 1832-1900 ***5900.10*** *p88*
Normile, Dennis; Pennsylvania, 1868 ***6058.10*** *p77*
Normyle, Honore; Vermont, 1910 ***5900.10*** *p54*
Norn, John; Savannah, Georgia, 1775 ***1640.10*** *p167*
Norpel, Johann; America, 1739 ***2856.30*** *p328*
Norrice, Charles; Quebec, 1858 ***9196.15*** *p46*
Norrie, Adam; New York, 1836 ***8197.10*** *p77*
Norrie, George; Manitoba, 1883 ***1640.13*** *p95*
Norrie, John Sanderson; Toronto, 1898 ***1640.13*** *p95*
Norrie, Robert; Georgia, 1698 ***1640.13*** *p95*
Norringsworth, James; Virginia, 1667-1668 ***6212.30*** *p39*
Norrington, John; Maryland, 1681 ***2524.55*** *p162*
Norrington, William; Virginia, 1697 ***1224.1*** *p42*
Norris, Mr.; Quebec, 1857 ***9196.15*** *p25*
Norris, Mrs.; Quebec, 1857 ***9196.15*** *p25*
Norris, Andrew; Boston, 1753 ***1224.2*** *p85*
Norris, Ann 17; Baltimore, 1775 ***1220.25*** *p116*
Norris, Frances 31; Ontario, 1871 ***1823.15*** *p204*
Norris, Henry; New York, 1836 ***8197.10*** *p266*
Norris, Henry Lee; New Jersey, 1900 ***1640.13*** *p95*
Norris, Hugh 17; Maryland, 1775 ***1220.25*** *p120*
Norris, Isaac; Philadelphia, 1767 ***1224.2*** *p85*
Norris, James; Virginia, 1677 ***6212.30*** *p53*
Norris, John; Virginia, 1664 ***6212.30*** *p11*
Norris, John; Virginia, 1671-1672 ***6212.30*** *p47*
Norris, John 57; Ontario, 1871 ***1823.22*** *p118*
Norris, Marian Schaeffer; New York, 1890 ***1640.13*** *p95*
Norris, Richard 30; Ontario, 1871 ***1823.22*** *p118*
Norris, Thomas; Maryland, 1661 ***2524.55*** *p162*
Norris, Thomas; Maryland, 1663 ***2524.55*** *p162*
Norris, Thomas; Maryland, 1666 ***2524.55*** *p162*
Norris, Thomas; New York, 1803 ***8197.10*** *p15*
Norris, William; New York, 1802 ***8197.10*** *p23*
Norris, William; Ontario, 1871 ***1823.28*** *p77*
Norris, William 60; Ontario, 1871 ***1823.15*** *p204*
Norris, William Richard; New York, 1837 ***8197.10*** *p96*
Norrish, Thomas; Maryland, 1666 ***2524.55*** *p162*
Norrison, John 36; Maryland, 1775 ***1220.25*** *p113*
Norry, Catharine; Portsmouth, New Hampshire, 1804 ***1224.3*** *p49*
Norsworthy, Henry 32; Ontario, 1871 ***1823.15*** *p204*
Norsworthy, Samuel; New York, 1807 ***8197.10*** *p47*
Nort, Georg; Port uncertain, 1751 ***2856.30*** *p327*
Norten, John; Maryland, 1663 ***2524.55*** *p162*
Norten, Smith 18; Ontario, 1861 ***2896.27*** *p43*
Norten, Toby; Virginia, 1665-1666 ***6212.30*** *p23*
North, Francis Thomas; New York, 1838 ***8197.10*** *p266*
North, George; Pennsylvania, 1777 ***4629.10*** *p29*
North, John; Pennsylvania, 1777 ***4629.10*** *p9*
North, John; Virginia, 1666 ***6212.30*** *p29*
North, Joseph; Virginia, 1667-1668 ***6212.30*** *p38*
North, Margaret Burgey; Vermont, 1835-1911 ***5900.10*** *p609*
North, Margery; Maryland, 1681 ***2524.55*** *p162*
North, Richard; Virginia, 1666 ***6212.30*** *p26*
North, Ridgeby; Virginia, 1666 ***6212.30*** *p27*
North, Samuel; Pennsylvania, 1777 ***4629.10*** *p15*
North, Sarah 27; Maryland, 1775 ***1220.25*** *p110*
North, Stephen; Boston, 1723 ***1224.2*** *p85*
North, Thomas; Virginia, 1666-1667 ***6212.30*** *p34*
North, William; Virginia, 1667-1668 ***6212.30*** *p39*
Northcott, Thomas 23; Ontario, 1871 ***1823.22*** *p118*
Northcutt, William 61; Ontario, 1871 ***1823.22*** *p118*
Northeimer, Bernard; New York, 1839 ***8197.10*** *p266*
Northey, William 37; Maryland, 1775 ***1220.25*** *p121*
Northgate, Lewis; Virginia, 1666 ***6212.30*** *p25*
Nortman, Mary; Maryland, 1910 ***3259.35*** *p42*
Norton, Mrs.; Maryland, 1655 ***2524.55*** *p162*
Norton, Mrs.; Maryland, 1659 ***2524.55*** *p162*
Norton, Alfred 19; Ontario, 1871 ***1823.28*** *p77*
Norton, Ann 79; Vermont, 1894 ***5900.10*** *p95*
Norton, Anne; Maryland, 1680 ***2524.55*** *p162*
Norton, Bernard 82; Vermont, 1923 ***5900.10*** *p95*
Norton, Bridget 36; Vermont, 1868 ***5900.10*** *p561*
Norton, Catherine; Vermont, 1828-1899 ***5900.10*** *p350*
Norton, Cordelia 9; Ontario, 1861 ***2896.27*** *p64*
Norton, Edmund; Maryland, 1664 ***2524.55*** *p162*
Norton, Elizabeth 75; Vermont, 1925 ***5900.10*** *p95*
Norton, Francis 21; Ontario, 1871 ***1823.28*** *p77*
Norton, George 37; Ontario, 1871 ***1823.28*** *p77*
Norton, Helen Clark; Vermont, 1824-1918 ***5900.10*** *p321*
Norton, J. 59; Alaska, 1917 ***9196.1*** *p49*
Norton, J. 59; Whitehorse, Yukon, 1917 ***9196.1*** *p49*
Norton, James; New York, 1780 ***1224.2*** *p85*
Norton, James; Virginia, 1664 ***6212.30*** *p10*
Norton, Jeffry; Virginia, 1664 ***6212.30*** *p5*
Norton, Jno; Virginia, 1665-1666 ***6212.30*** *p22*
Norton, John; Maryland, 1663 ***2524.55*** *p162*
Norton, John; Vermont, 1845-1915 ***5900.10*** *p311*
Norton, John 11; Ontario, 1861 ***2896.27*** *p46*
Norton, John 21; Georgia, 1774 ***1220.25*** *p47*
Norton, John 30; Maryland, 1774 ***1220.25*** *p39*
Norton, Julia 41; Vermont, 1898 ***5900.10*** *p95*
Norton, Kathrine; Vermont, 1862-1895 ***5900.10*** *p350*
Norton, Margaret 56; Vermont, 1890 ***5900.10*** *p569*
Norton, Margaret 77; Vermont, 1933 ***5900.10*** *p95*
Norton, Margaret Moriarty; Vermont, 1850-1926 ***5900.10*** *p349*
Norton, Martha; New York, New York, 1815 ***1224.3*** *p57*
Norton, Martha 7; Ontario, 1861 ***2896.27*** *p46*
Norton, Mary 15; Ontario, 1861 ***2896.27*** *p65*
Norton, Mary D. 16; Vermont, 1860 ***5900.10*** *p95*
Norton, Mary Houghton; New England, 1653 ***1224.1*** *p31*
Norton, Matilda J. 5; Ontario, 1861 ***2896.27*** *p46*
Norton, Michael 50; Vermont, 1901 ***5900.10*** *p95*
Norton, Michael 60; Vermont, 1870 ***5900.10*** *p95*
Norton, Mike 56; Vermont, 1882 ***5900.10*** *p96*
Norton, Nathan 42; Ontario, 1871 ***1823.28*** *p77*
Norton, Nathaniel 26; Maryland, 1774 ***1220.25*** *p84*
Norton, Patrick; Vermont, 1851-1901 ***5900.10*** *p350*
Norton, Patrick 67; Vermont, 1925 ***5900.10*** *p95*
Norton, Peter 77; Vermont, 1920 ***5900.10*** *p95*
Norton, Robert 23; Grenada, 1774 ***1220.25*** *p37*
Norton, Rose 78; Vermont, 1925 ***5900.10*** *p95*
Norton, Samuel; New York, 1815 ***1224.3*** *p57*
Norton, Samuel; New York, New York, 1791 ***1224.2*** *p85*
Norton, Sara; Virginia, 1664 ***6212.30*** *p9*
Norton, Susan 55; Vermont, 1885 ***5900.10*** *p96*
Norton, Tho; Virginia, 1665-1666 ***6212.30*** *p22*
Norton, Thomas; Vermont, 1848-1926 ***5900.10*** *p349*
Norton, Thomas 63; Ontario, 1871 ***1823.15*** *p204*
Norton, Thomas Frederick 27; Philadelphia, 1774 ***1220.25*** *p35*
Norton, Tobias; Maryland, 1658 ***2524.55*** *p162*
Norton, Tobias; Virginia, 1658 ***1224.1*** *p42*
Norton, William; New York, 1834 ***8197.10*** *p266*
Norton, William 75; Ontario, 1871 ***1823.22*** *p118*
Norton, William H.; Vermont, 1855-1884 ***5900.10*** *p321*
Norton, William K.; Vermont, 1822-1891 ***5900.10*** *p321*
Norvaki, Jaskwas; Maryland, 1910 ***3259.35*** *p42*
Norves, Toby; Virginia, 1666-1667 ***6212.30*** *p32*
Norvich, August; Maryland, 1910 ***3259.35*** *p42*
Norwich, Esther Dent; Vermont, 1819-1905 ***5900.10*** *p496*
Norwich, Jean; Virginia, 1666-1667 ***6212.30*** *p34*
Norwich, Robt; Virginia, 1666-1667 ***6212.30*** *p34*
Norwood, Andrew *SEE* Norwood, John
Norwood, John *SEE* Norwood, John
Norwood, John; Maryland, 1650 ***2524.55*** *p162*
With wife
Child: Andrew
Child: John
Norwood, John; Maryland, 1658 ***2524.55*** *p162*
With wife
Norwood, Thomas; Virginia, 1679 ***1224.1*** *p42*
Nosal, Joseph; Maryland, 1910 ***3259.35*** *p42*
Nosek, James; Maryland, 1910 ***3259.35*** *p42*
Noskes, George; Maryland, 1665 ***2524.55*** *p114*
Nosworthy, Edw; Virginia, 1666 ***6212.30*** *p28*
Nosworthy, Joan; Virginia, 1664 ***6212.30*** *p10*
Noter, Edwd; Virginia, 1690-1691 ***6212.30*** *p58*
Noth, Henry 31; Ontario, 1871 ***1823.15*** *p204*
Nothgate, John 55; Ontario, 1871 ***1823.15*** *p204*
Notley, Edw; Virginia, 1664 ***6212.30*** *p14*
Notley, Peter 27; Maryland, 1774 ***1220.25*** *p39*
Notman, Mrs.; Quebec, 1856 ***9196.15*** *p11*
Notres, Tho; Virginia, 1665-1666 ***6212.30*** *p23*
Nott, Edward; Virginia, 1664 ***6212.30*** *p9*
Nott, Edward; Virginia, 1706 ***1224.2*** *p66*
Nott, John 69; Ontario, 1871 ***1823.15*** *p204*
Nott, Thomas 24; Ontario, 1871 ***1823.15*** *p204*
Nottingham, John; Maryland, 1658 ***2524.55*** *p162*
Nottingham, Thomas; Maryland, 1674 ***2524.55*** *p162*
Nottingham, Thomas; Maryland, 1675 ***2524.55*** *p162*
Nottley, Mary; Maryland, 1681 ***2524.55*** *p162*
Notz, Johann Leonhard; America, 1738 ***2856.30*** *p327*
With wife & children
Nourse, Elizabeth; Missouri, 1847 ***1224.3*** *p13*
Nourse, Sarah Fouace; Philadelphia, 1785 ***1224.2*** *p85*
Nourse, Thomas; New York, 1807 ***8197.10*** *p47*
Novak, August; Maryland, 1910 ***3259.35*** *p42*
Novak, Edward; Maryland, 1910 ***3259.35*** *p42*
Novak, Irene; Maryland, 1910 ***3259.35*** *p43*
Novak, Martin; Maryland, 1910 ***3259.35*** *p43*
Novak, Mary A. Spellman; Vermont, 1854-1919 ***5900.10*** *p447*
Novak, Michael; Maryland, 1910 ***3259.35*** *p43*
Novak, Peter; Maryland, 1910 ***3259.35*** *p43*
Novak, Peter P.; Maryland, 1910 ***3259.35*** *p43*
Novakosky, Wladislow; Maryland, 1910 ***3259.35*** *p43*
Novakowski, Casmar J.; Maryland, 1910 ***3259.35*** *p43*
Novecinskie, Wanston; Maryland, 1910 ***3259.35*** *p43*
Novitnski, Walter; Maryland, 1910 ***3259.35*** *p43*
Novocinskie, Peter; Maryland, 1910 ***3259.35*** *p43*
Novotny, Wenceslaus; Maryland, 1910 ***3259.35*** *p43*
Novrzchauski, Walter; Maryland, 1910 ***3259.35*** *p43*
Novuk, Augustus 40; Ontario, 1871 ***1823.28*** *p77*
Novyzmska, Joseph; Maryland, 1910 ***3259.35*** *p43*
Nowacki, Adam; Maryland, 1910 ***3259.35*** *p43*
Nowacki, Ignacy; Maryland, 1910 ***3259.35*** *p43*
Nowak, Alberta; Maryland, 1910 ***3259.35*** *p43*
Nowak, Antonie; Maryland, 1910 ***3259.35*** *p43*
Nowak, Baltazar; Maryland, 1910 ***3259.35*** *p43*
Nowak, Casper; Maryland, 1910 ***3259.35*** *p43*
Nowak, Cebbe; Maryland, 1910 ***3259.35*** *p43*
Nowak, Ignacy; Maryland, 1910 ***3259.35*** *p43*
Nowak, James; Maryland, 1910 ***3259.35*** *p43*
Nowak, John; Maryland, 1910 ***3259.35*** *p43*
Nowak, Joseph; Maryland, 1910 ***3259.35*** *p43*
Nowak, Joseph S.; Maryland, 1910 ***3259.35*** *p43*
Nowak, Jozefee; Maryland, 1910 ***3259.35*** *p43*
Nowak, Katiazyna; Maryland, 1910 ***3259.35*** *p43*
Nowak, Ludyander; Maryland, 1910 ***3259.35*** *p43*
Nowak, Martin; Maryland, 1910 ***3259.35*** *p43*
Nowak, Michel; Maryland, 1910 ***3259.35*** *p43*
Nowak, Stanislaw; Maryland, 1910 ***3259.35*** *p43*
Nowak, Stansilaus; Maryland, 1910 ***3259.35*** *p43*
Nowak, Stephen; Maryland, 1910 ***3259.35*** *p43*
Nowak, Thomas; Maryland, 1910 ***3259.35*** *p43*
Nowak, Valeria; Maryland, 1910 ***3259.35*** *p43*
Nowak, William; Maryland, 1910 ***3259.35*** *p43*
Nowakewski, Andrew; Maryland, 1910 ***3259.35*** *p43*
Nowakowska, Agnes; Maryland, 1910 ***3259.35*** *p43*
Nowakowski, Antone; Maryland, 1910 ***3259.35*** *p43*
Nowakowski, Frank; Maryland, 1910 ***3259.35*** *p43*
Nowakowski, John; Maryland, 1910 ***3259.35*** *p43*
Nowakowski, Joseph; Maryland, 1910 ***3259.35*** *p43*
Nowakowski, Szcsepan; Maryland, 1910 ***3259.35*** *p43*
Nowakowski, Wladyslaw; Maryland, 1910 ***3259.35*** *p43*

O

Oak, Margret 70; Ontario, 1871 ***1823.15*** *p205*
Oak, Mary 46; Ontario, 1871 ***1823.15*** *p205*
Oakden, John 35; Ontario, 1871 ***1823.28*** *p78*
Oakden, William; Virginia, 1666-1667 ***6212.30*** *p33*
Oakden, William 48; Ontario, 1871 ***1823.28*** *p78*
Oake, Thomas; Virginia, 1666 ***6212.30*** *p25*
Oakeland, Alice; Virginia, 1665-1666 ***6212.30*** *p25*
Oakeland, Tho; Virginia, 1666 ***6212.30*** *p25*
Oakeley, John 19; Virginia, 1773 ***1220.25*** *p29*
Oakes, B. A.; Quebec, 1857 ***9196.15*** *p14*
Oakes, Edward; Maryland, 1655-1656 ***2524.55*** *p163*
Oakes, Edward 27; Vermont, 1866 ***5900.10*** *p319*
Oakes, George 58; Ontario, 1871 ***1823.15*** *p205*
Oakes, Thomas; New York, 1794 ***8197.10*** *p4*
Oakes, William 23; Maryland, 1774 ***1220.25*** *p52*
Oakley, Robert 36; Ontario, 1871 ***1823.22*** *p119*
Oakley, Samuel 36; Ontario, 1871 ***1823.22*** *p119*
Oakley, Samuel 38; Ontario, 1871 ***1823.22*** *p119*
Oakley, Samuel 40; Ontario, 1871 ***1823.22*** *p119*
Oakley, William Smith; Kentucky, 1825 ***1224.3*** *p57*
Oakley, William Smith; New York, 1818 ***8197.10*** *p267*
Oakly, William; Virginia, 1664 ***6212.30*** *p11*
Oakly, William 39; Ontario, 1871 ***1823.15*** *p205*
Oaks, Edward 70; Ontario, 1871 ***1823.22*** *p119*
Oaks, John; Vermont, 1838-1910 ***5900.10*** *p69*
Oaks, Nora Brown; Vermont, 1837-1919 ***5900.10*** *p69*
Oaslter, James 31; Ontario, 1871 ***1823.28*** *p78*
Oastler, Andrew 28; Ontario, 1871 ***1823.28*** *p78*
Oately, Christopher; Maryland, 1649-1650 ***2524.55*** *p163*
Oately, Christopher; Maryland, 1659 ***2524.55*** *p163*
Oately, Christopher; Maryland, 1663 ***2524.55*** *p163*
Oately, Mary; Maryland, 1677-1681 ***2524.55*** *p163*
Oates, Edward; New York, 1802 ***8197.10*** *p23*
Oates, Ellen; Vermont, 1860-1949 ***5900.10*** *p398*
Oates, Mary McDonnell 52; Vermont, 1890 ***5900.10*** *p385*
Oates, Patrick 76; Vermont, 1909 ***5900.10*** *p385*
Oates, Richard; Pennsylvania, 1777 ***4629.10*** *p11*
Oats, Richard 38; Ontario, 1871 ***1823.28*** *p78*
Obbetosoway, George 45; Ontario, 1871 ***1823.28*** *p78*
Obbetossway, Mrs. George 47; Ontario, 1871 ***1823.28*** *p78*
Obbetossway, Kitty 28; Ontario, 1871 ***1823.28*** *p78*
O'Beirne, Rebecca; Philadelphia, n.d. ***1224.3*** *p57*
Obeley, John Peter 25; Maryland, 1774 ***1220.25*** *p62*
Obelmann, Johann Henrich; America, 1748 ***2856.30*** *p329*
Obelmann, Michael; Port uncertain, 1754 ***2856.30*** *p329*
Obenauer, Leopold; Port uncertain, 1782 ***2856.30*** *p329*
Oberacker, Hans Georg; Port uncertain, 1739 ***2856.30*** *p329*
Oberbeck, Andreas; America, 1732 ***2856.30*** *p329*
With wife 2 sons & 2 daughters
Oberdorf, Franz Joh. C.; America, 1776-1799 ***2856.30*** *p329*
Oberlaender, Heinrich; New York, 1837 ***8197.10*** *p96*
Oberle, Johann Georg; Port uncertain, 1752 ***2856.30*** *p329*
Oberle, Josef; America, 1740 ***2856.30*** *p329*
Oberle, Susanna; America, 1752 ***2856.30*** *p329*
With husband
Oberlein, Adam; Port uncertain, 1735 ***2856.30*** *p329*
Obermayer, Georg; Port uncertain, 1746 ***2856.30*** *p329*
Obermoser, Jerg; Port uncertain, 1771 ***2856.30*** *p329*
O'Bern, Patrick 50; Ontario, 1871 ***1823.15*** *p204*
Oberrieder, Michael; America, 1758 ***2856.30*** *p329*
With wife & 3 children
Obert, Bertram; Maryland, 1646 ***2524.55*** *p163*
Obert, Peter; America, 1753 ***2856.30*** *p329*
Obery, William; Maryland, 1670 ***2524.55*** *p163*
Obholtzer, Johann Georg; Port uncertain, 1738 ***2856.30*** *p329*
Obojski, Alexander; Maryland, 1910 ***3259.35*** *p44*
Oboncpak, Stumac; Maryland, 1910 ***3259.35*** *p44*
Oborne, Thomas Watts 35; Maryland, 1774 ***1220.25*** *p53*
O'Boyle, James 45; Ontario, 1871 ***1823.28*** *p78*
Obrecht, Martin; Port uncertain, 1788 ***2856.30*** *p329*
Obrian, Archibald 24; Virginia, 1773 ***1220.25*** *p29*
O'Brian, Brian 24; Maryland, 1775 ***1220.25*** *p116*
Obrian, David 55; Ontario, 1871 ***1823.28*** *p78*
O'Brian, Ellen; Vermont, 1827-1895 ***5900.10*** *p157*
O'Brian, Henry 21; Ontario, 1871 ***1823.28*** *p78*
Obrian, Henry 66; Ontario, 1871 ***1823.28*** *p78*
O'Brian, Jennett 62; Ontario, 1871 ***1823.28*** *p78*
O'Brian, John; New York, 1838 ***8197.10*** *p147*
Obrian, Johnson 26; Ontario, 1871 ***1823.15*** *p205*
O'Brian, Michael; New York, 1837 ***8197.10*** *p96*
O'Brian, Michael; Pennsylvania, 1785 ***4629.10*** *p48*
Obrian, Mortimer; Maryland, 1671 ***2524.55*** *p163*
O'Brian, Patrick 25; Philadelphia, 1774 ***1220.25*** *p35*
O'Brian, Patrick 51; Ontario, 1871 ***1823.15*** *p204*
Obrian, Robt 32; Ontario, 1871 ***1823.15*** *p205*
O'Brian, Thomas 27; Philadelphia, 1774 ***1220.25*** *p35*
O'Brien, Albert J. 10 months; Vermont, n.d. ***5900.10*** *p162*
O'Brien, Alice 48; Vermont, 1884 ***5900.10*** *p229*
O'Brien, Alice 60; Vermont, 1879 ***5900.10*** *p404*
O'Brien, Amelia; Vermont, n.d. ***5900.10*** *p160*
O'Brien, Amelia A.; Vermont, 1852-1912 ***5900.10*** *p602*
Obrien, Ann 38; Ontario, 1871 ***1823.15*** *p205*
O'Brien, Annie; Vermont, 1849-1916 ***5900.10*** *p593*
O'Brien, Bridget; Vermont, 1837-1924 ***5900.10*** *p424*
O'Brien, Bridget; Vermont, 1842-1917 ***5900.10*** *p541*
O'Brien, Bridget; Vermont, 1847-1896 ***5900.10*** *p388*
O'Brien, Bridget; Vermont, 1847-1914 ***5900.10*** *p63*
O'Brien, Bridget; Vermont, 1869-1925 ***5900.10*** *p255*
O'Brien, Bridget 55; Ontario, 1861 ***2896.27*** *p74*
O'Brien, Bridget 64; Vermont, 1890 ***5900.10*** *p262*
O'Brien, Bridget Callahan; Vermont, 1856-1924 ***5900.10*** *p551*
O'Brien, Bridget Dolan 66; Vermont, 1899 ***5900.10*** *p600*
O'Brien, Bridget Fogarty 65; Vermont, 1899 ***5900.10*** *p381*
O'Brien, Bridget Keefe; Vermont, 1855-1904 ***5900.10*** *p159*
O'Brien, Bridget M. Deady 76; Vermont, 1898 ***5900.10*** *p165*
O'Brien, Bridget Meagher; Vermont, 1837-1910 ***5900.10*** *p581*
O'Brien, Bridget Smith 30; Vermont, 1874 ***5900.10*** *p564*
O'Brien, Bryan; New York, 1839 ***8197.10*** *p136*
O'Brien, Catharine; Vermont, 1891 ***5900.10*** *p215*
O'Brien, Catharine 50; Vermont, 1864 ***5900.10*** *p67*
O'Brien, Catharine 77; Vermont, 1866 ***5900.10*** *p67*
O'Brien, Catherine; Vermont, 1841-1904 ***5900.10*** *p223*
O'Brien, Catherine; Vermont, 1857-1928 ***5900.10*** *p262*
O'Brien, Catherine 16; Ontario, 1861 ***2896.27*** *p74*
O'Brien, Catherine 25; Vermont, 1848 ***5900.10*** *p348*
O'Brien, Catherine 65; Vermont, 1913 ***5900.10*** *p192*
O'Brien, Catherine 67; Vermont, 1870 ***5900.10*** *p362*
O'Brien, Catherine 74; Vermont, 1887 ***5900.10*** *p178*
O'Brien, Catherine 77; Vermont, 1875 ***5900.10*** *p577*
O'Brien, Catherine 80; Ontario, 1871 ***1823.15*** *p204*
Obrien, Catherine 80; Ontario, 1871 ***1823.15*** *p205*
O'Brien, Catherine E.; Vermont, 1858-1934 ***5900.10*** *p59*
O'Brien, Catherine Horigan 70; Vermont, 1892 ***5900.10*** *p551*
O'Brien, Catherine Lally; Vermont, 1814-1899 ***5900.10*** *p601*
O'Brien, Catherine Murphy; Vermont, 1869-1927 ***5900.10*** *p255*
O'Brien, Catherine O'Donnell; Vermont, 1852-1919 ***5900.10*** *p385*
O'Brien, Catherine Ryan; Vermont, 1830-1878 ***5900.10*** *p63*
O'Brien, Catie 3; Vermont, 1878 ***5900.10*** *p97*
O'Brien, Charles; New York, 1837 ***8197.10*** *p319*
O'Brien, Charles; New York, 1839 ***8197.10*** *p136*
Obrien, Charles 30; Ontario, 1871 ***1823.22*** *p119*
O'Brien, Charles 67; Ontario, 1871 ***1823.28*** *p78*
O'Brien, Charlotte Foley 73; Vermont, 1913 ***5900.10*** *p564*
O'Brien, Cornelius; Vermont, 1857-1937 ***5900.10*** *p408*
O'Brien, Cornelius; Vermont, 1897 ***5900.10*** *p408*
O'Brien, Dan 26; Ontario, 1871 ***1823.28*** *p78*
O'Brien, Daniel; New York, 1827-1834 ***8197.10*** *p309*
O'Brien, Daniel; New York, 1837 ***8197.10*** *p95*
O'Brien, Daniel; New York, 1840 ***8197.10*** *p191*
O'Brien, Daniel; Vermont, 1824-1910 ***5900.10*** *p63*
O'Brien, Daniel; Vermont, 1857-1930 ***5900.10*** *p159*
O'Brien, Daniel 98; Vermont, 1905 ***5900.10*** *p437*
O'Brien, Daniel J.; Vermont, 1855-1929 ***5900.10*** *p192*
Obrien, David 26; Ontario, 1871 ***1823.15*** *p205*
O'Brien, Denis; New York, 1839 ***8197.10*** *p136*
Obrien, Dennis 65; Ontario, 1871 ***1823.22*** *p119*
O'Brien, Dennis 67; Vermont, 1899 ***5900.10*** *p381*
O'Brien, Eddie 1 day; Vermont, n.d. ***5900.10*** *p162*
O'Brien, Edward; Vermont, 1833-1909 ***5900.10*** *p562*
O'Brien, Edward E.; Vermont, n.d. ***5900.10*** *p160*
O'Brien, Elesebath 35; Ontario, 1871 ***1823.28*** *p78*
O'Brien, Eliza; Vermont, 1834-1921 ***5900.10*** *p241*
O'Brien, Elizabeth 80; Vermont, 1843 ***5900.10*** *p601*
O'Brien, Ellen; Vermont, 1839-1909 ***5900.10*** *p162*
O'Brien, Ellen; Vermont, 1846-1925 ***5900.10*** *p55*
O'Brien, Ellen; Vermont, 1865 ***5900.10*** *p264*
O'Brien, Ellen 44; Vermont, 1891 ***5900.10*** *p201*
Obrien, Ellen 50; Ontario, 1871 ***1823.15*** *p205*
O'Brien, Ellen 76; Vermont, 1881 ***5900.10*** *p323*
O'Brien, Ellen Cantlow 73; Vermont, 1909 ***5900.10*** *p117*
O'Brien, Ellen M.; Vermont, 1855-1940 ***5900.10*** *p466*
O'Brien, Francis; Vermont, 1829-1915 ***5900.10*** *p546*
O'Brien, Hannah Bradley; Vermont, 1857-1938 ***5900.10*** *p192*
O'Brien, Hannah McNamara; Vermont, 1856-1929 ***5900.10*** *p592*
O'Brien, Hannah Ward; Vermont, 1902 ***5900.10*** *p408*
Obrien, Honoura 43; Ontario, 1871 ***1823.28*** *p78*
O'Brien, James; New York, 1839 ***8197.10*** *p268*
O'Brien, James; Vermont, 1846-1928 ***5900.10*** *p553*
O'Brien, James; Vermont, 1854 ***5900.10*** *p95*
O'Brien, James 65; Vermont, 1880 ***5900.10*** *p67*
Obrien, James 77; Ontario, 1871 ***1823.15*** *p205*
O'Brien, James 98; Vermont, 1872 ***5900.10*** *p264*
O'Brien, James E.; Vermont, 1871-1926 ***5900.10*** *p59*
Obrien, Jane 70; Ontario, 1871 ***1823.15*** *p205*
O'Brien, Jane Burke; Vermont, 1856-1937 ***5900.10*** *p161*
O'Brien, Jeanette; Vermont, 1851-1920 ***5900.10*** *p600*
O'Brien, Jeremiah; Vermont, 1820-1910 ***5900.10*** *p178*
O'Brien, Jeremiah; Vermont, 1850-1928 ***5900.10*** *p555*
O'Brien, Jeremiah 33; Vermont, 1890 ***5900.10*** *p178*
O'Brien, Jeremiah 71; Ontario, 1871 ***1823.22*** *p118*
O'Brien, Jeremiah 78; Vermont, n.d. ***5900.10*** *p165*
O'Brien, Jeremiah J.; Vermont, 1885-1960 ***5900.10*** *p256*

O'Brien, Jermiah 70; Ontario, 1871 ***1823.15*** *p204*
O'Brien, Jerry 19; Vermont, 1889 ***5900.10*** *p249*
O'Brien, Jno; Vermont, n.d. ***5900.10*** *p449*
O'Brien, Joanna 54; Vermont, 1894 ***5900.10*** *p468*
O'Brien, John *SEE* O'Brien, Morris
O'Brien, John; New York, 1827-1831 ***8197.10*** *p305*
O'Brien, John; New York, 1832 ***8197.10*** *p299*
O'Brien, John; Vermont, 1808-1892 ***5900.10*** *p387*
O'Brien, John; Vermont, 1837-1923 ***5900.10*** *p223*
O'Brien, John; Vermont, 1844-1917 ***5900.10*** *p408*
O'Brien, John; Vermont, 1849-1933 ***5900.10*** *p385*
O'Brien, John; Vermont, 1850-1896 ***5900.10*** *p409*
O'Brien, John; Vermont, 1867-1929 ***5900.10*** *p255*
O'Brien, John 11; Vermont, 1872 ***5900.10*** *p381*
O'Brien, John 19; Vermont, 1870 ***5900.10*** *p338*
O'Brien, John 37; Vermont, 1855 ***5900.10*** *p67*
O'Brien, John 40; Ontario, 1871 ***1823.28*** *p78*
O'Brien, John 42; Vermont, 1874 ***5900.10*** *p227*
O'Brien, John 50; Ontario, 1871 ***1823.28*** *p78*
O'Brien, John 51; Ontario, 1871 ***1823.15*** *p204*
O'Brien, John 58; Ontario, 1871 ***1823.28*** *p78*
O'Brien, John 60; Vermont, 1871 ***5900.10*** *p249*
O'Brien, John 65; Vermont, 1876 ***5900.10*** *p600*
O'Brien, John 66; Vermont, 1900 ***5900.10*** *p117*
O'Brien, John 76; Vermont, 1878 ***5900.10*** *p577*
O'Brien, John, Sr. 63; Ontario, 1871 ***1823.28*** *p78*
O'Brien, John S.; Vermont, 1852-1935 ***5900.10*** *p147*
O'Brien, John W.; Vermont, 1865-1924 ***5900.10*** *p162*
O'Brien, Judy 69; Vermont, 1880 ***5900.10*** *p611*
O'Brien, Julia; Vermont, 1821-1901 ***5900.10*** *p484*
O'Brien, Julia 71; Vermont, 1892 ***5900.10*** *p201*
O'Brien, Julia 103; Vermont, 1880 ***5900.10*** *p83*
O'Brien, Julia A. Benway; Vermont, 1858-1941 ***5900.10*** *p408*
O'Brien, Julia Donovan; Vermont, 1822-1858 ***5900.10*** *p75*
O'Brien, Julia Roach; Vermont, 1815-1899 ***5900.10*** *p388*
O'Brien, Katherine; Vermont, 1855-1919 ***5900.10*** *p250*
O'Brien, Katie 2 days; Vermont, n.d. ***5900.10*** *p162*
O'Brien, Lawrence 86; Vermont, 1881 ***5900.10*** *p213*
O'Brien, Lewis; New York, 1838 ***8197.10*** *p147*
O'Brien, Lucy J.; Vermont, 1845-1933 ***5900.10*** *p555*
O'Brien, Mamie H. Blackburn 26; Vermont, 1898 ***5900.10*** *p600*
O'Brien, Marey 40; Ontario, 1871 ***1823.28*** *p78*
O'Brien, Margaret; Vermont, 1846-1918 ***5900.10*** *p484*
O'Brien, Margaret; Vermont, 1848-1912 ***5900.10*** *p546*
O'Brien, Margaret 38; Vermont, 1887 ***5900.10*** *p250*
O'Brien, Margaret 69; Vermont, 1877 ***5900.10*** *p251*
O'Brien, Margaret 70; Vermont, 1887 ***5900.10*** *p466*
O'Brien, Margaret Conlin; Vermont, 1852-1923 ***5900.10*** *p464*
O'Brien, Margaret Hayes; Vermont, 1837-1910 ***5900.10*** *p63*
O'Brien, Margaret Sheehan 59; Vermont, 1913 ***5900.10*** *p60*
Obrien, Margery 70; Ontario, 1871 ***1823.15*** *p205*
O'Brien, Martin; Vermont, 1839-1907 ***5900.10*** *p581*
O'Brien, Martin 63; Vermont, 1872 ***5900.10*** *p250*
O'Brien, Mary; Vermont, 1806-1889 ***5900.10*** *p470*
O'Brien, Mary; Vermont, 1836-1909 ***5900.10*** *p484*
O'Brien, Mary; Vermont, 1837-1897 ***5900.10*** *p617*
O'Brien, Mary; Vermont, 1840-1879 ***5900.10*** *p408*
O'Brien, Mary; Vermont, 1842-1915 ***5900.10*** *p387*
O'Brien, Mary; Vermont, 1858-1945 ***5900.10*** *p120*
O'Brien, Mary 2 months; Vermont, 1878 ***5900.10*** *p201*
O'Brien, Mary 19; Ontario, 1861 ***2896.27*** *p74*
O'Brien, Mary 19; Vermont, 1876 ***5900.10*** *p201*
Obrien, Mary 20; Ontario, 1871 ***1823.22*** *p119*
O'Brien, Mary 38; Vermont, 1855 ***5900.10*** *p348*
O'Brien, Mary 67; Vermont, 1887 ***5900.10*** *p601*
O'Brien, Mary 70; Vermont, 1890 ***5900.10*** *p77*
O'Brien, Mary 72; Vermont, 1903 ***5900.10*** *p214*
O'Brien, Mary 83; Vermont, 1903 ***5900.10*** *p437*
O'Brien, Mary 92; Vermont, 1898 ***5900.10*** *p600*
O'Brien, Mary A.; Vermont, 1832-1915 ***5900.10*** *p408*
O'Brien, Mary A.; Vermont, 1833-1862 ***5900.10*** *p160*
O'Brien, Mary A.; Vermont, 1843-1927 ***5900.10*** *p98*
O'Brien, Mary A. Dwyer 68; Vermont, 1898 ***5900.10*** *p590*
O'Brien, Mary Ahern; Vermont, 1832-1913 ***5900.10*** *p59*
O'Brien, Mary Ann; Vermont, 1904 ***5900.10*** *p50*
O'Brien, Mary Ballard; Vermont, n.d. ***5900.10*** *p546*
O'Brien, Mary Crahan; Vermont, 1842-1884 ***5900.10*** *p562*
O'Brien, Mary Cushing; Vermont, 1852 ***5900.10*** *p593*
O'Brien, Mary E.; Vermont, 1854-1943 ***5900.10*** *p420*
O'Brien, Mary E. Brown; Vermont, 1862-1921 ***5900.10*** *p147*
O'Brien, Mary Gunshannon; Vermont, 1849-1877 ***5900.10*** *p546*
O'Brien, Mary Henley; Vermont, 1852-1929 ***5900.10*** *p409*
O'Brien, Mary J.; Vermont, 1859-1936 ***5900.10*** *p257*
O'Brien, Mary M.; Vermont, 1855-1928 ***5900.10*** *p552*
O'Brien, Mary Sullivan; Vermont, 1857-1927 ***5900.10*** *p95*
O'Brien, Mary Toohey 34; Vermont, 1899 ***5900.10*** *p425*
O'Brien, Mathew 72; Vermont, 1878 ***5900.10*** *p404*
O'Brien, Maurice; Maine, 1775-1781 ***4628.40*** *p48*
Obrien, Maurice 80; Ontario, 1871 ***1823.15*** *p205*
O'Brien, Michael; Vermont, 1828-1896 ***5900.10*** *p408*
O'Brien, Michael; Vermont, 1844-1924 ***5900.10*** *p609*
O'Brien, Michael; Vermont, 1854-1930 ***5900.10*** *p183*
O'Brien, Michael 30; Vermont, 1859 ***5900.10*** *p275*
O'Brien, Michael 36; Ontario, 1871 ***1823.28*** *p78*
O'Brien, Michael 55; Ontario, 1871 ***1823.28*** *p78*
O'Brien, Michael 76; Vermont, 1892 ***5900.10*** *p201*
O'Brien, Michael 88; Vermont, 1888 ***5900.10*** *p60*
O'Brien, Michael C.; Vermont, 1855-1926 ***5900.10*** *p551*
O'Brien, Michael Morgan; Pennsylvania, 1781 ***4629.10*** *p43*
O'Brien, Morgan; Vermont, 1841-1914 ***5900.10*** *p98*
O'Brien, Morris; Maine, 1740-1750 ***4628.40*** *p77*
With 4 sons
Son: John
Son: William
O'Brien, Nancy; Vermont, 1806-1888 ***5900.10*** *p544*
O'Brien, Nancy 62; Vermont, 1886 ***5900.10*** *p271*
O'Brien, Nancy O'Neill; Vermont, 1852-1929 ***5900.10*** *p553*
O'Brien, Nellie; Vermont, 1858-1922 ***5900.10*** *p275*
O'Brien, Nicholas; New York, 1840 ***8197.10*** *p192*
O'Brien, Patrick; New York, 1807 ***8197.10*** *p328*
O'Brien, Patrick; New York, 1823 ***8197.10*** *p267*
O'Brien, Patrick; New York, 1840 ***8197.10*** *p268*
O'Brien, Patrick; New York, New York, 1851 ***1825.45*** *p56*
O'Brien, Patrick; Ontario, 1871 ***1823.28*** *p78*
O'Brien, Patrick; Vermont, n.d. ***5900.10*** *p155*
O'Brien, Patrick; Vermont, 1842-1920 ***5900.10*** *p593*
O'Brien, Patrick 22; Vermont, 1860 ***5900.10*** *p363*
O'Brien, Patrick 35; Ontario, 1871 ***1823.28*** *p78*
Obrien, Patrick 35; Ontario, 1871 ***1823.28*** *p78*
Obrien, Patrick 45; Ontario, 1871 ***1823.22*** *p119*
Obrien, Patrick 46; Ontario, 1871 ***1823.15*** *p205*
O'Brien, Patrick 50; Ontario, 1871 ***1823.28*** *p78*
O'Brien, Patrick 52; Ontario, 1871 ***1823.28*** *p78*
O'Brien, Patrick 63; Vermont, 1887 ***5900.10*** *p600*
Obrien, Patrick 68; Ontario, 1871 ***1823.28*** *p78*
O'Brien, Richard 36; Ontario, 1871 ***1823.28*** *p78*
O'Brien, Richard 46; Vermont, 1881 ***5900.10*** *p468*
O'Brien, Robert; Vermont, 1848-1928 ***5900.10*** *p552*
O'Brien, Sara A.; Vermont, 1850-1932 ***5900.10*** *p275*
O'Brien, Sarah Powers; Vermont, 1860-1913 ***5900.10*** *p183*
O Brien, Stephen 33; Ontario, 1871 ***1823.22*** *p118*
O'Brien, Thomas; New York, 1824-1829 ***8197.10*** *p305*
O'Brien, Thomas; New York, 1826 ***8197.10*** *p268*
O'Brien, Thomas; New York, 1837 ***8197.10*** *p95*
O'Brien, Thomas; Vermont, 1810-1888 ***5900.10*** *p601*
O'Brien, Thomas; Vermont, 1830-1914 ***5900.10*** *p59*
O'Brien, Thomas; Vermont, 1853-1893 ***5900.10*** *p425*
O'Brien, Thomas; Vermont, 1857-1930 ***5900.10*** *p592*
O'Brien, Thomas 8; Vermont, 1867 ***5900.10*** *p600*
O'Brien, Thomas 26; Vermont, 1864 ***5900.10*** *p577*
O'Brien, Timothy; Vermont, 1823 ***5900.10*** *p551*
Obrien, Timothy 42; Ontario, 1871 ***1823.22*** *p119*
O'Brien, Timothy 69; Vermont, 1909 ***5900.10*** *p564*
O'Brien, Timothy F.; New York, 1839 ***8197.10*** *p137*
O'Brien, William *SEE* O'Brien, Morris
O'Brien, William; New York, 1840 ***8197.10*** *p191*
O'Brien, William; Vermont, 1804-1879 ***5900.10*** *p147*
O'Brien, William; Vermont, 1840-1904 ***5900.10*** *p162*
O'Brien, William; Vermont, 1844-1905 ***5900.10*** *p63*
O'Brien, William; Vermont, 1852-1923 ***5900.10*** *p464*
Obrien, William 23; Ontario, 1871 ***1823.28*** *p78*
O'Brien, William 68; Vermont, 1898 ***5900.10*** *p577*
O'Brien, William 75; Vermont, 1887 ***5900.10*** *p262*
O'Brien, William A.; Vermont, 1860-1928 ***5900.10*** *p59*
O'Brine, Ann; Vermont, 1845 ***5900.10*** *p225*
O'Brine, Bridget Doyle 31; Vermont, 1849 ***5900.10*** *p612*
O'Brine, Catharine 19; Vermont, 1846 ***5900.10*** *p601*
O'Brine, Catherine; Vermont, 1840-1934 ***5900.10*** *p269*
O'Brine, Elizabeth; Vermont, 1808-1892 ***5900.10*** *p458*
O'Brine, Ellen; Vermont, 1847-1916 ***5900.10*** *p144*
O'Brine, John 34; Vermont, 1849 ***5900.10*** *p160*
O'Brine, John 40; Ontario, 1871 ***1823.28*** *p78*
O'Brine, John 68; Vermont, 1857 ***5900.10*** *p147*
O'Brine, Margaret 77; Vermont, 1915 ***5900.10*** *p587*
O'Brine, Margret 70; Ontario, 1871 ***1823.28*** *p78*
O'Brine, Mary; Vermont, 1835-1878 ***5900.10*** *p288*
O'Brine, Mary; Vermont, 1900 ***5900.10*** *p476*
O'Brine, Mary 47; Vermont, 1846 ***5900.10*** *p147*
O'Brine, Mary 92; Vermont, 1894 ***5900.10*** *p410*
Obrine, Patrick 48; Ontario, 1871 ***1823.28*** *p78*
O'Brine, Patrick 62; Ontario, 1871 ***1823.28*** *p78*
O'Brine, Patrick 76; Vermont, 1846 ***5900.10*** *p601*
Obrine, Thomas 30; Ontario, 1871 ***1823.28*** *p78*
Obrine, Thomas 40; Ontario, 1871 ***1823.28*** *p78*
O'Brine, William; Vermont, 1852-1918 ***5900.10*** *p224*
O'Brine, William 37; Vermont, 1850 ***5900.10*** *p611*
O'Brion, Bridget 69; Vermont, 1855 ***5900.10*** *p601*
Obrion, James 47; Ontario, 1871 ***1823.28*** *p78*
O'Brion, Mary Mullen 21; Vermont, 1851 ***5900.10*** *p606*
Obry, Earnest 31; Ontario, 1871 ***1823.28*** *p78*
O'Bryan, Ann 71; Vermont, 1903 ***5900.10*** *p188*
Obryan, Bryan; Maryland, 1682 ***2524.55*** *p163*
O'Bryan, Cathrine; Vermont, 1834-1911 ***5900.10*** *p90*
O'Bryan, James; Pennsylvania, 1777 ***4629.10*** *p15*
O'Bryan, John; Pennsylvania, 1777 ***4629.10*** *p10*
O'Bryan, Mathias; Maryland, 1659 ***2524.55*** *p163*
O'Bryen, Patrick; New York, 1823 ***8197.10*** *p267*
O'Byrne, Bridget; Vermont, 1850-1924 ***5900.10*** *p190*
O'Byrne, Ellen; Vermont, 1836-1915 ***5900.10*** *p412*
O'Byrne, Patrick; Vermont, 1833-1920 ***5900.10*** *p412*
O'Cahell, James; Maryland, 1678 ***2524.55*** *p163*
O'Cahett, James; Maryland, 1678 ***2524.55*** *p163*
O'Callaghan, Alice; Vermont, n.d. ***5900.10*** *p146*
O'Callanon, Denis; Maryland, 1658 ***2524.55*** *p163*
O'Canavan, . . . 67; Ontario, 1861 ***2896.26*** *p31*
Ochab, Andrew; Maryland, 1910 ***3259.35*** *p44*
Ocho, Catherine 50; Kansas, 1876-1910 ***9079.10*** *p24*
Ocho, Philip 55; Kansas, 1876-1910 ***9079.10*** *p24*
Ochs, Agnes Catharina; Port uncertain, 1786 ***2856.30*** *p329*
Ochs, Anna Maria; Port uncertain, 1769 ***2856.30*** *p329*
Ochs, Anna Maria; Port uncertain, 1786 ***2856.30*** *p329*
Ochs, Georg; America, 1739 ***2856.30*** *p329*
With 5 children
Ochs, Maria Catharina; Port uncertain, 1787 ***2856.30*** *p329*
Ochs, Marianna; Port uncertain, 1760 ***2856.30*** *p329*
Ochs, Niklas; Port uncertain, 1752 ***2856.30*** *p329*
Ochsner, Martin; Port uncertain, 1766 ***2856.30*** *p329*
Ochterlony, Patrick; Maryland, 1758 ***1640.13*** *p96*
Ockerman, Jane 39; Ontario, 1861 ***2896.25*** *p42*
Ockerman, Mary Jane 1; Ontario, 1861 ***2896.25*** *p42*
Ockerman, Sarah 13; Ontario, 1861 ***2896.25*** *p42*
Ockerman, Wm M. 14; Ontario, 1861 ***2896.25*** *p53*
Ockershanson, John 25; Virginia, 1773 ***1220.25*** *p30*
O'Clair, Julia B.; Vermont, 1856-1920 ***5900.10*** *p552*
O'Connel, Ellen; Vermont, n.d. ***5900.10*** *p55*
O'Connell, Abigail Lyons; Vermont, 1818-1871 ***5900.10*** *p266*
O'Connell, Anastasia; Vermont, 1857-1929 ***5900.10*** *p84*
O'Connell, Annie; Vermont, n.d. ***5900.10*** *p55*
Oconnell, Bernard 34; Ontario, 1871 ***1823.15*** *p205*
O'Connell, Bridget; Vermont, 1828-1903 ***5900.10*** *p93*
O'Connell, Bridget 35; Vermont, 1888 ***5900.10*** *p270*
O'Connell, Catherine; Vermont, n.d. ***5900.10*** *p53*
O'Connell, Catherine; Vermont, 1854-1889 ***5900.10*** *p391*
O'Connell, Catherine 44; Vermont, 1891 ***5900.10*** *p251*
O'Connell, Catherine Welsh; Vermont, n.d. ***5900.10*** *p55*
O'Connell, Daniel 50; Ontario, 1871 ***1823.22*** *p118*
O'Connell, Daniel J.; Vermont, 1858-1921 ***5900.10*** *p318*
O'Connell, Dennis 76; Vermont, 1893 ***5900.10*** *p270*
O'Connell, Elizabeth McMahon 54; Vermont, 1846 ***5900.10*** *p240*
O'Connell, Ella J. Prouty; Vermont, 1851-1911 ***5900.10*** *p108*
O'Connell, Ellen; Vermont, 1812-1889 ***5900.10*** *p460*
O'Connell, Ellen Griffin 79; Vermont, 1905 ***5900.10*** *p405*
O'Connell, George D.; New York, 1828-1834 ***8197.10*** *p305*
O'Connell, Hannorah 65; Vermont, 1883 ***5900.10*** *p270*
O'Connell, Jane; Vermont, 1865-1928 ***5900.10*** *p59*
O'Connell, Jeremiah; Vermont, 1840-1905 ***5900.10*** *p391*
O'Connell, Joanna Kiely; Vermont, 1845-1914 ***5900.10*** *p403*
O'Connell, John; New York, 1822 ***8197.10*** *p267*
O'Connell, John; New York, 1829 ***8197.10*** *p303*
O'Connell, John; Vermont, n.d. ***5900.10*** *p55*
O'Connell, John; Vermont, 1848-1917 ***5900.10*** *p108*
O'Connell, John 21; Vermont, 1871 ***5900.10*** *p249*
O'Connell, John 25; Vermont, 1885 ***5900.10*** *p405*
O'Connell, John 46; Vermont, 1892 ***5900.10*** *p398*
O'Connell, John 80; Vermont, 1893 ***5900.10*** *p53*
O'Connell, John J.; Vermont, 1850-1922 ***5900.10*** *p318*
O'Connell, Julia 80; Vermont, 1897 ***5900.10*** *p359*
O'Connell, Katie 17; Vermont, 1896 ***5900.10*** *p246*
O'Connell, Margaret; Vermont, 1843 ***5900.10*** *p474*
O'Connell, Margaret; Vermont, 1852-1925 ***5900.10*** *p352*
O'Connell, Margaret Carey; Vermont, 1861 ***5900.10*** *p318*
O'Connell, Margaret M.; Vermont, 1861-1940 ***5900.10*** *p318*
O'Connell, Mary; Vermont, 1856-1922 ***5900.10*** *p89*

O'Connell, Mary E.; Vermont, 1844-1897 ***5900.10*** *p52*
O'Connell, Mary Hennessy; Vermont, 1826-1900 ***5900.10*** *p79*
O'Connell, Mary Noonan 63; Vermont, 1888 ***5900.10*** *p571*
O'Connell, Maurice 10; Vermont, 1878 ***5900.10*** *p521*
O'Connell, Michael; Vermont, 1815-1891 ***5900.10*** *p266*
O'Connell, Michael; Vermont, 1847-1899 ***5900.10*** *p52*
O'Connell, Nellie; Vermont, n.d. ***5900.10*** *p318*
O'Connell, Patrick; Vermont, 1838-1904 ***5900.10*** *p474*
O'Connell, Patrick 70; Vermont, 1880 ***5900.10*** *p405*
Oconnell, Peter 60; Ontario, 1871 ***1823.15*** *p205*
O'Connell, Peter M.; Vermont, 1827-1905 ***5900.10*** *p403*
O'Connell, Theresa Mullen; Vermont, 1834-1919 ***5900.10*** *p473*
O'Connell, Thomas; Vermont, 1821-1899 ***5900.10*** *p79*
O'Connell, Thomas; Vermont, 1834-1904 ***5900.10*** *p473*
O'Conner, Bridget 70; Vermont, 1896 ***5900.10*** *p109*
Oconner, Daniel 74; Ontario, 1871 ***1823.22*** *p119*
O'Conner, Ellen O'Brian; Vermont, 1827-1895 ***5900.10*** *p157*
O'Conner, Hannah; Vermont, 1835-1877 ***5900.10*** *p502*
O'Conner, Helen 30; Vermont, 1863 ***5900.10*** *p502*
O'Conner, James 40; Vermont, 1899 ***5900.10*** *p47*
O'Conner, John; Vermont, 1807-1880 ***5900.10*** *p157*
O'Conner, John 40; Ontario, 1871 ***1823.28*** *p78*
O'Conner, Patrick; Pennsylvania, 1845 ***6058.10*** *p21*
O'Conner, Thomas 32; Ontario, 1871 ***1823.15*** *p204*
O'Conner, William 44; Ontario, 1871 ***1823.28*** *p78*
O'Conner, William 51; Ontario, 1871 ***1823.28*** *p78*
Oconners, Robert 34; Ontario, 1871 ***1823.28*** *p78*
O'Connor, Mr.; Vermont, 1821-1903 ***5900.10*** *p307*
O'Connor, Mrs.; Vermont, 1832-1903 ***5900.10*** *p307*
O'Connor, Andrew 53; Ontario, 1871 ***1823.22*** *p118*
O'Connor, Ann; Vermont, 1827-1903 ***5900.10*** *p350*
O'Connor, Ann 79; Vermont, 1908 ***5900.10*** *p63*
O'Connor, Ann 80; Ontario, 1871 ***1823.22*** *p118*
O'Connor, Anna; Vermont, n.d. ***5900.10*** *p168*
O'Connor, Anna Stacey Lee 45; Vermont, 1896 ***5900.10*** *p101*
O'Connor, Annie Cummings; Vermont, 1837-1910 ***5900.10*** *p591*
O'Connor, Annie Howard; Vermont, 1840-1902 ***5900.10*** *p65*
O'Connor, Annie Quinn 80; Vermont, 1933 ***5900.10*** *p593*
Oconnor, Arther 45; Ontario, 1871 ***1823.15*** *p205*
O'Connor, Bernard; New York, 1807 ***8197.10*** *p47*
O'Connor, Bridget; Vermont, 1846-1918 ***5900.10*** *p109*
O'Connor, Bridget 62; Vermont, 1884 ***5900.10*** *p404*
O'Connor, Bridget 75; Vermont, 1864 ***5900.10*** *p316*
O'Connor, Bridget 87; Vermont, 1884 ***5900.10*** *p61*
O'Connor, Bridget Brown; Vermont, 1828-1898 ***5900.10*** *p60*
O'Connor, Bryan J.; Vermont, 1856-1940 ***5900.10*** *p68*
O'Connor, Catherine; Vermont, 1829-1918 ***5900.10*** *p107*
O'Connor, Catherine; Vermont, 1841-1882 ***5900.10*** *p329*
O'Connor, Catherine 32; Vermont, 1874 ***5900.10*** *p111*
O'Connor, Catherine 72; Vermont, 1921 ***5900.10*** *p277*
O'Connor, Catherine Casey; Vermont, 1865-1950 ***5900.10*** *p124*
O'Connor, Catherine Martin; Vermont, 1822-1886 ***5900.10*** *p122*
O'Connor, Charles 28; Dominica, 1774 ***1220.25*** *p127*
Oconnor, Charles 30; Ontario, 1871 ***1823.28*** *p78*
Oconnor, Charles 50; Ontario, 1871 ***1823.22*** *p119*
O'Connor, Daniel; New York, 1840 ***8197.10*** *p191*
O'Connor, Daniel; New York, 1840 ***8197.10*** *p268*
O'Connor, Delia; Vermont, 1860-1923 ***5900.10*** *p68*
O'Connor, Dennis; New York, 1806 ***8197.10*** *p267*
O'Connor, Dennis 28; Ontario, 1871 ***1823.28*** *p78*
O'Connor, E.; Portland, Maine, 1858 ***9196.15*** *p27*
O'Connor, Edmund; Vermont, 1850-1870 ***5900.10*** *p122*
O'Connor, Edward M. C.; Pennsylvania, 1868 ***6058.10*** *p76*
O'Connor, Eliza W.; New York, 1837 ***8197.10*** *p96*
O'Connor, Ellen 36; Vermont, 1844 ***5900.10*** *p146*
O'Connor, Ellen Leonard; Vermont, 1854-1940 ***5900.10*** *p126*
O'Connor, Hannah Cray; Vermont, n.d. ***5900.10*** *p67*
O'Connor, Hannorah 83; Vermont, 1904 ***5900.10*** *p251*
O'Connor, Hannorah Hallsey; Vermont, 1843-1925 ***5900.10*** *p272*
O'Connor, James; New York, 1831 ***8197.10*** *p268*
O'Connor, James; New York, 1837 ***8197.10*** *p95*
O'Connor, James; Vermont, 1829-1902 ***5900.10*** *p314*
O'Connor, James; Vermont, 1858-1891 ***5900.10*** *p60*
O'Connor, James 60; Ontario, 1871 ***1823.28*** *p78*
Oconnor, James 68; Ontario, 1871 ***1823.28*** *p78*
O'Connor, James 69; Ontario, 1871 ***1823.15*** *p204*
O'Connor, James 69; Ontario, 1871 ***1823.28*** *p78*
O'Connor, James 76; Vermont, 1899 ***5900.10*** *p251*
O'Connor, Jeremiah; New York, 1831 ***8197.10*** *p366*
O'Connor, Johanna 71; Vermont, 1885 ***5900.10*** *p54*
O'Connor, Johannah; Vermont, 1827-1917 ***5900.10*** *p69*
O'Connor, John; New York, 1828 ***8197.10*** *p299*
O'Connor, John; New York, 1837 ***8197.10*** *p96*
O'Connor, John; Pennsylvania, 1848 ***6058.10*** *p25*
O'Connor, John; Vermont, 1809-1901 ***5900.10*** *p591*
O'Connor, John; Vermont, 1847-1933 ***5900.10*** *p551*
O'Connor, John 40; Vermont, 1881 ***5900.10*** *p315*
O'Connor, John 50; Vermont, 1887 ***5900.10*** *p61*
O'Connor, John 56; Vermont, 1897 ***5900.10*** *p551*
O'Connor, John 86; Vermont, 1936 ***5900.10*** *p106*
O'Connor, Joseph; New York, 1826 ***8197.10*** *p298*
O'Connor, Joseph James; New York, 1819 ***8197.10*** *p267*
O'Connor, Julia 53; Vermont, 1863 ***5900.10*** *p198*
O'Connor, Lena; Vermont, 1866-1896 ***5900.10*** *p307*
O'Connor, Luke; New York, 1836 ***8197.10*** *p268*
O'Connor, Luke; Vermont, 1824-1896 ***5900.10*** *p218*
O'Connor, Maranda L.; Vermont, 1829-1893 ***5900.10*** *p315*
O'Connor, Margaret; Vermont, 1817-1849 ***5900.10*** *p606*
O'Connor, Margaret; Vermont, 1836-1909 ***5900.10*** *p58*
O'Connor, Margaret; Vermont, 1858-1911 ***5900.10*** *p324*
O'Connor, Margaret 54; Vermont, 1887 ***5900.10*** *p521*
O'Connor, Margaret Henchie 70; Vermont, 1885 ***5900.10*** *p104*
O'Connor, Martin 60; Ontario, 1871 ***1823.28*** *p78*
O'Connor, Martin 62; Vermont, 1907 ***5900.10*** *p515*
O'Connor, Mary; Vermont, n.d. ***5900.10*** *p122*
O'Connor, Mary; Vermont, 1826-1904 ***5900.10*** *p218*
O'Connor, Mary; Vermont, 1849-1886 ***5900.10*** *p551*
O'Connor, Mary; Vermont, 1849-1912 ***5900.10*** *p359*
O'Connor, Mary; Vermont, 1876 ***5900.10*** *p104*
O'Connor, Mary 34; Vermont, 1871 ***5900.10*** *p341*
O'Connor, Mary 45; Vermont, 1882 ***5900.10*** *p107*
O'Connor, Mary 75; Vermont, 1897 ***5900.10*** *p61*
O'Connor, Mary Ann Koan 77; Vermont, 1891 ***5900.10*** *p589*
O'Connor, Mary Butler 43; Vermont, 1893 ***5900.10*** *p466*
O'Connor, Mary C.; Vermont, 1856-1937 ***5900.10*** *p122*
O'Connor, Mary Halpin; Vermont, 1841-1909 ***5900.10*** *p314*
O'Connor, Mary Heffron 75; Vermont, 1931 ***5900.10*** *p106*
O'Connor, Mary Kelly 66; Vermont, 1866 ***5900.10*** *p449*
O'Connor, Mary Tomey 42; Vermont, 1875 ***5900.10*** *p101*
O'Connor, Maurice; Vermont, 1822-1898 ***5900.10*** *p122*
O'Connor, Michael; Vermont, 1821-1886 ***5900.10*** *p60*
O'Connor, Michael; Vermont, 1833-1906 ***5900.10*** *p57*
O'Connor, Michael 87; Vermont, 1902 ***5900.10*** *p404*
O'Connor, Michael J.; Vermont, n.d. ***5900.10*** *p67*
O'Connor, Patrick; New York, 1827 ***8197.10*** *p268*
O'Connor, Patrick; New York, 1838 ***8197.10*** *p147*
O'Connor, Patrick; New York, 1840 ***8197.10*** *p192*
O'Connor, Patrick 68; Vermont, 1886 ***5900.10*** *p42*
O'Connor, Patrick 86; Vermont, 1924 ***5900.10*** *p466*
O'Connor, Patrick John; New York, 1821 ***8197.10*** *p267*
O'Connor, Peter 18; Vermont, 1862 ***5900.10*** *p198*
O'Connor, Peter 47; Vermont, 1863 ***5900.10*** *p198*
O'Connor, Richard; New York, 1839 ***8197.10*** *p136*
O'Connor, Rose Doon 40; Vermont, 1831 ***5900.10*** *p515*
O'Connor, Sarah; Vermont, 1864-1936 ***5900.10*** *p307*
O'Connor, Sarah Ellen; Vermont, 1855-1876 ***5900.10*** *p315*
O'Connor, Simon 42; Vermont, 1862 ***5900.10*** *p66*
Oconnor, Stephen 58; Ontario, 1871 ***1823.28*** *p78*
O'Connor, Susan B.; Vermont, 1859-1933 ***5900.10*** *p276*
O'Connor, Terrence 52; Vermont, 1887 ***5900.10*** *p272*
O'Connor, Thomas; New York, 1807 ***8197.10*** *p47*
O'Connor, Thomas; Vermont, 1835-1876 ***5900.10*** *p65*
O'Connor, Thomas; Vermont, 1852-1885 ***5900.10*** *p126*
O'Connor, Thomas 45; Vermont, 1876 ***5900.10*** *p104*
O'Connor, William; New York, 1840 ***8197.10*** *p191*
O'Connor, William John 88; Vermont, 1935 ***5900.10*** *p589*
O'Connors, Andrew; New York, 1827 ***8197.10*** *p346*
O'Conol, Mary 48; Vermont, 1883 ***5900.10*** *p64*
Octoby, Robert 44; Ontario, 1871 ***1823.15*** *p205*
O'Daniell, Mrs.; Maryland, 1663 ***2524.55*** *p163*
O'Day, Anna; Vermont, 1858-1908 ***5900.10*** *p515*
O'Day, Annie 52; Vermont, 1892 ***5900.10*** *p77*
O'Day, Bridget; Vermont, n.d. ***5900.10*** *p87*
O'Day, Bridget 62; Vermont, 1888 ***5900.10*** *p362*
O'Day, Catharine; Vermont, n.d. ***5900.10*** *p344*
O'Day, Daniel; Vermont, 1850-1932 ***5900.10*** *p256*
O'Day, Delia; Vermont, 1865-1930 ***5900.10*** *p515*
O'Day, Dennis; Vermont, 1847-1881 ***5900.10*** *p591*
O'Day, Frank; Vermont, 1864-1920 ***5900.10*** *p515*
O'Day, Johanna; Vermont, 1918 ***5900.10*** *p85*
O'Day, John; Vermont, 1847-1918 ***5900.10*** *p515*
O'Day, John 27; Ontario, 1871 ***1823.28*** *p78*
O'Day, John 58; Ontario, 1871 ***1823.28*** *p78*
O'Day, Lizzie 37; Vermont, 1897 ***5900.10*** *p362*
O'Day, Margaret; Vermont, 1786-1891 ***5900.10*** *p438*
O'Day, Margaret 57; Vermont, 1916 ***5900.10*** *p486*
O'Day, Margaret Cummings; Vermont, 1855-1932 ***5900.10*** *p256*
O'Day, Martin 54; Vermont, 1893 ***5900.10*** *p332*
O'Day, Mary; Vermont, 1857-1860 ***5900.10*** *p515*
O'Day, Mary 91; Vermont, 1924 ***5900.10*** *p595*
O'Day, Michael; Vermont, 1851-1917 ***5900.10*** *p515*
O'Day, Michael; Vermont, 1854-1920 ***5900.10*** *p256*
O'Day, Michael 76; Vermont, 1888 ***5900.10*** *p549*
O'Day, Nora 81; Vermont, 1909 ***5900.10*** *p445*
O'Day, Patrick; Vermont, n.d. ***5900.10*** *p362*
O'Day, Patrick; Vermont, 1849-1877 ***5900.10*** *p515*
O'Day, Patrick; Vermont, 1892 ***5900.10*** *p77*
Odbert, Richard 34; Ontario, 1871 ***1823.15*** *p205*
Odea, Bridget 24; Ontario, 1871 ***1823.15*** *p205*
O'Dea, Ellen; Vermont, 1850-1936 ***5900.10*** *p81*
O'Dea, Joan 48; Vermont, 1878 ***5900.10*** *p251*
O'Dea, John 71; Vermont, 1894 ***5900.10*** *p251*
Odea, Pat 21; Ontario, 1871 ***1823.15*** *p205*
Odea, Pat 33; Ontario, 1871 ***1823.15*** *p205*
O'deare, Teage; Virginia, 1671-1672 ***6212.30*** *p46*
O'Dell, Almira; Vermont, 1843-1906 ***5900.10*** *p495*
O'Dell, Kate McDonough; Vermont, 1834-1903 ***5900.10*** *p265*
Odell, Miluchtowoth 63; Ontario, 1871 ***1823.15*** *p205*
O'Den, Thomas 49; Ontario, 1871 ***1823.15*** *p204*
Odenbreit, Anna Maria; Port uncertain, 1766 ***2856.30*** *p329*
Odenbreit, Catharina; Port uncertain, 1765 ***2856.30*** *p329*
Odenbreit, Georg; Port uncertain, 1785 ***2856.30*** *p330*
With wife & 4 children
Odenbreit, Peter; Port uncertain, 1785 ***2856.30*** *p329*
With wife
Odenbreith, Catharina; Port uncertain, 1740 ***2856.30*** *p330*
Odenbreith, Elisabeth; Port uncertain, 1740 ***2856.30*** *p330*
Odenbreith, Johann Peter; Port uncertain, 1739 ***2856.30*** *p330*
Odenbreith, Peter; Port uncertain, 1738 ***2856.30*** *p330*
Odernheimer, Johann Peter; Port uncertain, 1749 ***2856.30*** *p330*
Odernheimer, Johann Philipp; America, 1785 ***2856.30*** *p330*
Odernheimer, Johann Philipp; Port uncertain, 1742 ***2856.30*** *p330*
Odeway, Isaac; Maryland, 1779 ***1224.2*** *p85*
Odger, Elinor *SEE* Odger, Wm.
Odger, Elinor; Maryland, 1673 ***2524.55*** *p163*
Odger, Mary *SEE* Odger, Wm.
Odger, Mary; Maryland, 1673 ***2524.55*** *p163*
Odger, Wm.; Maryland, 1675 ***2524.55*** *p163*
Wife: Elinor
Daughter: Mary
Odi, Michael; Port uncertain, 1771 ***2856.30*** *p330*
O'Donahue, Mary; Vermont, 1863-1940 ***5900.10*** *p360*
O'Donnel, Daniel 7; Ontario, 1861 ***2896.27*** *p24*
O'Donnel, Edward 40; Ontario, 1861 ***2896.27*** *p24*
O'Donnel, Mary; Vermont, 1837-1880 ***5900.10*** *p587*
O'Donnel, Mary 42; Ontario, 1861 ***2896.27*** *p24*
O'Donnell, Anthony; New York, New York, 1820 ***8197.10*** *p137*
O'Donnell, Bessie; Vermont, 1837-1929 ***5900.10*** *p585*
O'Donnell, Bridget 84; Vermont, 1897 ***5900.10*** *p267*
O'Donnell, Bryan; New York, 1838 ***8197.10*** *p378*
O'Donnell, Catharine Doude 59; Vermont, 1900 ***5900.10*** *p113*
O'Donnell, Catherine; Vermont, 1837-1913 ***5900.10*** *p586*
O'Donnell, Catherine; Vermont, 1852-1919 ***5900.10*** *p385*
O'Donnell, Catherine; Vermont, 1860-1942 ***5900.10*** *p71*
O'Donnell, Catherine 38; Vermont, 1880 ***5900.10*** *p497*
O'Donnell, Catherine 86; Vermont, 1909 ***5900.10*** *p103*
O'Donnell, Catherine Casey; Vermont, 1833-1901 ***5900.10*** *p136*
O'Donnell, Daniel 45; Ontario, 1861 ***2896.27*** *p18*
O'Donnell, Elizabeth Gregory; Vermont, 1845-1880 ***5900.10*** *p76*
O'Donnell, Ellen 18; Vermont, 1873 ***5900.10*** *p382*
O'Donnell, Ellen 42; Vermont, 1873 ***5900.10*** *p65*
O'Donnell, Ellen Carmody 44; Vermont, 1869 ***5900.10*** *p320*
O'Donnell, Eugene 40; Vermont, 1883 ***5900.10*** *p113*
O'Donnell, Hannah Kennelly 66; Vermont, 1905 ***5900.10*** *p167*
O'Donnell, James; New York, 1827 ***8197.10*** *p346*
O'Donnell, James; Vermont, 1850-1924 ***5900.10*** *p387*
O'Donnell, James 81; Vermont, 1925 ***5900.10*** *p167*
O'Donnell, James Delaney; New York, 1812 ***8197.10*** *p267*
O'Donnell, Jennie F.; Vermont, 1854-1917 ***5900.10*** *p148*
O'Donnell, Jeremiah; New York, 1830 ***8197.10*** *p361*

O'Hara, John; Pennsylvania, 1779 ***4629.10*** *p40*
O'Hara, Mary; Vermont, 1856-1922 ***5900.10*** *p116*
O'Hara, Mary Flynn 34; Vermont, 1883 ***5900.10*** *p577*
O'Hara, Michael; New York, 1831 ***8197.10*** *p314*
Ohara, Michael 70; Ontario, 1871 ***1823.15*** *p206*
O'Hara, Patrick; New York, 1840 ***8197.10*** *p268*
Ohara, Thomas 40; Ontario, 1871 ***1823.15*** *p206*
O'Hara, Thomas 46; Ontario, 1871 ***1823.22*** *p118*
O'Hare, Ann 60; Vermont, 1890 ***5900.10*** *p93*
O'Hare, Bessie; Vermont, 1858-1958 ***5900.10*** *p93*
O'Hare, Bridget; Vermont, 1825-1896 ***5900.10*** *p54*
O'Hare, Hugh 74; Ontario, 1871 ***1823.28*** *p78*
O'Hare, James; New York, 1840 ***8197.10*** *p191*
O'Hare, James 84; Vermont, 1900 ***5900.10*** *p93*
O'Hare, John; New York, 1840 ***8197.10*** *p384*
O'Hare, Lilian A. Wells; Vermont, 1866-1936 ***5900.10*** *p321*
O'Hare, Terrance; Vermont, n.d. ***5900.10*** *p284*
O'Hare, William B.; Vermont, 1848-1910 ***5900.10*** *p321*
O'Harra, Bryan; Pennsylvania, 1779 ***4629.10*** *p40*
O'Harra, Bryan 78; Ontario, 1871 ***1823.22*** *p118*
O'Harra, Jeremiah 25; Ontario, 1871 ***1823.22*** *p118*
O'Harra, John 45; Ontario, 1871 ***1823.22*** *p118*
O'Harra, Margaret; Vermont, 1795-1871 ***5900.10*** *p515*
O'Harrah, Bryon; Pennsylvania, 1777 ***4629.10*** *p24*
O'Harror, Biddy 35; Ontario, 1861 ***2896.25*** *p39*
O'Harror, James 5; Ontario, 1861 ***2896.25*** *p39*
O'Harror, Mary A. 9; Ontario, 1861 ***2896.25*** *p39*
O'Harror, Thomas 2; Ontario, 1861 ***2896.25*** *p39*
O'Harror, Thomas 36; Ontario, 1861 ***2896.25*** *p39*
O'Hear, Alice McMahan 75; Vermont, 1883 ***5900.10*** *p232*
O'Hear, Daniel; Vermont, 1809-1861 ***5900.10*** *p279*
O'Hear, Edward 50; Ontario, 1871 ***1823.28*** *p78*
O'Hear, Elizabeth Sloan 70; Vermont, 1901 ***5900.10*** *p604*
O'Hear, Ellen 69; Vermont, 1899 ***5900.10*** *p279*
O'Hear, Katherine; Vermont, 1854-1917 ***5900.10*** *p492*
O'Hear, Mary L.; Vermont, 1887 ***5900.10*** *p604*
O'Hear, Nancy; Vermont, 1812-1879 ***5900.10*** *p279*
O'Hear, Peter 101; Vermont, 1879 ***5900.10*** *p232*
O'Hear, Rose; Vermont, 1862-1949 ***5900.10*** *p604*
O'Hear, Sarah 88; Vermont, 1912 ***5900.10*** *p226*
O'Heare, James; Vermont, 1854-1923 ***5900.10*** *p487*
O'Heare, John B.; Vermont, 1860-1923 ***5900.10*** *p487*
O'Heare, Mary Fee 71; Vermont, 1904 ***5900.10*** *p487*
O'Heare, Patrick; Vermont, 1868-1937 ***5900.10*** *p487*
O'Heare, Thomas 76; Vermont, 1903 ***5900.10*** *p487*
O'Hearn, Edmund J.; Vermont, 1865-1915 ***5900.10*** *p92*
O'Hearn, Edward 52; Vermont, 1910 ***5900.10*** *p547*
O'Hearn, Ellen Cullen; Vermont, 1830-1890 ***5900.10*** *p92*
O'Hearn, James; Pennsylvania, 1867 ***6058.10*** *p57*
O'Hearn, James; Vermont, 1826-1876 ***5900.10*** *p446*
O'Hearn, John; Vermont, 1863-1864 ***5900.10*** *p92*
O'Hearn, Katie; Vermont, 1868-1875 ***5900.10*** *p92*
O'Hearn, Margaret; Vermont, 1860-1937 ***5900.10*** *p92*
O'Hearn, Mary Barry; Vermont, 1827-1889 ***5900.10*** *p446*
O'Hearn, Michael; Vermont, 1859-1881 ***5900.10*** *p92*
O'Hearn, Morris; Vermont, 1856-1875 ***5900.10*** *p92*
O'Hearn, Nellie; Vermont, 1862-1868 ***5900.10*** *p92*
O'Hearn, Patrick; Vermont, 1827-1883 ***5900.10*** *p92*
O'Hearne, John 68; Vermont, 1884 ***5900.10*** *p209*
O'Hearne, Margaret; Vermont, 1901 ***5900.10*** *p209*
O'Heer, Matty 60; Vermont, 1850 ***5900.10*** *p497*
O'Heere, Bridget Hanna; Vermont, 1823-1884 ***5900.10*** *p278*
O'Heere, Bridget Hanna 62; Vermont, 1884 ***5900.10*** *p280*
Oheere, Daniel; Vermont, 1853-1934 ***5900.10*** *p278*
O'Heere, Elizabeth; Vermont, n.d. ***5900.10*** *p278*
Oheere, Elizabeth; Vermont, 1843-1918 ***5900.10*** *p278*
Oheere, Ellen; Vermont, 1848-1934 ***5900.10*** *p278*
Oheere, Emma; Vermont, 1881-1908 ***5900.10*** *p278*
O'Heere, James; Vermont, n.d. ***5900.10*** *p278*
O'Heere, John; Vermont, 1853-1921 ***5900.10*** *p278*
O'Heere, Mary; Vermont, n.d. ***5900.10*** *p278*
Oheere, Michael; Vermont, 1846-1936 ***5900.10*** *p278*
O'Heere, Thomas; Vermont, 1822-1915 ***5900.10*** *p278*
O'Heir, Daniel; Vermont, 1829 ***5900.10*** *p13*
O'Heir, Thomas; Vermont, 1825 ***5900.10*** *p13*
O'Henley, Alexander *SEE* O'Henley, John
O'Henley, Allan; Ontario, 1850-1859 ***4537.37*** *p82*
Child: John
Child: Neil
Child: Angus
Child: Murdo
Child: Janet
Wife: Janet MacDonald
O'Henley, Allan; Ontario, 1851 ***4537.32*** *p90*
Wife: Janet MacDonald
Child: Janet
Child: Angus
Child: Neil
Child: Murdo
O'Henley, Allan; Port uncertain, 1850-1859 ***4537.37*** *p132*
Child: Angus
Wife: Kirsty MacDonald
Child: Neil
Child: Donald
Child: Margaret
Child: John
Child: Mary
O'Henley, Angus *SEE* O'Henley, Allan
O'Henley, Angus *SEE* O'Henley, Donald
O'Henley, Angus *SEE* O'Henley, John
O'Henley, Ann *SEE* O'Henley, John
O'Henley, Ann *SEE* O'Henley, Malcolm
O'Henley, Ann; Ontario, 1850-1859 ***4537.37*** *p57*
O'Henley, Ann; Ontario, 1851 ***4537.32*** *p38*
O'Henley, Ann; Port uncertain, 1850-1859 ***4537.37*** *p110*
O'Henley, Archie *SEE* O'Henley, Murdo
O'Henley, Catherine *SEE* O'Henley, Donald
O'Henley, Catherine *SEE* O'Henley, John
O'Henley, Catherine *SEE* O'Henley, Kirsty MacDonald
O'Henley, Catherine *SEE* O'Henley, Murdo
O'Henley, Catherine *SEE* O'Henley, Sarah
O'Henley, Catherine; Port uncertain, 1840-1849 ***4537.37*** *p115*
O'Henley, Catherine MacDonald *SEE* O'Henley, John
O'Henley, Catherine Morrison *SEE* O'Henley, John
O'Henley, Colin *SEE* O'Henley, Malcolm
O'Henley, Donald *SEE* O'Henley, Allan
O'Henley, Donald *SEE* O'Henley, Janet MacInnes
O'Henley, Donald *SEE* O'Henley, John
O'Henley, Donald *SEE* O'Henley, Kirsty MacDonald
O'Henley, Donald *SEE* O'Henley, Malcolm
O'Henley, Donald *SEE* O'Henley, Marion
O'Henley, Donald *SEE* O'Henley, Sarah
O'Henley, Donald; Ontario, 1840-1849 ***4537.37*** *p82*
Wife: Kirsty MacLellan
Child: Mary
Child: Catherine
Child: Angus
O'Henley, Dougal *SEE* O'Henley, John
O'Henley, Effie; Port uncertain, 1840-1849 ***4537.37*** *p118*
O'Henley, Finlay *SEE* O'Henley, Murdo
O'Henley, Flora Johnston *SEE* O'Henley, John
O'Henley, Isabella MacDonald *SEE* O'Henley, John
O'Henley, Janet *SEE* O'Henley, Allan
O'Henley, Janet *SEE* O'Henley, John
O'Henley, Janet MacDonald *SEE* O'Henley, Allan
O'Henley, Janet MacInnes; Port uncertain, 1850-1859 ***4537.37*** *p132*
Child: Murdo
Child: John
Child: Donald
O'Henley, Jessie *SEE* O'Henley, Malcolm
O'Henley, John *SEE* O'Henley, Allan
O'Henley, John *SEE* O'Henley, Janet MacInnes
O'Henley, John *SEE* O'Henley, John
O'Henley, John *SEE* O'Henley, Murdo
O'Henley, John; Ontario, 1848 ***4537.37*** *p83*
Wife: Catherine Morrison
Child: Mary
Child: Donald
Child: Michael
Child: Angus
O'Henley, John; Ontario, 1848 ***4537.37*** *p83*
Wife: Mary MacIntyre
Child: John
Child: Janet
Child: Kirsty
Child: Neil
Child: Michael
Child: Marion
O'Henley, John; Ontario, 1850-1859 ***4537.37*** *p83*
With wife
Child: Donald
Child: Ann
Child: Malcolm
Child: Dougal
O'Henley, John; Ontario, 1851 ***4537.32*** *p90*
With wife
Child: Donald
Child: Dougal
Child: Ann
Child: Malcolm
O'Henley, John; Port uncertain, 1850-1859 ***4537.37*** *p132*
Wife: Catherine MacDonald
Child: Neil
Child: Angus
Child: John
Child: Ranald
Child: Alexander
O'Henley, John; Port uncertain, 1850-1859 ***4537.37*** *p132*
Wife: Flora Johnston
Child: Kirsty
Child: Ann
Child: Mary
Child: Marion
Child: Catherine
O'Henley, John; Port uncertain, 1850-1859 ***4537.37*** *p132*
Wife: Isabella MacDonald
Child: Malcolm
Child: Mary
Child: Alexander
O'Henley, Kirsty *SEE* O'Henley, John
O'Henley, Kirsty *SEE* O'Henley, Marion
O'Henley, Kirsty; Ontario, 1849 ***4537.37*** *p80*
O'Henley, Kirsty MacDonald *SEE* O'Henley, Allan
O'Henley, Kirsty MacDonald *SEE* O'Henley, Murdo
O'Henley, Kirsty MacDonald; Ontario, 1849 ***4537.37*** *p82*
Child: Marion
Child: Donald
Child: Catherine
Child: Mary
O'Henley, Kirsty MacLellan *SEE* O'Henley, Donald
O'Henley, Malcolm *SEE* O'Henley, John
O'Henley, Malcolm; Port uncertain, 1850-1859 ***4537.37*** *p132*
Sibling: Jessie
Sibling: Donald
Sibling: Mary
Sibling: Ann
Sibling: Colin
O'Henley, Margaret *SEE* O'Henley, Allan
O'Henley, Margaret; Saskatchewan, 1884 ***4537.37*** *p97*
O'Henley, Marion *SEE* O'Henley, John
O'Henley, Marion *SEE* O'Henley, Kirsty MacDonald
O'Henley, Marion *SEE* O'Henley, Murdo
O'Henley, Marion; Ontario, 1849 ***4537.37*** *p53*
O'Henley, Marion; Port uncertain, 1840-1849 ***4537.37*** *p132*
Child: Kirsty
Child: Donald
O'Henley, Marion; Port uncertain, 1850-1859 ***4537.37*** *p108*
O'Henley, Mary *SEE* O'Henley, Allan
O'Henley, Mary *SEE* O'Henley, Donald
O'Henley, Mary *SEE* O'Henley, John
O'Henley, Mary *SEE* O'Henley, Kirsty MacDonald
O'Henley, Mary *SEE* O'Henley, Malcolm
O'Henley, Mary *SEE* O'Henley, Murdo
O'Henley, Mary; Ontario, 1850-1859 ***4537.37*** *p38*
O'Henley, Mary; Ontario, 1851 ***4537.32*** *p17*
O'Henley, Mary MacIntyre *SEE* O'Henley, John
O'Henley, Michael *SEE* O'Henley, John
O'Henley, Murdo *SEE* O'Henley, Allan
O'Henley, Murdo *SEE* O'Henley, Janet MacInnes
O'Henley, Murdo; Ontario, 1850-1859 ***4537.37*** *p83*
Wife: Kirsty MacDonald
Child: Archie
Child: Catherine
Child: Rachel
Child: Marion
Child: John
Child: Neil
Child: Sarah
Child: Mary
Child: Finlay
O'Henley, Murdo; Ontario, 1851 ***4537.32*** *p90*
Wife: Kirsty MacDonald
Child: Archie
Child: Mary
Child: Sarah
Child: Neil
Child: John
Child: Marion
Child: Rachel
Child: Catherine
Child: Finlay
O'Henley, Neil *SEE* O'Henley, Allan
O'Henley, Neil *SEE* O'Henley, John
O'Henley, Neil *SEE* O'Henley, Murdo
O'Henley, Rachel *SEE* O'Henley, Murdo
O'Henley, Ranald *SEE* O'Henley, John
O'Henley, Sarah *SEE* O'Henley, Murdo
O'Henley, Sarah; Port uncertain, 1840-1849 ***4537.37*** *p133*
Child: Donald
Child: Catherine
O'Heren, Ward 85; Vermont, 1881 ***5900.10*** *p613*
O'Heren, William; New York, 1837 ***8197.10*** *p96*
O'Hern, Bridget; Vermont, 1840-1915 ***5900.10*** *p547*
O'Hern, David; New York, 1828 ***8197.10*** *p268*

O'Hern, David; New York, 1831 ***8197.10*** *p67*
O'Heron, John 17; Vermont, 1873 ***5900.10*** *p209*
O'Heron, William; New York, 1837 ***8197.10*** *p96*
Ohl, George; New York, 1807 ***8197.10*** *p47*
Ohl, Nicolas; America, 1751 ***2856.30*** *p330*
Ohlen, Henry George 16; New York, 1775 ***1220.25*** *p94*
Ohlenschlager, Georg Peter; Port uncertain, 1737 ***2856.30*** *p330*
With wife & 4 children
Ohler, Daniel; Port uncertain, 1783 ***2856.30*** *p330*
Ohler, Johann Philipp; Port uncertain, 1766 ***2856.30*** *p330*
Ohler, Johann Thomas; Port uncertain, 1752 ***2856.30*** *p330*
Ohler, Johann Thomas; Port uncertain, 1784 ***2856.30*** *p330*
Ohler, Philipp Jakob; America, 1768 ***2856.30*** *p330*
Ohliger, Michael; Port uncertain, 1783 ***2856.30*** *p330*
With wife & 2 sons
Ohligschlager, Johann; Port uncertain, 1763 ***2856.30*** *p330*
Ohlinger, Eberhard; Port uncertain, 1766 ***2856.30*** *p330*
Ohlinger, Johann Wendel; Port uncertain, 1764 ***2856.30*** *p330*
Ohlinger, Mrs. Valentin; Port uncertain, 1746 ***2856.30*** *p330*
Ohlson, William 29; Maryland, 1774 ***1220.25*** *p77*
Ohlweyler, Philipp; Port uncertain, 1756 ***2856.30*** *p330*
Ohnweiler, Friedrich; Port uncertain, 1795 ***2856.30*** *p330*
Ohnweiler, Friedrich; Port uncertain, 1796 ***2856.30*** *p330*
O'Horow, Arthur; Pennsylvania, 1778 ***4629.10*** *p32*
Oitiex, John; Maryland, 1910 ***3259.35*** *p44*
O'Kane, Anna J. Reavy; Vermont, 1869-1932 ***5900.10*** *p324*
O'Kane, Bridget; Vermont, 1856-1926 ***5900.10*** *p326*
O'Kane, Bridget 62; Vermont, 1800-1899 ***5900.10*** *p512*
O'Kane, Charles; Vermont, 1845-1923 ***5900.10*** *p278*
O'Kane, Charles 68; Vermont, 1875 ***5900.10*** *p514*
O'Kane, Daniel; Vermont, 1851-1930 ***5900.10*** *p324*
O'Kane, Eliza; Vermont, 1853-1909 ***5900.10*** *p326*
O'Kane, Ellen; Vermont, 1847-1914 ***5900.10*** *p514*
O'Kane, Harry A.; Vermont, 1855-1901 ***5900.10*** *p517*
Okane, Joseph; Maryland, 1662 ***2524.55*** *p164*
O'Kane, Margaret; Vermont, 1807-1889 ***5900.10*** *p515*
O'Kane, Margaret McGee 56; Vermont, 1906 ***5900.10*** *p324*
O'Kane, Mary; Vermont, 1839-1919 ***5900.10*** *p514*
O'Kane, Mary Birney 79; Vermont, 1890 ***5900.10*** *p514*
O'Kane, Mary McCarty; Vermont, 1852-1925 ***5900.10*** *p278*
O'Kane, Michael 50; Ontario, 1871 ***1823.28*** *p78*
OKane, Roger; Virginia, 1672 ***6212.30*** *p49*
Oke, John 36; Ontario, 1871 ***1823.15*** *p206*
Oke, Samuel 34; Ontario, 1871 ***1823.15*** *p206*
Oke, Thomas 30; Ontario, 1871 ***1823.15*** *p206*
Oke, Thomas 62; Ontario, 1871 ***1823.15*** *p206*
Oke, Thomas 73; Ontario, 1871 ***1823.15*** *p206*
Oke, William 70; Ontario, 1871 ***1823.22*** *p119*
O'Keefe, Ann Banahan; Vermont, 1840-1894 ***5900.10*** *p508*
O'Keefe, Catherine 75; Vermont, 1882 ***5900.10*** *p104*
O'Keefe, Catherine Banahan 63; Vermont, 1914 ***5900.10*** *p506*
O'Keefe, D. H. 1; Ontario, 1861 ***2896.26*** *p28*
O'Keefe, Daniel 29; Ontario, 1861 ***2896.26*** *p28*
O'Keefe, Denis 55; Vermont, 1896 ***5900.10*** *p506*
O'Keefe, Denis 79; Vermont, 1871 ***5900.10*** *p506*
O'Keefe, Ed 61; Alaska, 1916 ***9196.1*** *p7*
O'Keefe, Ed 61; Yukon, 1916 ***9196.1*** *p7*
O'Keefe, Ellen 19; Vermont, 1879 ***5900.10*** *p412*
O'Keefe, George 6; Vermont, 1881 ***5900.10*** *p450*
O'Keefe, J. F. 3; Ontario, 1861 ***2896.26*** *p28*
O'Keefe, Johanna; Vermont, 1829-1911 ***5900.10*** *p353*
O'Keefe, John; Vermont, 1834-1888 ***5900.10*** *p508*
O'Keefe, John; Vermont, 1853-1916 ***5900.10*** *p395*
O'Keefe, John 19; Vermont, 1874 ***5900.10*** *p412*
O'Keefe, Lizzie 2; Vermont, 1881 ***5900.10*** *p450*
O'Keefe, Luke; Vermont, 1857-1923 ***5900.10*** *p394*
O'Keefe, Margaret; Vermont, 1863-1911 ***5900.10*** *p236*
O'Keefe, Margaret; Vermont, 1863-1931 ***5900.10*** *p395*
O'Keefe, Mary; Vermont, 1852-1935 ***5900.10*** *p394*
O'Keefe, Mary Dundon; Vermont, n.d. ***5900.10*** *p393*
O'Keefe, Mary Flood 26; Vermont, 1882 ***5900.10*** *p181*
O'Keefe, Mary L. Downes 20; Vermont, 1871 ***5900.10*** *p258*
O'Keefe, Mary Morisey 74; Vermont, 1868 ***5900.10*** *p506*
O'Keefe, Mary O'Neil 76; Vermont, 1902 ***5900.10*** *p412*
O'Keefe, Michael; Vermont, 1826-1906 ***5900.10*** *p353*
O'Keefe, Michael; Vermont, 1850-1895 ***5900.10*** *p461*
O'Keefe, Michael 34; Vermont, 1882 ***5900.10*** *p181*
O'Keefe, Thomas 40; Vermont, 1895 ***5900.10*** *p393*
O'Keefe, Timothy 47; Vermont, 1871 ***5900.10*** *p412*
O'Keeffe, Ellen Roche 60; Vermont, 1885 ***5900.10*** *p290*
O'Keeffe, Eugene 17 *SEE* O'Keeffe, Margaret
O'Keeffe, James 56; Vermont, 1915 ***5900.10*** *p290*
O'Keeffe, James 66; Vermont, 1885 ***5900.10*** *p290*
O'Keeffe, Jeane 13 *SEE* O'Keeffe, Margaret
O'Keeffe, Johanna 21 *SEE* O'Keeffe, Margaret
O'Keeffe, Margaret 50; New York, New York, 1849 ***1825.45*** *p50*
Son: Eugene 17
Daughter: Johanna 21
Daughter: Nano 23
Daughter: Jeane 13
O'Keeffe, Nano 23 *SEE* O'Keeffe, Margaret
O'Keeffe, Patrick; Vermont, 1849-1949 ***5900.10*** *p290*
O'Keff, Patrick 40; Ontario, 1871 ***1823.15*** *p204*
O'Keiff, Michael; New York, 1836 ***8197.10*** *p76*
Okeley, Ann; Maryland, 1671 ***2524.55*** *p164*
Okeley, Margrett; Maryland, 1678 ***2524.55*** *p164*
Okeley, Thomas; Maryland, 1671 ***2524.55*** *p164*
Okell, George 24; Maryland, 1775 ***1220.25*** *p105*
Okell, Joseph; New York, 1821 ***8197.10*** *p267*
O'Kelly, . . .; South Carolina, 1750-1770 ***4628.40*** *p98*
Okelly, Edw D. 27; Ontario, 1871 ***1823.28*** *p79*
Okely, James; Virginia, 1667-1668 ***6212.30*** *p39*
Okely, Sisly; Virginia, 1665 ***6212.30*** *p20*
Okenton, William; Maryland, 1665 ***2524.55*** *p164*
Oker, Abraham; Died enroute, 1667 ***1224.1*** *p43*
Oker, Matthew 40; Ontario, 1871 ***1823.28*** *p79*
O'Kerry, Dennough; Maryland, 1659 ***2524.55*** *p164*
Okey, John; Maryland, 1666 ***2524.55*** *p244*
Okeyne, Joseph; Maryland, 1662 ***2524.55*** *p164*
Okley, Margrett; Maryland, 1678 ***2524.55*** *p164*
Okoniczka, Michel; Maryland, 1910 ***3259.35*** *p44*
Okonski, Andrew; Maryland, 1910 ***3259.35*** *p44*
Okuniewsky, John; Maryland, 1910 ***3259.35*** *p44*
Olaham, Philip; Maryland, 1668 ***2524.55*** *p164*
Olandman, Denham; Maryland, 1665 ***2524.55*** *p138*
O'Langlin, Brien 60; Ontario, 1871 ***1823.15*** *p204*
Olaniski, Wladistaw; Maryland, 1910 ***3259.35*** *p44*
O'Lara, John 51; Vermont, 1862 ***5900.10*** *p345*
O'Lara, Mary 47; Vermont, 1861 ***5900.10*** *p345*
O'Laughlin, Elizabeth Kennedy; Vermont, 1838-1894 ***5900.10*** *p472*
O'Laughlin, Ellen Carroll 66; Vermont, 1910 ***5900.10*** *p443*
O'Laughlin, J. 77; Vermont, 1900 ***5900.10*** *p497*
O'Laughlin, John; Vermont, n.d. ***5900.10*** *p421*
O'Laughlin, Thos 40; Ontario, 1871 ***1823.15*** *p204*
Old, John; Virginia, 1803 ***1640.13*** *p96*
Old, John 16; Maryland, 1774 ***1220.25*** *p57*
Old, John 30; Halifax, Nova Scotia, 1774 ***1220.25*** *p138*
Oldaker, William 22; Philadelphia, 1774 ***1220.25*** *p82*
Oldall, Mrs.; Portland, Maine, 1858 ***9196.15*** *p29*
Oldall, Francis; Portland, Maine, 1858 ***9196.15*** *p29*
Oldden, Benjamin; Pennsylvania, 1776 ***4629.10*** *p53*
Olden, John; Pennsylvania, 1777 ***4629.10*** *p23*
Oldenberg, Fredrick 52; Ontario, 1871 ***1823.28*** *p79*
Oldenbough, August 42; Ontario, 1871 ***1823.28*** *p79*
Olderidge, Ann *SEE* Olderidge, William
Olderidge, Elizabeth *SEE* Olderidge, William
Olderidge, William; Maryland, 1662 ***2524.55*** *p164*
Wife: Elizabeth
Daughter: Ann
Oldershao, Mr.; Quebec, 1856 ***9196.15*** *p6*
Oldershao, L.; Quebec, 1856 ***9196.15*** *p6*
Oldfeild, Henry; Maryland, 1673 ***2524.55*** *p164*
Oldfield, Samuel 26; Ontario, 1871 ***1823.28*** *p79*
Oldfield, William 49; Ontario, 1871 ***1823.15*** *p206*
Oldham, John L. 43; Ontario, 1871 ***1823.28*** *p79*
Oldham, Thomas M.; New York, 1839 ***8197.10*** *p268*
Oldis, Marmaduke; Maryland, 1667 ***2524.55*** *p164*
Oldmixon, Mary; Philadelphia, 1838 ***1224.3*** *p58*
Olds, Cyrena A.; Vermont, 1850-1938 ***5900.10*** *p607*
Olds, John 60; Ontario, 1871 ***1823.15*** *p206*
Oldstaff, Margaret; Maryland, 1664 ***2524.55*** *p164*
With 2 children
Oldsworth, John; Maryland, 1666 ***2524.55*** *p164*
O'Leary, Annie N.; Vermont, 1877 ***5900.10*** *p65*
O'Leary, Bridget; Vermont, 1842-1885 ***5900.10*** *p439*
O'Leary, Catherine; Vermont, 1860-1876 ***5900.10*** *p315*
O'Leary, Charles 62; Vermont, 1876 ***5900.10*** *p367*
O'Leary, Cornelius 63; Vermont, 1884 ***5900.10*** *p585*
O'Leary, Daniel 90; Vermont, 1897 ***5900.10*** *p169*
O'Leary, Dennis; New York, 1840 ***8197.10*** *p320*
O'Leary, Elennor McCarty 81; Vermont, 1913 ***5900.10*** *p367*
O'Leary, Elizabeth; Vermont, 1857 ***5900.10*** *p315*
O'Leary, Elizabeth Coffey; Vermont, 1842-1915 ***5900.10*** *p465*
Oleary, James 30; Ontario, 1871 ***1823.28*** *p79*
O'Leary, Jeremiah; Vermont, 1815-1900 ***5900.10*** *p315*
O'Leary, Jeremiah, Jr.; Vermont, 1855-1873 ***5900.10*** *p315*
O'Leary, Joanna; Vermont, 1843-1916 ***5900.10*** *p570*
O'Leary, Johannah Grady; Vermont, 1860-1911 ***5900.10*** *p422*
O'Leary, John; New York, 1836 ***8197.10*** *p77*
O'Leary, John; Vermont, 1806-1865 ***5900.10*** *p439*
Oleary, John 47; Ontario, 1871 ***1823.28*** *p79*
O'Leary, John 69; Ontario, 1871 ***1823.22*** *p118*
O'Leary, Julia 97; Vermont, 1905 ***5900.10*** *p585*
O'Leary, Margaret 30; Vermont, 1881 ***5900.10*** *p423*
O'Leary, Margaret Buckley 78; Vermont, 1891 ***5900.10*** *p169*
O'Leary, Margaret Sweeney 63; Vermont, 1891 ***5900.10*** *p426*
O'Leary, Mary; Vermont, 1823-1913 ***5900.10*** *p53*
O'Leary, Mary; Vermont, 1833-1878 ***5900.10*** *p177*
O'Leary, Mary; Vermont, 1840-1863 ***5900.10*** *p315*
O'Leary, Mary Keogh; Vermont, 1820-1892 ***5900.10*** *p315*
O'Leary, Mary L.; Vermont, 1816-1913 ***5900.10*** *p364*
O'Leary, Michael 33; Ontario, 1871 ***1823.22*** *p119*
Oleary, Michael 63; Ontario, 1871 ***1823.28*** *p79*
O'Leary, Nancy Dwyer 74; Vermont, 1901 ***5900.10*** *p466*
O'Leary, Nora 34; Vermont, 1886 ***5900.10*** *p169*
O'Leary, Patrick; Vermont, 1839-1915 ***5900.10*** *p465*
O'Leary, Timothy; New York, 1821 ***8197.10*** *p267*
O'Leary, Timothy; Vermont, 1847-1922 ***5900.10*** *p422*
O'Leary, Timothy 68; Ontario, 1871 ***1823.22*** *p119*
O'Leary, Timothy 78; Vermont, 1879 ***5900.10*** *p65*
O'Leary, Timothy 78; Vermont, 1879 ***5900.10*** *p466*
O'Leary, Timothy 82; Vermont, 1908 ***5900.10*** *p426*
Olek, Bawel; Maryland, 1910 ***3259.35*** *p44*
Olek, Mikolay; Maryland, 1910 ***3259.35*** *p44*
Olendrowicz, Felix; Maryland, 1910 ***3259.35*** *p44*
Olenik, Julius; Maryland, 1910 ***3259.35*** *p44*
Olerious, John 70; Ontario, 1871 ***1823.22*** *p119*
Oles, Alexander; Maryland, 1910 ***3259.35*** *p44*
Oles, Anthony; Maryland, 1910 ***3259.35*** *p44*
Oles, Frank; Maryland, 1910 ***3259.35*** *p44*
Oles, Jacob; Maryland, 1910 ***3259.35*** *p44*
Oles, Joseph; Maryland, 1910 ***3259.35*** *p44*
Oles, Peter; Maryland, 1910 ***3259.35*** *p44*
Olezewski, Michal; Maryland, 1910 ***3259.35*** *p44*
Olies, Pauline; Maryland, 1910 ***3259.35*** *p44*
Oliphant, Ann Hay; Colorado, 1892 ***1640.13*** *p96*
Oliphant, James; Georgia, 1775 ***1640.10*** *p167*
Oliphant, James 34; Georgia, 1775 ***1220.25*** *p125*
Oliphant, Jemima; Charleston, South Carolina, 1804 ***1640.13*** *p96*
Oliphant, John; Georgia, 1698 ***1640.13*** *p96*
Oliphant, John 73; Ontario, 1871 ***1823.15*** *p206*
Oliphant, Laurence; Georgia, 1698 ***1640.13*** *p96*
Oliphant, Margaret; Jamaica, 1800 ***1640.13*** *p96*
Oliphant, Thomas; Georgia, 1698 ***1640.13*** *p96*
Oliphant, W.; Mobile, Alabama, 1822-1845 ***1640.10*** *p168*
Olive, John; Maryland, 1673 ***2524.55*** *p164*
Olive, John; Maryland, 1673 ***2524.55*** *p201*
Olive, John; Maryland, 1679 ***2524.55*** *p164*
Olive, Peter; Maryland, 1665 ***2524.55*** *p164*
Oliver, Mr.; Quebec, 1856 ***9196.15*** *p6*
Oliver, Mr.; Quebec, 1857 ***9196.15*** *p20*
Oliver, Mr.; Quebec, 1858 ***9196.15*** *p44*
Oliver, Mrs.; Quebec, 1857 ***9196.15*** *p21*
Oliver, Aaron 40; Ontario, 1871 ***1823.22*** *p119*
Oliver, Alexander 50; Ontario, 1871 ***1823.15*** *p206*
Oliver, Benjamin 19; Ontario, 1861 ***2896.28*** *p19*
Oliver, Catherine 19; Ontario, 1861 ***2896.27*** *p35*
Oliver, Catherine 33; Kansas, 1910 ***9079.10*** *p51*
Oliver, Dorothy; Virginia, 1676 ***6212.30*** *p53*
Oliver, Emmile 40; Ontario, 1871 ***1823.15*** *p206*
Oliver, F. F.; Portland, Maine, 1858 ***9196.15*** *p30*
Oliver, Frances 40; Ontario, 1871 ***1823.15*** *p206*
Oliver, Francis 50; Ontario, 1871 ***1823.15*** *p206*
Oliver, Irmima 42; Ontario, 1871 ***1823.15*** *p206*
Oliver, Isaac 22; Ontario, 1861 ***2896.28*** *p45*
Oliver, James; Maryland, 1663 ***2524.55*** *p164*
Oliver, James; Savannah, Georgia, 1808 ***1640.10*** *p168*
Oliver, James 18; Maryland, 1775 ***1220.25*** *p115*
Oliver, James 53; Ontario, 1871 ***1823.15*** *p206*
Oliver, Jane 38; Ontario, 1871 ***1823.15*** *p206*
Oliver, John; Cuba, 1854 ***1224.3*** *p58*
Oliver, John; New York, 1807 ***8197.10*** *p330*
Oliver, John; New York, 1807 ***8197.10*** *p332*
Oliver, John; Died enroute, 1854 ***1224.3*** *p58*
Oliver, John 17; Maryland, 1774 ***1220.25*** *p84*
Oliver, John 33; Maryland, 1775 ***1220.25*** *p120*
Oliver, John 50; Ontario, 1871 ***1823.15*** *p206*
Oliver, John W.; New York, 1839 ***8197.10*** *p136*
Oliver, Joseph; Virginia, 1688 ***1224.1*** *p43*
Oliver, Joseph 45; Ontario, 1871 ***1823.28*** *p79*
Oliver, Matthew 32; Virginia, 1774 ***1220.25*** *p93*
Oliver, Richard 19; Nova Scotia, 1774 ***1220.25*** *p137*
Oliver, Richard 50; Ontario, 1871 ***1823.22*** *p120*

Oliver, Richard 61; Ontario, 1871 ***1823.22*** *p120*
Oliver, Robert; Virginia, 1664 ***6212.30*** *p14*
Oliver, Robt; Virginia, 1665-1666 ***6212.30*** *p21*
Oliver, T.; Quebec, 1857 ***9196.15*** *p23*
Oliver, Thomas; Maryland, 1663 ***2524.55*** *p214*
Oliver, Thomas; Savannah, Georgia, 1774 ***1640.10*** *p168*
With wife & 2 children
Oliver, Thomas 29; Savannah, Georgia, 1774 ***1220.25*** *p139*
With wife & 2 children
Oliver, Thomas 50; Ontario, 1871 ***1823.22*** *p120*
Oliver, Thomas 54; Ontario, 1871 ***1823.22*** *p120*
Oliver, Vincent; Virginia, 1678 ***6212.30*** *p54*
Oliver, William; New York, 1807 ***8197.10*** *p47*
Oliver, William 53; Ontario, 1871 ***1823.28*** *p79*
Oljewski, John; Maryland, 1910 ***3259.35*** *p44*
Olkofski, George; Maryland, 1910 ***3259.35*** *p44*
Olkoski, Michael; Maryland, 1910 ***3259.35*** *p44*
Ollier, Jane; Charles Town, South Carolina, 1737 ***1224.2*** *p86*
Ollier, Ponz; Charles Town, South Carolina, 1737 ***1224.2*** *p86*
Olliman, Henry; Pennsylvania, 1840 ***6058.10*** *p17*
Ollis, Lowry; Maryland, 1681 ***2524.55*** *p164*
Olliver, William 38; Ontario, 1871 ***1823.15*** *p206*
Olmer, Hans Adam; America, 1738 ***2856.30*** *p330*
Oloni, Bernard 52; Ontario, 1871 ***1823.15*** *p206*
Oloni, Eletia 87; Ontario, 1871 ***1823.15*** *p206*
O'Loughlin, Anne 18; Vermont, 1865 ***5900.10*** *p614*
Oloughlin, John 49; Ontario, 1871 ***1823.15*** *p206*
O'Loughlin, Mary Ladon 67; Vermont, 1877 ***5900.10*** *p614*
O'Loughlin, Michael 71; Vermont, 1872 ***5900.10*** *p614*
Olschinsky, John; Maryland, 1910 ***3259.35*** *p44*
Olsen, Andrew 20; British Columbia, 1909 ***9196.1*** *p26*
Olsen, Andrew 20; Washington, 1909 ***9196.1*** *p26*
Olsen, Andrew Julius; New York, 1838 ***8197.10*** *p147*
Olsen, Con 36; Juneau, Alaska, 1917 ***9196.1*** *p45*
Olsen, Con 36; Whitehorse, Yukon, 1917 ***9196.1*** *p45*
Olsen, J... 38; Vancouver, British Columbia, 1910 ***9196.1*** *p15*
Olsen, O. 35; Alaska, 1912 ***9196.1*** *p38*
Olsen, O. 35; Whitehorse, Yukon, 1912 ***9196.1*** *p38*
Olsen, Ole 22; British Columbia, 1911 ***9196.1*** *p34*
Olsen, Ole 22; Washington, 1911 ***9196.1*** *p34*
Olsen, Pete 59; Seattle, 1917 ***9196.1*** *p51*
Olsen, Pete 59; Yukon, 1917 ***9196.1*** *p51*
Olsen, Richard; New York, 1805 ***8197.10*** *p30*
Olsen, Stephen E. 52; Ontario, 1871 ***1823.22*** *p120*
Olshewska, Mary; Maryland, 1910 ***3259.35*** *p44*
Olshewski, Antoni; Maryland, 1910 ***3259.35*** *p44*
Olshiskie, John; Maryland, 1910 ***3259.35*** *p44*
Olski, James; Maryland, 1910 ***3259.35*** *p44*
Olson, F. 30; Alaska, 1917 ***9196.1*** *p53*
Olson, F. 30; Whitehorse, Yukon, 1917 ***9196.1*** *p53*
Olson, Lear; New York, 1807 ***8197.10*** *p327*
Olson, T. 29; Alaska, 1917 ***9196.1*** *p47*
Olson, T. 29; Whitehorse, Yukon, 1917 ***9196.1*** *p47*
Olsyski, Thomas; Maryland, 1910 ***3259.35*** *p44*
Olszewski, August; Maryland, 1910 ***3259.35*** *p44*
Olszewski, Joseph; Maryland, 1910 ***3259.35*** *p44*
Olszewski, Michael; Maryland, 1910 ***3259.35*** *p44*
Olszewski, Peter; Maryland, 1910 ***3259.35*** *p44*
Olszewsky, John; Maryland, 1910 ***3259.35*** *p44*
Olszewsky, Stanislaw; Maryland, 1910 ***3259.35*** *p44*
Olszewsky, Wladislaw; Maryland, 1910 ***3259.35*** *p44*
Oltman, Maggie; Maryland, 1910 ***3259.35*** *p44*
O'Lunge, Daniel; Maryland, 1659 ***2524.55*** *p164*
Olvis, Jno; Virginia, 1666 ***6212.30*** *p25*
Olwell, James; New York, 1831 ***8197.10*** *p365*
Olwell, James; New York, 1831 ***8197.10*** *p370*
Olyniesak, M. Ambrose; Maryland, 1910 ***3259.35*** *p44*
O'Maher, Timothy; New York, 1831 ***8197.10*** *p268*
O'Malley, Bridget Durkin; Vermont, 1908 ***5900.10*** *p145*
O'Malley, Ellen 34; Vermont, 1875 ***5900.10*** *p601*
O'Malley, John; Vermont, 1916 ***5900.10*** *p145*
O'Malley, Julia Ellen Canty; Vermont, 1851-1951 ***5900.10*** *p509*
O'Malley, Patrick F.; Vermont, 1840-1912 ***5900.10*** *p509*
Omar, Jery 31; Alaska, 1912 ***9196.1*** *p20*
Omar, Jery 31; British Columbia, 1912 ***9196.1*** *p20*
O'Mara, Anna; Vermont, n.d. ***5900.10*** *p144*
O'Mara, Catharine 38; Vermont, 1875 ***5900.10*** *p263*
O'Mara, Ellen; Vermont, 1846-1914 ***5900.10*** *p79*
O'Mara, Ellen Sullivan 63; Vermont, 1899 ***5900.10*** *p428*
O'Mara, James; Vermont, 1813-1893 ***5900.10*** *p306*
O'Mara, Johanna; Vermont, 1821-1904 ***5900.10*** *p306*
O'Mara, John; New York, 1825 ***8197.10*** *p267*
O'Mara, John; New York, 1828 ***8197.10*** *p65*
O'Mara, John; Vermont, 1837-1903 ***5900.10*** *p144*
O'Mara, John; Vermont, 1855-1914 ***5900.10*** *p77*
O'Mara, Lawrence; Vermont, n.d. ***5900.10*** *p144*
O'Mara, Margaret; Vermont, 1869-1969 ***5900.10*** *p144*
O'Mara, Mary; Vermont, 1837-1906 ***5900.10*** *p80*
O'Mara, Mary; Vermont, 1838-1903 ***5900.10*** *p144*
O'Mara, Mary F. Patton 31; Vermont, 1883 ***5900.10*** *p294*
O'Mara, Mary Powers; Vermont, 1859-1923 ***5900.10*** *p77*
O'Mara, Maurice; New York, 1828-1831 ***8197.10*** *p369*
O'Mara, Thomas; Vermont, n.d. ***5900.10*** *p144*
O'Mara, Timothy; Vermont, 1822-1904 ***5900.10*** *p428*
Omaro, Patrick 55; Ontario, 1871 ***1823.15*** *p206*
O'Marrah, Bridget; Vermont, 1821-1891 ***5900.10*** *p506*
O'Meara, Delia; Vermont, n.d. ***5900.10*** *p495*
O'Meara, Edwd 38; Ontario, 1871 ***1823.28*** *p78*
O'Meara, James; New York, 1828 ***8197.10*** *p268*
O'Meara, James 35; Ontario, 1871 ***1823.28*** *p78*
O'Meara, Jeremiah; New York, 1831 ***8197.10*** *p366*
O'Meara, Mary; Vermont, 1825-1909 ***5900.10*** *p158*
Omeara, Michl 50; Ontario, 1871 ***1823.28*** *p79*
Omeara, Patrick 38; Ontario, 1871 ***1823.28*** *p79*
Omeara, William 42; Ontario, 1871 ***1823.28*** *p79*
Omeely, Bryan; Maryland, 1664 ***2524.55*** *p164*
O'Melia, Anthony 49; Ontario, 1871 ***1823.22*** *p119*
O'Melia, John 42; Ontario, 1871 ***1823.22*** *p119*
O'Melia, Patrick 41; Ontario, 1871 ***1823.22*** *p119*
O'Mersh, Thomas; Maryland, 1652-1659 ***2524.55*** *p164*
Omley, John; Pennsylvania, 1777 ***4629.10*** *p10*
Onail, Catherin 68; Ontario, 1871 ***1823.28*** *p79*
O'Nale, Herege; Maryland, 1659 ***2524.55*** *p164*
O'Nale, Huege; Maryland, 1659 ***2524.55*** *p159*
O'Nale, Hugh; Maryland, 1659 ***2524.55*** *p164*
Onangisse, Joseph 42; Ontario, 1871 ***1823.28*** *p79*
Onay, Annie 73; Ontario, 1871 ***1823.15*** *p206*
Onchard, John 31; Baltimore, 1775 ***1220.25*** *p118*
O'Neal, Anne 20 *SEE* O'Neal, Bernard
O'Neal, Bernard 13 *SEE* O'Neal, Bernard
O'Neal, Bernard 45; New York, New York, 1847 ***1825.45*** *p19*
Wife: Betty 40
Son: Bernard 13
Son: John 16
Daughter: Anne 20
O'Neal, Betty 40 *SEE* O'Neal, Bernard
O'Neal, Charles 29; Ontario, 1871 ***1823.22*** *p119*
O'Neal, Daniel 60; Ontario, 1871 ***1823.22*** *p119*
O'Neal, James; Canada, 1756-1760 ***4628.40*** *p45*
O'Neal, John 16 *SEE* O'Neal, Bernard
Oneal, John 32; Ontario, 1871 ***1823.28*** *p79*
O'Neale, Charles *SEE* O'Neale, Hugh
O'Neale, Daniel *SEE* O'Neale, Hugh
O'Neale, Hugh; Maryland, 1667 ***2524.55*** *p164*
Wife: Mary
Child: Charles
Child: Joy
Child: Daniel
Oneale, John; Virginia, 1682 ***1224.1*** *p41*
O'Neale, Joy *SEE* O'Neale, Hugh
O'Neale, Mary *SEE* O'Neale, Hugh
O'Neil, . . .; Vermont, 1869 ***5900.10*** *p139*
Oneil, Ann 15; Ontario, 1871 ***1823.28*** *p79*
O'Neil, Anna; Vermont, 1842-1872 ***5900.10*** *p481*
O'Neil, Anna C.; Vermont, 1849-1935 ***5900.10*** *p183*
O'Neil, Anna M.; Vermont, 1849-1862 ***5900.10*** *p345*
O'Neil, Anna M. Conline; Vermont, 1852-1913 ***5900.10*** *p447*
O'Neil, Annie; Vermont, n.d. ***5900.10*** *p322*
Oneil, Arthur 32; Ontario, 1871 ***1823.22*** *p120*
O'Neil, Bernard 84; Vermont, 1876 ***5900.10*** *p231*
O'Neil, Bridget; Vermont, n.d. ***5900.10*** *p584*
O'Neil, Bridget; Vermont, 1845-1892 ***5900.10*** *p462*
O'Neil, Bridget 62; Vermont, 1887 ***5900.10*** *p295*
O'Neil, Bridget Hurley 28; Vermont, 1869 ***5900.10*** *p139*
O'Neil, Catharine 39; Vermont, 1855 ***5900.10*** *p347*
O'Neil, Catherine; Vermont, n.d. ***5900.10*** *p333*
O'Neil, Catherine; Vermont, 1833-1926 ***5900.10*** *p478*
O'Neil, Catherine Baker; Vermont, 1897 ***5900.10*** *p103*
O'neil, Catherine Keenan 86; Vermont, 1880 ***5900.10*** *p477*
O'Neil, Caturah; Ontario, 1861 ***2896.28*** *p64*
Oneil, Charles 42; Ontario, 1871 ***1823.15*** *p206*
O'Neil, Charles 96; Vermont, 1876 ***5900.10*** *p477*
O'Neil, Con 85; Vermont, 1890 ***5900.10*** *p294*
O'Neil, Daniel; Vermont, 1822-1899 ***5900.10*** *p614*
O'Neil, Dinah; Vermont, 1812-1897 ***5900.10*** *p138*
O'Neil, Duncan 24; Maryland, 1774 ***1220.25*** *p3*
O'Neil, E. 23; Ontario, 1861 ***2896.28*** *p2*
Oneil, E. 40; Ontario, 1871 ***1823.28*** *p79*
O'Neil, Edmond 62; Vermont, 1901 ***5900.10*** *p139*
O'Neil, Edward 78; Vermont, 1895 ***5900.10*** *p584*
Oneil, Eliza 45; Ontario, 1871 ***1823.15*** *p206*
Oneil, Elizabeth 67; Ontario, 1871 ***1823.15*** *p206*
O'Neil, Ellen 27; Vermont, 1839 ***5900.10*** *p153*
O'Neil, Ellen 67; Vermont, 1883 ***5900.10*** *p477*
O'Neil, Ellen 80; Vermont, 1886 ***5900.10*** *p387*
O'Neil, Ellen Dixon; Vermont, 1842-1915 ***5900.10*** *p99*
O'Neil, Francis 48; Vermont, 1874 ***5900.10*** *p514*
O'Neil, Helen; Vermont, 1860-1947 ***5900.10*** *p560*
O'Neil, Hugh; New York, 1806 ***8197.10*** *p267*
O'Neil, James; New York, 1831 ***8197.10*** *p268*
O'Neil, James; New York, 1840 ***8197.10*** *p191*
O'Neil, James; Vermont, n.d. ***5900.10*** *p322*
O'Neil, James; Vermont, 1885 ***5900.10*** *p103*
O'Neil, James 39; Vermont, 1895 ***5900.10*** *p584*
O'Neil, James 46; Vermont, 1869 ***5900.10*** *p514*
Oneil, James 70; Ontario, 1871 ***1823.28*** *p79*
O'Neil, James C.; New York, 1826 ***8197.10*** *p268*
O'Neil, John; New York, 1825 ***8197.10*** *p267*
O'Neil, John; New York, 1826 ***8197.10*** *p337*
O'Neil, John; New York, 1834 ***8197.10*** *p72*
O'Neil, John; Pennsylvania, 1868 ***6058.10*** *p74*
O'Neil, John; Vermont, 1846-1928 ***5900.10*** *p137*
O'Neil, John; Vermont, 1846-1933 ***5900.10*** *p99*
O'Neil, John; Vermont, 1852-1935 ***5900.10*** *p447*
O'Neil, John; Vermont, 1857-1911 ***5900.10*** *p552*
O'Neil, John; Vermont, 1906 ***5900.10*** *p387*
O'Neil, John 45; Ontario, 1871 ***1823.15*** *p204*
O'Neil, John 46; Ontario, 1871 ***1823.22*** *p119*
O'Neil, John 63; Vermont, 1873 ***5900.10*** *p586*
O'Neil, Julia 26; Ontario, 1871 ***1823.15*** *p204*
O'Neil, Katie E. 10 months; Vermont, 1876 ***5900.10*** *p586*
O'Neil, M. Kelty; Vermont, 1826-1926 ***5900.10*** *p334*
O'Neil, Margaret; Vermont, 1829-1913 ***5900.10*** *p152*
O'Neil, Margaret; Vermont, 1855-1908 ***5900.10*** *p339*
O'Neil, Margaret 20; Vermont, 1872 ***5900.10*** *p412*
O'Neil, Margaret 51; Vermont, 1905 ***5900.10*** *p97*
O'Neil, Margaret 75; Vermont, n.d. ***5900.10*** *p514*
O'Neil, Margaret Crowley; Vermont, 1850-1925 ***5900.10*** *p137*
O'Neil, Maria Culligan; Vermont, 1858-1940 ***5900.10*** *p552*
O'Neil, Mary; Vermont, 1837-1910 ***5900.10*** *p271*
O'Neil, Mary; Vermont, 1838-1911 ***5900.10*** *p114*
O'Neil, Mary; Vermont, 1846-1921 ***5900.10*** *p93*
O'Neil, Mary; Vermont, 1847-1934 ***5900.10*** *p485*
O'Neil, Mary; Vermont, 1860-1934 ***5900.10*** *p400*
O'Neil, Mary 28; Vermont, 1886 ***5900.10*** *p584*
O'Neil, Mary 52; Vermont, 1880 ***5900.10*** *p534*
O'Neil, Mary 54; Ontario, 1871 ***1823.15*** *p204*
O'Neil, Mary 60; Vermont, 1877 ***5900.10*** *p540*
O'Neil, Mary 74; Vermont, 1906 ***5900.10*** *p233*
O'Neil, Mary 76; Vermont, 1902 ***5900.10*** *p412*
O'Neil, Mary 82; Vermont, 1888 ***5900.10*** *p366*
O'Neil, Mary A. Fean 19; Vermont, 1886 ***5900.10*** *p399*
O'Neil, Mary Baker 85; Vermont, 1927 ***5900.10*** *p139*
O'Neil, Mary E. Bray 23; Vermont, 1870 ***5900.10*** *p509*
O'Neil, Mary Foley; Vermont, 1834-1934 ***5900.10*** *p488*
O'Neil, Mary Frokey 51; Vermont, 1878 ***5900.10*** *p611*
O'Neil, Mary Gleeson 67; Vermont, 1893 ***5900.10*** *p584*
O'Neil, Michael; Vermont, 1919 ***5900.10*** *p97*
O'Neil, Owen; New York, 1824 ***8197.10*** *p267*
O'Neil, Patrick; Vermont, n.d. ***5900.10*** *p322*
O'Neil, Patrick; Vermont, 1814-1894 ***5900.10*** *p131*
Oneil, Patrick 34; Ontario, 1871 ***1823.15*** *p206*
O'Neil, Patrick 51; Ontario, 1871 ***1823.22*** *p119*
O'Neil, Patrick H.; New York, 1838 ***8197.10*** *p146*
O'Neil, Peter; Vermont, 1808-1884 ***5900.10*** *p138*
O'Neil, Richard 38; Vermont, 1875 ***5900.10*** *p141*
O'Neil, Richard 40; Ontario, 1871 ***1823.15*** *p204*
O'Neil, Rose Harrision 72; Vermont, 1875 ***5900.10*** *p231*
Oneil, Susan 23; Ontario, 1871 ***1823.15*** *p206*
Oneil, Terance 34; Ontario, 1871 ***1823.22*** *p120*
O'Neil, Thomas; New York, 1802 ***8197.10*** *p24*
O'Neil, Thomas; Vermont, 1848-1910 ***5900.10*** *p488*
O'Neil, Thomas 36; Ontario, 1871 ***1823.15*** *p204*
O'Neil, Thomas J.; Vermont, 1850-1870 ***5900.10*** *p344*
O'Neil, Timothy; New York, 1834 ***8197.10*** *p72*
O'Neil, Timothy 52; Ontario, 1871 ***1823.22*** *p119*
O'Neil, William; New York, 1838 ***8197.10*** *p146*
O'Neil, William; Vermont, 1825-1900 ***5900.10*** *p334*
O'Neil, William 41; Vermont, 1864 ***5900.10*** *p498*
O'Neil, William 54; Ontario, 1871 ***1823.15*** *p204*
O'Neil, William 69; Vermont, 1891 ***5900.10*** *p536*
O'Neile, Thomas; New York, 1840 ***8197.10*** *p192*
O'Neill, Ann; Vermont, 1848-1911 ***5900.10*** *p50*
O'Neill, Ann 65; Vermont, 1861 ***5900.10*** *p229*
O'Neill, Ann 82; Vermont, 1903 ***5900.10*** *p295*
O'Neill, Ann Carrigan; Vermont, 1837-1901 ***5900.10*** *p231*
O'Neill, Anne 20 *SEE* O'Neill, Bernard
Oneill, Barnard; Pennsylvania, 1831 ***6058.10*** *p10*
O'Neill, Bernard 13 *SEE* O'Neill, Bernard
O'Neill, Bernard 45; New York, New York, 1847 ***1825.45*** *p19*
Wife: Betty 40
Son: John 16

Daughter: Anne 20
Son: Bernard 13
O'Neill, Betty 40 *SEE* O'Neill, Bernard
O'Neill, Bridget G. Nowland; Vermont, 1831-1875 ***5900.10*** *p123*
O'Neill, Catharine Lane 76; Vermont, 1900 ***5900.10*** *p370*
O'Neill, Catherine; Vermont, 1854-1926 ***5900.10*** *p67*
O'Neill, Catherine 1; Vermont, 1850 ***5900.10*** *p471*
O'Neill, Cornelius; New York, 1827 ***8197.10*** *p345*
O'Neill, Daniel; Vermont, 1866-1902 ***5900.10*** *p253*
O'Neill, Daniel 81; Vermont, 1878 ***5900.10*** *p471*
O'Neill, Edward P.; Vermont, 1854-1915 ***5900.10*** *p123*
O'Neill, Elizabeth; Vermont, 1828-1910 ***5900.10*** *p471*
O'Neill, Elizabeth 7; Vermont, 1864 ***5900.10*** *p471*
O'Neill, Elizabeth 18; Vermont, 1864 ***5900.10*** *p372*
O'Neill, Ellen; Vermont, 1855-1912 ***5900.10*** *p532*
O'Neill, Ellen 56; Vermont, 1867 ***5900.10*** *p364*
O'Neill, Ellen 56; Vermont, 1867 ***5900.10*** *p369*
O'Neill, Ellen 65; Vermont, 1900 ***5900.10*** *p295*
O'Neill, Ellen Crowley; Vermont, 1853-1941 ***5900.10*** *p588*
O'Neill, Ellen Hughes; Vermont, 1857-1930 ***5900.10*** *p591*
O'Neill, Ellen Shortell; Vermont, 1820-1899 ***5900.10*** *p579*
O'Neill, Francis; New York, 1837 ***8197.10*** *p96*
O'Neill, Francis; Vermont, 1832-1854 ***5900.10*** *p515*
O'Neill, Francis; Vermont, 1864-1931 ***5900.10*** *p123*
O'Neill, Francis 47; Ontario, 1871 ***1823.15*** *p204*
O'Neill, Harry; Vermont, 1842-1913 ***5900.10*** *p138*
O'Neill, Harry; Vermont, 1842-1914 ***5900.10*** *p170*
O'Neill, Helen; Vermont, 1863-1932 ***5900.10*** *p123*
O'Neill, Hugh; Albany, New York, 1832 ***6058.10*** *p48*
O'Neill, Hugh; New York, 1832 ***8197.10*** *p368*
O'Neill, Hugh 48; Ontario, 1871 ***1823.22*** *p119*
O'Neill, J. H. 26; Vermont, 1880 ***5900.10*** *p173*
O'Neill, James; New York, 1826 ***8197.10*** *p268*
O'Neill, James; New York, 1837 ***8197.10*** *p96*
O'Neill, James; New York, 1838 ***8197.10*** *p268*
O'Neill, James; Vermont, 1820-1849 ***5900.10*** *p515*
O'Neill, James; Vermont, 1844-1922 ***5900.10*** *p174*
O'Neill, James 17; Vermont, 1863 ***5900.10*** *p294*
O'Neill, James 56; Vermont, 1871 ***5900.10*** *p50*
O'Neill, James 80; Vermont, 1904 ***5900.10*** *p576*
O'Neill, Jane 29; Vermont, 1859 ***5900.10*** *p345*
O'Neill, Jeremiah 82; Vermont, 1894 ***5900.10*** *p370*
O'Neill, John; America, 1792 ***1224.2*** *p86*
O'Neill, John; New York, 1840 ***8197.10*** *p192*
O'Neill, John; Vermont, 1789-1834 ***5900.10*** *p515*
O'Neill, John; Vermont, 1823-1908 ***5900.10*** *p471*
O'Neill, John; Vermont, 1831-1895 ***5900.10*** *p231*
O'Neill, John; Vermont, 1866-1928 ***5900.10*** *p123*
O'Neill, John 16 *SEE* O'Neill, Bernard
O'Neill, John 42; Ontario, 1871 ***1823.22*** *p119*
O'Neill, John 84; Vermont, 1895 ***5900.10*** *p294*
O'Neill, Julia 82; Vermont, 1908 ***5900.10*** *p576*
O'Neill, Katie 10; Vermont, 1866 ***5900.10*** *p173*
O'Neill, M. Belle King; Vermont, 1929 ***5900.10*** *p549*
O'Neill, Margaret; Vermont, 1848-1890 ***5900.10*** *p579*
O'Neill, Margaret; Vermont, 1858-1935 ***5900.10*** *p472*
O'Neill, Margaret C.; Vermont, 1861-1936 ***5900.10*** *p123*
O'Neill, Margaret Maguire 79; Vermont, 1887 ***5900.10*** *p589*
O'Neill, Margaret O'Harra; Vermont, 1795-1871 ***5900.10*** *p515*
O'Neill, Margaret Sheridan; Vermont, 1839-1895 ***5900.10*** *p253*
Oneill, Margret 35; Ontario, 1871 ***1823.22*** *p120*
O'Neill, Mary; Vermont, 1846-1910 ***5900.10*** *p589*
O'Neill, Mary; Vermont, 1855-1925 ***5900.10*** *p356*
O'Neill, Mary; Vermont, 1923 ***5900.10*** *p550*
O'Neill, Mary 84; Vermont, 1902 ***5900.10*** *p50*
O'Neill, Mary 85; Vermont, 1899 ***5900.10*** *p294*
O'Neill, Mary A.; Vermont, 1857-1903 ***5900.10*** *p123*
O'Neill, Mary A. Casey; Vermont, 1861-1943 ***5900.10*** *p174*
O'Neill, Mary A. O'Reilly; Vermont, 1884 ***5900.10*** *p138*
O'Neill, Mary A. O'Reilly; Vermont, 1884 ***5900.10*** *p170*
O'Neill, Mary Ann 19; Vermont, 1851 ***5900.10*** *p471*
O'Neill, Mattie 22; Vermont, 1890 ***5900.10*** *p550*
O'Neill, Michael; Vermont, 1822-1893 ***5900.10*** *p579*
O'Neill, Michael; Vermont, 1840-1912 ***5900.10*** *p253*
O'Neill, Michael; Vermont, 1848-1878 ***5900.10*** *p515*
O'Neill, Michael; Vermont, 1850-1931 ***5900.10*** *p591*
O'Neill, Nancy; Vermont, 1852-1929 ***5900.10*** *p553*
O'Neill, Nary; Vermont, n.d. ***5900.10*** *p325*
O'Neill, Nellie; Vermont, 1861-1872 ***5900.10*** *p580*
O'Neill, Nellie 7; Vermont, 1876 ***5900.10*** *p173*
O'Neill, Patrick; Vermont, 1821-1907 ***5900.10*** *p123*
O'Neill, Patrick 2; Vermont, 1871 ***5900.10*** *p173*
O'Neill, Patrick 5; Vermont, 1864 ***5900.10*** *p173*
O'Neill, Patrick 79; Vermont, 1887 ***5900.10*** *p364*
O'Neill, Patrick H.; Vermont, 1864-1948 ***5900.10*** *p550*
O'Neill, Robert J.; Vermont, 1860-1951 ***5900.10*** *p550*
O'Neill, Sara Dufey 51; Vermont, 1848 ***5900.10*** *p471*
O'Neill, Sarah; Vermont, 1803-1847 ***5900.10*** *p147*
O'Neill, Susanna 83; Vermont, 1900 ***5900.10*** *p295*
O'Neill, Suzanna; Vermont, 1840-1912 ***5900.10*** *p158*
O'Neill, Thomas; New York, 1827 ***8197.10*** *p268*
O'Neill, Thomas; Vermont, 1820-1899 ***5900.10*** *p173*
O'Neill, Thomas; Vermont, 1855-1921 ***5900.10*** *p588*
O'Neill, Thomas; Vermont, 1857-1888 ***5900.10*** *p579*
O'Neill, Thomas 69; Vermont, 1888 ***5900.10*** *p550*
O'Neill, Thomas C.; Vermont, 1943 ***5900.10*** *p548*
O'Neill, Will 32; Vermont, 1887 ***5900.10*** *p550*
O'Neill, William; Vermont, n.d. ***5900.10*** *p325*
O'Neill, William; Vermont, 1844-1924 ***5900.10*** *p158*
O'Neill, William; Vermont, 1852-1935 ***5900.10*** *p515*
O'Neill, William; Vermont, 1867-1933 ***5900.10*** *p123*
O'Neill, William D. 3; Vermont, 1864 ***5900.10*** *p471*
Onerdonk, Elizabeth 19; Ontario, 1861 ***2896.25*** *p17*
Onerdonk, Harriet C. 16; Ontario, 1861 ***2896.25*** *p17*
Onerdonk, John 49; Ontario, 1861 ***2896.25*** *p17*
Onerdonk, John R. 4; Ontario, 1861 ***2896.25*** *p17*
Onerdonk, Sarah M. 13; Ontario, 1861 ***2896.25*** *p17*
Onerdonk, W. T. 11; Ontario, 1861 ***2896.25*** *p17*
Onerdonk, William H. 21; Ontario, 1861 ***2896.25*** *p17*
Oneretti, Thomas; New York, 1840 ***8197.10*** *p268*
Onesby, Sarah; Maryland, 1679 ***2524.55*** *p164*
Onesby, Stephen; Maryland, 1679 ***2524.55*** *p164*
Oney, William; Vermont, 1831-1903 ***5900.10*** *p442*
O'Niel, Catharine 24; Vermont, 1857 ***5900.10*** *p605*
O'Niel, Cornelius; Pennsylvania, 1777 ***4629.10*** *p20*
O'Niel, Elizabeth 26; Vermont, 1862 ***5900.10*** *p605*
O'Niel, Michael 67; Vermont, 1894 ***5900.10*** *p86*
O'Niel, Patrick 51; Ontario, 1871 ***1823.15*** *p205*
Onion, John; Maryland, 1681 ***2524.55*** *p164*
Onion, Joseph 48; Ontario, 1871 ***1823.22*** *p120*
Onions, John; Maryland, 1681 ***2524.55*** *p164*
Onions, John; New York, 1816 ***1224.3*** *p58*
Onions, Josephus; Pennsylvania, 1844 ***6058.10*** *p20*
Onions, Thomas; Pennsylvania, 1844 ***6058.10*** *p19*
Onoleme, Jno; Virginia, 1672 ***6212.30*** *p49*
Onongst, Michael; Pennsylvania, 1777 ***4629.10*** *p15*
Onoziski, Martin; Maryland, 1910 ***3259.35*** *p44*
Onquetto, Michel 71; Ontario, 1871 ***1823.28*** *p79*
Onslow, John; Virginia, 1664 ***6212.30*** *p7*
Onsman, Thomas 19; Maryland, 1774 ***1220.25*** *p39*
Onstler, Henry; Pennsylvania, 1816-1825 ***6058.10*** *p7*
Onwin, John 17; Virginia, 1773 ***1220.25*** *p29*
Onwin, Richard; New York, New York, 1840 ***1224.3*** *p58*
Oodle, Joshua; Ontario, 1861 ***2896.25*** *p13*
Ooser, Anna Maria; Port uncertain, 1767 ***2856.30*** *p331*
Openlander, Gutlup; Pennsylvania, 1836 ***6058.10*** *p12*
Opie, Thomas; Virginia, 1703 ***1224.2*** *p86*
Oppenheimer, David; New York, 1840 ***8197.10*** *p191*
Oppermann, Maria Elisabeth; Port uncertain, 1755 ***2856.30*** *p331*
Oppermannin, Maria Elisabeth; Port uncertain, 1755 ***2856.30*** *p331*
O'Ragan, Louise 18; Ontario, 1861 ***2896.25*** *p11*
O'Ragan, Thomas 85; Ontario, 1861 ***2896.25*** *p11*
Oram, Valentine; Maryland, 1680 ***2524.55*** *p164*
Oram, William; New York, 1830 ***8197.10*** *p361*
Orams, Frederick 42; Ontario, 1871 ***1823.15*** *p206*
Orange, Thomas; New York, New York, 1824 ***1224.3*** *p58*
Orange, William; Norfolk, Virginia, n.d. ***1224.2*** *p86*
Orbe, Francis; Maryland, 1682 ***2524.55*** *p164*
Orberston, William; Maryland, 1658 ***2524.55*** *p165*
Orberton, Sarah; Maryland, 1661 ***2524.55*** *p165*
Orberton, Sarah; Maryland, 1665 ***2524.55*** *p165*
Orbetsky, Adam 45; Ontario, 1871 ***1823.28*** *p79*
Orchard, John; Virginia, 1690-1691 ***6212.30*** *p59*
Orchard, William; Maryland, 1650-1654 ***2524.55*** *p165*
Orchard, William; Maryland, 1659 ***2524.55*** *p165*
Orcher, John; Maryland, 1665 ***2524.55*** *p165*
Orcott, Silas 67; Ontario, 1861 ***2896.26*** *p29*
Ord, Mr.; Quebec, 1857 ***9196.15*** *p20*
Ord, Ms.; Ontario, 1871 ***1823.15*** *p206*
Ord, James; Pennsylvania, 1786 ***4629.10*** *p55*
Ord, John, Jr.; Pennsylvania, 1777 ***4629.10*** *p15*
Ord, Lewis; Portland, Maine, 1858 ***9196.15*** *p27*
Ord, Mrs. Lewis; Portland, Maine, 1858 ***9196.15*** *p27*
Ord, Walter; Georgia, 1734 ***1640.10*** *p168*
Ordakowski, Frantz; Maryland, 1910 ***3259.35*** *p44*
Ordaskowka, Teleska; Maryland, 1910 ***3259.35*** *p44*
Ordronan, John; New York, 1816 ***8197.10*** *p59*
Ords, Lewis 42; Ontario, 1871 ***1823.15*** *p206*
O'Reagan, Mary; Vermont, 1854-1927 ***5900.10*** *p137*
Oreck, William; Virginia, 1706 ***1224.2*** *p86*
O'Reilley, Ellen 24; Vermont, 1894 ***5900.10*** *p240*
O'Reilly, Andrew 42; Ontario, 1861 ***2896.27*** *p64*
O'Reilly, Ann; Vermont, 1837-1922 ***5900.10*** *p193*
O'Reilly, Bernard 45; Ontario, 1871 ***1823.22*** *p119*
O'Reilly, Bridget 3; Vermont, 1862 ***5900.10*** *p232*
O'Reilly, Bridget 43; Ontario, 1861 ***2896.27*** *p64*
O'Reilly, Charles; Vermont, 1824-1910 ***5900.10*** *p415*
O'Reilly, Edward; New York, 1836 ***8197.10*** *p77*
O'Reilly, Edward; New York, 1837 ***8197.10*** *p95*
O'Reilly, James 19; Ontario, 1861 ***2896.27*** *p64*
O'Reilly, James 70; Ontario, 1871 ***1823.22*** *p119*
O'Reilly, John; Vermont, n.d. ***5900.10*** *p154*
O'Reilly, Mary 14; Ontario, 1861 ***2896.27*** *p64*
O'Reilly, Mary A.; Vermont, 1884 ***5900.10*** *p138*
O'Reilly, Mary A.; Vermont, 1884 ***5900.10*** *p170*
O'Reilly, Robert; New York, 1838 ***8197.10*** *p318*
O'Reilly, William; New York, 1836 ***8197.10*** *p77*
Orford, Tho; Virginia, 1667 ***6212.30*** *p36*
Organ, Timothy; Philadelphia, 1790 ***4629.10*** *p60*
Orgram, William D.; Pennsylvania, 1858 ***6058.10*** *p40*
Orian, Christina; Port uncertain, 1784 ***2856.30*** *p331*
Orianin, Christina; Port uncertain, 1784 ***2856.30*** *p331*
O'Rielly, Anne; Vermont, 1846-1892 ***5900.10*** *p580*
O'Rielly, Bridget 60; Ontario, 1871 ***1823.15*** *p205*
O'Rielly, John 24; Ontario, 1871 ***1823.15*** *p205*
O'Rielly, Patrick 40; Ontario, 1871 ***1823.15*** *p205*
O'Rielly, Patrick C.; New York, 1838 ***8197.10*** *p146*
O'Riely, Christopher 45; Ontario, 1871 ***1823.22*** *p119*
O'Riley, Andrew 29; Vermont, 1867 ***5900.10*** *p104*
O'Riley, Anna 6; Ontario, 1861 ***2896.27*** *p70*
O'Riley, Bartholomew 73; Vermont, 1906 ***5900.10*** *p104*
O'Riley, Catherine 8; Ontario, 1861 ***2896.27*** *p70*
O'Riley, Catherine O'Keefe 75; Vermont, 1882 ***5900.10*** *p104*
O'Riley, Daniel 17; Vermont, 1868 ***5900.10*** *p104*
O'Riley, Ellen 40; Ontario, 1861 ***2896.28*** *p24*
O'Riley, Hugh 29; Ontario, 1861 ***2896.27*** *p70*
O'Riley, James 2; Ontario, 1861 ***2896.27*** *p70*
O'Riley, Jeremiah 32; Vermont, 1876 ***5900.10*** *p104*
O'Riley, Jeremiah 78; Vermont, 1882 ***5900.10*** *p104*
O'Riley, Julia 64; Vermont, 1907 ***5900.10*** *p104*
O'Riley, M. 19; Ontario, 1861 ***2896.28*** *p8*
O'Riley, Michael 33; Ontario, 1871 ***1823.15*** *p205*
O'Riley, Michael 36; Ontario, 1861 ***2896.28*** *p24*
O'Riley, P.; Vermont, n.d. ***5900.10*** *p449*
O'Riley, Patrick; Pennsylvania, 1868 ***6058.10*** *p76*
O'Riley, Patrick 88; Ontario, 1871 ***1823.22*** *p119*
O'Riley, Thomas 1; Ontario, 1861 ***2896.28*** *p24*
O'Riley, Thomas 50; Ontario, 1871 ***1823.22*** *p119*
Oriott, Tho; Virginia, 1664 ***6212.30*** *p9*
Orkird, John 30; Nova Scotia, 1774 ***1220.25*** *p136*
Orkney, Mr.; Portland, Maine, 1858 ***9196.15*** *p30*
Orland, Fran; Virginia, 1671-1672 ***6212.30*** *p47*
Orland, James; Virginia, 1667 ***6212.30*** *p35*
Orlefaski, William; Maryland, 1910 ***3259.35*** *p44*
Orlekowski, Joseph; Maryland, 1910 ***3259.35*** *p44*
Orlington, Rich; Virginia, 1666-1667 ***6212.30*** *p34*
Orloski, Edward; Maryland, 1910 ***3259.35*** *p44*
Orlowska, Rose; Maryland, 1910 ***3259.35*** *p44*
Orlowski, Lottie; Maryland, 1910 ***3259.35*** *p44*
Orlton, Griffith; New York, 1816 ***1224.3*** *p58*
Orly, William; Virginia, 1665 ***6212.30*** *p19*
Ormerod, Mr.; Quebec, 1858 ***9196.15*** *p40*
Ormiston, Mr.; Quebec, 1857 ***9196.15*** *p26*
Ormiston, John Andrew; America, 1883 ***1640.13*** *p96*
Ormiston, Thomas; Georgia, 1736 ***1640.10*** *p168*
Ormiston, Thomas; Savannah, Georgia, 1736 ***1640.10*** *p168*
Ormond, Helen; Florida, 1841 ***1640.10*** *p168*
Ormond, Johanna; Vermont, 1832-1904 ***5900.10*** *p187*
Ormond, Joseph 24; Virginia, 1774 ***1220.25*** *p45*
Ormond, Russell; Florida, 1841 ***1640.10*** *p168*
Ormsby, Eubule; Florida, 1768 ***1224.2*** *p86*
Ormsby, James 48; Ontario, 1871 ***1823.28*** *p79*
Ormston, Miss; Quebec, 1857 ***9196.15*** *p26*
Ormston, Peter 50; Ontario, 1871 ***1823.22*** *p120*
Orne, Robert; Maryland, 1673 ***2524.55*** *p165*
Orne, Susannah; Marblehead, Massachusetts, 1818 ***1224.3*** *p58*
Ornstein, Henry; Maryland, 1910 ***3259.35*** *p45*
O'Roark, Mary D.; Vermont, 1826-1895 ***5900.10*** *p484*
Oroneck, James; Maryland, 1650 ***2524.55*** *p165*
Oronski, Walter; Maryland, 1910 ***3259.35*** *p45*
O'Rooke, Mr.; Quebec, 1858 ***9196.15*** *p42*
O'Rooke, Mrs.; Quebec, 1858 ***9196.15*** *p42*
Orork, James 40; Ontario, 1871 ***1823.28*** *p79*
O'Rorke, Hugh; New York, 1839 ***8197.10*** *p268*
Orourck, James; Maryland, 1650 ***2524.55*** *p165*
Orourk, Peter 45; Ontario, 1871 ***1823.15*** *p206*
O'Rourke, Bernard; New York, 1826 ***8197.10*** *p268*
O'Rourke, Bernard; New York, 1829 ***8197.10*** *p352*
O'Rourke, Bridget; Vermont, 1813-1878 ***5900.10*** *p415*
O'Rourke, Catherine; Vermont, n.d. ***5900.10*** *p409*
O'Rourke, Catherine Campbell; Vermont, 1855-1936 ***5900.10*** *p462*
O'Rourke, Eleanor; Vermont, 1886-1949 ***5900.10*** *p560*
O'Rourke, Ellen Julia; Vermont, 1859-1926 ***5900.10*** *p429*

O'Rourke, James; Vermont, n.d. 5900.10 p409
O'Rourke, James Francis; New York, 1837 8197.10 p96
O'Rourke, Joanna O'Leary; Vermont, 1843-1916 5900.10 p570
O'Rourke, John; Vermont, n.d. 5900.10 p409
O'Rourke, John; Vermont, 1845-1915 5900.10 p462
Orourke, John 30; Ontario, 1871 1823.15 p206
O'Rourke, John J.; Vermont, 1839-1923 5900.10 p560
O'Rourke, Lawrence; Vermont, 1852-1934 5900.10 p462
O'Rourke, Margaret; Vermont, 1830-1902 5900.10 p316
O'Rourke, Margaret; Vermont, 1888-1964 5900.10 p560
O'Rourke, Mary; Vermont, n.d. 5900.10 p409
O'Rourke, Mary; Vermont, 1833-1922 5900.10 p404
O'Rourke, Mary; Vermont, 1842-1903 5900.10 p578
O'Rourke, Mary; Vermont, 1843-1931 5900.10 p255
O'Rourke, Mary; Vermont, 1851-1916 5900.10 p464
O'Rourke, Mary Conklin; Vermont, 1851-1927 5900.10 p560
O'Rourke, Owen; New York, 1827 8197.10 p342
O'Rourke, Patrick; Vermont, 1815-1901 5900.10 p462
O'Rourke, Patrick; Vermont, 1839-1904 5900.10 p462
O'Rourke, Richard; Vermont, n.d. 5900.10 p409
O'Rourke, Sarah; Vermont, 1849-1926 5900.10 p176
O'Rourke, Thomas; Vermont, n.d. 5900.10 p409
O'Rourke, Thomas; Vermont, 1840-1913 5900.10 p404
O'Rourke, William J.; Vermont, 1844-1913 5900.10 p570
Orowczynski, Frank; Maryland, 1910 3259.35 p45
Orpen, Edward; New York, 1838 8197.10 p147
Orpwood, John 25; Virginia, 1773 1220.25 p29
Orr, Annie 18; Ontario, 1871 1823.15 p206
Orr, Annie 60; Ontario, 1871 1823.15 p206
Orr, Arthur; New York, 1803 8197.10 p15
Orr, Catherine 29; Ontario, 1871 1823.15 p207
Orr, Charles; Alabama, 1833-1845 1640.10 p168
Orr, Gabrial 44; Ontario, 1871 1823.22 p120
Orr, George; Pennsylvania, 1779 4629.10 p33
Orr, James; Jamaica, 1750 1640.13 p97
Orr, James 36; Ontario, 1871 1823.22 p120
Orr, James 39; Ontario, 1871 1823.15 p207
Orr, James 39; Ontario, 1871 1823.22 p120
Orr, James 57; Ontario, 1871 1823.15 p207
Orr, Jean 73; Ontario, 1871 1823.22 p120
Orr, John; Quebec, 1886 1640.13 p97
Orr, John 25; Ontario, 1871 1823.15 p207
Orr, John 27; Ontario, 1871 1823.28 p79
Orr, John 42; Ontario, 1871 1823.22 p120
Orr, Johnston 43; Ontario, 1871 1823.15 p207
Orr, Joseph; New York, 1840 8197.10 p386
Orr, Mary 20; Ontario, 1871 1823.15 p207
Orr, Mary Ann 36; Ontario, 1871 1823.22 p120
Orr, Robert; New York, 1827 8197.10 p338
Orr, Robert; New York, 1840 8197.10 p386
Orr, Robert 16; Ontario, 1871 1823.15 p207
Orr, Robert 35; Ontario, 1871 1823.15 p207
Orr, Robert 38; Ontario, 1871 1823.22 p120
Orr, Robert 50; Ontario, 1871 1823.28 p79
Orr, Robert 57; Ontario, 1871 1823.15 p207
Orr, Robert 70; Ontario, 1871 1823.15 p207
Orr, Sarah 64; Ontario, 1871 1823.15 p207
Orr, William; New York, 1807 8197.10 p47
Orr, William 29; Ontario, 1871 1823.15 p207
Orr, William 36; Ontario, 1871 1823.22 p120
Orr, William 50; Ontario, 1871 1823.15 p207
Orrage, George 29; Virginia, 1774 1220.25 p91
Orrock, Alexander; Georgia, 1698 1640.13 p97
Orrock, John; Georgia, 1698 1640.13 p97
Orrok, Fergus Edgar; New York, 1900 1640.13 p97
Orry, William; Georgia, 1774 1640.10 p169
Orser, Mrs.; Ontario, 1861 2896.26 p29
Orser, Almira 11; Ontario, 1861 2896.27 p15
Orser, Asenath 41; Ontario, 1861 2896.25 p13
Orser, Darius 6; Ontario, 1861 2896.26 p21
Orser, David H. 7; Ontario, 1861 2896.27 p21
Orser, Deborah 57; Ontario, 1861 2896.27 p15
Orser, Elijah 29; Ontario, 1861 2896.27 p15
Orser, Elijah F. 10; Ontario, 1861 2896.27 p12
Orser, Elisha 65; Ontario, 1861 2896.27 p15
Orser, Emila 24; Ontario, 1861 2896.27 p15
Orser, Emily E. 7; Ontario, 1861 2896.27 p21
Orser, Esther S. 8; Ontario, 1861 2896.27 p12
Orser, Franklin 19; Ontario, 1861 2896.27 p21
Orser, Hannah 14; Ontario, 1861 2896.27 p15
Orser, Henry 36; Ontario, 1861 2896.27 p12
Orser, Jane 39; Ontario, 1861 2896.26 p21
Orser, Joanna 22; Ontario, 1861 2896.27 p21
Orser, John B. 1; Ontario, 1861 2896.27 p12
Orser, John B. 20; Ontario, 1861 2896.27 p21
Orser, Joseph 17; Ontario, 1861 2896.26 p21
Orser, Joseph J. 29; Ontario, 1861 2896.25 p13
Orser, Lovernia 27; Ontario, 1861 2896.27 p15
Orser, Lydia 52; Ontario, 1861 2896.27 p15
Orser, Manson W. 2; Ontario, 1861 2896.27 p12
Orser, Marshal E. 2; Ontario, 1861 2896.27 p12
Orser, Martha 9; Ontario, 1861 2896.26 p21
Orser, Mary 11; Ontario, 1861 2896.26 p21
Orser, Mary A. 14; Ontario, 1861 2896.27 p12
Orser, Matilda 13; Ontario, 1861 2896.26 p21
Orser, Mira E. 2; Ontario, 1861 2896.27 p21
Orser, Nathaniel 1; Ontario, 1861 2896.26 p21
Orser, Phebe 30; Ontario, 1861 2896.25 p13
Orser, Phoebe 30; Ontario, 1861 2896.27 p21
Orser, Randolph 8; Ontario, 1861 2896.25 p13
Orser, Samuel 73; Ontario, 1861 2896.25 p13
Orser, Sarah 35; Ontario, 1861 2896.27 p12
Orser, Sarah A. 22; Ontario, 1861 2896.27 p15
Orser, Stephen 27; Ontario, 1861 2896.27 p15
Orser, Victoria 4; Ontario, 1861 2896.26 p21
Orser, Willet H. 5; Ontario, 1861 2896.27 p21
Orser, William 18; Ontario, 1861 2896.27 p12
Orser, William C. 18; Ontario, 1861 2896.27 p15
Ort, Anna Juliana; Port uncertain, 1788 2856.30 p331
Ort, Mrs. Georg; Port uncertain, 1783 2856.30 p331
Ort, Johann Georg; Port uncertain, 1791 2856.30 p331
Ort, Niklas; Port uncertain, 1790 2856.30 p331
Orth, Mr.; America, 1749 2856.30 p331
Orth, Bastian; Port uncertain, 1761 2856.30 p10
Orth, Johann Adam; Port uncertain, 1786 2856.30 p331
Orth, Johann Dianich; America, 1749 2856.30 p331
Orth, Johann Nikolaus; Port uncertain, 1786 2856.30 p331
Orth, Lawrence; New York, 1840 8197.10 p191
Orthar, Simon; Virginia, 1667 6212.30 p37
Orthman, John 54; Ontario, 1871 1823.15 p207
Ortocki, Stanislaus; Maryland, 1910 3259.35 p45
Orton, James; Virginia, 1664 6212.30 p13
Orton, William; Virginia, 1664-1665 6212.30 p16
Ortowsky, Romildt; Maryland, 1910 3259.35 p45
Ortwein, Henry 40; Ontario, 1871 1823.15 p207
O'Rurke, Ellen 48; Ontario, 1871 1823.22 p119
O'Ryan, Mr.; Portland, Maine, 1858 9196.15 p27
O'Rylie, Francis 70; Ontario, 1871 1823.22 p119
O'Rylie, Philip 40; Ontario, 1871 1823.22 p119
Orzakowski, Frances; Maryland, 1910 3259.35 p45
Osawainis, Joseph 50; Ontario, 1871 1823.28 p79
Osawamik, J. B. 40; Ontario, 1871 1823.28 p79
Osawibiurse, Augustin 53; Ontario, 1871 1823.28 p79
Osbald, Jno; Virginia, 1664 6212.30 p11
Osberston, William; Maryland, 1658 2524.55 p165
Osborn, Abraham 16; Virginia, 1775 1220.25 p95
Osborn, Albert 17; Ontario, 1861 2896.28 p46
Osborn, Andrew 52; Ontario, 1871 1823.22 p120
Osborn, John; New York, 1808 8197.10 p54
Osborn, John; Pennsylvania, 1777 4629.10 p11
Osborn, Joseph; New York, New York, 1830 1224.3 p58
Osborn, Michael; New York, 1831 8197.10 p355
Osborn, Oliver; Virginia, 1665 6212.30 p17
Osborn, William; Jamaica, 1850 1640.13 p97
Osborne, . . .; Maryland, 1662 2524.55 p116
Osborne, Mrs.; Maryland, 1665 2524.55 p165
With child
Osborne, A. M. 7; Ontario, 1861 2896.28 p3
Osborne, Anna Boyce; Vermont, 1833-1912 5900.10 p287
Osborne, Bridget; Vermont, 1831-1865 5900.10 p364
Osborne, C. 9; Ontario, 1861 2896.25 p11
Osborne, Calvin 20; Ontario, 1861 2896.25 p11
Osborne, Catherine 17; Ontario, 1861 2896.25 p32
Osborne, Charles H. 11; Ontario, 1861 2896.25 p12
Osborne, Cordelia P. 7; Ontario, 1861 2896.25 p32
Osborne, Deborah 21; Ontario, 1861 2896.25 p11
Osborne, E. O. A. 4; Ontario, 1861 2896.28 p3
Osborne, Edward; Maryland, 1680 2524.55 p165
Osborne, Harriet 23; Ontario, 1861 2896.25 p32
Osborne, Henry; Maryland, 1668 2524.55 p165
Osborne, Henry N. 9; Ontario, 1861 2896.25 p3
Osborne, Horace G. 5; Ontario, 1861 2896.25 p12
Osborne, Isabel 30; Ontario, 1861 2896.25 p3
Osborne, J. C. 41; Ontario, 1861 2896.25 p3
Osborne, J. H. 1; Ontario, 1861 2896.28 p3
Osborne, J. H. 31; Ontario, 1861 2896.28 p3
Osborne, John 53; Ontario, 1861 2896.25 p32
Osborne, Jonas; Maryland, 1660 2524.55 p165
Osborne, Jonathan G. 21; Ontario, 1861 2896.25 p12
Osborne, Lydia M. 16; Ontario, 1861 2896.25 p12
Osborne, Margaret 22; Ontario, 1861 2896.25 p3
Osborne, Mary; Maryland, 1659 2524.55 p165
Osborne, Mary 44; Ontario, 1861 2896.25 p11
Osborne, Richard 19; Ontario, 1861 2896.25 p12
Osborne, Samuel; Carolina, 1683 1224.1 p43
Osborne, Sarah 1; Ontario, 1861 2896.25 p3
Osborne, Sarah 44; Ontario, 1861 2896.25 p11
Osborne, Sarah J. 14; Ontario, 1861 2896.25 p11
Osborne, T. N. 6; Ontario, 1861 2896.28 p3
Osborne, Thomas 34; Ontario, 1871 1823.28 p79
Osborne, Urio 17; Ontario, 1861 2896.25 p11
Osborne, Walter 13; Ontario, 1861 2896.25 p12
Osborne, Walton 13; Ontario, 1861 2896.25 p12
Osborne, William S. 19; Ontario, 1861 2896.25 p32
Osbourn, Catherine *SEE* Osbourn, Henry
Osbourn, Henry; Maryland, 1651 2524.55 p165
Wife: Catherine
Child: Rebecca
Osbourn, Rebecca *SEE* Osbourn, Henry
Osbourn, Thomas; Maryland, 1658 2524.55 p165
Osbourne, Caleb; Maryland, 1681 2524.55 p165
Osbourne, Henry; Pennsylvania, 1778 4629.10 p43
Osbrey, Elizabeth; New York, 1833 8197.10 p268
Osbrey, Thomas; New York, 1833 8197.10 p268
Osburn, Albert 16; Ontario, 1861 2896.28 p60
Osburn, Alfrad 15; Ontario, 1861 2896.28 p60
Osburn, Melisa 13; Ontario, 1861 2896.28 p60
Osburn, Sarah 12; Ontario, 1861 2896.28 p60
Osburn, William 20; Virginia, 1774 1220.25 p140
Osburne, Mary; Maryland, 1659 2524.55 p131
Osburne, Thomas; Maryland, 1672 2524.55 p165
Oseau, Frederick; New York, New York, 1853 6058.10 p61
O'Sellaway, John; Nova Scotia, 1745 4628.40 p45
Oser, Magdalena; Port uncertain, 1765 2856.30 p331
Osgood, B. S. 40; Ontario, 1871 1823.28 p79
Oshaughnessay, Michael; Ontario, 1871 1823.28 p79
Oshaughnessay, Michael 30; Ontario, 1871 1823.28 p79
Oshaughnessey, John 28; Ontario, 1871 1823.28 p79
Oshaughnessey, Michael 32; Ontario, 1871 1823.28 p79
O'Shaughnessy, Patrick 42; Ontario, 1871 1823.28 p78
O'Shea, Alice 33; Ontario, 1861 2896.27 p71
O'Shea, Bridget; Vermont, 1839-1916 5900.10 p432
O'Shea, Catherine; Vermont, 1845-1915 5900.10 p255
O'Shea, Daniel 61; Ontario, 1861 2896.27 p71
O'Shea, Dennis; Vermont, 1848-1929 5900.10 p429
O'Shea, Dennis 84; Vermont, 1903 5900.10 p421
O'Shea, Edmond; Vermont, 1832-1910 5900.10 p380
O'Shea, Ellen Julia O'Rourke; Vermont, 1859-1926 5900.10 p429
O'Shea, Mary 54; Vermont, 1879 5900.10 p421
O'Shea, Mary Walsh; Vermont, 1836-1906 5900.10 p380
O'Shea, Michael 35; Ontario, 1861 2896.27 p71
O'Shea, Patrick; New York, 1835 8197.10 p268
O'Shea, Susan 61; Ontario, 1861 2896.27 p71
O'Sheagh, Cornelius; Maryland, 1652-1658 2524.55 p165
Oshey, D. 34; Ontario, 1861 2896.27 p5
Oshey, Margot 2; Ontario, 1861 2896.27 p5
Oshey, Mary 7; Ontario, 1861 2896.27 p5
Oshey, Mary 26; Ontario, 1861 2896.27 p5
O'Shiel, William; New York, 1822 8197.10 p267
Oshkabewissens, Antoine 35; Ontario, 1871 1823.28 p79
Oshkabewissens, Francois 61; Ontario, 1871 1823.28 p79
Osland, Edward 43; Ontario, 1871 1823.22 p120
Osland, Thomas 49; Ontario, 1871 1823.22 p120
Osler, John 37; Ontario, 1871 1823.15 p207
Osman, John; Pennsylvania, 1777 4629.10 p12
Osmond, Thomas 40; Virginia, 1774 1220.25 p90
Osowsky, Stefan; Maryland, 1910 3259.35 p45
Ossett, Jane; Virginia, 1663 6212.30 p4
Ossin, Jane; Maryland, 1665 2524.55 p165
Ossipe, Anne; Virginia, 1664-1665 6212.30 p16
Ossley, Daniell; Maryland, 1673 2524.55 p165
Ossun, Jane; Maryland, 1665 2524.55 p165
Osswald, Jerg; Port uncertain, 1778 2856.30 p331
Osswald, Johann; America, 1738 2856.30 p331
Osswald, Peter; Port uncertain, 1734 2856.30 p331
Osswald, Wilhelm; America, 1741 2856.30 p331
Ostazowski, John; Maryland, 1910 3259.35 p45
Ostberg, E. 38; Alaska, 1917 9196.1 p46
Ostberg, E. 38; Whitehorse, Yukon, 1917 9196.1 p46
Ostenhaut, Henry J. 45; Ontario, 1871 1823.22 p120
Oster, . . .; Port uncertain, 1784 2856.30 p331
Oster, Anton; America, 1749 2856.30 p331
Oster, Maria Elisabeth; Port uncertain, 1791 2856.30 p331
Oster, Michael; America, 1783 2856.30 p331
Oster, Michael; Port uncertain, 1739 2856.30 p331
Oster, Peter; America, 1783 2856.30 p332
Oster, Peter; Port uncertain, 1739 2856.30 p331
Ostergun, John 29; Washington, 1914 9196.1 p66
Osterhout, Adala 25; Ontario, 1861 2896.28 p43
Osterhout, Catharine 50; Ontario, 1861 2896.28 p25
Osterhout, David 72; Ontario, 1871 1823.22 p120
Osterhout, H. 18; Ontario, 1861 2896.28 p4
Osterhout, Henrietta 24; Ontario, 1861 2896.28 p21
Osterhout, Henry 73; Ontario, 1871 1823.22 p120
Osterhout, Herbert 4; Ontario, 1861 2896.28 p21
Osterhout, John H. 65; Ontario, 1861 2896.28 p25
Osterhout, Louis A. 7; Ontario, 1861 2896.28 p21
Osterhout, Margaret 2; Ontario, 1861 2896.28 p21
Osterhout, Margaret 33; Ontario, 1861 2896.28 p21

Osterhout, Wilford 10; Ontario, 1861 ***2896.28*** *p21*
Osterhoute, David E. 5; Ontario, 1861 ***2896.27*** *p70*
Osterhoute, Elizabeth 27; Ontario, 1861 ***2896.27*** *p70*
Osterhoute, Mary C. 6; Ontario, 1861 ***2896.27*** *p70*
Osterhoute, Mary E. 72; Ontario, 1861 ***2896.27*** *p70*
Ostgen, Franz; Port uncertain, 1789 ***2856.30*** *p332*
Ostgen, Johann Heinrich; Port uncertain, 1763 ***2856.30*** *p332*
Ostgen, Nikolaus; Port uncertain, 1791 ***2856.30*** *p332*
Ostrand, Carls; New York, 1806 ***8197.10*** *p323*
O'Stronge, Eliza.; Maryland, 1652-1659 ***2524.55*** *p165*
Ostrosky, Frank; Maryland, 1910 ***3259.35*** *p45*
Ostrosky, Michael; Maryland, 1910 ***3259.35*** *p45*
Ostrowski, Anton; Maryland, 1910 ***3259.35*** *p45*
Ostrowski, Henry; Maryland, 1910 ***3259.35*** *p45*
Ostrowski, John; Maryland, 1910 ***3259.35*** *p45*
Ostrowsky, John; Maryland, 1910 ***3259.35*** *p45*
Osuch, John; Maryland, 1910 ***3259.35*** *p45*
O'Sullivan, Caroline; New York, New York, 1855 ***1224.3*** *p58*
O'Sullivan, Catherine; Vermont, 1841-1915 ***5900.10*** *p140*
O'Sullivan, D. 40; Alaska, 1917 ***9196.1*** *p48*
O'Sullivan, D. 40; Whitehorse, Yukon, 1917 ***9196.1*** *p48*
O'Sullivan, Daniel 40; Ontario, 1871 ***1823.22*** *p119*
O'Sullivan, Daniel 41; Vermont, 1873 ***5900.10*** *p218*
O'Sullivan, Daniel Joseph; Vermont, 1853-1918 ***5900.10*** *p186*
O'Sullivan, Dennis; New York, 1831 ***8197.10*** *p366*
O'Sullivan, Dennis M.; Vermont, 1841-1912 ***5900.10*** *p586*
O'Sullivan, Dennough; Maryland, 1659 ***2524.55*** *p165*
O'Sullivan, Esther Feeney; Vermont, 1862-1950 ***5900.10*** *p163*
O'Sullivan, Hannah Murphy; Vermont, 1842-1926 ***5900.10*** *p586*
O'Sullivan, Honora; Vermont, 1851-1924 ***5900.10*** *p144*
O'Sullivan, Jeremiah; Vermont, 1835-1919 ***5900.10*** *p140*
O'Sullivan, John; New York, 1825 ***1224.3*** *p58*
O'Sullivan, John; Vermont, 1826-1898 ***5900.10*** *p186*
O'Sullivan, John 46; Ontario, 1871 ***1823.15*** *p205*
O'Sullivan, Jonniah 55; Ontario, 1871 ***1823.15*** *p205*
O'Sullivan, Lucilla Frances; Vermont, 1934 ***5900.10*** *p184*
O'Sullivan, Margaret McAvoy; Vermont, 1833-1894 ***5900.10*** *p186*
O'Sullivan, Margaret Pickett 87; Vermont, 1907 ***5900.10*** *p218*
O'Sullivan, Mary; Vermont, 1800-1865 ***5900.10*** *p432*
Osullivan, Patrick 25; Ontario, 1871 ***1823.15*** *p207*
Osullivan, Patrick 81; Ontario, 1871 ***1823.15*** *p207*
O'Sullivan, Peter 40; Ontario, 1871 ***1823.15*** *p205*
O'Sullivan, Sarah A.; Vermont, 1838-1913 ***5900.10*** *p140*
O'Sullivan, Teage; Maryland, 1658 ***2524.55*** *p90*
O'Sullivan, Thomas W. 68; Vermont, 1911 ***5900.10*** *p163*
O'Sullivan, William Joseph; Vermont, 1855-1915 ***5900.10*** *p186*
Oswald, Christian 70; Ontario, 1871 ***1823.15*** *p207*
Oswald, Johann; Port uncertain, 1728 ***2856.30*** *p332*
Oswald, Johann; Port uncertain, 1764 ***2856.30*** *p332*
Oswald, Johann; Port uncertain, 1785 ***2856.30*** *p332*
Oswald, Johann; Port uncertain, 1786 ***2856.30*** *p332*
Oswald, Johann; Port uncertain, 1789 ***2856.30*** *p332*
Oswald, Maria; Port uncertain, 1784 ***2856.30*** *p332*
Oswald, Richard; Georgia, 1751 ***1640.10*** *p169*
Oswell, William; Mississippi, 1810-1845 ***1640.10*** *p169*
Oswin, Thomas; Virginia, 1721 ***1224.2*** *p86*
Oszakiewski, William; Maryland, 1910 ***3259.35*** *p45*
Oszewich, Jerome; Maryland, 1910 ***3259.35*** *p45*
Osziendek, John; Maryland, 1910 ***3259.35*** *p45*
Oszokowsky, August; Maryland, 1910 ***3259.35*** *p45*
Otaway, John; Virginia, 1665 ***6212.30*** *p18*
Otford, Jane *SEE* Otford, Thomas
Otford, Thomas; Maryland, 1679 ***2524.55*** *p165*
Wife: Jane
Other, Thomas; Virginia, 1665-1666 ***6212.30*** *p21*
Otis, Daniel; Vermont, 1853-1934 ***5900.10*** *p278*
Otis, Elizabeth; Vermont, 1843-1918 ***5900.10*** *p278*
Otis, Ellen; Vermont, 1848-1934 ***5900.10*** *p278*
Otis, Emma; Vermont, 1881-1908 ***5900.10*** *p278*
Otis, Michael; Vermont, 1846-1936 ***5900.10*** *p278*
Otley, Richard; Virginia, 1664 ***6212.30*** *p12*
O'Tole, Harry; Vermont, 1828-1889 ***5900.10*** *p299*
O'Tole, Mary Glass; Vermont, 1833-1908 ***5900.10*** *p299*
O'Tole, Michael; Vermont, 1855-1925 ***5900.10*** *p299*
O'Tool, Martin 44; Ontario, 1871 ***1823.28*** *p78*
Otram, Edward 34; Ontario, 1871 ***1823.22*** *p120*
Otrasir, Trage; Maryland, 1665 ***2524.55*** *p165*
Otrombe, Maria; Maryland, 1910 ***3259.35*** *p45*
O'Truce, Teagh; Maryland, 1652-1658 ***2524.55*** *p165*
Ott, Andreas; America, 1752 ***2856.30*** *p332*
Ott, Andreas; America, 1760 ***2856.30*** *p332*
Ott, Andreas; Port uncertain, 1749 ***2856.30*** *p332*
Ott, Andreas; Port uncertain, 1750 ***2856.30*** *p332*
Ott, Andreas; Port uncertain, 1771 ***2856.30*** *p332*
Ott, Anthony; New York, 1826 ***8197.10*** *p268*
Ott, Daniel; Port uncertain, 1784 ***2856.30*** *p332*
With wife & 3 children
Ott, Johann Nickel; Port uncertain, 1745 ***2856.30*** *p332*
Ott, Johann Nickel; Port uncertain, 1752 ***2856.30*** *p332*
Ott, Kathrine; Vermont, 1848-1917 ***5900.10*** *p89*
Ott, Valentin; Port uncertain, 1752 ***2856.30*** *p332*
Ott, William; Maryland, 1910 ***3259.35*** *p45*
Ottenbreit, Georg; Port uncertain, 1785 ***2856.30*** *p332*
With wife & 4 children
Otter, Edward; New York, 1807 ***8197.10*** *p47*
Otter, V. 27; Alaska, 1913 ***9196.1*** *p39*
Otter, V. 27; Yukon, 1913 ***9196.1*** *p39*
Otterson, James 31; Ontario, 1871 ***1823.28*** *p79*
Otterson, Sarah 70; Ontario, 1871 ***1823.28*** *p79*
Otterton, John; Virginia, 1654 ***1224.1*** *p43*
Ottey, Thomas 29; Ontario, 1871 ***1823.15*** *p207*
Ottignon, Catherine; New York, 1833 ***8197.10*** *p358*
Ottignon, Claude; New York, 1815 ***8197.10*** *p56*
Ottignon, Joseph; New York, 1838 ***8197.10*** *p146*
Ottilson, David 35; Ontario, 1871 ***1823.15*** *p207*
Ottin, Elis. Barbara; Port uncertain, 1743 ***2856.30*** *p333*
Ottman, Frank; Maryland, 1910 ***3259.35*** *p45*
Otto, Harriet 2; Ontario, 1871 ***1823.22*** *p120*
Otto, Henry 46; Ontario, 1871 ***1823.15*** *p207*
Otton, Mr.; Quebec, 1858 ***9196.15*** *p34*
Otton, Demas 55; Ontario, 1871 ***1823.22*** *p120*
Ottstadt, Catharina; Port uncertain, 1785 ***2856.30*** *p333*
Ottway, John; Died enroute, 1670 ***1224.1*** *p43*
Otway, Henry 42; Ontario, 1871 ***1823.15*** *p207*
Otway, Jane 80; Ontario, 1871 ***1823.15*** *p207*
Otway, Robert 49; Ontario, 1871 ***1823.15*** *p207*
Ouchterlony, Mary; Kingston, Jamaica, 1852 ***1640.13*** *p97*
Ouey, John; Virginia, 1667 ***6212.30*** *p35*
Ough, Joseph 61; Ontario, 1871 ***1823.22*** *p120*
Oughney, Patrick 50; Ontario, 1871 ***1823.28*** *p79*
Oughten, Robert; New York, 1837 ***8197.10*** *p96*
Oughtred, Jno; Virginia, 1666 ***6212.30*** *p26*
Ould, James 15; New York, 1775 ***1220.25*** *p94*
Ouldcastle, Ja; Virginia, 1665-1666 ***6212.30*** *p25*
Oulden, Nicholas; Maryland, 1658-1662 ***2524.55*** *p165*
Oulder, Mathew; Virginia, 1667-1668 ***6212.30*** *p38*
Ouldfeild, Alice; Virginia, 1666 ***6212.30*** *p25*
Oulihan, William 50; Ontario, 1871 ***1823.22*** *p121*
Oulson, Rasmus 45; Ontario, 1871 ***1823.28*** *p79*
Ouly, Johann Peter; Port uncertain, 1784 ***2856.30*** *p198*
With wife
Ourens, Thomas; Maryland, 1678 ***2524.55*** *p165*
Ousterhout, Benjamin 20; Ontario, 1861 ***2896.28*** *p54*
Ousterhout, Charles 48; Ontario, 1861 ***2896.28*** *p54*
Ousterhout, Clarra 8; Ontario, 1861 ***2896.28*** *p54*
Ousterhout, David 19; Ontario, 1861 ***2896.28*** *p54*
Ousterhout, Elizabeth 40; Ontario, 1861 ***2896.28*** *p54*
Ousterhout, Emily 17; Ontario, 1861 ***2896.28*** *p54*
Ousterhout, Maria 10; Ontario, 1861 ***2896.28*** *p54*
Ousterhout, Nancy 21; Ontario, 1861 ***2896.28*** *p54*
Ousterhout, Smith 15; Ontario, 1861 ***2896.28*** *p54*
Ousterhout, Stephen 12; Ontario, 1861 ***2896.28*** *p54*
Oustler, Henry; Pennsylvania, 1827 ***6058.10*** *p9*
Outred, William; Virginia, 1663 ***6212.30*** *p1*
Outrell, George; Virginia, 1667-1668 ***6212.30*** *p39*
Outwright, James; Virginia, 1666-1667 ***6212.30*** *p34*
Ovens, James; Baltimore, 1884 ***1640.13*** *p97*
Ovens, Thomas 24; Ontario, 1871 ***1823.22*** *p121*
Over, Andrew; Maryland, 1681 ***2524.55*** *p165*
Overbeck, Mr.; Port uncertain, 1732 ***2856.30*** *p86*
Overbeck, Andreas; America, 1732 ***2856.30*** *p333*
Overberry, Rich; Virginia, 1664 ***6212.30*** *p7*
Overend, Joseph 42; Ontario, 1871 ***1823.15*** *p207*
Overend, William; New York, 1821 ***8197.10*** *p267*
Overhultzer, Jacob 65; Ontario, 1871 ***1823.15*** *p207*
Overing, Henry John; Newport, Rhode Island, 1784 ***1224.2*** *p86*
Overington, John; Philadelphia Co., Pennsylvania, 1810 ***1224.3*** *p58*
Overton, Francis; Maryland, 1667 ***2524.55*** *p165*
Wife: Mary
Overton, Mary *SEE* Overton, Francis
Overton, Thomas; Maryland, 1658 ***2524.55*** *p165*
Overzee, Sarah *SEE* Overzee, Simon
Overzee, Simon; Maryland, 1650 ***2524.55*** *p166*
Wife: Sarah
With child
Oveton, Edward; Maryland, 1681 ***2524.55*** *p166*
Ovil, Moses 29; Ontario, 1861 ***2896.27*** *p63*
Owand, John 42; Ontario, 1871 ***1823.15*** *p207*
Owans, Mathew 37; Ontario, 1871 ***1823.15*** *p207*
Owans, Thomas; Jamaica, 1740 ***1640.13*** *p97*
Owczerzak, Joseph; Maryland, 1910 ***3259.35*** *p45*
Owen, David; Maryland, 1682 ***2524.55*** *p166*
Owen, David Dale; New York, 1829 ***8197.10*** *p268*
Owen, Edward; Philadelphia Co., Pennsylvania, 1821 ***1224.3*** *p58*
Owen, Edward 25; Ontario, 1871 ***1823.15*** *p207*
Owen, Edward W.; New York, 1838 ***8197.10*** *p268*
Owen, Elizabeth 54; Vermont, 1898 ***5900.10*** *p229*
Owen, Griffith; Pennsylvania, 1779 ***4629.10*** *p36*
Owen, Henry 54; Ontario, 1871 ***1823.22*** *p121*
Owen, James 21; Maryland, 1774 ***1220.25*** *p40*
Owen, James 21; Virginia, 1774 ***1220.25*** *p45*
Owen, Jane; Maryland, 1681 ***2524.55*** *p166*
Owen, John; Maryland, 1672 ***2524.55*** *p166*
Owen, Jonathan; Virginia, 1671 ***6212.30*** *p42*
Owen, Jonathon; Maryland, 1681 ***2524.55*** *p166*
Owen, Joseph; Virginia, 1709 ***1224.2*** *p86*
Owen, Mary; Maryland, 1656 ***2524.55*** *p166*
Owen, Patrick; New York, 1840 ***8197.10*** *p384*
Owen, Rich; Virginia, 1678 ***6212.30*** *p54*
Owen, Richard; Maryland, 1667 ***2524.55*** *p166*
Owen, Richard; Maryland, 1672 ***2524.55*** *p166*
Owen, Richard 40; Georgia, 1774 ***1220.25*** *p47*
Owen, Robert; Maryland, 1658 ***2524.55*** *p166*
Owen, Robert; Pennsylvania, 1777 ***4629.10*** *p19*
Owen, Thomas; Maryland, 1652 ***2524.55*** *p211*
Owen, Thomas; South Carolina, 1738 ***1224.2*** *p86*
Owen, William; California, 1850 ***1224.3*** *p58*
Owen, William; Carolina, 1690 ***1224.1*** *p43*
Owen, William; New York, 1807 ***8197.10*** *p47*
Owen, William; New York, 1838 ***8197.10*** *p146*
Owen, William; New York, 1840 ***8197.10*** *p383*
Owen, William; North Carolina, 1735 ***1224.2*** *p86*
Owen, William; Virginia, 1655 ***1224.1*** *p43*
Owen, William; Virginia, 1664 ***6212.30*** *p12*
Owen, William 27; Ontario, 1871 ***1823.28*** *p79*
Owenes, Ann 62; Ontario, 1871 ***1823.28*** *p79*
Owens, Ann; Maryland, 1674 ***2524.55*** *p166*
Owens, Ann 65; Vermont, 1896 ***5900.10*** *p558*
Owens, Ann 72; Vermont, 1888 ***5900.10*** *p236*
Owens, Ann 85; Vermont, 1883 ***5900.10*** *p51*
Owens, Bridget; Vermont, 1850-1928 ***5900.10*** *p442*
Owens, Bridget 50; Vermont, 1898 ***5900.10*** *p236*
Owens, Charlotte 24; Ontario, 1861 ***2896.28*** *p20*
Owens, Edward 6; Vermont, 1853 ***5900.10*** *p242*
Owens, Edward 31; Ontario, 1871 ***1823.22*** *p121*
Owens, Eliza 36; Ontario, 1861 ***2896.28*** *p41*
Owens, H. A.; Ontario, 1861 ***2896.27*** *p9*
Owens, Henry; New York, 1840 ***8197.10*** *p192*
Owens, James; New York, 1824 ***8197.10*** *p267*
Owens, James; New York, 1840 ***8197.10*** *p192*
Owens, James 32; Vermont, 1880 ***5900.10*** *p236*
Owens, James 35; Ontario, 1871 ***1823.28*** *p79*
Owens, James 39; Ontario, 1871 ***1823.15*** *p207*
Owens, James 57; Ontario, 1871 ***1823.22*** *p121*
Owens, John; New York, 1840 ***8197.10*** *p192*
Owens, John 30; Ontario, 1871 ***1823.22*** *p121*
Owens, John 36; Ontario, 1871 ***1823.28*** *p79*
Owens, Joseph 42; Ontario, 1871 ***1823.28*** *p79*
Owens, Julia 75; Vermont, 1891 ***5900.10*** *p484*
Owens, Katherine 60; Vermont, 1905 ***5900.10*** *p440*
Owens, Margaret 25; Ontario, 1871 ***1823.22*** *p121*
Owens, Margaret T. 43; Vermont, 1889 ***5900.10*** *p229*
Owens, Mary; Maryland, 1650 ***2524.55*** *p166*
Owens, Mary; Vermont, 1836-1904 ***5900.10*** *p423*
Owens, Mary E. 1; Ontario, 1861 ***2896.28*** *p20*
Owens, Mary J. Miles; Vermont, 1850-1918 ***5900.10*** *p47*
Owens, Matilda 21; Ontario, 1861 ***2896.28*** *p47*
Owens, Michael 75; Ontario, 1871 ***1823.22*** *p121*
Owens, Owen; Maryland, 1681 ***2524.55*** *p166*
Owens, Peter 56; Vermont, 1867 ***5900.10*** *p236*
Owens, Peter C.; Vermont, 1849-1928 ***5900.10*** *p47*
Owens, Pheby J. 20; Ontario, 1861 ***2896.28*** *p20*
Owens, Richard; Maryland, 1649 ***2524.55*** *p166*
Owens, Sarah J. 2; Vermont, 1854 ***5900.10*** *p242*
Owens, Thomas; New York, 1831 ***8197.10*** *p354*
Owens, Thomas 52; Ontario, 1871 ***1823.22*** *p121*
Owens, William; New York, 1834 ***8197.10*** *p315*
Owfeild, Jno; Virginia, 1664 ***6212.30*** *p8*
Owin, Hugh; Virginia, 1665-1666 ***6212.30*** *p21*
Owin, James; Virginia, 1664 ***6212.30*** *p6*
Owin, Timothy; Maryland, 1665 ***2524.55*** *p166*
Owins, Thomas; Virginia, 1664 ***6212.30*** *p7*
Owler, William 43; Ontario, 1871 ***1823.22*** *p121*
Ownens, Robert; Maryland, 1665 ***2524.55*** *p166*
Owner, Michael; Pennsylvania, 1777 ***4629.10*** *p22*
Owner, Michael; Pennsylvania, 1779 ***4629.10*** *p38*
Ownes, Bernard 30; Ontario, 1871 ***1823.28*** *p80*
Ownes, James 60; Ontario, 1871 ***1823.28*** *p80*
Ownes, Robert 38; Ontario, 1871 ***1823.28*** *p80*
Ownies, Yantee 34; Ontario, 1871 ***1823.28*** *p80*
Owozaczak, John; Maryland, 1910 ***3259.35*** *p45*
Oxenbridge, . . .; New England, 1686 ***1224.1*** *p35*
Oxenbrigg, John; Maryland, 1680 ***2524.55*** *p166*
Oxford, Joan; Virginia, 1666-1667 ***6212.30*** *p35*

P

Palmatier, Mary 24; Ontario, 1861 ***2896.26*** *p33*
Palmatier, Mary E. 1; Ontario, 1861 ***2896.26*** *p36*
Palmatier, Permila 6; Ontario, 1861 ***2896.25*** *p10*
Palmatier, Simon 19; Ontario, 1861 ***2896.25*** *p3*
Palmatier, Thomas 68; Ontario, 1861 ***2896.28*** *p39*
Palmatier, William 1; Ontario, 1861 ***2896.25*** *p10*
Palmer, Miss; Quebec, 1857 ***9196.15*** *p26*
Palmer, Mr.; Quebec, 1857 ***9196.15*** *p27*
Palmer, Mr.; Quebec, 1858 ***9196.15*** *p43*
Palmer, Mrs.; Quebec, 1858 ***9196.15*** *p43*
Palmer, Miss A.; Quebec, 1857 ***9196.15*** *p26*
Palmer, Aaron; Pennsylvania, 1786 ***4629.10*** *p54*
Palmer, Agnes 19; Ontario, 1861 ***2896.28*** *p35*
Palmer, Alfred 19; Ontario, 1871 ***1823.22*** *p121*
Palmer, Anthony; Leeward Islands, 1749 ***1224.2*** *p87*
Palmer, Anthony; Philadelphia, 1749 ***1224.2*** *p87*
Palmer, Arthur 3; Ontario, 1861 ***2896.28*** *p31*
Palmer, Benjamin 25; Philadelphia, 1774 ***1220.25*** *p81*
Palmer, Benjamin 29; Ontario, 1871 ***1823.28*** *p80*
Palmer, Byran 13; Ontario, 1861 ***2896.28*** *p31*
Palmer, Miss C.; Quebec, 1858 ***9196.15*** *p43*
Palmer, C. A. 38; Ontario, 1871 ***1823.28*** *p80*
Palmer, Catharine; Ontario, 1861 ***2896.28*** *p22*
Palmer, Charlotte 18; Maryland, 1775 ***1220.25*** *p97*
Palmer, David J.; Buffalo, New York, 1852 ***6058.10*** *p75*
Palmer, Edward 44; Baltimore, 1775 ***1220.25*** *p118*
Palmer, Ellen Nixon; Vermont, 1895 ***5900.10*** *p494*
Palmer, Francis; New York, 1840 ***8197.10*** *p272*
Palmer, Frederick 26; Ontario, 1871 ***1823.28*** *p80*
Palmer, Georg Michael; America, 1738 ***2856.30*** *p334*
Palmer, Georg Michael; Port uncertain, 1737 ***2856.30*** *p334*
Palmer, George T.; New York, 1838 ***8197.10*** *p146*
Palmer, Hamilton John 51; Vermont, 1892 ***5900.10*** *p494*
Palmer, Hannah 65; Ontario, 1861 ***2896.28*** *p35*
Palmer, Hannah Davis; Vermont, 1846-1922 ***5900.10*** *p494*
Palmer, Hen; Virginia, 1665-1666 ***6212.30*** *p22*
Palmer, Henrietta 15; Ontario, 1861 ***2896.28*** *p31*
Palmer, Isabella; Vermont, 1816-1888 ***5900.10*** *p495*
Palmer, Issabell; Maryland, 1665 ***2524.55*** *p167*
Palmer, Jacob; America, 1738 ***2856.30*** *p334*
Palmer, Jacob; Port uncertain, 1737 ***2856.30*** *p334*
Palmer, James 27; Virginia, 1774 ***1220.25*** *p74*
Palmer, James 60; Ontario, 1871 ***1823.22*** *p122*
Palmer, James J. 70; Ontario, 1861 ***2896.28*** *p35*
Palmer, James R. 14; Ontario, 1861 ***2896.28*** *p35*
Palmer, Jno; Virginia, 1664 ***6212.30*** *p15*
Palmer, Joanna M.; Vermont, 1829-1901 ***5900.10*** *p598*
Palmer, John; Jamaica, 1775 ***1220.25*** *p133*
Palmer, John; New York, 1821 ***8197.10*** *p269*
Palmer, John; Pennsylvania, 1777 ***4629.10*** *p24*
Palmer, John; Virginia, 1664 ***6212.30*** *p13*
Palmer, John 16; Maryland, 1775 ***1220.25*** *p101*
Palmer, John 31; Ontario, 1871 ***1823.28*** *p80*
Palmer, John 86; Vermont, 1889 ***5900.10*** *p494*
Palmer, John J.; New York, 1803 ***8197.10*** *p15*
Palmer, John Temple; Boston, 1822 ***1224.3*** *p59*
Palmer, Jos; Virginia, 1690-1691 ***6212.30*** *p59*
Palmer, Joseph 16; Philadelphia, 1774 ***1220.25*** *p80*
Palmer, Joseph 61; Ontario, 1871 ***1823.22*** *p122*
Palmer, Lucretia 32; Ontario, 1861 ***2896.28*** *p35*
Palmer, Ludwig; America, 1750 ***2856.30*** *p334*
Palmer, Lueretia 70; Ontario, 1871 ***1823.22*** *p122*
Palmer, Margaret Harvey 25; Vermont, 1865 ***5900.10*** *p602*
Palmer, Margarete; America, 1764 ***2856.30*** *p334*
Palmer, Margarett; Maryland, 1666 ***2524.55*** *p203*
Palmer, Martha 19; Ontario, 1861 ***2896.28*** *p22*
Palmer, Mary 42; Ontario, 1871 ***1823.22*** *p122*
Palmer, Mary 45; Ontario, 1871 ***1823.22*** *p122*
Palmer, Myron 43; Ontario, 1871 ***1823.22*** *p122*
Palmer, Nancy L. 7; Ontario, 1861 ***2896.28*** *p31*
Palmer, Nathaniel 22; Maryland, 1775 ***1220.25*** *p96*
Palmer, Peregrine; New York, 1832 ***1224.3*** *p59*
Palmer, Rachel 38; Ontario, 1861 ***2896.28*** *p43*
Palmer, Samuell; Virginia, 1665 ***6212.30*** *p17*
Palmer, Sarah 16; Ontario, 1861 ***2896.27*** *p29*
Palmer, Sarah A. 34; Ontario, 1861 ***2896.28*** *p31*
Palmer, Sarah F. 11; Ontario, 1861 ***2896.28*** *p31*
Palmer, Sebastian; New York, 1807 ***8197.10*** *p328*
Palmer, Solomon 9; Ontario, 1861 ***2896.28*** *p31*
Palmer, Stephen 26; Virginia, 1774 ***1220.25*** *p92*
Palmer, Thomas; Pennsylvania, 1777 ***4629.10*** *p20*
Palmer, Thomas; Virginia, 1663 ***6212.30*** *p2*
Palmer, Thomas; Virginia, 1768 ***1224.2*** *p87*
Palmer, Thomas 21; Baltimore, 1775 ***1220.25*** *p117*
Palmer, Thomas 28; Maryland, 1775 ***1220.25*** *p120*
Palmer, Thomas 33; Ontario, 1871 ***1823.28*** *p80*
Palmer, William; Maryland, 1655-1656 ***2524.55*** *p167*
Palmer, William; Maryland, 1661 ***2524.55*** *p167*
Palmer, William; Maryland, 1667 ***2524.55*** *p167*
Palmer, William; New York, 1802 ***8197.10*** *p24*
Palmer, William; New York, 1840 ***8197.10*** *p194*
Palmer, William; Pennsylvania, 1777 ***4629.10*** *p16*
Palmer, William; Pennsylvania, 1780 ***4629.10*** *p41*
Palmer, William 45; Ontario, 1871 ***1823.15*** *p208*
Palmer, William H. 2; Ontario, 1861 ***2896.28*** *p22*
Palmer, Wm.; Maryland, 1660 ***2524.55*** *p167*
Palmi, Jacob; Port uncertain, 1773 ***2856.30*** *p334*
With wife & children
Palmy, William; Virginia, 1663 ***6212.30*** *p2*
Palmytier, James 82; Ontario, 1861 ***2896.28*** *p5*
Palon, Jane 40; Ontario, 1871 ***1823.22*** *p122*
Palouc, P. 32; Alaska, 1912 ***9196.1*** *p37*
Palouc, P. 32; British Columbia, 1912 ***9196.1*** *p37*
Palpeman, Aaron 29; Virginia, 1773 ***1220.25*** *p28*
Palrim, John 21; Virginia, 1773 ***1220.25*** *p32*
Palterman, Thomas 46; Ontario, 1871 ***1823.15*** *p208*
Paltridge, Francis 34; Ontario, 1871 ***1823.15*** *p208*
Paltridge, William 19; Ontario, 1871 ***1823.15*** *p208*
Palucka, Katherine; Maryland, 1910 ***3259.35*** *p45*
Pampe, Frederick 22; Virginia, 1774 ***1220.25*** *p45*
Pancost, David; Pennsylvania, 1777 ***4629.10*** *p23*
Pandel, Martin 21; Maryland, 1774 ***1220.25*** *p78*
Pandert, Eva 25; Kansas, 1910 ***9079.10*** *p6*
Pandert, Henry 24; Kansas, 1887-1910 ***9079.10*** *p6*
Panes, Peter; Maryland, 1910 ***3259.35*** *p45*
Pangowish, Pierre 63; Ontario, 1871 ***1823.28*** *p80*
Panis, John; Maryland, 1910 ***3259.35*** *p45*
Panjewski, Charles; Maryland, 1910 ***3259.35*** *p45*
Pankhurst, Francis 20; Virginia, 1774 ***1220.25*** *p93*
Pankovich, Inkola 27; British Columbia, 1915 ***9196.1*** *p11*
Pankovich, Inkola 27; Washington, 1915 ***9196.1*** *p11*
Panos, Gus 27; Washington, 1911 ***9196.1*** *p33*
Pansack, Catherine; Maryland, 1910 ***3259.35*** *p45*
Pansh, William 50; Ontario, 1871 ***1823.15*** *p208*
Panson, Tobias; Maryland, 1664 ***2524.55*** *p167*
Panter, John; Maryland, 1668 ***2524.55*** *p167*
Pantezis, L. 23; Juneau, Alaska, 1917 ***9196.1*** *p45*
Pantezis, L. 23; Whitehorse, Yukon, 1917 ***9196.1*** *p45*
Panther, Elisabeth; America, 1738 ***2856.30*** *p334*
Panther, John; Maryland, 1668 ***2524.55*** *p167*
Panton, George; New York, n.d. ***1224.3*** *p59*
Panton, George; Nova Scotia, n.d. ***1224.3*** *p59*
Panton, James; New York, 1840 ***8197.10*** *p272*
Panton, William; Florida, 1804 ***1224.3*** *p59*
Panton, William; Savannah, Georgia, 1765 ***1640.10*** *p169*
Panushawski, Jan; Maryland, 1910 ***3259.35*** *p46*
Pany, J. S.; Quebec, 1858 ***9196.15*** *p35*
Panzer, Charles; New York, 1838 ***8197.10*** *p271*
Papadopulos, George 35; Alaska, 1912 ***9196.1*** *p20*
Papadopulos, George 35; British Columbia, 1912 ***9196.1*** *p20*
Papas, Jim 38; Juneau, Alaska, 1917 ***9196.1*** *p45*
Papas, Jim 38; Whitehorse, Yukon, 1917 ***9196.1*** *p45*
Pape, Carls; New York, 1840 ***8197.10*** *p192*
Papek, Joe 26; British Columbia, 1909 ***9196.1*** *p27*
Papek, Joe 26; Seattle, 1909 ***9196.1*** *p27*
Papierniak, Fred; Maryland, 1910 ***3259.35*** *p46*
Papil, John 61; Ontario, 1871 ***1823.15*** *p208*
Papkey, John 40; Ontario, 1871 ***1823.28*** *p80*
Papkey, Michael 72; Ontario, 1871 ***1823.28*** *p80*
Papkey, William 32; Ontario, 1871 ***1823.28*** *p80*
Papon, Peter; Philadelphia, 1793 ***4629.10*** *p69*
Pappenberger, Ad; America, 1733 ***2856.30*** *p334*
Pappenberger, Catharina; America, 1733 ***2856.30*** *p334*
Pappenberger, Christina; America, 1733 ***2856.30*** *p334*
Pappenberger, Elisabeth; America, 1733 ***2856.30*** *p334*
Pappenberger, Jurk, Sr.; America, 1733 ***2856.30*** *p334*
Pappenberger, Jurk, Jr.; America, 1733 ***2856.30*** *p334*
Pappett, Tho.; Maryland, 1664 ***2524.55*** *p167*
Pappi, John; New York, 1835 ***8197.10*** *p317*
Pappi, Luigi; New York, 1840 ***8197.10*** *p193*
Pappis, John; New York, 1835 ***8197.10*** *p317*
Papple, Alexander 36; Ontario, 1871 ***1823.15*** *p208*
Papple, William 30; Ontario, 1871 ***1823.15*** *p208*
Paptewski, John; Maryland, 1910 ***3259.35*** *p46*
Paquette, Catherine Griffin; Vermont, 1847-1906 ***5900.10*** *p289*
Paquin, Anthony; Philadelphia, 1793 ***4629.10*** *p75*
Par, Margaret 10; Ontario, 1861 ***2896.25*** *p40*
Paradise, Lucy; Virginia, 1815 ***1224.3*** *p59*
Parafu, Stepa 33; British Columbia, 1909 ***9196.1*** *p27*
Parafu, Stepa 33; Seattle, 1909 ***9196.1*** *p27*
Paramour, John *SEE* Paramour, John
Paramour, John; Maryland, 1673 ***2524.55*** *p167*
Wife: Mary
Son: Thomas
Son: John
Paramour, Mary *SEE* Paramour, John
Paramour, Mary; Maryland, 1674 ***2524.55*** *p167*
Paramour, Richard; Maryland, 1674 ***2524.55*** *p167*
Paramour, Thomas *SEE* Paramour, John
Parcival, Charles; Pennsylvania, 1777 ***4629.10*** *p13*
Parczynski, Sophie; Maryland, 1910 ***3259.35*** *p46*
Pardee, Henry J. 36; Ontario, 1871 ***1823.15*** *p208*
Pardo, Isaac Loper; New York, 1806 ***8197.10*** *p32*
Pardoe, Reginald 19; Ontario, 1871 ***1823.22*** *p122*
Pardue, John; Maryland, 1681 ***2524.55*** *p167*
Pare, Marceline; Vermont, 1864-1923 ***5900.10*** *p291*
Pareman, Mary; Maryland, 1665 ***2524.55*** *p167*
Paremski, John; Maryland, 1910 ***3259.35*** *p46*
Parent, Esther 24 *SEE* Parent, T. P.
Parent, T. P. 25; Virginia, 1774 ***1220.25*** *p93*
Wife: Esther 24
Paresall, William 59; Ontario, 1871 ***1823.22*** *p122*
Parfitt, Charles; New York, 1837 ***8197.10*** *p100*
Parham, Joseph; Boston, 1701 ***1224.2*** *p88*
Parimski, Joseph; Maryland, 1910 ***3259.35*** *p46*
Parinski, Frank; Maryland, 1910 ***3259.35*** *p46*
Parinski, Louis; Maryland, 1910 ***3259.35*** *p46*
Paris, Benjamin 37; Maryland, 1774 ***1220.25*** *p41*
Paris, John 63; Ontario, 1871 ***1823.28*** *p80*
Paris, John Anthony 33; Pennsylvania, 1794 ***4629.10*** *p63*
Parish, George; New York, 1839 ***1224.3*** *p59*
Parish, George; New York, 1839 ***8197.10*** *p271*
Park, Mr.; Quebec, 1858 ***9196.15*** *p34*
Park, Elizabeth Watson Chambers; Savannah, Georgia, 1770 ***1224.2*** *p87*
Park, Henry 45; Ontario, 1871 ***1823.15*** *p208*
Park, James; New York, 1830 ***8197.10*** *p354*
Park, James 33; Ontario, 1871 ***1823.28*** *p80*
Park, Jane 68; Ontario, 1871 ***1823.22*** *p122*
Park, John 57; Ontario, 1871 ***1823.28*** *p80*
Park, Patrick; Georgia, 1698 ***1640.13*** *p98*
Park, Thomas 40; Ontario, 1871 ***1823.15*** *p208*
Park, Toly; Pennsylvania, 1786 ***4629.10*** *p49*
Park, W. N. 38; Ontario, 1871 ***1823.28*** *p80*
Parke, Mr.; Quebec, 1857 ***9196.15*** *p22*
Parke, Cuthbert; Philadelphia, 1847 ***1224.3*** *p59*
Parke, Daniel; Virginia, 1679 ***1224.1*** *p43*
Parke, Graves; Virginia, 1731 ***1224.2*** *p87*
Parke, James 50; Ontario, 1871 ***1823.15*** *p208*
Parke, Robert; Maryland, 1664 ***2524.55*** *p167*
Parke, Robert 67; Ontario, 1871 ***1823.15*** *p208*
Parke, Roger 21; Maryland, 1775 ***1220.25*** *p120*
Parke, Theophilus; Pennsylvania, 1777 ***4629.10*** *p15*
Parke, Thomas; New York, 1780 ***1224.2*** *p87*
Parker, Mr.; Quebec, 1856 ***9196.15*** *p7*
Parker, A. D.; Quebec, 1858 ***9196.15*** *p47*
Parker, Alvira McBride; Vermont, 1855-1904 ***5900.10*** *p375*
Parker, Andrew; Pennsylvania, 1778 ***4629.10*** *p34*
Parker, Andrew 38; Ontario, 1871 ***1823.28*** *p80*
Parker, Ann; Vermont, 1848-1917 ***5900.10*** *p578*
Parker, Archilas 15; Philadelphia, 1774 ***1220.25*** *p43*
Parker, Benjamin; Boston, 1772 ***1224.2*** *p87*
Parker, Betsay 94; Ontario, 1871 ***1823.28*** *p80*
Parker, Edith *SEE* Parker, Noah
Parker, Edm; Virginia, 1666 ***6212.30*** *p30*
Parker, Edward; Maryland, 1648 ***2524.55*** *p167*
Parker, Edward; Maryland, 1658 ***2524.55*** *p167*
Parker, Edward; Virginia, 1681-1682 ***6212.30*** *p56*
Parker, Elizabeth 9 *SEE* Parker, Mary
Parker, Elizabeth 33 *SEE* Parker, Joseph
Parker, George; New York, 1838 ***8197.10*** *p146*
Parker, George; New York, 1860 ***1640.13*** *p98*
Parker, George; Ontario, 1876 ***1640.13*** *p98*
Parker, George; Pennsylvania, 1777 ***4629.10*** *p14*
Parker, George; Savannah, Georgia, 1799 ***1640.10*** *p169*
Parker, Henry; Maryland, 1664 ***2524.55*** *p167*
Parker, Ire 52; Ontario, 1871 ***1823.28*** *p80*
Parker, J.; Quebec, 1857 ***9196.15*** *p25*
Parker, Mrs. J.; Quebec, 1857 ***9196.15*** *p25*
Parker, James; New England, 1644 ***1224.1*** *p43*
Parker, James; New York, 1821 ***8197.10*** *p270*
Parker, James 2 *SEE* Parker, Mary
Parker, James 25; Ontario, 1871 ***1823.15*** *p208*
Parker, James 48; Ontario, 1871 ***1823.15*** *p208*
Parker, Jno; Virginia, 1664 ***6212.30*** *p13*
Parker, Jno; Virginia, 1665-1666 ***6212.30*** *p23*
Parker, Jno; Virginia, 1668-1669 ***6212.30*** *p41*
Parker, John; Albany, New York, 1799 ***1224.2*** *p87*
Parker, John; Maryland, 1660 ***2524.55*** *p167*
Parker, John; Maryland, 1665 ***2524.55*** *p167*
Parker, John; Maryland, 1682 ***2524.55*** *p167*
Parker, John; New York, 1821 ***8197.10*** *p269*
Parker, John; New York, 1839 ***8197.10*** *p137*
Parker, John; New York, 1839 ***8197.10*** *p320*
Parker, John; Pennsylvania, 1750 ***1224.2*** *p87*
Parker, John; Pennsylvania, 1777 ***4629.10*** *p10*
Parker, John; Pennsylvania, 1777 ***4629.10*** *p30*
Parker, John; Pennsylvania, 1868 ***6058.10*** *p73*
Parker, John; Virginia, 1671 ***6212.30*** *p45*
Parker, John; Virginia, 1690-1691 ***6212.30*** *p59*
Parker, John; Virginia, 1701 ***1224.2*** *p87*
Parker, John 3 *SEE* Parker, William

Parker, John 24; Maryland, 1774 ***1220.25*** *p70*
Parker, John 26; Ontario, 1871 ***1823.15*** *p208*
Parker, John 29; Ontario, 1871 ***1823.28*** *p80*
Parker, John N.; Vermont, 1849-1913 ***5900.10*** *p375*
Parker, Joseph; Charles Town, South Carolina, 1785 ***1224.2*** *p87*
Parker, Joseph; New York, 1839 ***8197.10*** *p320*
Parker, Joseph 19; Ontario, 1871 ***1823.28*** *p80*
Parker, Joseph 33; Nova Scotia, 1774 ***1220.25*** *p15*
Wife: Elizabeth 33
Child: William 2
Parker, Joseph 60; Ontario, 1871 ***1823.15*** *p208*
Parker, Joseph 66; Ontario, 1871 ***1823.15*** *p208*
Parker, Joshua; New York, 1837 ***8197.10*** *p375*
Parker, Josiah; North America, 1796 ***1224.2*** *p87*
Parker, Judith; New England, 1649 ***1224.1*** *p44*
Parker, Katherine; Maryland, 1673 ***2524.55*** *p167*
Parker, Margaret; Vermont, 1818-1890 ***5900.10*** *p350*
Parker, Margaret 14; Ontario, 1871 ***1823.22*** *p122*
Parker, Martha A. Doolin; Vermont, 1855-1906 ***5900.10*** *p286*
Parker, Mary; Vermont, 1822-1906 ***5900.10*** *p349*
Parker, Mary; Virginia, 1663-1664 ***6212.30*** *p5*
Parker, Mary 38 *SEE* Parker, William
Parker, Mary 40; Halifax, Nova Scotia, 1775 ***1220.25*** *p22*
Child: James 2
Child: Elizabeth 9
Parker, Mary 74; Nova Scotia, 1774 ***1220.25*** *p14*
Parker, Mathew; Vermont, 1838-1912 ***5900.10*** *p578*
Parker, Michael; New York, 1840 ***8197.10*** *p192*
Parker, Noah; Maryland, 1665 ***2524.55*** *p168*
Wife: Edith
Parker, Phillip; Virginia, 1665-1666 ***6212.30*** *p22*
Parker, Richard; Maryland, 1681 ***2524.55*** *p168*
Parker, Richard 62; Ontario, 1871 ***1823.15*** *p208*
Parker, Robert; New York, 1821 ***8197.10*** *p270*
Parker, Robert 21; Maryland, 1774 ***1220.25*** *p61*
Parker, Robert 45; Ontario, 1871 ***1823.28*** *p80*
Parker, Robt; Virginia, 1663 ***6212.30*** *p4*
Parker, Robt; Virginia, 1668-1669 ***6212.30*** *p40*
Parker, Samuel; New York, 1827 ***8197.10*** *p345*
Parker, Samuell; Maryland, 1658 ***2524.55*** *p168*
Parker, Sarah 19; Virginia, 1774 ***1220.25*** *p91*
Parker, Thomas; Maryland, 1658 ***2524.55*** *p168*
Parker, Thomas; Maryland, 1663 ***2524.55*** *p168*
Parker, Thomas; Maryland, 1680 ***2524.55*** *p168*
Parker, Thomas; Maryland, 1681 ***2524.55*** *p168*
Parker, Thomas; New England, 1650 ***1224.1*** *p43*
Parker, Thomas; Pennsylvania, 1779 ***4629.10*** *p40*
Parker, Thomas; Vermont, 1826 ***5900.10*** *p349*
Parker, Thomas 50; Ontario, 1871 ***1823.15*** *p208*
Parker, Walter; Virginia, 1664 ***6212.30*** *p15*
Parker, William; Maryland, 1658 ***2524.55*** *p168*
With family
Parker, William; Maryland, 1665 ***2524.55*** *p168*
Parker, William; New York, 1830 ***8197.10*** *p361*
Parker, William; New York, 1834 ***8197.10*** *p271*
Parker, William; New York, New York, 1855 ***1224.3*** *p59*
Parker, William; Pennsylvania, 1777 ***4629.10*** *p19*
Parker, William; Vermont, 1781-1838 ***5900.10*** *p349*
Parker, William 2 *SEE* Parker, Joseph
Parker, William 17; Ontario, 1871 ***1823.22*** *p122*
Parker, William 19; Maryland, 1774 ***1220.25*** *p41*
Parker, William 22; Virginia, 1773 ***1220.25*** *p30*
Parker, William 25; Virginia, 1773 ***1220.25*** *p31*
Parker, William 31; Nova Scotia, 1774 ***1220.25*** *p14*
Wife: Mary 38
Child: John 3
Parker, William 40; Ontario, 1871 ***1823.28*** *p80*
Parker, William 68; Ontario, 1871 ***1823.15*** *p208*
Parker, William H.; New York, 1840 ***8197.10*** *p193*
Parker, William T.; New York, 1838 ***8197.10*** *p146*
Parkes, Mr.; Quebec, 1858 ***9196.15*** *p31*
Parkes, Hen; Virginia, 1677 ***6212.30*** *p54*
Parkes, John; Virginia, 1630 ***1224.1*** *p44*
Parket, Ellin; Virginia, 1663 ***6212.30*** *p3*
Parkhurst, George; Died enroute, 1635 ***1224.1*** *p44*
Parkhurst, John 26; Maryland, 1774 ***1220.25*** *p40*
Parkhurst, Mary 63; Vermont, 1882 ***5900.10*** *p402*
Parkin, James; Maryland, 1663 ***2524.55*** *p168*
Parkin, John; New York, 1777 ***1224.2*** *p87*
Parkin, Thomas; New York, New York, 1795 ***1224.2*** *p87*
Parkin, Thomas 54; Ontario, 1871 ***1823.28*** *p80*
Parkins, Miss; Quebec, 1858 ***9196.15*** *p38*
Parkins, Joseph Wilfred; New Jersey, 1843 ***1224.3*** *p59*
Parkinson, Mr.; Portland, Maine, 1858 ***9196.15*** *p29*
Parkinson, Christopher; New York, 1840 ***8197.10*** *p194*
Parkinson, Elizabeth; Maryland, 1678 ***2524.55*** *p168*
Parkinson, Francis; Maryland, 1658 ***2524.55*** *p168*
Parkinson, Henry; New Hampshire, n.d. ***4628.40*** *p76*
Parkinson, Henry; New Hampshire, 1725 ***4628.40*** *p47*
Parkinson, John 34; Maryland, 1774 ***1220.25*** *p84*
Parkinson, Thomas 61; Ontario, 1871 ***1823.15*** *p208*
Parks, Mrs.; Quebec, 1858 ***9196.15*** *p41*
Parks, Benjamin A. 4; Ontario, 1861 ***2896.27*** *p26*
Parks, Catherine 48; Ontario, 1861 ***2896.25*** *p31*
Parks, Frederick; New York, 1822-1834 ***8197.10*** *p305*
Parks, George 45; Ontario, 1871 ***1823.15*** *p208*
Parks, Hannah 90; Ontario, 1871 ***1823.15*** *p208*
Parks, Hester Ann 21; Ontario, 1861 ***2896.27*** *p44*
Parks, Ira E. 1; Ontario, 1861 ***2896.27*** *p44*
Parks, James; New York, 1807 ***8197.10*** *p47*
Parks, Janes 60; Ontario, 1871 ***1823.15*** *p208*
Parks, Jerimiah 37; Ontario, 1871 ***1823.15*** *p208*
Parks, Jessie A. 13; Ontario, 1871 ***1823.22*** *p122*
Parks, John; New York, 1802 ***8197.10*** *p269*
Parks, John 28; Ontario, 1871 ***1823.15*** *p208*
Parks, John 70; Ontario, 1871 ***1823.15*** *p209*
Parks, Joseph; Pennsylvania, 1777 ***4629.10*** *p23*
Parks, Phebeyann 26; Ontario, 1861 ***2896.27*** *p26*
Parks, Robert 56; Ontario, 1871 ***1823.22*** *p122*
Parks, Roland; Westfield, Massachusetts, 1830 ***1224.3*** *p59*
Parks, Samuel 19; Ontario, 1861 ***2896.27*** *p64*
Parks, William H.; Ontario, 1861 ***2896.27*** *p44*
Parle, Edw; Virginia, 1674 ***6212.30*** *p52*
Parlett, George 30; Ontario, 1871 ***1823.28*** *p80*
Parliament, Adaline 18; Ontario, 1861 ***2896.25*** *p5*
Parliament, Adam L. 5; Ontario, 1861 ***2896.25*** *p62*
Parliament, Adeline 16; Ontario, 1861 ***2896.28*** *p29*
Parliament, Agnes 36; Ontario, 1861 ***2896.25*** *p5*
Parliament, Charles H. 2; Ontario, 1861 ***2896.25*** *p12*
Parliament, David 21; Ontario, 1861 ***2896.25*** *p62*
Parliament, Edwin 3; Ontario, 1861 ***2896.25*** *p67*
Parliament, Elen J. 4; Ontario, 1861 ***2896.25*** *p12*
Parliament, Elizabeth 34; Ontario, 1861 ***2896.25*** *p12*
Parliament, Emily 13; Ontario, 1861 ***2896.25*** *p67*
Parliament, Emma 14; Ontario, 1861 ***2896.25*** *p5*
Parliament, Flavious 8; Ontario, 1861 ***2896.25*** *p67*
Parliament, George 13; Ontario, 1861 ***2896.25*** *p62*
Parliament, George M. 16; Ontario, 1861 ***2896.25*** *p12*
Parliament, Gilford 12; Ontario, 1861 ***2896.25*** *p67*
Parliament, Hannah 46; Ontario, 1861 ***2896.25*** *p61*
Parliament, Henry 17; Ontario, 1861 ***2896.25*** *p61*
Parliament, Henry 24; Ontario, 1861 ***2896.25*** *p12*
Parliament, Jane 42; Ontario, 1861 ***2896.25*** *p62*
Parliament, John H. 8; Ontario, 1861 ***2896.25*** *p12*
Parliament, Lette 1; Ontario, 1861 ***2896.25*** *p67*
Parliament, Margaret 1; Ontario, 1861 ***2896.25*** *p62*
Parliament, Mariah 37; Ontario, 1861 ***2896.25*** *p67*
Parliament, Martha 30; Ontario, 1861 ***2896.25*** *p56*
Parliament, Mary 56; Ontario, 1861 ***2896.25*** *p12*
Parliament, Mary A. 4; Ontario, 1861 ***2896.25*** *p56*
Parliament, Mary E. 10; Ontario, 1861 ***2896.25*** *p12*
Parliament, Peter 9; Ontario, 1861 ***2896.25*** *p4*
Parliament, Philana 21; Ontario, 1861 ***2896.25*** *p61*
Parliament, Samuel 14; Ontario, 1861 ***2896.25*** *p62*
Parliament, Samuel 36; Ontario, 1861 ***2896.25*** *p67*
Parliament, Sary Ann 18; Ontario, 1861 ***2896.25*** *p62*
Parliament, Sherwood 10; Ontario, 1861 ***2896.25*** *p67*
Parliament, Victoria 15; Ontario, 1861 ***2896.25*** *p61*
Parliament, Wellington 16; Ontario, 1861 ***2896.25*** *p5*
Parliament, Wendle 8; Ontario, 1861 ***2896.25*** *p62*
Parliament, Wesley 12; Ontario, 1861 ***2896.25*** *p61*
Parliament, William 7; Ontario, 1861 ***2896.25*** *p4*
Parlour, Edw; Virginia, 1701-1702 ***6212.30*** *p61*
Parlow, Elizabeth 70; Ontario, 1871 ***1823.22*** *p122*
Parlow, John 30; Virginia, 1774 ***1220.25*** *p88*
Parmentier, Charles; Philadelphia, 1793 ***4629.10*** *p76*
Parmphe, Robert; Maryland, 1661 ***2524.55*** *p168*
Parnel, James; Pennsylvania, 1725 ***1224.2*** *p87*
Parnell, Honora Conway; Vermont, 1841-1913 ***5900.10*** *p378*
Parnell, John; Vermont, 1829-1909 ***5900.10*** *p378*
Parnell, Lawrence 27; Vermont, 1861 ***5900.10*** *p294*
Parnell, Margaret 62; Vermont, 1868 ***5900.10*** *p294*
Parnell, Mary A. 41; Vermont, 1882 ***5900.10*** *p293*
Parnell, Michael 74; Vermont, 1865 ***5900.10*** *p294*
Parnell, Moses; Long Island, 1756 ***1224.2*** *p87*
Parnes, Francis; Maryland, 1657 ***2524.55*** *p168*
Parnes, Richard; Maryland, 1680 ***2524.55*** *p168*
Parnham, A. 18; Ontario, 1861 ***2896.27*** *p11*
Parnish, Robert; Maryland, 1661 ***2524.55*** *p168*
Parott, Peter; Maryland, 1668 ***2524.55*** *p168*
Parr, Anne; Virginia, 1671 ***6212.30*** *p43*
Parr, Anne 88; Ontario, 1871 ***1823.15*** *p209*
Parr, Chloe Ann 16; Ontario, 1861 ***2896.28*** *p21*
Parr, David 32; Ontario, 1871 ***1823.28*** *p80*
Parr, Elgin 10; Ontario, 1861 ***2896.28*** *p21*
Parr, George 32; Ontario, 1871 ***1823.28*** *p80*
Parr, Henry; Boston, 1753 ***1224.2*** *p88*
Parr, James; Pennsylvania, 1778 ***4629.10*** *p32*
Parr, John; New York, 1836 ***8197.10*** *p77*
Parr, John 23; Ontario, 1861 ***2896.28*** *p28*
Parr, John 45; Ontario, 1871 ***1823.15*** *p209*
Parr, John Raynor 2; Ontario, 1861 ***2896.28*** *p21*
Parr, Jotham 14; Ontario, 1861 ***2896.28*** *p21*
Parr, Nathaniel 45; Baltimore, 1775 ***1220.25*** *p118*
Parr, Phebe Ann 31; Ontario, 1861 ***2896.28*** *p21*
Parr, Sarah H. 6; Ontario, 1861 ***2896.28*** *p21*
Parr, Thomas 40; Ontario, 1871 ***1823.28*** *p80*
Parr, Washington 12; Ontario, 1861 ***2896.28*** *p21*
Parr, Young 53; Ontario, 1871 ***1823.15*** *p209*
Parre, Anne; Virginia, 1671 ***6212.30*** *p44*
Parree, Patrick; Maryland, 1682 ***2524.55*** *p168*
Parrest, William; Maryland, 1667 ***2524.55*** *p178*
Parrett, Thomas 63; Ontario, 1871 ***1823.28*** *p80*
Parriot, Robert; Virginia, 1664 ***6212.30*** *p11*
Parris, Dorothy Noyes; New England, 1699 ***1224.1*** *p42*
Parris, Margaret Higgins; Vermont, 1855-1924 ***5900.10*** *p428*
Parrish, Edward; Maryland, 1655 ***2524.55*** *p175*
Parrish, John, Jr.; Pennsylvania, 1777 ***4629.10*** *p23*
Parrish, Robert; Pennsylvania, 1777 ***4629.10*** *p23*
Parrit, Henry 55; Ontario, 1871 ***1823.22*** *p122*
Parro, David; Vermont, 1831-1892 ***5900.10*** *p396*
Parro, Rosella Dalton; Vermont, 1835-1890 ***5900.10*** *p396*
Parrott, Mr.; Quebec, 1857 ***9196.15*** *p22*
Parrott, Benjamin 32; Virginia, 1773 ***1220.25*** *p29*
Parrott, Francis; Maryland, 1655 ***2524.55*** *p168*
Parrott, John; Maryland, 1665 ***2524.55*** *p168*
Parrott, Lawrence; Maryland, 1662 ***2524.55*** *p200*
Parrott, Richard; New York, 1827 ***8197.10*** *p298*
Parrott, Richard, Jr.; Maryland, 1673 ***2524.55*** *p168*
Parrott, Thomas 21; Baltimore, 1775 ***1220.25*** *p118*
Parrott, Thomas 41; Ontario, 1871 ***1823.15*** *p209*
Parrott, Thomas 46; Ontario, 1871 ***1823.22*** *p122*
Parrott, William; Maryland, 1658 ***2524.55*** *p168*
With family
Parrum, Joseph; Boston, 1701 ***1224.2*** *p88*
Parry, Elizabeth; Maryland, 1658 ***2524.55*** *p168*
Parry, Jas 36; Alaska, 1917 ***9196.1*** *p49*
Parry, Jas 36; Whitehorse, Yukon, 1917 ***9196.1*** *p49*
Parry, John; Maryland, 1658 ***2524.55*** *p168*
Parry, John; Virginia, 1638 ***1224.1*** *p44*
Parry, John 22; Virginia, 1774 ***1220.25*** *p93*
Parry, Samuel; New York, 1838 ***8197.10*** *p146*
Parry, William; New York, 1838 ***8197.10*** *p127*
Parry, William Henry; New York, 1830 ***8197.10*** *p363*
Parset, John 16; Maryland, 1775 ***1220.25*** *p10*
Parsevall, John; Maryland, 1659 ***2524.55*** *p168*
Parsley, John 23; Philadelphia, 1774 ***1220.25*** *p63*
Parslow, John; New Jersey, 1845 ***1224.3*** *p59*
Parson, Alis 40; Ontario, 1861 ***2896.27*** *p11*
Parson, Charles 25; Ontario, 1871 ***1823.28*** *p80*
Parson, Ema 5; Ontario, 1861 ***2896.27*** *p11*
Parson, Lavena 10; Ontario, 1861 ***2896.27*** *p11*
Parson, Loiza 3; Ontario, 1861 ***2896.27*** *p11*
Parson, M. Ann 15; Ontario, 1861 ***2896.27*** *p11*
Parson, Sarah; Maryland, 1675 ***2524.55*** *p168*
Parson, William 42; Ontario, 1861 ***2896.27*** *p11*
Parsons, Ms. 60; Ontario, 1871 ***1823.22*** *p122*
Parsons, Benjamin 50; Ontario, 1871 ***1823.22*** *p122*
Parsons, Daniel; New York, 1831 ***8197.10*** *p368*
Parsons, Edward 29; Ontario, 1871 ***1823.28*** *p80*
Parsons, Edward Lambert; Jamestown, Virginia, 1778 ***1224.2*** *p88*
Parsons, Elias S. 52; Ontario, 1871 ***1823.28*** *p80*
Parsons, Elizabeth; Maryland, 1680 ***2524.55*** *p168*
Parsons, Humphrey; Boston, 1696 ***1224.1*** *p44*
Parsons, J. D.; Quebec, 1858 ***9196.15*** *p45*
Parsons, James 25; Virginia, 1774 ***1220.25*** *p87*
Parsons, James 60; Ontario, 1871 ***1823.15*** *p209*
Parsons, John; Maryland, 1681 ***2524.55*** *p168*
Parsons, John 42; Ontario, 1871 ***1823.15*** *p209*
Parsons, John 47; Ontario, 1871 ***1823.22*** *p122*
Parsons, John Temple; Maryland, 1778 ***1224.2*** *p88*
Parsons, Joseph; Boston, 1696 ***1224.1*** *p44*
Parsons, Margaret; New York, 1831 ***8197.10*** *p67*
Parsons, Mary 23; Philadelphia, 1774 ***1220.25*** *p44*
Parsons, Mary 62; Ontario, 1871 ***1823.15*** *p209*
Parsons, Mary Ewer; Boston, 1818 ***1224.3*** *p59*
Parsons, Richard; Maryland, 1664 ***2524.55*** *p168*
Parsons, Robert; Virginia, 1655 ***1224.1*** *p44*
Parsons, Thomas; Maryland, 1664 ***2524.55*** *p168*
Parsons, Thomas; Maryland, 1669 ***2524.55*** *p168*
Parsons, Thomas; Virginia, 1671 ***6212.30*** *p44*
Parsons, Thomas 18; Ontario, 1871 ***1823.22*** *p122*
Parsons, W. J. 27; Ontario, 1871 ***1823.28*** *p80*
Parsons, William 41; Ontario, 1871 ***1823.28*** *p80*
Parsons, William 46; Ontario, 1871 ***1823.15*** *p209*
Parsons, William 53; Ontario, 1871 ***1823.15*** *p209*
Parsonson, John; New York, 1830 ***8197.10*** *p312*
Part, Joseph 42; Ontario, 1871 ***1823.15*** *p209*
Partemer, Philipp; Port uncertain, 1724 ***2856.30*** *p334*

Partenmes, Peter; Port uncertain, 1760 ***2856.30*** *p334*
Parthemer, Friedrich; America, 1744 ***2856.30*** *p335*
With family
Parthemer, Friedrich; Port uncertain, 1744 ***2856.30*** *p334*
With family
Parton, Francis; Newfoundland, 1811 ***1224.3*** *p59*
Parton, Francis; Salem, Massachusetts, 1811 ***1224.3*** *p59*
Parton, George 32; British Columbia, 1910 ***9196.1*** *p31*
Parton, George 32; Seattle, 1910 ***9196.1*** *p31*
Parton, William 39; Ontario, 1871 ***1823.28*** *p80*
Partrick, William 22; Baltimore, 1775 ***1220.25*** *p119*
Partridge, Daniel; New York, 1838 ***8197.10*** *p379*
Partridge, Isaac 35; Ontario, 1871 ***1823.22*** *p122*
Partridge, John; New York, New York, 1827 ***1224.3*** *p59*
Partridge, Richard; Maryland, 1665 ***2524.55*** *p168*
Partridge, Samuel; Rappahannock, Virginia, 1676 ***1224.1*** *p44*
Partridge, Stephen; New York, 1840 ***8197.10*** *p193*
Partridge, William; New York, 1832 ***8197.10*** *p357*
Parts, Francis; New York, 1830 ***8197.10*** *p313*
Partszer, Jonas; New York, New York, 1853 ***6058.10*** *p47*
Partzer, Jonas; New York, New York, 1853 ***6058.10*** *p47*
Parvis, Elizabeth; Maryland, 1656 ***2524.55*** *p168*
Parvy, Charles; Maryland, 1682 ***2524.55*** *p168*
Parvy, Elizabeth; Maryland, 1678 ***2524.55*** *p169*
Parvy, Elizabeth; Maryland, 1682 ***2524.55*** *p169*
Parvy, John; Maryland, 1678 ***2524.55*** *p169*
Parvy, John; Maryland, 1682 ***2524.55*** *p169*
Paryns, Adam; Maryland, 1910 ***3259.35*** *p46*
Pascall, Elizabeth *SEE* Pascall, James
Pascall, George *SEE* Pascall, James
Pascall, George; Maryland, 1651 ***2524.55*** *p169*
Wife: Maudley
Pascall, George; Maryland, 1666 ***2524.55*** *p169*
Pascall, James *SEE* Pascall, James
Pascall, James; Maryland, 1652 ***2524.55*** *p169*
Wife: Elizabeth
Son: James
Son: George
Pascall, Maudley *SEE* Pascall, George
Paschall, Edward; Pennsylvania, 1777 ***4629.10*** *p18*
Paschall, Elizabeth *SEE* Paschall, George
Paschall, George; Maryland, 1651 ***2524.55*** *p169*
Relative: James
Wife: Elizabeth
Paschall, James *SEE* Paschall, George
Pasco, William 29; Virginia, 1774 ***1220.25*** *p93*
Pascoe, Nicholas Jasper; New York, 1836 ***8197.10*** *p271*
Pascol, John; Portland, Maine, 1858 ***9196.15*** *p29*
Pasela, Jacob; Maryland, 1910 ***3259.35*** *p46*
Pasey, William H. 53; Ontario, 1871 ***1823.15*** *p209*
Pashby, Thomas; Vermont, 1844-1908 ***5900.10*** *p152*
Pashby, Thomas; Vermont, 1844-1908 ***5900.10*** *p182*
Pashley, John; New York, 1839 ***8197.10*** *p138*
Pashley, John, Jr.; New York, 1840 ***8197.10*** *p193*
Pashley, Samuel; New York, 1839 ***8197.10*** *p138*
Pashley, William 70; Halifax, Nova Scotia, 1774 ***1220.25*** *p138*
Pashly, James; Virginia, 1665-1666 ***6212.30*** *p21*
Pasint, Stephina; Maryland, 1910 ***3259.35*** *p46*
Paska, Harry; Maryland, 1910 ***3259.35*** *p46*
Paskow, Frank; Maryland, 1910 ***3259.35*** *p46*
Pasnsna, Stanislaw; Maryland, 1910 ***3259.35*** *p46*
Passage, Johann Georg; America, 1732 ***2856.30*** *p335*
Passage, Johann Georg; America, 1744 ***2856.30*** *p335*
Passapae, John Davis; Baltimore, n.d. ***1224.3*** *p60*
Passapae, John Davis; Valparaiso, Chile, 1853 ***1224.3*** *p60*
Passapae, Joseph; Baltimore, n.d. ***1224.3*** *p60*
Passapae, Joseph; Peru, 1849 ***1224.3*** *p60*
Passell, Eliza; Virginia, 1664-1665 ***6212.30*** *p15*
Passell, Sara; Virginia, 1664-1665 ***6212.30*** *p15*
Passey, Samuel; Philadelphia, 1829 ***1224.3*** *p62*
Passfield, John; New York, 1807 ***8197.10*** *p47*
Passmor, William 58; Ontario, 1871 ***1823.15*** *p209*
Passmore, Mr.; Quebec, 1857 ***9196.15*** *p13*
Passmore, John 28; Ontario, 1871 ***1823.15*** *p209*
Passmore, John 39; Ontario, 1871 ***1823.15*** *p209*
Passmore, William; New York, 1821 ***8197.10*** *p269*
Passmore, William 28; Ontario, 1871 ***1823.15*** *p209*
Pasternak, William; Maryland, 1910 ***3259.35*** *p46*
Pasternik, John; Maryland, 1910 ***3259.35*** *p46*
Paston, John; America, 1711 ***1224.2*** *p88*
Pastree, George; Boston, 1751 ***1224.2*** *p88*
Pastree, Margaret; Boston, 1751 ***1224.2*** *p88*
Paszke, Jacob; Maryland, 1910 ***3259.35*** *p46*
Paszkewich, Frank; Maryland, 1910 ***3259.35*** *p46*
Paszkiewicz, Michael; Maryland, 1910 ***3259.35*** *p46*
Patarski, John; Maryland, 1910 ***3259.35*** *p46*
Patasik, Watesky; Maryland, 1910 ***3259.35*** *p46*
Patch, Mrs.; Quebec, 1856 ***9196.15*** *p9*
Patchell, Edward; Pennsylvania, 1806 ***6058.10*** *p1*
Pate, John; Virginia, 1673 ***1224.1*** *p44*
Pate, McDowall; New York, 1828 ***8197.10*** *p271*
Pate, Richard; Virginia, 1657 ***1224.1*** *p44*
Pate, Wm. McDowell; New York, 1839 ***8197.10*** *p138*
Pateet, Thomas; Maryland, 1639 ***2524.55*** *p169*
Patelsky, Andrew; Maryland, 1910 ***3259.35*** *p46*
Paterlange, John 21; Maryland, 1774 ***1220.25*** *p79*
Paterson, Miss; Quebec, 1857 ***9196.15*** *p14*
Paterson, Miss; Quebec, 1858 ***9196.15*** *p44*
Paterson, Mr.; Quebec, 1857 ***9196.15*** *p14*
Paterson, Mr.; Quebec, 1857 ***9196.15*** *p26*
Paterson, Alexander 21; Ontario, 1871 ***1823.15*** *p209*
Paterson, Alexander Baird; New York, 1886 ***1640.13*** *p98*
Paterson, Angus; Nova Scotia, 1840-1849 ***4537.35*** *p37*
Wife: Margaret MacLeod
Child: Sam
Child: John
Child: Kirsty
Child: Duncan
Child: Rachel
Child: Mary
Paterson, Catherine; Nova Scotia, 1820-1829 ***4537.35*** *p37*
Paterson, Catherine; Nova Scotia, 1840-1849 ***4537.35*** *p31*
Paterson, Clara A. 12; Ontario, 1861 ***2896.27*** *p29*
Paterson, Donald *SEE* Paterson, Norman
Paterson, Donald; Port uncertain, 1840-1849 ***4537.35*** *p86*
With wife
Child: James
Paterson, Donald; Port uncertain, 1840-1849 ***4537.37*** *p133*
Paterson, Duncan *SEE* Paterson, Angus
Paterson, Effie; Nova Scotia, 1840-1849 ***4537.35*** *p20*
Paterson, Elioner; Maryland, 1651 ***2524.55*** *p169*
Paterson, Elizabeth; New York, 1853 ***1640.13*** *p98*
Paterson, George, Sr. 62; Ontario, 1871 ***1823.22*** *p122*
Paterson, Hugh 60; Ontario, 1871 ***1823.28*** *p80*
Paterson, Isaac; New York, 1823 ***8197.10*** *p270*
Paterson, Jacob; Maryland, 1677 ***2524.55*** *p169*
Paterson, James *SEE* Paterson, Donald
Paterson, James; Quebec, 1857 ***9196.15*** *p26*
Paterson, James 39; Ontario, 1871 ***1823.15*** *p209*
Paterson, James 54; Ontario, 1871 ***1823.28*** *p80*
Paterson, James 67; Ontario, 1871 ***1823.15*** *p209*
Paterson, Jane 22; Virginia, 1774 ***1220.25*** *p88*
Paterson, Janet; Montreal, 1889 ***1640.13*** *p98*
Paterson, John *SEE* Paterson, Angus
Paterson, John *SEE* Paterson, Margaret
Paterson, John; Canada, 1882 ***1640.13*** *p98*
Paterson, John 70; Ontario, 1871 ***1823.15*** *p209*
Paterson, John 73; Ontario, 1871 ***1823.22*** *p122*
Paterson, Kirsty *SEE* Paterson, Angus
Paterson, Margaret; Port uncertain, 1840-1849 ***4537.37*** *p133*
Child: John
Child: Mary
Paterson, Margaret MacLeod *SEE* Paterson, Angus
Paterson, Marion; Nova Scotia, 1828 ***4537.35*** *p36*
Paterson, Mary *SEE* Paterson, Angus
Paterson, Mary *SEE* Paterson, Margaret
Paterson, Norman; Nova Scotia, 1820-1829 ***4537.35*** *p37*
Brother: Donald
Paterson, P.; Quebec, 1856 ***9196.15*** *p8*
Paterson, Rachel *SEE* Paterson, Angus
Paterson, Robert; Charles Town, South Carolina, 1781 ***1224.2*** *p88*
Paterson, Robert; New York, 1802 ***8197.10*** *p24*
Paterson, Robert 65; Ontario, 1871 ***1823.15*** *p209*
Paterson, Sam *SEE* Paterson, Angus
Paterson, Samuel 66; Ontario, 1871 ***1823.22*** *p122*
Paterson, Stephen; New York, 1794 ***8197.10*** *p1*
Paterson, Thomas; Maryland, 1651 ***2524.55*** *p169*
Paterson, Thomas 23; Maryland, 1774 ***1220.25*** *p78*
Paterson, Timothy 41; Ontario, 1871 ***1823.28*** *p80*
Paterson, William 21; Maryland, 1774 ***1220.25*** *p47*
Paterson, William 34; Halifax, Nova Scotia, 1774 ***1220.25*** *p138*
Pateshall, Richard; Boston, 1763 ***1224.2*** *p88*
Pateshall, Robert; Boston, 1763 ***1224.2*** *p88*
Patison, Jonathan 19; Fort Cumberland, Nova Scotia, 1774 ***1220.25*** *p15*
Patison, William; Windward Islands, 1848 ***1640.13*** *p98*
Patmore, Richard 17; Maryland, 1774 ***1220.25*** *p60*
Paton, George; New York, 1828 ***8197.10*** *p350*
Paton, George 38; Ontario, 1871 ***1823.15*** *p209*
Paton, James; New York, 1839 ***8197.10*** *p137*
Paton, Robert; New York, 1807 ***8197.10*** *p47*
Patrick, . . .; New Hampshire, 1641-1660 ***4628.40*** *p44*
Patrick, Miss; Quebec, 1857 ***9196.15*** *p25*
Patrick, Ann *SEE* Patrick, Roger
Patrick, Edward; New York, 1855 ***1224.3*** *p60*
Patrick, Eleanor 21; Maryland, 1774 ***1220.25*** *p59*
Patrick, Jane; New York, 1891 ***1640.13*** *p98*
Patrick, John *SEE* Patrick, Roger
Patrick, John; Maryland, 1670 ***2524.55*** *p169*
Patrick, John; Maryland, 1671 ***2524.55*** *p169*
Patrick, Joshua; Vermont, 1828-1901 ***5900.10*** *p459*
Patrick, Peter 60; Ontario, 1871 ***1823.15*** *p209*
Patrick, Roger; Maryland, 1673 ***2524.55*** *p169*
Daughter-In-Law: Sarah Harrison
Wife: Ann
Son: John
Patrick, Sarah Harrison *SEE* Patrick, Roger
Patrick, Sary Fitts; Virginia, 1703-1704 ***6212.30*** *p63*
Patrick, William 50; Ontario, 1871 ***1823.22*** *p122*
Patridge, Edward; Maryland, 1673 ***2524.55*** *p169*
Patridge, John; Maryland, 1652 ***2524.55*** *p169*
Patro, George; Maryland, 1910 ***3259.35*** *p46*
Patry, Pierre; Quebec, 1858 ***9196.15*** *p35*
Patten, Ann 56; Ontario, 1871 ***1823.22*** *p123*
Patten, Dennis; New York, 1821 ***8197.10*** *p270*
Patten, Edward 81; Ontario, 1871 ***1823.28*** *p80*
Patten, Ellen Madigan; Vermont, 1847-1917 ***5900.10*** *p584*
Patten, James; Pennsylvania, 1786 ***4629.10*** *p49*
Patten, John; Havana, 1765 ***1224.2*** *p88*
Patten, John; Vermont, 1831-1906 ***5900.10*** *p581*
Patten, John J.; Vermont, 1838-1918 ***5900.10*** *p584*
Patten, Margaret Devlin 68; Vermont, 1898 ***5900.10*** *p581*
Patten, Mary; New York, 1811 ***1224.3*** *p60*
Patten, Stephen 34; Ontario, 1871 ***1823.15*** *p209*
Patten, William; New York, 1838 ***8197.10*** *p146*
Patten, Wm; Virginia, 1664 ***6212.30*** *p15*
Pattenson, John 30; New York, 1775 ***1220.25*** *p143*
With wife & 3 children
Pattenson, Thomas 27; New York, 1775 ***1220.25*** *p143*
With wife & child
Patterson, A., Sr.; Vermont, 1824-1888 ***5900.10*** *p549*
Patterson, A. J., Jr.; Vermont, 1856-1934 ***5900.10*** *p549*
Patterson, Agnes 40; Ontario, 1871 ***1823.15*** *p209*
Patterson, Albert 20; Ontario, 1861 ***2896.28*** *p36*
Patterson, Alexander; New York, 1825 ***8197.10*** *p270*
Patterson, Alexander; Philadelphia, 1855 ***6058.10*** *p45*
Patterson, Alexander 2; Vermont, 1851 ***5900.10*** *p524*
Patterson, Alexander 24; Ontario, 1871 ***1823.22*** *p123*
Patterson, Alva A. 10; Ontario, 1861 ***2896.27*** *p29*
Patterson, Annie C. Slattery; Vermont, 1849-1914 ***5900.10*** *p446*
Patterson, Archibald 54; Ontario, 1871 ***1823.15*** *p209*
Patterson, Arthur; New York, 1840 ***8197.10*** *p193*
Patterson, Betsy 76; Ontario, 1861 ***2896.25*** *p14*
Patterson, Catherine 53; Ontario, 1871 ***1823.15*** *p209*
Patterson, Charles; Vermont, 1846-1905 ***5900.10*** *p511*
Patterson, Charles 22; Ontario, 1861 ***2896.28*** *p36*
Patterson, Charles 44; Ontario, 1871 ***1823.28*** *p80*
Patterson, Christenia 44; Ontario, 1871 ***1823.22*** *p123*
Patterson, David; New York, 1837 ***8197.10*** *p374*
Patterson, David 26; Ontario, 1871 ***1823.28*** *p80*
Patterson, David 32; Ontario, 1871 ***1823.15*** *p209*
Patterson, David 59; Ontario, 1871 ***1823.22*** *p123*
Patterson, David 70; Ontario, 1871 ***1823.15*** *p209*
Patterson, David W.; Vermont, 1851-1923 ***5900.10*** *p554*
Patterson, Donald 32; Ontario, 1871 ***1823.15*** *p209*
Patterson, Edward 6 months; Vermont, 1854 ***5900.10*** *p524*
Patterson, Elizabeth; Vermont, 1853-1900 ***5900.10*** *p551*
Patterson, Ephraim; New York, 1840 ***8197.10*** *p387*
Patterson, George 52; Ontario, 1871 ***1823.15*** *p209*
Patterson, George D., Sr.; Vermont, 1846-1935 ***5900.10*** *p446*
Patterson, H. 20; Ontario, 1861 ***2896.28*** *p12*
Patterson, Harriet S. Mooney; Vermont, 1844-1931 ***5900.10*** *p493*
Patterson, Henry L. 32; Vermont, 1864 ***5900.10*** *p493*
Patterson, Isabella 73; Ontario, 1871 ***1823.28*** *p80*
Patterson, James; Cuba, 1857 ***1640.13*** *p98*
Patterson, James; Georgia, 1809-1812 ***1640.10*** *p169*
Patterson, James; New York, 1815 ***8197.10*** *p269*
Patterson, James; New York, 1819 ***8197.10*** *p269*
Patterson, James; New York, 1825 ***8197.10*** *p270*
Patterson, James; New York, 1840 ***8197.10*** *p192*
Patterson, James 39; Ontario, 1871 ***1823.28*** *p80*
Patterson, James 45; Ontario, 1871 ***1823.15*** *p209*
Patterson, James 58; Ontario, 1861 ***2896.28*** *p36*
Patterson, John; Connecticut, 1765 ***1224.2*** *p88*
Patterson, John; Havana, 1765 ***1224.2*** *p88*
Patterson, John; Maryland, 1682 ***2524.55*** *p169*
Patterson, John; New York, 1821 ***8197.10*** *p270*
Patterson, John; Pennsylvania, 1777 ***4629.10*** *p9*
Patterson, John; Pennsylvania, 1777 ***4629.10*** *p17*
Patterson, John 18; Ontario, 1861 ***2896.28*** *p36*
Patterson, John 20; Ontario, 1871 ***1823.15*** *p209*

Patterson, John 22; Virginia, 1773 1220.25 p29
Patterson, John 41; Ontario, 1871 1823.15 p209
Patterson, John 45; Ontario, 1871 1823.28 p80
Patterson, John 48; Ontario, 1871 1823.15 p209
Patterson, John 59; Ontario, 1871 1823.28 p80
Patterson, John 60; Ontario, 1871 1823.15 p209
Patterson, John 62; Ontario, 1871 1823.15 p209
Patterson, John 73; Ontario, 1871 1823.22 p123
Patterson, John 77; Ontario, 1871 1823.28 p80
Patterson, John 80; Ontario, 1871 1823.28 p80
Patterson, Jonas; Georgia, 1699 1640.13 p99
Patterson, Livingston; South Carolina, 1831 1640.13 p98
Patterson, M. 44; Ontario, 1861 2896.28 p12
Patterson, Margaret Ann 20; Ontario, 1871 1823.15 p209
Patterson, Mary; Vermont, 1880 5900.10 p551
Patterson, Mary 60; Ontario, 1871 1823.28 p81
Patterson, Mary Fay 47; Vermont, 1861 5900.10 p524
Patterson, Michael 46; Ontario, 1871 1823.15 p209
Patterson, Michael 61; Ontario, 1871 1823.28 p81
Patterson, Neal 30; Ontario, 1871 1823.15 p210
Patterson, Oscar M.; Vermont, 1840-1888 5900.10 p493
Patterson, Peter 58; Ontario, 1871 1823.15 p210
Patterson, Robert; New York, 1837 8197.10 p374
Patterson, Robert; Ontario, 1854 1640.13 p98
Patterson, Robert 25; Ontario, 1871 1823.22 p123
Patterson, Robert 33; Ontario, 1871 1823.15 p210
Patterson, Robert 44; Ontario, 1871 1823.15 p210
Patterson, Robert 70; Ontario, 1861 2896.25 p32
Patterson, Robert 75; Ontario, 1871 1823.28 p81
Patterson, Rosa McManus 68; Vermont, 1887 5900.10 p527
Patterson, Samuel; Charleston, South Carolina, 1838 1640.13 p98
Patterson, Samuel 50; Ontario, 1871 1823.28 p81
Patterson, Simon, Jr.; Georgia, 1801 1640.10 p169
Patterson, Thomas; Jamaica, 1813 1640.13 p98
Patterson, Thomas; New York, 1840 8197.10 p272
Patterson, William; New Jersey, 1775-1781 4628.40 p69
Patterson, William; New York, 1821 8197.10 p270
Patterson, William; Savannah, Georgia, 1762 1640.10 p169
Patterson, William 17; Ontario, 1861 2896.28 p36
Patterson, William 24; Maryland, 1775 1220.25 p98
Patterson, William 27; Ontario, 1871 1823.28 p81
Patterson, William 35; Ontario, 1861 2896.28 p12
Patterson, William 45; Ontario, 1871 1823.22 p123
Patterson, William 56; Ontario, 1871 1823.28 p81
Patterson, Winifred E.; Vermont, 1860-1935 5900.10 p549
Patterson, Wm 32; Ontario, 1871 1823.15 p210
Patteson, James 63; Ontario, 1871 1823.28 p81
Pattin, William; Pennsylvania, 1786 4629.10 p49
Pattingall, A. 12; Ontario, 1861 2896.28 p6
Pattingall, A. 18; Ontario, 1861 2896.28 p6
Pattingall, Allen 51; Ontario, 1861 2896.28 p6
Pattingall, B. 13; Ontario, 1861 2896.28 p6
Pattingall, E. 2; Ontario, 1861 2896.28 p14
Pattingall, E. 17; Ontario, 1861 2896.28 p6
Pattingall, E. 44; Ontario, 1861 2896.28 p6
Pattingall, G. 15; Ontario, 1861 2896.28 p6
Pattingall, J. 22; Ontario, 1861 2896.28 p6
Pattingall, L. D. 17; Ontario, 1861 2896.28 p6
Pattingall, P. H. 19; Ontario, 1861 2896.28 p14
Pattingall, S. 27; Ontario, 1861 2896.28 p14
Pattingall, Wm 63; Ontario, 1861 2896.28 p6
Pattinger, John; New York, New York, 1820 1224.3 p61
Pattingill, Maria 29; Ontario, 1861 2896.28 p32
Pattison, Alex; Virginia, 1697 6212.30 p60
Pattison, Bridget 40; New York, 1775 1220.25 p142
With child
Pattison, Catherine 48; Ontario, 1871 1823.28 p81
Pattison, George; Virginia, 1722 1224.2 p88
Pattison, John; South Carolina, 1742 1224.2 p88
Pattison, John 50; Ontario, 1871 1823.15 p210
Pattison, Robert; New York, 1830 8197.10 p353
Pattison, William; New York, 1824 8197.10 p270
Pattison, William; Windward Islands, 1843 1640.13 p99
Pattle, Eliza Henrietta; New York, New York, 1854 1224.3 p60
Pattoin, Jas; Quebec, 1856 9196.15 p10
Patton, Mr.; Quebec, 1856 9196.15 p9
Patton, Catherine Sweeney 67; Vermont, 1881 5900.10 p294
Patton, Charles 61; Ontario, 1871 1823.28 p81
Patton, David 37; Ontario, 1871 1823.15 p210
Patton, Esther 77; Ontario, 1871 1823.15 p210
Patton, Grace 74; Ontario, 1871 1823.22 p123
Patton, Henry; Georgia, 1698 1640.13 p99
Patton, J.; Quebec, 1857 9196.15 p20
Patton, James 54; Ontario, 1871 1823.15 p210
Patton, John; New York, 1837 8197.10 p101
Patton, John 52; Ontario, 1871 1823.22 p123
Patton, John 56; Ontario, 1871 1823.15 p210
Patton, Maggie 54; Vermont, 1901 5900.10 p517
Patton, Mary F. 31; Vermont, 1883 5900.10 p294
Patton, Mary Petifer; Savannah, Georgia, 1775 1224.2 p88
Patton, Michal 40; Ontario, 1871 1823.22 p123
Patton, Robert; New York, 1837 8197.10 p101
Patton, Robert; Pennsylvania, 1777 4629.10 p20
Patton, Thomas; New York, 1840 8197.10 p192
Patton, Thomas; Pennsylvania, 1777 4629.10 p13
Patton, Thomas; Pennsylvania, 1777 4629.10 p32
Patton, William 42; Ontario, 1871 1823.15 p210
Patton, William 56; Ontario, 1871 1823.15 p210
Pattullo, David; New York, 1870 1640.13 p99
Paty, Mr.; Quebec, 1858 9196.15 p32
Patywield, August 47; Ontario, 1871 1823.28 p81
Paul, A.; Quebec, 1858 9196.15 p47
Paul, Alexander; New York, 1840 8197.10 p193
Paul, Barbara; Port uncertain, 1757 2856.30 p335
Paul, Christina; Port uncertain, 1770 2856.30 p335
Paul, Elizabeth J.; Vermont, 1849-1910 5900.10 p398
Paul, George; Jamaica, 1834 1640.13 p99
Paul, James 51; Ontario, 1871 1823.28 p81
Paul, Johann; Port uncertain, 1766 2856.30 p335
Paul, John; New York, 1807 8197.10 p47
Paul, Mary Kelley; Vermont, 1852-1918 5900.10 p553
Paul, Michael; New York, 1837 8197.10 p101
Paul, Michael; Port uncertain, 1768 2856.30 p335
Paul, Paul; Pennsylvania, 1777 4629.10 p11
Paul, Samuel 23; Ontario, 1871 1823.28 p81
Paul, Stephen; New England, 1696 1224.1 p44
Paul, William; Pennsylvania, 1779 4629.10 p38
Paulding, Alice McCue 57; Vermont, 1904 5900.10 p595
Paulen, H.; Quebec, 1858 9196.15 p45
Pauler, Martial; New York, 1808 8197.10 p54
Paulet, Wm; Virginia, 1664 6212.30 p15
Pauli, Johann Nickel; Port uncertain, 1738 2856.30 p335
Paulin, Christina; Port uncertain, 1770 2856.30 p335
Paulin, James 41; Ontario, 1871 1823.15 p210
Paulmier, Francis; New York, 1828 8197.10 p298
Paulsen, George O. Peter; New York, 1840 8197.10 p193
Paulsen, John Christian; New York, 1838 8197.10 p146
Paulson, Mr.; Quebec, 1858 9196.15 p42
Paulson, Edward 42; Alaska, 1913 9196.1 p22
Paulson, Edward 42; British Columbia, 1913 9196.1 p22
Paulson, James 43; Virginia, 1775 1220.25 p109
Paulukofsky, William J.; Maryland, 1910 3259.35 p46
Paulus, Andreas; America, 1749 2856.30 p335
With wife & 2 children
Paulus, Gustav Ludwig Henry; New York, 1834 8197.10 p271
Paulus, Gustavus Ludwig Henry; New York, 1839 8197.10 p138
Paulus, Johann Adam; Port uncertain, 1747 2856.30 p335
Paulus, Johann Michael; America, 1742 2856.30 p335
Paulus, Maria Catharina; Port uncertain, 1749 2856.30 p335
Pauwels, Edward 42; Ontario, 1871 1823.22 p123
Pavlovich, Nicola 49; Alaska, 1917 9196.1 p51
Pavlovich, Nicola 49; British Columbia, 1917 9196.1 p51
Pawaski, Edward; Maryland, 1910 3259.35 p46
Pawel, Daniel 16; Ontario, 1871 1823.22 p123
Pawelcyk, Thomas; Maryland, 1910 3259.35 p46
Pawer, James 52; Ontario, 1871 1823.28 p81
Pawlak, Andrew; Maryland, 1910 3259.35 p46
Pawlak, Frances; Maryland, 1910 3259.35 p46
Pawlak, Frank A.; Maryland, 1910 3259.35 p46
Pawlak, Helena; Maryland, 1910 3259.35 p46
Pawlak, James; Maryland, 1910 3259.35 p46
Pawlak, John P.; Maryland, 1910 3259.35 p46
Pawlak, Josef; Maryland, 1910 3259.35 p46
Pawlak, Peter; Maryland, 1910 3259.35 p46
Pawlik, Stanislw; Maryland, 1910 3259.35 p46
Pawlofski, Peter; Maryland, 1910 3259.35 p46
Pawson, Elizabeth 63; Ontario, 1871 1823.15 p210
Pawson, Isaac 41; Ontario, 1871 1823.15 p210
Pawtanski, Stanislaw; Maryland, 1910 3259.35 p46
Paxon, Israel; Pennsylvania, 1786 4629.10 p53
Paxton, Charles; Boston, n.d. 1224.2 p88
Paxton, James; New York, 1807 8197.10 p47
Paxton, John; Louisville, Kentucky, 1861 1640.13 p99
Paxton, Wentworth; Boston, 1751 1224.2 p88
Pay, Jane; Maryland, 1682 2524.55 p169
Payant, Mary; Vermont, 1842-1925 5900.10 p488
Payler, John; Maryland, 1664 2524.55 p166
Payler, Wm; Virginia, 1671-1672 6212.30 p47
Payley, Mr.; Quebec, 1857 9196.15 p15
Payne, Miss; Quebec, 1857 9196.15 p26
Payne, Anna; Vermont, 1854-1954 5900.10 p186
Payne, Charles 27; Ontario, 1871 1823.15 p210
Payne, Charles 42; Ontario, 1871 1823.22 p123
Payne, David 38; Philadelphia, 1774 1220.25 p86
Payne, David 44; Ontario, 1861 2896.27 p45
Payne, David H. 8; Ontario, 1861 2896.27 p45
Payne, Edmund; Maryland, 1708 1224.2 p88
Payne, Edward J.; Pennsylvania, 1868 6058.10 p77
Payne, Elen 38; Ontario, 1861 2896.27 p45
Payne, Francis 25; Philadelphia, 1774 1220.25 p66
Payne, Fridrick 25; Ontario, 1871 1823.28 p81
Payne, George; Maryland, 1661 2524.55 p169
Payne, George 21; Maryland, 1774 1220.25 p63
Payne, Henry; Maryland, 1664 2524.55 p169
Payne, Hugh; Maryland, 1666 2524.55 p171
Payne, James 64; Ontario, 1871 1823.15 p210
Payne, James A. 10; Ontario, 1861 2896.27 p45
Payne, Jean; Virginia, 1808 1224.3 p60
Payne, John; Maryland, 1660 2524.55 p169
Payne, John; Maryland, 1661 2524.55 p169
Payne, John 40; Ontario, 1871 1823.28 p81
Payne, Mary E. 6; Ontario, 1861 2896.27 p45
Payne, Mathew; Pennsylvania, 1686 1224.1 p44
Payne, Richard 24; Ontario, 1871 1823.28 p81
Payne, Richard 27; Maryland, 1774 1220.25 p41
Payne, Robert; New England, 1645 1224.1 p63
Payne, Samuel C. 40; Ontario, 1871 1823.22 p123
Payne, Sarah J. 12; Ontario, 1861 2896.27 p45
Payne, Thomas 22; Philadelphia, 1774 1220.25 p82
Payne, Thomas 28; Maryland, 1774 1220.25 p41
Payne, Thos 45; Ontario, 1871 1823.15 p210
Payne, William 13; Ontario, 1871 1823.22 p123
Payne, William 21; Virginia, 1774 1220.25 p45
Payne, William 33; Virginia, 1774 1220.25 p53
Payne, William 47; Ontario, 1871 1823.28 p81
Payne, William 49; Ontario, 1871 1823.15 p210
Payne, William 64; Ontario, 1871 1823.28 p81
Payne, William E. 3; Ontario, 1861 2896.27 p45
Payne, William L. 54; Ontario, 1871 1823.22 p123
Paynter, Alice; Maryland, 1662 2524.55 p169
Paynter, Joseph 78; Ontario, 1871 1823.28 p81
Paynter, Lovell; Philadelphia, 1741 1224.2 p89
Paynter, Mather; Maryland, 1658 2524.55 p169
Paynter, Nicholas; Maryland, 1685 1224.1 p44
Paynter, Thomas 33; Ontario, 1871 1823.28 p81
Payovich, J. 27; Alaska, 1917 9196.1 p48
Payovich, J. 27; Whitehorse, Yukon, 1917 9196.1 p48
Payr, Frances; Maryland, 1659 2524.55 p87
Paytin, John; New York, 1838 8197.10 p127
Payton, Tho; Virginia, 1665-1666 6212.30 p22
Pazolt, Thomas; New York, 1840 8197.10 p194
Pczydyzceski, Antonina; Maryland, 1910 3259.35 p46
Peacake, Doris *SEE* Peacake, John
Peacake, George *SEE* Peacake, John
Peacake, John *SEE* Peacake, John
Peacake, John; Maryland, 1671 2524.55 p169
Son: George
Daughter: Doris
Son: John
Daughter: Sarah
Peacake, Sarah *SEE* Peacake, John
Peacey, Emily Ann; Ontario, 1871 1823.22 p123
Peacey, Levi 47; Ontario, 1871 1823.22 p123
Peachy, Mary; Virginia, 1717 1224.2 p89
Peacock, Christopher 31; Ontario, 1871 1823.28 p81
Peacock, Eliz; Virginia, 1674 6212.30 p52
Peacock, Elizabeth; Maryland, 1660-1661 2524.55 p170
Peacock, Elizabeth; Virginia, 1664 6212.30 p6
Peacock, Elizabeth 34 *SEE* Peacock, John
Peacock, George 51; Ontario, 1871 1823.15 p210
Peacock, Hannah; America, 1785 1640.13 p99
Peacock, Jane 46; Ontario, 1871 1823.15 p210
Peacock, John 39; Maryland, 1774 1220.25 p84
Wife: Elizabeth 34
Peacock, Richard; Maryland, 1663 2524.55 p51
Peacock, Robert 24; Maryland, 1774 1220.25 p78
Peacock, Robert 47; Ontario, 1871 1823.15 p210
Peacock, Thomas 77; Ontario, 1871 1823.22 p123
Peacock, William Robert; New York, 1838 8197.10 p271
Peacock Roe Clas, John; Maryland, 1658 2524.55 p176
Pead, Elizabeth *SEE* Pead, Timothy
Pead, Jane *SEE* Pead, Timothy
Pead, Timothy; Maryland, 1680 2524.55 p170
Wife: Elizabeth
Daughter: Jane
Pead, Timothy; Virginia, 1671 6212.30 p42
Peak, Samuel; Boston, 1753 1224.2 p89
Peake, Anne; Maryland, 1682 2524.55 p170
Peake, Christopher; Virginia, 1726 1224.2 p89
Peake, Patrick 60; Ontario, 1871 1823.22 p123
Peake, Samuel 57; Ontario, 1871 1823.28 p81
Peake, Thomas; Virginia, 1664 6212.30 p13
Peakeman, William; Maryland, 1682 2524.55 p170
Peakstone, Eleanor 26; Georgia, 1775 1220.25 p126
Peal, Edgar 33; Ontario, 1871 1823.15 p210
Peale, Anne; Virginia, 1671 6212.30 p42
Peale, Tho; Virginia, 1665 6212.30 p22
Peale, Tho; Virginia, 1665-1666 6212.30 p23

Pealing, Dianna 12; Ontario, 1861 ***2896.27*** *p14*
Pealing, Dudly 9; Ontario, 1861 ***2896.27*** *p14*
Pealing, Elinnda 7; Ontario, 1861 ***2896.27*** *p14*
Pealing, John 1; Ontario, 1861 ***2896.27*** *p14*
Pealing, Luther 4; Ontario, 1861 ***2896.27*** *p14*
Pealing, Mary 26; Ontario, 1861 ***2896.27*** *p14*
Pealing, Robert 90; Ontario, 1861 ***2896.27*** *p16*
Pean, John 38; Ontario, 1871 ***1823.28*** *p81*
Peans, James; Maryland, 1910 ***3259.35*** *p46*
Pearce, Mr.; Quebec, 1858 ***9196.15*** *p39*
Pearce, Mrs.; Quebec, 1858 ***9196.15*** *p39*
Pearce, Charles; New York, 1839 ***8197.10*** *p271*
Pearce, Edward; Pennsylvania, 1827 ***6058.10*** *p9*
Pearce, George 17; Maryland, 1774 ***1220.25*** *p62*
Pearce, James 64; Ontario, 1871 ***1823.22*** *p123*
Pearce, Jane 36; Ontario, 1861 ***2896.27*** *p50*
Pearce, Jno; Virginia, 1703 ***6212.30*** *p62*
Pearce, John 45; Ontario, 1861 ***2896.27*** *p50*
Pearce, Richard; Maryland, 1659-1662 ***2524.55*** *p170*
Pearce, Robert 15; Virginia, 1774 ***1220.25*** *p87*
Pearce, William; Maryland, 1671 ***2524.55*** *p170*
Pearces, Tho; Virginia, 1672 ***6212.30*** *p48*
Pearle, James; Maryland, 1664 ***2524.55*** *p170*
Pearle, Richard; Virginia, 1668 ***1224.1*** *p44*
Pearle, Wm; Virginia, 1663 ***6212.30*** *p4*
Pearman, Ann; Albany, New York, 1785 ***1224.2*** *p89*
Pearn, James 49; Ontario, 1871 ***1823.22*** *p123*
Pearn, Samuel; New York, 1834-1839 ***8197.10*** *p138*
Pearne, George; New York, 1838 ***1224.3*** *p60*
Pearsaul, Cynthia 22; Ontario, 1861 ***2896.25*** *p61*
Pearsaul, Sara T. 3; Ontario, 1861 ***2896.25*** *p61*
Pearsaul, Wellington 2; Ontario, 1861 ***2896.25*** *p61*
Pearse, John; Virginia, 1671 ***6212.30*** *p42*
Pearse, Samuel 12; Philadelphia, 1774 ***1220.25*** *p3*
Pearse, William 23; Maryland, 1774 ***1220.25*** *p78*
Pearse, William 33; Philadelphia, 1774 ***1220.25*** *p3*
With wife & 2 children
Pearsill, David 25; Ontario, 1861 ***2896.27*** *p43*
Pearsill, Freeman 15; Ontario, 1861 ***2896.27*** *p43*
Pearsill, Matilda J. 8; Ontario, 1861 ***2896.27*** *p43*
Pearsill, Oliver 47; Ontario, 1861 ***2896.27*** *p43*
Pearsill, Philip James 13; Ontario, 1861 ***2896.27*** *p43*
Pearsill, Philoann 21; Ontario, 1861 ***2896.27*** *p43*
Pearsill, Smith A. 19; Ontario, 1861 ***2896.27*** *p43*
Pearsill, Thomas S. 17; Ontario, 1861 ***2896.27*** *p43*
Pearsol, Benjamin 54; Ontario, 1861 ***2896.28*** *p61*
Pearsol, Hannah 10; Ontario, 1861 ***2896.28*** *p61*
Pearsol, Hellen 27; Ontario, 1861 ***2896.28*** *p61*
Pearsol, Lara 2; Ontario, 1861 ***2896.28*** *p61*
Pearsol, Lara 23; Ontario, 1861 ***2896.28*** *p61*
Pearsol, Margaret 29; Ontario, 1861 ***2896.28*** *p62*
Pearsol, Maria 6; Ontario, 1861 ***2896.28*** *p62*
Pearsol, Martha C. 2; Ontario, 1861 ***2896.28*** *p62*
Pearsol, Raial 15; Ontario, 1861 ***2896.28*** *p61*
Pearsol, Rebecca 13; Ontario, 1861 ***2896.28*** *p61*
Pearsol, Robert 21; Ontario, 1861 ***2896.28*** *p61*
Pearsol, Samuel 4; Ontario, 1861 ***2896.28*** *p62*
Pearsol, William 60; Ontario, 1861 ***2896.28*** *p61*
Pearson, Mr.; Quebec, 1856 ***9196.15*** *p7*
Pearson, Mr.; Quebec, 1857 ***9196.15*** *p16*
Pearson, Mr.; Quebec, 1858 ***9196.15*** *p33*
Pearson, Mr.; Tobago, West Indies, 1775 ***1220.25*** *p133*
Pearson, Mrs.; Quebec, 1857 ***9196.15*** *p16*
Pearson, Aaron 5; Ontario, 1861 ***2896.25*** *p69*
Pearson, Ann 19; Georgia, 1775 ***1220.25*** *p126*
Pearson, Christopher 20; Nova Scotia, 1774 ***1220.25*** *p136*
Pearson, David 3; Ontario, 1861 ***2896.25*** *p69*
Pearson, Esther 36 *SEE* Pearson, Nicholas
Pearson, Francis 40; Ontario, 1871 ***1823.15*** *p210*
Pearson, George 19; Ontario, 1871 ***1823.28*** *p81*
Pearson, George 27; Philadelphia, 1774 ***1220.25*** *p23*
Pearson, James; New York, 1840 ***8197.10*** *p386*
Pearson, John; Maryland, 1681 ***2524.55*** *p170*
Pearson, John; Virginia, 1766 ***1224.2*** *p89*
Pearson, John 40; Baltimore, 1775 ***1220.25*** *p118*
Pearson, John S.; New York, 1839 ***8197.10*** *p380*
Pearson, Joseph; Maryland, 1726 ***1224.2*** *p89*
Pearson, Joseph; New York, 1830 ***8197.10*** *p271*
Pearson, Nicholas 40; Halifax, Nova Scotia, 1774 ***1220.25*** *p138*
Wife: Esther 36
With child 1
With child 10
With child 6
Pearson, Richard; New York, 1730 ***1224.2*** *p89*
Pearson, Robert 52; Ontario, 1871 ***1823.15*** *p210*
Pearson, Sarah 23; Ontario, 1861 ***2896.25*** *p69*
Pearson, Thomas; New York, 1831 ***8197.10*** *p271*
Pearson, Thomas; New York, 1840 ***8197.10*** *p192*
Pearson, Thomas 23; Maryland, 1774 ***1220.25*** *p77*
Pearson, Thomas 27; Tobago, West Indies, 1775 ***1220.25*** *p129*
Pearson, William 28; Nova Scotia, 1774 ***1220.25*** *p136*
Pearson, William 48; Ontario, 1871 ***1823.15*** *p210*
Pearson, William 50; Ontario, 1871 ***1823.22*** *p123*
Pearsons, John 57; Ontario, 1871 ***1823.22*** *p123*
Pease, James 58; Ontario, 1871 ***1823.15*** *p210*
Pease, James L. 29; Ontario, 1871 ***1823.15*** *p210*
Pease, Robert 50; Ontario, 1871 ***1823.15*** *p210*
Pease, Thomas 60; Ontario, 1871 ***1823.15*** *p210*
Peasor, Mary; Maryland, 1682 ***2524.55*** *p170*
Peaster, Peter 67; Ontario, 1871 ***1823.22*** *p123*
Peat, John 41; Ontario, 1871 ***1823.22*** *p123*
Peate, John; Virginia, 1673 ***1224.1*** *p44*
Peate, William 20; Maryland, 1774 ***1220.25*** *p69*
Peather, Mary *SEE* Peather, Richard
Peather, Richard; Maryland, 1663 ***2524.55*** *p170*
Wife: Mary
Daughter: Mary
Peato, Humphry; Maryland, 1674 ***2524.55*** *p172*
Peaverbe, George; Virginia, 1674-1675 ***6212.30*** *p53*
Pecher, Anton; New York, 1838 ***8197.10*** *p110*
Peck, Anna 55; Ontario, 1861 ***2896.25*** *p49*
Peck, E. 28; Ontario, 1861 ***2896.25*** *p49*
Peck, Edward; New England, 1676 ***1224.1*** *p44*
Peck, Eliza 38; Ontario, 1861 ***2896.25*** *p49*
Peck, Francis 26; Ontario, 1871 ***1823.22*** *p123*
Peck, Helen 15 *SEE* Peck, Richard
Peck, Henry 23; Ontario, 1861 ***2896.25*** *p49*
Peck, Isaac 13 *SEE* Peck, Richard
Peck, James H. 36; Ontario, 1861 ***2896.25*** *p49*
Peck, Jane 17 *SEE* Peck, Richard
Peck, Jane 42 *SEE* Peck, Richard
Peck, John 25; Ontario, 1871 ***1823.15*** *p210*
Peck, John 45; Ontario, 1871 ***1823.15*** *p210*
Peck, John G. 17; Ontario, 1861 ***2896.25*** *p49*
Peck, Joseph 2 *SEE* Peck, Richard
Peck, Joshua 18; Maryland, 1774 ***1220.25*** *p72*
Peck, Leonard 61; Ontario, 1871 ***1823.15*** *p210*
Peck, Lucy Ann 9; Ontario, 1861 ***2896.25*** *p49*
Peck, M. A. 26; Ontario, 1861 ***2896.25*** *p49*
Peck, M. J. 26; Ontario, 1861 ***2896.25*** *p49*
Peck, Mary 20 *SEE* Peck, Richard
Peck, Nancy 24; Ontario, 1861 ***2896.25*** *p49*
Peck, Richard 5 *SEE* Peck, Richard
Peck, Richard 46; Nova Scotia, 1774 ***1220.25*** *p13*
Peck, Richard 47; Halifax, Nova Scotia, 1775 ***1220.25*** *p22*
Wife: Jane 42
Child: Richard 5
Child: Rose 7
Child: Joseph 2
Child: Mary 20
Child: Helen 15
Child: Isaac 13
Child: Robert 10
Child: Jane 17
Peck, Richard Denny; New York, 1838 ***8197.10*** *p146*
Peck, Robert 10 *SEE* Peck, Richard
Peck, Rose 7 *SEE* Peck, Richard
Peck, S. W. 19; Ontario, 1861 ***2896.25*** *p49*
Peck, William; Maryland, 1668 ***2524.55*** *p42*
Peck, William 24; Ontario, 1871 ***1823.15*** *p210*
Peck, William 52; Ontario, 1871 ***1823.15*** *p210*
Peck, William 55; Ontario, 1871 ***1823.22*** *p123*
Peck, William 60; Ontario, 1861 ***2896.25*** *p49*
Peckam, Hen; Virginia, 1664 ***6212.30*** *p8*
Peckard, Anne; Maryland, 1666 ***2524.55*** *p170*
Pecke, Anne; New England, 1658 ***1224.1*** *p44*
Pecke, Hen; Virginia, 1672 ***6212.30*** *p50*
Pecket, Edward 55; Ontario, 1871 ***1823.15*** *p210*
Pecket, John; Maryland, 1672 ***2524.55*** *p170*
Peckett, Edward 11; Fort Cumberland, Nova Scotia, 1774 ***1220.25*** *p16*
Peckett, Giles 41; Fort Cumberland, Nova Scotia, 1774 ***1220.25*** *p17*
Wife: Mary 38
Child: James 16
Child: Margaret 5
Child: William 1
Child: John 7
Peckett, James 16 *SEE* Peckett, Giles
Peckett, John 7 *SEE* Peckett, Giles
Peckett, Margaret 5 *SEE* Peckett, Giles
Peckett, Mary 38 *SEE* Peckett, Giles
Peckett, William 1 *SEE* Peckett, Giles
Peckharness, John; New York, New York, 1796 ***1224.2*** *p86*
Peckman, Tho; Virginia, 1671-1672 ***6212.30*** *p46*
Pecknell, Elizabeth; New York, New York, 1786 ***1224.2*** *p89*
Pecksman, Ann 24; Ontario, 1871 ***1823.22*** *p123*
Pedden, James; Georgia, 1699 ***1640.13*** *p99*
Pedder, Mary *SEE* Pedder, Richard
Pedder, Richard; Maryland, 1673 ***2524.55*** *p170*
Wife: Mary
Daughter: Mary
Pedder, William 24; Virginia, 1774 ***1220.25*** *p55*
Pedder, Wm; Virginia, 1693-1694 ***6212.30*** *p60*
Peddie, Robert; Antigua (Antego), 1841 ***1640.13*** *p99*
Peddle, George; Pennsylvania, 1777 ***4629.10*** *p13*
Pedersen, A.; Illinois, 1890 ***6688.10*** *p36*
Pedersen, Anders; Illinois, 1886 ***6688.10*** *p66*
Pedersen, Anders; Illinois, 1893 ***6688.10*** *p66*
Pedersen, Anders; Illinois, 1896 ***6688.10*** *p66*
Pedersen, James; New York, 1831 ***8197.10*** *p271*
Pederson, A. 23; Alaska, 1918 ***9196.1*** *p54*
Pederson, A. 23; Whitehorse, Yukon, 1918 ***9196.1*** *p54*
Pederson, Andreas; Boston, 1873 ***6688.10*** *p62*
Pedlar, George 29; Ontario, 1871 ***1823.15*** *p211*
Pedler, Joshua 69; Ontario, 1871 ***1823.15*** *p211*
Pedley, Charles 50; Ontario, 1871 ***1823.22*** *p123*
Pedley, Nich; Virginia, 1665-1666 ***6212.30*** *p21*
Pedon, Robert; New York, 1839 ***8197.10*** *p138*
Pedroita, Charles; New York, 1840 ***8197.10*** *p272*
Peebles, Captain; Quebec, 1857 ***9196.15*** *p13*
Peebles, Elizabeth 28; Ontario, 1871 ***1823.22*** *p124*
Peebles, Hugh 36; Nova Scotia, 1774 ***1220.25*** *p137*
Peebles, James 65; Ontario, 1871 ***1823.22*** *p124*
Peebles, Mat; Quebec, 1858 ***9196.15*** *p40*
Peek, Mary 37; Ontario, 1861 ***2896.27*** *p41*
Peek, Thomas 41; Ontario, 1861 ***2896.27*** *p41*
Peel, Adam 96; Kansas, 1901-1910 ***9079.10*** *p47*
Peel, Christina 68; Kansas, 1910 ***9079.10*** *p47*
Peel, Frederick 37; Kansas, 1910 ***9079.10*** *p47*
Peel, John; New York, New York, 1800 ***1224.3*** *p60*
Peel, John 30; New York, 1775 ***1220.25*** *p143*
Peel, John A.; New York, 1837 ***8197.10*** *p100*
Peel, William; Pennsylvania, 1777 ***4629.10*** *p9*
Peele, Elizabeth; Maryland, 1685 ***1224.1*** *p44*
Peele, Robert; Maryland, 1734 ***1224.2*** *p89*
Peele, Samuel; Maryland, 1733 ***1224.2*** *p89*
Peele, Sarah; Virginia, 1671-1672 ***6212.30*** *p45*
Peeples, James; Pennsylvania, 1842 ***6058.10*** *p18*
Peer, Henry; Maryland, 1658 ***2524.55*** *p170*
Peer, Thomas; Virginia, 1670 ***1224.1*** *p45*
Peerce, David; Maryland, 1669 ***2524.55*** *p170*
Peerce, Rachel; Maryland, 1672 ***2524.55*** *p170*
Peere, Henry; Maryland, 1658 ***2524.55*** *p170*
Peers, Joseph; Long Island, 1783 ***1224.2*** *p89*
Peerson, Ann; Maryland, 1674 ***2524.55*** *p170*
Peet, Joseph; Philadelphia, 1797 ***1224.2*** *p89*
Peete, Mr.; Quebec, 1857 ***9196.15*** *p17*
Peete, Mrs.; Quebec, 1857 ***9196.15*** *p17*
Peever, David 32; Ontario, 1871 ***1823.28*** *p81*
Peever, James 42; Ontario, 1871 ***1823.28*** *p81*
Peever, William 45; Ontario, 1871 ***1823.28*** *p81*
Peever, William 59; Ontario, 1871 ***1823.28*** *p81*
Pegg, C. G. 23; Alaska, 1918 ***9196.1*** *p55*
Pegg, C. G. 23; Yukon, 1918 ***9196.1*** *p55*
Pegg, Jeremiah 85; Ontario, 1871 ***1823.22*** *p124*
Peggs, Anna; Vermont, 1856-1935 ***5900.10*** *p518*
Pegnom, William 43; Ontario, 1871 ***1823.22*** *p124*
Pegoneiasang, J. Bte 61; Ontario, 1871 ***1823.28*** *p81*
Pehalk, Ellen 21; Ontario, 1871 ***1823.22*** *p124*
Pehawanakwed, Paul 42; Ontario, 1871 ***1823.28*** *p81*
Peianowski, Michael; Maryland, 1910 ***3259.35*** *p46*
Peirce, Ann; Virginia, 1674-1675 ***6212.30*** *p53*
Peirce, Edm; Virginia, 1665-1666 ***6212.30*** *p22*
Peirce, Edmond; Virginia, 1664 ***6212.30*** *p13*
Peirce, Edmond; Virginia, 1666-1667 ***6212.30*** *p33*
Peirce, Frances *SEE* Peirce, Robert
Peirce, George; Virginia, 1671 ***6212.30*** *p42*
Peirce, John; Maryland, 1680 ***2524.55*** *p170*
Peirce, Lydia *SEE* Peirce, Thomas
Peirce, Rich; Virginia, 1672 ***6212.30*** *p50*
Peirce, Robert; Maryland, 1669 ***2524.55*** *p170*
Wife: Frances
Peirce, Tho; Virginia, 1665-1666 ***6212.30*** *p22*
Peirce, Thomas; Maryland, 1667 ***2524.55*** *p170*
Wife: Lydia
Peirce, Thomas; Virginia, 1666 ***6212.30*** *p28*
Peireey, Joseph 61; Ontario, 1871 ***1823.28*** *p81*
Peiroy, Thomas; Virginia, 1666 ***6212.30*** *p28*
Peirpoint, Amis *SEE* Peirpoint, Henry
Peirpoint, Elizabeth *SEE* Peirpoint, Henry
Peirpoint, Henry; Maryland, 1665 ***2524.55*** *p170*
Wife: Elizabeth
Son: Amis
Peirsey, Abraham; Virginia, 1625 ***1224.1*** *p19*
Peirson, Ann 19; Ontario, 1871 ***1823.15*** *p211*
Peirson, John 21; Ontario, 1871 ***1823.15*** *p211*
Peirson, Mary; Maryland, 1673 ***2524.55*** *p170*
Peitz, Anna Elisabeth; Port uncertain, 1775 ***2856.30*** *p335*
Peitz, Peter; Port uncertain, 1754 ***2856.30*** *p335*
Peive, John 23; Ontario, 1871 ***1823.15*** *p211*
Peiz, Philipp; Port uncertain, 1774 ***2856.30*** *p335*

Pekroff, B. 23; Washington, 1915 ***9196.1*** *p67*
Pelczar, Michael; Maryland, 1910 ***3259.35*** *p46*
Pele, John 21; Virginia, 1774 ***1220.25*** *p87*
Pele, Mary; Virginia, 1671 ***6212.30*** *p45*
Pelham, . . .; Boston, 1737 ***4628.40*** *p114*
Pelham, Hen; Virginia, 1664 ***6212.30*** *p8*
Pelham, Jabez Clinton; New York, 1837 ***8197.10*** *p101*
Pelham, Jabez Clinton; New York, 1840 ***8197.10*** *p193*
Pelham, Mary 31 *SEE* Pelham, William
Pelham, Penelope; Boston, 1790 ***1224.2*** *p89*
Pelham, Peter; Virginia, 1790 ***1224.2*** *p89*
Pelham, William; Boston, 1790 ***1224.2*** *p89*
Pelham, William 34; Virginia, 1774 ***1220.25*** *p90*
Wife: Mary 31
Peling, Joseph 48; Ontario, 1871 ***1823.22*** *p124*
Peliser, John 43; Ontario, 1871 ***1823.22*** *p124*
Pell, Alfred 37; Ontario, 1871 ***1823.28*** *p81*
Pell, H. P.; Quebec, 1856 ***9196.15*** *p8*
Pell, Samuel 39; Ontario, 1871 ***1823.28*** *p81*
Pell, William; Maryland, 1648 ***2524.55*** *p170*
Pell, William; Maryland, 1677 ***2524.55*** *p22*
Pellet, Joseph 63; Ontario, 1871 ***1823.22*** *p124*
Pelletier, Rev.; Quebec, 1858 ***9196.15*** *p35*
Pelletier, Joseph 67; Ontario, 1871 ***1823.28*** *p81*
Pelletier, M.; Quebec, 1856 ***9196.15*** *p8*
Pellett, Rosetta 20; Philadelphia, 1774 ***1220.25*** *p63*
Pelley, James; New Jersey, 1825 ***1224.3*** *p60*
Pellin, Thomas; Maryland, 1681 ***2524.55*** *p170*
Pellow, Henry 25; Ontario, 1871 ***1823.22*** *p124*
Pellow, William F. 33; Ontario, 1871 ***1823.15*** *p211*
Pelly, John; New York, 1827 ***8197.10*** *p347*
Peltz, John; Maryland, 1910 ***3259.35*** *p46*
Peltz, Marcin; Maryland, 1910 ***3259.35*** *p46*
Pember, Charles; Maryland, 1656 ***2524.55*** *p170*
Pember, Fran; Virginia, 1671-1672 ***6212.30*** *p47*
Pemberton, Mr.; Portland, Maine, 1858 ***9196.15*** *p30*
Pemberton, Mr.; Quebec, 1858 ***9196.15*** *p33*
Pemberton, Mrs.; Quebec, 1858 ***9196.15*** *p33*
Pemberton, Charles 16; Philadelphia, 1774 ***1220.25*** *p80*
Pemberton, Edward 30; Virginia, 1773 ***1220.25*** *p29*
Pemberton, Jacob; New York, 1838 ***8197.10*** *p146*
Pemberton, Thomas 20; Virginia, 1773 ***1220.25*** *p29*
Pembroke, Daniel; Vermont, 1806-1898 ***5900.10*** *p338*
Pembroke, John 24; Philadelphia, 1775 ***1220.25*** *p9*
Pembroke, Katherine; Vermont, 1854-1938 ***5900.10*** *p360*
Pembroke, Margaret; Vermont, 1861-1939 ***5900.10*** *p360*
Pembroke, Margaret Brown; Vermont, 1829-1898 ***5900.10*** *p360*
Pembroke, Mary Reardon; Vermont, 1821-1893 ***5900.10*** *p338*
Pembroke, Michael; Vermont, 1825-1880 ***5900.10*** *p360*
Pembroke, Michael; Vermont, 1863-1940 ***5900.10*** *p360*
Pembroke, Morris; Virginia, 1667-1668 ***6212.30*** *p39*
Pembroke, Nicholas; New York, 1832 ***8197.10*** *p368*
Pembroke, Owen; Virginia, 1667-1668 ***6212.30*** *p39*
Pembroke, Thomas B.; Vermont, 1866-1931 ***5900.10*** *p360*
Pemell, Jeffery; Virginia, 1664 ***6212.30*** *p9*
Pemow, Mary 19; Ontario, 1861 ***2896.28*** *p30*
Pemry, Thomas; Maryland, 1681 ***2524.55*** *p170*
Pemsel, Hans Georg; America, 1751 ***2856.30*** *p29*
With wife & children
Pemsel, Hans Georg; Port uncertain, 1752 ***2856.30*** *p29*
With wife & children
Pemwick, Walter 43; Ontario, 1871 ***1823.15*** *p211*
Penasanabic, Susan 62; Ontario, 1871 ***1823.28*** *p81*
Pencak, Mary; Maryland, 1910 ***3259.35*** *p46*
Pence, Edward 65; Ontario, 1871 ***1823.15*** *p211*
Pence, Thomas 32; Ontario, 1871 ***1823.15*** *p211*
Pencoast, Edward; Virginia, 1671 ***6212.30*** *p44*
Pendan, Nicholas; New York, 1837 ***8197.10*** *p101*
Pendarins, Richard; Virginia, 1666 ***6212.30*** *p27*
Pendarins, Wm; Virginia, 1666 ***6212.30*** *p27*
Pender, Mr.; Quebec, 1856 ***9196.15*** *p8*
Pender, Lawrence 29; Vermont, 1894 ***5900.10*** *p331*
Pender, Martin 28; Ontario, 1871 ***1823.22*** *p124*
Pender, Mary 39; Vermont, 1893 ***5900.10*** *p331*
Pender, Mary 82; Vermont, 1898 ***5900.10*** *p331*
Pender, Patrick 90; Vermont, 1905 ***5900.10*** *p331*
Pendergast, . . .; New Hampshire, 1641-1660 ***4628.40*** *p44*
Pendergast, Ann 67; Vermont, 1889 ***5900.10*** *p88*
Pendergast, Bridget 88; Vermont, 1899 ***5900.10*** *p387*
Pendergast, Catherine Kelley 40; Vermont, 1862 ***5900.10*** *p245*
Pendergast, James 52; Vermont, 1868 ***5900.10*** *p43*
Pendergast, Margaret; Vermont, 1835-1910 ***5900.10*** *p428*
Pendergast, Margaret 68; Vermont, 1891 ***5900.10*** *p430*
Pendergast, Mary; Vermont, 1830-1914 ***5900.10*** *p575*
Pendergast, Mary 19; Vermont, 1877 ***5900.10*** *p43*
Pendergast, Thomas 78; Vermont, 1901 ***5900.10*** *p430*
Pendergras, Thomas; Maryland, 1676 ***2524.55*** *p170*
Pendergrass, Catherine 60; Ontario, 1871 ***1823.22*** *p124*
Pendergrass, Honor; Maryland, 1681 ***2524.55*** *p170*
Pendergrass, Thomas; Virginia, 1699 ***1224.1*** *p45*
Penders, Henry; Vermont, 1831-1899 ***5900.10*** *p400*
Penders, Margaret Healey; Vermont, 1839-1926 ***5900.10*** *p400*
Penders, Mary Ann Clifford; Vermont, 1857-1933 ***5900.10*** *p393*
Pendleton, Samuel 22; Philadelphia, 1774 ***1220.25*** *p66*
Pendors, John 25; Vermont, 1876 ***5900.10*** *p267*
Pendred, Elizabeth 48; Ontario, 1871 ***1823.22*** *p124*
Pendrich, William; Georgia, 1734 ***1640.10*** *p169*
Penell, John; Vermont, 1829-1910 ***5900.10*** *p515*
Penell, Mary Ann Dooling; Vermont, 1837-1897 ***5900.10*** *p515*
Penell, Rosa E.; Vermont, 1866-1906 ***5900.10*** *p515*
Penessewahbai, Antoine 45; Ontario, 1871 ***1823.28*** *p81*
Penessewonquet, Antoine 34; Ontario, 1871 ***1823.28*** *p81*
Penewfsky, Zegmond; Maryland, 1910 ***3259.35*** *p46*
Penfold, Thomas; Virginia, 1671-1672 ***6212.30*** *p47*
Penfound, Henry 56; Ontario, 1871 ***1823.15*** *p211*
Pengelly, William 49; Ontario, 1871 ***1823.15*** *p211*
Penhale, John 46; Ontario, 1871 ***1823.15*** *p211*
Penhole, William 40; Ontario, 1871 ***1823.15*** *p211*
Penifold, Thomas 16; Maryland, 1775 ***1220.25*** *p120*
Penington, Rachael; Maryland, 1677 ***2524.55*** *p170*
Penington, Rich; Virginia, 1665-1666 ***6212.30*** *p22*
Penjstone, Francis; Virginia, 1664 ***6212.30*** *p11*
Penman, Archibald; Florida, 1785-1845 ***1640.10*** *p169*
Penman, James; Charles Town, South Carolina, n.d. ***1224.2*** *p89*
Penman, James; Florida, 1766 ***1640.10*** *p169*
Penman, Robert Patterson; Fort Wayne, Indiana, 1899 ***1640.13*** *p99*
Penn, John; Pennsylvania, 1777 ***4629.10*** *p23*
Penn, John; Philadelphia, 1796 ***1224.2*** *p89*
Penn, John; Virginia, 1671-1672 ***6212.30*** *p47*
Penn, Samuel 24; Philadelphia, 1774 ***1220.25*** *p86*
Penn, William; Maryland, 1697 ***1224.1*** *p45*
Penna, Joseph Joaquim; New York, 1819 ***8197.10*** *p269*
Pennecoat, John; Maryland, 1671 ***2524.55*** *p170*
Pennell, Edw; Virginia, 1664 ***6212.30*** *p9*
Penney, John 53; Ontario, 1871 ***1823.15*** *p211*
Penney, Robertson 51; Ontario, 1871 ***1823.15*** *p211*
Penney, Sophia McCullough; Vermont, 1855-1936 ***5900.10*** *p512*
Penney, William Honeycombe; New York, 1840 ***1224.3*** *p60*
Pennian, George 37; Ontario, 1871 ***1823.15*** *p211*
Pennicoate, John; Maryland, 1674 ***2524.55*** *p172*
Pennie, Elizabeth A.; Vermont, 1848-1923 ***5900.10*** *p374*
Penning, James; Virginia, 1665 ***6212.30*** *p17*
Penninger, Johann Nikol; Port uncertain, 1751 ***2856.30*** *p335*
Penninger, Margarete; Port uncertain, 1751 ***2856.30*** *p481*
Pennington, Benj.; Pennsylvania, 1776 ***4629.10*** *p52*
Pennington, Elizabeth *SEE* Pennington, Willm.
Pennington, James; Maryland, 1679 ***1224.1*** *p45*
Pennington, John 24; Ontario, 1871 ***1823.15*** *p211*
Pennington, John 35; Baltimore, 1775 ***1220.25*** *p117*
Pennington, Oliver 45; Ontario, 1871 ***1823.15*** *p211*
Pennington, Rich; Virginia, 1666-1667 ***6212.30*** *p32*
Pennington, Sarah 23; Philadelphia, 1774 ***1220.25*** *p23*
Pennington, Thomas 28; Ontario, 1871 ***1823.15*** *p211*
Pennington, William 55; Ontario, 1871 ***1823.15*** *p211*
Pennington, William L. 24; Ontario, 1871 ***1823.15*** *p211*
Pennington, Willm.; Maryland, 1658 ***2524.55*** *p171*
Wife: Elizabeth
Pennistone, Nicholas *SEE* Pennistone, William
Pennistone, Sarah *SEE* Pennistone, William
Pennistone, William; Maryland, 1666 ***2524.55*** *p171*
Relative: Nicholas
Relative: Sarah
Penno, Henry 34; Ontario, 1871 ***1823.28*** *p81*
Pennock, Ann; Ontario, 1861 ***2896.25*** *p9*
Pennock, Ann 25; Ontario, 1861 ***2896.28*** *p28*
Pennock, Catherine 61; Ontario, 1861 ***2896.28*** *p30*
Pennock, Elizabeth 27; Ontario, 1861 ***2896.25*** *p8*
Pennock, Elizabeth 62; Ontario, 1861 ***2896.25*** *p10*
Pennock, Ella 1; Ontario, 1861 ***2896.25*** *p8*
Pennock, Ida 6; Ontario, 1861 ***2896.28*** *p30*
Pennock, John 32; Ontario, 1861 ***2896.25*** *p10*
Pennock, Louis J. 22; Ontario, 1861 ***2896.28*** *p30*
Pennock, Mary; Ontario, 1861 ***2896.25*** *p9*
Pennock, Mary 25; Ontario, 1861 ***2896.25*** *p10*
Pennock, Mary 28; Ontario, 1861 ***2896.28*** *p30*
Pennock, Richard 10; Ontario, 1861 ***2896.28*** *p30*
Pennock, Zelma 8; Ontario, 1861 ***2896.28*** *p30*
Pennoyer, Robert; New England, 1671 ***1224.1*** *p45*
Penny, Amial 13; Ontario, 1861 ***2896.27*** *p52*
Penny, Charles 15; Maryland, 1775 ***1220.25*** *p98*
Penny, Clystey 9; Ontario, 1861 ***2896.27*** *p52*
Penny, Elizabeth 15; Ontario, 1861 ***2896.27*** *p52*
Penny, Helen R. 3; Ontario, 1861 ***2896.27*** *p52*
Penny, James 17; Ontario, 1861 ***2896.27*** *p52*
Penny, Joane; Maryland, 1663 ***2524.55*** *p171*
Penny, John; Philadelphia, 1779 ***1224.2*** *p90*
Penny, John 28; Philadelphia, 1774 ***1220.25*** *p44*
Penny, Milton A. 6; Ontario, 1861 ***2896.27*** *p52*
Penny, Noah 41; Ontario, 1861 ***2896.27*** *p52*
Penny, R.; Portland, Maine, 1857 ***9196.15*** *p13*
Penny, Samuel 19; Maryland, 1775 ***1220.25*** *p112*
Penny, Thomas; New York, 1802 ***8197.10*** *p24*
Penny, Wm.; Maryland, 1649-1650 ***2524.55*** *p171*
Pennycook, Robert; Jamaica, 1826 ***1640.13*** *p99*
Peno, Andrew; New York, 1840 ***8197.10*** *p193*
Penpraise, Honnor 45; Ontario, 1871 ***1823.22*** *p124*
Penrice, Elizabeth; Maryland, 1675 ***2524.55*** *p171*
Penrice, Hannah; Maryland, 1675 ***2524.55*** *p171*
Penrice, Robert; Maryland, 1675 ***2524.55*** *p171*
Penrose, John; Virginia, 1666 ***6212.30*** *p27*
Penrose, Jonathan; Pennsylvania, 1777 ***4629.10*** *p29*
Penrose, Jonathan; Pennsylvania, 1779 ***4629.10*** *p39*
Penrose, Joseph; Pennsylvania, 1777 ***4629.10*** *p6*
Penrose, William; Philadelphia, 1793 ***4629.10*** *p76*
Penry, Morgan; Maryland, 1674 ***2524.55*** *p171*
Pensax, Samuel; Maryland, 1657 ***2524.55*** *p171*
Pensax, Samuel; Maryland, 1659 ***2524.55*** *p171*
Pensiorz, Frank; Maryland, 1910 ***3259.35*** *p46*
Penson, Richard 42; Ontario, 1871 ***1823.28*** *p81*
Penter, Elizabeth; Virginia, 1663-1664 ***6212.30*** *p4*
Pentigrew, William 26; Ontario, 1871 ***1823.15*** *p211*
Pentland, John 49; Ontario, 1871 ***1823.15*** *p211*
Pentland, Mary 72; Ontario, 1871 ***1823.15*** *p211*
Pentland, William J. 55; Ontario, 1871 ***1823.22*** *p124*
Pentlow, William B.; New York, 1840 ***8197.10*** *p192*
Pentony, Michael; New York, 1840 ***8197.10*** *p193*
Penwarden, David 30; Ontario, 1871 ***1823.15*** *p211*
Penwarden, Thomas 48; Ontario, 1871 ***1823.15*** *p211*
Penzel, Maria Catharina; Port uncertain, 1746 ***2856.30*** *p336*
Penzer, Valentin; New York, 1836 ***8197.10*** *p271*
Peock, James; St. Vincent, 1812 ***1640.13*** *p99*
Peon, Jose Maria; New York, 1827 ***8197.10*** *p343*
People, John; Maryland, 1682 ***2524.55*** *p171*
Peoples, David 73; Ontario, 1871 ***1823.22*** *p124*
Peoples, John; Pennsylvania, 1835 ***6058.10*** *p22*
Peper, Elizabeth 78; Ontario, 1871 ***1823.22*** *p124*
Peper, Joseph 21; Maryland, 1775 ***1220.25*** *p100*
Peplow, Richard 18; Philadelphia, 1775 ***1220.25*** *p107*
Pepper, Joseph; Pennsylvania, 1786 ***4629.10*** *p52*
Pepperell, Andrew; Portsmouth, New Hampshire, n.d. ***1224.2*** *p90*
Pepperell, William; Massachusetts, 1768 ***1224.2*** *p90*
Perce, Frances; Maryland, 1670 ***2524.55*** *p171*
Perce, Thomas; Maryland, 1660 ***2524.55*** *p171*
Percey, Richard; Virginia, 1654 ***1224.1*** *p45*
Percha, Nicholas 50; Ontario, 1871 ***1823.28*** *p81*
Perches, William 32; Maryland, 1775 ***1220.25*** *p99*
Percie, Thomas; Maryland, 1660 ***2524.55*** *p171*
Percival, Henry 65; Ontario, 1871 ***1823.28*** *p81*
Percival, James, Sr.; New York, 1840 ***8197.10*** *p192*
Percival, James, Jr.; New York, 1840 ***8197.10*** *p192*
Percival, John 25; Maryland, 1775 ***1220.25*** *p114*
Percival, Pearce; New York, 1829-1837 ***8197.10*** *p300*
Percon, Edward; Maryland, 1680 ***2524.55*** *p171*
Percy, Thomas 51; Ontario, 1871 ***1823.15*** *p211*
Perdrian, Lewis; Carolina, 1697 ***1224.1*** *p45*
Perdrian, Peter; Carolina, 1693 ***1224.1*** *p45*
Perdue, Ellen 48; Alaska, 1917 ***9196.1*** *p7*
Perdue, Ellen 48; Yukon, 1917 ***9196.1*** *p7*
Perdue, Henry 40; Ontario, 1871 ***1823.15*** *p211*
Perdue, Stephen; Maryland, 1659 ***2524.55*** *p183*
Perdue, Thomas 60; Ontario, 1871 ***1823.15*** *p211*
Perelly, Elizabeth 73; Ontario, 1871 ***1823.22*** *p124*
Perfect, Sarah 50; Ontario, 1871 ***1823.28*** *p81*
Perira, Emanuel; New York, 1780 ***1224.2*** *p90*
Perke, Robert; Maryland, 1679 ***2524.55*** *p171*
Perke, Willm; Maryland, 1672 ***2524.55*** *p171*
Perkerson, John; Pennsylvania, 1786 ***4629.10*** *p53*
Perkin, Charles 36; Ontario, 1871 ***1823.15*** *p211*
Perkin, Henry 44; Ontario, 1871 ***1823.15*** *p211*
Perkin, Henry 74; Ontario, 1871 ***1823.15*** *p211*
Perkin, Honner 75; Ontario, 1871 ***1823.15*** *p211*
Perkin, James 34; Ontario, 1871 ***1823.22*** *p124*
Perkin, James 53; Ontario, 1871 ***1823.22*** *p124*
Perkin, John 30; Ontario, 1871 ***1823.22*** *p124*
Perkin, Joseph; Pennsylvania, 1779 ***4629.10*** *p41*
Perkin, Richard 40; Ontario, 1871 ***1823.15*** *p212*
Perkin, Richard 40; Ontario, 1871 ***1823.22*** *p124*
Perkin, William 52; Ontario, 1871 ***1823.15*** *p212*
Perkins, Mr.; Quebec, 1858 ***9196.15*** *p46*
Perkins, Mrs.; Quebec, 1858 ***9196.15*** *p46*
Perkins, Catherine; Charles Town, South Carolina, 1746 ***1224.2*** *p90*
Perkins, Daniel; Maryland, 1672 ***2524.55*** *p171*

Perkins, Edward; Maryland, 1665 ***2524.55*** *p14*
Perkins, James; Maryland, 1663 ***2524.55*** *p168*
Perkins, John; New York, 1777 ***1224.2*** *p87*
Perkins, John; New York, 1831 ***8197.10*** *p271*
Perkins, John; New York, 1832 ***8197.10*** *p314*
Perkins, Joshua N.; New York, 1829 ***8197.10*** *p65*
Perkins, Nathaniel; New York, 1779 ***1224.2*** *p90*
Perkins, Richard 73; Ontario, 1871 ***1823.15*** *p212*
Perkins, Thomas; Pennsylvania, 1777 ***4629.10*** *p6*
Perkinson, Mary; Vermont, 1822-1907 ***5900.10*** *p213*
Perkinson, Samil 28; Ontario, 1871 ***1823.15*** *p212*
Perkle, James 22; Maryland, 1774 ***1220.25*** *p77*
Perkowski, Joseph; Maryland, 1910 ***3259.35*** *p46*
Perling, William; Ontario, 1871 ***1823.22*** *p124*
Perm, John 35; Ontario, 1871 ***1823.15*** *p212*
Perm, Lawrance 57; Ontario, 1871 ***1823.15*** *p212*
Perm, Thomas 44; Ontario, 1871 ***1823.15*** *p212*
Permaine, Henry; Virginia, 1663 ***6212.30*** *p2*
Perman, George; Charleston, South Carolina, n.d. ***1224.3*** *p60*
Perndt, Adam; America, 1769 ***2856.30*** *p336*
Pernie, Peter; New York, 1821 ***8197.10*** *p269*
Perofrank, Jno; Virginia, 1677 ***6212.30*** *p53*
Peronneau, Mary Coffin; Charleston, South Carolina, 1849 ***1224.3*** *p60*
Peros, R. 28; Alaska, 1916 ***9196.1*** *p43*
Peros, R. 28; Whitehorse, Yukon, 1916 ***9196.1*** *p43*
Perovich, Zeke 32; British Columbia, 1913 ***9196.1*** *p23*
Perovich, Zeke 32; Juneau, Alaska, 1913 ***9196.1*** *p23*
Perrault, Mr.; Quebec, 1857 ***9196.15*** *p16*
Perrault, Mr.; Quebec, 1858 ***9196.15*** *p31*
Perrault, Antoine 58; Ontario, 1871 ***1823.28*** *p81*
Perreau, John; Philadelphia, 1791-1792 ***4629.10*** *p66*
Perreeve, William; Maryland, 1682 ***2524.55*** *p171*
Perrey, Johann Georg; Port uncertain, 1755 ***2856.30*** *p336*
Perri, Jeremiah; Virginia, 1690-1691 ***6212.30*** *p59*
Perrigo, Rebecca 25; Ontario, 1871 ***1823.28*** *p82*
Perriman, Henry 22; Maryland, 1774 ***1220.25*** *p84*
Perriman, Richard 33; Maryland, 1774 ***1220.25*** *p71*
Perrin, T.; Portland, Maine, 1857 ***9196.15*** *p13*
Perring, John 22; Philadelphia, 1774 ***1220.25*** *p3*
Perrini, P. 28; Alaska, 1912 ***9196.1*** *p38*
Perrini, P. 28; Whitehorse, Yukon, 1912 ***9196.1*** *p38*
Perris, Thomas 21; Philadelphia, 1774 ***1220.25*** *p67*
Perrisher, Charles 24; Ontario, 1871 ***1823.28*** *p82*
Perro, James 49; Ontario, 1871 ***1823.28*** *p82*
Perrogalli, Goetan; Pennsylvania, 1785 ***4629.10*** *p44*
Perroneau, Alexander; Charles Town, South Carolina, 1781 ***1224.2*** *p90*
Perroneau, Ann; Charles Town, South Carolina, 1787 ***1224.2*** *p90*
Perroneau, Henry; Charles Town, South Carolina, n.d. ***1224.2*** *p90*
Perroneau, Henry; Charles Town, South Carolina, 1755 ***1224.2*** *p90*
Perrot, Anthony Savimin; New York, 1830 ***8197.10*** *p362*
Perry, Mr.; Quebec, 1857 ***9196.15*** *p21*
Perry, Mrs.; Quebec, 1857 ***9196.15*** *p21*
Perry, Annie M. 75; Vermont, 1910 ***5900.10*** *p117*
Perry, Avery 64; Ontario, 1871 ***1823.22*** *p124*
Perry, Benj.; Pennsylvania, 1781 ***4629.10*** *p42*
Perry, C. P. 75; Ontario, 1871 ***1823.22*** *p124*
Perry, Constant; Maryland, 1677 ***2524.55*** *p171*
Perry, David; Pennsylvania, 1777 ***4629.10*** *p31*
Perry, George; Maryland, 1675 ***2524.55*** *p171*
Perry, George 18; Ontario, 1871 ***1823.15*** *p212*
Perry, George 23; Maryland, 1774 ***1220.25*** *p37*
Perry, Isaac 17; Philadelphia, 1774 ***1220.25*** *p63*
Perry, Jane McLaws; Salt Lake City, 1895 ***1640.13*** *p99*
Perry, John; Pennsylvania, 1868 ***6058.10*** *p64*
Perry, John; Vermont, 1838-1916 ***5900.10*** *p285*
Perry, John; Virginia, 1629 ***1224.1*** *p45*
Perry, John; Virginia, 1666-1667 ***6212.30*** *p34*
Perry, John 16; Maryland, 1774 ***1220.25*** *p6*
Perry, Joseph C. 59; Vermont, 1897 ***5900.10*** *p117*
Perry, Julia 79; Vermont, 1903 ***5900.10*** *p510*
Perry, Mary L. Breo; Vermont, 1843-1910 ***5900.10*** *p285*
Perry, Patrick 48; Ontario, 1871 ***1823.28*** *p82*
Perry, Peter; New York, 1803 ***8197.10*** *p15*
Perry, Robert; New York, 1827 ***1224.3*** *p60*
Perry, Robert; Virginia, 1652 ***1224.1*** *p45*
Perry, Robert 20; Virginia, 1774 ***1220.25*** *p89*
Perry, Robert 38; Ontario, 1871 ***1823.15*** *p212*
Perry, Robert D. 27; Ontario, 1871 ***1823.28*** *p82*
Perry, Sarah; Maryland, 1667 ***2524.55*** *p171*
Perry, Sarah; Maryland, 1677 ***2524.55*** *p171*
Perry, Thomas; Virginia, 1670 ***1224.1*** *p45*
Perry, William; New York, 1821 ***8197.10*** *p269*
Perry, William Henry; New York, 1812-1834 ***8197.10*** *p309*
Perry, Wm; Virginia, 1671-1672 ***6212.30*** *p47*
Perryman, Mary; Maryland, 1671 ***2524.55*** *p171*
Perryman, Thomas; Pennsylvania, 1807 ***1224.3*** *p60*
Perryn, Mr.; Quebec, 1857 ***9196.15*** *p14*
Perryn, Mrs.; Quebec, 1857 ***9196.15*** *p15*
Persch, Johann; Port uncertain, 1783 ***2856.30*** *p336*
Persch, Maria Eva; Port uncertain, 1751 ***2856.30*** *p336*
Persch, Mathias; Port uncertain, 1766 ***2856.30*** *p336*
Persett, Wm.; Maryland, 1641 ***2524.55*** *p171*
Persey, Abraham; Virginia, 1633 ***1224.1*** *p45*
Pershon, John; Pennsylvania, 1778 ***4629.10*** *p32*
Persick, John 24; Ontario, 1871 ***1823.28*** *p82*
Persick, Valente 67; Ontario, 1871 ***1823.28*** *p82*
Person, Andreas; Maryland, 1671 ***2524.55*** *p171*
Person, Andrew; Detroit, 1880 ***6688.10*** *p66*
Person, Charles; Maryland, 1673 ***2524.55*** *p171*
Person, Daniel; Maryland, 1681 ***2524.55*** *p171*
Person, S. H. 60; Ontario, 1871 ***1823.28*** *p82*
Person, Welle; Maryland, 1671 ***2524.55*** *p171*
Persons, Caroline 25; Ontario, 1871 ***1823.28*** *p82*
Persons, John; Maryland, 1682 ***2524.55*** *p171*
Persons, Mary E.; Vermont, 1858-1940 ***5900.10*** *p506*
Persons, Phillip; Virginia, 1664 ***6212.30*** *p9*
Persons, Wilbur; Vermont, 1851-1928 ***5900.10*** *p506*
Pert, James; Maryland, 1678 ***2524.55*** *p171*
Perth, Joseph 55; Ontario, 1871 ***1823.22*** *p124*
Pertnier, John; Maryland, 1665 ***2524.55*** *p129*
Pervey, Robert 41; Ontario, 1871 ***1823.28*** *p82*
Pervis, George 28; Ontario, 1871 ***1823.28*** *p82*
Peschier, Madam 25; Grenada, 1774-1775 ***1220.25*** *p128*
Peschier, John 31; Grenada, 1774-1775 ***1220.25*** *p128*
Pescod, Joseph 48; New York, 1775 ***1220.25*** *p142*
With wife & 5 children
Pessimout, Ann; Maryland, 1673 ***2524.55*** *p171*
Pessinger, Wuenafeld; New York, 1840 ***8197.10*** *p193*
Pesson, Jno; Virginia, 1664 ***6212.30*** *p15*
Pestana, Manuel; New York, 1807 ***8197.10*** *p47*
Pestiaux, Amedee; New York, 1838 ***8197.10*** *p127*
Pestle, William; Maryland, 1665 ***2524.55*** *p171*
Peston, Thomas; Virginia, 1664 ***6212.30*** *p15*
Peszozynska, Anton; Maryland, 1910 ***3259.35*** *p46*
Petchell, Tho; Virginia, 1664 ***6212.30*** *p15*
Petegrew, George 34; Ontario, 1871 ***1823.28*** *p82*
Petegrew, James 32; Ontario, 1871 ***1823.28*** *p82*
Petegrew, Mathew 26; Ontario, 1871 ***1823.28*** *p82*
Peteorski, Annie; Maryland, 1910 ***3259.35*** *p46*
Peter, Mr.; America, 1732 ***2856.30*** *p186*
Peter, Anna Maria; America, 1727 ***2856.30*** *p336*
With husband
Peter, Anna Maria; America, 1727 ***2856.30*** *p336*
Peter, Anna Martha; America, 1765 ***2856.30*** *p336*
Peter, Catharina; America, 1733 ***2856.30*** *p336*
With husband & son
Peter, Mrs. Gg. Phil.; America, 1752 ***2856.30*** *p336*
With 6 children
Peter, Hans, The Younger; America, 1732 ***2856.30*** *p336*
Peter, Hendrik; America, 1733 ***2856.30*** *p337*
With wife & son
Peter, Henrich; Port uncertain, 1752 ***2856.30*** *p336*
With wife
Peter, Jerg; America, 1727 ***2856.30*** *p337*
With wife & son
Peter, Josef; Port uncertain, 1765 ***2856.30*** *p337*
With wife & son
Peter, Palser; Baltimore, 1843 ***3437.14*** *p18*
Peter, Peter; Port uncertain, 1717 ***2856.30*** *p336*
Peter, Thomas; America, 1738 ***2856.30*** *p336*
Peter, Wilhelm; Port uncertain, 1788 ***2856.30*** *p336*
Peter, William; Philadelphia, 1853 ***1224.3*** *p60*
Peter, William 35; Ontario, 1871 ***1823.15*** *p212*
Peterkin, Alexander; Jamaica, 1775 ***1220.25*** *p133*
Peterkin, Anthony; Maryland, 1673 ***2524.55*** *p172*
Peterkin, Donald 52; Ontario, 1871 ***1823.22*** *p125*
Peterkin, Elizabeth 54; Ontario, 1871 ***1823.28*** *p82*
Peterkin, John; New York, 1839 ***8197.10*** *p272*
Peterkin, John 56; Ontario, 1871 ***1823.22*** *p125*
Petermann, Anna Maria; Port uncertain, 1777 ***2856.30*** *p337*
Petermann, E. Ackva *SEE* Petermann, Jakob
Petermann, Georg; Port uncertain, 1771 ***2856.30*** *p337*
Petermann, Jakob; America, 1773 ***2856.30*** *p337*
Wife: E. Ackva
Peters, Mr.; Quebec, 1858 ***9196.15*** *p38*
Peters, Catherine; Vermont, 1835-1895 ***5900.10*** *p89*
Peters, Charles 60; Ontario, 1871 ***1823.22*** *p125*
Peters, Edwin 34; Ontario, 1871 ***1823.22*** *p125*
Peters, Evelyn; Vermont, 1853-1955 ***5900.10*** *p556*
Peters, Forbes 25; Ontario, 1871 ***1823.28*** *p82*
Peters, Henry; Maryland, 1649 ***2524.55*** *p171*
Peters, Henry; Pennsylvania, 1777 ***4629.10*** *p9*
Peters, James; New York, 1831 ***8197.10*** *p355*
Peters, James 46; Ontario, 1871 ***1823.15*** *p212*
Peters, Janet; Mobile, Alabama, 1809-1845 ***1640.10*** *p170*
Peters, Jas; Quebec, 1856 ***9196.15*** *p11*
Peters, John; Canada, 1790 ***1224.2*** *p90*
Peters, John; New York, 1802 ***8197.10*** *p24*
Peters, John; New York, 1807 ***8197.10*** *p48*
Peters, John; Vermont, 1790 ***1224.2*** *p90*
Peters, John; Virginia, 1759 ***1224.2*** *p90*
Peters, John 57; Ontario, 1871 ***1823.15*** *p212*
Peters, Mary; Vermont, 1857-1930 ***5900.10*** *p89*
Peters, Randall; Maryland, 1672 ***2524.55*** *p172*
Peters, Reese; Pennsylvania, 1777 ***4629.10*** *p14*
Peters, Richard; Pennsylvania, 1777 ***4629.10*** *p8*
Peters, Thomas; Pennsylvania, 1777 ***4629.10*** *p10*
Peters, Thomas; Pennsylvania, 1777 ***4629.10*** *p26*
Peters, Thomas; Pennsylvania, 1779 ***4629.10*** *p38*
Peters, William 15; Virginia, 1774 ***1220.25*** *p90*
Peters, William 39; Ontario, 1871 ***1823.22*** *p125*
Petersen, A.; Illinois, 1900 ***6688.10*** *p34*
Petersen, A.; Iowa, 1860 ***6688.10*** *p34*
Petersen, A.; Iowa, 1880 ***6688.10*** *p34*
Petersen, A. G.; New York, 1868 ***6688.10*** *p35*
Petersen, A. L.; Iowa, 1880 ***6688.10*** *p35*
Petersen, A. T.; Iowa, 1860 ***6688.10*** *p35*
Petersen, Andrew P.; New York, 1881 ***6688.10*** *p37*
Petersen, Eric Eiegod; New York, 1827 ***8197.10*** *p337*
Petersen, George Christopher; New York, 1825 ***8197.10*** *p270*
Petersen, George Christopher; New York, 1827 ***8197.10*** *p337*
Petersen, John 34; British Columbia, 1911 ***9196.1*** *p35*
Petersen, John 34; Seattle, 1911 ***9196.1*** *p35*
Petersen, Ole 32; British Columbia, 1911 ***9196.1*** *p35*
Petersen, Ole 32; Washington, 1911 ***9196.1*** *p35*
Petersheim, Anton; America, 1749 ***2856.30*** *p337*
Peterson, A.; Illinois, 1872 ***6688.10*** *p34*
Peterson, A.; Illinois, 1876 ***6688.10*** *p34*
Peterson, A.; Illinois, 1880 ***6688.10*** *p34*
Peterson, A.; Illinois, 1888 ***6688.10*** *p34*
Peterson, A.; Illinois, 1900 ***6688.10*** *p36*
Peterson, A.; Iowa, 1857 ***6688.10*** *p36*
Peterson, A.; Iowa, 1860 ***6688.10*** *p36*
Peterson, A.; Iowa, 1891 ***6688.10*** *p34*
Peterson, A.; New York, 1884 ***6688.10*** *p36*
Peterson, A. C.; Illinois, 1880 ***6688.10*** *p36*
Peterson, A. D.; Illinois, 1875 ***6688.10*** *p36*
Peterson, A. E.; Illinois, 1873 ***6688.10*** *p36*
Peterson, A. F.; Illinois, 1878 ***6688.10*** *p35*
Peterson, A. F.; Iowa, 1875 ***6688.10*** *p35*
Peterson, A. G.; Illinois, 1856-1900 ***6688.10*** *p35*
Peterson, A. Gustave; Illinois, 1890 ***6688.10*** *p35*
Peterson, A. H.; Wisconsin, 1856 ***6688.10*** *p36*
Peterson, A. John; Iowa, 1890 ***6688.10*** *p36*
Peterson, A. John; Iowa, 1892 ***6688.10*** *p35*
Peterson, A. L.; Illinois, 1890 ***6688.10*** *p35*
Peterson, A. P.; Iowa, 1886 ***6688.10*** *p35*
Peterson, A. R.; Iowa, 1878 ***6688.10*** *p35*
Peterson, A. V.; Illinois, 1886 ***6688.10*** *p35*
Peterson, A. Victor; Illinois, 1893 ***6688.10*** *p61*
Peterson, A. W.; Illinois, 1888 ***6688.10*** *p61*
Peterson, Abaraham W. 13; Ontario, 1861 ***2896.27*** *p12*
Peterson, Amelia 32; Kansas, 1892-1910 ***9079.10*** *p6*
Peterson, Anders; Illinois, 1894 ***6688.10*** *p66*
Peterson, Anders; New York, 1874 ***6688.10*** *p61*
Peterson, Anders; New York, 1881 ***6688.10*** *p61*
Peterson, Anders Johan; Illinois, 1879-1900 ***6688.10*** *p61*
Peterson, Anders Y.; Illinois, 1888 ***6688.10*** *p62*
Peterson, Andreas; Boston, 1873 ***6688.10*** *p62*
Peterson, Andres; Illinois, 1875 ***6688.10*** *p62*
Peterson, Andrew *SEE* Peterson, Cornelius
Peterson, Andrew; Boston, 1846-1880 ***6688.10*** *p62*
Peterson, Andrew; DeKalb Co., Illinois, 1891 ***6688.10*** *p64*
Peterson, Andrew; Detroit, 1880 ***6688.10*** *p66*
Peterson, Andrew; Dubuque Co., Iowa, 1877 ***6688.10*** *p39*
Peterson, Andrew; Illinois, 1870 ***6688.10*** *p63*
Peterson, Andrew; Illinois, 1872 ***6688.10*** *p63*
Peterson, Andrew; Illinois, 1872 ***6688.10*** *p64*
Peterson, Andrew; Illinois, 1872 ***6688.10*** *p65*
Peterson, Andrew; Illinois, 1874 ***6688.10*** *p39*
Peterson, Andrew; Illinois, 1875 ***6688.10*** *p39*
Peterson, Andrew; Illinois, 1875 ***6688.10*** *p63*
Peterson, Andrew; Illinois, 1875 ***6688.10*** *p64*
Peterson, Andrew; Illinois, 1876 ***6688.10*** *p39*
Peterson, Andrew; Illinois, 1876 ***6688.10*** *p40*
Peterson, Andrew; Illinois, 1876 ***6688.10*** *p63*
Peterson, Andrew; Illinois, 1876 ***6688.10*** *p64*
Peterson, Andrew; Illinois, 1877 ***6688.10*** *p62*
Peterson, Andrew; Illinois, 1879 ***6688.10*** *p40*
Peterson, Andrew; Illinois, 1880 ***6688.10*** *p62*
Peterson, Andrew; Illinois, 1880 ***6688.10*** *p66*
Peterson, Andrew; Illinois, 1881 ***6688.10*** *p62*
Peterson, Andrew; Illinois, 1882 ***6688.10*** *p38*
Peterson, Andrew; Illinois, 1882 ***6688.10*** *p40*
Peterson, Andrew; Illinois, 1884 ***6688.10*** *p40*
Peterson, Andrew; Illinois, 1884 ***6688.10*** *p64*

Peterson, Andrew; Illinois, 1886 6688.10 p64
Peterson, Andrew; Illinois, 1886 6688.10 p65
Peterson, Andrew; Illinois, 1887 6688.10 p39
Peterson, Andrew; Illinois, 1887 6688.10 p64
Peterson, Andrew; Illinois, 1888 6688.10 p39
Peterson, Andrew; Illinois, 1888 6688.10 p40
Peterson, Andrew; Illinois, 1888 6688.10 p61
Peterson, Andrew; Illinois, 1888 6688.10 p62
Peterson, Andrew; Illinois, 1888 6688.10 p63
Peterson, Andrew; Illinois, 1888 6688.10 p64
Peterson, Andrew; Illinois, 1888 6688.10 p65
Peterson, Andrew; Illinois, 1889 6688.10 p63
Peterson, Andrew; Illinois, 1889 6688.10 p65
Peterson, Andrew; Illinois, 1890 6688.10 p63
Peterson, Andrew; Illinois, 1890 6688.10 p65
Peterson, Andrew; Illinois, 1891 6688.10 p64
Peterson, Andrew; Illinois, 1891 6688.10 p65
Peterson, Andrew; Illinois, 1892 6688.10 p39
Peterson, Andrew; Illinois, 1892 6688.10 p62
Peterson, Andrew; Illinois, 1892 6688.10 p65
Peterson, Andrew; Illinois, 1894 6688.10 p40
Peterson, Andrew; Illinois, 1894 6688.10 p62
Peterson, Andrew; Illinois, 1894 6688.10 p63
Peterson, Andrew; Illinois, 1894 6688.10 p65
Peterson, Andrew; Illinois, 1895 6688.10 p65
Peterson, Andrew; Illinois, 1896 6688.10 p62
Peterson, Andrew; Iowa, 1874 6688.10 p39
Peterson, Andrew; Iowa, 1875 6688.10 p38
Peterson, Andrew; Iowa, 1876 6688.10 p39
Peterson, Andrew; Iowa, 1886 6688.10 p38
Peterson, Andrew; Iowa, 1887 6688.10 p38
Peterson, Andrew; Iowa, 1891 6688.10 p39
Peterson, Andrew 21; Alaska, 1913 9196.1 p23
Peterson, Andrew 21; British Columbia, 1913 9196.1 p23
Peterson, Andrew F.; Illinois, 1876 6688.10 p39
Peterson, Andrew F.; Illinois, 1888 6688.10 p38
Peterson, Andrew G.; Illinois, 1876 6688.10 p38
Peterson, Andrew G.; Illinois, 1880 6688.10 p37
Peterson, Andrew G.; Illinois, 1889 6688.10 p37
Peterson, Andrew G.; Iowa, 1875 6688.10 p38
Peterson, Andrew Gust; Illinois, 1876 6688.10 p38
Peterson, Andrew Gustaf; Illinois, 1889 6688.10 p38
Peterson, Andrew J.; Illinois, 1885 6688.10 p38
Peterson, Andrew J.; Indiana, 1884 6688.10 p37
Peterson, Andrew L.; Illinois, 1890 6688.10 p37
Peterson, Andrew M.; Illinois, 1876 6688.10 p37
Peterson, Andrew P.; America, 1869 6688.10 p37
Peterson, Andrew P.; Illinois, 1875 6688.10 p37
Peterson, Andrew P.; Illinois, 1879 6688.10 p37
Peterson, Andrew P.; Illinois, 1884 6688.10 p37
Peterson, Andrew P.; Illinois, 1888 6688.10 p37
Peterson, Andrew P.; New York, 1881 6688.10 p37
Peterson, Andrew W.; Illinois, 1882 6688.10 p36
Peterson, Androw M.; Illinois, 1876 6688.10 p36
Peterson, Anthony; Maryland, 1673 2524.55 p172
Peterson, Bridget E. Ferran; Vermont, 1836-1912 5900.10 p341
Peterson, Catherine E. 3; Ontario, 1861 2896.25 p22
Peterson, Charles; New York, 1826 8197.10 p270
Peterson, Cornelius; Maryland, 1664 2524.55 p172
  Brother: Andrew
  Sister: Earee
Peterson, E. 25; Alaska, 1912 9196.1 p39
Peterson, E. 25; Whitehorse, Yukon, 1912 9196.1 p39
Peterson, Earee *SEE* Peterson, Cornelius
Peterson, Elizabeth 39; Ontario, 1861 2896.25 p43
Peterson, Emily 11; Ontario, 1861 2896.25 p22
Peterson, Emily J. 20; Ontario, 1861 2896.28 p37
Peterson, F. E. 14; Ontario, 1861 2896.25 p43
Peterson, George; New York, 1839 8197.10 p138
Peterson, Gilbert; Virginia, 1724 1224.2 p90
Peterson, H. 28; Alaska, 1917 9196.1 p46
Peterson, H. 28; Whitehorse, Yukon, 1917 9196.1 p46
Peterson, Hans; New York, 1827 8197.10 p346
Peterson, Harold; British Columbia, 1910 9196.1 p15
Peterson, Harold; San Francisco, 1910 9196.1 p15
Peterson, Henry 43; Ontario, 1861 2896.27 p12
Peterson, Hiram 9; Ontario, 1861 2896.27 p14
Peterson, Jacob; Maryland, 1677 2524.55 p169
Peterson, Jacob E. 13; Ontario, 1861 2896.25 p22
Peterson, James W. 18; Ontario, 1861 2896.25 p43
Peterson, Jane Ann 28; Ontario, 1861 2896.25 p43
Peterson, John; New York, 1807 8197.10 p328
Peterson, John 43; British Columbia, 1909 9196.1 p28
Peterson, John 43; Washington, 1909 9196.1 p28
Peterson, John A. 15; Ontario, 1861 2896.25 p22
Peterson, M. 80; Ontario, 1861 2896.26 p9
Peterson, Manson 5; Ontario, 1861 2896.25 p22
Peterson, Margaret; Maryland, 1667 2524.55 p172
  Son: Peter
Peterson, Margaret 64; Ontario, 1861 2896.25 p43
Peterson, Mary 42; Ontario, 1861 2896.27 p14
Peterson, Mathias; Maryland, 1665 2524.55 p172
Peterson, N. A. 32; Ontario, 1861 2896.25 p43
Peterson, Nancy 17; Ontario, 1861 2896.25 p43
Peterson, Nicholas; New York, 1803 8197.10 p15
Peterson, Oliver 10; Ontario, 1861 2896.27 p14
Peterson, Peter *SEE* Peterson, Margaret
Peterson, Peter; Maryland, 1666 2524.55 p172
Peterson, Peter; Virginia, 1672 6212.30 p51
Peterson, Peter J. 17; Ontario, 1861 2896.25 p22
Peterson, Ransom 5; Ontario, 1861 2896.25 p22
Peterson, Robert; New York, 1837 8197.10 p101
Peterson, Robert H. 10; Ontario, 1861 2896.25 p24
Peterson, Robert N. 10; Ontario, 1861 2896.25 p22
Peterson, S. W. 26; Ontario, 1861 2896.25 p43
Peterson, Sarah 41; Ontario, 1861 2896.27 p12
Peterson, Sarah M. 1; Ontario, 1861 2896.27 p14
Peterson, William; Vermont, 1834-1906 5900.10 p341
Peterson, William 2; Ontario, 1861 2896.28 p37
Peterson, William A. 8; Ontario, 1861 2896.27 p12
Peterson, William Asa 18; Ontario, 1861 2896.25 p22
Pether, Mary 21; America, 1774 1220.25 p37
Petherick, Daniel 24; Ontario, 1871 1823.22 p125
Petherick, Daniel 57; Ontario, 1871 1823.22 p125
Petherick, William 58; Ontario, 1871 1823.22 p125
Pethero, Ann 28; Ontario, 1861 2896.27 p17
Pethick, Elizabeth 36; Ontario, 1871 1823.15 p212
Petifer, Mary; Savannah, Georgia, 1775 1224.2 p88
Petit, Mrs.; Maryland, 1642 2524.55 p172
Petit, Abraham Clement; Maryland, 1668 2524.55 p172
  Wife: Jertsuyt
  Daughter: Rachel
  Daughter: Barbary
Petit, Barbary *SEE* Petit, Abraham Clement
Petit, Jertsuyt *SEE* Petit, Abraham Clement
Petit, Rachel *SEE* Petit, Abraham Clement
Petit, Thomas; Maryland, 1641 2524.55 p172
  With wife
Petite, Catherine; Maryland, 1645 2524.55 p172
Petite, Thomas; Maryland, 1639 2524.55 p169
Petoe, Humphrey; Maryland, 1670 2524.55 p172
Petoe, Humphry; Maryland, 1674 2524.55 p172
Petri, Mrs.; Port uncertain, 1752 2856.30 p337
Petri, Catharina; Port uncertain, 1785 2856.30 p337
Petri, Franz; Port uncertain, 1749 2856.30 p337
Petri, Franziska; Port uncertain, 1764 2856.30 p337
Petri, Jakob; Port uncertain, 1747 2856.30 p337
Petri, Johann Jakob; Port uncertain, 1733 2856.30 p337
Petri, John William; New York, 1826 8197.10 p270
Petri, Jonas; Port uncertain, 1775 2856.30 p337
Petri, Man Philip; America, 1743 2856.30 p337
Petri, Margarete; Port uncertain, 1788 2856.30 p337
Petri, Maria Catharina; Port uncertain, 1775 2856.30 p337
Petri, Mathes; Port uncertain, 1733 2856.30 p337
Petri, Nickel; America, 1749 2856.30 p337
Petri, Nickel; England, 1756 2856.30 p337
Petri, Valentin; America, 1749 2856.30 p337
Petrie, Ann Perroneau; Charles Town, South Carolina, 1787 1224.2 p90
Petrie, Frederick Henry; Virginia, 1846 1224.3 p60
Petrie, James 20; Ontario, 1871 1823.15 p212
Petrie, John; New York, 1840 8197.10 p192
Petrie, John; Virginia, 1672 6212.30 p49
Petrie, John 30; Tobago, West Indies, 1775 1220.25 p129
Petrie, Peter; Savannah, Georgia, 1774 1640.10 p170
Petroski, Theodore; Maryland, 1910 3259.35 p46
Petrosky, Frank; Maryland, 1910 3259.35 p47
Petrosska, Kasimer; Maryland, 1910 3259.35 p47
Petrovich, M. 26; Alaska, 1916 9196.1 p44
Petrovich, M. 26; Whitehorse, Yukon, 1916 9196.1 p44
Petrowicz, Joe; Maryland, 1910 3259.35 p47
Petrowitz, Stanislaus; Maryland, 1910 3259.35 p47
Petry, Mr.; Quebec, 1858 9196.15 p36
Petry, Mr.; Port uncertain, 1787 2856.30 p338
Petry, Mr.; Port uncertain, 1788 2856.30 p338
Petry, A. H.; Quebec, 1858 9196.15 p38
Petry, Johann Michael; New York, 1837 8197.10 p100
Petsch, Mr.; America, 1764 2856.30 p71
Petsch, Anna Maria; America, 1764 2856.30 p338
Petsch, Johann Georg; Port uncertain, 1751 2856.30 p338
Petsch, Paul; America, 1764 2856.30 p338
  With wife & 4 children
Petshotski, Mike; Maryland, 1910 3259.35 p47
Pett, George; Maryland, 1681 2524.55 p172
Pett, Peter; Virginia, 1664 6212.30 p13
Pett, Peter; Virginia, 1665-1666 6212.30 p21
Pett, Thomas; Maryland, 1635 2524.55 p172
Pettengell, Frederick; South Carolina, 1843 1224.3 p60
Pettengell, William Henn; South Carolina, 1843 1224.3 p61
Pettenger, George 42; Ontario, 1871 1823.15 p212
Petter, Robert; New York, 1828 8197.10 p349
Petters, Christopher; Virginia, 1671-1672 6212.30 p45
Pettersen, Anders John; Illinois, 1887 6688.10 p61
Petterson, Anders; Illinois, 1896 6688.10 p66
Petterson, Andreas; Illinois, 1886 6688.10 p61
Petterson, Andrew; Illinois, 1876 6688.10 p38
Petterson, Andrew; Illinois, 1882 6688.10 p38
Petterson, Andrew; Illinois, 1888 6688.10 p65
Petterson, Andrew J.; Illinois, 1884 6688.10 p38
Petterson, Andrew P.; Illinois, 1888 6688.10 p37
Petterson, Gilbert; Virginia, 1724 1224.2 p90
Pettes, Catherine; Vermont, 1831-1910 5900.10 p594
Pettes, Fredrick; Vermont, 1831-1907 5900.10 p594
Pettet, Phebe 65; Ontario, 1871 1823.22 p125
Pettey, William 53; Ontario, 1871 1823.22 p125
Pettibone, James 60; Ontario, 1871 1823.22 p125
Pettigrew, James; New York, 1837 8197.10 p101
Pettigrew, John; Georgia, 1757 1640.10 p170
Pettigrew, Robert; New York, 1826 8197.10 p334
Pettigrew, Robert 56; Ontario, 1871 1823.22 p125
Pettingall, Arnet 55; Ontario, 1861 2896.28 p23
Pettingall, Charles 23; Ontario, 1861 2896.28 p23
Pettingall, Ellen 23; Ontario, 1861 2896.28 p25
Pettingall, Hannah 1; Ontario, 1861 2896.28 p25
Pettingall, Henry M. 17; Ontario, 1861 2896.28 p23
Pettingall, Margery 19; Ontario, 1861 2896.28 p23
Pettingall, Martin 70; Ontario, 1861 2896.28 p23
Pettingall, Mary J. 13; Ontario, 1861 2896.28 p23
Pettingall, Mellville 20; Ontario, 1861 2896.28 p25
Pettingall, Phila A. 10; Ontario, 1861 2896.28 p23
Pettingall, Robert 19; Ontario, 1861 2896.28 p23
Pettingall, Susan 60; Ontario, 1861 2896.28 p23
Pettingell, E. 24; Ontario, 1861 2896.26 p3
Pettingell, W. G. 3; Ontario, 1861 2896.26 p3
Pettinger, John; New York, New York, 1820 1224.3 p61
Pettingill, Amanda 23; Ontario, 1861 2896.28 p26
Pettingill, Wm 24; Ontario, 1861 2896.28 p26
Pettipoole, Ann *SEE* Pettipoole, William
Pettipoole, William *SEE* Pettipoole, William
Pettipoole, William; Maryland, 1665 2524.55 p172
  Wife: Ann
  Son: William
Pettis, Henry; Virginia, 1665-1666 6212.30 p21
Pettit, Agnes 13; Ontario, 1861 2896.27 p30
Pettit, Amanda 34; Ontario, 1861 2896.28 p24
Pettit, Amanda 39; Ontario, 1861 2896.27 p69
Pettit, Anna Mary 4; Ontario, 1861 2896.28 p24
Pettit, Anne 26; Ontario, 1861 2896.27 p43
Pettit, Daniel H. 14; Ontario, 1861 2896.27 p27
Pettit, Dorcas 42; Ontario, 1861 2896.27 p27
Pettit, Elisa 57; Ontario, 1861 2896.27 p69
Pettit, Emma 6; Ontario, 1861 2896.28 p44
Pettit, Emma F. 2; Ontario, 1861 2896.27 p37
Pettit, Frances H. 10; Ontario, 1861 2896.27 p27
Pettit, Freeman 7; Ontario, 1861 2896.28 p24
Pettit, Hannah 53; Ontario, 1861 2896.28 p46
Pettit, Harriet E. 17; Ontario, 1861 2896.28 p43
Pettit, Henry A. 15; Ontario, 1861 2896.27 p69
Pettit, Hiram; Ontario, 1861 2896.28 p43
Pettit, Isaac; Ontario, 1861 2896.28 p45
Pettit, James; New York, 1821 8197.10 p269
Pettit, James; New York, 1840 8197.10 p272
Pettit, Jane 5; Ontario, 1861 2896.27 p37
Pettit, Joseph 8; Ontario, 1861 2896.27 p43
Pettit, Margaret 24; Ontario, 1861 2896.28 p43
Pettit, Mary 8; Ontario, 1861 2896.27 p37
Pettit, Mary A. 7; Ontario, 1861 2896.28 p43
Pettit, Mary Ann 40; Ontario, 1861 2896.28 p43
Pettit, Mary S. 17; Ontario, 1861 2896.27 p27
Pettit, Miles 21; Ontario, 1861 2896.27 p37
Pettit, Patrick; New York, 1833 8197.10 p271
Pettit, Phebe 4; Ontario, 1861 2896.27 p43
Pettit, Phebe 15; Ontario, 1861 2896.27 p27
Pettit, Phebe 27; Ontario, 1861 2896.28 p44
Pettit, Phebe 52; Ontario, 1861 2896.28 p25
Pettit, Philip 22; Ontario, 1861 2896.27 p29
Pettit, Phoebe 53; Ontario, 1861 2896.27 p37
Pettit, Phoebe J. 17; Ontario, 1861 2896.27 p30
Pettit, Ruby F. 4; Ontario, 1861 2896.28 p43
Pettit, Sally 37; Ontario, 1861 2896.27 p37
Pettit, Samuel 1; Ontario, 1861 2896.27 p43
Pettit, Sarah 7; Ontario, 1861 2896.27 p27
Pettit, Sarah 66; Ontario, 1861 2896.28 p44
Pettit, Sylvanus 8; Ontario, 1861 2896.27 p27
Pettit, Sylvanus 57; Ontario, 1861 2896.27 p37
Pettit, Thomas; New York, 1838 8197.10 p146
Pettit, Thomas; Virginia, 1663 6212.30 p3
Pettit, William 3; Ontario, 1861 2896.27 p27
Pettit, Willis M. 8; Ontario, 1861 2896.28 p43
Pettit, Wm James 3; Ontario, 1861 2896.28 p44
Pettitt, Tho; Virginia, 1672 6212.30 p49
Petty, Francis; Died enroute, 1693 1224.1 p45
Petty, George 45; Ontario, 1871 1823.15 p212
Petty, John 25; Grenada, 1774 1220.25 p58

Petty, John 50; Ontario, 1871 ***1823.15*** *p212*
Petty, William 60; Ontario, 1871 ***1823.22*** *p125*
Pettycoate, John; Maryland, 1674 ***2524.55*** *p172*
Pettygrove, Jesse 51; Ontario, 1871 ***1823.22*** *p125*
Pettyt, J. P. 30; Maryland, 1775 ***1220.25*** *p114*
Peuscher, George; New York, 1835 ***8197.10*** *p310*
Pevenor, Alex 40; Ontario, 1871 ***1823.15*** *p212*
Pever, James 35; Ontario, 1871 ***1823.28*** *p82*
Pever, James 68; Ontario, 1871 ***1823.28*** *p82*
Pever, John 33; Ontario, 1871 ***1823.28*** *p82*
Pever, Robert 34; Ontario, 1871 ***1823.28*** *p82*
Pevie, Rich; Virginia, 1672 ***6212.30*** *p49*
Pew, Elias; Pennsylvania, 1777 ***4629.10*** *p21*
Pew, George; New York, 1840 ***8197.10*** *p192*
Pew, Margret; Virginia, 1703-1704 ***6212.30*** *p62*
Pewell, Ursula; Maryland, 1672 ***2524.55*** *p172*
Pexson, Walter; Maryland, 1662 ***2524.55*** *p172*
Peye, Anne; Virginia, 1671-1672 ***6212.30*** *p46*
Peytecote, James; Maryland, 1670 ***2524.55*** *p172*
Peyton, Henry; New York, 1838 ***8197.10*** *p146*
Pezwol, John; Maryland, 1910 ***3259.35*** *p47*
Pfaff, Conrad 40; Ontario, 1871 ***1823.15*** *p212*
Pfaff, Henry 43; Ontario, 1871 ***1823.15*** *p212*
Pfaff, Henry 49; Ontario, 1871 ***1823.15*** *p212*
Pfaff, Johann; Port uncertain, 1744 ***2856.30*** *p338*
Pfaff, Johann Theobald; Port uncertain, 1770 ***2856.30*** *p338*
Pfaff, John 52; Ontario, 1871 ***1823.15*** *p212*
Pfaff, Ursula 77; Ontario, 1871 ***1823.15*** *p212*
Pfaffenberg, Georg; America, 1733 ***2856.30*** *p338*
With wife & children
Pfahl, Lorenz; America, 1771 ***2856.30*** *p338*
Pfahl, Lorenz; America, 1789 ***2856.30*** *p338*
Pfaltzgraf, Peter; New York, 1806 ***8197.10*** *p323*
Pfalzer, Georg; Port uncertain, 1784 ***2856.30*** *p338*
Pfalzgraf, Georg; America, 1784 ***2856.30*** *p338*
Pfalzgraf, Jakob; America, 1784 ***2856.30*** *p338*
Pfalzgraf, Peter; Port uncertain, 1752 ***2856.30*** *p338*
Pfalzgraf, Peter; Port uncertain, 1764 ***2856.30*** *p338*
Pfalztrager, Philipp; Port uncertain, 1791 ***2856.30*** *p338*
Pfander, Andreas; Port uncertain, 1748 ***2856.30*** *p341*
Pfannenbecker, Lothar; America, 1749 ***2856.30*** *p338*
Pfarr, Friedrich; Port uncertain, 1763 ***2856.30*** *p338*
Pfass, Johann; Port uncertain, 1744 ***2856.30*** *p338*
Pfautz, Hans Michael; America, 1727 ***2856.30*** *p338*
Pfautz, Hans Michael; America, 1727 ***2856.30*** *p339*
Pfautz, Hans Michael; America, 1737 ***2856.30*** *p338*
Pfautz, Johann Georg; Port uncertain, 1744 ***2856.30*** *p338*
Pfeffel, Peter Carl; New York, 1842 ***1224.3*** *p61*
Pfeffel, Peter Charles; New York, 1839 ***8197.10*** *p272*
Pfeffer, Anna Maria; Port uncertain, 1751 ***2856.30*** *p339*
Pfeifer, George; New York, 1837 ***8197.10*** *p101*
Pfeifer, Martin; Port uncertain, 1754 ***2856.30*** *p339*
Pfeifer, Mathias; Port uncertain, 1744 ***2856.30*** *p339*
Pfeifer, Mathias; Port uncertain, 1784 ***2856.30*** *p339*
Pfeifer, Wilhelm; Port uncertain, 1788 ***2856.30*** *p339*
Pfeiffer, Cath. Elisabeth; Port uncertain, 1781 ***2856.30*** *p339*
Pfeiffer, Catharina; America, 1749 ***2856.30*** *p340*
Pfeiffer, Catharina; Port uncertain, 1794 ***2856.30*** *p339*
Pfeiffer, Elisabeth; Port uncertain, 1747 ***2856.30*** *p339*
Pfeiffer, Franz Josef; Port uncertain, 1792 ***2856.30*** *p339*
Pfeiffer, Franziska; Port uncertain, 1772 ***2856.30*** *p339*
Pfeiffer, Friedrich; New York, 1837 ***8197.10*** *p100*
Pfeiffer, Hans Adam; Port uncertain, 1751 ***2856.30*** *p339*
With children
Pfeiffer, Hans Adam; Port uncertain, 1769 ***2856.30*** *p339*
Pfeiffer, Jacob; America, 1737 ***2856.30*** *p339*
With wife
Pfeiffer, Jacob; America, 1741 ***2856.30*** *p339*
Pfeiffer, Johann; Port uncertain, 1747 ***2856.30*** *p339*
Pfeiffer, Karl; Port uncertain, 1783 ***2856.30*** *p339*
With wife & 4 daughters
Pfeiffer, Karl; Port uncertain, 1786 ***2856.30*** *p339*
With wife & 4 daughters
Pfeiffer, Maria Elisabeth; Port uncertain, 1776 ***2856.30*** *p339*
Pfeiffer, Mathias; Port uncertain, 1784 ***2856.30*** *p339*
Pfeiffer, Mathis; Port uncertain, 1736 ***2856.30*** *p339*
Pfeiffer, Mathis; Port uncertain, 1769 ***2856.30*** *p339*
Pfeiffer, Michael; America, 1745 ***2856.30*** *p339*
Pfeiffer, Michael; Port uncertain, 1741 ***2856.30*** *p339*
Pfeiffer, Mrs. Peter; Port uncertain, 1744 ***2856.30*** *p339*
Pfeiffer, Philipp; Port uncertain, 1784 ***2856.30*** *p339*
Pfeifferin, Catharina; America, 1749 ***2856.30*** *p340*
Pfeil, Catharina; Port uncertain, 1787 ***2856.30*** *p340*
Pfeil, Catharina Munster; Port uncertain, 1787 ***2856.30*** *p318*
Pfeil, Friedrich; Port uncertain, 1742 ***2856.30*** *p340*
Pfeil, Hans Matthaus; America, 1736 ***2856.30*** *p340*
With wife
Pfeil, Heinrich; Port uncertain, 1788 ***2856.30*** *p340*
Pfeil, Henry 42; Ontario, 1871 ***1823.15*** *p212*
Pfeil, Johann; America, 1741 ***2856.30*** *p340*
Pfeil, Johann; Port uncertain, 1776 ***2856.30*** *p340*
Pfeil, Maria Elisabeth; Port uncertain, 1756 ***2856.30*** *p340*
Pfeil, Mathias; America, 1733 ***2856.30*** *p340*
With wife
Pfeil, Mathias; America, 1737 ***2856.30*** *p340*
Pfeill, Hans Matthaus; America, 1737 ***2856.30*** *p341*
Pfenninger, Anna Elisabeth; Port uncertain, 1793 ***2856.30*** *p340*
Pfetsch, A.; America, 1790 ***2856.30*** *p227*
Pfetsch, Anna; America, 1790 ***2856.30*** *p340*
With husband
Pfetsch, Christina; America, 1752 ***2856.30*** *p340*
With husband & daughter
Pfetsch, Christina; America, 1752 ***2856.30*** *p340*
Husband: Freym.
With daughter
Pfetsch, Freym. *SEE* Pfetsch, Christina
Pfetsch, Georg; America, 1752 ***2856.30*** *p340*
Pfhal, John Otto; Seattle, 1917 ***9196.1*** *p57*
Pfhal, John Otto; Victoria, British Columbia, 1917 ***9196.1*** *p57*
Pfifer, Yan; Maryland, 1910 ***3259.35*** *p47*
Pfirrmann, Charles; New York, 1840 ***8197.10*** *p272*
Pfister, Jacob; Port uncertain, 1770 ***2856.30*** *p340*
Pfisterer, Hans Adam; Port uncertain, 1750 ***2856.30*** *p340*
With wife & 5 children
Pfisterer, Jacob; Port uncertain, 1761 ***2856.30*** *p340*
Pfistner, Jacob; Port uncertain, 1761 ***2856.30*** *p340*
Pfitzer, Henrich; Port uncertain, 1764 ***2856.30*** *p340*
Pfleger, Michael; Port uncertain, 1802 ***2856.30*** *p340*
Pfleger, Michael; Port uncertain, 1805 ***2856.30*** *p340*
Pflieger, Anna Maria; America, 1751 ***2856.30*** *p340*
With husband
Pflieger, Anna Maria; America, 1757 ***2856.30*** *p340*
With wife
Pfliehinger, Peter; America, 1787 ***2856.30*** *p340*
Pflug, Aurelius; Port uncertain, 1764 ***2856.30*** *p340*
Pflug, Aurelius; Port uncertain, 1794 ***2856.30*** *p340*
Pflug, Johann Adam; Port uncertain, 1754 ***2856.30*** *p340*
Pflug, Josef; Port uncertain, 1764 ***2856.30*** *p340*
Pflug, Josef; Port uncertain, 1794 ***2856.30*** *p340*
Pfluger, Hans; America, 1752 ***2856.30*** *p340*
Pfluger, John Jacob; New York, 1839 ***8197.10*** *p272*
Pfluger, Sebastian; Port uncertain, 1785 ***2856.30*** *p340*
Pfluger, Simon; Port uncertain, 1764 ***2856.30*** *p340*
Pflukus, Friedrich; New York, 1837 ***8197.10*** *p100*
Pfoersch, Henrich; New York, 1834 ***8197.10*** *p319*
Pfohl, Cath. Sybilla; Port uncertain, 1751 ***2856.30*** *p341*
Pfohlin, Cath. Sybilla; Port uncertain, 1751 ***2856.30*** *p341*
Pfordt, Peter; Port uncertain, 1760 ***2856.30*** *p341*
Pfotrer, George; New York, 1832 ***8197.10*** *p271*
Pfrang, Georg, The Older; America, 1764 ***2856.30*** *p341*
With wife & 4 children
Pfrommer, Gottlieb Friedrich; New York, 1839 ***8197.10*** *p271*
Pfrommer, Philip; New York, 1839 ***8197.10*** *p271*
Pfundheller, Lorenz; Port uncertain, 1770 ***2856.30*** *p341*
Pfundheller, Lorenz; Port uncertain, 1781 ***2856.30*** *p341*
Pfunter, Barbara; Port uncertain, 1772 ***2856.30*** *p341*
Phailen, John 26; Ontario, 1871 ***1823.28*** *p82*
Phailen, Philip 37; Ontario, 1871 ***1823.15*** *p212*
Phain, Francis 16; Maryland, 1775 ***1220.25*** *p107*
Phair, Edward 45; Ontario, 1871 ***1823.15*** *p212*
Phair, William 44; Ontario, 1871 ***1823.15*** *p212*
Phalan, Timothy 21; Maryland, 1774 ***1220.25*** *p59*
Phalen, Annie Bowen 54; Vermont, 1893 ***5900.10*** *p214*
Phalen, Catherine; Vermont, 1870-1873 ***5900.10*** *p579*
Phalen, Ellen; Vermont, 1851-1905 ***5900.10*** *p532*
Phalen, Margaret; Vermont, 1864-1951 ***5900.10*** *p394*
Phalen, Mary 66; Vermont, 1874 ***5900.10*** *p384*
Phalen, Mary A.; Vermont, 1857-1940 ***5900.10*** *p579*
Phalen, Mathew; Vermont, 1891-1963 ***5900.10*** *p579*
Phalen, Michael 45; Vermont, 1849 ***5900.10*** *p384*
Phalen, Patrick 56; Vermont, 1893 ***5900.10*** *p214*
Phalen, Sarah; Vermont, 1849-1932 ***5900.10*** *p218*
Phaup, Benjamin 38; Philadelphia, 1774 ***1220.25*** *p67*
Phealan, Michael; New York, 1837 ***8197.10*** *p319*
Phealan, Michael; New York, 1840 ***8197.10*** *p192*
Pheasant, Rachel; Maryland, 1798 ***1224.2*** *p7*
Pheasant, Samuel 22; Maryland, 1774 ***1220.25*** *p47*
Pheipo, Marks; Maryland, 1641 ***2524.55*** *p172*
Phelan, Alice Dunne; Vermont, 1853-1925 ***5900.10*** *p300*
Phelan, John, Jr.; New York, 1836 ***8197.10*** *p77*
Phelan, Mary; Vermont, 1819-1912 ***5900.10*** *p474*
Phelan, Mary E.; Vermont, n.d. ***5900.10*** *p130*
Phelan, Mary Mulhall; Vermont, 1795-1882 ***5900.10*** *p474*
Phelan, Owen; New York, 1840 ***8197.10*** *p193*
Phelan, Patrick; Vermont, 1845-1904 ***5900.10*** *p300*
Phelan, Patrick 40; Ontario, 1871 ***1823.15*** *p212*
Phelan, Peter 84; Ontario, 1871 ***1823.15*** *p212*
Phelp, Cudbeard; Maryland, 1654 ***2524.55*** *p172*
Wife: Mary
Child: Darby
Child: Cuthbert
Phelp, Cuthbert *SEE* Phelp, Cudbeard
Phelp, Darby *SEE* Phelp, Cudbeard
Phelp, Jane; Maryland, 1658 ***2524.55*** *p172*
Phelp, John 24; Maryland, 1774 ***1220.25*** *p74*
Phelp, John 44; Ontario, 1871 ***1823.22*** *p125*
Phelp, Mary *SEE* Phelp, Cudbeard
Phelpes, Thomas; Maryland, 1669 ***2524.55*** *p172*
Phelps, Mr.; Quebec, 1858 ***9196.15*** *p38*
Phelps, Alfred; Vermont, 1851-1923 ***5900.10*** *p414*
Phelps, Cuthbert *SEE* Phelps, Cuthbert
Phelps, Cuthbert; Maryland, 1654 ***2524.55*** *p172*
Wife: Mary
Child: Cuthbert
Child: Darby
Phelps, Darby *SEE* Phelps, Cuthbert
Phelps, Edward; Virginia, 1678 ***1224.1*** *p45*
Phelps, Edwin; Ohio, 1854 ***1224.3*** *p61*
Phelps, Elizabeth *SEE* Phelps, Walter
Phelps, Emma; Vermont, 1860-1952 ***5900.10*** *p463*
Phelps, Manerva 17; Ontario, 1861 ***2896.28*** *p58*
Phelps, Mary *SEE* Phelps, Cuthbert
Phelps, Olive Dwire; Vermont, 1852-1932 ***5900.10*** *p414*
Phelps, Rebecca *SEE* Phelps, Walter
Phelps, Thomas; Maryland, 1650 ***2524.55*** *p207*
Phelps, Thomas; Maryland, 1658 ***2524.55*** *p172*
Phelps, Thomas; Maryland, 1668 ***2524.55*** *p172*
Phelps, Walter; Maryland, 1680 ***2524.55*** *p172*
Wife: Elizabeth
Mother: Rebecca
Phelps, William; Maryland, 1675 ***2524.55*** *p172*
Pheney, John; Vermont, 1857-1872 ***5900.10*** *p291*
Pheney, Margaret; Vermont, 1808-1890 ***5900.10*** *p291*
Pheney, Patrick; Vermont, 1816-1868 ***5900.10*** *p291*
Phepol, Mary 21; Maryland, 1775 ***1220.25*** *p104*
Pheyl, Hans Matthaus; America, 1737 ***2856.30*** *p341*
Pheypoe, Mark; Maryland, 1649 ***2524.55*** *p172*
Philary, Denis; New York, 1822 ***8197.10*** *p270*
Philben, Martin; New York, 1840 ***8197.10*** *p193*
Philby, Stephen; Virginia, 1671 ***6212.30*** *p43*
Philip, Alexander Brockie; Belize, 1897 ***1640.13*** *p99*
Philip, Peter 30; Ontario, 1871 ***1823.15*** *p212*
Philip, William; New York, 1828 ***8197.10*** *p348*
Philipp, Christian; Port uncertain, 1790 ***2856.30*** *p341*
Philipp, Christian; Port uncertain, 1792 ***2856.30*** *p341*
Philipp, Georg; America, 1745 ***2856.30*** *p341*
With wife & 3 children
Philipp, Heinrich; Port uncertain, 1755 ***2856.30*** *p341*
Philipp, Johann; Port uncertain, 1755 ***2856.30*** *p341*
Philipp, Johann Adam; Port uncertain, 1747 ***2856.30*** *p341*
Philipp, Johann Georg; Port uncertain, 1741 ***2856.30*** *p341*
Philippi, H.; Port uncertain, 1790 ***2856.30*** *p290*
Philippi, Johann Peter; Port uncertain, 1746 ***2856.30*** *p341*
Philipps, Mrs.; Maryland, 1675 ***2524.55*** *p172*
Philipps, Caleb; New England, 1693 ***1224.1*** *p45*
Philipps, Erasmus John; New York, 1780 ***1224.2*** *p90*
Philipps, Maria Elisabeth; Port uncertain, 1738 ***2856.30*** *p341*
Philipps, William; Boston, 1727 ***1224.2*** *p91*
Philippsin, Maria Elisabeth; Port uncertain, 1738 ***2856.30*** *p341*
Philippus, Johann; Port uncertain, 1754 ***2856.30*** *p341*
Philips, Alexander; Pennsylvania, 1785 ***4629.10*** *p45*
Philips, Ann 22; Virginia, 1774 ***1220.25*** *p88*
Philips, C. 48; Ontario, 1861 ***2896.28*** *p3*
Philips, Caroline 6; Ontario, 1861 ***2896.25*** *p63*
Philips, Catharine 23; Ontario, 1861 ***2896.28*** *p23*
Philips, Daniel 15; Ontario, 1861 ***2896.25*** *p63*
Philips, Elizabeth; Maryland, 1680 ***2524.55*** *p172*
Philips, Elizabeth 20; Ontario, 1861 ***2896.28*** *p23*
Philips, Elizabeth 32; Ontario, 1861 ***2896.25*** *p63*
Philips, Frederick; New York, n.d. ***1224.2*** *p90*
Philips, Frederick; New York, n.d. ***1224.3*** *p61*
Philips, Frederick; New York, 1831 ***1224.3*** *p61*
Philips, George 9; Ontario, 1861 ***2896.25*** *p63*
Philips, Hannah 33; Ontario, 1861 ***2896.27*** *p68*
Philips, Hedward 34; Ontario, 1871 ***1823.28*** *p82*
Philips, Henry 31; Ontario, 1871 ***1823.22*** *p126*
Philips, Hugh 40; Ontario, 1871 ***1823.15*** *p212*
Philips, J. G. 6; Ontario, 1861 ***2896.25*** *p36*
Philips, James 20; Ontario, 1861 ***2896.27*** *p25*
Philips, James 23; Virginia, 1774 ***1220.25*** *p88*
Philips, James 28; Ontario, 1871 ***1823.15*** *p212*
Philips, John; Maryland, 1672 ***2524.55*** *p172*
Philips, John; Pennsylvania, 1775 ***1224.2*** *p91*
Philips, John 13; Ontario, 1861 ***2896.25*** *p63*
Philips, John 15; Maryland, 1774 ***1220.25*** *p7*

Pierce, Nathiel 21; Ontario, 1871 1823.15 p213
Pierce, Nathiel 65; Ontario, 1871 1823.15 p213
Pierce, Patrick 56; Ontario, 1871 1823.22 p126
Pierce, Philip 52; Ontario, 1871 1823.28 p82
Pierce, Robert; Maryland, 1635 2524.55 p174
Pierce, Thomas; New York, 1807 8197.10 p48
Pierce, Thomas 40; Ontario, 1871 1823.15 p213
Pierce, Thomas Will.; Pennsylvania, 1777 4629.10 p24
Pierce, William; Maryland, 1671 2524.55 p170
Pierce, William; New York, 1807 8197.10 p47
Pierce, William 48; Ontario, 1871 1823.28 p82
Piercy, Robert; Maryland, 1635 2524.55 p174
Pierepoint, Jabis; Maryland, 1665 2524.55 p170
Pierginski, William; Maryland, 1910 3259.35 p47
Pieroth, Mathes; Port uncertain, 1724 2856.30 p341
Pieroth, Mathes; Port uncertain, 1725 2856.30 p341
Pierpoint, Wm; Virginia, 1665-1666 6212.30 p22
Pierre, Big 35; Ontario, 1871 1823.28 p82
Pierrot, Mathes; Port uncertain, 1724 2856.30 p341
Pierrot, Mathes; Port uncertain, 1725 2856.30 p341
Pierson, Mrs.; Ontario, 1861 2896.27 p28
Pierson, Aaron 29; Ontario, 1861 2896.25 p49
Pierson, Bryant 32; Ontario, 1861 2896.25 p49
Pierson, Caroline 34; Ontario, 1861 2896.28 p33
Pierson, David 63; Ontario, 1861 2896.25 p49
Pierson, James 6; Ontario, 1861 2896.28 p33
Pierson, James 77; Ontario, 1861 2896.28 p34
Pierson, John; New York, 1830 8197.10 p360
Pierson, Joseph 34; Halifax, Nova Scotia, 1774 1220.25 p138
Pierson, Joseph 60; Ontario, 1861 2896.28 p31
Pierson, M. 12; Ontario, 1861 2896.25 p49
Pierson, S. J. 25; Ontario, 1861 2896.25 p49
Pierson, Sarah J. 2; Ontario, 1861 2896.28 p33
Pierson, Thomas; New York, 1807 8197.10 p326
Pierson, William R. 5; Ontario, 1861 2896.28 p33
Pieshaska, Joseph; Maryland, 1910 3259.35 p47
Pietnak, Casemer; Maryland, 1910 3259.35 p47
Pietrick, John; Maryland, 1910 3259.35 p47
Pietrok, Joseph; Maryland, 1910 3259.35 p47
Pietronska, Michael; Maryland, 1910 3259.35 p47
Pietrowiak, Josef; Maryland, 1910 3259.35 p47
Pietrowiak, Marcin; Maryland, 1910 3259.35 p47
Pietrowicak, John; Maryland, 1910 3259.35 p47
Piezczynski, Stanislaw; Maryland, 1910 3259.35 p47
Pigeon, Dorothy; Maryland, 1681 2524.55 p174
Pigeon, Philip; Maryland, 1682 2524.55 p174
Piggott, George; Jamaica, 1743 1224.2 p91
Piggott, George; Virginia, 1665 6212.30 p20
Pignatel, John B.; New York, 1822 8197.10 p62
Pignolet, Louis; New York, 1825 8197.10 p270
Pignolet, Louis; New York, 1830 8197.10 p67
Pihlstrom, Adolphus Peter; New York, 1816 8197.10 p269
Pik, Johann; Port uncertain, 1773 2856.30 p342
Pik, Johann; Port uncertain, 1779 2856.30 p342
Pikard, Elizabeth *SEE* Pikard, Nicholas
Pikard, Nicholas; Maryland, 1659 2524.55 p174
Wife: Elizabeth
Pike, Ann; Maryland, 1637 2524.55 p174
Pike, Edm; Virginia, 1664 6212.30 p9
Pike, Edward 33; Ontario, 1871 1823.15 p213
Pike, Humphrey; Maryland, 1658 2524.55 p174
Pike, John; New York, New York, 1793 1224.2 p91
Pike, Mary; Maryland, 1650 2524.55 p174
Pike, Robert 75; Ontario, 1871 1823.22 p126
Pike, Samuel 53; Ontario, 1871 1823.15 p213
Pike, Thomas; New York, 1840 8197.10 p192
Piker, Thomas; Virginia, 1666 6212.30 p29
Pikersky, Mathias 49; Ontario, 1871 1823.28 p82
Pilachowski, John; Maryland, 1910 3259.35 p47
Pilarski, Andrew J.; Maryland, 1910 3259.35 p47
Pilarski, Angelica; Maryland, 1910 3259.35 p47
Pilarski, Jan; Maryland, 1910 3259.35 p47
Pilarski, Joseph; Maryland, 1910 3259.35 p47
Pilashowsky, Frank; Maryland, 1910 3259.35 p47
Pilatske, John; Ontario, 1871 1823.28 p82
Pilawski, Caszmer; Maryland, 1910 3259.35 p47
Pile, Mrs.; Maryland, 1648 2524.55 p174
Husband: John
Pile, Jane 40; Ontario, 1871 1823.22 p126
Pile, John *SEE* Pile, Mrs.
Pile, John; Maryland, 1658 2524.55 p174
Pile, John; New York, 1827 8197.10 p343
Pile, John; Virginia, 1665 6212.30 p19
Pile, Mary; Maryland, 1650 2524.55 p174
Pilgir, Jacob 51; Ontario, 1871 1823.28 p82
Pilgrim, Henry 58; Ontario, 1871 1823.28 p82
Pilgrim, William 51; Ontario, 1871 1823.28 p82
Pilkington, Samuel; Maryland, 1682 2524.55 p174
Pilkington, William; New York, 1839 8197.10 p137
Pilkington, William; Virginia, 1641 1224.1 p45
Pillage, James 33; Ontario, 1871 1823.22 p126
Pillar, Charles 25; Baltimore, 1775 1220.25 p118
Piller, Vinzenz; America, 1738 2856.30 p342
Pillin, Dan; New York, 1838 8197.10 p318
Pilling, James; New York, 1830 8197.10 p271
Pillmen, William 50; Ontario, 1871 1823.15 p213
Pillon, Honora 55; Vermont, 1893 5900.10 p418
Pillory, Joseph; New York, 1840 8197.10 p272
Pillow, William; New York, 1835 8197.10 p70
Piluch, Frank; Maryland, 1910 3259.35 p47
Piluk, John; Maryland, 1910 3259.35 p47
Pilzak, Victor; Maryland, 1910 3259.35 p47
Pim, Margaret 38; Ontario, 1871 1823.28 p82
Pimett, John; Maryland, 1666 2524.55 p174
Pimm, Richard; Maryland, 1667 2524.55 p174
Pimpel, Balthasar; Port uncertain, 1751 2856.30 p342
Pinard, Mary Maloney 57; Vermont, 1881 5900.10 p501
Pinch, John; Ontario, 1892 1640.13 p100
Pinch, John 34; Ontario, 1871 1823.22 p126
Pinchin, Thomas; Maryland, 1670 2524.55 p174
Pinchnikowski, Lukas; Maryland, 1910 3259.35 p47
Pinchot, Constantine Cirile, Jr.; New York, 1826 8197.10 p333
Pinchsoski, Joseph; Maryland, 1910 3259.35 p47
Pinchuerski, Felix; Maryland, 1910 3259.35 p47
Pinckney, Mr.; Quebec, 1858 9196.15 p41
Pinckney, Charles; Charles Town, South Carolina, 1769 1224.2 p91
Pinckney, Charles Cotesworth; Charleston, South Carolina, 1827 1224.3 p61
Pincock, John 27; Maryland, 1774 1220.25 p52
Pincombe, Richard 40; Ontario, 1871 1823.15 p213
Pindar, Charles; New York, 1812 8197.10 p269
Pindar, Martin; New York, 1803 8197.10 p15
Pinder, George 21; Maryland, 1775 1220.25 p103
Pinder, Margaret; Barbados, 1842 1640.13 p100
Pinder, Mathew; Virginia, 1675 1224.1 p46
Pinder, Thomas 16; Maryland, 1775 1220.25 p120
Pinders, Catherine O'Connell 44; Vermont, 1891 5900.10 p251
Pinders, Thomas 67; Vermont, 1914 5900.10 p251
Pindletton, John; Maryland, 1680 2524.55 p174
Pine, Amelia 40; Ontario, 1861 2896.28 p62
Pine, Benjamin 24; Ontario, 1861 2896.28 p61
Pine, Benjamin 61; Ontario, 1861 2896.28 p61
Pine, Charles; Maryland, 1680 2524.55 p174
Pine, Eben 21; Ontario, 1861 2896.28 p61
Pine, Edward; Virginia, 1666 6212.30 p31
Pine, Elias 26; Ontario, 1861 2896.28 p61
Pine, Elizabeth 6; Ontario, 1861 2896.28 p58
Pine, Herbert 1; Ontario, 1861 2896.28 p58
Pine, Jacob 53; Ontario, 1861 2896.28 p61
Pine, James 33; Ontario, 1861 2896.28 p61
Pine, John; Maryland, 1667 2524.55 p174
Pine, Joseph 45; Ontario, 1861 2896.28 p61
Pine, Lazarus; Pennsylvania, 1777 4629.10 p7
Pine, Margaret 29; Ontario, 1861 2896.28 p62
Pine, Martha 22; Ontario, 1861 2896.28 p61
Pine, Peter; New York, 1838 8197.10 p146
Pine, Rebecca 26; Ontario, 1861 2896.28 p58
Pine, Richard 9; Ontario, 1861 2896.28 p62
Pine, Robert Edge; Philadelphia, 1789 1224.2 p92
Pine, S. 18; Ontario, 1861 2896.28 p61
Pine, Stephen; New York, n.d. 1224.2 p92
Pinecombe, Mary 64; Ontario, 1871 1823.15 p213
Pinecombe, Robert 39; Ontario, 1871 1823.15 p213
Pinel, Hannah 43; Ontario, 1871 1823.28 p82
Pinett, John; Maryland, 1666 2524.55 p174
Pinger, Johann; Port uncertain, 1776 2856.30 p342
Pinger, Sontag; Port uncertain, 1726 2856.30 p342
Pingley, Christin 41; Ontario, 1871 1823.15 p213
Pinheiro, Joaquim; New York, 1837 8197.10 p101
Pinhorne, John; Halifax, Nova Scotia, 1765 1224.2 p92
Pinhorne, Mary; New York, New York, 1740 1224.2 p92
Pininski, William; Maryland, 1910 3259.35 p47
Pink, Alexander 61; Ontario, 1871 1823.22 p126
Pink, Edward 32; Virginia, 1774 1220.25 p94
Pink, Thomas 27; Ontario, 1871 1823.28 p82
Pink, William; New York, 1840 8197.10 p193
Pinkerton, Henry; New York, 1840 8197.10 p193
Pinkerton, James 6; Ontario, 1871 1823.28 p82
Pinkerton, John 15; Ontario, 1871 1823.28 p82
Pinkerton, Mary Catherine 7; Ontario, 1871 1823.28 p82
Pinkerton, Robert; Georgia, 1699 1640.13 p100
Pinkerton, Robert 60; Ontario, 1871 1823.28 p82
Pinkny, Michael 42; Nova Scotia, 1774 1220.25 p136
Pinkoski, Joseph; Maryland, 1910 3259.35 p47
Pinkowski, Joseph; Maryland, 1910 3259.35 p47
Pinley, Dorothy; Maryland, 1663 2524.55 p58
Pinley, Dorothy; Maryland, 1664 2524.55 p60
Pinley, Dorothy; Maryland, 1672 2524.55 p174
Pinley, Thomas; Maryland, 1663 2524.55 p58
Pinley, Thomas; Maryland, 1664 2524.55 p60
Pinley, Thomas; Maryland, 1672 2524.55 p174
Pinnar, Thomas; Maryland, 1672 2524.55 p174
Pinnell, Edward 77; Ontario, 1871 1823.22 p126
Pinner, Ann *SEE* Pinner, Richard
Pinner, Hester 17; Ontario, 1861 2896.27 p70
Pinner, John 11; Ontario, 1871 1823.22 p126
Pinner, Mary Jane 13; Ontario, 1871 1823.22 p127
Pinner, Moses; Maryland, 1669 2524.55 p84
Pinner, Richard *SEE* Pinner, Richard
Pinner, Richard; Maryland, 1667 2524.55 p174
Wife: Ann
Son: Richard
Son: William
Pinner, Richard 9; Ontario, 1871 1823.22 p127
Pinner, Thomas; Maryland, 1674 2524.55 p174
Pinner, Thomas 15; Ontario, 1871 1823.22 p127
Pinner, William *SEE* Pinner, Richard
Pinner, Wm.; Maryland, 1663-1664 2524.55 p174
Pinneski, Henry; Maryland, 1910 3259.35 p47
Pinney, Jane Crosby 71; Vermont, 1907 5900.10 p301
Pinney, Mary E.; Vermont, 1854-1941 5900.10 p188
Pinney, Oscar H.; Vermont, 1852-1911 5900.10 p188
Pinney, Samuel L. 73; Vermont, 1910 5900.10 p301
Pinnfry, Elizabeth; Maryland, 1668 2524.55 p175
Pinnicki, Peter; Maryland, 1910 3259.35 p47
Pinning, Emma 20; Ontario, 1871 1823.15 p213
Pinning, John 18; Ontario, 1871 1823.15 p213
Pinnkett, Mrs.; Quebec, 1858 9196.15 p47
Pinol, Emanuel J.; New York, 1832 8197.10 p368
Pinsent, John 16; Philadelphia, 1774 1220.25 p42
Pinsonuault, A.; Quebec, 1858 9196.15 p45
Pinte, Joseph 15; Maryland, 1774 1220.25 p53
Piorinski, Ben; Maryland, 1910 3259.35 p47
Piornoski, Michael; Maryland, 1910 3259.35 p47
Piowinski, William; Maryland, 1910 3259.35 p47
Piowtkowsky, Anna; Maryland, 1910 3259.35 p47
Pipe, Mr.; Quebec, 1858 9196.15 p46
Pipe, Mrs.; Quebec, 1858 9196.15 p46
Piper, Ann; Maryland, 1655 2524.55 p175
Piper, Charles 59; Ontario, 1871 1823.28 p82
Piper, Edward; New York, 1840 8197.10 p386
Piper, George; New York, 1838 8197.10 p146
Piper, Henry; Pennsylvania, 1777 4629.10 p16
Piper, Hugh; Virginia, 1666 6212.30 p27
Piper, James 44; Ontario, 1871 1823.15 p213
Piper, James 60; Ontario, 1871 1823.15 p213
Piper, Mary A. 66; Ontario, 1871 1823.22 p127
Piper, Richard 67; Ontario, 1871 1823.22 p127
Piper, Samuel 55; Ontario, 1871 1823.15 p213
Piper, Thomas 25; Ontario, 1871 1823.15 p213
Piper, Thomas 51; Ontario, 1871 1823.15 p213
Piper, William; Maryland, 1655 2524.55 p175
Piper, William; Maryland, 1682 2524.55 p175
Piper, William; New York, 1840 8197.10 p386
Piper, William 66; Ontario, 1871 1823.15 p213
Pipes, Jonathan 20; Fort Cumberland, Nova Scotia, 1774 1220.25 p17
Pipes, William 22; Fort Cumberland, Nova Scotia, 1774 1220.25 p17
Pipes, William 49; Fort Cumberland, Nova Scotia, 1774 1220.25 p17
Pipher, E. 14; Ontario, 1861 2896.28 p2
Pipher, J. 11; Ontario, 1861 2896.28 p2
Pipher, L. 9; Ontario, 1861 2896.28 p2
Pipher, L. 40; Ontario, 1861 2896.28 p2
Pipher, M. A. 17; Ontario, 1861 2896.28 p2
Pipher, S. 36; Ontario, 1861 2896.28 p2
Pipher, William 3; Ontario, 1861 2896.28 p2
Pirce, Sibella; Maryland, 1656 2524.55 p175
Pirie, Jane 14; Ontario, 1871 1823.22 p127
Pirie, John 47; Ontario, 1871 1823.22 p127
Pirie, Robert 69; Ontario, 1871 1823.22 p127
Pirnie, John; New York, 1820 8197.10 p269
Piroth, Anna Catharina; Port uncertain, 1731 2856.30 p342
Piroth, Johann Bernard; Port uncertain, 1739 2856.30 p342
Pirrie, Alexander; Augusta, Georgia, 1797 1640.10 p170
Pirson, Joseph P.; New York, 1811 8197.10 p269
Pirsson, Joseph Poole; New York, New York, 1848 1224.3 p61
Pirsson, William; New York, 1833 8197.10 p358
Pis, Antonio; Maryland, 1910 3259.35 p47
Pisani, Andrew; New York, 1815 8197.10 p269
Pisarek, Trzeslaw; Maryland, 1910 3259.35 p47
Pisarsky, Stanislaus; Maryland, 1910 3259.35 p47
Piscauf, Joseph 45; Ontario, 1871 1823.28 p82
Piscauf, Laurince 38; Ontario, 1871 1823.28 p82
Piscon, John; Maryland, 1910 3259.35 p47
Piscor, Mary; Maryland, 1910 3259.35 p48
Piscor, Michael; Maryland, 1910 3259.35 p48
Piskarski, Alexandra; Maryland, 1910 3259.35 p48
Piskor, John; Maryland, 1910 3259.35 p48

Piskor, Joseph; Maryland, 1910 ***3259.35*** *p48*
Piskor, Michael; Maryland, 1910 ***3259.35*** *p48*
Piskor, Wojsuch; Maryland, 1910 ***3259.35*** *p48*
Pistor, Peter 59; Ontario, 1871 ***1823.15*** *p213*
Pistorius, Christof; Port uncertain, 1729 ***2856.30*** *p342*
Piszczako, Andrew; Maryland, 1910 ***3259.35*** *p48*
Pitcairn, David; Jamaica, 1730 ***1640.13*** *p100*
Pitcarthy, Robert; New York, 1807 ***8197.10*** *p48*
Pitcher, James; New York, 1800 ***1224.3*** *p61*
Pitcher, James; New York, New York, 1783 ***1224.2*** *p92*
Pitel, Henry; Maryland, 1910 ***3259.35*** *p48*
Pitherell, Thomas; Maryland, 1667 ***2524.55*** *p173*
Pithouse, Mary; Virginia, 1665 ***6212.30*** *p17*
Pitkin, Daniel; Hartford, Connecticut, 1765 ***1224.2*** *p92*
Pitkin, James; Connecticut, 1765 ***1224.2*** *p92*
Pitkin, James; Havana, 1765 ***1224.2*** *p92*
Pitkin, Thomas 15; New York, 1775 ***1220.25*** *p94*
Pitman, Henry; Carolina, 1701 ***1224.2*** *p92*
Pitman, William 24; Maryland, 1774 ***1220.25*** *p77*
Pitscottie, Colin; Georgia, 1699 ***1640.13*** *p100*
Pitt, George; Virginia, 1666 ***6212.30*** *p31*
Pitt, James 23; Philadelphia, 1775 ***1220.25*** *p9*
Pitt, John; New York, 1840 ***8197.10*** *p193*
Pitt, Samuel Grove; Michigan, 1854 ***1224.3*** *p61*
Pitt, Stephen 15; Maryland, 1775 ***1220.25*** *p103*
Pitt, Thomas; Virginia, 1665-1666 ***6212.30*** *p23*
Pitt, William; Pennsylvania, 1777 ***4629.10*** *p11*
Pittaluga, Luigi; New York, 1826 ***8197.10*** *p332*
Pittman, Alice; Maryland, 1663 ***2524.55*** *p175*
Pittman, Frances; Virginia, 1665 ***6212.30*** *p17*
Pittman, Joseph; Virginia, 1665 ***6212.30*** *p17*
Pittman, Thomas; Virginia, 1665 ***6212.30*** *p17*
Pitts, William 32; Maryland, 1775 ***1220.25*** *p98*
Pitty, Hebart; Maryland, 1652 ***2524.55*** *p175*
Pitty, Hobar; Maryland, 1659 ***2524.55*** *p175*
Pitza, Joseph; Maryland, 1910 ***3259.35*** *p48*
Piveyer, Samuel 22; Baltimore, 1775 ***1220.25*** *p118*
Pizzal, Conrad; Baltimore, 1847 ***6058.10*** *p43*
Pizzal, Henry; Pennsylvania, 1863 ***6058.10*** *p46*
Placco, John 56; Ontario, 1871 ***1823.22*** *p127*
Place, Henry; Maryland, 1659 ***2524.55*** *p175*
Place, James 22; Maryland, 1774 ***1220.25*** *p41*
Place, Paul Richards; New York, 1794 ***8197.10*** *p4*
Place, Symond; Maryland, 1657 ***2524.55*** *p175*
Plackovich, B. 30; Alaska, 1916 ***9196.1*** *p44*
Plackovich, B. 30; Whitehorse, Yukon, 1916 ***9196.1*** *p44*
Plaine, James; Savannah, Georgia, 1798 ***1640.10*** *p170*
Plaine, James; Savannah, Georgia, 1798 ***1640.13*** *p100*
Plaine, John F.; New York, 1803 ***8197.10*** *p15*
Plaisted, Francis; Boston, 1733 ***1224.2*** *p92*
Planck, John; North America, 1795 ***1224.2*** *p92*
Plane, Bartholomew; New York, 1807 ***8197.10*** *p329*
Plant, James 36; Ontario, 1871 ***1823.15*** *p213*
Plantz, Ludwig; Port uncertain, 1764 ***2856.30*** *p342*
Plasch, Jonas; America, 1789 ***2856.30*** *p41*
Plaskett, Mr.; Quebec, 1857 ***9196.15*** *p14*
Plaskitt, Joshua, Jr.; New York, 1818 ***8197.10*** *p269*
Plat, Carsten; New York, 1840 ***8197.10*** *p193*
Plat, Henry; New York, 1840 ***8197.10*** *p193*
Platas, Antonio; Baton Rouge, Louisiana, 1831 ***1224.3*** *p61*
Plate, Caleb E. 16; Ontario, 1861 ***2896.27*** *p31*
Plate, Elisa J. 10; Ontario, 1861 ***2896.27*** *p31*
Plate, Emily 46; Ontario, 1861 ***2896.27*** *p31*
Plate, Emily E. 6; Ontario, 1861 ***2896.27*** *p31*
Plate, Helen 18; Ontario, 1861 ***2896.27*** *p31*
Plate, Henry E. 14; Ontario, 1861 ***2896.27*** *p31*
Plate, Mary 12; Ontario, 1861 ***2896.27*** *p31*
Platefeild, Adam; Maryland, 1671 ***2524.55*** *p175*
Platt, A. 25; Ontario, 1861 ***2896.26*** *p13*
Platt, A. P. 15; Ontario, 1861 ***2896.25*** *p28*
Platt, Adaline 14; Ontario, 1861 ***2896.28*** *p46*
Platt, Alva 16; Ontario, 1861 ***2896.28*** *p46*
Platt, Daniel 72; Ontario, 1871 ***1823.22*** *p127*
Platt, David 15; Ontario, 1861 ***2896.26*** *p19*
Platt, E. 34; Ontario, 1861 ***2896.26*** *p13*
Platt, Frederick 44; Ontario, 1871 ***1823.15*** *p214*
Platt, George 2; Ontario, 1861 ***2896.26*** *p19*
Platt, H. A. 22; Ontario, 1861 ***2896.25*** *p28*
Platt, H. M. 17; Ontario, 1861 ***2896.25*** *p28*
Platt, J. 29; Ontario, 1861 ***2896.26*** *p13*
Platt, J. S. 1; Ontario, 1861 ***2896.26*** *p13*
Platt, James; Pennsylvania, 1811 ***6058.10*** *p3*
Platt, John 21; Philadelphia, 1774 ***1220.25*** *p68*
Platt, L. 33; Ontario, 1861 ***2896.26*** *p13*
Platt, Louis P.; Maryland, 1910 ***3259.35*** *p48*
Platt, Luther 18; Ontario, 1861 ***2896.26*** *p19*
Platt, Malissa 20; Ontario, 1861 ***2896.26*** *p19*
Platt, Marah 48; Ontario, 1861 ***2896.26*** *p19*
Platt, Milton 22; Ontario, 1861 ***2896.26*** *p19*
Platt, Niklas; Port uncertain, 1785 ***2856.30*** *p342*
With wife & 5 children
Platt, Orinda 24; Ontario, 1861 ***2896.26*** *p19*
Platt, Priscilla 43; Ontario, 1861 ***2896.28*** *p46*
Platt, Ralph; New York, 1802 ***8197.10*** *p24*
Platt, Richard; New York, 1807 ***8197.10*** *p47*
Platt, Rowland; Virginia, 1664 ***6212.30*** *p14*
Platt, S. 10; Ontario, 1861 ***2896.25*** *p28*
Platt, S. 55; Ontario, 1861 ***2896.26*** *p13*
Platt, S. E. 23; Ontario, 1861 ***2896.26*** *p13*
Platt, Samuel 49; Ontario, 1871 ***1823.15*** *p214*
Platt, Sarah 1; Ontario, 1861 ***2896.28*** *p46*
Platt, Susan 20; Ontario, 1861 ***2896.28*** *p46*
Platt, Thomas; New York, 1831 ***8197.10*** *p314*
Platt, Thomas 20; Maryland, 1774 ***1220.25*** *p64*
Platteicher, Isaac; Port uncertain, 1694 ***2856.30*** *p342*
Platteicher, Isaac; Port uncertain, 1742 ***2856.30*** *p342*
Platteicher, Martin; America, 1737 ***2856.30*** *p343*
Platteicher, Martin; Port uncertain, 1737 ***2856.30*** *p343*
Platters, William; Maryland, 1661 ***2524.55*** *p74*
Platts, Christopher; Maryland, 1700 ***1224.2*** *p92*
Platts, Elizabeth; Maryland, 1663 ***2524.55*** *p26*
Platts, John; Maryland, 1663 ***2524.55*** *p26*
Platz, Anna Maria; Port uncertain, 1783 ***2856.30*** *p343*
Platz, John; New Jersey, 1835 ***8197.10*** *p146*
Platzer, Miss; America, 1753 ***2856.30*** *p343*
Platzer, John 46; Ontario, 1871 ***1823.15*** *p214*
Platzier, John 38; Ontario, 1871 ***1823.15*** *p214*
Plaxton, George; Barbados, 1736 ***1224.2*** *p92*
Plaxton, George; Salem, Massachusetts, 1736 ***1224.2*** *p92*
Playford, Samuel 50; Ontario, 1871 ***1823.15*** *p214*
Playford, Thomas 51; Ontario, 1871 ***1823.15*** *p214*
Playsted, Edward; Virginia, 1701 ***1224.2*** *p92*
Playter, Sarah B. 75; Ontario, 1871 ***1823.28*** *p83*
Pleasants, James; Cuba, 1821 ***1224.3*** *p61*
Pleasants, James; Richmond, Virginia, n.d. ***1224.3*** *p61*
Pleden, John 29; Maryland, 1774 ***1220.25*** *p57*
Pledge, Mary 21; Maryland, 1775 ***1220.25*** *p114*
Pleete, John 32; Ontario, 1871 ***1823.28*** *p83*
Plenderleath, Gabriel George; New York, 1827 ***1224.3*** *p62*
Plesc, Jonas; America, 1789 ***2856.30*** *p41*
Plesto, Edward; Maryland, 1727 ***1224.2*** *p92*
Pletzer, Catherine 47; Ontario, 1871 ***1823.15*** *p214*
Pletzer, George 36; Ontario, 1871 ***1823.15*** *p214*
Pleughs, John 35; Ontario, 1871 ***1823.15*** *p214*
Plewa, Wojciech; Maryland, 1910 ***3259.35*** *p48*
Plewacka, Joseph; Maryland, 1910 ***3259.35*** *p48*
Plewacki, Stanislaus; Maryland, 1910 ***3259.35*** *p48*
Plewacki, Thomas; Maryland, 1910 ***3259.35*** *p48*
Plewes, George 38; Ontario, 1871 ***1823.15*** *p214*
Plewes, Robert 45; Ontario, 1871 ***1823.15*** *p214*
Plews, James, Sr. 62; Ontario, 1871 ***1823.22*** *p127*
Plews, Robert 57; Ontario, 1871 ***1823.22*** *p127*
Pleydell, John; Virginia, 1665 ***6212.30*** *p19*
Pleydell, Robert; Virginia, 1666-1667 ***6212.30*** *p34*
Pleyl, Samuel; Port uncertain, 1747 ***2856.30*** *p343*
Plichta, Frank; Maryland, 1910 ***3259.35*** *p48*
Plimoth, Mary; Virginia, 1667 ***6212.30*** *p36*
Plimsoll, Mr.; Quebec, 1857 ***9196.15*** *p19*
Plitzeir, Conrad 37; Ontario, 1871 ***1823.15*** *p214*
Ploachvex, Paul; Maryland, 1910 ***3259.35*** *p48*
Plomley, Mary; Maryland, 1681 ***2524.55*** *p175*
Ploof, F.; Vermont, 1858-1938 ***5900.10*** *p194*
Ploof, K. Bresnehan; Vermont, 1853-1929 ***5900.10*** *p194*
Ploss, Mary 60; Ontario, 1871 ***1823.28*** *p83*
Plott, Anna Magdalena; America, 1741 ***2856.30*** *p343*
Plott, Garret; America, 1741 ***2856.30*** *p343*
Plott, Gorg; America, 1741 ***2856.30*** *p343*
Plott, Johann Philipp; America, 1741 ***2856.30*** *p343*
Plott, Philipp; America, 1741 ***2856.30*** *p343*
With wife & child
Plotzak, Joseph; Maryland, 1910 ***3259.35*** *p48*
Ploughton, Alexander 27; Virginia, 1774 ***1220.25*** *p75*
Plowden, Catherine; Carolina, 1718 ***1224.2*** *p92*
Plowden, Edmund; America, 1659 ***1224.1*** *p46*
Plowden, Frances; Carolina, 1717 ***1224.2*** *p92*
Plowman, Joseph; Pennsylvania, 1777 ***4629.10*** *p13*
Plowman, Wm.; Maryland, 1681 ***2524.55*** *p175*
Plowright, Samuel; New York, 1840 ***8197.10*** *p193*
Ploydon, Jno; Virginia, 1664 ***6212.30*** *p15*
Plplnske, Jacob 20; Ontario, 1871 ***1823.28*** *p83*
Pluchta, Thomas; Maryland, 1910 ***3259.35*** *p48*
Pluciak, Frank P.; Maryland, 1910 ***3259.35*** *p48*
Plucinski, Agness; Maryland, 1910 ***3259.35*** *p48*
Pluckett, Richard; Maryland, 1682 ***2524.55*** *p175*
Pluffie, James 80; Ontario, 1871 ***1823.28*** *p83*
Plug, George 44; Ontario, 1871 ***1823.15*** *p214*
Plum, Andrew P.; Maryland, 1910 ***3259.35*** *p48*
Plum, John 45; Vermont, 1883 ***5900.10*** *p239*
Plum, Joseph S.; Maryland, 1910 ***3259.35*** *p48*
Plumbe, Frances Margaretta; Iowa, 1857 ***1224.3*** *p62*
Plumber, John 33; Maryland, 1775 ***1220.25*** *p121*
Plumber, William 52; Ontario, 1871 ***1823.28*** *p83*
Plumer, Richard; Maryland, 1653 ***2524.55*** *p175*
Plummer, Benjamin; Portsmouth, New Hampshire, 1741 ***1224.2*** *p92*
Plummer, John 28; Ontario, 1871 ***1823.28*** *p83*
Plummer, Joseph; New York, 1837 ***8197.10*** *p100*
Plummer, Richard; New York, 1794 ***8197.10*** *p1*
Plummer, Richard 51; Ontario, 1871 ***1823.28*** *p83*
Plummer, Samuel; Maryland, 1682 ***2524.55*** *p175*
Plummer, Samuel Aggs; Philadelphia, 1829 ***1224.3*** *p62*
Plummer, Thomas; Maryland, 1659 ***2524.55*** *p175*
Plumton, Daniel 1; Ontario, 1861 ***2896.27*** *p49*
Plumton, Horace 66; Ontario, 1871 ***1823.22*** *p127*
Plumton, James 41; Ontario, 1871 ***1823.22*** *p127*
Plumton, Joseph 31; Ontario, 1861 ***2896.27*** *p49*
Plumton, William 45; Ontario, 1871 ***1823.22*** *p127*
Plunckett, Rose A. 31; Vermont, 1875 ***5900.10*** *p594*
Plunket, David; Baltimore, 1818 ***1224.3*** *p62*
Plunket, John 52; Ontario, 1871 ***1823.15*** *p214*
Plunket, Oliver; New York, 1837 ***8197.10*** *p101*
Plunkett, . . . 18; Tortola, 1773-1774 ***1220.25*** *p32*
Plunkett, Alexander; Pennsylvania, 1777 ***4629.10*** *p8*
Plunkett, Alexander; Pennsylvania, 1777 ***4629.10*** *p45*
Plunkett, Bridget; Vermont, 1836-1904 ***5900.10*** *p325*
Plunkett, Edward; New York, 1840 ***8197.10*** *p192*
Plunkett, Ellen; Vermont, 1840-1912 ***5900.10*** *p325*
Plunkett, James; Vermont, 1843-1908 ***5900.10*** *p325*
Plunkett, John; Vermont, 1840-1883 ***5900.10*** *p325*
Plunkett, Mary Kirk; Vermont, 1804-1877 ***5900.10*** *p325*
Plunkett, Patrick; Vermont, 1805-1875 ***5900.10*** *p325*
Plunkett, Patrick C.; New York, 1806 ***8197.10*** *p323*
Plunkett, Roseanna 50; Ontario, 1871 ***1823.22*** *p127*
Plunkett, Thomas; Vermont, 1838-1875 ***5900.10*** *p325*
Pluph, Gilbart 32; Ontario, 1871 ***1823.28*** *p83*
Pluse, Catherine 35; Ontario, 1861 ***2896.25*** *p21*
Pluse, H. E. 47; Ontario, 1861 ***2896.25*** *p21*
Plusinski, Peter C.; Maryland, 1910 ***3259.35*** *p48*
Pnier, John 62; Ontario, 1871 ***1823.15*** *p214*
Pnocian, Feliks; Maryland, 1910 ***3259.35*** *p48*
Poaly, Edward; Maryland, 1651 ***2524.55*** *p175*
Poar, Nicholas; Maryland, 1679 ***2524.55*** *p175*
Poast, Filo 19; Ontario, 1861 ***2896.27*** *p13*
Poast, Jane 73; Ontario, 1861 ***2896.27*** *p13*
Pobocki, Maryana; Maryland, 1910 ***3259.35*** *p48*
Pochoricka, George; Maryland, 1910 ***3259.35*** *p48*
Pockett, Elizabeth; Vermont, 1837-1875 ***5900.10*** *p268*
Pockett, James 30; Ontario, 1871 ***1823.22*** *p127*
Pockett, John; Vermont, 1832-1903 ***5900.10*** *p268*
Pockh, Anna; Port uncertain, 1730 ***2856.30*** *p343*
Pocock, George 32; Ontario, 1871 ***1823.15*** *p214*
Pocock, Joseph; Rochester, New York, 1856 ***1224.3*** *p62*
Pocock, Sarah; Charleston, South Carolina, 1856 ***1224.3*** *p62*
Pocock, William 21; Maryland, 1775 ***1220.25*** *p119*
Pode, Mr.; Quebec, 1857 ***9196.15*** *p23*
Pode, Mrs.; Quebec, 1857 ***9196.15*** *p23*
Pode, Abraham 57; Ontario, 1871 ***1823.15*** *p214*
Podom, Frank; New York, New York, 1888 ***3437.14*** *p123*
Podoski, John; Maryland, 1910 ***3259.35*** *p48*
Podvin, John 21; Maryland, 1774 ***1220.25*** *p58*
Poe, Alexander 36; Ontario, 1871 ***1823.22*** *p127*
Poff, Henery 38; Ontario, 1871 ***1823.28*** *p83*
Poff, Mary 55; Ontario, 1871 ***1823.28*** *p83*
Poff, Peter 60; Ontario, 1871 ***1823.28*** *p83*
Poff, Thomas 41; Ontario, 1871 ***1823.28*** *p83*
Poffard, Mrs.; Quebec, 1857 ***9196.15*** *p25*
Poffel, Michael; Maryland, 1910 ***3259.35*** *p48*
Poffel, Steny; Maryland, 1910 ***3259.35*** *p48*
Pogelski, Stephan; Maryland, 1910 ***3259.35*** *p48*
Pogson, George; Charleston, South Carolina, 1816 ***1224.3*** *p62*
Pogson, George; North America, 1798 ***1224.2*** *p93*
Pogue, Andrew 30; Ontario, 1871 ***1823.22*** *p127*
Pogue, Isaiah 60; Ontario, 1871 ***1823.22*** *p127*
Pogue, James 26; Ontario, 1861 ***2896.25*** *p38*
Pogue, James 45; Ontario, 1871 ***1823.22*** *p127*
Pogue, Maria 30; Ontario, 1871 ***1823.22*** *p127*
Poinsett, Fanny; Charleston, South Carolina, 1806 ***1224.3*** *p62*
Pointer, Francis; Maryland, 1651 ***2524.55*** *p175*
Pointius, Johann David; Port uncertain, 1774 ***2856.30*** *p343*
Pointius, Johann Philipp; Port uncertain, 1774 ***2856.30*** *p343*
Pointkowski, Anton; Maryland, 1910 ***3259.35*** *p48*
Poiteuin, Sebastian; New England, 1716 ***1224.2*** *p93*
Poitevin, Sebastian; New England, 1716 ***1224.2*** *p93*
Poizer, Thomas; Florida, 1767 ***1224.2*** *p93*
Pokorvki, Mary; Maryland, 1910 ***3259.35*** *p48*
Pokrywka, Paul; Maryland, 1910 ***3259.35*** *p48*
Pokyfke, John 38; Ontario, 1871 ***1823.28*** *p83*
Polack, Nathan; New York, 1835 ***8197.10*** *p70*
Polack, William L.; New York, 1835 ***8197.10*** *p98*
Polack, William N.; New York, 1838 ***8197.10*** *p146*

Polak, Thomas; Maryland, 1910 *3259.35 p48*
Poland, John; Maryland, 1665 *2524.55 p175*
Polanowski, Sigman; Maryland, 1910 *3259.35 p48*
Polasheck, Victor; Maryland, 1910 *3259.35 p48*
Polax, Lawrence; Maryland, 1659 *2524.55 p197*
Polczynske, Maltaus; Maryland, 1910 *3259.35 p48*
Pole, Edward; Pennsylvania, 1777 *4629.10 p6*
Polegreen, Wallace; New York, 1838 *8197.10 p146*
Polehill, Jno; Virginia, 1666-1667 *6212.30 p32*
Polek, Agnes; Maryland, 1910 *3259.35 p48*
Polek, Michal; Maryland, 1910 *3259.35 p48*
Polek, Szymon; Maryland, 1910 *3259.35 p48*
Poletton, John 24; Ontario, 1871 *1823.15 p214*
Poley, Sr.; Port uncertain, 1764 *2856.30 p343*
Polharchaid, David 64; Ontario, 1871 *1823.15 p214*
Polheim, Johann Theodor; America, 1654 *2856.30 p343*
Polich, Frank; Maryland, 1910 *3259.35 p48*
Polick, Marria 74; Ontario, 1871 *1823.15 p214*
Polick, Thomas 50; Ontario, 1871 *1823.28 p83*
Polik, Peter M.; Maryland, 1910 *3259.35 p48*
Polinski, John; Maryland, 1910 *3259.35 p48*
Polislack, Igniski; Maryland, 1910 *3259.35 p48*
Politowicz, Martin; Maryland, 1910 *3259.35 p48*
Politowski, John; Maryland, 1910 *3259.35 p48*
Polk, . . .; South Carolina, 1750-1770 *4628.40 p98*
Polkinghorne, John 27; Ontario, 1871 *1823.22 p127*
Polkinghorne, Richard 61; Ontario, 1871 *1823.22 p127*
Polkowski, James; Maryland, 1910 *3259.35 p48*
Pollack, James 47; Ontario, 1871 *1823.15 p214*
Pollack, Louise; Maryland, 1910 *3259.35 p48*
Pollak, Simon; New York, 1837 *8197.10 p101*
Pollan, John 46; Ontario, 1871 *1823.15 p214*
Pollan, Simon 24; Ontario, 1871 *1823.15 p214*
Pollan, William 70; Ontario, 1871 *1823.15 p214*
Pollard, Mr.; Quebec, 1856 *9196.15 p8*
Pollard, Amos; Virginia, 1666 *6212.30 p31*
Pollard, Edmund 59; Ontario, 1871 *1823.15 p214*
Pollard, Edward; Maryland, 1681 *2524.55 p175*
Pollard, Edward; New Hampshire, 1841 *1224.3 p62*
Pollard, Francis; Grenada, 1800 *1224.3 p62*
Pollard, Hugh; Maryland, 1670 *2524.55 p175*
Pollard, James 43; Ontario, 1871 *1823.15 p214*
Pollard, John; Maryland, 1679 *2524.55 p175*
Pollard, John; Maryland, 1680 *2524.55 p175*
Pollard, John; Philadelphia, 1809 *1224.3 p62*
Pollard, John 59; Ontario, 1871 *1823.15 p214*
Pollard, John Dobey; New York, 1821 *8197.10 p269*
Pollard, Rebecca; Maryland, 1666 *2524.55 p179*
Pollard, Richard 31; Ontario, 1871 *1823.15 p214*
Pollard, Suzan; Maryland, 1664 *2524.55 p175*
Pollard, Thomas 55; Ontario, 1871 *1823.15 p214*
Pollard, William 28; Philadelphia, 1774 *1220.25 p44*
Pollard, William 33; Ontario, 1871 *1823.15 p214*
Pollard, William 37; Ontario, 1871 *1823.15 p214*
Pollard, William 51; Ontario, 1871 *1823.22 p127*
Pollard, William 60; Ontario, 1871 *1823.15 p214*
Polleck, James 50; Ontario, 1871 *1823.15 p214*
Pollen, William; Maryland, 1649 *2524.55 p175*
Pollenbach, Anton; Port uncertain, 1748 *2856.30 p343*
Pollett, John; Maryland, 1656 *2524.55 p175*
Polley, Albert M. 35; Ontario, 1871 *1823.15 p214*
Polley, Mary 50; Ontario, 1871 *1823.15 p214*
Polley, Richard 28; Ontario, 1871 *1823.28 p83*
Polley, William 17; Ontario, 1861 *2896.25 p47*
Polley, William 35; Ontario, 1871 *1823.28 p83*
Polleys, Captain; Quebec, 1857 *9196.15 p18*
Pollich, Hilgard; America, 1754 *2856.30 p343*
Pollick, Margerat 40; Ontario, 1871 *1823.15 p214*
Pollick, Marshall 44; Ontario, 1871 *1823.15 p214*
Pollinger, Johann; Port uncertain, 1741 *2856.30 p346*
Pollock, Abram 53; Ontario, 1871 *1823.28 p83*
Pollock, Allan; Virginia, 1816 *1640.13 p100*
Pollock, Andrew 52; Ontario, 1871 *1823.15 p214*
Pollock, Archibald 40; Ontario, 1871 *1823.22 p127*
Pollock, Charles 32; Ontario, 1871 *1823.22 p127*
Pollock, Charlotte 48; Ontario, 1871 *1823.15 p214*
Pollock, Elizabeth; New Brunswick, 1895 *1640.13 p100*
Pollock, George 35; Ontario, 1871 *1823.15 p214*
Pollock, Henery 49; Ontario, 1871 *1823.22 p127*
Pollock, Henry 73; Ontario, 1871 *1823.15 p214*
Pollock, Hugh; New York, 1792-1840 *8197.10 p192*
Pollock, James; New York, 1839 *8197.10 p380*
Pollock, James 41; Ontario, 1871 *1823.15 p214*
Pollock, James 60; Ontario, 1871 *1823.15 p214*
Pollock, John 38; Ontario, 1871 *1823.15 p215*
Pollock, John 60; Ontario, 1871 *1823.15 p215*
Pollock, John 77; Ontario, 1871 *1823.15 p214*
Pollock, M. A.; America, 1876 *1640.13 p100*
Pollock, Margaret 30; Ontario, 1871 *1823.15 p215*
Pollock, Mary 39; Ontario, 1871 *1823.15 p215*
Pollock, Mary Jane 48; Ontario, 1871 *1823.15 p215*
Pollock, R.; Quebec, 1857 *9196.15 p22*
Pollock, Robert; America, 1811 *1640.13 p100*
Pollock, Robert 28; Ontario, 1871 *1823.15 p215*
Pollock, Robert 40; Ontario, 1871 *1823.15 p215*
Pollock, Samuel; New York, 1838 *8197.10 p271*
Pollock, Samuel; New York, 1840 *8197.10 p193*
Pollock, Samuel 59; Ontario, 1871 *1823.15 p215*
Pollock, Thomas; Boston, 1838 *1224.3 p62*
Pollock, Thomas; New York, 1803 *8197.10 p15*
Pollock, Thomas 40; Ontario, 1871 *1823.15 p215*
Pollock, William 46; Ontario, 1871 *1823.22 p127*
Pollock, William 68; Ontario, 1871 *1823.22 p127*
Polly, Robert 70; Ontario, 1871 *1823.22 p127*
Polman, Ida 15; Ontario, 1871 *1823.28 p83*
Polo, Casimiro; New York, 1837 *8197.10 p101*
Polonowicz, Stephen; Maryland, 1910 *3259.35 p49*
Polson, Mr.; Quebec, 1857 *9196.15 p23*
Polson, John; Georgia, 1761 *1640.10 p171*
Polson, Pete 47; British Columbia, 1909 *9196.1 p28*
Polson, Pete 47; Washington, 1909 *9196.1 p28*
Polten, Anne 35; Ontario, 1871 *1823.28 p83*
Polton, Richd.; Maryland, 1680 *2524.55 p175*
Poluchowski, Alexander; Maryland, 1910 *3259.35 p49*
Poluczinska, Macey; Maryland, 1910 *3259.35 p49*
Polwart, John; Georgia, 1734 *1640.10 p171*
Polwarth, James; New York, 1838 *8197.10 p271*
Polwarth, James; New York, 1840 *8197.10 p194*
Polydras, Henry; Maryland, 1910 *3259.35 p49*
Pomatowski, Bronislaw; Maryland, 1910 *3259.35 p49*
Pomeraing, Ernest 33; Ontario, 1871 *1823.28 p83*
Pomeray, Thomas 61; Ontario, 1871 *1823.15 p215*
Pomeroy, Henry 70; Ontario, 1871 *1823.22 p128*
Pomeroy, Hugh; Virginia, 1666 *6212.30 p28*
Pomeroy, Louisa N. 27; Ontario, 1871 *1823.22 p128*
Pomeroy, Robert; Philadelphia, 1790 *1224.2 p93*
Pomeroy, Saml; Virginia, 1676 *6212.30 p53*
Pomeroy, William 37; Ontario, 1871 *1823.15 p215*
Pomeroy, William 61; Ontario, 1871 *1823.22 p128*
Pomfast, Hannah Middleton; New England, 1650 *1224.1 p39*
Pomfrett, James; Maryland, 1681 *2524.55 p175*
Pomfrey, William 38; Maryland, 1775 *1220.25 p108*
Pommer, Hans Georg; Port uncertain, 1745 *2856.30 p343*
Pomp, . . .; America, 1766 *2856.30 p343*
Pomroy, John 40; Ontario, 1871 *1823.15 p215*
Pon, Mrs.; Quebec, 1857 *9196.15 p19*
Ponay, George 27; Maryland, 1774 *1220.25 p58*
Pond, Eva M. 41; Vermont, 1890 *5900.10 p305*
Pond, Robt; Virginia, 1667 *6212.30 p36*
Pond, Samuel; Virginia, 1698 *1224.1 p46*
Ponds, Frank; Maryland, 1910 *3259.35 p49*
Ponds, Petronela; Maryland, 1910 *3259.35 p49*
Poni, Charles; New York, 1806 *8197.10 p32*
Ponsford, Mr.; Quebec, 1858 *9196.15 p38*
Ponsford, James; New York, 1807 *8197.10 p47*
Ponsonby, Richard; New Bern, North Carolina, 1837 *1224.3 p62*
Pontious, William; New York, New York, 1881 *3437.14 p152*
Pontius, Adam; America, 1747 *2856.30 p344*
With wife & children
Pontius, Georg Heinrich; Port uncertain, 1769 *2856.30 p343*
Pontius, Jakob; Port uncertain, 1747 *2856.30 p344*
With wife & children
Pontius, Johann David; America, 1766 *2856.30 p343*
Pontius, Johann David; America, 1780 *2856.30 p344*
Pontius, Johann David; Port uncertain, 1777 *2856.30 p343*
Pontius, Johann Friedric; America, 1739 *2856.30 p344*
Pontius, Johann Philipp; America, 1766 *2856.30 p344*
Pontius, Johann Philipp; America, 1780 *2856.30 p344*
Pontius, Johann Philipp; Port uncertain, 1777 *2856.30 p344*
Pontius, Karl; Port uncertain, 1755 *2856.30 p344*
Pontius, Mrs. Peter; America, 1738 *2856.30 p344*
Pontius, William; New York, New York, 1881 *3437.14 p152*
Ponton, Archibald; Bahamas, 1799 *1640.13 p100*
Pontzius, David; America, 1768 *2856.30 p344*
Pontzius, Martin; America, 1768 *2856.30 p344*
Ponwarden, David 74; Ontario, 1871 *1823.15 p215*
Pool, Hannah 24; Montreal, 1775 *1220.25 p110*
Pool, Samuel; New York, 1819 *8197.10 p269*
Pool, William; Pennsylvania, 1777 *4629.10 p11*
Poole, Mr.; Quebec, 1858 *9196.15 p36*
Poole, Mrs.; Maryland, 1665 *2524.55 p175*
Poole, Ann; Virginia, 1690-1691 *6212.30 p59*
Poole, Edw; Virginia, 1664 *6212.30 p15*
Poole, Eliz; Virginia, 1688 *6212.30 p57*
Poole, Elizabeth; New York, New York, 1839 *1224.3 p67*
Poole, Hendrick; Maryland, 1650 *2524.55 p175*
Poole, Henry; Virginia, 1666 *6212.30 p29*
Poole, Henry 21; Maryland, 1775 *1220.25 p105*
Poole, Hugh; Maryland, 1682 *2524.55 p175*
Poole, Jane; Boston, 1685 *1224.1 p42*
Poole, John 25; Ontario, 1871 *1823.28 p83*
Poole, Joseph; Pennsylvania, 1785 *4629.10 p48*
Poole, Joseph 71; Ontario, 1871 *1823.22 p128*
Poole, Martin; Maryland, 1660 *2524.55 p175*
Poole, Richard; Dominica, 1790 *1224.2 p93*
Poole, Richard; Florida, n.d. *1224.2 p93*
Poole, Susan; Virginia, 1666 *6212.30 p25*
Poole, Theophilus; Boston, 1685 *1224.1 p42*
Poole, Thomas; Long Island, 1778 *1224.2 p93*
Poole, William 45; Ontario, 1871 *1823.22 p128*
Pooler, Sarah; Vermont, 1833-1909 *5900.10 p518*
Pooley, John; Maryland, 1673 *2524.55 p175*
Pooley, Mary; Maryland, 1672 *2524.55 p176*
Poones, Daniel 80; Ontario, 1871 *1823.15 p215*
Poor, Nicholas; Maryland, 1679 *2524.55 p175*
Poore, Elen; Maryland, 1681 *2524.55 p176*
Poore, Thomas; Maryland, 1681 *2524.55 p176*
Poorman, Charles Fredrick 76; Ontario, 1871 *1823.28 p83*
Poorman, Ida 15; Ontario, 1871 *1823.28 p83*
Poorman, Polena Charlotte 50; Ontario, 1871 *1823.28 p83*
Poorman, Powell 19; Ontario, 1871 *1823.28 p83*
Popa, Nick 40; Alaska, 1917 *9196.1 p48*
Popa, Nick 40; Whitehorse, Yukon, 1917 *9196.1 p48*
Pope, Mrs.; Maryland, 1648 *2524.55 p176*
Pope, Alexander; Jamaica, 1787 *1224.2 p93*
Pope, Alexander; Philadelphia, 1787 *1224.2 p93*
Pope, Annis; Maryland, 1658 *2524.55 p176*
Pope, Charles; America, 1830 *1224.3 p62*
Pope, Charles; New York, 1834 *8197.10 p68*
Pope, Charles 49; Ontario, 1871 *1823.15 p215*
Pope, Charles 50; Ontario, 1871 *1823.15 p215*
Pope, Charles, Jr.; New York, 1832 *8197.10 p271*
Pope, Codlip 46; Ontario, 1871 *1823.15 p215*
Pope, Daniel; Maryland, 1681 *2524.55 p176*
Pope, Francis; Maryland, 1639 *2524.55 p176*
Pope, Francis; Maryland, 1645 *2524.55 p176*
Pope, Francis; Newport, Rhode Island, 1749 *1224.2 p93*
Pope, Francis; Rhode Island, 1788 *1224.2 p93*
Pope, George 46; Ontario, 1871 *1823.15 p215*
Pope, Henry; Maryland, 1658 *2524.55 p176*
Pope, Jno; Virginia, 1681-1682 *6212.30 p56*
Pope, John 14; Maryland, 1774 *1220.25 p8*
Pope, John 21; Maryland, 1774 *1220.25 p2*
Pope, John 45; Ontario, 1871 *1823.15 p215*
Pope, John 55; Ontario, 1871 *1823.22 p128*
Pope, Mary; Maryland, 1680 *2524.55 p176*
Pope, Mary; Newport, Rhode Island, 1749 *1224.2 p93*
Pope, Mary; Vermont, 1856-1920 *5900.10 p166*
Pope, Math; Virginia, 1674 *6212.30 p52*
Pope, Nathaniel; Maryland, 1639 *2524.55 p176*
Pope, Robert; Maryland, 1669 *2524.55 p84*
Pope, Robert 39; Ontario, 1871 *1823.28 p83*
Pope, Thomas 44; Ontario, 1871 *1823.28 p83*
Pope, Thomas 47; Ontario, 1871 *1823.22 p128*
Pope, Thomas 50; Ontario, 1871 *1823.15 p215*
Pope, William 18; Maryland, 1774 *1220.25 p7*
Popiel, Joseph; Maryland, 1910 *3259.35 p49*
Popiotek, Stanislau; Maryland, 1910 *3259.35 p49*
Popjoy, William; Maryland, 1682 *2524.55 p176*
Poplac, Frank 28; British Columbia, 1910 *9196.1 p31*
Poplac, Frank 28; Washington, 1910 *9196.1 p31*
Popletone, Samuel 53; Ontario, 1871 *1823.15 p215*
Poplett, Elizabeth 28; Virginia, 1774 *1220.25 p90*
Popnacky, Joseph; Maryland, 1910 *3259.35 p49*
Popowick, Wladislow; Maryland, 1910 *3259.35 p49*
Popowski, Peter; Maryland, 1910 *3259.35 p49*
Popplesdorf, Albertus; Pennsylvania, 1777 *4629.10 p13*
Popplestone, John 50; Ontario, 1871 *1823.15 p215*
Popplewell, Mr.; Quebec, 1857 *9196.15 p18*
Poppye, Thomas; Maryland, 1670 *2524.55 p176*
Popuski, Ludwik; Maryland, 1910 *3259.35 p49*
Porcher, James; South Carolina, 1824 *1224.3 p62*
Porcheska, Andrew; Maryland, 1910 *3259.35 p49*
Pordage, George; Boston, 1691 *1224.1 p46*
Pore, J. C.; Quebec, 1856 *9196.15 p10*
Poremski, Matus; Maryland, 1910 *3259.35 p49*
Porenski, Frank; Maryland, 1910 *3259.35 p49*
Porger, Franz Nickel; Port uncertain, 1792 *2856.30 p344*
Porger, Johann; Port uncertain, 1792 *2856.30 p344*
Porger, Johann Jacob; Port uncertain, 1792 *2856.30 p344*
Porger, Maria Juliane; Port uncertain, 1792 *2856.30 p344*
Porger, Sophia Catharin; Port uncertain, 1792 *2856.30 p344*
Porle, Rebecca; Maryland, 1667 *2524.55 p219*
Poro Roe Clas, John; Maryland, 1658 *2524.55 p176*
Porrill, Joseph 63; Ontario, 1871 *1823.22 p128*
Porsch, Mr.; America, 1764 *2856.30 p346*
With brother

Porsch, Johann Georg; Port uncertain, 1771 ***2856.30*** *p346*
Port, James; Maryland, 1665 ***2524.55*** *p176*
Port, John; Maryland, 1665 ***2524.55*** *p176*
Portal, John 87; Vermont, 1911 ***5900.10*** *p328*
Portal, John A.; New York, 1830 ***8197.10*** *p362*
Portal, Juan Antonio; New York, 1829 ***8197.10*** *p352*
Portal, Margaret Tierney 83; Vermont, 1904 ***5900.10*** *p328*
Portall, Eliza 9; Vermont, 1862 ***5900.10*** *p328*
Portankiewicz, Ignacy; Maryland, 1910 ***3259.35*** *p49*
Porteate, Robert; Maryland, 1658 ***2524.55*** *p176*
Porteous, Clarisa 71; Ontario, 1871 ***1823.28*** *p83*
Porteous, George; Alabama, 1811-1845 ***1640.10*** *p171*
Porteous, John 67; Ontario, 1871 ***1823.28*** *p83*
Porteous, Mary Jane 24; Ontario, 1871 ***1823.28*** *p83*
Porteous, Robert; New York, 1828 ***8197.10*** *p271*
Porteous, Robert; New York, 1840 ***8197.10*** *p193*
Porteous, Samuel; Trinidad, 1889 ***1640.13*** *p100*
Porteous, Simon; Georgia, 1775 ***1640.10*** *p171*
Porteous, Thomas B.; New York, New York, 1854 ***6058.10*** *p70*
Porteous, William 60; Ontario, 1871 ***1823.15*** *p215*
Porter, Alexander 27; Ontario, 1871 ***1823.15*** *p215*
Porter, Alexander 37; Ontario, 1871 ***1823.15*** *p215*
Porter, Andrew 27; Ontario, 1871 ***1823.22*** *p128*
Porter, Ann; Maryland, 1649 ***2524.55*** *p176*
Porter, Anne 18; Ontario, 1861 ***2896.27*** *p19*
Porter, Betsey; Vermont, n.d. ***5900.10*** *p189*
Porter, David; Pennsylvania, 1868 ***6058.10*** *p73*
Porter, Edward W. 2; Ontario, 1861 ***2896.25*** *p2*
Porter, Elmira 58; Ontario, 1871 ***1823.28*** *p83*
Porter, Francis *SEE* Porter, Peter
Porter, Frederick; Boston, 1762 ***1224.2*** *p93*
Porter, Frederick; New York, 1840 ***8197.10*** *p272*
Porter, George; New York, New York, 1860 ***6058.10*** *p57*
Porter, George 48; Ontario, 1871 ***1823.15*** *p215*
Porter, Hannah 23; Ontario, 1861 ***2896.25*** *p2*
Porter, Hen; Virginia, 1663 ***6212.30*** *p4*
Porter, Hen; Virginia, 1665-1666 ***6212.30*** *p23*
Porter, Hen; Virginia, 1666-1667 ***6212.30*** *p32*
Porter, Henry; Maryland, 1681 ***2524.55*** *p176*
Porter, Henry; Virginia, 1664 ***6212.30*** *p13*
Porter, Henry 65; Ontario, 1871 ***1823.22*** *p128*
Porter, Hugh 11; Ontario, 1861 ***2896.25*** *p57*
Porter, James; New York, 1840 ***8197.10*** *p194*
Porter, James 40; Ontario, 1871 ***1823.15*** *p215*
Porter, Jane; Maryland, 1680 ***2524.55*** *p176*
Porter, Joan; Maryland, 1651 ***2524.55*** *p176*
Porter, John; New York, 1823 ***8197.10*** *p270*
Porter, John; New York, 1838 ***8197.10*** *p127*
Porter, John 2; Ontario, 1861 ***2896.25*** *p57*
Porter, John 40; Ontario, 1871 ***1823.15*** *p215*
Porter, John 45; Ontario, 1871 ***1823.15*** *p215*
Porter, John 47; Ontario, 1871 ***1823.15*** *p215*
Porter, John 50; Ontario, 1871 ***1823.15*** *p215*
Porter, M. A.; America, 1876 ***1640.13*** *p100*
Porter, Margaret 5; Ontario, 1861 ***2896.25*** *p57*
Porter, Margaret J. 4; Ontario, 1861 ***2896.25*** *p2*
Porter, Martha 7; Ontario, 1861 ***2896.25*** *p57*
Porter, Mary; Vermont, 1816-1892 ***5900.10*** *p189*
Porter, Mary Jane 18; Ontario, 1861 ***2896.25*** *p57*
Porter, Nancy 70; Ontario, 1871 ***1823.15*** *p215*
Porter, Patience; Maryland, 1665 ***2524.55*** *p238*
Porter, Patience; Maryland, 1674 ***2524.55*** *p176*
Porter, Peter; Maryland, 1659 ***2524.55*** *p176*
Wife: Francis
Porter, Richard; Pennsylvania, 1777 ***4629.10*** *p25*
Porter, Richard; Virginia, 1663 ***6212.30*** *p1*
Porter, Richard; Virginia, 1666 ***6212.30*** *p28*
Porter, Richard 32; Ontario, 1871 ***1823.15*** *p215*
Porter, Robert 27; Ontario, 1861 ***2896.25*** *p2*
Porter, Robert 39; Ontario, 1871 ***1823.28*** *p83*
Porter, Robert 42; Ontario, 1871 ***1823.15*** *p215*
Porter, Samuel; Pennsylvania, 1786 ***4629.10*** *p54*
Porter, Samuel 35; Ontario, 1871 ***1823.15*** *p215*
Porter, Sarah 9; Ontario, 1861 ***2896.25*** *p57*
Porter, Sary 40; Ontario, 1861 ***2896.25*** *p57*
Porter, Sudney C. 19; Ontario, 1861 ***2896.27*** *p29*
Porter, Tho; Virginia, 1673 ***6212.30*** *p51*
Porter, Thomas; New York, 1724 ***1224.2*** *p93*
Porter, Thomas; New York, 1836 ***8197.10*** *p77*
Porter, Thomas; Virginia, 1673 ***6212.30*** *p51*
Porter, William; Maryland, 1649 ***2524.55*** *p176*
With wife
Porter, William 13; Ontario, 1861 ***2896.25*** *p57*
Porter, William 18; Ontario, 1871 ***1823.15*** *p215*
Porter, William 48; Ontario, 1871 ***1823.15*** *p215*
Porter, William H.; New York, 1827 ***8197.10*** *p271*
Porter, Wm; Virginia, 1673 ***6212.30*** *p51*
Porterfield, Alexander; New York, 1807 ***8197.10*** *p47*
Porterfield, James 47; Ontario, 1871 ***1823.15*** *p215*
Porterfield, John 41; Ontario, 1871 ***1823.15*** *p215*
Porterfield, Peter 36; Ontario, 1871 ***1823.15*** *p215*
Porteus, Edward; Virginia, 1700 ***1224.2*** *p93*
Porteus, Simon 49; Georgia, 1775 ***1220.25*** *p125*
Porteus, Thomas B.; New York, New York, 1854 ***6058.10*** *p70*
Porth, Johann Philipp; Port uncertain, 1780 ***2856.30*** *p344*
Portias, William 40; Ontario, 1871 ***1823.15*** *p215*
Portiener, Catharina; Port uncertain, 1771 ***2856.30*** *p344*
Portilla, Ramon de la; New York, 1838 ***8197.10*** *p271*
Portin, Elisabeth; Port uncertain, 1740 ***2856.30*** *p344*
Portious, William 52; Ontario, 1871 ***1823.28*** *p83*
Portley, John; New York, 1828 ***8197.10*** *p349*
Portman, Robert; Virginia, 1654 ***1224.1*** *p46*
Portner, Johann Georg; Port uncertain, 1752 ***2856.30*** *p344*
With wife & children
Portous, Robert 43; Ontario, 1871 ***1823.28*** *p83*
Portwood, Elizabeth; Maryland, 1680 ***2524.55*** *p176*
Portwood, John; Maryland, 1680 ***2524.55*** *p176*
Porulewski, John; Maryland, 1910 ***3259.35*** *p49*
Pory, Tho; Virginia, 1663 ***6212.30*** *p4*
Porzki, Tomaz; Maryland, 1910 ***3259.35*** *p49*
Poschinger, Joseph Jacob; New York, 1824 ***8197.10*** *p270*
Posey, Mrs.; Maryland, 1643 ***2524.55*** *p176*
Posey, Francis; Maryland, 1640 ***2524.55*** *p176*
Posilwaitt, George 73; Ontario, 1871 ***1823.15*** *p215*
Posnaniak, Martin; Maryland, 1910 ***3259.35*** *p49*
Possert, Johann; Port uncertain, 1744 ***2856.30*** *p344*
Post, Albert W. 13; Ontario, 1861 ***2896.28*** *p64*
Post, Almira D. 8; Ontario, 1861 ***2896.28*** *p53*
Post, Ann E. 7; Ontario, 1861 ***2896.25*** *p37*
Post, Anne M. 15; Ontario, 1861 ***2896.28*** *p57*
Post, Catherine 33; Ontario, 1861 ***2896.25*** *p37*
Post, Catherine 33; Ontario, 1861 ***2896.28*** *p64*
Post, Charles 42; Ontario, 1861 ***2896.28*** *p52*
Post, Charles H. 17; Ontario, 1861 ***2896.28*** *p53*
Post, Charlotte A. 49; Ontario, 1861 ***2896.28*** *p52*
Post, Clarah 27; Ontario, 1861 ***2896.28*** *p58*
Post, Elen 16; Ontario, 1861 ***2896.27*** *p11*
Post, Eunice 80; Ontario, 1861 ***2896.25*** *p37*
Post, Friedrich; Port uncertain, 1785 ***2856.30*** *p344*
With wife & child
Post, George W. 15; Ontario, 1861 ***2896.28*** *p53*
Post, Irvine W. 12; Ontario, 1861 ***2896.28*** *p57*
Post, Jacob 81; Ontario, 1861 ***2896.28*** *p64*
Post, James 27; Ontario, 1861 ***2896.28*** *p52*
Post, James R. 13; Ontario, 1861 ***2896.28*** *p53*
Post, Jamima 44; Ontario, 1861 ***2896.28*** *p57*
Post, John 90; Ontario, 1861 ***2896.25*** *p37*
Post, Magdalena; Port uncertain, 1785 ***2856.30*** *p344*
Post, Marshal W. 5; Ontario, 1861 ***2896.28*** *p53*
Post, Martha J. 19; Ontario, 1861 ***2896.28*** *p57*
Post, Mary 69; Ontario, 1861 ***2896.28*** *p52*
Post, Mary 71; Ontario, 1861 ***2896.28*** *p64*
Post, Mary E. 5; Ontario, 1861 ***2896.28*** *p64*
Post, Mary E. 18; Ontario, 1861 ***2896.28*** *p53*
Post, Mary M. 1; Ontario, 1861 ***2896.28*** *p52*
Post, Nathan 12; Ontario, 1861 ***2896.25*** *p37*
Post, Oliver 7; Ontario, 1861 ***2896.28*** *p57*
Post, Peter Wm 23; Ontario, 1861 ***2896.28*** *p57*
Post, Rebecca 9; Ontario, 1861 ***2896.28*** *p57*
Post, Rinar T. 21; Ontario, 1861 ***2896.28*** *p57*
Post, Robert 11, Ontario, 1861 ***2896.27*** *p11*
Post, S. E. 3; Ontario, 1861 ***2896.26*** *p24*
Post, Samantha 11; Ontario, 1861 ***2896.28*** *p64*
Post, Samuel J. 17; Ontario, 1861 ***2896.28*** *p57*
Post, Saphrenus 1; Ontario, 1861 ***2896.28*** *p64*
Post, Sarah 23; Ontario, 1861 ***2896.27*** *p11*
Post, Semantha 1; Ontario, 1861 ***2896.26*** *p24*
Post, Thomas 66; Ontario, 1861 ***2896.27*** *p11*
Post, Thursa M. 21; Ontario, 1861 ***2896.28*** *p52*
Post, Walter 1; Ontario, 1861 ***2896.28*** *p57*
Post, Walter 10; Ontario, 1861 ***2896.25*** *p37*
Post, Wilferd A. 2; Ontario, 1861 ***2896.28*** *p53*
Post, William H. 9; Ontario, 1861 ***2896.28*** *p64*
Post, William S. 5; Ontario, 1861 ***2896.25*** *p37*
Postanowicz, Roch; Maryland, 1910 ***3259.35*** *p49*
Posthtewaite, Thomas 45; Ontario, 1871 ***1823.22*** *p128*
Postlethwaite, Mr.; Quebec, 1857 ***9196.15*** *p17*
Postlethwaite, George; New York, New York, 1803 ***1224.3*** *p62*
Poston, E.; Quebec, 1857 ***9196.15*** *p24*
Postuszny, Wadyslaw; Maryland, 1910 ***3259.35*** *p49*
Poswiatowski, Charles; Maryland, 1910 ***3259.35*** *p49*
Poszko, Henry; Maryland, 1910 ***3259.35*** *p49*
Potaskiewicz, Walter; Maryland, 1910 ***3259.35*** *p49*
Poteraj, Stephen; Maryland, 1910 ***3259.35*** *p49*
Poth, Maria Magdalena; Port uncertain, 1784 ***2856.30*** *p344*
Pothell, David; Virginia, 1665-1666 ***6212.30*** *p22*
Potocki, Stephen; Maryland, 1910 ***3259.35*** *p49*
Potonralska, Michel; Maryland, 1910 ***3259.35*** *p49*
Potovin, Sebastian; New England, 1716 ***1224.2*** *p93*
Potroki, James; Maryland, 1910 ***3259.35*** *p49*
Potrsysky, Leon; Maryland, 1910 ***3259.35*** *p49*
Potrzuski, Frank; Maryland, 1910 ***3259.35*** *p49*
Pots, Ellen 60; Ontario, 1871 ***1823.22*** *p128*
Pott, Mr.; Quebec, 1858 ***9196.15*** *p46*
Pott, Adam; Port uncertain, 1749 ***2856.30*** *p344*
Pott, Ann; Maryland, 1649-1650 ***2524.55*** *p176*
Pott, Eliza *SEE* Pott, John
Pott, John; Maryland, 1658 ***2524.55*** *p176*
Wife: Eliza
Pott, Mary; Maryland, 1681 ***2524.55*** *p176*
Pott, Richd; Virginia, 1671-1672 ***6212.30*** *p46*
Potten, John; Havana, 1765 ***1224.2*** *p88*
Potter, Amos 55; Ontario, 1871 ***1823.22*** *p128*
Potter, Ann; Maryland, 1664 ***2524.55*** *p176*
Potter, Austin 26; Ontario, 1871 ***1823.28*** *p83*
Potter, Betsy 6; Ontario, 1861 ***2896.25*** *p59*
Potter, Bridget 34; Vermont, 1874 ***5900.10*** *p133*
Potter, Carl 33; Ontario, 1871 ***1823.28*** *p83*
Potter, Catherine 37; Ontario, 1861 ***2896.25*** *p59*
Potter, Cynthia 4; Ontario, 1861 ***2896.25*** *p59*
Potter, Ellen; Vermont, 1855-1926 ***5900.10*** *p333*
Potter, Frederick 42; Ontario, 1871 ***1823.28*** *p83*
Potter, George; Virginia, 1666 ***6212.30*** *p30*
Potter, Henry; Maryland, 1649 ***2524.55*** *p176*
Potter, James; Kansas, 1876 ***1640.13*** *p100*
Potter, James 42; Ontario, 1871 ***1823.15*** *p216*
Potter, James 65; Ontario, 1871 ***1823.15*** *p216*
Potter, Jesse 22; Ontario, 1861 ***2896.25*** *p59*
Potter, John 36; Ontario, 1871 ***1823.15*** *p216*
Potter, John 44; Ontario, 1871 ***1823.28*** *p83*
Potter, John 57; Ontario, 1871 ***1823.28*** *p83*
Potter, John W. 37; Ontario, 1871 ***1823.28*** *p83*
Potter, Joseph; Maryland, 1910 ***3259.35*** *p49*
Potter, Keziah 64; Ontario, 1861 ***2896.25*** *p59*
Potter, Lyndia 1; Ontario, 1861 ***2896.25*** *p59*
Potter, Mary; Vermont, 1848-1948 ***5900.10*** *p215*
Potter, Matilda 8; Ontario, 1861 ***2896.25*** *p59*
Potter, Richard 20; Ontario, 1871 ***1823.28*** *p83*
Potter, Richard 50; Ontario, 1871 ***1823.22*** *p128*
Potter, Samuel 12; Ontario, 1861 ***2896.25*** *p59*
Potter, Thomas 21; Virginia, 1774 ***1220.25*** *p56*
Potter, Thomas 53; Ontario, 1871 ***1823.28*** *p83*
Potter, Thomas 58; Ontario, 1871 ***1823.15*** *p216*
Potter, Wilford 10; Ontario, 1861 ***2896.25*** *p59*
Potter, William; Maryland, 1668 ***2524.55*** *p176*
Potter, X. P.; Virginia, 1666 ***6212.30*** *p29*
Pottinger, James; New York, 1764 ***1224.2*** *p93*
Pottinger, James 15; Philadelphia, 1774 ***1220.25*** *p82*
Pottinger, John; New York, New York, 1820 ***1224.3*** *p61*
Pottlander, Johann Adam; Port uncertain, 1738 ***2856.30*** *p346*
Potts, George 36; Ontario, 1871 ***1823.22*** *p129*
Potts, George 63; Ontario, 1871 ***1823.22*** *p128*
Potts, John; Virginia, 1668-1669 ***6212.30*** *p40*
Potts, John, Jr.; Pennsylvania, 1779 ***4629.10*** *p41*
Potts, Joseph; Maryland, 1777 ***1224.2*** *p93*
Potts, Joseph; Philadelphia, 1773 ***1224.2*** *p93*
Potts, Joseph 62; Ontario, 1871 ***1823.22*** *p129*
Potts, Joseph, Jr.; Pennsylvania, 1785 ***4629.10*** *p48*
Potts, Ralph Henry; New York, 1825 ***8197.10*** *p297*
Potts, Robert 59; Ontario, 1871 ***1823.22*** *p129*
Potts, Stephen 37; Ontario, 1871 ***1823.22*** *p129*
Potts, Theophilus; Virginia, 1678 ***1224.1*** *p46*
Potts, Tho; Virginia, 1674-1675 ***6212.30*** *p53*
Potts, Thomas; New York, New York, 1852 ***6058.10*** *p69*
Potts, William; Pennsylvania, 1777 ***4629.10*** *p11*
Potts, William I.; New York, 1837 ***8197.10*** *p101*
Potts, William J.; New York, 1840 ***8197.10*** *p385*
Potts, William T. 38; Ontario, 1871 ***1823.15*** *p216*
Potuyanski, Michail; Maryland, 1910 ***3259.35*** *p49*
Potz, Johann Adam; Port uncertain, 1749 ***2856.30*** *p345*
Potzalska, Jacob; Maryland, 1910 ***3259.35*** *p49*
Poule, Julia 76; Vermont, 1896 ***5900.10*** *p434*
Pouleson, Clare *SEE* Pouleson, Michael
Pouleson, Cosine *SEE* Pouleson, Michael
Pouleson, Geo. *SEE* Pouleson, Michael
Pouleson, John *SEE* Pouleson, Michael
Pouleson, Mary *SEE* Pouleson, Michael
Pouleson, Michael *SEE* Pouleson, Michael
Pouleson, Michael; Maryland, 1661 ***2524.55*** *p177*
Wife: Mary
Relative: Cosine
Relative: John
Relative: Geo.
Relative: Clare
Relative: Mary
Relative: Michael
Relative: Paul
Pouleson, Paul *SEE* Pouleson, Michael
Poullan, Thomas; Maryland, 1680 ***2524.55*** *p177*

Pouls, Paul; Virginia, 1684 1224.1 p46
Poulson, Andrew; Maryland, 1662 2524.55 p177
Poulson, Anguett; Maryland, 1664 2524.55 p107
Poulson, Isabel; Virginia, 1701 1224.2 p43
Poulson, Paul; Virginia, 1684 1224.1 p46
Poulter, Edward; Maryland, 1672 2524.55 p177
Poulter, Edward; Maryland, 1678 2524.55 p177
Poulter, Mathew; Maryland, 1681 2524.55 p177
Poulter, Samuel 39; Virginia, 1774 1220.25 p87
Poulter, Thomas; Virginia, 1663 1224.1 p60
Pound, Edward 19; Maryland, 1774 1220.25 p57
Pound, Edward 32; Maryland, 1774 1220.25 p46
Pounder, John 66; Ontario, 1871 1823.28 p83
Poupore, Sarah 65; Ontario, 1871 1823.28 p83
Pour, Thomas; America, 1737 2856.30 p345
Pourie, Alexander; Georgia, 1698 1640.13 p100
Pourridge, Thomas; Maryland, 1662 2524.55 p30
Pourridge, Thomas; Maryland, 1662 2524.55 p177
Pouse, William; Maryland, 1673 2524.55 p177
Pouvroy, John; Georgia, 1734 1640.10 p171
Pouvroy, Martha; Georgia, 1734 1640.10 p171
Poveroski, Alexander; Maryland, 1910 3259.35 p49
Povey, James 29; Philadelphia, 1774 1220.25 p86
Povey, John; New York, 1831 8197.10 p271
Povinski, Lawrence; Maryland, 1910 3259.35 p49
Pow, David; Savannah, Georgia, 1804 1640.10 p171
Powderly, Ann 88; Vermont, 1922 5900.10 p434
Powderly, Elizabeth; Vermont, 1842-1929 5900.10 p434
Powderly, William 52; Vermont, 1896 5900.10 p138
Powele, Edgar; Virginia, 1668-1669 6212.30 p41
Powell, Ann *SEE* Powell, Thomas
Powell, Ann 21; Baltimore, 1775 1220.25 p119
Powell, Elizabeth *SEE* Powell, Thomas
Powell, Elizabeth; Maryland, 1671 2524.55 p177
Powell, Ephraim 72; Ontario, 1871 1823.22 p129
Powell, Even; Virginia, 1663 6212.30 p2
Powell, Frederick; Pennsylvania, 1777 4629.10 p10
Powell, George; Maryland, 1663-1664 2524.55 p177
Powell, George; Maryland, 1673 2524.55 p177
Powell, George; Maryland, 1674 2524.55 p177
Powell, George W.; New York, 1826 8197.10 p270
Powell, Howell *SEE* Powell, Thomas
Powell, Howell; New York, New York, 1842 1224.3 p62
Powell, Hugh; Philadelphia, 1771 1224.2 p93
Powell, James; Maryland, 1747 1224.2 p93
Powell, James; Virginia, 1664-1665 6212.30 p16
Powell, James 21; Maryland, 1774 1220.25 p74
Powell, James 22; Maryland, 1774 1220.25 p71
Powell, Jane; Virginia, 1663 6212.30 p2
Powell, Jane; Virginia, 1667 6212.30 p37
Powell, John; Boston, n.d. 1224.2 p94
Powell, John; Maryland, 1664 2524.55 p177
Powell, John; Maryland, 1668 2524.55 p177
Powell, John; Maryland, 1681 2524.55 p177
Powell, John; New England, 1673 1224.1 p46
Powell, John; Virginia, 1671-1672 6212.30 p45
Powell, John 36; Virginia, 1774 1220.25 p46
Powell, John 55; Ontario, 1871 1823.15 p216
Powell, John Parry; St. Louis, 1841 1224.3 p62
Powell, Jonathan 66; Ontario, 1871 1823.22 p129
Powell, Joseph; New York, 1833 1224.3 p62
Powell, Joseph 25; Maryland, 1773-1774 1220.25 p34
Powell, Lawrence; Pennsylvania, 1777 4629.10 p22
Powell, Lenord; Virginia, 1665 6212.30 p17
Powell, Lydia 21; Philadelphia, 1774 1220.25 p43
Powell, Margarett; Maryland, 1671 2524.55 p177
Powell, Mary; Maryland, 1653 2524.55 p82
Powell, Mary; Maryland, 1659 2524.55 p83
Powell, Mary; Maryland, 1679 2524.55 p177
Powell, Mary 33; Jamaica, 1774 1220.25 p85
Powell, Orrien 51; Ontario, 1871 1823.22 p129
Powell, Penelope 23; Maryland, 1775 1220.25 p97
Powell, Ralph; Maryland, 1667 2524.55 p177
Powell, Richard; Pennsylvania, 1777 4629.10 p16
Powell, Richard; Virginia, 1654 1224.1 p46
Powell, Richard 21; Maryland, 1774 1220.25 p37
Powell, Samuel; Pennsylvania, 1777 4629.10 p21
Powell, Samuel 60; Ontario, 1871 1823.28 p83
Powell, Sara; Virginia, 1665 6212.30 p17
Powell, Sarah; Maryland, 1675 2524.55 p177
Powell, Sarah 21; Maryland, 1775 1220.25 p111
Powell, Simon 56; Ontario, 1871 1823.15 p216
Powell, Thomas; Maryland, 1661 2524.55 p177
Relative: Howell
Relative: Ann
Relative: Elizabeth
Relative: Ann
Powell, Thomas; Maryland, 1668 2524.55 p177
Wife: Ann
Powell, Thomas 53; Ontario, 1871 1823.15 p216
Powell, Walter; Maryland, 1658 2524.55 p177
Powell, William; Maryland, 1666 2524.55 p177
Powell, William; Maryland, 1667 2524.55 p177
Powell, William; Maryland, 1678 2524.55 p177
Powell, William; Maryland, 1679 2524.55 p177
Powell, William; New York, 1830 8197.10 p353
Powell, William; Pennsylvania, 1779 4629.10 p39
Powell, William; Virginia, 1651 1224.1 p46
Powell, William 15; Philadelphia, 1774 1220.25 p42
Powell, William 36; Ontario, 1871 1823.28 p83
Power, Miss; Quebec, 1858 9196.15 p37
Power, Andrew 15; Maryland, 1775 1220.25 p120
Power, Anstas; Maryland, 1682 2524.55 p177
Power, Edmund; New York, 1827 8197.10 p343
Power, Edward; Georgia, 1698 1640.13 p101
Power, Edward; Maryland, 1682 2524.55 p177
Power, Edward 45; Ontario, 1871 1823.28 p83
Power, Ellen 32; Vermont, 1857 5900.10 p368
Power, Emily; New York, 1856 1224.3 p63
Power, John; Maryland, 1682 2524.55 p178
Power, John; New York, 1818-1834 8197.10 p309
Power, John; New York, 1835 8197.10 p98
Power, John 32; Ontario, 1871 1823.28 p83
Power, Katharine; Maryland, 1682 2524.55 p178
Power, Lucy; Virginia, 1769 1224.2 p94
Power, Margaret 50; Ontario, 1871 1823.28 p83
Power, Mary; Vermont, 1852-1939 5900.10 p310
Power, Morris 50; Ontario, 1871 1823.28 p83
Power, Nicholas; New York, 1839 8197.10 p137
Power, Patrick; Pennsylvania, 1861 6058.10 p65
Power, Peter 55; Ontario, 1871 1823.28 p83
Power, Sarah 75; Ontario, 1871 1823.28 p83
Power, Thomas; America, 1737 2856.30 p345
Power, Thomas; Virginia, 1686 1224.1 p46
Power, Thomas 51; Ontario, 1871 1823.28 p83
Power, William 18; Philadelphia, 1774 1220.25 p6
Power, William 24; Maryland, 1775 1220.25 p108
Power, William 52; Ontario, 1871 1823.28 p83
Powers, Abraham; Pennsylvania, 1778 4629.10 p32
Powers, Alexander; Vermont, 1858-1902 5900.10 p166
Powers, Anastasia; Vermont, 1838-1899 5900.10 p351
Powers, Ann; Vermont, 1887 5900.10 p207
Powers, Ann 58; Vermont, 1876 5900.10 p350
Powers, Anna B.; Vermont, 1859-1935 5900.10 p489
Powers, Anna E. Markham; Vermont, 1852-1949 5900.10 p96
Powers, Anna Statia; Vermont, 1822-1895 5900.10 p155
Powers, Bridget; Vermont, 1841-1903 5900.10 p563
Powers, Bridget Cullinan; Vermont, 1850-1910 5900.10 p93
Powers, Bridget G. 37; Vermont, 1866 5900.10 p157
Powers, Bridget Mulvaney; Vermont, 1836-1914 5900.10 p475
Powers, Bridget Ward; Vermont, 1857-1940 5900.10 p492
Powers, Catharine Tinney; Vermont, 1830-1896 5900.10 p311
Powers, Catherine; Vermont, n.d. 5900.10 p139
Powers, Catherine; Vermont, 1816-1904 5900.10 p179
Powers, Catherine 55; Vermont, 1879 5900.10 p170
Powers, Edward; Vermont, 1833-1910 5900.10 p88
Powers, Edward E. 40; Vermont, 1893 5900.10 p566
Powers, Elisabeth 22; Vermont, 1870 5900.10 p157
Powers, Eliza 65; Ontario, 1871 1823.22 p129
Powers, Elizabeth; Vermont, 1848-1930 5900.10 p352
Powers, Ellen; Vermont, 1841-1904 5900.10 p144
Powers, Ellen Flynn; Vermont, 1831-1914 5900.10 p483
Powers, Ellenor 72; Vermont, 1846 5900.10 p160
Powers, Francis G. 70; Vermont, 1885 5900.10 p350
Powers, Hanora 85; Vermont, 1883 5900.10 p85
Powers, Harriet; Vermont, 1849-1899 5900.10 p133
Powers, Honore Normyle; Vermont, 1910 5900.10 p54
Powers, J. Bernard; Vermont, 1866-1946 5900.10 p392
Powers, Jabez 63; Ontario, 1871 1823.22 p129
Powers, Jacob; Pennsylvania, 1778 4629.10 p32
Powers, James; New York, 1838 8197.10 p146
Powers, James; New York, 1840 8197.10 p193
Powers, James 33; Ontario, 1871 1823.28 p83
Powers, James 83; Vermont, 1890 5900.10 p85
Powers, James E.; Vermont, 1863-1924 5900.10 p394
Powers, James S.; Vermont, 1841-1903 5900.10 p489
Powers, Jeffrey 43; Vermont, 1884 5900.10 p571
Powers, John; Vermont, 1828-1890 5900.10 p311
Powers, John; Vermont, 1828-1898 5900.10 p93
Powers, John; Vermont, 1848-1916 5900.10 p354
Powers, John; Vermont, 1878 5900.10 p246
Powers, John 36; Vermont, 1870 5900.10 p54
Powers, John 65; Vermont, 1866 5900.10 p157
Powers, John E. 89; Vermont, 1917 5900.10 p397
Powers, John W.; Vermont, 1846-1922 5900.10 p96
Powers, Joseph; Philadelphia, 1794 4629.10 p82
Powers, Julia Boyle; Vermont, 1879 5900.10 p247
Powers, Julia O'Brien; Vermont, 1821-1901 5900.10 p484
Powers, Katherine Cunningham; Vermont, 1843-1903 5900.10 p74
Powers, Kittie 33; Vermont, 1888 5900.10 p157
Powers, Lizzie L. 20; Vermont, 1880 5900.10 p350
Powers, Louisa S.; Vermont, 1852-1922 5900.10 p555
Powers, Margaret; Vermont, 1843-1916 5900.10 p89
Powers, Margaret Burke; Vermont, 1849-1924 5900.10 p394
Powers, Margaret Cummins; Vermont, 1860-1938 5900.10 p166
Powers, Margaret Mooney 54; Vermont, 1896 5900.10 p397
Powers, Margaret Mulqueen 75; Vermont, 1889 5900.10 p98
Powers, Mary; Vermont, 1859-1923 5900.10 p77
Powers, Mary; Vermont, 1861-1942 5900.10 p397
Powers, Mary 60; Vermont, 1875 5900.10 p157
Powers, Mary 70; Vermont, 1893 5900.10 p192
Powers, Mary 75; Vermont, 1903 5900.10 p137
Powers, Mary E.; Vermont, 1874-1953 5900.10 p354
Powers, Mary Ferry; Vermont, 1849-1897 5900.10 p392
Powers, Mary Haher; Vermont, 1841-1924 5900.10 p579
Powers, Mary Jones; Vermont, 1850-1921 5900.10 p354
Powers, Mary Mooney 34; Vermont, 1872 5900.10 p571
Powers, Mary Russell 35; Vermont, 1857 5900.10 p160
Powers, Michael; Vermont, 1845-1925 5900.10 p579
Powers, Michael C.; Vermont, 1829-1916 5900.10 p483
Powers, Michael D.; Vermont, 1837-1914 5900.10 p475
Powers, Michael J. 73; Vermont, 1920 5900.10 p489
Powers, Nancy 63; Vermont, 1902 5900.10 p489
Powers, Nora; Vermont, 1867-1964 5900.10 p351
Powers, Patrick; New York, 1822 8197.10 p270
Powers, Patrick; New York, 1827 8197.10 p344
Powers, Patrick; New York, 1831 8197.10 p366
Powers, Pierre; New York, 1837 8197.10 p101
Powers, Richard 55; Vermont, 1897 5900.10 p87
Powers, Robert 73; Vermont, 1848 5900.10 p160
Powers, Sarah; Vermont, 1860-1913 5900.10 p183
Powers, Thomas; New York, 1802 8197.10 p24
Powers, Thomas; Vermont, 1831-1909 5900.10 p351
Powers, Thomas; Vermont, 1842-1895 5900.10 p74
Powers, Thomas 21; Vermont, 1873 5900.10 p157
Powers, Thomas 76; Vermont, 1895 5900.10 p98
Powers, William; Vermont, 1842-1910 5900.10 p133
Powers, William; Vermont, 1852-1935 5900.10 p492
Powers, William M.; Vermont, 1857-1888 5900.10 p409
Powill, Howill 54; Ontario, 1871 1823.15 p216
Powis, Henry; New York, 1829 8197.10 p303
Powlak, Martin; Maryland, 1910 3259.35 p49
Powles, Thomas; Ohio, 1856 1224.3 p63
Powley, John; New York, 1828 8197.10 p348
Powling, Benjamin; Illinois, 1855 1224.3 p63
Powrie, John; Georgia, 1734 1640.10 p171
Powrie, Martha; Georgia, 1734 1640.10 p171
Powse, William; Maryland, 1673 2524.55 p178
Powys, Thomas; Boston, 1684 1224.1 p46
Poyntel, William 21; Baltimore, 1775 1220.25 p117
Poyntell, John; Pennsylvania, 1785 4629.10 p48
Poyntell, William; Philadelphia, 1812 1224.3 p63
Poyntell, William 21; Maryland, 1775 1220.25 p103
Poynter, Abigaile; Maryland, 1674 2524.55 p178
Poynter, Frances; Maryland, 1674 2524.55 p178
Poynter, Thomas; Maryland, 1674 2524.55 p178
Poynter, William; Maryland, 1674 2524.55 p178
Poyntill, William; Pennsylvania, 1777 4629.10 p28
Poyton, James 40; Philadelphia, 1774 1220.25 p80
Pozenski, Wojciech; Maryland, 1910 3259.35 p49
Pozniak, William; Maryland, 1910 3259.35 p49
Pozybylowski, Wladyslaw; Maryland, 1910 3259.35 p49
Prade, James; Virginia, 1666 6212.30 p27
Prady, Nicholas; Maryland, 1673 2524.55 p178
Pragowski, Michael; Maryland, 1910 3259.35 p49
Prags, Franz Ignaz; Port uncertain, 1772 2856.30 p346
Prance, Emely Cushing; Vermont, 1844-1909 5900.10 p349
Prance, John; Vermont, 1841-1925 5900.10 p349
Prancke, Maria Elisabeth; Port uncertain, 1764 2856.30 p345
Prankay, Agustus 31; Ontario, 1871 1823.28 p83
Pratesy, Maximilian; New York, 1826 8197.10 p271
Pratt, Alexander; Bermuda, 1888 1640.13 p101
Pratt, Alexander 21; Ontario, 1871 1823.22 p129
Pratt, Caleb; Boston, 1748 1224.2 p94
Pratt, George; Portland, Maine, 1858 9196.15 p29
Pratt, George 22; Virginia, 1774 1220.25 p76
Pratt, George 50; Ontario, 1871 1823.22 p129
Pratt, George 60; Ontario, 1871 1823.22 p129
Pratt, Horace Southworth; Alabama, 1843 1224.3 p63
Pratt, James 32; Ontario, 1871 1823.15 p216
Pratt, James 45; Ontario, 1871 1823.15 p216
Pratt, Jane Farley; Alabama, 1843 1224.3 p63
Pratt, John; Texas, 1812-1845 1640.10 p171
Pratt, John 28; Ontario, 1871 1823.15 p216
Pratt, John 36; Ontario, 1871 1823.22 p129
Pratt, John 45; Ontario, 1871 1823.22 p129

Pratt, John 73; Ontario, 1871 ***1823.22*** *p129*
Pratt, Josiah; Boston, 1767 ***1224.2*** *p94*
Pratt, Margaret; New England, 1686 ***1224.1*** *p19*
Pratt, Margarett; Maryland, 1656 ***2524.55*** *p40*
Pratt, Mary; Maryland, 1649 ***2524.55*** *p178*
Pratt, Matthew; Pennsylvania, 1777 ***4629.10*** *p24*
Pratt, Matthew; Pennsylvania, 1779 ***4629.10*** *p35*
Pratt, Rebecca 70; Ontario, 1871 ***1823.15*** *p216*
Pratt, Richard 40; Ontario, 1871 ***1823.15*** *p216*
Pratt, Robert; New York, 1836 ***8197.10*** *p271*
Pratt, Robert; New York, 1839 ***8197.10*** *p138*
Pratt, Samuel; Boston, 1767 ***1224.2*** *p94*
Pratt, Silas 33; Ontario, 1871 ***1823.15*** *p216*
Pratt, Thomas; Georgia, 1698 ***1640.13*** *p101*
Pratt, Thomas; Virginia, 1667-1668 ***6212.30*** *p38*
Pratt, Thomas 61; Ontario, 1871 ***1823.22*** *p129*
Preaut, Henry; New York, 1838 ***8197.10*** *p146*
Prebbel, Stephen 54; Ontario, 1871 ***1823.28*** *p83*
Prebble, John; New York, 1830 ***8197.10*** *p313*
Prebius, Johann Nicolaus; Port uncertain, 1788 ***2856.30*** *p345*
Precious, George 43; Ontario, 1871 ***1823.22*** *p129*
Precious, Harry 28; Ontario, 1871 ***1823.22*** *p129*
Precious, Joseph 38; Ontario, 1871 ***1823.22*** *p129*
Precious, Thomas 82; Ontario, 1871 ***1823.22*** *p129*
Prediger, Andrew 75; Kansas, 1901-1910 ***9079.10*** *p17*
Prediger, Frederic 33; Kansas, 1900-1910 ***9079.10*** *p17*
Prediger, Mary 25; Kansas, 1886-1910 ***9079.10*** *p17*
Predix, Gabriel; Virginia, 1697 ***1224.1*** *p46*
Predix, Tampefer; Maryland, 1673 ***2524.55*** *p178*
Predix, Thompson; Maryland, 1675 ***2524.55*** *p178*
Preece, Henry; California, 1850 ***1224.3*** *p63*
Preedom, Charles G.; Vermont, 1841-1904 ***5900.10*** *p398*
Preedom, Elizabeth J. Paul; Vermont, 1849-1910 ***5900.10*** *p398*
Preest, Robert; Maryland, 1674 ***2524.55*** *p178*
Preg, Catharina; Port uncertain, 1623 ***2856.30*** *p345*
Pregelt, Georg; Port uncertain, 1698 ***2856.30*** *p345*
With wife
Prehal, John; New York, 1840 ***8197.10*** *p192*
Preia, Anthony; New York, 1827 ***8197.10*** *p340*
Preier, Regina; Port uncertain, 1730 ***2856.30*** *p345*
With child
Preis, Juliana; America, 1749 ***2856.30*** *p345*
Preis, William 57; Ontario, 1871 ***1823.15*** *p216*
Preist, Robert; Maryland, 1663 ***2524.55*** *p178*
Preist, William; Maryland, 1671 ***2524.55*** *p178*
Preistly, Mary; Virginia, 1672 ***6212.30*** *p50*
Premo, Julia; Vermont, 1846-1880 ***5900.10*** *p336*
Premry, Thomas; Virginia, 1667-1668 ***6212.30*** *p39*
Prendergast, Baby; Vermont, 1870 ***5900.10*** *p211*
Prendergast, Frank; Vermont, 1852-1891 ***5900.10*** *p545*
Prendergast, Mary; New York, 1823 ***8197.10*** *p270*
Prendergast, Michael; New York, 1826 ***8197.10*** *p335*
Prendiville, Joana 43; Vermont, 1883 ***5900.10*** *p329*
Prenifskie, Mikel; Maryland, 1910 ***3259.35*** *p49*
Prentice, Mr.; Quebec, 1858 ***9196.15*** *p39*
Prentis, Alice; New England, 1701 ***1224.2*** *p94*
Prentis, John; New London, Connecticut, 1746 ***1224.2*** *p94*
Prentki, Frank; Maryland, 1910 ***3259.35*** *p49*
Prenzel, Adam; America, 1749 ***2856.30*** *p345*
Preschatt, Thomas; Maryland, 1664 ***2524.55*** *p178*
Prescott, Henry 39; Maryland, 1775 ***1220.25*** *p102*
Prescourt, Wm.; Maryland, 1635-1641 ***2524.55*** *p178*
Presley, Henry; Maryland, 1658 ***2524.55*** *p178*
Preslidge, Edw; Virginia, 1663 ***6212.30*** *p2*
Presly, Peter; Virginia, 1663 ***6212.30*** *p2*
Pressel, Michael; Port uncertain, 1755 ***2856.30*** *p345*
Pressett, John 20; Maryland, 1774 ***1220.25*** *p3*
Pressler, Eva; Port uncertain, 1749 ***2856.30*** *p345*
Pressler, Johann; Port uncertain, 1749 ***2856.30*** *p345*
Pressler, Magdalena; Port uncertain, 1749 ***2856.30*** *p345*
Pressure, Julius 34; Kansas, 1910 ***9079.10*** *p53*
Pressure, Katherine 28; Kansas, 1910 ***9079.10*** *p53*
Prest, James Abbey; New York, 1818 ***8197.10*** *p269*
Prest, Nicholas; Maryland, 1681 ***2524.55*** *p178*
Prest, William; Maryland, 1667 ***2524.55*** *p178*
Presta, Charles; Maryland, 1672 ***2524.55*** *p178*
Prester, Catharine 15; Kansas, 1900-1910 ***9079.10*** *p18*
Prester, Catharine 38; Kansas, 1900-1910 ***9079.10*** *p18*
Prester, Daniel 34; Kansas, 1900-1910 ***9079.10*** *p18*
Prester, David 12; Kansas, 1900-1910 ***9079.10*** *p18*
Prester, Gottfred 9; Kansas, 1900-1910 ***9079.10*** *p18*
Prestill, Edward; Virginia, 1671 ***6212.30*** *p43*
Preston, Mrs.; Maryland, 1650 ***2524.55*** *p178*
Preston, Ann 29; Ontario, 1861 ***2896.26*** *p33*
Preston, Ann Kerwan; Vermont, 1834-1878 ***5900.10*** *p336*
Preston, Bridget; Vermont, 1871 ***5900.10*** *p469*
Preston, Charles; Maryland, 1673 ***2524.55*** *p171*
Preston, Edward 38; Maryland, 1774 ***1220.25*** *p72*
Preston, Elizabeth; Vermont, 1846-1915 ***5900.10*** *p93*
Preston, Ellen M. Devine; Vermont, 1854-1892 ***5900.10*** *p336*
Preston, Esabella 63; Ontario, 1861 ***2896.26*** *p33*
Preston, George 21; Maryland, 1773-1774 ***1220.25*** *p34*
Preston, George, Jr.; Georgia, 1737 ***1640.10*** *p171*
Preston, Helen 72; Ontario, 1861 ***2896.27*** *p31*
Preston, James; Pennsylvania, 1786 ***4629.10*** *p55*
Preston, James; Texas, 1892 ***1640.13*** *p101*
Preston, James 32; Ontario, 1871 ***1823.15*** *p216*
Preston, Jno; Virginia, 1665-1666 ***6212.30*** *p23*
Preston, John; Virginia, 1666-1667 ***6212.30*** *p32*
Preston, Julia; Vermont, 1858-1928 ***5900.10*** *p487*
Preston, Louis 33; Vermont, 1862 ***5900.10*** *p245*
Preston, Mary 24; Ontario, 1861 ***2896.25*** *p65*
Preston, Mary 31; Vermont, 1863 ***5900.10*** *p245*
Preston, Philip; Vermont, 1834-1904 ***5900.10*** *p336*
Preston, Reuben; Virginia, 1671-1672 ***6212.30*** *p47*
Preston, Richard; Maryland, 1670 ***1224.1*** *p46*
Preston, Richard; Vermont, 1862-1885 ***5900.10*** *p336*
Preston, Thomas; Pennsylvania, 1777 ***4629.10*** *p10*
Preston, William 48; Ontario, 1871 ***1823.15*** *p216*
Prestwood, Joan; Virginia, 1666 ***6212.30*** *p31*
Preswick, Mary; New York, 1815 ***1224.3*** *p63*
Preter, John 47; Ontario, 1871 ***1823.15*** *p216*
Pretious, Ann; Maryland, 1672 ***2524.55*** *p178*
Pretty, Mr.; Quebec, 1856 ***9196.15*** *p10*
Pretty, Henry 55; Ontario, 1871 ***1823.22*** *p129*
Preturyki, Tomasz; Maryland, 1910 ***3259.35*** *p49*
Preuss, Mr.; America, 1749 ***2856.30*** *p341*
Preuss, Johann Nicol; America, 1749 ***2856.30*** *p345*
With wife & child
Prevost, Mr.; Quebec, 1857 ***9196.15*** *p19*
Prevost, William; Cincinnati, 1830 ***1224.3*** *p63*
Prewitt, Robert; New England, 1697 ***1224.1*** *p46*
Preyl, Jacob; Port uncertain, 1771 ***2856.30*** *p52*
With wife
Price, Mr.; Quebec, 1857 ***9196.15*** *p20*
Price, Mr.; Quebec, 1858 ***9196.15*** *p34*
Price, Mrs.; Quebec, 1858 ***9196.15*** *p34*
Price, Ann; Maryland, 1662 ***2524.55*** *p178*
Price, Anna; Maryland, 1660 ***2524.55*** *p178*
Price, Anth; Virginia, 1672 ***6212.30*** *p50*
Price, Bridget; Vermont, 1857 ***5900.10*** *p404*
Price, Bridget M.; Vermont, 1860-1921 ***5900.10*** *p353*
Price, Catherine *SEE* Price, John
Price, Catherine; Vermont, 1842-1925 ***5900.10*** *p328*
Price, Cesar *SEE* Price, John
Price, Charles; Maryland, 1673 ***2524.55*** *p178*
Price, Constantine; New York, 1834 ***8197.10*** *p358*
Price, David 37; Ontario, 1871 ***1823.28*** *p84*
Price, David, Sr. 50; Ontario, 1871 ***1823.28*** *p84*
Price, Dorothy; Maryland, 1665 ***2524.55*** *p178*
Price, Edward; Maryland, 1667 ***2524.55*** *p178*
Price, Edward; Maryland, 1668 ***2524.55*** *p178*
Price, Edward; Maryland, 1714 ***1224.2*** *p94*
Price, Edward 33; Virginia, 1773 ***1220.25*** *p31*
Price, Elizabeth; Maryland, 1668 ***2524.55*** *p178*
Price, Elizabeth; Maryland, 1682 ***2524.55*** *p178*
Price, Ellis; New York, 1833 ***8197.10*** *p358*
Price, Ellistyne 28; Ontario, 1871 ***1823.15*** *p216*
Price, Enoch 35; Ontario, 1871 ***1823.28*** *p84*
Price, F. 50; Alaska, 1917 ***9196.1*** *p50*
Price, F. 50; Yukon, 1917 ***9196.1*** *p50*
Price, Frances *SEE* Price, John
Price, Francis; Maryland, 1714 ***1224.2*** *p94*
Price, George; Maryland, 1656 ***2524.55*** *p178*
Price, George; Pennsylvania, 1777 ***4629.10*** *p9*
Price, Herbert; Virginia, 1665-1666 ***6212.30*** *p21*
Price, Hopkin; Virginia, n.d. ***1224.1*** *p46*
Price, Hugh 15; Philadelphia, 1774 ***1220.25*** *p79*
Price, Humphry; Maryland, 1681 ***2524.55*** *p178*
Price, J.; Quebec, 1856 ***9196.15*** *p6*
Price, James; Maryland, 1663 ***2524.55*** *p179*
Price, James; Maryland, 1666 ***2524.55*** *p178*
Wife: Suzan
Price, James; Maryland, 1670 ***2524.55*** *p179*
Price, James; Maryland, 1681 ***2524.55*** *p179*
Price, James; Virginia, 1668-1669 ***6212.30*** *p40*
Price, James 24; Ontario, 1871 ***1823.15*** *p216*
Price, James 32; Ontario, 1871 ***1823.28*** *p84*
Price, James 40; Ontario, 1871 ***1823.15*** *p216*
Price, Jenkin; Maryland, 1658 ***2524.55*** *p179*
Wife: Martha
Child: Margarett
Child: John
Price, Jenkin; Maryland, 1671-1677 ***2524.55*** *p179*
Price, Johann Nicol; America, 1749 ***2856.30*** *p345*
Price, John *SEE* Price, Jenkin
Price, John; Maryland, 1637 ***2524.55*** *p179*
Price, John; Maryland, 1641 ***2524.55*** *p179*
Price, John; Maryland, 1651 ***2524.55*** *p179*
Wife: Frances
Child: Cesar
Child: Catherine
Price, John; Maryland, 1666 ***2524.55*** *p179*
Price, John; Maryland, 1675 ***2524.55*** *p179*
Wife: Sarah
Price, John; Maryland, 1682 ***2524.55*** *p179*
Price, John; Maryland, 1910 ***3259.35*** *p49*
Price, John; New York, 1834 ***8197.10*** *p358*
Price, John; New York, 1839 ***8197.10*** *p127*
Price, John; South Carolina, 1753 ***1224.2*** *p94*
Price, John; Virginia, 1665 ***6212.30*** *p19*
Price, John; Virginia, 1668 ***1224.1*** *p46*
Price, John 18; Philadelphia, 1774 ***1220.25*** *p34*
Price, John 22; Maryland, 1775 ***1220.25*** *p113*
Price, Jonah; Virginia, 1664 ***6212.30*** *p7*
Price, Joseph B.; New York, 1838 ***8197.10*** *p127*
Price, Juliana; America, 1749 ***2856.30*** *p345*
Price, Katherine; Maryland, 1666 ***2524.55*** *p179*
Price, Lewis; Virginia, 1665 ***6212.30*** *p19*
Price, Margaret; Maryland, 1672 ***2524.55*** *p179*
Price, Margaret; Virginia, 1671-1672 ***6212.30*** *p45*
Price, Margaret A. 13; Ontario, 1871 ***1823.28*** *p84*
Price, Margarett *SEE* Price, Jenkin
Price, Maria; Vermont, 1857-1932 ***5900.10*** *p333*
Price, Martha *SEE* Price, Jenkin
Price, Mary; Maryland, 1652 ***2524.55*** *p179*
Price, Mary; Maryland, 1665 ***2524.55*** *p179*
Price, Mary; Maryland, 1673 ***2524.55*** *p179*
Price, Mary 67; Ontario, 1871 ***1823.28*** *p84*
Price, Michael; Vermont, 1820-1904 ***5900.10*** *p337*
Price, Nathaniel 22; Maryland, 1774 ***1220.25*** *p38*
Price, Penelope; Maryland, 1644 ***2524.55*** *p179*
Price, Philip; Pennsylvania, 1776 ***4629.10*** *p53*
Price, Rice 30; Maryland, 1775 ***1220.25*** *p109*
Price, Richard; Maryland, 1666 ***2524.55*** *p244*
Price, Richard; Virginia, 1630 ***1224.1*** *p47*
Price, Robert; Maryland, 1681 ***2524.55*** *p179*
Price, Robt; Virginia, 1664 ***6212.30*** *p7*
Price, Roger; Maryland, 1671 ***2524.55*** *p179*
Price, Roger; Virginia, 1672 ***1224.1*** *p47*
Price, Samuel 25; Maryland, 1775 ***1220.25*** *p108*
Price, Sarah *SEE* Price, John
Price, Suzan *SEE* Price, James
Price, Thomas; Maryland, 1668 ***2524.55*** *p179*
Price, Thomas; Maryland, 1672 ***2524.55*** *p179*
Price, Thomas; Maryland, 1680 ***2524.55*** *p179*
Price, Thomas 22; Maryland, 1774 ***1220.25*** *p74*
Price, Thomas 40; Maryland, 1774 ***1220.25*** *p61*
Price, Thomas 41; Ontario, 1871 ***1823.15*** *p216*
Price, Thomas 45; Ontario, 1871 ***1823.15*** *p216*
Price, Thomas 51; Ontario, 1871 ***1823.15*** *p216*
Price, Timothy; New York, 1807 ***8197.10*** *p326*
Price, William; Maryland, 1662 ***2524.55*** *p179*
Price, William; Maryland, 1663 ***2524.55*** *p179*
Price, William; New York, 1818 ***1224.3*** *p63*
Price, William; Pennsylvania, 1777 ***4629.10*** *p6*
Price, William; Virginia, 1671-1672 ***6212.30*** *p45*
Price, William 19; Maryland, 1774 ***1220.25*** *p39*
Price, William 50; Ontario, 1871 ***1823.15*** *p216*
Price, Wm; Virginia, 1668-1669 ***6212.30*** *p41*
Price, Wm; Virginia, 1693-1694 ***6212.30*** *p60*
Prichard, Mrs.; Maryland, 1659 ***2524.55*** *p179*
Prichard, Alfred 36; Ontario, 1871 ***1823.28*** *p84*
Prichard, David; Maryland, 1649 ***2524.55*** *p179*
Prichard, James; New York, 1840 ***1224.3*** *p63*
Prichard, John; Maryland, 1675 ***2524.55*** *p179*
Prichard, John; Maryland, 1742 ***1224.2*** *p94*
Prichard, Thomas 20; Ontario, 1871 ***1823.28*** *p84*
Prichard, William; Pennsylvania, 1826 ***6058.10*** *p14*
Prichett, Henry; Maryland, 1653 ***2524.55*** *p179*
Prichett, Hester; Maryland, 1676 ***2524.55*** *p180*
Prichlett, William; Maryland, 1664 ***2524.55*** *p179*
Prichocki, John J.; Maryland, 1910 ***3259.35*** *p49*
Pricker, John 22; Maryland, 1775 ***1220.25*** *p96*
Prickett, Miles; Virginia, 1627 ***1224.1*** *p47*
Pridaux, Mr.; Quebec, 1857 ***9196.15*** *p17*
Priddis, Mr.; Quebec, 1858 ***9196.15*** *p41*
Prideaus, John; Virginia, 1666 ***6212.30*** *p28*
Prideaux, Rich; Virginia, 1666 ***6212.30*** *p27*
Pridham, John 35; Ontario, 1871 ***1823.15*** *p216*
Priebe, Fredrick 44; Ontario, 1871 ***1823.28*** *p84*
Pries, Philipp; Port uncertain, 1777 ***2856.30*** *p53*
Priest, Charles; Maryland, 1675 ***2524.55*** *p179*
Priest, Charles; Maryland, 1681 ***2524.55*** *p179*
Priest, Francis; New York, 1838 ***8197.10*** *p127*
Priest, Henry; New York, New York, 1815 ***1224.3*** *p63*
Priest, John; Pennsylvania, 1777 ***4629.10*** *p11*
Priest, Joseph 19; Maryland, 1775 ***1220.25*** *p119*
Priest, Robert; Pennsylvania, 1777 ***4629.10*** *p24*
Priestly, Benjamin; Maryland, 1681 ***2524.55*** *p179*
Priex, John; New York, New York, 1852 ***3437.14*** *p1*

Prijs, Annie; Maryland, 1910 ***3259.35*** *p49*
Pril, John; Maryland, 1910 ***3259.35*** *p49*
Prime, Abbigail; Maryland, 1670 ***2524.55*** *p180*
Prime, Anne; Virginia, 1671-1672 ***6212.30*** *p46*
Prime, Richard Airey; New Orleans, 1818 ***1224.3*** *p63*
Primer, Ann *SEE* Primer, Richard
Primer, Richard *SEE* Primer, Richard
Primer, Richard; Maryland, 1667 ***2524.55*** *p174*
Wife: Ann
Son: William
Son: Richard
Primer, Thomas; Maryland, 1675 ***2524.55*** *p180*
Primer, William *SEE* Primer, Richard
Primerose, Catharine; Charleston, South Carolina, 1841 ***1224.3*** *p63*
Primerose, Robert; Charleston, South Carolina, 1825 ***1224.3*** *p63*
Primmer, Adam; Pennsylvania, 1777 ***4629.10*** *p16*
Primmer, Peter; Pennsylvania, 1777 ***4629.10*** *p16*
Primrose, Dorothy; Maryland, 1682 ***2524.55*** *p180*
Primrose, Edward; Augusta, Georgia, 1808 ***1640.10*** *p172*
Primrose, William 39; Maryland, 1775 ***1220.25*** *p101*
Primrose, William 43; Maryland, 1775 ***1220.25*** *p97*
Primus, John; Virginia, 1697 ***1224.1*** *p47*
Prince, Captain; Quebec, 1857 ***9196.15*** *p26*
Prince, Abbigail; Maryland, 1670 ***2524.55*** *p180*
Prince, Adam 35; Ontario, 1871 ***1823.28*** *p84*
Prince, Adam 74; Ontario, 1871 ***1823.28*** *p84*
Prince, Edward; Maryland, 1675 ***2524.55*** *p180*
Prince, Francis 35; Ontario, 1871 ***1823.28*** *p84*
Prince, John 75; Ontario, 1871 ***1823.28*** *p84*
Prince, Joseph 40; Ontario, 1871 ***1823.28*** *p84*
Prince, Joseph 59; Ontario, 1871 ***1823.28*** *p84*
Prince, Michael 32; Ontario, 1871 ***1823.28*** *p84*
Prince, Michael 47; Ontario, 1871 ***1823.28*** *p84*
Prince, Richard; Virginia, 1664 ***6212.30*** *p11*
Prindle, Timothy F.; New York, 1839 ***8197.10*** *p137*
Prine, Charles 40; Ontario, 1871 ***1823.15*** *p216*
Pringle, Alexander 60; Ontario, 1871 ***1823.22*** *p130*
Pringle, Andrew 39; Ontario, 1871 ***1823.15*** *p216*
Pringle, George 28; Philadelphia, 1774 ***1220.25*** *p43*
Pringle, Henry Timbral; Savannah, Georgia, 1867 ***1640.10*** *p172*
Pringle, Hugh 45; Ontario, 1871 ***1823.15*** *p216*
Pringle, James; New York, 1840 ***8197.10*** *p386*
Pringle, James 39; Ontario, 1871 ***1823.15*** *p216*
Pringle, James 73; Ontario, 1871 ***1823.22*** *p130*
Pringle, John; Pennsylvania, 1777 ***4629.10*** *p13*
Pringle, John 27; Maryland, 1775 ***1220.25*** *p114*
Pringle, John 30; Maryland, 1774 ***1220.25*** *p69*
Pringle, R.; Georgia, 1752 ***1640.10*** *p172*
Pringle, Walter; St. Kitts, 1760 ***1640.13*** *p101*
Pringley, John 45; Ontario, 1871 ***1823.22*** *p130*
Pringley, William 10; Ontario, 1871 ***1823.22*** *p130*
Pringley, William 32; Maryland, 1774 ***1220.25*** *p65*
Prinn, Nicholas; Virginia, 1684 ***1224.1*** *p47*
Prinoch, Jonathan 21; Maryland, 1774 ***1220.25*** *p57*
Prinse, Angas 76; Ontario, 1861 ***2896.27*** *p3*
Print, John 21; Maryland, 1774 ***1220.25*** *p71*
Printz, Catharina; Port uncertain, 1733 ***2856.30*** *p345*
Printz, Johann; America, 1754 ***2856.30*** *p345*
With wife & children
Prinz, Peter; Port uncertain, 1754 ***2856.30*** *p335*
Prior, Miss; Quebec, 1858 ***9196.15*** *p37*
Prior, Benjamin 22; Maryland, 1774 ***1220.25*** *p71*
Prior, Daniel 20; Ontario, 1871 ***1823.15*** *p216*
Prior, Elizabeth Dagnan; Vermont, 1838-1913 ***5900.10*** *p487*
Prior, Ellen; Vermont, 1830-1905 ***5900.10*** *p506*
Prior, Hugh; New York, 1840 ***8197.10*** *p272*
Prior, James; Newport, Rhode Island, 1769 ***1224.2*** *p94*
Prior, Jno; Portland, Maine, 1858 ***9196.15*** *p28*
Prior, John; New York, 1840 ***8197.10*** *p192*
Prior, John 21; Ontario, 1871 ***1823.15*** *p216*
Prior, Jone *SEE* Prior, Thomas
Prior, Katherine 53; Vermont, 1890 ***5900.10*** *p505*
Prior, Margaret 55; Vermont, 1899 ***5900.10*** *p505*
Prior, Thomas; Maryland, 1665 ***2524.55*** *p180*
Wife: Jone
Prior, Thomas; Vermont, 1836-1908 ***5900.10*** *p487*
Prior, Thomas 26; Ontario, 1871 ***1823.15*** *p216*
Prior, Walter 32; Maryland, 1774 ***1220.25*** *p85*
Prisby, Mary 40; Ontario, 1871 ***1823.22*** *p130*
Prise, John; Died enroute, 1677 ***1224.1*** *p46*
Prisketon, John 44; Ontario, 1871 ***1823.15*** *p216*
Priss, Blasius; Port uncertain, 1764 ***2856.30*** *p345*
Pritchard, Abraham; Maryland, 1662 ***2524.55*** *p85*
Pritchard, Elizabeth; Virginia, 1691 ***1224.1*** *p47*
Pritchard, George; New York, 1840 ***8197.10*** *p193*
Pritchard, Hugh 35; Ontario, 1871 ***1823.15*** *p216*
Pritchard, Owen R.; Vermont, 1849-1914 ***5900.10*** *p195*
Pritchard, Pollidore; Maryland, 1664 ***2524.55*** *p180*
With wife & daughter
Pritchard, Richard; New York, 1836 ***8197.10*** *p271*
Pritchard, Richard; New York, 1839 ***8197.10*** *p137*
Pritchard, Thomas; Maryland, 1672 ***2524.55*** *p180*
Pritchard, Warren 40; Ontario, 1871 ***1823.28*** *p84*
Pritchatt, Elizabeth *SEE* Pritchatt, Thomas
Pritchatt, Jane *SEE* Pritchatt, Thomas
Pritchatt, Thomas; Maryland, 1654 ***2524.55*** *p180*
Wife: Elizabeth
Daughter: Jane
Pritchet, Griffin; Virginia, 1701-1702 ***6212.30*** *p61*
Pritchett, Ann; Maryland, 1664 ***2524.55*** *p180*
Pritchett, Hester; Maryland, 1676 ***2524.55*** *p180*
Pritchett, William; Maryland, 1658 ***2524.55*** *p180*
With wife
Pritsch, John; Philadelphia, 1882 ***3437.14*** *p138*
Pritts, Benedict; Virginia, 1681 ***1224.1*** *p47*
Pritzen, Wendel; America, 1754 ***2856.30*** *p345*
Pritzius, Johann Adam; America, 1751 ***2856.30*** *p53*
Pritzius, Johann Adam; America, 1758 ***2856.30*** *p53*
Pritzius, Wendel; America, 1754 ***2856.30*** *p345*
Privaly, John; New York, 1807 ***8197.10*** *p47*
Prive, Friedrich; Port uncertain, 1754 ***2856.30*** *p345*
Prive, Honora Kerin; Vermont, 1830-1875 ***5900.10*** *p337*
Prix, Johann; New York, New York, 1852 ***3437.14*** *p1*
Prizbylski, Michael; Maryland, 1910 ***3259.35*** *p49*
Proberts, John; Philadelphia, 1742 ***1224.2*** *p94*
Probst, Jakob; Port uncertain, 1783 ***2856.30*** *p345*
Probst, Johann; Port uncertain, 1756 ***2856.30*** *p345*
Probst, Johann Michael; Port uncertain, 1742 ***2856.30*** *p345*
Proby, Jacob; Pennsylvania, 1777 ***4629.10*** *p19*
Proby, Richard; Maryland, 1654 ***2524.55*** *p180*
Probyen, Louise 32; Ontario, 1871 ***1823.28*** *p84*
Procarione, J. 38; Alaska, 1914 ***9196.1*** *p41*
Proch, Ludwig; New York, 1830 ***8197.10*** *p361*
Prockter, John; Virginia, 1703-1704 ***6212.30*** *p63*
Proctor, Mr.; Quebec, 1858 ***9196.15*** *p37*
Proctor, Abraham 48; Ontario, 1871 ***1823.15*** *p216*
Proctor, Charles 47; Ontario, 1871 ***1823.15*** *p216*
Proctor, Elizabeth 71; Ontario, 1871 ***1823.22*** *p130*
Proctor, Francis, Sr.; Pennsylvania, 1779 ***4629.10*** *p37*
Proctor, Francis, Jr.; Pennsylvania, 1781 ***4629.10*** *p42*
Proctor, John; Virginia, 1664 ***6212.30*** *p6*
Proctor, Levi; Vermont, 1848-1887 ***5900.10*** *p133*
Proctor, Mary Welch; Vermont, 1847-1925 ***5900.10*** *p133*
Proctor, Richard 32; Ontario, 1871 ***1823.28*** *p84*
Proctor, Robert 71; Ontario, 1871 ***1823.15*** *p217*
Proctor, Samuel; Pennsylvania, 1777 ***4629.10*** *p10*
Prodakowski, Adolph; Maryland, 1910 ***3259.35*** *p49*
Profit, Charles; New Orleans, 1805 ***1640.10*** *p172*
Proforke, Rob.; Maryland, 1663 ***2524.55*** *p180*
Progers, Thomas 23; Virginia, 1774 ***1220.25*** *p46*
Prole, George; New York, 1844 ***1224.3*** *p63*
Prondfoot, Robert 44; Ontario, 1871 ***1823.15*** *p217*
Proom, William 21; Maryland, 1774 ***1220.25*** *p2*
Prophet, John 38; Ontario, 1871 ***1823.28*** *p84*
Propp, Eva 31; Kansas, 1910 ***9079.10*** *p43*
Propp, Fred 44; Kansas, 1896-1910 ***9079.10*** *p43*
Propp, George 19; Kansas, 1910 ***9079.10*** *p43*
Propp, Jacob 22; Kansas, 1910 ***9079.10*** *p43*
Proseski, Helen; Maryland, 1910 ***3259.35*** *p50*
Prosser, John; Maryland, 1662 ***2524.55*** *p85*
Prosser, Mathias; Virginia, 1667 ***1224.1*** *p47*
Proster, Thomas; Maryland, 1635-1640 ***2524.55*** *p180*
Prosybylska, Frances; Maryland, 1910 ***3259.35*** *p50*
Prothniki, Frank; Maryland, 1910 ***3259.35*** *p50*
Protopski, John; Maryland, 1910 ***3259.35*** *p50*
Protrsewitz, Piotr; Maryland, 1910 ***3259.35*** *p50*
Proud, George 37; Ontario, 1871 ***1823.22*** *p130*
Proud, William 22; Maryland, 1774 ***1220.25*** *p70*
Proudfoot, Alex 33; British Columbia, 1913 ***9196.1*** *p58*
Proudfoot, Alex 33; Seattle, 1913 ***9196.1*** *p58*
Proudfoot, Alexander 54; Ontario, 1871 ***1823.28*** *p84*
Proudfoot, John 66; Ontario, 1871 ***1823.15*** *p217*
Proudfort, John 24; Virginia, 1774 ***1220.25*** *p87*
Proudlove, John 37; Ontario, 1871 ***1823.15*** *p217*
Proudlove, Sarah 35; Ontario, 1871 ***1823.15*** *p217*
Prout, Frank 30; Ontario, 1871 ***1823.28*** *p84*
Prout, Jane 32; Ontario, 1871 ***1823.15*** *p217*
Prout, John 30; Ontario, 1871 ***1823.15*** *p217*
Prout, Margret 60; Ontario, 1871 ***1823.28*** *p84*
Prout, Robert; Charles Town, South Carolina, n.d. ***1224.2*** *p94*
Prout, Robert; Halifax, Nova Scotia, 1783 ***1224.2*** *p94*
Prout, William 46; Ontario, 1871 ***1823.22*** *p130*
Prouty, Ella J.; Vermont, 1851-1911 ***5900.10*** *p108*
Provan, Matthew; Mississippi, 1823 ***1640.10*** *p172*
Proverton, Edward; Virginia, 1671 ***6212.30*** *p43*
Provit, Don 21; Alaska, 1912 ***9196.1*** *p19*
Provit, Don 21; British Columbia, 1912 ***9196.1*** *p19*
Provo, John; New York, 1807 ***8197.10*** *p48*
Provoast, Elias; New York, 1691 ***1224.1*** *p47*
Prowce, George; Maryland, 1663 ***2524.55*** *p180*
Prowell, Joseph; Guyana, n.d. ***1224.3*** *p63*
Prowell, Joseph; Philadelphia, 1806 ***1224.3*** *p63*
Prownelow, Rich; Virginia, 1664 ***6212.30*** *p15*
Prowse, Charles; Maryland, 1673 ***2524.55*** *p180*
Wife: Mary
Son: William
Prowse, Mary *SEE* Prowse, Charles
Prowse, William *SEE* Prowse, Charles
Prowse, William 32; Ontario, 1871 ***1823.15*** *p217*
Prozniesky, Frank; Maryland, 1910 ***3259.35*** *p50*
Prsybyle, John; Maryland, 1910 ***3259.35*** *p50*
Pruchniecka, Catherine; Maryland, 1910 ***3259.35*** *p50*
Pruchniewski, Valent; Maryland, 1910 ***3259.35*** *p50*
Prudhomme, John Francis Eugene; New York, 1812-1834 ***8197.10*** *p68*
Prudhomme, Lewis, Jr.; Philadelphia, 1792 ***4629.10*** *p72*
Prug, Jakob; Port uncertain, 1764 ***2856.30*** *p346*
Pruitt, Benjamin; Virginia, 1690 ***6212.30*** *p58*
Prunder, Cath. Elisabeth; Philadelphia, 1729 ***2856.30*** *p346*
With husband 2 sons & daughter
Prunder, Josef; Philadelphia, 1729 ***2856.30*** *p346*
With wife 2 sons & daughter
Prunet, John Peter; Philadelphia, 1793 ***4629.10*** *p68*
Prunsin, Maria; Port uncertain, 1740 ***2856.30*** *p346*
With husband & 4 children
Prunty, Patrick 54; Ontario, 1871 ***1823.28*** *p84*
Pruss, Charles 47; Ontario, 1871 ***1823.28*** *p84*
Prusterowicz, John; Maryland, 1910 ***3259.35*** *p50*
Prybus, John 28; Ontario, 1871 ***1823.15*** *p217*
Pryce, Charles; Savannah, Georgia, 1780 ***1224.2*** *p94*
Prydyziewski, Joseph; Maryland, 1910 ***3259.35*** *p50*
Pryer, James; Virginia, 1672 ***6212.30*** *p49*
Pryor, Charles; Pennsylvania, 1779 ***4629.10*** *p37*
Pryor, Joane *SEE* Pryor, Thomas
Pryor, John; Pennsylvania, 1777 ***4629.10*** *p10*
Pryor, Joseph 36; Ontario, 1871 ***1823.22*** *p130*
Pryor, Norton; Pennsylvania, 1777 ***4629.10*** *p9*
Pryor, Norton, Jr.; Pennsylvania, 1786 ***4629.10*** *p49*
Pryor, Thomas; Maryland, 1662 ***2524.55*** *p180*
Pryor, Thomas; Maryland, 1666 ***2524.55*** *p180*
Wife: Joane
Pryor, Thomas; Pennsylvania, 1777 ***4629.10*** *p6*
Pryor, William; Virginia, 1647 ***1224.1*** *p47*
Pryzbulski, Frank; Maryland, 1910 ***3259.35*** *p50*
Przybilski, Frank; Maryland, 1910 ***3259.35*** *p50*
Przybis, Antonia; Maryland, 1910 ***3259.35*** *p50*
Przybylski, John; Maryland, 1910 ***3259.35*** *p50*
Przybylski, Michael; Maryland, 1910 ***3259.35*** *p50*
Przybylski, Stanislaw; Maryland, 1910 ***3259.35*** *p50*
Przybzlski, Joseph; Maryland, 1910 ***3259.35*** *p50*
Przyleylski, Joseph A.; Maryland, 1910 ***3259.35*** *p50*
Przylsyewski, Mateusz; Maryland, 1910 ***3259.35*** *p50*
Pszhnewski, Michael; Maryland, 1910 ***3259.35*** *p50*
Psihas, John 27; Juneau, Alaska, 1917 ***9196.1*** *p45*
Psihas, John 27; Whitehorse, Yukon, 1917 ***9196.1*** *p45*
Ptotosyk, Vincent; Maryland, 1910 ***3259.35*** *p50*
Ptussysky, Marczys; Maryland, 1910 ***3259.35*** *p50*
Pubalski, Woliryan; Maryland, 1910 ***3259.35*** *p50*
Publ, Bernhard; Port uncertain, 1785 ***2856.30*** *p56*
Puc, Anton; Maryland, 1910 ***3259.35*** *p50*
Puckett, Ellnor; Virginia, 1663 ***6212.30*** *p4*
Puckridge, Moses 29; Virginia, 1774 ***1220.25*** *p93*
Puczyski, Anton; Maryland, 1910 ***3259.35*** *p50*
Puddington, Comfort *SEE* Puddington, George
Puddington, George; Maryland, 1649 ***2524.55*** *p180*
Relative: Jane
Relative: Comfort
Relative: Mary
Puddington, Jane *SEE* Puddington, George
Puddington, Mary *SEE* Puddington, George
Puderford, Jane 21; Georgia, 1774 ***1220.25*** *p48*
Pudge, Elizabeth; Maryland, 1665 ***2524.55*** *p180*
Pue, William; Maryland, 1676 ***2524.55*** *p180*
Puffer, Elizabeth 78; Ontario, 1871 ***1823.22*** *p130*
Puffer, George; New York, 1837 ***1224.3*** *p63*
Puffer, Matilda Brown; New York, 1837 ***1224.3*** *p64*
Pug, Frank; Maryland, 1910 ***3259.35*** *p50*
Pugh, Christina; Virginia, 1864 ***1640.13*** *p101*
Pugh, Eliza; Philadelphia, 1838 ***1224.3*** *p64*
Pugh, Frederick 51; Ontario, 1871 ***1823.22*** *p130*
Pugh, Henry C. 62; Ontario, 1871 ***1823.15*** *p217*
Pugh, John; New York, New York, 1894 ***3437.14*** *p165*
Pugh, William 52; Ontario, 1871 ***1823.28*** *p84*
Pugley, John 43; Ontario, 1871 ***1823.15*** *p217*
Pugsley, William 36; Ontario, 1871 ***1823.15*** *p217*
Puhl, Wilhelm Van; America, 1791 ***2856.30*** *p346*
Puick, J. 30; Alaska, 1912 ***9196.1*** *p38*
Puick, J. 30; Whitehorse, Yukon, 1912 ***9196.1*** *p38*
Puin, Charles; Maryland, 1669 ***2524.55*** *p180*
Puisell, John 33; Ontario, 1871 ***1823.15*** *p217*
Pukalski, Joseph; Maryland, 1910 ***3259.35*** *p50*

Pula, Cunegunda E.; Maryland, 1910 ***3259.35*** *p50*
Pulforth, Robert; Maryland, 1681 ***2524.55*** *p180*
Pulham, Miss; Quebec, 1858 ***9196.15*** *p33*
Pullard, Susan 78; Ontario, 1871 ***1823.28*** *p84*
Pullen, Thomas 21; Philadelphia, 1774 ***1220.25*** *p63*
Pulley, Edward 30; Baltimore, 1775 ***1220.25*** *p117*
Pulleyblank, Richard 42; Ontario, 1871 ***1823.22*** *p130*
Pullich, Henrich; Port uncertain, 1780 ***2856.30*** *p346*
Pullin, John; Pennsylvania, 1777 ***4629.10*** *p15*
Pullin, Peter; Pennsylvania, 1777 ***4629.10*** *p12*
Pullin, Richard; Maryland, 1667 ***2524.55*** *p14*
Pulling, Richard; Maryland, 1665 ***2524.55*** *p180*
Pulse, Levi 50; Ontario, 1871 ***1823.28*** *p84*
Pulte, Johan; New York, 1839 ***8197.10*** *p271*
Pultz, Michael, The Younger; America, 1737 ***2856.30*** *p44*
Pulver, Biddy 11; Ontario, 1861 ***2896.25*** *p36*
Pulver, David 8; Ontario, 1861 ***2896.25*** *p36*
Pulver, Eliza 16; Ontario, 1861 ***2896.25*** *p36*
Pulver, Henry 18; Ontario, 1861 ***2896.25*** *p36*
Pulver, Jakob; Port uncertain, 1790 ***2856.30*** *p346*
With wife
Pulver, Sarah 11; Ontario, 1861 ***2896.25*** *p36*
Pumfred, Samll; Virginia, 1671-1672 ***6212.30*** *p47*
Pumphrey, Rebecca; Maryland, 1680 ***2524.55*** *p180*
Punfield, Samuel; Baltimore, 1801 ***1224.3*** *p64*
Puntin, Jane; Virginia, 1671-1672 ***6212.30*** *p46*
Pural, William; Maryland, 1910 ***3259.35*** *p50*
Purbeck, Jno; Virginia, 1664 ***6212.30*** *p7*
Purcel, Ellen 80; Ontario, 1871 ***1823.28*** *p84*
Purcel, Nicholas 23; Tortola, 1774 ***1220.25*** *p85*
Purcell, Agnes A.; Vermont, 1858-1944 ***5900.10*** *p380*
Purcell, Alice; Vermont, 1830-1900 ***5900.10*** *p273*
Purcell, Andrew 86; Vermont, 1892 ***5900.10*** *p452*
Purcell, Ann; Vermont, 1841-1899 ***5900.10*** *p74*
Purcell, Ann Tunney 72; Vermont, 1898 ***5900.10*** *p128*
Purcell, Anthony J. 42; Vermont, 1904 ***5900.10*** *p452*
Purcell, Bridget; Vermont, 1863-1904 ***5900.10*** *p421*
Purcell, Catherine Dumphrey; Vermont, 1855-1906 ***5900.10*** *p425*
Purcell, Dominick; New York, 1802 ***8197.10*** *p24*
Purcell, Ellen; Vermont, 1857-1943 ***5900.10*** *p81*
Purcell, Ellen Rugg; Vermont, 1855-1955 ***5900.10*** *p379*
Purcell, Hanora; Vermont, 1817-1899 ***5900.10*** *p81*
Purcell, Hanora Gallagher; Vermont, 1831-1918 ***5900.10*** *p379*
Purcell, James; Vermont, 1852-1929 ***5900.10*** *p425*
Purcell, James; Vermont, 1854-1907 ***5900.10*** *p380*
Purcell, James 26; Ontario, 1871 ***1823.28*** *p84*
Purcell, James 59; Vermont, 1880 ***5900.10*** *p213*
Purcell, Mrs. James 56; Vermont, 1884 ***5900.10*** *p213*
Purcell, James W.; Vermont, 1857-1957 ***5900.10*** *p379*
Purcell, Johanna 61; Vermont, 1889 ***5900.10*** *p302*
Purcell, John; New York, 1837 ***8197.10*** *p100*
Purcell, Kate; Vermont, 1865-1949 ***5900.10*** *p451*
Purcell, Kate I. Noonan 59; Vermont, 1926 ***5900.10*** *p452*
Purcell, Margaret Godey 72; Vermont, 1892 ***5900.10*** *p218*
Purcell, Mary; Vermont, 1844-1888 ***5900.10*** *p82*
Purcell, Mary 73; Vermont, 1899 ***5900.10*** *p452*
Purcell, Mary Dewitt; Vermont, 1904 ***5900.10*** *p380*
Purcell, Mary Foley; Vermont, 1856-1936 ***5900.10*** *p213*
Purcell, Mary J.; Vermont, 1858-1943 ***5900.10*** *p94*
Purcell, Michael 62; Vermont, 1884 ***5900.10*** *p302*
Purcell, Michael 87; Vermont, 1903 ***5900.10*** *p128*
Purcell, Patrick; Vermont, 1855-1934 ***5900.10*** *p213*
Purcell, Patrick 70; Vermont, 1893 ***5900.10*** *p380*
Purcell, Susan; Vermont, 1861-1925 ***5900.10*** *p151*
Purcell, Thomas; New York, 1838 ***8197.10*** *p146*
Purcell, Thomas; Vermont, 1826-1912 ***5900.10*** *p379*
Purcell, Thomas 23; Ontario, 1871 ***1823.15*** *p217*
Purcell, Thomas 78; Vermont, 1875 ***5900.10*** *p379*
Purcell, William; Vermont, 1814-1902 ***5900.10*** *p273*
Purcell, William 35; Ontario, 1871 ***1823.28*** *p84*
Purchase, James; Arkansas, 1851 ***1224.3*** *p64*
Purcil, Henry 50; Ontario, 1871 ***1823.28*** *p84*
Purckes, Sarah; Maryland, 1666 ***2524.55*** *p180*
Purdie, John; Georgia, 1734 ***1640.10*** *p172*
Purdy, Benjamin 79; Ontario, 1871 ***1823.22*** *p130*
Purdy, David; New York, 1827 ***1224.3*** *p64*
Purdy, David; Quebec, 1790 ***1224.2*** *p94*
Purdy, Dorcas 71; Ontario, 1871 ***1823.22*** *p130*
Purdy, Gilbert; New York, 1790 ***1224.2*** *p94*
Purdy, James 74; Ontario, 1871 ***1823.22*** *p130*
Purdy, James 84; Ontario, 1871 ***1823.22*** *p130*
Purdy, John 41; Ontario, 1871 ***1823.15*** *p217*
Purdy, Robert; Pennsylvania, 1777 ***4629.10*** *p11*
Purdy, Thomas 17; Georgia, 1775 ***1220.25*** *p124*
Purdy, Unus 69; Ontario, 1871 ***1823.22*** *p130*
Purdy, William 32; Ontario, 1871 ***1823.15*** *p217*
Puree, Eliza 23; Ontario, 1871 ***1823.15*** *p217*
Puree, John 28; Ontario, 1871 ***1823.15*** *p217*
Puree, Susanah 25; Ontario, 1871 ***1823.15*** *p217*
Purefy, Francis; Maryland, 1657 ***2524.55*** *p181*
Purellio, Camlin 18; Maryland, 1775 ***1220.25*** *p97*
Purfield, Lawrence; Pennsylvania, 1777 ***4629.10*** *p17*
Purford, William; Virginia, 1664-1665 ***6212.30*** *p16*
Purgold, Caspar; Port uncertain, 1785 ***2856.30*** *p346*
Purkis, George; New England, 1682 ***1224.1*** *p47*
Purle, James; Virginia, 1703-1704 ***6212.30*** *p63*
Purnell, Elizabeth; Maryland, 1673 ***2524.55*** *p181*
Purner, William 38; Ontario, 1871 ***1823.15*** *p217*
Purois, Peter 32; Virginia, 1774 ***1220.25*** *p55*
Purper, Anna Maria; Port uncertain, 1786 ***2856.30*** *p346*
Purper, Maria Elisabeth; Port uncertain, 1777 ***2856.30*** *p346*
Purpur, Miss; Port uncertain, 1769 ***2856.30*** *p346*
Purpur, Otto; Port uncertain, 1755 ***2856.30*** *p346*
Purpus, Marianna; Port uncertain, 1776 ***2856.30*** *p346*
Pursell, Edmond; Maryland, 1680 ***2524.55*** *p181*
Pursell, Eliza; Virginia, 1690-1691 ***6212.30*** *p59*
Pursell, James 30; Ontario, 1871 ***1823.15*** *p217*
Pursell, John; Maryland, 1678 ***2524.55*** *p181*
Pursell, Mathew 35; Ontario, 1871 ***1823.15*** *p217*
Purser, James 21; Virginia, 1774 ***1220.25*** *p55*
Purser, Matthew 65; Ontario, 1871 ***1823.22*** *p130*
Purtel, Bridget; Vermont, 1859-1953 ***5900.10*** *p408*
Purtel, Martin; Vermont, 1856-1939 ***5900.10*** *p408*
Purtell, Edmund 11; Ontario, 1861 ***2896.28*** *p51*
Purtell, Eliza 8; Ontario, 1861 ***2896.28*** *p51*
Purtell, Honora; Vermont, 1818-1891 ***5900.10*** *p216*
Purtell, Jane 13; Ontario, 1861 ***2896.28*** *p51*
Purtell, Joanna 43; Ontario, 1861 ***2896.28*** *p51*
Purtell, John 3; Ontario, 1861 ***2896.28*** *p51*
Purtell, Patrick 6; Ontario, 1861 ***2896.28*** *p51*
Purtell, Patrick 45; Ontario, 1861 ***2896.28*** *p51*
Purtell, Thomas 15; Ontario, 1861 ***2896.28*** *p51*
Purveor, Henry; Maryland, 1657 ***2524.55*** *p181*
Purves, Ann; Mississippi, 1812-1845 ***1640.10*** *p172*
Purves, Burridge; Mississippi, 1837 ***1640.10*** *p172*
Purves, George; Arkansas, 1900 ***1640.13*** *p101*
Purves, James; California, 1888 ***1640.13*** *p101*
Purves, John; Mississippi, 1850 ***1640.10*** *p172*
Purves, John Archibald; Toronto, 1877 ***1640.13*** *p101*
Purves, John Home; Pensacola, Florida, 1827 ***1640.10*** *p172*
Purves, Robert; South Carolina, 1833 ***1640.10*** *p173*
Purves, William; Mississippi, 1842 ***1640.10*** *p173*
Purves, William; New York, 1813 ***8197.10*** *p58*
Purviance, John; Pennsylvania, 1777 ***4629.10*** *p6*
Purvis, Andrew 67; Ontario, 1871 ***1823.15*** *p217*
Purvis, Burridge; America, 1837 ***1640.13*** *p101*
Purvis, James 39; Ontario, 1871 ***1823.15*** *p217*
Purvis, James 47; Ontario, 1871 ***1823.15*** *p217*
Purvis, Jessie 40; Ontario, 1871 ***1823.22*** *p130*
Purvis, William; Charleston, South Carolina, 1842 ***1640.13*** *p101*
Purvis, William; Mississippi, 1867 ***1640.13*** *p101*
Pusa, Jakub 44; British Columbia, 1917 ***9196.1*** *p51*
Pusa, Jakub 44; Juneau, Alaska, 1917 ***9196.1*** *p51*
Puser, George; New York, 1840 ***8197.10*** *p385*
Pussell, John 21; Maryland, 1775 ***1220.25*** *p115*
Putawski, Michael; Maryland, 1910 ***3259.35*** *p50*
Putnam, Mrs.; Ontario, 1861 ***2896.26*** *p27*
Putnam, Agness; Vermont, 1850-1922 ***5900.10*** *p422*
Putnam, Flora; Ontario, 1861 ***2896.26*** *p27*
Putnam, George; Ontario, 1861 ***2896.26*** *p27*
Putnam, Henry; Massachusetts, 1763 ***1224.2*** *p94*
Putnam, John; Connecticut, 1763 ***1224.2*** *p94*
Putnam, John; Havana, 1763 ***1224.2*** *p94*
Putnam, John Chandler; Boston, 1840 ***1224.3*** *p64*
Putnam, Maybell; Ontario, 1861 ***2896.26*** *p27*
Putnam, Thomas; Died enroute, 1659 ***1224.1*** *p47*
Puza, Andrew; Maryland, 1910 ***3259.35*** *p50*
Puzycki, Peter; Maryland, 1910 ***3259.35*** *p50*
Pyatt, Francis; New York, 1840 ***8197.10*** *p194*
Pybus, John 70; Ontario, 1871 ***1823.15*** *p217*
Pye, Capt.; Quebec, 1856 ***9196.15*** *p5*
Pye, Captain; Quebec, 1858 ***9196.15*** *p36*
Pye, David; New York, 1826 ***8197.10*** *p335*
Pye, Edward Henry; Maryland, 1826 ***1224.3*** *p64*
Pye, George; New York, 1807 ***8197.10*** *p331*
Pye, John 24; Philadelphia, 1774 ***1220.25*** *p86*
Pye, Mary 32; Ontario, 1861 ***2896.28*** *p47*
Pye, Sarah 61; Ontario, 1861 ***2896.28*** *p47*
Pye, Thomas; New York, 1802 ***8197.10*** *p24*
Pye, William 63; Ontario, 1861 ***2896.28*** *p47*
Pyerden, John 32; Philadelphia, 1774 ***1220.25*** *p86*
Pyes, John; Maryland, 1910 ***3259.35*** *p50*
Pygnas, Francis; Maryland, 1910 ***3259.35*** *p50*
Pykaegowski, Ignac; Maryland, 1910 ***3259.35*** *p50*
Pyke, John; Philadelphia, 1704 ***1224.2*** *p91*
Pym, Mr.; Quebec, 1858 ***9196.15*** *p36*
Pym, Mrs.; Quebec, 1858 ***9196.15*** *p36*
Pym, John 45; Ontario, 1871 ***1823.15*** *p217*
Pymer, Albert 7; Ontario, 1861 ***2896.28*** *p65*
Pymer, David; New York, 1807 ***8197.10*** *p47*
Pymer, Elizabeth 48; Ontario, 1861 ***2896.28*** *p65*
Pymer, Ester 16; Ontario, 1861 ***2896.28*** *p65*
Pymer, George 11; Ontario, 1861 ***2896.28*** *p65*
Pymer, Jane 14; Ontario, 1861 ***2896.28*** *p65*
Pymer, John 54; Ontario, 1861 ***2896.28*** *p65*
Pymer, Loretta 2; Ontario, 1861 ***2896.28*** *p65*
Pymer, Mary 26; Ontario, 1861 ***2896.28*** *p65*
Pymer, Robert 4; Ontario, 1861 ***2896.28*** *p65*
Pymer, Susan 19; Ontario, 1861 ***2896.28*** *p65*
Pymm, William 41; Ontario, 1871 ***1823.15*** *p217*
Pynchon, John; New England, 1662 ***1224.1*** *p47*
Pyne, John; Maryland, 1682 ***2524.55*** *p181*
Pyne, Thomas; New York, 1839 ***8197.10*** *p271*
Pyshop, Henry; Maryland, 1673 ***2524.55*** *p181*
Pyther, Ann *SEE* Pyther, William
Pyther, William *SEE* Pyther, William
Pyther, William; Maryland, 1658 ***2524.55*** *p181*
Pyther, William; Maryland, 1659 ***2524.55*** *p181*
Wife: Ann
Son: William
Pzerothoski, John; Maryland, 1910 ***3259.35*** *p50*

Q

Quack, Margarete; Port uncertain, 1750 ***2856.30*** *p347*
Quack, Nickel; Port uncertain, 1744 ***2856.30*** *p347*
Quackenbush, Hester M. 3; Ontario, 1861 ***2896.25*** *p7*
Quackenbush, Luis; Ontario, 1861 ***2896.25*** *p58*
Quackenbush, Martin S. 1; Ontario, 1861 ***2896.25*** *p7*
Quackenbush, Mary J.; Ontario, 1861 ***2896.25*** *p58*
Quackenbush, Mary J. 23; Ontario, 1861 ***2896.25*** *p7*
Quackenbush, Newton 25; Ontario, 1861 ***2896.25*** *p21*
Quackin, Margarete; Port uncertain, 1750 ***2856.30*** *p347*
Quackinbush, George 26; Ontario, 1861 ***2896.28*** *p64*
Quackinbush, Janet 23; Ontario, 1861 ***2896.28*** *p64*
Quackinbush, Martin 21; Ontario, 1861 ***2896.28*** *p47*
Quackinbush, Peter 27; Ontario, 1861 ***2896.28*** *p64*
Quade, August 22; Ontario, 1871 ***1823.28*** *p84*
Quade, August 51; Ontario, 1871 ***1823.28*** *p84*
Quahan, Anastania 17; Ontario, 1871 ***1823.28*** *p84*
Quahan, Yoin 15; Ontario, 1871 ***1823.28*** *p84*
Quaid, Andrew 58; Ontario, 1871 ***1823.15*** *p217*
Quaiff, George, Sr. 35; Ontario, 1861 ***2896.26*** *p20*
Quaiff, John 9; Ontario, 1861 ***2896.26*** *p19*
Quaiff, Margaret 12; Ontario, 1861 ***2896.26*** *p19*
Quaiff, Sarah 30; Ontario, 1861 ***2896.26*** *p19*
Quaiff, William 31; Ontario, 1861 ***2896.26*** *p19*
Quail, William; New York, 1822 ***8197.10*** *p62*
Quain, Ellen Elvidge; Vermont, 1860-1954 ***5900.10*** *p504*
Quain, Patrick; Vermont, 1855-1928 ***5900.10*** *p504*
Quaine, Alice; Maryland, 1678 ***2524.55*** *p181*
Quait, William 40; Ontario, 1871 ***1823.28*** *p84*
Quality, Joseph; Pennsylvania, 1777 ***4629.10*** *p13*
Quality, Joseph; Pennsylvania, 1779 ***4629.10*** *p36*
Qualters, Catherine 70; Vermont, 1922 ***5900.10*** *p62*
Qualters, Mary; Vermont, 1854-1924 ***5900.10*** *p588*
Qualy, Timothy 20; Ontario, 1871 ***1823.28*** *p84*
Quandt, Hurman 50; Ontario, 1871 ***1823.15*** *p217*
Quane, Alice; Maryland, 1678 ***2524.55*** *p181*
Quarles, Aaron; Virginia, 1771 ***1224.2*** *p94*
Quarles, William; Maryland, 1659 ***2524.55*** *p181*
Quarrie, Mr.; Quebec, 1858 ***9196.15*** *p46*
Quarrie, Mrs.; Quebec, 1858 ***9196.15*** *p46*
Quast, Anna Catharina; Port uncertain, 1766 ***2856.30*** *p347*
Quast, Gotlip 43; Ontario, 1871 ***1823.28*** *p84*
Quast, Johann; America, 1778 ***2856.30*** *p347*
Quast, Johann; America, 1781 ***2856.30*** *p347*
Quast, Johann; Port uncertain, 1780 ***2856.30*** *p347*
Quast, William 87; Ontario, 1871 ***1823.28*** *p84*
Quayle, John; New York, 1839 ***8197.10*** *p142*
Queely, Dorothy; St. Kitts, 1777 ***1640.13*** *p101*
Queen, Allan; New York, 1806 ***8197.10*** *p30*
Queen, Jane 74; Vermont, 1898 ***5900.10*** *p600*
Queen, John; New York, 1821 ***8197.10*** *p272*
Queenliven, Bridget 23; Ontario, 1871 ***1823.28*** *p84*
Quegly, John 48; Ontario, 1871 ***1823.28*** *p84*
Quelet, George; New York, 1839 ***8197.10*** *p142*
Quenszer, Martin; America, 1754 ***2856.30*** *p347*
Quenzer, Eva; America, 1764 ***2856.30*** *p347*
Quenzer, Eva; Port uncertain, 1763 ***2856.30*** *p347*
Quesnel, Catherine *SEE* Quesnel, Paul
Quesnel, Noel 38; Philadelphia, 1789 ***4629.10*** *p57*
Quesnel, Paul; Philadelphia, 1789 ***4629.10*** *p57*
Wife: Catherine
Quest, Bridget Foley 29; Vermont, 1871 ***5900.10*** *p582*
Quevedo, John; New York, 1838 ***8197.10*** *p377*
Quevell, Peter; Virginia, 1664 ***6212.30*** *p8*
Quicfe, Samuel S. 48; Ontario, 1871 ***1823.28*** *p84*
Quick, Agness 71; Ontario, 1871 ***1823.15*** *p217*
Quick, Johann Niklas; America, 1764 ***2856.30*** *p347*
Quick, Soloman 46; Ontario, 1871 ***1823.15*** *p217*
Quick, William 69; Ontario, 1871 ***1823.22*** *p131*
Quicley, Margret 60; Ontario, 1871 ***1823.15*** *p218*
Quig, Michael; New York, 1821 ***8197.10*** *p272*
Quigg, Bernard; New York, 1840 ***8197.10*** *p187*
Quigg, Edward; New York, 1837 ***8197.10*** *p104*
Quigg, William; New York, 1840 ***8197.10*** *p188*
Quigley, Austas; Maryland, 1678 ***2524.55*** *p181*
Quigley, Bridget; Vermont, 1841-1934 ***5900.10*** *p272*
Quigley, Daniel; New York, 1807 ***8197.10*** *p326*
Quigley, Hugh; New York, 1839 ***8197.10*** *p380*
Quigley, James; Vermont, 1834-1907 ***5900.10*** *p217*
Quigley, James; Vermont, 1856-1873 ***5900.10*** *p252*
Quigley, James 40; Ontario, 1871 ***1823.15*** *p218*
Quigley, James 42; Ontario, 1871 ***1823.22*** *p131*
Quigley, John; Maryland, 1672 ***2524.55*** *p181*
Quigley, John; Maryland, 1673 ***2524.55*** *p181*
Quigley, Julia; Vermont, 1847-1902 ***5900.10*** *p252*
Quigley, Mary; Vermont, 1820-1931 ***5900.10*** *p272*
Quigley, Mary 95; Ontario, 1871 ***1823.15*** *p218*
Quigley, Mary A. Hynes; Vermont, 1856-1926 ***5900.10*** *p419*
Quigley, Michael 29; Ontario, 1871 ***1823.28*** *p84*
Quigley, Patrick 63; Ontario, 1871 ***1823.22*** *p131*
Quigley, Patrick 75; Ontario, 1871 ***1823.15*** *p218*
Quigley, Philip; Vermont, 1842-1912 ***5900.10*** *p256*
Quigley, Rose McGee; Vermont, 1832-1904 ***5900.10*** *p217*
Quigley, Thomas 25; Ontario, 1871 ***1823.15*** *p218*
Quigley, Thomas 45; Ontario, 1871 ***1823.15*** *p218*
Quigly, Catherine 32; Ontario, 1871 ***1823.28*** *p84*
Quigly, Elizabeth Moore; Virginia, 1789 ***1224.2*** *p94*
Quigly, Michael 29; Ontario, 1871 ***1823.28*** *p84*
Quill, Timothy; New York, 1837 ***8197.10*** *p104*
Quillaine, Daniel; Maryland, 1667 ***2524.55*** *p181*
Relative: Lidean
Quillaine, Lidean *SEE* Quillaine, Daniel
Quilley, Donnel; Maryland, 1682 ***2524.55*** *p181*
Quillinan, Christiana; Vermont, 1838-1894 ***5900.10*** *p534*
Quillinan, John; Vermont, 1835-1912 ***5900.10*** *p534*
Quillinan, Margaret Ryan 79; Vermont, 1877 ***5900.10*** *p259*
Quillins, Margarett; Maryland, 1682 ***2524.55*** *p181*
Quilter, John; Vermont, 1820-1898 ***5900.10*** *p219*
Quilter, Mary Toohey; Vermont, 1836-1921 ***5900.10*** *p219*
Quilty, Mary 75; Vermont, 1891 ***5900.10*** *p411*
Quilty, Thomas 60; Ontario, 1871 ***1823.28*** *p84*
Quim, Lawrence 24; Ontario, 1871 ***1823.28*** *p84*
Quin, Anne 45; Ontario, 1871 ***1823.15*** *p218*
Quin, Daniel; New York, 1836 ***8197.10*** *p272*
Quin, Daniel 30; Ontario, 1871 ***1823.15*** *p218*
Quin, Edward C.; New York, 1828 ***8197.10*** *p349*
Quin, James; New York, 1839 ***8197.10*** *p272*
Quin, James; Pennsylvania, 1864 ***6058.10*** *p48*
Quin, James 60; Ontario, 1871 ***1823.28*** *p84*
Quin, John; New York, 1809 ***8197.10*** *p272*
Quin, John; New York, 1840 ***8197.10*** *p188*
Quin, John 30; Ontario, 1871 ***1823.28*** *p84*
Quin, John 45; Ontario, 1871 ***1823.15*** *p218*
Quin, John 70; Ontario, 1871 ***1823.15*** *p218*
Quin, Matthew; New York, 1840 ***8197.10*** *p384*
Quin, Patrick; New York, 1839 ***8197.10*** *p272*
Quin, Patrick 40; Ontario, 1871 ***1823.22*** *p131*
Quin, Thomas; New York, 1837 ***8197.10*** *p104*
Quin, Timothy 55; Ontario, 1871 ***1823.15*** *p218*
Quin, William 35; Ontario, 1871 ***1823.22*** *p131*
Quince, Francis; Virginia, 1671 ***6212.30*** *p44*
Quincy, Josiah, Jr.; Portland, Maine, 1858 ***9196.15*** *p29*
Quinder, Antonio; New York, 1830 ***8197.10*** *p354*
Quine, Mary Ann 32; Vermont, 1875 ***5900.10*** *p287*
Quinlan, Alice 16; Vermont, 1875 ***5900.10*** *p202*
Quinlan, Anna Murphy; Vermont, 1870-1958 ***5900.10*** *p202*
Quinlan, Bridget Dwyer; Vermont, 1826-1873 ***5900.10*** *p561*
Quinlan, Bridget Harrington 49; Vermont, 1880 ***5900.10*** *p538*
Quinlan, Charles; Vermont, n.d. ***5900.10*** *p561*
Quinlan, Daniel 50; Ontario, 1871 ***1823.15*** *p218*
Quinlan, Denis; New York, 1837 ***8197.10*** *p104*
Quinlan, Dennis; Vermont, 1857-1859 ***5900.10*** *p202*
Quinlan, Ellen M.; Vermont, 1868-1960 ***5900.10*** *p202*
Quinlan, James 77; Vermont, 1887 ***5900.10*** *p538*
Quinlan, Johannah 78; Vermont, 1876 ***5900.10*** *p557*
Quinlan, John; Vermont, 1813-1912 ***5900.10*** *p202*
Quinlan, John; Vermont, 1853-1914 ***5900.10*** *p452*
Quinlan, John 27; Ontario, 1871 ***1823.28*** *p84*
Quinlan, Joseph; Vermont, 1861-1937 ***5900.10*** *p202*
Quinlan, Katy 3; Vermont, 1865 ***5900.10*** *p202*
Quinlan, Maleechy 42; Ontario, 1871 ***1823.15*** *p218*
Quinlan, Margaret Hannan; Vermont, 1851-1923 ***5900.10*** *p559*
Quinlan, Margaret Harvey; Vermont, 1834-1919 ***5900.10*** *p202*
Quinlan, Mary A.; Vermont, 1859-1916 ***5900.10*** *p202*
Quinlan, Mary McDonald; Vermont, 1855-1931 ***5900.10*** *p452*
Quinlan, Mathew 39; Vermont, 1887 ***5900.10*** *p559*
Quinlan, Michael; Vermont, 1840-1920 ***5900.10*** *p202*
Quinlan, Michael 22; Vermont, 1875 ***5900.10*** *p538*
Quinlan, Michiel 30; Ontario, 1871 ***1823.15*** *p218*
Quinlan, Pat 76; Ontario, 1871 ***1823.22*** *p131*
Quinlan, Patrick 65; Vermont, 1881 ***5900.10*** *p538*
Quinlan, William; Vermont, 1844-1905 ***5900.10*** *p202*
Quinlen, Judath 37; Vermont, 1853 ***5900.10*** *p154*
Quinley, Patrick; New York, 1839 ***8197.10*** *p272*
Quinlin, Patrick; New York, 1839 ***8197.10*** *p272*
Quinn, Anastasia Finnegan; Vermont, 1851-1887 ***5900.10*** *p255*
Quinn, Ann; Vermont, 1839-1907 ***5900.10*** *p151*
Quinn, Ann; Vermont, 1842-1903 ***5900.10*** *p273*
Quinn, Ann 81; Vermont, 1895 ***5900.10*** *p483*
Quinn, Ann Nerney; Vermont, 1840-1890 ***5900.10*** *p567*
Quinn, Anne 3 *SEE* Quinn, Catherine
Quinn, Annie; Vermont, 1805-1880 ***5900.10*** *p133*
Quinn, Annie 80; Vermont, 1933 ***5900.10*** *p593*
Quinn, Bid Hayes; Vermont, 1858-1933 ***5900.10*** *p133*
Quinn, Bridget 46; Vermont, 1892 ***5900.10*** *p266*
Quinn, Bridget Collins 87; Vermont, 1917 ***5900.10*** *p564*
Quinn, Catharine; Vermont, 1810-1884 ***5900.10*** *p480*
Quinn, Catherine 17; New York, New York, 1847 ***1825.45*** *p19*
Quinn, Catherine 30; New York, New York, 1847 ***1825.45*** *p19*
Son: Hugh 6
Daughter: Anne 3
Son: John 1
Son: James 8
Quinn, Catherine 30; Vermont, 1861 ***5900.10*** *p336*
Quinn, Catherine 40; Ontario, 1871 ***1823.22*** *p131*
Quinn, Catherine 45; Vermont, 1883 ***5900.10*** *p515*
Quinn, Charles; Vermont, 1853-1923 ***5900.10*** *p472*
Quinn, Daniel 72; Vermont, 1875 ***5900.10*** *p472*
Quinn, Dennis; Vermont, 1869-1920 ***5900.10*** *p261*
Quinn, Donald 34; Ontario, 1871 ***1823.15*** *p218*
Quinn, Edward 80; Vermont, 1918 ***5900.10*** *p564*

R

Raikes, Mr.; Quebec, 1857 ***9196.15*** *p22*
Raikes, Mr.; Quebec, 1858 ***9196.15*** *p37*
Raikes, Mr.; Quebec, 1858 ***9196.15*** *p45*
Railey, Mrs.; Quebec, 1858 ***9196.15*** *p34*
Railey, Jessie Johnston; New Orleans, 1899 ***1640.13*** *p102*
Railley, Mr.; Quebec, 1856 ***9196.15*** *p6*
Raillie, John; Georgia, 1820 ***1640.10*** *p173*
Raimus, Julious 33; Ontario, 1871 ***1823.28*** *p85*
Rain, Peter; Pennsylvania, 1779 ***4629.10*** *p38*
Rainborowe, Martha; New England, 1642 ***1224.1*** *p48*
Rainer, James 41; Ontario, 1871 ***1823.15*** *p218*
Rainer, William 45; Ontario, 1871 ***1823.22*** *p131*
Raines, Francis; Maryland, 1665 ***2524.55*** *p14*
Rainey, John; New York, 1840 ***8197.10*** *p383*
Rainey, Mary A. Goyet; Vermont, 1850-1901 ***5900.10*** *p507*
Rainey, Thomas; Ontario, 1861 ***2896.28*** *p59*
Rainey, Thomas G.; Vermont, 1839-1923 ***5900.10*** *p507*
Rains, Jane; Virginia, 1668-1669 ***6212.30*** *p41*
Rains, William 82; Ontario, 1871 ***1823.28*** *p85*
Rainy, William; Jamaica, 1847 ***1640.13*** *p102*
Rairdon, Margaret 75; Vermont, 1864 ***5900.10*** *p366*
Raisnie, George 63; Ontario, 1871 ***1823.22*** *p131*
Raistrick, George; New York, 1839 ***8197.10*** *p276*
Raithby, George 49; Ontario, 1871 ***1823.15*** *p218*
Raitt, Alexander; Maine, n.d. ***1224.3*** *p64*
Raizler, Anton; America, 1770 ***2856.30*** *p348*
Raizler, Anton; America, 1771 ***2856.30*** *p348*
Raizler, Hans Martin; America, 1770 ***2856.30*** *p348*
Raizler, Hans Martin; America, 1771 ***2856.30*** *p348*
Raizler, Johann; America, 1770 ***2856.30*** *p348*
Raizler, Johann; America, 1771 ***2856.30*** *p348*
Raizler, Karl *SEE* Raizler, Rosina
Raizler, Karl; America, 1770 ***2856.30*** *p348*
Raizler, Karl; America, 1770 ***2856.30*** *p348*
Wife: Rosina
With 5 sons
Raizler, Karl; America, 1771 ***2856.30*** *p348*
Raizler, Karl; America, 1771 ***2856.30*** *p348*
Wife: Rosina
With 5 sons
Raizler, Rosina *SEE* Raizler, Karl
Raizler, Rosina; America, 1770 ***2856.30*** *p348*
Husband: Karl
With 5 sons
Raizler, Rosina; America, 1771 ***2856.30*** *p348*
Husband: Karl
With 5 sons
Raizler, Wendel; America, 1770 ***2856.30*** *p348*
Raizler, Wendel; America, 1771 ***2856.30*** *p348*
Rajisky, Andy; Maryland, 1910 ***3259.35*** *p51*
Rak, John; Maryland, 1910 ***3259.35*** *p51*
Rake, Robert; Maryland, 1664 ***2524.55*** *p181*
Rakestraw, Joseph; Pennsylvania, 1776 ***4629.10*** *p52*
Rakocevich, D. 26; Alaska, 1917 ***9196.1*** *p50*
Rakocevich, D. 26; Yukon, 1917 ***9196.1*** *p50*
Rakocevich, P. 36; Alaska, 1917 ***9196.1*** *p50*
Rakocevich, P. 36; Yukon, 1917 ***9196.1*** *p50*
Rakowicz, Wladyslaw; Maryland, 1910 ***3259.35*** *p51*
Rakowski, Viola; Maryland, 1910 ***3259.35*** *p51*
Rakowski, Vola; Maryland, 1910 ***3259.35*** *p51*
Rakowsky, Adolph; Maryland, 1910 ***3259.35*** *p51*
Ralajezak, Michael; Maryland, 1910 ***3259.35*** *p51*
Raleigh, Bridget Lanan 84; Vermont, 1920 ***5900.10*** *p584*
Raleigh, Bridget T.; Vermont, 1854-1931 ***5900.10*** *p115*
Raleigh, Catherine 44; Vermont, 1889 ***5900.10*** *p566*
Raleigh, Catherine Agnes; Vermont, 1866-1889 ***5900.10*** *p115*
Raleigh, Catherine Clifford 60; Vermont, 1917 ***5900.10*** *p585*
Raleigh, Catherine Frawley 70; Vermont, 1903 ***5900.10*** *p115*
Raleigh, Gilbert; Virginia, 1664 ***6212.30*** *p15*
Raleigh, John 56; Vermont, 1895 ***5900.10*** *p566*
Raleigh, Mary; Vermont, 1849-1905 ***5900.10*** *p441*
Raleigh, Mary; Vermont, 1858-1905 ***5900.10*** *p115*
Raleigh, Maurice 56; Vermont, 1873 ***5900.10*** *p574*
Raleigh, Maurice 60; Vermont, 1873 ***5900.10*** *p566*
Raleigh, Patrick 31; Vermont, 1885 ***5900.10*** *p584*
Raleigh, Patrick 76; Vermont, 1893 ***5900.10*** *p115*
Raleigh, Richard 86; Vermont, 1910 ***5900.10*** *p584*
Ralf, George; Quebec, 1857 ***9196.15*** *p15*
Ralph, James 55; Ontario, 1871 ***1823.28*** *p85*
Ralph, Joseph 27; Boston, 1774 ***1220.25*** *p62*
Ralph, Richard 44; Ontario, 1871 ***1823.15*** *p218*
Ralph, Tho; Virginia, 1677 ***6212.30*** *p54*
Ralph, Thomas 38; Ontario, 1871 ***1823.15*** *p218*
Ralston, George; Savannah, Georgia, 1794-1812 ***1640.10*** *p173*
Ram, Mathew; Maryland, 1662 ***2524.55*** *p181*
Ramage, James 36; Ontario, 1871 ***1823.15*** *p218*
Ramans, Sarah; Maryland, 1653 ***2524.55*** *p181*
Rambach, Marianna; Port uncertain, 1796 ***2856.30*** *p348*
Ramer, Nicholas; New York, New York, 1846 ***6058.10*** *p30*
Rames, Mary; Virginia, 1698 ***6212.30*** *p61*
Ramford, William; Maryland, 1665 ***2524.55*** *p181*
Ramm, William 67; Ontario, 1871 ***1823.22*** *p131*
Ramo, Jakob; Port uncertain, 1751 ***2856.30*** *p349*
Ramp, Johann Nickel; Port uncertain, 1759 ***2856.30*** *p349*
Ramp, Michael; Port uncertain, 1764 ***2856.30*** *p357*
With wife & 3 children
Ramp, Wendel; Canada, 1750 ***2856.30*** *p349*
Ramppan, Francis Joseph; New York, 1827 ***8197.10*** *p337*
Ramsay, Mr.; Quebec, 1857 ***9196.15*** *p21*
Ramsay, Mrs.; Quebec, 1857 ***9196.15*** *p18*
Ramsay, Mrs.; Quebec, 1857 ***9196.15*** *p21*
Ramsay, Professor; Quebec, 1857 ***9196.15*** *p18*
Ramsay, Alexander; New Orleans, 1815 ***1640.10*** *p173*
Ramsay, Allan; Quebec, 1858 ***9196.15*** *p33*
Ramsay, Betsy 56; Ontario, 1871 ***1823.22*** *p131*
Ramsay, Charles; America, 1761 ***1224.2*** *p95*
Ramsay, Charles 16; Ontario, 1871 ***1823.15*** *p218*
Ramsay, Daniel 43; Ontario, 1871 ***1823.28*** *p85*
Ramsay, David; Augusta, Georgia, 1799 ***1640.10*** *p174*
Ramsay, David; Charlottetown, Prince Edward Island, 1883 ***1640.13*** *p102*
Ramsay, Elizabeth *SEE* Ramsay, James
Ramsay, George; St. Vincent, 1775 ***1640.13*** *p102*
Ramsay, James; Charleston, South Carolina, 1802-1812 ***1640.10*** *p174*
Ramsay, James; Charleston, South Carolina, 1833 ***1224.3*** *p65*
Ramsay, James; New York, 1745 ***1224.2*** *p95*
Ramsay, James; Texas, 1814-1845 ***1640.10*** *p174*
Wife: Elizabeth
Ramsay, James 40; Ontario, 1871 ***1823.15*** *p218*
Ramsay, John; New York, 1761 ***1224.2*** *p95*
Ramsay, John; New York, 1826 ***8197.10*** *p298*
Ramsay, Thomas; Savannah, Georgia, 1805 ***1640.10*** *p174*
Ramsay, William 22; Virginia, 1774 ***1220.25*** *p87*
Ramsden, John; Maryland, 1681 ***2524.55*** *p181*
Ramsey, Alex 55; Ontario, 1871 ***1823.15*** *p218*
Ramsey, Alexander; New York, 1840 ***8197.10*** *p276*
Ramsey, Betty 85; Vermont, 1875 ***5900.10*** *p503*
Ramsey, David 39; Ontario, 1871 ***1823.22*** *p132*
Ramsey, James 40; Ontario, 1871 ***1823.15*** *p218*
Ramsey, John; New York, 1821 ***8197.10*** *p273*
Ramsey, Peter 62; Ontario, 1871 ***1823.15*** *p218*
Ramsey, Steven; Maryland, 1658 ***2524.55*** *p181*
Ramsey, Thomas; Maryland, 1658 ***2524.55*** *p181*
Ramsey, Thomas; Virginia, 1671-1672 ***6212.30*** *p45*
Ramsey, Thomas 17; Jamaica, 1773 ***1220.25*** *p28*
Ramsie, Eliz.; Maryland, 1654 ***2524.55*** *p181*
Ramsie, William; Maryland, 1650 ***2524.55*** *p181*
Ramsy, Joan; Virginia, 1665 ***6212.30*** *p20*
Ramsy, John; Virginia, 1666-1667 ***6212.30*** *p34*
Ramus, August R.; Maryland, 1910 ***3259.35*** *p51*
Ran, Frederick; Pennsylvania, 1777 ***4629.10*** *p16*
Ran, Martha; Maryland, 1662 ***2524.55*** *p181*
Ranale, Hugh 69; Ontario, 1871 ***1823.15*** *p218*
Rance, Mary 30; Ontario, 1871 ***1823.15*** *p219*
Rance, Samuel 40; Ontario, 1871 ***1823.15*** *p219*
Ranck, J. M.; America, 1740 ***2856.30*** *p416*
Ranck, Johann Michael; America, 1740 ***2856.30*** *p349*
Rand, Martha; Maryland, 1662 ***2524.55*** *p181*
Rand, Mathew; Maryland, 1662 ***2524.55*** *p181*
Rand, Thomas 22; Virginia, 1774 ***1220.25*** *p45*
Randal, Robert 21; Maryland, 1774 ***1220.25*** *p72*
Randal, Thomas; New York, 1807 ***8197.10*** *p48*
Randall, Ann 30 *SEE* Randall, John
Randall, Christ 42; Vancouver, British Columbia, 1913 ***9196.1*** *p58*
Randall, Christ 42; Washington, 1913 ***9196.1*** *p58*
Randall, Christopher; Maryland, 1660 ***2524.55*** *p182*
Randall, Eliza Gaberie 66; Vermont, 1889 ***5900.10*** *p222*
Randall, Elizabeth; Maryland, 1673 ***2524.55*** *p182*
Randall, Francis 72; Vermont, 1890 ***5900.10*** *p222*
Randall, Herbert; Virginia, 1665 ***6212.30*** *p22*
Randall, John 19; Philadelphia, 1774 ***1220.25*** *p67*
Randall, John 23; Philadelphia, 1774 ***1220.25*** *p66*
Randall, John 27; Philadelphia, 1774 ***1220.25*** *p67*
Randall, John 40; Maryland, 1774 ***1220.25*** *p57*
Wife: Ann 30
Randall, Margaret; Ontario, 1844 ***1640.13*** *p102*
Randall, Richard; Virginia, 1693 ***1224.1*** *p48*
Randall, Robert; Virginia, 1726 ***1224.2*** *p95*
Randall, William; New York, 1829 ***8197.10*** *p275*
Randall, William; New York, 1831 ***8197.10*** *p67*
Randen, Geo.; Maryland, 1657 ***2524.55*** *p182*
Randhill, Vincent; Virginia, 1664 ***6212.30*** *p8*
Randolph, Benjamin; Virginia, 1818 ***1224.3*** *p65*
Randolph, Edward; Virginia, 1703 ***1224.2*** *p95*
Randolph, Edw'd F.; Pennsylvania, 1781 ***4629.10*** *p42*
Randolph, Peter; Virginia, 1768 ***1224.2*** *p95*
Rands, George 34; Ontario, 1871 ***1823.15*** *p219*
Rands, William 33; Maryland, 1775 ***1220.25*** *p102*
Rands, William 42; Ontario, 1871 ***1823.15*** *p219*
Raney, Abraham 28; New York, 1774 ***1220.25*** *p141*
Ranger, Sisly; Virginia, 1667 ***6212.30*** *p36*
Rankeiller, Thomas; Georgia, 1699 ***1640.13*** *p102*
Rankelin, Mrs.; Port uncertain, 1751 ***2856.30*** *p349*
Ranken, John; Georgia, 1699 ***1640.13*** *p102*
Rankie, John 35; Ontario, 1871 ***1823.15*** *p219*
Rankie, William 40; Ontario, 1871 ***1823.15*** *p219*
Rankin, Aaron 24; Ontario, 1861 ***2896.26*** *p18*
Rankin, Aramenta 14; Ontario, 1861 ***2896.26*** *p18*
Rankin, Calvin 21; Ontario, 1861 ***2896.26*** *p18*
Rankin, Catharine 23; Ontario, 1861 ***2896.26*** *p19*
Rankin, Catherine 14; Ontario, 1861 ***2896.26*** *p18*
Rankin, George Nicholas; New York, 1834 ***8197.10*** *p275*
Rankin, Hanah 54; Ontario, 1861 ***2896.26*** *p19*
Rankin, J. E.; Quebec, 1856 ***9196.15*** *p11*
Rankin, John; New York, 1794 ***8197.10*** *p4*
Rankin, John; New York, 1827 ***8197.10*** *p275*
Rankin, July Ann 14; Ontario, 1861 ***2896.26*** *p19*
Rankin, Mahala 17; Ontario, 1861 ***2896.26*** *p18*
Rankin, Mathew 37; Ontario, 1871 ***1823.28*** *p85*
Rankin, Rachel E. 24; Ontario, 1861 ***2896.26*** *p18*
Rankin, Robert; Canada, 1756-1760 ***4628.40*** *p46*
Rankin, Robert; New York, 1803 ***8197.10*** *p16*
Rankin, Robert; New York, 1834-1845 ***1640.10*** *p174*
Rankin, Rose 11; Ontario, 1861 ***2896.26*** *p19*
Rankin, Rosel 1; Ontario, 1861 ***2896.26*** *p18*
Rankin, Samuel 8; Ontario, 1861 ***2896.26*** *p18*
Rankin, Samuel 37; Ontario, 1871 ***1823.28*** *p85*
Rankin, Sarah A. 20; Ontario, 1861 ***2896.26*** *p19*
Rankin, Sarahfine 10; Ontario, 1861 ***2896.26*** *p18*
Rankin, Thomas 39; Ontario, 1871 ***1823.28*** *p85*
Rankin, Thomas 51; Ontario, 1861 ***2896.26*** *p18*
Rankin, Thomas A. 19; Ontario, 1861 ***2896.26*** *p18*
Rankin, William; New York, 1839 ***8197.10*** *p134*
Rankinhorn, Michael; Pennsylvania, 1777 ***4629.10*** *p9*
Rankins, James; New York, New York, 1849 ***6058.10*** *p48*
Ranlyn, Christina; Port uncertain, 1765 ***2856.30*** *p349*
Rann, George W.; Vermont, 1831-1896 ***5900.10*** *p350*
Rann, Margaret Murphy 69; Vermont, 1902 ***5900.10*** *p350*
Rannels, William 54; Ontario, 1871 ***1823.22*** *p132*
Ranney, Mary 70; Ontario, 1871 ***1823.22*** *p132*
Ranney, William 38; Ontario, 1871 ***1823.22*** *p132*
Rannie, Alexander 34; Ontario, 1871 ***1823.22*** *p132*
Rannie, J.; Quebec, 1857 ***9196.15*** *p26*
Ranolds, Samuel; South Carolina, 1732 ***1224.2*** *p96*
Rans, Wm.; Maryland, 1682 ***2524.55*** *p182*
Ranscom, Laurance; Virginia, 1666-1667 ***6212.30*** *p32*
Ransford, Randall; Maryland, 1656 ***2524.55*** *p182*
Ransford, William; Maryland, 1663 ***2524.55*** *p182*
Ransom, B.; Quebec, 1857 ***9196.15*** *p14*
Ransom, Daniel 34; Ontario, 1871 ***1823.15*** *p219*
Ransom, Emma; Vermont, 1857-1922 ***5900.10*** *p243*
Ransom, Susanna 65; Ontario, 1871 ***1823.15*** *p219*
Ransom, Thomas 30; Ontario, 1871 ***1823.15*** *p219*
Ranson, Robert 48; Ontario, 1871 ***1823.28*** *p85*
Ranson, William 35; Maryland, 1775 ***1220.25*** *p116*
Ranstom, Laurance; Virginia, 1665-1666 ***6212.30*** *p22*
Rant, John 40; Philadelphia, 1774 ***1220.25*** *p88*
Rantio, Oskar 26; Washington, 1913 ***9196.1*** *p60*
Rantowl, Alexander; Savannah, Georgia, 1736 ***1640.10*** *p175*
Rantzum, Ferdinand; New York, 1840 ***8197.10*** *p302*
Rapallo, Anthony; New York, 1816 ***8197.10*** *p59*
Rapelye, James R.; New York, 1834 ***8197.10*** *p75*
Raper, Mrs.; Maryland, 1651 ***2524.55*** *p182*
Raper, Barney; New York, 1831 ***8197.10*** *p355*
Raper, George; Maryland, 1651 ***2524.55*** *p182*
Raper, Robert; Charles Town, South Carolina, 1789 ***1224.2*** *p95*
Raphael, Solomon; New York, 1839 ***8197.10*** *p134*
Rapier, John; Maryland, 1682 ***2524.55*** *p182*
Rapner, Langhorne Benton; New York, 1806 ***8197.10*** *p32*
Rapp, Andrew; New York, New York, 1845 ***6058.10*** *p28*
Rapp, Ap.; America, 1723 ***2856.30*** *p123*
Rapp, Apollonia; America, 1723 ***2856.30*** *p349*
With husband
Rapp, Barbara; Port uncertain, 1796 ***2856.30*** *p349*
Rapp, Bernhard; America, 1755 ***2856.30*** *p349*
Rapp, Bernhard; Port uncertain, 1749 ***2856.30*** *p349*
Rapp, Christopher; Pennsylvania, 1786 ***4629.10*** *p51*
Rapp, Friedrich; New York, 1839 ***8197.10*** *p276*
Rapp, Godfrey; Pennsylvania, 1777 ***4629.10*** *p10*
Rapp, Hans Adam; Port uncertain, 1771 ***2856.30*** *p349*
Rapp, J. B. Henry; New York, 1807 ***8197.10*** *p48*

Rapp, Johann Valentin; Port uncertain, 1749 2856.30 p349
Rapp, John; Baltimore, 1838 1224.3 p65
Rapp, Margarete; Port uncertain, 1786 2856.30 p349
Rapp, Martin; New York, 1840 8197.10 p276
Rapp, Mary Catharine Martha Berard; New York, 1839 8197.10 p135
Rapp, Matthias; New York, 1837 8197.10 p102
Rapp, Michael; Port uncertain, 1754 2856.30 p349
Rapp, Philipp; America, 1755 2856.30 p349
Rapp, Philipp; Port uncertain, 1749 2856.30 p349
Rapp, Therese; Port uncertain, 1785 2856.30 p349
Rappe, Johann Michael; Port uncertain, 1773 2856.30 p349
Rappington, Rowland; Virginia, 1667-1668 6212.30 p39
Rapple, Konrad; America, 1734 2856.30 p373
Rapprish, Carl 40; Ontario, 1871 1823.28 p85
Raps, George 28; Ontario, 1871 1823.15 p219
Rapson, Isaac 41; Ontario, 1871 1823.15 p219
Rapson, James 71; Ontario, 1871 1823.15 p219
Rapson, Mary 13; Ontario, 1871 1823.28 p85
Rapson, Phillip 44; Ontario, 1871 1823.15 p219
Raquai, Miss; America, 1770 2856.30 p317
Raquai, Miss; Port uncertain, 1743 2856.30 p322
Raquai, Miss; Port uncertain, 1769 2856.30 p322
Raquai, Miss; Port uncertain, 1770 2856.30 p322
Rarden, Robert 22; Ontario, 1861 2896.27 p61
Rarich, Godfrey; Pennsylvania, 1786 4629.10 p53
Rarridge, John; Maryland, 1670 2524.55 p102
Ras, Joseph; Maryland, 1910 3259.35 p51
Rasch, Martin; Port uncertain, 1788 2856.30 p349
Raser, Johann Jacob; Port uncertain, 1784 2856.30 p349
Rash, Frank 65; Vermont, 1894 5900.10 p509
Rash, Joe 35; Seattle, 1914 9196.1 p63
Rash, John; Virginia, 1666 6212.30 p27
Rash, Peter; America, 1749 2856.30 p358
Rashly, Jonas; Virginia, 1666 6212.30 p27
Rasines, Anthony; New York, 1838 8197.10 p147
Rasmusson, Walter 33; San Francisco, 1917 9196.1 p52
Rasmusson, Walter 33; Whitehorse, Yukon, 1917 9196.1 p52
Rason, Richard; Maryland, 1665 2524.55 p57
Rason, Thomas; Maryland, 1681 2524.55 p182
Raspin, Samuell; Maryland, 1675 2524.55 p182
Rass, Alester; Maryland, 1651 2524.55 p182
Rass, Alester; Maryland, 1651 2524.55 p190
Rassaler, Emmila 17; Ontario, 1871 1823.15 p219
Rassey, James 24; Maryland, 1774 1220.25 p38
Rastsky, Frank; Maryland, 1910 3259.35 p51
Raszeja, Joseph A.; Maryland, 1910 3259.35 p51
Rataczak, Thomas; Maryland, 1910 3259.35 p51
Rataczyk, John; Maryland, 1910 3259.35 p51
Ratajcyak, Andrew; Maryland, 1910 3259.35 p51
Ratazak, Anthony J.; Maryland, 1910 3259.35 p51
Ratcherly, Miles; Virginia, 1666-1667 6212.30 p34
Ratclife, Sarah; Maryland, 1666 2524.55 p178
Ratcliff, Elizabeth 77; Ontario, 1871 1823.15 p219
Ratcliff, James; Boston, 1781 1224.2 p95
Ratcliff, Joseph 27; Ontario, 1871 1823.15 p219
Ratcliffe, Mrs.; Maryland, 1673 2524.55 p182
Ratcliffe, Charles *SEE* Ratcliffe, Charles
Ratcliffe, Charles; Maryland, 1677 2524.55 p182
Wife: Eliza.
Child: Charles
Child: Rachel
Child: Eliza.
Ratcliffe, Charles; Virginia, 1663-1664 6212.30 p5
Ratcliffe, Eliza. *SEE* Ratcliffe, Charles
Ratcliffe, Emanuel; Maryland, 1673 2524.55 p182
Ratcliffe, John; Maryland, 1678 2524.55 p182
Ratcliffe, John; New York, 1856 1224.3 p65
Ratcliffe, John; Died enroute, 1611 1224.1 p52
Ratcliffe, John 77; Ontario, 1871 1823.15 p219
Ratcliffe, Rachel *SEE* Ratcliffe, Charles
Ratcliffe, Robert; Maryland, 1681 2524.55 p182
Ratclive, James 53; Ontario, 1871 1823.15 p219
Rate, George; Portland, Oregon, 1895 1640.13 p102
Ratfeild, Ann; Maryland, 1671 2524.55 p182
Ratfeild, Ann; Maryland, 1676 2524.55 p182
Ratfeile, Ann; Maryland, 1671 2524.55 p182
Ratford, Francis; Maryland, 1664 2524.55 p182
Rath, Charles 30; Ontario, 1871 1823.28 p85
Rath, George 35; Ontario, 1871 1823.15 p219
Rath, Henry 56; Ontario, 1871 1823.15 p219
Rath, James 44; Ontario, 1871 1823.15 p219
Rath, John 45; Ontario, 1871 1823.15 p219
Rathbone, Joseph; New York, 1840 8197.10 p189
Rathborn, Robt; Virginia, 1664 6212.30 p5
Ratheal, James; Maryland, 1661 2524.55 p182
With wife
Ratheram, Edward; New York, 1836 8197.10 p276
Ratheram, James; New York, 1836 8197.10 p276
Rathgaren, John; New York, 1838 8197.10 p147
Rathgeber, Gabriel; Port uncertain, 1770 2856.30 p349
Rathgeber, Gabriel; Port uncertain, 1775 2856.30 p349
Rathmacher, Anna Barbara; Port uncertain, 1775 2856.30 p349
Rathmacher, Philipp; Port uncertain, 1771 2856.30 p349
Rathmacher, Ulrich; America, 1748 2856.30 p349
Rathmacher, Ulrich; Port uncertain, 1747 2856.30 p349
Rathuer, August 23; Seattle, 1913 9196.1 p60
Rathville, John 58; Ontario, 1871 1823.15 p219
Rathvon, Friedrich; America, 1740 2856.30 p350
With wife & 2 children
Rathwell, Catherine 38; Ontario, 1871 1823.28 p85
Rathwell, Edw; Virginia, 1665-1666 6212.30 p23
Rathwell, John 40; Ontario, 1871 1823.28 p85
Rathwell, Richard 31; Ontario, 1871 1823.28 p85
Rathwell, William 22; Ontario, 1871 1823.15 p219
Rathwell, William 51; Ontario, 1871 1823.15 p219
Rathwill, William 51; Ontario, 1871 1823.15 p219
Ratican, Bernard; New York, 1838 8197.10 p147
Ratican, Walter 77; Vermont, 1848 5900.10 p383
Ratka, Catherine 49; Kansas, 1878-1910 9079.10 p23
Ratka, Samuel 51; Kansas, 1878-1910 9079.10 p23
Ratkovich, J. 45; Alaska, 1917 9196.1 p47
Ratkovich, J. 45; Yukon, 1917 9196.1 p47
Ratoyczak, Henry; Maryland, 1910 3259.35 p51
Ratszezek, Michael; Maryland, 1910 3259.35 p51
Rattenbury, Isaac 66; Ontario, 1871 1823.15 p219
Rattenbury, Mary 57; Ontario, 1871 1823.15 p219
Rattenbury, William 65; Ontario, 1871 1823.15 p219
Rattler, Mr.; Quebec, 1857 9196.15 p26
Rattray, Miss; Quebec, 1857 9196.15 p26
Rattray, Rev.; Quebec, 1857 9196.15 p26
Rattray, Alexander; Georgia, 1734 1640.10 p174
Rattsby, James; Virginia, 1667-1668 6212.30 p38
Ratyczak, Michael; Maryland, 1910 3259.35 p51
Ratz, Anna Maria; Port uncertain, 1744 2856.30 p350
Ratz, Jacob; America, 1755 2856.30 p350
Ratz, Jacob, Jr.; America, 1754 2856.30 p350
Ratz, Jerg Jacob; America, 1754 2856.30 p350
Ratz, Philipp; Port uncertain, 1754 2856.30 p350
Ratzler, Anton; America, 1759 2856.30 p350
Ratzler, Anton; America, 1761 2856.30 p350
Ratzler, Anton; America, 1762 2856.30 p350
Ratzler, Hans Martin; America, 1759 2856.30 p350
Ratzler, Hans Martin; America, 1761 2856.30 p350
Ratzler, Hans Martin; America, 1762 2856.30 p350
Ratzler, Johann; America, 1759 2856.30 p350
Ratzler, Johann; America, 1761 2856.30 p350
Ratzler, Johann; America, 1762 2856.30 p350
Ratzler, Karl *SEE* Ratzler, Rosina
Ratzler, Karl; America, 1759 2856.30 p350
Ratzler, Karl; America, 1759 2856.30 p350
Wife: Rosina
With 5 sons
Ratzler, Karl; America, 1761 2856.30 p350
Ratzler, Karl; America, 1761 2856.30 p350
Wife: Rosina
With 5 sons
Ratzler, Karl; America, 1762 2856.30 p350
Ratzler, Karl; America, 1762 2856.30 p350
Wife: Rosina
With 5 sons
Ratzler, Rosina *SEE* Ratzler, Karl
Ratzler, Rosina; America, 1759 2856.30 p350
Husband: Karl
With 5 sons
Ratzler, Rosina; America, 1761 2856.30 p350
Husband: Karl
With 5 sons
Ratzler, Rosina; America, 1762 2856.30 p350
Husband: Karl
With 5 sons
Ratzler, Wendel; America, 1759 2856.30 p350
Ratzler, Wendel; America, 1761 2856.30 p350
Ratzler, Wendel; America, 1762 2856.30 p350
Rau, Abraham; Port uncertain, 1769 2856.30 p350
Rau, Anna Margarete; Port uncertain, 1751 2856.30 p350
Rau, Cath. Elisabeth; Port uncertain, 1761 2856.30 p363
Rau, Matthaus; Port uncertain, 1764 2856.30 p350
Raub, Caspar; America, 1769 2856.30 p350
Raubach, Christian; Port uncertain, 1785 2856.30 p350
Rauber, Jakob; Port uncertain, 1761 2856.30 p373
With wife & 5 children
Rauch, Augustina; Port uncertain, 1775 2856.30 p350
Rauch, Barbara; Port uncertain, 1737 2856.30 p350
Rauch, Bechtold; America, 1744 2856.30 p351
With wife & 5 children
Rauch, Bernhard; America, 1738 2856.30 p350
Rauch, Georg; America, 1739 2856.30 p351
With 3 children
Rauch, Hans; Port uncertain, 1612 2856.30 p351
With wife & son
Rauch, Hans Georg; Port uncertain, 1751 2856.30 p350
Rauch, Heinrich; Port uncertain, 1775 2856.30 p350
Rauch, Jakob; America, 1738 2856.30 p350
Rauch, Johann; Port uncertain, 1763 2856.30 p350
Rauch, Johann Adam; America, 1748 2856.30 p350
Rauch, Johann Adam; Port uncertain, 1756 2856.30 p350
Rauch, Nikolaus; America, 1749 2856.30 p351
With wife & 5 children
Rauch, Stefan; Port uncertain, 1784 2856.30 p350
Rauckes, Sarah; Maryland, 1666 2524.55 p182
Raue, Johann Christof; Port uncertain, 1759 2856.30 p351
With wife & 2 children
Rauer, Augustus; New York, 1840 8197.10 p189
Rauer, Wendel; Port uncertain, 1732 2856.30 p351
Rauguth, Anna Christina; Port uncertain, 1756 2856.30 p351
Rauguth, Maria Margarete; Port uncertain, 1762 2856.30 p351
Rauh, Friedrich; America, 1749 2856.30 p351
With wife & 5 children
Rauh, Johanna; Port uncertain, 1716 2856.30 p351
Rauh, Lorenz; America, 1738 2856.30 p351
Raukin, Walter 48; Ontario, 1871 1823.15 p219
Raupp, Martin; Port uncertain, 1739 2856.30 p351
Raupp, Michael; America, 1751 2856.30 p351
Raus, Wm.; Maryland, 1682 2524.55 p106
Rausch, A. M. *SEE* Rausch, Peter
Rausch, Georg Caspar; America, 1742 2856.30 p351
With wife & children
Rausch, Peter; America, 1736 2856.30 p351
Wife: A. M.
With son & 2 daughters
Rausch, Petronella; Port uncertain, 1766 2856.30 p351
Rausch, Wilhelm; America, 1738 2856.30 p351
Rauscher, Michael; America, 1772 2856.30 p351
Rauscher, Wilhelm; America, 1738 2856.30 p351
Raush, Peter; America, 1737 2856.30 p351
Rauss, Johann Martin; America, 1749 2856.30 p351
With wife & 2 children
Rautenbusch, Anna Maria; Port uncertain, 1783 2856.30 p351
With father
Ravaud, Ferdinand; New York, 1708 1224.2 p95
Ravaud, Susannah; Perth Amboy, New Jersey, 1746 1224.2 p64
Raveille, Severe; Philadelphia, 1792 4629.10 p83
Raven, Baldur; New York, 1861 6058.10 p61
Raven, Catherine; Vermont, n.d. 5900.10 p604
Raven, Cornelius B.; New York, 1838 8197.10 p147
Raven, Jane; Maryland, 1672 2524.55 p182
Raven, Mary Ann White 62; Vermont, 1893 5900.10 p604
Raven, Mary Nicholas; New England, 1687 1224.1 p10
Raven, Patrick 60; Vermont, 1890 5900.10 p604
Ravens, Richard; Maryland, 1659-1664 2524.55 p187
Ravens, Richard; Maryland, 1665 2524.55 p187
Raveret, Augustus; New York, 1840 8197.10 p188
Ravery, John 60; Ontario, 1871 1823.22 p132
Ravey, Ann Rooney 67; Vermont, 1898 5900.10 p49
Ravey, Anna; Vermont, 1857-1933 5900.10 p407
Ravey, Catherine; Vermont, 1825-1899 5900.10 p550
Ravey, Francis; Vermont, 1825-1899 5900.10 p49
Ravey, Henry; Vermont, 1820-1895 5900.10 p550
Ravey, James 42; Vermont, 1865 5900.10 p530
Ravin, Julia Murphy 89; Vermont, 1905 5900.10 p602
Ravin, William 52; Vermont, 1880 5900.10 p602
Ravis, Jane; Virginia, 1668-1669 6212.30 p41
Ravon, Pierre Andre; Philadelphia, 1793 4629.10 p76
Raw, Peter 35; Ontario, 1871 1823.15 p219
Raw, Robert; Pennsylvania, 1868 6058.10 p73
Rawa, Antone; Maryland, 1910 3259.35 p51
Rawdon, Maurice; Virginia, 1665-1666 6212.30 p21
Rawicki, Joseph; Maryland, 1910 3259.35 p51
Rawinic, John; Maryland, 1910 3259.35 p51
Rawland, D. Wilson 55; Ontario, 1871 1823.28 p85
Rawlens, Michael 46; Ontario, 1871 1823.15 p219
Rawley, A. 23; Ontario, 1861 2896.28 p8
Rawling, Robt; Virginia, 1665-1666 6212.30 p23
Rawling, Robt; Virginia, 1666-1667 6212.30 p32
Rawlings, Robert; St. Christopher, 1775 1220.25 p132
With family
Rawlins, Alice; Virginia, 1673 6212.30 p51
Rawlins, Anthony; Maryland, 1645 2524.55 p182
With wife & child
Rawlins, Edward; New York, 1678 1224.1 p48
Rawlins, Elizabeth 19; Philadelphia, 1774 1220.25 p42
Rawlins, George; Virginia, 1654 1224.1 p48
Rawlins, Joan; Maryland, 1645 2524.55 p182
Rawlins, Joseph; Baltimore, 1797 1224.2 p95
Rawlins, Mary; Maryland, 1677 2524.55 p182
Rawlins, Philadelphia; Maryland, 1663 2524.55 p182
Rawlins, Roger; Virginia, 1673 6212.30 p51
Rawlins, Rowland; Maryland, 1651 2524.55 p133

Rawlins, Thomas C.; New York, 1836 ***8197.10*** *p275*
Rawlins, Walter; Maryland, 1681 ***2524.55*** *p182*
Rawlinson, Charles; Maryland, 1641 ***2524.55*** *p183*
Rawlinson, Charles; Maryland, 1649 ***2524.55*** *p182*
Rawlinson, Charles; Maryland, 1658 ***2524.55*** *p183*
Rawlison, Tho.; Maryland, 1681 ***2524.55*** *p183*
Rawly, John; Virginia, 1666-1667 ***6212.30*** *p34*
Raworth, Morris; New York, 1839 ***8197.10*** *p276*
Rawson, Edward; New England, 1655 ***1224.1*** *p57*
Rawson, Elisha 63; Ontario, 1871 ***1823.22*** *p132*
Rawson, Hannah 65; Ontario, 1871 ***1823.22*** *p132*
Rawson, Joseph 50; Ontario, 1871 ***1823.15*** *p219*
Rawson, Robert 23; Ontario, 1871 ***1823.28*** *p85*
Rawson, Thomas 25; Ontario, 1871 ***1823.28*** *p85*
Rawson, William 51; Ontario, 1871 ***1823.28*** *p85*
Ray, Mr.; Quebec, 1857 ***9196.15*** *p18*
Ray, Mr.; Quebec, 1858 ***9196.15*** *p35*
Ray, Alexander *SEE* Ray, Alexander
Ray, Alexander; Maryland, 1664 ***2524.55*** *p183*
Wife: Joane
Child: Hannah
Child: Sarah
Child: Marah
Child: Alexander
Child: Joane
Ray, Elizabeth; Maryland, 1653 ***2524.55*** *p183*
Ray, Ellen; Vermont, 1824-1898 ***5900.10*** *p409*
Ray, George; New York, 1840 ***8197.10*** *p189*
Ray, Hannah *SEE* Ray, Alexander
Ray, Henry 16; Philadelphia, 1774 ***1220.25*** *p42*
Ray, Isabel; Florida, 1804-1838 ***1640.10*** *p174*
Ray, James; Pennsylvania, 1815 ***6058.10*** *p5*
Ray, James 48; Ontario, 1871 ***1823.15*** *p219*
Ray, James H.; New York, 1822 ***8197.10*** *p274*
Ray, Joane *SEE* Ray, Alexander
Ray, Marah *SEE* Ray, Alexander
Ray, Margret; Virginia, 1664 ***6212.30*** *p6*
Ray, Mary; Maryland, 1681 ***2524.55*** *p183*
Ray, Mathew; Virginia, 1664 ***6212.30*** *p9*
Ray, Robert; Pennsylvania, 1786 ***4629.10*** *p50*
Ray, Samuel 86; Ontario, 1871 ***1823.22*** *p132*
Ray, Sarah *SEE* Ray, Alexander
Ray, Tho; Virginia, 1664 ***6212.30*** *p9*
Ray, W. A. Y. 60; Ontario, 1871 ***1823.15*** *p219*
Ray, William; New York, New York, 1827 ***6058.10*** *p22*
Ray, William 51; Ontario, 1871 ***1823.15*** *p219*
Ray, Wm; Virginia, 1664-1665 ***6212.30*** *p16*
Raycroft, Eliza A. 29; Vermont, 1876 ***5900.10*** *p365*
Raycroft, William 63; Vermont, 1903 ***5900.10*** *p365*
Raydon, William; Philadelphia, 1696 ***1224.1*** *p48*
Rayford, Emanuell; Maryland, 1659 ***2524.55*** *p183*
Rayler, George; New York, New York, 1857 ***3437.14*** *p121*
Raylln, Johann Georg; America, 1750 ***2856.30*** *p358*
With wife
Rayment, Elizabeth; New England, 1651 ***1224.1*** *p48*
Rayment, John; New England, 1651 ***1224.1*** *p48*
Rayment, John; Died enroute, 1630 ***1224.1*** *p48*
Rayment, William; New England, 1651 ***1224.1*** *p48*
Raymond, Mrs.; Maryland, 1670 ***2524.55*** *p183*
Raymond, Agust 21; Ontario, 1871 ***1823.28*** *p85*
Raymond, M.; Ontario, 1861 ***2896.25*** *p13*
Raymond, Virginia; Vermont, 1846-1934 ***5900.10*** *p279*
Raymus, Fredrick 67; Ontario, 1871 ***1823.28*** *p85*
Raymus, William 30; Ontario, 1871 ***1823.28*** *p85*
Rayn, James 50; Ontario, 1871 ***1823.28*** *p85*
Raynard, Samuell; Maryland, 1674 ***2524.55*** *p183*
Raynells, Arthur 23; Virginia, 1773 ***1220.25*** *p31*
Rayner, James; New York, 1823 ***8197.10*** *p274*
Rayner, John; New England, 1682 ***1224.1*** *p48*
Raynes, Capt.; Quebec, 1856 ***9196.15*** *p7*
Raynes, Captain; Portland, Maine, 1858 ***9196.15*** *p29*
Raynes, Captain; Quebec, 1858 ***9196.15*** *p35*
Raynes, Mrs.; Quebec, 1858 ***9196.15*** *p35*
Raynes, Arthur 54; Ontario, 1871 ***1823.22*** *p132*
Raynolds, Ann; Maryland, 1637 ***2524.55*** *p183*
Raynor, Arnoldi; Ontario, 1861 ***2896.28*** *p23*
Raynor, Chloe 44; Ontario, 1861 ***2896.28*** *p23*
Raynor, Edna 21; Ontario, 1861 ***2896.28*** *p23*
Raynor, Edw; Virginia, 1664-1665 ***6212.30*** *p16*
Raynor, George U. 6; Ontario, 1861 ***2896.28*** *p23*
Raynor, Jane E. 21; Ontario, 1861 ***2896.28*** *p23*
Raynor, Jotham 2; Ontario, 1861 ***2896.28*** *p24*
Raynor, Leticia J. 28; Ontario, 1861 ***2896.28*** *p23*
Raynor, Sarah 24; Ontario, 1861 ***2896.28*** *p24*
Raynor, Sarah A. 4; Ontario, 1861 ***2896.28*** *p23*
Raynor, Sharlotte 19; Ontario, 1861 ***2896.28*** *p23*
Raynsr., Barnaby; Maryland, 1655 ***2524.55*** *p183*
Raysborough, Susanna; Maryland, 1668 ***2524.55*** *p183*
Rayson, John 45; Ontario, 1871 ***1823.15*** *p219*
Rayzhal, Wojcach; Maryland, 1910 ***3259.35*** *p51*
Razler, Anton; America, 1772 ***2856.30*** *p373*
Razler, Anton; America, 1773 ***2856.30*** *p373*
Razler, Hans Martin; America, 1772 ***2856.30*** *p373*
Razler, Hans Martin; America, 1773 ***2856.30*** *p373*
Razler, Johann; America, 1772 ***2856.30*** *p373*
Razler, Johann; America, 1773 ***2856.30*** *p373*
Razler, Karl *SEE* Razler, Rosina
Razler, Karl; America, 1772 ***2856.30*** *p373*
Razler, Karl; America, 1772 ***2856.30*** *p373*
Wife: Rosina
With 5 sons
Razler, Karl; America, 1773 ***2856.30*** *p373*
Razler, Karl; America, 1773 ***2856.30*** *p373*
Wife: Rosina
With 5 sons
Razler, Rosina *SEE* Razler, Karl
Razler, Rosina; America, 1772 ***2856.30*** *p373*
Husband: Karl
With 5 sons
Razler, Rosina; America, 1773 ***2856.30*** *p373*
Husband: Karl
With 5 sons
Razler, Wendel; America, 1772 ***2856.30*** *p373*
Razler, Wendel; America, 1773 ***2856.30*** *p373*
Raznard, John 29; Ontario, 1871 ***1823.15*** *p219*
Razynski, Aitor; Maryland, 1910 ***3259.35*** *p51*
Rdowsky, Frank; Maryland, 1910 ***3259.35*** *p51*
Rea, Mr.; Quebec, 1858 ***9196.15*** *p34*
Rea, Mrs.; Quebec, 1858 ***9196.15*** *p34*
Rea, Arthur; New York, 1828 ***8197.10*** *p275*
Rea, James; New York, 1821 ***8197.10*** *p273*
Rea, James; New York, 1833 ***8197.10*** *p304*
Rea, John 28; Ontario, 1871 ***1823.15*** *p219*
Rea, Robert; New York, 1803 ***8197.10*** *p16*
Rea, William; New York, 1807 ***8197.10*** *p332*
Rea, William 39; Ontario, 1871 ***1823.15*** *p219*
Read, Miss; Quebec, 1856 ***9196.15*** *p10*
Read, Miss; Quebec, 1857 ***9196.15*** *p23*
Read, Mr.; Quebec, 1858 ***9196.15*** *p32*
Read, Mrs.; Maryland, 1652 ***2524.55*** *p183*
Read, Mrs.; Quebec, 1858 ***9196.15*** *p32*
Read, Adam 33; Ontario, 1871 ***1823.15*** *p219*
Read, Andrew 23; Ontario, 1871 ***1823.15*** *p219*
Read, Chas; Quebec, 1856 ***9196.15*** *p10*
Read, Daniel 65; Ontario, 1871 ***1823.15*** *p220*
Read, Elizabeth; Maryland, 1681 ***2524.55*** *p183*
Read, George; Delaware, n.d. ***4628.40*** *p49*
Read, George; Maryland, 1658 ***2524.55*** *p183*
With wife
Read, George; Maryland, 1663 ***2524.55*** *p51*
Read, George; Maryland, 1681 ***2524.55*** *p183*
Read, George; Virginia, 1685 ***1224.1*** *p48*
Read, James; New York, 1840 ***8197.10*** *p190*
Read, James; Pennsylvania, 1777 ***4629.10*** *p9*
Read, James; South Carolina, 1791 ***1224.2*** *p96*
Read, James 20; Maryland, 1774 ***1220.25*** *p83*
Read, James 30; Ontario, 1871 ***1823.28*** *p85*
Read, Jane; Maryland, 1665 ***2524.55*** *p183*
Read, John; Maryland, 1658 ***2524.55*** *p183*
Read, John; New York, 1835 ***8197.10*** *p275*
Read, John; Virginia, 1663 ***6212.30*** *p2*
Read, John; Virginia, 1671-1672 ***6212.30*** *p47*
Read, John; Virginia, 1688 ***1224.1*** *p48*
Read, John 41; Ontario, 1871 ***1823.28*** *p85*
Read, Margaret 27; British Columbia, 1912 ***9196.1*** *p17*
Read, Margaret 27; California, 1912 ***9196.1*** *p17*
Read, Mary 16; Virginia, 1774 ***1220.25*** *p88*
Read, Miriam; Maryland, 1681 ***2524.55*** *p183*
Read, Robt; Quebec, 1856 ***9196.15*** *p10*
Read, S.; Quebec, 1857 ***9196.15*** *p17*
Read, Mrs. S.; Quebec, 1857 ***9196.15*** *p17*
Read, Samuel; Pennsylvania, 1777 ***4629.10*** *p22*
Read, Samuel 50; Ontario, 1871 ***1823.15*** *p220*
Read, Thomas; Pennsylvania, 1777 ***4629.10*** *p10*
Read, Timothy; Maryland, 1681 ***2524.55*** *p183*
Read, William; New England, 1692 ***1224.1*** *p48*
Read, William; Pennsylvania, 1777 ***4629.10*** *p23*
Read, William 15; Maryland, 1774 ***1220.25*** *p7*
Reade, Alexander; Virginia, 1767 ***1224.2*** *p95*
Reade, Charles; New York, 1819 ***8197.10*** *p61*
Reade, Eliza; New York, 1819 ***8197.10*** *p61*
Reade, Elizabeth *SEE* Reade, Thomas
Reade, George *SEE* Reade, Thomas
Reade, Hayden; New York, 1796 ***1224.2*** *p96*
Reade, Joseph 25; Philadelphia, 1774 ***1220.25*** *p67*
Reade, Mary Ann; New York, 1819 ***8197.10*** *p61*
Reade, Thomas; Maryland, 1658 ***2524.55*** *p183*
Wife: Elizabeth
Child: Elizabeth
Child: George
Child: William
Reade, Thomas; Maryland, 1659 ***2524.55*** *p183*
Wife: Elizabeth
Child: William
Child: Elizabeth
Reade, Thomas; Died enroute, 1663 ***1224.1*** *p48*
Reade, William *SEE* Reade, Thomas
Reading, John 40; Dominica, 1774 ***1220.25*** *p127*
Reading, Richard; New York, 1851 ***1224.3*** *p65*
Reading, William 24; Maryland, 1775 ***1220.25*** *p113*
Readshaw, Christianna 45; Ontario, 1871 ***1823.22*** *p132*
Ready, Anne 4; Vermont, 1851 ***5900.10*** *p145*
Ready, Bernard 40; Ontario, 1871 ***1823.22*** *p132*
Ready, Bridget; Vermont, n.d. ***5900.10*** *p177*
Ready, Bridget Early 73; Vermont, 1891 ***5900.10*** *p145*
Ready, Bryan 76; Vermont, 1891 ***5900.10*** *p145*
Ready, David; Pennsylvania, 1868 ***6058.10*** *p74*
Ready, Elizabeth; Vermont, 1860-1919 ***5900.10*** *p95*
Ready, Elizabeth 7; Vermont, 1863 ***5900.10*** *p145*
Ready, Ellen; Vermont, 1839-1909 ***5900.10*** *p186*
Ready, James 40; Ontario, 1871 ***1823.28*** *p85*
Ready, Jane Melody; Vermont, 1847-1904 ***5900.10*** *p167*
Ready, John; New York, 1838 ***8197.10*** *p276*
Ready, John; Vermont, 1841-1909 ***5900.10*** *p167*
Ready, John 30; Ontario, 1871 ***1823.28*** *p85*
Ready, John 44; Ontario, 1871 ***1823.28*** *p85*
Ready, Kate; Vermont, 1849-1932 ***5900.10*** *p177*
Ready, Margaret; Vermont, 1845-1877 ***5900.10*** *p138*
Ready, Margaret; Vermont, 1845-1877 ***5900.10*** *p170*
Ready, Margaret Farrell; Vermont, 1834-1913 ***5900.10*** *p150*
Ready, Mary 18; Vermont, 1863 ***5900.10*** *p145*
Ready, Mathias 80; Ontario, 1871 ***1823.22*** *p132*
Ready, Nancy 27; Vermont, 1872 ***5900.10*** *p161*
Ready, Patrick 65; Ontario, 1871 ***1823.28*** *p85*
Ready, Patrick C. 38; Vermont, 1907 ***5900.10*** *p162*
Ready, Thomas; Georgia, 1734 ***1640.10*** *p174*
Ready, William 50; Vermont, 1883 ***5900.10*** *p150*
Reagan, Bartholomew 78; Vermont, 1889 ***5900.10*** *p137*
Reagan, Daniel 25; Ontario, 1871 ***1823.15*** *p220*
Reagan, David 65; Vermont, 1904 ***5900.10*** *p137*
Reagan, Ellen; Vermont, 1825-1897 ***5900.10*** *p508*
Reagan, Ellen; Vermont, 1834-1921 ***5900.10*** *p487*
Reagan, Ellen; Vermont, 1853-1933 ***5900.10*** *p216*
Reagan, Ellen Coffey; Vermont, 1835-1920 ***5900.10*** *p216*
Reagan, Hannah 1; Vermont, 1866 ***5900.10*** *p209*
Reagan, Hanora; Vermont, 1827-1864 ***5900.10*** *p150*
Reagan, Jeremiah; Vermont, 1826-1889 ***5900.10*** *p216*
Reagan, Johannah; Vermont, 1847-1921 ***5900.10*** *p137*
Reagan, John; Vermont, 1851-1921 ***5900.10*** *p486*
Reagan, Mary 70; Ontario, 1871 ***1823.15*** *p220*
Reagan, Mary Cotter 74; Vermont, 1887 ***5900.10*** *p137*
Reagan, Michael 17; Ontario, 1871 ***1823.22*** *p132*
Reagan, Patrick; Vermont, 1832-1895 ***5900.10*** *p487*
Reaghan, Ann 19; Ontario, 1861 ***2896.27*** *p20*
Reaghan, Margaret 50; Ontario, 1861 ***2896.27*** *p20*
Reaghan, Mary 20; Ontario, 1861 ***2896.27*** *p20*
Real, Hannah 75; Vermont, 1930 ***5900.10*** *p506*
Real, John; Vermont, 1822-1867 ***5900.10*** *p502*
Real, Levy; New York, 1837 ***8197.10*** *p102*
Real, Lewis; New York, 1837 ***8197.10*** *p102*
Real, Mary Fogerty 54; Vermont, 1887 ***5900.10*** *p245*
Real, Mary Ryan; Vermont, 1828-1866 ***5900.10*** *p502*
Real, Michael 55; Vermont, 1883 ***5900.10*** *p244*
Real, Thomas; New York, 1830 ***8197.10*** *p312*
Realy, Philomy; Maryland, 1682 ***2524.55*** *p183*
Reanier, George; New York, 1840 ***8197.10*** *p190*
Rearden, James 50; Ontario, 1871 ***1823.15*** *p220*
Rearden, Margaret Kearney 19; Vermont, 1858 ***5900.10*** *p575*
Rearden, Mary 70; Ontario, 1871 ***1823.15*** *p220*
Reardon, Agnes; Vermont, 1868-1953 ***5900.10*** *p495*
Reardon, Honora; Vermont, 1835-1907 ***5900.10*** *p432*
Reardon, J. W.; Vermont, 1852-1938 ***5900.10*** *p495*
Reardon, Joanna Brown; Vermont, 1837-1872 ***5900.10*** *p432*
Reardon, Johanna; Vermont, 1809-1860 ***5900.10*** *p58*
Reardon, John; Pennsylvania, 1868 ***6058.10*** *p77*
Reardon, John; Vermont, 1827-1905 ***5900.10*** *p432*
Reardon, Margaret; Vermont, 1853-1910 ***5900.10*** *p338*
Reardon, Mary; Vermont, 1821-1893 ***5900.10*** *p338*
Reardon, Owen; Vermont, 1844-1917 ***5900.10*** *p437*
Reardon, Mrs. Owen; Vermont, 1843-1921 ***5900.10*** *p437*
Reass, Mathias; Pennsylvania, 1829-1834 ***6058.10*** *p12*
Reassig, Amelia 1; Kansas, 1910 ***9079.10*** *p46*
Reassig, Elizabeth 32; Kansas, 1910 ***9079.10*** *p46*
Reassig, George W. 35; Kansas, 1909-1910 ***9079.10*** *p46*
Reaver, Philip; Pennsylvania, 1786 ***4629.10*** *p51*
Reaves, Ann; Maryland, 1671 ***2524.55*** *p183*
Reaves, Ann; Maryland, 1678 ***2524.55*** *p183*
Reaves, Francis; Maryland, 1671 ***2524.55*** *p183*
Reaves, Francis; Maryland, 1678 ***2524.55*** *p183*
Reaves, Humphrey; Maryland, 1678 ***2524.55*** *p184*
Reaves, Humphry; Maryland, 1671 ***2524.55*** *p184*
Reaves, John; Virginia, 1671-1672 ***6212.30*** *p47*
Reavey, Catherine 61; Vermont, 1861 ***5900.10*** *p530*
Reavey, Charles; Vermont, 1832-1918 ***5900.10*** *p509*

Reavey, Mary Cahill; Vermont, 1841-1920 ***5900.10*** *p536*
Reavey, Mary Kerrigan; Vermont, 1833-1900 ***5900.10*** *p509*
Reavey, Terrence; Vermont, n.d. ***5900.10*** *p530*
Reavey, William; Vermont, 1834-1919 ***5900.10*** *p536*
Reavoly, Robert 29; Ontario, 1871 ***1823.15*** *p220*
Reavy, Anna J.; Vermont, 1869-1932 ***5900.10*** *p324*
Reay, James B.; Vermont, 1847-1920 ***5900.10*** *p374*
Reay, Nancy McBride 43; Vermont, 1891 ***5900.10*** *p374*
Reb, Josef; Port uncertain, 1751 ***2856.30*** *p351*
Rebaud, Joseph; Pennsylvania, 1786 ***4629.10*** *p54*
Reber, Elisabeth; Port uncertain, 1791 ***2856.30*** *p352*
Rebermack, George; New York, New York, 1888 ***3437.14*** *p129*
Rebetskie, Joseph; Maryland, 1910 ***3259.35*** *p51*
Rebholz, Michael; Port uncertain, 1791 ***2856.30*** *p352*
Reblaus, Christof; America, 1754 ***2856.30*** *p352*
Reblaus, Christof; Port uncertain, 1754 ***2856.30*** *p352*
Reblaus, Jacob; Port uncertain, 1754 ***2856.30*** *p352*
With wife
Reble, Adam; Port uncertain, 1752 ***2856.30*** *p352*
Reble, Christof; America, 1754 ***2856.30*** *p352*
With family
Reble, Jacob; America, 1744 ***2856.30*** *p352*
Reble, Jacob; America, 1748 ***2856.30*** *p352*
Reble, Jacob; America, 1754 ***2856.30*** *p352*
Reblin, Jacob, Jr.; America, 1750 ***2856.30*** *p352*
Rebold, Adam; Port uncertain, 1729 ***2856.30*** *p352*
Rebold, Philipp; Port uncertain, 1749 ***2856.30*** *p352*
Rebold, Philipp; Port uncertain, 1779 ***2856.30*** *p352*
Rebold, Philipp; Port uncertain, 1788 ***2856.30*** *p352*
Rebrasius, Joseph; New York, 1839 ***8197.10*** *p134*
Rebrowski, John; Maryland, 1910 ***3259.35*** *p51*
Rebstock, Georg; Cayenne, 1763 ***2856.30*** *p352*
With family
Rech, Andreas; Port uncertain, 1788 ***2856.30*** *p352*
Rech, Gertrud; Port uncertain, 1784 ***2856.30*** *p352*
Rech, Johann; Port uncertain, 1790 ***2856.30*** *p352*
Rech, Magdalena; Port uncertain, 1760 ***2856.30*** *p352*
Rech, Michael; Port uncertain, 1758 ***2856.30*** *p352*
Rechier, Jacob 57; Ontario, 1871 ***1823.15*** *p220*
Rechner, Anna Eva; America, 1724 ***2856.30*** *p352*
Rechner, Anna Eva; America, 1728 ***2856.30*** *p352*
Rechuba, Andrew; Maryland, 1910 ***3259.35*** *p51*
Recka, Mary; Maryland, 1910 ***3259.35*** *p51*
Recke, Johann Georg; America, 1744 ***2856.30*** *p352*
Reckel, Jost; Port uncertain, 1785 ***2856.30*** *p352*
Reco, Mary 50; Ontario, 1871 ***1823.28*** *p85*
Recosky, Stanaslus 35; Ontario, 1871 ***1823.28*** *p85*
Recroft, Charles 58; Ontario, 1871 ***1823.28*** *p85*
Rectewald, Anna Catharina; Port uncertain, 1751 ***2856.30*** *p352*
Rectewald, Anna Maria; Port uncertain, 1752 ***2856.30*** *p352*
Rectewald, Johann Jakob; Port uncertain, 1759 ***2856.30*** *p352*
Rectewald, Wendel; Port uncertain, 1753 ***2856.30*** *p352*
With family
Reczensky, Bronislaw; Maryland, 1910 ***3259.35*** *p51*
Redd, Eliz; Virginia, 1702 ***6212.30*** *p62*
Reddan, Daniel 57; Ontario, 1871 ***1823.28*** *p85*
Reddick, A. D. 1; Ontario, 1861 ***2896.25*** *p31*
Reddick, Albert 18; Ontario, 1861 ***2896.25*** *p58*
Reddick, Allis 1; Ontario, 1861 ***2896.25*** *p31*
Reddick, Caroline 10; Ontario, 1861 ***2896.25*** *p31*
Reddick, Catherine 5; Ontario, 1861 ***2896.25*** *p31*
Reddick, Catherine 27; Ontario, 1861 ***2896.25*** *p40*
Reddick, Charles 18; Ontario, 1861 ***2896.25*** *p31*
Reddick, George 12; Ontario, 1861 ***2896.25*** *p31*
Reddick, Hiram 25; Ontario, 1861 ***2896.25*** *p58*
Reddick, M. A. 7; Ontario, 1861 ***2896.25*** *p40*
Reddick, Margaret 25; Ontario, 1861 ***2896.25*** *p31*
Reddick, Matilda 3; Ontario, 1861 ***2896.25*** *p31*
Reddick, Matilda 21; Ontario, 1861 ***2896.25*** *p31*
Reddick, Philip 15; Ontario, 1861 ***2896.25*** *p31*
Reddick, Seamore 15; Ontario, 1861 ***2896.25*** *p58*
Reddick, Semantha 20; Ontario, 1861 ***2896.25*** *p58*
Reddick, Semantha 20; Ontario, 1861 ***2896.25*** *p71*
Reddick, Walter 23; Ontario, 1861 ***2896.25*** *p31*
Reddick, Walter 38; Ontario, 1871 ***1823.22*** *p132*
Reddick, William 3; Ontario, 1861 ***2896.25*** *p31*
Reddicliffe, Ann Cole; Illinois, 1853 ***1224.3*** *p19*
Reddin, Anne 87; Vermont, 1923 ***5900.10*** *p115*
Reddin, Mary; Vermont, 1861-1893 ***5900.10*** *p117*
Reddin, Mary O'Hara; Vermont, 1856-1922 ***5900.10*** *p116*
Reddin, Mathew M.; Vermont, 1878-1936 ***5900.10*** *p116*
Reddin, Niel; New York, 1839 ***8197.10*** *p380*
Reddin, William; Vermont, 1844-1901 ***5900.10*** *p116*
Redding, Bartholomew; Vermont, 1845-1918 ***5900.10*** *p118*
Redding, Charles; Pennsylvania, 1777 ***4629.10*** *p16*
Redding, Edward; Maryland, 1681 ***2524.55*** *p184*
Redding, Ellen M. Mack; Vermont, 1850-1932 ***5900.10*** *p118*
Redding, John 21; Maryland, 1774 ***1220.25*** *p7*
Reddington, Margaret 33; Vermont, 1862 ***5900.10*** *p155*
Reddington, Mary; Vermont, 1852-1913 ***5900.10*** *p132*
Reddy, Ellen; Vermont, 1850-1924 ***5900.10*** *p531*
Reddy, Margaret; Vermont, 1852-1935 ***5900.10*** *p531*
Reddy, Patrick; New York, 1821 ***8197.10*** *p273*
Redel, Johann; Port uncertain, 1756 ***2856.30*** *p352*
Redelmuher, Georg; Port uncertain, 1760 ***2856.30*** *p352*
Reden, Bridget 17; Ontario, 1861 ***2896.27*** *p36*
Redenbach, Johann Gorg; America, 1749 ***2856.30*** *p352*
Redfern, Edwin 52; Ontario, 1871 ***1823.22*** *p132*
Redfern, Henry 26; Ontario, 1871 ***1823.22*** *p132*
Redfern, James 24; Ontario, 1871 ***1823.22*** *p132*
Redford, Anna 74; Ontario, 1871 ***1823.22*** *p132*
Redford, Benjamin 80; Ontario, 1871 ***1823.22*** *p132*
Redford, Robert; Georgia, 1734 ***1640.10*** *p174*
Redfort, Ellen; Maryland, 1664 ***2524.55*** *p231*
Redgley, Thomas; Maryland, 1670 ***2524.55*** *p184*
Redick, Cindrilla 18; Ontario, 1861 ***2896.27*** *p13*
Reding, John; Maryland, 1678 ***2524.55*** *p184*
Reding, Richard; Maryland, 1673 ***2524.55*** *p184*
Redington, Thomas 76; Vermont, 1882 ***5900.10*** *p155*
Redland, Robt; Virginia, 1667 ***6212.30*** *p37*
Redlich, August Charles; New York, 1840 ***8197.10*** *p190*
Redman, Bridget 5; Ontario, 1861 ***2896.27*** *p61*
Redman, Catharine 26; Ontario, 1861 ***2896.28*** *p25*
Redman, Charles 50; Ontario, 1871 ***1823.15*** *p220*
Redman, Daniel 60; Ontario, 1861 ***2896.27*** *p61*
Redman, Dority 56; Ontario, 1861 ***2896.27*** *p61*
Redman, Edward 18; Ontario, 1861 ***2896.28*** *p25*
Redman, Edward 39; Ontario, 1871 ***1823.28*** *p85*
Redman, Frederick 64; Ontario, 1871 ***1823.28*** *p85*
Redman, Jeremiah; New York, 1840 ***8197.10*** *p190*
Redman, John; Pennsylvania, 1777 ***4629.10*** *p21*
Redman, John 23; Ontario, 1861 ***2896.28*** *p25*
Redman, John, Jr.; Pennsylvania, 1779 ***4629.10*** *p36*
Redman, Margaret 17; Ontario, 1861 ***2896.27*** *p61*
Redman, Marsella 14; Ontario, 1861 ***2896.27*** *p61*
Redman, Mary 21; Ontario, 1861 ***2896.27*** *p72*
Redman, Mary Adelia 2; Ontario, 1861 ***2896.27*** *p72*
Redman, Michael 11; Ontario, 1861 ***2896.27*** *p61*
Redman, Patrick 26; Ontario, 1861 ***2896.27*** *p70*
Redman, Richard; Pennsylvania, 1777 ***4629.10*** *p8*
Redman, Rose 60; Ontario, 1861 ***2896.28*** *p25*
Redman, W.; Quebec, 1858 ***9196.15*** *p45*
Redman, William 20; Ontario, 1861 ***2896.27*** *p61*
Redmon, Ann 17; Ontario, 1861 ***2896.27*** *p71*
Redmon, Bridget 23; Vermont, 1869 ***5900.10*** *p141*
Redmond, Alice E. Kennedy; Vermont, 1835-1904 ***5900.10*** *p129*
Redmond, Ann 43; Ontario, 1871 ***1823.15*** *p220*
Redmond, Bernard 46; Ontario, 1871 ***1823.15*** *p220*
Redmond, Charles 36; Ontario, 1871 ***1823.15*** *p220*
Redmond, Charles F.; New York, 1830 ***8197.10*** *p360*
Redmond, Edward; Philadelphia, 1804 ***1224.3*** *p65*
Redmond, Frederick 32; Ontario, 1871 ***1823.28*** *p85*
Redmond, H. 21; Ontario, 1861 ***2896.28*** *p15*
Redmond, J. 27; Ontario, 1861 ***2896.28*** *p15*
Redmond, James; New York, 1808 ***8197.10*** *p54*
Redmond, James; Vermont, 1800-1873 ***5900.10*** *p166*
Redmond, John 34; Ontario, 1871 ***1823.15*** *p220*
Redmond, John 53; Ontario, 1871 ***1823.15*** *p220*
Redmond, John R.; Vermont, 1837-1906 ***5900.10*** *p129*
Redmond, Mary 72; Ontario, 1871 ***1823.15*** *p220*
Redmond, Mary Cavanaugh; Vermont, 1811-1873 ***5900.10*** *p166*
Redmond, Patrick; New York, 1806 ***8197.10*** *p32*
Redmond, Patrick 21; Maryland, 1773-1774 ***1220.25*** *p33*
Redmond, Patrick 34; Ontario, 1871 ***1823.15*** *p220*
Redner, A. A. 17; Ontario, 1861 ***2896.25*** *p30*
Redner, Catherine 69; Ontario, 1861 ***2896.25*** *p30*
Redner, D. R. 2; Ontario, 1861 ***2896.25*** *p30*
Redner, George 6; Ontario, 1861 ***2896.25*** *p35*
Redner, Henry P. 32; Ontario, 1861 ***2896.25*** *p30*
Redner, Hulda 20; Ontario, 1861 ***2896.25*** *p30*
Redner, James 23; Ontario, 1861 ***2896.25*** *p53*
Redner, Jane A. 35; Ontario, 1861 ***2896.25*** *p30*
Redner, L. L. 17; Ontario, 1861 ***2896.25*** *p53*
Redner, Lettie 45; Ontario, 1861 ***2896.25*** *p36*
Redner, M. 11; Ontario, 1861 ***2896.25*** *p30*
Redner, M. C. 13; Ontario, 1861 ***2896.25*** *p30*
Redner, M. J. 13; Ontario, 1861 ***2896.25*** *p53*
Redner, Mary 15; Ontario, 1861 ***2896.25*** *p36*
Redner, Nancy 36; Ontario, 1861 ***2896.25*** *p30*
Redner, P. M. 21; Ontario, 1861 ***2896.25*** *p53*
Redner, Peter 72; Ontario, 1861 ***2896.25*** *p30*
Redner, Peter D. 22; Ontario, 1861 ***2896.25*** *p30*
Redner, S. C. 8; Ontario, 1861 ***2896.25*** *p30*
Redner, Sarah A. 10; Ontario, 1861 ***2896.25*** *p30*
Redner, Susan 51; Ontario, 1861 ***2896.25*** *p53*
Redner, William H. 16; Ontario, 1861 ***2896.25*** *p53*
Rednick, Janina; Maryland, 1910 ***3259.35*** *p51*
Redpath, Alex 27; Washington, 1914 ***9196.1*** *p64*
Redpath, George 23; Ontario, 1871 ***1823.22*** *p132*
Redpath, George 50; Ontario, 1871 ***1823.22*** *p132*
Redpeth, John 30; Maryland, 1775 ***1220.25*** *p116*
Wife: Mary 31
Redpeth, Mary 31 *SEE* Redpeth, John
Redrup, Abel; Ohio, 1849 ***1224.3*** *p65*
Redshaw, James; Maryland, 1681 ***2524.55*** *p184*
Redurus, Frederick 25; Ontario, 1871 ***1823.15*** *p220*
Redwood, Abraham; Newport, Rhode Island, n.d. ***1224.2*** *p96*
Redwood, Langford; New York, 1844 ***1224.3*** *p65*
Redy, Bartholomew 65; Vermont, 1876 ***5900.10*** *p56*
Redy, Catherine Sullivan 33; Vermont, 1863 ***5900.10*** *p56*
Redy, Margaret 23; Vermont, 1874 ***5900.10*** *p56*
Redzensky, Antony; Maryland, 1910 ***3259.35*** *p51*
Reeb, Catharina; Port uncertain, 1785 ***2856.30*** *p352*
Reeb, Jakob; Port uncertain, 1736 ***2856.30*** *p352*
Reeber, Maria Catharina; Port uncertain, 1745 ***2856.30*** *p353*
Reeber, Matthaus; Port uncertain, 1786 ***2856.30*** *p353*
Reeby, John 24; Baltimore, 1775 ***1220.25*** *p117*
Reece, C. L. 6; Ontario, 1861 ***2896.25*** *p46*
Reece, Eliza Ann 28; Ontario, 1861 ***2896.25*** *p46*
Reece, Hugh; Maryland, 1681 ***2524.55*** *p184*
Reece, L. A. 8; Ontario, 1861 ***2896.25*** *p46*
Reece, Thomas; Philadelphia, 1777 ***1224.2*** *p96*
Reece, Thomas 19; Maryland, 1774 ***1220.25*** *p7*
Reece, William F. 5; Ontario, 1861 ***2896.25*** *p46*
Reed, Miss; Quebec, 1856 ***9196.15*** *p6*
Reed, Mr.; Quebec, 1858 ***9196.15*** *p36*
Reed, Mrs.; Quebec, 1858 ***9196.15*** *p36*
Reed, Abigael; New England, 1656 ***1224.1*** *p48*
Reed, Adam 35; Ontario, 1871 ***1823.28*** *p85*
Reed, Alexander 35; Ontario, 1871 ***1823.22*** *p132*
Reed, Ann 9 *SEE* Reed, George
Reed, C.; Quebec, 1857 ***9196.15*** *p15*
Reed, C. W. 5; Ontario, 1861 ***2896.25*** *p47*
Reed, Candace 17; Ontario, 1861 ***2896.26*** *p17*
Reed, Catherine 32; Ontario, 1861 ***2896.25*** *p47*
Reed, Clara 36; Ontario, 1871 ***1823.15*** *p220*
Reed, Daniel 82; Vermont, 1906 ***5900.10*** *p389*
Reed, E. B.; Quebec, 1857 ***9196.15*** *p15*
Reed, Eliza 60; Ontario, 1871 ***1823.15*** *p220*
Reed, Elizabeth 28 *SEE* Reed, William
Reed, Ferdinand; America, 1749 ***2856.30*** *p353*
Reed, George; New England, 1656 ***1224.1*** *p48*
Reed, George; Pennsylvania, 1777 ***4629.10*** *p28*
Reed, George 1 *SEE* Reed, George
Reed, George 16; Maryland, 1774 ***1220.25*** *p59*
Reed, George 33; Fort Cumberland, Nova Scotia, 1774 ***1220.25*** *p16*
Wife: Hannah 33
Child: George 1
Child: Ann 9
Child: Isabella 4
Child: John 6
Reed, George Chambers; New York, 1810 ***8197.10*** *p57*
Reed, Hannah 33 *SEE* Reed, George
Reed, Henry; Virginia, 1664 ***6212.30*** *p10*
Reed, Hester *SEE* Reed, Walter
Reed, Hester; Maryland, 1680 ***2524.55*** *p184*
Reed, Hugh 23; Virginia, 1774 ***1220.25*** *p87*
Reed, Isaac; Boston, 1695 ***1224.1*** *p48*
Reed, Isaac 30; Virginia, 1774 ***1220.25*** *p38*
Reed, Isabella 4 *SEE* Reed, George
Reed, James; New Orleans, 1839 ***1640.10*** *p174*
Reed, James; New York, 1831 ***8197.10*** *p275*
Reed, James; New York, 1839 ***8197.10*** *p380*
Reed, James; Pennsylvania, 1777 ***4629.10*** *p14*
Reed, James 27; Jamaica, 1774 ***1220.25*** *p82*
Reed, James 34; Ontario, 1871 ***1823.15*** *p220*
Reed, James 37; Ontario, 1861 ***2896.26*** *p17*
Reed, Jamison 33; Ontario, 1871 ***1823.15*** *p220*
Reed, Johann Philipp; America, 1727 ***2856.30*** *p360*
Reed, Johann Philipp; Port uncertain, 1729 ***2856.30*** *p360*
Reed, John; Maryland, 1675 ***2524.55*** *p184*
Reed, John; New York, 1820-1834 ***8197.10*** *p305*
Reed, John; New York, 1831 ***8197.10*** *p275*
Reed, John; Pennsylvania, 1777 ***4629.10*** *p20*
Reed, John 6 *SEE* Reed, George
Reed, John 26; Fort Cumberland, Nova Scotia, 1774 ***1220.25*** *p16*
Reed, John 29; Ontario, 1871 ***1823.28*** *p85*
Reed, John 30; Maryland, 1774 ***1220.25*** *p73*
Reed, John 32; Maryland, 1774 ***1220.25*** *p37*
Reed, John 48; Vermont, 1906 ***5900.10*** *p305*
Reed, John 78; Vermont, 1896 ***5900.10*** *p305*
Reed, Joseph; New England, 1775-1781 ***4628.40*** *p68*
Reed, Joseph; New York, 1837 ***8197.10*** *p101*
Reed, Joseph; Pennsylvania, 1775-1781 ***4628.40*** *p69*
Reed, Joseph; Pennsylvania, 1777 ***4629.10*** *p29*

Reed, Joseph 23; Virginia, 1774 ***1220.25*** *p93*
Reed, Joseph 52; Ontario, 1861 ***2896.26*** *p17*
Reed, Joshua; New York, 1840 ***8197.10*** *p190*
Reed, Julia Sullivan 69; Vermont, 1909 ***5900.10*** *p389*
Reed, Katharine; Maryland, 1681 ***2524.55*** *p184*
Reed, Lucy; Virginia, 1694 ***1224.1*** *p16*
Reed, M. A. 2; Ontario, 1861 ***2896.25*** *p47*
Reed, Mahala 23; Ontario, 1861 ***2896.27*** *p34*
Reed, Margaret 1; New York, 1774 ***1220.25*** *p141*
Reed, Margaret 25; New York, 1774 ***1220.25*** *p141*
Reed, Maria 48; Ontario, 1871 ***1823.22*** *p132*
Reed, Mariah 19; Ontario, 1861 ***2896.26*** *p17*
Reed, Mary; Maryland, 1681 ***2524.55*** *p184*
Reed, Mary 67; Vermont, 1884 ***5900.10*** *p305*
Reed, Mary P. 52; Ontario, 1871 ***1823.15*** *p220*
Reed, Michael; Vermont, 1848-1932 ***5900.10*** *p305*
Reed, Owen; Pennsylvania, 1836 ***6058.10*** *p12*
Reed, Philip 40; Ontario, 1871 ***1823.15*** *p220*
Reed, R. J. 7; Ontario, 1861 ***2896.25*** *p47*
Reed, Ralph; New England, 1656 ***1224.1*** *p48*
Reed, Sarah 36; Ontario, 1861 ***2896.26*** *p17*
Reed, Thomas; Maryland, 1682 ***2524.55*** *p184*
Reed, Thomas; New York, 1802 ***1224.3*** *p65*
Reed, Thomas 40; Philadelphia, 1775 ***1220.25*** *p122*
Reed, Thor; New York, 1832 ***8197.10*** *p356*
Reed, Walter *SEE* Reed, Walter
Reed, Walter; Maryland, 1681 ***2524.55*** *p184*
Wife: Hester
Daughter: Hester
Son: Walter
Reed, William 14; New York, 1774 ***1220.25*** *p141*
Reed, William 21; Maryland, 1775 ***1220.25*** *p120*
Reed, William 30; Nova Scotia, 1774 ***1220.25*** *p136*
Sister: Elizabeth 28
Reed, William 36; New York, 1774 ***1220.25*** *p141*
Reed, William 41; Ontario, 1871 ***1823.15*** *p220*
Reed, William 56; Ontario, 1871 ***1823.15*** *p220*
Reed, William H. 63; Ontario, 1871 ***1823.15*** *p220*
Reed, Wm W. 95; Ontario, 1871 ***1823.15*** *p220*
Reedle, John; Pennsylvania, 1779 ***4629.10*** *p35*
Reedy, Bridgit 54; Vermont, 1908 ***5900.10*** *p411*
Reedy, Bridgit 58; Vermont, 1884 ***5900.10*** *p411*
Reedy, Catherine 81; Vermont, 1911 ***5900.10*** *p433*
Reedy, Catherine McLaughlin; Vermont, 1844-1873 ***5900.10*** *p416*
Reedy, John 71; Vermont, 1890 ***5900.10*** *p411*
Reedy, Margaret M. Boland; Vermont, 1852-1935 ***5900.10*** *p432*
Reedy, Martin 57; Vermont, 1905 ***5900.10*** *p411*
Reedy, Michael; Vermont, 1847-1892 ***5900.10*** *p432*
Reedy, Patrick 19; Vermont, 1874 ***5900.10*** *p411*
Reedy, Patrick 65; Vermont, 1895 ***5900.10*** *p433*
Reekie, George 72; Ontario, 1871 ***1823.28*** *p85*
Reeks, Nicholas; Maryland, 1734 ***1224.2*** *p96*
Reel, Andrew; New York, 1837 ***8197.10*** *p102*
Reeman, James 60; Ontario, 1871 ***1823.28*** *p85*
Reen, Bridget 41 *SEE* Reen, Darby
Reen, Darby 51; New York, New York, 1851 ***1825.45*** *p52*
Wife: Bridget 41
Son: John 12
Son: Tade 19
Daughter: Mary 6
Daughter: Ellen 5
Son: Michael 15
Son: Jerry 9
Reen, Denis 25; New York, New York, 1850 ***1825.45*** *p52*
Brother: Tade 22
Reen, Ellen 5 *SEE* Reen, Darby
Reen, Jerry 9 *SEE* Reen, Darby
Reen, John 12 *SEE* Reen, Darby
Reen, Mary 6 *SEE* Reen, Darby
Reen, Michael 15 *SEE* Reen, Darby
Reen, Tade 19 *SEE* Reen, Darby
Reen, Tade 22 *SEE* Reen, Denis
Rees, David 22; Virginia, 1774 ***1220.25*** *p76*
Rees, Henry 29; Maryland, 1774 ***1220.25*** *p62*
Rees, John; New York, 1807 ***8197.10*** *p49*
Rees, John; New York, 1821 ***8197.10*** *p273*
Rees, John; New York, 1826 ***8197.10*** *p297*
Rees, Thomas; New York, 1807 ***8197.10*** *p48*
Rees, Thomas A.; New York, 1840 ***8197.10*** *p190*
Rees, Valentine; Pennsylvania, 1777 ***4629.10*** *p10*
Rees, William; New York, 1807 ***8197.10*** *p49*
Reese, Jacob; Pennsylvania, 1777 ***4629.10*** *p25*
Reese, Jacob; Pennsylvania, 1787 ***4629.10*** *p56*
Reese, Lewis; Pennsylvania, 1779 ***4629.10*** *p35*
Reese, Martin 39; Ontario, 1871 ***1823.28*** *p85*
Reesner, Henry; Pennsylvania, 1859 ***6058.10*** *p38*
Reest, Johann Georg; America, 1752 ***2856.30*** *p353*
Reeve, Ann; Baltimore, 1848 ***1224.3*** *p26*
Reeve, Francis; Maryland, 1672 ***2524.55*** *p184*
Reeve, George; Virginia, 1689 ***1224.1*** *p48*
Reeve, James; Died enroute, 1714 ***1224.2*** *p96*
Reeve, Jane Bowhill; Powhatan Co., Virginia, 1900 ***1640.13*** *p102*
Reeve, John; Maryland, 1654 ***2524.55*** *p184*
Reeve, Stephen; New York, New York, 1838 ***1224.3*** *p65*
Reeve, Thomas; New York, 1837 ***8197.10*** *p102*
Reeve, Wm; Virginia, 1672-1673 ***6212.30*** *p51*
Reeves, Annie C. 36; British Columbia, 1918 ***9196.1*** *p71*
Reeves, Annie C. 36; California, 1918 ***9196.1*** *p71*
Reeves, Bridget McGrath; Vermont, 1851-1925 ***5900.10*** *p555*
Reeves, Charles; New York, 1834 ***8197.10*** *p75*
Reeves, Charlotte; Charles Town, South Carolina, 1789 ***1224.2*** *p96*
Reeves, Edward 12; Vermont, 1873 ***5900.10*** *p346*
Reeves, Elizabeth; Maryland, 1682 ***2524.55*** *p184*
Reeves, Elizabeth; Pennsylvania, 1854 ***1224.3*** *p65*
Reeves, George; Virginia, 1689 ***1224.1*** *p48*
Reeves, Joseph 17; America, 1774 ***1220.25*** *p36*
Reeves, Joseph 31; Maryland, 1775 ***1220.25*** *p105*
Reeves, Richard 21; Maryland, 1774 ***1220.25*** *p70*
Reeves, Thomas; New York, 1838 ***8197.10*** *p147*
Reeves, Thomas; Vermont, 1850-1926 ***5900.10*** *p555*
Reeves, Thomas 50; Vermont, 1864 ***5900.10*** *p346*
Refane, Ann 22; Virginia, 1774 ***1220.25*** *p88*
Regan, Mrs. 50; Ontario, 1871 ***1823.28*** *p85*
Regan, Abbie F. Smith; Vermont, 1853-1915 ***5900.10*** *p457*
Regan, Andrew 70; Ontario, 1861 ***2896.27*** *p20*
Regan, Anna; Vermont, 1869-1960 ***5900.10*** *p391*
Regan, Bridget 70; Vermont, 1914 ***5900.10*** *p272*
Regan, Catharine 20; Ontario, 1871 ***1823.28*** *p85*
Regan, Catherine Ryan; Vermont, 1856-1937 ***5900.10*** *p252*
Regan, Cornelius, Jr. 76; Vermont, 1902 ***5900.10*** *p480*
Regan, Daniel 60; Ontario, 1871 ***1823.28*** *p85*
Regan, Darby; Virginia, 1668-1669 ***6212.30*** *p41*
Regan, Dora Cleary; Vermont, 1822-1899 ***5900.10*** *p508*
Regan, Ella; Vermont, 1856-1913 ***5900.10*** *p455*
Regan, Ellen; Vermont, 1863 ***5900.10*** *p351*
Regan, Frances 53; Ontario, 1871 ***1823.15*** *p220*
Regan, Hannah 80; Vermont, 1910 ***5900.10*** *p252*
Regan, James; New York, 1839 ***8197.10*** *p276*
Regan, Jane Ryan; Vermont, 1824-1902 ***5900.10*** *p411*
Regan, Jeremiah 23; Maryland, 1775 ***1220.25*** *p111*
Regan, Jerry; Vermont, 1819-1869 ***5900.10*** *p508*
Regan, John; Vermont, 1824-1907 ***5900.10*** *p397*
Regan, John; Vermont, 1847-1895 ***5900.10*** *p252*
Regan, John 33; Ontario, 1871 ***1823.15*** *p220*
Regan, John 62; Vermont, 1891 ***5900.10*** *p252*
Regan, John 85; Vermont, 1887 ***5900.10*** *p456*
Regan, Katharine; Maryland, 1682 ***2524.55*** *p184*
Regan, Margery 81; Vermont, 1895 ***5900.10*** *p456*
Regan, Mary 40; Ontario, 1861 ***2896.27*** *p20*
Regan, Mary Ann Erwin; Vermont, 1824-1881 ***5900.10*** *p457*
Regan, Mary Ann Geelan; Vermont, 1826-1912 ***5900.10*** *p397*
Regan, Mary Rooney; Vermont, 1818-1886 ***5900.10*** *p271*
Regan, Michael; Vermont, 1832-1905 ***5900.10*** *p411*
Regan, Michael 23; Vermont, 1872 ***5900.10*** *p481*
Regan, Patrick; New York, 1840 ***8197.10*** *p189*
Regan, Patrick; Vermont, 1818-1891 ***5900.10*** *p271*
Regan, Patrick 40; Ontario, 1871 ***1823.28*** *p85*
Regan, Patrick 52; Ontario, 1871 ***1823.22*** *p133*
Regan, Robert A.; Vermont, 1848-1927 ***5900.10*** *p457*
Regan, Roger 21; Maryland, 1775 ***1220.25*** *p120*
Regan, Thomas; New York, 1837 ***8197.10*** *p101*
Regan, William; New York, 1804 ***8197.10*** *p28*
Regan, William; Vermont, 1817-1893 ***5900.10*** *p457*
Regan, William John 6 months; Vermont, 1851 ***5900.10*** *p456*
Regan, Winifred; Vermont, 1850-1911 ***5900.10*** *p271*
Regel, Anna Barbara; Port uncertain, 1731 ***2856.30*** *p353*
Regelmann, Hans Martin; America, 1740 ***2856.30*** *p353*
With wife & children
Regelmann, Hans Martin; America, 1741 ***2856.30*** *p353*
Regley, Thomas; Maryland, 1670 ***2524.55*** *p184*
Regly, Christian 36; Ontario, 1871 ***1823.15*** *p220*
Regulska, Thomas; Maryland, 1910 ***3259.35*** *p51*
Rehble, Christof; America, 1754 ***2856.30*** *p373*
Rehe, Leonhard; Port uncertain, 1770 ***2856.30*** *p353*
Rehm, Franziska; Port uncertain, 1770 ***2856.30*** *p353*
Rehmi, Johann; Port uncertain, 1759 ***2856.30*** *p353*
Rehn, Johann; Port uncertain, 1752 ***2856.30*** *p353*
With wife & children
Reibel, Matthaus; Port uncertain, 1766 ***2856.30*** *p353*
Reibelt, Johann Franz; Port uncertain, 1792 ***2856.30*** *p353*
Reiber, Abraham; America, 1749 ***2856.30*** *p353*
Reiblen, Johann; America, 1752 ***2856.30*** *p353*
Reibold, Maria Magdalena; America, 1763 ***2856.30*** *p353*
Reibold, Maria Magdalena; America, 1789 ***2856.30*** *p353*
Reibold, Niklas; America, 1752 ***2856.30*** *p353*
With wife & 2 children
Reibold, Ursula; Port uncertain, 1736 ***2856.30*** *p353*
Reibolt, John; Pennsylvania, 1777 ***4629.10*** *p9*
Reich, Augusta; Port uncertain, 1793 ***2856.30*** *p353*
Reich, Matthaus; America, 1751 ***2856.30*** *p353*
Reich, Philipp Jakob; England, 1773 ***2856.30*** *p353*
Reich, Solomon; New York, 1840 ***8197.10*** *p277*
Reichard, Aglai Constance *SEE* Reichard, Frederick
Reichard, Frederick; New York, 1831 ***8197.10*** *p67*
Wife: Aglai Constance
Reichard, Frederick; New York, 1839 ***8197.10*** *p276*
Reichard, Magdalena; Port uncertain, 1759 ***2856.30*** *p353*
Reiche, Stefan; Port uncertain, 1759 ***2856.30*** *p354*
Reichel, Hans Georg; America, 1753 ***2856.30*** *p354*
Reichel, Michael; America, 1764 ***2856.30*** *p354*
Reichenbach, Peter; Port uncertain, 1741 ***2856.30*** *p354*
Reichenbacher, Adam; America, 1750 ***2856.30*** *p354*
Reichenbacher, Philipp Jacob; Port uncertain, 1751 ***2856.30*** *p354*
With wife & child
Reichenberger, Johann; Port uncertain, 1791 ***2856.30*** *p354*
With wife & 5 children
Reichert, Anna Maria; Port uncertain, 1784 ***2856.30*** *p354*
Reichert, Gottlieb; Port uncertain, 1774 ***2856.30*** *p354*
Reichert, Gottlieb; Port uncertain, 1794 ***2856.30*** *p354*
Reichert, Jakob; America, 1751 ***2856.30*** *p354*
Reichert, Jakob; Port uncertain, 1777 ***2856.30*** *p354*
Reichert, Johann Adam; America, 1749 ***2856.30*** *p354*
With wife & 6 children
Reichert, Salome; Port uncertain, 1749 ***2856.30*** *p354*
Reichert, Thomas; Canada, 1750 ***2856.30*** *p354*
With wife
Reichhardt, Franz; Port uncertain, 1740 ***2856.30*** *p354*
Reichhardt, Michael; Port uncertain, 1740 ***2856.30*** *p354*
Reichle, Grun. *SEE* Reichle, Johann Georg
Reichle, Johann Georg; America, 1752 ***2856.30*** *p354*
Wife: Grun.
With 4 children
Reid, Mr.; Quebec, 1857 ***9196.15*** *p15*
Reid, Mrs. 30; Ontario, 1861 ***2896.26*** *p28*
Reid, Mrs. 37; Ontario, 1861 ***2896.26*** *p28*
Reid, Mrs. 42; Ontario, 1861 ***2896.26*** *p30*
Reid, Mrs. 49; Ontario, 1861 ***2896.26*** *p29*
Reid, Mrs. 50; Ontario, 1861 ***2896.26*** *p26*
Reid, Adam 43; Ontario, 1871 ***1823.15*** *p220*
Reid, Albert 13; Ontario, 1861 ***2896.26*** *p26*
Reid, Alexander; New York, 1835 ***8197.10*** *p275*
Reid, Alexander 46; Ontario, 1871 ***1823.15*** *p220*
Reid, Andrew; Charles Town, South Carolina, 1784 ***1224.2*** *p95*
Reid, Ann 26; Ontario, 1871 ***1823.28*** *p85*
Reid, Archibald 1; Ontario, 1861 ***2896.26*** *p28*
Reid, C. 14; Ontario, 1861 ***2896.25*** *p34*
Reid, Candas 17; Ontario, 1861 ***2896.26*** *p30*
Reid, Caroline 6; Ontario, 1861 ***2896.26*** *p28*
Reid, Charles 44; Ontario, 1871 ***1823.28*** *p85*
Reid, D.; Mobile, Alabama, 1814-1845 ***1640.10*** *p174*
Wife: Jane
Reid, David 35; Ontario, 1871 ***1823.15*** *p221*
Reid, David 60; Ontario, 1871 ***1823.15*** *p220*
Reid, David Boswell; America, 1863 ***1640.13*** *p102*
Reid, E. J. 10; Ontario, 1861 ***2896.26*** *p26*
Reid, E. Jane 14; Ontario, 1861 ***2896.26*** *p26*
Reid, E. Jane 15; Ontario, 1861 ***2896.26*** *p29*
Reid, Ebenezer; Kingston, Jamaica, 1843 ***1640.13*** *p102*
Reid, Elisa 20; Ontario, 1871 ***1823.15*** *p221*
Reid, Elizabeth 27; Ontario, 1871 ***1823.22*** *p133*
Reid, Ephriam 51; Ontario, 1871 ***1823.28*** *p85*
Reid, Francis Chalmers; Ontario, 1877 ***1640.13*** *p103*
Reid, George; New York, 1838 ***8197.10*** *p276*
Reid, George; New York, 1840 ***8197.10*** *p189*
Reid, George; Savannah, Georgia, 1807-1812 ***1640.10*** *p175*
Reid, Grace 50; Ontario, 1871 ***1823.15*** *p221*
Reid, H. A. 26; Ontario, 1861 ***2896.25*** *p34*
Reid, H. M. 4; Ontario, 1861 ***2896.26*** *p26*
Reid, Hellen 17; Ontario, 1861 ***2896.26*** *p28*
Reid, Henery 56; Ontario, 1871 ***1823.28*** *p85*
Reid, Hugh 17; Ontario, 1861 ***2896.26*** *p29*
Reid, James; America, 1843 ***1640.13*** *p103*
Reid, James; New York, 1803 ***8197.10*** *p16*
Reid, James; New York, 1807 ***8197.10*** *p48*
Reid, James; New York, 1831 ***8197.10*** *p314*
Reid, James; Savannah, Georgia, 1757 ***1640.10*** *p175*
Reid, James 15; Ontario, 1861 ***2896.26*** *p28*
Reid, James 21; Ontario, 1871 ***1823.28*** *p85*
Reid, James 45; Ontario, 1871 ***1823.15*** *p221*
Reid, James 47; Ontario, 1861 ***2896.26*** *p30*
Reid, James Hope; New York, 1848 ***1640.10*** *p175*
Reid, James W. 5; Ontario, 1861 ***2896.26*** *p28*

Reid, Jane *SEE* Reid, D.
Reid, Jane; Jamaica, 1829 ***1640.13*** *p103*
Reid, John; Georgia, 1736 ***1640.10*** *p175*
Reid, John; Maryland, 1675 ***2524.55*** *p184*
Reid, John; New York, 1794 ***8197.10*** *p4*
Reid, John; New York, 1803 ***8197.10*** *p16*
Reid, John; New York, 1807 ***8197.10*** *p48*
Reid, John; New York, 1826 ***8197.10*** *p297*
Reid, John; New York, 1835 ***8197.10*** *p275*
Reid, John; New York, 1839 ***8197.10*** *p276*
Reid, John 45; Ontario, 1871 ***1823.15*** *p221*
Reid, John 81; Ontario, 1871 ***1823.15*** *p221*
Reid, John E. 4; Ontario, 1861 ***2896.26*** *p28*
Reid, John Hope; New York, 1833 ***8197.10*** *p299*
Reid, Lucinda 2; Ontario, 1861 ***2896.26*** *p28*
Reid, M. Jane 4; Ontario, 1861 ***2896.26*** *p28*
Reid, Mahala 20; Ontario, 1861 ***2896.25*** *p61*
Reid, Margaratt 13; Ontario, 1861 ***2896.26*** *p28*
Reid, Margaret; Montreal, 1884 ***1640.13*** *p103*
Reid, Margaret 16; Ontario, 1861 ***2896.26*** *p26*
Reid, Mariah 20; Ontario, 1861 ***2896.26*** *p26*
Reid, Martha 17; Ontario, 1861 ***2896.26*** *p30*
Reid, Mary; Canada, 1871 ***1640.13*** *p103*
Reid, Mary 8; Ontario, 1861 ***2896.26*** *p28*
Reid, Mary 40; Ontario, 1871 ***1823.15*** *p221*
Reid, Mary Dunn; Vermont, 1854-1912 ***5900.10*** *p43*
Reid, Mary E. 10; Ontario, 1861 ***2896.26*** *p26*
Reid, Robert; Alabama, 1817-1845 ***1640.10*** *p175*
Reid, Robert; Jamaica, 1835 ***1640.13*** *p103*
Reid, Robert; Jamaica, 1846 ***1640.13*** *p103*
Reid, Robert; New London, Connecticut, 1876 ***1640.13*** *p103*
Reid, Robert 21; Ontario, 1861 ***2896.26*** *p29*
Reid, Robert 32; Ontario, 1871 ***1823.15*** *p221*
Reid, Robert 34; Ontario, 1871 ***1823.28*** *p85*
Reid, Robert 37; Ontario, 1871 ***1823.28*** *p85*
Reid, Robert 40; Ontario, 1861 ***2896.26*** *p28*
Reid, Robert 55; Ontario, 1871 ***1823.15*** *p221*
Reid, Robert 55; Ontario, 1871 ***1823.22*** *p133*
Reid, Robert 66; Ontario, 1871 ***1823.15*** *p221*
Reid, S. E. 6; Ontario, 1861 ***2896.26*** *p26*
Reid, Samuel 34; Ontario, 1871 ***1823.15*** *p221*
Reid, Samuel 35; Ontario, 1871 ***1823.15*** *p221*
Reid, Sarah A. 17; Ontario, 1861 ***2896.26*** *p18*
Reid, Stephen 14; Ontario, 1861 ***2896.26*** *p30*
Reid, Thomas; Alabama, 1822-1846 ***1640.10*** *p175*
Reid, Thomas; Georgia, 1698 ***1640.13*** *p103*
Reid, Thomas; Vermont, 1848-1911 ***5900.10*** *p43*
Reid, Thomas 60; Ontario, 1861 ***2896.26*** *p29*
Reid, W. J. 13; Ontario, 1861 ***2896.26*** *p29*
Reid, Walter 23; Ontario, 1871 ***1823.15*** *p221*
Reid, William; Georgia, 1740 ***1640.10*** *p175*
Reid, William; New York, 1823-1831 ***8197.10*** *p369*
Reid, William; Portland, Maine, 1857 ***9196.15*** *p12*
Reid, William 36; Ontario, 1871 ***1823.22*** *p133*
Reid, William 48; Ontario, 1871 ***1823.28*** *p85*
Reid, William 52; Ontario, 1871 ***1823.15*** *p221*
Reid, William 61; Ontario, 1861 ***2896.26*** *p26*
Reid, William 62; Ontario, 1871 ***1823.15*** *p221*
Reid, William 66; Ontario, 1871 ***1823.15*** *p221*
Reide, John; Maryland, 1675 ***2524.55*** *p184*
Reidenbach, Henrich; Port uncertain, 1738 ***2856.30*** *p354*
With wife & 8 children
Reidenbach, Michael; America, 1764 ***2856.30*** *p354*
Reidenbach, Peter; America, 1741 ***2856.30*** *p354*
Reidenbach, Peter; America, 1764 ***2856.30*** *p354*
Reider, Peter; New York, New York, 1888 ***3437.14*** *p155*
Reidy, Johann Jakob; America, 1739 ***2856.30*** *p354*
Reif, Johann Jacob; Port uncertain, 1796 ***2856.30*** *p354*
Reiff, Barbara; Port uncertain, 1753 ***2856.30*** *p354*
Reiff, Maria; Port uncertain, 1694 ***2856.30*** *p184*
Reiff, Maria; Port uncertain, 1694 ***2856.30*** *p355*
With husband
Reiff, Wilhelm; Port uncertain, 1754 ***2856.30*** *p354*
Reihlin, Bernhard; Port uncertain, 1628 ***2856.30*** *p359*
Reiley, Charles 38; Vermont, 1848 ***5900.10*** *p386*
Reiley, Hannah 84; Ontario, 1871 ***1823.15*** *p221*
Reiley, James; New York, 1837 ***8197.10*** *p102*
Reiley, James 64; Vermont, 1856 ***5900.10*** *p456*
Reiley, John; New York, 1836 ***8197.10*** *p75*
Reiley, John 19; New York, 1775 ***1220.25*** *p94*
Reiley, Mary 74; Vermont, 1869 ***5900.10*** *p456*
Reiley, Mary Ann 17; Vermont, 1847 ***5900.10*** *p456*
Reiley, Michael 61; Ontario, 1871 ***1823.15*** *p221*
Reiley, Patrick 25; Virginia, 1773 ***1220.25*** *p29*
Reiley, Patrick 69; Ontario, 1871 ***1823.15*** *p221*
Reilley, Honor 89; Vermont, 1876 ***5900.10*** *p450*
Reilly, Alexander; New York, 1802 ***8197.10*** *p24*
Reilly, Andrew; New York, 1837 ***8197.10*** *p103*
Reilly, Ann; Vermont, 1838-1909 ***5900.10*** *p444*
Reilly, Ann 52; Vermont, 1885 ***5900.10*** *p298*
Reilly, Bridget 75; Vermont, 1878 ***5900.10*** *p613*
Reilly, Bridget Kilgalan; Vermont, 1830-1902 ***5900.10*** *p205*
Reilly, Charles; Charleston, South Carolina, 1807 ***1224.3*** *p65*
Reilly, Charles 38; Vermont, 1848 ***5900.10*** *p390*
Reilly, Daniel 45; Ontario, 1871 ***1823.28*** *p85*
Reilly, Edward 19; New York, 1827-1828 ***8197.10*** *p309*
Reilly, Farrel; New York, 1830 ***8197.10*** *p275*
Reilly, Francis; New York, 1840 ***8197.10*** *p188*
Reilly, Hugh; New York, 1834 ***8197.10*** *p315*
Reilly, Hugh; New York, 1838 ***8197.10*** *p147*
Reilly, James; New York, 1839 ***8197.10*** *p134*
Reilly, James 56; Vermont, 1875 ***5900.10*** *p390*
Reilly, John; New York, 1794 ***8197.10*** *p4*
Reilly, John; New York, 1829 ***8197.10*** *p275*
Reilly, John; New York, 1839 ***8197.10*** *p276*
Reilly, John 26; Maryland, 1774 ***1220.25*** *p78*
Reilly, Joseph; New York, 1837 ***8197.10*** *p101*
Reilly, Margaret Corly; Vermont, 1825-1861 ***5900.10*** *p205*
Reilly, Marlow 42; Ontario, 1871 ***1823.28*** *p85*
Reilly, Mary McGuire; Vermont, 1805-1878 ***5900.10*** *p444*
Reilly, Michael; New York, 1822 ***8197.10*** *p274*
Reilly, Michael; New York, 1825 ***8197.10*** *p274*
Reilly, Michael; New York, 1832 ***8197.10*** *p275*
Reilly, Michael; New York, 1840 ***8197.10*** *p190*
Reilly, Myles; New York, 1820 ***8197.10*** *p273*
Reilly, Patrick; New York, 1837 ***8197.10*** *p102*
Reilly, Patrick 22; Philadelphia, 1774 ***1220.25*** *p43*
Reilly, Patrick 67; Vermont, 1879 ***5900.10*** *p390*
Reilly, Peter 32; Ontario, 1871 ***1823.15*** *p221*
Reilly, Richard; New York, 1840 ***8197.10*** *p188*
Reilly, Robert 48; Ontario, 1871 ***1823.28*** *p85*
Reilly, Roger; Vermont, 1845-1915 ***5900.10*** *p444*
Reilly, Sally; Vermont, 1818-1897 ***5900.10*** *p615*
Reilly, Thomas; New York, 1823 ***8197.10*** *p274*
Reilly, Thomas; New York, 1837 ***8197.10*** *p101*
Reilly, Thomas; New York, 1840 ***8197.10*** *p188*
Reilly, Thomas; Pennsylvania, 1865 ***6058.10*** *p50*
Reilly, William; Pennsylvania, 1865 ***6058.10*** *p50*
Reilly, William; Vermont, 1815-1906 ***5900.10*** *p205*
Reilly, William 35; Philadelphia, 1774 ***1220.25*** *p44*
Reily, George 60; Ontario, 1871 ***1823.28*** *p85*
Reily, John; Pennsylvania, 1777 ***4629.10*** *p7*
Reily, John; Pennsylvania, 1787 ***4629.10*** *p51*
Reily, John P.; New York, 1823 ***8197.10*** *p274*
Reily, Patrick 28; Ontario, 1871 ***1823.28*** *p85*
Reily, William; New York, 1827 ***8197.10*** *p275*
Reimer, Fridrick; New York, 1831 ***8197.10*** *p367*
Reimer, John Peter; New York, 1807 ***8197.10*** *p49*
Rein, Catherine 18; Kansas, 1910 ***9079.10*** *p14*
Rein, Elizabeth 55; Kansas, 1910 ***9079.10*** *p14*
Rein, George 31; Kansas, 1891-1910 ***9079.10*** *p31*
Rein, George 54; Kansas, 1892-1910 ***9079.10*** *p14*
Rein, Henry 21; Kansas, 1910 ***9079.10*** *p14*
Reinacher, Friedrich; Port uncertain, 1790 ***2856.30*** *p355*
Reinalds, Jno; Virginia, 1665-1666 ***6212.30*** *p22*
Reinbic, Christopher; Maryland, 1910 ***3259.35*** *p51*
Reinbold, Barbara; Port uncertain, 1783 ***2856.30*** *p355*
Reinbold, Fidel; Port uncertain, 1787 ***2856.30*** *p355*
Reinbold, Franziska; Port uncertain, 1793 ***2856.30*** *p355*
Reinbold, Josef; Port uncertain, 1774 ***2856.30*** *p355*
Reinbold, Melchior; Port uncertain, 1784 ***2856.30*** *p355*
Reiner, Augustus; New York, 1813 ***8197.10*** *p272*
Reiner, Christopher; Pennsylvania, 1778 ***4629.10*** *p32*
Reiner, Margarete; Port uncertain, 1752 ***2856.30*** *p355*
Reinhard, Dietrich; Port uncertain, 1778 ***2856.30*** *p355*
Reinhard, Jacob; Port uncertain, 1791 ***2856.30*** *p355*
With wife
Reinhard, Jakob; Port uncertain, 1756 ***2856.30*** *p355*
Reinhard, Johann Niklas; Canada, 1751 ***2856.30*** *p355*
With wife & children
Reinhard, John; New York, 1837 ***8197.10*** *p102*
Reinhard, John; Pennsylvania, 1779 ***4629.10*** *p38*
Reinhard, Konrad; Port uncertain, 1784 ***2856.30*** *p355*
Reinhard, Maria Catharina; Port uncertain, 1769 ***2856.30*** *p355*
Reinhard, Mathias; Port uncertain, 1754 ***2856.30*** *p355*
Reinhardt, Alexander 24; Kansas, 1886-1910 ***9079.10*** *p36*
Reinhardt, Anna Maria; Port uncertain, 1771 ***2856.30*** *p355*
Reinhardt, Catharina; Port uncertain, 1759 ***2856.30*** *p355*
Reinhardt, Catherina 48; Kansas, 1886-1910 ***9079.10*** *p36*
Reinhardt, Christian; Port uncertain, 1738 ***2856.30*** *p355*
Reinhardt, Emelia 26; Kansas, 1886-1910 ***9079.10*** *p36*
Reinhardt, George 71; Kansas, 1887-1910 ***9079.10*** *p34*
Reinhardt, Johann Michael; Port uncertain, 1744 ***2856.30*** *p355*
Reinhardt, Mary E. 68; Kansas, 1887-1910 ***9079.10*** *p34*
Reinhart, Frank 30; Ontario, 1871 ***1823.15*** *p221*
Reinhart, George, Jr.; Pennsylvania, 1787 ***4629.10*** *p55*
Reinhart, John Martin; New York, New York, 1884 ***3437.14*** *p189*
Reinhart, Martin; America, 1754 ***2856.30*** *p355*
With wife & 4 children
Reinhart, Wilhelm; Port uncertain, 1749 ***2856.30*** *p355*
Reinheimer, Valentin; Port uncertain, 1764 ***2856.30*** *p355*
Reinhirdl, Alexander 25; Kansas, 1886-1910 ***9079.10*** *p30*
Reinhirdl, Katie 24; Kansas, 1886-1910 ***9079.10*** *p30*
Reinhold, Casper; New York, 1825 ***8197.10*** *p274*
Reinhold, Johann; Port uncertain, 1766 ***2856.30*** *p355*
Reinhold, Johann Jaob; America, 1766 ***2856.30*** *p355*
Reinke, Henry 66; Ontario, 1871 ***1823.15*** *p221*
Reinold, Charles; New York, 1806 ***8197.10*** *p323*
Reinolds, Robert; Maryland, 1681 ***2524.55*** *p184*
Reinsperger, Mr.; America, 1749 ***2856.30*** *p355*
Wife: A. Cath
Reinsperger, A. Cath *SEE* Reinsperger, Mr.
Reinstadler, Martin; Port uncertain, 1782 ***2856.30*** *p355*
Reintzel, Konrad; America, 1762 ***2856.30*** *p355*
Reiny, John; Maryland, 1676 ***2524.55*** *p184*
Wife: Mary
Reiny, John; Maryland, 1676 ***2524.55*** *p184*
Reiny, Mary *SEE* Reiny, John
Reiny, Mary; Maryland, 1676 ***2524.55*** *p184*
Reipert, Anton; Port uncertain, 1791 ***2856.30*** *p355*
Reippel, Georg; Port uncertain, 1755 ***2856.30*** *p355*
Reirdan, Daniel; Maryland, 1682 ***2524.55*** *p184*
Reirdan, David; Maryland, 1682 ***2524.55*** *p184*
Reirdan, Mathew; Maryland, 1682 ***2524.55*** *p184*
Reirdan, Teague; Maryland, 1682 ***2524.55*** *p184*
Reirdan, Thomas; Maryland, 1682 ***2524.55*** *p184*
Reis, Andreas; New York, 1837 ***8197.10*** *p103*
Reis, Georg; America, 1738 ***2856.30*** *p355*
Reis, Joseph; New York, 1837 ***8197.10*** *p103*
Reisch, Anton; Port uncertain, 1720 ***2856.30*** *p356*
Reisch, Anton; Port uncertain, 1748 ***2856.30*** *p356*
Reisch, Margarete; Port uncertain, 1614 ***2856.30*** *p356*
With daughter
Reisch, Matthaus; America, 1751 ***2856.30*** *p353*
Reisch, Philipp; Port uncertain, 1716 ***2856.30*** *p356*
Reisel, Simon; Port uncertain, 1754 ***2856.30*** *p356*
Reiser, Henry; Baltimore, 1847 ***6058.10*** *p38*
Reiser, Herman M.; Pennsylvania, 1868 ***6058.10*** *p62*
Reiser, Johann; Port uncertain, 1788 ***2856.30*** *p356*
Reiser, Nicolas; America, 1749 ***2856.30*** *p356*
With wife & children
Reisinger, Jakob; Port uncertain, 1749 ***2856.30*** *p356*
Reisinger, Johann Jakob; America, 1749 ***2856.30*** *p356*
Reiss, Conrad; New York, New York, 1855 ***6058.10*** *p40*
Reiss, Georg; Port uncertain, 1783 ***2856.30*** *p356*
Reiss, John Henry; New York, 1806 ***8197.10*** *p32*
Reiss, Mathias; Pennsylvania, 1829-1834 ***6058.10*** *p12*
Reisser, Johann; Port uncertain, 1766 ***2856.30*** *p356*
Reisser, Magdalena; America, 1751 ***2856.30*** *p356*
Reissig, Anna 9; Kansas, 1910 ***9079.10*** *p14*
Reissig, Eva 52; Kansas, 1877-1910 ***9079.10*** *p14*
Reissig, Frederic 53; Kansas, 1877-1910 ***9079.10*** *p14*
Reissig, George 40; Kansas, 1897-1910 ***9079.10*** *p53*
Reissner, Jakob; Port uncertain, 1749 ***2856.30*** *p356*
Reissner, Johann Jakob; America, 1749 ***2856.30*** *p356*
Reister, Jacob; America, 1752 ***2856.30*** *p356*
Reister, Jacob; America, 1752 ***2856.30*** *p356*
With wife & children
Reister, Jacob; Port uncertain, 1764 ***2856.30*** *p356*
Reistow, Charles 53; Ontario, 1871 ***1823.28*** *p85*
Reitenbach, Apollonia; Port uncertain, 1796 ***2856.30*** *p356*
Reitenbach, Barbara; America, 1780 ***2856.30*** *p356*
Reitenbach, Wilhelm; Port uncertain, 1790 ***2856.30*** *p356*
Reith, William 51; Ontario, 1871 ***1823.15*** *p221*
Reither, Jacob; Port uncertain, 1748 ***2856.30*** *p356*
Reitz, Anna Margarete; Port uncertain, 1748 ***2856.30*** *p356*
Reitz, Francis Joseph; New York, 1834 ***8197.10*** *p372*
Reitz, George 69; Ontario, 1871 ***1823.15*** *p221*
Reitz, John 25; Ontario, 1871 ***1823.15*** *p221*
Reives, William 59; Ontario, 1871 ***1823.22*** *p133*
Reiz, Catharina; Port uncertain, 1752 ***2856.30*** *p356*
Reizin, Catharina; Port uncertain, 1752 ***2856.30*** *p356*
Rejski, James; Maryland, 1910 ***3259.35*** *p51*
Rekerry, Alice; Virginia, 1671 ***6212.30*** *p43*
Rekiel, Walter; Maryland, 1910 ***3259.35*** *p51*
Relfe, Margret; Maryland, 1673 ***2524.55*** *p184*
Relihan, Daniel B. 41; Vermont, 1899 ***5900.10*** *p62*
Relihan, Hannah M. Keefe 72; Vermont, 1922 ***5900.10*** *p62*
Relihan, Jeremiah; Vermont, 1854-1938 ***5900.10*** *p589*
Relihan, Margaret Sheehan; Vermont, 1854-1904 ***5900.10*** *p589*
Relin, Magdalena; Port uncertain, 1769 ***2856.30*** *p356*
Relinin, Magdalena; Port uncertain, 1769 ***2856.30*** *p356*

Relion, John Baptist; Philadelphia, 1793 ***4629.10*** *p72*
Rellis, Bridget 27; Ontario, 1861 ***2896.27*** *p71*
Rellis, C. 42; Ontario, 1861 ***2896.28*** *p9*
Rellis, J. 18; Ontario, 1861 ***2896.28*** *p9*
Rellis, John 35; Ontario, 1861 ***2896.27*** *p71*
Rellis, M. 22; Ontario, 1861 ***2896.28*** *p9*
Rellis, Peter 50; Ontario, 1861 ***2896.28*** *p9*
Relly, Edward 63; Ontario, 1871 ***1823.15*** *p221*
Relton, Donald 46; Ontario, 1871 ***1823.15*** *p221*
Rembis, Agnes; Maryland, 1910 ***3259.35*** *p51*
Remcke, Jakob; America, 1748 ***2856.30*** *p356*
Remele, Ambrosius; America, 1749 ***2856.30*** *p356*
Remelius, Hans Michael; Port uncertain, 1752 ***2856.30*** *p357*
Rementon, John; Maryland, 1671 ***2524.55*** *p184*
Remer, Nicholas; New York, New York, 1846 ***6058.10*** *p30*
Remfry, John 37; Ontario, 1871 ***1823.28*** *p85*
Remig, Johann Wendel; Port uncertain, 1786 ***2856.30*** *p357*
Reminger, Johann Georg; America, 1742 ***2856.30*** *p357*
Remington, Jonathan; New England, 1751 ***1224.2*** *p96*
Remle, Niklas; America, 1731 ***2856.30*** *p357*
Remmergen, John; New York, 1840 ***8197.10*** *p190*
Remminger, Wendel; America, 1750 ***2856.30*** *p357*
Remmington, Frederick 38; Ontario, 1871 ***1823.28*** *p85*
Remnant, John; Alexandria, Virginia, 1793 ***1224.2*** *p96*
Remnant, John; Virginia, 1743 ***1224.2*** *p96*
Remnant, John 23; Maryland, 1774 ***1220.25*** *p74*
Remond, John; Pennsylvania, 1779 ***4629.10*** *p41*
Remonda, John 30; Maryland, 1774 ***1220.25*** *p84*
Remp, Maria Catharina; Port uncertain, 1790 ***2856.30*** *p357*
Remp, Michael; Port uncertain, 1764 ***2856.30*** *p357*
With wife & 3 children
Rempy, Jakob; America, 1741 ***2856.30*** *p357*
Remsen, Peter; New York, New York, 1792 ***1224.2*** *p96*
Remshard, Daniel; America, 1751 ***2856.30*** *p357*
With family
Remsshardt, Christian; America, 1786 ***2856.30*** *p357*
Remus, Tulious; Ontario, 1871 ***1823.28*** *p85*
Renalds, Thomas; Virginia, 1666 ***6212.30*** *p28*
Renaud, Charlotte; Philadelphia, 1804 ***1224.3*** *p65*
Renaud, Ignace; Portland, Maine, 1857 ***9196.15*** *p11*
Renber, Michael, Jr. 34; Kansas, 1907-1910 ***9079.10*** *p14*
Renber, Mollie 36; Kansas, 1910 ***9079.10*** *p14*
Renber, Pauline 4; Kansas, 1910 ***9079.10*** *p14*
Renchen, Mathew; New York, 1840 ***8197.10*** *p276*
Renck, Georg Adam; Port uncertain, 1785 ***2856.30*** *p357*
Renck, Johann; America, 1764 ***2856.30*** *p357*
With wife & children
Rendall, Mary; Maryland, 1675 ***2524.55*** *p184*
Rendczilski, Helena; Maryland, 1910 ***3259.35*** *p51*
Rendell, Abraham; New York, 1832 ***8197.10*** *p102*
Rendell, Mortlock 34; Ontario, 1871 ***1823.22*** *p133*
Render, Henry 58; Ontario, 1871 ***1823.15*** *p221*
Renehan, Mary Ryan 70; Vermont, 1895 ***5900.10*** *p586*
Renehan, William 69; Vermont, 1892 ***5900.10*** *p586*
Renet, Hypolite; New York, 1837 ***8197.10*** *p103*
Renfrew, Clara; Vermont, 1861-1909 ***5900.10*** *p206*
Renfrew, David 40; Ontario, 1871 ***1823.28*** *p85*
Renihan, Lauretta R.; Vermont, 1947 ***5900.10*** *p183*
Renihan, Nellie A.; Vermont, 1935 ***5900.10*** *p183*
Renik, Joseph; Maryland, 1910 ***3259.35*** *p51*
Reninger, Edm; Virginia, 1666 ***6212.30*** *p25*
Renkowska, Sophia; Maryland, 1910 ***3259.35*** *p51*
Renn, Richard; Maryland, 1672 ***2524.55*** *p184*
Renner, Catharina; America, 1732 ***2856.30*** *p357*
Renner, Hans Valentin; America, 1732 ***2856.30*** *p357*
Renner, Henry; New York, 1837 ***8197.10*** *p102*
Renner, Jakob; America, 1754 ***2856.30*** *p357*
Renner, Jakob; Port uncertain, 1764 ***2856.30*** *p357*
Renner, Jakob, Jr.; America, 1754 ***2856.30*** *p357*
Renner, Jerg; Port uncertain, 1738 ***2856.30*** *p357*
With wife & children
Renner, Johann; Port uncertain, 1752 ***2856.30*** *p357*
Renner, Johann Jakob; America, 1754 ***2856.30*** *p357*
With wife & children
Renner, Johann Jurg; America, 1754 ***2856.30*** *p357*
Renner, Margarete; America, 1732 ***2856.30*** *p357*
Renner, Michael; Port uncertain, 1751 ***2856.30*** *p357*
Renner, Peter; Port uncertain, 1764 ***2856.30*** *p357*
Renner, Valentin; America, 1732 ***2856.30*** *p357*
Rennet, Robert; Pennsylvania, 1777 ***4629.10*** *p17*
Rennie, Archibald 56; Ontario, 1871 ***1823.15*** *p221*
Rennie, John 25; Georgia, 1773-1774 ***1220.25*** *p32*
Rennie, William; North America, 1866 ***1640.13*** *p103*
Rennie, William 40; Ontario, 1871 ***1823.28*** *p85*
Renninger, Wendel; America, 1750 ***2856.30*** *p357*
Rennitt, Elizabeth; Maryland, 1665 ***2524.55*** *p184*
Renny, John; Maryland, 1672 ***2524.55*** *p184*
Wife: Mary
Renny, Mary *SEE* Renny, John
Renolds, Elizabeth 17; Ontario, 1871 ***1823.22*** *p133*
Renolds, George; Virginia, 1703-1704 ***6212.30*** *p63*
Renolds, George 77; Ontario, 1871 ***1823.15*** *p221*
Renolds, Richard 41; Ontario, 1871 ***1823.15*** *p221*
Renouf, Charles; New York, 1807 ***8197.10*** *p330*
Rensch, Konrad; Port uncertain, 1791 ***2856.30*** *p357*
Rensch, Leonhard, Jr.; Port uncertain, 1791 ***2856.30*** *p357*
With wife & 4 children
Rensha, John; Maryland, 1661 ***2524.55*** *p185*
Renshaw, John; Maryland, 1663 ***2524.55*** *p107*
Renshaw, John; Maryland, 1672 ***2524.55*** *p185*
Renshaw, Richard; Pennsylvania, 1779 ***4629.10*** *p41*
Renson, Maria Elisabeth; Port uncertain, 1733 ***2856.30*** *p357*
Renter, Madame; Quebec, 1857 ***9196.15*** *p24*
Renton, Joseph; Virginia, 1742 ***1224.2*** *p96*
Rentschler, Christina; Port uncertain, 1753 ***2856.30*** *p357*
Rentzen, George 40; Ontario, 1871 ***1823.15*** *p221*
Renwick, James; New York, 1840 ***8197.10*** *p190*
Renwick, James 36; Ontario, 1871 ***1823.22*** *p133*
Renwick, Jane 47; Ontario, 1871 ***1823.22*** *p133*
Renwick, John 28; Ontario, 1871 ***1823.22*** *p133*
Renwick, John 30; Ontario, 1871 ***1823.15*** *p221*
Renwick, Robert 39; Ontario, 1871 ***1823.15*** *p221*
Renwick, William; New York, 1794 ***8197.10*** *p4*
Renwick, William; New York, New York, 1816 ***1224.3*** *p65*
Reny, John; Maryland, 1672 ***2524.55*** *p184*
Wife: Mary
Reny, Mary *SEE* Reny, John
Reny, William 35; Ontario, 1871 ***1823.28*** *p86*
Renz, Jakob; Port uncertain, 1752 ***2856.30*** *p357*
Renz, Maria; Port uncertain, 1756 ***2856.30*** *p357*
Renz, Matthaus; Port uncertain, 1750 ***2856.30*** *p357*
Renzen, Mrs. Martin; Port uncertain, 1752 ***2856.30*** *p357*
Reo, Victor 26; Ontario, 1871 ***1823.28*** *p86*
Reocaja, Anton; Maryland, 1910 ***3259.35*** *p51*
Reosthski, Frank; Maryland, 1910 ***3259.35*** *p51*
Reppmann, Konrad; America, 1738 ***2856.30*** *p358*
Repps, Hans; Port uncertain, 1790 ***2856.30*** *p211*
Resch, Johann; America, 1753 ***2856.30*** *p358*
Resch, Johann; Port uncertain, 1750 ***2856.30*** *p358*
Resch, Peter; America, 1749 ***2856.30*** *p358*
Resch, Peter; Port uncertain, 1749 ***2856.30*** *p358*
With wife & children
Reschin, Maria; Port uncertain, 1783 ***2856.30*** *p358*
Resner, Andrew 57; Kansas, 1879-1910 ***9079.10*** *p22*
Resner, Chritine 57; Kansas, 1878-1910 ***9079.10*** *p22*
Resnor, Amy 11; Ontario, 1861 ***2896.28*** *p60*
Resnor, Betsy 31; Ontario, 1861 ***2896.28*** *p60*
Resnor, John 2; Ontario, 1861 ***2896.28*** *p60*
Resnor, P. 5; Ontario, 1861 ***2896.28*** *p60*
Ressel, Jung Jakob; America, 1738 ***2856.30*** *p358*
With family
Resslin, Joachim; Port uncertain, 1614 ***2856.30*** *p358*
Restead, James 40; British Columbia, 1913 ***9196.1*** *p21*
Restead, James 40; Spokane, Washington, 1913 ***9196.1*** *p21*
Resteineyer, Ernst 47; Ontario, 1871 ***1823.15*** *p221*
Restle, Martin; America, 1751 ***2856.30*** *p358*
Restley, John 21; Baltimore, 1775 ***1220.25*** *p117*
Retajezsak, Joseph; Maryland, 1910 ***3259.35*** *p51*
Retallack, Simon 22; Maryland, 1774 ***1220.25*** *p73*
Retallic, Betsy 22; Ontario, 1871 ***1823.22*** *p133*
Retallick, Stephen 58; Ontario, 1871 ***1823.22*** *p133*
Retchiak, William; Maryland, 1910 ***3259.35*** *p51*
Rethisch, Catharina; Port uncertain, 1711 ***2856.30*** *p358*
With 2 sons
Retmann, Konrad; America, 1738 ***2856.30*** *p358*
Retowsky, James; Maryland, 1910 ***3259.35*** *p51*
Retsch, Elisabeth; Port uncertain, 1785 ***2856.30*** *p358*
Retschin, Elisabeth; Port uncertain, 1785 ***2856.30*** *p358*
Retseuoto, J. 30; Alaska, 1910 ***9196.1*** *p9*
Retseuoto, J. 30; Yukon, 1910 ***9196.1*** *p9*
Rettalick, Samuel 49; Ontario, 1871 ***1823.22*** *p133*
Rettalick, Thomas 80; Ontario, 1871 ***1823.22*** *p133*
Rettich, Magdalena; Port uncertain, 1766 ***2856.30*** *p358*
Rettin, Theobald; Port uncertain, 1793 ***2856.30*** *p358*
Retting, Mr.; Port uncertain, 1791 ***2856.30*** *p358*
With wife
Rettinger, Mr.; Port uncertain, 1791 ***2856.30*** *p358*
With wife
Rettkowski, William; Maryland, 1910 ***3259.35*** *p51*
Retty, John 55; Ontario, 1871 ***1823.28*** *p86*
Retza, Peter 50; Ontario, 1871 ***1823.28*** *p86*
Reubel, John; New York, 1840 ***8197.10*** *p190*
Reuder, John 73; Ontario, 1871 ***1823.15*** *p221*
Reudy, David; Pennsylvania, 1868 ***6058.10*** *p74*
Reuhlin, Bernhard; Port uncertain, 1628 ***2856.30*** *p359*
Reuler, Barbara; America, 1752 ***2856.30*** *p358*
Reuning, Louis; New York, 1839 ***8197.10*** *p276*
Reuschle, Johann; America, 1750 ***2856.30*** *p358*
With wife & 2 children
Reuschlin, Johann; America, 1750 ***2856.30*** *p358*
With wife & 2 children
Reusse, Christian; Port uncertain, 1768 ***2856.30*** *p358*
Reusser, Christian; Port uncertain, 1768 ***2856.30*** *p358*
Reusser, Magdalena; America, 1751 ***2856.30*** *p356*
Reuter, . . .; America, 1749 ***2856.30*** *p358*
With sibling
Reuter, . . .; America, 1790 ***2856.30*** *p358*
With sibling
Reuter, Wilhelm; America, 1767 ***2856.30*** *p358*
Reuth, Jakob; Port uncertain, 1783 ***2856.30*** *p358*
Reuther, Anna Maria; Port uncertain, 1779 ***2856.30*** *p358*
Reuther, Hans; America, 1749 ***2856.30*** *p358*
Reuther, Hans; America, 1751 ***2856.30*** *p358*
With wife & children
Reuther, Hans; America, 1751 ***2856.30*** *p363*
With wife
Reuther, Hans; Port uncertain, 1747 ***2856.30*** *p358*
Reuther, Nicolaus; Port uncertain, 1752 ***2856.30*** *p358*
Reutmeyer, Michael; America, 1766 ***2856.30*** *p358*
With wife
Reutone, Mr.; Quebec, 1858 ***9196.15*** *p36*
Reutone, Mrs.; Quebec, 1858 ***9196.15*** *p36*
Reve, Andrew; Maryland, 1674 ***2524.55*** *p185*
Revell, Ann *SEE* Revell, Randall
Revell, Hannah *SEE* Revell, Randall
Revell, Katherine *SEE* Revell, Randall
Revell, Katherine, Jr. *SEE* Revell, Randall
Revell, Randall; Maryland, 1663 ***2524.55*** *p185*
Relative: Katherine, Jr.
Relative: Hannah
Relative: Katherine
Relative: Randall, Jr.
Relative: Ann
Revell, Randall, Jr. *SEE* Revell, Randall
Revely, Edward 32; Dominica, 1774 ***1220.25*** *p128*
Revero, Manuel; Philadelphia, 1791 ***4629.10*** *p62*
Reves, Mikel; Maryland, 1910 ***3259.35*** *p51*
Revi, Katherine Grant 37; Vermont, 1881 ***5900.10*** *p212*
Revi, Thomas 69; Vermont, 1913 ***5900.10*** *p212*
Revill, Richard; New York, 1839 ***8197.10*** *p134*
Revitts, William 49; Ontario, 1871 ***1823.28*** *p86*
Revus, Jno; Virginia, 1665-1666 ***6212.30*** *p22*
Rewerke, Cornelius; Maryland, 1675 ***2524.55*** *p190*
Rewes, Frank; Maryland, 1910 ***3259.35*** *p51*
Rewner, Thomas; Maryland, 1651 ***2524.55*** *p185*
Rex, Henry; Maryland, 1681 ***2524.55*** *p185*
Rey, Alexander *SEE* Rey, Alexander
Rey, Alexander; Maryland, 1664 ***2524.55*** *p183*
Wife: Joane
Child: Hannah
Child: Marah
Child: Sarah
Child: Joane
Child: Alexander
Rey, Hannah *SEE* Rey, Alexander
Rey, Joane *SEE* Rey, Alexander
Rey, Marah *SEE* Rey, Alexander
Rey, Sarah *SEE* Rey, Alexander
Reybold, Philip; Pennsylvania, 1777 ***4629.10*** *p11*
Reybolt, Jacob 45; Maryland, 1774 ***1220.25*** *p51*
Reych, William 21; Philadelphia, 1775 ***1220.25*** *p122*
Reycroft, John 60; Ontario, 1871 ***1823.22*** *p133*
Reyer, Anna Catharina; America, 1749 ***2856.30*** *p358*
Reyer, Christof; America, 1749 ***2856.30*** *p358*
Reyers, Edward; Pennsylvania, 1777 ***4629.10*** *p7*
Reyes, Mary; Virginia, 1690-1691 ***6212.30*** *p58*
Reyff, Margarete; Port uncertain, 1750 ***2856.30*** *p358*
Reylin, Barbara; America, 1752 ***2856.30*** *p358*
Reyling, Johann Georg; America, 1750 ***2856.30*** *p358*
With wife
Reyms, Mary; Virginia, 1666 ***6212.30*** *p31*
Reymuth, Johann Philipp; America, 1764 ***2856.30*** *p359*
Reynalds, James; Virginia, 1664-1665 ***6212.30*** *p16*
Reynalds, James 39; Ontario, 1871 ***1823.28*** *p86*
Reynaud, Nicholas Joseph; New York, 1840 ***8197.10*** *p276*
Reynell, Emily; Louisville, Kentucky, 1845 ***1224.3*** *p65*
Reynell, Thomas; Virginia, 1666 ***6212.30*** *p31*
Reynett, Isabella 22; Ontario, 1871 ***1823.15*** *p221*
Reynold, Edward; Maryland, 1672 ***2524.55*** *p185*
Reynold, Rowland; New York, 1794 ***8197.10*** *p4*
Reynolds, Miss; Quebec, 1857 ***9196.15*** *p22*
Reynolds, Miss; Quebec, 1858 ***9196.15*** *p36*
Reynolds, Mr.; Quebec, 1857 ***9196.15*** *p22*
Reynolds, Mr.; Quebec, 1857 ***9196.15*** *p23*
Reynolds, Mr.; Quebec, 1857 ***9196.15*** *p26*
Reynolds, Mrs.; Portland, Maine, 1858 ***9196.15*** *p30*
Reynolds, Mrs.; Quebec, 1857 ***9196.15*** *p22*
Reynolds, A. 12; Ontario, 1861 ***2896.28*** *p17*
Reynolds, Albert E.; Vermont, 1849-1925 ***5900.10*** *p167*
Reynolds, Alexander; Georgia, 1740 ***1640.10*** *p175*
Reynolds, Alexander; New York, 1807 ***8197.10*** *p329*

Reynolds, Alice Waters 71; Vermont, 1886 ***5900.10*** *p535*
Reynolds, Andrew 5 *SEE* Reynolds, Thomas
Reynolds, Andrew 25; Ontario, 1871 ***1823.22*** *p133*
Reynolds, Andrew 27 *SEE* Reynolds, Thomas
Reynolds, Ann; Maryland, 1674 ***2524.55*** *p185*
Reynolds, Ann E. 4; Ontario, 1861 ***2896.27*** *p15*
Reynolds, Anna; Vermont, 1855-1946 ***5900.10*** *p92*
Reynolds, B. 52; Ontario, 1861 ***2896.28*** *p17*
Reynolds, Bernard; Vermont, 1865-1918 ***5900.10*** *p71*
Reynolds, Bernard 34; Ontario, 1871 ***1823.28*** *p86*
Reynolds, Bishop 23; Ontario, 1861 ***2896.28*** *p11*
Reynolds, Bridget; Vermont, 1824-1898 ***5900.10*** *p468*
Reynolds, Bridget; Vermont, 1831-1884 ***5900.10*** *p426*
Reynolds, Bridget 14; New York, New York, 1847 ***1825.45*** *p20*
Reynolds, Bridget 35; Vermont, 1874 ***5900.10*** *p538*
Reynolds, Bridget 60 *SEE* Reynolds, James
Reynolds, Bridget 60 *SEE* Reynolds, Thomas
Reynolds, Bridget A.; Vermont, 1925 ***5900.10*** *p94*
Reynolds, Miss C. E.; Quebec, 1857 ***9196.15*** *p22*
Reynolds, Caroline 16; Ontario, 1861 ***2896.26*** *p19*
Reynolds, Caroline 25; Ontario, 1861 ***2896.27*** *p57*
Reynolds, Catharine 21; Philadelphia, 1774 ***1220.25*** *p42*
Reynolds, Catherine; Vermont, 1811-1901 ***5900.10*** *p342*
Reynolds, Catherine; Vermont, 1825-1914 ***5900.10*** *p535*
Reynolds, Catherine; Vermont, 1854-1935 ***5900.10*** *p71*
Reynolds, Catherine 2; New York, New York, 1847 ***1825.45*** *p20*
Reynolds, Charles 59; Ontario, 1871 ***1823.22*** *p133*
Reynolds, Christopher; New York, 1839 ***8197.10*** *p382*
Reynolds, Daniel; New York, 1807 ***8197.10*** *p48*
Reynolds, David 14; Ontario, 1861 ***2896.27*** *p67*
Reynolds, Davis 24; Ontario, 1861 ***2896.28*** *p15*
Reynolds, Domnick 56; Ontario, 1871 ***1823.15*** *p222*
Reynolds, Dorothy *SEE* Reynolds, George
Reynolds, E. 17; Ontario, 1861 ***2896.28*** *p17*
Reynolds, Edward 37; Ontario, 1871 ***1823.28*** *p86*
Reynolds, Elizabeth; Maryland, 1665 ***2524.55*** *p185*
Reynolds, Elizabeth; Vermont, 1871 ***5900.10*** *p528*
Reynolds, Ellen 32; Vermont, 1877 ***5900.10*** *p528*
Reynolds, Ellen 71; Vermont, 1881 ***5900.10*** *p92*
Reynolds, Ellen 75; Vermont, 1883 ***5900.10*** *p528*
Reynolds, Emma 15; Ontario, 1861 ***2896.27*** *p66*
Reynolds, Emma L. 1; Ontario, 1861 ***2896.27*** *p15*
Reynolds, F. 6; Ontario, 1861 ***2896.28*** *p17*
Reynolds, Francis 22; Maryland, 1775 ***1220.25*** *p99*
Reynolds, Francis 43; Ontario, 1871 ***1823.22*** *p133*
Reynolds, G.; Portland, Maine, 1858 ***9196.15*** *p30*
Reynolds, George; Maryland, 1655 ***2524.55*** *p185*
Wife: Dorothy
Reynolds, George 21; Ontario, 1861 ***2896.26*** *p19*
Reynolds, George 47; Ontario, 1871 ***1823.15*** *p222*
Reynolds, H.; Quebec, 1857 ***9196.15*** *p22*
Reynolds, H. 60; Ontario, 1861 ***2896.28*** *p11*
Reynolds, Hanah Shea 26; Vermont, 1853 ***5900.10*** *p245*
Reynolds, Hanna; Portland, Maine, 1858 ***9196.15*** *p30*
Reynolds, Hannah; Maryland, 1665 ***2524.55*** *p185*
Son: John
Son: Thomas
Reynolds, Helen C.; Vermont, 1839-1927 ***5900.10*** *p552*
Reynolds, Helen M. 4; Ontario, 1861 ***2896.27*** *p15*
Reynolds, Henry 17; Ontario, 1861 ***2896.26*** *p19*
Reynolds, J.; Portland, Maine, 1858 ***9196.15*** *p30*
Reynolds, J. 28; Ontario, 1861 ***2896.28*** *p16*
Reynolds, J. 60; Ontario, 1861 ***2896.27*** *p9*
Reynolds, Miss J.; Quebec, 1857 ***9196.15*** *p22*
Reynolds, James; Pennsylvania, 1777 ***4629.10*** *p22*
Reynolds, James; Portland, Maine, 1858 ***9196.15*** *p30*
Reynolds, James; Vermont, 1833-1891 ***5900.10*** *p528*
Reynolds, James; Vermont, 1837-1915 ***5900.10*** *p550*
Reynolds, James 8 *SEE* Reynolds, Thomas
Reynolds, James 19; Vermont, 1871 ***5900.10*** *p526*
Reynolds, James 20; Vermont, 1862 ***5900.10*** *p525*
Reynolds, James 28; New York, New York, 1847 ***1825.45*** *p20*
Mother: Bridget 60
Brother: John 24
Brother: Joseph 22
Reynolds, James H. 4; Ontario, 1861 ***2896.27*** *p57*
Reynolds, Jane 5; Vermont, 1870 ***5900.10*** *p528*
Reynolds, Joanna; Vermont, 1847-1923 ***5900.10*** *p532*
Reynolds, John *SEE* Reynolds, Hannah
Reynolds, John; Maryland, 1656 ***2524.55*** *p185*
Reynolds, John; New York, 1807 ***8197.10*** *p328*
Reynolds, John; New York, 1840 ***8197.10*** *p190*
Reynolds, John; Ontario, 1871 ***1823.22*** *p133*
Reynolds, John; Pennsylvania, 1777 ***4629.10*** *p13*
Reynolds, John; Pennsylvania, 1779 ***4629.10*** *p36*
Reynolds, John; Vermont, 1859-1923 ***5900.10*** *p92*
Reynolds, John; Virginia, 1690-1691 ***6212.30*** *p59*
Reynolds, John 6 *SEE* Reynolds, Thomas
Reynolds, John 22; Maryland, 1774 ***1220.25*** *p84*
Reynolds, John 24 *SEE* Reynolds, James
Reynolds, John 30; Ontario, 1871 ***1823.22*** *p133*
Reynolds, John 48; Ontario, 1871 ***1823.28*** *p86*
Reynolds, John 49; Ontario, 1871 ***1823.28*** *p86*
Reynolds, John 50; Ontario, 1871 ***1823.15*** *p222*
Reynolds, John 57; Ontario, 1871 ***1823.15*** *p222*
Reynolds, John 78; Vermont, 1891 ***5900.10*** *p92*
Reynolds, John H. 28; Ontario, 1861 ***2896.26*** *p19*
Reynolds, John R. 65; Ontario, 1871 ***1823.22*** *p133*
Reynolds, Jonathan 44; Ontario, 1871 ***1823.22*** *p133*
Reynolds, Joseph; Vermont, 1895 ***5900.10*** *p511*
Reynolds, Joseph 22 *SEE* Reynolds, James
Reynolds, Joseph 27; Ontario, 1861 ***2896.27*** *p57*
Reynolds, Joseph 61; Ontario, 1861 ***2896.27*** *p15*
Reynolds, Joshua; Maryland, 1653 ***2524.55*** *p185*
Reynolds, Julia; Vermont, 1845-1911 ***5900.10*** *p545*
Reynolds, L. 10; Ontario, 1861 ***2896.28*** *p17*
Reynolds, Lackey; New York, 1816 ***8197.10*** *p59*
Reynolds, Louisa 35; Ontario, 1861 ***2896.27*** *p15*
Reynolds, Lowisa P. 12; Ontario, 1861 ***2896.27*** *p15*
Reynolds, M. 28; Ontario, 1861 ***2896.28*** *p17*
Reynolds, M. M. 4; Ontario, 1861 ***2896.28*** *p17*
Reynolds, Margarett; Maryland, 1659 ***2524.55*** *p185*
Reynolds, Martha; Maryland, 1668 ***2524.55*** *p185*
Reynolds, Martha; Maryland, 1673 ***2524.55*** *p185*
Reynolds, Martha A. Sheridan; Vermont, 1852-1921 ***5900.10*** *p167*
Reynolds, Mary *SEE* Reynolds, Thomas
Reynolds, Mary; Vermont, 1804-1873 ***5900.10*** *p342*
Reynolds, Mary 21; Ontario, 1861 ***2896.26*** *p19*
Reynolds, Mary 30 *SEE* Reynolds, Thomas
Reynolds, Mary 77; Vermont, 1897 ***5900.10*** *p342*
Reynolds, Mary 79; Ontario, 1871 ***1823.22*** *p133*
Reynolds, Mary Ann; Vermont, 1853-1919 ***5900.10*** *p531*
Reynolds, Mary Jane; Vermont, 1850-1895 ***5900.10*** *p459*
Reynolds, Mary Kelty; Vermont, 1846-1884 ***5900.10*** *p550*
Reynolds, Michael; Vermont, n.d. ***5900.10*** *p100*
Reynolds, Michael; Vermont, n.d. ***5900.10*** *p535*
Reynolds, Michael; Vermont, 1796-1858 ***5900.10*** *p342*
Reynolds, Michael; Vermont, 1825-1889 ***5900.10*** *p535*
Reynolds, Michael 9; New York, New York, 1848 ***1825.45*** *p20*
Reynolds, Michael 39; Ontario, 1871 ***1823.28*** *p86*
Reynolds, Patrick 48; Vermont, 1892 ***5900.10*** *p92*
Reynolds, Peter 71; Vermont, 1913 ***5900.10*** *p531*
Reynolds, Peter 75; Vermont, 1887 ***5900.10*** *p528*
Reynolds, Phebe A.; Ontario, 1861 ***2896.28*** *p36*
Reynolds, Phebe S. 10; Ontario, 1861 ***2896.27*** *p15*
Reynolds, Rachel E. 28; Ontario, 1861 ***2896.27*** *p15*
Reynolds, Rhoda 30; Ontario, 1861 ***2896.26*** *p19*
Reynolds, Richard; Maryland, 1659 ***2524.55*** *p185*
Reynolds, Richard 19; Philadelphia, 1775 ***1220.25*** *p9*
Reynolds, Rosannah 17; Ontario, 1861 ***2896.27*** *p15*
Reynolds, Rose Ann 67; Vermont, 1906 ***5900.10*** *p531*
Reynolds, Ruben 58; Ontario, 1861 ***2896.26*** *p19*
Reynolds, S. 30; Ontario, 1861 ***2896.28*** *p17*
Reynolds, Sarah; Vermont, 1845-1927 ***5900.10*** *p554*
Reynolds, Sarah 51; Ontario, 1861 ***2896.27*** *p9*
Reynolds, Sarah P. 15; Ontario, 1861 ***2896.27*** *p15*
Reynolds, Stephen 46; Ontario, 1871 ***1823.22*** *p133*
Reynolds, T. J. 8; Ontario, 1861 ***2896.28*** *p17*
Reynolds, Thomas *SEE* Reynolds, Hannah
Reynolds, Thomas 2 *SEE* Reynolds, Thomas
Reynolds, Thomas 33; New York, New York, 1848 ***1825.45*** *p20*
Wife: Mary 30
Son: James 8
Son: Thomas 2
Brother: Andrew 27
Mother: Bridget 60
Daughter: Mary
Son: John 6
Son: Andrew 5
Reynolds, Thomas 40; New York, New York, 1847 ***1825.45*** *p20*
Reynolds, W.; Portland, Maine, 1858 ***9196.15*** *p30*
Reynolds, Walter 53; Ontario, 1871 ***1823.22*** *p133*
Reynolds, Welthan 11; Ontario, 1861 ***2896.27*** *p15*
Reynolds, William; Maryland, 1680-1681 ***2524.55*** *p185*
Reynolds, William; New York, 1821 ***8197.10*** *p273*
Reynolds, William; New York, 1837 ***8197.10*** *p101*
Reynolds, William; Pennsylvania, 1788 ***4629.10*** *p56*
Reynolds, William; Philadelphia, 1853 ***1224.3*** *p65*
Reynolds, William 28; Ontario, 1861 ***2896.27*** *p33*
Reynolds, William 31; Ontario, 1871 ***1823.28*** *p86*
Reynolds, William 57; Ontario, 1871 ***1823.15*** *p222*
Reynolds, William H. 11; Vermont, 1861 ***5900.10*** *p525*
Reynolds, William W. 7; Ontario, 1861 ***2896.27*** *p15*
Reynolds, Willie E.; Vermont, 1878-1890 ***5900.10*** *p550*
Reynolds, Willm.; Maryland, 1663 ***2524.55*** *p185*
Reynolds, Y. Henry E.; Quebec, 1857 ***9196.15*** *p22*
Reynsbottom, Isaac 16; Maryland, 1775 ***1220.25*** *p116*
Reys, Hans Georg; America, 1748 ***2856.30*** *p359*
With wife
Reyss, Catharina; Port uncertain, 1759 ***2856.30*** *p359*
Rhein, Anna Maria; Port uncertain, 1741 ***2856.30*** *p359*
Rhein, Johann Henrich; Port uncertain, 1747 ***2856.30*** *p359*
Rheinegger, Anton; Port uncertain, 1720 ***2856.30*** *p359*
Rheingans, Christina; Port uncertain, 1777 ***2856.30*** *p359*
Rheingans, Johann Georg; Port uncertain, 1758 ***2856.30*** *p359*
Rheingans, Konrad; Port uncertain, 1764 ***2856.30*** *p359*
Rheingraf, Peter; Port uncertain, 1720 ***2856.30*** *p359*
Rheinhard, Barbara; America, 1732 ***2856.30*** *p359*
Rheinhard, Barbara; America, 1752 ***2856.30*** *p359*
Rheinhard, Barbara; Port uncertain, 1733 ***2856.30*** *p359*
Rheinhard, Johann; Port uncertain, 1711 ***2856.30*** *p359*
Rheinhard, Johann Georg; Port uncertain, 1739 ***2856.30*** *p359*
Rheinhard, Magdalene; Port uncertain, 1747 ***2856.30*** *p359*
Rheinhard, Margarete; Port uncertain, 1747 ***2856.30*** *p359*
Rheinhard, Margarete; Port uncertain, 1766 ***2856.30*** *p359*
Rheinhard, Mathis; Port uncertain, 1760 ***2856.30*** *p359*
Rheinhard, Philipp; America, 1732 ***2856.30*** *p359*
Rheinhard, Philipp; America, 1752 ***2856.30*** *p359*
Rheinhard, Philipp; Port uncertain, 1733 ***2856.30*** *p359*
Rheinheimer, Philipp; Port uncertain, 1746 ***2856.30*** *p359*
Rheins, Gerhard; Port uncertain, 1748 ***2856.30*** *p359*
With wife & children
Rheinschmidt, Mrs. Andreas; Port uncertain, 1737 ***2856.30*** *p359*
Rheinschmidt, Anna Christina; Port uncertain, 1739 ***2856.30*** *p359*
Rhenoh, Janet; Savannah, Georgia, 1775 ***1640.10*** *p175*
Rherer, Hans; Port uncertain, 1764 ***2856.30*** *p386*
Rhind, John; Jamaica, 1789 ***1640.13*** *p103*
Rhoads, Joseph; Pennsylvania, 1777 ***4629.10*** *p7*
Rhode, Nicholas 24; Ontario, 1871 ***1823.28*** *p86*
Rhodes, Abraham; Maryland, 1664 ***2524.55*** *p185*
Rhodes, Barb. Muller *SEE* Rhodes, Johann
Rhodes, Elizabeth *SEE* Rhodes, John
Rhodes, Frances; Maryland, 1673 ***2524.55*** *p185*
Rhodes, James; New York, 1827 ***8197.10*** *p275*
Rhodes, Jane Sinnott 40; Vermont, 1874 ***5900.10*** *p51*
Rhodes, Johann; America, 1719 ***2856.30*** *p359*
Wife: Barb. Muller
Rhodes, John *SEE* Rhodes, John
Rhodes, John; Maryland, 1665 ***2524.55*** *p185*
Wife: Elizabeth
Child: Mary
Child: Veronoka
Child: Elizabeth
Child: Martha
Child: John
Rhodes, John; Maryland, 1670 ***2524.55*** *p185*
Rhodes, John 22; Maryland, 1774 ***1220.25*** *p61*
Rhodes, John 36; Maryland, 1774 ***1220.25*** *p62*
Rhodes, Martha *SEE* Rhodes, John
Rhodes, Mary *SEE* Rhodes, John
Rhodes, Nathaniel; Virginia, 1697 ***1224.1*** *p48*
Rhodes, Nicholas; Virginia, 1664 ***6212.30*** *p5*
Rhodes, Samuel; New York, 1819 ***8197.10*** *p273*
Rhodes, Veronoka *SEE* Rhodes, John
Rhodon, Mathew; Maryland, 1639 ***2524.55*** *p186*
Rhodt, Bernhard; Port uncertain, 1738 ***2856.30*** *p359*
Rhodt, Chrisian; America, 1751 ***2856.30*** *p359*
With father & mother
Rhone, Elizabeth Gary; Vermont, 1804-1875 ***5900.10*** *p156*
Rhone, Francis; Vermont, 1802-1880 ***5900.10*** *p156*
Rhone, Francis Patrick; Vermont, 1835-1876 ***5900.10*** *p156*
Rhone, James E. 39; Vermont, 1881 ***5900.10*** *p156*
Rhone, John; Vermont, 1833-1834 ***5900.10*** *p156*
Rhone, Mary 43; Vermont, 1904 ***5900.10*** *p156*
Rhone, William H.; Vermont, 1845-1848 ***5900.10*** *p156*
Rhynas, Lrns 53; Ontario, 1871 ***1823.15*** *p222*
Rianer, Frederick 51; Ontario, 1871 ***1823.15*** *p222*
Rians, John; New York, 1836 ***8197.10*** *p75*
Riass, Mathias; Pennsylvania, 1829-1834 ***6058.10*** *p12*
Riba, Jacinto; New York, 1830 ***8197.10*** *p361*
Ribbe, Ann 27; Ontario, 1861 ***2896.25*** *p69*
Ribbe, Arvilla 1; Ontario, 1861 ***2896.25*** *p69*
Ribbe, Henry 39; Ontario, 1861 ***2896.25*** *p69*
Ribbe, Mary 4; Ontario, 1861 ***2896.25*** *p69*
Ribbe, Mary 37; Ontario, 1861 ***2896.25*** *p69*
Ribbe, Sarah 6; Ontario, 1861 ***2896.25*** *p69*
Ribbel, Nicholas; Pennsylvania, 1777 ***4629.10*** *p19*
Ribicky, Stanislaw; Maryland, 1910 ***3259.35*** *p52*
Ribrand, Rowland; Virginia, 1667 ***6212.30*** *p36*
Ricard, Francis; New England, 1773 ***1224.2*** *p96*

Ricard, John; New York, 1807 8197.10 p330
Ricard, John B.; New York, 1830 8197.10 p313
Ricard, Polin 21; Maryland, 1774 1220.25 p62
Rice, Miss; Quebec, 1858 9196.15 p34
Rice, Bernard; New York, 1840 8197.10 p276
Rice, Bertie D.; Vermont, 1873-1965 5900.10 p480
Rice, Bridget; Vermont, 1836-1914 5900.10 p580
Rice, Catherine Neagle 69; Vermont, 1885 5900.10 p289
Rice, David; Annapolis, Maryland, 1724 1224.2 p96
Rice, Edward; New York, 1839 8197.10 p134
Rice, Edward; Vermont, 1845-1916 5900.10 p310
Rice, Edward; Virginia, 1665-1666 6212.30 p24
Rice, Elizabeth; Vermont, 1845-1918 5900.10 p288
Rice, Gilbert Cuthbert; New York, 1827 8197.10 p345
Rice, Hugh; Vermont, 1837-1899 5900.10 p288
Rice, James 62; Vermont, 1902 5900.10 p442
Rice, James 73; Ontario, 1871 1823.28 p86
Rice, John; Maryland, 1657 2524.55 p186
Rice, John; Maryland, 1663 2524.55 p220
Rice, John; Maryland, 1910 3259.35 p52
Rice, John; New York, 1806 8197.10 p322
Rice, John; New York, 1840 8197.10 p188
Rice, John; Vermont, 1830-1903 5900.10 p288
Rice, John; Vermont, 1832-1899 5900.10 p580
Rice, Jonathan; Vermont, 1810-1895 5900.10 p457
Rice, Lazarus; New York, 1839 8197.10 p134
Rice, Lizzie 30; Vermont, 1882 5900.10 p289
Rice, Luther 60; Ontario, 1871 1823.15 p222
Rice, Margaret; Vermont, 1854-1930 5900.10 p48
Rice, Margaret; Vermont, 1854-1930 5900.10 p292
Rice, Mary; Vermont, 1839-1920 5900.10 p310
Rice, Mary; Vermont, 1861-1920 5900.10 p579
Rice, Mary O'Brine; Vermont, 1835-1878 5900.10 p288
Rice, Patrick; New York, 1828 8197.10 p348
Rice, Patrick; New York, 1839 8197.10 p382
Rice, Peter; New York, 1840 8197.10 p189
Rice, Philip; Pennsylvania, 1777 4629.10 p9
Rice, Sadie L. Hogan; Vermont, 1880-1966 5900.10 p480
Rice, Sarah 71; Ontario, 1871 1823.15 p222
Rice, Sarah Erwin; Vermont, 1818-1899 5900.10 p457
Rice, Sephen Henry 26; Ontario, 1871 1823.15 p222
Rice, Thomas 17; Maryland, 1775 1220.25 p113
Rice, Timothy; Virginia, 1666 6212.30 p25
Rice, William 26; Virginia, 1773 1220.25 p28
Rice, Zoe; Vermont, 1809-1851 5900.10 p457
Rich, Jeremiah; Virginia, 1682 1224.1 p48
Rich, John; Virginia, 1666-1667 6212.30 p34
Rich, Joseph 18; Philadelphia, 1774 1220.25 p67
Richard, Cousin 29; Grenada, 1774 1220.25 p128
Richard, David 24; Ontario, 1871 1823.15 p222
Richard, Edith 20; Ontario, 1861 2896.27 p20
Richard, Frederick; New York, 1826 8197.10 p275
Richard, Jane 38; Ontario, 1871 1823.22 p133
Richard, John 22; Maryland, 1775 1220.25 p102
Richard, John 53; Ontario, 1871 1823.22 p133
Richard, John F.; New York, 1831 8197.10 p366
Richard, Maggie 37; Ontario, 1871 1823.22 p133
Richard, Mary 65; Ontario, 1861 2896.27 p20
Richard, Morris; Pennsylvania, 1850 6058.10 p28
Richards, Miss; Quebec, 1856 9196.15 p7
Richards, Mr.; Quebec, 1856 9196.15 p7
Richards, Alexander; Virginia, 1703-1704 6212.30 p63
Richards, Alfred D. 17; Ontario, 1861 2896.26 p32
Richards, Ann 53; Ontario, 1861 2896.26 p32
Richards, Ann E. 10; Ontario, 1861 2896.26 p32
Richards, Benjamin 35; Virginia, 1773 1220.25 p29
Richards, C. 9; Ontario, 1861 2896.27 p7
Richards, Calista 25; Ontario, 1861 2896.25 p72
Richards, Charles 26; Ontario, 1871 1823.22 p133
Richards, David 45; Ontario, 1871 1823.28 p86
Richards, David 60; Ontario, 1871 1823.15 p222
Richards, Edith 20; Ontario, 1861 2896.26 p20
Richards, Edward; New York, 1807 8197.10 p48
Richards, Edward; Portland, Maine, 1858 9196.15 p28
Richards, Edward 22; Maryland, 1775 1220.25 p104
Richards, Edward 24; Ontario, 1871 1823.28 p86
Richards, Eliza 19; Ontario, 1861 2896.27 p8
Richards, George; New York, 1828 8197.10 p350
Richards, George; Vermont, 1856-1943 5900.10 p543
Richards, H. E. 15; Ontario, 1861 2896.27 p7
Richards, Herbert A. 26; Ontario, 1871 1823.28 p86
Richards, Isaiah 22; Ontario, 1871 1823.28 p86
Richards, J. 17; Ontario, 1861 2896.27 p7
Richards, James; Pennsylvania, 1777 4629.10 p23
Richards, James G. 6; Ontario, 1861 2896.25 p72
Richards, Jane 22; Maryland, 1775 1220.25 p104
Richards, John; Maryland, 1663 2524.55 p219
Richards, John; Maryland, 1667 2524.55 p165
Richards, John; Maryland, 1680 2524.55 p186
Richards, John; New York, 1838 8197.10 p147
Richards, John; Pennsylvania, 1777 4629.10 p17
Richards, John; Virginia, 1745 1224.2 p96
Richards, John 21; Ontario, 1861 2896.27 p10
Richards, John 33; Ontario, 1871 1823.28 p86
Richards, John 40; Ontario, 1871 1823.28 p86
Richards, John 44; Ontario, 1871 1823.22 p133
Richards, John Henry; New York, 1831 8197.10 p364
Richards, Joseph; New York, 1839 8197.10 p134
Richards, L. 5; Ontario, 1861 2896.27 p7
Richards, M. 12; Ontario, 1861 2896.27 p7
Richards, M. E. 11; Ontario, 1861 2896.27 p10
Richards, M. E. 67; Ontario, 1861 2896.27 p10
Richards, Margaret; Vermont, 1827-1910 5900.10 p490
Richards, Margaret M. 1; Ontario, 1861 2896.25 p72
Richards, Marsh 17; Ontario, 1861 2896.27 p10
Richards, Mary; Maryland, 1667 2524.55 p165
Richards, Mary M. 13; Ontario, 1861 2896.26 p32
Richards, Nellie M. Tennian; Vermont, 1858-1898 5900.10 p543
Richards, Richard 35; Ontario, 1871 1823.28 p86
Richards, Robert; Virginia, 1681-1682 6212.30 p56
Richards, S. 7; Ontario, 1861 2896.27 p7
Richards, Sampson 33; Ontario, 1871 1823.28 p86
Richards, Samuel; Virginia, 1668 1224.1 p49
Richards, Samuel 16; Maryland, 1775 1220.25 p100
Richards, Thomas; Maryland, 1681 2524.55 p186
Richards, Thomas; New York, 1803 8197.10 p15
Richards, Thomas; Virginia, 1677 1224.1 p49
Richards, Thomas 22; Virginia, 1774 1220.25 p45
Richards, Thomas 46; Ontario, 1871 1823.22 p133
Richards, Thomas 48; Ontario, 1871 1823.28 p86
Richards, Thomas 64; Ontario, 1871 1823.22 p133
Richards, William; Carolina, 1722 1224.2 p96
Richards, William; Pennsylvania, 1777 4629.10 p8
Richards, William 34; Ontario, 1871 1823.28 p86
Richards, William 39; Ontario, 1871 1823.28 p86
Richards, William 54; Ontario, 1871 1823.28 p86
Richards, William 70; Ontario, 1871 1823.22 p133
Richards, William, Jr.; New York, 1825-1834 8197.10 p309
Richards, William A. 3; Ontario, 1861 2896.25 p72
Richards, William Fayting; North America, n.d. 1224.3 p65
Richards, William H. 22; Ontario, 1861 2896.26 p32
Richards, William S., Jr.; New York, 1837 8197.10 p318
Richardson, . . .; Boston, 1765 4628.40 p114
Richardson, Miss; Quebec, 1858 9196.15 p44
Richardson, Mr.; Quebec, 1857 9196.15 p20
Richardson, Mr.; Quebec, 1858 9196.15 p44
Richardson, Mr.; St. Kitts, 1774 1220.25 p131
Richardson, Adam 21; America, 1774 1220.25 p36
Richardson, Ann; Chicago, 1796 1640.13 p103
Richardson, Anne; Maryland, 1682 2524.55 p186
Richardson, Anne 56; Ontario, 1871 1823.15 p222
Richardson, Anne 60; Ontario, 1871 1823.28 p86
Richardson, Annie 82; Vermont, 1900 5900.10 p431
Richardson, Anthony; Virginia, 1656 1224.1 p49
Richardson, Cattien 49; Ontario, 1871 1823.15 p222
Richardson, Charles 23; Philadelphia, 1774 1220.25 p50
Richardson, Charles 68; Ontario, 1871 1823.22 p134
Richardson, David; Maryland, 1681 2524.55 p186
Wife: Elizabeth
Son: John
Richardson, David; Pennsylvania, 1777 4629.10 p13
Richardson, E. P.; Vermont, 1820-1932 5900.10 p203
Richardson, Elbert 10; Ontario, 1871 1823.22 p134
Richardson, Elizabeth SEE Richardson, David
Richardson, Enock; Pennsylvania, 1776 4629.10 p53
Richardson, Francis 31; Ontario, 1871 1823.15 p222
Richardson, Frederick 41; Ontario, 1871 1823.28 p86
Richardson, Frederick 60; Ontario, 1871 1823.15 p222
Richardson, George; Portland, Maine, 1858 9196.15 p29
Richardson, George 61; Ontario, 1871 1823.15 p222
Richardson, Henry 40; Ontario, 1871 1823.22 p134
Richardson, Isabelah 46; Ontario, 1871 1823.22 p134
Richardson, James; New York, 1802 8197.10 p24
Richardson, James 40; Ontario, 1871 1823.15 p222
Richardson, Jeremiah; New York, 1826 8197.10 p275
Richardson, Jno.; Pennsylvania, 1777 4629.10 p30
Richardson, John SEE Richardson, David
Richardson, John; Maryland, 1682 2524.55 p186
Richardson, John; New York, 1794 8197.10 p4
Richardson, John; New York, 1807 8197.10 p48
Richardson, John; New York, 1825-1834 8197.10 p310
Richardson, John; New York, New York, 1858 6058.10 p63
Richardson, John 24; Virginia, 1775 1220.25 p110
Richardson, John 28; Nova Scotia, 1774 1220.25 p136
Richardson, John 30; Ontario, 1871 1823.15 p222
Richardson, John 49; Ontario, 1871 1823.15 p222
Richardson, John 58; Ontario, 1871 1823.28 p86
Richardson, John Morgan; New York, 1837 8197.10 p276
Richardson, Joseph; New York, 1840 8197.10 p190
Richardson, Joseph 35; Ontario, 1871 1823.15 p222
Richardson, Julia; Vermont, 1857-1911 5900.10 p207
Richardson, Julius 71; Ontario, 1871 1823.22 p134
Richardson, Lawrence; Maryland, 1649 2524.55 p186
Wife: Sarah
Daughter: Sarah
Richardson, Margaret; Virginia, 1671-1672 6212.30 p45
Richardson, Margret 73; Ontario, 1871 1823.22 p134
Richardson, Martha A.; Vermont, 1840-1894 5900.10 p460
Richardson, Martha O'Donnell; Vermont, 1843-1903 5900.10 p465
Richardson, Martin 35; Ontario, 1871 1823.15 p222
Richardson, Mary McCue; Vermont, 1833-1899 5900.10 p203
Richardson, Michael; Maryland, 1681 2524.55 p186
Richardson, Moses 78; Ontario, 1871 1823.28 p86
Richardson, Nicholas 69; Ontario, 1871 1823.22 p134
Richardson, Ralph 35; South Carolina, 1774 1220.25 p83
Richardson, Richard; Pennsylvania, 1700 1224.2 p96
Richardson, Richard 18; Maryland, 1774 1220.25 p52
Richardson, Robert; New York, 1807 8197.10 p48
Richardson, Robert; Virginia, 1664-1665 6212.30 p15
Richardson, Robert 30; Ontario, 1871 1823.15 p222
Richardson, Robert 47; Ontario, 1871 1823.15 p222
Richardson, Samuel; Vermont, 1839-1917 5900.10 p465
Richardson, Samuel 22; Maryland, 1774 1220.25 p73
Richardson, Samuel 23; Ontario, 1871 1823.28 p86
Richardson, Sarah SEE Richardson, Lawrence
Richardson, Simon; Maryland, 1662 2524.55 p186
Richardson, Thomas; Maryland, 1681 2524.55 p186
Richardson, Thomas 26; Ontario, 1871 1823.15 p222
Richardson, Thomas 30; Philadelphia, 1774 1220.25 p50
Richardson, Thomas 40; Ontario, 1871 1823.15 p222
Richardson, Thomas 65; Ontario, 1871 1823.22 p134
Richardson, Wilhemenia 41; Vancouver, British Columbia, 1918 9196.1 p71
Richardson, Wilhemenia 41; Washington, 1918 9196.1 p71
Richardson, William; Maryland, 1732 1224.2 p96
Richardson, William; Pensacola, Florida, 1769 1224.2 p96
Richardson, William 20; Barbados, 1774 1220.25 p62
Richardson, William 22; Maryland, 1774 1220.25 p71
Richardson, William 31; Ontario, 1871 1823.15 p222
Richardson, William 44; Ontario, 1871 1823.22 p134
Richardson, William 47; Ontario, 1871 1823.15 p222
Richardson, William 47; Ontario, 1871 1823.28 p86
Richardson, William H.; New York, 1803 8197.10 p16
Richart, Hans; Port uncertain, 1694 2856.30 p359
Richart, Morris; Pennsylvania, 1850 6058.10 p28
Richee, Alice SEE Richee, William
Richee, Eve SEE Richee, William
Richee, John SEE Richee, William
Richee, William; Maryland, 1665 2524.55 p186
Wife: Alice
Child: Eve
Child: John
Richell, Jno; Virginia, 1665-1666 6212.30 p23
Richens, John; Maryland, 1680 2524.55 p186
Richer, John 22; Maryland, 1774 1220.25 p64
Richers, Carsten; New York, 1826 8197.10 p274
Richers, Hannah; New York, 1831 8197.10 p370
Richers, Henry; New York, 1821-1831 8197.10 p370
Richers, Hinrich; New York, 1821 8197.10 p273
Riches, George 24; Jamaica, 1775 1220.25 p144
Riches, George 24; St. Christopher, 1775 1220.25 p144
Riches, John 23; St. Christopher, 1775 1220.25 p144
Richeson, Frances; Maryland, 1666 2524.55 p186
Richeson, Mark; Maryland, 1653 2524.55 p186
Richeson, Thomas; Maryland, 1654 2524.55 p186
Richey, . . .; Boston, 1765 4628.40 p114
Richey, John; Pennsylvania, 1838 6058.10 p15
Richey, John 55; Ontario, 1871 1823.22 p134
Richey, John 64; Ontario, 1871 1823.15 p222
Richey, Samuel; Pennsylvania, 1864 6058.10 p49
Richey, Thomas; New York, 1803 8197.10 p16
Richford, Marke; Maryland, 1676 2524.55 p186
Richie, Hugh 38; Ontario, 1871 1823.28 p86
Richie, James 60; Ontario, 1871 1823.28 p86
Richie, Robert 54; Ontario, 1871 1823.28 p86
Richison, John; Virginia, 1703-1704 6212.30 p62
Richison, Thomas; Virginia, 1703-1704 6212.30 p62
Richl, Peter; New York, 1837 8197.10 p102
Richler, Mr.; America, 1738 2856.30 p35
Richloe, Samuel; Maryland, 1633 2524.55 p186
Richman, Francis Henry; Philadelphia, n.d. 1224.3 p65
Richmezolski, Stanolau; Maryland, 1910 3259.35 p52
Richmond, Mr.; Quebec, 1858 9196.15 p42
Richmond, Mrs.; Quebec, 1858 9196.15 p42
Richmond, George; Boston, 1819 1224.3 p65
Richmond, George; New York, 1840 8197.10 p190
Richmond, James 50; Ontario, 1871 1823.22 p134
Richmond, Jane; Virginia, 1666 6212.30 p29

Richmond, Jessie 39; Ontario, 1871 1823.22 p134
Richmond, John; New York, 1839 8197.10 p276
Richmond, John 33; Ontario, 1871 1823.15 p222
Richmond, John 42; Ontario, 1871 1823.22 p134
Richmond, Margaret; Virginia, 1685 1224.1 p49
Richmond, Margret; Virginia, 1690 6212.30 p58
Richmond, Robert 30; Ontario, 1871 1823.15 p222
Richmond, Thomas; Ontario, 1877 1640.13 p103
Richmond, Volney 46; Alaska, 1917 9196.1 p7
Richmond, Volney 46; Yukon, 1917 9196.1 p7
Richter, Frederick; New York, 1835 8197.10 p316
Richter, Johann; America, 1738 2856.30 p359
With wife 2 sons & 2 daughters
Richter, Johann Heinrich; America, 1738 2856.30 p359
Richter, Johann Jacob; America, 1738 2856.30 p359
Richter, Joseph; Maryland, 1910 3259.35 p52
Richter, Margaret; New York, 1838 8197.10 p147
Richter, Maria Christina; America, 1738 2856.30 p359
Richter, Sus. Catharina; America, 1738 2856.30 p359
Richtschnaid, Maria Catharina; Port uncertain, 1733 2856.30 p359
Richum, Phoebe 57; Ontario, 1871 1823.22 p134
Rick, Thomas 67; Ontario, 1871 1823.15 p222
Rickabrod, John; Pennsylvania, 1825 6058.10 p8
Rickard, Thomas; New York, 1840 8197.10 p188
Rickard, William; St. Vincent, 1835 1640.13 p103
Rickards, John; Virginia, 1671-1672 6212.30 p45
Rickbeil, John 28; Ontario, 1871 1823.15 p222
Rickbeil, John 49; Ontario, 1871 1823.15 p222
Rickemann, Daniel; America, 1752 2856.30 p360
Ricker, Elizabeth 25; Grenada, 1776 1220.25 p129
Ricker, John Peter 30; Grenada, 1776 1220.25 p129
Rickers, Hannah; New York, 1831 8197.10 p355
Rickert, Johann Georg; Port uncertain, 1752 2856.30 p360
Rickert, Johann Georg; Port uncertain, 1786 2856.30 p360
Ricketts, James; Maryland, 1673 2524.55 p186
Ricketts, James Jervis; Philadelphia, 1843 1224.3 p66
Ricketts, W. H. 19; Jamaica, 1773 1220.25 p28
Rickey, Alfred; Vermont, 1849-1920 5900.10 p156
Rickey, Catherine Martin; Vermont, 1850-1938 5900.10 p156
Rickh, Martin; America, 1754 2856.30 p360
Rickin, Margarett; Maryland, 1661 2524.55 p186
Ricord, Alexander; New York, 1809 8197.10 p55
Ricouard, Eugene; Pennsylvania, 1861-1867 6058.10 p58
Ricroft, Martin; Maryland, 1671 2524.55 p186
Ridd, Andrew 48; Ontario, 1871 1823.15 p222
Ridd, Francis; New York, 1833 1224.3 p66
Riddall, Jane *SEE* Riddall, Walter
Riddall, Katherine *SEE* Riddall, Walter
Riddall, Walter *SEE* Riddall, Walter
Riddall, Walter; Maryland, 1680 2524.55 p186
Wife: Katherine
Child: Jane
Child: Walter
Riddel, James 56; Ontario, 1871 1823.15 p222
Riddell, Mr.; Quebec, 1858 9196.15 p33
Riddell, Mrs.; Quebec, 1858 9196.15 p33
Riddell, George 56; Ontario, 1871 1823.22 p134
Riddell, James; Georgia, 1698 1640.13 p103
Riddell, Mary 23; Ontario, 1871 1823.15 p223
Riddell, Susanna; Virginia, 1790 1224.2 p97
Riddell, Thomas; Georgia, 1699 1640.13 p103
Ridden, Bernard; New York, 1831 8197.10 p364
Ridden, Martin; New York, 1804 8197.10 p28
Ridder, Jno; Virginia, 1681-1682 6212.30 p56
Ridder, John; Maryland, 1661 2524.55 p186
Riddie, Richard 25; St. Kitts, 1774-1775 1220.25 p129
Riddle, George; New York, 1807 8197.10 p48
Riddle, Susanna; Missouri, 1850 1224.3 p66
Ride, Hans Otto; America, 1739 2856.30 p360
With wife & 3 children
Ride, Johann Jakob; America, 1739 2856.30 p360
Rideing, Tho.; Maryland, 1681 2524.55 p186
Rider, Robert; Maryland, 1660 2524.55 p187
Rider, Robert; Maryland, 1665 2524.55 p187
Rider, Robert; Maryland, 1668 2524.55 p187
Ridge, Anne; Virginia, 1665 6212.30 p17
Ridge, Earnest William 22; Ontario, 1871 1823.28 p86
Ridge, Jonathan; Maryland, 1656 2524.55 p187
Ridge, Jonathan 22; Maryland, 1774 1220.25 p84
Ridge, Mary; Virginia, 1665 6212.30 p17
Ridge, Morgan; Pennsylvania, 1777 4629.10 p24
Ridgely, Robert; Maryland, 1670 2524.55 p187
Ridgley, Elizabeth Howard *SEE* Ridgley, Henry
Ridgley, Henry; Maryland, 1659-1664 2524.55 p187
Wife: Elizabeth Howard
Ridgly, Elizabeth Howard *SEE* Ridgly, Henry
Ridgly, Henry; Maryland, 1665 2524.55 p187
Wife: Elizabeth Howard
Ridgway, Mary 29; Maryland, 1775 1220.25 p12
Ridiz, Anna 58; Kansas, 1910 9079.10 p51
Ridiz, Henry 60; Kansas, 1900-1910 9079.10 p51
Ridiz, John 30; Kansas, 1900-1910 9079.10 p51
Ridiz, Mary 27; Kansas, 1910 9079.10 p51
Ridler, Mrs.; Port uncertain, 1790 2856.30 p360
Ridley, Drew 22; Maryland, 1774 1220.25 p52
Ridley, George; New York, 1802 8197.10 p24
Ridley, John; Pennsylvania, 1838 6058.10 p15
Ridley, Joseph 40; Ontario, 1871 1823.15 p223
Ridley, Matthew; Baltimore, 1806 1224.3 p66
Ridont, Mr.; Quebec, 1857 9196.15 p22
Ridont, Mrs.; Quebec, 1857 9196.15 p22
Ridout, Mr.; Quebec, 1856 9196.15 p10
Ridout, Isabella 60; Ontario, 1871 1823.15 p223
Ridout, Joseph; Savannah, Georgia, 1811 1640.10 p175
Ridpeth, John 30; Maryland, 1775 1220.25 p100
Ridy, Hans Otto; America, 1739 2856.30 p360
With wife & 3 children
Ridy, Johann Jakob; America, 1739 2856.30 p360
Rieb, Johann; Port uncertain, 1737 2856.30 p360
Riebel, Anna 19; Kansas, 1910 9079.10 p10
Riebel, Mrs. Georg; Port uncertain, 1743 2856.30 p360
Riebel, George 23; Kansas, 1910 9079.10 p10
Rieck, Arend Hinrich; New York, 1839 8197.10 p135
Ried, Andreas; Port uncertain, 1790 2856.30 p360
Ried, David 45; Ontario, 1871 1823.15 p223
Ried, Ferdinand; Port uncertain, 1749 2856.30 p360
Wife: M. Cath.
Ried, Hans Georg; America, 1752 2856.30 p360
With wife & 5 children
Ried, James 29; Ontario, 1871 1823.15 p223
Ried, James 31; Ontario, 1871 1823.15 p223
Ried, John 29; Ontario, 1871 1823.15 p223
Ried, M. Cath. *SEE* Ried, Ferdinand
Ried, Robert 40; Ontario, 1871 1823.15 p223
Ried, Robert 72; Ontario, 1871 1823.15 p223
Ried, Robert 73; Ontario, 1871 1823.15 p223
Ried, Samuel 24; Ontario, 1871 1823.15 p223
Riede, John; Maryland, 1680 2524.55 p187
Rieder, Henry; New York, 1840 8197.10 p277
Rieder, Mrs. Johann; Port uncertain, 1769 2856.30 p360
Riedinger, Christia Muller; America, 1774 2856.30 p360
Riedinger, Peter; America, 1770 2856.30 p360
Riedmuller, Christof; Port uncertain, 1732 2856.30 p360
Riedmuller, Christof; Port uncertain, 1762 2856.30 p360
Riedt, Johann Philipp; America, 1727 2856.30 p360
Riedt, Johann Philipp; Port uncertain, 1729 2856.30 p360
Riedy, Widow 45; Ontario, 1871 1823.15 p223
Riedy, William 28; Ontario, 1871 1823.15 p223
Riefmacher, Andreas; Port uncertain, 1790 2856.30 p360
Riegel, Miss; Port uncertain, 1791 2856.30 p360
With sister
Riegel, Daniel; Port uncertain, 1774 2856.30 p360
Riegel, David; America, 1733 2856.30 p360
Riegel, Gertrony; America, 1733 2856.30 p360
Riegel, Johann; America, 1733 2856.30 p360
Riegel, Johann; America, 1733 2856.30 p360
With wife & children
Riegel, Johann; Port uncertain, 1783 2856.30 p360
Riegel, Johann, Jr.; America, 1733 2856.30 p360
Riegel, Karl; Port uncertain, 1796 2856.30 p360
Riegel, Maria Elisabeth; Port uncertain, 1765 2856.30 p360
Riegel, Michael; Port uncertain, 1795 2856.30 p360
Riegel, Michael; Port uncertain, 1796 2856.30 p360
Riegel, Peter; Port uncertain, 1784 2856.30 p360
Riegel, Sara; America, 1733 2856.30 p360
Rieger, Mr.; America, 1765 2856.30 p361
With brother
Rieger, Anna Maria; Port uncertain, 1768 2856.30 p360
Rieger, Bartle; Port uncertain, 1750 2856.30 p360
Rieger, Franz Theobald; Port uncertain, 1688 2856.30 p361
Rieger, Thomas; Port uncertain, 1697 2856.30 p361
Rieglin, Anna Elisabeth; Port uncertain, 1757 2856.30 p361
Rieglin, Anna Elisabeth; Port uncertain, 1776 2856.30 p361
Rieglin, Elisabeth; Port uncertain, 1763 2856.30 p361
Rieglin, Elisabeth; Port uncertain, 1768 2856.30 p361
Riehle, Ignaz; Port uncertain, 1795 2856.30 p361
Riel, Edward 74; Vermont, 1902 5900.10 p396
Riel, Hannora Lynch 53; Vermont, 1890 5900.10 p396
Riel, William 16; Ontario, 1871 1823.22 p134
Rieley, John 47; Ontario, 1871 1823.15 p223
Rieley, Thomas 55; Ontario, 1871 1823.15 p223
Rielly, Lawrance 60; Ontario, 1871 1823.28 p86
Rielly, Owen 51; Ontario, 1871 1823.15 p223
Rielly, Patrick; New York, 1821 8197.10 p273
Riely, Patrick; New York, 1837 8197.10 p103
Riely, Thomas 57; Ontario, 1871 1823.28 p86
Riely, William 57; Ontario, 1871 1823.15 p223
Rieman, George 37; Ontario, 1871 1823.15 p223
Riemensperger, Anna Barbara; Port uncertain, 1764 2856.30 p361
Riemensperger, Johann Adam; America, 1747 2856.30 p361
With wife
Riemer, Andreas; Port uncertain, 1764 2856.30 p361
Rien, Michael; Pennsylvania, 1779 4629.10 p38
Rienhand, Henry 42; Kansas, 1887-1910 9079.10 p7
Rienhand, Lizzie 34; Kansas, 1892-1910 9079.10 p7
Riensset, Mary Hays; North Carolina, 1744 1224.2 p97
Ries, Barbara; Port uncertain, 1768 2856.30 p361
Riese, Rudolph; New York, 1838 8197.10 p276
Rieser, Herman M.; Pennsylvania, 1868 6058.10 p62
Rieser, Julius M.; New York, New York, 1858 6058.10 p54
Riesner, Herman M.; Pennsylvania, 1868 6058.10 p38
Riess, Conrad; New York, New York, 1855 6058.10 p40
Riess, Martin; Port uncertain, 1739 2856.30 p361
Riess, Matthaus; Port uncertain, 1749 2856.30 p361
Riess, Melchior; America, 1749 2856.30 p361
With wife & 4 children
Riester, Jacob; Port uncertain, 1764 2856.30 p356
Rieth, Lorenz; Port uncertain, 1736 2856.30 p361
Riethammer, Barbara; Port uncertain, 1748 2856.30 p361
Riethammer, Maria; Port uncertain, 1748 2856.30 p361
Rietter, Christina; Port uncertain, 1764 2856.30 p361
Riettinger, Wilhelm; Port uncertain, 1793 2856.30 p361
Rifbrooke, Suzan; Maryland, 1664 2524.55 p187
Rife, Joseph 48; Ontario, 1871 1823.15 p223
Riffee, Jacob; Pennsylvania, 1777 4629.10 p8
Riffel, Henrich; Port uncertain, 1732 2856.30 p361
With children
Riffel, Jakob; Port uncertain, 1739 2856.30 p361
With wife & 6 children
Rigal, . . .; America, 1797 2856.30 p361
Rigal, . . .; America, 1801 2856.30 p361
Rigbey, Thomas; New York, 1838 8197.10 p147
Rigby, Alex; Virginia, 1665-1666 6212.30 p23
Rigby, Constance; Maryland, 1660 2524.55 p187
Rigby, Jno; Virginia, 1665-1666 6212.30 p23
Rigby, John; New York, New York, 1894 3437.14 p151
Rigby, John; Virginia, 1666-1667 6212.30 p32
Rigby, William 52; Ontario, 1871 1823.22 p134
Rigdel, Catharine 22; Maryland, 1775 1220.25 p105
Rigdon, William; Pennsylvania, 1777 4629.10 p14
Rigel, Georg; Port uncertain, 1748 2856.30 p361
Rigge, Francis; Maryland, 1659 2524.55 p187
Riggen, Darby; Maryland, 1681 2524.55 p187
Wife: Elizabeth
Child: Nathaniel
Child: Jonathan
Child: Mary
Child: John
Riggen, Elizabeth *SEE* Riggen, Darby
Riggen, John *SEE* Riggen, Darby
Riggen, Jonathan *SEE* Riggen, Darby
Riggen, Mary *SEE* Riggen, Darby
Riggen, Nathaniel *SEE* Riggen, Darby
Riggen, Teague; Maryland, 1672 2524.55 p187
Riggles, Mary; Maryland, 1675 2524.55 p187
Riggs, Abram; Virginia, 1698 6212.30 p61
Riggs, William; Vermont, 1855 1224.3 p66
Righby, Jno; Virginia, 1702 6212.30 p62
Right, Adam 32; Ontario, 1871 1823.15 p223
Right, Edw; Virginia, 1679-1680 6212.30 p54
Right, Edwd; Virginia, 1671 6212.30 p42
Right, George 58; Ontario, 1871 1823.15 p223
Right, Henry 30; Ontario, 1871 1823.15 p223
Right, Johan; New York, 1807 8197.10 p48
Right, John 18; Ontario, 1861 2896.27 p13
Right, Richard 73; Ontario, 1871 1823.15 p223
Right, Robert; Maryland, 1671 2524.55 p187
Right, Solloman; Maryland, 1672 2524.55 p187
Right, William; Maryland, 1665 2524.55 p57
Right, William 31; Maryland, 1774 1220.25 p72
Right, William 42; Ontario, 1871 1823.15 p223
Righter, Johann; America, 1738 2856.30 p361
Rightmeyer, Mary 22; Ontario, 1861 2896.27 p7
Rightmeyer, W. A. 2; Ontario, 1861 2896.27 p7
Rightmyer, C. 35; Ontario, 1861 2896.28 p16
Rightmyer, H. 15; Ontario, 1861 2896.28 p16
Rightmyer, J. 10; Ontario, 1861 2896.28 p16
Rightmyer, L. 9; Ontario, 1861 2896.28 p16
Rightmyer, M. 17; Ontario, 1861 2896.28 p16
Rightmyer, M. M. 1; Ontario, 1861 2896.28 p16
Rightmyer, S. A. 7; Ontario, 1861 2896.28 p16
Rightmyer, S. C. 12; Ontario, 1861 2896.28 p16
Rigler, John Andrew; New York, 1835 8197.10 p317
Rigney, Margaret; Vermont, 1828-1906 5900.10 p212
Rigney, Michael; New York, 1837 8197.10 p102
Rihl, Mr.; Port uncertain, 1781 2856.30 p406
Rihm, Franz; Port uncertain, 1775 2856.30 p361

Rihmersperger, Johann Adam; America, 1764 ***2856.30*** *p361*
With wife
Rikowski, Ignacy; Maryland, 1910 ***3259.35*** *p52*
Riland, Jeffry; Virginia, 1667 ***6212.30*** *p37*
Rilaye, Ann; Maryland, 1664 ***2524.55*** *p187*
Rilee, Thomas; Maryland, 1662 ***2524.55*** *p187*
Riley, Mr.; Quebec, 1856 ***9196.15*** *p10*
Riley, Mr.; Vermont, n.d. ***5900.10*** *p37*
Riley, Ann 74; Vermont, 1878 ***5900.10*** *p367*
Riley, Ann M. 86; Vermont, 1932 ***5900.10*** *p446*
Riley, Barney A.; Vermont, 1843-1893 ***5900.10*** *p546*
Riley, Bartholomew; New York, 1829 ***8197.10*** *p352*
Riley, Benjamin 37; Ontario, 1871 ***1823.15*** *p223*
Riley, Bernard; New York, New York, 1854 ***6058.10*** *p40*
Riley, Bridget; Vermont, 1829-1897 ***5900.10*** *p205*
Riley, Bridget 56; Vermont, 1884 ***5900.10*** *p85*
Riley, Bridget 78; Vermont, 1903 ***5900.10*** *p301*
Riley, Bridget McNiff; Vermont, 1836-1913 ***5900.10*** *p426*
Riley, Bridgid L. Haughian; Vermont, 1847-1927 ***5900.10*** *p406*
Riley, Catherine; Vermont, 1815-1904 ***5900.10*** *p231*
Riley, Catherine; Vermont, 1844-1904 ***5900.10*** *p77*
Riley, Catherine E. Hynes; Vermont, 1858-1935 ***5900.10*** *p598*
Riley, Catherine Roach 79; Vermont, 1889 ***5900.10*** *p598*
Riley, Catherine Steele; Vermont, 1835-1893 ***5900.10*** *p227*
Riley, Charles; New York, 1839 ***8197.10*** *p134*
Riley, Cleora P. Dunton; Vermont, 1829-1901 ***5900.10*** *p276*
Riley, Daniel; Vermont, 1822-1902 ***5900.10*** *p227*
Riley, Daniel W.; Vermont, 1855-1932 ***5900.10*** *p67*
Riley, Dennis; Vermont, 1852-1915 ***5900.10*** *p216*
Riley, Edward Cat; New York, 1831 ***8197.10*** *p363*
Riley, Elizabeth 56; Vermont, 1889 ***5900.10*** *p135*
Riley, Ellen A. Ryan; Vermont, 1857-1929 ***5900.10*** *p67*
Riley, Fannie; Vermont, 1833-1870 ***5900.10*** *p77*
Riley, Francis; New York, 1840 ***8197.10*** *p189*
Riley, Frankie J. 6 months; Vermont, 1870 ***5900.10*** *p341*
Riley, George 10; Ontario, 1861 ***2896.27*** *p28*
Riley, George 33; Ontario, 1871 ***1823.15*** *p223*
Riley, Hannah; Vermont, n.d. ***5900.10*** *p545*
Riley, Hattie; Vermont, 1865-1934 ***5900.10*** *p227*
Riley, Henry; New York, 1831 ***8197.10*** *p364*
Riley, Henry; Pennsylvania, 1811 ***6058.10*** *p4*
Riley, Hugh; Vermont, 1882 ***5900.10*** *p543*
Riley, Isabella; Vermont, 1816-1893 ***5900.10*** *p455*
Riley, James; New York, 1837 ***8197.10*** *p276*
Riley, James; New York, 1838 ***8197.10*** *p147*
Riley, James; New York, 1838 ***8197.10*** *p276*
Riley, James; New York, 1840 ***8197.10*** *p190*
Riley, James; Vermont, 1828-1906 ***5900.10*** *p240*
Riley, James; Vermont, 1851-1918 ***5900.10*** *p138*
Riley, James 45; Vermont, 1860 ***5900.10*** *p238*
Riley, James 85; Vermont, 1906 ***5900.10*** *p85*
Riley, James A.; Vermont, 1851-1913 ***5900.10*** *p170*
Riley, James M.; Vermont, 1854-1919 ***5900.10*** *p65*
Riley, James T.; Vermont, 1846-1956 ***5900.10*** *p426*
Riley, James W.; Vermont, 1843-1914 ***5900.10*** *p134*
Riley, Jane 82; Vermont, 1893 ***5900.10*** *p457*
Riley, Jane McMahon; Vermont, 1856-1896 ***5900.10*** *p46*
Riley, Jerry; Vermont, 1834-1908 ***5900.10*** *p103*
Riley, Johanna; Vermont, 1856-1933 ***5900.10*** *p138*
Riley, Johanna; Vermont, 1856-1933 ***5900.10*** *p170*
Riley, Johannah; Vermont, n.d. ***5900.10*** *p545*
Riley, John; New York, 1827-1834 ***8197.10*** *p309*
Riley, John; New York, 1837 ***8197.10*** *p101*
Riley, John; Vermont, n.d. ***5900.10*** *p545*
Riley, John; Vermont, 1824-1886 ***5900.10*** *p63*
Riley, John; Vermont, 1837-1925 ***5900.10*** *p406*
Riley, John; Vermont, 1853-1926 ***5900.10*** *p310*
Riley, John 21; Jamaica, 1774 ***1220.25*** *p60*
Riley, John 35; Vermont, 1884 ***5900.10*** *p301*
Riley, John 58; Vermont, 1914 ***5900.10*** *p193*
Riley, John H.; Vermont, 1852-1900 ***5900.10*** *p227*
Riley, Joseph 40; Ontario, 1871 ***1823.15*** *p223*
Riley, Julia; Vermont, 1855-1912 ***5900.10*** *p387*
Riley, Kate Meehan; Vermont, 1842-1920 ***5900.10*** *p464*
Riley, Katherine; Vermont, 1850-1932 ***5900.10*** *p92*
Riley, Katie M. 47; Vermont, 1888 ***5900.10*** *p598*
Riley, Lawrence; Vermont, 1829-1893 ***5900.10*** *p77*
Riley, Lucy Stone 56; Vermont, 1913 ***5900.10*** *p193*
Riley, M. John; Vermont, 1814-1895 ***5900.10*** *p310*
Riley, Malinda 58; Vermont, 1884 ***5900.10*** *p456*
Riley, Mame; Vermont, n.d. ***5900.10*** *p545*
Riley, Margaret; Vermont, n.d. ***5900.10*** *p545*
Riley, Margaret; Vermont, 1882 ***5900.10*** *p543*
Riley, Margaret 36; Vermont, 1865 ***5900.10*** *p395*
Riley, Margaret A.; Vermont, 1864-1943 ***5900.10*** *p546*
Riley, Margaret Collins; Vermont, 1837-1915 ***5900.10*** *p63*
Riley, Martin; Vermont, 1852-1923 ***5900.10*** *p46*
Riley, Mary; Vermont, 1811-1863 ***5900.10*** *p157*
Riley, Mary; Vermont, 1848-1890 ***5900.10*** *p401*
Riley, Mary; Vermont, 1885 ***5900.10*** *p191*
Riley, Mary 72; Vermont, 1913 ***5900.10*** *p465*
Riley, Mary A. 24; Vermont, 1879 ***5900.10*** *p545*
Riley, Mary Ann; Vermont, 1843-1923 ***5900.10*** *p382*
Riley, Mary Ann Brown; Vermont, 1854-1942 ***5900.10*** *p46*
Riley, Mary Holland; Vermont, 1855-1955 ***5900.10*** *p426*
Riley, Mary O'Connor 34; Vermont, 1871 ***5900.10*** *p341*
Riley, Mary Roch; Vermont, 1850-1911 ***5900.10*** *p310*
Riley, Mary Stone; Vermont, 1864-1938 ***5900.10*** *p216*
Riley, Miles; New York, 1838 ***8197.10*** *p318*
Riley, Murty J.; Vermont, 1834-1911 ***5900.10*** *p598*
Riley, O. H.; Vermont, 1853-1893 ***5900.10*** *p276*
Riley, Owen; New York, 1840 ***8197.10*** *p188*
Riley, Patrick; New York, 1838 ***8197.10*** *p147*
Riley, Patrick; New York, 1838 ***8197.10*** *p320*
Riley, Patrick; New York, 1840 ***8197.10*** *p188*
Riley, Patrick; Vermont, 1831-1883 ***5900.10*** *p426*
Riley, Patrick; Vermont, 1835-1912 ***5900.10*** *p464*
Riley, Philip; New York, 1837 ***8197.10*** *p102*
Riley, Phillip; New York, 1840 ***8197.10*** *p190*
Riley, Richard; New York, 1840 ***8197.10*** *p277*
Riley, Rose Ann 24; Vermont, 1874 ***5900.10*** *p232*
Riley, Sarah Killen; Vermont, 1839-1908 ***5900.10*** *p240*
Riley, Susan; Vermont, 1842-1924 ***5900.10*** *p304*
Riley, Susan 37; Vermont, 1881 ***5900.10*** *p505*
Riley, T. D. 67; Vermont, 1888 ***5900.10*** *p51*
Riley, Thomas; New York, 1840 ***8197.10*** *p189*
Riley, Thomas; Vermont, 1840-1899 ***5900.10*** *p304*
Riley, Thomas 75; Vermont, 1872 ***5900.10*** *p367*
Riley, Victoria 44; Vermont, 1894 ***5900.10*** *p194*
Riley, William; New York, 1840 ***8197.10*** *p190*
Riley, William 66; Ontario, 1871 ***1823.15*** *p223*
Riley, William J.; Vermont, 1823-1899 ***5900.10*** *p276*
Riley, William J. 2; Vermont, 1870 ***5900.10*** *p341*
Riley B., Margaret 82; Vermont, 1932 ***5900.10*** *p596*
Riluk, Joseph; Maryland, 1910 ***3259.35*** *p52*
Rimer, Edward 25; Philadelphia, 1774 ***1220.25*** *p26*
Rimerman, John 48; Ontario, 1871 ***1823.15*** *p223*
Rimes, Edward; New York, 1704 ***1224.2*** *p100*
Rimmer, Mr.; Quebec, 1857 ***9196.15*** *p15*
Rimmer, Mr.; Quebec, 1858 ***9196.15*** *p44*
Rimmer, Mrs.; Quebec, 1858 ***9196.15*** *p44*
Rimmersperger, Anna Barbara; Port uncertain, 1764 ***2856.30*** *p362*
Rimmon, George 15; Ontario, 1861 ***2896.25*** *p71*
Rimmon, Jane 1; Ontario, 1861 ***2896.25*** *p71*
Rimmon, Lida Ann 9; Ontario, 1861 ***2896.25*** *p71*
Rimmon, Mary 19; Ontario, 1861 ***2896.25*** *p71*
Rimmon, Matilda 13; Ontario, 1861 ***2896.25*** *p71*
Rimmon, Susan 17; Ontario, 1861 ***2896.25*** *p71*
Rimmon, Walter 11; Ontario, 1861 ***2896.25*** *p71*
Rimmore, Gilbert; Virginia, 1683 ***6212.30*** *p56*
Rimus, Ann Barrett; Virginia, 1755 ***1224.2*** *p97*
Rinck, Angelika; America, 1752 ***2856.30*** *p362*
Rinck, Georg Adam; America, 1785 ***2856.30*** *p362*
Rinck, Jakob; Port uncertain, 1782 ***2856.30*** *p362*
Rinck, Johann; Port uncertain, 1785 ***2856.30*** *p362*
Rinck, Philipp; Port uncertain, 1783 ***2856.30*** *p362*
With wife & daughter
Rinckert, Elisabeth; America, 1764 ***2856.30*** *p362*
Rinckin, Angelika; America, 1752 ***2856.30*** *p362*
Rinds, Frances 55; Ontario, 1871 ***1823.15*** *p223*
Rineheart, Safield 26; Ontario, 1871 ***1823.28*** *p86*
Riners, Joan; Virginia, 1664 ***6212.30*** *p9*
Rines, John; Virginia, 1666 ***6212.30*** *p31*
Ring, Alice Cooper; Vermont, 1827-1901 ***5900.10*** *p550*
Ring, Edmond 62; Ontario, 1871 ***1823.28*** *p86*
Ring, James; New York, 1818 ***1224.3*** *p66*
Ring, Johann; Port uncertain, 1785 ***2856.30*** *p362*
Ring, John; New York, 1840 ***1224.3*** *p66*
Ring, John; Died enroute, 1637 ***1224.1*** *p49*
Ring, John H.; Vermont, 1858-1927 ***5900.10*** *p550*
Ring, Margaret 82; Vermont, 1883 ***5900.10*** *p139*
Ring, Mary L. McMahon; Vermont, 1862 ***5900.10*** *p550*
Ring, Philipp; Port uncertain, 1783 ***2856.30*** *p362*
With wife & daughter
Ring, Thomas; Vermont, 1830-1893 ***5900.10*** *p550*
Ring, Zebedee; New York, 1828 ***8197.10*** *p349*
Ringall, Peter 35; British Columbia, 1911 ***9196.1*** *p34*
Ringall, Peter 35; Washington, 1911 ***9196.1*** *p34*
Ringeiss, Kilian; Port uncertain, 1729 ***2856.30*** *p362*
With wife & children
Ringel, Anna Dorothea; America, 1727 ***2856.30*** *p362*
With husband
Ringer, Mr.; Quebec, 1858 ***9196.15*** *p41*
Ringer, Anna Dorothea; America, 1727 ***2856.30*** *p362*
With husband
Ringer, Robert 27; Maryland, 1774 ***1220.25*** *p60*
Ringerspacher, Oswald; Canada, 1751 ***2856.30*** *p362*
With wife
Ringfahrt, Johann Peter; Port uncertain, 1784 ***2856.30*** *p362*
Ringland, G.; Portland, Maine, 1858 ***9196.15*** *p30*
Ringle, Charles 46; Ontario, 1871 ***1823.28*** *p86*
Ringle, Julious 34; Ontario, 1871 ***1823.28*** *p86*
Ringrose, Michael; Pennsylvania, 1868 ***6058.10*** *p64*
Ringsby, Mary; Virginia, 1666 ***6212.30*** *p25*
Ringshausen, Georg; New York, 1838 ***8197.10*** *p320*
Ringwaldt, Hans Georg; Cayenne, 1764 ***2856.30*** *p362*
Ringwood, Thomas; New York, 1802 ***8197.10*** *p24*
Rinkler, Georg Michael; America, 1751 ***2856.30*** *p362*
Rinley, Mirea 40; Ontario, 1871 ***1823.15*** *p223*
Rinn, Ellen Cassidy 35; Vermont, 1875 ***5900.10*** *p584*
Rinn, Francis; New York, 1837 ***8197.10*** *p102*
Rinnard, Thomas 48; Ontario, 1871 ***1823.15*** *p223*
Rinnel, Herman 56; Ontario, 1871 ***1823.15*** *p223*
Rinney, Patrick 22; Virginia, 1774 ***1220.25*** *p89*
Rinnington, John; Virginia, 1664 ***6212.30*** *p7*
Rinolls, Darius; Maryland, 1680 ***2524.55*** *p187*
Rinseland, Ditmar; New York, 1838 ***8197.10*** *p147*
Rintoul, Alexander; Savannah, Georgia, 1736 ***1640.10*** *p175*
Rioch, Kenneth; Boston, 1802 ***1224.3*** *p66*
Riordan, Eliza McGarry; Vermont, 1861-1891 ***5900.10*** *p97*
Riordan, Ellen 61; Vermont, 1881 ***5900.10*** *p562*
Riordan, Ellen 61; Vermont, 1881 ***5900.10*** *p576*
Riordan, Eugene; Vermont, 1857-1916 ***5900.10*** *p97*
Riordan, James; Vermont, 1848-1880 ***5900.10*** *p511*
Riordan, Jeremiah; Vermont, 1850-1892 ***5900.10*** *p390*
Riordan, Jerry; Vermont, 1828-1910 ***5900.10*** *p390*
Riordan, John 88; Vermont, 1906 ***5900.10*** *p561*
Riordan, John 88; Vermont, 1906 ***5900.10*** *p576*
Riordan, Mary; Vermont, 1838-1910 ***5900.10*** *p390*
Riordan, Nellie 73; Vermont, 1882 ***5900.10*** *p593*
Riordan, Thomas 29; Vermont, 1861 ***5900.10*** *p232*
Riordian, Ellen 75; Vermont, 1906 ***5900.10*** *p66*
Ripamonti, Andrea; New York, 1823 ***8197.10*** *p274*
Ripley, Mr.; Quebec, 1857 ***9196.15*** *p20*
Ripley, John; Florida, 1773 ***1224.2*** *p97*
Ripley, William 22; Carolina, 1774 ***1220.25*** *p85*
Ripp, Henrica; Port uncertain, 1788 ***2856.30*** *p362*
With husband
Ripp, Henrica; Port uncertain, 1789 ***2856.30*** *p362*
With husband
Rippel, Georg; Port uncertain, 1755 ***2856.30*** *p362*
Rippeler, Johann Georg; America, 1768 ***2856.30*** *p362*
Ripperger, Friedrich; Port uncertain, 1774 ***2856.30*** *p362*
Rippington, John 23; Ontario, 1871 ***1823.28*** *p86*
Risbrooke, Mary; Maryland, 1636 ***2524.55*** *p187*
Riscall, Margaret 101; Ontario, 1871 ***1823.15*** *p223*
Risch, Anna Barbara; America, 1746 ***2856.30*** *p362*
Risch, Anna Maria; America, 1697 ***2856.30*** *p362*
With husband
Risch, Eva Elisabeth; America, 1758 ***2856.30*** *p362*
Risch, Eva Marg. *SEE* Risch, Jakob
Risch, Jakob; America, 1697 ***2856.30*** *p362*
Wife: Eva Marg.
Risch, Jakob; Port uncertain, 1775 ***2856.30*** *p362*
Risch, Johann Friedric; America, 1750 ***2856.30*** *p362*
Risch, Johann Friedric; Port uncertain, 1750 ***2856.30*** *p362*
With wife & children
Risch, Luise; Port uncertain, 1700-1799 ***2856.30*** *p362*
Riser, Julius M.; New York, New York, 1858 ***6058.10*** *p54*
Rish, John 38; Philadelphia, 1774 ***1220.25*** *p67*
Risha, John; Virginia, 1681 ***6212.30*** *p55*
Rishton, Jeffry; Virginia, 1665-1666 ***6212.30*** *p22*
Rishton, Jeffry; Virginia, 1666-1667 ***6212.30*** *p32*
Risky, William 37; Ontario, 1871 ***1823.28*** *p86*
Risly, John; Virginia, 1665 ***6212.30*** *p18*
Rison, Thomas 77; Ontario, 1871 ***1823.22*** *p134*
Rispen, Matthew; New York, 1807 ***8197.10*** *p46*
Risque, Charles; Pennsylvania, 1777 ***4629.10*** *p19*
Risser, Julius M.; New York, New York, 1858 ***6058.10*** *p54*
Rissig, Christina 28; Kansas, 1891-1910 ***9079.10*** *p28*
Rissig, George 28; Kansas, 1889-1910 ***9079.10*** *p28*
Rist, Catharina; Port uncertain, 1791 ***2856.30*** *p363*
Rist, Josef; Port uncertain, 1736 ***2856.30*** *p363*
Rist, Josef; Port uncertain, 1760 ***2856.30*** *p363*
Riswig, Isaac W. 37; Kansas, 1899-1910 ***9079.10*** *p36*
Ritchie, Master; Quebec, 1858 ***9196.15*** *p34*
Ritchie, Miss; Quebec, 1857 ***9196.15*** *p18*
Ritchie, Mr.; Quebec, 1856 ***9196.15*** *p7*
Ritchie, Mr.; Quebec, 1857 ***9196.15*** *p18*
Ritchie, Mr.; Quebec, 1858 ***9196.15*** *p34*
Ritchie, Mrs.; Quebec, 1858 ***9196.15*** *p34*
Ritchie, Adam; Pennsylvania, 1777 ***4629.10*** *p15*
Ritchie, Alexander; New York, 1823 ***8197.10*** *p62*

Robinson, Edward 50; Ontario, 1871 ***1823.22*** *p135*
Robinson, Elizabeth; Maryland, 1660 ***2524.55*** *p189*
Robinson, Elizabeth; Mississippi, 1822-1845 ***1640.10*** *p177*
Robinson, Elizabeth 9 *SEE* Robinson, William
Robinson, Elizabeth 30 *SEE* Robinson, William
Robinson, Elizabeth 53; Ontario, 1871 ***1823.15*** *p225*
Robinson, Esther; Vermont, 1844 ***5900.10*** *p376*
Robinson, Francis; Maryland, 1664 ***2524.55*** *p189*
Robinson, Francis 3 *SEE* Robinson, William
Robinson, G. C. 34; Ontario, 1871 ***1823.28*** *p87*
Robinson, George; New York, 1840 ***8197.10*** *p277*
Robinson, George; New York, New York, 1802 ***1224.3*** *p66*
Robinson, George; Pennsylvania, 1777 ***4629.10*** *p20*
Robinson, George 3; Ontario, 1861 ***2896.25*** *p3*
Robinson, George 40; Ontario, 1871 ***1823.22*** *p135*
Robinson, George 42; Ontario, 1871 ***1823.15*** *p226*
Robinson, George 63; Ontario, 1871 ***1823.22*** *p135*
Robinson, George H.; Vermont, 1850-1942 ***5900.10*** *p89*
Robinson, Hannah 44; Vermont, 1871 ***5900.10*** *p377*
Robinson, Henry; New York, 1828 ***8197.10*** *p332*
Robinson, Henry; New York, 1834 ***8197.10*** *p75*
Robinson, Henry; New York, 1840 ***8197.10*** *p189*
Robinson, Henry 33; Ontario, 1871 ***1823.28*** *p87*
Robinson, Henry G.; New York, 1831 ***8197.10*** *p355*
Robinson, Hugh 90; Ontario, 1871 ***1823.15*** *p226*
Robinson, Isaac; Texas, 1836 ***1640.10*** *p177*
Robinson, Isaac; Texas, 1836 ***1640.10*** *p178*
Robinson, Isabella 38; Ontario, 1871 ***1823.15*** *p226*
Robinson, Ja; Virginia, 1667-1668 ***6212.30*** *p38*
Robinson, James; Maryland, 1669 ***2524.55*** *p189*
Robinson, James; Maryland, 1679 ***2524.55*** *p189*
Robinson, James; Mississippi, 1809-1845 ***1640.10*** *p178*
Wife: Margaret
Robinson, James; New York, 1834 ***8197.10*** *p75*
Robinson, James; Pennsylvania, 1777 ***4629.10*** *p20*
Robinson, James; Virginia, 1671 ***6212.30*** *p42*
Robinson, James 17; Virginia, 1775 ***1220.25*** *p106*
Robinson, James 18; Ontario, 1861 ***2896.25*** *p25*
Robinson, James 33; Ontario, 1871 ***1823.28*** *p87*
Robinson, James 36; Maryland, 1775 ***1220.25*** *p99*
Robinson, James 42; Ontario, 1871 ***1823.15*** *p226*
Robinson, James 49; Ontario, 1871 ***1823.15*** *p226*
Robinson, James 49; Ontario, 1871 ***1823.28*** *p87*
Robinson, James 51; Ontario, 1871 ***1823.15*** *p226*
Robinson, James 53; Ontario, 1871 ***1823.28*** *p87*
Robinson, James 65; Ontario, 1871 ***1823.22*** *p135*
Robinson, Jane; Maryland, 1666 ***2524.55*** *p189*
Robinson, Jenny 9 *SEE* Robinson, John
Robinson, Jno; Virginia, 1664 ***6212.30*** *p11*
Robinson, Jno; Virginia, 1674 ***6212.30*** *p52*
Robinson, Joane *SEE* Robinson, William
Robinson, John; Maryland, 1674 ***2524.55*** *p189*
Robinson, John; Maryland, 1676 ***2524.55*** *p189*
Robinson, John; Maryland, 1678 ***2524.55*** *p189*
Robinson, John; Maryland, 1680 ***2524.55*** *p189*
Robinson, John; New York, 1837 ***8197.10*** *p102*
Robinson, John; Ontario, 1855 ***1640.13*** *p105*
Robinson, John; Pennsylvania, 1777 ***4629.10*** *p31*
Robinson, John; Pennsylvania, 1785 ***4629.10*** *p48*
Robinson, John; Virginia, 1671 ***6212.30*** *p43*
Robinson, John 15; Grenada, 1774 ***1220.25*** *p89*
Robinson, John 17; Maryland, 1775 ***1220.25*** *p113*
Robinson, John 23; Maryland, 1774 ***1220.25*** *p70*
Robinson, John 28; Nova Scotia, 1774 ***1220.25*** *p135*
Robinson, John 30; America, 1774 ***1220.25*** *p36*
Robinson, John 30; Maryland, 1774 ***1220.25*** *p61*
Robinson, John 33; Ontario, 1871 ***1823.28*** *p87*
Robinson, John 40; Nova Scotia, 1774 ***1220.25*** *p135*
Robinson, John 41; Nova Scotia, 1774 ***1220.25*** *p135*
With wife & 6 children
Robinson, John 43; Ontario, 1871 ***1823.22*** *p135*
Robinson, John 44; Ontario, 1871 ***1823.15*** *p226*
Robinson, John 47; Halifax, Nova Scotia, 1775 ***1220.25*** *p22*
Child: Ann 15
Child: Jenny 9
Robinson, John 50; Ontario, 1871 ***1823.15*** *p226*
Robinson, John 58; Ontario, 1871 ***1823.28*** *p87*
Robinson, John 67; Ontario, 1871 ***1823.22*** *p135*
Robinson, John, II; Maryland, 1676 ***2524.55*** *p189*
Robinson, Jonas; Virginia, 1663 ***6212.30*** *p1*
Robinson, Jonathan 5 *SEE* Robinson, William
Robinson, Jone *SEE* Robinson, William
Robinson, Joseph; Charlottetown, Prince Edward Island, 1808 ***1224.3*** *p66*
Robinson, Joseph; New York, 1778 ***1224.2*** *p98*
Robinson, Joseph; Pennsylvania, 1777 ***4629.10*** *p26*
Robinson, Joseph; South Carolina, n.d. ***1224.3*** *p66*
Robinson, Joseph; South Carolina, 1784 ***1224.2*** *p98*
Robinson, Joseph 50; Ontario, 1871 ***1823.22*** *p135*
Robinson, Josephine 7; Ontario, 1861 ***2896.25*** *p3*
Robinson, Joshua 12; New York, 1774 ***1220.25*** *p25*
Robinson, Josiah; Pennsylvania, 1777 ***4629.10*** *p17*
Robinson, Lawrence; Virginia, 1671 ***6212.30*** *p43*
Robinson, Miss M.; Quebec, 1858 ***9196.15*** *p41*
Robinson, Margaret *SEE* Robinson, James
Robinson, Margaret; America, 1835 ***1224.3*** *p77*
Robinson, Margaret 28; Ontario, 1861 ***2896.25*** *p3*
Robinson, Margaret 73; Ontario, 1871 ***1823.15*** *p226*
Robinson, Martha 23; Philadelphia, 1774 ***1220.25*** *p63*
Robinson, Martin 27; Maryland, 1775 ***1220.25*** *p104*
Robinson, Mary *SEE* Robinson, William
Robinson, Mary; Maryland, 1681 ***2524.55*** *p189*
Robinson, Mary; Virginia, 1671-1672 ***6212.30*** *p46*
Robinson, Mary 20; Philadelphia, 1774 ***1220.25*** *p23*
Robinson, Mary 26; Maryland, 1775 ***1220.25*** *p112*
Robinson, Mary 35 *SEE* Robinson, William
Robinson, Mary Ann; Vermont, 1840-1919 ***5900.10*** *p85*
Robinson, Mary Flood; Vermont, 1812-1887 ***5900.10*** *p89*
Robinson, Mary O'Connell; Vermont, 1856-1922 ***5900.10*** *p89*
Robinson, Maximilian; Died enroute, 1695 ***1224.1*** *p49*
Robinson, Melinda McKenney; Vermont, 1820-1887 ***5900.10*** *p281*
Robinson, Morris; New York, 1840 ***8197.10*** *p188*
Robinson, Neill C.; West Indies, 1863 ***1640.13*** *p106*
Robinson, Patrick; Maryland, 1666 ***2524.55*** *p205*
Robinson, Peter; New York, 1821 ***8197.10*** *p273*
Robinson, Peter; New York, 1826 ***8197.10*** *p297*
Robinson, Peter; Pennsylvania, 1777 ***4629.10*** *p17*
Robinson, Richard; Maryland, 1675 ***2524.55*** *p189*
Robinson, Richard; New England, 1732 ***1224.2*** *p98*
Robinson, Robert; Maryland, 1673 ***2524.55*** *p189*
Robinson, Robert; Pennsylvania, 1777 ***4629.10*** *p31*
Robinson, Samuel; Boston, 1664 ***1224.1*** *p49*
Robinson, Samuel; Pennsylvania, 1777 ***4629.10*** *p31*
Robinson, Samuel 16; Philadelphia, 1774 ***1220.25*** *p35*
Robinson, Sarah; Illinois, 1851 ***1224.3*** *p66*
Robinson, Solomon; Pennsylvania, 1777 ***4629.10*** *p20*
Robinson, Susannah; Maryland, 1677-1681 ***2524.55*** *p189*
Robinson, Tho.; Maryland, 1681 ***2524.55*** *p189*
Robinson, Thomas; Delaware, n.d. ***1224.2*** *p98*
Robinson, Thomas; Maryland, 1653 ***2524.55*** *p189*
Robinson, Thomas; Maryland, 1668 ***2524.55*** *p189*
Robinson, Thomas; Maryland, 1675 ***2524.55*** *p189*
Robinson, Thomas; Maryland, 1681 ***2524.55*** *p189*
Robinson, Thomas; New York, 1804 ***8197.10*** *p28*
Robinson, Thomas; New York, 1824 ***8197.10*** *p273*
Robinson, Thomas; New York, 1834 ***8197.10*** *p274*
Robinson, Thomas; New York, 1840 ***8197.10*** *p188*
Robinson, Thomas; New York, 1840 ***8197.10*** *p276*
Robinson, Thomas; New York, 1840 ***8197.10*** *p277*
Robinson, Thomas; Nova Scotia, 1788 ***1224.2*** *p98*
Robinson, Thomas; Vermont, 1798-1893 ***5900.10*** *p89*
Robinson, Thomas; Virginia, 1666 ***6212.30*** *p27*
Robinson, Thomas 22; Maryland, 1774 ***1220.25*** *p70*
Robinson, Thomas 26; Ontario, 1871 ***1823.28*** *p87*
Robinson, Thomas 35; Ontario, 1871 ***1823.28*** *p87*
Robinson, Thomas 40; Ontario, 1871 ***1823.15*** *p226*
Robinson, Thomas 61; Ontario, 1871 ***1823.15*** *p226*
Robinson, Thomas 62; Ontario, 1871 ***1823.15*** *p226*
Robinson, Walter; Tobago, West Indies, 1774 ***1220.25*** *p132*
Robinson, William *SEE* Robinson, William
Robinson, William; Maryland, 1664 ***2524.55*** *p189*
Relative: Jone
Relative: Mary
Relative: William
Robinson, William; Maryland, 1666 ***2524.55*** *p189*
Relative: Joane
Relative: Mary
Relative: William
Robinson, William; Maryland, 1675 ***2524.55*** *p189*
Robinson, William; Maryland, 1697 ***1224.1*** *p49*
Robinson, William; New York, 1807 ***8197.10*** *p48*
Robinson, William; New York, 1825 ***8197.10*** *p274*
Robinson, William; Pennsylvania, 1777 ***4629.10*** *p11*
Robinson, William; Pennsylvania, 1777 ***4629.10*** *p31*
Robinson, William; South Carolina, 1730 ***1224.2*** *p98*
Robinson, William; Vermont, 1818-1864 ***5900.10*** *p281*
Robinson, William 2 *SEE* Robinson, William
Robinson, William 25; Virginia, 1774 ***1220.25*** *p94*
Robinson, William 32; Halifax, Nova Scotia, 1774 ***1220.25*** *p138*
Wife: Mary 35
Robinson, William 42; Halifax, Nova Scotia, 1775 ***1220.25*** *p22*
Wife: Elizabeth 30
Child: Jonathan 5
Child: Francis 3
Child: William 2
Child: Elizabeth 9
Robinson, William 42; Ontario, 1871 ***1823.15*** *p226*
Robinson, William 46; Ontario, 1871 ***1823.15*** *p226*
Robinson, William 51; Ontario, 1871 ***1823.15*** *p226*
Robinson, William 52; Ontario, 1871 ***1823.15*** *p226*
Robinson, Wm 24; Ontario, 1871 ***1823.28*** *p87*
Robinson, Wm J. 50; Ontario, 1861 ***2896.25*** *p3*
Robinstone, A.; Mobile, Alabama, 1825-1845 ***1640.10*** *p178*
Robison, Alexander 68; Ontario, 1871 ***1823.15*** *p226*
Robison, Andrew; Montreal, 1842 ***1640.13*** *p106*
Robison, Augusta L. 5; Ontario, 1861 ***2896.28*** *p40*
Robison, C. A. 30; Ontario, 1861 ***2896.25*** *p44*
Robison, Edward 9; Ontario, 1861 ***2896.28*** *p40*
Robison, Edward 53; Ontario, 1871 ***1823.22*** *p135*
Robison, Eliza 24; Ontario, 1861 ***2896.28*** *p40*
Robison, G. R. 6; Ontario, 1861 ***2896.25*** *p44*
Robison, George 19; Ontario, 1861 ***2896.28*** *p40*
Robison, H. J. 9; Ontario, 1861 ***2896.25*** *p44*
Robison, Harriet 7; Ontario, 1861 ***2896.28*** *p40*
Robison, Henry 21; Ontario, 1871 ***1823.28*** *p87*
Robison, Jane 13; Ontario, 1861 ***2896.28*** *p40*
Robison, Jane 49; Ontario, 1861 ***2896.28*** *p40*
Robison, Jno; Virginia, 1690-1691 ***6212.30*** *p59*
Robison, John; Maryland, 1678 ***2524.55*** *p189*
Robison, John 16; Ontario, 1871 ***1823.22*** *p135*
Robison, M. E. 4; Ontario, 1861 ***2896.25*** *p44*
Robison, Margaret V. 9; Ontario, 1861 ***2896.28*** *p40*
Robison, Mary 41; Ontario, 1861 ***2896.28*** *p40*
Robison, Matthew 17; Ontario, 1861 ***2896.28*** *p40*
Robison, N. J. 22; Ontario, 1861 ***2896.25*** *p52*
Robison, Nancy J. 12; Ontario, 1861 ***2896.28*** *p40*
Robison, R. A. 2; Ontario, 1861 ***2896.25*** *p44*
Robison, Rosalin 2; Ontario, 1861 ***2896.28*** *p40*
Robison, William 22; Ontario, 1861 ***2896.28*** *p40*
Robison, William 55; Ontario, 1871 ***1823.15*** *p226*
Robison, William 68; Ontario, 1871 ***1823.15*** *p226*
Robitson, E. A. 14; Ontario, 1861 ***2896.27*** *p6*
Robitson, F. J. 7; Ontario, 1861 ***2896.27*** *p6*
Robitson, George 11; Ontario, 1861 ***2896.27*** *p6*
Robitson, M. 33; Ontario, 1861 ***2896.27*** *p6*
Robler, Frederick; Pennsylvania, 1836 ***6058.10*** *p12*
Roblin, A. 1; Ontario, 1861 ***2896.25*** *p28*
Roblin, A. 9; Ontario, 1861 ***2896.27*** *p6*
Roblin, A. 23; Ontario, 1861 ***2896.25*** *p28*
Roblin, A. M. 2; Ontario, 1861 ***2896.27*** *p6*
Roblin, Donald 7; Ontario, 1861 ***2896.25*** *p69*
Roblin, Edward; Ontario, 1861 ***2896.25*** *p69*
Roblin, Eliza 15; Ontario, 1861 ***2896.25*** *p36*
Roblin, G. 5; Ontario, 1861 ***2896.25*** *p28*
Roblin, H. 27; Ontario, 1861 ***2896.25*** *p28*
Roblin, Henrietta 9; Ontario, 1861 ***2896.25*** *p32*
Roblin, Huldah 50; Ontario, 1861 ***2896.25*** *p69*
Roblin, J. 7; Ontario, 1861 ***2896.27*** *p6*
Roblin, John 28; Ontario, 1861 ***2896.25*** *p28*
Roblin, L. 29; Ontario, 1861 ***2896.27*** *p6*
Roblin, Mary 81; Ontario, 1861 ***2896.25*** *p32*
Roblin, Mary J. 14; Ontario, 1861 ***2896.28*** *p64*
Roblin, Nancy 51; Ontario, 1861 ***2896.25*** *p32*
Roblin, Prudence 21; Ontario, 1861 ***2896.25*** *p12*
Roblin, Rodger 16; Ontario, 1861 ***2896.25*** *p69*
Roblin, S. 54; Ontario, 1861 ***2896.25*** *p28*
Roblin, W. 4; Ontario, 1861 ***2896.27*** *p6*
Roblin, William 16; Ontario, 1861 ***2896.25*** *p28*
Robotham, George; Maryland, 1672 ***2524.55*** *p189*
Robotham, George; Maryland, 1698 ***1224.1*** *p49*
Robotham, John; Virginia, 1677 ***1224.1*** *p49*
Robson, Andrew 47; Ontario, 1871 ***1823.22*** *p135*
Robson, Ann Smith; Vermont, n.d. ***5900.10*** *p496*
Robson, Charles 29; Ontario, 1871 ***1823.28*** *p87*
Robson, Eleanor *SEE* Robson, Robert
Robson, Eleanor 6 *SEE* Robson, Robert
Robson, Frances Appleton; Vermont, 1838-1916 ***5900.10*** *p496*
Robson, George 27; Ontario, 1871 ***1823.22*** *p135*
Robson, George 55; Ontario, 1871 ***1823.22*** *p135*
Robson, Henery 45; Ontario, 1871 ***1823.15*** *p226*
Robson, Henry 64; Ontario, 1871 ***1823.22*** *p135*
Robson, Isaac; Virginia, 1710 ***1224.2*** *p98*
Robson, James *SEE* Robson, Robert
Robson, James 4 *SEE* Robson, Robert
Robson, Jane *SEE* Robson, Robert
Robson, Jane 28 *SEE* Robson, Robert
Robson, John 37; Ontario, 1871 ***1823.15*** *p226*
Robson, John T.; Vermont, 1834-1920 ***5900.10*** *p496*
Robson, Libbie S. Wright 22; Vermont, 1867 ***5900.10*** *p453*
Robson, Margaret L. Hogan 47; Vermont, 1892 ***5900.10*** *p497*
Robson, Mary *SEE* Robson, Robert
Robson, Mary 1 *SEE* Robson, Robert
Robson, Nicholas 35; Ontario, 1871 ***1823.15*** *p226*
Robson, Robert; Georgia, 1775 ***1640.10*** *p178*
Wife: Jane
Child: Eleanor

Child: Mary
Child: James
Robson, Robert 28; Georgia, 1775 ***1220.25*** *p125*
Wife: Jane 28
Child: Eleanor 6
Child: Mary 1
Child: James 4
Robson, Robert 28; Ontario, 1871 ***1823.22*** *p136*
Robson, Robert 61; Ontario, 1871 ***1823.22*** *p136*
Robson, W. R. 60; Vermont, 1890 ***5900.10*** *p497*
Robson, William; Vermont, 1794-1888 ***5900.10*** *p496*
Robson, William 34; Ontario, 1871 ***1823.22*** *p136*
Roby, Anthony; Carolina, 1688 ***1224.1*** *p49*
Roby, Mary; Maryland, 1682 ***2524.55*** *p189*
Robyns, Edward; Virginia, 1647 ***1224.1*** *p49*
Roch, Hannah; Vermont, 1842-1923 ***5900.10*** *p314*
Roch, Mary; Vermont, 1850-1911 ***5900.10*** *p310*
Roch, Peter; America, 1753 ***2856.30*** *p364*
With wife son & family
Roch, Peter; America, 1753 ***2856.30*** *p369*
Roche, Mr.; Quebec, 1858 ***9196.15*** *p31*
Roche, Mrs.; Quebec, 1858 ***9196.15*** *p31*
Roche, Ann; Vermont, 1878-1927 ***5900.10*** *p193*
Roche, Anna M.; Vermont, 1859-1924 ***5900.10*** *p69*
Roche, Ellen; Vermont, 1850-1940 ***5900.10*** *p68*
Roche, Ellen 48; Vermont, 1894 ***5900.10*** *p270*
Roche, Ellen 60; Vermont, 1885 ***5900.10*** *p290*
Roche, George; Philadelphia, 1794 ***4629.10*** *p82*
Roche, James; Pennsylvania, 1777 ***4629.10*** *p22*
Roche, James; Virginia, 1652 ***1224.1*** *p49*
Roche, Johanna; Vermont, 1835-1897 ***5900.10*** *p68*
Roche, John; New York, 1838 ***8197.10*** *p276*
Roche, John 76; Vermont, 1889 ***5900.10*** *p247*
Roche, John F.; Vermont, 1848-1913 ***5900.10*** *p69*
Roche, Julia E.; Vermont, 1853-1909 ***5900.10*** *p163*
Roche, Patrick; South Carolina, 1726 ***1224.2*** *p98*
Roche, Patrick; Vermont, 1837-1909 ***5900.10*** *p270*
Roche, Stephen; New York, 1826 ***8197.10*** *p274*
Rochford, Bridget Farrell; Vermont, 1855-1893 ***5900.10*** *p311*
Rochford, Bridget Kane; Vermont, 1835-1901 ***5900.10*** *p311*
Rochford, Catherine Crowley 40; Vermont, 1898 ***5900.10*** *p108*
Rochford, James; Vermont, n.d. ***5900.10*** *p122*
Rochford, John; Vermont, 1820-1896 ***5900.10*** *p311*
Rochford, Mary; Vermont, 1891-1892 ***5900.10*** *p311*
Rochford, Mary O'Connor; Vermont, n.d. ***5900.10*** *p122*
Rochford, Patrick J.; Vermont, 1862-1897 ***5900.10*** *p311*
Rochin, Mary 60; Ontario, 1871 ***1823.22*** *p136*
Rochinger, Friedrich; Port uncertain, 1765 ***2856.30*** *p373*
Rochowiak, Michael; Maryland, 1910 ***3259.35*** *p52*
Rochowicz, Joseph; Maryland, 1910 ***3259.35*** *p52*
Rock, Caspar; Port uncertain, 1764 ***2856.30*** *p364*
Rock, George 57; Ontario, 1871 ***1823.15*** *p226*
Rock, James; New York, 1837 ***8197.10*** *p101*
Rock, James; Vermont, 1825-1904 ***5900.10*** *p539*
Rock, James; Vermont, 1840-1931 ***5900.10*** *p285*
Rock, Margaret Valley; Vermont, 1845-1923 ***5900.10*** *p285*
Rock, Mary Addel Stebbins; Vermont, 1829-1904 ***5900.10*** *p539*
Rock, Michael; New York, 1837 ***8197.10*** *p101*
Rock, Thomas; Maryland, 1680 ***2524.55*** *p189*
Rock, Thomas; Virginia, 1664 ***6212.30*** *p12*
Rock, William 16; Maryland, 1774 ***1220.25*** *p46*
Rock, William 77; Ontario, 1871 ***1823.15*** *p226*
Rocke, Thomas; Maryland, 1665 ***2524.55*** *p189*
Rockel, Jost; Port uncertain, 1785 ***2856.30*** *p352*
Rockenbach, Magdalena; Port uncertain, 1794 ***2856.30*** *p364*
Rockenbach, Maria Christina; Port uncertain, 1792 ***2856.30*** *p364*
Rockenbach, Susanna; Port uncertain, 1793 ***2856.30*** *p364*
Rockenberger, Johann Georg; Port uncertain, 1790 ***2856.30*** *p364*
Rockenberger, Johann Georg; Port uncertain, 1791 ***2856.30*** *p364*
Rockenbrodt, Anton; Port uncertain, 1767 ***2856.30*** *p364*
Rockes, Charles; Maryland, 1665 ***2524.55*** *p189*
Rockett, John; New York, 1826 ***8197.10*** *p337*
Rockhold, Robert; Maryland, 1649-1650 ***2524.55*** *p189*
Rockhould, John; Maryland, 1649 ***2524.55*** *p189*
Rockhould, Robert *SEE* Rockhould, Robert
Rockhould, Robert; Maryland, 1659 ***2524.55*** *p189*
Wife: Sarah
Son: Thomas
Son: Robert
Rockhould, Sarah *SEE* Rockhould, Robert
Rockhould, Sarah, Jr.; Maryland, 1659 ***2524.55*** *p190*
Rockhould, Thomas *SEE* Rockhould, Robert
Rocklitz, Christian; Maryland, 1910 ***3259.35*** *p52*
Rockwell, John; New England, 1638 ***1224.1*** *p49*
Rockwell, Prudence; Maryland, 1681 ***2524.55*** *p190*
Rockwell, Richard; New England, 1638 ***1224.1*** *p49*
Rockwell, William; New England, 1638 ***1224.1*** *p49*
Rockwood, Margaret E. Elliott; Vermont, 1865-1931 ***5900.10*** *p386*
Rockwood, William A.; Vermont, 1853-1935 ***5900.10*** *p386*
Rocufskie, Nellie; Maryland, 1910 ***3259.35*** *p52*
Roda, Eval 7; Ontario, 1871 ***1823.28*** *p87*
Roda, Mina 8; Ontario, 1871 ***1823.28*** *p87*
Roda, Zachariah; New York, 1840 ***8197.10*** *p277*
Rodaway, Aaron Miller; Philadelphia, 1852 ***1224.3*** *p66*
Rodd, Jno; Virginia, 1665-1666 ***6212.30*** *p23*
Rodd, John 74; Ontario, 1871 ***1823.15*** *p226*
Rodd, Thomas; Virginia, 1665-1666 ***6212.30*** *p23*
Rodd, William 20; Philadelphia, 1774 ***1220.25*** *p43*
Rodd, William 50; Ontario, 1871 ***1823.15*** *p226*
Roddam, Lucy; New York, 1751 ***1224.2*** *p98*
Roddan, Edward 60; Ontario, 1871 ***1823.28*** *p87*
Rodden, Mr.; Quebec, 1856 ***9196.15*** *p11*
Rodden, Charles 50; Ontario, 1871 ***1823.28*** *p87*
Roddick, Catherine 55; Ontario, 1871 ***1823.15*** *p226*
Roddick, George 73; Ontario, 1871 ***1823.22*** *p136*
Roddick, James 26; Maryland, 1773-1774 ***1220.25*** *p33*
Roddick, John 48; Ontario, 1871 ***1823.15*** *p226*
Roddick, William 54; Ontario, 1871 ***1823.22*** *p136*
Roddin, Robt 37; Ontario, 1871 ***1823.28*** *p87*
Roddy, Anne O'Rielly; Vermont, 1846-1892 ***5900.10*** *p580*
Roddy, Bernard T.; Vermont, 1854-1919 ***5900.10*** *p241*
Roddy, Catharine 77; Vermont, 1888 ***5900.10*** *p235*
Roddy, James; Vermont, 1840-1892 ***5900.10*** *p400*
Roddy, James; Vermont, 1844-1927 ***5900.10*** *p284*
Roddy, John 66; Ontario, 1871 ***1823.22*** *p136*
Roddy, Lucy R. Fanton; Vermont, 1857-1949 ***5900.10*** *p241*
Roddy, Margaret Norton 56; Vermont, 1890 ***5900.10*** *p569*
Roddy, Maria; Vermont, 1846-1918 ***5900.10*** *p284*
Roddy, Mary 27; Vermont, 1886 ***5900.10*** *p569*
Roddy, Mary Curry; Vermont, 1844-1913 ***5900.10*** *p400*
Roddy, Mary E.; Vermont, 1850-1932 ***5900.10*** *p224*
Roddy, Michael 24; Vermont, 1869 ***5900.10*** *p235*
Roddy, Michael 46; Vermont, 1882 ***5900.10*** *p569*
Roddy, Michael 80; Vermont, 1884 ***5900.10*** *p235*
Roddy, Owen 3; Vermont, 1853 ***5900.10*** *p235*
Roddy, Patrick; Vermont, 1842-1894 ***5900.10*** *p580*
Roddy, Terrence 24; Vermont, 1862 ***5900.10*** *p235*
Roddy, Thomas 35; Ontario, 1871 ***1823.22*** *p136*
Rode, William; New York, 1828 ***8197.10*** *p298*
Rodel, Christian; Port uncertain, 1791 ***2856.30*** *p373*
Rodel, Christian; Port uncertain, 1792 ***2856.30*** *p373*
Rodel, Elisabeth; Port uncertain, 1756 ***2856.30*** *p373*
Rodel, Michael; Port uncertain, 1751 ***2856.30*** *p364*
Rodel, Philipp; Port uncertain, 1722 ***2856.30*** *p373*
Rodelin, Elisabeth; Port uncertain, 1756 ***2856.30*** *p373*
Roden, Charles; New York, 1811 ***8197.10*** *p57*
Rodenbach, Maria Eva; Port uncertain, 1759 ***2856.30*** *p364*
Rodenhauser, Andreas, The Younger; America, 1748 ***2856.30*** *p364*
Rodenstetter, Margarete; Port uncertain, 1735 ***2856.30*** *p364*
Roder, Mrs. Adam; America, 1737 ***2856.30*** *p373*
Roder, Mrs. Adam; Port uncertain, 1726 ***2856.30*** *p373*
Roderer, Valentin; America, 1752 ***2856.30*** *p373*
Rodes, John; Maryland, 1662 ***2524.55*** *p190*
Rodes, Mathew; Philadelphia, 1793 ***4629.10*** *p74*
Rodger, Mathew 63; Ontario, 1871 ***1823.15*** *p226*
Rodger, William; New York, 1803 ***8197.10*** *p16*
Rodgers, Mr.; Quebec, 1857 ***9196.15*** *p17*
Rodgers, James; South Carolina, 1764 ***1224.2*** *p98*
Rodgers, James 40; Ontario, 1871 ***1823.22*** *p136*
Rodgers, Joseph; New York, 1818 ***8197.10*** *p272*
Rodgers, Margret 67; Ontario, 1871 ***1823.15*** *p226*
Rodgers, Paterick 62; Ontario, 1871 ***1823.15*** *p226*
Rodgers, Robert H.; Ontario, 1871 ***1823.28*** *p87*
Rodgers, Solomon 45; Ontario, 1871 ***1823.15*** *p226*
Rodian, Roger; Virginia, 1667-1668 ***6212.30*** *p39*
Rodick, Archibald 28; Ontario, 1871 ***1823.15*** *p226*
Rodie, William; New York, 1840 ***8197.10*** *p189*
Rodler, Mrs.; Port uncertain, 1790 ***2856.30*** *p374*
Rodlin, Anna Margarete; Port uncertain, 1759 ***2856.30*** *p374*
Rodling, Christiana; Virginia, 1676 ***1224.1*** *p49*
Rodman, Thomas; New York, 1806 ***8197.10*** *p32*
Rodman, Thomas Rotch; Havana, 1810 ***1224.3*** *p66*
Rodman, Thomas Rotch; New Bedford, Massachusetts, n.d. ***1224.3*** *p66*
Rodney, Glema A.; Vermont, n.d. ***5900.10*** *p337*
Rodney, Louis 58; Vermont, 1888 ***5900.10*** *p337*
Rodney, Mathew; New York, 1836 ***8197.10*** *p75*
Rodolph, Cotty 34; Ontario, 1871 ***1823.28*** *p87*
Rodra, Hans Georg; Port uncertain, 1736 ***2856.30*** *p364*
Rodrian, Margarete; Port uncertain, 1796 ***2856.30*** *p364*
Rodrie, Thomas; Georgia, 1699 ***1640.13*** *p106*
Rodrigues, Bernardo Jose; New York, 1840 ***8197.10*** *p276*
Rodriguez, Vincente; New York, 1816 ***8197.10*** *p59*
Rodt, Clara; America, 1764 ***2856.30*** *p364*
Rodth, Anna Margarete; Port uncertain, 1764 ***2856.30*** *p364*
Rodth, Anna Margarete; Port uncertain, 1767 ***2856.30*** *p364*
Rodth, Helena; Port uncertain, 1764 ***2856.30*** *p364*
Rodth, Helena; Port uncertain, 1767 ***2856.30*** *p364*
Rodtler, Elis. Margarete; Port uncertain, 1773 ***2856.30*** *p374*
Rody, William; Ontario, 1861 ***2896.27*** *p72*
Roe, Ann 35; Maryland, 1775 ***1220.25*** *p101*
Roe, Anne; Virginia, 1667 ***1224.1*** *p13*
Roe, Benjaman 45; Ontario, 1871 ***1823.15*** *p226*
Roe, Charles S.; New York, 1839 ***8197.10*** *p134*
Roe, Dennis Mack; Virginia, 1668-1669 ***6212.30*** *p41*
Roe, Edward; Maryland, 1666 ***2524.55*** *p190*
Relative: Mary
Relative: Elizabeth
Roe, Edward; New York, 1838 ***8197.10*** *p276*
Roe, Elizabeth *SEE* Roe, Edward
Roe, George; Virginia, 1667-1668 ***6212.30*** *p39*
Roe, George 8; Ontario, 1861 ***2896.25*** *p12*
Roe, George 38; Ontario, 1871 ***1823.28*** *p87*
Roe, J. P.; Quebec, 1857 ***9196.15*** *p20*
Roe, Mrs. J. P.; Quebec, 1857 ***9196.15*** *p20*
Roe, James; Virginia, 1666 ***6212.30*** *p26*
Roe, James 30; Ontario, 1871 ***1823.15*** *p226*
Roe, James 45; Ontario, 1871 ***1823.22*** *p136*
Roe, Jisse 38; Ontario, 1871 ***1823.15*** *p226*
Roe, John; Maryland, 1682 ***2524.55*** *p190*
Roe, John; Ohio, 1849 ***1224.3*** *p66*
Roe, John 31; Ontario, 1871 ***1823.15*** *p226*
Roe, John 59; Ontario, 1871 ***1823.28*** *p87*
Roe, John 67; Ontario, 1871 ***1823.15*** *p226*
Roe, Joseph 15; Philadelphia, 1774 ***1220.25*** *p35*
Roe, Laurance; Virginia, 1666 ***6212.30*** *p26*
Roe, Lewis; Virginia, 1667 ***6212.30*** *p37*
Roe, Luke; Virginia, 1665-1666 ***6212.30*** *p25*
Roe, Mark; Maryland, 1657 ***2524.55*** *p190*
Roe, Mary *SEE* Roe, Edward
Roe, Nathan 7; Ontario, 1861 ***2896.25*** *p12*
Roe, Orlando 11; Ontario, 1861 ***2896.25*** *p12*
Roe, Richard 39; Ontario, 1871 ***1823.15*** *p226*
Roe, Robert; Virginia, 1671-1672 ***6212.30*** *p47*
Roe, Roger 23; Philadelphia, 1775 ***1220.25*** *p8*
Roe, Samuel 26; Ontario, 1871 ***1823.15*** *p227*
Roe, Sarah; Ohio, 1847 ***1224.3*** *p67*
Roe, Thomas; New York, 1827-1834 ***8197.10*** *p310*
Roe, Thomas; New York, 1840 ***8197.10*** *p277*
Roe, William 30; Ontario, 1871 ***1823.15*** *p227*
Roebanski, Henry; Maryland, 1910 ***3259.35*** *p52*
Roebelin, John; New York, 1807 ***8197.10*** *p48*
Roedding, Eckhardh 60; Ontario, 1871 ***1823.15*** *p227*
Roedding, Justus 35; Ontario, 1871 ***1823.15*** *p227*
Roedel, Christian; Port uncertain, 1791 ***2856.30*** *p364*
Roedel, Christian; Port uncertain, 1792 ***2856.30*** *p364*
Roeder, Catharina 51; Ontario, 1871 ***1823.15*** *p227*
Roeder, Henry 18; Ontario, 1871 ***1823.15*** *p227*
Roeder, Jacob 36; Ontario, 1871 ***1823.15*** *p227*
Roeder, Philip 29; Ontario, 1871 ***1823.15*** *p227*
Roedeull, Anna Barbara; America, 1751 ***2856.30*** *p370*
Roeff, Augustus; New York, 1835 ***8197.10*** *p188*
Roemer, Adam; Baltimore, 1850 ***6058.10*** *p41*
Roemer, David; New York, 1807 ***8197.10*** *p49*
Roemer, George; New York, New York, 1853 ***6058.10*** *p38*
Roemer, Hermann; New York, New York, 1852 ***6058.10*** *p36*
Roes, John Joseph; New York, 1821 ***8197.10*** *p273*
Roessger, Ernst; New York, New York, 1888 ***3437.14*** *p147*
Roessyer, Ernest; New York, New York, 1888 ***3437.14*** *p147*
Roesthski, Frank; Maryland, 1910 ***3259.35*** *p52*
Roetter, Adam; Port uncertain, 1764 ***2856.30*** *p364*
Roetz, A. M.; America, 1764 ***2856.30*** *p242*
Roetz, Anna Maria; America, 1764 ***2856.30*** *p364*
With husband
Roevoy, Henry 15; Ontario, 1861 ***2896.25*** *p58*
Roewerke, Cornelius; Maryland, 1675 ***2524.55*** *p190*
Rofs, Samuel 62; Ontario, 1871 ***1823.28*** *p87*
Rogan, Catherine; Vermont, 1811-1904 ***5900.10*** *p146*
Rogan, Cornelius; Maryland, 1663 ***2524.55*** *p190*
Rogan, John; New York, 1827 ***8197.10*** *p275*
Roger, Charles 42; Ontario, 1871 ***1823.15*** *p227*
Roger, David 51; Ontario, 1871 ***1823.15*** *p227*

Roger, J. D.; Quebec, 1856 ***9196.15*** *p8*
Roger, Nikolaus; Port uncertain, 1718 ***2856.30*** *p364*
Roger, Nikolaus; Port uncertain, 1725 ***2856.30*** *p364*
Roger, Ralph 39; Ontario, 1871 ***1823.15*** *p227*
Roger, Robert 44; Ontario, 1871 ***1823.15*** *p227*
Rogers, . . .; New England, 1669 ***1224.1*** *p16*
Rogers, Mr.; Quebec, 1858 ***9196.15*** *p46*
Rogers, Mrs.; Quebec, 1858 ***9196.15*** *p46*
Rogers, Agnes 16; Ontario, 1861 ***2896.27*** *p29*
Rogers, Ann; Charleston, South Carolina, 1805 ***1224.3*** *p67*
Rogers, Ann Sloan 89; Vermont, 1891 ***5900.10*** *p474*
Rogers, Anthony; New York, 1704 ***1224.2*** *p98*
Rogers, Barbara 18; Ontario, 1861 ***2896.27*** *p56*
Rogers, Benjamin H.; New York, 1839 ***8197.10*** *p134*
Rogers, Catharine Mulheron; Vermont, n.d. ***5900.10*** *p238*
Rogers, Catherine; Vermont, 1834-1906 ***5900.10*** *p488*
Rogers, Daniel; Maryland, 1671 ***2524.55*** *p190*
Rogers, Daniel; New York, 1840 ***8197.10*** *p277*
Rogers, Edward; New York, 1794 ***8197.10*** *p4*
Rogers, Elizabeth; Maryland, 1673 ***2524.55*** *p190*
Son: Thomas
Son: Francis
Son: John
Rogers, Fanny; New York, 1841 ***1224.3*** *p67*
Rogers, Francis *SEE* Rogers, Elizabeth
Rogers, Francis; Maryland, 1634 ***2524.55*** *p190*
Rogers, Fred W. 54; Ontario, 1871 ***1823.22*** *p136*
Rogers, Henry; Maryland, 1679 ***2524.55*** *p190*
Wife: Jane
Daughter: Juce
Rogers, Hester; Maryland, 1682 ***2524.55*** *p190*
Rogers, Hugh 61; Ontario, 1871 ***1823.15*** *p227*
Rogers, James; New York, 1840 ***8197.10*** *p277*
Rogers, James; Vermont, 1832-1910 ***5900.10*** *p280*
Rogers, James 29; Vermont, 1866 ***5900.10*** *p238*
Rogers, James 30; Ontario, 1861 ***2896.28*** *p21*
Rogers, James 46; Ontario, 1871 ***1823.15*** *p227*
Rogers, Jane *SEE* Rogers, Henry
Rogers, Jane; Vermont, 1844-1905 ***5900.10*** *p488*
Rogers, Jane 44; Ontario, 1871 ***1823.22*** *p136*
Rogers, John *SEE* Rogers, Elizabeth
Rogers, John; New England, 1670 ***1224.1*** *p16*
Rogers, John; New York, 1778 ***1224.2*** *p98*
Rogers, John; New York, 1807 ***8197.10*** *p327*
Rogers, John 25; Ontario, 1871 ***1823.28*** *p87*
Rogers, John Morris; New York, New York, 1846 ***1224.3*** *p67*
Rogers, John O.; Vermont, 1825-1905 ***5900.10*** *p307*
Rogers, John P.; Vermont, 1840-1905 ***5900.10*** *p488*
Rogers, John S. 58; Vermont, 1904 ***5900.10*** *p474*
Rogers, Joseph; New York, 1823 ***8197.10*** *p62*
Rogers, Joseph; New York, 1823 ***8197.10*** *p274*
Rogers, Joseph; New York, 1840 ***8197.10*** *p190*
Rogers, Joseph 45; Ontario, 1871 ***1823.15*** *p227*
Rogers, Joshua 17; Maryland, 1774 ***1220.25*** *p60*
Rogers, Juce *SEE* Rogers, Henry
Rogers, Margaret; New England, 1678 ***1224.1*** *p49*
Rogers, Margaret; Vermont, 1826-1888 ***5900.10*** *p470*
Rogers, Margaret; Vermont, 1847-1921 ***5900.10*** *p217*
Rogers, Margaret Crane; New England, 1655 ***1224.1*** *p16*
Rogers, Mary; Maryland, 1673 ***2524.55*** *p190*
Rogers, Mary; New York, 1844 ***1224.3*** *p74*
Rogers, Mary; Virginia, 1671 ***6212.30*** *p44*
Rogers, Mary Callahan; Vermont, 1839-1884 ***5900.10*** *p280*
Rogers, Maurice; Pennsylvania, 1777 ***4629.10*** *p14*
Rogers, Moses 28; Dominica, 1774 ***1220.25*** *p127*
Rogers, Mrs. Nathaniel; New England, 1659 ***1224.1*** *p16*
Rogers, Nicholas; Maryland, 1681 ***2524.55*** *p190*
Rogers, Patrick; New York, 1838 ***8197.10*** *p147*
Rogers, Patrick 60; Vermont, 1901 ***5900.10*** *p217*
Rogers, Patrick 69; Vermont, 1875 ***5900.10*** *p238*
Rogers, Reuth; Virginia, 1677 ***6212.30*** *p53*
Rogers, Rich.; Maryland, 1681 ***2524.55*** *p190*
Rogers, Robert; Maryland, 1682 ***2524.55*** *p190*
Rogers, Robert 55; Ontario, 1871 ***1823.22*** *p136*
Rogers, Rosana A.; Vermont, 1842-1906 ***5900.10*** *p488*
Rogers, Rose S. 68; Vermont, 1919 ***5900.10*** *p474*
Rogers, Samuel; Boston, 1805 ***1224.3*** *p67*
Rogers, Samuel; Boston, 1833 ***1224.3*** *p67*
Rogers, Sarah 68; Ontario, 1871 ***1823.22*** *p136*
Rogers, Terence 52; Vermont, 1852 ***5900.10*** *p474*
Rogers, Theophilus; Maryland, 1650 ***2524.55*** *p190*
Rogers, Tho; Virginia, 1664 ***6212.30*** *p7*
Rogers, Thomas *SEE* Rogers, Elizabeth
Rogers, Thomas; Georgia, n.d. ***1224.2*** *p98*
Rogers, Thomas; New York, 1832 ***8197.10*** *p275*
Rogers, Thomas 52; Ontario, 1871 ***1823.15*** *p227*
Rogers, W. P.; Portland, Maine, 1858 ***9196.15*** *p31*
Rogers, William; New York, 1836 ***8197.10*** *p75*
Rogers, William; New York, New York, 1829 ***1224.3*** *p67*
Rogers, William; Pennsylvania, 1777 ***4629.10*** *p20*
Rogers, William 21; Maryland, 1775 ***1220.25*** *p113*
Rogerson, Isaac 28; Ontario, 1871 ***1823.15*** *p227*
Rogerson, J. N.; Quebec, 1858 ***9196.15*** *p35*
Rogerson, John; Quebec, 1861 ***1640.13*** *p106*
Rogerson, Joseph 41; Ontario, 1871 ***1823.28*** *p87*
Rogerson, Robert 26; Ontario, 1871 ***1823.15*** *p227*
Rogerson, Robert L. A. 52; Ontario, 1871 ***1823.15*** *p227*
Rogerson, Soloman 42; Ontario, 1871 ***1823.15*** *p227*
Rogowsky, Dominek; Maryland, 1910 ***3259.35*** *p52*
Rogza, Walenti; Maryland, 1910 ***3259.35*** *p52*
Rohan, John 24; Ontario, 1871 ***1823.22*** *p136*
Rohan, Margaret; Vermont, 1796-1878 ***5900.10*** *p504*
Rohan, Martin C.; Vermont, 1836-1900 ***5900.10*** *p401*
Rohan, Mary 29; Ontario, 1871 ***1823.22*** *p136*
Rohan, Patrick 43; Ontario, 1871 ***1823.22*** *p136*
Rohan, Sarah K.; Vermont, 1847-1899 ***5900.10*** *p401*
Rohbausch, Bernhard; America, 1750 ***2856.30*** *p364*
Rohbausch, Bernhard; Port uncertain, 1750 ***2856.30*** *p365*
With wife & 2 children
Rohbausch, Christof; America, 1752 ***2856.30*** *p364*
Rohbausch, Mrs. Christof; Port uncertain, 1752 ***2856.30*** *p364*
Rohbausch, Eva Barbara; Port uncertain, 1751 ***2856.30*** *p364*
Rohde, George; New York, 1803 ***8197.10*** *p16*
Roheleder, Philipp Jakob; Canada, 1753 ***2856.30*** *p365*
Rohl, George 57; Kansas, 1910 ***9079.10*** *p1*
Rohl, Jakob; Port uncertain, 1771 ***2856.30*** *p365*
Rohleder, Airprocessa 3; Kansas, 1909-1910 ***9079.10*** *p37*
Rohleder, Antone 9; Kansas, 1909-1910 ***9079.10*** *p37*
Rohleder, Mary 48; Kansas, 1909-1910 ***9079.10*** *p37*
Rohleder, Nicholas 11; Kansas, 1909-1910 ***9079.10*** *p37*
Rohleder, Nicholas 46; Kansas, 1909-1910 ***9079.10*** *p36*
Rohloff, Michael; Ontario, 1871 ***1823.28*** *p87*
Rohm, Franziska; Port uncertain, 1770 ***2856.30*** *p353*
Rohm, Johann; America, 1752 ***2856.30*** *p374*
With wife & children
Rohmer, Henrich; America, 1738 ***2856.30*** *p365*
Rohmer, Henrich; Port uncertain, 1754 ***2856.30*** *p365*
Rohr, Augustus William; New York, 1836 ***8197.10*** *p275*
Rohr, Augustus William; New York, 1837 ***8197.10*** *p102*
Rohr, Augustus Wm.; New York, 1839 ***8197.10*** *p134*
Rohr, John G.; New York, 1826 ***8197.10*** *p334*
Rohr, Rudolf; America, 1752 ***2856.30*** *p365*
Rohrer, Johann; America, 1738 ***2856.30*** *p374*
With wife & children
Rohrer, Johann; America, 1738 ***2856.30*** *p374*
Rohrer, Johann; America, 1749 ***2856.30*** *p365*
Rohrer, Johann Gottfrie; America, 1738 ***2856.30*** *p374*
Rohrich, Johann Jakob; Port uncertain, 1739 ***2856.30*** *p365*
Rohrig, Ludwig; Port uncertain, 1783 ***2856.30*** *p374*
With wife & son
Rohrmann, Johann; America, 1700-1799 ***2856.30*** *p365*
Rohrmann, Johann; England, 1767 ***2856.30*** *p365*
Rohski, Joseph; Maryland, 1910 ***3259.35*** *p52*
Roily, Richard 28; Philadelphia, 1774 ***1220.25*** *p80*
Roke, Joseph 3; Ontario, 1861 ***2896.27*** *p17*
Roke, Josephine 36; Ontario, 1861 ***2896.27*** *p17*
Roke, Lasham 8; Ontario, 1861 ***2896.27*** *p17*
Roke, Leo 14; Ontario, 1861 ***2896.27*** *p17*
Roke, Mary 7; Ontario, 1861 ***2896.27*** *p17*
Roke, Ogile 13; Ontario, 1861 ***2896.27*** *p17*
Roke, Sarah 15; Ontario, 1861 ***2896.27*** *p17*
Rokold, Frank; Maryland, 1910 ***3259.35*** *p52*
Rolak, Edward; Maryland, 1910 ***3259.35*** *p52*
Roland, Johan Adam; New York, 1803 ***8197.10*** *p16*
Role, John; Virginia, 1703 ***6212.30*** *p62*
Roles, Thomas; Virginia, 1665 ***6212.30*** *p18*
Rolfe, Elizabeth Poole; New York, New York, 1839 ***1224.3*** *p67*
Rolfe, John P.; New York, 1834 ***8197.10*** *p372*
Rolfe, Mary 20; Jamaica, 1775 ***1220.25*** *p113*
Rolffe, John; Virginia, 1630 ***1224.1*** *p49*
Roll, Friedrich; Port uncertain, 1745 ***2856.30*** *p365*
With wife
Roll, Gottlieb; Pennsylvania, 1777 ***4629.10*** *p10*
Roll, Johann; Port uncertain, 1770 ***2856.30*** *p365*
Roll, John; Virginia, 1665 ***6212.30*** *p17*
Roll, John; Virginia, 1666 ***6212.30*** *p29*
Roll, John 22; Maryland, 1774 ***1220.25*** *p65*
Rolland, Michael 60; Ontario, 1871 ***1823.15*** *p227*
Rolland, William 26; Ontario, 1871 ***1823.15*** *p227*
Rollans, Edward 70; Ontario, 1871 ***1823.28*** *p87*
Rolle, Georg; Port uncertain, 1764 ***2856.30*** *p365*
Roller, Johann; Port uncertain, 1751 ***2856.30*** *p365*
Roller, Johann; Port uncertain, 1781 ***2856.30*** *p365*
Roller, Leonard; Port uncertain, 1767 ***2856.30*** *p365*
Rolles, Mrs. Christian; Port uncertain, 1769 ***2856.30*** *p365*
Rolles, Mrs. Christian; Port uncertain, 1770 ***2856.30*** *p365*
Rolles, Francis; Maryland, 1724 ***1224.2*** *p98*
Rolling, Mary 67; Ontario, 1871 ***1823.22*** *p136*
Rolling, Michael; Port uncertain, 1751 ***2856.30*** *p365*
Rollings, Mr.; Quebec, 1857 ***9196.15*** *p19*
Rollington, Jacob; Virginia, 1667-1668 ***6212.30*** *p38*
Rollington, Tho; Virginia, 1667 ***6212.30*** *p36*
Rollins, Daniel; Vermont, 1856-1936 ***5900.10*** *p386*
Rollins, Edward 40; Ontario, 1871 ***1823.15*** *p227*
Rollins, Ellen P.; Vermont, 1866-1924 ***5900.10*** *p387*
Rollins, Isaac 50; Ontario, 1871 ***1823.15*** *p227*
Rollo, Mr.; Portland, Maine, 1858 ***9196.15*** *p30*
Rollo, Granville 53; Ontario, 1871 ***1823.22*** *p136*
Rollo, Henry C.; Vermont, 1848-1913 ***5900.10*** *p492*
Rollo, Jane Miles; Vermont, 1844-1916 ***5900.10*** *p492*
Rollo, John; Portland, Maine, 1858 ***9196.15*** *p29*
Rollof, Joseph 38; Ontario, 1871 ***1823.28*** *p87*
Rolls, Mr.; Portland, Maine, 1858 ***9196.15*** *p30*
Rolls, Mrs.; Portland, Maine, 1858 ***9196.15*** *p30*
Rolls, Mrs.; Quebec, 1858 ***9196.15*** *p46*
Rolls, William; Portland, Maine, 1858 ***9196.15*** *p29*
Rollwagen, Philippe; New York, 1837 ***8197.10*** *p102*
Rolly, Patrick 30; Ontario, 1871 ***1823.15*** *p227*
Rolly, Rowland; Virginia, 1665 ***6212.30*** *p17*
Rolph, Jemima Hopwood; New York, 1844 ***1224.3*** *p67*
Rolph, John 15; Philadelphia, 1774 ***1220.25*** *p81*
Rolph, Thomas 21; Philadelphia, 1774 ***1220.25*** *p81*
Rolph, William 22; Maryland, 1774 ***1220.25*** *p41*
Rolshausen, Karl; Port uncertain, 1740 ***2856.30*** *p365*
With wife
Rolsloff, Michael 46; Ontario, 1871 ***1823.28*** *p87*
Rolston, George; Pennsylvania, 1777 ***4629.10*** *p20*
Rolston, James; Philadelphia, 1837 ***6058.10*** *p48*
Rolston, Richard 63; Ontario, 1871 ***1823.22*** *p136*
Rolston, William; Pennsylvania, 1777 ***4629.10*** *p17*
Rolston, William James 2; Ontario, 1871 ***1823.22*** *p136*
Roluski, Stefana; Maryland, 1910 ***3259.35*** *p52*
Romaine, Mrs.; Quebec, 1856 ***9196.15*** *p9*
Romaine, R.; Quebec, 1856 ***9196.15*** *p9*
Roman, James 63; Ontario, 1871 ***1823.28*** *p87*
Roman, Walenty; Maryland, 1910 ***3259.35*** *p52*
Romanis, Robert; New York, 1818 ***8197.10*** *p272*
Romano, John; Maryland, 1910 ***3259.35*** *p52*
Rome, Andrew; St. Vincent, 1822 ***1640.13*** *p106*
Rome, Elizabeth 52; Ontario, 1871 ***1823.22*** *p137*
Rome, James 41; Ontario, 1871 ***1823.15*** *p227*
Romel, Maria Elisabeth; Port uncertain, 1733 ***2856.30*** *p365*
Romentz, Johann Friedric; Port uncertain, 1769 ***2856.30*** *p365*
Romer, A. E. Wagner *SEE* Romer, Konrad
Romer, Anna Maria; Port uncertain, 1746 ***2856.30*** *p374*
With 2 children
Romer, Anton; Port uncertain, 1752 ***2856.30*** *p374*
Romer, Anton; Port uncertain, 1785 ***2856.30*** *p374*
Romer, Anton; Port uncertain, 1786 ***2856.30*** *p374*
Romer, Caspar; Port uncertain, 1750 ***2856.30*** *p365*
Romer, Christian Franz; Port uncertain, 1752 ***2856.30*** *p374*
Romer, Georg; Port uncertain, 1763 ***2856.30*** *p374*
Romer, Georg; Port uncertain, 1785 ***2856.30*** *p374*
Romer, Georg; Port uncertain, 1786 ***2856.30*** *p374*
Romer, Johann Jakob; Port uncertain, 1752 ***2856.30*** *p365*
Romer, Konrad; Port uncertain, 1768 ***2856.30*** *p374*
Wife: A. E. Wagner
Romer, Konrad; Port uncertain, 1785 ***2856.30*** *p374*
Romer, Mrs. Peter; Port uncertain, 1747 ***2856.30*** *p365*
With 2 daughters
Romich, Anna Barbara; America, 1769 ***2856.30*** *p250*
Romich, Anna Barbara Kuhn; America, 1774 ***2856.30*** *p374*
Romich, Anna Barbara Kuhn; Port uncertain, 1769 ***2856.30*** *p374*
Romig, Georg; Port uncertain, 1725 ***2856.30*** *p365*
Romiger, Johann Georg; America, 1742 ***2856.30*** *p365*
Rominger, Johann Georg; America, 1742 ***2856.30*** *p357*
Rominski, Joseph; Maryland, 1910 ***3259.35*** *p52*
Rominsky, Casmier; Maryland, 1910 ***3259.35*** *p52*
Romman, William; Philadelphia, 1722 ***1224.2*** *p98*
Rommel, Christian Bernard; Philadelphia, 1834 ***8197.10*** *p148*
Rommel, John Christian Frederick; New York, 1794 ***8197.10*** *p4*
Rommel, Valentin; Port uncertain, 1777 ***2856.30*** *p365*
With wife & children
Rommel, Wilhelm; Port uncertain, 1784 ***2856.30*** *p365*
Ron, Jacob; Pennsylvania, 1777 ***4629.10*** *p12*
Ron, Leonard; Pennsylvania, 1786 ***4629.10*** *p52*
Ronald, Mr.; Quebec, 1858 ***9196.15*** *p37*
Ronald, George; Cape Fear, North Carolina, 1741 ***1640.13*** *p106*
Ronald, John 50; Ontario, 1871 ***1823.28*** *p87*
Ronald, William; Georgia, 1699 ***1640.13*** *p106*
Ronalds, Edmund Hugh; Florida, 1895 ***1640.13*** *p106*
Ronalds, Robert; New York, 1825 ***8197.10*** *p274*

Ronaldson, Mr.; Quebec, 1858 **9196.15** *p40*
Ronaldson, Janet; Philadelphia, 1834 **1640.13** *p106*
Ronan, Catharine; Vermont, 1833-1908 **5900.10** *p275*
Ronan, Sarah M.; Vermont, 1837-1926 **5900.10** *p490*
Ronen, James; New York, 1828 **8197.10** *p63*
Wife: Margaret
Ronen, Margaret *SEE* Ronen, James
Roney, Henery 49; Ontario, 1871 **1823.28** *p87*
Roney, Jeremiah; Maryland, 1818 **6058.10** *p10*
Roney, William 21; Maryland, 1774 **1220.25** *p65*
Ronney, Thomas; Maryland, 1637 **2524.55** *p190*
Ronognolo, J. 35; Alaska, 1912 **9196.1** *p37*
Ronognolo, J. 35; British Columbia, 1912 **9196.1** *p37*
Ronold, James; New York, New York, 1850 **6058.10** *p35*
Ronson, James 49; Ontario, 1871 **1823.28** *p88*
Rontier, Rev.; Quebec, 1858 **9196.15** *p35*
Rood, John; Maryland, 1679 **2524.55** *p190*
Rood, William 73; Ontario, 1871 **1823.15** *p227*
Rooe, John; Virginia, 1663 **6212.30** *p2*
Roofey, David; Maryland, 1667 **2524.55** *p190*
With wife
Daughter: Elizabeth
Roofey, Elizabeth *SEE* Roofey, David
Rook, John 34; Ontario, 1871 **1823.28** *p88*
Rooke, John; New York, 1794 **8197.10** *p4*
Rooke, John Bolton; Charles Town, South Carolina, 1802 **1224.3** *p67*
Rooke, Wm; Virginia, 1665-1666 **6212.30** *p21*
Rookes, Sarah; Maryland, 1667 **2524.55** *p190*
Rooklige, David 41; Ontario, 1871 **1823.15** *p227*
Rooklige, John 32; Ontario, 1871 **1823.15** *p227*
Rooks, George; Maryland, 1666 **2524.55** *p190*
Rookwood, John; Maryland, 1642 **2524.55** *p190*
Rookwood, Thomas; Maryland, 1642 **2524.55** *p190*
Rooney, A. B.; Vermont, 1854-1922 **5900.10** *p49*
Rooney, Anastasia Callan 39; Vermont, 1887 **5900.10** *p478*
Rooney, Ann 67; Vermont, 1872 **5900.10** *p240*
Rooney, Ann 67; Vermont, 1898 **5900.10** *p49*
Rooney, Anne Kirk; Vermont, 1849-1920 **5900.10** *p285*
Rooney, Annie; Vermont, 1850-1900 **5900.10** *p505*
Rooney, Barnard 63; Vermont, 1884 **5900.10** *p239*
Rooney, Bernard; New York, 1840 **8197.10** *p189*
Rooney, Bernard G.; Vermont, 1844-1916 **5900.10** *p285*
Rooney, Bridget 72; Vermont, 1916 **5900.10** *p560*
Rooney, Bridget A.; Vermont, 1856-1942 **5900.10** *p505*
Rooney, Bridget King; Vermont, 1847-1873 **5900.10** *p227*
Rooney, C. 25; Ontario, 1861 **2896.28** *p9*
Rooney, Catherine 17; Vermont, 1878 **5900.10** *p294*
Rooney, Daniel; New York, 1822-1834 **8197.10** *p305*
Rooney, Daniel 60; Ontario, 1871 **1823.22** *p137*
Rooney, Elizabeth; Vermont, 1849-1908 **5900.10** *p185*
Rooney, Ellen King; Vermont, 1845-1884 **5900.10** *p227*
Rooney, Ellen M.; Vermont, 1849-1897 **5900.10** *p242*
Rooney, Ellen McLaughlin; Vermont, 1838-1912 **5900.10** *p419*
Rooney, Felix 52; Vermont, 1874 **5900.10** *p505*
Rooney, Felix 60; Ontario, 1871 **1823.22** *p137*
Rooney, Hanora; Vermont, 1813-1871 **5900.10** *p166*
Rooney, Hugh; New York, 1821 **8197.10** *p273*
Rooney, James; New York, 1821 **8197.10** *p273*
Rooney, James; Vermont, 1795-1882 **5900.10** *p227*
Rooney, James; Vermont, 1814-1890 **5900.10** *p228*
Rooney, James H.; Vermont, 1836-1917 **5900.10** *p487*
Rooney, James T. 28; Vermont, 1881 **5900.10** *p228*
Rooney, John; New York, 1823 **8197.10** *p274*
Rooney, John 33; Ontario, 1871 **1823.22** *p137*
Rooney, John 56; Vermont, 1845 **5900.10** *p239*
Rooney, Julia; Vermont, 1854-1946 **5900.10** *p490*
Rooney, Margaret; Vermont, 1828-1910 **5900.10** *p395*
Rooney, Martin 40; San Francisco, 1917 **9196.1** *p52*
Rooney, Martin 40; Yukon, 1917 **9196.1** *p52*
Rooney, Mary; Vermont, 1818-1886 **5900.10** *p271*
Rooney, Mary 60; Ontario, 1871 **1823.22** *p137*
Rooney, Mary A. Coakley; Vermont, 1860-1923 **5900.10** *p505*
Rooney, Mary Breen; Vermont, 1823-1907 **5900.10** *p228*
Rooney, Mary Callan; Vermont, 1850-1921 **5900.10** *p487*
Rooney, Mary Condon; Vermont, 1833-1909 **5900.10** *p461*
Rooney, Mary J. Gaffney 34; Vermont, 1884 **5900.10** *p559*
Rooney, Mary Kelley 70; Vermont, 1896 **5900.10** *p505*
Rooney, Nancy; Vermont, 1840-1916 **5900.10** *p276*
Rooney, Nancy; Vermont, 1844-1922 **5900.10** *p241*
Rooney, Patrick; New York, 1826-1831 **8197.10** *p370*
Rooney, Patrick; New York, 1837 **8197.10** *p102*
Rooney, Patrick 40; Ontario, 1871 **1823.22** *p137*
Rooney, Patrick 48; Vermont, 1888 **5900.10** *p559*
Rooney, Patrick 55; Ontario, 1871 **1823.15** *p227*
Rooney, Patrick J. 30; Vermont, 1883 **5900.10** *p505*
Rooney, Rosa; Vermont, 1838-1867 **5900.10** *p227*
Rooney, Rose; Vermont, 1844-1917 **5900.10** *p276*
Rooney, Rose Brennan; Vermont, 1854-1939 **5900.10** *p241*
Rooney, Rossie D. Bennett; Vermont, 1863-1952 **5900.10** *p49*
Rooney, Sarah A.; Vermont, 1854-1942 **5900.10** *p505*
Rooney, Thomas; New York, 1831 **8197.10** *p364*
Rooney, Thomas; Vermont, 1822-1895 **5900.10** *p419*
Rooney, Thomas; Vermont, 1840-1894 **5900.10** *p227*
Rooney, William; New York, 1839 **8197.10** *p134*
Rooney, William; Vermont, 1842-1933 **5900.10** *p241*
Rooney, William J.; Vermont, 1858-1922 **5900.10** *p505*
Roony, John 38; Ontario, 1871 **1823.22** *p137*
Roop, Ambross; Virginia, 1666 **6212.30** *p31*
Roop, Richard 36; Ontario, 1871 **1823.15** *p227*
Roos, David; New York, 1807 **8197.10** *p48*
Roos, Elisabeth; Port uncertain, 1796 **2856.30** *p366*
Roos, Franz; America, 1754 **2856.30** *p366*
With wife & child
Roos, Heinrich; Port uncertain, 1792 **2856.30** *p366*
Roos, Johannetta; Port uncertain, 1789 **2856.30** *p366*
Roos, Maria Elisabeth; America, 1754 **2856.30** *p366*
Roos, Susanna Elisabe; Port uncertain, 1796 **2856.30** *p366*
Roosey, David; Maryland, 1667 **2524.55** *p190*
With wife
Daughter: Elizabeth
Roosey, Elizabeth *SEE* Roosey, David
Rooss, Johann Adam; Port uncertain, 1747 **2856.30** *p366*
Rooss, Johann Niklas; Port uncertain, 1782 **2856.30** *p366*
Rooss, Johann Niklas; Port uncertain, 1789 **2856.30** *p366*
Root, Ann 5; Ontario, 1861 **2896.27** *p23*
Root, Daniel; America, 1753 **2856.30** *p366*
Root, G. 2; Ontario, 1861 **2896.28** *p4*
Root, L. 25; Ontario, 1861 **2896.28** *p4*
Root, Mary A. 25; Ontario, 1861 **2896.27** *p23*
Root, William 21; Ontario, 1871 **1823.15** *p227*
Root, William S.; New York, 1820 **8197.10** *p371*
Rootes, Thomas Reade; Virginia, 1767 **1224.2** *p98*
Roots, August 47; Ontario, 1871 **1823.28** *p88*
Rop, Andrew 40; Ontario, 1871 **1823.22** *p137*
Rop, David 44; Ontario, 1871 **1823.15** *p227*
Ropain, John 31; Ontario, 1871 **1823.15** *p227*
Ropanski, Anthony; Maryland, 1910 **3259.35** *p52*
Ropeman, Joseph; Maryland, 1666 **2524.55** *p190*
Roper, A.; Quebec, 1856 **9196.15** *p9*
Roper, Catharine 32; Virginia, 1774 **1220.25** *p75*
Roper, James; New York, 1825 **8197.10** *p274*
Roper, John H. 37; Ontario, 1871 **1823.22** *p137*
Roper, Richard 70; Ontario, 1871 **1823.22** *p137*
Roper, Thomas; Virginia, 1624 **1224.1** *p49*
Roper, Virlinda; Maryland, 1658 **2524.55** *p190*
Roper, Virlinda; Maryland, 1658 **2524.55** *p207*
Ropes, Jonathan; Salem, Massachusetts, 1715 **1224.2** *p98*
Ropes, William; Salem, Massachusetts, 1715 **1224.2** *p98*
Ropina, Yem 30; Alaska, 1912 **9196.1** *p19*
Ropina, Yem 30; British Columbia, 1912 **9196.1** *p19*
Ropinskie, Bronstow; Maryland, 1910 **3259.35** *p52*
Ropler, George 46; Ontario, 1871 **1823.15** *p227*
Roploski, Joseph; Maryland, 1910 **3259.35** *p52*
Roppe, Annie Wynn; Vermont, 1853-1918 **5900.10** *p404*
Roppe, Edward; Vermont, 1861-1939 **5900.10** *p404*
Rorabach, C. 4; Ontario, 1861 **2896.27** *p1*
Rorabach, Mary 2; Ontario, 1861 **2896.27** *p1*
Rorabach, Mary 30; Ontario, 1861 **2896.27** *p1*
Roraback, George 63; Ontario, 1871 **1823.22** *p137*
Roraback, Julia 60; Ontario, 1871 **1823.22** *p137*
Rorabeck, H. 24; Ontario, 1861 **2896.28** *p12*
Rorabeck, James 2; Ontario, 1861 **2896.27** *p30*
Rorabeck, Reuben 3; Ontario, 1861 **2896.27** *p30*
Rorabeck, Sarah 32; Ontario, 1861 **2896.27** *p30*
Rorabeck, Thomas 58; Ontario, 1871 **1823.22** *p137*
Rorbownczka, Pahel; Maryland, 1910 **3259.35** *p52*
Rorison, James 49; Ontario, 1871 **1823.28** *p88*
Rork, Mary 90; Ontario, 1861 **2896.26** *p24*
Rorke, Catherine 17; Ontario, 1861 **2896.26** *p32*
Rorke, Edward 14; Ontario, 1861 **2896.26** *p32*
Rorke, Edward 62; Ontario, 1861 **2896.26** *p32*
Rorke, Esther 48; Ontario, 1861 **2896.27** *p39*
Rorke, John 8; Ontario, 1861 **2896.26** *p32*
Rorke, Margaret 53; Ontario, 1861 **2896.26** *p32*
Rorke, Thomas; New York, 1821 **8197.10** *p273*
Rorrie, Justus; New York, 1839 **8197.10** *p276*
Rortook, Mr.; Quebec, 1857 **9196.15** *p19*
Ros, Elisabeth; Port uncertain, 1766 **2856.30** *p366*
Rosa, John 22; Ontario, 1871 **1823.15** *p227*
Rosbach, Joseph; New York, 1807 **8197.10** *p329*
Rosborough, Mahala 67; Ontario, 1871 **1823.22** *p137*
Roscar, John; Virginia, 1666 **6212.30** *p27*
Rosch, Andreas; Port uncertain, 1766 **2856.30** *p374*
Rosch, Anna Maria; Port uncertain, 1712 **2856.30** *p374*
Rosch, Antoni; Port uncertain, 1720 **2856.30** *p374*
Rosch, Antoni; Port uncertain, 1748 **2856.30** *p374*
Rosch, Jacob Friedrich; Port uncertain, 1795 **2856.30** *p374*
Rosch, Jacob Friedrich; Port uncertain, 1796 **2856.30** *p374*
Rosch, Johann Martin; Port uncertain, 1795 **2856.30** *p374*
With wife & 4 children
Rosch, Johann Michael; America, 1754 **2856.30** *p374*
With wife & children
Roschardt, Anna Maria; Port uncertain, 1758 **2856.30** *p374*
Rosche, Christof; Port uncertain, 1764 **2856.30** *p374*
Rosche, Peter; America, 1754 **2856.30** *p374*
With wife & child
Roscielski, Frank R.; Maryland, 1910 **3259.35** *p52*
Rose, Master 1; Ontario, 1861 **2896.26** *p25*
Rose, Mr.; Quebec, 1856 **9196.15** *p6*
Rose, Mrs. 21; Ontario, 1861 **2896.26** *p25*
Rose, Mrs. 50; Ontario, 1861 **2896.26** *p25*
Rose, A. G. 2; Ontario, 1861 **2896.25** *p33*
Rose, A. J. 13; Ontario, 1861 **2896.25** *p8*
Rose, A. V. 3; Ontario, 1861 **2896.25** *p33*
Rose, Albert 10; Ontario, 1861 **2896.25** *p33*
Rose, Alexander; Georgia, 1757 **1640.10** *p178*
Rose, Alexander; Georgia, 1819 **1640.10** *p178*
Rose, Allen 63; Ontario, 1871 **1823.15** *p227*
Rose, Amanda 7; Ontario, 1861 **2896.27** *p28*
Rose, Amarilla 21; Ontario, 1861 **2896.25** *p36*
Rose, Ann Amelia 1; Ontario, 1861 **2896.27** *p28*
Rose, Bella 29; Ontario, 1871 **1823.15** *p227*
Rose, Charles 5; Ontario, 1861 **2896.27** *p28*
Rose, Christopher; Virginia, 1670 **1224.1** *p50*
Rose, David 8; Ontario, 1861 **2896.25** *p33*
Rose, David 21; Maryland, 1775 **1220.25** *p98*
Rose, Donald; Georgia, 1737 **1640.10** *p178*
Rose, Donald; Georgia, 1738 **1640.10** *p178*
Rose, Doratha 37; Ontario, 1861 **2896.25** *p33*
Rose, Duncan 32; Ontario, 1871 **1823.15** *p227*
Rose, George; New York, 1827 **8197.10** *p275*
Rose, George 10; Ontario, 1861 **2896.27** *p28*
Rose, George 18; Ontario, 1861 **2896.25** *p33*
Rose, George 55; Ontario, 1871 **1823.28** *p88*
Rose, Glema A.; Vermont, 1798-1880 **5900.10** *p338*
Rose, Gusta 16; Ontario, 1871 **1823.28** *p88*
Rose, Harriet; Vermont, 1832-1909 **5900.10** *p89*
Rose, Henry; New York, 1837 **8197.10** *p102*
Rose, Hiram 6; Ontario, 1861 **2896.25** *p33*
Rose, Hugh; New York, 1764 **1224.2** *p98*
Rose, Isabella; Canada, 1895 **1640.13** *p106*
Rose, Isibella 60; Ontario, 1871 **1823.15** *p227*
Rose, John; Jamaica, 1775 **1640.13** *p106*
Rose, John; New York, 1807 **8197.10** *p48*
Rose, John; New York, 1807 **8197.10** *p328*
Rose, John; New York, 1839 **8197.10** *p382*
Rose, John; Rhode Island, 1765 **1224.2** *p98*
Rose, John; Virginia, 1671 **6212.30** *p43*
Rose, John; Virginia, 1688 **1224.1** *p50*
Rose, John 12; Ontario, 1861 **2896.25** *p33*
Rose, John 22; Maryland, 1774 **1220.25** *p78*
Rose, John Pringle; California, 1889 **1640.13** *p106*
Rose, John Wallington; New Orleans, 1851 **1224.3** *p67*
Rose, M. A. 8; Ontario, 1861 **2896.25** *p33*
Rose, Martin 40; Ontario, 1871 **1823.28** *p88*
Rose, Mary 9; Ontario, 1861 **2896.27** *p28*
Rose, Mary 66; Ontario, 1861 **2896.25** *p33*
Rose, Michael; New York, 1840 **8197.10** *p189*
Rose, Nancy 3; Ontario, 1861 **2896.27** *p28*
Rose, Peter 78; Vermont, 1866 **5900.10** *p338*
Rose, Robert 20; Carolina, 1774 **1220.25** *p38*
Rose, Robert 48; Ontario, 1871 **1823.15** *p227*
Rose, Robert 78; Ontario, 1861 **2896.27** *p37*
Rose, S. A. 4; Ontario, 1861 **2896.25** *p33*
Rose, S. A. 6; Ontario, 1861 **2896.25** *p33*
Rose, Sarah Ann 30; Ontario, 1861 **2896.27** *p28*
Rose, Stephen 26; Virginia, 1775 **1220.25** *p109*
Rose, Sylvanus 14; Ontario, 1861 **2896.27** *p28*
Rose, Thomas; Havana, 1765 **1224.2** *p98*
Rose, Thomas; Rhode Island, 1765 **1224.2** *p98*
Rose, Waly C. 41; Ontario, 1861 **2896.25** *p33*
Rose, William; New Jersey, 1792 **1224.3** *p67*
Rose, William 1; Ontario, 1861 **2896.25** *p33*
Rose, William 23; Ontario, 1871 **1823.15** *p228*
Rose, William 30; Ontario, 1871 **1823.15** *p228*
Rose, William 57; Ontario, 1871 **1823.22** *p137*
Rose, William H. 16; Ontario, 1861 **2896.25** *p33*
Rose, William James; New York, New York, 1849 **1224.3** *p67*
Rosebush, C. R. 16; Ontario, 1861 **2896.25** *p43*
Rosebush, Lavin R. 54; Ontario, 1861 **2896.25** *p43*
Rosebush, Lewis R. 17; Ontario, 1861 **2896.25** *p43*
Rosebush, Sarah 37; Ontario, 1861 **2896.25** *p43*
Rosebush, William S. 9; Ontario, 1861 **2896.25** *p43*
Rosebush, Wm., Sr. 78; Ontario, 1861 **2896.25** *p43*
Rosenbaum, Frederick; New York, 1839 **8197.10** *p276*

Rosenberg, Jacob; Pennsylvania, 1863 ***6058.10*** *p49*
Rosenblack, John 69; Ontario, 1871 ***1823.22*** *p137*
Rosenburg, Jacob; Pennsylvania, 1863 ***6058.10*** *p49*
Rosenburger, Jacob; New York, 1840 ***8197.10*** *p189*
Rosendorf, David; New York, New York, 1858 ***6058.10*** *p53*
Rosendorf, Michael Jacob; New York, New York, 1857 ***6058.10*** *p54*
Rosenfeld, Samuel; New York, 1840 ***8197.10*** *p189*
Rosenlor, Charles A.; New York, 1838 ***8197.10*** *p148*
Rosenquest, John; New York, 1834 ***8197.10*** *p359*
Rosentein, Dr.; Quebec, 1857 ***9196.15*** *p15*
Rosentein, Mrs.; Quebec, 1857 ***9196.15*** *p15*
Rosenthall, Mr.; Quebec, 1858 ***9196.15*** *p46*
Roser, Adam; America, 1753 ***2856.30*** *p366*
Roser, Adam; Port uncertain, 1753 ***2856.30*** *p366*
With wife & 3 children
Roser, Anna Maria; Port uncertain, 1764 ***2856.30*** *p374*
Roser, Hans Georg; Port uncertain, 1754 ***2856.30*** *p366*
Roser, Susanna; Port uncertain, 1746 ***2856.30*** *p366*
Roserin, Anna Maria; Port uncertain, 1764 ***2856.30*** *p374*
Rosevear, James 35; Ontario, 1871 ***1823.22*** *p137*
Rosevear, Joseph 51; Ontario, 1871 ***1823.22*** *p137*
Rose Vear, Mathew 52; Ontario, 1871 ***1823.22*** *p137*
Rosevear, Matthew 77; Ontario, 1871 ***1823.22*** *p137*
Rosiak, Julian; Maryland, 1910 ***3259.35*** *p52*
Rosiak, Stanislaw; Maryland, 1910 ***3259.35*** *p52*
Rosier, William; Maryland, 1655 ***2524.55*** *p190*
Rosin, Anna Maria; Port uncertain, 1766 ***2856.30*** *p366*
Rosinska, Mary; Maryland, 1910 ***3259.35*** *p52*
Rosinski, Stanisllaus; Maryland, 1910 ***3259.35*** *p52*
Rosnowski, Stanislaw; Maryland, 1910 ***3259.35*** *p52*
Ross, Dr.; Quebec, 1857 ***9196.15*** *p13*
Ross, Miss; Quebec, 1857 ***9196.15*** *p27*
Ross, Mr.; Portland, Maine, 1858 ***9196.15*** *p47*
Ross, Mr.; Quebec, 1857 ***9196.15*** *p15*
Ross, Mr.; Quebec, 1857 ***9196.15*** *p22*
Ross, Mr.; Quebec, 1857 ***9196.15*** *p23*
Ross, Mr.; Quebec, 1858 ***9196.15*** *p35*
Ross, Mrs.; Quebec, 1857 ***9196.15*** *p22*
Ross, Mrs.; Quebec, 1857 ***9196.15*** *p27*
Ross, Alesander 34; Ontario, 1871 ***1823.15*** *p228*
Ross, Alescander 44; Ontario, 1871 ***1823.15*** *p228*
Ross, Alester; Maryland, 1651 ***2524.55*** *p190*
Ross, Alexander; Georgia, 1734 ***1640.10*** *p178*
Ross, Alexander; Georgia, 1819 ***1640.10*** *p179*
Ross, Alexander; New York, 1888 ***1640.13*** *p106*
Ross, Alexander 38; Ontario, 1871 ***1823.15*** *p228*
Ross, Alexander 43; Ontario, 1871 ***1823.15*** *p228*
Ross, Alexander 46; Ontario, 1871 ***1823.22*** *p137*
Ross, Alexander 56; Ontario, 1871 ***1823.15*** *p228*
Ross, Andrew; New York, 1802 ***8197.10*** *p24*
Ross, Andrew; Savannah, Georgia, 1804 ***1640.10*** *p179*
Ross, Andrew 36; Ontario, 1871 ***1823.15*** *p228*
Ross, Andrew 68; Ontario, 1871 ***1823.22*** *p137*
Ross, Angus; Ontario, 1849 ***4537.37*** *p84*
Wife: Catherine Morrison
Child: John
Child: Donald
Child: Mary
Child: Finlay
Child: Ann
Child: Isabella
Child: Ewen
Child: Marion
Ross, Ann *SEE* Ross, Angus
Ross, Archibald 37; Ontario, 1871 ***1823.15*** *p228*
Ross, Archie *SEE* Ross, Marion Morrison
Ross, Barbara; Washington, 1864 ***1640.13*** *p106*
Ross, Benjamin 21; Ontario, 1861 ***2896.25*** *p40*
Ross, Benjamin B. 67; Ontario, 1861 ***2896.25*** *p40*
Ross, Caroline S.; Vermont, 1839-1915 ***5900.10*** *p197*
Ross, Catherine 67; Ontario, 1861 ***2896.25*** *p40*
Ross, Catherine Morrison *SEE* Ross, Angus
Ross, Charles 24; Ontario, 1871 ***1823.28*** *p88*
Ross, Colin; Jamaica, 1779 ***1640.13*** *p106*
Ross, Colin 36; Ontario, 1871 ***1823.28*** *p88*
Ross, D. A.; Quebec, 1858 ***9196.15*** *p40*
Ross, Daniel; Georgia, 1738 ***1640.10*** *p179*
Ross, David; Baltimore, 1794 ***1640.13*** *p107*
Ross, David; Mississippi, 1783 ***1640.10*** *p179*
Ross, David; Richmond, Virginia, 1822 ***1224.3*** *p67*
Ross, David 44; Ontario, 1871 ***1823.28*** *p88*
Ross, David 46; Ontario, 1871 ***1823.22*** *p137*
Ross, David 48; Ontario, 1871 ***1823.15*** *p228*
Ross, David 55; Ontario, 1871 ***1823.15*** *p228*
Ross, David 62; Ontario, 1871 ***1823.22*** *p137*
Ross, Donald *SEE* Ross, Angus
Ross, Donald 49; Ontario, 1871 ***1823.15*** *p228*
Ross, Donald 55; Ontario, 1871 ***1823.15*** *p228*
Ross, Donald 58; Ontario, 1871 ***1823.15*** *p228*
Ross, Donald 58; Ontario, 1871 ***1823.22*** *p137*
Ross, Donald 61; Ontario, 1871 ***1823.15*** *p228*
Ross, Donald 71; Ontario, 1871 ***1823.15*** *p228*
Ross, Donilla 20; Ontario, 1871 ***1823.15*** *p228*
Ross, Edmund 60; Ontario, 1871 ***1823.15*** *p228*
Ross, Elizabeth; Virginia, 1768 ***1224.2*** *p99*
Ross, Elizabeth 34; Ontario, 1871 ***1823.15*** *p228*
Ross, Elizabeth 40; Ontario, 1871 ***1823.22*** *p137*
Ross, Emeline G. 34; Ontario, 1871 ***1823.22*** *p138*
Ross, Euphemia 38; Ontario, 1871 ***1823.22*** *p138*
Ross, Ewen *SEE* Ross, Angus
Ross, Finlay *SEE* Ross, Angus
Ross, Finley 52; Ontario, 1871 ***1823.15*** *p228*
Ross, Francis A.; New York, 1832 ***8197.10*** *p368*
Ross, Gassaway 56; Ontario, 1871 ***1823.28*** *p88*
Ross, Gavin 34; Ontario, 1871 ***1823.15*** *p228*
Ross, Gavin 82; Ontario, 1871 ***1823.15*** *p228*
Ross, George; Bahamas, 1863 ***1640.13*** *p107*
Ross, George; Mississippi, 1783 ***1640.10*** *p179*
Ross, George; North America, 1846 ***1640.13*** *p107*
Ross, George 38; Ontario, 1861 ***2896.25*** *p40*
Ross, George 47; Ontario, 1871 ***1823.15*** *p228*
Ross, Gilbert; Florida, 1767 ***1640.10*** *p179*
Ross, Helen 57; Ontario, 1871 ***1823.28*** *p88*
Ross, Hugh; Georgia, 1734 ***1640.10*** *p179*
Ross, Hugh; Georgia, 1736 ***1640.10*** *p179*
Ross, Hugh; Georgia, 1764 ***1640.10*** *p180*
Ross, Hugh; New England, 1708 ***1640.13*** *p107*
Ross, Hugh; Savannah, Georgia, 1758 ***1640.10*** *p179*
Ross, Hugh; Savannah, Georgia, 1762 ***1640.10*** *p179*
Ross, Hugh 29; Ontario, 1871 ***1823.22*** *p138*
Ross, Hugh 41; Ontario, 1871 ***1823.15*** *p228*
Ross, Hugh 41; Ontario, 1871 ***1823.22*** *p138*
Ross, Hugh 60; Ontario, 1871 ***1823.28*** *p88*
Ross, Isabella *SEE* Ross, Angus
Ross, Isabella 47; Ontario, 1871 ***1823.22*** *p138*
Ross, J.; Portland, Maine, 1858 ***9196.15*** *p29*
Ross, J.; Quebec, 1857 ***9196.15*** *p20*
Ross, J.; Quebec, 1858 ***9196.15*** *p42*
Ross, J. C.; Quebec, 1856 ***9196.15*** *p8*
Ross, James; Chicago, 1900 ***1640.13*** *p107*
Ross, James; Georgia, 1734 ***1640.10*** *p180*
Ross, James; Georgia, 1736 ***1640.10*** *p180*
Ross, James; New York, 1806 ***8197.10*** *p32*
Ross, James; New York, 1834 ***8197.10*** *p75*
Ross, James; New York, 1840 ***8197.10*** *p384*
Ross, James; Pennsylvania, 1777 ***4629.10*** *p45*
Ross, James 25; Ontario, 1861 ***2896.25*** *p40*
Ross, James 40; Ontario, 1871 ***1823.15*** *p228*
Ross, James 44; Ontario, 1871 ***1823.22*** *p138*
Ross, James 45; Ontario, 1871 ***1823.28*** *p88*
Ross, James 60; Ontario, 1871 ***1823.15*** *p228*
Ross, James 61; Ontario, 1871 ***1823.15*** *p228*
Ross, James 72; Ontario, 1871 ***1823.28*** *p88*
Ross, James Gibb; Quebec, 1890 ***1640.13*** *p107*
Ross, Jessie; New York, 1899 ***1640.13*** *p107*
Ross, Jessie 40; Ontario, 1871 ***1823.28*** *p88*
Ross, Johan 30; Ontario, 1871 ***1823.22*** *p138*
Ross, Johann; Port uncertain, 1765 ***2856.30*** *p366*
Ross, Johann Adam; Port uncertain, 1784 ***2856.30*** *p366*
Ross, Johann Philipp; Port uncertain, 1796 ***2856.30*** *p366*
Ross, John *SEE* Ross, Angus
Ross, John; Florida, 1775 ***1640.10*** *p180*
Ross, John; Georgia, 1760 ***1640.10*** *p180*
Ross, John; Jamaica, 1863 ***1640.13*** *p107*
Ross, John; Mobile, Alabama, 1820-1845 ***1640.10*** *p180*
Ross, John; Montreal, 1830-1839 ***1640.13*** *p107*
Ross, John; New England, 1770 ***1224.2*** *p99*
Ross, John; Pennsylvania, 1777 ***4629.10*** *p6*
Ross, John; Pennsylvania, 1780 ***4629.10*** *p43*
Ross, John; Quebec, 1856 ***9196.15*** *p5*
Ross, John; Virginia, 1664-1665 ***6212.30*** *p16*
Ross, John 34; Ontario, 1871 ***1823.15*** *p228*
Ross, John 41; Ontario, 1871 ***1823.15*** *p228*
Ross, John 49; Ontario, 1871 ***1823.15*** *p228*
Ross, John 55; Ontario, 1871 ***1823.22*** *p138*
Ross, John 59; Ontario, 1871 ***1823.28*** *p88*
Ross, John 60; Ontario, 1871 ***1823.15*** *p228*
Ross, John 65; Ontario, 1871 ***1823.15*** *p228*
Ross, John G.; New York, 1840 ***8197.10*** *p189*
Ross, John M. 66; Ontario, 1871 ***1823.28*** *p88*
Ross, Lexy; Ontario, 1862 ***4537.32*** *p81*
Ross, Lexy; Ontario, 1863 ***4537.35*** *p61*
Ross, Margaret; Illinois, 1836 ***1640.13*** *p107*
Ross, Margaret 20; Ontario, 1871 ***1823.15*** *p229*
Ross, Margaret 22; Ontario, 1871 ***1823.22*** *p138*
Ross, Marion *SEE* Ross, Angus
Ross, Marion *SEE* Ross, Marion Morrison
Ross, Marion Morrison; Quebec, 1880-1889 ***4537.35*** *p64*
Child: Archie
Child: Mary
Child: Sorley
Child: Marion
Child: Mary Ann
Ross, Martin A. 78; Vermont, 1914 ***5900.10*** *p401*
Ross, Mary *SEE* Ross, Angus
Ross, Mary *SEE* Ross, Marion Morrison
Ross, Mary; Falkland Islands, 1880-1889 ***4537.35*** *p76*
Ross, Mary; Port uncertain, 1840-1849 ***4537.37*** *p113*
Ross, Mary 56; Ontario, 1871 ***1823.15*** *p229*
Ross, Mary Ann *SEE* Ross, Marion Morrison
Ross, Neil 64; Ontario, 1871 ***1823.15*** *p229*
Ross, Phebe 23; Ontario, 1861 ***2896.25*** *p40*
Ross, Rebecca 73; Ontario, 1871 ***1823.22*** *p138*
Ross, Robert; New York, 1792 ***1224.2*** *p99*
Ross, Robert; Nova Scotia, 1785 ***1640.10*** *p180*
Ross, Robert; Pensacola, Florida, 1764 ***1640.10*** *p180*
Ross, Robert; Vermont, 1856-1901 ***5900.10*** *p414*
Ross, Robert 15; Maryland, 1774 ***1220.25*** *p74*
Ross, Robert 27; Ontario, 1861 ***2896.25*** *p40*
Ross, Robert 55; Ontario, 1871 ***1823.15*** *p229*
Ross, Roderick 47; Ontario, 1871 ***1823.15*** *p229*
Ross, Samuel; New York, 1831 ***8197.10*** *p365*
Ross, Samuel J. 31; Ontario, 1871 ***1823.28*** *p88*
Ross, Sellinda Dunbar 75; Vermont, 1939 ***5900.10*** *p401*
Ross, Sorley *SEE* Ross, Marion Morrison
Ross, Thomas; Georgia, 1766 ***1640.10*** *p180*
Ross, Thomas 40; Ontario, 1871 ***1823.15*** *p229*
Ross, W. R.; Quebec, 1858 ***9196.15*** *p45*
Ross, Walter 42; Ontario, 1871 ***1823.22*** *p138*
Ross, Walter 49; Ontario, 1871 ***1823.22*** *p138*
Ross, William; America, 1893 ***1640.13*** *p107*
Ross, William; Georgia, 1737 ***1640.10*** *p180*
Ross, William; Georgia, 1737 ***1640.10*** *p181*
Ross, William; Jamaica, 1802 ***1640.13*** *p107*
Ross, William; New York, 1782 ***1640.13*** *p107*
Ross, William; Pennsylvania, 1777 ***4629.10*** *p8*
Ross, William; Virginia, 1718 ***1224.2*** *p99*
Ross, William 24; Ontario, 1861 ***2896.28*** *p55*
Ross, William 25; Ontario, 1871 ***1823.22*** *p138*
Ross, William 37; Ontario, 1871 ***1823.15*** *p229*
Ross, William 40; Philadelphia, 1774 ***1220.25*** *p67*
Ross, William 41; Ontario, 1871 ***1823.15*** *p229*
Ross, William 41; Ontario, 1871 ***1823.22*** *p138*
Ross, William 49; Ontario, 1871 ***1823.15*** *p229*
Ross, William 50; Ontario, 1871 ***1823.28*** *p88*
Ross, William J.; New York, 1840 ***8197.10*** *p189*
Rossa, Julias 33; Ontario, 1871 ***1823.28*** *p88*
Rossalek, Joseph; Maryland, 1910 ***3259.35*** *p52*
Rossbausch, Eva Barbara; Port uncertain, 1751 ***2856.30*** *p366*
Rossberg, Mrs. Friedr.; America, 1786 ***2856.30*** *p366*
Rossberg, Mrs. Friedr.; America, 1793 ***2856.30*** *p366*
Rosse, Daniel; Maryland, 1663 ***2524.55*** *p190*
Rosse, Francis; Maryland, 1664 ***2524.55*** *p190*
Rosse, Nicholas; New York, 1806 ***8197.10*** *p32*
Rosse, Thomas; Virginia, 1666 ***6212.30*** *p26*
Rosse, Thomas 35; Maryland, 1775 ***1220.25*** *p10*
Rossel, Auguste; New York, 1808 ***8197.10*** *p54*
Rossel, Simon; Port uncertain, 1768 ***2856.30*** *p375*
Rosselot, Peter A.; New York, 1837 ***8197.10*** *p101*
Rosser, Jakob; America, 1770 ***2856.30*** *p367*
Rosseter, Elizabeth; New England, 1666 ***1224.1*** *p2*
Rossett, Geo.; Maryland, 1659 ***2524.55*** *p191*
Rossi, M. 26; Alaska, 1917 ***9196.1*** *p46*
Rossi, M. 26; Whitehorse, Yukon, 1917 ***9196.1*** *p46*
Rossiter, Eliza; Cleveland, Ohio, 1836 ***1224.3*** *p67*
Rossiter, John; Scranton, Pennsylvania, 1852 ***1224.3*** *p67*
Rossiter, Patrick 70; Ontario, 1871 ***1823.22*** *p138*
Rosskopf, Barbara; Port uncertain, 1765 ***2856.30*** *p367*
Rossle, Gabriel; America, 1751 ***2856.30*** *p375*
With wife & 3 children
Rossle, Gabriel; America, 1751 ***2856.30*** *p375*
Rossler, Gabriel; America, 1751 ***2856.30*** *p375*
With wife & 3 children
Rossler, Gabriel; America, 1751 ***2856.30*** *p375*
Rossler, Johann Georg; Port uncertain, 1771 ***2856.30*** *p375*
Rossler, Johann Georg; Port uncertain, 1772 ***2856.30*** *p375*
With wife
Rossmuller, Johann; Port uncertain, 1738 ***2856.30*** *p367*
Ross of Culgruff, George Clark; Canada, 1852 ***1640.13*** *p107*
Rosswag, Hans Martin; America, 1738 ***2856.30*** *p367*
Rosswag, Michael, The Old; America, 1737 ***2856.30*** *p367*
Rost, Hans Georg; Port uncertain, 1754 ***2856.30*** *p367*
Rost, P. 27; Alaska, 1912 ***9196.1*** *p37*
Rost, P. 27; Whitehorse, Yukon, 1912 ***9196.1*** *p37*
Rostek, Wladyslaw; Maryland, 1910 ***3259.35*** *p52*
Rostkowski, Edward; Maryland, 1910 ***3259.35*** *p52*
Rosunonufski, Joseph; Maryland, 1910 ***3259.35*** *p52*
Rosweiler, Jakob; New York, 1840 ***8197.10*** *p277*
Roswska, Frank; Maryland, 1910 ***3259.35*** *p52*
Rosyard, A. 25; Alaska, 1913 ***9196.1*** *p21*
Roszyk, Michael; Maryland, 1910 ***3259.35*** *p52*
Rotchford, Thomas 57; Ontario, 1871 ***1823.22*** *p138*

Rotchford, William; New York, 1821 ***8197.10*** *p273*
Roteler, Johann; Port uncertain, 1731 ***2856.30*** *p375*
Roteler, Johann; Port uncertain, 1771 ***2856.30*** *p375*
Roterdam, Francis; Virginia, 1665 ***6212.30*** *p18*
Roth, . . .; Port uncertain, 1792 ***2856.30*** *p367*
With 2 siblings
Roth, Mr.; America, 1750 ***2856.30*** *p367*
Roth, Mr.; America, 1758 ***2856.30*** *p367*
Roth, Anna Helena; Port uncertain, 1792 ***2856.30*** *p368*
Roth, Anna Maria; Port uncertain, 1731 ***2856.30*** *p367*
Roth, Anna Maria; Port uncertain, 1751 ***2856.30*** *p367*
Roth, Anna Maria; Port uncertain, 1752 ***2856.30*** *p367*
Roth, Anna Maria; Port uncertain, 1770 ***2856.30*** *p367*
Roth, Barb. Muller *SEE* Roth, Johann
Roth, Barbara; Port uncertain, 1731 ***2856.30*** *p367*
Roth, Barbara; Port uncertain, 1751 ***2856.30*** *p367*
Roth, Barbara; Port uncertain, 1769 ***2856.30*** *p367*
Roth, Catharina; Cayenne, 1764 ***2856.30*** *p368*
Roth, Christian; Port uncertain, 1764 ***2856.30*** *p367*
Roth, David; America, 1720 ***2856.30*** *p367*
Roth, Dorothea Margar; Port uncertain, 1789 ***2856.30*** *p367*
Roth, Elisabeth; America, 1751 ***2856.30*** *p367*
Roth, Franz David; Port uncertain, 1775 ***2856.30*** *p367*
Roth, Mrs. Georg; America, 1750 ***2856.30*** *p367*
Roth, J.; America, 1719 ***2856.30*** *p316*
Roth, J. P. 50; Alaska, 1914 ***9196.1*** *p42*
Roth, Jacob; America, 1751 ***2856.30*** *p367*
Roth, Jacob; America, 1751 ***2856.30*** *p368*
With wife
Roth, Johan Georg; New York, 1835 ***8197.10*** *p275*
Roth, Johann; America, 1719 ***2856.30*** *p368*
Wife: Barb. Muller
Roth, Johann; America, 1736 ***2856.30*** *p367*
Roth, Johann; Port uncertain, 1724 ***2856.30*** *p367*
Roth, Johann; Port uncertain, 1726 ***2856.30*** *p367*
Roth, Johann; Port uncertain, 1731 ***2856.30*** *p367*
Roth, Johann; Port uncertain, 1775 ***2856.30*** *p367*
Roth, Johann Daniel; America, 1767 ***2856.30*** *p367*
Roth, Johann Georg; America, 1751 ***2856.30*** *p367*
Roth, Johann Georg; Port uncertain, 1793 ***2856.30*** *p367*
Roth, Johann Jakob; America, 1740 ***2856.30*** *p367*
Roth, Johann Jakob; America, 1742 ***2856.30*** *p367*
Roth, Johann Jakob; America, 1775 ***2856.30*** *p367*
Roth, Johann Jakob; America, 1784 ***2856.30*** *p367*
Roth, Johann Jakob; Port uncertain, 1775 ***2856.30*** *p367*
Roth, Johann Nickel; Port uncertain, 1786 ***2856.30*** *p367*
Roth, Juliane; Port uncertain, 1775 ***2856.30*** *p367*
Roth, Juliane Cathari; Port uncertain, 1788 ***2856.30*** *p375*
Roth, Konrad; Port uncertain, 1755 ***2856.30*** *p367*
Roth, Konrad; Port uncertain, 1792 ***2856.30*** *p368*
Roth, Kunigunda; Port uncertain, 1746 ***2856.30*** *p367*
Roth, Lorenz; Port uncertain, 1768 ***2856.30*** *p367*
Roth, Margarete; Canada, 1761 ***2856.30*** *p368*
Roth, Margarete; Port uncertain, 1752 ***2856.30*** *p368*
Roth, Margarete; Port uncertain, 1758 ***2856.30*** *p367*
Roth, Margarete; Port uncertain, 1760 ***2856.30*** *p368*
Roth, Margarete; Port uncertain, 1792 ***2856.30*** *p368*
Roth, Maria; Port uncertain, 1775 ***2856.30*** *p368*
Roth, Maria Magdalena; Port uncertain, 1777 ***2856.30*** *p368*
Roth, Marianna; Port uncertain, 1763 ***2856.30*** *p368*
Roth, Martin; Port uncertain, 1763 ***2856.30*** *p368*
Roth, Melchior; Port uncertain, 1756 ***2856.30*** *p368*
Roth, Ottilia; America, 1750 ***2856.30*** *p368*
Roth, Philipp Georg; Port uncertain, 1785 ***2856.30*** *p368*
Roth, Vanantine 47; Ontario, 1871 ***1823.15*** *p229*
Roth, Wilhelm; Port uncertain, 1788 ***2856.30*** *p368*
Rothaass, Georg; Port uncertain, 1784 ***2856.30*** *p368*
With wife & 6 children
Rothaass, Georg; Port uncertain, 1785 ***2856.30*** *p368*
Rothach, Elisabeth; Port uncertain, 1773 ***2856.30*** *p368*
Rothacker, Daniel; Port uncertain, 1793 ***2856.30*** *p368*
Rothacker, Jacob; Port uncertain, 1745 ***2856.30*** *p368*
Rothaug, Johann; Port uncertain, 1784 ***2856.30*** *p368*
Rothaug, Ludwig; Port uncertain, 1789 ***2856.30*** *p368*
Rothaug, Ludwig; Port uncertain, 1793 ***2856.30*** *p368*
Rothaug, Philipp Peter; Port uncertain, 1789 ***2856.30*** *p368*
Rothaug, Philipp Peter; Port uncertain, 1793 ***2856.30*** *p368*
Rothbusch, Catharina; America, 1752 ***2856.30*** *p368*
With 3 children
Rothbusch, Catharina; America, 1752 ***2856.30*** *p368*
Rotheheffer, Andreas, The Younger; America, 1748 ***2856.30*** *p368*
Rothenberger, Johann; Port uncertain, 1780 ***2856.30*** *p368*
Rothenberger, Johann Philipp; Port uncertain, 1745 ***2856.30*** *p368*
Rothenberger, Magdalena; Port uncertain, 1759 ***2856.30*** *p368*
Rothenberger, Marianna; Port uncertain, 1765 ***2856.30*** *p368*
Rothenberger, Peter; Port uncertain, 1764 ***2856.30*** *p368*
Rothenbuch, Jakob; Port uncertain, 1763 ***2856.30*** *p369*
Rothenburg, Anna Eva; Port uncertain, 1768 ***2856.30*** *p369*
Rothenbusch, Maria Eva; Port uncertain, 1759 ***2856.30*** *p369*
Rothenhausler, Johann; Canada, 1766 ***2856.30*** *p369*
Rothenhaussler, Catharina; Port uncertain, 1727 ***2856.30*** *p369*
Rothenhoffer, Andreas, The Younger; America, 1738 ***2856.30*** *p369*
With wife
Rotherford, Mary; Virginia, 1664 ***6212.30*** *p12*
Rothermal, Lewis 45; Ontario, 1871 ***1823.15*** *p229*
Rothermel, Peter 39; Ontario, 1871 ***1823.15*** *p229*
Rothery, William; New York, 1808 ***8197.10*** *p54*
Rothgangel, Andrew; New York, 1806 ***8197.10*** *p32*
Rothgaven, John; New York, 1838 ***8197.10*** *p147*
Rothin, Juliane Cathari; Port uncertain, 1788 ***2856.30*** *p375*
Rothin, Ottilia; America, 1750 ***2856.30*** *p368*
Rothlerin, Eva; Port uncertain, 1765 ***2856.30*** *p369*
Rothley, Dionys; Port uncertain, 1786 ***2856.30*** *p369*
Rothmeyer, Johann Philipp; Port uncertain, 1736 ***2856.30*** *p369*
Rothmeyer, Johann Philipp; Port uncertain, 1737 ***2856.30*** *p369*
Rothweiler, Jacob; Port uncertain, 1737 ***2856.30*** *p369*
Rothwell, Miss; Quebec, 1857 ***9196.15*** *p26*
Rothwell, Mr.; Quebec, 1857 ***9196.15*** *p15*
Rothwell, Mr.; Quebec, 1858 ***9196.15*** *p40*
Rothwell, Rev.; Quebec, 1857 ***9196.15*** *p26*
Rothwell, Andrew 35; Ontario, 1871 ***1823.28*** *p88*
Rothwood, William; Maryland, 1681 ***2524.55*** *p191*
Rotkey, Fredrick 39; Ontario, 1871 ***1823.28*** *p88*
Rottelin, Jacob; Port uncertain, 1749 ***2856.30*** *p375*
Rottenbury, John 63; Ontario, 1871 ***1823.15*** *p229*
Rottenhofer, Jacob; America, 1751 ***2856.30*** *p369*
Rottenhofer, Jacob; Port uncertain, 1744 ***2856.30*** *p369*
Rotter, Adam; Port uncertain, 1764 ***2856.30*** *p375*
Rotter, Dionys; Port uncertain, 1786 ***2856.30*** *p369*
Rottermund, Baroness; Quebec, 1858 ***9196.15*** *p38*
Rottey, Dionys; Port uncertain, 1786 ***2856.30*** *p369*
Rottiers, John Nepomucene; New York, 1824 ***8197.10*** *p274*
Rottinger, Friedrich; Port uncertain, 1787 ***2856.30*** *p375*
Rottlin, Anna Eva; Port uncertain, 1765 ***2856.30*** *p375*
Rottoman, Morris; Virginia, 1667-1668 ***6212.30*** *p38*
Rotzel, Henrich; America, 1784 ***2856.30*** *p375*
Rotzler, Johann; Port uncertain, 1765 ***2856.30*** *p375*
Rouatt, James 39; Ontario, 1871 ***1823.15*** *p229*
Rouatt, William 72; Ontario, 1871 ***1823.15*** *p229*
Rouault, Joseph; New York, 1807 ***8197.10*** *p48*
Roued, Kate 55; Ontario, 1871 ***1823.22*** *p138*
Roueh, John 51; Ontario, 1871 ***1823.15*** *p229*
Rouen, Bridget Riley; Vermont, 1829-1897 ***5900.10*** *p205*
Rouen, Edward 27; Vermont, 1884 ***5900.10*** *p205*
Rouen, John; Vermont, 1867-1900 ***5900.10*** *p205*
Rouen, Michael 61; Vermont, 1895 ***5900.10*** *p205*
Rouen, Tom; Vermont, 1855-1899 ***5900.10*** *p205*
Rough, Miss; Quebec, 1858 ***9196.15*** *p35*
Rough, William; Maryland, 1666 ***2524.55*** *p191*
Roughton, Miss; Quebec, 1858 ***9196.15*** *p33*
Rougier, Paul 34; Ontario, 1871 ***1823.28*** *p88*
Rouh, Anthony; Pennsylvania, 1839 ***6058.10*** *p16*
Rouhier, Alphonse; New York, 1830 ***8197.10*** *p360*
Rouke, Patrick 65; Ontario, 1871 ***1823.15*** *p229*
Rouking, John; Pennsylvania, 1777 ***4629.10*** *p22*
Rouks, Charles 36; Ontario, 1871 ***1823.28*** *p88*
Roulsi, Frederick; New York, New York, 1847 ***3437.14*** *p14*
Roulski, Stefana; Maryland, 1910 ***3259.35*** *p52*
Roulsten, James 13; Ontario, 1861 ***2896.27*** *p4*
Roulsten, Jane 46; Ontario, 1861 ***2896.27*** *p4*
Roulsten, John 15; Ontario, 1861 ***2896.27*** *p4*
Roun, Ferdinand 84; Ontario, 1871 ***1823.28*** *p88*
Roun, Herman 21; Ontario, 1871 ***1823.28*** *p88*
Round, George; Mobile, Alabama, 1850 ***1224.3*** *p67*
Round, James; Maryland, 1680 ***2524.55*** *p191*
Rounde, George; Virginia, 1654 ***1224.1*** *p50*
Rounds, Joseph A. 63; Vermont, 1917 ***5900.10*** *p439*
Rounds, Margaret A. Sullivan 70; Vermont, n.d. ***5900.10*** *p439*
Rountree, J.; Quebec, 1858 ***9196.15*** *p40*
Rourk, John; Vermont, 1829-1913 ***5900.10*** *p429*
Rourke, Ann 73; Vermont, 1909 ***5900.10*** *p315*
Rourke, Catherine 70; Vermont, 1889 ***5900.10*** *p316*
Rourke, Catherine Conors 75; Vermont, 1883 ***5900.10*** *p461*
Rourke, Edward 59; Ontario, 1871 ***1823.28*** *p88*
Rourke, Elizabeth 70; Vermont, 1892 ***5900.10*** *p316*
Rourke, Ellen; Vermont, 1847-1930 ***5900.10*** *p82*
Rourke, Ellen McGarl 83; Vermont, 1913 ***5900.10*** *p134*
Rourke, Eugene J. 59; Vermont, 1913 ***5900.10*** *p316*
Rourke, Honora; Vermont, 1828-1882 ***5900.10*** *p316*
Rourke, James 65; Vermont, 1849 ***5900.10*** *p316*
Rourke, Jeremiah 50; Ontario, 1871 ***1823.15*** *p229*
Rourke, John 45; Ontario, 1871 ***1823.15*** *p229*
Rourke, John 62; Vermont, 1861 ***5900.10*** *p72*
Rourke, Lizzie A. 32; Vermont, 1885 ***5900.10*** *p559*
Rourke, Mary; Vermont, 1822-1901 ***5900.10*** *p315*
Rourke, Mary 68; Vermont, 1888 ***5900.10*** *p212*
Rourke, Mary 69; Vermont, 1875 ***5900.10*** *p72*
Rourke, Mary Ann; Vermont, 1850-1880 ***5900.10*** *p316*
Rourke, Michael 34; Vermont, 1886 ***5900.10*** *p461*
Rourke, Owen 84; Vermont, 1905 ***5900.10*** *p316*
Rourke, Patrick; New York, 1837 ***8197.10*** *p103*
Rourke, Patrick; New York, 1839 ***8197.10*** *p276*
Rourke, Patrick 60; Ontario, 1871 ***1823.15*** *p229*
Rourke, Patrick 74; Vermont, 1901 ***5900.10*** *p134*
Rourke, Thomas; New York, 1829 ***8197.10*** *p359*
Rourke, Thomas 36; Ontario, 1871 ***1823.15*** *p229*
Rourke, William 35; Ontario, 1871 ***1823.15*** *p229*
Rousby, Christopher; Maryland, 1685 ***1224.1*** *p50*
Rousby, John *SEE* Rousby, John
Rousby, John; Maryland, 1675 ***2524.55*** *p191*
Wife: Mary
Son: John
Rousby, John; Maryland, 1678 ***2524.55*** *p191*
Rousby, John; Maryland, 1679 ***2524.55*** *p191*
Wife: Mary
Son: John
Rousby, John; Maryland, 1680 ***2524.55*** *p191*
Rousby, Mary *SEE* Rousby, John
Rousby, Mary; Maryland, 1673 ***2524.55*** *p191*
Rouse, Adam; Virginia, 1667 ***6212.30*** *p37*
Rouse, Emanuel; Pennsylvania, 1777 ***4629.10*** *p16*
Rouse, Gravel; Maryland, 1658 ***2524.55*** *p191*
Rouse, Henry; Virginia, 1665-1666 ***6212.30*** *p24*
Rouse, Jeffry; Virginia, 1666 ***6212.30*** *p26*
Rouse, Joan; Virginia, 1667-1668 ***6212.30*** *p38*
Rouse, John; Virginia, 1667 ***6212.30*** *p37*
Rouse, John 79; Ontario, 1871 ***1823.15*** *p229*
Rouse, Michael; Virginia, 1667 ***6212.30*** *p37*
Rouse, Rich; Virginia, 1666 ***6212.30*** *p27*
Rouse, Samuell; Virginia, 1664 ***6212.30*** *p7*
Rouse, Thomas; Virginia, 1663 ***6212.30*** *p1*
Rouse, William 17; Maryland, 1774 ***1220.25*** *p77*
Roush, Mathias; Pennsylvania, 1779 ***4629.10*** *p38*
Rouske, Carl 60; Ontario, 1871 ***1823.28*** *p88*
Rouske, Vilamena 60; Ontario, 1871 ***1823.28*** *p88*
Rously, John *SEE* Rously, John
Rously, John; Maryland, 1675 ***2524.55*** *p191*
Wife: Mary
Son: John
Rously, Mary *SEE* Rously, John
Rousseau, Peter; New York, 1803 ***8197.10*** *p16*
Route, James; Maryland, 1681 ***2524.55*** *p191*
Route, Robert; South Carolina, 1725 ***1224.2*** *p99*
Routh, John 22; Nova Scotia, 1774 ***1220.25*** *p13*
Routledge, Charles 26; Ontario, 1871 ***1823.15*** *p229*
Routlidge, Diana 2 *SEE* Routlidge, William
Routlidge, Joseph 18 months *SEE* Routlidge, William
Routlidge, Sarah 27 *SEE* Routlidge, William
Routlidge, William 30; Nova Scotia, 1774 ***1220.25*** *p14*
Wife: Sarah 27
Child: Diana 2
Child: Joseph 18 months
Routly, Mathew 48; Ontario, 1871 ***1823.15*** *p229*
Roux, Earnest 9; Ontario, 1871 ***1823.28*** *p88*
Roux, John 51; Ontario, 1871 ***1823.28*** *p88*
Row, Ann; Maryland, 1670 ***2524.55*** *p191*
Row, Edmond; Maryland, 1665 ***2524.55*** *p191*
Row, Edward; Maryland, 1665 ***2524.55*** *p191*
Row, Isaack; Maryland, 1665 ***2524.55*** *p49*
Row, John 21; Philadelphia, 1775 ***1220.25*** *p107*
Row, Phillip; Maryland, 1670 ***2524.55*** *p191*
Row, Robert; Virginia, 1664 ***6212.30*** *p5*
Rowalewski, Joseph; Maryland, 1910 ***3259.35*** *p52*
Rowan, James; Pennsylvania, 1777 ***4629.10*** *p11*
Rowan, John; Canada, 1756-1760 ***4628.40*** *p45*
Rowan, John 34; Ontario, 1871 ***1823.28*** *p88*
Rowan, Matthew; North Carolina, 1775-1781 ***4628.40*** *p69*
Rowan, Thomas; Pennsylvania, 1777 ***4629.10*** *p16*
Rowan, Thos 45; Ontario, 1871 ***1823.28*** *p88*
Rowbotham, Joseph; Virginia, 1703 ***1224.2*** *p99*
Rowcliffe, James 30; Ontario, 1871 ***1823.15*** *p229*
Rowcliffe, John 35; Ontario, 1871 ***1823.15*** *p229*
Rowcliffe, John 60; Ontario, 1871 ***1823.15*** *p229*
Rowden, James 40; Ontario, 1871 ***1823.15*** *p229*
Rowden, Richard 29; Ontario, 1871 ***1823.15*** *p229*
Rowden, Thomas 17; Philadelphia, 1774 ***1220.25*** *p4*
Rowe, Allice E. 1; Ontario, 1861 ***2896.25*** *p21*

Rowe, Catherine 27; Ontario, 1861 ***2896.25*** *p21*
Rowe, Charles 19; Ontario, 1861 ***2896.25*** *p25*
Rowe, Charles 51; Ontario, 1871 ***1823.15*** *p229*
Rowe, Daniel 21; Ontario, 1871 ***1823.22*** *p138*
Rowe, Daniel 48; Ontario, 1871 ***1823.22*** *p138*
Rowe, Edmond; Maryland, 1665 ***2524.55*** *p191*
Rowe, Edward 13; Ontario, 1861 ***2896.25*** *p25*
Rowe, Edward 37; Ontario, 1871 ***1823.22*** *p138*
Rowe, Eleanor 36; Ontario, 1861 ***2896.27*** *p27*
Rowe, Ellen 28; Ontario, 1861 ***2896.25*** *p21*
Rowe, Frederick 43; Ontario, 1871 ***1823.22*** *p138*
Rowe, George 7; Ontario, 1861 ***2896.25*** *p15*
Rowe, George 38; Ontario, 1871 ***1823.22*** *p138*
Rowe, George 38; Ontario, 1871 ***1823.28*** *p88*
Rowe, Hannah A. 33; Ontario, 1861 ***2896.25*** *p15*
Rowe, Henry 5; Ontario, 1861 ***2896.25*** *p15*
Rowe, Henry 34; Ontario, 1871 ***1823.15*** *p229*
Rowe, Henry 60; Ontario, 1871 ***1823.22*** *p138*
Rowe, Hiram 2; Ontario, 1861 ***2896.25*** *p15*
Rowe, James; New Brunswick, n.d. ***1224.3*** *p67*
Rowe, James 19; Vermont, 1873 ***5900.10*** *p295*
Rowe, James 27; Ontario, 1871 ***1823.22*** *p138*
Rowe, Joanna 65; Vermont, 1894 ***5900.10*** *p295*
Rowe, Johanner 3; Vermont, 1890 ***5900.10*** *p295*
Rowe, John; Maryland, 1681 ***2524.55*** *p191*
Rowe, John; New York, 1806 ***8197.10*** *p32*
Rowe, John; New York, 1839 ***8197.10*** *p134*
Rowe, John 3; Ontario, 1861 ***2896.25*** *p15*
Rowe, John 43; Ontario, 1871 ***1823.15*** *p229*
Rowe, John 48; Ontario, 1871 ***1823.15*** *p229*
Rowe, John 70; Ontario, 1861 ***2896.25*** *p25*
Rowe, John 78; Ontario, 1871 ***1823.22*** *p138*
Rowe, Joseph 15; Ontario, 1861 ***2896.25*** *p25*
Rowe, Joseph 61; Ontario, 1861 ***2896.25*** *p15*
Rowe, Lucy 70; Ontario, 1871 ***1823.22*** *p138*
Rowe, Marcus 55; Ontario, 1871 ***1823.22*** *p138*
Rowe, Margaret 4; Ontario, 1861 ***2896.25*** *p21*
Rowe, Mary 38; Ontario, 1871 ***1823.22*** *p138*
Rowe, Patrick E.; Vermont, 1815-1909 ***5900.10*** *p295*
Rowe, Rebecca 14; Ontario, 1861 ***2896.27*** *p27*
Rowe, Richard 52; Ontario, 1871 ***1823.28*** *p88*
Rowe, Samuel 43; Ontario, 1871 ***1823.28*** *p88*
Rowe, Thomas 40; Ontario, 1871 ***1823.15*** *p229*
Rowe, Thomas 45; Ontario, 1871 ***1823.15*** *p229*
Rowe, Thomas 45; Ontario, 1871 ***1823.22*** *p138*
Rowe, Thomas 46; Ontario, 1871 ***1823.28*** *p88*
Rowe, Thomas S.; Vermont, 1849-1900 ***5900.10*** *p295*
Rowe, Wesley 1; Ontario, 1861 ***2896.25*** *p21*
Rowe, William 33; Ontario, 1871 ***1823.22*** *p138*
Rowe, William 39; Ontario, 1871 ***1823.28*** *p88*
Rowe, William 67; Vermont, 1867 ***5900.10*** *p295*
Rowel, William 58; Ontario, 1871 ***1823.15*** *p229*
Rowell, Annie E. Winters; Vermont, 1854-1924 ***5900.10*** *p336*
Rowell, George; Maryland, 1660 ***2524.55*** *p191*
Rowell, Jno; Virginia, 1669-1670 ***6212.30*** *p41*
Rowell, John; Virginia, 1672 ***6212.30*** *p49*
Rowell, Mary 50; Ontario, 1871 ***1823.22*** *p138*
Rowen, Ellen Burke; Vermont, 1860-1905 ***5900.10*** *p203*
Rowen, Mary Sinon 55; Vermont, 1920 ***5900.10*** *p206*
Rowen, Patrick; Vermont, 1846-1906 ***5900.10*** *p203*
Rowen, Richard W.; Vermont, 1860-1935 ***5900.10*** *p206*
Rowen, Sophia; Vermont, 1865-1928 ***5900.10*** *p43*
Rowestown, John 28; Ontario, 1871 ***1823.15*** *p229*
Rowin, James; Philadelphia, 1793 ***4629.10*** *p83*
Rowland, Charles 21; Maryland, 1774 ***1220.25*** *p73*
Rowland, Charles 23; Virginia, 1774 ***1220.25*** *p94*
Rowland, Edward; Maryland, 1681 ***2524.55*** *p191*
Rowland, Elinour; Maryland, 1659 ***2524.55*** *p175*
Rowland, Elizabeth; Maryland, 1665 ***2524.55*** *p191*
Rowland, Ellen; Vermont, 1900 ***5900.10*** *p426*
Rowland, Henry; Maryland, 1681 ***2524.55*** *p191*
Rowland, Hugh; Maryland, 1651 ***2524.55*** *p191*
Rowland, James 22; Maryland, 1775 ***1220.25*** *p100*
Rowland, John; New England, 1714 ***1224.2*** *p99*
Rowland, Peter; Virginia, 1674 ***1224.1*** *p50*
Rowland, Thomas; Sacramento, California, 1853 ***1224.3*** *p67*
Rowland, Thomas 37; Maryland, 1775 ***1220.25*** *p104*
Rowlands, James 29; New England, 1774 ***1220.25*** *p56*
Rowlandson, Richard 40; New York, 1774 ***1220.25*** *p24*
Rowlatt, James 23; Virginia, 1774 ***1220.25*** *p53*
Rowlen, Barbery 5; Ontario, 1861 ***2896.25*** *p60*
Rowlen, Charles 31; Ontario, 1861 ***2896.25*** *p60*
Rowlen, Margaret Ann 12; Ontario, 1861 ***2896.25*** *p60*
Rowlen, Mary Ann 67; Ontario, 1861 ***2896.25*** *p60*
Rowlen, William H. 10; Ontario, 1861 ***2896.25*** *p60*
Rowles, Allice; Maryland, 1659 ***2524.55*** *p191*
Rowles, Christopher; Maryland, 1649 ***2524.55*** *p191*
Rowles, Christopher; Maryland, 1659 ***2524.55*** *p191*
Rowles, James; Virginia, 1667 ***6212.30*** *p37*
Rowles, Jaspher; Virginia, 1665 ***6212.30*** *p20*
Rowles, Peter; Maryland, 1670 ***2524.55*** *p191*
Rowles, Walter; Maryland, 1670 ***2524.55*** *p191*
Rowley, Barrett; Vermont, 1864-1907 ***5900.10*** *p323*
Rowley, Elizabeth; Maryland, 1663 ***2524.55*** *p191*
Rowley, Elizabeth; Vermont, 1838-1923 ***5900.10*** *p323*
Rowley, George; Philadelphia, 1802 ***1224.3*** *p67*
Rowley, Hanora 29; Vermont, 1860 ***5900.10*** *p227*
Rowley, John 29; Virginia, 1774 ***1220.25*** *p90*
Rowley, John 70; Vermont, 1871 ***5900.10*** *p227*
Rowley, Joseph; Pennsylvania, 1845 ***6058.10*** *p21*
Rowley, Mary; Vermont, 1831-1909 ***5900.10*** *p530*
Rowley, Patrick; Vermont, 1836-1918 ***5900.10*** *p323*
Rowley, Teresa; Vermont, n.d. ***5900.10*** *p323*
Rowlson, Matthew; Virginia, 1688 ***1224.1*** *p50*
Rowly, Christopher; Maryland, 1656 ***2524.55*** *p191*
Rowly, Margret; Virginia, 1667 ***6212.30*** *p35*
Rowly, Mosses; Virginia, 1667 ***6212.30*** *p35*
Rowly, Susan; Virginia, 1666-1667 ***6212.30*** *p34*
Rownder, Joshua; Virginia, 1667-1668 ***6212.30*** *p39*
Roworth, John 21; Baltimore, 1775 ***1220.25*** *p118*
Rows, John; Maryland, 1677 ***2524.55*** *p191*
Rowse, Math.; Maryland, 1658 ***2524.55*** *p191*
Rowse, Thomas; Virginia, 1665 ***6212.30*** *p18*
Rowtcliff, Thomas 60; Ontario, 1871 ***1823.15*** *p229*
Rowzee, Lewis; Virginia, 1655 ***1224.1*** *p50*
Rowzee, Ralph; Virginia, 1655 ***1224.1*** *p50*
Roxberry, Edgar; Virginia, 1666 ***6212.30*** *p25*
Roxburgh, Alexander; Ontario, 1847 ***1640.13*** *p107*
Roxbury, James; Virginia, 1667-1668 ***6212.30*** *p38*
Roxby, John; Virginia, 1666-1667 ***6212.30*** *p33*
Roxby, Margret; Virginia, 1663 ***6212.30*** *p1*
Roxby, Michaell; Virginia, 1666 ***6212.30*** *p26*
Roxell, Miles; Virginia, 1667-1668 ***6212.30*** *p39*
Roxford, James; Virginia, 1664-1665 ***6212.30*** *p16*
Roxford, Jean; Virginia, 1667 ***6212.30*** *p36*
Roxford, Tho; Virginia, 1665-1666 ***6212.30*** *p25*
Roy, Captain; Quebec, 1857 ***9196.15*** *p18*
Roy, Captain; Quebec, 1857 ***9196.15*** *p25*
Roy, Mr.; Quebec, 1857 ***9196.15*** *p20*
Roy, Mr.; Quebec, 1858 ***9196.15*** *p44*
Roy, A.; Portland, Maine, 1858 ***9196.15*** *p29*
Roy, A.; Quebec, 1858 ***9196.15*** *p42*
Roy, Alexander; New York, 1794 ***8197.10*** *p4*
Roy, Ebinezar 35; Ontario, 1871 ***1823.15*** *p229*
Roy, Elizabeth; Virginia, 1666-1667 ***6212.30*** *p34*
Roy, James; Augusta, Georgia, 1818 ***1640.10*** *p181*
Roy, James; Windsor, Ontario, 1874 ***1640.13*** *p108*
Roy, John; New York, 1803 ***8197.10*** *p16*
Roy, Mary; Vermont, 1853-1929 ***5900.10*** *p593*
Roy, Mary Hagan 64; Vermont, 1900 ***5900.10*** *p608*
Roy, William; New York, 1828 ***8197.10*** *p350*
Roy, William 39; Maryland, 1773-1774 ***1220.25*** *p33*
Roy, Xavier; New York, 1840 ***8197.10*** *p188*
Royall, Edmond; Maryland, 1673 ***2524.55*** *p191*
Royall, Edmund; Maryland, 1665 ***2524.55*** *p192*
Royall, Edmund; Maryland, 1672 ***2524.55*** *p191*
Royall, Edward; Maryland, 1679 ***2524.55*** *p192*
Royall, Elizabeth; Maryland, 1674 ***2524.55*** *p192*
Royall, Isabell; Maryland, 1673 ***2524.55*** *p192*
Royall, Isabella; Maryland, 1679 ***2524.55*** *p192*
Royall, Jane; Maryland, 1664 ***2524.55*** *p192*
Royall, Joseph; Boston, 1710 ***1224.2*** *p99*
Royall, Thomas; Maryland, 1670 ***2524.55*** *p192*
Royle, Margaret; Maryland, 1668 ***2524.55*** *p192*
Royle, William; Virginia, 1852 ***1224.3*** *p67*
Royse, John; Died enroute, 1686 ***1224.1*** *p50*
Roystan, Cathrine; Vermont, 1854-1857 ***5900.10*** *p604*
Roystan, Cathrine Curley; Vermont, 1819-1883 ***5900.10*** *p604*
Roystan, Eliza 47; Vermont, 1891 ***5900.10*** *p604*
Roystan, George; Vermont, 1808 ***5900.10*** *p604*
Roystan, George; Vermont, 1856-1857 ***5900.10*** *p604*
Roystan, George P.; Vermont, 1858 ***5900.10*** *p604*
Roystan, James E. 43; Vermont, 1893 ***5900.10*** *p604*
Roystan, Mary J.; Vermont, 1852-1915 ***5900.10*** *p406*
Roystan, Mary L. O'Hear; Vermont, 1887 ***5900.10*** *p604*
Roystan, Michael; Vermont, 1847-1921 ***5900.10*** *p603*
Roystan, Rose O'Hear; Vermont, 1862-1949 ***5900.10*** *p604*
Royston, Catharine; Vermont, 1808-1880 ***5900.10*** *p605*
Royston, Mary; Maryland, 1678 ***2524.55*** *p192*
Royston, Robert; Maryland, 1661 ***2524.55*** *p192*
Royston, William; Vermont, 1842-1927 ***5900.10*** *p603*
Rozenfeld, Julian; New York, 1839 ***8197.10*** *p134*
Rozler, Anna Maria Elis; Port uncertain, 1792 ***2856.30*** *p369*
Rozmus, Anna; Maryland, 1910 ***3259.35*** *p52*
Roznamak, Frank; Maryland, 1910 ***3259.35*** *p52*
Rozynkowski, Julian K.; New York, 1840 ***8197.10*** *p188*
Rte, James; Virginia, 1665-1666 ***6212.30*** *p21*
Ruane, Mary; Vermont, 1828-1898 ***5900.10*** *p582*
Ruane, Mary 80; Vermont, 1874 ***5900.10*** *p465*
Rub, Johann; America, 1787 ***2856.30*** *p369*
Rub, Nicolas; Port uncertain, 1784 ***2856.30*** *p369*
Rubardo, Defondina; Philadelphia, 1793 ***4629.10*** *p67*
Rubb, Jakob; America, 1752 ***2856.30*** *p369*
With wife & 3 children
Rubb, John; Pennsylvania, 1776 ***4629.10*** *p53*
Rubeck, . . .; Port uncertain, 1751 ***2856.30*** *p369*
Ruben, Christian; New York, 1839 ***8197.10*** *p276*
Ruben, George; New York, 1840 ***8197.10*** *p188*
Rubenacker, Johann; Port uncertain, 1764 ***2856.30*** *p369*
Rubenacker, Johann; Port uncertain, 1764 ***2856.30*** *p372*
Rubennich, Henrich; Port uncertain, 1741 ***2856.30*** *p372*
Rubidge, Thomas 37; Maryland, 1774 ***1220.25*** *p79*
Rubin, Eva; Port uncertain, 1794 ***2856.30*** *p372*
Rublein, Anna Elisabeth; Port uncertain, 1752 ***2856.30*** *p372*
Rublin, Anna Elisabeth; Port uncertain, 1752 ***2856.30*** *p372*
Rubridge, Mr.; Quebec, 1858 ***9196.15*** *p38*
Rubsom, Jacob; Pennsylvania, 1777 ***4629.10*** *p13*
Ruby, Anthelme; New York, 1834 ***8197.10*** *p275*
Ruch, Peter; America, 1753 ***2856.30*** *p369*
Ruck, . . .; Port uncertain, 1754 ***2856.30*** *p369*
Ruck, Adam; Port uncertain, 1781 ***2856.30*** *p369*
Ruck, Martin; America, 1754 ***2856.30*** *p360*
Ruckenbrodt, Barbara; Port uncertain, 1770 ***2856.30*** *p369*
Ruckhenbrodt, Philipp; Port uncertain, 1746 ***2856.30*** *p369*
Ruckstoll, Barbara; America, 1725 ***2856.30*** *p372*
Ruckstoll, Barbara; America, 1725 ***2856.30*** *p373*
Ruckstoll, Barbara; America, 1754 ***2856.30*** *p373*
Ruckstoll, Hendrycke; America, 1725 ***2856.30*** *p373*
Ruckstoll, Hendrycke; America, 1754 ***2856.30*** *p373*
Ruckstoll, Olive; America, 1725 ***2856.30*** *p373*
Ruckstoll, Olive; America, 1754 ***2856.30*** *p373*
Ruckstoll, Salomon, Sr.; America, 1725 ***2856.30*** *p369*
Ruckstoll, Salomon, Sr.; America, 1754 ***2856.30*** *p369*
Ruckstoll, Salomon, Jr.; America, 1725 ***2856.30*** *p369*
Ruckstoll, Salomon, Jr.; America, 1754 ***2856.30*** *p369*
Ruckstuhl, Anna Barbara; America, 1725 ***2856.30*** *p372*
Ruckstuhl, Anna Barbara; America, 1754 ***2856.30*** *p372*
Ruckstuhl, Barbara; America, 1725 ***2856.30*** *p372*
Ruckstuhl, Barbara; America, 1725 ***2856.30*** *p373*
Ruckstuhl, Barbara; America, 1754 ***2856.30*** *p373*
Ruckstuhl, Hendrycke; America, 1725 ***2856.30*** *p373*
Ruckstuhl, Hendrycke; America, 1754 ***2856.30*** *p373*
Ruckstuhl, Maria Barbara; America, 1725 ***2856.30*** *p372*
Ruckstuhl, Maria Barbara; America, 1754 ***2856.30*** *p372*
Ruckstuhl, Olive; America, 1725 ***2856.30*** *p373*
Ruckstuhl, Olive; America, 1754 ***2856.30*** *p373*
Rudd, Amos 25; Philadelphia, 1775 ***1220.25*** *p9*
Rudd, Charles; Maryland, 1752 ***1224.2*** *p99*
Rudd, John 53; Ontario, 1871 ***1823.15*** *p230*
Rudd, Stephen; New York, 1807 ***8197.10*** *p49*
Rudd, William 51; Ontario, 1871 ***1823.15*** *p230*
Ruddell, George 45; Ontario, 1871 ***1823.15*** *p230*
Rudden, Garrett; Maryland, 1661 ***2524.55*** *p192*
With 3 sons
Wife: Mary
Rudden, Mary *SEE* Rudden, Garrett
Rudder, Thomas; Maryland, 1661 ***2524.55*** *p192*
Ruddoch, Thomas; Tobago, West Indies, 1790 ***1640.13*** *p108*
Ruddy, John; Springfield, Massachusetts, 1856 ***1224.3*** *p68*
Ruddy, Patrick 67; Ontario, 1871 ***1823.28*** *p88*
Ruden, Jaques; New York, 1803 ***8197.10*** *p16*
Rudfearne, Margaret; Maryland, 1660 ***2524.55*** *p192*
Rudge, Jonathan; New Orleans, 1805 ***1224.3*** *p68*
Rudhall, Jno; Virginia, 1665-1666 ***6212.30*** *p23*
Rudhart, Benedikt; Port uncertain, 1763 ***2856.30*** *p370*
Rudi, Ernst; America, 1727 ***2856.30*** *p370*
Rudinger, Wilhelm; Port uncertain, 1793 ***2856.30*** *p373*
Rudisilli, Mr.; America, 1752 ***2856.30*** *p483*
Rudisilli, Anna Barbara; America, 1751 ***2856.30*** *p370*
Rudisilli, Philipp; America, 1727 ***2856.30*** *p370*
With wife
Rudisillie, Johann Jakob; America, 1752 ***2856.30*** *p370*
Rudisillie, Johann Jakob; Port uncertain, 1761 ***2856.30*** *p370*
With wife
Rudkin, Thomas 28; Virginia, 1774 ***1220.25*** *p75*
Rudmicki, Antoni; Maryland, 1910 ***3259.35*** *p52*
Rudolph, Heinrich; Port uncertain, 1784 ***2856.30*** *p370*
Rudolph, John; Pennsylvania, 1777 ***4629.10*** *p24*
Rudolph, Magdalena; Port uncertain, 1772 ***2856.30*** *p370*
Rudolph, Mathes; Port uncertain, 1764 ***2856.30*** *p370*
With wife & 6 children
Rudolph, Wendel; Port uncertain, 1796 ***2856.30*** *p370*
Rudsdell, Joseph 15; Philadelphia, 1774 ***1220.25*** *p81*
Rudt, Ernst; America, 1727 ***2856.30*** *p370*
Rudty, Konrad; America, 1747 ***2856.30*** *p370*
Rudzinski, Frank; Maryland, 1910 ***3259.35*** *p52*
Rudzynski, Adam; Maryland, 1910 ***3259.35*** *p52*

Rue, Benjamin; Pennsylvania, 1777 ***4629.10*** *p15*
Rue, Thomas; Pennsylvania, 1777 ***4629.10*** *p10*
Ruecch, Regine; Port uncertain, 1712 ***2856.30*** *p370*
Ruef, Georg Friedrich; America, 1764 ***2856.30*** *p370*
With wife
Ruef, Jerg Josef; Port uncertain, 1723 ***2856.30*** *p370*
Rueff, Jacob, The Younger; Port uncertain, 1752 ***2856.30*** *p370*
Rueff, Ulrich; Port uncertain, 1684 ***2856.30*** *p370*
Rueff, Ulrich; Port uncertain, 1714 ***2856.30*** *p370*
Ruegerin, Mrs. Jost; Port uncertain, 1749 ***2856.30*** *p370*
With daughter
Ruesch, Regine; Port uncertain, 1712 ***2856.30*** *p370*
Rueserin, Barbara; Port uncertain, 1744 ***2856.30*** *p370*
Ruess, Hans; Port uncertain, 1692 ***2856.30*** *p370*
Ruf, Adolph; New York, 1807 ***8197.10*** *p48*
Ruf, Catharina; Port uncertain, 1745 ***2856.30*** *p370*
Ruf, Mrs. J. Georg; Port uncertain, 1774 ***2856.30*** *p370*
Ruf, Jacob; Port uncertain, 1796 ***2856.30*** *p370*
Ruf, Johann; Port uncertain, 1745 ***2856.30*** *p370*
Ruf, Michael; America, 1764 ***2856.30*** *p370*
Ruf, Michael; Port uncertain, 1795 ***2856.30*** *p370*
Ruf, Michael; Port uncertain, 1796 ***2856.30*** *p370*
Rufer, Johann; Port uncertain, 1793 ***2856.30*** *p370*
Ruff, A. 50; Kansas, 1892-1910 ***9079.10*** *p45*
Ruff, Andrew, Jr. 26; Kansas, 1896-1910 ***9079.10*** *p9*
Ruff, Anna Maria; America, 1743 ***2856.30*** *p370*
Ruff, Catherine 46; Kansas, 1910 ***9079.10*** *p42*
Ruff, Daniel; Port uncertain, 1774 ***2856.30*** *p370*
Ruff, Daniel; Port uncertain, 1778 ***2856.30*** *p370*
Ruff, Eva E. 22; Kansas, 1899-1910 ***9079.10*** *p9*
Ruff, Friedrich; Port uncertain, 1761 ***2856.30*** *p370*
Ruff, Georg; Port uncertain, 1752 ***2856.30*** *p370*
Ruff, George 20; Kansas, 1910 ***9079.10*** *p45*
Ruff, George 53; Kansas, 1910 ***9079.10*** *p42*
Ruff, Jacob; Port uncertain, 1744 ***2856.30*** *p370*
With wife & daughter
Ruff, Jacob, Jr.; America, 1738 ***2856.30*** *p370*
With wife & 5 children
Ruff, Johann Daniel; Port uncertain, 1751 ***2856.30*** *p370*
Ruff, Maria Barbara; Port uncertain, 1744 ***2856.30*** *p370*
Ruff, Sofia 51; Kansas, 1892-1910 ***9079.10*** *p45*
Ruffie, James; Ontario, 1871 ***1823.28*** *p88*
Rugel, Firedrich; Port uncertain, 1745 ***2856.30*** *p373*
With wife & 2 children
Rugel, Friedrich; Port uncertain, 1745 ***2856.30*** *p373*
With wife & 2 children
Ruger, Anna Maria; Port uncertain, 1747 ***2856.30*** *p373*
Rugg, Ellen; Vermont, 1855-1955 ***5900.10*** *p379*
Rugge, Honoh; Virginia, 1672 ***6212.30*** *p50*
Ruggles, Timothy; Massachusetts, n.d. ***1224.2*** *p99*
Ruggles, Timothy; Nova Scotia, 1796 ***1224.2*** *p99*
Rugutin, Elis. Margarete; Port uncertain, 1788 ***2856.30*** *p370*
Ruhl, Charles; New York, 1837 ***8197.10*** *p102*
Ruhlin, Johann Valentin; Port uncertain, 1768 ***2856.30*** *p373*
Ruin, Winniford 43; Vermont, 1877 ***5900.10*** *p205*
Rulance, Alexander; Maryland, 1910 ***3259.35*** *p52*
Rule, Anthony; Virginia, 1671-1672 ***6212.30*** *p47*
Rule, Thomas 27; Maryland, 1773-1774 ***1220.25*** *p33*
Rule, William; Maryland, 1665 ***2524.55*** *p192*
With wife
Rull, Adam; Maryland, 1910 ***3259.35*** *p52*
Ruller, Mathes; Port uncertain, 1786 ***2856.30*** *p373*
Ruller, Mathies; Port uncertain, 1784 ***2856.30*** *p373*
Rulski, Marie; Maryland, 1910 ***3259.35*** *p52*
Rumanski, Peter; Maryland, 1910 ***3259.35*** *p53*
Rumball, Benjamin 52; Ontario, 1871 ***1823.15*** *p230*
Rumball, Ebenezer 41; Ontario, 1871 ***1823.15*** *p230*
Rumball, Samuel 49; Ontario, 1871 ***1823.15*** *p230*
Rumball, William 42; Ontario, 1871 ***1823.15*** *p230*
Rumbi, Johann Nickel; Port uncertain, 1764 ***2856.30*** *p370*
Rumbold, Thomas; Boston, 1727 ***1224.2*** *p99*
Rumbrowski, Joseph; Maryland, 1910 ***3259.35*** *p53*
Rumbunck, Annie; Maryland, 1910 ***3259.35*** *p53*
Rumford, William 22; Maryland, 1775 ***1220.25*** *p108*
Rumley, Johan; New York, 1778 ***1224.2*** *p99*
Rumly, Jno; Virginia, 1679 ***6212.30*** *p54*
Rummel, Georg; Port uncertain, 1790 ***2856.30*** *p370*
Rummel, Jaj; America, 1750 ***2856.30*** *p370*
Rummel, Johann Jakob; America, 1750 ***2856.30*** *p371*
With wife & child
Rummel, Jorg Philipp; America, 1750 ***2856.30*** *p371*
Rummel, Michael; America, 1749 ***2856.30*** *p371*
Rumming, I. 29; Alaska, 1916 ***9196.1*** *p44*
Rumming, I. 29; Whitehorse, Yukon, 1916 ***9196.1*** *p44*
Rummlin, Anna Catharina; Port uncertain, 1792 ***2856.30*** *p371*
Rumner, Mury 76; Ontario, 1871 ***1823.22*** *p138*
Rumper, Elizabeth; Maryland, 1665 ***2524.55*** *p192*
Rumsey, James; Maryland, 1678 ***2524.55*** *p192*
Rumsie, Eliz.; Maryland, 1660 ***2524.55*** *p192*
Runals, Sarah A. 20; Ontario, 1861 ***2896.27*** *p68*
Runanski, Peter; Maryland, 1910 ***3259.35*** *p53*
Runcie, John T.; New York, 1840 ***8197.10*** *p189*
Runciman, Andrew 54; Ontario, 1871 ***1823.22*** *p138*
Runciman, David 35; Ontario, 1871 ***1823.15*** *p230*
Runciman, Robert 47; Ontario, 1871 ***1823.15*** *p230*
Runciman, William 45; Ontario, 1871 ***1823.22*** *p138*
Runcimon, Anges 49; Ontario, 1871 ***1823.15*** *p230*
Runckel, Johann Jakob; America, 1748 ***2856.30*** *p371*
Runckel, Nikol; Port uncertain, 1743 ***2856.30*** *p371*
Runckel, Wendel; America, 1749 ***2856.30*** *p371*
Rundle, Abel 13; Ontario, 1861 ***2896.27*** *p57*
Rundle, Abraham 44; Ontario, 1861 ***2896.27*** *p51*
Rundle, Ann 38; Ontario, 1861 ***2896.27*** *p51*
Rundle, Caroline A. 14; Ontario, 1861 ***2896.27*** *p51*
Rundle, Daniel; Philadelphia, 1795 ***1224.2*** *p99*
Rundle, Elen E. 9; Ontario, 1861 ***2896.27*** *p51*
Rundle, Elizabeth 36; Ontario, 1861 ***2896.27*** *p57*
Rundle, Elizabeth Ann 14; Ontario, 1861 ***2896.27*** *p57*
Rundle, Henry 52; Ontario, 1871 ***1823.22*** *p138*
Rundle, Mariah J. 12; Ontario, 1861 ***2896.27*** *p51*
Rundle, Richard; Pennsylvania, 1777 ***4629.10*** *p21*
Rundle, Richard; Pennsylvania, 1779 ***4629.10*** *p41*
Rundle, Stephen 50; Ontario, 1871 ***1823.22*** *p138*
Rundle, William 1; Ontario, 1861 ***2896.27*** *p51*
Rundle, William 38; Ontario, 1861 ***2896.27*** *p57*
Runer, Lewis; Pennsylvania, 1785 ***4629.10*** *p48*
Runnalls, John 64; Ontario, 1871 ***1823.22*** *p139*
Runnalls, Thomas 48; Ontario, 1871 ***1823.22*** *p139*
Runnells, Oliver 60; Ontario, 1871 ***1823.22*** *p139*
Running, Tom 30; British Columbia, 1917 ***9196.1*** *p52*
Running, Tom 30; Juneau, Alaska, 1917 ***9196.1*** *p52*
Runshort, Francis; Virginia, 1672 ***6212.30*** *p51*
Runtz, Carilina 14; Ontario, 1871 ***1823.28*** *p88*
Runtz, William 48; Ontario, 1871 ***1823.28*** *p88*
Runze, Johann; America, 1777 ***2856.30*** *p373*
Ruoff, Johann Georg; America, 1751 ***2856.30*** *p371*
Rupert, Gottfried; Port uncertain, 1740 ***2856.30*** *p371*
Rupert, Jakob; America, 1740 ***2856.30*** *p371*
With wife & 3 children
Rupp, Miss; Port uncertain, 1795 ***2856.30*** *p371*
Rupp, Anna Christina; Port uncertain, 1787 ***2856.30*** *p371*
Rupp, Bernard; America, 1744 ***2856.30*** *p371*
With wife & children
Rupp, Christian; America, 1747 ***2856.30*** *p371*
Rupp, Christian; Port uncertain, 1747 ***2856.30*** *p371*
Rupp, Franz Ludwig; America, 1734 ***2856.30*** *p371*
Rupp, Jakob; Port uncertain, 1796 ***2856.30*** *p371*
Rupp, Martin; New York, 1835 ***8197.10*** *p316*
Rupp, Michael; New York, 1839 ***8197.10*** *p134*
Rupp, Weiprecht; America, 1749 ***2856.30*** *p371*
With wife
Ruppele, August Leonhard; America, 1772 ***2856.30*** *p373*
Ruppele, August Leonhard; Port uncertain, 1771 ***2856.30*** *p373*
Ruppele, Johann Georg; America, 1768 ***2856.30*** *p362*
Ruppenthal, Franz Jakob; Port uncertain, 1783 ***2856.30*** *p372*
With 3 sons & 4 daughters
Ruppert, Anna Christina; Port uncertain, 1791 ***2856.30*** *p372*
Ruppert, Johann Henrich; America, 1766 ***2856.30*** *p372*
Rupperter, Johann Philipp; America, 1789 ***2856.30*** *p372*
Rupperter, Johann Philipp; Port uncertain, 1774 ***2856.30*** *p372*
Rupperti, Leonard; Port uncertain, 1754 ***2856.30*** *p372*
Rupprecht, Anna Catharina; Port uncertain, 1765 ***2856.30*** *p372*
Ruprecht, Benoni; Port uncertain, 1788 ***2856.30*** *p372*
Ruprecht, John; New York, 1834 ***8197.10*** *p75*
Ruren, Miss; Quebec, 1857 ***9196.15*** *p22*
Rusakey, Michael; Maryland, 1910 ***3259.35*** *p53*
Rusaw, Catherine 30; Ontario, 1861 ***2896.26*** *p39*
Rusaw, Mary 2; Ontario, 1861 ***2896.26*** *p39*
Rusaw, Sophronia 4; Ontario, 1861 ***2896.26*** *p39*
Rusbach, Henrich; Port uncertain, 1764 ***2856.30*** *p372*
Rusch, Peter Martin; Port uncertain, 1794 ***2856.30*** *p372*
Rusch, Peter Martin; Port uncertain, 1824 ***2856.30*** *p372*
Ruschel, Friedrich; Port uncertain, 1752 ***2856.30*** *p372*
Ruschinyki, Mary; Maryland, 1910 ***3259.35*** *p53*
Ruse, John 46; Ontario, 1871 ***1823.22*** *p139*
Rusell, Thomas 28; Ontario, 1871 ***1823.15*** *p230*
Rush, A. 4; Ontario, 1861 ***2896.25*** *p51*
Rush, Angenora 6; Ontario, 1861 ***2896.25*** *p51*
Rush, Benjamin; Pennsylvania, 1777 ***4629.10*** *p11*
Rush, C. 2; Ontario, 1861 ***2896.25*** *p51*
Rush, Daniel F. 32; Ontario, 1861 ***2896.25*** *p51*
Rush, David 37; Ontario, 1861 ***2896.25*** *p51*
Rush, Edward; Vermont, 1823-1886 ***5900.10*** *p183*
Rush, Edward J.; Vermont, 1856-1862 ***5900.10*** *p183*
Rush, George L.; Vermont, 1858-1861 ***5900.10*** *p183*
Rush, Hiram 28; Ontario, 1861 ***2896.25*** *p51*
Rush, James C. 67; Ontario, 1861 ***2896.25*** *p51*
Rush, Jane 32; Ontario, 1861 ***2896.25*** *p51*
Rush, Joanna Barrett; Vermont, 1835-1921 ***5900.10*** *p183*
Rush, John 67; Ontario, 1861 ***2896.25*** *p53*
Rush, L. 23; Ontario, 1861 ***2896.25*** *p51*
Rush, Laughlin; New York, 1839 ***8197.10*** *p134*
Rush, Luke 49; Ontario, 1871 ***1823.15*** *p230*
Rush, M. A. 12; Ontario, 1861 ***2896.25*** *p53*
Rush, M. A. 25; Ontario, 1861 ***2896.25*** *p51*
Rush, M. J. 8; Ontario, 1861 ***2896.25*** *p51*
Rush, Mary; Vermont, 1868-1954 ***5900.10*** *p136*
Rush, Patrick; New York, 1831 ***8197.10*** *p367*
Rush, S. J. 6; Ontario, 1861 ***2896.25*** *p51*
Rush, Warren S. 52; Ontario, 1871 ***1823.22*** *p139*
Rush, William; Pennsylvania, 1777 ***4629.10*** *p8*
Rush, William; Pennsylvania, 1779 ***4629.10*** *p36*
Rushang, William; Maryland, 1910 ***3259.35*** *p53*
Rushell, Mr.; Quebec, 1857 ***9196.15*** *p17*
Rushell, Mrs.; Quebec, 1857 ***9196.15*** *p17*
Rushell, Jno; Virginia, 1666-1667 ***6212.30*** *p32*
Rushells, George; Maryland, 1671 ***2524.55*** *p192*
Rusher, Daniell; Virginia, 1659 ***1224.1*** *p50*
Rusher, George; New York, 1808 ***8197.10*** *p54*
Rushforth, William; New York, 1802 ***8197.10*** *p24*
Rushton, William L.; New York, 1817-1834 ***8197.10*** *p306*
Rushy, Mary; Maryland, 1681 ***2524.55*** *p192*
Rusill, William 42; Ontario, 1871 ***1823.15*** *p230*
Rusin, Fulryel; Maryland, 1910 ***3259.35*** *p53*
Rusin, Jozefa; Maryland, 1910 ***3259.35*** *p53*
Rusinsky, Andrew; Maryland, 1910 ***3259.35*** *p53*
Rusk, Charles 57; Ontario, 1871 ***1823.28*** *p88*
Rusk, Hugh; Baltimore, 1829 ***1224.3*** *p68*
Rusk, James 28; Ontario, 1871 ***1823.28*** *p88*
Ruska, Frank; Maryland, 1910 ***3259.35*** *p53*
Ruske, Peter; Virginia, 1656 ***1224.1*** *p50*
Ruskey, Fredrick 45; Ontario, 1871 ***1823.28*** *p88*
Ruski, James; Maryland, 1910 ***3259.35*** *p53*
Rusoler, John 32; Ontario, 1871 ***1823.28*** *p88*
Russ, Anton; Port uncertain, 1795 ***2856.30*** *p372*
Russ, Bertha 29; British Columbia, 1917 ***9196.1*** *p69*
Russ, Bertha 29; Washington, 1917 ***9196.1*** *p69*
Russ, Christian; New York, 1840 ***8197.10*** *p188*
Russ, Friedrich; Port uncertain, 1751 ***2856.30*** *p372*
Russ, Horace; New York, 1840 ***8197.10*** *p321*
Russ, Johann Daniel; Port uncertain, 1751 ***2856.30*** *p370*
Russ, Jonathan 73; Ontario, 1871 ***1823.22*** *p139*
Russ, Sidney George; New York, 1840 ***8197.10*** *p277*
Russea, Richard D.; New York, 1840 ***8197.10*** *p157*
Russel, Adam; Maryland, 1910 ***3259.35*** *p53*
Russel, Andrew 24; Maryland, 1774 ***1220.25*** *p85*
Russel, David 25; Boston, 1774 ***1220.25*** *p51*
Russel, Henry 24; Ontario, 1871 ***1823.15*** *p230*
Russel, Herbert 3; Ontario, 1861 ***2896.27*** *p49*
Russel, Hugh 40; Ontario, 1871 ***1823.28*** *p88*
Russel, James 24; Philadelphia, 1775 ***1220.25*** *p107*
Russel, Johann; Port uncertain, 1738 ***2856.30*** *p373*
Russel, John 36; Ontario, 1861 ***2896.27*** *p49*
Russel, Patrick 4; Ontario, 1861 ***2896.27*** *p20*
Russel, Phebe A. 1; Ontario, 1861 ***2896.27*** *p49*
Russel, Robert 19; Ontario, 1871 ***1823.28*** *p88*
Russel, Rose 64; Ontario, 1861 ***2896.27*** *p20*
Russel, Thomas 17; Maryland, 1774 ***1220.25*** *p6*
Russell, Captain; Quebec, 1857 ***9196.15*** *p18*
Russell, Miss; Quebec, 1856 ***9196.15*** *p5*
Russell, Miss; Quebec, 1857 ***9196.15*** *p23*
Russell, Mr.; Quebec, 1856 ***9196.15*** *p10*
Russell, Mr.; Quebec, 1857 ***9196.15*** *p16*
Russell, Mr.; Quebec, 1857 ***9196.15*** *p25*
Russell, Mr.; Quebec, 1858 ***9196.15*** *p39*
Russell, Mrs.; Quebec, 1856 ***9196.15*** *p9*
Russell, Adam; America, 1878 ***1640.13*** *p108*
Russell, Alexander; Manitoba, 1897 ***1640.13*** *p108*
Russell, Alexander 37; Ontario, 1871 ***1823.22*** *p139*
Russell, Alexander 41; Ontario, 1871 ***1823.22*** *p139*
Russell, Andrew 75; Ontario, 1871 ***1823.22*** *p139*
Russell, Ann *SEE* Russell, Nicholas
Russell, Arthur; Pennsylvania, 1851 ***6058.10*** *p28*
Russell, Calvin F. 69; Ontario, 1871 ***1823.28*** *p88*
Russell, Catharine M. 71; Vermont, 1864 ***5900.10*** *p171*
Russell, Catherine 55; Ontario, 1871 ***1823.22*** *p139*
Russell, Catherine 77; Ontario, 1871 ***1823.15*** *p230*
Russell, Christopher; Maryland, 1658 ***2524.55*** *p192*
Russell, David 25; Ontario, 1871 ***1823.15*** *p230*
Russell, Edmond; Vermont, 1799-1865 ***5900.10*** *p149*
Russell, Edward; Maryland, 1661 ***2524.55*** *p68*
Russell, Edward; Maryland, 1668 ***2524.55*** *p192*
Russell, Edward; Maryland, 1675 ***2524.55*** *p192*
Russell, Edward; Virginia, 1666-1667 ***6212.30*** *p33*
Russell, Edward 40; Ontario, 1871 ***1823.22*** *p139*
Russell, Elizabeth; Marblehead, Massachusetts, 1772 ***1224.2*** *p99*

Russell, Elizabeth; Marblehead, Massachusetts, 1803 ***1224.3*** *p68*
Russell, Emily; Vermont, 1817-1879 ***5900.10*** *p199*
Russell, Erastus 60; Ontario, 1871 ***1823.22*** *p139*
Russell, G.; Quebec, 1858 ***9196.15*** *p45*
Russell, Geo; Virginia, 1672 ***6212.30*** *p50*
Russell, George; Georgia, 1698 ***1640.13*** *p108*
Russell, George; Maryland, 1671 ***2524.55*** *p192*
Russell, George; Pennsylvania, 1852 ***6058.10*** *p30*
Russell, George 42; Ontario, 1871 ***1823.28*** *p88*
Russell, Hellen McCummins 42; Vermont, 1883 ***5900.10*** *p282*
Russell, Henry; South Carolina, 1734 ***1224.2*** *p99*
Russell, Isabella 65; Ontario, 1871 ***1823.28*** *p88*
Russell, Mrs. J.; Quebec, 1857 ***9196.15*** *p13*
Russell, J. J.; Quebec, 1857 ***9196.15*** *p14*
Russell, James; Augusta, Georgia, 1819 ***1640.10*** *p181*
Russell, James; Charleston, South Carolina, 1810 ***1224.3*** *p68*
Russell, James; Georgia, 1699 ***1640.13*** *p108*
Russell, James; New York, 1818 ***8197.10*** *p272*
Russell, James; New York, 1840 ***8197.10*** *p189*
Russell, James; San Francisco, 1898 ***1640.13*** *p108*
Russell, James; Vermont, 1833-1907 ***5900.10*** *p149*
Russell, James 29; Ontario, 1871 ***1823.15*** *p230*
Russell, James 39; Ontario, 1871 ***1823.28*** *p88*
Russell, James 41; Ontario, 1871 ***1823.22*** *p139*
Russell, James 44; Ontario, 1871 ***1823.22*** *p139*
Russell, James 52; Ontario, 1871 ***1823.15*** *p230*
Russell, James R. 15; Ontario, 1861 ***2896.25*** *p55*
Russell, John; Boston, 1771 ***1640.13*** *p108*
Russell, John; Brunswick, North Carolina, 1753 ***1224.2*** *p99*
Russell, John; Maryland, 1659 ***2524.55*** *p192*
Russell, John; Maryland, 1665 ***2524.55*** *p192*
Russell, John; Maryland, 1678 ***2524.55*** *p192*
Russell, John; Pennsylvania, 1808 ***6058.10*** *p2*
Russell, John 40; Ontario, 1871 ***1823.15*** *p230*
Russell, John 50; Ontario, 1871 ***1823.15*** *p230*
Russell, John 59; Ontario, 1861 ***2896.25*** *p55*
Russell, John 66; Ontario, 1871 ***1823.22*** *p139*
Russell, Joshna 30; Ontario, 1871 ***1823.15*** *p230*
Russell, Katharine; Maryland, 1682 ***2524.55*** *p192*
Russell, Louise M.; Vermont, 1852-1928 ***5900.10*** *p194*
Russell, Margaret; Vermont, 1799-1883 ***5900.10*** *p149*
Russell, Margaret; Vermont, 1845-1864 ***5900.10*** *p149*
Russell, Mary; Windward Islands, 1818 ***1640.13*** *p108*
Russell, Mary 35; Vermont, 1857 ***5900.10*** *p160*
Russell, Mary 70; Ontario, 1871 ***1823.15*** *p230*
Russell, Mary A.; Vermont, 1834-1917 ***5900.10*** *p149*
Russell, Mary A.; Vermont, 1856-1919 ***5900.10*** *p407*
Russell, Matilda 56; Vermont, 1886 ***5900.10*** *p199*
Russell, Matthew; Missouri, 1897 ***1640.13*** *p108*
Russell, Matthew; New York, 1835 ***8197.10*** *p275*
Russell, Nancy Hanley; Vermont, 1834-1901 ***5900.10*** *p534*
Russell, Nicholas; Maryland, 1662 ***2524.55*** *p192*
Daughter: Ann
Russell, P. C. 31; Ontario, 1871 ***1823.22*** *p139*
Russell, Patrick 75; Vermont, 1868 ***5900.10*** *p171*
Russell, Phebe; Maryland, 1672 ***2524.55*** *p192*
Russell, R. S.; Philadelphia, 1839 ***6058.10*** *p45*
Russell, Richard; Pennsylvania, 1842 ***6058.10*** *p18*
Russell, Robert; New York, 1807 ***8197.10*** *p48*
Russell, Robert 49; Ontario, 1871 ***1823.15*** *p230*
Russell, Robert 61; Ontario, 1871 ***1823.15*** *p230*
Russell, Robert H.; New York, New York, 1836 ***6058.10*** *p29*
Russell, S. B. 28; Ontario, 1861 ***2896.25*** *p55*
Russell, Samuel; New York, 1827 ***8197.10*** *p343*
Russell, Stephen John; Pennsylvania, 1848 ***6058.10*** *p24*
Russell, Thomas; Boston, 1810 ***1224.3*** *p68*
Russell, Thomas; Maryland, 1672 ***2524.55*** *p192*
Russell, Thomas; Maryland, 1673 ***2524.55*** *p192*
Russell, Thomas; New York, 1840 ***8197.10*** *p277*
Russell, Thomas 21; Vermont, 1863 ***5900.10*** *p149*
Russell, Timothy; Pennsylvania, 1785 ***4629.10*** *p67*
Russell, Walter E. 84; Vermont, 1903 ***5900.10*** *p534*
Russell, Wellington 22; Ontario, 1861 ***2896.25*** *p55*
Russell, William; Kansas, 1881 ***1640.13*** *p108*
Russell, William; Maryland, 1663 ***2524.55*** *p192*
Russell, William; New York, 1838 ***8197.10*** *p276*
Russell, William; New York, 1840 ***8197.10*** *p188*
Russell, William; Savannah, Georgia, n.d. ***1224.2*** *p99*
Russell, William; Savannah, Georgia, 1819 ***1640.10*** *p181*
Russell, William 26; Ontario, 1861 ***2896.25*** *p55*
Russell, William 32; Ontario, 1871 ***1823.15*** *p230*
Russell, William 45; Ontario, 1871 ***1823.28*** *p89*
Russell, William 46; Ontario, 1871 ***1823.28*** *p89*
Russell, William 49; Ontario, 1871 ***1823.22*** *p139*
Russell, William 70; Ontario, 1871 ***1823.22*** *p139*
Russell, William 71; Ontario, 1871 ***1823.28*** *p89*
Russelsom, John 50; Ontario, 1871 ***1823.28*** *p89*
Russey, Miss; Quebec, 1856 ***9196.15*** *p7*
Russig, Christina 25; Kansas, 1910 ***9079.10*** *p43*
Russig, F. G. 24; Kansas, 1910 ***9079.10*** *p43*
Rust, Carl; Pennsylvania, 1860 ***6058.10*** *p43*
Rust, Johann; Port uncertain, 1732 ***2856.30*** *p373*
Rust, Stephen 28; Virginia, 1774 ***1220.25*** *p89*
Ruston, David 43; Ontario, 1871 ***1823.15*** *p230*
Rusty, Pawel; Maryland, 1910 ***3259.35*** *p53*
Ruszke, Vincent; Maryland, 1910 ***3259.35*** *p53*
Rut, J. J. 23; British Columbia, 1909 ***9196.1*** *p27*
Rut, J. J. 23; Seattle, 1909 ***9196.1*** *p27*
Rutford, Daniel 40; Ontario, 1871 ***1823.15*** *p230*
Ruth, Christian; America, 1733 ***2856.30*** *p372*
With wife & children
Ruth, Christian; America, 1737 ***2856.30*** *p372*
Ruth, Georg; America, 1741 ***2856.30*** *p372*
Ruth, Peter; America, 1733 ***2856.30*** *p372*
With wife & children
Ruth, Peter; America, 1737 ***2856.30*** *p372*
Rutherford, Mr. 44; Ontario, 1871 ***1823.22*** *p139*
Rutherford, Alexander; New York, 1834 ***1640.13*** *p108*
Rutherford, Andrew 64; Ontario, 1871 ***1823.15*** *p230*
Rutherford, Archie 29; Ontario, 1871 ***1823.22*** *p139*
Rutherford, Charles 22; Boston, 1774 ***1220.25*** *p124*
Rutherford, Ebenezer; Jamaica, 1804 ***1640.13*** *p108*
Rutherford, Francis 60; Ontario, 1861 ***2896.25*** *p70*
Rutherford, George; Georgia, 1698 ***1640.13*** *p108*
Rutherford, George 57; Ontario, 1871 ***1823.22*** *p139*
Rutherford, H. A. 33; Alaska, 1918 ***9196.1*** *p55*
Rutherford, H. A. 33; Whitehorse, Yukon, 1918 ***9196.1*** *p55*
Rutherford, Isaac 47; Ontario, 1871 ***1823.15*** *p230*
Rutherford, James; Georgia, 1757 ***1640.10*** *p181*
Rutherford, James 32; Ontario, 1871 ***1823.15*** *p230*
Rutherford, James 56; Ontario, 1871 ***1823.22*** *p139*
Rutherford, John; Alabama, 1827-1845 ***1640.10*** *p181*
Rutherford, John; America, 1840 ***1640.13*** *p108*
Rutherford, John; Georgia, 1734 ***1640.10*** *p181*
Rutherford, John; New Jersey, 1841 ***1224.3*** *p68*
Rutherford, John 21; Maryland, 1774 ***1220.25*** *p78*
Rutherford, John 33; Ontario, 1871 ***1823.15*** *p230*
Rutherford, John 34; Ontario, 1871 ***1823.22*** *p139*
Rutherford, John 44; Ontario, 1871 ***1823.15*** *p230*
Rutherford, John Murray; Toronto, 1898 ***1640.13*** *p108*
Rutherford, Margaret 50; Ontario, 1871 ***1823.15*** *p230*
Rutherford, Margaret Craig; Manitoba, 1900 ***1640.13*** *p109*
Rutherford, Peter 40; Ontario, 1871 ***1823.15*** *p230*
Rutherford, Robert 50; Ontario, 1871 ***1823.15*** *p230*
Rutherford, Robert 60; Ontario, 1871 ***1823.22*** *p139*
Rutherford, Samuel 64; Ontario, 1871 ***1823.15*** *p230*
Rutherford, Thomas 54; Ontario, 1871 ***1823.22*** *p139*
Rutherford, Thomas Scott; St. Louis, 1900 ***1640.13*** *p109*
Rutherford, W. E.; Alabama, 1826-1845 ***1640.10*** *p181*
Rutherford, Walter 51; Ontario, 1871 ***1823.22*** *p139*
Rutherford, William; Louisiana, 1816-1850 ***1640.10*** *p181*
Rutherford, William; Northwest Territories, 1897 ***1640.13*** *p109*
Ruthren, William 37; Ontario, 1871 ***1823.22*** *p139*
Ruthtra, Arthur; Virginia, 1667 ***1224.1*** *p50*
Ruthven, James Virgo; Jamaica, 1830 ***1640.13*** *p109*
Ruti, Konrad; America, 1747 ***2856.30*** *p370*
Rutkauski, Joseph; Maryland, 1910 ***3259.35*** *p53*
Rutkauski, Koven; Maryland, 1910 ***3259.35*** *p53*
Rutkowski, Anton; Maryland, 1910 ***3259.35*** *p53*
Rutkowski, Florjan; Maryland, 1910 ***3259.35*** *p53*
Rutkowski, Joseph; Maryland, 1910 ***3259.35*** *p53*
Rutkowski, Stanislaw; Maryland, 1910 ***3259.35*** *p53*
Rutkowsky, Paul; Maryland, 1910 ***3259.35*** *p53*
Rutland, Margaret; Maryland, 1654 ***2524.55*** *p192*
Rutland, Thomas; Virginia, 1667 ***6212.30*** *p35*
Rutledge, Andy 47; Ontario, 1871 ***1823.15*** *p230*
Rutledge, David J.; Vermont, 1857-1928 ***5900.10*** *p266*
Rutledge, Delia N. 71; Vermont, 1905 ***5900.10*** *p94*
Rutledge, Edward; South Carolina, n.d. ***4628.40*** *p48*
Rutledge, George; Vermont, 1828-1891 ***5900.10*** *p94*
Rutledge, James 66; Ontario, 1871 ***1823.15*** *p230*
Rutledge, John; South Carolina, 1775-1781 ***4628.40*** *p69*
Rutledge, John 24; Ontario, 1871 ***1823.28*** *p89*
Rutledge, John M. 37; Ontario, 1871 ***1823.15*** *p230*
Rutledge, Joseph 40; Ontario, 1871 ***1823.15*** *p231*
Rutledge, Mary E. McGuire; Vermont, 1863-1918 ***5900.10*** *p266*
Rutledge, Robert 45; Ontario, 1871 ***1823.15*** *p231*
Rutledge, Sarah Motte; Charleston, South Carolina, 1852 ***1224.3*** *p68*
Rutledge, Susanna 65; Ontario, 1871 ***1823.15*** *p231*
Rutledge, Thompson 30; Ontario, 1871 ***1823.15*** *p231*
Rutledge, William 33; Ontario, 1871 ***1823.28*** *p89*
Rutledge, William 38; Ontario, 1871 ***1823.15*** *p231*
Rutley, F. A.; Quebec, 1858 ***9196.15*** *p31*
Rutlidg, Edward; Maryland, 1670 ***2524.55*** *p28*
Rutlidge, Christopher 41; Ontario, 1871 ***1823.15*** *p231*
Rutlidge, Edward 75; Ontario, 1871 ***1823.15*** *p231*
Rutlidge, James 35; Ontario, 1871 ***1823.15*** *p231*
Rutsch, Martin; Port uncertain, 1809 ***2856.30*** *p372*
Rutschi, Elias; Port uncertain, 1768 ***2856.30*** *p372*
Rutschska, Joseph; Maryland, 1910 ***3259.35*** *p53*
Rutson, Thomas 46; Ontario, 1871 ***1823.15*** *p231*
Ruttan, A. J. 36; Ontario, 1861 ***2896.25*** *p34*
Ruttan, Aaron 32; Ontario, 1861 ***2896.27*** *p7*
Ruttan, C. 13; Ontario, 1861 ***2896.25*** *p34*
Ruttan, Catherine 76; Ontario, 1861 ***2896.27*** *p7*
Ruttan, John 40; Ontario, 1861 ***2896.27*** *p7*
Ruttan, M. 10; Ontario, 1861 ***2896.25*** *p34*
Ruttan, W. 7; Ontario, 1861 ***2896.25*** *p34*
Ruttan, W. S. 17; Ontario, 1861 ***2896.25*** *p34*
Rutter, Mrs.; Ontario, 1861 ***2896.28*** *p63*
Rutter, Andrew 22; Ontario, 1861 ***2896.28*** *p44*
Rutter, David; Pennsylvania, 1785 ***4629.10*** *p48*
Rutter, Elisa 21; Ontario, 1861 ***2896.27*** *p66*
Rutter, Fanny 24; Ontario, 1861 ***2896.28*** *p44*
Rutter, Jacob; Pennsylvania, 1777 ***4629.10*** *p22*
Rutter, James W. 18; Ontario, 1861 ***2896.28*** *p44*
Rutter, Jonah 2; Ontario, 1861 ***2896.27*** *p66*
Rutter, Mary 1; Ontario, 1861 ***2896.27*** *p66*
Rutter, Mary E. 27; Ontario, 1861 ***2896.28*** *p44*
Rutter, Phebe 62; Ontario, 1861 ***2896.28*** *p44*
Rutter, Thomas; Virginia, 1666-1667 ***6212.30*** *p34*
Rutter, William; Ontario, 1861 ***2896.28*** *p63*
Ruttergerod, Friedrich; New York, 1838 ***8197.10*** *p276*
Ruttle, Henry 30; Ontario, 1871 ***1823.15*** *p231*
Rutty, Robert; Maryland, 1669 ***2524.55*** *p192*
Rutzbeek, H. 25; Alaska, 1914 ***9196.1*** *p42*
Rutzer, Ernie 27; British Columbia, 1913 ***9196.1*** *p21*
Rutzer, Ernie 27; Juneau, Alaska, 1913 ***9196.1*** *p21*
Rutzler, Frederick; New York, 1840 ***8197.10*** *p188*
Ruxby, George 80; Ontario, 1871 ***1823.22*** *p139*
Ruzakowski, Adam; Maryland, 1910 ***3259.35*** *p53*
Ruzminski, Casemer; Maryland, 1910 ***3259.35*** *p53*
Ryal, William S. 67; Ontario, 1871 ***1823.22*** *p140*
Ryan, Miss; Quebec, 1857 ***9196.15*** *p14*
Ryan, Miss; Quebec, 1858 ***9196.15*** *p33*
Ryan, Mr.; Quebec, 1856 ***9196.15*** *p10*
Ryan, Mr.; Quebec, 1857 ***9196.15*** *p14*
Ryan, Abbie H.; Vermont, 1873-1916 ***5900.10*** *p499*
Ryan, Agnes; Vermont, 1866-1894 ***5900.10*** *p439*
Ryan, Anastasia; Vermont, 1831-1920 ***5900.10*** *p373*
Ryan, Andrew; New York, 1840 ***8197.10*** *p277*
Ryan, Andrew 60; Ontario, 1871 ***1823.28*** *p89*
Ryan, Ann 7; Vermont, 1859 ***5900.10*** *p229*
Ryan, Ann 23; Ontario, 1871 ***1823.15*** *p231*
Ryan, Ann 43; Ontario, 1871 ***1823.15*** *p231*
Ryan, Ann 50; Vermont, 1870 ***5900.10*** *p540*
Ryan, Ann 62; Vermont, 1924 ***5900.10*** *p579*
Ryan, Ann 82; Vermont, 1907 ***5900.10*** *p561*
Ryan, Ann Murphy 62; Vermont, 1887 ***5900.10*** *p485*
Ryan, Anna; Vermont, 1849-1931 ***5900.10*** *p245*
Ryan, Anna Larkin 68; Vermont, 1887 ***5900.10*** *p467*
Ryan, Annette M. Spaulding; Vermont, 1849-1894 ***5900.10*** *p243*
Ryan, Anstais 2; Vermont, 1856 ***5900.10*** *p363*
Ryan, Anstais 8; Vermont, 1849 ***5900.10*** *p363*
Ryan, Bridged Heaphy; Vermont, 1829-1912 ***5900.10*** *p119*
Ryan, Bridget; Vermont, 1832-1911 ***5900.10*** *p536*
Ryan, Bridget; Vermont, 1840-1881 ***5900.10*** *p543*
Ryan, Bridget; Vermont, 1860-1938 ***5900.10*** *p252*
Ryan, Bridget 18; Vermont, 1882 ***5900.10*** *p259*
Ryan, Bridget 53; Vermont, 1873 ***5900.10*** *p165*
Ryan, Bridget 74; Vermont, 1894 ***5900.10*** *p380*
Ryan, Bridget Brannan 68; Vermont, 1886 ***5900.10*** *p229*
Ryan, Bridget Hogan; Vermont, 1859-1916 ***5900.10*** *p274*
Ryan, Bridget Keogh; Vermont, 1840-1897 ***5900.10*** *p537*
Ryan, Bridget M. 18; Vermont, 1865 ***5900.10*** *p165*
Ryan, Bridget Murphy; Vermont, 1846-1885 ***5900.10*** *p539*
Ryan, Bridget Murphy; Vermont, 1862-1936 ***5900.10*** *p439*
Ryan, Caleb 44; Ontario, 1871 ***1823.15*** *p231*
Ryan, Catharine 71; Vermont, 1905 ***5900.10*** *p342*
Ryan, Catharine Costello; Vermont, 1837-1917 ***5900.10*** *p83*
Ryan, Catherine; Vermont, 1830-1878 ***5900.10*** *p63*
Ryan, Catherine; Vermont, 1842-1906 ***5900.10*** *p613*
Ryan, Catherine; Vermont, 1846-1915 ***5900.10*** *p273*
Ryan, Catherine; Vermont, 1848-1910 ***5900.10*** *p238*
Ryan, Catherine; Vermont, 1856-1937 ***5900.10*** *p252*
Ryan, Catherine; Vermont, 1859 ***5900.10*** *p229*
Ryan, Catherine; Vermont, 1861-1917 ***5900.10*** *p394*
Ryan, Catherine 17; Vermont, 1872 ***5900.10*** *p259*
Ryan, Catherine 29; Vermont, 1876 ***5900.10*** *p412*
Ryan, Catherine 64; Vermont, 1884 ***5900.10*** *p167*
Ryan, Catherine 65; Vermont, 1883 ***5900.10*** *p613*
Ryan, Catherine 74; Vermont, 1886 ***5900.10*** *p370*

Ryan, Catherine 75; Vermont, 1890 ***5900.10*** *p136*
Ryan, Catherine 75; Vermont, 1911 ***5900.10*** *p445*
Ryan, Catherine 76; Ontario, 1871 ***1823.22*** *p140*
Ryan, Catherine Belford; Vermont, 1800-1852 ***5900.10*** *p238*
Ryan, Catherine Drew; Vermont, 1847-1915 ***5900.10*** *p90*
Ryan, Catherine Green; Vermont, 1847-1926 ***5900.10*** *p380*
Ryan, Catherine Griffin 41; Vermont, 1872 ***5900.10*** *p613*
Ryan, Catherine Healy; Vermont, 1848-1917 ***5900.10*** *p129*
Ryan, Catherine Heffron 70; Vermont, 1907 ***5900.10*** *p539*
Ryan, Cornelius; New York, 1807 ***8197.10*** *p327*
Ryan, Cornelius; Vermont, 1853-1920 ***5900.10*** *p195*
Ryan, Dan 36; Seattle, 1913 ***9196.1*** *p58*
Ryan, Dan 36; Vancouver, British Columbia, 1913 ***9196.1*** *p58*
Ryan, Daniel; Vermont, 1855-1904 ***5900.10*** *p274*
Ryan, Daniel 54; Vermont, 1810 ***5900.10*** *p493*
Ryan, David 38; Vermont, 1861 ***5900.10*** *p360*
Ryan, Dennis; Vermont, 1818-1899 ***5900.10*** *p439*
Ryan, Dennis; Vermont, 1848-1914 ***5900.10*** *p582*
Ryan, Dennis 87; Vermont, 1876 ***5900.10*** *p614*
Ryan, Dennis M.; Vermont, 1858-1910 ***5900.10*** *p439*
Ryan, E.; Quebec, 1858 ***9196.15*** *p33*
Ryan, Edmond; Vermont, 1827-1900 ***5900.10*** *p367*
Ryan, Edmond 72; Ontario, 1871 ***1823.28*** *p89*
Ryan, Edward; Vermont, 1834-1902 ***5900.10*** *p244*
Ryan, Edward; Vermont, 1836-1917 ***5900.10*** *p350*
Ryan, Edward; Vermont, 1856-1936 ***5900.10*** *p439*
Ryan, Edward 12; Vermont, 1865 ***5900.10*** *p543*
Ryan, Edward 21; Philadelphia, 1774 ***1220.25*** *p6*
Ryan, Edward 38; Ontario, 1871 ***1823.15*** *p231*
Ryan, Edward 38; Ontario, 1871 ***1823.28*** *p89*
Ryan, Edward 48; Ontario, 1871 ***1823.28*** *p89*
Ryan, Edward 51; Vermont, 1880 ***5900.10*** *p265*
Ryan, Edward 64; Vermont, 1888 ***5900.10*** *p485*
Ryan, Edward 70; Vermont, 1886 ***5900.10*** *p539*
Ryan, Elizabeth 64; Vermont, 1885 ***5900.10*** *p556*
Ryan, Elizabeth Boland 80; Vermont, 1911 ***5900.10*** *p259*
Ryan, Elizabeth M.; Vermont, 1842-1909 ***5900.10*** *p491*
Ryan, Ella M.; Vermont, 1848-1924 ***5900.10*** *p435*
Ryan, Ellen; Vermont, 1831-1914 ***5900.10*** *p473*
Ryan, Ellen; Vermont, 1853-1898 ***5900.10*** *p204*
Ryan, Ellen 36; Vermont, 1899 ***5900.10*** *p259*
Ryan, Ellen 48; Ontario, 1871 ***1823.22*** *p140*
Ryan, Ellen 60; Ontario, 1871 ***1823.15*** *p231*
Ryan, Ellen 82; Vermont, 1889 ***5900.10*** *p85*
Ryan, Ellen A.; Vermont, 1857-1929 ***5900.10*** *p67*
Ryan, Ellen B. Connell; Vermont, 1857-1888 ***5900.10*** *p359*
Ryan, Ellen Brennan; Vermont, 1861-1939 ***5900.10*** *p235*
Ryan, Ellen Clarke; Vermont, 1837-1853 ***5900.10*** *p477*
Ryan, Ellen H.; Vermont, 1849-1941 ***5900.10*** *p553*
Ryan, Ellen Hayes 65; Vermont, 1884 ***5900.10*** *p58*
Ryan, Ellen Kennedy; Vermont, 1834-1873 ***5900.10*** *p476*
Ryan, Ellen Leahy; Vermont, 1827-1916 ***5900.10*** *p367*
Ryan, Francis 43; Vermont, 1867 ***5900.10*** *p143*
Ryan, Francis 53; Vermont, 1897 ***5900.10*** *p235*
Ryan, Francis 68; Vermont, 1868 ***5900.10*** *p226*
Ryan, George; New York, 1821 ***8197.10*** *p273*
Ryan, George; Pennsylvania, 1778 ***4629.10*** *p32*
Ryan, George; Vermont, n.d. ***5900.10*** *p260*
Ryan, George 15; Maryland, 1775 ***1220.25*** *p108*
Ryan, George 67; Ontario, 1871 ***1823.15*** *p231*
Ryan, H.; Vermont, 1837-1904 ***5900.10*** *p554*
Ryan, Hannah 30; Vermont, 1898 ***5900.10*** *p259*
Ryan, Hanora; Vermont, 1852-1865 ***5900.10*** *p439*
Ryan, Hanora Leahy 89; Vermont, 1907 ***5900.10*** *p363*
Ryan, Hanorah; Vermont, 1849-1903 ***5900.10*** *p394*
Ryan, Harriett 16; Ontario, 1871 ***1823.15*** *p231*
Ryan, Helena E.; Vermont, 1859-1926 ***5900.10*** *p435*
Ryan, Henry; America, 1790 ***4628.40*** *p29*
Ryan, Henry C.; Vermont, 1853-1915 ***5900.10*** *p159*
Ryan, J. D.; Vermont, 1859-1939 ***5900.10*** *p240*
Ryan, James; New York, 1826 ***8197.10*** *p275*
Ryan, James; New York, 1827 ***8197.10*** *p346*
Ryan, James; New York, 1838 ***8197.10*** *p276*
Ryan, James; Pennsylvania, 1864-1868 ***6058.10*** *p62*
Ryan, James; Vermont, 1830-1877 ***5900.10*** *p203*
Ryan, James; Vermont, 1854-1923 ***5900.10*** *p89*
Ryan, James 16; Vermont, 1869 ***5900.10*** *p189*
Ryan, James 47; Vermont, 1899 ***5900.10*** *p582*
Ryan, James 48; Ontario, 1871 ***1823.15*** *p231*
Ryan, James 78; Vermont, 1888 ***5900.10*** *p363*
Ryan, James 93; Vermont, 1894 ***5900.10*** *p229*
Ryan, James B.; Vermont, 1820-1889 ***5900.10*** *p615*
Ryan, James B., Jr.; Vermont, 1857-1878 ***5900.10*** *p615*
Ryan, James D.; Vermont, 1866-1937 ***5900.10*** *p553*
Ryan, James F.; Vermont, 1862-1917 ***5900.10*** *p271*
Ryan, Jane; Vermont, 1824-1902 ***5900.10*** *p411*
Ryan, Jane; Vermont, 1827-1893 ***5900.10*** *p435*
Ryan, Jane; Vermont, 1853-1925 ***5900.10*** *p275*
Ryan, Jane; Vermont, 1853-1932 ***5900.10*** *p249*
Ryan, Jane 5; Vermont, 1859 ***5900.10*** *p229*
Ryan, Jane 61; Vermont, 1898 ***5900.10*** *p137*
Ryan, Jennie A.; Vermont, 1875-1904 ***5900.10*** *p48*
Ryan, Jeremiah 31; Ontario, 1871 ***1823.28*** *p89*
Ryan, Johanna; Vermont, 1840-1882 ***5900.10*** *p143*
Ryan, Johanna; Vermont, 1852-1913 ***5900.10*** *p578*
Ryan, Johanna Mahar; Vermont, 1856-1956 ***5900.10*** *p582*
Ryan, Johanna Todd; Vermont, 1837-1890 ***5900.10*** *p581*
Ryan, Johannah 25; Ontario, 1871 ***1823.22*** *p140*
Ryan, Johannah Dwyer 55; Vermont, 1911 ***5900.10*** *p582*
Ryan, John; Canada, 1756-1760 ***4628.40*** *p45*
Ryan, John; New York, 1831 ***8197.10*** *p364*
Ryan, John; New York, 1840 ***8197.10*** *p276*
Ryan, John; New York, 1864 ***6058.10*** *p69*
Ryan, John; Vermont, 1830-1901 ***5900.10*** *p172*
Ryan, John; Vermont, 1833-1866 ***5900.10*** *p560*
Ryan, John; Vermont, 1836-1908 ***5900.10*** *p491*
Ryan, John; Vermont, 1839-1909 ***5900.10*** *p409*
Ryan, John; Vermont, 1842-1910 ***5900.10*** *p275*
Ryan, John; Vermont, 1843-1871 ***5900.10*** *p80*
Ryan, John; Vermont, 1843-1904 ***5900.10*** *p308*
Ryan, John; Vermont, 1844-1930 ***5900.10*** *p380*
Ryan, John; Vermont, 1846 ***5900.10*** *p150*
Ryan, John; Vermont, 1849-1906 ***5900.10*** *p195*
Ryan, John; Vermont, 1867-1911 ***5900.10*** *p172*
Ryan, John 26; Ontario, 1871 ***1823.15*** *p231*
Ryan, John 28; Vermont, 1851 ***5900.10*** *p191*
Ryan, John 31; Ontario, 1871 ***1823.15*** *p231*
Ryan, John 32; Ontario, 1871 ***1823.15*** *p231*
Ryan, John 35; Vermont, 1867 ***5900.10*** *p265*
Ryan, John 40; Ontario, 1871 ***1823.28*** *p89*
Ryan, John 45; Vermont, 1866 ***5900.10*** *p58*
Ryan, John 50; Ontario, 1871 ***1823.28*** *p89*
Ryan, John 55; Ontario, 1871 ***1823.15*** *p231*
Ryan, John 58; Ontario, 1871 ***1823.15*** *p231*
Ryan, John 60; Ontario, 1871 ***1823.15*** *p231*
Ryan, John 60; Ontario, 1871 ***1823.22*** *p140*
Ryan, John 62; Vermont, 1905 ***5900.10*** *p568*
Ryan, John 69; Vermont, 1889 ***5900.10*** *p467*
Ryan, John 75; Vermont, 1881 ***5900.10*** *p260*
Ryan, John B.; Vermont, 1859-1944 ***5900.10*** *p379*
Ryan, John F.; Vermont, 1853-1885 ***5900.10*** *p615*
Ryan, John F.; Vermont, 1854-1926 ***5900.10*** *p499*
Ryan, John H.; Vermont, 1844-1916 ***5900.10*** *p508*
Ryan, John J.; Vermont, 1854-1917 ***5900.10*** *p439*
Ryan, John J., Jr.; Vermont, 1857-1924 ***5900.10*** *p552*
Ryan, John M.; Vermont, 1832-1913 ***5900.10*** *p259*
Ryan, John P.; Vermont, 1846-1924 ***5900.10*** *p592*
Ryan, John W.; Vermont, 1847-1923 ***5900.10*** *p553*
Ryan, Joseph; Vermont, 1828-1910 ***5900.10*** *p271*
Ryan, Josephine Meigher; Vermont, 1865-1949 ***5900.10*** *p195*
Ryan, Julia; Vermont, 1816-1888 ***5900.10*** *p248*
Ryan, Julia; Vermont, 1831-1884 ***5900.10*** *p290*
Ryan, Julia; Vermont, 1859-1865 ***5900.10*** *p172*
Ryan, Julia A.; Vermont, 1875-1899 ***5900.10*** *p172*
Ryan, Julia A. Quirk; Vermont, 1844-1931 ***5900.10*** *p444*
Ryan, Kate; Vermont, n.d. ***5900.10*** *p409*
Ryan, Kate Waters; Vermont, 1838-1889 ***5900.10*** *p203*
Ryan, Katherine; Vermont, 1850-1922 ***5900.10*** *p308*
Ryan, Katie 75; Vermont, 1875 ***5900.10*** *p297*
Ryan, Lavinia; Vermont, 1854-1938 ***5900.10*** *p409*
Ryan, Lawrence; New York, 1804 ***8197.10*** *p28*
Ryan, Lawrence Francis; Vermont, 1848-1898 ***5900.10*** *p260*
Ryan, Lou Jane; Vermont, 1871-1929 ***5900.10*** *p553*
Ryan, Loude Forcier; Vermont, 1847-1921 ***5900.10*** *p379*
Ryan, Louisa 11; Ontario, 1871 ***1823.15*** *p231*
Ryan, Lucy A. McCarthy; Vermont, 1856-1923 ***5900.10*** *p548*
Ryan, Miss M.; Quebec, 1858 ***9196.15*** *p33*
Ryan, Margaret; Vermont, 1829-1902 ***5900.10*** *p548*
Ryan, Margaret; Vermont, 1829-1915 ***5900.10*** *p534*
Ryan, Margaret; Vermont, 1835-1919 ***5900.10*** *p238*
Ryan, Margaret 45; Vermont, 1898 ***5900.10*** *p259*
Ryan, Margaret 51; Vermont, 1877 ***5900.10*** *p421*
Ryan, Margaret 76; Vermont, 1878 ***5900.10*** *p331*
Ryan, Margaret 78; Vermont, 1883 ***5900.10*** *p226*
Ryan, Margaret 79; Vermont, 1877 ***5900.10*** *p259*
Ryan, Margaret Carroll; Vermont, 1826-1890 ***5900.10*** *p615*
Ryan, Margaret Coleman 70; Vermont, 1859 ***5900.10*** *p342*
Ryan, Margaret J.; Vermont, 1861-1929 ***5900.10*** *p327*
Ryan, Margaret Miles 41; Vermont, 1874 ***5900.10*** *p241*
Ryan, Margaret S.; Vermont, 1863-1950 ***5900.10*** *p240*
Ryan, Margery 24; Vermont, 1879 ***5900.10*** *p495*
Ryan, Margret 18; Ontario, 1861 ***2896.26*** *p36*
Ryan, Maria Burke; Vermont, 1845-1933 ***5900.10*** *p271*
Ryan, Mary; Vermont, 1798-1877 ***5900.10*** *p615*
Ryan, Mary; Vermont, 1816-1908 ***5900.10*** *p413*
Ryan, Mary; Vermont, 1828-1866 ***5900.10*** *p502*
Ryan, Mary; Vermont, 1828-1912 ***5900.10*** *p610*
Ryan, Mary; Vermont, 1838-1907 ***5900.10*** *p243*
Ryan, Mary; Vermont, 1840-1885 ***5900.10*** *p557*
Ryan, Mary; Vermont, 1841-1916 ***5900.10*** *p256*
Ryan, Mary; Vermont, 1849-1937 ***5900.10*** *p106*
Ryan, Mary; Vermont, 1854-1928 ***5900.10*** *p396*
Ryan, Mary; Vermont, 1859-1946 ***5900.10*** *p204*
Ryan, Mary; Vermont, 1870-1888 ***5900.10*** *p439*
Ryan, Mary 15; Vermont, 1859 ***5900.10*** *p229*
Ryan, Mary 40; Vermont, 1877 ***5900.10*** *p251*
Ryan, Mary 40; Vermont, 1881 ***5900.10*** *p81*
Ryan, Mary 48; Vermont, 1890 ***5900.10*** *p273*
Ryan, Mary 50; Ontario, 1861 ***2896.26*** *p36*
Ryan, Mary 60; Ontario, 1871 ***1823.22*** *p140*
Ryan, Mary 60; Vermont, 1878 ***5900.10*** *p188*
Ryan, Mary 63; Vermont, 1891 ***5900.10*** *p614*
Ryan, Mary 65; Vermont, 1889 ***5900.10*** *p265*
Ryan, Mary 67; Vermont, 1876 ***5900.10*** *p614*
Ryan, Mary 70; Ontario, 1871 ***1823.22*** *p140*
Ryan, Mary 70; Vermont, 1895 ***5900.10*** *p586*
Ryan, Mary 80; Vermont, 1896 ***5900.10*** *p83*
Ryan, Mary 80; Vermont, 1910 ***5900.10*** *p557*
Ryan, Mary A.; Vermont, 1880-1953 ***5900.10*** *p578*
Ryan, Mary A. Fitzgerald; Vermont, 1855-1884 ***5900.10*** *p508*
Ryan, Mary A. Keefe; Vermont, 1858-1925 ***5900.10*** *p444*
Ryan, Mary A. Kelley; Vermont, 1854-1886 ***5900.10*** *p148*
Ryan, Mary Ann 18; Vermont, 1857 ***5900.10*** *p238*
Ryan, Mary Bradshaw 83; Vermont, 1902 ***5900.10*** *p393*
Ryan, Mary Browne; Vermont, 1855-1900 ***5900.10*** *p432*
Ryan, Mary E.; Vermont, 1851-1926 ***5900.10*** *p593*
Ryan, Mary E. 34; Vermont, 1908 ***5900.10*** *p313*
Ryan, Mary J. 40; Vermont, 1897 ***5900.10*** *p259*
Ryan, Mary M.; Vermont, 1844-1938 ***5900.10*** *p335*
Ryan, Mary McKenna; Vermont, 1828-1900 ***5900.10*** *p439*
Ryan, Mary McLure; Vermont, 1839-1899 ***5900.10*** *p350*
Ryan, Mary O'Brien; Vermont, 1836-1909 ***5900.10*** *p484*
Ryan, Mary O'Neil; Vermont, 1837-1910 ***5900.10*** *p271*
Ryan, Mary R.; Vermont, 1851-1873 ***5900.10*** *p615*
Ryan, Mary Stapleton; Vermont, 1842-1906 ***5900.10*** *p244*
Ryan, Mary T. 31; Vermont, 1888 ***5900.10*** *p379*
Ryan, Mary Torphey 72; Vermont, 1884 ***5900.10*** *p260*
Ryan, Mary Ward; Vermont, 1857-1929 ***5900.10*** *p592*
Ryan, Mathew 43; Vermont, 1885 ***5900.10*** *p188*
Ryan, Matthew 54; Vermont, n.d. ***5900.10*** *p409*
Ryan, Mchail 60; Ontario, 1871 ***1823.15*** *p231*
Ryan, Michael; New York, 1827 ***8197.10*** *p340*
Ryan, Michael; New York, 1837 ***8197.10*** *p319*
Ryan, Michael; New York, 1840 ***8197.10*** *p190*
Ryan, Michael; Pennsylvania, 1779 ***4629.10*** *p41*
Ryan, Michael; Vermont, 1873-1874 ***5900.10*** *p172*
Ryan, Michael 30; Ontario, 1871 ***1823.15*** *p231*
Ryan, Michael 43; Vermont, 1881 ***5900.10*** *p83*
Ryan, Michael 47; Ontario, 1871 ***1823.28*** *p89*
Ryan, Michael 53; Ontario, 1861 ***2896.25*** *p50*
Ryan, Michael 54; Vermont, 1887 ***5900.10*** *p260*
Ryan, Michael 55; Ontario, 1871 ***1823.22*** *p140*
Ryan, Michael 60; Ontario, 1871 ***1823.28*** *p89*
Ryan, Michael 64; Vermont, 1894 ***5900.10*** *p484*
Ryan, Michael 70; Ontario, 1871 ***1823.28*** *p89*
Ryan, Michael 75; Vermont, 1880 ***5900.10*** *p195*
Ryan, Michael 79; Vermont, 1896 ***5900.10*** *p393*
Ryan, Michael J.; Vermont, 1857-1939 ***5900.10*** *p48*
Ryan, Michael P.; Vermont, 1852-1906 ***5900.10*** *p444*
Ryan, Michael W.; Vermont, 1847-1889 ***5900.10*** *p539*
Ryan, Nancy; Vermont, 1854-1921 ***5900.10*** *p552*
Ryan, Nancy Barney 40; Vermont, 1855 ***5900.10*** *p190*
Ryan, Nancy Hogan 42; Vermont, 1870 ***5900.10*** *p207*
Ryan, Nancy O'Brien 62; Vermont, 1886 ***5900.10*** *p271*
Ryan, Nellie E.; Vermont, 1869-1916 ***5900.10*** *p552*
Ryan, Nora J. 76; Vermont, 1924 ***5900.10*** *p162*
Ryan, Owen E.; Vermont, 1854-1881 ***5900.10*** *p148*
Ryan, Patrick; New York, 1834 ***8197.10*** *p372*
Ryan, Patrick; New York, 1837 ***8197.10*** *p375*
Ryan, Patrick; Vermont, 1820-1886 ***5900.10*** *p539*
Ryan, Patrick; Vermont, 1824-1899 ***5900.10*** *p434*
Ryan, Patrick; Vermont, 1829-1907 ***5900.10*** *p119*
Ryan, Patrick; Vermont, 1832-1915 ***5900.10*** *p476*
Ryan, Patrick; Vermont, 1845-1903 ***5900.10*** *p578*
Ryan, Patrick 16; Ontario, 1861 ***2896.26*** *p36*
Ryan, Patrick 21; Vermont, 1862 ***5900.10*** *p260*
Ryan, Patrick 22; New York, 1833-1840 ***8197.10*** *p189*
Ryan, Patrick 28; Ontario, 1871 ***1823.28*** *p89*
Ryan, Patrick 42; Ontario, 1871 ***1823.22*** *p140*
Ryan, Patrick 60; Ontario, 1871 ***1823.22*** *p140*
Ryan, Patrick 63; Vermont, 1897 ***5900.10*** *p81*
Ryan, Patrick 72; Ontario, 1871 ***1823.28*** *p89*

S

S, David 62; Ontario, 1871 ***1823.22*** *p140*
Saal, Anna Margarete; Port uncertain, 1765 ***2856.30*** *p376*
Saala, Johann Peter; Port uncertain, 1771 ***2856.30*** *p376*
Saalin, Anna Margarete; Port uncertain, 1765 ***2856.30*** *p376*
Saam, Johann; Port uncertain, 1737 ***2856.30*** *p376*
With family
Saam, Johann; Port uncertain, 1773 ***2856.30*** *p376*
Saam, Johann Jacob; Port uncertain, 1739 ***2856.30*** *p376*
Saam, Konrad; Port uncertain, 1741 ***2856.30*** *p376*
Saam, Maria Elisabeth; Port uncertain, 1746 ***2856.30*** *p376*
Saamin, Elisabeth; Port uncertain, 1764 ***2856.30*** *p379*
Saamin, Maria Catharina; Port uncertain, 1763 ***2856.30*** *p379*
Saar, Aran 27; Ontario, 1871 ***1823.28*** *p89*
Saar, Charles; Ontario, 1871 ***1823.28*** *p89*
Sabatier, Richard; Massachusetts, 1819 ***1224.3*** *p68*
Sabauski, A. 39; Alaska, 1910 ***9196.1*** *p9*
Sabauski, A. 39; Yukon, 1910 ***9196.1*** *p9*
Sabbin, Willm; Virginia, 1671-1672 ***6212.30*** *p47*
Sabel, Konrad; Port uncertain, 1769 ***2856.30*** *p453*
Sabes, George 36; Ontario, 1861 ***2896.27*** *p63*
Sabin, Thomas 15; Antigua (Antego), 1774 ***1220.25*** *p90*
Sabine, William; Boston, 1776 ***1224.2*** *p100*
Sabines, Miss; Quebec, 1858 ***9196.15*** *p40*
Sabins, Daniel 62; Ontario, 1871 ***1823.22*** *p140*
Sabins, William C. 36; Ontario, 1871 ***1823.22*** *p140*
Sabo, Andrew 30; Seattle, 1911 ***9196.1*** *p34*
Sabolefsky, John; Maryland, 1910 ***3259.35*** *p53*
Saboroski, John; Maryland, 1910 ***3259.35*** *p53*
Sabouren, Daniel 21; Virginia, 1774 ***1220.25*** *p86*
Sacarce, Isaac 3; Ontario, 1861 ***2896.25*** *p47*
Sacarce, Margaret 6; Ontario, 1861 ***2896.25*** *p47*
Sacarce, Mary 38; Ontario, 1861 ***2896.25*** *p47*
Sachenreuter, Johann Christia; Port uncertain, 1792 ***2856.30*** *p376*
Sachs, Adam 47; Ontario, 1871 ***1823.15*** *p232*
Sachs, Alexander; New York, 1838 ***8197.10*** *p149*
Sachs, Anna Catharina; Port uncertain, 1789 ***2856.30*** *p376*
Sachs, Daniel 45; Ontario, 1871 ***1823.15*** *p232*
Sachs, Johann; America, 1763 ***2856.30*** *p376*
With wife & son
Sachs, Johann Daniel; America, 1751 ***2856.30*** *p376*
With wife & children
Sachs, Maria Catharina; Port uncertain, 1789 ***2856.30*** *p376*
Sachs, Urban; America, 1763 ***2856.30*** *p376*
With wife son & daughter
Sachsenheimer, George; New York, 1837 ***8197.10*** *p106*
Sachss, Maria Elisabeth; Port uncertain, 1755 ***2856.30*** *p376*
Sachssin, Maria Elisabeth; Port uncertain, 1755 ***2856.30*** *p376*
Sack, August 28; Ontario, 1871 ***1823.28*** *p89*
Sack, Georg; Port uncertain, 1729 ***2856.30*** *p376*
Sack, Martan 40; Ontario, 1871 ***1823.28*** *p89*
Sack, William 36; Ontario, 1871 ***1823.28*** *p89*
Sacker, Jno; Virginia, 1665-1666 ***6212.30*** *p21*
Sackfeild, William; Maryland, 1664 ***2524.55*** *p205*
Sacklow, Eliz; Virginia, 1671 ***6212.30*** *p44*
Sackmeister, Bernard; New York, 1837 ***8197.10*** *p106*
Sackmeister, Bernhard; New York, 1834 ***8197.10*** *p319*
Sacksmith, B. 21; Ontario, 1861 ***2896.28*** *p15*
Sackville, George 59; Ontario, 1871 ***1823.22*** *p140*
Sackville, James 65; Ontario, 1871 ***1823.22*** *p140*
Sacock, James; Pennsylvania, 1866 ***6058.10*** *p56*
Sacolitch, Belle 40; British Columbia, 1909 ***9196.1*** *p27*
Sacolitch, Belle 40; Seattle, 1909 ***9196.1*** *p27*
Saconen, Barnard 48; Ontario, 1871 ***1823.15*** *p232*
Sacribusky, Powl 40; Ontario, 1871 ***1823.28*** *p89*
Sacrosinski, Frank; Maryland, 1910 ***3259.35*** *p53*
Sacy, Daniel 42; Ontario, 1871 ***1823.28*** *p89*
Sacye, William; Maryland, 1663 ***2524.55*** *p193*
Sadbury, Ralph; Virginia, 1672 ***6212.30*** *p49*
Saddler, James 40; Ontario, 1871 ***1823.15*** *p232*
Saddler, Jonathon 45; Ontario, 1871 ***1823.28*** *p89*
Saddler, Robert 55; Ontario, 1871 ***1823.28*** *p89*
Sadfosky, William; Maryland, 1910 ***3259.35*** *p54*
Sadgebury, James; New York, 1826 ***8197.10*** *p336*
Sadicoff, Deomisie 37; British Columbia, 1913 ***9196.1*** *p21*
Sadinchiski, Alex; Maryland, 1910 ***3259.35*** *p54*
Sadleir, Hugh B.; New York, 1823 ***8197.10*** *p281*
Sadler, Andrew; Maryland, 1910 ***3259.35*** *p54*
Sadler, Edw; Virginia, 1667 ***6212.30*** *p37*
Sadler, George 26; Philadelphia, 1774 ***1220.25*** *p82*
Sadler, Henry; New York, 1794 ***8197.10*** *p2*
Sadler, James; Virginia, 1667 ***6212.30*** *p37*
Sadler, John; Maryland, 1657 ***2524.55*** *p193*
Sadler, John; Maryland, 1669 ***2524.55*** *p193*
Sadler, John; Maryland, 1910 ***3259.35*** *p54*
Sadler, John; New York, 1794 ***8197.10*** *p2*
Sadler, Mary; New England, 1647 ***1224.1*** *p50*
Sadler, Matthias; Pennsylvania, 1781 ***4629.10*** *p42*
Sadler, Mickell; Virginia, 1693-1694 ***6212.30*** *p60*
Sadler, Renall; Virginia, 1671 ***6212.30*** *p42*
Sadler, Robert; Virginia, 1665-1666 ***6212.30*** *p21*
Sadler, Robert 56; Ontario, 1871 ***1823.15*** *p232*
Sadler, Robt; Virginia, 1665-1666 ***6212.30*** *p21*
Sadler, William 21; Maryland, 1775 ***1220.25*** *p111*
Sadler, William Coats; Pennsylvania, 1777 ***4629.10*** *p28*
Sadler, Wm; Virginia, 1664 ***6212.30*** *p15*
Sadlier, Alice 89; Vermont, 1927 ***5900.10*** *p123*
Sadlier, John 67; Vermont, 1879 ***5900.10*** *p123*
Sadlier, Mary Davern 88; Vermont, 1894 ***5900.10*** *p123*
Sadlo, Samuel; New York, 1832 ***8197.10*** *p357*
Sadowski, Joseph; Maryland, 1910 ***3259.35*** *p54*
Sadowski, Mary R.; Maryland, 1910 ***3259.35*** *p54*
Sadowski, Michael F.; Maryland, 1910 ***3259.35*** *p54*
Sadowski, Vincent; Maryland, 1910 ***3259.35*** *p54*
Sadowski, Wiktor; Maryland, 1910 ***3259.35*** *p54*
Sadowsky, Frank; Maryland, 1910 ***3259.35*** *p54*
Safegar, Susanna; Maryland, 1674 ***2524.55*** *p193*
Saffeta, Frank; Maryland, 1910 ***3259.35*** *p54*
Saffill, Jane; Virginia, 1663 ***6212.30*** *p4*
Saffin, Thomas; Boston, 1688 ***1224.1*** *p50*
Safford, Cora Alice; Vermont, 1854-1899 ***5900.10*** *p308*
Saffron, John 40; Ontario, 1871 ***1823.28*** *p89*
Safroski, Kazimer; Maryland, 1910 ***3259.35*** *p54*
Sagar, Louace 51; Ontario, 1871 ***1823.28*** *p89*
Sagar, M. 12; Ontario, 1861 ***2896.25*** *p47*
Sagar, M. E. 9; Ontario, 1861 ***2896.25*** *p47*
Sagar, Margaret 37; Ontario, 1861 ***2896.25*** *p47*
Sagawa, C. 31; Alaska, 1910 ***9196.1*** *p9*
Sagawa, C. 31; Yukon, 1910 ***9196.1*** *p9*
Sage, Annabelle Murray; Vermont, 1838-1924 ***5900.10*** *p443*
Sage, Charles 37; Ontario, 1871 ***1823.15*** *p232*
Sage, J.; Georgia, 1852 ***1640.10*** *p181*
Sage, James; Vermont, 1825-1911 ***5900.10*** *p443*
Sage, Philipp; Virginia, 1691 ***1224.1*** *p50*
Sager, Hannah Kennedy; Vermont, 1836-1913 ***5900.10*** *p164*
Sager, Maria Catharina Klein; America, 1765 ***2856.30*** *p230*
Sagger, Mr.; Quebec, 1857 ***9196.15*** *p14*
Saghorn, Henry; New York, 1837 ***8197.10*** *p106*
Sago, John; New York, 1806 ***8197.10*** *p33*
Sagoff, M. 28; Alaska, 1917 ***9196.1*** *p45*
Sagoff, M. 28; Whitehorse, Yukon, 1917 ***9196.1*** *p45*
Sagor, Peter; Maryland, 1656 ***2524.55*** *p193*
Sagory, Charles Constants; New York, 1815 ***8197.10*** *p56*
Sahgahnuckke, Thos 42; Ontario, 1871 ***1823.28*** *p89*
Sahling, Jacob; Port uncertain, 1763 ***2856.30*** *p376*
Sahlinger, Jacob; Port uncertain, 1763 ***2856.30*** *p376*
Sailer, Hans Jakob; America, 1752 ***2856.30*** *p376*
With wife & 2 children
Sailer, Hans Jakob; America, 1765 ***2856.30*** *p376*
With 3 brothers
Sailer, Martin; Port uncertain, 1757 ***2856.30*** *p376*
Saili, Wendel; New York, 1840 ***8197.10*** *p199*
Sailler, Friedrich; Port uncertain, 1785 ***2856.30*** *p376*
Sailor, Matura 41; Ontario, 1861 ***2896.28*** *p56*
Sailor, Phebe A. 16; Ontario, 1861 ***2896.28*** *p56*
Sailor, Sarah 13; Ontario, 1861 ***2896.28*** *p56*
Sailsbury, Jonathan 40; Ontario, 1871 ***1823.22*** *p140*
Saim, William 51; Ontario, 1871 ***1823.22*** *p140*
Sainsser, Hans Jakob; Port uncertain, 1749 ***2856.30*** *p376*
Sainsser, Maria; Port uncertain, 1749 ***2856.30*** *p376*
St. Clair, John; New Jersey, 1769 ***1224.2*** *p100*
St. George, Rose A.; Vermont, 1857-1932 ***5900.10*** *p96*
St. George, William; New York, 1839 ***8197.10*** *p383*
St. John, George 62; Ontario, 1871 ***1823.22*** *p151*
St. John, James 50; Ontario, 1871 ***1823.15*** *p250*
St. Johns, Julie E.; Vermont, 1846-1913 ***5900.10*** *p474*
St. Jurjo, Joseph de Rivera; New York, 1838 ***8197.10*** *p148*
Saint Laurent, Andrew Clement Desenclosde; Philadelphia, 1793 ***4629.10*** *p68*
St. Lawrence, . . .; Boston, 1737 ***4628.40*** *p114*
St. Marie, Alexis; New York, 1817 ***8197.10*** *p278*
St. Paul, Bries; New York, 1827 ***8197.10*** *p342*
St. Pierre, Amelia; Vermont, 1862-1937 ***5900.10*** *p225*
Saircki, Mike; Maryland, 1910 ***3259.35*** *p54*
Saird, James 45; Ontario, 1871 ***1823.15*** *p232*
Saiudge, William; Maryland, 1668 ***2524.55*** *p193*
Sakalowisky, Joseph; Maryland, 1910 ***3259.35*** *p54*
Sakosky, John; Maryland, 1910 ***3259.35*** *p54*
Salarski, Andrew; Maryland, 1910 ***3259.35*** *p54*
Salathee, Emanuel; America, 1730 ***2856.30*** *p376*
Salazar, Peter Goncalias; New York, 1793 ***8197.10*** *p1*
Salberry, Samuell; Maryland, 1657 ***2524.55*** *p238*
Salborg, Jonas M.; New York, 1819 ***8197.10*** *p278*
Salde, Emanuel; America, 1730 ***2856.30*** *p376*
Saldler, William 49; Ontario, 1871 ***1823.15*** *p232*
Sale, Joseph 30; Maryland, 1775 ***1220.25*** *p102*
Sale, Nathaniel; Charles Town, South Carolina, 1711 ***1224.2*** *p100*
Saler, Augusta Maria; Port uncertain, 1793 ***2856.30*** *p376*
Salesbury, Mrs.; Maryland, 1662 ***2524.55*** *p193*
Salfer, Albert 23; Ontario, 1871 ***1823.28*** *p89*
Salinski, Annie; Maryland, 1910 ***3259.35*** *p54*
Salisbury, Charles; Georgia, 1775 ***1640.10*** *p181*
Salisbury, Charles 30; Georgia, 1775 ***1220.25*** *p126*
Child: Robert 11
Child: Thomas 10
Salisbury, John; Maryland, 1670 ***2524.55*** *p193*
With wife
Salisbury, Nicholas; Boston, 1749 ***1224.2*** *p100*
Salisbury, Robert 11 *SEE* Salisbury, Charles
Salisbury, Thomas 10 *SEE* Salisbury, Charles

Salisbury, Thomas 36; Maryland, 1774 ***1220.25*** *p59*
Salisbury, William; Maryland, 1682 ***2524.55*** *p193*
Salkald, John 38; Ontario, 1871 ***1823.15*** *p232*
Salkeld, Francis; Virginia, 1666 ***6212.30*** *p29*
Salkeld, George; New Orleans, 1834 ***1224.3*** *p68*
Salkeld, Isaac 46; Ontario, 1871 ***1823.15*** *p232*
Salkeld, John 83; Ontario, 1871 ***1823.15*** *p232*
Sallame, Hermane; Maryland, 1666 ***2524.55*** *p193*
Sallary, Mary; Maryland, 1681 ***2524.55*** *p193*
Sallenge, John; Maryland, 1665 ***2524.55*** *p108*
Sallers, Robt; Virginia, 1664 ***6212.30*** *p9*
Sallitt, William; Charles Town, South Carolina, 1784 ***1224.2*** *p100*
Salloway, Henry; New York, 1838 ***8197.10*** *p150*
Sallows, James 63; Ontario, 1871 ***1823.15*** *p232*
Salman, James 48; Ontario, 1871 ***1823.28*** *p89*
Salmon, Mrs.; Maryland, 1649 ***2524.55*** *p193*
Salmon, Ann; Virginia, 1679-1680 ***6212.30*** *p54*
Salmon, Barbara 82; Vermont, 1915 ***5900.10*** *p419*
Salmon, Elizabeth 16; Newfoundland, 1774 ***1220.25*** *p1*
Salmon, Jno; Virginia, 1665 ***6212.30*** *p22*
Salmon, John 15; Maryland, 1774 ***1220.25*** *p83*
Salmon, John 16; Maryland, 1775 ***1220.25*** *p112*
Salmon, John 17; Philadelphia, 1774 ***1220.25*** *p66*
Salmon, John 38; Vermont, 1866 ***5900.10*** *p419*
Salmon, Margaret; Vermont, 1856-1915 ***5900.10*** *p439*
Salmon, Mary 24; Ontario, 1871 ***1823.28*** *p89*
Salmon, Michael; New York, 1777 ***1224.2*** *p100*
Salmon, Stephen; Maryland, 1633 ***2524.55*** *p193*
Salmon, Thomas; Maryland, 1670 ***2524.55*** *p193*
Salmon, Thomas; New York, 1834 ***8197.10*** *p315*
Salmon, Thomas 20; Ontario, 1871 ***1823.28*** *p89*
Salmond, David; Toronto, 1879 ***1640.13*** *p110*
Salmonson, Frederick; New York, 1854 ***1224.3*** *p68*
Salomon, Jonas; New York, 1831 ***8197.10*** *p367*
Salonen, Richard; New York, 1837 ***8197.10*** *p106*
Salor, Patrick 28; Ontario, 1871 ***1823.28*** *p89*
Salsbury, Job.; Virginia, 1664 ***6212.30*** *p5*
Salschoska, Helena; Maryland, 1910 ***3259.35*** *p54*
Salt, Ben; Virginia, 1672 ***6212.30*** *p49*
Salt, Benjamin; Virginia, 1668-1669 ***6212.30*** *p41*
Salt, John; Maryland, 1656 ***2524.55*** *p193*
Salt, John; Maryland, 1663 ***2524.55*** *p193*
Salt, Thomas 60; Ontario, 1871 ***1823.15*** *p232*
Saltarsh, Rebecca; Maryland, 1667 ***2524.55*** *p193*
Salter, Mr.; Canada, 1858 ***9196.15*** *p45*
Salter, Abigail; New England, 1654 ***1224.1*** *p51*
Salter, Daniel; Died enroute, 1610-1699 ***1224.1*** *p50*
Salter, Hannah; New England, 1654 ***1224.1*** *p51*
Salter, Ja; Virginia, 1671 ***6212.30*** *p44*
Salter, James; Alabama, 1820-1848 ***1640.10*** *p182*
Salter, James; Ohio, 1846 ***1224.3*** *p68*
Salter, John; Maryland, 1631-1685 ***2524.55*** *p193*
Salter, John; Maryland, 1657 ***2524.55*** *p193*
Salter, John; Pennsylvania, 1777 ***4629.10*** *p25*
Salter, John; Virginia, 1668-1669 ***6212.30*** *p40*
Salter, John, Jr.; Pennsylvania, 1787 ***4629.10*** *p52*
Salter, Mary Burns; Vermont, 1859-1910 ***5900.10*** *p379*
Salter, Robert 21; Virginia, 1774 ***1220.25*** *p87*
Salter, William; New York, New York, 1858 ***3437.14*** *p81*
Saltern, William 63; Ontario, 1871 ***1823.22*** *p140*
Salton, William 42; Virginia, 1774 ***1220.25*** *p46*
Saltonstall, Mary; Massachusetts, 1748 ***1224.2*** *p100*
Saltus, Susan Zoe; Vermont, 1835-1907 ***5900.10*** *p134*
Saluza, Christobal Garcia; New York, 1826 ***8197.10*** *p334*
Salvador, Joseph; Charles Town, South Carolina, 1788 ***1224.2*** *p100*
Salvatore, Felix; Alaska, 1910 ***9196.1*** *p37*
Salver, Thomas 30; Philadelphia, 1774 ***1220.25*** *p81*
Salvor, Hen.; Maryland, 1661 ***2524.55*** *p193*
Salwey, Anthony; Maryland, 1672 ***1224.1*** *p51*
Salzgeber, Dietrich; America, 1738 ***2856.30*** *p376*
With wife
Salzgeber, Dietrich; America, 1745 ***2856.30*** *p376*
With wife
Salzmann, Franz; America, 1752 ***2856.30*** *p376*
Salzmann, Hans; America, 1752 ***2856.30*** *p376*
Samann, Barbara; Port uncertain, 1795 ***2856.30*** *p453*
Samann, Jonathan; Port uncertain, 1769 ***2856.30*** *p453*
Sambs, Elisabeth; America, 1744 ***2856.30*** *p376*
Sames, Anne; Maryland, 1682 ***2524.55*** *p193*
Samin, Anna Barbara; Port uncertain, 1773 ***2856.30*** *p376*
Samine, George; Maryland, 1681 ***2524.55*** *p193*
Samlanski, Frank; Maryland, 1910 ***3259.35*** *p54*
Samm, Andreas; America, 1749 ***2856.30*** *p376*
Samme, James; Maryland, 1658 ***2524.55*** *p193*
Sammes, Margarett; Maryland, 1652-1653 ***2524.55*** *p193*
Sammon, Andrew 60; Ontario, 1871 ***1823.28*** *p89*
Sammon, Annie 10; Ontario, 1871 ***1823.28*** *p89*
Sammon, Bridget 12; Ontario, 1871 ***1823.28*** *p89*
Sammon, Daniel 14; Ontario, 1871 ***1823.28*** *p89*
Sammon, Ellen; Vermont, 1855-1929 ***5900.10*** *p274*
Sammon, James 11; Ontario, 1871 ***1823.28*** *p89*
Sammon, Joseph; Maryland, 1677-1681 ***2524.55*** *p193*
Sammon, Margaret; Vermont, 1844-1914 ***5900.10*** *p562*
Sammon, Mary Murphy 65; Vermont, 1888 ***5900.10*** *p447*
Sammon, Mary Walsh; Vermont, 1854-1931 ***5900.10*** *p195*
Sammon, Michael 5; Ontario, 1871 ***1823.28*** *p89*
Sammon, Michael 35; Ontario, 1871 ***1823.28*** *p89*
Sammon, Patrick T.; Vermont, 1855-1928 ***5900.10*** *p195*
Sammon, Thomas 7; Ontario, 1871 ***1823.28*** *p89*
Sammonds, Thomas 24; Maryland, 1775 ***1220.25*** *p99*
Sammony, George 16; Philadelphia, 1774 ***1220.25*** *p43*
Samms, Richard 22; Maryland, 1774 ***1220.25*** *p5*
Samon, Jno; Virginia, 1665-1666 ***6212.30*** *p24*
Sampell, James 32; Virginia, 1775 ***1220.25*** *p109*
Sample, John; Philadelphia, 1794 ***4629.10*** *p81*
Father: Samuel
Mother: Margaret
Sample, John 36; Ontario, 1871 ***1823.28*** *p89*
Sample, John 45; Ontario, 1871 ***1823.15*** *p232*
Sample, John 62; Ontario, 1871 ***1823.28*** *p89*
Sample, John 78; Ontario, 1871 ***1823.15*** *p232*
Sample, Margaret *SEE* Sample, John
Sample, Robert 35; Ontario, 1871 ***1823.15*** *p232*
Sample, Samuel *SEE* Sample, John
Sample, Samuel 56; Ontario, 1871 ***1823.15*** *p232*
Sample, William; Maryland, 1653 ***2524.55*** *p193*
Sample, William 35; Ontario, 1871 ***1823.28*** *p89*
Sampson, Alice *SEE* Sampson, Richard
Sampson, Edward; Maryland, 1665 ***2524.55*** *p193*
Sampson, Henry; Florida, 1772 ***1224.2*** *p100*
Sampson, Henry; Maryland, 1657 ***2524.55*** *p193*
Sampson, Isaack *SEE* Sampson, Richard
Sampson, John; California, 1851 ***1224.3*** *p68*
Sampson, Moses; New York, 1838 ***8197.10*** *p149*
Sampson, Rachael 23; Maryland, 1775 ***1220.25*** *p109*
Sampson, Richard *SEE* Sampson, Richard
Sampson, Richard; Maryland, 1682 ***2524.55*** *p193*
Wife: Alice
Son: Isaack
Son: Richard
Sampson, Robert; Maryland, 1667 ***2524.55*** *p194*
Sampson, Thomas; Maryland, 1659 ***2524.55*** *p51*
Sampson, William; Maryland, 1655 ***2524.55*** *p194*
Sampson, William; New York, 1806 ***8197.10*** *p277*
Sampson, William; New York, 1808 ***8197.10*** *p277*
Sampson, William; New York, 1810 ***8197.10*** *p277*
Sams, Elisabeth; America, 1744 ***2856.30*** *p376*
Samson, Richard; Pennsylvania, 1785 ***4629.10*** *p48*
Samson, Rosan 65; Ontario, 1871 ***1823.28*** *p89*
Samssel, Paul; America, 1739 ***2856.30*** *p376*
With wife & 2 children
Samuel, Agnes 50; Ontario, 1871 ***1823.22*** *p141*
Samuel, David; New York, 1828 ***8197.10*** *p282*
Samuel, David; New York, 1828-1835 ***8197.10*** *p310*
Samuel, Gilbert 21; Maryland, 1775 ***1220.25*** *p99*
Samuel, John 73; Ontario, 1871 ***1823.15*** *p232*
Samuel, Robert 22; Philadelphia, 1774 ***1220.25*** *p86*
Samuels, Charles; New York, 1840 ***8197.10*** *p195*
Samuels, R. A.; Quebec, 1858 ***9196.15*** *p41*
Samwaies, Jonathan; Virginia, 1663 ***6212.30*** *p4*
Samwell, George 39; Ontario, 1871 ***1823.15*** *p232*
Sanbatch, John 13; Grenada, 1774 ***1220.25*** *p85*
Sanborn, Catherine Lacey; Vermont, 1863-1949 ***5900.10*** *p186*
Sanborn, Ezra A. 61; Ontario, 1871 ***1823.22*** *p141*
Sanborn, Margaret I.; Vermont, 1849-1914 ***5900.10*** *p456*
Sanborn, Moses L.; Vermont, 1853-1911 ***5900.10*** *p186*
Sanbourn, Ruben 49; Ontario, 1871 ***1823.15*** *p232*
Sanburn, Adelainde 2; Ontario, 1861 ***2896.27*** *p30*
Sanburn, Allen 46; Ontario, 1861 ***2896.27*** *p30*
Sanburn, Elgin 11; Ontario, 1861 ***2896.27*** *p30*
Sanburn, Isabella 8; Ontario, 1861 ***2896.27*** *p30*
Sanburn, James 88; Ontario, 1871 ***1823.28*** *p89*
Sanburn, Rachel 17; Ontario, 1861 ***2896.27*** *p30*
Sanches, Anthony; Philadelphia, 1793 ***4629.10*** *p82*
Sanchy, William; Maryland, 1661 ***2524.55*** *p194*
Sanckey, Wm.; Maryland, 1660 ***2524.55*** *p194*
Sanckley, Richard; Virginia, 1675 ***1224.1*** *p51*
Sand, Christina Elisa; America, 1765 ***2856.30*** *p376*
Sandall, Peter; Maryland, 1651 ***2524.55*** *p194*
Sandall, Peter; Maryland, 1668 ***2524.55*** *p194*
Sandall, Samuell; Maryland, 1658 ***2524.55*** *p194*
Sandaver, John; New York, 1838 ***8197.10*** *p284*
Sandberg, Charles; New York, New York, 1882 ***3437.14*** *p182*
Sandel, Daniel; America, 1754 ***2856.30*** *p377*
Sandel, Peter; America, 1752 ***2856.30*** *p377*
With wife & child
Sandel, Valentin; America, 1768 ***2856.30*** *p377*
Sandele, Andreas; Port uncertain, 1781 ***2856.30*** *p453*
Sandele, Andreas; Port uncertain, 1801 ***2856.30*** *p453*
Sandeon, August 44; Montana, 1917 ***9196.1*** *p52*
Sandeon, August 44; Yukon, 1917 ***9196.1*** *p52*
Sander, Philipp; America, 1752 ***2856.30*** *p377*
Sander, William; New York, 1839 ***8197.10*** *p285*
Sandercock, William 38; Ontario, 1871 ***1823.22*** *p141*
Sanderman, Christopher Henry; Pennsylvania, 1776 ***4629.10*** *p53*
Sanders, Miss; Quebec, 1857 ***9196.15*** *p17*
Sanders, Mrs.; Quebec, 1856 ***9196.15*** *p9*
Sanders, Abraham; Maryland, 1657 ***2524.55*** *p194*
Sanders, Abraham 40; Ontario, 1871 ***1823.15*** *p232*
Sanders, Ann; Maryland, 1652 ***2524.55*** *p57*
Sanders, C.; Quebec, 1856 ***9196.15*** *p9*
Sanders, Daniel 27; Maryland, 1775 ***1220.25*** *p102*
Sanders, Edward William; Havana, 1849 ***1224.3*** *p68*
Sanders, Edward William; Texas, n.d. ***1224.3*** *p68*
Sanders, Emanuel 40; Ontario, 1871 ***1823.28*** *p89*
Sanders, Francis 36; Ontario, 1871 ***1823.15*** *p232*
Sanders, Francis M. 36; Ontario, 1871 ***1823.28*** *p89*
Sanders, George 31; Ontario, 1871 ***1823.22*** *p141*
Sanders, George 43; Ontario, 1871 ***1823.15*** *p232*
Sanders, Isibelia 23; Ontario, 1871 ***1823.22*** *p141*
Sanders, John; New York, 1807 ***8197.10*** *p50*
Sanders, John; South Carolina, 1747 ***1224.2*** *p101*
Sanders, John 15; Virginia, 1774 ***1220.25*** *p46*
Sanders, John 21; Maryland, 1774 ***1220.25*** *p3*
Sanders, John 29; Ontario, 1871 ***1823.22*** *p141*
Sanders, John 37; Ontario, 1871 ***1823.15*** *p232*
Sanders, John 38; Ontario, 1871 ***1823.15*** *p232*
Sanders, John 40; Ontario, 1871 ***1823.15*** *p232*
Sanders, John 41; Ontario, 1871 ***1823.15*** *p232*
Sanders, Lovett; Boston, 1710 ***1224.2*** *p101*
Sanders, Richard; Virginia, 1664 ***6212.30*** *p12*
Sanders, Richard; Virginia, 1677 ***6212.30*** *p53*
Sanders, Richard; Virginia, 1679-1680 ***6212.30*** *p54*
Sanders, Richard 34; Ontario, 1871 ***1823.15*** *p232*
Sanders, Roxana 20; Philadelphia, 1774 ***1220.25*** *p63*
Sanders, Samll; Virginia, 1664 ***6212.30*** *p9*
Sanders, Samuel 31; Ontario, 1871 ***1823.15*** *p232*
Sanders, Samuel 36; Ontario, 1871 ***1823.15*** *p232*
Sanders, Samuel 67; Ontario, 1871 ***1823.15*** *p232*
Sanders, Simon 30; Ontario, 1871 ***1823.15*** *p232*
Sanders, Tho; Virginia, 1664 ***6212.30*** *p11*
Sanders, Thomas 18; Virginia, 1774 ***1220.25*** *p55*
Sanders, Thomas 31; Ontario, 1871 ***1823.15*** *p233*
Sanders, Thomas 33; Ontario, 1871 ***1823.15*** *p233*
Sanders, Thomas 55; Ontario, 1871 ***1823.15*** *p233*
Sanders, William; New York, 1805 ***8197.10*** *p30*
Sanders, William; Newfoundland, 1774 ***1220.25*** *p1*
Sanders, William 22; Maryland, 1775 ***1220.25*** *p111*
Sanders, William 36; Ontario, 1871 ***1823.15*** *p233*
Sanders, William 39; Ontario, 1871 ***1823.15*** *p233*
Sanders, William 68; Ontario, 1871 ***1823.15*** *p233*
Sanders, William H. 33; Ontario, 1871 ***1823.15*** *p233*
Sanderson, Aaron 60; Ontario, 1871 ***1823.22*** *p141*
Sanderson, Ann; Maryland, 1663 ***2524.55*** *p194*
Sanderson, Ann; Maryland, 1668 ***2524.55*** *p194*
Sanderson, Ann J. 2; Ontario, 1861 ***2896.27*** *p42*
Sanderson, Christophr 60; Ontario, 1871 ***1823.15*** *p233*
Sanderson, David 38; Ontario, 1871 ***1823.15*** *p233*
Sanderson, Edward Fisher; New York, 1831 ***8197.10*** *p299*
Sanderson, Emma 25; Ontario, 1871 ***1823.22*** *p141*
Sanderson, Henry 50; Ontario, 1871 ***1823.15*** *p233*
Sanderson, James 35; Ontario, 1871 ***1823.15*** *p233*
Sanderson, James 50; Ontario, 1871 ***1823.15*** *p233*
Sanderson, Jane 62; Ontario, 1871 ***1823.22*** *p141*
Sanderson, Janes 40; Ontario, 1871 ***1823.15*** *p233*
Sanderson, John; Virginia, 1663 ***6212.30*** *p1*
Sanderson, John 40; Ontario, 1871 ***1823.15*** *p233*
Sanderson, John 45; Carolina, 1774 ***1220.25*** *p85*
Sanderson, John 45; Ontario, 1871 ***1823.15*** *p233*
Sanderson, John Pinder; Philadelphia, 1791 ***4629.10*** *p80*
Sanderson, Joseph 31; Ontario, 1871 ***1823.15*** *p233*
Sanderson, Robert 35; Ontario, 1871 ***1823.15*** *p233*
Sanderson, Robert 70; Ontario, 1871 ***1823.15*** *p233*
Sanderson, Thomas; New York, 1838 ***8197.10*** *p150*
Sanderson, Thomas 40; Ontario, 1871 ***1823.15*** *p233*
Sanderson, Thos 40; Ontario, 1871 ***1823.15*** *p233*
Sanderson, William; Georgia, 1699 ***1640.13*** *p110*
Sanderson, William 40; Ontario, 1871 ***1823.15*** *p233*
Sanderson, William 44; Ontario, 1871 ***1823.28*** *p89*
Sanderson, William 73; Ontario, 1871 ***1823.22*** *p141*
Sanderson, Wm 22; Ontario, 1871 ***1823.28*** *p89*
Sandfield, Robert; Maryland, 1675 ***2524.55*** *p194*
Sandford, John; Virginia, 1704 ***1224.2*** *p100*
Sandford, Samuel; Virginia, 1710 ***1224.2*** *p100*
Sandford, Thomas James Harris; Ohio, 1825 ***1224.3*** *p68*
Sandham, Andrew; New York, 1832 ***8197.10*** *p368*
Sandicock, John 30; Ontario, 1871 ***1823.22*** *p141*
Sandis, Richard; Virginia, 1666-1667 ***6212.30*** *p32*
Sandish, John; Maryland, 1661 ***2524.55*** *p208*

Sandlant, William 21; Maryland, 1774 ***1220.25*** *p61*
Sandlett, Henry; Maryland, 1654 ***2524.55*** *p194*
Sando, Marten 25; Alaska, 1913 ***9196.1*** *p23*
Sandome, William; Maryland, 1660 ***2524.55*** *p194*
Sandown, William; Maryland, 1660 ***2524.55*** *p194*
Sandrih, Ole 28; Canada, 1913 ***9196.1*** *p21*
Sandrih, Ole 28; North Dakota, 1913 ***9196.1*** *p21*
Sandritter, Michael; America, 1731 ***2856.30*** *p377*
Sandry, Peter 37; Ontario, 1871 ***1823.22*** *p141*
Sands, Archibald 38; Ontario, 1871 ***1823.15*** *p233*
Sands, Elizabeth Kelley 69; Vermont, 1911 ***5900.10*** *p471*
Sands, Geo; Virginia, 1664 ***6212.30*** *p10*
Sands, Geo; Virginia, 1665-1666 ***6212.30*** *p22*
Sands, George; New York, 1803 ***8197.10*** *p16*
Sands, James; Virginia, 1669-1670 ***6212.30*** *p41*
Sands, John; Virginia, 1671 ***6212.30*** *p44*
Sands, John; Virginia, 1672 ***6212.30*** *p49*
Sands, Joseph; New York, 1830 ***8197.10*** *p312*
Sands, Joseph; New York, 1840 ***8197.10*** *p197*
Sands, Joseph; New York, 1840 ***8197.10*** *p286*
Sands, Patrick 55; Vermont, 1896 ***5900.10*** *p471*
Sands, Thomas; New York, 1824 ***8197.10*** *p281*
Sands, William; Georgia, 1699 ***1640.13*** *p110*
Sanduskey, August; Maryland, 1910 ***3259.35*** *p54*
Sandy, George 26; Ontario, 1871 ***1823.15*** *p233*
Sandy, James 60; Ontario, 1871 ***1823.15*** *p233*
Sandys, Richard; Maryland, 1681 ***2524.55*** *p194*
Saneafft, Thomas; Maryland, 1678 ***2524.55*** *p194*
Sanen, Elizabeth; Maryland, 1679 ***2524.55*** *p194*
Sanfert, George; Maryland, 1910 ***3259.35*** *p54*
Sanford, Casie 56; Ontario, 1871 ***1823.22*** *p141*
Sanford, Richard; Virginia, 1683 ***1224.1*** *p51*
Sanger, Hanerich; New York, 1807 ***8197.10*** *p51*
Sanger, Hermann; America, 1754 ***2856.30*** *p453*
With wife & child
Sanger, Richard; Philadelphia, 1737 ***1224.2*** *p101*
Sanger, Stephen 40; Philadelphia, 1774 ***1220.25*** *p43*
Sanghier, Dorothy *SEE* Sanghier, George
Sanghier, Dorothy; Maryland, 1659 ***2524.55*** *p194*
Sanghier, George; Maryland, 1650 ***2524.55*** *p194*
With family
Sanghier, George; Maryland, 1659 ***2524.55*** *p194*
Wife: Dorothy
Sanghoffe, Eva 52; Kansas, 1892-1910 ***9079.10*** *p37*
Sanghoffe, Godfried 73; Kansas, 1892-1910 ***9079.10*** *p37*
Sanghoffe, Reinhardt 31; Kansas, 1892-1910 ***9079.10*** *p37*
Sangster, James; Maryland, 1681 ***2524.55*** *p194*
Sangster, James 57; Ontario, 1871 ***1823.15*** *p233*
Sangster, John 21; Virginia, 1773 ***1220.25*** *p29*
Sangster, John 32; Ontario, 1871 ***1823.15*** *p233*
Sangster, William 19; Montserrat, 1774 ***1220.25*** *p91*
Sanils, Nancy 46; Ontario, 1871 ***1823.22*** *p141*
Sanis, James; New York, 1827 ***8197.10*** *p339*
Sankt Georg, Philipp; Port uncertain, 1763 ***2856.30*** *p377*
Sankt Georgen, Anna Catharina; Port uncertain, 1763 ***2856.30*** *p377*
Sannders, Mr.; Quebec, 1858 ***9196.15*** *p43*
Sannemann, Diedrick; New York, 1839 ***8197.10*** *p139*
Sanner, Carl; New York, New York, 1886 ***3437.14*** *p149*
Sanpoginaes, B. 31; Alaska, 1917 ***9196.1*** *p44*
Sanpoginaes, B. 31; Yukon, 1917 ***9196.1*** *p44*
Sans, Joseph; Pennsylvania, 1777 ***4629.10*** *p27*
Sansaskie, Annie; Maryland, 1910 ***3259.35*** *p54*
Sansom, Joseph; Philadelphia, 1828 ***1224.3*** *p69*
Sansom, Luke 26; Maryland, 1774 ***1220.25*** *p53*
Sanson, William 44; Ontario, 1871 ***1823.15*** *p233*
Sanston, James; Maryland, 1680-1681 ***2524.55*** *p194*
Sanstrom, Dan 48; British Columbia, 1911 ***9196.1*** *p34*
Sanstrom, Dan 48; Washington, 1911 ***9196.1*** *p34*
Santerin, Jacobina; Virginia, 1775 ***1220.25*** *p123*
Santini, John; New York, 1833 ***8197.10*** *p283*
Santos, Margaret; Vermont, 1844-1896 ***5900.10*** *p378*
Santwaak, Johanis; New York, 1839 ***8197.10*** *p140*
Santwack, Johanis; New York, 1839 ***8197.10*** *p140*
Santwaik, Johanis; New York, 1836 ***8197.10*** *p283*
Saphir, George; Maryland, 1649-1650 ***2524.55*** *p194*
Sapsford, Ed W. 37; British Columbia, 1918 ***9196.1*** *p72*
Sapsford, Ed W. 37; Washington, 1918 ***9196.1*** *p72*
Sarbach, John; New York, 1834 ***8197.10*** *p319*
Sareither, Thomas; Port uncertain, 1738 ***2856.30*** *p377*
Saren, Catharina; Port uncertain, 1769 ***2856.30*** *p453*
Saret, John B.; New York, 1830 ***8197.10*** *p362*
Sargant, Thomas, Jr.; New York, 1840 ***8197.10*** *p197*
Sargant, W. J. 40; Ontario, 1871 ***1823.22*** *p141*
Sargeant, Albert 15; Ontario, 1861 ***2896.27*** *p57*
Sargeant, George A. 46; Ontario, 1861 ***2896.27*** *p57*
Sargeant, John 22; Ontario, 1861 ***2896.27*** *p57*
Sargeant, Joseph; Pennsylvania, 1785 ***4629.10*** *p48*
Sargeant, Marshall 12; Ontario, 1861 ***2896.27*** *p57*
Sargeant, Thomas; New York, 1838 ***8197.10*** *p284*
Sargeant, Thomas; New York, 1840 ***8197.10*** *p196*
Sargeant, Walter 18; Ontario, 1861 ***2896.27*** *p57*
Sargeant, William J. 39; Ontario, 1871 ***1823.22*** *p141*
Sargeaunt, John; Philadelphia, 1822 ***1224.3*** *p69*
Sargent, Mr.; Quebec, 1857 ***9196.15*** *p14*
Sargent, Ann Eliza Hanley; Vermont, 1840-1916 ***5900.10*** *p303*
Sargent, John 57; Ontario, 1871 ***1823.22*** *p141*
Sargent, John Henman 51; Vermont, 1886 ***5900.10*** *p303*
Sargent, William 48; Ontario, 1871 ***1823.22*** *p141*
Sargent, William 61; Ontario, 1871 ***1823.22*** *p141*
Sargent, William Clark; New York, 1839 ***8197.10*** *p140*
Sargent, Willis 54; Ontario, 1871 ***1823.22*** *p141*
Sargeson, William; Maryland, 1663 ***2524.55*** *p194*
Sargison, John 33; Ontario, 1871 ***1823.22*** *p141*
Sargison, Joseph 69; Ontario, 1871 ***1823.28*** *p89*
Sargison, William; Maryland, 1670 ***2524.55*** *p194*
Sargison, William; Maryland, 1671 ***2524.55*** *p194*
Sargood, John 21; Maryland, 1774 ***1220.25*** *p74*
Sarjeant, Mr.; Quebec, 1856 ***9196.15*** *p9*
Sarjeant, Mr.; Quebec, 1858 ***9196.15*** *p37*
Sarjeant, Mrs.; Quebec, 1858 ***9196.15*** *p37*
Sarjeant, Samual 59; Ontario, 1871 ***1823.15*** *p233*
Sarjeant, Thomas; New York, 1826 ***8197.10*** *p281*
Sarony, Adolphus; New York, 1831 ***8197.10*** *p355*
Sarratt, George 27; Virginia, 1774 ***1220.25*** *p94*
Sarreuther, Thomas; Port uncertain, 1738 ***2856.30*** *p377*
Sarrures, John 60; Ontario, 1871 ***1823.15*** *p233*
Sars, F. 51; Alaska, 1910 ***9196.1*** *p9*
Sars, F. 51; Yukon, 1910 ***9196.1*** *p9*
Sarsennt, Henry; Maryland, 1674 ***2524.55*** *p194*
Sarsfield, Elizabeth 80; Ontario, 1871 ***1823.28*** *p89*
Sarsnett, Henry; Maryland, 1674 ***2524.55*** *p194*
Sartan, Thomas; Pennsylvania, 1777 ***4629.10*** *p13*
Sarti, Antonio; Boston, 1851 ***1224.3*** *p69*
Sarum, John; Virginia, 1664 ***6212.30*** *p9*
Sarvice, David; Pennsylvania, 1864 ***6058.10*** *p48*
Sarvir, Joseph 15; Ontario, 1871 ***1823.28*** *p89*
Sash, Mary; New England, 1711 ***1224.2*** *p101*
Sasiadek, Thomas; Maryland, 1910 ***3259.35*** *p54*
Sass, James; Maryland, 1910 ***3259.35*** *p54*
Sass, Jozef; Maryland, 1910 ***3259.35*** *p54*
Sassan, David L.; New York, 1840 ***8197.10*** *p195*
Sassay, Emmanuel Edmond Aimie; Philadelphia, 1793 ***4629.10*** *p73*
Sasseen, David L.; New York, 1840 ***8197.10*** *p195*
Sassenberg, George A.; New York, 1803 ***8197.10*** *p17*
Sastain, James; New York, New York, 1868 ***3437.14*** *p102*
Satchell, James; New York, 1837 ***8197.10*** *p106*
Satchell, Richard; New York, 1840 ***8197.10*** *p387*
Satchell, Robt; Virginia, 1663 ***6212.30*** *p3*
Satchwell, Jeremiah; Pennsylvania, 1785 ***4629.10*** *p47*
Satchwell, Thomas 17; Maryland, 1775 ***1220.25*** *p120*
Satchwell, William; Bermuda, n.d. ***1224.2*** *p101*
Satchwell, William; Philadelphia, 1786 ***1224.2*** *p101*
Satowski, Alex; Maryland, 1910 ***3259.35*** *p54*
Satthafer, Peter; New Orleans, 1853 ***3437.14*** *p15*
Sattler, Barbara; Port uncertain, 1761 ***2856.30*** *p377*
Sattler, Catharina; Port uncertain, 1761 ***2856.30*** *p377*
Satur, Mary; South Carolina, 1737 ***1224.2*** *p86*
Satzer, . . .; Port uncertain, 1778 ***2856.30*** *p377*
Saubere, Samuel; Philadelphia, 1849 ***1224.3*** *p69*
Sauberlich, Anna Maria; America, 1790 ***2856.30*** *p453*
Sauberlich, Barbara; America, 1750 ***2856.30*** *p453*
Sauberlich, Michael, America, 1740 ***2856.30*** *p453*
With wife & children
Saudtner, Johann Adam; Port uncertain, 1748 ***2856.30*** *p377*
With wife & 4 children
Sauer, Anna; Port uncertain, 1739 ***2856.30*** *p377*
Sauer, Anna Magdalena; Port uncertain, 1745 ***2856.30*** *p377*
Sauer, Elisabeth; Port uncertain, 1740 ***2856.30*** *p377*
Sauer, Friedrich; America, 1744 ***2856.30*** *p377*
Sauer, Friedrich; America, 1744 ***2856.30*** *p379*
Sauer, Friedrich, The Younger; America, 1744 ***2856.30*** *p379*
Sauer, Johann; Port uncertain, 1700-1799 ***2856.30*** *p377*
Sauer, Johann Nikolaus; Port uncertain, 1794 ***2856.30*** *p377*
Sauer, John; New York, 1840 ***8197.10*** *p285*
Sauer, Juliana; Port uncertain, 1803 ***2856.30*** *p377*
Sauer, Martin; England, 1756 ***2856.30*** *p377*
Sauer, Regina; Port uncertain, 1744 ***2856.30*** *p378*
Sauer, Wilhelm; America, 1740 ***2856.30*** *p378*
With wife & 5 children
Sauerbek, Anna; Port uncertain, 1743 ***2856.30*** *p378*
Saueressig, Johann Mathes; Port uncertain, 1778 ***2856.30*** *p378*
With wife
Saueressig, Johann Mathes; Port uncertain, 1780 ***2856.30*** *p378*
Saueressig, Johann Mathes; Port uncertain, 1780 ***2856.30*** *p378*
With wife
Sauerhebe, Mr.; America, 1788 ***2856.30*** *p456*
Sauerheber, Jakob; America, 1764 ***2856.30*** *p378*
Sauerheber, Johann; America, 1787 ***2856.30*** *p378*
With wife
Sauerheber, Johann; Port uncertain, 1791 ***2856.30*** *p378*
Sauerheber, Johann; Port uncertain, 1792 ***2856.30*** *p378*
Sauerheber, John; America, 1794 ***2856.30*** *p378*
Sauerhoffer, Christof; Port uncertain, 1774 ***2856.30*** *p378*
Sauermilch, Martin; Port uncertain, 1747 ***2856.30*** *p378*
Sauermilch, Martin; Port uncertain, 1758 ***2856.30*** *p378*
Sauermilch, Martin; Port uncertain, 1778 ***2856.30*** *p378*
Sauermilch, Peter; Port uncertain, 1747 ***2856.30*** *p378*
Sauermilch, Peter; Port uncertain, 1758 ***2856.30*** *p378*
Sauermilch, Peter; Port uncertain, 1778 ***2856.30*** *p378*
Saughier, Mrs.; Maryland, 1647 ***2524.55*** *p194*
Saughier, Dorothy *SEE* Saughier, George
Saughier, Dorothy; Maryland, 1659 ***2524.55*** *p194*
Saughier, George; Maryland, 1650 ***2524.55*** *p194*
With family
Saughier, George; Maryland, 1659 ***2524.55*** *p194*
Wife: Dorothy
Saughnau, James; Ontario, 1871 ***1823.28*** *p90*
Saul, Ann; Maryland, 1669 ***2524.55*** *p194*
Saul, Ann; Maryland, 1676 ***2524.55*** *p194*
Saul, Jakob; Port uncertain, 1768 ***2856.30*** *p378*
Saul, John 13 *SEE* Saul, John
Saul, John 37; Virginia, 1774 ***1220.25*** *p92*
Wife: Mary 21
Child: John 13
Child: S. L. 17
Saul, Mary 21 *SEE* Saul, John
Saul, S. L. 17 *SEE* Saul, John
Saule, Oliver; Virginia, 1666 ***6212.30*** *p28*
Saultry, Mary; Vermont, 1817-1902 ***5900.10*** *p532*
Saunder, John; Maryland, 1667 ***2524.55*** *p194*
Saunders, Mr.; Quebec, 1858 ***9196.15*** *p36*
Saunders, Ann; Maryland, 1665 ***2524.55*** *p186*
Saunders, Donald; Ontario, 1851 ***4537.32*** *p91*
Wife: Margaret MacLeod
Child: James
Child: Robert
Child: Mary
Child: Effie
Saunders, Edward 40; Ontario, 1871 ***1823.28*** *p90*
Saunders, Edwin 24; Ontario, 1871 ***1823.15*** *p233*
Saunders, Edwin 45; Ontario, 1871 ***1823.28*** *p90*
Saunders, Effie *SEE* Saunders, Donald
Saunders, Effie *SEE* Saunders, James
Saunders, Elias 18; Ontario, 1871 ***1823.15*** *p233*
Saunders, Ellen *SEE* Saunders, James
Saunders, Francis Williams; Mexico, 1886 ***1640.13*** *p110*
Saunders, Henry 58; Ontario, 1871 ***1823.15*** *p233*
Saunders, Israel; Connecticut, 1763 ***1224.2*** *p101*
Saunders, Israel; Havana, 1763 ***1224.2*** *p101*
Saunders, James *SEE* Saunders, Donald
Saunders, James; Ontario, 1863 ***4537.32*** *p91*
Wife: Janet Morrison
Child: Effie
Child: Ellen
Child: Margaret
Saunders, James 30; Ontario, 1871 ***1823.15*** *p233*
Saunders, James 48; Ontario, 1871 ***1823.15*** *p233*
Saunders, Janet Morrison *SEE* Saunders, James
Saunders, Jno; Portland, Maine, 1858 ***9196.15*** *p28*
Saunders, John; Maryland, 1667 ***2524.55*** *p194*
Saunders, John; Pennsylvania, 1785 ***4629.10*** *p48*
Saunders, John 38; Ontario, 1871 ***1823.28*** *p90*
Saunders, John 42; Virginia, 1773 ***1220.25*** *p28*
Saunders, Jonathan; Virginia, 1702 ***1224.2*** *p101*
Saunders, Joseph; Pennsylvania, 1777 ***4629.10*** *p16*
Saunders, Katherine E.; Vermont, 1850-1916 ***5900.10*** *p419*
Saunders, Margaret *SEE* Saunders, James
Saunders, Margaret MacLeod *SEE* Saunders, Donald
Saunders, Margaret Smith; Ontario, 1851 ***4537.32*** *p91*
Saunders, Mary *SEE* Saunders, Donald
Saunders, Mary; Maryland, 1680 ***2524.55*** *p194*
Saunders, Mary A. 34; Vermont, 1889 ***5900.10*** *p419*
Saunders, Nora A.; Vermont, 1857-1923 ***5900.10*** *p420*
Saunders, Robert *SEE* Saunders, Donald
Saunders, Samuel 19; Ontario, 1871 ***1823.28*** *p90*
Saunders, Thomas; Maryland, 1663 ***2524.55*** *p18*
Saunders, Thomas; Newport, Rhode Island, 1765 ***1224.2*** *p101*
Saunders, Thomas; Virginia, 1723 ***1224.2*** *p101*
Saunders, William; Philadelphia, 1792 ***1224.2*** *p101*
Saunders, William 48; Ontario, 1871 ***1823.15*** *p233*
Saunders, William Edward; New York, 1834 ***8197.10*** *p283*

Saunders, William Edward; New York, 1840 8197.10 p196
Saunier, Claudius Antoine; New York, 1816 8197.10 p60
Saunier, Francis; New York, 1816 8197.10 p60
Saur, Georg; Port uncertain, 1761 2856.30 p378
Sauraft, Thomas; Maryland, 1678 2524.55 p194
Saurin, Anna Magdalena; Port uncertain, 1745 2856.30 p377
Saurin, Maria Elisabeth; Port uncertain, 1747 2856.30 p378
Saurin, Regina; Port uncertain, 1744 2856.30 p378
Saurwein, Hans; Port uncertain, 1733 2856.30 p378
Sausbery, Ann; Maryland, 1673 2524.55 p194
Sausbery, John; Maryland, 1673 2524.55 p194
Sauser, Johann; Port uncertain, 1714 2856.30 p378
Sausseleer, David; Virginia, 1775 1220.25 p123
Sausville, Julie; Vermont, 1850-1936 5900.10 p90
Sauter, Miss; America, 1746 2856.30 p317
Sauter, Miss; Port uncertain, 1784 2856.30 p378
Sauter, A. M.; America, 1754 2856.30 p102
Sauter, Anna Margarete; America, 1754 2856.30 p378
With husband
Sauter, Barbara; America, 1750 2856.30 p378
Sauter, Barbara; America, 1755 2856.30 p378
Sauter, Heinrich; America, 1754 2856.30 p378
Sauter, Heinrich; America, 1754 2856.30 p378
With son & daughter
Sauter, Heinrich; America, 1764 2856.30 p378
Wife: Ottilia
With 2 children
Sauter, Heinrich; Port uncertain, 1764 2856.30 p378
With wife & 2 children
Sauter, Johan; America, 1749 2856.30 p378
Sauter, Johann; America, 1775 2856.30 p378
Sauter, Johann; Port uncertain, 1727 2856.30 p378
Sauter, Maria; Port uncertain, 1693 2856.30 p378
With husband & 2 sons
Sauter, Martha; America, 1746 2856.30 p378
Sauter, Martha; America, 1749 2856.30 p378
Sauter, Ottilia *SEE* Sauter, Heinrich
Sauther, Georg; America, 1764 2856.30 p378
Sauthinark, A. O. 48; Alaska, 1917 9196.1 p48
Sauthinark, A. O. 48; Whitehorse, Yukon, 1917 9196.1 p48
Sautteer, Johan Michale; Virginia, 1775 1220.25 p123
Savage, . . .; Boston, 1765 4628.40 p115
Savage, Miss; Quebec, 1857 9196.15 p25
Savage, Miss; Quebec, 1858 9196.15 p46
Savage, Mr.; Quebec, 1857 9196.15 p25
Savage, Mrs.; Quebec, 1857 9196.15 p25
Savage, Mrs.; Quebec, 1858 9196.15 p41
Savage, Miss A.; Quebec, 1857 9196.15 p25
Savage, Alce; Maryland, 1663 2524.55 p195
Savage, Alice; Vermont, 1857-1923 5900.10 p285
Savage, Annie; Vermont, 1856-1902 5900.10 p284
Savage, Anthony 9 *SEE* Savage, John
Savage, Daniel; New York, 1837 8197.10 p107
Savage, David; Vermont, 1849-1937 5900.10 p56
Savage, Dorothy; Maryland, 1661 2524.55 p195
Savage, Elizabeth; Maryland, 1660 2524.55 p195
Savage, Elizabeth 55 *SEE* Savage, John
Savage, Ellen Keefe; Vermont, 1849-1929 5900.10 p56
Savage, Frederick 29; Ontario, 1871 1823.28 p90
Savage, Griffin; Virginia, 1663 6212.30 p2
Savage, Hannah; Vermont, n.d. 5900.10 p329
Savage, Hugh; Vermont, 1857-1943 5900.10 p284
Savage, Isabella 67; Ontario, 1871 1823.15 p233
Savage, J. 13; Ontario, 1861 2896.28 p12
Savage, James 60; Ontario, 1871 1823.28 p90
Savage, John; Maryland, 1662 2524.55 p195
Savage, John; New York, 1840 8197.10 p321
Savage, John; Vermont, n.d. 5900.10 p56
Savage, John 36; Virginia, 1774 1220.25 p54
Savage, John 40; Fort Cumberland, Nova Scotia, 1774 1220.25 p17
Wife: Elizabeth 55
Child: Anthony 9
Savage, John 57; Ontario, 1871 1823.15 p233
Savage, John J. 14; Ontario, 1861 2896.27 p20
Savage, John M. 73; Ontario, 1871 1823.28 p90
Savage, Joseph 22; Philadelphia, 1774 1220.25 p80
Savage, Miss L.; Quebec, 1857 9196.15 p25
Savage, Lemuel; Pennsylvania, 1777 4629.10 p27
Savage, Mary; Virginia, 1677 6212.30 p54
Savage, Mary A.; Vermont, 1852-1910 5900.10 p285
Savage, Nora; Vermont, 1866-1929 5900.10 p54
Savage, Patrick; New York, 1840 8197.10 p199
Savage, Patrick; Norfolk, Virginia, 1818 1224.3 p69
Savage, Patrick 65; Vermont, 1865 5900.10 p501
Savage, Perez; Salem, Massachusetts, 1702 1224.2 p101
Savage, Rebecca; Maryland, 1681 2524.55 p195
Savage, Richard 26; San Francisco, 1913 9196.1 p62
Savage, Robert; New York, 1829 8197.10 p351
Savage, Rowland; Virginia, 1666 6212.30 p27
Savage, Thomas; Maryland, 1661 2524.55 p195
Savage, Thomas; Maryland, 1676 2524.55 p195
Savage, Thomas; Portland, Maine, 1858 9196.15 p29
Savage, Thomas 33; Maryland, 1775 1220.25 p109
Savage, Walter; Virginia, 1664 6212.30 p9
Savage, William 18; Maryland, 1774 1220.25 p41
Savage, William 42; Ontario, 1871 1823.15 p234
Savatier, John 21; Maryland, 1774 1220.25 p47
Saven, Louis 35; Alaska, 1917 9196.1 p50
Saven, Louis 35; Yukon, 1917 9196.1 p50
Savich, M. 35; Alaska, 1917 9196.1 p53
Savich, M. 35; Whitehorse, Yukon, 1917 9196.1 p53
Saviche, Matias; Los Angeles, 1853 1224.3 p69
Savidge, Geo; Virginia, 1666-1667 6212.30 p34
Savidge, Wm; Virginia, 1666 6212.30 p26
Savigny, Elizabeth 21; Philadelphia, 1774 1220.25 p82
Savill, George 51; Ontario, 1871 1823.15 p234
Savilla, Michael 58; Ontario, 1871 1823.22 p141
Savin, Charles 24; Maryland, 1774 1220.25 p83
Savon, John *SEE* Savon, William
Savon, William; Maryland, 1664 2524.55 p195
With wife
Son: John
Savory, Nicholas; Maryland, 1682 2524.55 p195
Sawcer, Benjamin; Maryland, 1666 2524.55 p195
Sawcer, Benjamin; Maryland, 1674 2524.55 p195
Sawer, Friedrich; America, 1744 2856.30 p379
Sawer, Friedrich, The Younger; America, 1744 2856.30 p379
Sawer, Henery 33; Ontario, 1871 1823.28 p90
Sawers, George; Missouri, 1866 1640.13 p110
Sawers, John; Richmond, Virginia, 1832 1640.13 p110
Sawers, William; Georgia, 1800 1640.10 p182
Sawicki, Andrew; Maryland, 1910 3259.35 p54
Sawicky, Adolph; Maryland, 1910 3259.35 p54
Sawitzki, George; Maryland, 1910 3259.35 p54
Sawle, Nicholas; Virginia, 1666 6212.30 p29
Sawoski, Frank; Maryland, 1910 3259.35 p54
Sawosky, Joseph; Maryland, 1910 3259.35 p54
Sawser, Anne; Maryland, 1682 2524.55 p195
Sawser, Benjamin; Maryland, 1682 2524.55 p195
Sawska, Andrew; Maryland, 1910 3259.35 p54
Sawski, Marian; Maryland, 1910 3259.35 p54
Sawtell, Edelia M.; Vermont, 1822-1864 5900.10 p607
Sawyer, Mr.; Quebec, 1857 9196.15 p22
Sawyer, Benjamin; Maryland, 1679 2524.55 p195
Sawyer, Charles Henry; New York, 1826 8197.10 p282
Sawyer, Henry R.; New York, 1840 8197.10 p286
Sawyer, Herbert 32; British Columbia, 1910 9196.1 p29
Sawyer, Herbert 32; Washington, 1910 9196.1 p29
Sawyer, James; Pennsylvania, 1785 4629.10 p48
Sawyer, Jennie R. McWain; Vermont, 1852-1910 5900.10 p308
Sawyer, Levi 67; Ontario, 1871 1823.22 p141
Sawyer, Merritt A.; Vermont, 1852-1926 5900.10 p308
Sawyer, William 35; Maryland, 1775 1220.25 p101
Sax, Franz Anton; Port uncertain, 1753 2856.30 p379
Sax, Johann Georg; Port uncertain, 1749 2856.30 p379
Sax, Johann Niklas; Port uncertain, 1793 2856.30 p379
Saxon, George; Albany, New York, 1781 1224.2 p101
Saxton, Jerimy; Maryland, 1665 2524.55 p195
Say, John; Virginia, 1663 6212.30 p2
Say, Mary; Maryland, 1682 2524.55 p195
Sayer, Miss; Quebec, 1857 9196.15 p19
Sayer, Mr.; Quebec, 1858 9196.15 p45
Sayer, A. A. 1; Ontario, 1861 2896.25 p45
Sayer, A. L. 10; Ontario, 1861 2896.25 p45
Sayer, Albert 21; Ontario, 1861 2896.25 p49
Sayer, Anna 57; Ontario, 1861 2896.25 p45
Sayer, C. N. 6; Ontario, 1861 2896.25 p45
Sayer, Charles 20; Ontario, 1861 2896.28 p47
Sayer, David 29; Ontario, 1861 2896.25 p45
Sayer, E. 26; Ontario, 1861 2896.25 p45
Sayer, Edward 57; Ontario, 1871 1823.28 p90
Sayer, George 15; Ontario, 1861 2896.25 p49
Sayer, H. 38; Ontario, 1861 2896.25 p49
Sayer, Henry 19; Ontario, 1861 2896.25 p45
Sayer, J. 8; Ontario, 1861 2896.25 p45
Sayer, J. H. 12; Ontario, 1861 2896.25 p45
Sayer, John; Virginia, 1686 1224.1 p51
Sayer, John 27; Georgia, 1774 1220.25 p48
Sayer, M. A. 9; Ontario, 1861 2896.25 p45
Sayer, Maria Elisabeth; Port uncertain, 1764 2856.30 p379
Sayer, Mary Ann 33; Ontario, 1861 2896.25 p45
Sayer, Nancy 18; Ontario, 1861 2896.25 p45
Sayer, P. A. 18; Ontario, 1861 2896.25 p49
Sayer, Ralp; Virginia, 1671-1672 6212.30 p47
Sayer, S. E. 3; Ontario, 1861 2896.25 p45
Sayer, Touissaint M. 51; Ontario, 1871 1823.28 p90
Sayer, William 27; Maryland, 1775 1220.25 p115
Sayer, William H. 21; Ontario, 1861 2896.25 p45
Sayers, Mrs. 52; Ontario, 1861 2896.26 p30
Sayers, George 24; Ontario, 1871 1823.28 p90
Sayers, Gillaspie 53; Ontario, 1861 2896.26 p30
Sayers, James; Pennsylvania, 1777 4629.10 p15
Sayers, Martha Jane 30; Ontario, 1861 2896.26 p30
Sayers, Matilda 25; Ontario, 1861 2896.26 p31
Sayers, Rebecca 27; Ontario, 1861 2896.26 p31
Sayes, James; Maryland, 1681 2524.55 p195
Saygor, William; Maryland, 1665 2524.55 p195
Sayler, Johann; Port uncertain, 1728 2856.30 p379
Sayler, Ludwig; Port uncertain, 1696 2856.30 p379
Sayles, Marshall 52; Ontario, 1871 1823.22 p141
Sayller, Peter; Port uncertain, 1732 2856.30 p379
Saylor, Anne E. 6; Ontario, 1861 2896.27 p40
Saylor, Caroline 36; Ontario, 1861 2896.27 p40
Saylor, Catherine 29; Ontario, 1861 2896.27 p30
Saylor, Charles 6; Ontario, 1861 2896.27 p42
Saylor, Charles 12; Ontario, 1861 2896.27 p40
Saylor, David 7; Ontario, 1861 2896.27 p30
Saylor, James V. 2; Ontario, 1861 2896.27 p42
Saylor, Jemima 72; Ontario, 1861 2896.27 p30
Saylor, Mary E. 4; Ontario, 1861 2896.27 p42
Saylor, Ruth 29; Ontario, 1861 2896.27 p42
Saylor, Samuel 11; Ontario, 1861 2896.27 p30
Saylor, Sarah E. 9; Ontario, 1861 2896.27 p40
Saynhaysen, Felte; America, 1754 2856.30 p379
Saynhisin, Felte; America, 1754 2856.30 p379
Saynish, Lewis; New York, 1825 8197.10 p281
Sayre, Charles 21; Ontario, 1861 2896.28 p33
Sayre, Fannie 13; Ontario, 1861 2896.28 p33
Sayre, Sarah E. 19; Ontario, 1861 2896.28 p33
Sayre, William 15; Ontario, 1861 2896.28 p33
Sayres, Brook 42; Ontario, 1861 2896.26 p33
Sayres, John 5; Ontario, 1861 2896.26 p33
Sayres, Margret 11; Ontario, 1861 2896.26 p33
Sayres, Martha 2; Ontario, 1861 2896.26 p33
Sayrs, James 14; Ontario, 1861 2896.26 p35
Sayrs, John 50; Ontario, 1861 2896.26 p39
Sayrs, Mahaly 9; Ontario, 1861 2896.26 p35
Sayrs, Mahaly 16; Ontario, 1861 2896.26 p35
Sayrs, Maria 12; Ontario, 1861 2896.26 p35
Sayrs, Mary 45; Ontario, 1861 2896.26 p39
Sayrs, William 2; Ontario, 1861 2896.26 p35
Sayther, Fran; Virginia, 1671-1672 6212.30 p46
Sazger, Therese; Port uncertain, 1773 2856.30 p379
Scaben, Mrs. Peter; Port uncertain, 1786 2856.30 p379
Scablehorne, Sarah; Maryland, 1681 2524.55 p107
Scablehorne, Sarah; Maryland, 1681 2524.55 p195
Scadamore, James; Virginia, 1665-1666 6212.30 p23
Scaife, Elizabeth; New York, 1844 1224.3 p69
Scaife, Sarah Fell; New York, 1844 1224.3 p69
Scales, Ralph; Virginia, 1688 6212.30 p58
Scallin, Andrew; New York, 1830 8197.10 p282
Scallion, Ellen 30; Ontario, 1871 1823.15 p234
Scammell, Mr.; Quebec, 1858 9196.15 p32
Scammell, Mrs.; Quebec, 1858 9196.15 p32
Scammon, Julia; Vermont, 1850-1899 5900.10 p175
Scandrett, James; South Carolina, 1770 1224.2 p101
Scandrill, Phillip; Virginia, 1671-1672 6212.30 p47
Scanlan, Bridget 81; Vermont, 1901 5900.10 p433
Scanlan, Catherine Tully; Vermont, 1829-1909 5900.10 p93
Scanlan, David P. 78; Vermont, 1903 5900.10 p61
Scanlan, Denis; New York, 1837 8197.10 p105
Scanlan, Dennis; Vermont, 1833-1889 5900.10 p93
Scanlan, Joanna Lawlor 76; Vermont, 1909 5900.10 p61
Scanlan, Johann 27; Ontario, 1871 1823.28 p90
Scanlan, John; New York, 1840 8197.10 p198
Scanlan, John J.; Vermont, 1858-1913 5900.10 p433
Scanlan, Patrick 65; Vermont, 1880 5900.10 p433
Scanlan, Thomas; Vermont, 1856-1905 5900.10 p93
Scanlan, William; New York, 1840 8197.10 p321
Scanlan, William John; New York, 1826 8197.10 p281
Scanlen, Bridget 1; Vermont, 1875 5900.10 p99
Scanlen, Ellen; Vermont, 1820-1898 5900.10 p219
Scanlen, Mary 2; Vermont, 1874 5900.10 p99
Scanlin, Barney; New York, 1822 8197.10 p280
Scanlin, Barney; New York, 1827 8197.10 p282
Scanlin, Bartley; New York, 1840 8197.10 p196
Scanlon, Ellen 74; Vermont, 1877 5900.10 p72
Scanlon, Frank 73; Vermont, 1906 5900.10 p444
Scanlon, James 66; Vermont, 1916 5900.10 p484
Scanlon, Johanna 29; Vermont, 1884 5900.10 p61
Scanlon, Margaret; Vermont, 1851-1934 5900.10 p478
Scanlon, Mary; Vermont, 1834-1898 5900.10 p461
Scanlon, Mary; Vermont, 1853-1930 5900.10 p492
Scanlon, Mary; Vermont, 1860-1960 5900.10 p61
Scanlon, Mary Drum 32; Vermont, 1853 5900.10 p484
Scanlon, Mary Ward 62; Vermont, 1915 5900.10 p484
Scanlon, Patrick 87; Vermont, 1896 5900.10 p484
Scanlon, Thomas; New York, 1826 8197.10 p281
Scanlon, William; Vermont, 1843-1923 5900.10 p478
Scannel, Hanorah; Vermont, 1860-1911 5900.10 p395

Scannell, Daniel; New York, 1822 8197.10 p280
Scannell, Hanora Barry; Vermont, 1816-1905 5900.10 p586
Scannell, Jeremiah; Vermont, 1816-1884 5900.10 p586
Scantlebury, Joanna; New York, 1854 1224.3 p4
Scantlebury, Joseph; New York, 1831 8197.10 p282
Scapes, John; Maryland, 1658 2524.55 p195
Scarborough, Dennis *SEE* Scarborough, Mathew
Scarborough, Hannah *SEE* Scarborough, Mathew
Scarborough, James 25; Maryland, 1774 1220.25 p83
Scarborough, John; New York, 1834 8197.10 p319
Scarborough, Mathew; Maryland, 1680 2524.55 p195
Wife: Hannah
Child: Hannah
Child: Dennis
Scarbrough, Mathew; Virginia, 1664 6212.30 p10
Scarburgh, Charles; Virginia, 1672 6212.30 p48
Scarburgh, Edm; Virginia, 1672 6212.30 p49
Scarburgh, Thomas; Virginia, 1671-1672 6212.30 p47
Scarburgh, Ursila; Virginia, 1672 6212.30 p49
Scarburgh, Ursila, Jr.; Virginia, 1672 6212.30 p49
Scarey, James; Vermont, 1828-1904 5900.10 p353
Scarey, Julia Howe; Vermont, 1837-1907 5900.10 p353
Scarf, John 34; Maryland, 1775 1220.25 p103
Scarf, Robert 46; Ontario, 1871 1823.22 p141
Scarfe, Nicholas; Maryland, 1681 2524.55 p195
Scarilou, Patrick 65; Ontario, 1871 1823.15 p234
Scarlet, Susan; Virginia, 1667 6212.30 p37
Scarlett, Edward 19; Ontario, 1871 1823.22 p141
Scarlett, Edward 50; Ontario, 1871 1823.22 p141
Scarlett, John 68; Ontario, 1871 1823.22 p141
Scarlett, John S. 26; Ontario, 1871 1823.28 p90
Scarlett, Margaret 15; Ontario, 1871 1823.22 p141
Scarlett, Samuel 53; Ontario, 1871 1823.15 p234
Scarlett, Susan 17; Ontario, 1871 1823.22 p142
Scarr, George 21; Maryland, 1775 1220.25 p111
Scarry, Mary; Vermont, 1834-1920 5900.10 p48
Scarth, Isaac; Virginia, 1728 1224.2 p101
Scarth, Thomas; New York, 1835 8197.10 p283
Scatch, John 27; Ontario, 1871 1823.15 p234
Scawen, Wm; Virginia, 1666 6212.30 p27
Scea, Catherine 28; Ontario, 1861 2896.25 p13
Scea, George 3; Ontario, 1861 2896.25 p13
Scea, Henry S. 1; Ontario, 1861 2896.25 p13
Scea, Sophia 72; Ontario, 1861 2896.25 p13
Sceavey, Captain; Quebec, 1858 9196.15 p40
Scele, Bridget; Vermont, n.d. 5900.10 p498
Scenters, James; Alabama, 1831-1845 1640.10 p182
Scerf, John 43; Ontario, 1871 1823.15 p234
Scesth, Christian 28; Ontario, 1871 1823.15 p234
Sceszek, Martin; Maryland, 1910 3259.35 p54
Schaab, Paul; Port uncertain, 1752 2856.30 p379
Schaad, Henrich; Port uncertain, 1774 2856.30 p379
Schaaf, Georg; Port uncertain, 1790 2856.30 p379
Schaaf, Johann Georg; Port uncertain, 1757 2856.30 p379
Schaaka, Henry; Philadelphia, 1839 6058.10 p18
Schaake, Elizabeth 62; Ontario, 1871 1823.15 p234
Schab, John; Maryland, 1910 3259.35 p54
Schababerle, Friedrich; Port uncertain, 1765 2856.30 p379
Schaber, Elisabeth; Port uncertain, 1751 2856.30 p421
Schabler, Johann; America, 1747 2856.30 p379
With 2 children & mother
Schablin, Christian; Port uncertain, 1696 2856.30 p401
Schachtele, Michael; America, 1771 2856.30 p421
Schachter, Andreas; America, 1753 2856.30 p421
Schack, Andrew 22; Kansas, 1909-1910 9079.10 p10
Schack, Jakob; Port uncertain, 1770 2856.30 p381
Schack, Johann; America, 1751 2856.30 p379
Schack, Otto W. C.; New York, 1840 8197.10 p198
Schack, Rosa 19; Kansas, 1909-1910 9079.10 p10
Schad, J.; America, 1744 2856.30 p476
Schad, Johann Adam; America, 1738 2856.30 p379
Schade, Johann; America, 1744 2856.30 p379
Schade, John 34; Ontario, 1871 1823.15 p234
Schadel, Maria; Port uncertain, 1785 2856.30 p421
Schader, Charles 26; Ontario, 1871 1823.15 p234
Schader, Christina 64; Ontario, 1871 1823.15 p234
Schader, John 66; Ontario, 1871 1823.15 p234
Schadka, Henry; Philadelphia, 1839 6058.10 p18
Schaefer, Frederick 52; Ontario, 1871 1823.15 p234
Schaefer, Jakob; Port uncertain, 1785 2856.30 p379
Schaefer, Wilhelm; Port uncertain, 1767 2856.30 p379
Schaeffer, Alphonse; New York, 1837 8197.10 p106
Schaeffer, Andreas; Port uncertain, 1791 2856.30 p379
Schaeffer, Andreas; Port uncertain, 1792 2856.30 p379
Schaeffer, Anna Maria; Port uncertain, 1780 2856.30 p380
Schaeffer, Daniel; Port uncertain, 1773 2856.30 p379
Schaeffer, Francis C.; New York, 1838 8197.10 p149
Schaeffer, Friedrich; Port uncertain, 1764 2856.30 p380
Schaeffer, Herman; New York, 1828 8197.10 p282
Schaeffer, Johann Michael; America, 1752 2856.30 p380
Schaeffer, Josef; Port uncertain, 1791 2856.30 p380
Schaeffer, Josef; Port uncertain, 1792 2856.30 p380
Schaeffer, Konrad; New York, 1840 8197.10 p385
Schaeffer, Marie 36; Kansas, 1910 9079.10 p43
Schaeffer, Michael; Port uncertain, 1766 2856.30 p380
Schaeffer, Michael; Port uncertain, 1774 2856.30 p380
Schaeffer, Nicholas; New York, 1838 8197.10 p148
Schaefferin, Anna Maria; Port uncertain, 1780 2856.30 p380
Schaeffler, Marie 36; Kansas, 1910 9079.10 p5
Schaer, Jakob; Port uncertain, 1770 2856.30 p381
Schafer, Adam; Port uncertain, 1769 2856.30 p422
With wife
Schafer, Alexander; America, 1789 2856.30 p422
Schafer, Andreas; Port uncertain, 1791 2856.30 p421
Schafer, Anna; Port uncertain, 1736 2856.30 p421
Schafer, Anna Barbara; America, 1789 2856.30 p422
Schafer, Anna Maria; America, 1789 2856.30 p422
Schafer, Catharina Maurer; America, 1764 2856.30 p422
With husband & 4 children
Schafer, Christian; America, 1774 2856.30 p421
Schafer, Friedrich; Port uncertain, 1755 2856.30 p421
Schafer, Georg Heinrich; Port uncertain, 1783 2856.30 p421
Schafer, Mrs. H. 45; Alaska, 1912 9196.1 p18
Schafer, Mrs. H. 45; British Columbia, 1912 9196.1 p18
Schafer, Hans Georg; Port uncertain, 1765 2856.30 p421
Schafer, Henry 54; Alaska, 1913 9196.1 p20
Schafer, Henry 54; British Columbia, 1913 9196.1 p20
Schafer, Jakob; America, 1774 2856.30 p421
Schafer, Jakob; Port uncertain, 1754 2856.30 p421
Schafer, Johann; Port uncertain, 1773 2856.30 p421
Schafer, Lewis; New York, 1839 8197.10 p284
Schafer, Magdalena; Port uncertain, 1736 2856.30 p421
Schafer, Meyer; New York, 1838 8197.10 p284
Schafer, Michael; America, 1764 2856.30 p422
With wife & children
Schafer, Michael; Port uncertain, 1736 2856.30 p421
Schafer, Nikolaus; America, 1749 2856.30 p422
With wife & children
Schafer, Peter; Port uncertain, 1748 2856.30 p421
Schafer, Theobald; New York, 1839 8197.10 p140
Schafer, Thiel; Port uncertain, 1794 2856.30 p422
With wife & 2 children
Schaffel, Heinrich; Port uncertain, 1771 2856.30 p422
With wife & 2 children
Schaffer, Andreas; Port uncertain, 1748 2856.30 p422
Schaffer, Anna Cath. Elis.; Port uncertain, 1754 2856.30 p423
Schaffer, Anna Margarete; America, 1749 2856.30 p422
Schaffer, Anna Margarete; Port uncertain, 1751 2856.30 p422
Schaffer, Bernhard; America, 1738 2856.30 p422
Schaffer, Casimir; Maryland, 1910 3259.35 p54
Schaffer, Caspar; New York, 1840 8197.10 p195
Schaffer, Christof; Port uncertain, 1792 2856.30 p422
Schaffer, Diebold; Port uncertain, 1748 2856.30 p422
Schaffer, Francis C.; New York, 1838 8197.10 p149
Schaffer, Franz; Port uncertain, 1750 2856.30 p422
Schaffer, Fritz; America, 1749 2856.30 p422
Schaffer, Hendrik Bartol; America, 1738 2856.30 p422
Schaffer, Isaac; America, 1749 2856.30 p422
Schaffer, Jacob; New York, 1840 8197.10 p196
Schaffer, Jakob; America, 1749 2856.30 p422
Schaffer, Johann; Port uncertain, 1740 2856.30 p422
Schaffer, Johann Hermann; America, 1738 2856.30 p422
Schaffer, Johann Nickel; America, 1749 2856.30 p422
With wife & children
Schaffer, Johann Nikolaus; America, 1749 2856.30 p422
Schaffer, Johann Nikolaus; America, 1752 2856.30 p422
Schaffer, Konrad; Port uncertain, 1792 2856.30 p422
Schaffer, Lukas; Port uncertain, 1783 2856.30 p422
Schaffer, Michael; America, 1749 2856.30 p422
Schaffer, Michael; America, 1752 2856.30 p423
Schaffer, Paul; America, 1738 2856.30 p422
Schaffer, Paul, Sr.; America, 1738 2856.30 p422
Schaffer, Paul, Jr.; America, 1738 2856.30 p422
Schaffer, Wendel; Port uncertain, 1792 2856.30 p422
Schafferin, Anna Cath. Elis.; Port uncertain, 1754 2856.30 p423
Schaffhauser, Martin; Port uncertain, 1756 2856.30 p380
Schaffner, Catharina; Port uncertain, 1756 2856.30 p380
Schaffner, Christian; Port uncertain, 1764 2856.30 p380
Schaffnerin, Catharina; Port uncertain, 1756 2856.30 p380
Schafler, Lorenz; Port uncertain, 1782 2856.30 p423
Schaib, Jacob; Port uncertain, 1660 2856.30 p380
With wife & children
Schaibel, Konrad; Port uncertain, 1769 2856.30 p380
Schaible, John; New York, 1840 8197.10 p194
Schaider, Peter; Port uncertain, 1785 2856.30 p380
Schaidlin, Balthasar; America, 1744 2856.30 p383
Schala, Joseph 60; Ontario, 1871 1823.28 p90
Schalaski, Anna; Maryland, 1910 3259.35 p54
Schalck, Jakob; Port uncertain, 1770 2856.30 p380
Schalit, A. M.; Port uncertain, 1767 2856.30 p293
Schalit, Anna Margarete; Port uncertain, 1765 2856.30 p380
With husband
Schall, Christine 20; Ontario, 1871 1823.15 p234
Schall, Edward 27; Ontario, 1871 1823.15 p234
Schall, Frederick Edwin; New York, 1840 8197.10 p198
Schall, Tobias; America, 1784 2856.30 p380
With wife & son
Schaller, Adam; Port uncertain, 1764 2856.30 p380
Wife: M. Eva
With 5 children
Schaller, Christian; America, 1741 2856.30 p423
With wife & children
Schaller, Johann; America, 1738 2856.30 p380
Schaller, Johann; Port uncertain, 1737 2856.30 p380
Schaller, M. Eva *SEE* Schaller, Adam
Schaller, Marianna; Port uncertain, 1766 2856.30 p380
Schaller, Valentin; Port uncertain, 1749 2856.30 p380
With wife & children
Schallmeyer, Josef; Port uncertain, 1772 2856.30 p380
Schallmeyer, Simon; Port uncertain, 1780 2856.30 p380
Schallmeyer, Simon; Port uncertain, 1781 2856.30 p380
Schalter, Franz Balthasar; America, 1768 2856.30 p380
Schalter, Franz Balthasar; Port uncertain, 1754 2856.30 p380
Schalter, Franz Baltzer; America, 1754 2856.30 p380
Schalus, Valentin; America, 1764 2856.30 p380
Schanck, Theobald; America, 1740 2856.30 p381
Schans, Johann; Port uncertain, 1749 2856.30 p381
Schantz, . . .; America, 1749 2856.30 p381
Schantz, Andreas; America, 1719 2856.30 p381
Schantz, Christian 63; Ontario, 1871 1823.15 p234
Schantz, Jacob; America, 1737 2856.30 p381
Schantz, Jacob; Port uncertain, 1795 2856.30 p381
Schantz, Jacob; Port uncertain, 1796 2856.30 p381
Schantzenbach, Anna Margarete; Port uncertain, 1745 2856.30 p381
Schantzlin, Josua; Port uncertain, 1750 2856.30 p381
Schanz, Daniel; America, 1771 2856.30 p381
With wife
Schanz, Diederich; Port uncertain, 1752 2856.30 p381
Schanz, Johann; America, 1739 2856.30 p381
Schanzenbach, Maria Margarete; Port uncertain, 1794 2856.30 p381
Schapeler, Georg; Port uncertain, 1716 2856.30 p381
Schapeler, Georg; Port uncertain, 1736 2856.30 p381
Schapeler, Konrad; Port uncertain, 1721 2856.30 p381
Schapeler, Konrad; Port uncertain, 1736 2856.30 p381
Schaper, Henry; New York, 1835 8197.10 p71
Schappeler, Konrad; Port uncertain, 1721 2856.30 p381
Schappeler, Konrad; Port uncertain, 1752 2856.30 p381
Schappert, Johann; Port uncertain, 1758 2856.30 p381
Schardong, Maria; Port uncertain, 1778 2856.30 p381
Schardong, Maria Catharina; Port uncertain, 1778 2856.30 p381
Schardong, Nickel; Port uncertain, 1774 2856.30 p381
Schardongin, Maria; Port uncertain, 1778 2856.30 p381
Schardongin, Maria Catharina; Port uncertain, 1778 2856.30 p381
Scharfer, Johann; Port uncertain, 1790 2856.30 p381
Scharff, Gertrud; Port uncertain, 1765 2856.30 p381
Scharmann, Peter; Port uncertain, 1766 2856.30 p381
Scharp, Bernard; Port uncertain, 1749 2856.30 p381
Scharth, Jakob; Port uncertain, 1770 2856.30 p381
Scharth, Jakob; Port uncertain, 1770 2856.30 p381
With wife & 2 children
Schatt, Philipp; Port uncertain, 1764 2856.30 p381
Schatz, Jacob 52; Ontario, 1871 1823.15 p234
Schatz, Peter; America, 1738 2856.30 p382
Schatzel, Heinrich; Port uncertain, 1750 2856.30 p423
Schatzler, Magdalena; Port uncertain, 1736 2856.30 p423
Schaub, Balthasar; Port uncertain, 1765 2856.30 p382
Schaub, Henrich; America, 1764 2856.30 p382
Schaub, Henrich; America, 1770 2856.30 p382
Schaub, Maria Dorothea; America, 1770 2856.30 p382
Schaub, Marianna; Port uncertain, 1765 2856.30 p382
Schaub, Susanna Cathari; America, 1770 2856.30 p382
Schaubhut, Tobias; America, 1792 2856.30 p382
Schaubhut, Tobias; America, 1794 2856.30 p382
Schaubhut, Tobias; Port uncertain, 1792 2856.30 p382
Schaublin, Heinrich; Port uncertain, 1743 2856.30 p423
Schauer, Jacob; America, 1751 2856.30 p382
With family
Schauer, Philipp; America, 1751 2856.30 p382
Schaufe, Catherine 26; Ontario, 1871 1823.15 p234
Schaufelin, Elisabeth; Port uncertain, 1791 2856.30 p423
Schauffer, Friedrich; New York, 1840 8197.10 p285
Schauffler, Hans Georg; America, 1750 2856.30 p382

Schmitt, Peter; Port uncertain, 1784 ***2856.30*** *p400*
Schmitt, Peter; Port uncertain, 1784 ***2856.30*** *p401*
With wife & 2 sons
Schmitt, Peter; Port uncertain, 1786 ***2856.30*** *p401*
With wife 3 sons & 3 daughters
Schmitt, Philipp; America, 1738 ***2856.30*** *p400*
Schmitt, Mrs. Philipp; America, 1764 ***2856.30*** *p400*
With 2 children
Schmitt, Philipp Jakob; America, 1749 ***2856.30*** *p401*
With wife & child
Schmitt, Sophia; America, 1749 ***2856.30*** *p400*
Schmitt, Susanna Ritter; Port uncertain, 1790 ***2856.30*** *p363*
Schmitt, Theobald; America, 1738 ***2856.30*** *p400*
Schmitt, Valentin; Port uncertain, 1732 ***2856.30*** *p401*
With wife & children
Schmitterger, Frank 47; Kansas, 1891-1910 ***9079.10*** *p8*
Schmitterger, Maggie 60; Kansas, 1891-1910 ***9079.10*** *p8*
Schmittin, Anna Maria; America, 1752 ***2856.30*** *p401*
Schmittin, Catharina; Port uncertain, 1779 ***2856.30*** *p401*
Schmittin, Elisabeth; Port uncertain, 1774 ***2856.30*** *p401*
Schmittin, Eva Barbara; Port uncertain, 1729 ***2856.30*** *p401*
Schmittin, Maria; Port uncertain, 1721 ***2856.30*** *p401*
Schmittin, Veronika; Port uncertain, 1745 ***2856.30*** *p401*
Schmitz, Franz Jacob; San Francisco, 1853 ***1224.3*** *p69*
Schmitz, Maria Catharina; Port uncertain, 1793 ***2856.30*** *p401*
Schmitzer, George Michael; New York, 1802 ***8197.10*** *p24*
Schmiz, Maria Catharina; Port uncertain, 1793 ***2856.30*** *p401*
Schmoll, Ludewick; New York, 1807 ***8197.10*** *p49*
Schmoll, Niklas; Port uncertain, 1784 ***2856.30*** *p401*
Schmults, John; New York, 1840 ***8197.10*** *p285*
Schmutteler, Stefan; America, 1752 ***2856.30*** *p401*
Schmutzig, Anna Maria; Port uncertain, 1784 ***2856.30*** *p280*
Schmutzig, Anna Maria Blasin; Port uncertain, 1784 ***2856.30*** *p401*
Schmyer, Philipp; America, 1733 ***2856.30*** *p401*
With wife & children
Schmyer, Philipp; America, 1750 ***2856.30*** *p401*
Schnack, Charles 49; Ontario, 1871 ***1823.15*** *p234*
Schnakenberg, Claus; New York, 1839 ***8197.10*** *p284*
Schnancia, Martin 32; Ontario, 1871 ***1823.15*** *p234*
Schnapper, Jacob; America, 1753 ***2856.30*** *p401*
Schnatterbeck, Sebastian; New York, 1837 ***8197.10*** *p105*
Schnaufer, John; New York, 1835 ***8197.10*** *p310*
Schnebel, Christian; Port uncertain, 1696 ***2856.30*** *p401*
Schnebel, Johann; Port uncertain, 1748 ***2856.30*** *p401*
Schnebele, Isaac; America, 1749 ***2856.30*** *p401*
Schneck, Albert; America, 1751 ***2856.30*** *p401*
Schneck, Hans Georg; America, 1765 ***2856.30*** *p402*
Schneck, Joh. Albrecht Le; America, 1751 ***2856.30*** *p402*
Schneck, Joh. Albrecht Le; America, 1752 ***2856.30*** *p402*
Schneck, Joh. Albrecht Le; America, 1752 ***2856.30*** *p402*
With wife
Schneck, Johann Georg; America, 1765 ***2856.30*** *p402*
Schneckh, Georg; America, 1765 ***2856.30*** *p402*
With wife & children
Schneewalder, Andreas; Port uncertain, 1779 ***2856.30*** *p402*
Schneibel, Johann Georg; Port uncertain, 1792 ***2856.30*** *p402*
Schneibel, Josef; Port uncertain, 1772 ***2856.30*** *p402*
Schneickert, Christof; Port uncertain, 1784 ***2856.30*** *p402*
Schneid, Jakob; Port uncertain, 1734 ***2856.30*** *p402*
Schneid, Johann Nickel; Port uncertain, 1753 ***2856.30*** *p402*
Schneid, Johann Peter; Port uncertain, 1769 ***2856.30*** *p402*
Schneidemann, Georg Friedrich; America, 1752 ***2856.30*** *p402*
With wife & family
Schneider, . . .; Port uncertain, 1793 ***2856.30*** *p404*
Schneider, Adam; New York, 1837 ***8197.10*** *p105*
Schneider, Adam; Port uncertain, 1778 ***2856.30*** *p402*
Schneider, Adam; Port uncertain, 1785 ***2856.30*** *p402*
Schneider, Anna; Port uncertain, 1781 ***2856.30*** *p406*
With husband
Schneider, Anna Christina; Port uncertain, 1756 ***2856.30*** *p402*
Schneider, Anna Margarete Niederaue; America, 1752 ***2856.30*** *p405*
Schneider, Anna Maria; America, 1745 ***2856.30*** *p405*
Schneider, Anna Maria; Port uncertain, 1762 ***2856.30*** *p402*
Schneider, Anna Maria; Port uncertain, 1767 ***2856.30*** *p402*
Schneider, Anna Ottilia; Port uncertain, 1759 ***2856.30*** *p402*
Schneider, Anna Ursula; Port uncertain, 1747 ***2856.30*** *p402*
Schneider, Anton; Port uncertain, 1763 ***2856.30*** *p402*
Schneider, Barbara; Port uncertain, 1769 ***2856.30*** *p402*
Schneider, Caspar; America, 1744 ***2856.30*** *p402*
Schneider, Caspar; America, 1749 ***2856.30*** *p406*
With wife & children
Schneider, Cath. Elisabeth; Port uncertain, 1792 ***2856.30*** *p402*
Schneider, Catharina; America, 1745 ***2856.30*** *p405*
Schneider, Catharina; Port uncertain, 1797 ***2856.30*** *p475*
Schneider, Catharina Engel; Port uncertain, 1784 ***2856.30*** *p405*
With 5 children
Schneider, Charles 51; Ontario, 1871 ***1823.28*** *p90*
Schneider, Christian; Port uncertain, 1756 ***2856.30*** *p402*
Schneider, Christiana Mari; Port uncertain, 1783 ***2856.30*** *p402*
Schneider, Christina; America, 1777 ***2856.30*** *p402*
Schneider, Christina; England, 1777 ***2856.30*** *p402*
Schneider, Daniel; America, 1738 ***2856.30*** *p402*
Schneider, Daniel; Port uncertain, 1770 ***2856.30*** *p402*
Schneider, Dominik; Port uncertain, 1728 ***2856.30*** *p402*
Schneider, Dominik; Port uncertain, 1748 ***2856.30*** *p402*
Schneider, Elis. Margarete; Port uncertain, 1745 ***2856.30*** *p402*
Schneider, Elisabeth; Port uncertain, 1762 ***2856.30*** *p402*
Schneider, Elizabeth 15; Kansas, 1899-1910 ***9079.10*** *p36*
Schneider, Eva; Port uncertain, 1756 ***2856.30*** *p402*
Schneider, Eva A. 38; Kansas, 1899-1910 ***9079.10*** *p36*
Schneider, Eva Maria; Port uncertain, 1700-1799 ***2856.30*** *p406*
Schneider, Francis; New York, 1838 ***8197.10*** *p148*
Schneider, Gabriel; Port uncertain, 1791 ***2856.30*** *p402*
Schneider, Georg; Port uncertain, 1777 ***2856.30*** *p402*
Schneider, Georg Friedrich; America, 1753 ***2856.30*** *p406*
With wife & 2 children
Schneider, George; New York, New York, 1852 ***6058.10*** *p42*
Schneider, Gottfried Jacob; New York, 1840 ***8197.10*** *p285*
Schneider, Hans; Port uncertain, 1733 ***2856.30*** *p406*
With wife
Schneider, Hans Jakob; America, 1741 ***2856.30*** *p406*
With family
Schneider, Hans Jost; America, 1741 ***2856.30*** *p406*
With family
Schneider, Hans Nikolaus; Port uncertain, 1767 ***2856.30*** *p403*
Schneider, Hans Nikolaus; Port uncertain, 1787 ***2856.30*** *p403*
Schneider, Hans Wendel; America, 1754 ***2856.30*** *p403*
Schneider, Hans Wendel; Port uncertain, 1754 ***2856.30*** *p403*
Schneider, Heinrich; America, 1741 ***2856.30*** *p406*
With wife & children
Schneider, Heinrich; Port uncertain, 1760 ***2856.30*** *p403*
Schneider, Heinrich Peter; Port uncertain, 1773 ***2856.30*** *p403*
Schneider, Henr. Balthasar; America, 1753 ***2856.30*** *p403*
Schneider, Henrich; America, 1763 ***2856.30*** *p403*
Schneider, Henrich; Port uncertain, 1771 ***2856.30*** *p403*
Schneider, Jacob; America, 1744 ***2856.30*** *p405*
Schneider, Jacob; America, 1755 ***2856.30*** *p406*
With wife & 2 children
Schneider, Jacob; New York, 1840 ***8197.10*** *p196*
Schneider, Jacob; New York, New York, 1856 ***3437.14*** *p35*
Schneider, Jakob; America, 1749 ***2856.30*** *p406*
With wife & 2 children
Schneider, Jakob; America, 1755 ***2856.30*** *p406*
With wife & 2 children
Schneider, Jakob; America, 1763 ***2856.30*** *p403*
Schneider, Jakob; America, 1764 ***2856.30*** *p403*
Schneider, Jakob; America, 1767 ***2856.30*** *p403*
Schneider, Jakob; America, 1790 ***2856.30*** *p403*
Schneider, Jakob; Port uncertain, 1734 ***2856.30*** *p402*
Schneider, Jakob; Port uncertain, 1767 ***2856.30*** *p403*
Schneider, Jakob; Port uncertain, 1793 ***2856.30*** *p403*
Schneider, Mrs. Jakob; Port uncertain, 1744 ***2856.30*** *p406*
With children
Schneider, Johann; Port uncertain, 1730 ***2856.30*** *p403*
Schneider, Johann; Port uncertain, 1741 ***2856.30*** *p403*
Schneider, Johann; Port uncertain, 1745 ***2856.30*** *p403*
Schneider, Johann; Port uncertain, 1751 ***2856.30*** *p403*
Schneider, Miss Johann; America, 1764 ***2856.30*** *p403*
Schneider, Johann Ernst; New York, 1807 ***8197.10*** *p51*
Schneider, Johann Konrad; Port uncertain, 1759 ***2856.30*** *p403*
Schneider, Johann Nikolaus; America, 1764 ***2856.30*** *p403*
Schneider, Johann Peter; America, 1764 ***2856.30*** *p403*
Schneider, Johann Peter; Port uncertain, 1783 ***2856.30*** *p406*
With wife 2 sons & daughter
Schneider, Johann Valentin; America, 1764 ***2856.30*** *p403*
Schneider, John; America, 1764 ***2856.30*** *p403*
Schneider, John 37; Ontario, 1871 ***1823.15*** *p234*
Schneider, John F. 37; Kansas, 1899-1910 ***9079.10*** *p36*
Schneider, Josef; Port uncertain, 1740 ***2856.30*** *p403*
Schneider, Josef; Port uncertain, 1769 ***2856.30*** *p403*
Schneider, Justus; Port uncertain, 1787 ***2856.30*** *p406*
With wife
Schneider, K.; Port uncertain, 1784 ***2856.30*** *p27*
Schneider, Karl; Port uncertain, 1737 ***2856.30*** *p403*
Schneider, Karl; Port uncertain, 1774 ***2856.30*** *p403*
Schneider, Karl; Port uncertain, 1777 ***2856.30*** *p403*
Schneider, Karl; Port uncertain, 1784 ***2856.30*** *p406*
With wife
Schneider, Karl; Port uncertain, 1787 ***2856.30*** *p403*
Schneider, Konrad; America, 1740 ***2856.30*** *p403*
Schneider, Konrad; Port uncertain, 1780 ***2856.30*** *p403*
Schneider, Lorenz; Port uncertain, 1739 ***2856.30*** *p403*
Schneider, Margarete; Port uncertain, 1792 ***2856.30*** *p404*
Schneider, Maria Anna; Port uncertain, 1781 ***2856.30*** *p404*
Schneider, Maria Catharina; Port uncertain, 1788 ***2856.30*** *p404*
Schneider, Maria Charlotte; Port uncertain, 1751 ***2856.30*** *p407*
Schneider, Maria Dorothea; Port uncertain, 1763 ***2856.30*** *p404*
Schneider, Maria Dorothea; Port uncertain, 1790 ***2856.30*** *p404*
Schneider, Maria Elisabeth; America, 1753 ***2856.30*** *p404*
Schneider, Martin; America, 1753 ***2856.30*** *p404*
Schneider, Martin; America, 1753 ***2856.30*** *p406*
With wife & 2 children
Schneider, Matthaus; Port uncertain, 1771 ***2856.30*** *p404*
Schneider, Max; Port uncertain, 1741 ***2856.30*** *p404*
Schneider, Michael; America, 1744 ***2856.30*** *p405*
Schneider, Michael; America, 1746 ***2856.30*** *p406*
With wife & children
Schneider, Michael; Port uncertain, 1783 ***2856.30*** *p404*
Schneider, Michael, Sr.; America, 1753 ***2856.30*** *p404*
Schneider, Michael, Jr.; America, 1751 ***2856.30*** *p404*
Schneider, Michael, Jr.; America, 1744 ***2856.30*** *p406*
With wife & 2 children
Schneider, Michel; America, 1763 ***2856.30*** *p404*
Schneider, Nickel; Port uncertain, 1738 ***2856.30*** *p404*
Schneider, Nickel; Port uncertain, 1760 ***2856.30*** *p404*
Schneider, Nickel; Port uncertain, 1766 ***2856.30*** *p404*
Schneider, Nickel; Port uncertain, 1788 ***2856.30*** *p404*
Schneider, Nikklaus; America, 1784 ***2856.30*** *p404*
Schneider, Ottilia; America, 1764 ***2856.30*** *p406*
With husband & 6 children
Schneider, Peter; America, 1738 ***2856.30*** *p407*
With wife & 3 children
Schneider, Peter; America, 1739 ***2856.30*** *p407*
With wife & 3 children
Schneider, Peter; Port uncertain, 1742 ***2856.30*** *p404*
Schneider, Peter; Port uncertain, 1743 ***2856.30*** *p404*
Schneider, Peter; Port uncertain, 1760 ***2856.30*** *p404*
Schneider, Peter; Port uncertain, 1764 ***2856.30*** *p404*
Schneider, Peter; Port uncertain, 1793 ***2856.30*** *p404*
Schneider, Petronella; Port uncertain, 1750 ***2856.30*** *p407*
Schneider, Philipp; America, 1740 ***2856.30*** *p404*
Schneider, Philipp; America, 1741 ***2856.30*** *p404*
Schneider, Philipp; America, 1750 ***2856.30*** *p404*
Schneider, Philipp Jakob; Port uncertain, 1775 ***2856.30*** *p404*
Schneider, Rosina; America, 1744 ***2856.30*** *p404*
Schneider, Sebastian; Port uncertain, 1766 ***2856.30*** *p404*
Schneider, Seyfried; America, 1752 ***2856.30*** *p407*
With wife & 8 children
Schneider, Simon; Port uncertain, 1784 ***2856.30*** *p404*
Schneider, Stefan; Port uncertain, 1788 ***2856.30*** *p404*
Schneider, Susanna; America, 1744 ***2856.30*** *p404*
Schneider, Susanna; Port uncertain, 1744 ***2856.30*** *p404*
Schneider, Theobald; America, 1749 ***2856.30*** *p407*
With wife & 4 children
Schneider, Valentin; Port uncertain, 1741 ***2856.30*** *p404*
Schneider, Mrs. Valentin; Port uncertain, 1745 ***2856.30*** *p405*
Schneider, Wendel; America, 1744 ***2856.30*** *p406*
With wife & 2 children
Schneider, Wendel; America, 1747 ***2856.30*** *p405*
With daughter
Schneider, Wendelin; America, 1742 ***2856.30*** *p406*
With wife & children
Schneider, Wilhelm; Port uncertain, 1787 ***2856.30*** *p406*
Schneider, Wilhelm; Port uncertain, 1788 ***2856.30*** *p406*
Schneider, Wilhelm; Port uncertain, 1789 ***2856.30*** *p406*
Schneider, William 34; Ontario, 1871 ***1823.15*** *p234*

Schneiderin, . . .; England, 1778 ***2856.30*** *p407*
Schneiderin, Maria Charlotte; Port uncertain, 1751 ***2856.30*** *p407*
Schneiderin, Petronella; Port uncertain, 1750 ***2856.30*** *p407*
Schneidmann, Eva; America, 1752 ***2856.30*** *p407*
Schneidmann, Georg Friedrich; America, 1752 ***2856.30*** *p402*
With wife & family
Schneidmann, Sebastian; America, 1749 ***2856.30*** *p407*
With wife & children
Schneiss, Anna Elisabeth; Port uncertain, 1746 ***2856.30*** *p407*
Schneiss, Anna Sophia; Port uncertain, 1783 ***2856.30*** *p407*
Schneiss, Maria Elisabeth; Port uncertain, 1787 ***2856.30*** *p407*
Schneissin, Anna Elisabeth; Port uncertain, 1746 ***2856.30*** *p407*
Schneissin, Anna Sophia; Port uncertain, 1783 ***2856.30*** *p407*
Schneizhoffer, Andreas; Port uncertain, 1754 ***2856.30*** *p407*
Schnell, Anna Catharina; Port uncertain, 1768 ***2856.30*** *p407*
Schnell, Anna Christina; Port uncertain, 1784 ***2856.30*** *p407*
Schnell, Anna Elisabeth; Port uncertain, 1787 ***2856.30*** *p407*
Schnell, Anna Maria; Port uncertain, 1778 ***2856.30*** *p407*
Schnell, Henrich; America, 1735 ***2856.30*** *p407*
Schnell, Iss; Port uncertain, 1739 ***2856.30*** *p407*
Schnell, Johann Martin; Port uncertain, 1794 ***2856.30*** *p407*
Schnell, John 26; Ontario, 1871 ***1823.15*** *p234*
Schnell, John H. 55; Ontario, 1871 ***1823.15*** *p234*
Schnell, Sara; Port uncertain, 1796 ***2856.30*** *p407*
Schnepf, Sebastian; Port uncertain, 1791 ***2856.30*** *p407*
Schnerrer, Hans Michael; America, 1754 ***2856.30*** *p407*
With wife & 10 children
Schnerrer, Hans Michael; America, 1754 ***2856.30*** *p407*
Schnetzer, Franziska; Port uncertain, 1782 ***2856.30*** *p407*
Schnider, Jacob; New York, New York, 1856 ***3437.14*** *p35*
Schnip, John; New York, 1823 ***8197.10*** *p62*
Schnitt, Adam 50; Ontario, 1871 ***1823.15*** *p234*
Schnittinger, Anna Catharina; Port uncertain, 1784 ***2856.30*** *p407*
Schnittinger, Maria Agathe; Port uncertain, 1791 ***2856.30*** *p407*
Schnitz, Maria Catharina; Port uncertain, 1790 ***2856.30*** *p408*
Schnizer, Josef; Port uncertain, 1746 ***2856.30*** *p408*
Schnopf, Hans Martin; Port uncertain, 1732 ***2856.30*** *p408*
Schnorr, Jakob; Port uncertain, 1779 ***2856.30*** *p408*
Schnur, Maria Catharina; America, 1747 ***2856.30*** *p408*
Schnur, Martin; Port uncertain, 1752 ***2856.30*** *p408*
Schnurer, Georg Jacob; America, 1737 ***2856.30*** *p408*
Schnyder, Charles; New York, 1840 ***8197.10*** *p285*
Scho, George; New York, 1835 ***8197.10*** *p283*
Schoalla, Robert; Georgia, 1698 ***1640.13*** *p110*
Schoals, Elizabeth 26 *SEE* Schoals, John
Schoals, John; New York, 1828 ***8197.10*** *p63*
Wife: Elizabeth 26
Schober, Christopher; New York, 1840 ***8197.10*** *p286*
Schober, Johann; Port uncertain, 1764 ***2856.30*** *p408*
Schober, Maria Martha; Port uncertain, 1791 ***2856.30*** *p178*
Schoch, Anna; Port uncertain, 1697 ***2856.30*** *p408*
Schoch, Anna; Port uncertain, 1698 ***2856.30*** *p408*
Schoch, Anna Magdalena; America, 1749 ***2856.30*** *p408*
Schoch, Anthony; America, 1767 ***2856.30*** *p408*
Schoch, Anton; America, 1787 ***2856.30*** *p408*
Schoch, Christian 34; Ontario, 1871 ***1823.15*** *p234*
Schoch, Maria; Port uncertain, 1759 ***2856.30*** *p408*
Schoch, Michael; Port uncertain, 1695 ***2856.30*** *p408*
Schoch, Michael 81; Ontario, 1871 ***1823.15*** *p234*
Schoefert, Alexander; America, 1738 ***2856.30*** *p408*
Schoeffberger, Anthony; New York, 1838 ***8197.10*** *p284*
Schoeller, Adam; Port uncertain, 1793 ***2856.30*** *p408*
Schoemel, Johann; Port uncertain, 1775 ***2856.30*** *p408*
Schoenauer, Johann; Port uncertain, 1780 ***2856.30*** *p408*
Schoenewald, Jakob; Port uncertain, 1783 ***2856.30*** *p408*
Schoenhoffer, Miss; Port uncertain, 1785 ***2856.30*** *p408*
Schoenling, Henrich; Port uncertain, 1788 ***2856.30*** *p408*
Schoenmann, Henrich Adam; Port uncertain, 1767 ***2856.30*** *p408*
Schoepflin, Hans Georg; Port uncertain, 1767 ***2856.30*** *p408*
Schoeweiler, Johann; Port uncertain, 1777 ***2856.30*** *p408*
Schof, Jakob; America, 1737 ***2856.30*** *p408*
Schoffel, Heinrich; Port uncertain, 1771 ***2856.30*** *p423*
With wife & 2 children
Schoffel, Michael; Port uncertain, 1786 ***2856.30*** *p423*
Schoffel, Sophie Salome; Port uncertain, 1795 ***2856.30*** *p423*
Schofield, Elizabeth; Maryland, 1681 ***2524.55*** *p195*
Schofield, John; New York, 1821 ***8197.10*** *p279*
Schofield, John; New York, 1827 ***8197.10*** *p342*
Schofield, Mary Ann 48; Ontario, 1871 ***1823.28*** *p90*
Schofield, William 26; Ontario, 1871 ***1823.28*** *p90*
Schol, Christina; Port uncertain, 1784 ***2856.30*** *p408*
With husband
Scholar, Hannah 25; Baltimore, 1775 ***1220.25*** *p117*
Scholard, James 48; Ontario, 1871 ***1823.28*** *p90*
Scholer, Mr.; America, 1764 ***2856.30*** *p408*
With wife
Scholer, Johann Georg; Port uncertain, 1753 ***2856.30*** *p408*
Scholes, James; New York, New York, 1850 ***1224.3*** *p69*
Scholey, George 51; Ontario, 1871 ***1823.28*** *p90*
Scholey, Hariat 44; Ontario, 1871 ***1823.28*** *p90*
Scholl, Andreas; America, 1749 ***2856.30*** *p408*
Scholl, Andreas; America, 1753 ***2856.30*** *p409*
Scholl, Balthasar; Port uncertain, 1752 ***2856.30*** *p409*
Scholl, E.; Port uncertain, 1737 ***2856.30*** *p42*
Scholl, Elisabeth; America, 1737 ***2856.30*** *p409*
Scholl, Frederick; Pennsylvania, 1779 ***4629.10*** *p36*
Scholl, Georg; Port uncertain, 1744 ***2856.30*** *p409*
With family
Scholl, Jakob; America, 1752 ***2856.30*** *p409*
Scholl, Jakob; America, 1752 ***2856.30*** *p423*
Scholl, Jakob; America, 1753 ***2856.30*** *p384*
Scholl, Johann Heinrich; America, 1752 ***2856.30*** *p409*
Scholl, Johann Michael; Port uncertain, 1765 ***2856.30*** *p423*
Scholl, Johann Nikolaus; Port uncertain, 1782 ***2856.30*** *p409*
With wife & 6 children
Scholl, Josef; Port uncertain, 1782 ***2856.30*** *p409*
Scholl, Lorenz; Port uncertain, 1775 ***2856.30*** *p409*
Scholl, Maria Barbara; America, 1752 ***2856.30*** *p409*
Scholl, Samuel; Port uncertain, 1782 ***2856.30*** *p409*
With wife & 5 children
Scholl, Theobald; Port uncertain, 1782 ***2856.30*** *p409*
With wife & 7 children
Schollasch, Christian; America, 1750 ***2856.30*** *p409*
With wife & 2 children
Schollenberger, Jakob; Port uncertain, 1794 ***2856.30*** *p409*
Schollenkircher, Balthasar; Port uncertain, 1766 ***2856.30*** *p409*
Schollhorn, Therese; Port uncertain, 1755 ***2856.30*** *p423*
Scholtenburg, Leon A. C.; New York, 1837 ***8197.10*** *p105*
Scholterer, Johann; Port uncertain, 1723 ***2856.30*** *p409*
Scholthes, Nickel; Port uncertain, 1744 ***2856.30*** *p409*
Scholvain, Frederick 40; Ontario, 1871 ***1823.28*** *p90*
Schomaclar, John; Indiana, 1881-1884 ***3437.14*** *p203*
Schomberg, Romam 21; Boston, 1774 ***1220.25*** *p48*
Schon, Margarete; Port uncertain, 1762 ***2856.30*** *p423*
Schonberger, Georg; Port uncertain, 1748 ***2856.30*** *p423*
Schonberger, Georg; Port uncertain, 1788 ***2856.30*** *p423*
Schonberger, Leopold; Port uncertain, 1765 ***2856.30*** *p423*
Schonberger, Leopold; Port uncertain, 1797 ***2856.30*** *p423*
Schone, Michael; Pennsylvania, 1865-1868 ***6058.10*** *p76*
Schoneberger, Anna Catharina; Port uncertain, 1792 ***2856.30*** *p423*
Schoneberger, Anna Gertrud; Port uncertain, 1791 ***2856.30*** *p423*
Schonenberger, Antoni; Port uncertain, 1739 ***2856.30*** *p423*
Schonenberger, Antoni; Port uncertain, 1769 ***2856.30*** *p423*
Schonenberger, Susanna; Port uncertain, 1785 ***2856.30*** *p423*
Schonher, Henry; New York, 1830 ***8197.10*** *p359*
Schonherr, Anna Barbara; Port uncertain, 1742 ***2856.30*** *p423*
Schonherr, Josef; Port uncertain, 1746 ***2856.30*** *p423*
Schonherr, Josef; Port uncertain, 1747 ***2856.30*** *p423*
Schoninger, Michael; Port uncertain, 1751 ***2856.30*** *p423*
Schonneberger, Jorg Albrecht; Port uncertain, 1757 ***2856.30*** *p423*
Schonnenberg, Maria Elisabeth; Port uncertain, 1750 ***2856.30*** *p409*
Schonsiegel, Georg; Port uncertain, 1774 ***2856.30*** *p424*
With wife & 2 children
Schonsiegel, Jakob; Port uncertain, 1775 ***2856.30*** *p424*
Schonthaler, Anna Catharina; Port uncertain, 1743 ***2856.30*** *p424*
Schonthaler, Anna Maria; Port uncertain, 1745 ***2856.30*** *p424*
Schonweiler, Eva Catharina; Port uncertain, 1767 ***2856.30*** *p424*
Schoof, Fredrick 36; Ontario, 1871 ***1823.28*** *p90*
Schoolcraft, Horatio J.; Vermont, 1858-1928 ***5900.10*** *p517*
Schoolcraft, Mary Donaldson; Vermont, 1850-1943 ***5900.10*** *p517*
Schools, James 56; Ontario, 1871 ***1823.22*** *p142*
Schools, James 68; Ontario, 1871 ***1823.22*** *p142*
Schooss, Johann Henrich; England, 1784 ***2856.30*** *p409*
Schop, Jakob; America, 1737 ***2856.30*** *p409*
Schop, Nickolous 27; Ontario, 1871 ***1823.15*** *p234*
Schopf, Miss; America, 1727 ***2856.30*** *p370*
Schopf, Anna Maria; America, 1727 ***2856.30*** *p409*
Schopf, Johann Dietrich; America, 1754 ***2856.30*** *p409*
Schopflin, Anna; Port uncertain, 1733 ***2856.30*** *p424*
Schopflin, Hans; Port uncertain, 1762 ***2856.30*** *p424*
Schopflin, Johann; Port uncertain, 1781 ***2856.30*** *p424*
Schopp, Barbara 64; Ontario, 1871 ***1823.15*** *p234*
Schopp, Catharina; America, 1737 ***2856.30*** *p409*
Schopp, Jakob; America, 1738 ***2856.30*** *p409*
Schopp, Jakob; America, 1756 ***2856.30*** *p409*
Schopp, Jakob; America, 1762 ***2856.30*** *p409*
Schopp, John 36; Ontario, 1871 ***1823.15*** *p234*
Schopp, Joseph 35; Ontario, 1871 ***1823.15*** *p234*
Schopp, Joseph 65; Ontario, 1871 ***1823.15*** *p234*
Schopp, Lorenz; Port uncertain, 1744 ***2856.30*** *p409*
Schopp, Peter; America, 1738 ***2856.30*** *p409*
Schopp, Peter; America, 1756 ***2856.30*** *p409*
Schopp, Peter; America, 1762 ***2856.30*** *p409*
Schopp, Philipp; England, 1790 ***2856.30*** *p409*
Schorer, Christian; Port uncertain, 1791 ***2856.30*** *p410*
Schorg, Johan Michael; Port uncertain, 1764 ***2856.30*** *p410*
Schorin, Christina; Port uncertain, 1768 ***2856.30*** *p410*
Schorp, Barbara; Port uncertain, 1776 ***2856.30*** *p410*
Schorp, Veronika; America, 1771 ***2856.30*** *p410*
Schorr, Maria Catharina; Port uncertain, 1760 ***2856.30*** *p410*
Schorr, Maria Elisabeth; Port uncertain, 1775 ***2856.30*** *p410*
Schorr, Martin; Port uncertain, 1747 ***2856.30*** *p410*
Schorr, Michael; Port uncertain, 1790 ***2856.30*** *p410*
Schorrberger, Franz Leonhard; Port uncertain, 1751 ***2856.30*** *p410*
Schott, Florence; New York, 1835 ***8197.10*** *p283*
Schott, Hans Peter; America, 1754 ***2856.30*** *p410*
Schott, Johann; Port uncertain, 1781 ***2856.30*** *p410*
Schott, Johann Paul; America, 1753 ***2856.30*** *p410*
Schott, Johann Paul; America, 1754 ***2856.30*** *p410*
Schott, John P. 30; St. Kitts, 1774 ***1220.25*** *p44*
Schott, Ludwig; America, 1754 ***2856.30*** *p410*
Schott, Nikol; Port uncertain, 1783 ***2856.30*** *p410*
Schott, Paul; America, 1783 ***2856.30*** *p410*
Schottenmuller, Josef; Port uncertain, 1752 ***2856.30*** *p410*
Schottin, Hans Georg; Port uncertain, 1753 ***2856.30*** *p424*
With 3 children
Schotto, Johann Nickel; America, 1739 ***2856.30*** *p410*
Schotts, Fredrick 52; Ontario, 1871 ***1823.28*** *p90*
Schouborg, Ann; New York, 1857 ***1224.3*** *p69*
Schouppert, Jean; Port uncertain, 1784 ***2856.30*** *p410*
With wife
Schovich, Paul Ralph; New York, 1823 ***8197.10*** *p63*
Schrader, Louis; Pennsylvania, 1867 ***6058.10*** *p57*
Schrader, Peter 48; Ontario, 1871 ***1823.15*** *p234*
Schramm, Henrich; Port uncertain, 1783 ***2856.30*** *p410*
Schramm, Jakob; America, 1749 ***2856.30*** *p411*
With wife & 3 children
Schramm, Johann Theobald; America, 1769 ***2856.30*** *p410*
Schramm, Johann Theobald; America, 1781 ***2856.30*** *p410*
Schramm, Johann Theobald; America, 1788 ***2856.30*** *p410*
Schramm, Sigmund; Port uncertain, 1750 ***2856.30*** *p410*
Schramm, Sigmund; Port uncertain, 1780 ***2856.30*** *p411*
Schranck, Philipp Georg; Port uncertain, 1776 ***2856.30*** *p411*
Schrea, Catharine 27; Kansas, 1902-1910 ***9079.10*** *p18*
Schrea, George 30; Kansas, 1896-1910 ***9079.10*** *p18*
Schredler, Friedr. Arnold; America, 1738 ***2856.30*** *p412*
Schredor, August 34; Ontario, 1871 ***1823.15*** *p235*
Schregle, Heinrich; Port uncertain, 1761 ***2856.30*** *p411*
Schreiber, Miss; Quebec, 1857 ***9196.15*** *p17*
Schreiber, Mr.; Quebec, 1857 ***9196.15*** *p17*
Schreiber, Franz; Port uncertain, 1788 ***2856.30*** *p411*
Schreiber, Georg Adam; America, 1741 ***2856.30*** *p411*
Schreiber, Georg Adam; America, 1765 ***2856.30*** *p411*
Schreiber, Jakob; America, 1749 ***2856.30*** *p411*
Schreiber, Johann; Port uncertain, 1744 ***2856.30*** *p411*

Schreiber, Johann, Jr.; Port uncertain, 1737 ***2856.30*** *p411*
Schreiber, Johann Adam; America, 1749 ***2856.30*** *p411*
With wife & 3 children
Schreiber, Lorenz; America, 1741 ***2856.30*** *p411*
With wife & children
Schreiber, Philipp; Port uncertain, 1748 ***2856.30*** *p411*
Schreiber, Valentin; Port uncertain, 1748 ***2856.30*** *p411*
Schreiner, Abraham; America, 1739 ***2856.30*** *p411*
Schreiner, Abraham; America, 1751 ***2856.30*** *p411*
Schreiner, Anton; America, 1749 ***2856.30*** *p411*
With wife & child
Schreiner, Johann Adam; Port uncertain, 1751 ***2856.30*** *p411*
Schreiner, Johann Jakob; America, 1741 ***2856.30*** *p411*
Schreiner, John 23; Ontario, 1871 ***1823.15*** *p235*
Schreiner, Lawrence; New York, 1840 ***8197.10*** *p196*
Schreiner, Lisa; Port uncertain, 1785 ***2856.30*** *p411*
Schreiner, Michael; Port uncertain, 1766 ***2856.30*** *p411*
With wife & 4 children
Schreiner, Valentin; Port uncertain, 1790 ***2856.30*** *p411*
Schrepf, Johann Paul; Port uncertain, 1742 ***2856.30*** *p411*
Schrest, Andreas; Port uncertain, 1757 ***2856.30*** *p411*
Schreyer, Caspar; America, 1747 ***2856.30*** *p411*
Schreyer, Elisabeth; Port uncertain, 1762 ***2856.30*** *p411*
Schreyer, Johann Adam; America, 1738 ***2856.30*** *p411*
Schreyer, John; New York, 1826 ***8197.10*** *p282*
Schreyer, Peter; Port uncertain, 1755 ***2856.30*** *p412*
Schriber, Anna 53; Kansas, 1885-1910 ***9079.10*** *p17*
Schriber, George 55; Kansas, 1877-1910 ***9079.10*** *p17*
Schrimpf, Wenzel; New York, 1837 ***8197.10*** *p105*
Schroader, William 40; Ontario, 1871 ***1823.15*** *p235*
Schrock, Elisabeth; Port uncertain, 1781 ***2856.30*** *p412*
Schrock, Friedrich; Port uncertain, 1795 ***2856.30*** *p412*
Schrock, Friedrich; Port uncertain, 1796 ***2856.30*** *p412*
Schrod, Matthaus; America, 1741 ***2856.30*** *p412*
With wife & children
Schroder, Catharina; Port uncertain, 1781 ***2856.30*** *p412*
Schroder, Christian; Port uncertain, 1752 ***2856.30*** *p412*
Schroder, Frederick 30; Ontario, 1871 ***1823.15*** *p235*
Schroder, Friedr. Arnold; America, 1738 ***2856.30*** *p412*
Schroder, Jacob 59; Ontario, 1871 ***1823.15*** *p235*
Schroder, M.; Port uncertain, 1781 ***2856.30*** *p137*
Schroder, Maria; Port uncertain, 1781 ***2856.30*** *p137*
Schroder, Maria; Port uncertain, 1781 ***2856.30*** *p412*
With husband
Schroder, Sebastian; America, 1749 ***2856.30*** *p412*
With wife & child
Schrodi, Jacob; Port uncertain, 1695 ***2856.30*** *p412*
Schrodi, Jacob; Port uncertain, 1726 ***2856.30*** *p412*
Schroeder, Carl 34; British Columbia, 1913 ***9196.1*** *p23*
Schroeder, Carl 34; Washington, 1913 ***9196.1*** *p23*
Schroeder, Christian 41; Ontario, 1871 ***1823.15*** *p235*
Schroeder, Konrad; Port uncertain, 1744 ***2856.30*** *p412*
With wife
Schroeder, Michael; Maryland, 1910 ***3259.35*** *p54*
Schrof, Endrebas; New York, New York, 1855 ***3437.14*** *p30*
Schroher, Johann Henrich; Port uncertain, 1755 ***2856.30*** *p412*
Schron, Bernard; Port uncertain, 1742 ***2856.30*** *p412*
Schrorfner, Valentin; New York, 1838 ***8197.10*** *p320*
Schrot, Margarete; Port uncertain, 1747 ***2856.30*** *p412*
Schrot, Theodor; Port uncertain, 1794 ***2856.30*** *p412*
Schroter, Anna; America, 1751 ***2856.30*** *p412*
Schrotz, . . .; Port uncertain, 1751 ***2856.30*** *p412*
Schrowinski, Adelbert; Maryland, 1910 ***3259.35*** *p54*
Schu, Anna Elisabeth; Port uncertain, 1790 ***2856.30*** *p412*
Schub, August 24; Washington, 1914 ***9196.1*** *p65*
Schub, Peter; Port uncertain, 1768 ***2856.30*** *p412*
Schubar, Johann; America, 1752 ***2856.30*** *p412*
With wife & child
Schublin, Jacob; America, 1750 ***2856.30*** *p413*
Schuch, Christian; America, 1739 ***2856.30*** *p413*
Schuch, Christian; America, 1739 ***2856.30*** *p413*
With wife & 7 children
Schuch, Eva Maria; Port uncertain, 1752 ***2856.30*** *p413*
Schuch, M. El.; America, 1753 ***2856.30*** *p415*
Schuch, Maria Elisabeth; America, 1753 ***2856.30*** *p413*
Schuch, Maria Elisabeth; Port uncertain, 1775 ***2856.30*** *p413*
Schuch, Maria Margarete; Port uncertain, 1776 ***2856.30*** *p413*
Schuch, Martin; America, 1751 ***2856.30*** *p413*
Schuch, Valentin; Port uncertain, 1731 ***2856.30*** *p413*
Schuchardt, John Jacob; New York, 1836-1838 ***8197.10*** *p300*
Schuck, Martin; America, 1751 ***2856.30*** *p413*
Schuck, Martin; America, 1751 ***2856.30*** *p413*
With wife & 4 sons
Schuck, Martin; Port uncertain, 1754 ***2856.30*** *p413*
Schuck, Michael; Port uncertain, 1764 ***2856.30*** *p413*
Schuck, Peter; Port uncertain, 1751 ***2856.30*** *p413*
Schuck, Peter; Port uncertain, 1784 ***2856.30*** *p414*
Schucker, Margarete; Port uncertain, 1796 ***2856.30*** *p413*
Schudwjcheska, John; Maryland, 1910 ***3259.35*** *p54*
Schueler, Benedikt; Port uncertain, 1712 ***2856.30*** *p413*
Schueler, Benedikt; Port uncertain, 1754 ***2856.30*** *p413*
Schuellin, Anna Maria; Port uncertain, 1751 ***2856.30*** *p420*
Schuellin, Anton; Port uncertain, 1751 ***2856.30*** *p420*
Schuellin, Johann Ernst; Port uncertain, 1751 ***2856.30*** *p420*
Schuemacher, Peter; Port uncertain, 1748 ***2856.30*** *p413*
Schuemann, Johann Adam; Port uncertain, 1744 ***2856.30*** *p413*
Schufzler, Frederick; New York, 1828 ***8197.10*** *p282*
Schug, Christian; America, 1739 ***2856.30*** *p429*
Schug, Elis. Catharina; Port uncertain, 1785 ***2856.30*** *p413*
Schug, Peter; America, 1753 ***2856.30*** *p413*
With wife & children
Schuh, Johann Georg; New York, 1835 ***8197.10*** *p317*
Schuh, Maria Catharina; Port uncertain, 1770 ***2856.30*** *p413*
Schuh, Mrs. Nikol; Port uncertain, 1789 ***2856.30*** *p413*
Schuh, Peter; Port uncertain, 1756 ***2856.30*** *p413*
With wife & children
Schuhe, Balthasar; Port uncertain, 1745 ***2856.30*** *p413*
Schuhe, Mathias; Port uncertain, 1745 ***2856.30*** *p413*
Schuhe, Peter; Port uncertain, 1765 ***2856.30*** *p413*
Schuhemacher, Henrich; America, 1754 ***2856.30*** *p413*
Schuhemann, Johann Adam; Port uncertain, 1744 ***2856.30*** *p413*
Schuhler, Anna Eva; Port uncertain, 1769 ***2856.30*** *p414*
Schuhler, Michael; America, 1752 ***2856.30*** *p420*
Schuhmacher, Andreas; Port uncertain, 1762 ***2856.30*** *p414*
Schuhmacher, Andreas; Port uncertain, 1782 ***2856.30*** *p414*
Schuhmacher, Angelika; America, 1752 ***2856.30*** *p414*
Schuhmacher, Jakob; America, 1752 ***2856.30*** *p414*
With wife & 3 children
Schuhmacher, Leonhard; Port uncertain, 1768 ***2856.30*** *p414*
Schuhmacher, Michael; Port uncertain, 1762 ***2856.30*** *p414*
With wife 2 sons & 2 daughters
Schuhmacher, Salome; Port uncertain, 1747 ***2856.30*** *p414*
Schuhriehmer, Johann Heinrich; Port uncertain, 1756 ***2856.30*** *p414*
Schuk, Christina; Port uncertain, 1738 ***2856.30*** *p414*
Schuk, Christina; Port uncertain, 1738 ***2856.30*** *p420*
Schukin, Christina; Port uncertain, 1738 ***2856.30*** *p414*
Schukin, Christina; Port uncertain, 1738 ***2856.30*** *p420*
Schukt, Edward; New York, 1836 ***8197.10*** *p317*
Schul, Johann Michael; America, 1750 ***2856.30*** *p420*
Schulby, Christian 49; Ontario, 1871 ***1823.15*** *p235*
Schulby, Henry 25; Ontario, 1871 ***1823.15*** *p235*
Schuld, Peter; Port uncertain, 1784 ***2856.30*** *p414*
Schuld, Peter; Port uncertain, 1785 ***2856.30*** *p414*
Schulenbergh, A. R. 27; Ontario, 1871 ***1823.28*** *p90*
Schuler, Miss; America, 1767 ***2856.30*** *p460*
Schuler, George Frederick; New York, 1837 ***8197.10*** *p284*
Schuler, Hans Georg; America, 1737 ***2856.30*** *p414*
Schuler, Jakob; America, 1737 ***2856.30*** *p420*
With wife & 8 children
Schuler, Johann Jakob; America, 1742 ***2856.30*** *p414*
With wife & 2 children
Schuler, Johann Melchior; Port uncertain, 1792 ***2856.30*** *p414*
Schuler, Maria Elisabeth; Port uncertain, 1771 ***2856.30*** *p414*
Schuler, Maria Gertrud; Port uncertain, 1772 ***2856.30*** *p414*
Schull, Johann Bernard; Port uncertain, 1752 ***2856.30*** *p414*
Schullen, Johann Bernard; Port uncertain, 1752 ***2856.30*** *p414*
Schulliner, Frederick; New York, New York, 1863 ***3437.14*** *p89*
Schulth, Eva; Port uncertain, 1765 ***2856.30*** *p14*
Schultheis, Galle; Port uncertain, 1712 ***2856.30*** *p414*
Schultheis, Galle; Port uncertain, 1743 ***2856.30*** *p414*
Schultheiss, Hans Adam; Port uncertain, 1762 ***2856.30*** *p414*
Schultheiss, Johann; Port uncertain, 1736 ***2856.30*** *p414*
Schultheiss, Maria Catharina; Port uncertain, 1765 ***2856.30*** *p414*
Schultz, Adam; Maryland, 1910 ***3259.35*** *p55*
Schultz, Anton; Maryland, 1910 ***3259.35*** *p55*
Schultz, August 31; Ontario, 1871 ***1823.28*** *p90*
Schultz, Daniel John; New York, 1831 ***8197.10*** *p364*
Schultz, Elizabeth 36; Ontario, 1871 ***1823.15*** *p235*
Schultz, Ernest 34; Ontario, 1871 ***1823.28*** *p90*
Schultz, Frank; Maryland, 1910 ***3259.35*** *p55*
Schultz, Frank R.; Maryland, 1910 ***3259.35*** *p55*
Schultz, Heinrich; New York, 1840 ***8197.10*** *p286*
Schultz, Jakob; Port uncertain, 1728 ***2856.30*** *p414*
Schultz, Joseph; Maryland, 1910 ***3259.35*** *p55*
Schultz, Martin; Maryland, 1910 ***3259.35*** *p55*
Schulz, Hennerich; Port uncertain, 1785 ***2856.30*** *p414*
Schulz, Johann; Port uncertain, 1789 ***2856.30*** *p414*
Schulz, Mrs. Peter; Port uncertain, 1785 ***2856.30*** *p414*
Schulz, Valentin; America, 1770 ***2856.30*** *p414*
Schulz, Vicenty; Maryland, 1910 ***3259.35*** *p55*
Schulze, Frank; Maryland, 1910 ***3259.35*** *p55*
Schumacher, Ms.; America, 1739 ***2856.30*** *p415*
With husband
Schumacher, Mrs. Abraham; Port uncertain, 1789 ***2856.30*** *p415*
Schumacher, Anna Barbara; America, 1749 ***2856.30*** *p415*
Schumacher, Antoin 28; British Columbia, 1910 ***9196.1*** *p31*
Schumacher, Antoin 28; Seattle, 1910 ***9196.1*** *p31*
Schumacher, Barthel; America, 1749 ***2856.30*** *p415*
Schumacher, Christoffel; Port uncertain, 1752 ***2856.30*** *p415*
Schumacher, Daniel; America, 1749 ***2856.30*** *p415*
Schumacher, Elizabeth 62; Ontario, 1871 ***1823.15*** *p235*
Schumacher, Eva Florina; America, 1789 ***2856.30*** *p415*
With husband
Schumacher, Hans Jakob; America, 1749 ***2856.30*** *p415*
Schumacher, Hans Jerg; America, 1749 ***2856.30*** *p415*
Schumacher, Jacob F.; New York, 1807 ***8197.10*** *p50*
Schumacher, Jakob; America, 1749 ***2856.30*** *p415*
Schumacher, John 34; Ontario, 1871 ***1823.15*** *p235*
Schumacher, Konrad; Port uncertain, 1771 ***2856.30*** *p415*
Schumacher, Peter Jakob; Port uncertain, 1783 ***2856.30*** *p415*
Schumacher, Rudolf; America, 1752 ***2856.30*** *p415*
Schumann, Karl; Port uncertain, 1764 ***2856.30*** *p415*
Schumann, Maria Magdalena; Port uncertain, 1790 ***2856.30*** *p415*
Schumentz, Christian 35; Ontario, 1871 ***1823.28*** *p90*
Schumm, Samuel; Port uncertain, 1783 ***2856.30*** *p415*
Schumpff, Anthony; New York, 1840 ***8197.10*** *p196*
Schup, Henrich; America, 1753 ***2856.30*** *p415*
Wife: M. El. Schuch
Schup, M. El. Schuch *SEE* Schup, Henrich
Schup, Maria Elisabeth Schuch; America, 1753 ***2856.30*** *p413*
Schupf, Jakob; Port uncertain, 1752 ***2856.30*** *p415*
Schupp, Peter; Port uncertain, 1768 ***2856.30*** *p412*
Schuppe, Georg Heinrich; Port uncertain, 1747 ***2856.30*** *p415*
Schuppe, Georg Heinrich; Port uncertain, 1749 ***2856.30*** *p415*
Schurandt, William 36; Ontario, 1871 ***1823.28*** *p90*
Schurck, Jakob; America, 1738 ***2856.30*** *p420*
Schurck, Moris; New York, 1837 ***8197.10*** *p106*
Schuriwer, Michael; Port uncertain, 1765 ***2856.30*** *p415*
Schurk, Balthazar; New York, 1837 ***8197.10*** *p105*
Schusick, Joseph 35; Ontario, 1871 ***1823.28*** *p90*
Schussele, Martin; Port uncertain, 1760 ***2856.30*** *p420*
Schussele, Martin; Port uncertain, 1794 ***2856.30*** *p420*
Schussler, Miss; America, 1759 ***2856.30*** *p421*
Schussler, Elisabeth; Port uncertain, 1774 ***2856.30*** *p420*
Schusslerin, Catharina; Port uncertain, 1762 ***2856.30*** *p421*
Schuster, . . .; America, 1740 ***2856.30*** *p416*
With 3 siblings
Schuster, Franz; America, 1747 ***2856.30*** *p416*
With wife & children
Schuster, George Joseph; Pennsylvania, 1865 ***6058.10*** *p50*
Schuster, Gerhard; America, 1744 ***2856.30*** *p416*
With wife & 3 children
Schuster, Jakob; America, 1749 ***2856.30*** *p416*
With wife & 2 children
Schuster, Jakob; America, 1752 ***2856.30*** *p415*
Schuster, Jakob; America, 1752 ***2856.30*** *p416*
With wife & 3 children
Schuster, Jakob; Port uncertain, 1756 ***2856.30*** *p415*
Schuster, Jakob; Port uncertain, 1768 ***2856.30*** *p415*
Schuster, Johann; Port uncertain, 1792 ***2856.30*** *p415*
Schuster, Maria Elisabeth; America, 1784 ***2856.30*** *p415*
Schuster, Maria Elisabeth; Port uncertain, 1754 ***2856.30*** *p415*
Schuster, Mathes; Port uncertain, 1764 ***2856.30*** *p415*
Schuster, Nikol; Port uncertain, 1740-1749 ***2856.30*** *p415*
Schuster, Peter; America, 1754 ***2856.30*** *p415*
Schuster, Philipp Jakob; America, 1773 ***2856.30*** *p415*
Schuster, Philipp Jakob; America, 1784 ***2856.30*** *p416*
Schutt, Charles 23; Ontario, 1871 ***1823.28*** *p90*
Schutt, Fredrick 28; Ontario, 1871 ***1823.28*** *p90*

Schutt, Jacob; America, 1750 ***2856.30*** *p421*
Schutt, William 21; Ontario, 1871 ***1823.28*** *p90*
Schuttenwurfler, Judith; Port uncertain, 1773 ***2856.30*** *p416*
Schutter, Sebastian; Port uncertain, 1770 ***2856.30*** *p421* With 3 children
Schuttes, Carrel 44; Ontario, 1871 ***1823.28*** *p90*
Schuttler, Jacob; America, 1780 ***2856.30*** *p421*
Schuttler, Sebastian; Port uncertain, 1770 ***2856.30*** *p416* With 3 children
Schuttler, Sebastian; Port uncertain, 1770 ***2856.30*** *p421* With 3 children
Schutz, Anna Maria; Port uncertain, 1750 ***2856.30*** *p421*
Schutz, Cath. Elisabeth; Port uncertain, 1790 ***2856.30*** *p421*
Schutz, Cath. Elisabeth; Port uncertain, 1796 ***2856.30*** *p421*
Schutz, Georg; America, 1736 ***2856.30*** *p421* With wife 3 sons & 2 daughters
Schutz, Georg; Port uncertain, 1735 ***2856.30*** *p421*
Schutz, Georg Heinrich; Port uncertain, 1770 ***2856.30*** *p421*
Schutz, Henrich; Port uncertain, 1783 ***2856.30*** *p421*
Schutz, John; New York, 1838 ***8197.10*** *p148*
Schutz, Konrad; Port uncertain, 1753 ***2856.30*** *p421*
Schutz, Konrad; Port uncertain, 1783 ***2856.30*** *p421*
Schutz, Konrad; Port uncertain, 1788 ***2856.30*** *p421*
Schutzin, Anna Maria; Port uncertain, 1750 ***2856.30*** *p421*
Schuwalski, George; Maryland, 1910 ***3259.35*** *p55*
Schuy, Christian; America, 1739 ***2856.30*** *p429*
Schuyler, John Cortlandt; North America, 1797 ***1224.2*** *p101*
Schuz, Colestin; Port uncertain, 1796 ***2856.30*** *p421*
Schuz, Mathes; Port uncertain, 1751 ***2856.30*** *p416*
Schwaab, Thaddaus; America, 1818 ***2856.30*** *p416* With family
Schwab, Anna Barbara; America, 1740 ***2856.30*** *p416* With husband
Schwab, Anna Margarete; Port uncertain, 1781 ***2856.30*** *p416*
Schwab, Anna Maria; Port uncertain, 1775 ***2856.30*** *p416*
Schwab, Bartholomaus; Port uncertain, 1754 ***2856.30*** *p416*
Schwab, Christopher; New York, 1823 ***8197.10*** *p280*
Schwab, Christopher; New York, 1831 ***8197.10*** *p67*
Schwab, Elisabeth; America, 1752 ***2856.30*** *p416* With 2 sons
Schwab, Friedrich; New York, 1837 ***8197.10*** *p105*
Schwab, Georg; Port uncertain, 1736 ***2856.30*** *p416*
Schwab, Georg; Port uncertain, 1737 ***2856.30*** *p416*
Schwab, Georg Adam; America, 1789 ***2856.30*** *p416*
Schwab, Georg Adam; Port uncertain, 1783 ***2856.30*** *p416*
Schwab, Georg Michael; Port uncertain, 1755 ***2856.30*** *p416* With wife & children
Schwab, Henrich; America, 1752 ***2856.30*** *p416*
Schwab, Jacob; Port uncertain, 1737 ***2856.30*** *p416*
Schwab, Jakob Bernhard; America, 1752 ***2856.30*** *p416*
Schwab, Johan; New York, 1834 ***8197.10*** *p69*
Schwab, Johann Adam; America, 1752 ***2856.30*** *p416*
Schwab, Johann Philipp; America, 1749 ***2856.30*** *p416*
Schwab, Josef; America, 1720 ***2856.30*** *p416*
Schwab, Maria Barbara; Port uncertain, 1761 ***2856.30*** *p416*
Schwab, Martin; Port uncertain, 1714 ***2856.30*** *p416*
Schwab, Matheis; Port uncertain, 1749 ***2856.30*** *p416*
Schwab, Matheis; Port uncertain, 1779 ***2856.30*** *p416*
Schwab, Peter; Port uncertain, 1714 ***2856.30*** *p416*
Schwab, Rudolph; New York, 1840 ***8197.10*** *p199*
Schwab, Wilhelm; Port uncertain, 1714 ***2856.30*** *p416*
Schwabin, Anna Margarete; Port uncertain, 1781 ***2856.30*** *p416*
Schwabin, Elisabeth; America, 1752 ***2856.30*** *p416* With 2 sons
Schwagert, Samuel; Port uncertain, 1751 ***2856.30*** *p416*
Schwal, Friedrich; New York, 1837 ***8197.10*** *p105*
Schwalbach, Elis. Margarete; Port uncertain, 1770 ***2856.30*** *p416*
Schwald, Catharina; Port uncertain, 1765 ***2856.30*** *p416*
Schwald, Georg; Port uncertain, 1762 ***2856.30*** *p416*
Schwald, Jacob; Port uncertain, 1764 ***2856.30*** *p416*
Schwall, Anton; Port uncertain, 1776 ***2856.30*** *p416*
Schwall, Johann, The Old; Port uncertain, 1781 ***2856.30*** *p417*
Schwalm, William 24; Ontario, 1871 ***1823.15*** *p235*
Schwalm, William 51; Ontario, 1871 ***1823.15*** *p235*
Schwamberger, Anna Maria; Port uncertain, 1785 ***2856.30*** *p417* With husband
Schwan, Apollonia; America, 1752 ***2856.30*** *p417* With 2 children
Schwancis, Michael 24; Ontario, 1871 ***1823.15*** *p235*
Schwander, Peter; America, 1738 ***2856.30*** *p417*
Schwann, Georg; Port uncertain, 1780 ***2856.30*** *p417*
Schwapp, Joseph 22; Ontario, 1871 ***1823.28*** *p90*
Schwartz, Amallia 14; Kansas, 1902-1910 ***9079.10*** *p27*
Schwartz, Balthasar; America, 1752 ***2856.30*** *p417* With wife
Schwartz, Barbara; America, 1737 ***2856.30*** *p417*
Schwartz, Bertha 11; Kansas, 1906-1910 ***9079.10*** *p11*
Schwartz, Daniel; America, 1743 ***2856.30*** *p417*
Schwartz, Daniel; America, 1754 ***2856.30*** *p417* With wife
Schwartz, Elizabeth 36; Kansas, 1906-1910 ***9079.10*** *p11*
Schwartz, Henrich; America, 1738 ***2856.30*** *p417*
Schwartz, Henry 6; Kansas, 1906-1910 ***9079.10*** *p11*
Schwartz, Henry 38; Kansas, 1906-1910 ***9079.10*** *p11*
Schwartz, Jacob; New York, 1839 ***8197.10*** *p284*
Schwartz, Jacob 42; Kansas, 1902-1910 ***9079.10*** *p27*
Schwartz, Jakob; Port uncertain, 1738 ***2856.30*** *p417*
Schwartz, Johann; Port uncertain, 1745 ***2856.30*** *p417*
Schwartz, John George; New York, 1840 ***8197.10*** *p194*
Schwartz, Katie 13; Kansas, 1906-1910 ***9079.10*** *p11*
Schwartz, Martin; America, 1738 ***2856.30*** *p417*
Schwartz, Mary E. 41; Kansas, 1902-1910 ***9079.10*** *p27*
Schwartz, Michael; New York, 1840 ***8197.10*** *p196*
Schwartz, Michael 43; Ontario, 1871 ***1823.15*** *p235*
Schwartz, Nickel; America, 1743 ***2856.30*** *p417*
Schwartz, Paul; Port uncertain, 1766 ***2856.30*** *p417*
Schwartz, Paul; Port uncertain, 1768 ***2856.30*** *p417*
Schwartz, Peter; Port uncertain, 1736 ***2856.30*** *p417*
Schwartz, Rebekka; Port uncertain, 1755 ***2856.30*** *p417*
Schwartz, Simon; America, 1743 ***2856.30*** *p417*
Schwartz, Steven; Maryland, 1910 ***3259.35*** *p55*
Schwartz, Theobald; America, 1752 ***2856.30*** *p417* With wife & child
Schwartzwalder, Christian; New York, 1838 ***8197.10*** *p150*
Schwarz, Anna; America, 1744 ***2856.30*** *p417*
Schwarz, Anna Margarete; America, 1765 ***2856.30*** *p418*
Schwarz, Anna Maria; America, 1765 ***2856.30*** *p418*
Schwarz, Apoll.; Port uncertain, 1770 ***2856.30*** *p73*
Schwarz, Apollonia; Port uncertain, 1765 ***2856.30*** *p418*
Schwarz, C.; America, 1742 ***2856.30*** *p298*
Schwarz, Caspar; Port uncertain, 1765 ***2856.30*** *p417*
Schwarz, Cath. Magdalena; Port uncertain, 1772 ***2856.30*** *p417*
Schwarz, Catharina; America, 1742 ***2856.30*** *p418*
Schwarz, Elisabeth; Port uncertain, 1768 ***2856.30*** *p417*
Schwarz, Hans Martin; America, 1744 ***2856.30*** *p418* With wife & 4 children
Schwarz, Hans Michael; America, 1740 ***2856.30*** *p418* With wife & children
Schwarz, Hans Wendel; America, 1738 ***2856.30*** *p417*
Schwarz, Henrich; America, 1754 ***2856.30*** *p418* With wife & children
Schwarz, Henrich; Port uncertain, 1754 ***2856.30*** *p417*
Schwarz, Jacob; America, 1750 ***2856.30*** *p418* With wife & 5 children
Schwarz, Jacob; America, 1751 ***2856.30*** *p417*
Schwarz, Johann; America, 1768 ***2856.30*** *p417*
Schwarz, Johann; America, 1769 ***2856.30*** *p418*
Schwarz, Johann; Port uncertain, 1764 ***2856.30*** *p417*
Schwarz, Johann; Port uncertain, 1765 ***2856.30*** *p417*
Schwarz, Johann; Port uncertain, 1769 ***2856.30*** *p418*
Schwarz, Johann; Port uncertain, 1772 ***2856.30*** *p418*
Schwarz, Johann; Port uncertain, 1791 ***2856.30*** *p418*
Schwarz, Johann Adam; Port uncertain, 1784 ***2856.30*** *p418*
Schwarz, Johann Adam; Port uncertain, 1787 ***2856.30*** *p418*
Schwarz, Josef; America, 1744 ***2856.30*** *p418*
Schwarz, Josef; Port uncertain, 1730 ***2856.30*** *p418*
Schwarz, Margarete; America, 1744 ***2856.30*** *p418*
Schwarz, Michael; Port uncertain, 1742 ***2856.30*** *p418*
Schwarz, Nikolaus; Port uncertain, 1786 ***2856.30*** *p418*
Schwarz, Nikolaus; Port uncertain, 1787 ***2856.30*** *p418*
Schwarz, Susanna Margare; America, 1765 ***2856.30*** *p418*
Schwarz, Theobald; America, 1764 ***2856.30*** *p418* With sister
Schwarz, Valentin; America, 1765 ***2856.30*** *p418*
Schwarzbach, Adam; America, 1749 ***2856.30*** *p418*
Schwarzenberger, Anton; Port uncertain, 1746 ***2856.30*** *p418*
Schwarzin, Apollonia; Port uncertain, 1765 ***2856.30*** *p418*
Schwarzmuller, Josef; Port uncertain, 1790 ***2856.30*** *p418* With wife
Schwarzwaelder, Charles; New York, 1840 ***8197.10*** *p196*
Schwarzwalder, Johann; America, 1738 ***2856.30*** *p418*
Schwede, . . .; Port uncertain, 1796 ***2856.30*** *p418*
Schweder, Eva; Port uncertain, 1765 ***2856.30*** *p418*
Schweich, Maria Barbara; America, 1742 ***2856.30*** *p418*
Schweichert, Georg Konrad; America, 1751 ***2856.30*** *p418*
Schweickard, Jacob; Philadelphia, 1741 ***2856.30*** *p418*
Schweickert, Georg Michael; Port uncertain, 1757 ***2856.30*** *p419*
Schweickert, Johann Michael; Port uncertain, 1787 ***2856.30*** *p419*
Schweickert, Peter; Port uncertain, 1724 ***2856.30*** *p419*
Schweickhardt, Jakob; America, 1727 ***2856.30*** *p419*
Schweickhardt, Philipp; America, 1727 ***2856.30*** *p419*
Schweid, Henrich; America, 1737 ***2856.30*** *p419*
Schweig, Philipp; Port uncertain, 1787 ***2856.30*** *p419*
Schweigert, Nikol; Port uncertain, 1760 ***2856.30*** *p419*
Schweigert, Samuel; America, 1751 ***2856.30*** *p419*
Schweigli, Mrs. Andreas; Port uncertain, 1769 ***2856.30*** *p419*
Schwein, Maria Anna; Port uncertain, 1738 ***2856.30*** *p419*
Schweinin, Maria Anna; Port uncertain, 1738 ***2856.30*** *p419*
Schweisguth, Johann; Port uncertain, 1730 ***2856.30*** *p419*
Schweiss, Georg Adam; Port uncertain, 1752 ***2856.30*** *p419*
Schweitzer, Balthasar; Port uncertain, 1784 ***2856.30*** *p419*
Schweitzer, Friedr.; Port uncertain, 1784 ***2856.30*** *p419*
Schweizer, Jacob; America, 1864 ***2856.30*** *p419*
Schwellenback, Anthony; Philadelphia, 1793 ***4629.10*** *p69*
Schwemmling, Michael; Port uncertain, 1763 ***2856.30*** *p419*
Schwenck, Georg Michael; Port uncertain, 1778 ***2856.30*** *p419* With wife & 2 children
Schwendemann, Jacob; America, 1738 ***2856.30*** *p419*
Schwender, Christian; Port uncertain, 1768 ***2856.30*** *p419*
Schwenk, Peter; Port uncertain, 1784 ***2856.30*** *p419*
Schweppler, Johann; Port uncertain, 1784 ***2856.30*** *p420*
Schwer, Johann; America, 1749 ***2856.30*** *p420*
Schwer, Wilhelm; Port uncertain, 1749 ***2856.30*** *p420*
Schwerdle, Johann Georg; Port uncertain, 1792 ***2856.30*** *p420*
Schwertle, Johann Georg; Port uncertain, 1792 ***2856.30*** *p420*
Schwerzler, Jacob; Port uncertain, 1737 ***2856.30*** *p420*
Schwickert, Jakob; Port uncertain, 1796 ***2856.30*** *p420*
Schwickert, Maria Catharina; Port uncertain, 1775 ***2856.30*** *p420*
Schwickert, Valentin; Port uncertain, 1787 ***2856.30*** *p420*
Schwind, Georg Ludwig; Port uncertain, 1768 ***2856.30*** *p420* With wife
Schwindelhurn, Anna Maria; Port uncertain, 1753 ***2856.30*** *p420*
Schwingel, Hans Nickel; America, 1740 ***2856.30*** *p420* With wife & 4 children
Schwingel, Hans Nickel; America, 1740 ***2856.30*** *p420*
Schwinn, Nikol; Port uncertain, 1785 ***2856.30*** *p420* With wife
Schybilski, Joseph; Maryland, 1910 ***3259.35*** *p55*
Schymoshik, Martin; Maryland, 1910 ***3259.35*** *p55*
Scidimore, Thomas; Virginia, 1703-1704 ***6212.30*** *p62*
Scilla, Barbary; Maryland, 1668 ***2524.55*** *p195*
Sckovowica, Antonie; Maryland, 1910 ***3259.35*** *p55*
Sclatten, James; Pennsylvania, 1778 ***4629.10*** *p45*
Scobie, Charles 66; Ontario, 1871 ***1823.15*** *p235*
Scobie, George; New York, 1840 ***8197.10*** *p198*
Scobie, John G. M.; New York, 1839 ***8197.10*** *p140*
Scobie, William 40; Ontario, 1871 ***1823.15*** *p235*
Scoble, John; New York, 1839 ***8197.10*** *p140*
Scolari, Giobani; New York, 1835 ***8197.10*** *p317*
Scoles, John; New York, 1807 ***8197.10*** *p49*
Scollick, John 32; Ontario, 1871 ***1823.28*** *p90*
Sconers, Edward; Virginia, 1671-1672 ***6212.30*** *p47*
Scoon, Alexander 35; Ontario, 1871 ***1823.22*** *p142*
Score, Edwin 55; Ontario, 1871 ***1823.22*** *p142*
Scot, James 19; Ontario, 1871 ***1823.15*** *p235*
Scot, James 38; Ontario, 1871 ***1823.15*** *p235*
Scot, James 78; Ontario, 1871 ***1823.15*** *p235*
Scot, John 45; Ontario, 1871 ***1823.15*** *p235*
Scot, Thomas; Maryland, 1673 ***2524.55*** *p195*
Scotch, Denam; Virginia, 1663 ***6212.30*** *p4*
Scotchmer, Alfred 30; Ontario, 1871 ***1823.15*** *p235*
Scotchmerr, John 60; Ontario, 1871 ***1823.15*** *p235*
Scotchmerr, Mary 56; Ontario, 1871 ***1823.15*** *p235*
Scote, Alescander 14; Ontario, 1871 ***1823.15*** *p235*
Scoti, Franz; Port uncertain, 1784 ***2856.30*** *p424*
Scotland, James 21; Virginia, 1774 ***1220.25*** *p75*
Scotland, Robert 27; Maryland, 1775 ***1220.25*** *p101*
Scotney, Susanna 19; Maryland, 1775 ***1220.25*** *p98*
Scott, . . .; Maryland, 1660 ***2524.55*** *p195*
Scott, Miss; Quebec, 1858 ***9196.15*** *p35*
Scott, Miss 1; Ontario, 1861 ***2896.28*** *p62*
Scott, Mr.; Quebec, 1856 ***9196.15*** *p6*
Scott, Mr.; Quebec, 1857 ***9196.15*** *p23*

Shandly, Ann Gleason 70; Vermont, 1881 ***5900.10*** *p505*
Shandly, Margaret Earley; Vermont, 1838-1910 ***5900.10*** *p505*
Shandzey, Edward; Pennsylvania, 1786 ***4629.10*** *p52*
Shane, Michael 61; Ontario, 1871 ***1823.28*** *p91*
Shane, Samuel; New York, New York, 1857 ***3437.14*** *p80*
Shanewolf, Frederick; New York, 1803 ***8197.10*** *p17*
Shank, Dieble; America, 1741 ***2856.30*** *p429*
Shank, Matthew; New York, 1711 ***1224.2*** *p102*
Shank, Peter; Maryland, 1910 ***3259.35*** *p55*
Shanklin, Gilbert 55; Ontario, 1871 ***1823.15*** *p237*
Shanks, James; New York, 1834 ***8197.10*** *p69*
Shanks, John; Maryland, 1640 ***2524.55*** *p198*
Shanley, Alice Barrett 52; Vermont, 1880 ***5900.10*** *p525*
Shanley, Barnabus 88; Vermont, 1872 ***5900.10*** *p525*
Shanley, Catherine; Vermont, 1856-1922 ***5900.10*** *p151*
Shanley, Catherine 38; Vermont, 1854 ***5900.10*** *p524*
Shanley, Edward; New York, 1834 ***8197.10*** *p372*
Shanley, Edward; Vermont, 1846-1904 ***5900.10*** *p127*
Shanley, Elizabeth Cross; Vermont, 1847-1915 ***5900.10*** *p159*
Shanley, Ellen Harran; Vermont, 1848-1880 ***5900.10*** *p135*
Shanley, Ellen Reynolds 32; Vermont, 1877 ***5900.10*** *p528*
Shanley, Ellen Splain 26; Vermont, 1880 ***5900.10*** *p534*
Shanley, Frances Gallagher; Vermont, 1852-1920 ***5900.10*** *p127*
Shanley, Frederick; Vermont, 1853-1953 ***5900.10*** *p526*
Shanley, Frederick 3; Vermont, 1853 ***5900.10*** *p525*
Shanley, James; Vermont, 1823-1904 ***5900.10*** *p526*
Shanley, James; Vermont, 1840-1904 ***5900.10*** *p528*
Shanley, James; Vermont, 1847-1896 ***5900.10*** *p127*
Shanley, James C.; Vermont, 1858-1958 ***5900.10*** *p526*
Shanley, Joan; Vermont, 1853-1931 ***5900.10*** *p531*
Shanley, John; New York, 1838 ***8197.10*** *p378*
Shanley, John; Vermont, 1832-1862 ***5900.10*** *p530*
Shanley, Julia; Vermont, 1856-1956 ***5900.10*** *p526*
Shanley, Lawrence 14; Vermont, 1868 ***5900.10*** *p171*
Shanley, Leonard 45; Ontario, 1871 ***1823.15*** *p237*
Shanley, Lewis J.; Vermont, 1861-1901 ***5900.10*** *p526*
Shanley, Malachi; Vermont, 1848-1913 ***5900.10*** *p159*
Shanley, Maria; Vermont, 1865-1866 ***5900.10*** *p526*
Shanley, Maria Hanley; Vermont, 1825-1902 ***5900.10*** *p526*
Shanley, Martha F. Flynn; Vermont, 1863-1911 ***5900.10*** *p529*
Shanley, Mary A.; Vermont, 1834-1919 ***5900.10*** *p335*
Shanley, Mary Rowley; Vermont, 1831-1909 ***5900.10*** *p530*
Shanley, Michael 11; Vermont, 1864 ***5900.10*** *p171*
Shanley, Patrick 55; Vermont, 1872 ***5900.10*** *p171*
Shanley, Rose Anna 85; Vermont, 1870 ***5900.10*** *p525*
Shanley, Thomas; Vermont, 1861-1901 ***5900.10*** *p530*
Shanley, Thomas 68; Vermont, 1888 ***5900.10*** *p525*
Shanley, William; Vermont, 1850-1950 ***5900.10*** *p526*
Shanly, Barnaby 18; Vermont, 1844 ***5900.10*** *p524*
Shanly, Mary 33; Vermont, 1845 ***5900.10*** *p524*
Shannahan, Daniel 45; Ontario, 1871 ***1823.15*** *p237*
Shannahan, Mary 70; Ontario, 1871 ***1823.15*** *p237*
Shannahon, Elisa 44; Ontario, 1871 ***1823.15*** *p237*
Shannasey, Sarah Cosgrove; Vermont, 1839-1917 ***5900.10*** *p239*
Shannasey, Timothy 34; Vermont, 1873 ***5900.10*** *p239*
Shannessy, Patrick; New York, 1838 ***8197.10*** *p284*
Shannon, Ada Samantha 10; Vermont, 1861 ***5900.10*** *p520*
Shannon, Alexander B.; Ontario, 1871 ***1823.28*** *p91*
Shannon, Bridget Finnerty 56; Vermont, 1852 ***5900.10*** *p228*
Shannon, Catherine; Vermont, 1814-1895 ***5900.10*** *p602*
Shannon, Catherine Harvey; Vermont, 1838-1875 ***5900.10*** *p222*
Shannon, Christopher 44; Ontario, 1871 ***1823.15*** *p237*
Shannon, Edward 41; Ontario, 1871 ***1823.15*** *p237*
Shannon, Elizabeth Brady; Vermont, 1836-1910 ***5900.10*** *p192*
Shannon, Ellen C. 5; Ontario, 1861 ***2896.28*** *p54*
Shannon, Florence C.; Vermont, 1857-1937 ***5900.10*** *p455*
Shannon, Hanora Griffin; Vermont, 1856-1934 ***5900.10*** *p428*
Shannon, Isabella 60; Ontario, 1871 ***1823.28*** *p91*
Shannon, James; New York, 1807 ***8197.10*** *p329*
Shannon, James 44; Ontario, 1871 ***1823.15*** *p237*
Shannon, James 65; Vermont, 1894 ***5900.10*** *p519*
Shannon, Jane; Vermont, 1862 ***5900.10*** *p520*
Shannon, John; New York, 1806 ***8197.10*** *p30*
Shannon, John; Pennsylvania, 1812 ***6058.10*** *p4*
Shannon, John; Vermont, 1847-1934 ***5900.10*** *p428*
Shannon, John 35; Ontario, 1861 ***2896.28*** *p54*
Shannon, John 53; Ontario, 1871 ***1823.22*** *p143*
Shannon, M. 95; Ontario, 1861 ***2896.26*** *p7*
Shannon, Margaret 1; Ontario, 1861 ***2896.28*** *p54*
Shannon, Margaret T. Owens 43; Vermont, 1889 ***5900.10*** *p229*
Shannon, Mary 27; Ontario, 1861 ***2896.28*** *p54*
Shannon, Mary A.; Vermont, 1845-1926 ***5900.10*** *p386*
Shannon, Mary A. 3; Ontario, 1861 ***2896.28*** *p54*
Shannon, Matthew; Vermont, 1822-1884 ***5900.10*** *p222*
Shannon, Patrick 84; Vermont, 1877 ***5900.10*** *p228*
Shannon, Paulina Austin 71; Vermont, 1899 ***5900.10*** *p520*
Shannon, Richard 58; Ontario, 1871 ***1823.28*** *p91*
Shannon, Robert 26; New York, 1774 ***1220.25*** *p141*
Shannon, Robert 73; Vermont, 1903 ***5900.10*** *p47*
Shannon, Samuel; New York, 1826 ***8197.10*** *p332*
Shannon, Susan M. 28; Vermont, 1879 ***5900.10*** *p289*
Shannon, Thomas 30; Ontario, 1871 ***1823.15*** *p237*
Shannon, Thomas 49; Ontario, 1871 ***1823.22*** *p143*
Shannon, Thomas 93; Vermont, 1881 ***5900.10*** *p520*
Shannon, William 51; Ontario, 1871 ***1823.22*** *p143*
Shannon, William 57; Ontario, 1871 ***1823.15*** *p237*
Shannon, William 57; Vermont, 1895 ***5900.10*** *p380*
Shannon, William 58; Ontario, 1871 ***1823.15*** *p237*
Shanon, Martha 70; Ontario, 1871 ***1823.15*** *p237*
Shanty, Kate 48; Vermont, 1901 ***5900.10*** *p310*
Shapcoate, Phillip; Virginia, 1666 ***6212.30*** *p31*
Shapcott, W. S.; Quebec, 1858 ***9196.15*** *p31*
Shapgood, Jonas; Maryland, 1673 ***2524.55*** *p198*
Shapgood, Susana; Maryland, 1673 ***2524.55*** *p198*
Shapleigh, Phillip; Maryland, 1672 ***2524.55*** *p198*
Shapten, James 58; Ontario, 1871 ***1823.22*** *p143*
Shapter, Thomas, Jr.; New York, 1802 ***8197.10*** *p24*
Shapton, James 72; Ontario, 1871 ***1823.15*** *p238*
Shapton, Thomas; New York, New York, 1856 ***1224.3*** *p70*
Shapton, Thomas 32; Ontario, 1871 ***1823.15*** *p238*
Shark, Thomas 30; Philadelphia, 1774 ***1220.25*** *p68*
Sharkey, Ann; Vermont, 1805-1887 ***5900.10*** *p237*
Sharkey, Arthur 36; Ontario, 1871 ***1823.15*** *p238*
Sharkey, Bridget; Vermont, 1829-1863 ***5900.10*** *p237*
Sharkey, John; Vermont, 1795-1876 ***5900.10*** *p237*
Sharkey, Mary; Vermont, 1847-1935 ***5900.10*** *p237*
Sharkey, Mary 68; Vermont, 1879 ***5900.10*** *p232*
Sharkey, R. H.; Vermont, 1844-1911 ***5900.10*** *p237*
Sharman, Edward 43; Ontario, 1871 ***1823.15*** *p238*
Sharman, George 30; Ontario, 1871 ***1823.15*** *p238*
Sharman, Robert 22; Maryland, 1775 ***1220.25*** *p113*
Sharman, Robert 37; Ontario, 1871 ***1823.15*** *p238*
Sharman, William 63; Ontario, 1871 ***1823.15*** *p238*
Sharmanaw, Toney 35; Ontario, 1871 ***1823.15*** *p238*
Sharmon, Robert; Ontario, 1871 ***1823.22*** *p143*
Sharp, Mr.; Quebec, 1858 ***9196.15*** *p43*
Sharp, Alexander; New York, 1807 ***8197.10*** *p332*
Sharp, Alexander; New York, 1822 ***8197.10*** *p280*
Sharp, Annie 19; Ontario, 1871 ***1823.28*** *p91*
Sharp, Edward; New York, 1828-1834 ***8197.10*** *p306*
Sharp, Elizabeth; New Bern, North Carolina, 1781 ***1224.2*** *p102*
Sharp, Godfrey 46; Ontario, 1871 ***1823.22*** *p143*
Sharp, Henry David; New York, 1823 ***8197.10*** *p280*
Sharp, Jacob 60; Ontario, 1871 ***1823.22*** *p143*
Sharp, James; New Orleans, 1829 ***1640.10*** *p184*
Sharp, James; New York, 1802 ***8197.10*** *p24*
Sharp, James 26; Ontario, 1871 ***1823.28*** *p91*
Sharp, Jane; Virginia, 1703 ***6212.30*** *p62*
Sharp, Jannett 72; Ontario, 1871 ***1823.28*** *p91*
Sharp, John; Canada, 1712 ***1224.2*** *p102*
Sharp, John; Pennsylvania, 1780 ***4629.10*** *p43*
Sharp, John 44; Ontario, 1871 ***1823.15*** *p238*
Sharp, John 47; Ontario, 1871 ***1823.28*** *p91*
Sharp, John 62; Ontario, 1871 ***1823.28*** *p91*
Sharp, Nehemiah; Pennsylvania, 1786 ***4629.10*** *p53*
Sharp, Neil 65; Ontario, 1871 ***1823.15*** *p238*
Sharp, Nicholas; New York, 1807 ***8197.10*** *p330*
Sharp, Ralph 48; Ontario, 1871 ***1823.15*** *p238*
Sharp, Robert 32; Ontario, 1871 ***1823.28*** *p91*
Sharp, Robert 50; Ontario, 1871 ***1823.28*** *p91*
Sharp, Robert H. 56; Ontario, 1871 ***1823.22*** *p143*
Sharp, T. 40; Alaska, 1917 ***9196.1*** *p48*
Sharp, T. 40; Whitehorse, Yukon, 1917 ***9196.1*** *p48*
Sharp, Thomas; Philadelphia, 1740 ***1224.2*** *p102*
Sharp, Thomas 30; St. Vincent, 1775 ***1220.25*** *p129*
Sharp, Thomas 40; Ontario, 1871 ***1823.15*** *p238*
Sharp, Walter 38; Ontario, 1871 ***1823.28*** *p91*
Sharp, William; Florida, 1764 ***1224.2*** *p102*
Sharp, William; Pennsylvania, 1780 ***4629.10*** *p43*
Sharp, William 15; Ontario, 1871 ***1823.28*** *p91*
Sharp, William 35; Ontario, 1871 ***1823.15*** *p238*
Sharp, William 70; Ontario, 1871 ***1823.15*** *p238*
Sharpbone, Ellex; Virginia, 1671-1672 ***6212.30*** *p47*
Sharpcross, Richard; New York, 1838 ***8197.10*** *p150*
Sharpe, James 49; Ontario, 1871 ***1823.28*** *p91*
Sharpe, James 74; Ontario, 1871 ***1823.28*** *p91*
Sharpe, John; New England, 1667 ***1224.1*** *p52*
Sharpe, John; New York, 1802 ***8197.10*** *p24*
Sharpe, Robert; Virginia, 1666 ***1224.1*** *p52*
Sharpe, Simon; America, 1659 ***1224.1*** *p52*
Sharpe, Thomas; Virginia, 1678 ***1224.1*** *p52*
Sharpen, Marcia 13; Ontario, 1871 ***1823.15*** *p238*
Sharpin, James 41; Ontario, 1871 ***1823.15*** *p238*
Sharpin, Richard 36; Ontario, 1871 ***1823.15*** *p238*
Sharples, James; New York, New York, 1811 ***1224.3*** *p70*
Sharpley, John; Maryland, 1669 ***2524.55*** *p198*
Sharpman, John 50; Ontario, 1871 ***1823.15*** *p238*
Sharpney, Elizabeth; Maryland, 1681 ***2524.55*** *p198*
Sharrow, George 26; Nova Scotia, 1774 ***1220.25*** *p135*
Sharwin, Richard; New York, New York, 1783 ***1224.2*** *p103*
Sharwood, James; Pennsylvania, 1777 ***4629.10*** *p25*
Shatney, Rose 38; Vermont, 1877 ***5900.10*** *p203*
Shaughnassy, John; New York, 1840 ***8197.10*** *p286*
Shaughnassy, John 46; Ontario, 1871 ***1823.22*** *p144*
Shaughnassy, Mary 48; Ontario, 1871 ***1823.22*** *p144*
Shaughness, James; New York, 1838 ***8197.10*** *p149*
Shaughness, Simon 50; Ontario, 1871 ***1823.28*** *p91*
Shaughnessy, Catherine Ahearn 78; Vermont, 1918 ***5900.10*** *p64*
Shaughnessy, John; New York, 1838 ***8197.10*** *p284*
Shaughnessy, Margaret King; Vermont, 1850-1927 ***5900.10*** *p56*
Shaughnessy, Mary 60; Ontario, 1871 ***1823.28*** *p91*
Shaughnessy, Patrick; Vermont, 1835-1912 ***5900.10*** *p56*
Shaughnessy, Thomas 79; Vermont, 1923 ***5900.10*** *p64*
Shaughnesy, Michael 55; Ontario, 1871 ***1823.22*** *p144*
Shauts, Thomas; New York, 1839 ***8197.10*** *p140*
Shaven, William 30; Ontario, 1871 ***1823.15*** *p238*
Shaver, Michael 58; Ontario, 1871 ***1823.28*** *p91*
Shaves, Isaac; New York, 1824 ***8197.10*** *p281*
Shaves, William; New York, 1824 ***8197.10*** *p281*
Shaw, Mr.; Quebec, 1857 ***9196.15*** *p17*
Shaw, Mr.; Quebec, 1858 ***9196.15*** *p40*
Shaw, Mrs.; Quebec, 1857 ***9196.15*** *p26*
Shaw, A. James 32; Ontario, 1871 ***1823.15*** *p238*
Shaw, Alexander; Jamaica, 1869 ***1640.13*** *p113*
Shaw, Alexander; Nova Scotia, 1820-1829 ***4537.35*** *p37*
Wife: Sarah
Child: Angus
Child: Kirsty
Child: John
Child: Ann
Child: Norman
Shaw, Alexander; Tobago, West Indies, 1832 ***1640.13*** *p113*
Shaw, Alexander L.; New York, 1840 ***8197.10*** *p195*
Shaw, Andrew 46; Ontario, 1871 ***1823.22*** *p144*
Shaw, Angus *SEE* Shaw, Alexander
Shaw, Angus; Quebec, 1870-1879 ***4537.35*** *p64*
Wife: Ann MacDonald
Child: Ann
Child: Duncan
Child: Kenneth
Child: Donald J.
Shaw, Angus 30; Ontario, 1871 ***1823.15*** *p238*
Shaw, Ann *SEE* Shaw, Alexander
Shaw, Ann *SEE* Shaw, Angus
Shaw, Ann *SEE* Shaw, John
Shaw, Ann; Nova Scotia, 1820-1829 ***4537.35*** *p23*
Shaw, Ann; Nova Scotia, 1840-1849 ***4537.35*** *p21*
Shaw, Ann; Nova Scotia, 1840-1849 ***4537.35*** *p35*
Shaw, Ann Elizabeth; Vermont, 1828-1910 ***5900.10*** *p402*
Shaw, Ann MacDonald *SEE* Shaw, Angus
Shaw, Anna; Florida, 1796-1845 ***1640.10*** *p184*
Shaw, Catherine *SEE* Shaw, John
Shaw, Catherine 53; Ontario, 1871 ***1823.15*** *p238*
Shaw, Catherine MacCusbic *SEE* Shaw, Evander
Shaw, Charles 47; Ontario, 1871 ***1823.15*** *p238*
Shaw, Charles 48; Ontario, 1871 ***1823.15*** *p238*
Shaw, Daniel 46; Ontario, 1871 ***1823.28*** *p91*
Shaw, Donald *SEE* Shaw, Evander
Shaw, Donald *SEE* Shaw, John
Shaw, Donald J. *SEE* Shaw, Angus
Shaw, Duncan *SEE* Shaw, Angus
Shaw, Duncan; Falkland Islands, 1890-1899 ***4537.35*** *p77*
Shaw, Effie *SEE* Shaw, John
Shaw, Effie Fraser *SEE* Shaw, Neil
Shaw, Euphemith 32; Ontario, 1871 ***1823.15*** *p238*
Shaw, Evander *SEE* Shaw, John
Shaw, Evander; Nova Scotia, 1850-1859 ***4537.35*** *p37*
Child: John
Child: Donald
Child: Kirsty
Child: Sarah
Wife: Catherine MacCusbic
Child: Mary
Shaw, Franklin B.; Vermont, 1824-1898 ***5900.10*** *p598*

Shaw, George 23; Ontario, 1871 ***1823.15*** *p238*
Shaw, Isabella 74; Ontario, 1871 ***1823.15*** *p238*
Shaw, James; Georgia, 1820 ***1640.10*** *p184*
Shaw, James 36; Ontario, 1871 ***1823.22*** *p144*
Shaw, James 49; Ontario, 1871 ***1823.15*** *p238*
Shaw, James 50; Ontario, 1871 ***1823.22*** *p144*
Shaw, James 54; Ontario, 1871 ***1823.22*** *p144*
Shaw, James Allan; Nova Scotia, 1860 ***1640.13*** *p113*
Shaw, James Southby; Missouri, 1847 ***1224.3*** *p70*
Shaw, Jane; Virginia, 1664 ***6212.30*** *p10*
Shaw, Janet *SEE* Shaw, John
Shaw, Jeremiah 57; Ontario, 1871 ***1823.15*** *p239*
Shaw, Jessie *SEE* Shaw, Norman
Shaw, Joan; Virginia, 1664 ***6212.30*** *p12*
Shaw, Joanna M. Palmer; Vermont, 1829-1901 ***5900.10*** *p598*
Shaw, John *SEE* Shaw, Alexander
Shaw, John *SEE* Shaw, Evander
Shaw, John *SEE* Shaw, John
Shaw, John; Grenada, 1794 ***1640.13*** *p113*
Shaw, John; New England, 1693 ***1224.1*** *p52*
Shaw, John; Nova Scotia, 1820-1829 ***4537.35*** *p38*
Wife: Mary MacLeod
Child: Mary
Child: Ann
Child: Evander
Child: Kirsty
Child: Donald
Child: Catherine
Child: John
Child: Janet
Shaw, John; Nova Scotia, 1840-1849 ***4537.35*** *p38*
Wife: Kirsty MacCusbic
Child: Effie
Child: John
Child: Mary
Shaw, John; Pennsylvania, 1779 ***4629.10*** *p41*
Shaw, John; Philadelphia, 1793 ***4629.10*** *p66*
Shaw, John; Philadelphia, 1794 ***4629.10*** *p84*
Shaw, John; Virginia, 1666-1667 ***6212.30*** *p33*
Shaw, John; Port uncertain, 1840-1849 ***4537.35*** *p86*
Wife: Marion
Child: Marion
Child: John
Shaw, John 22; Baltimore, 1775 ***1220.25*** *p118*
Shaw, John 32; Ontario, 1871 ***1823.15*** *p238*
Shaw, John 38; Ontario, 1871 ***1823.15*** *p238*
Shaw, John 54; Ontario, 1871 ***1823.28*** *p91*
Shaw, John 64; Ontario, 1871 ***1823.22*** *p144*
Shaw, John 65; Ontario, 1871 ***1823.28*** *p91*
Shaw, Joseph; New York, 1830 ***8197.10*** *p282*
Shaw, Joseph; New York, 1830 ***8197.10*** *p314*
Shaw, Joseph; New York, 1831 ***8197.10*** *p363*
Shaw, Joseph; New York, 1832 ***8197.10*** *p303*
Shaw, Joseph, Jr.; New York, 1830 ***8197.10*** *p282*
Shaw, Joseph B.; New York, New York, 1856 ***6058.10*** *p49*
Shaw, Kemeys; New York, 1802 ***8197.10*** *p24*
Shaw, Kenneth *SEE* Shaw, Angus
Shaw, Kirsty *SEE* Shaw, Alexander
Shaw, Kirsty *SEE* Shaw, Evander
Shaw, Kirsty *SEE* Shaw, John
Shaw, Kirsty; Nova Scotia, 1840-1849 ***4537.35*** *p17*
Shaw, Kirsty MacCusbic *SEE* Shaw, John
Shaw, Kirsty Morrison *SEE* Shaw, Michael
Shaw, Lachlan; South Carolina, 1761 ***1640.13*** *p113*
Shaw, Lachlan; South Carolina, 1765 ***1224.2*** *p103*
Shaw, M. N. 24; Ontario, 1871 ***1823.22*** *p144*
Shaw, Margaret; Nova Scotia, 1820-1829 ***4537.35*** *p11*
Shaw, Margaret MacLeod *SEE* Shaw, Roderick
Shaw, Marion *SEE* Shaw, John
Shaw, Mary *SEE* Shaw, Evander
Shaw, Mary *SEE* Shaw, John
Shaw, Mary; Manitoba, 1888 ***4537.35*** *p66*
Shaw, Mary; Nova Scotia, 1840-1849 ***4537.35*** *p23*
Shaw, Mary 50; Ontario, 1871 ***1823.15*** *p238*
Shaw, Mary MacLeod *SEE* Shaw, John
Shaw, Matthew Holfred 22; Maryland, 1773-1774 ***1220.25*** *p33*
Shaw, Michael; Nova Scotia, 1825 ***4537.35*** *p38*
Wife: Kirsty Morrison
Child: Sarah
Shaw, Michael 87; Vermont, 1882 ***5900.10*** *p597*
Shaw, Neil; Saskatchewan, 1880-1889 ***4537.35*** *p70*
Wife: Effie Fraser
Shaw, Norman *SEE* Shaw, Alexander
Shaw, Norman; Port uncertain, 1840-1849 ***4537.35*** *p86*
Wife: Jessie
Shaw, Owen 21; Philadelphia, 1774 ***1220.25*** *p69*
Shaw, R. D.; Mississippi, 1799-1831 ***1640.10*** *p184*
Shaw, Rachel; Nova Scotia, 1826-1829 ***4537.35*** *p36*
Shaw, Richard; Virginia, 1700 ***1224.2*** *p103*
Shaw, Robert 21; Maryland, 1774 ***1220.25*** *p59*
Shaw, Roderick; America, 1850-1859 ***4537.35*** *p77*
Wife: Margaret MacLeod
Shaw, Rosina; Vermont, 1828-1914 ***5900.10*** *p597*
Shaw, Samuel; Virginia, 1700 ***1224.2*** *p103*
Shaw, Samuel 28; Ontario, 1871 ***1823.15*** *p238*
Shaw, Sarah *SEE* Shaw, Alexander
Shaw, Sarah *SEE* Shaw, Evander
Shaw, Sarah *SEE* Shaw, Michael
Shaw, Sarah 68; Ontario, 1871 ***1823.22*** *p144*
Shaw, Sarah 72; Vermont, 1866 ***5900.10*** *p598*
Shaw, Sarah A.; Vermont, 1856-1933 ***5900.10*** *p598*
Shaw, Sarah Eliza 57; Vermont, 1900 ***5900.10*** *p598*
Shaw, Susan D.; Vermont, 1830-1909 ***5900.10*** *p598*
Shaw, Thomas; Pennsylvania, 1777 ***4629.10*** *p13*
Shaw, Thomas 76; Ontario, 1871 ***1823.22*** *p144*
Shaw, William; Alabama, 1798-1845 ***1640.10*** *p184*
Shaw, William; Georgia, 1809 ***1640.10*** *p184*
Shaw, William; Maryland, 1672 ***2524.55*** *p198*
Shaw, William; New York, 1802 ***8197.10*** *p24*
Shaw, William; New York, 1804 ***8197.10*** *p28*
Shaw, William; New York, 1821 ***8197.10*** *p63*
Shaw, William; Pennsylvania, 1777 ***4629.10*** *p16*
Shaw, William; Pennsylvania, 1777 ***4629.10*** *p21*
Shaw, William; Pennsylvania, 1845 ***6058.10*** *p21*
Shaw, William; South Carolina, 1774 ***1224.2*** *p103*
Shaw, William; Vermont, 1831-1900 ***5900.10*** *p402*
Shaw, William; Vermont, 1854-1909 ***5900.10*** *p402*
Shaw, William; Virginia, 1703-1704 ***6212.30*** *p62*
Shaw, William 21; Maryland, 1775 ***1220.25*** *p115*
Shaw, William 47; Ontario, 1871 ***1823.22*** *p144*
Shaw, Wm.; Pennsylvania, 1779 ***4629.10*** *p40*
Shaw, Wm; Virginia, 1671-1672 ***6212.30*** *p47*
Shawe, Robert; London, England, 1818 ***1640.13*** *p113*
Shawe, William; Maryland, 1659 ***2524.55*** *p198*
Shay, Abigail E.; Vermont, 1845-1892 ***5900.10*** *p272*
Shay, Allen 30; Ontario, 1871 ***1823.28*** *p91*
Shay, Ellen; Vermont, 1852-1914 ***5900.10*** *p503*
Shay, Fred 36; Ontario, 1871 ***1823.28*** *p91*
Shay, John 60; Ontario, 1871 ***1823.22*** *p144*
Shay, Philip 64; Ontario, 1871 ***1823.28*** *p91*
Shazepanski, Kiel; Maryland, 1910 ***3259.35*** *p55*
Shazepanski, Walerian; Maryland, 1910 ***3259.35*** *p55*
Shea, Andrew; New York, 1840 ***8197.10*** *p195*
Shea, Annie 6; Vermont, 1861 ***5900.10*** *p306*
Shea, Bartholomew; New York, 1830 ***8197.10*** *p282*
Shea, Bartholomew; New York, 1831 ***8197.10*** *p365*
Shea, Catherine; Vermont, 1826-1911 ***5900.10*** *p220*
Shea, Catherine Holland; Vermont, 1855-1937 ***5900.10*** *p69*
Shea, Christina Higgins; Vermont, 1837-1892 ***5900.10*** *p107*
Shea, Dennis; Vermont, 1833-1908 ***5900.10*** *p552*
Shea, Ellen; Vermont, 1833-1915 ***5900.10*** *p251*
Shea, Francis 44; Ontario, 1871 ***1823.22*** *p144*
Shea, George; Philadelphia, 1789 ***4629.10*** *p60*
Shea, Hanah 26; Vermont, 1853 ***5900.10*** *p245*
Shea, Hannah Conner; Vermont, 1839-1913 ***5900.10*** *p552*
Shea, Hanora Haley 56; Vermont, 1868 ***5900.10*** *p502*
Shea, Jeremiah; Vermont, 1855-1930 ***5900.10*** *p69*
Shea, Jeremiah 60; Ontario, 1871 ***1823.28*** *p91*
Shea, Johanna; Vermont, 1841-1923 ***5900.10*** *p175*
Shea, John; New York, New York, 1848 ***1825.45*** *p56*
With 2 brothers & sister
Shea, John; Vermont, 1847-1904 ***5900.10*** *p127*
Shea, John; Vermont, 1851-1911 ***5900.10*** *p306*
Shea, John 29; Ontario, 1871 ***1823.15*** *p239*
Shea, John 32; Ontario, 1871 ***1823.15*** *p239*
Shea, John 49; Ontario, 1871 ***1823.15*** *p239*
Shea, John A.; New York, New York, 1828 ***8197.10*** *p194*
Shea, John Joseph; Vermont, 1862-1922 ***5900.10*** *p377*
Shea, Julia 20; Ontario, 1871 ***1823.22*** *p144*
Shea, Katie 19; Vermont, 1866 ***5900.10*** *p306*
Shea, Margaret; Vermont, n.d. ***5900.10*** *p370*
Shea, Margaret; Vermont, 1849-1936 ***5900.10*** *p306*
Shea, Mary; Vermont, 1831-1906 ***5900.10*** *p115*
Shea, Mary 85; Vermont, 1901 ***5900.10*** *p306*
Shea, Mary Farrell 75; Vermont, 1888 ***5900.10*** *p503*
Shea, Mary Walsh; Vermont, 1862-1932 ***5900.10*** *p127*
Shea, Michael; Maryland, 1678 ***2524.55*** *p198*
Shea, Michael; Vermont, 1836-1898 ***5900.10*** *p107*
Shea, Michael 69; Vermont, 1881 ***5900.10*** *p503*
Shea, Michael 70; Vermont, 1892 ***5900.10*** *p306*
Shea, Peter 50; Ontario, 1871 ***1823.15*** *p239*
Shea, Thomas; Pennsylvania, 1845 ***6058.10*** *p23*
Shea, Timothy; New York, 1840 ***8197.10*** *p199*
Shea, Timothy C.; Vermont, 1832-1905 ***5900.10*** *p113*
Sheahan, Mrs. 60; Ontario, 1871 ***1823.28*** *p91*
Sheahan, Catherine 67; Vermont, 1873 ***5900.10*** *p141*
Sheahan, Patrick 70; Ontario, 1871 ***1823.28*** *p91*
Sheahan, Philip 40; Ontario, 1871 ***1823.22*** *p144*
Sheails, Matthew; New York, 1826 ***8197.10*** *p333*
Sheale, Richard; Virginia, 1664 ***6212.30*** *p10*
Shean, Timothy 31; Maryland, 1774 ***1220.25*** *p51*
Shear, John 55; Ontario, 1871 ***1823.15*** *p239*
Shearer, Alex 56; Ontario, 1871 ***1823.22*** *p144*
Shearer, Alexander; New York, 1840 ***8197.10*** *p194*
Shearer, Ann 56; Ontario, 1871 ***1823.22*** *p144*
Shearer, Archibald; New York, 1837 ***8197.10*** *p284*
Shearer, Archibald; New York, 1840 ***8197.10*** *p196*
Shearer, Donald; Georgia, 1736 ***1640.10*** *p184*
Shearer, Elizabeth; Ontario, 1871 ***1823.22*** *p144*
Shearer, Ennis 60; Ontario, 1871 ***1823.15*** *p239*
Shearer, James 69; Ontario, 1871 ***1823.22*** *p144*
Shearer, Margret 74; Ontario, 1871 ***1823.28*** *p91*
Shearer, Mathew 53; Ontario, 1871 ***1823.22*** *p144*
Shearer, Thomas 50; Ontario, 1871 ***1823.22*** *p144*
Shearer, William; Boston, 1763 ***1224.2*** *p103*
Shears, David R. 75; Ontario, 1871 ***1823.22*** *p144*
Shears, James 19; Ontario, 1861 ***2896.25*** *p23*
Shears, Jane 14; Ontario, 1861 ***2896.25*** *p23*
Shears, Joana 10; Ontario, 1861 ***2896.25*** *p23*
Shears, Laney 38; Ontario, 1861 ***2896.25*** *p23*
Shears, Pheba 87; Ontario, 1861 ***2896.25*** *p23*
Shears, Phebe E. 11; Ontario, 1861 ***2896.25*** *p20*
Shears, Sarah A. 18; Ontario, 1861 ***2896.25*** *p23*
Shears, Sarah J. 23; Ontario, 1861 ***2896.25*** *p20*
Shebagizi, John 70; Ontario, 1871 ***1823.28*** *p91*
Shebagizi, William 38; Ontario, 1871 ***1823.28*** *p91*
Shebrick, William 43; Ontario, 1871 ***1823.28*** *p91*
Shed, Thomas; Pennsylvania, 1777 ***4629.10*** *p18*
Shedacker, William; Pennsylvania, 1777 ***4629.10*** *p7*
Shedden, Mr.; Quebec, 1857 ***9196.15*** *p18*
Shedden, Robert; New York, 1794 ***8197.10*** *p2*
Shedden, William Ralston; New York, 1852 ***1224.3*** *p70*
Shedel, John J.; New York, 1838 ***8197.10*** *p284*
Shee, Burtle; Pennsylvania, 1779 ***4629.10*** *p41*
Shee, Edmund; Pennsylvania, 1867 ***6058.10*** *p58*
Shee, John; Pennsylvania, 1777 ***4629.10*** *p8*
Shee, Richard; New York, 1821 ***8197.10*** *p280*
Shee, Walter; Pennsylvania, 1777 ***4629.10*** *p7*
Sheedy, Bridget Connor 49; Vermont, 1875 ***5900.10*** *p468*
Sheedy, John 47; Ontario, 1871 ***1823.28*** *p91*
Sheedy, Margaret 31; Vermont, 1868 ***5900.10*** *p412*
Sheedy, Martin 45; Ontario, 1871 ***1823.28*** *p91*
Sheedy, Mary; Vermont, 1856-1910 ***5900.10*** *p445*
Sheedy, Michael; New York, 1833 ***8197.10*** *p283*
Sheedy, Michael; New York, 1836 ***8197.10*** *p78*
Sheedy, Patrick 75; Vermont, 1883 ***5900.10*** *p468*
Sheeham, Dennis 39; Maryland, 1774 ***1220.25*** *p65*
Sheehan, Bridget; Vermont, 1838-1912 ***5900.10*** *p127*
Sheehan, Bridget; Vermont, 1847-1907 ***5900.10*** *p174*
Sheehan, Bridget; Vermont, 1854-1918 ***5900.10*** *p161*
Sheehan, Bridget; Vermont, 1859-1936 ***5900.10*** *p413*
Sheehan, Bridget A.; Vermont, 1853-1938 ***5900.10*** *p438*
Sheehan, Catherine; Vermont, 1865-1934 ***5900.10*** *p413*
Sheehan, Catherine 80; Vermont, 1880 ***5900.10*** *p413*
Sheehan, Daniel; Vermont, 1814-1898 ***5900.10*** *p182*
Sheehan, Dennis 87; Vermont, 1890 ***5900.10*** *p413*
Sheehan, Edward; Vermont, n.d. ***5900.10*** *p248*
Sheehan, Edward; Vermont, 1862-1918 ***5900.10*** *p413*
Sheehan, Ellen; Vermont, 1841-1922 ***5900.10*** *p535*
Sheehan, Ellen; Vermont, 1869-1934 ***5900.10*** *p413*
Sheehan, Ellen 78; Vermont, 1901 ***5900.10*** *p418*
Sheehan, Ellen Cunningham 96; Vermont, 1926 ***5900.10*** *p197*
Sheehan, Ellen Fitzgerald; Vermont, 1829-1919 ***5900.10*** *p107*
Sheehan, Hannah; Vermont, 1822-1897 ***5900.10*** *p401*
Sheehan, Hanora 64; Vermont, 1887 ***5900.10*** *p161*
Sheehan, Ida L. Hughes; Vermont, 1865-1926 ***5900.10*** *p187*
Sheehan, James 77; Vermont, 1896 ***5900.10*** *p613*
Sheehan, Jane Collins 47; Vermont, 1876 ***5900.10*** *p613*
Sheehan, Jeremiah 55; Vermont, 1864 ***5900.10*** *p105*
Sheehan, Joanna; Vermont, 1816-1901 ***5900.10*** *p182*
Sheehan, John; Pennsylvania, 1868 ***6058.10*** *p65*
Sheehan, John; Vermont, n.d. ***5900.10*** *p57*
Sheehan, John; Vermont, 1830-1906 ***5900.10*** *p486*
Sheehan, John; Vermont, 1838-1884 ***5900.10*** *p277*
Sheehan, John 42; Vermont, 1883 ***5900.10*** *p413*
Sheehan, John 65; Vermont, 1893 ***5900.10*** *p197*
Sheehan, Katherine; Vermont, 1848-1935 ***5900.10*** *p187*
Sheehan, Katherine 80; Vermont, 1874 ***5900.10*** *p105*
Sheehan, Lawrence; Vermont, 1824-1909 ***5900.10*** *p107*
Sheehan, Margaret; Vermont, 1839-1891 ***5900.10*** *p267*
Sheehan, Margaret; Vermont, 1854-1904 ***5900.10*** *p589*
Sheehan, Margaret 59; Vermont, 1913 ***5900.10*** *p60*
Sheehan, Maria 4; Vermont, 1854 ***5900.10*** *p162*
Sheehan, Martin; Vermont, 1854-1916 ***5900.10*** *p413*
Sheehan, Mary A. Donovan; Vermont, 1838-1906 ***5900.10*** *p486*
Sheehan, Nora M. Gallagher; Vermont, 1850-1930 ***5900.10*** *p277*

Sheehan, Patrick; Vermont, 1836-1921 ***5900.10*** *p174*
Sheehan, Patrick; Vermont, 1853-1923 ***5900.10*** *p438*
Sheehan, Patrick 60; Ontario, 1871 ***1823.28*** *p91*
Sheehan, Patrick 60; Vermont, 1883 ***5900.10*** *p161*
Sheehan, Patrick E.; Vermont, 1858-1923 ***5900.10*** *p187*
Sheehan, Peter; Vermont, 1858-1906 ***5900.10*** *p413*
Sheehan, Timothy; Pennsylvania, 1868 ***6058.10*** *p65*
Sheehan, William F.; Vermont, 1859-1893 ***5900.10*** *p161*
Sheehey, James; Vermont, 1852-1903 ***5900.10*** *p474*
Sheehey, John; New York, 1830 ***8197.10*** *p282*
Sheehey, Margaret Donovan; Vermont, 1850-1922 ***5900.10*** *p474*
Sheehy, Ann Melledy 70; Vermont, 1898 ***5900.10*** *p190*
Sheehy, Bridget; Vermont, 1885 ***5900.10*** *p85*
Sheehy, Deborah H.; Vermont, 1845-1911 ***5900.10*** *p136*
Sheehy, James; Vermont, 1831-1925 ***5900.10*** *p536*
Sheehy, John; Vermont, n.d. ***5900.10*** *p190*
Sheehy, John 84; Vermont, 1897 ***5900.10*** *p140*
Sheehy, Mary Marlow 60; Vermont, 1890 ***5900.10*** *p536*
Sheehy, William; New York, 1821 ***8197.10*** *p279*
Sheele, Captaine; Maryland, 1680 ***2524.55*** *p198*
Sheen, Patrick 21; Maryland, 1775 ***1220.25*** *p108*
Sheep, . . .; Maryland, 1631-1685 ***2524.55*** *p198*
Sheep, Lancelot; Maryland, 1646 ***2524.55*** *p128*
Sheer, Alex; New York, New York, 1846 ***6058.10*** *p27*
Sheer, Peter; Pennsylvania, 1823 ***6058.10*** *p8*
Sheeran, Ellen Finney; Vermont, 1837-1921 ***5900.10*** *p170*
Sheeran, John; Vermont, 1841-1923 ***5900.10*** *p170*
Sheeran, William; New York, 1834 ***8197.10*** *p372*
Sheerer, David; Pennsylvania, 1777 ***4629.10*** *p32*
Sheffeild, James; Virginia, 1665-1666 ***6212.30*** *p23*
Sheffer, Alexander; America, 1738 ***2856.30*** *p408*
Sheffield, H. D.; Quebec, 1858 ***9196.15*** *p34*
Sheffield, Thomas; Virginia, 1622 ***1224.1*** *p52*
Shehane, William; Maryland, 1681 ***2524.55*** *p198*
Sheik, Martin 52; Ontario, 1871 ***1823.15*** *p239*
Sheild, Geo.; Maryland, 1660 ***2524.55*** *p198*
Sheilds, Danl 52; Ontario, 1871 ***1823.28*** *p91*
Sheilds, Frederick 25; Ontario, 1871 ***1823.28*** *p91*
Sheilds, Mary 62; Ontario, 1871 ***1823.28*** *p91*
Sheilds, Michael 50; Ontario, 1871 ***1823.28*** *p91*
Sheilk, Caspar; America, 1738 ***2856.30*** *p382*
Sheille, George; Maryland, 1670 ***2524.55*** *p198*
Shelder, Nik; America, 1740 ***2856.30*** *p429*
Sheldon, Austin 96; Vermont, 1898 ***5900.10*** *p200*
Sheldon, Edward A. 32; Vermont, 1869 ***5900.10*** *p582*
Sheldon, J. W.; Vermont, 1779-1866 ***5900.10*** *p454*
Sheldon, James; Virginia, 1664 ***6212.30*** *p9*
Sheldon, Martha; Vermont, n.d. ***5900.10*** *p200*
Sheldon, Mary; Vermont, 1831-1917 ***5900.10*** *p582*
Sheldon, William; Virginia, 1664 ***6212.30*** *p8*
Shele, William; Virginia, 1666-1667 ***6212.30*** *p34*
Sheles, Mary 88; Ontario, 1871 ***1823.15*** *p239*
Shelinger, Frederick; Pennsylvania, 1817-1827 ***6058.10*** *p7*
Shell, Richard; New York, 1857 ***1224.3*** *p70*
Shelle, Susanna; Virginia, 1677 ***6212.30*** *p53*
Shelley, Anna Downs; Vermont, 1855-1928 ***5900.10*** *p272*
Shelley, Caleb; Vermont, 1819-1904 ***5900.10*** *p50*
Shelley, John; New York, 1839 ***8197.10*** *p285*
Shelley, John; Virginia, 1664 ***6212.30*** *p8*
Shelley, Mary; Vermont, 1852-1919 ***5900.10*** *p50*
Shelley, Mary Lawrence; Vermont, 1825-1898 ***5900.10*** *p50*
Shelley, Stephen 37; Ontario, 1871 ***1823.15*** *p239*
Shelley, William; Vermont, 1853-1907 ***5900.10*** *p272*
Shelling, Sarah; Virginia, 1665-1666 ***6212.30*** *p25*
Shellito, Tho; Virginia, 1672 ***6212.30*** *p50*
Shellito, Thomas; Maryland, 1670 ***2524.55*** *p198*
Shelly, William; New York, 1838 ***8197.10*** *p284*
Shelton, James; New York, 1833 ***8197.10*** *p283*
Shelton, Mary; Maryland, 1681 ***2524.55*** *p198*
Shelton, William 32; Ontario, 1871 ***1823.15*** *p239*
Shelts, Samuel 22; Ontario, 1871 ***1823.15*** *p239*
Shelvey, Gilbert 37; Vermont, 1883 ***5900.10*** *p389*
Shelvey, James 26; Vermont, 1878 ***5900.10*** *p389*
Shelvey, Kate 73; Vermont, 1910 ***5900.10*** *p381*
Shelvey, Margaret; Vermont, 1840-1924 ***5900.10*** *p387*
Shelvey, Margaret 75; Vermont, 1882 ***5900.10*** *p389*
Shelvey, Mary Murphy 40; Vermont, 1886 ***5900.10*** *p389*
Shelvey, Mary Starr; Vermont, 1850-1939 ***5900.10*** *p431*
Shelvey, Patrick 47; Vermont, 1881 ***5900.10*** *p389*
Shelvey, Thomas 37; Vermont, 1887 ***5900.10*** *p431*
Shelvey, Thomas 72; Vermont, 1871 ***5900.10*** *p389*
Shemans, Benjamin; Carolina, 1723 ***1224.2*** *p103*
Shenat, John 45; Ontario, 1871 ***1823.15*** *p239*
Shenirn, Elizabeth 50; Maryland, 1774 ***1220.25*** *p37*
Shennon, John 47; Ontario, 1871 ***1823.28*** *p91*
Shepard, Catharine 77; Vermont, 1876 ***5900.10*** *p514*
Shepard, Gideon 71; Ontario, 1871 ***1823.22*** *p144*
Shepard, Jeanette O'Brien; Vermont, 1851-1920 ***5900.10*** *p600*
Shepard, John J.; Vermont, 1847-1923 ***5900.10*** *p600*
Shepard, Mary; Maryland, 1643 ***2524.55*** *p198*
Shepard, William; Maryland, 1643 ***2524.55*** *p198*
Shephard, John; New York, 1836 ***8197.10*** *p78*
Shephard, John 23; Virginia, 1775 ***1220.25*** *p109*
Shephard, Roger 27; Maryland, 1775 ***1220.25*** *p111*
Shephard, Samuel; New York, 1834 ***8197.10*** *p283*
Shephard, Samuel; New York, 1836 ***8197.10*** *p78*
Shepheard, Isaac; Maryland, 1681 ***2524.55*** *p198*
Shepheard, Nicholas; Maryland, 1675 ***2524.55*** *p198*
Shepheard, Tho; Virginia, 1670 ***6212.30*** *p42*
Shepheard, Wm; Virginia, 1664 ***6212.30*** *p10*
Shepherd, Abram; Mobile, Alabama, 1805-1845 ***1640.10*** *p184*
Shepherd, David; New Orleans, 1847 ***1640.10*** *p184*
Shepherd, Elizabeth 36; New York, 1774 ***1220.25*** *p24*
Child: Molly 4
Child: John 2
Shepherd, George 49; Ontario, 1871 ***1823.15*** *p239*
Shepherd, Helen; Mobile, Alabama, 1815-1841 ***1640.10*** *p184*
Shepherd, John 2 *SEE* Shepherd, Elizabeth
Shepherd, John 22; Philadelphia, 1774 ***1220.25*** *p43*
Shepherd, Joseph; Florida, 1769 ***1224.2*** *p103*
Shepherd, Matthew 65; Ontario, 1871 ***1823.15*** *p239*
Shepherd, Molly 4 *SEE* Shepherd, Elizabeth
Shepherd, Samuel 16; Philadelphia, 1774 ***1220.25*** *p4*
Shepherd, William 21; Maryland, 1773-1774 ***1220.25*** *p33*
Shepherd, William 53; Ontario, 1871 ***1823.28*** *p91*
Sheppard, Abigall; Maryland, 1669 ***2524.55*** *p198*
Sheppard, Dorothy 72; Ontario, 1871 ***1823.15*** *p239*
Sheppard, Ellinor *SEE* Sheppard, John
Sheppard, George; Pennsylvania, 1777 ***4629.10*** *p10*
Sheppard, George G.; New York, 1836 ***8197.10*** *p283*
Sheppard, Jacob; New York, 1840 ***8197.10*** *p197*
Sheppard, James 35; Ontario, 1871 ***1823.15*** *p239*
Sheppard, John; Maryland, 1669 ***2524.55*** *p198*
Wife: Ellinor
Sheppard, John; Pennsylvania, 1779 ***4629.10*** *p36*
Sheppard, John 32; Ontario, 1871 ***1823.15*** *p239*
Sheppard, John 68; Ontario, 1871 ***1823.15*** *p239*
Sheppard, Lewis; Maryland, 1665 ***2524.55*** *p198*
Sheppard, Mary; Maryland, 1647 ***2524.55*** *p198*
Sheppard, Rowland; Maryland, 1681 ***2524.55*** *p198*
Sheppard, Susannah Mary Lestourgeon; Illinois, 1857 ***1224.3*** *p70*
Sheppard, William; New York, 1839 ***1224.3*** *p70*
Shepperd, Catherine 76; Ontario, 1871 ***1823.15*** *p239*
Shepperd, James 33; Ontario, 1871 ***1823.15*** *p239*
Shepperd, James Nutley; Key West, Florida, 1846 ***1224.3*** *p70*
Shepperd, John 42; Ontario, 1871 ***1823.15*** *p239*
Shepperd, John 45; Ontario, 1871 ***1823.15*** *p239*
Shepperd, John 48; Ontario, 1871 ***1823.15*** *p239*
Sheppey, Mary Mills *SEE* Sheppey, Richard
Sheppey, Richard; Maryland, 1665 ***2524.55*** *p198*
Wife: Mary Mills
Shepphard, Mary; Maryland, 1646 ***2524.55*** *p66*
Sheppherd, James 24; Ontario, 1871 ***1823.15*** *p239*
Shera, Ann 25; Ontario, 1861 ***2896.27*** *p64*
Shera, Fureta 5; Ontario, 1861 ***2896.27*** *p64*
Sherbrook, James 40; Ontario, 1871 ***1823.15*** *p239*
Sherclif, Mrs.; Maryland, 1649 ***2524.55*** *p198*
Sherclif, John; Maryland, 1646 ***2524.55*** *p198*
Sherer, Henry; New York, 1807 ***8197.10*** *p50*
Sherer, Robert; Pennsylvania, 1777 ***4629.10*** *p29*
Sherffil, Manly 23; Ontario, 1871 ***1823.22*** *p144*
Sherica, Thomas; Maryland, 1676 ***2524.55*** *p209*
Sheridan, . . .; Vermont, n.d. ***5900.10*** *p179*
Sheridan, Ann; Vermont, 1847-1889 ***5900.10*** *p437*
Sheridan, Ann 75; Ontario, 1871 ***1823.22*** *p144*
Sheridan, Ann Cline; Vermont, 1810-1892 ***5900.10*** *p219*
Sheridan, Ann Kelly; Vermont, 1843-1905 ***5900.10*** *p219*
Sheridan, Anna S. McDermot; Vermont, 1816-1892 ***5900.10*** *p451*
Sheridan, Anne; Vermont, 1863-1920 ***5900.10*** *p69*
Sheridan, Anne G.; Vermont, 1833-1917 ***5900.10*** *p70*
Sheridan, Anora; Vermont, 1843-1930 ***5900.10*** *p388*
Sheridan, Bridget Kelley; Vermont, 1853-1931 ***5900.10*** *p161*
Sheridan, Catherine 68; Vermont, 1882 ***5900.10*** *p179*
Sheridan, Catherine A. Falloon; Vermont, 1858-1914 ***5900.10*** *p390*
Sheridan, Catherine Carey; Vermont, 1820-1900 ***5900.10*** *p441*
Sheridan, Daniel; Vermont, 1795-1888 ***5900.10*** *p219*
Sheridan, Daniel; Vermont, 1871-1872 ***5900.10*** *p209*
Sheridan, Delia M. Daniels; Vermont, 1927 ***5900.10*** *p61*
Sheridan, Edward 50; Vermont, 1903 ***5900.10*** *p175*
Sheridan, Eliza 62; Vermont, 1896 ***5900.10*** *p564*
Sheridan, Ellen 12; Vermont, 1853 ***5900.10*** *p188*
Sheridan, Ellen Jane 15; Ontario, 1871 ***1823.28*** *p92*
Sheridan, Ellen Lee; Vermont, 1839-1918 ***5900.10*** *p277*
Sheridan, Ellen Splain 51; Vermont, 1907 ***5900.10*** *p175*
Sheridan, Helen 23; British Columbia, 1911 ***9196.1*** *p35*
Sheridan, Helen 23; Seattle, 1911 ***9196.1*** *p35*
Sheridan, Helen McGarry; Vermont, 1879-1929 ***5900.10*** *p451*
Sheridan, James; New York, 1837 ***8197.10*** *p105*
Sheridan, James; New York, 1837-1840 ***8197.10*** *p300*
Sheridan, James; Vermont, 1810-1882 ***5900.10*** *p451*
Sheridan, James; Vermont, 1829 ***5900.10*** *p13*
Sheridan, James; Vermont, 1836-1890 ***5900.10*** *p219*
Sheridan, James 74; Vermont, 1902 ***5900.10*** *p564*
Sheridan, James E.; Vermont, 1857-1929 ***5900.10*** *p441*
Sheridan, Jane M.; Vermont, 1858-1929 ***5900.10*** *p69*
Sheridan, Johanna Nevins; Vermont, 1839-1908 ***5900.10*** *p491*
Sheridan, John; New York, 1838 ***8197.10*** *p149*
Sheridan, John; New York, 1840 ***8197.10*** *p197*
Sheridan, John; Vermont, 1795-1873 ***5900.10*** *p441*
Sheridan, John; Vermont, 1842-1903 ***5900.10*** *p608*
Sheridan, John; Vermont, 1851-1937 ***5900.10*** *p179*
Sheridan, John 68; Vermont, 1912 ***5900.10*** *p61*
Sheridan, John D. 74; Vermont, 1901 ***5900.10*** *p519*
Sheridan, John E.; Vermont, 1849-1926 ***5900.10*** *p147*
Sheridan, Maggie McGee 42; Vermont, 1902 ***5900.10*** *p608*
Sheridan, Margaret; Vermont, 1839-1895 ***5900.10*** *p253*
Sheridan, Margaret; Vermont, 1855-1869 ***5900.10*** *p441*
Sheridan, Maria; Vermont, 1844-1900 ***5900.10*** *p219*
Sheridan, Martha A.; Vermont, 1852-1921 ***5900.10*** *p167*
Sheridan, Martin; Vermont, 1835-1916 ***5900.10*** *p219*
Sheridan, Martin B.; Vermont, 1809-1854 ***5900.10*** *p390*
Sheridan, Mary; Vermont, 1855-1930 ***5900.10*** *p179*
Sheridan, Mary 68; Vermont, 1899 ***5900.10*** *p441*
Sheridan, Mary A.; Vermont, 1856-1900 ***5900.10*** *p147*
Sheridan, Mary E. Hammel; Vermont, 1860-1938 ***5900.10*** *p441*
Sheridan, Mary Hayes; Vermont, 1841-1905 ***5900.10*** *p219*
Sheridan, Mary Hoyt 47; Vermont, 1891 ***5900.10*** *p280*
Sheridan, Mary Keenan; Vermont, 1836-1916 ***5900.10*** *p48*
Sheridan, Mary McNerny; Vermont, 1843-1905 ***5900.10*** *p608*
Sheridan, Mathew; New York, 1821 ***8197.10*** *p279*
Sheridan, Mathew; New York, 1822 ***8197.10*** *p280*
Sheridan, Michael; New York, 1837 ***8197.10*** *p106*
Sheridan, Owen E.; Vermont, 1823-1904 ***5900.10*** *p283*
Sheridan, Patrick 30; Vermont, 1865 ***5900.10*** *p280*
Sheridan, Patrick 62; Ontario, 1871 ***1823.28*** *p92*
Sheridan, Patrick 75; Vermont, 1896 ***5900.10*** *p179*
Sheridan, Peter; New York, 1836 ***8197.10*** *p78*
Sheridan, Sarah Jane; Vermont, 1867 ***5900.10*** *p209*
Sheridan, Thomas; New York, New York, 1863 ***3437.14*** *p108*
Sheridan, Thomas; Vermont, 1838-1911 ***5900.10*** *p219*
Sheridan, Thomas 36; Ontario, 1871 ***1823.28*** *p92*
Sheridan, Thomas 54; Ontario, 1871 ***1823.15*** *p239*
Sheridan, Thomas 55; Ontario, 1871 ***1823.15*** *p239*
Sheridan, Thomas 71; Vermont, 1915 ***5900.10*** *p608*
Sheridan, Thos 52; Ontario, 1871 ***1823.28*** *p92*
Sheridan, Timothy; Vermont, 1846-1870 ***5900.10*** *p441*
Sheridan, William; Vermont, 1837-1907 ***5900.10*** *p48*
Sheridan, William; Vermont, 1842-1923 ***5900.10*** *p491*
Sheridan, William J.; Vermont, 1856-1923 ***5900.10*** *p451*
Sheridan, Winefred 60; Vermont, 1875 ***5900.10*** *p161*
Sheriff, Charles N. 18; Ontario, 1861 ***2896.28*** *p32*
Sheriff, Margaret 37; Ontario, 1861 ***2896.28*** *p32*
Sheriff, Sarah M. 16; Ontario, 1861 ***2896.28*** *p32*
Sherley, William; Virginia, 1750 ***1224.2*** *p103*
Sherleys, Robert; Maryland, 1633 ***2524.55*** *p198*
Sherlock, A. J.; Vermont, 1831-1888 ***5900.10*** *p487*
Sherlock, Ann M.; Vermont, 1845-1930 ***5900.10*** *p403*
Sherlock, Edward; New York, New York, 1819 ***8197.10*** *p342*
Sherlock, Esther Ellen; Vermont, 1852-1907 ***5900.10*** *p488*
Sherlock, James; New York, 1807 ***8197.10*** *p51*
Sherlock, James; New York, 1838 ***8197.10*** *p149*
Sherlock, James; Virginia, 1710 ***1224.2*** *p103*
Sherlock, James 68; Ontario, 1871 ***1823.28*** *p92*
Sherlock, John; Vermont, 1848-1913 ***5900.10*** *p403*
Sherlock, Lucy A.; Vermont, 1861-1952 ***5900.10*** *p403*
Sherlock, Mary; Vermont, 1831-1906 ***5900.10*** *p84*
Sherlock, Michael; Vermont, 1838-1899 ***5900.10*** *p218*
Sherlock, Sarah Carney 38; Vermont, 1869 ***5900.10*** *p210*
Sherlock, Sarah Phalen; Vermont, 1849-1932 ***5900.10*** *p218*
Sherly, Elizabeth; Maryland, 1676 ***2524.55*** *p198*
Sherly, Henry; Virginia, 1667 ***6212.30*** *p37*
Sherman, Amos; New York, 1808 ***8197.10*** *p54*

Shontell, Augustus 67; Vermont, 1907 5900.10 p361
Shontell, Mary Cole 49; Vermont, 1890 5900.10 p361
Shooe, Andrew; Maryland, 1651 2524.55 p199
Shook, Christian; America, 1739 2856.30 p429
Shoolbred, Mary; Charleston, South Carolina, 1820 1224.3 p71
Shoowis, J.; Quebec, 1858 9196.15 p35
Shope, Bernhart; America, 1753 2856.30 p429
Shope, Johann Jerick; America, 1739 2856.30 p429
Shopperd, Edward 45; Ontario, 1871 1823.15 p241
Shopperd, George 50; Ontario, 1871 1823.15 p241
Shopperd, James 59; Ontario, 1871 1823.15 p241
Shore, Henry 36; Ontario, 1871 1823.22 p145
Shore, Thomas; New York, 1834 8197.10 p371
Shorey, Albert 19; Ontario, 1861 2896.27 p29
Shorey, Joseph; Vermont, 1824-1891 5900.10 p334
Shorey, Mary E. King; Vermont, 1831-1905 5900.10 p334
Shork, Christian; America, 1739 2856.30 p429
Shorkey, Francis; Vermont, 1855-1955 5900.10 p312
Shorkey, Selina; Vermont, 1857-1892 5900.10 p312
Shorland, Thomas; New York, 1820 8197.10 p279
Shorland, Thomas; New York, 1823 8197.10 p62
Short, Abraham; Virginia, 1667-1668 6212.30 p38
Short, Francis; New York, 1803 8197.10 p17
Short, Jacob 23; Ontario, 1871 1823.15 p241
Short, James; Pennsylvania, 1777 4629.10 p20
Short, James; Virginia, 1774 1224.2 p103
Short, James; Virginia, 1787 1640.13 p113
Short, Jno; Virginia, 1666 6212.30 p25
Short, John; Illinois, 1842 1224.3 p71
Short, John; New York, 1828 8197.10 p282
Short, John; Virginia, 1671-1672 6212.30 p46
Short, John 21; Maryland, 1774 1220.25 p69
Short, John 33; Philadelphia, 1774 1220.25 p43
Short, Martha; Virginia, 1681 6212.30 p55
Short, Mary; Michigan, 1856 1224.3 p71
Short, Saml; Virginia, 1663 6212.30 p4
Short, Samuel 28; Maryland, 1775 1220.25 p10
Short, Samuell; Virginia, 1668-1669 6212.30 p40
Short, Thomas 35; Ontario, 1871 1823.15 p241
Short, William 41; Ontario, 1871 1823.22 p145
Short, William 46; Ontario, 1871 1823.15 p241
Shortell, Ellen; Vermont, 1820-1899 5900.10 p579
Shorter, Mary McAnaney 56; Vermont, 1890 5900.10 p436
Shorthouse, Thomas; New York, 1791 4629.10 p80
Shortis, Edward; New York, 1839 8197.10 p285
Shortland, Thomas; New York, 1827 8197.10 p346
Shortreed, Thomas 52; Ontario, 1871 1823.28 p92
Shortreid, John; Virginia, 1792 1640.13 p113
Shortricke, William; York, Virginia, 1669 1224.1 p52
Shorts, Amy 12; Ontario, 1861 2896.28 p65
Shorts, Eke; Maryland, 1910 3259.35 p56
Shorts, George 15; Ontario, 1861 2896.28 p65
Shorts, Hannah 19; Ontario, 1871 1823.22 p145
Shorts, John 9; Ontario, 1861 2896.28 p65
Shorts, Phebe 37; Ontario, 1861 2896.28 p65
Shorts, Richard 4; Ontario, 1861 2896.28 p65
Shortsleeve, Dennis; Vermont, 1841-1923 5900.10 p299
Shortsleeve, Elmira Goddard; Vermont, 1841-1924 5900.10 p299
Shoto, John 23; Washington, 1911 9196.1 p33
Shott, Stephen; Maryland, 1680 2524.55 p199
Shottly, Henry; Virginia, 1667-1668 6212.30 p38
Shouldice, Christfer 65; Ontario, 1871 1823.28 p92
Shouldice, Dennis; Vermont, 1851-1910 5900.10 p425
Shouldice, John; Vermont, 1856-1924 5900.10 p425
Shouldice, Julia Hogan; Vermont, 1864-1900 5900.10 p425
Shouldice, Leonard 32; Ontario, 1871 1823.15 p241
Shouldice, Margaret; Vermont, 1856-1906 5900.10 p425
Shouldice, Maria Hogan; Vermont, 1862-1927 5900.10 p425
Shoulist, Thomas 52; Ontario, 1871 1823.28 p92
Shoults, Rosannah 36; Ontario, 1861 2896.27 p55
Shoultze, Charles 35; Ontario, 1871 1823.28 p92
Shoultze, Charles 45; Ontario, 1871 1823.28 p92
Shoultze, John 37; Ontario, 1871 1823.28 p92
Shoulz, Lewis 42; Ontario, 1871 1823.15 p241
Shoun, Johann; America, 1741 2856.30 p429
Shove, John 29; Maryland, 1775 1220.25 p112
Shoveler, Sarah; Philadelphia, 1800 1224.3 p71
Showell, Arthur; Carolina, 1683 1224.1 p52
Showell, Jonathan; Maryland, 1672 2524.55 p199
Showell, Mary; Maryland, 1672 2524.55 p199
Shower, Nathaniel; Boston, 1761 1224.2 p104
Showers, Christopher; Baltimore, 1847 6058.10 p32
Showry, Elizabeth; Ontario, 1861 2896.28 p52
Showry, Norris; Ontario, 1861 2896.28 p52
Showwainoshe, Joseph 70; Ontario, 1871 1823.28 p92
Shrader, John 36; Ontario, 1871 1823.15 p241
Shrauder, John; New York, 1807 8197.10 p50
Shreder, Jacob; Pennsylvania, 1777 4629.10 p14
Shreinen, Charles 65; Ontario, 1871 1823.15 p241
Shrewsbury, Thomas 57; Ontario, 1871 1823.22 p145
Shriefe, Anne; Maryland, 1682 2524.55 p199
Shrimpton, . . .; Boston, 1661 1224.1 p52
Shrimpton, John; Virginia, 1667-1668 6212.30 p38
Shrimpton, Samuel; Boston, 1700 1224.2 p104
Shrine, Alexander; Maryland, 1673 2524.55 p199
Shriver, Michael; Pennsylvania, 1777 4629.10 p10
Shriver, Samuel; Maryland, 1676 2524.55 p199
Shropshire, Mrs.; Maryland, 1658 2524.55 p47
Husband: Thomas
Shropshire, Robert 26; Maryland, 1774 1220.25 p51
Shropshire, Thomas *SEE* Shropshire, Mrs.
Shrott, Joseph; New York, 1836 8197.10 p319
Shrubb, Thomas; Maryland, 1654 2524.55 p199
Shrubsole, William; South Carolina, 1759 1224.2 p104
Shruder, August 40; Ontario, 1871 1823.28 p92
Shruder, William 51; Ontario, 1871 1823.28 p92
Shryber, Johann, Jr.; America, 1738 2856.30 p429
Shubeck, Joseph; Maryland, 1910 3259.35 p56
Shubrick, Richard; Charles Town, South Carolina, 1777 1224.3 p71
Shubrick, Sarah; South Carolina, 1842 1224.3 p73
Shudiman, Jeremiah; Maryland, 1657 2524.55 p199
Shudinam, Jeremiah; Maryland, 1657 2524.55 p199
Shufelt, Alzina 4; Ontario, 1861 2896.25 p5
Shufelt, Catherine L. 9; Ontario, 1861 2896.25 p5
Shufelt, Elizabeth 19; Ontario, 1861 2896.25 p5
Shufelt, John 7; Ontario, 1861 2896.25 p5
Shufelt, Laner 16; Ontario, 1861 2896.25 p5
Shufelt, Laner 79; Ontario, 1861 2896.25 p5
Shufelt, Mary A. 18; Ontario, 1861 2896.25 p5
Shufelt, Mary J. 11; Ontario, 1861 2896.25 p5
Shuffle, Albert 8; Ontario, 1861 2896.27 p17
Shuffle, Franklin 4; Ontario, 1861 2896.27 p17
Shuffle, Hariet A. 6; Ontario, 1861 2896.27 p17
Shufflebottom, Thomas; Portland, Maine, 1858 9196.15 p29
Shular, Almira 5; Ontario, 1861 2896.25 p10
Shular, Mary Ann 30; Ontario, 1861 2896.25 p10
Shular, Mary E. 1; Ontario, 1861 2896.25 p10
Shulavane, Jane; Maryland, 1671 2524.55 p199
Shuler, Catharine 61; Ontario, 1861 2896.25 p10
Shuler, William 71; Ontario, 1861 2896.25 p10
Shules, Richard 45; Ontario, 1871 1823.15 p241
Shultesky, George; Maryland, 1910 3259.35 p56
Shults, William 25; Ontario, 1871 1823.28 p92
Shultz, Andy; Maryland, 1910 3259.35 p56
Shultz, Christopher; Pennsylvania, 1779 4629.10 p38
Shulze, Paul 23; Alaska, 1916 9196.1 p6
Shulze, Paul 23; Yukon, 1916 9196.1 p6
Shum, Edward; Vermont, 1826-1906 5900.10 p545
Shum, Julia Reynolds; Vermont, 1845-1911 5900.10 p545
Shupreave, Edeth; Maryland, 1681 2524.55 p199
Shurinski, Pawel; Maryland, 1910 3259.35 p56
Shurley, Ralph; Virginia, 1694 1224.1 p52
Shurlin, Roger; Maryland, 1675 2524.55 p199
Shurlock, Robert; Pennsylvania, 1831 1224.3 p71
Shurn, May 38; Ontario, 1871 1823.22 p145
Shurn, Phebe 42; Ontario, 1871 1823.22 p145
Shurrie, James 48; Ontario, 1871 1823.15 p241
Shurt, Abraham; New England, 1658 1224.1 p52
Shuscoskey, Fred 48; Ontario, 1871 1823.28 p92
Shuster, George Joseph; Pennsylvania, 1865 6058.10 p50
Shut, Hans Peter; America, 1754 2856.30 p410
Shut, Ludwig; America, 1754 2856.30 p410
Shute, Joseph 20; Virginia, 1775 1220.25 p95
Shute, Thomas 50; Ontario, 1871 1823.15 p241
Shute, William; Pennsylvania, 1779 4629.10 p37
Shuter, J.; Quebec, 1857 9196.15 p17
Shutle, Henry 60; Ontario, 1871 1823.15 p241
Shutly, John 48; Ontario, 1871 1823.28 p92
Shutly, Mary 46; Ontario, 1871 1823.28 p92
Shutte, George 21; Ontario, 1871 1823.28 p92
Shuttleworth, Mr.; Quebec, 1857 9196.15 p17
Shuttleworth, Mrs.; Quebec, 1857 9196.15 p17
Shuttling, John; Maryland, 1666 2524.55 p11
Shutz, Georg; America, 1737 2856.30 p429
Shutz, John; New York, 1838 8197.10 p148
Shymansky, Edward; Maryland, 1910 3259.35 p56
Shymborska, Mary; Maryland, 1910 3259.35 p56
Siarin, Catharina; Port uncertain, 1769 2856.30 p453
Sibbal, Henry; Pennsylvania, 1863 6058.10 p46
Sibbald, George; Georgia, 1807 1640.10 p185
Sibbald, George; Pennsylvania, 1837 6058.10 p13
Sibbald, James; Pennsylvania, 1831-1834 6058.10 p11
Sibbald, John; Pennsylvania, 1777 4629.10 p24
Sibbald, Robert 52; Ontario, 1871 1823.15 p241
Sibbet, Peter; Virginia, 1678 1224.1 p52
Sibbet, Robert; Manitoba, 1737 1224.2 p104
Siberry, Thomas 63; Ontario, 1871 1823.28 p92
Sibery, William 17; Virginia, 1774 1220.25 p45
Sibiska, Alexander; Maryland, 1910 3259.35 p56
Sibiski, John; Maryland, 1910 3259.35 p56
Sibistowicz, Frank; Maryland, 1910 3259.35 p56
Sibler, Matthaus; America, 1832 2856.30 p429
With wife
Siblewski, Michael; Maryland, 1910 3259.35 p56
Sibley, George; New Jersey, 1876 1640.13 p113
Sibstowicz, Karol; Maryland, 1910 3259.35 p56
Sichrist, John 39; Ontario, 1871 1823.15 p241
Sichrist, Michel 35; Ontario, 1871 1823.15 p241
Sick, Anna Maria; Port uncertain, 1760 2856.30 p429
Sick, Johann Jacob; Port uncertain, 1769 2856.30 p429
Sickamore, John; Maryland, 1662 2524.55 p199
Sickelsin, Catharina; Port uncertain, 1739 2856.30 p429
Sickh, Anna Maria; Port uncertain, 1716 2856.30 p429
Sickh, Christof; Port uncertain, 1724 2856.30 p429
Sickhinger, Eva Catharina; Port uncertain, 1738 2856.30 p429
Sickin, Anna Maria; Port uncertain, 1760 2856.30 p429
Sickinger, Jacob; Port uncertain, 1776 2856.30 p429
Sickle, John David; Pennsylvania, 1777 4629.10 p28
Sickle, Lawrence; Pennsylvania, 1779 4629.10 p41
Sicklemore, John; Died enroute, 1611 1224.1 p52
Sickora, Joseph; Maryland, 1910 3259.35 p56
Sicks, John; Maryland, 1662 2524.55 p199
Wife: Sibella
Sicks, Sibella *SEE* Sicks, John
Sicksmith, James; Maryland, 1675 2524.55 p199
Sidall, Eliza.; Maryland, 1678 2524.55 p137
Siddons, Josiah; Pennsylvania, 1787 4629.10 p56
Side, William; Pennsylvania, 1777 4629.10 p12
Sidell, Ralph 29; Fort Cumberland, Nova Scotia, 1774 1220.25 p19
Sidey, David 43; Ontario, 1871 1823.22 p145
Sidey, David 88; Ontario, 1871 1823.22 p145
Sidey, James 51; Ontario, 1871 1823.22 p145
Sidey, Jennett 60; Ontario, 1871 1823.22 p145
Sidey, John 61; Ontario, 1871 1823.22 p145
Sidey, John S. 35; Ontario, 1871 1823.22 p145
Sidey, Peter 38; Ontario, 1871 1823.22 p145
Sidie, Thomas; Maryland, 1667 2524.55 p199
Sidney, Albert 50; Ontario, 1871 1823.15 p241
Sieb, Catharina; Port uncertain, 1696 2856.30 p429
Siebel, August; Ontario, 1871 1823.28 p92
Sieber, . . .; Maryland, 1910 3259.35 p56
Sieber, George 45; Ontario, 1871 1823.15 p241
Sieber, Philipp; Port uncertain, 1738 2856.30 p429
Siebert, Anna Maria; Port uncertain, 1747 2856.30 p429
Siebert, Henry; New York, 1837 8197.10 p106
Siebert, Jacob; New York, 1840 8197.10 p199
Siebert, John; New York, 1837 8197.10 p107
Siebert, John; New York, 1840 8197.10 p199
Siebert, Josef; Port uncertain, 1780 2856.30 p429
Siebert, Josef; Port uncertain, 1781 2856.30 p429
Siebert, Silvester; New York, 1839 8197.10 p285
Sieberth, Marianna; Port uncertain, 1753 2856.30 p429
Siebler, Bernhard; America, 1744 2856.30 p429
Siebler, Margarete Catha; America, 1753 2856.30 p429
Siebler, Michael; America, 1737 2856.30 p429
Siebler, Susanna; America, 1753 2856.30 p429
Siedlecki, Alex R.; Maryland, 1910 3259.35 p56
Sieds, Peter; Maryland, 1663 2524.55 p199
Siegel, Anna Maria; Port uncertain, 1777 2856.30 p429
Siegel, Johann; Port uncertain, 1780 2856.30 p429
Siegel, Maria Margarete; America, 1752 2856.30 p429
Siegele, Hans Georg; Port uncertain, 1748 2856.30 p429
Siegenthaler, Josef; America, 1784 2856.30 p429
Siegenthaler, Margarete; Port uncertain, 1786 2856.30 p429
Sieger, Johann; Port uncertain, 1751 2856.30 p425
Sieger, Michael; Port uncertain, 1742 2856.30 p430
With wife
Siegler, David; America, 1752 2856.30 p430
Siegler, Hans Jerrik; America, 1727 2856.30 p430
Siegler, Jerg; America, 1752 2856.30 p430
Siegmund, John, Sr.; Maryland, 1910 3259.35 p56
Siegmunt, James; Maryland, 1910 3259.35 p56
Siegrist, Anna Maria; Port uncertain, 1744 2856.30 p430
Siegrist, Anna Maria; Port uncertain, 1754 2856.30 p430
Siegrist, Hans Georg; America, 1700-1799 2856.30 p430
Siegrist, Hans Georg; Port uncertain, 1751 2856.30 p430
With wife & 3 children
Siegrist, Hans Georg; Port uncertain, 1752 2856.30 p430
With wife & 3 children
Siegrist, Margarete; Port uncertain, 1754 2856.30 p430
Siegrist, Maria; America, 1744 2856.30 p430
Son: Wendel
Siegrist, Mrs. Matthaus; America, 1744 2856.30 p430
Siegrist, Wendel *SEE* Siegrist, Maria
Siejak, Alexander; Maryland, 1910 3259.35 p56
Siekierki, Frank; Maryland, 1910 3259.35 p56
Siekierski, Martin; Maryland, 1910 3259.35 p56

Sieling, F. J. 48; Minnesota, 1915 ***9196.1*** *p67*
Siemanski, George; Maryland, 1910 ***3259.35*** *p56*
Siemon, Walrob; New York, 1802 ***8197.10*** *p25*
Sienkiewicz, Wincenty; Maryland, 1910 ***3259.35*** *p56*
Sierak, Antoni; Maryland, 1910 ***3259.35*** *p56*
Siess, Friedrich; America, 1744 ***2856.30*** *p430*
Siess, Wolfgang; America, 1744 ***2856.30*** *p430*
Sieveking, John Henry; New York, 1812 ***8197.10*** *p278*
Sievers, John Frederick; New York, 1827 ***8197.10*** *p282*
Sieverty, Bertrem 35; British Columbia, 1915 ***9196.1*** *p67*
Sieverty, Bertrem 35; Washington, 1915 ***9196.1*** *p67*
Siewierski, Peter M.; Maryland, 1910 ***3259.35*** *p56*
Siewierski, Roman; Maryland, 1910 ***3259.35*** *p56*
Siewiski, Sophia; Maryland, 1910 ***3259.35*** *p56*
Sifert, Ludwig; New York, 1840 ***8197.10*** *p285*
Sigai, Frank; Maryland, 1910 ***3259.35*** *p56*
Sigey, Samuell; Maryland, 1680 ***2524.55*** *p199*
Sigg, Kunigunda; Port uncertain, 1737 ***2856.30*** *p430*
Siggins, William; Pennsylvania, 1811 ***6058.10*** *p4*
Sigismund, Mrs. Jakob; America, 1731 ***2856.30*** *p430*
Siglar, Frederik; America, 1743 ***2856.30*** *p430*
Sigler, Rosalia; Port uncertain, 1737 ***2856.30*** *p430*
Sigmann, Josef; America, 1751 ***2856.30*** *p430*
Sigmund, Bernhard; America, 1730 ***2856.30*** *p430*
Sigmundt, Anna Eva; Port uncertain, 1733 ***2856.30*** *p430*
Signett, George; Virginia, 1671 ***6212.30*** *p44*
Signey, Samuell; Maryland, 1680 ***2524.55*** *p199*
Sigrist, Anna Apollonia; America, 1744 ***2856.30*** *p430*
Sigrist, Anna Apollonia; Port uncertain, 1765 ***2856.30*** *p430*
Sigurdson, Bald...n 63; British Columbia, 1916 ***9196.1*** *p16*
Sigurdson, Bald...n 63; Washington, 1916 ***9196.1*** *p16*
Sijltevig, K. T. 53; Alaska, 1918 ***9196.1*** *p54*
Sijltevig, K. T. 53; Yukon, 1918 ***9196.1*** *p54*
Sikellem, Elizabeth; Maryland, 1668 ***2524.55*** *p199*
Sikes, John; Maryland, 1910 ***3259.35*** *p56*
Sikoski, Victor; Maryland, 1910 ***3259.35*** *p56*
Sikowski, John; Maryland, 1910 ***3259.35*** *p56*
Silas, Frederick 48; Ontario, 1871 ***1823.28*** *p92*
Silbereisen, L.; Port uncertain, 1784 ***2856.30*** *p430*
Silbernagtin, Catharina; Port uncertain, 1777 ***2856.30*** *p430*
Silk, James; Vermont, 1820-1894 ***5900.10*** *p87*
Silk, James; Vermont, 1855-1936 ***5900.10*** *p87*
Silk, James 21; Baltimore, 1775 ***1220.25*** *p117*
Silk, John; Pennsylvania, 1868 ***6058.10*** *p70*
Silk, Margaret; Vermont, 1861-1942 ***5900.10*** *p87*
Silk, Mary; Vermont, 1825-1903 ***5900.10*** *p87*
Silk, Mary; Vermont, 1849-1932 ***5900.10*** *p87*
Silk, Michael; Pennsylvania, 1868 ***6058.10*** *p71*
Silk, Sarah 43; Vermont, 1860-1869 ***5900.10*** *p77*
Sillars, Alexander 40; Ontario, 1871 ***1823.15*** *p241*
Siller, Robert 40; Ontario, 1871 ***1823.15*** *p241*
Sillers, Archibald 36; Ontario, 1871 ***1823.15*** *p241*
Sillers, Henry 21; Ontario, 1871 ***1823.15*** *p241*
Sillers, John 33; Ontario, 1871 ***1823.15*** *p241*
Sillers, William 25; Ontario, 1871 ***1823.15*** *p241*
Sillib, Henry 44; Ontario, 1871 ***1823.28*** *p92*
Sillivan, William; Maryland, 1681 ***2524.55*** *p199*
Silly, Barbara; Maryland, 1655 ***2524.55*** *p199*
Silon, John; New York, 1807 ***8197.10*** *p49*
Silus, Caraline 21; Ontario, 1871 ***1823.28*** *p92*
Silva, Francis J.; New York, 1838 ***8197.10*** *p150*
Silva, Joaquim Jose Duarte; New York, 1840 ***8197.10*** *p285*
Silva, Lewis B.; New York, 1840 ***8197.10*** *p197*
Silva, Manuel; New York, 1834 ***8197.10*** *p316*
Silva, Manuel; New York, 1839 ***8197.10*** *p140*
Silver, Mr.; Quebec, 1858 ***9196.15*** *p44*
Silver, James 32; Maryland, 1774 ***1220.25*** *p39*
Silverhead, Joshua; Maryland, 1681 ***2524.55*** *p200*
Silverlock, James; Virginia, 1666-1667 ***6212.30*** *p33*
Silverlocks, Ja; Virginia, 1663 ***6212.30*** *p4*
Silverwood, John 51; Ontario, 1871 ***1823.28*** *p92*
Silverwood, Samuel 19; Ontario, 1871 ***1823.28*** *p92*
Silvester, Charles 59; Ontario, 1871 ***1823.22*** *p146*
Silvester, Grissell Brinley; New England, 1661 ***1224.1*** *p9*
Silvester, Henry; Virginia, 1664 ***6212.30*** *p12*
Silvester, John; New York, 1763 ***1224.2*** *p104*
Silvester, Joseph Hooper; America, 1846 ***1224.3*** *p71*
Silvester, Thomas; Pennsylvania, 1777 ***4629.10*** *p10*
Sim, Francis 33; America, 1774 ***1220.25*** *p36*
Sim, James 52; Ontario, 1871 ***1823.22*** *p146*
Sim, Jane 24 *SEE* Sim, William
Sim, William 24; North Carolina, 1774 ***1220.25*** *p49*
Wife: Jane 24
Simanok, Gim; Maryland, 1910 ***3259.35*** *p56*
Simcin, Wm; Virginia, 1698 ***6212.30*** *p61*
Sime, Archibald; Georgia, 1699 ***1640.13*** *p113*
Simes, Eleanor; Maryland, 1682 ***2524.55*** *p200*
Simes, Judith; Maryland, 1681 ***2524.55*** *p200*
Simile, William 45; Ontario, 1871 ***1823.15*** *p241*
Simington, James 33; Ontario, 1871 ***1823.28*** *p92*
Siminski, Matthew; Maryland, 1910 ***3259.35*** *p56*
Simister, Joseph; New York, 1821 ***8197.10*** *p279*
Simkin, Wm; Virginia, 1690-1691 ***6212.30*** *p59*
Simkins, Jno; Virginia, 1688 ***6212.30*** *p58*
Simley, Ann; Maryland, 1667 ***2524.55*** *p200*
Simm, Mary Ann; Vermont, 1817-1904 ***5900.10*** *p406*
Simmens, John 28; Ontario, 1871 ***1823.28*** *p92*
Simmens, Margaret 2; Ontario, 1871 ***1823.28*** *p92*
Simmer, Sarah 22; New York, 1774 ***1220.25*** *p24*
Simmermann, Andrew; America, 1727 ***2856.30*** *p430*
Simmes, Ann *SEE* Simmes, Francis
Simmes, Francis; Maryland, 1663 ***2524.55*** *p200*
Relative: Ann
Simmes, Sarah; New England, 1641 ***1224.1*** *p51*
Simmington, William 65; Ontario, 1871 ***1823.28*** *p92*
Simmins, Frank; Maryland, 1910 ***3259.35*** *p56*
Simmins, Richard 62; Ontario, 1871 ***1823.15*** *p241*
Simmonds, Henry 22; Maryland, 1774 ***1220.25*** *p41*
Simmonds, John 37; Ontario, 1871 ***1823.15*** *p241*
Simmonds, Mary 16; Maryland, 1775 ***1220.25*** *p111*
Simmonite, George; New York, 1826 ***8197.10*** *p281*
Simmons, Mr.; Portland, Maine, 1858 ***9196.15*** *p28*
Simmons, Mr.; Quebec, 1858 ***9196.15*** *p45*
Simmons, Mrs.; Portland, Maine, 1858 ***9196.15*** *p28*
Simmons, Catherine Fitzgerald; Vermont, 1844-1910 ***5900.10*** *p339*
Simmons, Charles; Maryland, 1910 ***3259.35*** *p56*
Simmons, Frances 70; Ontario, 1871 ***1823.22*** *p146*
Simmons, George; Maryland, 1650 ***2524.55*** *p200*
Simmons, Henry 32; Ontario, 1871 ***1823.22*** *p146*
Simmons, Jack; Mississippi, 1820-1845 ***1640.10*** *p185*
Simmons, James C.; Vermont, 1830-1898 ***5900.10*** *p339*
Simmons, Jeremiah; Pennsylvania, 1777 ***4629.10*** *p16*
Simmons, John; Maryland, 1676 ***2524.55*** *p200*
Simmons, John; Maryland, 1682 ***2524.55*** *p200*
Simmons, John; New York, 1840 ***8197.10*** *p197*
Simmons, Joseph 22; Maryland, 1774 ***1220.25*** *p52*
Simmons, L.; Ontario, 1861 ***2896.26*** *p4*
Simmons, Michael; New York, 1833 ***8197.10*** *p283*
Simmons, Nathan; Pennsylvania, 1777 ***4629.10*** *p6*
Simmons, Rose 70; Ontario, 1871 ***1823.15*** *p241*
Simmons, Saunders; Maryland, 1664 ***2524.55*** *p200*
Simmons, Thomas; Maryland, 1665 ***2524.55*** *p200*
Simmons, Thomas 21; Maryland, 1774 ***1220.25*** *p57*
Simmons, Thomas 29; Maryland, 1774 ***1220.25*** *p5*
Simmonson, Peter; Pennsylvania, 1777 ***4629.10*** *p26*
Simmouce, Robert 30; Ontario, 1871 ***1823.15*** *p242*
Simms, Jacob; Trinidad, 1823 ***1640.13*** *p113*
Simms, John C.; New York, 1827 ***8197.10*** *p347*
Simms, Marmaduke; Maryland, 1666 ***2524.55*** *p200*
Simms, Robert B., Sr.; New York, 1834 ***8197.10*** *p283*
Simms, Robert B., Sr.; New York, 1838 ***8197.10*** *p149*
Simms, Robert B., Jr.; New York, 1834 ***8197.10*** *p69*
Simon, Mr.; Quebec, 1858 ***9196.15*** *p33*
Simon, Ms. 71; Ontario, 1871 ***1823.22*** *p146*
Simon, Adam; New York, New York, 1857 ***6058.10*** *p60*
Simon, Anastazy; Maryland, 1910 ***3259.35*** *p56*
Simon, Anna; Port uncertain, 1737 ***2856.30*** *p430*
Simon, Mrs. Caspar; Port uncertain, 1761 ***2856.30*** *p430*
Simon, Elisabeth; Port uncertain, 1784 ***2856.30*** *p431*
Simon, George; New York, 1838 ***8197.10*** *p148*
Simon, Henrich; Port uncertain, 1754 ***2856.30*** *p430*
Simon, Henry; New York, 1815-1834 ***8197.10*** *p306*
Simon, Jakob; America, 1741 ***2856.30*** *p430*
Simon, Jakob; America, 1749 ***2856.30*** *p430*
Simon, Johann Jakob; America, 1760 ***2856.30*** *p430*
Simon, John; Philadelphia, 1793 ***4629.10*** *p74*
Simon, Joseph; Maryland, 1910 ***3259.35*** *p56*
Simon, Joseph; New York, 1807 ***8197.10*** *p49*
Simon, Joseph 60; Ontario, 1871 ***1823.28*** *p92*
Simon, Leopold; New York, 1838 ***8197.10*** *p148*
Simon, Michael; New York, New York, 1863 ***3437.14*** *p87*
Simon, Michael; Port uncertain, 1731 ***2856.30*** *p430*
Simon, Michael; Port uncertain, 1761 ***2856.30*** *p430*
Simon, Nicholas; New York, 1833 ***8197.10*** *p358*
Simon, Nickel; America, 1738 ***2856.30*** *p430*
Simon, Niklas; America, 1749 ***2856.30*** *p431*
Simon, Nikol; Port uncertain, 1755 ***2856.30*** *p431*
With wife
Simon, Peter; America, 1738 ***2856.30*** *p431*
Simon, Peter; Port uncertain, 1784 ***2856.30*** *p431*
Simon, Philipp; Port uncertain, 1767 ***2856.30*** *p431*
With wife & children
Simonds, Andrew 60; Vermont, 1880 ***5900.10*** *p431*
Simonds, Catherine 59; Vermont, 1887 ***5900.10*** *p431*
Simonds, James F. 32; Vermont, 1885 ***5900.10*** *p431*
Simonds, Jennie E. 34; Vermont, 1885 ***5900.10*** *p431*
Simonds, Jno; Virginia, 1666 ***6212.30*** *p26*
Simonds, John 82; Ontario, 1861 ***2896.25*** *p31*
Simonds, Martha 62; Ontario, 1861 ***2896.25*** *p31*
Simonds, Nellie; Vermont, 1868-1945 ***5900.10*** *p550*
Simonds, Thomas; Maryland, 1640 ***2524.55*** *p200*
Simone, Alex 30; Seattle, 1912 ***9196.1*** *p36*
Simonis, T. 32; Alaska, 1912 ***9196.1*** *p17*
Simonis, T. 32; British Columbia, 1912 ***9196.1*** *p17*
Simons, Catherine 30; Ontario, 1861 ***2896.25*** *p6*
Simons, Cynthia 27; Ontario, 1861 ***2896.27*** *p49*
Simons, Francis C.; New York, New York, 1856 ***3437.14*** *p54*
Simons, George 64; Ontario, 1871 ***1823.15*** *p242*
Simons, Henry 59; Ontario, 1861 ***2896.25*** *p68*
Simons, James; New York, 1837 ***8197.10*** *p105*
Simons, James; Virginia, 1665-1666 ***6212.30*** *p24*
Simons, James 65; Ontario, 1871 ***1823.15*** *p242*
Simons, John; Maryland, 1681 ***2524.55*** *p200*
Simons, Joseph G. 4; Ontario, 1861 ***2896.25*** *p6*
Simons, Marion 30; Ontario, 1871 ***1823.15*** *p242*
Simons, Mary J. 10; Ontario, 1861 ***2896.25*** *p6*
Simons, Olive 55; Ontario, 1861 ***2896.25*** *p69*
Simons, Olive L. 6; Ontario, 1861 ***2896.25*** *p6*
Simons, Paul 18; New York, 1775 ***1220.25*** *p94*
Simons, Philip N. 8; Ontario, 1861 ***2896.25*** *p6*
Simons, Samuel 1; Ontario, 1861 ***2896.25*** *p6*
Simons, William H. 11; Ontario, 1861 ***2896.25*** *p6*
Simonson, Peter; Pennsylvania, 1779 ***4629.10*** *p41*
Simonton, James 25; Ontario, 1871 ***1823.22*** *p146*
Simple, William; Pennsylvania, 1777 ***4629.10*** *p11*
Simple, William 20; Ontario, 1871 ***1823.22*** *p146*
Simpson, . . .; Maryland, 1631-1685 ***2524.55*** *p200*
Simpson, Mr.; Portland, Maine, 1858 ***9196.15*** *p30*
Simpson, Mr.; Quebec, 1856 ***9196.15*** *p10*
Simpson, Mr.; Quebec, 1857 ***9196.15*** *p13*
Simpson, Mr.; Quebec, 1858 ***9196.15*** *p36*
Simpson, Mr.; Quebec, 1858 ***9196.15*** *p38*
Simpson, Mr.; Quebec, 1858 ***9196.15*** *p43*
Simpson, Mrs.; Quebec, 1856 ***9196.15*** *p10*
Simpson, Mrs.; Quebec, 1858 ***9196.15*** *p36*
Simpson, Adam; Mississippi, 1815-1845 ***1640.10*** *p185*
Simpson, Albert 19; Ontario, 1861 ***2896.27*** *p51*
Simpson, Alexande; Georgia, 1698 ***1640.13*** *p113*
Simpson, Alexander; Norfolk, Virginia, 1771 ***1224.2*** *p104*
Simpson, Alexander 36; Ontario, 1871 ***1823.22*** *p146*
Simpson, Amanda 15; Ontario, 1861 ***2896.27*** *p51*
Simpson, Andrew; New York, 1835 ***8197.10*** *p317*
Simpson, Andrew; New York, 1838 ***8197.10*** *p148*
Simpson, Andrew 33; Ontario, 1871 ***1823.15*** *p242*
Simpson, Ann 24; Philadelphia, 1774 ***1220.25*** *p23*
Simpson, Ann 86; Ontario, 1871 ***1823.15*** *p242*
Simpson, Anna Jean; Savannah, Georgia, 1774 ***1640.10*** *p185*
Simpson, Anna M.; Vermont, 1856-1935 ***5900.10*** *p446*
Simpson, Catharine 23; Virginia, 1774 ***1220.25*** *p89*
Simpson, Charles 22; Fort Cumberland, Nova Scotia, 1774 ***1220.25*** *p15*
Simpson, Charles 25; Ontario, 1871 ***1823.22*** *p146*
Simpson, Charles O. 24; Ontario, 1861 ***2896.28*** *p34*
Simpson, David; London, England, 1756 ***1640.13*** *p114*
Simpson, David; New York, 1802 ***8197.10*** *p25*
Simpson, David; Pennsylvania, 1785 ***4629.10*** *p48*
Simpson, Deborah 33; Ontario, 1861 ***2896.27*** *p51*
Simpson, Deborah A. 19; Ontario, 1861 ***2896.28*** *p34*
Simpson, Edmund; New York, 1810 ***8197.10*** *p277*
Simpson, Edward; Maryland, 1666 ***2524.55*** *p46*
Simpson, Edward 56; Ontario, 1871 ***1823.15*** *p242*
Simpson, Edward 75; Ontario, 1871 ***1823.15*** *p242*
Simpson, Elizabeth *SEE* Simpson, John
Simpson, Elizabeth; Maryland, 1663 ***2524.55*** *p200*
Simpson, Elizabeth; Maryland, 1670 ***2524.55*** *p200*
Simpson, Frances; New York, n.d. ***1224.3*** *p71*
Simpson, Francis 22; Virginia, 1774 ***1220.25*** *p45*
Simpson, Frederick Godwin; New York, New York, 1857 ***1224.3*** *p71*
Simpson, George; Grenada, 1775 ***1640.13*** *p114*
Simpson, George; New York, 1802 ***8197.10*** *p25*
Simpson, George 43; Ontario, 1871 ***1823.15*** *p242*
Simpson, George 47; Ontario, 1871 ***1823.22*** *p146*
Simpson, Grace 46; Ontario, 1871 ***1823.15*** *p242*
Simpson, Henry; Maryland, 1650 ***2524.55*** *p200*
Simpson, Henry; Virginia, 1704 ***1224.2*** *p104*
Simpson, Hugh 48; Ontario, 1871 ***1823.15*** *p242*
Simpson, Hugh 50; Ontario, 1871 ***1823.28*** *p92*
Simpson, Huldah 54; Ontario, 1861 ***2896.27*** *p51*
Simpson, J.; Savannah, Georgia, 1768 ***1640.10*** *p185*
Simpson, J. H.; Quebec, 1858 ***9196.15*** *p41*
Simpson, James; New York, 1837 ***8197.10*** *p106*
Simpson, James; New York, 1838 ***8197.10*** *p378*
Simpson, James; New York, 1840 ***8197.10*** *p198*
Simpson, James 22; Ontario, 1861 ***2896.27*** *p51*
Simpson, James 30; Ontario, 1871 ***1823.15*** *p242*
Simpson, James 34; Maryland, 1775 ***1220.25*** *p98*
Simpson, Jane; America, 1836 ***1640.13*** *p114*
Simpson, Jane; Virginia, 1688 ***6212.30*** *p57*
Simpson, Jeremy; Maryland, 1668 ***2524.55*** *p200*

Simpson, John; Georgia, 1774 1640.10 p185
Simpson, John; Georgia, 1791 1224.2 p104
Simpson, John; Maryland, 1675 2524.55 p200
Wife: Elizabeth
Simpson, John; New Orleans, 1843 1640.10 p185
Simpson, John; New York, 1784 1640.13 p114
Simpson, John; New York, 1802 8197.10 p25
Simpson, John; New York, 1838 8197.10 p284
Simpson, John; New York, 1840 8197.10 p198
Simpson, John; Savannah, Georgia, 1760 1640.10 p185
Simpson, John; Savannah, Georgia, 1788 1224.2 p104
Simpson, John; Savannah, Georgia, 1788 1640.10 p185
Simpson, John; Virginia, 1683 1224.1 p53
Simpson, John 22; Baltimore, 1775 1220.25 p118
Simpson, John 27; Philadelphia, 1774 1220.25 p6
Simpson, John 33; Ontario, 1871 1823.22 p146
Simpson, John 35; Ontario, 1871 1823.28 p92
Simpson, John 47; Ontario, 1871 1823.28 p92
Simpson, John 50; Ontario, 1871 1823.15 p242
Simpson, John 56; Ontario, 1871 1823.22 p146
Simpson, John 86; Ontario, 1871 1823.22 p146
Simpson, John H. 49; Ontario, 1871 1823.28 p92
Simpson, Jonathan; Boston, n.d. 1224.2 p104
Simpson, Jonathan; North America, 1787 1224.2 p126
Simpson, Joseph; Toronto, 1899 1640.13 p114
Simpson, Joseph 28; Virginia, 1775 1220.25 p95
Simpson, Martha McIntyre; Vermont, 1858-1934 5900.10 p497
Simpson, Mary; Maryland, 1680 2524.55 p200
Simpson, Mary 25; Fort Cumberland, Nova Scotia, 1774 1220.25 p16
Simpson, Mary 71; Ontario, 1871 1823.15 p242
Simpson, Mary J. 29; Ontario, 1861 2896.27 p51
Simpson, Mathew 35; Maryland, 1775 1220.25 p111
Simpson, Mathew 48; Maryland, 1774 1220.25 p84
Simpson, Patrick; South Carolina, 1791 1640.13 p114
Simpson, Patrick; South Carolina, 1792 1224.2 p104
Simpson, Paul; Maryland, 1647 2524.55 p200
Simpson, Paul; Maryland, 1659 2524.55 p200
Simpson, Peter 50; Virginia, 1774 1220.25 p140
Simpson, Peter B.; Pennsylvania, 1842 6058.10 p18
Simpson, Rebecca 64; Ontario, 1861 2896.28 p34
Simpson, Richard; Maryland, 1671 2524.55 p200
Simpson, Robert; New York, 1819 8197.10 p278
Simpson, Robert; New York, 1838 8197.10 p284
Simpson, Robert 31; Virginia, 1774 1220.25 p86
Simpson, Samuel; New York, 1827 1224.3 p71
Simpson, Samuel 63; Ontario, 1871 1823.28 p92
Simpson, Thomas; Maryland, 1650 2524.55 p200
Simpson, Thomas; Maryland, 1654 2524.55 p214
Simpson, Thomas; Maryland, 1658 2524.55 p200
Simpson, Thomas; New York, 1807 8197.10 p50
Simpson, Thomas; Ohio, 1854 1224.3 p71
Simpson, Thomas 30; Ontario, 1871 1823.15 p242
Simpson, Thomas 33; Ontario, 1871 1823.15 p242
Simpson, Thomas 36; Maryland, 1775 1220.25 p120
Simpson, Thomas 42; Ontario, 1871 1823.15 p242
Simpson, Thomas 47; Ontario, 1871 1823.15 p242
Simpson, Thomas 54; Ontario, 1871 1823.15 p242
Simpson, Thoms 83; Ontario, 1871 1823.22 p146
Simpson, Walter 21; Maryland, 1773-1774 1220.25 p33
Simpson, Willett 12; Ontario, 1861 2896.28 p34
Simpson, William; Georgia, 1699 1640.13 p114
Simpson, William; Georgia, 1763 1640.10 p186
Simpson, William; Georgia, 1772 1640.10 p186
Simpson, William; Maryland, 1666 2524.55 p200
Simpson, William; New York, 1802 8197.10 p25
Simpson, William; New York, 1837 8197.10 p106
Simpson, William; New York, 1837 8197.10 p284
Simpson, William; New York, 1838 8197.10 p149
Simpson, William; New York, 1839 8197.10 p140
Simpson, William; New York, 1840 8197.10 p385
Simpson, William 43; Ontario, 1871 1823.15 p242
Simpson, William 52; Ontario, 1871 1823.22 p146
Simpson, William 57; Ontario, 1871 1823.15 p242
Simpson, William 66; Ontario, 1871 1823.22 p146
Simpson, William B.; Pennsylvania, 1836 6058.10 p14
Simpson, William R.; Vermont, 1855-1932 5900.10 p497
Sims, Andrew 46; Ontario, 1871 1823.15 p242
Sims, David; New York, 1838 8197.10 p318
Sims, Fredk Lloyd 50; Ontario, 1871 1823.28 p92
Sims, George; New York, 1840 8197.10 p198
Sims, James 35; Maryland, 1773-1774 1220.25 p33
Sims, Joseph; Pennsylvania, 1779 4629.10 p39
Sims, Mary Ann 37; Ontario, 1871 1823.28 p92
Sims, Robt; Virginia, 1674-1675 6212.30 p53
Sims, Thomas 21; Philadelphia, 1775 1220.25 p122
Sims, William; Cuba, 1860 1640.13 p114
Simson, Esibella 47; Ontario, 1871 1823.15 p242
Simson, Hester; New England, 1665 1224.1 p53
Simson, James 31; Ontario, 1871 1823.15 p242
Simson, Jno; Virginia, 1701-1702 6212.30 p61
Simson, John; Virginia, 1690-1691 6212.30 p59
Simson, John; Virginia, 1727 1224.2 p104
Simson, Robert; New York, 1840 8197.10 p198
Simson, Thomas; Georgia, 1699 1640.13 p114
Simson, Thomas; Jamaica, 1729 1224.2 p104
Simson, Thomas; New York, 1729 1224.2 p104
Simspon, Wemyss 46; Ontario, 1871 1823.28 p92
Sinckler, Avary; Maryland, 1681 2524.55 p200
Sinckler, George; Maryland, 1673 2524.55 p200
Sinckler, Jane *SEE* Sinckler, John
Sinckler, John; Maryland, 1655 2524.55 p200
Wife: Jane
Sinckler, John; Virginia, 1697 1224.1 p53
Sinckler, Ursula; Maryland, 1681 2524.55 p200
Sincklow, Jane *SEE* Sincklow, John
Sincklow, John; Maryland, 1655 2524.55 p200
Wife: Jane
Sinclair, . . .; Savannah, Georgia, 1737 1640.10 p187
Sinclair, Mrs. 66; Ontario, 1871 1823.15 p242
Sinclair, Alexander; Savannah, Georgia, 1809-1812 1640.10 p186
Sinclair, Archibald; Georgia, 1734 1640.10 p186
Sinclair, Archibald; Savannah, Georgia, 1737 1640.10 p186
Sinclair, Benjamin W.; Savannah, Georgia, 1842 1640.10 p186
Sinclair, Charles 28; Ontario, 1871 1823.22 p146
Sinclair, Collin 37; Ontario, 1871 1823.15 p242
Sinclair, D.; Quebec, 1858 9196.15 p37
Sinclair, Daniel; New York, 1838 8197.10 p149
Sinclair, David; Jamaica, 1733 1640.13 p114
Sinclair, Diana 21; Jamaica, 1773-1774 1220.25 p32
Sinclair, Duncan; New York, 1807 8197.10 p50
Sinclair, George; New York, 1829 8197.10 p278
Sinclair, Henry; Boston, 1777 1224.2 p104
Sinclair, J.; Portland, Maine, 1858 9196.15 p30
Sinclair, James; Savannah, Georgia, 1775 1640.10 p186
Sinclair, Jane 54; Ontario, 1871 1823.22 p147
Sinclair, John; Florida, 1767 1640.10 p187
Sinclair, John; Georgia, 1699 1640.13 p114
Sinclair, John; Georgia, 1736 1640.10 p186
Sinclair, John; New York, 1839 8197.10 p285
Sinclair, John 33; Ontario, 1871 1823.15 p242
Sinclair, John 36; Ontario, 1871 1823.15 p242
Sinclair, John 45; Ontario, 1871 1823.22 p147
Sinclair, Margaret; Savannah, Georgia, 1775 1640.10 p187
Sinclair, Peter 61; Ontario, 1871 1823.15 p242
Sinclair, Samuel 34; Ontario, 1871 1823.15 p242
Sinclair, Thomas 33; Ontario, 1871 1823.15 p242
Sinclair, William; Florida, 1767 1640.10 p187
Sinclair, William; Georgia, 1735 1640.10 p187
Sinclair, William 39; Ontario, 1871 1823.15 p242
Sinclair, William T.; New York, 1838 8197.10 p149
Sinclear, Dugal 19; Ontario, 1871 1823.28 p93
Sinclear, Henry; Boston, 1777 1224.2 p104
Sinden, F. 23; Ontario, 1861 2896.28 p4
Sinden, H. M. 1; Ontario, 1861 2896.28 p4
Sinden, T. 27; Ontario, 1861 2896.28 p4
Sines, Isabill 15; Ontario, 1871 1823.22 p147
Sinetowski, Joseph; Maryland, 1910 3259.35 p56
Singcleare, Magnis; Virginia, 1703-1704 6212.30 p63
Singer, Rev.; Quebec, 1856 9196.15 p8
Singer, Anna Maria; Port uncertain, 1764 2856.30 p431
Singer, Fred 24; Ontario, 1871 1823.28 p93
Singer, Ignaz; Port uncertain, 1795 2856.30 p431
Singer, John; Pennsylvania, 1776 4629.10 p52
Single, William 14; Philadelphia, 1774 1220.25 p4
Singleton, Charles 30; Maryland, 1775 1220.25 p102
Singleton, George; New York, 1838 8197.10 p284
Singleton, James; Pennsylvania, 1777 4629.10 p24
Singleton, John; Maryland, 1662 2524.55 p200
Singleton, John; Maryland, 1682 2524.55 p200
Wife: Mary
Singleton, John; New York, 1802 8197.10 p25
Singleton, Margaret 76; Ontario, 1871 1823.22 p147
Singleton, Mary *SEE* Singleton, John
Singleton, Robert 51; Ontario, 1871 1823.28 p93
Singleton, William 15; Maryland, 1774 1220.25 p61
Singleton, William 63; Ontario, 1871 1823.15 p242
Singleton, Willm.; Maryland, 1662 2524.55 p200
Sinhouse, Jane *SEE* Sinhouse, John
Sinhouse, Jane; Maryland, 1673 2524.55 p200
Sinhouse, John; Maryland, 1672 2524.55 p201
Wife: Jane
Daughter: Mary
Sinhouse, Mary *SEE* Sinhouse, John
Sinicich, John 45; Alaska, 1913 9196.1 p13
Sinicich, John 45; British Columbia, 1913 9196.1 p13
Siniddocke, Mary; Maryland, 1664 2524.55 p201
Sinister, Thomas; Maryland, 1679 2524.55 p201
Sinn, Mrs.; Port uncertain, 1805 2856.30 p431
Sinn, Christina; Port uncertain, 1764 2856.30 p431
Sinn, Frederick 29; Ontario, 1871 1823.28 p93
Sinn, Johann Friedric; America, 1751 2856.30 p431
Sinn, Peter; Port uncertain, 1778 2856.30 p431
Sinn, Peter; Port uncertain, 1782 2856.30 p431
Sinnett, Mary; Maryland, 1675 2524.55 p201
Sinnick, Edwd; Virginia, 1671-1672 6212.30 p47
Sinnot, Ellenor Roach 78; Vermont, 1884 5900.10 p51
Sinnot, Moses 49; Vermont, 1854 5900.10 p51
Sinnot, William M.; Vermont, 1850-1910 5900.10 p50
Sinnott, Agness; Vermont, 1850-1909 5900.10 p50
Sinnott, Bridget 33; Ontario, 1871 1823.22 p147
Sinnott, Christina; Vermont, 1845-1928 5900.10 p51
Sinnott, Ellenor 25; Vermont, 1864 5900.10 p51
Sinnott, Jane 40; Vermont, 1874 5900.10 p51
Sinnott, John; New York, 1821 8197.10 p279
Sinnott, John E. 81; Vermont, 1918 5900.10 p51
Sinnott, John F. 25; Vermont, 1863 5900.10 p559
Sinnott, Margaret 23; Vermont, 1874 5900.10 p51
Sinnott, Margaret 67; Vermont, 1888 5900.10 p618
Sinnott, Martin 61; Vermont, 1886 5900.10 p618
Sinnott, Mary E.; Vermont, 1830-1906 5900.10 p50
Sinnott, Mary J.; Vermont, 1848-1926 5900.10 p503
Sinnott, Moses 49; Vermont, 1854 5900.10 p230
Sinnott, Sarah 28; Vermont, 1886 5900.10 p51
Sinon, James; Vermont, 1851-1940 5900.10 p277
Sinon, John 69; Vermont, 1903 5900.10 p206
Sinon, Julia A. Burke 36; Vermont, 1895 5900.10 p206
Sinon, Mary 55; Vermont, 1920 5900.10 p206
Sinon, Mary Ann; Vermont, 1854-1928 5900.10 p277
Sinon, Patrick; Vermont, n.d. 5900.10 p539
Sinsgreen, John 35; Philadelphia, 1774 1220.25 p42
Sinskey, Arthur; Maryland, 1910 3259.35 p56
Sinski, Lawrence; Maryland, 1910 3259.35 p56
Sinsky, Catherine; Maryland, 1910 3259.35 p56
Sinton, William 21; Fort Cumberland, Nova Scotia, 1774 1220.25 p19
Sinvingly, James 37; Ontario, 1871 1823.15 p242
Siovens, Mary 17; Maryland, 1775 1220.25 p97
Sipel, George 47; Ontario, 1871 1823.15 p242
Sippel, Henry 41; Ontario, 1871 1823.15 p242
Sippet, Albert; New York, 1840 8197.10 p196
Sipple, Conrad; Baltimore, 1847 6058.10 p43
Sirgrist, Anna Elisabeth; Port uncertain, 1749 2856.30 p431
Siri, Christof; Port uncertain, 1750 2856.30 p431
Siri, Christof; Port uncertain, 1753 2856.30 p431
Siri, Christof; Port uncertain, 1764 2856.30 p431
Sirrey, William, Sr.; New York, 1840 8197.10 p197
Sisiecki, Charles K.; Maryland, 1910 3259.35 p56
Siskey, Charles; Pennsylvania, 1777 4629.10 p31
Sissell, John; Maryland, 1665 2524.55 p210
Sisson, Mr.; Quebec, 1856 9196.15 p9
Sisson, Deliverance; Portsmouth, 1765 1224.2 p104
Sisson, Francis *SEE* Sisson, John
Sisson, James; Maryland, 1661 2524.55 p201
Sisson, Joane; Maryland, 1663 2524.55 p201
Sisson, John; Maryland, 1659-1660 2524.55 p201
Wife: Francis
Sisson, William; Newport, Rhode Island, 1765 1224.2 p104
Sisson, William 21; Maryland, 1774 1220.25 p84
Sisters, Mary A.; Vermont, 1863-1951 5900.10 p407
Sitgreaves, William; Pennsylvania, 1777 4629.10 p21
Sitken, Mary 18; Ontario, 1861 2896.27 p11
Sito, Robert; Maryland, 1910 3259.35 p56
Sitterle, Franz; Port uncertain, 1760 2856.30 p431
Sitzler, Barbara; America, 1750 2856.30 p426
Sitzler, Barbara; America, 1750 2856.30 p428
Sitzler, Barbara; America, 1755 2856.30 p428
Sitzler, Barbara Sauter; America, 1750 2856.30 p378
Sitzler, Barbara Sauter; America, 1755 2856.30 p378
Sivan, William; Virginia, 1664 6212.30 p12
Sivan, Wm; Virginia, 1665-1666 6212.30 p22
Sivear, James 26; Ontario, 1871 1823.28 p93
Siveen, Robert 43; Ontario, 1871 1823.15 p242
Sivell, Mary; Maryland, 1681 2524.55 p201
Siveller, Alice; Maryland, 1651 2524.55 p138
Siveright, Mr.; Quebec, 1858 9196.15 p40
Sivewright, David; Jamaica, 1847 1640.13 p114
Sivewright, Henrietta Home; New Brunswick, 1884 1640.13 p114
Sivich, T. 38; Alaska, 1917 9196.1 p47
Sivich, T. 38; Whitehorse, Yukon, 1917 9196.1 p47
Siwierski, Joseph; Maryland, 1910 3259.35 p56
Siwinski, George W. L.; Maryland, 1910 3259.35 p56
Siwinski, Walter B.; Maryland, 1910 3259.35 p56
Sixby, M. E.; Vermont, 1836-1919 5900.10 p607
Sixt, Josef; Port uncertain, 1768 2856.30 p432
Sjoska, M. 36; British Columbia, 1912 9196.1 p15
Skahen, Lilie; Vermont, 1884 5900.10 p180
Skahen, Nora; Vermont, 1885 5900.10 p179
Skahen, Thomas 26; Vermont, 1885 5900.10 p179
Skalinsky, Frak; Maryland, 1910 3259.35 p57
Skalinsky, Teophil; Maryland, 1910 3259.35 p57

Skalska, Veroneka; Maryland, 1910 ***3259.35 p57***
Skarbex, Jasenty; Maryland, 1910 ***3259.35 p57***
Skeane, Bridget 70; Vermont, 1875 ***5900.10 p615***
Skebo, Frank 60; Ontario, 1871 ***1823.28 p93***
Skeen, John; New York, 1820 ***8197.10 p278***
Skeetah, Alexander 62; Ontario, 1871 ***1823.28 p93***
Skeffington, Bernard 26; New York, 1827-1830 ***8197.10 p198***
Skeglo, Jacob 30; Ontario, 1871 ***1823.28 p93***
Skehan, Edmund; Vermont, 1842-1893 ***5900.10 p88***
Skehan, Margaret; Vermont, 1862-1895 ***5900.10 p88***
Skellton, Jno; Virginia, 1666 ***6212.30 p29***
Skelly, Bridget Grady 83; Vermont, 1902 ***5900.10 p479***
Skelly, James 35; Ontario, 1871 ***1823.28 p93***
Skelly, John 71; Vermont, 1871 ***5900.10 p479***
Skelly, Margaret 80; Vermont, 1884 ***5900.10 p501***
Skelly, William 29; Maryland, 1775 ***1220.25 p110***
Skelson, William; Maryland, 1679 ***2524.55 p201***
Skelton, Ann 18; Fort Cumberland, Nova Scotia, 1774 ***1220.25 p16***
Skelton, Jane 36 *SEE* Skelton, John
Skelton, John 25; Nova Scotia, 1774 ***1220.25 p137***
Skelton, John 38; Annapolis, Nova Scotia, 1775 ***1220.25 p22***
Wife: Jane 36
Skelton, Ralph; Jamaica, 1775 ***1220.25 p133***
Skelton, Robert; New York, 1692 ***1224.1 p12***
Skelton, Thomas 35; Nova Scotia, 1774 ***1220.25 p135***
Skelton, William; Maryland, 1679 ***2524.55 p201***
Skelvinski, John; Maryland, 1910 ***3259.35 p57***
Skene, Ann; Boston, 1773 ***1224.2 p104***
Skene, Ann; Nova Scotia, 1773 ***1224.2 p104***
Skene, Robert; Maryland, 1736 ***1640.13 p114***
Skerret, James; Pennsylvania, 1787 ***4629.10 p56***
Sketton, George 42; Ontario, 1871 ***1823.15 p242***
Sketton, George 69; Ontario, 1871 ***1823.15 p242***
Sketton, Thomas 28; Ontario, 1871 ***1823.15 p242***
Skey, George; California, 1853 ***1224.3 p71***
Skidmore, Edward; Maryland, 1658 ***2524.55 p201***
Wife: Mary
Skidmore, Edward; Maryland, 1659 ***2524.55 p201***
Wife: Mary
Skidmore, Joyce; Maryland, 1663 ***2524.55 p201***
Skidmore, Mary *SEE* Skidmore, Edward
Skidmore, Mary; Maryland, 1682 ***2524.55 p201***
Skidmore, Nicholas; Maryland, 1682 ***2524.55 p201***
Skien, Jane 51; Ontario, 1871 ***1823.22 p147***
Skiffington, Bernard 26; New York, 1827-1830 ***8197.10 p198***
Skillin, James; New York, 1836 ***8197.10 p78***
Skillin, William; New York, 1836 ***8197.10 p78***
Skillinger, Eneas; Pennsylvania, 1777 ***4629.10 p11***
Skillington, Mary; Maryland, 1660 ***2524.55 p201***
Skillington, Thomas; Maryland, 1653 ***2524.55 p201***
Skillinson, Mary; Maryland, 1660 ***2524.55 p201***
Skillinson, Thomas; Maryland, 1653 ***2524.55 p201***
Skiner, Alice *SEE* Skiner, Robert
Skiner, Mary *SEE* Skiner, Robert
Skiner, Nathaniel *SEE* Skiner, Robert
Skiner, Nathaniel; Maryland, 1679 ***2524.55 p201***
Skiner, Robert *SEE* Skiner, Robert
Skiner, Robert; Maryland, 1673 ***2524.55 p201***
Wife: Alice
Son: Nathaniel
Daughter: Mary
Son: Robert
Skiner, Robert; Maryland, 1679 ***2524.55 p201***
Skinner, Miss; Quebec, 1857 ***9196.15 p23***
Skinner, Mrs.; Quebec, 1856 ***9196.15 p8***
Skinner, Alexander; St. Augustine, Florida, 1800 ***1224.3 p71***
Skinner, Alexander; St. Augustine, Florida, 1800 ***1640.10 p187***
Skinner, Alice *SEE* Skinner, Robert
Skinner, Arvesta J. Conner; Vermont, 1829-1899 ***5900.10 p500***
Skinner, Augustine; Maryland, 1667 ***2524.55 p84***
Skinner, Charles 28; Maryland, 1774 ***1220.25 p68***
Skinner, Cortlandt; New Jersey, n.d. ***1224.2 p104***
Skinner, Elizabeth; Maryland, 1670 ***2524.55 p201***
Skinner, Elizabeth 20; Maryland, 1774 ***1220.25 p59***
Skinner, Harris; Vermont, 1824-1899 ***5900.10 p500***
Skinner, Henry 27; Ontario, 1871 ***1823.15 p243***
Skinner, Henry 50; Ontario, 1871 ***1823.22 p147***
Skinner, James; Pennsylvania, 1777 ***4629.10 p16***
Skinner, James 22; Maryland, 1774 ***1220.25 p2***
Skinner, James 65; Ontario, 1871 ***1823.22 p147***
Skinner, James 68; Ontario, 1871 ***1823.22 p147***
Skinner, Jane *SEE* Skinner, John
Skinner, John; Maryland, 1670 ***2524.55 p201***
Skinner, John; Philadelphia, 1789 ***4629.10 p58***
Wife: Jane
Skinner, John; Vermont, 1837-1880 ***5900.10 p519***
Skinner, John 24; Philadelphia, 1789 ***4629.10 p58***
Skinner, John 40; Ontario, 1871 ***1823.15 p243***
Skinner, Margret 36; Ontario, 1871 ***1823.15 p243***
Skinner, Mary *SEE* Skinner, Robert
Skinner, Mathew 40; Maryland, 1775 ***1220.25 p96***
Skinner, Nathaniel *SEE* Skinner, Robert
Skinner, Nathaniel; Maryland, 1679 ***2524.55 p201***
Skinner, Peter 46; Ontario, 1871 ***1823.22 p147***
Skinner, Richard; Florida, 1775 ***1224.2 p105***
Skinner, Richard; New Orleans, 1817 ***1224.3 p71***
Skinner, Robert *SEE* Skinner, Robert
Skinner, Robert; Maryland, 1673 ***2524.55 p201***
Wife: Alice
Daughter: Mary
Son: Robert
Son: Nathaniel
Skinner, Robert; Maryland, 1679 ***2524.55 p201***
Skinner, S. A.; Quebec, 1856 ***9196.15 p8***
Skinner, Samuel 38; Ontario, 1871 ***1823.15 p243***
Skinner, Samuel 40; Ontario, 1861 ***2896.27 p18***
Skinner, Samul 40; Ontario, 1871 ***1823.15 p243***
Skinner, Stephen; Nova Scotia, 1822 ***1224.3 p71***
Skinner, Thomas; Maryland, 1664 ***2524.55 p201***
Skinner, Thomas; Maryland, 1706 ***1224.2 p105***
Skinner, William Stephens; Boston, 1845 ***1224.3 p71***
Skinning, James 60; Ontario, 1871 ***1823.15 p243***
Skippen, John 57; Ontario, 1871 ***1823.28 p93***
Skirrey, William 27; Philadelphia, 1774 ***1220.25 p35***
Skivington, Patrick; New York, 1836 ***8197.10 p78***
Sklodowski, Browislaw; Maryland, 1910 ***3259.35 p57***
Skoccynaski, Annie; Maryland, 1910 ***3259.35 p57***
Skoole, Charity; Maryland, 1658 ***2524.55 p201***
Skottowe, Thomas; Charles Town, South Carolina, n.d. ***1224.2 p105***
Skoturski, Martin S.; Maryland, 1910 ***3259.35 p57***
Skraupa, Francis; Maryland, 1910 ***3259.35 p57***
Skraupa, Wincenty; Maryland, 1910 ***3259.35 p57***
Skroch, Mathews; Maryland, 1910 ***3259.35 p57***
Skroger, James 16; America, 1774 ***1220.25 p36***
Skrydlewski, Woinech; Maryland, 1910 ***3259.35 p57***
Skrzynski, Jaruza W.; Maryland, 1910 ***3259.35 p57***
Skuce, Richard 56; Ontario, 1871 ***1823.28 p93***
Skudsen, Olaf 45; British Columbia, 1911 ***9196.1 p15***
Skulich, Peter 34; Alaska, 1912 ***9196.1 p20***
Skulich, Peter 34; British Columbia, 1912 ***9196.1 p20***
Skull, Sarah; New York, 1839 ***1224.3 p71***
Skull, William; Baltimore, 1788 ***1224.2 p105***
Skwinut, Tadesuz; Maryland, 1910 ***3259.35 p57***
Skworski, George; Maryland, 1910 ***3259.35 p57***
Skynner, Henry; St. Augustine, Florida, 1781 ***1224.2 p105***
Skynski, Christinia; Maryland, 1910 ***3259.35 p57***
Skyring, Col.; Quebec, 1857 ***9196.15 p24***
Skyring, Mrs.; Quebec, 1857 ***9196.15 p24***
Slack, Mr.; Quebec, 1857 ***9196.15 p16***
Slack, Ann; Maryland, 1658 ***2524.55 p201***
Slack, Ann 19; Baltimore, 1775 ***1220.25 p119***
Slack, Eliza Mary; Vermont, 1839-1928 ***5900.10 p607***
Slack, George 57; Ontario, 1871 ***1823.15 p243***
Slack, James W.; New York, 1834 ***8197.10 p283***
Slack, James W. 49; Ontario, 1871 ***1823.28 p93***
Slack, Robert; Maryland, 1657 ***2524.55 p201***
Sladden, Benjamin; Maryland, 1667 ***2524.55 p201***
Slade, Miss; Portland, Maine, 1857 ***9196.15 p12***
Slade, Alfred 39; Ontario, 1871 ***1823.22 p147***
Slade, Alice L.; Vermont, 1862-1927 ***5900.10 p594***
Slade, Daniel 36; Maryland, 1774 ***1220.25 p68***
Slade, George 29; Ontario, 1871 ***1823.28 p93***
Slade, John 33; Maryland, 1774 ***1220.25 p73***
Slade, Mary; Maryland, 1649 ***2524.55 p202***
Slade, Thomas; Portland, Maine, 1857 ***9196.15 p12***
Slade, Thomas 22; Maryland, 1775 ***1220.25 p99***
Slade, William 28; Ontario, 1871 ***1823.22 p147***
Sladen, Charles; New York, 1840 ***8197.10 p197***
Slahery, John 46; Ontario, 1871 ***1823.15 p243***
Slake, . . .; Maryland, 1656 ***2524.55 p202***
Slammon, Michael; Vermont, 1837-1907 ***5900.10 p512***
Slammon, Rachel Dugan; Vermont, 1844-1915 ***5900.10 p512***
Slammon, Sarah J. 36; Vermont, 1880 ***5900.10 p223***
Slamon, Anna 23; Vermont, 1869 ***5900.10 p512***
Slamon, Bridget Redmon 23; Vermont, 1869 ***5900.10 p141***
Slamon, Catharine 29; Vermont, 1869 ***5900.10 p512***
Slamon, Francis 28; Vermont, 1871 ***5900.10 p513***
Slamon, James 37; Vermont, 1872 ***5900.10 p513***
Slamon, James 60; Ontario, 1871 ***1823.22 p147***
Slamon, Mary 72; Vermont, 1875 ***5900.10 p512***
Slamon, Mary Corley 57; Vermont, 1889 ***5900.10 p141***
Slamon, Thomas 62; Vermont, 1894 ***5900.10 p141***
Slamon, William 80; Vermont, 1875 ***5900.10 p512***
Slankensee, Mr.; Portland, Maine, 1858 ***9196.15 p29***
Slanski, John; Maryland, 1910 ***3259.35 p57***
Slany, Joane; New England, 1649 ***1224.1 p53***
Slareo, William 66; Ontario, 1871 ***1823.22 p147***
Slaska, Frank; Maryland, 1910 ***3259.35 p57***
Slaska, Teofil; Maryland, 1910 ***3259.35 p57***
Slater, Christopher 72; Ontario, 1871 ***1823.22 p147***
Slater, Henry 39; Ontario, 1871 ***1823.28 p93***
Slater, J. C. 47; Ontario, 1871 ***1823.28 p93***
Slater, John 27; Maryland, 1775 ***1220.25 p101***
Slater, Mary; New York, 1705 ***1224.2 p105***
Slater, Mary Mayow; New York, 1680 ***1224.1 p39***
Slater, Samuel; New York, 1832 ***8197.10 p368***
Slater, William; New York, 1821-1834 ***8197.10 p310***
Slater, William 66; Ontario, 1871 ***1823.22 p147***
Slater, Wm 62; Ontario, 1871 ***1823.15 p243***
Slatery, John; Pennsylvania, 1777 ***4629.10 p25***
Slatery, Patk 29; Ontario, 1871 ***1823.28 p93***
Slatter, William; Kingston, Jamaica, 1760 ***1224.2 p105***
Slatter, William; Norfolk, Virginia, 1760 ***1224.2 p105***
Slattery, Agnes 83; Vermont, 1941 ***5900.10 p450***
Slattery, Andrew; New York, 1804 ***8197.10 p28***
Slattery, Ann 59; Vermont, 1891 ***5900.10 p565***
Slattery, Annie C.; Vermont, 1849-1914 ***5900.10 p446***
Slattery, Bridget; Vermont, 1847-1923 ***5900.10 p588***
Slattery, Bridget; Vermont, 1903 ***5900.10 p417***
Slattery, Bridget Flood; Vermont, 1847-1889 ***5900.10 p89***
Slattery, Catherine 82; Vermont, 1919 ***5900.10 p450***
Slattery, Ellen Howard; Vermont, 1835-1853 ***5900.10 p54***
Slattery, James; Vermont, 1835-1884 ***5900.10 p54***
Slattery, James 5; Vermont, n.d. ***5900.10 p450***
Slattery, John R. 49; Vermont, 1884 ***5900.10 p450***
Slattery, Joseph; Vermont, 1826-1888 ***5900.10 p336***
Slattery, Julia; Vermont, n.d. ***5900.10 p450***
Slattery, Julia 30; Vermont, 1875 ***5900.10 p450***
Slattery, Julia 66; Vermont, 1892 ***5900.10 p167***
Slattery, Kitty; Vermont, n.d. ***5900.10 p450***
Slattery, Maggie; Vermont, n.d. ***5900.10 p450***
Slattery, Margaret; Vermont, 1850-1923 ***5900.10 p433***
Slattery, Mary; Vermont, 1815-1870 ***5900.10 p417***
Slattery, Mary 20; Vermont, 1877 ***5900.10 p450***
Slattery, Mary A. 73; Vermont, 1922 ***5900.10 p122***
Slattery, Mary Gleason 56; Vermont, 1866 ***5900.10 p449***
Slattery, Mary V.; Vermont, 1855-1926 ***5900.10 p55***
Slattery, Matthew 82; Vermont, 1917 ***5900.10 p450***
Slattery, Michael 20; Vermont, 1871 ***5900.10 p449***
Slattery, Michael 28; Vermont, 1860 ***5900.10 p210***
Slattery, Patrick; Vermont, 1812-1878 ***5900.10 p417***
Slattery, Patrick; Vermont, 1846-1900 ***5900.10 p336***
Slattery, Roderick 70; Ontario, 1871 ***1823.15 p243***
Slattery, Rody; Vermont, n.d. ***5900.10 p450***
Slattery, Sarah 40; Vermont, 1915 ***5900.10 p450***
Slattery, Timothy; New York, 1838 ***8197.10 p149***
Slattery, Timothy; Vermont, n.d. ***5900.10 p450***
Slattery, Timothy 12; Vermont, n.d. ***5900.10 p450***
Slattery, Timothy 84; Vermont, 1880 ***5900.10 p449***
Slattery, William F.; Vermont, 1845-1915 ***5900.10 p89***
Slaughter, Mr.; Quebec, 1856 ***9196.15 p6***
Slaughter, Mrs.; Quebec, 1856 ***9196.15 p6***
Slaughter, John; Maryland, 1682 ***2524.55 p202***
Slaughter, John; Pennsylvania, 1786 ***4629.10 p49***
Slaughter, Richard Hampton; Pensacola, Florida, 1842 ***1224.3 p72***
Slaughter, Sophia Mary; Louisiana, 1842 ***1224.3 p72***
Slaven, C., Sr. 48; Ontario, 1861 ***2896.28 p7***
Slaven, Edward 77; Ontario, 1871 ***1823.22 p147***
Slaven, F. 17; Ontario, 1861 ***2896.28 p7***
Slaven, J. 14; Ontario, 1861 ***2896.28 p7***
Slaven, James 56; Ontario, 1861 ***2896.28 p7***
Slaven, Patrick; New York, 1840 ***8197.10 p194***
Slavin, James; New York, 1835 ***8197.10 p284***
Slawinska, Stephan; Maryland, 1910 ***3259.35 p57***
Slawska, Julja; Maryland, 1910 ***3259.35 p57***
Slay, John; Pennsylvania, 1781 ***4629.10 p42***
Slay, Joseph; Pennsylvania, 1781 ***4629.10 p42***
Slayd, William; Maryland, 1649 ***2524.55 p202***
Slayd, William; Maryland, 1663 ***2524.55 p202***
Slayter, Henry; Virginia, 1665-1666 ***6212.30 p22***
Slayter, Henry; Virginia, 1666-1667 ***6212.30 p32***
Sleater, George 35; Ontario, 1871 ***1823.28 p93***
Sleavon, Elisa 48; Ontario, 1861 ***2896.26 p36***
Sleavon, Frederick 5; Ontario, 1861 ***2896.26 p38***
Sleavon, Henry 9; Ontario, 1861 ***2896.26 p38***
Sleavon, James 19; Ontario, 1861 ***2896.26 p36***
Sleavon, Mary 21; Ontario, 1861 ***2896.26 p36***
Sleavon, Milow 18; Ontario, 1861 ***2896.26 p36***
Sleavon, Moses 16; Ontario, 1861 ***2896.26 p36***
Sleavon, Patrick 63; Ontario, 1861 ***2896.26 p36***
Sleavon, William 11; Ontario, 1861 ***2896.26 p38***
Slebioda, Michael; Maryland, 1910 ***3259.35 p57***
Sleclenski, Ignatz; Maryland, 1910 ***3259.35 p57***
Slee, John 22; Fort Cumberland, Nova Scotia, 1774 ***1220.25 p17***

Slee, William 51; Ontario, 1871 ***1823.15*** *p243*
Sleep, Samuel 65; Ontario, 1871 ***1823.22*** *p147*
Sleeth, James; New York, 1807 ***8197.10*** *p325*
Sleigh, Joseph; Boston, 1740 ***1224.2*** *p105*
Sleight, Nary 20; Ontario, 1861 ***2896.28*** *p33*
Sleiman, Gabriel; Georgia, 1699 ***1640.13*** *p115*
Sleith, Thomas 40; Ontario, 1871 ***1823.28*** *p93*
Sleman, James; New York, 1815-1834 ***8197.10*** *p305*
Slemon, Samuel 37; Ontario, 1871 ***1823.15*** *p243*
Slennis, Edward 49; Alaska, 1917 ***9196.1*** *p8*
Slennis, Edward 49; Yukon, 1917 ***9196.1*** *p8*
Slesson, John; New York, 1803 ***8197.10*** *p16*
Slevin, James; New York, 1840 ***8197.10*** *p199*
Slewka, Alexander; Maryland, 1910 ***3259.35*** *p57*
Sleyewski, Sophia; Maryland, 1910 ***3259.35*** *p57*
Slight, M. 55; Ontario, 1861 ***2896.28*** *p14*
Slight, Nancy 16; Ontario, 1861 ***2896.28*** *p45*
Slight, William 42; Ontario, 1871 ***1823.15*** *p243*
Sliminski, John S.; Maryland, 1910 ***3259.35*** *p57*
Slingsby, Mary; Virginia, 1667 ***6212.30*** *p37*
Slipper, Joseph; New York, 1802 ***8197.10*** *p25*
Slipper, Thomas M.; New York, 1807 ***8197.10*** *p330*
Slipski, Andrew; Maryland, 1910 ***3259.35*** *p57*
Slite, Sarah 11; Ontario, 1861 ***2896.28*** *p45*
Sliter, Robert; Panama, 1716 ***1224.2*** *p105*
Sloan, Ann 89; Vermont, 1891 ***5900.10*** *p474*
Sloan, Arthur 50; Ontario, 1871 ***1823.22*** *p147*
Sloan, Bernard; Vermont, 1830 ***5900.10*** *p13*
Sloan, Bridget 23; Vermont, 1876 ***5900.10*** *p234*
Sloan, Bridget 87; Vermont, 1893 ***5900.10*** *p223*
Sloan, David A.; Vermont, 1849-1910 ***5900.10*** *p291*
Sloan, Dennis 58; Vermont, 1900 ***5900.10*** *p279*
Sloan, Edward 87; Vermont, 1897 ***5900.10*** *p226*
Sloan, Edward E.; Vermont, 1852-1917 ***5900.10*** *p278*
Sloan, Elizabeth; Salt Lake City, 1888 ***1640.13*** *p115*
Sloan, Elizabeth; Vermont, 1854-1925 ***5900.10*** *p241*
Sloan, Elizabeth; Vermont, 1855-1928 ***5900.10*** *p257*
Sloan, Elizabeth 28; Ontario, 1871 ***1823.15*** *p243*
Sloan, Elizabeth 70; Vermont, 1901 ***5900.10*** *p604*
Sloan, Ellen; Vermont, 1828-1865 ***5900.10*** *p263*
Sloan, Ellen 37; Vermont, 1865 ***5900.10*** *p263*
Sloan, Ellen Flynn; Vermont, 1842-1910 ***5900.10*** *p241*
Sloan, Ellen Quinn; Vermont, 1837-1914 ***5900.10*** *p246*
Sloan, George; Alabama, 1820-1845 ***1640.10*** *p187*
Sloan, Hugh 47; Vermont, 1899 ***5900.10*** *p439*
Sloan, James 40; Ontario, 1871 ***1823.15*** *p243*
Sloan, John; New York, 1806 ***8197.10*** *p33*
Sloan, John; New York, 1818 ***8197.10*** *p278*
Sloan, John 60; Vermont, 1901 ***5900.10*** *p405*
Sloan, Margaret Mackrel 90; Vermont, 1929 ***5900.10*** *p405*
Sloan, Mary 44; Vermont, 1896 ***5900.10*** *p453*
Sloan, Mary E. Hanna; Vermont, 1859 ***5900.10*** *p278*
Sloan, Mary Maloy 77; Vermont, 1889 ***5900.10*** *p279*
Sloan, Mary Nolan; Vermont, 1855-1955 ***5900.10*** *p291*
Sloan, Mary O'Rourke; Vermont, 1843-1931 ***5900.10*** *p255*
Sloan, Nancy 67; Vermont, 1914 ***5900.10*** *p241*
Sloan, Patrick; Vermont, 1827-1907 ***5900.10*** *p246*
Sloan, Patrick; Vermont, 1846-1912 ***5900.10*** *p241*
Sloan, Patrick; Vermont, 1855-1938 ***5900.10*** *p52*
Sloan, Phoebe E. Moran; Vermont, 1846-1915 ***5900.10*** *p52*
Sloan, Richard 77; Vermont, 1889 ***5900.10*** *p279*
Sloan, Robert 26; Ontario, 1871 ***1823.15*** *p243*
Sloan, Rose Callahan 54; Vermont, 1909 ***5900.10*** *p439*
Sloan, S. 40; Ontario, 1871 ***1823.15*** *p243*
Sloan, Samuel; New York, 1840 ***8197.10*** *p196*
Sloan, Sarah O'Hear 86; Vermont, 1912 ***5900.10*** *p226*
Sloan, Terrance; Vermont, 1840-1922 ***5900.10*** *p255*
Sloan, Thomas 62; Ontario, 1871 ***1823.15*** *p243*
Sloan, William; Vermont, 1824 ***5900.10*** *p13*
Sloan, William 26; Ontario, 1871 ***1823.15*** *p243*
Sloan, William 30; Vermont, 1910 ***5900.10*** *p291*
Sloane, Mr.; Quebec, 1856 ***9196.15*** *p10*
Sloane, Alexander; New Orleans, 1794-1835 ***1640.10*** *p187*
Sloane, Anthony; New Orleans, 1844 ***1640.10*** *p187*
Sloane, Peter; New Orleans, 1849 ***1640.10*** *p187*
Sloe, Mary; Maryland, 1664 ***2524.55*** *p202*
Sloggart, William 79; Ontario, 1871 ***1823.22*** *p147*
Sloggett, Richard 53; Ontario, 1871 ***1823.22*** *p147*
Sloman, William 36; Ontario, 1871 ***1823.15*** *p243*
Slone, James; Boston, 1737 ***1224.2*** *p105*
Slone, John 40; Ontario, 1871 ***1823.28*** *p93*
Slone, Mary 92; Vermont, 1896 ***5900.10*** *p222*
Slone, William 55; Ontario, 1871 ***1823.15*** *p243*
Sloon, Isabella 50; Ontario, 1871 ***1823.15*** *p243*
Sloon, Walter 47; Ontario, 1871 ***1823.15*** *p243*
Slooper, Thomas 32; Ontario, 1871 ***1823.28*** *p93*
Sloper, Ann; Maryland, 1672 ***2524.55*** *p211*
Sloper, Christopher; Maryland, 1672 ***2524.55*** *p211*
Slopp, F. Y. 35; Washington, 1914 ***9196.1*** *p65*
Slorach, James; New York, 1782 ***1224.2*** *p105*
Slough, William; Carolina, 1703 ***1224.2*** *p105*
Slough, William; Virginia, 1708 ***1224.2*** *p105*
Sloway, Anna 35; Vermont, 1879 ***5900.10*** *p573*
Slowcuna, John 16; Antigua (Antego), 1775 ***1220.25*** *p97*
Slowick, John; Maryland, 1910 ***3259.35*** *p57*
Slowik, Felix; Maryland, 1910 ***3259.35*** *p57*
Slowrekurski, Josef; Maryland, 1910 ***3259.35*** *p57*
Sluce, Susan; Virginia, 1681-1682 ***6212.30*** *p56*
Sluriton, Miss; Quebec, 1857 ***9196.15*** *p16*
Sluzewski, Frank; Maryland, 1910 ***3259.35*** *p57*
Sluzewski, John S.; Maryland, 1910 ***3259.35*** *p57*
Sly, Agness 64; Ontario, 1871 ***1823.22*** *p147*
Sly, John 18; Maryland, 1774 ***1220.25*** *p5*
Sly, Robert 66; Ontario, 1871 ***1823.15*** *p243*
Slytler, Andrew 36; Ontario, 1871 ***1823.15*** *p243*
Slytler, Elizabeth 79; Ontario, 1871 ***1823.15*** *p243*
Smael, William; New York, 1807 ***8197.10*** *p50*
Smaile, John; New York, 1725 ***1224.2*** *p105*
Smaill, James 45; Ontario, 1871 ***1823.15*** *p243*
Smaldon, John 29; Ontario, 1871 ***1823.15*** *p243*
Smaldon, John 63; Ontario, 1871 ***1823.15*** *p243*
Smaldon, William 24; Ontario, 1871 ***1823.15*** *p243*
Smale, Elizabeth 31; Ontario, 1871 ***1823.15*** *p243*
Smale, Mary Ann 76; Ontario, 1871 ***1823.22*** *p147*
Smale, Robert 26; Ontario, 1871 ***1823.15*** *p243*
Smale, Thomas 24; Ontario, 1871 ***1823.15*** *p243*
Smale, William; New York, 1838 ***8197.10*** *p150*
Smale, William 50; Ontario, 1871 ***1823.15*** *p243*
Small, Mr.; Quebec, 1857 ***9196.15*** *p18*
Small, Mrs.; Quebec, 1857 ***9196.15*** *p18*
Small, Christian; New York, 1802 ***8197.10*** *p25*
Small, Daniel; Charles Town, South Carolina, 1772 ***1224.2*** *p105*
Small, George 45; Ontario, 1871 ***1823.28*** *p93*
Small, James; New York, 1838 ***8197.10*** *p148*
Small, John; New York, 1840 ***8197.10*** *p195*
Small, John 47; Vermont, 1874 ***5900.10*** *p250*
Small, Judeth; Virginia, 1666-1667 ***6212.30*** *p35*
Small, Mary; Alabama, 1783-1845 ***1640.10*** *p188*
Small, Matthew 48; Ontario, 1871 ***1823.28*** *p93*
Small, Samuel; Pennsylvania, 1817 ***6058.10*** *p6*
Small, Samuel, Jr. 21; Pennsylvania, 1818-1826 ***6058.10*** *p7*
Smallacomb, George 32; Ontario, 1871 ***1823.15*** *p243*
Smallacombe, John 42; Ontario, 1871 ***1823.15*** *p243*
Smallard, Ann; Maryland, 1656 ***2524.55*** *p202*
Smallay, Robert; Virginia, 1621 ***1224.1*** *p53*
Smallbone, William 64; Ontario, 1871 ***1823.28*** *p93*
Smallcombe, William 30; Ontario, 1871 ***1823.15*** *p243*
Smallee, Edward; Virginia, 1671-1672 ***6212.30*** *p46*
Smallee, John; Virginia, 1671-1672 ***6212.30*** *p46*
Smalley, Mrs.; Portland, Maine, 1857 ***9196.15*** *p12*
Smalley, James 84; Vermont, 1873 ***5900.10*** *p455*
Smalley, Richard; Portland, Maine, 1857 ***9196.15*** *p12*
Smalley, Susan MacFarland 75; Vermont, 1879 ***5900.10*** *p455*
Smallman, John; Pennsylvania, 1779 ***4629.10*** *p39*
Smallpeice, Hannah 46; Ontario, 1871 ***1823.28*** *p93*
Smallpeice, Thomas 51; Ontario, 1871 ***1823.28*** *p93*
Smallwood, Hester *SEE* Smallwood, James
Smallwood, James; Maryland, 1667 ***2524.55*** *p202*
Wife: Hester
Smallwood, Thomas; Maryland, 1670 ***2524.55*** *p202*
Smally, William; Virginia, 1668-1669 ***6212.30*** *p41*
Smart, David 28; Ontario, 1871 ***1823.22*** *p147*
Smart, Eleanor; Maryland, 1681 ***2524.55*** *p202*
Smart, James; Pennsylvania, 1777 ***4629.10*** *p14*
Smart, James 50; Ontario, 1871 ***1823.22*** *p147*
Smart, Jane 23; Maryland, 1774 ***1220.25*** *p83*
Smart, John; Maryland, 1720 ***1224.2*** *p105*
Smart, Joseph; New York, 1833 ***8197.10*** *p358*
Smart, William 49; Ontario, 1871 ***1823.15*** *p244*
Smarte, Tho.; Maryland, 1681 ***2524.55*** *p202*
Smeath, Francis 45; Ontario, 1871 ***1823.15*** *p244*
Smeaton, Alexander; Portland, Maine, 1857 ***9196.15*** *p12*
Smedberg, Charles Gustavus; New York, 1824 ***8197.10*** *p297*
Smedley, Henry 27; Ontario, 1871 ***1823.22*** *p147*
Smednury, C.; Quebec, 1856 ***9196.15*** *p10*
Smee, Thomas 31; Maryland, 1774 ***1220.25*** *p64*
Smeed, Mr.; Quebec, 1858 ***9196.15*** *p45*
Smelcer, John 45; Ontario, 1871 ***1823.15*** *p244*
Smell, Edmond 55; Ontario, 1871 ***1823.15*** *p244*
Smellie, George William; Florida, 1875 ***1640.13*** *p115*
Smellie, Patrick; Savannah, Georgia, 1768 ***1640.10*** *p188*
Smeltzer, Able 44; Ontario, 1871 ***1823.15*** *p244*
Smeyer, Elisabeth; America, 1733 ***2856.30*** *p432*
Smeyer, Johann; America, 1733 ***2856.30*** *p432*
Smeyer, Maria; America, 1733 ***2856.30*** *p432*
Smeyer, Philipp; America, 1733 ***2856.30*** *p432*
Smialek, Francis; Maryland, 1910 ***3259.35*** *p57*
Smichlaw, Thomas; Maryland, 1675 ***2524.55*** *p202*
Smick, Peter; Pennsylvania, 1777 ***4629.10*** *p8*
Smidley, Henry; Maryland, 1669 ***2524.55*** *p202*
Smiglawski, Leonard; Maryland, 1910 ***3259.35*** *p57*
Smiglawski, Sophia; Maryland, 1910 ***3259.35*** *p57*
Smile, Robert 35; Ontario, 1871 ***1823.15*** *p244*
Smiley, Jemima 19; Ontario, 1871 ***1823.22*** *p147*
Smiley, Margaret 59; Ontario, 1871 ***1823.15*** *p244*
Smilie, Isabella 65; Ontario, 1871 ***1823.15*** *p244*
Smilie, James 36; Ontario, 1871 ***1823.15*** *p244*
Smiling, Frederick 37; Ontario, 1871 ***1823.28*** *p93*
Smillie, James 38; Ontario, 1871 ***1823.15*** *p244*
Smissaert, Gilbert; New York, 1812 ***8197.10*** *p278*
Smith, . . .; Virginia, 1674 ***6212.30*** *p52*
Smith, Capt.; Quebec, 1857 ***9196.15*** *p16*
Smith, Master; Portland, Maine, 1858 ***9196.15*** *p27*
Smith, Miss; Portland, Maine, 1858 ***9196.15*** *p27*
Smith, Miss; Quebec, 1856 ***9196.15*** *p7*
Smith, Miss; Quebec, 1857 ***9196.15*** *p22*
Smith, Miss; Quebec, 1858 ***9196.15*** *p36*
Smith, Miss 3; Ontario, 1861 ***2896.25*** *p60*
Smith, Mr.; Quebec, 1856 ***9196.15*** *p6*
Smith, Mr.; Quebec, 1856 ***9196.15*** *p7*
Smith, Mr.; Quebec, 1856 ***9196.15*** *p8*
Smith, Mr.; Quebec, 1856 ***9196.15*** *p10*
Smith, Mr.; Quebec, 1856 ***9196.15*** *p11*
Smith, Mr.; Quebec, 1857 ***9196.15*** *p18*
Smith, Mr.; Quebec, 1857 ***9196.15*** *p19*
Smith, Mr.; Quebec, 1857 ***9196.15*** *p24*
Smith, Mr.; Quebec, 1858 ***9196.15*** *p32*
Smith, Mr.; Quebec, 1858 ***9196.15*** *p33*
Smith, Mr.; Quebec, 1858 ***9196.15*** *p35*
Smith, Mr.; Quebec, 1858 ***9196.15*** *p36*
Smith, Mrs.; Maryland, 1661 ***2524.55*** *p202*
Smith, Mrs.; Quebec, 1857 ***9196.15*** *p19*
Smith, Mrs.; Quebec, 1858 ***9196.15*** *p33*
Smith, A. 16; Ontario, 1861 ***2896.26*** *p12*
Smith, A. 18; Ontario, 1861 ***2896.28*** *p4*
Smith, A. E.; Quebec, 1856 ***9196.15*** *p11*
Smith, Abbie F.; Vermont, 1853-1915 ***5900.10*** *p457*
Smith, Abraham 35; Ontario, 1871 ***1823.15*** *p244*
Smith, Abraham Lynsen; New York, 1827 ***1224.3*** *p72*
Smith, Adam; Pennsylvania, 1777 ***4629.10*** *p13*
Smith, Adam 33; Ontario, 1871 ***1823.15*** *p244*
Smith, Adelaide; Quebec, 1858 ***9196.15*** *p31*
Smith, Adelia 7; Ontario, 1861 ***2896.28*** *p30*
Smith, Agnes; Vermont, 1868-1962 ***5900.10*** *p533*
Smith, Agness; Maryland, 1910 ***3259.35*** *p57*
Smith, Albert 25; Ontario, 1871 ***1823.28*** *p93*
Smith, Alexander *SEE* Smith, Kirsty MacKenzie
Smith, Alexander *SEE* Smith, Neil
Smith, Alexander; New Orleans, 1848 ***1640.10*** *p188*
Smith, Alexander; New York, 1837 ***8197.10*** *p106*
Smith, Alexander; New York, New York, 1799 ***1224.2*** *p105*
Smith, Alexander; Ontario, 1849 ***4537.37*** *p84*
Wife: Margaret MacEachan
Child: Catherine
Child: John
Child: Margaret
Child: Mary
Child: Allan
Child: Eliza
Smith, Alexander; Ontario, 1863 ***4537.32*** *p91*
Wife: Mary
Child: Catherine
Child: Kirsty
Smith, Alexander 26; Ontario, 1871 ***1823.15*** *p244*
Smith, Alexander 37; Ontario, 1871 ***1823.15*** *p244*
Smith, Alexander 51; Ontario, 1871 ***1823.15*** *p244*
Smith, Alexander 55; Ontario, 1871 ***1823.15*** *p244*
Smith, Alexander 56; Ontario, 1871 ***1823.15*** *p244*
Smith, Alexander 63; Ontario, 1871 ***1823.15*** *p244*
Smith, Alexander 75; Ontario, 1871 ***1823.15*** *p244*
Smith, Alexina; Alabama, 1832-1845 ***1640.10*** *p188*
Smith, Alferd 30; Ontario, 1871 ***1823.28*** *p93*
Smith, Alford 5; Ontario, 1861 ***2896.27*** *p2*
Smith, Alfred; Vermont, 1846-1922 ***5900.10*** *p71*
Smith, Alice; Vermont, 1864-1879 ***5900.10*** *p544*
Smith, Alice Alice; Maryland, 1654 ***2524.55*** *p202*
Smith, Alice Cooley; Vermont, 1858-1893 ***5900.10*** *p554*
Smith, Allan *SEE* Smith, Alexander
Smith, Allan *SEE* Smith, Neil
Smith, Allen; Maryland, 1663 ***2524.55*** *p202*
Smith, Amos L. 16; Ontario, 1861 ***2896.27*** *p65*
Smith, Andrew; Barbados, 1822 ***1640.13*** *p115*
Smith, Andrew 24; Philadelphia, 1774 ***1220.25*** *p42*
Smith, Andrew 51; Ontario, 1871 ***1823.15*** *p244*
Smith, Andrew 59; Ontario, 1871 ***1823.28*** *p93*
Smith, Angus *SEE* Smith, John
Smith, Angus *SEE* Smith, Neil
Smith, Angus *SEE* Smith, Norman

Smith, Angus; Ontario, 1851 ***4537.32*** *p92*
Wife: Mary MacRitchie
Child: Malcolm
Child: Donald
Child: Mary
Child: Marion
Child: Catherine
Child: John
Smith, Angus 28; Ontario, 1871 ***1823.15*** *p244*
Smith, Ann *SEE* Smith, George
Smith, Ann *SEE* Smith, John
Smith, Ann *SEE* Smith, Kenneth
Smith, Ann *SEE* Smith, Malcolm
Smith, Ann *SEE* Smith, Norman
Smith, Ann; Illinois, 1852 ***1224.3*** *p72*
Smith, Ann; Maryland, 1659 ***2524.55*** *p202*
Smith, Ann; Maryland, 1665 ***2524.55*** *p202*
Smith, Ann; Maryland, 1668 ***2524.55*** *p202*
Smith, Ann; Maryland, 1672 ***2524.55*** *p202*
Smith, Ann; Mobile, Alabama, 1818-1845 ***1640.10*** *p188*
Smith, Ann; Ontario, 1863 ***4537.32*** *p47*
Smith, Ann; Ontario, 1880-1889 ***4537.32*** *p44*
Smith, Ann; Vermont, n.d. ***5900.10*** *p496*
Smith, Ann; Virginia, 1681-1682 ***6212.30*** *p56*
Smith, Ann; Virginia, 1703-1704 ***6212.30*** *p62*
Smith, Ann 21; Maryland, 1775 ***1220.25*** *p114*
Smith, Ann MacAulay *SEE* Smith, Malcolm
Smith, Ann MacKay *SEE* Smith, Kenneth
Smith, Ann Matheson *SEE* Smith, John
Smith, Anna M.; Vermont, n.d. ***5900.10*** *p180*
Smith, Anna M.; Vermont, 1857-1893 ***5900.10*** *p86*
Smith, Anne; Virginia, 1684-1685 ***6212.30*** *p57*
Smith, Anne 28; Ontario, 1871 ***1823.15*** *p244*
Smith, Annie; Vermont, 1855-1934 ***5900.10*** *p533*
Smith, Annie 66; Vermont, 1917 ***5900.10*** *p609*
Smith, Anthon; New York, 1807 ***8197.10*** *p50*
Smith, Anthony 32; Ontario, 1871 ***1823.15*** *p244*
Smith, Anthony S.; New York, 1863 ***6058.10*** *p77*
Smith, Anto; Virginia, 1665-1666 ***6212.30*** *p21*
Smith, Anton; New York, 1840 ***8197.10*** *p285*
Smith, Arthur A.; New York, 1838 ***8197.10*** *p284*
Smith, Arthur Everard; Omaha, Nebraska, 1893 ***1640.13*** *p115*
Smith, B. 18; Ontario, 1861 ***2896.27*** *p6*
Smith, Barbara; Quebec, 1858 ***9196.15*** *p35*
Smith, Bartholomew 29; Vermont, 1872 ***5900.10*** *p580*
Smith, Baswell; Maryland, 1682 ***2524.55*** *p202*
Smith, Bengeman 18; Ontario, 1871 ***1823.28*** *p93*
Smith, Benjamin; Charles Town, South Carolina, 1791 ***1224.2*** *p105*
Smith, Benjamin; New York, 1827 ***8197.10*** *p344*
Smith, Benjamin 24; Virginia, 1773 ***1220.25*** *p29*
Smith, Benjamin F.; Vermont, 1839-1922 ***5900.10*** *p310*
Smith, Bernard; New York, 1821 ***8197.10*** *p279*
Smith, Bernard; New York, 1837 ***8197.10*** *p106*
Smith, Bernard J.; Vermont, 1890-1916 ***5900.10*** *p323*
Smith, Boselle 42; Ontario, 1871 ***1823.22*** *p147*
Smith, Boyd; New Orleans, 1844 ***1224.3*** *p72*
Smith, Bridget; Vermont, 1862-1954 ***5900.10*** *p533*
Smith, Bridget 30; Vermont, 1874 ***5900.10*** *p564*
Smith, Bridget Bellew; Vermont, 1921 ***5900.10*** *p271*
Smith, Bridget McGroaty; Vermont, 1840-1906 ***5900.10*** *p85*
Smith, Brooke; Philadelphia, 1788 ***1224.2*** *p106*
Smith, C. 1; Ontario, 1861 ***2896.28*** *p12*
Smith, C. 4; Ontario, 1861 ***2896.28*** *p12*
Smith, Carl 27; Ontario, 1871 ***1823.28*** *p93*
Smith, Caroline; Michigan, 1847 ***1224.3*** *p72*
Smith, Caroline A. 30; Ontario, 1861 ***2896.28*** *p30*
Smith, Catharine 33; Ontario, 1861 ***2896.27*** *p55*
Smith, Catherine *SEE* Smith, Alexander
Smith, Catherine *SEE* Smith, Angus
Smith, Catherine *SEE* Smith, Kenneth
Smith, Catherine *SEE* Smith, Kirsty MacKenzie
Smith, Catherine *SEE* Smith, Neil
Smith, Catherine *SEE* Smith, Norman
Smith, Catherine; Ontario, 1851 ***4537.32*** *p21*
Smith, Catherine; Ontario, 1851 ***4537.37*** *p54*
Smith, Catherine; Vermont, 1871-1943 ***5900.10*** *p533*
Smith, Catherine 28; Ontario, 1861 ***2896.27*** *p30*
Smith, Catherine Collins; Vermont, 1851-1885 ***5900.10*** *p584*
Smith, Catherine Farmer; Vermont, n.d. ***5900.10*** *p180*
Smith, Catherine MacLeod *SEE* Smith, John
Smith, Cel 4; Ontario, 1861 ***2896.27*** *p6*
Smith, Characy 34; Ontario, 1861 ***2896.25*** *p36*
Smith, Charles; Maryland, 1678 ***2524.55*** *p202*
Smith, Charles; New York, 1797 ***8197.10*** *p8*
Smith, Charles; Pennsylvania, 1786 ***4629.10*** *p47*
Smith, Charles 7; Ontario, 1861 ***2896.27*** *p2*
Smith, Charles 12; Ontario, 1861 ***2896.27*** *p42*
Smith, Charles 15; Philadelphia, 1774 ***1220.25*** *p42*
Smith, Charles 24; Maryland, 1775 ***1220.25*** *p103*
Smith, Charles 31; Ontario, 1871 ***1823.22*** *p147*
Smith, Charles 36; Ontario, 1871 ***1823.15*** *p244*
Smith, Charles C.; New York, 1840 ***8197.10*** *p285*
Smith, Charles E.; Vermont, 1850-1886 ***5900.10*** *p107*
Smith, Charleton 36; Baltimore, 1775 ***1220.25*** *p117*
Smith, Charlotte 23; Ontario, 1871 ***1823.15*** *p244*
Smith, Christina 50; Ontario, 1871 ***1823.15*** *p244*
Smith, Christopher; New York, 1731 ***1224.2*** *p106*
Smith, Christopher; Vermont, 1834-1887 ***5900.10*** *p547*
Smith, Christopher 35; Carolina, 1774 ***1220.25*** *p91*
Wife: Esther
Smith, Colin 27; Ontario, 1871 ***1823.15*** *p244*
Smith, Conrad; Pennsylvania, 1777 ***4629.10*** *p19*
Smith, Cornelius 8; Ontario, 1861 ***2896.25*** *p35*
Smith, Cornelius 14; Ontario, 1861 ***2896.27*** *p46*
Smith, Cornilurs 33; Ontario, 1871 ***1823.15*** *p244*
Smith, Cossimer; Baltimore, 1841 ***6058.10*** *p48*
Smith, D. C. 10; Ontario, 1861 ***2896.26*** *p5*
Smith, Dan 39; Alaska, 1916 ***9196.1*** *p6*
Smith, Dan 39; Yukon, 1916 ***9196.1*** *p6*
Smith, Daniel; Maryland, 1669 ***2524.55*** *p202*
Smith, Daniel; Maryland, 1674 ***2524.55*** *p202*
Smith, Daniel; Maryland, 1676 ***2524.55*** *p202*
Smith, Daniel; New Jersey, 1766 ***1224.2*** *p106*
Smith, Daniel; New York, 1830 ***8197.10*** *p282*
Smith, Daniel; Pennsylvania, 1777 ***4629.10*** *p12*
Smith, Daniel; Pennsylvania, 1786 ***4629.10*** *p49*
Smith, Daniel 21; Maryland, 1774 ***1220.25*** *p57*
Smith, Daniel 30; Maryland, 1774 ***1220.25*** *p39*
Smith, Daniel 38; Maryland, 1774 ***1220.25*** *p84*
Smith, Daniel 56; Ontario, 1871 ***1823.22*** *p147*
Smith, Dan'l; Pennsylvania, 1781 ***4629.10*** *p42*
Smith, David *SEE* Smith, Kenneth
Smith, David; Louisiana, 1813 ***1640.10*** *p188*
Smith, David; Louisiana, 1829 ***1640.10*** *p188*
Smith, David; Maryland, 1671 ***2524.55*** *p202*
Smith, David; New York, 1807 ***8197.10*** *p50*
Smith, David; Norfolk, Virginia, 1811 ***1224.3*** *p72*
Smith, David; Pennsylvania, 1777 ***4629.10*** *p15*
Smith, David 21; Jamaica, 1774 ***1220.25*** *p85*
Smith, David 23; Virginia, 1774 ***1220.25*** *p55*
Smith, David 48; Ontario, 1871 ***1823.15*** *p244*
Smith, Dennis 42; Vermont, 1883 ***5900.10*** *p91*
Smith, Dinah 15; Ontario, 1861 ***2896.28*** *p43*
Smith, Donald *SEE* Smith, Angus
Smith, Donald *SEE* Smith, Hugh
Smith, Donald *SEE* Smith, Malcolm
Smith, Donald *SEE* Smith, Neil
Smith, Donald; Ontario, 1855 ***4537.32*** *p92*
Wife: Mary MacAulay
Child: Murdo
Child: John
Child: Duncan
Smith, Duncan *SEE* Smith, Donald
Smith, Duncan; Georgia, 1816-1843 ***1640.10*** *p188*
Smith, Ebenezer; New York, 1840 ***8197.10*** *p194*
Smith, Edm; Virginia, 1665-1666 ***6212.30*** *p21*
Smith, Edmond; Maryland, 1658 ***2524.55*** *p202*
Smith, Edmond; Maryland, 1665 ***2524.55*** *p113*
Smith, Edmond; Rhode Island, 1765 ***1224.2*** *p106*
Smith, Edw; Virginia, 1665-1666 ***6212.30*** *p21*
Smith, Edward; Maryland, 1672 ***2524.55*** *p203*
Smith, Edward; Maryland, 1682 ***2524.55*** *p203*
Smith, Edward; New York, 1758 ***1224.2*** *p106*
Smith, Edward; New York, 1819 ***8197.10*** *p278*
Smith, Edward; Virginia, 1663 ***6212.30*** *p1*
Smith, Edward 3; Ontario, 1861 ***2896.25*** *p60*
Smith, Edward 34; Maryland, 1774 ***1220.25*** *p39*
Smith, Edward S.; New York, 1840 ***8197.10*** *p320*
Smith, Effie; Ontario, 1863 ***4537.32*** *p86*
Smith, Elisha 27; Ontario, 1861 ***2896.27*** *p17*
Smith, Eliza *SEE* Smith, Alexander
Smith, Eliza 5; Ontario, 1861 ***2896.25*** *p60*
Smith, Eliza 25; Ontario, 1871 ***1823.28*** *p93*
Smith, Eliza 48; Ontario, 1871 ***1823.15*** *p244*
Smith, Elizabeth *SEE* Smith, Robert
Smith, Elizabeth; Connecticut, 1786 ***1224.2*** *p106*
Smith, Elizabeth; Maryland, 1656 ***2524.55*** *p203*
Smith, Elizabeth; Maryland, 1668 ***2524.55*** *p203*
Smith, Elizabeth; Maryland, 1672 ***2524.55*** *p203*
Smith, Elizabeth; Maryland, 1674 ***2524.55*** *p203*
Smith, Elizabeth; New Jersey, 1848 ***1224.3*** *p56*
Smith, Elizabeth; New York, 1785 ***1224.2*** *p106*
Smith, Elizabeth; Vermont, 1832-1909 ***5900.10*** *p244*
Smith, Elizabeth; Vermont, 1866-1878 ***5900.10*** *p533*
Smith, Elizabeth 7 *SEE* Smith, Nathaniel
Smith, Elizabeth 9; Ontario, 1861 ***2896.27*** *p2*
Smith, Elizabeth 9; Ontario, 1861 ***2896.27*** *p41*
Smith, Elizabeth 25; Maryland, 1774 ***1220.25*** *p40*
Smith, Elizabeth 27; Ontario, 1861 ***2896.25*** *p60*
Smith, Elizabeth 37; Ontario, 1861 ***2896.27*** *p47*
Smith, Elizabeth 44; Ontario, 1861 ***2896.25*** *p54*
Smith, Elizabeth 52 *SEE* Smith, Nathaniel
Smith, Elizabeth 58; Ontario, 1871 ***1823.15*** *p244*
Smith, Elizabeth 63; Ontario, 1871 ***1823.28*** *p93*
Smith, Elizabeth 67; Ontario, 1871 ***1823.15*** *p244*
Smith, Elizabeth B.; Vermont, 1837-1915 ***5900.10*** *p159*
Smith, Elizabeth Sloan; Vermont, 1854-1925 ***5900.10*** *p241*
Smith, Ellen; Vermont, 1859-1937 ***5900.10*** *p533*
Smith, Ellen 26; Ontario, 1871 ***1823.15*** *p244*
Smith, Ellen 26; Vermont, 1880 ***5900.10*** *p107*
Smith, Ellen 72; Vermont, 1891 ***5900.10*** *p472*
Smith, Ellen G.; Vermont, 1859-1937 ***5900.10*** *p452*
Smith, Ellinour; Maryland, 1651 ***2524.55*** *p204*
Smith, Ephraim; New York, 1838 ***8197.10*** *p149*
Smith, Esther *SEE* Smith, Christopher
Smith, Esther; Maryland, 1663 ***2524.55*** *p203*
Smith, Esther 16; Maryland, 1774 ***1220.25*** *p59*
Smith, F. 7; Ontario, 1861 ***2896.28*** *p12*
Smith, Franc; Virginia, 1681 ***6212.30*** *p55*
Smith, Francis; Maryland, 1658 ***2524.55*** *p203*
Smith, Francis; Maryland, 1659 ***2524.55*** *p203*
Smith, Francis; New York, 1806 ***8197.10*** *p33*
Smith, Francis; Pennsylvania, 1786 ***4629.10*** *p49*
Smith, Francis; Vermont, 1786-1860 ***5900.10*** *p329*
Smith, Francis; Virginia, 1664 ***6212.30*** *p11*
Smith, Francis A.; Vermont, 1826-1902 ***5900.10*** *p517*
Smith, Franciska; Maryland, 1910 ***3259.35*** *p57*
Smith, Frankie J.; Vermont, 1889 ***5900.10*** *p323*
Smith, Fred 30; Ontario, 1871 ***1823.28*** *p93*
Smith, Frederick; Charles Town, South Carolina, 1839 ***1224.3*** *p72*
Smith, Frederick 27; Ontario, 1871 ***1823.15*** *p245*
Smith, Fredrick 19; Ontario, 1871 ***1823.28*** *p93*
Smith, G. 22; Ontario, 1861 ***2896.28*** *p63*
Smith, Miss G.; Portland, Maine, 1858 ***9196.15*** *p27*
Smith, Geo; Quebec, 1856 ***9196.15*** *p6*
Smith, George *SEE* Smith, John
Smith, George; Baltimore, 1840 ***6058.10*** *p36*
Smith, George; Maryland, 1658-1663 ***2524.55*** *p20*
Smith, George; Maryland, 1666 ***2524.55*** *p203*
Wife: Ann
Smith, George; Maryland, 1680 ***2524.55*** *p203*
Smith, George; New York, 1763 ***1224.2*** *p106*
Smith, George; New York, 1807 ***8197.10*** *p50*
Smith, George; New York, 1835 ***8197.10*** *p283*
Smith, George; New York, 1838 ***8197.10*** *p149*
Smith, George; New York, 1839 ***8197.10*** *p140*
Smith, George; New York, 1840 ***8197.10*** *p198*
Smith, George; New York, 1857 ***1640.13*** *p115*
Smith, George; New York, 1888 ***1640.13*** *p115*
Smith, George; Ontario, 1891 ***1640.13*** *p115*
Smith, George; Pennsylvania, 1777 ***4629.10*** *p10*
Smith, George; Pennsylvania, 1777 ***4629.10*** *p11*
Smith, George; Vermont, 1822-1897 ***5900.10*** *p290*
Smith, George; Virginia, 1664 ***6212.30*** *p7*
Smith, George; Virginia, 1729 ***1224.2*** *p106*
Smith, George 2 *SEE* Smith, John
Smith, George 16; Ontario, 1861 ***2896.27*** *p32*
Smith, George 18; Virginia, 1774 ***1220.25*** *p93*
Smith, George 21; Ontario, 1871 ***1823.15*** *p245*
Smith, George 21; Philadelphia, 1774 ***1220.25*** *p81*
Smith, George 23; Maryland, 1775 ***1220.25*** *p103*
Smith, George 28; Ontario, 1871 ***1823.28*** *p93*
Smith, George 30; Ontario, 1871 ***1823.22*** *p148*
Smith, George 44; Ontario, 1871 ***1823.28*** *p93*
Smith, George 48; Ontario, 1871 ***1823.15*** *p245*
Smith, George 56; Ontario, 1871 ***1823.15*** *p245*
Smith, George 69; Ontario, 1871 ***1823.22*** *p148*
Smith, George 86; Ontario, 1871 ***1823.22*** *p148*
Smith, George, II; Maryland, 1666 ***2524.55*** *p203*
Smith, George Clement Fearn; Philadelphia, 1844 ***1224.3*** *p72*
Smith, George H. 4; Ontario, 1861 ***2896.25*** *p54*
Smith, George H. 12; Ontario, 1861 ***2896.27*** *p41*
Smith, Gerret; New York, 1821 ***8197.10*** *p280*
Smith, Grace 27; Baltimore, 1775 ***1220.25*** *p119*
Smith, Grace 30; New York, 1774 ***1220.25*** *p26*
Smith, Graham 27; Ontario, 1871 ***1823.22*** *p148*
Smith, H.; Quebec, 1856 ***9196.15*** *p7*
Smith, H. S.; Quebec, 1858 ***9196.15*** *p34*
Smith, Hamilton 25; Ontario, 1871 ***1823.15*** *p245*
Smith, Hamilton 41; Ontario, 1871 ***1823.15*** *p245*
Smith, Hanna 20; Ontario, 1871 ***1823.28*** *p93*
Smith, Hannah *SEE* Smith, John
Smith, Hannah 10; Ontario, 1861 ***2896.25*** *p60*
Smith, Harry; Vermont, 1865-1923 ***5900.10*** *p327*
Smith, Harry 14; Ontario, 1871 ***1823.28*** *p93*
Smith, Henry; Maryland, 1668 ***2524.55*** *p203*
Smith, Henry; New York, 1840 ***8197.10*** *p197*
Smith, Henry; New York, 1840 ***8197.10*** *p198*
Smith, Henry; Pennsylvania, 1703 ***1224.2*** *p106*
Smith, Henry; Pennsylvania, 1777 ***4629.10*** *p13*
Smith, Henry; Virginia, 1664 ***6212.30*** *p6*
Smith, Henry; Virginia, 1665-1666 ***6212.30*** *p23*

Smith, Henry; Virginia, 1667 ***6212.30*** *p37*
Smith, Henry; Virginia, 1703-1704 ***6212.30*** *p62*
Smith, Henry 24; Virginia, 1774 ***1220.25*** *p56*
Smith, Henry 30; Maryland, 1774 ***1220.25*** *p53*
Smith, Henry 30; Ontario, 1871 ***1823.28*** *p93*
Smith, Henry 32; Ontario, 1871 ***1823.15*** *p245*
Smith, Henry 34; Ontario, 1871 ***1823.22*** *p148*
Smith, Henry 36; Ontario, 1871 ***1823.15*** *p245*
Smith, Henry 38; Ontario, 1871 ***1823.15*** *p245*
Smith, Henry 40; Ontario, 1871 ***1823.15*** *p245*
Smith, Henry 40; Ontario, 1871 ***1823.28*** *p93*
Smith, Henry 43; Ontario, 1871 ***1823.22*** *p148*
Smith, Henry 48; Ontario, 1871 ***1823.15*** *p245*
Smith, Henry 61; Ontario, 1871 ***1823.22*** *p148*
Smith, Henry 65; Ontario, 1871 ***1823.15*** *p245*
Smith, Henry A. 5; Ontario, 1861 ***2896.25*** *p60*
Smith, Henry K.; New York, 1831 ***8197.10*** *p364*
Smith, Henry L. E.; Vermont, 1862-1937 ***5900.10*** *p334*
Smith, Hermon 41; Ontario, 1871 ***1823.15*** *p245*
Smith, Hugh; New York, 1840 ***8197.10*** *p285*
Smith, Hugh; Ontario, 1840-1849 ***4537.37*** *p84*
Brother: Donald
Smith, Hugh 28; Ontario, 1871 ***1823.15*** *p245*
Smith, Hugh 28; Philadelphia, 1774 ***1220.25*** *p67*
Smith, Hugh 38; Ontario, 1861 ***2896.27*** *p41*
Smith, Hugh 48; Ontario, 1871 ***1823.28*** *p93*
Smith, Hugh 58; Ontario, 1871 ***1823.22*** *p148*
Smith, Hugh 75; Ontario, 1871 ***1823.28*** *p93*
Smith, Isaac; New York, 1832 ***8197.10*** *p357*
Smith, Isaac 40; Ontario, 1871 ***1823.28*** *p93*
Smith, Isabel 80; Ontario, 1871 ***1823.22*** *p148*
Smith, Isabell; Maryland, 1663 ***2524.55*** *p203*
Smith, Isabella *SEE* Smith, Kenneth
Smith, Isabella; Portland, Maine, 1858 ***9196.15*** *p47*
Smith, Isabella 47; Ontario, 1871 ***1823.22*** *p148*
Smith, Miss J.; Quebec, 1858 ***9196.15*** *p44*
Smith, J. Adam; Vermont, 1844-1908 ***5900.10*** *p148*
Smith, J. C. 14; Ontario, 1861 ***2896.25*** *p54*
Smith, J. H. 24; Seattle, 1917 ***9196.1*** *p51*
Smith, J. H. 24; Whitehorse, Yukon, 1917 ***9196.1*** *p51*
Smith, J. John 58; Ontario, 1871 ***1823.15*** *p245*
Smith, J. L.; Quebec, 1857 ***9196.15*** *p20*
Smith, Mrs. J. L.; Quebec, 1857 ***9196.15*** *p20*
Smith, Jacob; New York, 1802 ***8197.10*** *p25*
Smith, Jacob 36; Ontario, 1871 ***1823.15*** *p245*
Smith, Jacob 74; Ontario, 1871 ***1823.22*** *p148*
Smith, James; America, n.d. ***4628.40*** *p49*
Smith, James; Georgia, 1734 ***1640.10*** *p188*
Smith, James; Maryland, 1663 ***2524.55*** *p203*
With wife
Smith, James; Nashville, Tennessee, 1835 ***1640.10*** *p188*
Smith, James; New Jersey, 1733 ***1224.2*** *p106*
Smith, James; New York, 1797 ***1224.2*** *p106*
Smith, James; New York, 1807 ***8197.10*** *p50*
Smith, James; New York, 1822 ***8197.10*** *p280*
Smith, James; New York, 1825 ***8197.10*** *p281*
Smith, James; New York, 1833 ***8197.10*** *p283*
Smith, James; New York, 1836 ***8197.10*** *p78*
Smith, James; New York, 1837 ***8197.10*** *p107*
Smith, James; New York, 1838 ***8197.10*** *p149*
Smith, James; New York, 1839 ***8197.10*** *p140*
Smith, James; New York, 1839 ***8197.10*** *p284*
Smith, James; New York, 1840 ***8197.10*** *p195*
Smith, James; Ohio, 1896 ***1640.13*** *p115*
Smith, James; Ontario, 1895 ***1640.13*** *p115*
Smith, James; Pennsylvania, 1777 ***4629.10*** *p17*
Smith, James; Pennsylvania, 1785 ***4629.10*** *p48*
Smith, James; Portland, Maine, 1857 ***9196.15*** *p12*
Smith, James; Quebec, 1857 ***9196.15*** *p25*
Smith, James; Savannah, Georgia, 1817 ***1640.10*** *p188*
Smith, James; South Carolina, 1820 ***1224.3*** *p72*
Smith, James; Tobago, West Indies, 1853 ***1640.13*** *p115*
Smith, James; Vermont, 1846-1915 ***5900.10*** *p554*
Smith, James; Vermont, 1848 ***5900.10*** *p316*
Smith, James; Vermont, 1864-1888 ***5900.10*** *p533*
Smith, James; Virginia, 1666 ***6212.30*** *p28*
Smith, James; Virginia, 1666 ***6212.30*** *p29*
Smith, James; Virginia, 1666-1667 ***6212.30*** *p33*
Smith, James; Virginia, 1785 ***1224.2*** *p106*
Smith, James 16; Ontario, 1861 ***2896.28*** *p50*
Smith, James 16; Ontario, 1871 ***1823.15*** *p245*
Smith, James 20; Ontario, 1861 ***2896.27*** *p6*
Smith, James 21; Carolina, 1774 ***1220.25*** *p76*
Smith, James 22; Ontario, 1861 ***2896.27*** *p42*
Smith, James 23; Virginia, 1773 ***1220.25*** *p31*
Smith, James 32; Ontario, 1871 ***1823.15*** *p245*
Smith, James 35; Ontario, 1871 ***1823.28*** *p93*
Smith, James 39; Ontario, 1871 ***1823.15*** *p245*
Smith, James 43; Ontario, 1871 ***1823.28*** *p93*
Smith, James 46; Ontario, 1871 ***1823.15*** *p245*
Smith, James 50; Ontario, 1871 ***1823.15*** *p245*
Smith, James 54; Ontario, 1871 ***1823.28*** *p93*
Smith, James 55; Ontario, 1871 ***1823.22*** *p148*
Smith, James 60; Ontario, 1871 ***1823.15*** *p245*
Smith, James 63; Ontario, 1871 ***1823.15*** *p245*
Smith, James 63; Ontario, 1871 ***1823.22*** *p148*
Smith, James 64; Ontario, 1871 ***1823.15*** *p245*
Smith, James 73; Ontario, 1871 ***1823.28*** *p93*
Smith, James, Jr.; New York, 1837 ***8197.10*** *p107*
Smith, James E. 2; Ontario, 1861 ***2896.25*** *p54*
Smith, James Edward 31; Maryland, 1775 ***1220.25*** *p115*
Smith, James F.; Portland, Maine, 1858 ***9196.15*** *p27*
Smith, James P.; Vermont, 1859-1907 ***5900.10*** *p442*
Smith, James T.; New York, 1825 ***8197.10*** *p281*
Smith, Jane *SEE* Smith, John
Smith, Jane *SEE* Smith, Neil
Smith, Jane; Vermont, 1849-1939 ***5900.10*** *p532*
Smith, Jane 16; Ontario, 1871 ***1823.15*** *p245*
Smith, Jane 18; Ontario, 1861 ***2896.27*** *p40*
Smith, Jane 36; Ontario, 1871 ***1823.22*** *p148*
Smith, Jane B. McCue; Vermont, 1844-1920 ***5900.10*** *p464*
Smith, Jane Lilley; Jamaica, 1750 ***1224.2*** *p106*
Smith, Jane Lilley; Philadelphia, 1750 ***1224.2*** *p106*
Smith, Jane McKinney; Vermont, 1833-1905 ***5900.10*** *p517*
Smith, Jane Sexton; Vermont, 1847-1924 ***5900.10*** *p472*
Smith, Janet; Ontario, 1851 ***4537.37*** *p35*
Smith, Jean; Virginia, 1666 ***6212.30*** *p26*
Smith, Jehosaphat; Boston, 1678 ***1224.1*** *p53*
Smith, Jennie Howley; Vermont, 1858-1919 ***5900.10*** *p323*
Smith, Jeremiah; Pennsylvania, 1777 ***4629.10*** *p24*
Smith, Jessey 80; Ontario, 1871 ***1823.22*** *p148*
Smith, Jessie; Alabama, 1828-1845 ***1640.10*** *p188*
Smith, Jessie 37; Ontario, 1871 ***1823.22*** *p148*
Smith, Jno; Virginia, 1664 ***6212.30*** *p7*
Smith, Jno; Virginia, 1665-1666 ***6212.30*** *p21*
Smith, Jno; Virginia, 1668-1669 ***6212.30*** *p41*
Smith, Jno; Virginia, 1673 ***6212.30*** *p51*
Smith, Joan; Virginia, 1667-1668 ***6212.30*** *p39*
Smith, Job; New York, 1838 ***8197.10*** *p149*
Smith, Job E. 14; Ontario, 1861 ***2896.27*** *p40*
Smith, Joe 37; Alaska, 1917 ***9196.1*** *p48*
Smith, Joe 37; Yukon, 1917 ***9196.1*** *p48*
Smith, Johanna Ryan; Vermont, 1840-1882 ***5900.10*** *p143*
Smith, John *SEE* Smith, Alexander
Smith, John *SEE* Smith, Angus
Smith, John *SEE* Smith, Donald
Smith, John *SEE* Smith, John
Smith, John *SEE* Smith, Kenneth
Smith, John *SEE* Smith, Kirsty MacKenzie
Smith, John *SEE* Smith, Malcolm
Smith, John *SEE* Smith, Neil
Smith, John; America, 1815 ***1640.13*** *p115*
Smith, John; Baltimore, 1840 ***6058.10*** *p36*
Smith, John; Baltimore, 1840 ***6058.10*** *p43*
Smith, John; Boston, 1698 ***1224.1*** *p53*
Smith, John; Carolina, 1683 ***1224.1*** *p53*
Smith, John; Connecticut, 1764 ***1224.2*** *p106*
Smith, John; Georgia, 1699 ***1640.13*** *p115*
Smith, John; Hartford, Connecticut, 1732 ***1224.2*** *p106*
Smith, John; Havana, 1764 ***1224.2*** *p106*
Smith, John; Jamaica, 1872 ***1640.13*** *p115*
Smith, John; Maryland, 1653 ***2524.55*** *p203*
Smith, John; Maryland, 1658 ***2524.55*** *p203*
Smith, John; Maryland, 1659 ***2524.55*** *p203*
Smith, John; Maryland, 1660 ***2524.55*** *p203*
Smith, John; Maryland, 1661 ***2524.55*** *p203*
Wife: Rebecca
Son: John, Jr.
Relative: Ann
Relative: George
Smith, John; Maryland, 1665 ***2524.55*** *p203*
Smith, John; Maryland, 1666 ***2524.55*** *p203*
Wife: Hannah
Daughter: Hannah
Smith, John; Maryland, 1667 ***2524.55*** *p114*
Smith, John; Maryland, 1669 ***2524.55*** *p203*
Smith, John; Maryland, 1680 ***2524.55*** *p203*
Wife: Martha
Smith, John; Maryland, 1681 ***2524.55*** *p203*
Smith, John; Maryland, 1682 ***2524.55*** *p203*
Smith, John; Maryland, 1727 ***1224.2*** *p106*
Smith, John; Maryland, 1775 ***1640.10*** *p189*
Smith, John; New England, 1651 ***1224.1*** *p54*
Smith, John; New York, 1802 ***8197.10*** *p25*
Smith, John; New York, 1807 ***8197.10*** *p49*
Smith, John; New York, 1807 ***8197.10*** *p50*
Smith, John; New York, 1827 ***8197.10*** *p341*
Smith, John; New York, 1831 ***8197.10*** *p365*
Smith, John; New York, 1832 ***8197.10*** *p314*
Smith, John; New York, 1832 ***8197.10*** *p357*
Smith, John; New York, 1838 ***8197.10*** *p148*
Smith, John; New York, 1839 ***8197.10*** *p139*
Smith, John; New York, 1839 ***8197.10*** *p140*
Smith, John; New York, 1839 ***8197.10*** *p141*
Smith, John; New York, 1840 ***8197.10*** *p198*
Smith, John; New York, 1898 ***1640.13*** *p115*
Smith, John; Ontario, 1855 ***4537.32*** *p93*
Wife: Ann Matheson
Child: Angus
Child: John
Smith, John; Ontario, 1861 ***2896.28*** *p43*
Smith, John; Ontario, 1863 ***4537.32*** *p93*
Wife: Catherine MacLeod
Child: Murdo
Child: Malcolm
Child: Angus
Smith, John; Pennsylvania, 1689 ***1224.1*** *p53*
Smith, John; Pennsylvania, 1777 ***4629.10*** *p22*
Smith, John; Pennsylvania, 1786 ***4629.10*** *p50*
Smith, John; Pennsylvania, 1835 ***6058.10*** *p11*
Smith, John; Philadelphia, n.d. ***1224.2*** *p106*
Smith, John; Philadelphia, 1789 ***4629.10*** *p57*
Wife: Jane
Smith, John; Philadelphia, 1789 ***4629.10*** *p58*
Wife: Mary
Smith, John; Philadelphia, 1802 ***6058.10*** *p7*
Smith, John; Philadelphia, 1856 ***1224.3*** *p72*
Smith, John; Vermont, n.d. ***5900.10*** *p180*
Smith, John; Vermont, 1822-1898 ***5900.10*** *p532*
Smith, John; Vermont, 1851-1929 ***5900.10*** *p533*
Smith, John; Virginia, 1663 ***6212.30*** *p1*
Smith, John; Virginia, 1663 ***6212.30*** *p4*
Smith, John; Virginia, 1664 ***6212.30*** *p13*
Smith, John; Virginia, 1664-1665 ***6212.30*** *p16*
Smith, John; Virginia, 1666-1667 ***6212.30*** *p33*
Smith, John; Virginia, 1667 ***6212.30*** *p37*
Smith, John; Virginia, 1698 ***6212.30*** *p60*
Smith, John 4 *SEE* Smith, John
Smith, John 16; Maryland, 1775 ***1220.25*** *p107*
Smith, John 17; Maryland, 1774 ***1220.25*** *p37*
Smith, John 18 *SEE* Smith, Nathaniel
Smith, John 21; Maryland, 1774 ***1220.25*** *p40*
Smith, John 21; Maryland, 1774 ***1220.25*** *p51*
Smith, John 21; Maryland, 1774 ***1220.25*** *p59*
Smith, John 21; Maryland, 1775 ***1220.25*** *p97*
Smith, John 22; Carolina, 1774 ***1220.25*** *p74*
Smith, John 22; Philadelphia, 1789 ***4629.10*** *p58*
Smith, John 22; Virginia, 1774 ***1220.25*** *p91*
Wife: Mary 22
Smith, John 23; Ontario, 1871 ***1823.28*** *p93*
Smith, John 24; Maryland, 1774 ***1220.25*** *p69*
Smith, John 26; Ontario, 1871 ***1823.15*** *p245*
Smith, John 26; Ontario, 1871 ***1823.28*** *p93*
Smith, John 27; Virginia, 1774 ***1220.25*** *p92*
Smith, John 28; Fort Cumberland, Nova Scotia, 1774 ***1220.25*** *p17*
Smith, John 28; Maryland, 1775 ***1220.25*** *p120*
Smith, John 29; Nova Scotia, 1774 ***1220.25*** *p13*
Wife: Mary 25
Child: William 1
Child: George 2
Child: John 4
Smith, John 29; Pensacola, Florida, 1774 ***1220.25*** *p2*
Smith, John 35; Ontario, 1871 ***1823.15*** *p245*
Smith, John 37; Ontario, 1871 ***1823.28*** *p93*
Smith, John 40; Grenada, 1774 ***1220.25*** *p128*
Smith, John 40; Ontario, 1871 ***1823.28*** *p93*
Smith, John 41; Ontario, 1871 ***1823.15*** *p245*
Smith, John 42; Maryland, 1774 ***1220.25*** *p41*
Smith, John 42; Maryland, 1775 ***1220.25*** *p115*
Smith, John 45; Ontario, 1871 ***1823.15*** *p245*
Smith, John 46; Ontario, 1871 ***1823.22*** *p148*
Smith, John 49; Ontario, 1871 ***1823.28*** *p93*
Smith, John 52; Ontario, 1871 ***1823.28*** *p93*
Smith, John 56; Ontario, 1871 ***1823.15*** *p245*
Smith, John 60; Ontario, 1871 ***1823.22*** *p148*
Smith, John 63; Ontario, 1871 ***1823.15*** *p245*
Smith, John 63; Ontario, 1871 ***1823.28*** *p93*
Smith, John 68; Ontario, 1871 ***1823.28*** *p93*
Smith, John 70; Ontario, 1871 ***1823.22*** *p148*
Smith, John, Jr. *SEE* Smith, John
Smith, John D.; New York, 1807 ***8197.10*** *p51*
Smith, John E. 33; Ontario, 1861 ***2896.25*** *p32*
Smith, John Edward; New York, 1855 ***1224.3*** *p60*
Smith, John F. 9; Ontario, 1861 ***2896.27*** *p41*
Smith, John J. 63; Ontario, 1861 ***2896.28*** *p54*
Smith, John Laxon; Louisiana, 1840 ***1224.3*** *p72*
Smith, John Malcolm; Ontario, 1856 ***1640.13*** *p115*
Smith, John Murray; America, 1870 ***1640.13*** *p116*
Smith, John N.; New York, 1824 ***8197.10*** *p297*
Smith, John N.; New York, 1840 ***8197.10*** *p198*
Smith, John Preston; New York, 1839 ***8197.10*** *p285*
Smith, John R. 7; Ontario, 1861 ***2896.27*** *p55*
Smith, John Ravenscraft; New York, 1828 ***8197.10*** *p350*
Smith, John T.; Vermont, 1845-1911 ***5900.10*** *p472*
Smith, John W.; New York, 1827 ***8197.10*** *p338*

Smith, Jonithan A. 5; Ontario, 1861 ***2896.27*** *p55*
Smith, Joseph; America, 1763 ***1224.2*** *p107*
Smith, Joseph; New York, 1825 ***8197.10*** *p281*
Smith, Joseph; New York, 1838 ***8197.10*** *p379*
Smith, Joseph; New York, New York, 1795 ***1224.2*** *p107*
Smith, Joseph; New York, New York, 1795 ***1224.3*** *p72*
Smith, Joseph 16; Philadelphia, 1774 ***1220.25*** *p67*
Smith, Joseph 20; Virginia, 1774 ***1220.25*** *p74*
Smith, Joseph 24; Virginia, 1774 ***1220.25*** *p87*
Smith, Joseph 31; Maryland, 1774 ***1220.25*** *p64*
Smith, Joseph 32; Ontario, 1871 ***1823.28*** *p93*
Smith, Joseph 35; Ontario, 1871 ***1823.28*** *p93*
Smith, Joseph 60; Ontario, 1871 ***1823.28*** *p93*
Smith, Joseph H.; Vermont, 1813-1895 ***5900.10*** *p499*
Smith, Joseph Harris; New Orleans, 1850 ***1640.10*** *p189*
Smith, Joshua; Virginia, 1663 ***6212.30*** *p4*
Smith, Judith; New England, 1650 ***1224.1*** *p55*
Smith, Judson D. 63; Vermont, 1906 ***5900.10*** *p456*
Smith, Julia; Vermont, 1863-1948 ***5900.10*** *p333*
Smith, Julia E.; Vermont, 1840-1889 ***5900.10*** *p545*
Smith, Julia Ryan; Vermont, 1831-1884 ***5900.10*** *p290*
Smith, Kate; Vermont, 1853-1877 ***5900.10*** *p544*
Smith, Katherine *SEE* Smith, William
Smith, Katherine L. Finnegan; Vermont, 1858-1888 ***5900.10*** *p290*
Smith, Kenneth *SEE* Smith, Malcolm
Smith, Kenneth; Ontario, 1863 ***4537.32*** *p93*
Child: Kirsty
Child: David
Child: Isabella
Child: Catherine
Child: John
Wife: Ann MacKay
Child: Ann
Smith, Kenneth 24; Ontario, 1871 ***1823.15*** *p245*
Smith, Kenneth 42; Ontario, 1871 ***1823.15*** *p245*
Smith, Kirsty *SEE* Smith, Alexander
Smith, Kirsty *SEE* Smith, Kenneth
Smith, Kirsty *SEE* Smith, Malcolm
Smith, Kirsty; Ontario, 1851 ***4537.32*** *p44*
Smith, Kirsty Campbell *SEE* Smith, Neil
Smith, Kirsty MacDonald *SEE* Smith, Norman
Smith, Kirsty MacKenzie; Ontario, 1855 ***4537.32*** *p92*
Child: Alexander
Child: Malcolm
Child: Mary
Child: Catherine
Child: John
Smith, L.; Quebec, 1857 ***9196.15*** *p24*
Smith, Linda S.; Vermont, 1870-1926 ***5900.10*** *p326*
Smith, Livingston; South Carolina, 1831 ***1640.13*** *p116*
Smith, Lizzie 25; Kansas, 1906-1910 ***9079.10*** *p40*
Smith, Lot 45; Ontario, 1861 ***2896.27*** *p6*
Smith, Lucy S. 17; Ontario, 1861 ***2896.25*** *p38*
Smith, Luis 27; Ontario, 1861 ***2896.25*** *p62*
Smith, Luther 1; Ontario, 1861 ***2896.25*** *p60*
Smith, Lyman 9; Ontario, 1861 ***2896.28*** *p30*
Smith, Lyman 70; Ontario, 1861 ***2896.28*** *p30*
Smith, Lynoretta 12; Ontario, 1861 ***2896.28*** *p30*
Smith, M.; Portland, Maine, 1858 ***9196.15*** *p30*
Smith, M. 11; Ontario, 1861 ***2896.28*** *p12*
Smith, M. 18; Ontario, 1861 ***2896.28*** *p13*
Smith, M. A. 35; Ontario, 1861 ***2896.27*** *p2*
Smith, M. E. 24; Ontario, 1861 ***2896.28*** *p12*
Smith, Malcolm *SEE* Smith, Angus
Smith, Malcolm *SEE* Smith, John
Smith, Malcolm *SEE* Smith, Kirsty MacKenzie
Smith, Malcolm *SEE* Smith, Malcolm
Smith, Malcolm; Ontario, 1855 ***4537.32*** *p93*
Wife: Ann MacAulay
Child: Marion
Child: Kenneth
Child: Donald
Child: Malcolm
Child: Ann
Child: Kirsty
Smith, Malcolm; Ontario, 1855 ***4537.32*** *p94*
Wife: Ann
Child: Marion
Smith, Malcolm; Ontario, 1855 ***4537.32*** *p94*
Wife: Margaret MacIver
Child: Donald
Child: Malcolm
Child: Norman
Child: John
Smith, Malcolm 34; Ontario, 1871 ***1823.28*** *p93*
Smith, Malcolm 52; Ontario, 1871 ***1823.15*** *p245*
Smith, Malcolm 61; Ontario, 1871 ***1823.15*** *p245*
Smith, Margaret *SEE* Smith, Alexander
Smith, Margaret; New York, 1876 ***1640.13*** *p116*
Smith, Margaret; Ontario, 1851 ***4537.32*** *p91*
Smith, Margaret; Ontario, 1855 ***4537.32*** *p59*
Smith, Margaret; Vermont, 1849-1921 ***5900.10*** *p563*
Smith, Margaret 18; Ontario, 1871 ***1823.15*** *p246*
Smith, Margaret 22; Philadelphia, 1774 ***1220.25*** *p42*
Smith, Margaret A.; Vermont, 1845-1918 ***5900.10*** *p545*
Smith, Margaret M. Harris; Vermont, 1855-1917 ***5900.10*** *p334*
Smith, Margaret MacEachan *SEE* Smith, Alexander
Smith, Margaret MacIver *SEE* Smith, Malcolm
Smith, Margarett; Maryland, 1681 ***2524.55*** *p203*
Smith, Margery; Virginia, 1667 ***6212.30*** *p37*
Smith, Margret; Virginia, 1667 ***6212.30*** *p37*
Smith, Margret; Virginia, 1667-1668 ***6212.30*** *p38*
Smith, Margt 27; Ontario, 1871 ***1823.15*** *p246*
Smith, Marguerite; Vermont, 1782-1863 ***5900.10*** *p329*
Smith, Marguerite Nadon; Vermont, 1849-1928 ***5900.10*** *p71*
Smith, Marion *SEE* Smith, Angus
Smith, Marion *SEE* Smith, Malcolm
Smith, Marion *SEE* Smith, Norman
Smith, Marion; Ontario, 1855 ***4537.32*** *p51*
Smith, Marks; America, 1738 ***2856.30*** *p432*
Smith, Martha *SEE* Smith, John
Smith, Martha; Chicago, 1847 ***1224.3*** *p72*
Smith, Martha 15; Maryland, 1775 ***1220.25*** *p98*
Smith, Martin; New York, 1831 ***8197.10*** *p283*
Smith, Martin F.; Maryland, 1910 ***3259.35*** *p57*
Smith, Mary *SEE* Smith, Alexander
Smith, Mary *SEE* Smith, Angus
Smith, Mary *SEE* Smith, John
Smith, Mary *SEE* Smith, Kirsty MacKenzie
Smith, Mary; Alabama, 1844-1845 ***1640.10*** *p189*
Smith, Mary; Maryland, 1657 ***2524.55*** *p204*
Smith, Mary; Maryland, 1679 ***2524.55*** *p204*
Smith, Mary; New England, 1682 ***1224.1*** *p53*
Smith, Mary; Ontario, 1863 ***4537.32*** *p8*
Smith, Mary; Ontario, 1863 ***4537.32*** *p42*
Smith, Mary; Vermont, 1839-1906 ***5900.10*** *p486*
Smith, Mary; Vermont, 1847-1875 ***5900.10*** *p536*
Smith, Mary; Vermont, 1847-1908 ***5900.10*** *p290*
Smith, Mary; Vermont, 1851-1896 ***5900.10*** *p193*
Smith, Mary; Vermont, 1852-1911 ***5900.10*** *p318*
Smith, Mary; Vermont, 1853-1884 ***5900.10*** *p533*
Smith, Mary; Vermont, 1858-1942 ***5900.10*** *p490*
Smith, Mary 7; Ontario, 1861 ***2896.25*** *p60*
Smith, Mary 22 *SEE* Smith, John
Smith, Mary 25 *SEE* Smith, John
Smith, Mary 25; Maryland, 1775 ***1220.25*** *p20*
Smith, Mary 26; Fort Cumberland, Nova Scotia, 1774 ***1220.25*** *p17*
Smith, Mary 26; Ontario, 1861 ***2896.25*** *p32*
Smith, Mary 35; Ontario, 1871 ***1823.15*** *p246*
Smith, Mary 48; Ontario, 1871 ***1823.22*** *p148*
Smith, Mary 51; Ontario, 1871 ***1823.15*** *p246*
Smith, Mary A.; Vermont, 1857-1940 ***5900.10*** *p442*
Smith, Mary A.; Vermont, 1861-1944 ***5900.10*** *p292*
Smith, Mary Bresnehan; Vermont, 1845-1923 ***5900.10*** *p609*
Smith, Mary Dryden; Ontario, 1871 ***1640.13*** *p116*
Smith, Mary E.; Vermont, n.d. ***5900.10*** *p180*
Smith, Mary E. 4; Ontario, 1861 ***2896.27*** *p41*
Smith, Mary H.; Vermont, 1833-1921 ***5900.10*** *p442*
Smith, Mary M. Erwin 28; Vermont, 1875 ***5900.10*** *p456*
Smith, Mary MacAulay *SEE* Smith, Donald
Smith, Mary Mack; Vermont, 1840-1912 ***5900.10*** *p316*
Smith, Mary MacRitchie *SEE* Smith, Angus
Smith, Mary Maria; New York, New York, 1847 ***1224.3*** *p75*
Smith, Mary McElroy; Vermont, 1821-1911 ***5900.10*** *p532*
Smith, Mary Moynihan; Vermont, 1854-1917 ***5900.10*** *p129*
Smith, Mary Power; Vermont, 1852-1939 ***5900.10*** *p310*
Smith, Mathew; Maryland, 1658 ***2524.55*** *p204*
Smith, Mathew; Maryland, 1671 ***2524.55*** *p204*
Smith, Mathew; Maryland, 1673 ***2524.55*** *p204*
Smith, Mathew; Maryland, 1676 ***2524.55*** *p204*
Smith, Mathew 46; Ontario, 1871 ***1823.15*** *p246*
Smith, Mathias; Maryland, 1663 ***2524.55*** *p204*
Smith, Matthew; Carolina, 1771 ***1640.13*** *p116*
Smith, Matthew; Maryland, 1658 ***2524.55*** *p218*
Smith, Michael; Louisiana, 1801 ***1640.10*** *p189*
Smith, Michael; Vermont, 1857-1900 ***5900.10*** *p289*
Smith, Michael J.; Vermont, 1853-1917 ***5900.10*** *p464*
Smith, Micheal 40; Ontario, 1871 ***1823.15*** *p246*
Smith, Mike 22; British Columbia, 1910 ***9196.1*** *p29*
Smith, Mike 22; Seattle, 1910 ***9196.1*** *p29*
Smith, Murdo *SEE* Smith, Donald
Smith, Murdo *SEE* Smith, John
Smith, Murdo *SEE* Smith, Norman
Smith, N. 30; Ontario, 1861 ***2896.28*** *p12*
Smith, N. J. 6; Ontario, 1861 ***2896.25*** *p36*
Smith, Nancy 37; Ontario, 1861 ***2896.25*** *p60*
Smith, Nathaniel; New York, 1803 ***8197.10*** *p16*
Smith, Nathaniel 22 *SEE* Smith, Nathaniel
Smith, Nathaniel 52; Fort Cumberland, Nova Scotia, 1774 ***1220.25*** *p15*
Wife: Elizabeth 52
Child: Nathaniel 22
Child: John 18
Child: Robert 9
Child: Rachael 22
Child: Elizabeth 7
Smith, Neil; Ontario, 1855 ***4537.32*** *p94*
Wife: Kirsty Campbell
Child: Allan
Child: John
Child: Angus
Child: Jane
Child: Catherine
Child: Donald
Child: Alexander
Smith, Neil 32; Ontario, 1871 ***1823.15*** *p246*
Smith, Nicholas; Vermont, 1833-1903 ***5900.10*** *p143*
Smith, Nicholas; Vermont, 1861-1962 ***5900.10*** *p533*
Smith, Nicholas; Virginia, 1710 ***1224.2*** *p107*
Smith, Nicholas Winter; New York, 1820 ***8197.10*** *p278*
Smith, Norman *SEE* Smith, Malcolm
Smith, Norman; Ontario, 1851 ***4537.32*** *p94*
Wife: Kirsty MacDonald
Child: Catherine
Child: Angus
Child: Marion
Child: Ann
Child: Murdo
Smith, Norman 35; Ontario, 1871 ***1823.15*** *p246*
Smith, Norman 36; Ontario, 1871 ***1823.15*** *p246*
Smith, Norman W.; Vermont, 1822-1899 ***5900.10*** *p598*
Smith, Olive; Maryland, 1682 ***2524.55*** *p204*
Smith, Oliver; Virginia, 1686 ***1224.1*** *p53*
Smith, Oliver 62; Ontario, 1871 ***1823.15*** *p246*
Smith, Owen; New York, 1827 ***8197.10*** *p338*
Smith, Owen 40; Ontario, 1871 ***1823.15*** *p246*
Smith, Patrick; New York, 1837 ***8197.10*** *p106*
Smith, Patrick; Vermont, 1828-1876 ***5900.10*** *p442*
Smith, Patrick; Vermont, 1868-1889 ***5900.10*** *p544*
Smith, Paul 14; Ontario, 1861 ***2896.27*** *p66*
Smith, Paul 15; Ontario, 1861 ***2896.27*** *p42*
Smith, Perley J.; Vermont, 1891 ***5900.10*** *p323*
Smith, Peter; Maryland, 1682 ***2524.55*** *p204*
Smith, Peter; New York, 1837 ***8197.10*** *p107*
Smith, Peter; Vermont, n.d. ***5900.10*** *p180*
Smith, Peter 34; Ontario, 1871 ***1823.22*** *p149*
Smith, Peter 45; Ontario, 1871 ***1823.22*** *p149*
Smith, Peter J.; Vermont, 1857-1942 ***5900.10*** *p323*
Smith, Phebe; Virginia, 1676 ***1224.1*** *p54*
Smith, Philip; New York, 1837 ***8197.10*** *p107*
Smith, Philip; Vermont, 1823-1901 ***5900.10*** *p544*
Smith, Phillip; Virginia, 1664 ***6212.30*** *p6*
Smith, R. C.; Quebec, 1857 ***9196.15*** *p25*
Smith, Rachael 22 *SEE* Smith, Nathaniel
Smith, Randall; Maryland, 1650 ***2524.55*** *p204*
Smith, Rebecca *SEE* Smith, John
Smith, Rich; Virginia, 1677 ***6212.30*** *p54*
Smith, Richard; Maryland, 1649 ***2524.55*** *p204*
Smith, Richard; Maryland, 1669 ***2524.55*** *p204*
Smith, Richard; Virginia, 1680 ***1224.1*** *p54*
Smith, Richard; Virginia, 1804 ***1224.3*** *p72*
Smith, Richard 13; Ontario, 1861 ***2896.25*** *p54*
Smith, Richard 34; Ontario, 1871 ***1823.22*** *p149*
Smith, Richard 65; Ontario, 1871 ***1823.15*** *p246*
Smith, Robert; America, 1756 ***1224.2*** *p107*
Smith, Robert; Jamaica, 1778 ***1224.2*** *p107*
Smith, Robert; Maryland, 1649 ***2524.55*** *p204*
Smith, Robert; Maryland, 1658 ***2524.55*** *p204*
Smith, Robert; Maryland, 1666 ***2524.55*** *p204*
Wife: Rose
Daughter: Elizabeth
Smith, Robert; Maryland, 1671 ***2524.55*** *p204*
Smith, Robert; Maryland, 1674 ***2524.55*** *p204*
Smith, Robert; Maryland, 1680 ***2524.55*** *p204*
Smith, Robert; Maryland, 1707 ***1224.2*** *p107*
Smith, Robert; New York, 1821 ***8197.10*** *p279*
Smith, Robert; Pennsylvania, 1777 ***4629.10*** *p7*
Smith, Robert; Savannah, Georgia, 1778 ***1224.2*** *p107*
Smith, Robert; South Carolina, 1842 ***1224.3*** *p72*
Smith, Robert; Virginia, 1665-1666 ***6212.30*** *p24*
Smith, Robert; Virginia, 1690-1691 ***6212.30*** *p59*
Smith, Robert 5; Ontario, 1861 ***2896.28*** *p30*
Smith, Robert 9 *SEE* Smith, Nathaniel
Smith, Robert 20; Virginia, 1774 ***1220.25*** *p140*
Smith, Robert 24; Baltimore, 1775 ***1220.25*** *p117*
Smith, Robert 31; Ontario, 1871 ***1823.15*** *p246*
Smith, Robert 33; Ontario, 1871 ***1823.15*** *p246*
Smith, Robert 33; Ontario, 1871 ***1823.22*** *p149*
Smith, Robert 34; Ontario, 1871 ***1823.22*** *p149*
Smith, Robert 44; Ontario, 1871 ***1823.22*** *p149*
Smith, Robert 55; Ontario, 1871 ***1823.15*** *p246*

Smyth, Allice; Maryland, 1658 ***2524.55*** *p205*
Smyth, Allice; Maryland, 1659 ***2524.55*** *p201*
Smyth, Ann; Maryland, 1659 ***2524.55*** *p205*
Smyth, Hannah *SEE* Smyth, Peter
Smyth, James *SEE* Smyth, Peter
Smyth, James; Carolina, 1791 ***1224.2*** *p106*
Smyth, John; New York, 1807 ***8197.10*** *p277*
Smyth, John; Philadelphia, 1794 ***4629.10*** *p81*
Smyth, Mary *SEE* Smyth, William
Smyth, Paul; New York, 1840 ***8197.10*** *p195*
Smyth, Peter *SEE* Smyth, Peter
Smyth, Peter; America, 1757 ***1224.2*** *p107*
Smyth, Peter; Maryland, 1660 ***2524.55*** *p205*
Wife: Hannah
Child: Robert
Child: James
Child: Peter
Smyth, Robert *SEE* Smyth, Peter
Smyth, Robert 60; Ontario, 1871 ***1823.15*** *p247*
Smyth, Samuel 29; Ontario, 1871 ***1823.28*** *p94*
Smyth, Sarah; North America, 1791 ***1224.2*** *p107*
Smyth, William; Maryland, 1663 ***2524.55*** *p205*
Wife: Mary
Smyth, William 45; Ontario, 1871 ***1823.28*** *p94*
Smyth, William James; Illinois, 1870 ***1640.13*** *p116*
Smythe, Samuel; Baltimore, n.d. ***1224.3*** *p73*
Smythies, William; New York, New York, 1785 ***1224.2*** *p107*
Snacks, Thomas 32; Ontario, 1871 ***1823.15*** *p247*
Snagg, William; Virginia, 1665 ***6212.30*** *p19*
Snail, Elizabeth; Maryland, 1666 ***2524.55*** *p205*
Snaith, Isaac; New York, New York, 1818 ***8197.10*** *p196*
Snale, Elizabeth; Maryland, 1666 ***2524.55*** *p205*
Snape, Robert 38; Virginia, 1774 ***1220.25*** *p92*
Snape, Timothy; Died enroute, 1629 ***1224.1*** *p54*
Snasdell, Christopher; Maryland, 1663 ***2524.55*** *p205*
Snayle, Elizabeth; Maryland, 1672 ***2524.55*** *p205*
Snead, Charles; Virginia, 1709 ***6212.30*** *p63*
Snead, Elizabeth; Virginia, 1709 ***6212.30*** *p63*
Snead, Frances; Virginia, 1709 ***6212.30*** *p63*
Snead, Henry 21; Maryland, 1774 ***1220.25*** *p71*
Snead, James; Virginia, 1709 ***6212.30*** *p63*
Snead, Robert; Virginia, 1709 ***6212.30*** *p63*
Snead, Robert, Jr.; Virginia, 1709 ***6212.30*** *p63*
Snead, William 18; Philadelphia, 1775 ***1220.25*** *p8*
Sneadon, Cuthbert; Maryland, 1682 ***2524.55*** *p205*
Sneath, Jacob; New York, 1785 ***1224.2*** *p107*
Sneath, John; New York, 1828 ***8197.10*** *p282*
Sneciak, Walenty; Maryland, 1910 ***3259.35*** *p57*
Sneddon, James; New York, 1851 ***1640.10*** *p189*
Sneddon, Jane *SEE* Sneddon, William
Sneddon, William; Alabama, 1824-1848 ***1640.10*** *p189*
Wife: Jane
Sneder, John; Pennsylvania, 1777 ***4629.10*** *p7*
Sneider, Jacob; New York, 1834 ***8197.10*** *p373*
Sneider, John 21; Kansas, 1910 ***9079.10*** *p52*
Sneidmiller, John 13; Kansas, 1910 ***9079.10*** *p44*
Sneidmiller, John 40; Kansas, 1902-1910 ***9079.10*** *p44*
Sneidmiller, Kate 37; Kansas, 1910 ***9079.10*** *p44*
Sneidmiller, Liddia 10; Kansas, 1910 ***9079.10*** *p44*
Sneidmiller, Lizzie 12; Kansas, 1910 ***9079.10*** *p44*
Sneigowska, Henry; Maryland, 1910 ***3259.35*** *p57*
Snelgrove, John S. 40; Ontario, 1871 ***1823.22*** *p149*
Snell, Mr.; Quebec, 1857 ***9196.15*** *p15*
Snell, Catherine; South Carolina, 1743 ***1224.2*** *p107*
Snell, Elizabeth 1 *SEE* Snell, Major
Snell, Elizabeth 24; New York, 1774 ***1220.25*** *p24*
Snell, Elon 42; Ontario, 1871 ***1823.15*** *p247*
Snell, Ephraim 45; Ontario, 1871 ***1823.15*** *p247*
Snell, George 47; Ontario, 1871 ***1823.15*** *p247*
Snell, George 70; Ontario, 1871 ***1823.15*** *p247*
Snell, Humphrey 49; Ontario, 1871 ***1823.15*** *p247*
Snell, James 35; Ontario, 1871 ***1823.22*** *p149*
Snell, James 51; Ontario, 1871 ***1823.15*** *p247*
Snell, James 55; Ontario, 1871 ***1823.15*** *p247*
Snell, John; Maryland, 1669 ***2524.55*** *p205*
Snell, John; Maryland, 1669 ***2524.55*** *p209*
Snell, John 33; Ontario, 1871 ***1823.15*** *p247*
Snell, John 50; Ontario, 1871 ***1823.15*** *p247*
Snell, Major 36; New York, 1774 ***1220.25*** *p24*
Child: Elizabeth 1
Snell, Margarett; Maryland, 1675 ***2524.55*** *p205*
Snell, Richard 16; Philadelphia, 1774 ***1220.25*** *p4*
Snell, William; San Antonio, Texas, 1876 ***1640.13*** *p116*
Snell, William 40; Ontario, 1871 ***1823.15*** *p247*
Snell, William 42; Ontario, 1871 ***1823.15*** *p247*
Snell, William 45; Ontario, 1871 ***1823.15*** *p247*
Snell, William 45; Ontario, 1871 ***1823.22*** *p149*
Snell, William 46; Ontario, 1871 ***1823.15*** *p247*
Snell, Wm 40; Ontario, 1871 ***1823.28*** *p94*
Snellick, Wm.; Maryland, 1667 ***2524.55*** *p205*
Snelling, Mr.; Quebec, 1857 ***9196.15*** *p22*
Snelling, Israel; Maryland, 1681 ***2524.55*** *p205*
Sneyd, Jane 57; Ontario, 1871 ***1823.15*** *p247*
Snidely, Fredrick 34; Ontario, 1871 ***1823.28*** *p94*
Snider, Alletta 32; Ontario, 1861 ***2896.25*** *p2*
Snider, Ann Jane; Vermont, 1830-1910 ***5900.10*** *p603*
Snider, Anna 14; Ontario, 1861 ***2896.25*** *p56*
Snider, Charles 36; Ontario, 1871 ***1823.28*** *p94*
Snider, David 44; Ontario, 1871 ***1823.28*** *p94*
Snider, David 47; Ontario, 1861 ***2896.25*** *p56*
Snider, Debrah 58; Ontario, 1861 ***2896.25*** *p35*
Snider, Elizabeth 49; Ontario, 1861 ***2896.25*** *p56*
Snider, Emilia A. 10; Ontario, 1861 ***2896.25*** *p2*
Snider, G. 7; Ontario, 1861 ***2896.25*** *p28*
Snider, George; Pennsylvania, 1779 ***4629.10*** *p41*
Snider, George 32; Ontario, 1861 ***2896.25*** *p34*
Snider, Georgina 4; Ontario, 1861 ***2896.27*** *p7*
Snider, H. M. 11; Ontario, 1861 ***2896.25*** *p34*
Snider, Hellen 7; Ontario, 1861 ***2896.25*** *p56*
Snider, Henry 33; Ontario, 1861 ***2896.25*** *p2*
Snider, Henryetta 2; Ontario, 1861 ***2896.25*** *p30*
Snider, Hirum 20; Ontario, 1861 ***2896.25*** *p56*
Snider, J. A. 16; Ontario, 1861 ***2896.25*** *p34*
Snider, Jerusha 18; Ontario, 1861 ***2896.25*** *p35*
Snider, John 15; Ontario, 1861 ***2896.27*** *p10*
Snider, John 21; Ontario, 1861 ***2896.25*** *p35*
Snider, John 21; Ontario, 1861 ***2896.25*** *p56*
Snider, L. A. 8; Ontario, 1861 ***2896.25*** *p34*
Snider, M. S. 14; Ontario, 1861 ***2896.25*** *p34*
Snider, Maran 13; Ontario, 1861 ***2896.27*** *p10*
Snider, Maranda 19; Ontario, 1861 ***2896.25*** *p56*
Snider, Maria; Ontario, 1861 ***2896.28*** *p41*
Snider, Maria 27; Ontario, 1861 ***2896.25*** *p7*
Snider, Mary A. 28; Ontario, 1861 ***2896.25*** *p30*
Snider, Mary E. 5; Ontario, 1861 ***2896.25*** *p2*
Snider, Mary E. 11; Ontario, 1861 ***2896.25*** *p56*
Snider, Peter; Pennsylvania, 1777 ***4629.10*** *p10*
Snider, Randolph 38; Ontario, 1871 ***1823.28*** *p94*
Snider, Sarah 43; Ontario, 1861 ***2896.25*** *p34*
Snider, Sarah E. 2; Ontario, 1861 ***2896.25*** *p2*
Snider, Sarah S. 18; Ontario, 1861 ***2896.25*** *p35*
Snider, Silva 23; Ontario, 1861 ***2896.25*** *p56*
Snider, Susan G. 9; Ontario, 1861 ***2896.25*** *p56*
Snider, Willet 23; Ontario, 1861 ***2896.25*** *p35*
Snider, William; Ontario, 1861 ***2896.28*** *p41*
Snider, William F. 2; Ontario, 1861 ***2896.25*** *p7*
Sniegowski, Charles; Maryland, 1910 ***3259.35*** *p57*
Snip, John; New York, 1818 ***8197.10*** *p278*
Snodden, Stewart 71; Ontario, 1871 ***1823.28*** *p94*
Snodgrass, Mrs.; Quebec, 1856 ***9196.15*** *p8*
Snodgrass, Rev.; Quebec, 1856 ***9196.15*** *p8*
Snodgrass, Alexander 40; Ontario, 1871 ***1823.22*** *p150*
Snodgrass, John 56; Ontario, 1871 ***1823.22*** *p150*
Snodgrass, Neal; Norfolk, Virginia, 1785 ***1224.2*** *p107*
Snodgrass, Neil; Virginia, 1782 ***1640.13*** *p116*
Snook, James; New York, 1821 ***8197.10*** *p280*
Snook, John; New York, 1819 ***8197.10*** *p278*
Snook, Joseph 26; Maryland, 1774 ***1220.25*** *p57*
Snooks, Martin 50; Ontario, 1871 ***1823.15*** *p247*
Snow, Alexander; Vermont, 1835-1904 ***5900.10*** *p301*
Snow, Bridget; Vermont, 1835-1914 ***5900.10*** *p301*
Snow, Edward E.; Vermont, 1840-1908 ***5900.10*** *p142*
Snow, Ellen; Vermont, 1844-1911 ***5900.10*** *p142*
Snow, Frank; Vermont, 1848-1934 ***5900.10*** *p299*
Snow, John 46; Maryland, 1774 ***1220.25*** *p52*
Snow, John 48; Ontario, 1871 ***1823.22*** *p150*
Snow, John 57; Ontario, 1871 ***1823.15*** *p247*
Snow, Lucy McMahon; Vermont, 1858-1940 ***5900.10*** *p299*
Snow, Marmaduke; Maryland, 1638 ***2524.55*** *p205*
Snow, Mary Finnisey 47; Vermont, 1889 ***5900.10*** *p142*
Snow, Mary McEnany; Vermont, 1845-1925 ***5900.10*** *p307*
Snow, Melcas Kelway; New England, 1651 ***1224.1*** *p34*
Snow, Richard; Virginia, 1664 ***6212.30*** *p7*
Snow, Robert; New York, 1794 ***8197.10*** *p2*
Snow, Valentine; Maryland, 1659 ***2524.55*** *p205*
Snow, William; New York, 1794 ***8197.10*** *p2*
Snow, William; Virginia, 1667 ***6212.30*** *p35*
Snowden, Barnard 54; Ontario, 1871 ***1823.15*** *p247*
Snowden, Edward 50; Ontario, 1871 ***1823.15*** *p247*
Snowden, Isaac; Pennsylvania, 1779 ***4629.10*** *p35*
Snowden, Pickering 23; Nova Scotia, 1774 ***1220.25*** *p15*
Snowden, Ralph 19; New York, 1774 ***1220.25*** *p24*
Snowden, Robert 60; Ontario, 1871 ***1823.15*** *p247*
Snowe, Thomas; Maryland, 1653 ***2524.55*** *p205*
Snowton, Robt; Virginia, 1664 ***6212.30*** *p15*
Snuvre, William 22; Maryland, 1775 ***1220.25*** *p99*
Snyder, Frederick; New York, 1840 ***8197.10*** *p197*
Snyder, George; Pennsylvania, 1840 ***6058.10*** *p16*
Snyder, Jacob; New York, 1807 ***8197.10*** *p331*
Snyder, John; Pennsylvania, 1777 ***4629.10*** *p28*
Snyder, Joseph; New York, 1821 ***8197.10*** *p280*
Snyder, Joseph; Pennsylvania, 1836 ***6058.10*** *p14*
Snyder, Philip; Pennsylvania, 1781 ***4629.10*** *p42*
Soanes, Anne 78; Ontario, 1871 ***1823.15*** *p247*
Sobezak, Martin; Maryland, 1910 ***3259.35*** *p57*
Sobieski, Louis; Maryland, 1910 ***3259.35*** *p57*
Sobiloska, Dominic; Maryland, 1910 ***3259.35*** *p58*
Sobolewski, Frank; Maryland, 1910 ***3259.35*** *p58*
Sobolewski, John; Maryland, 1910 ***3259.35*** *p58*
Sobotka, Antonina; Maryland, 1910 ***3259.35*** *p58*
Sobousnski, Josef; Maryland, 1910 ***3259.35*** *p58*
Soboz, George; Maryland, 1910 ***3259.35*** *p58*
Sobus, Frank; Maryland, 1910 ***3259.35*** *p58*
Sobus, Peter; Maryland, 1910 ***3259.35*** *p58*
Sobusz, Leon; Maryland, 1910 ***3259.35*** *p58*
Sobusz, Michael; Maryland, 1910 ***3259.35*** *p58*
Socha, Joseph; Maryland, 1910 ***3259.35*** *p58*
Socki, Antonie; Maryland, 1910 ***3259.35*** *p58*
Soder, Nikolaus; America, 1743 ***2856.30*** *p432*
Sodij, Valentin; Port uncertain, 1734 ***2856.30*** *p432*
Soduskey, Mathias 45; Ontario, 1871 ***1823.28*** *p94*
Soffel, Maria Barbara; America, 1764 ***2856.30*** *p432*
With husband
Sofnoka, Michael; Maryland, 1910 ***3259.35*** *p58*
Softley, Edward 71; Ontario, 1871 ***1823.15*** *p247*
Soher, J. 37; Alaska, 1913 ***9196.1*** *p39*
Soher, J. 37; Yukon, 1913 ***9196.1*** *p39*
Sohl, Franz; America, 1749 ***2856.30*** *p432*
Sohl, Henrich; Port uncertain, 1738 ***2856.30*** *p432*
Sohl, Henry 55; Ontario, 1871 ***1823.15*** *p247*
Sohling, Johann; Port uncertain, 1772 ***2856.30*** *p432*
Sohn, Franz Karl; Port uncertain, 1791 ***2856.30*** *p432*
Sohne, Andreas; Port uncertain, 1778 ***2856.30*** *p432*
Sohns, Daniel; Port uncertain, 1746 ***2856.30*** *p432*
Sohns, Johann Daniel; America, 1746 ***2856.30*** *p432*
With wife
Sohns, Philipp Nickhel; Port uncertain, 1746 ***2856.30*** *p432*
Sohr, Josef; Port uncertain, 1691 ***2856.30*** *p432*
Sohr, Josef; Port uncertain, 1721 ***2856.30*** *p432*
Sohu, J. 37; Alaska, 1913 ***9196.1*** *p39*
Sohu, J. 37; Yukon, 1913 ***9196.1*** *p39*
Sojka, Joseph; Maryland, 1910 ***3259.35*** *p58*
Sojka, Stanislaw; Maryland, 1910 ***3259.35*** *p58*
Sokewski, Stanislaw; Maryland, 1910 ***3259.35*** *p58*
Soldan, Conrad 59; Ontario, 1871 ***1823.15*** *p247*
Soldan, Henry 55; Ontario, 1871 ***1823.15*** *p247*
Soldner, John; New York, 1840 ***8197.10*** *p195*
Sole, John 17; Virginia, 1774 ***1220.25*** *p55*
Sole, John T.; New York, 1835 ***8197.10*** *p283*
Soler, George 37; Ontario, 1871 ***1823.15*** *p247*
Soles, C. 18; Ontario, 1861 ***2896.28*** *p4*
Soley, Henry 27; Philadelphia, 1774 ***1220.25*** *p35*
Solinski, Joseph; Maryland, 1910 ***3259.35*** *p58*
Soliskie, Hypolyt; Maryland, 1910 ***3259.35*** *p58*
Soliskey, Joseph; Maryland, 1910 ***3259.35*** *p58*
Solkeild, William; Maryland, 1664 ***2524.55*** *p205*
Solkowsky, Michael; Maryland, 1910 ***3259.35*** *p58*
Sollicoffre, John 17; Philadelphia, 1774 ***1220.25*** *p79*
Solme, Peter; Virginia, 1663 ***6212.30*** *p4*
Solme, Peter; Virginia, 1666-1667 ***6212.30*** *p34*
Solmons, Ralph; Maryland, 1655 ***2524.55*** *p175*
Soloman, George 75; Ontario, 1871 ***1823.15*** *p247*
Soloman, Jesse 16; Ontario, 1871 ***1823.28*** *p94*
Solomon, Catherine E.; Vermont, 1868-1944 ***5900.10*** *p607*
Solomon, Daniel B.; New York, 1840 ***8197.10*** *p195*
Solomon, Hannah Driscoll; Vermont, 1832-1924 ***5900.10*** *p607*
Solomon, Heym; Pennsylvania, 1777 ***4629.10*** *p28*
Solomon, James 53; Ontario, 1871 ***1823.28*** *p94*
Solomon, John L.; Vermont, 1830-1908 ***5900.10*** *p607*
Solomon, Joseph 35; Ontario, 1871 ***1823.28*** *p94*
Solomon, S.; Ontario, 1861 ***2896.25*** *p13*
Solomon, Solomon B.; New York, 1830 ***8197.10*** *p360*
Solomons, Solomon; Pennsylvania, 1777 ***4629.10*** *p30*
Solomons, Solomon; Savannah, Georgia, 1770 ***1224.2*** *p108*
Solter, John; Pennsylvania, 1777 ***4629.10*** *p25*
Soltys, Henry; Maryland, 1910 ***3259.35*** *p58*
Soltzsiak, Anastza; Maryland, 1910 ***3259.35*** *p58*
Somer, Edward; Maryland, 1665 ***2524.55*** *p61*
Somerby, . . .; Portland, Maine, 1858 ***9196.15*** *p29*
Somerby, Frances; Portland, Maine, 1858 ***9196.15*** *p29*
Somerby, Jane; Portland, Maine, 1858 ***9196.15*** *p29*
Somerby, Mary; Portland, Maine, 1858 ***9196.15*** *p29*
Somerby, Thomas; Portland, Maine, 1858 ***9196.15*** *p29*
Somerby, William; Portland, Maine, 1858 ***9196.15*** *p29*
Somerford, Jeffery; Maryland, 1667 ***2524.55*** *p205*
Somers, Charles; Virginia, 1702 ***1224.2*** *p108*
Somers, George; Died enroute, 1611 ***1224.1*** *p54*
Somers, John; Maryland, 1680 ***2524.55*** *p205*
Somers, John; Pennsylvania, 1786 ***4629.10*** *p50*
Somers, John; Virginia, 1672 ***1224.1*** *p54*
Somers, John 45; Ontario, 1871 ***1823.22*** *p150*
Somers, Mathew; Virginia, 1667-1668 ***6212.30*** *p38*

Spaid, Jacob; Pennsylvania, 1836 ***6058.10*** *p10*
Spain, Biddy 30; New York, New York, 1852 ***1825.45*** *p59*
Sister: Catherine 25
Spain, Catherine 25 *SEE* Spain, Biddy
Spak, Mark; Maryland, 1910 ***3259.35*** *p58*
Spalding, Franklin 31; Ontario, 1871 ***1823.22*** *p150*
Spalding, James; Florida, 1769 ***1640.10*** *p190*
Spalding, James; Georgia, 1760 ***1640.10*** *p190*
Spalding, John; Connecticut, 1764 ***1224.2*** *p108*
Spalding, John; Havana, 1764 ***1224.2*** *p108*
Spalding, Katherine; Maryland, 1674 ***2524.55*** *p206*
Spalsie, John; Georgia, 1699 ***1640.13*** *p116*
Spang, Adam; Port uncertain, 1788 ***2856.30*** *p433*
Spanger, Philipp; Port uncertain, 1791 ***2856.30*** *p433*
Spangle, Godfrey; Pennsylvania, 1777 ***4629.10*** *p15*
Spangler, George; Pennsylvania, 1777 ***4629.10*** *p8*
Spaniard, Jno; Virginia, 1668-1669 ***6212.30*** *p40*
Spannagel, Gabriel; Canada, 1752 ***2856.30*** *p433*
Spannagel, Ludwig; Canada, 1752 ***2856.30*** *p433*
Spannagel, Melchior; Port uncertain, 1764 ***2856.30*** *p433*
With family
Spannagel, Philipp; America, 1751 ***2856.30*** *p433*
Spaque, Obed 48; Ontario, 1871 ***1823.15*** *p249*
Spara, Frank; Maryland, 1910 ***3259.35*** *p58*
Sparham, Mr.; Portland, Maine, 1858 ***9196.15*** *p47*
Sparhawk, John; Pennsylvania, 1777 ***4629.10*** *p8*
Sparhawk, Susannah; New York, New York, 1800 ***1224.3*** *p73*
Sparhawke, . . .; New England, 1653 ***1224.1*** *p54*
Spark, Silvester 35; Alaska, 1908 ***9196.1*** *p36*
Spark, Silvester 35; Yukon, 1908 ***9196.1*** *p36*
Spark, William 13; Ontario, 1871 ***1823.28*** *p94*
Sparke, Jonathan; Virginia, 1666 ***6212.30*** *p31*
Sparke, Walter; Maryland, 1659 ***2524.55*** *p206*
Sparke, William; Maryland, 1662 ***2524.55*** *p206*
Sparkeman, Brazil; Maryland, 1681 ***2524.55*** *p206*
Sparkes, Arthur; Virginia, 1665-1666 ***6212.30*** *p21*
Sparkes, Edward; Maryland, 1682 ***2524.55*** *p206*
Sparkes, Jno; Virginia, 1663 ***6212.30*** *p4*
Sparkes, Tho.; Maryland, 1682 ***2524.55*** *p206*
Sparkes, William; Maryland, 1673 ***2524.55*** *p206*
Sparkes, William; New York, New York, 1821 ***1224.3*** *p73*
Sparks, Abraham 45; Ontario, 1871 ***1823.28*** *p94*
Sparks, Alex 48; Ontario, 1871 ***1823.15*** *p248*
Sparks, George 44; Ontario, 1871 ***1823.15*** *p248*
Sparks, James; Pennsylvania, 1777 ***4629.10*** *p22*
Sparks, James; Pennsylvania, 1779 ***4629.10*** *p40*
Sparks, James 22; Ontario, 1871 ***1823.15*** *p248*
Sparks, James 46; Ontario, 1871 ***1823.15*** *p248*
Sparks, Jno; Virginia, 1668-1669 ***6212.30*** *p40*
Sparks, John; New York, 1802 ***8197.10*** *p25*
Sparks, Richard; Pennsylvania, 1785 ***4629.10*** *p48*
Sparks, William; Maryland, 1662 ***2524.55*** *p206*
Sparling, Ann 55; Ontario, 1871 ***1823.15*** *p248*
Sparling, George 42; Ontario, 1871 ***1823.28*** *p94*
Sparling, Isabella 59; Ontario, 1871 ***1823.15*** *p248*
Sparling, James 51; Ontario, 1871 ***1823.15*** *p248*
Sparling, John 42; Ontario, 1871 ***1823.28*** *p94*
Sparling, John 63; Ontario, 1871 ***1823.15*** *p248*
Sparling, Joseph 37; Ontario, 1871 ***1823.28*** *p94*
Sparling, Joseph 57; Ontario, 1871 ***1823.15*** *p248*
Sparling, Philip 47; Ontario, 1871 ***1823.15*** *p249*
Sparling, Richard 29; Ontario, 1871 ***1823.15*** *p249*
Sparling, Richard 33; Ontario, 1871 ***1823.15*** *p249*
Sparling, Richard 54; Ontario, 1871 ***1823.15*** *p249*
Sparling, Wm 37; Ontario, 1871 ***1823.28*** *p94*
Sparow, John 36; Ontario, 1871 ***1823.15*** *p249*
Sparr, John Henry Godfrey; New York, 1832 ***8197.10*** *p283*
Sparrow, Catherine; Maryland, 1656 ***2524.55*** *p206*
Sparrow, Edwin; New Jersey, 1857 ***1224.3*** *p73*
Sparrow, Elizabeth *SEE* Sparrow, Thomas
Sparrow, Elizabeth; Maryland, 1649 ***2524.55*** *p206*
Sparrow, Jean; Virginia, 1667-1668 ***6212.30*** *p38*
Sparrow, Margaret 54; Ontario, 1871 ***1823.15*** *p249*
Sparrow, Samuel; Charleston, South Carolina, 1801 ***1224.3*** *p73*
Sparrow, Thomas *SEE* Sparrow, Thomas
Sparrow, Thomas; Maryland, 1649 ***2524.55*** *p206*
Wife: Elizabeth
Child: Thomas
Child: Elizabeth
Sparrow, Thomas; Maryland, 1649 ***2524.55*** *p206*
Sparrow, William 22; Philadelphia, 1774 ***1220.25*** *p80*
Spath, Charles 56; Ontario, 1871 ***1823.15*** *p249*
Spath, Maria; Port uncertain, 1749 ***2856.30*** *p437*
Spath, Marianna; Port uncertain, 1760 ***2856.30*** *p437*
Spath, Peter 29; Jamaica, 1773 ***1220.25*** *p31*
Spatz, Mr.; America, 1750 ***2856.30*** *p433*
With wife & 5 children
Spatz, Adam; Port uncertain, 1783 ***2856.30*** *p433*
With wife 3 sons & 4 daughters
Spatz, Friedrich; Port uncertain, 1783 ***2856.30*** *p433*
Spatz, Jacob; America, 1750 ***2856.30*** *p433*
Spatz, Lorenz, Jr.; America, 1750 ***2856.30*** *p433*
With wife & 5 children
Spaulding, Annette M.; Vermont, 1849-1894 ***5900.10*** *p243*
Spaulding, John; Connecticut, 1764 ***1224.2*** *p108*
Spaulding, John; Havana, 1764 ***1224.2*** *p108*
Spaulding, Matilda J.; Vermont, n.d. ***5900.10*** *p244*
Spavinder, George; Baltimore, 1846 ***6058.10*** *p20*
Spavinder, George; Pennsylvania, 1847 ***6058.10*** *p23*
Spayd, Jacob; Pennsylvania, 1836 ***6058.10*** *p10*
Spaz, Georg Michael; America, 1752 ***2856.30*** *p433*
With wife & child
Spaz, Georg Michael; America, 1752 ***2856.30*** *p433*
Speagel, Samuel; America, 1741 ***2856.30*** *p434*
Speake, Thomas; Maryland, 1658 ***2524.55*** *p206*
Speakman, John 20; Maryland, 1775 ***1220.25*** *p121*
Speakman, S.; Portland, Maine, 1858 ***9196.15*** *p28*
Spear, Andrew; Pennsylvania, 1817 ***6058.10*** *p5*
Spear, Maria Erwin 67; Vermont, 1894 ***5900.10*** *p456*
Spear, Noah 83; Vermont, 1907 ***5900.10*** *p457*
Spear, Peter; Pennsylvania, 1817 ***6058.10*** *p5*
Spearing, William; Havana, 1763 ***1224.2*** *p108*
Spearing, William; New York, 1763 ***1224.2*** *p108*
Spears, Agnes M.; Vermont, 1888-1905 ***5900.10*** *p278*
Spears, Ann; Vermont, 1831-1913 ***5900.10*** *p224*
Spears, Barney; Vermont, 1835-1913 ***5900.10*** *p223*
Spears, Ellen O'Hear 69; Vermont, 1899 ***5900.10*** *p279*
Spears, Gilbert 47; Ontario, 1871 ***1823.15*** *p249*
Spears, Helen 62; Vermont, 1890 ***5900.10*** *p533*
Spears, James; Vermont, 1856-1914 ***5900.10*** *p278*
Spears, James 76; Vermont, 1878 ***5900.10*** *p222*
Spears, John 87; Vermont, 1919 ***5900.10*** *p279*
Spears, Mary Houston; Vermont, 1835-1905 ***5900.10*** *p223*
Spears, Mary Slone 92; Vermont, 1896 ***5900.10*** *p222*
Spears, Rosa McGue; Vermont, 1860-1954 ***5900.10*** *p278*
Spears, Thomas 79; Ontario, 1871 ***1823.22*** *p150*
Spec, Mr.; Quebec, 1857 ***9196.15*** *p24*
Speccot, Jno; Virginia, 1666 ***6212.30*** *p30*
Specer, John; Maryland, 1665 ***2524.55*** *p206*
Specht, Daniel; America, 1754 ***2856.30*** *p434*
With wife & 2 children
Specht, Elisabeth; Port uncertain, 1754 ***2856.30*** *p434*
Specht, Georg Jakob; Port uncertain, 1779 ***2856.30*** *p434*
Specht, Johann; Port uncertain, 1784 ***2856.30*** *p434*
Specht, John; Pennsylvania, 1777 ***4629.10*** *p12*
Spechtin, Elisabeth; Port uncertain, 1754 ***2856.30*** *p434*
Speck, Barbara; America, 1749 ***2856.30*** *p434*
With children
Speck, Francis; New York, 1794 ***8197.10*** *p2*
Speck, Franz; America, 1752 ***2856.30*** *p434*
With wife & 3 children
Speck, Johann; America, 1752 ***2856.30*** *p434*
Speck, Johann; Port uncertain, 1752 ***2856.30*** *p434*
With wife & 2 children
Speck, Martin; America, 1738 ***2856.30*** *p434*
Speck, Martin; Port uncertain, 1737 ***2856.30*** *p434*
Speckh, Catharina; Port uncertain, 1759 ***2856.30*** *p434*
Speckh, Jacob; Port uncertain, 1771 ***2856.30*** *p434*
Speckhher, Christina; Port uncertain, 1759 ***2856.30*** *p434*
Speckhlin, Barbara; Port uncertain, 1711 ***2856.30*** *p434*
Specknell, Jno; Virginia, 1664 ***6212.30*** *p5*
Spedden, George; Maryland, 1910 ***3259.35*** *p58*
Speed, Charles; Rhode Island, 1759 ***1224.2*** *p108*
Speede, John; Maryland, 1662 ***2524.55*** *p206*
Speedil, John 32; Ontario, 1871 ***1823.28*** *p94*
Speelman, John; Pennsylvania, 1777 ***4629.10*** *p31*
Speer, Alex; New York, New York, 1846 ***6058.10*** *p27*
Speer, Jacob; Pennsylvania, 1818 ***6058.10*** *p6*
Speer, John; New York, New York, 1852 ***6058.10*** *p41*
Speer, Peter; New York, New York, 1852 ***6058.10*** *p41*
Speers, Joseph 68; Ontario, 1871 ***1823.15*** *p249*
Speers, William S.; New York, 1838 ***8197.10*** *p149*
Spees, Henry; Pennsylvania, 1777 ***4629.10*** *p6*
Speicher, Georg; Port uncertain, 1788 ***2856.30*** *p434*
Speicher, Johann; Port uncertain, 1788 ***2856.30*** *p434*
Speid, John 23; Ontario, 1871 ***1823.28*** *p94*
Speidler, August 23; Ontario, 1871 ***1823.28*** *p94*
Speigel, Enos; Pennsylvania, 1868 ***6058.10*** *p72*
Speight, Frederick 50; Ontario, 1871 ***1823.15*** *p249*
Speight, Henry; New York, 1821 ***8197.10*** *p279*
Speiran, Hartwill 38; Ontario, 1871 ***1823.15*** *p249*
Speiran, Luke 35; Ontario, 1871 ***1823.15*** *p249*
Speirman, Catherine O'Brien 65; Vermont, 1913 ***5900.10*** *p192*
Speirs, Elizabeth 22; Virginia, 1774 ***1220.25*** *p93*
Spekcot, John; Virginia, 1666 ***6212.30*** *p27*
Spellicy, Bridget McMahon 68; Vermont, 1885 ***5900.10*** *p332*
Spellicy, James 32; Vermont, 1890 ***5900.10*** *p332*
Spellicy, John 92; Vermont, 1886 ***5900.10*** *p332*
Spellicy, Patrick 38; Vermont, 1892 ***5900.10*** *p332*
Spellman, James; Maryland, 1651 ***2524.55*** *p206*
Spellman, John O.; Vermont, 1854-1927 ***5900.10*** *p425*
Spellman, Katherine 76; Vermont, 1890 ***5900.10*** *p615*
Spellman, Mary 75; Vermont, 1898 ***5900.10*** *p417*
Spellman, Mary A.; Vermont, 1854-1919 ***5900.10*** *p447*
Spellman, Thomas 61; Vermont, 1877 ***5900.10*** *p417*
Spellman, William P.; Vermont, 1849-1912 ***5900.10*** *p425*
Spelman, Henry; Virginia, 1613 ***1224.1*** *p51*
Spelman, Thomas; Virginia, 1627 ***1224.1*** *p54*
Spence, Andrew; New York, 1840 ***8197.10*** *p196*
Spence, Ann *SEE* Spence, David
Spence, Barbara *SEE* Spence, James
Spence, Charles 47; Ontario, 1871 ***1823.15*** *p249*
Spence, David; Augusta, Georgia, 1827 ***1640.10*** *p190*
Spence, David; Maryland, 1667 ***2524.55*** *p206*
Wife: Ann
Spence, Finley 35; Ontario, 1871 ***1823.28*** *p94*
Spence, Gavin; New York, 1807 ***8197.10*** *p50*
Spence, George; New York, 1838 ***8197.10*** *p284*
Spence, George; New York, 1840 ***8197.10*** *p197*
Spence, George; Ontario, 1871 ***1823.22*** *p150*
Spence, George 26; Ontario, 1871 ***1823.28*** *p94*
Spence, Gilbert 32; Ontario, 1871 ***1823.28*** *p94*
Spence, Helen *SEE* Spence, James
Spence, Henry; New York, 1807 ***8197.10*** *p51*
Spence, Henry 25; Virginia, 1773 ***1220.25*** *p31*
Spence, Henry 52; Ontario, 1871 ***1823.15*** *p249*
Spence, Jacob 57; Ontario, 1871 ***1823.28*** *p94*
Spence, James *SEE* Spence, James
Spence, James; Savannah, Georgia, 1774 ***1640.10*** *p190*
Wife: Mary Gorne
Child: James
Child: Helen
Child: Barbara
Spence, James 41; Virginia, 1775 ***1220.25*** *p110*
Spence, James 54; Ontario, 1871 ***1823.15*** *p249*
Spence, Jane *SEE* Spence, William
Spence, John; Alabama, 1810-1845 ***1640.10*** *p191*
Wife: Mary
Spence, John; British Columbia, 1866 ***1640.13*** *p117*
Spence, John; Georgia, 1699 ***1640.13*** *p117*
Spence, John; Georgia, 1736 ***1640.10*** *p190*
Spence, John; Quebec, 1829 ***1640.13*** *p117*
Spence, John; Savannah, Georgia, 1774 ***1640.10*** *p191*
Spence, John 33; Ontario, 1871 ***1823.28*** *p94*
Spence, Margaret; Ontario, 1884 ***1640.13*** *p117*
Spence, Margret 21; Ontario, 1871 ***1823.22*** *p150*
Spence, Mary *SEE* Spence, John
Spence, Mary *SEE* Spence, William
Spence, Mary; Vermont, 1855-1922 ***5900.10*** *p277*
Spence, Mary Ann; Vermont, 1846-1929 ***5900.10*** *p170*
Spence, Mary Gorne *SEE* Spence, James
Spence, Moses 69; Ontario, 1871 ***1823.28*** *p94*
Spence, Patrick; Virginia, 1710 ***1224.2*** *p108*
Spence, Philip 14; Antigua (Antego), 1774 ***1220.25*** *p90*
Spence, Violet 44; Ontario, 1871 ***1823.28*** *p94*
Spence, William *SEE* Spence, William
Spence, William; Alabama, 1840 ***1640.10*** *p191*
Wife: Jane
Child: Jane
Child: William
Child: Mary
Spence, William; Ontario, 1896 ***1640.13*** *p117*
Spence, William 23; Maryland, 1774 ***1220.25*** *p59*
Spence, William 25; Ontario, 1871 ***1823.15*** *p249*
Spence, William 60; Ontario, 1871 ***1823.15*** *p249*
Spence, William 66; Ontario, 1871 ***1823.28*** *p94*
Spencer, Miss; Quebec, 1857 ***9196.15*** *p21*
Spencer, Miss A.; Quebec, 1856 ***9196.15*** *p10*
Spencer, Abel 39; Ontario, 1871 ***1823.28*** *p94*
Spencer, Abigail 53; Ontario, 1861 ***2896.26*** *p4*
Spencer, Albert 16; Ontario, 1861 ***2896.26*** *p4*
Spencer, Ambrose Hall; Los Angeles, 1896 ***1640.13*** *p117*
Spencer, Anto; Virginia, 1664 ***6212.30*** *p11*
Spencer, Asa H. 24; Ontario, 1861 ***2896.25*** *p56*
Spencer, Benjamin 21; Maryland, 1774 ***1220.25*** *p40*
Spencer, C. A. 6; Ontario, 1861 ***2896.26*** *p16*
Spencer, C. J. 39; Ontario, 1861 ***2896.26*** *p7*
Spencer, Carrie A. 2; Ontario, 1861 ***2896.28*** *p49*
Spencer, Cory 49; Ontario, 1871 ***1823.22*** *p150*
Spencer, D. C. 9; Ontario, 1861 ***2896.26*** *p16*
Spencer, D. C. 55; Ontario, 1861 ***2896.26*** *p4*
Spencer, D. J. 13; Ontario, 1861 ***2896.25*** *p31*
Spencer, David 29; Ontario, 1861 ***2896.28*** *p21*
Spencer, David 37; Ontario, 1871 ***1823.15*** *p249*
Spencer, E. 33; Ontario, 1861 ***2896.26*** *p8*
Spencer, E. R. 5; Ontario, 1861 ***2896.26*** *p8*
Spencer, Eliza 21; Ontario, 1861 ***2896.26*** *p20*

Spencer, Elizabeth 3; Ontario, 1861 ***2896.25*** *p6*
Spencer, Emily A. 5; Ontario, 1861 ***2896.25*** *p6*
Spencer, Fanny 24; Ontario, 1861 ***2896.26*** *p20*
Spencer, Francis; Maryland, 1665 ***2524.55*** *p206*
Wife: Suzan
Spencer, Fred 3; Ontario, 1861 ***2896.28*** *p23*
Spencer, Frederick; New York, 1835 ***8197.10*** *p283*
Spencer, George 16; Ontario, 1861 ***2896.25*** *p31*
Spencer, George 24; Ontario, 1871 ***1823.22*** *p150*
Spencer, J. F. 10; Ontario, 1861 ***2896.26*** *p8*
Spencer, James 34; Antigua (Antego), 1775 ***1220.25*** *p104*
Spencer, James 45; Ontario, 1871 ***1823.22*** *p150*
Spencer, James R. 32; Ontario, 1861 ***2896.26*** *p4*
Spencer, Jemima 40; Ontario, 1861 ***2896.25*** *p31*
Spencer, Jno; Virginia, 1665-1666 ***6212.30*** *p24*
Spencer, John; New York, 1840 ***8197.10*** *p197*
Spencer, John; Savannah, Georgia, 1761 ***1224.2*** *p108*
Spencer, John; Vermont, 1834-1910 ***5900.10*** *p164*
Spencer, John 42; Ontario, 1871 ***1823.22*** *p150*
Spencer, John S.; New York, 1836 ***8197.10*** *p283*
Spencer, Joseph; Pennsylvania, 1779 ***4629.10*** *p37*
Spencer, Joseph 16; Philadelphia, 1774 ***1220.25*** *p4*
Spencer, Julius 34; Ontario, 1871 ***1823.22*** *p150*
Spencer, M. M. 14; Ontario, 1861 ***2896.26*** *p16*
Spencer, M. O. 18; Ontario, 1861 ***2896.26*** *p4*
Spencer, Magnes 49; Ontario, 1871 ***1823.15*** *p249*
Spencer, Mary; Vermont, 1858-1871 ***5900.10*** *p164*
Spencer, Mary 13; New York, New York, 1848 ***1825.45*** *p40*
Spencer, Mary 19; Philadelphia, 1774 ***1220.25*** *p23*
Spencer, Mary E.; Ontario, 1861 ***2896.28*** *p23*
Spencer, Mary J. 23; Ontario, 1861 ***2896.28*** *p49*
Spencer, Mary McDonald; Vermont, 1826-1911 ***5900.10*** *p164*
Spencer, Mottrom; Virginia, 1703 ***1224.2*** *p108*
Spencer, Nicholas; Virginia, 1686 ***1224.1*** *p54*
Spencer, Nicholas; Virginia, 1700 ***1224.2*** *p108*
Spencer, Paul; New York, 1803 ***8197.10*** *p16*
Spencer, Phebe 20; Ontario, 1861 ***2896.28*** *p21*
Spencer, Robert; Virginia, 1665 ***6212.30*** *p19*
Spencer, Rosina 56; Ontario, 1871 ***1823.22*** *p150*
Spencer, Samuel 17; Ontario, 1861 ***2896.25*** *p56*
Spencer, Sarah 25; Ontario, 1861 ***2896.28*** *p23*
Spencer, Sinderila 28; Ontario, 1861 ***2896.25*** *p6*
Spencer, Susan 21; Ontario, 1861 ***2896.28*** *p21*
Spencer, Suzan *SEE* Spencer, Francis
Spencer, T. D. 6; Ontario, 1861 ***2896.25*** *p31*
Spencer, Thomas; Augusta, Georgia, 1764 ***1224.2*** *p108*
Spencer, Thomas 30; Baltimore, 1775 ***1220.25*** *p118*
Spencer, W. S. 12; Ontario, 1861 ***2896.26*** *p16*
Spencer, William; Maryland, 1665 ***2524.55*** *p206*
Spencer, William; Maryland, 1768 ***1224.2*** *p108*
Spencer, William; New York, 1803 ***8197.10*** *p16*
Spencer, William 13; Ontario, 1861 ***2896.25*** *p56*
Spencer, William 15; Philadelphia, 1774 ***1220.25*** *p35*
Spencer, William 25; Maryland, 1775 ***1220.25*** *p111*
Spencer, William 37; Ontario, 1871 ***1823.28*** *p94*
Spendelove, Roger; Boston, 1776 ***1224.2*** *p108*
Spendelow, Charles; Virginia, 1756 ***1224.2*** *p108*
Spengler, Anna Catharina; Port uncertain, 1777 ***2856.30*** *p434*
Spengler, B.; America, 1732 ***2856.30*** *p363*
Spengler, Baltzer; America, 1732 ***2856.30*** *p435*
Wife: M. Ritter
Spengler, C.; America, 1727 ***2856.30*** *p511*
Spengler, Caspar; America, 1727 ***2856.30*** *p435*
Wife: J. Ziegler
Spengler, Caspar; America, 1727 ***2856.30*** *p437*
Spengler, Caspar; America, 1744 ***2856.30*** *p434*
Spengler, Georg; Port uncertain, 1749 ***2856.30*** *p434*
Spengler, Hans; Port uncertain, 1623 ***2856.30*** *p434*
With wife 2 sons daughter & mother
Spengler, Hans Georg; America, 1732 ***2856.30*** *p434*
Spengler, Henrich; America, 1732 ***2856.30*** *p434*
Spengler, J. Ziegler *SEE* Spengler, Caspar
Spengler, Jerg; America, 1732 ***2856.30*** *p434*
Spengler, Jerrich; America, 1732 ***2856.30*** *p436*
Spengler, Johann Caspar; Port uncertain, 1746 ***2856.30*** *p434*
Spengler, Karl; Port uncertain, 1755 ***2856.30*** *p434*
Spengler, Karl; Port uncertain, 1783 ***2856.30*** *p434*
Spengler, Karl; Port uncertain, 1791 ***2856.30*** *p434*
Spengler, M. Ritter *SEE* Spengler, Baltzer
Spengler, Margarete; Port uncertain, 1766 ***2856.30*** *p434*
Spengler, Maria Justina; Port uncertain, 1758 ***2856.30*** *p434*
Spengler, Schweickard; Port uncertain, 1785 ***2856.30*** *p434*
With wife & 5 children
Spenlove, Ann; North America, 1792 ***1224.2*** *p109*
Sperberg, Fredrick 33; Ontario, 1871 ***1823.28*** *p94*
Sperberg, William 55; Ontario, 1871 ***1823.28*** *p94*
Spernon, Joseph; Maryland, 1681 ***2524.55*** *p206*
Sperrmaine, Launce; Virginia, 1700 ***1224.2*** *p109*
Speth, Anton; Port uncertain, 1750 ***2856.30*** *p435*
Speth, Johann; Port uncertain, 1780 ***2856.30*** *p435*
Speth, Johanna; Port uncertain, 1771 ***2856.30*** *p435*
Speth, Maria Barbara; Port uncertain, 1781 ***2856.30*** *p435*
Speurs, Jannet 50; Ontario, 1871 ***1823.15*** *p249*
Speyer, Christian Frederick; New York, 1817 ***8197.10*** *p278*
Speyer, Eliza; New York, 1833 ***8197.10*** *p68*
Speyer, George William; New York, 1833 ***8197.10*** *p68*
Speyer, John; New York, 1816 ***1224.3*** *p73*
Speyer, Philip; New York, 1840 ***8197.10*** *p285*
Spicen, John 54; Ontario, 1871 ***1823.15*** *p249*
Spicer, Benjamin 26; Ontario, 1871 ***1823.22*** *p151*
Spicer, Edw; Virginia, 1663-1664 ***6212.30*** *p5*
Spicer, Jacob; Pennsylvania, 1779 ***4629.10*** *p40*
Spicer, Margaret; Maryland, 1679 ***2524.55*** *p206*
Spicer, Math; Virginia, 1692-1693 ***6212.30*** *p59*
Spicer, Robert 46; Ontario, 1871 ***1823.15*** *p249*
Spicer, William 75; Ontario, 1871 ***1823.15*** *p249*
Spickh, Peter; Port uncertain, 1746 ***2856.30*** *p435*
Spiegel, Josef; Port uncertain, 1728 ***2856.30*** *p435*
Spiegel, Magdalena; Port uncertain, 1724 ***2856.30*** *p435*
Spiegel, Michael; America, 1736 ***2856.30*** *p435*
With wife & son
Spiegel, Michael; America, 1737 ***2856.30*** *p435*
Spiegel, Samuel; America, 1738 ***2856.30*** *p435*
With wife & 2 children
Spiegle, Enos; Pennsylvania, 1868 ***6058.10*** *p72*
Spiehlberger, Hans Georg; America, 1753 ***2856.30*** *p435*
With wife & children
Spieler, Anna Dorothea; Port uncertain, 1758 ***2856.30*** *p435*
Spielerin, Maria Margarete; Port uncertain, 1760 ***2856.30*** *p435*
Spielmann, Johann; Port uncertain, 1728 ***2856.30*** *p435*
Spielmann, Johann Jacob; Port uncertain, 1756 ***2856.30*** *p435*
Spielmann, Maria Barbara; Port uncertain, 1761 ***2856.30*** *p435*
Spielmann, Mathis; Port uncertain, 1761 ***2856.30*** *p435*
Spier, Frederick Albert; New York, 1838 ***8197.10*** *p284*
Spiers, Mrs.; Quebec, 1857 ***9196.15*** *p25*
Spies, John; New York, 1837 ***8197.10*** *p107*
Spies, M. M.; America, 1739 ***2856.30*** *p128*
Spies, Maria Magdalena; America, 1738 ***2856.30*** *p435*
Spies, Martin; Port uncertain, 1749 ***2856.30*** *p435*
Spies, Michael; Port uncertain, 1785 ***2856.30*** *p435*
Spies, Susanna; Port uncertain, 1785 ***2856.30*** *p435*
Spies, Wolfgang; America, 1744 ***2856.30*** *p435*
With wife & 7 children
Spiess, Daniel; America, 1754 ***2856.30*** *p435*
Spiess, Daniel; Port uncertain, 1753 ***2856.30*** *p435*
Spiess, Georg; Port uncertain, 1624 ***2856.30*** *p436*
Spiess, Jacob; Port uncertain, 1624 ***2856.30*** *p435*
Spiess, Johann; Port uncertain, 1786 ***2856.30*** *p435*
Spiess, Maria Margarete; Port uncertain, 1773 ***2856.30*** *p435*
Spihler, Anna Maria; Port uncertain, 1756 ***2856.30*** *p436*
Spike, George; Maryland, 1661 ***2524.55*** *p206*
Spillane, Catherine; Vermont, 1835-1916 ***5900.10*** *p464*
Spillane, Catherine 26; Vermont, 1860 ***5900.10*** *p369*
Spillane, Ellen 37; Vermont, 1893 ***5900.10*** *p180*
Spillane, Eugene 17; Vermont, 1872 ***5900.10*** *p369*
Spillane, Hanora Holland; Vermont, 1837-1924 ***5900.10*** *p359*
Spillane, Honora Sullivan 69; Vermont, 1888 ***5900.10*** *p180*
Spillane, John 42; Vermont, 1912 ***5900.10*** *p369*
Spillane, John D. 82; Vermont, 1888 ***5900.10*** *p180*
Spillane, Julia Finn 88; Vermont, 1911 ***5900.10*** *p369*
Spillane, Michael; Vermont, 1832-1924 ***5900.10*** *p359*
Spillane, Patrick 38; Vermont, 1896 ***5900.10*** *p180*
Spillane, Patrick 76; Vermont, 1901 ***5900.10*** *p369*
Spillane, Richard 15; Ontario, 1871 ***1823.28*** *p94*
Spillane, Theresa Farrell; Vermont, 1855-1936 ***5900.10*** *p149*
Spiller, Joel M.; New York, 1840 ***8197.10*** *p198*
Spilman, Philip; Pennsylvania, 1777 ***4629.10*** *p11*
Spilmann, Maria Margarete; Port uncertain, 1790 ***2856.30*** *p436*
Spilsbury, F. B. 53; Ontario, 1871 ***1823.22*** *p151*
Spiltbury, Margaret; Maryland, 1674 ***2524.55*** *p206*
Spincke, Elinor; Maryland, 1673 ***2524.55*** *p207*
Spindler, Gertrud; Port uncertain, 1751 ***2856.30*** *p436*
Spindler, Paul; Port uncertain, 1733 ***2856.30*** *p436*
Spindler, Paul; Port uncertain, 1753 ***2856.30*** *p436*
Spinestowicz, Anna; Maryland, 1910 ***3259.35*** *p58*
Spingen, C. 21; Maryland, 1774 ***1220.25*** *p84*
Spingler, Balster; America, 1732 ***2856.30*** *p436*
Spingler, Jerrich; America, 1732 ***2856.30*** *p436*
Spink, James; Savannah, Georgia, 1822 ***1640.10*** *p191*
Spink, Margarett *SEE* Spink, Thomas
Spink, Thomas; Maryland, 1667 ***2524.55*** *p207*
Wife: Margarett
Spinks, Jacob 36; Ontario, 1871 ***1823.22*** *p151*
Spinks, Thomas 43; Ontario, 1871 ***1823.22*** *p151*
Spinner, Elizabeth *SEE* Spinner, Jacob
Spinner, Hannah *SEE* Spinner, Jacob
Spinner, Jacob; Maryland, 1665 ***2524.55*** *p207*
Wife: Hannah
Child: Elizabeth
Child: Margarett
Child: Thomas
Relative: Suzan
Spinner, Johann P.; America, 1801 ***2856.30*** *p436*
Spinner, Margarett *SEE* Spinner, Jacob
Spinner, Suzan *SEE* Spinner, Jacob
Spinner, Thomas *SEE* Spinner, Jacob
Spinola, Francisco; New York, 1832 ***8197.10*** *p368*
Spinolla, John L.; New York, 1818 ***8197.10*** *p278*
Spira, Elisabeth; Port uncertain, 1747 ***2856.30*** *p436*
Spira, Valentin; Port uncertain, 1764 ***2856.30*** *p436*
With wife & children
Spirain, Elisabeth; Port uncertain, 1747 ***2856.30*** *p436*
Spirar, Ursula; Port uncertain, 1738 ***2856.30*** *p436*
Spirarin, Ursula; Port uncertain, 1738 ***2856.30*** *p436*
Spiry, Peter; America, 1754 ***2856.30*** *p436*
With wife & 7 children
Spittal, William; Jamaica, 1837 ***1640.13*** *p117*
Spitzer, Heinrich; Port uncertain, 1764 ***2856.30*** *p436*
Spitzer, Henrich; Port uncertain, 1747 ***2856.30*** *p436*
Spitzer, Henrich; Port uncertain, 1764 ***2856.30*** *p436*
Spitzer, Henrich; Port uncertain, 1784 ***2856.30*** *p436*
Spitzer, Johann Andreas; America, 1764 ***2856.30*** *p436*
Spitzer, Johann Heinrich; America, 1764 ***2856.30*** *p436*
Spitzhirn, Eva; Port uncertain, 1771 ***2856.30*** *p436*
Spitznagel, Balthasar; America, 1774 ***2856.30*** *p436*
Spitznagel, Elisabeth; America, 1774 ***2856.30*** *p436*
Spitznagel, Elisabeth; Port uncertain, 1773 ***2856.30*** *p436*
Spitznagel, Gertrud; America, 1774 ***2856.30*** *p436*
Spitznagel, Gertrud; Port uncertain, 1773 ***2856.30*** *p436*
Splain, Agnes 16; Vermont, 1881 ***5900.10*** *p534*
Splain, Alice; Vermont, 1886 ***5900.10*** *p534*
Splain, Anne 20; Vermont, 1875 ***5900.10*** *p534*
Splain, Bridget; Vermont, 1839-1918 ***5900.10*** *p174*
Splain, Bridget O'Byrne; Vermont, 1850-1924 ***5900.10*** *p190*
Splain, Catherine; Vermont, 1863-1935 ***5900.10*** *p161*
Splain, Daniel 15; Vermont, 1881 ***5900.10*** *p534*
Splain, Daniel 75; Vermont, 1903 ***5900.10*** *p534*
Splain, Eliza 20; Vermont, 1881 ***5900.10*** *p534*
Splain, Ellen 26; Vermont, 1880 ***5900.10*** *p534*
Splain, Ellen 51; Vermont, 1907 ***5900.10*** *p175*
Splain, James 1; Vermont, 1882 ***5900.10*** *p534*
Splain, Katie 24; Vermont, 1881 ***5900.10*** *p534*
Splain, Mary 1; Vermont, 1885 ***5900.10*** *p534*
Splain, Mary O'Neil 52; Vermont, 1880 ***5900.10*** *p534*
Splaine, Lawrence; Vermont, 1828-1916 ***5900.10*** *p359*
Splan, Ann 78; Ontario, 1871 ***1823.15*** *p249*
Splatt, Ann; South Carolina, 1742 ***1224.2*** *p13*
Sployd, Cornelius L.; Vermont, 1857-1919 ***5900.10*** *p355*
Sployd, Julia L. Donahue; Vermont, 1857-1947 ***5900.10*** *p355*
Spochaeq, Michael; Maryland, 1910 ***3259.35*** *p58*
Spohn, Henrich; Port uncertain, 1731 ***2856.30*** *p436*
Spohn, Johann Jacob; Port uncertain, 1744 ***2856.30*** *p436*
Spohn, Johann Jacob; Port uncertain, 1745 ***2856.30*** *p436*
Spohn, Peter; America, 1749 ***2856.30*** *p436*
With wife
Spohn, Sara; Port uncertain, 1752 ***2856.30*** *p436*
Spohucz, John; Maryland, 1910 ***3259.35*** *p58*
Spon, Peter; Port uncertain, 1749 ***2856.30*** *p436*
Sponheimer, Johann; Port uncertain, 1748 ***2856.30*** *p436*
Spooner, Charles 46; Ontario, 1871 ***1823.15*** *p249*
Spooner, Ebenezer B.; Vermont, 1839-1914 ***5900.10*** *p282*
Spooner, John; Boston, 1764 ***1224.2*** *p109*
Spooner, John; Boston, 1769 ***1224.2*** *p109*
Spooner, Martha McKinney; Vermont, 1845-1892 ***5900.10*** *p282*
Spooner, Thomas 50; Ontario, 1871 ***1823.15*** *p249*
Sporer, Therese; Port uncertain, 1779 ***2856.30*** *p436*
Sporney, Julia; Maryland, 1910 ***3259.35*** *p58*
Sporny, Frank; Maryland, 1910 ***3259.35*** *p58*
Sporny, James W.; Maryland, 1910 ***3259.35*** *p58*
Sporny, Martin; Maryland, 1910 ***3259.35*** *p58*
Spotswood, Alexander; Virginia, 1742 ***1224.2*** *p109*
Spotswood, Jane 56; Ontario, 1871 ***1823.28*** *p94*
Spotswood, William 60; Ontario, 1871 ***1823.28*** *p94*
Spotton, Arthur 29; Ontario, 1871 ***1823.15*** *p249*
Spotton, John 30; Ontario, 1871 ***1823.15*** *p249*
Sprage, Edward 33; Ontario, 1871 ***1823.28*** *p94*
Sprague, Mrs.; Quebec, 1858 ***9196.15*** *p39*
Sprague, Douglass 1; Ontario, 1861 ***2896.25*** *p70*

Sprague, Drusilla 18; Ontario, 1861 ***2896.25*** *p60*
Sprague, George 1; Ontario, 1861 ***2896.25*** *p70*
Sprague, George 15; Ontario, 1861 ***2896.25*** *p60*
Sprague, Hiram 28; Ontario, 1871 ***1823.15*** *p249*
Sprague, Jane 21; Ontario, 1861 ***2896.25*** *p60*
Sprague, Jasper 3; Ontario, 1861 ***2896.25*** *p70*
Sprague, John; Boston, 1776 ***1224.2*** *p109*
Sprague, John 23; Boston, 1775 ***1220.25*** *p106*
Sprague, Lawrence 17; Ontario, 1861 ***2896.25*** *p60*
Sprague, Lette 23; Ontario, 1861 ***2896.25*** *p70*
Sprague, Levina 5; Ontario, 1861 ***2896.25*** *p61*
Sprague, Mary 23; Ontario, 1861 ***2896.25*** *p70*
Sprague, Silvenus 53; Ontario, 1861 ***2896.25*** *p60*
Sprague, Sylvanus, Sr. 92; Ontario, 1861 ***2896.25*** *p61*
Sprandal, Charles; New York, New York, 1860 ***6058.10*** *p46*
Sprandle, Charles; New York, New York, 1860 ***6058.10*** *p46*
Sprankenbach, Peter; Port uncertain, 1749 ***2856.30*** *p436*
With wife & 5 children
Spratley, Benjamin; Virginia, 1783 ***1224.2*** *p109*
Spratlin, James; Virginia, 1672 ***6212.30*** *p50*
Spratt, John; New York, 1806 ***8197.10*** *p33*
Spratt, William; New York, 1804 ***8197.10*** *p28*
Sprauer, Barbara; Port uncertain, 1763 ***2856.30*** *p437*
Sprauer, Barbara; Port uncertain, 1764 ***2856.30*** *p437*
Sprauer, Franz Simon; Port uncertain, 1763 ***2856.30*** *p437*
Spray, John 15; Maryland, 1775 ***1220.25*** *p120*
Spreadborough, George 36; Ontario, 1871 ***1823.28*** *p94*
Spreadborough, William 42; Ontario, 1871 ***1823.28*** *p94*
Sprengart, Philippina; Port uncertain, 1782 ***2856.30*** *p437*
Sprenger, Leopold; Port uncertain, 1752 ***2856.30*** *p437*
Sprengler, Adam; America, 1749 ***2856.30*** *p437*
Sprengler, Judith; Port uncertain, 1733 ***2856.30*** *p437*
Sprentall, Francis 66; Ontario, 1871 ***1823.22*** *p151*
Sprentall, Samuel 68; Ontario, 1871 ***1823.22*** *p151*
Spreuer, Peter; Port uncertain, 1722 ***2856.30*** *p437*
Spreull, Samuel; Toronto, 1881 ***1640.13*** *p117*
Spreyer, Anna Elisabeth; Port uncertain, 1754 ***2856.30*** *p437*
Spreyer, Johann Thiel; Port uncertain, 1751 ***2856.30*** *p437*
Spreyer, Peter; Port uncertain, 1744 ***2856.30*** *p437*
Spreyer, Philipp; Port uncertain, 1766 ***2856.30*** *p437*
Sprie, James 31; Virginia, 1774 ***1220.25*** *p90*
Sprigg, Catherine *SEE* Sprigg, Thomas
Sprigg, Nathaniel; Maryland, 1658 ***2524.55*** *p207*
Sprigg, Thomas; Maryland, 1658 ***2524.55*** *p207*
Wife: Catherine
Spriggs, James; Pennsylvania, 1777 ***4629.10*** *p13*
Spriggs, Thomas 23; Maryland, 1774 ***1220.25*** *p61*
Sprin, Patrick 58; Ontario, 1871 ***1823.15*** *p249*
Spring, Anna; Maryland, 1910 ***3259.35*** *p58*
Spring, Jessie 38; Ontario, 1871 ***1823.15*** *p249*
Spring, William 24; Philadelphia, 1775 ***1220.25*** *p9*
Spring, Wm; Portland, Maine, 1858 ***9196.15*** *p30*
Springbelt, Ann 32; Ontario, 1871 ***1823.28*** *p94*
Springbitt, John Edward 27; Ontario, 1871 ***1823.28*** *p94*
Springer, Benjamin; St. Augustine, Florida, n.d. ***1224.2*** *p109*
Springer, Herbert; Virginia, 1664 ***6212.30*** *p9*
Springer, John 47; Ontario, 1871 ***1823.28*** *p95*
Springer, Maria; America, 1752 ***2856.30*** *p437*
With husband & 4 children
Springer, Philip; Pennsylvania, 1777 ***4629.10*** *p9*
Springfort, Jakob; America, 1764 ***2856.30*** *p437*
Springler, Judith; America, 1727 ***2856.30*** *p437*
Springweiler, Catharina; Port uncertain, 1739 ***2856.30*** *p437*
Springweiler, Franz Josef; Port uncertain, 1790 ***2856.30*** *p437*
Sprinkhorn, Henry 52; Ontario, 1871 ***1823.22*** *p151*
Sproat, Agness 76; Ontario, 1871 ***1823.15*** *p249*
Sproat, Andrew 26; Ontario, 1871 ***1823.15*** *p249*
Sproat, David 35; Ontario, 1871 ***1823.15*** *p249*
Sproat, George 46; Ontario, 1871 ***1823.15*** *p249*
Sproat, John 50; Ontario, 1871 ***1823.15*** *p249*
Sproat, Joseph 27; Ontario, 1871 ***1823.15*** *p249*
Sproat, William 48; Ontario, 1871 ***1823.15*** *p249*
Sproat, Wm 38; Ontario, 1871 ***1823.28*** *p95*
Sprogell, Lodwick; Pennsylvania, 1777 ***4629.10*** *p7*
Sprole, Catherine 15; Ontario, 1861 ***2896.25*** *p54*
Sprole, John 40; Ontario, 1871 ***1823.15*** *p250*
Sprossi, Eorg; Port uncertain, 1752 ***2856.30*** *p437*
Sprot, James 42; Ontario, 1871 ***1823.15*** *p250*
Sprott, Margaret; Westmoreland Co., Pennsylvania, 1900 ***1640.13*** *p121*
Sproul, David; New York, 1840 ***8197.10*** *p285*
Sproul, Margaret 59; Ontario, 1871 ***1823.15*** *p250*
Sproule, Adam 45; Boston, 1774 ***1220.25*** *p54*
Sproule, Andrew; Norfolk, Virginia, 1779 ***1640.13*** *p117*
Sproull, Joseph; New York, 1804 ***8197.10*** *p277*
Sprowle, Andrew; Virginia, 1782 ***1224.2*** *p109*
Spruch, Christina; Port uncertain, 1775 ***2856.30*** *p437*
Spruchin, Christina; Port uncertain, 1775 ***2856.30*** *p437*
Sprung, Anninthia 20; Ontario, 1861 ***2896.25*** *p63*
Sprung, Bethene V. 3; Ontario, 1861 ***2896.25*** *p63*
Sprung, Catherine 31; Ontario, 1861 ***2896.28*** *p56*
Sprung, Daniel 32; Ontario, 1861 ***2896.25*** *p66*
Sprung, David E. 5; Ontario, 1861 ***2896.25*** *p64*
Sprung, David H. 9; Ontario, 1861 ***2896.28*** *p56*
Sprung, F. A. 15; Ontario, 1861 ***2896.28*** *p56*
Sprung, George 23; Ontario, 1861 ***2896.25*** *p66*
Sprung, George W. 7; Ontario, 1861 ***2896.25*** *p64*
Sprung, Hannah 49; Ontario, 1861 ***2896.25*** *p66*
Sprung, Hulda 2; Ontario, 1861 ***2896.25*** *p66*
Sprung, Israel 18; Ontario, 1861 ***2896.25*** *p66*
Sprung, Jane 33; Ontario, 1861 ***2896.28*** *p56*
Sprung, Jesse 2; Ontario, 1861 ***2896.25*** *p63*
Sprung, Letty Ann 21; Ontario, 1861 ***2896.25*** *p66*
Sprung, Lucinda 29; Ontario, 1861 ***2896.25*** *p64*
Sprung, Manly 19; Ontario, 1861 ***2896.25*** *p66*
Sprung, Margaret 61; Ontario, 1861 ***2896.25*** *p66*
Sprung, Mary L. 7; Ontario, 1861 ***2896.28*** *p56*
Sprung, R. M. 10; Ontario, 1861 ***2896.28*** *p56*
Sprung, S. M. 5; Ontario, 1861 ***2896.28*** *p56*
Sprung, Sarah E. 12; Ontario, 1861 ***2896.28*** *p56*
Sprung, Suffrona 11; Ontario, 1861 ***2896.25*** *p66*
Sprung, Thomas 4; Ontario, 1861 ***2896.25*** *p66*
Sprunnca, Wm; Virginia, 1698 ***6212.30*** *p61*
Spry, Arthur; Virginia, 1666 ***6212.30*** *p27*
Spry, Christopher; Maryland, 1670 ***2524.55*** *p207*
Spry, Ellen 16; Ontario, 1871 ***1823.15*** *p250*
Spry, Lydia Ann; Vermont, 1855-1921 ***5900.10*** *p591*
Spry, William; Virginia, 1666 ***6212.30*** *p28*
Sprye, Joan *SEE* Sprye, Oliver
Sprye, Joan; Maryland, 1658 ***2524.55*** *p207*
Sprye, Mary *SEE* Sprye, Oliver
Sprye, Mary; Maryland, 1658 ***2524.55*** *p207*
Sprye, Oliver *SEE* Sprye, Oliver
Sprye, Oliver; Maryland, 1649-1650 ***2524.55*** *p207*
Sprye, Oliver; Maryland, 1650 ***2524.55*** *p207*
Wife: Joan
Child: Mary
Child: Oliver
Sprye, Oliver; Maryland, 1678 ***2524.55*** *p207*
Spuess, Georg; Port uncertain, 1624 ***2856.30*** *p436*
Spuhl, William 46; Ontario, 1871 ***1823.15*** *p250*
Spuhler, Philipp Jakob; Port uncertain, 1788 ***2856.30*** *p437*
Spurne, John; Maryland, 1651 ***2524.55*** *p207*
Spurr, Henry; Virginia, 1666 ***6212.30*** *p27*
Spurton, Mathew; Virginia, 1666-1667 ***6212.30*** *p34*
Spurzheim, Gaspar; Boston, 1835 ***1224.3*** *p73*
Squance, William 53; Ontario, 1871 ***1823.15*** *p250*
Square, Robert; Maryland, 1910 ***3259.35*** *p58*
Squiar, Samuel 21; Maryland, 1775 ***1220.25*** *p97*
Squier, Euphemia 78; Ontario, 1871 ***1823.22*** *p151*
Squier, Joseph B.; Vermont, 1850-1945 ***5900.10*** *p444*
Squiers, William 58; Ontario, 1871 ***1823.15*** *p250*
Squire, Mr.; Quebec, 1857 ***9196.15*** *p27*
Squire, Anson B. 9; Ontario, 1861 ***2896.25*** *p1*
Squire, Daniel; New York, 1786 ***1224.2*** *p109*
Squire, Gibb 64; Ontario, 1861 ***2896.25*** *p2*
Squire, Harriet A. 37; Ontario, 1861 ***2896.25*** *p1*
Squire, Harriet Louisa Miles; Philadelphia, 1844 ***1224.3*** *p73*
Squire, Henry 18; Ontario, 1861 ***2896.25*** *p2*
Squire, J. G. 8; Ontario, 1861 ***2896.25*** *p1*
Squire, Jenna 2; Ontario, 1861 ***2896.25*** *p1*
Squire, Orrilla 63; Ontario, 1861 ***2896.25*** *p2*
Squires, George 22; Maryland, 1775 ***1220.25*** *p101*
Squires, Sarah 41; Ontario, 1871 ***1823.22*** *p151*
Sqyne, William; Maryland, 1663 ***2524.55*** *p207*
Srak, William 46; Ontario, 1871 ***1823.22*** *p151*
Srebna, Kosstancsyja; Maryland, 1910 ***3259.35*** *p58*
Srebomiski, Andrea; Maryland, 1910 ***3259.35*** *p58*
Srebomiski, Constanty; Maryland, 1910 ***3259.35*** *p58*
Srendzewski, James; Maryland, 1910 ***3259.35*** *p58*
Sring, John 80; Ontario, 1871 ***1823.22*** *p151*
Sroka, Mary; Maryland, 1910 ***3259.35*** *p58*
Sroka, Mary S.; Maryland, 1910 ***3259.35*** *p58*
Staab, Johann; Port uncertain, 1773 ***2856.30*** *p437*
Staab, Michael; Port uncertain, 1742 ***2856.30*** *p437*
Staalschmid, Peter; Port uncertain, 1784 ***2856.30*** *p437*
Staat, Franz; New York, 1835 ***8197.10*** *p310*
Stabel, Lebald; Port uncertain, 1779 ***2856.30*** *p437*
Stabel, Sebastian; Port uncertain, 1750 ***2856.30*** *p437*
Stacey, Enne; Maryland, 1665 ***2524.55*** *p207*
Stacey, Jeremiah 19; Virginia, 1774 ***1220.25*** *p46*
Stacey, Nathaniel 36; Maryland, 1774 ***1220.25*** *p7*
Stacey, Sarah 24; Philadelphia, 1774 ***1220.25*** *p63*
Stacey, Thomas 48; Ontario, 1871 ***1823.15*** *p250*
Stacey, Thomas F. 24; Ontario, 1871 ***1823.15*** *p250*
Stacey, William; Maryland, 1665 ***2524.55*** *p207*
Stachan, Thomas 40; Ontario, 1871 ***1823.15*** *p250*
Stacharowski, Lena; Maryland, 1910 ***3259.35*** *p58*
Stachlelski, Ignatius; Maryland, 1910 ***3259.35*** *p58*
Stachowak, Mary; Maryland, 1910 ***3259.35*** *p59*
Stachowicz, Joseph; Maryland, 1910 ***3259.35*** *p59*
Stachowski, Andrew; Maryland, 1910 ***3259.35*** *p59*
Stachowski, Frank; Maryland, 1910 ***3259.35*** *p59*
Stachowski, John; Maryland, 1910 ***3259.35*** *p59*
Stack, Miss; Quebec, 1856 ***9196.15*** *p11*
Stack, Edmond 65; Vermont, 1880 ***5900.10*** *p363*
Stack, Ellen Riordian 75; Vermont, 1906 ***5900.10*** *p66*
Stack, Garret; New York, 1834 ***8197.10*** *p372*
Stack, Hanorah 37; Vermont, 1885 ***5900.10*** *p369*
Stack, Honora; Vermont, 1857-1911 ***5900.10*** *p369*
Stack, James 65; Vermont, 1879 ***5900.10*** *p369*
Stack, James R.; Vermont, 1858-1940 ***5900.10*** *p369*
Stack, John; New York, 1840 ***8197.10*** *p195*
Stack, John; Vermont, 1855-1904 ***5900.10*** *p369*
Stack, John 21; Vermont, 1874 ***5900.10*** *p363*
Stack, John 43; Ontario, 1871 ***1823.28*** *p95*
Stack, John 60; Ontario, 1871 ***1823.28*** *p95*
Stack, Julia; Vermont, 1858-1927 ***5900.10*** *p369*
Stack, Julia 63; Vermont, 1885 ***5900.10*** *p369*
Stack, Margaret; Vermont, 1843-1901 ***5900.10*** *p119*
Stack, Margaret; Vermont, 1852-1931 ***5900.10*** *p412*
Stack, Mary; Vermont, 1848-1905 ***5900.10*** *p358*
Stack, Mary 95; Vermont, 1921 ***5900.10*** *p66*
Stack, Mary Daly 30; Vermont, 1859 ***5900.10*** *p363*
Stack, Michael 30; Ontario, 1871 ***1823.28*** *p95*
Stack, Michael 67; Vermont, 1891 ***5900.10*** *p66*
Stack, Patrick 40; Ontario, 1871 ***1823.28*** *p95*
Stackhouse, Wm 62; Ontario, 1871 ***1823.15*** *p250*
Stackoski, Martin; Maryland, 1910 ***3259.35*** *p59*
Stackowicz, Joseph; Maryland, 1910 ***3259.35*** *p59*
Stackowski, Anthony; Maryland, 1910 ***3259.35*** *p59*
Stackowski, Michal; Maryland, 1910 ***3259.35*** *p59*
Stackpole, Joseph; New York, 1827 ***8197.10*** *p340*
Stackpool, John Massy 41; Ontario, 1871 ***1823.28*** *p95*
Stacy, Mrs.; Maryland, 1661 ***2524.55*** *p207*
Stacy, Bridget Doyle; Vermont, 1843-1905 ***5900.10*** *p201*
Stacy, Edward; Maryland, 1678 ***2524.55*** *p207*
Stacy, John 32; Ontario, 1871 ***1823.22*** *p151*
Stacy, Julia D.; Vermont, 1835-1857 ***5900.10*** *p157*
Stacy, Peter; Vermont, 1826-1909 ***5900.10*** *p201*
Stacy, Richard 43; Ontario, 1871 ***1823.15*** *p250*
Stacy, Samuel; New England, 1716 ***1224.2*** *p109*
Stacy, Sarah; Maryland, 1662 ***2524.55*** *p207*
Stadarowski, Feliex; Maryland, 1910 ***3259.35*** *p59*
Stade, Charles; Maryland, 1650 ***2524.55*** *p207*
Stadler, Catharina Wegerer; Port uncertain, 1795 ***2856.30*** *p438*
Stadler, Christof; Port uncertain, 1751 ***2856.30*** *p438*
Stadler, Jacob; Port uncertain, 1711 ***2856.30*** *p438*
Stadler, Jakob; Port uncertain, 1720 ***2856.30*** *p438*
Stadler, Johann Georg; Port uncertain, 1751 ***2856.30*** *p438*
Stadler, Melchior; Port uncertain, 1617 ***2856.30*** *p438*
Stadranowski, Felix; Maryland, 1910 ***3259.35*** *p59*
Stadtler, Adam; Port uncertain, 1762 ***2856.30*** *p438*
Stadtler, Michael; Port uncertain, 1762 ***2856.30*** *p438*
Stadziki, Adam; Maryland, 1910 ***3259.35*** *p59*
Stafafitza, Verla; Maryland, 1910 ***3259.35*** *p59*
Stafal, Martin; New York, New York, 1845 ***6058.10*** *p26*
Staff, James; New York, 1837 ***8197.10*** *p106*
Staff, Maria Catharina; Port uncertain, 1739 ***2856.30*** *p438*
Staffon, Henry 42; Ontario, 1871 ***1823.15*** *p255*
Stafford, A. 1; Ontario, 1861 ***2896.25*** *p30*
Stafford, E. A. 4; Ontario, 1861 ***2896.25*** *p30*
Stafford, H. G. 8; Ontario, 1861 ***2896.25*** *p30*
Stafford, J. C. 10; Ontario, 1861 ***2896.25*** *p30*
Stafford, James; Maryland, 1681 ***2524.55*** *p207*
Stafford, James; Vermont, 1801-1874 ***5900.10*** *p133*
Stafford, James 41; Ontario, 1871 ***1823.15*** *p250*
Stafford, John; Maryland, 1660 ***2524.55*** *p207*
Stafford, John 15; Maryland, 1774 ***1220.25*** *p7*
Stafford, Mary; New York, 1827 ***8197.10*** *p341*
Stafford, Michael 33; Ontario, 1871 ***1823.15*** *p250*
Stafford, Nicholas; New York, 1821 ***8197.10*** *p279*
Stafford, S. J. 4; Ontario, 1861 ***2896.25*** *p30*
Stafford, S. J. 29; Ontario, 1861 ***2896.25*** *p30*
Stafford, Stephen; Maryland, 1658 ***2524.55*** *p207*
Stafford, Tho; Virginia, 1666 ***6212.30*** *p30*
Stagg, Thomas; Virginia, 1652 ***1224.1*** *p55*
Stagga, Charles 35; Ontario, 1871 ***1823.28*** *p95*
Staggemeyer, Philip Henry; New York, 1834 ***8197.10*** *p316*
Staggwell, Ruth *SEE* Staggwell, Thomas
Staggwell, Thomas *SEE* Staggwell, Thomas
Staggwell, Thomas; Maryland, 1659 ***2524.55*** *p207*
Wife: Ruth
Son: Thomas
Stagwell, Ruth *SEE* Stagwell, Thomas

Stapleton, Mary 32; Vermont, 1880 ***5900.10*** *p584*
Stapleton, Mary 34; Ontario, 1861 ***2896.25*** *p26*
Stapleton, Mary 38; Ontario, 1861 ***2896.25*** *p19*
Stapleton, Mary 50; Ontario, 1861 ***2896.28*** *p49*
Stapleton, Mary A. 30; Ontario, 1861 ***2896.28*** *p35*
Stapleton, Mary Raftery 70; Vermont, 1913 ***5900.10*** *p198*
Stapleton, Melissa 17; Ontario, 1861 ***2896.28*** *p29*
Stapleton, Mellissa 15; Ontario, 1861 ***2896.28*** *p35*
Stapleton, Michael; Vermont, 1823-1895 ***5900.10*** *p312*
Stapleton, N. J. 5; Ontario, 1861 ***2896.25*** *p19*
Stapleton, Patrick; Vermont, 1828-1883 ***5900.10*** *p545*
Stapleton, Patrick 24; Vermont, 1873 ***5900.10*** *p566*
Stapleton, Patrick Henry; Vermont, 1854-1885 ***5900.10*** *p312*
Stapleton, Peter D. 40; Ontario, 1861 ***2896.28*** *p49*
Stapleton, Robert 3; Ontario, 1861 ***2896.25*** *p19*
Stapleton, Sarah 33; Ontario, 1861 ***2896.25*** *p19*
Stapleton, Seymour 21; Ontario, 1861 ***2896.28*** *p55*
Stapleton, Stinson 14; Ontario, 1861 ***2896.25*** *p26*
Stapleton, Susanna 35; Virginia, 1775 ***1220.25*** *p103*
Stapleton, Thomas B.; Vermont, 1880 ***5900.10*** *p296*
Stapleton, Victoria 18; Ontario, 1861 ***2896.28*** *p35*
Stapleton, William 3; Ontario, 1861 ***2896.27*** *p68*
Stapleton, William 71; Ontario, 1861 ***2896.28*** *p49*
Stapleton, William H. 9; Ontario, 1861 ***2896.25*** *p26*
Stapley, Jo; Virginia, 1671 ***6212.30*** *p44*
Staplicky, Stephen; Maryland, 1910 ***3259.35*** *p59*
Stapp, Agnes; Port uncertain, 1773 ***2856.30*** *p438*
Stapylton, Francis Samuel; New York, 1779 ***1224.2*** *p110*
Star, Sarah 86; Vermont, 1912 ***5900.10*** *p361*
Starck, Anton; Port uncertain, 1732 ***2856.30*** *p438*
Starck, Augustin; Port uncertain, 1794 ***2856.30*** *p438*
Starck, Georg; Port uncertain, 1748 ***2856.30*** *p439*
Starck, Henry; New York, 1840 ***8197.10*** *p196*
Starck, Johann; Port uncertain, 1790 ***2856.30*** *p439*
Starck, Magdalena; Port uncertain, 1771 ***2856.30*** *p439*
Starckher, Franz Josef; Port uncertain, 1758 ***2856.30*** *p439*
Stares, Alfred Guildford; New York, 1856 ***1224.3*** *p74*
Stares, Bennett; Maryland, 1666 ***2524.55*** *p208*
Stark, Adam Bertram; America, 1893 ***1640.13*** *p117*
Stark, Ellen 13; Vermont, n.d. ***5900.10*** *p60*
Stark, Ellen 13; Vermont, 1877 ***5900.10*** *p60*
Stark, Eva; Port uncertain, 1700-1799 ***2856.30*** *p439*
Stark, Georg; Port uncertain, 1700-1799 ***2856.30*** *p439*
Stark, Hans Georg; Port uncertain, 1787 ***2856.30*** *p439*
Stark, James; Georgia, 1806 ***1640.10*** *p191*
Stark, Johann; America, 1764 ***2856.30*** *p439*
Stark, Johann; Port uncertain, 1791 ***2856.30*** *p439*
Stark, Johann; Port uncertain, 1792 ***2856.30*** *p439*
Stark, John 52; Ontario, 1871 ***1823.15*** *p251*
Stark, Samuel 50; Ontario, 1871 ***1823.15*** *p251*
Stark, Thomas 39; Ontario, 1871 ***1823.15*** *p251*
Stark, William 50; Vermont, 1876 ***5900.10*** *p60*
Starke, Henry; Maryland, 1669 ***2524.55*** *p208*
Starke, John; Maryland, 1679 ***2524.55*** *p208*
Starkey, Arthur 23; Ontario, 1871 ***1823.28*** *p95*
Starkey, Charles P.; New York, 1806 ***8197.10*** *p323*
Starkey, Katherine; Maryland, 1664 ***2524.55*** *p208*
Starkey, Nathaniell; Virginia, 1703-1704 ***6212.30*** *p62*
Starks, C. 10; Ontario, 1861 ***2896.26*** *p30*
Starks, David 14; Ontario, 1861 ***2896.26*** *p30*
Starlin, Filian 18; Ontario, 1861 ***2896.26*** *p20*
Starnes, Mr.; Quebec, 1857 ***9196.15*** *p18*
Starns, Louis 35; Ontario, 1871 ***1823.28*** *p95*
Starr, Ann; Vermont, 1823-1907 ***5900.10*** *p393*
Starr, Ann 70; Vermont, 1892 ***5900.10*** *p361*
Starr, Anna; New London, Connecticut, 1838 ***1224.3*** *p74*
Starr, Annie; Vermont, 1863-1954 ***5900.10*** *p588*
Starr, Annie Richardson 82; Vermont, 1900 ***5900.10*** *p431*
Starr, Bridget; Vermont, 1835-1912 ***5900.10*** *p586*
Starr, Bridget Carroll; Vermont, 1834-1918 ***5900.10*** *p257*
Starr, Bridget Cleary 81; Vermont, 1879 ***5900.10*** *p618*
Starr, Bridget Osborne; Vermont, 1831-1865 ***5900.10*** *p364*
Starr, Catherine K.; Vermont, 1830-1886 ***5900.10*** *p588*
Starr, Catherine O'Donnell; Vermont, 1837-1913 ***5900.10*** *p586*
Starr, Delia Steele; Vermont, 1866-1931 ***5900.10*** *p248*
Starr, Dennis; Vermont, 1837-1907 ***5900.10*** *p247*
Starr, Dennis, Jr.; Vermont, 1861-1900 ***5900.10*** *p247*
Starr, John; Vermont, 1828-1897 ***5900.10*** *p586*
Starr, John 10 days; Vermont, 1867 ***5900.10*** *p247*
Starr, Josephine Gregory; Vermont, 1854-1911 ***5900.10*** *p274*
Starr, Julia; Vermont, 1855-1861 ***5900.10*** *p248*
Starr, Julia; Vermont, 1862-1870 ***5900.10*** *p248*
Starr, Julia Ryan; Vermont, 1816-1888 ***5900.10*** *p248*
Starr, Margaret Maloney; Vermont, 1843-1914 ***5900.10*** *p247*
Starr, Mary; Vermont, 1850-1939 ***5900.10*** *p431*
Starr, Michael; Vermont, 1859-1861 ***5900.10*** *p248*
Starr, Michael R.; Vermont, 1825-1892 ***5900.10*** *p588*
Starr, Nancy; Vermont, 1852-1924 ***5900.10*** *p432*
Starr, Nancy 97; Vermont, 1914 ***5900.10*** *p587*
Starr, Nora; Vermont, 1796-1871 ***5900.10*** *p247*
Starr, Patrick; Vermont, 1811-1893 ***5900.10*** *p248*
Starr, Patrick 96; Vermont, 1880 ***5900.10*** *p431*
Starr, Timothy; Vermont, 1849-1904 ***5900.10*** *p274*
Starr, Timothy 74; Vermont, 1889 ***5900.10*** *p431*
Starr, William P.; Vermont, 1853-1937 ***5900.10*** *p248*
Starret, Samuel; Pennsylvania, 1779 ***4629.10*** *p35*
Starritt, Hannah 53; Ontario, 1871 ***1823.28*** *p95*
Starzynski, John; Maryland, 1910 ***3259.35*** *p59*
Starzynski, Joseph; Maryland, 1910 ***3259.35*** *p59*
Stashalyski, Joseph; Maryland, 1910 ***3259.35*** *p59*
Stasiak, Victoria; Maryland, 1910 ***3259.35*** *p59*
Stasiak, William; Maryland, 1910 ***3259.35*** *p59*
Staskowsak, Martin; Maryland, 1910 ***3259.35*** *p59*
Stassen, Franz Karl; Port uncertain, 1791 ***2856.30*** *p439*
Staszak, Michael; Maryland, 1910 ***3259.35*** *p59*
States, John; Portland, Maine, 1858 ***9196.15*** *p31*
Statner, Bernhard; Port uncertain, 1783 ***2856.30*** *p451*
Stats, Sarah 28; Ontario, 1871 ***1823.22*** *p152*
Statthafer, Peter; New Orleans, 1853 ***3437.14*** *p15*
Stattler, Catharina; Port uncertain, 1766 ***2856.30*** *p439*
Staub, Johann; Port uncertain, 1730 ***2856.30*** *p439*
Stauber, Agathe; Port uncertain, 1800 ***2856.30*** *p439*
Stauber, Franz Josef; Port uncertain, 1800 ***2856.30*** *p439*
Staubus, Conrad 36; Ontario, 1871 ***1823.15*** *p251*
Stauch, Burkhard; Port uncertain, 1762 ***2856.30*** *p439*
Staud, Abraham; America, 1739 ***2856.30*** *p439*
With family
Staud, Anna Barbara; America, 1738 ***2856.30*** *p439*
Staud, Anna Elisabeth; America, 1738 ***2856.30*** *p439*
Staud, Anna Magdalena; America, 1742 ***2856.30*** *p439*
Staud, Cath. Christina; America, 1742 ***2856.30*** *p439*
Staud, Georg; America, 1739 ***2856.30*** *p439*
Staud, Gorg; America, 1749 ***2856.30*** *p439*
Staud, Johann; America, 1749 ***2856.30*** *p439*
Staud, Johann; Port uncertain, 1784 ***2856.30*** *p439*
Staud, Michael; America, 1749 ***2856.30*** *p439*
Staud, Peter; America, 1738 ***2856.30*** *p439*
Staudacher, Caspar; Port uncertain, 1784 ***2856.30*** *p439*
Staudacher, Georg; Port uncertain, 1747 ***2856.30*** *p439*
Staudacher, Georg; Port uncertain, 1767 ***2856.30*** *p439*
Staudacher, Johann; Port uncertain, 1747 ***2856.30*** *p439*
Staudacher, Johann; Port uncertain, 1767 ***2856.30*** *p439*
Staudenmayer, Hans; America, 1752 ***2856.30*** *p439*
Staudenmayer, Johann; America, 1752 ***2856.30*** *p439*
With wife & 3 children
Staudenmayer, Johann Jakob; Port uncertain, 1763 ***2856.30*** *p439*
With wife & 6 children
Staudenmayer, Magdalena; America, 1752 ***2856.30*** *p439*
Stauder, Hans Erhard; Port uncertain, 1728 ***2856.30*** *p440*
Stauder, Theobald; Port uncertain, 1762 ***2856.30*** *p440*
With wife & children
Stauderin, Maria Eva; Port uncertain, 1778 ***2856.30*** *p440*
Staudin, Anna Magdalena; America, 1742 ***2856.30*** *p439*
Staudin, Cath. Christina; America, 1742 ***2856.30*** *p439*
Staudinger, Franz Josef; Port uncertain, 1766 ***2856.30*** *p440*
Staudinger, Johann; Port uncertain, 1774 ***2856.30*** *p440*
Staudt, Miss; Port uncertain, 1784 ***2856.30*** *p175*
Staudt, Daniel; America, 1738 ***2856.30*** *p440*
Staudt, Johann Jakob; Port uncertain, 1765 ***2856.30*** *p440*
Stauff, Anna Maria; Port uncertain, 1756 ***2856.30*** *p440*
Stauff, Daniel; America, 1770 ***2856.30*** *p440*
Stauffer, Christina; America, 1774 ***2856.30*** *p440*
Stauffer, Jakob; America, 1774 ***2856.30*** *p440*
Stauffer, Ulrich; America, 1738 ***2856.30*** *p440*
Staufter, Christian; America, 1749 ***2856.30*** *p440*
Staugel, John 40; Ontario, 1871 ***1823.15*** *p251*
Staunton, John; New York, 1840 ***8197.10*** *p285*
Staunton, Moses; Toronto, 1878 ***1640.13*** *p117*
Staunton, Patrick; New York, 1836 ***8197.10*** *p302*
Staussin, Elisabeth; Port uncertain, 1781 ***2856.30*** *p440*
Staut, Maria Catharina; Port uncertain, 1768 ***2856.30*** *p440*
Stautt, Jakob; America, 1739 ***2856.30*** *p440*
Stautt, Johann; America, 1739 ***2856.30*** *p440*
Stautt, Michael; America, 1739 ***2856.30*** *p440*
Stauzki, Anafly; Maryland, 1910 ***3259.35*** *p59*
Stavar, Nels 30; British Columbia, 1909 ***9196.1*** *p28*
Stavar, Nels 30; Washington, 1909 ***9196.1*** *p28*
Stavely, Adam; Maryland, 1649 ***2524.55*** *p209*
Stavely, Giles; Maryland, 1682 ***2524.55*** *p209*
Stavely, James 46; Ontario, 1871 ***1823.15*** *p251*
Stavely, Richard 30; Nova Scotia, 1774 ***1220.25*** *p14*
Stavely, Robert 26; Halifax, Nova Scotia, 1774 ***1220.25*** *p138*
Stavely, Robert 26; Nova Scotia, 1774 ***1220.25*** *p14*
Stawinska, John; Maryland, 1910 ***3259.35*** *p59*
Stay, Mary; Vermont, 1857-1921 ***5900.10*** *p174*
Staynes, Thomas; Maryland, 1671 ***2524.55*** *p209*
Staynes, Thomas; Maryland, 1676 ***2524.55*** *p209*
Staynestreet, Thomas; Maryland, 1662 ***2524.55*** *p211*
Staynton, John; Virginia, 1690-1691 ***6212.30*** *p59*
Steacy, George 45; Ontario, 1871 ***1823.15*** *p251*
Stead, Benjamin; South Carolina, n.d. ***1224.2*** *p110*
Stead, Edward; New York, 1831 ***8197.10*** *p282*
Stead, Elizabeth 26; New York, 1774 ***1220.25*** *p73*
Steady, Hannah Coriveau; Vermont, 1838-1916 ***5900.10*** *p288*
Steady, Jeremiah G.; Vermont, 1826-1911 ***5900.10*** *p288*
Steady, Leonard; Vermont, 1853-1925 ***5900.10*** *p288*
Steady, Mary Dunn; Vermont, 1855-1932 ***5900.10*** *p288*
Steapleton, John 39; Ontario, 1871 ***1823.28*** *p95*
Stear, Nicholas 47; Maryland, 1775 ***1220.25*** *p104*
Stearns, Dolly A. Megee; Vermont, 1818-1893 ***5900.10*** *p282*
Stearns, Eldad B. 75; Vermont, 1888 ***5900.10*** *p282*
Stearns, Margaret Keenan; Vermont, 1843-1912 ***5900.10*** *p512*
Steavens, Herrman 20; Ontario, 1861 ***2896.27*** *p11*
Stebbins, Anthony; Vermont, 1847-1926 ***5900.10*** *p69*
Stebbins, Emma Lalor; Vermont, 1863-1939 ***5900.10*** *p420*
Stebbins, Mary Addel; Vermont, 1829-1904 ***5900.10*** *p539*
Stebbins, Peter; Vermont, 1846-1931 ***5900.10*** *p420*
Stebbins, Rachel; Vermont, 1834-1924 ***5900.10*** *p199*
Stebbins, Timothy; Vermont, 1825-1913 ***5900.10*** *p199*
Stebbins, Tressa Tucker 59; Vermont, 1909 ***5900.10*** *p69*
Stebil, Abraham; New York, 1840 ***8197.10*** *p285*
Steck, Johan; New York, 1807 ***8197.10*** *p50*
Steckle, Nikol; Port uncertain, 1722 ***2856.30*** *p440*
Stect, John 48; Ontario, 1871 ***1823.15*** *p251*
Stedell, Henry 26; Philadelphia, 1774 ***1220.25*** *p3*
Stedman, Charles; Pennsylvania, 1777 ***4629.10*** *p22*
Stedman, James; Savannah, Georgia, 1768 ***1640.10*** *p191*
Stedman, Lewis; Virginia, 1665 ***6212.30*** *p20*
Stedman, Solomon; Boston, 1697 ***1224.1*** *p55*
Stedman, William; Georgia, 1758 ***1640.10*** *p191*
Stedot, John; Pennsylvania, 1786 ***4629.10*** *p51*
Steeb, Johann; Port uncertain, 1773 ***2856.30*** *p437*
Steeblin, Elisabeth; Port uncertain, 1746 ***2856.30*** *p440*
Steed, Abraham; Maryland, 1665 ***2524.55*** *p209*
Steed, Edward 25; Maryland, 1774 ***1220.25*** *p84*
Steed, William; Maryland, 1665 ***2524.55*** *p209*
Steed, William 62; Ontario, 1871 ***1823.22*** *p152*
Steeg, Michael; Port uncertain, 1788 ***2856.30*** *p440*
Steeger, Andreas; America, 1753 ***2856.30*** *p440*
With wife & children
Steel, Miss; Quebec, 1857 ***9196.15*** *p22*
Steel, Mrs.; Quebec, 1856 ***9196.15*** *p8*
Steel, Agnus 58; Ontario, 1871 ***1823.28*** *p95*
Steel, Alexander 26; Maryland, 1774 ***1220.25*** *p54*
Steel, Allen; Boston, 1754 ***1224.2*** *p110*
Steel, Allen; New York, 1837 ***8197.10*** *p106*
Steel, Ann 12; Ontario, 1861 ***2896.28*** *p28*
Steel, Cintha 6; Ontario, 1861 ***2896.27*** *p5*
Steel, Daniel 22; Ontario, 1861 ***2896.27*** *p5*
Steel, Elizabeth 80; Vermont, 1876 ***5900.10*** *p280*
Steel, Emily 9; Ontario, 1861 ***2896.27*** *p5*
Steel, George; Pennsylvania, 1786 ***4629.10*** *p54*
Steel, George 53; Ontario, 1871 ***1823.15*** *p251*
Steel, Hugh; Philadelphia, 1757 ***1640.13*** *p117*
Steel, J. D.; Alabama, 1814-1845 ***1640.10*** *p192*
Steel, James; Pennsylvania, 1778 ***4629.10*** *p32*
Steel, James 38; Ontario, 1871 ***1823.28*** *p95*
Steel, John; Charles Town, South Carolina, 1745 ***1224.2*** *p110*
Steel, John; Georgia, 1699 ***1640.13*** *p117*
Steel, John; Pennsylvania, 1777 ***4629.10*** *p22*
Steel, John 46; Nova Scotia, 1774 ***1220.25*** *p135*
With son
Steel, John 94; Vermont, 1882 ***5900.10*** *p280*
Steel, Margaret 16; Ontario, 1861 ***2896.27*** *p5*
Steel, Martha 47; Ontario, 1861 ***2896.28*** *p28*
Steel, Mary 40; Ontario, 1861 ***2896.27*** *p5*
Steel, Robert 59; Ontario, 1871 ***1823.15*** *p251*
Steel, Sarah 20; Ontario, 1861 ***2896.27*** *p5*
Steel, Thomas 18; Ontario, 1861 ***2896.27*** *p5*
Steel, William 11; Ontario, 1861 ***2896.27*** *p5*
Steele, Agnes 46; Ontario, 1871 ***1823.15*** *p251*
Steele, Alexander *SEE* Steele, Donald
Steele, Alexander *SEE* Steele, John
Steele, Alexander; Canada, 1892 ***1640.13*** *p117*
Steele, Alexander; Ontario, 1840-1849 ***4537.37*** *p84*
Wife: Catherine MacIsaac
Child: Kirsty
Child: Angus
Child: Flora
Child: Catherine

Steele, Alexander; Ontario, 1849 ***4537.32*** *p95*
Wife: Catherine MacIsaac
Child: Flora
Child: Catherine
Child: Kirsty
Child: Angus
Steele, Alexander; Ontario, 1851 ***4537.37*** *p85*
Wife: Catherine Morrison
Child: Charlotte
Child: Donald
Child: Dougal
Child: Michael
Child: Jessie
Steele, Alexander; Saskatchewan, 1884 ***4537.37*** *p104*
Wife: Annabella Kennedy
Child: Ann
Child: Marion
Child: Hugh
Child: John
Child: Isabella
Steele, Allan *SEE* Steele, Catherine
Steele, Allan *SEE* Steele, John
Steele, Angus *SEE* Steele, Alexander
Steele, Angus *SEE* Steele, Donald
Steele, Angus *SEE* Steele, James
Steele, Angus *SEE* Steele, John
Steele, Ann *SEE* Steele, Alexander
Steele, Ann *SEE* Steele, Donald
Steele, Ann *SEE* Steele, John
Steele, Ann; Ontario, 1789-1900 ***4537.37*** *p62*
Steele, Ann; Ontario, 1849 ***4537.32*** *p40*
Steele, Ann; Port uncertain, 1840-1849 ***4537.37*** *p127*
Steele, Ann 72; Vermont, 1906 ***5900.10*** *p568*
Steele, Ann MacMillan *SEE* Steele, John
Steele, Annabella Kennedy *SEE* Steele, Alexander
Steele, Catherine *SEE* Steele, Alexander
Steele, Catherine *SEE* Steele, Donald
Steele, Catherine *SEE* Steele, John
Steele, Catherine; Ontario, 1840-1849 ***4537.37*** *p87*
Steele, Catherine; Ontario, 1849 ***4537.32*** *p96*
Steele, Catherine; Ontario, 1851 ***4537.37*** *p59*
Steele, Catherine; Vermont, 1835-1893 ***5900.10*** *p227*
Steele, Catherine; Port uncertain, 1840-1849 ***4537.37*** *p133*
Child: Mary
Child: Allan
Steele, Catherine; Port uncertain, 1850-1859 ***4537.37*** *p106*
Steele, Catherine MacInnes *SEE* Steele, Donald
Steele, Catherine MacIsaac *SEE* Steele, Alexander
Steele, Catherine Morrison *SEE* Steele, Alexander
Steele, Catherine Walker *SEE* Steele, Peter
Steele, Charles; New York, 1807 ***8197.10*** *p49*
Steele, Charlotte *SEE* Steele, Alexander
Steele, Delia; Vermont, 1866-1931 ***5900.10*** *p248*
Steele, Donald *SEE* Steele, Alexander
Steele, Donald *SEE* Steele, Donald
Steele, Donald *SEE* Steele, John
Steele, Donald *SEE* Steele, Peter
Steele, Donald; Nova Scotia, 1848 ***4537.37*** *p20*
Wife: Margaret MacDonald
Child: Roderick
Child: Donald
Child: Margaret
Child: Alexander
Child: Malcolm
Steele, Donald; Ontario, 1849 ***4537.37*** *p85*
Child: Ann
Child: Lachlan
Child: Donald
Wife: Jessie Cumming
Child: Angus
Child: John
Steele, Donald; Port uncertain, 1840-1849 ***4537.37*** *p133*
Wife: Catherine MacInnes
Child: Donald
Child: John
Child: Mary
Child: Catherine
Steele, Donald; Port uncertain, 1840-1849 ***4537.37*** *p133*
Wife: Flora Cameron
Child: Neil
Child: John
Child: Sarah
Steele, Dougal *SEE* Steele, Alexander
Steele, Edward; Illinois, 1855 ***1224.3*** *p74*
Steele, Elizabeth; Vermont, 1831-1914 ***5900.10*** *p491*
Steele, Finlay *SEE* Steele, John
Steele, Flora *SEE* Steele, Alexander
Steele, Flora *SEE* Steele, James
Steele, Flora; Saskatchewan, 1884 ***4537.37*** *p98*
Steele, Flora Cameron *SEE* Steele, Donald
Steele, George; Alabama, 1810-1845 ***1640.10*** *p191*
Steele, Hugh *SEE* Steele, Alexander
Steele, Isabella *SEE* Steele, Alexander
Steele, James; Nova Scotia, 1840-1849 ***4537.37*** *p21*
Wife: Mary MacIsaac
Child: Flora
Child: Angus
Steele, Janet *SEE* Steele, John
Steele, Jessie *SEE* Steele, Alexander
Steele, Jessie Cumming *SEE* Steele, Donald
Steele, Jno.; Pennsylvania, 1784 ***4629.10*** *p44*
Steele, John *SEE* Steele, Alexander
Steele, John *SEE* Steele, Donald
Steele, John *SEE* Steele, John
Steele, John *SEE* Steele, Peter
Steele, John; Nova Scotia, 1840-1849 ***4537.37*** *p21*
Wife: Marion MacKinnon
Child: Finlay
Child: Donald
Child: Lachlan
Steele, John; Ontario, 1840-1849 ***4537.37*** *p85*
Wife: Ann MacMillan
Child: Mary
Child: Donald
Steele, John; Ontario, 1848 ***4537.37*** *p85*
Wife: Mary MacIsaac
Child: John
Child: Roderick
Steele, John; Ontario, 1849 ***4537.32*** *p95*
Wife: Ann MacMillan
Child: Donald
Child: Mary
Steele, John; Ontario, 1849 ***4537.32*** *p95*
Wife: Mary MacIsaac
Child: Roderick
Child: Alexander
Child: John
Steele, John; Vermont, 1829 ***5900.10*** *p13*
Steele, John; Virginia, 1638 ***1224.1*** *p55*
Steele, John; Port uncertain, 1840-1849 ***4537.37*** *p133*
Wife: Margaret MacDonald
Child: Ann
Child: Angus
Child: Allan
Child: John
Child: Mary
Child: Janet
Child: Kirsty
Child: Catherine
Steele, John 53; Ontario, 1871 ***1823.22*** *p152*
Steele, Kirsty *SEE* Steele, Alexander
Steele, Kirsty *SEE* Steele, John
Steele, Kirsty; Port uncertain, 1850-1859 ***4537.37*** *p118*
Steele, Lachlan *SEE* Steele, Donald
Steele, Lachlan *SEE* Steele, John
Steele, Malcolm *SEE* Steele, Donald
Steele, Margaret *SEE* Steele, Donald
Steele, Margaret; Ontario, 1850-1859 ***4537.37*** *p55*
Steele, Margaret; Ontario, 1851 ***4537.32*** *p38*
Steele, Margaret MacDonald *SEE* Steele, Donald
Steele, Margaret MacDonald *SEE* Steele, John
Steele, Marion *SEE* Steele, Alexander
Steele, Marion MacKinnon *SEE* Steele, John
Steele, Mary *SEE* Steele, Catherine
Steele, Mary *SEE* Steele, Donald
Steele, Mary *SEE* Steele, John
Steele, Mary *SEE* Steele, Peter
Steele, Mary; Ontario, 1840-1849 ***4537.37*** *p79*
Steele, Mary; Ontario, 1849 ***4537.32*** *p82*
Steele, Mary; Ontario, 1850-1859 ***4537.37*** *p33*
Steele, Mary 51; Ontario, 1871 ***1823.15*** *p251*
Steele, Mary MacIsaac *SEE* Steele, James
Steele, Mary MacIsaac *SEE* Steele, John
Steele, Mathew; Virginia, 1667-1668 ***6212.30*** *p39*
Steele, Michael *SEE* Steele, Alexander
Steele, Neil *SEE* Steele, Donald
Steele, Penny; Port uncertain, 1850-1859 ***4537.37*** *p122*
Steele, Peter; Ontario, 1849 ***4537.37*** *p86*
Wife: Catherine Walker
Child: Donald
Child: Rachel
Child: Roderick
Child: John
Child: Mary
Steele, Peter W.; New York, 1840 ***8197.10*** *p194*
Steele, Rachel *SEE* Steele, Peter
Steele, Robert; New York, 1803 ***8197.10*** *p16*
Steele, Roderick *SEE* Steele, Donald
Steele, Roderick *SEE* Steele, John
Steele, Roderick *SEE* Steele, Peter
Steele, Sarah *SEE* Steele, Donald
Steele, William; Alabama, 1826-1845 ***1640.10*** *p192*
Steele, William; Maryland, 1682 ***2524.55*** *p209*
Steelman, Frederick; Pennsylvania, 1777 ***4629.10*** *p14*
Steels, Henry 80; Ontario, 1871 ***1823.22*** *p152*
Steen, John; New York, 1840 ***8197.10*** *p196*
Steen, John 35; Ontario, 1871 ***1823.15*** *p251*
Steen, John 37; Ontario, 1871 ***1823.22*** *p152*
Steen, Robert 49; Ontario, 1871 ***1823.15*** *p251*
Steep, George 40; Ontario, 1871 ***1823.15*** *p251*
Steep, Henry 50; Ontario, 1871 ***1823.15*** *p251*
Steep, Michael 51; Ontario, 1871 ***1823.28*** *p95*
Steep, Peter 38; Ontario, 1871 ***1823.15*** *p251*
Steep, William 39; Ontario, 1871 ***1823.15*** *p251*
Steepe, John 40; Ontario, 1871 ***1823.15*** *p251*
Steeple, George; New York, 1829 ***8197.10*** *p352*
Steeps, William 32; Ontario, 1871 ***1823.15*** *p251*
Steer, Deborah 21; Ontario, 1861 ***2896.27*** *p29*
Steer, W.; Quebec, 1857 ***9196.15*** *p23*
Steer, William 72; Ontario, 1871 ***1823.22*** *p152*
Steere, Mary; Vermont, 1843-1885 ***5900.10*** *p479*
Steers, Benjamin; New York, 1840 ***8197.10*** *p285*
Steevens, David; Maryland, 1651 ***2524.55*** *p209*
Steevens, Thomas; New Orleans, 1823 ***1224.3*** *p74*
Stefan, Mary; Maryland, 1910 ***3259.35*** *p59*
Stefankiewicz, Valentine; Maryland, 1910 ***3259.35*** *p59*
Stefanski, Ignatius T.; Maryland, 1910 ***3259.35*** *p59*
Stefanski, Mary; Maryland, 1910 ***3259.35*** *p59*
Stefanski, Matias; Maryland, 1910 ***3259.35*** *p59*
Stefanski, Michael; Maryland, 1910 ***3259.35*** *p59*
Stefanski, Raymond; Maryland, 1910 ***3259.35*** *p59*
Stefanski, Thomas; Maryland, 1910 ***3259.35*** *p60*
Stefenski, I.; Maryland, 1910 ***3259.35*** *p60*
Steff, Mrs. Christof; Port uncertain, 1783 ***2856.30*** *p440*
Steffan, Christian; America, 1737 ***2856.30*** *p440*
Steffan, Wendel; America, 1737 ***2856.30*** *p440*
Steffen, George; Maryland, 1910 ***3259.35*** *p60*
Steffen, Johann Christof; Port uncertain, 1758 ***2856.30*** *p440*
Steffen, Margaretha; America, 1758 ***2856.30*** *p440*
Steffen, Nicol; Port uncertain, 1771 ***2856.30*** *p440*
Steffenson, Erick; New York, 1820 ***8197.10*** *p278*
Steffi, Mrs. Christof; Port uncertain, 1783 ***2856.30*** *p440*
Steffin, Anna Eva; Port uncertain, 1790 ***2856.30*** *p440*
Steger, Conrad; Pennsylvania, 1779 ***4629.10*** *p36*
Stegge, Thomas; Virginia, 1652 ***1224.1*** *p55*
Stegge, Thomas; Virginia, 1671 ***1224.1*** *p55*
Stegmayer, Philipp; Port uncertain, 1752 ***2856.30*** *p440*
Stehelin, Thomas; Boston, 1777 ***1224.2*** *p110*
Stehle, Michael; Port uncertain, 1733 ***2856.30*** *p441*
Steidelberger, Nikolaus; Port uncertain, 1748 ***2856.30*** *p441*
Steiger, Andreas; America, 1766 ***2856.30*** *p441*
Steiger, Franz Xaver; Port uncertain, 1790 ***2856.30*** *p441*
Steiger, Jacob; Port uncertain, 1729 ***2856.30*** *p441*
Steiger, Johann; Port uncertain, 1749 ***2856.30*** *p441*
Steiger, Johanna; Port uncertain, 1741 ***2856.30*** *p441*
Steiger, Josef; Port uncertain, 1790 ***2856.30*** *p441*
Steimel, Johann; Port uncertain, 1764 ***2856.30*** *p442*
With family
Steimitz, George; New Orleans, 1856 ***3437.14*** *p41*
Steimour, John 30; Ontario, 1871 ***1823.15*** *p251*
Stein, Andreas; Port uncertain, 1790 ***2856.30*** *p441*
Stein, Christian; Port uncertain, 1734 ***2856.30*** *p441*
Stein, Christof; Port uncertain, 1791 ***2856.30*** *p441*
Stein, Diederick; New York, 1839 ***8197.10*** *p140*
Stein, Henrich; America, 1745 ***2856.30*** *p441*
Stein, Johann; Port uncertain, 1793 ***2856.30*** *p441*
Stein, Johann Elias; Port uncertain, 1744 ***2856.30*** *p442*
With wife son & 3 daughters
Stein, Johann Esajas; America, 1744 ***2856.30*** *p442*
With wife son & 3 daughters
Stein, Johann Martin; America, 1750 ***2856.30*** *p441*
Stein, Johann Michael; America, 1742 ***2856.30*** *p441*
Stein, Johann Michael; Port uncertain, 1742 ***2856.30*** *p441*
Stein, John F.; New York, 1830 ***8197.10*** *p67*
Stein, John Frederick; New York, 1828 ***8197.10*** *p282*
Stein, Maria Elisabeth; Port uncertain, 1788 ***2856.30*** *p441*
Stein, Marianna; Port uncertain, 1774 ***2856.30*** *p441*
Stein, Michael; Port uncertain, 1789 ***2856.30*** *p441*
Stein, Mrs. Nikol; America, 1741 ***2856.30*** *p441*
With family
Stein, Peter; Port uncertain, 1748 ***2856.30*** *p441*
Stein, Regina; Port uncertain, 1774 ***2856.30*** *p441*
Stein, Robert; Maryland, 1910 ***3259.35*** *p60*
Stein, Sabina; Port uncertain, 1754 ***2856.30*** *p441*
Stein, Wm 51; Ontario, 1871 ***1823.28*** *p95*
Steinart, Annie 43; Kansas, 1879-1910 ***9079.10*** *p13*
Steinart, Conrad 46; Kansas, 1879-1910 ***9079.10*** *p13*
Steinart, Eva 45; Kansas, 1879-1910 ***9079.10*** *p13*
Steinart, George J. 54; Kansas, 1876-1910 ***9079.10*** *p13*
Steinart, Jacob 40; Kansas, 1878-1910 ***9079.10*** *p13*
Steinart, John F. 49; Kansas, 1879-1910 ***9079.10*** *p13*
Steinart, Pauline 36; Kansas, 1891-1910 ***9079.10*** *p13*
Steinbach, Jakob; Port uncertain, 1778 ***2856.30*** *p442*

Steinbach, Johann Jakob; Port uncertain, 1750 ***2856.30*** *p442*
Stein Bach, Johannes; New York, 1807 ***8197.10*** *p50*
Steinback, Andreas; Port uncertain, 1771 ***2856.30*** *p442*
Steinbek, Andreas; Port uncertain, 1771 ***2856.30*** *p442*
Steinberger, Anna Catharina; Port uncertain, 1784 ***2856.30*** *p442*
With husband & 4 children
Steinberger, Marquard; Port uncertain, 1784 ***2856.30*** *p442*
With wife & 4 children
Steinborn, Christian; Port uncertain, 1732 ***2856.30*** *p442*
Steinbrenner, Frederick W.; New York, 1821 ***8197.10*** *p280*
Steinbrenner, Frederick William; New York, 1827 ***8197.10*** *p282*
Steinbrick, Reinhold 33; Ontario, 1871 ***1823.28*** *p95*
Steinbronn, Johann Heinrich; Port uncertain, 1755 ***2856.30*** *p442*
Steinbronner, Anna; Port uncertain, 1768 ***2856.30*** *p442*
Steinbronner, Anna Maria; Port uncertain, 1729 ***2856.30*** *p442*
Steinbronner, Nikolaus; Port uncertain, 1754 ***2856.30*** *p442*
Steinel, Johann; Port uncertain, 1764 ***2856.30*** *p442*
With family
Steiner, G. J.; Pennsylvania, 1833 ***6058.10*** *p11*
Steiner, George; New York, New York, 1850 ***6058.10*** *p53*
Steiner, Jakob; Port uncertain, 1754 ***2856.30*** *p442*
Steiner, Johann; Port uncertain, 1769 ***2856.30*** *p442*
Steinhagen, Charles 31; Ontario, 1871 ***1823.15*** *p251*
Steinhauer, Daniel; Port uncertain, 1764 ***2856.30*** *p442*
Steinhause, Mr.; America, 1767 ***2856.30*** *p309*
Steinhauser, Johann Nikolaus; America, 1754 ***2856.30*** *p442*
With wife
Steinhauser, Johann Nikolaus; Port uncertain, 1767 ***2856.30*** *p442*
With wife
Steinhauser, Maria; Port uncertain, 1613 ***2856.30*** *p442*
With husband & 2 children
Steinheuser, Jonas; America, 1754 ***2856.30*** *p442*
Steinheuser, Jonas; Port uncertain, 1767 ***2856.30*** *p442*
Steiniger, August; New York, 1839 ***8197.10*** *p140*
Steinkonig, Jakob; Port uncertain, 1747 ***2856.30*** *p442*
With wife & children
Steinle, Andrew 56; Kansas, 1908-1910 ***9079.10*** *p18*
Steinle, Andrew H. 35; Kansas, 1887-1910 ***9079.10*** *p16*
Steinle, Anna 18; Kansas, 1908-1910 ***9079.10*** *p18*
Steinle, Anna 35; Kansas, 1894-1910 ***9079.10*** *p39*
Steinle, Catharine 18; Kansas, 1891-1910 ***9079.10*** *p18*
Steinle, Catharine 47; Kansas, 1908-1910 ***9079.10*** *p18*
Steinle, Catherine 38; Kansas, 1900-1910 ***9079.10*** *p16*
Steinle, D. Peter 33; Kansas, 1887-1910 ***9079.10*** *p16*
Steinle, David 7; Kansas, 1908-1910 ***9079.10*** *p18*
Steinle, David 14; Kansas, 1899-1910 ***9079.10*** *p17*
Steinle, David 15; Kansas, 1900-1910 ***9079.10*** *p16*
Steinle, David 38; Kansas, 1891-1910 ***9079.10*** *p39*
Steinle, David 61; Kansas, 1887-1910 ***9079.10*** *p17*
Steinle, David C. 44; Kansas, 1878-1910 ***9079.10*** *p38*
Steinle, David W. 38; Kansas, 1888-1910 ***9079.10*** *p37*
Steinle, Fred G. 24; Kansas, 1893-1910 ***9079.10*** *p17*
Steinle, Frederic, Sr. 74; Kansas, 1899-1910 ***9079.10*** *p17*
Steinle, George 24; Kansas, 1902-1910 ***9079.10*** *p18*
Steinle, Godfreid D. 38; Kansas, 1900-1910 ***9079.10*** *p16*
Steinle, Gotfreid 13; Kansas, 1900-1910 ***9079.10*** *p16*
Steinle, Gottfreid 57; Kansas, 1899-1910 ***9079.10*** *p17*
Steinle, Gottfried 25; Kansas, 1899-1910 ***9079.10*** *p17*
Steinle, Gottfried 45; Kansas, 1887-1910 ***9079.10*** *p15*
Steinle, J. F. 46; Kansas, 1878-1910 ***9079.10*** *p38*
Steinle, Julia 12; Kansas, 1899-1910 ***9079.10*** *p17*
Steinle, Julia 30; Kansas, 1897-1910 ***9079.10*** *p37*
Steinle, Julia 56; Kansas, 1887-1910 ***9079.10*** *p17*
Steinle, Julia 61; Kansas, 1893-1910 ***9079.10*** *p17*
Steinle, Katie 38; Kansas, 1886-1910 ***9079.10*** *p38*
Steinle, Maria 22; Kansas, 1887-1910 ***9079.10*** *p17*
Steinle, Maria 57; Kansas, 1899-1910 ***9079.10*** *p17*
Steinle, Mary 41; Kansas, 1881-1910 ***9079.10*** *p38*
Steinle, Mary 50; Kansas, 1875-1910 ***9079.10*** *p37*
Steinle, Mary C. 43; Kansas, 1892-1910 ***9079.10*** *p15*
Steinle, Mollie 17; Kansas, 1899-1910 ***9079.10*** *p17*
Steinle, Peter 54; Kansas, 1876-1910 ***9079.10*** *p37*
Steinle, Rachael 36; Kansas, 1887-1910 ***9079.10*** *p15*
Steinle, Reinhart 43; Kansas, 1892-1910 ***9079.10*** *p15*
Steinle, Reinhart 63; Kansas, 1893-1910 ***9079.10*** *p17*
Steinler, Stoffel; America, 1749 ***2856.30*** *p442*
Steinmann, Anna Barbara; Port uncertain, 1729 ***2856.30*** *p442*
Steinmann, Anna Maria; Port uncertain, 1751 ***2856.30*** *p442*
Steinmann, Hans Jakob; Port uncertain, 1716 ***2856.30*** *p442*
Steinmann, Johann Niklas; Port uncertain, 1738 ***2856.30*** *p442*
Steinmann, Michael; America, 1754 ***2856.30*** *p442*
With wife & 6 children
Steinmayer, Johann Georg; Port uncertain, 1749 ***2856.30*** *p442*
Steinmayer, Mathis; Port uncertain, 1730 ***2856.30*** *p442*
Steinmayer, Melchior; America, 1738 ***2856.30*** *p442*
Steinmetz, Anna Margarete; Port uncertain, 1784 ***2856.30*** *p442*
Steinmitz, George; New Orleans, 1856 ***3437.14*** *p41*
Steinmitz, George; New Orleans, 1856 ***3437.14*** *p53*
Steinmuller, Johann Adam; Port uncertain, 1753 ***2856.30*** *p443*
Steinmuller, Johann Adam; Port uncertain, 1790 ***2856.30*** *p443*
Steinmuller, Johann Adam; Port uncertain, 1791 ***2856.30*** *p443*
Steinwank, Christian 20; Kansas, 1907-1910 ***9079.10*** *p7*
Steinwender, Anna Catharina; Port uncertain, 1784 ***2856.30*** *p443*
With husband & 4 children
Steinwender, Daniel; America, 1752 ***2856.30*** *p443*
With family
Steinwender, Marquard; Port uncertain, 1784 ***2856.30*** *p443*
With wife & 4 children
Steirly, James C. R.; New York, New York, 1867 ***6058.10*** *p70*
Steirly, John R.; New York, 1862 ***6058.10*** *p66*
Steiss, John Y. 36; Ontario, 1871 ***1823.15*** *p251*
Steitly, Johannes, Jr.; America, 1753 ***2856.30*** *p443*
Steitz, Elisabeth; Port uncertain, 1789 ***2856.30*** *p443*
Husband: Henzig
Steitz, Henzig *SEE* Steitz, Elisabeth
Steitz, Ludwig; New York, 1825 ***8197.10*** *p281*
Steitz, Maria Margarete; Port uncertain, 1789 ***2856.30*** *p443*
Stejer, Theobald; Port uncertain, 1741 ***2856.30*** *p443*
Stelarbe, Tho.; Maryland, 1663-1664 ***2524.55*** *p209*
Stelk, Claus 60; Ontario, 1871 ***1823.15*** *p251*
Stelk, Henry 26; Ontario, 1871 ***1823.15*** *p251*
Stell, Ezekiel; New York, 1840 ***8197.10*** *p199*
Stell, James; Pennsylvania, 1777 ***4629.10*** *p18*
Stell, John; Maryland, 1669 ***2524.55*** *p205*
Stell, John; Maryland, 1669 ***2524.55*** *p209*
Stellbaur, Josef; Port uncertain, 1796 ***2856.30*** *p443*
Stellbaur, Josef; Port uncertain, 1805 ***2856.30*** *p443*
Stelle, James; Maryland, 1679 ***2524.55*** *p209*
Stellwagen, Anna Apollonia; Port uncertain, 1741 ***2856.30*** *p443*
Stellwagen, Anna Elisabeth; Port uncertain, 1774 ***2856.30*** *p443*
Stellwagen, Heinrich Quart; America, 1741 ***2856.30*** *p443*
With wife & children
Stellwagen, Jakob; America, 1767 ***2856.30*** *p443*
Stellwagen, Jakob; Port uncertain, 1767 ***2856.30*** *p443*
Stellwagen, Jakob; Port uncertain, 1768 ***2856.30*** *p443*
Stellwagen, Johann; Port uncertain, 1774 ***2856.30*** *p443*
Stellwagen, Johann; Port uncertain, 1783 ***2856.30*** *p443*
Stellwagen, Johann; Port uncertain, 1784 ***2856.30*** *p443*
Stellwagen, Sara; Port uncertain, 1774 ***2856.30*** *p443*
Stellwagin, Anna Elisabeth; America, 1766 ***2856.30*** *p443*
Stellwagin, Anna Elisabeth; Port uncertain, 1766 ***2856.30*** *p443*
Stelmaszek, Frank; Maryland, 1910 ***3259.35*** *p60*
Stelter, Frederick; New York, 1840 ***8197.10*** *p196*
Stelzel, Adam; Port uncertain, 1783 ***2856.30*** *p443*
Stelzer, Mrs. Matthaus; America, 1788 ***2856.30*** *p443*
Stemler, Elisabeth; Port uncertain, 1765 ***2856.30*** *p443*
Stemmler, Miss; America, 1759 ***2856.30*** *p55*
Stemmler, Ms.; America, 1759 ***2856.30*** *p444*
With husband
Stemmler, Jakob; Port uncertain, 1769 ***2856.30*** *p444*
Stemmlin, Catharina; Port uncertain, 1774 ***2856.30*** *p444*
Stemner, Michael; Pennsylvania, 1777 ***4629.10*** *p9*
Stemperin, Petronella; Port uncertain, 1754 ***2856.30*** *p444*
Stempson, William; Maryland, 1681 ***2524.55*** *p209*
Stemski, John; Maryland, 1910 ***3259.35*** *p60*
Steneck, Johann Henry; New York, 1839 ***8197.10*** *p140*
Stengel, August 22; Kansas, 1900-1910 ***9079.10*** *p30*
Stengel, David; New York, 1835 ***8197.10*** *p283*
Stenger, Johann Adam; America, 1747 ***2856.30*** *p444*
Stengin, Elisabeth; Port uncertain, 1729 ***2856.30*** *p444*
Stenhouse, George; Georgia, 1698 ***1640.13*** *p117*
Stenhouse, Jas; Quebec, 1858 ***9196.15*** *p38*
Stenson, Andy 61; Ontario, 1871 ***1823.15*** *p251*
Stenson, Louis 21; Alaska, 1913 ***9196.1*** *p22*
Stenson, Louis 21; British Columbia, 1913 ***9196.1*** *p22*
Stent, Joseph W.; New York, 1839 ***8197.10*** *p139*
Stent, William; Virginia, 1680 ***1224.1*** *p55*
Stenzel, Alexander 21; Kansas, 1899-1910 ***9079.10*** *p35*
Stenzel, Amelia 29; Kansas, 1910 ***9079.10*** *p45*
Stenzel, Fredrick W. 11; Kansas, 1899-1910 ***9079.10*** *p35*
Stenzel, Jacob 22; Kansas, 1907-1910 ***9079.10*** *p35*
Stenzel, Jacob 32; Kansas, 1910 ***9079.10*** *p45*
Stenzel, John 25; Kansas, 1910 ***9079.10*** *p45*
Stenzel, John 59; Kansas, 1899-1910 ***9079.10*** *p35*
Stenzel, Mollie 18; Kansas, 1907-1910 ***9079.10*** *p35*
Stenzel, Sharlotte 57; Kansas, 1899-1910 ***9079.10*** *p35*
Stenzel, Victor 15; Kansas, 1899-1910 ***9079.10*** *p35*
Step, John 36; Ontario, 1871 ***1823.15*** *p251*
Stepanski, Anton; Maryland, 1910 ***3259.35*** *p60*
Stephan, Christina; Port uncertain, 1734 ***2856.30*** *p444*
Stephan, Christina; Port uncertain, 1735 ***2856.30*** *p444*
Stephan, Jakob; America, 1744 ***2856.30*** *p444*
With wife & child
Stephan, Johann Karl; Port uncertain, 1787 ***2856.30*** *p444*
Stephan, Josef; Port uncertain, 1730 ***2856.30*** *p444*
Stephan, Josef; Port uncertain, 1762 ***2856.30*** *p444*
Stephan, Philipp; America, 1737 ***2856.30*** *p444*
With wife & children
Stephanski, Michael; Maryland, 1910 ***3259.35*** *p60*
Stephen, Mr.; Quebec, 1857 ***9196.15*** *p18*
Stephen, Mr.; Quebec, 1857 ***9196.15*** *p22*
Stephen, Mrs.; Quebec, 1857 ***9196.15*** *p22*
Stephen, Alexander; Virginia, 1770 ***1224.2*** *p110*
Stephen, Alexander Reid; Texas, 1879 ***1640.13*** *p118*
Stephen, James; Ontario, 1857 ***1640.13*** *p118*
Stephen, James 26; Ontario, 1871 ***1823.28*** *p95*
Stephen, James 37; Ontario, 1871 ***1823.28*** *p95*
Stephen, John *SEE* Stephen, William
Stephen, John; Virginia, 1770 ***1224.2*** *p110*
Stephen, John 46; Ontario, 1871 ***1823.22*** *p152*
Stephen, Magdelan *SEE* Stephen, William
Stephen, William *SEE* Stephen, William
Stephen, William; Maryland, 1651 ***2524.55*** *p209*
Wife: Magdelan
Child: John
Child: William
Stephen, William; Pensacola, Florida, 1774 ***1640.10*** *p192*
Stephen, William; Texas, 1879 ***1640.13*** *p118*
Stephen, William 7; Ontario, 1871 ***1823.15*** *p251*
Stephens, Mr.; Quebec, 1856 ***9196.15*** *p6*
Stephens, Mrs.; Quebec, 1856 ***9196.15*** *p6*
Stephens, Alexander; New York, 1838 ***8197.10*** *p318*
Stephens, Alida 7; Ontario, 1861 ***2896.27*** *p53*
Stephens, Angelia 9; Ontario, 1861 ***2896.27*** *p53*
Stephens, B. Gilbert 51; Ontario, 1871 ***1823.15*** *p251*
Stephens, Cha; Virginia, 1668-1669 ***6212.30*** *p40*
Stephens, Charles; Maryland, 1682 ***2524.55*** *p209*
Stephens, Charles 38; Ontario, 1871 ***1823.28*** *p95*
Stephens, Christopher; Maryland, 1659 ***2524.55*** *p209*
Stephens, Dan'l; Pennsylvania, 1785 ***4629.10*** *p44*
Stephens, Donald; Georgia, 1741 ***1640.10*** *p192*
Stephens, Dorothy 22 *SEE* Stephens, William
Stephens, Edward; New York, 1809 ***8197.10*** *p277*
Stephens, Elizabeth *SEE* Stephens, John
Stephens, Emanuel 26; Ontario, 1871 ***1823.22*** *p152*
Stephens, Emanuel 43; Ontario, 1871 ***1823.22*** *p152*
Stephens, Frances; Virginia, 1670 ***1224.1*** *p22*
Stephens, Frederick 37; Ontario, 1871 ***1823.22*** *p152*
Stephens, George 65; Ontario, 1871 ***1823.22*** *p152*
Stephens, Henry; New York, 1832 ***8197.10*** *p357*
Stephens, Hugh 22; Maryland, 1775 ***1220.25*** *p99*
Stephens, James; New York, 1768 ***1224.2*** *p110*
Stephens, James 47; Ontario, 1871 ***1823.22*** *p152*
Stephens, James Wilson; New York, 1825 ***8197.10*** *p297*
Stephens, John; Cuba, 1743 ***1224.2*** *p110*
Stephens, John; Maryland, 1670 ***2524.55*** *p209*
Wife: Elizabeth
Child: Elizabeth
Child: Judith
Stephens, John; New York, 1743 ***1224.2*** *p110*
Stephens, John; Pennsylvania, 1776 ***4629.10*** *p53*
Stephens, John 24; Philadelphia, 1774 ***1220.25*** *p2*
Stephens, John C.; New York, 1838 ***8197.10*** *p375*
Stephens, John George; Los Angeles, 1898 ***1640.13*** *p121*
Stephens, Judith *SEE* Stephens, John
Stephens, Lawrance; Maryland, 1658 ***2524.55*** *p209*
Stephens, Lucy Ann 30; Ontario, 1861 ***2896.27*** *p53*
Stephens, Mary 80; Ontario, 1871 ***1823.22*** *p152*
Stephens, Michael 46; Ontario, 1871 ***1823.15*** *p251*
Stephens, Moses 30; Ontario, 1871 ***1823.22*** *p152*
Stephens, Newdigate; Savannah, Georgia, 1772 ***1224.2*** *p110*
Stephens, Patrick 24; Maryland, 1775 ***1220.25*** *p115*
Stephens, Patrick 31; Ontario, 1871 ***1823.15*** *p251*
Stephens, Peter 60; Ontario, 1871 ***1823.22*** *p152*
Stephens, Richard; New York, 1781 ***1224.2*** *p110*
Stephens, Richard 50; Ontario, 1871 ***1823.28*** *p95*
Stephens, Richd; Virginia, 1671 ***6212.30*** *p42*
Stephens, Robert 22; Philadelphia, 1774 ***1220.25*** *p68*
Stephens, Robert 51; Ontario, 1871 ***1823.15*** *p251*
Stephens, Thomas 26; Philadelphia, 1774 ***1220.25*** *p2*
Stephens, Thomas 60; Ontario, 1871 ***1823.22*** *p152*

Stephens, William; Virginia, 1684 *1224.1 p55*
Stephens, William 22; Virginia, 1774 *1220.25 p88*
Wife: Dorothy 22
Stephens, William 23; Pensacola, Florida, 1774 *1220.25 p75*
Stephens, William 37; Ontario, 1871 *1823.15 p251*
Stephens, William 40; Ontario, 1871 *1823.22 p152*
Stephens, William 55; Ontario, 1871 *1823.22 p152*
Stephenson, Mr.; Portland, Maine, 1858 *9196.15 p28*
Stephenson, Charles; New York, 1838 *8197.10 p149*
Stephenson, Christopher *SEE* Stephenson, William
Stephenson, Connant; Maryland, 1662 *2524.55 p209*
Stephenson, David; Quebec, 1856 *9196.15 p5*
Stephenson, David 77; Ontario, 1871 *1823.22 p152*
Stephenson, Elena 21; Ontario, 1871 *1823.22 p152*
Stephenson, Enoch; New York, New York, 1753 *1224.2 p110*
Stephenson, Frances *SEE* Stephenson, William
Stephenson, Francis; Illinois, 1861 *6058.10 p55*
Stephenson, Isaac; New York, 1840 *8197.10 p321*
Stephenson, John; New York, 1840 *8197.10 p195*
Stephenson, John; New York, 1856 *1224.3 p74*
Stephenson, John 13; Ontario, 1861 *2896.25 p26*
Stephenson, John 25; Ontario, 1871 *1823.15 p252*
Stephenson, John 27; Maryland, 1775 *1220.25 p103*
Stephenson, John 56; Ontario, 1871 *1823.15 p252*
Stephenson, John 64; Ontario, 1861 *2896.25 p26*
Stephenson, Joseph 58; Ontario, 1871 *1823.22 p152*
Stephenson, Mary *SEE* Stephenson, William
Stephenson, Mary; Vermont, 1833-1941 *5900.10 p447*
Stephenson, Max 36; Ontario, 1871 *1823.15 p252*
Stephenson, Robert 50; Ontario, 1871 *1823.15 p251*
Stephenson, Thomas; New York, 1821 *8197.10 p280*
Stephenson, Thomas 22; America, 1774 *1220.25 p36*
Stephenson, Victoria 7; Ontario, 1861 *2896.25 p26*
Stephenson, William; Jamaica, 1835 *1640.13 p118*
Stephenson, William; Maryland, 1654 *2524.55 p209*
With wife
Child: Christopher
Child: Mary
Child: Frances
Stepheson, Alexander 70; Ontario, 1871 *1823.28 p95*
Stepheson, Ambrose 59; Ontario, 1871 *1823.15 p252*
Stepheson, Donald 40; Ontario, 1871 *1823.28 p95*
Stepheson, James 60; Ontario, 1871 *1823.28 p95*
Stepheson, Rapheal 57; Ontario, 1871 *1823.15 p252*
Stephton, Fortree; Virginia, 1665-1666 *6212.30 p21*
Stepik, Sam 25; Alaska, 1912 *9196.1 p19*
Stepik, Sam 25; British Columbia, 1912 *9196.1 p19*
Stepkin, Charles; Virginia, 1689 *1224.1 p55*
Stepkings, Elizabeth; Maryland, 1682 *2524.55 p209*
Stepleton, Patrick 40; Ontario, 1871 *1823.15 p252*
Stepney, James 16; Baltimore, 1775 *1220.25 p119*
Steppin, Anna Margarete; Port uncertain, 1764 *2856.30 p444*
Sterck, Johann Martin; Port uncertain, 1795 *2856.30 p444*
Sterford, William; Maryland, 1669 *2524.55 p209*
Sterica, Thomas; Maryland, 1676 *2524.55 p209*
Sterica, Thomas; Maryland, 1680 *2524.55 p209*
Sterk, William 59; Ontario, 1871 *1823.15 p252*
Sterkel, Friedrich; Port uncertain, 1757 *2856.30 p444*
Sterkel, Johann; Port uncertain, 1773 *2856.30 p444*
Sterling, Mr.; Quebec, 1858 *9196.15 p42*
Sterling, Alexan 75; Ontario, 1871 *1823.15 p252*
Sterling, Alexander 38; Ontario, 1871 *1823.15 p252*
Sterling, Alice; Maryland, 1674 *2524.55 p209*
Sterling, Archibald 45; Ontario, 1871 *1823.15 p252*
Sterling, David 40; Ontario, 1871 *1823.15 p252*
Sterling, George 45; Ontario, 1871 *1823.15 p252*
Sterling, John; Maryland, 1674 *2524.55 p209*
Sterling, John 45; Ontario, 1871 *1823.15 p252*
Sterling, Robert 42; Ontario, 1871 *1823.15 p252*
Sterling, Thomas; Maryland, 1658 *2524.55 p209*
Sterling, William; New York, 1802 *8197.10 p25*
Sterling, William 35; Ontario, 1871 *1823.15 p252*
Sterling, William 45; Ontario, 1871 *1823.15 p252*
Sterling, William 60; Ontario, 1871 *1823.15 p252*
Sternberge, Detmorus; Maryland, 1658 *2524.55 p208*
Sternbor, Renscoe; Maryland, 1658 *2524.55 p208*
Sternbor, Tobias; Maryland, 1658 *2524.55 p209*
Sterne, Thomas; Maryland, 1663 *2524.55 p209*
Sterner, Hans Georg; Port uncertain, 1749 *2856.30 p444*
Sternigle, John 50; Ontario, 1871 *1823.15 p252*
Sterriker, Hannah 12; Nova Scotia, 1774 *1220.25 p14*
Sterry, William; Boston, 1685 *1224.1 p55*
Stese, Joseph; New York, 1838 *8197.10 p150*
Stetford, Eliza; Virginia, 1665 *6212.30 p19*
Stettner, Bernhard; Port uncertain, 1783 *2856.30 p451*
Stetz, John; Maryland, 1910 *3259.35 p60*
Stetzenbach, Miss; Port uncertain, 1784 *2856.30 p478*
Stetzenbach, Maria Christina; Port uncertain, 1784 *2856.30 p444*
With husband
Steuart, James; Charles Town, South Carolina, 1755 *1224.2 p111*
Steuart, William; New York, 1821 *8197.10 p279*
Steudle, Johannes, Jr.; Port uncertain, 1753 *2856.30 p444*
With wife & 7 children
Steuer, John; New York, 1830 *8197.10 p312*
Steurwaldin, Maria Eva; America, 1749 *2856.30 p444*
Steven, John 59; Ontario, 1871 *1823.15 p252*
Steven, Mimile 28; British Columbia, 1910 *9196.1 p29*
Steven, Mimile 28; Washington, 1910 *9196.1 p29*
Steven, William; Jamaica, 1740 *1640.13 p118*
Stevens, Mrs.; Maryland, 1666 *2524.55 p210*
Stevens, Mrs.; Quebec, 1856 *9196.15 p9*
Stevens, A.; Ontario, 1861 *2896.26 p8*
Stevens, A. 10; Ontario, 1861 *2896.28 p8*
Stevens, A. 73; Ontario, 1861 *2896.26 p8*
Stevens, Ann 79; Vermont, 1893 *5900.10 p422*
Stevens, Barnaby *SEE* Stevens, William
Stevens, C. 18; Ontario, 1861 *2896.26 p7*
Stevens, Charles *SEE* Stevens, Charles
Stevens, Charles; Maryland, 1666 *2524.55 p210*
Wife: Suzan
Child: Elizabeth
Child: Suzan
Child: Sarah
Child: Charles
Stevens, Charles; New York, New York, 1857 *1224.3 p74*
Stevens, Charles 22; Virginia, 1774 *1220.25 p88*
Stevens, Clement William; Florida, 1839 *1224.3 p74*
Stevens, David; Maryland, 1651 *2524.55 p210*
Stevens, David; New York, 1834 *8197.10 p283*
Stevens, David 60; Ontario, 1871 *1823.22 p152*
Stevens, E. 4; Ontario, 1861 *2896.26 p8*
Stevens, E. 14; Ontario, 1861 *2896.26 p7*
Stevens, E. 23; Ontario, 1861 *2896.26 p7*
Stevens, E. J. 4; Ontario, 1861 *2896.26 p7*
Stevens, Edward *SEE* Stevens, William
Stevens, Edward; Maryland, 1673 *2524.55 p210*
Wife: Ruth
Stevens, Edward; Maryland, 1673 *2524.55 p210*
Stevens, Edward; Virginia, 1694 *1224.1 p55*
Stevens, Eliza J. 8; Ontario, 1861 *2896.28 p30*
Stevens, Elizabeth *SEE* Stevens, Charles
Stevens, Elizabeth *SEE* Stevens, John
Stevens, Elizabeth *SEE* Stevens, William
Stevens, Francis; Maryland, 1666 *2524.55 p17*
Stevens, George; New York, New York, 1857 *6058.10 p62*
Stevens, George; Pennsylvania, 1777 *4629.10 p26*
Stevens, Godeip 25; Ontario, 1871 *1823.15 p252*
Stevens, Griffith; Maryland, 1672 *2524.55 p210*
Stevens, H. 64; Ontario, 1861 *2896.26 p8*
Stevens, H. A. 9; Ontario, 1861 *2896.27 p4*
Stevens, H. G. 6; Ontario, 1861 *2896.27 p4*
Stevens, Henry 38; Ontario, 1871 *1823.15 p252*
Stevens, J. D.; Quebec, 1856 *9196.15 p9*
Stevens, James; New York, 1840 *8197.10 p196*
Stevens, Jno; Virginia, 1663 *6212.30 p2*
Stevens, John; Maryland, 1651 *2524.55 p210*
Stevens, John; Maryland, 1666 *2524.55 p17*
Stevens, John; Maryland, 1670 *2524.55 p209*
Child: Jude
Wife: Elizabeth
Child: Elizabeth
Stevens, John; Virginia, 1666-1667 *6212.30 p33*
Stevens, John 21; Maryland, 1775 *1220.25 p96*
Stevens, John 26; Maryland, 1774 *1220.25 p38*
Stevens, John 45; Ontario, 1871 *1823.15 p252*
Stevens, John 55; Ontario, 1871 *1823.15 p252*
Stevens, Joseph 42; Ontario, 1871 *1823.15 p252*
Stevens, Jude *SEE* Stevens, John
Stevens, L. 12; Ontario, 1861 *2896.26 p7*
Stevens, Lambert 51; Ontario, 1861 *2896.27 p4*
Stevens, Lewis; Maryland, 1666 *2524.55 p210*
Stevens, Lewis; Maryland, 1672 *2524.55 p210*
Stevens, M. 15; Ontario, 1861 *2896.28 p8*
Stevens, M. A. 24; Ontario, 1861 *2896.27 p4*
Stevens, M. C. 6; Ontario, 1861 *2896.26 p7*
Stevens, M. E. 8; Ontario, 1861 *2896.26 p7*
Stevens, Mary; Maryland, 1672 *2524.55 p210*
Stevens, Mary; Maryland, 1681 *2524.55 p210*
Stevens, Mary A. 40; Vermont, 1887 *5900.10 p422*
Stevens, Michael; New York, 1838 *8197.10 p149*
Stevens, Michall; Maryland, 1669 *2524.55 p210*
Stevens, Nathaniel; Virginia, 1679 *1224.1 p55*
Stevens, Oliver 18; Virginia, 1774 *1220.25 p93*
Stevens, Ontario Brook Bridges; New Jersey, 1852 *1224.3 p74*
Stevens, Ontario Brook Bridges; Ontario, n.d. *1224.3 p74*
Stevens, R. 28; Ontario, 1861 *2896.26 p8*
Stevens, R. 63; Ontario, 1861 *2896.26 p7*
Stevens, Rebecca 28; Ontario, 1861 *2896.28 p30*
Stevens, Richard; Maryland, 1665 *2524.55 p210*
Stevens, Richard; New York, 1807 *8197.10 p332*
Stevens, Richard; Virginia, 1663 *6212.30 p3*
Stevens, Robert; South Carolina, 1722 *1224.2 p110*
Stevens, Robert 26; Philadelphia, 1774 *1220.25 p42*
Stevens, Ruth *SEE* Stevens, Edward
Stevens, Ruth; Maryland, 1673 *2524.55 p210*
Stevens, S. 1; Ontario, 1861 *2896.26 p8*
Stevens, S. 21; Ontario, 1861 *2896.26 p7*
Stevens, Sarah *SEE* Stevens, Charles
Stevens, Seaborne *SEE* Stevens, William
Stevens, Suzan *SEE* Stevens, Charles
Stevens, Thomas; Maryland, 1680 *2524.55 p210*
Stevens, Thomas; New York, 1807 *8197.10 p49*
Stevens, William; Maryland, 1665 *2524.55 p210*
Relative: Barnaby
Stevens, William; Maryland, 1665 *2524.55 p210*
Wife: Elizabeth
Stevens, William; Maryland, 1667 *2524.55 p210*
Wife: Elizabeth
Child: Edward
Child: Seaborne
Stevens, William; Pennsylvania, 1779 *4629.10 p36*
Stevens, William; Pennsylvania, 1779 *4629.10 p37*
Stevens, William; Virginia, 1651 *1224.1 p55*
Stevens, William 28; Ontario, 1871 *1823.15 p252*
Stevens, William 33; Ontario, 1871 *1823.15 p252*
Stevens, William 45; Ontario, 1871 *1823.15 p252*
Stevens, William 71; Ontario, 1871 *1823.15 p252*
Stevens, William George 37; Maryland, 1773-1774 *1220.25 p33*
Stevens, Wm; Virginia, 1671-1672 *6212.30 p45*
Stevenson, Mr.; Quebec, 1858 *9196.15 p42*
Stevenson, Mrs.; Quebec, 1857 *9196.15 p23*
Stevenson, Abigail E. Shay; Vermont, 1845-1892 *5900.10 p272*
Stevenson, Agnes; San Francisco, 1887 *1640.13 p118*
Stevenson, Alexander 23; Ontario, 1871 *1823.22 p152*
Stevenson, Alexander 28; Maryland, 1773-1774 *1220.25 p33*
Stevenson, Alexander 51; Ontario, 1871 *1823.22 p153*
Stevenson, Andrew McMath; San Francisco, 1891 *1640.13 p118*
Stevenson, Ann 76; Ontario, 1871 *1823.22 p153*
Stevenson, Anne 11; Ontario, 1861 *2896.28 p48*
Stevenson, Archibald; America, 1887 *1640.13 p118*
Stevenson, Archibald 4; Ontario, 1861 *2896.28 p48*
Stevenson, Cornelius; New York, New York, 1806 *1224.3 p74*
Stevenson, Edward 32; Ontario, 1871 *1823.15 p252*
Stevenson, Elizabeth 9; Ontario, 1861 *2896.28 p48*
Stevenson, Elizabeth 32; Ontario, 1861 *2896.28 p48*
Stevenson, F. J.; Quebec, 1858 *9196.15 p38*
Stevenson, Fred 43; Ontario, 1871 *1823.22 p153*
Stevenson, George 28; Ontario, 1871 *1823.22 p153*
Stevenson, George 58; Ontario, 1871 *1823.15 p252*
Stevenson, George Goude; New York, 1827 *8197.10 p282*
Stevenson, George Goude; New York, 1833 *8197.10 p68*
Stevenson, H. 46; Ontario, 1861 *2896.28 p16*
Stevenson, Hamilton; Jamaica, 1783 *1640.13 p118*
Stevenson, Henry; Jamaica, 1845 *1640.13 p118*
Stevenson, J. 10; Ontario, 1861 *2896.28 p16*
Stevenson, J. B.; Portland, Maine, 1858 *9196.15 p29*
Stevenson, J. B.; Quebec, 1858 *9196.15 p40*
Stevenson, James; Georgia, 1698 *1640.13 p118*
Stevenson, James; Jamaica, 1844 *1640.13 p118*
Stevenson, James; New York, 1802 *8197.10 p25*
Stevenson, James; New York, 1840 *8197.10 p197*
Stevenson, James; Pennsylvania, 1780 *4629.10 p41*
Stevenson, James; Salem, Massachusetts, 1728 *1224.2 p110*
Stevenson, James; Tobago, West Indies, 1848 *1640.13 p118*
Stevenson, James 37; Ontario, 1871 *1823.22 p153*
Stevenson, James 50; Ontario, 1871 *1823.15 p252*
Stevenson, James 51; Ontario, 1871 *1823.28 p95*
Stevenson, James B.; Portland, Maine, 1857 *9196.15 p11*
Stevenson, Jean; Jamaica, 1783 *1640.13 p118*
Stevenson, John; Albany, New York, 1810 *1224.3 p74*
Stevenson, John; Georgia, 1699 *1640.13 p118*
Stevenson, John; Georgia, 1751 *1640.10 p192*
Stevenson, John; New York, 1839 *8197.10 p140*
Stevenson, John; Vermont, 1841-1917 *5900.10 p272*
Stevenson, John 75; Ontario, 1871 *1823.22 p153*
Stevenson, Joseph 25; Virginia, 1773 *1220.25 p29*
Stevenson, Joseph 29; Ontario, 1871 *1823.15 p252*
Stevenson, M. 12; Ontario, 1861 *2896.28 p16*
Stevenson, Mary Rogers; New York, 1844 *1224.3 p74*
Stevenson, Mathew 53; Ontario, 1871 *1823.28 p95*

Stewart, Mary D. O'Roark; Vermont, 1826-1895 ***5900.10*** *p484*
Stewart, Mary E. Collins; Vermont, 1859-1955 ***5900.10*** *p485*
Stewart, Mary Riley; Vermont, 1848-1890 ***5900.10*** *p401*
Stewart, Mathew; Vermont, 1844-1925 ***5900.10*** *p401*
Stewart, Mathew W.; Georgia, 1801-1812 ***1640.10*** *p195*
Stewart, Michael 5 *SEE* Stewart, Bridget
Stewart, Neil; Halifax, Nova Scotia, 1793 ***1640.13*** *p120*
Stewart, Nicholas; Vermont, 1855-1926 ***5900.10*** *p485*
Stewart, Patrick 25; New York, New York, 1847 ***1825.45*** *p20*
Sister: Catherine
Stewart, Patrick 55; Vermont, 1884 ***5900.10*** *p436*
Stewart, Pete; Ontario, 1871 ***1823.28*** *p96*
Stewart, Peter; New York, 1827 ***8197.10*** *p282*
Stewart, Peter; New York, 1836 ***1224.3*** *p75*
Stewart, Peter 25; Ontario, 1871 ***1823.15*** *p254*
Stewart, Peter 50; Ontario, 1871 ***1823.15*** *p254*
Stewart, Peter 62; Ontario, 1871 ***1823.15*** *p254*
Stewart, Peter 80; Ontario, 1871 ***1823.22*** *p153*
Stewart, Randall; North Carolina, 1806-1844 ***1640.10*** *p195*
Stewart, Richard 20; Maryland, 1774 ***1220.25*** *p64*
Stewart, Richard 41; Ontario, 1871 ***1823.28*** *p96*
Stewart, Richard 45; Ontario, 1871 ***1823.28*** *p96*
Stewart, Richard 54; Ontario, 1871 ***1823.15*** *p254*
Stewart, Robert; Georgia, 1757 ***1640.10*** *p195*
Stewart, Robert; Georgia, 1763 ***1640.10*** *p195*
Stewart, Robert; Mississippi, 1807-1834 ***1640.10*** *p195*
Stewart, Robert; New York, 1840 ***8197.10*** *p197*
Stewart, Robert; Petersburg, Virginia, 1816 ***1640.13*** *p120*
Stewart, Robert; Savannah, Georgia, 1762 ***1640.10*** *p195*
Stewart, Robert 6; Ontario, 1861 ***2896.25*** *p59*
Stewart, Robert 34; Ontario, 1871 ***1823.28*** *p96*
Stewart, Robert 36; Ontario, 1871 ***1823.15*** *p254*
Stewart, Robert 38; Ontario, 1871 ***1823.28*** *p96*
Stewart, Robert 40; Ontario, 1871 ***1823.15*** *p254*
Stewart, Robert 45; Ontario, 1871 ***1823.28*** *p96*
Stewart, Robert 61; Vermont, 1874 ***5900.10*** *p205*
Stewart, Robert 78; Ontario, 1871 ***1823.15*** *p254*
Stewart, Roderick 40; Ontario, 1871 ***1823.28*** *p96*
Stewart, Roger; Georgia, 1844 ***1640.10*** *p195*
Stewart, Samuel; Pennsylvania, 1777 ***4629.10*** *p13*
Stewart, Sarah; Alabama, 1785-1845 ***1640.10*** *p196*
Stewart, Sarah 12; Ontario, 1861 ***2896.25*** *p59*
Stewart, Thomas; Georgia, 1826 ***1640.10*** *p196*
Stewart, Thomas; New York, 1803 ***8197.10*** *p17*
Stewart, Thomas; Pennsylvania, 1777 ***4629.10*** *p26*
Stewart, Thomas 18; Philadelphia, 1774 ***1220.25*** *p43*
Stewart, Thomas 48; Ontario, 1871 ***1823.15*** *p254*
Stewart, Thomas 60; Ontario, 1871 ***1823.22*** *p153*
Stewart, Thomas 66; Vermont, 1895 ***5900.10*** *p440*
Stewart, William; Boston, 1729 ***1224.2*** *p111*
Stewart, William; Cuba, 1791 ***1640.13*** *p120*
Stewart, William; Georgia, 1775 ***1640.10*** *p196*
Stewart, William; Jamaica, 1775 ***1220.25*** *p133*
Stewart, William; New York, 1794 ***8197.10*** *p2*
Stewart, William; New York, 1831 ***8197.10*** *p283*
Stewart, William; New York, 1840 ***8197.10*** *p285*
Stewart, William 20; Ontario, 1871 ***1823.15*** *p254*
Stewart, William 24; Georgia, 1775 ***1220.25*** *p125*
Stewart, William 34; Ontario, 1871 ***1823.15*** *p254*
Stewart, William 42; Ontario, 1871 ***1823.15*** *p254*
Stewart, William 45; Ontario, 1871 ***1823.15*** *p254*
Stewart, William 54; Ontario, 1871 ***1823.15*** *p254*
Stewart, William 54; Ontario, 1871 ***1823.22*** *p153*
Stewart, William 60; Ontario, 1871 ***1823.15*** *p254*
Stewart, William John 42; Ontario, 1871 ***1823.22*** *p153*
Stewkley, Tho; Virginia, 1664 ***6212.30*** *p15*
Stewonski, Frank; Maryland, 1910 ***3259.35*** *p60*
Steyer, Arnolt; Port uncertain, 1747 ***2856.30*** *p444*
With wife & 4 children
Steyer, Elisabeth; Port uncertain, 1746 ***2856.30*** *p444*
Steyert, Magdalena; Port uncertain, 1769 ***2856.30*** *p444*
Steyerwald, Martin; Port uncertain, 1749 ***2856.30*** *p444*
With 3 sisters
Steyner, Mr.; Quebec, 1857 ***9196.15*** *p16*
Steziska, John; Maryland, 1910 ***3259.35*** *p60*
Sthamer, William; New York, 1836 ***8197.10*** *p283*
Stibbins, Ralph 40; Nova Scotia, 1774 ***1220.25*** *p136*
With 3 children
Stich, Georg Friedrich; Port uncertain, 1775 ***2856.30*** *p445*
Stich, Johann Philipp; Port uncertain, 1788 ***2856.30*** *p445*
Stich, Michael; Port uncertain, 1773 ***2856.30*** *p445*
Stick, Jakob; America, 1749 ***2856.30*** *p445*
Stick, Michael; America, 1749 ***2856.30*** *p445*
Stickels, Sarah 26; Ontario, 1861 ***2896.25*** *p6*
Stickle, Geo.; Maryland, 1657 ***2524.55*** *p210*
Stickler, Peter 43; Ontario, 1871 ***1823.28*** *p96*
Stickles, John 53; Ontario, 1871 ***1823.22*** *p153*
Stickney, Barney H.; Vermont, 1826-1905 ***5900.10*** *p500*
Stickney, Caleb; Newburyport, Massachusetts, 1801 ***1224.3*** *p75*
Stickney, Mary L. Webber; Vermont, 1844-1900 ***5900.10*** *p500*
Stickney, Sarah; Newbury, Massachusetts, 1801 ***1224.3*** *p15*
Stickney, William; Salem, Massachusetts, 1835 ***1224.3*** *p75*
Sticzynski, Joseph P.; Maryland, 1910 ***3259.35*** *p60*
Sticzynski, Martin; Maryland, 1910 ***3259.35*** *p60*
Stidelfe, Jno; Virginia, 1664 ***6212.30*** *p7*
Stiebel, Bernhard; Baltimore, 1848 ***1224.3*** *p75*
Stieben, John 28; Kansas, 1900-1910 ***9079.10*** *p12*
Stiedle, Anna Maria; Port uncertain, 1764 ***2856.30*** *p445*
Stief, Anna Christina; America, 1752 ***2856.30*** *p445*
Stief, Anna Clara; America, 1752 ***2856.30*** *p445*
Stief, Anna Margarete; America, 1752 ***2856.30*** *p445*
Stief, Christina; America, 1749 ***2856.30*** *p445*
Stief, Frederick H.; New York, 1839 ***8197.10*** *p285*
Stief, Heinr. *SEE* Stief, Regina
Stief, Heinrich; America, 1749 ***2856.30*** *p445*
Stief, Heinrich; America, 1749 ***2856.30*** *p445*
Wife: Reg.
With son & daughter
Stief, Reg. *SEE* Stief, Heinrich
Stief, Regina; America, 1749 ***2856.30*** *p445*
Husband: Heinr.
With son & daughter
Stiefenhofer, Anna Catharina; Port uncertain, 1756 ***2856.30*** *p445*
Stieffenhoffer, Johann Jakob; Port uncertain, 1752 ***2856.30*** *p445*
Stiefin, Maria Sofia; Port uncertain, 1777 ***2856.30*** *p445*
Stiefvater, Jacob; Port uncertain, 1710 ***2856.30*** *p445*
Stiefvater, Jacob; Port uncertain, 1766 ***2856.30*** *p445*
Stieg, Daniel; Port uncertain, 1773 ***2856.30*** *p445*
Stiehin, Maria Sofia; Port uncertain, 1777 ***2856.30*** *p445*
Stiehl, Diederich; Port uncertain, 1756 ***2856.30*** *p445*
Stiehl, Wilhelm Henrich; Port uncertain, 1756 ***2856.30*** *p445*
With wife & 5 children
Stiep, John 26; Ontario, 1871 ***1823.28*** *p96*
Stier, . . .; Port uncertain, 1764 ***2856.30*** *p445*
With 3 siblings
Stierling, Johann; Port uncertain, 1746 ***2856.30*** *p445*
Stierling, Johann; Port uncertain, 1786 ***2856.30*** *p445*
Stierling, Johann Adam; Port uncertain, 1746 ***2856.30*** *p445*
Stierling, Johann Adam; Port uncertain, 1786 ***2856.30*** *p445*
Stierly, James C. R.; New York, New York, 1867 ***6058.10*** *p70*
Stierly, John R.; New York, 1862 ***6058.10*** *p66*
Stiff, Henry; New York, 1838 ***8197.10*** *p311*
Stiffe, William; Virginia, 1673 ***1224.1*** *p55*
Stigelmayer, Maria Catharina; Port uncertain, 1755 ***2856.30*** *p445*
Stigelmayerin, Maria Catharina; Port uncertain, 1755 ***2856.30*** *p445*
Stihlin, Mrs.; America, 1751 ***2856.30*** *p445*
With 2 children
Stihlin, Anna Elisabeth; Port uncertain, 1752 ***2856.30*** *p445*
Stiker, James; Virginia, 1690-1691 ***6212.30*** *p59*
Stikkers, Edward 35; Ontario, 1871 ***1823.22*** *p153*
Stile, George; Virginia, 1666-1667 ***6212.30*** *p33*
Stile, James 22; Baltimore, 1775 ***1220.25*** *p117*
Stiles, Mrs.; Maryland, 1648 ***2524.55*** *p210*
Stiles, Bartholomew 40; Ontario, 1871 ***1823.22*** *p153*
Stiles, George; Maryland, 1665 ***2524.55*** *p210*
Stiles, Nathaniell; Maryland, 1665 ***2524.55*** *p210*
Stiles, Richard; Pennsylvania, 1785 ***4629.10*** *p48*
Stiles, Richard 42; Ontario, 1871 ***1823.22*** *p153*
Stiles, Tho; Virginia, 1665-1666 ***6212.30*** *p22*
Stiles, Thomas; Pennsylvania, 1777 ***4629.10*** *p13*
Stilk, David 55; Ontario, 1871 ***1823.15*** *p254*
Still, Abraham; America, 1750 ***2856.30*** *p445*
With wife & 4 children
Still, Adam; New York, 1815-1834 ***8197.10*** *p310*
Still, Heinrich; America, 1733 ***2856.30*** *p445*
Still, James 21; Maryland, 1775 ***1220.25*** *p97*
Still, John; Virginia, 1666-1667 ***6212.30*** *p33*
Stille, John; Pennsylvania, 1777 ***4629.10*** *p28*
Stille, John; Pennsylvania, 1779 ***4629.10*** *p39*
Stillemunckel, Hans Georg; Port uncertain, 1752 ***2856.30*** *p445*
With wife & 2 children
Stillemunckes, Johann; Port uncertain, 1754 ***2856.30*** *p445*
With wife & 2 children
Stillemunnckes, Margarete; Port uncertain, 1755 ***2856.30*** *p445*
Stiller, Valentine; Indiana, 1881-1884 ***3437.14*** *p204*
Stilles, George; Maryland, 1665 ***2524.55*** *p210*
Stillman, Robert 68; Ontario, 1871 ***1823.22*** *p153*
Stills, Robert; Maryland, 1664 ***2524.55*** *p76*
Stillwell, George 35; Ontario, 1871 ***1823.22*** *p153*
Stillwell, John; Pennsylvania, 1785 ***4629.10*** *p48*
Stimble, Matthias; Pennsylvania, 1777 ***4629.10*** *p11*
Stimble, Nicholas; Pennsylvania, 1777 ***4629.10*** *p10*
Stimble, Philip; Pennsylvania, 1777 ***4629.10*** *p10*
Stimmel, Albrecht; America, 1754 ***2856.30*** *p446*
With wife & 8 children
Stimson, William; Maryland, 1667 ***2524.55*** *p84*
Stinchcomb, John; Maryland, 1672 ***2524.55*** *p210*
Stine, Charles; Pennsylvania, 1777 ***4629.10*** *p26*
Stinehour, Henry 80; Vermont, 1867 ***5900.10*** *p282*
Stinehour, Margaret Corigan 55; Vermont, 1873 ***5900.10*** *p282*
Stiner, Martin; Pennsylvania, 1836 ***6058.10*** *p11*
Stinert, Catherine 43; Kansas, 1877-1910 ***9079.10*** *p13*
Stinert, George 52; Kansas, 1878-1910 ***9079.10*** *p12*
Stink, Thomas 46; Ontario, 1871 ***1823.15*** *p254*
Stinnens, Jno; Virginia, 1666-1667 ***6212.30*** *p33*
Stinson, Dr.; Quebec, 1858 ***9196.15*** *p34*
Stinson, Miss; Quebec, 1858 ***9196.15*** *p34*
Stinson, Mrs.; Quebec, 1858 ***9196.15*** *p34*
Stinson, Adda M. 6; Ontario, 1861 ***2896.27*** *p65*
Stinson, Ann 26; Vermont, 1867 ***5900.10*** *p529*
Stinson, Benjamin 9; Ontario, 1861 ***2896.27*** *p70*
Stinson, Brayton 4; Ontario, 1861 ***2896.27*** *p52*
Stinson, Catherine 18; Ontario, 1861 ***2896.27*** *p63*
Stinson, Catherine 40; Ontario, 1871 ***1823.22*** *p153*
Stinson, Catherine 62; Vermont, 1897 ***5900.10*** *p533*
Stinson, Charles W.; Quebec, 1858 ***9196.15*** *p34*
Stinson, D. G. 10; Ontario, 1861 ***2896.27*** *p63*
Stinson, David 75; Ontario, 1861 ***2896.27*** *p63*
Stinson, Effa 32; Ontario, 1861 ***2896.27*** *p70*
Stinson, Elizabeth 14; Ontario, 1861 ***2896.28*** *p29*
Stinson, Elizabeth 15; Ontario, 1861 ***2896.27*** *p70*
Stinson, Elizabeth 57; Ontario, 1861 ***2896.27*** *p59*
Stinson, Elizabeth 70; Ontario, 1861 ***2896.27*** *p70*
Stinson, Elizabeth Morris 54; Vermont, 1897 ***5900.10*** *p526*
Stinson, Francis 6; Ontario, 1861 ***2896.27*** *p70*
Stinson, Freeman 23; Ontario, 1861 ***2896.27*** *p63*
Stinson, George 40; Ontario, 1871 ***1823.15*** *p254*
Stinson, George 41; Ontario, 1861 ***2896.27*** *p70*
Stinson, Hugh; New York, 1838 ***8197.10*** *p148*
Stinson, J. D. 16; Ontario, 1861 ***2896.27*** *p63*
Stinson, J. Henry; Quebec, 1858 ***9196.15*** *p34*
Stinson, James H. 1; Ontario, 1861 ***2896.27*** *p65*
Stinson, Jane 12; Ontario, 1861 ***2896.27*** *p63*
Stinson, John 5; Ontario, 1861 ***2896.27*** *p70*
Stinson, John 46; Ontario, 1871 ***1823.15*** *p254*
Stinson, John J.; Quebec, 1858 ***9196.15*** *p34*
Stinson, Lyda 53; Ontario, 1861 ***2896.27*** *p63*
Stinson, Margaret 11; Ontario, 1861 ***2896.27*** *p70*
Stinson, Mary 28; Ontario, 1861 ***2896.27*** *p65*
Stinson, Mary A. 18; Ontario, 1861 ***2896.27*** *p63*
Stinson, Rachel F. 7; Ontario, 1861 ***2896.27*** *p63*
Stinson, Robert 29; Ontario, 1871 ***1823.28*** *p96*
Stinson, Sarah 25; Ontario, 1861 ***2896.27*** *p52*
Stinson, Sarah A. 37; Ontario, 1861 ***2896.27*** *p63*
Stinson, Thomas 3; Ontario, 1861 ***2896.27*** *p63*
Stinson, William; New York, 1837 ***8197.10*** *p106*
Stinson, William 42; Ontario, 1871 ***1823.28*** *p96*
Stinson, William 43; Ontario, 1871 ***1823.15*** *p254*
Stinson, William 60; Ontario, 1871 ***1823.15*** *p254*
Stinson, William 74; Ontario, 1871 ***1823.15*** *p254*
Stinson, William H. 13; Ontario, 1861 ***2896.27*** *p70*
Stirk, Benjamin; Georgia, 1761 ***1640.10*** *p196*
Stirk, Mrs. John Williamson; Savannah, Georgia, 1819 ***1640.10*** *p196*
Stirling, Miss; Quebec, 1857 ***9196.15*** *p17*
Stirling, Mrs.; Quebec, 1857 ***9196.15*** *p17*
Stirling, Alexander; Georgia, 1699 ***1640.13*** *p120*
Stirling, Alexander; Louisiana, 1812 ***1640.10*** *p196*
Stirling, David 35; Ontario, 1871 ***1823.28*** *p96*
Stirling, George; Georgia, 1749 ***1224.2*** *p111*
Stirling, George; Georgia, 1749 ***1640.10*** *p196*
Stirling, Georgina 76; Ontario, 1871 ***1823.15*** *p254*
Stirling, Hugh; Georgia, 1734 ***1640.10*** *p196*
Stirling, James; Georgia, 1761 ***1640.10*** *p197*
Stirling, James; Montreal, 1861 ***1640.13*** *p120*
Stirling, John; New York, 1840 ***8197.10*** *p198*
Stirling, Robert; Georgia, 1707 ***1640.13*** *p120*
Stirling, William; Georgia, 1734 ***1640.10*** *p197*
Stirling, William; New York, 1838 ***8197.10*** *p284*
Stirling, William; New York, 1840 ***8197.10*** *p198*
Stisi, Joseph; New York, 1838 ***8197.10*** *p150*
Stister, Sarah; Maryland, 1650 ***2524.55*** *p210*
Stitt, Ann 56; Ontario, 1871 ***1823.15*** *p254*
Stitt, David; New York, 1822 ***8197.10*** *p280*
Stitt, Joseph 54; Ontario, 1871 ***1823.15*** *p254*
Stitzer, Konrad; Port uncertain, 1756 ***2856.30*** *p446*

Stixon, John; Virginia, 1663 ***6212.30*** *p2*
Stoake, John; Maryland, 1667 ***2524.55*** *p210*
Stoakes, Elizabeth *SEE* Stoakes, William
Stoakes, John *SEE* Stoakes, William
Stoakes, William *SEE* Stoakes, William
Stoakes, William; Maryland, 1660 ***2524.55*** *p211*
Wife: Elizabeth
Daughter: Elizabeth
Son: William
Son: John
Stoakes, William 16; Maryland, 1774 ***1220.25*** *p76*
Stobbs, Charles 19; New York, 1774 ***1220.25*** *p25*
Stober, Jacob; Port uncertain, 1739 ***2856.30*** *p446*
Stober, Joachim; America, 1738 ***2856.30*** *p446*
Stober, Joachim; Port uncertain, 1737 ***2856.30*** *p446*
Stober, Martin; Port uncertain, 1770 ***2856.30*** *p446*
Stober, Michael; Port uncertain, 1737 ***2856.30*** *p446*
Stober, Philipp; Port uncertain, 1737 ***2856.30*** *p446*
Stober, Valentin; America, 1737 ***2856.30*** *p446*
Stober, Valentin; Port uncertain, 1737 ***2856.30*** *p446*
Stobie, Alexander 21; Ontario, 1871 ***1823.15*** *p254*
Stobie, Janet 50; Ontario, 1871 ***1823.15*** *p254*
Stobo, Alexander; New York, 1840 ***8197.10*** *p195*
Stock, Benedikt; Port uncertain, 1788 ***2856.30*** *p451*
Stock, Hans Adam; America, 1741 ***2856.30*** *p446*
Stock, Johann; America, 1753 ***2856.30*** *p446*
Stock, Johann; Port uncertain, 1753 ***2856.30*** *p446*
Stock, Johann Adam; Port uncertain, 1751 ***2856.30*** *p446*
Stock, John; Maryland, 1676 ***2524.55*** *p211*
Stock, John 53; Ontario, 1871 ***1823.22*** *p153*
Stock, Mary 73; Ontario, 1871 ***1823.22*** *p153*
Stock, Zacariah 73; Ontario, 1871 ***1823.22*** *p153*
Stockall, John; Maryland, 1682 ***2524.55*** *p211*
Stockdale, Joseph 24; Fort Cumberland, Nova Scotia, 1774 ***1220.25*** *p17*
Stockdale, Richard 16; Ontario, 1861 ***2896.28*** *p55*
Stockdale, Richard 24; Ontario, 1871 ***1823.22*** *p153*
Stockdell, William; Maryland, 1659 ***2524.55*** *p211*
Stockden, Willm.; Maryland, 1651 ***2524.55*** *p211*
Stockel, A. Cath. *SEE* Stockel, Paul
Stockel, Anna Barbara; Port uncertain, 1750 ***2856.30*** *p446*
Stockel, Nicolas; Port uncertain, 1750 ***2856.30*** *p451*
Stockel, Paul; Port uncertain, 1743 ***2856.30*** *p451*
Wife: A. Cath.
Stockel, Ulerich; America, 1738 ***2856.30*** *p451*
Stockell, William 19; Philadelphia, 1774 ***1220.25*** *p76*
Stockemeyer, Anton; Port uncertain, 1688 ***2856.30*** *p446*
Stockemeyer, Anton; Port uncertain, 1712 ***2856.30*** *p446*
Stocker, Edward; Maryland, 1654 ***2524.55*** *p211*
Stocker, Elisabeth; Port uncertain, 1758 ***2856.30*** *p446*
Stocker, Ephraim; Virginia, 1679 ***1224.1*** *p55*
Stockert, Franz; Port uncertain, 1732 ***2856.30*** *p451*
With wife & 2 children
Stockes, Wm; Virginia, 1665-1666 ***6212.30*** *p24*
Stockett, Elizabeth; Maryland, 1665 ***2524.55*** *p211*
Stockett, Francis; Maryland, 1658 ***2524.55*** *p211*
Brother: Thomas
Brother: Henry
Stockett, Henry *SEE* Stockett, Francis
Stockett, Thomas *SEE* Stockett, Francis
Stockey, James; New York, 1838 ***8197.10*** *p150*
Stockey, Peter; New York, 1838 ***8197.10*** *p149*
Stockheimer, Philipp; America, 1738 ***2856.30*** *p446*
With wife & children
Stockhle, Johann; Port uncertain, 1733 ***2856.30*** *p452*
Stockin, James 25; Virginia, 1774 ***1220.25*** *p53*
Stockle, . . .; America, 1752 ***2856.30*** *p452*
Stockle, Balthasar; Port uncertain, 1751 ***2856.30*** *p452*
Stockle, Johann; Port uncertain, 1745 ***2856.30*** *p452*
Stockle, Johann; Port uncertain, 1779 ***2856.30*** *p452*
Stockle, Johann Friedric; America, 1752 ***2856.30*** *p452*
Stocklen, Jacob; Port uncertain, 1757 ***2856.30*** *p446*
Stockley, America *SEE* Stockley, Woodman
Stockley, Anne; Maryland, 1653 ***2524.55*** *p211*
Stockley, Eliza; Virginia, 1664 ***6212.30*** *p6*
Stockley, James *SEE* Stockley, Woodman
Stockley, John; Virginia, 1664 ***6212.30*** *p6*
Stockley, William 26; Virginia, 1774 ***1220.25*** *p92*
Stockley, Woodman; Maryland, 1652 ***2524.55*** *p211*
Wife: America
Son: James
Stocklin, Anna Barbara; Port uncertain, 1750 ***2856.30*** *p446*
Stocklin, Anna Maria; Port uncertain, 1788 ***2856.30*** *p452*
Stocklin, Johann; Port uncertain, 1730 ***2856.30*** *p452*
Stocklin, Johann; Port uncertain, 1732 ***2856.30*** *p452*
Stocklin, Johann Georg; America, 1790 ***2856.30*** *p452*
Stocklinin, Anna Barbara; Port uncertain, 1750 ***2856.30*** *p446*
Stocklinski, John; Maryland, 1910 ***3259.35*** *p60*
Stockman, Joseph; Virginia, 1664 ***6212.30*** *p15*
Stockman, William; Pennsylvania, 1840 ***6058.10*** *p17*
Stocks, Conrad 36; Ontario, 1871 ***1823.15*** *p254*
Stocks, Henry; New York, 1838 ***8197.10*** *p150*
Stocks, James 50; Ontario, 1871 ***1823.28*** *p96*
Stockton, James 20; Ontario, 1871 ***1823.15*** *p254*
Stockton, Richard; Pennsylvania, 1787 ***4629.10*** *p56*
Stockwell, James; Boston, n.d. ***1224.3*** *p75*
Stockwell, William 23; Maryland, 1774 ***1220.25*** *p64*
Stoda, Andrew M.; Maryland, 1910 ***3259.35*** *p60*
Stodart, A.; Alabama, 1808-1845 ***1640.10*** *p197*
Stodart, D.; Alabama, 1806-1845 ***1640.10*** *p197*
Stodart, Daniel; New York, 1838 ***8197.10*** *p284*
Stoddard, William; Boston, 1780 ***1224.2*** *p111*
Stoddart, D.; Quebec, 1856 ***9196.15*** *p10*
Stoddart, David; Panama, 1831 ***1640.13*** *p120*
Stoddart, David 25; Ontario, 1871 ***1823.15*** *p254*
Stoddart, Edward; New York, 1808 ***8197.10*** *p54*
Stoddart, John 56; Ontario, 1871 ***1823.15*** *p254*
Stoddart, Walter G.; New York, 1829 ***8197.10*** *p352*
Stoddart, William 22; Virginia, 1774 ***1220.25*** *p141*
Stodena, Agnes; Maryland, 1910 ***3259.35*** *p60*
Stodhart, Samuel Lake; Maine, 1851 ***1224.3*** *p75*
Stoeck, Henrich; Port uncertain, 1755 ***2856.30*** *p446*
Stoffel, Johann Wendel; Port uncertain, 1752 ***2856.30*** *p446*
Stofkoni, Gabriel; Maryland, 1910 ***3259.35*** *p60*
Stogdill, William 68; Ontario, 1871 ***1823.15*** *p255*
Stohr, Jacob; Port uncertain, 1734 ***2856.30*** *p452*
Stohr, Jacob; Port uncertain, 1735 ***2856.30*** *p452*
Stohr, Johann; Port uncertain, 1731 ***2856.30*** *p452*
Stojewsky, Antony; Maryland, 1910 ***3259.35*** *p60*
Stokberger, George; Pennsylvania, 1778 ***4629.10*** *p32*
Stokbergur, Mathias; Pennsylvania, 1778 ***4629.10*** *p32*
Stokely, William; Maryland, 1652 ***2524.55*** *p211*
Stoker, Charles 48; Ontario, 1871 ***1823.28*** *p96*
Stokes, Bridget O'Neil; Vermont, 1845-1892 ***5900.10*** *p462*
Stokes, Edward 74; Ontario, 1871 ***1823.28*** *p96*
Stokes, Henry; New York, 1834 ***8197.10*** *p69*
Stokes, Henry 24; Ontario, 1871 ***1823.28*** *p96*
Stokes, James 14; Maryland, 1773-1774 ***1220.25*** *p33*
Stokes, John; Pennsylvania, 1717 ***1224.2*** *p111*
Stokes, John; Vermont, 1837-1888 ***5900.10*** *p462*
Stokes, Margaret Donahoe; Vermont, n.d. ***5900.10*** *p129*
Stokes, Michael 34; Vermont, 1893 ***5900.10*** *p129*
Stokes, Thomas; New York, 1806 ***8197.10*** *p33*
Stokes, Thomas; New York, 1837 ***8197.10*** *p106*
Stokes, Thomas 35; Ontario, 1871 ***1823.15*** *p255*
Stokes, Thomas 41; Ontario, 1871 ***1823.15*** *p255*
Stokes, Thomas 61; Ontario, 1871 ***1823.15*** *p255*
Stokley, America *SEE* Stokley, Woodman
Stokley, James *SEE* Stokley, Woodman
Stokley, Woodman; Maryland, 1652 ***2524.55*** *p211*
Wife: America
Son: James
Stokowski, Bolestar; Maryland, 1910 ***3259.35*** *p60*
Stoler, Jacob; New York, 1839 ***8197.10*** *p285*
Stolinski, Alexander; Maryland, 1910 ***3259.35*** *p60*
Stolinski, Michler; Maryland, 1910 ***3259.35*** *p60*
Stolion, Jane; New England, 1647 ***1224.1*** *p56*
Stoll, Anna Margarete; Port uncertain, 1748 ***2856.30*** *p446*
Stoll, Anna Margarete; Port uncertain, 1754 ***2856.30*** *p446*
Stoll, J. Friedr. Albert; Port uncertain, 1751 ***2856.30*** *p446*
Stoll, Jacob; Port uncertain, 1708 ***2856.30*** *p446*
Stoll, Jacob; Port uncertain, 1749 ***2856.30*** *p446*
Stoll, Johann Georg; Port uncertain, 1756 ***2856.30*** *p446*
Stoll, Josef; Port uncertain, 1770 ***2856.30*** *p446*
Stollenwerk, Lewis Augustus; New York, 1805 ***8197.10*** *p30*
Stollenwerk, Peter; New York, 1805 ***8197.10*** *p30*
Stoller, Robt; Virginia, 1664 ***6212.30*** *p9*
Stollery, Phebe 65; Ontario, 1871 ***1823.22*** *p154*
Stolls, Mathew 45; Ontario, 1871 ***1823.15*** *p255*
Stolpee, John; Virginia, 1692 ***1224.1*** *p56*
Stolpys, John; Virginia, 1692 ***1224.1*** *p56*
Stoltz, John; New York, 1807 ***8197.10*** *p51*
Stoltz, Konrad; America, 1741 ***2856.30*** *p446*
Stoltz, Peter; New York, 1835 ***8197.10*** *p316*
Stoltz, Peter; New York, 1837 ***8197.10*** *p106*
Stoltz, Peter; New York, 1837 ***8197.10*** *p107*
Stoltzenberger, Hans Philipp; Port uncertain, 1728 ***2856.30*** *p446*
Stoltzenberger, Josef; Port uncertain, 1733 ***2856.30*** *p446*
Stoltzenberger, Josef; Port uncertain, 1734 ***2856.30*** *p447*
Stoltzerin, Elisabeth; Port uncertain, 1734 ***2856.30*** *p447*
Stolz, Jacob; Port uncertain, 1789 ***2856.30*** *p447*
Stolz, Johannes; New York, 1838 ***8197.10*** *p148*
Stolz, Sofia; Maryland, 1910 ***3259.35*** *p60*
Stone, . . .; New England, 1636 ***1224.1*** *p51*
Stone, Mr.; Quebec, 1856 ***9196.15*** *p7*
Stone, Mrs.; Maryland, 1651 ***2524.55*** *p211*
Stone, A.; Quebec, 1856 ***9196.15*** *p10*
Stone, Andrew; Vermont, 1839-1878 ***5900.10*** *p134*
Stone, Charles; New York, 1839 ***8197.10*** *p141*
Stone, Charles 21; Maryland, 1774 ***1220.25*** *p85*
Stône, Charles 35; Ontario, 1871 ***1823.15*** *p255*
Stone, David; Vermont, 1829-1896 ***5900.10*** *p215*
Stone, Edward; Maryland, 1649 ***2524.55*** *p211*
Stone, Edward 20; America, 1774 ***1220.25*** *p35*
Stone, Ellen; Vermont, 1846-1917 ***5900.10*** *p331*
Stone, Emery; Vermont, n.d. ***5900.10*** *p409*
Stone, Francis; Maryland, 1658 ***2524.55*** *p211*
Stone, Frankie 13 months; Vermont, 1862 ***5900.10*** *p211*
Stone, Henry; Vermont, 1828-1913 ***5900.10*** *p378*
Stone, Henry; Virginia, 1664 ***6212.30*** *p14*
Stone, Henry 21; Virginia, 1774 ***1220.25*** *p87*
Stone, Hugh; Maryland, 1680 ***2524.55*** *p211*
Stone, James 51; Ontario, 1871 ***1823.15*** *p255*
Stone, Jno; Virginia, 1665-1666 ***6212.30*** *p21*
Stone, John; Maryland, 1681 ***2524.55*** *p211*
Stone, John; Vermont, 1838-1896 ***5900.10*** *p331*
Stone, John; Virginia, 1737 ***1224.2*** *p111*
Stone, John 49; Ontario, 1871 ***1823.28*** *p96*
Stone, Joseph 56; Vermont, n.d. ***5900.10*** *p561*
Stone, Joseph 72; Ontario, 1871 ***1823.22*** *p154*
Stone, Lucy 56; Vermont, 1913 ***5900.10*** *p193*
Stone, Margaret Harris; Vermont, 1836-1916 ***5900.10*** *p134*
Stone, Mary; Vermont, 1864-1938 ***5900.10*** *p216*
Stone, Mary Credy; Vermont, 1825-1902 ***5900.10*** *p378*
Stone, Mary J. 4; Ontario, 1861 ***2896.27*** *p49*
Stone, Mary Maria Smith; New York, New York, 1847 ***1224.3*** *p75*
Stone, Mary Ritchie; Vermont, 1839-1901 ***5900.10*** *p215*
Stone, Mary V.; Vermont, n.d. ***5900.10*** *p141*
Stone, Mathew; Maryland, 1659 ***2524.55*** *p211*
Stone, Nathan 75; Ontario, 1871 ***1823.22*** *p154*
Stone, Richard 16; Philadelphia, 1774 ***1220.25*** *p3*
Stone, Robert; New York, 1803 ***8197.10*** *p17*
Stone, Rosana 3; Ontario, 1861 ***2896.27*** *p49*
Stone, Rosealth 3; Ontario, 1861 ***2896.27*** *p49*
Stone, Samuel 70; Ontario, 1871 ***1823.22*** *p154*
Stone, Thomas; Maryland, 1662 ***2524.55*** *p211*
Stone, Thomas; Maryland, 1675 ***2524.55*** *p211*
Stone, Thomas 50; Ontario, 1871 ***1823.22*** *p154*
Stone, Thomas H. 6; Ontario, 1861 ***2896.27*** *p49*
Stone, William; Philadelphia, 1788 ***1224.2*** *p111*
Stone, William; Virginia, 1637 ***1224.1*** *p28*
Stone, William; Virginia, 1676 ***1224.1*** *p56*
Stone, William 18; Philadelphia, 1774 ***1220.25*** *p82*
Stone, William 35; Ontario, 1861 ***2896.27*** *p49*
Stone, William W.; New York, 1840 ***8197.10*** *p197*
Stone, Wm.; Maryland, 1678 ***2524.55*** *p138*
Stoneburg, Abner 8; Ontario, 1861 ***2896.28*** *p36*
Stoneburg, Phebe 26; Ontario, 1861 ***2896.28*** *p36*
Stoneburg, Stephen 5; Ontario, 1861 ***2896.28*** *p36*
Stoneburgh, Catherine 60; Ontario, 1861 ***2896.25*** *p22*
Stoneburgh, Charles 22; Ontario, 1861 ***2896.25*** *p26*
Stoneburgh, Clarisa 64; Ontario, 1871 ***1823.22*** *p154*
Stoneburgh, Daniel 20; Ontario, 1861 ***2896.25*** *p26*
Stoneburgh, George 20; Ontario, 1861 ***2896.25*** *p22*
Stoneburgh, Peter 77; Ontario, 1871 ***1823.22*** *p154*
Stoneburgh, William A. 25; Ontario, 1861 ***2896.25*** *p26*
Stoneburner, Leonard; Pennsylvania, 1777 ***4629.10*** *p15*
Stonehouse, Alfred 42; Ontario, 1871 ***1823.15*** *p255*
Stonehouse, Henry 44; Ontario, 1871 ***1823.15*** *p255*
Stonehouse, Ja; Virginia, 1664 ***6212.30*** *p15*
Stonehouse, James 52; Ontario, 1871 ***1823.15*** *p255*
Stoneman, William 33; Ontario, 1871 ***1823.28*** *p96*
Stonemetz, John; Pennsylvania, 1779 ***4629.10*** *p38*
Stonemeyer, Bastian; Pennsylvania, 1777 ***4629.10*** *p21*
Stoner, Robert; Maryland, 1658 ***2524.55*** *p211*
Stoner, Stephen; New York, New York, 1849 ***6058.10*** *p35*
Stonestreet, Elizabeth; Maryland, 1668 ***2524.55*** *p211*
Stonestreet, Thomas; Maryland, 1662 ***2524.55*** *p211*
Stoney, Henry; New York, 1840 ***8197.10*** *p195*
Stonier, Mary Ann Hardwick; New York, 1850 ***1224.3*** *p75*
Stony, Tho; Virginia, 1668-1669 ***6212.30*** *p41*
Stoodley, Robert 54; Ontario, 1871 ***1823.28*** *p96*
Stooke, Richard; America, 1808 ***1224.3*** *p75*
Stooke, Thomas S.; New York, 1838 ***8197.10*** *p148*
Stoope, Henry; Maryland, 1649 ***2524.55*** *p211*
Stoope, Henry; Maryland, 1651 ***2524.55*** *p211*
Stoope, Henry; Maryland, 1658 ***2524.55*** *p211*
Stoots, George; Pennsylvania, 1777 ***4629.10*** *p11*
Stooz, Konrad; Port uncertain, 1759 ***2856.30*** *p447*
Stopczenski, Frank; Maryland, 1910 ***3259.35*** *p60*
Stope, Andre; Virginia, 1672 ***6212.30*** *p49*
Stopfel, Johann Nikolaus; Port uncertain, 1772 ***2856.30*** *p452*
Stopfel, Maria Eva; Port uncertain, 1785 ***2856.30*** *p447*
Stopffin, Rosina; Port uncertain, 1779 ***2856.30*** *p447*
Stopford, John; Maryland, 1681 ***2524.55*** *p211*

Strenzel, Catharina; Port uncertain, 1764 ***2856.30*** *p448*
Strenzel, Johann Daniel; Port uncertain, 1757 ***2856.30*** *p448*
Strenzlin, Anna Maria; Port uncertain, 1755 ***2856.30*** *p448*
Stresman, Fredrick 43; Ontario, 1871 ***1823.28*** *p96*
Stretch, William; Pennsylvania, 1777 ***4629.10*** *p30*
Streton, George; Pennsylvania, 1779 ***4629.10*** *p38*
Stretten, James 42; Ontario, 1871 ***1823.15*** *p255*
Stretton, Henry; New Orleans, 1853 ***1224.3*** *p76*
Stretton, John 33; Ontario, 1871 ***1823.15*** *p255*
Streusel, George; New York, 1807 ***8197.10*** *p50*
Stribel, Jacob; America, 1752 ***2856.30*** *p448*
Striby, Jacob; America, 1752 ***2856.30*** *p448*
Strick, Andrew; New York, New York, 1848 ***6058.10*** *p33*
Strickelberger, Maria Magdalena; Port uncertain, 1733 ***2856.30*** *p448*
Stricker, Christian; Port uncertain, 1764 ***2856.30*** *p448*
Stricker, Elizabeth 62; Ontario, 1861 ***2896.26*** *p36*
Stricker, Emaly 5; Ontario, 1861 ***2896.26*** *p36*
Stricker, Eva M. 38; Kansas, 1902-1910 ***9079.10*** *p26*
Stricker, Frederick 8; Kansas, 1910 ***9079.10*** *p26*
Stricker, Godfried 13; Kansas, 1910 ***9079.10*** *p26*
Stricker, Henry 11; Kansas, 1910 ***9079.10*** *p26*
Stricker, Henry 40; Kansas, 1902-1910 ***9079.10*** *p26*
Stricker, Jamima 88; Ontario, 1861 ***2896.27*** *p59*
Stricker, Malissa 22; Ontario, 1861 ***2896.26*** *p36*
Stricker, Mary J. 8; Ontario, 1861 ***2896.27*** *p59*
Stricker, Matury J. 14; Ontario, 1861 ***2896.27*** *p59*
Stricker, Peter; Port uncertain, 1785 ***2856.30*** *p448*
Stricker, Phebe 27; Ontario, 1861 ***2896.26*** *p36*
Stricker, Samson 26; Ontario, 1861 ***2896.26*** *p36*
Stricker, Sophia 34; Ontario, 1861 ***2896.27*** *p59*
Stricklan, Benjamin 15; Virginia, 1775 ***1220.25*** *p110*
Strickland, Edward 14; Virginia, 1775 ***1220.25*** *p142*
Strickland, John; Baltimore, 1797 ***1224.2*** *p112*
Strickland, John 22; Maryland, 1775 ***1220.25*** *p100*
Strickland, Walter; Virginia, 1665 ***6212.30*** *p20*
Stride, Joseph; Pennsylvania, 1779 ***4629.10*** *p41*
Striebel, Georg; America, 1752 ***2856.30*** *p448*
Striebich, Josef; Port uncertain, 1775 ***2856.30*** *p448*
Strieby, Jacob; America, 1752 ***2856.30*** *p448*
Strieska, Mary; Maryland, 1910 ***3259.35*** *p60*
Strigler, Magdalena; Port uncertain, 1795 ***2856.30*** *p448*
Striker, Eliza 45; Ontario, 1861 ***2896.27*** *p51*
Striker, Henry; New York, 1807 ***8197.10*** *p50*
Striker, Hiram 23; Ontario, 1861 ***2896.26*** *p38*
Striker, James 20; Ontario, 1861 ***2896.27*** *p51*
Striker, Martha 54; Ontario, 1861 ***2896.27*** *p42*
Strimbeck, John; Pennsylvania, 1777 ***4629.10*** *p18*
Stringer, John 65; Ontario, 1871 ***1823.28*** *p96*
Stringer, Joseph 31; Ontario, 1871 ***1823.28*** *p96*
Stringer, Rowland; Virginia, 1690 ***1224.1*** *p56*
Stringers, William 70; Ontario, 1871 ***1823.28*** *p96*
Strippel, Nicholas; New York, 1819 ***8197.10*** *p278*
Strissler, Wendel; Port uncertain, 1753 ***2856.30*** *p448*
Strobel, Catharina; Port uncertain, 1793 ***2856.30*** *p448*
Strobel, Christof; Port uncertain, 1754 ***2856.30*** *p448*
Strobel, Jacob Heinrich; America, 1752 ***2856.30*** *p448*
Strobel, Johann; Port uncertain, 1766 ***2856.30*** *p448*
Strobel, Simon; Port uncertain, 1749 ***2856.30*** *p448*
Strobridge, Christopher; Virginia, 1671 ***6212.30*** *p43*
Strode, Margret; Virginia, 1666-1667 ***6212.30*** *p32*
Strodthoff, Diedrich; New York, 1837 ***8197.10*** *p107*
Stroebel, John C.; New York, 1807 ***8197.10*** *p49*
Strog, Dorothy; Maryland, 1666 ***2524.55*** *p212*
Stroginski, Carl; Maryland, 1910 ***3259.35*** *p60*
Stroh, Anna Maria; Port uncertain, 1760 ***2856.30*** *p448*
Stroh, Franz; Port uncertain, 1786 ***2856.30*** *p448*
Stroh, Karl; Port uncertain, 1764 ***2856.30*** *p448*
Strohe, Nickel; Port uncertain, 1743 ***2856.30*** *p449*
Strohe, Ranz; Port uncertain, 1712 ***2856.30*** *p449*
Strohefuss, Anna Margarete; Port uncertain, 1745 ***2856.30*** *p449*
Strohefuss, Johann Heinrich; Port uncertain, 1763 ***2856.30*** *p449*
Stroher, Anna Maria; Port uncertain, 1748 ***2856.30*** *p449*
Stroher, Maria Catharina; Port uncertain, 1748 ***2856.30*** *p449*
Stroher, Matthaus; America, 1748 ***2856.30*** *p449*
Stroher, Matthaus; Port uncertain, 1748 ***2856.30*** *p449*
Strohm, Johann; America, 1769 ***2856.30*** *p449*
Strohm, Johann; Port uncertain, 1784 ***2856.30*** *p449*
Strohm, Maria Eva; Port uncertain, 1785 ***2856.30*** *p449*
Strohmayer, Christian; Port uncertain, 1732 ***2856.30*** *p449*
Strohmayer, Christian; Port uncertain, 1762 ***2856.30*** *p449*
Strole, Nicholas; New York, 1840 ***8197.10*** *p197*
Strom, L. 27; Alaska, 1918 ***9196.1*** *p55*
Strom, L. 27; Yukon, 1918 ***9196.1*** *p55*
Stromsky, Alexander; Maryland, 1910 ***3259.35*** *p60*
Stronach, Catherine *SEE* Stronach, John
Stronach, John; Georgia, 1738 ***1640.10*** *p197*
Wife: Catherine
Stronach, Michael; Georgia, 1738 ***1640.10*** *p198*
Strond, Samuel; Maryland, 1671 ***2524.55*** *p212*
Strong, Mr.; Quebec, 1857 ***9196.15*** *p21*
Strong, Mrs.; Quebec, 1857 ***9196.15*** *p21*
Strong, Charles; Maryland, 1681 ***2524.55*** *p212*
Strong, Duncan; New York, 1821 ***8197.10*** *p279*
Strong, Ellen; Vermont, 1884-1900 ***5900.10*** *p413*
Strong, Frances 100; Vermont, 1888 ***5900.10*** *p414*
Strong, George; Maryland, 1658 ***2524.55*** *p212*
Strong, George; Maryland, 1659 ***2524.55*** *p221*
Strong, George 33; Ontario, 1871 ***1823.15*** *p256*
Strong, George 52; Ontario, 1871 ***1823.15*** *p256*
Strong, George 59; Ontario, 1871 ***1823.15*** *p256*
Strong, Hugh 41; Ontario, 1871 ***1823.22*** *p154*
Strong, James 49; Ontario, 1871 ***1823.15*** *p256*
Strong, Janet; Iowa, 1897 ***1640.13*** *p121*
Strong, John; Maryland, 1651 ***2524.55*** *p212*
Strong, John; New York, 1839 ***8197.10*** *p140*
Strong, John; Virginia, 1666 ***6212.30*** *p26*
Strong, John 25; Maryland, 1774 ***1220.25*** *p77*
Strong, John 48; Ontario, 1871 ***1823.15*** *p256*
Strong, Joseph W.; Vermont, 1856-1932 ***5900.10*** *p407*
Strong, Mary A. Sisters; Vermont, 1863-1951 ***5900.10*** *p407*
Strong, Matthew; Pennsylvania, 1777 ***4629.10*** *p11*
Strong, Peter; Vermont, 1860-1914 ***5900.10*** *p413*
Strong, Peter; Virginia, 1663 ***6212.30*** *p1*
Strong, Thomas; New York, 1818 ***8197.10*** *p61*
Strong, Thomas 38; Ontario, 1871 ***1823.15*** *p256*
Strong, Thomas J.; Alabama, 1826 ***1224.3*** *p76*
Strong, Valentine 39; Virginia, 1774 ***1220.25*** *p94*
Strong, William; New York, 1828 ***1224.3*** *p76*
Strong, William 35; Ontario, 1871 ***1823.15*** *p256*
Strong, William G. 52; Ontario, 1871 ***1823.22*** *p154*
Stronge, George; Maryland, 1653 ***2524.55*** *p212*
Stronge, Hannah; Maryland, 1656 ***2524.55*** *p212*
Strosinski, Victor; Maryland, 1910 ***3259.35*** *p60*
Strothers, A.; Pensacola, Florida, 1781 ***1640.10*** *p198*
Strotz, Balthasar; America, 1744 ***2856.30*** *p449*
Stroube, Helena Murphy; Vermont, n.d. ***5900.10*** *p476*
Stroud, David 35; Ontario, 1871 ***1823.15*** *p256*
Stroud, George 55; Ontario, 1871 ***1823.22*** *p154*
Stroud, James; Maryland, 1663 ***2524.55*** *p212*
Wife: Rebecca
Daughter: Mary
Stroud, James 33; Ontario, 1871 ***1823.15*** *p256*
Stroud, Mary *SEE* Stroud, James
Stroud, Michael 58; Ontario, 1871 ***1823.28*** *p96*
Stroud, Michel 71; Ontario, 1871 ***1823.15*** *p256*
Stroud, Rebecca *SEE* Stroud, James
Stroud, William; Virginia, 1666 ***6212.30*** *p30*
Stroud, William 21; Maryland, 1774 ***1220.25*** *p41*
Stroup, John; Pennsylvania, 1777 ***4629.10*** *p13*
Strowbridge, Cristop; Virginia, 1663 ***6212.30*** *p2*
Strozyszkowski, Andy; Maryland, 1910 ***3259.35*** *p60*
Strub, Andreas; Port uncertain, 1749 ***2856.30*** *p449*
Strub, Andreas; Port uncertain, 1750 ***2856.30*** *p449*
With wife son & daughter
Strubel, Mrs. Andreas; America, 1741 ***2856.30*** *p449*
With children
Strubel, Anna; America, 1752 ***2856.30*** *p449*
Strubel, Anna Maria; America, 1751 ***2856.30*** *p449*
Strubel, Apollonia; America, 1752 ***2856.30*** *p449*
Strubel, Catharina; America, 1752 ***2856.30*** *p449*
Strubel, Jacob; America, 1752 ***2856.30*** *p449*
With wife & 4 children
Strubel, Johann; America, 1752 ***2856.30*** *p449*
Strubel, Melchior; Port uncertain, 1706-1799 ***2856.30*** *p449*
Strubel, Ulrich; America, 1752 ***2856.30*** *p449*
Strubing, Johann Martin; Port uncertain, 1718 ***2856.30*** *p449*
Struck, John; New York, 1807 ***8197.10*** *p49*
Strucker, Peter; Port uncertain, 1785 ***2856.30*** *p449*
With wife & 4 children
Struckmann, Henry Christian; New York, 1837 ***8197.10*** *p105*
Strudwick, Henry 33; Baltimore, 1775 ***1220.25*** *p118*
Strudwick, Martha; North Carolina, 1820 ***1224.3*** *p76*
Strudwick, Samuel; Wilmington, North Carolina, 1797 ***1224.2*** *p112*
Strudwick, William Francis; North Carolina, 1820 ***1224.3*** *p76*
Strugala, Jacob; Maryland, 1910 ***3259.35*** *p60*
Strugi, Mike 40; British Columbia, 1910 ***9196.1*** *p29*
Strugi, Mike 40; Washington, 1910 ***9196.1*** *p29*
Struhl, Johann; Port uncertain, 1783 ***2856.30*** *p449*
Strumlin, Maria Eva; Port uncertain, 1773 ***2856.30*** *p449*
Strunckh, Johann Adam; Port uncertain, 1749 ***2856.30*** *p449*
Strunckh, Weymar; America, 1744 ***2856.30*** *p449*
With wife & children
Strunckh, Weymar; Port uncertain, 1743 ***2856.30*** *p449*
With wife & children
Strunofsky, Stanislaw; Maryland, 1910 ***3259.35*** *p60*
Strunsky, August; Maryland, 1910 ***3259.35*** *p60*
Struthers, Mrs.; Quebec, 1858 ***9196.15*** *p36*
Struthers, Gavin 46; Ontario, 1871 ***1823.15*** *p256*
Struthers, Hugh 56; Ontario, 1871 ***1823.15*** *p256*
Struthers, Jane 73; Ontario, 1871 ***1823.28*** *p96*
Struthers, Jean 52; Ontario, 1871 ***1823.15*** *p256*
Struthers, John; Georgia, 1790 ***1640.10*** *p198*
Struthers, William; Georgia, 1762 ***1640.10*** *p198*
Struthers, William; New York, 1807 ***8197.10*** *p50*
Struthes, John 55; Ontario, 1871 ***1823.15*** *p256*
Struttle, Mary; Maryland, 1682 ***2524.55*** *p212*
Strybing, Henry; New York, 1836 ***8197.10*** *p317*
Stryhusz, Stanislaus; Maryland, 1910 ***3259.35*** *p60*
Stryntryser, Johann; America, 1754 ***2856.30*** *p449*
Stryntryser, Johann; Port uncertain, 1767 ***2856.30*** *p449*
Strzegowski, Mikolay; Maryland, 1910 ***3259.35*** *p60*
Strzelcik, Marcin; Maryland, 1910 ***3259.35*** *p60*
Strzelewsky, Herman; Maryland, 1910 ***3259.35*** *p60*
Stuard, James 22; Maryland, 1773-1774 ***1220.25*** *p33*
Stuard, James 25; Ontario, 1871 ***1823.28*** *p96*
Stuart, Ann Murry 91; Vermont, 1881 ***5900.10*** *p213*
Stuart, Anne 4; Ontario, 1861 ***2896.25*** *p71*
Stuart, Bridget 17 *SEE* Stuart, John
Stuart, Bridget 32 *SEE* Stuart, George
Stuart, Bridget 43 *SEE* Stuart, William
Stuart, Bridget Gilooly; Vermont, 1849-1942 ***5900.10*** *p442*
Stuart, C.; Quebec, 1857 ***9196.15*** *p18*
Stuart, Catherine 15 *SEE* Stuart, John
Stuart, Catherine 25 *SEE* Stuart, Patrick
Stuart, Charles; Canada, 1874 ***1640.13*** *p121*
Stuart, Charles; Carolina, 1718 ***1640.13*** *p121*
Stuart, Charles; Florida, 1767 ***1640.10*** *p198*
Stuart, Charles; Florida, 1781 ***1224.2*** *p111*
Stuart, Charles; Georgia, 1800 ***1640.10*** *p198*
Stuart, Charles; Philadelphia, 1809 ***1224.3*** *p75*
Stuart, Charles 6 *SEE* Stuart, George
Stuart, Charles 14 *SEE* Stuart, William
Stuart, Charles 50; Ontario, 1871 ***1823.28*** *p96*
Stuart, Christopher; Carolina, 1718 ***1640.13*** *p121*
Stuart, Colquhoun 67; Ontario, 1871 ***1823.15*** *p256*
Stuart, Daniel; New York, 1802 ***8197.10*** *p25*
Stuart, David *SEE* Stuart, William
Stuart, David Knox; New Orleans, 1851 ***1640.10*** *p198*
Stuart, David Knox; New Orleans, 1851 ***1640.13*** *p121*
Stuart, E.; Quebec, 1856 ***9196.15*** *p6*
Stuart, Edward 37; Ontario, 1861 ***2896.25*** *p71*
Stuart, Eliza 10 *SEE* Stuart, William
Stuart, Elizabeth; Virginia, 1671-1672 ***6212.30*** *p47*
Stuart, Ellen 18 *SEE* Stuart, James
Stuart, Ellen 60 *SEE* Stuart, James
Stuart, Ellen Fox; Vermont, n.d. ***5900.10*** *p213*
Stuart, Finley 13; Ontario, 1861 ***2896.26*** *p34*
Stuart, Francis; New York, 1779 ***1224.2*** *p111*
Stuart, George *SEE* Stuart, William
Stuart, George 20 *SEE* Stuart, James
Stuart, George 40; New York, New York, 1847 ***1825.45*** *p20*
Wife: Bridget 32
Daughter: Mary 10
Son: John 4
Son: Charles 6
Stuart, Hugh; New York, 1812 ***1224.3*** *p75*
Stuart, Isaac; America, 1821 ***1224.3*** *p75*
Stuart, James; America, 1781 ***1224.2*** *p111*
Stuart, James; Georgia, 1774 ***1640.10*** *p198*
Stuart, James; New York, 1837 ***8197.10*** *p319*
Stuart, James 48; Ontario, 1871 ***1823.15*** *p256*
Stuart, James 50; Ontario, 1861 ***2896.26*** *p34*
Stuart, James 63; New York, New York, 1847 ***1825.45*** *p20*
Wife: Ellen 60
Son: George 20
Daughter: Ellen 18
Stuart, James, Jr. 19; Ontario, 1861 ***2896.26*** *p34*
Stuart, James O. 40; Ontario, 1871 ***1823.15*** *p256*
Stuart, Jane 16; Ontario, 1861 ***2896.26*** *p34*
Stuart, Jane 50; Ontario, 1861 ***2896.26*** *p34*
Stuart, John; Carolina, 1718 ***1640.13*** *p121*
Stuart, John; Charleston, South Carolina, 1748 ***1640.10*** *p199*
Stuart, John; New York, 1838 ***8197.10*** *p379*
Stuart, John; Pensacola, Florida, 1783 ***1224.2*** *p111*
Stuart, John; Savannah, Georgia, 1760 ***1640.10*** *p199*
Stuart, John; Vermont, 1834-1907 ***5900.10*** *p442*
Stuart, John 4 *SEE* Stuart, George
Stuart, John 6; Ontario, 1861 ***2896.25*** *p71*

Stuart, John 21; New York, New York, 1847 **1825.45** *p20*
Sister: Bridget 17
Sister: Catherine 15
Stuart, John 29; Ontario, 1871 **1823.15** *p256*
Stuart, John 47; Ontario, 1871 **1823.22** *p154*
Stuart, John A. 4; Ontario, 1861 **2896.28** *p46*
Stuart, John S. 82; Vermont, 1891 **5900.10** *p213*
Stuart, Joseph 9; Ontario, 1861 **2896.28** *p19*
Stuart, Joseph 48; Ontario, 1871 **1823.22** *p154*
Stuart, Margaret; Vermont, 1824-1861 **5900.10** *p213*
Stuart, Margaret; Vermont, 1900 **5900.10** *p88*
Stuart, Mary *SEE* Stuart, William
Stuart, Mary; Vermont, 1828-1901 **5900.10** *p78*
Stuart, Mary 3; Ontario, 1861 **2896.28** *p32*
Stuart, Mary 10 *SEE* Stuart, George
Stuart, May 65; Ontario, 1871 **1823.22** *p154*
Stuart, Michael *SEE* Stuart, William
Stuart, Michael 12 *SEE* Stuart, William
Stuart, Patrick 18; New York, New York, 1847 **1825.45** *p20*
Sister: Catherine 25
Stuart, Peter; Augusta, Georgia, 1862 **1640.10** *p199*
Stuart, Rachel *SEE* Stuart, William
Stuart, Rebecca A. 22; Ontario, 1861 **2896.27** *p66*
Stuart, Richard; New York, 1839 **8197.10** *p141*
Stuart, Robert; New York, 1802 **8197.10** *p25*
Stuart, Ruth; Boston, 1752 **1224.2** *p111*
Stuart, Sally *SEE* Stuart, William
Stuart, Sally; Savannah, Georgia, 1767 **1640.10** *p199*
Stuart, Thomas 21; Ontario, 1871 **1823.28** *p96*
Stuart, William; Louisiana, 1797 **1640.10** *p199*
Son: George
Daughter: Sally
Daughter: Rachel
Daughter: Mary
Son: David
Son: Michael
Stuart, William; Montreal, 1871 **1640.13** *p121*
Stuart, William; New York, 1840 **8197.10** *p195*
Stuart, William 8 *SEE* Stuart, William
Stuart, William 29; Ontario, 1871 **1823.22** *p154*
Stuart, William 47; New York, New York, 1847 **1825.45** *p21*
Wife: Bridget 43
Son: Charles 14
Son: Michael 12
Daughter: Eliza 10
Son: William 8
Stuart, William 55; Ontario, 1871 **1823.22** *p154*
Stuazinska, John; Maryland, 1910 **3259.35** *p60*
Stubanist, Catharina; Port uncertain, 1733 **2856.30** *p449*
Stubbins, Henry W. 36; Ontario, 1871 **1823.15** *p256*
Stubbins, James 38; Ontario, 1871 **1823.15** *p256*
Stubbins, Jane 65; Ontario, 1871 **1823.15** *p256*
Stubbins, Mary Jane 31; Ontario, 1871 **1823.15** *p256*
Stubbins, Thomas 71; Ontario, 1871 **1823.15** *p256*
Stubbs, Miss; Quebec, 1857 **9196.15** *p24*
Stubbs, Edward; New York, 1807 **8197.10** *p277*
Stubbs, Fredrick 23; Ontario, 1871 **1823.28** *p96*
Stubbs, Joseph; Maryland, 1681 **2524.55** *p212*
Stubbs, Joseph 42; Ontario, 1871 **1823.15** *p256*
Stubbs, Katharin; Virginia, 1664-1665 **6212.30** *p15*
Stubbs, Lydia 27; Ontario, 1861 **2896.26** *p1*
Stubbs, M. J. 1; Ontario, 1861 **2896.26** *p1*
Stubbs, Sarah; Maryland, 1681 **2524.55** *p212*
Stubbs, William; New York, 1807 **8197.10** *p277*
Stubbs, Wilson 12; Ontario, 1861 **2896.26** *p1*
Stubelin, Maria Christina; Port uncertain, 1793 **2856.30** *p451*
Stubenrauch, . . .; Port uncertain, 1779 **2856.30** *p449*
With brother
Stubenrauch, . . .; Port uncertain, 1782 **2856.30** *p449*
With brother
Stubenrauch, Karl Heinrich; Port uncertain, 1780 **2856.30** *p449*
Stubenroth, Abraham; Port uncertain, 1782 **2856.30** *p449*
Stuber, A. M. Altomus *SEE* Stuber, Johann Peter
Stuber, Friedrich; Port uncertain, 1764 **2856.30** *p451*
With wife & 5 children
Stuber, Johann; America, 1749 **2856.30** *p450*
With son & 6 children
Stuber, Johann Peter; America, 1739 **2856.30** *p450*
Wife: A. M. Altomus
Stuber, Johann Wilhelm; America, 1752 **2856.30** *p450*
With wife & 5 children
Stuber, Maria Juliana; Port uncertain, 1745 **2856.30** *p450*
Stuber, Theobald; Port uncertain, 1756 **2856.30** *p451*
Stubi, Xaver; Port uncertain, 1792 **2856.30** *p451*
Stubler, Jakob; America, 1749 **2856.30** *p451*
Stublewski, Andrew; Maryland, 1910 **3259.35** *p60*
Stubs, Edward 65; Ontario, 1871 **1823.28** *p97*
Stuchal, John; Pennsylvania, 1777 **4629.10** *p31*
Stuck, Anna Christina; America, 1741 **2856.30** *p450*
Stuckert, Michael; Port uncertain, 1779 **2856.30** *p450*
Stuckert, Michael; Port uncertain, 1788 **2856.30** *p450*
Stuckfield, Joseph; New York, 1840 **8197.10** *p198*
Stucki, Johann; America, 1751 **2856.30** *p450*
Stucki, Johann; America, 1751 **2856.30** *p450*
With wife & 3 children
Stucklin, Mr.; America, 1751 **2856.30** *p451*
With wife
Stuctzinski, Charles; Maryland, 1910 **3259.35** *p60*
Studdard, William 56; Ontario, 1871 **1823.28** *p97*
Studds, Frederick; New York, 1840 **8197.10** *p195*
Study, Francis; Pennsylvania, 1830 **6058.10** *p9*
Studzinski, John; Maryland, 1910 **3259.35** *p60*
Studzinski, Mary M.; Maryland, 1910 **3259.35** *p60*
Studzinski, Michael; Maryland, 1910 **3259.35** *p60*
Stuffels, David 10; Ontario, 1861 **2896.26** *p35*
Stuffels, Elen 18; Ontario, 1861 **2896.26** *p35*
Stuffels, Elizabeth 16; Ontario, 1861 **2896.26** *p35*
Stuffels, Hanah 47; Ontario, 1861 **2896.26** *p35*
Stuffels, July Ann 19; Ontario, 1861 **2896.26** *p35*
Stuffels, Margret 7; Ontario, 1861 **2896.26** *p35*
Stuffels, Sarah 4; Ontario, 1861 **2896.26** *p35*
Stuffels, Thomas 21; Ontario, 1861 **2896.26** *p35*
Stufflebeam, Clayton M.; Vermont, 1853-1924 **5900.10** *p455*
Stufflebeam, Florence C. Shannon; Vermont, 1857-1937 **5900.10** *p455*
Stuhler, Anna Maria; Port uncertain, 1784 **2856.30** *p257*
Stuhlfaud, Maria Sara; Port uncertain, 1770 **2856.30** *p159*
Stuhlfauth, Nikolaus; Port uncertain, 1770 **2856.30** *p450*
Stukely, Francis; Maryland, 1663 **2524.55** *p212*
Stultz, George; New York, 1836 **8197.10** *p283*
Stultz, George; New York, 1838 **8197.10** *p149*
Stultz, Johannes; New York, 1838 **8197.10** *p148*
Stulz, George; New York, 1838 **8197.10** *p149*
Stum, Adam; America, 1749 **2856.30** *p450*
Stum, Hilgert; Port uncertain, 1738 **2856.30** *p450*
Stumkeller, Anna Catharina; America, 1749 **2856.30** *p450*
With husband
Stumm, Anna Catharina; Port uncertain, 1746 **2856.30** *p450*
Stumm, Johann; Port uncertain, 1745 **2856.30** *p450*
Stumm, Johann Heinrich; Port uncertain, 1753 **2856.30** *p450*
Stumm, Johann Konrad; Port uncertain, 1745 **2856.30** *p450*
Stumm, Johann Nikolaus; Port uncertain, 1771 **2856.30** *p450*
Stumm, Johann Peter; Port uncertain, 1745 **2856.30** *p450*
Stumm, Margarete; America, 1749 **2856.30** *p450*
With 4 children
Stumm, Margarete; Port uncertain, 1746 **2856.30** *p450*
Stumm, Margarete; Port uncertain, 1778 **2856.30** *p450*
Stumm, Maria Elisabeth; Port uncertain, 1758 **2856.30** *p450*
Stumm, Maria Gertrud; Port uncertain, 1755 **2856.30** *p450*
Stumm, Maria Ursula; Port uncertain, 1746 **2856.30** *p450*
Stumm, Philipp; Port uncertain, 1764 **2856.30** *p450*
With wife children & father
Stumm, Susanna; Port uncertain, 1757 **2856.30** *p450*
Stumpf, Mrs.; Port uncertain, 1795 **2856.30** *p450*
Stumpf, Anna Elisabeth; Port uncertain, 1773 **2856.30** *p450*
Stumpf, Charles; New York, 1840 **8197.10** *p196*
Stumpf, Paul Henrich; Port uncertain, 1754 **2856.30** *p450*
Stumpf, Reinhard; Port uncertain, 1787 **2856.30** *p450*
Stumpff, Mary C. 33; Kansas, 1889-1910 **9079.10** *p39*
Stumpfin, Mrs.; Port uncertain, 1795 **2856.30** *p450*
Stumph, Anna Maria; Port uncertain, 1743 **2856.30** *p451*
Stumphin, Anna Maria; Port uncertain, 1743 **2856.30** *p451*
Stumpp, Anton; Port uncertain, 1775 **2856.30** *p451*
Stunt, William Henry; New York, 1831 **8197.10** *p283*
Stupanus, Johann; Port uncertain, 1795 **2856.30** *p451*
Stupanus, Johann; Port uncertain, 1796 **2856.30** *p451*
Stupenski, Annie; Maryland, 1910 **3259.35** *p60*
Stuppel, Christian 14; Kansas, 1905-1910 **9079.10** *p41*
Stuppel, Henry 34; Kansas, 1906-1910 **9079.10** *p41*
Stuppel, Jacob 11; Kansas, 1905-1910 **9079.10** *p41*
Stuppel, Laura 5; Kansas, 1905-1910 **9079.10** *p41*
Stuppel, Lizzie 34; Kansas, 1905-1910 **9079.10** *p41*
Stuppy, Johann Georg; Port uncertain, 1755 **2856.30** *p451*
Sturcke, Carl Joh. Quintus Friedrich; New York, 1839 **8197.10** *p284*
Sturcken, Henry; New York, 1823 **8197.10** *p281*
Sturdy, Hugh 70; Ontario, 1871 **1823.15** *p256*
Sturdy, John 44; Ontario, 1871 **1823.15** *p256*
Sturdy, John 59; Ontario, 1871 **1823.15** *p256*
Sturdy, Margaret 58; Ontario, 1871 **1823.15** *p256*
Sturdy, Robert; Virginia, 1715 **1224.2** *p112*
Sturdy, Thomas 60; Ontario, 1871 **1823.22** *p154*
Sturdy, William; Virginia, 1715 **1224.2** *p112*
Sturge, Thomas; New York, 1853 **1224.3** *p76*
Sturgen, Tomasine; Maryland, 1658 **2524.55** *p212*
Sturgeon, Mr.; Quebec, 1857 **9196.15** *p15*
Sturgeon, Agnes 72; Ontario, 1871 **1823.15** *p256*
Sturgeon, Bridgett Eagleton; Vermont, 1844-1940 **5900.10** *p602*
Sturgeon, Peter; Vermont, 1854-1948 **5900.10** *p602*
Sturgeon, Robert 40; Ontario, 1871 **1823.15** *p256*
Sturgeon, William; Pennsylvania, 1777 **4629.10** *p19*
Sturges, Henry; Maryland, 1697 **1224.1** *p56*
Sturges, Robert; New York, 1838 **8197.10** *p284*
Sturgis, Amos; Pennsylvania, 1777 **4629.10** *p26*
Sturgis, Geo; Virginia, 1668-1669 **6212.30** *p41*
Sturgis, Jno; Virginia, 1663-1664 **6212.30** *p5*
Sturm, Anna Elisabeth; Port uncertain, 1768 **2856.30** *p451*
Sturm, Anna Maria; Port uncertain, 1765 **2856.30** *p451*
Sturm, Johann; America, 1737 **2856.30** *p451*
Sturm, Margarete; America, 1749 **2856.30** *p451*
With 4 children
Sturm, Maria; Port uncertain, 1743 **2856.30** *p451*
Sturm, Peter; Port uncertain, 1785 **2856.30** *p451*
Sturm, Simon; Port uncertain, 1765 **2856.30** *p451*
Sturman, Mrs.; Maryland, 1648 **2524.55** *p212*
Sturman, Anne *SEE* Sturman, Thomas
Sturman, Elizabeth *SEE* Sturman, Thomas
Sturman, John *SEE* Sturman, Thomas
Sturman, Richard; Virginia, 1672 **1224.1** *p56*
Sturman, Thomas; Maryland, 1640 **2524.55** *p212*
With wife
Daughter: Anne
Daughter: Elizabeth
Son: John
Sturmfels, Johann Georg; Port uncertain, 1734 **2856.30** *p451*
Sturmtal, Anna Margarete; Port uncertain, 1791 **2856.30** *p451*
Sturmy, William; Maryland, 1677-1678 **2524.55** *p212*
Sturnby, Richard; Maryland, 1671 **2524.55** *p212*
Sturt, Thomas; Virginia, 1765 **1224.2** *p112*
Stut, William; Maryland, 1669 **2524.55** *p212*
Stuteville, Charles 22; Maryland, 1774 **1220.25** *p76*
Stuthers, Stephen 63; Ontario, 1871 **1823.15** *p256*
Stuthers, William 56; Ontario, 1871 **1823.15** *p256*
Stuttson, Joshua; Pennsylvania, 1777 **4629.10** *p12*
Stutz, Caspar; Port uncertain, 1733 **2856.30** *p451*
Stutzlin, Peter; Port uncertain, 1739 **2856.30** *p451*
Stutzmann, Johann Jakob; America, 1727 **2856.30** *p451*
Stutzmann, Johann Jakob; America, 1772 **2856.30** *p451*
Stutzmann, Johann Jakob; America, 1773 **2856.30** *p451*
Stutzmann, Peter; America, 1741 **2856.30** *p451*
Stuzensky, Walenty; Maryland, 1910 **3259.35** *p60*
Style, Elizabeth; New England, 1665 **1224.1** *p56*
Styles, Meichacl 73; Ontario, 1871 **1823.15** *p256*
Styles, Reuben 40; Maryland, 1774 **1220.25** *p61*
Styles, Samuel; Maryland, 1663 **2524.55** *p212*
Styles, Simon 55; Ontario, 1871 **1823.15** *p256*
Styles, William; Maryland, 1649 **2524.55** *p212*
Stzneckski, Martin; Maryland, 1910 **3259.35** *p60*
Suber, J. 34; British Columbia, 1910 **9196.1** *p28*
Suber, J. 34; Washington, 1910 **9196.1** *p28*
Subinska, Peter F.; Maryland, 1910 **3259.35** *p60*
Succor, John; Maryland, 1659 **2524.55** *p83*
Sucford, Ann 66; Ontario, 1871 **1823.15** *p256*
Sucford, Joseph 66; Ontario, 1871 **1823.15** *p256*
Such, George; Virginia, 1671-1672 **6212.30** *p46*
Such, James; New York, 1839 **8197.10** *p284*
Suckley, George; New York, 1794 **8197.10** *p2*
Suckofska, Sophia; Maryland, 1910 **3259.35** *p60*
Sudberry, Henry *SEE* Sudberry, Peter
Sudberry, James *SEE* Sudberry, Peter
Sudberry, John *SEE* Sudberry, Peter
Sudberry, Margarett *SEE* Sudberry, Peter
Sudberry, Peter *SEE* Sudberry, Peter
Sudberry, Peter; Maryland, 1663 **2524.55** *p212*
Wife: Margarett
Son: Peter
Son: William
Son: Henry
Son: John
Son: Richard
Son: James
Sudberry, Richard *SEE* Sudberry, Peter
Sudberry, William *SEE* Sudberry, Peter
Suddevan, Jeremiah; Maryland, 1654 **2524.55** *p212*
Suder, Christian; America, 1733 **2856.30** *p452*
Sudowski, Andy; Maryland, 1910 **3259.35** *p61*
Sudowski, Frances; Maryland, 1910 **3259.35** *p61*

Sudowski, John; Maryland, 1910 ***3259.35*** *p61*
Sudwan, Jeremiah; Maryland, 1654 ***2524.55*** *p212*
Sudward, Elizabeth *SEE* Sudward, James
Sudward, James; Maryland, 1658 ***2524.55*** *p212*
Wife: Mary
Child: Elizabeth
Sudward, Mary *SEE* Sudward, James
Sueton, John; Maryland, 1663 ***2524.55*** *p212*
Suffern, Anthony 34; Ontario, 1871 ***1823.28*** *p97*
Suffern, James 63; Ontario, 1871 ***1823.28*** *p97*
Suffrin, George 18; New York, 1775 ***1220.25*** *p94*
Sugars, William 21; Maryland, 1775 ***1220.25*** *p97*
Sugden, Charles 21; Ontario, 1871 ***1823.28*** *p97*
Suggett, Ann 14 *SEE* Suggett, Mary
Suggett, Christopher 10 *SEE* Suggett, Mary
Suggett, John 8 *SEE* Suggett, Mary
Suggett, Mary 12 *SEE* Suggett, Mary
Suggett, Mary 40; Nova Scotia, 1774 ***1220.25*** *p15*
Child: Ann 14
Child: Mary 12
Child: Christopher 10
Child: John 8
Suggett, William 18; Nova Scotia, 1774 ***1220.25*** *p15*
Suggitt, Jane; Virginia, 1771 ***1224.2*** *p112*
Suggitt, John; Virginia, 1771 ***1224.2*** *p112*
Suher, Anna Eva; Port uncertain, 1774 ***2856.30*** *p452*
Suhr, Peter Christof; Port uncertain, 1785 ***2856.30*** *p452*
With wife & 3 children
Suilivan, John; New Hampshire, n.d. ***4628.40*** *p76*
Sujet, Maria Ursula; Port uncertain, 1740 ***2856.30*** *p452*
Sujetin, Maria Ursula; Port uncertain, 1740 ***2856.30*** *p452*
Suki, Joseph; Maryland, 1910 ***3259.35*** *p61*
Sul, John; Maryland, 1910 ***3259.35*** *p61*
Sulaven, John 36; Ontario, 1861 ***2896.26*** *p32*
Sulaven, Mary 29; Ontario, 1861 ***2896.26*** *p32*
Sulavin, Patrick 102; Ontario, 1871 ***1823.28*** *p97*
Sulavin, Timothy 54; Ontario, 1871 ***1823.28*** *p97*
Sulch, Antoni; Maryland, 1910 ***3259.35*** *p61*
Sulear, George; Pennsylvania, 1777 ***4629.10*** *p31*
Sulevin, John 50; Ontario, 1871 ***1823.15*** *p256*
Sulivan, Bridget 40; Ontario, 1871 ***1823.22*** *p155*
Sulivan, Catherine 35; Ontario, 1871 ***1823.15*** *p257*
Sulivan, John 43; Ontario, 1871 ***1823.15*** *p256*
Sulivan, John 52; Ontario, 1871 ***1823.22*** *p155*
Sulivan, John 77; Ontario, 1871 ***1823.15*** *p256*
Sulivan, Katharine; Maryland, 1681 ***2524.55*** *p212*
Sulivan, Martin; New York, 1836 ***8197.10*** *p301*
Sulivan, Michael 32; Ontario, 1871 ***1823.28*** *p97*
Sulivan, Michael 55; Ontario, 1871 ***1823.15*** *p256*
Sulivan, Patrick 35; Ontario, 1871 ***1823.15*** *p257*
Sulivan, Thomas 56; Ontario, 1871 ***1823.15*** *p257*
Sulivan, Thos 30; Ontario, 1871 ***1823.28*** *p97*
Sulivan, Timothy 56; Ontario, 1871 ***1823.22*** *p155*
Sulivan, Timothy 61; Vermont, 1875 ***5900.10*** *p330*
Sulivant, Juliana; Maryland, 1671 ***2524.55*** *p212*
Suliven, Dan 61; Ontario, 1861 ***2896.27*** *p3*
Suliven, M. A. 49; Ontario, 1861 ***2896.27*** *p3*
Sullavan, Jeremiah 70; Ontario, 1871 ***1823.28*** *p97*
Sullavan, Marey 71; Ontario, 1871 ***1823.28*** *p97*
Sullavin, Daniel 34; Ontario, 1871 ***1823.28*** *p97*
Sullivan, . . .; New Hampshire, 1641-1660 ***4628.40*** *p44*
Sullivan, . . .; New York, New York, 1855 ***1825.45*** *p52*
Sullivan, Miss; Quebec, 1858 ***9196.15*** *p39*
Sullivan, Mr.; Quebec, 1858 ***9196.15*** *p39*
Sullivan, Abby 31; Vermont, 1862 ***5900.10*** *p58*
Sullivan, Agnes; Vermont, n.d. ***5900.10*** *p121*
Sullivan, Agnes C. McEnany; Vermont, 1863-1937 ***5900.10*** *p487*
Sullivan, Andrew 51; Ontario, 1871 ***1823.28*** *p97*
Sullivan, Ann J. 65; Vermont, 1911 ***5900.10*** *p184*
Sullivan, Anna B.; Vermont, 1860-1932 ***5900.10*** *p96*
Sullivan, Anna G. 83; Vermont, 1959 ***5900.10*** *p313*
Sullivan, Anna Manning; Vermont, 1848-1888 ***5900.10*** *p302*
Sullivan, Annie 21; Vermont, 1894 ***5900.10*** *p378*
Sullivan, Arthur A. 50; Vermont, 1915 ***5900.10*** *p439*
Sullivan, Bartholomew 76; Vermont, 1886 ***5900.10*** *p61*
Sullivan, Betsey; Vermont, 1832-1912 ***5900.10*** *p109*
Sullivan, Bridget; Vermont, 1841-1873 ***5900.10*** *p371*
Sullivan, Bridget; Vermont, 1856-1918 ***5900.10*** *p327*
Sullivan, Bridget; Vermont, 1867-1921 ***5900.10*** *p371*
Sullivan, Bridget 47; Vermont, 1880 ***5900.10*** *p364*
Sullivan, Bridget 59; Vermont, 1883 ***5900.10*** *p469*
Sullivan, Bridget 64; Vermont, 1887 ***5900.10*** *p106*
Sullivan, Bridget 72; Vermont, 1930 ***5900.10*** *p439*
Sullivan, Bridget Doherty; Vermont, 1811-1903 ***5900.10*** *p371*
Sullivan, Bridget Lynch; Vermont, 1851-1881 ***5900.10*** *p76*
Sullivan, Bridget Ryan; Vermont, 1840-1881 ***5900.10*** *p543*
Sullivan, Catharine; Vermont, 1840-1871 ***5900.10*** *p616*
Sullivan, Catharine 67; Vermont, 1894 ***5900.10*** *p121*
Sullivan, Catharine 78; Vermont, 1898 ***5900.10*** *p431*
Sullivan, Catherine; Vermont, 1834-1901 ***5900.10*** *p145*
Sullivan, Catherine; Vermont, 1840-1912 ***5900.10*** *p438*
Sullivan, Catherine 15; Vermont, 1859 ***5900.10*** *p57*
Sullivan, Catherine 24; Ontario, 1861 ***2896.27*** *p4*
Sullivan, Catherine 33; Vermont, 1863 ***5900.10*** *p56*
Sullivan, Catherine 48; Vermont, 1876 ***5900.10*** *p614*
Sullivan, Catherine Conners 23; Vermont, 1862 ***5900.10*** *p473*
Sullivan, Catherine Gallivan 77; Vermont, 1883 ***5900.10*** *p298*
Sullivan, Catherine Lawlor; Vermont, 1846-1912 ***5900.10*** *p442*
Sullivan, Catherine Murphy; Vermont, 1826-1905 ***5900.10*** *p475*
Sullivan, Charles E.; Vermont, 1854-1918 ***5900.10*** *p492*
Sullivan, Cornelius 37; Ontario, 1871 ***1823.28*** *p97*
Sullivan, Cornelius 40; Ontario, 1871 ***1823.28*** *p97*
Sullivan, Cornelius 51; Vermont, 1877 ***5900.10*** *p121*
Sullivan, Cornelius 59; Vermont, 1905 ***5900.10*** *p121*
Sullivan, Cornelius 60; Vermont, 1894 ***5900.10*** *p58*
Sullivan, Dan 4 *SEE* Sullivan, Pat
Sullivan, Daniel; Canada, 1756-1760 ***4628.40*** *p46*
Sullivan, Daniel; New York, 1829 ***8197.10*** *p312*
Sullivan, Daniel; New York, 1837 ***8197.10*** *p106*
Sullivan, Daniel; Vermont, 1808-1887 ***5900.10*** *p473*
Sullivan, Daniel; Vermont, 1812-1893 ***5900.10*** *p313*
Sullivan, Daniel; Vermont, 1837-1902 ***5900.10*** *p141*
Sullivan, Daniel; Vermont, 1841-1903 ***5900.10*** *p489*
Sullivan, Daniel; Vermont, 1854-1924 ***5900.10*** *p489*
Sullivan, Daniel; Vermont, 1860-1910 ***5900.10*** *p145*
Sullivan, Daniel; Vermont, 1873-1940 ***5900.10*** *p120*
Sullivan, Daniel; Vermont, 1879 ***5900.10*** *p143*
Sullivan, Daniel 20; Ontario, 1861 ***2896.27*** *p4*
Sullivan, Daniel 23; Vermont, 1877 ***5900.10*** *p192*
Sullivan, Daniel 58; Vermont, 1868 ***5900.10*** *p249*
Sullivan, Daniel D. 40; Vermont, 1882 ***5900.10*** *p315*
Sullivan, Daniel F.; Vermont, 1852-1939 ***5900.10*** *p485*
Sullivan, Daniel F. D.; Vermont, 1849-1921 ***5900.10*** *p118*
Sullivan, Darby; Canada, 1756-1760 ***4628.40*** *p45*
Sullivan, Deborah 40; Ontario, 1871 ***1823.28*** *p97*
Sullivan, Denis; New York, 1837 ***8197.10*** *p107*
Sullivan, Dennis; Canada, 1756-1760 ***4628.40*** *p45*
Sullivan, Dennis; Vermont, 1866-1884 ***5900.10*** *p371*
Sullivan, Dennis 13; Vermont, 1860 ***5900.10*** *p315*
Sullivan, Dennis 26; Maryland, 1775 ***1220.25*** *p108*
Sullivan, Dennis 40; Ontario, 1871 ***1823.15*** *p257*
Sullivan, Dennis 54; Ontario, 1871 ***1823.28*** *p97*
Sullivan, Dennis J.; Vermont, 1844-1914 ***5900.10*** *p442*
Sullivan, Dinnis 60; Ontario, 1871 ***1823.28*** *p97*
Sullivan, Edward; Vermont, 1852-1928 ***5900.10*** *p94*
Sullivan, Elizabeth; Vermont, 1862-1881 ***5900.10*** *p371*
Sullivan, Elizabeth 18; Vermont, 1867 ***5900.10*** *p368*
Sullivan, Elizabeth 59; Vermont, 1894 ***5900.10*** *p249*
Sullivan, Elizabeth Hurley; Vermont, 1828-1901 ***5900.10*** *p489*
Sullivan, Elizabeth M.; Vermont, 1889-1971 ***5900.10*** *p120*
Sullivan, Ellen; Vermont, 1816-1874 ***5900.10*** *p427*
Sullivan, Ellen; Vermont, 1837-1907 ***5900.10*** *p339*
Sullivan, Ellen; Vermont, 1850-1942 ***5900.10*** *p115*
Sullivan, Ellen 21; Ontario, 1871 ***1823.28*** *p97*
Sullivan, Ellen 24; Vermont, 1877 ***5900.10*** *p364*
Sullivan, Ellen 30 *SEE* Sullivan, John
Sullivan, Ellen 34; Vermont, 1874 ***5900.10*** *p381*
Sullivan, Ellen 40; Ontario, 1861 ***2896.27*** *p36*
Sullivan, Ellen 63; Vermont, 1899 ***5900.10*** *p428*
Sullivan, Ellen 64; Vermont, 1886 ***5900.10*** *p61*
Sullivan, Ellen 73; Vermont, 1879 ***5900.10*** *p540*
Sullivan, Ellen 82; Vermont, 1905 ***5900.10*** *p94*
Sullivan, Ellen Cavanaugh 70; Vermont, 1893 ***5900.10*** *p341*
Sullivan, Ellen Lavery 64; Vermont, 1906 ***5900.10*** *p379*
Sullivan, Ellen Leonard; Vermont, 1847-1911 ***5900.10*** *p461*
Sullivan, Ellen M. O'Brien; Vermont, 1855-1940 ***5900.10*** *p466*
Sullivan, Ellen O'Brien; Vermont, 1846-1925 ***5900.10*** *p55*
Sullivan, Ellen Reagan; Vermont, 1853-1933 ***5900.10*** *p216*
Sullivan, Ellen Sheehan 78; Vermont, 1901 ***5900.10*** *p418*
Sullivan, Elmira 55; Vermont, 1899 ***5900.10*** *p170*
Sullivan, Franciece; Vermont, 1871-1891 ***5900.10*** *p371*
Sullivan, Frank C.; Vermont, 1837-1925 ***5900.10*** *p76*
Sullivan, Frank P.; Vermont, 1836-1936 ***5900.10*** *p296*
Sullivan, Genevieve Rivet; Vermont, 1830-1911 ***5900.10*** *p462*
Sullivan, Hannah; Vermont, 1822-1846 ***5900.10*** *p381*
Sullivan, Hannah; Vermont, 1841-1921 ***5900.10*** *p58*
Sullivan, Hannah; Vermont, 1845-1869 ***5900.10*** *p473*
Sullivan, Hannah; Vermont, 1860-1952 ***5900.10*** *p304*
Sullivan, Hannah Carty 73; Vermont, 1879 ***5900.10*** *p378*
Sullivan, Hannie; Vermont, n.d. ***5900.10*** *p331*
Sullivan, Hanora; Vermont, 1821-1906 ***5900.10*** *p55*
Sullivan, Hanora 72; Vermont, 1913 ***5900.10*** *p54*
Sullivan, Helen M.; Vermont, 1886-1975 ***5900.10*** *p120*
Sullivan, Honora 69; Vermont, 1888 ***5900.10*** *p180*
Sullivan, Honora O'Sullivan; Vermont, 1851-1924 ***5900.10*** *p144*
Sullivan, Humphrey; New Hampshire, n.d. ***4628.40*** *p76*
Sullivan, Humphrey C.; Vermont, 1850-1926 ***5900.10*** *p313*
Sullivan, J. 55; Alaska, 1918 ***9196.1*** *p56*
Sullivan, J. 55; British Columbia, 1918 ***9196.1*** *p56*
Sullivan, James; Massachusetts, 1775-1781 ***4628.40*** *p69*
Sullivan, James; New York, 1833 ***8197.10*** *p283*
Sullivan, James; New York, 1839 ***8197.10*** *p285*
Sullivan, James; Vermont, 1815-1894 ***5900.10*** *p317*
Sullivan, James; Vermont, 1830-1925 ***5900.10*** *p55*
Sullivan, James; Vermont, 1852-1906 ***5900.10*** *p458*
Sullivan, James; Vermont, 1867-1870 ***5900.10*** *p145*
Sullivan, James; Vermont, 1884-1971 ***5900.10*** *p120*
Sullivan, James 49; Vermont, 1877 ***5900.10*** *p112*
Sullivan, James 55; Vermont, 1860 ***5900.10*** *p315*
Sullivan, James 59; Ontario, 1871 ***1823.28*** *p97*
Sullivan, James 75; Vermont, 1934 ***5900.10*** *p94*
Sullivan, James 80; Vermont, 1892 ***5900.10*** *p94*
Sullivan, James C.; Vermont, 1866-1927 ***5900.10*** *p121*
Sullivan, James P.; Vermont, 1854-1920 ***5900.10*** *p446*
Sullivan, Jane 9; Ontario, 1861 ***2896.27*** *p36*
Sullivan, Jeramiah; New York, 1840 ***8197.10*** *p285*
Sullivan, Jeremiah; Vermont, 1825-1879 ***5900.10*** *p475*
Sullivan, Jeremiah 27; Ontario, 1871 ***1823.28*** *p97*
Sullivan, Jeremiah 31; Ontario, 1871 ***1823.15*** *p257*
Sullivan, Jeremiah 46; Ontario, 1861 ***2896.27*** *p36*
Sullivan, Jeremiah 48; Vermont, 1863 ***5900.10*** *p100*
Sullivan, Jeremiah 73; Vermont, 1910 ***5900.10*** *p504*
Sullivan, Jeremiah M.; New York, 1838 ***8197.10*** *p148*
Sullivan, Jerry 64; Vermont, 1867 ***5900.10*** *p72*
Sullivan, Joanna 49; Ontario, 1871 ***1823.22*** *p155*
Sullivan, Joanna F.; Vermont, 1851-1888 ***5900.10*** *p170*
Sullivan, Johanna; Vermont, 1833-1912 ***5900.10*** *p59*
Sullivan, Johanna; Vermont, 1844-1905 ***5900.10*** *p141*
Sullivan, Johanna; Vermont, 1848-1916 ***5900.10*** *p592*
Sullivan, Johanna F. McMahon; Vermont, 1851-1883 ***5900.10*** *p138*
Sullivan, Johanna Murphy 85; Vermont, 1876 ***5900.10*** *p57*
Sullivan, John; New Hampshire, 1775-1781 ***4628.40*** *p69*
Sullivan, John; New York, 1837 ***8197.10*** *p105*
Sullivan, John; New York, 1839 ***8197.10*** *p284*
Sullivan, John; New York, 1840 ***8197.10*** *p198*
Sullivan, John; Pennsylvania, 1777 ***4629.10*** *p22*
Sullivan, John; Vermont, 1820-1894 ***5900.10*** *p489*
Sullivan, John; Vermont, 1823-1872 ***5900.10*** *p538*
Sullivan, John; Vermont, 1837-1872 ***5900.10*** *p421*
Sullivan, John; Vermont, 1844-1896 ***5900.10*** *p466*
Sullivan, John; Vermont, 1850-1885 ***5900.10*** *p145*
Sullivan, John; Vermont, 1855-1949 ***5900.10*** *p61*
Sullivan, John; Vermont, 1860-1889 ***5900.10*** *p102*
Sullivan, John; Vermont, 1865-1891 ***5900.10*** *p371*
Sullivan, John 6 months *SEE* Sullivan, John
Sullivan, John 10; Vermont, 1866 ***5900.10*** *p112*
Sullivan, John 12 *SEE* Sullivan, Pat
Sullivan, John 27; Vermont, 1842 ***5900.10*** *p151*
Sullivan, John 30; Ontario, 1871 ***1823.28*** *p97*
Sullivan, John 32; Ontario, 1871 ***1823.28*** *p97*
Sullivan, John 35; New York, New York, 1849 ***1825.45*** *p53*
Son: John 6 months
Wife: Ellen 30
Sullivan, John 36; Ontario, 1871 ***1823.28*** *p97*
Sullivan, John 40; Ontario, 1871 ***1823.15*** *p257*
Sullivan, John 40; Ontario, 1871 ***1823.28*** *p97*
Sullivan, John 45; Vermont, 1894 ***5900.10*** *p435*
Sullivan, John 48; Vermont, 1869 ***5900.10*** *p418*
Sullivan, John 55; Ontario, 1871 ***1823.28*** *p97*
Sullivan, John 72; Vermont, 1914 ***5900.10*** *p379*
Sullivan, John 92; Vermont, 1892 ***5900.10*** *p341*
Sullivan, John B.; New York, 1840 ***8197.10*** *p301*
Sullivan, John D.; Vermont, 1920 ***5900.10*** *p120*
Sullivan, John F. 47; Vermont, 1897 ***5900.10*** *p473*
Sullivan, John J. 42; Vermont, 1893 ***5900.10*** *p162*
Sullivan, John O. 82; Vermont, 1885 ***5900.10*** *p298*
Sullivan, John R.; Vermont, 1842-1925 ***5900.10*** *p298*
Sullivan, Joseph; Vermont, 1904 ***5900.10*** *p118*
Sullivan, Joseph 83; Vermont, 1924 ***5900.10*** *p184*
Sullivan, Judith; Vermont, 1852-1896 ***5900.10*** *p168*
Sullivan, Judy 1 *SEE* Sullivan, Pat
Sullivan, Judy 43 *SEE* Sullivan, Pat
Sullivan, Julia; Vermont, 1847-1908 ***5900.10*** *p75*
Sullivan, Julia 69; Vermont, 1909 ***5900.10*** *p389*
Sullivan, Julia A. Lyons; Vermont, 1839-1919 ***5900.10*** *p76*

Sullivan, Julia C.; Vermont, 1842-1919 ***5900.10*** *p298*
Sullivan, Julia M.; Vermont, 1854-1947 ***5900.10*** *p57*
Sullivan, Kate 35; Vermont, 1898 ***5900.10*** *p58*
Sullivan, Katherine; Vermont, 1829-1904 ***5900.10*** *p424*
Sullivan, Katherine Sweeney; Vermont, 1827-1902 ***5900.10*** *p381*
Sullivan, Katie; Vermont, n.d. ***5900.10*** *p112*
Sullivan, Katie 18; Vermont, 1878 ***5900.10*** *p112*
Sullivan, Katie 19; Vermont, 1864 ***5900.10*** *p109*
Sullivan, Lawrence 24; Ontario, 1871 ***1823.28*** *p97*
Sullivan, Lillian 73; Vermont, 1879 ***5900.10*** *p542*
Sullivan, M. A. 80; Vermont, 1918 ***5900.10*** *p504*
Sullivan, Maggie 27; Vermont, 1878 ***5900.10*** *p309*
Sullivan, Maggie A.; Vermont, 1857-1946 ***5900.10*** *p304*
Sullivan, Margaret; Vermont, 1818-1846 ***5900.10*** *p543*
Sullivan, Margaret; Vermont, 1831-1895 ***5900.10*** *p437*
Sullivan, Margaret; Vermont, 1835-1906 ***5900.10*** *p156*
Sullivan, Margaret; Vermont, 1839-1915 ***5900.10*** *p296*
Sullivan, Margaret; Vermont, 1842-1928 ***5900.10*** *p380*
Sullivan, Margaret 19; Vermont, 1857 ***5900.10*** *p76*
Sullivan, Margaret 53; Vermont, 1883 ***5900.10*** *p317*
Sullivan, Margaret 67; New York, New York, 1851 ***1825.45*** *p56*
Sullivan, Margaret 75; Vermont, 1889 ***5900.10*** *p109*
Sullivan, Margaret 78; Vermont, 1892 ***5900.10*** *p306*
Sullivan, Margaret A.; Vermont, 1857-1909 ***5900.10*** *p446*
Sullivan, Margaret A. 70; Vermont, n.d. ***5900.10*** *p439*
Sullivan, Margaret Callahan 65; Vermont, 1890 ***5900.10*** *p438*
Sullivan, Margaret E.; Vermont, 1853-1880 ***5900.10*** *p381*
Sullivan, Margaret G.; Vermont, 1864-1943 ***5900.10*** *p492*
Sullivan, Margaret Holleran; Vermont, 1855-1902 ***5900.10*** *p275*
Sullivan, Margaret Rogers; Vermont, 1826-1888 ***5900.10*** *p470*
Sullivan, Margarette; Vermont, 1811-1901 ***5900.10*** *p300*
Sullivan, Mary; Vermont, 1809-1877 ***5900.10*** *p473*
Sullivan, Mary; Vermont, 1834-1908 ***5900.10*** *p432*
Sullivan, Mary; Vermont, 1835-1907 ***5900.10*** *p421*
Sullivan, Mary; Vermont, 1837-1907 ***5900.10*** *p405*
Sullivan, Mary; Vermont, 1839-1912 ***5900.10*** *p427*
Sullivan, Mary; Vermont, 1840-1916 ***5900.10*** *p507*
Sullivan, Mary; Vermont, 1841-1923 ***5900.10*** *p60*
Sullivan, Mary; Vermont, 1853-1920 ***5900.10*** *p301*
Sullivan, Mary; Vermont, 1854-1908 ***5900.10*** *p306*
Sullivan, Mary; Vermont, 1857-1927 ***5900.10*** *p95*
Sullivan, Mary; Vermont, 1865-1936 ***5900.10*** *p61*
Sullivan, Mary; Vermont, 1871-1932 ***5900.10*** *p174*
Sullivan, Mary; Vermont, 1883 ***5900.10*** *p144*
Sullivan, Mary 25; New York, New York, 1849 ***1825.45*** *p53*
Sullivan, Mary 27; Ontario, 1861 ***2896.27*** *p4*
Sullivan, Mary 28; Vermont, 1870 ***5900.10*** *p210*
Sullivan, Mary 33; Vermont, 1855 ***5900.10*** *p347*
Sullivan, Mary 42; Vermont, 1871 ***5900.10*** *p575*
Sullivan, Mary 45; Vermont, 1870 ***5900.10*** *p192*
Sullivan, Mary 48; Vermont, 1863 ***5900.10*** *p305*
Sullivan, Mary 90; Vermont, 1928 ***5900.10*** *p541*
Sullivan, Mary 92; Vermont, 1884 ***5900.10*** *p415*
Sullivan, Mary A.; Vermont, n.d. ***5900.10*** *p94*
Sullivan, Mary A.; Vermont, 1852-1932 ***5900.10*** *p102*
Sullivan, Mary A. 46; Vermont, 1884 ***5900.10*** *p298*
Sullivan, Mary A. 56; Ontario, 1861 ***2896.27*** *p4*
Sullivan, Mary Ann McCarthy; Vermont, 1854-1900 ***5900.10*** *p485*
Sullivan, Mary B.; Vermont, 1852-1918 ***5900.10*** *p80*
Sullivan, Mary Brosnahan; Vermont, 1849-1917 ***5900.10*** *p121*
Sullivan, Mary Carney 78; Vermont, 1918 ***5900.10*** *p313*
Sullivan, Mary Casey 70; Vermont, 1913 ***5900.10*** *p315*
Sullivan, Mary Clifford 47; Vermont, 1876 ***5900.10*** *p261*
Sullivan, Mary E.; Vermont, 1851-1893 ***5900.10*** *p313*
Sullivan, Mary E.; Vermont, 1858-1921 ***5900.10*** *p158*
Sullivan, Mary E. 48; Vermont, 1909 ***5900.10*** *p563*
Sullivan, Mary E. Erving; Vermont, 1853-1889 ***5900.10*** *p361*
Sullivan, Mary J.; Vermont, 1871-1949 ***5900.10*** *p118*
Sullivan, Mary J. McSorley; Vermont, 1850-1909 ***5900.10*** *p475*
Sullivan, Mary J. Purcell; Vermont, 1858-1943 ***5900.10*** *p94*
Sullivan, Mary Johnson; Vermont, 1829-1898 ***5900.10*** *p145*
Sullivan, Mary L.; Vermont, 1857-1928 ***5900.10*** *p313*
Sullivan, Mary Malloy 75; Vermont, 1873 ***5900.10*** *p614*
Sullivan, Mary Twomey; Vermont, 1814-1893 ***5900.10*** *p313*
Sullivan, Mathias; Vermont, 1840-1907 ***5900.10*** *p121*
Sullivan, Matthew; Vermont, 1864-1899 ***5900.10*** *p102*
Sullivan, Maurice; Vermont, 1810-1888 ***5900.10*** *p381*
Sullivan, Maurice; Vermont, 1815-1907 ***5900.10*** *p145*
Sullivan, Maurice; Vermont, 1824-1910 ***5900.10*** *p462*
Sullivan, May 14 *SEE* Sullivan, Pat
Sullivan, Michael; New York, 1821 ***8197.10*** *p280*
Sullivan, Michael; New York, 1838 ***8197.10*** *p149*
Sullivan, Michael; New York, 1840 ***8197.10*** *p199*
Sullivan, Michael; Vermont, 1817-1911 ***5900.10*** *p361*
Sullivan, Michael; Vermont, 1829-1911 ***5900.10*** *p302*
Sullivan, Michael; Vermont, 1829-1923 ***5900.10*** *p543*
Sullivan, Michael; Vermont, 1838-1915 ***5900.10*** *p357*
Sullivan, Michael; Vermont, 1846-1883 ***5900.10*** *p475*
Sullivan, Michael; Vermont, 1863-1865 ***5900.10*** *p371*
Sullivan, Michael 3; Vermont, 1865 ***5900.10*** *p112*
Sullivan, Michael 8 *SEE* Sullivan, Pat
Sullivan, Michael 14; Ontario, 1861 ***2896.27*** *p36*
Sullivan, Michael 19; Vermont, 1862 ***5900.10*** *p57*
Sullivan, Michael 32; Vermont, 1898 ***5900.10*** *p378*
Sullivan, Michael 38; Vermont, 1875 ***5900.10*** *p138*
Sullivan, Michael 57; Ontario, 1871 ***1823.28*** *p97*
Sullivan, Michael 68; Vermont, 1896 ***5900.10*** *p378*
Sullivan, Michael, Sr. 84; Vermont, 1882 ***5900.10*** *p378*
Sullivan, Michael F.; Vermont, 1854-1933 ***5900.10*** *p487*
Sullivan, Michael H.; Vermont, 1836-1907 ***5900.10*** *p144*
Sullivan, Morris; New York, 1840 ***8197.10*** *p197*
Sullivan, Mortimer 55; Vermont, 1873 ***5900.10*** *p438*
Sullivan, Nancy Collins; Vermont, 1845-1936 ***5900.10*** *p357*
Sullivan, Nellie McAllister; Vermont, 1844-1926 ***5900.10*** *p298*
Sullivan, Nora D. 12; Vermont, 1869 ***5900.10*** *p364*
Sullivan, Nora J. Ryan 76; Vermont, 1924 ***5900.10*** *p162*
Sullivan, Nora Welch; Vermont, 1842-1910 ***5900.10*** *p489*
Sullivan, Owen; Vermont, 1836-1914 ***5900.10*** *p60*
Sullivan, Pat 7 *SEE* Sullivan, Pat
Sullivan, Pat 50; New York, New York, 1850 ***1825.45*** *p53*
Wife: Judy 43
Son: Dan 4
Son: Michael 8
Son: John 12
Daughter: May 14
Daughter: Judy 1
Son: Pat 7
Sullivan, Patrick; New York, 1834 ***8197.10*** *p372*
Sullivan, Patrick; New York, 1836 ***8197.10*** *p319*
Sullivan, Patrick; Vermont, 1848-1918 ***5900.10*** *p379*
Sullivan, Patrick 1; Vermont, 1866 ***5900.10*** *p112*
Sullivan, Patrick 30; Ontario, 1871 ***1823.28*** *p97*
Sullivan, Patrick 30; Seattle, 1913 ***9196.1*** *p60*
Sullivan, Patrick 58; Ontario, 1871 ***1823.28*** *p97*
Sullivan, Patrick 60; Vermont, 1863 ***5900.10*** *p305*
Sullivan, Patrick 60; Vermont, 1891 ***5900.10*** *p470*
Sullivan, Patrick 61; Ontario, 1871 ***1823.15*** *p257*
Sullivan, Patrick 63; Ontario, 1861 ***2896.27*** *p4*
Sullivan, Patrick 64; Vermont, 1875 ***5900.10*** *p473*
Sullivan, Patrick 66; Ontario, 1871 ***1823.15*** *p257*
Sullivan, Patrick 83; Vermont, 1897 ***5900.10*** *p306*
Sullivan, Patrick M. 51; Vermont, 1890 ***5900.10*** *p57*
Sullivan, Philip 19; Maryland, 1774 ***1220.25*** *p3*
Sullivan, Phillips 77; Ontario, 1871 ***1823.22*** *p155*
Sullivan, Rebecca; Vermont, 1840-1878 ***5900.10*** *p187*
Sullivan, Richard 10; Vermont, 1863 ***5900.10*** *p365*
Sullivan, Robert; Maryland, 1663 ***2524.55*** *p212*
Sullivan, Roger 60; Ontario, 1871 ***1823.15*** *p257*
Sullivan, Rose; Vermont, 1871-1894 ***5900.10*** *p112*
Sullivan, Sarah Hurley; Vermont, 1826-1911 ***5900.10*** *p538*
Sullivan, Susan 55; Vermont, 1874 ***5900.10*** *p475*
Sullivan, Thomas; Vermont, n.d. ***5900.10*** *p112*
Sullivan, Thomas; Vermont, 1844-1908 ***5900.10*** *p275*
Sullivan, Thomas; Vermont, 1856-1905 ***5900.10*** *p216*
Sullivan, Thomas 4; Ontario, 1861 ***2896.27*** *p36*
Sullivan, Thomas 17; Maryland, 1774 ***1220.25*** *p7*
Sullivan, Thomas 44; Ontario, 1871 ***1823.28*** *p97*
Sullivan, Thomas 56; Vermont, 1897 ***5900.10*** *p485*
Sullivan, Thomas 63; Vermont, 1903 ***5900.10*** *p313*
Sullivan, Thomas 65; Vermont, 1905 ***5900.10*** *p341*
Sullivan, Thomas J. 21; Vermont, 1878 ***5900.10*** *p112*
Sullivan, Timothy; New York, 1838 ***8197.10*** *p148*
Sullivan, Timothy; Vermont, n.d. ***5900.10*** *p315*
Sullivan, Timothy; Vermont, 1843-1903 ***5900.10*** *p313*
Sullivan, Timothy 18; Vermont, 1862 ***5900.10*** *p306*
Sullivan, Timothy 33; Vermont, 1884 ***5900.10*** *p249*
Sullivan, Timothy 63; Vermont, 1876 ***5900.10*** *p431*
Sullivan, Valentine; Canada, 1756-1760 ***4628.40*** *p46*
Sullivan, William; New York, 1839 ***8197.10*** *p284*
Sullivan, William; Vermont, 1845-1921 ***5900.10*** *p461*
Sullivan, William 22; Vermont, 1865 ***5900.10*** *p100*
Sullivan, William 45; Ontario, 1871 ***1823.28*** *p97*
Sullivan, Winifred; Vermont, 1826-1903 ***5900.10*** *p60*
Sulliven, Jarimiah 50; Ontario, 1871 ***1823.15*** *p257*
Sully, William 21; Maryland, 1774 ***1220.25*** *p2*
Sulowski, John; Maryland, 1910 ***3259.35*** *p61*
Sulzbacher, Anna Eva; America, 1750 ***2856.30*** *p452*
Sulzbacher, Martin; Port uncertain, 1730 ***2856.30*** *p452*
Sulzbacherin, Anna Eva; America, 1750 ***2856.30*** *p452*
Sulzer, Josef; Port uncertain, 1729 ***2856.30*** *p452*
Sulzer, Josef; Port uncertain, 1769 ***2856.30*** *p452*
Sumdio, S. 23; Washington, 1914 ***9196.1*** *p65*
Sumek, Andrzef; Maryland, 1910 ***3259.35*** *p61*
Sumer, Charles; Maryland, 1671 ***2524.55*** *p212*
Sumers, James; Virginia, 1665 ***6212.30*** *p20*
Sumers, Margaret; Virginia, 1674 ***6212.30*** *p52*
Sumerson, John; Maryland, 1667 ***2524.55*** *p212*
Sumfield, Ann 30; Philadelphia, 1774 ***1220.25*** *p68*
With child
Sumfield, Frederick; Pennsylvania, 1777 ***4629.10*** *p11*
Sumfleth, Jacob; New York, 1838 ***8197.10*** *p284*
Summach, Carl 44; Ontario, 1871 ***1823.28*** *p97*
Summer, David; Maryland, 1679 ***2524.55*** *p212*
Summer, John; Maryland, 1669 ***2524.55*** *p212*
Summer, Joseph; Maryland, 1676 ***2524.55*** *p212*
Summer, Peter; Pennsylvania, 1777 ***4629.10*** *p10*
Summerhays, Thos 20; Ontario, 1871 ***1823.15*** *p257*
Summers, Anne; Virginia, 1671-1672 ***6212.30*** *p47*
Summers, Bridget 52; Vermont, 1873 ***5900.10*** *p79*
Summers, Catharine 77; Vermont, 1905 ***5900.10*** *p45*
Summers, Daniel; Pennsylvania, 1777 ***4629.10*** *p9*
Summers, Elizabeth 66; Ontario, 1871 ***1823.15*** *p257*
Summers, James 25; Ontario, 1871 ***1823.15*** *p257*
Summers, John; Virginia, 1671-1672 ***6212.30*** *p47*
Summers, John 20; Philadelphia, 1774 ***1220.25*** *p67*
Summers, John 24; Maryland, 1774 ***1220.25*** *p40*
Summers, Louis 40; Ontario, 1871 ***1823.28*** *p97*
Summers, Patrick; Vermont, 1835-1884 ***5900.10*** *p45*
Summers, Patrick 50; Ontario, 1871 ***1823.22*** *p155*
Summers, Richard 29; Ontario, 1871 ***1823.15*** *p257*
Summers, Thomas; New York, 1839 ***8197.10*** *p140*
Summers, Thomas 38; Ontario, 1871 ***1823.22*** *p155*
Summers, William; New York, 1807 ***8197.10*** *p49*
Summerskill, John 49; Ontario, 1871 ***1823.28*** *p97*
Summerville, Edward 54; Ontario, 1871 ***1823.22*** *p155*
Summerville, J. 31; Ontario, 1871 ***1823.15*** *p257*
Summerville, James 34; Ontario, 1871 ***1823.22*** *p155*
Summerville, James 45; Ontario, 1871 ***1823.15*** *p257*
Summerville, Robt 57; Ontario, 1871 ***1823.22*** *p155*
Summerville, Saml 32; Ontario, 1871 ***1823.28*** *p97*
Summerville, Wm 26; Ontario, 1871 ***1823.28*** *p97*
Sumner, Captain; Quebec, 1858 ***9196.15*** *p38*
Sumner, John; Maryland, 1671 ***2524.55*** *p212*
Sumons, John; Maryland, 1665 ***2524.55*** *p212*
Sundam, Richard; Maryland, 1677 ***2524.55*** *p213*
Sunday, John 74; Ontario, 1871 ***1823.22*** *p155*
Sundercock, Thomas 58; Ontario, 1871 ***1823.15*** *p257*
Sunderland, Angus 45; Ontario, 1871 ***1823.28*** *p97*
Sunderland, John; New York, 1837 ***8197.10*** *p283*
Sundheimer, Maria Catharina; Port uncertain, 1753 ***2856.30*** *p452*
Sundon, William; Virginia, 1665 ***6212.30*** *p19*
Sunlider, Peter; Pennsylvania, 1777 ***4629.10*** *p28*
Sunmary, John 21; Maryland, 1775 ***1220.25*** *p121*
Sunsden, Robert 41; Ontario, 1871 ***1823.15*** *p257*
Sunss, Catharina; Port uncertain, 1768 ***2856.30*** *p452*
Sunton, John 27; Ontario, 1871 ***1823.15*** *p257*
Super, Philip; Pennsylvania, 1777 ***4629.10*** *p28*
Super, Philip; Pennsylvania, 1779 ***4629.10*** *p41*
Superius, Dun; Virginia, 1672 ***6212.30*** *p51*
Superius, Rebecca; Virginia, 1672 ***6212.30*** *p51*
Superius, Sarah; Virginia, 1672 ***6212.30*** *p51*
Superius, Susannah; Virginia, 1672 ***6212.30*** *p51*
Suple, Eleanor; Maryland, 1682 ***2524.55*** *p213*
Suple, Garrett; Maryland, 1682 ***2524.55*** *p213*
Suple, Mary; Maryland, 1682 ***2524.55*** *p213*
Suple, Wakeman; Maryland, 1682 ***2524.55*** *p213*
Suplee, Andrew; Pennsylvania, 1777 ***4629.10*** *p12*
Suppin, Catharina; Port uncertain, 1794 ***2856.30*** *p452*
Supple, Bartholemaw; Vermont, 1850-1912 ***5900.10*** *p70*
Supple, Garret; Virginia, 1668-1669 ***6212.30*** *p40*
Supple, John 66; Ontario, 1871 ***1823.28*** *p97*
Supple, Joseph 17; Ontario, 1871 ***1823.15*** *p257*
Supple, Margarett; Maryland, 1681 ***2524.55*** *p213*
Supple, Mary; Vermont, 1844-1919 ***5900.10*** *p70*
Supple, Mary T. Pierce; Vermont, 1847-1924 ***5900.10*** *p70*
Suppll, Mary 79; Vermont, 1903 ***5900.10*** *p337*
Suppile, Catherine Nathan; Vermont, 1838-1911 ***5900.10*** *p335*
Suppile, James; Vermont, 1837-1914 ***5900.10*** *p335*
Suppnick, A. 44; Alaska, 1917 ***9196.1*** *p45*
Suppnick, A. 44; Whitehorse, Yukon, 1917 ***9196.1*** *p45*
Supuczynski, John J.; Maryland, 1910 ***3259.35*** *p61*
Surberin, Anna Maria; Port uncertain, 1739 ***2856.30*** *p452*
With husband
Suringhousen, William; Pennsylvania, 1777 ***4629.10*** *p14*
Surman, Frederick 40; Ontario, 1871 ***1823.28*** *p97*

Surman, John; Pennsylvania, 1744 ***1224.2*** *p112*
Surncsznski, Wojciecu; Maryland, 1910 ***3259.35*** *p61*
Surnowski, Antonie; Maryland, 1910 ***3259.35*** *p61*
Surr, George 19; Georgia, 1775 ***1220.25*** *p122*
Surrs, John; Maryland, 1682 ***2524.55*** *p213*
Surtees, Thomas; New York, 1794 ***8197.10*** *p2*
Surtus, Thomas; New York, 1794 ***8197.10*** *p2*
Surtyr, J.; Quebec, 1858 ***9196.15*** *p35*
Susans, John; Long Island, 1783 ***1224.2*** *p112*
Sushan, William; Georgia, 1698 ***1640.13*** *p121*
Suske, Jacob 45; Ontario, 1871 ***1823.28*** *p97*
Suss, Anna Maria; America, 1760 ***2856.30*** *p453*
Suss, Balthasar; Port uncertain, 1736 ***2856.30*** *p453*
With wife & 6 children
Suss, Georg; Port uncertain, 1751 ***2856.30*** *p453*
Suss, Johann Adam; Port uncertain, 1767 ***2856.30*** *p453*
Suss, Michael; Port uncertain, 1768 ***2856.30*** *p453*
Susse, Johann; Port uncertain, 1770 ***2856.30*** *p452*
Susz, Balthasar; America, 1737 ***2856.30*** *p453*
Suszynski, Andrew A.; Maryland, 1910 ***3259.35*** *p61*
Sutch, Robert 40; Ontario, 1871 ***1823.15*** *p257*
Sutchliffe, Lister 40; Ontario, 1871 ***1823.28*** *p97*
Suter, Francis 20; Maryland, 1774 ***1220.25*** *p59*
Suter, John; Pennsylvania, 1777 ***4629.10*** *p10*
Sutham, Richard 27; Ontario, 1871 ***1823.15*** *p257*
Sutherby, Charles 38; Ontario, 1871 ***1823.15*** *p257*
Sutherland, Mr.; Quebec, 1857 ***9196.15*** *p18*
Sutherland, Mrs.; Quebec, 1858 ***9196.15*** *p42*
Sutherland, Alexander; Georgia, 1736 ***1640.10*** *p199*
Sutherland, Alexander; Mobile, Alabama, 1857 ***1640.10*** *p199*
Sutherland, Alexander 21; Ontario, 1871 ***1823.22*** *p155*
Sutherland, Alexander 50; Ontario, 1871 ***1823.28*** *p97*
Sutherland, Alexander Smith; New Orleans, 1828 ***1640.10*** *p199*
Sutherland, Alexander Smith; New York, 1828 ***1224.3*** *p76*
Sutherland, Archibald 28; Ontario, 1871 ***1823.28*** *p97*
Sutherland, Christy 74; Ontario, 1871 ***1823.15*** *p257*
Sutherland, David 42; Ontario, 1871 ***1823.28*** *p97*
Sutherland, Donald; Jamaica, 1801 ***1640.13*** *p121*
Sutherland, Donald 55; Ontario, 1871 ***1823.15*** *p257*
Sutherland, Ebenezer; New York, 1783 ***1224.2*** *p112*
Sutherland, Elizabeth 60; Ontario, 1871 ***1823.22*** *p155*
Sutherland, Francis; Savannah, Georgia, 1775 ***1640.10*** *p199*
Sutherland, George G.; Louisiana, 1850 ***1640.10*** *p200*
Sutherland, Henry; Texas, 1830-1845 ***1640.10*** *p200*
Sutherland, James 17; Ontario, 1871 ***1823.15*** *p257*
Sutherland, James 18; Virginia, 1774 ***1220.25*** *p45*
Sutherland, James 19; Ontario, 1871 ***1823.22*** *p155*
Sutherland, James 27; Ontario, 1871 ***1823.22*** *p155*
Sutherland, James 43; Ontario, 1871 ***1823.15*** *p257*
Sutherland, James 51; Ontario, 1871 ***1823.15*** *p257*
Sutherland, James 51; Ontario, 1871 ***1823.28*** *p97*
Sutherland, Janet 45; Ontario, 1861 ***2896.25*** *p1*
Sutherland, John; New York, 1888 ***1640.13*** *p121*
Sutherland, John 28; Maryland, 1775 ***1220.25*** *p96*
Sutherland, John 55; Ontario, 1871 ***1823.22*** *p155*
Sutherland, John 71; Ontario, 1871 ***1823.28*** *p97*
Sutherland, Martin 32; Ontario, 1871 ***1823.15*** *p257*
Sutherland, Neil 35; Ontario, 1871 ***1823.15*** *p257*
Sutherland, Patrick; Georgia, 1748 ***1640.10*** *p200*
Sutherland, Robert; Georgia, 1736 ***1640.10*** *p200*
Sutherland, Robert; Georgia, 1741 ***1640.10*** *p200*
Sutherland, Robert 26; Ontario, 1871 ***1823.15*** *p257*
Sutherland, William; Savannah, Georgia, 1775 ***1640.10*** *p200*
Sutherland, William; Savannah, Georgia, 1806 ***1640.10*** *p200*
Sutherland, William 21; Ontario, 1871 ***1823.28*** *p97*
Sutherland, William Smith; California, 1867 ***1640.13*** *p122*
Sutherland, Wm 72; Ontario, 1871 ***1823.28*** *p97*
Suthvan, D.; Portland, Maine, 1858 ***9196.15*** *p28*
Sutledge, J.; Quebec, 1856 ***9196.15*** *p9*
Sutliff, Edwan 50; Ontario, 1871 ***1823.28*** *p97*
Sutliff, Thomas 60; Ontario, 1871 ***1823.28*** *p97*
Sutliff, Thos 34; Ontario, 1871 ***1823.28*** *p97*
Sutliffe, Harry; Ontario, 1871 ***1823.22*** *p155*
Sutor, Rudolf; Port uncertain, 1748 ***2856.30*** *p452*
Sutor, Simon; Port uncertain, 1762 ***2856.30*** *p452*
Sutorski, James; Maryland, 1910 ***3259.35*** *p61*
Suttaby, William 25; Ontario, 1871 ***1823.28*** *p97*
Sutte, Edmond; Maryland, 1657 ***2524.55*** *p213*
Sutter, James; New York, 1840 ***8197.10*** *p195*
Sutter, James; Pennsylvania, 1777 ***4629.10*** *p19*
Sutter, Johann Georg; Port uncertain, 1784 ***2856.30*** *p452*
Sutter, Maria Elisabeth; Port uncertain, 1756 ***2856.30*** *p452*
Sutter, Maria Magdalena; Port uncertain, 1792 ***2856.30*** *p452*
Sutter, Michael; Port uncertain, 1763 ***2856.30*** *p452*
Sutter, Peter; Pennsylvania, 1777 ***4629.10*** *p22*
Sutterin, Ernst Jacob; Port uncertain, 1737 ***2856.30*** *p452*
Sutterin, Ernst Jacob; Port uncertain, 1769 ***2856.30*** *p452*
Sutterin, Maria Elisabeth; Port uncertain, 1756 ***2856.30*** *p452*
Sutterlin, Christian; Port uncertain, 1761 ***2856.30*** *p453*
Sutterlin, Elisabeth; Port uncertain, 1736 ***2856.30*** *p452*
Sutterlin, Euphrosyne; Port uncertain, 1769 ***2856.30*** *p453*
Sutterlin, Hans Georg; Port uncertain, 1739 ***2856.30*** *p453*
Sutterlin, Martin; Port uncertain, 1728 ***2856.30*** *p452*
Suttie, David; Georgia, 1698 ***1640.13*** *p122*
Suttle, Ann; Maryland, 1666 ***2524.55*** *p213*
Suttle, John; Maryland, 1675 ***2524.55*** *p213*
Sutton, Andrew 21; New York, 1774 ***1220.25*** *p49*
Sutton, Bartholomew; Pennsylvania, 1777 ***4629.10*** *p25*
Sutton, Edgar; Virginia, 1667 ***6212.30*** *p37*
Sutton, Edm; Virginia, 1664 ***6212.30*** *p15*
Sutton, Edward 16; Maryland, 1775 ***1220.25*** *p98*
Sutton, Edward 47; Ontario, 1871 ***1823.28*** *p97*
Sutton, George; New York, 1830 ***8197.10*** *p353*
Sutton, Henry; Virginia, 1703 ***1224.2*** *p112*
Sutton, Henry 25; Ontario, 1871 ***1823.28*** *p97*
Sutton, James; Pennsylvania, 1786 ***4629.10*** *p55*
Sutton, John; Virginia, 1651 ***1224.1*** *p56*
Sutton, John; Virginia, 1671 ***6212.30*** *p44*
Sutton, John 19; Philadelphia, 1774 ***1220.25*** *p26*
Sutton, John 22; Philadelphia, 1775 ***1220.25*** *p9*
Sutton, John 43; New York, 1775 ***1220.25*** *p142*
Sutton, John P. 31; Ontario, 1871 ***1823.28*** *p97*
Sutton, Lidia; Virginia, 1673 ***6212.30*** *p51*
Sutton, Peter; New York, 1807 ***8197.10*** *p50*
Sutton, Phillip; Maryland, 1673 ***2524.55*** *p213*
Sutton, Richard 40; Ontario, 1871 ***1823.28*** *p97*
Sutton, Samuel; Pennsylvania, 1777 ***4629.10*** *p10*
Sutton, Samuel 30; Ontario, 1871 ***1823.28*** *p97*
Sutton, Samuel 32; Ontario, 1871 ***1823.28*** *p97*
Sutton, Thomas; Virginia, 1665-1666 ***6212.30*** *p23*
Sutton, Thomas; Virginia, 1666-1667 ***6212.30*** *p32*
Sutton, William; Maryland, 1658 ***2524.55*** *p213*
Sutton, William; New York, 1839 ***8197.10*** *p285*
Suttrel, Alexander 29; Ontario, 1871 ***1823.15*** *p257*
Suvak, John; Maryland, 1910 ***3259.35*** *p61*
Suwalski, John M.; Maryland, 1910 ***3259.35*** *p61*
Suwalski, Stephan; Maryland, 1910 ***3259.35*** *p61*
Suwczensky, Stanislaw; Maryland, 1910 ***3259.35*** *p61*
Suwlenski, Head; Maryland, 1910 ***3259.35*** *p61*
Suzarzinski, Joseph; Maryland, 1910 ***3259.35*** *p61*
Swabey, Joseph; Pennsylvania, 1777 ***4629.10*** *p24*
Swaffield, Agustine 47; Ontario, 1871 ***1823.15*** *p257*
Swaffield, William 37; Ontario, 1871 ***1823.15*** *p257*
Swain, John; Pennsylvania, 1777 ***4629.10*** *p14*
Swain, John 32; Ontario, 1871 ***1823.22*** *p155*
Swaine, Henry; Maryland, 1670 ***2524.55*** *p213*
Swaine, John; Virginia, 1700 ***1224.2*** *p112*
Swainy, Thomas; Maryland, 1682 ***2524.55*** *p213*
Swales, Alfred 15; Ontario, 1861 ***2896.25*** *p40*
Swales, Charles 21; Ontario, 1861 ***2896.25*** *p40*
Swales, Henry 23; Ontario, 1861 ***2896.25*** *p28*
Swallow, James 24; Philadelphia, 1774 ***1220.25*** *p73*
Swallow, John H. 46; Ontario, 1871 ***1823.15*** *p257*
Swallow, Samuel; Maryland, 1678 ***2524.55*** *p213*
Swalwell, Joann 41; Ontario, 1871 ***1823.28*** *p97*
Swaly, Robert; Maryland, 1649-1658 ***2524.55*** *p213*
Swan, Andrew 46; Ontario, 1871 ***1823.15*** *p257*
Swan, Betsey 76; Ontario, 1871 ***1823.15*** *p257*
Swan, Charles 54; Ontario, 1871 ***1823.28*** *p97*
Swan, Clifford 21; Nova Scotia, 1774 ***1220.25*** *p136*
Swan, Elizabeth; Maryland, 1661 ***2524.55*** *p213*
Swan, Eva 21; Kansas, 1910 ***9079.10*** *p48*
Swan, James; Savannah, Georgia, 1817 ***1640.10*** *p200*
Swan, John; New England, 1701 ***1224.2*** *p113*
Swan, John; Pennsylvania, 1777 ***4629.10*** *p12*
Swan, John 29; Kansas, 1908-1910 ***9079.10*** *p48*
Swan, Joseph 67; Ontario, 1871 ***1823.22*** *p155*
Swan, Mark; Maryland, 1653-1661 ***2524.55*** *p225*
Swan, Mary; South Carolina, 1784 ***1224.2*** *p113*
Swan, Peter 40; Maryland, 1775 ***1220.25*** *p106*
Swan, Samuel; New York, 1826 ***8197.10*** *p282*
Swan, Thomas; New York, 1828 ***8197.10*** *p350*
Swan, Thomas; Virginia, 1691 ***1224.1*** *p56*
Swan, Violetta; Maryland, 1657 ***2524.55*** *p213*
Swan, William; New York, 1802 ***8197.10*** *p25*
Swan, William; New York, 1807 ***8197.10*** *p277*
Swan, William; New York, 1837 ***8197.10*** *p106*
Swan, William; New York, 1838 ***8197.10*** *p150*
Swan, William H. 52; Ontario, 1871 ***1823.15*** *p257*
Swan, William J.; New York, 1840 ***8197.10*** *p197*
Swanczyk, Peter; Maryland, 1910 ***3259.35*** *p61*
Swaney, Bryan; Maryland, 1682 ***2524.55*** *p213*
Swaney, Edward; Maryland, 1682 ***2524.55*** *p213*
Swaney, Thurless; Maryland, 1682 ***2524.55*** *p213*
Swanhoski, Martin; Maryland, 1910 ***3259.35*** *p61*
Swanick, Thomas 32; Maryland, 1775 ***1220.25*** *p104*
Swann, Allex.; Virginia, 1671 ***6212.30*** *p42*
Swann, Samuel; Maryland, 1681 ***2524.55*** *p213*
Swann, Thomas; Tennessee, 1832-1845 ***1640.10*** *p201*
Swann, William; Virginia, 1664 ***6212.30*** *p12*
Swanne, Margaret; Virginia, 1646 ***1224.1*** *p11*
Swanpiper, Christopher 32; Ontario, 1871 ***1823.28*** *p97*
Swansen, John E. 35; Washington, 1914 ***9196.1*** *p66*
Swanson, August 45; British Columbia, 1911 ***9196.1*** *p34*
Swanson, August 45; Washington, 1911 ***9196.1*** *p34*
Swanson, E. 33; Alaska, 1914 ***9196.1*** *p40*
Swanson, Francis; Maryland, 1665 ***2524.55*** *p213*
Swanson, George 46; Ontario, 1871 ***1823.15*** *p257*
Swanson, H. 35; British Columbia, 1913 ***9196.1*** *p62*
Swanson, H. 35; Washington, 1913 ***9196.1*** *p62*
Swanson, John 40; British Columbia, 1911 ***9196.1*** *p35*
Swanson, John 40; Seattle, 1911 ***9196.1*** *p35*
Swanson, N. 32; Alaska, 1917 ***9196.1*** *p49*
Swanson, N. 32; Whitehorse, Yukon, 1917 ***9196.1*** *p49*
Swanson, O. J. 58; British Columbia, 1913 ***9196.1*** *p22*
Swanson, O. J. 58; San Francisco, 1913 ***9196.1*** *p22*
Swanson, Ronald 21; Washington, 1915 ***9196.1*** *p67*
Swanson, S. 23; Alaska, 1914 ***9196.1*** *p40*
Swanson, Samuel; Maryland, 1682 ***2524.55*** *p213*
Swanston, Edward; Maryland, 1674 ***2524.55*** *p213*
Swanston, Thomas; St. Kitts, 1874 ***1640.13*** *p122*
Swantike, Swann; Maryland, 1682 ***2524.55*** *p213*
Swanton, Ann; New York, 1833 ***8197.10*** *p358*
Swanton, Ann 92; Vermont, 1889 ***5900.10*** *p475*
Swanton, John; New York, 1810 ***8197.10*** *p277*
Swanton, Matthew 26; New York, 1836-1840 ***8197.10*** *p195*
Swanton, Michael; Virginia, 1664 ***6212.30*** *p14*
Swanton, Thomas; New York, 1831 ***8197.10*** *p283*
Swanton, William; Vermont, 1894 ***5900.10*** *p460*
Swanwick, Mary; Alexandria, Virginia, 1821 ***1224.3*** *p76*
Swanwick, Thomas; Illinois, 1843 ***1224.3*** *p76*
Swap, George; Pennsylvania, 1779 ***4629.10*** *p33*
Swart, Henry; Virginia, 1666 ***6212.30*** *p26*
Swarts, Aron; New York, 1803 ***8197.10*** *p17*
Swarts, Hans Michael; America, 1741 ***2856.30*** *p452*
Swartswalter, Johann; America, 1738 ***2856.30*** *p452*
Swartz, Charles 60; Ontario, 1871 ***1823.28*** *p97*
Swatzfager, Henry; Pennsylvania, 1840 ***6058.10*** *p17*
Swayne, Charles; New York, 1785 ***1224.2*** *p112*
Swayne, Elizabeth; Virginia, 1671-1672 ***6212.30*** *p46*
Swayne, John; Maryland, 1668 ***2524.55*** *p213*
Swcoski, William; Maryland, 1910 ***3259.35*** *p61*
Sweatman, Susanna 22; Maryland, 1775 ***1220.25*** *p115*
Sweatnam, Edward; Maryland, 1673 ***2524.55*** *p213*
Sweatnam, John *SEE* Sweatnam, Richard
Sweatnam, Mary *SEE* Sweatnam, Richard
Sweatnam, Richard; Maryland, 1677 ***2524.55*** *p213*
Wife: Mary
Son: John
Swedden, Miss; Quebec, 1856 ***9196.15*** *p7*
Swedman, George Douglas; New York, 1830 ***8197.10*** *p362*
Sweenan, Richard 28; Maryland, 1774 ***1220.25*** *p52*
Sweeney, Ada Kiley; Vermont, 1874-1943 ***5900.10*** *p496*
Sweeney, Alexander; New York, 1840 ***8197.10*** *p321*
Sweeney, Alexander 64; Vermont, 1891 ***5900.10*** *p273*
Sweeney, Ann; Vermont, 1831-1903 ***5900.10*** *p414*
Sweeney, Catherine 21; Vermont, 1867 ***5900.10*** *p209*
Sweeney, Catherine 67; Vermont, 1881 ***5900.10*** *p294*
Sweeney, Catherine Connolly 69; Vermont, 1874 ***5900.10*** *p209*
Sweeney, Daniel E.; Vermont, 1853-1910 ***5900.10*** *p338*
Sweeney, Edward 27; Vermont, 1867 ***5900.10*** *p367*
Sweeney, Elizabeth; Vermont, 1847-1880 ***5900.10*** *p431*
Sweeney, Ellen; Vermont, 1846-1919 ***5900.10*** *p428*
Sweeney, Eugene; New York, 1834 ***8197.10*** *p69*
Sweeney, Eugene 21; Vermont, 1871 ***5900.10*** *p563*
Sweeney, Francis 82; Vermont, 1911 ***5900.10*** *p338*
Sweeney, George; Vermont, 1838-1913 ***5900.10*** *p257*
Sweeney, Hannah; Vermont, 1842-1890 ***5900.10*** *p425*
Sweeney, Hanora Grogen 82; Vermont, 1914 ***5900.10*** *p68*
Sweeney, James; Vermont, 1850-1923 ***5900.10*** *p433*
Sweeney, Jeremiah 2; Vermont, 1856 ***5900.10*** *p563*
Sweeney, Jeremiah 67; Vermont, 1880 ***5900.10*** *p209*
Sweeney, John; New York, 1837 ***8197.10*** *p105*
Sweeney, John; Vermont, 1850-1917 ***5900.10*** *p217*
Sweeney, John; Vermont, 1856-1903 ***5900.10*** *p487*
Sweeney, John 70; Vermont, 1884 ***5900.10*** *p574*
Sweeney, John 82; Vermont, 1889 ***5900.10*** *p483*
Sweeney, John B.; Vermont, 1848-1925 ***5900.10*** *p496*
Sweeney, John H.; Vermont, 1864-1894 ***5900.10*** *p332*
Sweeney, Julia 75; Vermont, 1897 ***5900.10*** *p574*
Sweeney, Julia Preston; Vermont, 1858-1928 ***5900.10*** *p487*
Sweeney, Katherine; Vermont, 1827-1902 ***5900.10*** *p381*

Sweeney, Margaret; Vermont, 1839-1914 ***5900.10*** *p366*
Sweeney, Margaret 63; Vermont, 1891 ***5900.10*** *p426*
Sweeney, Margaret Slattery; Vermont, 1850-1923 ***5900.10*** *p433*
Sweeney, Mary; Vermont, 1834-1926 ***5900.10*** *p76*
Sweeney, Mary; Vermont, 1848 ***5900.10*** *p217*
Sweeney, Mary Connell; Vermont, 1853-1924 ***5900.10*** *p338*
Sweeney, Mary Hurley 53; Vermont, 1885 ***5900.10*** *p338*
Sweeney, Mary J. 65; Vermont, 1898 ***5900.10*** *p273*
Sweeney, Michael; New York, 1839 ***8197.10*** *p381*
Sweeney, Michael; Vermont, n.d. ***5900.10*** *p603*
Sweeney, Michael; Vermont, 1845-1907 ***5900.10*** *p431*
Sweeney, Owen 66; Vermont, 1878 ***5900.10*** *p209*
Sweeney, Sarah; Vermont, 1842-1911 ***5900.10*** *p257*
Sweeney, T. S.; Vermont, 1837-1911 ***5900.10*** *p425*
Sweeney, Thomas; Vermont, 1832-1904 ***5900.10*** *p414*
Sweeney, Thomas 75; Vermont, 1903 ***5900.10*** *p68*
Sweeny, Bernard; Pennsylvania, 1868 ***6058.10*** *p71*
Sweeny, Daniel; New York, 1836 ***8197.10*** *p78*
Sweeny, Edward; Pennsylvania, 1819 ***6058.10*** *p7*
Sweeny, Francis; Pennsylvania, 1862-1868 ***6058.10*** *p67*
Sweeny, George; New York, 1838 ***8197.10*** *p376*
Sweeny, George A.; Vermont, 1853-1892 ***5900.10*** *p494*
Sweeny, Hamilton F.; Vermont, 1865 ***5900.10*** *p494*
Sweeny, Isabella Palmer; Vermont, 1816-1888 ***5900.10*** *p495*
Sweeny, Isabelle 60; Ontario, 1871 ***1823.28*** *p97*
Sweeny, James 36; Ontario, 1871 ***1823.28*** *p97*
Sweeny, John 33; Ontario, 1871 ***1823.28*** *p97*
Sweeny, Joseph D. 15; Vermont, 1863 ***5900.10*** *p494*
Sweeny, Lelen Wheeler; Vermont, 1852-1905 ***5900.10*** *p494*
Sweeny, Michael; New York, 1835 ***8197.10*** *p283*
Sweeny, Michael 55; Ontario, 1871 ***1823.15*** *p258*
Sweeny, Morgan 30; Maryland, 1774 ***1220.25*** *p40*
Sweeny, Myles; New York, 1821 ***8197.10*** *p279*
Sweeny, Owen; New York, 1839 ***8197.10*** *p284*
Sweeny, Patrick; New York, 1837 ***8197.10*** *p105*
Sweeny, Patrick A.; Vermont, 1809-1887 ***5900.10*** *p495*
Sweeny, Ralph; Pennsylvania, 1868 ***6058.10*** *p74*
Sweeny, Thos 40; Ontario, 1871 ***1823.28*** *p97*
Sweeny, William H. 20; Vermont, 1861 ***5900.10*** *p494*
Sweers, Cornelius; Pennsylvania, 1777 ***4629.10*** *p9*
Sweet, Catherine 59; Ontario, 1871 ***1823.15*** *p258*
Sweet, Charles 20; Ontario, 1871 ***1823.28*** *p97*
Sweet, Jared 80; Ontario, 1871 ***1823.22*** *p155*
Sweet, John 43; Ontario, 1871 ***1823.15*** *p258*
Sweet, Richard 42; Ontario, 1871 ***1823.15*** *p258*
Sweet, Robert 32; Ontario, 1871 ***1823.15*** *p258*
Sweet, Thomas; Maryland, 1679 ***2524.55*** *p213*
Sweet, William 38; Ontario, 1871 ***1823.15*** *p258*
Sweet, William 62; Ontario, 1871 ***1823.15*** *p258*
Sweet, William 71; Ontario, 1871 ***1823.15*** *p258*
Sweetelad, Thomas; Maryland, 1661 ***2524.55*** *p213*
Sweethall, Dorothy; Maryland, 1665 ***2524.55*** *p213*
Sweetman, James 41; Ontario, 1871 ***1823.22*** *p155*
Sweetman, John; New York, 1807 ***8197.10*** *p277*
Sweetman, John I. 33; Ontario, 1871 ***1823.15*** *p258*
Sweetman, Rachel 44; Ontario, 1871 ***1823.28*** *p97*
Sweetman, William 53; Ontario, 1871 ***1823.28*** *p97*
Sweetman, William 82; Ontario, 1871 ***1823.22*** *p155*
Sweetman, William P. 18; Ontario, 1871 ***1823.28*** *p97*
Sweitzer, John; Pennsylvania, 1803-1817 ***6058.10*** *p6*
Swell, George 53; Ontario, 1871 ***1823.15*** *p258*
Sweney, Edmond; Pennsylvania, 1777 ***4629.10*** *p20*
Sweney, John; New York, 1805 ***8197.10*** *p277*
Sweney, Mary 60; Vermont, 1859 ***5900.10*** *p526*
Swenor, John; Vermont, 1815-1890 ***5900.10*** *p460*
Swenroy, Darby; Maryland, 1680 ***2524.55*** *p213*
Swett, Joseph; Boston, 1696 ***1224.1*** *p56*
Swiderski, Antony; Maryland, 1910 ***3259.35*** *p61*
Swiec, Andrew; Maryland, 1910 ***3259.35*** *p61*
Swierski, Frank A.; Maryland, 1910 ***3259.35*** *p61*
Swietoslawa, Mary; Maryland, 1910 ***3259.35*** *p61*
Swift, Mr.; Quebec, 1856 ***9196.15*** *p11*
Swift, Benjamin; Nantucket, Massachusetts, 1805 ***1224.3*** *p77*
Swift, Dean 48; Ontario, 1871 ***1823.15*** *p258*
Swift, John; New York, 1840 ***8197.10*** *p198*
Swift, John; Philadelphia, 1714 ***1224.2*** *p113*
Swift, Joseph; New York, 1840 ***8197.10*** *p198*
Swift, Joseph; Pennsylvania, 1777 ***4629.10*** *p22*
Swift, Joseph; Pennsylvania, 1779 ***4629.10*** *p41*
Swift, Joseph; Pennsylvania, 1810 ***1224.3*** *p77*
Swift, Michael; New York, 1836 ***8197.10*** *p78*
Swift, Thomas; Boston, 1722 ***1224.2*** *p113*
Swift, Thomas 56; Ontario, 1871 ***1823.22*** *p155*
Swift, William; New York, 1840 ***8197.10*** *p198*
Swigon, Kasper; Maryland, 1910 ***3259.35*** *p61*
Swigty, Martin; Maryland, 1910 ***3259.35*** *p61*
Swillivant, Dardey; Maryland, 1671 ***2524.55*** *p213*
Swillivant, Jaimes; Maryland, 1671 ***2524.55*** *p213*
Swinbank, George 44; Ontario, 1871 ***1823.15*** *p258*
Swindell, Master; Quebec, 1858 ***9196.15*** *p33*
Swindell, Miss; Quebec, 1858 ***9196.15*** *p33*
Swindell, Mrs.; Quebec, 1858 ***9196.15*** *p33*
Swindell, Daniell; Maryland, 1663 ***2524.55*** *p213*
Swindlehurst, Abraham 34; Ontario, 1871 ***1823.15*** *p258*
Swindon, Edward; Maryland, 1662 ***2524.55*** *p213*
Swine, Bryan; Virginia, 1703-1704 ***6212.30*** *p63*
Swineford, Mr.; Quebec, 1857 ***9196.15*** *p20*
Swineford, Mrs.; Quebec, 1857 ***9196.15*** *p20*
Swiney, Briant; Maryland, 1680 ***2524.55*** *p214*
Swiney, John; New York, 1806 ***8197.10*** *p277*
Swiney, Mary; Maryland, 1680 ***2524.55*** *p214*
Swinfen, Francis; Maryland, 1664 ***2524.55*** *p214*
Swinfen, Francis; Maryland, 1667 ***2524.55*** *p214*
Swinkels, Joseph; Indiana, 1882-1884 ***3437.14*** *p191*
Swinnerton, Sarah; New Jersey, 1845 ***1224.3*** *p77*
Swinney, Jeremy; Georgia, 1738 ***1640.10*** *p201*
Swinsen, Francis; Maryland, 1664 ***2524.55*** *p214*
Swinton, Alexander; Georgia, 1699 ***1640.13*** *p122*
Swinton, Robert; Maryland, 1677-1681 ***2524.55*** *p214*
Swinton, William; Georgia, 1763 ***1640.10*** *p201*
Swisk, Bessie; Maryland, 1910 ***3259.35*** *p61*
Swiss, Jane 39; Ontario, 1871 ***1823.15*** *p258*
Switcher, Christopher 68; Ontario, 1871 ***1823.15*** *p258*
Switkowska, Anna; Maryland, 1910 ***3259.35*** *p61*
Switzer, Miss 1; Ontario, 1861 ***2896.26*** *p9*
Switzer, Ann 19; Ontario, 1861 ***2896.27*** *p56*
Switzer, C. O. 6; Ontario, 1861 ***2896.26*** *p9*
Switzer, Henry 50; Ontario, 1871 ***1823.15*** *p258*
Switzer, J. 8; Ontario, 1861 ***2896.26*** *p9*
Switzer, James 57; Ontario, 1871 ***1823.15*** *p258*
Switzer, Joseph 65; Ontario, 1871 ***1823.28*** *p98*
Switzer, M. J. 28; Ontario, 1861 ***2896.26*** *p9*
Switzer, Martin 50; Ontario, 1871 ***1823.28*** *p98*
Switzer, S. A. 4; Ontario, 1861 ***2896.26*** *p9*
Switzler, Jacob; Pennsylvania, 1815 ***6058.10*** *p5*
Switzler, Johannas; Pennsylvania, 1815 ***6058.10*** *p5*
Swjateski, Andrew; Maryland, 1910 ***3259.35*** *p61*
Sword, James; Virginia, 1703-1704 ***6212.30*** *p63*
Sword, John 21; Ontario, 1871 ***1823.28*** *p98*
Sword, Thomas 56; Ontario, 1871 ***1823.28*** *p98*
Sworder, William 26; Philadelphia, 1774 ***1220.25*** *p35*
Sworecki, Martin; Maryland, 1910 ***3259.35*** *p61*
Sycks, Richard 55; Ontario, 1871 ***1823.22*** *p155*
Syckukauski, Apolinary; Maryland, 1910 ***3259.35*** *p61*
Sycoski, Marion; Maryland, 1910 ***3259.35*** *p61*
Syfrayson, Marcus; Maryland, 1658 ***2524.55*** *p214*
Sygmont, Jan; Maryland, 1910 ***3259.35*** *p61*
Sykes, Mr.; Portland, Maine, 1857 ***9196.15*** *p13*
Sykes, Mrs.; Portland, Maine, 1857 ***9196.15*** *p13*
Sykes, Bernard; Virginia, 1682 ***1224.1*** *p56*
Sykes, Robert 33; Ontario, 1871 ***1823.22*** *p155*
Sykes, William; Pennsylvania, 1777 ***4629.10*** *p25*
Sykes, William; Pennsylvania, 1786 ***4629.10*** *p49*
Sykes, William 64; Ontario, 1871 ***1823.22*** *p155*
Sylvazkski, Joseph; Maryland, 1910 ***3259.35*** *p61*
Sylverin, Mr.; Port uncertain, 1742 ***2856.30*** *p452*
With wife & 5 children
Sylvester, Christian; New York, 1832 ***8197.10*** *p357*
Sylvester, John 43; Ontario, 1871 ***1823.22*** *p155*
Sylvester, Sylvester Joseph; Philadelphia, 1826 ***8197.10*** *p300*
Sylvoys, Mary 37; Ontario, 1871 ***1823.28*** *p98*
Sym, Hugh; Georgia, 1770 ***1640.10*** *p201*
Sym, James 27; Ontario, 1871 ***1823.15*** *p258*
Symborsky, Joseph; Maryland, 1910 ***3259.35*** *p61*
Syme, Andrew; New Orleans, 1821 ***1224.3*** *p77*
Syme, Andrew; New Orleans, 1821 ***1640.10*** *p201*
Syme, Andrew; New York, 1817 ***8197.10*** *p278*
Syme, John; Georgia, 1699 ***1640.13*** *p122*
Symes, G. B.; Quebec, 1858 ***9196.15*** *p33*
Symes, Robert; America, 1813 ***1224.3*** *p77*
Symes, William 21; Virginia, 1774 ***1220.25*** *p54*
Symington, James; Savannah, Georgia, 1807 ***1640.10*** *p201*
Symington, James 49; Ontario, 1871 ***1823.15*** *p258*
Symington, Jane 53; Ontario, 1871 ***1823.22*** *p155*
Symington, Mary; New York, 1887 ***1640.13*** *p122*
Symington, Thomas 38; Ontario, 1871 ***1823.22*** *p155*
Symington, William 43; Ontario, 1871 ***1823.28*** *p98*
Symmes, Ebenezer; Boston, 1779 ***1224.2*** *p113*
Symmonds, Jos 34; Ontario, 1871 ***1823.15*** *p258*
Symmons, Mr.; Portland, Maine, 1858 ***9196.15*** *p27*
Symmons, John; Maryland, 1674 ***2524.55*** *p214*
Symms, Job 43; Ontario, 1871 ***1823.15*** *p258*
Symms, Richard 49; Ontario, 1871 ***1823.15*** *p258*
Symon, Henry 20; Ontario, 1871 ***1823.15*** *p258*
Symon, Lawrence 49; Ontario, 1871 ***1823.22*** *p155*
Symond, Mary; Maryland, 1676 ***2524.55*** *p214*
Symonds, Anthony *SEE* Symonds, Lawrence
Symonds, George; Maryland, 1663 ***2524.55*** *p214*
Symonds, George 70; Ontario, 1871 ***1823.15*** *p258*
Symonds, John 21; Baltimore, 1775 ***1220.25*** *p118*
Symonds, Lawrence; Maryland, 1663 ***2524.55*** *p214*
Wife: Seth
Son-In-Law: Anthony
Symonds, Mary; Maryland, 1679 ***2524.55*** *p214*
Symonds, Seth *SEE* Symonds, Lawrence
Symonds, William; Maryland, 1672 ***2524.55*** *p214*
Symonds, William; New England, 1693 ***1224.1*** *p56*
Symons, Mrs.; Quebec, 1858 ***9196.15*** *p37*
Sympson, Elizabeth; Maryland, 1662 ***2524.55*** *p214*
Sympson, Thomas; Maryland, 1654 ***2524.55*** *p214*
Sympson, Thomas; Maryland, 1659 ***2524.55*** *p214*
Synnot, Dorothy; Maryland, 1678 ***2524.55*** *p214*
Sypieska, Agnieska; Maryland, 1910 ***3259.35*** *p61*
Syri, Christof; Port uncertain, 1750 ***2856.30*** *p431*
Syri, Christof; Port uncertain, 1753 ***2856.30*** *p431*
Syri, Christof; Port uncertain, 1764 ***2856.30*** *p431*
Syring, Anton; Port uncertain, 1757 ***2856.30*** *p453*
Syring, Anton; Port uncertain, 1791 ***2856.30*** *p453*
Syversen, Gus 31; Alaska, 1917 ***9196.1*** *p47*
Syversen, Gus 31; Whitehorse, Yukon, 1917 ***9196.1*** *p47*
Szachezenski, Stamslus; Maryland, 1910 ***3259.35*** *p61*
Szambursky, Teofil; Maryland, 1910 ***3259.35*** *p61*
Szamski, Peter; Maryland, 1910 ***3259.35*** *p61*
Szaska, Joseph; Maryland, 1910 ***3259.35*** *p61*
Szatkowsky, Wojczech; Maryland, 1910 ***3259.35*** *p61*
Szaworski, Aldys; Maryland, 1910 ***3259.35*** *p61*
Szcerbicki, Frank; Maryland, 1910 ***3259.35*** *p61*
Szczepanski, Alexander; Maryland, 1910 ***3259.35*** *p61*
Szczepanski, Frank; Maryland, 1910 ***3259.35*** *p61*
Szczepanski, Lawrence; Maryland, 1910 ***3259.35*** *p61*
Szczeswik, Anton; Maryland, 1910 ***3259.35*** *p61*
Szczurowski, Alexander; Maryland, 1910 ***3259.35*** *p61*
Szczypinki, Frank; Maryland, 1910 ***3259.35*** *p62*
Szdebzki, Martin; Maryland, 1910 ***3259.35*** *p62*
Szeliga, Adam; Maryland, 1910 ***3259.35*** *p62*
Szemborski, Gus; Maryland, 1910 ***3259.35*** *p62*
Szerublewski, Frank; Maryland, 1910 ***3259.35*** *p62*
Szezerbicki, Peter; Maryland, 1910 ***3259.35*** *p62*
Szinski, John; Maryland, 1910 ***3259.35*** *p62*
Szlunczka, Tomas; Maryland, 1910 ***3259.35*** *p62*
Szmare, Valentine; Maryland, 1910 ***3259.35*** *p62*
Szmencky, Daniel; Maryland, 1910 ***3259.35*** *p62*
Szmiaki, Henry; Maryland, 1910 ***3259.35*** *p62*
Szok, Peter; Maryland, 1910 ***3259.35*** *p62*
Szozech, Henry; Maryland, 1910 ***3259.35*** *p62*
Szpakowski, Nikonor; Maryland, 1910 ***3259.35*** *p62*
Szpolura, John; Maryland, 1910 ***3259.35*** *p62*
Sztoda, Joseph; Maryland, 1910 ***3259.35*** *p62*
Szucknisky, Boleslaw; Maryland, 1910 ***3259.35*** *p62*
Szucknisky, Peter; Maryland, 1910 ***3259.35*** *p62*
Szwesecky, John; Maryland, 1910 ***3259.35*** *p62*
Szwinski, Harry; Maryland, 1910 ***3259.35*** *p62*
Szyczukowski, Ignacy; Maryland, 1910 ***3259.35*** *p62*
Szykowna, Victoria; Maryland, 1910 ***3259.35*** *p62*
Szymacki, Frank; Maryland, 1910 ***3259.35*** *p62*
Szymanowski, Frances; Maryland, 1910 ***3259.35*** *p62*
Szymanowski, Joseph; Maryland, 1910 ***3259.35*** *p62*
Szymanowski, Theodor; Maryland, 1910 ***3259.35*** *p62*
Szymanska, Mariana; Maryland, 1910 ***3259.35*** *p62*
Szymanski, Agnes; Maryland, 1910 ***3259.35*** *p62*
Szymanski, Andrew; Maryland, 1910 ***3259.35*** *p62*
Szymanski, John B.; Maryland, 1910 ***3259.35*** *p62*
Szymanski, Joseph; Maryland, 1910 ***3259.35*** *p62*
Szymanski, Leon; Maryland, 1910 ***3259.35*** *p62*
Szymanski, Michael; Maryland, 1910 ***3259.35*** *p62*
Szymanski, Peter; Maryland, 1910 ***3259.35*** *p62*
Szymanski, Rose; Maryland, 1910 ***3259.35*** *p62*
Szymanski, Walter; Maryland, 1910 ***3259.35*** *p62*
Szymansky, Joseph; Maryland, 1910 ***3259.35*** *p62*
Szymansky, Michael; Maryland, 1910 ***3259.35*** *p62*
Szymborski, John; Maryland, 1910 ***3259.35*** *p62*
Szymek, John; Maryland, 1910 ***3259.35*** *p62*
Szymiski, Anton; Maryland, 1910 ***3259.35*** *p62*
Szymkowiak, Antonia; Maryland, 1910 ***3259.35*** *p62*
Szymkowiak, John; Maryland, 1910 ***3259.35*** *p62*
Szymyewski, Stanislaus S.; Maryland, 1910 ***3259.35*** *p62*
Szymzowski, Mary; Maryland, 1910 ***3259.35*** *p62*
Szynkowak, Jacob; Maryland, 1910 ***3259.35*** *p62*
Szyzewski, Mary; Maryland, 1910 ***3259.35*** *p62*

T

Taaffe, James; New York, 1832 ***8197.10*** *p357*
Taback, Joseph; Maryland, 1910 ***3259.35*** *p62*
Tabb, . . .; Boston, 1765 ***4628.40*** *p115*
Tabb, Joyles; Maryland, 1680 ***2524.55*** *p214*
Tabbot, Zibodie D. 66; Ontario, 1871 ***1823.15*** *p258*
Taber, Gideon; Rhode Island, 1765 ***1224.2*** *p113*
Taber, Henry; New York, 1826 ***8197.10*** *p288*
Taber, James; New York, 1838 ***8197.10*** *p150*
Taber, Stephen; Rhode Island, 1765 ***1224.2*** *p113*
Tabert, Martha 12; Ontario, 1871 ***1823.28*** *p98*
Tabert, Matilda 18; Ontario, 1871 ***1823.28*** *p98*
Tabor, Jennie A.; Vermont, 1858-1906 ***5900.10*** *p243*
Tabula, Frederick; Maryland, 1910 ***3259.35*** *p62*
Taburg, Henery 20; Ontario, 1871 ***1823.28*** *p98*
Tachowski, Stanisla; Maryland, 1910 ***3259.35*** *p63*
Tackaberry, John; Pennsylvania, 1826 ***8197.10*** *p78*
Tackberry, Benjamin 77; Ontario, 1871 ***1823.15*** *p258*
Tackberry, Elizabeth 80; Ontario, 1871 ***1823.15*** *p258*
Tackberry, John 48; Ontario, 1871 ***1823.15*** *p258*
Tackberry, Joseph 40; Ontario, 1871 ***1823.15*** *p258*
Tacker, John 39; Philadelphia, 1775 ***1220.25*** *p9*
Tadayewski, John; Maryland, 1910 ***3259.35*** *p63*
Tadowski, Clement; Maryland, 1910 ***3259.35*** *p63*
Taff, Alpheus 18; Ontario, 1861 ***2896.25*** *p32*
Taff, David 14; Ontario, 1861 ***2896.25*** *p32*
Taff, Esmerelda 4; Ontario, 1861 ***2896.25*** *p39*
Taff, Margaret 1; Ontario, 1861 ***2896.25*** *p39*
Taff, Mary 57; Ontario, 1861 ***2896.25*** *p32*
Taff, Mary A. 24; Ontario, 1861 ***2896.25*** *p39*
Taff, Samuel 21; Ontario, 1861 ***2896.25*** *p39*
Taffe, Christof; Port uncertain, 1775 ***2856.30*** *p454*
Taffe, Johann Adam; Port uncertain, 1777 ***2856.30*** *p454*
Taft, Elizabeth 24; Ontario, 1861 ***2896.27*** *p70*
Taft, Joseph 21; Maryland, 1774 ***1220.25*** *p69*
Tag, Miss; America, 1772 ***2856.30*** *p454*
Tag, Anna Elisabeth; America, 1776 ***2856.30*** *p454*
With husband
Tag, Anna Elisabeth; America, 1787 ***2856.30*** *p454*
With husband
Taggart, Bella; Vermont, 1844-1926 ***5900.10*** *p403*
Taggart, Robert; Pennsylvania, 1777 ***4629.10*** *p7*
Taggart, Thomas 60; Ontario, 1871 ***1823.15*** *p258*
Taggert, John; New York, 1807 ***8197.10*** *p331*
Taggert, Robert; New York, 1840 ***8197.10*** *p386*
Taggert, Roland 56; Ontario, 1871 ***1823.15*** *p258*
Taggort, John; Pennsylvania, 1777 ***4629.10*** *p18*
Tague, Ann 47; Vermont, 1853 ***5900.10*** *p153*
Tague, Bridget McMahan; Vermont, 1840-1881 ***5900.10*** *p51*
Tague, John; Vermont, 1844-1915 ***5900.10*** *p51*
Taigle, Jon.; Maryland, 1675 ***2524.55*** *p214*
Tailfer, Patrick; Georgia, 1734 ***1640.10*** *p201*
Tailhen, Mr.; Quebec, 1858 ***9196.15*** *p42*
Tailor, Adam 62; Ontario, 1871 ***1823.22*** *p156*
Tailor, Alexander 50; Ontario, 1871 ***1823.15*** *p258*
Tailor, Ephraim 60; Ontario, 1871 ***1823.15*** *p258*
Tailor, John; Virginia, 1663 ***6212.30*** *p1*
Tailor, John 42; Ontario, 1871 ***1823.15*** *p258*
Tailor, John 63; Ontario, 1871 ***1823.15*** *p258*
Tailor, John 80; Ontario, 1871 ***1823.22*** *p156*
Tailor, John B. 47; Ontario, 1871 ***1823.15*** *p258*
Tailor, Margret 75; Ontario, 1871 ***1823.15*** *p258*
Tailor, Robt; Virginia, 1690 ***6212.30*** *p58*
Tailor, Tho.; Maryland, 1680-1681 ***2524.55*** *p214*
Tailor, Thomas 46; Ontario, 1871 ***1823.15*** *p258*
Taine, Gabriell; Maryland, 1661 ***2524.55*** *p214*
Taine, Mary; Maryland, 1677 ***2524.55*** *p214*
Tais, Charles; Savannah, Georgia, 1768 ***1640.10*** *p201*
Tait, David; Florida, 1769 ***1640.10*** *p201*
Tait, David 64; Ontario, 1861 ***2896.25*** *p47*
Tait, Elizabeth; Savannah, Georgia, 1775 ***1640.10*** *p202*
Tait, George; New York, 1794 ***8197.10*** *p1*
Tait, George; New York, New York, 1819 ***1224.3*** *p77*
Tait, George 36; Ontario, 1871 ***1823.15*** *p259*
Tait, James; Alabama, 1847 ***1640.10*** *p202*
Tait, James; Boston, 1774 ***1224.2*** *p113*
Tait, James; Georgia, 1698 ***1640.13*** *p123*
Tait, James 45; Ontario, 1871 ***1823.22*** *p156*
Tait, John 18; Maryland, 1775 ***1220.25*** *p120*
Tait, John 22; Ontario, 1861 ***2896.25*** *p47*
Tait, Peter; Tobago, West Indies, 1860 ***1640.13*** *p123*
Tait, Robert; Antigua (Antego), 1845 ***1640.13*** *p123*
Tait, Robert; Florida, 1700-1799 ***1640.10*** *p202*
Tait, Robert 40; Ontario, 1871 ***1823.28*** *p98*
Tait, Robert 48; Ontario, 1871 ***1823.15*** *p259*
Tait, Samuel 49; Ontario, 1871 ***1823.28*** *p98*
Tait, Sinclair 71; Ontario, 1871 ***1823.15*** *p259*
Tait, William 56; Ontario, 1871 ***1823.28*** *p98*
Tait, William 76; Ontario, 1871 ***1823.22*** *p156*
Takamise, Antoine 61; Ontario, 1871 ***1823.28*** *p98*
Takman, Carl 38; Ontario, 1871 ***1823.28*** *p98*
Takwadjwon, J. Bte 43; Ontario, 1871 ***1823.28*** *p98*
Takwadjwon, Louis 39; Ontario, 1871 ***1823.28*** *p98*
Talar, Thinous 39; Ontario, 1871 ***1823.15*** *p259*
Talbot, Benidict; Virginia, 1690-1691 ***6212.30*** *p59*
Talbot, Edward 57; Ontario, 1871 ***1823.15*** *p259*
Talbot, George; Maryland, 1680 ***2524.55*** *p214*
Talbot, Henrietta; Boston, 1799 ***1224.2*** *p113*
Talbot, James; Pennsylvania, 1777 ***4629.10*** *p25*
Talbot, John 79; Ontario, 1871 ***1823.15*** *p259*
Talbot, Joseph; New York, 1838 ***8197.10*** *p289*
Talbot, Robert 40; Ontario, 1871 ***1823.15*** *p259*
Talbot, Samuel White; New York, 1829 ***8197.10*** *p299*
Talbot, Thomas 38; Ontario, 1871 ***1823.15*** *p259*
Talbot, Valentine; New York, 1793 ***8197.10*** *p1*
Talbot, Whitton; New York, 1840 ***8197.10*** *p289*
Talbot, William Henry; New York, 1785 ***1224.2*** *p113*
Talbott, Henry; Maryland, 1660 ***2524.55*** *p214*
Talbott, Jno; Virginia, 1664 ***6212.30*** *p15*
Talbutt, Albutt; Maryland, 1663 ***2524.55*** *p10*
Talcoate, Francis; Virginia, 1668-1669 ***6212.30*** *p40*
Talcott, Noah; New York, 1843 ***1224.3*** *p77*
Talen, B. 24; Alaska, 1917 ***9196.1*** *p45*
Talen, B. 24; Whitehorse, Yukon, 1917 ***9196.1*** *p45*
Talent, James; New York, 1840 ***8197.10*** *p200*
Talford, William 37; Ontario, 1871 ***1823.15*** *p259*
Talier, James; Virginia, 1698 ***1224.1*** *p18*
Talin, Wladimir Appollonius; New York, 1838 ***8197.10*** *p320*
Tall, Anthony; Maryland, 1668 ***2524.55*** *p214*
Wife: Elizabeth
Daughter: Elizabeth
Son: Anthony, Jr.
Tall, Anthony, Jr. *SEE* Tall, Anthony
Tall, Elizabeth *SEE* Tall, Anthony
Tall, James; Maryland, 1682 ***2524.55*** *p214*
Talldersby, Thomas; Maryland, 1649 ***2524.55*** *p214*
Talle, Anthony; Maryland, 1662 ***2524.55*** *p214*
Talle, Elizabeth; Maryland, 1663 ***2524.55*** *p214*
Son: Philip
Talle, Philip *SEE* Talle, Elizabeth
Tallian, Mr.; Quebec, 1858 ***9196.15*** *p41*
Talliday, Mrs. G.; Quebec, 1856 ***9196.15*** *p8*
Tallier, Rev.; Quebec, 1857 ***9196.15*** *p24*
Talling, Charles 28; Ontario, 1871 ***1823.22*** *p156*
Tallner, Michael; New York, New York, 1853 ***3437.14*** *p67*
Tallon, Mary Anne 44; Ontario, 1871 ***1823.28*** *p98*
Tallon, Patrick 37; Ontario, 1871 ***1823.28*** *p98*
Tally, Michael; New York, 1821 ***8197.10*** *p287*
Tally, Thomas; Virginia, 1671 ***6212.30*** *p42*
Talmage, Joseph 76; Ontario, 1871 ***1823.22*** *p156*
Talmie, John 45; Ontario, 1871 ***1823.22*** *p156*
Talor, Arther 54; Ontario, 1871 ***1823.28*** *p98*
Tame, Edward 21; Maryland, 1774 ***1220.25*** *p54*
Tamer, Thomas 21; Maryland, 1774 ***1220.25*** *p78*
Tamley, James 25; Ontario, 1871 ***1823.15*** *p259*
Tamlyn, George; New York, 1853 ***1224.3*** *p77*
Tamlyn, John E. 37; Ontario, 1871 ***1823.15*** *p259*
Tammion, Stephen; Maryland, 1633 ***2524.55*** *p214*
Tamoff, P. 41; Alaska, 1917 ***9196.1*** *p45*
Tamoff, P. 41; Whitehorse, Yukon, 1917 ***9196.1*** *p45*
Tampakis, Gust 33; Washington, 1913 ***9196.1*** *p61*
Tampkins, John; New York, 1840 ***8197.10*** *p200*
Tanch, Joseph 35; Maryland, 1775 ***1220.25*** *p98*
Tandyside, Mrs. G.; Quebec, 1856 ***9196.15*** *p8*
Tang, Fredrick 14; Ontario, 1871 ***1823.28*** *p98*
Tang, Lissee 14; Ontario, 1871 ***1823.28*** *p98*
Tangl, Hans; Port uncertain, 1742 ***2856.30*** *p454*
Tangney, John J. 25; Vermont, 1870 ***5900.10*** *p475*
Tankard, John; Maryland, 1681 ***2524.55*** *p214*
Tankard, William 21; Maryland, 1774 ***1220.25*** *p62*
Tannahill, Mr.; Quebec, 1857 ***9196.15*** *p17*
Tannahill, Mrs.; Quebec, 1857 ***9196.15*** *p17*
Tanner, Anna Maria; Port uncertain, 1745 ***2856.30*** *p454*
Tanner, Bartolomaus; America, 1744 ***2856.30*** *p454*
Tanner, Elwin E. 21; Ontario, 1871 ***1823.28*** *p98*
Tanner, Henry 60; Ontario, 1871 ***1823.22*** *p156*
Tanner, Jno; Virginia, 1666 ***6212.30*** *p28*
Tanner, Jno; Virginia, 1666 ***6212.30*** *p31*
Tanner, John; Maryland, 1670 ***2524.55*** *p214*
Tanner, Joseph; New York, 1840 ***8197.10*** *p199*
Tanner, Magdalena; Port uncertain, 1790 ***2856.30*** *p454*
Tanner, Paull; Virginia, 1703-1704 ***6212.30*** *p62*
Tannor, William; Maryland, 1661 ***2524.55*** *p214*
Tannus, Ar.; Maryland, 1670 ***2524.55*** *p215*
Tanocka, L. 39; British Columbia, 1911 ***9196.1*** *p14*
Tanocka, L. 39; Buenos Aires, 1911 ***9196.1*** *p14*
Tanterson, Dorin 34; Ontario, 1871 ***1823.28*** *p98*
Tanterson, Jemina 28; Ontario, 1871 ***1823.28*** *p98*
Tantphaeus, Peter; Port uncertain, 1744 ***2856.30*** *p454*
Taparich, Chas A. 27; Alaska, 1913 ***9196.1*** *p23*
Taparich, Chas A. 27; British Columbia, 1913 ***9196.1*** *p23*
Tapin, James Alfred; Pensacola, Florida, 1801 ***1224.3*** *p77*
Tapley, John 44; Maryland, 1775 ***1220.25*** *p108*
Taplin, Isaac 16; Maryland, 1775 ***1220.25*** *p112*
Tapp, Ann 16; Maryland, 1774 ***1220.25*** *p83*
Tapp, Anthony 27; Maryland, 1774 ***1220.25*** *p41*
Tapp, Eliza 28; Ontario, 1871 ***1823.15*** *p259*
Tapp, Thomas 19; Ontario, 1871 ***1823.15*** *p259*
Tappen, David; East New Jersey, 1754 ***1224.2*** *p113*
Tapper, John; New York, 1828 ***8197.10*** *p349*
Tappey, William 26; Maryland, 1774 ***1220.25*** *p47*
Tapscott, George Loveless; Texas, 1840 ***1224.3*** *p77*
Tapscott, Job 72; Ontario, 1871 ***1823.22*** *p156*
Tapscott, Samuel 32; Ontario, 1871 ***1823.22*** *p156*
Tapson, George 34; Ontario, 1871 ***1823.15*** *p259*
Tarbell, Julia M. Farwell; Vermont, 1844-1908 ***5900.10*** *p300*
Tarbell, Martin M.; Vermont, 1841-1893 ***5900.10*** *p300*
Tarberet, Mr.; Quebec, 1858 ***9196.15*** *p45*

Taylor, John; Maryland, 1671 2524.55 p215
Taylor, John; New York, 1794 8197.10 p1
Taylor, John; New York, 1802 8197.10 p25
Taylor, John; New York, 1807 8197.10 p51
Taylor, John; New York, 1831 8197.10 p355
Taylor, John; North America, 1794 1640.13 p123
Taylor, John; Ontario, 1882 1640.13 p123
Taylor, John; Pennsylvania, 1777 4629.10 p15
Taylor, John; Pennsylvania, 1777 4629.10 p26
Taylor, John; Pennsylvania, 1777 4629.10 p27
Taylor, John; Pennsylvania, 1777 4629.10 p30
Taylor, John; Pennsylvania, 1779 4629.10 p41
Taylor, John; Savannah, Georgia, 1772 1224.2 p114
Taylor, John; Savannah, Georgia, 1772 1640.10 p203
Taylor, John; Virginia, 1665 1224.1 p57
Taylor, John; West Indies, 1784 1640.13 p123
Taylor, John 15; Philadelphia, 1774 1220.25 p4
Taylor, John 21; Maryland, 1775 1220.25 p110
Taylor, John 21; Maryland, 1775 1220.25 p116
Taylor, John 21; Virginia, 1774 1220.25 p93
Taylor, John 24; Ontario, 1871 1823.22 p156
Taylor, John 26; Ontario, 1871 1823.28 p98
Taylor, John 33; Maryland, 1774 1220.25 p77
Taylor, John 40; Ontario, 1871 1823.28 p98
Taylor, John 42; Ontario, 1871 1823.15 p260
Taylor, John 44; Ontario, 1871 1823.15 p260
Taylor, John 45; Ontario, 1871 1823.28 p98
Taylor, John 46; Ontario, 1871 1823.15 p260
Taylor, John 49; Ontario, 1871 1823.15 p260
Taylor, John 49; Ontario, 1871 1823.22 p156
Taylor, John 56; Ontario, 1871 1823.15 p260
Taylor, John 60; Ontario, 1871 1823.15 p260
Taylor, John 67; Ontario, 1871 1823.15 p260
Taylor, John Chisim; Kentucky, 1854 1224.3 p78
Taylor, John L.; New York, 1829 8197.10 p351
Taylor, John N. 24; Ontario, 1871 1823.28 p98
Taylor, John Rae; New York, 1885 1640.13 p123
Taylor, John Swanston; Quebec, 1873 1640.13 p123
Taylor, Joseph; Georgia, 1737 1640.10 p203
Taylor, Joseph; Maryland, 1666 2524.55 p179
Taylor, Joseph; Maryland, 1709 1224.2 p114
Taylor, Joseph 12; Ontario, 1871 1823.22 p156
Taylor, Joseph 41; Ontario, 1871 1823.15 p260
Taylor, Joseph 45; Ontario, 1871 1823.28 p98
Taylor, Joseph 63; Ontario, 1871 1823.28 p98
Taylor, Joyce; Maryland, 1681 2524.55 p216
Taylor, Kazia 34; Ontario, 1871 1823.22 p156
Taylor, Lancelot 26; Maryland, 1774 1220.25 p40
Taylor, Lewis; Pennsylvania, 1779 4629.10 p37
Taylor, Lyman 44; Ontario, 1871 1823.22 p156
Taylor, Malc 55; Ontario, 1861 2896.27 p6
Taylor, Malcolm 74; Ontario, 1871 1823.15 p260
Taylor, Margarett *SEE* Taylor, John
Taylor, Martha *SEE* Taylor, Richard
Taylor, Mary *SEE* Taylor, John
Taylor, Mary *SEE* Taylor, Robert
Taylor, Mathew 30; Ontario, 1871 1823.15 p260
Taylor, Merrit 22; Ontario, 1861 2896.26 p26
Taylor, Michael 23; Fort Cumberland, Nova Scotia, 1774 1220.25 p17
Taylor, Michael 45; Fort Cumberland, Nova Scotia, 1774 1220.25 p16
Wife: Ann 26
Taylor, Michael 47; Vermont, 1878 5900.10 p344
Taylor, Michael 48; Ontario, 1871 1823.22 p156
Taylor, Nancy 18; Ontario, 1871 1823.22 p156
Taylor, Nich; Virginia, 1666 6212.30 p26
Taylor, Patrick H.; New York, 1826 8197.10 p333
Taylor, Peter 61; Ontario, 1871 1823.15 p260
Taylor, Peter Burnet; New York, 1899 1640.13 p123
Taylor, Precival 47; Ontario, 1871 1823.28 p98
Taylor, R. A. 7; Ontario, 1861 2896.26 p29
Taylor, Richard; Maryland, 1665 2524.55 p216
Wife: Martha
Taylor, Richard; Maryland, 1681 2524.55 p216
Taylor, Richard; Virginia, 1664 6212.30 p11
Taylor, Richard 25; Philadelphia, 1774 1220.25 p23
Taylor, Richard 42; Ontario, 1871 1823.15 p260
Taylor, Robert *SEE* Taylor, John
Taylor, Robert *SEE* Taylor, Robert
Taylor, Robert; Charleston, South Carolina, 1782 4629.10 p68
Taylor, Robert; Maryland, 1651 2524.55 p216
Wife: Mary
Taylor, Robert; Maryland, 1652 2524.55 p216
With wife
Son: Robert
Son: Samll.
Taylor, Robert; Maryland, 1658 2524.55 p216
With family
Taylor, Robert; Maryland, 1667 2524.55 p216
Wife: Mary
Taylor, Robert; Maryland, 1672 2524.55 p216
Taylor, Robert; New York, 1807 8197.10 p51
Taylor, Robert; Pennsylvania, 1785 4629.10 p48
Taylor, Robert; Virginia, 1656 1224.1 p57
Taylor, Robert 26; Philadelphia, 1774 1220.25 p43
Taylor, Robert 28; Nova Scotia, 1774 1220.25 p136
Taylor, Robert 33; Ontario, 1871 1823.15 p260
Taylor, Robert 44; Ontario, 1871 1823.15 p260
Taylor, Robert 44; Ontario, 1871 1823.22 p156
Taylor, Robert 60; Ontario, 1871 1823.15 p260
Taylor, Robert B.; New York, 1831 8197.10 p366
Taylor, Robt; Virginia, 1666 6212.30 p26
Taylor, Rose; Maryland, 1682 2524.55 p216
Taylor, S. J. 14; Ontario, 1861 2896.27 p1
Taylor, Saml; Virginia, 1690 6212.30 p58
Taylor, Samll. *SEE* Taylor, Robert
Taylor, Samll.; Maryland, 1652 2524.55 p216
Taylor, Samll; Virginia, 1671-1672 6212.30 p47
Taylor, Samuel; Pennsylvania, 1777 4629.10 p7
Taylor, Samuel; Virginia, 1641 1224.1 p57
Taylor, Samuel 28; Virginia, 1774 1220.25 p91
Taylor, Samuel 34; Ontario, 1871 1823.28 p98
Taylor, Sara Hamilton; Vermont, 1848-1918 5900.10 p579
Taylor, Sarah *SEE* Taylor, John
Taylor, Simon 21; Maryland, 1775 1220.25 p96
Taylor, Solomon 25; Virginia, 1774 1220.25 p89
Wife: Ann 27
Taylor, Soutel 75; Ontario, 1871 1823.15 p260
Taylor, Susan 35; Ontario, 1871 1823.22 p157
Taylor, Suzan *SEE* Taylor, George
Taylor, Thomas; Maryland, 1658 2524.55 p216
Taylor, Thomas; Maryland, 1661 2524.55 p37
Taylor, Thomas; Maryland, 1665 2524.55 p216
Taylor, Thomas; Maryland, 1674 2524.55 p216
Wife: Elizabeth
Daughter: Ann
Taylor, Thomas; New York, 1807 8197.10 p51
Taylor, Thomas; New York, 1833 8197.10 p288
Taylor, Thomas; New York, New York, 1858 6058.10 p70
Taylor, Thomas; Philadelphia, 1794 4629.10 p81
Taylor, Thomas; Virginia, 1663-1664 6212.30 p5
Taylor, Thomas; Virginia, 1703-1704 6212.30 p62
Taylor, Thomas 21; Philadelphia, 1774 1220.25 p80
Taylor, Thomas 22; Georgia, 1775 1220.25 p126
Taylor, Thomas 30; Ontario, 1871 1823.22 p157
Taylor, Thomas 37; Ontario, 1871 1823.15 p260
Taylor, Thomas 40; Ontario, 1871 1823.15 p260
Taylor, Thomas 43; Ontario, 1871 1823.28 p98
Taylor, Thomas 45; Ontario, 1871 1823.15 p260
Taylor, Thomas 54; Ontario, 1871 1823.15 p260
Taylor, Thomas 59; Ontario, 1871 1823.22 p157
Taylor, Thomas Matthew; South Carolina, 1807 1224.3 p78
Taylor, William; Georgia, 1738 1640.10 p203
Taylor, William; Maryland, 1658 2524.55 p216
Taylor, William; Maryland, 1663 2524.55 p216
Taylor, William; Maryland, 1667 2524.55 p216
Taylor, William; New Orleans, 1842 1640.10 p203
Taylor, William; New York, 1803 8197.10 p15
Taylor, William; New York, 1837 8197.10 p105
Taylor, William; New York, 1863 6058.10 p68
Taylor, William; New York, New York, 1845 1224.3 p78
Taylor, William; Pennsylvania, 1777 4629.10 p20
Taylor, William; Pennsylvania, 1785 4629.10 p48
Taylor, William; Perth Amboy, New Jersey, 1808 1224.3 p78
Taylor, William; Vermont, 1849-1928 5900.10 p443
Taylor, William 21; Maryland, 1774 1220.25 p39
Taylor, William 28; Ontario, 1871 1823.15 p260
Taylor, William 31; Ontario, 1871 1823.28 p98
Taylor, William 33; Ontario, 1871 1823.15 p260
Taylor, William 36; Ontario, 1871 1823.22 p157
Taylor, William 41; Ontario, 1871 1823.22 p157
Taylor, William 43; Ontario, 1871 1823.28 p98
Taylor, William 54; Ontario, 1871 1823.22 p157
Taylor, William 60; Ontario, 1871 1823.22 p157
Taylor, William 61; Ontario, 1871 1823.22 p157
Taylor, William 72; Ontario, 1871 1823.15 p260
Taylor, William Blackwell; New York, New York, 1857 1224.3 p78
Taylor, William Swain; New York, New York, n.d. 1224.3 p78
Taylor, Wm; Virginia, 1673 6212.30 p51
Taylor, Wm S. 41; Ontario, 1871 1823.15 p260
Taylour, George; Maryland, 1670 2524.55 p216
Taylour, Joseph; Maryland, 1667 2524.55 p165
Taylour, Thomas; Maryland, 1672 2524.55 p216
Taylrs, Cecelia; Maryland, 1910 3259.35 p63
Tayton, Mary 18; St. Kitts, 1774-1775 1220.25 p129
Tchingewak, Antoine 47; Ontario, 1871 1823.28 p98
Tea, Robert; Virginia, 1709 1224.2 p114
Teace, George; Pennsylvania, 1786 4629.10 p51
Teachout, Hanibal 65; Ontario, 1871 1823.22 p157
Teage, Cicily; Maryland, 1671 2524.55 p216
Teage, Sheily; Maryland, 1670 2524.55 p216
Teagle, John; New England, 1711 1224.2 p114
Teagle, Nathaniell; Maryland, 1673 2524.55 p216
Teague, Bridget; Vermont, 1845-1926 5900.10 p240
Teague, Bridget McEnaney 68; Vermont, 1890 5900.10 p237
Teague, Catherine 80; Vermont, 1891 5900.10 p155
Teague, Catherine Kennedy; Vermont, 1845-1919 5900.10 p222
Teague, Hanna McCarthy 36; Vermont, 1847 5900.10 p146
Teague, Hannah 35; Vermont, 1845 5900.10 p235
Teague, James; Vermont, 1843-1925 5900.10 p240
Teague, Mary Branon; Vermont, 1861 5900.10 p237
Teague, Mathew; Vermont, 1835-1916 5900.10 p240
Teague, Matthew 42; Vermont, 1847 5900.10 p146
Teague, Patrick 44; Vermont, 1859 5900.10 p237
Teague, Rosa 22; Vermont, 1865 5900.10 p232
Teague, Terence 68; Vermont, 1865 5900.10 p235
Teague, William; Vermont, 1861-1961 5900.10 p221
Teahan, Bridget; Vermont, 1843-1918 5900.10 p355
Teait, George; New York, 1794 8197.10 p1
Teal, Thomas G.; New York, 1840 8197.10 p200
Tear, William 31; New York, 1775 1220.25 p94
Teare, Samuel; Virginia, 1695 1224.1 p57
Teas, James 51; Ontario, 1871 1823.15 p260
Teas, Mary 56; Ontario, 1871 1823.15 p260
Teas, Sarah 91; Ontario, 1871 1823.15 p260
Teasdale, J. M. 51; Ontario, 1871 1823.22 p157
Teasdale, John 20; Maryland, 1774 1220.25 p60
Teasdale, William Robert; New York, 1838 8197.10 p151
Tease, William; New York, 1839 8197.10 p137
Teasel, Jacob; Pennsylvania, 1786 4629.10 p54
Teatter, John 38; Ontario, 1871 1823.15 p260
Tebo, Joseph 48; Ontario, 1871 1823.28 p98
Teckford, John 38; Ontario, 1871 1823.15 p260
Teckle, Elizabeth 40 *SEE* Teckle, John
Teckle, John 42; Halifax, Nova Scotia, 1774 1220.25 p138
Wife: Elizabeth 40
Teclaw, Ignacy; Maryland, 1910 3259.35 p63
Tedden, Miss; Quebec, 1858 9196.15 p40
Tedejefski, Michael; Maryland, 1910 3259.35 p63
Teelon, Bridget Cooley; Vermont, 1854-1900 5900.10 p430
Teelon, Catherine; Vermont, 1839-1899 5900.10 p584
Teelon, Thomas; Vermont, 1836-1910 5900.10 p430
Teeple, Silvester 40; Ontario, 1871 1823.15 p260
Teesdale, James; New York, 1808 8197.10 p54
Teffoe, Daniel 24; Philadelphia, 1775 1220.25 p107
Teggert, John 70; Ontario, 1871 1823.15 p260
Teggert, Joseph 25; Ontario, 1871 1823.15 p260
Teggert, Rynisce 60; Ontario, 1871 1823.15 p260
Teggert, William 33; Ontario, 1871 1823.15 p260
Tegil, August 45; Ontario, 1871 1823.28 p98
Tegiosh, Peter 75; Ontario, 1871 1823.28 p98
Tehan, Elizabeth; Vermont, 1859-1948 5900.10 p58
Tehan, Mary; Vermont, 1841-1914 5900.10 p356
Tehan, Mary; Vermont, 1847-1934 5900.10 p335
Tehan, Patrick; Vermont, 1856-1923 5900.10 p58
Tehean, Daniel 67; Vermont, 1875 5900.10 p344
Tehkummah, Frances 42; Ontario, 1871 1823.28 p98
Tehkummah, Louis 56; Ontario, 1871 1823.28 p98
Teige, Elizabeth; Virginia, 1672 6212.30 p49
Teigs, Gustav 28; Ontario, 1871 1823.28 p98
Teigs, John 58; Ontario, 1871 1823.28 p98
Teirney, John 42; Ontario, 1871 1823.28 p98
Teitler, Jacob; New York, 1840 8197.10 p383
Telakowicz, John; Maryland, 1910 3259.35 p63
Telfair, Edward; America, 1766 1640.10 p203
Telfair, Edward; Georgia, 1770 1640.10 p203
Telfair, W.; Louisiana, 1764 1640.10 p203
Telfair, William; Georgia, 1770 1640.10 p203
Telfe, James; Maryland, 1637 2524.55 p216
Telfer, Dorothy 1; Ontario, 1871 1823.28 p98
Telfer, Joseph W. 49; Ontario, 1871 1823.28 p98
Telfer, Thomas 57; Ontario, 1871 1823.15 p260
Telford, Bridgett McDormitt; Vermont, 1826-1907 5900.10 p514
Telford, John 16; Virginia, 1774 1220.25 p140
Telford, Peter; Vermont, 1827-1892 5900.10 p514
Teller, Frank; Maryland, 1910 3259.35 p63
Telliard, John; Maryland, 1668 2524.55 p216
Telocleowki, Jan; Maryland, 1910 3259.35 p63
Telor, John; Pennsylvania, 1778 4629.10 p32
Telsch, Franziska; Port uncertain, 1731 2856.30 p77
Telteng, John 26; Philadelphia, 1774 1220.25 p3
Tema, Mary; Maryland, 1910 3259.35 p63
Temby, Edwin 34; British Columbia, 1917 9196.1 p71

Temby, Edwin 34; Washington, 1917 ***9196.1*** *p71*
Tempa, Geo 30; Seattle, 1913 ***9196.1*** *p61*
Tempel, Jacob; America, 1746 ***2856.30*** *p454*
Tempel, Jacob; Port uncertain, 1746 ***2856.30*** *p454*
Tempel, Konrad; Port uncertain, 1783 ***2856.30*** *p454*
Tempelmann, John C.; America, 1700-1799 ***2856.30*** *p454*
Tempest, James; Pennsylvania, 1777 ***4629.10*** *p29*
Tempest, James; Pennsylvania, 1779 ***4629.10*** *p38*
Templar, John 17; Maryland, 1775 ***1220.25*** *p10*
Temple, . . .; Boston, 1765 ***4628.40*** *p115*
Temple, Charles 40; Ontario, 1871 ***1823.28*** *p98*
Temple, Edward; Virginia, 1664 ***6212.30*** *p8*
Temple, Elizabeth; Boston, 1816 ***1224.3*** *p78*
Temple, Fred 34; Kansas, 1900-1910 ***9079.10*** *p49*
Temple, John; America, 1799 ***1224.3*** *p78*
Temple, John; New York, 1799 ***1224.2*** *p114*
Temple, Joseph; Virginia, 1762 ***1224.2*** *p114*
Temple, Lea 32; Kansas, 1910 ***9079.10*** *p49*
Temple, Margarett; Maryland, 1663 ***2524.55*** *p216*
Temple, Peter 31; Ontario, 1871 ***1823.22*** *p157*
Temple, Peter 37; Ontario, 1871 ***1823.22*** *p157*
Temple, Richd.; Maryland, 1654 ***2524.55*** *p216*
Temple, Robert; Boston, 1717 ***4628.40*** *p114*
Temple, Robert 33; Maryland, 1774 ***1220.25*** *p46*
Temple, William; Virginia, 1767 ***1224.2*** *p114*
Templeman, John; Pennsylvania, 1780 ***4629.10*** *p43*
Templeman, William 28; Carolina, 1774 ***1220.25*** *p74*
Templeton, Hugh 78; Ontario, 1871 ***1823.15*** *p261*
Templeton, James; Wisconsin, 1878 ***1640.13*** *p124*
Templeton, John 42; Ontario, 1871 ***1823.15*** *p261*
Templeton, Sarah 26; Ontario, 1871 ***1823.15*** *p260*
Templeton, Thomas; Chicago, 1882 ***1640.13*** *p124*
Templing, George H. 48; Kansas, 1888-1910 ***9079.10*** *p27*
Templing, Gerorg 35; Kansas, 1891-1910 ***9079.10*** *p24*
Templing, Mary E. 33; Kansas, 1892-1910 ***9079.10*** *p24*
Templing, Teffir 38; Kansas, 1876-1910 ***9079.10*** *p27*
Templton, Edward 52; Ontario, 1871 ***1823.15*** *p261*
Tenail, John 31; Ontario, 1871 ***1823.15*** *p261*
Tenand, Richard; Maryland, 1658 ***2524.55*** *p216*
Tenant, James; Virginia, 1729 ***1224.2*** *p114*
Tench, Francis *SEE* Tench, John
Tench, Jane *SEE* Tench, John
Tench, John; Maryland, 1669 ***2524.55*** *p216*
  Relative: Jane
  Relative: Francis
Tench, Michaell; Virginia, 1666-1667 ***6212.30*** *p34*
Tenet, Peter; New York, 1806 ***8197.10*** *p33*
Teney, James 34; Ontario, 1871 ***1823.22*** *p157*
Tengley, Evi 60; Ontario, 1871 ***1823.15*** *p261*
Tennant, Betty 16; Virginia, 1774 ***1220.25*** *p140*
Tennant, Joshua 40; Ontario, 1871 ***1823.15*** *p261*
Tennant, Mary 20; Ontario, 1871 ***1823.28*** *p99*
Tennant, Peter 50; Ontario, 1871 ***1823.22*** *p157*
Tennant, Rich'd 80; Ontario, 1871 ***1823.28*** *p99*
Tennent, Joseph; New York, 1840 ***8197.10*** *p200*
Tennent, W.; New York, 1810 ***8197.10*** *p289*
Tennet, William 35; Ontario, 1871 ***1823.22*** *p157*
Tennian, Nellie M.; Vermont, 1858-1898 ***5900.10*** *p543*
Tennien, Alice A.; Vermont, 1855-1928 ***5900.10*** *p444*
Tennien, Catharine; Vermont, 1827-1932 ***5900.10*** *p384*
Tennien, Catherine 60; Vermont, 1871 ***5900.10*** *p97*
Tennien, Catherine 79; Vermont, 1910 ***5900.10*** *p94*
Tennien, James 78; Vermont, 1932 ***5900.10*** *p94*
Tennien, Patrick; Vermont, 1792-1882 ***5900.10*** *p97*
Tennien, Rose; Vermont, 1848-1880 ***5900.10*** *p97*
Tennien, Thomas 49; Vermont, 1865 ***5900.10*** *p384*
Tennien, Thomas F.; Vermont, 1840-1916 ***5900.10*** *p389*
Tennien, William 29; Vermont, 1892 ***5900.10*** *p94*
Tennison, Rowland; Maryland, 1682 ***2524.55*** *p216*
Tenny, Arthur J.; Vermont, 1849-1917 ***5900.10*** *p496*
Tensh, John; Maryland, 1656 ***2524.55*** *p216*
Tepham, Thomas; New York, 1821 ***8197.10*** *p287*
Tephug, James 37; Ontario, 1871 ***1823.15*** *p261*
Teriff, Mary 71; Ontario, 1871 ***1823.15*** *p261*
Teril, Eleanor 50; Ontario, 1861 ***2896.28*** *p58*
Teril, John A. 13; Ontario, 1861 ***2896.28*** *p58*
Teril, Mary A. 22; Ontario, 1861 ***2896.28*** *p58*
Teril, William 16; Ontario, 1861 ***2896.28*** *p58*
Terman, Antonia; Philadelphia, 1789 ***4629.10*** *p59*
  Wife: Catherine
Terman, Catherine *SEE* Terman, Antonia
Terman, Michael 50; Philadelphia, 1789 ***4629.10*** *p59*
Terme, Denis; Philadelphia, 1793 ***4629.10*** *p74*
Ternan, Arthur; New York, 1837 ***8197.10*** *p104*
Ternen, James; New York, 1821 ***8197.10*** *p287*
Terney, Catherine 3; Ontario, 1861 ***2896.27*** *p60*
Terney, Helen 1; Ontario, 1861 ***2896.27*** *p60*
Terney, Luke 35; Ontario, 1861 ***2896.27*** *p60*
Terney, Mary 26; Ontario, 1861 ***2896.27*** *p60*
Ternian, Sarah 40; Ontario, 1871 ***1823.15*** *p261*
Terra, Kaspar; New York, 1839 ***8197.10*** *p289*
Terrell, Elinr; Virginia, 1671 ***6212.30*** *p43*
Terrell, James; Maryland, 1682 ***2524.55*** *p216*
Terrell, James; New York, 1838 ***8197.10*** *p151*
Terrell, John 75; Ontario, 1861 ***2896.27*** *p32*
Terrett, Nicholas; Maryland, 1674 ***2524.55*** *p216*
Terricker, Thomas; Maryland, 1663 ***2524.55*** *p216*
Terrie, John; Maryland, 1667 ***2524.55*** *p217*
Terrier, Charles 31; Maryland, 1774 ***1220.25*** *p83*
Terrier, Jane 27; Ontario, 1861 ***2896.27*** *p17*
Terriere, Daniel; New York, 1840 ***8197.10*** *p200*
Terriere, Edward; New York, 1840 ***8197.10*** *p199*
Terriker, Thomas; Maryland, 1663 ***2524.55*** *p216*
Terrill, Allice 18; Ontario, 1861 ***2896.27*** *p30*
Terrill, Sarah J. 15; Ontario, 1861 ***2896.27*** *p30*
Terrill, Sarah J. 16; Ontario, 1861 ***2896.27*** *p29*
Terrill, Thomas; Maryland, 1665 ***2524.55*** *p217*
Terrill, Timothy; Virginia, 1664 ***6212.30*** *p11*
Terron, Samuel; New England, 1790 ***1224.2*** *p114*
Terry, A. 6; Ontario, 1861 ***2896.28*** *p15*
Terry, A. B. 3; Ontario, 1861 ***2896.28*** *p5*
Terry, Agnes 32; Ontario, 1861 ***2896.28*** *p25*
Terry, Alexander 34; Ontario, 1871 ***1823.15*** *p261*
Terry, Bridget; Vermont, 1828-1914 ***5900.10*** *p412*
Terry, Ellen 2; Ontario, 1861 ***2896.28*** *p25*
Terry, G. J. 16; Ontario, 1861 ***2896.28*** *p3*
Terry, George; New York, 1807 ***8197.10*** *p51*
Terry, George 30; Ontario, 1871 ***1823.28*** *p99*
Terry, Hannah J. 7; Ontario, 1861 ***2896.27*** *p46*
Terry, Harriet L. 4; Ontario, 1861 ***2896.28*** *p25*
Terry, Henry 69; Ontario, 1871 ***1823.22*** *p157*
Terry, J. H. 18; Ontario, 1861 ***2896.28*** *p3*
Terry, James 70; Vermont, 1881 ***5900.10*** *p200*
Terry, John 19; Ontario, 1861 ***2896.25*** *p13*
Terry, John 50; Ontario, 1871 ***1823.22*** *p157*
Terry, Jonas; Virginia, 1672 ***6212.30*** *p48*
Terry, K. E. 4; Ontario, 1861 ***2896.28*** *p15*
Terry, Lavina 45; Ontario, 1871 ***1823.22*** *p157*
Terry, M. 34; Ontario, 1861 ***2896.28*** *p3*
Terry, M. Emma 7; Ontario, 1861 ***2896.28*** *p3*
Terry, P. A. 9; Ontario, 1861 ***2896.28*** *p3*
Terry, R. 33; Ontario, 1861 ***2896.28*** *p15*
Terry, Rebecca 8; Ontario, 1861 ***2896.28*** *p25*
Terry, S. 14; Ontario, 1861 ***2896.28*** *p3*
Terry, S. A. 17; Ontario, 1861 ***2896.28*** *p15*
Terry, S. E. 11; Ontario, 1861 ***2896.28*** *p15*
Terry, S. T. 11; Ontario, 1861 ***2896.28*** *p3*
Terry, Silvester W. 11; Ontario, 1861 ***2896.27*** *p46*
Terry, Sophiah E. 9; Ontario, 1861 ***2896.27*** *p46*
Terry, T. C. 1; Ontario, 1861 ***2896.28*** *p15*
Terry, Thomas; Maryland, 1671 ***2524.55*** *p217*
Terry, William 22; Virginia, 1774 ***1220.25*** *p90*
Terry, Zebedee; New England, 1795 ***1224.2*** *p114*
Terson, Andreas; Maryland, 1661 ***2524.55*** *p217*
  Wife: Katherine
  Daughter: Ann
Terson, Ann *SEE* Terson, Andreas
Terson, Katherine *SEE* Terson, Andreas
Tervis, William 52; Ontario, 1871 ***1823.15*** *p261*
Terwiliger, Lewis W. 15; Ontario, 1861 ***2896.27*** *p14*
Terwiliger, Phebe Ann 22; Ontario, 1861 ***2896.27*** *p14*
Terwiliger, William 26; Ontario, 1861 ***2896.27*** *p14*
Terwilligar, Catharine 75; Ontario, 1861 ***2896.27*** *p55*
Terwilligar, David W. 1; Ontario, 1861 ***2896.27*** *p49*
Terwilligar, Elizabeth M. 25; Ontario, 1861 ***2896.27*** *p23*
Terwilligar, Eve 40; Ontario, 1861 ***2896.27*** *p49*
Terwilligar, Frank W. 2; Ontario, 1861 ***2896.27*** *p23*
Terwilligar, George 11; Ontario, 1861 ***2896.27*** *p49*
Terwilligar, Jane 33; Ontario, 1861 ***2896.27*** *p48*
Terwilligar, John 82; Ontario, 1861 ***2896.25*** *p63*
Terwilligar, Joseph 18; Ontario, 1861 ***2896.27*** *p49*
Terwilligar, Mary 7; Ontario, 1861 ***2896.25*** *p63*
Terwilligar, Mary C. 14; Ontario, 1861 ***2896.27*** *p49*
Terwilligar, Matura; Ontario, 1861 ***2896.28*** *p57*
Terwilligar, Obadiser 19; Ontario, 1861 ***2896.25*** *p63*
Terwilligar, Sarah 42; Ontario, 1861 ***2896.25*** *p63*
Terwilligar, Sarah J. 16; Ontario, 1861 ***2896.27*** *p49*
Terwilligar, Stephen 7; Ontario, 1861 ***2896.27*** *p49*
Terwilligar, Victoria 15; Ontario, 1861 ***2896.25*** *p63*
Terwilligar, William 9; Ontario, 1861 ***2896.27*** *p49*
Tesch, Anna Catharina; Port uncertain, 1765 ***2856.30*** *p454*
Tesch, Niklas; Port uncertain, 1734 ***2856.30*** *p454*
  With wife & children
Teschen, Georg; Port uncertain, 1758 ***2856.30*** *p454*
  With son
Teschen, Georg; Port uncertain, 1763 ***2856.30*** *p455*
  With son
Tessero, Susan; Virginia, 1665 ***6212.30*** *p17*
Testard, Ernest; New York, 1831 ***8197.10*** *p367*
Tester, Jane 22; Maryland, 1775 ***1220.25*** *p99*
Tester, Stephen 22; Maryland, 1775 ***1220.25*** *p99*
Testill, Joshua 27; Maryland, 1774 ***1220.25*** *p61*
Tetevide, Francois; Quebec, 1858 ***9196.15*** *p34*
Tetmash, Jane *SEE* Tetmash, John
Tetmash, John; Maryland, 1662 ***2524.55*** *p220*
  Wife: Jane
Teto, Manuel; New York, 1807 ***8197.10*** *p51*
Tetu, Mr.; Quebec, 1858 ***9196.15*** *p44*
Tetu, L.; Quebec, 1858 ***9196.15*** *p44*
Teuber, Josef; Port uncertain, 1771 ***2856.30*** *p455*
Teuckesbury, William; Maryland, 1672 ***2524.55*** *p217*
Teutsch, Christof; America, 1758 ***2856.30*** *p455*
Teutsch, Georg Adam; Port uncertain, 1770 ***2856.30*** *p455*
Tevars, Thomas; Virginia, 1671 ***6212.30*** *p43*
Tevivdale, John 36; Ontario, 1871 ***1823.28*** *p99*
Tevlin, James; New York, 1837 ***8197.10*** *p104*
Tew, Richard; Newport, Rhode Island, 1674 ***1224.1*** *p57*
Tewes, Jacobin; Virginia, 1672 ***6212.30*** *p49*
Tewesly, Henry 44; Ontario, 1871 ***1823.15*** *p261*
Tewey, Martin; Vermont, 1836-1915 ***5900.10*** *p593*
Tewey, Mary Mooney; Vermont, 1845-1912 ***5900.10*** *p593*
Tewsley, James 70; Ontario, 1871 ***1823.15*** *p261*
Textor, Adam; America, 1769 ***2856.30*** *p455*
Tezich, B. 22; Alaska, 1917 ***9196.1*** *p48*
Tezich, B. 22; Whitehorse, Yukon, 1917 ***9196.1*** *p48*
Thaaham, William 64; Ontario, 1871 ***1823.15*** *p261*
Thacker, Gilbert; Virginia, 1666 ***6212.30*** *p29*
Thackeray, N. T.; Portland, Maine, 1857 ***9196.15*** *p12*
Thackray, Richard 41; Ontario, 1871 ***1823.28*** *p99*
Thackrey, William 66; Ontario, 1871 ***1823.22*** *p157*
Thadlett, John; Maryland, 1674 ***2524.55*** *p217*
Thager, Charles B. 13; Ontario, 1871 ***1823.22*** *p157*
Thailowicz, John; Maryland, 1910 ***3259.35*** *p63*
Thain, John 34; Ontario, 1871 ***1823.22*** *p157*
Thain, Margaret 79; Ontario, 1871 ***1823.15*** *p261*
Thairjames, Thomas 21; Virginia, 1773 ***1220.25*** *p29*
Thale, Carl 19; Maryland, 1774 ***1220.25*** *p77*
Thaler, Adam 52; Ontario, 1871 ***1823.15*** *p261*
Thalhofer, Ernst; Port uncertain, 1795 ***2856.30*** *p455*
Thalhofer, Ernst; Port uncertain, 1796 ***2856.30*** *p455*
Thalhofer, Friedrich; Port uncertain, 1795 ***2856.30*** *p455*
Thalhofer, Friedrich; Port uncertain, 1796 ***2856.30*** *p455*
Thally, Charles; New York, 1827 ***8197.10*** *p288*
Thamann, Antoine; New York, 1840 ***8197.10*** *p199*
Thane, Geo; Virginia, 1672 ***6212.30*** *p50*
Thane, Walter 28; Ontario, 1871 ***1823.22*** *p157*
Thanner, Friedrich; Port uncertain, 1790 ***2856.30*** *p455*
Tharges, Martha 49; Ontario, 1871 ***1823.15*** *p261*
Tharp, William; Pennsylvania, 1777 ***4629.10*** *p8*
Thasier, Antwain 78; Ontario, 1861 ***2896.27*** *p66*
Thasier, Elisa 45; Ontario, 1861 ***2896.27*** *p66*
Thatcher, Anthony; New England, 1641 ***1224.1*** *p57*
Thatcher, Bartholomew; New Jersey, 1818 ***1224.3*** *p78*
Thatcher, Thomas; New York, 1838 ***8197.10*** *p289*
Thawburn, James 65; Ontario, 1871 ***1823.15*** *p261*
Thayer, Mr.; Quebec, 1857 ***9196.15*** *p20*
Thayer, Arodi; Dorchester, Massachusetts, 1832 ***1224.3*** *p78*
Thayer, C. S. 28; Alaska, 1912 ***9196.1*** *p38*
Thayer, C. S. 28; Whitehorse, Yukon, 1912 ***9196.1*** *p38*
Thayer, Eva; Vermont, 1865-1941 ***5900.10*** *p499*
Thayer, Isaiah 71; Ontario, 1871 ***1823.22*** *p157*
Thayer, John; Connecticut, 1819 ***1224.3*** *p78*
Thayer, Nathaniel 79; Ontario, 1871 ***1823.22*** *p157*
Theabo, Samuel 56; Ontario, 1871 ***1823.28*** *p99*
Thearns, Thomas 30; Ontario, 1871 ***1823.15*** *p261*
Theato, Johann Michael; America, 1745 ***2856.30*** *p455*
Thebaud, Andre Augustus; New York, 1815 ***8197.10*** *p56*
Theem, Konrad; Port uncertain, 1753 ***2856.30*** *p455*
Theis, Anna Maria; Port uncertain, 1773 ***2856.30*** *p455*
Theis, Delila *SEE* Theis, Jacob
Theis, Dorothea; Port uncertain, 1775 ***2856.30*** *p455*
Theis, Gertrud; Port uncertain, 1774 ***2856.30*** *p455*
Theis, Jacob; America, 1772 ***2856.30*** *p455*
  Wife: Delila
Theis, Johann; Port uncertain, 1782 ***2856.30*** *p455*
Theis, Johann; Port uncertain, 1783 ***2856.30*** *p455*
Theisin, Anna Maria; Port uncertain, 1773 ***2856.30*** *p455*
Theiss, Dor. Engel *SEE* Theiss, Jakob
Theiss, Jakob; America, 1771 ***2856.30*** *p455*
  Wife: Dor. Engel
Theiss, Jakob; America, 1772 ***2856.30*** *p455*
  Wife: Dor. Engel
Theiss, Jakob; America, 1773 ***2856.30*** *p455*
  Wife: Dor. Engel
Theiss, Jakob; America, 1774 ***2856.30*** *p455*
  Wife: Dor. Engel
Theiss, Jakob; America, 1792 ***2856.30*** *p455*
Theiss, Johann; Port uncertain, 1779 ***2856.30*** *p455*
Theiss, Johann Georg; America, 1764 ***2856.30*** *p455*
Theiss, Johann Peter; Port uncertain, 1764 ***2856.30*** *p455*
Theiss, Margarete Cath.; America, 1748 ***2856.30*** *p455*
Theiss, Mrs. Mattheiss; America, 1738 ***2856.30*** *p455*
Theleball, Elizabeth; Virginia, 1680 ***1224.1*** *p13*

Thelwall, David; Illinois, 1767 ***1224.2*** *p114*
Theobald, Adam; Port uncertain, 1745 ***2856.30*** *p456*
Theobald, Catharina; America, 1787 ***2856.30*** *p456*
Theobald, George 37; Ontario, 1871 ***1823.15*** *p261*
Theobald, Jakob; America, 1740 ***2856.30*** *p456*
Theobald, Johann Jakob; Port uncertain, 1744 ***2856.30*** *p456*
Theobald, Maria Catharina; America, 1788 ***2856.30*** *p456*
With husband
Theobold, Mary *SEE* Theobold, William
Theobold, William; Maryland, 1681 ***2524.55*** *p217*
Wife: Mary
Theodorick, Thomas; Maryland, 1655 ***2524.55*** *p217*
Therasson, Lewis; New York, 1806 ***8197.10*** *p33*
Therberge, Mr.; Quebec, 1857 ***9196.15*** *p16*
Theriat, Augustus R.; New York, 1823 ***8197.10*** *p287*
Theriat, Augustus R.; New York, 1828 ***8197.10*** *p63*
Thesser, Charles 27; Ontario, 1871 ***1823.15*** *p261*
Thesser, Henry 21; Ontario, 1871 ***1823.15*** *p261*
Thesser, Ricky 25; Ontario, 1871 ***1823.15*** *p261*
Theuerkauff, Anna; Port uncertain, 1790 ***2856.30*** *p456*
Theuerkauff, Charlotte; Port uncertain, 1790 ***2856.30*** *p456*
Thexton, Geo 22; Ontario, 1871 ***1823.15*** *p261*
Thexton, Thomas; Maryland, 1672 ***2524.55*** *p217*
Thibaudeau, Mr.; Quebec, 1858 ***9196.15*** *p40*
Thibault, Francis Adrian; Philadelphia, 1792 ***4629.10*** *p71*
Thibaut, Nikolaus; Port uncertain, 1784 ***2856.30*** *p456*
With family
Thickett, William; New York, 1840 ***8197.10*** *p200*
Thickson, John 26; Ontario, 1871 ***1823.22*** *p157*
Thiel, Anna Elisabeth; Port uncertain, 1745 ***2856.30*** *p456*
Thiel, George 45; Ontario, 1871 ***1823.15*** *p261*
Thiel, Johann; Port uncertain, 1763 ***2856.30*** *p456*
Thiel, Johann; Port uncertain, 1765 ***2856.30*** *p456*
Thiel, Margarete; Port uncertain, 1764 ***2856.30*** *p456*
Thielen, Peter; Port uncertain, 1793 ***2856.30*** *p456*
Thiemann, Adam 51; Ontario, 1871 ***1823.28*** *p99*
Thierison, Francis D. 10; Ontario, 1861 ***2896.27*** *p29*
Thinin, Fredrick 32; Ontario, 1871 ***1823.15*** *p261*
Thinn, Frederick; Virginia, 1664 ***6212.30*** *p12*
Thinn, James; Virginia, 1664 ***6212.30*** *p15*
Thinn, Wm; Virginia, 1664 ***6212.30*** *p7*
Thirain, Elisabeth; America, 1764 ***2856.30*** *p462*
With husband
Third, Elizabeth 77; Ontario, 1871 ***1823.22*** *p157*
Third, Will'm 38; Ontario, 1871 ***1823.28*** *p99*
Thirde, James Young; Ontario, 1884 ***1640.13*** *p124*
Thirey, Beavis 25; Baltimore, 1775 ***1220.25*** *p118*
Thiring, Anthony; Florida, 1767 ***1224.2*** *p114*
Thirk, Alexander 42; Ontario, 1871 ***1823.22*** *p157*
Thirsk, John 53; Ontario, 1871 ***1823.15*** *p261*
Thirston, John 52; Ontario, 1871 ***1823.22*** *p157*
Thiss, Thomas 43; Ontario, 1871 ***1823.28*** *p99*
Thodd, Thomas 35; Ontario, 1871 ***1823.15*** *p261*
Thode, William Denton; New York, 1832 ***8197.10*** *p288*
Tholl, Anton; Port uncertain, 1724 ***2856.30*** *p84*
With wife & 5 children
Thom, Christian; New York, 1825 ***8197.10*** *p297*
Thom, Edward 29; Ontario, 1871 ***1823.15*** *p261*
Thom, James 43; Ontario, 1871 ***1823.15*** *p261*
Thom, William; Canada, 1860 ***1640.13*** *p124*
Thom, William 38; Ontario, 1871 ***1823.15*** *p262*
Thoma, Christina 56; Ontario, 1871 ***1823.28*** *p99*
Thoma, Gotlip 20; Ontario, 1871 ***1823.28*** *p99*
Thoma, Johann Henrich; Port uncertain, 1742 ***2856.30*** *p456*
Thomadu, Tillie; Maryland, 1910 ***3259.35*** *p63*
Thoman, Margarete; Port uncertain, 1751 ***2856.30*** *p456*
With husband
Thomas, . . .; Boston, 1737 ***4628.40*** *p114*
Thomas, . . .; Maryland, 1666 ***2524.55*** *p218*
Thomas, Miss; Quebec, 1858 ***9196.15*** *p33*
Thomas, Mr.; Portland, Maine, 1858 ***9196.15*** *p31*
Thomas, Mr.; Quebec, 1858 ***9196.15*** *p33*
Thomas, Mr.; Quebec, 1858 ***9196.15*** *p46*
Thomas, A. H. 29; Ontario, 1871 ***1823.28*** *p99*
Thomas, Alexander 68; Ontario, 1871 ***1823.22*** *p157*
Thomas, Ann *SEE* Thomas, David
Thomas, Ann; Maryland, 1673 ***2524.55*** *p217*
Thomas, Ann; Maryland, 1679 ***2524.55*** *p217*
Thomas, Anna Catharina; Port uncertain, 1747 ***2856.30*** *p457*
With husband
Thomas, Anna Elisabeth; Port uncertain, 1754 ***2856.30*** *p456*
Thomas, Arthur; New York, New York, 1784 ***1224.2*** *p114*
Thomas, Asa 50; Ontario, 1861 ***2896.28*** *p57*
Thomas, B. Thomas 37; Ontario, 1871 ***1823.22*** *p157*
Thomas, Bartholomew; Virginia, 1673 ***1224.1*** *p57*
Thomas, Benjamin; New York, 1807 ***8197.10*** *p331*
Thomas, Benjamin; Pennsylvania, 1786 ***4629.10*** *p50*
Thomas, Blanch; Maryland, 1672 ***2524.55*** *p217*
Thomas, Blanch; Maryland, 1676 ***2524.55*** *p217*
Thomas, Brun 57; Ontario, 1871 ***1823.28*** *p99*
Thomas, C. 26; Ontario, 1861 ***2896.28*** *p9*
Thomas, Caleb *SEE* Thomas, Phil.ip
Thomas, Cerlinda 9; Ontario, 1861 ***2896.28*** *p57*
Thomas, Charles; Maryland, 1677 ***2524.55*** *p217*
Thomas, Charles; Vermont, 1855-1934 ***5900.10*** *p243*
Thomas, Charles; Washington, 1893 ***1640.13*** *p124*
Thomas, Charles 23; Ontario, 1871 ***1823.15*** *p262*
Thomas, Christopher; Maryland, 1664 ***2524.55*** *p217*
Wife: Elizabeth
Child: Suzan
Child: Katherine
Thomas, Daniel; Port uncertain, 1768 ***2856.30*** *p456*
Thomas, Daniel; Port uncertain, 1768 ***2856.30*** *p457*
Thomas, David; Carolina, 1711 ***1224.2*** *p114*
Thomas, David; Maryland, 1650 ***2524.55*** *p217*
Thomas, David; Maryland, 1650 ***2524.55*** *p217*
Wife: Ann
Thomas, David; Maryland, 1682 ***2524.55*** *p217*
Thomas, David; New York, 1807 ***8197.10*** *p51*
Thomas, Edward; Maryland, 1662 ***2524.55*** *p217*
Thomas, Edward; Maryland, 1676 ***2524.55*** *p217*
Thomas, Edward; South Carolina, 1738 ***1224.2*** *p114*
Thomas, Eliza 40; Ontario, 1871 ***1823.22*** *p157*
Thomas, Elizabeth *SEE* Thomas, Christopher
Thomas, Elizabeth *SEE* Thomas, Phil.ip
Thomas, Elizabeth *SEE* Thomas, Thomas
Thomas, Elizabeth 21; Philadelphia, 1774 ***1220.25*** *p63*
Thomas, Elizabeth 48; Ontario, 1871 ***1823.22*** *p157*
Thomas, Evan; Maryland, 1668 ***2524.55*** *p217*
Thomas, Evan; Maryland, 1675 ***2524.55*** *p217*
Thomas, Evan; New York, 1802 ***8197.10*** *p25*
Thomas, Evan; Pennsylvania, 1777 ***4629.10*** *p26*
Thomas, Francis *SEE* Thomas, William
Thomas, George 22; Virginia, 1774 ***1220.25*** *p88*
Thomas, George 25; Ontario, 1871 ***1823.22*** *p157*
Thomas, George 26; Philadelphia, 1774 ***1220.25*** *p69*
Wife: Mary 32
With child
Thomas, George 30; Philadelphia, 1775 ***1220.25*** *p9*
Thomas, Hamilton 20; Ontario, 1861 ***2896.28*** *p57*
Thomas, Henrich Peter; Port uncertain, 1778 ***2856.30*** *p457*
Thomas, Henry 43; Ontario, 1871 ***1823.15*** *p262*
Thomas, Hugh; Maryland, 1672 ***2524.55*** *p217*
Thomas, Hugh; Maryland, 1676 ***2524.55*** *p217*
Thomas, Hugh; Virginia, 1671-1672 ***6212.30*** *p47*
Thomas, J. 31; Ontario, 1861 ***2896.26*** *p10*
Thomas, Jakob; Port uncertain, 1731 ***2856.30*** *p457*
Thomas, Jakob; Port uncertain, 1748 ***2856.30*** *p457*
With wife & 3 children
Thomas, James *SEE* Thomas, Thomas
Thomas, James; New York, 1807 ***8197.10*** *p331*
Thomas, James; Philadelphia, 1712 ***1224.2*** *p115*
Thomas, James 16; Grenada, 1774 ***1220.25*** *p128*
Thomas, James 22; Maryland, 1774 ***1220.25*** *p74*
Thomas, James 35; Ontario, 1871 ***1823.15*** *p262*
Thomas, Jno; Virginia, 1671 ***6212.30*** *p44*
Thomas, Jno 42; Mexico, 1911 ***9196.1*** *p15*
Thomas, Johann; America, 1764 ***2856.30*** *p457*
With wife & children
Thomas, Johann Adam; Port uncertain, 1754 ***2856.30*** *p457*
Thomas, Johann Gerhard; Port uncertain, 1754 ***2856.30*** *p457*
Thomas, Johann Nikolaus; Port uncertain, 1748 ***2856.30*** *p457*
With wife & 6 children
Thomas, Johann Peter; Port uncertain, 1754 ***2856.30*** *p457*
Thomas, John *SEE* Thomas, Philip
Thomas, John *SEE* Thomas, William
Thomas, John; Maryland, 1663 ***2524.55*** *p217*
Thomas, John; Maryland, 1673 ***2524.55*** *p217*
Thomas, John; Maryland, 1679 ***2524.55*** *p217*
Thomas, John; Maryland, 1680 ***2524.55*** *p217*
Thomas, John; Maryland, 1681 ***2524.55*** *p217*
Thomas, John; Maryland, 1681 ***2524.55*** *p218*
Thomas, John; New York, 1838 ***8197.10*** *p377*
Thomas, John; Pennsylvania, 1777 ***4629.10*** *p23*
Thomas, John; Pennsylvania, 1779 ***4629.10*** *p36*
Thomas, John; Vermont, 1841-1925 ***5900.10*** *p225*
Thomas, John; Virginia, 1666 ***6212.30*** *p29*
Thomas, John; Died enroute, 1849 ***1224.3*** *p78*
Thomas, John 24; Ontario, 1871 ***1823.15*** *p262*
Thomas, John 26; Philadelphia, 1775 ***1220.25*** *p107*
Thomas, John 28; Maryland, 1774 ***1220.25*** *p41*
Thomas, John 29; Maryland, 1775 ***1220.25*** *p10*
Thomas, John 30; Philadelphia, 1775 ***1220.25*** *p9*
Thomas, John 35; Ontario, 1871 ***1823.28*** *p99*
Thomas, John 42; Maryland, 1774 ***1220.25*** *p71*
Thomas, John 42; Maryland, 1775 ***1220.25*** *p105*
Thomas, John 63; Vermont, 1859 ***5900.10*** *p229*
Thomas, John 82; Ontario, 1871 ***1823.22*** *p157*
Thomas, John, Jr.; New York, 1829 ***8197.10*** *p359*
Thomas, John Chew; Pennsylvania, 1786 ***4629.10*** *p53*
Thomas, John R.; New York, 1807 ***8197.10*** *p51*
Thomas, John W. 33; Ontario, 1871 ***1823.28*** *p99*
Thomas, Jonathan; New York, 1838 ***8197.10*** *p151*
Thomas, Juilian Burnell; Vermont, 1840-1922 ***5900.10*** *p225*
Thomas, Katherine *SEE* Thomas, Christopher
Thomas, L.; St. John, New Brunswick, 1857 ***9196.15*** *p12*
Thomas, Lorenz; Port uncertain, 1752 ***2856.30*** *p457*
Thomas, Manly 15; Ontario, 1861 ***2896.28*** *p57*
Thomas, Margarett; Maryland, 1676 ***2524.55*** *p218*
Thomas, Maria Catharina; Port uncertain, 1785 ***2856.30*** *p457*
Thomas, Martha Bixby; Vermont, 1857-1909 ***5900.10*** *p225*
Thomas, Mary *SEE* Thomas, Philip
Thomas, Mary *SEE* Thomas, William
Thomas, Mary; Maryland, 1658 ***2524.55*** *p38*
Thomas, Mary; Maryland, 1661 ***2524.55*** *p218*
Thomas, Mary 17; Ontario, 1871 ***1823.22*** *p157*
Thomas, Mary 27; Ontario, 1871 ***1823.28*** *p99*
Thomas, Mary 32 *SEE* Thomas, George
Thomas, Mary 62; Vermont, 1859 ***5900.10*** *p229*
Thomas, Mary Jane 23; Ontario, 1861 ***2896.28*** *p57*
Thomas, Matilda Russell 56; Vermont, 1886 ***5900.10*** *p199*
Thomas, Michael; Maryland, 1661 ***2524.55*** *p114*
Thomas, Michael; Philadelphia, 1729 ***2856.30*** *p457*
With wife & 7 children
Thomas, Michel; Philadelphia, 1730 ***2856.30*** *p457*
Thomas, Mitch 67; Ontario, 1861 ***2896.25*** *p66*
Thomas, Morris; Virginia, 1666 ***6212.30*** *p26*
Thomas, Nathaniel Ray; Massachusetts, 1789 ***1224.2*** *p115*
Thomas, Nellie Driscoll; Vermont, 1861-1882 ***5900.10*** *p243*
Thomas, Nicholas *SEE* Thomas, Philip
Thomas, Nicholas 43; Ontario, 1871 ***1823.22*** *p157*
Thomas, Patrick 27; Virginia, 1774 ***1220.25*** *p87*
Thomas, Paul; Maryland, 1680-1681 ***2524.55*** *p218*
Thomas, Peter; America, 1748 ***2856.30*** *p457*
With wife & 6 children
Thomas, Peter; America, 1751 ***2856.30*** *p457*
With wife & 6 children
Thomas, Peter; Port uncertain, 1785 ***2856.30*** *p457*
Thomas, Phil.ip; Maryland, 1651 ***2524.55*** *p218*
Wife: Sarah
Child: Sarah
Child: Elizabeth
Child: Caleb
Child: Phill
Thomas, Philip; Maryland, 1678 ***2524.55*** *p218*
Wife: Mary
Child: Nicholas
Child: John
Child: Susann
Child: William
Thomas, Phill *SEE* Thomas, Phil.ip
Thomas, Pierre; New York, 1817 ***8197.10*** *p287*
Thomas, Prince 35; Ontario, 1871 ***1823.28*** *p99*
Thomas, Quirin; Port uncertain, 1771 ***2856.30*** *p457*
Thomas, Richard; New York, 1838 ***8197.10*** *p151*
Thomas, Richard; Pennsylvania, 1777 ***4629.10*** *p24*
Thomas, Richard 36; Virginia, 1773 ***1220.25*** *p30*
Thomas, Richard 45; Ontario, 1871 ***1823.22*** *p158*
Thomas, Robert; Maryland, 1650 ***2524.55*** *p218*
Thomas, Robert 73; Ontario, 1871 ***1823.28*** *p99*
Thomas, Samuel 10; Ontario, 1861 ***2896.28*** *p35*
Thomas, Sarah *SEE* Thomas, Phil.ip
Thomas, Sarah; Maryland, 1682 ***2524.55*** *p43*
Thomas, Sarah; Maryland, 1682 ***2524.55*** *p218*
Thomas, Sarah 24; Ontario, 1861 ***2896.28*** *p57*
Thomas, Sarah 26; Ontario, 1861 ***2896.28*** *p35*
Thomas, Sarah Driscoll; Vermont, 1856-1925 ***5900.10*** *p243*
Thomas, Steve 21; Washington, 1915 ***9196.1*** *p67*
Thomas, Susann *SEE* Thomas, Philip
Thomas, Susanna; Port uncertain, 1733 ***2856.30*** *p457*
Thomas, Suzan *SEE* Thomas, Christopher
Thomas, Thomas; Maryland, 1651 ***2524.55*** *p218*
Wife: Elizabeth
Son: James
Thomas, Thomas; Maryland, 1658 ***2524.55*** *p218*
With wife
Thomas, Thomas; Maryland, 1658 ***2524.55*** *p218*
Wife: Elizabeth
Son: James

Thomas, Thomas; Maryland, 1658 ***2524.55*** *p218*
Thomas, Thomas; Maryland, 1666 ***2524.55*** *p204*
Thomas, Thomas 17; Philadelphia, 1774 ***1220.25*** *p4*
Thomas, Thomas 47; Ontario, 1871 ***1823.15*** *p262*
Thomas, W. H. 35; Ontario, 1871 ***1823.28*** *p99*
Thomas, Walter; Maryland, 1664 ***2524.55*** *p218*
Thomas, Walter; Maryland, 1671 ***2524.55*** *p218*
Thomas, Walter; Maryland, 1681 ***2524.55*** *p218*
Thomas, William *SEE* Thomas, Philip
Thomas, William; Dominica, 1773 ***1220.25*** *p28*
Thomas, William; Maryland, 1655 ***2524.55*** *p30*
Thomas, William; Maryland, 1669 ***2524.55*** *p218*
Wife: Francis
Child: John
Child: Mary
Thomas, William; Maryland, 1674 ***2524.55*** *p218*
Thomas, William; Maryland, 1681 ***2524.55*** *p218*
Thomas, William; New York, 1824 ***8197.10*** *p288*
Thomas, William; Virginia, 1660 ***1224.1*** *p57*
Thomas, William 15; Baltimore, 1775 ***1220.25*** *p119*
Thomas, William 20; Philadelphia, 1774 ***1220.25*** *p72*
Thomas, William 28; Ontario, 1871 ***1823.15*** *p262*
Thomas, William 36; Ontario, 1871 ***1823.28*** *p99*
Thomas, William 50; Ontario, 1871 ***1823.22*** *p158*
Thomas, William 60; Ontario, 1871 ***1823.22*** *p158*
Thomas, Wm; Virginia, 1668-1669 ***6212.30*** *p41*
Thomass, Maria Gertrud; Port uncertain, 1753 ***2856.30*** *p457*
Thombush, John; Maryland, 1662 ***2524.55*** *p218*
Thome, Hans Michael; America, 1748 ***2856.30*** *p457*
With wife & 5 children
Thomes, Simeon 33; Ontario, 1871 ***1823.15*** *p262*
Thomlinson, Robert; Boston, 1741 ***1224.2*** *p116*
Thompkin, Giles; Maryland, 1651 ***2524.55*** *p218*
Thompkins, Anne; Virginia, 1671 ***6212.30*** *p42*
Thompkins, Benjamin; Maryland, 1681 ***2524.55*** *p218*
Thompkins, Sarah; Maryland, 1669 ***2524.55*** *p218*
Thompson, . . .; Boston, 1765 ***4628.40*** *p115*
Thompson, Miss; Quebec, 1858 ***9196.15*** *p35*
Thompson, Mr.; Quebec, 1856 ***9196.15*** *p7*
Thompson, Mr.; Quebec, 1858 ***9196.15*** *p39*
Thompson, Mr.; Quebec, 1858 ***9196.15*** *p43*
Thompson, Mrs.; Maryland, 1647 ***2524.55*** *p218*
Thompson, Mrs.; Portland, Maine, 1858 ***9196.15*** *p47*
Thompson, Mrs.; Quebec, 1856 ***9196.15*** *p10*
Thompson, Mrs.; Quebec, 1857 ***9196.15*** *p15*
Thompson, Mrs.; Quebec, 1858 ***9196.15*** *p39*
Thompson, Mrs. 53; Ontario, 1861 ***2896.26*** *p25*
Thompson, Mrs. 55; Ontario, 1871 ***1823.15*** *p262*
Thompson, Abner 41; Ontario, 1871 ***1823.15*** *p262*
Thompson, Adam; Pennsylvania, 1777 ***4629.10*** *p10*
Thompson, Alexander; New York, 1807 ***8197.10*** *p327*
Thompson, Alexander 40; Ontario, 1871 ***1823.22*** *p158*
Thompson, Alexander 43; Ontario, 1871 ***1823.15*** *p262*
Thompson, Alexander 45; Ontario, 1871 ***1823.15*** *p262*
Thompson, Alexander 70; Ontario, 1871 ***1823.28*** *p99*
Thompson, Alice 21; Ontario, 1861 ***2896.25*** *p64*
Thompson, Allice *SEE* Thompson, Peter
Thompson, Andrew; Pennsylvania, 1779 ***4629.10*** *p41*
Thompson, Andrew 40; Nova Scotia, 1774 ***1220.25*** *p136*
Wife: Mary 32
Son: William 9
Thompson, Andrew 40; Ontario, 1871 ***1823.28*** *p99*
Thompson, Ann; Maryland, 1667 ***2524.55*** *p218*
Thompson, Ann; Maryland, 1674 ***2524.55*** *p218*
Thompson, Ann 22; Ontario, 1871 ***1823.15*** *p262*
Thompson, Ann 62; Ontario, 1871 ***1823.15*** *p262*
Thompson, Anna; Charleston, South Carolina, 1841 ***1224.3*** *p78*
Thompson, Anna M. 14; Ontario, 1861 ***2896.27*** *p20*
Thompson, Anne *SEE* Thompson, Barnard
Thompson, Anne; Maryland, 1665 ***2524.55*** *p219*
Thompson, Anthony; Maryland, 1672 ***2524.55*** *p218*
Thompson, Anthony 20; Fort Cumberland, Nova Scotia, 1774 ***1220.25*** *p16*
Thompson, Archd 49; Ontario, 1871 ***1823.28*** *p99*
Thompson, Archibald; Alabama, 1805-1845 ***1640.10*** *p204*
Thompson, Archibald; New York, 1806 ***8197.10*** *p322*
Thompson, Arthur; Maryland, 1665 ***2524.55*** *p219*
Thompson, Arthur 40; Ontario, 1871 ***1823.22*** *p158*
Thompson, Mrs. B. 25; Ontario, 1861 ***2896.26*** *p26*
Thompson, Barnard; Virginia, 1667 ***2524.55*** *p218*
Wife: Joyce
Child: Eliz.
Child: Anne
Thompson, Benjamin 27; Virginia, 1774 ***1220.25*** *p45*
Thompson, Betsy; Quebec, 1858 ***9196.15*** *p35*
Thompson, Catherine; Vermont, 1851-1900 ***5900.10*** *p423*
Thompson, Catherine 37; Ontario, 1871 ***1823.22*** *p158*
Thompson, Charles G. 17; Ontario, 1861 ***2896.27*** *p20*
Thompson, Charles S.; Pennsylvania, 1867 ***6058.10*** *p57*
Thompson, Christopher; Virginia, 1687 ***1224.1*** *p57*
Thompson, Clare; Maryland, 1667 ***2524.55*** *p218*
Thompson, Cornelius 25; Maryland, 1774 ***1220.25*** *p77*
Thompson, D.; Quebec, 1857 ***9196.15*** *p22*
Thompson, David; Pennsylvania, 1777 ***4629.10*** *p8*
Thompson, David; Virginia, 1679 ***1224.1*** *p57*
Thompson, David 24; Ontario, 1871 ***1823.22*** *p158*
Thompson, David 65; Ontario, 1871 ***1823.22*** *p158*
Thompson, David A. 20; Ontario, 1861 ***2896.27*** *p20*
Thompson, Edward; New York, 1903 ***8197.10*** *p15*
Thompson, Edward 31; Maryland, 1774 ***1220.25*** *p61*
Thompson, Edward 43; Ontario, 1871 ***1823.28*** *p99*
Thompson, Eliz. *SEE* Thompson, Barnard
Thompson, Elizabeth; Maryland, 1674 ***2524.55*** *p218*
Thompson, Elizabeth; Vermont, 1832-1901 ***5900.10*** *p168*
Thompson, Elizabeth 60; Ontario, 1871 ***1823.15*** *p262*
Thompson, Elizabeth 66; Ontario, 1861 ***2896.25*** *p60*
Thompson, Elizabeth 80; Ontario, 1871 ***1823.15*** *p262*
Thompson, Elizabeth 85; Ontario, 1871 ***1823.22*** *p158*
Thompson, Emaly 2; Ontario, 1861 ***2896.26*** *p26*
Thompson, Emily 12; Ontario, 1861 ***2896.25*** *p64*
Thompson, Emma 21; Ontario, 1861 ***2896.27*** *p20*
Thompson, Emma J. 5; Ontario, 1861 ***2896.27*** *p20*
Thompson, Miss F.; Quebec, 1858 ***9196.15*** *p45*
Thompson, Felix 36; Ontario, 1871 ***1823.15*** *p262*
Thompson, Flora 39; Ontario, 1871 ***1823.15*** *p262*
Thompson, Frances *SEE* Thompson, James
Thompson, Francis; New York, 1802 ***8197.10*** *p25*
Thompson, G. 45; Alaska, 1916 ***9196.1*** *p7*
Thompson, G. 45; Yukon, 1916 ***9196.1*** *p7*
Thompson, Geo; Quebec, 1856 ***9196.15*** *p6*
Thompson, George *SEE* Thompson, Peter
Thompson, George; Maryland, 1659 ***2524.55*** *p218*
Thompson, George; Maryland, 1661 ***2524.55*** *p218*
Thompson, George; New York, 1811 ***8197.10*** *p287*
Thompson, George; New York, 1840 ***8197.10*** *p386*
Thompson, George; New York, New York, 1841 ***1224.3*** *p78*
Thompson, George; Pennsylvania, 1779 ***4629.10*** *p37*
Thompson, George 1; Ontario, 1861 ***2896.25*** *p64*
Thompson, George 47; Ontario, 1871 ***1823.22*** *p158*
Thompson, George 50; Ontario, 1871 ***1823.28*** *p99*
Thompson, George 62; Ontario, 1871 ***1823.22*** *p158*
Thompson, George 65; Ontario, 1871 ***1823.28*** *p99*
Thompson, George 70; Ontario, 1871 ***1823.15*** *p262*
Thompson, George 75; Ontario, 1871 ***1823.15*** *p262*
Thompson, Georgie E.; Vermont, 1866-1944 ***5900.10*** *p455*
Thompson, Hannah 19; Maryland, 1775 ***1220.25*** *p109*
Thompson, Hannah 69; Ontario, 1871 ***1823.15*** *p262*
Thompson, Harriet 31; Ontario, 1871 ***1823.15*** *p262*
Thompson, Henry; Boston, 1686 ***1224.1*** *p57*
Thompson, Henry; Maryland, 1672 ***2524.55*** *p218*
Thompson, Henry; New York, 1813 ***8197.10*** *p58*
Thompson, Henry; New York, 1837 ***8197.10*** *p105*
Thompson, Henry 22; Ontario, 1871 ***1823.28*** *p99*
Thompson, Hester 16; Ontario, 1861 ***2896.25*** *p34*
Thompson, Honor; Maryland, 1681 ***2524.55*** *p218*
Thompson, Isaac; Connecticut, 1765 ***1224.2*** *p115*
Thompson, Isaac; Havana, 1765 ***1224.2*** *p115*
Thompson, Isaac; Portland, Maine, 1858 ***9196.15*** *p47*
Thompson, J.; Quebec, 1857 ***9196.15*** *p15*
Thompson, J.; Quebec, 1857 ***9196.15*** *p23*
Thompson, J.; Quebec, 1858 ***9196.15*** *p35*
Thompson, J.; Quebec, 1858 ***9196.15*** *p39*
Thompson, J. 26; Alaska, 1912 ***9196.1*** *p39*
Thompson, J. 26; Yukon, 1912 ***9196.1*** *p39*
Thompson, J. S.; Quebec, 1858 ***9196.15*** *p35*
Thompson, James; Maine, 1862 ***6058.10*** *p58*
Thompson, James; Maryland, 1656 ***2524.55*** *p218*
Wife: Jane
Daughter: Frances
Thompson, James; Maryland, 1665 ***2524.55*** *p219*
Thompson, James; New York, 1830 ***8197.10*** *p360*
Thompson, James; New York, 1837 ***8197.10*** *p104*
Thompson, James; New York, 1839 ***8197.10*** *p381*
Thompson, James; Pennsylvania, 1777 ***4629.10*** *p19*
Thompson, James; Vermont, 1854-1932 ***5900.10*** *p43*
Thompson, James 25; New York, 1774 ***1220.25*** *p49*
Thompson, James 25; Ontario, 1871 ***1823.15*** *p262*
Thompson, James 28; Ontario, 1871 ***1823.15*** *p262*
Thompson, James 30; Maryland, 1775 ***1220.25*** *p116*
Thompson, James 30; Ontario, 1871 ***1823.15*** *p262*
Thompson, James 32; New York, 1774 ***1220.25*** *p4*
With wife & 4 children
Thompson, James 37; Ontario, 1871 ***1823.22*** *p158*
Thompson, James 38; Philadelphia, 1774 ***1220.25*** *p69*
Thompson, James 40; Ontario, 1871 ***1823.15*** *p262*
Thompson, James 45; Ontario, 1871 ***1823.15*** *p262*
Thompson, James 50; Ontario, 1871 ***1823.15*** *p262*
Thompson, James 50; Ontario, 1871 ***1823.28*** *p99*
Thompson, James 60; Ontario, 1871 ***1823.15*** *p262*
Thompson, James 76; Ontario, 1871 ***1823.22*** *p158*
Thompson, Jane *SEE* Thompson, James
Thompson, Jane *SEE* Thompson, Peter
Thompson, Jane 24; Ontario, 1871 ***1823.15*** *p262*
Thompson, Janet; Quebec, 1858 ***9196.15*** *p35*
Thompson, Jeane; Maryland, 1669 ***2524.55*** *p45*
Thompson, Jennitt 59; Ontario, 1871 ***1823.15*** *p262*
Thompson, Jeremiah; New York, 1807 ***8197.10*** *p51*
Thompson, Jno.; Pennsylvania, 1785 ***4629.10*** *p44*
Thompson, John; Boston, 1751 ***1224.2*** *p115*
Thompson, John; Georgia, 1734 ***1640.10*** *p204*
Thompson, John; Maryland, 1681 ***2524.55*** *p219*
Thompson, John; New York, 1794 ***8197.10*** *p1*
Thompson, John; New York, 1840 ***8197.10*** *p200*
Thompson, John; New York, New York, 1850 ***6058.10*** *p34*
Thompson, John; Pennsylvania, 1777 ***4629.10*** *p7*
Thompson, John; Pennsylvania, 1777 ***4629.10*** *p9*
Thompson, John; Pennsylvania, 1786 ***4629.10*** *p49*
Thompson, John; Pennsylvania, 1808 ***6058.10*** *p2*
Thompson, John; Virginia, 1699 ***1224.1*** *p57*
Thompson, John 5; Ontario, 1861 ***2896.26*** *p26*
Thompson, John 17; Jamaica, 1774 ***1220.25*** *p86*
Thompson, John 21; Maryland, 1774 ***1220.25*** *p64*
Thompson, John 22; Maryland, 1774 ***1220.25*** *p61*
Thompson, John 32; Fort Cumberland, Nova Scotia, 1774 ***1220.25*** *p18*
Thompson, John 32; Maryland, 1774 ***1220.25*** *p57*
Thompson, John 33; Ontario, 1871 ***1823.28*** *p99*
Thompson, John 35; Ontario, 1871 ***1823.15*** *p262*
Thompson, John 38; Ontario, 1871 ***1823.28*** *p99*
Thompson, John 39; Ontario, 1871 ***1823.28*** *p99*
Thompson, John 42; Ontario, 1871 ***1823.28*** *p99*
Thompson, John 45; Ontario, 1871 ***1823.15*** *p262*
Thompson, John 47; Ontario, 1871 ***1823.22*** *p158*
Thompson, John 48; Ontario, 1871 ***1823.15*** *p262*
Thompson, John 49; Ontario, 1871 ***1823.28*** *p99*
Thompson, John 50; Ontario, 1871 ***1823.15*** *p262*
Thompson, John 54; Ontario, 1871 ***1823.22*** *p158*
Thompson, John 57; Ontario, 1861 ***2896.27*** *p20*
Thompson, John 68; Ontario, 1871 ***1823.28*** *p99*
Thompson, Joseph; Florida, 1781 ***1224.2*** *p115*
Thompson, Joseph; Maryland, 1668 ***2524.55*** *p19*
Thompson, Joseph; New York, 1840 ***8197.10*** *p385*
Thompson, Joseph 11; Ontario, 1861 ***2896.25*** *p64*
Thompson, Joseph 26; Fort Cumberland, Nova Scotia, 1774 ***1220.25*** *p18*
Thompson, Joseph 30; Virginia, 1774 ***1220.25*** *p93*
Thompson, Joseph 55; Ontario, 1871 ***1823.22*** *p158*
Thompson, Joyce *SEE* Thompson, Barnard
Thompson, Lamt R. 23; Ontario, 1871 ***1823.28*** *p99*
Thompson, Lawrence 25; Maryland, 1774 ***1220.25*** *p39*
Thompson, Margaret 20; Ontario, 1871 ***1823.15*** *p262*
Thompson, Margaret 63; Ontario, 1871 ***1823.15*** *p262*
Thompson, Margaret Cullinan; Vermont, 1851-1906 ***5900.10*** *p43*
Thompson, Margret 42; Ontario, 1871 ***1823.15*** *p262*
Thompson, Marinus 19; Ontario, 1861 ***2896.26*** *p25*
Thompson, Martha J. 24; Ontario, 1861 ***2896.27*** *p20*
Thompson, Mary *SEE* Thompson, Peter
Thompson, Mary *SEE* Thompson, Walter
Thompson, Mary; Pennsylvania, 1777 ***4629.10*** *p20*
Thompson, Mary 24; Maryland, 1775 ***1220.25*** *p97*
Thompson, Mary 26; Maryland, 1774 ***1220.25*** *p84*
Thompson, Mary 32 *SEE* Thompson, Andrew
Thompson, Mary 55; Ontario, 1871 ***1823.15*** *p262*
Thompson, Mary 55; Ontario, 1871 ***1823.28*** *p99*
Thompson, Mary 75; Vermont, 1868 ***5900.10*** *p262*
Thompson, Mary O'Halloran; Vermont, 1826-1907 ***5900.10*** *p423*
Thompson, Mathew 24; Ontario, 1871 ***1823.22*** *p158*
Thompson, Melvin 13; Ontario, 1861 ***2896.26*** *p25*
Thompson, Michael; New York, 1839 ***8197.10*** *p289*
Thompson, Nellie E. Ryan; Vermont, 1869-1916 ***5900.10*** *p552*
Thompson, Nelson 9; Ontario, 1861 ***2896.25*** *p64*
Thompson, Peter; Alabama, 1838-1845 ***1640.10*** *p204*
Wife: Mary
Daughter: Mary
Thompson, Peter; New York, 1827 ***8197.10*** *p340*
Thompson, Peter; Pennsylvania, 1777 ***4629.10*** *p22*
Thompson, Peter; Virginia, 1667 ***2524.55*** *p219*
Wife: Jane
Child: Allice
Child: George
Thompson, Peter; Virginia, 1671-1672 ***6212.30*** *p47*
Thompson, Peter 54; Ontario, 1871 ***1823.22*** *p158*
Thompson, R.; Quebec, 1858 ***9196.15*** *p35*
Thompson, Mrs. R.; Quebec, 1858 ***9196.15*** *p35*
Thompson, Ralph; New York, 1828 ***8197.10*** *p288*
Thompson, Richard; Maryland, 1636 ***2524.55*** *p219*
With wife & child
Thompson, Richard; Maryland, 1681 ***2524.55*** *p219*
Thompson, Richard; Pennsylvania, 1786 ***4629.10*** *p55*

Thompson, Richard 15; Philadelphia, 1774 ***1220.25*** *p67*
Thompson, Richard 22; Maryland, 1774 ***1220.25*** *p39*
Thompson, Richard 25; Fort Cumberland, Nova Scotia, 1774 ***1220.25*** *p19*
Thompson, Richard 30; Nova Scotia, 1774 ***1220.25*** *p14*
Thompson, Richard 34; Philadelphia, 1775 ***1220.25*** *p122*
Thompson, Richard 50; Ontario, 1871 ***1823.15*** *p263*
Thompson, Robert; New York, 1803 ***8197.10*** *p15*
Thompson, Robert; New York, 1821 ***8197.10*** *p287*
Thompson, Robert 2; Ontario, 1861 ***2896.25*** *p4*
Thompson, Robert 18; Ontario, 1861 ***2896.25*** *p64*
Thompson, Robert 23; Ontario, 1871 ***1823.15*** *p263*
Thompson, Robert 24; Ontario, 1871 ***1823.15*** *p263*
Thompson, Robert 25; Ontario, 1871 ***1823.28*** *p99*
Thompson, Robert 40; Ontario, 1871 ***1823.15*** *p263*
Thompson, Robert 50; Ontario, 1871 ***1823.15*** *p263*
Thompson, Robert 60; Ontario, 1871 ***1823.15*** *p263*
Thompson, Robert 73; Ontario, 1871 ***1823.22*** *p158*
Thompson, Rolph 38; Ontario, 1871 ***1823.15*** *p263*
Thompson, Samuel; New London, Connecticut, 1765 ***1224.2*** *p115*
Thompson, Samuel; New York, 1821 ***8197.10*** *p287*
Thompson, Sarah; Quebec, 1858 ***9196.15*** *p39*
Thompson, Sarah 4; Ontario, 1861 ***2896.25*** *p4*
Thompson, Sarah 20; Ontario, 1861 ***2896.26*** *p19*
Thompson, Sarah 35; Ontario, 1861 ***2896.25*** *p4*
Thompson, Sarah 65; Ontario, 1871 ***1823.28*** *p99*
Thompson, Theodore 56; Ontario, 1871 ***1823.22*** *p158*
Thompson, Thomas; Carolina, 1706 ***1224.2*** *p115*
Thompson, Thomas; Georgia, 1775 ***1640.10*** *p204*
Thompson, Thomas; New York, 1837 ***8197.10*** *p374*
Thompson, Thomas; Pennsylvania, 1777 ***4629.10*** *p22*
Thompson, Thomas 15; Philadelphia, 1775 ***1220.25*** *p107*
Thompson, Thomas 23; Maryland, 1775 ***1220.25*** *p111*
Thompson, Thomas 29; Georgia, 1775 ***1220.25*** *p126*
Thompson, Thomas 51; Ontario, 1861 ***2896.25*** *p64*
Thompson, Thomas 53; Ontario, 1871 ***1823.15*** *p263*
Thompson, Thomas H. 58; Ontario, 1871 ***1823.15*** *p263*
Thompson, Thomas M.; New York, 1826 ***8197.10*** *p334*
Thompson, Thos B. 53; Ontario, 1861 ***2896.25*** *p4*
Thompson, Truman 45; Ontario, 1871 ***1823.22*** *p158*
Thompson, W. P.; Quebec, 1858 ***9196.15*** *p34*
Thompson, Walter; Alabama, 1821-1845 ***1640.10*** *p205*
Wife: Mary
Thompson, William; Maryland, 1658 ***2524.55*** *p219*
Thompson, William; Maryland, 1673 ***2524.55*** *p219*
Thompson, William; Maryland, 1674 ***2524.55*** *p219*
Thompson, William; Maryland, 1681 ***2524.55*** *p219*
Thompson, William; New England, 1775-1781 ***4628.40*** *p68*
Thompson, William; New York, 1803 ***8197.10*** *p15*
Thompson, William; New York, 1834 ***8197.10*** *p371*
Thompson, William; New York, 1854 ***1224.3*** *p78*
Thompson, William; Vermont, 1853-1942 ***5900.10*** *p552*
Thompson, William 9 *SEE* Thompson, Andrew
Thompson, William 21; Virginia, 1774 ***1220.25*** *p90*
Thompson, William 30; Virginia, 1774 ***1220.25*** *p74*
Thompson, William 34; Ontario, 1871 ***1823.15*** *p263*
Thompson, William 39; Ontario, 1871 ***1823.15*** *p263*
Thompson, William 40; Ontario, 1871 ***1823.15*** *p263*
Thompson, William 46; Ontario, 1871 ***1823.15*** *p263*
Thompson, William 47; Ontario, 1871 ***1823.15*** *p263*
Thompson, William 60; Ontario, 1871 ***1823.15*** *p263*
Thompson, William 65; Ontario, 1871 ***1823.15*** *p263*
Thompson, William A.; New York, 1839 ***8197.10*** *p137*
Thompson, William Dick; Ontario, 1895 ***1640.13*** *p124*
Thompson, William H.; New York, 1820-1834 ***8197.10*** *p310*
Thompson, William Stallard 60; Ontario, 1871 ***1823.28*** *p99*
Thompson, Wm 42; Ontario, 1871 ***1823.28*** *p99*
Thompson, Wm 52; Ontario, 1871 ***1823.22*** *p158*
Thompson, Xpher.; Virginia, 1671 ***6212.30*** *p42*
Thompson, Zachary; Barbados, 1676 ***2524.55*** *p219*
Thompson, Zachary; Maryland, 1676 ***2524.55*** *p219*
Thoms, Christian; New York, 1820 ***8197.10*** *p287*
Thoms, Christopher 50; Ontario, 1871 ***1823.15*** *p263*
Thomson, Mr.; Quebec, 1857 ***9196.15*** *p19*
Thomson, Mrs.; Quebec, 1857 ***9196.15*** *p19*
Thomson, Agnes; Jamaica, 1850 ***1640.13*** *p124*
Thomson, Alesander 36; Ontario, 1871 ***1823.15*** *p263*
Thomson, Alexander; Charles Town, South Carolina, 1783 ***1224.2*** *p115*
Thomson, Alexander; Jamaica, 1783 ***1224.2*** *p115*
Thomson, Alexander; New York, 1798 ***1224.2*** *p115*
Thomson, Alexander; New York, 1807 ***8197.10*** *p51*
Thomson, Alexander; New York, 1838 ***8197.10*** *p151*
Thomson, Alexander; Savannah, Georgia, 1770 ***1640.10*** *p203*
Thomson, Alexander 32; Ontario, 1871 ***1823.28*** *p99*
Thomson, Andrew; Florida, 1841 ***1640.10*** *p204*
Thomson, Andrew; Georgia, 1698 ***1640.13*** *p124*
Thomson, Andrew; New York, 1803 ***8197.10*** *p287*
Thomson, Andrew; Virginia, 1724 ***1224.2*** *p115*
Thomson, Andrew; Virginia, 1727 ***1640.13*** *p124*
Thomson, Andrew 30; Ontario, 1871 ***1823.15*** *p263*
Thomson, Ann; New Jersey, 1801 ***1224.3*** *p78*
Thomson, Daniel; Georgia, 1740 ***1640.10*** *p204*
Thomson, David; Georgia, 1698 ***1640.13*** *p124*
Thomson, David; New York, 1829 ***8197.10*** *p352*
Thomson, David; Virginia, 1749 ***1224.2*** *p115*
Thomson, Dugald; Jamaica, 1823 ***1640.13*** *p124*
Thomson, Eleazr; Virginia, 1673 ***6212.30*** *p51*
Thomson, Emily Ida; Michigan, 1882 ***1640.13*** *p124*
Thomson, George; Georgia, 1734 ***1640.10*** *p204*
Thomson, George; Savannah, Georgia, 1768 ***1640.10*** *p204*
Thomson, George; Virginia, 1674-1675 ***6212.30*** *p53*
Thomson, George 35; Ontario, 1871 ***1823.28*** *p99*
Thomson, George 41; Ontario, 1871 ***1823.22*** *p158*
Thomson, George 63; Ontario, 1871 ***1823.15*** *p263*
Thomson, George H. 57; Ontario, 1871 ***1823.22*** *p158*
Thomson, Gilbert 53; Ontario, 1871 ***1823.15*** *p263*
Thomson, Henry; Georgia, 1698 ***1640.13*** *p124*
Thomson, Henry Lawson; New York, 1880 ***1640.13*** *p124*
Thomson, J. E.; Quebec, 1857 ***9196.15*** *p27*
Thomson, James; Carolina, 1738 ***1224.2*** *p115*
Thomson, James; Georgia, 1698 ***1640.13*** *p124*
Thomson, James; Georgia, 1699 ***1640.13*** *p124*
Thomson, James; Georgia, 1807 ***1640.10*** *p204*
Thomson, James; Jamaica, 1829 ***1640.13*** *p125*
Thomson, James; Kansas, 1884 ***1640.13*** *p125*
Thomson, James; Quebec, 1889 ***1640.13*** *p125*
Thomson, James 50; Ontario, 1871 ***1823.15*** *p263*
Thomson, Jean; Illinois, 1853 ***1640.13*** *p125*
Thomson, Jessie; Chicago, 1893 ***1640.13*** *p125*
Thomson, Job; Connecticut, 1764 ***1224.2*** *p115*
Thomson, John; Alabama, 1811-1845 ***1640.10*** *p204*
Thomson, John; Canada, 1830 ***1640.13*** *p125*
Thomson, John; Illinois, 1884 ***1640.13*** *p125*
Thomson, John; New York, 1808 ***8197.10*** *p54*
Thomson, John; New York, 1832 ***8197.10*** *p288*
Thomson, John; New York, 1840 ***8197.10*** *p200*
Thomson, John 37; Ontario, 1871 ***1823.28*** *p99*
Thomson, John 73; Ontario, 1871 ***1823.22*** *p158*
Thomson, John W.; New York, 1839 ***8197.10*** *p289*
Thomson, M. 50; Ontario, 1861 ***2896.28*** *p12*
Thomson, Maria; Washington, District of Columbia, 1889 ***1640.13*** *p125*
Thomson, Marion; St. Kitts, 1818 ***1640.13*** *p125*
Thomson, Mary; Chicago, 1896 ***1640.13*** *p125*
Thomson, Mich'll.; Maryland, 1677 ***2524.55*** *p219*
Thomson, Nancy 67; Ontario, 1871 ***1823.22*** *p158*
Thomson, Owen; Maryland, 1672 ***2524.55*** *p219*
Thomson, Patrick; Bahamas, 1720 ***1640.13*** *p125*
Thomson, Ralph; New York, 1804 ***8197.10*** *p28*
Thomson, Richard; New York, 1816 ***8197.10*** *p60*
Thomson, Robert; New York, 1802 ***8197.10*** *p25*
Thomson, Robert 40; Ontario, 1871 ***1823.15*** *p263*
Thomson, Robert 50; Ontario, 1871 ***1823.15*** *p263*
Thomson, Robert 75; Ontario, 1871 ***1823.22*** *p158*
Thomson, Rodger; Virginia, 1671-1672 ***6212.30*** *p47*
Thomson, Samuel; Virginia, 1694 ***1224.1*** *p58*
Thomson, Thomas; Louisiana, 1824-1845 ***1640.10*** *p204*
Thomson, Thomas 18; Virginia, 1774 ***1220.25*** *p87*
Thomson, Thomas 38; New York, 1774 ***1220.25*** *p25*
Thomson, Walter; Georgia, 1699 ***1640.13*** *p125*
Thomson, William; Connecticut, 1764 ***1224.2*** *p115*
Thomson, William; Georgia, 1699 ***1640.13*** *p125*
Thomson, William; Havana, 1764 ***1224.2*** *p115*
Thomson, William; Kingston, Jamaica, 1783 ***1640.13*** *p125*
Thomson, William; New York, 1830 ***8197.10*** *p288*
Thomson, William; New York, 1839 ***8197.10*** *p289*
Thomson, William 42; Nova Scotia, 1774 ***1220.25*** *p136*
Thomson, William Conn; New York, 1867 ***1640.13*** *p126*
Thomson, William S.; New York, 1839 ***8197.10*** *p137*
Thomson, Wm; Portland, Maine, 1858 ***9196.15*** *p29*
Thon, Jacob 48; Ontario, 1871 ***1823.15*** *p263*
Thonges, Nickel; America, 1764 ***2856.30*** *p458*
Thooft, Bernardus; New York, 1822 ***8197.10*** *p62*
Thorblane, Ja; Virginia, 1665 ***6212.30*** *p22*
Thorburn, Andrew; Detroit, 1849 ***1640.13*** *p126*
Thorburn, John; New York, 1807 ***8197.10*** *p51*
Thorch, Laurance; Virginia, 1665-1666 ***6212.30*** *p21*
Thore, Jos; Virginia, 1688 ***6212.30*** *p57*
Thoresby, John 26; Philadelphia, 1774 ***1220.25*** *p43*
Thorey, Tho; Virginia, 1664 ***6212.30*** *p13*
Thorn, Alex 50; British Columbia, 1914 ***9196.1*** *p24*
Thorn, Alex 50; Oregon, 1914 ***9196.1*** *p24*
Thorn, Alice 5; Ontario, 1861 ***2896.28*** *p46*
Thorn, Catherine 6; Ontario, 1861 ***2896.28*** *p44*
Thorn, Elizabeth; Albany, New York, 1820 ***1224.3*** *p78*
Thorn, G. C. 45; Ontario, 1871 ***1823.22*** *p158*
Thorn, Isaac J.; New York, 1840 ***8197.10*** *p200*
Thorn, James 21; Ontario, 1861 ***2896.28*** *p2*
Thorn, M. E.; Ontario, 1861 ***2896.28*** *p2*
Thorn, Margaret; Ontario, 1861 ***2896.28*** *p44*
Thorn, Marshall 10; Ontario, 1861 ***2896.28*** *p44*
Thorn, Mary 3; Ontario, 1861 ***2896.28*** *p44*
Thorn, Merium 59; Ontario, 1861 ***2896.28*** *p44*
Thorn, Nancy M. 20; Ontario, 1861 ***2896.27*** *p44*
Thorn, Priscilla 38; Ontario, 1861 ***2896.28*** *p44*
Thorn, Richard; New York, 1840 ***8197.10*** *p200*
Thorn, Samuel 18; Ontario, 1861 ***2896.28*** *p59*
Thorn, Sarah F. 18; Ontario, 1861 ***2896.28*** *p44*
Thorn, Seth 1; Ontario, 1861 ***2896.28*** *p44*
Thorn, Sophiah 19; Ontario, 1861 ***2896.28*** *p44*
Thorn, Theresa 25; Ontario, 1861 ***2896.28*** *p46*
Thornber, John 35; Virginia, 1773 ***1220.25*** *p29*
Thornborrow, George; New Jersey, 1897 ***1640.13*** *p126*
Thornbury, Ann; Virginia, 1703 ***6212.30*** *p62*
Thornbush, Jno; Virginia, 1664 ***6212.30*** *p7*
Thorndale, Anthony 25; Maryland, 1774 ***1220.25*** *p70*
Thorndike, Alice; New England, 1672 ***1224.1*** *p58*
Thorndike, Martha; New England, 1672 ***1224.1*** *p58*
Thorndon, Mary; Maryland, 1659 ***2524.55*** *p201*
Thorne, Chas; Quebec, 1856 ***9196.15*** *p10*
Thorne, Ellen Morris; Vermont, 1833-1910 ***5900.10*** *p493*
Thorne, Henry; Virginia, 1664 ***6212.30*** *p13*
Thorne, John; Vermont, 1857-1946 ***5900.10*** *p355*
Thorne, John T. 40; Ontario, 1871 ***1823.22*** *p158*
Thorne, Joseph; Virginia, 1668-1669 ***6212.30*** *p40*
Thorne, Mary; Vermont, 1862-1943 ***5900.10*** *p355*
Thorne, Moses; Maryland, 1675 ***2524.55*** *p219*
Thorne, Parley; Maryland, 1680 ***2524.55*** *p219*
Thorne, Ralph; Maryland, 1674 ***2524.55*** *p219*
Thorne, Stephen 70; Ontario, 1871 ***1823.22*** *p159*
Thorne, Thomas; Vermont, 1836-1890 ***5900.10*** *p493*
Thorne, Thomas; Virginia, 1703-1704 ***6212.30*** *p62*
Thorne, Willm.; Maryland, 1663 ***2524.55*** *p219*
Wife: Winifred
Thorne, Winifred *SEE* Thorne, Willm.
Thornhill, Hen; Virginia, 1665-1666 ***6212.30*** *p23*
Thornhill, John; Pennsylvania, 1779 ***4629.10*** *p36*
Thornhill, Joseph; Pennsylvania, 1777 ***4629.10*** *p22*
Thornton, Miss; Quebec, 1856 ***9196.15*** *p6*
Thornton, Miss; Quebec, 1858 ***9196.15*** *p37*
Thornton, Mr.; Quebec, 1857 ***9196.15*** *p17*
Thornton, Mrs.; Quebec, 1857 ***9196.15*** *p17*
Thornton, Andrew; Vermont, 1855-1929 ***5900.10*** *p578*
Thornton, Benjamin; Pennsylvania, 1779 ***4629.10*** *p36*
Thornton, Bessie B.; Vermont, 1884-1950 ***5900.10*** *p578*
Thornton, Bridget Holleran; Vermont, 1859-1943 ***5900.10*** *p578*
Thornton, David 38; Ontario, 1871 ***1823.28*** *p99*
Thornton, Edward R.; Vermont, 1858-1926 ***5900.10*** *p578*
Thornton, George; Buffalo, New York, 1843 ***1224.3*** *p78*
Thornton, John 30; Philadelphia, 1774 ***1220.25*** *p86*
Thornton, John 48; Ontario, 1871 ***1823.15*** *p263*
Thornton, Matthew; New Hampshire, n.d. ***4628.40*** *p49*
Thornton, Moses 57; Ontario, 1871 ***1823.22*** *p159*
Thornton, Patrick; New York, 1821 ***8197.10*** *p287*
Thornton, Richard 35; Ontario, 1871 ***1823.28*** *p99*
Thornton, Robert; New York, 1839 ***1224.3*** *p79*
Thornton, William 47; Ontario, 1871 ***1823.15*** *p263*
Thorogood, Mary; Virginia, 1754 ***1224.2*** *p128*
Thoroughgood, Ann; Maryland, 1664 ***2524.55*** *p219*
Thoroughgood, Frances *SEE* Thoroughgood, Thomas
Thoroughgood, Thomas; Maryland, 1665 ***2524.55*** *p219*
Wife: Frances
Thorowgood, Frances; Maryland, 1664 ***2524.55*** *p219*
Husband: Thomas
Thorowgood, Joseph; Carolina, 1685 ***1224.1*** *p58*
Thorowgood, Thomas *SEE* Thorowgood, Frances
Thorp, Annie L. McGee; Vermont, n.d. ***5900.10*** *p451*
Thorp, George 30; Ontario, 1871 ***1823.15*** *p263*
Thorp, Henry 42; Ontario, 1871 ***1823.15*** *p263*
Thorp, William; Virginia, 1665 ***6212.30*** *p20*
Thorp, Zephaniah; New York, 1838 ***8197.10*** *p150*
Thorpe, Catherine; America, 1695 ***1224.1*** *p58*
Thorpe, Sarah; Charles Town, South Carolina, 1737 ***1224.2*** *p115*
Thorpe, Thomas; Virginia, 1724 ***1224.2*** *p115*
Thorpe, William; Nevada, 1848 ***1224.3*** *p79*
Thorreither, Jakob; Port uncertain, 1771 ***2856.30*** *p457*
Thors, Georg; Port uncertain, 1784 ***2856.30*** *p457*
Thors, Georg; Port uncertain, 1785 ***2856.30*** *p457*
Thorsbey, Bridgett; Maryland, 1639 ***2524.55*** *p219*
Thorton, William; Pennsylvania, 1777 ***4629.10*** *p20*
Thoser, Johann Michael; America, 1742 ***2856.30*** *p457*
Thourson, Alexander; Maryland, 1659 ***2524.55*** *p219*
Thouvenin, John C.; New York, 1830 ***8197.10*** *p362*
Thowrson, Andrew; Maryland, 1659 ***2524.55*** *p219*
Thracey, John 21; Ontario, 1861 ***2896.28*** *p35*
Thraley, John 58; Ontario, 1871 ***1823.28*** *p100*
Thrasher, Mary; New England, 1680 ***1224.1*** *p58*

Thrdior, William 37; Ontario, 1871 ***1823.15*** *p263*
Threadgold, Sarah 20; Norfolk, Virginia, 1774 ***1220.25*** *p20*
Thretfull, Stephen; Maryland, 1660 ***2524.55*** *p219*
Thrichy, Elizabeth; Virginia, 1681 ***6212.30*** *p56*
Thrift, Joan; Virginia, 1678 ***6212.30*** *p54*
Thrift, William; Maryland, 1663 ***2524.55*** *p219*
Throckmorton, John; Virginia, 1670 ***1224.1*** *p45*
Throckmorton, Richard Samuel; New York, New York, 1851 ***1224.3*** *p79*
Throop, Bennett 35; Ontario, 1871 ***1823.22*** *p159*
Throop, Sarah 37; Ontario, 1871 ***1823.22*** *p159*
Throughgood, Frances *SEE* Throughgood, Thomas
Throughgood, Thomas; Maryland, 1665 ***2524.55*** *p219*
Wife: Frances
Thrower, Samuel 27; Ontario, 1871 ***1823.15*** *p263*
Thud, John 67; Ontario, 1871 ***1823.22*** *p159*
Thuell, Samuel 42; Ontario, 1871 ***1823.15*** *p263*
Thuerson, Albert 3; Ontario, 1861 ***2896.25*** *p2*
Thuerson, Anna 1; Ontario, 1861 ***2896.25*** *p2*
Thuerson, Anna 8; Ontario, 1861 ***2896.25*** *p1*
Thuerson, George 7; Ontario, 1861 ***2896.25*** *p1*
Thuerson, Mary A. 28; Ontario, 1861 ***2896.25*** *p1*
Thum, Augush 46; Ontario, 1871 ***1823.15*** *p264*
Thum, George; Pennsylvania, 1777 ***4629.10*** *p14*
Thumbell, Samuell; Maryland, 1680 ***2524.55*** *p219*
Thunell, Elizabeth; Rhode Island, 1765 ***1224.2*** *p115*
Thunell, William; Havana, 1765 ***1224.2*** *p115*
Thure, William 41; Ontario, 1871 ***1823.28*** *p100*
Thurison, Adelia 3; Ontario, 1861 ***2896.28*** *p39*
Thurison, Frances A. 13; Ontario, 1861 ***2896.28*** *p31*
Thurison, Francis 1; Ontario, 1861 ***2896.28*** *p39*
Thurison, James 9; Ontario, 1861 ***2896.28*** *p31*
Thurison, John R. P. 11; Ontario, 1861 ***2896.28*** *p31*
Thurison, Mary A. 33; Ontario, 1861 ***2896.28*** *p31*
Thurkettle, Eliza; Virginia, 1666 ***6212.30*** *p25*
Thurkey, John; New York, 1807 ***8197.10*** *p50*
Thurland, Edw; Virginia, 1664 ***6212.30*** *p7*
Thurlow, John 40; Ontario, 1871 ***1823.15*** *p264*
Thurman, Susanna; New York, New York, 1760 ***1224.2*** *p115*
Thurmur, John; Maryland, 1669 ***1224.1*** *p58*
Thurn, Barbara; Vermont, 1855-1914 ***5900.10*** *p356*
Thurn, Ethelonia; Vermont, 1848-1925 ***5900.10*** *p355*
Thurow, Charles 35; Ontario, 1871 ***1823.28*** *p100*
Thurry, Jno; Virginia, 1673 ***6212.30*** *p51*
Thursby, William 28; Nova Scotia, 1774 ***1220.25*** *p15*
Thurston, David; Pennsylvania, 1777 ***4629.10*** *p18*
Thurston, Joshua; New York, 1830 ***8197.10*** *p288*
Thurston, Joshua; New York, 1834 ***8197.10*** *p69*
Thurston, Peter; New York, 1803 ***8197.10*** *p15*
Thurston, Robert; Died enroute, 1678 ***1224.1*** *p58*
Thurston, Samll; Virginia, 1671-1672 ***6212.30*** *p48*
Thurtell, Mr.; Quebec, 1858 ***9196.15*** *p36*
Thurtell, Mrs.; Quebec, 1858 ***9196.15*** *p35*
Thurtell, Mrs.; Quebec, 1858 ***9196.15*** *p36*
Thurticle, Edmund; Maryland, 1659 ***2524.55*** *p219*
Thuy, Konrad; America, 1740 ***2856.30*** *p458*
With wife & 5 children
Thuy, Konrad; America, 1740 ***2856.30*** *p458*
With wife & children
Thwaites, Jane; Salt Lake City, 1895 ***1640.13*** *p126*
Thwaits, Richard 63; Ontario, 1871 ***1823.15*** *p264*
Thwid, Wojciech; Maryland, 1910 ***3259.35*** *p63*
Thy, John 70; Vermont, 1888 ***5900.10*** *p203*
Thymothy, Mabella; Maryland, 1682 ***2524.55*** *p220*
Thymothy, William; Maryland, 1682 ***2524.55*** *p220*
Thynne, John 55; Ontario, 1871 ***1823.15*** *p264*
Thyri, Georg; Port uncertain, 1764 ***2856.30*** *p458*
Tibbert, Mary; Vermont, 1863-1924 ***5900.10*** *p117*
Tibbett, William 38; Ontario, 1871 ***1823.28*** *p100*
Tibbin, William; Maryland, 1665 ***2524.55*** *p114*
Tibbotts, Catheryn *SEE* Tibbotts, Clement
Tibbotts, Clement; Maryland, 1654 ***2524.55*** *p219*
Wife: Catheryn
Daughter: Catheryn
Tibbs, William 56; Ontario, 1871 ***1823.22*** *p159*
Tibbutt, Christopher 28; Ontario, 1871 ***1823.15*** *p264*
Tibbutt, Fredrick 33; Ontario, 1871 ***1823.15*** *p264*
Tibbutt, Wallgate 40; Ontario, 1871 ***1823.15*** *p264*
Tibells, Thomas; Maryland, 1675 ***2524.55*** *p219*
Tiberson, Jane 21; Philadelphia, 1774 ***1220.25*** *p82*
Tibley, Jacob; Pennsylvania, 1786 ***4629.10*** *p54*
Tibout, Andrew; Pennsylvania, 1777 ***4629.10*** *p25*
Tice, Adalaide 7; Ontario, 1861 ***2896.25*** *p58*
Tice, Alzina 5; Ontario, 1861 ***2896.25*** *p63*
Tice, Anne; New England, 1649 ***1224.1*** *p58*
Tice, E. P. 9; Ontario, 1861 ***2896.25*** *p37*
Tice, Electa Ann 10; Ontario, 1861 ***2896.25*** *p58*
Tice, Elizabeth 18; Ontario, 1861 ***2896.25*** *p62*
Tice, Elizabeth 44; Ontario, 1861 ***2896.25*** *p58*
Tice, George 13; Ontario, 1861 ***2896.25*** *p58*
Tice, George 14; Ontario, 1861 ***2896.25*** *p62*
Tice, J. C. 28; Alaska, 1913 ***9196.1*** *p23*
Tice, J. C. 28; British Columbia, 1913 ***9196.1*** *p23*
Tice, James 19; Ontario, 1861 ***2896.25*** *p62*
Tice, Jesse 4; Ontario, 1861 ***2896.25*** *p58*
Tice, John 24; Maryland, 1774 ***1220.25*** *p64*
Tice, John 90; Ontario, 1871 ***1823.22*** *p159*
Tice, Olive 37; Ontario, 1861 ***2896.25*** *p62*
Tice, P. J. 5; Ontario, 1861 ***2896.25*** *p37*
Tice, Randle 22; Ontario, 1861 ***2896.25*** *p71*
Tice, Ranille 22; Ontario, 1861 ***2896.25*** *p58*
Tice, Sarah 13; Ontario, 1861 ***2896.25*** *p62*
Tice, Sarah 33; Ontario, 1861 ***2896.25*** *p37*
Tice, Susannah; Cincinnati, 1826 ***1224.3*** *p79*
Tice, T. 21; Ontario, 1861 ***2896.25*** *p63*
Tice, William 18; Ontario, 1861 ***2896.25*** *p58*
Tice, William H. 18; Ontario, 1861 ***2896.25*** *p6*
Ticeley, Mr.; Quebec, 1857 ***9196.15*** *p17*
Tichbborne, Mary; Maryland, 1654 ***2524.55*** *p219*
Tichcombe, William; Maryland, 1668 ***2524.55*** *p219*
Tichenor, Henry; New York, 1838 ***8197.10*** *p151*
Tichoruts, Joseph; Maryland, 1910 ***3259.35*** *p63*
Tickamore, John; Maryland, 1661 ***2524.55*** *p219*
Ticker, Philip 42; Philadelphia, 1774 ***1220.25*** *p68*
Tickerell, Thomas; Maryland, 1669 ***2524.55*** *p220*
Tickewell, Thomas; Maryland, 1669 ***2524.55*** *p45*
Tickford, Alfred 44; Ontario, 1871 ***1823.15*** *p264*
Tickner, Isaac 24; Virginia, 1774 ***1220.25*** *p55*
Tickner, William; New York, 1838 ***8197.10*** *p151*
Tidd, Thomas; Maryland, 1668 ***2524.55*** *p220*
Tidd, William 21; Maryland, 1775 ***1220.25*** *p101*
Tide, Andrew; Maryland, 1659 ***2524.55*** *p220*
Tidell, Sarah; Maryland, 1650 ***2524.55*** *p220*
Tider, Robert; Virginia, 1666 ***6212.30*** *p31*
Tidestry, Amelia 40; Ontario, 1871 ***1823.22*** *p159*
Tidy, David 52; Ontario, 1871 ***1823.15*** *p264*
Tie, Frank 58; Vermont, 1915 ***5900.10*** *p252*
Tie, Parmilie 31; Vermont, 1889 ***5900.10*** *p252*
Tiebant, Ann 21; Philadelphia, 1774 ***1220.25*** *p42*
Tiebant, Peter 30; Philadelphia, 1774 ***1220.25*** *p42*
Tiebendorf, Johann; America, 1727 ***2856.30*** *p458*
Tiedemann, Frederick 45; Ontario, 1871 ***1823.15*** *p264*
Tief, William; New York, 1837 ***8197.10*** *p105*
Tiefenbach, Jacob; Port uncertain, 1771 ***2856.30*** *p458*
With wife
Tieffenbach, Caspar; America, 1749 ***2856.30*** *p458*
With wife & 4 children
Tieffenbach, Caspar; America, 1750 ***2856.30*** *p458*
With wife & 3 children
Tielmann, Johann; Port uncertain, 1792 ***2856.30*** *p458*
Tieman, William 35; Ontario, 1871 ***1823.15*** *p264*
Tiemann, Anthon; New York, 1807 ***8197.10*** *p51*
Tienkiewicz, John; Maryland, 1910 ***3259.35*** *p63*
Tier, Packer; Quebec, 1857 ***9196.15*** *p25*
Tiernan, Ann 65; Vermont, 1886 ***5900.10*** *p451*
Tiernan, Annie; Vermont, 1860-1925 ***5900.10*** *p447*
Tiernan, Catherine A.; Vermont, 1857-1935 ***5900.10*** *p442*
Tiernan, Elizabeth; Vermont, 1864-1933 ***5900.10*** *p398*
Tiernan, John; Vermont, 1848-1914 ***5900.10*** *p546*
Tiernan, Julia; Vermont, 1827-1901 ***5900.10*** *p546*
Tiernan, Julius William; New York, 1819 ***8197.10*** *p287*
Tiernan, Katherine; Vermont, 1853-1940 ***5900.10*** *p398*
Tiernan, Lawrence; Vermont, 1807-1884 ***5900.10*** *p546*
Tiernan, Margaret Hickey; Vermont, 1852-1925 ***5900.10*** *p546*
Tiernan, Michael G.; Vermont, 1856-1928 ***5900.10*** *p442*
Tiernay, Mary A.; Vermont, 1849-1911 ***5900.10*** *p382*
Tierney, Annie T. Moriarty; Vermont, 1867-1920 ***5900.10*** *p552*
Tierney, Bridget; Vermont, 1861-1873 ***5900.10*** *p506*
Tierney, Bridget 63; Vermont, 1875 ***5900.10*** *p328*
Tierney, Bridget Gleason; Vermont, 1854-1923 ***5900.10*** *p506*
Tierney, Bridget O'Marrah; Vermont, 1821-1891 ***5900.10*** *p506*
Tierney, Christopher 45; Ontario, 1871 ***1823.28*** *p100*
Tierney, Edward; Vermont, 1861-1875 ***5900.10*** *p506*
Tierney, Ellen 49; Vermont, 1889 ***5900.10*** *p226*
Tierney, James; Vermont, 1830-1896 ***5900.10*** *p311*
Tierney, James; Vermont, 1852-1924 ***5900.10*** *p141*
Tierney, James 38; Vermont, 1855 ***5900.10*** *p359*
Tierney, John; Vermont, 1832-1896 ***5900.10*** *p238*
Tierney, John 34; Ontario, 1871 ***1823.28*** *p100*
Tierney, Joseph; Vermont, 1833-1885 ***5900.10*** *p475*
Tierney, Kate 71; Vermont, 1898 ***5900.10*** *p290*
Tierney, Katherine Leonard; Vermont, 1861-1902 ***5900.10*** *p505*
Tierney, Katie Agnes; Vermont, 1880-1883 ***5900.10*** *p506*
Tierney, Maggie; Vermont, n.d. ***5900.10*** *p304*
Tierney, Margaret 83; Vermont, 1904 ***5900.10*** *p328*
Tierney, Margaret Howrigan; Vermont, 1837-1929 ***5900.10*** *p238*
Tierney, Martha 72; Vermont, 1920 ***5900.10*** *p402*
Tierney, Martin; Vermont, 1844-1902 ***5900.10*** *p552*
Tierney, Mary; Vermont, 1842-1907 ***5900.10*** *p47*
Tierney, Mary 57; Vermont, 1872 ***5900.10*** *p475*
Tierney, Mary 67; Vermont, 1871 ***5900.10*** *p238*
Tierney, Mary A. Andrews; Vermont, 1853-1925 ***5900.10*** *p475*
Tierney, Mary Farley; Vermont, 1830-1893 ***5900.10*** *p311*
Tierney, Mary Ward; Vermont, 1836-1894 ***5900.10*** *p421*
Tierney, Matilda Lavalley; Vermont, 1861-1938 ***5900.10*** *p141*
Tierney, Michael; Vermont, 1826-1892 ***5900.10*** *p421*
Tierney, Michael J.; Vermont, 1858-1928 ***5900.10*** *p505*
Tierney, Patrick; Vermont, 1814-1878 ***5900.10*** *p506*
Tierney, Patrick 70; Vermont, 1867 ***5900.10*** *p238*
Tierney, Terrence 45; Ontario, 1871 ***1823.22*** *p159*
Tierney, Thomas E.; Vermont, 1856-1908 ***5900.10*** *p552*
Tierney, Thomas J.; Vermont, 1854-1925 ***5900.10*** *p506*
Tierney, Thomas M.; Vermont, 1843-1890 ***5900.10*** *p475*
Tierney, Thomas Raymond; Vermont, 1892-1893 ***5900.10*** *p506*
Ties, John; Maryland, 1910 ***3259.35*** *p63*
Tiffanan, Patrick; New York, 1826 ***8197.10*** *p288*
Tiffany, Sarah; Vermont, 1817-1893 ***5900.10*** *p475*
Tiffin, John 40; Ontario, 1871 ***1823.15*** *p264*
Tiffin, Joseph 76; Ontario, 1871 ***1823.15*** *p264*
Tigh, Elizabeth 19; Ontario, 1871 ***1823.15*** *p264*
Tighe, Darby; Vermont, 1833-1908 ***5900.10*** *p565*
Tighe, Darby 75; Vermont, 1908 ***5900.10*** *p565*
Tighe, Edward 30; Ontario, 1871 ***1823.15*** *p264*
Tighe, Edward 60; Ontario, 1871 ***1823.15*** *p264*
Tighe, Ellen; Vermont, 1800-1875 ***5900.10*** *p565*
Tighe, Katherine; Vermont, 1864-1955 ***5900.10*** *p422*
Tighe, Margaret McGowan; Vermont, 1836-1903 ***5900.10*** *p565*
Tighe, Mary 45; Ontario, 1871 ***1823.22*** *p159*
Tighe, Michael; Vermont, 1851-1870 ***5900.10*** *p565*
Tighe, Patrick; Vermont, 1831-1914 ***5900.10*** *p565*
Tiley, Christian; Pennsylvania, 1777 ***4629.10*** *p20*
Tilford, William; New York, 1802 ***8197.10*** *p25*
Tilgerin, Gottfried Paul; Port uncertain, 1748 ***2856.30*** *p458*
With child
Tilgerin, Gottfried Paul; Port uncertain, 1749 ***2856.30*** *p458*
With child
Tilghman, James; Pennsylvania, 1777 ***4629.10*** *p24*
Tilghman, Mary *SEE* Tilghman, Richard
Tilghman, Richard; Maryland, 1659 ***2524.55*** *p220*
Tilghman, Richard; Maryland, 1663 ***2524.55*** *p220*
Wife: Mary
Child: Mary
Child: William
Tilghman, Richd.; Maryland, 1657 ***2524.55*** *p220*
Tilghman, Samll.; Maryland, 1657 ***2524.55*** *p220*
Tilghman, Samuel; Maryland, 1659 ***2524.55*** *p220*
Tilghman, William *SEE* Tilghman, Richard
Tilian, Gian; Philadelphia, 1786 ***4629.10*** *p61*
Tiller, John 39; Ontario, 1871 ***1823.15*** *p264*
Tiller, William 53; Ontario, 1871 ***1823.15*** *p264*
Tilley, Isabel Harris; New England, 1700 ***1224.2*** *p52*
Tilley, James; Havana, 1765 ***1224.2*** *p115*
Tilley, James; Rhode Island, 1765 ***1224.2*** *p115*
Tilley, John; New York, 1832 ***8197.10*** *p368*
Tilley, Linius 35; Ontario, 1871 ***1823.22*** *p159*
Tilley, William; Newport, Rhode Island, 1765 ***1224.2*** *p115*
Tilley, William 21; Virginia, 1774 ***1220.25*** *p89*
Tillghman, Richard; Maryland, 1659 ***2524.55*** *p220*
Tillich, Heinrich; America, 1785 ***2856.30*** *p458*
Tillison, Roda A. 20; Ontario, 1861 ***2896.27*** *p67*
Tillitson, Daniel 55; Ontario, 1871 ***1823.22*** *p159*
Tillor, George 51; Ontario, 1871 ***1823.22*** *p159*
Tillotson, John 3; Ontario, 1861 ***2896.25*** *p61*
Tillotson, Mary 73; Ontario, 1861 ***2896.25*** *p61*
Tillotson, Susan 30; Ontario, 1861 ***2896.25*** *p61*
Tillwood, William 17; Maryland, 1775 ***1220.25*** *p103*
Tilly, Samuel; New York, 1839 ***8197.10*** *p137*
Tilman, Peter; New York, 1840 ***8197.10*** *p199*
Tilney, Ann; Maryland, 1656 ***2524.55*** *p220*
Tilor, Robert; Maryland, 1664 ***2524.55*** *p220*
Tilsley, Thomas; Maryland, 1664 ***2524.55*** *p220*
Tilson, John; Boston, 1757 ***1224.2*** *p115*
Tilston, Mr.; Quebec, 1858 ***9196.15*** *p32*
Tilston, Mrs.; Quebec, 1858 ***9196.15*** *p32*
Tilton, William; Pennsylvania, 1777 ***4629.10*** *p30*
Timbers, Catharine 55; Vermont, 1809-1899 ***5900.10*** *p382*
Timbers, Mary; Vermont, 1824-1856 ***5900.10*** *p547*
Timberton, Anthony; Maryland, 1670 ***2524.55*** *p220*
Timbiewicz, Frank; Maryland, 1910 ***3259.35*** *p63*

Timins, Elizabeth; Alabama, 1825-1843 ***1640.10*** *p205*
Husband: P. H.
Timins, P. H. *SEE* Timins, Elizabeth
Timins, Peter; Maryland, 1682 ***2524.55*** *p220*
Timlin, Edward; New York, 1839 ***8197.10*** *p289*
Timlin, Fanny 25; Ontario, 1871 ***1823.22*** *p159*
Timlin, James 38; Ontario, 1871 ***1823.22*** *p159*
Timlin, James 60; Ontario, 1871 ***1823.22*** *p159*
Timlin, John 51; Ontario, 1871 ***1823.22*** *p159*
Timlin, Michael 67; Ontario, 1871 ***1823.22*** *p159*
Timlin, Thomas 25; Ontario, 1871 ***1823.22*** *p159*
Timlin, Thomas 50; Ontario, 1871 ***1823.22*** *p159*
Timmins, Patrick; New York, 1826 ***8197.10*** *p288*
Timmins, Sarah 21; Maryland, 1774 ***1220.25*** *p78*
Timmoney, James; New York, 1826 ***8197.10*** *p288*
Timmons, Ann; Vermont, 1830-1901 ***5900.10*** *p328*
Timmons, John; Vermont, n.d. ***5900.10*** *p83*
Timmons, Marty; Vermont, n.d. ***5900.10*** *p83*
Timony, Daniel; New York, 1837 ***8197.10*** *p104*
Timothy, Mabella; Maryland, 1682 ***2524.55*** *p220*
Timothy, William; Maryland, 1682 ***2524.55*** *p220*
Tims, Richard; New York, 1837-1840 ***8197.10*** *p302*
Tims, William; Maryland, 1666 ***2524.55*** *p220*
Timson, William; Virginia, 1736 ***1224.2*** *p116*
Tindall, Mr.; Quebec, 1857 ***9196.15*** *p16*
Tindall, Mrs.; Quebec, 1857 ***9196.15*** *p16*
Tindall, Allisica 67; Ontario, 1871 ***1823.15*** *p264*
Tindall, Ann; Pennsylvania, 1839 ***1224.3*** *p79*
Tindall, George 26; Ontario, 1871 ***1823.15*** *p264*
Tindall, William 42; Ontario, 1871 ***1823.15*** *p264*
Tine, John; Virginia, 1684-1685 ***6212.30*** *p57*
Tine, John; Virginia, 1703-1704 ***6212.30*** *p62*
Tinehant, Joseph; New York, 1807 ***8197.10*** *p51*
Tinel, Matilda 14; Ontario, 1861 ***2896.28*** *p27*
Tiney, William 34; Ontario, 1871 ***1823.15*** *p264*
Tinga, Caroline 55; Ontario, 1871 ***1823.28*** *p100*
Tingey, August 21; Ontario, 1871 ***1823.28*** *p100*
Tingle, John; Maryland, 1673 ***2524.55*** *p220*
Tingle, William 15; Philadelphia, 1775 ***1220.25*** *p10*
Tingman, John; Mobile, Alabama, 1811-1845 ***1640.10*** *p205*
Tinkle, A. 45; Ontario, 1871 ***1823.15*** *p264*
Tinklebaugh, Hariet 17; Ontario, 1861 ***2896.28*** *p60*
Tinklepaugh, Anetta 19; Ontario, 1861 ***2896.28*** *p60*
Tinklepaugh, Henry 7; Ontario, 1861 ***2896.28*** *p61*
Tinklepaugh, Henry 46; Ontario, 1861 ***2896.28*** *p60*
Tinklepaugh, Jane 15; Ontario, 1861 ***2896.28*** *p60*
Tinklepaugh, John 3; Ontario, 1861 ***2896.28*** *p61*
Tinklepaugh, Malcolm 5; Ontario, 1861 ***2896.28*** *p61*
Tinklepaugh, Mary 42; Ontario, 1861 ***2896.28*** *p60*
Tinklepaugh, Osker 13; Ontario, 1861 ***2896.28*** *p60*
Tinklepaugh, Thadeus 12; Ontario, 1861 ***2896.28*** *p60*
Tinley, John; Georgia, 1746 ***1640.10*** *p205*
Tinney, Mr.; Quebec, 1857 ***9196.15*** *p20*
Tinney, Mrs.; Quebec, 1857 ***9196.15*** *p20*
Tinney, Catharine; Vermont, 1830-1896 ***5900.10*** *p311*
Tinney, Henry 56; Ontario, 1871 ***1823.22*** *p159*
Tinney, John 28; Ontario, 1871 ***1823.22*** *p159*
Tinney, John 46; Ontario, 1871 ***1823.22*** *p159*
Tinney, John 48; Ontario, 1871 ***1823.22*** *p159*
Tinney, Joseph 57; Ontario, 1871 ***1823.22*** *p159*
Tinney, Richard 18; Ontario, 1871 ***1823.22*** *p159*
Tinney, William 27; Ontario, 1871 ***1823.22*** *p159*
Tinney, William 37; Ontario, 1871 ***1823.22*** *p159*
Tinny, A. 49; Ontario, 1861 ***2896.28*** *p12*
Tinny, William 48; Ontario, 1861 ***2896.28*** *p12*
Tinsdale, Robert 15; Ontario, 1861 ***2896.25*** *p25*
Tinsley, Seth; Maryland, 1657 ***2524.55*** *p220*
Tiplen, Thomas; Pennsylvania, 1786 ***4629.10*** *p54*
Tipper, Mr.; Quebec, 1857 ***9196.15*** *p17*
Tippet, Charles 22; Ontario, 1871 ***1823.15*** *p264*
Tippet, Harry 14; Ontario, 1871 ***1823.15*** *p264*
Tippet, Mary Ann 20; Ontario, 1871 ***1823.15*** *p264*
Tippin, Francis; Virginia, 1664 ***6212.30*** *p12*
Tipping, Elizabeth; Maryland, 1672 ***2524.55*** *p220*
Tipple, James; Maryland, 1660 ***2524.55*** *p220*
Tippling, Thomas 27; Ontario, 1871 ***1823.15*** *p264*
Tirell, John; Virginia, 1666-1667 ***6212.30*** *p34*
Tireman, William; Buffalo, New York, 1842 ***6058.10*** *p29*
Tirnes, George; Pennsylvania, 1778 ***4629.10*** *p34*
Tirolff, Josef; Port uncertain, 1757 ***2856.30*** *p458*
Tirrey, Daniel; New York, 1839 ***8197.10*** *p382*
Tirrey, Elizabeth; Maryland, 1680 ***2524.55*** *p220*
Tirrey, John; New York, 1839 ***8197.10*** *p382*
Tisbery, Thomas; Maryland, 1652-1659 ***2524.55*** *p220*
Tischbein, Elisabeth; Port uncertain, 1729 ***2856.30*** *p458*
Tischbeinin, Elisabeth; Port uncertain, 1729 ***2856.30*** *p458*
Tischler, Bernhard; Port uncertain, 1738 ***2856.30*** *p458*
Tisdale, George 32; Ontario, 1871 ***1823.15*** *p264*
Tisdale, James; Boston, 1796 ***1224.3*** *p79*
Tisdale, James 38; Ontario, 1871 ***1823.15*** *p264*
Tisdale, James 70; Ontario, 1871 ***1823.15*** *p264*
Tisdall, Fitzgerald; New York, 1838 ***8197.10*** *p151*
Tisdell, George 76; Ontario, 1871 ***1823.22*** *p159*
Tiskolski, James; Maryland, 1910 ***3259.35*** *p63*
Titchner, John 62; Ontario, 1871 ***1823.28*** *p100*
Titcomb, Thomas 25; Maryland, 1774 ***1220.25*** *p84*
Titford, Charles 30; Ontario, 1871 ***1823.22*** *p159*
Titien, Benjamin; New York, 1840 ***8197.10*** *p200*
Titmarsh, John; Maryland, 1655-1656 ***2524.55*** *p220*
Titmash, Jane *SEE* Titmash, John
Titmash, John; Maryland, 1662 ***2524.55*** *p220*
Wife: Jane
Titmatch, John; Maryland, 1653-1658 ***2524.55*** *p220*
Titon, Peter; Maryland, 1665 ***2524.55*** *p114*
Tittel, David 34; Kansas, 1888-1910 ***9079.10*** *p23*
Tittel, Fred 63; Kansas, 1889-1910 ***9079.10*** *p25*
Tittel, Frederick 38; Kansas, 1889-1910 ***9079.10*** *p25*
Tittel, Jacob 33; Kansas, 1889-1910 ***9079.10*** *p25*
Tittel, Malla 33; Kansas, 1889-1910 ***9079.10*** *p25*
Tittel, Margerett 63; Kansas, 1889-1910 ***9079.10*** *p25*
Tittel, Mary 28; Kansas, 1905-1910 ***9079.10*** *p25*
Tittermann, Charles Edward; New York, 1836 ***8197.10*** *p288*
Tittermary, John; Pennsylvania, 1777 ***4629.10*** *p26*
Tittermary, Richard; Pennsylvania, 1779 ***4629.10*** *p40*
Tittermerry, Richard; Pennsylvania, 1777 ***4629.10*** *p27*
Titus, Almeda 9; Ontario, 1861 ***2896.28*** *p43*
Titus, Caleb 13; Ontario, 1861 ***2896.28*** *p43*
Titus, Deborah 2; Ontario, 1861 ***2896.28*** *p43*
Titus, James B.; Vermont, 1846-1916 ***5900.10*** *p447*
Titus, Jane Eliza 21; Ontario, 1861 ***2896.28*** *p24*
Titus, Mary 11; Ontario, 1861 ***2896.28*** *p43*
Titus, Mary Wynne; Vermont, 1846-1913 ***5900.10*** *p447*
Titus, Sarah 31; Ontario, 1861 ***2896.28*** *p43*
Titus, Sarah A. 3; Ontario, 1861 ***2896.28*** *p24*
Tivanan, Bridget; Vermont, 1796-1880 ***5900.10*** *p45*
Tivisman, Francis; Virginia, 1664 ***6212.30*** *p13*
Tizard, John; Virginia, 1663 ***6212.30*** *p4*
Tizard, John; Virginia, 1668-1669 ***6212.30*** *p40*
Tler, Stephen; Pennsylvania, 1777 ***4629.10*** *p15*
Tlewes, William 40; Ontario, 1871 ***1823.15*** *p264*
Tobe, Anna Maria; Port uncertain, 1756 ***2856.30*** *p458*
Toben, Cornelius 70; Ontario, 1871 ***1823.22*** *p159*
Tober, Rachel; New England, 1705 ***1224.2*** *p66*
Tobias, Henry; New York, 1847 ***1224.3*** *p79*
Tobias, Tobias J.; New York, 1830 ***8197.10*** *p362*
Tobin, Mrs.; St. John, New Brunswick, 1857 ***9196.15*** *p12*
Tobin, Alice Carver; Vermont, 1835-1885 ***5900.10*** *p549*
Tobin, Ann; Vermont, 1844-1880 ***5900.10*** *p133*
Tobin, B. 13; Ontario, 1861 ***2896.28*** *p5*
Tobin, B. 50; Ontario, 1861 ***2896.28*** *p5*
Tobin, Bridget Terry; Vermont, 1828-1914 ***5900.10*** *p412*
Tobin, C. 15; Ontario, 1861 ***2896.28*** *p5*
Tobin, Christopher C.; Vermont, 1847-1915 ***5900.10*** *p556*
Tobin, E. 57; Ontario, 1861 ***2896.28*** *p5*
Tobin, Ellen 65; Vermont, 1861 ***5900.10*** *p73*
Tobin, Emma Jane 18; Vermont, 1857 ***5900.10*** *p556*
Tobin, J. 11; Ontario, 1861 ***2896.28*** *p5*
Tobin, James 32; Ontario, 1871 ***1823.15*** *p264*
Tobin, James 72; Vermont, 1896 ***5900.10*** *p411*
Tobin, Jane M. Mann; Vermont, 1856-1905 ***5900.10*** *p556*
Tobin, Joanna; Vermont, 1829-1912 ***5900.10*** *p491*
Tobin, John; New York, 1830-1840 ***8197.10*** *p200*
Tobin, John; Vermont, 1838-1922 ***5900.10*** *p412*
Tobin, Joseph 55; Ontario, 1871 ***1823.28*** *p100*
Tobin, M. 5; Ontario, 1861 ***2896.28*** *p5*
Tobin, M. 16; Ontario, 1861 ***2896.28*** *p5*
Tobin, M. 17; Ontario, 1861 ***2896.28*** *p17*
Tobin, M. 19; Ontario, 1861 ***2896.28*** *p5*
Tobin, Margaret Whalen; Vermont, 1839-1909 ***5900.10*** *p552*
Tobin, Martin 41; Vermont, 1894 ***5900.10*** *p229*
Tobin, Mary; Vermont, 1835-1921 ***5900.10*** *p520*
Tobin, Mary 60; Vermont, 1889 ***5900.10*** *p411*
Tobin, Mary A. O'Flanegan 88; Vermont, 1914 ***5900.10*** *p517*
Tobin, Mary Upton; Vermont, 1806-1878 ***5900.10*** *p556*
Tobin, Michael 18; New York, 1775 ***1220.25*** *p94*
Tobin, Patrick; Canada, 1756-1760 ***4628.40*** *p45*
Tobin, Patrick; New York, 1840 ***8197.10*** *p289*
Tobin, Patrick; Vermont, 1798-1873 ***5900.10*** *p556*
Tobin, Patrick; Vermont, 1833-1908 ***5900.10*** *p552*
Tobin, Richard; Maryland, 1659 ***2524.55*** *p220*
Tobin, Richard; New York, 1828 ***8197.10*** *p288*
Tobin, Sarah J. Chase; Vermont, 1852-1936 ***5900.10*** *p517*
Tobin, Theabold M.; Vermont, 1847-1918 ***5900.10*** *p517*
Tobin, William 50; Ontario, 1871 ***1823.22*** *p159*
Tobin, William 70; Vermont, 1889 ***5900.10*** *p517*
Tocher, Alexander; Colorado, 1896 ***1640.13*** *p126*
Tocher, Miss E.; Quebec, 1857 ***9196.15*** *p19*
Tod, Alexander; Maryland, 1666 ***2524.55*** *p220*
Tod, Alexander; Mississippi, 1813-1849 ***1640.10*** *p205*
Tod, Alexander; Pennsylvania, 1777 ***4629.10*** *p22*
Tod, Alexander; Pennsylvania, 1779 ***4629.10*** *p39*
Tod, Elizabeth; Maryland, 1665 ***2524.55*** *p61*
Tod, James; New York, 1839 ***8197.10*** *p137*
Tod, Lindsay; Florida, 1820 ***1640.10*** *p205*
Tod, Matthew; St. Louis, 1869 ***1640.13*** *p126*
Tod, Robert; Maryland, 1665 ***2524.55*** *p61*
Tod, William Robert; New York, 1889 ***1640.13*** *p126*
Todd, Alexander; New Orleans, 1819-1845 ***1640.10*** *p205*
Todd, Andrew; Georgia, 1734 ***1640.10*** *p205*
Todd, Ann *SEE* Todd, Thomas
Todd, Ann; Vermont, 1817-1894 ***5900.10*** *p454*
Todd, Catherine McKelvey; Vermont, 1845-1919 ***5900.10*** *p510*
Todd, Christophr; Virginia, 1674-1675 ***6212.30*** *p53*
Todd, Cornelius; Maryland, 1654 ***2524.55*** *p220*
Todd, Ellen; Vermont, 1835-1914 ***5900.10*** *p511*
Todd, Frances *SEE* Todd, Thomas
Todd, Francis; Maryland, 1658 ***2524.55*** *p221*
Todd, George 16; America, 1774 ***1220.25*** *p36*
Todd, Humphrey; Boston, 1714 ***1224.2*** *p116*
Todd, James 61; Ontario, 1871 ***1823.15*** *p264*
Todd, Johanna *SEE* Todd, Thomas
Todd, Johanna; Vermont, 1837-1890 ***5900.10*** *p581*
Todd, John *SEE* Todd, Thomas
Todd, John; Pennsylvania, 1786 ***4629.10*** *p54*
Todd, John; Vermont, 1799-1881 ***5900.10*** *p501*
Todd, John D.; Vermont, 1844-1920 ***5900.10*** *p510*
Todd, M. A. 45; Ontario, 1861 ***2896.28*** *p12*
Todd, Margaret Skelly 80; Vermont, 1884 ***5900.10*** *p501*
Todd, Mary Ann 84; Vermont, 1866 ***5900.10*** *p456*
Todd, Rachael 19; New York, 1774 ***1220.25*** *p20*
Todd, Richard 21; South Carolina, 1775 ***1220.25*** *p142*
Todd, Richard J.; New York, 1834 ***8197.10*** *p69*
Todd, Robert *SEE* Todd, Thomas
Todd, Samuel; Jamaica, 1755 ***1224.2*** *p116*
Todd, Samuel; New Hampshire, 1755 ***1224.2*** *p116*
Todd, Samuel; New York, 1829 ***8197.10*** *p288*
Todd, Thomas; Baltimore, 1678 ***1224.1*** *p58*
Todd, Thomas; Maryland, 1669 ***2524.55*** *p221*
Wife: Ann
Child: John
Child: Johanna
Child: Frances
Child: Ann
Child: Robert
Todd, Thomas 40; Ontario, 1871 ***1823.22*** *p160*
Todd, Walter 57; Ontario, 1871 ***1823.22*** *p160*
Todd, William; Vermont, 1759-1830 ***5900.10*** *p242*
Todhunter, Sarah Anne; Germantown, Pennsylvania, 1853 ***1224.3*** *p79*
Todman, C. 37; Ontario, 1861 ***2896.28*** *p4*
Todman, James 70; Ontario, 1861 ***2896.28*** *p43*
Todman, Jno C. 5; Ontario, 1861 ***2896.28*** *p4*
Todman, M. H. 2; Ontario, 1861 ***2896.28*** *p4*
Todvaine, Nich.; Maryland, 1675 ***2524.55*** *p221*
Toft, Ann; Virginia, 1668-1669 ***6212.30*** *p40*
Tohieff, S. 27; Alaska, 1917 ***9196.1*** *p45*
Tohieff, S. 27; Whitehorse, Yukon, 1917 ***9196.1*** *p45*
Toke, Nich; Virginia, 1665-1666 ***6212.30*** *p21*
Token, William; Maryland, 1663 ***2524.55*** *p221*
Tolburt, Richard; Maryland, 1682 ***2524.55*** *p221*
Tole, Henry; Maryland, 1671 ***2524.55*** *p221*
Tole, Roger; Maryland, 1663 ***2524.55*** *p221*
Tole, Susan 60; Ontario, 1871 ***1823.15*** *p264*
Tolfrey, Martha; New York, New York, 1842 ***1224.3*** *p79*
Tolfrey, Sarah Anne; New York, 1842 ***1224.3*** *p79*
Tolfrey, William; Toronto, 1842 ***1224.3*** *p79*
Tolle, Henry; New York, 1839 ***8197.10*** *p137*
Tolley, Margarett *SEE* Tolley, Thomas
Tolley, Thomas *SEE* Tolley, Thomas
Tolley, Thomas; Maryland, 1661 ***2524.55*** *p221*
Wife: Margarett
Son: Thomas
Tollpett, Magdalena; Port uncertain, 1756 ***2856.30*** *p465*
Tollson, William; Maryland, 1659 ***2524.55*** *p221*
Tolme, Alexander 33; New York, 1774 ***1220.25*** *p4*
Tolmie, Alexander; Georgia, 1736 ***1640.10*** *p205*
Tolmie, Colin; New York, 1804 ***8197.10*** *p28*
Tolmie, Phebe; New York, 1796 ***1224.2*** *p116*
Tolodz, John; Maryland, 1910 ***3259.35*** *p63*
Tolsman, Zeb 37; Ontario, 1871 ***1823.15*** *p264*
Tolson, John 30; Virginia, 1774 ***1220.25*** *p87*
Tolson, Rich; Virginia, 1666 ***6212.30*** *p30*
Tolson, William; Maryland, 1659 ***2524.55*** *p221*
Tom, Black; Virginia, 1668-1669 ***6212.30*** *p41*
Tom, James 50; Ontario, 1871 ***1823.15*** *p264*
Tomaliki, Thomas S.; Maryland, 1910 ***3259.35*** *p63*
Tomanson, John; Portland, Maine, 1858 ***9196.15*** *p30*
Tomas, Even John; Virginia, 1681 ***6212.30*** *p56*

Tomashewski, Theodor; Maryland, 1910 3259.35 p63
Tomaszeski, Michal; Maryland, 1910 3259.35 p63
Tomaszewski, Dominican; Maryland, 1910 3259.35 p63
Tomaszewsky, Antony; Maryland, 1910 3259.35 p63
Tomenwski, Andrew; Maryland, 1910 3259.35 p63
Tomes, Francis; New York, 1816 8197.10 p287
Tomes, James; New York, 1840 8197.10 p321
Tomey, John; New York, 1830 8197.10 p361
Tomey, Mary 42; Vermont, 1875 5900.10 p101
Tomkin, Jno; Virginia, 1665-1666 6212.30 p23
Tomkins, John 32; Philadelphia, 1774 1220.25 p67
Tomkins, Joshua; Maryland, 1680 2524.55 p221
Tomkins, Michael; Maryland, 1672 2524.55 p221
Tomkins, Rowles; Maryland, 1668 2524.55 p221
Tomkins, William; Maryland, 1672 2524.55 p221
Tomkins, William; Maryland, 1681 2524.55 p221
Tomkins, William 27; Ontario, 1871 1823.15 p264
Tomkinson, Mrs.; Maryland, 1651 2524.55 p221
Tomlin, Arthur; Virginia, 1667 6212.30 p37
Tomlin, Henry; Virginia, 1664 6212.30 p5
Tomlin, Henry; Virginia, 1666 6212.30 p26
Tomlin, John Henry 31; Ontario, 1871 1823.28 p100
Tomlin, Luke; Virginia, 1666-1667 6212.30 p34
Tomlin, Mark; Virginia, 1666 6212.30 p25
Tomlin, Thomas 54; Ontario, 1871 1823.22 p160
Tomling, James 25; Virginia, 1774 1220.25 p92
Tomlins, George; Maryland, 1664 2524.55 p221
Tomlins, George; New York, 1840 8197.10 p200
Tomlins, James; Baltimore, 1827 1224.3 p79
Tomlins, Sarah; Philadelphia, 1856 1224.3 p79
Tomlinson, Barnard; New York, 1807 8197.10 p51
Tomlinson, D.; Quebec, 1858 9196.15 p37
Tomlinson, E.; Quebec, 1858 9196.15 p36
Tomlinson, Edward; Virginia, 1743 1224.2 p116
Tomlinson, George; New York, 1831 8197.10 p288
Tomlinson, Henry; New York, 1833 8197.10 p288
Tomlinson, John; Maryland, 1658 2524.55 p221
Tomlinson, John Edge; New Bern, North Carolina, 1793 1224.2 p116
Tomlinson, Joseph Hale; New York, 1831 8197.10 p288
Tomlinson, Mary 60; Ontario, 1871 1823.28 p100
Tomlinson, Mathew; Virginia, 1667 6212.30 p36
Tomlinson, Richard 34; Maryland, 1775 1220.25 p108
Tomlinson, Roger; Virginia, 1667-1668 6212.30 p39
Tomlison, John 54; Ontario, 1871 1823.15 p264
Tomonovich, L. 28; Alaska, 1912 9196.1 p38
Tomonovich, L. 28; Whitehorse, Yukon, 1912 9196.1 p38
Tompkins, Mr.; Quebec, 1857 9196.15 p15
Tompkins, Caleb 75; Ontario, 1871 1823.22 p160
Tompkins, Daniel 11; Ontario, 1861 2896.25 p67
Tompkins, Fanny 30; Ontario, 1861 2896.25 p67
Tompkins, Joshua; Maryland, 1680 2524.55 p221
Tompkins, Myron 54; Ontario, 1871 1823.28 p100
Tompkins, Russell; Pennsylvania, 1750 1224.2 p116
Tompkins, William; Virginia, 1663-1664 6212.30 p5
Tompset, Allice 7; Ontario, 1861 2896.28 p59
Tompset, Emma J. 6; Ontario, 1861 2896.28 p59
Tompset, George 9; Ontario, 1861 2896.28 p59
Tompset, Harriet 41; Ontario, 1861 2896.28 p59
Tompset, James 41; Ontario, 1861 2896.28 p59
Tompset, James C. 11; Ontario, 1861 2896.28 p59
Tompset, Jesse 16; Ontario, 1861 2896.28 p59
Tompset, Walter 2; Ontario, 1861 2896.28 p59
Tompsett, C. 13; Ontario, 1861 2896.26 p3
Tompsett, D. 4; Ontario, 1861 2896.26 p3
Tompsett, George 41; Ontario, 1861 2896.26 p3
Tompsett, Jessie 1; Ontario, 1861 2896.26 p4
Tompsett, John 35; Ontario, 1861 2896.27 p51
Tompsett, Joseph J. 12; Ontario, 1861 2896.27 p51
Tompsett, Margaret J. 4; Ontario, 1861 2896.27 p51
Tompsett, Sarah E. 9; Ontario, 1861 2896.27 p51
Tompsett, W. 7; Ontario, 1861 2896.26 p3
Tompsett, W. 35; Ontario, 1861 2896.26 p3
Tompson, Mrs.; Maryland, 1647 2524.55 p221
Tompson, Alfred; New York, 1838 8197.10 p151
Tompson, Cristop; Virginia, 1663 6212.30 p2
Tompson, George 80; Ontario, 1861 2896.27 p11
Tompson, Jacob; Virginia, 1699 1224.1 p57
Tompson, John; Virginia, 1664 6212.30 p6
Tompson, Katherine; Virginia, 1665-1666 6212.30 p23
Tompson, Mary; Virginia, 1663 6212.30 p3
Tompson, Mary 75; Ontario, 1861 2896.27 p11
Tompson, Stephen; Virginia, 1665 6212.30 p19
Tomras, William 30; Ontario, 1871 1823.28 p100
Toms, Henry 48; Ontario, 1871 1823.22 p160
Toms, Thomas 35; Ontario, 1871 1823.22 p160
Toms, William; Virginia, 1681 1224.1 p58
Tomsey, Alexander; New York, 1840 8197.10 p387
Tomsit, Benjamin 28; Ontario, 1861 2896.27 p59
Tomsit, George 5; Ontario, 1861 2896.27 p59
Tomsit, Mary 2; Ontario, 1861 2896.27 p59
Tomsit, Roda 27; Ontario, 1861 2896.27 p59
Tone, Richard; New York, 1831 8197.10 p366
Tone, William Theobald Wolfe; New York, 1816 8197.10 p287
Tonehouse, Richard 46; Ontario, 1871 1823.15 p264
Toner, Bryan; New York, 1821 8197.10 p287
Toner, Timothy; New York, 1827 8197.10 p346
Tong, Friendship; Maryland, 1649 2524.55 p221
Tongue, Herbert; New York, 1840 8197.10 p200
Tonkins, James 37; Ontario, 1871 1823.15 p264
Tonly, Miss; Quebec, 1857 9196.15 p26
Tonnell, Tho.; Maryland, 1651 2524.55 p221
Tonnell, Thomas; Maryland, 1650 2524.55 p221
Tonney, Patrick 76; Ontario, 1871 1823.22 p160
Tonor, William 40; Ontario, 1871 1823.28 p100
Tonstall, John; Maryland, 1685 1224.1 p58
Tonte, Robert; Virginia, 1688 1224.1 p58
Toogood, Mary; Maryland, 1651 2524.55 p221
Toohey, Ann; Vermont, 1843-1907 5900.10 p420
Toohey, Anthony 70; Ontario, 1871 1823.28 p100
Toohey, Bridget; Vermont, 1846-1913 5900.10 p420
Toohey, Catharine 73; Vermont, 1908 5900.10 p267
Toohey, Eleanor Kelly; Vermont, 1842-1923 5900.10 p425
Toohey, Ellen; Vermont, 1857-1887 5900.10 p420
Toohey, James 62; Vermont, 1915 5900.10 p421
Toohey, Julia 3; Vermont, 1874 5900.10 p493
Toohey, Margaret Ryan 51; Vermont, 1877 5900.10 p421
Toohey, Maria Kennedy 66; Vermont, 1923 5900.10 p421
Toohey, Martin 60; Vermont, 1894 5900.10 p267
Toohey, Mary; Vermont, 1809-1872 5900.10 p420
Toohey, Mary; Vermont, 1828-1903 5900.10 p260
Toohey, Mary; Vermont, 1836-1921 5900.10 p219
Toohey, Mary 34; Vermont, 1899 5900.10 p425
Toohey, Mary A. 50; Vermont, 1903 5900.10 p275
Toohey, Michael; Vermont, 1940 5900.10 p275
Toohey, Michael J.; New York, 1821 8197.10 p287
Toohey, Michael J.; New York, 1827 8197.10 p345
Toohey, Patrick 75; Vermont, 1892 5900.10 p421
Toohey, Thomas; Vermont, 1811-1881 5900.10 p420
Toohey, Thomas; Vermont, 1842-1928 5900.10 p425
Took, Ann 21; Dominica, 1773-1774 1220.25 p127
Took, William 30; Ontario, 1871 1823.15 p264
Tooke, Nich; Virginia, 1664 6212.30 p14
Tooker, Edward; Virginia, 1665 6212.30 p20
Tooker, Jno; Virginia, 1664 6212.30 p15
Tookey, James 47; Ontario, 1871 1823.28 p100
Tool, Jeremiah; New York, 1828 8197.10 p288
Tool, John 22; Maryland, 1775 1220.25 p96
Tool, Martin; New York, 1831 8197.10 p288
Toole, . . .; New Hampshire, 1641-1660 4628.40 p44
Toole, Edward; New York, 1839 8197.10 p289
Toole, Elizabeth; Vermont, 1827-1905 5900.10 p80
Toole, Michael; New York, 1837 8197.10 p104
Toole, William; New York, 1837 8197.10 p104
Tooley, Edwin 40; Ontario, 1871 1823.15 p265
Tooley, John; New York, 1838 8197.10 p289
Tooley, Susannah Fry; New York, New York, 1854 1224.3 p79
Toombs, Blemi 66; Ontario, 1871 1823.15 p265
Toombs, Francis 35; Ontario, 1871 1823.15 p265
Toombs, Zophia 1; Ontario, 1871 1823.15 p265
Toomey, Bridget O'Leary; Vermont, 1842-1885 5900.10 p439
Toomey, John; Vermont, 1846-1903 5900.10 p119
Toomey, John; Vermont, 1854-1924 5900.10 p512
Toomey, Margaret T. Murphy; Vermont, 1833-1897 5900.10 p83
Toomey, Mary; Vermont, 1801-1887 5900.10 p132
Toomey, Mary A. Martin; Vermont, 1846-1916 5900.10 p119
Toomey, Mary O'Donnell; Vermont, 1841-1908 5900.10 p115
Toomey, Patrick; Vermont, 1834-1894 5900.10 p439
Toomey, Thomas; Vermont, 1824-1903 5900.10 p83
Toomy, Daniel; New York, 1835 8197.10 p288
Toomy, John 27; Baltimore, 1775 1220.25 p117
Toomy, Lawrence; Pennsylvania, 1785 4629.10 p44
Toony, John; New York, 1840 8197.10 p200
Toothacre, Edward 22; Maryland, 1775 1220.25 p113
Toozer, Judith; New England, 1666 1224.1 p54
Top, Edward; Virginia, 1665 6212.30 p19
Tope, Abraham; Maryland, 1659 2524.55 p221
Tope, Edw; Virginia, 1664 6212.30 p15
Topham, Christopher; South Carolina, 1737 1224.2 p116
Topham, J. 32; Alaska, 1918 9196.1 p55
Topham, J. 32; Yukon, 1918 9196.1 p55
Topham, John 64; Ontario, 1871 1823.15 p265
Topham, Richard 29; Nova Scotia, 1774 1220.25 p136
With wife & child
Topham, Thomas; New York, 1821 8197.10 p287
Topinard, Antoine; New York, 1839 8197.10 p289
Topkoski, Andrew; Maryland, 1910 3259.35 p63
Toply, Christopher; Maryland, 1673 2524.55 p221
Topolski, Waclaw; Maryland, 1910 3259.35 p63
Topolsky, Mary; Maryland, 1910 3259.35 p63
Topp, Mrs.; Quebec, 1858 9196.15 p42
Topp, Rev.; Quebec, 1858 9196.15 p42
Toppen, David; East New Jersey, 1754 1224.2 p113
Topping, . . .; New England, 1658 1224.1 p58
Topping, James; Portland, Maine, 1858 9196.15 p29
Topping, John 23; Philadelphia, 1774 1220.25 p81
Topping, William; New York, 1718 1224.2 p116
Torain, H. 22; Alaska, 1912 9196.1 p37
Torain, H. 22; Whitehorse, Yukon, 1912 9196.1 p37
Toral, Sarah 52; Ontario, 1871 1823.15 p265
Torbett, James 37; Ontario, 1871 1823.15 p265
Torensky, Woetczek; Maryland, 1910 3259.35 p63
Torff, Wilhelm; America, 1764 2856.30 p459
Torker, Tomasse 41; Washington, 1911 9196.1 p33
Torkington, Joseph; Virginia, 1653 1224.1 p58
Torningham, Ellinor; Maryland, 1654 2524.55 p127
Torpay, Edward; New York, 1840 8197.10 p200
Torpey, Bridget; Vermont, 1792-1882 5900.10 p465
Torpey, Margaret; Vermont, 1830-1903 5900.10 p465
Torphey, Mary 72; Vermont, 1884 5900.10 p260
Torr, Hans Georg; America, 1747 2856.30 p463
With wife
Torrance, Mr.; Quebec, 1857 9196.15 p21
Torrance, Mr.; Quebec, 1857 9196.15 p23
Torrance, Mrs.; Quebec, 1857 9196.15 p21
Torrance, Mrs.; Quebec, 1857 9196.15 p23
Torrance, James 43; Ontario, 1871 1823.15 p265
Torrance, Janet 39; Ontario, 1871 1823.15 p265
Torrance, John; New York, 1858 1640.13 p126
Torrance, John 43; Ontario, 1871 1823.15 p265
Torrance, John 55; Ontario, 1871 1823.15 p265
Torrance, John 56; Ontario, 1871 1823.15 p265
Torrans, William 38; Ontario, 1871 1823.28 p100
Torrant, James 40; Ontario, 1871 1823.15 p265
Torry, George; Mississippi, 1789-1845 1640.10 p206
Torry, Jane Haviland; New England, 1671 1224.1 p28
Tortel, Mr.; Quebec, 1858 9196.15 p45
Tory, Catherine 37; Ontario, 1861 2896.25 p70
Tory, Isaac 8; Ontario, 1861 2896.25 p70
Tory, Mary 5; Ontario, 1861 2896.25 p70
Toschenski, Alexander; Maryland, 1910 3259.35 p63
Totney, John; Maryland, 1651 2524.55 p221
Tott, Hannah 65; Ontario, 1871 1823.15 p265
Totten, Elizabeth 54; Ontario, 1871 1823.15 p265
Totten, George 57; Ontario, 1871 1823.15 p265
Tottey, Robert; Maryland, 1649 2524.55 p221
Totton, John; Pennsylvania, 1777 4629.10 p12
Touchburn, Henry 70; Ontario, 1871 1823.15 p265
Touchburn, William 73; Ontario, 1871 1823.15 p265
Touchstone, Mary; Maryland, 1682 2524.55 p221
Touchstone, Mary; Maryland, 1978 2524.55 p221
Touchstone, Richard; Maryland, 1682 2524.55 p221
Touey, Elizabeth; Maryland, 1679 2524.55 p221
Touey, Samuel; Maryland, 1679 2524.55 p221
Touffle, Leo 23; Kansas, 1910 9079.10 p44
Tough, Charles 58; Ontario, 1871 1823.15 p265
Tough, John 36; Ontario, 1871 1823.15 p265
Tough, John 60; Ontario, 1871 1823.28 p100
Touhey, Mary; Vermont, 1810-1897 5900.10 p218
Touhill, Nora 50; Vermont, 1910 5900.10 p108
Touhy, Ellen 60; Vermont, 1882 5900.10 p573
Touhy, John; Vermont, 1812-1887 5900.10 p215
Touhy, Thomas; Vermont, 1847-1877 5900.10 p215
Toulmin, Mr.; Quebec, 1857 9196.15 p22
Toulmin, Mrs.; Quebec, 1857 9196.15 p22
Toulmin, Harry; Alabama, 1825 1224.3 p79
Toulson, John; Virginia, 1656 1224.1 p59
Toumine, Lucas; New York, 1828 8197.10 p288
Toumy, John; New York, 1828 8197.10 p312
Toun, John; New York, 1839 8197.10 p137
Toupet, Nicholas F.; New York, 1834 8197.10 p69
Tourje, Philip 80; Ontario, 1871 1823.22 p160
Tourje, William 57; Ontario, 1871 1823.22 p160
Tours, Peter 44; Ontario, 1871 1823.15 p265
Tousa, Mathias; Maryland, 1633 2524.55 p221
Toussaint, Louis; New York, 1840 8197.10 p200
Toutles, Andrew; Maryland, 1663 2524.55 p221
Tovey, Nicholas; Maryland, 1675 1224.1 p59
Tovey, William; New York, 1800 1224.3 p79
Tow, John 28; Philadelphia, 1774 1220.25 p67
Toward, Henry; Georgia, 1698 1640.13 p126
Towart, Robert; New York, 1836 1640.13 p126
Towe, Jost; America, 1741 2856.30 p459
With wife & children
Towe, R. W.; Quebec, 1856 9196.15 p5
Towell, Cornelius; New York, 1710 1224.2 p116
Towell, Joseph; Nova Scotia, 1725 1224.2 p116
Towell, Mary 5; Ontario, 1871 1823.28 p100
Towell, Thomas; Maryland, 1682 2524.55 p222
Towen, Thomas; Virginia, 1671-1672 6212.30 p47

Towensend, Angus 32; Ontario, 1871 ***1823.22*** *p160*
Tower, Ann; Virgin Islands, 1843 ***1640.13*** *p126*
Tower, Benjamin; Pennsylvania, 1777 ***4629.10*** *p10*
Tower, Judith; New England, 1659 ***1224.1*** *p32*
Tower, Maria D. Banahan; Vermont, 1848-1924 ***5900.10*** *p504*
Tower, Owen N.; Vermont, 1854-1925 ***5900.10*** *p504*
Towers, Bridget O'Brien; Vermont, 1869-1925 ***5900.10*** *p255*
Towers, Dennis; Vermont, 1849 ***5900.10*** *p255*
Towers, James 49; Ontario, 1871 ***1823.15*** *p265*
Towers, Thomas A. P. 28; Ontario, 1871 ***1823.28*** *p100*
Towers, William 44; Ontario, 1871 ***1823.15*** *p265*
Towes, Michaell; Virginia, 1667 ***6212.30*** *p36*
Towhill, Deborah; Maryland, 1651 ***2524.55*** *p222*
Towhill, Maudlin; Maryland, 1651 ***2524.55*** *p222*
Towin, Anna Catharina; America, 1741 ***2856.30*** *p459*
Towl, John 45; Ontario, 1871 ***1823.15*** *p265*
Towle, George; New York, 1757 ***1224.2*** *p116*
Towle, George 46; Ontario, 1871 ***1823.15*** *p265*
Towle, Kate 80; Vermont, 1910 ***5900.10*** *p226*
Towle, Roger; Maryland, 1663 ***2524.55*** *p222*
Towler, William H.; Pennsylvania, 1868 ***6058.10*** *p73*
Towlon, Geo 30; British Columbia, 1910 ***9196.1*** *p31*
Towlon, Geo 30; Seattle, 1910 ***9196.1*** *p31*
Towmans, John; Pennsylvania, 1835 ***6058.10*** *p12*
Town, Christiana 32; Maryland, 1775 ***1220.25*** *p111*
Town, Harvey 48; Ontario, 1871 ***1823.22*** *p160*
Town, Mary E.; Vermont, 1844-1906 ***5900.10*** *p374*
Towne, John; New York, 1839 ***8197.10*** *p137*
Towne, Mary Hunt; Vermont, 1844-1931 ***5900.10*** *p285*
Townehill, Deborah; Maryland, 1651 ***2524.55*** *p222*
Townehill, Maudlin; Maryland, 1651 ***2524.55*** *p222*
Townesen, John; Maryland, 1682 ***2524.55*** *p222*
Townesend, Rebecca; Virginia, 1672 ***6212.30*** *p49*
Towney, John; Maryland, 1659 ***2524.55*** *p222*
Towney, Michael; Maryland, 1659 ***2524.55*** *p222*
Townhover, Adam; New York, 1840 ***8197.10*** *p199*
Towning, Charles 36; Ontario, 1871 ***1823.28*** *p100*
Townley, Henry 18; Maryland, 1775 ***1220.25*** *p104*
Townly, Nich; Virginia, 1665-1666 ***6212.30*** *p22*
Towns, Robert 39; Ontario, 1871 ***1823.15*** *p265*
Townsan, Luther 15; Ontario, 1861 ***2896.26*** *p18*
Townsen, Polly 19; Ontario, 1861 ***2896.26*** *p19*
Townsend, A. 51; Ontario, 1861 ***2896.28*** *p56*
Townsend, Andrew James; New York, 1840 ***8197.10*** *p289*
Townsend, Ann 17; Ontario, 1861 ***2896.28*** *p56*
Townsend, Ann 79; Ontario, 1871 ***1823.22*** *p160*
Townsend, Bety 80; Ontario, 1871 ***1823.22*** *p160*
Townsend, David 18; Ontario, 1871 ***1823.28*** *p100*
Townsend, Elijaih 24; Ontario, 1871 ***1823.15*** *p265*
Townsend, Elizabeth *SEE* Townsend, John
Townsend, Elizabeth 47 *SEE* Townsend, James
Townsend, Emily; Portland, Maine, 1857 ***9196.15*** *p11*
Townsend, Henry 76; Ontario, 1871 ***1823.22*** *p160*
Townsend, J. 13; Ontario, 1861 ***2896.26*** *p14*
Townsend, James 10 *SEE* Townsend, James
Townsend, James 24; America, 1774 ***1220.25*** *p36*
Townsend, James 41; St. John Island, 1775 ***1220.25*** *p121*
Child: John 19
Child: James 10
Child: Richard 13
Child: Lucy 18
Child: Mary 5
Wife: Elizabeth 47
Townsend, James 48; Ontario, 1871 ***1823.15*** *p265*
Townsend, James 54; Ontario, 1871 ***1823.15*** *p265*
Townsend, Joane; Virginia, 1661 ***1224.1*** *p39*
Townsend, John; Maryland, 1667 ***2524.55*** *p222*
Wife: Elizabeth
Daughter: Elizabeth
Townsend, John; Virginia, 1671-1672 ***6212.30*** *p47*
Townsend, John 19 *SEE* Townsend, James
Townsend, Jonathan 5; Ontario, 1861 ***2896.28*** *p56*
Townsend, Joseph 23; Maryland, 1774 ***1220.25*** *p53*
Townsend, Joseph 50; Ontario, 1871 ***1823.15*** *p265*
Townsend, L. 16; Ontario, 1861 ***2896.26*** *p14*
Townsend, L. A. 17; Ontario, 1861 ***2896.28*** *p60*
Townsend, Lucy 18 *SEE* Townsend, James
Townsend, Mary; Virginia, 1694 ***1224.1*** *p59*
Townsend, Mary 5 *SEE* Townsend, James
Townsend, Mary E. 12; Ontario, 1861 ***2896.28*** *p56*
Townsend, P. 19; Ontario, 1861 ***2896.26*** *p14*
Townsend, Patrick; Boston, 1702 ***1224.2*** *p116*
Townsend, Patrick; West Indies, 1702 ***1224.2*** *p116*
Townsend, Phebe J. 22; Ontario, 1861 ***2896.28*** *p56*
Townsend, Richard; Maryland, 1674 ***2524.55*** *p222*
Townsend, Richard 13 *SEE* Townsend, James
Townsend, Richard 60; Ontario, 1871 ***1823.15*** *p265*
Townsend, S. 17; Ontario, 1861 ***2896.26*** *p14*
Townsend, S. 18; Ontario, 1861 ***2896.26*** *p1*
Townsend, Thomas; Pennsylvania, 1777 ***4629.10*** *p10*
Townsend, W. 10; Ontario, 1861 ***2896.26*** *p14*
Townsend, W. 57; Ontario, 1861 ***2896.26*** *p14*
Townsend, W. M. 41; Ontario, 1871 ***1823.15*** *p265*
Townsend, William 16; Maryland, 1775 ***1220.25*** *p111*
Townsend, William 43; Ontario, 1871 ***1823.15*** *p265*
Townshend, John 37; Ontario, 1871 ***1823.15*** *p265*
Townsinn, Tho; Virginia, 1674-1675 ***6212.30*** *p53*
Townson, Fredrick 39; Ontario, 1871 ***1823.28*** *p100*
Towny, John; Maryland, 1659 ***2524.55*** *p222*
Towny, Michael; Maryland, 1659 ***2524.55*** *p222*
Towse, Elizabeth *SEE* Towse, Robert
Towse, Mary *SEE* Towse, Robert
Towse, Robert *SEE* Towse, Robert
Towse, Robert; Maryland, 1663 ***2524.55*** *p222*
Wife: Elizabeth
Child: Mary
Child: Robert
Child: Elizabeth
Towsey, John; Boston, 1709 ***1224.2*** *p116*
Toy, Dennis; New York, 1839 ***8197.10*** *p137*
Toy, Elias; Pennsylvania, 1777 ***4629.10*** *p27*
Toy, Frederick 43; Ontario, 1871 ***1823.28*** *p100*
Toy, Joseph; Pennsylvania, 1777 ***4629.10*** *p10*
Toyle, James; New York, 1837 ***8197.10*** *p104*
Tozer, James 36; Ontario, 1871 ***1823.22*** *p160*
Tozer, Joseph; Philadelphia, 1781 ***1224.2*** *p116*
Trabel, Martin; America, 1749 ***2856.30*** *p459*
Traber, Ludwig; America, 1750 ***2856.30*** *p459*
Tracey, Alice; Vermont, 1902 ***5900.10*** *p84*
Tracey, Bridget Lyons; Vermont, 1915 ***5900.10*** *p84*
Tracey, Dennis; Vermont, 1883 ***5900.10*** *p84*
Tracey, Hannora Morrissey; Vermont, 1828-1909 ***5900.10*** *p76*
Tracey, Katherine J.; Vermont, 1855-1913 ***5900.10*** *p353*
Tracey, Patrick 60; Vermont, 1870 ***5900.10*** *p76*
Tracey, Thomas; Vermont, 1896 ***5900.10*** *p84*
Tracey, Timothy; Maryland, 1673 ***2524.55*** *p222*
Tracey, Zachary 30; Ontario, 1871 ***1823.28*** *p100*
Trackly, Sara; Virginia, 1666-1667 ***6212.30*** *p34*
Tracy, Mr.; Quebec, 1857 ***9196.15*** *p21*
Tracy, Andrew 84; Vermont, 1874 ***5900.10*** *p290*
Tracy, Andrew E.; Vermont, 1852-1926 ***5900.10*** *p290*
Tracy, Catherine; Vermont, 1812-1870 ***5900.10*** *p539*
Tracy, Catherine; Vermont, 1857-1881 ***5900.10*** *p540*
Tracy, Catherine 29; Vermont, 1883 ***5900.10*** *p290*
Tracy, Delia; Vermont, 1840-1897 ***5900.10*** *p289*
Tracy, Francis; Pennsylvania, 1811 ***6058.10*** *p4*
Tracy, Jane; Vermont, 1837-1895 ***5900.10*** *p595*
Tracy, John 24; Ontario, 1871 ***1823.28*** *p100*
Tracy, John 30; Ontario, 1871 ***1823.22*** *p160*
Tracy, Joseph 29; Ontario, 1871 ***1823.28*** *p100*
Tracy, Julia Hannon 85; Vermont, 1895 ***5900.10*** *p289*
Tracy, Kate; Vermont, 1845-1919 ***5900.10*** *p432*
Tracy, Lawrence P. 70; Vermont, 1874 ***5900.10*** *p76*
Tracy, Martin; New York, 1839 ***8197.10*** *p289*
Tracy, Mary A. 65; Vermont, 1891 ***5900.10*** *p76*
Tracy, Mary Folan 64; Vermont, 1894 ***5900.10*** *p290*
Tracy, Patrick; New York, 1831 ***8197.10*** *p367*
Tracy, Peter 70; Vermont, 1890 ***5900.10*** *p290*
Tracy, Robert 35; Ontario, 1871 ***1823.15*** *p265*
Tracy, Thomas; New York, 1802 ***8197.10*** *p25*
Tracy, Thomas C.; Vermont, 1865-1942 ***5900.10*** *p290*
Trahearne, George; Maryland, 1673 ***2524.55*** *p222*
Traherne, Michael; Virginia, 1658 ***1224.1*** *p59*
Traiaczewski, Henry; Maryland, 1910 ***3259.35*** *p63*
Traiell, James; Virginia, 1718 ***1224.2*** *p116*
Trail, Janet; Savannah, Georgia, 1775 ***1640.10*** *p206*
Trail, Robert; Augusta, Georgia, 1779 ***1640.10*** *p206*
Traill, George; North America, 1759 ***1224.2*** *p116*
Traill, Henrietta 27; Ontario, 1871 ***1823.22*** *p160*
Trainer, Bernard 45; Ontario, 1871 ***1823.15*** *p265*
Trainer, Bridget Sloan 87; Vermont, 1893 ***5900.10*** *p223*
Trainer, Catherine; Vermont, 1843-1897 ***5900.10*** *p548*
Trainer, Margaret; Vermont, 1810-1880 ***5900.10*** *p228*
Trainer, Owen; Vermont, 1832-1870 ***5900.10*** *p228*
Trainer, Patrick; Vermont, 1794-1875 ***5900.10*** *p228*
Trainer, Patrick 69; Ontario, 1871 ***1823.22*** *p160*
Trainer, Peter; New York, 1840 ***8197.10*** *p200*
Trainor, Anna Fitzpatrick; Vermont, 1833-1901 ***5900.10*** *p508*
Trainor, Cathrine; Vermont, 1832-1858 ***5900.10*** *p565*
Trainor, Patrick; Vermont, 1831-1908 ***5900.10*** *p508*
Trainor, Thomas E. 5; Vermont, 1868 ***5900.10*** *p508*
Traiteur, Johann; America, 1785 ***2856.30*** *p459*
Traiteur, Peter; Port uncertain, 1785 ***2856.30*** *p459*
Trajaunowiski, Joeseph; Maryland, 1910 ***3259.35*** *p63*
Trake, George; Maryland, 1665 ***2524.55*** *p18*
Trakes, Maxwell; Richmond, Virginia, 1852 ***1640.13*** *p126*
Tramner, Joseph 32; Nova Scotia, 1774 ***1220.25*** *p136*
With wife & child
Tran, John 20; Virginia, 1774 ***1220.25*** *p45*
Traner, Thomas; New York, 1826 ***8197.10*** *p288*
Trang, John 39; Ontario, 1871 ***1823.15*** *p265*
Trang, Margaretha 78; Ontario, 1871 ***1823.15*** *p265*
Trankle, Christian; America, 1832 ***2856.30*** *p462*
Trap, Parenborn; America, 1741 ***2856.30*** *p459*
Trapp, Johann David; Port uncertain, 1762 ***2856.30*** *p459*
With daughters
Trapp, Johann Otto; Port uncertain, 1734 ***2856.30*** *p459*
Traquair, James; Georgia, 1698 ***1640.13*** *p126*
Trarbach, Johann Michel; Port uncertain, 1791 ***2856.30*** *p459*
Trarback, Michael; Port uncertain, 1751 ***2856.30*** *p459*
With wife & 10 children
Trask, Isaac; Pennsylvania, 1777 ***4629.10*** *p19*
Trasy, Edward 45; Ontario, 1871 ***1823.22*** *p160*
Traub, Mr.; America, 1793 ***2856.30*** *p459*
With brother & son
Traub, Jakob; America, 1754 ***2856.30*** *p459*
Traub, Jakob Adam; America, 1754 ***2856.30*** *p459*
Traub, Jakob Adam; America, 1756 ***2856.30*** *p459*
Traub, Johann; America, 1754 ***2856.30*** *p459*
Traub, Johann; America, 1756 ***2856.30*** *p459*
Traub, Paul; America, 1749 ***2856.30*** *p459*
Traub, Philipp; Port uncertain, 1749 ***2856.30*** *p459*
Traub, Rupert; Port uncertain, 1749 ***2856.30*** *p459*
Traub'sche, . . .; Port uncertain, 1802 ***2856.30*** *p459*
Trautmann, Adam; New York, 1838 ***8197.10*** *p318*
Trautmann, Fourier; Port uncertain, 1786 ***2856.30*** *p460*
Trautmann, Georg; Port uncertain, 1788 ***2856.30*** *p460*
Trautt, Ann 58; Ontario, 1871 ***1823.22*** *p160*
Trauttenbach, Michael; Port uncertain, 1770 ***2856.30*** *p460*
Trautwein, Dionys; Port uncertain, 1764 ***2856.30*** *p460*
Trautwein, Eva Maria; Port uncertain, 1780 ***2856.30*** *p460*
Trautz, Christina; Port uncertain, 1744 ***2856.30*** *p460*
Travanion, Hugh; Virginia, 1666 ***6212.30*** *p28*
Travers, Mr.; Quebec, 1858 ***9196.15*** *p34*
Travers, Mrs.; Quebec, 1858 ***9196.15*** *p38*
Travers, Ellen Gleason; Vermont, 1834-1934 ***5900.10*** *p424*
Travers, James; New York, 1827 ***8197.10*** *p288*
Travers, James; New York, 1827 ***8197.10*** *p338*
Travers, John; New York, 1837 ***8197.10*** *p104*
Travers, John; Vermont, 1824-1924 ***5900.10*** *p424*
Travers, John; Vermont, 1838-1922 ***5900.10*** *p552*
Travers, Martha Kinsella; Vermont, 1845-1920 ***5900.10*** *p552*
Travers, Patrick; New York, 1840 ***8197.10*** *p200*
Travethan, Mary; Virginia, 1754 ***1224.2*** *p128*
Traweek, Robert; Virginia, 1730 ***1224.2*** *p117*
Trawinski, Joseph F.; Maryland, 1910 ***3259.35*** *p63*
Trawinsky, Maczy; Maryland, 1910 ***3259.35*** *p63*
Traxeller, Jeremiah; Pennsylvania, 1779 ***4629.10*** *p40*
Traxeller, Joseph; Pennsylvania, 1777 ***4629.10*** *p26*
Traxeller, Joseph; Pennsylvania, 1779 ***4629.10*** *p40*
Trayck, Humphry; Virginia, 1671-1672 ***6212.30*** *p46*
Traynor, Bridget; Vermont, 1838-1915 ***5900.10*** *p425*
Traynor, Catherine M.; Vermont, 1842-1910 ***5900.10*** *p261*
Traynor, Elizabeth; Vermont, 1869-1935 ***5900.10*** *p261*
Traynor, Hugh; New York, 1840 ***8197.10*** *p199*
Traynor, James; Vermont, 1864-1865 ***5900.10*** *p261*
Traynor, Patrick; Vermont, 1818-1906 ***5900.10*** *p425*
Traynor, Thomas; Vermont, 1831-1905 ***5900.10*** *p261*
Traynor, Thomas; Vermont, 1879-1889 ***5900.10*** *p261*
Trdski, Adam; Maryland, 1910 ***3259.35*** *p63*
Treacy, James 23; Ontario, 1871 ***1823.28*** *p100*
Treacy, Patrick; New York, 1830 ***8197.10*** *p360*
Treahey, Eliza; Vermont, 1856-1896 ***5900.10*** *p267*
Treahey, Hannah 34; Vermont, 1887 ***5900.10*** *p258*
Treahey, James; Vermont, 1847-1900 ***5900.10*** *p257*
Treahey, Mary; Vermont, 1851-1924 ***5900.10*** *p257*
Treahey, Mary Boland 69; Vermont, 1888 ***5900.10*** *p257*
Treat, John; Massachusetts, 1765 ***1224.2*** *p117*
Treaton, Ann; Maryland, 1675 ***2524.55*** *p222*
Trebel, Martin; Port uncertain, 1785 ***2856.30*** *p460*
Trebilcock, Paul 51; Ontario, 1871 ***1823.22*** *p160*
Treble, Philip; Pennsylvania, 1840 ***6058.10*** *p16*
Trecour, Johann; Port uncertain, 1739 ***2856.30*** *p460*
With wife & 2 children
Tredin, William; Virginia, 1666 ***6212.30*** *p27*
Tredrea, William 45; Ontario, 1871 ***1823.28*** *p100*
Tree, Isaack; Maryland, 1663 ***2524.55*** *p222*
Tree, John Philip; New York, 1839 ***8197.10*** *p137*
Tree, Mary A.; Vermont, 1861-1932 ***5900.10*** *p399*
Treely, John; Maryland, 1682 ***2524.55*** *p222*
Treffen, John; Maryland, 1679 ***2524.55*** *p222*
Treffing, Anna Maria; Port uncertain, 1777 ***2856.30*** *p460*
Treffzer, Friedrich; Port uncertain, 1775 ***2856.30*** *p460*
Trefy, Thomas; Virginia, 1666 ***6212.30*** *p27*
Tregan, Joan; Virginia, 1666-1667 ***6212.30*** *p32*

Tregent, Henry Wakeman; New York, 1839 ***8197.10*** *p289*
Tregenza, John 27; Ontario, 1871 ***1823.28*** *p100*
Tregenza, Thomas 50; Ontario, 1871 ***1823.28*** *p100*
Tregon, John; Virginia, 1666-1667 ***6212.30*** *p32*
Treianowski, Joseph; Maryland, 1910 ***3259.35*** *p63*
Treibelbiss, A. Marg *SEE* Treibelbiss, Philipp
Treibelbiss, Jakob; America, 1733 ***2856.30*** *p460*
Treibelbiss, Jakob; America, 1763 ***2856.30*** *p460*
Treibelbiss, Philipp; America, 1741 ***2856.30*** *p460*
Wife: A. Marg
Treier, Michael; Port uncertain, 1775 ***2856.30*** *p460*
Trein, Johann Georg; America, 1787 ***2856.30*** *p460*
Trein, Johann Niklas; America, 1767 ***2856.30*** *p460*
With wife
Treiner, Peter; New York, 1840 ***8197.10*** *p200*
Treitler, Crescentia; Port uncertain, 1784 ***2856.30*** *p460*
Treitler, Crescentia; Port uncertain, 1785 ***2856.30*** *p460*
Trelany, John; Virginia, 1666 ***6212.30*** *p27*
Treleven, Jane 83; Ontario, 1871 ***1823.15*** *p265*
Treleven, Richard 48; Ontario, 1871 ***1823.15*** *p265*
Treleven, Thomas 53; Ontario, 1871 ***1823.15*** *p265*
Trelevin, John 49; Ontario, 1871 ***1823.15*** *p265*
Trelivan, William 36; Ontario, 1871 ***1823.22*** *p160*
Treloar, Thomas 41; Ontario, 1871 ***1823.28*** *p100*
Treloar, Thomas 66; Ontario, 1871 ***1823.28*** *p100*
Tremaiden, Jno.; Maryland, 1681 ***2524.55*** *p222*
Tremain, Edw; Virginia, 1666 ***6212.30*** *p31*
Tremain, Thomas 25; Ontario, 1871 ***1823.22*** *p160*
Treman, Tho; Virginia, 1666 ***6212.30*** *p28*
Tremayne, Edward; New York, 1837 ***8197.10*** *p105*
Tremble, James 45; Ontario, 1871 ***1823.15*** *p266*
Tremble, John 72; Ontario, 1871 ***1823.15*** *p266*
Trembreth, Thomas 31; Ontario, 1871 ***1823.28*** *p100*
Tremelling, William 33; Ontario, 1871 ***1823.28*** *p100*
Tremiticke, Mr.; Quebec, 1857 ***9196.15*** *p23*
Trempp, Michael; Port uncertain, 1735 ***2856.30*** *p460*
Trempp, Michael; Port uncertain, 1758 ***2856.30*** *p460*
Trenanion, Charles; Virginia, 1666 ***6212.30*** *p28*
Trench, Alexander; South Carolina, 1733 ***1224.2*** *p117*
Trenchard, Henry; Virginia, 1666 ***6212.30*** *p20*
Trenchard, Tho; Virginia, 1666 ***6212.30*** *p31*
Trend, Henry; Maryland, 1675 ***2524.55*** *p222*
Trenear, Joseph 67; Ontario, 1871 ***1823.22*** *p160*
Trenham, James 22; Carolina, 1774 ***1220.25*** *p85*
Trenham, N. J. 30; Ontario, 1871 ***1823.28*** *p100*
Trenicarski, Pelagia; Maryland, 1910 ***3259.35*** *p63*
Trenor, Thomas; Vermont, 1798 ***5900.10*** *p3*
Trent, James; Pennsylvania, 1699 ***1224.1*** *p59*
Trente, Bernor; Virginia, 1673 ***6212.30*** *p51*
Trentein, Joannes; Virginia, 1775 ***1220.25*** *p122*
Trentle, Frederick; Virginia, 1775 ***1220.25*** *p123*
Trentle, Peter; Virginia, 1775 ***1220.25*** *p123*
Tress, Ignaz; Port uncertain, 1785 ***2856.30*** *p461*
Tress, Mathias; Port uncertain, 1741 ***2856.30*** *p461*
Tress, Mathias; Port uncertain, 1786 ***2856.30*** *p461*
Tressler, Daniel; Port uncertain, 1783 ***2856.30*** *p461*
Tretheway, James 38; Ontario, 1871 ***1823.28*** *p100*
Tretheway, Paul 40; Ontario, 1871 ***1823.28*** *p100*
Tretheway, Samuel 44; Ontario, 1871 ***1823.28*** *p100*
Trethewey, Thomas 30; Ontario, 1871 ***1823.28*** *p100*
Trett, Joseph 34; Ontario, 1871 ***1823.15*** *p266*
Tretter, Elisabeth; Port uncertain, 1785 ***2856.30*** *p461*
Tretter, Elisabeth; Port uncertain, 1786 ***2856.30*** *p461*
Tretter, Johann; Port uncertain, 1763 ***2856.30*** *p461*
Treuser, Jacob; Port uncertain, 1795 ***2856.30*** *p461*
Treutler, Anton; Port uncertain, 1785 ***2856.30*** *p461*
Treutler, Anton; Port uncertain, 1786 ***2856.30*** *p461*
Treutler, Egid; Port uncertain, 1781 ***2856.30*** *p461*
Treutling, Philipp Ludwig; Port uncertain, 1788 ***2856.30*** *p461*
Trevett, Russell; Marblehead, Massachusetts, 1803 ***1224.3*** *p79*
Trevillian, Francis; New York, New York, 1778 ***1224.2*** *p117*
Trevillian, John 46; Ontario, 1871 ***1823.28*** *p100*
Trevin, Hugh 23; Ontario, 1871 ***1823.28*** *p100*
Trevisa, William; Virginia, 1666 ***6212.30*** *p27*
Trevithick, John 49; Ontario, 1871 ***1823.15*** *p266*
Trevithick, Maria 73; Ontario, 1871 ***1823.15*** *p266*
Trevithick, William 46; Ontario, 1871 ***1823.15*** *p266*
Trevor, Tho; Virginia, 1664 ***6212.30*** *p7*
Trew, Mr.; Quebec, 1858 ***9196.15*** *p43*
Trew, Henry; Virginia, 1661 ***1224.1*** *p59*
Trewbinskey, Powel 58; Ontario, 1871 ***1823.28*** *p100*
Trewes, Wm; Virginia, 1672 ***6212.30*** *p49*
Trewin, William 46; Ontario, 1871 ***1823.15*** *p266*
Treyer, Jacob; Port uncertain, 1756 ***2856.30*** *p461*
Trian, Samuell; Virginia, 1666-1667 ***6212.30*** *p33*
Trible, Elizabeth 56; Ontario, 1871 ***1823.15*** *p266*
Trible, Samuel 29; Ontario, 1871 ***1823.15*** *p266*
Trice, Jasper; Virginia, 1665-1666 ***6212.30*** *p21*
Trich, Valentin; Port uncertain, 1772 ***2856.30*** *p461*
Trick, John 38; Ontario, 1871 ***1823.15*** *p266*
Tricket, William; Pennsylvania, 1777 ***4629.10*** *p21*
Trickett, Sarah; New York, New York, 1810 ***1224.3*** *p79*
Trieb, Anna Barbara; America, 1750 ***2856.30*** *p461*
Trieb, Jakob; America, 1750 ***2856.30*** *p461*
Trieber, Anna Barbara; America, 1750 ***2856.30*** *p461*
Trieber, Jakob; America, 1750 ***2856.30*** *p461*
Triebuir, Frederick 45; Ontario, 1871 ***1823.15*** *p266*
Trien, Miss; Portland, Maine, 1857 ***9196.15*** *p13*
Trienan, Thos 24; Ontario, 1871 ***1823.15*** *p266*
Trier, Jakob; America, 1753 ***2856.30*** *p461*
Trier, Joseph; New York, 1837 ***8197.10*** *p104*
Tries, Jakob; America, 1752 ***2856.30*** *p461*
Trig, John 70; Ontario, 1861 ***2896.26*** *p21*
Trigg, John; Maryland, 1675 ***2524.55*** *p222*
Trigge, Mr.; Quebec, 1858 ***9196.15*** *p35*
Triggs, Joseph 33; Maryland, 1775 ***1220.25*** *p121*
Triggs, Richard; Maryland, 1682 ***2524.55*** *p222*
Trimble, James N.; New York, 1840 ***8197.10*** *p199*
Trimley, Thomas 27; Philadelphia, 1774 ***1220.25*** *p66*
Trinble, John 49; Ontario, 1871 ***1823.15*** *p266*
Trinble, William 26; Ontario, 1871 ***1823.15*** *p266*
Trinian, Thomas 56; Ontario, 1871 ***1823.15*** *p266*
Trinler, Catharina; Port uncertain, 1767 ***2856.30*** *p461*
Trion, Henrich; Port uncertain, 1780 ***2856.30*** *p461*
Trion, Henrich; Port uncertain, 1783 ***2856.30*** *p461*
Trion, Johann Ludwig; Port uncertain, 1780 ***2856.30*** *p461*
Trion, Johann Ludwig; Port uncertain, 1783 ***2856.30*** *p461*
Trip, Mary 58; Ontario, 1871 ***1823.22*** *p160*
Trip, S. 21; Ontario, 1861 ***2896.25*** *p29*
Tripp, Mr.; Quebec, 1857 ***9196.15*** *p20*
Tripp, Adolph 32; Alaska, 1910 ***9196.1*** *p9*
Tripp, Adolph 32; Yukon, 1910 ***9196.1*** *p9*
Tripp, David 16; Ontario, 1861 ***2896.28*** *p22*
Tripp, George W. 2; Ontario, 1861 ***2896.28*** *p28*
Tripp, Hanah 25; Ontario, 1861 ***2896.28*** *p28*
Tripp, James S. 4; Ontario, 1861 ***2896.28*** *p28*
Tripp, John 24; Ontario, 1861 ***2896.28*** *p28*
Tripp, Lettia 60; Ontario, 1861 ***2896.28*** *p28*
Tripp, Margaret 30; Ontario, 1861 ***2896.28*** *p28*
Tripp, Mary 2; Ontario, 1861 ***2896.28*** *p28*
Tripp, Rebecca 28; Ontario, 1861 ***2896.28*** *p28*
Tripp, Sarah 25; Ontario, 1861 ***2896.28*** *p28*
Tripp, Stanley 1; Ontario, 1861 ***2896.28*** *p28*
Tripp, Thomas 28; Ontario, 1861 ***2896.28*** *p28*
Tripp, Victoria 5; Ontario, 1861 ***2896.28*** *p28*
Trippas, Francis; Maryland, 1666 ***2524.55*** *p222*
Trippes, Ann; Maryland, 1659 ***2524.55*** *p222*
Trippey, Margaret; Maryland, 1669 ***2524.55*** *p222*
Trippey, Nicholas; Maryland, 1669 ***2524.55*** *p222*
Trisczynsky, Jacob; Maryland, 1910 ***3259.35*** *p63*
Trissell, Charles; Virginia, 1671 ***6212.30*** *p45*
Trissell, Hescott; Virginia, 1671 ***6212.30*** *p45*
Trissell, Thomas; Maryland, 1658 ***2524.55*** *p222*
Trites, John 56; Ontario, 1871 ***1823.15*** *p266*
Trites, Peter; Pennsylvania, 1777 ***4629.10*** *p13*
Tritheway, Robert; New York, 1838 ***8197.10*** *p151*
Trivett, James; New York, 1802 ***8197.10*** *p25*
Trivett, Thomas 57; Ontario, 1871 ***1823.15*** *p266*
Trohear, Joseph; New York, 1781 ***1224.2*** *p117*
Troke, Martha; New York, New York, 1840 ***1224.3*** *p79*
Trolan, William; New York, 1840 ***8197.10*** *p200*
Troll, Bastian; Port uncertain, 1612 ***2856.30*** *p461*
Tromball, Robert; Boston, 1716 ***1224.2*** *p117*
Trombel, Robert; Boston, 1716 ***1224.2*** *p117*
Tromhold, Martin; Pennsylvania, 1841 ***6058.10*** *p17*
Tron, Christian; America, 1737 ***2856.30*** *p87*
Troope, Edward; Maryland, 1660 ***2524.55*** *p222*
Tropczynski, Albert; Maryland, 1910 ***3259.35*** *p63*
Tropea, F. 29; Alaska, 1918 ***9196.1*** *p55*
Tropea, F. 29; Yukon, 1918 ***9196.1*** *p55*
Tropf, Friedrich; America, 1737 ***2856.30*** *p461*
With wife & 2 children
Troster, John; Maryland, 1658 ***2524.55*** *p222*
Troter, Mary; Maryland, 1682 ***2524.55*** *p222*
Trotman, Mary; Virginia, 1663 ***6212.30*** *p3*
Trotman, Mary; Virginia, 1671-1672 ***6212.30*** *p45*
Trotman, Samuel 16; Maryland, 1774 ***1220.25*** *p7*
Trott, Jane; Maryland, 1682 ***2524.55*** *p222*
Trott, Joshua 83; Ontario, 1871 ***1823.28*** *p100*
Trott, Samuel 40; Ontario, 1871 ***1823.15*** *p266*
Trotter, George; America, 1842 ***1640.13*** *p126*
Trotter, Henry 26; New York, 1774 ***1220.25*** *p26*
Trotter, Jonathan; New York, 1828 ***8197.10*** *p288*
Trotton, Francis; Maryland, 1661 ***2524.55*** *p222*
Troup, George; Savannah, Georgia, 1789 ***1640.10*** *p206*
Troup, Hans Adam; America, 1754 ***2856.30*** *p461*
Troup, James; Georgia, 1699 ***1640.13*** *p126*
Trouse, Thomas; Maryland, 1663 ***2524.55*** *p242*
Trout, Balzer; Pennsylvania, 1777 ***4629.10*** *p15*
Troutford, Augustin; Virginia, 1667-1668 ***6212.30*** *p39*
Trouth, Tofel; Maryland, 1910 ***3259.35*** *p63*
Troutman, John Jacob; New York, 1839 ***8197.10*** *p137*
Trouton, James; Virginia, 1667-1668 ***6212.30*** *p39*
Trouts, Ja; Virginia, 1665-1666 ***6212.30*** *p21*
Trouts, Jno; Virginia, 1664 ***6212.30*** *p14*
Troutwine, William; New York, 1806 ***8197.10*** *p30*
Trovosky, Adolph; Maryland, 1910 ***3259.35*** *p63*
Trowell, Edward; Maryland, 1659 ***2524.55*** *p222*
Troy, James 29; Vermont, 1876 ***5900.10*** *p62*
Troy, Jane; Vermont, 1823-1917 ***5900.10*** *p57*
Troy, Nicholas; New York, 1838 ***8197.10*** *p151*
Troy, Patrick 66; Ontario, 1871 ***1823.15*** *p266*
Troy, Philip; New York, 1828-1831 ***8197.10*** *p310*
Troy, Thomas 32; Ontario, 1871 ***1823.15*** *p266*
Truber, Eleazer; Pennsylvania, 1777 ***4629.10*** *p26*
Trucker, Henry; Virginia, 1664 ***6212.30*** *p14*
Truckle, Elizabeth; Maryland, 1654 ***2524.55*** *p222*
Truczowski, Maria; Maryland, 1910 ***3259.35*** *p63*
Trudden, Margaret; Vermont, 1829-1909 ***5900.10*** *p311*
Truden, Patrick; New York, 1831 ***8197.10*** *p366*
True, John; Maryland, 1664 ***2524.55*** *p222*
True, Richd.; Maryland, 1658 ***2524.55*** *p222*
True, William; Maryland, 1674 ***2524.55*** *p222*
Truefitt, Henry Paul; Philadelphia, 1864 ***1640.13*** *p127*
Truefitt, Jane Cass; Philadelphia, 1832 ***1224.3*** *p79*
Trueland, Mary 83; Vermont, 1892 ***5900.10*** *p297*
Truelove, James; New York, 1823 ***8197.10*** *p287*
Trueman, Ann *SEE* Trueman, James
Trueman, James; Maryland, 1672 ***2524.55*** *p223*
Wife: Ann
Daughter: Ann
Daughter: Mary
Daughter: Martha
Trueman, Martha *SEE* Trueman, James
Trueman, Mary *SEE* Trueman, James
Trueman, Thomas; Maryland, 1651 ***2524.55*** *p223*
Truemner, Andrew 42; Ontario, 1871 ***1823.15*** *p266*
Truemner, John Joseph 50; Ontario, 1871 ***1823.15*** *p266*
Truemner, Justus 49; Ontario, 1871 ***1823.15*** *p266*
Trukaski, Frank; Maryland, 1910 ***3259.35*** *p63*
Truland, James 75; Vermont, 1885 ***5900.10*** *p297*
Truland, Mary Ann McElroy 38; Vermont, 1888 ***5900.10*** *p297*
Truman, A. 1; Ontario, 1861 ***2896.27*** *p7*
Truman, Ann 58 *SEE* Truman, William
Truman, Evan; Pennsylvania, 1786 ***4629.10*** *p49*
Truman, G. 4; Ontario, 1861 ***2896.27*** *p7*
Truman, Hannah; Vermont, 1792-1890 ***5900.10*** *p373*
Truman, R. F.; Pennsylvania, 1867 ***6058.10*** *p60*
Truman, William; Maryland, 1678 ***2524.55*** *p223*
Truman, William 22 *SEE* Truman, William
Truman, William 52; Fort Cumberland, Nova Scotia, 1774 ***1220.25*** *p17*
Wife: Ann 58
Son: William 22
Truman, Y. 28; Ontario, 1861 ***2896.27*** *p7*
Trumball, Samuel; Died enroute, 1659 ***1224.1*** *p59*
Trumbell, Michael; Maryland, 1675 ***2524.55*** *p223*
Trumber, Ludwig; New York, 1839 ***8197.10*** *p137*
Trumner, Adam 24; Ontario, 1871 ***1823.15*** *p266*
Trumner, Cathrine 70; Ontario, 1871 ***1823.15*** *p266*
Trumner, Wiegard 57; Ontario, 1871 ***1823.15*** *p266*
Trump, Jacob; Pennsylvania, 1777 ***4629.10*** *p25*
Trump, John; Pennsylvania, 1777 ***4629.10*** *p25*
Trumpler, Konrad; Port uncertain, 1784 ***2856.30*** *p461*
With wife
Trumpo, Susan 42; Ontario, 1861 ***2896.26*** *p19*
Trumpour, A.; Ontario, 1861 ***2896.28*** *p62*
Trumpour, A. 2; Ontario, 1861 ***2896.28*** *p10*
Trumpour, Adalaid 19; Ontario, 1861 ***2896.28*** *p49*
Trumpour, Adelaide 17; Ontario, 1861 ***2896.27*** *p30*
Trumpour, Andrew 25; Ontario, 1861 ***2896.28*** *p46*
Trumpour, Catharine 18; Ontario, 1861 ***2896.28*** *p46*
Trumpour, Catherine 16; Ontario, 1861 ***2896.27*** *p66*
Trumpour, Catherine 18; Ontario, 1861 ***2896.27*** *p29*
Trumpour, Catherine 73; Ontario, 1861 ***2896.27*** *p66*
Trumpour, Catherine J. 4; Ontario, 1861 ***2896.27*** *p66*
Trumpour, D. A. 6; Ontario, 1861 ***2896.28*** *p10*
Trumpour, Eliza Jane 19; Ontario, 1861 ***2896.28*** *p46*
Trumpour, Elizabeth 38; Ontario, 1861 ***2896.27*** *p66*
Trumpour, Emily 6; Ontario, 1861 ***2896.28*** *p46*
Trumpour, George A. 18; Ontario, 1861 ***2896.27*** *p67*
Trumpour, H. E. 8; Ontario, 1861 ***2896.28*** *p10*
Trumpour, Hermon 21; Ontario, 1861 ***2896.28*** *p49*
Trumpour, Hiram 13; Ontario, 1861 ***2896.27*** *p66*
Trumpour, Jehiel 21; Ontario, 1861 ***2896.27*** *p67*
Trumpour, Johiel 22; Ontario, 1861 ***2896.27*** *p29*
Trumpour, July 42; Ontario, 1861 ***2896.27*** *p66*
Trumpour, L. M. 10; Ontario, 1861 ***2896.28*** *p10*
Trumpour, Lidia 13; Ontario, 1861 ***2896.28*** *p46*
Trumpour, M. A. 27; Ontario, 1861 ***2896.28*** *p10*
Trumpour, Marshal 14; Ontario, 1861 ***2896.28*** *p49*
Trumpour, P. M. 4; Ontario, 1861 ***2896.28*** *p10*

Turinger, Martin; Port uncertain, 1739 ***2856.30*** *p462*
Turinger, Martin; Port uncertain, 1769 ***2856.30*** *p462*
Turk, Timothy 65; Ontario, 1871 ***1823.15*** *p266*
Turk, William; New York, 1839 ***8197.10*** *p137*
Turkinton, Johnson 53; Ontario, 1871 ***1823.22*** *p161*
Turley, Henry; New York, 1806 ***8197.10*** *p33*
Turling, Andrew; Maryland, 1673 ***2524.55*** *p223*
Turlock, Joseph; New York, 1806 ***8197.10*** *p322*
Turmak, Jacob; Maryland, 1910 ***3259.35*** *p64*
Turnbell, Isabella 23; Ontario, 1871 ***1823.15*** *p267*
Turnbell, Isabelle 24; Ontario, 1871 ***1823.15*** *p267*
Turnbull, Andrew; Florida, 1767 ***1640.10*** *p206*
Turnbull, Andrew 30; Ontario, 1871 ***1823.28*** *p101*
Turnbull, Andrew 31; Ontario, 1871 ***1823.15*** *p267*
Turnbull, Andrew 35; Ontario, 1871 ***1823.15*** *p267*
Turnbull, Ann; Savannah, Georgia, 1774 ***1640.10*** *p206*
Turnbull, Catherine; California, 1888 ***1640.13*** *p127*
Turnbull, David 55; Ontario, 1871 ***1823.15*** *p267*
Turnbull, George; Grenada, 1809 ***1640.13*** *p127*
Turnbull, George; New Haven, Connecticut, 1826 ***1224.3*** *p80*
Turnbull, George; New York, New York, 1812 ***1224.3*** *p80*
Turnbull, Henry 45; Ontario, 1871 ***1823.15*** *p267*
Turnbull, James; Antigua (Antego), 1817 ***1640.13*** *p127*
Turnbull, James; Georgia, 1734 ***1640.10*** *p207*
Turnbull, James; New York, 1837 ***8197.10*** *p289*
Turnbull, James; New York, 1837 ***8197.10*** *p374*
Turnbull, James 39; Ontario, 1871 ***1823.15*** *p267*
Turnbull, James 55; Ontario, 1871 ***1823.22*** *p161*
Turnbull, Jane; Florida, 1767 ***1640.10*** *p207*
Turnbull, John James 16; Ontario, 1871 ***1823.28*** *p101*
Turnbull, Margaret; Florida, 1767 ***1640.10*** *p207*
Turnbull, Mary; Florida, 1767 ***1640.10*** *p207*
Turnbull, Mary 63; Ontario, 1871 ***1823.15*** *p267*
Turnbull, Nicholas; Florida, 1767 ***1640.10*** *p207*
Turnbull, Peter; Montserrat, 1809 ***1640.13*** *p127*
Turnbull, Robert 50; Ontario, 1871 ***1823.15*** *p267*
Turnbull, Thomas; Antigua (Antego), 1817 ***1640.13*** *p127*
Turnbull, Thomas; New York, 1807 ***8197.10*** *p51*
Turnbull, Thomas 80; Ontario, 1871 ***1823.15*** *p267*
Turnbull, Walter 47; Ontario, 1871 ***1823.15*** *p267*
Turnbull, William; Georgia, 1698 ***1640.13*** *p127*
Turnbull, William 33; Ontario, 1871 ***1823.15*** *p267*
Turnbull, William 36; Ontario, 1871 ***1823.15*** *p267*
Turnbull, William 58; Ontario, 1871 ***1823.15*** *p267*
Turnbull, William 64; Ontario, 1871 ***1823.15*** *p267*
Turneck, John; Maryland, 1675 ***2524.55*** *p223*
Turner, Miss; Quebec, 1856 ***9196.15*** *p10*
Turner, Mr.; Quebec, 1856 ***9196.15*** *p5*
Turner, Mrs.; Quebec, 1856 ***9196.15*** *p34*
Turner, A. P. 28; Alaska, 1912 ***9196.1*** *p18*
Turner, A. P. 28; British Columbia, 1912 ***9196.1*** *p18*
Turner, Ann *SEE* Turner, Daniell
Turner, Ann; South Carolina, 1817 ***1224.3*** *p81*
Turner, Ann 21; Philadelphia, 1774 ***1220.25*** *p44*
Turner, Ann J.; Vermont, 1849-1938 ***5900.10*** *p490*
Turner, Arthur; Maryland, 1648 ***2524.55*** *p224*
Wife: Mary
Turner, Arthur; Maryland, 1649 ***2524.55*** *p224*
With wife
Turner, Barnard; North America, 1758 ***1224.2*** *p117*
Turner, Bonham; Maryland, 1672 ***2524.55*** *p224*
Turner, Bonham; Maryland, 1673 ***2524.55*** *p224*
Turner, Catharine 58; Vermont, 1870 ***5900.10*** *p482*
Turner, Charles 66; Vermont, 1926 ***5900.10*** *p319*
Turner, Constance *SEE* Turner, Daniell
Turner, Daniel 22; Virginia, 1774 ***1220.25*** *p46*
Turner, Daniel 62; Ontario, 1871 ***1823.22*** *p161*
Turner, Daniell; Maryland, 1674 ***2524.55*** *p224*
Wife: Ann
Daughter: Constance
Turner, David *SEE* Turner, David
Turner, David; Mississippi, 1814-1849 ***1640.10*** *p207*
Wife: Margaret
Son: William
Son: David
Turner, David; Savannah, Georgia, 1807 ***1640.10*** *p207*
Turner, David 40; Ontario, 1871 ***1823.15*** *p267*
Turner, Donald 44; Ontario, 1871 ***1823.15*** *p267*
Turner, Edward *SEE* Turner, William
Turner, Edward; Maryland, 1651 ***2524.55*** *p224*
Turner, Edward; Maryland, 1681 ***2524.55*** *p224*
Turner, Edward 45; Ontario, 1871 ***1823.15*** *p267*
Turner, Edward 82; Ontario, 1871 ***1823.15*** *p267*
Turner, Elizabeth; Vermont, 1845-1927 ***5900.10*** *p183*
Turner, Elizabeth 73; Ontario, 1871 ***1823.15*** *p267*
Turner, Emma; Maryland, 1651 ***2524.55*** *p224*
Turner, Fanny 24; Ontario, 1861 ***2896.26*** *p22*
Turner, Francis 33; Virginia, 1774 ***1220.25*** *p87*
Turner, G. A.; Quebec, 1858 ***9196.15*** *p35*
Turner, George; Maryland, 1682 ***2524.55*** *p224*
Turner, George 50; Ontario, 1871 ***1823.28*** *p101*
Turner, Ginny 77; Ontario, 1871 ***1823.15*** *p267*
Turner, Hannah; Charleston, South Carolina, 1811 ***1224.3*** *p80*
Turner, Henry; Maryland, 1680 ***2524.55*** *p224*
Turner, Henry 24; Maryland, 1775 ***1220.25*** *p116*
Turner, J.; Quebec, 1856 ***9196.15*** *p5*
Turner, J. J. 43; Vermont, 1890 ***5900.10*** *p485*
Turner, James; Georgia, 1699 ***1640.13*** *p127*
Turner, James; Maryland, 1681 ***2524.55*** *p224*
Turner, Jane; Maryland, 1663 ***2524.55*** *p224*
Turner, John *SEE* Turner, William
Turner, John; Maryland, 1659 ***2524.55*** *p224*
Turner, John; Maryland, 1673 ***2524.55*** *p224*
With wife
Turner, John; Maryland, 1673 ***2524.55*** *p224*
Turner, John; Maryland, 1724 ***1224.2*** *p117*
Turner, John; New York, 1783 ***1224.2*** *p117*
Turner, John; Savannah, Georgia, 1821 ***1640.10*** *p207*
Turner, John 21; Baltimore, 1775 ***1220.25*** *p118*
Turner, John 21; Maryland, 1774 ***1220.25*** *p71*
Turner, John 22; Maryland, 1774 ***1220.25*** *p84*
Turner, John 25; Virginia, 1773 ***1220.25*** *p28*
Turner, John 27; Virginia, 1774 ***1220.25*** *p45*
Turner, John 40; Ontario, 1871 ***1823.15*** *p267*
Turner, John 43; Ontario, 1871 ***1823.22*** *p161*
Turner, John 47; Ontario, 1871 ***1823.22*** *p161*
Turner, John 50; Ontario, 1871 ***1823.15*** *p267*
Turner, John, Jr.; Maryland, 1671 ***2524.55*** *p224*
Turner, Jon; Virginia, 1674-1675 ***6212.30*** *p53*
Turner, Jonas 25; Philadelphia, 1774 ***1220.25*** *p80*
Turner, Joseph; Pennsylvania, 1777 ***4629.10*** *p23*
Turner, Joseph; Pennsylvania, 1779 ***4629.10*** *p40*
Turner, Joseph, Jr.; Pennsylvania, 1777 ***4629.10*** *p23*
Turner, Joseph, Jr.; Pennsylvania, 1779 ***4629.10*** *p39*
Turner, Joseph Prentiss; New York, 1821 ***8197.10*** *p287*
Turner, Kate; Vermont, 1845-1927 ***5900.10*** *p310*
Turner, Katherine; Maryland, 1673 ***2524.55*** *p224*
Turner, Louis Paulo; Canada, 1844 ***1640.13*** *p127*
Turner, Margaret *SEE* Turner, David
Turner, Margret 4; Ontario, 1871 ***1823.15*** *p267*
Turner, Margret 40; Ontario, 1871 ***1823.15*** *p267*
Turner, Mary *SEE* Turner, Arthur
Turner, Mary; Maryland, 1673 ***2524.55*** *p224*
Turner, Mary; Virginia, 1690-1691 ***6212.30*** *p58*
Turner, Mary 68; Ontario, 1861 ***2896.28*** *p36*
Turner, Mary Lapan 75; Vermont, 1910 ***5900.10*** *p485*
Turner, Nancy Grant 55; Vermont, 1933 ***5900.10*** *p319*
Turner, Peter; New York, 1817 ***8197.10*** *p60*
Turner, Richard; Virginia, 1664-1665 ***6212.30*** *p15*
Turner, Richard 21; Maryland, 1774 ***1220.25*** *p58*
Turner, Richard 21; Maryland, 1774 ***1220.25*** *p71*
Turner, Richard D.; Vermont, 1845-1919 ***5900.10*** *p183*
Turner, Robert; Alabama, 1815-1845 ***1640.10*** *p207*
Turner, Robert; Montreal, 1836 ***1640.13*** *p127*
Turner, Samuel 30; Ontario, 1871 ***1823.15*** *p267*
Turner, Stephen 24; Maryland, 1775 ***1220.25*** *p120*
Turner, Thomas; Maryland, 1658 ***2524.55*** *p224*
Turner, Thomas; New York, 1807 ***8197.10*** *p51*
Turner, Thomas; New York, 1837 ***8197.10*** *p374*
Turner, Thomas; New York, 1840 ***8197.10*** *p199*
Turner, Thomas 22; Maryland, 1774 ***1220.25*** *p73*
Turner, Thomas 37; Ontario, 1871 ***1823.28*** *p101*
Turner, William *SEE* Turner, David
Turner, William *SEE* Turner, William
Turner, William; Maryland, 1652 ***2524.55*** *p224*
With wife
Son: John
Son: William
Son: Edward
Turner, William; Maryland, 1678 ***2524.55*** *p224*
Turner, William; New York, 1818 ***8197.10*** *p287*
Turner, William; New York, 1825-1831 ***8197.10*** *p369*
Turner, William; New York, 1837 ***8197.10*** *p105*
Turner, William; Pennsylvania, 1779 ***4629.10*** *p40*
Turner, William; Philadelphia Co., Pennsylvania, 1852 ***1224.3*** *p80*
Turner, William; Virginia, 1671 ***6212.30*** *p45*
Turner, William 16; Maryland, 1775 ***1220.25*** *p104*
Turner, William 17; Philadelphia, 1774 ***1220.25*** *p63*
Turner, William 22; Maryland, 1774 ***1220.25*** *p71*
Turner, William 32; Ontario, 1871 ***1823.28*** *p101*
Turner, William 45; Maryland, 1775 ***1220.25*** *p111*
Turner, William 70; Ontario, 1871 ***1823.15*** *p267*
Turner, William G.; New York, 1840 ***8197.10*** *p200*
Turner, Wm; Virginia, 1672 ***6212.30*** *p49*
Turner, Zachariah; New York, New York, 1835 ***1224.3*** *p80*
Turney, John; New York, 1838 ***8197.10*** *p150*
Turney, John H.; Vermont, 1855-1925 ***5900.10*** *p333*
Turney, Maria Price; Vermont, 1857-1932 ***5900.10*** *p333*
Turney, Mathew 46; Ontario, 1871 ***1823.22*** *p161*
Turney, Michael 65; Vermont, 1880 ***5900.10*** *p413*
Turnin, William 37; Ontario, 1871 ***1823.22*** *p161*
Turnipseed, Katie 22; Kansas, 1910 ***9079.10*** *p48*
Turnley, John 24; Philadelphia, 1774 ***1220.25*** *p23*
Turnor, James; Virginia, 1667-1668 ***6212.30*** *p38*
Turnor, Mary; Virginia, 1665-1666 ***6212.30*** *p23*
Turnor, Robert; Maryland, 1681 ***2524.55*** *p224*
Turnor, Sarah; Virginia, 1663 ***6212.30*** *p2*
Turnor, William; Virginia, 1664 ***6212.30*** *p13*
Turnor, William; Virginia, 1667 ***6212.30*** *p37*
Turnstra, A. 32; Alaska, 1914 ***9196.1*** *p24*
Turow, Peter; Maryland, 1910 ***3259.35*** *p64*
Turpin, James; Virginia, 1678 ***1224.1*** *p59*
Turpin, William; Maryland, 1672 ***2524.55*** *p224*
Turriff, Isabella; West Indies, 1881 ***1640.13*** *p127*
Turtle, James; Maryland, 1660 ***2524.55*** *p224*
Turtle, John 23; Virginia, 1774 ***1220.25*** *p91*
Turtle, Thomas 21; Virginia, 1773 ***1220.25*** *p29*
Turtus, George 49; Ontario, 1871 ***1823.28*** *p101*
Turvey, George 76; Ontario, 1861 ***2896.28*** *p19*
Turvey, Hannah 18; Ontario, 1861 ***2896.28*** *p19*
Turvey, Jane 46; Ontario, 1861 ***2896.28*** *p19*
Turvey, William 57; Ontario, 1871 ***1823.15*** *p267*
Turvile, Arcadia *SEE* Turvile, William
Turvile, Margery *SEE* Turvile, William
Turvile, William *SEE* Turvile, William
Turvile, William; Maryland, 1678 ***2524.55*** *p224*
Wife: Margery
Daughter: Arcadia
Son: William
Turvill, John; Virginia, 1664 ***6212.30*** *p13*
Turvy, George 58; Ontario, 1871 ***1823.15*** *p267*
Turzenska, Charles; New York, 1839 ***8197.10*** *p137*
Tusfryi, Louisa 14; Ontario, 1871 ***1823.15*** *p267*
Tushner, John 50; Ontario, 1871 ***1823.28*** *p101*
Tusko, John 35; Ontario, 1871 ***1823.28*** *p101*
Tuson, Chas; Virginia, 1672 ***6212.30*** *p51*
Tustine, Rebecca; Maryland, 1674 ***2524.55*** *p225*
Tute, James 19; Virginia, 1774 ***1220.25*** *p54*
Tute, John; Virginia, 1738 ***1224.2*** *p117*
Tute, Mary; Maryland, 1663 ***2524.55*** *p225*
Tutt, George 40; Ontario, 1871 ***1823.22*** *p161*
Tutt, James 60; Ontario, 1871 ***1823.15*** *p267*
Tuttle, Andrew 4; Ontario, 1861 ***2896.26*** *p39*
Tuttle, Andrew 62; Ontario, 1861 ***2896.26*** *p39*
Tuttle, Beley J. 1; Ontario, 1861 ***2896.26*** *p39*
Tuttle, Byran 8; Ontario, 1861 ***2896.26*** *p39*
Tuttle, Calvin 57; Ontario, 1871 ***1823.22*** *p161*
Tuttle, Emaline 27; Ontario, 1861 ***2896.26*** *p39*
Tuttle, Hanah 34; Ontario, 1861 ***2896.26*** *p39*
Tuttle, Hariet 8; Ontario, 1861 ***2896.26*** *p39*
Tuttle, Henry 40; Ontario, 1861 ***2896.26*** *p34*
Tuttle, James Albert 3; Ontario, 1861 ***2896.26*** *p39*
Tuttle, John 11; Ontario, 1861 ***2896.26*** *p39*
Tuttle, Leonard 61; Ontario, 1871 ***1823.22*** *p161*
Tuttle, Mary 4; Ontario, 1861 ***2896.26*** *p39*
Tuttle, Perlina 1; Ontario, 1861 ***2896.26*** *p39*
Tutton, William 30; Ontario, 1871 ***1823.15*** *p267*
Twaddel, Samuel; New York, 1840 ***8197.10*** *p200*
Twaddle, Alexander; New York, 1840 ***8197.10*** *p289*
Twaddle, James; New York, 1839 ***8197.10*** *p289*
Twaddle, Robert; New York, 1839 ***8197.10*** *p289*
Twamley, George 45; Ontario, 1871 ***1823.15*** *p267*
Twan, Mark; Maryland, 1653-1661 ***2524.55*** *p225*
Twardouski, Marya; Maryland, 1910 ***3259.35*** *p64*
Twardowicz, Peter S.; Maryland, 1910 ***3259.35*** *p64*
Twardowski, Mateurs; Maryland, 1910 ***3259.35*** *p64*
Twatt, Magnus; Canada, 1801 ***1640.13*** *p127*
Twckaswska, Katie; Maryland, 1910 ***3259.35*** *p64*
Twedy, John 28; Baltimore, 1775 ***1220.25*** *p117*
Tweed, Thomas 66; Ontario, 1871 ***1823.22*** *p162*
Tweed, William 41; Ontario, 1871 ***1823.22*** *p162*
Tweedie, Elizabeth 42; Ontario, 1871 ***1823.15*** *p267*
Tweedie, Isabella; Louisiana, 1824-1845 ***1640.10*** *p207*
Tweedie, Janet; Louisiana, 1824-1845 ***1640.10*** *p208*
Tweedly, Robert 22; Ontario, 1871 ***1823.15*** *p267*
Tweeley, George *SEE* Tweeley, Robert
Tweeley, Mary *SEE* Tweeley, Robert
Tweeley, Robert *SEE* Tweeley, Robert
Tweeley, Robert; Maryland, 1678 ***2524.55*** *p225*
Wife: Mary
Son: Robert
Son: George
Tweelie, George *SEE* Tweelie, Robert
Tweelie, Mary *SEE* Tweelie, Robert
Tweelie, Robert *SEE* Tweelie, Robert
Tweelie, Robert; Maryland, 1678 ***2524.55*** *p225*
Wife: Mary
Son: Robert
Son: George
Tweit, Edmund O. 47; Seattle, 1917 ***9196.1*** *p52*
Tweit, Edmund O. 47; Yukon, 1917 ***9196.1*** *p52*
Twelves, Godfrey; Pennsylvania, 1777 ***4629.10*** *p25*
Twentyman, Mr.; Quebec, 1857 ***9196.15*** *p22*

U

Uban, George; New York, 1832 ***8197.10*** *p356*
Uban, John; New York, 1831 ***8197.10*** *p356*
Uber, Michael; Pennsylvania, 1777 ***4629.10*** *p10*
Uecker, Philipp; Port uncertain, 1750 ***2856.30*** *p26*
Uekele, Bernhard; America, 1756 ***2856.30*** *p464*
Uekele, Johann Friedric; Port uncertain, 1770 ***2856.30*** *p464*
Uff, Maria; Port uncertain, 1764 ***2856.30*** *p464*
Uffer, Andreas; Port uncertain, 1802 ***2856.30*** *p464*
With family
Uglow, James; New York, 1840 ***8197.10*** *p200*
Uhl, Adam; Port uncertain, 1764 ***2856.30*** *p464*
Uhl, Caspar; Port uncertain, 1786 ***2856.30*** *p464*
Uhl, Christian; Port uncertain, 1783 ***2856.30*** *p464*
Uhl, Christof; Port uncertain, 1749 ***2856.30*** *p464*
Uhl, Franz; Port uncertain, 1764 ***2856.30*** *p464*
Uhl, John; New York, 1838 ***8197.10*** *p320*
Uhl, Lorenz; Port uncertain, 1736 ***2856.30*** *p464*
Uhl, Lorenz; Port uncertain, 1768 ***2856.30*** *p464*
Uhl, Philipp Johann; Port uncertain, 1786 ***2856.30*** *p464*
Uhl, Wendel; America, 1746 ***2856.30*** *p464*
With wife & children
Uhle, Christian; Port uncertain, 1783 ***2856.30*** *p464*
Uhler, Andrew; America, 1785 ***2856.30*** *p464*
Uhrich, Philipp; Port uncertain, 1783 ***2856.30*** *p464*
Uhrig, Johann; America, 1742 ***2856.30*** *p464*
Uhrig, Johann; America, 1748 ***2856.30*** *p464*
Uhrig, Valentin; America, 1742 ***2856.30*** *p464*
Uhrig, Valentin; America, 1748 ***2856.30*** *p464*
Ukele, Philipp; Port uncertain, 1794 ***2856.30*** *p464*
Ulamowicz, Stanislaus; Maryland, 1910 ***3259.35*** *p64*
Ulenicka, Frances; Maryland, 1910 ***3259.35*** *p64*
Uletowsky, Alexander; Maryland, 1910 ***3259.35*** *p64*
Ullmer, Georg; America, 1769 ***2856.30*** *p464*
With wife & 5 children
Ullmer, Hans Adam; Port uncertain, 1737 ***2856.30*** *p464*
With wife son & 4 daughters
Ullrich, Christina; Port uncertain, 1763 ***2856.30*** *p464*
Ullrich, Michael; America, 1737 ***2856.30*** *p465*
Ullrich, Peter; America, 1788 ***2856.30*** *p465*
Ullrich, Peter; America, 1790 ***2856.30*** *p465*
Ullrich, Peter; America, 1805 ***2856.30*** *p465*
Ullrich, Peter; America, 1816 ***2856.30*** *p465*
Ullrich, Peter; Port uncertain, 1787 ***2856.30*** *p465*
Ullrich, Valentin; Port uncertain, 1740 ***2856.30*** *p465*
Ullrich, Valentin; Port uncertain, 1780 ***2856.30*** *p465*
Ully, Johann Peter; Port uncertain, 1784 ***2856.30*** *p198*
With wife
Ulm, Catharina; Philadelphia, 1752 ***2856.30*** *p465*
Ulm, Johann; Mississippi, 1737 ***2856.30*** *p465*
With wife & 5 children
Ulm, Margarete; Philadelphia, 1752 ***2856.30*** *p465*
Ulm, Martin; Philadelphia, 1752 ***2856.30*** *p465*
Ulmanijawski, Mary A.; Maryland, 1910 ***3259.35*** *p64*
Ulmer, Henrich; America, 1752 ***2856.30*** *p465*
With wife & 4 children
Ulmer, Jacob; America, 1769 ***2856.30*** *p465*
With children
Ulmer, Johann; America, 1752 ***2856.30*** *p465*
Ulrich, Anna Catharina; Port uncertain, 1774 ***2856.30*** *p465*
Ulrich, Anna Dorothea; Port uncertain, 1759 ***2856.30*** *p465*
Ulrich, Anna Margarete; Port uncertain, 1759 ***2856.30*** *p465*
Ulrich, August L.; New York, 1819 ***8197.10*** *p289*
Ulrich, Catharina; Port uncertain, 1764 ***2856.30*** *p465*
Ulrich, Georg; America, 1751 ***2856.30*** *p465*
Ulrich, Georg; Port uncertain, 1751 ***2856.30*** *p465*
Ulrich, Hans Adam; America, 1738 ***2856.30*** *p465*
Ulrich, Hans Adam; Port uncertain, 1737 ***2856.30*** *p465*
Ulrich, Henrich; Port uncertain, 1764 ***2856.30*** *p465*
Ulrich, Jacob; New York, 1840 ***8197.10*** *p200*
Ulrich, Jakob; Port uncertain, 1751 ***2856.30*** *p465*
Ulrich, Johann; Port uncertain, 1771 ***2856.30*** *p465*
Ulrich, Johann Leonhard; Port uncertain, 1750 ***2856.30*** *p465*
Ulrich, Magdalena Tollpett; Port uncertain, 1756 ***2856.30*** *p465*
Ulrich, Mathias; America, 1765 ***2856.30*** *p465*
Ulrich, Michael; Port uncertain, 1762 ***2856.30*** *p465*
Ulrich, Peter; America, 1765 ***2856.30*** *p465*
Ulrich, Peter; America, 1790 ***2856.30*** *p465*
Ulrich, Peter; Port uncertain, 1754 ***2856.30*** *p465*
With wife & child
Ulrich, Philipp; America, 1749 ***2856.30*** *p465*
Ulrick, Henry; New York, 1824 ***8197.10*** *p312*
Ulrick, Henry; New York, 1829 ***8197.10*** *p303*
Uminia, Sophia; Maryland, 1910 ***3259.35*** *p64*
Ummel, Akob; America, 1749 ***2856.30*** *p465*
Ummell, Elizabeth 21; Maryland, 1775 ***1220.25*** *p115*
Ummell, George 32; Maryland, 1775 ***1220.25*** *p115*
Ummenhofer, Michael; Port uncertain, 1738 ***2856.30*** *p465*
Ummenhofer, Michael; Port uncertain, 1739 ***2856.30*** *p465*
Uncik, Frank; Maryland, 1910 ***3259.35*** *p64*
Underberge, George 36; Alaska, 1914 ***9196.1*** *p11*
Underdowns, C. 26; Ontario, 1861 ***2896.26*** *p15*
Underdowns, J. 1; Ontario, 1861 ***2896.26*** *p15*
Underdowns, J. 26; Ontario, 1861 ***2896.26*** *p15*
Underhill, Edward; Maryland, 1661 ***2524.55*** *p225*
Underhill, Elizabeth; Maryland, 1661 ***2524.55*** *p225*
Underhill, John; Maryland, 1659 ***2524.55*** *p225*
Wife: Mary
Underhill, John; Virginia, 1664 ***6212.30*** *p14*
Underhill, Mary *SEE* Underhill, John
Underlea, Michael; Pennsylvania, 1777 ***4629.10*** *p10*
Underwood, Anthony; Maryland, 1682 ***2524.55*** *p225*
Underwood, David 21; Philadelphia, 1774 ***1220.25*** *p66*
Underwood, Edward 39; Ontario, 1871 ***1823.15*** *p268*
Underwood, Elizabeth; Maryland, 1650 ***2524.55*** *p225*
Underwood, Francis Henry; America, 1894 ***1640.13*** *p128*
Underwood, James 27; Maryland, 1774 ***1220.25*** *p78*
Underwood, John; Maryland, 1682 ***2524.55*** *p225*
Underwood, John 39; Ontario, 1871 ***1823.15*** *p268*
Underwood, John 49; Ontario, 1871 ***1823.15*** *p268*
Underwood, John 50; Ontario, 1871 ***1823.22*** *p162*
Underwood, John 76; Ontario, 1871 ***1823.15*** *p268*
Underwood, Martha; South Carolina, 1754 ***1224.2*** *p118*
Underwood, Thomas; Maryland, 1650 ***2524.55*** *p225*
Underwood, Walter 47; Ontario, 1871 ***1823.22*** *p162*
Underwood, Wm; Virginia, 1667 ***6212.30*** *p37*
Ungemach, Seibert; New York, 1840 ***8197.10*** *p289*
Unger, Jacob; New York, 1838 ***8197.10*** *p289*
Unger, Maria; Port uncertain, 1771 ***2856.30*** *p466*
Ungerer, Eva Dorothea; America, 1792 ***2856.30*** *p466*
Ungerer, Jakob; America, 1733 ***2856.30*** *p466*
Ungerer, Jakob; Port uncertain, 1759 ***2856.30*** *p466*
Ungerer, Johann Michael; America, 1753 ***2856.30*** *p466*
Ungerer, Johann Michael; America, 1759 ***2856.30*** *p466*
Ungerer, Johann Wolfgang; America, 1792 ***2856.30*** *p466*
With wife & children
Ungerer, Maria; America, 1774 ***2856.30*** *p466*
Ungerin, Maria; America, 1741 ***2856.30*** *p466*
Unit, Ted 52; British Columbia, 1909 ***9196.1*** *p26*
Unit, Ted 52; Washington, 1909 ***9196.1*** *p26*
Unruh, . . .; America, 1771 ***2856.30*** *p466*
Unruh, Anna Catharina; America, 1734 ***2856.30*** *p466*
With husband
Unruhe, Jakob; Port uncertain, 1783 ***2856.30*** *p466*
Unschutz, Amelia 3; Kansas, 1909-1910 ***9079.10*** *p19*
Unschutz, Carl 43; Kansas, 1909-1910 ***9079.10*** *p19*
Unschutz, Catharine 12; Kansas, 1909-1910 ***9079.10*** *p19*
Unschutz, Christian 7; Kansas, 1909-1910 ***9079.10*** *p19*
Unschutz, Theadora 43; Kansas, 1909-1910 ***9079.10*** *p19*
Unseld, David; America, 1751 ***2856.30*** *p466*
Unseld, Lucia; America, 1749 ***2856.30*** *p466*
Unseld, Michael, The Younger; America, 1767 ***2856.30*** *p466*
Unser, Georg Nikolaus; Port uncertain, 1765 ***2856.30*** *p466*
Unser, Margarete; Port uncertain, 1763 ***2856.30*** *p466*
Unser, Nikolaus; Port uncertain, 1764 ***2856.30*** *p466*
Upe, Richard; Maryland, 1637 ***2524.55*** *p139*
Upgate, John; Maryland, 1663 ***2524.55*** *p226*
Uphomoe, Stephen 11; Ontario, 1871 ***1823.15*** *p268*
Upington, Walter; Maryland, 1692 ***1224.1*** *p59*
Upjohn, Edward 17; Philadelphia, 1774 ***1220.25*** *p67*
Upjohn, James 15; Philadelphia, 1774 ***1220.25*** *p66*
Uppord, John 21; Maryland, 1774 ***1220.25*** *p77*
Upshott, Elizabeth *SEE* Upshott, John
Upshott, John; Maryland, 1672 ***2524.55*** *p226*
Wife: Elizabeth
Child: Elizabeth
Child: Sarah
Upshott, Sarah *SEE* Upshott, John
Upton, Mr.; Quebec, 1857 ***9196.15*** *p24*
Upton, Mrs.; Quebec, 1857 ***9196.15*** *p24*
Upton, Arthur; Virginia, 1667 ***6212.30*** *p35*
Upton, Eliza; Virginia, 1666 ***6212.30*** *p25*
Upton, Elizabeth; Maryland, 1673 ***2524.55*** *p226*
Upton, James; Virginia, 1665-1666 ***6212.30*** *p24*
Upton, James 64; Ontario, 1871 ***1823.22*** *p162*
Upton, Jno; Virginia, 1666 ***6212.30*** *p26*
Upton, John 57; Ontario, 1871 ***1823.15*** *p268*
Upton, Mary; Vermont, 1806-1878 ***5900.10*** *p556*
Upton, Mary; Virginia, 1664 ***6212.30*** *p5*
Upton, Richard 57; Ontario, 1871 ***1823.22*** *p162*
Upton, William 50; Ontario, 1871 ***1823.28*** *p101*
Upton, William 55; Ontario, 1871 ***1823.22*** *p162*
Urbacz, Franciska; Maryland, 1910 ***3259.35*** *p64*
Urban, Anna Elisabeth; Port uncertain, 1753 ***2856.30*** *p466*
Urban, Georg; America, 1752 ***2856.30*** *p466*
With son
Urban, Johann; Port uncertain, 1782 ***2856.30*** *p466*
Urban, Joseph; Maryland, 1910 ***3259.35*** *p64*
Urbanauski, Antonia; Maryland, 1910 ***3259.35*** *p64*
Urbani, Francis; New York, 1840 ***8197.10*** *p321*
Urbanowics, John; Maryland, 1910 ***3259.35*** *p64*
Urbanowski, Franciszad; Maryland, 1910 ***3259.35*** *p64*
Urbanowski, Frank; Maryland, 1910 ***3259.35*** *p64*
Urbanski, John; Maryland, 1910 ***3259.35*** *p64*
Urbanski, Michael; Maryland, 1910 ***3259.35*** *p64*
Urbanski, Peter; Maryland, 1910 ***3259.35*** *p64*
Urbanski, Samuel; Maryland, 1910 ***3259.35*** *p65*
Urbanski, Wadysaw; Maryland, 1910 ***3259.35*** *p65*
Urbaynski, Anna; Maryland, 1910 ***3259.35*** *p65*
Ure, Rev. 48; Ontario, 1871 ***1823.15*** *p268*
Ureck, John; New York, 1833 ***8197.10*** *p358*
Uren, John; New York, 1819 ***8197.10*** *p289*
Urgehart, Aneas; Pennsylvania, 1779 ***4629.10*** *p40*
Urguhart, Eneas; Pennsylvania, 1777 ***4629.10*** *p22*

V

Vaass, Peter; Port uncertain, 1756 ***2856.30*** *p467*
Vaber, Hans; America, 1722 ***1224.2*** *p118*
Vache, John; New York, 1795 ***8197.10*** *p6*
Vacher, Mr.; Quebec, 1858 ***9196.15*** *p47*
Vacy, Ann 40; Ontario, 1871 ***1823.15*** *p268*
Vade, Frederick 34; Ontario, 1871 ***1823.15*** *p268*
Vaer, Mr.; Quebec, 1856 ***9196.15*** *p6*
Vagerski, Frank; Maryland, 1910 ***3259.35*** *p65*
Vagierski, Celia; Maryland, 1910 ***3259.35*** *p65*
Vahhan, Elizabeth *SEE* Vahhan, Rice
Vahhan, Mary *SEE* Vahhan, Rice
Vahhan, Rebecca *SEE* Vahhan, Rice
Vahhan, Rice; Maryland, 1668 ***2524.55*** *p226*
Wife: Rebecca
Child: Elizabeth
Child: Mary
Vail, Emma 20; Ontario, 1861 ***2896.25*** *p25*
Vail, Willam 45; Ontario, 1871 ***1823.28*** *p101*
Vaillant, Anthony; New York, 1831 ***8197.10*** *p364*
Vaines, M. A. 26; Virginia, 1774 ***1220.25*** *p94*
Vair, James 53; Ontario, 1871 ***1823.22*** *p162*
Vaissiere, Victor; New York, 1822 ***8197.10*** *p290*
Valantine, John 23; Jamaica, 1774 ***1220.25*** *p37*
Valentin, Mr.; America, 1700-1799 ***2856.30*** *p467*
With wife & 7 children
Valentin, Anna Maria; Port uncertain, 1755 ***2856.30*** *p467*
Valentine, Emma 27; Ontario, 1871 ***1823.15*** *p268*
Valentine, M. A. 48; Ontario, 1861 ***2896.26*** *p5*
Valentine, Richard; New York, 1840 ***8197.10*** *p290*
Valentine, Theophilus; New York, 1838 ***8197.10*** *p150*
Valentine, W. 55; Ontario, 1861 ***2896.26*** *p5*
Valentine, William H. 16; Ontario, 1861 ***2896.27*** *p29*
Valiquette, Anna Monahan; Vermont, 1856-1935 ***5900.10*** *p419*
Valiquette, Edward A.; Vermont, 1851-1924 ***5900.10*** *p419*
Valiquette, Mary Ann Daly; Vermont, 1827-1881 ***5900.10*** *p419*
Valleau, Deborah; Ontario, 1861 ***2896.28*** *p64*
Valleau, E. 28; Ontario, 1861 ***2896.28*** *p64*
Valleau, Eli 1; Ontario, 1861 ***2896.28*** *p64*
Valleau, Hellen 6; Ontario, 1861 ***2896.28*** *p61*
Valleau, Hiram 23; Ontario, 1861 ***2896.28*** *p64*
Valleau, Ida 3; Ontario, 1861 ***2896.28*** *p64*
Valleau, Irvin 21; Ontario, 1861 ***2896.28*** *p64*
Valleau, Martha 6; Ontario, 1861 ***2896.28*** *p64*
Valleau, Martha 58; Ontario, 1861 ***2896.28*** *p64*
Valleau, Mary C. 16; Ontario, 1861 ***2896.28*** *p64*
Valleau, Polly 4; Ontario, 1861 ***2896.28*** *p61*
Vallence, Guido; Virginia, 1666 ***6212.30*** *p26*
Valley, Elizabeth *SEE* Valley, Thomas
Valley, John *SEE* Valley, Thomas
Valley, Margaret; Vermont, 1845-1923 ***5900.10*** *p285*
Valley, Margarett *SEE* Valley, Thomas
Valley, Rachell *SEE* Valley, Thomas
Valley, Thomas; Maryland, 1665 ***2524.55*** *p226*
Wife: Elizabeth
Child: Margarett
Child: Elizabeth
Child: Rachell
Child: John
Valliano, T. 22; Alaska, 1917 ***9196.1*** *p51*
Valliano, T. 22; Yukon, 1917 ***9196.1*** *p51*
Vallier, Joseph; New York, 1820 ***8197.10*** *p290*
Valliere De St. Real, Mr.; Quebec, 1858 ***9196.15*** *p36*
Valliere De St. Real, Mrs.; Quebec, 1858 ***9196.15*** *p36*
Vallon, Peter; Maryland, 1680 ***2524.55*** *p226*
Valloo, Lewis; New York, 1803 ***8197.10*** *p15*
Valnant, Susanna 22; Maryland, 1775 ***1220.25*** *p115*
Valondek, Frank; Maryland, 1910 ***3259.35*** *p65*
Valpey, John; New York, 1831 ***8197.10*** *p368*
Valton, Peter; Maryland, 1680 ***2524.55*** *p226*
Valuck, Jacob 56; Ontario, 1871 ***1823.28*** *p101*
Vanalstine, Mrs. 77; Ontario, 1861 ***2896.26*** *p24*
Vanalstine, Alonzo 15; Ontario, 1861 ***2896.27*** *p8*
Vanalstine, C. 3; Ontario, 1861 ***2896.26*** *p14*
Vanalstine, C. 7; Ontario, 1861 ***2896.26*** *p14*
Vanalstine, C. 15; Ontario, 1861 ***2896.26*** *p14*
Vanalstine, Mrs. C. 29; Ontario, 1861 ***2896.26*** *p24*
Vanalstine, Cor's 87; Ontario, 1861 ***2896.26*** *p24*
Vanalstine, Dy 37; Ontario, 1861 ***2896.27*** *p8*
Vanalstine, E. 32; Ontario, 1861 ***2896.26*** *p14*
Vanalstine, E. M. 5; Ontario, 1861 ***2896.26*** *p14*
Vanalstine, Flora 5; Ontario, 1861 ***2896.27*** *p8*
Vanalstine, G. 11; Ontario, 1861 ***2896.26*** *p14*
Vanalstine, H. 17; Ontario, 1861 ***2896.26*** *p14*
Vanalstine, J. 19; Ontario, 1861 ***2896.26*** *p14*
Vanalstine, L. 9; Ontario, 1861 ***2896.26*** *p14*
Van Alstine, Lambert; Pennsylvania, 1790 ***1224.2*** *p118*
Vanalstine, Me 7; Ontario, 1861 ***2896.27*** *p8*
Vanalstine, Sam 1; Ontario, 1861 ***2896.27*** *p8*
Vanalstine, Sarah 10; Ontario, 1861 ***2896.27*** *p8*
Vanalstine, T. E. 2; Ontario, 1861 ***2896.26*** *p24*
Vanalstine, Thomas 3; Ontario, 1861 ***2896.27*** *p8*
Vanalstine, W. H. 21; Ontario, 1861 ***2896.28*** *p53*
Van Arx, Samuel Jacob; New York, 1835 ***8197.10*** *p316*
Van Arx, Samuel James; New York, 1837 ***8197.10*** *p311*
Vanatter, John 62; Ontario, 1861 ***2896.28*** *p63*
Van Baerle, Thomas John; Ontario, 1837 ***1640.13*** *p128*
Vanblaricum, Sarah 36; Ontario, 1871 ***1823.22*** *p162*
Vanblauman, Peter 50; Ontario, 1871 ***1823.22*** *p162*
Van Bockel, Andrew J.; New York, 1805 ***8197.10*** *p30*
Van Camp, Peter; Albany, New York, 1790 ***1224.2*** *p118*
Vancamps, Charles; New York, 1811 ***8197.10*** *p57*
Vance, C. 14; Ontario, 1861 ***2896.27*** *p9*
Vance, C. 30; Ontario, 1861 ***2896.27*** *p9*
Vance, F. D. 1; Ontario, 1861 ***2896.27*** *p9*
Vance, Ellice 6; Ontario, 1861 ***2896.28*** *p21*
Vance, F. 7; Ontario, 1861 ***2896.27*** *p9*
Vance, George 2; Ontario, 1861 ***2896.27*** *p9*
Vance, J. 16; Ontario, 1861 ***2896.27*** *p9*
Vance, J. 18; Ontario, 1861 ***2896.27*** *p9*
Vance, James 46; Ontario, 1861 ***2896.28*** *p21*
Vance, James 61; Ontario, 1871 ***1823.15*** *p268*
Vance, John 13; Ontario, 1861 ***2896.28*** *p21*
Vance, John 46; Ontario, 1871 ***1823.28*** *p101*
Vance, Lawrence; Pennsylvania, 1777 ***4629.10*** *p27*
Vance, M. 12; Ontario, 1861 ***2896.27*** *p9*
Vance, Robert; Ontario, 1861 ***2896.27*** *p9*
Vance, Robert 40; Ontario, 1861 ***2896.27*** *p9*
Vance, T. 10; Ontario, 1861 ***2896.27*** *p9*
Vance, Thomas; New York, 1832-1840 ***8197.10*** *p201*
Vance, W. F. 21; Ontario, 1861 ***2896.27*** *p9*
Vance, W. M. 20; Ontario, 1861 ***2896.27*** *p9*
Vance, W. S. 1; Ontario, 1861 ***2896.27*** *p9*
Vance, William; New York, New York, 1841 ***6058.10*** *p35*
Vance, William 59; Ontario, 1861 ***2896.27*** *p9*
Van Cleaf, Daniel 30; Ontario, 1861 ***2896.27*** *p43*
Van Cleaf, Hannah 23; Ontario, 1861 ***2896.27*** *p43*
Van Cleaf, Hannah 61; Ontario, 1861 ***2896.27*** *p43*
Van Cleaf, Phebe A. 20; Ontario, 1861 ***2896.27*** *p43*
Vancleif, Daniel 21; Ontario, 1861 ***2896.25*** *p33*
Vanclief, Cath. 55; Ontario, 1861 ***2896.26*** *p32*
Vanclief, Christy 4; Ontario, 1861 ***2896.28*** *p60*
Van Clief, D. 20; Ontario, 1861 ***2896.28*** *p17*
Vanclief, Daniel; Ontario, 1861 ***2896.28*** *p65*
Vanclief, Daniel 21; Ontario, 1861 ***2896.28*** *p60*
Vanclief, Deborah 24; Ontario, 1861 ***2896.28*** *p60*
Vanclief, George 11; Ontario, 1861 ***2896.28*** *p60*
Vanclief, Hannah 30; Ontario, 1861 ***2896.27*** *p3*
Vanclief, Jacob 19; Ontario, 1861 ***2896.28*** *p50*
Vanclief, Jesse 19; Ontario, 1861 ***2896.28*** *p60*
Vanclief, John 7; Ontario, 1861 ***2896.26*** *p6*
Vanclief, John 13; Ontario, 1861 ***2896.28*** *p60*
Vanclief, L. 14; Ontario, 1861 ***2896.26*** *p7*
Vanclief, Leslie 4; Ontario, 1861 ***2896.26*** *p6*
Vanclief, M. A. 31; Ontario, 1861 ***2896.26*** *p6*
Vanclief, Sarah 8; Ontario, 1861 ***2896.28*** *p60*
Vanclief, Sarah 43; Ontario, 1861 ***2896.28*** *p60*
Vanclief, Susan 17; Ontario, 1861 ***2896.28*** *p60*
Vanclief, William H. 22; Ontario, 1861 ***2896.28*** *p60*
Van Court, John 60; Ontario, 1861 ***2896.25*** *p8*
Vancourt, Michael; Pennsylvania, 1777 ***4629.10*** *p29*
Van Court, Nancy Ann 19; Ontario, 1861 ***2896.25*** *p8*
Vandan, Mrs.; Maryland, 1650 ***2524.55*** *p226*
Vandefort, Michael Powleson; Maryland, 1663 ***2524.55*** *p226*
Van den Heuvell, Kornelis Wilhelm; New York, 1794 ***8197.10*** *p6*
Vanderburgh, Richard; Long Island, 1829 ***1224.3*** *p80*
Vanderdy, . . . 28; Grenada, 1774 ***1220.25*** *p127*
Vanderen, Charles; Pennsylvania, 1779 ***4629.10*** *p41*
Vanderince, Perlina 75; Ontario, 1861 ***2896.28*** *p34*
Van der Linden, John Jacob De Jung; New York, 1807 ***8197.10*** *p52*
Vandermark, Ferdenand; New York, 1864 ***6058.10*** *p53*
Van Der Sluys, Peter; New York, 1803 ***8197.10*** *p15*
Vandewater, Anna 30; Ontario, 1861 ***2896.27*** *p33*
Vandewater, Henrey 18; Ontario, 1871 ***1823.28*** *p101*
Vandewater, James H. 9; Ontario, 1861 ***2896.27*** *p33*
Vandewater, Juliann 2; Ontario, 1861 ***2896.27*** *p33*
Vandewater, Malvina 8; Ontario, 1861 ***2896.27*** *p33*
Vandewater, Robert 5; Ontario, 1861 ***2896.27*** *p33*
Vandewater, Sarah J. 6; Ontario, 1861 ***2896.27*** *p33*
Vandewater, William E. 4; Ontario, 1861 ***2896.27*** *p33*
Vandihider, Peter 81; Ontario, 1861 ***2896.25*** *p4*
Vandike, Joseph; Pennsylvania, 1779 ***4629.10*** *p37*
Vandosme, Abraham 21; Maryland, 1774 ***1220.25*** *p47*
Vandrel, Jacob; New England, 1709 ***1224.2*** *p118*
Van Duisburg, Henry Anthony Charles; New York, 1815 ***8197.10*** *p289*
Vandusen, Agnes 24; Ontario, 1861 ***2896.25*** *p61*
Vandusen, Ann 26; Ontario, 1861 ***2896.27*** *p14*
Vandusen, E. D. 16; Ontario, 1861 ***2896.26*** *p2*
Vandusen, Ella 2; Ontario, 1861 ***2896.25*** *p61*
Vandusen, G. A. 9; Ontario, 1861 ***2896.26*** *p2*
Vandusen, Mary A. 1; Ontario, 1861 ***2896.25*** *p9*
Vandusen, Permilia 52; Ontario, 1861 ***2896.27*** *p14*
Vandusen, Philip; Ontario, 1861 ***2896.28*** *p54*
Vandusen, R. 14; Ontario, 1861 ***2896.26*** *p2*
Vandusen, Rebecca 21; Ontario, 1861 ***2896.27*** *p30*
Vandusen, Sarah A. 24; Ontario, 1861 ***2896.25*** *p9*
Vandusen, Sintha 35; Ontario, 1861 ***2896.26*** *p2*
Vandusen, William W. 3; Ontario, 1861 ***2896.25*** *p9*
Vandyke, Elizabeth 4; Ontario, 1861 ***2896.27*** *p72*
Van Dyke, John; New Jersey, 1812 ***1224.3*** *p80*
Vandyke, Mary 34; Ontario, 1861 ***2896.27*** *p72*
Vandyne, Douw; Long Island, n.d. ***1224.2*** *p118*
Vane, Walter; Virginia, 1665-1666 ***6212.30*** *p22*
Van Egmond, August 47; Ontario, 1871 ***1823.15*** *p268*
Van Egmond, Constant 64; Ontario, 1871 ***1823.15*** *p268*
Van Egmond, Edward 59; Ontario, 1871 ***1823.15*** *p268*

Van Egmond, Leopold 53; Ontario, 1871 1823.15 p268
Van Egmond, Susan 85; Ontario, 1871 1823.15 p268
Van Egmond, William 44; Ontario, 1871 1823.15 p268
Van Einden, . . .; Maryland, 1631-1685 2524.55 p226
Van Einden, Francis; Maryland, 1635 2524.55 p226
VanEmarson, Harman; Maryland, 1680-1681 2524.55 p226
Vanenden, Francis; Maryland, 1635 2524.55 p226
Van Ewigen, Meynart Albert; New York, 1807 8197.10 p52
Vangeson, Mrs. 72; Ontario, 1861 2896.26 p24
Vangeson, Garret 75; Ontario, 1861 2896.26 p24
Vanhack, John; Maryland, 1651 2524.55 p226
Vanhesle, Margarite; Maryland, 1685 2524.55 p226
VanHeyst, Abraham; Maryland, 1669 2524.55 p17
Van Heyst, Gertrayt; Maryland, 1669 2524.55 p17
VanHeyst, Rynier; Maryland, 1669 2524.55 p17
Van Horn, Caniff 2; Ontario, 1861 2896.28 p28
Van Horn, Cornelia 2; Ontario, 1861 2896.28 p26
Vanhorn, John 20; Ontario, 1861 2896.27 p65
Van Horn, Lydia J. 20; Ontario, 1861 2896.28 p26
Van Horn, Nancy 61; Ontario, 1861 2896.28 p28
Van Horn, Nancy M. 21; Ontario, 1861 2896.28 p28
Van Horn, Paul 29; Ontario, 1861 2896.28 p28
Van Horn, Townsend 21; Ontario, 1861 2896.28 p24
Van Horne, Cornelius Garret; New York, New York, 1770 1224.2 p118
Vaningen, Abraham J. 43; Ontario, 1871 1823.22 p162
Van Ingen, Wiliam 68; Ontario, 1871 1823.22 p162
Vann, John; Virginia, 1665 6212.30 p18
Vanners, Francis; New York, 1838 8197.10 p150
Vannorman, Elizabeth 32; Ontario, 1861 2896.27 p73
Vannorman, Garrick 59; Ontario, 1861 2896.27 p73
Vannorman, Seymour 1; Ontario, 1861 2896.27 p73
Vannost, John; Pennsylvania, 1779 4629.10 p37
Vannovous, Mr.; Quebec, 1857 9196.15 p26
Vanorman, A. 5; Ontario, 1861 2896.25 p41
Vanorman, Allen 21; Ontario, 1861 2896.25 p10
Vanorman, Annie 8; Ontario, 1861 2896.28 p38
Vanorman, Ben 1; Ontario, 1861 2896.25 p34
Vanorman, Catherine 20; Ontario, 1861 2896.25 p10
Vanorman, Fanny 31; Ontario, 1861 2896.25 p41
Vanorman, Frederick 1; Ontario, 1861 2896.28 p38
Vanorman, Jacob 75; Ontario, 1861 2896.25 p10
Vanorman, M. 23; Ontario, 1861 2896.25 p34
Vanorman, Nelson 6; Ontario, 1861 2896.28 p38
Vanorman, Philip 5; Ontario, 1861 2896.28 p38
Vanost, Isaac; Pennsylvania, 1777 4629.10 p25
Vanosten, Jacob; Pennsylvania, 1777 4629.10 p27
Vanplanke, Gillcon; Virginia, 1672 6212.30 p50
Vanreid, Henry; Pennsylvania, 1777 4629.10 p23
Vanreynegom, Francis W.; New York, 1802 8197.10 p26
Vans, Samuel; Boston, 1709 1224.2 p118
Van Salzen, Cordt; New York, 1826 8197.10 p290
Van Santin, H. G.; Portland, Maine, 1858 9196.15 p28
Van Seggern, Christian; New York, 1827 8197.10 p290
VanSickle, Andrew; Pennsylvania, 1861-1864 6058.10 p49
Vansickler, E. 4; Ontario, 1861 2896.26 p4
Vansickler, E. 22; Ontario, 1861 2896.26 p4
Vansickler, M. N. 1; Ontario, 1861 2896.26 p4
Vansiclin, Zerdem 78; Ontario, 1871 1823.22 p163
Vanslycke, Marcillus 55; Ontario, 1871 1823.22 p163
Vansoldt, Abraham; Virginia, 1665 1224.1 p60
Vanstan, John; New York, 1837 8197.10 p104
Vanston, John 22; Ontario, 1871 1823.15 p268
Vanston, John 45; Ontario, 1871 1823.15 p268
Vanstone, James 36; Ontario, 1871 1823.15 p268
Vanstone, James 51; Ontario, 1871 1823.15 p268
Vanstone, Samuel 40; Ontario, 1871 1823.15 p268
Vanstone, William 42; Ontario, 1871 1823.15 p268
Van Swieten, Ouzeel; New York, 1703 1224.2 p118
Vantassel, Ellen 26; Ontario, 1871 1823.15 p269
Vanusin, John; Pennsylvania, 1777 4629.10 p12
Vanuxen, James; Pennsylvania, 1777 4629.10 p29
Vanvalkenburgh, Ann 20; Ontario, 1861 2896.25 p70
Van Veen, Karst Jans; New York, 1836 8197.10 p78
Van Veghten, John; Havana, 1764 1224.2 p118
Van Veghten, John; New York, 1764 1224.2 p118
Van Veightin, John; Havana, 1764 1224.2 p118
Van Veightin, John; New York, 1764 1224.2 p118
Vanvolkenburg, John 60; Ontario, 1871 1823.22 p163
Vanwart, James 30; Ontario, 1861 2896.25 p58
Vanwart, James 75; Ontario, 1861 2896.25 p63
Vanwart, John 50; Ontario, 1861 2896.25 p58
Vanwart, Mary Ann 72; Ontario, 1861 2896.25 p63
Vanwort, Daniel 15; Ontario, 1861 2896.25 p37
Vanwort, E. 1; Ontario, 1861 2896.25 p54
Vanwort, Eunice 45; Ontario, 1861 2896.25 p37
Vanwort, George 13; Ontario, 1861 2896.25 p28
Vanwort, George 14; Ontario, 1861 2896.25 p54
Vanwort, J. 10; Ontario, 1861 2896.25 p54
Vanwort, J. 46; Ontario, 1861 2896.25 p28
Vanwort, James 13; Ontario, 1861 2896.25 p37
Vanwort, John 19; Ontario, 1861 2896.25 p37
Vanwort, L. C. 10; Ontario, 1861 2896.25 p28
Vanwort, L. J. 16; Ontario, 1861 2896.25 p28
Vanwort, M. 8; Ontario, 1861 2896.25 p54
Vanwort, M. 37; Ontario, 1861 2896.25 p54
Vanwort, M. E. 6; Ontario, 1861 2896.25 p28
Vanwort, Mary 11; Ontario, 1861 2896.25 p37
Vanwort, Mary 24; Ontario, 1861 2896.25 p64
Vanwort, S. J. 17; Ontario, 1861 2896.25 p54
Vanwort, Sophia 21; Ontario, 1861 2896.25 p37
Van Wyck, Elizabeth; Baltimore, 1821 1224.3 p80
Van Wyck, Elizabeth Linnington; Baltimore, 1819 1224.3 p80
Varco, Alfred F. 41; Ontario, 1871 1823.22 p163
Varco, Anna 55; Ontario, 1871 1823.22 p163
Varcoe, John 64; Ontario, 1871 1823.15 p269
Varcoe, William 42; Ontario, 1871 1823.22 p163
Varey, Joseph; New York, 1818 8197.10 p289
Varisellas, V. 32; Alaska, 1917 9196.1 p48
Varisellas, V. 32; Whitehorse, Yukon, 1917 9196.1 p48
Varisellaz, Victor 26; Alaska, 1912 9196.1 p18
Varlett, Sarah; Virginia, 1671-1672 6212.30 p45
Varley, Elizabeth; Maryland, 1673 2524.55 p226
Varley, Isabell; Maryland, 1673 2524.55 p226
Varley, Margaret 35; New York, 1775 1220.25 p143
With 2 children
Varnett, James; Virginia, 1672 6212.30 p49
Varney, John 60; Ontario, 1871 1823.28 p101
Varney, Levi 42; Ontario, 1861 2896.27 p56
Varney, Ruth E. 19; Ontario, 1861 2896.27 p56
Varrel, William 24; Ontario, 1871 1823.28 p101
Vasakowski, Joseph; Maryland, 1910 3259.35 p65
Vasques, Joaquim Jose; New York, 1828 8197.10 p348
Vass, Charles; Georgia, 1698 1640.13 p128
Vass, William; New York, 1796 8197.10 p7
Vassall, William; Barbados, 1657 1224.1 p60
Vassau, Alicia; Vermont, 1845-1903 5900.10 p318
Vassler, Catharina; Port uncertain, 1764 2856.30 p471
Vauce, William 35; Ontario, 1871 1823.15 p269
Vaughan, . . .; New Hampshire, 1641-1660 4628.40 p44
Vaughan, Mrs.; Maryland, 1649 2524.55 p226
Vaughan, Mrs.; Maryland, 1658 2524.55 p226
Vaughan, Bruerton; Maryland, 1674 2524.55 p226
Vaughan, Bruerton; Maryland, 1677 2524.55 p227
Vaughan, Charles; Maine, 1842 1224.3 p80
Vaughan, Elizabeth *SEE* Vaughan, Rice
Vaughan, Elizabeth; Maryland, 1675 2524.55 p227
Vaughan, Ellen 47; Vermont, 1876 5900.10 p99
Vaughan, Ellinge; Maryland, 1662 2524.55 p227
Vaughan, Frances Western; Maine, 1842 1224.3 p80
Vaughan, Henry P.; New York, 1836 8197.10 p319
Vaughan, Hugh 28; Virginia, 1774 1220.25 p94
Vaughan, Jane; Virginia, 1665 6212.30 p18
Vaughan, Jane 19; Philadelphia, 1774 1220.25 p42
Vaughan, Jane Jones; Maryland, 1681 1224.1 p60
Vaughan, John; Maryland, 1672 2524.55 p227
Vaughan, John; Maryland, 1673 2524.55 p227
Vaughan, John 23; Maryland, 1774 1220.25 p54
Vaughan, Martha Underwood; South Carolina, 1754 1224.2 p118
Vaughan, Mary *SEE* Vaughan, Rice
Vaughan, Morris; Virginia, 1667 6212.30 p37
Vaughan, Petrus Wynard; New York, 1845 1224.3 p81
Vaughan, Rebecca *SEE* Vaughan, Rice
Vaughan, Rice; Maryland, 1668 2524.55 p226
Wife: Rebecca
Child: Mary
Child: Elizabeth
Vaughan, Robert; Maryland, 1649 2524.55 p227
With wife
Vaughan, Thomas; Maryland, 1663 2524.55 p227
Vaughan, Thomas; New York, 1803 8197.10 p15
Vaughan, Thomas, Jr.; Maryland, 1678 2524.55 p227
Vaughan, William; Virginia, 1665 6212.30 p20
Vaughan, William 22; Philadelphia, 1775 1220.25 p8
Vaughan, William 28; Ontario, 1871 1823.28 p101
Vaughan, William 32; Maryland, 1774 1220.25 p37
Vaughn, Mary; Vermont, 1819-1913 5900.10 p619
Vaulotte, James 17; Philadelphia, 1775 1220.25 p107
Vaun, Roger; New York, 1839 8197.10 p142
Vaupell, George F.; New York, 1830 8197.10 p67
Vauthey, Louis 33; Baltimore, 1834-1836 8197.10 p78
Vautier, Daniel 22; Philadelphia, 1774 1220.25 p42
Vaux, David; Maryland, 1670 2524.55 p227
Vaux, James; Pennsylvania, 1777 4629.10 p23
Vaux, Walter; Virginia, 1665 6212.30 p18
Vavasser, Richard; Philadelphia, 1778 1224.2 p118
Vawter, Ellis; Maryland, 1664 2524.55 p227
Vawter, Thomas; Maryland, 1664 2524.55 p227
Veale, John; New York, 1840 8197.10 p290
Veatch, William; Georgia, 1699 1640.13 p128
Veck, Johann; America, 1697 2856.30 p467
With wife & children
Veckel, Hannah 20; Fort Cumberland, Nova Scotia, 1774 1220.25 p15
Veckel, Mary 20; Fort Cumberland, Nova Scotia, 1774 1220.25 p15
Vedulich, Antonio 45; British Columbia, 1909 9196.1 p27
Vedulich, Antonio 45; Seattle, 1909 9196.1 p27
Vegele, Johann; Canada, 1751 2856.30 p467
Vegnall, Timo; Virginia, 1665-1666 6212.30 p23
Vegsey, John 35; Ontario, 1871 1823.15 p269
Vehner, Georg; Port uncertain, 1738 2856.30 p467
With 3 children
Veikovich, E. 39; Alaska, 1917 9196.1 p53
Veikovich, E. 39; Whitehorse, Yukon, 1917 9196.1 p53
Veil, John 50; Ontario, 1871 1823.15 p269
Veille, Isaac; New York, 1824 8197.10 p290
Veit, Anna Margarete; Port uncertain, 1755 2856.30 p467
Veitch, Captain; Quebec, 1858 9196.15 p35
Veitch, James; Maryland, 1658 2524.55 p227
Veith, Anna Maria; America, 1774 2856.30 p467
Veith, Apollonia; America, 1774 2856.30 p467
Veith, Friedrich; New York, 1836 8197.10 p290
Veith, Jacob; New York, 1836 8197.10 p290
Veith, John Adam; New York, 1836 8197.10 p290
Veith, Magdalena; Port uncertain, 1765 2856.30 p467
Veitin, Anna Margarete; Port uncertain, 1755 2856.30 p467
Velden, Maria Elisabeth; Port uncertain, 1766 2856.30 p467
Veldin, Ottilia; Port uncertain, 1760 2856.30 p467
Velepsky, Frank; Maryland, 1910 3259.35 p65
Velovski, John 28; Seattle, 1910 9196.1 p29
Velten, Albert; Port uncertain, 1750 2856.30 p467
With wife & 5 children
Velten, El. Cath. *SEE* Velten, Matheiss
Velten, El. Cath. *SEE* Velten, Peter
Velten, Elis. Catharina; America, 1709 2856.30 p326
Husband: P.
With son
Velten, Elis. Catharina; Port uncertain, 1712 2856.30 p326
Husband: P.
With son
Velten, Elis. Catharina; Port uncertain, 1793 2856.30 p467
Velten, Johann Meinhard; America, 1709 2856.30 p467
With parents
Velten, Johann Meinhard; Port uncertain, 1712 2856.30 p467
With parents
Velten, Johann Peter; America, 1748 2856.30 p467
Velten, Martin; Port uncertain, 1790 2856.30 p467
Velten, Matheiss; America, 1739 2856.30 p467
Wife: El. Cath.
With child
Velten, P. *SEE* Velten, Elis. Catharina
Velten, Peter; America, 1709 2856.30 p467
With wife & son
Velten, Peter; America, 1709 2856.30 p467
Wife: El. Cath.
With son
Velten, Peter; America, 1717 2856.30 p467
Wife: El. Cath.
With son
Velten, Peter; Port uncertain, 1712 2856.30 p467
With wife & son
Velti, Catharina; Port uncertain, 1773 2856.30 p467
Velti, Maria Catharina; Port uncertain, 1773 2856.30 p467
Veltin, Georg; America, 1738 2856.30 p467
With wife & 2 children
Velzant, Frances; Maryland, 1910 3259.35 p65
Velzant, Stanislaw; Maryland, 1910 3259.35 p65
Venables, Thomas; Philadelphia, 1752 1224.2 p118
Venaken, Mathias; Maryland, 1665 2524.55 p227
Vence, Francis; Philadelphia, 1794 4629.10 p78
Venda, Henry 40; Ontario, 1871 1823.15 p269
Venechizki, Frank; Maryland, 1910 3259.35 p65
Veners, Francis; New York, 1838 8197.10 p150
Venizelos, L. 38; Juneau, Alaska, 1917 9196.1 p45
Venizelos, L. 38; Whitehorse, Yukon, 1917 9196.1 p45
Venizelos, P. 45; Juneau, Alaska, 1917 9196.1 p45
Venizelos, P. 45; Whitehorse, Yukon, 1917 9196.1 p45
Venner, Samuel; America, n.d. 1224.3 p80
Vent, Frederick 43; Ontario, 1871 1823.28 p101
Ventland, Ludway 33; Ontario, 1871 1823.28 p101
Ventress, Mark 35; Ontario, 1871 1823.22 p163
Venzelas, I. 38; Alaska, 1916 9196.1 p43
Venzelas, I. 38; Whitehorse, Yukon, 1916 9196.1 p43
Verbass, Jakob; America, 1770 2856.30 p467

Verdier, Francis Jean Charles; New York, 1794 ***8197.10*** *p3*
Vere, John Weir; St. Vincent, 1781 ***1640.13*** *p128*
Verelle, Hypollite; New York, 1838 ***8197.10*** *p150*
Veren, Mary; New England, 1658 ***1224.1*** *p51*
Verge, Magdalena; Port uncertain, 1712 ***2856.30*** *p468*
Verier, Jno; Virginia, 1664 ***6212.30*** *p14*
Verier, Jno; Virginia, 1665 ***6212.30*** *p22*
Verity, W. H. 41; Ontario, 1871 ***1823.15*** *p269*
Verman, John; Virginia, 1666 ***6212.30*** *p27*
Vermilyea, Ann Jennett A. 7; Ontario, 1861 ***2896.28*** *p24*
Vermilyea, Edna Adell 2; Ontario, 1861 ***2896.28*** *p24*
Vermilyea, Jane 29; Ontario, 1861 ***2896.28*** *p24*
Vermilyea, Jane 30; Ontario, 1861 ***2896.28*** *p24*
Vermilyea, M. 60; Ontario, 1861 ***2896.28*** *p3*
Vermilyea, R. A. 20; Ontario, 1861 ***2896.28*** *p3*
Vermylea, Jane 22; Ontario, 1861 ***2896.28*** *p20*
Vernan, Thomas 22; Carolina, 1774 ***1220.25*** *p38*
Vernes, Philip; Pennsylvania, 1777 ***4629.10*** *p13*
Vernon, Christopher; Maryland, 1724 ***1224.2*** *p118*
Vernon, Daniel; Maryland, 1675 ***2524.55*** *p227*
Vernon, Edw; Virginia, 1664 ***6212.30*** *p9*
Vernon, Francis; New England, 1656 ***1224.1*** *p60*
Vernon, George; Virginia, 1666 ***6212.30*** *p29*
Vernon, Henry; Virginia, 1664 ***6212.30*** *p11*
Vernon, Jno; Virginia, 1664 ***6212.30*** *p8*
Vernon, Job; Pennsylvania, 1781 ***4629.10*** *p42*
Vernon, Margaret 48; Ontario, 1871 ***1823.22*** *p163*
Vernon, Robert; New York, 1831 ***8197.10*** *p365*
Vernon, Thomas; Savannah, Georgia, 1784 ***1224.2*** *p118*
Verolier, Francis Jean Charles; New York, 1794 ***8197.10*** *p3*
Verren, Antoine Francois; New York, 1831 ***8197.10*** *p290*
Verret, Mr.; Quebec, 1858 ***9196.15*** *p31*
Verson, John; Maryland, 1657 ***2524.55*** *p227*
Vertris, John; Virginia, 1665 ***6212.30*** *p17*
Vertue, James; North America, 1799 ***1640.13*** *p128*
Vertue, Robert 24; Ontario, 1871 ***1823.15*** *p269*
Verty, Thomas; New York, 1838 ***8197.10*** *p150*
Very, Joseph; New York, 1827 ***8197.10*** *p347*
Vesal, Catherine 19; Philadelphia, 1774 ***1220.25*** *p43*
Vesar, Lewis 23; America, 1774 ***1220.25*** *p36*
Vessell, Daick; Virginia, 1672 ***6212.30*** *p51*
Vessey, Nathaniel; Maryland, 1675 ***2524.55*** *p227*
Vetal, Frank; Vermont, 1882-1901 ***5900.10*** *p216*
Vetal, Mary L.; Vermont, 1842-1887 ***5900.10*** *p216*
Vetch, James 36; Ontario, 1871 ***1823.15*** *p269*
Vetter, Miss; Port uncertain, 1734 ***2856.30*** *p468*
Vetter, Adam; America, 1752 ***2856.30*** *p468*
Vetter, Anna Maria; Port uncertain, 1746 ***2856.30*** *p468*
Vetter, Eva; Port uncertain, 1734 ***2856.30*** *p468*
Vetter, Hans; America, 1765 ***2856.30*** *p468*
Vetter, Johann; Port uncertain, 1751 ***2856.30*** *p468*
Vetter, Marianna; Port uncertain, 1760 ***2856.30*** *p468*
Vetter, Peter; Port uncertain, 1746 ***2856.30*** *p468*
Vetter, Philipp; Port uncertain, 1734 ***2856.30*** *p468*
Vetter, Susanna; Port uncertain, 1777 ***2856.30*** *p468*
Vetterlin, Daniel; Port uncertain, 1798 ***2856.30*** *p468*
Vetterlin, Daniel; Port uncertain, 1799 ***2856.30*** *p468*
Vial, Mr.; Quebec, 1857 ***9196.15*** *p16*
Vial, Mrs.; Quebec, 1857 ***9196.15*** *p27*
Viall, Charles 19; Grenada, 1774 ***1220.25*** *p58*
Viand, Augustino Domique 30; Philadelphia, 1789 ***4629.10*** *p56*
Wife: Mary
Viand, Mary *SEE* Viand, Augustino Domique
Viant, Catherine 52; Ontario, 1861 ***2896.25*** *p7*
Vicary, George 30; Ontario, 1871 ***1823.28*** *p101*
Vicary, Walter 34; Ontario, 1871 ***1823.28*** *p101*
Viccary, Joshua; Maryland, 1673 ***2524.55*** *p227*
Vich, N. 23; Alaska, 1912 ***9196.1*** *p38*
Vich, N. 23; British Columbia, 1912 ***9196.1*** *p38*
Vichtner, Mattheis; America, 1738 ***2856.30*** *p468*
With wife & daughter
Vicke, Martin 48; Ontario, 1871 ***1823.15*** *p269*
Vickers, Mrs.; Portland, Maine, 1858 ***9196.15*** *p28*
Vickers, Rev.; Portland, Maine, 1858 ***9196.15*** *p28*
Vickers, Francis; Maryland, 1678 ***2524.55*** *p227*
Vickers, J. R.; Portland, Maine, 1858 ***9196.15*** *p28*
Vicks, John 28; Ontario, 1871 ***1823.15*** *p269*
Victor, Theodore; New York, 1827 ***8197.10*** *p344*
Viczek, Bronislow; Maryland, 1910 ***3259.35*** *p65*
Vidal, Mr.; Quebec, 1858 ***9196.15*** *p38*
Vidal, Beaufort; Quebec, 1858 ***9196.15*** *p38*
Vidal, Jean Baptiste; New York, 1831 ***8197.10*** *p365*
Vidal, John B.; New York, 1831 ***8197.10*** *p369*
Vidal, Laurent; Philadelphia, 1793 ***4629.10*** *p71*
Vidal, O.; Quebec, 1858 ***9196.15*** *p38*
Videan, George 46; Ontario, 1871 ***1823.15*** *p269*
Videl, Eli; New York, 1838 ***8197.10*** *p150*
Videl, James; New York, 1838 ***8197.10*** *p150*
Vidler, Mary 23; America, 1774 ***1220.25*** *p35*
Vieland, Martin; Virginia, 1775 ***1220.25*** *p123*
Vielhauer, Miss; America, 1778 ***2856.30*** *p468*
Vielhauer, Adam, The Younger; Port uncertain, 1773 ***2856.30*** *p468*
Vielhauer, Adam, The Younger; Port uncertain, 1774 ***2856.30*** *p468*
Vienz, Jacob; New York, 1838 ***8197.10*** *p150*
Vier, Johann Jakob; Port uncertain, 1750 ***2856.30*** *p468*
Vierer, Heinrich; Port uncertain, 1783 ***2856.30*** *p468*
Vigars, John 50; Ontario, 1871 ***1823.28*** *p101*
Vigars, William 29; Ontario, 1871 ***1823.28*** *p101*
Vigelius, Anton Michael; Port uncertain, 1749 ***2856.30*** *p468*
With wife & children
Viger, I. I.; Portland, Maine, 1858 ***9196.15*** *p29*
Viger, J. L.; Quebec, 1858 ***9196.15*** *p39*
Vigers, William R.; New York, 1810 ***8197.10*** *p57*
Viggory, Thomas; New England, 1690 ***1224.1*** *p60*
Vigne, Anthony; Philadelphia, 1792 ***4629.10*** *p70*
Vihart, H.; Quebec, 1857 ***9196.15*** *p17*
Vilac, John; New York, 1812 ***8197.10*** *p57*
Vilhar, Gertrud; Port uncertain, 1750 ***2856.30*** *p468*
Vilhar, Johann; Port uncertain, 1750 ***2856.30*** *p468*
Vilhauer, Michael; Port uncertain, 1751 ***2856.30*** *p468*
Vilicky, Stanislow; Maryland, 1910 ***3259.35*** *p65*
Villar, Anton; America, 1744 ***2856.30*** *p468*
With wife
Villers, Samuel; Maryland, 1681 ***2524.55*** *p227*
Villhars, Miss; America, 1778 ***2856.30*** *p468*
Villhars, Adam, The Younger; Port uncertain, 1773 ***2856.30*** *p468*
Villhars, Adam, The Younger; Port uncertain, 1774 ***2856.30*** *p468*
Vimcard, Elizabeth 64; Ontario, 1871 ***1823.15*** *p269*
Vina, Jane; Virginia, 1663-1664 ***6212.30*** *p5*
Vinane, Jack 26; Ontario, 1861 ***2896.27*** *p59*
Vincent, . . .; Boston, 1765 ***4628.40*** *p115*
Vincent, Miss; Quebec, 1857 ***9196.15*** *p18*
Vincent, Mr.; Quebec, 1857 ***9196.15*** *p14*
Vincent, Mrs.; Quebec, 1857 ***9196.15*** *p14*
Vincent, Rev.; Quebec, 1857 ***9196.15*** *p25*
Vincent, A.; Quebec, 1857 ***9196.15*** *p14*
Vincent, Abram; Virginia, 1663 ***6212.30*** *p1*
Vincent, Adelaide 10; Ontario, 1861 ***2896.28*** *p33*
Vincent, Arnold 9; Ontario, 1861 ***2896.27*** *p48*
Vincent, Catherine A. 2; Ontario, 1861 ***2896.25*** *p16*
Vincent, Charles; Maryland, 1669 ***2524.55*** *p227*
Vincent, Charles A. 1; Ontario, 1861 ***2896.27*** *p48*
Vincent, Eliza 29; Ontario, 1861 ***2896.28*** *p19*
Vincent, Elizabeth A. 19; Ontario, 1861 ***2896.27*** *p48*
Vincent, Francis; Maryland, 1671 ***2524.55*** *p227*
Vincent, Francis; Virginia, 1664 ***6212.30*** *p7*
Vincent, Francis; Virginia, 1665-1666 ***6212.30*** *p22*
Vincent, Francis S. 6; Ontario, 1861 ***2896.28*** *p33*
Vincent, Gershom 78; Ontario, 1861 ***2896.27*** *p16*
Vincent, Hannah 24; Ontario, 1861 ***2896.25*** *p16*
Vincent, Hiram J. 25; Ontario, 1861 ***2896.27*** *p48*
Vincent, Irvin 7; Ontario, 1861 ***2896.27*** *p52*
Vincent, Jane; Maryland, 1676 ***2524.55*** *p227*
Vincent, Jemima Ann 16; Ontario, 1861 ***2896.27*** *p38*
Vincent, Jeremiah 14; Ontario, 1861 ***2896.27*** *p48*
Vincent, Joane; Maryland, 1668 ***2524.55*** *p227*
Vincent, Joane; Maryland, 1681 ***2524.55*** *p227*
Vincent, John; Maryland, 1665 ***2524.55*** *p227*
Vincent, John 12; Ontario, 1871 ***1823.15*** *p269*
Vincent, John 64; Ontario, 1871 ***1823.15*** *p269*
Vincent, Johnathan 17; Ontario, 1861 ***2896.27*** *p48*
Vincent, Johnathan 64; Ontario, 1861 ***2896.27*** *p48*
Vincent, Julia A. 9; Ontario, 1861 ***2896.28*** *p33*
Vincent, Levi 30; Ontario, 1861 ***2896.27*** *p48*
Vincent, Louisa 31; Ontario, 1861 ***2896.27*** *p38*
Vincent, Martha Boscawen Evelyn; Charleston, South Carolina, 1815 ***1224.3*** *p81*
Vincent, Mary 40; Ontario, 1861 ***2896.28*** *p33*
Vincent, Mary 78; Ontario, 1861 ***2896.27*** *p16*
Vincent, Mary J. 9; Ontario, 1861 ***2896.27*** *p52*
Vincent, Mary McGrath; Vermont, 1829-1881 ***5900.10*** *p330*
Vincent, Melezena 1; Ontario, 1861 ***2896.27*** *p48*
Vincent, Nancy 24; Ontario, 1861 ***2896.27*** *p48*
Vincent, Nicholas; Charleston, South Carolina, 1818 ***1224.3*** *p81*
Vincent, Rufus 13; Ontario, 1861 ***2896.28*** *p33*
Vincent, Samuel 23; Maryland, 1774 ***1220.25*** *p85*
Vincent, Sarah 32; Ontario, 1861 ***2896.27*** *p52*
Vincent, Susan 23; Ontario, 1861 ***2896.27*** *p48*
Vincent, Susannah E. 44; Ontario, 1861 ***2896.28*** *p19*
Vincent, William 3; Ontario, 1861 ***2896.27*** *p48*
Vincent, William 25; Maryland, 1775 ***1220.25*** *p107*
Vincent, William 38; Ontario, 1871 ***1823.15*** *p269*
Vincent, William Burton 1; Ontario, 1861 ***2896.27*** *p38*
Vincent, William F. 4; Ontario, 1861 ***2896.27*** *p48*
Vine, Amy; Maryland, 1663 ***2524.55*** *p227*
Vine, D. B. 57; Ontario, 1871 ***1823.15*** *p269*
Vine, Hugh; Virginia, 1672 ***6212.30*** *p50*
Vineberg, Hiram 16; Ontario, 1871 ***1823.28*** *p101*
Vines, Richard 58; Ontario, 1871 ***1823.15*** *p269*
Vinich, M. 26; Alaska, 1912 ***9196.1*** *p38*
Vinich, M. 26; Whitehorse, Yukon, 1912 ***9196.1*** *p38*
Vinju, Jan; New York, 1807 ***8197.10*** *p52*
Vink, Petrus Wynard; New York, 1845 ***1224.3*** *p81*
Vinnig, James 36; Ontario, 1871 ***1823.15*** *p269*
Vinning, Mrs.; Quebec, 1857 ***9196.15*** *p27*
Vino, James 41; Seattle, 1911 ***9196.1*** *p34*
Vinson, Christian *SEE* Vinson, Niles
Vinson, Ellen *SEE* Vinson, Niles
Vinson, John; Maryland, 1657 ***2524.55*** *p227*
Vinson, Niles; Maryland, 1670 ***2524.55*** *p227*
Wife: Ellen
Daughter: Christian
Vint, James 60; Ontario, 1871 ***1823.15*** *p269*
Vinzent, Roessler 37; Ontario, 1871 ***1823.15*** *p269*
Violet, . . . 30; Dominica, 1774 ***1220.25*** *p128*
Vion, Peter; New England, 1755 ***1224.2*** *p119*
Virden, Charles 69; Ontario, 1871 ***1823.22*** *p163*
Virgania, Ellias; Virginia, 1663 ***6212.30*** *p2*
Virgin, John 21; Maryland, 1774 ***1220.25*** *p65*
Virtue, Daniel; Jamaica, 1823 ***1640.13*** *p128*
Virtue, David; New York, 1807 ***8197.10*** *p325*
Visniewski, Vicenty; Maryland, 1910 ***3259.35*** *p65*
Visser, Hans Nichel; America, 1739 ***2856.30*** *p113*
Visser, Herman 17; Ontario, 1871 ***1823.28*** *p102*
Vitora, Peter 35; Seattle, 1911 ***9196.1*** *p34*
Vittie, James 32; Ontario, 1871 ***1823.15*** *p269*
Vittle, William F.; New York, 1834 ***8197.10*** *p72*
Vitty, John A.; New York, 1834-1837 ***8197.10*** *p300*
Vitzel, John 37; Ontario, 1871 ***1823.28*** *p102*
Vivan, Gerald; Quebec, 1857 ***9196.15*** *p15*
Vivcoe, Henry 30; Ontario, 1871 ***1823.15*** *p269*
Vivers, Richard; Virginia, 1664 ***6212.30*** *p11*
Vivian, Captain; Quebec, 1857 ***9196.15*** *p13*
Vivian, Gerald 35; Ontario, 1871 ***1823.22*** *p163*
Vivian, Henry 51; Ontario, 1871 ***1823.28*** *p102*
Vivian, John 43; Ontario, 1871 ***1823.28*** *p102*
Vizer, Henry; Virginia, 1667 ***1224.1*** *p60*
Voaux, Campell 30; Dominica, 1774 ***1220.25*** *p128*
Voby, M. 45; Alaska, 1918 ***9196.1*** *p55*
Voby, M. 45; Whitehorse, Yukon, 1918 ***9196.1*** *p55*
Vock, Johann Adam; Port uncertain, 1789 ***2856.30*** *p469*
Vodack, Mary; Maryland, 1910 ***3259.35*** *p65*
Vodden, Vaughan; Philadelphia, 1892 ***3437.14*** *p159*
Vodden, William 53; Ontario, 1871 ***1823.15*** *p269*
Voeck, Johann Michael; Port uncertain, 1753 ***2856.30*** *p469*
Voeck, Johann Michael; Port uncertain, 1774 ***2856.30*** *p469*
Voeck, Johann Michael; Port uncertain, 1779 ***2856.30*** *p469*
Voeck, Johann Michael; Port uncertain, 1781 ***2856.30*** *p469*
Voedall, Edmond; Virginia, 1666-1667 ***6212.30*** *p33*
Voegler, Michael; Port uncertain, 1758 ***2856.30*** *p469*
Voegler, Michael; Port uncertain, 1775 ***2856.30*** *p469*
Voelker, Catherine 55; Ontario, 1871 ***1823.15*** *p269*
Voelker, Georg Christian; America, 1772 ***2856.30*** *p469*
Voelker, Henry 56; Ontario, 1871 ***1823.15*** *p269*
Vogel, Anna 9; Kansas, 1902-1910 ***9079.10*** *p37*
Vogel, Annie 20; Kansas, 1910 ***9079.10*** *p44*
Vogel, Anton; Port uncertain, 1771 ***2856.30*** *p469*
Vogel, Charolotte 49; Kansas, 1910 ***9079.10*** *p43*
Vogel, Christian; Port uncertain, 1729 ***2856.30*** *p469*
Vogel, Christina 23; Kansas, 1910 ***9079.10*** *p47*
Vogel, David 13; Kansas, 1902-1910 ***9079.10*** *p37*
Vogel, David 42; Kansas, 1902-1910 ***9079.10*** *p37*
Vogel, Franziska; Port uncertain, 1782 ***2856.30*** *p469*
Vogel, Georg; America, 1749 ***2856.30*** *p469*
Vogel, Henry 25; Kansas, 1910 ***9079.10*** *p43*
Vogel, Jacob 23; Kansas, 1908-1910 ***9079.10*** *p47*
Vogel, Jacob 53; Kansas, 1906-1910 ***9079.10*** *p43*
Vogel, John; New York, 1839 ***8197.10*** *p142*
Vogel, Katherine 15; Kansas, 1910 ***9079.10*** *p44*
Vogel, Katie 18; Kansas, 1910 ***9079.10*** *p43*
Vogel, Katie 38; Kansas, 1902-1910 ***9079.10*** *p37*
Vogel, Marianna; Port uncertain, 1782 ***2856.30*** *p469*
Vogel, Mary 11; Kansas, 1910 ***9079.10*** *p44*
Vogel, Mary 16; Kansas, 1902-1910 ***9079.10*** *p37*
Vogel, Minnie 28; Kansas, 1910 ***9079.10*** *p43*
Vogel, Mollie 20; Kansas, 1910 ***9079.10*** *p45*
Vogel, Moltie 16; Kansas, 1910 ***9079.10*** *p43*
Vogele, Johann; Port uncertain, 1795 ***2856.30*** *p471*
Vogele, Johann; Port uncertain, 1796 ***2856.30*** *p471*
Vogeler, Johann; Canada, 1751 ***2856.30*** *p467*
Vogelin, Elisabeth; Port uncertain, 1764 ***2856.30*** *p471*
Vogell, Wilhelm; New York, 1807 ***8197.10*** *p42*
Vogelmann, Melcher; America, 1749 ***2856.30*** *p469*
Vogelmann, Mellicher; America, 1749 ***2856.30*** *p469*

W

Waal, Christina; Port uncertain, 1739 ***2856.30*** *p472*
With husband & 3 children
Wabanosse, Onisime 52; Ontario, 1871 ***1823.28*** *p102*
Waberton, William 46; Ontario, 1871 ***1823.15*** *p269*
Wabikekeke, Henry 67; Ontario, 1871 ***1823.28*** *p102*
Wabikijig, Michel 57; Ontario, 1871 ***1823.28*** *p102*
Wabinsky, John; Maryland, 1910 ***3259.35*** *p65*
Wachacki, Stanislaw; Maryland, 1910 ***3259.35*** *p65*
Wachjnski, Alexander; Maryland, 1910 ***3259.35*** *p65*
Wachlet, Moses; Pennsylvania, 1868 ***6058.10*** *p61*
Wachowiak, John; Maryland, 1910 ***3259.35*** *p65*
Wachs, Johann; Port uncertain, 1753 ***2856.30*** *p472*
Wachsmith, Christian; New York, New York, 1855 ***6058.10*** *p40*
Wachsmith, Edward; New York, New York, 1857 ***6058.10*** *p48*
Wachtel, Mark; New York, New York, 1857 ***6058.10*** *p45*
Wachtel, Moses; Pennsylvania, 1868 ***6058.10*** *p61*
Wachter, Georg; Port uncertain, 1790 ***2856.30*** *p505*
Wachter, Johann Georg; America, 1761 ***2856.30*** *p505*
Wack, Anna Elisabeth; Port uncertain, 1752 ***2856.30*** *p472*
Wack, Georg; America, 1782 ***2856.30*** *p472*
Wack, Georg; Port uncertain, 1773 ***2856.30*** *p472*
Wack, Georg; Port uncertain, 1784 ***2856.30*** *p472*
Wackenhauser, Blasius; Port uncertain, 1765 ***2856.30*** *p472*
Wacker, Abraham; Port uncertain, 1751 ***2856.30*** *p472*
Wacker, Justus; New York, 1805 ***8197.10*** *p30*
Wacker, Mathis; Port uncertain, 1752 ***2856.30*** *p472*
Wackher, Franziska; Port uncertain, 1763 ***2856.30*** *p472*
Wacksmith, Edward; New York, New York, 1857 ***6058.10*** *p48*
Waclawsky, John; Maryland, 1910 ***3259.35*** *p65*
Wacotorwski, Joseph; Maryland, 1910 ***3259.35*** *p65*
Wacznek, Budnz; Maryland, 1910 ***3259.35*** *p65*
Waczynski, Antone; Maryland, 1910 ***3259.35*** *p65*
Waddel, Archibald 39; Ontario, 1871 ***1823.22*** *p164*
Waddell, Alexander 44; Ontario, 1871 ***1823.22*** *p164*
Waddell, Alexander 68; Ontario, 1871 ***1823.22*** *p164*
Waddell, Andrew 41; Ontario, 1871 ***1823.15*** *p269*
Waddell, Andrew 46; Ontario, 1871 ***1823.22*** *p164*
Waddell, Archibald 57; Ontario, 1871 ***1823.22*** *p164*
Waddell, Duncan; Nova Scotia, 1893 ***1640.13*** *p129*
Waddell, Elizabeth 53; Ontario, 1871 ***1823.22*** *p164*
Waddell, George; Denver, Colorado, 1899 ***1640.13*** *p129*
Waddell, James; New York, 1821 ***8197.10*** *p292*
Waddell, John 52; Ontario, 1871 ***1823.15*** *p269*
Waddell, Robert N. 58; Ontario, 1871 ***1823.22*** *p164*
Waddell, Thomas; Georgia, 1699 ***1640.13*** *p129*
Waddell, William 42; Ontario, 1871 ***1823.22*** *p164*
Wadden, Thomas; Virginia, 1666 ***6212.30*** *p29*
Waddingham, James; Portland, Maine, 1857 ***9196.15*** *p12*
Waddington, John; Philadelphia, 1815 ***1224.3*** *p81*
Waddington, William 47; Ontario, 1871 ***1823.15*** *p269*
Waddle, George; Maryland, 1654 ***2524.55*** *p227*
Waddle, James; Pennsylvania, 1777 ***4629.10*** *p31*
Waddle, Robert; Pennsylvania, 1777 ***4629.10*** *p31*
Waddle, Robert 50; Ontario, 1871 ***1823.28*** *p102*
Waddle, William; Maryland, 1662 ***2524.55*** *p227*
Waddle, William; Pennsylvania, 1778 ***4629.10*** *p32*
Waddle, William 45; Ontario, 1871 ***1823.22*** *p164*
Waddy, Elizabeth; Maryland, 1664 ***2524.55*** *p151*
Waddy, Jane *SEE* Waddy, Thomas
Waddy, Thomas; Maryland, 1665 ***2524.55*** *p228*
Wife: Jane
Waddylove, Amy *SEE* Waddylove, Nicholas
Waddylove, Comfort *SEE* Waddylove, Nicholas
Waddylove, Nicholas; Maryland, 1659 ***2524.55*** *p228*
Wife: Amy
Daughter: Comfort
Daughter: Temperance
Daughter: Patience
Daughter: Amy
Waddylove, Patience *SEE* Waddylove, Nicholas
Waddylove, Temperance *SEE* Waddylove, Nicholas
Wade, Mr.; Quebec, 1856 ***9196.15*** *p7*
Wade, Mr.; Quebec, 1857 ***9196.15*** *p21*
Wade, Mr.; Quebec, 1857 ***9196.15*** *p25*
Wade, Mr.; Quebec, 1858 ***9196.15*** *p45*
Wade, Mrs.; Quebec, 1858 ***9196.15*** *p36*
Wade, Mrs.; Quebec, 1858 ***9196.15*** *p45*
Wade, Abraham 75; Ontario, 1871 ***1823.22*** *p164*
Wade, Andrew; Maryland, 1657 ***2524.55*** *p228*
Wade, Edward; New York, 1807 ***8197.10*** *p52*
Wade, Ellen Fitzgerald; Vermont, 1844-1911 ***5900.10*** *p291*
Wade, Farrell; Pennsylvania, 1779 ***4629.10*** *p37*
Wade, George 35; Ontario, 1871 ***1823.15*** *p269*
Wade, James 25; Maryland, 1775 ***1220.25*** *p99*
Wade, James 40; Ontario, 1871 ***1823.15*** *p269*
Wade, John; Georgia, 1734 ***1640.10*** *p208*
Wade, John; New York, 1807 ***8197.10*** *p52*
Wade, John 33; Ontario, 1871 ***1823.22*** *p164*
Wade, John 40; Ontario, 1871 ***1823.22*** *p164*
Wade, John 67; Ontario, 1871 ***1823.22*** *p164*
Wade, Joseph; Boston, 1692 ***1224.1*** *p60*
Wade, Kate; Vermont, 1845-1885 ***5900.10*** *p549*
Wade, Mark; Quebec, 1858 ***9196.15*** *p34*
Wade, Mark 31; Ontario, 1871 ***1823.15*** *p269*
Wade, Mark Edward 53; Ontario, 1871 ***1823.15*** *p269*
Wade, Mary Atkins; Maryland, 1660 ***1224.1*** *p60*
Wade, Peter; Pennsylvania, 1777 ***4629.10*** *p22*
Wade, Robert; Maryland, 1667 ***2524.55*** *p228*
Wade, Thomas 16; Philadelphia, 1774 ***1220.25*** *p43*
Wade, Thomas 37; Ontario, 1871 ***1823.22*** *p164*
Wade, William; Died enroute, 1682 ***1224.1*** *p60*
Wade, William 19; Philadelphia, 1774 ***1220.25*** *p42*
Wade, William 30; Ontario, 1871 ***1823.22*** *p164*
Wade, William 35; Ontario, 1871 ***1823.22*** *p164*
Wade, William 47; Ontario, 1871 ***1823.15*** *p269*
Wade, Wm; Virginia, 1664 ***6212.30*** *p9*
Wade, Zachary; Maryland, 1658 ***2524.55*** *p228*
With wife
Wade, Zachary; Maryland, 1662 ***2524.55*** *p228*
Wademan, Peace; Pennsylvania, 1777 ***4629.10*** *p18*
Wadick, Jane 78; Vermont, 1878 ***5900.10*** *p526*
Wadington, William 22; Ontario, 1871 ***1823.28*** *p102*
Wadkinson, Richard; Virginia, 1701 ***6212.30*** *p61*
Wadland, William 20; Ontario, 1871 ***1823.15*** *p270*
Wadle, Thomas; Maryland, 1673 ***2524.55*** *p228*
Wadlen, Richard 56; Ontario, 1871 ***1823.15*** *p270*
Wadlin, Henry 21; Ontario, 1871 ***1823.15*** *p270*
Wadlow, Mrs.; Quebec, 1858 ***9196.15*** *p36*
Wadshaski, John; Maryland, 1910 ***3259.35*** *p65*
Wadson, Abraham; Maryland, 1661 ***2524.55*** *p228*
Wadson, William; Maryland, 1661 ***2524.55*** *p232*
Wadsword, Robert 28; Ontario, 1871 ***1823.22*** *p164*
Wadsworth, Ellinor; Maryland, 1666 ***2524.55*** *p113*
Wadsworth, Henry; New York, 1818 ***8197.10*** *p291*
Wadsworth, Henry; New York, 1821 ***8197.10*** *p292*
Wadsworth, James; New York, 1819 ***8197.10*** *p292*
Wadup, Ann Turner; South Carolina, 1817 ***1224.3*** *p81*
Waesh, James; New York, 1807 ***8197.10*** *p52*
Waewyzisak, Jacob; Maryland, 1910 ***3259.35*** *p65*
Wafers, Jno; Virginia, 1676 ***6212.30*** *p53*
Waffenschmid, Philipp; America, 1770 ***2856.30*** *p472*
Wafford, Francis; Maryland, 1681 ***2524.55*** *p228*
Wafler, Frederick; New York, New York, 1862 ***3437.14*** *p98*
Wagendorf, Peter; Port uncertain, 1735 ***2856.30*** *p472*
Wageneck, Johann Peter; Port uncertain, 1731 ***2856.30*** *p472*
Wagener, Henry; New York, 1829 ***8197.10*** *p294*
Wagenknecht, Anna Maria; Port uncertain, 1780 ***2856.30*** *p472*
Wagenmacher, Christian; New York, 1838 ***8197.10*** *p152*
Wagenseil, Christof; America, 1750 ***2856.30*** *p472*
Wagenska, Anna; Maryland, 1910 ***3259.35*** *p65*
Wager, John; Pennsylvania, 1777 ***4629.10*** *p10*
Wager, Thomas 19; Maryland, 1775 ***1220.25*** *p103*
Wagg, Humphry; Maryland, 1668 ***2524.55*** *p228*
Waggay, Fetonia; Maryland, 1910 ***3259.35*** *p65*
Waggner, W. Couras 37; Ontario, 1871 ***1823.15*** *p270*
Waggoner, Peter; Pennsylvania, 1776 ***4629.10*** *p53*
Waghorn, Caroline 25; Ontario, 1861 ***2896.27*** *p69*
Waghorne, Ann; New York, 1751 ***1224.2*** *p119*
Wagmann, Bernhard; Port uncertain, 1785 ***2856.30*** *p472*
With wife & 2 children
Wagnar, Charles 35; Ontario, 1871 ***1823.28*** *p102*
Wagner, Miss; Port uncertain, 1784 ***2856.30*** *p410*
Wagner, A. E.; Port uncertain, 1768 ***2856.30*** *p374*
Wagner, Abraham; Port uncertain, 1752 ***2856.30*** *p475*
With wife
Wagner, Adam 29; Kansas, 1889-1910 ***9079.10*** *p43*
Wagner, Adam 42; Kansas, 1895-1910 ***9079.10*** *p52*
Wagner, Ambrosius; Port uncertain, 1758 ***2856.30*** *p474*
With family
Wagner, Andreas; America, 1752 ***2856.30*** *p472*
Wagner, Anna Catharina; Port uncertain, 1773 ***2856.30*** *p474*
Wagner, Anna Elisabeth; Port uncertain, 1794 ***2856.30*** *p472*
Wagner, Anna Eva, Port uncertain, 1775 ***2856.30*** *p472*
Wagner, Anna Margarete; Port uncertain, 1769 ***2856.30*** *p472*
Wagner, Anna Maria; America, 1754 ***2856.30*** *p472*
Wagner, Benjamine 27; Kansas, 1909-1910 ***9079.10*** *p31*
Wagner, Caspar; America, 1751 ***2856.30*** *p472*
Wagner, Catrina 66; Ontario, 1871 ***1823.15*** *p270*
Wagner, Christina; Port uncertain, 1755 ***2856.30*** *p475*
With husband
Wagner, Christof; Port uncertain, 1733 ***2856.30*** *p472*
Wagner, Conrad 34; Ontario, 1871 ***1823.15*** *p270*
Wagner, Conrad 36; Ontario, 1871 ***1823.15*** *p270*
Wagner, Conrad 42; Ontario, 1871 ***1823.15*** *p270*
Wagner, Elis. Margarete; Port uncertain, 1785 ***2856.30*** *p472*
Wagner, Eva Catharina; Port uncertain, 1784 ***2856.30*** *p472*
Wagner, Francis; New York, 1835 ***8197.10*** *p317*
Wagner, Franz; Port uncertain, 1784 ***2856.30*** *p474*
Wagner, Franz; Port uncertain, 1785 ***2856.30*** *p475*
With wife
Wagner, Georg; America, 1732 ***2856.30*** *p472*
Wagner, Georg; America, 1772 ***2856.30*** *p475*
With wife
Wagner, Georg; Port uncertain, 1700-1799 ***2856.30*** *p475*
Wagner, Georg; Port uncertain, 1764 ***2856.30*** *p475*
With wife
Wagner, Georg Michael; Port uncertain, 1742 ***2856.30*** *p472*

Wagner, Hans; Port uncertain, 1717 2856.30 p472
Wagner, Hans; Port uncertain, 1747 2856.30 p472
Wagner, Henry 14; Kansas, 1902-1910 9079.10 p32
Wagner, Henry 37; Kansas, 1902-1910 9079.10 p32
Wagner, Jacob; America, 1737 2856.30 p475
With wife & 5 children
Wagner, Jacob; America, 1738 2856.30 p472
Wagner, Jacob 20; Kansas, 1891-1910 9079.10 p25
Wagner, Jacob 48; Kansas, 1891-1910 9079.10 p25
Wagner, Jakob; America, 1744 2856.30 p475
With wife & 7 children
Wagner, Jakob; America, 1790 2856.30 p472
Wagner, Jakob; Port uncertain, 1785 2856.30 p475
With wife
Wagner, Jerg; Port uncertain, 1781 2856.30 p472
Wagner, Jno. Christian; Pennsylvania, 1778 4629.10 p34
Wagner, Johann; America, 1738 2856.30 p473
Wagner, Johann; America, 1749 2856.30 p472
Wagner, Johann; America, 1751 2856.30 p473
Wagner, Johann; America, 1755 2856.30 p473
Wagner, Johann; Port uncertain, 1680 2856.30 p473
Wagner, Johann; Port uncertain, 1738 2856.30 p473
Wagner, Johann; Port uncertain, 1749 2856.30 p472
Wagner, Johann; Port uncertain, 1751 2856.30 p473
Wagner, Johann; Port uncertain, 1764 2856.30 p473
Wagner, Johann Andreas; Port uncertain, 1751 2856.30 p475
With wife & 2 children
Wagner, Johann Georg; America, 1755 2856.30 p473
Wagner, Johann Georg; Port uncertain, 1755 2856.30 p473
Wagner, Johann Jakob; America, 1742 2856.30 p475
With wife & 7 children
Wagner, Johann Jakob; America, 1785 2856.30 p474
Wagner, Johann Karl; Port uncertain, 1795 2856.30 p473
Wagner, Johann Michael; America, 1753 2856.30 p473
Wagner, Johann Michael; Port uncertain, 1774 2856.30 p473
Wagner, Johann Nikolaus; America, 1756 2856.30 p473
Wagner, Johann Nikolaus; America, 1788 2856.30 p473
Wagner, Johann Nikolaus; Port uncertain, 1747 2856.30 p473
Wagner, Johann Nikolaus; Port uncertain, 1755 2856.30 p473
Wagner, Johann Peter; America, 1748 2856.30 p473
Wagner, Johann Peter; America, 1754 2856.30 p473
Wagner, Johann Peter; Port uncertain, 1747 2856.30 p473
Wagner, Johann Peter; Port uncertain, 1759 2856.30 p473
Wagner, John; Maryland, 1910 3259.35 p65
Wagner, John; New York, 1837 8197.10 p103
Wagner, John 30; Ontario, 1871 1823.28 p102
Wagner, John 36; Ontario, 1871 1823.15 p270
Wagner, John Frederick; New York, 1838 8197.10 p295
Wagner, Karl; Port uncertain, 1784 2856.30 p473
Wagner, Karl; Port uncertain, 1789 2856.30 p473
Wagner, Katie 36; Kansas, 1902-1910 9079.10 p32
Wagner, Katie 37; Kansas, 1910 9079.10 p52
Wagner, Konrad; Port uncertain, 1780 2856.30 p473
Wagner, Lizzie 73; Kansas, 1910 9079.10 p31
Wagner, Margarete; Port uncertain, 1737 2856.30 p473
Wagner, Maria; Port uncertain, 1746 2856.30 p473
Wagner, Maria Barbara; Port uncertain, 1775 2856.30 p473
Wagner, Maria Catharina; Port uncertain, 1760 2856.30 p473
Wagner, Maria Eva; Port uncertain, 1750 2856.30 p473
Wagner, Mary M. 48; Kansas, 1891-1910 9079.10 p25
Wagner, Matheiss; America, 1755 2856.30 p473
Wagner, Matheiss; Port uncertain, 1749 2856.30 p473
Wagner, Matteis; America, 1749 2856.30 p473
Wagner, Michael; Port uncertain, 1780 2856.30 p473
Wagner, Michael; Port uncertain, 1781 2856.30 p473
Wagner, Michael; Port uncertain, 1795 2856.30 p473
Wagner, Molly 9; Kansas, 1902-1910 9079.10 p32
Wagner, Peter; America, 1785 2856.30 p474
Wagner, Peter; Port uncertain, 1759 2856.30 p473
Wagner, Peter; Port uncertain, 1778 2856.30 p473
Wagner, Philipp; Port uncertain, 1785 2856.30 p474
Wagner, Reinhard; Port uncertain, 1736 2856.30 p474
Wagner, Rosina; Port uncertain, 1773 2856.30 p474
Wagner, Mrs. Simon; America, 1738 2856.30 p474
Wagner, Susanna; Port uncertain, 1752 2856.30 p474
With husband
Wagner, Therese; Port uncertain, 1778 2856.30 p474
Wagner, Thomas; Maryland, 1910 3259.35 p65
Wagner, Valentin; Port uncertain, 1757 2856.30 p474
Wagner, Valentin; Port uncertain, 1785 2856.30 p474
Wagner, Valentin; Port uncertain, 1821 2856.30 p474
Wagnor, William 27; Ontario, 1871 1823.28 p102
Wagoner, Elizabeth 34; Kansas, 1910 9079.10 p53
Wagoner, Jacob 35; Kansas, 1910 9079.10 p53
Wagoner, John; New York, 1834 8197.10 p69
Wagoner, John 40; Ontario, 1871 1823.15 p270
Wagoner, Lena 8; Kansas, 1910 9079.10 p53
Wagoner, Mollie 10; Kansas, 1910 9079.10 p53
Wagosh, J. Bte 48; Ontario, 1871 1823.28 p102
Wagstaff, Charles Eden; Boston, 1853 1224.3 p81
Wagstaff, Daniel; Delaware, 1830 1224.3 p81
Wahbekezhik, Michelle 50; Ontario, 1871 1823.28 p102
Wahbonggai, Louis 47; Ontario, 1871 1823.28 p102
Wahcowsai, Pierre 55; Ontario, 1871 1823.28 p102
Wahegijy, Francois 37; Ontario, 1871 1823.28 p102
Wahl, Andreas; Port uncertain, 1783 2856.30 p475
Wahl, Anton; Port uncertain, 1785 2856.30 p475
Wahl, Anton; Port uncertain, 1786 2856.30 p475
Wahl, Hans Georg, Jr.; Port uncertain, 1753 2856.30 p475
Wahl, Jakob; Port uncertain, 1751 2856.30 p475
Wahl, Johann; Port uncertain, 1749 2856.30 p475
Wahl, Johann Adam; Port uncertain, 1752 2856.30 p2
With wife & 2 children
Wahl, Johann Adam; Port uncertain, 1752 2856.30 p475
With wife & 3 children
Wahl, Josef; Port uncertain, 1770 2856.30 p475
With wife
Wahl, Magdalena; Port uncertain, 1747 2856.30 p475
Wahl, Maria; Port uncertain, 1724 2856.30 p475
Wahl, Peter; Port uncertain, 1749 2856.30 p475
Wahn, Friedrich; America, 1735 2856.30 p475
Wahowiak, Katarzyna; Maryland, 1910 3259.35 p65
Wahsaikezhik, Paul 45; Ontario, 1871 1823.28 p102
Waiblin, Catharina Schneider; Port uncertain, 1797 2856.30 p475
Waicop, Richard; Virginia, 1665 6212.30 p19
Waight, John; Maryland, 1658 2524.55 p228
Wailes, Mr.; Quebec, 1858 9196.15 p32
Wainman, John 48; Ontario, 1871 1823.22 p164
Wainwright, Miss; Quebec, 1857 9196.15 p23
Wainwright, Mr.; Quebec, 1857 9196.15 p23
Wainwright, Mr., Jr.; Quebec, 1857 9196.15 p23
Wainwright, Mrs.; Quebec, 1857 9196.15 p23
Wainwright, Mrs.; Quebec, 1858 9196.15 p31
Wainwright, Isaac; Pennsylvania, 1785 4629.10 p48
Wainwright, John 25; Savannah, Georgia, 1775 1220.25 p139
Wainwright, Jonathan; Pennsylvania, 1785 4629.10 p48
Wait, Griffin 62; Ontario, 1871 1823.22 p164
Wait, John T. 36; Ontario, 1871 1823.28 p102
Wait, Joseph 63; Ontario, 1871 1823.22 p164
Wait, Lorain 81; Ontario, 1871 1823.22 p164
Wait, Mary 85; Ontario, 1871 1823.22 p164
Wait, Samuel 88; Ontario, 1871 1823.22 p164
Wait, William; Virginia, 1668-1669 6212.30 p40
Waitcliffe, Cornelius 35; Ontario, 1871 1823.22 p164
Waite, John 50; New York, 1775 1220.25 p142
With wife & 6 children
Waite, Richard 54; Ontario, 1871 1823.15 p270
Waite, Robert; New York, 1840 8197.10 p203
Waite, William; New York, 1813 8197.10 p58
Waite, William; Virginia, 1671 1224.1 p60
Wajek, Dora; Maryland, 1910 3259.35 p65
Wakalin, John; New York, 1831 8197.10 p364
Wake, Miss; Quebec, 1857 9196.15 p15
Wake, George Daniel; New York, 1857 1224.3 p81
Wakefield, David 56; Ontario, 1871 1823.15 p270
Wakefield, James 44; Ontario, 1871 1823.15 p270
Wakefield, John; Maryland, 1651 2524.55 p228
Wakefield, Nicholas; Maryland, 1676 2524.55 p228
Wakefield, Rosetta 38; Ontario, 1871 1823.28 p102
Wakefield, Wm.; Maryland, 1682 2524.55 p228
Wakeford, Elizah 30; Ontario, 1871 1823.15 p270
Wakeford, Thomas 46; Ontario, 1871 1823.15 p270
Wakegijy, Alexander 41; Ontario, 1871 1823.28 p102
Wakegijy, Louis 64; Ontario, 1871 1823.28 p102
Wakeham, Miss; Quebec, 1858 9196.15 p41
Wakelyn, Henry; Maryland, 1659 2524.55 p228
Waklam, William; New York, 1827 8197.10 p294
Waklin, Charles 73; Ontario, 1871 1823.15 p270
Wakly, John 22; Ontario, 1871 1823.22 p164
Wakowiak, Peter; Maryland, 1910 3259.35 p65
Walace, William 56; Ontario, 1871 1823.15 p270
Walazewski, Lizzie; Maryland, 1910 3259.35 p65
Walbank, Edward; Philadelphia, 1735 1224.2 p119
Walber, Peter; Port uncertain, 1730 2856.30 p475
With wife & children
Walbridge, Elias 18; Ontario, 1861 2896.25 p40
Walbridge, Emma 20; Ontario, 1861 2896.25 p40
Walbridge, Henry; Baltimore, 1825 1224.3 p81
Walbridge, John F. 9; Ontario, 1861 2896.25 p40
Walbridge, Mary 46; Ontario, 1861 2896.25 p40
Walbridge, Mary E. 13; Ontario, 1861 2896.25 p40
Walbridge, Samuel 15; Ontario, 1861 2896.25 p40
Walbridge, Thomas 7; Ontario, 1861 2896.25 p40
Walbridge, William S. 4; Ontario, 1861 2896.25 p40
Walbrooke, Jno; Virginia, 1664-1665 6212.30 p16
Walbrooke, Rebecca; Virginia, 1664 6212.30 p7
Walburn, Mary 18; Ontario, 1871 1823.15 p270
Walbusky, Frank; Maryland, 1910 3259.35 p65
Walcker, Bernard; Port uncertain, 1736 2856.30 p476
Walcott, John; Maryland, 1649 2524.55 p228
Walcuk, Edward; Maryland, 1910 3259.35 p65
Wald, Anna Maria; America, 1757 2856.30 p505
Wald, Edward; Maryland, 1670 2524.55 p228
Wife: Elizabeth
Wald, Elizabeth *SEE* Wald, Edward
Waldenmeier, Andreas; America, 1770 2856.30 p476
Walder, Daniel; America, 1713 1224.2 p119
Waldhauer, Andreas; America, 1738 2856.30 p476
With wife & 8 children
Waldhauer, Caspar; America, 1744 2856.30 p476
With family
Waldhauer, Johann Georg; Port uncertain, 1788 2856.30 p476
Waldhauer, Josef; Port uncertain, 1762 2856.30 p476
Waldhuber, Conrad; Canada, 1763 2856.30 p476
With wife 3 sons & 2 daughters
Waldie, Elizabeth 7; Ontario, 1861 2896.25 p26
Waldie, Euphemia 5; Ontario, 1861 2896.25 p26
Waldie, John 45; Ontario, 1871 1823.22 p164
Waldie, Thomas 30; Ontario, 1861 2896.25 p25
Waldie, Thomas 40; Ontario, 1871 1823.22 p164
Waldie, Thomas, Jr. 5; Ontario, 1861 2896.25 p25
Waldin, Anna Maria; America, 1757 2856.30 p505
Waldmann, Catharina; America, 1744 2856.30 p284
Waldmann, Catharina; America, 1744 2856.30 p476
With husband
Waldmann, Christian; Port uncertain, 1766 2856.30 p476
Waldmann, Christmann; Port uncertain, 1776 2856.30 p476
Waldmann, Philipp Peter; Port uncertain, 1766 2856.30 p476
Waldo, Daniel; America, 1713 1224.2 p119
Waldo, Francis; Massachusetts, n.d. 1224.2 p119
Waldo, Samuel; Massachusetts, 1803 1224.3 p81
Waldon, Henry 40; Ontario, 1871 1823.22 p164
Waldon, Lionell; Virginia, 1665-1666 6212.30 p21
Waldren, James 74; Ontario, 1871 1823.22 p164
Waldron, Miss; Quebec, 1858 9196.15 p36
Waldron, Cornelius 84; Ontario, 1871 1823.22 p165
Walds, Mr.; Quebec, 1857 9196.15 p13
Waldvogel, Martin; Port uncertain, 1756 2856.30 p476
Wale, James; England, 1692 1640.13 p129
Wale, Joseph 30; Maryland, 1775 1220.25 p97
Wale, Patrick; New York, 1802 8197.10 p9
Wale, Phill; Virginia, 1690-1691 6212.30 p58
Wale, Wm; Virginia, 1678 6212.30 p54
Wale, Wm; Virginia, 1684-1685 6212.30 p57
Walecki, Piort; Maryland, 1910 3259.35 p65
Waler, Alice *SEE* Waler, John
Waler, John; Maryland, 1665 2524.55 p236
Wife: Alice
Son: William
Daughter: Major
Waler, Major *SEE* Waler, John
Waler, William *SEE* Waler, John
Wales, J. B.; Portland, Maine, 1858 9196.15 p31
Wales, Maria 75; Ontario, 1871 1823.15 p270
Wales, Wojciech; Maryland, 1910 3259.35 p65
Waley, John; Maryland, 1670 2524.55 p228
Walford, Ester 32; Ontario, 1871 1823.28 p102
Walford, John; New York, New York, 1844 1224.3 p81
Walford, John; Virginia, 1663 6212.30 p2
Walford, Stiren 59; Ontario, 1871 1823.28 p102
Walford, William; New York, 1840 8197.10 p203
Walgate, Mrs.; Quebec, 1857 9196.15 p15
Walgin, Margarete; Port uncertain, 1787 2856.30 p476
With husband
Walk, Marg.; Port uncertain, 1779 2856.30 p158
Walk, Margarete; Port uncertain, 1787 2856.30 p476
With husband
Walken, Fenwick 43; Ontario, 1871 1823.15 p270
Walker, . . .; Boston, 1737 4628.40 p114
Walker, Captain; Quebec, 1857 9196.15 p17
Walker, Master; Quebec, 1857 9196.15 p26
Walker, Miss; Quebec, 1857 9196.15 p25
Walker, Miss; Quebec, 1858 9196.15 p35
Walker, Mr.; Portland, Maine, 1858 9196.15 p30
Walker, Mr.; Quebec, 1857 9196.15 p18
Walker, Mr.; Quebec, 1857 9196.15 p22
Walker, Mr.; Quebec, 1858 9196.15 p35
Walker, Mr.; Quebec, 1858 9196.15 p38
Walker, Mr.; Quebec, 1858 9196.15 p40
Walker, Mr.; Quebec, 1858 9196.15 p42
Walker, Mrs.; Quebec, 1857 9196.15 p19
Walker, Mrs.; Quebec, 1858 9196.15 p42
Walker, Mrs. 28; Ontario, 1861 2896.26 p30
Walker, Adam; Georgia, 1698 1640.13 p129

Walker, Alexander; Georgia, 1751 ***1640.10*** *p208*
Walker, Alexander; Port uncertain, 1840-1849 ***4537.37*** *p133*
Wife: Joan Campbell
Child: Donald
Child: Jessie
Child: Mary
Child: Ann
Walker, Alexander 24; Ontario, 1871 ***1823.15*** *p270*
Walker, Andrew; Georgia, 1738 ***1640.10*** *p208*
Walker, Andrew; Pennsylvania, 1781 ***4629.10*** *p42*
Walker, Andrew 29; Ontario, 1871 ***1823.15*** *p270*
Walker, Andrew 61; Ontario, 1871 ***1823.15*** *p270*
Walker, Angus *SEE* Walker, Angus
Walker, Angus *SEE* Walker, Donald
Walker, Angus *SEE* Walker, Ewen
Walker, Angus *SEE* Walker, Michael
Walker, Angus; Ontario, 1849 ***4537.37*** *p86*
Wife: Ann MacCormick
Child: Hugh
Child: Neil
Child: Mary
Child: Angus
Walker, Ann *SEE* Walker, Alexander
Walker, Ann *SEE* Walker, Donald
Walker, Ann *SEE* Walker, Robert
Walker, Ann; Ontario, 1840-1849 ***4537.37*** *p46*
Walker, Ann; Port uncertain, 1840-1849 ***4537.37*** *p131*
Walker, Ann 30 *SEE* Walker, James
Walker, Ann 57; Ontario, 1871 ***1823.15*** *p270*
Walker, Ann MacCormick *SEE* Walker, Angus
Walker, Ann Morrison *SEE* Walker, James
Walker, Anne; Maryland, 1682 ***2524.55*** *p228*
Walker, Anne; Vermont, 1842-1897 ***5900.10*** *p289*
Walker, Bartholomew; Virginia, 1678 ***1224.1*** *p60*
Walker, Bartholomew 28; Virginia, 1773 ***1220.25*** *p29*
Walker, Benjamin *SEE* Walker, Daniel
Walker, Bridget 36; Vermont, 1873 ***5900.10*** *p410*
Walker, Catharan; Maryland, 1658 ***2524.55*** *p228*
Walker, Catherie *SEE* Walker, Donald
Walker, Catherine *SEE* Walker, Ewen
Walker, Catherine *SEE* Walker, James
Walker, Catherine *SEE* Walker, Michael
Walker, Catherine; Ontario, 1849 ***4537.37*** *p86*
Walker, Catherine; Port uncertain, 1840-1849 ***4537.37*** *p116*
Walker, Catherine 24; Vermont, 1861 ***5900.10*** *p177*
Walker, Catherine MacKinnon *SEE* Walker, Ewen
Walker, Catherine Steele *SEE* Walker, Ewen
Walker, Chapman; Virginia, 1737 ***1224.2*** *p119*
Walker, Charles; Maryland, 1680 ***2524.55*** *p228*
Walker, Christina; Virginia, 1861 ***1640.13*** *p129*
Walker, Christopher; Maryland, 1652-1658 ***2524.55*** *p228*
Walker, Christopher 24; Ontario, 1871 ***1823.15*** *p270*
Walker, Daniel; Maryland, 1670 ***2524.55*** *p228*
Son: Benjamin
Walker, Daniel; New York, 1837 ***8197.10*** *p295*
Walker, Daniel; Virginia, 1672 ***1224.1*** *p60*
Walker, Daniell; Maryland, 1674 ***2524.55*** *p228*
Walker, David; New York, 1834 ***8197.10*** *p68*
Walker, David 53; Ontario, 1871 ***1823.15*** *p270*
Walker, David 63; Ontario, 1871 ***1823.15*** *p270*
Walker, David 68; Ontario, 1871 ***1823.15*** *p270*
Walker, Donald *SEE* Walker, Alexander
Walker, Donald; Ontario, 1840-1849 ***4537.37*** *p86*
With wife
Child: Hugh
Child: Finlay
Child: Ann
Walker, Donald; Ontario, 1849 ***4537.32*** *p96*
With wife
Child: Hugh
Child: Finlay
Child: Ann
Walker, Donald; Port uncertain, 1840-1849 ***4537.37*** *p133*
Wife: Margaret
Child: Angus
Child: Catherie
Walker, Dougal *SEE* Walker, Ewen
Walker, Duncan 50; Ontario, 1871 ***1823.15*** *p270*
Walker, Edward; Virginia, 1664 ***6212.30*** *p12*
Walker, Edward 20; Virginia, 1774 ***1220.25*** *p90*
Walker, Edward 32; Virginia, 1775 ***1220.25*** *p95*
Walker, Elijah 35; Ontario, 1871 ***1823.15*** *p270*
Walker, Elisabeth 62; Ontario, 1871 ***1823.15*** *p270*
Walker, Eliz; Virginia, 1688 ***6212.30*** *p57*
Walker, Eliza E. 2; Ontario, 1861 ***2896.26*** *p30*
Walker, Elizabeth; Maryland, 1673 ***2524.55*** *p228*
Walker, Elizabeth; Maryland, 1682 ***2524.55*** *p228*
Walker, Ellen; Vermont, 1851-1930 ***5900.10*** *p71*
Walker, Ellen 17; Ontario, 1871 ***1823.15*** *p270*
Walker, Ellen 42; Ontario, 1871 ***1823.15*** *p270*
Walker, Emma 20; Ontario, 1871 ***1823.22*** *p165*
Walker, Emma 31; Ontario, 1871 ***1823.15*** *p270*
Walker, Esther; Vermont, 1856-1937 ***5900.10*** *p52*
Walker, Ewen; Ontario, 1840-1849 ***4537.37*** *p87*
Wife: Catherine Steele
Child: Neil
Child: Angus
Child: Dougal
Child: Marion
Child: John
Child: Flora
Walker, Ewen; Ontario, 1849 ***4537.32*** *p96*
Wife: Catherine Steele
Child: Dougal
Child: John
Child: Neil
Child: Angus
Child: Marion
Child: Flora
Walker, Ewen; Ontario, 1849 ***4537.37*** *p86*
Wife: Catherine MacKinnon
Child: Catherine
Child: Kirsty
Walker, Finlay *SEE* Walker, Donald
Walker, Flora *SEE* Walker, Ewen
Walker, Flower; Maryland, 1709 ***1224.2*** *p119*
Walker, Frances; Maryland, 1673 ***2524.55*** *p228*
Walker, George; Georgia, 1698 ***1640.13*** *p129*
Walker, George; Maryland, 1666 ***2524.55*** *p42*
Walker, George; New England, 1706 ***1224.2*** *p119*
Walker, George; New Orleans, 1851 ***1640.13*** *p129*
Walker, George; New York, 1807 ***8197.10*** *p53*
Walker, George; Portland, Maine, 1858 ***9196.15*** *p28*
Walker, George; Virginia, 1719 ***1224.2*** *p119*
Walker, George 30; Ontario, 1871 ***1823.15*** *p270*
Walker, George 34; Ontario, 1871 ***1823.28*** *p102*
Walker, George 36; Ontario, 1871 ***1823.15*** *p270*
Walker, George 53; Ontario, 1871 ***1823.15*** *p270*
Walker, George 66; Ontario, 1871 ***1823.22*** *p165*
Walker, George C.; New Orleans, 1851 ***1640.10*** *p208*
Walker, George Henry; Pennsylvania, 1850 ***1224.3*** *p81*
Walker, Henery 13; Ontario, 1871 ***1823.15*** *p270*
Walker, Henry; Maryland, 1666 ***2524.55*** *p42*
Walker, Henry; Philadelphia, 1829 ***1224.3*** *p81*
Walker, Henry; Vermont, 1831-1881 ***5900.10*** *p484*
Walker, Henry 38; New York, 1827-1837 ***8197.10*** *p104*
Walker, Henry J. 26; Ontario, 1871 ***1823.22*** *p165*
Walker, Hugh *SEE* Walker, Angus
Walker, Hugh *SEE* Walker, Donald
Walker, Jabez 33; Ontario, 1871 ***1823.15*** *p270*
Walker, James; Georgia, 1751 ***1640.10*** *p208*
Walker, James; Jamaica, 1826 ***1640.13*** *p129*
Walker, James; Jamaica, 1827 ***1640.13*** *p129*
Walker, James; Maryland, 1648 ***2524.55*** *p228*
Walker, James; Maryland, 1658 ***2524.55*** *p228*
Walker, James; Pennsylvania, 1808 ***6058.10*** *p2*
Walker, James; Port uncertain, 1850-1859 ***4537.37*** *p133*
Wife: Ann Morrison
Child: Roderick
Child: Catherine
Child: Mary
Child: Marion
Child: Margaret
Walker, James 11; New York, 1774 ***1220.25*** *p20*
Walker, James 23; Maryland, 1775 ***1220.25*** *p101*
Walker, James 27; Ontario, 1871 ***1823.15*** *p271*
Walker, James 30; Philadelphia, 1774 ***1220.25*** *p55*
Wife: Ann 30
Walker, James 34; Ontario, 1871 ***1823.15*** *p271*
Walker, James 48; Ontario, 1871 ***1823.15*** *p271*
Walker, James 50; Ontario, 1871 ***1823.15*** *p271*
Walker, James 66; Ontario, 1871 ***1823.15*** *p271*
Walker, James Dennistoun; Antigua (Antego), 1886 ***1640.13*** *p129*
Walker, Jane 19; Ontario, 1871 ***1823.15*** *p271*
Walker, Jane 52; Ontario, 1871 ***1823.22*** *p165*
Walker, Jane 62; Ontario, 1871 ***1823.22*** *p165*
Walker, Janet; Ontario, 1849 ***4537.37*** *p79*
Walker, Jessie *SEE* Walker, Alexander
Walker, Joan Campbell *SEE* Walker, Alexander
Walker, John *SEE* Walker, Ewen
Walker, John; Bahamas, 1792 ***1640.13*** *p129*
Walker, John; Maryland, 1652-1659 ***2524.55*** *p166*
Walker, John; Maryland, 1665 ***2524.55*** *p98*
Walker, John; Maryland, 1673 ***2524.55*** *p228*
Walker, John; New York, 1805 ***8197.10*** *p30*
Walker, John; New York, 1808 ***8197.10*** *p54*
Walker, John; New York, 1838 ***8197.10*** *p152*
Walker, John; Pennsylvania, 1777 ***4629.10*** *p13*
Walker, John; St. John, New Brunswick, 1871 ***1640.13*** *p129*
Walker, John; Vermont, 1855-1943 ***5900.10*** *p70*
Walker, John; Virginia, 1679 ***6212.30*** *p54*
Walker, John; Virginia, 1772 ***1224.2*** *p119*
Walker, John 30; Ontario, 1871 ***1823.15*** *p271*
Walker, John 34; Ontario, 1871 ***1823.15*** *p271*
Walker, John 35; Ontario, 1871 ***1823.15*** *p271*
Walker, John 37; Ontario, 1871 ***1823.15*** *p271*
Walker, John 45; Ontario, 1871 ***1823.15*** *p271*
Walker, John 50; Ontario, 1871 ***1823.15*** *p271*
Walker, John 51; Ontario, 1871 ***1823.15*** *p271*
Walker, John 57; Ontario, 1871 ***1823.28*** *p102*
Walker, John 63; Ontario, 1871 ***1823.22*** *p165*
Walker, John 74; Ontario, 1871 ***1823.15*** *p271*
Walker, Joseph; Maryland, 1676 ***2524.55*** *p228*
Walker, Joseph; New York, 1822 ***8197.10*** *p62*
Walker, Joseph; New York, 1822 ***8197.10*** *p293*
Walker, Joseph; Pennsylvania, 1776 ***4629.10*** *p52*
Walker, Joseph 30; Philadelphia, 1774 ***1220.25*** *p55*
Wife: Mary 28
Walker, Joseph, Jr.; New York, 1807 ***8197.10*** *p52*
Walker, Joseph James; New York, 1838 ***8197.10*** *p152*
Walker, Justice 40; Philadelphia, 1774 ***1220.25*** *p86*
With wife 30
Walker, Kirsty *SEE* Walker, Ewen
Walker, M. S. 6; Ontario, 1861 ***2896.26*** *p30*
Walker, Malcolm *SEE* Walker, Michael
Walker, Margaret *SEE* Walker, Donald
Walker, Margaret *SEE* Walker, James
Walker, Margret 80; Ontario, 1871 ***1823.15*** *p271*
Walker, Marion *SEE* Walker, Ewen
Walker, Marion *SEE* Walker, James
Walker, Marion; Ontario, 1850-1859 ***4537.37*** *p37*
Walker, Marion; Ontario, 1850-1859 ***4537.37*** *p39*
Walker, Marion; Ontario, 1851 ***4537.32*** *p17*
Walker, Marion; Port uncertain, 1840-1849 ***4537.37*** *p121*
Walker, Marvin 24; Ontario, 1871 ***1823.15*** *p271*
Walker, Mary *SEE* Walker, Alexander
Walker, Mary *SEE* Walker, Angus
Walker, Mary *SEE* Walker, James
Walker, Mary 28 *SEE* Walker, Joseph
Walker, Mary 65; Ontario, 1871 ***1823.15*** *p271*
Walker, Mary O'Neil; Vermont, 1847-1934 ***5900.10*** *p485*
Walker, Mary Scanlon; Vermont, 1853-1930 ***5900.10*** *p492*
Walker, Mathew 24; Nova Scotia, 1774 ***1220.25*** *p135*
Walker, Michael; Nova Scotia, 1840-1849 ***4537.37*** *p21*
Wife: Penny MacEachan
Child: Sam
Child: Angus
Child: Neil
Child: Catherine
Child: Malcolm
Walker, Micle 35; Ontario, 1871 ***1823.15*** *p271*
Walker, Murray 49; Ontario, 1871 ***1823.15*** *p271*
Walker, Nathen L.; Vermont, 1849-1917 ***5900.10*** *p492*
Walker, Neil *SEE* Walker, Angus
Walker, Neil *SEE* Walker, Ewen
Walker, Neil *SEE* Walker, Michael
Walker, Penny MacEachan *SEE* Walker, Michael
Walker, Peter F. 43; Ontario, 1871 ***1823.15*** *p271*
Walker, R. E.; Pennsylvania, 1868 ***6058.10*** *p72*
Walker, Ralph; New York, 1807 ***8197.10*** *p326*
Walker, Richard; Maryland, 1681 ***2524.55*** *p228*
Walker, Richard; Maryland, 1682 ***2524.55*** *p228*
Walker, Richard; Virginia, 1664 ***6212.30*** *p11*
Walker, Richard 38; Nova Scotia, 1774 ***1220.25*** *p136*
Walker, Robert; Alabama, 1832-1845 ***1640.10*** *p208*
Wife: Ann
Son: William
Walker, Robert; California, 1898 ***1640.13*** *p129*
Walker, Robert; Georgia, 1825 ***1640.10*** *p208*
Walker, Robert; Haiti, 1876 ***1640.13*** *p129*
Walker, Robert; New York, 1827 ***8197.10*** *p294*
Walker, Robert; Virginia, 1782 ***1224.2*** *p119*
Walker, Robert 22; Ontario, 1871 ***1823.15*** *p271*
Walker, Robert 38; Ontario, 1871 ***1823.15*** *p271*
Walker, Robert 40; Ontario, 1871 ***1823.22*** *p165*
Walker, Robert 42; Ontario, 1871 ***1823.22*** *p165*
Walker, Robert 46; Ontario, 1871 ***1823.15*** *p271*
Walker, Robert 48; Ontario, 1871 ***1823.15*** *p271*
Walker, Robert 54; Ontario, 1871 ***1823.15*** *p271*
Walker, Robt; Virginia, 1666 ***6212.30*** *p31*
Walker, Roderick *SEE* Walker, James
Walker, Sam *SEE* Walker, Michael
Walker, Samuel; Pennsylvania, 1777 ***4629.10*** *p23*
Walker, Samuel 27; Ontario, 1871 ***1823.15*** *p271*
Walker, Samuel 35; Ontario, 1871 ***1823.15*** *p271*
Walker, Samuel 36; Ontario, 1871 ***1823.15*** *p271*
Walker, Samuel 42; Ontario, 1871 ***1823.15*** *p271*
Walker, Samuel 57; Ontario, 1871 ***1823.15*** *p271*
Walker, Samuel B.; New York, New York, 1850 ***6058.10*** *p70*
Walker, Stephen 27; Maryland, 1775 ***1220.25*** *p104*
Walker, Susan; Vermont, 1840-1915 ***5900.10*** *p597*
Walker, Thomas; Boston, 1784 ***1224.2*** *p119*

Walker, Thomas; Maryland, 1676 ***2524.55*** *p229*
Walker, Thomas; New England, 1675 ***1224.1*** *p60*
Walker, Thomas; New York, 1794 ***8197.10*** *p3*
Walker, Thomas; New York, 1797 ***8197.10*** *p8*
Walker, Thomas 34; Ontario, 1871 ***1823.15*** *p271*
Walker, Thomas 38; Ontario, 1871 ***1823.15*** *p271*
Walker, Thomas 44; Ontario, 1871 ***1823.15*** *p271*
Walker, Thomas 59; Ontario, 1871 ***1823.22*** *p165*
Walker, Timothy; Jamaica, 1775 ***1220.25*** *p133*
Walker, Tristram 27; Fort Cumberland, Nova Scotia, 1774 ***1220.25*** *p18*
Walker, W. H.; Quebec, 1858 ***9196.15*** *p38*
Walker, Wadin 15; Ontario, 1871 ***1823.15*** *p271*
Walker, William *SEE* Walker, Robert
Walker, William; Georgia, 1698 ***1640.13*** *p130*
Walker, William; Maryland, 1662 ***2524.55*** *p229*
Walker, William; New York, 1803 ***8197.10*** *p17*
Walker, William; New York, 1805-1834 ***8197.10*** *p310*
Walker, William; New York, 1834 ***8197.10*** *p69*
Walker, William; Vermont, 1838-1896 ***5900.10*** *p289*
Walker, William 22; Ontario, 1871 ***1823.15*** *p271*
Walker, William 24; Maryland, 1775 ***1220.25*** *p100*
Walker, William 26; St. Vincent, 1775 ***1220.25*** *p129*
Walker, William 33; Ontario, 1871 ***1823.15*** *p271*
Walker, William 44; Ontario, 1871 ***1823.28*** *p102*
Walker, William 45; Ontario, 1871 ***1823.15*** *p271*
Walker, William 56; Ontario, 1871 ***1823.22*** *p165*
Walker, William G. 50; Ontario, 1871 ***1823.15*** *p271*
Walker, William J.; New York, 1840 ***8197.10*** *p201*
Walkering, T.; Quebec, 1857 ***9196.15*** *p13*
Walkerton, Joanna; Maryland, 1665 ***2524.55*** *p229*
Walkingshaw, James 66; Ontario, 1871 ***1823.15*** *p271*
Walkington, Thomas 50; Ontario, 1871 ***1823.15*** *p271*
Walkins, H. T. 40; British Columbia, 1912 ***9196.1*** *p15*
Walkins, H. T. 40; San Francisco, 1912 ***9196.1*** *p15*
Walkinshaw, George 44; Ontario, 1871 ***1823.22*** *p165*
Walkowiak, John; Maryland, 1910 ***3259.35*** *p65*
Walkowiak, Vincent; Maryland, 1910 ***3259.35*** *p65*
Wall, Alice; Maryland, 1675 ***2524.55*** *p229*
Wall, Ann 46; Vermont, 1880 ***5900.10*** *p474*
Wall, Anna; New England, 1673 ***1224.1*** *p60*
Wall, Annie; Vermont, 1859 ***5900.10*** *p521*
Wall, Bridget; Vermont, n.d. ***5900.10*** *p165*
Wall, Bridget 63; Vermont, 1885 ***5900.10*** *p533*
Wall, Daniel; Vermont, 1839-1907 ***5900.10*** *p181*
Wall, Daniel; Vermont, 1849-1929 ***5900.10*** *p533*
Wall, Daniel 76; Vermont, 1881 ***5900.10*** *p533*
Wall, Edward; Maryland, 1663 ***2524.55*** *p229*
Wall, Edward 50; Ontario, 1871 ***1823.15*** *p271*
Wall, Elizabeth 19; Georgia, 1775 ***1220.25*** *p126*
Wall, Ellen; Vermont, 1851-1915 ***5900.10*** *p538*
Wall, Frank 21; Seattle, 1914 ***9196.1*** *p66*
Wall, Frank 21; Vancouver, British Columbia, 1914 ***9196.1*** *p66*
Wall, James; New York, 1840 ***8197.10*** *p201*
Wall, James; Vermont, 1853 ***5900.10*** *p521*
Wall, James 29; Vermont, 1879 ***5900.10*** *p619*
Wall, James 56; Ontario, 1871 ***1823.15*** *p271*
Wall, Johann Heinrich; New York, 1834 ***8197.10*** *p319*
Wall, John; Charles Town, South Carolina, 1786 ***1224.2*** *p119*
Wall, John; New York, 1779 ***1224.2*** *p119*
Wall, John 22; Vermont, 1865 ***5900.10*** *p619*
Wall, John 30; New York, 1813-1826 ***8197.10*** *p298*
Wall, John 35; Maryland, 1774 ***1220.25*** *p39*
Wall, Joseph; Pennsylvania, 1752 ***1224.2*** *p119*
Wall, Joseph 30; Ontario, 1871 ***1823.28*** *p102*
Wall, Margaret; Maryland, 1669 ***2524.55*** *p229*
Wall, Margaret Mitten; Vermont, 1872 ***5900.10*** *p181*
Wall, Mary 18; Vermont, 1860 ***5900.10*** *p521*
Wall, Mary Grace 74; Ontario, 1871 ***1823.15*** *p271*
Wall, Michael 24; Philadelphia, 1774 ***1220.25*** *p67*
Wall, Richard 55; Ontario, 1871 ***1823.15*** *p271*
Wall, Robert; Pennsylvania, 1777 ***4629.10*** *p20*
Wall, Samuel; New England, 1799 ***1224.2*** *p120*
Wall, Stephen; New York, 1810 ***8197.10*** *p291*
Wall, Thomas; Georgia, 1733 ***1640.10*** *p209*
Wall, William; Virginia, 1663 ***6212.30*** *p4*
Wall, William 23; Maryland, 1774 ***1220.25*** *p74*
Wall, William 42; Ontario, 1871 ***1823.22*** *p165*
Wall, Wm; Virginia, 1665-1666 ***6212.30*** *p23*
Wall, Wm; Virginia, 1666-1667 ***6212.30*** *p32*
Wallace, Adam; Maryland, 1910 ***3259.35*** *p65*
Wallace, Alex 52; Ontario, 1871 ***1823.15*** *p272*
Wallace, Anastasia; Vermont, 1849-1923 ***5900.10*** *p254*
Wallace, Andrew J. B.; New York, 1824 ***8197.10*** *p293*
Wallace, Archibald; New York, 1840 ***8197.10*** *p385*
Wallace, Betsay 80; Ontario, 1871 ***1823.28*** *p102*
Wallace, Burton; Pennsylvania, 1776 ***4629.10*** *p53*
Wallace, David 40; Ontario, 1871 ***1823.22*** *p165*
Wallace, Edward; New York, 1838 ***8197.10*** *p295*
Wallace, Edward H. 63; Vermont, 1900 ***5900.10*** *p226*
Wallace, Elizabeth Nisbit; South Carolina, 1762 ***1224.2*** *p120*
Wallace, Ellen 86; Vermont, 1903 ***5900.10*** *p455*
Wallace, Francis 18; Georgia, 1775 ***1220.25*** *p124*
Wallace, Hannah 61; Vermont, 1874 ***5900.10*** *p556*
Wallace, Hugh; New York, New York, n.d. ***1224.2*** *p120*
Wallace, James; Georgia, 1798 ***1224.2*** *p120*
Wallace, James; Georgia, 1798 ***1640.10*** *p209*
Wallace, James; New York, 1809 ***8197.10*** *p9*
Wallace, James; New York, 1809 ***8197.10*** *p291*
Wallace, James; New York, 1840 ***8197.10*** *p203*
Wallace, James; Pennsylvania, 1786 ***4629.10*** *p51*
Wallace, James; Savannah, Georgia, 1829 ***1224.3*** *p82*
Wallace, James 15; Ontario, 1871 ***1823.15*** *p272*
Wallace, James 32; Ontario, 1871 ***1823.28*** *p102*
Wallace, James 41; Ontario, 1871 ***1823.28*** *p102*
Wallace, James 48; Ontario, 1871 ***1823.28*** *p102*
Wallace, James 55; Ontario, 1871 ***1823.15*** *p272*
Wallace, Jane 68; Ontario, 1871 ***1823.22*** *p165*
Wallace, Jane 70; Ontario, 1871 ***1823.15*** *p272*
Wallace, Jeremiah 49; Ontario, 1871 ***1823.15*** *p272*
Wallace, John; Canada, 1854 ***1640.13*** *p130*
Wallace, John; Georgia, 1698 ***1640.13*** *p130*
Wallace, John; Georgia, 1699 ***1640.13*** *p130*
Wallace, John; New York, 1838 ***8197.10*** *p376*
Wallace, John; New York, New York, 1858 ***6058.10*** *p52*
Wallace, John; Vermont, 1842-1924 ***5900.10*** *p394*
Wallace, John 22; Virginia, 1775 ***1220.25*** *p142*
Wallace, John 30; Ontario, 1871 ***1823.15*** *p272*
Wallace, John 31; Ontario, 1871 ***1823.15*** *p272*
Wallace, John 34; Ontario, 1871 ***1823.15*** *p272*
Wallace, John 59; Ontario, 1871 ***1823.28*** *p102*
Wallace, John 74; Ontario, 1871 ***1823.28*** *p102*
Wallace, John 78; Vermont, 1875 ***5900.10*** *p226*
Wallace, Joseph 20; Ontario, 1871 ***1823.15*** *p272*
Wallace, Joseph 61; Ontario, 1871 ***1823.15*** *p272*
Wallace, Joseph K.; Vermont, 1838-1908 ***5900.10*** *p237*
Wallace, Joseph W.; Vermont, 1839-1918 ***5900.10*** *p236*
Wallace, Margaret Morrissey; Vermont, 1795-1884 ***5900.10*** *p226*
Wallace, Margaret O'Keefe; Vermont, 1863-1911 ***5900.10*** *p236*
Wallace, Mary 60; Ontario, 1871 ***1823.15*** *p272*
Wallace, Mary Cassin; Vermont, 1851-1935 ***5900.10*** *p226*
Wallace, Mary O'Keefe; Vermont, 1852-1935 ***5900.10*** *p394*
Wallace, Michael; Vermont, 1828-1901 ***5900.10*** *p45*
Wallace, Norman; Savannah, Georgia, 1803-1812 ***1640.10*** *p209*
Wallace, Patrick; Vermont, 1847-1927 ***5900.10*** *p254*
Wallace, Patrick 26; Ontario, 1871 ***1823.15*** *p272*
Wallace, Peter 91; Ontario, 1871 ***1823.15*** *p272*
Wallace, Robert; Mobile, Alabama, 1867 ***1640.10*** *p209*
Wallace, Robert; New York, 1802 ***8197.10*** *p26*
Wallace, Robert; New York, 1814 ***8197.10*** *p58*
Wallace, Robert 68; Ontario, 1871 ***1823.15*** *p272*
Wallace, Robert 74; Vermont, 1856 ***5900.10*** *p556*
Wallace, Samuel 41; Ontario, 1871 ***1823.15*** *p272*
Wallace, Samuel 52; Ontario, 1871 ***1823.22*** *p165*
Wallace, Sarah J.; Vermont, 1840-1883 ***5900.10*** *p519*
Wallace, Septimus 17; Ontario, 1871 ***1823.15*** *p272*
Wallace, Thomas; New York, 1812 ***8197.10*** *p58*
Wallace, Thomas; New York, 1840 ***8197.10*** *p201*
Wallace, Thomas; New York, 1840 ***8197.10*** *p202*
Wallace, Thomas 17; Ontario, 1871 ***1823.15*** *p272*
Wallace, Thomas 23; Ontario, 1871 ***1823.22*** *p165*
Wallace, Thomas 45; Ontario, 1871 ***1823.15*** *p272*
Wallace, William; Georgia, 1733 ***1640.10*** *p209*
Wallace, William; New Haven, Connecticut, 1831 ***1224.3*** *p82*
Wallace, William; West Indies, n.d. ***1224.3*** *p82*
Wallace, William 24; Virginia, 1775 ***1220.25*** *p142*
Wallace, William 33; Ontario, 1871 ***1823.15*** *p272*
Wallace, William 50; Ontario, 1871 ***1823.15*** *p272*
Wallace, William 69; Ontario, 1871 ***1823.28*** *p102*
Wallace, William Alexander; New York, New York, 1840 ***1224.3*** *p82*
Wallace, William Oxford; South Carolina, 1790 ***1224.2*** *p120*
Wallach, Samuel; New York, 1821 ***8197.10*** *p293*
Wallas, Mr.; Quebec, 1858 ***9196.15*** *p32*
Wallas, Mrs.; Quebec, 1858 ***9196.15*** *p32*
Wallas, Mary; Maryland, 1910 ***3259.35*** *p65*
Wallas, Thomas 30; Ontario, 1871 ***1823.28*** *p102*
Wallbridge, Alice 16; Ontario, 1861 ***2896.25*** *p35*
Wallbridge, Alis 38; Ontario, 1861 ***2896.25*** *p32*
Wallbridge, Cintha 19; Ontario, 1861 ***2896.25*** *p35*
Wallbridge, E. 10; Ontario, 1861 ***2896.25*** *p35*
Wallbridge, Elias 55; Ontario, 1861 ***2896.25*** *p32*
Wallbridge, Ellen 2; Ontario, 1861 ***2896.25*** *p32*
Wallbridge, M. J. 13; Ontario, 1861 ***2896.25*** *p35*
Wallbridge, Martha 43; Ontario, 1861 ***2896.25*** *p35*
Wallbridge, Mary 5; Ontario, 1861 ***2896.25*** *p35*
Wallbridge, Mary 18; Ontario, 1861 ***2896.25*** *p32*
Wallbrooke, Jonah; Virginia, 1665-1666 ***6212.30*** *p24*
Wallbrunn, Freiherr von; Port uncertain, 1725 ***2856.30*** *p476*
Wallder, Mary; Virginia, 1666-1667 ***6212.30*** *p32*
Walldorf, Mr.; Port uncertain, 1745 ***2856.30*** *p476*
With brother
Wallece, Thomas 26; Ontario, 1871 ***1823.15*** *p272*
Waller, Alexander 25; Kansas, 1910 ***9079.10*** *p14*
Waller, Amelia 5; Kansas, 1910 ***9079.10*** *p14*
Waller, Anna 22; Kansas, 1910 ***9079.10*** *p14*
Waller, Annie 16; Ontario, 1861 ***2896.28*** *p38*
Waller, Edward; Virginia, 1666-1667 ***6212.30*** *p32*
Waller, Elizabeth 38; Ontario, 1861 ***2896.28*** *p18*
Waller, Elizabeth A. 85; Ontario, 1871 ***1823.22*** *p165*
Waller, Frances; Virginia, 1672 ***6212.30*** *p49*
Waller, Frederic 50; Kansas, 1905-1910 ***9079.10*** *p14*
Waller, George A. 4; Ontario, 1861 ***2896.28*** *p18*
Waller, Henry; New York, 1835 ***1224.3*** *p82*
Waller, Isaack; Maryland, 1681 ***2524.55*** *p229*
Waller, Isabelle 9; Ontario, 1861 ***2896.28*** *p18*
Waller, John; Maryland, 1668 ***2524.55*** *p229*
Waller, John; Virginia, 1666 ***6212.30*** *p25*
Waller, John W. 3; Ontario, 1861 ***2896.28*** *p18*
Waller, Joseph 18; Ontario, 1861 ***2896.28*** *p39*
Waller, Julian E. 50; Kansas, 1910 ***9079.10*** *p14*
Waller, Lydia 16; Kansas, 1910 ***9079.10*** *p14*
Waller, Maria 9; Kansas, 1910 ***9079.10*** *p14*
Waller, Pheby J. 6; Ontario, 1861 ***2896.28*** *p18*
Waller, Rebecca 1; Ontario, 1861 ***2896.28*** *p18*
Waller, Robert J. 7; Ontario, 1861 ***2896.28*** *p18*
Waller, Sarah E. 11; Ontario, 1861 ***2896.28*** *p18*
Waller, Thomas; Maryland, 1675 ***2524.55*** *p229*
Waller, Thomas; Virginia, 1666-1667 ***6212.30*** *p34*
Waller, Thomas 21; Ontario, 1861 ***2896.28*** *p56*
Waller, Thomas 26; Maryland, 1774 ***1220.25*** *p59*
Waller, Thomas 47; Ontario, 1861 ***2896.28*** *p18*
Waller, Tobias; Port uncertain, 1734 ***2856.30*** *p476*
Wallern, James 21; Tobago, West Indies, 1775 ***1220.25*** *p129*
Walleson, Edward; New York, 1838 ***8197.10*** *p152*
Wallet, William; Maryland, 1672 ***2524.55*** *p229*
Wallewein, Barbara; Port uncertain, 1795 ***2856.30*** *p476*
With husband & 4 children
Walley, Elizabeth *SEE* Walley, Thomas
Walley, John *SEE* Walley, Thomas
Walley, Margarett *SEE* Walley, Thomas
Walley, Rachell *SEE* Walley, Thomas
Walley, Thomas; Maryland, 1665 ***2524.55*** *p226*
Wife: Elizabeth
Child: Rachell
Child: Elizabeth
Child: John
Child: Margarett
Walley, Thomas; Maryland, 1665 ***2524.55*** *p229*
Wallin, Anne; New England, 1699 ***1224.1*** *p17*
Wallin, Samuel, Jr.; New York, 1838 ***8197.10*** *p152*
Walling, Jean; Virginia, 1667-1668 ***6212.30*** *p38*
Walling, John; Virginia, 1667-1668 ***6212.30*** *p38*
Wallingford, Rebecca; Virginia, 1665 ***6212.30*** *p18*
Wallington, George; Pennsylvania, 1787 ***4629.10*** *p56*
Wallington, Hartly; Virginia, 1664 ***6212.30*** *p7*
Wallington, John; Pennsylvania, 1787 ***4629.10*** *p56*
Wallis, Alexander 53; Ontario, 1871 ***1823.22*** *p165*
Wallis, Alfred; New York, 1827 ***8197.10*** *p339*
Wallis, Bridgett *SEE* Wallis, Thomas
Wallis, Charles 22; Philadelphia, 1774 ***1220.25*** *p80*
Wallis, Edward; Virginia, 1663 ***6212.30*** *p3*
Wallis, Elizabeth; Vermont, 1826-1892 ***5900.10*** *p198*
Wallis, Ellen Lyons; Vermont, 1832-1894 ***5900.10*** *p198*
Wallis, Esther Cross; Vermont, 1823-1855 ***5900.10*** *p198*
Wallis, George J.; Vermont, 1844-1865 ***5900.10*** *p198*
Wallis, Hammond; New York, 1817-1834 ***8197.10*** *p305*
Wallis, Henry; Virginia, 1664 ***6212.30*** *p15*
Wallis, James; Vermont, 1822-1902 ***5900.10*** *p198*
Wallis, James 23; Maryland, 1774 ***1220.25*** *p57*
Wallis, John 17; Maryland, 1774 ***1220.25*** *p69*
Wallis, John 21; Philadelphia, 1775 ***1220.25*** *p107*
Wallis, John 42; Ontario, 1871 ***1823.15*** *p272*
Wallis, John, Jr.; New York, 1839 ***8197.10*** *p135*
Wallis, Jonah; Virginia, 1665 ***6212.30*** *p19*
Wallis, Josiah; New York, 1779 ***1224.2*** *p120*
Wallis, Mary; Maryland, 1681 ***2524.55*** *p229*
Wallis, Mary 47; Ontario, 1871 ***1823.22*** *p165*
Wallis, Thomas; Maryland, 1681 ***2524.55*** *p229*
Wife: Bridgett
Wallis, William; Georgia, 1733 ***1640.10*** *p209*
Wallis, William; Vermont, 1820-1886 ***5900.10*** *p198*
Wallop, John; Virginia, 1690 ***6212.30*** *p58*
Wallop, Rebecca; Virginia, 1690 ***6212.30*** *p58*
Wallows, Thomas; Virginia, 1663 ***6212.30*** *p1*
Wallrapp, Nikolai; Port uncertain, 1771 ***2856.30*** *p476*

Ward, Elizabeth 22 *SEE* Ward, William
Ward, Elizabeth C.; Vermont, 1867-1967 ***5900.10*** *p472*
Ward, Elizabeth C. Whyte; Vermont, 1859-1934 ***5900.10*** *p490*
Ward, Elizabeth Callan; Vermont, 1845-1906 ***5900.10*** *p478*
Ward, Elizabeth Callan; Vermont, 1846-1906 ***5900.10*** *p500*
Ward, Elizabeth Steele; Vermont, 1831-1914 ***5900.10*** *p491*
Ward, Elizabeth Witty; Nebraska, 1893 ***1640.13*** *p130*
Ward, Ellen; Vermont, 1838-1907 ***5900.10*** *p140*
Ward, Ellen Dilworth; Vermont, 1818-1886 ***5900.10*** *p303*
Ward, Ellen M.; Vermont, 1854-1928 ***5900.10*** *p89*
Ward, F. 5; Ontario, 1861 ***2896.28*** *p4*
Ward, Frank 66; Vermont, 1909 ***5900.10*** *p184*
Ward, Gabriel 70; Vermont, 1898 ***5900.10*** *p193*
Ward, George; New York, 1838 ***8197.10*** *p151*
Ward, George 17; Ontario, 1871 ***1823.28*** *p102*
Ward, George 22; Maryland, 1774 ***1220.25*** *p79*
Ward, George 45; Ontario, 1871 ***1823.22*** *p166*
Ward, Hannah; Vermont, 1902 ***5900.10*** *p408*
Ward, Henrietta E. Collins; Vermont, 1857-1935 ***5900.10*** *p598*
Ward, Henrietta E. Collins; Vermont, 1857-1935 ***5900.10*** *p599*
Ward, Henry; Maryland, 1665 ***2524.55*** *p230*
Ward, Henry; Pennsylvania, 1771 ***1224.2*** *p120*
Ward, Henry; Virginia, 1659 ***1224.1*** *p61*
Ward, Henry 36; Maryland, 1774 ***1220.25*** *p47*
Ward, Henry 52; Ontario, 1871 ***1823.22*** *p166*
Ward, Henry 77; Vermont, 1903 ***5900.10*** *p597*
Ward, Henry B.; Pennsylvania, 1866 ***6058.10*** *p52*
Ward, Hugh; New York, 1804 ***8197.10*** *p28*
Ward, Hugh; New York, 1806 ***8197.10*** *p33*
Ward, Hugh 81; Vermont, 1889 ***5900.10*** *p601*
Ward, Isabella; Maryland, 1665 ***2524.55*** *p230*
Ward, Isabella 20; Ontario, 1871 ***1823.15*** *p273*
Ward, James; Maryland, 1662 ***2524.55*** *p230*
Ward, James; New York, 1827 ***8197.10*** *p293*
Ward, James; Vermont, 1872-1895 ***5900.10*** *p303*
Ward, James 20; Ontario, 1861 ***2896.27*** *p60*
Ward, James 21; Maryland, 1775 ***1220.25*** *p109*
Ward, James 28; Halifax, Nova Scotia, 1774 ***1220.25*** *p138*
Ward, James 58; Vermont, 1854 ***5900.10*** *p198*
Ward, James 80; Vermont, 1914 ***5900.10*** *p123*
Ward, James H.; Vermont, 1855-1926 ***5900.10*** *p490*
Ward, James J. 47; Vermont, 1867 ***5900.10*** *p239*
Ward, James S.; Vermont, 1857-1913 ***5900.10*** *p599*
Ward, Johanna Sullivan; Vermont, 1848-1916 ***5900.10*** *p592*
Ward, John; New York, 1836 ***8197.10*** *p301*
Ward, John; Pennsylvania, 1868 ***6058.10*** *p63*
Ward, John; Vermont, 1854-1920 ***5900.10*** *p598*
Ward, John; Vermont, 1856-1923 ***5900.10*** *p88*
Ward, John 21; Ontario, 1871 ***1823.15*** *p273*
Ward, John 27; Maryland, 1774 ***1220.25*** *p8*
Ward, John 27; New York, 1774 ***1220.25*** *p26*
Ward, John 42; Ontario, 1871 ***1823.28*** *p103*
Ward, John 45; Ontario, 1871 ***1823.15*** *p273*
Ward, John 54; Ontario, 1871 ***1823.15*** *p273*
Ward, John 57; Ontario, 1871 ***1823.15*** *p273*
Ward, John 59; Ontario, 1871 ***1823.22*** *p166*
Ward, John 59; Ontario, 1871 ***1823.28*** *p103*
Ward, John 72; Vermont, 1897 ***5900.10*** *p597*
Ward, John, Sr.; New York, 1840 ***8197.10*** *p202*
Ward, John H.; Vermont, 1854-1920 ***5900.10*** *p599*
Ward, Joseph 19; Vermont, 1879 ***5900.10*** *p341*
Ward, Joseph George 38; Ontario, 1871 ***1823.15*** *p273*
Ward, Kattie 31; Vermont, 1887 ***5900.10*** *p601*
Ward, Lewis; Pennsylvania, 1777 ***4629.10*** *p27*
Ward, Lewis; Vermont, 1836-1884 ***5900.10*** *p42*
Ward, M. 7; Ontario, 1861 ***2896.28*** *p4*
Ward, M. 12; Ontario, 1861 ***2896.28*** *p4*
Ward, Margaret *SEE* Ward, Andrew
Ward, Margaret E.; Vermont, 1858-1884 ***5900.10*** *p44*
Ward, Mark; Pennsylvania, 1817-1826 ***6058.10*** *p7*
Ward, Mary; Maryland, 1681 ***2524.55*** *p230*
Ward, Mary; Vermont, 1836-1894 ***5900.10*** *p421*
Ward, Mary; Vermont, 1853-1881 ***5900.10*** *p44*
Ward, Mary; Vermont, 1854-1906 ***5900.10*** *p88*
Ward, Mary; Vermont, 1857-1929 ***5900.10*** *p592*
Ward, Mary 25; Vermont, 1852 ***5900.10*** *p239*
Ward, Mary 62; Vermont, 1915 ***5900.10*** *p484*
Ward, Mary A.; Vermont, 1859-1911 ***5900.10*** *p599*
Ward, Mary Ann W. 57; Ontario, 1871 ***1823.22*** *p166*
Ward, Mary E.; Vermont, 1845-1917 ***5900.10*** *p184*
Ward, Mary Flynn; Vermont, 1852-1930 ***5900.10*** *p88*
Ward, Matthew; Maryland, 1671 ***2524.55*** *p230*
Ward, Matthew 66; Ontario, 1871 ***1823.15*** *p273*
Ward, Michaell; Virginia, 1668-1669 ***6212.30*** *p40*
Ward, Moses; New York, 1816 ***1224.3*** *p82*
Ward, Moses 18 months *SEE* Ward, William
Ward, Nathaniell; Maryland, 1661 ***2524.55*** *p230*
Ward, Patrick; New York, 1826 ***8197.10*** *p9*
Ward, Patrick; New York, 1840 ***8197.10*** *p203*
Ward, Patrick; New York, 1840 ***8197.10*** *p385*
Ward, Patrick; Vermont, 1831-1911 ***5900.10*** *p491*
Ward, Patrick; Vermont, 1832-1920 ***5900.10*** *p592*
Ward, Patrick 64; Ontario, 1871 ***1823.22*** *p166*
Ward, Patrick K.; Vermont, 1830-1902 ***5900.10*** *p44*
Ward, Pearson; South Carolina, 1786 ***1224.2*** *p120*
Ward, Peter 15; Ontario, 1871 ***1823.28*** *p103*
Ward, Peter 33; Ontario, 1871 ***1823.15*** *p273*
Ward, Peter 77; Vermont, 1867 ***5900.10*** *p239*
Ward, Philip; Vermont, 1841-1913 ***5900.10*** *p159*
Ward, Rebeccah; Maryland, 1680 ***2524.55*** *p230*
Ward, Richard; Vermont, 1848-1924 ***5900.10*** *p500*
Ward, Richard; Virginia, 1664 ***6212.30*** *p14*
Ward, Richard 40; Ontario, 1871 ***1823.15*** *p273*
Ward, Robert 17; Maryland, 1774 ***1220.25*** *p7*
Ward, Robt.; Maryland, 1665 ***2524.55*** *p230*
Ward, Robt; Virginia, 1665-1666 ***6212.30*** *p24*
Ward, Samuel; Pennsylvania, 1777 ***4629.10*** *p15*
Ward, Samuel; Vermont, 1848-1869 ***5900.10*** *p303*
Ward, Samuel Chandler; New York, 1798 ***1224.2*** *p120*
Ward, Sarah A. 54; Vermont, 1907 ***5900.10*** *p560*
Ward, Stewart 44; Ontario, 1871 ***1823.15*** *p273*
Ward, Susan 26; Ontario, 1871 ***1823.28*** *p103*
Ward, Susan Murphy 90; Vermont, 1894 ***5900.10*** *p601*
Ward, Thomas; Maryland, 1658 ***2524.55*** *p230*
Ward, Thomas; Maryland, 1679 ***2524.55*** *p230*
Ward, Thomas; Maryland, 1680 ***2524.55*** *p230*
Ward, Thomas; New York, 1802 ***8197.10*** *p26*
Ward, Thomas; New York, 1836 ***8197.10*** *p76*
Ward, Thomas; New York, 1840 ***8197.10*** *p295*
Ward, Thomas 19; Maryland, 1774 ***1220.25*** *p70*
Ward, Thomas 37; Ontario, 1871 ***1823.15*** *p273*
Ward, Thomas 39; Philadelphia, 1775 ***1220.25*** *p121*
Ward, Thomas 69; Vermont, 1909 ***5900.10*** *p310*
Ward, W. Sherman 39; Ontario, 1871 ***1823.28*** *p103*
Ward, William; Maryland, 1663 ***2524.55*** *p230*
Ward, William; Maryland, 1666 ***2524.55*** *p230*
Ward, William; Maryland, 1668 ***2524.55*** *p230*
Ward, William; Maryland, 1680 ***2524.55*** *p230*
Ward, William; New York, 1840 ***8197.10*** *p202*
Ward, William 18; Maryland, 1774 ***1220.25*** *p70*
Ward, William 18; Maryland, 1774 ***1220.25*** *p73*
Ward, William 19; Maryland, 1774 ***1220.25*** *p69*
Ward, William 24; Nova Scotia, 1774 ***1220.25*** *p13*
Wife: Elizabeth 22
Son: Moses 18 months
Ward, Winnifred; Vermont, 1825-1911 ***5900.10*** *p178*
Wardell, Christopher; New York, 1828 ***8197.10*** *p348*
Wardell, Joseph 44; Ontario, 1871 ***1823.28*** *p103*
Wardell, Michaell; Virginia, 1703-1704 ***6212.30*** *p62*
Warden, Daniel; New York, 1840 ***8197.10*** *p296*
Warden, John 60; Ontario, 1871 ***1823.15*** *p273*
Warden, William; Charles Town, South Carolina, 1746 ***1224.2*** *p120*
Warden, William 21; Virginia, 1774 ***1220.25*** *p75*
Warden, Wm; Virginia, 1665 ***6212.30*** *p19*
Warder, Jeremiah; Philadelphia, 1842 ***1224.3*** *p82*
Warder, John; Maryland, 1673 ***2524.55*** *p230*
Warder, Margery; Maryland, 1673 ***2524.55*** *p230*
Wardlaw, A.; Portland, Maine, 1857 ***9196.15*** *p12*
Wardlaw, Ralph; Pensacola, Florida, 1766 ***1640.10*** *p209*
Wardle, Thomas; New York, 1827 ***8197.10*** *p346*
Wardle, William 28; Ontario, 1871 ***1823.28*** *p103*
Wardleigh, George; Vermont, 1852-1926 ***5900.10*** *p284*
Wardleigh, Margaret; Vermont, 1930 ***5900.10*** *p284*
Wardlow, James; New York, 1837 ***8197.10*** *p103*
Wardner, Andrew; Maryland, 1662 ***2524.55*** *p230*
Wardner, Sarah *SEE* Wardner, Thomas
Wardner, Thomas; Maryland, 1667 ***2524.55*** *p230*
Wife: Sarah
Wardrop, John; Maryland, 1767 ***1224.2*** *p121*
Wardrop, John; Virginia, 1791 ***1640.13*** *p130*
Wardrop, Joseph; Georgia, 1734 ***1640.10*** *p209*
Wardrop, William; West Indies, 1848 ***1640.13*** *p130*
Wardrope, Robert; Portland, Maine, 1857 ***9196.15*** *p12*
Wardrope, William; Georgia, 1812 ***1640.10*** *p210*
Wardt, Johann Karl; Port uncertain, 1755 ***2856.30*** *p479*
Ware, Cornelius; Maryland, 1661 ***2524.55*** *p68*
Ware, David; Pennsylvania, 1777 ***4629.10*** *p23*
Ware, Jno; Virginia, 1668-1669 ***6212.30*** *p41*
Ware, John; Boston, 1694 ***1224.1*** *p61*
Ware, John 23; Maryland, 1773-1774 ***1220.25*** *p33*
Ware, Jonathan; Savannah, Georgia, 1805 ***1640.10*** *p210*
Ware, Kazie 78; Ontario, 1871 ***1823.22*** *p166*
Ware, Robert 15; Jamaica, 1774 ***1220.25*** *p44*
Ware, Roger; Virginia, 1663 ***6212.30*** *p2*
Wareham, Dennis; New York, 1807 ***8197.10*** *p52*
Wareham, James; New York, 1839 ***8197.10*** *p135*
Wareham, John; New York, 1823 ***1224.3*** *p82*
Warelock, Thomas; Maryland, 1679 ***2524.55*** *p230*
Warga, Joseph; Maryland, 1910 ***3259.35*** *p66*
Warge, Thomas 27; Jamaica, 1774 ***1220.25*** *p92*
Wargrave, Will.; Maryland, 1670 ***2524.55*** *p230*
Warick, Thomas 62; Ontario, 1871 ***1823.15*** *p273*
Warielewka, Theodore; Maryland, 1910 ***3259.35*** *p66*
Waring, Abigail 12; Ontario, 1861 ***2896.27*** *p31*
Waring, Adam H. 2; Ontario, 1861 ***2896.27*** *p31*
Waring, Agnes 8; Ontario, 1861 ***2896.27*** *p31*
Waring, Ann 15; Ontario, 1861 ***2896.27*** *p39*
Waring, Charles R.; New York, 1806 ***8197.10*** *p33*
Waring, Edmund; New York, 1840 ***8197.10*** *p202*
Waring, Ellen; Boston, 1827 ***1224.3*** *p82*
Waring, Frances 43; Ontario, 1861 ***2896.27*** *p35*
Waring, George 8; Ontario, 1861 ***2896.27*** *p35*
Waring, Jacob; Maryland, 1681 ***2524.55*** *p230*
Waring, James; New York, 1829 ***8197.10*** *p294*
Waring, John 18; Ontario, 1861 ***2896.27*** *p35*
Waring, Mary Ann 39; Ontario, 1861 ***2896.27*** *p31*
Waring, Mragaret 16; Ontario, 1861 ***2896.27*** *p35*
Waring, Richard 54; Ontario, 1871 ***1823.15*** *p273*
Waring, Sampson; Maryland, 1659 ***2524.55*** *p230*
Waring, Sarah; South Carolina, 1760 ***1224.2*** *p121*
Waring, Sarah Ann 16; Ontario, 1861 ***2896.27*** *p31*
Waring, Thomas 12; Ontario, 1861 ***2896.27*** *p35*
Waring, Thomas 50; Ontario, 1861 ***2896.27*** *p35*
Waring, William E. 6; Ontario, 1861 ***2896.27*** *p31*
Wark, George 38; Ontario, 1871 ***1823.28*** *p103*
Wark, Isaac; New York, 1838 ***8197.10*** *p295*
Wark, Isaac; New York, 1840 ***8197.10*** *p201*
Wark, James 54; Ontario, 1871 ***1823.28*** *p103*
Wark, John; Georgia, 1775 ***1640.10*** *p210*
Wark, John; New York, 1802 ***8197.10*** *p26*
Wark, John 30; Georgia, 1775 ***1220.25*** *p125*
Wark, John 60; Ontario, 1871 ***1823.28*** *p103*
Wark, Mary Ann 34; Ontario, 1871 ***1823.28*** *p103*
Wark, Myra 56; Ontario, 1871 ***1823.28*** *p103*
Warkman, Robert; Virginia, 1670 ***1224.1*** *p24*
Warle, Steven; Maryland, 1662 ***2524.55*** *p230*
Warmald, W. E.; Pennsylvania, 1838 ***6058.10*** *p15*
Warmdorf, Anna; Ontario, 1871 ***1823.28*** *p103*
Warmdorf, Fredrick 23; Ontario, 1871 ***1823.28*** *p103*
Warmdorf, Louisa 23; Ontario, 1871 ***1823.28*** *p103*
Warmer, Tho; Virginia, 1664-1665 ***6212.30*** *p16*
Warminski, Mike; Maryland, 1910 ***3259.35*** *p66*
Warminski, Stanislaus; Maryland, 1910 ***3259.35*** *p66*
Warmock, Mary 72; Ontario, 1871 ***1823.15*** *p273*
Warmor, Benjamin 28; Ontario, 1871 ***1823.15*** *p273*
Warmsly, Ruth 74; Ontario, 1871 ***1823.15*** *p273*
Warn, John W. 50; Ontario, 1871 ***1823.22*** *p166*
Warneker, Anthony; New York, 1821 ***8197.10*** *p292*
Warner, Miss; Quebec, 1858 ***9196.15*** *p42*
Warner, Mrs.; Quebec, 1856 ***9196.15*** *p10*
Warner, Andrew; Maryland, 1651 ***2524.55*** *p230*
Wife: Mary
Daughter: Isabell
Warner, Charles 21; Maryland, 1775 ***1220.25*** *p99*
Warner, Ebenezer 61; Ontario, 1871 ***1823.28*** *p103*
Warner, Francis 74; Ontario, 1871 ***1823.22*** *p166*
Warner, George 37; Ontario, 1871 ***1823.15*** *p273*
Warner, Isabell *SEE* Warner, Andrew
Warner, James; Maryland, 1650 ***2524.55*** *p231*
Wife: Joan
Child: Joan
Warner, James 31; Maryland, 1775 ***1220.25*** *p111*
Warner, Jeremiah; New York, 1803 ***8197.10*** *p17*
Warner, Jno; Virginia, 1664 ***6212.30*** *p15*
Warner, Joan *SEE* Warner, James
Warner, John; New York, 1840 ***8197.10*** *p202*
Warner, John T.; New York, 1840 ***8197.10*** *p203*
Warner, Joseph, Jr.; Pennsylvania, 1786 ***4629.10*** *p51*
Warner, Mary *SEE* Warner, Andrew
Warner, Michael; Maryland, 1910 ***3259.35*** *p66*
Warner, Nathaniel; Boston, 1746 ***1224.2*** *p121*
Warner, Robert 27; Virginia, 1775 ***1220.25*** *p95*
Warner, Thomas 21; Maryland, 1775 ***1220.25*** *p105*
Warner, William 49; Ontario, 1871 ***1823.15*** *p274*
Warner, William S. 42; Vermont, 1888 ***5900.10*** *p259*
Warnett, Thomas; Virginia, 1630 ***1224.1*** *p61*
Warnick, Thomas 63; Ontario, 1871 ***1823.22*** *p166*
Warnoc, Eliza 40; Ontario, 1871 ***1823.15*** *p274*
Warnock, John 45; Ontario, 1871 ***1823.28*** *p103*
Warnock, John 80; Ontario, 1871 ***1823.15*** *p274*
Warnock, Samuel 53; Ontario, 1871 ***1823.15*** *p274*
Warnsley, John; Died enroute, 1698 ***1224.1*** *p61*
Warowsci, Adam; Maryland, 1910 ***3259.35*** *p66*
Warr, Laura 12; Ontario, 1871 ***1823.22*** *p166*
Warrack, James; Georgia, 1690-1699 ***1640.13*** *p130*
Warrall, John; Maryland, 1674 ***2524.55*** *p231*
Warre, Francis Whitehead; New York, 1846 ***1224.3*** *p82*
Warre, John; Maryland, 1673 ***2524.55*** *p231*
Warreck, John; Maryland, 1670 ***2524.55*** *p127*

Warren, Amy 38; Ontario, 1861 ***2896.27*** *p22*
Warren, Anna Wignell; Philadelphia, 1813 ***1224.3*** *p82*
Warren, Bertha E. 5; Ontario, 1861 ***2896.27*** *p22*
Warren, Charlotte Susannah Clare; Galveston, Texas, 1855 ***1224.3*** *p82*
Warren, Deborah 66; Ontario, 1861 ***2896.27*** *p22*
Warren, Eliza J. 26; Ontario, 1861 ***2896.27*** *p22*
Warren, Ellen; Maryland, 1664 ***2524.55*** *p231*
Warren, Esther 3; Ontario, 1861 ***2896.27*** *p12*
Warren, George 14; Philadelphia, 1775 ***1220.25*** *p106*
Warren, George 55; Ontario, 1871 ***1823.15*** *p274*
Warren, H. 22; Ontario, 1871 ***1823.28*** *p103*
Warren, Henry; Virginia, 1667 ***6212.30*** *p37*
Warren, Humphrey *SEE* Warren, Humphrey
Warren, Humphrey; Maryland, 1662 ***2524.55*** *p231*
Son: Humphrey
Warren, James; Maryland, 1666 ***2524.55*** *p145*
Warren, James; Maryland, 1666 ***2524.55*** *p231*
Warren, James; New York, 1807 ***8197.10*** *p331*
Warren, James; Virginia, 1664-1665 ***6212.30*** *p16*
Warren, James; Virginia, 1672-1673 ***6212.30*** *p51*
Warren, James 42; British Columbia, 1911 ***9196.1*** *p36*
Warren, James 42; Seattle, 1911 ***9196.1*** *p36*
Warren, John; Albany, New York, 1722 ***1224.2*** *p121*
Warren, John; Maryland, 1646 ***2524.55*** *p231*
With wife
Warren, John; Missouri, 1855 ***1224.3*** *p82*
Warren, Johnson 16; Ontario, 1871 ***1823.15*** *p274*
Warren, L. 30; Alaska, 1910 ***9196.1*** *p9*
Warren, L. 30; Yukon, 1910 ***9196.1*** *p9*
Warren, Mariah L. 9; Ontario, 1861 ***2896.27*** *p22*
Warren, Mary; Virginia, 1671 ***6212.30*** *p42*
Warren, Mary Asina 14; Ontario, 1861 ***2896.27*** *p22*
Warren, Medcalf 37; Ontario, 1861 ***2896.27*** *p12*
Warren, Paul D. 2; Ontario, 1861 ***2896.27*** *p22*
Warren, Rachel 36; Ontario, 1861 ***2896.27*** *p12*
Warren, Samuel; Detroit, 1850 ***1224.3*** *p82*
Warren, Sintha Ann 11; Ontario, 1861 ***2896.27*** *p12*
Warren, Stephen; Virginia, 1672-1673 ***6212.30*** *p51*
Warren, Thomas; Boston, 1850 ***1224.3*** *p82*
Warren, Thomas 31; Maryland, 1774 ***1220.25*** *p78*
Warren, Thomas 68; Ontario, 1871 ***1823.28*** *p103*
Warren, Valentine; Maryland, 1660 ***2524.55*** *p231*
Warren, William; Maryland, 1657 ***2524.55*** *p231*
Warren, William; New York, 1840 ***8197.10*** *p202*
Warren, William 46; Ontario, 1871 ***1823.22*** *p166*
Warren, Wm; Virginia, 1671 ***6212.30*** *p42*
Warrender, William; Georgia, 1698 ***1640.13*** *p130*
Warrin, Ann; Maryland, 1673 ***2524.55*** *p19*
Warring, M. E. 10; Ontario, 1861 ***2896.26*** *p5*
Warrington, Godfry; Virginia, 1667-1668 ***6212.30*** *p38*
Warrington, Henry; Virginia, 1667-1668 ***6212.30*** *p39*
Warrock, Francis 20; Ontario, 1871 ***1823.28*** *p103*
Warrwicke, Henry; Maryland, 1657 ***2524.55*** *p231*
Wart, Bernhard; America, 1738 ***2856.30*** *p479*
Wart, Bernhard; America, 1739 ***2856.30*** *p479*
Wart, Bernhard; America, 1779 ***2856.30*** *p479*
Wartzner, William; New York, New York, 1854 ***3437.14*** *p100*
Warwall, M. A. 32; Dominica, 1773 ***1220.25*** *p28*
Warwick, John; Virginia, 1666 ***6212.30*** *p29*
Warwick, John 29; Virginia, 1774 ***1220.25*** *p140*
Warwick, John 48; Ontario, 1871 ***1823.15*** *p274*
Warwick, Robert 41; Ontario, 1871 ***1823.15*** *p274*
Warwick, Thomas 40; Ontario, 1871 ***1823.15*** *p274*
Warzinski, Marcin; Maryland, 1910 ***3259.35*** *p66*
Wasbe, John; Maryland, 1668 ***2524.55*** *p229*
Wasek, Mary; Maryland, 1910 ***3259.35*** *p66*
Wasekegeg, Joseph 38; Ontario, 1871 ***1823.28*** *p103*
Wasekegig, Edouard 62; Ontario, 1871 ***1823.28*** *p103*
Wasekegig, Louis 42; Ontario, 1871 ***1823.28*** *p103*
Wasen, Philipp; Port uncertain, 1751 ***2856.30*** *p479*
Wash, Joseph; Virginia, 1664 ***6212.30*** *p9*
Washal, Stefania; Maryland, 1910 ***3259.35*** *p66*
Washbourne, John; Virginia, 1690 ***6212.30*** *p58*
Washburn, Joel 64; Ontario, 1871 ***1823.22*** *p166*
Washby, Hen; Virginia, 1665-1666 ***6212.30*** *p22*
Washfeild, Robert; Maryland, 1668 ***2524.55*** *p231*
Washford, John; Virginia, 1666-1667 ***6212.30*** *p35*
Washford, Lewis; Virginia, 1667 ***6212.30*** *p37*
Washileski, Andrew; Maryland, 1910 ***3259.35*** *p66*
Washington, Henry; Virginia, 1664 ***6212.30*** *p13*
Washington, John 51; Ontario, 1871 ***1823.15*** *p274*
Washington, Laurence; Virginia, 1677 ***1224.1*** *p61*
Washington, Laurence; Virginia, 1700 ***1224.2*** *p121*
Washington, Thomas; Pennsylvania, 1777 ***4629.10*** *p6*
Washtel, Mark; New York, New York, 1857 ***6058.10*** *p45*
Washton, Harriet 60; Ontario, 1871 ***1823.15*** *p274*
Wasielewski, Joseph; Maryland, 1910 ***3259.35*** *p66*
Wasieliski, James; Maryland, 1910 ***3259.35*** *p66*
Wasiewski, Adam; Maryland, 1910 ***3259.35*** *p66*
Wasik, Ignacy; Maryland, 1910 ***3259.35*** *p66*
Wasilewski, John; Maryland, 1910 ***3259.35*** *p66*
Wasilumski, Stanislaw; Maryland, 1910 ***3259.35*** *p66*
Waskiewcki, Teofil; Maryland, 1910 ***3259.35*** *p66*
Waskiewicz, John; Maryland, 1910 ***3259.35*** *p66*
Waskiewiz, Monka; Maryland, 1910 ***3259.35*** *p66*
Wasmont, Christian 68; Ontario, 1871 ***1823.28*** *p103*
Wasmont, Mary 50; Ontario, 1871 ***1823.28*** *p103*
Wasmund, Theyodore 33; Ontario, 1871 ***1823.28*** *p103*
Wasowicz, Ignacy; Maryland, 1910 ***3259.35*** *p66*
Wassel, George 17; Virginia, 1775 ***1220.25*** *p109*
Wassermann, Heindrick; New York, 1836 ***8197.10*** *p295*
Wassner, Eva; Port uncertain, 1765 ***2856.30*** *p479*
Wasson, William; Virginia, 1733 ***1224.2*** *p121*
Wassondau, Augustus 36; Ontario, 1871 ***1823.15*** *p274*
Wastenays, John 20; Virginia, 1773 ***1220.25*** *p31*
Waszak, Joseph; Maryland, 1910 ***3259.35*** *p66*
Waszkevicz, Vincent; Maryland, 1910 ***3259.35*** *p66*
Waszkiewitz, Michael; Maryland, 1910 ***3259.35*** *p66*
Watahzski, Joseph; Maryland, 1910 ***3259.35*** *p66*
Watcher, John 45; Ontario, 1871 ***1823.15*** *p274*
Watchie, Elizabeth Cahill; Vermont, 1850-1917 ***5900.10*** *p310*
Watchie, Joseph; Vermont, 1852-1926 ***5900.10*** *p310*
Watchka, Lizzie; Maryland, 1910 ***3259.35*** *p66*
Waterbury, Lucretia 77; Ontario, 1861 ***2896.25*** *p38*
Waterfeild, Wm; Virginia, 1693-1694 ***6212.30*** *p60*
Waterhouse, Miss; Portland, Maine, 1858 ***9196.15*** *p27*
Waterland, Mary; Virginia, 1677 ***6212.30*** *p53*
Waterling, Water; Maryland, 1658 ***2524.55*** *p231*
Waterlow, Elizabeth; Maryland, 1631-1685 ***2524.55*** *p46*
Waterman, Ellen *SEE* Waterman, Nicholas
Waterman, Nicholas; Maryland, 1659 ***2524.55*** *p232*
Wife: Ellen
Waters, Alice 71; Vermont, 1886 ***5900.10*** *p535*
Waters, Andrew 24; Ontario, 1871 ***1823.22*** *p166*
Waters, Arabella Strachey; Virginia, 1687 ***1224.1*** *p56*
Waters, Bernard; New York, 1840 ***8197.10*** *p201*
Waters, Catherine 13; Vermont, 1866 ***5900.10*** *p364*
Waters, Catherine 64; Vermont, 1864 ***5900.10*** *p230*
Waters, Dominick; New York, 1792-1840 ***8197.10*** *p203*
Waters, Edward; Maryland, 1665 ***2524.55*** *p231*
Waters, Edward; Virginia, 1630 ***1224.1*** *p61*
Waters, Elizabeth; Maryland, 1748 ***1224.2*** *p121*
Waters, Ellen McCarty; Vermont, 1826-1891 ***5900.10*** *p205*
Waters, Francis; Maryland, 1676 ***2524.55*** *p231*
Waters, George 69; Ontario, 1871 ***1823.22*** *p166*
Waters, Henry 55; Ontario, 1871 ***1823.22*** *p167*
Waters, Humphrey; New York, 1809 ***1224.3*** *p82*
Waters, James; New York, 1829 ***8197.10*** *p352*
Waters, Jane 75; Ontario, 1871 ***1823.15*** *p274*
Waters, John; Jamaica, 1834 ***1640.13*** *p130*
Waters, John; Maryland, 1667 ***2524.55*** *p219*
Waters, John; New York, 1838 ***8197.10*** *p151*
Waters, John; Vermont, 1807-1889 ***5900.10*** *p205*
Waters, Kate; Vermont, 1838-1889 ***5900.10*** *p203*
Waters, Kate; Vermont, 1857-1939 ***5900.10*** *p206*
Waters, Letitia 23; Philadelphia, 1774 ***1220.25*** *p43*
Waters, Mary; Vermont, 1834-1904 ***5900.10*** *p429*
Waters, Owen; Pennsylvania, 1785 ***4629.10*** *p48*
Waters, P. C.; Vermont, n.d. ***5900.10*** *p448*
Waters, Patrick; New York, 1826 ***8197.10*** *p335*
Waters, Philip; New York, 1844 ***8197.10*** *p10*
Waters, Richard; Maryland, 1722 ***1224.2*** *p121*
Waters, Richard; Maryland, 1748 ***1224.2*** *p121*
Waters, Sampson; Maryland, 1674 ***2524.55*** *p231*
Waters, Thomas; New York, 1828 ***8197.10*** *p348*
Waters, Thomas 16; Maryland, 1775 ***1220.25*** *p115*
Waters, Thomas 24; Norfolk, Virginia, 1774 ***1220.25*** *p19*
Waters, Timothy; New York, 1839 ***8197.10*** *p295*
Waters, William; Maryland, 1681 ***2524.55*** *p231*
Waters, William; New York, 1831 ***8197.10*** *p294*
Waters, William; Virginia, 1722 ***1224.2*** *p121*
Waters, William 40; Ontario, 1871 ***1823.22*** *p167*
Waters, William 48; Ontario, 1871 ***1823.15*** *p274*
Waterson, Anne; Virginia, 1664 ***6212.30*** *p14*
Waterson, Benjamin Joseph; New York, 1839 ***8197.10*** *p135*
Waterson, Catherine; New Jersey, 1800-1858 ***1224.3*** *p83*
Waterson, Francis; Maryland, 1671 ***2524.55*** *p231*
Waterstone, James R.; New York, 1867 ***1640.13*** *p130*
Watersworth, John 33; Nova Scotia, 1774 ***1220.25*** *p14*
Waterton, Anne; Guyana, n.d. ***1224.3*** *p83*
Waterton, Anne; New York, New York, 1834 ***1224.3*** *p83*
Waterton, John; Maryland, 1670 ***2524.55*** *p231*
Waterway, Anthony; Maryland, 1672 ***2524.55*** *p231*
Waterworth, George 45; New York, 1774 ***1220.25*** *p20*
Watfield, James 22; New York, 1774 ***1220.25*** *p25*
Wathen, John; Maryland, 1674 ***2524.55*** *p231*
Watkin, Gifford; Virginia, 1637 ***1224.1*** *p61*
Watkin, James; Virginia, 1679 ***6212.30*** *p54*
Watkin, William; Pennsylvania, 1777 ***4629.10*** *p17*
Watkins, Mrs.; Portland, Maine, 1858 ***9196.15*** *p47*
Watkins, Anne; Maryland, 1659 ***2524.55*** *p231*
Watkins, Charles; South Carolina, 1742 ***1224.2*** *p121*
Watkins, Elijah; Cleveland, Ohio, 1857 ***1224.3*** *p83*
Watkins, Eliza; Canada, 1866 ***1640.13*** *p130*
Watkins, Frederick; New York, 1840 ***8197.10*** *p203*
Watkins, George; Maryland, 1681 ***2524.55*** *p231*
Watkins, George; Virginia, 1673 ***1224.1*** *p61*
Watkins, Henry; Maryland, 1681 ***2524.55*** *p231*
Watkins, Henry 27; Ontario, 1871 ***1823.28*** *p103*
Watkins, John; Maryland, 1663 ***2524.55*** *p231*
Watkins, John L.; New York, 1839 ***8197.10*** *p135*
Watkins, Joseph 46; Ontario, 1871 ***1823.15*** *p274*
Watkins, Marshall; Virginia, 1668-1669 ***6212.30*** *p41*
Watkins, Mary 70; Ontario, 1871 ***1823.15*** *p274*
Watkins, Richard; Virginia, 1666 ***6212.30*** *p26*
Watkins, Sedina 77; Ontario, 1871 ***1823.15*** *p274*
Watkins, Sybill; Maryland, 1669 ***2524.55*** *p170*
Watkins, Thomas; Maryland, 1652-1659 ***2524.55*** *p231*
Watkins, Thomas 21; Philadelphia, 1775 ***1220.25*** *p106*
Watkins, Thomas 65; Ontario, 1871 ***1823.15*** *p274*
Watkinshaw, Mr.; Quebec, 1858 ***9196.15*** *p35*
Watkinson, Mr.; Quebec, 1858 ***9196.15*** *p32*
Watkinson, Mrs.; Quebec, 1858 ***9196.15*** *p32*
Watkinson, Cornelius *SEE* Watkinson, Cornelius
Watkinson, Cornelius; Maryland, 1670 ***2524.55*** *p232*
Wife: Jane
Son: Cornelius
Watkinson, Ebeneser 36; Ontario, 1871 ***1823.28*** *p103*
Watkinson, Jane *SEE* Watkinson, Cornelius
Watkinson, John 18; New York, 1774 ***1220.25*** *p24*
Watkinson, Peter; Virginia, 1672 ***6212.30*** *p48*
Watkinson, Peter; Virginia, 1690-1691 ***6212.30*** *p58*
Watkinson, Samuel; Connecticut, 1819 ***1224.3*** *p83*
Watley, Joseph 22; Philadelphia, 1774 ***1220.25*** *p81*
Watlin, John; Maryland, 1672 ***2524.55*** *p232*
Watlin, John; Maryland, 1676 ***2524.55*** *p232*
Watling, William 40; Ontario, 1871 ***1823.15*** *p274*
Watmough, Jonathan; New York, 1836 ***8197.10*** *p76*
Watne, Hans 30; British Columbia, 1913 ***9196.1*** *p21*
Watne, Hans 30; Spokane, Washington, 1913 ***9196.1*** *p21*
Watowski, John; Maryland, 1910 ***3259.35*** *p66*
Wats, Jane; Maryland, 1665 ***2524.55*** *p233*
Wats, Jane; Maryland, 1672 ***2524.55*** *p232*
Watson, Miss; Quebec, 1856 ***9196.15*** *p5*
Watson, Mr.; Quebec, 1856 ***9196.15*** *p6*
Watson, Mr.; Quebec, 1858 ***9196.15*** *p45*
Watson, Mrs.; Quebec, 1858 ***9196.15*** *p36*
Watson, Abb 7; Ontario, 1861 ***2896.27*** *p6*
Watson, Abigail F. 20; Ontario, 1861 ***2896.27*** *p35*
Watson, Abraham; Maryland, 1661 ***2524.55*** *p228*
Watson, Abraham; Virginia, 1663 ***6212.30*** *p1*
Watson, Adam 46; Ontario, 1871 ***1823.22*** *p167*
Watson, Agnes Anderson; Vermont, 1848-1930 ***5900.10*** *p375*
Watson, Alexander; America, 1857 ***1640.13*** *p130*
Watson, Alexander; New York, 1836 ***8197.10*** *p76*
Watson, Alexander 44; Virginia, 1774 ***1220.25*** *p86*
Watson, Alexander 48; Ontario, 1871 ***1823.15*** *p274*
Watson, Andrew; Georgia, 1775 ***1640.10*** *p210*
Watson, Andrew 21; Georgia, 1775 ***1220.25*** *p126*
Watson, Andrew 45; Georgia, 1775 ***1220.25*** *p126*
Watson, Ann 20; Baltimore, 1775 ***1220.25*** *p117*
Watson, Ann 50; Ontario, 1861 ***2896.27*** *p55*
Watson, Anna Bell 2; Ontario, 1861 ***2896.27*** *p35*
Watson, Beatrice L. 2; Ontario, 1871 ***1823.28*** *p103*
Watson, C. L. 12; Ontario, 1861 ***2896.27*** *p6*
Watson, Catherine; Maryland, 1669 ***2524.55*** *p232*
Watson, Catherine O'Donnell 38; Vermont, 1880 ***5900.10*** *p497*
Watson, Charles; Georgia, 1746 ***1640.10*** *p210*
Watson, Charles 23; Virginia, 1773 ***1220.25*** *p29*
Watson, Charles 39; Ontario, 1871 ***1823.22*** *p167*
Watson, Christian 39; Ontario, 1871 ***1823.15*** *p274*
Watson, David 32; Ontario, 1871 ***1823.15*** *p274*
Watson, David 38; Ontario, 1871 ***1823.15*** *p274*
Watson, Denise; Maryland, 1669 ***2524.55*** *p232*
Watson, Douglas 2 *SEE* Watson, George
Watson, Eleanor; Maryland, 1682 ***2524.55*** *p232*
Watson, Eliza 13; Ontario, 1871 ***1823.15*** *p274*
Watson, Elizabeth; Maryland, 1681 ***2524.55*** *p232*
Watson, Elizabeth; Savannah, Georgia, 1770 ***1224.2*** *p87*
Watson, Frances; Maryland, 1678 ***2524.55*** *p233*
Watson, Francis; Virginia, 1713 ***1224.2*** *p121*
Watson, Francis 18; Annapolis, Nova Scotia, 1775 ***1220.25*** *p22*
Watson, Francis 49; Ontario, 1871 ***1823.22*** *p167*
Watson, G.; Quebec, 1856 ***9196.15*** *p9*
Watson, George; Jamaica, 1835 ***1640.13*** *p130*
Watson, George; Virginia, 1664 ***6212.30*** *p11*
Watson, George 21; Ontario, 1871 ***1823.15*** *p274*
Watson, George 29; Maryland, 1775 ***1220.25*** *p116*

Watson, George 36; Georgia, 1775 ***1220.25*** *p125*
Wife: Mary 33
Child: Isabella 10
Child: Mary 5
Child: Douglas 2
Child: Thomas 12
Watson, George 45; Ontario, 1871 ***1823.28*** *p103*
Watson, George 49; Ontario, 1871 ***1823.15*** *p274*
Watson, Grace; Maryland, 1669 ***2524.55*** *p232*
Watson, Henry; Maryland, 1767 ***1224.2*** *p121*
Watson, Henry J.; Vermont, 1835-1904 ***5900.10*** *p496*
Watson, Hopper 29; Ontario, 1871 ***1823.15*** *p274*
Watson, Hugh; Georgia, 1736 ***1640.10*** *p210*
Watson, Hugh; Kansas, 1898 ***1640.13*** *p130*
Watson, Hugh; New York, 1822 ***8197.10*** *p293*
Watson, Isabella; Jamaica, 1834 ***1640.13*** *p130*
Watson, Isabella; New York, 1894 ***1640.13*** *p131*
Watson, Isabella 10 *SEE* Watson, George
Watson, J.; Quebec, 1856 ***9196.15*** *p11*
Watson, J.; Quebec, 1858 ***9196.15*** *p46*
Watson, James; Nebraska, 1900 ***1640.13*** *p131*
Watson, James; New Orleans, 1839 ***1640.10*** *p210*
Watson, James; New York, 1840 ***8197.10*** *p202*
Watson, James; Toronto, 1845 ***1640.13*** *p131*
Watson, James 27; Ontario, 1871 ***1823.28*** *p103*
Watson, James 38; Alberta, 1915 ***9196.1*** *p68*
Watson, James 38; Montana, 1915 ***9196.1*** *p68*
Watson, James 39; Ontario, 1871 ***1823.15*** *p274*
Watson, James 50; Ontario, 1871 ***1823.15*** *p274*
Watson, James 57; Ontario, 1871 ***1823.15*** *p274*
Watson, James 61; Ontario, 1871 ***1823.28*** *p103*
Watson, James 65; Ontario, 1871 ***1823.22*** *p167*
Watson, James 74; Ontario, 1871 ***1823.22*** *p167*
Watson, Jane *SEE* Watson, Peter
Watson, Jane 37; Ontario, 1871 ***1823.15*** *p274*
Watson, Janet; New York, 1859 ***1640.13*** *p131*
Watson, Janet; Ontario, 1834 ***1640.13*** *p131*
Watson, Jmes; Georgia, 1698 ***1640.13*** *p131*
Watson, John *SEE* Watson, Peter
Watson, John; America, 1789 ***1224.2*** *p121*
Watson, John; Charleston, South Carolina, 1756 ***1640.13*** *p131*
Watson, John; Maryland, 1746 ***1224.2*** *p121*
Watson, John; New York, 1831 ***8197.10*** *p355*
Watson, John; New York, 1838 ***8197.10*** *p295*
Watson, John; North Carolina, 1759 ***1224.2*** *p121*
Watson, John; Rhode Island, 1789 ***1224.2*** *p121*
Watson, John; Virginia, 1677 ***1224.1*** *p61*
Watson, John 19; Ontario, 1871 ***1823.28*** *p103*
Watson, John 33; Fort Cumberland, Nova Scotia, 1774 ***1220.25*** *p17*
Watson, John 43; Ontario, 1871 ***1823.28*** *p103*
Watson, John 45; Ontario, 1871 ***1823.28*** *p103*
Watson, John James; New York, 1853 ***1224.3*** *p83*
Watson, Joseph; Pennsylvania, 1776 ***4629.10*** *p53*
Watson, Julia McLeod; Vermont, 1845-1899 ***5900.10*** *p516*
Watson, Margarett; Maryland, 1669 ***2524.55*** *p232*
Watson, Marion; Toronto, 1877 ***1640.13*** *p131*
Watson, Martin 22; Ontario, 1871 ***1823.28*** *p103*
Watson, Mary *SEE* Watson, Peter
Watson, Mary 5 *SEE* Watson, George
Watson, Mary 33 *SEE* Watson, George
Watson, Mary 36; Ontario, 1871 ***1823.22*** *p167*
Watson, Mary 52; Ontario, 1861 ***2896.27*** *p6*
Watson, Matthew; Vermont, 1850-1891 ***5900.10*** *p375*
Watson, Nicholas; South Carolina, 1793 ***1224.2*** *p121*
Watson, Nicholas 15; Montreal, 1775 ***1220.25*** *p106*
Watson, Peter *SEE* Watson, Peter
Watson, Peter; Maryland, 1680 ***2524.55*** *p232*
Wife: Jane
Child: Mary
Child: Peter
Child: John
Watson, Peter 42; Maryland, 1775 ***1220.25*** *p106*
Watson, Philip; New England, 1697 ***1224.1*** *p61*
Watson, Rebecca; New England, 1652 ***1224.1*** *p61*
Watson, Richard; Maryland, 1652 ***2524.55*** *p232*
Watson, Richard 30; Ontario, 1871 ***1823.28*** *p103*
Watson, Robert 28; Maryland, 1774 ***1220.25*** *p79*
Watson, Robert 61; Ontario, 1871 ***1823.22*** *p167*
Watson, Robert 71; Ontario, 1871 ***1823.22*** *p167*
Watson, Robert 85; Ontario, 1871 ***1823.15*** *p274*
Watson, Robert, Sr. 57; Ontario, 1871 ***1823.15*** *p274*
Watson, Roberts; Maryland, 1669 ***2524.55*** *p232*
Watson, Robt; Virginia, 1665-1666 ***6212.30*** *p21*
Watson, Rudee; Maryland, 1669 ***2524.55*** *p232*
Watson, Sara; Virginia, 1677 ***6212.30*** *p53*
Watson, Sarah A. Mooney; Vermont, 1841-1904 ***5900.10*** *p496*
Watson, Saran Ann; Vermont, 1841-1904 ***5900.10*** *p496*
Watson, Tho; Virginia, 1664 ***6212.30*** *p9*
Watson, Thomas; Maryland, 1672 ***2524.55*** *p232*
Watson, Thomas; New York, 1805 ***8197.10*** *p30*
Watson, Thomas; New York, 1840 ***8197.10*** *p203*
Watson, Thomas 12 *SEE* Watson, George
Watson, Thomas 26; Ontario, 1871 ***1823.22*** *p167*
Watson, Thomas 27; Ontario, 1871 ***1823.15*** *p275*
Watson, Thomas 44; Ontario, 1871 ***1823.22*** *p167*
Watson, Thomas 61; Ontario, 1871 ***1823.15*** *p274*
Watson, Thomas 73; Ontario, 1861 ***2896.27*** *p66*
Watson, Thomas George; New York, 1826 ***8197.10*** *p293*
Watson, Walter; New York, 1836 ***8197.10*** *p295*
Watson, William; Carolina, 1686 ***1224.1*** *p61*
Watson, William; Florida, 1782 ***1224.2*** *p122*
Watson, William; Maryland, 1661 ***2524.55*** *p232*
Watson, William; Maryland, 1678 ***2524.55*** *p233*
Watson, William; Maryland, 1682 ***2524.55*** *p232*
Watson, William; Pennsylvania, 1777 ***4629.10*** *p19*
Watson, William; St. Augustine, Florida, 1818 ***1640.10*** *p211*
Watson, William; South Carolina, 1781 ***1640.10*** *p210*
Watson, William; Vermont, 1840-1912 ***5900.10*** *p136*
Watson, William; Virginia, 1663 ***6212.30*** *p3*
Watson, William; Virginia, 1703-1704 ***6212.30*** *p62*
Watson, William; Died enroute, 1659 ***1224.1*** *p61*
Watson, William 26; Grenada, 1775-1776 ***1220.25*** *p126*
Watson, William 32; Ontario, 1871 ***1823.15*** *p275*
Watson, William 35; Ontario, 1871 ***1823.22*** *p167*
Watson, William 45; Ontario, 1871 ***1823.15*** *p275*
Watson, William 57; Ontario, 1871 ***1823.15*** *p275*
Watson, William 57; Ontario, 1871 ***1823.22*** *p167*
Watson, William W. 67; Vermont, 1890 ***5900.10*** *p497*
Watson, Willm.; Maryland, 1661 ***2524.55*** *p37*
Watson, Wm.; Pennsylvania, 1777 ***4629.10*** *p17*
Watt, Mr.; Quebec, 1857 ***9196.15*** *p14*
Watt, Mr.; Quebec, 1857 ***9196.15*** *p19*
Watt, Alexander; Florida, 1785 ***1640.10*** *p211*
Watt, Alexander 35; Ontario, 1871 ***1823.15*** *p275*
Watt, David 50; Ontario, 1871 ***1823.22*** *p167*
Watt, Ebenezer; New Jersey, 1881 ***1640.13*** *p131*
Watt, Fred 37; Ontario, 1871 ***1823.28*** *p103*
Watt, George 42; Ontario, 1871 ***1823.28*** *p103*
Watt, George 44; Ontario, 1871 ***1823.15*** *p275*
Watt, George 85; Ontario, 1871 ***1823.15*** *p275*
Watt, James; Alabama, 1805-1845 ***1640.10*** *p211*
Watt, James; New York, 1806 ***8197.10*** *p33*
Watt, James 37; Ontario, 1871 ***1823.15*** *p275*
Watt, James 38; Ontario, 1871 ***1823.22*** *p167*
Watt, James, Jr.; New York, 1833 ***8197.10*** *p295*
Watt, Jane Ann 37; Ontario, 1871 ***1823.22*** *p167*
Watt, John; Georgia, 1698 ***1640.13*** *p131*
Watt, John; Pittsburgh, 1837 ***1224.3*** *p83*
Watt, John 30; Ontario, 1871 ***1823.15*** *p275*
Watt, John 36; Ontario, 1871 ***1823.15*** *p275*
Watt, Margaret 24; Ontario, 1871 ***1823.22*** *p167*
Watt, Margaret 42; Ontario, 1871 ***1823.15*** *p275*
Watt, Mary; Savannah, Georgia, 1804 ***1640.10*** *p211*
Watt, Richard 22; Ontario, 1871 ***1823.15*** *p275*
Watt, Robert; Pennsylvania, 1828 ***6058.10*** *p9*
Watt, Robert 23; Ontario, 1871 ***1823.15*** *p275*
Watt, Robert 23; Ontario, 1871 ***1823.28*** *p103*
Watt, Robert 47; Ontario, 1871 ***1823.22*** *p167*
Watt, Thomas; Georgia, 1698 ***1640.13*** *p131*
Watt, Thomas 36; Ontario, 1871 ***1823.22*** *p167*
Watt, William; Georgia, 1765 ***1640.10*** *p211*
Watt, William; New York, 1838 ***8197.10*** *p295*
Watt, William 36; Ontario, 1871 ***1823.22*** *p167*
Watt, William 54; Ontario, 1871 ***1823.15*** *p275*
Watt, Zacariah 34; Ontario, 1871 ***1823.28*** *p103*
Wattakajia, Joseph 25; Ontario, 1871 ***1823.28*** *p103*
Watter, John; Virginia, 1666 ***6212.30*** *p26*
Watterman, Ellen *SEE* Watterman, Nicholas
Watterman, Nicholas; Maryland, 1659 ***2524.55*** *p232*
Wife: Ellen
Watters, John 42; Ontario, 1871 ***1823.15*** *p275*
Watters, John 59; Ontario, 1871 ***1823.22*** *p167*
Watters, Martin 50; Ontario, 1871 ***1823.15*** *p275*
Watterson, William; New York, 1826 ***8197.10*** *p9*
Watterton, John; Maryland, 1667 ***2524.55*** *p232*
Wattin, Thomas 60; Ontario, 1871 ***1823.15*** *p275*
Wattkins, William; Maryland, 1664 ***2524.55*** *p232*
Watto, John 60; Ontario, 1871 ***1823.28*** *p103*
Watton, Thomas 22; Baltimore, 1775 ***1220.25*** *p118*
Watts, Miss; Quebec, 1857 ***9196.15*** *p18*
Watts, Miss; Quebec, 1858 ***9196.15*** *p46*
Watts, Mr.; Quebec, 1858 ***9196.15*** *p46*
Watts, Anne *SEE* Watts, George
Watts, Anne; Maryland, 1676 ***2524.55*** *p232*
Watts, David 54; Ontario, 1871 ***1823.22*** *p167*
Watts, Edward; Virginia, 1669 ***1224.1*** *p62*
Watts, Elionor; Maryland, 1662 ***2524.55*** *p232*
Watts, Elizabeth; Maryland, 1708 ***1224.2*** *p122*
Watts, Gabriell; Maryland, 1660 ***2524.55*** *p232*
Watts, George *SEE* Watts, George
Watts, George; Maryland, 1665 ***2524.55*** *p232*
Wife: Anne
Child: William
Child: John
Child: Anne
Child: George
Watts, George; Maryland, 1666 ***2524.55*** *p232*
Wife: Joyce
Watts, George; Maryland, 1675 ***2524.55*** *p232*
Watts, Hannah 45; Ontario, 1871 ***1823.15*** *p275*
Watts, J. B.; Quebec, 1856 ***9196.15*** *p9*
Watts, Mrs. J. B.; Quebec, 1856 ***9196.15*** *p9*
Watts, James; New York, 1839 ***8197.10*** *p135*
Watts, James; Virginia, 1666-1667 ***6212.30*** *p35*
Watts, Jane; Maryland, 1665 ***2524.55*** *p233*
Watts, Jane E.; Vermont, 1816-1902 ***5900.10*** *p494*
Watts, Jno; Virginia, 1665-1666 ***6212.30*** *p21*
Watts, Joane; Maryland, 1659 ***2524.55*** *p233*
Watts, Joane; Maryland, 1663 ***2524.55*** *p233*
Watts, John *SEE* Watts, George
Watts, John; Maryland, 1679 ***2524.55*** *p233*
Watts, John; Maryland, 1736 ***1224.2*** *p122*
Watts, John; New York, n.d. ***1224.2*** *p122*
Watts, John; New York, 1834 ***8197.10*** *p69*
Watts, John; New York, 1838 ***8197.10*** *p295*
Watts, John; Virginia, 1671-1672 ***6212.30*** *p45*
Watts, John 22; Philadelphia, 1774 ***1220.25*** *p80*
Watts, Joyce *SEE* Watts, George
Watts, Mary; Maryland, 1682 ***2524.55*** *p233*
Watts, Mary; New York, 1852 ***1224.3*** *p83*
Watts, Mat 45; Ontario, 1871 ***1823.15*** *p275*
Watts, Robert; New York, 1802 ***8197.10*** *p26*
Watts, Robert; New York, 1852 ***1224.3*** *p83*
Watts, Robert 58; Ontario, 1871 ***1823.15*** *p275*
Watts, Silas; Pennsylvania, 1777 ***4629.10*** *p17*
Watts, William *SEE* Watts, George
Watts, William; New York, 1807 ***8197.10*** *p52*
Watts, William; New York, 1818 ***8197.10*** *p291*
Watts, William; Virginia, 1640 ***1224.1*** *p61*
Watts, William 23; Maryland, 1774 ***1220.25*** *p70*
Wattson, Charles; Maryland, 1682 ***2524.55*** *p233*
Wattson, Frances; Maryland, 1678 ***2524.55*** *p233*
Wattson, Katherine; Maryland, 1649 ***2524.55*** *p233*
Wattson, William; Maryland, 1659 ***2524.55*** *p233*
Wattson, William; Maryland, 1665 ***2524.55*** *p233*
Wattson, William; Maryland, 1678 ***2524.55*** *p233*
Wattyen, Conrad; New York, 1826 ***8197.10*** *p293*
Watus, Mary 30; Ontario, 1871 ***1823.15*** *p275*
Watz, Jacob 46; Ontario, 1871 ***1823.15*** *p275*
Waudby, Thomas 52; Ontario, 1871 ***1823.15*** *p275*
Waugh, Catharine 35; Vermont, 1851 ***5900.10*** *p522*
Waugh, David; Virginia, 1694 ***1224.1*** *p62*
Waugh, Edward; Alabama, 1822-1845 ***1640.10*** *p211*
Waugh, George 35; Ontario, 1871 ***1823.28*** *p103*
Waugh, Patrick; Vermont, 1848-1920 ***5900.10*** *p285*
Waughey, Samuel 39; Ontario, 1871 ***1823.15*** *p275*
Wauke, Jno; Virginia, 1664 ***6212.30*** *p15*
Waukowski, William; Maryland, 1910 ***3259.35*** *p66*
Waules, Richd.; Maryland, 1666 ***2524.55*** *p233*
Waurrighm, Henry 46; Ontario, 1871 ***1823.15*** *p275*
Wawrzymak, Andreas; Maryland, 1910 ***3259.35*** *p66*
Wawrzymick, Joseph; Maryland, 1910 ***3259.35*** *p66*
Waxmoth, Christian; New York, New York, 1855 ***6058.10*** *p40*
Way, Mr.; Portland, Maine, 1858 ***9196.15*** *p47*
Way, A. 20; Ontario, 1861 ***2896.25*** *p29*
Way, Alpheus 13; Ontario, 1861 ***2896.25*** *p59*
Way, Amarilla 23; Ontario, 1861 ***2896.25*** *p61*
Way, Amos 21; Ontario, 1861 ***2896.25*** *p59*
Way, Auston 17; Ontario, 1861 ***2896.25*** *p73*
Way, Benjamin 10; Ontario, 1861 ***2896.25*** *p59*
Way, Catherine 26; Ontario, 1861 ***2896.25*** *p72*
Way, Catherine 54; Ontario, 1861 ***2896.25*** *p59*
Way, Clarence 6; Ontario, 1861 ***2896.25*** *p68*
Way, Coleman 1; Ontario, 1861 ***2896.25*** *p72*
Way, Conrad; Pennsylvania, 1777 ***4629.10*** *p10*
Way, Conrad 4; Ontario, 1861 ***2896.25*** *p61*
Way, Corintha 7; Ontario, 1861 ***2896.25*** *p72*
Way, Cornelia 12; Ontario, 1861 ***2896.25*** *p68*
Way, Cornelia 76; Ontario, 1861 ***2896.25*** *p67*
Way, E. 35; Ontario, 1861 ***2896.25*** *p28*
Way, F. A. 5; Ontario, 1861 ***2896.25*** *p37*
Way, George 1; Ontario, 1861 ***2896.25*** *p61*
Way, George 10; Ontario, 1861 ***2896.25*** *p73*
Way, Gilbert 28; Ontario, 1861 ***2896.25*** *p66*
Way, Harriet 15; Ontario, 1861 ***2896.25*** *p68*
Way, Hester 35; Ontario, 1861 ***2896.25*** *p73*
Way, J. 1; Ontario, 1861 ***2896.25*** *p29*
Way, John 19; Ontario, 1861 ***2896.25*** *p59*
Way, John B. 78; Ontario, 1861 ***2896.25*** *p67*
Way, John W. 26; Ontario, 1861 ***2896.25*** *p37*
Way, Justus 15; Ontario, 1861 ***2896.25*** *p73*
Way, Laura E. 17; Ontario, 1861 ***2896.25*** *p71*

Way, Lucinda 17; Ontario, 1861 ***2896.25*** *p59*
Way, Mary; Virginia, 1671-1672 ***6212.30*** *p46*
Way, Mary A. 10; Ontario, 1861 ***2896.25*** *p66*
Way, Naomi 39; Ontario, 1861 ***2896.25*** *p68*
Way, P. A. 28; Ontario, 1861 ***2896.25*** *p37*
Way, Reuben 4; Ontario, 1861 ***2896.25*** *p72*
Way, Reuben 14; Ontario, 1861 ***2896.25*** *p68*
Way, Richard; New England, 1736 ***1224.2*** *p122*
Way, Robert 65; Ontario, 1871 ***1823.15*** *p275*
Way, Sarah 18; Ontario, 1861 ***2896.25*** *p73*
Way, Sarah 25; Ontario, 1861 ***2896.25*** *p66*
Way, Sarah 41; Ontario, 1861 ***2896.25*** *p68*
Way, Sarah 56; Ontario, 1861 ***2896.25*** *p71*
Way, Wallace 1; Ontario, 1861 ***2896.25*** *p68*
Way, Wellington 16; Ontario, 1861 ***2896.25*** *p68*
Way, William 1; Ontario, 1861 ***2896.25*** *p73*
Way, William 6; Ontario, 1861 ***2896.25*** *p72*
Way, William 33; Ontario, 1871 ***1823.15*** *p275*
Wayd, Andrew; Maryland, 1657 ***2524.55*** *p228*
Wayde, Peter; Virginia, 1672 ***6212.30*** *p50*
Waydmann, Johann; America, 1729 ***2856.30*** *p479*
With wife son & 2 daughters
Waydmann, Mathew; America, 1733 ***2856.30*** *p479*
Waydmann, Matthias; America, 1732 ***2856.30*** *p479*
With wife & 2 children
Waydmann, Matthias; America, 1733 ***2856.30*** *p479*
Wayer, Frank; Maryland, 1910 ***3259.35*** *p66*
Wayht, John; Maryland, 1651 ***2524.55*** *p233*
Wayle, Margaret; Maryland, 1654 ***2524.55*** *p233*
Waymaster, Fred 21; Kansas, 1892-1910 ***9079.10*** *p31*
Waymaster, Fred 45; Kansas, 1892-1910 ***9079.10*** *p19*
Waymaster, Henry 18; Kansas, 1892-1910 ***9079.10*** *p19*
Waymaster, Henry 24; Kansas, 1892-1910 ***9079.10*** *p19*
Waymaster, Mary 19; Kansas, 1908-1910 ***9079.10*** *p31*
Waymaster, Mary 44; Kansas, 1892-1910 ***9079.10*** *p19*
Waymcole, John; Maryland, 1676 ***2524.55*** *p233*
Waymouth, William 34; Ontario, 1871 ***1823.15*** *p275*
Wayne, Anthony; New England, 1775-1781 ***4628.40*** *p68*
Wayne, Wm; Virginia, 1671 ***6212.30*** *p42*
Waztowicz, Martin J.; Maryland, 1910 ***3259.35*** *p66*
Wazuriak, Andrew; Maryland, 1910 ***3259.35*** *p66*
Wdzrecyny, Stanislaus; Maryland, 1910 ***3259.35*** *p66*
Weant, Johannes; Baltimore, 1848 ***6058.10*** *p25*
Wear, William 44; Ontario, 1871 ***1823.22*** *p167*
Weare, Peter; New England, 1685 ***1224.1*** *p62*
Weare, Samuel; Quebec, 1858 ***9196.15*** *p44*
Weaser, William; Pennsylvania, 1786 ***4629.10*** *p53*
Weatherald, Ann 76; Ontario, 1871 ***1823.15*** *p275*
Weatherald, Thomas 37; Ontario, 1871 ***1823.15*** *p275*
Weatherby, Peter; New York, 1827 ***8197.10*** *p294*
Weatherby, Peter; New York, 1833 ***8197.10*** *p68*
Weatherfield, John 20; Virginia, 1773 ***1220.25*** *p29*
Weatherhead, George 41; Ontario, 1871 ***1823.15*** *p275*
Weatherhead, William; New England, 1710 ***1224.2*** *p122*
Weatherley, Robert; Detroit, 1848 ***1224.3*** *p83*
Weatherley, Thomas 21; Virginia, 1773 ***1220.25*** *p28*
Weatherly, Herbert; Washington, 1892 ***1640.13*** *p131*
Weatherly, Jannet; Maryland, 1673 ***2524.55*** *p233*
Weatherman, W.; Quebec, 1857 ***9196.15*** *p16*
Weatherspoon, David; Georgia, 1775 ***1640.10*** *p211*
Weatherspoon, David 23; Georgia, 1775 ***1220.25*** *p126*
Weatherston, Lucke 55; Ontario, 1871 ***1823.22*** *p167*
Weatherton, William 21; Maryland, 1774 ***1220.25*** *p64*
Weaver, Adam; Pennsylvania, 1777 ***4629.10*** *p7*
Weaver, Casper; Pennsylvania, 1778 ***4629.10*** *p32*
Weaver, Charles; Pennsylvania, 1833 ***6058.10*** *p11*
Weaver, Edward; Philadelphia, 1824 ***1224.3*** *p83*
Weaver, Henry; Pennsylvania, 1787 ***4629.10*** *p55*
Weaver, Israel 42; Ontario, 1871 ***1823.28*** *p103*
Weaver, Jacob; Pennsylvania, 1777 ***4629.10*** *p10*
Weaver, Jacob; Pennsylvania, 1777 ***4629.10*** *p27*
Weaver, Jno; Virginia, 1667-1668 ***6212.30*** *p38*
Weaver, Job; Havana, 1765 ***1224.2*** *p122*
Weaver, Job; Rhode Island, 1765 ***1224.2*** *p122*
Weaver, John; Maryland, 1682 ***2524.55*** *p233*
Weaver, John; Maryland, 1705 ***1224.2*** *p122*
Weaver, John; Maryland, 1740 ***1224.2*** *p26*
Weaver, John; Pennsylvania, 1777 ***4629.10*** *p24*
Weaver, John 74; Ontario, 1871 ***1823.22*** *p167*
Weaver, Marshall 29; Ontario, 1871 ***1823.22*** *p167*
Weaver, Meinrad; New York, 1836 ***8197.10*** *p319*
Weaver, Nicholas; Pennsylvania, 1777 ***4629.10*** *p9*
Weaver, Peter 63; Ontario, 1871 ***1823.22*** *p167*
Weaver, Rich; Virginia, 1665-1666 ***6212.30*** *p21*
Weaver, Robert; Virginia, 1665-1666 ***6212.30*** *p25*
Weaver, Robert; Virginia, 1667 ***6212.30*** *p36*
Weaver, Sarah 27; Ontario, 1871 ***1823.22*** *p167*
Weaver, Tho; Virginia, 1666-1667 ***6212.30*** *p34*
Weaver, William; Maryland, 1660 ***2524.55*** *p233*
Web, John; Maryland, 1910 ***3259.35*** *p66*
Webb, Mrs.; Maryland, 1659 ***2524.55*** *p233*
Webb, Mrs.; Nevis, 1774 ***1220.25*** *p34*
Webb, A. C. 28; Ontario, 1871 ***1823.22*** *p167*
Webb, Alexander F. W.; New York, 1838 ***8197.10*** *p152*
Webb, Alice; Maryland, 1657 ***2524.55*** *p233*
Webb, Anne; Maryland, 1658 ***2524.55*** *p233*
Webb, Anne; Vermont, n.d. ***5900.10*** *p386*
Webb, Calibray; Maryland, 1681 ***2524.55*** *p233*
Webb, Christopher; Maryland, 1654 ***2524.55*** *p233*
Webb, Edmond; Maryland, 1659 ***2524.55*** *p233*
Webb, Edmond; Virginia, 1664 ***6212.30*** *p14*
Webb, Edward; New York, 1839 ***1224.3*** *p83*
Webb, Edward Jackson; New York, 1829 ***8197.10*** *p66*
Webb, Eliza; Mobile, Alabama, 1827 ***1224.3*** *p5*
Webb, Geo 40; Washington, 1909 ***9196.1*** *p25*
Webb, George; Nevis, 1774 ***1220.25*** *p34*
Webb, George; New York, 1837 ***8197.10*** *p374*
Webb, Gilbert; New York, 1824 ***1224.3*** *p83*
Webb, Giles; Virginia, 1656 ***1224.1*** *p15*
Webb, Giles; Virginia, 1715 ***1224.2*** *p122*
Webb, Is. 24; Maryland, 1774 ***1220.25*** *p2*
Webb, James; St. Augustine, Florida, 1780 ***1224.2*** *p122*
Webb, James 39; Ontario, 1871 ***1823.22*** *p168*
Webb, John; Maryland, 1681 ***2524.55*** *p233*
Webb, John; New York, 1817 ***8197.10*** *p60*
Webb, John; New York, 1840 ***8197.10*** *p202*
Webb, John; Pennsylvania, 1777 ***4629.10*** *p16*
Webb, John 21; Virginia, 1773 ***1220.25*** *p31*
Webb, John 40; Ontario, 1871 ***1823.15*** *p275*
Webb, John 41; Ontario, 1871 ***1823.22*** *p168*
Webb, John 52; Ontario, 1871 ***1823.15*** *p275*
Webb, Jonathan 62; Ontario, 1871 ***1823.22*** *p168*
Webb, Jone; Maryland, 1665 ***2524.55*** *p237*
Webb, Joseph 34; Ontario, 1871 ***1823.22*** *p168*
Webb, Nicholas; Maryland, 1665 ***2524.55*** *p233*
Webb, Peter 39; Maryland, 1774 ***1220.25*** *p54*
Webb, Richard; Boston, 1731 ***1224.2*** *p122*
Webb, Richard; Jamaica, 1731 ***1224.2*** *p122*
Webb, Richard; Virginia, 1667 ***6212.30*** *p37*
Webb, Robert; Virginia, 1659 ***1224.1*** *p62*
Webb, Tho.; Maryland, 1681 ***2524.55*** *p233*
Webb, Thomas; Maryland, 1658 ***2524.55*** *p233*
Webb, Thomas; Virginia, 1671 ***6212.30*** *p43*
Webb, Thomas 25; Ontario, 1871 ***1823.15*** *p275*
Webb, Thomas 43; Ontario, 1871 ***1823.15*** *p275*
Webb, William; Maryland, 1681 ***2524.55*** *p233*
Webb, William; Maryland, 1711 ***1224.2*** *p122*
Webb, William; New Orleans, 1848 ***1224.3*** *p83*
Webb, William; New York, 1838 ***8197.10*** *p152*
Webb, William; Pennsylvania, 1777 ***4629.10*** *p7*
Webb, William; Pennsylvania, 1777 ***4629.10*** *p24*
Webb, William; Pennsylvania, 1779 ***4629.10*** *p38*
Webb, William; South Carolina, 1751 ***1224.2*** *p122*
Webber, Catharine 50; Ontario, 1871 ***1823.15*** *p275*
Webber, Charles; New York, 1839 ***8197.10*** *p295*
Webber, Chas 40; Alaska, 1914 ***9196.1*** *p24*
Webber, Edward 45; Ontario, 1871 ***1823.28*** *p103*
Webber, George; New York, New York, 1851 ***6058.10*** *p54*
Webber, George 21; Maryland, 1774 ***1220.25*** *p57*
Webber, George 35; Ontario, 1871 ***1823.15*** *p275*
Webber, George 70; Ontario, 1871 ***1823.22*** *p168*
Webber, Henry 25; Philadelphia, 1774 ***1220.25*** *p35*
Webber, John; Pennsylvania, 1785 ***4629.10*** *p48*
Webber, John 21; Philadelphia, 1774 ***1220.25*** *p66*
Webber, John 48; Ontario, 1871 ***1823.28*** *p103*
Webber, Mary; Maryland, 1678 ***2524.55*** *p233*
Webber, Mary L.; Vermont, 1844-1900 ***5900.10*** *p500*
Webber, Matilda 14; Ontario, 1871 ***1823.28*** *p103*
Webber, Sarah 65; Ontario, 1871 ***1823.22*** *p168*
Webber, Stephen; Massachusetts, 1805 ***1224.3*** *p83*
Webber, William 22; Ontario, 1871 ***1823.28*** *p103*
Webber, William 24; Ontario, 1871 ***1823.15*** *p275*
Webber, William 35; Ontario, 1871 ***1823.22*** *p168*
Webber, Wm; Virginia, 1666 ***6212.30*** *p29*
Weber, . . .; America, 1776 ***2856.30*** *p481*
Weber, . . .; America, 1780 ***2856.30*** *p481*
Weber, Andreas; Port uncertain, 1777 ***2856.30*** *p479*
Weber, Anna Eva; Port uncertain, 1754 ***2856.30*** *p482*
Weber, Anna Margarete; Port uncertain, 1754 ***2856.30*** *p479*
Weber, Anna Maria; Port uncertain, 1754 ***2856.30*** *p482*
Weber, Anna Maria; Port uncertain, 1774 ***2856.30*** *p479*
Weber, Anna Sara; Port uncertain, 1734 ***2856.30*** *p479*
Weber, Anton; Maryland, 1910 ***3259.35*** *p66*
Weber, Barbara; Port uncertain, 1785 ***2856.30*** *p479*
Weber, Bernhard; Port uncertain, 1791 ***2856.30*** *p479*
Weber, Burkhard; Port uncertain, 1755 ***2856.30*** *p479*
Weber, Carolin 65; Ontario, 1871 ***1823.28*** *p103*
Weber, Catharina; Port uncertain, 1772 ***2856.30*** *p479*
Weber, Catharina; Port uncertain, 1786 ***2856.30*** *p479*
Weber, Charlotte; Port uncertain, 1783 ***2856.30*** *p479*
Weber, Christian; America, 1759 ***2856.30*** *p479*
Weber, Christian; America, 1764 ***2856.30*** *p479*
Weber, Conrad 25; Ontario, 1871 ***1823.15*** *p275*
Weber, Daniel; Peru, 1802 ***2856.30*** *p479*
Weber, Daniel; Port uncertain, 1787 ***2856.30*** *p479*
Weber, Dewalt; America, 1741 ***2856.30*** *p479*
Weber, Elis. *SEE* Weber, Michael
Weber, Elisabeth; Port uncertain, 1784 ***2856.30*** *p212*
Weber, Elisabeth Karlsin; Port uncertain, 1763 ***2856.30*** *p481*
Weber, Elizabeth 57; Ontario, 1871 ***1823.15*** *p275*
Weber, Erhard; America, 1754 ***2856.30*** *p479*
Weber, Erhard; Port uncertain, 1754 ***2856.30*** *p482*
With wife & 4 children
Weber, Frank; Maryland, 1910 ***3259.35*** *p66*
Weber, Frederick; New York, 1830 ***8197.10*** *p294*
Weber, G. 37; Washington, 1914 ***9196.1*** *p66*
Weber, Georg Ludwig; Port uncertain, 1749 ***2856.30*** *p480*
Weber, George; Baltimore, 1832 ***8197.10*** *p152*
Weber, George; New York, New York, 1851 ***6058.10*** *p54*
Weber, Hans; America, 1764 ***2856.30*** *p480*
Weber, Hans; America, 1769 ***2856.30*** *p480*
Weber, Hans Adam; Port uncertain, 1738 ***2856.30*** *p480*
Weber, Hans Georg; Port uncertain, 1764 ***2856.30*** *p482*
With wife & 2 children
Weber, Heinrich; Port uncertain, 1744 ***2856.30*** *p480*
Weber, Henrich; America, 1749 ***2856.30*** *p482*
With wife & 3 children
Weber, Henry; America, 1749 ***2856.30*** *p480*
Weber, Jacob 44; Ontario, 1871 ***1823.15*** *p275*
Weber, Jakob; America, 1742 ***2856.30*** *p480*
Weber, Jakob; Port uncertain, 1778 ***2856.30*** *p480*
Weber, Jakob; Port uncertain, 1783 ***2856.30*** *p480*
Weber, Jakob; Port uncertain, 1788 ***2856.30*** *p480*
Weber, Jakob; Port uncertain, 1789 ***2856.30*** *p480*
Weber, Jakob; Port uncertain, 1793 ***2856.30*** *p480*
Weber, Jakob; Port uncertain, 1794 ***2856.30*** *p480*
Weber, Jakob; Port uncertain, 1795 ***2856.30*** *p480*
Weber, Johann; Port uncertain, 1714 ***2856.30*** *p481*
Weber, Johann; Port uncertain, 1765 ***2856.30*** *p480*
Weber, Johann; Port uncertain, 1771 ***2856.30*** *p480*
Weber, Johann Daniel; America, 1749 ***2856.30*** *p480*
Weber, Johann Peter; America, 1756 ***2856.30*** *p480*
Weber, Johann Peter; Port uncertain, 1754 ***2856.30*** *p480*
Weber, Johann Peter; Port uncertain, 1790 ***2856.30*** *p480*
Weber, Johann Thiel; Port uncertain, 1751 ***2856.30*** *p480*
Weber, Johann Valentin; America, 1749 ***2856.30*** *p480*
Weber, Johann Wilhelm; America, 1764 ***2856.30*** *p480*
Weber, John; New York, 1807 ***8197.10*** *p52*
Weber, Josef; Port uncertain, 1741 ***2856.30*** *p482*
With wife & 2 children
Weber, Josef; Port uncertain, 1743 ***2856.30*** *p481*
With wife
Weber, Josef; Port uncertain, 1752 ***2856.30*** *p480*
Weber, Joseph; Maryland, 1910 ***3259.35*** *p66*
Weber, Karl; Port uncertain, 1764 ***2856.30*** *p480*
Weber, Konrad; Port uncertain, 1775 ***2856.30*** *p480*
Weber, Leonard; Port uncertain, 1752 ***2856.30*** *p480*
Weber, Leonhard; Port uncertain, 1714 ***2856.30*** *p481*
Weber, Magdalena; America, 1753 ***2856.30*** *p480*
Weber, Magdalena; America, 1784 ***2856.30*** *p480*
Weber, Margarete Penninger; Port uncertain, 1751 ***2856.30*** *p481*
Weber, Maria Catharina; Port uncertain, 1789 ***2856.30*** *p480*
Weber, Maria Christian; Port uncertain, 1752 ***2856.30*** *p482*
Weber, Maria Eva; America, 1764 ***2856.30*** *p480*
Weber, Martin; Port uncertain, 1770 ***2856.30*** *p480*
Weber, Michael; America, 1737 ***2856.30*** *p481*
Weber, Michael; America, 1741 ***2856.30*** *p480*
Weber, Michael; New England, 1766 ***2856.30*** *p482*
Wife: Elis.
With 3 children
Weber, Michael; Pennsylvania, 1848 ***6058.10*** *p24*
Weber, Michael; Port uncertain, 1738 ***2856.30*** *p480*
Weber, Michael; Port uncertain, 1775 ***2856.30*** *p482*
With wife & children
Weber, Niklas; America, 1752 ***2856.30*** *p482*
With wife & son
Weber, Niklas; Port uncertain, 1786 ***2856.30*** *p481*
Weber, Niklas; Port uncertain, 1790 ***2856.30*** *p481*
Weber, Nikolaus; Port uncertain, 1782 ***2856.30*** *p481*
Weber, Ottilia; Port uncertain, 1785 ***2856.30*** *p481*
Weber, Peter; America, 1741 ***2856.30*** *p481*
Weber, Peter; Port uncertain, 1736 ***2856.30*** *p481*
Weber, Peter; Port uncertain, 1783 ***2856.30*** *p482*
With wife 6 sons & 3 daughters
Weber, R. T.; Maryland, 1910 ***3259.35*** *p66*
Weber, Theobald; America, 1764 ***2856.30*** *p481*
Weber, Theobald; Port uncertain, 1774 ***2856.30*** *p481*
Weber, Thomas A.; Maryland, 1910 ***3259.35*** *p66*
Weber, Vincent J.; Maryland, 1910 ***3259.35*** *p67*
Weberin, Anna Eva; Port uncertain, 1754 ***2856.30*** *p482*

Weberin, Anna Maria; Port uncertain, 1754 2856.30 p482
Weberin, Maria Christian; Port uncertain, 1752 2856.30 p482
Weberruss, Anna Margarete; America, 1752 2856.30 p482
With 6 children
Weberruss, Konrad; America, 1752 2856.30 p482
With wife & children
Weberuss, Konrad; America, 1752 2856.30 p482
With wife & children
Webham, Jno; Virginia, 1677 6212.30 p54
Webikamigud, Joseph 46; Ontario, 1871 1823.28 p103
Weblan, Wm; Virginia, 1674-1675 6212.30 p53
Weble, George 48; Ontario, 1871 1823.15 p275
Webley, Lillian O.; Vermont, 1883-1913 5900.10 p487
Webster, Agnes; Mobile, Alabama, 1735-1845 1640.10 p211
Webster, Alexander 18; Ontario, 1871 1823.15 p275
Webster, B. 10; Ontario, 1861 2896.28 p5
Webster, Charles 36; Quebec, 1774 1220.25 p75
Wife: Jenna 33
With 3 children
Webster, D. H. 5; Ontario, 1861 2896.28 p11
Webster, Daniel 40; Ontario, 1871 1823.15 p275
Webster, Daniel 48; Ontario, 1861 2896.28 p5
Webster, Daniel 73; Ontario, 1871 1823.15 p275
Webster, David; Virginia, 1767 1224.2 p122
Webster, Dorothy; Maryland, 1673 2524.55 p233
Webster, E. H. 8; Ontario, 1861 2896.28 p11
Webster, Edward; Maryland, 1679 2524.55 p233
Webster, Elizabeth 58; Ontario, 1871 1823.15 p275
Webster, George; Buffalo, New York, 1898 3437.14 p183
Webster, George 46; Ontario, 1871 1823.15 p275
Webster, Hamilton Ball 31; Ontario, 1871 1823.22 p168
Webster, Henry 31; Ontario, 1871 1823.15 p276
Webster, James; Virginia, 1766 1224.2 p122
Webster, James 22; Norfolk, Virginia, 1774 1220.25 p20
Webster, James 33; Ontario, 1871 1823.15 p276
Webster, James 39; Ontario, 1871 1823.15 p276
Webster, James 47; Ontario, 1871 1823.15 p276
Webster, Jane 16; Ontario, 1871 1823.15 p276
Webster, Jenna 33 *SEE* Webster, Charles
Webster, John; Maryland, 1660 2524.55 p233
Webster, John; Maryland, 1665 2524.55 p233
Webster, John; Maryland, 1671 1224.1 p62
Webster, John 25; Nova Scotia, 1774 1220.25 p13
Webster, John 40; Ontario, 1871 1823.15 p276
Webster, Joseph 19; Philadelphia, 1774 1220.25 p35
Webster, Joseph 35; Ontario, 1871 1823.15 p276
Webster, Joshua 76; Ontario, 1871 1823.22 p168
Webster, L. 1; Ontario, 1861 2896.28 p11
Webster, M. 25; Ontario, 1861 2896.28 p5
Webster, M. 28; Ontario, 1861 2896.28 p11
Webster, Marke; Maryland, 1649 2524.55 p233
Webster, Mary 20; Maryland, 1774 1220.25 p58
With 3 children
Webster, Mathew 33; Nova Scotia, 1774 1220.25 p136
With wife & 3 children
Webster, Paletiah, Jr.; Pennsylvania, 1777 4629.10 p10
Webster, Pelatiah; Pennsylvania, 1777 4629.10 p24
Webster, Pelatiah; Pennsylvania, 1779 4629.10 p37
Webster, Richard; Virginia, 1667-1668 6212.30 p39
Webster, Robert; Jamaica, 1846 1640.13 p131
Webster, Robert 37; Ontario, 1871 1823.15 p276
Webster, S. 4; Ontario, 1861 2896.28 p5
Webster, Samuel 28; Ontario, 1871 1823.22 p168
Webster, Thomas 30; Ontario, 1871 1823.15 p276
Webster, Thomas 50; Philadelphia, 1774 1220.25 p20
Webster, Thomas 84; Ontario, 1871 1823.22 p168
Webster, William; Georgia, 1740 1640.10 p211
Webster, William 17; Ontario, 1861 2896.28 p5
Webster, William 23; Maryland, 1773-1774 1220.25 p33
Webster, William 24; Ontario, 1871 1823.15 p276
Webster, William 32; Ontario, 1871 1823.15 p276
Webster, William 33; Nova Scotia, 1774 1220.25 p135
Webster, William 46; Ontario, 1871 1823.15 p276
Webster, William 50; Ontario, 1871 1823.22 p168
Webstor, Geo.; Maryland, 1657 2524.55 p233
Websto'r, Humphry; Maryland, 1653 2524.55 p234
Weburgh, William; New York, 1840 8197.10 p203
Weckemann, Johann; Port uncertain, 1768 2856.30 p482
Weckemann, Johann; Port uncertain, 1788 2856.30 p482
Wecker, Mathes; America, 1752 2856.30 p482
With wife & 5 sons
Weddel, James; New York, 1877 1640.13 p131
Wedderburn, Alexander; Florida, 1774 1640.10 p211
Wedderburn, David; Florida, 1767 1640.10 p211
Weddill, Christian; Maryland, 1673 2524.55 p234
Weddill, Roger; Maryland, 1673 2524.55 p234
Wedekend, Charles; Pennsylvania, 1840 6058.10 p18
Wedekind, Frank; Baltimore, 1843 6058.10 p30
Wedekind, Henry; New York, 1837 8197.10 p295
Wedekind, Henry; New York, 1839 8197.10 p135
Wedekind, Justina Regina; Port uncertain, 1767 2856.30 p482
Wedel, Mr.; America, 1752 2856.30 p391
Wedel, Anna Maria; America, 1752 2856.30 p482
With child
Wedel, Caspar; America, 1737 2856.30 p482
Wedel, Eva Cath.; America, 1752 2856.30 p61
Wedel, Eva Catharina; America, 1752 2856.30 p482
With husband
Wedel, Georg Albrecht; America, 1752 2856.30 p482
With wife & 2 children
Wedel, Georg Albrecht; America, 1764 2856.30 p482
Wedel, J. Ptr.; America, 1764 2856.30 p180
Wedel, Joh. Michael, The Younger; America, 1726 2856.30 p482
Wedel, Johann Peter; America, 1764 2856.30 p482
With wife
Wedel, M. C.; America, 1752 2856.30 p319
Wedel, Maria Catharina; America, 1752 2856.30 p482
With husband & 3 daughters
Wedel, Michael; America, 1726 2856.30 p482
Wedel, Peter; America, 1764 2856.30 p482
Wedel, Peter; America, 1764 2856.30 p482
With wife & 5 children
Wedel, Peter; America, 1790 2856.30 p482
Wedel, Peter; America, 1791 2856.30 p482
Wedenpuhl, Mrs. Daniel; Port uncertain, 1795 2856.30 p482
With 2 sons
Wederstone, James R.; New York, 1867 1640.13 p131
Wedert, Susanna; Port uncertain, 1739 2856.30 p482
Wedge, Ann 50; Ontario, 1871 1823.15 p276
Weeb, Bengamin O. 32; Ontario, 1871 1823.28 p103
Weeber, Miss; Port uncertain, 1792 2856.30 p482
Weeber, Mr.; Port uncertain, 1761 2856.30 p483
Weeber, Anna Maria; Port uncertain, 1769 2856.30 p482
Weeber, Anna Maria; Port uncertain, 1791 2856.30 p482
Weeber, Barbara; Port uncertain, 1769 2856.30 p482
Weeber, Catharina; Port uncertain, 1753 2856.30 p483
Weeber, Catharina; Port uncertain, 1763 2856.30 p483
Weeber, Catharina; Port uncertain, 1793 2856.30 p483
Weeber, Christina; Port uncertain, 1741 2856.30 p483
Weeber, Christof; America, 1751 2856.30 p483
Weeber, Christof; America, 1752 2856.30 p483
Weeber, Christof; Port uncertain, 1751 2856.30 p483
With wife & child
Weeber, Gottfried; America, 1733 2856.30 p483
With wife & children
Weeber, Gottfried; America, 1741 2856.30 p483
Weeber, Hans David; America, 1744 2856.30 p483
Weeber, Hans Martin; Port uncertain, 1755 2856.30 p483
Weeber, Hans Martin; Port uncertain, 1791 2856.30 p483
Weeber, Hermann; America, 1744 2856.30 p483
With children
Weeber, Hermann; Port uncertain, 1744 2856.30 p483
With children
Weeber, Johann; Port uncertain, 1765 2856.30 p483
Weeber, Johann; Port uncertain, 1766 2856.30 p483
Weeber, Karl; Port uncertain, 1784 2856.30 p483
Weeber, Ludwig; Port uncertain, 1751 2856.30 p483
Weeber, Maria Catharina; Port uncertain, 1753 2856.30 p483
Weeber, Maria Elisabeth; Port uncertain, 1791 2856.30 p483
Weeber, Michael; America, 1751 2856.30 p483
Weeber, Michael; America, 1751 2856.30 p483
With wife & child
Weeber, Michael; America, 1764 2856.30 p483
Weeber, Michael; Port uncertain, 1783 2856.30 p483
With wife 2 sons & 3 daughters
Weed, John W. 50; Ontario, 1871 1823.22 p168
Weeden, Joseph 39; Maryland, 1774 1220.25 p54
Weederman, Dora 35; Kansas, 1907-1910 9079.10 p30
Weederman, John 6; Kansas, 1907-1910 9079.10 p30
Weederman, John 42; Kansas, 1907-1910 9079.10 p30
Weederman, Lizzie 3; Kansas, 1907-1910 9079.10 p30
Weedham, John 16; Virginia, 1774 1220.25 p91
Weedon, Ann; Maryland, 1692 1224.1 p62
Weedon, John; Boston, 1699 1224.1 p62
Weedon, William; Maryland, 1692 1224.1 p62
Weejan, Jane 39; Ontario, 1871 1823.15 p276
Weekes, Anna 5; Ontario, 1861 2896.25 p10
Weekes, Charles 36; Ontario, 1871 1823.15 p276
Weekes, Charlotte 51; Ontario, 1861 2896.25 p8
Weekes, Elicy A. J. 4; Ontario, 1861 2896.25 p8
Weekes, Elizabeth; Maryland, 1670 2524.55 p234
Weekes, Elizabeth Hobbs; Middlesex Co., Virginia, 1698 1224.1 p30
Weekes, Freeman 15; Ontario, 1861 2896.25 p9
Weekes, George M. 20; Ontario, 1861 2896.25 p8
Weekes, Hady A. 11; Ontario, 1861 2896.25 p8
Weekes, Isaac 26; Ontario, 1861 2896.25 p11
Weekes, James G. 3; Ontario, 1861 2896.25 p10
Weekes, John; Maryland, 1681 2524.55 p234
Weekes, John 16; Ontario, 1861 2896.25 p8
Weekes, L. A. 11; Ontario, 1861 2896.25 p8
Weekes, Randolph 11; Ontario, 1861 2896.25 p9
Weekes, Samuel 13; Ontario, 1861 2896.25 p9
Weekes, Samuel J. 15; Ontario, 1861 2896.25 p8
Weekes, Sarah C. 17; Ontario, 1861 2896.25 p9
Weekes, Sarah E. 22; Ontario, 1861 2896.25 p8
Weekes, Solomon 45; Ontario, 1861 2896.25 p9
Weekes, Solomon, Jr. 21; Ontario, 1861 2896.25 p9
Weekes, Thomas G. 7; Ontario, 1861 2896.25 p10
Weekes, W. H. 26; Ontario, 1861 2896.25 p8
Weekes, William 67; Ontario, 1871 1823.15 p276
Weekman, James 25; Maryland, 1774 1220.25 p60
Weeks, Ada 7; Ontario, 1861 2896.27 p19
Weeks, Agnes 8; Ontario, 1861 2896.28 p31
Weeks, Allan 27; Ontario, 1861 2896.28 p31
Weeks, B. 9; Ontario, 1861 2896.26 p8
Weeks, C. 59; Ontario, 1861 2896.26 p8
Weeks, Charles 22; Ontario, 1861 2896.28 p33
Weeks, Charley W. 10; Ontario, 1861 2896.28 p42
Weeks, Daniel 17; Ontario, 1861 2896.28 p41
Weeks, Daniel 20; Ontario, 1861 2896.28 p42
Weeks, Eleanor 83; Ontario, 1861 2896.28 p41
Weeks, Elias 3; Ontario, 1861 2896.28 p31
Weeks, Ellen 10; Ontario, 1861 2896.27 p19
Weeks, F. 28; Ontario, 1861 2896.26 p8
Weeks, Fairman 19; Ontario, 1861 2896.28 p31
Weeks, Fannie E. 18; Ontario, 1861 2896.28 p42
Weeks, Frances 23; Ontario, 1861 2896.28 p52
Weeks, Frederick 1; Ontario, 1861 2896.28 p52
Weeks, George 8; Ontario, 1861 2896.28 p42
Weeks, George 20; Ontario, 1861 2896.28 p33
Weeks, George 26; Ontario, 1861 2896.28 p31
Weeks, Harriet 20; Ontario, 1861 2896.28 p31
Weeks, Heman 6; Ontario, 1861 2896.28 p42
Weeks, Herman 4; Ontario, 1861 2896.28 p41
Weeks, J. 42; Ontario, 1861 2896.26 p15
Weeks, James H. 12; Ontario, 1861 2896.28 p41
Weeks, Jane 14; Ontario, 1861 2896.27 p19
Weeks, John; Maryland, 1672 2524.55 p234
Weeks, John; Maryland, 1682 2524.55 p234
Weeks, John 12; Ontario, 1861 2896.28 p31
Weeks, John 22; Philadelphia, 1774 1220.25 p6
Weeks, L. 7; Ontario, 1861 2896.26 p8
Weeks, Lydia 35; Ontario, 1861 2896.28 p41
Weeks, Lydia A. 13; Ontario, 1861 2896.28 p42
Weeks, Mahala 18; Ontario, 1861 2896.28 p31
Weeks, Margaret 11; Ontario, 1861 2896.28 p42
Weeks, Martha; Maryland, 1674 2524.55 p234
Weeks, Mary J. 15; Ontario, 1861 2896.28 p42
Weeks, Morris 22; Ontario, 1861 2896.28 p42
Weeks, Nancy A. 25; Ontario, 1861 2896.28 p42
Weeks, Phebe A. 10; Ontario, 1861 2896.28 p31
Weeks, Randell 9; Ontario, 1861 2896.28 p42
Weeks, Robert 16; Ontario, 1861 2896.28 p39
Weeks, Sarah 7; Ontario, 1861 2896.27 p19
Weeks, Sarah 34; Ontario, 1861 2896.28 p31
Weeks, Sarah 43; Ontario, 1861 2896.28 p42
Weeks, Sarah J. 2; Ontario, 1861 2896.28 p31
Weeks, Selim 5; Ontario, 1861 2896.28 p42
Weeks, Solomon 3; Ontario, 1861 2896.28 p42
Weeks, Solomon 20; Ontario, 1861 2896.28 p42
Weeks, Stephen 16; Ontario, 1861 2896.28 p31
Weeks, T. 10; Ontario, 1861 2896.26 p8
Weeks, Thankful; Vermont, 1793-1876 5900.10 p500
Weeks, Thomas; New York, 1840 8197.10 p202
Weeks, Webster 1; Ontario, 1861 2896.28 p41
Weeks, William 3; Ontario, 1861 2896.28 p42
Weeks, Wrenselaer S. 24; Ontario, 1861 2896.25 p21
Weekwark, John 28; Ontario, 1871 1823.28 p103
Weems, Rachael Morris; Maryland, 1797 1224.2 p122
Weese, A. 5; Ontario, 1861 2896.25 p50
Weese, A. M. 2; Ontario, 1861 2896.25 p51
Weese, Adam 54; Ontario, 1861 2896.25 p50
Weese, C. A. L. 11; Ontario, 1861 2896.25 p48
Weese, C. R. 31; Ontario, 1861 2896.25 p50
Weese, C. W. 22; Ontario, 1861 2896.25 p53
Weese, D. 13; Ontario, 1861 2896.25 p51
Weese, E. 36; Ontario, 1861 2896.25 p48
Weese, E. E. 2; Ontario, 1861 2896.25 p50
Weese, E. T. 3; Ontario, 1861 2896.25 p50
Weese, F. 21; Ontario, 1861 2896.25 p51
Weese, F. 31; Ontario, 1861 2896.25 p51
Weese, F. V. 2; Ontario, 1861 2896.25 p53
Weese, Fanny B. 16; Ontario, 1861 2896.25 p51
Weese, G. W. 5; Ontario, 1861 2896.25 p50
Weese, H. A. 11; Ontario, 1861 2896.25 p51
Weese, H. M. 24; Ontario, 1861 2896.25 p53
Weese, H. W. 17; Ontario, 1861 2896.25 p53
Weese, Hannah 39; Ontario, 1861 2896.25 p17

Weese, Hannah E. 8; Ontario, 1861 2896.25 p50
Weese, J. A. 43; Ontario, 1861 2896.25 p51
Weese, J. G. 12; Ontario, 1861 2896.25 p50
Weese, J. H. 10; Ontario, 1861 2896.25 p50
Weese, J. J. 3; Ontario, 1861 2896.25 p50
Weese, J. L. 3; Ontario, 1861 2896.25 p53
Weese, Jemima 24; Ontario, 1861 2896.25 p53
Weese, L. 4; Ontario, 1861 2896.25 p53
Weese, L. 7; Ontario, 1861 2896.25 p50
Weese, L. 16; Ontario, 1861 2896.25 p50
Weese, L. A. 8; Ontario, 1861 2896.25 p51
Weese, M. C. 7; Ontario, 1861 2896.25 p50
Weese, M. C. 12; Ontario, 1861 2896.25 p51
Weese, M. J. 22; Ontario, 1861 2896.25 p53
Weese, M. J. 32; Ontario, 1861 2896.25 p50
Weese, M. M. 11; Ontario, 1861 2896.25 p53
Weese, Margaret 6; Ontario, 1861 2896.25 p17
Weese, Margaret 79; Ontario, 1861 2896.25 p54
Weese, Marinda 14; Ontario, 1861 2896.25 p17
Weese, N. J. 12; Ontario, 1861 2896.25 p50
Weese, P. A. 32; Ontario, 1861 2896.25 p50
Weese, P. L. 9; Ontario, 1861 2896.25 p50
Weese, Polly 52; Ontario, 1861 2896.25 p53
Weese, R. C. 7; Ontario, 1861 2896.25 p50
Weese, R. C. 17; Ontario, 1861 2896.25 p48
Weese, S. 8; Ontario, 1861 2896.25 p51
Weese, S. C. 3; Ontario, 1861 2896.25 p53
Weese, S. E. 37; Ontario, 1861 2896.25 p50
Weese, S. M. 10; Ontario, 1861 2896.25 p51
Weese, Sabra 8; Ontario, 1861 2896.25 p51
Weese, Sarah Ann 2; Ontario, 1861 2896.25 p17
Weese, Selidona 5; Ontario, 1861 2896.25 p17
Weese, W. 3; Ontario, 1861 2896.25 p51
Weese, W. R. 14; Ontario, 1861 2896.25 p50
Weese, W. S. 9; Ontario, 1861 2896.25 p50
Weese, William H. 14; Ontario, 1861 2896.25 p48
Weese, William S. 13; Ontario, 1861 2896.25 p50
Wege, Henry; New York, New York, 1860 6058.10 p61
Wegerer, Catharina; Port uncertain, 1795 2856.30 p438
Wegerli, Miss; Port uncertain, 1761 2856.30 p370
Wegerlin, Anna Barbara; America, 1752 2856.30 p483
With husband
Wegielska, Agnes; Maryland, 1910 3259.35 p67
Weglewicz, Joseph; Maryland, 1910 3259.35 p67
Wegrocki, Ramond; Maryland, 1910 3259.35 p67
Wegurth, John; Maryland, 1910 3259.35 p67
Wehelon, William 56; Ontario, 1871 1823.15 p276
Wehler, Jakob; Port uncertain, 1764 2856.30 p483
Wehr, Anna Margarete; Port uncertain, 1794 2856.30 p483
Wehr, Anna Maria; Port uncertain, 1751 2856.30 p484
Wehr, Friedrich; Port uncertain, 1789 2856.30 p483
Wehr, Johann; Port uncertain, 1791 2856.30 p484
Wehr, Peter; Port uncertain, 1781 2856.30 p484
Wehrer, Peter; America, 1735 2856.30 p484
Wehrin, Anna Maria; Port uncertain, 1751 2856.30 p484
Weiand, Maria; Port uncertain, 1777 2856.30 p484
Weibens, Frederick; New York, 1837 8197.10 p104
Weichel, Konrad; America, 1774 2856.30 p484
Weick, Johann Heinrich; America, 1738 2856.30 p484
Weick, Magdalena; America, 1736 2856.30 p484
Weickersheim, . . .; Port uncertain, 1729 2856.30 p484
Weickhel, Wilhelm; Port uncertain, 1747 2856.30 p484
With wife
Weickhert, Sebastian; Port uncertain, 1740 2856.30 p484
Weicksel, Henry; Pennsylvania, 1854 6058.10 p32
Weid, Charles; Savannah, Georgia, 1808 1640.10 p212
Weidemann, Johann; Port uncertain, 1765 2856.30 p484
Weidemann, Martin; America, 1748 2856.30 p484
Weidenbach, Johann Wilhelm; Port uncertain, 1747 2856.30 p484
Weidmann, Jacob Heinrich; America, 1736 2856.30 p484
With wife son & daughter
Weidmann, Jeremias; Port uncertain, 1767 2856.30 p484
With wife & children
Weidmann, Philipp; Port uncertain, 1785 2856.30 p484
Weidner, Peter; New York, 1838 8197.10 p295
Weierbacher, Johann; America, 1753 2856.30 p484
Weierbacher, Johann; Port uncertain, 1754 2856.30 p484
Weiffenbach, Caspar; Port uncertain, 1765 2856.30 p484
Weigand, Anna Dorothea; Port uncertain, 1731 2856.30 p484
Weigand, Anna Maria; Port uncertain, 1785 2856.30 p484
Weigand, Hans Georg; America, 1744 2856.30 p484
Weigand, Konrad; America, 1748 2856.30 p484
With wife & children
Weigand, Thomas; Port uncertain, 1773 2856.30 p484
Weightman, Johannes; Philadelphia, 1729 2856.30 p484
Weightman, Thomas; New York, 1827 8197.10 p341
Weignad, Johannes; Baltimore, 1848 6058.10 p25
Weiher, Johann; America, 1752 2856.30 p485
Weiher, Johann Adam; America, 1749 2856.30 p485
Weiher, Johann Peter; America, 1749 2856.30 p485
Weihnacht, Johann Adam; Port uncertain, 1752 2856.30 p485
Weil, Ferdinand; New York, 1840 8197.10 p204
Weil, Henry; New York, 1839 8197.10 p135
Weil, John 30; Alaska, 1917 9196.1 p50
Weil, John 30; Yukon, 1917 9196.1 p50
Weil, Peter 64; Ontario, 1871 1823.15 p276
Weil, Sam 35; Alaska, 1917 9196.1 p49
Weil, Sam 35; Whitehorse, Yukon, 1917 9196.1 p49
Weil, Tom 30; Alaska, 1917 9196.1 p49
Weil, Tom 30; Yukon, 1917 9196.1 p49
Weiland, Adelaide 16; Ontario, 1871 1823.15 p276
Weiland, Frederick 23; Ontario, 1871 1823.15 p276
Weilding, Robt; Virginia, 1666-1667 6212.30 p35
Weiler, Andreas; America, 1785 2856.30 p485
With wife
Weiler, Jorg; America, 1744 2856.30 p485
Weiler, Michael; America, 1749 2856.30 p485
Weilgant, Hattie; Maryland, 1910 3259.35 p67
Weilhard, Johann; Port uncertain, 1750 2856.30 p485
Weimar, Heinrich; New York, 1837 8197.10 p103
Weimar, Justus 60; Ontario, 1871 1823.15 p276
Weimer, Jakob; America, 1751 2856.30 p485
Weimer, Jakob; America, 1759 2856.30 p485
Weimer, Joseph; New York, 1834 8197.10 p316
Weimert, Nikolaus; America, 1749 2856.30 p485
With wife & children
Wein, Frederick 70; Ontario, 1871 1823.15 p276
Wein, Godfried 35; Ontario, 1871 1823.15 p276
Wein, Matthew 33; Ontario, 1871 1823.15 p276
Weinacher, Margarete; America, 1748 2856.30 p485
With husband
Weinacher, Margarete; Port uncertain, 1737 2856.30 p485
With husband
Weinand, Jakob; Port uncertain, 1754 2856.30 p485
With children
Weinbrenner, Peter; Canada, 1774 2856.30 p485
Weinert, Johann Nikolaus; Canada, 1754 2856.30 p485
Weinert, Johann Nikolaus; Port uncertain, 1784 2856.30 p485
Weingarten, Jakob; Port uncertain, 1736 2856.30 p485
Weinheimer, Anna Margarete; Port uncertain, 1756 2856.30 p485
Weinheimer, Jakob; Port uncertain, 1783 2856.30 p485
Weinholdt, Joseph 30; Ontario, 1871 1823.28 p103
Weinkauf, Andreas; Port uncertain, 1741 2856.30 p485
Weinmann, Andreas; America, 1766 2856.30 p485
Weinmann, Andreas; America, 1768 2856.30 p485
Weinmann, Andreas; Canada, 1752 2856.30 p485
Weinmann, Christof; Port uncertain, 1744 2856.30 p485
Weinmann, Georg; Port uncertain, 1772 2856.30 p485
Weinmann, Mathes; America, 1752 2856.30 p485
Weinmann, Peter; America, 1752 2856.30 p485
Weinmar, Melchior; America, 1752 2856.30 p485
Weinmaster, Anna 22; Kansas, 1900-1910 9079.10 p31
Weinmaster, David 30; Kansas, 1882-1910 9079.10 p31
Weinmaster, Fred 28; Kansas, 1900-1910 9079.10 p31
Weinmuller, Mr.; America, 1738 2856.30 p397
Weinmuller, Caspar; Port uncertain, 1756 2856.30 p486
With wife & 3 children
Weinmuller, Johann; America, 1738 2856.30 p486
Weinmuller, Konrad; America, 1738 2856.30 p486
With wife
Weinsheimer, Heinrich Peter; Port uncertain, 1762 2856.30 p486
Weinsheimer, Philipp; Port uncertain, 1786 2856.30 p486
With wife & 3 children
Weintz, John; New York, 1840 8197.10 p203
Weinz, Christian; New York, 1838-1840 8197.10 p201
Weinz, Michael; Port uncertain, 1783 2856.30 p490
With wife son & daughter
Weipler, Jakob; Port uncertain, 1727 2856.30 p486
Weir, Anthony 65; Ontario, 1871 1823.28 p103
Weir, David 47; Ontario, 1871 1823.15 p276
Weir, Edward; New York, 1802 8197.10 p26
Weir, Edward 25; Ontario, 1871 1823.22 p168
Weir, George; Canada, 1837 1640.13 p132
Weir, George; New York, 1803 8197.10 p17
Weir, Hugh 40; Ontario, 1871 1823.22 p168
Weir, James 31; Ontario, 1871 1823.15 p276
Weir, James 60; Ontario, 1871 1823.22 p168
Weir, Janett 37; Ontario, 1871 1823.28 p103
Weir, John; Georgia, 1699 1640.13 p132
Weir, John 24; Ontario, 1871 1823.15 p276
Weir, John 40; British Columbia, 1910 9196.1 p31
Weir, John 40; Seattle, 1910 9196.1 p31
Weir, John 62; Ontario, 1871 1823.22 p168
Weir, Joseph 30; Ontario, 1871 1823.15 p276
Weir, Lancelot 75; Ontario, 1871 1823.22 p168
Weir, Mary 85; Ontario, 1871 1823.22 p168
Weir, Robert; New York, 1802 8197.10 p26
Weir, Robert 33; Ontario, 1871 1823.15 p276
Weir, Thomas; London, England, 1740 1640.13 p132
Weir, Thomas 22; Ontario, 1871 1823.28 p103
Weir, Thomas 38; Ontario, 1871 1823.28 p103
Weir, William; St. Vincent, 1795 1640.13 p132
Weir, William; Savannah, Georgia, 1768 1640.10 p212
Weir, William 52; Ontario, 1871 1823.15 p276
Weirich, Ernst; Port uncertain, 1783 2856.30 p486
Weirich, Maria Elisabeth; Port uncertain, 1775 2856.30 p486
Weis, Abraham; Port uncertain, 1751 2856.30 p486
Weis, Adolf; America, 1738 2856.30 p486
Weis, Charles; Pennsylvania, 1851 6058.10 p28
Weis, Eva; Port uncertain, 1764 2856.30 p486
Weis, Franziska; Port uncertain, 1764 2856.30 p486
Weis, George; Pennsylvania, 1851 6058.10 p28
Weis, Helena; Port uncertain, 1752 2856.30 p486
Weis, Jacob; Pennsylvania, 1777 4629.10 p22
Weis, Johann Wilhelm; America, 1781 2856.30 p486
Weis, John; New York, New York, 1847 6058.10 p35
Weis, Michael; America, 1755 2856.30 p486
Weis, Niklas; America, 1751 2856.30 p486
Weis, Niklas; America, 1752 2856.30 p486
With wife & 3 children
Weis, Philipp; America, 1764 2856.30 p486
With son
Weis, Philipp; Port uncertain, 1783 2856.30 p486
Weisang, . . .; Port uncertain, 1770 2856.30 p486
Weise, Christopher 65; Ontario, 1871 1823.15 p276
Weise, John 40; Ontario, 1871 1823.15 p276
Weise, John 45; Alaska, 1917 9196.1 p54
Weise, John 45; Yukon, 1917 9196.1 p54
Weise, Julius 35; Ontario, 1871 1823.15 p276
Weiseburger, Jacob; America, 1752 2856.30 p486
Weisenbacher, Helena; Port uncertain, 1753 2856.30 p486
Weisenbacher, Jacob; America, 1744 2856.30 p486
Weisenbacher, Michael; America, 1769 2856.30 p486
Weisenberger, Hans Michael; America, 1744 2856.30 p486
Weisenbergh, Eliza 61; Ontario, 1871 1823.28 p103
Weisenbergh, Gottllilp 71; Ontario, 1871 1823.28 p103
Weisenbuhler, Barbara; Port uncertain, 1773 2856.30 p486
Weiser, Johann; Port uncertain, 1780 2856.30 p486
Weiser, Marianna; Port uncertain, 1736 2856.30 p486
Weiser, Tiberi; Port uncertain, 1740 2856.30 p486
Weiser, Tiberi; Port uncertain, 1769 2856.30 p486
Weiseugk, Michl; Maryland, 1910 3259.35 p67
Weisgerber, Jacob; New York, 1840 8197.10 p295
Weisman, Augustus; New York, 1837 8197.10 p103
Weiss, A. E.; Port uncertain, 1787 2856.30 p222
Weiss, Abraham; America, 1737 2856.30 p488
Weiss, Abraham; America, 1749 2856.30 p488
With 6 children
Weiss, Absalom; Port uncertain, 1771 2856.30 p487
Weiss, Adam Friedrich; America, 1752 2856.30 p487
Weiss, Adam Friedrich; America, 1771 2856.30 p487
Weiss, Adam Friedrich; America, 1774 2856.30 p487
Weiss, Andreas; America, 1754 2856.30 p487
Weiss, Andreas; Port uncertain, 1753 2856.30 p487
Weiss, Andreas; Port uncertain, 1787 2856.30 p487
Weiss, Anna Maria; America, 1750 2856.30 p487
Weiss, Barbara; Port uncertain, 1743 2856.30 p487
Weiss, Barbara; Port uncertain, 1773 2856.30 p487
Weiss, Catharina; America, 1700-1799 2856.30 p487
Weiss, Catharina; Port uncertain, 1769 2856.30 p487
Weiss, Christian; America, 1752 2856.30 p488
With wife & 4 children
Weiss, Christian; America, 1753 2856.30 p488
With wife & 4 children
Weiss, Christian Ernest; New York, 1834 8197.10 p295
Weiss, Christina Marge; Port uncertain, 1743 2856.30 p488
Weiss, Christof; Port uncertain, 1771 2856.30 p487
Weiss, Daniel; America, 1754 2856.30 p488
Weiss, Elis. C. Fritz *SEE* Weiss, Johann Wilhelm
Weiss, Ernst Friedrich; America, 1752 2856.30 p488
With wife & children
Weiss, Franz; America, 1733 2856.30 p487
Weiss, Georg; Port uncertain, 1771 2856.30 p487
Weiss, Georg Friedrich; Port uncertain, 1781 2856.30 p487
Weiss, Hans Adam; Port uncertain, 1731 2856.30 p487
Weiss, Hans Jerg; America, 1750 2856.30 p487
Weiss, Hans Martin; Port uncertain, 1731 2856.30 p487
Weiss, Hans Peter; America, 1741 2856.30 p488
Weiss, J. Wilh.; America, 1754 2856.30 p123
Weiss, Jacob; America, 1738 2856.30 p487
Weiss, Jacob; Port uncertain, 1767 2856.30 p487
Weiss, Jacob, Jr.; America, 1750 2856.30 p487

Weiss, Jacob, Jr.; America, 1750 ***2856.30*** *p488*
With wife & children
Weiss, Jakob; Port uncertain, 1770 ***2856.30*** *p487*
Weiss, Joachim; Port uncertain, 1773 ***2856.30*** *p487*
Weiss, Johann; America, 1750 ***2856.30*** *p487*
Weiss, Johann; Port uncertain, 1752 ***2856.30*** *p487*
Weiss, Johann Wilhelm; America, 1754 ***2856.30*** *p488*
Wife: Elis. C. Fritz
Weiss, Johann Wilhelm; Port uncertain, 1783 ***2856.30*** *p488*
Weiss, Josef; Port uncertain, 1743 ***2856.30*** *p487*
Weiss, Konrad; America, 1752 ***2856.30*** *p487*
Weiss, Konrad; Port uncertain, 1752 ***2856.30*** *p487*
Weiss, Konrad; Port uncertain, 1774 ***2856.30*** *p487*
Weiss, Leonhard; America, 1727 ***2856.30*** *p487*
Weiss, Louis F.; Maryland, 1910 ***3259.35*** *p67*
Weiss, Ludwig; America, 1775 ***2856.30*** *p487*
Weiss, Ludwig; Port uncertain, 1766 ***2856.30*** *p487*
Weiss, Margarete; Port uncertain, 1764 ***2856.30*** *p487*
Weiss, Margarete; Port uncertain, 1769 ***2856.30*** *p487*
Weiss, Maria Agnes; Port uncertain, 1747 ***2856.30*** *p487*
Weiss, Maria Eva; Port uncertain, 1766 ***2856.30*** *p487*
Weiss, Martin; America, 1750 ***2856.30*** *p487*
Weiss, Matheis; Port uncertain, 1764 ***2856.30*** *p487*
Weiss, Melchior; Port uncertain, 1777 ***2856.30*** *p487*
Weiss, Michael; America, 1731 ***2856.30*** *p488*
With wife & children
Weiss, Michael; America, 1742 ***2856.30*** *p487*
Weiss, Peter; Port uncertain, 1724 ***2856.30*** *p487*
Weiss, Philipp; America, 1753 ***2856.30*** *p487*
Weiss, Philipp; America, 1753 ***2856.30*** *p488*
With wife & 2 children
Weiss, Philipp; America, 1753 ***2856.30*** *p504*
Weissbrod, Georg; Port uncertain, 1735 ***2856.30*** *p488*
Weisseler, Barbara; America, 1750 ***2856.30*** *p488*
Weisseler, Jacob Friedrich; America, 1750 ***2856.30*** *p488*
Weissenbach, Caspar; Port uncertain, 1765 ***2856.30*** *p488*
Weissenburger, Magdalena; Port uncertain, 1774 ***2856.30*** *p488*
Weissgerber, Elis. Barbara; America, 1741 ***2856.30*** *p488*
Weissin, Christina Marge; Port uncertain, 1743 ***2856.30*** *p488*
Weisskopf, Johann Georg; Port uncertain, 1770 ***2856.30*** *p488*
Weisslogel, Johann, The Younger; Port uncertain, 1793 ***2856.30*** *p488*
Weissmann, Heinrich Adam; America, 1784 ***2856.30*** *p488*
Weissmann, Michael; America, 1750 ***2856.30*** *p488*
Weissmann, Nickel; America, 1750 ***2856.30*** *p488*
Weissmann, Peter; America, 1754 ***2856.30*** *p488*
Weissmann, Peter; America, 1775 ***2856.30*** *p488*
Weissmann, Peter; America, 1780 ***2856.30*** *p488*
Weiter, Jakob; Port uncertain, 1781 ***2856.30*** *p488*
Weitersberger, Johann Peter; America, 1742 ***2856.30*** *p488*
Weites, Christian; Maryland, 1665 ***2524.55*** *p234*
Weithner, Catharina; America, 1738 ***2856.30*** *p488*
With 3 daughters
Weitig, Marianna; Port uncertain, 1764 ***2856.30*** *p488*
Weitner, Catharina; America, 1738 ***2856.30*** *p488*
With 3 daughters
Weitnerin, Catharina; America, 1738 ***2856.30*** *p488*
With 3 daughters
Weittmann, Andreas; America, 1738 ***2856.30*** *p488*
Weitzel, Adam; New York, New York, 1855 ***6058.10*** *p46*
Weland, William 33; Ontario, 1871 ***1823.15*** *p276*
Welapski, Frank; Maryland, 1910 ***3259.35*** *p67*
Welbanks, Calvin 26; Ontario, 1861 ***2896.26*** *p35*
Welbanks, Deborah 11; Ontario, 1861 ***2896.26*** *p32*
Welbanks, E. Jane 10; Ontario, 1861 ***2896.26*** *p25*
Welbanks, George 7; Ontario, 1861 ***2896.26*** *p32*
Welbanks, Lewis 9; Ontario, 1861 ***2896.26*** *p32*
Welbanks, Susan 33; Ontario, 1861 ***2896.26*** *p32*
Welberks, Richard; Maryland, 1666 ***2524.55*** *p234*
Welberry, Elizabeth; Maryland, 1659 ***2524.55*** *p234*
Welch, Miss; Quebec, 1858 ***9196.15*** *p36*
Welch, Alice; Maryland, 1663 ***2524.55*** *p234*
Welch, Annie; Vermont, 1850-1903 ***5900.10*** *p68*
Welch, Annie; Vermont, 1857-1958 ***5900.10*** *p420*
Welch, Annie B.; Vermont, 1874 ***5900.10*** *p143*
Welch, Anthony; New York, 1839 ***8197.10*** *p295*
Welch, Bernard; Maryland, 1657 ***2524.55*** *p234*
Welch, Betsey Mullaney; Vermont, 1865 ***5900.10*** *p436*
Welch, Bridget Griffin 79; Vermont, 1907 ***5900.10*** *p73*
Welch, Carnmen 49; Ontario, 1871 ***1823.15*** *p276*
Welch, Catherine; Vermont, 1832-1912 ***5900.10*** *p547*
Welch, Catherine Conway 55; Vermont, 1888 ***5900.10*** *p506*
Welch, Catherine Foran; Vermont, 1851-1930 ***5900.10*** *p137*
Welch, Catherine Kelley; Vermont, 1841-1918 ***5900.10*** *p83*
Welch, Christopher; New York, 1837 ***8197.10*** *p104*
Welch, David; Nova Scotia, 1745 ***4628.40*** *p45*
Welch, David; Vermont, 1844-1917 ***5900.10*** *p98*
Welch, Dennis; Vermont, 1834-1904 ***5900.10*** *p127*
Welch, E. D.; Vermont, 1851-1925 ***5900.10*** *p420*
Welch, Edward; Canada, 1756-1760 ***4628.40*** *p45*
Welch, Ellen; Vermont, n.d. ***5900.10*** *p482*
Welch, Ellen; Vermont, 1839-1913 ***5900.10*** *p596*
Welch, Ellen; Vermont, 1867-1967 ***5900.10*** *p462*
Welch, Ellen 72; Vermont, 1899 ***5900.10*** *p96*
Welch, Ellen 75; Vermont, 1892 ***5900.10*** *p410*
Welch, Ellen 98; Vermont, 1901 ***5900.10*** *p116*
Welch, Ellen J.; Vermont, 1857-1896 ***5900.10*** *p44*
Welch, Fanny; Quebec, 1858 ***9196.15*** *p36*
Welch, Francis; New York, New York, n.d. ***1224.2*** *p123*
Welch, Hannah 68; Vermont, 1900 ***5900.10*** *p220*
Welch, Hannah Geary; Vermont, 1840-1916 ***5900.10*** *p127*
Welch, Hanora; Vermont, 1855-1933 ***5900.10*** *p80*
Welch, Henry; Vermont, 1830-1905 ***5900.10*** *p334*
Welch, Henry 93; Vermont, 1907 ***5900.10*** *p96*
Welch, J.; Alabama, 1812-1845 ***1640.10*** *p212*
Welch, J. Y.; Quebec, 1858 ***9196.15*** *p42*
Welch, James; New York, 1840 ***8197.10*** *p202*
Welch, Johanna Leonard; Vermont, 1846-1929 ***5900.10*** *p126*
Welch, John; New York, 1844 ***8197.10*** *p10*
Welch, John; Vermont, 1846-1890 ***5900.10*** *p126*
Welch, John; Vermont, 1926 ***5900.10*** *p436*
Welch, John 31; Virginia, 1773 ***1220.25*** *p29*
Welch, John 35; Ontario, 1871 ***1823.22*** *p168*
Welch, John 60; Vermont, 1882 ***5900.10*** *p220*
Welch, John 82; Vermont, 1890 ***5900.10*** *p410*
Welch, John T.; Vermont, 1840-1915 ***5900.10*** *p95*
Welch, John W.; Vermont, 1858-1925 ***5900.10*** *p70*
Welch, Joseph; Maryland, 1910 ***3259.35*** *p67*
Welch, Joseph; Vermont, 1846-1935 ***5900.10*** *p291*
Welch, Katherine; Vermont, 1850-1923 ***5900.10*** *p125*
Welch, Lawrence; Vermont, 1860-1929 ***5900.10*** *p377*
Welch, Marceline Pare; Vermont, 1864-1923 ***5900.10*** *p291*
Welch, Margaret; Vermont, 1840-1906 ***5900.10*** *p334*
Welch, Margret; Virginia, 1667-1668 ***6212.30*** *p39*
Welch, Mary; Vermont, 1806-1881 ***5900.10*** *p137*
Welch, Mary; Vermont, 1847-1925 ***5900.10*** *p133*
Welch, Mary; Vermont, 1855-1943 ***5900.10*** *p70*
Welch, Mary 30; Vermont, 1879 ***5900.10*** *p98*
Welch, Mary 33; Vermont, 1878 ***5900.10*** *p469*
Welch, Mary 63; Vermont, 1878 ***5900.10*** *p411*
Welch, Mary 70; Ontario, 1871 ***1823.15*** *p276*
Welch, Mary 95; Vermont, 1881 ***5900.10*** *p121*
Welch, Mary A. 20; Vermont, 1874 ***5900.10*** *p143*
Welch, Mary A. McGuire 46; Vermont, 1894 ***5900.10*** *p95*
Welch, Mary Ann; Maryland, 1856 ***1224.3*** *p83*
Welch, Michael; Vermont, 1840-1920 ***5900.10*** *p83*
Welch, Michael 40; Vermont, 1878 ***5900.10*** *p73*
Welch, Nancy 83; Vermont, 1930 ***5900.10*** *p96*
Welch, Nathaniel 32; Virginia, 1774 ***1220.25*** *p38*
Welch, Nora; Vermont, 1842-1910 ***5900.10*** *p489*
Welch, Patrick; Vermont, 1845-1914 ***5900.10*** *p137*
Welch, Richard; New York, 1835 ***8197.10*** *p71*
Welch, Richard; Virginia, 1664 ***6212.30*** *p6*
Welch, Richard 26; Vermont, 1867 ***5900.10*** *p331*
Welch, Richard 71; Vermont, 1858 ***5900.10*** *p343*
Welch, Rose A. Boyle; Vermont, 1836-1913 ***5900.10*** *p592*
Welch, Thomas; Canada, 1756-1760 ***4628.40*** *p46*
Welch, Thomas; Virginia, 1667-1668 ***6212.30*** *p38*
Welch, Thomas M. 30; Vermont, 1885 ***5900.10*** *p410*
Welch, W. P.; Vermont, 1850-1915 ***5900.10*** *p283*
Welch, William; New York, 1807 ***8197.10*** *p53*
Welch, William 17; Maryland, 1775 ***1220.25*** *p101*
Welcher, Henry; Virginia, 1672 ***6212.30*** *p48*
Welchman, Edward; Illinois, 1845 ***1224.3*** *p83*
Welcke, Georg; America, 1744 ***2856.30*** *p489*
With wife & 2 children
Welcker, Georg; America, 1744 ***2856.30*** *p489*
With wife & 2 children
Welcomb, Tho; Virginia, 1665-1666 ***6212.30*** *p23*
Welcome, Philip; Vermont, 1821-1901 ***5900.10*** *p253*
Welcome, Rose; Vermont, 1835-1916 ***5900.10*** *p253*
Weld, Ann; Virginia, 1691 ***6212.30*** *p59*
Weld, George; Virginia, 1664 ***6212.30*** *p12*
Weld, John; Virginia, 1664 ***6212.30*** *p11*
Welde, Jakob; America, 1752 ***2856.30*** *p489*
Welde, Jakob; America, 1760 ***2856.30*** *p489*
With wife
Welde, Jakob; Port uncertain, 1791 ***2856.30*** *p489*
Weldon, Andrew 12 *SEE* Weldon, Ann
Weldon, Andrew 63; Ontario, 1861 ***2896.25*** *p22*
Weldon, Ann 1 *SEE* Weldon, Ann
Weldon, Ann 38; Fort Cumberland, Nova Scotia, 1774 ***1220.25*** *p19*
Child: Andrew 12
Child: Ann 1
Child: Elizabeth 8
Child: Thomas 4
Weldon, Elizabeth 8 *SEE* Weldon, Ann
Weldon, John; New York, 1837 ***8197.10*** *p104*
Weldon, Peter; New York, 1803 ***8197.10*** *p17*
Weldon, Thomas; New York, 1830 ***8197.10*** *p360*
Weldon, Thomas 4 *SEE* Weldon, Ann
Weldtele, Xaver; Port uncertain, 1781 ***2856.30*** *p489*
Welend, James 31; Ontario, 1871 ***1823.15*** *p276*
Welfore, Lewis; Virginia, 1664-1665 ***6212.30*** *p16*
Welizcinski, William; Maryland, 1910 ***3259.35*** *p67*
Welker, Jakob; America, 1768 ***2856.30*** *p489*
Welker, Jakob; America, 1777 ***2856.30*** *p489*
Welker, Johann; America, 1768 ***2856.30*** *p489*
Welkowski, Teoble; Maryland, 1910 ***3259.35*** *p67*
Well, John 62; Ontario, 1871 ***1823.15*** *p276*
Well, Moses 24; Ontario, 1871 ***1823.22*** *p168*
Wellbrook, Robt; Virginia, 1699 ***6212.30*** *p61*
Wellecker, Rudolf; America, 1727 ***2856.30*** *p497*
Weller, Abraham 18; Ontario, 1861 ***2896.25*** *p28*
Weller, Emma 19; Ontario, 1861 ***2896.28*** *p32*
Weller, Francis; Pennsylvania, 1777 ***4629.10*** *p26*
Weller, Francis 26; Philadelphia, 1774 ***1220.25*** *p67*
Weller, William H. 46; Ontario, 1871 ***1823.22*** *p168*
Welleven, Same; Maryland, 1665 ***2524.55*** *p234*
Wellin, Anna Maria; America, 1727 ***2856.30*** *p489*
Welling, Henry F.; New York, 1792-1840 ***8197.10*** *p350*
Welling, John 21; Maryland, 1775 ***1220.25*** *p96*
Wellington, Elizabeth U. 91; Ontario, 1871 ***1823.22*** *p168*
Wellington, Lizzy 14; Ontario, 1871 ***1823.22*** *p169*
Wellington, Neil 49; Ontario, 1871 ***1823.22*** *p169*
Wellington, William 55; Ontario, 1871 ***1823.22*** *p169*
Wellington, William T. 35; Ontario, 1871 ***1823.22*** *p169*
Wellman, Thomas; New York, 1840 ***8197.10*** *p201*
Wellmar, Mrs. Stefan; America, 1744 ***2856.30*** *p489*
With 2 children
Wells, . . .; Maryland, 1678 ***2524.55*** *p234*
Wells, Major; Quebec, 1856 ***9196.15*** *p10*
Wells, Alfred 44; Ontario, 1871 ***1823.22*** *p169*
Wells, Ann *SEE* Wells, Richard
Wells, Annie 10; Ontario, 1861 ***2896.28*** *p46*
Wells, Benjamin *SEE* Wells, Richard
Wells, Charles 46; Ontario, 1871 ***1823.15*** *p276*
Wells, Christopher 26; Ontario, 1861 ***2896.28*** *p22*
Wells, Daniel 20; Maryland, 1774 ***1220.25*** *p64*
Wells, E.; Portland, Maine, 1858 ***9196.15*** *p30*
Wells, Edward; Maryland, 1652 ***2524.55*** *p234*
Wells, Elizabeth *SEE* Wells, Richard
Wells, Elizabeth; Maryland, 1652 ***2524.55*** *p234*
Wells, Elizabeth; Maryland, 1661-1662 ***2524.55*** *p75*
Wells, Elizabeth 68; Ontario, 1871 ***1823.15*** *p276*
Wells, Frances *SEE* Wells, Richard
Wells, Francis; Virginia, 1709 ***1224.2*** *p123*
Wells, George *SEE* Wells, Richard
Wells, George 18; Ontario, 1871 ***1823.15*** *p276*
Wells, H.; Quebec, 1857 ***9196.15*** *p22*
Wells, H.; Quebec, 1858 ***9196.15*** *p45*
Wells, Henry 47; Ontario, 1871 ***1823.22*** *p169*
Wells, Henry 56; Ontario, 1871 ***1823.15*** *p276*
Wells, James; Pennsylvania, 1777 ***4629.10*** *p13*
Wells, Jeffry; Virginia, 1664 ***6212.30*** *p14*
Wells, Jeffry; Virginia, 1665-1666 ***6212.30*** *p24*
Wells, Jno; Virginia, 1663 ***6212.30*** *p4*
Wells, John *SEE* Wells, Richard
Wells, John; Maryland, 1663 ***2524.55*** *p234*
Wells, John; Nashville, Tennessee, 1821-1845 ***1640.10*** *p212*
Wells, John; Pennsylvania, 1777 ***4629.10*** *p22*
Wells, John; Virginia, 1668-1669 ***6212.30*** *p40*
Wells, John 55; Ontario, 1871 ***1823.28*** *p104*
Wells, Joseph; Virginia, 1671-1672 ***6212.30*** *p47*
Wells, Josephine 4; Ontario, 1861 ***2896.28*** *p39*
Wells, Lilian A.; Vermont, 1866-1936 ***5900.10*** *p321*
Wells, Mary *SEE* Wells, Richard
Wells, Michael; Pennsylvania, 1777 ***4629.10*** *p19*
Wells, Paterick 48; Ontario, 1871 ***1823.15*** *p276*
Wells, Patrick; Maryland, 1663 ***2524.55*** *p234*
Wells, Rachel 76; Ontario, 1871 ***1823.22*** *p169*
Wells, Ralph; Maryland, 1674 ***2524.55*** *p234*
Wells, Richard *SEE* Wells, Richard
Wells, Richard; Maryland, 1652-1653 ***2524.55*** *p234*
Wife: Frances
Child: Ann
Child: Mary
Child: Frances
Child: Elizabeth
Child: William
Child: John

Child: Robert
Child: Benjamin
Child: George
Child: Richard
Wells, Richard; Maryland, 1665 ***2524.55*** *p234*
Wells, Richard; Maryland, 1668 ***1224.1*** *p62*
Wells, Robert *SEE* Wells, Richard
Wells, Samuel; Pennsylvania, 1777 ***4629.10*** *p25*
Wells, Tho; Virginia, 1664 ***6212.30*** *p12*
Wells, Tho; Virginia, 1666 ***6212.30*** *p25*
Wells, Thomas 60; Ontario, 1871 ***1823.15*** *p277*
Wells, William *SEE* Wells, Richard
Wells, Zorobabell; Maryland, 1661-1662 ***2524.55*** *p75*
Wellwood, John 59; Ontario, 1871 ***1823.15*** *p277*
Wellwood, John 60; Ontario, 1871 ***1823.22*** *p169*
Wellwood, Joseph 70; Ontario, 1871 ***1823.22*** *p169*
Wellwood, William 62; Ontario, 1871 ***1823.22*** *p169*
Welmore, Catharine 29; Jamaica, 1775 ***1220.25*** *p113*
Welsby, Joseph; Pennsylvania, 1858 ***6058.10*** *p40*
Welsby, Matthew; Pennsylvania, 1858 ***6058.10*** *p40*
Welsch, Johann; Port uncertain, 1793 ***2856.30*** *p489*
Welsch, Mathias; Port uncertain, 1793 ***2856.30*** *p489*
Welsh, Andrew; Maryland, 1682 ***2524.55*** *p234*
Welsh, Anna; Vermont, 1815-1887 ***5900.10*** *p507*
Welsh, Bertha 52; Vermont, 1876 ***5900.10*** *p586*
Welsh, Bridget; Vermont, 1838-1923 ***5900.10*** *p114*
Welsh, Bridget; Vermont, 1855-1926 ***5900.10*** *p119*
Welsh, Bridget 41; Vermont, 1880 ***5900.10*** *p222*
Welsh, C. 33; Ontario, 1861 ***2896.26*** *p14*
Welsh, Catherine; Vermont, n.d. ***5900.10*** *p55*
Welsh, Charlotte; Philadelphia, 1842 ***1224.3*** *p83*
Welsh, Cornelius; Pennsylvania, 1866 ***6058.10*** *p51*
Welsh, Daniel; Nova Scotia, 1745 ***4628.40*** *p44*
Welsh, David 58; Ontario, 1871 ***1823.15*** *p277*
Welsh, Elizabeth; Vermont, 1839-1909 ***5900.10*** *p588*
Welsh, Elizabeth; Vermont, 1839-1909 ***5900.10*** *p592*
Welsh, Elizabeth 79; Ontario, 1871 ***1823.15*** *p277*
Welsh, Ellen C.; Vermont, 1836-1863 ***5900.10*** *p462*
Welsh, Ellen Green 65; Vermont, 1907 ***5900.10*** *p380*
Welsh, J.; Quebec, 1858 ***9196.15*** *p45*
Welsh, J. 34; Ontario, 1861 ***2896.26*** *p14*
Welsh, James; New York, 1824 ***8197.10*** *p293*
Welsh, James; New York, 1828 ***8197.10*** *p294*
Welsh, James; New York, 1840 ***8197.10*** *p201*
Welsh, James; New York, 1840 ***8197.10*** *p203*
Welsh, James; Pennsylvania, 1777 ***4629.10*** *p13*
Welsh, James; Pennsylvania, 1867 ***6058.10*** *p57*
Welsh, James 34; Ontario, 1871 ***1823.28*** *p104*
Welsh, James 38; Ontario, 1871 ***1823.15*** *p277*
Welsh, James 40; Ontario, 1871 ***1823.22*** *p169*
Welsh, James Henry; Montreal, 1893 ***1640.13*** *p132*
Welsh, Jeremiah; New York, 1825 ***8197.10*** *p293*
Welsh, John; Maryland, 1673 ***2524.55*** *p234*
Welsh, John; New York, 1829 ***8197.10*** *p294*
Welsh, John; New York, 1836 ***8197.10*** *p317*
Welsh, John; Nova Scotia, 1745 ***4628.40*** *p44*
Welsh, John; Pennsylvania, 1777 ***4629.10*** *p26*
Welsh, John; Pennsylvania, 1777 ***4629.10*** *p28*
Welsh, John; Virginia, 1667 ***6212.30*** *p36*
Welsh, John 29; Ontario, 1871 ***1823.15*** *p277*
Welsh, John 74; Ontario, 1871 ***1823.15*** *p277*
Welsh, John Miller; Massachusetts, 1893 ***1640.13*** *p132*
Welsh, Julian; Maryland, 1668 ***2524.55*** *p234*
Welsh, Juliana; Maryland, 1671 ***2524.55*** *p234*
Welsh, Katharin; Maryland, 1682 ***2524.55*** *p234*
Welsh, Martin; Pennsylvania, 1864 ***6058.10*** *p69*
Welsh, Mary 82; Ontario, 1871 ***1823.15*** *p277*
Welsh, Mary Owens; Vermont, 1836-1904 ***5900.10*** *p423*
Welsh, Michael; Vermont, 1834-1905 ***5900.10*** *p423*
Welsh, Michael 35; Ontario, 1871 ***1823.28*** *p104*
Welsh, Morris; Maryland, 1671 ***2524.55*** *p234*
Welsh, Patrick; New York, 1838 ***8197.10*** *p151*
Welsh, Patrick 61; Vermont, 1877 ***5900.10*** *p586*
Welsh, Richard; New York, 1837 ***8197.10*** *p103*
Welsh, Richard 40; Ontario, 1871 ***1823.22*** *p169*
Welsh, Richard 58; Ontario, 1871 ***1823.15*** *p277*
Welsh, Robert; New York, 1836-1840 ***8197.10*** *p300*
Welsh, Robert 38; Ontario, 1871 ***1823.28*** *p104*
Welsh, Samuel; Pennsylvania, 1809 ***6058.10*** *p3*
Welsh, T. L. 6; Ontario, 1861 ***2896.26*** *p14*
Welsh, Terrence; New York, 1837 ***8197.10*** *p374*
Welsh, Thomas; New York, 1838 ***8197.10*** *p151*
Welsh, Thomas; Pennsylvania, 1864 ***6058.10*** *p63*
Welsh, Thomas 32; Ontario, 1871 ***1823.15*** *p277*
Welsh, Thomas 37; Ontario, 1871 ***1823.22*** *p169*
Welsh, Thomas 40; Ontario, 1871 ***1823.15*** *p277*
Welsh, Thomas 41; Ontario, 1871 ***1823.22*** *p169*
Welsh, Thomas 64; Ontario, 1871 ***1823.15*** *p277*
Welsh, William; New Jersey, 1775-1781 ***4628.40*** *p69*
Welsh, William; New York, 1834 ***8197.10*** *p315*
Welsh, William 30; Maryland, 1775 ***1220.25*** *p112*
Welsh, William 35; Ontario, 1871 ***1823.15*** *p277*
Welsh, William 48; Ontario, 1871 ***1823.28*** *p104*
Welshman, Robert; New York, 1803 ***8197.10*** *p17*
Welt, George; Maryland, 1657 ***2524.55*** *p234*
Welt, George; Maryland, 1668 ***2524.55*** *p234*
Welt, James; Maryland, 1655 ***2524.55*** *p234*
Weltherin, Anna Maria; Port uncertain, 1760 ***2856.30*** *p489*
Welti, Benedict; New York, 1838 ***8197.10*** *p152*
Weltin, Johann; Port uncertain, 1765 ***2856.30*** *p489*
Welton, C. 50; Ontario, 1861 ***2896.26*** *p12*
Welton, Charles 35; Ontario, 1871 ***1823.28*** *p104*
Welton, E. 16; Ontario, 1861 ***2896.26*** *p12*
Welton, E. 18; Ontario, 1861 ***2896.26*** *p12*
Welton, J. 13; Ontario, 1861 ***2896.26*** *p12*
Welton, J. 51; Ontario, 1861 ***2896.26*** *p12*
Welton, Levi 66; Ontario, 1871 ***1823.22*** *p169*
Welton, M. A. 15; Ontario, 1861 ***2896.26*** *p12*
Welts, Robert *SEE* Welts, Robert
Welts, Robert; Maryland, 1680 ***2524.55*** *p234*
Wife: Ruth
Son: William
Son: Robert
Welts, Ruth *SEE* Welts, Robert
Welts, William *SEE* Welts, Robert
Welty, Nicholas; New York, 1838 ***8197.10*** *p152*
Weltzenberger, Simon; Port uncertain, 1742 ***2856.30*** *p489*
Welwood, Thomas; New York, 1840 ***8197.10*** *p296*
Welz, Michael; America, 1738 ***2856.30*** *p489*
Welzant, Charles W.; Maryland, 1910 ***3259.35*** *p67*
Wemyss, James; Georgia, 1699 ***1640.13*** *p132*
Wemyss, John; Georgia, 1698 ***1640.13*** *p132*
Wemyss, Walter; Savannah, Georgia, 1804 ***1640.10*** *p212*
Wenam, Ailse; Maryland, 1668 ***2524.55*** *p235*
Wenckh, Michael; Port uncertain, 1742 ***2856.30*** *p489*
Wenckh, Michael; Port uncertain, 1754 ***2856.30*** *p489*
Wend, John 32; Ontario, 1871 ***1823.15*** *p277*
Wendecker, Nikolaus; Port uncertain, 1785 ***2856.30*** *p489*
Wendel, Catharina; Port uncertain, 1791 ***2856.30*** *p489*
Wendel, Johann Peter; Port uncertain, 1738 ***2856.30*** *p489*
Wendel, Mathias; Port uncertain, 1785 ***2856.30*** *p489*
Wendel, Michael; Port uncertain, 1764 ***2856.30*** *p489*
Wendel, Nikolaus; Port uncertain, 1778 ***2856.30*** *p489*
Wendelin, Catharina; Port uncertain, 1753 ***2856.30*** *p489*
Wendelin, Catharina; Port uncertain, 1791 ***2856.30*** *p489*
Wendelin, Christof; Port uncertain, 1749 ***2856.30*** *p489*
Wendelinger, Christina; Port uncertain, 1732 ***2856.30*** *p490*
Wendell, John; New York, 1840 ***8197.10*** *p201*
Wendelus, Jan; Maryland, 1910 ***3259.35*** *p67*
Wendl, Niklas; Port uncertain, 1785 ***2856.30*** *p490*
Wendlin, Eva; Port uncertain, 1779 ***2856.30*** *p490*
Wendlin, Johann Leonard; Port uncertain, 1751 ***2856.30*** *p490*
Wendling, Anna Catharina; Port uncertain, 1754 ***2856.30*** *p490*
Wendling, Johann; Port uncertain, 1754 ***2856.30*** *p490*
Wendling, Johann Michael; Port uncertain, 1741 ***2856.30*** *p490*
Wendling, Johann Philipp; Port uncertain, 1760 ***2856.30*** *p490*
Wendling, Johann Simon; Port uncertain, 1751 ***2856.30*** *p490*
Wendlinger, Christof; Port uncertain, 1784 ***2856.30*** *p490*
Wendlinger, Marianna; Port uncertain, 1748 ***2856.30*** *p490*
Wenedgski, Peter; Maryland, 1910 ***3259.35*** *p67*
Weneski, Ludwig; Maryland, 1910 ***3259.35*** *p67*
Wengen, Ludwig; Port uncertain, 1776 ***2856.30*** *p490*
Wengenroth, Johann Friedric; Port uncertain, 1759 ***2856.30*** *p490*
Wengert, Cath.; America, 1743 ***2856.30*** *p32*
Wengert, Catharina; America, 1743 ***2856.30*** *p490*
With husband
Wengielska, Rozalia; Maryland, 1910 ***3259.35*** *p67*
Wengler, Mathis; Port uncertain, 1700 ***2856.30*** *p478*
Wengler, Mathis; Port uncertain, 1732 ***2856.30*** *p478*
Wenham, Ann 15; Ontario, 1861 ***2896.27*** *p51*
Wenham, Elen 37; Ontario, 1861 ***2896.27*** *p51*
Wenham, George W. 8; Ontario, 1861 ***2896.27*** *p51*
Wenham, Tho; Virginia, 1664 ***6212.30*** *p11*
Wenham, Thomas Smith; New York, 1833 ***8197.10*** *p294*
Wenham, Thomas Smith; New York, 1837 ***8197.10*** *p103*
Wenham, William; Maryland, 1659 ***2524.55*** *p235*
Wenham, William 55; Ontario, 1861 ***2896.27*** *p51*
Wenick, John 29; British Columbia, 1910 ***9196.1*** *p31*
Wenick, John 29; Seattle, 1910 ***9196.1*** *p31*
Wenk, Jacob; Philadelphia, 1846 ***6058.10*** *p20*
Wenrer, Catharina; Port uncertain, 1737 ***2856.30*** *p490*
Wenserot, Johann Wendel; America, 1749 ***2856.30*** *p479*
Wenss, Michael; Port uncertain, 1783 ***2856.30*** *p490*
With wife son & daughter
Went, Christian; Maryland, 1669 ***2524.55*** *p170*
Went, Christopher; New York, 1796 ***8197.10*** *p7*
Wentherhead, Robert 26; Virginia, 1774 ***1220.25*** *p87*
Wentworth, Ella 43; Kansas, 1910 ***9079.10*** *p5*
Wentworth, John; Portsmouth, New Hampshire, n.d. ***1224.3*** *p84*
Wentworth, William S.; New York, 1840 ***8197.10*** *p204*
Wentz, Georg; Port uncertain, 1747 ***2856.30*** *p490*
Wentz, Mandus; America, 1750 ***2856.30*** *p490*
Wentz, Martin; America, 1750 ***2856.30*** *p490*
With wife
Wentz, Martin; Port uncertain, 1750 ***2856.30*** *p490*
With wife
Wentzel, Peter; New York, 1840 ***8197.10*** *p202*
Wentzer, Georg; Port uncertain, 1747 ***2856.30*** *p490*
Wenz, Elisabeth; Port uncertain, 1758 ***2856.30*** *p491*
Wenz, Jakob; Port uncertain, 1764 ***2856.30*** *p490*
Wenz, Johann Jakob; Port uncertain, 1759 ***2856.30*** *p490*
Wenz, Johann Melchior; Port uncertain, 1756 ***2856.30*** *p490*
Wenz, Lorenz; Port uncertain, 1765 ***2856.30*** *p490*
Wenz, Maria Catharina; Port uncertain, 1739 ***2856.30*** *p490*
Wenz, Matthaus; Port uncertain, 1761 ***2856.30*** *p491*
Wenz, Matthaus; Port uncertain, 1764 ***2856.30*** *p491*
Wenzel, Mrs. Konrad; Port uncertain, 1731 ***2856.30*** *p491*
With children
Werbald, Juliana Philipp; America, 1784 ***2856.30*** *p491*
Werbald, Michael; America, 1784 ***2856.30*** *p491*
Werckhin, Anna Elisabeth; Port uncertain, 1758 ***2856.30*** *p491*
Werczynski, Francis; Maryland, 1910 ***3259.35*** *p67*
Werden, A. 6; Ontario, 1861 ***2896.26*** *p1*
Werden, Asa 82; Ontario, 1861 ***2896.26*** *p1*
Werden, C. 4; Ontario, 1861 ***2896.26*** *p10*
Werden, Catherine 57; Ontario, 1861 ***2896.27*** *p32*
Werden, E. A. 28; Ontario, 1861 ***2896.26*** *p1*
Werden, Elias 10; Ontario, 1861 ***2896.27*** *p28*
Werden, Elly 25; Ontario, 1861 ***2896.26*** *p1*
Werden, Emma 8; Ontario, 1861 ***2896.27*** *p28*
Werden, Emma C. 20; Ontario, 1861 ***2896.27*** *p32*
Werden, Eugene 2; Ontario, 1861 ***2896.26*** *p1*
Werden, Francis C. 14; Ontario, 1861 ***2896.27*** *p32*
Werden, G. A. 16; Ontario, 1861 ***2896.26*** *p4*
Werden, H. 6; Ontario, 1861 ***2896.26*** *p10*
Werden, Hanover 12; Ontario, 1861 ***2896.27*** *p28*
Werden, L. A. 19; Ontario, 1861 ***2896.26*** *p4*
Werden, Louisa 16; Ontario, 1861 ***2896.27*** *p28*
Werden, M. G. 25; Ontario, 1861 ***2896.27*** *p32*
Werden, Montalbert B. 19; Ontario, 1861 ***2896.27*** *p38*
Werden, Philip 18; Ontario, 1861 ***2896.27*** *p28*
Werden, Phoebe Ann 23; Ontario, 1861 ***2896.27*** *p32*
Werden, Rachel; Ontario, 1861 ***2896.27*** *p28*
Werden, Robert 4; Ontario, 1861 ***2896.26*** *p1*
Werden, Rudolphus 14; Ontario, 1861 ***2896.27*** *p38*
Werden, S. 31; Ontario, 1861 ***2896.26*** *p10*
Werden, Sully 14; Ontario, 1861 ***2896.27*** *p28*
Werden, Tallman 4; Ontario, 1861 ***2896.27*** *p28*
Werden, Theresa 16; Ontario, 1861 ***2896.27*** *p53*
Werden, Theressa J. 17; Ontario, 1861 ***2896.27*** *p38*
Werden, W. A. 26; Ontario, 1861 ***2896.27*** *p32*
Werden, Walter 6; Ontario, 1861 ***2896.27*** *p28*
Werden, Wealthy Ann 43; Ontario, 1861 ***2896.27*** *p38*
Werden, Wilford M. 10; Ontario, 1861 ***2896.27*** *p32*
Werden, William 43; Ontario, 1861 ***2896.26*** *p4*
Werdon, Laney 27; Ontario, 1861 ***2896.27*** *p4*
Werdon, Pheby 3; Ontario, 1861 ***2896.27*** *p4*
Werdowski, Thomas; Maryland, 1910 ***3259.35*** *p67*
Werges, Benedict; Port uncertain, 1764 ***2856.30*** *p491*
With wife son & 4 daughters
Werieski, Theodora; Maryland, 1910 ***3259.35*** *p67*
Werle, Johann Henrich; Port uncertain, 1769 ***2856.30*** *p491*
Werle, Niklas; Port uncertain, 1774 ***2856.30*** *p491*
Werlowski, Adam; Maryland, 1910 ***3259.35*** *p67*
Wern, Jakob; America, 1764 ***2856.30*** *p491*
Werner, Anna Catharina; America, 1744 ***2856.30*** *p492*
With 3 children
Werner, Clara 18; Kansas, 1909-1910 ***9079.10*** *p10*
Werner, Elisabeth; Port uncertain, 1729 ***2856.30*** *p491*
Werner, Georg; Port uncertain, 1771 ***2856.30*** *p491*
Werner, George 30; Kansas, 1909-1910 ***9079.10*** *p10*
Werner, Helena; Maryland, 1910 ***3259.35*** *p67*
Werner, Henry 43; Ontario, 1871 ***1823.15*** *p277*
Werner, Jacob; Port uncertain, 1760 ***2856.30*** *p491*
Werner, Jacob; Port uncertain, 1765 ***2856.30*** *p491*
With 2 children
Werner, Johann; America, 1752 ***2856.30*** *p491*
With wife & children
Werner, Johann; America, 1752 ***2856.30*** *p492*
With wife & 7 children
Werner, Johann; Port uncertain, 1726 ***2856.30*** *p491*
Werner, Johann Georg; America, 1752 ***2856.30*** *p491*
Werner, Louisa; America, 1750 ***2856.30*** *p491*
Werner, Ludwig; America, 1751 ***2856.30*** *p491*

Werner, Margarete; Port uncertain, 1779 ***2856.30*** *p491*
Werner, Martin; Port uncertain, 1686 ***2856.30*** *p491*
Werner, Martin; Port uncertain, 1732 ***2856.30*** *p491*
Werner, Philip; New York, 1837 ***8197.10*** *p103*
Werner, Philipp; Port uncertain, 1741 ***2856.30*** *p491*
Werner, Sebastian; Port uncertain, 1756 ***2856.30*** *p491*
Werner, Theobald; America, 1744 ***2856.30*** *p491*
Werner, Viktor; Port uncertain, 1738 ***2856.30*** *p491*
Werner, Wilhelm; America, 1785 ***2856.30*** *p492*
Werner, Wilhelm; Port uncertain, 1785 ***2856.30*** *p491*
Werner, Wilhelm; Port uncertain, 1786 ***2856.30*** *p491*
Wernersbach, Heinrich; America, 1763 ***2856.30*** *p492*
With wife & 3 daughters
Wernet, Michael; Port uncertain, 1775 ***2856.30*** *p492*
Wernsin, Mituna; Port uncertain, 1769 ***2856.30*** *p492*
Werrmann, Johann; Port uncertain, 1783 ***2856.30*** *p492*
Werry, Thomas 54; Ontario, 1871 ***1823.15*** *p277*
Werry, William 32; Ontario, 1871 ***1823.15*** *p277*
Wersin, Marianna; Port uncertain, 1769 ***2856.30*** *p492*
Wert, Frederick 27; Ontario, 1871 ***1823.15*** *p277*
Wert, Mary 72; Ontario, 1871 ***1823.15*** *p277*
Wert, Philip; Pennsylvania, 1777 ***4629.10*** *p7*
Wertes, Christian; Maryland, 1665 ***2524.55*** *p234*
Werth, John Jacob; New York, 1796 ***8197.10*** *p7*
Wesby, Jacob; Pennsylvania, 1786 ***4629.10*** *p50*
Weselek, Frank; Maryland, 1910 ***3259.35*** *p67*
Weselon, Henry 42; Ontario, 1871 ***1823.15*** *p277*
Wesemann, Henry; New York, 1840 ***8197.10*** *p201*
Wesgen, Friedlin; Port uncertain, 1749 ***2856.30*** *p492*
Weshett, Margaret 28; Quebec, 1774 ***1220.25*** *p75*
Wesils, Phebe 73; Ontario, 1861 ***2896.25*** *p6*
Wesley, Ann 44 *SEE* Wesley, Mary
Wesley, Charles 25; Philadelphia, 1774 ***1220.25*** *p88*
Wesley, Elizabeth 13; Philadelphia, 1774 ***1220.25*** *p88*
Wesley, James W. 5; Ontario, 1861 ***2896.27*** *p51*
Wesley, Joseph 15; Philadelphia, 1774 ***1220.25*** *p88*
Wesley, Mary 22; Philadelphia, 1774 ***1220.25*** *p88*
Mother: Ann 44
Weslowski, Bronslaw; Maryland, 1910 ***3259.35*** *p67*
Wesman, Maryanna; Maryland, 1910 ***3259.35*** *p67*
Wesolek, Joseph W.; Maryland, 1910 ***3259.35*** *p67*
Weson, Thomas; Maryland, 1640 ***2524.55*** *p235*
Wessau, Konrad; New York, 1840 ***8197.10*** *p321*
Wessels, Hannah 24; Ontario, 1861 ***2896.27*** *p67*
Wessels, John 22; Ontario, 1861 ***2896.25*** *p32*
Wessels, Thomas 21; Ontario, 1861 ***2896.25*** *p70*
Wessenbacher, Michael; America, 1769 ***2856.30*** *p492*
With 6 children
Wessenburg, William 38; Ontario, 1871 ***1823.15*** *p277*
Wessle, Anton; Port uncertain, 1769 ***2856.30*** *p492*
Wessner, Salome; America, 1771 ***2856.30*** *p492*
West, Mr.; Quebec, 1857 ***9196.15*** *p20*
West, Bartholomew; New York, 1822 ***8197.10*** *p293*
West, Beal; New York, 1838 ***8197.10*** *p152*
West, Charles; Pennsylvania, 1777 ***4629.10*** *p9*
West, Charles; Virginia, 1671-1672 ***6212.30*** *p47*
West, Charles 19; Ontario, 1871 ***1823.28*** *p104*
West, Edward; Maryland, 1656 ***2524.55*** *p235*
West, Edward; Maryland, 1665 ***2524.55*** *p235*
West, Edward; Maryland, 1676 ***2524.55*** *p235*
West, Eliza.; Maryland, 1682 ***2524.55*** *p235*
West, Eliza 40; Ontario, 1871 ***1823.15*** *p277*
West, Elizabeth *SEE* West, William
West, Francis; Virginia, 1634 ***1224.1*** *p62*
West, George 26; Philadelphia, 1774 ***1220.25*** *p67*
West, Hannah; Pennsylvania, 1819 ***1224.3*** *p84*
West, Henry; Virginia, 1670 ***1224.1*** *p50*
West, James; New York, 1821 ***8197.10*** *p292*
West, James; New York, New York, 1817 ***8197.10*** *p335*
West, James; Virginia, 1665 ***6212.30*** *p22*
West, James 59; Ontario, 1871 ***1823.22*** *p169*
West, John; Maryland, 1649 ***2524.55*** *p235*
West, John; Maryland, 1653 ***2524.55*** *p235*
West, John; Maryland, 1668 ***2524.55*** *p235*
West, John; Maryland, 1682 ***2524.55*** *p235*
West, John; New York, 1691 ***1224.1*** *p62*
West, John; Pennsylvania, 1838 ***6058.10*** *p15*
West, John 35; Maryland, 1774 ***1220.25*** *p64*
West, Joseph; Maryland, 1681 ***2524.55*** *p235*
West, Joseph; Pennsylvania, 1777 ***4629.10*** *p19*
West, Joseph 21; Maryland, 1774 ***1220.25*** *p53*
West, Joseph 44; Maryland, 1774 ***1220.25*** *p78*
West, Joseph 56; Ontario, 1871 ***1823.28*** *p104*
West, Mary *SEE* West, William
West, Nath; Virginia, 1665-1666 ***6212.30*** *p22*
West, Nathaniel; Virginia, 1666-1667 ***6212.30*** *p32*
West, Peter; Maryland, 1668 ***2524.55*** *p235*
West, Ralph; Maryland, 1654 ***2524.55*** *p235*
West, Richard; Virginia, 1664 ***6212.30*** *p8*
West, Richard 66; Ontario, 1871 ***1823.15*** *p277*
West, Robert 45; Ontario, 1871 ***1823.15*** *p277*
West, Silas; Nantucket, Massachusetts, n.d. ***1224.3*** *p84*
West, Smith 45; Ontario, 1861 ***2896.27*** *p18*
West, Thomas; New York, 1794 ***8197.10*** *p3*
West, Thomas; Pennsylvania, 1779 ***4629.10*** *p40*
West, Thomas 45; Ontario, 1871 ***1823.22*** *p169*
West, Thomas 51; Ontario, 1871 ***1823.28*** *p104*
West, William *SEE* West, William
West, William; Maryland, 1672 ***2524.55*** *p235*
Wife: Elizabeth
Relative: William
Relative: Mary
West, William; Pennsylvania, 1786 ***4629.10*** *p51*
West, William; Virginia, 1672 ***6212.30*** *p48*
West, William; Virginia, 1687 ***1224.1*** *p62*
West, William; Died enroute, 1616 ***1224.1*** *p62*
West, William 25; Philadelphia, 1775 ***1220.25*** *p10*
West, William 33; Ontario, 1871 ***1823.22*** *p169*
West, William 59; Ontario, 1871 ***1823.22*** *p169*
West, William, Jr.; Pennsylvania, 1777 ***4629.10*** *p28*
West, William B.; New York, 1832 ***8197.10*** *p294*
Westa, William; New York, 1837 ***8197.10*** *p103*
Westacott, George 50; Ontario, 1871 ***1823.15*** *p277*
Westall, William; New York, 1837 ***8197.10*** *p103*
Westbe, Edward; Maryland, 1640 ***2524.55*** *p235*
Westbery, Edward; Maryland, 1640 ***2524.55*** *p235*
Westbrooke, Geo; Virginia, 1664 ***6212.30*** *p7*
Westby, Miss; Quebec, 1858 ***9196.15*** *p44*
Westcoate, Elizabeth; Virginia, 1660 ***1224.1*** *p5*
Westcomb, John; Maryland, 1667 ***2524.55*** *p235*
Westcome, John; Maryland, 1665 ***2524.55*** *p235*
Westcott, Ernest August Steven; New York, 1840 ***8197.10*** *p202*
Westcott, George 50; Ontario, 1871 ***1823.15*** *p277*
Westcott, George 54; Ontario, 1871 ***1823.15*** *p277*
Westcott, Henry 48; Ontario, 1871 ***1823.15*** *p277*
Westcott, John; Pennsylvania, 1777 ***4629.10*** *p12*
Westcott, John 16; Ontario, 1871 ***1823.28*** *p104*
Westcott, John 44; Ontario, 1871 ***1823.28*** *p104*
Westcott, John 50; Ontario, 1871 ***1823.15*** *p277*
Westcott, Mary Anne 2; Ontario, 1871 ***1823.28*** *p104*
Westcott, William 31; Ontario, 1871 ***1823.15*** *p277*
Westcott, William 39; Ontario, 1871 ***1823.15*** *p277*
Westenberger, Adam; Port uncertain, 1791 ***2856.30*** *p492*
Westenberger, Johann Christof; America, 1744 ***2856.30*** *p492*
Westenfelder, Helena; Port uncertain, 1761 ***2856.30*** *p492*
Westenhofer, Thomas; Port uncertain, 1790 ***2856.30*** *p492*
Westenwick, . . . 36; Alaska, 1913 ***9196.1*** *p39*
Westenwick, . . . 36; Whitehorse, Yukon, 1913 ***9196.1*** *p39*
Westerband, Abraham; Maryland, 1662 ***2524.55*** *p235*
Westerfelt, Ira 18; Ontario, 1861 ***2896.25*** *p33*
Westerfelt, James 15; Ontario, 1861 ***2896.25*** *p33*
Westerfelt, Margaret 12; Ontario, 1861 ***2896.25*** *p33*
Westerfelt, Mary 44; Ontario, 1861 ***2896.25*** *p33*
Westerfelt, Pete 20; Ontario, 1861 ***2896.25*** *p38*
Westerfelt, W. J. 9; Ontario, 1861 ***2896.25*** *p33*
Westerhead, Mr.; Quebec, 1856 ***9196.15*** *p7*
Westerhead, Mrs.; Quebec, 1856 ***9196.15*** *p7*
Westerich, Johann; Port uncertain, 1783 ***2856.30*** *p492*
Westerich, Peter; Port uncertain, 1783 ***2856.30*** *p492*
Westerman, James; New York, 1832 ***8197.10*** *p294*
Westerman, Joseph; New York, 1832 ***8197.10*** *p294*
Westermann, Augustin; Port uncertain, 1750 ***2856.30*** *p492*
With wife & 2 children
Westermann, Jacob; Port uncertain, 1738 ***2856.30*** *p492*
Westermann, Margarete; Port uncertain, 1764 ***2856.30*** *p492*
Western, Ann; New York, 1803 ***8197.10*** *p17*
Western, James 35; Ontario, 1871 ***1823.22*** *p169*
Western, Thomas 50; Ontario, 1871 ***1823.22*** *p169*
Westeway, Samuel 29; Ontario, 1871 ***1823.15*** *p277*
Westfall, Catherine 21; Ontario, 1861 ***2896.25*** *p23*
Westfall, Colina 72; Ontario, 1871 ***1823.15*** *p277*
Westfall, Diederich; New York, 1840 ***8197.10*** *p203*
Westfall, Frederick 36; Ontario, 1871 ***1823.15*** *p277*
Westfall, Frederick 76; Ontario, 1871 ***1823.15*** *p277*
Westgate, James; Virginia, 1663 ***6212.30*** *p1*
Westhoffer, Valentin; America, 1731 ***2856.30*** *p492*
Westhorp, Richard; New York, 1828 ***8197.10*** *p294*
Westhrope, John; Virginia, 1656 ***1224.1*** *p62*
Westill, George *SEE* Westill, George
Westill, George; Maryland, 1659 ***2524.55*** *p235*
Son: George
Westington, Constantine 51; Ontario, 1871 ***1823.22*** *p169*
Westington, William 58; Ontario, 1871 ***1823.22*** *p169*
Westlake, Edward; Maryland, 1694 ***1224.1*** *p62*
Westlake, Edward 28; Ontario, 1871 ***1823.15*** *p277*
Westlake, John *SEE* Westlake, John
Westlake, John; Maryland, 1664 ***2524.55*** *p235*
Wife: Magdalen
Son-In-Law: John
Westlake, John 50; Ontario, 1871 ***1823.22*** *p169*
Westlake, Magdalen *SEE* Westlake, John
Westlake, Mathew 67; Ontario, 1871 ***1823.15*** *p277*
Westlake, Richard; New York, 1838 ***8197.10*** *p152*
Westlake, William 28; Maryland, 1775 ***1220.25*** *p97*
Westlake, William 37; Ontario, 1871 ***1823.15*** *p278*
Westland, David Douglas; Mexico, 1900 ***1640.13*** *p132*
Westland, Henry 20; Ontario, 1871 ***1823.15*** *p278*
Westland, Nathaniel; West New Jersey, 1710 ***1224.2*** *p123*
Westley, Ambrose; Charles Town, South Carolina, 1763 ***1224.2*** *p123*
Westley, Henry J.; New York, 1840 ***8197.10*** *p296*
Westley, William 22; Maryland, 1774 ***1220.25*** *p37*
Westlocke, John *SEE* Westlocke, John
Westlocke, John; Maryland, 1664 ***2524.55*** *p235*
Wife: Magdalen
Son-In-Law: John
Westlocke, Magdalen *SEE* Westlocke, John
Westloke, John *SEE* Westloke, John
Westloke, John; Maryland, 1664 ***2524.55*** *p235*
Wife: Magdalen
Son-In-Law: John
Westloke, Magdalen *SEE* Westloke, John
Westly, Edw; Virginia, 1664 ***6212.30*** *p10*
Westmiller, Hermen 56; Ontario, 1871 ***1823.28*** *p104*
Westome, John; Maryland, 1665 ***2524.55*** *p235*
Weston, Mr.; Quebec, 1856 ***9196.15*** *p10*
Weston, Edward; Maryland, 1665 ***2524.55*** *p235*
Weston, Francis; Virginia, 1664 ***6212.30*** *p7*
Weston, Francis Marion; South Carolina, 1855 ***1224.3*** *p84*
Weston, Job; New York, 1840 ***8197.10*** *p384*
Weston, John; Maryland, 1675 ***2524.55*** *p235*
Weston, Lucy; Vermont, 1851-1927 ***5900.10*** *p224*
Weston, Mary 71; Vermont, 1884 ***5900.10*** *p237*
Weston, Mildred; South Carolina, 1825 ***1224.3*** *p84*
Weston, Thomas; Maryland, 1640 ***2524.55*** *p235*
Weston, Thomas; Maryland, 1666 ***2524.55*** *p235*
Weston, Walter 27; Alaska, 1914 ***9196.1*** *p24*
Westoras, James; Maryland, 1658 ***2524.55*** *p235*
Westott, Ema 14; Ontario, 1871 ***1823.28*** *p104*
Westover, Betsey; Vermont, 1841-1930 ***5900.10*** *p520*
Westover, Bridget Cowan; Vermont, 1846-1920 ***5900.10*** *p600*
Westphal, Peter 24; Virginia, 1773 ***1220.25*** *p29*
Westra, Michael; Maryland, 1681 ***2524.55*** *p235*
Westroff, Mr.; Quebec, 1857 ***9196.15*** *p27*
Westrop, Philip; New York, 1837 ***8197.10*** *p374*
Westrope, Elizabeth; Maryland, 1668 ***2524.55*** *p160*
Westrope, Susanna; Virginia, 1690-1691 ***6212.30*** *p59*
Westwater, John; New York, 1837 ***8197.10*** *p374*
Weszka, Adam; Maryland, 1910 ***3259.35*** *p67*
Wesznewsky, Antoni; Maryland, 1910 ***3259.35*** *p67*
Wetbridge, Grace; Maryland, 1653 ***2524.55*** *p235*
Wetheral, Henry 40; Virginia, 1775 ***1220.25*** *p95*
Wetheral, Thomas 30; Norfolk, Virginia, 1774 ***1220.25*** *p20*
Wetherald, James; Philadelphia, 1791-1792 ***4629.10*** *p65*
Wethered, Henry; Boston, 1763 ***1224.2*** *p123*
Wetherel, Charles; New York, 1827 ***8197.10*** *p343*
Wetherel, John 15; Philadelphia, 1774 ***1220.25*** *p80*
Wetherell, S. 31; Virginia, 1773 ***1220.25*** *p28*
Wetherell, Thomas; Maryland, 1648 ***2524.55*** *p236*
Wetherer, Gabrell; Maryland, 1672 ***2524.55*** *p236*
Wetherhead, Thomas; Maryland, 1677 ***2524.55*** *p236*
Wetherill, Thomas; Pennsylvania, 1786 ***4629.10*** *p50*
Wetherly, James; Maryland, 1670 ***2524.55*** *p236*
Wetherspoon, William 26; Ontario, 1871 ***1823.15*** *p278*
Wetherup, Nancy 80; Vermont, 1874 ***5900.10*** *p71*
Wetherup, William 70; Vermont, 1881 ***5900.10*** *p71*
Wethoffer, Nicholas 26; Ontario, 1871 ***1823.28*** *p104*
Wetmore, Margaret; Ohio, 1885 ***1640.13*** *p132*
Wetmore, Mary Malone 47; Vermont, 1895 ***5900.10*** *p381*
Wetsch, Jakob; Port uncertain, 1770 ***2856.30*** *p492*
Wetter, Therese; Port uncertain, 1765 ***2856.30*** *p492*
Wetterer, Christina; Port uncertain, 1768 ***2856.30*** *p492*
Wetterer, Philipp; Port uncertain, 1768 ***2856.30*** *p492*
Wetterhan, Johann; Port uncertain, 1750 ***2856.30*** *p492*
Wetterich, Paul; Port uncertain, 1799 ***2856.30*** *p492*
Wettle, Johann Jacob; Port uncertain, 1756 ***2856.30*** *p492*
Wetton, Charles; New York, 1844 ***8197.10*** *p10*
Wetz, Daniel; New York, 1838 ***8197.10*** *p152*
Wetzel, Henry 26; Ontario, 1871 ***1823.15*** *p278*
Wetzel, Johann Adam; America, 1750 ***2856.30*** *p493*
With wife & children
Wetzel, Josef; Port uncertain, 1733 ***2856.30*** *p492*
Wetzel, Josef; Port uncertain, 1758 ***2856.30*** *p492*
Wetzel, Ludwig Daniel; New York, 1817 ***8197.10*** *p291*
Wetzel, Peter; Port uncertain, 1804 ***2856.30*** *p492*
Wetzstein, Andreas; America, 1751 ***2856.30*** *p493*
With wife & 2 children

Whelan, Thos 45; Ontario, 1871 ***1823.28*** *p104*
Whelan, Thos 73; Ontario, 1871 ***1823.28*** *p104*
Whelan, William H.; Vermont, 1850-1888 ***5900.10*** *p109*
Wheldon, Thersea 40; Ontario, 1871 ***1823.15*** *p278*
Wheling, E. E. 10; Ontario, 1861 ***2896.26*** *p2*
Whenham, James 26; Ontario, 1871 ***1823.15*** *p278*
Wheret, John Gamlin; New York, 1839 ***8197.10*** *p135*
Wherrett, Samuel 25; Maryland, 1774 ***1220.25*** *p78*
Wherrott, William; Maryland, 1675 ***2524.55*** *p236*
Whestle, James; Maryland, 1649 ***2524.55*** *p236*
Whetham, John 40; New York, 1775 ***1220.25*** *p123*
Whettum, Ja; Virginia, 1663 ***6212.30*** *p4*
Whey, Henry; Georgia, 1740 ***1640.10*** *p212*
Wheyley, Katherin; Virginia, 1671-1672 ***6212.30*** *p45*
Whicford, James 62; Ontario, 1871 ***1823.15*** *p278*
Whichead, James 50; Ontario, 1871 ***1823.22*** *p170*
Whielock, Robert 25; Philadelphia, 1774 ***1220.25*** *p67*
Whiett, Mary; Maryland, 1678 ***2524.55*** *p247*
Whight, Rich; Virginia, 1664 ***6212.30*** *p5*
Whilachin, Michael 37; Ontario, 1871 ***1823.28*** *p104*
Whilhelme, Christian; Virginia, 1630 ***1224.1*** *p63*
Whimsett, Edward 36; Ontario, 1871 ***1823.22*** *p170*
Whimsett, George 43; Ontario, 1871 ***1823.22*** *p170*
Whinfell, John; Maryland, 1658 ***2524.55*** *p237*
With 3 children
Whinfield, John; Maryland, 1658 ***2524.55*** *p237*
With 3 children
Whingle, Nicholas 45; Ontario, 1871 ***1823.28*** *p104*
Whingtown, Charlote 20; Ontario, 1871 ***1823.15*** *p278*
Whinley, Thomas; Maryland, 1670 ***2524.55*** *p237*
Whinley, Thomas; Maryland, 1673 ***2524.55*** *p237*
Whinyeard, Thomas; Maryland, 1661 ***2524.55*** *p237*
Whiram, Elizabeth 65; Ontario, 1871 ***1823.15*** *p278*
Whisker, Robert; Maryland, 1680 ***2524.55*** *p237*
Whistler, Richard; Maryland, 1679 ***2524.55*** *p237*
Whitaker, Frances; Georgia, 1812 ***1640.10*** *p212*
Whitaker, Joseph; New York, 1840 ***8197.10*** *p201*
Whitaker, Rebecca 35; Barbados, 1774 ***1220.25*** *p69*
Whitaker, Robert; New York, 1783 ***1224.2*** *p123*
Whitborn, John; South Carolina, 1760 ***1224.2*** *p123*
Whitby, Henry 40; Ontario, 1871 ***1823.22*** *p170*
Whitby, Jonathan 16; Maryland, 1774 ***1220.25*** *p72*
Whitcher, John; Maryland, 1668 ***2524.55*** *p237*
Whitchurch, Hen; Virginia, 1664 ***6212.30*** *p7*
Whitco, Thomas; Maryland, 1665 ***2524.55*** *p237*
White, Miss; Portland, Maine, 1858 ***9196.15*** *p29*
White, Miss; Quebec, 1857 ***9196.15*** *p24*
White, Mr.; Quebec, 1857 ***9196.15*** *p24*
White, Mr.; Quebec, 1858 ***9196.15*** *p35*
White, Mr.; Quebec, 1858 ***9196.15*** *p45*
White, Mrs.; Quebec, 1857 ***9196.15*** *p24*
White, Mrs. A.; Alabama, 1805-1845 ***1640.10*** *p212*
White, Aaron 28; Ontario, 1861 ***2896.28*** *p37*
White, Agnes A.; Vermont, 1863-1923 ***5900.10*** *p122*
White, Albert 19; Ontario, 1861 ***2896.28*** *p37*
White, Alexander; Vermont, 1847-1902 ***5900.10*** *p592*
White, Ambross; Virginia, 1670 ***6212.30*** *p42*
White, Andrew; Jamaica, 1854 ***1640.13*** *p132*
White, Andrew; Ontario, 1832 ***1640.13*** *p132*
White, Andrew 85; Ontario, 1871 ***1823.22*** *p170*
White, Ann; Virginia, 1667 ***6212.30*** *p35*
White, Ann 14 *SEE* White, Bridget
White, Anne; Virginia, 1664 ***6212.30*** *p15*
White, Anne; Virginia, 1667-1668 ***6212.30*** *p39*
White, Anne 16; New York, New York, 1848 ***1825.45*** *p40*
White, Anne M.; Vermont, 1860-1862 ***5900.10*** *p383*
White, Annie; Portland, Maine, 1858 ***9196.15*** *p29*
White, Annie Ferguson; Vermont, 1817-1904 ***5900.10*** *p249*
White, Archibald; New York, 1806 ***8197.10*** *p324*
White, Archibald; New York, 1807 ***8197.10*** *p52*
White, Auzabel 16; Ontario, 1861 ***2896.28*** *p32*
White, Mrs. B. A. 65; Vermont, 1908 ***5900.10*** *p136*
White, Bartho; Virginia, 1666 ***6212.30*** *p28*
White, Benjamin; Boston, 1774 ***1224.2*** *p123*
White, Betty; Cleveland, Ohio, 1836 ***1224.3*** *p84*
White, Biddy 15 *SEE* White, John
White, Bridget; Vermont, 1825-1898 ***5900.10*** *p461*
White, Bridget 3 *SEE* White, Thomas
White, Bridget 8 *SEE* White, Bridget
White, Bridget 16 *SEE* White, Mary
White, Bridget 34; Vermont, 1871 ***5900.10*** *p480*
White, Bridget 36; New York, New York, 1849 ***1825.45*** *p40*
Son: John 6
Daughter: Bridget 8
Daughter: Margaret 10
Daughter: Mary 16
Son: Pat 16
White, Bridget 39; New York, New York, 1849 ***1825.45*** *p40*
Daughter: Ann 14
Daughter: Catherine 6
Daughter: Mary 15
Daughter: Sally 19
White, Bridget 41 *SEE* White, John
White, Bridget 62; Ontario, 1871 ***1823.22*** *p170*
White, C. H.; Quebec, 1858 ***9196.15*** *p31*
White, Catherine 6 *SEE* White, Bridget
White, Catherine 70; Vermont, 1893 ***5900.10*** *p272*
White, Catherine Laduke; Vermont, 1824-1895 ***5900.10*** *p361*
White, Catherine Laxton; Cincinnati, 1845 ***1224.3*** *p84*
White, Charles; Georgia, 1840 ***1224.3*** *p84*
White, Charles; New York, 1793 ***8197.10*** *p3*
White, Charles 21; Maryland, 1774 ***1220.25*** *p39*
Wife: Martha 21
White, Charles H.; Vermont, 1867-1868 ***5900.10*** *p383*
White, Charlotte; Portland, Maine, 1858 ***9196.15*** *p29*
White, Christopher; Pennsylvania, 1786 ***4629.10*** *p51*
White, Christopher 50; Ontario, 1871 ***1823.22*** *p170*
White, Clara 58; Ontario, 1861 ***2896.28*** *p60*
White, Clarissa 17; Ontario, 1861 ***2896.27*** *p58*
White, Dan 1; Ontario, 1861 ***2896.28*** *p60*
White, Daniel; Albany, New York, 1841 ***1224.3*** *p84*
White, David; New York, New York, 1850 ***6058.10*** *p49*
White, E. B. 4; Ontario, 1861 ***2896.28*** *p53*
White, E. B. 46; Ontario, 1861 ***2896.28*** *p53*
White, Edward; New York, 1840 ***8197.10*** *p10*
White, Edward; Vermont, 1825-1908 ***5900.10*** *p361*
White, Edward; Virginia, 1665 ***6212.30*** *p20*
White, Eliza; Virginia, 1665 ***6212.30*** *p19*
White, Eliza 21; Ontario, 1871 ***1823.28*** *p104*
White, Eliza 55; Vermont, 1892 ***5900.10*** *p604*
White, Elizabeth *SEE* White, John
White, Elizabeth; Maryland, 1658 ***2524.55*** *p237*
White, Elizabeth; New Jersey, 1785 ***1224.2*** *p123*
White, Elizabeth 28; Jamaica, 1773 ***1220.25*** *p23*
White, Elizabeth 38; Ontario, 1861 ***2896.27*** *p58*
White, Elizabeth 41; Vermont, 1895 ***5900.10*** *p488*
White, Elizabeth A.; Vermont, 1868-1953 ***5900.10*** *p532*
White, Ellen Farrell; Vermont, 1846-1924 ***5900.10*** *p491*
White, George; New York, 1792-1840 ***8197.10*** *p322*
White, George; Pennsylvania, 1777 ***4629.10*** *p12*
White, George 21; Vermont, 1878 ***5900.10*** *p480*
White, George 36; Ontario, 1871 ***1823.15*** *p278*
White, George 47; Ontario, 1871 ***1823.15*** *p278*
White, George 51; Ontario, 1871 ***1823.15*** *p278*
White, George A. 6; Ontario, 1861 ***2896.28*** *p60*
White, George B. 6; Ontario, 1861 ***2896.28*** *p32*
White, George H.; Vermont, 1853-1929 ***5900.10*** *p532*
White, Gilbert J. 6; Ontario, 1861 ***2896.27*** *p44*
White, Gratiana *SEE* White, John
White, H. B. 37; Ontario, 1871 ***1823.22*** *p170*
White, H. E. 6; Ontario, 1861 ***2896.28*** *p53*
White, Hannah M. 16; Ontario, 1861 ***2896.27*** *p44*
White, Henry; Maryland, 1659 ***2524.55*** *p237*
White, Henry; Pennsylvania, 1777 ***4629.10*** *p30*
White, Henry; Pennsylvania, 1779 ***4629.10*** *p41*
White, Henry 30; Maryland, 1775 ***1220.25*** *p108*
White, Henry W. 13; Ontario, 1861 ***2896.27*** *p68*
White, Hepzibah *SEE* White, John
White, Honor 28 *SEE* White, Thomas
White, Hugh; Maryland, 1655 ***2524.55*** *p237*
White, Isaac; Pennsylvania, 1777 ***4629.10*** *p14*
White, J. S. 23; Ontario, 1861 ***2896.28*** *p60*
White, James; Boston, 1668 ***1224.1*** *p63*
White, James; New York, 1803 ***8197.10*** *p17*
White, James; New York, 1807 ***8197.10*** *p52*
White, James; New York, 1837 ***8197.10*** *p103*
White, James; North America, 1785 ***1224.2*** *p123*
White, James; Pennsylvania, 1777 ***4629.10*** *p17*
White, James; Portland, Maine, 1858 ***9196.15*** *p29*
White, James; Vermont, 1820-1893 ***5900.10*** *p383*
White, James; Virginia, 1663 ***6212.30*** *p2*
White, James; Virginia, 1664-1665 ***6212.30*** *p16*
White, James; Virginia, 1694 ***1224.1*** *p63*
White, James 13 *SEE* White, Mary
White, James 19; Ontario, 1861 ***2896.28*** *p31*
White, James 22; Ontario, 1871 ***1823.15*** *p278*
White, James 41; Ontario, 1871 ***1823.15*** *p278*
White, James 50; Ontario, 1871 ***1823.15*** *p278*
White, James 61; Ontario, 1871 ***1823.22*** *p170*
White, James 66; Ontario, 1871 ***1823.28*** *p104*
White, James 71; Ontario, 1871 ***1823.28*** *p104*
White, James, Jr.; Portland, Maine, 1858 ***9196.15*** *p29*
White, Mrs. James; Portland, Maine, 1858 ***9196.15*** *p29*
White, James M. 2; Ontario, 1861 ***2896.28*** *p32*
White, Jane; Vermont, 1824-1896 ***5900.10*** *p423*
White, Jane 3 *SEE* White, John
White, Jane 16; Ontario, 1861 ***2896.27*** *p29*
White, Jane 20; Ontario, 1861 ***2896.28*** *p60*
White, Jane Gribbon; Vermont, 1842-1906 ***5900.10*** *p592*
White, Jemima E. 4; Ontario, 1861 ***2896.27*** *p58*
White, Jerome; Maryland, 1665 ***2524.55*** *p237*
White, Jerry; Vermont, 1856-1921 ***5900.10*** *p96*
White, Jno; Virginia, 1664 ***6212.30*** *p12*
White, John; Boston, 1679 ***1224.1*** *p63*
White, John; Boston, 1796 ***1224.2*** *p123*
White, John; Maryland, 1663 ***2524.55*** *p237*
White, John; Maryland, 1666 ***2524.55*** *p237*
White, John; Maryland, 1680 ***2524.55*** *p237*
Wife: Mary
Daughter: Elizabeth
Daughter: Mary
Daughter: Gratiana
Daughter: Susannah
White, John; New York, 1813 ***8197.10*** *p291*
White, John; New York, 1838 ***8197.10*** *p151*
White, John; New York, 1840 ***8197.10*** *p296*
White, John; Pennsylvania, 1837 ***6058.10*** *p13*
White, John; Vermont, 1844-1911 ***5900.10*** *p491*
White, John; Virginia, 1666 ***6212.30*** *p25*
White, John; Virginia, 1667 ***6212.30*** *p36*
White, John; Virginia, 1676 ***1224.1*** *p63*
White, John; Died enroute, 1857 ***1224.3*** *p84*
Wife: Hepzibah
Child: Elizabeth
White, John 1; Ontario, 1861 ***2896.28*** *p32*
White, John 6 *SEE* White, Bridget
White, John 8 *SEE* White, Mary
White, John 16 *SEE* White, John
White, John 17; Ontario, 1861 ***2896.27*** *p69*
White, John 18 *SEE* White, Pat
White, John 22; Philadelphia, 1774 ***1220.25*** *p80*
White, John 30; Ontario, 1871 ***1823.15*** *p278*
White, John 35; America, 1774 ***1220.25*** *p36*
White, John 35; Ontario, 1871 ***1823.22*** *p170*
White, John 40; Ontario, 1871 ***1823.28*** *p104*
White, John 46; Ontario, 1871 ***1823.22*** *p170*
White, John 49; Ontario, 1871 ***1823.22*** *p170*
White, John 50; New York, New York, 1848 ***1825.45*** *p41*
Wife: Bridget 41
Son: Martin 12
Son: Pat 14
Daughter: Jane 3
Daughter: Nancy 18
Daughter: Mary 20
Daughter: Biddy 15
Son: Michael 6
Son: John 16
White, John 50; Ontario, 1871 ***1823.15*** *p278*
White, John 57; Ontario, 1871 ***1823.15*** *p278*
White, John 70; Vermont, 1886 ***5900.10*** *p272*
White, John 77; Vermont, 1877 ***5900.10*** *p480*
White, John C. 1; Ontario, 1861 ***2896.28*** *p53*
White, John E.; Vermont, 1855-1858 ***5900.10*** *p383*
White, John M.; Vermont, 1862 ***5900.10*** *p383*
White, John V. 11; Ontario, 1861 ***2896.27*** *p68*
White, John W. 8; Ontario, 1861 ***2896.27*** *p44*
White, Joseph; Pennsylvania, 1777 ***4629.10*** *p14*
White, Joseph; Vermont, 1845-1925 ***5900.10*** *p392*
White, Joseph 29; Ontario, 1871 ***1823.22*** *p170*
White, Joseph 62; Ontario, 1871 ***1823.22*** *p170*
White, Joseph W. 3; Ontario, 1861 ***2896.28*** *p32*
White, Josias; Maryland, 1663 ***2524.55*** *p237*
White, Justis 44; Ontario, 1861 ***2896.27*** *p68*
White, Justis 60; Ontario, 1871 ***1823.22*** *p170*
White, Kate; Vermont, 1858-1908 ***5900.10*** *p383*
White, Katherine; Maryland, 1665 ***2524.55*** *p132*
White, Katherine; Vermont, 1848-1910 ***5900.10*** *p249*
White, Katie A. 20; Vermont, 1873 ***5900.10*** *p453*
White, Lionel 22; Philadelphia, 1774 ***1220.25*** *p42*
White, Luke; Virginia, 1666 ***6212.30*** *p25*
White, Lydia 37; Ontario, 1861 ***2896.27*** *p44*
White, Maggie 20; Vermont, 1862 ***5900.10*** *p480*
White, Margaret; Virginia, 1666-1667 ***6212.30*** *p32*
White, Margaret 7 *SEE* White, Thomas
White, Margaret 10 *SEE* White, Bridget
White, Margaret 22 *SEE* White, Michael
White, Margaret 30; Ontario, 1861 ***2896.28*** *p55*
White, Marian 26; Ontario, 1861 ***2896.27*** *p65*
White, Marmaduke John Horton; New York, New York, 1846 ***1224.3*** *p84*
White, Martha 21 *SEE* White, Charles
White, Martin 12 *SEE* White, John
White, Mary *SEE* White, John
White, Mary; Maryland, 1637 ***2524.55*** *p237*
White, Mary; Maryland, 1663 ***2524.55*** *p137*
White, Mary; New York, New York, 1790 ***1224.2*** *p123*
White, Mary; Vermont, 1816-1909 ***5900.10*** *p274*
White, Mary; Vermont, 1823-1901 ***5900.10*** *p381*
White, Mary; Vermont, 1830-1893 ***5900.10*** *p383*
White, Mary; Vermont, 1834-1906 ***5900.10*** *p274*

White, Mary; Vermont, 1845-1910 ***5900.10*** *p442*
White, Mary; Virginia, 1664 ***6212.30*** *p10*
White, Mary; Virginia, 1665 ***6212.30*** *p19*
White, Mary; Virginia, 1666 ***6212.30*** *p26*
White, Mary 5 *SEE* White, Mary
White, Mary 15 *SEE* White, Bridget
White, Mary 16 *SEE* White, Bridget
White, Mary 20 *SEE* White, John
White, Mary 20; Nova Scotia, 1774 ***1220.25*** *p135*
White, Mary 38; New York, New York, 1852 ***1825.45*** *p59*
Son: James 13
Daughter: Bridget 16
Daughter: Mary 5
Son: John 8
White, Mary 50; Ontario, 1871 ***1823.22*** *p170*
White, Mary 60; Ontario, 1861 ***2896.28*** *p37*
White, Mary 60; Ontario, 1871 ***1823.15*** *p278*
White, Mary 78; Vermont, 1881 ***5900.10*** *p196*
White, Mary A.; Vermont, 1872-1961 ***5900.10*** *p340*
White, Mary A. 42; Ontario, 1861 ***2896.27*** *p69*
White, Mary Ann 16; Ontario, 1871 ***1823.28*** *p104*
White, Mary Ann 62; Vermont, 1893 ***5900.10*** *p604*
White, Mary E. 11; Ontario, 1861 ***2896.27*** *p42*
White, Mary E. 14; Ontario, 1861 ***2896.27*** *p44*
White, Mary E. 23; Ontario, 1861 ***2896.28*** *p55*
White, Mary E. Difley; Vermont, 1849-1904 ***5900.10*** *p579*
White, Mary Nolan 73; Vermont, 1883 ***5900.10*** *p480*
White, Mary Smith; Vermont, 1847-1908 ***5900.10*** *p290*
White, Michael; New York, 1838 ***8197.10*** *p377*
White, Michael; Pennsylvania, 1830 ***6058.10*** *p17*
White, Michael; Pennsylvania, 1866 ***6058.10*** *p56*
White, Michael; Virginia, 1663 ***6212.30*** *p1*
White, Michael 6 *SEE* White, John
White, Michael 6 *SEE* White, Thomas
White, Michael 21; New York, New York, 1849 ***1825.45*** *p41*
Sister: Margaret 22
White, Morris 13; Ontario, 1871 ***1823.28*** *p104*
White, Moses 74; Ontario, 1861 ***2896.27*** *p65*
White, Mulberry 50; Ontario, 1871 ***1823.15*** *p278*
White, N. 24; Ontario, 1861 ***2896.28*** *p4*
White, N. 26; Ontario, 1861 ***2896.28*** *p55*
White, Nancy 18 *SEE* White, John
White, Nicholas; Virginia, 1663 ***6212.30*** *p2*
White, Pat 14 *SEE* White, John
White, Pat 16 *SEE* White, Bridget
White, Pat 26; New York, New York, 1848 ***1825.45*** *p41*
Brother: John 18
White, Patrick; New York, New York, 1849 ***6058.10*** *p37*
White, Patrick; Pennsylvania, 1867 ***6058.10*** *p59*
White, Patrick; Vermont, 1812-1872 ***5900.10*** *p249*
White, Peter; New York, 1807 ***8197.10*** *p52*
White, Peter 18; Maryland, 1775 ***1220.25*** *p98*
White, Peter, Sr. 76; Ontario, 1871 ***1823.28*** *p104*
White, Phebe C. 3; Ontario, 1861 ***2896.27*** *p42*
White, Phebe J. 32; Ontario, 1861 ***2896.27*** *p42*
White, Philip 44; Ontario, 1871 ***1823.15*** *p278*
White, Phillip; Virginia, 1671-1672 ***6212.30*** *p46*
White, Rachel 27; Ontario, 1861 ***2896.28*** *p60*
White, Ralph; Maryland, 1670 ***2524.55*** *p237*
White, Rebecca *SEE* White, Richard
White, Rebecca S. 13; Ontario, 1861 ***2896.27*** *p44*
White, Rephen; Maryland, 1653-1661 ***2524.55*** *p237*
White, Rich; Virginia, 1664 ***6212.30*** *p9*
White, Richard; Maryland, 1665 ***2524.55*** *p237*
Relative: Rebecca
Relative: William
White, Richard; Virginia, 1667 ***6212.30*** *p36*
White, Richard; Virginia, 1677 ***6212.30*** *p54*
White, Richard M. 10; Ontario, 1861 ***2896.27*** *p44*
White, Robert; Maryland, 1672 ***2524.55*** *p237*
White, Robert; New York, 1774 ***1224.2*** *p123*
White, Robert 46; Ontario, 1871 ***1823.15*** *p278*
White, Robert 53; Ontario, 1871 ***1823.22*** *p170*
White, Robert H. 26; Ontario, 1871 ***1823.28*** *p104*
White, Robert N.; New York, 1840 ***8197.10*** *p201*
White, Rose Hart; Vermont, 1869-1938 ***5900.10*** *p96*
White, Rowland; Virginia, 1667-1668 ***6212.30*** *p38*
White, Sally 19 *SEE* White, Bridget
White, Samps; Virginia, 1664 ***6212.30*** *p11*
White, Samuel 79; Ontario, 1871 ***1823.15*** *p278*
White, Sarah; Maryland, 1653 ***2524.55*** *p237*
White, Sarah; Vermont, 1821-1908 ***5900.10*** *p249*
White, Sarah 23; Vermont, 1882 ***5900.10*** *p453*
White, Sarah 65; Ontario, 1861 ***2896.28*** *p55*
White, Sarah Husband 65; Vermont, 1888 ***5900.10*** *p453*
White, Silomey 31; Ontario, 1861 ***2896.28*** *p32*
White, Sophiah H. 4; Ontario, 1861 ***2896.27*** *p42*
White, Stephen 71; Ontario, 1861 ***2896.27*** *p54*
White, Stephen H. 9; Ontario, 1861 ***2896.27*** *p69*
White, Stephen W. 27; Ontario, 1861 ***2896.27*** *p65*
White, Susannah *SEE* White, John
White, Theodorick; Virginia, 1663 ***6212.30*** *p2*
White, Theresa; Portland, Maine, 1858 ***9196.15*** *p29*
White, Thomas; Georgia, 1798 ***1224.2*** *p123*
White, Thomas; Maryland, 1635-1636 ***2524.55*** *p237*
White, Thomas; New York, 1838 ***8197.10*** *p151*
White, Thomas; New York, 1839 ***8197.10*** *p381*
White, Thomas; New York, New York, 1822 ***1224.3*** *p84*
White, Thomas; Philadelphia, 1786 ***1224.2*** *p123*
White, Thomas; Vermont, 1836-1869 ***5900.10*** *p290*
White, Thomas 26; New York, New York, 1849 ***1825.45*** *p41*
Wife: Honor 28
Son: Michael 6
Daughter: Bridget 3
Daughter: Margaret 7
White, Thomas 27; Vermont, 1871 ***5900.10*** *p480*
White, Thomas 32; Ontario, 1871 ***1823.15*** *p278*
White, Thomas 42; Virginia, 1775 ***1220.25*** *p95*
White, Thomas 47; Ontario, 1871 ***1823.22*** *p170*
White, Thomas 48; Ontario, 1871 ***1823.15*** *p278*
White, Thomas 52; Ontario, 1871 ***1823.15*** *p278*
White, Thomas 66; Ontario, 1861 ***2896.28*** *p55*
White, Timothy; Virginia, 1665-1666 ***6212.30*** *p25*
White, Townsend; Pennsylvania, 1777 ***4629.10*** *p24*
White, Turns 24; Baltimore, 1775 ***1220.25*** *p117*
White, W. H. 21; Vermont, 1889 ***5900.10*** *p136*
White, William *SEE* White, Richard
White, William; Charles Town, South Carolina, 1795 ***1224.2*** *p123*
White, William; Maryland, 1678 ***2524.55*** *p237*
White, William; New England, 1722 ***1224.2*** *p123*
White, William; New York, 1832 ***8197.10*** *p314*
White, William; New York, 1832 ***8197.10*** *p368*
White, William; New York, New York, 1887 ***3437.14*** *p163*
White, William; Pennsylvania, 1777 ***4629.10*** *p11*
White, William; Virginia, 1627 ***1224.1*** *p63*
White, William; Virginia, 1682 ***1224.1*** *p63*
White, William; Virginia, 1697 ***1224.1*** *p63*
White, William 16; Barbados, 1774 ***1220.25*** *p62*
White, William 31; Ontario, 1871 ***1823.28*** *p104*
White, William 41; Ontario, 1871 ***1823.22*** *p170*
White, William 59; Ontario, 1871 ***1823.28*** *p104*
White, William 85; Vermont, 1904 ***5900.10*** *p453*
White, William H. 27; Ontario, 1861 ***2896.27*** *p48*
White, William McAntchon 72; Ontario, 1871 ***1823.15*** *p278*
White, William R.; Alabama, 1806-1845 ***1640.10*** *p212*
White, William W. 9; Ontario, 1861 ***2896.27*** *p68*
White, Wm; Portland, Maine, 1858 ***9196.15*** *p29*
Whiteall, George; Pennsylvania, 1777 ***4629.10*** *p14*
Whiteby, Jerod 64; Ontario, 1871 ***1823.15*** *p278*
Whitefield, George; Georgia, 1771 ***1224.2*** *p124*
Whitefield, Margaret 62; Ontario, 1871 ***1823.15*** *p278*
Whiteford, Adam 43; Ontario, 1871 ***1823.15*** *p279*
Whiteford, Ellen 70; Ontario, 1871 ***1823.15*** *p279*
Whiteford, George 35; Ontario, 1871 ***1823.15*** *p279*
Whiteford, John 38; Ontario, 1871 ***1823.15*** *p279*
Whiteford, Sarah 63; Ontario, 1871 ***1823.15*** *p279*
Whitehair, Jane 41; Ontario, 1871 ***1823.22*** *p170*
Whitehaire, Robert; Virginia, 1674 ***1224.1*** *p63*
Whitehall, Robert; North Carolina, 1769 ***1224.2*** *p124*
Whitehead, Charles 53; Ontario, 1871 ***1823.15*** *p279*
Whitehead, George; New York, 1837 ***8197.10*** *p103*
Whitehead, Ja; Virginia, 1667 ***6212.30*** *p37*
Whitehead, James 27; Virginia, 1773 ***1220.25*** *p29*
Whitehead, Job 27; Maryland, 1774 ***1220.25*** *p8*
Whitehead, John; Maryland, 1658-1663 ***2524.55*** *p20*
Whitehead, John; Maryland, 1680 ***2524.55*** *p237*
Whitehead, John; New York, 1807 ***8197.10*** *p52*
Whitehead, John; New York, 1840 ***8197.10*** *p201*
Whitehead, John; South Carolina, 1717 ***1224.2*** *p124*
Whitehead, John 24; Ontario, 1871 ***1823.15*** *p279*
Whitehead, John 38; Ontario, 1871 ***1823.15*** *p279*
Whitehead, John James 29; Vermont, 1854 ***5900.10*** *p198*
Whitehead, Joseph 56; Ontario, 1871 ***1823.15*** *p279*
Whitehead, Richard; Connecticut, 1645 ***1224.1*** *p63*
Whitehead, Richard; Virginia, 1679 ***1224.1*** *p63*
Whitehead, Samuel; Maryland, 1682 ***2524.55*** *p237*
Whitehead, Samuel; New York, 1816 ***8197.10*** *p60*
Whitehead, William 27; Maryland, 1774 ***1220.25*** *p7*
Whitehead, William 36; Ontario, 1871 ***1823.15*** *p279*
Whiteheart, George; Maryland, 1681 ***2524.55*** *p237*
Whitehill, Edward; Virginia, 1663-1664 ***6212.30*** *p4*
Whitehill, Robert; Pennsylvania, 1777 ***4629.10*** *p20*
Whitehorne, George; Boston, 1722 ***1224.2*** *p124*
Whitehorne, John; Maryland, 1682 ***2524.55*** *p237*
Whitehouse, Joseph; New York, 1838 ***8197.10*** *p152*
Whitehurst, Thomas; Brunswick, North Carolina, 1766 ***1224.2*** *p124*
Whitehust, Thomas; Brunswick, North Carolina, 1766 ***1224.2*** *p124*
Whiteing, Elizabeth; Maryland, 1673 ***2524.55*** *p237*
Whiteing, John; Maryland, 1673 ***2524.55*** *p237*
Whitelaw, David; California, 1850 ***1640.13*** *p132*
Whitelaw, John 47; Ontario, 1871 ***1823.22*** *p170*
Whitelock, Isaac 47; Ontario, 1871 ***1823.15*** *p279*
Whitely, Andrew 40; Ontario, 1871 ***1823.15*** *p279*
Whitely, Baptist 64; Ontario, 1871 ***1823.15*** *p279*
Whitely, James 50; Ontario, 1871 ***1823.15*** *p279*
Whitely, Jane 88; Ontario, 1871 ***1823.15*** *p279*
Whitely, John 40; Ontario, 1871 ***1823.15*** *p279*
Whitely, Joseph 38; Ontario, 1871 ***1823.15*** *p279*
Whitely, Mark 42; Ontario, 1871 ***1823.15*** *p279*
Whitely, Noble 67; Ontario, 1871 ***1823.15*** *p279*
Whitely, Robert 45; Ontario, 1871 ***1823.15*** *p279*
Whitely, Thomas 47; Ontario, 1871 ***1823.15*** *p279*
Whitely, William 59; Ontario, 1871 ***1823.15*** *p279*
Whitem, Clanne; Maryland, 1665 ***2524.55*** *p237*
Whiteman, Charles 31; Ontario, 1871 ***1823.15*** *p279*
Whiteman, John; New York, 1798 ***1224.2*** *p124*
Whiteman, John; Pennsylvania, 1777 ***4629.10*** *p11*
Whiteman, John 43; Ontario, 1871 ***1823.15*** *p279*
Whiteman, Thomas 39; Ontario, 1871 ***1823.15*** *p279*
Whitemarsh, Levi 7; Ontario, 1861 ***2896.26*** *p20*
Whitemarsh, Sam'l 34; Ontario, 1861 ***2896.26*** *p20*
Whitemarsh, Serepta 2; Ontario, 1861 ***2896.26*** *p20*
Whiteside, Edward; New York, 1829 ***8197.10*** *p294*
Whiteside, John 50; Ontario, 1871 ***1823.28*** *p104*
Whiteside, Peter; Pennsylvania, 1777 ***4629.10*** *p28*
Whiteside, Peter; Pennsylvania, 1779 ***4629.10*** *p38*
Whiteside, Richard 26; Ontario, 1871 ***1823.28*** *p104*
Whiteside, Thomas 66; Ontario, 1871 ***1823.15*** *p279*
Whitew, Samuel; Maryland, 1675 ***2524.55*** *p237*
Whitewe, Samuell; Maryland, 1675 ***2524.55*** *p237*
Whitewith, William 22; Maryland, 1775 ***1220.25*** *p111*
Whitewyn, John; Virginia, 1671 ***6212.30*** *p43*
Whitfeild, Fasy; Maryland, 1672 ***2524.55*** *p237*
Whitfeild, William; Maryland, 1673 ***2524.55*** *p237*
Whitfield, George; Georgia, 1774 ***1640.13*** *p132*
Whitfield, George T.; New York, 1834 ***8197.10*** *p295*
Whitfield, Hannah 81; Ontario, 1871 ***1823.15*** *p279*
Whitfield, John 42; Ontario, 1871 ***1823.15*** *p279*
Whitfield, Thomas; America, 1779 ***1224.2*** *p124*
Whitfield, Thomas 49; Ontario, 1871 ***1823.15*** *p279*
Whitfield, William 35; Ontario, 1871 ***1823.28*** *p104*
Whitford, John; Havana, 1765 ***1224.2*** *p124*
Whitford, John; Rhode Island, 1765 ***1224.2*** *p124*
Whitham, William 23; Ontario, 1871 ***1823.15*** *p279*
Whithy, Nicholas; New York, 1804 ***8197.10*** *p28*
Whiticoo, Samuell; Maryland, 1670 ***2524.55*** *p237*
Whitiman, James 61; Ontario, 1871 ***1823.15*** *p279*
Whiting, James; Virginia, 1665-1666 ***6212.30*** *p24*
Whiting, John 22; Ontario, 1871 ***1823.15*** *p280*
Whiting, Richard 31; Ontario, 1871 ***1823.15*** *p280*
Whiting, Robt.; Maryland, 1665 ***2524.55*** *p238*
Whiting, Sara; Virginia, 1667-1668 ***6212.30*** *p39*
Whiting, William 24; Virginia, 1774 ***1220.25*** *p93*
Whitla, R. J. 23; Ontario, 1871 ***1823.28*** *p104*
Whitley, Alce; Maryland, 1666 ***2524.55*** *p11*
Whitley, Archie 12; Ontario, 1861 ***2896.28*** *p53*
Whitley, Edmond 67; Ontario, 1871 ***1823.15*** *p280*
Whitley, Hannah 82; Ontario, 1871 ***1823.15*** *p280*
Whitley, John 52; Ontario, 1871 ***1823.22*** *p170*
Whitley, John 56; Ontario, 1871 ***1823.15*** *p280*
Whitley, Mary 45; Vermont, 1876 ***5900.10*** *p435*
Whitley, Patrick 45; Vermont, 1875 ***5900.10*** *p435*
Whitley, Roger; South Carolina, 1729 ***1224.2*** *p124*
Whitlock, . . .; Virginia, 1679 ***1224.1*** *p29*
Whitlock, Isaac 50; Ontario, 1871 ***1823.15*** *p280*
Whitlock, John 64; Ontario, 1871 ***1823.15*** *p280*
Whitlock, Siles 53; Ontario, 1871 ***1823.15*** *p280*
Whitlock, Thomas; Virginia, 1680 ***1224.1*** *p63*
Whitlock, William 58; Ontario, 1871 ***1823.15*** *p280*
Whitlow, George 90; Vermont, 1881 ***5900.10*** *p301*
Whitly, Arthur; Maryland, 1682 ***2524.55*** *p238*
Whitly, James 76; Ontario, 1871 ***1823.15*** *p280*
Whitly, Jeffery; Virginia, 1663 ***6212.30*** *p3*
Whitly, Martin 27; Ontario, 1871 ***1823.15*** *p280*
Whitman, Eva E. 32; Kansas, 1899-1910 ***9079.10*** *p30*
Whitman, Johannes; Philadelphia, 1729 ***2856.30*** *p494*
Whitman, John 35; Kansas, 1900-1910 ***9079.10*** *p52*
Whitman, Mary 37; Kansas, 1910 ***9079.10*** *p52*
Whitmers, Major; Quebec, 1857 ***9196.15*** *p21*
Whitmore, Major; Quebec, 1858 ***9196.15*** *p44*
Whitmore, Andrew 15; Grenada, 1774 ***1220.25*** *p127*
Whitmore, Benjamin; New England, 1696 ***1224.1*** *p63*
Whitmore, Rich; Virginia, 1666-1667 ***6212.30*** *p33*
Whitmore, Thomas; Virginia, 1664 ***6212.30*** *p11*
Whitnell, Charles 48; Ontario, 1871 ***1823.28*** *p104*
Whitney, A. P. 53; Vermont, 1873 ***5900.10*** *p64*
Whitney, Eliza 35; Ontario, 1861 ***2896.25*** *p62*
Whitney, George Emery; Vermont, 1857-1909 ***5900.10*** *p118*
Whitney, Ichabod 3; Ontario, 1861 ***2896.25*** *p62*

Wilson, Anne E.; Vermont, 1868-1929 ***5900.10*** *p95*
Wilson, Arabella *SEE* Wilson, Thomas
Wilson, Archie *SEE* Wilson, Alexander
Wilson, Archie *SEE* Wilson, Angus
Wilson, Benjamin; Baltimore, 1828 ***1224.3*** *p86*
Wilson, Benjamin 34; Ontario, 1871 ***1823.15*** *p283*
Wilson, Betsey 56; Vermont, 1873 ***5900.10*** *p450*
Wilson, Byron 37; Ontario, 1871 ***1823.15*** *p283*
Wilson, C. W.; Quebec, 1857 ***9196.15*** *p13*
Wilson, Mrs. C. W.; Quebec, 1857 ***9196.15*** *p13*
Wilson, Campbell; New York, 1794 ***8197.10*** *p3*
Wilson, Catharine 23; Jamaica, 1774 ***1220.25*** *p40*
Wilson, Catherine *SEE* Wilson, Donald
Wilson, Catherine *SEE* Wilson, James
Wilson, Catherine *SEE* Wilson, Malcolm
Wilson, Catherine *SEE* Wilson, Ranald
Wilson, Catherine 58; Ontario, 1861 ***2896.25*** *p40*
Wilson, Charles; Georgia, 1698 ***1640.13*** *p134*
Wilson, Charles; Jamaica, 1843 ***1640.13*** *p134*
Wilson, Charles; New York, 1840 ***8197.10*** *p202*
Wilson, Charles 45; Ontario, 1871 ***1823.15*** *p283*
Wilson, Charles 52; Ontario, 1871 ***1823.15*** *p283*
Wilson, Christena 77; Ontario, 1871 ***1823.15*** *p283*
Wilson, Daniel; New York, New York, 1849 ***1224.3*** *p86*
Wilson, Daniel; Pennsylvania, 1839 ***6058.10*** *p15*
Wilson, Daniel 50; Ontario, 1871 ***1823.15*** *p283*
Wilson, David; Alabama, 1800-1845 ***1640.10*** *p214*
Wilson, David; Georgia, 1698 ***1640.13*** *p134*
Wilson, David 46; Ontario, 1871 ***1823.15*** *p283*
Wilson, David 52; Ontario, 1871 ***1823.28*** *p105*
Wilson, David 83; Ontario, 1871 ***1823.15*** *p283*
Wilson, David L.; Texas, 1836 ***1640.10*** *p214*
Wilson, Donald *SEE* Wilson, Alexander
Wilson, Donald *SEE* Wilson, Angus
Wilson, Donald *SEE* Wilson, Malcolm
Wilson, Donald *SEE* Wilson, Ranald
Wilson, Donald; Port uncertain, 1840-1849 ***4537.37*** *p134*
Wife: Marion
Child: Marion
Child: Catherine
Wilson, Donald; Port uncertain, 1850-1859 ***4537.37*** *p134*
Wife: Ann
Child: Ann
Child: George
Wilson, Edward; New York, 1818 ***8197.10*** *p291*
Wilson, Edward; New York, 1840 ***8197.10*** *p384*
Wilson, Effie *SEE* Wilson, Alexander
Wilson, Eleanor 63; Ontario, 1861 ***2896.27*** *p32*
Wilson, Elen 15; Ontario, 1861 ***2896.27*** *p61*
Wilson, Elizabeth *SEE* Wilson, George
Wilson, Elizabeth *SEE* Wilson, Mathew
Wilson, Elizabeth *SEE* Wilson, Robert
Wilson, Elizabeth; Barbados, 1841 ***1640.13*** *p134*
Wilson, Elizabeth; Maryland, 1673 ***2524.55*** *p243*
Wilson, Elizabeth; Maryland, 1679 ***2524.55*** *p243*
Wilson, Elizabeth 33; Ontario, 1861 ***2896.25*** *p2*
Wilson, Elizabeth Ready; Vermont, 1860-1919 ***5900.10*** *p95*
Wilson, Ellen 47; Ontario, 1871 ***1823.15*** *p283*
Wilson, Ellen M.; Vermont, 1849-1896 ***5900.10*** *p44*
Wilson, Ester 24; Ontario, 1871 ***1823.22*** *p172*
Wilson, F. C. 27; Ontario, 1871 ***1823.15*** *p283*
Wilson, Francis; New York, 1807 ***8197.10*** *p325*
Wilson, Francis 21; Maryland, 1774 ***1220.25*** *p3*
Wilson, George *SEE* Wilson, Donald
Wilson, George *SEE* Wilson, George
Wilson, George; Charleston, South Carolina, 1886 ***1640.13*** *p134*
Wilson, George; Georgia, 1699 ***1640.13*** *p134*
Wilson, George; Jamaica, 1834 ***1640.13*** *p134*
Wilson, George; Maryland, 1671 ***2524.55*** *p243*
Wife: Elizabeth
Child: William
Child: Mary
Child: Ann
Child: Elizabeth
Child: George
Wilson, George; New York, 1803 ***8197.10*** *p9*
Wilson, George; New York, 1807 ***8197.10*** *p52*
Wilson, George; Quebec, 1858 ***9196.15*** *p32*
Wilson, George 21; Ontario, 1861 ***2896.27*** *p17*
Wilson, George 30; Ontario, 1871 ***1823.15*** *p283*
Wilson, George 35; Ontario, 1871 ***1823.28*** *p105*
Wilson, George 40; Ontario, 1871 ***1823.15*** *p283*
Wilson, George 47; Ontario, 1861 ***2896.25*** *p40*
Wilson, George, Sr. 70; Ontario, 1871 ***1823.15*** *p283*
Wilson, Mrs. George; Quebec, 1858 ***9196.15*** *p32*
Wilson, Gormelia Beaton *SEE* Wilson, Malcolm
Wilson, Helen; Maryland, 1673 ***2524.55*** *p243*
Wilson, Helen 29; Ontario, 1871 ***1823.15*** *p283*
Wilson, Hellen; Maryland, 1676 ***2524.55*** *p243*
Wilson, Henery 51; Ontario, 1871 ***1823.15*** *p283*
Wilson, Henry; Maryland, 1673 ***2524.55*** *p243*
Wilson, Henry; Maryland, 1676 ***2524.55*** *p243*
Wilson, Henry; Maryland, 1910 ***3259.35*** *p68*
Wilson, Henry; Pennsylvania, 1777 ***4629.10*** *p24*
Wilson, Hiram 19; Ontario, 1861 ***2896.27*** *p61*
Wilson, Hugh; New York, 1831 ***8197.10*** *p294*
Wilson, Hugh; New York, 1845 ***8197.10*** *p10*
Wilson, Hugh 25; Virginia, 1774 ***1220.25*** *p54*
Wilson, Hugh 64; Ontario, 1871 ***1823.22*** *p172*
Wilson, Hugh W.; New York, 1840 ***8197.10*** *p384*
Wilson, Isaac; Virginia, 1664 ***6212.30*** *p6*
Wilson, J.; Mobile, Alabama, 1804-1845 ***1640.10*** *p214*
Wife: Ruth
Wilson, J.; Quebec, 1856 ***9196.15*** *p6*
Wilson, J.; Quebec, 1857 ***9196.15*** *p18*
Wilson, J.; Quebec, 1857 ***9196.15*** *p23*
Wilson, Mrs. J.; Quebec, 1857 ***9196.15*** *p18*
Wilson, J. G. 62; Ontario, 1861 ***2896.27*** *p32*
Wilson, James; Alexandria, Virginia, 1807 ***1224.3*** *p86*
Wilson, James; Dakota, 1874 ***1640.13*** *p134*
Wilson, James; Maryland, 1672 ***2524.55*** *p243*
Wilson, James; New York, 1804 ***8197.10*** *p28*
Wilson, James; New York, 1807 ***8197.10*** *p327*
Wilson, James; Ontario, 1861 ***2896.28*** *p57*
Wilson, James; Ontario, 1884 ***1640.13*** *p134*
Wilson, James; Pennsylvania, 1868 ***6058.10*** *p77*
Wilson, James; Prince Edward Island, 1848 ***4537.37*** *p27*
Wife: Marion MacLellan
Child: Catherine
Child: John
Child: Mary
Wilson, James; Tobago, West Indies, 1840 ***1640.13*** *p134*
Wilson, James; Vermont, 1857-1901 ***5900.10*** *p95*
Wilson, James 9; Ontario, 1861 ***2896.28*** *p55*
Wilson, James 19; Fort Cumberland, Nova Scotia, 1774 ***1220.25*** *p18*
Wilson, James 19; Ontario, 1871 ***1823.28*** *p105*
Wilson, James 21; Ontario, 1871 ***1823.22*** *p172*
Wilson, James 23; Baltimore, 1775 ***1220.25*** *p118*
Wilson, James 29; Ontario, 1871 ***1823.28*** *p105*
Wilson, James 30; Ontario, 1871 ***1823.28*** *p105*
Wilson, James 31; Ontario, 1861 ***2896.25*** *p2*
Wilson, James 31; Ontario, 1871 ***1823.15*** *p284*
Wilson, James 41; Ontario, 1871 ***1823.15*** *p284*
Wilson, James 42; Ontario, 1871 ***1823.15*** *p284*
Wilson, James 44; Ontario, 1871 ***1823.15*** *p284*
Wilson, James 50; Ontario, 1871 ***1823.28*** *p105*
Wilson, James 57; Ontario, 1871 ***1823.28*** *p105*
Wilson, James F.; New Orleans, 1789-1821 ***1640.10*** *p214*
Wilson, Jane; Savannah, Georgia, 1774 ***1640.10*** *p214*
Wilson, Jane 19; Ontario, 1861 ***2896.28*** *p55*
Wilson, Jane 22; Savannah, Georgia, 1774 ***1220.25*** *p139*
Wilson, Jane 25; Ontario, 1861 ***2896.27*** *p3*
Wilson, Jane 25; Ontario, 1861 ***2896.27*** *p32*
Wilson, Jane 43; Ontario, 1861 ***2896.28*** *p55*
Wilson, Jane 47; Ontario, 1871 ***1823.15*** *p284*
Wilson, Jane 80; Ontario, 1871 ***1823.28*** *p105*
Wilson, Jemima; Quebec, 1858 ***9196.15*** *p32*
Wilson, Jessie Gillies *SEE* Wilson, Ranald
Wilson, Jno; Virginia, 1665-1666 ***6212.30*** *p23*
Wilson, John *SEE* Wilson, James
Wilson, John *SEE* Wilson, Malcolm
Wilson, John *SEE* Wilson, Ranald
Wilson, John; Georgia, 1698 ***1640.13*** *p134*
Wilson, John; Jamaica, 1851 ***1640.13*** *p134*
Wilson, John; Maryland, 1669 ***2524.55*** *p218*
Wilson, John; Maryland, 1673 ***2524.55*** *p243*
Wilson, John; Maryland, 1677-1681 ***2524.55*** *p243*
Wilson, John; New York, 1796 ***8197.10*** *p7*
Wilson, John; New York, 1807 ***8197.10*** *p52*
Wilson, John; New York, 1821 ***8197.10*** *p292*
Wilson, John; New York, 1827 ***8197.10*** *p293*
Wilson, John; New York, 1831 ***8197.10*** *p67*
Wilson, John; New York, 1840 ***8197.10*** *p203*
Wilson, John; New York, New York, 1850 ***6058.10*** *p34*
Wilson, John; Philadelphia, 1793 ***4629.10*** *p66*
Wilson, John; Philadelphia, 1793 ***4629.10*** *p74*
Wilson, John; South Carolina, 1792 ***1224.2*** *p126*
Wilson, John; Trinidad, 1833 ***1640.13*** *p134*
Wilson, John; Virginia, 1700 ***1224.2*** *p126*
Wilson, John 16; Ontario, 1861 ***2896.27*** *p61*
Wilson, John 23; Maryland, 1774 ***1220.25*** *p53*
Wilson, John 24; Ontario, 1871 ***1823.15*** *p284*
Wilson, John 27; Ontario, 1871 ***1823.15*** *p284*
Wilson, John 29; Ontario, 1871 ***1823.15*** *p284*
Wilson, John 30; Ontario, 1871 ***1823.28*** *p105*
Wilson, John 32; Ontario, 1871 ***1823.28*** *p105*
Wilson, John 36; Ontario, 1871 ***1823.15*** *p284*
Wilson, John 37; Ontario, 1871 ***1823.28*** *p105*
Wilson, John 38; Ontario, 1871 ***1823.15*** *p284*
Wilson, John 39; Maryland, 1774 ***1220.25*** *p84*
Wilson, John 39; Maryland, 1775 ***1220.25*** *p102*
Wilson, John 41; Ontario, 1871 ***1823.15*** *p284*
Wilson, John 42; Ontario, 1871 ***1823.22*** *p172*
Wilson, John 45; Ontario, 1871 ***1823.28*** *p105*
Wilson, John 46; Nova Scotia, 1774 ***1220.25*** *p13*
Wilson, John 47; Ontario, 1861 ***2896.28*** *p55*
Wilson, John 48; Ontario, 1871 ***1823.28*** *p105*
Wilson, John 54; Ontario, 1871 ***1823.15*** *p284*
Wilson, John 56; Ontario, 1871 ***1823.15*** *p284*
Wilson, John 56; Ontario, 1871 ***1823.22*** *p172*
Wilson, John 63; Ontario, 1871 ***1823.22*** *p172*
Wilson, John 69; Ontario, 1871 ***1823.22*** *p172*
Wilson, John 84; Ontario, 1871 ***1823.15*** *p284*
Wilson, John, Jr. 32; Pennsylvania, 1818-1826 ***6058.10*** *p7*
Wilson, John Black; Pennsylvania, 1893 ***1640.13*** *p134*
Wilson, John Buchanan; New York, 1855 ***1640.13*** *p134*
Wilson, John W. 56; Ontario, 1871 ***1823.22*** *p172*
Wilson, Jonathan 60; Ontario, 1871 ***1823.15*** *p284*
Wilson, Joseph; New York, 1827 ***8197.10*** *p293*
Wilson, Joseph; New York, 1840 ***8197.10*** *p202*
Wilson, Joseph 15; Philadelphia, 1774 ***1220.25*** *p68*
Wilson, Joseph 45; Ontario, 1871 ***1823.15*** *p284*
Wilson, Joseph 53; Ontario, 1871 ***1823.28*** *p105*
Wilson, Mrs. L. 27; Alaska, 1914 ***9196.1*** *p41*
Wilson, Leatham; New York, 1840 ***8197.10*** *p385*
Wilson, M. Agnes; Vermont, 1862-1864 ***5900.10*** *p95*
Wilson, M. Ellen; Vermont, 1874-1932 ***5900.10*** *p95*
Wilson, Malcolm; Ontario, 1850-1859 ***4537.37*** *p87*
Wife: Margaret MacLeod
Child: John
Child: Donald
Child: Catherine
Child: Alexander
Child: Angus
Wilson, Malcolm; Ontario, 1851 ***4537.32*** *p96*
Wife: Margaret MacLeod
Child: Catherine
Child: John
Child: Alexander
Child: Donald
Child: Angus
Wilson, Malcolm; Port uncertain, 1840-1849 ***4537.37*** *p134*
Wife: Gormelia Beaton
Child: Marion
Child: Margaret
Child: Alexander
Wilson, Margaret *SEE* Wilson, Malcolm
Wilson, Margaret; Barbados, 1842 ***1640.13*** *p134*
Wilson, Margaret 12; Ontario, 1861 ***2896.28*** *p55*
Wilson, Margaret 29; Ontario, 1871 ***1823.15*** *p284*
Wilson, Margaret 40; Ontario, 1871 ***1823.15*** *p284*
Wilson, Margaret 70; Ontario, 1871 ***1823.22*** *p172*
Wilson, Margaret 80; Ontario, 1871 ***1823.15*** *p284*
Wilson, Margaret MacLeod *SEE* Wilson, Malcolm
Wilson, Margt; Virginia, 1671 ***6212.30*** *p42*
Wilson, Marion *SEE* Wilson, Alexander
Wilson, Marion *SEE* Wilson, Donald
Wilson, Marion *SEE* Wilson, Malcolm
Wilson, Marion MacLellan *SEE* Wilson, James
Wilson, Martha R. 47; Ontario, 1871 ***1823.22*** *p172*
Wilson, Martin; Vermont, 1866-1932 ***5900.10*** *p95*
Wilson, Mary *SEE* Wilson, Alexander
Wilson, Mary *SEE* Wilson, George
Wilson, Mary *SEE* Wilson, James
Wilson, Mary *SEE* Wilson, Thomas
Wilson, Mary; New York, 1852 ***1224.3*** *p86*
Wilson, Mary 22; Baltimore, 1775 ***1220.25*** *p119*
Wilson, Mary 25; St. Kitts, 1774 ***1220.25*** *p60*
Wilson, Mary 83; Ontario, 1871 ***1823.22*** *p172*
Wilson, Mary A. 7; Ontario, 1861 ***2896.27*** *p61*
Wilson, Mary Anglim 65; Vermont, 1893 ***5900.10*** *p95*
Wilson, Mathew; Maryland, 1667 ***2524.55*** *p243*
Wife: Elizabeth
Daughter: Elizabeth
Wilson, Mathew 70; Ontario, 1871 ***1823.28*** *p105*
Wilson, Matthew 24; Ontario, 1871 ***1823.28*** *p105*
Wilson, Mulleneauve 34; Ontario, 1871 ***1823.22*** *p172*
Wilson, Peter; Ontario, 1861 ***2896.28*** *p57*
Wilson, Peter; Vermont, 1829-1915 ***5900.10*** *p95*
Wilson, Peter 51; Ontario, 1871 ***1823.28*** *p105*
Wilson, Peter 55; Ontario, 1871 ***1823.15*** *p284*
Wilson, Peter 59; Ontario, 1871 ***1823.15*** *p284*
Wilson, Philip; New York, 1840 ***8197.10*** *p203*
Wilson, Philip; Savannah, Georgia, 1804 ***1640.10*** *p214*
Wilson, Ranald; Port uncertain, 1840-1849 ***4537.37*** *p134*
Wife: Catherine
Child: Donald
Wilson, Ranald; Port uncertain, 1850-1859 ***4537.37*** *p134*
Wife: Jessie Gillies
Child: John
Wilson, Richard; New England, 1640 ***1224.1*** *p64*
Wilson, Richard; New York, 1838 ***8197.10*** *p378*
Wilson, Richard; New York, 1840 ***8197.10*** *p201*
Wilson, Richard; Virginia, 1648 ***1224.1*** *p29*

Wilson, Richard 16; New York, 1774 ***1220.25*** *p24*
Wilson, Richard 21; Ontario, 1861 ***2896.27*** *p61*
Wilson, Richard 29; Ontario, 1871 ***1823.22*** *p173*
Wilson, Richard 40; Ontario, 1871 ***1823.28*** *p105*
Wilson, Robert; Georgia, 1698 ***1640.13*** *p135*
Wilson, Robert; Maryland, 1659 ***2524.55*** *p243*
Wilson, Robert; Maryland, 1676 ***2524.55*** *p243*
Wife: Elizabeth
Wilson, Robert; Montreal, 1881 ***1640.13*** *p135*
Wilson, Robert; New York, 1800 ***8197.10*** *p291*
Wilson, Robert; New York, 1838 ***8197.10*** *p295*
Wilson, Robert; New York, 1841 ***8197.10*** *p201*
Wilson, Robert; Philadelphia, 1873 ***1640.13*** *p135*
Wilson, Robert; Virginia, 1648 ***1224.1*** *p29*
Wilson, Robert; Virginia, 1651 ***1224.1*** *p64*
Wilson, Robert; Virginia, 1699 ***1224.1*** *p64*
Wilson, Robert 16; New York, 1774 ***1220.25*** *p24*
Wilson, Robert 27; Ontario, 1871 ***1823.22*** *p173*
Wilson, Robert 27; Ontario, 1871 ***1823.28*** *p105*
Wilson, Robert 34; Ontario, 1871 ***1823.15*** *p284*
Wilson, Robert 37; Ontario, 1871 ***1823.15*** *p284*
Wilson, Robert 38; Maryland, 1774 ***1220.25*** *p73*
Wilson, Robert 48; Ontario, 1871 ***1823.15*** *p284*
Wilson, Robert 49; Nova Scotia, 1774 ***1220.25*** *p135*
With wife & 7 children
Wilson, Robert 51; Ontario, 1871 ***1823.28*** *p105*
Wilson, Robert 59; Ontario, 1871 ***1823.15*** *p284*
Wilson, Robert 63; Ontario, 1871 ***1823.15*** *p284*
Wilson, Rueben W. 4; Ontario, 1861 ***2896.25*** *p2*
Wilson, Ruth *SEE* Wilson, J.
Wilson, Samuel; Nashville, Tennessee, 1835 ***1224.3*** *p86*
Wilson, Samuel; New York, 1838 ***8197.10*** *p295*
Wilson, Samuel; Pennsylvania, 1811 ***6058.10*** *p3*
Wilson, Samuel; Virginia, 1677 ***1224.1*** *p64*
Wilson, Samuel 21; Philadelphia, 1774 ***1220.25*** *p63*
Wilson, Samuel 26; Virginia, 1774 ***1220.25*** *p74*
Wilson, Samuel 41; Ontario, 1871 ***1823.15*** *p284*
Wilson, Samuel 52; Ontario, 1871 ***1823.22*** *p173*
Wilson, Samuel D.; New York, 1831 ***8197.10*** *p294*
Wilson, Samuel D.; New York, 1834 ***8197.10*** *p68*
Wilson, Sarah 11; Ontario, 1861 ***2896.27*** *p61*
Wilson, Sarah 18; Ontario, 1861 ***2896.28*** *p55*
Wilson, Sarah 22; Maryland, 1775 ***1220.25*** *p115*
Wilson, Sarah 23; Ontario, 1861 ***2896.27*** *p62*
Wilson, Sarah 59; Ontario, 1871 ***1823.22*** *p173*
Wilson, Sarah G. 54; Vermont, 1874 ***5900.10*** *p519*
Wilson, Sarah L. 1; Ontario, 1861 ***2896.25*** *p2*
Wilson, Stafford; New York, 1831 ***8197.10*** *p294*
Wilson, Stafford; New York, 1838 ***8197.10*** *p152*
Wilson, Steward 29; Ontario, 1861 ***2896.27*** *p3*
Wilson, Tho; Virginia, 1666 ***6212.30*** *p27*
Wilson, Tho; Virginia, 1702 ***6212.30*** *p62*
Wilson, Thomas; Maryland, 1673 ***2524.55*** *p243*
Wilson, Thomas; Maryland, 1676 ***2524.55*** *p243*
Wilson, Thomas; Maryland, 1681 ***2524.55*** *p243*
Relative: Arabella
Relative: Mary
Wilson, Thomas; New York, 1818 ***8197.10*** *p291*
Wilson, Thomas; New York, 1821 ***8197.10*** *p292*
Wilson, Thomas; New York, New York, 1850 ***6058.10*** *p34*
Wilson, Thomas; Rhode Island, 1781 ***1224.2*** *p126*
Wilson, Thomas; Vermont, 1859-1919 ***5900.10*** *p95*
Wilson, Thomas 13; Ontario, 1861 ***2896.27*** *p61*
Wilson, Thomas 18; Maryland, 1774 ***1220.25*** *p39*
Wilson, Thomas 22; Ontario, 1861 ***2896.28*** *p2*
Wilson, Thomas 26; Nova Scotia, 1774 ***1220.25*** *p135*
Wilson, Thomas 40; Ontario, 1871 ***1823.15*** *p284*
Wilson, Thomas 50; Fort Cumberland, Nova Scotia, 1774 ***1220.25*** *p18*
Wilson, Thomas 51; Ontario, 1871 ***1823.15*** *p284*
Wilson, Thomas 59; Ontario, 1861 ***2896.28*** *p2*
Wilson, Thomas 64; Ontario, 1871 ***1823.28*** *p105*
Wilson, Thomas L. 40; Ontario, 1871 ***1823.22*** *p173*
Wilson, Thos 32; Ontario, 1871 ***1823.28*** *p105*
Wilson, Timothy 44; Vermont, 1900 ***5900.10*** *p95*
Wilson, W.; Pennsylvania, 1781 ***4629.10*** *p42*
Wilson, W.; Portland, Maine, 1858 ***9196.15*** *p28*
Wilson, William *SEE* Wilson, George
Wilson, William; Illinois, 1885 ***1640.13*** *p135*
Wilson, William; Maryland, 1669 ***2524.55*** *p243*
Wilson, William; New York, 1794 ***8197.10*** *p3*
Wilson, William; New York, 1807 ***8197.10*** *p291*
Wilson, William; New York, 1827 ***8197.10*** *p294*
Wilson, William; New York, 1829 ***8197.10*** *p352*
Wilson, William; New York, 1831 ***8197.10*** *p354*
Wilson, William; Tobago, West Indies, 1831 ***1640.13*** *p135*
Wilson, William 22; Ontario, 1871 ***1823.15*** *p285*
Wilson, William 22; Virginia, 1774 ***1220.25*** *p91*
Wilson, William 23; Nova Scotia, 1774 ***1220.25*** *p135*
Wilson, William 23; Virginia, 1774 ***1220.25*** *p53*
Wilson, William 29; Maryland, 1775 ***1220.25*** *p99*
Wilson, William 36; Ontario, 1871 ***1823.15*** *p285*
Wilson, William 38; Carolina, 1774 ***1220.25*** *p38*
Wilson, William 38; Ontario, 1871 ***1823.28*** *p105*
Wilson, William 41; Ontario, 1871 ***1823.28*** *p105*
Wilson, William 43; Ontario, 1871 ***1823.22*** *p173*
Wilson, William 46; Ontario, 1871 ***1823.15*** *p284*
Wilson, William 46; Ontario, 1871 ***1823.28*** *p105*
Wilson, William 49; Ontario, 1871 ***1823.15*** *p285*
Wilson, William 57; Ontario, 1871 ***1823.15*** *p284*
Wilson, William 60; Ontario, 1861 ***2896.27*** *p61*
Wilson, William 60; Ontario, 1871 ***1823.15*** *p285*
Wilson, William 70; Ontario, 1871 ***1823.15*** *p285*
Wilson, William A. 6; Ontario, 1861 ***2896.25*** *p2*
Wilson, William F.; Detroit, 1862 ***3437.14*** *p91*
Wilstach, Charles; Pennsylvania, 1786 ***4629.10*** *p51*
Wilstack, Charles 35; Philadelphia, 1774 ***1220.25*** *p69*
Wiltberger, Jacob; Pennsylvania, 1788 ***4629.10*** *p56*
Wilton, Charles 52; Ontario, 1871 ***1823.22*** *p173*
Wilton, Jno; Virginia, 1663 ***6212.30*** *p2*
Wilton, Thomas 56; Ontario, 1871 ***1823.22*** *p173*
Wiltshire, F. B. 30; Alaska, 1917 ***9196.1*** *p49*
Wiltshire, F. B. 30; Yukon, 1917 ***9196.1*** *p49*
Wiltshire, John 21; Maryland, 1775 ***1220.25*** *p113*
Wimbles, Francis 31; Ontario, 1871 ***1823.22*** *p173*
Wimes, Sarah Ann 20; Ontario, 1871 ***1823.28*** *p105*
Wimmersheim, Franz Josef; Port uncertain, 1785 ***2856.30*** *p498*
Wimphenner, Mr.; Port uncertain, 1785 ***2856.30*** *p498*
Wimphenner, Ms.; Port uncertain, 1785 ***2856.30*** *p498*
Win, Louis; Maryland, 1910 ***3259.35*** *p68*
Win, Thomas; Maryland, 1656 ***2524.55*** *p243*
Winacher, Margarete; America, 1737 ***2856.30*** *p498*
With husband
Winacher, Margarete; America, 1748 ***2856.30*** *p498*
Winall, John; Maryland, 1652 ***2524.55*** *p244*
Winall, John; Maryland, 1666 ***2524.55*** *p243*
Winbeutel, Georg; Port uncertain, 1731 ***2856.30*** *p498*
Wincenty, John; Maryland, 1910 ***3259.35*** *p68*
Winch, Miss; Portland, Maine, 1858 ***9196.15*** *p30*
Winch, Elizabeth; Died enroute, 1661 ***1224.1*** *p65*
Winch, Richard 60; Ontario, 1871 ***1823.22*** *p173*
Winch, Thomas; Virginia, 1665 ***6212.30*** *p17*
Winchello, Miss; Quebec, 1858 ***9196.15*** *p34*
Winchester, Elspet 65; Ontario, 1871 ***1823.22*** *p173*
Winchester, John *SEE* Winchester, John
Winchester, John; Maryland, 1650 ***2524.55*** *p243*
Child: Mary
Child: John
With wife
Winchester, John; Maryland, 1658 ***2524.55*** *p243*
Winchester, Mary *SEE* Winchester, John
Winck, Burkard; Port uncertain, 1764 ***2856.30*** *p498*
Winck, Nikolaus; Port uncertain, 1764 ***2856.30*** *p498*
Winckauski, Stanisla; Maryland, 1910 ***3259.35*** *p68*
Winckelsog, Christof; Port uncertain, 1725 ***2856.30*** *p498*
Wincker, Johann; Port uncertain, 1740 ***2856.30*** *p498*
Winckler, Anna Maria; Port uncertain, 1746 ***2856.30*** *p498*
Winckler, Maria Clara; Port uncertain, 1769 ***2856.30*** *p498*
Winckler, Maria Magdalena; Port uncertain, 1767 ***2856.30*** *p498*
Wincklerin, Eva; Port uncertain, 1774 ***2856.30*** *p498*
Winckles, Edw; Maryland, 1672 ***2524.55*** *p243*
Winckles, Thomas; New York, 1836 ***8197.10*** *p317*
Wind, Christof; Port uncertain, 1764 ***2856.30*** *p498*
Wind, Daniell; Maryland, 1666 ***2524.55*** *p243*
Windeat, James; New York, 1836 ***8197.10*** *p295*
Windecker, Nikolaus; Port uncertain, 1785 ***2856.30*** *p489*
Winder, Bridgett *SEE* Winder, John
Winder, Friedrich; America, 1772 ***2856.30*** *p498*
Winder, Jane; Maryland, 1674 ***2524.55*** *p244*
Winder, John; Maryland, 1666 ***2524.55*** *p244*
Relative: Bridgett
Relative: Suzanna
Winder, John; Maryland, 1672 ***2524.55*** *p244*
Winder, Suzanna *SEE* Winder, John
Winderbank, Thomas 15; Maryland, 1775 ***1220.25*** *p100*
Windeyer, Mr.; Quebec, 1858 ***9196.15*** *p33*
Windeyer, Elizabeth Willcox; Iowa, 1856 ***1224.3*** *p86*
Windfeild, Thomas; Maryland, 1667 ***2524.55*** *p244*
Windlas, Richard; Maryland, 1665 ***2524.55*** *p244*
Windle, Mr.; Quebec, 1857 ***9196.15*** *p14*
Windle, James 65; Ontario, 1871 ***1823.28*** *p105*
Windle, John 60; Ontario, 1871 ***1823.28*** *p105*
Windle, Patrick 45; Ontario, 1871 ***1823.28*** *p105*
Windle, Susanna; Maryland, 1680 ***2524.55*** *p244*
Windle, William B.; New York, 1827 ***8197.10*** *p339*
Windmiller, Solomon; New York, 1820 ***8197.10*** *p291*
Windmuller, Solomon; New York, 1820 ***8197.10*** *p291*
Windore, John; Maryland, 1646 ***2524.55*** *p244*
Window, Elizabeth; Maryland, 1680 ***2524.55*** *p244*
Window, Thomas; Maryland, 1672 ***2524.55*** *p244*
Window, Thomas; Maryland, 1678 ***2524.55*** *p244*
Window, William; Maryland, 1680 ***2524.55*** *p244*
Window, William; Maryland, 1681 ***2524.55*** *p244*
Windram, Robert; Georgia, 1698 ***1640.13*** *p135*
Windsor, Alexander; Maryland, 1674 ***2524.55*** *p244*
Windsor, Jane; Maryland, 1675 ***2524.55*** *p244*
Windsor, Mary; Maryland, 1668 ***2524.55*** *p244*
Windsor, William H.; New York, 1840 ***8197.10*** *p203*
Windthauser, Elisabeth; Port uncertain, 1755 ***2856.30*** *p498*
Wine, Daniel; Maryland, 1667 ***2524.55*** *p244*
Wine, Elizabeth; Maryland, 1665 ***2524.55*** *p244*
Wine, Frederick 29; Ontario, 1871 ***1823.15*** *p285*
Winegood, Thomas; Maryland, 1661 ***2524.55*** *p244*
Winfield, Mr.; Grenada, 1775 ***1220.25*** *p133*
Winfield, Thomas; Virginia, 1722 ***1224.2*** *p126*
Wing, Anne; Vermont, 1856-1943 ***5900.10*** *p165*
Wing, George 74; Ontario, 1871 ***1823.15*** *p285*
Wing, Richard; Virginia, 1664 ***6212.30*** *p12*
Wing, Susanna 17; Maryland, 1775 ***1220.25*** *p109*
Wing, William 34; Ontario, 1871 ***1823.15*** *p285*
Wing, William 43; Ontario, 1871 ***1823.15*** *p285*
Wingard, Thomas; Port uncertain, 1773 ***2856.30*** *p484*
Wingasson, Abraham; New York, 1806 ***8197.10*** *p33*
Wingate, Mr.; Quebec, 1857 ***9196.15*** *p18*
Wingate, Mrs.; Quebec, 1857 ***9196.15*** *p18*
Wingate, Ezra 55; Ontario, 1871 ***1823.22*** *p173*
Wingatt, John; Virginia, 1665 ***6212.30*** *p19*
Wingert, Anna Maria; Port uncertain, 1778 ***2856.30*** *p498*
Wingert, Josef Peter; Port uncertain, 1756 ***2856.30*** *p498*
Wingert, Maria Catharina; Port uncertain, 1755 ***2856.30*** *p498*
Wingert, Maria Elisabeth; Port uncertain, 1757 ***2856.30*** *p498*
Wingerter, Jakob; Port uncertain, 1783 ***2856.30*** *p498*
Wingfield, John M. 32; Ontario, 1871 ***1823.28*** *p105*
Wingfield, William 30; Virginia, 1773 ***1220.25*** *p28*
Wingle, John 26; Ontario, 1871 ***1823.15*** *p285*
Wingle, Nicholas 55; Ontario, 1871 ***1823.15*** *p285*
Wingle, Patrick 60; Ontario, 1871 ***1823.28*** *p105*
Wingle, Thomas 40; Ontario, 1871 ***1823.28*** *p105*
Wingood, Tho; Virginia, 1665-1666 ***6212.30*** *p23*
Winham, William 17; Ontario, 1861 ***2896.27*** *p63*
Winiecki, Josef; Maryland, 1910 ***3259.35*** *p68*
Winiecki, Stanislaw; Maryland, 1910 ***3259.35*** *p68*
Winiecki, Tomasi; Maryland, 1910 ***3259.35*** *p68*
Winifride, Mr.; Maryland, 1638 ***2524.55*** *p244*
Winkel, Hans Georg; America, 1751 ***2856.30*** *p498*
Winkenwader, John 29; Ontario, 1871 ***1823.15*** *p285*
Winkenweather, John 65; Ontario, 1871 ***1823.15*** *p285*
Winkie, John C. 56; Ontario, 1871 ***1823.28*** *p105*
Winkie, William 36; Ontario, 1871 ***1823.28*** *p105*
Winkle, Frederick; Pennsylvania, 1786 ***4629.10*** *p52*
Winkler, F. P. 61; Alaska, 1917 ***9196.1*** *p49*
Winkler, F. P. 61; Yukon, 1917 ***9196.1*** *p49*
Winkler, John Frederick; New York, 1834 ***8197.10*** *p295*
Winkler, Margarete; Port uncertain, 1788 ***2856.30*** *p498*
Winkler, Veit; America, 1764 ***2856.30*** *p499*
With wife & children
Winkles, Edward; Maryland, 1682 ***2524.55*** *p244*
Winklewsky, John H.; Maryland, 1910 ***3259.35*** *p68*
Winn, David 17; Fort Cumberland, Nova Scotia, 1774 ***1220.25*** *p19*
Winn, Harriett 66; Ontario, 1871 ***1823.22*** *p173*
Winn, J. H.; Portland, Maine, 1857 ***9196.15*** *p12*
Winn, Joel 70; Ontario, 1871 ***1823.22*** *p173*
Winn, John 52; New York, New York, 1847 ***1825.45*** *p21*
Son: Patrick 22
Daughter: Mary 13
Winn, John 92; Ontario, 1871 ***1823.22*** *p173*
Winn, John 97; Vermont, 1890 ***5900.10*** *p412*
Winn, Mary 13 *SEE* Winn, John
Winn, Mary Clark 96; Vermont, 1903 ***5900.10*** *p412*
Winn, Patrick 22 *SEE* Winn, John
Winn, Thomas; New York, 1840 ***8197.10*** *p296*
Winn, William; Virginia, 1665 ***6212.30*** *p18*
Winn, William 27; Fort Cumberland, Nova Scotia, 1774 ***1220.25*** *p19*
Winne, John; Virginia, 1753 ***1224.2*** *p128*
Winne, Tho.; Maryland, 1663 ***2524.55*** *p244*
Winnhold, Friedrich; America, 1746 ***2856.30*** *p499*
Winniett, Charles; New York, 1804 ***1224.3*** *p86*
Winning, William; New York, 1821 ***8197.10*** *p292*
Winnington, Dorothy; Maryland, 1663 ***2524.55*** *p244*
Winnoll, John; Maryland, 1652 ***2524.55*** *p244*
Winnosky, John; Maryland, 1910 ***3259.35*** *p68*
Winrow, George; New York, 1836 ***8197.10*** *p76*
Winsel, Peter; New York, 1821 ***8197.10*** *p292*
Winship, Thomas 26; North Carolina, 1774 ***1220.25*** *p65*
Winski, John; Maryland, 1910 ***3259.35*** *p68*
Winskia, John; Maryland, 1910 ***3259.35*** *p68*
Winsley, Nicholas; Maryland, 1664 ***2524.55*** *p244*

Winslow, Anne *SEE* Winslow, William
Winslow, Curtha; Maryland, 1675 ***2524.55*** *p244*
Winslow, Edward; Vermont, 1844-1916 ***5900.10*** *p90*
Winslow, Hannah; Rhode Island, 1797 ***1224.2*** *p126*
Winslow, Isaac; New York, New York, 1780 ***1224.2*** *p126*
Winslow, John; Hingham, Massachusetts, 1776 ***1224.2*** *p126*
Winslow, Joshua; Boston, 1781 ***1224.2*** *p126*
Winslow, Mary *SEE* Winslow, William
Winslow, Mary; Boston, 1787 ***1224.2*** *p126*
Winslow, Mary Craven; Vermont, 1846-1937 ***5900.10*** *p90*
Winslow, William *SEE* Winslow, William
Winslow, William; Maryland, 1680 ***2524.55*** *p244*
Wife: Mary
Child: Anne
Child: William
Winsly, John; Virginia, 1667 ***6212.30*** *p37*
Winsom, Emily 23; Ontario, 1861 ***2896.28*** *p37*
Winson, Peter; New York, 1821 ***8197.10*** *p292*
Winsor, Elizabeth 25; Ontario, 1871 ***1823.22*** *p173*
Winsor, John; Maryland, 1676 ***2524.55*** *p244*
Winston, Jno; Virginia, 1666 ***6212.30*** *p31*
Winten, John 58; Ontario, 1871 ***1823.15*** *p285*
Wintent, William 22; Maryland, 1774 ***1220.25*** *p84*
Winter, Miss; Quebec, 1858 ***9196.15*** *p46*
Winter, Adam 7; Kansas, 1910 ***9079.10*** *p49*
Winter, Anna Margarete; Port uncertain, 1738 ***2856.30*** *p499*
Winter, Augusta 22; Kansas, 1910 ***9079.10*** *p46*
Winter, C. 8; Ontario, 1861 ***2896.26*** *p13*
Winter, Catherine 1; New York, New York, 1847 ***1825.45*** *p21*
Winter, Charles 25; Ontario, 1871 ***1823.28*** *p105*
Winter, Christian; Port uncertain, 1780 ***2856.30*** *p499*
Winter, Dehlia 4; Kansas, 1910 ***9079.10*** *p46*
Winter, E. 3; Ontario, 1861 ***2896.26*** *p13*
Winter, E. 14; Ontario, 1861 ***2896.26*** *p13*
Winter, E. A. 6; Ontario, 1861 ***2896.26*** *p13*
Winter, E. A. 13; Ontario, 1861 ***2896.26*** *p13*
Winter, Elizabeth; Alabama, 1821-1845 ***1640.10*** *p214*
Husband: F.
Winter, Elizabeth 19; Philadelphia, 1774 ***1220.25*** *p63*
Winter, F. *SEE* Winter, Elizabeth
Winter, Franz; Port uncertain, 1777 ***2856.30*** *p499*
Winter, Friedrich; America, 1752 ***2856.30*** *p499*
Winter, G. Y. 5; Ontario, 1861 ***2896.26*** *p13*
Winter, George 25; Kansas, 1910 ***9079.10*** *p46*
Winter, H. 40; Ontario, 1861 ***2896.26*** *p13*
Winter, H. C. 6; Ontario, 1861 ***2896.26*** *p13*
Winter, Hans Georg; America, 1732 ***2856.30*** *p499*
With wife
Winter, Hans Georg; America, 1733 ***2856.30*** *p499*
Winter, Honor 18 *SEE* Winter, Honor
Winter, Honor 60; New York, New York, 1847 ***1825.45*** *p21*
Son: Thomas 30
Daughter: Honor 18
Daughter: Margaret 24
Winter, Jacob 35; Kansas, 1910 ***9079.10*** *p49*
Winter, James; New York, 1826 ***8197.10*** *p293*
Winter, James 21; Philadelphia, 1774 ***1220.25*** *p63*
Winter, Johann; Port uncertain, 1789 ***2856.30*** *p499*
Winter, Johann Georg; America, 1767 ***2856.30*** *p499*
Winter, Johann Georg; Port uncertain, 1764 ***2856.30*** *p499*
Winter, Johann Georg; Port uncertain, 1771 ***2856.30*** *p499*
Winter, Johann Nikolaus; Port uncertain, 1748 ***2856.30*** *p499*
Winter, John; Charles Town, South Carolina, 1781 ***1224.2*** *p126*
Winter, John 28; Maryland, 1774 ***1220.25*** *p60*
Winter, Juliana Frideri; Port uncertain, 1797 ***2856.30*** *p499*
Winter, M. M. 13; Ontario, 1861 ***2896.26*** *p13*
Winter, Margaret 24 *SEE* Winter, Honor
Winter, Margarete; America, 1766 ***2856.30*** *p499*
With husband
Winter, Mary 19; Ontario, 1861 ***2896.27*** *p47*
Winter, Mary 37; Vermont, 1858 ***5900.10*** *p264*
Winter, Mollie 32; Kansas, 1910 ***9079.10*** *p49*
Winter, Paulina 2; Kansas, 1910 ***9079.10*** *p46*
Winter, Robert; Maryland, 1657 ***2524.55*** *p244*
Winter, Robert; Maryland, 1666 ***2524.55*** *p244*
Winter, Samuel Friedric; America, 1772 ***2856.30*** *p499*
Winter, Sarah 46; Ontario, 1871 ***1823.15*** *p285*
Winter, Stephen 21; Maryland, 1774 ***1220.25*** *p52*
Winter, Thomas; Maryland, 1657 ***2524.55*** *p244*
Winter, Thomas; Maryland, 1666 ***2524.55*** *p244*
Winter, Thomas; Maryland, 1677-1681 ***2524.55*** *p244*
Winter, Thomas; Pennsylvania, 1778 ***4629.10*** *p32*
Winter, Thomas 21; Carolina, 1774 ***1220.25*** *p75*
Winter, Thomas 30 *SEE* Winter, Honor
Winter, U. 18; Ontario, 1861 ***2896.26*** *p13*
Winterbottom, Cicero; New York, 1840 ***8197.10*** *p203*
Winterhoff, Rudolph; New York, 1845 ***8197.10*** *p10*
Winters, Annie E.; Vermont, 1854-1924 ***5900.10*** *p336*
Winters, Antonia; Maryland, 1910 ***3259.35*** *p68*
Winters, Catherine 1; New York, New York, 1847 ***1825.45*** *p21*
Winters, Cathrine 84; Ontario, 1871 ***1823.15*** *p285*
Winters, Cristian; Virginia, 1663 ***6212.30*** *p4*
Winters, Hanora 98; Vermont, 1879 ***5900.10*** *p428*
Winters, Henry 2; Vermont, 1850 ***5900.10*** *p348*
Winters, Honor 18 *SEE* Winters, Honor
Winters, Honor 60; New York, New York, 1847 ***1825.45*** *p21*
Son: Thomas 30
Daughter: Margaret 24
Daughter: Honor 18
Winters, John 57; Vermont, 1882 ***5900.10*** *p427*
Winters, John 60; Ontario, 1871 ***1823.28*** *p105*
Winters, John 66; Vermont, 1880 ***5900.10*** *p260*
Winters, Margaret 24 *SEE* Winters, Honor
Winters, Margaret 64; Vermont, 1893 ***5900.10*** *p417*
Winters, Mary 46; Vermont, 1872 ***5900.10*** *p260*
Winters, Mary Maloney 84; Vermont, 1919 ***5900.10*** *p428*
Winters, Nancy 63; Vermont, 1874 ***5900.10*** *p559*
Winters, Nancy 63; Vermont, 1874 ***5900.10*** *p568*
Winters, Sarah J. 58; Vermont, 1908 ***5900.10*** *p568*
Winters, Thomas 30 *SEE* Winters, Honor
Winters, Thomas 73; Vermont, 1891 ***5900.10*** *p417*
Wintert, Friedrich; Port uncertain, 1790 ***2856.30*** *p499*
Winterton, William; New York, 1807 ***8197.10*** *p52*
Winther, Georg; Port uncertain, 1752 ***2856.30*** *p499*
Winther, Melchior; Port uncertain, 1746 ***2856.30*** *p499*
Winther, Samuel; America, 1751 ***2856.30*** *p499*
With wife & 7 children
Winthrop, . . .; Boston, 1658 ***1224.1*** *p65*
Winthrop, Elizabeth; New England, 1659 ***1224.1*** *p32*
Winton, David; Georgia, 1699 ***1640.13*** *p135*
Wintringham, Thomas; New York, 1830 ***8197.10*** *p299*
Wintter, H. G.; America, 1752 ***2856.30*** *p22*
Wintter, Hans Georg; America, 1752 ***2856.30*** *p499*
With wife
Wintz, Christian; New York, 1838-1840 ***8197.10*** *p201*
Winz, Georg; America, 1764 ***2856.30*** *p499*
With wife & 6 children
Winz, Margarete; America, 1765 ***2856.30*** *p499*
Winz, Sybilla; America, 1765 ***2856.30*** *p499*
Winzel, Johann Niklas; Port uncertain, 1742 ***2856.30*** *p499*
Winzenty, Alfred; Maryland, 1910 ***3259.35*** *p68*
Winzin, Margarete; America, 1765 ***2856.30*** *p499*
Winzin, Sybilla; America, 1765 ***2856.30*** *p499*
Wiprecht, Ludwig; Maryland, 1910 ***3259.35*** *p68*
Wirch, Richard; Maryland, 1673 ***2524.55*** *p244*
Wirdeberger, Johann Adam; America, 1751 ***2856.30*** *p499*
Wirsching, Abraham; America, 1753 ***2856.30*** *p499*
Wirsching, Hans Georg; America, 1753 ***2856.30*** *p499*
With 2 children
Wirsing, Johann Jakob; Port uncertain, 1755 ***2856.30*** *p499*
Wirth, John H. G.; New York, 1803 ***8197.10*** *p17*
Wirth, Peter; Port uncertain, 1758 ***2856.30*** *p500*
Wirth, Regina; Port uncertain, 1798 ***2856.30*** *p500*
Wirths, Maria Juliana; Port uncertain, 1775 ***2856.30*** *p500*
Wirtsin, Anna Ursula; Port uncertain, 1754 ***2856.30*** *p500*
Wirtz, Jacob; New York, 1838 ***8197.10*** *p151*
Wirz, Paul; Port uncertain, 1751 ***2856.30*** *p500*
Wischler, Michael; New York, 1839 ***8197.10*** *p135*
Wischnehski, Fred; Maryland, 1910 ***3259.35*** *p68*
Wise, Benjamin 18; Maryland, 1775 ***1220.25*** *p109*
Wise, Charles 21; Virginia, 1774 ***1220.25*** *p75*
Wise, Edward; Pennsylvania, 1853 ***1224.3*** *p86*
Wise, Henrey 25; Ontario, 1871 ***1823.28*** *p105*
Wise, John; New York, 1749 ***1224.2*** *p126*
Wise, John; Virginia, 1685 ***1224.1*** *p65*
Wise, Lydia 21; Georgia, 1774 ***1220.25*** *p48*
Wise, Magdalena; America, 1733 ***2856.30*** *p500*
Wise, Martin; New York, 1840 ***8197.10*** *p203*
Wise, Michael; America, 1733 ***2856.30*** *p500*
Wise, Richard; Maryland, 1681 ***2524.55*** *p244*
Wise, Tho; Virginia, 1671-1672 ***6212.30*** *p47*
Wise, William 57; Ontario, 1871 ***1823.15*** *p285*
Wisedale, Margery; Maryland, 1657 ***2524.55*** *p40*
Wiseman, David 53; Ontario, 1871 ***1823.15*** *p285*
Wiseman, James; New York, 1832 ***8197.10*** *p356*
Wiseman, Michael; New York, 1827 ***8197.10*** *p345*
Wiseman, Philip; Pennsylvania, 1777 ***4629.10*** *p24*
Wiseman, Richard 24; Maryland, 1775 ***1220.25*** *p105*
Wiseman, Robt.; Maryland, 1656 ***2524.55*** *p244*
Wiseman, Robt; Virginia, 1665-1666 ***6212.30*** *p23*
Wiseman, Timothy 50; Ontario, 1871 ***1823.22*** *p173*
Wiser, A. M.; America, 1754 ***2856.30*** *p252*
Wiser, Anna Maria; Port uncertain, 1754 ***2856.30*** *p500*
Wiser, Ludwick; Pennsylvania, 1777 ***4629.10*** *p20*
Wisgau, Martin 37; Ontario, 1871 ***1823.28*** *p105*
Wishart, Mr.; Quebec, 1858 ***9196.15*** *p36*
Wishart, John; New York, 1796 ***8197.10*** *p7*
Wisher, James 49; Ontario, 1871 ***1823.22*** *p173*
Wishert, Wisenty; Maryland, 1910 ***3259.35*** *p68*
Wismerski, Mike; Maryland, 1910 ***3259.35*** *p68*
Wisnieski, Walter; Maryland, 1910 ***3259.35*** *p68*
Wisniewska, Agnes; Maryland, 1910 ***3259.35*** *p68*
Wisniewska, Antonina; Maryland, 1910 ***3259.35*** *p68*
Wisniewska, Mary; Maryland, 1910 ***3259.35*** *p68*
Wisniewska, Michalina; Maryland, 1910 ***3259.35*** *p68*
Wisniewski, Bernard; Maryland, 1910 ***3259.35*** *p68*
Wisniewski, Frank; Maryland, 1910 ***3259.35*** *p68*
Wisniewski, Ignacy; Maryland, 1910 ***3259.35*** *p68*
Wisniewski, Joseph; Maryland, 1910 ***3259.35*** *p68*
Wisniewski, Lawrence; Maryland, 1910 ***3259.35*** *p68*
Wisniewski, Marion; Maryland, 1910 ***3259.35*** *p68*
Wisniewski, Mary; Maryland, 1910 ***3259.35*** *p68*
Wisniewski, Stanislaus; Maryland, 1910 ***3259.35*** *p68*
Wisocki, Francis; Maryland, 1910 ***3259.35*** *p68*
Wisocky, Antoni; Maryland, 1910 ***3259.35*** *p68*
Wisomatey, Frank; Maryland, 1910 ***3259.35*** *p68*
Wissinger, John 37; Kansas, 1909-1910 ***9079.10*** *p10*
Wissinger, Leo 7; Kansas, 1909-1910 ***9079.10*** *p10*
Wissinger, Melcher; Pennsylvania, 1776 ***4629.10*** *p53*
Wisson, James 45; Ontario, 1871 ***1823.15*** *p285*
Wister, John, Jr.; Pennsylvania, 1777 ***4629.10*** *p22*
Wister, Richard, Jr.; Pennsylvania, 1777 ***4629.10*** *p22*
Wisuski, Amelia; Maryland, 1910 ***3259.35*** *p68*
Wisznevski, Jacob; Maryland, 1910 ***3259.35*** *p68*
Witcherly, Thomas; Maryland, 1677 ***2524.55*** *p244*
Withall, Samuel; Virginia, 1701 ***1224.2*** *p126*
Withards, Michael; Georgia, 1698 ***1640.13*** *p135*
Wither, William 20; Ontario, 1871 ***1823.15*** *p285*
Witherell, Addie M.; Vermont, 1867-1929 ***5900.10*** *p402*
Witherington, John 27; Maryland, 1774 ***1220.25*** *p5*
Witherley, William 27; Philadelphia, 1774 ***1220.25*** *p3*
Withers, Elinor; Maryland, 1673 ***2524.55*** *p244*
Withers, Hazard; Oswego, New York, 1763 ***1224.2*** *p126*
Withers, Henry; New York, 1839 ***8197.10*** *p381*
Withers, Henry; Virginia, 1658 ***1224.1*** *p65*
Withers, James 21; Maryland, 1774 ***1220.25*** *p74*
Withers, Jane 21; Virginia, 1774 ***1220.25*** *p54*
Withers, John; New York, 1839 ***8197.10*** *p382*
Witherspoon, J.; Georgia, 1764 ***1640.10*** *p215*
Witherspoon, James; New York, 1834 ***8197.10*** *p359*
Witherspoon, James 56; Ontario, 1871 ***1823.15*** *p285*
Witherup, John; Pennsylvania, 1785 ***4629.10*** *p48*
Witkofski, Joseph; Maryland, 1910 ***3259.35*** *p68*
Witkowski, Frances; Maryland, 1910 ***3259.35*** *p68*
Witkowsky, Stefan; Maryland, 1910 ***3259.35*** *p68*
Witlinger, Jacob; Port uncertain, 1713 ***2856.30*** *p500*
With wife & 3 children
Witney, Howard 60; Ontario, 1871 ***1823.22*** *p173*
Witomski, Eva; Maryland, 1910 ***3259.35*** *p68*
Witrowe, Robert; Maryland, 1675 ***2524.55*** *p245*
Witschger, Nicolaus; Port uncertain, 1751 ***2856.30*** *p500*
Witt, Frances 36; Ontario, 1871 ***1823.28*** *p105*
Witt, Fredrick 48; Ontario, 1871 ***1823.28*** *p105*
Witt, Jost; America, 1754 ***2856.30*** *p497*
Witte, Friederick; New York, 1837 ***8197.10*** *p104*
Witte, Henre; New York, 1838 ***8197.10*** *p295*
Wittepack, Casper; Pennsylvania, 1777 ***4629.10*** *p20*
Witterich, Martin; America, 1752 ***2856.30*** *p500*
Wittib, . . .; America, 1746 ***2856.30*** *p500*
Wittkowsky, Frank; Maryland, 1910 ***3259.35*** *p68*
Wittle, Magdalen; Maryland, 1646 ***2524.55*** *p238*
Wittmann, Benedikt; America, 1749 ***2856.30*** *p500*
Wittmann, Jhoann Henrich; Port uncertain, 1751 ***2856.30*** *p500*
Wittmann, Konrad; Port uncertain, 1790 ***2856.30*** *p500*
With wife & children
Wittmer, Benedikt; Port uncertain, 1733 ***2856.30*** *p500*
Wittmer, Konrad; Port uncertain, 1749 ***2856.30*** *p500*
Wittmer, Sebastian; America, 1761 ***2856.30*** *p500*
Wittner, Sebastian; Port uncertain, 1753 ***2856.30*** *p500*
Wittrock, Hans Christopher; New York, 1819 ***8197.10*** *p291*
Witts, Charles 49; Ontario, 1871 ***1823.15*** *p285*
Witts, Christina 68; Ontario, 1871 ***1823.28*** *p105*
Witts, Daniel 76; Ontario, 1871 ***1823.28*** *p105*
Witts, Herman 30; Ontario, 1871 ***1823.28*** *p105*
Witts, Michael 73; Ontario, 1871 ***1823.28*** *p105*
Witts, Neziah 18; Ontario, 1871 ***1823.15*** *p285*
Witts, William 42; Ontario, 1871 ***1823.28*** *p105*
Wittsien, Johes; New York, 1838 ***8197.10*** *p295*
Witty, John 32; Nova Scotia, 1774 ***1220.25*** *p135*

Woodrow, P. J. 16; Ontario, 1861 ***2896.26*** *p13*
Woodrow, S. 33; Ontario, 1861 ***2896.26*** *p10*
Woodrow, William 27; Ontario, 1861 ***2896.26*** *p1*
Woodruff, Lieut.; Quebec, 1857 ***9196.15*** *p14*
Woodruff, Daniel 31; Ontario, 1871 ***1823.15*** *p286*
Woodruff, James 42; Ontario, 1871 ***1823.22*** *p174*
Woodruff, John 65; Ontario, 1871 ***1823.22*** *p174*
Woodruff, Thomas 39; Ontario, 1871 ***1823.22*** *p174*
Woods, Mr.; Portland, Maine, 1858 ***9196.15*** *p47*
Woods, Mr.; Quebec, 1857 ***9196.15*** *p14*
Woods, Mrs.; Portland, Maine, 1858 ***9196.15*** *p47*
Woods, Mrs.; Quebec, 1857 ***9196.15*** *p14*
Woods, Andrew; Vermont, 1830-1911 ***5900.10*** *p224*
Woods, Ann 40; Ontario, 1871 ***1823.22*** *p174*
Woods, Ann 65; Ontario, 1871 ***1823.15*** *p286*
Woods, Ann Spears; Vermont, 1831-1913 ***5900.10*** *p224*
Woods, Benjamin; Pennsylvania, 1779 ***4629.10*** *p37*
Woods, Bridget E. Daley; Vermont, 1842-1909 ***5900.10*** *p65*
Woods, Caroline 37; Ontario, 1871 ***1823.22*** *p174*
Woods, Catharine 76; Vermont, 1894 ***5900.10*** *p223*
Woods, Charlotte 46; Ontario, 1871 ***1823.28*** *p106*
Woods, Eliza 24; Ontario, 1871 ***1823.28*** *p106*
Woods, Henry; Vermont, 1819-1887 ***5900.10*** *p481*
Woods, Henry; Vermont, 1849-1895 ***5900.10*** *p481*
Woods, Henry 30; Ontario, 1871 ***1823.15*** *p286*
Woods, James; New York, 1840 ***8197.10*** *p296*
Woods, James 65; Ontario, 1871 ***1823.15*** *p286*
Woods, John; Pennsylvania, 1822 ***6058.10*** *p8*
Woods, John 16; Maryland, 1775 ***1220.25*** *p115*
Woods, John 33; Ontario, 1871 ***1823.22*** *p174*
Woods, John 47; Ontario, 1871 ***1823.22*** *p174*
Woods, John 69; Ontario, 1871 ***1823.22*** *p174*
Woods, John 70; Vermont, 1870 ***5900.10*** *p74*
Woods, John M. 24; Vermont, 1871 ***5900.10*** *p287*
Woods, John T.; Vermont, 1842-1904 ***5900.10*** *p65*
Woods, Joseph; Philadelphia, n.d. ***1224.2*** *p127*
Woods, Julia; Vermont, 1821-1882 ***5900.10*** *p481*
Woods, Martha; Maryland, 1674 ***2524.55*** *p245*
Woods, Martha; Maryland, 1677 ***2524.55*** *p245*
Woods, Mary; Vermont, 1830-1900 ***5900.10*** *p473*
Woods, Mary; Vermont, 1906 ***5900.10*** *p78*
Woods, Mary 73; Vermont, 1902 ***5900.10*** *p297*
Woods, Mary A.; Vermont, 1857-1926 ***5900.10*** *p223*
Woods, Nancy Collins; Vermont, 1844-1900 ***5900.10*** *p224*
Woods, Neal 60; Vermont, 1866 ***5900.10*** *p280*
Woods, Patrick 45; Ontario, 1871 ***1823.15*** *p286*
Woods, Peter; New York, 1822 ***8197.10*** *p293*
Woods, R. 42; Alaska, 1917 ***9196.1*** *p47*
Woods, R. 42; Whitehorse, Yukon, 1917 ***9196.1*** *p47*
Woods, Rosa; Vermont, 1860-1901 ***5900.10*** *p224*
Woods, Thomas; New York, 1837 ***8197.10*** *p104*
Woods, Thomas 47; Ontario, 1871 ***1823.22*** *p174*
Woods, Thomas 60; Ontario, 1871 ***1823.15*** *p286*
Woods, Thomas 63; Ontario, 1871 ***1823.15*** *p286*
Woods, Thomas 77; Ontario, 1871 ***1823.22*** *p174*
Woods, William; New York, 1834 ***8197.10*** *p69*
Woods, William 37; Ontario, 1871 ***1823.22*** *p174*
Woods, William 41; Ontario, 1871 ***1823.28*** *p106*
Woodside, James; Massachusetts, 1746 ***1224.2*** *p127*
Woodside, James; West Indies, 1746 ***1224.2*** *p127*
Woodson, William 71; Ontario, 1871 ***1823.22*** *p174*
Woodstock, John 25; Maryland, 1775 ***1220.25*** *p116*
Woodsworth, E. J. 2; Ontario, 1861 ***2896.25*** *p52*
Woodsworth, N. S. 24; Ontario, 1861 ***2896.25*** *p52*
Woodsworth, Thomas 5; Ontario, 1861 ***2896.25*** *p52*
Woodville, John; Dominica, 1776 ***1224.2*** *p127*
Woodville, John; Philadelphia, 1776 ***1224.2*** *p127*
Woodward, Alce; Maryland, 1662 ***2524.55*** *p245*
Woodward, Elizabeth; New York, 1849 ***1224.3*** *p86*
Woodward, George; New York, 1837 ***8197.10*** *p374*
Woodward, John; New York, New York, 1850 ***1224.3*** *p86*
Woodward, Mary Jackson; Boston, 1646 ***1224.1*** *p32*
Woodward, Nich; Virginia, 1663 ***6212.30*** *p4*
Woodward, Samuel; Cape Fear, North Carolina, 1751 ***1224.2*** *p127*
Woodward, Thomas 21; Virginia, 1775 ***1220.25*** *p95*
Woody, Jane *SEE* Woody, Thomas
Woody, Robert 33; Ontario, 1871 ***1823.15*** *p286*
Woody, Thomas; Maryland, 1665 ***2524.55*** *p228*
Wife: Jane
Woodyer, Ann; Virginia, 1671 ***6212.30*** *p43*
Woodyer, Geo; Virginia, 1665-1666 ***6212.30*** *p24*
Woodyer, Jno; Virginia, 1664 ***6212.30*** *p13*
Woofendale, John; New York, 1807 ***8197.10*** *p53*
Wooffendale, Robert; New York, 1807 ***8197.10*** *p52*
Woog, Friedrich; Port uncertain, 1756 ***2856.30*** *p503*
Woog, Johann; Port uncertain, 1781 ***2856.30*** *p503*
Woolcott, John; Maryland, 1649 ***2524.55*** *p228*
Wooldrich, George; New York, 1811 ***8197.10*** *p57*
Wooldridge, John; New York, 1813 ***8197.10*** *p58*
Wooldridge, Maria Henrietta; St. Augustine, Florida, 1770 ***1224.2*** *p127*
Wooldridge, Nicholas; Maryland, 1651 ***2524.55*** *p245*
Woolett, Robert 16; Philadelphia, 1774 ***1220.25*** *p67*
Wooley, Mr.; Quebec, 1857 ***9196.15*** *p25*
Wooley, Mrs.; Quebec, 1857 ***9196.15*** *p25*
Wooley, Charles Hitch; St. Vincent, 1796 ***1640.13*** *p135*
Wooley, George 31; Ontario, 1871 ***1823.28*** *p106*
Wooley, William 47; Ontario, 1871 ***1823.15*** *p286*
Woolf, Anthony; New York, 1797 ***8197.10*** *p8*
Woolf, William 42; Ontario, 1871 ***1823.22*** *p174*
Woolfield, Charles 24; Ontario, 1871 ***1823.28*** *p106*
Woolford, Mary *SEE* Woolford, Roger
Woolford, Roger; Maryland, 1665 ***2524.55*** *p245*
Wife: Mary
Daughter: Mary
Woolgast, Cornelius *SEE* Woolgast, Otta
Woolgast, Elizabeth *SEE* Woolgast, Otta
Woolgast, Otta; Maryland, 1673 ***2524.55*** *p245*
Wife: Elizabeth
Son: Cornelius
Woollaston, Mr.; Quebec, 1858 ***9196.15*** *p38*
Woollaston, Mrs.; Quebec, 1858 ***9196.15*** *p38*
Woollen, Annie 71; Vermont, 1929 ***5900.10*** *p426*
Woollerton, Joan; Virginia, 1666-1667 ***6212.30*** *p35*
Woolley, William J.; New York, 1838 ***8197.10*** *p152*
Woolley, Wm; Virginia, 1665-1666 ***6212.30*** *p23*
Woollful, Charles; Pennsylvania, 1777 ***4629.10*** *p22*
Woollis, John; Maryland, 1674 ***2524.55*** *p245*
Woolsey, George; New York, 1794 ***8197.10*** *p3*
Woolsey, John; Maryland, 1666 ***2524.55*** *p245*
Woolthary, Henry; Maryland, 1649 ***2524.55*** *p245*
Woolthwith, Henry; Maryland, 1649 ***2524.55*** *p245*
Woore, Thomas; New York, 1837 ***8197.10*** *p103*
Woosencroft, James 23; Virginia, 1774 ***1220.25*** *p93*
Wooster, Abraham; Virginia, 1667-1668 ***6212.30*** *p39*
Worchezski, James; Maryland, 1910 ***3259.35*** *p69*
Worczonek, John; Maryland, 1910 ***3259.35*** *p70*
Worczynski, William; Maryland, 1910 ***3259.35*** *p70*
Word, John 26; Maryland, 1775 ***1220.25*** *p104*
Worden, Almira 37; Ontario, 1861 ***2896.26*** *p38*
Worden, Evalina 12; Ontario, 1861 ***2896.26*** *p38*
Worden, Gurana 10; Ontario, 1861 ***2896.26*** *p38*
Worden, Henry 55; Ontario, 1861 ***2896.26*** *p38*
Worden, Marcus 7; Ontario, 1861 ***2896.26*** *p38*
Worden, Martha Jane; Quebec, 1858 ***9196.15*** *p38*
Worden, Thersia 7; Ontario, 1861 ***2896.26*** *p38*
Worden, W. H. 23; Ontario, 1861 ***2896.25*** *p30*
Wore, Timothy; Virginia, 1666 ***6212.30*** *p25*
Worgan, Alice; Maryland, 1667 ***2524.55*** *p246*
Husband: William
Worgan, William *SEE* Worgan, Alice
Worham, Miss; Quebec, 1858 ***9196.15*** *p43*
Worisnicki, Virginia; Maryland, 1910 ***3259.35*** *p70*
Workeman, Anthony; Maryland, 1680 ***2524.55*** *p246*
Worker, James 23; Maryland, 1774 ***1220.25*** *p78*
Workham, Mrs.; Quebec, 1858 ***9196.15*** *p35*
Workman, Anthony; Maryland, 1673 ***2524.55*** *p246*
Workman, Anthony; Maryland, 1680 ***2524.55*** *p246*
Workman, Elizabeth; Maryland, 1680 ***2524.55*** *p246*
Workman, Hannah 77; Ontario, 1871 ***1823.22*** *p174*
Workman, John 29; Ontario, 1871 ***1823.15*** *p286*
Worland, John; Maryland, 1662 ***2524.55*** *p246*
World, Joshua; New York, 1840 ***8197.10*** *p321*
Worler, Francis; Virginia, 1669-1670 ***6212.30*** *p41*
Worlich, Johann Michael; America, 1751 ***2856.30*** *p505*
With wife & children
Worly, John; Maryland, 1681 ***2524.55*** *p246*
Worm, Daniel 55; Ontario, 1871 ***1823.15*** *p286*
Wormald, W. E.; Pennsylvania, 1838 ***6058.10*** *p15*
Wormeley, Ralph Randolph; Newport, Rhode Island, 1852 ***1224.3*** *p87*
Wormersly, Henry; New York, New York, 1832 ***6058.10*** *p34*
Wormington, John; Philadelphia, n.d. ***1224.2*** *p127*
Worner, Catharina *SEE* Worner, Sebastian
Worner, Catharina; Port uncertain, 1750 ***2856.30*** *p506*
Son: Sebastian
Worner, Ignaz; Port uncertain, 1796 ***2856.30*** *p505*
Worner, Johann; America, 1752 ***2856.30*** *p491*
With wife & children
Worner, Martin; Port uncertain, 1686 ***2856.30*** *p491*
Worner, Martin; Port uncertain, 1732 ***2856.30*** *p491*
Worner, Philipp Jacob; America, 1751 ***2856.30*** *p505*
Worner, Sebastian *SEE* Worner, Catharina
Worner, Sebastian; America, 1750 ***2856.30*** *p506*
Mother: Catharina
Wornersley, Henry; New York, New York, 1832 ***6058.10*** *p34*
Woroski, Frank; Maryland, 1910 ***3259.35*** *p70*
Worrall, Eliza; Virginia, 1667-1668 ***6212.30*** *p39*
Worrall, Elizabeth; Vermont, 1840-1900 ***5900.10*** *p417*
Worrell, Isaac; Pennsylvania, 1777 ***4629.10*** *p23*
Worrell, Isaiah; Pennsylvania, 1786 ***4629.10*** *p51*
Worrell, James; Pennsylvania, 1779 ***4629.10*** *p35*
Worrell, James; Virginia, 1666 ***6212.30*** *p25*
Worrell, Michaell; Virginia, 1664-1665 ***6212.30*** *p16*
Worrell, Peter; Pennsylvania, 1777 ***4629.10*** *p13*
Worrell, Robert; Pennsylvania, 1786 ***4629.10*** *p51*
Worrell, Wm; Virginia, 1668-1669 ***6212.30*** *p41*
Worris, Jacob; Maryland, 1910 ***3259.35*** *p70*
Worsell, Tho; Virginia, 1681 ***6212.30*** *p55*
Worsey, William; New York, 1796 ***8197.10*** *p7*
Worslake, John *SEE* Worslake, John
Worslake, John; Maryland, 1662 ***2524.55*** *p246*
Wife: Magdalen
Son: John
Worslake, Magdalen *SEE* Worslake, John
Worsley, Mary; Maryland, 1681 ***2524.55*** *p246*
Worstall, James; Pennsylvania, 1776 ***4629.10*** *p53*
Worston, Thomas; Maryland, 1672 ***2524.55*** *p246*
Wort, Martin; Pennsylvania, 1777 ***4629.10*** *p9*
Worth, Obed; Nantucket, Massachusetts, 1816 ***1224.3*** *p87*
Worth, Shubael; Nantucket, Massachusetts, 1806 ***1224.3*** *p87*
Worthington, Elizabeth Laugher; Hartford, Connecticut, n.d. ***1224.3*** *p87*
Worthington, John; Maryland, 1769 ***1224.2*** *p127*
Worthington, Thomas; Maryland, 1676 ***2524.55*** *p246*
Worthington, William; Maryland, 1771 ***1224.2*** *p127*
Worthy, Damaris; Virginia, 1663 ***6212.30*** *p4*
Worthy, John 42; Ontario, 1871 ***1823.15*** *p286*
Worthy, Thomas; New York, 1794 ***8197.10*** *p3*
Wortley, John; New England, 1712 ***1224.2*** *p127*
Wortman, Henry; New York, 1840 ***8197.10*** *p202*
Wortman, Robert; New York, 1797 ***8197.10*** *p8*
Wortmann, Henry; New York, 1838 ***8197.10*** *p295*
Worts, George; Pennsylvania, 1777 ***4629.10*** *p9*
Wortweier, Catharina; Port uncertain, 1795 ***2856.30*** *p506*
Wosinski, Alex; Maryland, 1910 ***3259.35*** *p70*
Woska, Jan; Maryland, 1910 ***3259.35*** *p70*
Wosle, Matthaus; Port uncertain, 1766 ***2856.30*** *p506*
Wosniak, Bartholomy; Maryland, 1910 ***3259.35*** *p70*
Wossinger, Anna Maria; America, 1744 ***2856.30*** *p506*
Wossinger, Johann; Port uncertain, 1752 ***2856.30*** *p506*
With wife & child
Wossinger, Matthaus; America, 1752 ***2856.30*** *p506*
Wossinger, Matthaus; America, 1752 ***2856.30*** *p506*
With wife & 4 children
Wotherspoon, Abraham; New York, 1840 ***8197.10*** *p201*
Wotherspoon, Elizabeth; New York, 1853 ***1640.13*** *p135*
Wotton, Anne; Maryland, 1698 ***1224.1*** *p65*
Wotton, Simon; Maryland, 1696 ***1224.1*** *p65*
Wouldhand, Ann; Maryland, 1680 ***2524.55*** *p246*
Wouldhand, William; Maryland, 1680 ***2524.55*** *p246*
Woushewsky, Stephen; Maryland, 1910 ***3259.35*** *p70*
Wousowicz, John; Maryland, 1910 ***3259.35*** *p70*
Wovakowski, Michael; Maryland, 1910 ***3259.35*** *p70*
Wowswick, J.; Portland, Maine, 1857 ***9196.15*** *p13*
Woyciak, Joseph; Maryland, 1910 ***3259.35*** *p70*
Woycke, Michel; Maryland, 1910 ***3259.35*** *p70*
Woycynski, Martin; Maryland, 1910 ***3259.35*** *p70*
Woyczynski, Antony; Maryland, 1910 ***3259.35*** *p70*
Woytle, Miss; Port uncertain, 1738 ***2856.30*** *p103*
Woytych, John B.; Maryland, 1910 ***3259.35*** *p70*
Wozel, Daniel; Port uncertain, 1718 ***2856.30*** *p506*
Wozinak, Walter; Maryland, 1910 ***3259.35*** *p70*
Woznak, James; Maryland, 1910 ***3259.35*** *p70*
Wozniak, Albert; Maryland, 1910 ***3259.35*** *p70*
Wozniak, Eva; Maryland, 1910 ***3259.35*** *p70*
Wozny, Leonard; Maryland, 1910 ***3259.35*** *p70*
Wozucki, Josef; Maryland, 1910 ***3259.35*** *p70*
Wragg, Mary Ann 59; Ontario, 1861 ***2896.25*** *p21*
Wragg, Samuel; Charles Town, South Carolina, 1750 ***1224.2*** *p127*
Wragg, William; Charles Town, South Carolina, 1779 ***1224.2*** *p127*
Wragg, William; Charles Town, South Carolina, 1779 ***1224.3*** *p87*
Wraight, Edmund; New York, New York, 1848 ***3437.14*** *p68*
Wraight, James; Maryland, 1657 ***2524.55*** *p246*
Wrapson, William; New York, 1838 ***8197.10*** *p152*
Wrath, Edward; Virginia, 1664 ***6212.30*** *p7*
Wrath, Edward; Virginia, 1664-1665 ***6212.30*** *p16*
Wrath, James; Maryland, 1667 ***2524.55*** *p114*
Wrath, John; Virginia, 1667 ***6212.30*** *p37*
Wrath, Mary; Virginia, 1666 ***6212.30*** *p26*
Wrath, Rebecca; Virginia, 1667 ***6212.30*** *p36*
Wrath, Richard; Virginia, 1666-1667 ***6212.30*** *p34*
Wraxall, Peter; New York, New York, 1762 ***1224.2*** *p128*
Wraxhall, William; Died enroute, 1630 ***1224.1*** *p65*
Wray, Charles; New York, 1839 ***8197.10*** *p135*
Wray, George 29; Ontario, 1871 ***1823.28*** *p106*
Wray, John; New York, 1839 ***8197.10*** *p135*

Wray, William 22; Ontario, 1871 1823.22 p174
Wreaks, Charles; New York, 1831 8197.10 p313
Wreaks, Henry; New York, 1831 8197.10 p313
Wreath, Parnell; Maryland, 1666 2524.55 p246
Wrede, Jakob; Port uncertain, 1752 2856.30 p503
Wren, Geo 34; British Columbia, 1911 9196.1 p36
Wren, Geo 34; Seattle, 1911 9196.1 p36
Wren, James; Maryland, 1659 2524.55 p246
Wren, Peter; Maryland, 1657 2524.55 p246
Wren, Roger 17; Virginia, 1774 1220.25 p46
Wren, Thomas 40; Ontario, 1871 1823.28 p106
Wrenshall, Fred C. 31; Ontario, 1871 1823.28 p106
Wrest, Eliz; Virginia, 1690-1691 6212.30 p59
Wrest, Milleson; Maryland, 1658 2524.55 p246
Wrey, James; Virginia, 1666 6212.30 p27
Wriey, Thomas 21; Maryland, 1774 1220.25 p58
Wright, . . .; Mobile, Alabama, 1764 1640.10 p215
Wright, Miss; Quebec, 1857 9196.15 p22
Wright, Mr.; Portland, Maine, 1858 9196.15 p28
Wright, Mr.; Quebec, 1856 9196.15 p6
Wright, Mr.; Quebec, 1857 9196.15 p13
Wright, Mr.; Quebec, 1857 9196.15 p21
Wright, Mrs.; Maryland, 1648 2524.55 p246
Wright, Mrs.; Portland, Maine, 1858 9196.15 p28
Wright, Mrs.; Quebec, 1856 9196.15 p6
Wright, Alexander 27; Maryland, 1775 1220.25 p105
Wright, Alexander 45; Ontario, 1871 1823.15 p286
Wright, Alfred Jas 65; Ontario, 1871 1823.22 p174
Wright, Amelia 22; Ontario, 1861 2896.26 p37
Wright, Andrew; Pennsylvania, 1777 4629.10 p25
Wright, Ann *SEE* Wright, Ishmaell
Wright, Ann 20; Virginia, 1774 1220.25 p87
Wright, Anne *SEE* Wright, Ishmael
Wright, Arthur; Maryland, 1651 2524.55 p246
Wright, Avelin; Maryland, 1651 2524.55 p246
Wright, Avelin; Maryland, 1652 2524.55 p140
Wright, Benjamin; Virginia, 1707 1224.2 p128
Wright, Camilla Elizabeth C.; New York, 1818 8197.10 p291
Wright, Catharine 19; Ontario, 1861 2896.28 p38
Wright, Charles 35; Ontario, 1871 1823.15 p286
Wright, Charles 48; Ontario, 1871 1823.15 p286
Wright, Charlet 13; Ontario, 1861 2896.27 p13
Wright, Chas; Portland, Maine, 1858 9196.15 p28
Wright, Christian 2; Ontario, 1861 2896.26 p37
Wright, David; Chicago, 1888 1640.13 p135
Wright, David 79; Ontario, 1871 1823.15 p286
Wright, David M. 64; Ontario, 1871 1823.22 p174
Wright, Edward; Maryland, 1681 2524.55 p246
Wright, Edward 14; Ontario, 1861 2896.27 p13
Wright, Edward 23; Maryland, 1774 1220.25 p71
Wright, Edward 28; Maryland, 1775 1220.25 p98
Wright, Edward 28; Maryland, 1775 1220.25 p101
Wright, Edwin; Kentucky, 1895 1640.13 p136
Wright, Eliza 16; Ontario, 1861 2896.27 p13
Wright, Elizabeth; Portland, Maine, 1858 9196.15 p28
Wright, Elizabeth 20; Virginia, 1774 1220.25 p87
Wright, Ellen 3; Ontario, 1861 2896.27 p22
Wright, Frances; Cincinnati, 1852 1640.13 p136
Wright, Frances; New York, 1818 8197.10 p291
Wright, Francis; Virginia, 1671-1672 6212.30 p45
Wright, Francis 92; Vermont, 1897 5900.10 p350
Wright, George; Maryland, 1665 2524.55 p246
Wife: Mary
Wright, George; New York, 1839 8197.10 p383
Wright, George 28; Ontario, 1871 1823.15 p287
Wright, George 36; Ontario, 1871 1823.15 p287
Wright, George 45; Ontario, 1871 1823.15 p286
Wright, George 47; Ontario, 1871 1823.15 p286
Wright, Gilbert 56; Ontario, 1871 1823.22 p174
Wright, Henry; Virginia, 1666-1667 6212.30 p33
Wright, Henry; Virginia, 1666-1667 6212.30 p34
Wright, Henry 21; Maryland, 1775 1220.25 p115
Wright, Hy; Portland, Maine, 1858 9196.15 p28
Wright, Isaac; Maryland, 1672 2524.55 p246
Wright, Isaac 35; Ontario, 1871 1823.15 p287
Wright, Ishmael; Maryland, 1658 2524.55 p246
Wife: Anne
Wright, Ishmaell; Maryland, 1651 2524.55 p246
Wife: Ann
Son: Ismael, Jr.
Wright, Ismael, Jr. *SEE* Wright, Ishmaell
Wright, Jacob 18; Ontario, 1861 2896.26 p37
Wright, James; America, 1859 1640.13 p136
Wright, James; Georgia, 1698 1640.13 p136
Wright, James; Illinois, 1861 6058.10 p68
Wright, James; Maryland, 1657 2524.55 p246
Wright, James; New York, 1803 8197.10 p17
Wright, James; New York, 1831 8197.10 p314
Wright, James 11; Ontario, 1861 2896.26 p37
Wright, James 22; Virginia, 1774 1220.25 p88
Wright, James 23; Ontario, 1871 1823.15 p287
Wright, James 26; Virginia, 1775 1220.25 p100
Wright, James 28; Virginia, 1774 1220.25 p92
Wright, James 38; Virginia, 1774 1220.25 p56
Wright, James 39; Ontario, 1871 1823.22 p174
Wright, James 47; Ontario, 1871 1823.28 p106
Wright, Jane; Maryland, 1631-1685 2524.55 p246
Wright, Jas; Portland, Maine, 1858 9196.15 p28
Wright, Jno.; Maryland, 1681 2524.55 p246
Wright, Jno; Virginia, 1666 6212.30 p29
Wright, Johanna E.; Vermont, 1828-1908 5900.10 p228
Wright, John; Georgia, 1698 1640.13 p136
Wright, John; Georgia, 1699 1640.13 p136
Wright, John; Maryland, 1672 2524.55 p246
Wright, John; Maryland, 1673 2524.55 p246
Wright, John; Maryland, 1703 1224.2 p128
Wright, John; New York, 1898 1640.13 p136
Wright, John; Pennsylvania, 1786 4629.10 p52
Wright, John; Pennsylvania, 1867 6058.10 p57
Wright, John; South Carolina, 1791 1224.2 p128
Wright, John; South Carolina, 1791 1224.3 p87
Wright, John; Vermont, 1855-1936 5900.10 p464
Wright, John 17; Ontario, 1861 2896.27 p13
Wright, John 22; America, 1774 1220.25 p36
Wright, John 23; Virginia, 1773 1220.25 p31
Wright, John 27; Ontario, 1871 1823.15 p287
Wright, John 29; Ontario, 1871 1823.22 p175
Wright, John 30; Maryland, 1774 1220.25 p84
Wright, John 35; Ontario, 1871 1823.22 p175
Wright, John 40; Ontario, 1871 1823.15 p287
Wright, John 41; New York, 1774 1220.25 p25
Wright, John 50; Ontario, 1871 1823.15 p287
Wright, John 50; Ontario, 1871 1823.22 p175
Wright, John 55; Ontario, 1871 1823.22 p175
Wright, John 60; Ontario, 1871 1823.22 p175
Wright, John 70; Ontario, 1871 1823.22 p175
Wright, John D. 45; Ontario, 1861 2896.27 p13
Wright, John E. 43; Ontario, 1871 1823.28 p106
Wright, John Joseph Thomas; New York, New York, 1855 1224.3 p87
Wright, John S.; New York, 1840 8197.10 p202
Wright, John Tenant; New York, 1827 8197.10 p345
Wright, John Tennent; New York, 1826 8197.10 p294
Wright, John W.; New York, 1821 8197.10 p292
Wright, Joseph; New York, 1830 8197.10 p353
Wright, Joseph 16; Philadelphia, 1774 1220.25 p81
Wright, Joseph 19; Maryland, 1774 1220.25 p51
Wright, Joseph 38; Ontario, 1871 1823.15 p287
Wright, Joseph 48; Ontario, 1871 1823.22 p175
Wright, Joseph Farrell; New York, 1840 8197.10 p296
Wright, Lavinia 15; Ontario, 1861 2896.26 p37
Wright, Levi; Savannah, Georgia, 1810 1640.10 p215
Wright, Lewis; Virginia, 1664-1665 6212.30 p16
Wright, Libbie S. 22; Vermont, 1867 5900.10 p453
Wright, Margaret; Vermont, n.d. 5900.10 p350
Wright, Margaret 30; Ontario, 1871 1823.28 p106
Wright, Martha 41; Ontario, 1861 2896.27 p13
Wright, Martin 53; Ontario, 1871 1823.28 p106
Wright, Mary *SEE* Wright, George
Wright, Mary; Maryland, 1648 2524.55 p246
Wright, Mary; Maryland, 1669 2524.55 p170
Wright, Mary; Virginia, 1754 1224.2 p128
Wright, Mary 42; Ontario, 1861 2896.26 p37
Wright, Mary 47; Ontario, 1871 1823.28 p106
Wright, Mary E.; Ontario, 1861 2896.28 p41
Wright, Mary E. 3; Ontario, 1861 2896.28 p38
Wright, Mary Ferguson; Vermont, 1861-1939 5900.10 p464
Wright, Mary M. 7; Ontario, 1861 2896.27 p13
Wright, Moses; Boston, 1744 1224.2 p128
Wright, Nancy 11; Ontario, 1861 2896.27 p13
Wright, Nathaniell; Maryland, 1670 2524.55 p246
Wright, Nicola Eliza; Jamaica, 1835 1640.13 p136
Wright, Patrick Ross 57; Ontario, 1871 1823.22 p175
Wright, Peter; Maryland, 1667 2524.55 p246
Wright, Peter; New Orleans, 1816 1224.3 p87
Wright, Peter; New York, 1840 8197.10 p295
Wright, Peter 51; Ontario, 1871 1823.22 p175
Wright, Peter 64; Ontario, 1871 1823.22 p175
Wright, Peter 69; Ontario, 1871 1823.22 p175
Wright, Phebe 9; Ontario, 1861 2896.27 p13
Wright, Phebe A.; Ontario, 1861 2896.28 p41
Wright, R. 52; Ontario, 1861 2896.26 p14
Wright, Ralph; Virginia, 1667-1668 6212.30 p38
Wright, Rebecca 61; Ontario, 1871 1823.15 p287
Wright, Richard 79; Ontario, 1871 1823.15 p287
Wright, Robert; America, 1829 1640.13 p136
Wright, Robert; Maryland, 1665 2524.55 p247
Wright, Robert; Virginia, 1667 6212.30 p35
Wright, Robert 30; Ontario, 1871 1823.22 p175
Wright, Robert 43; Ontario, 1871 1823.22 p175
Wright, Ruth; New York, 1839 8197.10 p10
Wright, S.; Portland, Maine, 1858 9196.15 p28
Wright, Samuel; New York, 1828 8197.10 p298
Wright, Samuel 36; Ontario, 1871 1823.15 p287
Wright, Samuel 38; Ontario, 1871 1823.15 p287
Wright, Samuel 53; Ontario, 1861 2896.27 p22
Wright, Sarah 53; Ontario, 1871 1823.22 p175
Wright, Sarah Hogan; Vermont, 1835-1920 5900.10 p453
Wright, Solomon; Maryland, 1680 2524.55 p247
Wright, Solomon; Pennsylvania, 1777 4629.10 p12
Wright, Sophia; Portland, Maine, 1858 9196.15 p28
Wright, Stephen Finley 4; Ontario, 1861 2896.27 p22
Wright, Susanna; Maryland, 1659 2524.55 p247
Wright, Tho.; Maryland, 1660 2524.55 p247
Wright, Thomas; Maryland, 1651 2524.55 p247
Wright, Thomas; Maryland, 1661 2524.55 p247
Wright, Thomas; Maryland, 1663 2524.55 p247
Wright, Thomas; Maryland, 1775 1220.25 p113
Wright, Thomas; New York, 1811 8197.10 p57
Wright, Thomas; Pennsylvania, 1777 4629.10 p23
Wright, Thomas; Virginia, 1665-1666 6212.30 p23
Wright, Thomas 22; Virginia, 1774 1220.25 p93
Wright, Thomas 35; Ontario, 1871 1823.28 p106
Wright, Thomas 44; Ontario, 1871 1823.28 p106
Wright, Thomas E. 2; Ontario, 1861 2896.27 p22
Wright, W. J. 21; Alaska, 1912 9196.1 p39
Wright, Walter 47; Ontario, 1871 1823.28 p106
Wright, Wesley; New York, 1839 8197.10 p382
Wright, Will.; Maryland, 1646 2524.55 p247
Wright, William; Boston, 1695 1224.1 p65
Wright, William; Maryland, 1668 2524.55 p247
Wright, William; Maryland, 1672 2524.55 p247
Wright, William; Maryland, 1673 2524.55 p247
Wright, William; Nova Scotia, 1719 1224.2 p128
Wright, William; Virginia, 1663 6212.30 p1
Wright, William; Virginia, 1664 6212.30 p8
Wright, William 18; Maryland, 1774 1220.25 p71
Wright, William 27; Maryland, 1775 1220.25 p115
Wright, William 33; Maryland, 1774 1220.25 p76
Wright, William 50; Ontario, 1871 1823.15 p287
Wright, William 52; Ontario, 1871 1823.22 p175
Wright, William 56; Ontario, 1871 1823.28 p106
Wright, William 59; Ontario, 1871 1823.15 p287
Wright, William 60; Ontario, 1871 1823.22 p175
Wright, William H.; Pennsylvania, 1868 6058.10 p71
Wright, William H.; Vermont, 1835-1915 5900.10 p453
Wright, William Lloyd; Quebec, 1896 1640.13 p136
Wright, Wm; Virginia, 1664 6212.30 p11
Wright, X. P.; Virginia, 1665-1666 6212.30 p20
Wrightman, J. 4; Ontario, 1861 2896.28 p3
Wrightman, M. 1; Ontario, 1861 2896.28 p3
Wrightman, S. 24; Ontario, 1861 2896.28 p3
Wrightman, Sam'l; Ontario, 1861 2896.28 p41
Wrightson, Elizabeth 20; Nova Scotia, 1774 1220.25 p13
Wrightson, John; Maryland, 1671 2524.55 p247
Wrightson, Robert 58; Ontario, 1871 1823.22 p175
Wrigley, Joseph; New York, 1840 8197.10 p386
Wring, Samuell; Virginia, 1664 6212.30 p11
Wringsly, James; Maryland, 1673 2524.55 p247
Wrinkle, Christopher; New York, 1839 8197.10 p379
Wrisburg, Daniel; New Jersey, 1778 1224.2 p128
Write, John; Maryland, 1669 2524.55 p247
Wroblewski, Joseph; Maryland, 1910 3259.35 p70
Wroth, Jno; Virginia, 1665-1666 6212.30 p23
Wroublewska, Maryanna; Maryland, 1910 3259.35 p70
Wroughton, Allina *SEE* Wroughton, William
Wroughton, Diana *SEE* Wroughton, William
Wroughton, Elizabeth *SEE* Wroughton, William
Wroughton, Johanna *SEE* Wroughton, William
Wroughton, Margaret *SEE* Wroughton, William
Wroughton, Thomas *SEE* Wroughton, William
Wroughton, William; Maryland, 1673 2524.55 p247
Wife: Johanna
Daughter: Diana
Daughter: Allina
Son: Thomas
Daughter: Margaret
Daughter: Elizabeth
Wry, Edgar J.; Vermont, 1843-1916 5900.10 p241
Wry, John 23; Nova Scotia, 1774 1220.25 p15
Wry, Mary McDonald; Vermont, 1840-1922 5900.10 p241
Wuerth, Christian; New York, 1837 8197.10 p103
Wuest, Magdalena; America, 1744 2856.30 p504
Wuhlin, Anna Maria; Port uncertain, 1755 2856.30 p504
Wuier, William 42; Ontario, 1871 1823.15 p287
Wujek, Frank; Maryland, 1910 3259.35 p70
Wujen, Adam; Maryland, 1910 3259.35 p70
Wulff, John; New York, 1840 8197.10 p296
Wulich, M. 28; Alaska, 1916 9196.1 p44
Wulich, M. 28; Whitehorse, Yukon, 1916 9196.1 p44
Wulle, Sebastian; America, 1771 2856.30 p503
With wife
Wulle, Sebastian; America, 1771 2856.30 p503
With wife & child

X

Y

Yablonski, Vincente; Maryland, 1910 ***3259.35*** *p70*
Yackoby, Woolf J.; New York, 1835 ***8197.10*** *p316*
Yaerky, John 50; Ontario, 1871 ***1823.15*** *p287*
Yager, J. G.; Pennsylvania, 1835 ***6058.10*** *p11*
Yakiweski, Victor; Maryland, 1910 ***3259.35*** *p70*
Yakuweski, Annie; Maryland, 1910 ***3259.35*** *p70*
Yale, James W.; Vermont, 1832-1912 ***5900.10*** *p321*
Yale, Mary A. Carrigan; Vermont, 1840-1920 ***5900.10*** *p321*
Yale, Thomas; New England, 1698 ***1224.1*** *p66*
Yallowley, Joshua; Bahamas, 1787 ***1224.2*** *p128*
Yallowley, Joshua; Florida, n.d. ***1224.2*** *p128*
Yamchowski, Peter; Maryland, 1910 ***3259.35*** *p70*
Yancovtz, Frank; Maryland, 1910 ***3259.35*** *p70*
Yandt, Fredrick 24; Ontario, 1871 ***1823.28*** *p106*
Yankewitz, Stanislaw; Maryland, 1910 ***3259.35*** *p70*
Yankiewicz, Marion; Maryland, 1910 ***3259.35*** *p70*
Yankowski, Stanislaw; Maryland, 1910 ***3259.35*** *p70*
Yanna, John Jacob; New York, 1840 ***8197.10*** *p194*
Yanni, John Jacob; New York, 1840 ***8197.10*** *p194*
Yanovak, Francis; Maryland, 1910 ***3259.35*** *p70*
Yardley, Edward; Virginia, 1676 ***1224.1*** *p66*
Yardley, Thomas; Maryland, 1660-1661 ***2524.55*** *p121*
Yardley, Thomas; Maryland, 1660-1661 ***2524.55*** *p247*
Yarham, James 69; Ontario, 1871 ***1823.22*** *p175*
Yarnall, Ezekial; Pennsylvania, 1785 ***4629.10*** *p48*
Yarnold, Benjamin; Augusta, Georgia, 1847 ***1224.3*** *p88*
Yarns, Naomi 22; Ontario, 1861 ***2896.28*** *p57*
Yarwood, Mrs. 28; Ontario, 1861 ***2896.26*** *p26*
Yarwood, A. S. 4; Ontario, 1861 ***2896.26*** *p26*
Yarwood, E. B. 6; Ontario, 1861 ***2896.26*** *p26*
Yarwood, Eliza 37; Ontario, 1861 ***2896.27*** *p52*
Yarwood, Harry 15; Ontario, 1861 ***2896.27*** *p57*
Yarwood, L. J. 1; Ontario, 1861 ***2896.26*** *p26*
Yarwood, Laura J. 6; Ontario, 1861 ***2896.27*** *p52*
Yarwood, Lucy A. 3; Ontario, 1861 ***2896.27*** *p52*
Yarwood, Maryly 16; Ontario, 1861 ***2896.27*** *p52*
Yarwood, Sarah E. 8; Ontario, 1861 ***2896.27*** *p52*
Yarwood, William G. 13; Ontario, 1861 ***2896.27*** *p52*
Yasaw, Elizabeth 60; Ontario, 1871 ***1823.22*** *p175*
Yasek, Joseph; Maryland, 1910 ***3259.35*** *p70*
Yaszensky, Andrew; Maryland, 1910 ***3259.35*** *p71*
Yate, John; Maryland, 1680 ***2524.55*** *p247*
Yate, Thomas 22; Nova Scotia, 1774 ***1220.25*** *p13*
Yateman, Mr.; Quebec, 1856 ***9196.15*** *p9*
Yateman, Erasmus; Maryland, 1667 ***2524.55*** *p247*
Yates, Mrs.; Maryland, 1652 ***2524.55*** *p247*
Yates, Humphry; Maryland, 1672 ***2524.55*** *p247*
Yates, James D.; New York, 1840 ***8197.10*** *p194*
Yates, Richard; Maryland, 1662 ***2524.55*** *p247*
With wife
Yates, Sidney; New York, 1827-1834 ***8197.10*** *p306*
Yates, Stephen 47; Ontario, 1871 ***1823.15*** *p287*
Yates, Thomas 21; Ontario, 1871 ***1823.28*** *p106*
Yauch, Catharina; Port uncertain, 1738 ***2856.30*** *p508*
With husband & children
Yazon, Frederiak W.; Maryland, 1910 ***3259.35*** *p71*
Yeager, Adam; Pennsylvania, 1777 ***4629.10*** *p10*
Yeager, Peter; New York, 1840 ***8197.10*** *p194*
Yeamans, Christopher; New York, 1687 ***1224.1*** *p66*
Yeamans, James; Virginia, 1665-1666 ***6212.30*** *p24*
Yeamans, Tho; Virginia, 1667 ***6212.30*** *p37*
Yeardley, George; Virginia, 1629 ***1224.1*** *p66*
Yearley, Eliza Ma 44; Ontario, 1871 ***1823.28*** *p106*
Yearly, Thomas 47; Ontario, 1871 ***1823.15*** *p287*
Yeason, Joane; Maryland, 1663 ***2524.55*** *p247*
Yeates, John 24; Maryland, 1774 ***1220.25*** *p71*
Yeates, John 24; Virginia, 1773 ***1220.25*** *p29*
Yeats, John 26; Baltimore, 1775 ***1220.25*** *p119*
Yeaveley, Thomas; New York, 1767 ***1224.2*** *p128*
Yegyansky, Gregzos; Maryland, 1910 ***3259.35*** *p71*
Yejenski, Joseph; Maryland, 1910 ***3259.35*** *p71*
Yekubick, Joseph; Maryland, 1910 ***3259.35*** *p71*
Yeldall, Anthony; Pennsylvania, 1777 ***4629.10*** *p26*
Yeldall, Anthony; Pennsylvania, 1779 ***4629.10*** *p40*
Yendraszkiewicz, Frank; Maryland, 1910 ***3259.35*** *p71*
Yenkosky, Valentine; Maryland, 1910 ***3259.35*** *p71*
Yenniski, Antone; Maryland, 1910 ***3259.35*** *p71*
Yentzer, John; Pennsylvania, 1777 ***4629.10*** *p16*
Yeo, George; Virginia, 1666 ***6212.30*** *p30*
Yeo, George 26; Ontario, 1871 ***1823.15*** *p287*
Yeo, Henry; Virginia, 1659 ***1224.1*** *p66*
Yeo, Henry 60; Ontario, 1871 ***1823.15*** *p287*
Yeo, James 21; Maryland, 1774 ***1220.25*** *p83*
Yeo, John; Virginia, 1663-1664 ***6212.30*** *p5*
Yeo, John 40; Ontario, 1871 ***1823.15*** *p287*
Yeo, Robert 49; Ontario, 1871 ***1823.15*** *p287*
Yeo, William; Virginia, 1665-1666 ***6212.30*** *p23*
Yeo, William 39; Ontario, 1871 ***1823.15*** *p287*
Yeo, William 44; Ontario, 1871 ***1823.15*** *p287*
Yeoman, David 48; Ontario, 1871 ***1823.22*** *p175*
Yeoman, Richard 22; Virginia, 1774 ***1220.25*** *p54*
Yeomans, Cristop; Virginia, 1664 ***6212.30*** *p6*
Yeomans, John; Maryland, 1681 ***2524.55*** *p247*
Yeomans, John 43; Ontario, 1871 ***1823.22*** *p175*
Yeomans, Phebe 23; Ontario, 1861 ***2896.26*** *p20*
Yerex, Agnes V. 3; Ontario, 1861 ***2896.27*** *p22*
Yerex, Ann 1; Ontario, 1861 ***2896.27*** *p22*
Yerex, David 15; Ontario, 1861 ***2896.27*** *p14*
Yerex, Eliza J. 6; Ontario, 1861 ***2896.27*** *p22*
Yerex, Elizabeth 34; Ontario, 1861 ***2896.27*** *p22*
Yerex, Frances 19; Ontario, 1861 ***2896.27*** *p14*
Yerex, George 19; Ontario, 1861 ***2896.27*** *p14*
Yerex, H. 6; Ontario, 1861 ***2896.26*** *p16*
Yerex, J. 17; Ontario, 1861 ***2896.26*** *p16*
Yerex, J. 24; Ontario, 1861 ***2896.26*** *p16*
Yerex, Jane 33; Ontario, 1861 ***2896.27*** *p14*
Yerex, Johnathan 15; Ontario, 1861 ***2896.27*** *p14*
Yerex, M. 67; Ontario, 1861 ***2896.26*** *p16*
Yerex, M. G. 18; Ontario, 1861 ***2896.26*** *p16*
Yerex, Phoebe A. 12; Ontario, 1861 ***2896.27*** *p22*
Yerex, Rhinard 29; Ontario, 1861 ***2896.27*** *p14*
Yerex, Sarah C. 10; Ontario, 1861 ***2896.27*** *p22*
Yerex, Silvi S. 8; Ontario, 1861 ***2896.27*** *p22*
Yerhak, Frank; Maryland, 1910 ***3259.35*** *p71*
Yerks, Fred'k 7; Ontario, 1861 ***2896.26*** *p39*
Yerrow, William 36; Baltimore, 1775 ***1220.25*** *p118*
Yerwood, R. 12; Ontario, 1861 ***2896.26*** *p8*
Yerwood, Samuel 68; Ontario, 1861 ***2896.26*** *p8*
Yetrymire, John 65; Ontario, 1871 ***1823.15*** *p287*
Yew, William 30; Ontario, 1871 ***1823.28*** *p106*
Yhlin, Jacob; Port uncertain, 1747 ***2856.30*** *p508*
Yickiski, Michals; Maryland, 1910 ***3259.35*** *p71*
Yiffard, Joseph 30; Baltimore, 1775 ***1220.25*** *p118*
Ylidge, Elizabeth; Maryland, 1665 ***2524.55*** *p247*
Yochill, James; New York, 1840 ***8197.10*** *p194*
Yohe, Paul F.; New York, 1838 ***8197.10*** *p152*
Yoke, Paul F.; New York, 1838 ***8197.10*** *p152*
Yokes, James; Maryland, 1910 ***3259.35*** *p71*
Yokild, Martin 25; Ontario, 1871 ***1823.28*** *p106*
Yokisch, William 38; Ontario, 1871 ***1823.28*** *p106*
Yokobata, Frank 42; Alaska, 1918 ***9196.1*** *p8*
Yokobata, Frank 42; Yukon, 1918 ***9196.1*** *p8*
Yonaitis, M. 40; Alaska, 1918 ***9196.1*** *p54*
Yonaitis, M. 40; Yukon, 1918 ***9196.1*** *p54*
Yonat, Stanislaw; Maryland, 1910 ***3259.35*** *p71*
Yonavik, Maggie; Maryland, 1910 ***3259.35*** *p71*
Yong, Charles; Maryland, 1673 ***2524.55*** *p247*
Yong, John; Maryland, 1651 ***2524.55*** *p247*
Yong, Wm; Virginia, 1671-1672 ***6212.30*** *p46*
Yonge, Philip; Georgia, n.d. ***1224.2*** *p128*
Yongs, A. 50; Ontario, 1861 ***2896.27*** *p7*
Yonka, Henry; Maryland, 1910 ***3259.35*** *p71*
Yonka, Martin; Maryland, 1910 ***3259.35*** *p71*
Yonkay, Fredrick 36; Ontario, 1871 ***1823.28*** *p106*
Yonkey, Charley; Maryland, 1910 ***3259.35*** *p71*
Yonkey, Gottlieb; Maryland, 1910 ***3259.35*** *p71*
Yonkey, William T.; Maryland, 1910 ***3259.35*** *p71*
Yonkowicki, James; Maryland, 1910 ***3259.35*** *p71*
Yonson, Francis; Maryland, 1660 ***2524.55*** *p248*
Yonstane, Lawrence; Maryland, 1681 ***2524.55*** *p248*
Yontoe, Andrew 25; Ontario, 1871 ***1823.28*** *p106*
Yontoe, August 40; Ontario, 1871 ***1823.28*** *p106*
Yontoe, Joseph 35; Ontario, 1871 ***1823.28*** *p106*
York, Edward; Pennsylvania, 1777 ***4629.10*** *p19*
York, Patience 18; Philadelphia, 1774 ***1220.25*** *p42*
Yorke, Charles; Virginia, 1664 ***6212.30*** *p9*
Yorke, Peter; Virginia, 1671-1672 ***6212.30*** *p45*
Yorke, R.; Quebec, 1858 ***9196.15*** *p36*
Yorke, William; Maryland, 1661 ***2524.55*** *p120*
Yorke, Wm; Virginia, 1664 ***6212.30*** *p14*
Yorkshire, William; Maryland, 1655-1656 ***2524.55*** *p248*
Yorston, David; North America, 1791 ***1224.2*** *p128*
Youkin, Frank; Maryland, 1910 ***3259.35*** *p71*
Youkin, Kasimierz; Maryland, 1910 ***3259.35*** *p71*
Youl, David 52; Ontario, 1871 ***1823.15*** *p287*
Youle, David 50; Ontario, 1871 ***1823.15*** *p288*
Youle, George; New York, 1778 ***1224.2*** *p128*
Youle, John; New York, 1792 ***8197.10*** *p1*
Youll, Mr.; Quebec, 1858 ***9196.15*** *p45*
Youlton, John 72; Ontario, 1871 ***1823.22*** *p175*
Youman, Thomas 38; Ontario, 1871 ***1823.22*** *p175*
Youmans, Ann M. 50; Ontario, 1861 ***2896.27*** *p62*
Youmans, Calvin M. 14; Ontario, 1861 ***2896.27*** *p62*
Youmans, Charles; Ontario, 1861 ***2896.28*** *p65*
Youmans, Charles R. 23; Ontario, 1861 ***2896.27*** *p62*
Youmans, D. P. 40; Ontario, 1861 ***2896.26*** *p7*
Youmans, E. F. 3; Ontario, 1861 ***2896.26*** *p7*
Youmans, Egerton 21; Ontario, 1861 ***2896.27*** *p62*
Youmans, Elisa A. 16; Ontario, 1861 ***2896.27*** *p62*
Youmans, H. 8; Ontario, 1861 ***2896.26*** *p7*
Youmans, J. C. 17; Ontario, 1861 ***2896.26*** *p7*
Youmans, L. 12; Ontario, 1861 ***2896.26*** *p7*
Youmans, Sarah C. 10; Ontario, 1861 ***2896.27*** *p62*
Youmans, W. 15; Ontario, 1861 ***2896.26*** *p7*
Young, Mr.; Quebec, 1857 ***9196.15*** *p26*
Young, Mrs.; Quebec, 1857 ***9196.15*** *p20*
Young, Mrs.; Quebec, 1858 ***9196.15*** *p43*
Young, A. E. 11; Ontario, 1861 ***2896.26*** *p4*
Young, A. M. 9; Ontario, 1861 ***2896.26*** *p4*
Young, A. M. 27; Ontario, 1861 ***2896.26*** *p3*
Young, Aaron 18; Ontario, 1861 ***2896.25*** *p16*
Young, Abraham; Virginia, 1667-1668 ***6212.30*** *p38*
Young, Abraham 8; Ontario, 1861 ***2896.25*** *p16*
Young, Adam 47; Ontario, 1871 ***1823.28*** *p106*
Young, Alex 46; Ontario, 1871 ***1823.15*** *p288*
Young, Alexander; Mobile, Alabama, 1828 ***1224.3*** *p88*
Young, Alexander; New York, 1834 ***8197.10*** *p71*
Young, Alexander; North America, 1816 ***1640.13*** *p137*
Young, Alexander; Pennsylvania, 1777 ***4629.10*** *p31*
Young, Alexander 22; Ontario, 1871 ***1823.15*** *p288*
Young, Alexander 51; Ontario, 1871 ***1823.15*** *p288*
Young, Alexander 60; Ontario, 1871 ***1823.15*** *p288*
Young, Almeda 6; Ontario, 1861 ***2896.25*** *p16*

Z

Zablotzky, Alexander; Maryland, 1910 ***3259.35*** *p71*
Zaboff, Z. 23; Alaska, 1917 ***9196.1*** *p46*
Zaboff, Z. 23; Whitehorse, Yukon, 1917 ***9196.1*** *p46*
Zaborowska, Annie; Maryland, 1910 ***3259.35*** *p71*
Zaccek, Simon; Maryland, 1910 ***3259.35*** *p71*
Zacheis, . . .; Port uncertain, 1736 ***2856.30*** *p509*
Zacheisin, . . .; Port uncertain, 1736 ***2856.30*** *p509*
Zachelska, George; Maryland, 1910 ***3259.35*** *p71*
Zacher, Martin; Port uncertain, 1791 ***2856.30*** *p509*
Zachmann, Ignaz; Port uncertain, 1751 ***2856.30*** *p509*
Zachorski, Edmand; Maryland, 1910 ***3259.35*** *p71*
Zackaruka, Mary; Maryland, 1910 ***3259.35*** *p71*
Zadonoski, Joseph; Maryland, 1910 ***3259.35*** *p71*
Zadzek, Charles 16; Ontario, 1871 ***1823.28*** *p107*
Zaezak, Rosalie; Maryland, 1910 ***3259.35*** *p71*
Zahn, Frederick; Pennsylvania, 1777 ***4629.10*** *p9*
Zahn, Jakob; Port uncertain, 1794 ***2856.30*** *p509*
Zahn, Johann Valentin; Port uncertain, 1769 ***2856.30*** *p509*
Zahneichel, Felte; America, 1754 ***2856.30*** *p509*
Zahneissen, Mrs. Valentin; America, 1754 ***2856.30*** *p509*
With 2 children
Zahneisser, Valentin; America, 1754 ***2856.30*** *p509*
With wife
Zahnleckerin, Sybilla Barbara; Port uncertain, 1796 ***2856.30*** *p509*
Zahringer, Jacob; New York, 1838 ***8197.10*** *p152*
Zaines, John; Virginia, 1660 ***1224.1*** *p66*
Zaisser, Johann Adam; Port uncertain, 1760 ***2856.30*** *p510*
Zajaczkowsky, Frank; Maryland, 1910 ***3259.35*** *p71*
Zaklski, Anton; Maryland, 1910 ***3259.35*** *p71*
Zakrgewski, Vincent; Maryland, 1910 ***3259.35*** *p71*
Zakroewski, Teofil; Maryland, 1910 ***3259.35*** *p71*
Zakrzewska, Frances; Maryland, 1910 ***3259.35*** *p71*
Zalaries, John; Maryland, 1661 ***2524.55*** *p248*
Zalenski, William J.; Maryland, 1910 ***3259.35*** *p71*
Zaliski, Felix; Maryland, 1910 ***3259.35*** *p71*
Zaliski, Michael; Maryland, 1910 ***3259.35*** *p71*
Zalla, Paul 42; Ontario, 1871 ***1823.22*** *p176*
Zaluski, John; Maryland, 1910 ***3259.35*** *p71*
Zamerski, Ignacy; Maryland, 1910 ***3259.35*** *p71*
Zamesky, Felix; Maryland, 1910 ***3259.35*** *p71*
Zametzer, John; Maryland, 1910 ***3259.35*** *p71*
Zaminski, Lawrence; Maryland, 1910 ***3259.35*** *p71*
Zamiski, Thomas; Maryland, 1910 ***3259.35*** *p71*
Zamisky, Michael; Maryland, 1910 ***3259.35*** *p71*
Zamoski, Frank; Maryland, 1910 ***3259.35*** *p72*
Zaner, Johann; America, 1743 ***2856.30*** *p516*
Zang, Stefan; Port uncertain, 1747 ***2856.30*** *p509*
With wife & children
Zanyzuski, James; Maryland, 1910 ***3259.35*** *p72*
Zapalowicz, Brinslaw; Maryland, 1910 ***3259.35*** *p72*
Zapantis, Jos 34; Juneau, Alaska, 1917 ***9196.1*** *p45*
Zapantis, Jos 34; Whitehorse, Yukon, 1917 ***9196.1*** *p45*
Zapfe, Christian 43; Ontario, 1871 ***1823.15*** *p289*
Zapflerin, Anna Maria; Port uncertain, 1775 ***2856.30*** *p516*
Zaphe, August 40; Ontario, 1871 ***1823.15*** *p289*
Zapolowiac, John; Maryland, 1910 ***3259.35*** *p72*
Zaporaski, Henry; Maryland, 1910 ***3259.35*** *p72*
Zarachowicz, Vincent; Maryland, 1910 ***3259.35*** *p72*
Zaralnisky, John; Maryland, 1910 ***3259.35*** *p72*
Zaransky, Josep; Maryland, 1910 ***3259.35*** *p72*
Zarmski, Michael; Maryland, 1910 ***3259.35*** *p72*
Zarnowsky, Frank; Maryland, 1910 ***3259.35*** *p72*
Zarnowsky, John; Maryland, 1910 ***3259.35*** *p72*
Zaroff, B. 25; Alaska, 1916 ***9196.1*** *p43*
Zaroff, B. 25; Whitehorse, Yukon, 1916 ***9196.1*** *p43*
Zaromski, John; Maryland, 1910 ***3259.35*** *p72*
Zarzok, Wince; Maryland, 1910 ***3259.35*** *p72*
Zasada, Vincent; Maryland, 1910 ***3259.35*** *p72*
Zaslowska, August; Maryland, 1910 ***3259.35*** *p72*
Zatrowski, Henry; Maryland, 1910 ***3259.35*** *p72*
Zaun, Catharina; Port uncertain, 1767 ***2856.30*** *p509*
Zaun, Johann Martin; America, 1741 ***2856.30*** *p509*
Zaun, Magdalena; Port uncertain, 1774 ***2856.30*** *p509*
Zaun, Magdalena; Port uncertain, 1775 ***2856.30*** *p509*
Zavigan, John 40; Ontario, 1871 ***1823.15*** *p289*
Zawadny, Peter; Maryland, 1910 ***3259.35*** *p72*
Zawatsky, John; Maryland, 1910 ***3259.35*** *p72*
Zawieja, Frank; Maryland, 1910 ***3259.35*** *p72*
Zawkoski, Frank; Maryland, 1910 ***3259.35*** *p72*
Zawo, Tekla; Maryland, 1910 ***3259.35*** *p72*
Zaworski, George; Maryland, 1910 ***3259.35*** *p72*
Zawut, Valentine; Maryland, 1910 ***3259.35*** *p72*
Zaxarkuw, Philip; Maryland, 1910 ***3259.35*** *p72*
Zazecky, Boleslaw; Maryland, 1910 ***3259.35*** *p72*
Zbinsky, Anthoney; Maryland, 1910 ***3259.35*** *p72*
Zborowski, Henry; Maryland, 1910 ***3259.35*** *p72*
Zborowski, Martin; Maryland, 1910 ***3259.35*** *p72*
Zborrauski, Mary H.; Maryland, 1910 ***3259.35*** *p72*
Zdanomaz, Joseph; Maryland, 1910 ***3259.35*** *p72*
Zea, Chormon 48; Ontario, 1871 ***1823.15*** *p289*
Zeamon, William 24; Ontario, 1871 ***1823.15*** *p289*
Zeander, Thekla; Maryland, 1910 ***3259.35*** *p72*
Zebell, Gustave 46; Ontario, 1871 ***1823.28*** *p107*
Zebell, William 53; Ontario, 1871 ***1823.28*** *p107*
Zebroi, Joseph; Maryland, 1910 ***3259.35*** *p72*
Zebroi, Stanislow; Maryland, 1910 ***3259.35*** *p72*
Zebrowski, Wladeslaw; Maryland, 1910 ***3259.35*** *p72*
Zech, John; Maryland, 1910 ***3259.35*** *p72*
Zecher, Konrad; Port uncertain, 1783 ***2856.30*** *p509*
Zechiel, Christof Peter; America, 1751 ***2856.30*** *p509*
Zechiel, Christof Peter; Port uncertain, 1750 ***2856.30*** *p509*
Zechiel, Christof Peter; Port uncertain, 1751 ***2856.30*** *p509*
Zechiel, Jacob; America, 1767 ***2856.30*** *p509*
Zechiel, Jacob; America, 1770 ***2856.30*** *p509*
Zegulski, Tom; Maryland, 1910 ***3259.35*** *p72*
Zehen, Michael; America, 1762 ***2856.30*** *p509*
Zehenbauer, Martin; Port uncertain, 1752 ***2856.30*** *p509*
Zehenbaum, Martin; Port uncertain, 1752 ***2856.30*** *p509*
Zehender, Jakob; Port uncertain, 1782 ***2856.30*** *p509*
With wife & 3 children
Zehnle, Agathe; America, 1846 ***2856.30*** *p509*
Zeide, John; Maryland, 1910 ***3259.35*** *p72*
Zeif, Leonhard; New York, 1807 ***8197.10*** *p53*
Zeiger, Leonhard; Port uncertain, 1784 ***2856.30*** *p509*
Zeigler, David; Pennsylvania, 1781 ***4629.10*** *p42*
Zeiher, Friedrich; Port uncertain, 1781 ***2856.30*** *p509*
Zeiler, Michael 46; Ontario, 1871 ***1823.15*** *p289*
Zeiller, Henery 35; Ontario, 1871 ***1823.15*** *p289*
Zeiner, Michael; Pennsylvania, 1779 ***4629.10*** *p38*
Zeisel, Johann Adam; Port uncertain, 1760 ***2856.30*** *p510*
Zeisler, Anna Catharina; Port uncertain, 1764 ***2856.30*** *p510*
Zeitvogel, Anton; Port uncertain, 1780 ***2856.30*** *p510*
Zeitza, Mr.; Quebec, 1858 ***9196.15*** *p45*
Zelenski, Stanislaus; Maryland, 1910 ***3259.35*** *p72*
Zelenski, Thomas; Maryland, 1910 ***3259.35*** *p72*
Zelensky, John; Maryland, 1910 ***3259.35*** *p72*
Zelensky, Julian; Maryland, 1910 ***3259.35*** *p72*
Zelichowski, Cieslaw; Maryland, 1910 ***3259.35*** *p72*
Zelichowski, Joseph; Maryland, 1910 ***3259.35*** *p72*
Zelielesky, Walter; Maryland, 1910 ***3259.35*** *p72*
Zelka, Anthony; Maryland, 1910 ***3259.35*** *p72*
Zelkin, Nicholas; New York, 1824 ***8197.10*** *p296*
Zell, Fredrick 43; Ontario, 1871 ***1823.28*** *p107*
Zell, Johann Nikolaus; America, 1740 ***2856.30*** *p510*
Zeller, Andreas; America, 1764 ***2856.30*** *p510*
Zeller, Bartel; America, 1743 ***2856.30*** *p510*
Zeller, Daniel 60; Ontario, 1871 ***1823.15*** *p289*
Zeller, Franz; America, 1775 ***2856.30*** *p510*
Zeller, Hannis; Port uncertain, 1781 ***2856.30*** *p510*
Zeller, Hans Mardin; America, 1752 ***2856.30*** *p510*
Zeller, Michael 46; Ontario, 1871 ***1823.15*** *p289*
Zellinger, George; Maryland, 1910 ***3259.35*** *p72*
Zellio, Frank 40; British Columbia, 1917 ***9196.1*** *p70*
Zellio, Frank 40; Washington, 1917 ***9196.1*** *p70*
Zellio, Marguerite 11; British Columbia, 1917 ***9196.1*** *p70*
Zellio, Marguerite 11; Washington, 1917 ***9196.1*** *p70*
Zellio, Mattie 35; British Columbia, 1917 ***9196.1*** *p70*
Zellio, Mattie 35; Washington, 1917 ***9196.1*** *p70*
Zellmann, Jost; Port uncertain, 1781 ***2856.30*** *p510*
Zemar, John 40; Ontario, 1871 ***1823.15*** *p289*
Zembrod, Anton; Port uncertain, 1757 ***2856.30*** *p510*
Zembrod, Anton; Port uncertain, 1797 ***2856.30*** *p510*
Zemmiar, Midall 54; Ontario, 1871 ***1823.15*** *p289*
Zendel, Conrad; Baltimore, 1840 ***6058.10*** *p22*
Zendel, Conrad; Pennsylvania, 1846 ***6058.10*** *p22*
Zendel, Henry Adam; Pennsylvania, 1845 ***6058.10*** *p23*
Zendle, Henry; Pennsylvania, 1845 ***6058.10*** *p23*
Zendruziak, Yzepan; Maryland, 1910 ***3259.35*** *p72*
Zenger, Johann; America, 1743 ***2856.30*** *p510*
Zenger, Johann; America, 1764 ***2856.30*** *p510*
Zenger, Simon; America, 1743 ***2856.30*** *p510*
Zenger, Simon; America, 1764 ***2856.30*** *p510*
Zengerle, Magdalene; Port uncertain, 1764 ***2856.30*** *p510*
Zengerle, Margarete; Port uncertain, 1764 ***2856.30*** *p510*
Zentner, Christof; America, 1749 ***2856.30*** *p510*
Zentner, Christof; Port uncertain, 1756 ***2856.30*** *p510*
Zepkowsky, Ignac; Maryland, 1910 ***3259.35*** *p72*
Zepp, Peter; Port uncertain, 1770 ***2856.30*** *p510*
Zerban, Henrich; America, 1792 ***2856.30*** *p510*
Zerembic, Maryanna; Maryland, 1910 ***3259.35*** *p72*
Zerfass, Maria Elisabeth; Port uncertain, 1784 ***2856.30*** *p510*
Zerfus, Nikolaus; Port uncertain, 1764 ***2856.30*** *p510*
Zersky, Joseph 43; Ontario, 1871 ***1823.28*** *p107*
Zesiky, George; Maryland, 1910 ***3259.35*** *p72*
Zesza, Marton; Maryland, 1910 ***3259.35*** *p73*
Zett, Georg; Port uncertain, 1766 ***2856.30*** *p510*
Zety, Abraham; America, 1752 ***2856.30*** *p510*
Zewski, Louis; Maryland, 1910 ***3259.35*** *p73*
Zglenichky, Michael; Maryland, 1910 ***3259.35*** *p73*
Zibert, Anthony 54; Ontario, 1871 ***1823.28*** *p107*
Zibulski, Anton; Maryland, 1910 ***3259.35*** *p73*
Zieber, Mrs. Ludwig; Port uncertain, 1785 ***2856.30*** *p511*
Zieber, Mrs. Ludwig; Port uncertain, 1786 ***2856.30*** *p511*
Ziegelbauer, Anna Catharina; Port uncertain, 1747 ***2856.30*** *p511*
Ziegener, Andres; Port uncertain, 1786 ***2856.30*** *p511*
Ziegler, Mr.; America, 1727 ***2856.30*** *p362*
Ziegler, Adam; Port uncertain, 1739 ***2856.30*** *p511*
Ziegler, Anna Eva; America, 1752 ***2856.30*** *p511*
Ziegler, Anna Maria; Port uncertain, 1770 ***2856.30*** *p511*
Ziegler, David; America, 1748-1799 ***2856.30*** *p511*
Ziegler, Georg; Port uncertain, 1764 ***2856.30*** *p511*
Ziegler, Hans Georg; America, 1727 ***2856.30*** *p511*
With wife
Ziegler, Hans Jerrik; America, 1727 ***2856.30*** *p511*
Ziegler, J.; America, 1727 ***2856.30*** *p435*

Ziegler, J. G.; America, 1727 2856.30 p362
Ziegler, Jacob; Port uncertain, 1793 2856.30 p511
Ziegler, Jakob; Port uncertain, 1750 2856.30 p511
Ziegler, Johann Ernst; America, 1772 2856.30 p511
Ziegler, Johann Friedric; America, 1767 2856.30 p511
Ziegler, Johann Leonhard; America, 1750 2856.30 p511
Ziegler, Johann Sebastia; America, 1774 2856.30 p511
Ziegler, Judith; America, 1727 2856.30 p511
With husband
Ziegler, Karl; America, 1751 2856.30 p511
Ziegler, Martin; America, 1743 2856.30 p511
Ziegler, Martin; America, 1751 2856.30 p511
Ziegler, Michael; America, 1752 2856.30 p511
With wife & 4 children
Ziegler, Michael; Port uncertain, 1786 2856.30 p511
Ziegler, Peter; Port uncertain, 1736 2856.30 p511
Ziegler, Philipp; America, 1727 2856.30 p511
With wife & 7 children
Ziegler, Sebastian; America, 1773 2856.30 p511
Ziegler, Susanna Meyer; America, 1742 2856.30 p301
Ziegler, Valentin; Port uncertain, 1764 2856.30 p511
Zieglerin, Margarete; Port uncertain, 1752 2856.30 p511
Zielinski, Frank; Maryland, 1910 3259.35 p73
Zielinski, Jacob; Maryland, 1910 3259.35 p73
Zielinski, Maciej; Maryland, 1910 3259.35 p73
Zielishowsky, Vicenty; Maryland, 1910 3259.35 p73
Zielska, Maryanna; Maryland, 1910 3259.35 p73
Zielski, Frank; Maryland, 1910 3259.35 p73
Ziemer, Eorg Peter; Port uncertain, 1789 2856.30 p512
Ziemski, Julian; Maryland, 1910 3259.35 p73
Ziendtek, Peter F.; Maryland, 1910 3259.35 p73
Zienowicz, Michael; Maryland, 1910 3259.35 p73
Zientek, John; Maryland, 1910 3259.35 p73
Zientek, Ozbrieto; Maryland, 1910 3259.35 p73
Zier, Georg; Port uncertain, 1770 2856.30 p511
Zigler, . . .; America, 1727 2856.30 p512
Zigler, Christian; America, 1752 2856.30 p511
Zigler, Ernst; America, 1771 2856.30 p511
Zigler, Ernst; America, 1787 2856.30 p511
Zigler, Philipp; America, 1727 2856.30 p425
Zihler, Anna Maria; Port uncertain, 1791 2856.30 p512
Ziller, John; Pennsylvania, 1817 6058.10 p5
Zillich, Henrich; Port uncertain, 1736 2856.30 p512
Zillich, Maria Barbara; Port uncertain, 1754 2856.30 p512
Zillichin, Maria Barbara; Port uncertain, 1754 2856.30 p512
Zillmann, Michael; Port uncertain, 1741 2856.30 p512
Zilsdorf, Mrs. Leonhard; Port uncertain, 1785 2856.30 p512
With 4 children
Zimkowski, Wladyslaw; Maryland, 1910 3259.35 p73
Zimmelmann, Jakob; America, 1768 2856.30 p512
Zimmer, Andreas; Port uncertain, 1755 2856.30 p512
Zimmer, Christoffel; Port uncertain, 1761 2856.30 p512
Zimmer, Elisabeth; Port uncertain, 1765 2856.30 p512
Zimmer, Elisabeth; Port uncertain, 1796 2856.30 p512
Zimmer, Eorg Peter; Port uncertain, 1789 2856.30 p512
Zimmer, Hans Adam; Port uncertain, 1760 2856.30 p512
Zimmer, Jacob; Port uncertain, 1750 2856.30 p512
Zimmer, Johann Georg; Port uncertain, 1749 2856.30 p512
Zimmer, Johann Niklas; Port uncertain, 1761 2856.30 p512
Zimmer, John 51; Ontario, 1871 1823.15 p289
Zimmer, Marg.; Port uncertain, 1750 2856.30 p317
Zimmer, Peter; Port uncertain, 1792 2856.30 p512
Zimmerer, Mathias; Port uncertain, 1786 2856.30 p512
Zimmerman, Chris 31; Ontario, 1871 1823.15 p289
Zimmerman, Godfrey; New York, 1806 8197.10 p324
Zimmerman, Goodly 70; Ontario, 1871 1823.28 p107
Zimmerman, Henery, Jr. 30; Ontario, 1871 1823.15 p289
Zimmerman, John Christian; New York, 1818 8197.10 p60
Zimmerman, Sophie 68; Ontario, 1871 1823.28 p107
Zimmerman, William; New York, New York, 1851 6058.10 p62
Zimmermann, Andreas; America, 1727 2856.30 p512
Zimmermann, Apollonia; America, 1752 2856.30 p514
With 4 children
Zimmermann, Catharina; America, 1749 2856.30 p160
Zimmermann, Catharina Hager; America, 1749 2856.30 p513
Zimmermann, David; America, 1740 2856.30 p512
Zimmermann, David; America, 1752 2856.30 p512
Zimmermann, David; America, 1752 2856.30 p514
With wife & 5 children
Zimmermann, Eva Catharina; America, 1754 2856.30 p513
Zimmermann, Franziska; Port uncertain, 1773 2856.30 p513
Zimmermann, Gabriel; Port uncertain, 1731 2856.30 p513
Zimmermann, Gerhard; America, 1740 2856.30 p513
Zimmermann, Gerhard; America, 1740 2856.30 p514
With wife & 8 children
Zimmermann, Hans Adam; Port uncertain, 1752 2856.30 p513
With wife & children
Zimmermann, Hans Georg; America, 1752 2856.30 p514
With wife & 3 children
Zimmermann, Hans Nickel; America, 1740 2856.30 p513
Zimmermann, J. Nikolaus, Jr.; America, 1756 2856.30 p513
With wife & son
Zimmermann, Jakob; Port uncertain, 1747 2856.30 p513
Zimmermann, Jakob; Port uncertain, 1751 2856.30 p513
Zimmermann, Johann; Port uncertain, 1796 2856.30 p513
Zimmermann, Johann Georg; Port uncertain, 1787 2856.30 p513
Zimmermann, Johann Jakob; Port uncertain, 1764 2856.30 p513
Zimmermann, Johann Niklas; America, 1751 2856.30 p513
With wife & children
Zimmermann, Johann Nikolaus; America, 1756 2856.30 p513
Zimmermann, Johann Nikolaus; America, 1757 2856.30 p514
With wife & 2 children
Zimmermann, Lorenz; America, 1740 2856.30 p513
Zimmermann, Luisa; Port uncertain, 1744 2856.30 p513
Zimmermann, Magdalena; America, 1752 2856.30 p513
Zimmermann, Maria Catharina; America, 1765 2856.30 p513
Zimmermann, Maria Elisabeth; America, 1765 2856.30 p513
With husband
Zimmermann, Maria Magdalena; Port uncertain, 1744 2856.30 p513
Zimmermann, Michael; America, 1752 2856.30 p513
Zimmermann, Michael; America, 1753 2856.30 p513
Zimmermann, Philipp; America, 1732 2856.30 p513
Zimmermann, Philipp; America, 1735 2856.30 p513
Zimmermann, Philipp Heinric; Port uncertain, 1794 2856.30 p513
Zimmermann, Willibald; Port uncertain, 1737 2856.30 p513
Zimmermann, Willibald; Port uncertain, 1767 2856.30 p513
Zimmermann Family ; America, 1763 2856.30 p513
Zimpel, Paul; Port uncertain, 1736 2856.30 p514
Zimpelmann, Barbara; America, 1753 2856.30 p514
With husband
Zimpelmann, Nikolaus; America, 1765 2856.30 p514
Zimpelmann, Rachel; Port uncertain, 1778 2856.30 p514
Zimski, James; Maryland, 1910 3259.35 p73
Zinck, Agathe; Port uncertain, 1725 2856.30 p514
With husband
Zinck, Christina; Port uncertain, 1739 2856.30 p514
Zingailski, Lippert; Maryland, 1910 3259.35 p73
Zinglmann, Anna Maria; Port uncertain, 1770 2856.30 p514
Zink, Michael; America, 1818 2856.30 p514
With 4 sons & 3 daughters
Zink, Philipp; New York, 1840 8197.10 p194
Zinkand, Sophia; Maryland, 1910 3259.35 p73
Zinkgraf, Georg; America, 1749 2856.30 p514
Zinn, Johann Nickel; Port uncertain, 1790 2856.30 p514
Zinsbuskie, Walter; Maryland, 1910 3259.35 p73
Zinski, Anthony; Maryland, 1910 3259.35 p73
Zinsmeister, Anna Elisabeth; Port uncertain, 1783 2856.30 p514
Zint, John; Maryland, 1910 3259.35 p73
Ziomek, Larence; Maryland, 1910 3259.35 p73
Ziomek, Wladyslaw; Maryland, 1910 3259.35 p73
Ziomek, Wojcich; Maryland, 1910 3259.35 p73
Ziornek, Peter; Maryland, 1910 3259.35 p73
Zipf, Jacob; Port uncertain, 1756 2856.30 p514
Zipperer, Peter; America, 1751 2856.30 p514
With wife & son
Zirmier, Jacob 45; Ontario, 1871 1823.15 p289
Ziwowski, Jacob; Maryland, 1910 3259.35 p73
Zmudzcijuski, Michal; Maryland, 1910 3259.35 p73
Zmudziewski, Jacob; Maryland, 1910 3259.35 p73
Zobrski, John; Maryland, 1910 3259.35 p73
Zoci, Justina; Virginia, 1775 1220.25 p122
Zock, Martin; Ontario, 1871 1823.28 p107
Zodhair, Mr.; Quebec, 1856 9196.15 p8
Zodhair, Mrs.; Quebec, 1856 9196.15 p8
Zoeller, Christian E.; New York, 1817 8197.10 p296
Zofiezynski, Szczepan; Maryland, 1910 3259.35 p73
Zogoff, D. 29; Alaska, 1916 9196.1 p43
Zogoff, D. 29; Whitehorse, Yukon, 1916 9196.1 p43
Zogribci, Wienty; Maryland, 1910 3259.35 p73
Zokoski, John; Maryland, 1910 3259.35 p73
Zokowski, John; Maryland, 1910 3259.35 p73
Zolkowski, John; Maryland, 1910 3259.35 p73
Zolkowski, Stanislaw; Maryland, 1910 3259.35 p73
Zoll, Jacob; Pennsylvania, 1777 4629.10 p18
Zoll, Jakob; America, 1740 2856.30 p427
Zoll, Johann Nikolaus; America, 1740 2856.30 p427
Zoll, Peter; America, 1740 2856.30 p427
Zoller, Bartel; America, 1743 2856.30 p510
Zoller, David; America, 1751 2856.30 p514
Zoller, David; Port uncertain, 1751 2856.30 p514
With wife & 3 children
Zoller, Eva; America, 1780 2856.30 p256
Zoller, Hans; Port uncertain, 1763 2856.30 p514
Zoller, Lorenz; America, 1743 2856.30 p516
Zoller, Maria Magdalena; Port uncertain, 1694 2856.30 p514
Zoller, Martin; Port uncertain, 1781 2856.30 p514
Zoller, Mrs. Martin; America, 1752 2856.30 p516
With 4 children
Zoller, Michael; Port uncertain, 1798 2856.30 p514
Zoller, Nickel; America, 1740 2856.30 p514
Zoller, Nik; America, 1740 2856.30 p516
Zollerin, Christina; America, 1771 2856.30 p516
Zollin, Susanna; America, 1764 2856.30 p514
With husband
Zollinger, Jakob; America, 1749 2856.30 p514
With wife & 5 children
Zollmann, Peter; Port uncertain, 1741 2856.30 p514
Zoloski, Felix; Maryland, 1910 3259.35 p73
Zomba, Joseph; Maryland, 1910 3259.35 p73
Zomba, Theodore; Maryland, 1910 3259.35 p73
Zonblesky, Joseph 53; Ontario, 1871 1823.28 p107
Zonger, Simmon; America, 1743 2856.30 p514
Zoranik, Joseph; Maryland, 1910 3259.35 p73
Zorn, George; Baltimore, 1855 6058.10 p45
Zorn, George; Pennsylvania, 1862 6058.10 p45
Zorn, John; Baltimore, 1855 6058.10 p45
Zorn, Martin; America, 1744 2856.30 p514
Zottmann, Anna Amalia; Port uncertain, 1771 2856.30 p515
Zottmann, Margarete; Port uncertain, 1764 2856.30 p515
Zouch, Jno; Virginia, 1665-1666 6212.30 p21
Zouch, John; Virginia, 1639 1224.1 p66
Zouch, Zouch; Maryland, 1666 2524.55 p248
Zouristowski, Boleslaus; Maryland, 1910 3259.35 p73
Zowodny, George; Maryland, 1910 3259.35 p73
Zrochowski, Helen; Maryland, 1910 3259.35 p73
Zrochowski, Stephen; Maryland, 1910 3259.35 p73
Zruissevich, A. 34; Alaska, 1914 9196.1 p41
Zuber, Magdalena; America, 1742 2856.30 p515
Zuber, Maria Catharina; Port uncertain, 1775 2856.30 p515
Zuber, Michael; America, 1752 2856.30 p515
With daughter
Zubia, Juan Miguel; New York, 1830 8197.10 p353
Zubrowska, Michael F.; Maryland, 1910 3259.35 p73
Zubrowski, Frank; Maryland, 1910 3259.35 p73
Zuchno, Caspar; Maryland, 1910 3259.35 p73
Zuchnowski, Stanislaus; Maryland, 1910 3259.35 p73
Zuchowski, Joseph; Maryland, 1910 3259.35 p73
Zuck, Christina; Port uncertain, 1754 2856.30 p515
Zuckin, Christina; Port uncertain, 1754 2856.30 p515
Zufelt, A. 17; Ontario, 1861 2896.25 p29
Zufelt, C. C. 8; Ontario, 1861 2896.25 p29
Zufelt, Delina 80; Ontario, 1861 2896.28 p40
Zufelt, Edda E. 19; Ontario, 1861 2896.28 p19
Zufelt, Emiline 16; Ontario, 1861 2896.28 p19
Zufelt, Florance 26; Ontario, 1861 2896.28 p52
Zufelt, Florance A. 8; Ontario, 1861 2896.28 p52
Zufelt, Henryetta 7; Ontario, 1861 2896.28 p52
Zufelt, Isabella 12; Ontario, 1861 2896.28 p19
Zufelt, J. R. 2; Ontario, 1861 2896.28 p10
Zufelt, John 5; Ontario, 1861 2896.28 p52
Zufelt, L. E. 28; Ontario, 1861 2896.28 p10
Zufelt, Lydia J. 31; Ontario, 1861 2896.28 p19
Zufelt, M. 35; Ontario, 1861 2896.25 p29
Zufelt, M. S. 4; Ontario, 1861 2896.28 p10
Zufelt, Melvina 14; Ontario, 1861 2896.28 p19
Zufelt, Norton 5; Ontario, 1861 2896.28 p19
Zufelt, Sarah M. 3; Ontario, 1861 2896.28 p52
Zufelt, W. J. 6; Ontario, 1861 2896.28 p10
Zugai, Valentine; Maryland, 1910 3259.35 p73
Zukaszewicz, Andrew; Maryland, 1910 3259.35 p74
Zukawski, Julian; Maryland, 1910 3259.35 p74
Zukoff, I. 22; Alaska, 1916 9196.1 p43
Zukoff, I. 22; Whitehorse, Yukon, 1916 9196.1 p43
Zukoff, J. 21; Alaska, 1916 9196.1 p43
Zukoff, J. 21; Whitehorse, Yukon, 1916 9196.1 p43